譲歩を表す
◇Of course（もちろん）➔本分
◇Many people say that …（多くの人は…と言う）➔振り返る
◇It is often said that …（…と言われる）➔概ね
◇certainly（たしかに）➔忘れる
◇indeed（たしかに）➔終身
◇apparently（一見すると）➔有益
◇surely（きっと）➔挙げる

逆接を表す
◇but（しかし）➔様々
◇however（しかし）➔生まれる
◇yet（しかし）➔遂げる
◇nevertheless（しかし）➔事実
◇Although …, ~（…だが〜）➔同時に
◇Despite …（…にかかわらず）➔依然

2.「本論」に用いるディスコースマーカー

定義をする
◇A means that [to] …（Aは…を意味する）➔男女
◇By …here I mean that ~（…によってここでは〜を意味する）➔進歩
◇A consists of …（Aは…から構成される）➔自然
◇A refers to …（Aは…を意味する）➔持続

抽象的内容を述べる
◇some（いくつかの）➔有り得る
◇certain（特定の）➔広告
◇in many ways（多くの点で）➔第一
◇one [two, three, …several]（1つ[2つ, 3つ, …いくつもの]）➔紹介する
◇following（以下の）➔提案する
◇as follows:（以下の通りである）➔何より

関連を表す
◇concerning …（…に関して）➔問題
◇as to …（…に関して）➔正確な
◇as for …（…については）➔費用
◇regarding …（…に関しては）➔家庭
◇with respect to …（…に関しては）➔差
◇in terms of …（…の面では）➔輸出

［▶後見返しへ］

ウィズダム和英辞典

THE WISDOM JAPANESE-ENGLISH DICTIONARY

小西友七=編修主幹

岸野英治・三宅胖=編修委員

三省堂

© Sanseido Co., Ltd. 2007

THE WISDOM JAPANESE-ENGLISH DICTIONARY

First Edition 2007

Printed in Japan

古今ことばの系譜　引用英訳出典
『枕草子』
Ivan Morris, trans. and ed., *The Pillow Book of Seishonagon* (Penguin Books, 1967)
『徒然草』
Donald Keene, trans., *Essays in Idleness: The Tsurezuregusa of Kenko* (Columbia University Press, 1998)
『奥の細道』
Nobuyuki Yuasa, trans., *The Narrow Road to the Deep North and Other Travel Sketches* (Penguin Books, 1966)
『坊っちゃん』
Burton Watson, trans., "Botchan," in *Modern Japanese Literature: An Anthology*, ed. Donald Keene (Charles E.Tuttle, 1957)
『三四郎』
Jay Rubin, trans., *Sanshiro: A Novel*, Michigan Classics in Japanese Studies, no. 23 (Ann Arbor: Center for Japanese Studies, The University of Michigan, 2002)
『どんぐりと山猫』
John Bester, trans., *Once and Forever: The Tales of Kenji Miyazawa* (Kodansha International Ltd., 1993, 1997)
『夜明け前』
William E.Naff, trans., *Before the Dawn* (University of Hawaii Press, 1987)
高橋尚子選手インタビュー
『ヘラルド朝日』2005 年 11 月 23 日付

まえがき

ことばは絶えず変化する．IT革命以来ここ10年，めまぐるしい国際情勢の変化の中で，特に英語の変化は著しい．国際化，グローバル化の流れに沿って，英語に World English(es) としての言語的展開など多数のバラエティを認めざるを得なくなってきており，それに応じて文法の規範性にも必然的に幅ができてきたといえる．

以上のような情勢を踏まえ，本辞典の編修にあたって留意した点は次の通りである．

1. authentic Japanese

本辞典の編修にあたっては，まず authentic Japanese を標榜した．これまでの和英辞典の用例は，先に英文ありきで，それを訳している傾向があった．つまり，英文の構造を伝えようとするあまり，直訳調のぎこちない日本語となっているものがいろいろと散見されていたのである．和英辞典は日本語から引く辞典である．その入口となる日本語がぎこちないのでは，その役割を十全に果たすことはできない．このような傾向を払拭し，自然な日本語を自然な英語に置き換えることの出来る和英辞典とすべく，以下のような工夫を行った．

(1) 国語辞典・日本語コーパスの徹底調査

最新の国語辞典を徹底調査し，慣用句・ことわざなどを大幅に取り入れた．また，各種日本語コーパスを活用し，日常的な表現の充実も図った．

(2) 日本語校閲

用例については，従来の英文校閲に加え，日本文についても専門家に校閲を依頼した．これにより，前述の「英文ありき」のぎこちない日本語を一掃し，自然な日本語の提示を徹底できたと考えている．

(3) 新語・カタカナ語の充実

最近現れてきた用語を積極的に取り入れた．(例：居住空間 a living space/セブンイレブン直営店 a 7-eleven operated store [《英》shop]) また，カタカナ語については，国立国語研究所「外来語」委員会編『外来語言い換え提案』なども取り入れ，充実を図った．特に和製英語については，その表記を《和製語》というレーベルを付けて示すことで注意を促した．

(4) 専門用語校閲

近年特に人気のある野球・サッカーの用語については，専門家に校閲を依頼し，日本語の直訳・説明的な訳ではない，生の英語を提示した．

2. ディスコース

本辞典では真に作文に必要な文章，つまりディスコースにも視点を置いた．従来の和英辞典は(単)文，つまりセンテンスが主であった．しかし，高校のライティング教科書にパラグラフライティングが導入されていることからもわかるように，現在の英作文はディスコース中心に移行している．このような流れを考えれば，和英辞典にもディスコースに関する情報を取り入れるのは当然のことといえよう．本辞典では以下のような工夫を行うことでディスコースに対応した．

(1) 談話文法の導入

ディスコース文を書くためには，そのための文法，すなわち談話文法の知識が必要になる．例えば，「私は数年間フランス語を習っていたが，パリでは私のフランス語が通じなかった」と言う場合，日本語につられて I had been learning French for several years, but *in Paris* I couldn't make myself understood. と副詞句を先頭に持ってきがちである．しかし，英語では I had been learning French for several years, but I couldn't make myself understood *in Paris*. と副詞句を後置する方が自然であり，文章のつながりがよくなるのである．本辞典の用例の執筆にあたっては，このような談話文法の概念を全面的に取り入れ，より自然な英語の提示を心がけた．

(2) レクシカルフレーズの重視

また，近年注目されるようになった「ツー」と言えば「カー」と無意識に反応して出てくるレクシカルフレーズ (lexical phrase) の表現の塊 (chunk) を身につけることも，自然な英文を発信するためには重要である．これらを構成する文には2つある．

    (a) 会話の受け答え中の決まり文句：「明日は10時にそちらに着きます」「着いたらお電話ください」 "I will be there at ten tomorrow." "When you arrive, just give me a

call."
(b) 独立した単文で定型化したもの：物分かりの悪い人だなあ Don't you see what's happening? (= You don't know anything about it. You are a fool.)

本辞典では，用例の随所にこのような表現を取り入れた．

(3) ディスコース文の解説
ディスコース文の用例をコラムとして掲載し，文の展開方法についての解説を加えた．ここで学んだディスコースの知識を活用することで，大学入試の自由英作文，さらには英語論文にも十分対応できると考えている．

3. 日本人の心のふるさとを映し出す辞書

さらに，後世に長く愛用される辞書を目指し，読んで興味をそそり，人口に膾炙されている名言名句を用例として積極的に取り入れた．特に，古今の文学作品中に現れ，今に語り継がれることばについては，ディスコース文として掲載し，適宜解説を加えた．(例：山路を登りながら，こう考えた．智に働けば角が立つ．情に棹させば流される．意地を通せば窮屈だ．とかくに人の世は住みにくい．(⇨『草枕』)) これらを通じて，単に英語を学ぶにとどまらず，日本人の心のふるさと，原風景をも感じていただきたい．それが日本文化発信の一助にもなると考えている．

4. 懇切丁寧な解説

本辞典のもう一つの大きな柱は，中級の高校生にも分かりやすい「懇切丁寧な解説」である．高校生が誤りやすい学習上のポイントについては煩を厭わず解説を加え，先生が生徒の英作文を添削する様を紙面上で再現しようとする試みは本辞典の姉妹書である『グランドセンチュリー和英辞典』でも行ってきたが，本辞典ではそれをさらに追求した．主な点は以下の通りである．

(1) 非文情報
「こうは言うがこうは言わない」，つまり日本人が誤りやすい項目についての記述を充実させた．(例) 教会で挙式の予定です Our wedding will be held in (×a) church./布地はメートルで切り売りする sell cloth by the [×a] meter

(2) 日英比較
日本語を直訳しただけでは意味にズレが生じるものについては，構文・文化両面から解説を加え，日本語と英語の発想の違いを意識し，より自然な英文を書くことが出来るようにした．

(3) 語法解説
語法の記述は詳しく扱った．記述の量の多いものは「解説」欄の囲み記事に，少ないものは煩を厭わず(⚠️ ...) で注記した．特に基本語については随所に最大限の語法解説・注記を入れた．

(4) 類語解説
英語は日本語と同様類語が非常に多い．そのため，語の選択が重要となる．本辞典では「使い分け」欄を設けて微妙なニュアンスを詳しく解説した．

(5) スピーチレベル
語の選択に際しては，類語のほかに言語的差異の問題がある．そのため《米》《英》《古》《書》《話》《俗》などのレーベルを設けて，選んだ語がその使われる地域，社会，時代，文体に合っているかを確認できるようにした．

(6) 連語関係
英文を作る際には語と語の繋がりを理解することが重要である．本辞典では，一つの語についてその前後，特に後にどんな語(句)が来るかを《　》を用いて示した．

(7) PC関係
政治的に妥当な言葉遣い(PC : Political Correctness)も円滑なコミュニケーションには重要である．用例作成にあたっては，この点にも十分に配慮した．(例) 自宅通学の学生 a student commuting from *his* [*her*, *his or her*] home.

(8) 発音・音調
オーラルコミュニケーションを意識し，発音・アクセントを誤りやすい語句については，適宜発音記号・アクセント記号を付した．また，文強勢やリズムなどの音調についても，必要に応じて情報を盛り込んだ．

以上，本辞典を現代の英語の変化や語法研究の成果を全面的に取り入れた「本格的な語法文法の辞典」としての性格と，高校生にも分かりやすい解説を随所にちりばめた「懇切丁寧な辞典」としての性格

を兼ね備えたものとすべく，スタッフ一同は編修作業に全身全霊を注いだ．Matthew Arnold の *Essays in Criticism* に記されている「世の中で知られ考えられた最善のものを学びとり，これを公正に後の世に伝える」義務が我々にはあると考えているからである．

　本辞典の編修にあたっては別紙の編修委員，校閲協力者，執筆者の御世話になった．また，三省堂辞書出版部外国語辞書第一編集室の山口守編集長を始め，担当の金子真一，安藤まりかの両氏には何から何まで本当に御世話になった．心より御礼申し上げたい．

　最後に，編者としては最善の情報を提供すべく本辞典を編修したが，思いがけぬ誤りや不備があるかと思う．今後さらなる工夫と改良に努力するつもりであるが，ご利用くださった方々のご叱正・ご助言をいただければ幸いである．

2006 年(平成 18 年)夏

小西　友七

本書の編集にご協力いただいた先生方　(五十音順)

青木　祥庫	浅見　伸裕	麻生　朋成	麻生　雄治	安倍富士男	新井　正子
安藤　克典	飯塚　仁	生田　省三	砂金　紀	泉　政満	一法師克也
井出　清	伊藤　剛	伊藤　正一	稲垣　康和	稲留　芳明	猪俣しのぶ
今井　茂	今井　康人	今田　祐之	今吉　正	宇都宮正朗	江藤　愉
遠藤　明緒	遠藤　満雄	大石　正昭	太田　亨	大村　雅三	岡本　裕子
岡本　泰	小川　心経	小栗　晶	長村　孝雄	小野　亮子	柿木　洋介
加藤　輝雄	加藤　雅仁	金子　章生	川島　智幸	川西　義広	菊池　徹
岸本　史雄	北尾　秀司	北堀　洋	草階　健樹	工藤　正宏	国重　徹
熊谷　祥生	黒川　佳子	毛谷　裕二	小泉　量裕	合田　和広	児島　敏郎
後藤　公英	後藤　隆之	木幡信一郎	小林　英治	小林　広美	根田　敬一
酒井　治	酒井　孝男	三入　勝憲	坂田有士郎	佐藤　修一	佐藤　一隆
佐藤　仁志	佐藤　昌功	三小田博昭	塩出　文昭	渋木　一義夫	清水　晃
下田　和男	白井　宏明	杉浦　雅則	鈴木　聡	鈴木　晃彦	鈴木　寿秀
鈴木　雅範	瀬下　篤	髙城　真	髙田　恵子	髙田　幸司	高橋　哲徳
竹内　耕治	田中　慎一	田並　正	谷口　信一	谷口　雅英	谷口　正博
田村　達朗	田原真由美	千葉　圭	千葉　健司	積川　淳一恵	鶴田　欽也
手塚　達也	土肥　穣治	東方　誠	冨田　雅文	豊田　一恵	苗代　直隆
長岡　秀一	中野　昭雄	長野　雅弘	中畑　義明	中林　義晴	中村　哲也
中村　弘之	永山　一夫	鍋damage島　和男	南條　敦史	西山　勝治	丹羽　和彦
布川　裕行	根岸　晃	野島　伸仁	橋見　誠一	畑　義則	原　博司
原子　彰	原田　和範	樋口　直人	平井　正朗	福﨑　穣司	福田　洋平
藤井　佳一	藤井　哲	藤井　良晴	藤田　鉄雄	藤田　正紀	藤塚　孝夫
伏原　一樹	二石　政家	船戸　宙治	古川　陽一	本田　敦久	前田　美智
前原　義明	牧野　知美	益田　和之	町田　一忠	松岡　正喜	松崎　親界
松田　聡	松宮　晃	松本　秀樹	水迫　達郎	三谷　徳彦	道中　博司
宮本　洋一	宮本　順紀	宗里　佳子	村松　誠	森　孝志	森田　信彦
森脇　将成	柳生　敏克	安河内清徳	柳澤　真平	山岸　光男	山口　章
山下　敏伸	山田　道務	山野井康雄	山本光一郎	山森　義弘	淀縄　義男
脇山　哲夫					

編修スタッフ

【編 修 主 幹】 小西友七

【編 修 委 員】 岸野 英治　　三宅　　胖

【校 閲 協 力 者】 石川慎一郎　　（類語）　　　　　今野 真二　　（日本文用例）
　　　　　　　　　佐藤 尚孝　　（野球用語）　　　曾我 邦子　　（英文用例）
　　　　　　　　　東本 貢司　　（サッカー用語）　Denise May Wright

【執　筆　者】 芦谷 民枝　　池田久美子　　石川慎一郎　　石田 修治　　大月みゆき
　　　　　　　　尾崎 恒夫　　岸野 英治　　香田 禮二　　小西 友七　　佐藤　　隆
　　　　　　　　佐藤 尚孝　　塩濱 久雄　　曾我 邦子　　月足亜由美　　都築 郷実
　　　　　　　　中嶋 孝雄　　中野 道雄　　成田あゆみ　　西田あおい　　萩原 裕子
　　　　　　　　長谷川文代　　東本 貢司　　東森めぐみ　　日比野克哉　　三島 隆二
　　　　　　　　三宅　　胖

【執 筆 協 力 者】 後藤 一章　　坂本 智香　　三木　望

【資 料 提 供 者】 有岡 佳子　　石川慎一郎　　磯野 市子　　木澤 直子　　中尾 桂子

装丁・見返し　　岡本 健+
校正・資料作成　井内 長俊　　小久保秀之　　小松久美子　　佐田 一郎　　諏訪間 怜
　　　　　　　　三田百合　　山口 英則　　文章工房・句読点
調　査　協　力　日本アイアール株式会社
挿　　　　絵　　小林 和夫

本書の使い方

1 見出し語

1-1 収録項目
成句・複合語・関連語などを含め,約88,000項目を収録した.

1-2 重要度表示
見出しのうち,重要語については赤で示し,重要度に応じて2種類の印をつけた.
‡Aランク (最重要語) 約1,000語
*Bランク (重要語) 約3,000語

1-3 配列
見出し語は五十音順により配列した. 細則は以下の通り.
(1) 長音符については,長音符を直前の文字に含まれる母音に置き換えて配列する.
　　コーヒー→「コオヒイ」　　**ブーツ**→「ブウツ」　　**デート**→「デエト」
(2) 同じかなが続く場合は,原則として以下の順で配列する.
　(a) ひらかな → 漢字 → カタカナ
　(b) 清音 → 濁音 → 半濁音
　(c) 直音 → 促音・拗音
　(d) 接頭語 → 接尾語
　(e) 品詞 (名詞 → 形容詞 → 副詞 → 動詞 → その他)
　(f) 漢字の画数が少ないもの → 多いもの
　(g) 送りがなが多いもの → 少ないもの
　(h) 最重要語 → 重要語 → 一般語

1-4 同音同字語
同音同字だが語源の異なる項目については,別々に立項し,見出し語に続けて意味区分を示した.
　　能　　［能力］　　　　カレー　　［料理］
　　能　　［能楽］　　　　カレー　　［フランスの都市］

1-5 棒見出し
同じ語幹を持つ語については,原則として同一の見出し内で扱い,2つ目以降の品詞は棒見出し (—) に続けて示した.
　　—勉強する 動:　**勉強** 名　の棒見出しとして示す
　　—軽く 副:　**軽い** 形　の棒見出しとして示す

1-6 品詞の表示
同一見出し語に複数の品詞がある場合は,そのそれぞれに品詞を示した.
本書で用いる品詞は以下の通り. 原則としてそれぞれ英語の品詞に対応している.

　　名 名詞　　形 形容詞　　副 副詞　　動 動詞
　　接 接続詞　　助 助動詞　　代 代名詞　　間 間投詞

日本語の助詞については,必要に応じて《副助詞》のように示した.

2 語源

2-1 語源の表示
外来語のうち,英語以外の言語が語源のものについては,見出し語に続けて ［<…語］ の形でその語源を示した.
　　アベック　［<フランス語］ ［[男女一組]］ a couple, a young couple.

2-2 英語の語源
英語の語源については,原則として本文の注記で扱う.

3 訳 語

3-1 示し方
(1) 訳語は，用例などと区別するためにゴシック体で示した．
(2) 訳語は，原則として使用頻度の高いものから示した．
(3) 複数の訳語がある場合は，コンマで区切って示した．ただし，意味・用法が大きく異なるものについては，セミコロンで区切り，必要に応じて意味・用法の差異に関する注記を示した．(⇨3-7〜8)

3-2 つづり字
原則として米つづりのみを示した．ただし，米英でつづりが大きく異なる場合は，英つづりも併記した．

3-3 名詞の訳語
(1) 名詞の訳語は，原則として単数形で示した．ただし，複数形でのみ用いる場合には複数形で示した．
(2) 可算名詞・不可算名詞については，不定冠詞の有無で示した．
  (a) a [an] がついている語: 可算名詞
  (b) (a [an]) がついている語: 可算・不可算の両方の用法がある名詞
  (c) a [an] がついていない語: 不可算名詞
(3) 可算名詞・不可算名詞を表すための不定冠詞は，他の訳語と区別するために本文と同じ書体で示した．

3-4 変化形の表示
(1) be 以外の不規則変化語(動詞・形容詞・副詞)には，アステリスクをつけることでその語が不規則変化することを示した．動詞・形容詞・副詞の不規則変化表は ⇨2093〜2097 ページ
(2) 名詞で不規則変化をするものは，その変化形を( )に入れて示した．
(3) 動詞のうち以下のものについては，その形を( )に入れて示した．
  (a) 語末の子音が重なるもの: drop (-pp-)
  (b) -ie が現在分詞で -ying となるもの: tie (〜d; tying)
  (c) -c で終わり変化形で -ck と -k が加わるもの: mimic (-icked; -icking)

3-5 説明的な訳
(1) 日本の風物に対する訳など，日本語に対応する英語がなく，説明的な訳を示す場合は，(説明的に)に続けて示した．
(2) 説明的な訳は，他の訳語と区別するために本文と同じ書体で示した．
和え物 aemono; (説明的に) vegetables, fish or seaweed with Japanese dressing.

3-6 和製英語
(1) 和製英語は，原則として訳語の最後に《和製語》に続けて示した．
(2) 和製英語は，他の訳語と区別するために本文と同じ書体で示した．
(3) 日本文化紹介などのためにあえて日本語の直訳を訳語として示す場合は，' ' に入れて示した．
ゴールデンウィーク 'Golden Week' holidays

3-7 訳語間の差異
各訳語に対する説明・直訳，またはニュアンスの差異を示す場合は，訳語の前に( )に入れて示した．
換気 ventilation; (通風) airing.

3-8 語義の区分
(1) 日本語の語義区分は〚 〛に入れて示した．
肝心な〚重要な〛important, vital;〚必要な〛essential;〚決定的な〛crucial.
(2) 特に大きな区分の場合は，語義番号で分け，意味区分を〚 〛に入れて示した．
決まり ❶〚規則〛a rule ... ❷〚区切り〛(a) settlement

3-9 INDEX (語義一覧)
語義番号が多数あり，かつ記述量の多い語については，見出しの直後に語義番号と語義を一覧できる囲み(INDEX)を示した．

4 用例

4-1 配列
(1) 用例は，訳語に続けて「句例 → 文例」の順で掲載した．
(2) 句例の開始位置は ● で示した．
(3) 文例の開始位置は ▶ で示した．

4-2 日本語の言い換え
日本文をそのまま直訳しても自然な英語にならない場合は，英訳への橋渡しとして日本語の言い換え表現を示した．言い換え表現の示し方は，原則として以下の通り．
(1) 言い換えが1つの場合：(＝　　)の形で日本文の該当箇所の直後に示す．
 控える ●隣の部屋で控える(＝待つ) *wait* in the next room.
(2) 言い換えが複数ある場合：(　　)の形で各英訳文の前に示す．
 引く ●カーテンを引く (閉める) *draw* a curtain; (下ろす) *lower* a curtain.

4-3 構造表記
用例が多数ある項目については，日本語の構造・コロケーションによって用例を区分した．主な構造のパターンは以下のとおり．
(1) 名　詞：　**音**　①【～音】　②【音は[が]】　③【音を】
(2) 動　詞：　**信じる**　①【…を信じる】　②【…であると信じる】
(3) 形容詞：　**危ない**　①【危ない～】　②【…が[は]危ない】
(4) 副　詞：　**決して**　【決して…ない】

4-4 会話例
(1) 会話例は，用例の最後にまとめて掲載した．
(2) 会話例の開始位置は 会話 で示した

5 成句・複合語

5-1 成句
(1) 慣用句・ことわざなどは成句として，各品詞の最後まとめて掲載した．
(2) 成句は，原則としてその先頭の要素の項に掲載した．
(3) 成句の見出しは，●に続けて「ゴシック体＋下線」の形で示した．
 危ない ●<u>**危ない橋を渡る**</u>

5-2 複合語
(1) 複合語は，見出し語の最後にまとめて掲載した．
(2) 複合語は，その先頭の要素の項に掲載した．
(3) 複合語の見出しは，●に続けてゴシック体で示した．
 生涯 ●**生涯教育**

6 用法解説

6-1 連語関係
(1) 訳語・用例には，必要に応じて連語関係(しばしば共起する前置詞・目的語となる語句など)を《　》に入れて示した．
 うれしい glad 《*at, about, of; to do; that* 節》
 昇進 (a) promotion 《*to*》
 プレッシャー ●プレッシャーをかける put pressure 《*on* him *to do*》．
(2) 動詞と共起する副詞については，「動詞…副詞」の形で示した．
 焼却する burn … up

6-2 注記
訳語・用例についての注記は，以下の形で示した．
(1) 語法・用法に関する注記： **!**
(2) 百科的な説明・語の背景・語源記事など： 参考
(3) 文化的な差異・背景などに関する情報： 事情
(4) 関連語・関連表現： 関連
(5) 特に分量の多い注記については，囲み記事として掲載した．

6-3 非文情報
日本人が犯しやすい「こうは言わない(方がよい)」誤文などについては，非文として × をつけて示した．
 海 ●海に泳ぎに行く go swimming in [×to] the *sea* [*ocean*].

7　発音・アクセント・音調

7-1　発音・アクセント　発音・アクセントの位置に注意が必要な訳語については，それぞれ発音記号・アクセント記号を示し，注意を喚起した．

7-2　文強勢と音調　文例・会話例のうち，音調に注意が必要な場合，または音調によって文の持つ意味が変わる場合には，音調に注意すべき語句の先頭に音調記号を示した．
本書で用いる音調記号は，以下のとおり．

（下降調）＼　　（上昇調）／　　（下降上昇調）∨　　（上昇下降調）∧

8　参照・他項目との関連

8-1　参照
(1) 参照先は（⇨　）で示した．
(2) 参照先は，原則として見出し語・棒見出しとする．それ以外の項目を参照させる場合は，見出し語・棒見出しに続けて具体的な参照先を［　］に入れて示す．
（⇨決まり❷［第2文例］）：「決まり」②の2番目の文例を参照

8-2　同意語・類義語・対義語　日本語の関連語（同意語・類義語・対義語）については，訳語の最後に以下のような形で示した．
(1) 同意語　（⓼　）
(2) 類義語　（㊣　）
(3) 対義語　（㊥　）

9　各種コラム

9-1　類語解説　類語解説には，以下の2種類がある．
(1) **使い分け**
1つの語義に多くの訳語があり，その使い分けについて解説が必要な場合は，囲み記事にしてその意味の差異・用法上の注意点などをくわしく解説した．

(2) **WORD CHOICE**　（日本語の発信キーワード120）
日本語教科書・作文コーパスから選定した日本語のキーワード120については，そのキーワードに相当する代表的な英語を挙げ，用例を示しながらその意味の差異などを解説した．また，必要に応じて頻度情報・共起情報なども示した．掲載項目の一覧は　⇨xiiページ

9-2　DISCOURSE　まとまった文章を書く際に必要な，論旨の流れや転換を示す表現（ディスコースマーカー）の使い方について，用例をもとに解説した．見返しの「ディスコースマーカー一覧」とともに活用されたい．

9-3　名言名句　日本の名作などから用例を採ったコラムには，以下の2種類がある．
(1) **翻訳のこころ**
中学・高校の国語教科書に掲載されている現代の小説・論説文から用例をセンテンス（文）単位で採り，英訳のポイントとともに日英の言語的・文化的差異を解説した．掲載項目の一覧は　⇨xiページ

(2) **古今ことばの系譜**
平安時代の枕草子から現代の高橋尚子選手のインタビューまで，その時代を映し出すようなことばをディスコース（文章）単位で採り，英訳のポイントを解説するとともに，日本人のこころの移り変わりをパノラマ的に感じることのできるコラムをめざした．掲載項目の一覧は　⇨xiページ

10　約物・各種記号

10-1　約物

( )	省略可能な部分
[ ]	言い換え部分
《 》	(1)　レーベル
	(2)　連語関係
	(3)　略語・記号: 《略 AZ》《元素記号 Ag》《...の略》
	(4)　訳語の前につく語法注記: 《集合的》《人が主語》
〖 〗	専門分野表示
〚 〛	(1)　日本語の語義区分
	(2)　カタカナ語の日本語対訳・定義
	(3)　日本語の定義
(⇨)	参照先
(↔)	英語の対義語

10-2　レーベル

(1)　使用場面による差異
　　《話》　　口語
　　《俗》　　俗語
　　《卑》　　卑語
　　《書》　　改まった語，文語

(2)　地域的差異
　　《米》　　　米国英語・用法
　　《英》　　　英国英語・用法
　　《和製語》　和製英語

(3)　時代的差異
　　《古》　　今はあまり用いられなくなった語
　　《まれ》　今は用いられることがまれな語

WORD CHOICE 日本語の発信キーワード 120 一覧

[名詞]

家	80	声	590	腹	1463
嘘	155	心	601	光	1492
海	170	言葉	619	人	1513
絵	183	子供	619	船	1583
音	237	ごみ	628	町	1700
顔	293	時代	727	店	1734
風	326	自転車	746	道	1738
形	332	写真	765	虫	1760
川	371	力	1094	目	1773
木	398	中心	1110	物	1811
気持ち	432	手	1169	山	1837
国	495	箱	1427	様子	1873
車	508	花	1450		

[動詞]

会う	7	聞く	407	飲む	1398
上げる	20	決める	431	乗る	1400
集める	39	比べる	503	入る	1416
歩く	60	困る	627	運ぶ	1428
言う	77	捜す	659	始まる	1430
行く	89	死ぬ	749	走る	1433
生まれる	169	調べる	840	働く	1440
置く	218	知る	843	光る	1492
起こる	223	進む	887	引く	1497
怒る	223	住む	901	増える	1552
教える	226	育てる	990	待つ	1702
落ちる	235	食べる	1067	守る	1714
思い出す	250	違う	1093	回る	1719
思う	252	使う	1138	見付ける	1740
終わる	262	作る	1148	見る	1750
買う	290	続く	1153	結ぶ	1764
帰る	292	出る	1201	持つ	1804
書く	303	跳ぶ	1276	求める	1809
掛ける	315	取る	1290	分かる	1960
変わる	374	流れる	1310	忘れる	1966
考える	378	泣く	1311	笑う	1971

[形容詞]

新しい	33	少ない	881	早い	1460
美しい	162	素晴らしい	896	速い	1461
嬉しい	176	高い	1034	広い	1539
おいしい	202	楽しい	1063	良い	1866
大きい	209	小さい	1090	悪い	1974
悲しい	347	強い	1164		
暗い	500	長い	1305		

翻訳のこころ 一覧

『猿が島』(太宰治)	965, 1086, 1723, 1899
『高瀬舟』(森鷗外)	603, 752, 810, 826, 1077
『注文の多い料理店』(宮沢賢治)	296, 426, 541, 685, 731, 1068, 1113, 1421, 1545, 1965
『「である」ことと「する」こと』(丸山真男)	82, 322, 553, 787, 1716
『デューク』(江國香織)	120, 177, 351, 613, 748, 757, 895, 1318, 1342, 1399, 1431, 1665, 1700, 1972
『なめとこ山の熊』(宮沢賢治)	69, 534, 874, 898, 1735
『蠅』(横光利一)	1096, 1768, 1853
『走れメロス』(太宰治)	158, 230, 499, 602, 668, 828, 846, 881, 1312, 1501, 1766, 1867, 1970
『ひよこの眼』(山田詠美)	240, 627, 1462, 1466, 1639, 1728, 1809
『水の東西』(山崎正和)	105, 673, 982, 1125, 1309, 1967
『みどりのゆび』(吉本ばなな)	31, 138, 508, 667, 671, 1198, 1218, 1235, 1484, 1895
『羅生門』(芥川龍之介)	85, 1155, 1234, 1235
『蘭』(竹西寛子)	220, 224, 628, 682, 1162, 1429, 1472, 1725, 1791, 1941
『レキシントンの幽霊』(村上春樹)	26, 63, 148, 313, 354, 406, 899, 1027, 1077, 1228, 1296, 1325, 1734, 1764
『檸檬』(梶井基次郎)	190, 473, 479, 886, 1000, 1256, 1734, 1737, 1761, 1833

古今ことばの系譜 一覧

[平安]	『枕草子』(清少納言)	1690, 1745
[鎌倉]	『方丈記』(鴨長明)	1641
	『平家物語』	1611
	『徒然草』(吉田兼好)	1167
[江戸]	『奥の細道』(松尾芭蕉)	219
[明治]	『鹿狩り』(国木田独歩)	702
	『坊ちゃん』(夏目漱石)	1638, 1664
	『草枕』(夏目漱石)	125, 271, 483
	『三四郎』(夏目漱石)	690
[大正]	『千曲川のスケッチ』(島崎藤村)	1097
[昭和]	『どんぐりと山猫』(宮沢賢治)	352, 1295
	『夜明け前』(島崎藤村)	1866
	『ごんぎつね』(新美南吉)	637, 1471
	『風立ちぬ』(堀辰雄)	327
	『嘘』(太宰治)	156
[平成]	高橋尚子選手インタビュー	1862

発音記号表

母音

1. 単母音

/i/	city, kit
/i:/	tea, piece
/e/	red, pet
/æ/	ant, ask, aunt
/ʌ/	cut, bus
/ɑ/	hot, ox
/ɑ:/	father, calm
/ɔ:/	all, call
/u/	cook, could
/u:/	school, new
/ə/	gentleman, ahead
/ər/	singer, paper
/ə:r/	girl, hurry

2. 二重母音

/ai/	kind, cry
/ei/	cake, eight
/ɔi/	oil, boy
/au/	out, cow
/ou/	go, oak
/eər/	air, there
/iər/	beer, ear
/ɑ:r/	art, car
/ɔ:r/	store, door
/uər/	poor, cure

子音

1. 破裂音

/p/	pin, top
/b/	bed, job
/t/	ten, hit
/d/	day, kid
/k/	key, cake
/g/	gift, bag

2. 破擦音

/tʃ/	child, match
/dʒ/	joke, bridge

3. 摩擦音

/f/	fish, enough
/v/	visit, give
/θ/	thing, both
/ð/	that, brother
/s/	sea, chess
/z/	zoo, noise
/ʃ/	ship, dash
/ʒ/	decision, measure
/h/	hat, who
/j/	yes, onion
/w/	way, one
/hw/	why, white
/r/	race, horror

4. 鼻音

/m/	milk, ham
/n/	net, can
/ŋ/	king, finger

5. 側音

/l/	lip, hotel

あ

ああ 〔(あのように) like that; (あれほど) so, 《話》(all) that (❗通例否定文・疑問文で). (⇨あんなに)) ▶彼はああやればよかったのに He should have done *that way [like that]*. (❗should have＋過去分詞で過去の行為・状態への後悔・非難を表す) ▶彼はああするより仕方なかった He had no choice but to do *that*./He couldn't do *otherwise*. ▶ああ言えばこう言うで口の減らない(=言葉に窮することがない)奴は He's never *at a loss for words*. ▶あの男はああ見えても金持ちだ He doesn't *look* a rich man, *but in fact* he is./(信じられないかもしれないが) *Believe it or not*, he is a rich man. (❗Don't be deceived by his appearance. He is a rich man. ともいえる)

ああ 感 ❶ [感嘆] oh /óu/, ah /ɑ́ː/. ●oh は驚き・恐怖・悲しみ・苦痛・いらだち・突然の喜びなどを, ah は同情・苦痛・後悔・嫌悪・喜びなどを表し, いずれも通例後にはコンマか感嘆符を伴う) ▶ああ驚いた *Oh*, what a surprise! ▶ああかわいそうに *Ah*, (you) poor fellow. ▶ああフランスへ行きたい *Oh*, I dó wish I could go to France. (❗do は wish を強調する)/*How* I wish to go to France! (⇨何と圏) ▶ああおなかがすいた《米話》 Am Í \hungry! (❗Yes/No 疑問文を下降調で読むと How \hungry (I ám)! に相当する感嘆文を表す)

会話「すぐに七面鳥を焼き始めるわね」「ああ待ち切れないわ」"I'll start roasting the turkey very soon." "*Wow*! 〔《米話》*Gee*!〕 I can't wait." (⇨わあ)

❷ [反応, 応答] oh, ah. ●ともに理解・同意・承認を表すが, ah の後には批評・反対意見などが続くこともある) ▶ああ今夜帰省されるのですね *Oh* [*Ah*], you're going home tonight! (❗oh は帰省すると知った[思い出した]場合に, 驚きもこめられる. ah は「そうだったのか」と納得した場合など) ▶ああそうそう思い出した *Oh*, *yes*, (now) I remember [×remembered]. (❗oh は yes, no を感嘆的に強調する) ▶ああ来た来た *Oh* [*Ah*], hére they \come. ▶「じゃあ, 元気でね」私がアーもウーも言わないうちに電話は切れた "Take care," she said, and hung up, before I had time to say [utter] a word. (❗「アーもウーも」は「一言も」の意. a word の a で表し ¬読むことで示す)

会話「このボタンを押せばいいのですよ」「ああ, なるほど」"Push this button here." "*Oh*, I see."

会話「ブラウンさんを知ってのですか」「I know Mr. Brown." "*Oh*, ╱do you?" (⇨そう ❷)

❸ [安心, あきらめ] ▶ああやっと着いた Well, \here we ╱are at last! (❗×here we arrived とはいわない) ▶ああ仕方がない *Oh* / well, it can't be helped. ▶あーあバスに乗りおくれた *Óh òh* [*Óh*, \my]! I've missed the bus. (❗軽い失望を表す) ▶あーあ, また雨だ *Oh, nó*! It's raining again! (❗強いらだちを表す)

❹ [肯定, 応答] 会話「疲れたかい」「ああ, 疲れた」"Are you tired?" "*Yes*, I am."

会話「かまわないだろ」「ああちっとも」"You dón't ∨mind, do you?" "*No, nót at \all." (❗この場合 yes とはならないことに注意)

❺ [呼びかけ] oh, 《書》O. ▶あーぼーイさん, お勘定を *Excuse me*, check 〔《米》[bill〕《英》], please. (事前 普通は呼びかけをせず目や手振りで合図し, 声をかけないと気付いてもらえないときに限り用いる. 女性には Miss! で注意を引く. Oh, waiter! などとは通例言わな

い)

ああいう such; like that. (⇨そんな)

アーカイブ 〔保存記録・記録保存館〕an archive. ●歴史(物)アーカイブズ historical *archives*. ●〔テープ・レコードなどの〕サウンドアーカイブズ sound *archives*.

アーカンソー 〔米国の州〕 Arkansas /ɑ́ːrkənsɔ̀ː/ (略 Ark. 郵便州名 AR).

アーキテクチャー 〔コンピュータ全体の設計思想〕architecture.

アーケード an arcade /ɑːrkéid/. ●アーケード式商店街 a shopping *arcade*.

アース 《米》a ground, 《英》an earth. ●テレビにアースを付ける *ground* 《米》 [*earth*《英》] a TV.

アーチ an arch; (アーチ道) an archway.

アーチェリー archery. ●アーチェリーの選手をする practice [do] *archery*. ●アーチェリーの選手 an archer.

アーティスト 〔芸術家〕an artist.

アーティチョーク 〔チョウセンアザミ〕〖植物〗an artichoke.

アート 〔芸術, 美術〕art. ●ポップアート pop *art*. ●モダンアート modern *art*.
●アート紙 art paper, coated paper. ●アートシアター an art house. ●アートディレクター an art director. ●アートフラワー 〔造花〕an artificial flower; 《和製語》an art flower.

アーバン 〔都会の〕urban.
●アーバンデザイン 〔都市設計〕urban design. ●アーバンライフ urban [city] life (↔rural [country] life).

アーミールック 〔迷彩服〕(a piece of) camouflaged /kǽməflɑ̀ːʒd/ clothes; 〖軍服〗army [military] clothes.

アーム 〔腕〕an arm.
●アームチェア 〔ひじかけいす〕(sit in) an armchair. ●アームレスト 〔ひじかけ〕an armrest. ●アームスリング 〔腕相撲〕arm wrestling. ●アームレット 〔腕飾り〕an armlet /ɑ́ːrmlət/.

アーメン 〔<ヘブライ語〕amen /ɑ́ːmén, éim-/.

アーモンド an almond.

アーリークロス 〔サッカー〕an early cross. (⇨クロス)
●ベッカム得意のアーリークロス a typical early cross from Beckham.

アール 〔面積の単位〕an are /éɑr/ (略 a.).

アールエッチ Rh (*rhesus* の略).
●Rh 因子 the Rh factor. ●Rh プラス Rh positive, Rh＋. ●Rh マイナス Rh negative, Rh−.

アールデコ 〔<フランス語〕art deco /ɑ́ːrt dékou/. (時に A- D-) ●アールデコ建築 *art deco* architecture.

アールヌーボー 〔<フランス語〕〖新芸術〗art nouveau /ɑ̀ːrt nuːvóu/.

＊あい 愛 (a) love (*for, of*); 〖情愛〗(an) affection 〔*for, toward*); 〔「恋情」の意では通例複数形で〕; 〖愛着〗an attachment (*to, for*).

> 使い分け love 最も意味の広い語で, 個人的愛情から宗教的愛情まで幅広く含意する.
> affection 人・物に対する主として私的で持続的な愛情.
> attachment 主に主義・事物などに対する強い愛着・執着, 時に非理性的な感情も含意する.

❶ 【〜(の愛)】●父[母]性愛 paternal [mater-

nal] *love*. ●盲目的な[深い; 真実の]愛 blind [deep; true] *love*. ●強い祖国愛 a great *love for [of]* one's country. ●子供を思う母の愛 a mother's *love* [*affection*] *for* her children; the *love* [*affection*] *of* a mother *for* her children.
②【愛が】▶太郎と花子の間に愛が芽ばえた *Love* grew between Taro and Hanako.
③【愛の】●愛の対象 the object of one's *love* [*affection*(*s*)]. ●愛のきずな the bonds of *affection*. ●愛の結晶 (説明的に) a child born to parents who love each other. ●愛のしるし a *love* token. ●愛のむちをふるう take a severe attitude toward 《him》 from love. (**!**「愛のむち」は loving severity). ●愛のない家庭 a *loveless* home. ●愛の手を差しのべる extend a *tender* [*loving*] hand 《*to* help him》.
④【愛に】●彼女の愛に報いる return [reciprocate, 《書》requite] her *love*. ▶彼は若い妻の愛におぼれている(=若い妻を溺愛(ﾃﾞｷｱｲ)している) He *loves* his young wife exceedingly./He *dotes on* his young wife.
⑤【愛を】●彼女に愛を告白する confess [declare] one's *love* to her. ●彼女の愛を勝ち取る win her *love* [*affection*(*s*)]. ●愛を込めて彼女の手を握る hold her hand *lovingly* [*affectionately*]. ▶彼は永遠の愛を誓った He swore eternal *love*.

あい 藍 〖色〗deep blue, (すみれ色系の青) indigo blue; 〖染料〗indigo. ●あい色の deep-blue; indigo-blue.
あいあいがさ 相合い傘 ●相合い傘で行く walk together under one umbrella; (傘をいっしょにさす) share an umbrella 《*with*》.
アイアン 〖ゴルフ〗an iron. ●アイアンショット an iron shot.
あいいく 愛育 ── 愛育する 動 bring up [《主に米》raise]《a child》with loving care.
あいいれない 相容れない (一致しない) incompatible 《*with*》; (共存できない) exclusive; (衝突する) conflicting. ▶資本主義と共産主義は相容れないものである Capitalism and communism are *incompatible with* each other./They are mutually *exclusive*. ▶彼らの利害関係は相容れなかった They had *conflicting* interests./(衝突した) Their interests *clashed*.
あいいん 愛飲 ── 愛飲する 動 drink 《sake》 habitually, always drink 《sake》.
●愛飲家[者] a habitual drinker 《*of*》.
あいうつ 相打ち,相撃ち,相討ち ── 相打ちする 動 strike [hit] each other at the same time.
アイエスオー 〖国際標準化機構〗ISO 《*International Organization for Standardization* の略》.
アイエスディーエヌ 〖統合デジタル通信網〗ISDN 《*Integrated Services Digital Network* の略》.
アイエスビーエヌ 〖国際標準図書番号〗ISBN 《*International Standard Book Number* の略》.
アイエムエフ 〖国際通貨基金〗the IMF 《the *International Monetary Fund* の略》.
アイエルオー 〖国際労働機関〗the ILO 《the *International Labour Organization* の略》.
あいえんか 愛煙家 a (cigarette) smoker.
あいえんきえん 合縁奇縁 a relationship determined by a strange quirk of fate.
アイオーシー 〖国際オリンピック委員会〗the IOC 《the *International Olympic Committee* の略》.
アイオワ 〖米国の州〗Iowa /áiəwə/ 《略 Ia. 郵便略 IA》.
あいか 哀歌 (悲歌) a sad song, a lament; (挽歌) an elegy.
あいかぎ 合い鍵 a duplicate key; 〖親鍵〗a master key, a passkey.

あいかた 合方 ❶〖歌舞伎でせりふに合わせて入れる三味線〗a samisen accompaniment to a kabuki recitative. ❷〖能の囃子方(ﾊﾔｼｶﾀ)〗an accompaniment to a No(h) chant.
あいかた 相方 〖漫才の相棒〗one's partner.
あいがも 合鴨 〖鳥〗an aigamo; (説明的に) a crossbreed between the wild duck and the domestic duck; 〖合鴨の肉〗duck (meat).
あいかわらず 相変わらず (これまでと同様) (as ...) as ever; (以前のように) (as ...) as before; (いつものように) as usual; (依然として) still; (いつも) always. ▶彼女は相変わらず若々しい She looks *as* young *as ever*./She *still* looks young. ▶彼は相変わらずだ(=全然変わっていない) He *hasn't changed at all*.
会話 「達夫はどんな様子だった」「まったく相変わらずだったよ」"How was Tatsuo looking?" "Just *the same as he always did*."
会話 「多少遅れると思う」「相変わらずだね」"I'm afraid I'm rather late." "*As ／ usual*." (**!** 皮肉っぽい口調で)
あいかん 哀感 a feeling of sadness, a sad feeling.
●哀感を込めて歌う sing *with pathos*.
あいかん 哀歓 ●人生の哀歓 the joys and sorrows of life.
あいがん 哀願 ●哀願するような目で見る give 《him》 a *pleading* [(訴えるような) an *appealing*] look. (⇒懇願)
あいがん 愛玩 ── 愛玩する 動 pet; make a pet of .... ●愛玩犬 a pet dog. ●愛玩動物 a pet.
あいぎ 合着,間着 a spring [an autumn] suit. (⇒合服)
あいきどう 合気道 *aikido*; (説明的に) a Japanese art of self-defense that takes advantage of the opponent's own movements.
あいきゃく 相客 (訪問先などの) a fellow guest; 〖ホテルなどの〗a fellow lodger, a roommate; 〖列車・船などの〗a fellow passenger. ●宿屋で見知らぬ人と相客になる share a room with a stranger at an inn.
アイキュー 〖知能指数〗IQ 《*intelligence quotient* の略》. (関連) EQ 感情指数)
あいきょう 愛嬌 图 charm; (やや書) amiability. (⇒愛想) ▶そいつは愛嬌だ That's just to please you.
●愛嬌をふりまく be (very) pleasant [(やや書) amiable] 《*to* everyone》.
── 愛嬌の[が]ある 形 〖魅力的な〗charming, engaging; 〖にぎやかで、人なつっこい〗friendly and cheerful, (やや書) amiable; 〖ユーモアのある〗humorous. ●愛嬌のある女の子[笑顔] a *charming* girl [smile]. ▶あの娘(ｺ)は目元に愛嬌がある The girl has *charming* [(かわいい) *cute*] eyes.
あいきょうしん 愛郷心 love for [of] one's home [hometown].
あいくち 匕首 (つばのない短刀) a dagger.
あいくち 合口 (話などがよく合うこと) congeniality. (⇒相性)
あいくるしい 愛くるしい (⇒愛らしい)
あいけん 愛犬 one's (pet) dog.
●愛犬家 a dog lover; a lover of dogs.
あいこ 相子 ●あいこになる (仕返しなどして同等である) be even 《*with*》; (貸し借りがない) be quits 《*with*》. ▶さあこれであいこだ Now, we are *even* [*quits*]./Now, I'm *even* [*quits*] *with* you.
あいこ 愛顧 patronage. ▶お客様のご愛顧を感謝いたします We would like to thank all of our customers for their *patronage*.
あいご 愛護 图 (保護) protection.

——愛護する 動 ●動物を愛護する（優しくする）be kind to animals;（害から守る）protect animals from harm.

あいこう 愛好 名 ●平和愛好国民 a peace-loving nation [people]. ●愛好家だ（⇨愛好家）
——愛好する 動 love, like.（⇨好き）

あいこうか 愛好家 a lover, a devotee;（スポーツ・有名人などの）a fan. ●音楽の愛好家を a music lover [ˣdevotée].（❗対象をせばめれば Wagner devotees のように devotee を用いることもできる） ●スポーツ愛好者を a lover [a devotee] of sport(s); a sports enthusiast [fan].

あいこうしゃ 愛好者（⇨愛好家）

あいこうしん 愛校心（have）school [college] spirit. ●愛校心をかき立てる whip up school spirit.

あいこく 愛国 love for [of] one's country. ●愛国者を a patriot /péɪtriət/. ●愛国心（⇨愛国心） ●彼は愛国の情に燃えている（＝熱烈に国を愛している）He loves his country passionately [deeply]./He is very patriotic.

あいこくしん 愛国心 patriotism; (a) patriótic spirit [sentiment]. ●国粋主義的愛国心 nationalism. ●狂信的愛国心 chauvinism. ●愛国心の強い青年 a patriotic young man [woman].

あいことなる 相異なる differ《from》. ●相異なる意見 different opinions.

あいことば 合い言葉（合図の言葉）a password;（標語）a slogan.

アイコン〘コンピュータ〙（click）an icon.

アイコンタクト（make）eye contact《with》.（参考 目と目の合図でお互いの意思疎通を図ること）

あいさい 愛妻 one's beloved /bɪlʌ́vɪd/ wife（複 wives）（❗one's devoted wife は「夫や子供に献身的な妻」の意）.
●愛妻家（献身的な）a devoted husband;（愛情を注ぐ）a loving husband.

あいさつ 挨拶 名 ❶〘言葉・敬礼による〙a greeting,《書》(a) salutation.〘話〙米英では "Hello." または "Hi."（主に米）と言ったり、握手・キス・軽い会釈などが普通で、おじぎ（bow）は日常的的ではない（⇨こんにちは） ●気軽にあいさつを交わす exchange friendly greetings（❗複数形に注意）; say hello to each other. ●「こんにちは」と言ったが彼女はあいさつを返さなかった "Hello," I said [I said hello], but she didn't return the [my, ˣher] greeting. ●何百人もの人が手を振って彼に別れのあいさつをした Hundreds of people waved him good-by. ●（子供に）ごあいさつは？ Where's your cap?

❷〘演説〙a speech,《やや書》an address. ●開会のあいさつを述べる give [《やや書》deliver] an opening speech [address]. ●彼女は卒業生にお別れのあいさつをした She gave [made,《やや書》delivered] a farewell speech to the graduates. ●主催者を代表して一言歓迎のごあいさつを申し上げます Allow me to say a word of welcome on behalf of the sponsor.

❸〘儀礼的な書状やその文句〙a greeting.（❗通例複数形で）●新年[時候]のあいさつ the New Year's [season's] greetings. ●あいさつ状 a greeting[❗s をつけるのは《英》] card. ●（あいさつ代わりに）as a token of one's meeting each other;（あいさつ代わりに）instead of saying hello.

——あいさつする 動 greet;（気軽に）say* hello《to》（⇨名❶）;（丁寧な言葉・しぐさなどで）《書・古》salute.
●彼はにこやかに客にあいさつした He greeted the guests with a smile. ●彼らは互いに帽子を上げていさつし合った They greeted [saluted] each other by raising their hats. ●彼女はだれにもあいさつしないで（＝さようならを言わないで）部屋を出た She left [got out of] the room without saying good-by to anybody. ●彼とは親しいわけではありません。あいさつする程度です I don't know him well. I just say hello.

あいし 哀史（悲話）a sad [a pathetic] story;（哀れな歴史）a tragic history. ●女工哀史 the sad story of (cotton) mill girls.

あいじ 愛児 one's dear [beloved /bɪlʌ́vɪd/] child（複 children）.

あいしゃ 愛車 one's car.（❗特に男性はこれを受ける代名詞として it の代わりに she を用いることで車に対する愛着を表す）

あいしゃせいしん 愛社精神 loyalty to one's company.

アイシャドー eye shadow. ●アイシャドーをつける[つけている] put on [wear] eye shadow.

あいしゅう 哀愁 sadness, sorrow;〘文学〙pathos.
●哀愁を感じる feel sorrow [sad]. ●哀愁を誘うドラの音 a gong that makes us feel sad. ●哀愁に満ちた（＝悲しげな）顔 a sorrowful face.

あいしょう 愛称 a nickname; a pet name.（⇨囲 あだ名）●「ボブ」は「ロバート」の愛称です "Bob" is a nickname [a pet name] for "Robert." ●「Old Eli」はエール大学の愛称です "Old Eli" is the nickname of [for] Yale University. ●彼の車の愛称は「スポーティ」だ His car's pet name is "Sporty."/His car is nicknamed "Sporty."

あいしょう 相性（引かれ合い）chemistry;（性格の適合性）compatibility. ●相性がよい be compatible; live well together. ●私は彼女とは相性がよくなかった I didn't get along [on] with her./There was no chemistry（＝good chemistry）between her and me./〘話〙I didn't hit it off with her.

あいしょう 愛唱 名 ●愛唱歌（⇨愛唱歌）.
——愛唱する 動 love to sing (a song).

あいしょう 愛誦 ——愛誦する 動 love to recite《a poem》.

あいじょう 愛情〘親子・自然・異性などへの愛〙(a) love《for, of》;〘温和で長く続く愛〙(an) affection《for》;〘愛着〙an attachment《to, for》.（⇨愛）
① 〘～の（愛）〙●子供に対する父親としての愛情 a father's love for his children. ●温かい[強い]愛情 warm [strong] affection.
② 〘愛情の～〙●愛情の深い人 a person of deep affection. ●愛情豊かな母 a loving [an affectionate] mother. ●愛情のこもった手紙 an affectionate letter. ●愛情のない結婚 a loveless marriage.
③ 〘愛情から〙●愛情からでなく金のために結婚する marry not for love but for money.
④ 〘愛情に〙●愛情に飢えた子供たちの世話をする look after love-starved children. ●彼女は愛情に満ちた家庭に育った She was brought up in a family (which was) filled with love.
⑤ 〘愛情を〙●愛情を込めて抱きしめる hug《her》with affection [affectionately, lovingly]. ●孤児たちに惜しみない愛情を注ぐ shower lots of affection on the orphans. ●彼は自分の息子に愛情を示したことは一度もなかった He has never shown his son any affection. ●彼は恋人に愛情を抱いていた He had a burning love for his girlfriend./He loved his girlfriend passionately. ●ほとんどの母親は自分の子供に愛情を感じるものだ Most mothers feel affection for [toward] their children. ●彼は父親に特に愛情を持っているわけではなかった He was not particularly attached to his father.

あいしょうか 愛唱歌 one's favorite song.

あいじん 愛人 〖男性が〗a lover; 〖女性が〗a love; (めかけ) a mistress. ▶「恋人」の意味では one's boyfriend, one's girlfriend が普通

アイス 〖氷〗ice; 〖アイスコーヒー〗(an) iced coffee (⇨アイスクリーム); 〖アイスキャンデー〗(⇨アイスキャンデー).

あいず 合図 [名] (手・音・頭などによる) a sign; (身ぶり・音・信号などによる) a signal; 〖手招きやうなずきなどして〗beckon. ▶ピストルの音が競走のスタートの合図です The sound of the pistol is the *signal for* the start of the race [*to* start *the* race].
—**合図する** [動] signal; sign; 〖身ぶりで〗motion; 〖手招きやうなずきなどして〗beckon. ▶彼は始めるよう合図した He *signaled* [*signed*] (*for* [*to*]) us *to* start./ He gave us a *sign* [a *signal*] *to* start./He *motioned* (*to*) us *to* start. ▶彼は準備ができたと私に合図した He *signaled* [*signed*] to me that he was ready. ▶彼らは私にすぐについて来るように合図した They *beckoned* me *to* follow quickly. ▶私は彼にあっちに行くように合図した I *motioned* [*手を振って*] *waved*] him (*to get*) away.

アイスアリーナ an ice《skating, hockey》arena.

アイスキャンデー 《米・商標》a Popsicle, 《英》an ice lolly, a lollipop; 〖和製語〗ice candy.

アイスクリーム (an) ice cream (❗(1) 個々の商品は [C]. (2) (an) ice は, 今では《英》ではシャーベット (sorbet, water ice) をさし,「アイスクリーム」の意味では《古》); (コーンつきの) an ice cream cone. (❗一すくいのアイスクリームは a *scoop* of ice cream という. 二すくいを double, 三すくいを triple ともいう)
[会話]「アイスクリームを(コーンに)二盛りください」「どれになさいますか」「バニラと, もう一つはチョコレートで」"Can I have one double *cone*?" (❗Two scoops of ice cream, please. ともいう) "What flavor(s) would you like?" "Vanilla and chocolate, please." (❗正確には "One scoop of vanilla and another of chocolate, please.")

アイスコーヒー iced coffee. (❗ice coffee ともいう)

アイスショー 〖アイススケートによるショー〗an ice show.

アイススケート ice skating. ▶アイススケートをする ice-skate. ▶アイススケート靴 (a pair of) (ice) skates.

アイスダンス ice dance, ice dancing.

アイスティー ice(d) tea 《*with* lemon》.

アイスバーン 〖<ドイツ語〗(スキー場) an icy slope; (道路) an icy street.

アイスピック an ice pick.

アイスペール an ice bucket.

アイスボックス 〖氷を使う冷蔵庫〗an icebox.

アイスホッケー ice hockey, 《米》hockey. (❗(1) 《英》では単に hockey といえば〖陸上の〗ホッケー (field hockey) をさす (⇨ホッケー). (2) 使用する円盤は a puck で, 選手は a puckster ともいう)

アイスランド 〖国名〗Iceland; (公式名) the Republic of Iceland. (首都 Reykjavik) ▶アイスランド人 an Icelander. ▶アイスランド語 Icelándic. ▶アイスランド(人[語])の Icelandic.

アイスリンク 〖スケート場〗an ice [a skating] rink. (⇨スケート)

あいする 愛する love; 〖親愛の情を持つ〗have~ [feel*] affection 《*for*》. (⇨好き) ▶私の愛する(=かわいい)子供たち my *dear* [*beloved*] children. ▶愛すべき男 a *lovable* man. ▶愛していると言う declare one's *love*.

①【(人)を愛する】 ▶おまえを愛する父より Your *loving* father. (❗手紙の結び) ▶彼は彼女を心から愛している He *loves* her dearly [very much]. ▶very much を love の前に置いて, ×He very much loves her. とはいえない)/He *is* very much *in* love

with her. (❗love は状態を表す動詞なので, 通例進行形にはしない. ただし一時の感情を強調している場合は可) ▶彼女は母親をとても愛している She *has* [*feels*] (a) great *affection for* her mother.

②【(物・事)を愛する】 ▶彼は心からジャズを愛している He loves jazz dearly [very much].

あいせき 哀惜 grief [sorrow] 《*over* his death》. ▶ご母堂様のご逝去の報に接し哀惜の念に堪えません The sad news of your mother's death has filled me with deepest *grief*.

あいせき 相席 —**相席する** [動] share a table 《*with*》. ▶相席してもいいですか May I *share this table with* you?

アイゼン 〖<ドイツ語〗a crampon, a climbing iron. (❗いずれも通例複数形で)

あいそ(う) 愛想 ●**愛想のない** ▶彼に愛想のない(=そっけない)返事をする give him a *curt* [a *blunt*] reply.
●**愛想のよい** (人なつっこい) friendly; (にぎやかで人なつっこい) (やや書) amiable /éimiəbl/; (感じのよい) pleasant; (つき合いがよい) sociable. ▶愛想のよい店員 a *friendly* [a *pleasant*] clerk. ▶彼に愛想よく話しかける speak to him *pleasantly* [*amiably*].
●**愛想よくする** make oneself pleasant [agreeable] 《*to* him》; (急に愛想よくなる) 〖話〗turn [switch] on the charm. ▶彼はだれにも愛想がいい He is *friendly* [*amiable, sociable*] to everyone. ▶彼女は愛想よく客を迎えた She gave a *friendly* [温かい] a *warm*] welcome to her guests./She welcomed her guests *pleasantly* [*warmly*]. (❗friendly ともいうが副詞形はまれ)
●**愛想笑い** ▶愛想笑いする give a *fake* smile.
●**愛想を言う** ▶彼に愛想を言う(=お世辞を言う) *flatter* him.
●**愛想を尽かす** ▶彼には本当に愛想が尽きた(=うんざりした) I *am* absolutely [*completely*] *disgusted* [〖話〗*fed up*] *with* him. (❗very disgusted とはあまりいわない) ▶長居しすぎて愛想を尽かされる(=飽きられたく)ない I don't want to *wear out* my *welcome*. ▶彼はあまりにもしつこかったので彼女に愛想を尽かされた He was *rejected* by his girlfriend because he was too persistent.

あいぞう 愛憎 love and hate [hatred]. ▶愛憎の入りまじった感情〖*have*〗mixed feelings of *love and hate* [*hatred*]. (❗特に《米》では hate が普通)

あいぞう 愛蔵 ▶愛蔵の絵画のコレクション one's collection of *cherished* paintings.
—**愛蔵する** [動] ▶骨董品を愛蔵する *cherish* [*treasure*] one's antiques.

アイソトープ 〖同位元素〗an isotope.

あいた 空いた, 開いた ⇨空く, 開く.

あいだ 間 ❶ [期間] (...の間) for ...; during ...; (...している間) while (+節); (...以内に) within ...; (二つの時点の間) between ....

[解説] for の次には a year, three days など「数詞＋単位時間」が来て, その間ずっと動作や状態が継続していることを示す. during の次には the vacation, one's life などの特定の期間を示す名詞が来て, その期間中の継続または時点を示す.

▶3 年の間 *for* [×during] three years. (❗「その 3 年間」なら *during* [×for] the three years) ▶私はそこに 1 週間の間滞在した I stayed there (*for*) a week. (❗for は継続を表す動詞の後ではしばしば省略される. ただし継続性のない動詞の否定文 (⇨[次例]) や, 文頭位では通例省略されない) ▶彼には 20 年もの間会っていない I haven't seen him *in* (《主に英》*for*) twenty years. (❗in は否定文, 最上級や first を含む文で用いられる) ▶留守の間にスミスさんという方がお昼

えになりました A Mr. Smith called *while* you were out./A Mr. Smith called *during* [*in*] your absence. (❗*while* を用いた前の方が口語的である) ▶ 3 日の間に(= 3 日以内)にその仕事をし終えなさい Finish the work *within* three days. ▶ 食事と食事の間にお菓子を食べすぎてはいけない Don't eat too much cake *between* meals [each meal and the next, ×each meal]. ▶ 図書館は 8 月 1 日から 10 日までの間休館です. その間私の家で勉強したらいい The library is closed *from* August 1 *to* [*until*,《米》*through*] 10. Meanwhile [*In the meantime*], you can study at my place. ▶ 生きている間は(=限り)あなたのご親切を決して忘れません As long as I live, I shall never forget your kindness.

【…(の)間ずっと】(初めから終わりまで) through …, throughout …, all through … (❗後の二つは through の強意形); (終わりまで) over …; (ある期間中) all the time. ▶ 彼は夏の間ずっとその店で働いた He worked at the store *through* [*throughout*, *all through*] the summer./He worked at the store *during* the whole summer. (❗whole がない場合「夏のある時期に」の意にもとられる)/He worked at the store *over* the summer. ▶ 私が話している間彼はずっとガムをかんでいた He was chewing gum *all the time* I was talking. (❗この all the time は接続詞的)

❷【間隔】(時間的・空間的) an interval; (空間的) space; (距離)(…にわたって) for …; (位置, 空間)(2 者の間で) between …; (集合体の中で) among …. ▶ 5 フィート間隔で(=ずつ間をおいて)立つ stand *at intervals* of five feet. ▶ 間に庭のある 2 軒の家 two houses with a yard *between* them [*in between*]. (❗後の between は副詞) ▶ 木々の間を駆け回る run around *among* [×in] trees. ▶ その村を通り過ぎると数百マイルの間砂漠が続きます After you pass the village, you'll find a desert spreading *for* hundreds of miles. ▶ 車間距離=前方の車との間)を十分に取っておきなさい Keep enough space *between* you and the car ahead. ▶ 太陽が雲の間から突然現れた The sun broke [All of a sudden the sun appeared] *through* the clouds.

❸【途中, 中間】 on the [one's] way; (中途に) halfway (*between*). ▶ 駅から家に帰るまでの間で(=途中) *on the* [*one's*] *way home from the station*. ▶ 東京までの間ずっと立ち通しでした I stood *all the way* to Tokyo. ▶ 地下鉄の梅田と難波の間で事故があったようです I hear there was a subway accident *halfway* [《どこか》*somewhere*] *between* Umeda and Namba.

❹【関係, 間柄】(2者の間で) between …; (3者以上の間で) among …. (❗3 者以上についても, あるものと周囲のものとの関係を個別的に表す場合は between を用いる) ● 間に立つ(=仲介する) act as go-between. (❗stand between は「間に立ってじゃまをする」の意) ● お金を兄弟の[兄と弟と私の]間で分ける divide the money *among* the brothers [*between* my older brother, my younger brother and me]. ● 両者の間を調停する mediate *between* the two parties. ▶ 彼は学生の間でとても人気がある He is very popular *with* [×*among*, ×*to*] his students. (⇨人気) ▶ 議長は委員の中[中]から選ばれる The chair is chosen *from* (*among*) the members. (❗among のない方が普通) ▶ 彼ら 2 人の間は(=お互いに)うまくいっていない They don't get along [on] with *each other*./They are on bad terms with *each other*.

あいたいする 相対する (向かい合う) face each other; (向かい合って立つ) stand* face to face 《*with*》. ● 相対する(=対立する)二つの意見 two *opposing* [*conflicting*] opinions.

あいだがら 間柄 [[血族などの]] (a) relationship, (a) relation (⇨交際上の) terms. ▶ 私は彼とは親しい間柄だ I am *on* friendly [good] *terms with* him. (❗(1) しばしば仲違いしたあとの関係に用いる. (2) 単に話をする程度であれば *speaking* terms) ▶ 彼らは師弟の間柄だ They are teacher and student. (❗冠詞はつけない)

会話 「彼とはどういう間柄ですか」「兄弟(の間柄)です」 "What's your *relationship* [What *relation* are you] *to* him?" "We are brothers."

あいたずさえる 相携える (協力する) collaborate, work together 《*with*》. ● 友人と相携えて企画を進める *collaborate with* a friend on the project.

アイダホ 〖米国の州〗Idaho /áidəhòu/《略 Id(a). 郵便略 ID》.

あいちゃく 愛着 an attachment 《*to, for*》; 〖愛情〗(a) love 《*for, of*》. ● 海への愛着 one's *love for* the sea. ● 特別な愛着を覚える feel a special *attachment* 《*for, to*》. ▶ 彼はこの町に強い愛着を持っている He has a great [a strong] *attachment to* this town./He is greatly [strongly] *attached to* this town.

あいちょう 哀調 ● 哀調を帯びた歌 a plaintive [死を悲しむ] a *mournful*] song. ● 哀調を帯びた笛の音(ね)に聞き入る listen to the *plaintive* [*mournful*] tone of the flute.

あいちょう 愛鳥 ● 愛鳥家 a bird lover [fancier]. ● 愛鳥週間 Bird Week.

あいつ 〖あの男〗that man 〖《話》guy〗; (彼) he; 〖あの女〗that woman; (彼女) she. ● あいつら (彼ら) they; (あの人たち) those people [《米話》guys] (❗複数形 guys は男女混合または女性のみのグループにも用いるが, この呼び分けを嫌う女性もいる).

あいついで 相次いで (次々と) one after another, one after the other (❗前の方は三つ以上の不特定のもの, 後の方は通例二つ以上の特定数のものについて用いる); (続けて) in (quick) succession. ▶ 彼らは相次いでやって来た They came *one after another*.

あいつぐ 相次ぐ ● 相次ぐ 3 件の事故 three successive accidents. (⇨相次いで)

あいづち 相づち ● 相づちを打つ(うなずく) nod 《*to, at*》; (同意する) chime in [chime in には「人の話に割り込む」の意もあるので注意]. ▶ 「なるほど」と私は相づちを打った "I see," I chimed in.

あいて 相手 ❶ 〖いっしょに物事をする人〗company (❗1 人または集合的に); a companion. ▶ 彼らはいっしょにいるにはおもしろい[おもしろくない]相手です They're good [poor, ×bad] *company*. (❗bad company は「つきあったら困る相手」「悪友」の意)/I like [don't like] their *company*. (❗前の company は companions に相当する集合名詞, 後の company は companionship と同じで, いっしょにいる状態を表す抽象名詞) ▶ それは相手次第だ It depends on who the opponent [companion, partner] is.

会話「一杯やるときは相手がほしいな」「じゃ私がお相手をしましょう」"When I have a drink, I want *company*." "Well, I'll keep you *company*, then."

❷ 〖行為の対象となる人〗(❗特定の訳語はなく, 目的語(の関係)で表す) ● いい話[勉強の競争]相手 a good *person* [*friend*] to talk to [study competitively with]. ● 相談相手 a *person* to consult. ● 遊び相手[仲間の](やや書) a playmate, a playfellow. ▶ 彼の結婚相手のアン Ann, who [《書》whom] he is going to get married to. ● 観光客相手に商売をする do business *among* tourists; (店を経営する) run a store *for* tourists. ▶彼はアメリカ人旅行者を相手にいつも自分の英語の練習をしている He is always practicing his English *with* [*on*] the American tourists. (❗(1) practice は「定期的に練習する」の意. (2) は状況に戸惑っている場合に用いる) ▶でも彼の娘さんには誰か相手(=好きな人)がいるんじゃないですか I guess his daughter has someone, who she's in love with. (❗特定の「相手」であることを強調するときは someone, who とする. 一般的には who を省略して someone she's in love with となる)

DISCOURSE
明快な言葉で書けば，相手はあなたが言いたいことを理解してくれるだろう You should write in a clear language *so that* readers may understand what you mean. (❗so that A may ... (A が…できるように)は因果関係を述べるときに用いるディスコースマーカー)

❸ [競技相手] an opponent (❗最も一般的. チームをさす場合は複数形で); a competitor; (対抗者) a rival (❗日本語の「ライバル」と異なり，強い敵対意識を含む); (自分より勝るとも劣らない好敵手) a match (*for*); (同じ立場 [ポジション] の人) a counterpart. ●彼の試合の対戦相手 his *opponent*(*s*) [*competitor*(*s*)] in the game. ●相手ディフェンス [サッカー] the opponent defence. ●彼はかつて私と同じ [地位] を張り合った相手 At one time, he was my *rival* for the same position. ▶水泳ではあいつはぼくの相手になんかならない He is no *match for me in* swimming. (❗(1) not a match より強意的. (2)「相手にとって不足はない」なら He is a good *match* for me.) ▶相手は5人だった It was five *against* me. ▶サー・アレックス・ファーガソンは相手の監督を気遣う発言をした Sir Alex Ferguson expressed his sympathy to his *counterpart*.

❹ [競技などでペアを組む相手] a partner. ●ダンスの相手 a dancing *partner*. ●テニスのダブルスで組む相手(=味方) a tennis *partner* (*playing against* the other pair). ●その少年は踊りの相手がいなかった The boy had no *partner* to dance with.

❺ [相手方の当事者] the other person [side, end] (❗小説で2人物の動きを描写するときによく用いられる); (訴訟・契約・婚姻などの)《書》the other party. ●お互いが相手の求めるものを持っていた Each of them had what *the other* wanted. ●相手の方がお出になりました《交換手の言葉》Here's *your party*. ▶電話の相手はしばらく何も言わなかった There was a short silence *on the other end* (of the line).

*アイデア [思いつき] an idea. (⇨考え❷) ●アイデアを思いつく hit on [upon] an *idea*. ▶彼はいいアイデアをよく出してくれる He often comes up with a good *idea* [*suggestion*].
●アイデア商品 novelties. ●アイデアマン a man of ideas; an idea [《英》an ideas] man.

アイディア (⇨アイデア)
アイティー [情報(通信)技術] IT (*information technology* の略).
●IT 革命 the IT revolution. ●IT 産業 the IT industry.
アイディーカード [身分証明書] an ID [an identification] card.
あいでどる 相手どる ●彼を相手どって訴訟を起こす bring an action *against* him. ●彼を相手どって損害賠償の訴えを起こす sue him for damages.
アイデンティティー [独自性，自己認識] (an) identity. ●自己のアイデンティティーを確認する ascertain one's *identity*.

あいとう 哀悼 [悔やみ]《やや書》condolence (❗「哀悼の言葉」の意では複数形で); (悲しみ)《やや書》sorrow. ●哀悼の手紙 a letter of *condolence*. ●哀悼の辞を述べる make a funeral speech. (⇨弔辞) ●彼の亡き妻に哀悼の意を捧げる mourn for his (deceased [dead]) wife. (❗deceased の方が遠回しで一般的) ●哀悼の意を表して黒の腕章をつけている wear a black armband as a sign of *mourning*.

あいどく 愛読 ── 愛読する 動 like reading; enjoy reading; (雑誌・新聞を) read* regularly; (予約購読する) subscribe (*to*). ▶私は『戦争と平和』を愛読している I *like* [*am fond of*] *reading War and Peace*. (❗彼の方が口語的でかつ強意的) ▶彼の小説は若者に人気がある(=愛読されている) His novels *are popular* among [with] young people.
●愛読者 an avid reader (of comic books); an admirer (*of* Keats); (本の虫というぐらいの読書好きな人) a bookworm; (雑誌などの予約購読者) a subscriber (*to The Times*) (❗a regular reader (*of The Times*) ともいう). ●愛読書 one's favorite book.

あいともなう 相伴う ❶ [連れ立つ] go [come] 《*with*》; (連れて行く [来る]) take [bring] 《him *to*》.
❷ [一緒に現れる] 名実相伴う (⇨名実 [成句])
アイドリング ●車のエンジンをアイドリングしたままにしておく leave the car engine *idling*.
●アイドリングストップ [停車時エンジン停止] (説明的に) the action of turning off an engine of a car while it is not moving; 《和製語》idling stop.
アイドル an idol. ●テレビのアイドル a TV *idol*. ▶彼女はティーンエイジャー[十代]のアイドルだ She is the *idol* of teenagers [a teenage *idol*].
●アイドル歌手 a pop idol; a singing idol.
アイドルタイム [遊休時間]《経営》idle time.
あいなめ [魚介] a (fat) greenling (魚 〜, 〜s). (❗その肉は Ⓤ)
*あいにく (不運にも) unfortunately; unluckily. (❗ともに文修飾副詞) ●あいにく明日は行けません *Unfortunately*, I won't be able to come tomorrow. ▶それを買いたいと思ったが，あいにくお金の持ち合わせがなかった I wanted to buy it, but *unfortunately* [*it was unfortunate* (*that*); (残念だった) *it was a pity* (*that*)] I didn't have any money on [with] me. (❗お金などの小物には on が普通) ●あいにく(=残念ですが)社長は留守です I'm sorry. Our boss is out./Our boss is out, *I'm afraid*. (❗I'm afraid は相手に都合の悪いことなどを切り出すときに用いる. 文頭に置いて I'm afraid our boss is out. ともいえる) ●あいにく(=…とは期待に反して)天気は悪かった *Contrary* to our expectations, the weather was bad. ●あいにくの大雨ですが，お出かけになりますか Will you go out *in spite of* the heavy rain? ▶それはあいにくですね That's too bad.
会話「ごいっしょにいかがですか」「そうしたいんですけど，あいにくだめなんです」"Will you join us?" "I'd like to, but *I'm afraid* I can't." (❗注意)
アイヌ an Ainu,《集合的》the Ainu(s). ●アイヌ語 Ainu. ●アイヌ(語)の Ainu.
『アイネ・クライネ・ナハト・ムジーク』 [＜ドイツ語] *A Little Night Music*. [参考] モーツァルト作曲のセレナーデ)
あいのり 相乗り 图 ●夫は近所の人と相乗り方式でマイカー通勤している My husband *carpools* to work with our neighbors. ●自家用車の輪番相乗り方式 car pool, そのグループは a car pool)
── 相乗りする 動 ●自転車に相乗りする(=いっしょに乗る) ride on a bicycle together. (❗「バイクに相乗り

る」は ride pillion. pillion (seat) は「(バイクの)後部座席」) ▶駅までタクシーに相乗りした We *shared a taxi to the station*.

アイバンク [角膜銀行] an eye bank. ▶アイバンクに登録する register at an *eye bank*.

あいはんする 相反する 動 [一致しない] disagree 《with》; [対立し争う] conflict 《with》; [背く] run* counter 《to》. ▶相反する感情 conflicting [(反対の) contrary] emotions. ▶君の報告は彼の言っていることと相反する Your reports *disagree with* what he says. ▶彼の利害は私の利害と相反する His interests *conflict with* [*run counter to*] mine.

アイピー [インターネット通信規格] IP 《Internet Protocol の略》.
• IP 電話 an IP phone.

アイビーリーグ the Ivy League. 《参考 米国北東部にある8つの名門大学の一群》

あいびき 合い挽き (説明的に) a mixture of ground beef and ground pork.

あいぶ 愛撫 名 a caress /kərés/; [ペッティング] petting. —— **愛撫する 動** [手で継続してやさしくなでる] fondle; [手で軽くやさしくなでる・キスする] caress; [ペッティングする] pet.

あいふく 合服, 間服 (スーツ) a spring [an autumn] suit; (衣服) spring [autumn] clothes.

あいふだ 合い札 (預り証) a check; (割り符) a tally. ▶荷物の合い札 (米) a baggage *check*, (英) a luggage *ticket*.

アイブロー [まゆ] an eyebrow /áibràu/; [鉛筆型のまゆ墨] an eyebrow pencil.

あいべや 相部屋 ▶彼と相部屋はいやだ(=部屋を共用したくない) I don't like *sharing* [*to share*] *a room with* him.

あいぼ 愛慕 名 love; [敬慕] adoration.
—— **愛慕する 動** ▶姉を愛慕する love [adore] one's older [(英) elder] sister.

あいぼう 相棒 (仕事などの) an associate, a partner; (仲間) a mate. (⇨友達) ▶商売の相棒 one's business *associate*.

あいぼし 相星 [相手と勝敗の数が同じであること] (説明的に) 《have》 the same number of wins and losses with one's opponent.

アイボリー [象牙] ivory. ▶アイボリー色の ivory-colored. ▶アイボリーホワイト *ivory* white.

あいま 合間 (間隔) an interval; (休止) a pause. ▶仕事の合間に (暇な時に) in one's spare [free] time; (休憩時間に) during recess. ▶話の合間に(=小休止に) during a *pause* in the conversation. ▶合間合間に(=ひまひまに) at *odd moments* [*times*]. ▶ショーの合間に彼女はうたた寝をした She napped *between* the shows.

*あいまい 曖昧 —— 曖昧な 形** [二つ以上の意味にとれる] ambiguous; [はっきりしない] unclear; [意味が不明瞭(めいりょう)で理解しにくい] obscure; [意味が漠然とした] vague; [言質を与えない] noncommittal; [回避的な] evasive; [不確実な] uncertain. ▶あいまいな(=どっちつかずの)返事をする make an *ambiguous* [(不明確な) a *vague*, (はっきりした意見を示さない) a *noncommittal*, (逃げ口上の) an *evasive*] answer. ▶あいまいな態度をとる take an *uncertain* attitude. ▶この論文にはあいまいな点が多い There are a lot of *ambiguities* in this paper [thesis]. (! paper は一般的な論文, thesis は学位論文) ▶彼の説明はあいまいで分かりにくかった His explanation was *ambiguous* [*obscure, not clear* (enough to understand)].
• 曖昧模糊(も) 曖昧模糊とした言い方 a *vague* expression.

—— **曖昧さ 名** (an) ambiguity; (an) obscurity; vagueness; uncertainty.

あいまって 相俟って ▶彼の語学力と商売の腕が相まって(=いっしょになって)その計画は成功した His language ability and his business skills *together* made [結合して] *combined to make*] the project a success.

あいみたがい 相身互い ▶失業しているときは相身互いだ(=助け合うべきだ) When we are out of work, we *should help each other*.

アイメイト [盲導犬] 《米》 a seeing eye dog, 《英》 a guide dog; [和製語] an eye mate.

あいよう 愛用 名 ▶彼の愛用のパイプ his *favorite* pipe.
—— **愛用する 動** (常用する) use ... habitually [regularly]. ▶友人の安田はいまだにカメラは例のニコンを愛用している My friend Yasuda still *loves using* the Nikon camera.

あいよく 愛欲 (欲情) sexual desire; (激しい肉欲) lust. ▶愛欲に駆られて to satisfy one's *sexual desire* [one's *lust*]; out of *lust*.

アイライン eyeliner; [和製語] eyeline. (! 鉛筆状の化粧品は 可) ▶アイラインを引く put on *eyeliner*.

あいらしい 愛らしい [愛くるしい] lovable; [かわいくて美しい] pretty; [小さくて, 幼くて] cute; [すてきな] lovely. ▶愛らしい少女 a *lovely* girl. ▶愛らしい目をしている have *lovely* [*charming*] eyes.

アイリス [植物] an iris /áiəris/.

アイルランド [国名] Ireland /áiərland/; [首都 Dublin] ▶アイルランド人 (特に男) an Irishman; (女) an Irishwoman; [集合的に] Irish people, the Irish. ▶アイルランド語 Irish. ▶アイルランド(人[語])の Irish.

あいろ 隘路 [狭い道] a narrow path; [障害] a bottleneck. ▶隘路を切り開く break [解決する] 《書》 resolve] a *bottleneck*.

アイロニー [皮肉, 反語] irony.

アイロン an iron /áiərn/. ▶アイロン台 an ironing-board. ▶アイロン不要の wash-and-wear 《shirts》. ▶アイロンをかけていない unpressed 《shirts》. ▶アイロンをかける iron [press] 《a shirt》; do the ironing 《of a shirt》. ▶シャツにアイロンをかけてしわをとる *iron out* the wrinkles *in* a shirt. ▶このズボンはアイロンのかかりがよい These pants *iron* easily [*well*]. ▶彼のワイシャツはきちんとアイロンがかかっていた His shirt *was* properly *ironed*.

あいわ 哀話 (悲話) a sad [a pathetic] story [tale].

アインシュタイン [ドイツ生まれの米国の物理学者] Einstein /áinstain/ 《Albert ～》.

あう 会う, 遭う

〔WORD CHOICE〕 **会う**
see 主に特定の時間(帯)に会うことを表す. ▶後で[明日]会いましょう I'll *see* you later [tomorrow].
meet 偶然の遭遇や, 予約された面会を表す. 主に特定の場所で会い, いくらか会話を交わすことを含意する. ▶ジョンとバス停で会い, 少し話をした I *met* John at the bus stop and talked a little with him.

頻度チャート

see ████████████████████████
meet ██████████
     20   40   60   80 100 (%)

❶ [初対面で知り合う] meet*. ▶お会いできてうれしく思います (紹介の後で) (It's) nice [(I'm) pleased] to

meet you.(❗2度目からは通例 meet ではなく see を用いる) ▶失礼ですが以前お会いしていませんか Excuse me. *Haven't* we *met* before [Don't I know you]?
会話「お会いできてうれしゅうございました」「こちらこそ。またお会いしたいのです」(別れ際に) "(It's) [It's been] ＼nice ／*meeting* you./(It's) nice to *have met* you." "Same here. I'm looking forward to *seeing* you again."
❷【出会う, 面会する】meet*; see*;《公式に》《主に米》meet with.... ▶バスで彼に会った I *saw* [met] him on a bus. ▶see では「私」はバスに乗っていたとは限らず, 単に「バスの中の彼を見かけた」の意にもなる) ▶あす友達と東京駅で会う予定だ I'm *seeing* [*meeting*] a friend at Tokyo Station tomorrow. ▶(1) この進行形はすでに取り決めた予定を表す. (2) meeting では「出迎えに行く」ともとれる) ▶私はこのごろよく〔時々〕彼に会う〔話〕I *see* a lot [something] of him these days. (「あまり〔全然〕会わない」は〔話〕I *don't see* much [I *see* nothing] of him.「長い間会っていない」は I *haven't seen* him for a long time.) ▶きのう偶然通りで昔の友達に会った Yesterday I *happened to meet* [see] an old friend on the street. (「偶然に会う」の意には come [run] across..., 〔話〕run [bump] into ... なども用いられる) ▶彼女があなたに会いたいと言っている(=面会を求めている) She's *asking for* you. ▶元気かい. 会いたいなあ How are you? I really *miss* you. (「私は〔いなくて寂しく思う〕」→)▶ねえ, こういう人がいるんだけど会うだけでも会ってみない？ I know someone (who) you might be interested in (meeting). Wouldn't you like to *meet* him just once? (❗(1)「会うだけでも」は「(とりあえず)一度だけでも」と考え, just once と訳す. (2) meeting を入れると一般的に商売や友人などして相手となり, 省略するとロマンチックな意味での相手となる)
会話「美津子さん, こんにちは」「健二さん, ここであなたに会うなんて思いがけないわ」"Hello, Mitsuko." "Fancy *meeting* you here, Kenji!"
❸【会合する】meet*; (寄り集まる)《やや話》get* together (❗)▶クラブのメンバーは毎月１度会います The club members *meet* (*together*) [*get together*] once a month. ▶どこで会いましょうか Where shall I《主に米》should; can} we *meet* [*get together*, ×see]? (《米》で shall を用いるのは堅い言い方)
❹【経験する】have*; (困難・反対などに)《やや書》meet* with..., 《書》encounter. ▶乗っ取られた飛行機で恐ろしい目にあう have a terrible experience on the hijacked plane. ▶彼はきのう交通事故にあった He *had* [met with, (巻き込まれ) was *involved in*] a car accident yesterday. ▶その提案は強硬な反対にあった The proposal *met with* a strong objection. ▶私は交通渋滞に巻き込まれた(=あった) I *was caught* [*was stuck*] *in* a traffic jam. (❗この場合 with の代わりに got が用いられることがある) ▶駅の近くでにわか雨にあった I *was caught in* [We *had*, ×I *had*] a shower near the station.
● 会うは別れの始め We never meet without a parting.

:**あう 合う** ❶【大きさ・型がぴったり合う】fit (-tt-). ▶もうこの服は合わない. 太ってきた This dress doesn't *fit* me any more. I'm getting fat. ▶君はもうすぐ大きくなってこのスーツが合うようになるだろう You'll soon grow into this suit. ▶マスターキーは建物の全部のドアに合う The master key *is good* [*works*] *for* all the doors in the building.
会話「あなた, そのズボン合う？」「ぴったりだ」"How do the pants《米》[trousers《英》] *fit*, darling?" "They *fit* just fine." (❗応答文は They're a good *fit*. ともいえる)
❷【...と調和する】go* (well*) with...; (色・柄が似ていて) match. ▶この帽子はあなたの服と合わない This hat doesn't *go* (*well*) *with* [*match, harmonize with*] your dress. (⇨似合う) ▶赤ワインは肉と合う Red wine *goes well with* meat. (❗match は食べ物にはあまり用いられない)
❸【...に適する】suit; (ふさわしい) be suitable (*for*); fit. ▶その赤いスカーフは彼女に合っている The red scarf *suits* her [*looks good on* her]. ▶この日本酒がお口に(=好みに)合うとよいのですが I hope this sake will *suit* [be *to*] your taste./(気に入る) I hope you (will) *like* this sake. ▶それはよかったね. きっとそちらの気候はあなたの体に合っているのよ That's great. The climate there must *suit* you [*suit* your health, *agree with* you, ×*agree with* your health]. (❗「食べ物」が主語の場合は agree with は合わないか否定文・疑問文で用いられる) ▶彼女のドレスはその場には合わなかった Her dress didn't *fit* [was not *appropriate for*] the occasion. ▶彼の思想は今の世の中には合わない His ideas *are not in* [*are out of*] *tune with* the modern world.
❹【一致する】agree《*with*＋人・意見など, *on*＋事》; (呼応して) correspond《*with, to*》. (⇨一致する) ▶この点で彼は彼女と意見が合った He *agreed with* [×*to*] her (opinion) on that point. ▶君の話は彼の話と合わない Your story doesn't *agree with* [*match, correspond with*] his./Your story *disagrees with* his. ▶その男は人相書きに合っている The man *corresponds to* [*answers* (*to*)] the description. ▶彼の言ったことは事実と合っている What he said *is true to* the fact. ▶チーム全員の息がぴったり合っている The whole team plays *in* perfect *harmony*.
❺【正しい】(正確である) be correct (↔incorrect); (正当である) be right (↔wrong). ●正しい〔類語〕● 合っている答えを出す give a *correct* [a *right*] answer. ▶道が合っているかどうか自信がなかった I wasn't sure I'd taken the *right* [×*correct*] street. ▶君の時計は合っているか *Is* your watch *right* [*correct*]?/Do you have the *right* [*correct*] time? ▶君の計算は合っている Your calculation *is correct* [×*right*]. (❗「数値の正しさ」には correct を用いる)

アウェー ● アウェーで【相手チームのグラウンドで】away.
● ホームアンドアウェー home-and-away.
● アウェーゲーム an away game. 《米》ロードゲーム.

アウター(ウェア)【外衣】outerwear.

アウト an out; 〔ゴルフ〕the front nine 〔参考〕前半の９ホール. ● ノーアウトで make no *out*. ● 走者をアウト [フォースアウト] にする get [force] a runner *out*. ● ツーアウトからのヒットで得点する score on a two-*out* single. ● ツーアウト満塁だ There are two *out*(*s*) and the bases are loaded. (⇨満塁) ● ランナーはけん制球でアウトになった The runner *was* (*put*) *out* on a pickoff play. ● 彼はセカンドゴロ[フライ; ライナー]を打ってアウトになった He grounded [flied; lined] *out* to second. ● 走者はタッチアウトになった The runner was tagged *out* [*out* on a tag].

アウトウェア 【外衣】outerwear, (和製語) out wear. (⇨ アウター(ウェア))

アウトオブバウンズ 【(ボール・選手が)場外に出ること】【球技】out of bounds.
● アウトオブバウンズエリア an out-of-bounds area. (⇨オービー)

アウトコース 〔陸上〕the outside track; 〔野球〕the outside (corner), (和製語) out course.

アウトコーナー〖野球〗the outside (corner). 《和製語》out corner. ▶アウトコーナーへ速球を投げる throw a fastball on the *outside*.

アウトサイダー〖部外者〗an outsider.

アウトサイド〖外角の(へ)〗〖野球〗outside. ▶アウトサイドの pitch. ▶アウトサイドに投げる throw *outside*; throw on the *outside*.

アウトステップ —— **アウトステップする** 動〖野球〗(打者の)step in the bucket.

アウトソーシング〖外部委託〗outsourcing.

アウトドア〖戸外の〗outdoor. (限定的)(⊗ インドア) ▶アウトドアスポーツ outdoor sports.

アウトバーン[＜ドイツ語]〖ドイツなどの高速道路〗an autobahn.

アウトハイ〖野球〗high and outside [away]. (日本語との語感の違いに注意)

アウトプット 名〖コンピュータ〗(an) óutput.
—— **アウトプットする** 動 output (data *into* a file).

アウトライトとりひき アウトライト取引〖外国為替の無条件取引〗〖経済〗an outright transaction.

アウトライン〖概略〗an óutline.
▶アウトラインフォント〖コンピュータ〗an outline font.
▶アウトラインプロセッサー 〖データを階層構造化するソフト〗〖コンピュータ〗an online processor.

アウトレット(ショップ)〖余剰在庫などを格安に販売する店〗an outlet (store).
▶アウトレットモール an outlet mall (参考 アウトレットショップが集まったショッピングセンター).

アウトロー ❶〖無法者〗an outlaw. ❷〖野球〗low and outside, down and away. (日本語との語感の違いに注意)

あうん 阿吽 ▶あうんの呼吸 perfect timing in a collaboration.

あえぐ 喘ぐ ❶〖息を切らす〗(運動で)pant; (驚き・恐怖などで)gasp; (苦しそうに息をする)breathe hard. ▶はあはあとひどくあえぐ *pant* heavily. ▶恐怖にあえぐ *gasp* with horror. ▶バスに飛び乗ったとき彼はあえいでいた He *was panting* [*breathing hard*] when he jumped on the bus. ▶「お願い」と彼女はあえぎながら言った "Please," she *gasped*. (⚠日本語に引かれて ×said gaspingly のようにいわない) ▶彼は出会ったクマについてあえぎながら何か言った He *gasped* (*out*) something about the bear he had encountered.
❷〖苦しむ〗▶我が社は多額の債務にあえいでいる Our company *is suffering from* heavy debts.

あえて 敢えて〖あえて…する〗(思い切って)dare to 《do》(⚠ (1) 否定文・疑問文・if [whether]節中では to はしばしば省略される (⇨[第1文例]). (2) 口語ではbe not afraid to do, have the courage to do の方が普通); (冒険を冒して)《書》venture to 《do》, (危険を冒して)risk 《doing》; (おこがましいことだが)《書》presume to 《do》(通例疑問文・否定文に用いる). ▶あえて嵐の中を出かけて行く *venture* (*to go*) out in the storm; (嵐にもかかわらず)go out *in spite of* the storm. ▶それが本当だということは知っていたが、あえてそう言わなかった I knew it was true, but I didn't *dare* (*to*) [I *dared* not] say so./I knew it was true, but I *was afraid* [I didn't *have the courage*, (言わない方がよいと思った) I thought it was better not] to say so. ▶あえて一つだけ忠告させていただいてよろしいですか May I *presume to* give you a single piece of advice? ▶あえて(＝わざわざ)空港まではお出迎えをする必要はありません You don't have to *bother* [*trouble*, *take the trouble*] *to* meet me at the airport. ▶あえて(＝どうしても)おっしゃるのなら早く上げましょう If you *insist*, I will tell it to you. ▶私はあえて(＝特に)その計画には反対しない I will not object to the plan *particularly*./I have no *particular* objection to the plan.

あえない 敢え無い(悲惨な)tragic; (みじめな)miserable; (はかない)transient. ▶あえない最期を遂げる die a *tragic* [*a miserable*] death. (⚠ death は同族目的語) ▶あえなく(＝あっけなく)我々は試合に敗れた We lost the game *all too easily*.

あえもの 和え物 aemono, (説明的に)vegetables, fish or seaweed with Japanese dressing.

あえる 和える dress, add dressing and mix. ▶たこを酢味噌であえる *dress* octopus with vinegared miso.

あえん 亜鉛 zinc(元素記号 Zn). ▶亜鉛めっきする galvanize.
▶亜鉛板 a zinc plate.

＊**あお 青**〖青色〗blue;〖空色〗azure /ǽʒər/;〖緑色〗green 事情 日本語では「青野菜」「青信号」などのような緑色のものにも「青」を用いるが, 英語では緑色のものには blue を用いない。▶青野菜 greens; green vegetables. ▶信号が赤から青に変わった The (traffic) light changed from red to *green* [×blue].

あおあお 青々 ▶青々とした(＝青葉の茂った)丘 a *lush green* [(書) *a verdant*] hill. ▶青々とした海原 the *blue* ocean.

\:**あおい 青い** 形〖青色の〗blue;〖緑の〗green 事情 英語の green はしばしば「未熟」、「嫉妬(ピ)・羨望(話)」のイメージを伴う;〖顔色が青白い〗pale. (⇨あおざめる) ▶青い鳥 a *blue* bird 〖書名〗*The Blue Bird*. ▶青い目をした子供 a *blue*-eyed child. ▶ドアを青い色に(＝青く)塗る paint the door *blue*. ▶そのリンゴはまだ青い The apple is still *green*./(十分熟していない) The apple is *not ripe* enough. ▶顔が青いよ。どうしたの You look *pale*. What's the matter?
—— **青くなる** 動 (青ざめる) turn [go*, 《主に米》become*, 《主に英》grow*, ×get] pale; go white (＝青ざめる); (色を失う) lose* color (⇨❷).

あおい 葵〖植物〗(ゼニアオイ)a mallow; (タチアオイ)a hollyhock.

あおいきといき 青息吐息 ▶青息吐息である have a hard [a rough] time (of it). ▶その会社は資金繰りがつかず青息吐息である The company *is in very serious trouble* [*having a very hard time*] for lack of funds.

あおいさんみゃく 『青い山脈』 *The Blue Mountain Range*. (参考 石坂洋次郎の小説)

あおいろしんこく 青色申告 a blue return.

あおかび 青黴 blue [green] mold. ▶青かびチーズ (a) *blue* cheese.

あおき 青木〖植物〗a Japanese laurel.

あおぎみる 仰ぎ見る〖見上げる〗look up 《at》;〖尊敬する〗respect, look up to. (⇨仰ぐ)

あおぎり 青桐〖植物〗a Chinese parasol tree.

＊**あおぐ 仰ぐ** ❶〖上方を見る〗look up 《at》. ▶彼は空を仰いだ He *looked up at* the sky.
❷〖尊敬する〗respect; (仰ぎ見る) look up to …. ▶彼らは彼を指導者と仰いでいる They *respect* [*look up to*] him as their leader.
❸〖求める〗ask for …. ▶彼の指示を仰ぐ ask for his instructions; ask him *for* instructions. ▶私は彼に援助を仰いだ I *asked* him for help./(彼に頼んだ) I *asked* him to help me. ▶日本は中東に石油の供給を仰いでいる(＝依存している) Japan *depends* [*is dependent*] *on* the Middle East *for* its supply of oil.

あおぐ 扇ぐ fan (-nn-). ▶火をあおいで燃え立たせる *fan* the fire into flame(s). ▶「ここは暑いわね」と言いながら彼女はせわしなく扇子であおいだ "It's hot in here," she said as she busily *fanned* herself. (⚠ with a fan は不要)

あおくさい 青臭い 〚未熟な〛inexperienced, raw; 《話》green; (考えなどが) crude. ●青臭い作品 a *crude* work. ▶ココナツの果汁は少し青臭いにおいがする The coconut milk smells a little *green*.

あおぐろい 青黒い dark green.

あおげら 青啄木鳥 〚鳥〛a Japanese green woodpecker.

あおさ 石蓴 〚植物〛sea lettuce.

あおざめる 青ざめる (怒り・恐怖などで) turn [go*] pale 《with》;(嫉妬(しっと)・羨望(せんぼう)で) turn [go] green [×blue] 《with》;(吐き気・恐怖に)《話》go pale [green] around the gills. ▶彼女はショックで[その知らせを聞いて] 青ざめた She *turned pale* with shock [at the news]./She *went white* with shock [to hear the news]. ▶彼は青ざめた顔をしている He *looks pale*./He *has a pale* [*a pallid*] *face*. (❗pallidは病気・衰弱などで「青ざめた」の意)

あおしお 青潮 (説明的に) seawater containing little oxygen.

あおしぎ 青鴫 〚鳥〛a solitary snipe.

あおじそ 青紫蘇 〚植物〛a green beefsteak plant.

あおじゃしん 青写真 a blueprint. ●家[平和のための]の青写真を作る make a *blueprint* of a house [for peace].

あおじろい 青白い ●青白い顔色 (have) a *pale* [a *pallid*] complexion. (❗pallidは「病的な青白い」)

あおしんごう 青信号 a green [×a blue] (traffic) light. (⇨信号) ▶その計画に青信号を出す(=許可を与える) give the *green light* to the project (❗この場合は〈give〉);allow the project to begin.

あおすじ 青筋 blue veins.
●青筋を立てる 青筋を立てて怒る 'The veins on one's forehead stand out with anger.'; turn livid (with rage); (かんかんになって怒る) get furious, (怒ってさっと赤くなる) flush an angry red, (おどけて)《Don't》burst a blood vessel.

あおそこひ 青底翳 〚「緑内障」の俗称〛〚医学〛glaucóma.

あおぞら 青空 a blue sky. (⇨空) ●青空のもとで under [the] *blue sky* (❗具体的な場面では the). ●青空市場 an open-air [an outdoor, a street] market. ●青空教室 (授業) (an) open-air class; (場所・建物) an open-air classroom.

あおた 青田 a green rice [puddy] field.
●青田買いする buy rice before it is reaped; (卒業前に雇用契約をする) make an employment contract with students long before they graduate.

あおだいしょう 青大将 〚動物〛a Japanese rat snake.

あおだたみ 青畳 a new *tatami* [straw] mat.

あおてんじょう 青天井 ❶〚青空〛a blue sky. (⇨青空) **❷**〚際限なく値上がりを続けること〛▶株価は青天井 Stock prices are *sky-high*.

あおな 青菜 greens; leafy green vegetables.
●青菜に塩 (wither like) greens sprinkled with salt; (人がしおれる) (比喩的に) be visibly discouraged; be crestfallen; be unhappy.

あおにさい 青二才 an inexperienced young man.
▶彼はまったくの青二才だ He's very *green*. (❗×a very green man とはいわない)

あおのり 青海苔 green laver. (⇨青苔)

あおば 青葉 green leaves. ●青葉のころ the season of *fresh leaves* [*greenery*]. ●青葉が出る come into *leaf*. ▶庭の木はすっかり青葉になった The trees in the garden are now in full *leaf*.

あおびょうたん 青瓢箪 a green [an unripe] gourd; 〚やせて顔色の悪い人〛a pale-looking lean person.

あおみ 青み 〚青さ〛blueness; 〚青野菜〛a green vegetable. ●青みがかった bluish.

あおみどろ 青味泥 〚植物〛spirogyra /spáiərədʒáiərə/.

あおむく 仰向く ●〚上の方を見る〛look up [upward]; 〚顔を上の方に向ける〛turn one's face up [upward]; 〚仰向けになる〛turn on one's back. ▶彼女は仰向いて彼にキスを求めた She *turned her face up* to him for a kiss.

あおむけ 仰向け ●仰向けに寝る lie *on one's back* (↔ on one's face). ●仰向けに倒れる fall flat *on one's back*.

あおむける 仰向ける turn 《it》up [upward].

あおむし 青虫 a green caterpillar.

あおもの 青物 〚野菜類〛vegetables; (緑色の野菜) greens, green things [stuff]; 〚背の青い魚〛(green-) blue fish (❗色の感じからアジ・イワシなどは silver [silvery] fish ともいわれる).

あおやぎ 青柳 〚青々と葉をつけた柳〛a leafy green willow; 〚バカガイのむき身〛the meat of surf clams.

あおりいか 陳泥烏賊 a bigfin reef squid. (❗通例単・複同形)

あおりたてる 煽り立てる (⇨煽る)

あおりどめ あおり止め (戸止め) a doorstop.

あおる 煽る fan (-nn-); (扇動する) stir (-rr-) ... up, 《書》incite; (燃え立たせる) kindle; (激情をかきたてる) inflame. ●けんかをあおる fan a quarrel. ●愛国心をあおる *inflame* 《his》patriotism. ●反日感情をあおる *fan* [*stir up*] anti-Japanese feeling. ▶強風にあおられて火は赤々と炎をなめつくした *Fanned* by strong winds, flames licked up the woods. ▶彼女の甘い香水の香りは彼の欲情をあおった The sweet perfume she wore *inflamed* [*kindled*] his passions.

*　**あか 赤** 〚色〛(a) red (❗種類をいうときは〚C〛); (深紅色) crimson; (緋(ひ)) scarlet; 〚共産主義者〛a Red, a communist. ●赤の広場 the *Red Square*. ●赤の他人 (⇨赤の他人) ▶彼女の帽子は濃い赤(=えんじ色)だった Her hat was a dark (↔a light) red.

*　**あか 垢** 〚汚れ〛dirt, (しみついた汚れ) grime; 〚耳のあか〛earwax; 〚湯あか〛fur. ●あかで汚れた dirty; grimy. ●あかを落として wash off the *dirt*. ▶彼は体中あかだらけだった He was covered with *dirt* all over.

あかあか 赤々 ●赤々と燃える火 a *bright* fire. ▶薪(まき)が暖炉で赤々と燃えている A log fire is burning *brightly* in the mantelpiece.

*　**あかい 赤い** 形 red (-dd-); (深紅色の) crimson; (緋(ひ)色の) scarlet. ●赤っぽい reddish. (⇨赤い) ●赤いバラ a *red* rose. ●赤い服を着た少女 a girl wearing a *red* dress; a girl (dressed) *in red*. ▶寒さで君のほおはまだ赤いよ Your cheeks are still *red* [*pink*] from the cold. ▶彼女は泣いて目が赤かった Her eyes were *red* from crying [weeping]. ▶彼の顔は熱で赤みがさしていた His face was *flushed* by a fever.

— **赤く** 副 ▶木の葉が陽を浴びて燃えるように赤く輝いていた The leaves glowed *red* in the sun. ▶彼女ははお紅をつけてほおを少し赤くした She *reddened* her cheeks a little with some blusher.

— **赤くなる** 動 turn [go*], 《主に米》become*, 《主に英》grow*, ×get] red; (恥ずかしさや当惑などで) blush; (興奮・当惑・怒り・熱などでぱっと) flush. (⇨真っ赤, 赤らめる) ▶ワイン1杯で顔が赤くなった A glass of wine *made* my face *red*./My face *got red* when I drank a glass of wine. ▶彼女は恥ずかしくて顔が赤くなった She *turned red* [*blushed*] with embarrassment.

●赤い羽根共同募金 the Red Feather Community Chest Campaign.

あかいまゆ 『赤い繭』 Red Cocoon. (⇨参) 安部公房の小説)
アカウンタビリティー 〖説明責任〗 accountability.
あかがい 赤貝 〖魚介〗an ark shell.
あがき 足掻き・最後のあがき the last struggle.
・あがきが取れない(身動きできない) cannot move; (手段・方法がない) be in a fix. ▶日本の政府は借金地獄であがきが取れない状態に陥っている The Japanese Government *is up to the ears* [*eyes, neck*] in debt. (⚠(1) is in debt up to … の語順も可. (2) 溺死(できし)寸前の状態をさすような比喩的表現)
あかぎれ a chap. (⚠通例複数形で)・手にあかぎれができている My hands *are chapped.*/I have *chapped* hands. ・私は冬にはあかぎれができやすい My skin *chaps* easily in winter.
あがく 足掻く struggle (*to do; for*). (⚠じたばたする) ▶その会社は生き残りをかけて必死にあがいている The company *is struggling desperately* [*making a desperate struggle*] *for* survival.
あかぐろい 赤黒い dark red.
あかげ 赤毛 red hair; (人) a person with red hair, (主に女性の)(話) a redhead.
あかげのアン 『赤毛のアン』 *Anne of Green Gables.* (⇨参) モンゴメリーの小説)
あかご 赤子 (⇨赤ん坊, 赤ちゃん)
・赤子の手をひねる[ねじる]よう as easy as twisting a baby's arm.
あかさび 赤錆 rust. (⇨錆, 錆びる)
あかし 証・彼に友情のあかし(=証拠)を求める demand *proof* of friendship from [*to* him]. ・身のあかしを立てる(=無罪を証明する) prove one's *innocence*.
****あかじ** 赤字 (a surplus; be in the black); 〖損失〗a loss. ・貿易収支の赤字 a trade *deficit*. (⚠「アメリカの対日貿易赤字」は the US trade *deficit* with Japan; the US-Japanese trade *deficit*) ・巨額の累積赤字 a huge [a high] cumulative *deficit*. ・財政赤字を削減する reduce the budget [fiscal] *deficit*. ・100万ドルの赤字を出す[埋める] show [make up for] a *deficit* of a million dollars. ▶我が家の家計は赤字だ[になった] Our family budget *is in* [*went into*] *the Red*. ・赤字を出し続けていたが彼はその施設を維持した He kept the institution going when it *was losing money*.
・赤字国債 (issue) deficit government bonds.
・赤字予算 (make [draw up]) a deficit budget.
・赤字路線 a deficit-ridden line.
アカシア [<ギリシャ語] 〖植物〗an acacia /əkéiʃə/.
あかしお 赤潮 a red tide.
あかしんごう 赤信号 a red (traffic) light. (⇨信号) ▶赤信号みんなで渡れば恐くない (ことわざ) There is safety in numbers.
あかす 明かす ❶〖夜を過ごす〗spend* a night (⇨過ごす❶); (寝ずに) sit* [stay] up all night. ・一晩泣き明かす cry the whole *night through*. ▶その夜我々は語り明かした We *spent the night* talking./We sat [stayed] *up all night* talking./We talked the night away./(一晩中話をした) We talked all night (long) [all the *night through*].
❷〖打ち明ける〗(話す) tell* (it *to him*); (暴露する) reveal [disclose, betray] (it *to him*). (⇨打ち明ける) ・種を明かす explain one's trick (*to* him).
あかず 開かず・開かずの踏切 a crossing whose door has *never been opend*.
あかず 飽かず・飽かず満月を眺める *never get tired of* gazing at a full moon; gaze at a full moon *untiringly*.
あかずきん 『赤頭巾』 *Little Red Riding-Hood*. (⇨参) ヨーロッパの昔話)
あかせる 飽かせる bore. (⇨飽きる) ・彼女は金にあかせて(=金をふんだんに遣って)ダイヤを買いあさった She bought all the diamonds she can *regardless of expense* [〖話〗*sparing no expense*].
あかだし 赤出し dark-brown *miso* soup.
あかちゃいろ 赤茶色 reddish brown.
あかちゃける 赤茶ける turn reddish brown; (変色する) be discolored. ・赤茶けた古い封筒 a *discolored* old envelope.
****あかちゃん** 赤ちゃん a baby. (⇨赤ん坊) ・ライオンの赤ちゃん a *baby* lion. ・赤ちゃん言葉で話す (赤ん坊が) speak *baby* talk; (大人が子供などに) use *baby* talk (*with*). ▶5月に赤ちゃんができるの I'm going to have [*expecting*] a *baby* in May.
あかちょうちん 赤提灯 an *akachochin*; (説明的に) a little drinking place [joint] with a red paper lantern hanging outside it.
あかチン 赤チン 〖商標〗Mercurochrome /mərkjúərəkròum/.
あかつき 暁 (a) dawn, 《やや書》daybreak. ・暁の空 a *dawning* sky. ・暁に at *dawn* [*daybreak*]. ▶その大学に合格したあかつきには東京で一人暮らしするつもりだ Once I've been accepted into the college, I'll start to live alone in Tokyo.
・暁闇 the darkness just before the dawn. (⚠ the darkness before the dawn は「長く続く悪い状況がもうすぐ終わること」の意)
あかつりあがったり 上がったり・冷夏で商売は上がったりだ Because of the cool summer, our business *has suffered terribly*./The cool summer *has ruined* our business.
あかつち 赤土 red earth; (赤い粘土) red clay.
アカデミー an academy.
・アカデミー賞 (win) an Academy Award [an Oscar]. (⇨参) Oscar は授賞者に与えられる青銅金めっきの小さな立像)
アカデミック ── アカデミックな 形 academic.
あかとんぼ 赤とんぼ 〖昆虫〗a red drágonfly.
あがなう 贖う (償う)〖書〗atone (*for*). (⇨償う)
あかぬけ 垢抜け・垢抜けした (しゃれた) stylish; (趣味のいい、気のきいた) sophisticated; (都会風の) urbane. ・垢抜けしない unrefined; unsophisticated; (田舎ぽい) rustic.
あかね 茜 ❶〖植物〗a madder, the madder plant. ❷〖色〗(深紅色) deep red. ▶西の空があかね色だった There was a *deep red* glow in the western sky.
あかのたにん 赤の他人 a complete [a perfect] stranger; quite a stranger. (⇨他人)
あかはじ 赤恥・赤恥をかく suffer open disgrace; be put to great shame; be humiliated.
あかはだか 赤裸・素っ裸の stark naked; (覆うものがない) bare. ・彼は商売に失敗して赤裸になった(=財産をすべて失った) He lost his business, *lock, stock, and barrel*. (⚠lock (発射装置), stock (木部), barrel (銃身)で銃全体を構成することから)
アカハラ 〖「アカデミックハラスメント」の略〗academic harassment. (⇨参) 学問的に上位の者が下位の者へのいじめ) (⇨セクハラ)
あかひげ 赤髭 a red beard; 〖人〗a red-bearded man.
あかふだ 赤札〖見切り品の札〗a "sale" tag;〖売約済みの札〗a "sold" tag.
アカプルコ 〖メキシコの都市〗Acapulco /ɑ̀ːkəpúlkou/.
アガペー [<ギリシャ語]〖神の愛〗agape /ɑːɡɑ́ːpei/.
アカペラ [<イタリア語]〖無伴奏合唱で〗[の]] a cappella /àːkəpélə/. ・アカペラで歌う人々 people

あかぼう 赤帽 (駅などの) a (baggage) porter, 《米》a redcap. ▶空港のポーターは a skycap ともいう)

あかみ 赤身 (肉の脂の少ない部分) lean meat; (魚の) red flesh. ●豚肉の赤身 lean pork. ●赤身の魚 red-fleshed; 〘魚介〙a red fish.

あかみ 赤味 ●赤味がかった slightly red, reddish; (顔)赤らむ. ▶夕日で空に赤味がさした The sky turned [《主に米》became] *reddish* in the setting sun. ▶彼女のほおに赤味がさしてきた Her cheeks are getting *flushed* [are becoming *rosy*]. (!*flushed* は「恥ずかし さ, 熱などで」, *rosy* は「元気になって」)

あかみそ 赤味噌 dark-brown *miso* [soybean paste].

あがめる 〘尊敬する〙respect; (深く)〘書〙revere; 〘崇拝する〙worship (-pp-). ●彼は皆から神のようにあがめられている He *is worshipped* as a god by everyone.

あからがお 赤ら顔 ●赤ら顔の少女 a girl with a *ruddy face*. (!健康そのもの, あるいは風にさらされたり日焼けしたりしての顔色をいう)

あからさま ── あからさまな 〘形〙(明白な) plain; (率直な) frank; (遠慮ない) candid; (あけっぴろげの) open; (単刀直入な) direct, straightforward. ●あからさまな敵対心 *frank* [*open*] hostility.
── あからさまに 〘副〙(明白に) plainly; (率直に) frankly; (遠慮なく) candidly; (あけっぴろげに) openly; (単刀直入に) directly, straightforwardly. ●あからさまに否定する make a *direct* denial of it. ●あからさまに言うと to be frank [*candid*, *plain*] *with* you; *frankly* speaking.

あからむ 明らむ (空が) (begin to) grow light; (夜が明け始める) dawn (!主語は day, morning, it).

あからめる 〘動〙(⇨赤くなる) ●妹ははずかしくてほおを赤らめた My sister flushed with pleasure./My sister flushed because she was so [very] happy. (!「恥ずかしく顔を赤らめる」は blush)

***あかり 明かり** ❶ 〘灯火〙 a light; (電気スタンドなど移動可能な) a lamp. (⇨ランプ)
① 【明かりが】 ▶遠くに町の明かりが見えた We could see the *lights* of a [the] city in the distance. ▶部屋には明かりがついていた[いなかった] The *light* was on [off] in the room./The room *was* [*wasn't*] *lighted*. (⇨〖次例 注〗) ▶彼の部屋は明かりがこうこうとついていた[暗かった] His room *was* brightly [dimly] *lit up*. (!lit, lighted については (⇨明るい 解説 (2)))
② 【明かりを】 ▶明かりをつける[消す] (スイッチで) turn on [off] the *light*; (火をつける) light [*put out*, (吹き消す) *blow out*] (a candle). ●明かりをつけっぱなしにしておく leave a *light* on [*burning*].
❷ 〘光〙light; a glow (!複数形にしない); a gleam.

┌─────────────────
│ 使い分け light 暗闇(ﾔﾐ)に対して物が見えるという光を表す一般的な語で, しばしば複合語としても用いる.
│ glow 炎・煙を出さずに燃えているものの柔らかな光.
│ gleam 小さなまたはわずかの間の穏やかな光.
└─────────────────

●たき火[暖炉]の明かり the *glow* from the fire [fireplace]. ●霧の中の灯台の明かり the *gleam* of a lighthouse in the fog. ●月[ランプ]の明かりで仕事をする work by the *light* of the moon [a lamp]. ●窓から明かりを取る let in [admit] *light* through a window.
●明かり取り (天窓の) a skylight; (戸・窓上部の) a fanlight.

あがり 上がり ❶ 〘収入〙(an) income; 〘売上高〙proceeds; 〘利潤〙a profit, a return. ●バザーの上がりの *proceeds from* a bazaar. ●投資で多くの上がりを得る get a good *profit* [*return*] *on* an investment.
❷ 〘お茶〙▶上がりください Tea, *please*. (参考 「上がり花」の略)

-あがり -上がり ●病み上がりの just recovered from sickness; (回復期にある) cònvaléscent. ●風呂上がり) (just) *after* a bath. ●軍人上がりの政治家 an *ex-serviceman* politician. (!ex- は軽蔑的な含みはない)

あがりおり 上がり降り 名 《やや書》áscent and déscent. (!対照強勢に注意)
── 上がり降りする 動 ●階段を上がり降りする go [歩いて] *walk*, (走って) *run*] *up and down* the stairs; 《書》*ascend and descend* the stairs.

あがりかまち 上がり框 the *agarikamachi*, (説明的に) (a piece of) wood that runs along the front edge of the entrance hall.

アガリクス 〘植物〙agáricus.

あがりこむ 上がり込む (入って行く) come* [go*] in, (⇨行く), walk [〘書〙step (-pp-)] in. (!in の代わりに具体的に into 〈his〉 house などとしてもよい) ●彼は帽子をかぶったままずかずかと部屋に上がり込んできた He *walked* right *into* the room with his hat on. ●太郎は花子のところにでも上がり込んで(=立ち寄って)いるんだろう I think Taro *has* probably *dropped in on* Hanako [*stopped by* Hanako's *place*].

あがりさがり 上がり下がり 名 ●物価の上がり下がり a *rise and fall* in prices. ●円相場の上がり下がり(=変動) *fluctuations* in the value of the yen.
── 上がり下がりする 動 go up and down; rise and fall.

あがりめ 上がり目 ❶ 〘つり上がった目〙▶彼女は上がり目だ She has *slant* [*almond*] *eyes*./Her eyes *slant slightly upward*. ❷ 〘物価などが上がり始めた状態〙▶物価は再び上がり目にある Prices *are showing an upward trend* again./Prices *have started to rise* [*go up*] again.

あがりゆ 上がり湯 (説明的に) hot water one uses to cleanse one's body just before one goes out of the bathroom.

:**あがる 上がる, 揚がる, 挙がる**
┌─────────────── INDEX ─────────┐
│ ❶ 高い所へ移動する   ❷ 中へ入る, 訪問する │
│ ❸ 出てくる   │
│ ❹ 価格・数量などが上昇する   │
│ ❺ 向上・昇進する   ❻ 終わる   │
│ ❼ 利益・成果などが得られる   │
│ ❽ 犯人・証拠などが見つかる   │
│ ❾ 揚げ物ができる   ❿ 声などが生じる   │
│ ⓫ 過度に緊張する   ⓬ 飲食する   │
└──────────────────────────────┘

❶ 【高い所へ移動する】(上へ行く) go* *up*, rise*; (登る) climb, 《書》 ascend (↔descend); (段を) step (-pp-) up, 《書》 mount.

┌─────────────────
│ 使い分け go up 「上がる, 登る」の意の最も一般的な語.
│ rise go up より文語的な語ではとんど同じ意味に用いられる.
│ climb 通例「手足を使って努力して一歩一歩高い所に登る」の意だが, 比喩的に単に「登る (go up)」の意味でも用いられる.
│ ascend 品位のある語で, climb と違い必ずしも努力や困難を含意せず,「徐々に, 堂々と」の意を含む.
└─────────────────

●屋根の上に上がる *go up* on a roof. ●演壇に上がる *step up onto* [*mount*] the platform [《書》the podium]. ▶エレベーターで塔に上がった I *went up* [*climbed*] the tower in an elevator. (**!** (1) climb では「よじ登った」の意になるため通例不可. (2)「5階に上がった」は I *took* an elevator *to* the fifth floor.) ▶彼は重い足どりで階段を上がった He *went up* [*climbed, mounted*] the stairs with a heavy tread. ▶太陽は東から上がる The sun *rises* [*climbs*] *in* [×*from*] the east. ▶〔飛行機が〕ぐんぐん空高く上がっていった The kite [*airplane*] *climbed* higher and higher into the sky. ▶幕が上がった The curtain *went up*. ▶たこが揚がっている The flag *is up*. ▶加地が右サイドを上がる Kaji *pushed up* [*went up*] on the right flank.

❷ 【中へ入る, 訪問する】 (中へ入る) come* [go*] in; (入学する) enter; (訪問する) come (*to*); (立ち寄る) call (*at*). ▶どうぞお上がりください Please *come in*. (**!** 強く促すときは *Dó* come in. ▶くだけた会話では Come *on* in. ともいう) ▶彼女はちょっと上がりになってお茶でもと言った She *asked* us *in* for a cup of tea. ▶彼女は今年小学校に上がる She will *enter* an elementary school this year. ▶あすそれをいただきに上がります I'll *come* [*call*] *for* it tomorrow.

❸ 【出てくる】 ●プールから上がる *come* [*get*, (よじ登って) *climb*] *out of* a swimming pool. ▶彼はふろから上がってつめを切った He clipped his nails after his bath [he took a bath].

❹ 【価格・数量などが上昇する】go* up, rise* (*前の方が口語的*); (急騰する) jump, shoot* up, soar, 《話》 skyrocket; (価格などが上げられる) be raised. ▶気温が34度まで上がった The temperature *has gone up* [*risen*] to 34 degrees. ▶新しい税の導入の結果, 物価が急に上がった Prices *went up* suddenly [*jumped, shot up*] as a result of the new tax. ▶家賃は来月から3,000円上がる The rent will *be up* [*be raised, be put up*] by 3,000 yen next month. ▶給料が5パーセント上がった I *got* a pay *raise* [《英》 *rise*] by 5 percent. (**!** I *got* a 5 percent pay *raise* [*rise*]. ともいう) I *had* my pay [*salary*] *raised* by 5 percent./My pay [*salary*] *increased* by 5 percent.

❺ 【向上・昇進する】(向上する) improve; (昇進する) be promoted, get* (a) promotion (⇨昇進). ●どんどん地位が上がる *get* [*gain, win*] rapid *promotion*. ▶彼の学校の成績が上がっている His school record *is improving*./His grades *are going up* [*are getting better*]. ▶今度の試験で20番上がった I *jumped* [*went up*] *over* twenty places in the last exam.

❻ 【終わる】 be over, end; (終える) finish; (やむ) stop (-pp-). ▶やっと梅雨が上がった(=明けた) At last the rainy season *is* [×*was*] *over*. ▶雨が上がった The rain *has stopped*./The rain *has stopped* raining./ 《話》 It *has let up*./(晴れた) It [The sky] *has cleared up*. ▶この仕事は年内に上がります This work will *be finished by* [*before*] the end of this year. ▶バッテリーが上がった(=切れた) The battery *has run down* [*is dead*].

❼ 【利益・成果などが得られる】 (もうける) make* a profit. ▶その事業で1,000万ほどの利益が上がった We *made* [*There was*] *a profit* of about ten million yen on that business. ▶罰を与えても彼にはほとんど何の効果も(上がら)なかった Punishment had almost no [*very little*] *effect on* him.

❽ 【犯人・証拠などが見つかる】 (逮捕される) be arrested; (確保される) be secured; (失った物が取り戻される) be recovered. ▶ついに犯人が挙がった The criminal *has been arrested* at last. ▶十分な証拠が挙がった Full evidence *has been secured* [*been obtained*]. ▶湖から水死体はまだ揚がっていない The drowned body *has not been recovered* [*been found*] from the lake yet.

❾ 【揚げ物にする】 be (deep-)fried, fry. (⇨あげる)
❿ ▶このエビはからっと揚がっている This prawn *fries* [*is fried*] crisply./This is a crisp-*fried* prawn.
⓫ 【声などが生じる】 ▶どっと笑い声が上がった There *was* a burst [a roar] of laughter./A burst of laughter *went up*. ▶火の手は台所から上がった The fire broke out [*started*] in the kitchen.
⓬ 【過度に緊張する】 get* nervous; 〖舞台負けする〗 get [have*, suffer from] stage fright; (慣用的に) have butterflies in one's stomach on the stage. ▶私はすっかり上がってしまって自分が何を言っているのかも分からなかった I was so *nervous* (that) I didn't even know what I was saying. ▶彼女と面と向かうといつも上がってしまう(=自意識過剰になる) I always *feel self-conscious* when I see her face to face.
⓭ 【飲食する】 ▶どうぞ果物をお上がりください Dó *have* some fruit./Please *help yourself to* the fruit. (▶ help oneself to ... は「自由に取って食べる」の意)

:**あかるい 明るい** 形 ❶ 【明輝】 light; bright.

使い分け **light** 特定の場所またはあたりが多くの自然の光を受けて明るいこと.
bright 発光体が強烈に輝いて明るいことや, 場所・日の光が光あふれて明るいこと.

▶あの部屋は明るい That room is *bright* [*light*]./It's *light* in that room. (**!** itは明暗を表す主語) ▶That is a *light* [(照明が十分な) a well-lit, a well-lighted] room.

[解説] (1) 最上級・比較級では形容詞のlightを用いず, bright や名詞のlight を用いる方が普通: あの部屋は私の家でいちばん明るい That is the *brightest* [*lightest*] room in my house./That room gets the most *light* in my house.
(2) light の分詞形容詞としては lighted も用いるが, 副詞を伴うときは lit が普通.

▶夫は明るいうちに帰ってくることはめったにない My husband seldom comes home while it is still *light* [暗くなる前に] before (it gets) dark]. ▶この電灯は明るい This lamp is *bright* [(十分な光を与える) gives a good (↔a bad) *light*]. ▶太陽が明るく輝いている The sun is shining *bright* [*brightly*]. (▶副詞の bright は主に shine や burn の後で用いる. 副詞に重点がある)

❷ 【明朗, 清潔】(陽気な) cheerful, sunny; (朗らかな) bright; (清潔な) clean; (公正な) fair. ●明るい雰囲気 *a cheerful* atmosphere. ●明るい笑顔で with *a bright* [*a cheerful, a sunny*] smile. ●明るい(=幸せな)家庭 *a happy* home [family]. ●明るい政治 *clean* politics. ●明るい気持ちになる feel *happy*. ▶彼は性格が明るい He is *cheerful* (by nature)./He has [is of] *a cheerful* [*a sunny*] disposition. ▶教室は明るい雰囲気で感じがよかった The classroom was *cheery* and pleasant.

❸ 【将来が】(有望な) bright; (バラ色の) rosy. ●明るい希望[見通し] a *bright* hope [prospect]. ●人生の明るい面を見る(=楽観する) look on the *bright* [*sunny*] (↔*dark*) side (of life [things]). ▶今のところ見通しはあまり明るくない Things don't look too *bright* right now. ▶君の将来は明るい You have a *bright* [a *rosy*] future before you./Your future is *bright* [*rosy*].

❹ 【精通している】(よく知っている) know*... very

あかるさ

well、(親しんでよく知っている) be familiar 《with》;(熟練・熟達している)《書》be well versed 《in》.▶彼は法律に明るい He knows law very well./He is familiar with [完全な知識がある] has a thorough /θə́ːrou/ knowledge of law. ● 明るい人なので話しやすい Law is familiar to him. は[法律にかかわったことがある(程度の意)](専門家だ) he is an expert [is a specialist] in law.
❺[色彩](淡い) light; pale;(鮮やかな) bright. ● 明るい色(薄い色) light colors;(鮮やかな色) bright [vivid] colors. ● 明るい色の服を着ている be dressed in bright (colored) clothes. ▶宵の明星は空でいちばん明るい星です The evening star is the brightest star in the sky.

── 明るくする[なる] 動 ─ (光などで) light*(up), lighten, brighten;(状況などを) brighten ...(up),(人・顔・状況・空模様を) brighten (up);(顔などが) light up, lighten. ● 部屋を明るくする light up a room. ▶彼がいたので家庭が明るくなった He brightened (up) our home. ▶空が明るくなってきた(=晴れてきた)The sky is clearing up [brightening (up), lightening]./(夜明けで)It's getting [growing] light. ▶見通しは明るくなってきた The prospects are brightening (up). ▶その知らせを聞くと彼女の顔は明るくなった Her face brightened (up) [lit up, lightened] at the news./She looked cheerful [happy] when she heard the news. (⇒形)

あかるさ 明るさ ❶[輝き](太陽などの) brightness;(目に映る明るさ) light. ● 月の明るさ the light of the moon. ▶この部屋の明るさはあの部屋の数倍ある This room is several times as light as that one.

❷[快活] cheerfulness. ● 明るさのない陰気な家 a somber house without cheerfulness. ● その後彼女はだんだん明るさを増した She got more and more cheerful after that.

あかるみ 明るみ ─ 明るみに出る(秘密などが) come to light. ▶その汚職事件はついに明るみに出た The scandal was made public [came to light, was brought to light] at last./The scandal was brought out into [was out in] the open at last.

あかんたい 亜寒帯 (北半球の) the subarctic zone,(南半球の) the subantarctic zone.

あかんべ ●あかんべをする(説明的に) pull down one's lower eyelid (as a gesture of rejection).
会話 「ちょっとお金を貸してよ」「あかんべだ」"Lend me some money." "No! (I don't want to.)"

:あかんぼう 赤ん坊 a baby; an infant.

> 使い分け baby 通例まだ歩いたりしゃべったりできない幼児をさす一般的な語。性別が不明かあるいは特に問題としない場合は it で受けるが、性別がはっきりしているか自分にとって身近な話題にするときは he か she で受ける。
> infant baby の堅い語。《英》では8歳以下の学童をさすこともある。

①[~赤ん坊] ● 生まれたての赤ん坊 a newborn baby. ● 男[女]の赤ん坊 a báby bòy [gìrl]. (▮通例 ×a boy [a girl] baby とはいわない)
②[赤ん坊(の)~] ● 赤ん坊のような顔 a baby face. ● 赤ん坊の世話をする baby-sit. ▶彼はいつも私を赤ん坊扱いする He always treats me like a baby. ▶彼は赤ん坊のころよく病気をした He was frequently ill when he was a baby [during babyhood].
③[赤ん坊が] ● 彼女に来月赤ん坊が生まれる予定です She is going to have a baby next month. (▮確実な予定なので ×She'll have .... とはいわない) ▶彼女に先週赤ん坊が生まれた She had a baby last week./She gave birth (to a baby) last week./A baby was born to her last week. (▮「赤ん坊が生まれた」は《話》では A baby arrived [came (along)]. のようにいう)
④[赤ん坊を] ● 赤ん坊を抱く hold one's baby in one's arms. ● 赤ん坊をひざの上で(揺すって)あやす cradle one's baby in one's lap. ● ぐずる赤ん坊をあやして寝かしつける lull a fretting baby to sleep. (▮sleep は名詞) ▶私は赤ん坊を母乳[ミルク]で育てた I fed my baby on my milk [on the bottle]./I breast-fed [bottle-fed] my baby.

:あき 秋 图 《米》the fall,《英・米書》(the) autumn. (参考) 南半球では3~5月)(⇒春) ▶去年[今年, 来年]の秋 last [this; next] fall [autumn]. ● さわやかな[肌寒い]秋 a crisp [a chilly] fall. ● 実りの秋(=収穫の季節) the harvest season. ● 食欲の秋 autumn, a season for a hearty [a good] appetite. ▶秋は読書に最適の季節だ The fall is the best season for reading. ▶秋には木々は紅葉する The leaves of trees turn red in the fall. ▶秋も深まった It is now well [deep] into the fall.
─ 秋の 形 autumn,《米》fall,《書・詩》autumnal /ɔːtʌ́mnl/. ● 秋の草花 autumn flowers. ● 秋の流行 fall fashions. ● 秋の夜長に読書を楽しむ enjoy reading during the long nights of the fall [on long autumn nights]. ▶秋の気配が感じられた There was a hint [a sign] of fall [autumn] in the air. (▮この場合通例冠詞無冠詞)
● 秋の日はつるべ落とし (秋は日が沈むのが早い) The day ends very fast in the fall.

あき 空き(空き部屋, 空いた所, 欠員);[勤め口] an opening. ▶このマンションは3階に空きが2, 3ある This apartment house has a few vacancies on the third floor. ▶販売部にいくつか空きがあったがすぐふさがった There were some openings in the Sales Department but they were soon filled.
会話 「教員の職を探しているんだけど」「実はうちの学校では4月から理科の先生の空きができるんだ」「じゃ校長との面談を取り計らってもらえないかしら」"I'm looking for a teaching position." "Actually, there's an opening for a science teacher at our school starting April." "Could you arrange an interview with your principal for me?"

あきあき 飽き飽き ── 飽き飽きする 動 [うんざりする]《話》get fed up 《with》,《話》get sick (and tired) 《of》;[退屈する] get bored 《with》;[もうたくさんである] have enough 《of》. (⇒飽きる) ▶同じ単調な仕事で飽き飽きしている I'm fed up with [I'm sick and tired of] the same monotonous work. ▶彼の長話には飽き飽きした I got bored with his long talk. (▮意味を強めるときは I got bored stiff [to death, to tears] with .... のようにいう)/His long talk was quite boring [tiresome, ×bored, ×tired]. ▶君のばかげた話には飽き飽きしたよ (I've had) enough of your nonsense.

あきかぜ 秋風 an autumn [《米》a fall,《書・詩》an autumnal] wind [breeze].
● 秋風が立つ[吹く] An autumn wind begins to blow./(心に) My love for him [her] cools (down).

あきかん 空き缶 an empty can. ● 空き缶を車の窓から捨てるな Don't throw away empty cans out of the car window.

あきぐち 秋口 ● 秋口に in early [at the beginning of] autumn [《米》fall].

あきさめ 秋雨 autumn [《米》fall] rain.
● 秋雨前線 an autumnal rain front.

あきす 空き巣 ▶井田さんの家が(留守中に)空き巣にやられた Mr. Ida had his house robbed [Mr. Ida's

あきぞら　秋空 ●秋空の下で under the (*clear, blue*) *sky of autumn*; under the (*clear, blue*) *autumn sky.*

house *was robbed*, There was a burglary at Mr. Ida's house] while he was away.
●空き巣ねらい (人) a sneak thief (❷ thieves).

あきたりない　飽き足りない ●彼の仕事ぶりは私に飽き足りない I am *not satisfied with* his work./His work *is not satisfactory* (to me). (⇨物足りない)

あきち　空き地 (1区画の) a vacant [an empty] lot; (空いた)土地 vacant land [ground]. (⇨更地)

あきっぽい　飽きっぽい ●彼は飽きっぽい He cannot keep up interest in anything./He soon *gets tired of* things he is doing./Nothing interests him for long.

あきない　商い [商売] business; [取引] dealing, trading; [貿易] trade; [証券の取引高] turnover, volume. ●大商い heavy *trading*. ●薄商い light [thin] *trading*. ●商い口(=顧客)を増やす increase the number of *customers* [*clients*].

あきなう　商う (取り引きする) deal* [trade] (*in* tea).

あきばれ　秋晴 nice fall [米] [fine autumn 《英》] weather. ●その日は秋晴れの上天気だった It was a very *beautiful autumn day*.

あきびん　空き瓶 an empty bottle.

あきま　空き間 ❶ [空き室] a vacancy, a vacant room; [貸し間] a room for rent 《米》 [to let 《英》]. (⇨空き) ❷ [すき間] (⇨隙間)

あきや　空き家 a vacant [an unoccupied] house (❷ houses /-ziz, 《米》 -siz/); [人もいない家具もない空っぽの] an empty house; (廃屋) an abandoned house. ●その家は3か月前から空き家になっている The house *has been vacant* [*has not been lived in*] for the past three months. (❷ live in の受身 (⇨住む))

*あきらか　明らか ── 明らかな 形 clear; obvious; evident; apparent /əpǽrənt/; plain; definite /défənət/; positive.

┌─ 使い分け ───────────────────┐
│ **clear** 細部まで明瞭で、誤解の余地がない │
│ こと。証拠・情報・兆候などの明白性をいう。 │
│ **obvious** 事例・理由などが明白であること. │
│ **evident** 根拠に基づき、客観的に明白であること. │
│ **apparent** 表面的にはっきり現れていて視覚的に明白 │
│ であること。または、確かな推測に基づき明白であること. │
│ 人気・目的・問題などに対して用いる. │
│ **plain** 簡素・単純で平明でわかりやすいこと. │
│ **definite** 事象などが確定的で疑いの余地がないこと. │
│ **positive** 強い確信を持つほど決定的で疑いのないこと. │
└───────────────────────────┘

●明らかな証拠 《a piece of》 *clear* [*definite, positive*] evidence. ●明らかな事実 an *evident* [an *obvious*, an *apparent*, a *plain*, a *positive*] fact. ▶彼が窓ガラスを割ったことは明らかだ It is *clear* [*evident, obvious, apparent, plain*] that he broke the window. (❷ (1) that 節内に should を用いな い。(2) that 節の代わりに不定詞を用いて、× *... for him to have broken the window*. とはいわない)/(明らかに彼は窓ガラスを割った) *Clearly* [*Evidently, Obviously*, 《まれ》 *Apparently*], he broke the window. (❷ 文修飾の副詞は通例文頭、時に文中に置かれ、後には平叙文が続き、疑問反文は続かない) ▶彼の意図はだれの目にも明らかだ His intention is *clear* [*evident, obvious, apparent, plain*] to everyone. ▶彼は明らかにそこへ行くのは嫌がる He'll *definitely* go there. (❷ ×*It is definite for him to go there.* はいわない) ▶それは火を見るより明らかだ It's (*as*) *plain as day*. ▶その結果を見れば明らかだ The result

speaks for itself.
── 明らかに 副 clearly; obviously; evidently; plainly. ▶君は明らかに間違っている You are *clearly* [*obviously*] *mistaken*./It is *clear* [*obvious*] that you are mistaken.
── 明らかになる 動 come* to light; (知られる) become* known; (...と分かる) prove* (to be), turn out (to be). ▶新たな事実が明らかになった New facts *have come to light* [*have been brought to light*]. ▶その人の名前は明らかになっていない His name *is not disclosed*, (明らかにされていない)《やや書》*is not revealed*. ▶この絵はにせ物であることが明らかになった This painting *has proved* [*turned out*] *to be* an imitation./It *has turned out that* this painting is an imitation [(話) a fake].
── 明らかにする 動 make*... clear, 《書》 clarify; (公にする) make... public; (立証する) prove*; (明示する) define. ▶事情を明らかにする *make* things *clear*; *clarify* things. ▶彼の有罪を明らかにする *prove* his guilt. ▶立場を明らかにする *define* one's position. ▶彼は自分の見解を明らかにすべきだ He should *make* his views *public*.

あきらめ　諦め resignation; [断念] abandonment. ●あきらめの悪い人 a bad loser. ▶あきらめが肝心だ *Resignation* (to one's fate) is essential.

あきらめる　諦める [途中で断念する] give(...) up (❷最も口語的), (...を完全に) abandon; [運命などを甘受する] resign oneself [be resigned] (*to*+图, to doing); [絶望する] despair. ▶あきらめるのはまだ早い It's too early to *give up* [×*abandon*]. (❷ *abandon* は他動詞なので不可) ▶私は新車を買うのをあきらめた I *gave up* [*abandoned, dropped*] the idea of buying [a plan to buy] a new car. (❷ *give up doing* は「...し続けるのをやめる」の意。したがってまだ始めていないことについて *I gave up buying...*. というのは不適当。また ×*I gave up to buy ...* は不可) ▶私は小説を書くことはあきらめた I *gave up on* writing novels. (❷ *I gave up writing...*. は単に「...を書くことをやめた」であるが、on を入れると強調的になり、「見切りをつける」つまり「才能がないとあきらめた」の感じになる) ▶彼は今シーズンの成績が振わなかったので二軍に落とされてもしかたがないとあきらめていた He made a poor showing this season and *was resigned to* being sent down to the minors. ▶彼のことは死んだものとあきらめよう Let's *give him up for* [*as*] *lost*. (❷ 目的語が代名詞の場合で ×*give up him* の語順は不可) ▶手を振ってもヘリコプターが気づかずに飛び去ってしまったので私たちはもう助からないとあきらめた After a helicopter flew away without noticing us waving, we *despaired of* being rescued. ▶彼女のことがあきらめきれない(=忘れられない) I can't forget (about) her. (❷ *about* は「具体的なあれやこれやを」の意を加え、悶々(ಠಠ)とした気持ちが強調される)/I can't put her out of my mind.

あきる　飽きる, 厭きる [興味を失う] lose interest (*in*); (興味・気力をなくす) get* tired (*of*) (❷肉体的な疲れも含むことが多い); get weary /wíəri/ (*of*) (❷ get tired より堅い言い方); (話) get fed up (*with*), 《話》 get sick (and tired) (*of*) (❷ get tired より強意的) ❷以上いずれも「飽きている」状態を表すときは get に代えて be tired (❷「たくさんである」 have* enough (*of*) (❷完了時制で用いる). (⇨飽き飽き) ●切手の収集にあきる *lose interest in* collecting stamps. ▶読書にあきた I *got tired* [*weary*] *of* reading. ▶君の愚痴は聞きあきた I'm *fed up with* [*I'm sick and tired of, I've had enough of*] your complaints./I'm *fed up* (*with*) [*sick and tired*

あきれかえる 呆れ返る ▶あきれかえってものも言えない、とはこのことである This is exactly the kind of situation where I was amazed [stunned] that I couldn't utter a word [was speechless]. (! stun は突然の出来事に驚く場合を表す)
会話 「彼はそれに1万円も払ったんだよ」「あきれかえるような値段だね」"He paid ten thousand yen for it." "It was a *ridiculous* price, wasn't it?"

アキレスけん アキレス腱 an Achilles(') tendon; 〔唯一の弱点〕 an Achilles(') heel. ▶アキレス腱を切る tear [rupture] an *Achilles*(') *tendon*.

あきれた 呆れた (⇨呆れる)

あきれはてる 呆れ果てる be disgusted and amazed.

*あきれる 呆れる 動 ❶〔驚く〕be amazed, be astonished, be astounded 《at, by; to do; that 節》. (!順に意味が強くなる) (⇨驚く) ●あきれるほど要領のない 〔抜け目のない〕男 an *amazingly* clever [shrewd] fellow. ▶彼女のあつかましさにはあきれた I was *amazed at* [*by*] her impudence./Her impudence *amazed* me [*was amazing* (*to* me)]. (! amazing は形容詞) ▶あきれて物も言えない I am speechless [struck dumb] *with amazement*.
❷〔愛想が尽きる〕be disgusted 《with, at, by》. ▶あいつの行動にはあきれる I am *disgusted with* [*at*, *by*] his conduct. (!with は行為の種類や内容を, at は行為そのものを問題にする. by は受身の意味が強い) (!disgusting は形容詞)
── あきれた 〔驚くべき〕amazing, astonishing; 〔愛想が尽きる〕disgusting; 〔ばかげた〕ridiculous; 〔途方もない〕extraordinary. ▶あきれた意気地ない *amazing* coward. ▶君が泳げないとはあきれたものだ It's *amazing* that you can't swim. ▶あいつはあきれた奴だ He is a *disgusting* fellow.
会話 「彼, 私を告訴するって言ってるわ」「あきれたもんだ」"He says he'll sue me." "The idea of it! (!強めて The very idea of it! ともいう)/What an (*extraordinary*) idea!"

あきんど 商人 a merchant. (⇨商人(しょうにん))

あく 空く, 開く 〔空になる〕(中身が) become empty, (場所などが) become vacant. ●空いている家(＝空き家) a *vacant* house. ●an *empty* house は「人もいない家具もない空っぽの家」の意 (⇨空き家) ▶角に空いた(＝上に何も置かれていない)テーブルが一つあった There was an *empty* table in the corner. ▶箱が空いた The box *became empty* [*was emptied*]. ▶席が二つ空いた Two seats *became vacant* [*empty*]. ▶この席は空いていますが座る人が決まっています This seat is vacant but taken. (!対照例に注意 (⇨会話)) ▶彼の辞職によって重要なポストが空いた His resignation *left* an important post *vacant* [*open*]. ▶英語教員のポストが一つ空いている(＝就職口がある) We have [There is] an *opening for* an English teacher. ▶少なくともその職は空いているでしょう The job at least would remain *open*.
会話 「あの…, この席は空いていますか」「いいえ, ふさがっています」"Excuse me. *Is* this seat *taken* [*occupied*]?" "Yes, it is." (!日本語に対応した "Is this seat *free* [*vacant*]?" "No, it isn't." より普通. vacant は主に「職」「地位」などに用いる場合が多い)
❷〔使わなくなる〕(終える) have* [be] done with ..., be through with ...; (使われていない) be not in use. ▶その雑誌が空いたら貸してください I'd like to borrow the magazine when you have done *with* [*have finished reading*] it. ▶次の日曜は車が空いています The car *won't be in use* next Sunday.
❸〔暇である〕be free. ▶今週は手が空かない I *am not free* 〔忙しい〕*am busy*〕this week./I *have* my *hands full* this week. ▶来週のそちらの空いてる日を教えてくれますか Could you tell me what days you're *free* next week?
❹〔開く〕(戸・店などが) open; (幕が) rise*. ●開いている窓 an *open* window. ▶風で戸が開いた The wind blew the door *open* 〔×opened〕. (!open は形容詞) ▶戸はどうしても開かない The door will not *open*. (!will not で強い拒絶を表す)/I can't *open* [*undo*] the door. (!undo はかんぬきなどに使って開けること)/(つかえて動かない) The door *is stuck*. ▶金庫はこの鍵(かぎ)で開きます You can *open* the safe with this key./This key *opens* the safe. (!×The safe *opens* with this key. とはいわない) ▶木曜日には9時まで開いている店もあります On Thursdays some stores *stay open* until nine. ▶幕がやっと開いた The curtain *rose* [*went up*] at last. ▶劇の第1幕が開いた The first act of the play *began* 〔×rose〕. ▶開いた口がふさがらなかった(＝びっくり仰天して口がきけなかった) I *was* speechless [*was dumbfounded*].
会話 「郵便局は何時に開きますか」「9時に開きます」"Can you tell me what time the post office *opens*?" "(It) opens" at nine."

あく 悪 〔邪悪〕(an) evil /íːvl/; 〔不正〕wrong; 〔悪徳〕(a) vice. ●悪 社会(必要)悪 a social [a necessary] *evil*. ●悪の温床 a hotbed of *vice*. ●悪の道に誘う tempt 《him》 into *evil* [*wrong*]. ●善をもって悪に報いる return good for *evil* [*evil* with good]. ▶彼は悪に染まってしまった He has taken to *bad ways*. ●悪人は死ぬかもしれないが, 悪は決して死なない (⇨悪人)

あく 灰汁 〔木灰を水に溶かして作ったアルカリ液〕lye; 〔野菜などの渋み〕a harsh [a bitter] taste; 〔煮汁に浮かぶあか〕(a) scum (複数形なし); 〔自己主張〕self-assertiveness. ●あく抜きをする remove *harshness* 《*from*》. ●あくを取る〔すくう〕remove [skim off] the *scum from*.
●あくが強い ▶彼はあくが強い He is *self-assertive*./(強い個性を持っている) He has a *very strong* [a *forceful*] *personality*.

アクアマリン an aquamarine. (参考 3月の誕生石)

アクアラング 〔商標〕an Aqualung; a scuba.

アクアリウム 〔水族館, 養魚池〕an aquarium /əkwέəriəm/.

あくい 悪意 ill will; (積極的な) malice 《toward》. ●悪意のあるうわさ話 *malicious* (⇔ innocent) gossip. ●悪意のないうそ a *white* lie. ●あることで彼に悪意を抱く bear *ill will* [*malice*] *toward* him *for* something. ●悪意でそれをする do it *out of* [*from*] *malice*. ●彼の言葉を悪意に(＝悪く)解釈する take his words *ill* 〔書〕*amiss*. ▶間違ったからといって彼を怒ないでね. 悪意はないのだから Don't yell at him for making mistakes. He *means well* (↔*ill*).

あくうん 悪運 ●悪運が強い(＝めっぽう運が強い) 《話》 have the *devil's* (own) *luck*, have the *luck of the devil*. ●悪運続きである have a run of *bad luck*.

あくえいきょう 悪影響 ●悪影響を及ぼす have a *bad influence* [*effect*] 《*on*》. (⇨影響)

あくえき 悪疫 (a) plague /pléig/.

あくか 悪貨 bad money. (⇨悪貨(ᵃᵏ))
あくかんじょう 悪感情 ●悪感情を持つ[抱く] have [《書》harbor] ill [bad] feeling 《toward》; 《強烈な反感》《やや書》have [feel] an antipathy 《to, toward》.
あくさい 悪妻 a bad wife.
あくざいりょう 悪材料 〔株式〕an adverse [an unfavorable, a negative] factor, negative [bad] news.
あくじ 悪事 〔悪い行為〕(a) wrongdoing;〔犯罪〕a crime. ●悪事を働く commit a wrongdoing [a crime].
  ●悪事千里を走る （ことわざ）Bad news travels fast. 〔❢この英語には「人は他人の不幸話が好きだ」という含みがある〕
あくじき 悪食 ●悪食(=いかもの食い)である eat bizarre [unusual] food.
*__あくしつ__ 悪質 ●悪質な(=不正な)業者 a dishonest [《話》a crooked, a corrupt, 《詐欺的な》a fraudulent] dealer. ●悪質な ❶ ●悪質な(=悪意のある)いたずら電話 a malicious prank phone call. ●悪質な(=凶悪な)犯罪 an atrocious crime.
あくしゅ 握手 ●handshaking; (1回の) a handshake. ●彼らは固い握手を交わして別れた They parted with a firm handshake.
  ── 握手する 動 ●私は彼女と握手した I shook hands with her [shook her hand, shook her by the hand]. (❢×I shook hand with her. とはいわない)
あくしゅう 悪臭 ●〔いやな〕a nasty, 《むっとする》a disgusting] smell [odor] (❢a smell, 特にan odor だけでもこの意を表す); 《むかつくような》a stink, a stench. (⇨におい, 臭気) ●ヘドロの鼻をつく悪臭 a penetrating smell of sludge. ▶腐ってきた生ごみの悪臭で私は吐き気がした The stench of rotting garbage made me feel sick.
あくしゅう 悪習 ●〔個人の〕a bad habit; 〔社会の〕a bad custom. ●悪習が身につく fall into a bad habit.
  ●悪習を直す get rid of a bad habit.
あくしゅみ 悪趣味 bad [poor, vulgar] taste. (❢a bad hobby とはいわない) ▶彼女の服はいつ見ても悪趣味だ What she wears is always in bad taste.
あくじゅんかん 悪循環 a vicious circle [《米》cycle]. ●悪循環を断ち切る break the vicious circle 《of》.
あくしょ 悪書 a bad [有害な] a harmful, [好ましくない] an undesirable] book.
あくじょ 悪女 ❶〔性質のよくない女〕a bad [ひどく悪い] a wicked] woman. ❷〔醜い女〕an ugly woman.
  ●悪女の深情け An ugly woman has an abundance of love and affection.
アクション〔行動〕(an) action; 〔演技〕acting.
  ●アクション映画 an action film. ●アクションプログラム〔実行計画〕an action program.
あくせい 悪性 ●悪性の風邪 a bad cold.
  ●悪性腫瘍 a malignant (↔a benign) tumor.
あくせい 悪政 bad government; misrule; 〔失政〕misgovernment. ●悪政に苦しむ suffer from misrule.
あくぜい 悪税 a bad [《不当な》an unreasonable] tax.
あくせく〔忙しく〕busily; 〔熱心に〕(very) hard. ●あくせく働く work busily [very hard]. ●あくせくする(=忙しい) be very busy 《doing》. ●あくせくしない(=のんきな性格の人 an easygoing type of person.
アクセサリー ❶〔宝石などの装身具〕《集合的》jewelry /dʒúːəlri/. ●an accéssory は特に婦人用の靴・帽子・ハンドバッグなどを指す) ●アクセサリーを着けている[着ける] wear [put on] jewelry [×accessories].
  ❷〔周辺機器〕〔コンピュータ〕an accessory, a peripheral.
アクセシビリティー〔利用しやすさ〕accessibility.
アクセス 图 ❶〔接続・交通手段・参入〕access. ▶そのホテルは駅からのアクセスがよい The hotel is within easy access of [×from] the station.
  ❷〔情報への接続など〕〔コンピュータ〕access. ●不正アクセス an unlawful [an illegal] access. ●1日に100件のアクセスがある receive 100 hits [accesses] a day.
  ── アクセスする 動 〔コンピュータ〕have an access 《to a file》, access 《to a file》.
  ●アクセスコード an access cord. 〔参考〕ユーザーID・パスワードなど) ●アクセスタイム〔呼び出し時間〕access time. ●アクセスチャージ〔接続料金〕an access charge. ●アクセス道路 an access road. ●アクセスポイント〔接続基地〕an access point.
アクセル ❶〔車の加速装置〕an accelerator (pedal), 《米》a gas pedal. ●アクセルを踏む step on the accelerator 《米》gas]. ●アクセルを離す release the accelerator.
  ❷〔フィギュアスケートの1回転半ジャンプ〕 an axel /ǽksəl/. ●トリプルアクセル〔3回転半ジャンプ〕a triple axel.
アクセレレーター〔車の加速装置〕(⇨アクセル);〔処理速度を速くする装置〕〔コンピュータ〕an accelerator.
あくせん 悪銭 〔不正・不法の手段による利得〕ill-gotten gains; 《あぶく銭》easy money 《あぶく》. (❢後の方は宝くじで得た金なども含む)
  ●悪銭身につかず （ことわざ）Ill-got, ill-spent./Easy come, easy go.
あくせんくとう 悪戦苦闘 图 a desperate [a hard] struggle 《against》.
  ── 悪戦苦闘する 動 struggle (hard) 《with, against》; fight desperately 《against》. ●難問に悪戦苦闘する struggle 《hard》with [to solve] a difficult problem.
アクセント ❶〔高さ・強さの〕an accent; 〔強さの〕a stress; 〔アクセント記号〕an accent (mark). ●第1音節にアクセントをおく put [place] the accent [stress] on the first syllable; stress [accent] the first syllable. ●"elect"のアクセントは第2音節にある The accent [stress] in the word "elect" is [falls] on the second syllable.
  ❷〔強調点〕●えり元にアクセントをつける accentuate the collar of a blouse).
あくた 芥 〔「ごみ, ちり」の文語的表現〕(⇨ごみ, 塵(ᶜʰⁱ))
あくたい 悪態 ●悪態をつく〔「畜生!」などと〕curse; 〔ばかなど軽蔑した呼び名で〕call 《him》names. (⇨罵(ᵇⁿ)る)
あくだま 悪玉 (⇨悪役)
あくたれ 悪たれ 〔男の子〕a brat. ●悪たれ口をたたく use bad language; swear. (⇨憎まれ口)
アクティブ〔活動的な〕active.
  ●アクティブウィンドー〔選択中の画面〕〔コンピュータ〕an active window.
あくてん 悪天 (⇨悪天候)
あくてんこう 悪天候 bad weather. ●悪天候をついて出発する start in spite of bad [rough, stormy] weather.
あくどい〔ひどい〕vicious; 〔不正な〕dishonest; 〔けばけばしい〕gaudy. ●あくどい仕打ち a vicious treatment.
  ●あくどい商売 dishonest business. ●あくどい化粧 gaudy makeup.
あくとう 悪党 ●a villain /vílən/; 〔悪党仲間〕(a bunch of) villains. ▶この悪党め (You) devil./(You) son of a bitch.

あくどう 悪童 a bad [(わんぱくな) a naughty] boy; (悪がき)(軽蔑的な) a brat.

あくとく 悪徳 (a) vice (↔(a) virtue); (不道徳) immorality. ●悪徳(=不正を働いた)市長 a corrupt mayor.
●悪徳業者 (不正な業者) a dishonest dealer.
●悪徳商法 dishonest business.

あくなき 飽くなき ●飽くなき(=満足することのない)知識欲 an insatiable thirst for knowledge. ●世界平和を求めて飽くなき(=絶え間ない)努力をする make unceasing [(粘り強い) persistent] efforts for world peace.

あくにん 悪人 a bad [a wicked] person. (⇨悪い [悪い人間]) ▶悪人は死ぬかもしれないが, 悪は決して死なない Evil doers may die, but evil never does.

あぐねる (⇨困 倦(ﾂ)む) ●考えあぐねる (頭をしぼる) rack one's brain(s); (熟考する) think ... over.

あくび 欠伸 名 a yawn /jɔːn/. ●大あくびをする give a big [a heavy] yawn; yawn heavily. ●あくびをかみ殺す stifle 《やや書》 suppress, 《話》 bite back] a yawn. ●手であくびを隠す cover a yawn with one's hand.
—— **あくび(を)する** 動 yawn. ●あくびをしながらお休みと言う yawn good night.

あくひつ 悪筆 ▶彼は悪筆だ He has bad [poor, (とても読みにくい) illegible] handwriting./His handwriting is poor [illegible]./He writes in an illegible hand.

あくひょう 悪評 ●悪評のある人 a person with a bad reputation. ●悪評を買う get a bad reputation.

あくびょうどう 悪平等 inappropriate [mistaken, 《書》 injudicious] equality.

あくふう 悪風 ●世間の悪風に染まる become tainted with the bad ways of the world.

あくぶん 悪文 [文体] a bad style; [文章] poor writing. ▶彼は悪文を書く He has a bad written style [writes badly].

あくへい 悪弊 a vicious [(堕落した) a corrupt] practice. ●悪弊を断つ put an end to [(一掃する) sweep away] corrupt practices.

あくへき 悪癖 a bad habit (⇨癖(ｾ))

あくま 悪魔 名 [キリスト教での] the Devil, (魔王) Satan /séitn/; [人にとりついた] a demon. ●小悪魔 a little demon. ●悪魔にとりつかれている be possessed by a devil [a demon]. ●悪魔払いをする expel [drive out, (祈祷をして) exorcise] the devil [demon].
—— **悪魔的な** 形 Satanic; demoniac.

あくまでも 飽くまでも [最後まで] to the end [last]; [しつこく] persistently; [頑固に] stubbornly. ●あくまで戦う fight to the end [last]; fight it out. ●あくまでも自説を通す maintain one's opinion persistently; persist in one's opinion; (固執する) stick to one's opinion. ●それにあくまでも抵抗する resist it stubbornly; make stubborn resistance to it.

あくむ 悪夢 a nightmare (!比喩的にも用いる); a dreadful [a terrible] dream. ●悪夢のような体験をする have a nightmare. ●悪夢にうなされる be frightened by [troubled by] a nightmare. ●悪夢から覚める wake from a nightmare. ▶それは悪夢のような出来事だった The incident was like an evil dream.

あぐむ 倦む 攻めあぐむ(=攻撃に出られない) be unable to take the offensive. ▶彼女は息子の到着を待ちあぐんでいた She were tired [weary] of waiting for her son's arrival.

アクメ [<フランス語] [性的絶頂] (an) orgasm, a climax. (!英語の acme は [美しさなどの絶頂] の意)

あくめい 悪名 (悪評) a bad reputation [name].
▶彼は悪行で[ギャングとして]悪名高い (やや書) He is notorious for his evil deeds [as a gangster]. (!be famous for を悪いことで有名なものに用いるのは (古))

あくやく 悪役 the villain, 《米話》 the bad guy. ●悪役を演じる play a villain's role [part]; play the villain.

あくゆう 悪友 (好ましくない友人) an undesirable friend, (集合的) bad company. ●悪友(=よくない仲間)ができる get [fall] into bad company. ●悪友ととつきあう keep bad company. ▶彼とは20年来の悪友だ (反語的) He's been one of my best friends for twenty years [of twenty years' standing].

あくよう 悪用 —— **悪用する** 動 ●知識を悪用する put one's knowledge to wrong use. ●彼の名刺を悪用する(=不正な目的に使う) use his business card for evil [wrong] purposes.

あぐら 胡坐 ●あぐらをかく (!sit cross-legged は「足を組んで座る」の意); (ヨガ・座禅などで) sit in a lotus position. ●過去の栄光にあぐらをかく rest [sit back] on one's laurels.
●あぐら鼻 a nose with large or wide nostrils.

あくらつ 悪辣 —— **悪辣な** 形 (悪人がする) villainous; (下劣な) mean; (ずるくて悪い) crafty, wily. ●悪らつな手段で by crafty means.

あくりょう 悪霊 ●悪霊にとりつかれる be possessed by an evil spirit. ●悪霊を追い払う exorcise [expel] the evil spirit.

あくりょく 握力 (a) grip. ●握力が強い[弱い] have a strong [a weak] grip.
●握力計 a hand-dynamometer.

アクリル ●アクリル樹脂 acrylic resin. ●アクリル繊維 acrylic fiber. ●アクリルプラスチック acrylic plastic.

あくる- 明くる- [その次の] the next; [その後に続く] the following. ●明くる日に the next [following] day. (⇨翌日)

あくれい 悪例 a bad example [(先例) precedent].
●悪例を残す set a bad example.

あくろ 悪路 a bad [(でこぼこの) a rough, (雨でどろどろの) a muddy] road. ●名代(ﾀﾞｲ)の悪路をジープで飛ばす drive a jeep along the notorious road.

アクロバット [曲芸] acrobatics.

-あけ -明け ●休会明けの(=後の)国会 a new session of the Diet after recess. ▶今年の梅雨明けはまだです(=梅雨はまだ終わっていない) The rainy season is not over yet this year.

あげ 揚げ (油揚げ)(a piece of) thin deep-fried bean curd.

あげあし 揚げ足 ●揚げ足を取る (話) nitpick (at him).
●揚げ足取り (話) nitpicking; (人) (話) a nitpicker.

あけがた 明け方 ●明け方(に) (夜明けに) at dawn (⇨夜明け); (早朝に) in the early morning. ●明け方まで話し込む talk until the break [crack] of dawn.

あぐ 挙句 ●事業は何度も事業に失敗した挙げ句(=後)破産した After many failures in business he went bankrupt.
●挙げ句の果て ▶私は疲れて腹ぺこだった. 挙げ句の果てに雨まで降り出した I was tired and hungry, and, to crown [top, cap] it all, it began to rain. (!いずれも口語的)

あけくれる 明け暮れる ● 悲しみに明け暮れる(=日々を過ごす)*spend* one's *days* in (one's) sorrow. ● 研究に明け暮れる *spend all* one's *hours* on studies [(研究以外何もしない) *do nothing but* study] *day in and day out*. (❗自然科学などの研究なら spend all hours doing research ... ともいえる)

あげさげ 上げ下げ ❶ [上下に動かすこと] ▶旗を上げ下げする *raise and lower* a flag. ❷ [物価などの変動] (a) fluctuation. (⇨変動)

あげしお 上げ潮 the flood tide. (⇨潮) ▶上げ潮に乗って入港する enter harbor *on the flood tide*. ▶上げ潮に乗る(=時流に乗る) *go with the tide*.

あけすけ 明け透け ── **あけすけな** 形 frank; (隠さない) open; (遠慮のない) unreserved.
── **あけすけに** 副 frankly; openly. (⇨率直)

あげぜんすえぜん 上げ膳据え膳 ▶上げ膳据え膳の男 a man who won't lift a finger in the house.

あげぞこ 上げ底 ▶この箱は上げ底になっている There's a *raised* [(にせの) a *false*] *bottom* to this box.

あけたて 開け閉て ▶母は戸の開け閉てまでいちいちうるさい My mother nags me about trivial matters such as *opening or closing* a door.

あけっぱなし 開けっ放し ▶ドアを開けっ放しにしておく *leave* the door *open*; (開いた状態に保っておく) *keep* the door *open*. ▶開けっ放しの(=開けっ広げな)性格の人 a *frank* [an *outspoken*] person.

あけっぴろげ 開けっ広げ ── **開けっ広げな** 形 (誠実で言うべきことは言う) frank; (隠しごとのない) open. ▶彼女は開けっ広げな性格でクラスの人気者である She is very *straightforward* [*outspoken*] and everyone in the class likes her. (❗She has an open nature. は「彼女は寛大な心の持ち主だ (She is broad-minded.)」の意)

あげつらう 論う ▶ (いろいろとけちをつける) criticize, complain about [of]..., 《今は堅い》find fault [×faults] with 《him [one's work]》.

あげて 挙げて (⇨挙げる⓮)

あけてもくれても 明けても暮れても [[「1日中」の強調形]] day in and day out; day in, day out; night and day. ▶明けても暮れても思うのは彼女のことばかり I think of her *night and day*. ▶彼は明けても暮れてもテレビばかり見ている He *is always* watching TV [*is watching* TV *all the time*]. (❗進行形とともに always, all the time を用いると通例非難を暗示)

あけのこる 明け残る ▶月がまだ明け残っている The moon still *lingers in the morning sky*.

あけのみょうじょう 明けの明星 the morning star, the daystar.

あげは(ちょう) 揚羽(蝶) [昆虫] a swallowtail (butterfly).

あけはなす 開け放す ▶窓を開け放す (ぱっと開く) *throw* [*fling*] a window *open*; (広く開ける) *open* a window *wide* [×widely]; (全部の窓を開ける) *open all* the windows; (開けておく) *keep* [*leave*] a window *open*. (⇨開(ぁ)く❺)

あけび 木通,通草 [植物] akebia, akebi; chocolate vines.

あけぼの 曙 ❶ [明け方] (a) dawn, daybreak. ❷ [始まり] the dawn, the beginning. ▶文明のあけぼの the dawn of civilization.

あげまく 揚げ幕 (花道への出入り口の幕) *agemaku*; (説明的に) the curtain that separates the backstage and the passageway in the Noh theater.

あげもの 揚げ物 deep-fried food. ▶野菜の揚げ物をする *deep-fry* vegetables. (❗fry vegetables は通例「野菜をいためる」の意)

あけやらぬ 明けやらぬ ▶いまだ明けやらぬ空 the sky *just before dawn*.

あける 明ける ❶ [明け方になる] break*; (白み始める) dawn. ▶(明けても暮れても)夜が明けた (The) day [(The) morning, (The) dawn] *broke* [*has broken*]. (❗(1)×Night broke. とはいわない。(2) 日常会話では It's morning. (朝だ)や Morning has come [is here]. (朝がきた)のようにいう方が普通) ❷ [年が] ▶私は年が明けたらすぐその仕事に取りかかるつもりだ I'll get to the work as soon as the new year *begins* [*at the beginning of* the new year]. ❸ [終わる] ▶梅雨が明けた The rainy season *is* [×was] *over*.

:あける 空ける,開ける ❶ [空にする] (容器の中味を) empty (↔fill); (注ぐ) pour; (場所を) leave*, (書) vacate; (飲み干す) drink* ... up (❗通例命令形で). ▶バケツの水を空ける *empty* (the water *out of*) a bucket. ▶ミルクをなべに空ける *pour* [*empty*] the milk *into* a pan. ▶アパートを空ける(=出て行く) *leave* [*move out of*] the apartment. ▶ホテルのお客様は午前10時までに部屋を空けてください Hotel guests are requested to *check out* [*leave*, *vacate*] their rooms before 10 a.m. (❗leave, vacate は実際の場面で用いることはまれ) ▶2人でウイスキーを1本空けた The two of us *drank* [*emptied*, *finished*] a bottle of whiskey. ❷ [場所・余白を作る] (空いた場所を作る) make* room 《for》; (道を空ける) make way 《for》; (残す) leave*; (空白にしておく) leave ... blank. ▶広い[狭い]余白を空ける(=余白を大きく[小さく]取る) *leave* a wide [a narrow] margin. ▶だれも老人が座る場所を空けようとする者はいなかった No one would *make room for* the old man to sit down. ▶そこにいた人たちは消防車のために道を空けた The people there *made way for* the fire engine. ▶ここを2ページ空けておきなさい *Leave* the two pages *blank*. ▶1行ずつ空けて(=1行おきに)書きなさい Write *on every other line*. ❸ [留守にする] be away (from home) (❗遠く離れて不在であることを表す); (ちょっと外出している) be out. ▶一晩家を空ける *stay out* all night. ▶彼は1週間家を空けます He will *be away* (*from home*) for a week. ▶彼らは休暇で家を空けた(=出かけた) They *went away* on holiday. ❹ [場所・時間を取っておく] (部屋などを) reserve; (時間などを) keep* [hold*] ... open. ▶その座席は老人用に空けてください Please *reserve* the seats *for* older [elderly] people. ▶私は土曜の午前中は学生たちのために空けてあります I *keep* Saturday mornings *open* [*free*] for my students./I have my *office hour* on [My *office hour is*] Saturday mornings. (《参考》米国の大学で学生が自由に教授に会える時間。しばしば研究室のドアに office hour と明示されている) ❺ [開(ひら)く] open (↔close); (開けておく) keep* [leave*] ... open. (❗open は意図的に, leave は放任の意。open は形容詞), (錠をはずす) unlock; (包み・荷物などを) unpack, undo*. ▶窓を開ける *open* [*raise*] a window. (❗raise は「上げて開ける」。スーツケースを開ける open 《開いて中の物を取り出す》*unpack*] a suitcase. ▶包みを開ける *undo* a package. ▶箱のふたを開ける *lift* the lid of a box; *take* the lid *off* a box; *open* a box. ▶引き出しを(引いて[すべらせて])開ける *pull* [*slide*] a drawer *out*. ▶手紙の封を破って開ける *tear* a letter *open*. (❗open は形容詞で, 破った結果の状態を表す) ▶「孝雄, そこのワインを開けてちょうだい」と彼女は言った "*Open* the wine bottle [*Uncork* the bottle of wine], Takao," she said [《古・まれ》said she]. ▶本の15ページを開けない *Open* your book(s) to [《英》at] page 15. ▶窓を開けておいてください Please *keep* [*leave*] the window *open* (↔closed). (!) keep は風を入れるなどの目的で窓を開けておくの状態を保つこと, leave は単に今開いている窓を閉めずに放っておくことを表す. open の代わりに ×opened は不可) ▶彼はドアを乱暴に[破って, さっと]開けた He *threw* [*broke*; *swung*] the door *open*. ▶口を大きく開けて「あー」と言ってらん Just say "ah" *with* your mouth wide *open*. ▶この鍵(か)でドアを開けてください Please *unlock* [*open the lock of*] the door with this key. ▶彼は電話帳をめくって「こ」の部分を開けた He *leafed through* a telephone directory to the Ko's.

❻ [穴を作る] make*; （ドリルで）drill; （きりなどで）bore; （パンチで）punch; （堀って）dig*; （切って）cut*; （焼いて）burn*; （破って）tear*; （虫などが）eat*. （!）▶ドリルで金属に穴を一つ空ける drill a metal to *make* a hole; *drill* a hole through [in] a metal; *make* a hole through [in] a metal with a drill. ▶切符を切ってもらう(＝穴を空けてもらう) *have* one's ticket *punched*.

::あげる 上げる, 挙げる, 揚げる INDEX

❶ 高い所へ移す　　❷ 与える
❸ …してあげる　　❹ 成果・利益などを得る
❺ 向上させる
❻ 価格・量などを上昇させる
❼ 見つけ出して・並べ立てて示す
❽ 大きな声などを出す　　❾ 食べた物を吐く
❿ 揚げ物をする　　⓫ ある費用で済ます
⓬ 中へ入らせる　　⓭ 終わりにする
⓮ すべてを結集する

WORD CHOICE　　上げる, 上がる

raise 頭・眉・目線などを軽く上げること. 比喩的に税金・基準などを引き上げることも表す. ●教育水準を引き上げる *raise* the educational standard.
lift 一定の肉体的・人為的努力を伴って, 頭・あご・腕・グラスなどを持ち上げること. ●容器のふたを持ち上げる *lift* the lid of bin.

頻度チャート

raise ▬▬▬▬▬▬▬▬▬
lift ▬▬
       20   40   60   80   100 (%)

❶ [高い所へ移す] (a) [持ち上げる] raise, put*…up; pull…up; lift (…up); hoist; heave*.

使い分け **raise** ものを上の方へ移動する動作をいうが, 自然な[予想どおりの]高さに移動することを含意する.
put…up raise とほぼ同じ意味のくだけた語.
pull…up put…up に引っ張って上げるという意味が加わったもの.
lift (up) raise とほぼ同じ意味だが, よりくだけた語で, 肉体的努力が必要なことを暗示する.
hoist 旗・重い物をロープ・機械などを使って上げること.
heave 重い物を努力して持ち上げること.

●いかりを上げる *weigh* anchor; *raise* [*pull up*] an anchor. ●船から荷をあげる *hoist* the cargo out of the ship; *unload* the ship; (桟橋に) *unload* the cargo onto the jetty. ●ブラインドを上げる *raise* the (window) shade(s). ▶数名の学生が質問をしようと手を上げた A few of the students *raised* [*put up*] their hand(s) to ask questions. (!) 各学生が上げる手は片手なので単数形の手が普通. cf. We have *a* nose.) ▶犯人は両手を上げて家から出てきた The criminal came out of the house with (his) arms *raised* [*put up*]. (!) 「with＋目的語＋補語」は付帯状況を表す. raised, put up は過去分詞) ▶みんなにその本が高く上げなさい[上げてほしさい] *Raise* [*Hold up*] the book so (that) everyone can see it. (!) 後の方は上げた高さのまま保つことをいう.《話》ではしばし用を省略する)　▶この箱を棚に[2階に]上げてくれませんか Could you *put* this box *up* on the shelf [*carry this box upstairs*]? ▶それを上げるにはジャッキを使わなければならなかった We had to use a jack to *lift* it. ▶その子はずり落ちてきたズボンを上げた That boy *pulled up* [(さっと) *jerked up*, 《主に米語》*hiked up*] his pants [*trousers* 《英》]. ▶手を上げろ(強盗などが) Hands *up*!/*Hold up* your hands! (!) 通例 ×Hold up! とはいわない) ▶彼女は読んでいる本から眼を上げた She *looked up* [*lifted her eyes*, *raised her eyes*] from the book she was reading.

(b) [敷いてある物を] take*…up (↔put down, lay).
●じゅうたんをあげる *roll* [*take*] *up* a carpet. (!) 「大きなじゅうたんをあげる」は通例 roll up. take [lift] up は小さなものについて用いる) ●布団をあげる(＝押し入れに片づける) *put* the bedding *away* (in the closet).
(c) [空中に] ●たこ揚げる *fly* a kite. ●気球を揚げる *launch* [*fly*] a balloon. ●旗を揚げる *put up* [*run up*, *raise*, *hoist*] a flag. ●花火を揚げる *set off* fireworks. ▶機械が火花をあげていたので止めた The machine *was throwing up* sparks and I turned it off.

❷ [与える] give*; （許可して与える）allow /əláu/; （与えようと申し出る）offer.

①《…を[に]あげる》 ▶これをあげます This is for you./Here's something for you. (!) 以上は直接的な I'll *give* this to you. より丁寧)/You can have this./(取っておいてください) Keep this.
会話「そのLP盤は値打ちものよ. 手放してはだめよ」「いい, あなたにあげる」"The LP is valuable. Hang onto it." "No. You take it."
②《A(人)にB(物)をあげる》（他の物でなくBを）give A B;（他の人にではなくAに）give B to A. ▶私はそれを彼女にあげた I *gave* it *to* her. (!) (1) A・Bも代名詞の場合, ×I gave her it. とは通例いわない. ただし I *gave* her that [this, one]. および指示代名詞や不定代名詞が続く場合は (2) gave または her に強勢がある) ▶あなたにもう一度チャンスをあげよう I'll *give* [*allow*] you one more [another] chance. ▶それをやるなら君に1万円あげよう I'll *give* you 10,000 yen if you do it./I'll *offer* you 10,000 yen for it. ▶その本はいらなかったので人にあげた I *gave* the book *away* [×*gave away the book*] (to someone) because I didn't need it. (!) give…away は「ただであげる」の意)
会話「あのマフラーはだれにあげたの」「田中君によ」"Who did you *give* that scarf *to*?" "I *gave* it [the scarf] *to* Tanaka." (!)(1) A に関係代名詞の先行詞となる場合も同様に to がある方が普通: 私があのマフラーをあげた人はアメリカ人です The person I *gave* that scarf *to* is American. (2) 答えとして ×I gave Tanaka it [the scarf]. は不適切)
会話「秀雄には誕生日に何をあげましたか」「おもちゃの電車」"What did you *give* Hideo for his birthday?" "I *gave* him a toy train." (!) この場合答えとして ×I gave a toy train to him. は不適切)

❸ [...してあげる]

解説 「...してあげる」は, Do you want [Would you like] me to do...? などの慣用的表現, You can do.... などのおだやかな許可を表す表現, give や help などの恩恵を与えることを含意する動詞などで表せるが, 恩恵を受ける対象となる人を表す (for) you などを明示することで表現できることもある.

▶彼女は弟に本を読んであげた She *read* the book *to* her brother./She *read* her brother the book. (! 前の方は前者に, 後の方は後者に重点がある (⇨ ② ②)) ▶彼に話してあげましょうか *Do you want* [*Would you like*] *me to* speak to him? (! 後の方が丁寧な言い方)/Shall I speak to him (*for you*)? ▶悪いけど君のを手伝ってあげられないんだ Sorry, but I can't *help* you *with* yours. ▶いつでも貸してあげますよ *You can borrow* [*use*] it any time. (! 直接的な I'll lend it to you any time. のように恩着せがましくない)
会話 「そのスーツケース持ってあげるよ」「ありがとう, でも重いわよ」 "*Let me* carry your suitcase." "Thank you, but you'll find it heavy."

❹ [成果・利益などを得る] (得る) get*; (産出する) produce; (得点などを) score; (勝ち取る・努力して得る) win*. ●すばらしい成果をあげる *get* [努力して] *obtain*, *achieve*] excellent results. ●その取り引きで5万円の利益を上げる *make a profit of* 50,000 yen on the deal. ▶その農場はかなりの収穫をあげた That farm *produced* a good harvest. ▶カープは初回に6点あげた The Carp *scored* [*earned*] six runs in the first inning. ▶我がチームは初めての勝利をあげた Our team *won* the game for the first time [*won* the first victory].

❺ [向上させる] improve. ▶英語の成績をあげるのにはどうしたらいいのか分からない I don't know how to *improve* my grade [to *get* a high grade] in English. ▶彼は最近テニスの腕をあげた He *has* really *improved* his tennis recently./His tennis *has improved* a lot recently. ▶彼は仕事の能率をあげるためにパソコンを買った He bought a personal computer to *improve* [*increase*] the efficiency of his job./He bought a personal computer to *make* his job more *efficient*. ▶彼は今度の受賞で男をあげた(= 高い信望を得た) He *won* [*gained*, (やっと) *acquired*, (築いた) *built up*] a high reputation for winning the prize.

❻ [価格・量などを上昇させる] (価格などを) raise, put*... up; (数量を) increase; (音量・熱量など) turn... up. ●スピードを上げる speed up; (車で) drive faster. ▶もし値段を上げれば必ず大騒ぎになるだろう If we *raise* [*put up*] the prices, people are sure to make a noise. ▶先月給料を10パーセント上げてもらった I got [They gave me] a ten percent (pay) *raise* last month./They *raised* [*increased*] my pay by 10 percent. ▶テレビのボリュームを上げてくれませんか Will you *turn up* (the volume on) the TV?

❼ [見つけ出して・並べ立てて示す] (示して見せる) show*; (挙げる) give, provide; (引用する) 《やや書》 cite; (列挙する) list, 《書》 enumerate; (名前などを) mention. ●証拠をあげる *give* [*show*, *introduce*, *produce*] evidence. ●例をあげる *give* [*show*, *provide*, *cite*] an example. ▶彼はそこへ行った理由をくつあげた He *gave* me some reasons for (his) going there. ▶日本の主な産業を3つあげられますか Can you *name* [*mention* (the names of)] three major industries in Japan? ▶強盗はまだあげられて(= 逮捕されて)いない The Robber *hasn't been arrested yet*./《やや書》 The robber *is still at large*. (! *at large* は「つかまっていない」の意)

‼ DISCOURSE
よい教師の資質とは何だろうか. きっと多くの人が, 特定教科の深い知識を挙げにるでしょう. しかし私は, 教職はそれだけでないと考える What are the qualities of a good teacher? **Surely**, many people will *name* the depth of knowledge about the particular subject one teaches. However, I would say there is more to teaching than that. (! surely (きっと)は譲歩を表すディスコースマーカー)

❽ [大きな声などを出す] ●痛くて大声をあげる *give* [《やや書》 *raise*, 《書》 *utter*] a cry of pain. (! (1) pain の代わりに anger [fear, delight, surprise] を用いると, それぞれ「怒って[恐くて, 喜んで, 驚いて]大声をあげる」の意になる. (2) cry [shout, raise one's voice] in pain より細かい声の描写が可能: 痛くて哀れな叫び声をあげる *give* a pitiful cry of pain) ▶彼女は彼女他の前に現れたのきキャッと声をあげた She *shrieked* [*screamed*] when he suddenly appeared. (! 前の方がかん高い声)

❾ [食べた物を吐く] ●《書》 throw*... up, vomit (! 前の方が口語的に); (俗) puke. ▶その子は夕食で食べたものをあげた That boy *has thrown up* [*vomited*] his dinner [what he ate at dinner]. ▶彼女はその映画を見てあげそうになった When she saw the movie, she felt like *throwing up* [*sick in her stomach*]./(婉曲的に) The movie *turned* her *stomach*. (! 遠回しには feel [have] an *upset stomach* ともいう)

❿ [揚げ物をする] (たっぷりの油で) deep-fry, fry ... in deep oil [fat]; (少しの油で) fry. (! fry は「油で炒(いた)める」の意にも用いる (⇨炒める)) ●夕食に魚を揚げる *deep-fry* [*fry*] fish for dinner. ▶彼女はてんぷらを揚げるのがうまい She is good at *frying tempura* [(揚げ物をするのが) *cooking* [*making*] *fried food*].

⓫ [ある費用で済ます] ▶もっと安くあげたい I'd like to *get* it *cheaper* [*at a lower price*]. ▶コンパを1人3,000円であげたい(= 3,000円以下で開きたい) We'd like to *have* a class party *for less than* [*for under*] 3,000 yen per head [person].

⓬ [中へ入らせる] (来・部屋などに) let* 《*him*》 in; (学校へ送り込む) send* 《*him*》 to school. ▶私に黙って友達を家にあげてはいけません You shouldn't *let* your friends *into* the house without my permission. ▶彼はこの春娘さんを東京の大学にあげた He *sent* his daughter *to* a college in Tokyo this spring.

⓭ [終わりにする] finish, get* [*have*]... done. (⇨終わり ③) ▶この仕事を月末までにあげなければならない I have to *finish* this job [*get* this job *done*] by the end of this month. (! 後の方は確定完了. (米)に多い) ▶彼は2週間で卒論を書き上げた(= 書き終えた) He *finished* writing [ˣto write] his graduation thesis in two weeks.

⓮ [すべてを結集する] ●総力を挙げる *concentrate* the greatest possible effort 《*on*》. ●全力を挙げて with all one's strength. (⇨全力) ▶町を挙げて(= 町じゅうの)その一行を歓迎した The whole town [*Everyone in the town*] welcomed that party.

あけわたす 明け渡す [敵などに引き渡す] surrender 《a castle》; [家・場所などを立ち退く] 《書》 vacate; move [clear] out of. ●屋敷を明け渡す *vacate* the house.

あご 顎 a chin (! 下あごの先端部); a jaw (! 通例下あごをさす. 「上下両あご」は jaws).

①《～あご》・上[下]あご the upper [lower] jaw. ・二重あご《have》a double chin.
②《あごで》・あごを突き出す stick [thrust] one's *chin* out.(事情 抵抗・がんばりの姿勢)・あごをはずす dislocate one's *jaw*《×chin》.(! 骨格を示す場合は jaw)・あごをなでる rub [stroke] one's *chin*.(事情 米英人の場合機嫌よく思考にふけっているときのしぐさ,ختخを rub より強い動作)・あごをなぐる hit 《him》on the *chin*. ▶彼はドアの方へあごをしゃくった He pointed to the door with his *chin*./He nodded toward the door.
・あごが落ちる ▶彼女が作る野菜スープはあごが落ちるほど(=口の中でとろけるように)おいしい The vegetable soup she makes just *melts in your mouth*.
・あごが干上がる ▶石油価格がいっこうに下がらない。このままだとおれたちは今にあごが干上がってしまうよ Oil prices aren't getting any lower. If things continue like this, we will soon *starve to death*. (! starve to death は「飢え死にする」の意で,「生活や商売が立ち行かなくなる」の誇張した口語表現)
・あごで使う order [《話》boss]《him》around.
・あごを出す ▶丸太をのこぎりで切ってあごを出した(=へとへとになった) I *was exhausted [was tired out] from* sawing the logs.(事情 米英ではあごを突き出すことは不屈の意志や挑戦的な態度を表す)

あこう(だい) 赤魚(鯛) 〖魚介〗a kind of red rockfish.

アコースティック ❶[電気による増幅をしない] acoustic /əkúːstɪk/. ❷[音響効果](放送・劇などの) sound effects;(講堂などの) acoustics /əkúːstɪks/(! 複数扱い).
・アコースティックギター《play》an acoustic guitar.

アコーディオン an accordion. ・アコーディオン奏者 an accordionist.
・アコーディオンカーテン an accordion [a folding] curtain. アコーディオンドア an accordion [a folding] door.

あこがれ 憧れ (a) longing 《*for*》(抑えがたい)《主に書》(a) yearning《*for*》;〖賞賛〗admiration《*for*》. ・こがれのパリ Paris one *has longed [yearned] to visit* for a long time. ▶その歌手は少女たちのあこがれの的 The singer is the *admiration* of girls [the object of girls' *dream(s)*].

*****あこがれる** 憧れる long《主に書》yearn》《*for; to do*》(! 後の方がより情緒的);[賛美する] admire.
・名声にあこがれる *long* [*yearn*] *for* fame. ▶彼女は女優にあこがれている She *longs* [*yearns*] *to* be an actress./Her dream is [It is her dream] to become an actress. ▶彼は私があこがれている作家です He is a writer I *admire* [心酔する) *adore*].

あこぎ 阿漕 ─ **あこぎな** 形 ・あこぎな(=あくどい)男 a *cruel and heartless* [《無情な》a *ruthless*, (どん欲な) a *greedy*] man.

あごひげ a beard /bíərd/. ・(手入れの行き届いた)あごひげをはやした人 a man with a (well-trimmed) *beard*; a *bearded* man. ・あごひげをはやす[はやしている] grow [have, wear] a *beard*.

あごやがい 阿古屋貝 〖魚介〗a pearl oyster.

：あさ 朝 (a) morning.

解説 (1) 冠詞に関して: morning は「気持ちのよい朝」では a pleasant morning のように不定冠詞をつけて用いるが,慣用的に「朝には」では in *the morning* のように定冠詞を伴ったり,「朝から晩まで」では from *morning* till night のように無冠詞で用いる。
(2) 時刻に関して: morning は通例日の出から正午までの時間をさす。evening の始まりは日没時か仕事などの終了時とされることもあり,通例 17-18 時くらいから就寝時または一般的な活動の終了する 21 時くらいまでをさすことが多い。下の図は時計の 12 時の位置に午前 0 時をとり,1 日 24 時間の各時間帯の名称を示したものである。

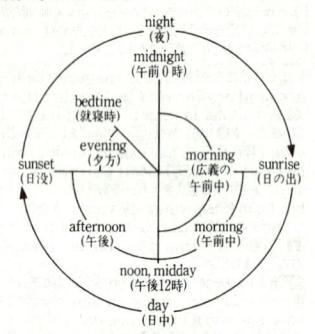

night (夜)
midnight (午前0時)
bedtime (就寝時)
evening (夕方)
sunset (日没)
afternoon (午後)
noon, midday (午後12時)
day (日中)
morning (午前中)
sunrise (日の出)
morning (広義の午前中)

(3) 前置詞に関して: 「朝に(は)」では in. 形容詞を伴った「(ある種の)朝に」や特定の日の「朝には」では on. ただし,時刻を伴う場合は in も可: 5 月 5 日の朝 10 時半に at 10:30 *on* [*in*] *the morning of* May 5. (⇒午前) tomorrow, yesterday, the next (その次の), the previous (その前の), this, every, one, some などが前につくと副詞句となり前置詞はつかない。

▶朝だ。起きる時間だ It's *morning*. Time to get up. (! 後の方は *It's time* … が省略されたもの) ▶すがすがしい朝の風だこと What a refreshing *morning* breeze! ▶もう朝の 4 時だ。寝なさい It's four o'clock *in the morning*. Go to bed. ▶彼女は朝は(いつもピアノを弾く She always plays the piano *in the morning*.(! 習慣的行為を表す場合は通例複数形)/She plays the piano 《×in》 every *morning*. ▶彼らはパリに 8 月 1 日 [日曜日] の朝到着した They arrived in Paris *on* [×in] *the morning of* August 1 [(*on*) Sunday *morning*]. (! Sunday morning の前の on は《主に米》ではしばしば省略される) ▶とても寒い朝早く,次の日の朝に出かけた He went hunting *on* a very cold *morning* [early *in the morning*, the next *morning*]. ▶明朝一番にそれをやります I'll do it first thing tomorrow *morning*./I'll do it first thing *in the morning* (tomorrow). (! 状況から明らかな場合 tomorrow は省略してよい) ▶今日は朝から降っている It has been raining since (this) *morning*. ▶朝は(=朝食は)トースト 1 枚ですませます I have just a slice of toast for *breakfast*. ▶電話切るぞ。明日は仕事で朝が早いんだ I'm hanging up. I must go to work very early tomorrow (morning).

あさ 麻 〖植物,繊維〗hemp;〖亜麻〗flax;〖布〗hemp cloth;《亜麻》linen;〖糸〗twine.

あざ 痣 (生まれつきの) a birthmark; (打撲などによる) a bruise /brúːz/;(打たれてできた目の周りの) a black eye. ▶彼はなぐられてあざができた He was beaten (till he was) *black and blue*. (! 通例( )内は省略する)

：あさい 浅い ❶[深さが] shallow (↔deep). ・浅い皿 [穴] a *shallow* dish [hole]. ・浅い浮き彫りの *low* relief. ▶この川はあそこで浅くなっている This river *becomes shallow* (浅瀬) the *shallows*] at that point. (! 前の方が普通)
❷[程度・状態が] (傷などが) slight; (眠りの) light (

sound); (色が) pale; (考えなどが) shallow. ●浅い緑 *pale* [*light*] green. ●考えの浅い人 a *shallow* (a deep) thinker; a *superficial* person. ●彼との交際は浅い I have a *slight* acquaintance [am *slightly* acquainted] with him. (❗(単なる知り合いだ) He's just an acquaintance. (❗後の方が口語的) 私の父は眠りが大変浅い My father is a very *light* sleeper. ●彼はまだ先生の経験が浅い(=あまり経験がない) He *doesn't* have *much* experience of teaching. ●私はローマ史については浅い(=うわべだけの)知識しかない I have only a *superficial* knowledge of Roman history./My knowledge of Roman history is poor. ●あの人はいっしょにいると面白いが、とても思慮の浅い人だ He's fun to be with, but he's very *superficial*.
❸ [時間が] (短い) short. ●この大学は創立以来まだ日が浅い It's *not* been [《ややまれ》 It's *not*] *long* since this college was founded./This college was founded *only a short time ago*./This college is *quite a new* [*a recent*] foundation. ●春はまだ浅い(=時はまだ早春である) It's still *early spring*./春になったばかりだ) Spring has just come.

あさいち 朝市 a morning open-air market.
あさがえり 朝帰り ── 朝帰りする 動 get home (early) in the morning; (外泊する) stay out all night.
あさがお 朝顔 〖植物〗 a morning glory. ●クウェートの空港の小便器は朝顔(=便器)の位置が異様に高い At Quait airport, men's urinals are (placed) unusually high on the wall.
あさがた 朝方 early in the morning, in the early morning. ●朝方(=夜明け方(ごろ))になって寝入る fall asleep *toward dawn*.
あさがた 朝型 ●あの人は朝型だ He is a *morning* (↔ *night*) *person*.
あさぎ 浅黄 (薄い黄色) pale [light] yellow.
あさぎ 浅葱 (薄い藍色) pale [light] blue.
あさくさのり 浅草海苔 (海藻) laver; (食品) (a sheet of) dried laver. (⇨海苔)
あさぐもり 朝曇り a cloudy morning.
あさぐろい 浅黒い rather dark, (少し黒く赤っぽい) swarthy. (❗後の方は不気味さを暗示することもある) ●浅黒い肌をしている have a (a) *rather dark* skin. (❗a swarthy fisherman a (a) *赤銅色の漁師*).
あざける 嘲る ridicule, 《書》deride, (やじったり冷やかして) jeer (at ...); (人の弱点などをあざけって) mock (at ...). ●彼らは彼の臆病(びょう)さをあざけった They *ridiculed* [*jeered* (at), *mocked* (at)] his cowardice.
あさごはん 朝御飯 breakfast. (⇨朝食)
あさせ 浅瀬 (海·川の) shallows, a shoal; (川の歩いて渡れる部分) a ford. ●(船が)浅瀬に乗り上げる be wrecked in the *shallows*; run ashore. ●浅瀬で遊ぶ play in the *shoals*.
あさぢえ 浅知恵 ●しろうとの浅知恵 the *shallow cleverness* of a layman.
あさつき 浅葱 〖植物〗 a chive. (❗通例複数形で)
あさって 明後日 the day after tomorrow. (❗《米話》 ではしばしば the を省略する) ●あさっての朝 the morning *after next*. ●あさって来れますか Can you come *the day after tomorrow*? ●英語では曜日表現が優先され「あさって」が金曜日であれば next Friday などということが多い) ●あすかあさって伺います I'll come to see you tomorrow or *the day after*. ●あらしが一晩じゅう吹き荒れた翌朝、田んぼに行ってみるとかかしがあさっての方向(=まったく違う方向)を向いて立っていた The morning after it stormed all night, I went to the rice field and found a scarecrow facing *in the completely wrong direction* there.
あさっぱら 朝っぱら ●朝っぱらから何をしているの What are you doing *early in the morning*?
あさつゆ 朝露 morning dew (↔ night dew).
あさで 浅手 (軽い傷) a slight wound [cut].
あざな 字 〖本名以外につけた名〗 a name received when one comes of age; 〖あだ名〗 (⇨あだ名).
あざなう 糾う twist 《a rope》; (織り合わせる) interweave.
あさなぎ 朝凪 a morning calm (on the sea).
あさなゆうな 朝な夕な morning and evening; (いつも) always.
あさね 朝寝 名 ●朝寝ふかしをする sleep late in the morning and stay up late at night. (❗keep late [bad] hours は「夜ふかしをする」または「朝寝をする」のどちらかの意)
── 朝寝する 動 sleep late in the morning; (遅く起きる) get up late; (うっかり寝過ごして) oversleep; (意図的に) 《米話》sleep in. ●朝寝して学校に遅れた I *overslept* and was late for school. ●翌日は休みだったので朝寝した I *slept in* because it was a holiday [xa vacation] (the) next day. (❗vacation は 1 日でなく長期の休み)
あさねぼう 朝寝坊 名 late rising; (人) a late riser.
── 朝寝坊する 動 (⇨朝寝)
あさはか 浅はか ── 浅はかな 形 (愚かな) silly, foolish (= 愚か); (無思慮な) thoughtless, (浅薄な) shallow, (やや書) superficial. ●浅はかな考え a *shallow* [*a foolish*] idea. ●彼を信じるなんて我ながら浅はかだった It was silly [*foolish, thoughtless*] of [xfor] me to trust him.
あさばん 朝晩 morning and evening. ●彼は朝晩犬を散歩させる He walks his dog *in the mornings and evenings*. (❗習慣を表す場合は通例複数形で)
あさひ 朝日 the rising [morning] sun. (⇨夕日) ●朝日がぐんぐん昇っていく The *sun* is rising quickly.
あさぶろ 朝風呂 ●朝風呂に入る take 《主に米》 [have 《英》] *a morning bath*.
あさぼらけ 朝ぼらけ (a) dawn, daybreak. (⇨夜明け)
あさましい 浅ましい ❶ 〖卑しい〗 (卑劣な) mean; (軽蔑すべき) contemptible; (顔を合わせるのが恥ずべき) shameful. ●浅ましい行為 *mean* [*contemptible, shameful*] behavior. ●彼は何と浅ましいやつだ What a *mean* [*a contemptible*] fellow he is!
❷ [みすぼらしい] (姿などが) shabby.
あざみ 薊 〖植物〗 a thistle. (参考 スコットランドの国花)
あさみどり 浅緑 (薄い緑色) pale [light] green.
あざむく 欺く deceive. (⇨だます) ●彼女は花をも欺く美しさだ(=花と同じように美しい) She is *as beautiful as a rose*. (事情 女性の美しさはよくバラにたとえられる)
あさめし 朝飯 breakfast. (⇨朝食)
あさめしまえ 朝飯前 ●そんなこと朝飯前だ That's *nothing* [*an easy job*, 《話》*a cinch*]. ●《口》決まり文句で That's child's play [a piece of cake]. ともいう)
あさもや 朝もや (薄い霧) (a) morning mist [かすみ haze]. ●朝もやに包まれる be covered in the *morning mist* [*haze*]. (⇨霧 ❶)
*あざやか 鮮やか ── 鮮やかな 形 ❶ [色·形·思い出などが] (鮮明な) vivid; (はっきり見える) clear; (明るい) bright, brilliant (❗後の方が強意的); (新鮮な) fresh. ●鮮やかな赤 *vivid* [*bright, brilliant*] red. ●鮮やかな輪郭 a *clear* outline. ●鮮やかな木の新緑 the *fresh* green of leaves. ●おんどりの尾は鮮やかな色をしていた The rooster's tail was *brightly* colored.

❷[技術・演技などが]（熟練した）skillful;（華々しい）brilliant;（優れた）excellent;（すばらしい）fine. ●鮮やかな演技をgive a *skillful* [a *fine*,《話》a *beautiful*] performance.
—— 鮮やかに 副 [はっきりと]vividly, clearly;［巧みに］skillfully;（見事に）brilliantly. ▶彼女の結婚式の日のことを今でも鮮やかに覚えているI still remember her wedding day *vividly* [*clearly*]./I still have a *vivid* [a *clear*] memory of her wedding day./Her wedding day is still *fresh* [*vivid*] in my memory.

あさやけ 朝焼け a morning glow; the glow (of the sky) at sunrise.

あさゆ 朝湯 (⇨朝風呂)

あさゆう 朝夕 morning and evening.（⇨朝晩）

あざらし 海豹 【動物】a seal（徴 ~(s)）. ●アザラシの（毛）皮 sealskin.

あさり a Japanese littleneck (clam); a clam（!二枚貝の総称）. ●アサリを掘る dig for *clams*.

あさる 漁る ［捜す］look [search, hunt]《*for*》;（ごみの中から）scavenge. ●食べ物はないかとごみ入れあさる *scavenge* for food *in* a garbage can [*in* a garbage can *for* food]. ●古本屋で稀覯(きこう)本をあさる *hunt* for rare books at secondhand bookstores.

あざわらう 嘲笑う ●他人の失敗をあざ笑うな Don't *laugh at* [*ridicule*, *jeer at*, *sneer at*] other people's failure.（⇨嘲(ちょう)，嘲笑(ちょうしょう)）

あし 足, 脚 ❶[人・動物・いすなどの脚部] a leg（!太もも付け根から足首まで（⇨❷）;（タコ・イカなどの）an arm.

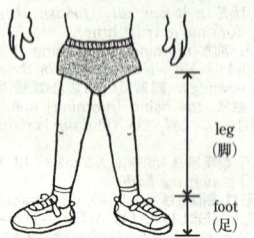

（足のイラスト：leg（脚）, foot（足））

①【～（の）足】●きれいな［太い；ほっそりした］足 nice [thick; slender] *legs*. ●昆虫の足 an insect's *legs*. ●テーブルの脚 the *legs* of a table.（!×the table's legs とはいわない）●グラスの足 the *stem* of a glass.
②【足が】●片方の足［右足］が不自由 be lame of one *leg* [*in* the right *leg*].（!前置詞の違いに注意）●足がすくむ（足すくむ）●彼は足が長い He has long *legs*.（!His *legs* are long. より普通）/He is long-*legged*. ●彼は足が達者（=健脚）だ He has strong（↔weak）*legs*./He's a good（↔a poor）walker. ●足が宙に浮くように感じた I felt as if I didn't have any *legs*. ●怖くて足がふるえた My *legs* trembled with fear.
③【足の】●4本脚の机 a four-*legged* desk. ●足の長い少女 a long-*legged* [a *leggy*] girl.（! *leggy* は子供・女性・子鹿などに用いる）●その部屋は足の踏み場もないほど散らかっていた The room was in such a mess that there was *no place to stand*.
④【足を】●足を組む cross one's *legs*. ●足を組んで座る sit (straight) with *legs* crossed《語源》日本と異なり、米英では男性の好ましい座り方とされ、女性は cross one's *ankles*;（あぐらかいて）sit cross-*legged*. ●足をくずす（=楽に座る）sit at ease. ●足を動かす move one's *legs* (and *feet*). ●足を休める rest one's *legs* [*feet*]. ▶彼は右足をけがした［折った］He injured [broke] his right *leg*. ▶彼は座って足を前へ伸ばした He sat down and stretched out his *legs*.（! stretch one's legs は「長時間座ったあと足をほぐすために散歩する」）
⑤【足で】●片足で立つ stand *on* one *leg*.

❷[足首から先] a foot（徴 feet）;（哺乳(ほにゅう)動物のつめのある）a paw;（牛馬などのひづめのある）a hoof 〜s, hooves.
①【足が】●くぎを踏んで足が痛い I stood on the nail, and have a sore *foot*. ▶彼女は足が大きい She has big *feet*. ▶足がむくんでいる My *feet* are swollen.
②【足の】●足の甲 one's instep. ●足の裏 the sole of one's *foot*. ●足の指 a toe. ▶彼は私を頭のてっぺんから足のつま先までしげしげと眺めた He looked me over from head to *foot* [from top to *toe*].
③【足を】●はしごに片足をかける put a *foot* on the ladder. ●足を(くるぶしを)くじく sprain one's *ankle* [*xfoot*]. ●疲れた足を引きずる drag one's weary *feet*. ●足を引っ込める pull one's *foot* [*feet*] in. ▶気をつけろよ，ぼくの足を踏んづけたんだ Be careful. You stepped on my *foot* [*toe*].（!「足を踏んでるよ」は You're on my *foot* [*toe*].）▶私は足をすべらせて転んだ I slipped [lost my footing]《on the wet grass》and fell. ▶彼女に足をひっかけられた She tripped me (up).
④【足で】●足でけるkick《him》with one's *foot*. ▶犬は足で地面を掘る習性がある A dog has a habit of digging the ground with its *paws*.
⑤【足から】▶靴は左足から先にはきますか Do you put your left shoe on before your right? ▶彼は足から先に川に飛び込んだ He plunged into the river *feet* first.

❸[歩行]（歩くこと）walking;（歩調）a pace.
①【足が】●足が速い walk [run] fast（↔slowly）, be a fast（↔a slow）walker [runner].
②【足を】●足を速める quicken（↔slacken）one's *pace*. ●足を踏みはずして階段からころぶ落ちる make a false *step* and fall down the stairs. ▶彼は足を止めた He stopped *walking* [×to walk].（⇨立ち止まる）
③【足で】●急ぎ足で歩く walk at a quick [a fast] *pace*. ▶そこへは君の足で20分で行ける You can get there in twenty minutes at your *pace* [×feet]. ▶会社を出るとその足で買い物に行った I went shopping *right after* I left the office.

❹[交通手段] ▶この村は足の便がいい［悪い］This village *is easy* [*hard*] *to reach* [*easily accessible* (by road)]. ▶JR のストで1万人以上の人が足を奪われた More than ten thousand people were inconvenienced [were deprived of their *means of transportation*] by JR's strike.
会話「足の便は？」「ええ、おやじの車を借りました」"Have you got (any) *transportation*?" "Yes, I borrowed my old man's car."

❺[訪問] ▶私は彼のところにたびたび足を運んだ I *called on* [*visited*] him very often [frequently].

●足が地につかない（嬉しくて舞い上がっている）be walking [floating] on air. ●足が地についていない（現実的でない）be not in contact with reality; be unrealistic;（実用的でない）be impractical.
●足がつく be traced [tracked] to one's crime.
●足が出る ▶今月は3万円足が出た（=予算をオーバーした）We *ran over* [*exceeded*] *the budget* this month by thirty thousand yen./(赤字は総額…

だった) The *budget deficit totaled* thirty thousand yen this month.▶3万円の旅費では足が出る(=まかなえない)だろう Thirty thousand yen *won't be able to cover* the traveling expenses.
- 足が遠のく ▶友人も彼から足が遠のく(=近づかなくなり)始めた His friends began to *keep* [*stay*] *away from* him.
- 足が生える ▶年末は出費がかさんでお金が足(=羽)も生えたようにあっという間になくなってしまう The expenses run up at the end of the year and my money *takes to itself wings*.(!慣用表現)
- 足が早い (食品などが腐る) go bad easily.
- 足が棒になる ▶歩いて足が棒になった I walked my *legs* off./I walked till my *legs* got stiff.
- 足が向く (知らず知らずの方へ行く) head for 《the pub》without realizing it. ▶足の向くまま(気の向くまま) walk around wherever one feels inclined to; (目的なく) (⇨[足にまかせる]).
- 足でかせぐ ▶足でかせいだ情報 information one gathered doing legwork. (!legwork は「実地調査や取材など足を使う仕事」の意) ▶足でヒットをかせぐ〘野球〙a leg hit. ▶足でヒットをかせぐ〘野球〙leg out a single; beat out an infield hit.
- 足にまかせる ▶足にまかせて野原を歩く (目的なく) walk around 〘(主に英)about〙*aimlessly* in [on] the fields; (足元向くままに) wander about in the fields as one's *feet* [*legs*] lead one.
- 足を洗う ▶男は泥棒稼業から足を洗った(=やめた) The man *quit* [*gave up*] the life of a thief. (!wash one's feet にはこの意はない)
- 足をすくう *trip* 〘*him*〙 *up*. (⇨[足下(あし)])
- 足を使う ▶足を使った戦法〘野球〙a running game.
- 足を取られる ▶彼はロープに足を取られて倒れた He caught his *foot* in [×by] the ropes and fell down.
- 足を伸ばす ▶エジンバラを訪れた際ネス湖まで足を伸ばした(=行った) When I visited Edinburgh, I *made a trip* [*went as far as*] Loch Ness.
- 足を引っ張る ▶彼は私の足を引っぱった(=じゃまをした) He *got in* my *way*./He *held* me *back*.
- 足を踏み入れる (中へ歩いて入る) step 《*into* a room》; (特定の社会・分野に) enter [go into] 《the judicial world》; (足跡を記す) set foot 《*on*, *in*》. ▶探検隊はついに北極圏[極地]に足を踏み入れた The expedition finally *set foot on* the Arctic Circle [*in* the polar regions].
- 足を向ける ▶彼は公園に足を向けた He *walked* toward [*in* the direction of] the park.

あし 葦 〘植物〙a reed.
- 葦笛 a reed pipe.

‡あじ 味 ❶〘食べ物の〙(a) taste; (風味)(米) (a) flavor (後の方は特に好ましい味や香りを暗示); (塩・香辛料の)(やや書) a savor. (!薄味, 味付け)
①【味が[は]】▶味がする 〘物が主語〙 taste 〘圏; *of* +物〙, have a ... taste [flavor, savor]. (!...は形容詞); 〘人が主語〙(can) taste. ▶これはいい[変な; 甘い; すっぱい]味がする This *tastes* good [*strange*; *sweet*; *sour*]. (!) (1) 副詞を用いて ×This fruit *tastes* well. などとはいえない. (2) 進行形は徐々に変化することを表す場合を除いて通例不可: だんだんひどい味になってきている It's *tasting* nastier and nastier./This *has a* good [*a strange*; *a sweet*; *a sour*] *taste*. ▶その食べ物は少しニンニクの味がした The food *tasted* slightly of garlic./The food *had a* slight *taste* [*savor*] of garlic./I could *taste* a bit of garlic in the food. ▶コショウを少し加えると味がよくなるだろう If you put in a little pepper, it will *taste* better./A little pepper will give it more *taste* [*improve* its *taste*]. ▶ワインの味が落ちた The wine has lost its *taste* [*flavor*, *savor*]./(気が抜けてしまった) The wine has become *stale* [*flat*].

会話「そのスープはどんな味がしますか」「シチューのような味がします」"What does the soup *taste like*?" "It *tastes like* stew."

会話「お味はいかがですか」「最高だ. 今回は最高の出来ね」「それはどうも」"How does it *taste* (to you)?" "Exquisite! You've really outdone yourself this time." "How kind of you to say so!"

②【味の】▶味のよい delicious, tasty (!(1) 前の方が意味が強い. (2) ×tasteful の意ではいわない); (ぴりっと辛くて) savory. (!おいしい) ▶味の薄い(=刺激の少ない)スープ a *bland* soup.

会話「どんな味のポテトチップがいいですか」「チーズ味をください」"What *flavor* of chips do you want?" "Can I have cheese(-*flavored*) chips, please?"

(!通例単に Cheese, please. という)

❸【味を】▶味をみる taste, have a *taste* 《*of*》. (⇨味見する) ▶味をつける (香辛料で) season; (調味料で) flavor, give flavor to .... ▶彼女は塩加減を確かめるためにスープの味をみた She *tasted* [*had a taste of*] the soup to see if it needed more salt. ▶塩を少し入してスープの味を調える *Season* the soup *with* a bit [a pinch] of salt.

❷【魅力】(a) charm; (趣) a flavor. ▶味のある(魅力のある) attractive; (おもしろい) interesting. ▶この陶器には素朴な味がある This porcelain has a simple [a rustic] *charm*. ▶その翻訳で原文の味はすっかり損なわれた The translation destroyed the *charm* [*flavor*] of the original. ▶彼はなかなか味のある(=高尚な)文を書く His writings are very *sophisticated*. ▶年を取るほど人生は味が出てくる The older you grow, the more *interesting* life becomes [the more *flavor* life has]. ▶この絵は見れば見るほど味が出てくる(=心を引きつける) This picture *grows on* me. ▶彼は若い時にたばこ[酒]の味を覚えた(=好きになった) He *took to* smoking [drinking] when he was young. (!×He took to smoke [drink]... とはいわない)

❸【経験】(an) experience; a taste. ▶彼は貧乏の味を知らない He has no *experience* [*taste*] of poverty./He doesn't really know what it is like to be poor.

- 味もそっけもない ▶彼は味もそっけもない返事をした He made a *curt* reply./(手紙で) His letter was *stiff and dry*.
- 味をしめる ▶うまくいったことに味をしめて, 彼は多額の金を株に投資した He got a *taste* of success and invested a lot of money in stocks.

あじ 鯵 〘魚介〙a horse mackerel 《複; ~s》.

*アジア Asia /éiʒə/, 〘書〙(東洋) the Orient. ▶アジア(人)の Asian; 〘書〙(東洋の) Oriental. ▶アジア人 an Asian; 〘やや古・軽蔑的〙an Oriental; 〘集合的〙*Asian* people, the Asians. ▶小アジア *Asia Minor*.
- アジア開発基金 the Asian Development Fund 《略 ADF》. ● アジア開発銀行 the Asian Development Bank 《略 ADB》. ● アジア競技大会 the Asian Games [Olympics]. ● アジア太平洋経済協力 the Asia-Pacific Economic Cooperation 《略 APEC》. ● アジア大陸 the Asian Continent.

あしあと 足跡 a footprint; (人や動物の行方を示す足跡) a track. (!いずれも通例複数形で) (⇨足跡(そくせき))
- 足跡を残す leave *footprints* 《*in* the sand; *on* the carpet》. ▶雪の上に真新しい足跡が残っていた

There were fresh *footprints* in the snow. ▶彼はクマの足跡をたどった He followed the bear's [bear] *tracks*.

アジェンダ【検討課題】an agenda.

あしおと 足音 (a) a footstep, a step (🅵通例複数形で); (踏むこと) a tread (🅵単数形で).
① 【〜足音】● うるさい[静かな], 軽快な; 重い足音 noisy [soft; light; heavy] *footsteps* ▶春の足音が聞こえる I feel spring approaching./The first signs of spring have appeared.
② 【足音が】● だれかが近づいて来る足音がした I heard someone's *footsteps* coming near me [approaching me]./I heard approaching *footsteps*. ▶行進する足音が聞こえた I heard the *tread* of marching feet.
③ 【足音を】● 足音をしのばせて歩く walk stealthily [with stealthy steps], 〈🅵抜き足, 忍び足〉 ▶たどたど足音を立てるな Don't walk noisily.

翻訳のこころ 僕は足音を立てないように廊下を歩いて, 階段の踊り場に出た (村上春樹『レキシントンの幽霊』) I walked down the hallway softly not to make a sound and came out onto the landing. (🅵足音は歩くときに出る音なので sound だけでもよい)

あしか 海驢【動物】a sea lion (🅵アシカ・トドの類の総称).
あしがかり 足掛かり (足場) a foothold; (a) footing. (⇨足場 ❷)
あしかけ 足掛け ▶ここに来てもう足掛け5年(=5年目)になる This is my fifth year here.
あしかせ 足枷【書】fetters, 《書》shackles (🅵比喩的にも用いる); (自由な発達・成長の) a straitjacket; (重荷) a burden (⇨足手まとい). ▶足かせをかけられている囚人 a prisoner (who is kept) in *fetters* [*shackles*].
あしがため 足固め ● 足固めをする [足を鍛える] strengthen one's legs; [将来に備える] prepare (for), make preparations (for).
あしからず 悪しからず ▶その会合に出席できませんが悪しからず I'm sorry I can't attend the meeting.
あしがる 足軽 a *samurai* of the lowest rank; (兵兵) an infantryman.
あしきり 足切り a cut-off. ● 足切り点 a *cut-off* (point). ▶本校は入試の足切りはありません Our college has no *cut-offs* in the entrance exams.
あしくせ 足癖 ❶ [歩き方・座り方の癖] ▶彼は足癖がよくない (歩き方が) He has a peculiar walk./(座り方が) He sits with his legs in a bad position.
❷ [相撲の足技] foot techniques.
あしくび 足首 an ankle. ▶足首をくじく sprain [twist] one's *ankle*.
あしげ 足蹴 ▶足蹴にする [ける] kick, give ... a kick; [ひどい仕打ちをする] treat ... very badly.
あじけない 味気ない (おもしろ味のない) tasteless, uninteresting, flat; (うんざりした) dull; (無価な, 無益な) useless, empty; (わびしい) dreary, sad, miserable. ▶人生が味気なくなる grow weary of life; (張り合いのないものと思う) feel one's life worthless; (むなしく思う) feel one's life empty. ▶西洋庭園は味気ない Compared with Japanese gardens, European ones seem to *lack artistic depth*.
あしこし 足腰 (体) one's body; (脚) one's legs. ▶足腰を鍛えるため運動する do exercises to strengthen one's body. ▶足腰が立つ be able to stand up; (老人が元気に活動できる) be able to move [get] around.
あじさい 紫陽花【植物】a hydrangea /haidréindʒiə/.

あしざま 悪し様 ● あしざまに言う speak badly 《米・英古》[ill of] 《やや書》of (him) (🅵主に忠言・忠告の場合に用いる); (悪意を持って悪く言う) malign.
あししげく 足繁く ▶足しげく図書館に通う *often visit* the library; *pay frequent visits* to the library.
アジスアベバ【エチオピアの首都】Addis Ababa /ǽdisæbəbə/.
アシスタント【助手】an assistant (to [×of] him).
アシスト 图 〈スポーツ〉 an assist. ──アシストする 動 assist.
あしずり 足摺り ── 足ずりする 動 stamp one's feet (in anger).
アジソンびょう アジソン病【医学】Addison's disease.
*あした 明日 tomorrow. (⇨明日 (ぁす)) ▶あしたがあるさ(=あしたはあしたの風が吹く) Tomorrow is another day. (⇨明日 会話)
あしだい 足代 (運賃) a fare, 《米》a carfare. (⇨交通 ①) ▶足代もばかにならない *Transportation* costs a lot.
あしたば 明日葉【植物】Japanese angelica; (説明的に) an edible wild plant with broad, soft leaves.
あじつけ 味付け 图 (a) seasoning. (🅵塩 (salt)・ニンニク (garlic)・香辛用植物 (herb) などのほか, コショウ (pepper) などの香辛料 (spice) による) ▶シチューの味付けを見る try the stew to see how it is *seasoned*. ▶彼女は味付けにレモンを使った She used lemon for *seasoning*. ▶この料理は味付けが濃すぎる There's too much *seasoning* in this food. (🅵甘みについては ×seasoning は不可)
── 味付けする 動 ▶そのスープを塩で味付けする *season* the soup *with* some salt; put [add] some salt to the soup. (🅵後の方は砂糖 (sugar) なども可)
あしてまとい 足手まとい ▶私は子供の足手まといになりたくない I don't want to be a *burden to* [(お荷物)) a drag on] my children.
アジト [<ロシア語] [隠れ家] a hiding place; a hideout; [地下活動指令所] the underground headquarters.
あしどめ 足止め ▶私たちは地震のため静岡駅で6時間足止めを食った We were held up [《やや書》detained] at Shizuoka Station by the earthquake for six hours.
あしどり 足取り ❶ [歩き方] a step, 《書》a gait (🅵後の方は通例単数形で); (歩調) a pace. ▶重い [軽い; 速い] 足取りで歩く walk with a heavy [a light; a fast] *step*. ▶彼の足取りは軽かった He was light on his *feet*.
❷ [犯人などの] (a) trace. ▶殺人犯の足取りをつかむ [たどる] find [follow] the *trace* of the murderer.
あしな 味な ● 味な(=気のきいた)ことを言う say *smart* things.
あしながおじさん『足ながおじさん』 *Daddy-Long-Legs*. (🅵参照) ウェブスターの児童文学作品)
あしながばち 足長蜂【昆虫】a long-legged wasp.
あしなみ 足並み (歩調) a step, a pace. (⇨歩調) ▶足並みをそろえて歩く walk *in step*. ▶足並みを合わせる keep *pace* [(in) *step*] (with). (🅵後の方は比喩的に用いることが多い) ▶足並みがそろっている be *in* (⇔ *out of*) *step* (with). (🅵比喩的に「協調している」の意でも用いる) ▶足並みをそろえる(=協調して行動する) act *in concert* (with). ▶足並みを乱す break *step*.
あしならし 足慣らし ❶ [歩く練習] ▶病後の足慣らしに2,3歩歩く *practice walking* for a few minutes after one's illness.

❷ 〖運動競技の下準備〗 a warm-up; (激しい) a workout. ●試合の前に足慣らしをする *warm up* [*have a warm-up*] before the game.

あしば 足場 ❶〖建築現場などの〗●建物の周りに足場を組む put up *scaffolding* [a *scaffold*] around the building.
❷〖足がかり〗a foothold, (a) footing. ●足場を探りながら険しい崖を下りる climb down a steep cliff, feeling if one has a *foothold* on it. ●政界でしっかりとした足場を固める get [gain] a firm *foothold* in the political world.
❸〖交通の便〗●その病院は郊外にあって足場が悪い The hospital *is not easily accessible* [*inconveniently located*] in the suburbs.

あしばや 足早 ── 足早に ● 足早に歩く walk quickly. ●足早に通り過ぎる pass by at a *quick step* [*pace*]; pass by with *quick steps*. ●後の方は足の運び方を強調した言い方）●人々が部屋から部屋へと足早に出入りしていた People were rushing [scurrying] from room to room. ●(リスが) ちょろちょろする」が本来の意味）

あしび 馬酔木 〖植物〗an *ashibi*, an (Japanese) andrómeda.

あしぶえ 葦笛 a reed pipe [flute].

あしふき 足拭き a foot towel; (バスマット) a bath mat.

あしぶみ 足踏み 图 ●足踏み状態である[になる] be at [come to] a temporary standstill; be stuck. ── **足踏みする** 動 (どしんどしんと) stomp. ●(足を暖めようと思って)寒空の下で足踏みする *stamp around* in the cold. ●(行進で)音楽に合わせて足踏みする *mark time* to the music.

あしまわり 足回り ●この車は小型で足回りがいい(=運転しやすい) This car is small and *easy to drive*.

あじみ 味見 图 tasting; (試食すること) sampling. ●味見スプーン a *tasting* spoon. 〖参考〗木製のものが多い
── **味見する** 動 taste. ●味見させて Let me have a *taste*. (⇨味 ❶ ③)

あしもと 足下 〖足のそばに〗at one's feet; 〖歩み〗a step.
① 〖足もとが[の]〗●足もとがかちかちに凍っていた It was frozen hard *underfoot*. ●酔っ払いは足もとがふらついていた The drunken man was unsteady *on his feet*./The drunken man walked *with unsteady steps*. ●足もとが悪い(=道がぬかるむ[すべりやすい]ので気をつけてね Watch your *step* [×steps]! The road is muddy [slippery]. (❗you が複数の相手の場合でも steps とはしない)
② 〖足もとに〗●足もとにパスを送る[出す] 〖サッカー〗pass straight to (the other player's) foot. ●彼の足もとに身を投げて彼女はさめざめと泣いた Throwing herself *at his feet*, she cried bitterly. ●暗いので足もとにご用心 Watch (米) [Mind (英)] your *step* [*footing*, ×steps] in the dark.
●足もとから鳥が立つ 解雇通知を受け取ると、彼は足もとから鳥が立つように(=急に)町から出て行った He left the town *abruptly* when he received the dismissal notice. ●足もとから鳥が立つようなこと(=まったく予期せぬことは)よく起こるものだ Completely *unexpected* things will often happen.
●足もとにつけこむ take advantage of 《(him)》《(his)》weakness.
●足もとに火がつく ●その会社は足もとに火がついていた(=倒産寸前であった) The company was on the verge of bankruptcy.
●足もとにも及ばない ●水泳では康介の足もとにも及ばないよ I'm no match for Kosuke at swimming.
●足もとにも寄りつけない ●英語では彼女の足もとにも寄りつけない(彼女にはかなわない) I *am no match for* her in English. (彼女の方がずっとできる) She is much better at English than I am. (話 me).
●足もとの明るいうちに ●足もとの明るい(=暗くならない)うちに家に帰りなさい Go home *before* (*it gets*) *dark*.
●足もとを見る ●彼に足もとを見られた(=弱みにつけ込まれた) He *took advantage of* my *weakness*.

あしゅら 阿修羅 Asura. ●阿修羅のごとき(=激怒した)形相 an *absolutely furious* look.

あしらう ❶〖扱う〗treat. ●彼を冷たくあしらう *treat* him coldly; 《話》give him the cold shoulder (❗×give the cold shoulder to him とは通例いわない); 《話》turn the cold shoulder to him; 《話》cold-shoulder him. ●その提案を鼻であしらう(=はなにしてはねつける) *spurn* the proposal. (話)*turn up* one's nose [*turn up* one's *nose*] *at* the proposal. ●彼は人のあしらい方がうまい He knows how to *treat* [*handle*] people.
❷〖取り合わせる〗(料理に添える) garnish. ●肉にパセリをあしらう *garnish* meat *with* parsley. ●彼女の服は青地に白の水玉をあしらったものです Her dress has white spots on a blue background.

アジリティ 〖サッカー〗agility. 〖参考〗素早い動きをこなす能力

アジる ●改革[反核]を叫んでアジる(=扇動する) *agitate for* reform [*against* nuclear armament].

あじろ 網代 〖竹・ヒノキを編んだもの〗wickerwork, basketwork; 〖魚を捕る仕掛け〗a wickerwork fish trap.

あじわい 味わい (a) taste; 〖風味、趣〗(a) flavor; artistic taste. (⇨味 ❷) ●味わいのある言葉 a *tasteful* remark; a remark *heavy with significance*. ●原文の味わいを伝える convey the *flavor* [*charm*] of the original.

あじわう 味わう 〖賞味する〗(ゆっくりと) savor, (少し) taste; 〖楽しむ〗enjoy; 〖鑑賞する〗appreciate; 〖経験する〗experience. ●ワインを味わう *savor* (the taste of) the wine; (試飲する) *taste* the wine. ●自由を味わう *enjoy* [*taste*] one's freedom. ●深い悲しみを味わう *experience* [*feel*] a deep sorrow. ●この詩を味わうには繊細な心が必要だ A *sensitive* mind is necessary to *appreciate* this poem.

あす 明日 tomorrow. (⇨今日) ●彼は「あす彼女に会います」と言った He said, "I'll meet her *tomorrow*."/He said that he would meet her *the next* [*following*] *day*. (❗間接話法で時制の一致が行われた場合 tomorrow は通例 the next [following] day, the day after となる)
① 〖あす(の)～〗●あすの新聞 *tomorrow*'s (news) papers. ●あすの今ごろは about this time *tomorrow*. ●あすの日本 the Japan of *tomorrow* [the future]; *tomorrow*'s [*future*'s] Japan. ●彼はあすの朝パリに出発する He is leaving for Paris (×on) *tomorrow* morning [night]. ●あす一番しをするつもりです I'm going to do it first thing *tomorrow*.
② 〖あすから[まで]〗●あすから仕事を始める begin one's work *tomorrow* [×from tomorrow]. ●出発をあすまで延期する put off one's departure until [till] *tomorrow*.
③ 〖あすは[が]〗●あすは日曜日です *Tomorrow is* Sunday. (❗(1) It is Sunday *tomorrow*. はまれ. (2) ×Tomorrow will be Sunday. とは通例いわない) ●あすは我が身だ This *could* happen to us [me].
会話「今朝は電車に乗り遅れるし、財布はなくすし、おまけにテストでDだった. なんという日なんだ」「まあ早く寝て睡眠を十分取ることよ. あすがあるさ」"I missed the

train this morning. I lost my purse and then I got a D on my test. What a day it was!" "Oh, well. Go to bed early and have a good sleep. *Tomorrow is another day*."

あずかりきん 預かり金 a deposit received, deposit money.

あずかりしょう 預かり証 (荷物の)《米》a (baggage) check,《英》a (baggage) ticket.

あずかりもの 預かり物 (預けられた物) something [(品物) an article] left in one's charge.

あずかる 預かる ❶ [保管[保護]する] keep*; look after ..., take* care of ....

> 使い分け keep 物をしばらく預かるの意の一般的な語.
> look after, take care of 主に幼児などを預かって面倒を見ることを意味するが, 物を預かる場合にも用いられる.

① 【〈物〉を預かる】 ▶ しばらくこのお金を預かっていただけますか Would you please *keep* this money for me for a while? ▶ 手荷物預かります (ホテル・劇場・駅などで)《米》Small parcels *are checked* here. ▶ コートをお預かりいたしましょうか Can I *take* your coat?/Let me *take* your coat.

② 【〈人〉を預かる】 ▶ 旅行中子供たちは私が預かってあげます I will *look after* [*take care of*,《米》*keep*] your children while you are traveling./You can *leave* your children *with* me while you're away on a journey. (❗ away を入れると親と子が離れている状態がはっきりする (⇨預ける))

❷ [責任下におく] take* charge of .... ▶ 家計を預かる (=切り盛りする) manage a household. ▶ 山田先生がそのクラスを預かっている Mr. Yamada is *in charge of* the class./The class *is in the charge of* Mr. Yamada. (❗ 前の方は「預かっている」という能動的な意味, 後の方は「預けられている」という受身的な意味 (⇨世話))

あずける 与える ❶ [参加する] take* part in ...,《やや書》participate in .... ▶ 利益にあずかる participate [(分け合う) share, have a share] in the profits. ▶ 健二はその計画にあずかった Kenji *took part* [*participated*] *in* the plan. ▶ それは私のあずかり知るところではない (=無関係だ) I have nothing to do with it./It is no concern of mine [none of my business].

❷ [目上から受ける] ▶ 結婚式のご招待にあずかりありがとうございます Thank you very much for inviting me to your wedding./(光栄に存じます) I am most honored to be invited to your wedding.

● **あずかって力がある** ▶ 彼は世界平和にあずかって力があった (=多大な貢献をした) He *made a great contribution to* world peace. ▶ この辞書は手紙を書くのにあずかって力がある (=大いに役立つ) This dictionary *is very useful for* writing letters.

あずき 小豆 【植物】adzuki beans. ● ゆであずき boiled *adzuki beans*. ● あずき色 blackish red.

アスキー [[米国情報交換標準コード]] ASCII (*American Standard Code for Information Interchange* の略).
● アスキーアート [[ASCII 文字を用いて描く絵]] ASCII art. ● アスキーファイル an ASCII file. ● アスキー文字 an ASCII character.

あずけいれ 預け入れ a deposit.
あずけいれる 預け入れる deposit (money *in* a

*****あずける** 預ける ❶ [物・人を] leave*; entrust, trust; [[物を一時的に]]《米》check; [[金銭を]] deposit, put*.

> 使い分け leave 人・物を預けていくこと.
> entrust, trust 大事な物・事を信頼して人に任せること. (⇨託す)
> deposit, put 主に銀行に預金すること.

① 【〈物〉を預ける】 ● スーツケースを駅に預ける *leave* one's suitcase *in* the station. ▶ 彼のような男にそんな大金を預けない方がいい You had better not *entrust* [*trust*] a man like him *with* such a large sum of money./You had better not [I'd advise you not to] *entrust* [(今はまれ) *trust*] such a large sum of money *to* a man like him. (❗ 前の文はお金に, 後の文は人に重点がある) ▶ 彼は銀行に 100 万円預けた He *deposited* [*put*] a million yen *in* the bank. (❗ (1) この文では ×leave, ×entrust は不可. (2) He *made a deposit of* a million yen .... ともいえる)

② 【〈人〉を預ける】 ● 子供を彼女に預ける *leave* one's child *with* her.

❷ [体の表現] ▶ 彼はしばらく背もたれに体をぐったり預けてじっとしていた Collapsing into the chair, he didn't move an inch for a while. (❗ 英語では椅子に座ったとき, その背もたれだけに体をあずけるという考えはない)

アスコットタイ 《米》an ascot,《英》a cravat.
あずさ 梓 【植物】(ヨグソミネバリ) a sweet birch, a black birch; (キササゲ) a catalpa, an Indian bean.
● 梓に上(ﾉﾎﾞ)す (⇨⇨ 出版する)
アスター 【植物】an aster.
アステリスク an ásterisk (*).
アステロイド [[小惑星]] an asteroid.
アストリンゼン(ト) 【薬学】(an) astringent; (化粧水) skin [face] lotion.
あすなろ 翌檜 【植物】a hiba arborvitae /ˈɑːrbərˌvaɪti/.
アスパラガス 【植物】asparagus /əspǽrəgəs/. ● アスパラガス 1 本 a stalk [a piece] of *asparagus*.
アスピリン (an) aspirin, [[錠剤он]] (©). ● アスピリンを 2 錠飲む take two *aspirins*.
アスファルト ásphalt. ● アスファルトで道を舗装する pave a road with *asphalt*; asphalt a road.
● アスファルトジャングル [[生存競争の厳しい大都会]] an asphalt jungle. ● アスファルト道路 an asphalt road [pavement].
アスベスト [[石綿]] asbestos /æsbéstəs/.
アスペルガー [<人名>] ● アスペルガー症候群 【精神医学】Asperger's [Asperger /ǽspərdʒər/] syndrome. [[参考]] 自閉症の一つ)
あずまや 東屋 (木陰の休憩所) a bower /báuər/; (木や枝やつるなどをからませた) an arbor; (眺めのある) a gazebo /gəzéibou/.
アスリート an athlete. (⇨スポーツマン)
アスレチック athlétics.
● アスレチッククラブ an athletics club.

*****あせ** 汗 [[人・動物の]] sweat /swét/. (❗ (1) 物の表面に生じる水滴をいう. (2)「汗をかくこと」の意では a 〜); (人の) perspiration /sweat より上品で堅い語. 通例動物や物には用いない).

① 【〜(の)汗】 ● 冷や汗 (a cold) sweat. (⇨冷や汗)
▶ 彼は額に玉の汗をかいていた Beads of *sweat* [*perspiration*] stood (out) on his forehead./There were beads of *sweat* [*perspiration*] on his forehead.

② 【汗(の)〜】 ● 汗一滴 a sweat. (❗ ×a drop of sweat とはいわない) ● 汗まみれの体 a sweaty [sweat-soaked] body. ● 汗だく, 汗みどろ ▶ 私は汗っかきだ (=すぐ汗をかく) I *sweat* [*perspire*] easily.

③【汗が】▶彼の額に玉のような汗が出ていた(=玉の汗をかいていた)(⇨引) ▶汗が彼の背中をだらだら流れていた *Sweat* was running [rolling, streaming] down his back./His back was running with *sweat*. ▶その部屋に入るとどっと汗を出した[汗がぐっと引いた] I broke out *in perspiration* [The *perspiration* stopped soon] the moment I entered the room. ▶彼のTシャツに汗がにじみ出ていた *Sweat* was oozing through his T-shirt. ▶彼女の額から汗がしたたっていた *Sweat* was dripping from [tricking down] her forehead.

④【汗を】●汗を流す (シャワーなどで) wash off one's *sweat*; (一生懸命に働く) work very hard; 《話》work like a horse [a dog] (!働き者は「元気ではりはりと」、like a dog は「なりふりかまわず」の意). ●額の汗をふく wipe the *sweat* [*perspiration*] off [from] one's forehead. ●手に汗を握る (⇨手【成句】)

●汗(と涙)の結晶 ▶この本は彼の汗と涙の結晶です This book is the fruit [product] of his *sweat and tears*./It took *sweat and tears* for him to write this book.

●汗をかく (人・馬などが) sweat, break a sweat; (人が)《書》perspire. ●びっしょり汗をかく *sweat* a lot; *sweat* buckets. ●(湿気で)汗をかいている壁 a *sweating* wall. ●(冷えて)汗をかいているビール缶 a *dewy* beer can. ●汗をかくことは体にはいい To *sweat* [×Sweats are] good for you [your health, the health]. ▶彼はテニスをしたと全身びっしょり汗をかいていた He *was sweating* [*perspiring*] all over after playing tennis./He was covered [was soaked] in *sweat* after playing tennis. ▶彼はテニスをしたあとポタポタ汗をたらしていた He was dripping (wet) with *sweat* after playing tennis.

あぜ 畦,畔 ［水田のうね］a ridge between rice field; ［鴨居(かもい)の溝の間の仕切り］a ridge between grooves. ●あぜ道 (⇨畦道)

アセアン ［東南アジア諸国連合］the ASEAN /ǽsiæn/ 《the *A*ssociation of *S*outheast *A*sian *N*ations の略》.

あせくさい 汗臭い ▶君、汗臭いよ You're *sweaty*.

あせぐら 校倉 ［三角柱の横材を組み上げて作った倉の説明に］a storehouse built by putting triangularly cut logs across each other.

アセスメント ［影響評価］assessment. ●環境アセスメント environmental *assessment*.

あせだく 汗だく ●汗だくである (一面の汗で) be covered in sweat; (ぽたぽた落ちる) be dripping with sweat. (⇨汗みどろ)

アセチレン ［化学］acetylene /əsétəliːn/.

あせとり 汗取り underwear ［《書》an undergarment] for soaking up sweat.

あせばむ 汗ばむ (⇨汗) ▶2,3分の歩きで少し汗ばんできた A few minutes' walk made me *sweat* [*perspire*] a little [a bit].

あせび 馬酔木 馬酔木(あせび).

あせみず 汗水 ▶汗水たらして働く work very hard; 《話》sweat blood.

あぜみち 畦道 ●(畑の)a footpath between fields [(田んぼの)rice paddies].

あせみどろ 汗みどろ ●汗みどろになる(=汗がしたたる) be dripping with sweat. ●汗みどろになって(=汗で汚れぬれになって)働く work *drenched* with *sweat*; *sweat a lot* from work.

あせも 汗疹 prickly heat, (a) heat rash. ●あせもができている have *prickly heat* (*on* one's *neck*).

あせり 焦り ［じりじりする気持ち］impatience; anxious eagerness; irritation; (急ぐこと) hurry. ▶1点を取ろうとするフランスに焦りが見える France [The French team] seems to be very eager to get a point. ●何をするにせよ焦りは禁物だ There's no hurry in doing anything.

あせる 焦る ● 急ぐ hurry, rush (!状態をいうときは be in a hurry [a rush]); ［待ち切れない]《書》make* haste; be impatient. ●焦らない be in no hurry; (冷静で)keep cool. ●成功を焦る(=熱望する) be too eager for success. ●焦らずゆっくりやりなさい Don't *hurry* [*rush*]./Take your time./Take it easy. ▶彼は試験が近いので焦っていた(=いらいらしていた) He *was irritated* [*nervous*] because the exam was drawing near.

あせる 褪せる ［色があせる］fade; [変色する]《やや書》discolor. ●色あせた服 a *faded* [a *discolored*] dress. ▶この生地は色があせない This material won't *fade* [*discolor*]. ▶晩秋にはこの美しい色あせて茶色になる These beautiful colors *fade* to brown in late autumn. ▶日に当たってカーテンの色があせた The sunlight *faded* [*discolored*] the curtains./The curtains *were faded* [*were discolored*] by the sun(light).

アゼルバイジャン ［国名］Azerbaijan /ɑːzərbaidʒáːn/; (公式名) the Republic of Azerbaijan. ●(首都)Baku ●アゼルバイジャン人 an Azerbaijani. ●アゼルバイジャン語 Azerbaijani. ●アゼルバイジャン(人)[語]の Azerbaijani.

アセロラ ［植物］an acerola.

あぜん 唖然 ▶そのことを聞くと彼はあぜんとしていた He *was speechless* [*dumbfounded*] when we told him about it. (!後の方が意味が強い)

アセンブラー ［アセンブリー言語の変換プログラム］［コンピュータ］an assembler. (⇨アセンブリー)

アセンブリー ［コンピュータ］an assembly. (参考 アセンブリー言語を機械語に変換すること)

●アセンブリー言語 assembly language. (参考 プログラミング用の言語)

あそこ ［その向こう］over there; (そこ) there (!通例 over there より近くをさす); [あの場所] that place. (⇨あちら, そこ) ▶バスはあそこの角で止まります The bus stops at that corner *over there*. ▶あそこから見た景色はとてもすばらしかった The view from *there* [*that place*] was absolutely wonderful.

会話 ｢田中さんはどこですか｣｢あそこにいます｣ "Where's Mr. Tanaka?" "He's (*over*) *there*."

会話 ｢私のノートがないわ｣｢ほら、あそこにあるじゃない｣ "My notebook is missing." "*There* it is."

会話 ｢あそこに住んでいらっしゃるのはあなたのご兄弟ですか｣｢ええ｣ "Is it your brother who lives *out there*?" "Yes." (!外をさという場合。上の場合は up there, 下の場合は down there, 内部の場合は in there という)

会話 ｢じゃああの店はどうだい｣｢あそこはあまりに高すぎるもの｣ "Well, what about that store?" "*Their* goods are far too expensive."

あそばせる 遊ばせる ［人を楽しませる］entertain; ［施設などを活用せずにおく］leave* (land) lying idle. ▶その工場で1か月間ストライキが行われた結果, 2万3千人以上の労働者を遊ばせる(=仕事をさせないでおく)ことになった A month-long strike at the plant *idled* more than 23,000 people.

あそび 遊び ❶ ［遊戯］play (↔work); a game. (⇨遊ぶ)

使い分け ▶ **play** 勉強・仕事に対して「遊び」一般をさすが、特に子供の遊びをいうことが多い。**game** かくれんぼ (hide-and-seek)や鬼ごっこ (tag)など一定のルールのあるものをいう。

あそびあるく

①【～遊び】● ままごと[泥んこ]遊びをする play house [with mud]. ● 火遊びをする play with matches. ● 子供の遊び a children's game. ● 小さい子供は活発な遊びが好きよ Young children enjoy energetic [lively] games. (!後の方は面白味のある意を含む)

②【遊び～】● 遊び心 (⇨遊び心). ● 遊び球を投げる『野球』throw a waste pitch [ball]; waste a pitch. ● 遊びざかりの(=活発な)子供が2人いる We have two lively [active] children. ● 彼は遊び半分で仕事をしている He works half-heartedly [wholeheartedly]./He plays at his job.

③【遊びが[は]】● 子供は生来遊びが好きです Children like playing by nature. ● 遊びは勉強と同じくらい重要だ Play is as important as study.

④【遊びに】● お母ちゃん、外へ遊びに行ってもいい? Mommy, can I go out to play? ● そうむきになるな。遊びにすぎないのだから Don't be so serious. It's just a game.

❷【娯楽】(楽しみ) (a) pleasure; (an) amusement (!前の方は仕事と対比しての楽しみ、後の方は没頭できる楽しみ); (気晴らし) a pastime. ● 悪い遊びを覚えると生涯を台無しにすることになる be apt to lead a life of dissipation. ● 神戸には仕事ではなく遊びで行った I went to Kobe for pleasure, not on business. ● 長崎は遊びに行くにはいいところですよ You can have a nice holiday in Nagasaki.

会話「こちらにはお仕事でいらしたのですか」「いいえ、遊びです」"Are you here on business?" "No, (I'm not,) I'm on vacation." (!日常会話では省略する方が普通)

❸【訪問】● 近いうちに遊びに来ませんか Won't you come and see [come to see, 《米話》come see] me soon? (!He came to see me yesterday. (彼がきのう遊びに来た)のように come が語形変化するときは通例 come to see を用いる。×come to play with me とはいわない)/Won't you come over (to my house) soon?

❹【機械部品などの】play. ● この車のハンドルには遊びがまったくない[多すぎる] There is no [too much] play in this steering wheel.

● 遊び着(子供の) a playsuit; (レジャー用の)《集合的》playclothes (!複数扱い). ● 遊び癖 (怠け癖) a habit of being lazy; (遊び回る癖)《参考》a habit of playing around. ● 遊び時間(学校の) (a) playtime; 《米》(a) recess. ● 遊び道具 (おもちゃ) a toy, 《書》a plaything; (ゲーム用品) a game. ● 遊び友達《相手》(特に子供の)《やや書》a playmate, a playfellow. (!「私は遊び相手がいない」は I have no playmates. より I have no friends to play with. の方が普通) ● 遊び人(ばくちうち) a gambler; (プレーボーイ) a playboy; a pleasure seeker. ● 遊び場(学校・公共の) a playground (参考)通例すべり台 (slide) やブランコ (swing) などの施設がある(遊び場所) a place to play (in) (!《話》では in は通例省略).

あそびあるく 遊び歩く go out here and there.
あそびごころ 遊び心 ● 遊び心にあふれた創作料理 a creative dish full of fun. ● 彼には遊び心がない He has no sense of humor [fun].
あそびほうける 遊び呆ける (子供が遊びに夢中で) be absorbed [deep] in play; (快楽にふける) be given to the pursuit of pleasure. ● 遊びほうけていないで少しは勉強もしろよ Stop loafing (around [about]) and study a bit. (!loaf (about [around]) は「仕事や勉強をしないでぶらぶらする」の意)
あそびまわる 遊び回る fool around [《英》about]; play around [《英》about] (a lot).

あたえる

あそぶ 遊ぶ ❶【遊戯する】play; (楽しむ) have* a good time; amuse [enjoy] oneself.

使い分け play 通例子供や動物が、また大人が子供といっしょに遊ぶ場合に用いる。大人の場合は状況によって次のように訳し分ける必要がある。
have a good time「楽しむ」の意の最も一般的な言い方。
amuse oneself, enjoy oneself やや堅い表現で、前の方は心のうさを晴らさせ、満足させるという積極的な意味を含むが、後の方は結果的に「楽しい」という意を暗示する。

● 人形[積木]で遊ぶ play with dolls [blocks]. ● テレビゲームで遊ぶ play a video game. ● トランプをして遊ぶ have a good time [enjoy (oneself)] playing cards. ● 友達と遊ぶ play with one's friend(s). ● 子供たちは裏庭で遊んでいた The children were playing [at play] in the backyard. ● よく学び、よく遊べ 'Work hard, play hard.'/《ことわざ》All work and no play makes Jack a dull boy. ● 昨夜仕事が終わってから新宿で遊んだ I had a good time [amused myself, enjoyed myself, ×played, (飲んだ) had a drink] at Shinjuku after work last night. (!単に「新宿に行った」と考えて I went to Shinjuku.... としてもよい) ● このところ仕事が忙しくて遊ぶ(=ゆっくりする)ひまがないんだ I'm much too busy to relax these days.

❷【何もしない】idle《time》away; (仕事がなくて遊んでいる) be idle; (のらくら暮らす)《話》loaf. ● 遊んでばかりもいられないので仕事を探したい I'd like to find a job because I can't be idle [(軽蔑的) fool around]. ● 彼は一生遊んで暮らした He idled his life away./He loafed through his life. ● その工場には遊んでいる機械が多い There are a lot of machines lying [sitting] idle in the factory.

❸【道楽する】● 彼は独身のときは相当遊んだ He spent a lot of time and money on pleasure [(放蕩(とう)な)生活をした]; 《やや書》led a very dissipated life, (女遊びをした) womanized] when he was single. (!play around《話》は既婚者などが「浮気をする」こと)

あだ 仇 ● 父の仇を打つ avenge one's father《on him》; avenge one's father's death《by doing》. (⇨復讐) ● 恩を仇で返す (⇨恩 [慣用])
あだ 徒 ● 彼の善意が彼女には徒となった His good intentions turned out harmful to her. ● 彼女はその美しさが徒となった Her beauty caused [was] her ruin.
あたい 値 图 (価値) value; 『数学』a value. (⇨価値) ● この一次方程式の x の値を求めよ What is the value of x in this linear equation?
— 値する 動 ● 彼の勇気ある行為は賞賛に値する His brave deed is worthy of praise./His brave deed deserves praise [to be praised]. ● 彼の提案は一考に値する His suggestion is worth considering [worthy of consideration]. (⇨価値 ③)
あたうかぎり 能う限り (⇨ 🔳 出来るだけ)
あたえる 与える ❶【渡して相手に持たせる】 (一般的に) give*; (贈呈する) present /prizént/; (賞などを) award; (称号などを) confer《-rr-》; (提供する) offer; (金品・権利などを) grant; (供給する) supply.

使い分け **give**「与える」の最も一般的な語。
present give より堅い語で、贈り物を公式に進呈すること。
award 審査などして十分考慮した上で賞などを与えること。
confer 堅い語で、通例地位の高い人が称号・学位な

どを授けること.
offer 援助などを提供すること.
grant やや堅い語で、通例金銭・権利などを要求に応じて与えること.
supply 足りない物を補充すること.

① 【...を与えられる】▶その罪人は恩赦を与えられた The criminal *was granted* an amnesty.▶洪水の被災者は食糧を与えられた The flood victims *were supplied* [*were provided*] *with* food.▶与えられた(=利用できる)時間を有効に使いなさい You should make good use of the time *available* [×*given to you*].

② 【人(人)に B(物)を与える】 **(a)** give* A B; give B to A.（!award, offer, grant も同じ構文をとる. ただし present と supply は通例 ～ A with B [B to A]）▶彼に小遣いを与える *give* him an allowance; *give* an allowance *to* him.▶大学は奨学金を与えた The university *awarded* him a scholarship [a scholarship *to* him]./He got a scholarship from the university.▶学校当局は彼に復学の機会を与えた The school authorities *gave* [*offered*] him the opportunity to come back to school./The school authorities *gave* [*offered*] *to* him the opportunity to come back to school.（!いずれも offer では彼がその機会を受け入れたかどうかは不明）▶校長は彼に休学の許可を与えた The principal *allowed* [《やや書》*permitted*] him to stay away from school./The headmaster *gave* [*granted*] him permission to stay away from school.

会話「彼にどんな任務を与えましたか」「特に何も与えませんでした」"What kind of task did you *give* him?" "I didn't *give* him anything in particular *to* him. は不適切. 一方 Who did you *give* to? に対する答えとしては I didn't *give* it to anyone. の文型が適切（⇨上げる **②** ②)）

(b) confer (-rr-) B on A. （!Bは勲章など）▶大学は彼に名誉学位を与えた The college *conferred* an honorary degree *on* [*upon*] him. （!× ... conferred him an honorary degree. とはいわない）

❷ [意図とは無関係に結果が相手に及ぶ] ▶よい印象を与える make [×*give*] a favorable impression (*on*).▶刺激を与える stimulate; *give* a stimulus (*to*).▶ショックを与える shock 《him》; *give* 《him》 a shock.▶...の感じを与える strike [impress] 《him》 as ....（!後の方が強意的）▶彼の演説は聴衆に多大な影響を与えた His speech *had* [×*gave*] a lot of influence *on* the audience.▶台風は農作物に多大な被害を与えた The typhoon *caused* [*did*, ×*gave*] a lot of damage *to* the crops.

あだおろそか 徒おろそか か (⇨徒や疎か)
あたかも 恰も as if [though] (+節); just like ....（⇨まるで ❶)

‡**あたたかい** 暖かい, 温かい 形 ❶ [温度が] warm (⇔ cool); (気候が温和な) mild.▶暖かい春の日 a *warm* [a *mild*] spring day.▶暖かい日 a *mild* winter.（!冬の暖かさには warm より mild が普通）▶暖かい手袋 *warm* gloves.▶暖かいファンヒーター a *warm* fan heater.▶今日はばかぽか暖かい It is nice and *warm* today.（!nice and は /náisən/ と読み,「快く」の意）▶日増しに暖かくなってきた It is getting *warmer* and *warmer* day by day.▶私は厚着しているので大変暖かい I wear heavy clothes [have heavy clothes on], so I am very *warm*.▶温かいうちに食べなさい Eat your food while it is *hot*.

（!飲食物には一般に hot を用いることが多い: *hot* [×*warm*] coffee. ただし本来冷たい状態で飲食するものは加熱の程度で warm も用いる: *warm* [*hot*] milk）

❷ [心が] (温情のある) warm; (親切な) kind; (心からの) hearty, 《やや書》cordial; (思いやりのある) warm-hearted.▶彼らから温かい歓迎を受ける receive a *warm* [a *hearty*, a *cordial*] welcome from them.▶温かく迎える give 《him》 a *warm* (=a cold) reception [welcome]; receive [welcome, greet] 《him》 *warmly*.▶彼女は心の温かい(=温かみのある)人だ (⇨温かみ)

❸ [その他の表現] ▶ふところが暖かい (⇨懐 [成句])

— **暖かさ 暖かさ, 温かさ** 图 [温情の] *warmth* a *warm* heart.▶部屋 [日差し] の暖かさ the *warmth* of the room [sun].

— **暖かみ, 温かみ** 图 (⇨暖かさ) ▶彼女は温かみのある人だ She is a *warm-hearted* woman./She has a *warm* [a *kind*] *heart*.（!「温かみのない人だ」は She has no *warmth*.）▶彼と握手したとき手の暖かみを感じた When I shook hands with him, I felt the *warmth* of his hand.

あたたまる 暖まる, 温まる [自然に暖まる] get* [become*] warm; [火にあたって] warm oneself (*at* a fire).▶心温まる heart-warming; (人の心を喜ばす) cheering.▶石油ストーブをつけるとすぐ部屋は暖まった I turned on the oil heater and the room soon *warmed* [*heated*] *up*.▶彼女は暖炉の火にあたって暖まった She *warmed* herself at the fire.

*‡**あたためる 温める, 暖める** ❶ [適温にする] warm; [直接火にかけて] heat. ▶シチューを温める *heat* [*warm*] (*up*) the stew.▶彼は火で手を暖めた He *warmed* his hands by [*at*] the fire. （!by は「そばによって」,at は「手をかざして」の意）▶私たちはストーブで部屋を暖めた We *heated* our room with the heater.

❷ [その他の表現] ▶旧交を温める *renew* one's old friendship.▶考えを温める keep one's thoughts to oneself.

翻訳のこころ アロエの愛情に包まれて、私は日の光の中で温められているような気がした(吉本ばなな『みどりのゆび』) I felt warm [*warmed*] in the sun, embraced by the aloe's love [the loving feeling of the aloe]. （! (1)「アロエの愛情」は、日本文の語順通り文頭に出すと理解されにくいので文末に置く. (2) warm が warmed より自然な表現）

アタッカー an attacker, (特にバレーボールの) a spiker.
アタック [攻撃] (an) attack; [挑戦] (a) challenge.
アタッシェケース [<フランス語] an attaché case.（!単独では /ətəʃéi/ だが, 複合語の場合は /ətəʃéi kèis/ とも読む）
アタッチメント [付属品] an attachment.▶ミシンのアタッチメント *attachments* to [×*for*] a sewing machine.

あだっぽい 婀娜っぽい ▶彼女はあだっぽい She is a *seductive* [*coquettish*] woman./She is a *charmer*.

あだな あだ名 a nickname.▶彼のあだ名は「カーリー」だ. 髪の毛がカールしているから His *nickname* is [He *is nicknamed*] "Curly" because he has (×a) curly hair./He had [got] the *nickname* (of) "Curly" for his curly hair.▶彼女をあだ名で呼んだ I called her by her *nickname*.

あたふた 副 (急いで) in a hurry, hurriedly, hastily; (忙しく) busily.▶彼女はあたふたと家へ戻って来た She came home *in a hurry*.

— **あたふたする** 動 ▶彼は客の応対で1日中あたふたした

いた He *was very busy* receiving visitors all day long.

アダプター an adapter, an adaptor.

あたま 頭 ❶〖首から上〗a head. (❗頭も含む上半体を言う)

①【頭が】● 頭がひどく[少し]痛い I have a bad [slight] *headache*./My *head* aches badly [a little]. ● 頭が重い My *head* feels heavy./I feel heavy *in the head*. ● 頭がくらくらする I feel my head *spin*./My head *is reeling*. ● 飲みすぎて頭が割れそうだ I drank too much and I have a splitting *head*.

②【頭の[から]】● 頭から(=まっさかさまに)池に落ちる fall *headfirst* [*headlong*] into the pond. ● 彼は私より頭の分だけ背が高い He is taller than I am by a *head*./He is a *head* taller than I am.

③【頭を】● 頭を上げる raise [lift] one's *head*. ● 頭をなでる pat 《his》 *head*. ● 頭を横[縦]に振る shake [nod] one's *head*. ● 彼の頭をなぐる hit him on the *head*; hit his *head*. ● 頭を撃たれる be shot in the *head*. ● 彼は恥じて頭を垂れた He hung his *head* in shame. ● 彼は頭を垂れ肩をすぼめて歩いていた He was walking, (with his) *head* hanging and shoulders hunched. (❗この hanging は自動詞) ● 彼は頭をかきながらその名前を思い出そうとした He tried to remember the name, scratching his *head*. (事情) 頭をかくのは米英人にとっては思案・困惑などを表すしぐさ

❷〖頭髪〗(one's) hair. ● 床屋で頭を刈ってもらう have one's *hair* cut at the barber's. ● 頭を洗う shampoo one's *hair*. ● 父の頭が白くなった My father's *hair* has turned gray [white].

❸〖頭脳〗brains, a head, (知性) (a) mind.

①【頭が】● 彼は頭がいい[切れる] He is *clever* [《主に米》*smart*, *bright*, *brilliant*, *intelligent*]. (❗*clever*, *smart* は時に「抜け目ない」の意も表すのに注意 (⇨賢い [類語]))/(明晰な頭脳を持つ) He has a clear *head* [*good*] *brains*, a brilliant *mind*, (切れる頭) a *sharp mind*. ● 彼は頭が悪い He is *weak in the head*./He has *no brains*./He is *stupid* [*dull*, 《英話》*thick*]. ● 奴は頭が変だ(=狂っている) That fellow is *out of* his *head* [*mind*]./That guy is *crazy* [*mad*]. ● その問題を解決するには頭がいる It requires *brains* [*intelligence*] to settle the problem. ● 頭がぼんやりしていたので正解を思いつかなかった My *mind* was foggy and I couldn't think of the answer. ● 頭が混乱してしっかり考えることができなかった My *thoughts* were chaotic [I was very confused] and I couldn't think clearly. ● 今いろんなことで頭がいっぱいだ I *have* so many things *on* my *mind* now. (❗*on* one's mind は「気にかかる, 頭を悩ます」意で, *on* one's mind は単に「考えている」の意) ● 母親たちは子供たちに最善の教育を受けさせることで頭がいっぱいだ(=夢中になっている) The mothers *are preoccupied with* the idea of getting their children the best education.

(会話)「両親は私が大学に行くのを望んでいるの」「あなたは頭がいいから行けるわよ」"Mom and dad want me to go to university." "Well, you're *bright* [*clever*] enough to get there."

②【頭の】● 頭の回転の早い人 a *quick-witted* (⇔a slow-witted) person; a *quick thinker*; a person who *has a quick mind*. ● 頭の中で計算する make a *mental* calculation. ● 彼はその光景を頭の中に描いた He formed a *mental* picture of the scene. ● そのことを頭の片隅に入れておきなさい Keep [Bear] that *in mind*.

③【頭に】● 彼は金のことしか頭にない(=金のこと以外何も考えない) He thinks of nothing but money./(ただ金だけに関心がある) He is only concerned with money./His sole concern is money.

④【頭を】● 頭を働かせる(=使う) (⇨〖成句〗) ● 答えを出そうと[ぞの名前を思い出そうと]頭をしぼる rack one's *brains* for the answer [to remember his name]. ● その問題に頭を悩ます bother one's *head* about the problem; rack one's *brains* over the problem; *puzzle* (one's *brains* [*mind*]) *over* the problem. ● 失敗するかもしれないという思いが私の頭をよぎった It flashed through [across] my *mind* that I might fail.

❹〖最初〗● 彼女は彼の言うことを頭から信用していなかった She didn't believe him *from the start* [(少しも) *at all*]. ● 彼は私の要求を頭から(=きっぱりと)はねつけた He refused my request *flatly* [*resolutely*].

❺〖人員〗a head. (⇨頭数, 一人頭)

● 頭が上がらない ● 数学にかけては彼に頭が上がらない(=かなわない) I *can't compete with* him in mathematics./I'm *no match for* him in mathematics. ● 彼は妻には頭が上がらない(=恐妻家である) He is just *a henpecked husband*.

● 頭が固い ● 父は頭が固い(頑固だ) My father is *stubborn* [《主に米》*hard-headed*]./(融通がきかない) My father is *inflexible* [(考えが古い) *old-fashioned in* his *ideas*]./(いつも同じ考え方をする) My father has a *one-track mind*.

● 頭隠して尻隠さず You dance in a net and think nobody sees you.

● 頭が下がる ● 彼の勇気に頭が下がる(=脱帽する) I (must) *take* my *hat off to*(賞賛する) *admire* him for his courage.

● 頭が低い (控えめな) modest; (えらぶらない) humble.

● 頭に浮かぶ (思いつく) come [(急に) spring] to ⟨x one's⟩ mind; come into [enter, cross] one's mind. (⇨思い付く, 思い出す)

● 頭にくる ● 彼の傲慢さが頭にきた He *drove* me *mad* [*crazy*, *out of* my *mind*] because he was arrogant./I *got mad at* him *for* [《米話》*got burned up about*] his arrogance./(事が主語) His arrogance *got* [*drove*, *made*] me *mad*./He was arrogant. That really *burned* me *up*.

● 頭に血が上る (かっとなる) get angry [《話》mad, furious]; fly into a rage; lose one's temper. (⇨かっとなる)

● 頭のてっぺんから足のつま先まで from head to foot; from top to toe. (❗無冠詞に注意)

● 頭の中が真っ白になる ● 私は突然頭の中が真っ白になった Suddenly my mind went blank [×pure white].

● 頭を痛める ● 彼は息子のことで頭を痛めている His son is giving him a hard time./(息子は頭痛の種だ) His son is a headache for him.

● 頭を抱える ● 彼はその問題をどう処理すべきか分からず頭を抱えた He did not know what to do with the problem, and held his *head* in his hands./(困り果てていた) He *was at* his *wit's end* ⟨about what to do⟩ with the problem.

● 頭を下げる (頭をぶつけないように) lower one's head; (おじぎする) bow [make a bow] 《*to* him, *before* the king》(❗深い敬意・忠誠を表す); (歌手などが拍手に対して) take a bow; (懇願する) beg. ● いくら頭を下げても(=頼んでも)私は出て行く I wouldn't stay if they *begged* me. (事情) 米英人は懇願するときに頭を下げるということはしないので, 直訳できない) ● こっちから彼に頭を下げる(=従う)ことはない We don't have to be submissive to him./(謝る) We need not apologize to him./It's not for us but

あたまうち / あたり

for him to apologize.
- **頭を使う** use one's brains [《話》head]. ● 頭を使う仕事 *mental* work, brainwork.
- **頭をひねる** (熱心に考える) think hard 《*of, about*》; (頭を悩ます) puzzle 《*over*》; (頭をしぼる) rack one's brain(s).
- **頭を冷やす** cool off; (気を落ち着ける) calm down.
- **頭を丸める** (頭髪を剃る) shave one's head; (僧侶になる) become a priest.

あたまうち 頭打ち ▶株式市場は頭打ちだ(=行きつくところまで行った) The stock market has gone *as far as it can go* [*天井値に達した*) *has reached the ceiling*].

あたまかず 頭数 ● 頭数(=人の数)を数える count the *number of people*; count *heads*. ● 頭数(=数)をそろえる[増す] make up [increase] the *number*.

あたまきん 頭金 ▶頭金として1万円払う pay ten thousand yen as a *down payment*; pay ten thousand yen *down*. ▶車の頭金を払った I *made a down payment* on the car.

あたまごし 頭越し ── **頭越しに** [副] over one's head. ▶彼は課長の頭越しに社長に話を持っていった He *bypassed* the section chief and spoke directly to the president.

あたまごなし 頭ごなし ● 頭ごなしに(=釈明する機会を与えずに)しかる tell 《him》 off [《書》 scold 《him》] *without* hearing his side of the story 《*giving* 《him》 *a chance to explain*》.

あたまだし 頭出し (磁気テープ・CDなどの) cueing. ▶このビデオは頭出しがとても簡単だ If you use this VCR, you will find it much easier to *cue* (*up*) a tape you want to watch.

あたまでっかち 頭でっかち ── **頭でっかちの** [形] (組織が) top-heavy; (理屈ばかりの) too theoretical. ● 頭でっかちの(=机上の)空論家 an armchair theorist.

あたままわり 頭割り ▶支払いは頭割りにしよう Let's split the bill. (⇨割り勘)

アダム Adam. [参考] 旧約聖書で, 神に創造された最初の人間)

アダム・スミス [スコットランドの経済学者] Adam Smith.

あだやおろそか 徒や疎か ● 彼をあだやおろそかに扱うわけにはいかない must treat him with proper respect.

あたら ▶あたら(=惜しくも)好機を逸した *Regrettably* [*To our regret*], we missed a good opportunity. ▶彼はあたら(=せっかくの)若い命を絶った He lost his *precious* life in his youth.

＊あたらしい 新しい [形]

WORD CHOICE 新しい

new 人・物事の新規性・清新性を表す最も一般的な語. ● 新しい技術を使う use *new* technology.
latest ファッション・書物・ニュースなどが最新のものであることを表す. ● コンピュータ技術に関する彼女の最も新しい本 her *latest* book on computer technology.
hot ニュース・話題などが最新のもので, 他の人がまだ知らず話題性が高いことを表す. ● 今日の新しいニュース today's *hot* news.

頻度チャート

new ████████████
latest ██████
hot ███
      20   40   60   80 100 (%)

new; (果物などが新鮮な) fresh; (設備などが最新の) up-to-date (-tt-); (いちばん最近の) the latest; (ニュースなどが最新の) hot (-tt-); (新奇な) novel. ▶車の新しいモデル a *new* model of a car. ● 新しい機械 a *new* (=まったくの) a *brand-new*] machine. ● 新しい証拠 *fresh* evidence. ● 新しい医療設備 *up-to-date* medical facilities. ● 私には新しい概念 a *novel* idea to me. ● 新しい(=次の)章を勉強する study a *new* [*a fresh*] chapter. ▶間もなく新しい年がやってくる Soon the *new* year comes around. ▶...*a new* year ... より普通) ▶彼は何でも新しい(=目新しいものが好きで He likes anything *new* [*novel*]. ▶この発明は世界史に新しい1ページを加えた This invention has added *a new page* to world history.

[会話] 「リプトンの紅茶はどこで手に入るかな」「そうねえ, あのスーパーマーケットには新しい品が置いてあるわよ」 "Where can I get Lipton tea?" "Well, that supermarket has a *fresh* supply."

── **新しく** ● 新しく開発された地域 a *newly* [(最近) a *recently*] developed region. ● コーヒーを新しく入れ直す make some *fresh* coffee. ● 新しくやり直す (=再出発する) have [make] a *fresh* start; start (all) over again; (書) start *afresh*. ▶この部屋はカーペットを新しくしました (=敷き替えた) We *have renewed* the carpet of [*had a new* carpet laid in] this room./We have replaced the carpet of this room with a new one.

あたらしいひとよめざめよ 『新しい人よ眼ざめよ』 *Rouse Up O Young Men of the New Age!* [参考] 大江健三郎の小説.

あたらしがりや 新しがり屋 a novelty seeker [hunter]; (流行に飛びつく人) a faddist.

あたらしがる 新しがる (新しいものを追う) hunt for [pursue] novelty; (流行を追う) be fashion-conscious.

あたらず 当たらず ● **当たらず障らず** (⇨当たり障り)
- **当たらずといえども遠からず** ▶(君の推測は)当たらずといえども遠からずだ Your guess is *almost right*./ That's a *near* guess. (⇨near ❸)

あたらない 当たらない [...するには及ばない] don't need (*to do*), need not (*do*) ([!]助動詞用法で堅い言い方); [(値しない) do* not deserve; [(適当でない] be not proper [fit, right]. ● 英雄と称するに当たらない *do not deserve* [*be unworthy of*] the name of a hero. ▶驚くには当たらない That's *nothing to be surprised at*./That is *hardly surprising*./ (まったく当然だ) That *is quite natural*. ▶彼の非難は当たらない(=場違いだ) His criticism *is out of place*.

あたり 辺り ❶ [近辺] a neighborhood, 《書》 the vicinity. (⇨付近, 近所) ● このあたりに in this *neighborhood*; around [*near*] here. ▶我々の住んでいるあたりは大変騒々しい We live in a very noisy *neighborhood*. ▶この前彼に会ったのはちょうどこのあたりでした It was right *around here* that I last saw him. ([!]last を文尾に置いてもよいが, この方が普通) ▶彼は立ち止まりあたりを見回した He paused and looked *around* 《him》. ▶あたり一面岩だらけだった There were rocks *all around* [*on all sides*].

[会話] 「彼女はこのあたりに住んでるの」「大阪駅の近くです」 "*Whereabouts* does she live?" "Near Osaka Station." ([!]正確な答えを期待しない聞き方. 正確にたずねるには What part of Osaka does she live? のように)

❷ [おそ] about, 《米》around. ▶来月の中ごろあたりに *about* the middle of next month. ▶彼は来週あたり(=来週のいつか)やってくるだろう He will come *sometime* next week. ▶このあたりで議論を打ち切ってはどうかと思う I think it's *about* time we ended this discussion.

● **あたりを払う**〖堂々とした〗impressive, imposing;〖威厳のある〗magnified, stately;〖荘厳な〗majestic. ▶彼の父は威風あたりを払う風貌の人だった His father looked truly *majestic*.

あたり 当たり ❶〖命中,的中,〖興業〗の大当たり〗a hit;〖成功〗a success. ● (⇨当たり年, 当たり外れ, 当たり屋, 当たり!)〖クイズなどで〗You've hit it!

❷〖野球で〗(ヒット) a hit ● 「ヒット」は「安打」の意だが, hit は「安打」と「打球」の両方をいう. ● いい当たりのゴロ a grounder *hit* well. ● 強い当たりのゴロ a hard-*hit* grounder. ● いい当たり! Good *hit*!

❸〖人・物に接したときの感じ〗● 当たりのよい〖人なつっこい〗friendly;〖気持ちのよい〗pleasant;〖自分の気質に合っていて快い〗agreeable. ● 当たりの柔らかい物腰をしている have a *mild* [a *smooth*] manner. ● (⇨人, 口当たり)

● 当たり役 a successful role [part].

-あたり〖…につき〗per; a. (❗後の方が口語的) ● 車で1時間あたり40マイルの速さで走る drive at (a speed of) 40 miles *an* [*per*, ×*per an*] hour. ● 1人あたりの米の消費量 the rice consumption *per* person [head];〖書〗the *per* capita consumption of rice.

あたりさわり 当たり障り ● 当たり障りのない(=言質を与えない)返事をする give a *noncommittal* answer [reply]; answer [reply] noncommittally. ● 当たり障りのない(=中立な)態度をとる take a *neutral* attitude. ● 当たり障りのない(=害のない)話題に変える change a subject to a *harmless*〖安全な〗a *safe*〗one.

あたりちらす 当たり散らす take* it out〖*on*〗. ▶彼は試合に負けたので私に当たり散らした He lost the game and *took it out*〖書〗*vented his anger*〗*on me.* (❗It は先行の文を受ける)

あたりどし 当たり年 one's (lucky) year. ▶今年はぼくの当たり年だった This has been my *year*./This has been a *lucky* [*good*] *year* for me. ▶昨年はブドウの当たり年(=が大豊作)だった We had a *bumper crop* of grapes last year./It was a *good year* for the grapes last year.

あたりはずれ 当たり外れ ● 当たり外れの多い(=危険度の高い)商売 a *risky* business. ● この商売では当たり外れが大きい The risks and the rewards are high in this business. ● ペンを買うときは慎重にね. 当たり外れがあるから(=よく書けないペンがあるから) Be careful when you buy a pen. Some pens don't write well.

あたりまえ 当たり前 ── 当たり前の形 ❶〖普通の〗ordinary;〖ありふれた〗common;〖通例の〗usual. (⇨普通) ● ごく当たり前の考え方 a very *ordinary* [*common*] way of thinking.

❷〖当然の〗natural. (⇨当然) ▶彼がそう言うのも当たり前だ It is *natural* for him to say so./It is *natural* that he *should* say so. ▶そのくらいの遅れは目下の状況では当たり前のことだ(=当然の成り行きだ) Such delays are *a matter of course* in these situations.

会話「また英語を落としたよ」「当たり前だ」"I flunked English again." "*No wonder*." (❗It's *no wonder that you flunked*.... の斜字体の部分が省略されたもの)

会話「Jリーグの試合見に行く?」「当たり前よ」"Are you going to see the J-League game?" "*You bet* [*Certainly*]!"

会話「助かりました」「あら, 当たり前のことをしたまでです」"Thank you for your help." "Oh, it was the least I could do."

会話「友達が私の歴史のレポートを写させてくれと言ってきかないのよ」「そんなこと していいわけないでしょ. あなたも本当なの?」「本当なの?」「本当なの?」「Are you sure?" "*Absolutely*."

あたりめ 当たりめ a dried cuttlefish. (⇨するめ)

あたりや 当たり屋 ❶〖運のいい人〗a lucky person,〖店〗a thriving [a flourishing] store.

❷〖安打を多く打つ人〗a good batter.

❸〖車にわざと当たって金などをゆすり取る人〗a car-accident faker.

:あたる 当たる

INDEX
❶ ぶつかる	❷ 命中する
❸ 予想などが的中する	❹ よい結果が出る
❺ 相当する	❻ きびしく扱う
❼ 困難などに立ち向かう	❽ 仕事などを引き受ける
❾ 割り当てられる	❿ 日光・風雨にさらされる
⓫ 害を受ける	⓬ 直接確かめてみる
⓭ 照合して調べる	

❶〖ぶつかる〗hit* 《*against, on*》; (触れる) touch; (雨・波などが) (続けざまに) beat*; (書) lash 《*against*》. ▶彼の手がテーブルに当たった His hand *hit* [*struck*] *against* the table. ▶球が彼の頭にあたった The ball *hit* [*struck*] him *on* the head./The ball *hit* [*struck*] his head. (⇨❷) ▶お互いにひじが当たらないようにもう少し間隔をあけて座りなさい Sit a little more apart from each other so that your elbows won't *touch*. ▶雨が窓ガラスに激しく当たっていた The rain *was beating* [*lashing*] hard *against* the windowpane. ▶波が激しく岩に当たって砕けた The waves *broke against* the rocks. ▶車が砂利をはねて私の顔に当たった The car threw gravel up and *into* my face.

会話「どうしたんだい」「気をつけろ, もうちょっとでそれが当たるところだったぞ」"What's the matter?" "Be careful. You nearly [almost] *hit* me with that."

❷〖命中する〗(矢・弾などが) hit*. ▶弾丸が彼の肩に当たった The bullet *hit* him *in* [×*into*] the shoulder./The bullet *hit* his shoulder. (❗前の方は人に, 後の方は体の部分に重点を置いた表現 ⇨❶ [第2文例]) ▶矢が的に当たった [当たらなかった] The arrow *hit* [*missed*] the target. ▶(まともに当たった [ひどくそれた]) The arrow *was right on* [*way off*] *target*. ▶(後の文では target は the がつかないのが普通) ▶当たった!〖話〗I got *hit*!

❸〖予想などが的中する〗(事実となる) come* true; (実現する) be fulfilled; (やや書) (正しいことが分かる) prove* right; (言い当てる) guess right (⇨当てる). ● よく当たる占い師 a *skilled* fortuneteller. ▶その予言が当たるとは思わない I don't think the prediction will *come true*. ▶天気予報が当たった The weather forecast *proved right* (↔*wrong*). ▶君の考えは当たったね You've *guessed right* (↔*wrong*)./Your *guess was right* (*on the mark*).

❹〖よい結果が出る〗(賞品などを勝ち取る) win*; (くじで引き当てる) *hit*; (芝居などが大当たりする) be a (big) *hit*; (事業などが成功する) be a (great) success. ● グアム島旅行が当たる *win* a trip to Guam. ▶彼は宝くじで5,000万円当たった He *won* fifty million yen in the lottery. ▶この芝居の映画化は当たった(=成功した) The film version of this play *came off well*.

❺ [相当する] (等しい) be equal [equivalent] 《to》; (一致・符合する) correspond 《to》; (ある日に) fall* 《on》. ▶1マイルは約1.6キロメートルに当たる One mile *is equal* [*equivalent*] *to* about 1.6 kilometers. (1.6 は one point six と読む) ▶米国の国務省は我が国の外務省に当たる The U.S. State Department *corresponds to* our Foreign Ministry./The State Department *is* the American *equivalent of* [*counterpart to*] our Foreign Ministry. ▶私の誕生日は今年は日曜に当たる My birthday *falls on* a Sunday this year. ▶×Sunday *falls on* my birthday this year. (とはいわない) ▶「桜」に当たる英語は何ですか What is the English *for* [the English *equivalent of*] "sakura"? (▶前の方が口語的。this English is the English word の意味なので the が必要)
会話 「あの人はあなたの何に当たりますか(=どんな関係ですか)」「おじです」"What *relation* is he *to* you?/ How *are* you *related to* him?" "He *is* my uncle."

❻ [きびしく扱う] (きつく当たる) be hard 《on》; (ひどい扱いをする) treat 《him》 harshly [badly]. ● 当たり散らす(=つらく散らす) ▶その少年にあまりつらく当たるな Don't *be* too *hard on* the boy. ▶彼女はしゅうとめにつらく当たった She *treated* her mother-in-law *harshly*.

❼ [困難などに立ち向かう] face, face up to ... (後の方が意図的); [対処する] meet*, deal* with .... ▶難局に当たる face (*up to*) [*meet, deal with*] a difficult situation. ▶当たって砕けろ(=一か八かやってみろ) Take a chance [*your chance*].

❽ [仕事など引き受ける] take*, (書) undertake*; [担当する] take charge of .... ▶私がそのやっかいな仕事に当たろう I'll *take* [*take charge of*] the troublesome job. ▶だれが今日の日直に当たって(=従事して)いますか Who's *on* day *duty* today?

❾ [割り当てられる] be assigned. ▶私たちは図書館の掃除が当たった We *were assigned* to clean the library./We *were assigned* the job of cleaning the library.

❿ [日光・風雨にさらされる] be exposed 《to》; [日が照る] shine* 《on》. ▶日の当たる[当たらない]場所にいる stay in [*out of*] the sun. ▶その写真は日が当たらないようにしなくてはならない The photograph should not *be exposed to* the sun. ▶日が海面に当たっていた The sun *was shining on* [×*in*] the sea. ▶この部屋は日がよく当たる(=日当たりがよい) This room *is sunny*./(日光を多量に受ける) This room *gets* plenty *of* (×*the*) *sun* [*sunshine*]. ▶彼女は火に当たって体を暖めた She warmed herself *at* [*by*] the fire. ▶水は日に当たっていたので暖かくなっていた The water was warm *from the sun*. ▶日に当たる(=日光浴をする)のは健康によい It is good for the health to *bask* [*sit*] *in the sun*.

⓫ [害を受ける] (人が食中毒にかかる) get* poisoned 《by》; (食物などが体に合わない) disagree 《with》; (影響を受ける) be affected 《by》; (果物などが打ち傷で傷む) get bruised. ●フグに当たる *get poisoned by* globefish. ▶暑さに当たる *be affected by* the heat; feel the heat (badly); *get sick from* [*because of*] the heat. ▶私は刺身を食べるとよく当たる Sashimi often *disagrees with* me. ▶この箱の桃は全部当たっている(=打ち傷がついている) All the peaches in this box *have bruises*.

⓬ [確かめてみる] (試す) try; (尋ねる) ask; (意見などを打診する) sound ... out; (確かめる) check with .... ▶その件について彼に当たってみよう I *myself* will *talk with* him about that matter. (▶myself は I を強調する)/I'll *meet* him *in person* ▶私には何とも言えません I can't give an answer until I *check it out with* the person himself [I *sound out* the person himself about it]. (▶himself is the person を強める)

会話 「申し訳ございませんが、すっかり売り切れてしまいました」「じゃあ、他に当たってみなくちゃならないわねえ」"We've quite sold out, I'm afraid." "Then I must *try* somewhere else, I suppose."

⓭ [照合して調べる] check. ▶原典に当たる *check* the original (text). ▶その単語は辞書に当たってみなさい *Look up* the word *in* the dictionary.

● 当たるも八卦当たらぬも八卦 Fortune is fickle and blind./Fortunetelling is a hit-or-miss business.

アダルト [成人, 大人] an adult.
●アダルト映画 a porn [a porno, (書) a pornographic] movie, an X-rated movie. ●アダルトサイト a porn site. ●アダルトチルドレン adult children (略 AC). (▶参考) 機能不全家族の中で育ったため大人になりきれない大人) ●アダルトビデオ a porn [a porno, (書) a pornographic] video, an X-rated video.

アチーブ(メント) [学力検査] an achievement test.
*あちこち around (...). (▶移動・分散を表す動詞とともに用いて); [あちらこちら] here and there; [行ったり来たり] up and down (...), to and fro (▶up and down より堅い語。以上三つは語順入れ替え不可: ×there and here, ×down and up, ×fro and to); [至る所] all over (...). ●あちこちそれを探す look *around* [▶*all over*, (口語) *all over the place*] for it. ▶日本のあちこち(=日本中)からの手紙 letters from *all over* Japan. ▶あちこち(=ある所からある所へと)旅行する travel *from place to place* (▶広範囲に) *extensively*, *widely*). ▶あちこちを見る look *this way or that* (*way*). ▶彼は公園をあちこち歩き回った He walked *around* (in) the park. (▶in を省略すると目的をもって歩き回る含みが強くなる) ▶町のあちこちにその広告が出ている The advertisement can be seen *here and there* in [*in different parts of*] the city. ▶私たちは広い通りをあちこち歩いた We walked *up and down* the broad street.

*あちら ❶ [あそこ] over there; (そこ) there; [あの方向] that way. (▶あそこ) ▶あちらへ着いたらお手紙を差し上げます I'll write when I get *there*. ▶川はあちらです The river is *that way* [(反対方向で) *the other way*]. ▶その本屋は通りのあちら側にあります The bookstore is *on the other side of* the street./(真向かいに) The bookstore is *across* [(米話) *across from*] the street.

❷ [あれ, あの(人)] that. ▶あちらを頂き(=買い)ます I'll take *that* (one). ▶あちらの(男性)は友人の山田君です *That* (gentleman) is my friend Yamada. (▶友人には Mr. Yamada としない) ▶あちら立てればこちら立たず You can't please everyone [*be* everybody's friends].

あちらこちら (あちこち) here and there. (▶あちこち)
●あちらこちらからやって来る come from *far and near* [*wide*]; come from *all over*. ▶床のあちらこちらに彼の服が散らばっている His clothes *are scattered* (*about*) on the floor.

あっ [注意喚起] look; listen; [驚きなど] oh (▶まあ); [痛み] ouch. (▶あっと) ▶あっ, 列車が入って来たよ *Look!* Here comes the *train!* (▶眼前の動作を表す言い方。×Here the train comes! とはいわない。ただし, 代名詞では Here *he* \comes! (あの人がやって来たよ)のように用いる) ▶あっ, ここにあった Oh, \here it

/is. ▶あっ, 切符がない Oh dear! [Dear me!] My ticket's gone. (❗あっ も女性に好まれる言い方)
▶あっ, 痛い Ouch!/It hurts!

あつあげ 厚揚げ deep-fried bean curd.

あつあつ 熱々 ▶熱々をお召し上がりください Please have it while it is *piping hot*. (⇨熱い ❸)

あつい 厚い 形 ❶ [物が] thick (↔thin); (厚く重い) heavy. ▶厚い本 a *thick* book. ▶厚い雲 *thick* [*heavy*] clouds. (❗heavy には「厚く重苦しい」という含みがある)

❷ [心情が] (親切な) kind; (温情ある) warm; (心からの) hearty; (手厚い) hospitable. (❗warm, hearty は通例限定的に用いる) ▶彼は友情に厚い人だ He is *kind* [*faithful*] to his friends.
▶厚いもてなしを受けた I received a *warm* [a *hearty*, a *hospitable*] welcome.

— **厚く** 副 thick(ly). ▶肉を厚く切って cut [slice] the meat *thick(ly)*. (❗thick の方は結果としての状態に重点がある); cut the meat into *thick* slices. ▶地面には落ち葉が厚く積もっていた The ground was *thickly* covered with leaves. (❗副詞の場合, 過去分詞の前では thick より thickly が好まれる) There was a *thick* layer of leaves on the ground. ▶ご援助厚くお礼申し上げます I am *very* grateful to you for your help./(心から) I thank you for your help *from the bottom of my heart*./Thank you *very much* (*indeed*) for your help.

あつい 暑い 〖気温が〗 hot (-tt-) (↔cold); (やや暑い) warm (↔cool); (蒸し暑い) sultry, 《話》 muggy. ▶今日は焼けつく〖うだる〗ように暑い It is broiling (《米》 boiling) *hot* today. (❗broiling, boiling は副詞的に hot を修飾する) ▶すごく暑い日になりそうだ It's going to be [We're going to have] a very *hot* day (《話》 a scorcher). ▶今年の夏[京都の夏]はとても暑い It is really *hot* this summer [in Kyoto in (the) summer]. (❗時[場所]を表す名詞を主語にして This summer is really *hot*./Kyoto is really *hot* in (the) summer. ともいえる) ▶運動をした後なのでとても暑い I feel [am] really *hot* after I exercised. ▶窓を開けてくれませんか, ここは暑すぎます Please open the window. I'm much too *warm* in here.

あつい 熱い ❶ [温度が] hot (-tt-) (↔cold); (加熱した) heated. ▶やけどするほどの熱い湯(=熱湯) scalding *hot* water. ▶焼きつくように熱い砂浜 a beach *hot* enough to burn. ▶ああ! Ouch! ▶ふろは熱めが好きだ I like my bath rather *hot*. (❗S+V+O+C の文型)

❷ [感情が] ▶彼女の熱いまなざし her *intent* gaze [stare]. ▶熱い期待を寄せる be (very) *eager* for ...; look forward to (*doing*)(❗進行形で用いる方が意味が強い). ▶熱い思いを語る talk with enthusiasm [enthusiastically]; talk eagerly. ▶2 人はとてもお熱い仲だ(=熱々だ) They are madly *in love with* each other.

あつえん 圧延 名 rolling. — **圧延する** 動 roll.
●圧延機 a rolling mill. ●圧延鋼 rolled steel.

あっか 悪化 名 deterioration.
— **悪化する** 動 become* [get*] worse, deteriorate; (深刻化する) become serious. ▶病人は症状が悪化した The sick person got worse [took a turn for the worse]. ▶事態が悪化しないように私たちはすぐに行動を起こした We took action immediately so that things wouldn't *get worse* [*deteriorate*, *worsen*]. ▶最近になって情勢はさらに悪化した The situation *has gone from bad to worse* lately.

DISCOURSE

地球環境が悪化していることは疑いない There is no doubt that the earth's environment is *getting worse*. (❗There is no doubt that ... (...に疑いの余地はない)は主張を表すディスコースマーカー)

あっか 悪貨 bad money.
●悪貨は良貨を駆逐する Bad money drives out good (money).

あつかい 扱い ❶ [操作] (使用(法)) use /júːs/; (機械などの) operation ▶操作過程に重点がある; (作業の) handling. ▶この機械は扱いがとても簡単だ This machine is really easy to *use* [*operate*]./It's really easy to *use* [*operate*] this machine.

❷ [処理] ▶こういった問題は扱いが難しい This kind of problem is hard to *deal with* [*handle*]./It's hard to *deal with* [*handle*] this kind of problem./(扱いには十分注意が必要だ) This kind of problem requires careful attention.

❸ [待遇] ▶特別扱いする give (him) special *treatment*. ▶子供扱いする *treat* (him) as [like] a child. ▶その店ではひどい扱いを受けた I *was* terribly *treated* [I got terrible *treatment*] at the store.
▶彼女は子供の扱いがうまい She is good (↔bad) *with* children./She *manages* [*handles*] children skillfully./《話》 She *has a way with* children.

あつかう 扱う 動 ❶ [待遇する] treat; (人を相手にする) deal* with ...; (うまく扱う) manage. ▶客を丁重に扱う *treat* one's guest courteously. ▶扱いやすい[にくい]客 an easy [a difficult] guest. ▶彼は私を大人として扱ってくれる He *treats* me *as* an adult.
▶彼は扱いにくい He is hard (↔easy) to *deal with* [*manage*, *handle*]./(気難しい) He is hard to please.

❷ [問題・事件などを処理する] deal* with ...; (取り扱う) handle; (論じる・報道する) cover. ▶扱いにくい問題 a matter hard to *deal with*; (微妙な問題) a *delicate* matter. ▶その本は 1890 年から現在までの出来事を扱っている The book *deals with* [*covers*] the events from 1890 up to the present. ▶新聞はその事件を大きく扱った The paper *featured* the affair./The paper *gave* massive *coverage* [the full *treatment*] to the affair./The affair *was played up* big (↔was played down) in the paper. ▶ここでは電報を扱っていません We don't *handle* [(受け付ける) *accept*] telegrams here.

❸ [操作する] operate; (動かす) work; (手で扱う) handle. ▶機械を注意深く扱う *operate* [*work*, *handle*] the machine carefully. ▶汚い手で本を扱うな Don't *handle* [×operate] books with dirty hands. ▶この機械は手荒に扱うと壊れる This machine doesn't allow rough *treatment* [*handling*]./(手荒に扱わないように) Be *gentle* with this machine.

会話 「ちょっと持ってもいい?」「そうねえ, じゃ大事に扱ってよ」 "May I hold it for a minute?" "Well, be careful [gentle] with it." (❗gentle は乱暴な扱いをしない)

❹ [売買する] (商品を扱う) deal* in .... ▶この店は食料品を扱っている This shop *deals in* [《やや話》 *carries*] groceries./We sell [deal in, ×carry] groceries (in this shop).

あつかましい 厚かましい impudent; (恥知らずな) shameless; (やりすぎな) pushy. (⇔ 図々しい) ▶彼は厚かましいやつだ He is an *impudent* [a *shameless*] fellow. ▶彼は厚かましくも私に仕事の世話を頼んできた He *had the impudence* [《話》 *nerve*] to ask me

あつかましさ for a job. ▶厚かましい(=無理な)お願いでしょうか Am I asking too much of you?/Is it too much to ask of you? ▶相当厚かましくないとそうはできない It takes a lot of *impudence* [《話》*nerve*, 《話》*brass*] to do that.

あつかましい 厚かましい *impudence*, (恥知らず) *shamelessness*.

あつがみ 厚紙 (厚い紙) *thick paper*; (ボール紙) *cardboard*, (薄い紙を重ね張り合わせた) *pasteboard*. (!) いずれも数えるときは a sheet [a piece] of ...)

あつがり 暑がり ▶彼はとても暑がりだ He is very *sensitive to the heat*.

あつがる 暑がる *complain about the heat*.

あつかん 熱燗 *hot sake*.

あっかん 圧巻 (最良の部分) *the best part*; (目玉) *the highlight*; (クライマックス) *the climax*.

あっかん 悪漢 *a villain* /vílən/; (無法者) *a scoundrel*. ● 悪漢小説 *a picaresque (novel)*.

あつぎ 厚着 ── 厚着する *put on thick layers of clothing*; *dress heavily* ▶厚着している *wear thick layers of clothing*; *be dressed heavily*. (⇒重ね着)

あつぎり 厚切り ▶厚切りのパン *thickly-sliced bread*; (1枚) *a thick slice* of bread.

あつくるしい 暑苦しい ▶暑苦しい日 *a sultry* [《話》*a muggy*] day. ▶暑苦しい(=暑くて息苦しい)部屋 *a hot and stuffy* room.
会話「きれいな人ね」「そう? ちょっと暑苦しい顔だなあ」 "She's pretty [beautiful]." "Do you think so? She's made-up a bit too much for me." (! make up は化粧やファッションについて用いる)

あっけ 呆気 ▶あっけにとられる *be stunned* [*shocked*] 《*at*; *to do*; *that*節》. (⇒びっくり, 驚き) ▶彼女の恥ずべき行いにあっけにとられ物も言えなかった I *was speechless* [*dumbfounded*] by her shameful conduct.

あっけい 悪計 *an evil scheme* [*design*], (陰謀) *a plot*.

あつげしょう 厚化粧 ── 厚化粧する *put on a lot of makeup*. ●厚化粧している *wear a lot of* [*too much*, *heavy*] *makeup*; *be too much* [*very much*, *heavily*] *made up*.

あっけない 呆気ない (期待はずれの) *disappointing*; (予想外の) *unexpected*; (不意な) *abrupt*. ▶あっけない幕切れ *an unexpected* [*abrupt*] *ending*. ▶そのボクシングの試合はあっけないくらいすぐ終わった The boxing match ended *all too soon*.
── あっけなく *disappointingly*; (予想外に) *unexpectedly*; (不意に) *abruptly*; (あまりに) *too*. ▶あっけなく勝つ [負ける] *win* [*lose*] *too easily*.

あっけらかんと ●あっけらかんとしている (まったくこだわりがない) *do not care at all*; (けろりとしている) *be* (*quite*) *nonchalant* 《*about*》; (開けっぴろげな) *be shamelessly frank* [*open*] 《*about*》. ▶彼は以前の恋人と過ごした日々のことをあっけらかんと話した He gave me an *open* account of his days with his former girlfriend, *as if he had nothing to hold back*.

あっこう 悪口 *abuse*. (⇒悪口(わるくち)) ▶アンは彼に悪口雑言(ごん)を浴びせた Ann called him names.

*****あつさ** 暑さ (the) *heat* (! 通例 the ～); *hot weather*. ▶7月の暑さ the *heat* of July. ●暑さを忘れる [逃れる] *forget* [*escape*] *the heat*. ▶この暑さには参った The *heat* has knocked me down./《話》The *heat* has really got me. (暑さで体が弱った) I got weak from [with] *the heat*. ▶寒さは平気だが暑さには耐えられない I don't mind the cold, but I cannot stand [bear] *the heat*. ▶この暑さでは外出する気がしない I don't feel like going out in this *heat* [*hot weather*]. ▶今日は今年一番の暑さだ It's the *hottest* day of the year. ▶今日はひどい暑さだった It was terribly *hot* today.
●暑寒さも彼岸まで Neither heat nor cold lasts until the equinox (days).

あつさ 厚さ *thickness*. ●壁の厚さ the *thickness* of a wall. ▶2インチの厚さの板 a board two inches *thick*; a two-inch-*thick* board.
会話「その氷の厚さはどのくらいですか」「5センチです」 "How *thick* is the ice?" "It's five centimeters *thick* [*in thickness*]."

あっさく 圧搾 图 *compression*. ── 圧搾する 動 *compress*.
●圧搾機 a *compressor*. ●圧搾空気 *compressed air*.

あっさつ 圧殺 ── 圧殺する 動 *crush* 《*him*》 *to death*. ▶権力者によって圧殺された(=抑圧された)自由主義 liberalism *crushed* [*suppressed*] by those in power.

あっさり 副 ❶【作り・様子が簡素に】*simply*, *plainly*. ▶部屋の飾りつけはあっさりとしていた The room was decorated *simply*.
❷【面倒な事などなしに】●あっさり試合に勝つ *win a game easily*; *have an easy win at a game*.
❸【すぐさま】*promptly*, *readily*. ▶彼はあっさり自分の間違いを認めた He *readily* admitted his error.
── あっさりした 形 *simple*, *plain*; *easy*. ●あっさりした料理 a *plain* dish. ●あっさりしたデザインはあっさりしていた The car had a *plain* design.

あっし 圧死 ── 圧死する 動 *be crushed to death*.

あつじ 厚地 *thick cloth*. ▶厚地の上着 a *thick* [*heavy*] coat.

あっしゅく 圧縮 图 (気体の) *compression*; (文章の) *condensation*. ── 圧縮する 動 *compress* 《*A into B*》; *condense*.
●圧縮ガス *compressed gas*.

あっしょう 圧勝 图 *an overwhelming* [*a sweeping*] *victory*; (選挙での) *a landslide* (*victory*).
●圧勝の試合 *a runaway game*.
── 圧勝する 動 ▶彼はその試合で圧勝した He *won an overwhelming victory* in the game./(やや話) He *ran away with* the game./(相手をこてんぱんに負かした) He *beat* his opponent *completely* in the game. ▶ジャイアンツはタイガースに10対1で圧勝した The Giants *wiped out* the Tigers, 10-1. ▶共和党が圧勝した The GOP *won a landslide victory* [*won by a landslide*] (in the election).

あっする 圧する (圧倒する) *overwhelm*. ▶米国は軍事力で他国を圧している America *overwhelms* other countries in military power.

あっせい 圧政 [[暴政]] *tyranny*; [[専制]] *despotism*.
●圧政に苦しむ *suffer under tyranny* [*despotism*].

*****あっせん** 斡旋 图 ▶彼に就職の斡旋を頼んだ I asked him to find me a job [a job for me]. ▶田中氏の斡旋(=尽力)でその会社に職を得た《書》He got a position in the company through the *good offices* [(仲介) the *agency*] of Mr. Tanaka.
── 斡旋する 動 ▶彼が就職を斡旋してくれた He *helped* me (*to*) *find a job*. (⇒世話する)
●斡旋収賄罪 *a bribery charge*; *the crime of accepting bribes in return for one's good offices*.

あっち (over) *there*. (⇒あちら)

あっちゃく 圧着 图 [[機械]] *pressure bonding* [*joining*]. ●熱圧着 *thermo-compression bonding*.
── 圧着する 動 ●ケースを板に圧着する *press fit a*

あって 厚手 ── 厚手の 形 thick; (衣類が) heavy.
 ▶厚手の布 [紙] thick cloth [paper].

あっと ●あっと驚かす astonish, startle; (口がきけないほど) leave 《him》 speechless; (はっとさせる) take 《his》 breath away.
 ●あっと言わせる ・世間をあっと言わせる astonish [startle] the world; (大評判となる) create a sensation.

あっというま あっという間 ── あっという間に (一瞬にして) in a flash; (たちまち) in an instant; (いつの間にか) before one knows it. ▶分かりません。あっという間の出来事でしたから I don't know. It happened *so fast* [*in an instant*]. ▶桜はあっという間に散ってしまった The cherry blossoms have gone *all too soon* [*before we knew it*]. ▶彼はあっという間にその問題を解いた He solved the problem *in no time* (*at all*).

***あっとう 圧倒** ── 圧倒的(な) 形 overwhelming; (強烈な) overpowering. ●圧倒的(な)多数で勝つ win by an *overwhelming* majority. ●圧倒的な勝利 (⇨圧勝) ▶チャンピオンの圧倒的(な)強さには敬服するばかりだ I simply admire the champion's *overwhelming* [*overpowering*] strength.
 ── 圧倒的に 副 overwhelmingly. ▶彼は圧倒的に強いHe is *overwhelmingly* powerful. ▶出席者は若い女性が圧倒的に多かった (=大部分若い女性だった) *Most* of those present were [Those present were *predominantly*] young women.
 ── 圧倒する 動 [断然優位な力[数]で] overwhelm; [より強い力で] overpower. ▶私たちは数において敵を圧倒した We *overwhelmed* the enemy in number. ▶ (敵より断然優位に立った) We *exceeded* the enemy *by far* in number.

アットホーム ●アットホームな雰囲気 a hom(e)y 《米話》 [a homely 《英》] atmosphere. ●homely は《英》では「素朴な、飾らない」など肯定的な意味だが、《米》では「醜い」の意

アットマーク @, at sign. (！ at mark とは通例いわない)

アッパーカット an úppercùt. ●アッパーカットを食わせる deliver an *uppercut* 《*to him, to his jaw*》; uppercut 《him》. ●アッパーカットを食らう take an *uppercut*.

アッパーミドル [中流階級の上層] the upper-middle class.

***あっぱく 圧迫** 名 (圧力) pressure; (重圧) oppression; (抑圧) suppression. ▶彼女は胸に圧迫を感じた (だれかに押されたりして) She felt the *pressure* on her chest. ●She felt pressure in the chest. だと「彼女は胸に不快な圧迫感があった」の意
 ── 圧迫する 動 (しいたげる) oppress; (抑圧する) suppress. ▶暴君は人民を圧迫した The tyrant *oppressed* his people. ▶政府は言論の自由を圧迫した The government *suppressed* freedom of speech. ▶インフレで家計が圧迫された (=家計を悪くした) Inflation *has worsened* [*affected*] the family budget.

あっぱれ あっぱれな 形 ádmirable; praiseworthy. (⇨見事, 立派) ●あっぱれなふるまい *admirable* [*praiseworthy*] behavior.

アップ ❶ [上がること] ●賃金アップ (get [ask for]) a (pay) raise 《米》 [rise 《英》]. ▶ガソリンの価格が5パーセントアップした Gas prices *have gone up* [*have risen*] by 5 percent. ●髪をアップにしている wear one's hair *up* [*upswept*]; have an *upswept* hairdo.
 ❷ [髪型] ●髪をアップにしている wear one's hair *up* [*upswept*]; have an *upswept* hairdo.
 ❸ [写真] a close-up /klóusʌp/. ●人の手の写真をアップで撮る take a *close-up* of a human hand; take a picture of a human hand *in close-up*.

あっぷあっぷ ●あっぷあっぷしている (溺れかけて) be gasping for air; be drowning /dráuniŋ/. ▶会社は多額の借金であっぷあっぷの状態にある Our company *is drowning* in debt /dét/.

アップグレード 名 [製品などの機能向上] upgrade.
 ── アップグレードする 動 ●コンピュータの機能をアップグレードする *upgrade* a computer system 《*by installing new software*》.

アップダウン [起伏の多い] up-and-down; /Apəndáun/; [起伏] úps and dówns; (和製語) up down.

アップツーデート [最新の] up-to-date. ●アップツーデートなファッション *up-to-date* [*the latest*] fashions.

アップデート 名 [データ・ファイルなどの更新] [コンピュータ] an update.
 ── アップデートする 動 update.

アップテンポ ●アップテンポのダンスミュージック an *up-tempo* dance music.

アップリケ [<フランス語] 名 appliqué /æpləkéi/.
 ── アップリケする 動 ●スカートにチューリップをアップリケする *appliqué* a skirt *with* tulips.

アップルパイ an apple pie.

アップロード 名 [ホストコンピュータへのデータの転送] an upload 《⇨download》.
 ── アップロードする 動 upload.

あつぼったい 厚ぼったい thick, heavy. ●厚ぼったいカーペット a *heavy* [a *thick*] cloth. ●厚ぼったい(=かさばった)封筒 a *bulky* envelope.

あつまり 集まり [集会] a meeting; (打ち解けた) a gathering; (家族的な集まり) [話] a get-together (⇨会); [参加状況] (an) attendance; [集団] a group. ●宗教的な集まり a religious *meeting* [*gathering*]. ●有志の集まり a *group* of volunteers. ●会議の集まりが悪かった [よかった] The meeting was poorly [well] attended. (⇨出席)

***あつまる 集まる** ❶ [寄り集まる] [散らばっていた人・物が1か所に集まる] gather; (会合・パーティー・飲酒など社交を目的として集まる) get* together; (会合する) meet*; (目的をもって公式に集まる) (やや書) assemble; (大勢の人が集まって混み合う) crowd; (動物・鳥・人などが群れをなして集まる) flock (together). (⇨群がる) ●その事故現場に人々が集まった People gathered in [crowded (together in), flocked to] the scene of the accident. ▶子供たちは話を聞こうと先生の周りに集まった The children *gathered* [*crowded*, *grouped*] *around* the teacher to hear his story. ▶みんな集まれ！ *Gather around*, all of you! ●あすの晩集まってそのことについて話し合おう Let's *get together* and talk about it tomorrow evening. ▶みんな集まりましたか(=ここにいますか) Is everybody here? ▶委員会は毎週土曜日に開かれる(=集まる) The committee *meet*(*s*) every Saturday. (！ meet(s) については ⇨委員会) ▶集まり散じて人は変われど、仰ぐは同じ理想の光 Our students may *come* and *go*, but our Ideal remains forever.
 ❷ [集中する] [興味・関心などが] center 《*on*》, focus 《*on*》; (目的を持って集められる) be collected. ●集まった金 the money *collected*; (献金) contributions. ▶今までにおよそ100万円集まった About a million yen *has been collected* so far. 《⇨集める ❶》 ▶注意がその司祭に集まった Attention (*was*) *centered on* the priest. (注目の的だった) The priest was the *center* [*focus*] of attention.

あつみ 厚み [厚さ] thickness. (⇨厚さ) ●非常に厚み(=深み)のある人 a man of great *depth*.

*あつめる 集める

WORD CHOICE 集める, 集まる

gather 散在している物・人を1か所に寄せ集めること。時に、副詞 up や together を伴う。●情報を集める *gather* information. ●友人たちを呼び集める *gather* friends *together*.

collect 同種の物・人などを計画的・組織的に選択して集めること。●税金[データ・金]を集める *collect* taxes [data; money].

assemble 集会などの目的で整然と人を一同に集めたり、部品をきちんと組んで機器を組み立てたりすること。●王に集められた同盟軍 the Allies *assembled* by the king.

頻度チャート

```
gather     ██████████████████████
collect    ███████████████████
assemble   ██████
           20  40  60  80  100 (%)
```

❶ [寄せ集める] (散在している物・人を1か所に) gather; (計画的に選択して集める) collect; (ある目的で人・物を) 《やや堅》assemble; (いっしょにする) get*... together; (資金などを) raise. ●情報を集める *gather* [*collect*] information. ●請願署名を集める *collect* petition signatures. ●被災者のために募金を集める *collect* [ˣ*gather*] money for the victims. ●その事業の資金を集める *raise* the funds [do fund-*raising*] for the undertaking. ●校長はすべての学生を講堂に集めた The principal *gathered* all the students (*together*) [*assembled* all the students] in the auditorium. ▶毎週月曜日にごみを集めに来る They *collect* our garbage every Monday. ▶落ち葉を集めて燃やしなさい *Gather* [*Sweep together*] fallen leaves and burn them.

会話 「君は何か集めてますか」「外国のコインをたくさん集めています」"Have you got any *collections*?" "I've got a large *collection* of foreign coins."

❷ [引きつける] (注意・客などを引き寄せる) draw*; (魅力による) attract. ●その計画は世間の注目を集めた The project *drew* [*attracted*] public attention. ▶孤児たちの境遇は世間の同情を集めた The orphans' circumstances *captured* the sympathy of the world. ▶そのロック歌手は最近若者の人気を集めている The rock singer *is getting popular* [*enjoying popularity*] among young people these days.

あつもの 羹 hot soup [broth].

●あつものに懲りてなますを吹く《ことわざ》A burnt child dreads the fire./Once bitten, twice shy.

あつやき 厚焼き ●厚焼きせんべい a thick Japanese rice cracker. ●厚焼きたまご a thick omelette.

アッラー (⇨アラー)

あつらえ 誂え ●あつらえのスーツ a made-to-order [《主に英》a made-to-measure] suit; a suit *made to order*. ▶このコートはあつらえだ This coat is *made to order*.

あつらえむき 誂え向き — あつらえ向きの 形 (ぴったりの) right; (理想的な) ideal; (申し分のない) perfect. ▶ハイキングにはあつらえ向きの日だ It's an *ideal* [a *perfect*] day for hiking. ▶これはあつらえ向きの品だ This is just the *right* thing [(まさにその品) the *very thing*] I've wanted.

あつらえる 誂える have 《a suit》made to order. (⇨

誂え)

*あつりょく 圧力 (a) pressure. (❗ 比喩的にも用いる)

●政治的圧力 political *pressure*. ●政府の圧力に屈する *give in to the pressure* of the government. ▶圧力を加えると気体の温度が上昇する *Pressure* can raise the temperature of gases. ▶彼らは私に調査を中止するよう圧力をかけた They *put pressure* [*brought pressure* (*to bear*)] on me to give up the investigation. (❗(1) 最終的には調査を中止したことを暗示。後の方が堅い表現。(2) 受身は通例 I を主語にしないで Pressure *was put* [*was brought*] on me to give up the investigation (by them). とする)/(私は調査を中止するよう圧力をかけられていた) I *was under pressure* (from them) *to* give up the investigation. (❗ 最終的に調査を中止したかどうかは不明)

●圧力がま a pressure cooker. ●圧力計 a pressure gauge; (気体用) a manometer /mənámətər/.
●圧力団体 a pressure group. (❗単・複両形扱い)

あつれき 軋轢 [摩擦] (a) friction. [不和] (a) discord; [争い] a conflict. ●二国間の軋轢 *friction* [*discord*] between the two countries.

あて 当て 图 ❶ [目的, 目標] a purpose; an aim; an object. (⇨目的, 目標) ●当てのない aimless. ●当てもなくさまよう wander about *aimlessly*. ▶彼はどこへ行くという当てがあったわけではなかった He was not going anywhere in particular. ▶どこに行く当てもなかった I had nowhere to go.

❷ [期待, 信頼] (expectation, 頼り) ●それについてはあまり当てにならない You can't *be too sure* about that.

— 当てにする 動 [頼る] rely [depend, 《やや話》count] on ...; [期待する] expect. ●私は彼の援助を当てにした I *relied on* him to help me./I *relied on* his help. ●彼は当てにできない He can't *be relied upon* [*be depended upon, be trusted*]./He is not a *reliable* [a *dependable*, a *trustworthy*] person. ●それは私が当てにしていたほどの金額ではなかった That's not as much money as I *expected*.

会話 「今晩返すよ」「当てにしていいかい」"I'll return it this evening." "Can I *count on* it [*that*]?"

-あて -宛て ●佐藤さんあての手紙 a letter *for* [*addressed to*] Mr. Sato. ●息子あてに手紙を書く write *to* one's son. ▶この手紙はだれあてですか Who is this letter *for*?/Who is this letter *addressed to*?

あてうま 当て馬 ❶ [種馬が来るまで仮にあてがわれる雄馬] (説明的に) a stallion brought near a mare to test whether the mare is ready to mate.
❷ [本命と勝負を争う馬] a rival horse.
❸ [相手のじゃまを目的に出される人] a stalking horse.

あてがいぶち 宛てがい扶持 (説明的に) an allowance given an employee [an apprentice] at his employer's [master's] discretion.

あてがう ❶ [与える] give*; (時間・金などをある目的のために) allow; (支給する) provide, furnish. ●彼に月10,000 円の小遣いをあてがう *allow* [*give*] him 10,000 yen a month for pocket money.

❷ [割り当てる] (仕事などを) assign; (仕事・時間・金などを) 《やや書》allot (-tt-); (資金などをある目的のために計上する) 《やや書》allocate. (❗順に堅い語) ●その仕事を彼にあてがう *assign* [*allot, allocate*] the task *to* him.

❸ [押し当てる] put*... (to); (手に持って) hold*... (to). (⇨当てる ❺) ●耳に両手をあてがって聴く listen with one's hands cupped *over* [*behind*] one's ears.

あてこすり 当て擦り (⇨当てつけ)

あてこする 当て擦る (⇨当てつける)

あてこむ 当て込む (頼りにする) count on [upon]...; (期待する) expect. ▶彼は値上がりを当て込んで広大な土地を買った He bought a large tract of land *in expectation of* its rise in value.

あてさき 宛て先 one's address. (⇨宛て名)

あてじ 当て字 (音への) a phonetic equivalent; (文字への) a substitute character.

あていりょう 当て推量 (だいたいの見当) a rough guess, guesswork; (当てずっぽう) a wild guess; (推測) a conjecture. ●当て推量で当てる (a *rough* [*wild*] *guess*); by guesswork. ●当て推量をする make a (*rough* [*wild*]) *guess* ⟨*at*⟩; hazard a *guess* [a *conjecture*].

あですがた 艶姿 ●芸者のあで姿 the *alluring figure* of a *geisha*.

あてずっぽう 当てずっぽう a (wild) guess. (⇨推測) ●彼の年齢を当てずっぽうで言う *guess* ⟨*at*⟩ his age; *make a guess at* his age. ▶当てずっぽうで言えば彼は40歳ぐらいだろう I'd say that, *at a guess*, he is about forty. (▮*at a guess* は文頭に置くことも可)

あてつけ 当てつけ (言葉) a snide /snáid/ remark, (話) a dig; (やや書) (an) insinuation. ●当てつけを言う (⇨当てつける) ▶あの冗談は私への当てつけだ That joke *is indirectly meant for* [*is actually directed at*, (話) *is a dig at*] me.

あてつける 当てつける (当てこする) make* a snide remark ⟨*about, on*⟩, hint at... (▮hint は不快感を暗示しない場合にも用いる); (話) have* [take*] a dig ⟨*at* him⟩, (やや書) insinuate. ●彼に不注意だと当てつけて言う *insinuate* [*make a snide remark about, hint at*] his carelessness. ▶気が変わりやすいのは女だけとは限らないと彼女は私に当てつけて言った She *insinuated* [*hinted*] *to me that* fickle creatures were not restricted [limited] to women.

あてど 当て所 ●当てどない旅 (aimless) wandering. ●当てどなく街をさまよう wander through the streets.

あてな 宛て名 (相手の氏名) one's name; (住所氏名) one's name and address (▮語順に注意). ●あて名の不明な(=判読できない)手紙 a *blind letter*. ●年賀状にあて名を書く *address* a New Year's card. ▶封筒のあて名ははっきり書いてください Please write your *name and address* /ədrés, (米) ǽdres/ *clearly* on the envelope./Please *address* /ədrés/ the envelope *clearly*. ▶この手紙のあて名は君になっている This letter *is addressed* to *you*./This letter is for *you*. ▶この手紙のあて名は間違っている This letter *is wrongly addressed*. ▶あて名変更などございましたらご連絡ください Please let us know if your *mailing details* require updating.

あてにげ 当て逃げ a hit and run, (口) 轢(ひ)き逃げ.

アテネ [ギリシャの首都] Athens /ǽθnz/.

アデノイド [医学] ádenoids. (▮複数扱い)

あてはずれ 当て外れ [期待外れ] (a) disappointment (⇨期待); [誤算] [書] (a) miscalculation.

あてはまる 当てはまる [適用される] apply ⟨*to*⟩; [有効である] hold* good [true] ⟨*in*＋事⟩, hold ⟨*for*＋人⟩; [いえる] be true ⟨*of*⟩; [満たす] fulfill. ▶この規則はその場合に当てはまらない This rule does not *apply to* [*hold good in*] the case. ▶同じことが他のだれにでも当てはまる The same is *true of* everybody else.

あてはめる 当てはめる [適用する] apply. ▶その方法をすべての場合に当てはめることはできない We cannot *apply* the method *to* all cases.

あでやか 艶やか —— 艶やかな 形 gorgeous, (話) stunning. ●身のこなしがあでやかな *elegant* [(魅惑的['には優美]) *fascinatingly elegant*] in one's manners.

あてられる 当てられる ▶彼は火山の毒気にあてられて倒れた He fell down [collapsed] after *being exposed* to [*breathing in*] *the poisonous gas from the volcano*. ▶新婚さんにあてられっぱなしだった The newly-married couple's display of love was embarrassing to me all along.

:あてる 当てる, 充てる ❶ [ぶつける] hit*, strike*. (▮後の方が強意的) ▶彼はその犬に石を当てた He *hit* the dog with a stone. ▶彼女は頭にボールを当てられた She *was* [*got*] *hit* [*was struck*] *on* the head by a ball.

❷ [くじで引き当てる] draw*; (賞金[品]を当てる) win*; [事業・興業などで山を当てる] make* a hit. ●くじで 3 等賞 (1,000 万円)を当てる *draw* ⟨*the* [*a*]⟩ *third prize* [*win ten million yen*] *in a lottery*. ▶彼はその仕事で一山当てた He *made a big hit in* [(話) *hit it big with*] that business.

❸ [推測する] guess, make* a guess ⟨*at*⟩. ▶彼はずばり言い当てた[当てそこなった] He *guessed right* [*wrong*]./He *made a good* [*a bad*] *guess*. (話) He *got it right* [*wrong*]. ▶私の年齢を正確に当てましたね You *guessed* ⟨*at*⟩ *my age correctly*./You *made a correct guess at* my age.

会話「彼女の今度の車は何色だか当ててごらん」「赤かしら」 "*Guess* what color her new car is." "Is it red?"

❹ [日光・風雨にさらす] expose; (空気に) air. ●それを日に当てる *put* it *in* the sun; *expose* it *to* the sun. ●雨の前の花を雨に当てないようにする(=雨から守る) *protect* the flower *from* rain. ▶衣類を時々風に当てて虫干ししなさい You must *air* your clothes once in a while.

❺ [押し当てる] (ある場所に置く) put* [place] ... ⟨*to, on, over, in*⟩ (1) 状況によって前置詞を使い分ける. (2) place は正確に特定の場所に置くこと); (手に持って) hold* ... ⟨*to*⟩. ●額に手を当てる *put* [*place*] *one's hand on one's forehead*. ●受話器を耳に当てる *hold* [*put*] *the receiver to one's ear*. ●両手を腰に当てて立っている stand with one's hands *on* one's hips ⟨⟨古⟩⟩ (with) arms akimbo. (▮one's hips は日本語の「腰」に近い意味で,「しり」 (buttocks) ではない) ▶彼は耳を壁に当てて聞いた He *put* his ear *to* [*against*] the wall./(押し当てて) He *pressed* his ear *against* [*to*] the wall. ▶彼女は目にハンカチを当てた She *held* [*put*] her handkerchief *to* her eyes. (▮*to* の代わりに *over* を用いると目をおおう感じになる)

❻ [割り当てる] (仕事・部屋などを) assign; (時間・お金などを) allot (-tt-). (⇨あてがう❷) ●読書に 1 日 2 時間充てる *allot* [*give*] (oneself) *two hours a day for reading*. ●1階を店，2階を住居に充てる have [run] a shop on the first floor and live on the second floor; use the first floor for a store and the second floor for a residence.

▶彼は収入の 10 パーセントをローンの返済に充てた He *allotted* 10 percent of his income *for* the loan repayments. ▶そのお金を中国旅行に充てたい(=取っておきたい) I want to *put* the money *aside* [(違う) *use* the money] *for* my trip to [︎of] China. ▶彼は趣味に充てる時間がほとんどない He has hardly any time *for* his hobbies.

❼ [授業で指名する] (求める) ask, (書) call on ⟨*to do*⟩. ▶私は当てられて教科書を読んだ I *was asked* [*was told*] *to* read the textbook and I did so.

あてる　宛てる address; (あて先を指示する) direct. (⇨ ~宛) ●...にあった手紙 a letter *addressed to...*; a letter *for....* ●この小包を下記住所にあててお送りください Please *direct* the parcel *to* the following address.

アテンションバリュー 〘広告注目度〙attention value.

あと　後　　　　　　　　　　　　　　　　**INDEX**
❶ 位置　　　　　　　❷ 時間
❸ 順序　　　　　　　❹ 残り
❺ 追加　　　　　　　❻ 将来, 今後
❼ 後継　　　　　　　❽ 去った後, 亡き後

❶【位置】 ① 〈後に[へ]〉(後方へ) back, backward; (後ろの位置に) behind (...); (...の後に続いて) after.... ●後にさがる draw [step] *back.* ●3歩後へさがる take three steps *back* [*backward*]. ●その犬は彼のすぐ後について歩いていた The dog was walking (close) *at his heels* [*close behind* him]. ●彼は遅れ後に残った[残された] He stayed [was left] *behind* alone. ●彼は東京を後にしてパリに向かった He *left* Tokyo *for* Paris. ●一歩も後には引かないぞ I will *hold* [*stand*] *my ground.*/(少しも譲れない) I can't *give* [*budge*] *an inch.* ●やっと頂上まで半分のところまで来たのだから，もう後には引けない(=引き返すわけにはいかない) Now that we have come halfway to the top at last, we won't go back.

② 〈後を〉 ●パレードのいちばん後を行く be the last in the parade; (しんがりをつとめる) 《やや書》 bring up the rear of [walk in the rear of] the parade. ●私の後をついてきなさい．道を教えてあげましょ *Follow* me and I'll show you the way. ●どうして私の後をつけ回すの Why do you keep *following* me *around*? ●刑事はその男の後をつけた The detective *shadowed* [《話》*tailed*] the man.

❷【時間】 ①〈後で〉(その後) later (on), afterward. ●じゃ, また後で (I'll) see you *later*. ●電話します I'll call you *later* (on) [*afterward*]. (事情) 英語では単なる別れのあいさつにとられる. 必ずかける場合は (I'll) *call* you around 8:30. などという）
[会話] 「今払わなくてはいけませんか」「後でけっこうです」 "Should I pay you now?" "*Later* will be fine." (❗ (1) later は「後で(支払うこと)」の表的主語. (2) You can *pay* ⁄ *later*. ともいえる. You can *páy* *later*. は「(...より)遅れて払ってもよい」の意となるので注意)

②【時間】+〈後に〉 ●ずいぶん後になって彼は本当のことを話してくれた He told me the truth much *later on* [*long afterward*, well *after* that]. ●彼はそれから1週間後にやって来た A week *later* [*afterward*] he came. (❗ 単に「1週間後に」では *After* a week.... となる）

③ 〈後+「時間」で [して]〉 (未来・過去のある時から...後に) ... after《+图, 節》; (今から...後に) in ...; ...before《+图, 節》. ●彼女は彼が出発した後すぐ[10分して] 到着した She arrived right [ten minutes] *after* he left. (❗ after によって時間的な順序関係が明白なので had left としないことが多い) ●後どのくらいで彼女は帰ってきますか How *soon* [How much *later*] will she be (coming) back? ●後10分ほどすれば彼女は帰ってくる She will be [come] back in [*x*after] about ten minutes./She will come back about ten minutes *from now.*/It will be about ten minutes *before* she comes back.

❸【順序】〈...の後に〉 after (...); (2者のうち後の方の) the latter (↔the former); (もっと後に) later; (最後

の) last; (次の) next. ●後の章で in a *later* chapter. ●彼の後から中へ入って来た *follow* him in; come in *after* [*behind*] him. ●後から参ります I'll come *after* you. ●ふろは食事の前それとも後が Will you take a bath before dinner or *after*? (⇨後回し) ●1年後の半分を京都で過ごした I spent *the latter* [*second*] half of the year in Kyoto. ●彼はついに彼らから入って来た He was *the last* (man) to come in. ●後の列車にどうにか間に合った I managed to catch *the next* train. ●今度はうまくやれよ. もう後(=次の機会)がないんだから You have to succeed now because there'll be no *next time*.

❹【残り】the rest. ●神戸まで電車で行き後は船で行った I went by train as far as Kobe and went *the rest* of the way by ship. ●後は(=その他のことは)私はあなたにまったく賛成です *For the rest*, I quite agree with you. ●後は私が引き受けます [=私に任せなさい] Leave *the rest* to me.

[会話] 「頂上まで後どのくらいあるの」「後3キロほどだ」 "How much farther do we have to go before we get to the top of the hill?" "(We have) about three kilometers *to go* [(さらに) *another* three kilometers or so, three *more* kilometers or so]." (❗ to go は名詞の後に置く.「(時間・距離などが) 残っている」の意 (⇨ [会話] 最終例))

❺【追加】(さらに) more; (程度・距離がそれ以上の[に]) further; (もう一つ[もうひとまとまり]の) another. ●あと三つ卵をください Please give me three *more* [*another* three] eggs. ●彼はそのことについて後は何も言わなかった He said nothing *more* [*further*] about it.

[会話] 「もっと要るだろうな」「あとどのくらい?」 "I'll want more than that." "How much [many] *more*?" (❗ much は量, many は数を問題にする場合)

[会話] 「(出かける用意に)あとどれくらいかかるんだい」「あと2, 3分よ」 "How much longer are you going to be?" "For a few *more* minutes." (❗ be long は「(人が)...するのに時間がかかる」の意)

[会話] 「試験をあと何日なの」「あと3日です」 "How many days *to go* before the exam?" "Three days." (❗ to go の前に are there または do you have が省略された言い方)

❻【将来, 今後】the [one's] future. ●後々のために備える provide for *the future*. ●後は運を天に任せよう Let's leave our *future* to Heaven. ●後のたたりが恐ろしいぞ(=ただではすまないよ) You can't *get away with it.*/You will *pay for it*.

❼【後継】 ●彼は森氏の後を継いで会長になった He *succeeded* Mr. Mori *as* president [*to* the presidency]./He *took over* as president when Mr. Mori retired. (❗ as に続く一人しかいない役職名は無冠詞) ●だが田中氏の後に座るのでしょうか Who will *take over from* Mr. Tanaka [(取って代わる) *take* Mr. Tanaka's *place*]?/《やや書》Who will *succeed* [*be a successor to*] Mr. Tanaka?

❽【去った後, 亡き後】 ●後に残った家族はどうしてよいか途方に暮れた The *bereaved* family didn't know what to do. ●彼は妻と2人の娘を後に残して死んだ He *left* his wife and two girls (after he died). (❗ ( )を省略すると「...のもとを去った」の意にもなる)/《やや書》He was *survived by* his wife and two daughters. (❗ survive は「...より長生きする」の意) ●留守中後を頼む(=いろいろなことをやってください) Please take care of *things* [my *affairs*] while I am away.

●後の祭り (⇨後の祭り)
●後は野となれ山となれ 《ことわざ》After me [us] the

deluge.(**!** deluge /délu:dʒ/ は「大洪水」で,「私がいなくなったら彼らが大いに悲しんでもかまわない」の意)
●後を追う・犬の後を追う run after a dog. ●父は母の後を追うように亡くなった My father died soon after my mother.
●後を引く・せんべいを食べたそう後を引く(=引き続き欲しくなる) Once I start eating rice crackers, I can't resist eating it. ●正月気分が後を引いている(=影響が残っている) I can't get rid of the New Year holiday mood./I am still in the New Year holiday mood.

＊あと 跡 ❶[形跡] a trace, 《やや書》 a vestige (**!** 通例否定文で); (通った跡) a track; (しるし) a sign; (傷・しみなどの) a mark; (傷跡) a scar. ●古代文明の跡 *traces* of ancient civilization. ●種痘(しゅとう)の跡 a vaccination *mark*. ●手術の跡 a surgical *scar*. ●英語に進歩の跡が見られない show no *sign* of progress in English. ●地面にタイヤの跡が残っていた *Traces* of tires [Tire *tracks*] were left on the ground. ●建物の跡には何も残っていなかった Not a *trace* [a *vestige*] of buildings remained. ●彼の論文には苦心の跡が見られる There are *traces* of effort [hard work] in his paper [thesis].
❷[行われた場所] a site. ●古戦場の跡 the *site* of an old battle. ▶立つ鳥跡を濁さず(ことわざ) It is an ill bird that fouls its own nest.(⇒立つ[成句])
❸[家督] ●父の跡を継ぐ take over from 《やや書》 succeed] one's father. (⇒継ぐ❶)
●跡を絶つ・この種の事件が跡を絶たない(=終わりがない) There is *no end* to these kind of cases./ (次々に起こる) These kind of cases *occur one after another*. ●弔問客が跡を絶たない Callers for condolence are coming one after another.

あとあし 後足 ●後足で立つ stand on its *hind* [back] *legs* (↔front legs); (特に馬が) rear up (in fear). ▶犬は後足で立って歩いた The dog walked on its *hind* [back] *legs*. ▶お世話になった人に後足で砂かけるようなことをしてはいけません You shouldn't do anything ungrateful to those who were kind [did favors] to you.

あとあじ 後味 an aftertaste. ●後味の悪い(=気持ちのよくない)出来事 an *uncomfortable* [不愉快な] *unpleasant*] event. ▶このケーキは後味がよい[悪い] This cake leaves a pleasant [an *unpleasant*] *aftertaste* (in the mouth). ▶そのことで私は後味の悪い思いをした That matter *left a bad taste in* my *mouth*./That matter *left an unpleasant aftertaste*./I *had an uncomfortable feeling* even after that matter was settled.

あとあと 後々 (将来) the future. ●後々の事を考える think about the *future*.

アドイン 〖ソフトに追加する拡張機能〗〖コンピュータ〗 an add-in.

あとおい 後追い ●後追い自殺 (commit) suicide immediately after another person's death.

あとおし 後押し ❶[後ろから押すこと] ●荷車を後押しする push a cart (from behind).
❷[後援] support, backing; (後援者) a supporter, a backer. ●彼の後押しをする support [give support to] him; back him (up).

アドオン 〖電気製品などの付属[付加]装置〗 an add-on.

アドオンほうしき アドオン方式 〖元利均等払い〗〖経済〗 an add-on system.

あとがき 後書き (本の) an afterword (**!** 主に著者以外の); (手紙・本などの) a postscript (**!** 追伸の場合は P.S., PS と略す). ●後書きを加える add a *P.S.*

あとかた 跡形 a trace, 《やや書》 a vestige. ▶津波でその建物は跡形もなかった After the tsunami, the building was gone without a *trace*./There was nothing left of the building after the tsunami.

あとかたづけ 後片付け ――後片付けをする 動 (きちんと整とんする) put (a room [things]) in order; (きれいに片付けて掃除をする) clean (a room) up; (食卓を片づける) clear [《米》 clear off] the table, clear away [《米》 off]; (皿を洗う) do [wash] the dishes, 《英》 wash up. (⇒洗う) ●夕食の後片付けをする *do the dishes and clear the table* after dinner.

あとがま 後釜 (後任) a successor 《to him》. ●A校長の後釜にすわる(=後任となる) *succeed* Mr. A as principal. (**!** 無冠詞に注意)

あとくされ 後腐れ ●後腐れがないように to avoid *trouble in the future* [*future trouble*].

あとくち 後口 (食後の舌に残る感じ) an aftertaste. (⇒後味)

あどけない (無邪気な) innocent; (外見上子供のような,子供らしい) childlike. ●あどけない考え[質問] a *childlike* idea [question]. ●子供のあどけない寝顔 the *innocent* face of a sleeping child. ▶彼女はまだあどけない顔をしている She still looks *childlike* [×innocent]. (**!** innocent は外面ではなく心の無邪気さをいう)/There is still something *childlike* about her.

あどけなさ innocence. ●その子のあどけなさ the *innocence* of the child.

あとさき 後先 ❶[位置] ●後先を見る look *before and after*.
❷[順序] order. ●後先を逆にする reverse the *order*. ●後先を考えずに without considering the consequences; (考えもなく) thoughtlessly; (無謀にも) recklessly. ●後先をよく考えて(=慎重に)行動する act *prudently*; *think carefully before* one acts. ▶話も後先になってしまいました... I should have told you this first, but....

あとざん 後産 the afterbirth.

あとしまつ 後始末 ――後始末をする 動 ❶[解決する] settle; (事態を収拾する) 《話》 pick up the pieces 《of》; (完済する) pay (one's debt) off. ●けんか[問題]の後始末をする *settle* the quarrel [matter]. ●倒産した会社の後始末をする(=業務整理をする) *wind up the affairs of* a bankrupt company.
❷[整とんする] put (a place) in order. (⇒後片付け)

あとずさり 後ずさり ――後ずさりする 動 move [step] back; (しり込みする) shrink away, back away 《from》; (精神的に)「しり込みする」は shrink 《from》. ●蛇に後ずさりする *shrink* [back] *away from* a snake. ▶彼は驚いて後ずさりした He *stepped back* in surprise.

あとぜめ 後攻め 〖野球〗 field first; bat last. (⇒後攻)

あとち 跡地 the site (of a demolished building).

あとぢえ 後知恵 ●後知恵ばかりで with the benefit of *hindsight*. ●下衆(げす)の後知恵 We are always wiser in *hindsight*.

あとつぎ 跡継ぎ [跡取り](⇒跡取り); [後継者] a successor (to the manager).

あとづける 跡付ける (跡をたどる) trace. ●歴史を跡づける *trace* the history.

あととり 跡取り (男性) an heir /éər/ 《to》; (女性) an heiress /éəris/. ●跡取り息子 a son and heir /sánəndéər/; 〖単数扱い〗.

あとにもさきにも 後にも先にも ●後にも先にもない(=古今を通じての)大学者 the *greatest scholar of all time*. ●後にも先にもそれほど愛した人は他にはなかった

あとのまつり

have never loved anyone else so much *before or since.* ▶後にも先にもたった1人の息子です He's the only son *that we have ever had.*

あとのまつり 後の祭り 〔会話〕「あんなこと言わなければよかった」「もう後の祭りだ(=遅すぎる)」"I shouldn't have said things like that." "It's too late now./It's too late to lock the stable door. (❗ after the horse is stolen と続くことわざ)/〔話〕A day after the fair." (❗「早すぎる」は A day before the fair.)

アドバイザー 〔助言者〕an adviser, 《ややまれ》an advisor.

アドバイス (先のことについての)《a piece [a bit, a word] of》advice /ədváis/ 《about, on》. (❗日本語の「アドバイス」より重大なニュアンスを持っていることが多い) (⇨忠告) ▶大学を選ぶことについてアドバイスをお願いできますか Could you give me some *advice about choosing universities?*
— **アドバイス(を)する** 動 advise /ədváiz/ 《him》; give 《him》advice. ▶彼はそこへ行かないようにアドバイスをしてくれた He *advised* me not to go there.

あとばら 後腹 (出産後の痛み) afterpains.

あとばらい 後払い 〔延期される支払い〕deferred payment.

アドバルーン an advertizing balloon [blimp]; 〔和製語〕an ad balloon. 〔参考〕日本で生まれたもので、米英ではほとんど使われない。blimp は飛行船状のもの) ▶アドバルーンを上げる hoist [fly] an *advertizing balloon.*

アドバンテージ 〔利点, 優位〕(an) advantage. ▶ホームアドバンテージ 〔ホームの地の利〕home advantage.

アトピー atopy /ǽtəpi/; 〔医学〕atopy. (❗米英では後の方をよく用いる) ▶アトピー性皮膚炎にかかっている be suffering from eczema [atopic dermatitis /eitápik dɜː́rmətáitəs/].

アドベンチャー 〔冒険〕(an) adventure.

アドホック 〔＜ラテン語〕〔特別な, 臨時の〕ad hoc. ▶災害対策本部をアドホックに設置する set up the *ad hoc* disaster relief headquarters; set up the disaster relief headquarters *on an ad hoc basis.*

あとまわし 後回し ▶難しい問題は後回しにしなさい Do the difficult problems later./(やさしいのから始めなさい) Begin with the easier problems. ▶その仕事は後回しでよい You can *put off* the job till later./The job can wait.

アドミッション 〔入場・入学などの許可〕(an) admission. ●アドミッションオフィス入試 (⇨AO入試)

アトム 〔原子〕an atom.

あとめ 跡目 ▶父の跡目を継いで(=後を継いで)社長になる *succeed* one's father as president; (代(ｶ)わりをする) *take the place of* one's father as president.

あともどり 後戻り ── **後戻りする** 動 〔元に戻る〕get [go] back; (ぐるりと向きを変える) turn back; 〔後ろへ移動する〕move back(ward); (病状・景気などが) go backward. ▶もう後戻りはできない There is no *turning back.* (❗慣用表現)

あとやく 後厄 (厄年の次の年) the year following an unlucky year.

アトラクション 〔呼び物に添える出し物〕a sideshow; 〔実演〕a show. (❗an attraction は「人を引きつける物」の意) (⇨呼び物)

アトラス ❶〔地図帳〕an atlas. ❷〔ギリシャ神話の巨人神の１人〕Atlas.

アトランタ 〔米国の都市〕Atlanta /ətlǽntə/.

アトランダム 〔無作為に〕at random. ▶アトランダムに選ぶ choose 《one》*at random.*

アトリエ 〔＜フランス語〕a studio (働 〜s); an atelier /ǽtəljéi/.

アドリブ an ad lib. ▶アドリブの[で]〔話〕ad lib. ▶実に見事なアドリブを言う make brilliant *ad libs.* ▶芝居でアドリブを言う *ad-lib* in a play. ▶アドリブでピアノを演奏する 〔話〕play the piano *ad lib.*

アドレス 图 an address /ədrés/, 《米》ǽdrès/. ▶Eメールアドレス an email [an e-mail] *address.*
— **アドレスする** 動 〔ゴルフ〕address /ədrés/.

アドレナリン 〔生化学〕adrénaline.

・**あな** 穴 ❶〔くぼみ〕a hole, a hollow, a pit, a gap, a cavity, an opening; 〔針の穴〕an eye.

〈使い分け〉**hole** 最も一般的で、貫通しているいないにかかわらず、また天然・人工、大小いずれにも用いられる。
hollow 固体の表面の空洞や土地のくぼみ。
pit 地面などに通例特定の目的で掘られた大きな穴。
gap 二つの物体の間の細長いすき間、壁などの割れ目。
cavity hole, hollow, pit の堅い語で、主に専門用語。歯にあいた穴には通例これを用いる。
opening 「開いた部分」の意で、天然・人工、大小を問わず用いる。

❶〔〜の穴〕▶塀の穴 a *hole* [an *opening*] in [xon] the fence. ▶木の幹の穴 a *hollow* in the tree. ▶針の穴 the *eye* [*hole*] of a needle. ▶鼻の穴 a nostril. (❗両方の穴は 〜s)
❷〔穴が〕▶歯に穴があいている There is [I have] a *cavity* [a *hole*] in my tooth.
❸〔穴に〕▶彼は誤って穴に落ちた He fell into the *pit* accidentally.
❹〔穴を〕▶穴をあける make a *hole*; (掘って) dig a *hole* [a *pit*]; (切って) cut a *hole*; (焼いて) burn a *hole*; (きりなどで) drill a *hole*; (穴あけ器で) punch a *hole*; (破って) tear a *hole*. ▶穴をふさぐ fill [応急的に] stop] a *hole* [a *gap*]. ▶穴をつくろう mend [patch] a *hole*. ▶地面に穴を掘る dig (a hole in) the ground. ▶フロンはオゾン層に穴をあける 'Chlorofluorocarbon /klɔ̀ːrouflúːəroukɑ́ːrbən/ eats a *hole* through the ozone layer.'/(激減させる) CFCs *deplete* the ozone layer. (❗略語 CFC の方が多く用いられる)
❷〔埋まらない所〕(欠員) a vacancy; (損失) a loss; (赤字) a déficit. ▶人員の穴を埋める fill the *vacant* post [the vacancy]. (⇨空白)
❸〔欠陥〕(完全を損なうもの) a flaw; (深刻な欠陥) a defect; 〔欠点, 誤り〕a fault; 〔弱点〕a weak point. (⇨欠陥, 弱点)

・**穴があったら入りたい** ▶きまりが悪くて穴があったら入りたかった I was so embarrassed that I wished I could disappear [I could sink through the floor].
・**穴のあくほど** ▶彼の顔を穴があくほど見つめる stare *hard* at his face; stare him *hard* in the [xhis] face.
・**穴をあける** ▶彼女は会社の帳簿に大穴をあけた(=彼女のせいで会社は大損をした) The company made *big losses* because of her.

アナーキスト 〔無政府主義者〕an anarchist.

あなうま 穴馬 a dark horse.

あなうめ 穴埋め ── **穴埋め(を)する** 動 〔欠損を〕make ... up; 〔空所を〕fill ... in; 〔臨時に代行する〕fill in 《for》. ▶損失[赤字]の穴埋めをする *make up* 《for》 the loss [deficit]. ▶主役が急病のため別の俳優がその穴埋めをした The leading actor suddenly got sick, so another actor *filled in* [*acted as a fill-in*] *for* him.
・**穴埋め問題** fill-in-the-blanks questions.

アナウンサー an annóuncer; (ニュース放送者) a

newscaster. ●ラジオ[テレビ]のアナウンサー a radio [a TV] announcer. ●女性アナウンサー a woman announcer. ●スポーツアナウンサー a sports announcer,《米》a sportscaster (❗スポーツ実況または スポーツニュースのアナウンサー).

アナウンス 图 (an) announcement. ▶245便の出発のアナウンスがあった The departure of Flight 245 was announced.
── **アナウンスする** 動 announce; make an announcement (of).

あながかり 穴かがり buttonhole darning. ●穴かがりをする darn a buttonhole.

あながち ▶安い料理があながちに(=必ずしも)味がよくないとは言えない Inexpensive food does not necessarily [always] taste bad. (⇨必ず❷②) ▶君の言うことはあながち(=完全には)間違っていない You are not altogether [wholly, quite] wrong.

あなぐま 穴熊 a badger.
あなぐら 穴倉 a cellar.
あなご 穴子〚魚介〛a conger eel, a conger.
あなじゃくし 穴杓子 a perforated ladle.

:**あなた** 代 (あなたが, に, を) you (❗日本語と異なり目上の人にも用いる); (あなたの) your; (あなたのもの) yours; (あなた自身) yourself. (⇨私(ぼ))
── **あなた** 图 (呼びかけ) dear, darling,《主に米話》honey.(❗いずれも愛情のこもった言い方で, 通例夫婦間・恋人同士で用いるが, 一般に女性が[女性に]親しみを込めて呼びかけるときにも用いる. dear と darling は親が子供に対しても用いる) ▶「あなた手伝ってよ」と彼女は夫に言った "Dear [Darling], please help me," she said to her husband.

あなたまかせ あなた任せ ▶あなた任せにする depend on [upon] others; rely on help from other people.

あなづり 穴釣り ●穴釣りをする fish through a small hole.

*****あなどる** 侮る (軽視する) make* light [〚書〛little] of ... (❗前の方は特に問題点について用いる); slight; (低く評価する) underestimate, (軽蔑する) despise,《話》look down on .... ●あなどりがたい(=手ごわい)チーム one's formidable team. ▶彼はその仕事をあなどって失敗した He made light [little] of the work and failed in it. ▶彼の実力をあなどってはいけない Don't underestimate him [his abilities]. ▶Don't make light of his abilities [×him]. ▶彼らは私をばかだと[ろくに英語もしゃべれないと]あなどった They made little [were disdainful] of me as a fool [because I didn't speak English well]. (⇨軽蔑する)

あなば 穴場 a good unknown spot [place] (for). ▶どこかフランス料理の穴場を教えていただけませんか Would [Could] you recommend me a good French-food restaurant which isn't known to the public? ▶このレストランは東京でも穴場の穴場といえるでしょう This restaurant is one of the best-kept secrets in Tokyo. (❗best-kept は well-kept の最上級で秘密が「まったく漏れていない」の意)

アナフィラキシー [<ドイツ語]〚医学〛Anaphylaxie.(参考) アレルギーの一種)
あなぼこ 穴ぼこ (路面の穴) a póthole. (⇨穴)
アナリスト [分析家] an analyst. ●財政アナリスト a financial analyst.
アナログ an analog(ue). (⇦ デジタル)
●アナログ型コンピュータ an analog(ue) computer.
●アナログ時計 an analog(ue) watch [clock].
アナロジー [類推] analogy.

:**あに** 兄 an older [〚米書・英〛an elder,《話》a big] brother. (❗big を用いるのは子供の場合 ⇨弟)

解説 英語では, 特に必要な場合以外は, 年の上下による区別をせず, 兄・弟ともに brother, 姉・妹は sister ですますのが普通. また「兄さん」「姉さん」と呼びかけるときは brother, sister は用いず, 通例 Tom とか Ann とか名前で呼ぶ. (⇨兄弟)
下の図で示すのは話し手の立場で A なら, B はいちばん上の弟, D 以下なら, いちばん上の兄となるが, 英語では B は常に oldest brother である. (❗oldest は3人以上の兄弟, 2人なら elder)

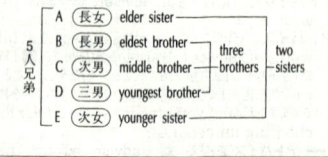

	A	〘長女〙	elder sister	
5人兄弟	B	〘長男〙	eldest brother	three brothers / two sisters
	C	〘次男〙	middle brother	
	D	〘三男〙	youngest brother	
	E	〘次女〙	younger sister	

▶私の兄[いちばん上の兄]は先週結婚した My older [oldest] brother got married last week.

あにき 兄貴 〚兄〛(⇨兄); 〚年長・先輩の人〛one's elder [senior]. ▶彼はぼくの兄貴のような存在だった He was a big brother to me.

あにでし 兄弟子 a senior student [fellow, disciple /dɪsáɪp(ə)l/]. (❗disciple は宗教的な「信奉者」の意味が強い)

アニマルセラピー 〚動物介在療法〛animal assisted therapy (の略 AAT).

アニメ(ーション) (動画) a cartoon,《書》an animated cartoon; (製作) animation.
●アニメ映画 an animated film. (❗この意味で ×animation とはいわないことに注意) ●アニメキャラクター a cartoon character. ●アニメ製作者 an animator.

アニュアルレポート 〚年次報告書〛an annual report.

あによめ 兄嫁 one's (older) sister-in-law (蹲 sisters-,《英語》~s); one's (older) brother's wife. (❗特に年長関係を明示する場合以外 older は通例省略される. (⇨兄))

:**あね** an older [〚米書・英〛an elder,《話》a big] sister. (⇨兄 解説) ●姉さん女房 a wife older [×elder] than her husband. (❗an older wife では「ひどく年をとった妻」の意となる)

あねき 姉貴 (⇨姉)
あねご 姉御 〚姉〛(⇨姉); 〚親分の妻〛the boss's wife,《女親分》a woman boss.
●姉御肌 (be) a big-sister type,《have》a big-sisterly disposition.

あねったい 亜熱帯 the subtropical zone(s); the subtropics. (⇨熱帯) ── 亜熱帯の 形 subtropical; semitropical.

アネモネ 〚植物〛an anémone,《詩語》a windflower.

:**あの** 〚指示的に〛that (❗複数名詞の前では those); [限定名詞の前で] the. (⇨この, この) ▶あの本を見せてください Show me that book, please. ▶あの音は何だろう What's that sound I hear? ▶私[美紀]のあの手袋はとても高かった Those gloves of mine [Miki's] were very expensive. ▶×my [Miki's] those gloves とはいわない) ▶彼を見たとたんあの男だと分かった The minute I saw him, I knew he was the man.

会話 「青いスーツを着たあの男の人はだれですか」「私のおじです」"Who's that man in the blue suit?" "He [×The man, ×That man] is my uncle." (❗前の名詞をくり返さず代名詞で he (男), she (女), it (物・事), they (複数)で受けるのが普通)

あの(う) [[思案]] well, let me [let's] see (⇨ええっと); [[呼びかけ]] 《女性に》 ma'am, 《男性に》 sir; 《くだけて》 oh, hello, hey (■hey は主に男性語で, 女性は hi を用いる), please (■「お願い」という気持ちをこめて); 《会話の始めに》 《米話》 say, 《英話》 I say; [[口ごもって]] er, uh, ah. ▶あの失礼ですが "Excuse me [Pardon (me)], (but)…. ▶後の方が丁寧な言い方. 音調の上昇部は平板に近い) ▶あのう実は Well, as a matter of fact, …. ▶あの, どうかしましたか Say, is anything wrong [the matter] with you? ▶あのう先生, ご質問の意味が分かりません Please, sir [《米》ma'am, 《英》Miss], I don't understand your question. (■(1) sir は男, ma'am, Miss は既婚未婚を問わず女の先生に対する敬語 ⇨先生 [語感]). (2) 暗に説明を求めている) ▶彼はあのう, その金をかけ事で, つまりあのう競馬で遣っていたんだ He was uh spending that kind of money on gambling, I mean, ah on horse races.

あのてこのて あの手この手 ●あの手この手を使って事態を収拾する use every possible [conceivable] means [every trick in the book] to save the situation.

あのね well; 《注意を促して》 listen; 《怒って》 look (here); 《会話の始めに》 《米話》 say, 《英話》 I say. ▶あのね, 私たち来春結婚します Listen, we are getting married next spring. ▶あのね, 君の言ってることは見当違いだよ Look (here), you're missing the point. ▶あのね, ベティ, ぼくは大学をやめなきゃならないんだ Say, Betty, I have to quit college. ▶あのね, こうしてはどうだろう I know what./I'll téll [Téll] you what. (■この後に提案が続く) [会話]「あのね」「えっ, 何なの」"Guess what! [(Do) you know what?]" "/What? /No, /what?]"

あのよ あの世 ●あの世へ行く go to the other world [the next world, the great beyond]; 《死ぬ》 die, 《婉曲的に》 pass away. (⇨死ぬ)

あのような like that. (⇨あんなに)

アノラック 《米》 a parka, 《英》 an anorak.

***アパート** (1世帯分の部屋)《米》 an apartment, 《英》 a flat; (建物全体)《米》 an apartment building [house], 《英》 a block of flats; (貧民街の安い) a tenement (house 《米》[block 《英》]). ▶アパートを捜しています [借りたい] I am looking for [would like to rent] an apartment [a flat] (in an apartment building).

アバウト ── アバウトな 形 (いいかげんな) sloppy; (大ざっぱな) rough.

あばく 暴く ❶[[悪事・秘密を]] expose, uncover. (⇨暴露する) ●陰謀をあばく expose the plot (to the public). ▶彼の正体はついにあばかれた He was at last unmasked./His mask was at last ripped away. (■後の方が口語的)
❷[[墓を]] open; (悪意から)《書》 violate.

あばずれ 阿婆擦れ 《話》 a real bitch; a minx; a shameless hussy.

あばた a pockmark. (■通例複数形で) ●あばた面 a pockmarked [a pocked, a pitted] face. ●月のあばた craters on the moon.
●あばたもえくぼ Love sees no faults./(恋は盲目)(ことわざ) Love is blind.

あばよ Bye!, So long! (⇨さよなら)

アパラチア ●アパラチア山脈 the Appalachian /æpəléɪtʃiən/ Mountains, the Appalachians.

あばら(ぼね) 肋(骨) (1本) a rib; (全体) the ribs. ●転落してあばら骨を折る break a rib when one falls.

あばらや あばら屋 (荒れはてた) a shabby [a tumbledown, a dilapidated] house; (我が家)《おどけて》 one's humble abode.

アパルトヘイト [<アフリカーンス語] [[南アの人種差別政策]] apartheid /əpáːt(h)èɪt/.

***あばれる 暴れる** [[乱暴な行動をする]] act violently [wild, 《話》rowdy]; [[もがく]] struggle; [[はしゃぎ回る]] romp about, run* about, 《激しく》 rampage; (台風などが荒れ狂う) rage; [[暴動を起こす]] riot. ▶彼は怒って暴れた He got angry and acted violently [wild, rowdy]. ▶泥棒は彼らの手の中から逃げようとして暴れた The thief struggled in their arms to get free. ▶家の中で暴れるな Don't romp about in the house. ▶馬が急に暴れ出した Suddenly the horse began to run about wildly [became unruly]. (■後の方は「制御できなくなる」の意.「暴れ馬」は an unruly horse) ▶暴走族が市内を暴れ回った The motorcycle gang rampaged through the city. ▶台風は西日本を暴れ回った The typhoon raged across the western part of Japan. ▶学生たちが暴れて警官隊と衝突した The students rioted and clashed with the police.

アパレル (衣料品)(集合的に) 《ladies'》 apparél.

あばれんぼう 暴れん坊 (⇨荒くれ男)

アバンギャルド [<フランス語] [[前衛派]] the avant-garde /à:va:ngá:rd/. (■単・複両扱い)

アバンゲール [<フランス語] [[戦前派]] the prewar generation. (■❽ アプレゲール)

アバンチュール [<フランス語] [[情事]] (have) a love affair (with).

アピール 名 (an) appeal. ●アピールを認める[却下する] sustain [deny] an appeal.
── アピールする 動 ❶[[懇願, 訴え]] ●審判に対してアピールする appeal [make an appeal] to the referee [umpire]. ●走者はアピールでアウトになった 《野球》 The runner was called out on appeal. ▶彼女はその計画の長所をアピールした(= 強調した) She emphasized [×appealed] the strong points of the plan.
❷[[魅力]] ▶その音楽は若者に全然アピールしない That music does not appeal to [attract] young people at all.

あびきょうかん 阿鼻叫喚 screaming in agony. ▶墜落事故の現場は阿鼻叫喚の巷」と化した The scene of the plane clash has changed [turned] into the very hell.

あひさん 亜砒酸 [化学] arseniöus ácid.

あびせたおし 浴びせ倒し [相撲] abisetaoshi; (backward) force-down.

あびせる 浴びせる ❶[[質問などを]] shower, fire. ▶彼らは彼に質問を浴びせた They showered him with questions./They showered questions on [(矢つぎ早に) shot questions at] him.
❷[[水などを]] dash (over, on). ●彼に水を浴びせる dash [shower, pour] water over him. (■ dash は勢いよく, shower は大量に, pour は続けざまに)

あひる 家鴨 a duck (狭義では雌をさす. 正式には a domestic duck); (雄) a drake; (子) a duckling. ▶アヒルがガーガー鳴く Ducks quack.

***あびる 浴びる** ❶[[水などをかける]] ▶夕食前にひとふろ浴びた I took [《英》had] a bath before dinner. ▶彼は浴びるように(=とてもたくさん)酒を飲んだ He drank a quantity of sake./He drank like a fish.
❷[[体中に受ける]] ▶彼女は暖かい日の光を浴びた(=日光浴をした)座っていた She sat basking in the warm sun [bathing in the warm sunshine]. ▶作業員たちは放射能を浴びた(=さらされた) The workers were exposed to [were showered with] radioactivity. ▶兵士たちは砲火を浴びた The soldiers were under fire.
❸[[非難・賞賛などを]] ●勇気ある行動によって賞賛を

ひる be showered with praise for one's courage. ▶彼は激しい非難を浴びた(=さらされた) He was subjected to severe criticism. ●その作家にわかに脚光を浴びた The writer suddenly *held the spotlight*.

あぶ 虻 a gadfly, a horsefly. (🖉虻蜂(はち)取らず ⇨虻蜂取らず)

アフガニスタン [国名] Afghanistan /æfgǽnəstæn/. (公式名) the Islamic Republic of Afghanistan. (首都 Kabul) ●アフガニスタン人 an Afghan. ●アフガニスタン(人)の Afghan.

あぶく a bubble; foam. (🖉後の方は小さな bubbles が集まったもの) ●息を吹き込んであぶくを立てる blow *bubbles*.
●あぶく銭 easy money. (🖉unearned money は「不労所得」 ⇨悪銭)

アブサン [<フランス語] absinth(e) /ǽbsinθ/. (参考 緑色の非常に強い蒸留酒)

アブストラクト [抜粋] an ábstract; [抽象芸術] abstract art. ●その作品はan abstract(だ) ●論文のアブストラクトを作る write [make] an *abstract* of a paper.

アフタ [医学] aphthae /ǽfθi:/. (🖉通例複数形で単数扱い)

アフターケア [術後・病気回復期の] aftercare; [アフターサービス] (⇨アフターサービス).

アフターサービス after-sale(s) service (🖉文脈により単に service でも表せる); [和製語] after service. ▶その店はアフターサービスが行き届いている The store provides [gives] very good *after-sales service*./The *service* is great at the store.

アフターファイブ after work. ●アフターファイブに英会話を習う learn English conversation *after work*.

アブダビ [アラブ首長国連邦の首都] Abu Dhabi /ɑ́:bu dɑ́:bi/.

:あぶない 危ない 形 ❶ [危険な] dangerous (⟷safe); (主に書) perilous; risky; (やや書) hazardous (🖉通例限定的に); (やや書) precarious. (⇨危険な)

> [使い分け] **dangerous** 危険性を表す最も一般的な語. 事柄・場所・試合・状況・任務などに対して用いる.
> **perilous** 生命の危険など, より重大な危険を表す.
> **risky** 事業・旅行・冒険など, 人の行動や試みが失敗の可能性が高いことを表す.
> **hazardous** 各種の状況・条件などの危険のほか, 特に, 廃棄物・ガスなど化学物質の危険性を表す.
> **precarious** 状況・地位・バランスなどが危ういことを表す.

① [危ない~] ●危ない所 a *dangerous* place. ●危ない(=冒険的な)商売 a *risky* business. ●危ないことをする(=危険を冒す) run [take] a *risk* [*risks*]; take a *chance* [*chances*]. ●男の女装は素敵だ. 女にはない危ない色気を感じる Those men wearing women's clothes are attractive. I feel a *dangerous* sex appeal around them, which women don't have.

② [...は[が]危ない] ●(あなたが)夜遅く1人で外出するのは危ない It is *dangerous* [(安全でない) *not safe*, *unsafe*] (for you) to go out alone late at night. ●彼女の命が危ない(=危険な状態にある) Her life is *in danger* [(危険にさらされて) *at stake*, *x*is *dangerous*]. ●危ない(=気をつけろ)! 車が来るよ! Look [Watch] *out*! There's a car coming! (🖉 (1) Careful! ともいうが, ×Dangerous! とはいわない. 掲示などで Danger! Keep away! (危険! 近寄るな!)とはいう. (2) これに対する応答は Thanks for warning me. (注意してくれてありがとう)など)

❷ [疑わしい] doubtful; (不確実な) uncertain; (不安定な) unsteady, (やや書) insecure; (信用できない) unreliable. ●危ない足場 an *unsteady* [an *insecure*] foothold. ●彼の合格は危ないものだ It is *doubtful* [*uncertain*] whether he will pass the exam.

❸ [間一髪の] (かろうじての) narrow; (きわどい) close. ●危ないところを助かる have a *narrow escape*; escape *by a hair's breadth*. ▶ああ危なかった. もう少しで車にひかれるところだった Wow, that was *close* [a *close call*, a *near thing*]—the car nearly ran me over.
●危ない橋を渡る 'cross a dangerous bridge'; (薄氷を踏む) walk [tread, skate] on thin ice; (危険を覚悟で物事を行う) take a chance.
── **危なく** 副 nearly; almost. (⇨危うく)

あぶなげ 危なげ ●危なげのない ●危なげない演技 a *sure* performance. ●危なげのない(=信頼できる)人物 a *reliable* [a *trustworthy*] person. ●危なげのない勝ち方をする win the game *without much difficulty*. ●危なげな(=不安定な)足取りで歩く walk with *unsteady* steps [(よろめく足で) on *shaky* legs]. ●危なげなく歩く walk *steadily*. ●危なげな手つきで(=不器用に)つめを切る cut one's nails *clumsily* [*in a clumsy manner*].

あぶなっかしい 危なっかしい risky, (話) chancy. ▶そいつはちょっと危なっかしい It's a bit *chancy*.

あぶはちとらず 虻蜂取らず ▶彼は全く決断力がない. 虻蜂取らずになるだろう He's so indecisive. He'll probably *fall between two stools*. (🖉「二つのいすのどちらにも座れない」の意)

あぶみ 鐙 a stirrup. (🖉通例複数形で)

•**あぶら 油・脂** oil; fat (🖉以上2語は種類をいうときに ⓒ); grease; lard.

> [使い分け] **oil** 潤滑油・調理油・燃料などとして用いられる鉱油・動物油・植物油の総称語.
> **grease** 溶けた動物の油・機械の潤滑油・頭髪用油など, どろっとした状態のもの.
> **fat** 動物・植物の脂肪で, 常温では固形で食用にする.
> **lard** 料理用に精製した豚の脂.

① [~油[脂]] ●サラダ[植物]油 salad [vegetable] *oil*. ●動物脂 animal *oil* [*fat*]. ●調理用の油 cooking *oil*.
② [油[脂] (の)~] ●油気のある[ない] 髪 *oily* [*unoily*] hair. (🖉*greasy* hair は「脂気の多いべたっとした髪」の意) ●油のしみ an *oil* stain. ●脂身 (⇨脂身) ▶油気の多いものは避けなさい Back away from *fatty* food.
③ [油が] ▶このバイクは油が切れている(注油が必要だ) This motorbike needs *oiling* [*to be oiled*]./(ガソリンが切れた) This motorbike has run out of *gas* (米) [*petrol* (英)].
④ [油を] ●髪に油をつける put *grease* [(*olive*) *oil*] on one's hair. (🖉*grease* ではべとべとした汚い感じを伴うので, olive oil のように種類を示す方が普通) ●機械に油をさした I *oiled* [*greased*, (やや書) *lubricated*] the machine./I put some *oil* into a machine.
⑤ [油[脂]で] ●油でよごれた指 *greasy* fingers. ●ソーセージを油でためるfry sausages (in *oil*). ●魚を油で揚げる fry fish (in deep *oil* [*fat*]); deep-fry fish. ▶お皿が脂でべとべとだ The dishes are *greasy*.
●油が切れる ▶彼は油が切れた(=活気がなくなっている)ようだ He looks *dull*./It seems to me that there are little *life* in him.
●脂が乗る ●脂が乗っている (魚が) be rich and

あぶらあげ

tender; (働き盛りだ) be in the prime (of life); (事業などが絶好調だ) be in full swing.
- 油を売る ▶彼は途中で油を売っている(=ぶらついている)《話》He *is loafing (around)* [(むだ話をしている)《米話》*shooting the bull*] on the way.
- 油を絞る ▶宿題を忘れて先生にさんざん油を絞られた(=ひどくしかられた)《話》My teacher *gave me a good talking-to* [*hauled me over the coals*] because I didn't do my homework.
- 油を注ぐ ▶彼の弁明は彼女の怒りに油を注いだ His excuse *added fuel to the fire* [*flames*] *of her rage*.
- 油かす oil cake. **油紙** oiled paper, oilpaper.
- 油差し an oilcan.

あぶらあげ 油揚げ (⇨油揚^(あぶらあげ))

あぶらあせ 脂汗 ▶脂汗を流す(恐怖・極度の心配などで汗が出る) break out in a (nervous [cold]) sweat; sweat like a pig. ▶蒸し暑くて自然と脂汗がしみ出た *Sweat oozed out in the sticky heat.*

あぶらえ 油絵 an oil painting.《話》an oil. (▮画法は Ⓤ) ●油絵の展覧会 an exhibition of *oils*. ●油絵をかく paint in *oils*.
- 油絵画家 an oil painter. **油絵の具** oil paints, oil colors, oils.

あぶらぎる 脂ぎる (脂っこくなる) become* greasy.
▶脂ぎった四十男 a *fatty* [a *greasy*] man of forty.

あぶらげ 油揚 (a piece of) thin deep-fried bean curd.

あぶらぜみ 油蝉 a large brown cicada /sikéida/.

あぶらっこい 脂っこい ▶脂っこい(=脂のつき過ぎた)食べ物を避ける back away from a *greasy* [a *fatty*, (揚げものなど) an *oily*] food. (▮a food that has too much *fat* などともいえる)

あぶらとりがみ 脂取り紙 〖美容〗an oil blotting paper. (▮メイク落としは a cleansing tissue)

あぶらみ 脂身 ▶この牛肉は脂身が多い This beef has a lot of *fat* in it [is very *fatty*].

あぶらむし 油虫 (アリマキ)a plant louse /láus/; (ゴキブリ)a cockroach.

***アフリカ** Africa /ǽfrikə/. ●アフリカ(人)の African. ●アフリカ人 an African. ●アフリカ大陸 the *African* Continent.

アプリケ appliqué. (⇨アップリケ)

アプリケーション 〖特定の作業のためのプログラム〗〖コンピュータ〗an application software.

あぶりだし 炙り出し ▶あぶり出しの絵 a picture drawn in invisible [*secret*] *ink*.

あぶる (肉などを直火で)《米》broil, (主に英)grill; (暖める) warm; (乾燥させる) dry. ●魚の干物(のり)を火であぶる *broil* dried fish [make a sheet of *nori* crisp] over a fire. ●手をたき火であぶる *warm* one's hands at [by, over] an open fire.

アプレ(ゲール) 〖フランス語〗〖戦後派〗the postwar generation. (⇨アバンゲール)

***あふれる 溢れる ❶** 〖こぼれ出る〗(流れ出る) overflow*; (コップなどの縁からあふれる) brim (-mm-) over 《with》(▮「(…で)あふれそうになる」の意). ●グラスからあふれそうなワイン a *brimming* glass of wine. ▶川があふれた The river *overflowed* (its banks). ▶ふろの水があふれているよ! The bath [bathwater] *is overflowing* [*running over*, *brimming over*]! ▶ビールがグラスからあふれた The beer *overflowed* [*flowed over*] the glass. (▮日本語の「から」にひかれて ✗*overflowed from …*としない) ▶人々は通りにあふれ出た The people *overflowed into* the street. ▶通りは買い物客であふれていた The street *was overflowing with* shoppers.
❷ 〖満ちている〗(満たされる) be filled 《with》; (いっ

ぱいである) be full 《of》. ▶彼の目には涙があふれていた His eyes *were filled with* [*were full of*] tears. ▶(わき出た) Tears *welled up* in his eyes. ▶この町は活気にあふれている This town *is full of* life. ▶彼の心は喜びにあふれていた He [His heart] *was brimming over* [*overflowing*] *with* happiness. (▮後の方が意味が強い)

あぶれる ▶仕事にあぶれて2週間になる I've *been out of work* for two weeks. ▶今日も仕事にあぶれた I *couldn't get a job* again today.

アフロ (⇨アフロヘア)

アプローチ 〖接近すること〗an approach 《to》; 〖ゴルフで〗an approach (shot). ●科学的アプローチ a scientific *approach*.
── **アプローチする** 〖接近する〗approach; 〖ゴルフで〗approach, play [hit] an approach shot.

アフロヘア an Afro 《~s》, an Afro hairstyle.

あべいちぞく 阿部一族 *The Abe Family.* (参考 森鷗外の小説)

アベイラビリティー 〖入手可能性, 有用性〗availability.

あべかわもち 安倍川餅 *abekawa-mochi*, (説明的に) toasted rice cake moistened and rolled in sweetened soybean flour.

あべこべ (正反対の) opposite 《to》; (内容が相対立する) contrary 《to》; (間違った) wrong. ●彼とあなたの話はまったくあべこべだ His story is quite *opposite to* yours. ▶その子は靴をあべこべにはいていた The boy wore his shoes *on the wrong feet*.

アペタイザー an appetizer. (⇨アペリティフ)

アベック [<フランス語] 〖男女一組〗a couple, a young couple.

アベニュー 〖大通り, 並木道〗an avenue. (▮New York 市では (✕the) Fifth *Avenue* (5番街)のように南北を走る通りをさす)

アベマリア [<ラテン語] Ave Maria /ɑ́:vei məri:ə/ (略 A.M.), Hail Mary.

アペリティフ [<フランス語] 〖食前酒〗an aperitif /əpèriti:f/ 《֎ ~s》. (▮前菜と食前酒の総称は an appetizer)

アベレージ (an) average. ●バッティングアベレージ 〖打率〗a batting *average*.

あへん 阿片 opium /óupiəm/. ●阿片吸飲者 an *opium* eater. ●阿片を吸う smoke *opium*.
- アヘン戦争 the Opium War.

アポ 〖約束〗an appointment. ●アポをとる[とってある] make [have] an *appointment* 《with》. ●アポなしで without an *appointment*.

アポイント(メント) (⇨アポ)

あほう 阿呆 a fool, an idiot. (⇨馬鹿^(ばか))

あほうどり 信天翁 〖鳥〗an albatross /ǽlbətrɔs/.

アポカド an avocado /ævəkɑ́:dou/ 《֎ ~s, ~es》.

アポストロフィー an apostrophe /əpɑ́strəfi/ (').

あほらしい 阿呆らしい (⇨馬鹿馬鹿^(ばか)しい)

アポロ 〖ギリシャ神話〗Apollo /əpɑ́lou/. (参考 音楽・医術・詩歌・予言の神) ●アポロ宇宙船11号 the Spaceship Apollo 11.

あま 尼 (尼僧) a nun 《↔ a monk》. (▮カトリック教の尼は a sister ともいう) ●尼になる become a *nun* [a *religious*]; enter a convent.
- 尼寺 a convent, (やや古) a nunnery.

あま 亜麻 〖植物〗flax. ●亜麻色 ivory yellow, yellowish light brown. ── 亜麻の 形 flaxen.
- 亜麻糸 linen thread.

あま 海女 an *ama* 《~s》; (説明的に) a professional woman diver who, usually without diving gear, collects abalones, turban shells, and seaweeds.

アマ an amateur. (⇨アマチュア)

あまあい 雨間 ▶雨あいに during a *lull* [*break*] *in the rain*.

あまあし 雨足, 雨脚 (降り去るさま) passing rain; (雨の筋) rain streaks. ▶夏の夕立はあまり足がはやい A summer shower comes and goes very quickly. ▶雨足がひどくなった(＝雨が激しく降りだした) It started *raining* harder.

:あまい 甘い ❶ [味・におい・音などが] sweet. ▶甘いリンゴ a *sweet* [*a sweet-tasting*] apple. ▶甘い音色 [メロディー] a *sweet* tone [melody]. ▶バラの甘い香りの sweet fragrance of roses. ▶甘い声 (＝美声) をしている have a *sweet* voice. (❗「甘ったるい声」は a sugary voice) ▶このケーキは私には甘すぎる This cake tastes [is] too *sweet* for me. (⇨味❶①) ▶彼女は甘いものには目がない She loves anything *sweet* [*sweet things*]./She has a *sweet tooth*. ▶私はいつもミルクで甘くして飲む I always *sweeten* my milk and drink it. ▶甘い言葉にだまされるな(話) Don't be tempted by *sweet* [*smooth*] talk.
❷ [考え・判断などが] (楽観的な) optimístic; (浅薄な) superficial; (安直な) easy. ▶甘い考え方 *wishful* thinking. ▶ひとりよがりな希望的な(観測) ▶甘い見方をする人 a *superficial* observer. ▶(投球の)甘い球 [野球] an easy [a hittable] pitch; a cookie. ▶彼が助けてくれると考えるのは少し甘いよ I think it rather *optimistic* to assume that he will help you. ▶世の中は君が考えているほど甘くない Things are not so *easy* [*rosy*] as you take [×are taking] them to be.
❸ [態度・評価などが] (気前のよい) generous; (寛容すぎる) permissive (❗特に性について用い, 通例限定的用法); (情け深い) lenient; (甘やかす) indulgent. ▶甘い親 an *indulgent* [*an indulging*, *a fond*] parent. ▶岸先生は点が甘い Mr. Kishi is *generous* [*lenient*] (↔*strict*) in giving grades./Mr. Kishi is a *soft* (↔*a hard*, *a strict*) grader. ▶彼は子供に甘すぎる He is too *indulgent to* [*easy with*] his children.
❹ [結び目などが] loose. ▶このねじは甘い[甘くなった] This screw is [has come] *loose*.

●**甘い汁を吸う** ▶彼だけが甘い汁を吸っている Only he gets the benefit [skims the cream (off the top)].

●**甘く見る** ▶彼は物事を甘く見すぎる He takes things too *easy*. ▶彼らを甘く見るな(＝過小評価するな) Don't *underestimate* them [*sell them short*]; they're a good team.

あまえ 甘え dependence. ▶今の子供は甘えがちだ Children today tend to be *dependent*.

*あまえる 甘える ❶ [甘ったれる] (赤ん坊のようにふるまう) behave like a baby; (取り入ろうとする) 《話》curry favor (*with*) (❗make up to は「利益を得るために おべんちゃらを言う」; (犬や猫が) fawn (*on*). ▶母に甘える seek a lot of affection from one's mother. ▶いつまでも甘えるな Don't *act like a baby*.
❷ [つけ込む] (人の好意に甘える) take* advantage of 《his》kindness; (頼る) depend on 《his》kindness. ▶先生に甘えすぎてはいけません You shouldn't *depend* [*rely*] too much *on* your teacher's kindness. ▶お言葉に甘えてそうさせていただきます I'll *accept* your kind [generous] offer.

あまえんぼう 甘えん坊 (甘えてねだる子) a wheedling child; (お母さん子) 《米話》a mama's [mummy's] boy, 《英話》a mother's boy. (❗甘やかされてだめになった子は⇨マザコン)

あまおと 雨音 the sound of the rain. ▶ばらばらと窓を打つ雨音 the *patter of rain* on the window.

あまがえる 雨蛙 a tree frog.

あまがさ 雨傘 an umbrella.

あまがっぱ 雨合羽 a raincoat; 《英》a waterproof.

あまからい 甘辛い salty-sweet.

あまかわ 甘皮 (みかんなどの) the endocarp; (爪の) the cuticle.
●**甘皮切り** (器具) a cuticle clipper.

あまぐ 雨具 (集合的に) rainwear. (❗実際には a raincoat とか an umbrella とか具体的にいうのが普通)

あまくさぼんいそほものがたり 『天草本伊曾保物語』 *Romanized Version of Aesop*. (参考) 室町時代の仮名草紙.

あまくだり 天下り ▶天下りの慣行 the long-held practice of sending retired high-ranking bureaucrats into top management of the semi-governmental corporations or private companies which are under the strong influence of government offices.
—— **天下りする 動** párachùte. (❗そのような役人は a parachutist. 主に新聞用法)

あまくち 甘口 ▶甘口のワイン *sweet* (↔*dry*) wine. ▶甘口のカレー a *mild* (↔*a hot*) curry.

あまぐつ 雨靴 (a pair of) rain shoes; (ゴム長靴の) rubber; 《米》wellington 《英》boots (⇨長靴); (半長オーバーシューズ) galoshes. (参考) ゴム製で防水・防寒用に耐えた.

あまぐも 雨雲 a rain cloud.

あまぐり 甘栗 *amaguri*; (説明的に) small Chinese sweet chestnuts roasted in sand with a sprinkle of syrup water.

あまごい 雨乞い ▶雨乞いをする pray for rain.

あまざけ 甘酒 *amazake*; (説明的に) a sweetened hot drink made using fermented rice or *sake* lees.

あまざらし 雨ざらし ▶雨ざらしの古いボート an old, weather-beaten boat. (❗weather-beaten は「雨・風・日光にさらされて傷んだ」の意) ▶材木は雨ざらしになっていた(＝雨にさらされていた) The lumber *was exposed to* [*was left in*] the rain.

あまじお 甘塩 —— 甘塩の形 lightly-salted. ▶甘塩のしゃけ a *lightly-salted* salmon.

あましょく 甘食 a sweet bun.

あます 余す ▶公判まで余すところ3日だ There are [We have] only three days *left* before the trial. ▶その物語は戦争の悲惨さを余すところなく伝えている The story *fully* [*thoroughly*] describes [portrays] the misery of war.

あますっぱい 甘酸っぱい (both) sweet and sour.

あまぞら 雨空 [雨が降り出しそうな空] a threatening sky; [雨が降っている空] a rainy sky.

アマゾン ▶アマゾン川 the Amazon /ǽməzən/.

あまた 数多 (⇨たくさん) ▶引く手あまた (⇨引く手)

あまだい 甘鯛 [魚介] a tilefish (複 ~, ~es).

あまだれ 雨垂れ (一滴) a raindrop. ▶雨垂れの音 the sound of *raindrops* falling; the drip(-drip) of the rain.
●**雨垂れ石をうがつ** (ことわざ) Constant dripping wears away a stone.

あまちゃ 甘茶 hydrangea tea.

アマチュア an amateur /ǽmət(ʃ)ʊər/ (↔a professional). ▶アマチュア選手 [ゴルファー] an *amateur* player [golfer].
●**アマチュア精神** (respect) the spirit of amateurism. ▶アマチュア無線 ham radio. ▶アマチュア無線家 a (radio) ham.

あまったるい 甘ったるい (⇨甘い) ▶甘ったるい声 a *sugary* voice. ▶そのケーキは甘ったるかった That cake was *too sweet* [*sugary*]. (❗×That was too

あまったれ / あまりにも

sweet [sugary] cake. とはいわない (⇨過ぎる❺))
あまったれ 甘ったれ (⇨甘えん坊)
あまったれる 甘ったれる (⇨甘える)
あまっちょろい 甘っちょろい ▶君はまだ甘っちょろいぞ(=未熟だ) You are still too green. ▶景気がそのうちよくなると考えるのは甘っちょろい(=希望的観測にすぎない) Expecting business will soon pick up is just wishful thinking.
あまでら 尼寺 a convent,《古》a nunnery.
あまど 雨戸 a (sliding) shutter,《米》a (sliding) storm window. ▶雨戸を立てる put the sliding shutters in place.
あまとう 甘党 ▶彼は甘党だ He has a sweet tooth./He likes sweet things. (❗ともに「酒が飲めない」の意はない) (⇨甘い❶)
あまなつ 甘夏 a sweet Chinese citron.
あまなっとう 甘納豆 amanatto,(説明的に) boiled and sweetened beans half dried and covered with powdered sugar.
あまねく 普く, 遍く [[広く]] extensively, widely; [[一般に]] generally; (普遍的に) universally. (⇨広い❷)
あまのがわ 天の川 the Milky Way; the Gálaxy.
あまのじゃく (つむじ曲がり) a contrary [《書》a perverse] person. ▶あまのじゃくな女でこちらが何を言ってもとにかく反対するのが楽しみなんだ She takes a perverse pleasure in upsetting everything I say.
あまみ 甘味 sweetness. ●はちみつで甘味をつける sweeten (it) with honey. ▶このブドウは甘味が足りない These grapes are not sweet enough [lack sweetness]. (❗前の方が普通)
あまみず 雨水 rainwater.
あまめ 甘目 ❶ [[味が]] (いつも[思っていた]より甘い) sweeter than usual [I expected]; (いくぶん甘い) rather sweet(er). ▶この料理は少し甘めだ This food is a little too sweet.
❷ [[判定・評価が]] more generous [lenient] than usual; rahter generous [lenient]. ▶この成績の評価はいつもより甘めのようだ These grades seem more lenient than usual. ▶このテストは甘めに採点されたうだ This test seems to have been marked rather generously.
あまもよう 雨模様 ▶雨模様の空 a watery [a threatening] sky. ▶雨模様だ(=雨が降りそうだ)(⇨雨②)
あまもり 雨漏り 图 a leak in the roof.
── 雨漏りする 動 leak.
あまやかす 甘やかす [[赤ん坊のように扱う]] baby (❗大人にも用いる); [[甘やかしてだめにする]] spoil*, pamper (❗後の方が堅い語); [[大事にしすぎる]] coddle; [[気ままにさせる]] indulge. ▶甘やかされた若者 a spoiled《米》[a spoilt《英》] young man. ▶子供を甘やかして育てる bring up one's child with indulgence. ▶彼を甘やかすな Don't baby him./Try not to spoil him./Don't be too permissive with [(過保護な) too protective toward] him.
あまやどり 雨宿り ── 雨宿りする 動 take shelter (from the rain); (雨がやむのを待つ)《米話》wait out the rain.
あまよけ 雨避け ❶ [[雨覆い]] a rain-cover; (避難所) a shelter. ❷ [[雨宿り]] (⇨雨宿り)
*__あまり__ 余り ❶ [[残余]] the rest (⇨残り),[[数学で]] (割り算の) remainder; (食事の) leftovers. ▶10割る3は3余り1です Ten divided by three is three with remainder one. (❗10 devided by 3 is 3, remainder 1. も可)
❷ [[以上]] more than ...; over ...; above ... (⇨以上); [[端数の]]《話》odd (❗10 の倍数の後で). ▶私はここに60年余り住んでいる I have lived here a

little over [more than] 60 years./I have lived here (for) 60 years odd. ▶この 60 odd は前の略. 60 odd people のように「60 人の変な人たち」の意にもとれるような場合は省略せずに 60 and odd people とする. 60-odd years は《話》で「60 何年か」の意で 61–69 年をさす
❸ [[過度]] ●あまりの(=あまりにも無理な)要求 an unreasonable [an excessive] request. (⇨あまりにも)
[〜の[する]あまり] ●急いだあまり in one's hurry. ▶うれしさのあまり跳び上がる jump for [with] joy. ▶彼がショックのあまり(=あまりにもショックだったので)口もきけなかった He was so shocked that he couldn't even speak./He was too shocked [×too much shocked] to speak. (ショックのために) He was speechless with shock. ▶彼女は彼に会いたいあまりにすぐ飛び出した She ran out immediately in her eagerness to meet him.
── **あまり(にも)** 副 [[形容詞・副詞・数量を表す名詞の前で]] too; [[動詞・過去分詞を修飾して]] too much; (過度に) excessively. (⇨過ぎる❺ 解説) ▶あまりたばこを吸いすぎると体に悪い Too much smoking is bad for your health./If you smoke too much [too many] cigarettes, you'll injure your health. ▶あまりにも話がうますぎる The story is (much) too good to be true. (❗too を強めるときは much か far を用い, very は用いない) ▶彼の動作はあまりにも見苦しい He is very, very awkward in his movements. (❗このように同じ強意語を反復して「あまりにも」の意を表せる)

① [あまりにも…なので] ▶このいすはあまりにも重いので動かせない This chair is so heavy (that) I can't move it. (❗口語ではしばしば that を省略する《非常に》)/This chair is too heavy for me to move (it) [too heavy to move]. (❗for me がないときはit は省略する)

② [あまり…でない] [[程度]] (形容詞・副詞を修飾して) not (...) very,《書》none too; (それほど…ない) not (...) so [《話》(all) that] (❗not very と異なり比較の概念を含む); (完全には…でない) not (...) quite (⇨まったく); [[数量]] (多くない) not (...) many [much] (❗複数可算名詞の前には many, 不可算名詞の前には much を用いる); (ほとんどない) hardly any, almost no (⇨ほとんど❷). ▶彼女はあまり裕福ではなかった She wasn't very [so,《話》(all) that] rich. ▶あまりそばに来ないで,風邪がうつりますよ Don't come too close or else you'll catch my cold. ▶私にはあまり友人がいない I don't have many friends./I have hardly any [almost no,《書》few] friends. ▶当地はあまり雪は降らない We don't have much snow here./We have hardly any [almost no,《書》little] snow here. ▶彼には最近あまり会わない I haven't seen much of him lately. ▶彼はあまりたいした役者ではない He's not quite an actor./He isn't much of an actor. ▶私はあまり映画には行かない I don't often [(めったに…しない) I seldom] go to the movies. ▶君の意見にはあまり賛成じゃない I can't really agree with you. (❗I really can't ...は「まったく賛成じゃない」の意) ▶本当のことを知って彼をあまり気の毒には思わなくなった I've learned of the truth and I feel less sympathetic to him.

会話 「彼女は歌はうまいですか」「あまり」"Is she a good singer?" "Not very." ❗ No, she isn't a very good singer. の省略した形)
あまりある 余りある ▶彼の悲しみは察するに余りある I can well imagine his grief. ▶彼の死は惜しんでもなお余りある We cannot lament [deplore] his death enough [too much]. (❗後の方が意味が強い)
あまりにも 余りにも (⇨余り 副)

アマリリス 〖植物〗an amarýllis.

あまる 余る ❶ 〖残る〗remain, be left (over). (!前の方は他のものが除かれた後もまだ残っているという状態で、後の方は残されるという動作の結果に重点がある) ●余った金 the money *left (over)*; (余分の金) *spare* [*surplus*] money. ▶8を3で割ると2余る If you divide 8 by 3, you *have* 2 *left over* [*have a remainder of* 2]. ●買い物をした後、金はほとんど余っていなかった I had little money *left* after shopping. / Little money *remained* [*was left over*] after shopping. (!(1) be left (over) の方が口語的。(2) ×Little money *was remaining* .... とはいわない)

會話「ノートは450円だ。まだ50円余ってるよ」「じゃあ鉛筆も買おう」"The notebook's 450 yen. We have an *extra* 50 yen." "Let's get a pencil as well."

❷ 〖有り余る〗be [have*] more than enough; (多過ぎる) be [have] too many [much]. ▶日本は米が余っている Japan has *more* rice *than is needed*./ Japan has *more than enough* rice. ●あの会社は人が余っている That firm *is overstaffed*.

❸ 〖限度を超える〗●私の手に余る (仕事などが) *be beyond* me [my ability]; (人・動物が) *be beyond* my control. ●目に余る(=堪えがたい)行為 the conduct one *can't stand* [*bear*, (認める) *approve*]. ●身に余る(=自分にはもったいない)光栄です It's an *undeserved* honor./I don't *deserve* such a great honor.

あまんじる 甘んじる (不十分ながら満足する) contént oneself 《with》; (あきらめて甘受する) reconcile /rékənsàil/ oneself 《to》. ●現状に甘んじている be content(ed) with [be reconciled to] the present situation. ●不当な扱いに甘んじる(堪える) tolerate [〖話〗put up with] unfair treatment; (甘んじて受ける) (やや話) take unfair treatment *lying down* (! 通例否定文で). ▶その競走で彼は2位に甘んじた(=残念ながら2位だった) It's a pity (that) he came in second in that race.

あみ 網 ❶ 〖糸や針金を編んだ〗a net, 《総称》netting; (投網(とあみ)) a cast(ing) net; (地引き網) a dragnet; (漁業の) a fishing net; (捕虫網) an insect net; (グローブ・ミットの網) webbing, a web. ●網にかかる be caught in a *net*. ●網を打つ cast [throw] a *net*. ●小鳥を捕るために網を張る lay [spread] a *net* to catch birds. ●網を引く draw a *net* ashore. ●目が1インチの網 a *net* with one inch *meshes* (! mesh は「網の目」の意). ●彼は網でたくさんの魚を捕った He caught a lot of fish in [with] a *net*./He netted a lot of fish.

❷ 〖その他の表現〗●捜査の網を張る spread a dragnet 《around him》. ●法の網をくぐる evade the law; escape from the clutches of the law.

あみ 醤蝦 〖動物〗a mysid shrimp. ●あみの佃煮 mysid shrimps boiled down in soy sauce and suger.

あみあげ(ぐつ) 編み上げ(靴) (a pair of) lace-ups.

あみいれ 編み機 a knitting machine.

あみじゃくし 網杓子 a skimmer, a ladle strainer.

あみだ 阿弥陀 〖仏教〗Amitabha /Amitá:ba/. ●(帽子を)あみだにかぶっている wear one's hat [cap etc.] on the back of one's head [pushed back on one's head; wear one's hat at an rakish angle (! rakish は「いなせな」の意).

あみだくじ 阿弥陀籤 draw lots to decide 《who pays how much [who is to do it]》. (事情) 米英には「あみだくじ」はない)

あみだす 編み出す 〖考え出す〗think* [work] ... out; (考案する) devise. ●新しい画法を編み出す *devise* [(創作する) *originate*] a new style of painting.

あみだな 網棚 〖列車・バスなどの〗a (luggage) rack. ●ブリーフケースを網棚に置く put a briefcase on a *luggage rack*.

あみと 網戸 〖戸の〗a screen door; 〖窓の〗a window screen. ●虫よけに窓に網戸を付ける *screen* the windows *against* insects.

アミノさん アミノ酸 an amino acid /əmí:nou ǽsid/.

あみのめ 網の目 a mesh (of a net). ▶網の目のように鉄道が全国中に広がっている A *network* of railroads covers the whole country.

あみぼう 編み棒 (編み針) a knitting needle [pin].

あみめ 網目 (網の一つの目) a mesh of a net. ●網目が2インチの網 a net *with* two-inch *meshes*.

あみもと 網元 a fishermen's boss.

あみもの 編みもの 图 〖編むこと〗knitting, (かぎ針編み) crochet /krouʃéi/; 〖編んだ作品〗(a piece of) knitting, knitted goods.

— 編みものをする 動 knit; crochet.

アミューズメント 〖娯楽〗amusement. ●アミューズメントパーク 《米》an *amusement* park.

アミラーゼ 〖生化学〗amylase /ǽməlèis/.

あむ 編む ❶ 〖衣類などを〗knit*, (かぎ針で) crochet; 〖かご・布・ひもなどを〗weave*; 〖髪の毛などをより合わせてひも状に〗(米) braid, (英) plait. ●編み針 (⇒編棒). ●毛糸でチョッキを編む *knit* a vest *out of* wool; *knit* wool *into* a vest. ●彼にセーターを編んであげる *knit* him a sweater; *knit* a sweater *for* him. ●髪をお下げに編んでいる wear one's hair in braids.

❷ 〖編集する〗辞書を編む *compile* a dictionary.

アムステルダム 〖オランダの首都〗Amsterdam /ǽmstərdæm/.

あめ 雨 (a) rain; (降水量) (a) rainfall; (にわか雨, 夕立) a shower.

> 解説 **(1)** rain はある期間の全般的な天気や雨量として見た場合は無冠詞, 1回の降雨としてとらえた場合には a がつく: この春は激しい雨が降った We had heavy *rain* last spring.(全般性)/昨夜は激しい雨が降った We had a heavy *rain* last night.(1回性)
>
> **(2)** 現に降っているか, 降りやんだ雨については the をつける: 雨は午後になって激しくなってきた The *rain* became heavier in the afternoon.
>
> **(3)** rains と複数形にすると大雨で, 熱帯地方の雨季や日本の梅雨には the rains となる: 梅雨が明けた The *rains* are [*The rainy season* is] over.
>
> **(4)** 日本の天気予報の「一時雨」は showers: 東京は曇り, 時々雨 Tokyo: cloudy, occasional *showers*.

①〖〜(の)雨〗 (!この場合通例 a がつく (⇒解説)) ●冷たい〖静かな; こぬか〗雨 a cold [a gentle; a fine] *rain*. ●土砂降り〖横ぐり〗の雨 a pouring [a driving] *rain*. ●にわか雨 a shower. ●質問の雨(比喩的) a *rain* [a *shower*] of questions. ●恵みの雨 a very welcome *rain*. ●暖かい春の雨だ It's a warm spring *rain*.

②〖雨は[が]〗 ▶今ひどく[しとしと]雨が降っています It's *raining* hard [*drizzling*] now. ▶あすは雨が降るだろう It will *rain* tomorrow./We will have *rain* tomorrow. (!話し手かある場所について述べるときは It より We を主語にする場合が多い) ▶雨が降り出した It began [started] to rain./The *rain* began [started] to fall. (!前の方が普通) ▶雨がやんだ The *rain* has stopped [〖話〗let up]./It has stopped raining. (!The rain is over. より普通) ▶雨はやみそうになかった The *rain* showed no sign of stopping [《話》letting up]. (❗The *rain* didn't seem to stop. は不自然)▶降りそうだ(＝雨模様だ)It looks like *rain*./It's likely to *rain*./It's going to *rain*. (❗今にも降って来そうな様子を暗示)It looks [seems] as if [《米話》] Looks like] it's going to *rain*. (❗It seems to rain. とはいわない（⇨一様）❷［類語，第 7 文例］))▶今年はあまり雨が降らなかった We haven't had much *rain* [*rainfall*] this year. ▶今朝から雨が降ったりやんだりしている It *has* been raining off and on [*on and off*] since this morning./The rain [It] *has been coming and going* since this morning. ▶雨がだんだん強くなってきた It's *raining* harder./The *rain* is getting heavier. ▶家を出た時は雨がひどく降っていたが，今は小降りになった It *was raining* hard when I left home, but now it *has let up*. ▶運転気をつけて．今晩は雨がひどいから Drive carefully. It's a very *rainy* [*wet*] night. (⇨③)

会話「前よりひどく降ってるよ」「天気予報によれば今ごろちら雨は上がって(＝晴れ上がって)いるはずなのに」"It's *raining* harder than ever." "And by now it should *have cleared up*, according to the weather forecast."

③【雨の】rainy, wet (-tt-). ●雨の日に on a *rainy* [a *wet*] day. (❗wet は霧などが深くてじめじめした状態も表す)●雨の多い地方 a *rainy* district. ●今日の雨の確率 the *rainfall* probability for today. ●雨の降らない夏 a *dry* summer. ●窓を打つ雨の音がする I can hear the *rain* pattering [the patter of *rain*] on the window.

④【雨に】●雨にぬれる get wet. ●雨にぬれた朝 a *wet* morning. ●雨に洗われた石だたみ a *rain-washed* stone pavement (丸い石を敷いた) cobbled stones]. ●また雨になるだろう(＝雨が降る)だろう (⇨②)●家に帰る途中雨にあった I *was caught in the rain* [*in a shower*] on my way home. (❗「にわか雨」の意では in *a* rain も用いられる)

⑤【雨の中を】●彼は雨の中をジョギングしていた He was jogging *in* [*through*] *the rain*. (❗through では「雨をついて」という感じが強調される．The の代わりにaは不可)▶雨の中を傘をささずに出かけると風邪をひくよ Don't go out *in the rain* without an umbrella, or you'll catch (a) cold.

⑥【雨で［のために］】●試合は雨で延期になった The game was put off *because of* (*the*) *rain*. (❗スポーツ界では in を省略するのが普通)●こう毎日雨ふりではいやになる All this *rain* every day makes me sick. ▶大雨のために外出できなかった We couldn't go out because we had a heavy *rain* [because of *the* heavy *rain*]. (❗前の方が口語的)/《物が主語》《書》The heavy *rain* prevented us from going out. ●雨のため試合が 6 回で流れた The game *was rained out* [《英》*off*] in the sixth inning.

●雨降って地固まる（ことわざ）After rain comes fair weather.

あめ 飴《米》(a) candy (❗集合的で ⓤ. 個々の飴当には種類をいうときは [c].《英》a sweet. ●飴の詰め合わせ 1 箱 a box of mixed *candies* [*sweets*]. ●飴をしゃぶる suck a *candy*. ▶飴はのどが痛いときにいいのよ．一ついかが *Candy* is good for a sore throat. Would you like a piece?

●飴と鞭（むち） ●飴と鞭の政策をとる have a carrot-and-stick policy (*toward*).

あめあがり 雨上がり ●雨上がりの好天気 fine weather (just) *after the rain*. (❗無冠詞に注意)

あめあられ 雨霰 ●雨あられと降りかかる銃弾 a *hail* [a *shower*] *of* bullets. ▶タイソンは相手に強打を雨あられと浴びせた Tyson delivered a *hail of* blows to his opponent.

アメーバ an amoeba,《米》an ameba /əmíːbə/ (⦿~s, -bae /-biː/).
●アメーバ赤痢 amoebic dysentery.

あめおとこ 雨男 （説明的に)《どどぎ》a man who never comes or goes out without being met by wet weather.

あめおんな 雨女 (説明的に)《どどぎ》a woman who never comes or goes out without being met by wet weather.

アメジスト 【紫水晶】an ámethyst. (参考 2 月の誕生石)

アメダス 【日本の地域気象観測システム】AMeDAS (*A*utomated *Me*teorological *D*ata *A*cquisition *S*ystem の略).

あめだま 飴玉（⇨飴）

あめつゆ 雨露 ●雨露をしのぐ have a roof over one's head; （やっと生きていく）keep body and soul together, scrape a living.

あめに 飴煮 food boild down in soy sauce and plenty of sugar.

アメニティ 【快適環境・快適さ】the amenity. (❗具体的な場所・設備を表す場合は常に amenities で用いる)
●アメニティ空間 an amenity space; a space with facilities for amenities. アメニティグッズ《bath》amenities.

あめもよう 雨模様（⇨雨(㊟)模様）

▸**アメリカ** ❶【アメリカ合衆国】America; （公式名）the United States of America《略 U.S.A., USA》. (❗(1)単数扱い. (2)▶とまどらわしいときや米人自身は the United States や the U.S. (主に印刷物かで)を用いることも多い. the States は米人が国外で自国を呼ぶ言い方)●アメリカ(人)の American. ●アメリカ人 an American; (集合的に) *American* people, the Americans. ●アメリカ海軍 the *U.S.* Navy. ▶彼はアメリカ人だ He's *American*./He's an *American*. (❗前の方が普通だが，国籍を強調するときは後の方を用いる)▶私はアメリカへ行ったことがない I've never been to *the United States* [*the US, the U.S., America*].

❷【アメリカ大陸】America; （南北アメリカ) North and South America, the Americas. ▶カナダは北アメリカにある Canada is in North *America*.
●アメリカンインディアン an American Indian. (❗今は a Native American というのが普通)●アメリカ英語 American English; （語法）(an) Americanism. ●アメリカザリガニ a crayfish. ●アメリカシロヒトリ 【昆虫】a fall webworm.

アメリカナイズ ― アメリカナイズする 動 Americanize. ▶戦後日本の生活様式は急速にアメリカナイズされた The Japanese lifestyle *was* rapidly *Americanized* after World War Ⅱ.

あめりかものがたり『あめりか物語』*American Stories*. (参考)永井荷風の短編小説集)

アメリカンコーヒー weak [mild] coffee;《和製語》American coffee.

『アメリカン・スクール』*American School*. (参考 小島信夫の小説)

アメリカンフットボール《米》football,《英》American football (❗《米》でもラグビーなどと明確に区別する場合には用いられる)

あめんぼ 【昆虫】a water strider.

あや 文，綾 ❶【模様・色合い】（模様）a design, a figure;（色合い）color.
❷【飾った言い回し】▶それは単なる言葉のあやだ It's just a *figure of speech*.

あやうい ❸[仕組み・筋道] ▶この事件にはいろいろなあや(=入り組んだ仕組み)がある This affair has many *complications*.

あやうい 危うい (⇨危ない)

あやうく 危うく ❶[もう少しで] nearly, almost. ▶ nearly はその状態に至らなかったのは不思議なくらいだったことを強調し, almost はその状態には至らなかったことを強調する) ▶危うくトラックにひかれるところだった I was *nearly* [*almost*] run over by a truck.
❷[かろうじて] barely; (やっと) narrowly. ▶彼女は危うく死を免れた She *narrowly* [*barely*] escaped death./She had a *narrow* [×*bare*] escape from death.

あやおり 綾織り twill.

あやかる ▶祖父にあやかって(=ちなんで)息子に一郎と名をつける name one's son Ichiro *after* [[米] *for*] one's grandfather. ▶私も君の幸運にあやかりたい I wish some of your luck would *rub off on* me. (**!** rub off on [upon] A 「(美点などが)こすれてAの上にこぼれ落ちる」の意)

あやしい 怪しい ❶[疑わしい] doubtful; (漠然と疑わしいと思う) dubious; (不審な) suspicious; (疑問のある) questionable (⇨疑わしい); (信頼できない) unreliable; (いかがわしい《話》 shady /ʃéidi/; (話などがうさん臭い)《話》fishy. ●怪しい人物 a *suspicious* [a *doubtful*, a *dubious*] character. ●怪しい情報源 an *unreliable* source. ●怪しい取り引きに関係している be mixed up in *shady* transactions. ▶彼が時間におくれずにやって来るかどうかは怪しいものだ I *doubt* [*wonder*] *if* [*whether*] he will come on time. (**!** doubt の方が積極的な疑惑を表す. wonder は「…かしらと思う」の意) ▶(嫌疑をかけて)彼が怪しいと思う I *suspect* him./I *am suspicious of* him./I have my *doubts about* him. ▶彼女がいつになく親切だったので怪しいと(=ありそうもない)思った She was unusually friendly, and I *was suspicious*.

会話「あの人と別れたなんて怪しいわ」「本当に別れたってば」"I *don't believe* you broke up with him." "I did leave him."

会話「でも太郎が手伝ってくれるのでしょ」「それがどうも怪しいんだよ(=ありそうもない)」"But Taro will help, won't he?" "It's *unlikely*."

❷[不思議な] (変な) strange; (神秘的な) mysterious. ▶階段を上ってくる怪しい足音がした I heard *strange* footsteps coming up the stairs.

❸[おぼつかない] (不器用な) clumsy, awkward; (下手な) poor; (不確かな) uncertain. ●怪しい手つきでリンゴをむく peel an apple with *clumsy* [*awkward*] hands. ●箸の扱い方が怪しい be awkward at handling chopsticks. ●怪しい(=あぶなげな)足取りで歩く walk with *unsteady* steps. ▶彼のフランス語は相当怪しい His French is very *poor* [(よくない) isn't *good*; (使わないので) is *rusty*]./(当てにならない) He is very *shaky* at French.

❹[その他の表現] ▶空模様が怪しい It *is likely to* rain [*looks like* rain]./The sky *is threatening*. ▶あの2人の(仲)は怪しい There *may be something going on* between the two./(愛し合っているようだ) They *may be in love* with each other./(不倫関係にあるようだ) They *may be having an affair*.

あやしげ 怪しげ (⇨怪しい) ●怪しげな男 a *suspicious*-[a *questionable*-]*looking* man. ●怪しげな《話》a *fishy* story. ●怪しげな包み a *mysterious-looking* parcel.

***あやしむ 怪しむ** [[疑う] doubt; suspect. (⇨疑う ❶ ❷, 怪しい)

あやす 赤ん坊を子守歌であやして寝かせる lull [soothe] a baby to sleep by singing a lullaby /lʌ́ləbài/. (**!** この sleep は名詞)

あやつりにんぎょう 操り人形 a puppet; a marionette. (⇨人形)

***あやつる 操る** [[動かす, 運転する]] work; (うまく操作する) manage; (扱う) handle; (操縦する) operate; (巧みに操作する) manipulate; (巧みに操る) maneuver; [[言語を自由に駆使する]] have* a command of …. ●人形を操る *work* [*manipulate*] a puppet (by strings). ●馬を操る *manage* [*handle, control*] a horse. ●船をうまく操ってドックに入れる *maneuver* a boat *into* the dock. ●英語を自由に操る *have a good command of* English; (流ちょうに話す) *speak* English *fluently* [*fluent* English]. ●政界を陰で操る *pull strings* in the political world. ▶彼女は彼を思いのままに操っている She *manages* [*manipulates*] him any way she wants.

あやとり 綾取り (play) cat's cradle.

あやぶむ 危ぶむ [[心配する]] worry [be worried] 《about, over》(**!** 《about》より口語的); be anxious 《about》, fear 《for》; [[疑う]] doubt. ▶彼の健康を危ぶむ *worry about* [*be anxious about, fear for*] his health. ▶彼女の成功を危ぶむ声もある Some people *are worried* [*fear*, ×*are anxious*] (*that*) she will fail./Some people *doubt* [*are doubtful of*] her success./Some people *doubt if* [*whether*] she will succeed.

あやふや ── **あやふやな** 形 (不確実な) uncertain; (はっきりしない) indefinite, equivocal; (漠然とした) vague; (信頼できない) unreliable. ●あやふやな態度をとる take an *uncertain* attitude. ●あやふやな答えをする give a *vague* [an *indefinite*, an *equivocal*] answer. ●あやふやな証言をする give (an) *unreliable* testimony.

***あやまち 過ち** a mistake; an error (**!** 前より堅い語); [[過失]] a fault. (⇨過失) ▶若気の過ち a youthful [×a young] *error* (=(愚行) folly). ●過ちを犯す make [×do] a *mistake*; commit [make] an *error*. ▶それは君の過ちではない It's not your *fault*. ▶同じ過ちを繰り返してはならない The same *mistake* should not be made again.

あやまつ 過つ ▶矢が的に命中した The arrow hit the mark *unerringly* [*with an unerring aim*].

あやまって 誤って (別のものと間違えて) by mistake; (うっかり) by accident. ●誤って違うバスに乗る get on the wrong bus *by mistake*. ▶彼は誤って川に落ちた He fell (over) into the stream *accidentally* [*by accident*, ×*by mistake*].

***あやまり 誤り** a mistake; an error. (⇨間違い [類語]) ●判断の誤り an *error* [×a mistake] of judgment. ●ささいな誤りをする make [×do] a slight mistake. ▶誤りがあれば正せ Correct *errors*(,) if any. ▶「too」は「to」の誤り "Too" is a mistake *for* "to."/(正誤表で) *For* "too" *read* "to." ▶彼は自分の誤りを認めた He admitted his *mistake* [that he *was mistaken*]./(法的・道徳的に) He admitted that he was *wrong* [*in the wrong*]. (⇨間違う ❶) ▶その報告は誤りである(=事実でない)ことが判明した The report turned out to be *false*.

***あやまる 誤る** 動 [[間違う, 間違える]] make* a mistake [an error]. (⇨間違う) ●判断を誤る make an *error* of judgment. ●タイミングを誤る *misjudge* the timing (*of*). ●人選を誤る *choose the wrong person* 《*for; to do*》. ●道(=職業選択)を誤る *miss* one's calling. ●身を誤る ruin oneself.

── **誤った** 形 wrong (↔right); false (↔true). (⇨間違った) ●誤った推測 a *wrong* guess. ●誤った情報 *false* information.

あやまる 謝る apologize 《to＋人, for＋事》; make* [offer] an apology. ▶彼は私に迷惑をかけたことを謝った He apologized [made an apology] to me for causing trouble. ▶彼は昨夜のことを謝ったが、心から(謝った)のではなかった He apologized [said he was very sorry] for last night, but he wasn't sincere about it.

あやめ 菖蒲〘植物〙an iris 《徽 ~es, irides /íridi:z/》.

あゆ 鮎 〘魚介〙an *ayu*, a sweetfish. (｡通例単・複同形)

あゆ 阿諛 flattery. (⇨おべっか)

あゆみ 歩み 〘歩くこと〙walking; 〘歩く速さ〙a pace; 〘歩く過程〙(進行) progress; (推移) a course; (経過) the passage 《of time》; 〘歴史〙a history. ●歩み(＝足並み)をそろえる keep *pace* 《with》. ●着実な歩み(＝進行)を重ねる make steady *progress*. ●月日の歩み(＝経過) the *passage* of time 《days, years》. ●歴史の歩み the *course* of history. ●本校50年の歩み the fifty years' *history* of this school. ▶近代化の歩みは遅々たるものだった Modernization advanced slowly.

あゆみより 歩み寄り (妥協) (a) compromise. ▶この論争は歩み寄りの余地がなさそうだ There seems to be no room for *compromise* in this dispute.

あゆみよる 歩み寄る ❶〘近寄る〙come* closer [nearer] 《to》; walk up 《to》; (つかつかと) step (-pp-) up 《to》. ▶彼は気色ばんで議長に歩み寄った He showed his anger and *walked* right *up to* the chairperson.
❷〘妥協する〙(make* a) compromise 《with＋人; over＋事; on＋決定条件》; (譲歩する) make concessions 《to》. ▶歩み寄って問題を解決する settle the matter *by* [*through*] *compromise*; *reach a compromise* over the matter; *meet* 《him》 *half way* on the matter.

あゆむ 歩む (⇨歩く)

あら (驚き・意外性などを表して) oh; oh dear, dear me (｡主に女性用語). ●あらほんと。知らなかったわ Oh, really? I didn't know that. ●あらご親切に。Oh, how kind of you! ●あら困ったわ。またかぎをなくしたわ Oh dear [Dear me]! I've lost my keys again. ●あらたいへん。花びんを割ってしまったわ Oh no, I've broken the vase! (｡「まさか, とんでもない」といった気持ちを表す)

あら 粗 ❶〘欠点〙a fault; (不備) a flaw; (不都合な点) a drawback; (欠陥) a defect. ▶彼女の理論には粗が目立つ There are lots of *flaws* [*drawbacks*] in her theory. ❷〘魚を料理した後に残る骨など〙the bony parts of fish.

アラー 〘イスラム教の唯一神〙Allah /á:lə/.

アラーム 〘警報装置〙an alarm; 〘目覚まし時計〙an alarm (clock).

あらあら 粗々に (ざっと) briefly.

あらあらしい 荒々しい (⇨荒い) ●荒々しい気性の人 a *violent*-tempered person. ●荒々しい語調で話す speak in a *harsh* tone; speak *harshly*. ●荒々しくドアを開ける[閉める] open [shut] the door *violently*; fling the door open [shut].

***あらい 荒い** ❶〘乱暴な〙rough; (荒っぽい) wild; (激しい) violent; (粗野な) rude. (⇨荒っぽい) ●語気が荒い speak in a *harsh* tone. ●金遣いが荒い人 an extravagant person; a spendthrift. ●荒々しく(人の) make 《him》 work *too hard*; (道具の) handle 《a tool》 *roughly*.
❷〘気性の激しい〙violent; 〘海・波の〙rough; wild. ●気が荒い have a *violent* temper; be *violent*-tempered. ●息遣いが荒い be breathing hard [heavily]. (⇨あえぐ) ●今日は波が荒い The sea is [The waves are] *rough* today.

***あらい 粗い** (きめの粗い) coarse; (表面がざらざらした) rough /rʌf/. ●目の粗い布地 *coarse* cloth. ●粒の粗い砂 *coarse* sand. ●きめの粗い皮膚 *rough* skin. ●目の粗い網 a *large*-meshed net; a net of *large* mesh.

あらい 洗い ❶〘洗うこと〙washing, wash. ●食器洗い(乾燥)機 a dishwasher. ●お手洗い a toilet. (⇨トイレ(ット)) ❷〘刺身〙thin slices of raw fish washed in cold water. ●洗い桶(洗濯の) a washtub; (皿洗いの)(米) a dishpan, (英) a washing-up bowl. ●洗い髪 freshly washed hair.

あらいあげる 洗い上げる ❶〘洗い終わる〙finish washing; (十分に洗う) wash well. ❷〘調べ上げる〙●殺人事件を洗い上げる *investigate* the murder case *thoroughly*; *make a thorough* [*a searching*] *investigation of* the murder case.

あらいぐま 洗い熊 a racóon, (米話) a coon.

あらいざらい 洗いざらい ●そのことを洗いざらいしゃべる tell [(白状する) confess] *everything* about it; (告白して) *make a clean breast of it*. ●秘密を洗いざらいしゃべる let out the *whole secret*.

あらいざらし 洗いざらし ●洗いざらしの(＝洗って色があせた)上着 a *washed-out* [*a faded*] jacket.

あらいそ 荒磯 a rough [(岩の多い) a rocky] coast [shoreline].

あらいだす 洗い出す ●いくつかの新しい事実を洗い出す *dig up* several new facts. ●彼は彼の過去を洗い出した We *dredged up* his past. ▶上り列車を待つ私の目の前に、浅間山が洗い出したような(＝はっきりときれいな)全景をあらわしていた A clear panoramic view of Mt. Asama was [spread out] in front of me, as I waited for a train for Tokyo.

あらいたてる 洗い立てる ●暗い過去を洗い立てる(＝暴き出す) *expose* [*disclose*] one's shady past.

あらいなおす 洗い直す (再検討する) reconsider; think* 《it》 all over again. ●計画を洗い直す(＝一からやり直す) *start* working on the plan *from the beginning* (*again*).

あらいながす 洗い流す ●過去の苦しい経験を洗い流す *wash away* one's past bitter experience. ▶その泥をすぐ洗い流しなさい *Wash* the mud *away* right now, please.

あらいはり 洗い張り ── 洗い張りする 動 (説明的に) stretch the pieces of a *kimono* on a board to dry after they were washed and starched.

あらいもの 洗い物 〘衣料の〙laundry, washing; 〘食器の〙(do [wash]) the dishes.

***あらう 洗う** ❶〘汚れを落とす〙wash (⇨洗濯(を)する); (すすいで) rinse ... (out) (⇨すすぐ); (ごしごしと) scrub (-bb-); (髪・カーペットなどを) shampóo; (傷などを) cleanse /klénz/. ●体を洗う wash oneself 《｡文脈上明らかなときは oneself は通例省略》; have a wash. (｡いずれも手・顔など体の一部分を洗うときにも用いる. ●食事の前に手を洗う *wash* [*have a wash*, 《米》*wash up*] before meals) ●車をよく洗う *wash* a car (*down*) well (｡down は大きな物を大量の水で洗う場合) ; *give* a car *a good wash*. (｡*give a good wash to a car* とはいわない) ●(食器)皿[食器]を洗う *do* [*wash*] the dishes. ●洗いたてのシャツ a *newly-washed* [*a freshly-washed*] shirt. ●手の汚れを洗い落とす *wash* the dirt *off* one's hands. (｡汚れが中にしみ込んだ場合は out of を用いる: シャツの汚れを洗い落とす *wash* the stain *out of* a shirt) ●手[浴槽]をごしごし洗う *scrub* one's hands [a bathtub]. ▶彼女は冷たい水[石けん]で顔を洗った She *washed* her face *in* cold water [*with* soap

あらうみ 荒海 a rough [a stormy] sea.
あらかじめ beforehand, in advance, 《主に米》ahead of time. (⇨前もって)
あらかせぎ 荒稼ぎ ── 荒稼ぎする 動 ●株で荒稼ぎする(=大金を稼ぐ) make a lot of money [突然大もうけする](話) make a killing on the stock market. (⇨儲け)
あらかた ▶その仕事はあらかた(=ほとんど)済んだ The work is almost [nearly] finished.
あらかべ 粗壁 a rough-surfaced [a rough-coated] wall.
アラカルト [<フランス語] ●アラカルトの[で] à la carte /à: lə ká:rt/.
あらくれおとこ 荒くれ男 a rough [a tough] fellow.
あらくれる 荒くれる (乱暴する) do violence 《to him》,(話) rough up 《him》,(荒々しくふるまう) behave roughly 《to him》.
あらけずり 粗削り ── 粗削りの 形 (木などが) rough-planed [-hewn]; (洗練されていない) unrefined; (粗野な) rough; (粗雑な) coarse. ▶粗削りの板 a rough [a rough-hewn] board. ▶粗削りなふるまい rough [coarse, unrefined] behavior.
あらげる 荒げる (⇨荒らげる)
あらごなし 粗ごなし (おおまかに処理しておくこと) rough preparations 《for》.
あらさがし 粗探し 图 fáultfinding,《話・軽蔑的》nitpicking.
── **あら探しをする** 動 find fault 《×faults》《with》(!) (1)「口に出して言う」ところまで含む.(2)criticize, complain of [about] より堅い言い方で,今はあまり用いない)《やや話》pick holes 《in》. ▶彼はいつも彼女のあら探しをしている He's always finding fault with [complaining about] her.
***あらし** 嵐 a storm; (強風) a windstorm; (暴風雨) a rainstorm.
①【~嵐】 ●激しい嵐 a heavy [a violent] storm;《書》a tempest.
②【嵐の~】 ●嵐の夜 a stormy night. ●嵐のような拍手 a storm of applause.
③【嵐に[に]】 ●海上で嵐にあう be (caught) in a storm at sea. ●一晩中嵐が吹き荒れた The storm blew all night./It stormed all night. ▶嵐が来るそうだ We are going to have a storm./There will be a storm. (!前の方は何らかの前兆がある場合,後の方は単なる予測として述べた場合) ▶嵐が吹きすさんでいる [静まった; 去った] The storm is raging [has calmed down; is over].
●**嵐の前の静けさ** ▶これは嵐の前の静けさにすぎない This is only the calm before the storm.
あらしがおか 『嵐が丘』 Wuthering /wʌðəriŋ/ Heights. (参考) エミリー・ブロンテの小説)
あらしごと 荒仕事 ●(骨の折れる仕事) hard work, (重労働) hard labor, toil.
❷(荒っぽい犯罪) (強盗) (commit) (a) burglary, (殺人) (commit) murder.
アラジン ▶『アラジンと魔法のランプ』 Aladdin and the Wonderful Lamp. (参考) 『アラビアンナイト』中の一編)
***あらす** 荒らす ●[めちゃめちゃにする] ruin; [破壊する] destroy; (手荒な手段で) wreck; [害する] damage, do* damage 《to》;[建物などを荒廃させる] devastate. ▶農作物が嵐のため荒らされた The crops were ruined by the storm./The storm did [caused] a lot of damage to the crops. ●公衆電話ボックスが暴徒に荒らされた The telephone booth was wrecked [was destroyed] by the mob. ▶強盗が部屋を荒らしていた The burglars left the room in a terrible mess.
❷[侵入して害を与える] (侵入する) invade; (建物に押し入って盗む)《米》burglarize,《英》burgle; (縄張りを荒らす) invade [intrude into] one's territory. ●事務所の金庫を荒らす burglarize the office safe.
あらず 有らず,在らず,非ず ▶あの人の心はここにあらず (=うわの空) だ He is absent-minded./He doesn't pay any attention to it./His mind is somewhere else.
  [会話] 「ジェーンはジムと婚約しているの?」「さにあらず さ(=違うよ)」"Is Jane engaged to Jim?" "It's not so."
アラスカ [米国の州] Alaska /əlǽskə/ 《略 Alas. 郵便略 AK》.
あらすじ 粗筋 [概略] an outline; [要約] a summary; [小説などの筋書き] a plot. ●その事件のあらすじを述べる give [draw] an outline [a summary] of the event. ●劇のあらすじを sketch out a plot of a drama.
あらせいとう [植物] a stock.
***あらそい** 争い ●[競争] competition 《with, against; for》. ●し烈な優勝争い a keen competition 《among the teams》 for the championship.
❷[闘争] (腕力・武力による) a fight (!比喩的にも用いる); (苦闘) a struggle 《with, against; for》; (衝突) a conflict 《with, between》; (反目による争い)《やや書》strife; [論争] (感情的・長期的な) (a) dispute; (公的な) a controversy; (議論) (an) argument; (口げんか) a quarrel 《with; about, over》; [不和] 《書》(a) discord. ●金をめぐる争い (have) a fight about money; (口論) (have) a quarrel over [about] money. ●土地の所有権をめぐる隣人との争い a dispute with one's neighbors over the ownership of the land. ●派閥争いに巻き込まれる be dragged into factional strife [a factional conflict, a factional dispute]. ●2国間の争いを平和的に解決する settle the conflict between the two nations peacefully. ●骨肉の争い 《×a》 family discord.
***あらそう** 争う ●[競争する] compete; [奮闘して]《やや書》contend 《with, against; for》. (⇨争い) ●議席を争う contend for [contest] a seat (in the Diet). ▶若い女の子たちは今や流行を追うものだ Young girls tend to compete with [against] each other to be (more) fashionable. ▶山田と田中は100メートル競走で1位を争った Yamada and Tanaka competed in the 100-meter dash for (the) first prize.
❷[けんかする] fight*; [口論かする] quarrel; [口論する] argue, [長期にわたって] dispute 《with; about, over》 (!後の方が堅い語). (⇨争い, 喧嘩 (%)) ●路上で警官と泥棒が激しく争っていた A policeman was fighting with [against] a masked man on the street. ●兄弟が遺産をめぐって争った The brothers quarreled [argued] 《with each

あらそえない　争えない ● 争えない(=争われぬ)事実 an undeniable [an indisputable] fact. ● 年は争えない You are not as young as you used to be./Age will tell. ▶やはり血筋は争えないものだ Blood will tell after all. (⇨血筋)

あらた　新た ── 新たな 形 new; (みずみずしい) fresh. ── 新たに 副 ●物事の認識を新たにする see the matter in a new light. ●感動を新たにする be impressed again [×be newly impressed]. ●新たにオープンした店(=新しい店) a new [a newly opened] store. ●装いを新たにした店 a remodeled store. ▶気分も新たに(=さわやかな気分で)彼は田舎から帰って来た He came back from the country feeling refreshed [fresh].

あらたか 霊験(_{れい})あらたか (⇨霊験[成句])

あらだてる　荒立てる ●声を荒立てる raise one's voice. ●そんなことをすれば事を荒立てることになる I'm afraid that would make things worse [difficult].

＊**あらたまる　改まる** ❶【変わる】be changed; change. ▶年号が平成と改まった The name of an era was changed to Heisei./The new era was named Heisei. ▶年が改まった The new year has begun. ❷【よくなる】(改善される) be improved; (改正される) be revised; (矯正される) be reformed, be corrected. ▶風紀が改まった Public morals have (been) improved. ▶規則が改まった The rules have been revised. ▶彼の生活態度が改まった He has reformed himself from his evil way of life. ❸【儀式ばる】be [become*] formal. ●改まった席で on a formal occasion. ●改まった顔をする look solemn [serious]. ●改まった物の言い方をする use formal language. ●そんなに改まるな Don't stand on ceremony.

あらためて　改めて ❶【別の折に】another time; (もう一度) again. ▶日を改めてまたまいります I'll come another [some other] time. ❷【特に】▶改めて言うことは何もありません I have nothing in particular to say. ❸【新に】▶改めて問題を提起します Let me bring forward a new question.

＊**あらためる　改める** ❶【変更する】(全体を) change, (一部を) alter; (改正する) revise. ●計画を改める change a plan. ●考え方を改める alter one's way of thinking. ●規則を改める revise the rule(s). ▶私は名前をトムと改めた I changed my name to Tom. ❷【直す】(改善する) improve; (矯正する) mend; reform; (訂正する) correct. ●体質[勉強法]を改める improve one's constitution [one's way of studying]. ●素行[欠点]を改める mend one's ways [one's fault(s)]. ●心を改める reform (oneself). ▶誤りがあれば改めなさい Correct errors(,) if any. ❸【調べる】examine, check; (公式に) inspect; 【数える】count. ●切符を改める examine the tickets. ●おつりを改める check the change. ●人数を改める count the number of people. ●死体を改める inspect a corpse. ❹【整える】●服装を改める dress well; dress oneself properly. ●言葉を改める(=改まった言葉を遣う) use formal language.

あら(っ) 〖驚きに〗oh; (~まあ) oh; (間違いに気づいて) oops /wúːps/; 〖注意喚起〗look. ●あら, 違うバスに乗ってしまった Oops! I'm on the wrong bus. ▶あら, あれは何ですか Look! What's that?

あらっぽい　荒っぽい (乱暴な) rough; (激しい) violent; (粗野な) rude. (⇨荒い) ●荒っぽい力仕事 rough work. ●荒っぽい態度 rough [rude] manners. ●言葉遣いが荒っぽい use rough [violent] language; (習慣的に) have a rough [a violent] tongue. ●荒っぽいことをする(=暴力を振るう) use violence. ●荒っぽく扱う handle (it [a child]) roughly. ●荒っぽい(=無謀な)運転をする drive recklessly.

あらて　新手 ❶【新人】a newcomer, a new worker [employee]. ❷【まだ戦わない軍勢】fresh groups of soldiers. ❸【新しい方法】a new way [method, (型) type] (of). ●新手の詐欺 a new type of fraud /frɔ́:d/. ●新手の資金集めの方法を考え出す think out a new method of raising funds.

あらなみ　荒波 rough [raging, angry] waves; rough [heavy] seas. (⇨波) ●岩に砕ける荒波 angry waves breaking on [against] the rocks. ●荒波に激しく揺れる be tossed wildly on the stormy sea. ▶荒波が立っていた The waves ran high.

あらなわ　荒縄, 粗縄 a straw rope.

あらに　粗煮 an arani; (説明的に) a dish made by boiling the bony parts of fish in soy sauce and sugar.

あらぬ (思いもよらない) unexpected; (途方もない) extraordinary; (不当な) unjust; (いつわりの) false; (わけのわからない) irrational. ●あらぬうわさを立てられる become the victim of a false rumor. ●彼女はその場の雰囲気でありもしないことを口走ってしまった She let out something irrational [terrible] influenced [(圧倒されて) overcome] by the atmosphere of the scene [place].

あらねつ　粗熱 most of the heat. ●粗熱をとる remove [get rid of] most of the heat; (冷ます) cool (it) off. ●焼きあがったばかりの食パンに粗熱をとってから切りなさい Cool off the bread hot from the oven before you slice it.

あらばこそ ●遠慮会釈もあらばこそ(=なくない) without the slightest reserve [(ちゅうちょ) hesitation].

アラバマ 〖米国の州〗Alabama /ˌæləbǽmə/ (略 Ala. 郵便略 AL).

アラビア　Arabia /əréibiə/. ●アラビアの (地理的に) Arabian /əréibiən/; (人種的に) Arab /ǽrəb/; (言語・文化的に) Arabic /ǽrəbik/. ●アラビア海 the Arabian Sea. ●アラビア語 Arabic. ●アラビア人 (古) an Arabian. (⇨アラブ)
●アラビアゴム gum arabic [acasia /əkéiʃə/]. ●アラビア数字 Arabic numerals [figures]. ●アラビア文字 Arabic script [characters].

『**アラビアンナイト**』*The Arabian* /əréibiən/ *Nights; The Arabian Nights' Entertainments; The Thousand and One Nights*. (〖参考〗アラビア語の説話集)

あらびき　粗びき ●粗びきの黒こしょう coarsely ground [a coarse grind of] black pepper.

アラブ 〖アラビア人〗an Arab; (アラブ〖民族〗) the Arabs. (⇨アラビア) ●アラブ諸国 the Arab nations. ●アラブ連盟 the Arab League.

アラブしゅちょうこくれんぽう　アラブ首長国連邦 the United Arab Emirates 《略 UAE》. (首都 Abu Dhabi)

アラベスク 〖アラビア風装飾模様〗(an) àrabésque.

あら(まあ) (⇨あら)

あらまき　新巻き a lightly salted salmon.

あらまし ●あらまし(=概要)を述べる give an outline

(要約) a summary] (*of*); give ... *in outline* [*summary*].
アラモード [＜フランス語] [最新流行の] à la mode, a la mode /ɑ̀ː lɑː móud/. バイアラモード [アイスクリームを添えたパイ] (a piece of) pie *à la mode*.
あらもの 荒物 hardware.
● 荒物屋 a hardware store.
*****あらゆる** [すべての] all; [どの一つも] every. (⇨すべて, 全部) ● あらゆる点で in *all* respects; in *every* respect. ● あらゆる手段を尽くす try *all* [*every*] possible means. (❗ means は単・複同形)
あららげる 荒らげる ● 声をあららげる raise one's voice. ▶ジムがまた遅刻したので部長は声をあららげた The manager *scolded* Jim *in an angry voice* [《米話》*bawled* Jim *out*] *for* being late again.
あらりえき 粗利益 a gross margin.
あらりょうじ 荒療治 ● 荒療治を行う perform *radical surgery*; [比喩的] take *drastic* [*radical*] *measures* (*to do*; *against*).
あられ 霰 ❶ [天候] hail. (❗ hail はあられ, ひょうの両方をさす) ● 雨あられのように飛んでくる弾丸 a *hail* of bullets. ▶昨夜あられがたくさん降った We had a lot of *hail* last night./It *hailed* a lot last night.
❷ [細かく切ったもの] ● チーズをあられに切る cut cheese into *small cubes*.
あられもない [あるべきでない] improper (*to*); [ふさわしくない] unbecoming (*to*, *for*); [みだらな] indecent. ▶高一の女子生徒があられもないシースルーの服を着て学校に来た A tenth-grade girl came to school, *improperly* dressed in a see-through dress.
あらわ 露 ── あらわに ● 肌もあらわに(=わずかに肌をおおう服装で)エルサレムの街を行く外国人観光客 *scantily-dressed* foreign tourists in Jerusalem. (⇨剥き出し) ● あらわに(=あからさまに)不満気な顔をあらわして *openly* show one's dissatisfaction. ● 敵意をあらわにして議案に反対する oppose the bill with *open* hostility. ▶両党間の対立があらわになった(=表面化した) Hostilities between the two parties *surfaced*.
あらわざ 荒技, 荒業 a rough technique; [荒仕事] rough work.
*****あらわす 表す, 現す** ❶ [表現する] express, (言葉で描写する) describe; (感情などを) show* (=示す); (意見などを書) signify. ● 言葉に表せない満足感 an *inexpressible* [an *indescribable*] sense of satisfaction; a sense of satisfaction *beyond expression* [*description*]. ● 驚きを顔に表す show one's surprise on one's face. ● 気持ちを外に表さない keep one's feelings *to oneself*. ▶彼はほほえんで賛成の意を表した He *expressed* [*gave expression to*, *signified*] his approval with a smile [*by smiling*]./He smiled his approval. ▶私の感謝の気持ちは言葉では表せません I cannot *express* [*put*] my gratitude in [*with*] words. (❗ put の方が口語的. put の場合, in の代わりに into も可)/I cannot find words to *express* my gratitude [how grateful I am].
❷ [意味する] represent; (略号などが) stand* for ..., (書) signify; [象徴する] symbolize; [証明する] show*. ● 地図でこの四角が私の家を表しています This square *represents* my house on the map. ● a.m. は何を表しているの？ What does *a.m. stand for*? ● これは太陽を表している This *symbolizes* the sun. ● この出来事は彼の愚かさを表している This incident *shows* [*proves*] his stupidity [that he is stupid, him to be stupid]. (❗ to be を用いる構文より that 節を用いる方が普通)
❸ [姿を現す] appear. (⇨現れる, 表れる ❶) ● ひょっこり姿を現す appear [《話》*show up*] unexpectedly.
あらわす 著す (書く) write*; (出版する) publish. ● 書物を著わす *write* [*publish*] a book.
あらわれ 表れ (an) expression; [発現][書] (a) manifestation; [反映] a reflection (*of*); [兆候] a sign (*of*); [感情・性質などの] a mark. ▶平静な返答ぶりは彼の忍耐強さの表れだ His calm reply is a *mark* of his patience.
:あらわれる 現れる, 表れる ❶ [出現する] appear, 《話》turn up, 《話》show* up; come* out (*from*), 《やや書》emerge (*from*, *out of*); arrive; come into existence [being]; come into view [in sight].

> [使い分け] **appear** 出現を表す最も一般的な語.
> **turn up** 突然に現れ出ること. その後に場所や時間などの情報を伴うことが多い.
> **show up** 人の目を引く形で現れること.
> **come out** 隠れていた物・人が明るみに現れること.
> **arrive** 遠くにあって見えなかった人・物が到来して姿を現すこと.
> **come into existence [being]** それまで存在しなかったものが新たに姿を現すこと.
> **come into view [sight]** 遠くにあって見えなかった物が近づいてきて姿を現すこと.

● (人が)現場に現れる *appear* [*arrive*] on the scene. ▶彼はパーティーに遅れて現れた He *appeared* [*turned up*, *showed up*] late for the party. ▶霧の中から突然船が現れた A boat suddenly *appeared* [There suddenly *appeared* a boat] out of the mist./A boat *burst* [suddenly *came*] into view through the mist. ▶太陽が水平線のかなたから現れた The sun *came out* [*emerged*] from beyond the horizon. ▶議会は 11 世紀に初めてできた(=現れた) Parliament *came into existence* in the 11th century.
❷ [表に出る] (感情などが) show* (itself); [隠れていたものが明らかになる] come* out, 《やや書》come to light; (おおっていたものがとれて)《やや書》reveal itself; (調査などによって)《やや書》emerge (*from*); [反映される]《やや書》be reflected (*in*). ●『平家物語』に現れた(=見られる)仏教思想 the Buddhist ideas which *are found* in *The Tale of the Heike*. ● 流行歌に表れた世相 aspects of society *reflected in* popular songs. ▶怒りが彼の顔に表れていた His anger *showed* (*itself*) [*was written*] on his face. ▶後の言い方では on の代わりに all over も可)/His face *showed* [*expressed*, *betrayed*] his anger. (❗ *betray* は「反意に反して」を含意する) ▶彼のうっ積した不満は暴力となって現れた His pent-up dissatisfaction *was expressed* in violent actions. ▶真相は必ず現れるものだ The truth always *comes out* [*comes to light*]. ▶調査の結果, 新しい事実が現れた A new fact *came out* [*emerged*] *from* the investigation. (❗ We found out a new fact from the investigation. の方が口語的) ▶霧が晴れてすばらしい景色が現れた The mist had cleared up and we were able to get a fine view. (❗ 次例より口語的)/The mist had cleared up to *reveal* a fine view. ▶薬の効果が現れ始めた The medicine is beginning to *take effect*.
あらんかぎり あらん限り ── あらん限りの [形] every; all. (⇨ある限り)
*****あり 蟻** an ant. ● 女王アリ a queen *ant*. ● 働きアリ a worker (*ant*). ● 羽アリ a winged *ant*. ● 白アリ a termite, a white *ant*. ● 台所にアリがいっぱいいる

アリア／ありがとう

There are [《話》There's] a lot of *ants* in the kitchen./The kitchen is full of *ants*./The kitchen is crawling with *ants*. (!*crawl with* は常に進行形で用いる)

●蟻の出る隙もない ▶その会場の警備はアリには出るすきもないほどだった The hall was very closely [tightly] guarded.

アリア [<イタリア語] [《音楽》] an aria /ɑ́ːriə/.

ありあまる 有り余る be [have*] more than enough. (⇨余る❷) ●精力が有り余っている have too much [an excess of] energy. ▶彼には有り余るほどの金がある He *has* more money *than* he can spend. ▶その老婦人にはあり余るほどの機知があった The older lady *was full of* wit.

ありあり ─ ありありと 副 (生き生きと) vividly; (はっきりと) clearly. ●ありありと描写する describe《it》*vividly*; give a *vivid* description 《of it》. ▶私は彼のうれしそうな顔をありありと覚えている I remember his happy face *vividly* [*clearly*].

ありあわせ 有り合わせ ▶有り合わせの物で昼食の支度をした I fixed lunch using anything I could find [anything that was available]. ▶有り合わせの金をすべてその人にやった I gave him all the money *I had on* [*with*] *me*./I gave him all the money *in* [*on*] *hand*.

アリーナ an arena. ●アイススケートアリーナ an ice-skating *arena*.

ありうる 有り得る possible; (大いに) probable. ▶彼女が間違っていることもありうる It's *possible* (that) she is wrong. (《話》では that は省略可)/She *may* be wrong. ▶ベテランの運転手でも事故を起こすことがありうる Even expert drivers *can* cause accidents./It is *possible* for even expert drivers to cause accidents. ▶そんなことはありえないよ It's *impossible*. (真実であるはずがない) It *can't* be true. (⇨はず②)

DISCOURSE

しかし, コンピュータ化には負の影響もありうる However, computerization *may have some* negative effects. (!*some* (いくつかの)は抽象的内容を述べるディスコースマーカー. 続けて負の影響の具体的内容を述べる)

ありか 在りか ▶その宝のありか(=どこにあるか)は分からない We don't know *where* the treasure *is* (*kept*).

ありかた 在り方 ▶大学のあり方が問われる時期に来ている Now is the time to question [call into question] *what* the universities *should* (*really*) *be*.

***ありがたい** 有り難い ❶[感謝する] be grateful, be thankful, appreciate, be obliged.

使い分け be grateful 主に人の親切や好意などに対する感謝.
be thankful 漠然と自然や神に対する感謝.
appreciate be grateful とほぼ同義. 人を目的語に取らないことに注意.
be obliged 堅い丁寧な言い方で商業文に多く見られる.

●ありがたく招待を受ける accept the invitation *with gratitude*. ▶ご推薦いただき心からありがたく存じます I *am* heartily *grateful* (*to you*) *for* your recommendation [*for* recommending me, *that* you recommended me]./I really *appreciate* your recommendation. (!×*appreciate* you とはいわない) ▶ぼくは幸運をありがたく思っている I *am thankful* [×*grateful*] *for* my good fortune. ▶ありがたいことに息子は助かりました I *am thankful* [×*grateful*] *that* my son was saved./*Thankfully*, my son was saved. ▶同封した書類にサインしていただければ大変ありがたく存じます We should *be* very much *obliged* if you would sign the enclosed document. (!商業文などによく用いられる堅い言い方) ▶申し込み用紙をお送りくださればありがたいのですが I would be *grateful* [×*glad*] if you could send me an application form. (!正式な要求を伝える方が *glad* は不可) ▶ありがたい《話》Thank God [Heaven(s)]!/God be blessed. ▶そう言ってくださるのはとてもありがたい It's very *kind of you* to say so./*How kind of you to say so*! ▶そんな音を立てないでくれるとありがたいのだが I *wish* you would stop making that noise.

❷[歓迎すべき] welcome. ●ありがたいお言葉 *gracious* words. ●ありがたくない客 an *unwelcome* guest. ▶あなたの協力は実にありがたい Your help will certainly be *welcome*. ●ありがたいことに(=幸運なことに)朝になって雨はやんだ *Fortunately* [*Luckily, By good luck*], the rain stopped in the morning.

ありがたがる 有り難がる (感謝する) be grateful 《*to; to do*》, appreciate; (尊ぶ) value. (⇨有り難い) ●ありがたがられない仕事 a *thankless* job [task]. ▶日本人は肩書きをありがたがる Japanese *value* [(重んじる) *make much of*] titles.

ありがたさ 有り難さ (⇨有り難み)

ありがたなみだ 有り難涙 ▶ありがた涙を流す shed tears of *gratitude*; weep for *gratitude*.

ありがたみ 有り難み ▶健康のありがたみ(=価値)を知る know [appreciate] the *value* (恵み) *blessing*] of health. ▶母のありがたみ(=いかに母の恩恵を受けているか)が分かるようになった I've come to appreciate *how much I owe* (*to*) my mother.

ありがためいわく 有り難迷惑 ▶彼のすることはありがた迷惑だ(=不必要な行為だ) What he does is an unwanted favor [利益とりむしろ害を与える) does more harm than good].

ありがち 有りがち ── ありがちな 形 (よく起こる) frequent. ●子供にありがちな病気 diseases *common* to children. ●彼にはありがちなことだが *as is often the case with* him. ▶冬には火事がありがちだ Fires are *frequent* in winter./Fires *often* break out in winter.

***ありがとう** thank you, thanks.

解説 軽く礼を言うときは Thank you. (/ŋkju/ ぐらいになることもある)またはそれよりくだけた言い方では Thanks. を用いる. 丁寧に礼を言うときは Thank you very much., ややくだけた言い方では Thanks a lot., やや堅い言い方の Many thanks. などを用いる. 米英人は, ささいな好意や家族など親しい間柄の人に対しても気軽にお礼の言葉を述べる.

▶きれいな絵はがきを送ってくださってありがとう Thanks a lot *for* the beautiful postcard you sent me. ▶ご招待ありがとうございます *Thank you* very much *for* inviting me [*for* your kind invitation]. (!×...for *your* inviting me. とはいわない)/It's very *kind of you* to invite me. ▶先日はご協力どうもありがとうございました *Thank you* very much [*We're* really *grateful*] *for* your cooperation the other day. (!(1) 後の方は通例援助などに対して用い, 贈り物に対しては用いない. (2)手紙などでは I am writing to *thank you* [to say how *grateful* we *are*] *for*..../《書》We would like to *thank you* [to express our *gratitude*] *for*.... とする)

会話 「(ドアを開けて待っていてくれた人に対して)ありがとう」「どういたしまして」 "*Thank you./\Thanks." "《やや書》Not at \all./\That's all right./《主

ありがね

米話）\Sure./《主に米》You're ˇwelcome." (!「ありがとう」を上がり調子で）と読むと、軽いぞんざいな響きがある。また Thank ˇyou. は「こちらこそありがとう」の意)
会話「手伝いましょうか」「ちょうど終わったところです。どうもありがとう」"Can I lend you a hand?" "I've just finished. Thánks júst the ／same [Thánk you véry ˊmuch]." \Thank you. より丁寧退する場合に用いる. No, thank you. より丁寧
会話「（プレゼントを渡すときに)これはあなたに」「わあ、どうもありがとう。これ欲しかったんですよ」"This is for you." "Oh great! Thánk you véry (só) \much./Thánks a \lot./Many \thanks. This is just what I wanted." (!(1) Thank you so much. は主に女性に好まれる. (2) さらに感謝の意を強めて ...very múch. ...véry múch indéed. のようにもいう. (3) お礼の言葉の前か後ろにちょっとした感想を添える方が丁寧

ありがね 有り金 ●有り金をはたいて自転車を買う spend all the money one has [all one's money] on a bike.

ありきたりの 在り来たりの 〚ありふれた〛common;〚普通の〛ordinary;〚陳腐な〛commonplace, hackneyed;〚型にはまった〛conventional. ●ありきたりの出来事 a common event.

ありくい 蟻食い 〚動物〛an anteater.

-ありげ -有り気 ●意味ありそうな様子でジムを見る cast a meaningful glance at Jim; glance meaningfully at Jim. ●彼は自信ありげなそぶりをしていた He looked confident.

アリゲーター 〚動物〛an álligàtor.

ありさま 有り様 〚状態〛a state, (a) condition;〚光景〛a sight. ●その村は悲惨なありさまだ The village is in a terrible state [condition]./Conditions [×States] in the village are terrible in the village. ●ありさまは何だ What's all this?/(人の苦境などに驚いて) What a state [a plight] you are in!/(乱雑さに驚いて) What a mess!

ありじごく 蟻地獄 〚昆虫〛(幼虫) a doodlebug; (成虫) an ant lion.

ありしひ 在りし日 ●在りし日(=過ぎ去った日)の楽しい思い出に生きる live on the happy memories of past [old] days. ●この写真を見ると在りし日(=生前)の母を思い出す This picture reminds me of my dead mother.

アリストテレス 〚古代ギリシャの哲学者〛Aristotle /ǽrəstɑ̀tl/.

ありそう(な) 有りそう(な) 〚十中八九ありそうな〛probable (↔improbable) 〚強調する副詞など〛quite, highly, most など); 〚十中五六ありそうな〛likely (↔unlikely). ●事故の最もありそうな原因 the most probable [likely] cause of an accident. ●ありそうな話 a likely 〚信じられる〛a believable] story. (! 前の方は語尾を上げぎみに読むと反語的に「怪しい話だ」の意になる) ●土地の値上がりがまたありそうだ It is probable [likely] that land prices will rise again./Land prices are likely [×probable] to rise again./Probably [Quite likely, ×Likely] land prices will rise again. (! この表現は通例 quite, most, very などの修飾を受け、単独では用いない) ●それはありそうなことだ That's a probability.

アリゾナ 〚米国の州〛Arizona /ærəzóunə/《略 Ariz. 郵便略 AZ》.

ありだか 有り高 〚現在の総量・総額〛amount in [on] hand, balance in hand.

ありたやき 有田焼き Arita ware [porcelain].

ありづか 蟻塚 an anthill.

ありつく 有り付く 〚見つける〛find*;〚手に入れる〛get*; ●長いこさがしてやっと仕事にありついた I found [got, (勝ち取る)《話》landed] a job after a long hunt. ●10時にようやく朝食にありついた I finally [At last I] got breakfast at ten. (! 後の方が強意的)

ありったけ 有りったけ ●ありったけの力を出す use 〚(やや書)〛exert] all one's strength. ●ありったけの声で叫ぶ shout at the top of one's voice (! 何人もの声を voices と表す場合 top は top あるいは tops となる); shout as loudly as possible.

ありてい 有体 ●ありていに言えば (率直に言えば) frankly (speaking), to be frank with you; (ぶっきらぼうに言えば) to put it bluntly.

ありとあらゆる 有りと有らゆる ●ありとあらゆる(種類の)人間 all kinds [sorts] of people; people of all kinds [sorts]. ●ありとあらゆる(=可能な限りすべての)方法を用いる use every possible method; leave no stone unturned (in a search for ...) (!「石を一つ一つ裏返して捜す」の意)

ありなし 有り無し (⇨有る無し)

＊ありのまま ── ありのままの 形 〚実体どおりの〛as A be (! A は先行する語またはその代名詞);〚飾らない〛plain, bare. ●日本のありのままの姿 Japan as it is; the true picture of Japan. ●彼にありのままの事実を述べる give him a plain [a bare] fact.

── **ありのままに 副** ●as A be;〚率直に〛frankly, plainly;〚正直に〛honestly. ●物事をありのままに見る see things as they are. ●ありのままに言えば to tell the truth; to be frank (with you); frankly speaking. ●その事件をありのままに報告する give an honest [a straightforward] account of the accident.

アリバイ 〚<ラテン語〛〚現場不在証明〛an álibi. ●完璧なアリバイ a perfect [a cast-iron] alibi. ●アリバイを作る〚でっちあげる; 崩す〛make [fake,《話》cook up; break, disprove] an alibi. ●アリバイを立証する prove (to have) an alibi; establish an alibi. ●彼にはその夜のアリバイがない [ある] He has no [an] alibi for the night.

ありふれた 〚普通に見かける〛common;〚よく見聞きされる〛familiar;〚日常の〛everyday;〚ありきたりの〛commonplace (! しばしばけなして). ●日常ありふれた出来事 common 〚everyday, ×every day] events. ●ありふれた映画の筋 a common plot of a movie. ●これは日本ではよくありふれた花です This is a very common flower in Japan. ●ホームレスは近ごろはごくありふれたものとなった Nowadays homeless people have become a very [an all too] familiar sight. (! 後の方は悪い状況に用いる)

ありまき 蟻巻 〚昆虫〛a plant louse, an aphid.

ありもしない 有りもしない ●ありもしない(=でたらめの)話をする tell a false 〚(架空の) a make-believe] story; (話をでっちあげる) make up [invent] a story.

ありゅう 亜流 (まねをする人) an imitator,《話》a copycat; (追随者) a follower.

ありゅうさんガス 亜硫酸ガス súlfur dióxide.

アリューシャン ●アリューシャン列島 the Aleutians /əlúːʃənz/; the Aleutian Island.

ある 在る, 有る   **INDEX**

❶ 存在する   ❷ 位置する
❸ 持っている   ❹ 数量が...ある
❺ 起こる, 行われる ❻ 手に入る
❼ 経験がある   ❽ 含まれている
❾ ...に存する

ある

❶ **[存在する]** (…がある) there is [are], be; (捜せば見つかる) be found; (現存する) exist.

解説 there is [are] の構文について
(1) 通例 there is [話]there's は /ðərz/, there are は /ðərər/ と読む。
(2) there is [are] は聞き手に対して新しい情報を伝える言い方で、後には通例不定名詞(句)がきて、the, this, my などを伴った特定的な名詞(句)はこない。
(3) there の後には、be 以外に exist, lie, live, remain, stand; arrive, come, go; happen, occur; appear, seem などの存在, 往来, 出来事, 状態を表す自動詞がくることもある。ただし通例肯定文に限られる。

▶テーブルの上にリンゴがある (一つ) *There is* [[話]*There's*] an apple on the table./(複数) *There are* [[話]*There're*] some apples on the table. (❗(1) この用法の there には「そこ」という場所の意味はない。「そこに」の意を表したいときは There's an apple [There are some apples] *there* /ðéər/. とする。(2) この場合 An apple is [Some apples are] on the table. は不自然) ▶1年は12か月ある *There are* twelve months in a year./A year *has* twelve months. ▶何か冷たい飲み物がありますか *Is there* [*Do* you *have*] anything cold to drink [any cold drinks]? ▶そのことについていくぶん疑いがあるようだ *There* seems [appears] to *be* some doubt about it. ▶昔かの丘の上に城があった *There* used to *be* a castle on that hill. ▶そんな習慣が世の中にあるとは思えない I don't believe (that) such a custom *exists* [*is found*] in the world.
会話 「木の下に何がありますか」「大きなベンチがあります」 "What *is* [×*are*] under the tree?" "A big bench (*is*)." (❗(1) この場合 *There is* a big bench …. は不自然。(2) 答えの文は は [話] では通例省略される)/"What *is* [×*are*] *there* under the tree?" "*There's* a big bench."
会話 「このリンゴはどれも甘いの?」「すっぱいのもあるよ」 "Are all these apples sweet?" "Some of them *are* sour /sáuər/." ▶この be 動詞は連結動詞で「…である」の意)

❷ **[位置する]** be, [書]be located [situated]; (建物などが) stand*; (家・都市・島などが) [やや書] lie*.
▶(その)鍵はテーブルの上にあった The key *was* on the table. (❗×There was the key on the table. とはいわない (⇨解説))/I *found* [*saw*] the key on the table. ▶私たちの学校は丘の上にある Our school *is* [*stands*, ×*is standing*] on the hill. (❗(1) 特に堂々とした建物であることを強調する場合を除いて is が普通。(2) 主語が移動可能で一時的に存在しているものであれば is standing 可: The bookcase *was standing* in the middle of the hall.) ▶その市は信濃川の西方にある The city *lies* [*is located*, *is situated*] (to the) west of the Shinano River.

❸ **[持っている]** have*, [話]have got, [書]possess. (⇨持つ) ▶ある限りの力を尽くす (⇨ある限り) ▶金はあればあるほど欲しくなる The more money we *have*, the more we want. ▶君に話したいことが山ほどある I *have* [*I've got*] a lot of things to tell you. ▶はがきと切手はありますか Do you *have* postcards and stamps? (❗店員に聞く場合は have の代わりに keep, carry, sell なども可) ▶彼にはたぐいまれな才能がある He *has* [*possesses*] incomparable talents./(授かっている) He *is gifted with* matchless [rare] talents.

❹ **[数量が…ある]** (重さが) weigh; (高さ・幅が) be; (長さ・大きさが) measure; (数が) number; (面積が) cover. ▶あなたの体重はどれくらいありますか How much [What] do you *weigh*?/What is your weight? ▶その橋は幅が11メートル長さが50メートルあります The bridge *is* 11 meters wide and 50 meters long. (❗is の代わりに measures も可) ▶英語のテストで君の間違いは全部で10あった Your errors in the English test *numbered* ten in all./*There were* ten errors in all in your English test. ▶その部屋は5平方メートルある The room *covers* [*measures*] five square meters [16.4 square feet].

❺ **[起こる, 行われる]** (偶然に起こる) happen, (生じる) [やや書] occur (-rr-); (行事などが行われる) take* place (⇨起こる), (開催される) be held, (会合・授業などが) meet*; (理論的にありうる) can* (*do*) (⇨有り得る). ▶昨夜近所で火事があった A fire *broke out* [*occurred*, ×*happened*] in my neighborhood last night./*There was* a fire last night in my neighborhood. ▶よくあることだ It could *happen* to anyone./It's the kind of thing that *happens* every day./It's just one of those things./It's an everyday occurrence. ▶正直が割に合わないことがよくあります It *often happens that* honesty doesn't pay. ▶例の音楽会はあしたある We'll *have* the concert tomorrow./The concert will *be held* tomorrow. ▶きのう取締役会があって, 彼が副社長に選ばれた The board of directors *met* yesterday and they chose him Vice-President. (❗they に注意) ▶そんなことがあるだろうか How *can* that *be*?/That's impossible. ▶当地では4月でもとても寒いことがある It *can be* very cold here even in April. ▶今日は4時間授業がある I *have* four classes today. ▶勝つこともあれば負けることもある *Sometimes* you win and *sometimes* you lose. ▶よくあるミスだ It is a *common* mistake.

❻ **[手に入る]** 《物が主語》 be got; (捜した結果見つけ出される) be found. ▶その本は丸善にあるよ You can get [*find*] the book at Maruzen's. ▶確かこのあたりに眼鏡を置いたんだ。あっ, あった I know I put [left] my glasses somewhere around here. Oh, I've *got* them.
会話 「ここにはよく来るの?」「機会がある度にね」 "Do you come here often?" "Every chance I *get*."

❼ **[経験がある]** ▶私はあの人に会ったことがある I've *met* him./I *have séen* him ＼*once*./I once ＼*saw* him. (❗前の once は「一度」, 後の once は無強勢で読み「昔, かつて」の意。ever を肯定文で用いて ×I have *ever* seen him once. とはいわない)
会話 「今までにアメリカへ行ったことがありますか」「はい, 一度あります [いいえ, 一度もありません]」 "*Have* you (*ever*) *been* [[米話]*Have* you *gone*] to America?" "Yes, (I have) once [No, never]."/"*Did* you *ever go* to America?" "Yes, (I did) once [No, never]."

❽ **[含まれている]** (成分として) be contained; (部分として) be included. ▶レモンにはビタミンCがたくさんある A lemon *contains* [×*includes*] a lot of vitamin C. ▶受験科目の中に英語がある English *is included* [×*is contained*] in the subjects of the examination.

❾ **[…に存する]** (本質的に) lie* [書] consist in …; (選択・決定などが) [書] rest with …. ▶人の価値は財産よりも人物にある A man's worth *lies* not so much *in* what he has as *in* what he is. ▶非は君にある It *is* you who [that] is to blame for it.

*ある 或る

certain; some /sʌ́m/; (一つの, 一人の) a, an; one (❗a, an より数を強調する); [(過去の時をさし

|解説| **certain** は分かってはいるが、はっきり言うのを避ける場合に用いる。**some** と不定冠詞 **a, an** は通例よく分からない場合に用い、単数可算名詞の前に置く。ただし、この some は通例 /sʌm/ と強勢が置かれ、話し手の無関心・軽蔑などを暗示することがあるため、堅い文脈では避けた方がよい。

▶彼とはある距離を置いている I keep him at *a distance*. ▶私はそれをいつもある所にしまっている I always keep that in a *certain* place. ▶ある人から電話があったよ *Some* man phoned you. ▶彼の話はある程度信用している I believe him to *some* [*a certain*] extent. ▶5月のある日[夜;日曜日;朝早く]彼は旅行に出かけた He set out on a trip *one* day [*one* evening; on *a* Sunday; early *one* morning] in May.

***あるいは** 接 ❶ [[または]]... or ...; (どちらか) either ... or ...; (...かどうか) whether ... or ... (⇨または) ▶彼がそう言ったかあるいは私の聞き違いかです He said so *or* I heard it wrong. (❗ wrong は「誤って」の意の副詞。この場合 wrongly は不可) ▶出かけますかあるいはやめますか Are you going out *or* not? ▶試験は来年の5月か6月、あるいは7月に行われます The examination will take place in May, June(,) *or* July next year. (❗ 最後に *or* を置く。コンマの有無は任意) ▶彼は私に賛成なのかあるいは反対なのか分からない I don't know *whether* he agrees with me (*or* not). (❗ (1) 間接疑問文では通例 or not を省略する。(2) whether 節が長い場合は or not を whether の直後に置くのが普通だがやや堅い言い方)

❷ [[一部は...また一部は...]] some ... and some ...; some ... and others ...; (⇨または) ▶人々は北海道から、あるいは九州から来ていた *Some* (people) were from Hokkaido *and some* [*others*] were from Kyushu.

—**あるいは** 副 [[もしかすると]] perhaps, maybe (❗ 後の方がくだけた語); [[ひょっとすると]] possibly; [[たぶん]] probably. (⇨もしかすると) ▶あるいは今日その店は休みかもしれない *Possibly* [*Perhaps, Probably*] the store is closed today. (❗ 話し手の確信の度合いは後の方ほど強くなる)

あるおんな『或る女』*A Certain Woman*. (参考 有島武郎の小説)

アルカイダ [[イスラム原理主義の過激派集団]] al Qaeda, Al Qaida /ǽlkáidə/.

あるかぎり ある限り ●ある限りの力を尽くす do [try] one's very best; (あらゆる手段を尽くす) try *all [every]* possible means. ●力のある限り to the best of one's power [ability]. ●命のある限り as long as one lives. (⇨有りったけ)

あるかせる 歩かせる walk. ●犬を歩かせる(=散歩させる) *walk* a dog. ●人を散歩に連れて行く take a dog for a walk の方が普通。●打者を四球で歩かせる *walk* a batter.

あるかなし 有るか無し few [little] or no; (あってもわずか) few [little], if any. ●有るか無いかの頭髪 *very thin* hair. ●間違いが有るか無いか There are *few*, *if any*, mistakes./There are *very few* [*hardly any*] mistakes.

あるがまま (⇨ありのまま)

アルカリ alkali /ǽlkəlài/.
●アルカリ性 alkalinity /ælkəlínəti/. アルカリ性の alkaline /ǽlkəlàin/. アルカリ電池 an alkaline cell.

アルカロイド [[植物塩基]] an álkaloid.

あるきまわる 歩き回る walk around [((主に英)) about]. ●部屋の中を歩き回る(=行ったり来たりする) *walk up and down* the room. ●世界中を歩き回る (=旅する) *travel around* [*all over*] the world. ▶彼はあちこち歩き回っていた He *was walking around* [*about*] here and there. ▶彼は息子を捜して町中を歩き回った He *walked around* (*in*) the town looking for his son. (❗ in を省略すると目的を持って歩き回る含みが強くなる)/He *walked* the streets looking for his son. (❗ 複数形に注意。受身は通例不可) ▶1,2 週間すればベッドを離れて歩き回れるようになりますよ You'll *be up and around* in a week or two.

アルキメデス [[古代ギリシャの数学者・物理学者]] Archimedes /ɑ̀ːrkəmíːdiːz/.

***あるく 歩く**

◨ WORD CHOICE ◨ **歩く**
walk 「歩く」の意の最も一般的な語. しばしば場所・方向を表す前置詞・副詞と共起する. ▶駅まで歩く *walk* to the station.
[[walk＋前 副]] out/in/to/away/into/on/up/through
step 短い距離を歩くこと. 特に、苦労して一歩を踏み出したり、慎重にゆっくり歩いたりする場合、一歩一歩の動きを意識する場合に用いる. ▶部屋の中に足を踏み入れる (=一歩歩いて部屋に入る) *step* into the room.
[[step＋前 副]] in/into/onto/back/forward
go on foot 移動手段として電車や乗り物を使わず「徒歩で行く」こと. go の代わりに move なども用いる. ▶数千人が公園まで歩いて移動した Thousands *moved on foot* to the park.

◨ 頻度チャート ◨
walk ██████████
step ████████
go on foot █

20 40 60 80 100 (%)

walk; (乗り物に乗らずに徒歩で) go* *on foot*; (短い距離をまたはある足取りで) step (-pp-). ●(走っていて)歩き出す drop [fall] into a *walk*; slow (down) to a *walk*. ●ストレートのフォアボールで歩く [野球] *walk* on four pitches.

① [[副＋歩く]] ●軽い足取りで歩く *walk* with light steps; *step* lightly. (❗ walk lightly は「さっと歩く」の意) ●3マイル歩く *walk* (*for*) three miles. (❗ for があれば「(全行程のうち) 3 マイルは」の意で歩くことで、なければ「(2 マイルでなく) 3 マイル」の意で距離に重点がある。したがって walk a mile in twenty minutes では for は用いない) ●はって歩く go [×walk] on one's hands and knees [on all fours]. (❗ 足を使わない移動には walk は用いない) ▶もう一歩も[これ以上は]歩けない I can't *walk* a step further [any further].

|関連| 大または歩く stride/足をひきずって歩く drag oneself/どしどしん歩く tramp/(疲れ果てて)とぼとぼ歩く plod; trudge/よたよた歩く totter/よちよち歩く toddle/よろめきながら歩く stagger/忍び足で歩く tiptoe/小走りに歩く trot/ふんぞり返って歩く strut.

② [[...を[に] 歩く]] ●通りを歩く *walk along* [*on*] the street. (❗ (1) along は「一方向に向かって」, on は「(芝生などでなく)道の上を」の意。(2) along の代わりに、話し手の関心の中心への移動には up, その逆では down を用いる) (3) 長時間または行ったり来たりで規則的に歩くときは walk the street(s) も可) (⇨歩き回る) ▶川沿いに歩く *walk along* a river.

●泥んこ道を歩く walk on [《書》tread] a muddy road. ●公園をぶらぶら歩こうよ Let's *stroll* [*take a stroll*] *in* the park. ③[歩いて] ●学校へ歩いて行く walk to school; go to school *on foot*. (!)後の方はバスなどでなく歩きでという他の手段との対照を明確にする場合に用いる) ●歩いて帰る walk home. ●通りを歩いて渡る walk across the street. ●大学に歩いて通える範囲内でアパートをさがす look for an apartment within *walking* distance of the college. ▶私の家から公園までは歩いて5分です It's five minutes' [a five(-) minute] *walk* from my house to the park. (!) *a* five minutes' walk は避けた方がよい. 公園を主語にして The park is ... from my house. のようにもいえる)/It takes five minutes to *walk* from my house to the park.

会話 「駅はここから遠いですか」「いいえ、歩いて行けますよ」"Is the station far from here?" "No, you can *walk* from here." (!)逆に「歩けばかなりありますよ」は "It'd be a good walk." のようにいう)

アルコール alcohol /ǽlkəhɔ(ː)l/; [酒類] alcoholic drinks, alcohol. (⇨酒) ●エチル[メチル]アルコール ethyl [methyl] *alcohol*. ●蒸留アルコール *distilled alcohol*. ●アルコール分 *alcoholic* content. ●アルコール度 alcoholicity. ●アルコール度数の低いビール low *alcohol* beer. ●アルコールを含まない飲物 non*alcoholic* drinks. ●アルコール抜きのパーティー a dry party; a party where no *alcoholic drinks* are served. ▶彼はアルコール類はいっさい口にしない He never has a *drink* [drinks (*alcohol*)]. (!) alcohol を省略する方が普通)/He never touches *alcohol* [*alcoholic drinks*, 《話》*the stuff*]. (!) the stuff は文脈から明らかな場合に用いる) ▶この軟膏にはアルコールは含まれていない This ointment has [contains] no *alcohol*.

●アルコール依存症 alcohol dependence. ●アルコール中毒者 (⇨アル中) ●アルコールランプ a spirit lamp. (!)×an alcohol lamp とはいわない)

アルゴリズム [数学・コンピュータ] algorithm.

あるじ 主 (⇨主人)

アルジェリア [国名] Algeria /ældʒíəriə/; (公式名) the People's Democratic Republic of Algeria. (首都 Algiers) ●アルジェリア人 an Algerian. ●アルジェリア(人)の Algérian.

あるしゅの ある種の ●ある種の道具 some kind [sort] *of* tool; a tool of *some kind* [*sort*]. (⇨種類)

アルゼンチン [国名] Argentina /ɑ̀ːrdʒəntíːnə/; (公式名) the Argentine /ɑ́ːrdʒəntàin/ Republic. (首都 Buenos Aires) ●アルゼンチン人 an Argentine. ●アルゼンチン(人)の Argentine.

アルちゅう アル中 [アルコール中毒] (中毒症) alcoholism; alcoholic poisoning; (婉曲的) (have) a drinking problem; (患者) an alcoholic; (婉曲的) a problem drinker.

アルツハイマー [医学] Álzhèimer's (disèase). (参考) 今は認知症という (⇨認知症) ▶彼はアルツハイマーにかかっている He has Alzheimer's.

アルデヒド [化学] aldehyde /ǽldəhàid/.

アルデンテ [<イタリア語] al dente. (参考) 歯ごたえのある食感)

アルト [<イタリア語] [音楽] alto /ǽltou/. ●アルトで[に]歌う sing *alto*. ●アルト歌手 an alto; an alto singer. ●アルトサックス an alto saxophone [《話》sax]. (⇨サキソホ(ー)ン)

あるときばらい ある時払い ▶ある時払い(の催促なし)でいいよ You can pay me *when* you *have* cash *in* hand [*at your convenience*].

あるなし 有る無し ▶能力の有る無しにかかわらずその仕事はやらなければならない You must do the job *whether* you are competent *or not*.

アルバイト [<ドイツ語] 图 (時間制の) a part-time job; (副業) a job on the side. (!)×a side job とはいわない) ●アルバイトの女子店員 a *part-time* shopgirl. ●アルバイト学生 a working student. ▶かつて、多くの大学生の生活がアルバイトなしでは成り立たない時代があった There was a time when many college [university] students could not survive without a *part-time job* [had to work *part-time* in order to survive].

── **アルバイト(を)する** 動 ▶彼はこの夏休みの間ウェーターのアルバイトをした He worked part-time [*had a part-time job*] as a waiter during this summer vacation.

アルパカ [動物] (an) alpaca /ælpǽkə/. (!)毛織物は U)

アルバトロス [ゴルフ] an albatross /ǽlbətrɔːs/, a double eagle. (参考) 基準打数より3打少なくホールアウトすること)

アルバニア [国名] Albania /ælbéiniə/; (公式名) the Republic of Albania. (首都 Tirana) ●アルバニア人 an Albanian. ●アルバニア語 Albanian. ●アルバニア(人[語])の Albanian.

アルバム an album. (レコード、CDなどを含む) ●写真アルバム a photo(graph) *album*. ●結婚式のアルバム a wedding *album*. ▶この写真をアルバムに入れておいて Put these pictures in the *album*.

アルハンブラ ●アルハンブラ宮殿 the Alhambra /ælhǽmbrə/.

アルピニスト [登山家] a mountaineer; [アルプスに登る人] an Alpinist /ǽlpənist/.

アルファ ❶ [ギリシャ文字] (an) alpha, α, A. ❷ [少しの上乗せ] ▶3万円プラスアルファの昇給を要求する demand a raise of 30,000 yen *plus something* (*extra*). (!) ×plus alpha は和製英語) ●アルファ線 [物理] an alpha ray.

アルファベット the alphabet. ●アルファベット順に alphabetically; in alphabetical order [sequence].

アルファルファ [植物] alfálfa.

アルプス the Alps. ●アルプスの Alpine. ●日本アルプス the Japan *Alps*. ▶アルプス山脈はヨーロッパで最も高い山脈です *The Alps* are the highest mountains in Europe.

アルプススタンド [和製語] the Alps stand; (説明的に) the stands between the infield stands and the bleachers at Koshien Stadium.

アルブミン [生化学] albumin /ælbjúːmən/. (参考) たんぱく質の一種)

あるべき ●教師のあるべき姿 what a teacher *should be*; a teacher as he [she] *should be*.

アルペジオ [<イタリア語] [音楽] an arpeggio.

アルペン [<ドイツ語] alpine /ǽlpàin/. ●アルペン種目 Alpine events. (参考) downhill (滑降), (giant) slalom ((大)回転)などで構成される) ●アルペンスキー alpine skiing. ●アルペンホルン an álpenhòrn.

アルマイト anodized aluminum. (!) Alumite は日本の商標名)

あるまじき ●彼の行為は教師にはあるまじきものだった His behavior was *not becoming for* [*unworthy of*] a teacher./It was *not becoming* behavior for a teacher.

アルマジロ [動物] an àrmadíllo. (複 ~s).

アルミ(ニウム) aluminum /əlúːmənəm/. 《元素記号 Al》.

●アルミ合金 (an) aluminum alloy. ●アルミサッシ an aluminum sash. ●アルミ箔(はく) (a piece of) aluminum foil.

アルメニア 〖国名〗Armenia /ɑːrmíːniə/; (公式名) the Republic of Armenia. (首都 Yerevan) ▶アルメニア人 an Armenian. ●アルメニア語 Armenian. ●アルメニア(人[語])の Armenian.

アルルのおんな『アルルの女』 *The Girl from Arles* /áːrl/. 〖参考〗(1) ドーデの戯曲. (2) ビゼーの管弦楽曲

あれ 〘代〙〖あの物, あの人, あの事〙that (複 those); 〖あの時〙then ▶〘これ〙これとあれとどちらが好きですか Which do you prefer, this one or *that* one [this (stuff) or *that*]? (❗前の方は可算名詞, 後の方は不可算名詞を示す) ▶あれは 2 年前の今日のことでした *That* was two years ago today. ▶あれから(=あの時以来)ずっとここに住んでいます I have lived here since *then* [*ever* since].

会話「あれは彼の本ですか」「そうです」"Is *that* his book?" "Yes, it is."/〘複数〙"Are *those* his books?" "Yes, they are." (❗ that は it, these は they で受ける. ×Yes, that is [those are]. とは通例いわない)

会話「あれはだれ?」「健だよ」"Who's *that*?" "It's [×He's] Ken." (❗that [those] を単独で人に用いるのは主語の場合に限る)

あれ 〘感〙〖注意喚起〙look, listen (⇨あっ); 〖驚き・困惑など〙oh; well; (oh) dear; 〖意外さ〙〘主に米〙why ▶〘まあ〙あれ, 鐘が鳴っている ↘*There* goes the ↗*bell*! (❗there は *that* と読み, 聞き手の注意を促す. 主語が代名詞の場合を除いて通例倒置構文となる. また進行形でないことに注意)

あれあれ (⇨あれ, ほら)

あれい 亜鈴 a dumbbell. ●a pair of dumbbells で一対) ●鉄アレイ an iron dumbbel.

アレキサンダー ●アレキサンダー大王 〖マケドニアの王〗Alexander /ǽligzændər/ the Great.

アレキサンドリア 〖エジプトの都市〗Alexandria /æligzǽndriə/.

あれきり since; since then [that time]. (⇨以来, それっきり) ▶あれきり彼女から便りがない I haven't heard from her *since then*. (あの時が便りがきた最後だった) That was *the last time* I heard from her.

あれくるう 荒れ狂う (人・風・波・戦争・病気などが) rage. (⇨荒れる) ▶風の荒れ狂う音 the *roar* of the wind. ▶海〖あらし〗は何日も荒れ狂った The sea [The storm] *raged* for many days. ▶今晩は風が荒れ狂っている The wind is *wild* tonight.

アレグロ 〖イタリア語〗〖軽快に速く〗〖音楽〗allegro /əléɡroʊ/.

あれこれ this and that; this, that and the other. ●あれこれ考える turn 〘it〙over in one's mind. ▶私たちは夜遅くまであれこれとしたをした We talked about *this and that* [×*that and this*] until late at night.

あれしき ▶あれしきの(=あんなつまらない)ことでめそめそする Stop crying over a *small* [a *trifle*] thing *like that*.

あれしょう 荒れ性 ●荒れ性の(=かさつような)肌 *dry* [(かさがさの) *rough*] skin. ▶私, ひどい荒れ性なんです I have very *dry* skin.

あれた 荒れた (⇨荒れる)

あれだけ (⇨あれほど)

あれち 荒れ地 (a) wasteland; (不毛の地) barren land, (土に書) a waste. (いずれもしばしば複数形で広がりを強調) ●荒れ地になっては lie *waste*.

あれっきり (⇨あれきり)

あれっぽっち ▶あれっぽっちの金では家は建てられない We cannot build a house with *so little* money [*such a small amount of* money].

あれで ▶あれでよくあの仕事が務まるものだ I wonder why people think he is equal to the job.

あれでは ▶あれでは(=それが事実なら)彼は死刑を免れない よ *If that is the case*, he cannot escape the death penalty.

あれでも 彼女はあれでも(=自分なりに)幸せなんだ She is happy *in her own way*.

あれの 荒れ野 the wilds. (⇨荒野(こうや))

あれはてる 荒れ果てる fall* into ruin. (⇨荒れる ❷) ●荒れ果てた古い建物 a *ruined* old building. ●荒れ果てた人心 the moral *decay* of the people.

あれほうだい 荒れ放題 ▶その家は荒れ放題になっている The house is *utterly neglected*.

あれほど 〖そんなに〗so (❗通例形容詞・副詞の前で (⇨ど)); such (❗通例形容詞を伴う名詞または程度を表す名詞の前で) ▶彼はあれほど勉強したのに入試に失敗した Though he worked *so* [×*such*] hard, he failed the entrance exam. ▶あれほどの人物はいない I have never seen *such* a great man *as that* [*he is*]. (❗... seen a great man *like that*. の方が口語的)/He is the greatest man [that] I have ever seen. ▶あれほど忠告したのに彼は私の言うことを聞かなかった He didn't listen to me in spite of [〖書〗despite] all my advice.

あれもよう 荒れ模様 stormy [rough] weather. ▶空は荒れ模様だ The sky looks *stormy*. ▶その会合はかなり荒れ模様だった The meeting was rather *stormy*.

あれやこれや 〖さまざまなこと〗〘話〙this and that (あれこれ); 〖さまざまな理由で〗〘話〙(what) with one thing and another (❗通例文頭で). ▶あれやこれやで昼食を食べるひまがなかった What with one thing and *another*, I had no time to have lunch.

あれよあれよ ▶あれよあれよという間に before [under] one's (very) eyes; before one knew what to do [what was happening]. ▶そのビルはあれよあれよという間に崩壊し, 跡形もなくなった The building collapsed *before our eyes* and crumbled to pieces at the bottom of the foundation.

あれる 荒れる ❶〖天候が〗be stormy; 〖海が〗be rough, be wild. (⇨荒れ狂う) ▶今日は天気がたいへん荒れている It is very *stormy* today. ▶海が荒れている The sea *is rough* [*wild*]. (❗「荒れた海」は a *rough* [a *wild*] sea)

❷〖荒廃する〗(土地が) lie* waste; (建物などが) fall* into ruin, be ruined. ▶荒れた(=ほったらかしの)庭 a *neglected* garden. ▶その空き地は荒れている The vacant land *lies waste*. ▶彼は建物を荒れるに任せた He let the building *fall into ruin* [*go to ruin*, *go to rack and ruin*]. (❗最後は慣用表現) ▶庭が激しい風で荒れてしまった The garden *was ruined* by the stormy wind. ▶その建物はすっかり荒れていた The building *was* [*lay*] *in ruins*.

❸〖皮膚が〗(ざらざらになる) become* [get*] rough. ▶家事をするので彼女の手は荒れてしまった Her hands *have become rough* from housework./ Housework *has roughened* her hands.

❹〖精神状態・行動が〗●荒れた生活を送る lead a *wild* life. ▶上司は今日は荒れている(=機嫌が悪い) Our boss is *in a bad temper* today. ▶彼は飲めば飲むほど荒れた(=乱暴になった) The more he drank, the *wilder* he grew. ▶きのうの組合の会合はたいへん荒れた Yesterday's union meeting *was rather stormy* /(収拾がつかなくなった) *got out of control*].

アレルギー an allergy /ǽlərdʒi/ 〘to〙. ●アレルギー専門医 an *allergy* specialist. ●その薬にアレルギー反応を

起こす have an *allergic* /ələ́ːrdʒik/ reaction to the medicine. ▶私は花粉アレルギー(の体質)です I am *allergic* [have an *allergy*] *to* pollens. ▶彼は数学アレルギーだ《おどけて》He's *allergic to* math《米》[maths《英》].

アレルゲン〖アレルギー起因物質〗(an) allergen /ǽlərdʒən/. ▶気管支喘息のアレルゲンにはスギ花粉, ハウスダスト, 動物の毛などがある Among the allergens that cause bronchial asthma are such things as cedar pollen, house dust, and the hair of some animals.

アレンジ图 (an) arrangement. ▶この曲はアレンジが実によい The *arrangement* of this song is very good.
— **アレンジする**動 ●交響曲をピアノ用にアレンジする *arrange* [*rewrite*] a symphony *for* (playing on) the piano. ▶バッハのアリアをジャズ[ポピュラー]風にアレンジする make [work out] a jazz [a popular] *arrangement* of a Bach aria /άːriə/.

あろうことか あろうことか彼は10代で死んだ *Quite unexpectedly* he died in his teens.

アロエ〖植物〗an aloe /ǽlou/.
アロハシャツ an aloha /əlóuhα:/ shirt.
アロマテラピー〖芳香療法〗aròmathérapy.

*****あわ 泡** foam (! foam は a bubble の集合体で常に Ⓤ); (ビールなどの)foam; (石けんの泡)lather, (soap) suds; (気泡)a bubble (!通例複数形で). ▶海面の泡 the *foam* on the sea. ●ビールの泡 the *foam* [*froth*] (on a glass) of beer. ▶牛乳の泡 *froth* の方が口語的). ●泡立て器(⇨泡立て器) ●ひと泡吹かせる(⇨一泡(成句)) ▶川面には泡が一面に浮かんでいた The surface of the river was covered with *foam*. ▶泡のよく立ったビールがほしい I'd like a *foamy* [*frothy*] glass of beer. ▶このシャンプーはよく泡が立つ This shampoo *lathers* well. ▶ビール[シャンペン]をグラスに注ぐと泡が立った The beer *foamed* [The champagne *bubbled*] in the glass as it was poured. ▶彼は口から泡を吹いている He's *running* [*foaming*] at the mouth.

●**泡を食う**(驚き慌てる) be upset; (慌てふためく) panic, get into panic. ▶ちょっと脅しただけなのに彼は泡を食って逃げていった I only threatened him a little, but he *panicked* and ran away.

あわ 粟〖植物〗millet.
あわい 淡い 〖色が薄い〗pale, light; 〖かすかな〗faint, slight. ●淡い期待 a *faint* [a *slight*] hope. ●淡い恋心 a *faint* feeling of love. ▶淡い月光を浴びて木は銀色に見えた The tree looked silvery in the *pale* moonlight.

> **翻訳のこころ** 玄関の縦長の窓からこぼれる明かりが, いかめしい感じのする広い玄関ホールを淡く照らしていた (村上春樹『レキシントンの幽霊』) The light through the tall window of [above] the entrance softly illuminated [lit] the large forbidding(-looking) entrance hall. (! (1) above the entrance は, 窓が玄関の高いところにある場合。(2) illuminate は「暗いところを照らす」の意)

あわせ 袷 a lined *kimono*.
あわせかがみ 合わせ鏡 ●合わせ鏡をする see one's back figure in two mirrors set against each other.
あわせず 合わせ酢 blended vinegar.
あわせて 合わせて, 併せて (全部で) in all, altogether (⇨合わせる) ; (同時に) and. ▶新年おめでとう. あわせてご多幸を祈ります A Happy New Year! *And* Best Wishes to All of You!
あわせめ 合わせ目 (継ぎ目) a joint; (縫い目) a seam.

あわせもつ 併せ持つ ●長所と短所を併せ持つ *have both* good points *and* weak points. ▶この車はスピードと安全性を併せ持っている(=兼ね備えている) This car *combines* speed *with* safety.

‡あわせる 合わせる, 併せる ❶ 〖合する〗(重ね合わせる) put ... together; (結合させる) join, combine, unite (! combine は緊密性, unite は一体化を強調する。いずれも join より堅い語); (混ぜ合わせる) merge. ●手を合わせる put [join] one's hands *together*; (指を組み合わせて) clasp one's hands 類語 しばしば祈り・絶望・感動などのしぐさ). ●力を合わせる join forces; *combine* (forces). ●(努力を結集する) *unite* [*combine*] one's efforts《with》. ●声を合わせて助けてと叫ぶ cry for help *in one voice*. ●声を合わせて歌う sing *in chorus*. ●心を合わせて(=結束して)働く work together *united* [*in agreement*]; 《やや書》 work *with one accord*. ▶彼は両党を併せて新党を結成した He *united* [*combined*] the two parties *into* a new one. ▶日本の人口はイギリスとフランスを合わせたより多い Japan's population is larger than that of Britain and France *put together* [*combined*].

❷ 〖合計する〗(加える) add; (総計する) sum (-mm-) [add] ... up; (総計すると...になる) add up to ..., total. ▶5に4を[4と5を]合わせると9になる *Add* 4 *to* 5, and you get 9. ▶私の借金を全部合わせると100万円になる My debts *add* [*sum*] *up to* one million yen. ▶全部合わせていくらですか(総額) How much is it *in all* [*altogether*]?/How much does it come to?/(総数) How many are they *in all* [*altogether*]?/(重さ) What is the *total* weight? ▶みんなの合わせて持ち金が5,000円しかない We have only 5,000 yen *among* [*between*] us.

❸ 〖適合させる〗(大きさなどを合わせる) fit (-tt-) ... 《to》; (釣り合わせる) match ... 《to》; (調整して合わせる) set ... 《for, to》; (器具などを調節する) adjust; (焦点を合わせる) focus ... 《on》; (テレビ・ラジオなどを局・番組に合わせる) tune ... 《to》. ●支出を収入に合わせる *fit* [*match*] one's spending *to* one's income; (収入内でやりくりする) make ends meet. ●目覚しを(時計を)7時に合わせる *set* the alarm (clock) *for* 7 (o'clock). ●時計をラジオの時報に合わせる *set* one's watch *by* the time-signal on the radio. ●眼鏡の度を合わせる *adjust* a pair of glasses *to* one's sight. ●人にカメラのピントを合わせる *focus* one's camera *on* a person. ●ラジオをお気に入りの局に合わせる *tune* the radio *to* one's favorite station. ●話を聞き手に合わせる *suit* one's speech *to* the listeners. ●足に合わせて靴を作る make shoes *to measure*. ▶このふたをあの箱と合わせてみたが合わなかった I tried to *fit* this lid *to* the box, but they didn't *match up* [〖合わせることができなかった〗I couldn't]. ▶当方はお客様のご要望に合わせて生産できます We can *tailor* our production *to* your needs.

❹ 〖照合する〗(正しいか調べる) check; (比較する) compare. ●訳文と原文を合わせる *check* a translation *against* [*with*] the original; *compare* a translation *with* the original.

❺ 〖調子をそろえる〗●音楽に合わせて足で軽く調子をとる tap one's foot *in time to* [*with*] the music. ▶音楽に合わせて踊ろう Let's dance to the music. ▶部長とは調子を合わせておいた方がいい You should *make yourself agreeable to* [〖協力するように見せかける〗 *play along with*] your manager.

あわせる 会わせる ▶どうか息子に会わせてください Please *allow* me *to see* [*let me see*] my son. ▶きみに会わせたい女の子がいるんだ I'd like you to *meet* a

あわせわざ 合わせ技 〘柔道〙 a double waza ari; (説明的に) one winning point gained by adding two technical points which are effective, but not effective enough to get one point.

***あわただしい** 形 (せきたてられた) hurried; (急いだ) hasty; (すばやい) quick; (忙しい) busy. ●あわただしい食事 a hurried [a hasty, a quick] meal. ●あわただしい1日 (have) a busy day. ●あわただしい(=ぎっしり詰まった)日程 a heavy [a tight, a full] schedule.
— **あわただしく** 副 in a hurry, hurriedly; quickly; hastily (⇨急ぐ); busily. ●あわただしく車[列車]に乗り込む hurry into a car [on a train]. ●彼はあわただしく出発した He left in a hurry [hurriedly, 《書》 in haste]./《書》 He made a hurried [a hasty] departure.

あわただしさ hurry; busyness /bíznəs/. ●都会生活のあわただしさの中で in the rush [bustle] of city [urban] life.

あわだつ 泡立つ (ぶくぶくと) bubble; (小泡のかたまりを作る) foam; (石けんなどが) lather. (⇨泡)

あわだつ 粟立つ ●蛇を見ただけで恐怖に肌があわだった The mere sight of the snake made my flesh creep with terror.

あわだてき 泡立て器 a whisk; (回転式の) an eggbeater, 《英》 an egg whisk.

あわだてる 泡立てる whip (-pp-), beat*. ●卵の白身を固くなるまで泡立てる beat (up) egg whites until (they become) stiff.

あわふためく 慌ふためく (⇨慌つ❶) ●あわふためいて(=ろうばいして)逃げる run away in a panic.

あわてもの 慌て者 (そそっかしい人) a hasty [不注意な] a careless, (考えなしの) a thoughtless] person.

***あわてる 慌てる** ❶[ろうばいする] be confused [bewildered, 《書・やや古》 confounded, upset] 《at, by》; (心の平静を失う) lose* one's presence of mind; (突然の恐怖や不安で) get* into panic, panic (-cked; -cking) 《at》. (⇨当惑する, まごつく)

使い分け	
be confused	事態を理解できないため、平静を失い、とまどうこと。
be bewildered	物事・事態などに対して、より強いとまどいを覚えること。
be confounded	事態を適切に理解できず、ひどくとまどうこと。
be upset	気持ちが動転して平静を失うこと。また、平静を保てないほどひどく立腹すること。

▶彼はその知らせにあわてた He was confused at [by] the news./He was upset by the news./The news confused [upset] him./The news threw him into confusion. ▶鍵(⊙)が見つからずひどくあわてた I was very upset about not finding the key. (❗この場合 upset は形容詞化しているので much では なく very で修飾する) ▶どんな事が起ころうと彼は決してあわてない No matter what happens, he never loses his presence of mind [loses his head]. ▶あわてるな。机の下に潜りなさい Don't panic [《話》 Don't get panicky], (冷静になりなさい) Be calm]! Get under your desk.
❷[急ぐ] hurry; rush. ●あわてて帰宅する hurry home. (❗ home は副詞) ●あわてて結論を出すto rush to a conclusion. ●あわてるな Don't hurry. [×Don't hurry up. とはいわない]/There's no hurry./《のんびりやる》 Take it easy./《ごゆっくり》 Take your time. ●電話が鳴って彼はあわてては出かけた When he got the phone call, he left hurriedly [in a hurry]. ●あわてていたのでバスを乗り違えた I took the wrong bus in my hurry. ▶あわてて部屋を出ようとして倒れた In my [a] hurry to leave the room I tripped over.

あわてんぼう 慌てん坊 (⇨慌て者)

あわび 鮑 〘魚介〙 an abalone /ǽbəlòuni/, an ear shell.

あわもり 泡盛 awamori, (説明的に) a kind of shochu, which is a specialty of Okinawa.

あわや ●あわやというところで(=ぎりぎり間に合って) in the nick of time. ●あわやと思う間もなく(=一瞬のうちに) in an instant; in the twinkling of an eye. ●あわやホームランというフライ a fly looking just like a home run. ▶あわやというところで衝突は回避された The crash was avoided in the nick of time. ▶あわや殴り合いになるところに彼が割って入った They were about to start fighting when he stepped in between them.

あわゆき 泡雪, 淡雪 ❶[泡のように消えやすい雪] a light snow. ❷[卵白で作る和菓子] awayuki; (説明的に) Japanese sweet jelly made of beaten egg white.

あわよくば ●あわよくば(=うまくいけば)優勝できるかもしれない If things go well [《運がよければ》 If I'm lucky], I may win the championship.

***あわれ 哀れ** 名 pity 《for》; (❗人の苦しみを気の毒に思う気持ち。時に弱者への優越感を含む); (やや書) compassion 《for, on》; (人の苦しみを分かち合おうとする気持ち ⇨同情); 〘悲哀〙 sorrow, 《書》 pathos; 〘はじめて〙 misery. ▶その悲しい話はみんなの哀れを誘った The sad story aroused everyone's pity.
— **哀れな** 形 (人・状態などが) pitiful, (やや書) pitiable; ((同情・光景などが)哀れを誘う) pathetic; (悲しい) sad; (みじめな) miserable. ●聞くも哀れな話 a pathetic [a sad] story to hear. ●哀れな死に方をする die miserably. ▶わなにかかったウサギは一上なく哀れな光景だった The rabbit caught in the trap was the most pitiful [pathetic] sight I'd ever seen.
— **哀れに** 副 ●哀れに思う feel pity for ... . ▶すすり泣く子を見てとても哀れに思った I felt a great pity [(×a) great compassion] for the sobbing child./I felt very sorry for the sobbing child. (❗この方が口語的) (⇨哀れむ) ●哀れにも彼の息子は事故死した His poor son was killed in an accident.

あわれっぽい 哀れっぽい ●哀れっぽい(=哀れを誘う)声で in a piteous [悲しそうな] plaintive] voice.

あわれみ 哀れみ pity; (慈悲から) compassion; 〘慈悲〙 mercy. (⇨哀れむ) ●こじきに哀れみをかける [take] pity on a beggar; (哀れに思う) feel pity for a beggar. ●哀れみを請う ask for [beg] 《his》 pity; beg 《him》 for mercy. ●哀れみを誘う泣き声 a pitiful [《書》 a piteous] cry. ●哀れみ深い婦人 a compassionate [(思いやりのある) a sympathetic] woman.

あわれむ 哀れむ 〘かわいそうに思う〙 feel* pity 《for》, pity; have* [take*] pity 《on》; 〘同情する〙 sympathize 《with》. (⇨哀れみ) ●哀れむ気持ちから out of pity 《for》. ▶あの人を哀れむのはもうやめた方がいい You'd better not pity [have pity on] him any more. ▶裁判官はその罪を犯した男を哀れんだ The judge sympathized with [(慈悲をかけた) had mercy on] the guilty man.

***あん 案** ❶[提案] a proposal, (示唆) a suggestion. ●[提案] 案を出す[撤回する] make [withdraw] a proposal. ▶だれかもっとよい案はありませんか Does anyone have a better suggestion [idea]?
❷[計画] a plan, [考え] an idea. (⇨計画, 考え) ●案を立てる[練る] make [elaborate] a plan. ●案に相違する ▶案に相違して彼は大成功した Contra-

ry to expectations [Quite unexpectedly], he made a great success.
●案にたがわず (⇨案の定)
あん 庵 a hermitage, a hermit's cell;(僧庵) a monastery.
あん 餡 sweetened bean paste.
●あんパン a bun filled with sweetened bean paste.
あんあん 暗暗 ▶暗暗のうちに[暗暗裏(り)に](=ひそかに)出会う meet together *in secret* [*secretly*].
***あんい 安易** ━━安易な 形 easy;[のんきな] easy-going (!日本語の「イージーゴーイング」のような悪い含みはない). ▶安易な生活《lead》an *easy* life.
━━安易に ▶安易に考える take (it) *lightly* (!通例否定文で).(熟考しない) do not think (it) well.
あんいつ 安逸 ▶安逸をむさぼる live in *idleness*; live a life of *idleness*; lead an *idle* life.
アンインストール 图 [ハードディスク内のソフトを削除すること][コンピュータ] uninstallation.
━━アンインストールする 動 uninstall (↔install).
あんうつ 暗鬱 gloom. ▶暗うつな気分になる feel *gloomy* 《about》.
あんうん 暗雲 a dark cloud. (⇨垂れ込める) ▶内閣の失政が日本経済に暗雲(= 暗い見通し)を招いている The misgovernment of the Cabinet is causing the Japanese economy *gloomy prospects*.
あんか 安価 cheapness, a low price.
━━安価な 形 cheap, low-priced. (⇨安い) ▶安価な品物 *cheap* goods. (!*cheap* はしばしば「安くて品質がよくない」の意を伴う)
あんか 行火 a heating pad.
アンカー ❶ ▶[リレーの最終走[泳]者] the last runner [swimmer] (of the team); an anchor, an anchorperson,(男の)an anchorman,(女の)an anchorwoman. ▶男子800メートルリレーの日本代表チームのアンカー the *anchorman* of the Japanese national team in the men's 800-meter relay.
❷ [建築用金具] an anchor bolt.
アンカーマン [報道番組の総合司会者](米) an anchor, an anchorperson,(男の)an anchorman,(女の)an anchorwoman. ▶口語では had を省略することが多い]口語では had を省略することが多い]彼女は10時の報道番組のアンカーマンを務めている She *anchors* [*is the anchorwoman of*] the ten o'clock news program.
***あんがい 案外** [思いがけなく] unexpectedly;[予想に反して] contrary to [against] (all) expectations;[驚くほどに] surprisingly. ▶私たちは案外早くそこへ着いた We got there *unexpectedly* early./(予想したより) We got there earlier *than* we (had) *expected*.(!口語では had を省略することが多い) [書] *Contrary to expectations*, we got there early. ▶彼女は案外若いのかもしれない She may be *younger than* we *think* she will be. (!will は推量を表す)
あんかけ 餡掛け *ankake*,(説明的に) food dressed with translucent, thick, starchy sauce.
あんかっしょく 暗褐色 dark brown,(a) dark brown color.
アンカラ [トルコの首都] Ankara /ǽŋkərə/.
あんかん 安閑 idleness. ▶今は安閑としている時ではない This is no time *sit* [*stand*] *idly by*.
あんき 暗記 图 ▶英語は暗記物の科目だ English is a *memory* subject.
━━暗記する 動 (記憶する) memorize;(そらで覚える) learn ... *by heart*. ▶その歌詞を暗記している know the lyrics *by heart*.
━━暗記力 a memory.
あんぎゃ 行脚 a walking tour;(巡拝)《make [go on]》a pilgrimage. ▶全国を行脚する *go on a walking tour of* the country; *travel* all over the country *on foot*. ▶講演行脚を *go on a lecture tour*.
あんきょ 暗渠（農場などの）an underdrain;（鉄道・道路などの）a culvert.
あんぐ 暗愚 [「ばか」の文語的表現] (⇨馬鹿)
アングラ ▶アングラ映画 [前衛的な映画][映画] an underground movie [film]. ▶アングラ経済 [地下経済] the underground money.
あんぐり ▶その子はあんぐり(と)口を開けてたこを見つめていた The child stared at the kite *with his mouth wide open* [(*with his mouth*) *agape*]. (⇨ぱっくり, ぽかんと)
アングロサクソン (人) an Anglo-Saxon;(民族) the Anglo-Saxons, the Anglo-Saxon race. ▶アングロサクソン (人) [語] の Anglo-Saxon.
アンケート [<フランス語] (用紙) a questionnaire /kwèstʃənéər/ 《about, on》. ▶アンケートを送る send out a *questionnaire*. ▶アンケートに記入する [答える] fill in [answer, reply to, respond to] a *questionnaire* (!(米) では fill in の代わりに fill out もよく用いる). ▶アンケートをお願いします (街頭で) May I ask you a few questions?
あんけん 案件 (事項) an item;(個々の訴訟事件) a case. ▶今回の議会日程の最初の案件 the first *item* on this agenda.
あんこう 鮟鱇 [魚介] an angler (fish) (億 ~, ~s).
あんごう 暗号 [] a code; (a) cipher. ▶暗号を解読する crack [break] a *code*; decode (a signal); decipher 《a message》.
▶暗号文 a coded message; a message (written) in cipher [code].
アンコール [<フランス語] an encore /ɑ́ŋkɔːr/;(もう一度と叫ぶ場合) Encore! ▶アンコールの叫び a call [a shout] *of encore*. ▶アンコールを求める[受ける] call for [get, receive] an *encore*. ▶アンコールに応じて1曲歌う[演奏する] sing [play] an *encore*. (!(1)単に「アンコールに応じる」は give [do] an *encore*. (2)アンコールで...を歌う sing ... *as* [*for*] *an encore*)
アンコールワット [カンボジアの寺院遺跡] Angkor Wat /ǽŋkɔːr wɑ́t/. (! Wat は「寺院」の意)
あんこく 暗黒 图 (暗闇(やみ)) darkness.
━━暗黒(の) 形 dark. ▶人生の暗黒面 the *dark* (↔ *bright*) side of life.
●暗黒街 the underworld. ▶暗黒時代 a *dark age*;(中世ヨーロッパの) the Dark Ages. ▶暗黒星雲 [天文] a dark nebula /nébjulə/. ▶暗黒大陸 the Dark Continent. ([参考]アフリカ大陸はかつて未開文明地と考えられ、このように呼ばれていたことから)
アンゴラ [国名] Angola /æŋɡóulə/;(公式名) the Republic of Angola.（首都 Luanda）●アンゴラ人 an Angolan. ▶アンゴラ(人)の Angolan.
アンゴラ [動物] (an) angora /æŋɡɔ́ːrə/. (!毛は U)
●アンゴラのセーター an *angora* sweater.
あんころもち 餡ころ餅 an *ankoro-mochi*, a rice cake covered with sweetened bean paste.
あんさつ 暗殺 assassination. ●暗殺者 an assássin. ▶王の暗殺を企てる plot the *assassination of* the king; plot to *assássinate* the king. ▶大統領はテロリストに暗殺された The President *was assassinated* by terrorists.
あんざん 安産 (have) an easy delivery [birth]. (⇨お産)
あんざん 暗算 图 mental arithmetic [calculation].
●暗算で答えを出す work out an answer in one's head [in *mental arithmetic*].

あんざんがん

── **暗算する** calculate mentally; calculate [do sums] in one's head.

あんざんがん 安山岩 andesite.

アンサンブル [＜フランス語] an ensemble /ɑːnˈsɑːmbl/.

あんし 暗視 ▶暗視カメラ an infrared camera.

あんじ 暗示 名 [示唆] (a) suggestion; [ヒント] a hint; [手がかり] a clue. ▶自己暗示 [心理学] auto-suggestion. ●暗示にかかりやすい be easily influenced by suggestion. ●「君は絶対に勝つ」と彼は暗示をかける make him believe that he will surely win.

── **暗示する** 動 [気づかせる] suggest; [ほのめかす] hint, give* [drop -pp-] a hint; [意味する] imply. ●あらしを暗示する旋律 (a) melody *suggestive of* a storm; (a) melody which *suggests* a storm.

あんしつ 暗室 a darkroom. (! a dark room は「暗い部屋」の意)

あんじゅう 安住 名 ●安住の地を求める seek a place for *peaceful living*.

── **安住する** 動 live in peace. ●現状に安住する(=満足する) be content with the present condition.

あんしゅつ 案出 ── **案出する** 動 devise, invent; think [work]... out. (⇨考え出す)

あんしょ 暗所 a dark place.
●暗所恐怖症 [医学] nyctophobia.

あんしょう 暗唱 名 (a) recitation. ●暗唱大会 a *recitation* contest. ── **暗唱する** 動 ●詩を暗唱する *recite* a poem.

あんしょう 暗礁 ❶ [海の] a reef (! 海面または海面近くにある細長く続く岩礁や砂礁); [岩礁] a rock (! しばしば複数形で). ▶船が暗礁に乗り上げた The ship struck [went on, ran on] a *reef* [*rocks*]. ❷ [行き詰まり] a deadlock. ●暗礁に乗り上げる ▶交渉は暗礁に乗り上げた The negotiations reached (a) *deadlock* [came to a *standstill*, ran on the *rocks*].

あんしょうばんごう 暗証番号 (キャッシュカードなどの) a PIN (number) (*personal identification number* の略).

あんじる 案じる (心配する) worry (about), be anxious (about). (⇨案ずる)

***あんしん** 安心 名 [安堵(あんど)] (a) relief; [心の平和] peace of mind; [不安のないこと] security; [安全] safety; [安楽] easiness; [信頼] confidence, trust. ▶彼といっしょだと安心感がある I *feel secure* with him.

── **安心する** 動 [ほっとする] be [feel*] relieved (*at; to do*); [気が楽である] feel easy (*at* (one's) *ease*); [落ち着いている] rest (! 否定文で). ●安心させる ease (his) mind; put [set] (his) mind at rest; (大丈夫だと納得させる) assure; (不安を取り除いて) reassure. ▶あなたが無事に家に着いたと聞いて大変安心しました I *was* very *relieved* (to hear) that you had got home safely./It was a great *relief* [It really *eased my mind*] to hear (that) you had got home safely. (! it は to 以下をさす) ▶そのことは安心しなさい Make yourself *easy* about it./(心配するな) Don't worry about it. ●できる限りのことはしますから安心してください You can *rest* [×feel] *as* I will do all I can./(やや書) You can *rest* [*Rest*] *assured* that I will do all I can. (! *rest* はいずれも「…のままである」の意) ▶その件が解決するまでは安心できない I cannot *rest* [I have no *peace of mind*] until the matter is settled. ▶船長は危険はないと言って乗客を安心させた The captain *assured* [*reassured*] the passengers *that* there was no danger.

会話 「母は快方に向かっています」「とっても安心しましたわ」"My mother's getting better." "What a *relief!*"

── **安心して** 副 ▶彼女の顔を見るまでは安心して寝られなかった I couldn't go to bed *with* an *easy mind* [*without* worry(*ing*)] until I saw her face. ▶ここをみんなが安心して(=安全に)住める町にしよう Let's make this a city where we can all live in *safety* [(平和[平穏]に) *in peace*]. ▶彼なら安心して車を貸せる I can *entrust* [*trust*] him *with* my car. (! 「信頼して預ける」の意では *entrust* の方が普通)/I can *entrust* [(今はまれ) *trust*] my car *to* him. (⇨預ける [預託])

あんず 杏 [植物] (実, 木) an apricot /ˈæprəkɑ̀t/.

***あんずる** 案ずる worry (*about*). (⇨案じる)
●案ずるより産むがやすし (ことわざ) Fear is often greater than the danger.

あんせい 安静 (a) rest. ●食後1時間安静にする (休む) have [take] an hour's rest after a meal; (静かに横になる) lie quietly for an hour after a meal. ▶医者は私に絶対安静を命じた The doctor ordered me to *take* a complete [an absolute] *rest*.
●安静療法 a rest cure.

‡**あんぜん** 安全 名 safety (↔*danger*); [危険に対する恐れや心配がないこと] security.
① [〜の安全] ●国家の安全 national *security*. ●公衆の安全 public *safety*. ▶運転手は乗客の安全に責任がある The driver is responsible for the *safety* of the passengers.
② [安全〜] ●交通安全週間 Traffic Safety Week. ●(競技などで) 安全圏内に入る get a *safe* lead. ▶安全第一 [標語] Safety first.
③ [安全を〜] ●身の安全を保障する [脅かす] guarantee [threaten] (his) *security*. ▶彼は常に安全を求め, 一か八かやるようなことはしない He always wants to *be safe*, and he never takes a chance.
── **安全な** 形 [危険のない] safe (*from*); [危険から守られている] secure (*from, against*). ●安全な場所 a *safe* place; a place of *safety*; a place *free from danger*. ●安全な要塞(ようさい) a *safe* fortress. ▶今では飛行機の旅は以前よりずっと安全である Air travel is much *safer* now than it used to be. ▶ここなら敵の攻撃に対し安全です We are *safe* [*secure*] *from* enemy attack here./This place is *safe* [*secure*] *from* enemy attack. ▶この湖でスケートをしても安全だ It is *safe* to skate on this lake./This lake is *safe* to skate on. ▶この塗料はベビーベッドに使っても安全ですか Is this paint *safe for* a crib? ▶彼の運転は安全だ He is a *safe* driver./He drives *safely*.

── **安全に** 副 safely, in safety; securely. ●きっちり安全に荷造りする pack (it) tight and *securely*. ●人間が宇宙でどのくらい安全に生きられるのかだれにも分からない Nobody knows how long human beings can *safely* live in space. ▶この宝石類は金庫に安全に保管されている The jewels are being kept *safe and secure* in the safe.
●安全運転 safe driving / 「安全運転をする」 drive safely). ●安全かみそり a safety razor.
●安全管理 safety management. ●安全対策 (take) safety measures. ●安全操業 safety operation. ●安全装置 a safety device; (銃の) a safety (catch). ●安全地帯 (車道にある歩行者用の)(米) a safety zone; a safety (米)[a safety (英)] island. ●安全ピン a safety pin. ●安全ベルト (飛行機・自動車などの) (fasten) a safety belt [a seat belt]. (! 後の方が普通) ●安全保障 security.

あんぜんパイ 安全パイ ❶【マージャンの】(説明的に) a (mah-jong) tile which one can safely discard from one's hand. ❷【人】▶彼は彼女にとって安全パイだと思われていた He was thought to be neither useful nor harmful to her. ▶彼は相手チームのピッチャーにとっては安全パイだと見なされている He is considered to be no threat by opposing pitchers to be no threat.

あんそくび 安息日 the Sabbath (day). (❗キリスト教では日曜日、ユダヤ教では土曜日、イスラム教では金曜日) ●安息日を守る keep [observe] (↔break) the Sabbath.

アンソロジー【名詩選集, 詞華集】an anthology.

あんだ 安打【野球】a hit; a safety. ●内野安打 an infield hit [single]. ●安打を打つ make a hit. ●3安打に抑える hold [the Giants] to three hits; pitch a three-hitter (over [against] the Giants). ●レフト前に安打を打つ hit a single to left. ●3打数2安打である go two for three. ▶彼は333打数100安打で3割を打った He hit .300, with 100 hits in 333 at-bats.

アンダーウエア【下着類】underwear.
アンダーシャツ an undershirt. (⇨シャツ)
アンダースロー【野球】an únderhand thrów [pitch];《和製語》underthrow. (⇨オーバースロー) ●アンダースロー投手 an underhand pitcher; a submariner. ●アンダースローで投げる throw ùnderhánd. (↔overhand). (❗投球·送球の両方に用いる)

アンダーハンド ― アンダーハンドの 形【野球】underhand. ●アンダーハンドの投球 an underhand pitch. ●アンダーハンドで投げる throw underhand.

アンダーライン【下線】an underline. ●その句にアンダーラインを引く underline the phrase. ●アンダーラインを引いた箇所 an underlined part.

あんたい 安泰 ▶我が国の安泰(=平和と安全) the peace and security of our country. ▶彼は会社での自分の地位は安泰だ(=安心していられる)と感じている He feels secure about his place [position] in the company.

あんたん 暗たん ●暗たんたる前途 gloomy [dark] prospects.

アンダンテ【<イタリア語】【歩く速さで】【音楽】andante /ɑːndɑ́ːnteɪ/.

あんち 安置 图 enshrinement.
── 安置する 動 ▶王の遺体が宮殿に安置された The king's body was laid in state in the palace. ●安置所 (神器などの) a place of enshrinement; (遺体の) a mortuary.

アンチー anti-. ●アンチ巨人の野球ファン an anti-Giants baseball fan; a Giant hater.

アンチック (⇨アンティーク)
アンチテーゼ【哲学】an antithesis /ænˈtɪθəsɪs/ (複 -ses /-siːz/). ●社会主義は資本主義のアンチテーゼである Socialism is the antithesis of capitalism.

あんちゃん 兄ちゃん【兄】(⇨兄);【若い男】a young man.
あんちゅうもさく 暗中模索 ▶よりよい方法はないかと暗中模索する grope for a better way in the dark.
あんちょく 安直 ── 安直な 形 ❶【安価な】cheap; (値のはらない) inexpensive. ❷【気楽な】easy. ▶私はその仕事を安直に引き受けた I readily accepted the offer of the job./I accepted the job without giving it much thought.

あんちょこ (虎の巻) a crib.
アンチョビー【魚介】an anchovy.

アンツーカー【<フランス語】【全天候型の】all-weather (tracks [tennis courts]).

あんてい 安定 图 stability (↔instability); (安定させること) stabilization; (足場·地位などの) steadiness;【均衡】(a) balance.
① 【〜(の)安定】●経済[社会]の安定 economic [social] stability. ●物価の安定 the stabilization of prices; price stabilization. ●ドルの安定 stability [stabilization] of the dollar.
② 【安定を】▶片足で立って安定を保つ[失う] keep [lose] one's balance on one leg. ●政治の安定を維持する maintain political stability. ●情緒の安定を欠く lack emotional stability.

── 安定した 形 stable (↔unstable); steady. ●安定した仕事[収入] a stable job [income]. ●安定したはしご [a steady] ladder. ●安定した(=釣り合いの取れた)心 a well-balanced mind.

── 安定する 動 ▶その国の経済は安定している The economy of the country is stable./The country has a stable economy. ▶患者の容態は安定した[している] The patient's condition stabilized [is stable]. ▶この2年間物価は安定している Prices have been steady [have held firm] for the past two years. ▶そのうち天候も安定するでしょう The weather will settle before long.

── 安定させる 動 stabilize. ●物価を安定させる stabilize prices. ●テーブルの脚を安定させる steady a table leg.
●安定感 a sense of stability. ●安定成長 stable growth. ●安定多数 a comfortable [a stable] majority. ●安定賃金 stable wages. ●安定通貨 a stable [a stabilized] currency.

アンティーク【骨董(とう)品】an antique /ænˈtiːk/. ●アンティークいす an antique chair.

アンティグアバーブーダ【国名】Antigua /ænˈtiːɡə/ and Barbuda /bɑːrˈbuːdə/. (❗公式名も同じ) (首都 St. John's)

アンデス ●アンデス山脈 the Andes /ˈændiːz/. (❗複数扱い)

アンテナ《米》an anténna,《英》an aerial. ●テレビアンテナ a TV antenna [aerial]. ●アンテナを立てる[張る] put up [stretch] an antenna. ●アンテナショップ【実験店舗】an antenna shop.

アンデルセン【デンマークの童話作家】Andersen /ˈændərsən/ (Hans Christian ~).

あんてん 暗転 图【演劇】a blackout.
── 暗転する 動 ▶(舞台が) black ... out; (事態が) worse, take a turn for the worse. ▶舞台はふたたび暗転して次のシーンに移った The stage was blacked out again and the scene changed.

あんど 安堵 图 (a) relief. ●安堵の胸をなでおろす breathe [give] a sigh of relief.
── 安堵する 動 ▶その知らせを聞いて安堵する be [feel] relieved at the news. (⇨安心する)

あんとう 暗闘 a secret feud, secret strife.
アンドラ【国名】Andorra /ænˈdɔːrə/; (公式名) the Principality of Andorra. (首都 Andorra la Vella) ●アンドラ人 an Andorran. ●アンドラ(人)の

アントレ【<フランス語】an entrée /ˈɑːntreɪ/. (參考 ディナーで本料理の最初の皿)

アンドロイド an android. (參考 外見·思考·行動が人間同様のロボット)

アンドロメダ ●アンドロメダ銀河【天文】the Andromeda galaxy. ●アンドロメダ座【天文】Andrómeda.

アントワープ【ベルギーの都市】Antwerp /ˈæntwɜːrp/.
あんどん 行灯 a paper-covered lamp stand.
あんな (⇨あんな(に))

あんない 案内

❶【連れて行ったり見せて歩くこと】guidance;【案内される人・本など】a guide. ●旅行[映画、買い物]案内 a travelers' [a movie; a shopping] guide. ●道案内をする (⇨動) 旅行案内所 a travel bureau. ●総合案内所 a general information desk [counter]. ▶彼が我々の案内役を務めた He acted as our *guide* [*a guide* for us]. ▶我々は秘書の案内でその工場を見て回った We made a tour of the factory *under the guidance of* [*guided by, led by*] the secretary. (⇨動)

❷【知らせ】(情報) information; (通知(状)) a notice. ●入学案内 a guidebook [a pamphlet] for applicants. ▶百貨店からバーゲンセールの案内があった I got *information about* sales from the department store. ▶次回会合のご案内を申し上げます We are pleased to *inform* you of [*notify* you of, *let* you *know about*] the next meeting. (❗inform, notify は堅い語. 特に notify は正式に通知することをいう) ▶ご案内申し上げます《場所放送など》(May I have your) attention, please. 案内放送は普通 Thank you. で締めくくる

❸【招待】(an) invitation. (⇨招待) ▶我が社の創立25周年記念を祝うレセプションにご案内申し上げます We cordially *invite* you [You *are* cordially *invited*] *to attend* the reception to celebrate the 25th anniversary of the founding of our company. (❗後の方が正式)

❹【取り次ぎ】 ▶私は受付で社長に案内を請うた I requested [asked] the receptionist to tell the president that I was there. (❗ask の方がくだけた語) ▶彼は案内もなく(=受付に断わりなしに)社長の部屋に入った He went into the President's room *without a* receptionist's *permission*.

— **案内する** 動 show*; guide; lead*; take*.

> [使い分け] **show** 同行して道順を示すこと. 通例 in, out, up のような方向を表す副詞や *into* a room (部屋の中へ), *to* one's seat (席へ), *up to* a room ((階)上の部屋へ)のような目的地を表す副詞句を伴う. また show (him) around [through, over] の形で用いて、いろいろ見せて回ることを表す.
> **guide** 進むべき道からはずれないよう事情を知った人が同行すること. 観光・登山などについて用いることが多い.
> **lead** リーダー・案内人などが、自ら先に立って個人や集団を先導すること.
> **take** 方向・方角を表す副詞句を伴い, 道順はともかくある目的地へ連れて行くこと.

●道を案内する show (him) the way; (先に立って) lead the way (*to*). ▶彼が町を案内してくれた He *showed* [*guided*] me *around* the city./He was my *guide around* the city. ▶彼は私を彼の部屋に案内した He *showed* me *to* [*into*] his room./He *showed* me his room. (❗(1) ×He showed his room *to* me. は不可. (2) 文脈から明らかな場合, 場所は省略可:「私の部屋はどこですか」「ご案内します」"Where's my room?" "I'll *show* you.")/(連れていった) He *took* me *to* his room.

[会話]「大きな工場ですね」「ご案内しましょう」「あら、それうれしいです」"What a big factory!" "Let me give you *a tour* [*show* you *around*]." "Oh, that would be great."

●案内係 [場所] [掲示] Information; the information desk [office]; 【人】an information desk clerk; (劇場などの) an usher /ʌ́ʃər/; (女の) (今はまれ) an usherette. ●案内広告 (新聞などで求人・貸家などの) a classified advertisement [《話》ad]. ●案内書 a guide(book) 《to Kyoto》.

●案内図 a (guide) map; (道案内板) a guideboard.

*あんな(に) ▶あんな風に言ってはいけない Don't say it *like that* [(*in*) *that way*]. (❗《話》では通例 in は省略する) ▶あそこなような質問には答えられない I can't answer *such* a question [a question *like that, that sort of* question]. (❗ [ ] の方が口語的 (⇨動)) ▶あんなご亭主のどこがいいの What do you like about *that* husband of yours? ▶この子は軽蔑の意を含み, 無強勢) ▶彼があんなに頑固だとは思わなかった I didn't expect that he would be *so* [《話》(*all*) *that*] stubborn. (❗that は通例疑問文・否定文で) ▶彼があんなに強いとは驚きだ It's surprising (to know) *how* strong he is. ▶彼を見てごらん. あんな所(=はるか上のあそこ)まで登ったよ Look at him! He has climbed way up *there*. ▶あんな大きな足の男ははじめてだ(=今まで見た中でいちばん大きな足をしている) He has the biggest feet I've ever seen.

あんに 暗に implicitly; (遠回しに) in a roundabout way. ●暗ににおわせる (言葉で) hint 《*at*; *that* 節》;(言葉・態度で) imply 《*that* 節》, suggest 《*that* 節》. ●暗に辞職をせまる *hint at* 〈his〉 resignation; *hint that* 〈he〉 may resign. (⇨匂わす❷)

あんにんどうふ 杏仁豆腐 (説明的に) cubes of apricot jelly and fruit floating in syrup.

あんねい 安寧 (public) peace; (安定) stability. ●国内の安寧秩序を保つ[乱す] maintain [disturb] *peace and order* in the country.

アンネのにっき『アンネの日記』 *A Diary of Anne Frank*. (❗[参考] アンネ・フランクの日記)

あんのじょう 案の定 (just) as one expected [feared] (❗後の方は好ましくない場合に用いる. この例では《書》); true to form [type]; 《話》sure enough. (⇨予)たして) ▶雨が降ると思ったが案の定降った We thought it would rain, and *sure enough* it did. ▶その計画は案の定不首尾に終わった *True to form*, the project ended in failure.

あんのん 安穏 ●安穏な生活 a *peaceful* [(平穏な) a *quiet*, 《やや書》a *tranquil*] life. ●安穏に暮らす live *in peace*. ●無事安穏を祈る pray for one's *safety*.

あんば 鞍馬 《米》a side horse, 《英》a pommel horse. (❗競技種目は the 〜)

あんばい ●いいあんばいに(=幸運にも) fortunately, luckily. (⇨幸運)

アンパイア an úmpire. (⇨審判) ●アンパイアをする act as *umpire* 《*in* a game》; *umpire* 《a game》.

アンバランス imbálance. (❗unbalance は「精神的な不安定」の意) ●(肉体的・精神的に)アンバランスな状態になって unbalanced. ●輸入と輸出のアンバランス the *imbalance* [×unbalance] *between* imports and exports.

あんぴ 安否 ●彼の安否を気づかう worry about his *safety*. ▶彼が君の安否を尋ねていたよ He *asked after* you [your health]. (❗健康状態を聞く場合)／He asked *how* you *were getting along* [*on*]. (❗無事に暮らしているかなどを聞く場合)

あんぶ 暗部 ●政界の暗部(=隠された部分) the *hidden* [*secret*] *parts* in the political world.

あんぷ 暗譜 ●暗譜でソナタを弾く play a sonata *from memory*.

アンプ [増幅器]【電気】an amplifier, 《話》an amp.

アンフェア — **アンフェアな** 形 《公平[公正]でない》unfair. ●アンフェアな判定 an *unfair* judgment. ●アンフェアな扱いを受ける be *unfairly* treated. ●アンフェアな手段を使う use an *unfair* [a *dishonest*] means. ▶彼にばかり責任を負わせるのはアンフェアだ It

あんぶん 案分, 按分 ── **案分する** 動 ● 彼らに利益金を案分する *divide* [*distribute*] the profits proportionally among them.
● 案分比例 proportional distribution.

あんぶん 案文 a draft.

アンペア an ampere (略 a, A, amp.). ● 10 アンペアの電流 a current of 10 *amperes*.

あんぽう 罨法 〖医学〗 fomentation.

あんぽじょうやく 安保条約 〖安全保障条約〗 a security treaty [pact]. ● 日米安保条約 the Japan-U.S. *Security Treaty*.

あんぽんたん 〖『ばか』の口語的表現〗 (⇨馬鹿)

あんま 按摩 图 〖術〗 massage; 〖あんま師〗(男性) a masseur /mæsə́ːr/; (女性) a masseuse /mæsə́ːz/.
── **按摩(を)する** 動 massage 《him》. ● あんまをしてもらう have [get] a *massage*; have oneself massaged. (⇨マッサージ)

あんまく 暗幕 a blackout curtain.

あんまり 〖『あまり』の強調表現〗 ▶ あんまり飛ばすな Don't drive *so* fast. ▶ これはあんまりだ(=ひどすぎる), もう我慢できない This is *too much*, I won't stand for it! ▶ 彼の要求はあんまりだ(=不当だ) His demand is *unreasonable* [*exorbitant, extravagant*]. ▶ そんなことをするとあんまりだ(=無情だ) It is *heartless* [*cruel, unkind*] of you to do it.
[翻訳のこころ] いくら物価の安い時だって熊の毛皮二枚で二円はあんまり安いとだれでも思う《宮沢賢治『なめとこ山の熊』》Anyone would think two yen for two bear skins is unreasonably [too] cheap, even at this time of low prices. (❗(1)「だれでも」は everyone にすると「あらゆる人」の意になるので注意. (2) unreasonably 〖法外に〗は「あんまり」の意の一般的な語. too は話者の意見が含まれる)

アンマン 〖ヨルダンの首都〗 Amman /əmάːn/.

あんみつ *anmitsu*;〖説明的に〗sweets consisting of tidbits 《米》[titbits 《英》] of some kinds of fruit, gelatin cubes, red beans, ice cream, and so on, topped with bean paste, served with ample syrup.

あんみん 安眠 图 a sound [a good] sleep. ● 安眠を妨害する disturb one's (*sound*) *sleep*.
── **安眠する** 動 have a sound [a good] sleep; sleep soundly [well].

あんもく 暗黙 ● 暗黙の了解 a *tacit* [an *implicit*] understanding;〖無言の同意〗an unspoken agreement. ● 暗黙のうちに彼の意見に同意する *tacitly* agree with [xto] his opinion.

アンモナイト 〖古生物〗 an ámmonite.

アンモニア 〖化学〗 ammónia.
● アンモニア水 ammonia (water).

アンモニウム 〖化学〗 ammonium /əmóuniəm/.

あんやく 暗躍 ── **暗躍する** 動 〖秘密工作する〗engage in secret maneuvers;〖舞台裏で行動する〗act behind the scenes.

あんやこうろ 『暗夜行路』 *A Dark Night's Passing*. (參考) 志賀直哉の小説

あんらく 安楽 comfort;〖気楽〗ease. ● 安楽な生活をする live *in comfort* [*comfortably*].
● 安楽いす an easy chair.

あんらくし 安楽死 mercy killing;〖専門的に〗euthanasia /jùːθənéiʒiə/. ● 愛犬を(医者に依頼して)安楽死させる have one's dog put to sleep. (❗婉曲的な言い方)

アンラッキー unlucky. ● 我々のチームにとってのアンラッキー(=不運な)シーズン an *unlucky* season for our team. ▶ 日本や中国では 4 はアンラッキーナンバー(=縁起の悪い数)だと考えられている In Japan and China, people consider that the number four is *unlucky*.

あんりゅう 暗流〖表面に現れない水の流れ〗an undercurrent. ● 政治の暗流〖=表面に現れないなりゆき〗に流される be influenced by politics.

あんるい 暗涙 ● 暗涙にむせぶ weep *in silence* [*secret*]; shed *silent* [*secret*] *tears*.

い

い 胃 图 a stomach.
① 【胃が】 ● 胃が丈夫だ[弱い] have a strong [a weak] *stomach*; (消化力が強い[弱い]) have a good [a poor, a weak] *digestion*. ▶彼は胃が弱い(=胃病だ) He has *stomach* trouble [a *stomach* disorder, a *stomach* complaint]. (!complaint はたいしたことのない状況に用いる) ▶胃が痛い I have a stomachache./My *stomach* aches [hurts]. (⇨痛む❶, きりきり❷) ▶昼食が遅かったのでまだ胃が重い I had a late lunch, so the food is still lying heavy on my *stomach*.
② 【胃の[に, を]】 ● 胃の調子が悪い have a *stomach* upset; have something wrong with one's *stomach*. ● 胃をこわす[落ち着かせる] 《物が主語》 upset [settle] one's *stomach*. ▶ステーキが胃にもたれている The steak is lying heavy on my *stomach*. (!進行形は一時的な状態を表す)
── **胃の** 形 gastric /gǽstrik/.

い 井 (井戸) a well. (⇨井戸, 井の中の蛙(ﾅﾜｽﾞ))
い 亥 the Boar.
● 亥年 〖十二支〗 the year of the Boar.(⇨干支(ｴﾄ) 関連)
い 医 (医術) medicine; (医学) medical science. ⇨医学
● 医は仁術 Medicine is a benevolent art./Medical services should be based on a doctor's empathy [sympathy, love] for his or her patients.
い 威 (虎の威を借るきつね ⇨虎 [成句])
い 異 (異議) (an) objection. (⇨異議) ● 異な strange. ⇨変な, 妙な
● 異を唱える[立てる] ▶私は立って, その計画に異を唱えた I stood up to raise [make; voice] an *objection* to the plan.
い 意 ● 意のままに(=好きなように)する do as one *likes* [*pleases*]. (⇨思い通り) ▶私は助力してくれたことに対し山口氏に感謝の意を表した I expressed my thanks to Mr. Yamaguchi for his help. ▶彼女は父親の意に反して彼と結婚をした She married him *against* her father's *will* [*wishes*]. ▶仕事を辞めようと意を決した I *decided* [*made up* my *mind*] to give up my job.
● 意に介さない ▶私は人がどう思おうと意に介さない I *don't care* [*mind*] what other people think of me.
● 意に叶(ｶﾅ)う ▶この絵なら彼の意にかなう(=彼は満足する)だろう He will *be satisfied with* this painting./This painting will *satisfy* him.
● 意のあるところ ▶意のあるところをおくみとりください Please take my *feelings* into consideration. (⇨汲む❷)
● 意を強くする be encouraged 《by his words》.
● 意を迎える ▶彼は上役の意を迎えるのに必死だった He was always trying hard to *please* [*humor*; *curry favor with*] his boss.

いあいぬき 居合い抜き a quick draw of a sword; (術, 曲芸) the art of drawing a sword quickly.
いあつ 威圧 图 (脅し・権力などによる抑圧》 coercion.
── **威圧的な** 形 その先生は私たちに威圧的な態度をとった The teacher took a *coercive* [(高圧的な) *high-handed*] attitude *toward* us.
── **威圧する** 動 ●彼を威圧して服従させる *coerce* [(恐れさせる) *overawe*] him *into* submission.
いアトニー 胃アトニー 〖医学〗 gastric atony, gastrotonia.
いあわせる 居合わせる happen [《書》 chance] to be (present) 《at, in, on》; *happen to be* there [on the spot]; *be* there *by chance*. ▶居合わせた人は絶叫した Those *present* [(見ている人)Onlookers] cried out.
いあん 慰安 《娯楽》 recreation; 《楽しみ》(an) amusement; 《慰め》(a) consolation. ● 慰安旅行に行く go on a *recreational* trip.
● 慰安婦 a comfort woman.

いい — INDEX

❶ 好ましい, 優れている ❷ ためになる
❸ 適した   ❹ 正しい
❺ 十分な   ❻ 親しい
❼ 好む   ❽ 健康な
❾ 幸運な   ❿ 数量・程度がかなりの
⓫ 不必要な   ⓬ 希望, 願望
⓭ かまわない   ⓮ 許可
⓯ 助言   ⓰ 同意, 承諾
⓱ 確認   ⓲ その他の表現

❶ 【好ましい, 優れている】 good*; nice; fine; pleasant /plézənt/; excellent. (⇨良い)

> **使い分け** good 質・程度・技術などの点で満足でき, 賞賛に値するものであること.
> **nice** 主にくだけた会話で, 話し手にとって楽しくなるようなものや, 気持ちのよい思いをさせるようなものの意味の広い語. 堅い書き言葉では意味によって *interesting*, *beautiful*, *pleasant* などの明確な語を用いる方がよい.
> **fine** 見た目や質が他のものより優れていること.
> **pleasant** 物事が人にとって楽しく愉快で心地よいこと. また, 人・行為などが愛想がよく好感が持てること.
> **excellent** 並はずれて質が高いこと.

● いい女 (美しい) a *beautiful* [a *good-looking*, a *lovely*, (かわいい) a *pretty*] woman; (魅力的な) an *attractive* [a *charming*] woman. (!*beautiful* は外面, *charming* は内面についていう. 特に *charming* は立場が上の者が下の者に対していう語 (⇨美人))
● いい男 (=器量のよい)男 a *handsome* [a *good-looking*] man; (魅力的な) an *attractive* [a *charming*] man. (⇨ハンサム) ● いい人 (⇨いい人)
● いい(=さわやかな)空気 *fresh* air. ● 涼しくていい風 a *nice* and *cool* (a *cool* and *pleasant*) *breeze*. (!*nice* and は /náisən(d)/ と発音する) ▶あれは実にいい映画だ That is a really *good* [*nice*, *fine*, *excellent*] *film*. ● 意志が強いのが彼のいいところだ His *good* point is that he is strong-willed. ▶いい天気ですね It's a *nice* [a *lovely*, a *beautiful*, (主に英) a *fine*] day, isn't it? (《英》 では *fine* を実際には晴れていなくても単に雨が止んだときに用いることがある)/It's *nice* [*good*, *beautiful*] weather, isn't it? (《話》 では単に *Nice* [*Lovely*, *Beautiful*] day, isn't it?/*Nice* [*Good*, *Beautiful*] weather, isn't it? ともいう) ▶おはよう. なんていい朝なんだろう. 生きていてよ

ったって気分になるよね Gòod mórning. And a *góod* mòrining it is! It makes you feel good to be alive, doesn't it? ▶その店で何でも買えるのはいいことだ It is good for us to be able to get anything [that we can get anything] at that store. ▶この本はあの本よりいい This book is *better* than that one./(すぐれている) This book is *superior to* [×than] that one. ▶それにはどうしたらいちばんいいですか What's the *best* way to do it? ▶借金が多ければ多いほど都合がいい, そこがインフレのいいところ(=利点)だ The more you owe, the better you do. That's *the beauty* of inflation. ▶私は彼女に自分のことをいいことも悪いことも洗いざらい話した I told her everything about me—*the good* and *the bad*.
会話「彼の作品どう思う?」「なかなかいい(=悪くはない)よ」"What's your opinion of his work?" "It's *not bad*." (!very good の婉曲的な言い方)
【…がいい】(!「…」にあたる見出し語を参照) ▶彼は学校の成績がとてもいい He is doing very *well* in school. (!well is good に対応する副詞)/(成績のいい学生である) He's a student with *good* grades. ▶ここは気候がいい(=穏やかだ) The climate is *mild* here.

❷[ためになる](健康などによい) good*; (効果的な) effective; (有益な) useful. ▶この草は切り傷にいい This herb is *good* [*effective*] *for* a cut. ▶早寝早起きは健康にいい Keeping [To keep] regular hours is *good for* [×to] your health. (!(1)主語には動名詞を用いる方が普通. (2) your は一般に「人の」の意. 代わりに the でも可)/It is *good for* your health to keep regular hours./Keeping regular hours *does* you *good*. (!do (...) good は「(...に)益をもたらす」の意) ▶お医者さんが山の空気が私の健康回復にいいだろうと言いました The doctor said that the mountain air would *help* me (*to*) get better.

❸[適した] good*; (人・目的・状況に合った) suitable; (最適の) right. ▶この本は初歩の人にいい This book is *good* [*suitable, useful*] *for* [*to*] beginners. ▶京都駅へ行くのはこの道でいいのですか Is this the *right* way to Kyoto Station? ▶ちょうどいい時に彼がやって来た You have come along just at [at just] the *right* time. ▶このセーターは私にはちょうどいい(=寸法が合う) This sweater *fits* me very well [is a good *fit*, 《話》*fits* me to a T]. ▶もう彼が帰ってきてもいいころだ It is about time (*that*) he came back [*for* him to come back]. (!that は通例省略する. that 節内は通例直説法過去) ▶あなたの都合のいい時を教えてください Please tell me when it will *suit* [*be convenient for*] you. (!人を主語にした ×you will suit [be convenient] は不可)

❹[正しい](人・行為などが道徳・宗教的に立派な) good*; (行為などが道徳・社会通念上正しい) right. ▶私はいいと思うことをやったまでだ I only did what I thought (was) *good* [*right*]. ▶その子はまだいいことと悪いことの区別がつかない The boy still doesn't know the difference between *right* and *wrong*. (!この right, wrong は名詞(⇒善し悪し))

❺[十分な] enough (⇒十分); (申し分ない) all right, 《話》OK; (用意のできた) ready; (間に合う) will* do; (...で我慢しておく) settle for .... ▶それだけいえばもういいだろう I think you've said *enough*. (!短かく「もういい」は That's *enough*./Enough said. ▶それくらいは理解できてもいい年だ You are old *enough* [×*enough old*] *to* understand it. ▶睡眠は1日8時間でいい It will be *enough* if you sleep (for) eight hours a day./Eight hours a day will be *enough* for us to sleep. ▶本当は大きい辞書が欲しいのですが, 今はその小さいやつでいいです I really want a large dictionary, but right now I'll *settle for* [*do with*] that small one.

会話「これでいい?」「とってもきれいに見えるよ」"*Will* this *do*?/Is this *all right* [《話》*OK*]?" "You look lovely, my dear."
会話「もう支度はいいですか」「まだです」"Are you *ready* now?" "No, not yet." (!かくれんぼの「もういいかい」「まあだだよ」も同様)
会話「コーヒーをもう少しいかが」「ええ, でもほんの少しだけ」「じゃ(欲しいところで入れたら)『いい』って言ってね」「そこで結構よ」"Would you care for some more coffee?" "Yes. Only a little." "OK. Then say *when*." "That's fine. Thanks."

❻[親しい](非常に親しい) good* (限定的に); (友好的な) friendly; (親密な) close. ▶彼らはいい友達だ They are *good* [*close, nice*] *friends*. ▶私は彼女と仲がいい I am *friendly with* her./I am *on friendly* [*good*] *terms with* her./She is a *good friend* of mine.

❼[好む] like; (より好む) prefer (-rr-). ▶彼女のどこがいいんだ What do you *like* about her? ▶彼女のように(=好きなように)させておけ Let him do as he *likes* [*pleases*,《書》*wishes*]./Let him *have* his *own way*. ▶車で行くより歩いて行く方がいい I *like* walking better [more] than riding./I *prefer* walking *to* [×*more than*] riding./I *prefer* to walk *rather than* (*to*) ride [×than riding]./I *would* [I'd,《話》I'd] rather walk *than* drive [×walking than driving].

会話「ステーキはどんな焼き具合がいいですか」「ミディアムがいいです」"How would you *like* your steak?" "I'd *like* it [mine] medium." (!単に Medium, please. と答えてもよい)

会話「てんぷらがいいですか, 刺身がいいですか」「てんぷらの方がいいです」"*Would* you *like* ✓tempura or ✓sashimi?" "I'd *prefer* tempura, please." (!would like [prefer] は「好き嫌い」ではなく, 特定場面での穏やかな「希望」を表す. その後に不定詞は続くが, 動名詞は不可: I'd like [prefer] to eat [×eating later].)

❽[健康な] well*; (大丈夫で) all right. ▶(いずれも通例叙述的に) 顔色がいいですね You look *well*. ▶(以前と比べて)今日はずっと気分がいい I feel much *better* today. ▶もうすっかりいい I'm quite *all right* now./I've got quite *well*.

❾[幸運な] lucky, (さい先のよい)《書》auspicious. ● 運のいい男 a *lucky* man. ▶いい日を選ぶ choose a *lucky* [an *auspicious*] day (*for* a wedding). ▶これは縁起のいい番号だ This is a *lucky* number. ▶いい具合に雨が上がったわ *Fortunately* [*Luckily*], the rain has stopped.

❿[数量・程度がかなりの] good*; (水準以上の) high. (⇒高い) ▶彼は試験でいい点を取った He got a *good* [a *high*] mark on the exam. ▶野菜がいい値で売れている Vegetables are selling at a *good* [a *high*] price. (!... at an *expensive* price は避けた方がよい) ▶この仕事はいい金になる(=もうかる)だろう This job will be *profitable* [*lucrative*]. (!前の方は「利益が高い」, 後の方は「ともかく多くのお金が入ってくる」) ▶いい年をして(=もう分別のある年なのだから)そんなことをするじゃない Now that you *are* old *enough* to know *better*, you shouldn't do that.

⓫[不必要な](必要としない) do* not need; (...する必要がない) do not have [need] to《do》,《主に英》need not《do》. ▶今日はいいです(ご用聞きなどに) We *don't need* anything [（注文はない）don't have any order] today. ▶今日は学校に行かなくていいよ You *don't have to* [*don't need to*, 《主に英》*need not*] go to school today./*It isn't necessary for you to* go to school today. (❗) 後の方が堅い言い方. (2) 簡単には We don't have school [No school] today. も可）▶別に急がなくてもいいよ There's no hurry about it.

⓬ [希望, 願望] （希望する）hope; （…であればいいのだが）wish. (❗) hope は未来のことで可能性のあることを, wish は現在または過去の事実に反するといか実現の可能性がほとんどない未来のことを望む場合に用いる) ▶お手伝いいただけるといいのですけど I'm *hoping* you will help me. / I *hope* より控えめな言い方. また I *hoped* [*was hoping*] you would .... はこの順にいっそう控えめで丁寧な頼み方になる) ▶ここに彼がいたらいいのになあ I *wish* (*that*) he were [was] here. (❗) (1) that は通例省略される. (2) that 節中の動詞は現在のことには通例仮定法過去を用いるが, 後の単純過去を用いている方が that 節中の内容に対する話し手の確信度が高い. 過去のことには通例仮定法過去完了を用いる. (⇨良い ❸) (2) *If only* he were here. はさらに強意的な表現）▶(彼がいなくて残念だ) I am sorry [Too bad] (that) he isn't here.

会話 「早く仕事が見つかるといいですね」「そうだといいのですけど」"I *hope* (that) you (will) find a job soon." "I do, too./Me, too." (❗) (1) 《話》では通例 that を省略する. (2) that 節中は未来の内容であっても現実感を込めて言いたい場合にはしばしば現在時制となるが, be 動詞のときは will be の方が普通.

⓭ [かまわない] I don't mind (*doing*);（気にしない）I don't care (*about*); （できる）can (*do*). ▶君といっしょなら雨にぬれたっていい I *don't mind getting* wet [ˣ*to get wet*] in the rain if I am with you. ▶彼らに何と言われてもいい I *don't care* (*about*) what they say [ˣwill say] about me. (❗) wh- 語の前では通例, 前置詞は省略される ▶そんなことどうでもいいよ *It doesn't matter* at all. (❗) matter は通例 it を主語にして「重要である」の意. 主に疑問文・否定文で用いる ▶私は今年の夏は休みなしでいい I *can do without* a vacation this summer. ▶お疲れでしたら私が代わりにそれをしてあげてもいいですよ I *could do* it for you if you're tired. (❗) could は仮定法過去で「やろうと思えばできるのだが」の意）▶休暇をとるのはいいけれど, その仕事はどうするつもりだい *It's all very well* [*all very fine*] *for you to* take a vacation, but what are you going to do about the task? (❗) 不満・不賛成を表すときの決まり文句）▶トラベラーズチェックでもいいですか (=を受け取っていただけますか) Do you *accept* traveler's checks?

会話 「紅茶とコーヒーのどちらがいいですか」「どちらでもいいです」"Tea or coffee?" "*I don't mind*./Either will do."

会話 「このスーツケースは 3 キロほどオーバーですけれど. まあいいでしょう」「いや, どうも. ありがとうございます」"Your suitcase is about three kilos overweight, but we'll just let it go." "Thanks a lot. I appreciate it." (❗) let it go は「その通過を認める」の意.

⓮ [許可] can*, may*. (⇨良い ❹)

解説 I （1）can, may ともに「…してもいい」と主語に許可を与えることを表すが, may は通例話し手の権威を暗示することから目下の者以外に対して使うのは避けた方がよく, 堅い書き言葉を除いて can の方が一般的. (2) may はこの用法では通例動作動詞を従え, 状態を表す言い方が続くと「…かもしれない」という可能性を表す. ただし, 主語が you 以外のときは動作動詞が続いていても許可か可能性かあいまい.

▶先生が帰ってもいいとおっしゃったんです（直接話法）My teacher said to me, "You *can* [*may*] go home." / You *may*.... は目上の者が目下の者に対して言う命令調の言い方. ただし, You can.... も文脈によって軽い命令となる)/(間接話法) My teacher said that I *could* [*might*] go home. (❗) might は可能性の意味にもとられるので could の方が好まれる (⇨解説 I)) /My teacher *permitted* [*allowed*] me to go home. (❗) permit は積極的な許可を与える場合に用いる) ▶だれが私のアルバムを見ていいと言ったの？ Who said you *could* look at my album? Stop it. ▶ここに座ってもいいですか *Can* [*Could, May*] I *sit here*(*, please*)? (❗) (1) この順に丁寧な言い方となる. (2) might は丁寧すぎてこびた言い方ともなるのであまり一般的でない)/*Would* [*Do*, ˣ*Don't*, ˣ*Will*] you mind if I sit here? (❗) (1) do より would の方が丁寧な言い方になる. くだけた言い方ではしばしば Would [Do] you が省略される. (2) ...mind my (話) me] sitting here? ともいえる.

解説 II (1) 許可を求める丁寧な言い方としては他に, I wonder if I *could* [*might*] sit here./Do you think I could sit here? などがある. くだけた言い方では Is it all right [OK] if I sit here? などが可.
(2) 許可の求めに対する答え方: （a）許可する場合ー Yes, certainly./(Yes,) of course./(Yes,) certainly you can./Yes, that's fine [all right]./By all means. くだけた言い方では《主に米話》Sure./That's OK [by [with] me]./That's は しばしば省略される）/Go (right) ahead./(Yes, I don't see) why not? など. 日本語の「えぇ, どうぞ」にひかれて ˣYes, please. とはいえない.
（b）許可しない場合ー(Sorry,) I'm afraid you can't./I'm sorry, it's taken. (❗) このように軽く理由を添える方が丁寧な言い方となる)/I'm afraid not./I'd rather you didn't. (❗) didn't と過去形になることに注意
（c）mind を用いた Would [Do] you *mind* if ...? は「もし…したらあなたはいやですか」の意なので, 許可する場合は, ＼No, not at ＼all./Of ＼course not./＼Certainly not./No, go ahead. などの ように否定の形で答えるのが原則. ただし Certainly./Sure. と答えることもある.
(3) Can [Could, May] I ...? の質問に対して助動詞を使って答える際, 許可する場合は Of course you *can* [*may*, ˣ*could*]., 許可しない場合は No, you *can't* [*may not*, ˣ*mayn't*, ˣ*could not*]. となるが, これらは子供や目下の者以外には失礼にあたることもあるので注意.

▶ちょっといいですか（話に割り込むときの前置き）*Could I say some words?*/（相談などを持ちかけるときの前置き）*Could you spare me* [*Do you have*] *a few minutes*?

⓯ [助言] should [ought to]《do》; had better 《do》; may [might] (just) as well《do》; it would [might] be better《to do》.

使い分け should 相手に助言・勧告を与える時に用いる最も一般的な語.
ought to should より公的・客観的な勧告に用いる. 時に強意的ニュアンスを持つ.
had better 助言に従わないと取り返しのつかないことになるような緊急事態における警告として用いる. 状況次第では脅迫にもなりかねないので目上の人には用いない方がよい.

> **may [might] (just) as well** 軽い助言に用いる. 比較的軽い内容の二つの選択肢があって「してもしなくても大した違いはないが, そうしても悪くはない」の意.
> **it would [might] be better to** 客観的に何かと比較してそうする方がいいことを表す. might を用いる方が控えめな言い方になる.

▶どうすればいいのか分からなかった I didn't know *what to do* [*what I should do*]. (◀後の方が口語的) ▶私たちは何をすればいいのですか, ここでぶらぶらしていればいいのですか What *are we supposed to* do? Hang around here? (◀「実際には何をすることがなさそうだが」の含みのある発言) ▶熱があるんだから, 学校は休んだ (=家にいる) 方がいい You *had better* [*should, ought to*] stay home [(学校の方を強調して) away from school] because you have a fever. (◀ You had better は (通例目上の人の) 命令に近い強い忠告で,《主に英》では however You'd better, さらにくだけて You better, Better となることがある. いずれも I think, Maybe, Perhaps などを文頭に加えていうと, 控えめな言い方になる) ▶ You'd *better not* [*shouldn't, oughtn't to*] go to school because you have a fever. (◀had not better は 《非標準》/*It is advisable for you to* [*that you* 《主に英》 *should*] stay away from school because you have a fever. (◀ I advise you that .... より It is *advisable that* .... の方が穏やかな言い方) ▶彼に尋ねるのが一番いい You *had best* ask him. ▶天気が悪いので家にいた方がいいのでは The weather is so bad that you *may* [*might*] as *well* stay at home. (◀ might を用いる方が穏やかな言い方) ▶私がそちらに出向いて直接お渡ししてもいいのですが I *might* as well come [×go] over and give you them. (◀「相手のいる所へ行く」は come) ▶どれが一番いいと思いますか Which do you *recommend*? ▶「ありがとう」くらい言えばいいのに You *might at least* say "Thank you." (◀「...してもいいのに (なぜしないのか)」の非難の意を含むくだけた言い方)

会話「行きましょうか」「しばらく待つ方がいい (=賢明だ) と思わない?」"Shall we go?" "Don't you think *it would be wiser to* wait a while?"

会話「まっすぐ京都へ行った方がいいと思いますか, それとも大阪を経由した方がいいと思いますか」「大阪で一晩過ごした方がいいです」"Do you think I *should* go directly to Kyoto or go by way of Osaka?" "*It would be better (for you) to* [*You'd be better to,* ×You had better] spend a night in Osaka." (◀had better は二つの活動を比較するときには用いない)

会話「どの燃料がいいと思いますか」「そうだなあ. 石油が一番安くつくと思う」"Which fuel do you *suggest*?" "Well, oil's the cheapest."

会話「学校に遅れちゃうよ」「早く起きればいいのよ (=起きるべきだったのに)」"I can't be in time for school." "You *should have got* [I *suggest* you ((主に英)) *should*) get] up earlier." (◀should の後に完了形を用いると実現しなかったことを表す)

会話「京都の人口を知りたいのですが」「この本で調べるといいですよ」"I'd like to know the population of Kyoto." "I *suggest* you go [《主に英》 *should* go] through this book." (◀相手に選択を任せて軽く勧める場合は You *could* [*might*] go through this book. も可)

❶⑥【同意, 承諾】(同意する) **agree** (*to*); (満足である) **be satisfied** (*with*). ▶それでは彼がいいとうまい He won't *say yes to* [*agree to, be satisfied with*] it.

会話「映画に行きましょうか」「行きましょう」"Let's go to the movies, shall we?" "Yes, *let's*." (◀否定の答えは No, let's not.)

会話「食事の前に一杯どう?」「いいね」"How about a drink before dinner?" "(That's) *great*./That'll be *nice*./(That) sounds *great*./(いい考えだ) (That's) a *good* idea."

会話「あしたの朝 9 時に来ていただけませんか」「ええ, いいですよ」"Would you come over here at 9 tomorrow morning?" "*Certainly.*/(*Yes,*) *of course.*"/"Would you mind coming over here at 9 tomorrow morning?" "*No, I wouldn't.*/*Certainly not.*/*Of* *course not.*" (◀ not で返答するのが原則だが, Certainly., Sure. などで答えることもある. (⇒⓮ 解説 Ⅱ))/"Well, *I don't see why not*." (◀消極的同意・承諾で「まあいいですよ」といった感じ)

会話「ごみを出してくださる?」「いいよ」"Could you take out the garbage for me?" "*All right* [《話》 *OK*,《主に米話》 *Sure*]./(喜んで) *With pleasure*./(お安いご用) *No problem*."

会話「7 時でいいかい」「いいよ」"Is seven o'clock *OK*?" "*Fine*."

会話「それ全部は運べないわよ」「そうね, じゃあできるだけたくさん運んで」"I can't carry all of it." "*Well, then carry as much as you can.*"

❶⑰【確認】▶次にこのボタンを押します. いいですね Next we press this button. *OK* [(*All*) *right*]? (◀ OK の方がくだけた言い方. 類例: じろじろ見ないでくれ. いいね Stop staring, *right*? (◀「分かったな」に近い)) ▶いいかい (=気をつけて, 僕の手を離すんじゃないよ) *Be careful* [《主に英》*Mind*] (*that*) you don't [×won't] let go (of) my hand./(よく聞け) *Listen* [*mind you*], don't let go (of) my hand. ▶ぼくがたがたれを したのは, いいかい, やらされたからだよ I only did it, /*mind yóu*, because I was forced to.

会話「でもニンジンは好きじゃないんだもの」「いいこと, 残さず食べなさいよ」"But I don't like the carrot." "*Eat it up. Yes?*" (◀子供に対して用いる)

会話「いいかい, 私が言ったことを忘れるなよ」「はい, パパ」"*Now remember what I've said.*" "Yes, Daddy."

会話「お座り」「一杯どう?」「いいんですか」"Have a seat [a drink]." "*Don't you mind if I do?*"

❶⑱【その他の表現】▶人生いいことばかりではない Life is not all *fun*. ▶今にいいこともあるさ Let's have *hopes* in the future./Let's not [《米》 Let's don't] be pessimistic. ▶まあ, いいや (=あきらめるよ) Well, I'll *give it up*. ▶いいぞ *Góod for* *you!*/*Fine!*/*Wéll* *done!*

会話「ありがとうございます」「いいんですよ」"Thank you." "\ ♥*That's OK* [*all right*]. (◀ OK の方が口語的)/*Never* /*mind*." (◀感謝・謝罪などに対する答えには (It's) no trouble at all./Forget (about) it., 丁寧な言い方は 《主に米》 You are welcome./(It is) my pleasure./(Please) don't mention it. などがある. 堅い言い方では Not at all. があるが,《主に米》のくだけた言い方では Sure./Uh-huh /Áhá/. などが用いられたり,《英》では笑ってうなずくだけで何も言わというのでも多い)

会話「本当にすみません」「いいんだよ」"I'm terribly sorry." "*That's all* /*right*./(心配するな) *Don't* /*worry* (*about* it.)/(これ以上そのことを考えるな) *Don't give it* another *thought*./(謝るには及ばない) *Don't apologize*."

イー ◀イード Nyah(h)/njá:/!
いいあい 言い合い a quarrel. (⇨言い争い)
いいあて 言い当てる guess right. (⇨当てる ❸)
いいあやまる 言い誤る make* a slip of the tongue; say*... by mistake.
いいあらそい 言い争い (口論) a quarrel; (意見の不一

致) an argument. (⇨口論)

いいあらそう 言い争う argue [quarrel]《with+人, about [over]+事》, have* an argument [a quarrel, 《話》a row /ráu/, 《婉曲的に》words 《with, about》(❗argue, have an argument は怒りを伴わない議論にも用いる). (長時間にわたって) dispute 《with, about》. ▶彼は子供の教育のことで妻と言い争った He argued [quarreled] with his wife about the education of [for] their children. ▶そんなささいなことで(彼と)言い争うべきでない You shouldn't dispute (with him) about [over] such trifles.

いいあらわす 言い表す (表現する) express; (述べる) describe. (⇨表現する) ●喜びを言葉で言い表す express one's joy in [×with] words. ●自分の考えを言い表す express oneself [one's opinion, one's views]. ●言い表せないほどの inexpressible. (⇨言い知れぬ) ▶ご親切に対する感謝の気持ちは言葉では言い表せません I can't express (to you) [tell you] how grateful I am for your kindness./《やや書》My gratitude for your kindness is beyond expression [words].

***いいえ** ❶[質問に対して] no (↔yes); (否定疑問文に対して) yes (↔no).

> 解説 no は肯定または否定の答えを求めるいわゆる Yes/No 疑問文に対して, 否定文の答えが続く場合に用いる. (⇨はい 解説)

▶彼は「いいえ」と答えた He answered no [in the negative]. (❗後の方は堅い言い方)
会話「彼女はあなたのお母さんですか」「いいえ, 違います」"Is she your mother?" "Nó, she \isn't [she \not]."(❗(1) No, she is not. は強調または堅い言い方で, 日常会話では短縮形の方が普通. (2) 単に No. のように答えるのはぶっきらぼうに響くので避ける. (3) No, she is my aunt (, as a matter of fact). (いいえ, おばなんです)のような答えも可. as a matter of fact は相手の言った内容を訂正する表現をやわらげる)
会話「忙しい?」「いいえ, 全然」"Are you busy?" "No, not at all." (❗否定の意味を強めるときは, at all, at first, in the least などをそえる)
会話「お酒は飲まれますか」「いいえ, 飲むというほどではありません」"Do you drink? "Oh, not really (=I don't really drink)."(❗really は not の後で用いて否定の調子をやわらげる)
会話「泳げないんですか」「いいえ, 泳げます」"Can't you swim?" "Yes [×No], I can."(❗日本語では「いいえ」となるが, 英語では疑問文が否定かどうかにかかわらず, 答えとして肯定が続く場合は, Yes となる. ただし, "You can't swim?" "Yes [No], I can." ("泳げないんでしょ」「いいえ, 泳げます」)のように否定を期待する平叙文の形をした否定形疑問文では, 肯定が続いても反論する意味で No を用いることができる)

❷[反論] (肯定文に対して) no; (否定文に対して) yes.
会話「彼はやぶ医者だよ」「いいえ, そんなことはありませんよ」"He is a quack." "Nó, he ∕isn't."(❗反論する場合は❶とは異なり, ∕または \を用いて語調をやわらげるのが一般的)
会話「ぼくは気にしていないよ」「いいえ, 気にしているよ」"I don't care." "Yés, you \do cáre."

❸[感謝・わびに対して] That's all right. (⇨どういたしまして)

❹[提案に対して] 会話 「お酒はいかがですか」「いいえ, 結構です. 今日は車なんです」"How would you like a drink?" "\Nó, ∕thank you. I'm driving today." (❗No. だけではぶっきらぼうすぎて失礼)

いいえてみょう 言い得て妙 ▶あの女性のことを鉄の女とは言い得て妙だ She is aptly called "the Iron Lady."

いいおとす 言い落とす forget* to say. (⇨言い忘れる)

いいかえ 言い換え, 言い替え a paraphrase, another way of saying 《a thing》. (⇨言い換える)

いいかえす 言い返す (反論する) refute; (怒って反論する) retort; (口答えする) answer 《him》back. ▶「何をばかな」と彼は鋭く言い返した "Nonsense!" he sharply retorted./He sharply retorted that what he [she] said was nonsense.

いいかえる 言い換える, 言い替える say* [put*]...(in) another way 《《話》では in を省略するのが普通》; (文章などを) paraphrase. ●言い換えれば in other words; to put it another way [differently]; (すなわち) that is (to say). ●その句をやさしい英語で言い換える paraphrase the phrase in easy English.

いいかお 好い顔 ❶[好意的な態度の表れた顔] ▶母は私があのバイクを乗り回すとあまりいい顔をしない Mother isn't very happy [pleased] about my riding around on that motorbike. ❷[有力な人] an influential person, 《話》 a big shot. ❸[よい表情] a good look. (⇨顔 ❷)

いいがかり 言いがかり (間違った非難) a false accusation. ▶(…したと)私に言いがかりをつける (=非難しようとする) try to accuse me of 《having done ...》.

いいかける 言いかける (言いそうになる) be about [be just going] to say; (言い始める) start to say. ▶私はウエーターに文句を言いかけてやめた. 大人気ないと思ったのだ I was about to complain to the waiter, but stopped myself. I thought it ungentlemanly. (❗My complaint to the waiter was just on the tip of my tongue, but I held it back, ... のようにもいえる. 「口先までで出かかった」の意)

いいかげん いい加減 ── いい加減な 形 ❶[適度の] (適当な) proper; (ちょうどよい) just right; (十分な) enough. ▶ふろはちょうどいい加減だ The bath is just the right temperature [just warm enough].
❷[でたらめな, 不徹底の] (無責任な) irresponsible; (でたらめな) random; (疑わしい) dubious, 《話》fishy; (当てにならない) unreliable; (根拠のない) groundless; (あいまいな) vague; (言質 (げんち) を与えない) 《やや書》noncommittal; (中途半端な) halfway. ●いい加減なことを言う say irresponsible [random] things; talk irresponsibly. ●いい加減な=うさんくさい話 a suspicious [a fishy] story. ●いい加減な情報 unreliable information. ●いい加減なうわさ a groundless rumor. ●いい加減な返事をする give a vague [a noncommittal] answer. ▶私はいい加減な仕事はしたくない I don't want to do a halfway job [《遊び半分で》《話》play at a job].

── いい加減に 副 ●いい加減に(=無作為に)選ぶ choose at random; make a random choice. ●物事をいい加減に(=中途半端に)するな Don't do things by halves [leave things half-done]. (❗by halves は通例否定文で用いる) ●冗談もいい加減にしろ (=もうたくさんだ) (I've had) enough of your jokes./That's enough joking. (❗Enough of ... は独立して成句的によく用いる：(それは)もういい加減にしろ Enough of that./(度を越すな) Don't go too far in your jokes. ▶いい加減(=かなり)くたびれた I am pretty [rather] tired.
会話 (電話で)「ちょっと切らないで待ってて」「いい加減にしろよ. おれだって忙しいんだぞ」"Hold on a minute." "Come \on. We don't have all day."

いいかた 言い方 a way of speaking [saying it]; 〖表現〗an expression. ●慣用的な言い方 an idio-

いいがたい 言い難い hard [difficult] to say [mention], indescribable, unspeakable. ▶言いがたい悲しみ indescribable [unspeakable, inexpressible] sorrow. ▶いわく言いがたし That's *hard to say*.

いいかわす 言い交わす ❶ [互いに言う] exchange《opinions, greetings, a few words》. (❗目的語は通例複数名詞) ❷ [口約束をする] make a verbal [an oral] promise. ❸ [結婚の約束をする] ▶彼らは言い交わした仲です They *have exchanged* marriage vows./(婚約している) They *are engaged*.

いいき いい気 いい気な 形 [のん気な] easygoing, carefree; [楽観的な] optimistic; [得意気な] (うぬぼれている) conceited; [高慢な] proud. ▶あいつはいい気なものだ He is extremely *carefree*.
── いい気になる ●成功していい気になっている *be conceited about* one's success; *be too proud of* one's success; (得意になっている) *be elated by* one's success.

いいきかせる 言い聞かせる (❛説得する, 諭す) ▶自分に言い聞かせる say to [tell] oneself 《to do; (that) 節》. ▶それは自分の間違いだったと彼は自身に言い聞かせようとした He tried to *tell himself that* it was his fault.

いいきみ いい気味 (⇨気味)

イーキュー ❶ [感情指数] EQ《*emotional quotient* の略》. (関連) IQ 知能指数 ❷ [教育指数] EQ《*educational quotient* の略》.

いいきる 言い切る assert. (⇨断言する)

いいぐさ 言い草 [言ったこと] what〈he〉said; [言い方] the way〈he〉said. (❗いずれも日本語にあるような非難する気持ちはない) ▶彼の言い草がしゃくにさわった I was irritated by [at] *what* he *said*.

イーグル [ゴルフ] an eagle. (参考) パーより二つ少ない打数でホールアウトすること)

いいくるめる 言いくるめる ▶彼を言いくるめて計画をやめさせる *coax* him *out of* his plan; *coax* him *to give [into giving]* up his plan. (⇨丸め込む)

いいこ 好い子 a good boy [girl]. ▶いい子だからもう寝なさい Go to [Get into] bed like a *good boy [girl]*. ▶どちらにもいい子になろうったってそうはいかないね You can't make both sides think well of you.

いいことに ▶彼は彼女がお人好しなのをいいことに (=利用して) 金をだまし取った He *took advantage of* her innocence [good nature] and cheated her out of her money.

いいこめる 言い込める talk [(米) argue]《him》down.

イーシー [欧州共同体] EC《the *European Community* の略》.

イージーオーダー ▶この上着はイージーオーダーで作りました I had this jacket *made to order without a fitting*. (❗×easy order は和製英語 ⇨オーダーメード)

イージーゴーイング ▶彼はイージーゴーイングな人だ He is the kind of person who takes everything a bit *too easy*./His (way of) thinking is *too easygoing*. (❗単に easy や easygoing だけでは日本語の持つマイナスのニュアンスが伴わない)

イージーリスニング [くつろぎで聴ける軽音楽] easy listening.

イージスかん イージス艦 an aegis /iːdʒɪs/.

いいしぶる 言い渋る ▶遅刻の理由を言い渋る (=言うのをためらう) *hesitate to* [(いやいやながら言う) *be reluctant to*] say why one is late.

いいしれぬ 言い知れぬ ▶言い知れぬ悲しみ [喜び] *indescribable [inexpressible, unspeakable]* sorrow [joy].

いいすぎ 言い過ぎ ▶…と言っても言い過ぎでない It is *not too much to say that* …./It is *no exaggeration to say that* ….▶それは言い過ぎだよ You've said more than enough./You've gone too far.

イースター [復活祭] Easter.

イースト [酵母] ▶イースト菌 a *yeast* fungus /fʌŋɡəs/. (⑱ fungi -gai/, ~es).

いいそこなう 言い損なう [失言する] make* a slip of the tongue [lip]; [言い忘れる] forget* to tell.

いいそびれる 言いそびれる fail to tell; [言う機会を逸する] miss a chance to tell.

いいだくだく 唯々諾々 ▶兵士は唯々諾々として (=従順に) 命令に従った The soldiers *obediently [submissively]* obeyed the order.

いいだこ 飯蛸 [動物] *octopus ocellatus*; (説明的に) a kind of small-sized octopus.

いいだしっぺ 言い出しっぺ ▶言い出しっぺにまずやってもらおう We will ask you to try it first. You brought it up first./You do it first because you made the suggestion.

いいたす 言い足す add. ▶「忘れずにお電話ください」と彼女は言い足した "Don't forget to call me (up)," she *added*.

いいだす 言い出す [言い始める] begin* to say [speak]; [提案する] suggest, propose (❗前の方が口語的で控えめな提案); [問題を持ち出す] bring* …up. ▶彼は何か言い出そうとしたが電話のベルにさえぎられた He began [was beginning] to say something, but he was interrupted by the telephone ring. ▶伝助は魚釣りに行こうと言い出した Densuke *suggested* that we (主に英) *should) go fishing.*/Densuke *suggested going [*to go] fishing.* ▶だれがそれを言い出したのですか Who *has brought* the matter *up*?

いいちがい 言い違い ▶言い違いをする (⇨言い誤る)

いいつくす 言い尽くす [すべてを言う] *tell* everything [all]《*about*》; leave* nothing unsaid; [十二分に言い表す] express (oneself) fully; (口頭で, 書いて) talk [write] fully《*about*》. ▶ご助力に対する感謝の気持ちは言い尽くせません I *cannot express* how grateful I am for your invaluable help. (⇨言葉 2)

いいつくろう 言い繕う explain《it》away; make* an excuse《for》. (❗gloss over …は「…のマイナス面はなるべく話さずプラス面を強調する」の意で, 「言い繕う」とは異なる) ▶遅れて着いたことをあれこれ言い繕う *make excuses for* coming late; *explain away* one's late arrival.

いいつけ 言い付け [命令] an order. (⇨命令) ▶彼の言いつけにそむく go against his *order*. ▶親の言いつけを守る (=親に従う) *obey* one's parents.

いいつける 言い付ける [命じる] order; tell* 《⇨命令する); [告げ口する] (話) tell on … (⇨告げ口). ▶彼女のことを先生に言いつけた go to her teacher and *tell on* [(米) *tattle on*] her; *tell* her teacher *on* her. ▶そんなことしたらお母さんに言いつけるからね Do that, and I'll *tell* your mother.

いいつたえ 言い伝え（伝承）(a) tradition;（伝説）(a) legend.（⇨伝説）▶言い伝えによるとこのあたりに寺があったそうだ According to (an old) *tradition*, [*Tradition* has it that, *Tradition* says that, *It has been said that*] there was a temple around here.

いいつたえる 言い伝える（伝説などを）hand ... down. ▶この悲話は大昔から（＝何世紀にもわたって）言い伝えられてきたものだ This sad story *has been handed down* to us through the centuries.

いいつのる 言い募る insist more and more heartedly [vehemently /víːəməntli/].

いいとおす 言い通す persist 《in》;（主張する）insist. ▶事故は自分のせいではないと彼は言い通した He *persisted in* saying [*insisted*] that the accident wasn't his fault.

いいとこ ❶[せいぜい] at (the) best;（多くても）at (the) most. ▶100メートル競走では彼はいいとこ2位だろう He may come in second *at (the) best* in the 100-meter dash.
❷[あまりにも] too. ▶彼女に朝食をベッドまで運ばせるなんて彼は横着もいいとこだ He's much *too* lazy, making her bring his breakfast to the bed./（何たる横着者だ）What a lazybones he is to make her bring his breakfast to the bed!

いいなおす 言い直す［言い改める］correct oneself;［別の表現をする］put* [express*] ⟨it⟩ in another way（⇨言い替える）.

いいなか 仲のいい ▶彼らはいい仲だ They love each other./They're in love (with each other)./They are *lovers*.（❗時に性的関係を暗示する）

いいなずけ 許婚（男性）one's fiancé;（女性）one's fiancée.（❗これらの語には「親の定めた相手」の意はない. 発音はいずれも /fìːɑːnséɪ/）

いいなり 言いなり ▶彼は彼女の言いなりになっている He does just *as* she tells him to./〘話〙He is *under her thumb*.（❗she を主語にすると, She has him *under her thumb*.）/〘話〙He is tied to her apron strings.

いいにくい 言い難い ▶言いにくそうに hésitatingly. ▶言いにくいことだが... I hesitate to say.../I *hate to say* [*tell* (you)], but .... ▶言いにくいんだけどそれをこわしてしまったの I'm afraid I've broken it.
会話「言いにくいのですが, 1年前にお貸しした本を返していただけませんか」「あらごめんなさい. すっかり忘れていたわ. 本棚のどこかに片付けたのよ」"*I hate to ask you*, *but* could you return the book you borrowed from me a year ago?" "Oh, sorry. I'd completely forgotten about it. I put it somewhere on my bookshelf."（❗ask は「頼む, お願いする」の意）

いいね 言い値 the ásking price. ●言い値で買う buy ⟨it⟩ at the ásking price [*the price asked*].

いいのがれ 言い逃れ［あいまいな回答］an evasive answer, an evasion;［言い訳］(an) excuse（⇨言い訳）. ▶それは単なる言い逃れだ That's a mere *excuse*. ▶彼は言い逃ればかりしている He is full of *evasions* [*excuses*]./He's always *giving evasive answers* [*making excuses*].（❗always を進行形と共に用いるといらだちの気持ちを表す）

いいのがれる 言い逃れる（あいまいな返事をする）give an evasive answer;（言い訳をする）make an excuse 《for》; explain away ⟨one's faults⟩.

いいのこす 言い残す ❶［言い置く］［残る人に言っておく］leave* a message [⟨a⟩ word] 《with him》;［遺言する］state in one's will 《that 節》.
❷［言わないでおく］leave* ⟨it⟩ unsaid [untold];（言い忘れる）forget* to say.（⇨言い忘れる）

いいはなつ 言い放つ ❶［きっぱりと言う］（公式に）言明する）declare;（断言する）assert. ▶彼はそんなことは言った覚えはないと言い放った He *flatly denied* having said so.
❷［無責任なことを言う］make an irresponsible remark.（⇨放言する）

いいはやす 言い囃す［盛んに言う］（⇨言いふらす）;［褒めちぎる］（⇨褒めちぎる, 褒める）

いいはる 言い張る insist 《on》;（主張する）claim.（⇨主張する）

いいひと ❶［好ましい人］a good person. ▶彼女のだんなさんはとてもいい人だ Her husband is a very *good* [*nice*, *pleasant*] person.（❗good, nice のような漠然とした言い方より具体的な friendly（気さくな）, cheerful（愉快な）, affectionate（人に対して優しい）, good-natured（人がよい）などを用いる方が好まれる）
❷［適した人］a suitable [a right] person. ▶アルバイトの帳簿係を探していますが, だれかいい人（＝働いてくれそうな人）いないでしょうか We're looking for a part-time bookkeeper. Do you know (of) anyone who might be *available* [(関心のある) *interested*]?（❗know は直接に知っている, know of は間接的に「...がいるのを知って[聞いて]いる」の意）
❸［恋人］（男）a boyfriend,（女）a girlfriend.

イーブイ［電気自動車］an EV; an electric vehicle.

いいふくめる 言い含める（入念な指示を与える）give* ⟨him⟩ careful instructions;（もって承知させる）talk ⟨him into ⟨doing⟩⟩; persuade ⟨him to do⟩. ▶娘は親に結婚するように言い含められた The daughter *was persuaded to* marry by her parents.

いいふらす 言いふらす（みんなに言う）tell* everybody ⟨about; that 節⟩;（うわさを広める）spread* [circulate] a rumor ⟨about; that 節⟩（❗ひょっとすると内容がうそかもしれないことを暗示）. ▶彼はもも子が春に結婚すると言いふらした He told everyone ⟨that⟩ [spread a rumor that] Momoko was getting married in the spring.

いいふるされた 言い古された overworked（陳腐な）hackneyed;（創造性のない）lacking in originality. ▶言い古された話 a *hackneyed* story. ▶'To be, or not to be'は言い古された句だが意味は今もはっきりしていない 'To be, or not to be' is an *overworked* phrase, but its meaning is still not clear.

いいぶん 言い分 (have) one's say;［意見］what one has to say, something to say;［不平］a complaint. ●自分の言い分を通す carry one's *point*. ●両方の言い分を聞く hear both *sides*. ●今度は彼に言い分を言わせてやれ Let him have his *say* now. ●彼の言い分を聞こう Let's hear *what he has to say*. ●そのことで何か言い分がありますか Do you have *anything to say* [any *complaints* to make] about that?
会話「彼が先に殴ったんです」「彼の言い分も聞いてみよう」"He hit me first." "I'll hear his *version*."（❗version は「ある個人の意見[説明]」の意）

イーブン［同点, 均等の］even. ●イーブンペースで走りきる run at an *even* pace till the end. ●イーブンパーでコースを回る〘ゴルフ〙go around the course in *even* par.

いいまかす 言い負かす ●人を言い負かす argue [talk] ⟨him⟩ down.

いいまわし 言い回し［表現］an expression;［表現法］a way of expressing ⟨it⟩;［慣用表現］an idiom. ●うまい言い回し a happy [a clever, an apt] *expression*. ●まずい言い回し a clumsy [a poor, an awkward] *expression*.

イーメール, Eメール (an) e-mail /íːmèɪl/.（❗E-mail,

《英》e-mailともつうる. 個々のメールは[C])●イーメールアドレス *an e-mail address.* ●1日に約10通のイーメールがくる *get [receive] about ten e-mails a day.* ●イーメールで送る *send 〈it〉 by e-mail; e-mail [〈英〉email].* ●くわしいことはイーメールでお知らせします *We'll e-mail you further information./Further information will be sent to you by e-mail.* ▶彼には電話でもイーメールでも連絡できなかった *I couldn't contact [get hold of] him by phone or e-mail.* ▶(イー)メールありがとう《返信の書き出し》*Thank you for your message.*

■ DISCOURSE ■
イーメールの利点は何だろうか. 1つは, 遠いところにいる人とやりとりできる点だ *What are the advantages of e-mail? One is that it enables people in distant places to communicate with each other easily.* (❗「疑問文→答え」のパターン. 序論でよく用いられる)

いいや (❗「いや」を強めた形. at all, a bit, in the least などをつける (⇨いや❶))

イーユー [[欧州連合]] EU (*the European Union* の略). ●EU加盟国 *EU member countries.*

いいよう 言い様 *a way of speaking.* (⇨言い方) ●言い様もないほど美しい *be indescribably beautiful; be beautiful beyond description.* ●何とも言い様のないひどひどい振る舞い *unspeakably bad behavior.* ▶ものも言い様で角が立つ *You'll sometimes make them angry, if you don't speak carefully.* (❗*Soft words turn away the wrath.* は上の意味を裏から言ったもの. 「静かな言葉は怒りを鎮める」の意. wrath 〖❗怒りの意の古い語〗)

いいよどむ 言い淀む ▶彼女はしばらく言いよどんでいたが,「はい」と答えた *She hesitated for a moment, and then she said "Yes."* (❗and の前のコンマに注意)

いいよる 言い寄る *make* advances [approaches] *to 〈her, him〉;* 《誘いかける》《話》*proposition 〈her〉.* ▶彼は会う女性みんなに言い寄った *He made advances to every woman he met.*

いいわけ 言い訳 图 *(an) excuse* /ɪksˈkjuːs/ *(for).* (⇨弁解, 口実) ●うまい[苦い, へたな]言い訳 *a good [a feeble, a lame; a poor] excuse.* ●もっともらしい[口先だけの]言い訳 *a plausible [a glib] excuse.* ▶経験不足は彼の無作法の言い訳にはならない *His lack of experience is no excuse for [does not excuse] his bad behavior.* ▶頭痛を言い訳にして彼は早く帰った *He used a headache as an excuse for leaving [to leave] early.* ▶君の行動は言い訳のしようがないものだった *Your conduct was inexcusable.*

——言い訳(を)する 動 *make* [*offer, give*] *an excuse (for), excuse* /ɪksˈkjuːz/ *oneself (for).* ▶彼はこの仕事は初めてだったと言って失敗の言い訳をした *He made an excuse [excused himself] for his failure by saying (that) he was new to this work./In excuse of his failure, he said (that) he was new to this work.* (❗このように具体的な言い訳の理由を示して用いることに注意) ▶彼は自分のふるまいに対してどんな言い訳をしたか *What excuse [(理由) reason] did he give for his behavior?* ▶言い訳するな *No excuses./Don't make up excuses.* (❗make up は「でっちあげる」の意) ▶言い訳しても始まらないよ. 実行に移さなければ *Excuses don't get the job done, but performers do.*

いいわすれる 言い忘れる *forget* to say [mention] 〈*it, that* 節〉; *leave* 〈*it*〉 *unsaid.* (❗後の方は「わざと言わない」の意もある) ▶何か言い忘れたことはありませんか *Have you left anything unsaid?*

いいわたす 言い渡す [[宣告する]] *sentence, condemn,* 《やや書》*pronounce;* [[告げる]] *tell;* [[命じる]] *order.* ●死刑を言い渡す *sentence [condemn] 〈him〉 to death* (❗前の方が普通); *pass [pronounce]* a death sentence *on [upon] 〈him〉.*

❖**いいん 委員** *a committee member, a member of a committee;* 《集合的》 *a committee* (❗複数扱いが普通); [クラスの] *a class monitor.* ●常任[運営; 実行]委員 *a member of a standing [a steering; an executive] committee.* (⇨委員会, 委員長) ▶彼は私たちの委員会の委員だ *He is our committee member./He is [sits] on [xin] our committee.* (❗on は所属を表す) ▶委員たちの間で意見が分かれた *The committee were divided in their opinions.*

いいん 医院 《米》*a doctor's [a physician's] office,* 《英》*a surgery;* 《特定分野の》*a clinic.* (⇨クリニック) ●山田医院 *Dr. Yamada's office.*

いいんかい 委員会 《一般の》*a committee;* 《調査会》*a commission;* 《幹部評議会》*a board* (❗いずれも単・複両扱い); 《会合》*a committee meeting.* ●運営[常任; 予算]委員会 *a steering [a standing; a budget] committee.* ●教育委員会 *a board of education.* ●委員会の決定に従う *follow a committee decision.* ●委員会の一員である *be on [xin] the committee;* *be a member of the committee.* (⇨委員) ●特別委員会を設ける *set up a special [an ad hoc] committee.* ●今日委員会が開かれる *The committee meet(s) today.* (❗《米》では通例単数扱い, 《英》では委員会全体に重点がある場合単数扱い, 構成委員に重点を置く場合複数扱い) ▶その法案は現在委員会で審議中です *The bill is in committee now.*

いいんちょう 委員長 *a chair, a chairperson,* 《男の》*chairman* (⇨議長), *a president* (❗*chairperson* と同じく労働組合の委員長に用いることもある); [クラスの] *a class president, the head of a class.* ●不破哲三日本共産党前委員長 *Tetsuzo Fuwa, ex-chairperson of the Japanese Communist Party.* ●EU委員長 *the president of the European Union.*

❖**いう 言う** **INDEX**

❶ 口で言う ❷ 表現する
❸ ある名称で呼ぶ ❹ 意見を述べる
❺ 主張する ❻ 意味する
❼ 言及する ❽ 命令する
❾ 依頼する ❿ 提案する
⓫ 認める ⓬ 否認する
⓭ 文句を言う ⓮ その他の表現

■ WORD CHOICE ■ 言う, 話す
say 口頭または心中で発言すること. 時に *quietly, softly, gently* などの副詞を伴う. ▶「やあ」と彼は言った *He said, "Hi."*
[[say+前]] to/of/about
tell 他人に向けて口頭で情報伝達すること. 主に他動詞で用い, 直接目的語には人・社会・機関などがくる. ▶その事件について君に話すよ *I'll tell you about that accident.*
[[tell+前]] of/about
speak 特定の言語や内容を人前で堂々と話すこと. ●聴衆に向けて話す *speak to an audience.*
[[speak+前]] to/of/for/with
talk 仲間内で気軽に話したり, 改まった場で問題を議論したりすること. ●現代文化について話す *talk about the modern culture.*
[[talk+前]] about/to/of/with

いう

頻度チャート

say ████████████████████
tell ██████████
speak ███
talk ██

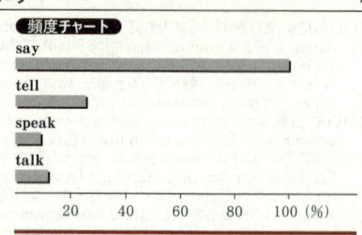

20　40　60　80　100 (%)

❶ [口で言う] (話す) speak*; (しゃべる, 語る) talk; (言葉を言う) say*; (伝える) tell*. (⇨[類語]) ▶まったく君の言うとおりだ What you *say* is quite right [true]./You're quite *right*.

①【(副)＋言う】 ●概して[率直に]言えば generally [frankly] *speaking*. (**!** 文頭では speaking がしばしば省略される) ●彼のことをよく[悪く]言う say good [bad] things about him; praise [criticize] him. (**!** 今は speak well [ill] of him より普通 (⇨褒める, 悪口)) ●大きな声で言ってくれ, 聞こえないぞ *Speak* (a little) louder [*Speak up*], we can't hear you. ▶何か私にご用があれば遠慮なく言ってください If you'd like me to do anything, just let me know [*say* the word]. ▶もう一度言ってもらえますか Could you *say* that again?/I beg your pardon? (**!** 後の方は聞き返すときのきわめて丁寧な表現. くだけた言い方では Beg pardon?, Pardon?とよくいう) ▶よく言うよ(＝よくそんなことが言えるね) How dare you *say* such a thing? ▶もっとはっきりと(＝明瞭に)言いなさい *Speak* more clearly. (黙っていないで) *Speak* up. ▶彼はなにかぼそぼそ言っていた He was *murmuring* something.

会話 「あいつ嫌いだ」「彼にそう言ったらどうなの?」"I hate him." "Why not *tell* him so [*that*]?" (⇨そう)

会話 「もっと早く来てほしかったなあ」「そう言ってくれればよかったのに」"I'd hoped you'd be here earlier." "You should *have told* me."

②【...を言う】 ●本当のことを言うと *tell* (you) [*speak*, ˣtalk, ˣsay] the truth. (⇨本当) ●わけのわからないことを言う *talk* nonsense. ●お祈りを言う *say* one's prayer. ●うそを言う *tell* [ˣsay, ˣspeak, ˣtalk] a lie [lies]. (**!** 一つの「うそ」にもしばしば lies を用いる) ●驚きのあまり何も言えない be *speechless* with astonishment; be dumb-founded. ▶その赤ん坊はまだものを言うことができない(＝言葉が話せない) The baby can't *speak* [*talk*, ˣsay, ˣtell] yet. (**!** speak の方が普通) ▶私もそれを言おうと思っていたところだ That's just what I'm going to *say*. ▶彼は言いたいことを言った (言いたい放題を言った) He *said* whatever he felt like *saying*. (率直に自分の意見を述べた) He *spoke* his mind./《話》He *had* his *say*. ▶ありのまま(＝事実のまま)を言いなさい *Tell* the plain truth./*Tell* it as it is./(正直に) Be honest and *tell* me the truth. ▶わがままを言うもんじゃない Don't be (so) selfish.

会話 「ちょっと, 見てよ, このおいしそうなパイ」「うん, そうだね. それで何を言おうとしていたかと言うと」"Wait. Look at this tasty-looking pie." "Uh-huh, yeah. So, back to what I *was saying*." (**!** 話を中断されて元へ戻すときのつなぎ表現)

③【A(人)にB(事)を言う】 say* B to A; tell* A B, tell B to A. ●彼女は彼に自分の名前を言った She *said* her name *to* him./She *told* him her name [her name *to* him]. (**!** say は単に自分の名前を相手に言うのに対して, tell は相手に教えるという含みがある)

▶彼は私にさよならを言った He *said* [ˣtold] good-by *to* me./《書》He *bade* me farewell [farewell *to* me]. ▶あなたに言いたいこと(＝話)がある I have something to *tell* [*say to*] you. ▶私は母親にこんなことを言われたことがある I've *been told* [ˣbeen said] this by my mother. ▶昨晩あったことを[何があったのかを](私に)言いなさい *Tell* me [(説明しない) *Describe to* me] what happened last night. (⇨ ⑤)

④【A(人に)Bについて[のことを]言う】 tell* (A) about [of] B; talk (to [with] A) about [of, on] B; speak* (with《主に》[to《主に英》] A) about [of, on] B. (**!** 通例 about は詳しく具体的な, of は抽象的な, on は専門的な事柄について話すときに用いる) ▶そのことをだれにも言わないでくれ Don't *tell* anyone *about* it./Don't *tell* [*mention*] it *to* anyone. (⇨❼)／それを秘密にしておいてくれ Keep it secret./Keep quiet about it. ▶彼はその問題について一言も言わなかった He didn't *say* [*speak*, ˣtalk, ˣtell] a word *about* the matter./He *said* [*told* (me), *spoke*, ˣtalked] nothing *about* the matter./(意見を述べなかった) He *made no remark* [*comment*] *on* the matter. (⇨❹) ▶君は何のことを言っているのですか What are you *talking* about? (**!** 全体に低い抑えた調子で言うと「何を言っているんだ, けしからんことを言うな」の意)

⑤【A(人に)...と言う】 say* (to A) (that)...; tell* A (that).... (**!** that 節の代わりに wh-節, wh-句なども用いられる) ▶秀雄は「今日は太郎と泳ぎに行った」と言った Hideo *said*, "I went swimming with Taro today."

解説 (1) 直接話法はだれが言った内容をそのまま正確に伝える形式, 書き言葉では "Taro and I went swimming today," Hideo *said* [*said* Hideo]./"Taro and I," Hideo *said* [*said* Hideo], "went swimming today." などの語順も可. また said Hideo (動詞＋主語) という語順は, 主語が人称代名詞でなく, かつ動詞が単純現在形や過去形の場合に限る. したがって ˣsaid he, ˣhas said Hideo などとはいわない.
(2) 間接話法はだれが言った内容を伝達する者の言葉によって客観的かつ間接的に伝える形式. 上の例文は状況に応じて Hideo *said* [ˣtold] (*that*) he had gone swimming [had gone to the beach for a swim] with Taro that day. などと言い換えが可. この場合 went → had gone, I → he のような動詞の時制と人称代名詞の変更に注意. ただし today → that day, here → there, this → that のような時・場所などを示す語の言い換えは伝達が発言と同じ日や場所で行われる場合にはしない: 今朝彼は「あした東京へ行く」と言っていた This morning he *said*, "I'm going to Tokyo tomorrow."/This morning he *said that* he was going to Tokyo tomorrow [ˣthe next day].

▶メアリーは私に「ゆうべここであなたのお母さんに会ったの」と言った "I met your mother here last night," Mary *said to* me [*told* me]./Mary *told* me [*said to* me] (*that*) she had met my mother there the night before. (**!** 聞き手を明示するときは, 直接話法では say, 間接話法では tell を用いる方が普通. また直接話法では の語順以外は伝達文の後ろに中間に置く. ただし最近では文頭でも用いるようになってきた)

▶「この辺では駐車するな」と彼は私に言った "Don't park around here," he *said to* me./(命じた) *ordered*, (注意した) *warned*] me./He *told* [*ordered*, *warned*] me not *to* park around here [there]. (**!** 注意された場所で彼が言ったとすれば here, 違う場所

いう

なら there) (⇨❽) ▶「たばこはやめるべきだ」と医者は彼に言った "You'd better give up smoking," the doctor *said to him.*/(忠告した) The doctor *advised* [(勧めた) *recommended*] him *to* give up smoking. ▶彼女は客に「お座りください」と言った "Please sit down [be seated]," she *said to* the guests. (!後の方が丁寧な言い方)/(頼んだ) She *asked* the guests *to* sit down. (⇨❾) ▶彼は私に「トランプをしよう」と言った "Let's play cards," he *said to me.*/(提案した) He *suggested* playing cards [*to* me] *that* we (should) play cards). (⇨❿) ▶彼女は彼に「音楽は好きですか」と言った "Do you like music?" she *said to him.*/(尋ねた) She *asked* him *if* [*whether*] he liked music. ▶×She said to him (*if* [*whether*]).... は不可) ▶彼女は「そこへは行きたくない」と言った She *said*, "I don't want to go there."/She *said* (*that*) she didn't want to go there. ▶She didn't say (that) she wanted to .... は「行きたいとは言わなかった」の意)/(拒んだ) She *refused* to go [×going) there. (!(1) refuse は未来のことを拒む表現. (2) この場合 ×She denied .... は不可 (⇨⓬))

❻【...と言っても(いい】 ▶彼は我が国が生んだ最大の科学者だと言ってもいいだろう You *could say* [言っても差し支えない]《書》It *may safely be said*] *that* he is the greatest scientist (that) our country has ever produced. ▶彼は詐欺師と言ってもいいくらいだ(=同然だ) He is *no better than* a fraud./He is *almost the same as* a fraud.

❼【...と言われる】 ▶私は父親似だとよく人に言われます I'm often *told* [×said] *that* I look like my father. (!通例 by people はつかない. It is said that..., I am said to.... は堅い書き言葉で用いる客観的表現でここでは不自然 (⇨[次例])) ▶彼はこの町一番の金持ちだと言われている People *say* [They *say*,《書》It *is said*, ×It is told] *that* he is the richest man in this town. (!(1) 前の二つではしばしば that が省略を. I hear(d) that.... と言える. (2)「...だとよく言われる」のように頻度にふれる際は People *often say* (*that*)..../It is *often said that....* となり, ×They often say (that).... は不可)/《書》He is said to be the richest man in this town. (!×They say him to be.... は不可)

❷【表現する】 express; put*（!通例様態の副詞(句)を伴う); (描写する) describe. (⇨言い方, 言い回し) ● 手短に言えば *to put* it briefly. ● ひと言で言えば *in a word*. ▶英語で思うことが言えますか Can you *express* yourself [your ideas] in English? ▶これを日本語でどう言えばいいのかわかりません I don't know how to *put* [*say*] it in Japanese. ▶なくしたカメラの特徴を詳しく言ってください *Describe* [×Describe about] your lost camera.

会話 「フランス語で『おはよう』はどう言うのですか」「ボンジュールと言います」 "How [×What] do you *say* 'Ohayo' in French?" "We *say* 'Bonjour.'"

❸【ある名称で呼ぶ】 call; (名前をつける) name. (!...と言う) ▶この花を英語で何と言いますか What do you *call* this flower in English?/What is the English (word) for this flower? (!the は省略不可) ▶私が臆病者だと言うのかい *Are* you *calling* me a coward?

会話 「例の新しいミュージカル見てきたわ」「(題名は)何というの?」 "I've just seen that new musical." "What's it *called*?"

❹【意見を述べる】 express [give*] one's opinion 《on, about》; (簡単な感想を述べる) remark [make* a *remark*] 《on, about》; (論評する) comment [make a *comment*] 《on》. (⇨❶ ④) ▶その件について彼は何と言っていますか What is his *opinion about* the matter? ▶何も言えません (報道陣の質問などに対して) No *comment*. ▶言わせてもらえばそれは有害無益だね *If you ask me* [*If I may say so*] it's worse than useless. (!日本語との言い方の違いに注意) ▶ちょっと待って, 最後まで言わせてください Wait! Just let me *finish*. ▶私にも一言, 言わせてください I hope you don't mind my interrupting you for a moment. (!決まり文句)

❺【主張する】(強く言い張る) insist; (事実であると主張する) claim; (公式に言明する) declare, state ... clearly [definitely]; (断言する)《書》affirm; (力説する) urge; (保証する) assure; (公言する)《書》profess. (⇨主張する) ▶彼は私といっしょに行くと言ってきかなかった He *insisted on* going with me. ▶彼は昨夜は家族と過ごしたと言っている He *claims* (*that*) he spent [*to* have spent] last night with his family. (!「と言っているが本当かな」の含みをもつ) ▶彼は我々を援助できないときっぱり言った He *declared* [*said flatly*] *that* he could not help us. ▶彼らは必ず時間どおりに来ると言った They *assured* me *that* they would be on time.

❻【意味する】 mean*; (暗に言う) imply. ▶私の言わんとすることがわかりますか Do you understand what I *mean* (*to say*)?/Do you understand me?/(要点がわかる) Do you get my *point*?/See what I *mean*? ▶君は何を言いたいのですか What do you *mean* (*by* that)? (!抗議の意にもなる)/What are you *trying to say*?/(話) What are you *driving at*?/(ほのめかしている) What are you *getting at*? ▶私は冗談のつもりで言ったのですが I *meant* it *for* [*as*] a joke./I was just kidding. ▶私が彼につれなくしているとでも言いたいのですか *Are* you *implying that* I've been unkind to him?

会話 「あのかわいい子見たかい」「ところでどの子のことを言ってるのさ」 "Did you see that pretty girl?" "Now which one do you *mean*?"

❼【言及する】 mention, refer (-rr-) to .... (!後の方が堅い語) (⇨❶ ④) ▶彼は手紙の中で君のことを言っていたよ He *mentioned* [*wrote about*] you in his letter. (!mention は「簡潔に触れる」こと. ×mention about... とはいわない) ▶これがきのう言っていた辞書です This is the dictionary I *told* you *about* [*mentioned*, *referred to*] yesterday. ▶君のことを言っているのですよ I'm *talking about* [*referring to*] you.

❽【命令する】 order; tell* (!order の方が強い命令); (忠告する) advise; (勧める) recommend. (⇨❶⑤) ▶私の言うとおりにしなさい Do as I *say* [*tell you*]. ▶言われたとおりにしなさい Do as you *are told*. (!後に to do が省略されている) ▶何度言ったらわかるの (=二度と言わせるな) Don't make me *say* it [*tell you*] again. (!親などが子供をしかる時に) ▶だから言わないことじゃない I *told* you so. (⇨それつ) ▶彼にいくら言っても(=忠告しても)むだです It is no use *giving* him any *advice*. ▶私も何とも言えません. 君自身の責任だからね I can't *advise* you. It's your own responsibility. ▶だれかその道の人の言うこと(=忠告)を聞いてくださいたらね! If only you'd *taken* some expert *advice*! (!If only is I wish より強い言い方)

❾【依頼する】(頼む) ask, request (!ask より改まった語 (⇨❶ ⑤)); (権利として強く要求する) demand. ▶彼は私に援助してほしいと言った He *asked* me *for* help [*to* help]./He *demanded* help *from* [*of*] me./He *demanded that* I ((主に英)) should) help him. (!×He demanded me to help him. とはいえない)

いうことなし / いえ

[会話]「今夜コンサートに行かない?」「もっと早く言ってくれればよかったのに」"How about a concert tonight?" "If only you'd *asked* me earlier."

❿ [提案する] suggest. (⇨❶⑤) ▶どこかいい場所はないでしょうか. それに時間も言っていただければ（会う約束をするとき）Will you *suggest* somewhere? And a time. (❗「予定の時間」の意では time は $\mathbb{C}$) ▶彼は私にもう一度考え直した方がよいのではないかと言った He *suggested* to me that I (《主に英》should) give it a second thought. (❗He *suggested* my giving .... ともいえるが, ×He suggested me to give .... は不可)

⓫ [認める] (しぶしぶ事実であると認める) admit (-tt-), acknowledge; (許可である)《やや書》permit (-tt-) ▶彼は自分が間違っていたと言った He *admitted* [*acknowledged*] that he was wrong. ▶父は家の中で絶対たばこを吸ってはいけないと言います Father never *permits* smoking [us *to* smoke] in the house.

⓬ [否認する] deny. ▶彼女はその男に会った覚えはないと言った She *denied* ever meeting [having met] him./She *denied* that she had ever met him. (❗deny は現在または過去の事実の否定を表す. この場合 She refused ....は不可) ▶⓭❶⓮以降での some/any, ever などの使用は否定文に準ずる)

⓭ [文句を言う] complain (*of, about; that* 節). ▶彼は隣家のピアノがうるさくて困ると言っている He's *complaining* of his neighbor's annoying piano.

⓮ [その他の表現] ▶そう言われてみると (⇨そういえば) ▶言うところの (⇨いわゆる) ▶言うもおろか (⇨言うまでもなく) ▶彼は言うこととすることが違う（=言行が一致しない）(⇨言行) ▶同じ事は彼にも言える The same thing can [×is able to] *be said about* him./(当てはまる) The same is *true of* [*goes for*] him. ▶言っていること と思っていることは別だ There are some things which should not *be said*. ▶彼女はその秘密を知っていると言わんばかりの口ぶりだった She talked *as if* [*though*] she knew the secret. ▶言っておくと聞く耳は持たないからね *I tell you* I won't listen. ▶言いたい人には言わせておく. 結果（=よい結果）を出すだけだから Let others *say* whatever they want to *say*. I'll just do my best to get [×show] results. (❗show は「（出た結果）を数字や表などを用いて提示する」の意味なので, ここでは不可) ▶言うでしょ（=ことわざにあるように），「たで食う虫も好きずき」って *As the saying goes*, "There's no accounting for taste."

[会話]「いつ引っ越してくるの」「すぐ. 何日とは言えないけど」"When are you moving in?" "Soon. Though I can't *name* the day."

● 言うに言われぬ ▶言うに言われぬ苦労があった I [Words] can't *express* how much I have suffered [hardship I've endured]. ▶苦労は消極的だが endure は積極的に打ち勝つ意）(⇨言い知れぬ) ▶言うに言われぬ美しい光景 a beautiful scene *beyond description*.

● 言うに事欠いて ▶言うに事欠いて彼は私をうそつき呼ばわりした *Of all things*, he called me a liar.

● 言うは易し, 行うは難し (ことわざ) Easier said than done.

● 言わぬが花 (言わないでおいた方がよい) It's better left unsaid.

いうことなし 言うことなし leave* nothing to be desired; be completely [very] satisfactory (*to* + 人); (人が主語) be completely [perfectly] satisfied (*with* + 事・人). ❗ satisfactory, satisfied は「（ある）水準に達していると認める」ぐらいの意味なので副詞を添えて意味を補強する必要がある)

いうなれば 言うなれば ▶あの人は, 言うなれば（=言わば）井の中の蛙のようなものだ He is, *so to speak* [*as it were*], a frog in the well.

いうまでもない 言うまでもない 囫 ▶彼がすぐれた芸術家であることは言うまでもなく *Needless to say*, he is an excellent artist./《書》*It goes without saying that* he is an excellent artist.

—— 言うまでもなく 囫 ▶彼は英語は言うまでもなくドイツ語やフランス語も話せる He can speak German and French, *not to mention* [*not to speak of*] English. (❗(1) 前の方が口語的. (2) to say nothing of は通例よくないことに用いる) ▶（英語だけでなく）He can speak German and French *as well as* English. ▶その子は走ることは言うまでもなく, 歩くことさえできない The child can't even walk, *much less* [*let alone*] run. (❗much less, let alone は主に否定文に用いる)

いえ 家

WORD CHOICE 家

house 住居用の家屋のこと. 直前に the や one's などを伴うことが多い. ▶その道沿いで一軒の小さい家を見つけた I've found a small *house* on the route.

home 家族とのふれあいのある家庭のこと. くつろぎ・団欒（だんらん）・暖かさ・安心感などを含意する. work at home (在宅勤務する) のように, しばしば職場の対照概念としての家をさす. ▶家に帰る go [come, return, get back] *home*.

頻度チャート

house ▬▬▬▬▬▬▬▬▬▬
home ▬▬▬▬▬▬▬
20   40   60   80   100 (%)

❶ [住居] a house (圈 houses /-ziz, 《米》-siz/); a home (⇨[類語]); 《話》a place. (⇨住居)

① [〜家] ▶広い [狭い] 家 a large [a small] *house*. ● ×wide, ×narrow は不可 ▶住みよい家 a cozy *house*. ▶木造２階建ての家 a two-story [a two-storied] wooden (frame) *house*. ▶赤い屋根に白い壁の家 a *house* with a red roof and white walls; a red-roofed and white-walled *house*. ▶小田さんの家でパーティーを開いた We had a party at the Oda *house* 《米》[at Oda's (*house*) 《英》]. (❗《米》では house の代わりに home も可.「小田太郎さんの家で」では ... at Taro's [Taro Oda's] (*house*)《話》place, 《米》home] のようにいう)

② [家が[は]] ▶彼の家は川のそばに建っている His *house* is [stands, ×is standing] by a river. (❗ stands は高々と目立つ場合) ▶彼には住む家がない He has no *house* to live in [*place* to live (in)]./He is *homeless*. ▶家は神戸です My *home* is in Kobe. (❗「郷里は神戸だ」の意にもなる) ▶（神戸に住んでいる）I live in Kobe.

③ [家の] ▶家の価格 hóuse prices. ▶家の外で遊ぶ play *outside* [*outdoors*]. (⇨中, 外) ▶家の中へ入る go into the *house*.

④ [家に[へ, で, まで, から]] ▶家にいる be [stay] (at) *home*. (❗《米話》では通例 at を省略するが, work at home (家で仕事をする) のように動作動詞の場合は省略不可; be [stày] in. (⇨留守)
● 家にこもる keep *at home*; keep *in* [*indoors*].
● (学校から) 家へ帰る途中 on one's way *home* (from school). ▶家で作ったトマト hòme-grown tomatoes. ▶家まで送る see (her) *home*. (⇨送る

❷ ▶私は夜はたいてい家にいてテレビを見ています I *stay in* almost every night and watch TV [television]. ▶彼が家に帰るまで待っています I'll wait until he is [comes, ×comes to] *home*. (⇨帰宅する) ▶あとで家から電話するよ I'll call you *from home* later. ▶ぼくはおばの家にやっかいになっている（同居）I live with my aunt./(一時の滞在) I am staying with my aunt. (⇨泊まる) (!いずれも ...at my aunt's. ともいえる) ▶あしたあなたの家へ行ってもいいかしら Can I come [×go] to your *house* [*place*] tomorrow? (⇨行く) ▶彼を家に入れてやれ Let him in [into the *house*]. ▶妻は町へ買い物に行ったが私は家に残って子供の面倒を見ていた My wife went shopping downtown and I stayed (at) *home*, looking after the children.

❺ 〖家を〗 ●家を持つ(借家暮らしでない) have one's (×own) *house*, have a *house* of one's own; 〖所帯を持つ〗 set up *house* [〖英〗*home*] (!無冠詞に注意). ●家を借りる rent a *house* (*from* him). ●家を貸す rent 〖米〗 [let〖英〗] a *house* (*to* him). ●家を出る leave the *house* [(one's) *home*]. (!ともに外出・独立・家出ほどのいずれにも用いる). ●京都に家を構える make one's *home* in Kyoto, 〖書〗 take up residence in Kyoto. (⇨一家) ▶彼らはなんてすばらしい家を買ったんだろう What a nice *house* [*place*] they've got! ▶ぼくは家を建てた I had my *house* built./I built my *house*. (!前の方は「人に依頼して建てて貰った」の意。後の方は「自分の手で建てた」の意にもなる (⇨建てる)) ▶彼は酔っぱらって一晩家をあけた(=外泊した) He got drunk and *stayed out* all night.

❷ 〖家庭、家族、家系〗 a [one's] *family*. ●家の資産 the property of the *family*. ●家を継ぐ succeed to one's *family* estate. ●家の中でだれが一番早起きですか Who gets up (the) earliest of your *family*? (!×in your whole family とはいわない) ●家のことは妻にまかせている I let my wife keep *house*. (!keep house は「家事を切り回す」の意) ▶彼は貧乏な家に生まれた He was born poor [into a poor *family*]./He comes from a poor *home* [*family*].

〖関連〗家のいろいろ：一戸建て a house; a detached house/二戸建ての一戸〖米〗a duplex (house)/〖英〗 a semidetached house/棟続きの一戸〖米〗 a row house; 〖英〗 a terrace(d) house (!いずれも二階建てが多い)/平屋建て a one-story[-storied] house/アパート〖マンション〗(全体)〖米〗an apártment hòuse,〖英〗a block of flats; (一戸)〖米〗an apartment,〖英〗a flat. (〖英〗では mansion は Belle Mansions (ベルマンション)の形でアパートの名に用いる。〖米〗では分譲マンション (の1戸) を a condominium /kàndəmíniəm/, 〖話〗 a condo /kándou/ (⑯ ~s) という)/大邸宅 a mansion,〖書〗a residence,/(田舎の) a cóuntry hòuse.

いえ『家』 *The Family*. (参考) 島崎藤村の小説
いえ (⇨いいえ)
いえい 遺影 portrait of a deceased person. (!写真あるいは肖像画)
いえい (⇨いやいや)
いえがら 家柄 〖家の格〗 the social standing of a family; 〖血筋〗(生まれ) birth, 〖家系〗(a) (family) stock (!複数形はない). ●家柄がよい He comes from a good *family* [(a) good *stock*]. ●from の代わりに of も可/He is a man of [×from] good *birth*. ●家柄(=家族環境)は問題ではない Your *family* background does not matter [is not the issue].
いえき 胃液 〖生理〗 gastric juices.

いえじ 家路 ●家路につく make [start] for *home*. ●家路を急ぐ hurry *home*. ●家路に向かうサラリーマンたち *homeward-bound* office workers.
イエス(キリスト) Jesus (Christ) /dʒíːzəs (kráist)/.
イエスマン (軽蔑的) a yesman (⑯ yesmen). (!男女共に用いる)
いえだに 家だに a house tick.
いえつき 家付き ●家付きの土地 land *with a house*. ●家付きの(=婿をもらう立場)の娘 an heiress.
いえで 家出 —— 家出する 動 run away [disappear] from home.
●家出少年[娘] a runaway boy [girl]; a young runaway.
いえてる 言えてる ●それは言えてる(まさにそのものずばりだ) That's it./You guessed right./You said it./You (just) hit the nail on the head./(同感だ) I agree with that.
いえども (接続助詞) (...であるけれども) though..., although...(後の方が堅い語); (さえ) even. ▶彼は若いといえども思慮分別がある *Though* [*Although*] (he is) young, he is prudent./(⑯) Young though [*as*, ×although] he is, he is prudent.
▶子供といえどもそのくらいのことはできる *Even* a child can do those things.
いえなみ 家並み a row of houses.
いえのころうとう 家の子郎党 〖政治家などの子分〗 one's followers [adherents].
イエメン 〖国名〗 Yemen /jémən/; (公式名) the Republic of Yemen. (首都 Sana'a) ●イエメン人 a Yemeni, Yemenite. ●イエメン(人)の Yemeni, Yemenite.
いえもち 家持ち ❶〖家を持っている人〗 the owner of a house; 〖所帯を持っている人〗 the head of a household (⇨所帯).
❷〖家計のやりくり〗 ●母は家持ちがいい Mother is good at *doing the house budget*./Mother is a *good homemaker*.
いえもと 家元 the head of a school (*of* Japanese dancing); 〖宗家〗 the head family (*of*).
いえやしき 家屋敷 the premises. (⇨屋敷)
いえる 癒える get well. (⇨治る)
イエローカード a yellow card. ●イエローカードで警告する caution by showing (a player) a *yellow card*; yellow-card. ▶マルケス、本日2枚目のイエロー(カード)で退場です Marquez was sent off on his second *yellow card* of the day.
イエローページ 〖職業別電話帳〗 the Yellow Pages. (⇨電話帳)
いえん 以遠 ●大阪以遠の駅 Osaka and the stations *beyond*.
●以遠権 〖航空〗 the beyond right.
いえん 胃炎 〖医学〗 gastritis /gæstráitəs/.
いおう 硫黄 〖米〗 sulfur,〖英〗 sulphur (元素記号 S).
●硫黄の sulfurous; sulphurous.
いおり 庵 a hermitage. ●庵を結ぶ(建てる) build a *hermitage*. ●(住む) live in a *hermitage*.
イオン 〖物理〗 an ion /áiən/. ●陰イオン a negative *ion*; an anion. ●陽イオン a positive *ion*; a cation.
●イオン結合 an iónic bond. ●イオン結晶 an ionic crystal.
*いか 以下 ❶[...より下] below....; [...より少ない] less than..., under.... (!いずれも厳密には...の数を含まず、「...未満」の意となる (⇨以上 ❸) 〖類語〗) ●ぼくの成績は平均以下に下った My results were *below* average. ▶彼の月収は20万円以下だ His monthly income is *less than* [*under*] 200,000 yen. ▶5歳以下の子供は入場無料です Admission

いか is free for children five *and under* [children *under* six, ×*under* five]. (❗上の例と異なり正確でなければならないので ×*under* five (5歳未満)は不可) ▶おまえは召使い以下だ You are *less than* a servant.
❷〖次に述べるもの〗the following (❗単・複両扱い); 〖その他のもの〗the rest (❗数えられない物をさすときは単数扱い。数えられる物をさすときは複数扱い)。●首相以下与党幹部 leaders of the ruling party the prime minister *down on*. ▶15ページ以下参照 See p. 15*ff*. (❗*ff* is *and the following pages* is *read*り) ●以下は彼の話[言葉]です The *following* is his story [are his words]. ▶以下省略 The *rest* is omitted. ●彼らの住所は以下のとおりです:… Their addresses are *as follows*: ….

いか 医科 〖医学〗medicine; 〖医学部〗a medical department [school].

いか 烏賊 〖動物〗(甲イカ) a cuttlefish; (甲のない) a squid. (❗いずれも通例単・複両形) ●イカの足 the arms [触手] tentacles] of a *cuttlefish*.

いが（クリなどの）a bur.

＊いがい 意外 ── 意外な 形 〖予期しない〗unexpected; 〖驚くべき〗surprising; 〖偶然の〗accidental; 〖変な〗strange. ●意外な成功 an *unexpected* [a *surprising*] success. ●意外な出会い an *accidental* meeting. ●再び彼にあそこで会うとはまったく意外なことだった(=会うことを予期しなかった) I *never expected to* see him there again./(最も会いそうもないと思った人だ) He is *the last person* I *expected to* see there again. ▶彼が試験に落ちたのは意外だ It's *surprising that* he failed the exam. ▶彼の成功は意外だった[ではなかった] His success was a *surprise* [did not come as a *surprise*].
会話「田中が負けたよ」「意外だね」 "Tanaka was beaten." "Isn't it *strange*!"

── 意外に 副 〖思いがけなく〗unexpectedly; 〖驚いたことに〗surprisingly, to one's surprise. ▶試験は意外にやさしかった The exam was *unexpectedly easy*./(思ったより) The exam was easier *than* I (*had*) *expected* [*thought*] (it *would be*). (❗《話》では had は省略することが多い) ▶意外にも計画は失敗した *Surprisingly* [*To our surprise*], the plan failed./*It was surprising* [*We were surprised*] *that* the plan failed (失敗に終わる) fell through].
会話「人がはねられるってことはないの」「もちろんあるさ。でも意外に少ないんだよ」"Don't people get hit?" "Sure. But you'd *be surprised* at how few."

＊いがい 以外 ❶〖…を除いて〗except…, but…; except for…;《古》save…. (⇨ほか❷) ▶私以外はみな疲れていた Everyone *except* [*but*, ×*except for*] me was tired./Everyone was tired *except* (*for*) [*but*] me. (❗全体を表す語と例外的要素が選ばれる場合は except for も可)/*Except for* [×Except, ×But] me, everyone was tired. (❗例外的要素を全体を表す語より前によく場合は通例 except for を用いる) ▶緊急[来客]のとき以外はその出入口は使いません We never use that gateway *except* in (an) *emergency* [*except when* we have guests]. ▶ただ待つ以外にどうしようもない I can do nothing *but* [*except, besides*] wait. (❗do が前にあるときは ×to wait とはしない)/There is nothing I can do *but* wait./I have no choice *but* to wait [*no other choice than* wait*ing*]./All [The only thing] I can do is (to) wait. (❗主語では to はしばしば省略される) ▶彼は SF 小説以外のものは書かない He writes *nothing but* science fiction./(…に限定している) He *confines himself to* (writing) science fiction. ▶何か小説以外の(=小説と異なった)本を読みたい I want to read some *other* book [some book *other*] *than* fiction. ▶ごめんなさいと言ったのよ。それ以外言いようがないじゃないの I've said I'm sorry. What *else* can I say? ▶君は東京以外(=の外)のどこかに住んだ方がよい You should live somewhere *outside of* Tokyo.

❷〖…に加えて〗besides…, in addition to…. (⇨ほか❸) ▶数学以外にもたくさん勉強することがある I have a lot of things to study *besides* [*in addition to*] mathematics. (❗*…except* that … では、「勉強するのはたくさんあるが、数学だけは勉強しない」の意となる)

いがい 遺骸 a corpse; a (dead) body;《婉曲的》one's mortal remains. (⇨遺体)

いがいが (⇨いがらっぽい)

いかいよう 胃潰瘍 〖医学〗(have) a stomach [a gastric] ulcer. (❗後の方は専門語)

＊いかが ❶〖尋ねて〗(どのように) how; (何) what. (⇨どう❷❸) ▶近ごろごきげんいかがですか How are you getting along these days?/(病人に) How are you feeling these days? ▶ロンドンの生活はいかがですか How do you like it in London?
会話「お帰りなさい。西海岸(の旅)はいかがでした」「すごくよかった」"Welcome back. How was [How did you like, What did you think of] the West Coast?" "(It was) terrific [fantastic]."

❷〖勧めて〗Would you like …?; Won't you have …?; (話) How [What] about …? (⇨どう❷) ▶一杯やっているところです。ご一緒にいかがですか I'm just having a drink. *Would you like to* [*Will you*] *join* me? (❗「一杯やりませんか」は *Would you like* (*to* have) *a drink*?) ▶今晩お食事でもいかがかと思いまして I wondered if you could have dinner with me tonight. (❗控えめ表現の I wonder if を過去形にしてさらに丁寧さを加える言い方) ▶しばらく様子を見られたらいかがでしょうか May [Could] I suggest *that* you ((≪主≫英) should) wait and see for some time? [I suggest …. より丁寧な言い方]

❸〖不賛成〗▶未成年者にたばこを勧めるのはいかがなものでしょうか(=良いとは思わない) I don't think (that) it's good to offer a cigarette to a minor.

いかがく 医化学 medical chemistry.

いかがわしい ●いかがわしい(=怪しげな)人物 a *suspicious* [《話》a *shady*, 《やや書》a *dubious*] character. ●いかがわしい(=問題となる)行動 *questionable conduct*. ●いかがわしい(=わいせつな)本 a *dirty* [an *obscene*, an *indecent*] book. ▶うわさでは彼にはいかがわしい過去があると They say he has a *past* [a skeleton in the closet]. (❗後の慣用句は家庭内のことに限らず、表に出したくないすべてのことに使える)

いかく 威嚇 图《書》(脅威); (脅迫) a menace; (脅迫) a threat ●脅し, 脅迫 ●威嚇射撃を行う *fire warning* shots. ▶猫は犬に威嚇の姿勢をとった The cat assumed a *threat* posture against the dog.
翻訳のこころ これは大げさな威嚇でもなければ空疎な説教でもありません（丸山真男『「である」ことと「する」こと』） This is neither an exaggerated *warning* nor a meaningless lecture. ❗ (1)「威嚇」は threat (脅し)でなく warning (警告)とする。(2)「説教」は lecture. sermon は通例「聖職者などによる道徳的・宗教的な話」なのでここでは不適切)

── 威嚇する 動 threaten; menace. ●彼を銃で威嚇する *threaten* him with a gun. (⇨脅かす)

いがく 医学 图 (医術, 医療) medicine; (科学としての) medical science. ●予防医学 preventive *medicine*. ●西洋医学 Western *medicine*. ●東洋医学

Oriental *medicine*; (漢方医学) Chinese *medicine*. ● 精神医学 psychiatry /saikáiətri/. ● 医学の進歩 advances in *medicine* [*medical science*]; *medical* advances. ▶医学はめざましく進歩している *Medical science* is making (a) great progress. ▶君は医学的にはまったく健康です *Medically* (speaking), you are in sound [*good*] health. ▶彼は医学生だ He is a *medical* student./(医学を勉強している) He is studying *medicine*.
— 医学の 形 medical.
● 医学界 medical circles. ● 医学雑誌 a medical journal. ● 医学実習生《米》an intern;《英》a houseman. ● 医学博士 (人) a doctor of medicine; (学位) Doctor of Medicine (略 M.D.,《まれ》D.M.). ● 医学部 the medical department (of a university). (❕米国では医学部は大学院のみで a medical school となるが, 医科大学の意もある) ● エール大学医学部 Yale University School of *Medicine* (❕日本の大学医学部の公式名もこの形式を取るのが普通)

いかくちょう 胃拡張 gastric dilatation;〖医学〗gastrectasia.

いかぐり 毬栗 〖くり〗chestnuts in a bur;〖頭〗a close-cropped head.

いかさま (にせ物) a fake; (詐欺) (a) fraud. ● いかさまをやる (勝負で) cheat, play *foul* /fául/. ● いかさま師 a cheat; (詐欺師) a swindler.

いかす 生かす ❶〖生きたままにしておく〗keep... alive; (許して) let*... live. ▶できるだけ長い間この魚を生かしておいてください Please *keep* this fish *alive* as long as possible. ▶あの殺人犯は生かしておけない We can't *let* the murderer *live*./(命を助けてやれない) We can't *allow* the murderer *to live*./(命を助けてやれない) We can't *spare the life of* the murderer. ▶政治家を生かすも殺すもマスコミ次第 The press can make or break a politician.
❷〖活用する〗(使用する) use; (利用する) make* use of...;(効果的に)〖書〗utilize. ▶経験を十分生かす *make* full *use of* one's experience; *put* one's experience *to good use*. ● 経験を仕事に生かす *put* one's experience *to work*. ● 核エネルギーを平和目的に生かして使う *utilize* nuclear energy for peaceful purposes. ▶英語を生かせる仕事を探しています I'm looking for a job in which I can *use* my English [I can *put* my English *to good use*]. ▶君はこの機会をうまく生かしなさい You'd better *make use of* [《書》*avail yourself of*] this opportunity.

いかす (人・物が)《俗》cool; (物が)《話》nifty;《米話》a macho neat. (⇨かっこいい) ● いかす男 a *cool* guy; a macho /máːtʃou/. (❕男女の区別なくセクシーな人を hot stuff というが, この場合は無冠詞)

いかすい 胃下垂 〖医学〗gastroptosis /gæstrəptóusis/.

いかだ 筏 a raft. ● いかだ乗り a raftsman. ● いかだを組む make [build] a *raft* (of logs); raft logs. ● いかだで川を下る go down a river by [on a] *raft*; raft down a river.

いかた 鋳型 a mold, a cast. ● 鋳型に注ぎ込む cast [pour] (metal) into a *mold*. ● (人などを)鋳型にはめる mold (them) into one and the same type.

いかだいがく 医科大学 a medical school [(やや古) college].

イカタル 胃カタル 〖医学〗gastric catarrh.

いかつい ▶いかつい顔 (=厳しい表情) a *stern* [(いかめしい) *a forbidding*] look. ● いかつい肩 (=角張った)肩の人 a person with *square* shoulders; a *square*-shouldered person.

いかなご 〖魚介〗a sand lance.

いかなる 如何なる every, any. ▶《どんな ❷》● いかなる(種類の)体罰にも反対である be against corporal punishment of *any* kind.

いかなるほしのもとに 『如何なる星の下に』*Beneath What Star*. (参考) 高見順の小説

いかに ❶〖どの程度〗how. ▶この写真で彼がいかに背が高いかがわかる This picture shows *how* tall he is. ❷〖どんなに...しても〗however, no matter how. (❕後の方が口語的) ▶彼がいかに力持ちでもその岩は動かせない *However* [*No matter how*] strong he is, he can't move the rock.

いかにも ❶〖まさに〗just;〖非常に〗very,《話》so. ● いかにも満足そうに with *great* satisfaction. (×very satisfactorily は不可) ▶それはいかにも彼の言いそうなことだ It is *just* like him to say so./(彼らしいことである) *Characteristically*, he said so. ▶彼のお世辞はいかにも見え見えだった His flattery was *very* [*so*] obvious, wasn't it? ▶彼の考え方はいかにも(=典型的に)日本的だ His way of thinking is *typically* Japanese.
❷〖なるほど〗indeed; (確かに) to be sure. (⇨なるほど)
会話「彼女こそ彼にとって理想の妻だ」「いかにもそのとおりだ」"She is an ideal wife for him." "Yes, *indeed*./That's *quite* right./You are *quite* right." (❕後の2文のうち, 前の方は相手の言った内容に, 後の方は人に言及した言い方)
会話「これは安すぎると思う」「いかにもごもっとも. でもそれより高いのを買う余裕はないんだよ」"In my opinion it's too cheap." "That's all very well, but I can't afford a more expensive one." (❕不満・不賛成を表すときの決まり文句)
❸〖あたかも〗as if [though]. (⇨まるで ❶)

いかばかり ▶彼女の悲しみはいかばかりであろうか I can imagine just *how* sad she is.

いがみあい いがみ合い (口論) a quarrel. (⇨いがみ合う)

いがみあう いがみ合う (口論する) quarrel; (争う) fight. ▶その兄弟はいつもいがみ合っている Those brothers *are* always *quarreling* [*at odds*] with each other./Those brothers *fight like cat and dog*. (❕「夫婦など近い関係にある2人がいっしょにいるといつも大声を張り上げてのけんかになる」の意)

いかめしい 〖重苦しい〗grave;〖厳しい〗stern;〖威厳のある〗dignified;〖近づきがたい〗forbidding;〖仰々しい〗high-sounding. ● いかめしい顔つき a *grave* [a *stern*] look. ● いかめしい制服姿で in a *dignified* uniform. ● いかめしい感じの建物 a building with a *dignified* [a *forbidding*] appearance. ● いかめしい肩書き a *high-sounding* title.

イカメラ 胃カメラ a gastrocamera;〖医学〗(胃内視鏡) a gastric fiberscope [endoscope].

いかもの (偽物) a fake. ● (=偽物) ▶彼はいかもの食いです He is an eater of *unusual* food./He has an *eccentric taste* in food.

いかよう — いかようにも ▶いかようなご注文でも承ります We accept *any* order.

いからせる 怒らせる ❶〖怒らせる〗make 《him》 angry. ❷〖いかめしくする〗▶肩をいからせる *square* one's shoulders.

いがらっぽい scratchy; (ざらっとした) rough; (むずがゆい) itchy. ▶のどがいがらっぽい I feel *scratchy* in the throat./I have a *scratchy* throat.

いかり 怒り anger 《at, for》;〖抑えられないほどの〗(a) rage 《at, against, over》;〖気も狂わんばかりの〗(a) fury;〖不正・卑劣な行為に対する〗indignation 《at》. (⇨憤概) ▶彼は怒り狂って(=かっとなって)花びんを私に投げつけた He threw the vase at me in a fit of

いかり anger [rage].
① 【怒りが】▶彼の怒りが爆発した His *anger* exploded./He exploded *with anger*. ▶彼が老人をけっているのを見て彼に対する怒りが胸にこみ上げてきた When I saw him kicking an old man, I became filled with *anger at* [*against*] him. ▶このような侮辱に対する彼の怒りはすさまじかった His *indignation* at these insults was fierce. ▶彼の怒りが次第に収まった His *anger* gradually cooled (down) [*subsided*]. ▶怒りは敵と思え Consider *anger* your enemy.
② 【怒りの】▶怒りのあまり口もきけなかった I was so *angry* that I was unable to speak./I was speechless *with anger*. ▶彼は怒りの声をあげた He gave a roar of *anger*./He roared *with anger*.
③ 【怒りに】▶怒りに燃える burn *with anger*. ●怒りに触れる⇒【怒りを買う】▶彼は怒りにかられて妻を殴った In a fit of *anger*, he hit his wife.
④ 【怒りを[で]】▶怒りを買う【招く】《書》incúr 《his》*anger*; 《感情を害する》offend. ▶怒りを抑える control [check] one's *anger*; keep (↔lose) one's temper. ▶彼に怒りをぶちまける vent one's *anger* on him. ▶怒りを覚える feel *anger*. ▶彼の声は怒りで震えていた His voice was trembling *with anger* [*rage*]. ▶彼が笑ったことで彼女は怒りをいっそうつのらせた He laughed, which made her even *angrier*.
● 怒り心頭に発する ▶怒り心頭に発して in a *rage* [a *fury*]. ▶彼は怒り心頭に発した He flew into a *rage* [a *fury*]./He went wild with *rage* 《at the news》.

いかり 錨 an anchor. (**!**慣用表現では通例無冠詞)
● 錨を上げる[下ろす] weigh [cast, drop] *anchor*.
● 錨を下ろして(=停泊している) be [lie] at *anchor*.

いかりがた 怒り肩 ▶怒り肩の女性 a square-shouldered woman. ▶私は怒り肩だ I have *square shoulders*. (⇔なで肩)

いかる 斑鳩 〔鳥〕 a Japanese grosbeak.

いかる 怒る get* angry. (⇒怒(ぃ)る)

いかれた (⇒いかれる)

いかれぽんち 《軽薄な男》 a frivolous man; 《奇人,変人》《話》a crank, an oddball, a weirdo. (**!**いずれも軽蔑的)

いかれる ▶いかれた(=使い古した)靴 *worn-out* shoes. ▶その温度計はいかれている(=狂っている) That thermometer is *wrong*. ▶あの男はいかれてる He's *crazy./He has gone off* his head [mind]. ▶あいつは彼女にいかれてる(=夢中だ) He's *crazy* [《話》*mad*] *about* her.

いかん ▶いかんによる depend on the result. (⇒因(ぃ)る, 次第) ▶年齢のいかんを問わず *irrespective of age*; *regardless of age*; *however old* [*young*] 《he is》.
● いかんせん (あいにく) unfortunately.
● いかんとも ▶それはいかんともしがたい It cannot be helped. / There is nothing we can do about it.

いかん 偉観 a magnificent [a grand] sight. (⇒壮観)

いかん 移管 — **移管する** 動 transfer 《-rr-》《*to*》.

いかん 遺憾 形 (a) regret. (⇒残念) ▶遺憾ながらご招待はお受けできません I *regret* [*I'm sorry*] *to say that* I cannot accept your invitation. ▶彼の言い方の方が口語的(=*Much*) *to my regret*, I cannot accept your invitation.
── **遺憾な事** a matter for *regret*. ▶君が多くの人に迷惑をかけたのは遺憾だ It is *regrettable* [*to be regretted*, *a matter for regret*] *that* you have troubled many people./(遺憾に思う)I *regret* [*feel regretful*] *that* you have troubled many people. ▶彼はその件に[会議に出席できないことに]遺憾の意を表した He expressed his *regret for the matter* [*at not being able to attend the meeting*].
── **遺憾に** 副 ▶…を誠に遺憾に思う I deeply *regret that* .... ▶遺憾なことに犯罪が増加傾向にある *Regrettably* [*Regretfully*], crime is on the increase.

いがん 依願 — **依願退職** retirement at one's own request. ▶依願退職する retire [resign one's post [job]] at one's own *request*.

いがん 胃癌 〔医学〕(have) stomach cancer. (⇒癌)

いかんなく 遺憾なく 〔〔申し分なく〕〕(most) satisfactorily; 〔〔十分に〕〕fully. ▶遺憾なく(=最大限に)実力を発揮する show [display] one's ability *to the full*.

:いき 息 〔〔呼吸する空気〕〕(a) breath /bréθ/; 〔〔呼吸〕〕breathing /brí:ðiŋ/. ▶窓ガラスは子供たちの息で曇っていた The windowpanes were clouded with the steam of the children's *breaths*.
① 【息が】▶彼はまだ息がある He is still *breathing* [《生きている》is still *alive*]. (**!**前の方は動詞 breathe /brí:ð/ の進行形) ▶彼は息が臭い He has bad [foul] *breath*./His *breath* smells bad [foul]. (**!**「口臭」は bad breath で b.b. とも略す) ▶早く走ったので息が切れた[息が上がった] I ran so fast that I was *out of breath* [*lost my breath*]./I was *panting heavily* after running fast. ▶ほんの少し泳いだだけで息が続かなくなった I swam only a little before my *breath* was almost finished.
② 【息の】▶息のあるうちに while one *is* (still) *alive*. ▶息の続く限り (最後のあえぎまで) to the last gasp;《生きている限り》as long as one *lives*.
③ 【息を】▶激しく息をする *breathe* hard [heavily]. ▶息を吸い込む[吐き出す] breathe in [out]; 《やや書》inhale [exhale]. ▶息を止める[凝らす] hold one's *breath*. ▶息を整える get one's *breath* back; (一息つく) catch one's *breath*. ▶息を切らして(=あえぎながら)たどりつく arrive *breathlessly* [*gasping for air*]. ▶眼鏡のレンズに息を吹きかける *breathe* on the lenses of one's glasses. ▶(寒いときに)両手を丸めて息を吹きかける cup one's hands and *breathe into* them. ▶彼はほっと息をついた He *breathed* [*gave*] a sigh of relief./He felt (greatly) relieved. ▶彼は大きく息を吸って水にもぐった He took a deep *breath* and dove under the water. ▶彼は息をつく(継ぐ)ために水面に姿を現した He surfaced to get his *breath*./He came up for air. ▶力を抜いて, 大きく息を吸って, 吐いて(医者が患者に対して)Relax. *Inhale* deeply. And out again. ▶泥棒は息をひそめて物陰に隠れていた The robber hid himself *holding his breath* [*with bated breath*].
④ 【息も】▶息も絶え絶えである try to catch one's *breath*; be (all) *out of breath*. (**!**all がある方が強意的) ▶息もつかずにしゃべる talk without taking a *breath*. ▶彼は息も絶え絶えにゴールに走り込んだ He reached the goal line *all out of breath*.
● 息が合う ▶息の合った夫婦[《テニスなどの》ペア]だ They make a *perfect couple* [*pair*]./The couple [pair] is *in* (↔*out of*) *harmony*. ▶彼らは息が合っていた(=仲よくやっていた) They *were getting along well* [《話》*hitting it off*] *with each other*./They were *in perfect harmony*./(⇒呼吸 ③)
● 息がかかる ▶彼には社長の息がかかっている He is backed up by his boss./He has the backing of

- **息が詰まる** ●息が詰まりそうな[=風通しが悪くむっとする]部屋 a *stuffy* room. ▶彼は食物がつかえて息が詰まった He *choked on* a piece of food. ▶煙で[満員電車]息が詰まりそうだった[=窒息しそうだった] I *was suffocating* in the smoke [in the jammed train]. (⇨息苦しい)
- **息が長い** ●息の長い(=長期にわたる)計画 a *long-term* plan. ●息の長い仕事をする do *lasting, meaningful* work. ▶イギリス人は息が長い(=長期的視点を持っている)というか、日本人とは世を計る物差しが違う British people generally *have* [*take*] *a long term outlook* and judge the times by a measure different from ours (in Japan). (❗「日本人とは…違う」は「日本人の物差しとは異なった」の意味で、us としないで ours (=our measure)とする)
- **息の根を止める** ●彼の息の根を止める(=殺す) *kill* him.
- **息もつかせず** ●その映画は息もつかせぬ激しいアクションシーンが満載だ That movie [film] has full of *breathtakingly* vigorous action.
- **息を殺す** hold [×kill] one's breath.
  - 翻訳のこころ 一人の男が、猫のように身を縮めて、息を殺しながら、上の様子をうかがっていた (芥川龍之介『羅生門』) A man was trying to figure out [guess] what was happening upstairs above, curling his back like a cat and *holding his breath*. (❗「上の様子」は what was happening で「何が起こっているか」とする。時制の一致で was となることに注意)
- **息をつく[抜く]** ●忙しくて息をつく[抜く](=一休みする)暇もない I am too busy to *take a* (*short*) *rest* [(くつろぐ) *relax*]./I'm so busy (that) I have no time to *breathe*. (❗ that を省略するのは《話》)
- **息をのむ** ●日の出の美しさに私は思わず息をのんだ The beauty of the rising sun *took my breath away*./I *caught my breath* at the beautiful sight of the rising sun. (❗「息をのむような景色」は breathtaking scenery)
- **息を引き取る** (死ぬ) die; (婉曲的) pass away; (書) breathe one's last.
- **息を吹き返す** ▶人工呼吸をすると、その溺死(でき)しかけていた子は息を吹き返した After (being given) artificial respiration, the half-drowned child *came to life* [(意識が回復した) *came around*, (よみがえった) *revived*].

いき 生き ●この魚はとっても生きがよい This fish is very *fresh*.

いき 行き ●東京行きの列車 a train (*bound*) *for* Tokyo; a Tokyo(-*bound*) train. ●九州方面行きのホーム a platform *for* [×*bound for*] Kyushu. (❗ bound for の主語は乗り物) ●行きは電車で帰りはタクシーにする go by train and come back by taxi. ●行きも帰りも歩く walk there and back; walk both ways. ▶あのバスはどこ行きですか Where *is* that bus (*bound*) *for*?/Where does that bus go to?

いき 粋 图 chic /ʃiːk/; smartness with a touch of refined sexiness.
— **粋な** 圏 smart; stylish; (特に女性[女性の服]が) chic; (洗練された) refined; (上品で気のきいた) neat.
●いきなレストラン a *chic* restaurant. ●いきな身なりをしている be *smartly* [*stylishly*] dressed. ●いきな計らいをする make smart [wise] arrangements. ▶彼女の和服姿は小にくらしいほどいきだ She wears her *kimono* with great *chic*.

いき 域 (程度) a level. ●名人の域に達する reach a masterly *level*. ●素人の域を出ない(=まだ素人の程度である) be still at the *level* of an amateur. ▶それは私の憶測の域を出ない(=単なる憶測である) That's *only* [*merely*] my guess.

いき 意気 ❶ [元気] spirits, heart; (士気) morale. ●意気盛んである be in high *spirits*; be elated. ●その知らせで意気を喪失する lose *heart* [*courage*] at the news. (⇨意気消沈, 意気投合, 意気揚々) ▶その意気だ！ おれがついているぞ That's the *spirit*! I'm right behind you.
❷ [心だて] mind; (決意) resolution. ●彼の意気に打たれる be moved [touched] by his firm *resolution*.

いき 遺棄 图 (権利・財産・家族などを) abandonment; (義務・家族などを) desertion.
— **遺棄する** 動 abandon; desert. ●死体を遺棄する *abandon* a corpse [a (dead) body]; *leave* a corpse *behind*. ●遺棄された車[船] an abandoned car [boat].

いき 威儀 (威厳) dignity.
●威儀を正して(威厳のあるふうに) in a dignified [(厳粛な) a solemn] manner.

いき 異義 a different meaning, another meaning.
●同音異義(語) (⇨同音異義)

いき 異議 (反対) (an) objection; (不同意) dissent; (抗議) (a) protest (*against*). (⇨反対, 抗議) ●異議を唱える raise [voice] an *objection* (*to*); (反対する) object (*to*); (抗議する) protest (*against*). ▶彼らはその案を実行することに異議を唱えた(=反対した) They *objected to* (carrying out) the plan. 会話「この件についてご異議ありませんか」「異議なし」「異議なしと認めます」 "Does anyone have any *objections to* this?" "No *objection*!" "We see no *objection* whatsoever."

いき 意義 ❶ [意味] (言葉の) (a) meaning, (個々の) a sense. (⇨意味)
❷ [重要性] (やや書) (a) significance; importance. ●歴史的意義のある事件 an event of historical *significance* [*importance*]. ●意義深い実験 a *significant* experiment. ▶彼らの参加でその大会は一層意義深いものとなった Their participation gave the convention a deeper *significance*.

いきあう 行き会う (偶然会う) happen to meet [see], meet*... by chance, 《話》 come* across .... (⇨会う)

いきあたりばったり 行き当たりばったり — **行き当たりばったりの** 圏 [無計画の] haphazard; [無原則の] random; [運まかせの] hit-and[or]-míss; [のんきな] hàppy-go-lúcky.
— **行き当たりばったりに** 圖 ●行き当たりばったりにやる do *haphazardly* [*in a haphazard way*]; do *at random*; do *hit and* [*or*] *miss*.

いきあたる 行き当たる come* to; hit*, run* into. ●私たちは川に行き当たるまで中を進んで行った We went on through the bush until we *hit* [*came to*] the river.

いきいき 生き生き (元気な) lively; (新鮮な) fresh; (鮮やかな) vivid. ▶彼女は生き生きとした表情をしている She looks *lively* [*full of life*]. ▶雨でアジサイの葉が生き生きしている The leaves of a hydrangea look *fresh* in the rain. ▶その本の人物描写は生き生きとして真に迫っている The book's characterizations are *vivid* and true to nature. ▶子供にお話をしてやっているときの実に生き生きとしている(=彼の最高の状態にある) He is really *at his best* telling stories to children. ▶この町が生き生きしてくる[=活気づく]のは暗くなってからです It is after dark when this town comes *alive*.

いきうつし 生き写し ▶浩は父親に生き写しだ Hiroshi

いきうま　生き馬　●生き馬の目を抜く is *the very image* [*a carbon copy*] *of his father*./(まったく似ている) Hiroshi *looks exactly like* his father.　●生き馬の目を抜くような競争 *cutthroat* competition.　▶彼は生き馬の目を抜くような男だ He is very *shrewd*.

いきうめ　生き埋め　●生き埋めにする *bury* 《him》 *alive*.　▶なだれで 3 人のスキーヤーが生き埋めになった Three skiers *were buried alive* by the avalanche.

いきえ　生き餌　live /láiv/ *bait*; (飼料) (a) *live feed*.

:いきおい　勢い　❶[力, 活気, 勢力] (実際の動作や動きに現れる) *force*（❗何らかの抵抗を克服しての移動・加速を暗示する）; (何かに影響を与える能力) *power*（❗人について用いると社会的・政治的権力をさす); (忍耐・抵抗のできる内に秘めた力) *strength*; (精力) *vigor*; (元気) *energy*; (勢力の拡大) *influence*.
①【勢いが】　▶風の勢いが少しずつ衰えてきた The wind has gradually lost its *force* [become weak in *force*]./The *force* of the wind has gradually become weak.　▶彼の球は勢いがある[ない] His pitching is *powerful* [*lacks power*].　▶勢いが余ってドアに頭をぶつけた He spent too much *energy* and knocked his head against the door.　▶山火事はまた勢いが強くなった(=燃え上がった) The forest fire blazed up again.
②【勢いのある】　(力強い) *forceful*; (元気の出る) *energetic*; (精力旺盛な) *vigorous*; (勢力のある) *influential*, *powerful*.　●勢いのある文体 a *vigorous* style.
③【勢いに[を]】　▶我が軍は敵の勢いに圧倒された Our troops were overwhelmed by the enemy's *strength*.　▶あらしは勢いを増してきた The storm has grown in *force*.
④【勢いで】　▶風がものすごい勢いで窓に吹き付けていた The wind was blowing against the windows *with* great *force*.　▶人口が非常な勢いで(=急速に)増加している The population is growing *rapidly* [*with rapidity*].　▶彼は酔った勢いで暴力を振るった He used violence *under the influence of* alcohol [because he was drunk].　▶そのチームは破竹の勢いで勝ち進んだ The team *carried everything* [*all*] *before it*.　▶怒った群衆はすさまじい勢いで鉄の門を破った The angry crowd broke the iron gate *with* great *violence*.
⑤【勢いよく】　*forcefully*, *energetically*, *vigorously*.（❗動詞表現で表されることもある）　▶植物が勢いよく(=元気よく)成長している The plants are growing *vigorously* [*with vigor*].　▶水が壊れたパイプから勢いよく流れ出ている The water is gushing out [大量に] *flowing out in large amount*] from the broken pipe.　▶彼は勢いよく部屋に飛び込んできた He rushed into the room.（❗rush は性急さを暗示する）

❷[はずみ] (a) *momentum*（❗-ta, ~s); (推進力) (an) *impetus*; (速度) *speed*.　▶彼の車は坂を下るにつれ勢いがついていた His car gathered *momentum* [*speed*] as it went down the hill./His car moved faster and faster down the hill.　▶(前の方より口語的) よい知らせを聞いてチームは勢いに乗った(=気分が高まった) Their *spirits* lifted [(活気づいた) *rose*] at the good news.　▶彼は勢いかって(=勇気を奮い起こして)彼女をデートに誘った Maki plucked up her courage and asked him out on a date.　▶私たちはゲームの後半で勢いを失い始めた We began to lose *momentum* in the second half of the game.　▶彼のホームランで我がチームは勢いづいた His home run gave our team a new *impetus*./(元気づいた) His home run cheered up our team./Our team was cheered when he hit a home run.

❸[成り行き]　●時の勢いに乗る[逆らう] go *with* [*against*] *the tide* (of the times).　▶ただ勢いをすれば金が足りなくなる If you waste your money, you'll be in need of it *as a* (*natural*) *result* [you'll be *naturally* in need of it].

いきおいこむ　勢い込む　●勢い込んで (元気よく) *with vigor*, *vigorously*; (強い興味を示して) *with enthusiasm*, *enthusiastically*.

いきおくれる　行き遅れる　▶彼女は行き遅れている She is *past marriageable age*.

いきがい　生き甲斐　a reason for living.　●生きがいのある人生 (生きる価値のある) a [one's] *life worth living*; (定まった目標のある) a [one's] *life with a definite purpose*.　●自分の人生に生きがいを見いだす find one's life *worth living*.　▶仕事が私の生きがいだ I (really) *live for* my work./My work is my *reason for living* [*being*].　▶私にはもう何の生きがいもない I no longer have *anything to live for*.

いきがい　域外　(区域の外) *outside the area* [*region, territory, district*].　(⇨域内)
●域外生産 *offshore production*.　●域外投資 an *offshore investment*.

いきかう　行き交う　*come and go*.　●行き交う人もない (=通りに人影のない) 真夏の昼下がり an early afternoon of a high summer's day when the streets are deserted.　▶歩道は行き交う人々で混雑していた The sidewalk were crowded with people *coming and going*.

いきかえり　行き帰り　●行き帰り歩く *walk both ways*.　●学校の行き帰りに on one's [the] *way to and from* school.

いきかえる　生き返る　*revive*; (息を吹き返す) *come* (*back*) *to life*.　●生きかえらせる bring 《him》 *back to life*.　▶水につけると花が生き返った The flower *revived* in water.　▶シャワーを浴びて生き返った心地だ I *feel refreshed* after a shower./A shower *has refreshed* me.

いきがかり　行き掛かり　▶行き掛かり上, 彼の申し出を断れなかった *Circumstances forced* me *to accept his offer*./I was compelled to accept his offer *by force of circumstance*.

いきがけ　行き掛け　●学校へ行き掛けに (=行く途中で) *on* one's *way to school*.

いきかた　生き方　*how to live*; (ライフスタイル) one's *lifestyle*, one's way of life [*living*].　●簡素な生き方を選ぶ choose simple *living* [a simple *way of life*].　▶いろいろの会に誘われれば入らざるを得ないのが町の生き方である When we're invited to join a variety of clubs, we cannot refuse their invitations. That's *the way of life* in a community.（❗英語の主語にあたる部分が長いときは，2 文に分けて前の文で述べたことを後の文の主語 that で表すと理解しやすくなる）

いきかた　行き方　(行く方法) a *way* (*to*); (接近方法) an *access* (*to*).　▶空港の行き方は三つある There are three *ways* [*accesses*] *to* the airport.　▶駅への行き方を教えてください Please tell me *how to get to* [*how* I can *get to*] the station.

いきがる　粋がる　●いきがることはない There's no need to *show off*.　●いきがるのはよせ Stop *putting on air*.

いきき　行き来　图 [往来] *coming and going*（❗語順に注意); [人・車の通行] *traffic*（⇨往来); [交際] association.　▶彼は近ごろ人との行き来を(=会うのを)避けているようだ He seems to avoid (seeing) people these days.

— **行き来する** 動 come* and go*; go back and forth (*between*); (交際する) (やや書) associate (*with*). ▶東京大阪間を行き来する *go back and forth between* Tokyo and Osaka. ▶彼らはお互い行き来する(=訪問する間柄だ) They are *on visiting* (*親しい*) *terms with* each other.

いきぎれ 息切れ ━━ **息切れする** 動 lose one's breath; (息切れしている) be out of breath (=息); [仕事などで] run out of steam. ▶彼は走ったあと息切れしていた He *was out of* [*was short of*] *breath* after running.

いきぐるしい 息苦しい [息をつまらせるような] choking; suffocating; [部屋から風通しの悪い] stuffy. ▶その部屋は風通しが悪くて息苦しかった The room was stuffy and I *could hardly breathe*./It was *stuffy and suffocating* in the room. ▶このセーターの首は息苦しい The neck of this sweater *chokes* [*is choking*] *me*. (▶後の方は着ているときにのみ言う) ▶日本にいると息苦しい。もう嫌だ I feel so *suffocated* living [staying] in Japan. I've just had it. (1) living は日本人、staying は日本人以外の場合に用いる。(2) have just had it は「もう我慢できない」の意のくだけた言い方)

いきごみ 意気込み [熱意] eagerness; [熱中] enthusiasm; [決意] determination. ▶大変意気込みで勉強する study *with great enthusiasm*. ▶意気込みをくじく dampen (*his*) *enthusiasm* [*determination*]. ▶その試合に勝とうとする彼らの意気込みは大変なものだった They *were* very *determined* [*very eager*] *to* win the game.

いきごむ 意気込む [しきりに...したがる] be eager (*to do*); [熱心である] be enthusiastic (*about*); [熱中している] be intent (*on*). ▶大いに意気込んで事業を始める start a business *with great enthusiasm*. ▶彼は博士号を取ろうと意気込んでいる He *is eager to get* [*is intent on getting*, (堅く決意している) *is* (*very*) *determined to get*] a doctor's degree.

いきさき 行き先 [所在] one's whereabouts (❗ 単・複両扱い); [行った所] the place where one is going [has gone]; [目的地] one's destination. ▶彼の行き先は分かりません I don't know his *whereabouts*./I don't know *where he is* [*has gone*]. ▶我々の行き先はパリだ Our *destination* is Paris. ▶行き先はどちらですか How *far are you going*? ▶Where are you going? は場合によっては失礼な言い方になるので注意)/May I ask your *destination*?

いきさつ 経緯 [込み入った事情] details. ▶事件のいきさつ the *details* [*whole story*] *of* the case. ▶この間(☆)のいきさつをお話ししましょう I'll tell you *what happened* [*how it happened*] *during this period*. (❗ it は漠然とした状況を指す)

いきざま 生き様 one's attitude toward [to] life.

いきじごく 生き地獄 [この世の地獄] (a) hell on earth.

いきしに 生き死に life and [or] death. (⇨生死, 死活)

いきじびき 生き字引 [言葉をよく知っている人] a walking dictionary; [博識な人] a walking encyclopedia.

いきしょうちん 意気消沈 ━━ **意気消沈する** 動 become depressed [downhearted, dejected]; [落胆する] be discouraged, lose heart. ▶意気消沈している be depressed [downhearted, dejected]; be in low spirits.

いきすぎ 行き過ぎ (度を越えること) excess; (極度) (an) extreme. ▶行き過ぎを是正する put right [(書) rectify] *the excesses*.

DISCOURSE 個人的な意見では、上記の見方は行き過ぎだ This view is, **in my opinion**, *going too far*. (❗ in my opinion(個人的な意見では)は主張を表すディスコースマーカー)

いきすぎる 行き過ぎる ▶郵便局を行き過ぎる(=通り過ぎる) *go* [*walk*] *past* the post office. ▶駅を二つ行き過ぎてしまった I *went* two stops *too far*. ▶何事においても行き過ぎはよくない(=度を越えてはいけない) Don't *go too far* [*go to extremes*] in anything.

いきすじ 粋筋 (花柳界) the world of *geisha*.

いきせききる 息急き切る pant [gasp] (for breath), 《話》 puff and blow [pant]. ▶私たちは息せききって丘を駆け上った We ran up the hill, *puffing and panting*.

いきた 生きた [生きている] live /láiv/ (❗ 限定的に); alive (❗ 叙述的に); living (❗ 限定的にも叙述的にも用い、前の2語より意味範囲が広い). ▶生きたネズミで実験する experiment on *live*, ×*alive*] mice; experiment on mice (which are) still *alive*. ▶生きた英語を学ぶ learn *living* [(実際使われている) *real*, (日常の) *everyday*] English. ▶彼は生きたまま埋められた He was buried *alive*. ▶生きた心地もしなかった My heart was in my mouth [boots]. (❗ My heart leaped into my mouth. はこの動作表現)/(命が縮むほどおどろいた) I was scared to death.

いきだおれ 行き倒れ a person lying dead by the roadside. ▶行き倒れになる collapse [fall down] and die by the roadside.

いきち 生き血 (life) blood. ▶生き血を吸う suck the *blood of a living animal*. ▶生き血を吸うような悪人だ He is a vampire [a bloodsucker].

いきち 閾値 [心理・生理] threshold. ▶あの人は苦痛[刺激] 閾値が高い[低い](=痛み[刺激]を感じにくい[やすい]) He has a high [low] *threshold* of pain [stimulus].

いきちがい 行き違い [すれ違い] crossing; [誤解] (a) misunderstanding. ▶彼女の手紙は彼との行き違いになった Her letter *crossed* his in the mail (主に米) [post (主に英)]./Her and his letters *crossed* in the mail (主に米) [(主に英) post]. ▶私と君の間に行き違いがあった There was some *misunderstanding* between you and me [(非標準) you and I, ×me and you].

いきづかい 息遣い ▶息遣いが荒い[早い] breathe hard [fast].

いきつぎ 息継ぎ (呼吸) breathing; (休憩) 《have》 a break, 《話》 a breather.

いきつく 行き着く (着く) arrive (*at*); reach. ▶行き着くところまで行く go as far as one [it] can go. ▶彼女はあの夜ボーイフレンドと行き着くところまで行ってしまった She *went all the way with* her boyfriend that night. (❗「性交する」の婉曲表現)

いきづく 息づく (生きている) live; be living; be alive /əláiv/. ▶4月、鎌倉は春らんまんで自然が息づいていた(=生き生きとしていた) In April, Kamakura *was very much alive* with cherry blossoms and other gifts of spring flowers from Mother Nature. ▶彼の体内に息づいていた(=生き続けていた)のは古代ペルシャ人の血であった It was the blood of an ancient Persian that *was running* in his body.

いきづくり 生き作り, 活き作り (⇨生け作り)

いきつけ 行きつけ (気に入りの) (one's) favorite. ▶彼の行きつけのバー his *favorite* bar; (パブ) 《英話》 his [the] local.

いきづまり 行き詰まり [交渉などの] (a) deadlock, (a) stalemate, (an) impasse /ímpæs/; [停止, 休

いきづまる 行き詰まる 〔息が詰まる〕 come to a standstill. ●行き詰まりを打開する break the deadlock.

いきづまる 行き詰まる reach (a) deadlock. ●〔交渉などが〕行き詰まっている be at a deadlock. ▶和平交渉は行き詰まった The peace negotiations reached (a) deadlock [(a) stalemate]./(決裂した) The peace negotiations broke down. ▶彼の商売は行き詰まった His business has come to a standstill [a dead end]. ▶その計画は資金不足で行き詰まっている The project remains at a standstill [is bogged down] for lack of funds.

いきづまる 息詰まる ●息詰まるような(=手に汗を握る)自動車レース a breathtaking [ぞくぞくさせる] a thrilling] car race. ●息詰まるような(=重苦しい)沈黙 oppressive silence. (!)その間の時間をさすときは[C])

いきとうごう 意気投合 ▶2人は会ってすぐに意気投合した They met for the first time and hit it off immediately.

いきどおり 憤り indignation. ▶その誘拐犯人に強い憤りを感じた I felt strong indignation against the kidnapper.

いきどおる 憤る get* angry. (⇨怒(2)る, 憤慨する)

いきとしいけるもの 生きとし生けるもの all living things [creatures]; all God's creatures.

いきとどく 行き届く 〔サービス・看護などが〕 give* (xa) good service [careful nursing]; (掃除などが) be neat and tidy; (手入れなどが) be well-kept, be looked after carefully; (注意などが) be thorough 《about》. ▶あのホテルはサービスが行き届いている The hotel gives good service. ▶彼の庭は手入れがよく行き届いている〔行き届いていない〕 His garden is well-kept [suffering from neglect]. (!)「手入れの行き届いた庭」は a well-kept garden. ▶彼は何事にも行き届いた人 He is very thorough about everything. ▶準備にいろいろ行き届かなかった点が多かった(=不満な点が多かった)と思います I'm afraid the preparation left a lot to be desired.

いきどまり 行き止まり 〔袋小路〕 a blind alley; a dead end. (!)共に比喩的にも用いられる) ▶この路地は行き止まりです This alley comes to a dead end./This is a dead-end alley.

いきない 域内 (区域の中) within the area [region, territory, district]. (⇨域外)
●域内貿易 intraregional trade, intra-trading.

いきながらえる 生き長らえる 〔生き続ける〕 go* on living, live on; 〔生き残る〕 survive.

いきなり (突然に) suddenly; (唐突に) abruptly; (予告なしに) without notice. (⇨突然) ●いきなり解雇されるbe fired without notice. ▶彼はいきなり逃げ出した He suddenly ran away. ▶ドライアイスは固体からいきなり(=間に他を介せずに)気体になる Dry ice goes directly from a solid to a vapor.

いきぬき 息抜き 図 (短い休み) a break, 《話》 a breather; (気晴らし) relaxation. ▶私は時々息抜きに絵をかく I sometimes paint for relaxation. ●絵をかくのはたいへん息抜きになる Painting is very relaxing. ▶息抜きに(=気分転換に)映画を見に行こう Let's go to the movies for a change.
── 息抜き(を)する 動 ●ちょっと息抜きをする take [have] a break [a breather].

いきぬく 生き抜く 〔生き延びる〕 live through...; 〔切り抜ける〕 come* through...; 〔生き残る〕 survive.
●二つの戦争を生き抜く live through [survive, come through] two wars.

いきのこり 生き残り a survivor.

いきのこる 生き残る survive. ●生き残った人 a survivor. ▶彼があの航空機事故で生き残ったのは奇跡である It is a miracle that he survived the air accident.

いきのびる 生き延びる 〔生き残る〕 survive; 〔より長く生きる〕 outlive. ▶激しい戦いを生き延びる survive [come through] the fierce battle.

いきはじ 生き恥 ●生き恥をさらす live in disgrace [dishonor], expose oneself to ridicule.

いきば(しょ) 行き場(所) ●行き場所がない I have nowhere [no place] to go. ▶騒音の件で不平の持って行き場がない I have no idea who I should complain to about the noise.

いきぼとけ 生き仏 a living Buddha; an extremely virtuous person; a saint, a saintly person.

いきまく 息巻く (ひどく怒っている) be enraged; (脅かす) threaten 《(to do)》. ●ただではおかぬと巻く threaten revenge.

いきむ 息む hold one's breath and strain one's stomach.

いきもの 生き物 a living thing; 《集合的》 life; (植物を除く) a (living) creature /kríːtʃər/. (⇨生物) ●密林の生き物を殺す destroy the life of the jungle. ▶政治は生き物、一寸先は闇だ[分からない] Politics is a living thing. You don't know what will happen next.

いきょ 依拠 ── 依拠する 動 be based 《on》; be founded 《on》.

いきょう 異教 (説明的に) a different religion; (正統宗教に対して) (a) heresy /hérəsi/.
●異教徒 (正統宗教から見て) a heretic; (主要宗教を信じない) a pagan /péign/, 《古》 a heathen.

いきょう 異郷 a foreign country 《書》 land; 《古》 a strange land.

いぎょう 医業 the medical profession; medicine. (⇨医学, 医者)

いぎょう 異形 形 (変な, 奇妙な) odd-looking; (怪奇な, 異様な) grotesque; (不気味な) weird. (⇨異様)

いぎょう 偉業 a great [顕著な] an outstanding] achievement.

いぎょう 遺業 ▶父の遺業を継ぐ carry on with the work left unfinished [undone] by one's father.

いきようよう 意気揚々 ●意気揚々としている be in high spirits. ●成功して意気揚々としている be elated by one's success. ●意気揚々と家路に向かって start for home in triumph [triumphantly]. ●意気揚々と行進する march in soaring triumph and glory.

いきょく 医局 a medical office.
●医局員 a member of the medical staff.

いきょく 委曲 (委細, 詳細) details, 《書》 particulars. (⇨委細, 詳細) ●委曲を尽くす explain ... in detail; give a full account 《of》; go into detail(s).

***イギリス** 〔国名〕 (Great) Britain; England; (公式名) the United Kingdom (of Great Britain and Northern Ireland) 《略 the U.K.》. (首都 London)
●イギリス(人)の British; English. (!)政治的文脈では British が好まれる)

> **解説** England は広義でイギリス全体をさすこともあるが、本来 England, Scotland, Wales, Northern Ireland などの国からなる (Great) Britain, the United Kingdom の一つであるため、他の地域出身者は (Great) Britain を好む。

【イギリス(の)〜】 ●イギリス英語 British English. ●イギリス政府 the British Government. ●イギリス海峡 the (English) Channel. ●イギリス人 an Englishman; (女性) an Englishwoman (!)この女性形はあまり用いられない);《集合的》 British people,

いきりだつ / いく

the British (!ともに複数扱い。Englishmen や English はイングランド人に限定して用い、この扱いをするのは避ける方がよい). ▶ イギリス連邦 the Commonwealth (of Nations). ▶ 彼はイギリス人だ He is *English*./England 出身者を含め広くは He is *British*./He is from *Britain*. のようにいう/(国籍を強調して) He is an *Englishman*. ▶ イギリス人は保守的な国民だ *The British* are a conservative people.

いきりたつ いきり立つ 〚たいへん怒る〛 get* very angry, 《話》 get mad (-dd-); 〚怒り狂う〛 be furious; 《やや書》 fly* into a rage. (⇨怒る)

いきりょう 生き霊 a wraith. ● 生霊に取りつかれる be possessed by [with] a wraith.

:いきる 生きる ❶ 〚生物が生存する〛 live (↔die); (困難な状況で) exist; (生きている) be living, be alive (↔be dead) (!alive は叙述用法のみ). ▶ 生きている魚 a *live* [a *living*, ×an *alive*] fish. (!live は /láɪv/ と発音する) ● 生きた見本 a *living* [×a live] example. ● 生きて帰る return *alive*. ▶ 人はみな生きる権利がある Everyone has a right to *live*. ▶ トラは肉を食べて生きている(=常食としている) Tigers *live on* [*by* eating] meat. ▶ 彼は100歳まで生きた He *lived* until [till] he was a hundred./He *lived to be* [*to the age of*] a hundred. ▶ 父はまだ生きています(=健在です) My father *is* still *alive* [*living*]. ▶ 「彼はもうあまり長くは生きられないでしょう」と医者は言った "He doesn't have long [a long time] to *live*," the doctor said. ▶ 彼が生きている間にそれを見られなかったのは残念だ It's a pity that he didn't *live* to see it. ▶ 生きているうちにナポリを見たい I want to see Naples /néɪplz/ while I *live* (while I *am alive*, (死ぬ前に) before I die]. (!次例より口語的)/I want to see Naples in my lifetime. ▶ 私が生きている限りあなたには不自由はさせない As long [×far] as I *am alive* [I *live*], you will have all you need. ▶ そのクマは生きているのか死んでいるのか Is the bear *alive* [*living*] or dead? ▶ 水なしでは生きた上で欠かせないものだ Water is essential to *life*./(水なしでは生きられない) Nobody can [could] *exist* [*live*] without water.

❷ 〚生活する, 暮らす〛 live, make* a [one's] living. (⇨生活する, 暮らす) ▶ この人たちは正直に生きている These people *live* [×are *living*] honestly./These people *lead* [*live*] an honest *life*. (!live a ... life はやや古風な堅い言い方) ▶ 彼はペン一本で生きている He *lives by* his pen [*writing*]. ▶ 彼は仕事一筋に生きた He *led* [《やや古》 *lived*] his *life* for his work./(仕事に一生を捧げた) He *devoted* his *life* to his work. ▶ 男はタフでなければ生きていない, しかし優しくなければ生きている資格はない A male must be tough to *survive* in this world. But he doesn't deserve to be alive, if he's not [unless he's] kind and gentle. (!(1) man は「人類」の意もあるので male とする方がよい. (2)「でなければ生きていけない」の二重否定は, 肯定文で表した方が分かりやすい. (3) 後の文では主要な主張を先にすることに注意)

❸ 〚物事が存続[現存]する〛 live; be [keep*] alive; (契約などが効力をもつ) be valid, be in effect. ● 生きている(=現在も続いている)伝統 a *living* tradition. ▶ 先生のその言葉は今なお私たちの心の中に生きている(=鮮やかに残っている) The teacher's words *remain fresh* [*still live, are still alive*] in our minds. ▶ この法律はまだ生きている This law is still *valid* [*in effect*]. /《やや書》 This law still *holds*.

❹ 〚生き生きする〛 come* to life. ▶ たった1語で文が生きてきた Just this one word *has made* the sentence *come to life* [*has brought* the sentence *to life*]. ▶ この写真はまるで生きているようだ This picture *is* really *lifelike*.

いきれ 生きれ (蒸し暑いこと) sultriness; (風通しの悪いこと) stuffiness.

いきわかれ 生き別れ ▶ 彼は息子と生き別れになった He *parted* from his son *never to see* him *again*./He *became separated* from his son *for life*.

いきわたる 行き渡る 〚影響・うわさなどが広がる〛 spread*; 〚普及している〛《書》prevail; 〚分配されるものがみんなに回る〛 go* around [round]. ▶ そのうわさは町中に行き渡った The rumor *has spread* throughout the city. ▶ 当時そういう考えが行き渡っていた Such ideas *prevailed* [*were widespread*] at that time. ▶ みんなに行き渡るだけのケーキがない There isn't enough cake to *go around*.

:いく 行く

WORD CHOICE 行く

go 話し手のいる場所を中心ととらえ, そこから他の場所へ移動すること. ▶ 公園に行くところなんだ I'm *going* to the park.
〚go＋前副〛to/on/back/out/into

come 聞き手のいる場所を中心ととらえ, そこに人がやってくる, または自分がそこに行くこと. ▶ ママ, 今行くよ I'm *coming*, mom.
〚come＋前副〛to/from/on/out/up

● 頻度チャート ●

```
go    ████████████████████████████
come  ██████████████████████
      20   40   60   80  100 (%)
```

❶ 〚おもむく〛 go*; (聞き手の所へ行く) come* (⇨類語); (乗り物を利用して行く) take*; (着く) get* to ...; (出発する) leave* 《for》; (出席する) attend; 〚訪問する〛 visit, (ちょっと) call 《on＋人, at＋場所》.

① 〚～へ行く〛 ▶ もう行かないといけません I must *go* now./(I think) I must *be going* now. (!進行形を用いると表現が和らぐ. 「そろそろおいとましなければいけません」の意) ▶ 今行きます (呼ばれたときの返事) (I'm) *coming* [×going].

② 〚(場所)へ[に, まで]行く〛 ▶ あっちへ行け *go away*. ▶ どこへ行きたいですか Where do you want to *go* [×go to, ×visit]? (!「どの国へ行きたいですか」なら What country do you want to *visit* (go to, ×go)?) ▶ あすそちらに行きます I'll *go* [*come*] there tomorrow. (!come では話している今またはあす, 聞き手がそこにいることが含みされている. go [come] の代わりに be を用いて I'll *be* there tomorrow. とか come の代わりに I'll *be with you* tomorrow. ともいえる) ▶ 次の日曜日君のところへ行くよ I'll *come over* [*come to* your house, *visit* you] next Sunday. ▶ すぐ彼のところへ行きなさい *Go and see* [《米》*Go see*] him right away. ▶ 日常会話では *Go to* see him ... より普通. ただし, go が活用変化したときは go (and)... の形は不可 (⇨③ **会話** [第3例]) ▶ 駅へ行く道(=行き方)を教えてくれませんか Could you tell [show, ×teach] me how to *get to* the station? (!(1) 「そこへ行く道」の場合は how to *get* (×to) there. tell は口で説明すること, show は地図を示す, 同行して案内すること. (2) 単に How do I get to the station? ともいえる) ▶ 彼はニューヨークに行くつもりだ He's *going (to go)* to New York. (!《英》では be going to go to はあまり普通でない. 《米》では両方とも用いられる) ▶ いつアメリカへ行きます(=出発しますか) When will you *leave* for America? ▶ この列車

ボストンまで行きますか Does this train *go to* Boston?/この列車はボストン行きですか Does this train *take* us to Boston?/(ボストン行きの列車ですか) *Is* this train (*bound*) *for* Boston? ▶彼は今ロンドンに行っています He *has gone* to London now. (ⓘ *have gone* to ...は「...へ行ってしまって今はここにはいない」ことを表す)/He *is* (*away*) *in* London now. ▶英国へ行ったことがありますか *Have* you ever *been* [《米話》 *Have* you ever *gone*] *to* England?/Did you ever *go to* England? ▶私は九州には行ったことがあるが,四国へは行ったことがない I *have been to* Kyushu, but (I *have*) never *been to* Shikoku.

③【...(し)に行く】▶きのうデパートへ買い物に行きました I *went* shopping *at* [*in*, ×*to*] the department store yesterday./I *went to* the department store to do some [the] shopping yesterday. (ⓘ (1)×I *went to* shopping .... (2) *go doing* (...しに行く)の構文の *do* には通例活動的な娯楽・スポーツなどを表す動詞が多い: *go studying*. 文脈によっては *come doing* の形も用いる (⇨ [類語]). なお,この構文の *doing* に続く前置詞は *do* の示す動詞によって決まる: 蔵王へスキーに行く *go skiing at* [×*to*] Zao./川へ魚釣りに行く *go fishing in* [*at*, ×*to*] the river./海岸に泳ぎに行く *go swimming* [*for* a *swim*] *at* the beach./湖にスケートに行く *go skating on* the lake. ▶この前のクラス会へ行きましたか (=出席しましたか) Did you *go to* [《やや書》 *attend*] the last class reunion?

会話「お茶に来ない?」「うん,すぐ行くよ」"Would you like to come over for a cup of tea?" "OK. I'll *be right over*."

会話「どこへ行っていたのですか」「成田空港に友達を見送りに行っていました」 "Where *have* you *been*?" "I *have been to* Narita Airport to see my friend off." (ⓘ *have been to* ...は「...へ行って戻って来たところだ」の意)

会話「メアリーを迎えに行くところなの」「私も行っていいかしら」「あなたが行ってくださればうれしいわ」"I'm *going to* [×*going* (*and*)] *meet* Mary." "Can I *come* too?" "I'd love you to *come*."

④【(手段)で行く】▶僕は東京へ飛行機で行きました I *flew* (*over*) *to* Tokyo./(飛行機を利用して) I *took* a plane *to* Tokyo. ▶彼は学校へ車で [歩いて] 行った He *drove* [*walked*] *to* school./He *went to* school by car [*on foot*]. (ⓘ (1) 前の方が普通. 後の方は特に手段を強調した言い方. (2) *drive* は自分が運転する場合に用いる)

⑤【...を行く】▶この通りを行くと駅に出ます *Go down* [*along*] this street, and you will come to the station./This street *takes* you [*leads* (*you*)] *to* the station. ▶どちらの道を行きましょうか Which road shall we *take*?

❷【運ぶ】(事が) *go**; (暮らし・成績などが) *do**; (計画などが) *work*; (仲よく暮らす) *get** *along* [*on*] (*well*) (*with*). ▶何もかもうまく行った Everything *went well* (↔*badly*)./Everything *came* [*turned*] *out all right*. ▶物事はそう思うようにはうまく行かないものだ Things don't always *go* as *smooth*(*ly*) [*well*] as we might expect. ▶彼の入学試験はうまくいったようだ He seems to *have done well* [(成功した) *have been successful*] in the entrance exam. ▶仕事はうまくいっていますか *Are* you *getting along* [*on*] (*well*) *with* your work?

❸【その他の表現】▶病院へ行く途中で花を買った I bought some flowers *on my* [*the*] *way to* the hospital. ▶その距離を3時間で行くのは大変だった I found it difficult to *cover* [*make*, *do*] the distance in three hours. ▶彼は妹をたばこを買いに店に行かせた He *sent* his sister *around* to the shop for some cigarettes. ▶パトカーが道を行ったり来たりしている A patrol car is running *up and down* (*in*) [*to and fro in*] the street. ▶ぼくの時計はどこへ行ったのか (=どうなったのか) What *has become of* my watch? ▶彼のすることすべてが思いどおりにいかなかった Everything he did *fell short of* (↔*came up to*) his expectations.

会話「彼らはみんなそれを間違えたんだよ」「でも太郎はもう少しってところまでいったんだよ」"They all got it wrong." "Well, Taro *came close*."

いくー 幾ー ⇨【何(%)ー】

イグアナ【動物】an iguana /ɪɡwάːnə/.

いくえ 幾重 ▶テントを幾重にも折りたたむ fold a tent *several times*. ▶幾重にも (=くり返して) 頼む ask *repeatedly* [(熱心に) *earnestly*]. ▶幾重にもわびを申し上げます Please accept my *humble* [*sincere*] apologies.

いくえいかい 育英会 a scholarship society. ▶日本育英会 the Japan *Scholarship Society*. (参考) 現在は日本学生支援機構 (the Japan Student Services Organization) に統合

いくさ 戦 (a) war; (局地的な) (a) battle. (⇨戦争,戦い)

いくさ 藺草【植物】a rush.

***いくじ 育児** childcare. ▶育児に追われる [専念する; 悩む] be busy with [be devoted to; be worried about] the *care of* one's baby.
● 育児休暇 childcare [《婉曲的》 maternity] leave. ● 育児室 a nursery. ● 育児書 a baby [×child] book; (説明的に) a book on childcare. ▶育児ノイローゼ (suffer from) an infant-care [(産後の) a postnatal] depression.

いくじ 意気地なし ▶意気地(気骨)がない He has *no backbone* [《話》 *guts*]. (ⓘ *backbone* は通例否定文で用いる)/(臆病だ) He is *cowardly* [*timid*].

いくじなし 意気地無し a coward (ⓘ 卑劣さを含む); a timid creature. ▶この意気地なし! You *coward*!

いくしゅ 育種 图 breeding plants or animals; developing new plants. ━━育種する 動 breed (plants [animals]).

いくせい 育成 育成 图 training; [栽培] cultivation. ━━育成する 動 (人を) train; (作物・植物を) grow; cultivate. (⇨育てる)

いくた 幾多 (多くの,多数)

:**いくつ 幾つ** ❶【何個】hòw mány (+複数名詞). ▶いくつクッキーを食べたの How many cookies did you eat? ▶(いすは) あといくついりますか How many more (chairs) do you need? ▶彼はいくつ情報を得ましたか *How many pieces of* information [×How many informations] did he get? (ⓘ 不可算名詞の場合は How many pieces of ...? などとする. *How much information* ...? では漠然と「どのくらいの量の情報か」の意となる)

会話「2ダースもらったよ」「いくつだって?」"They've given me a couple of dozen [×dozens]." "They've given you *how many*?"

❷【何歳】how old. ▶鈴木さんはあなたよりいくつ年上ですか *How much older* is Mr. Suzuki than you are?

会話「田中さんはおいくつですか」「60いくつかです」"*How old* is Mr. Tanaka? (ⓘ *What age is* ...? ともいえるがやや堅い言い方)/(何歳か知っていますか) Do you know *how old* Mr. Tanaka is?" "He's sixty-*something*." (ⓘ How old are you? と目上の人や女性に聞くのは失礼)

いくつか 幾つか some; several; a few.

使い分け **some** 通例肯定文、疑問否定文や勧誘・依頼文で、漠然と不特定な数量を表す。疑問文、条件文では代わりに通例 any を用いる。
several 3つ以上の少数を表す。3-6をさすことが多いが、文脈によってはそれ以上で多数のこともある。
a few few に対する肯定的意味で「数は少ないがある」の意。具体的な数は文脈による。

▶いくつか質問してもいいですか May I ask you *some* [*several*] questions?（**!** yes の答えを期待する文脈では疑問文でも any でなく some を用いる）▶彼の英語の手紙にはいくつかのスペルの間違いがあった There were *a few* spelling mistakes in his English letter. ▶彼らは冷蔵庫にあったいくつかのリンゴを分け合った They shared *the few* [*several*, ×*some*] apples that were in the refrigerator.（**!** (1) some は the, those, one's などの限定詞とともには用いられない. (2)「…リンゴをいくつか」なら some [several, a few] of the apples ... となる）

会話「「どこの学校に行ったの」「ええとね、いくつかの学校に行ってたんだよ」"Where did you go to school?" "Well, I went to *several* schools."

DISCOURSE
田舎暮らしにはいくつかのメリットがある。住居費は都会よりはるかに安い。…もう一つのメリットは地域のつながりがあることだ。最後に、アウトドアスポーツが好きなら田舎暮らしは大きなメリットです Living in the country has *certain* benefits. Housing costs are much lower than in urban areas. ... *Another* benefit is people have a stronger sense of community. ... *Finally*, there are a lot of [many] other benefits if you like outdoor sports.（another (次に), finally (最後には) は列挙の用いるディスコースマーカー）

いくつ(で)も 幾つ(で)も [多数の]《通例疑問文・否定文で》many（＋複数名詞）, much（＋不可算名詞）;《通例肯定文で》a lot of ...（＋多く）▶彼女はいくつも指輪を持っている She has *a lot of* [×*many*] rings. ▶彼はいくつも助言をくれた He gave me *a lot of* [《書》*much*] advice. ▶ジャガイモはもういくつも（＝少ししか）残っていない There are *only a few* potatoes left. ▶いくつでも好きなだけ(リンゴを)食べてよろしい You can eat *as many* (apples) *as you like*.（**!** ×... eat apples as many as ... は不可）

いくど 幾度 how often, how many times.（⇒何度）
いくどうおん 異口同音 [声をそろえて] in chorus, in unison. ▶彼らは異口同音に「あいつが悪い」と言った They said *in chorus* [*unison*], "He is to blame."/They chorused (*in unison*), "He is to blame."

イグニッション [点火装置] the ignition. ● イグニッションスイッチを入れる switch on *the ignition* (of a car). ● イグニッションキー an ignition key.

いくばく 幾許 ● いくばくもなく before long, soon.（⇒やがて、間もなく）● いくばくの金 a *small sum of* [*some, a little*] money; *what little* money one has. ▶彼の余命はいくばくもない His days *are numbered*./He *doesn't have long to live*./He will die *soon*.

いくび 猪首 図 a bull neck; a short thick neck.
— 猪首の 形 bullnecked.

いくひさしく 幾久しく forever. ▶幾久しくお幸せに I wish your happiness would last *forever*./I wish you everlasting happiness.

いくぶん 幾分（⇒幾らか）
いくもう 育毛 hair restoration; hastening the growth of hair. ● 育毛剤 (a) hair tonic.

*いくら 幾ら ❶ [金額]（品物などに対して）how much;（価格などの）what. ●おいくらですか *How much* is it?/*How much* are you asking (for it)?/*How much* do you charge (for it)?（**!** 以上いくらかの会話では単に How \much? と尋ねることも多い. 聞き返すときは /How much (did you say it was)? のように how の方を強く, 全体を上昇調でいう)/*What's* [×*How much is*] *the price?* ▶この机はいくらでしたか *How much* (money) [*What* (price)] did you pay for this desk?/*How much* (money) did this desk cost (you)?（⇒❷）▶新幹線で東京までの運賃はいくらですか *What's the fare to Tokyo by Shinkansen?* ▶あなたの年収はいくらですか *What is your annual income?*（**!** 以上2例では How much is ...? も用いられる）▶その労賃は1時間 [1日; 1週間]いくらで(＝1時間 [1日; 1週間]単位で)支払われる The wages are paid *by the hour* [*day*; *week*].（**!** ×*by an hour* [×*a day*; ×*a week*] は不可）

❷ [数量] how much《＋不可算名詞》; how many《＋複数名詞》; [距離] how far; [時間] how long（⇒掛かる）; [寸法] （長さ）how long; （高さ）how high [tall]; （幅）how wide; （深さ）how deep. ▶体重はいくらありますか *How much* do you weigh?/*What* [×*How much*] *is your weight?* ▶この箱にリンゴがいくらありますか *How many* apples are there in this box? ▶お金いくら持ってる *How much* money do you have? ▶4×7はいくら What's four times seven? ▶ここから君の学校までの距離はいくらありますか *How far* is it from here to your school?（**!** *How many miles* [*kilometers*] *is it ...?* や *What is the distance from ...?* より普通）▶新宿までの間に駅はいくらありますか *How many stations* [《バスの》*stops*] *are there from here to* [*before we get to*] *Shinjuku?*

❸ [譲歩]【いくら…でも [...しても]】（どんなに…しても）no matter how, however《前の方が口語的だ》;（多くても）at (the) most《数量を表す語句の前または後におく. 文脈に応じて most を他の語の最上級に変えて用いる》;（…にもかかわらず）in spite of [《書》despite] .... ▶彼女はいくら食べても太らない *No matter how* [*However*] *much she eats, she never gets fat*《（婉曲的に）gains weight》. ▶彼にいくら欠点があっても、私は彼が好きだ *Though* he has lots of faults [(どれほど多くの欠点があろうと) *No matter how* many faults he has], I still like him./*In spite of* [《書》*Despite*, 《主に書》*For all*] his faults, I still like him. ▶私の休暇はいくら長くても10日だ My vacation is ten days *at* (*the*) *most* [*at the longest*]. ▶いくら遅くても9時までにはそこへ着くでしょう We will get there by nine *at the latest*. ▶いくらなんでも（＝控えめに言っても）彼はあんまりだ He's gone too far, *to say the least* (*of it*). ▶君はいくら勉強してもしすぎることはない You *can't study hard enough*./You *can't study too hard*.

イクラ [＜ロシア語] salmon roe.
*いくらか 幾らか 副 [少し] a little,《話》a bit;（少しは）any《疑問文・条件文で、比較級または different, too などの前、さらに《米語》では動詞の後にも用いる》; [やや] rather,《やや書》somewhat （**!** 通例肯定文で）; [ある程度] to a certain [to some] extent.（**!** 少し❷）▶今日はいくらか気分がいい I feel *a little* [*bit*, *rather*,《米》*some*] *better* today.（**!** some は肯定文で叙述的用法に限る）▶天気がいくらかよくなったら彼を訪ねよう If the weather gets *any* better, I'll visit him. ▶私はそのニュースにいくらか当惑した I was *rather* [*a little*,《話》*kind of*] puzzled at

the news. ▶彼らはその問題についていくらか異なった見方をした They took a *somewhat* different view of the matter. ▶最近物価はいくらか下がったようです Prices seem to have dropped *to a certain extent [degree]* recently. ▶その事故は私にもいくらか(=部分的に)責任があった The accident was *partly [partially]* my fault.

— 幾らかの 形 **some** (!肯定文・疑問否定文や勧誘・依頼文で), **any** (!否定文・疑問文・条件文で); (少しの) **a little** (+不可算名詞), **a few** (+複数名詞), (いくつもの) **several**. (⇨幾つか[類語]) ▶貯金はいくらかありましたか Have you saved *a little* [*any*] money? (!*any* を *some* にすると「できたでしょうね」と yes の答えを期待した言い方になる) ▶バスには乗客がいくらか乗っていた There were *a few* [*some, several*] passengers *in* [*on*] the bus.

いくらでも 幾らでも ❶ [好きなだけ] as many [**much**] (...) **as one likes** [**wants**]. (! 可算名詞についていうときは many, 不可算名詞については much を用いる) ▶いくらでも(=好きなだけ)食べなさい Eat *as many* [*much*] *as you like.*/(食べられるだけ) Eat *as many* [*much*] *as you can.* ▶彼はいくらでも本が買える He can buy *as many* books *as* [*any number of*] books *he likes*. ▶君に金をいくらでもやろう I'll give you *as much* money *as* [*any amount of* money] *you want*.
❷ [制限なく多く] ▶労働力はいくらでもある There is an *unlimited* amount of labor available. ▶彼は本当にいくらでも(=非常にたくさん)持っている He has *a great many* [*a great number of*] books.
❸ [わずかでも] ▶(金額は)いくらでも結構です *Any* sum is acceptable. ▶寄付を頼むとき

いくらも 幾らも ❶ [否定] (数が) **not many**; (量が) **not much**; (時間が) **not long**; (距離が) **not far**. ▶いくらも時間がない There *isn't much* time left. ▶彼が死んでからいくらもたたない It's *not* been *long* 《主に米》[It's *not long* 《主に英》] since he died. ▶ここから公園まではいくらもない It *isn't far* from here to the park.
❷ [肯定] ▶そのような学生はいくらもいる There are *a lot of* [《書》*many*] such students.

いくん 遺訓 teachings. ▶父の遺訓を守った I followed [observed] the *teachings* of my late father.

*いけ 池 **a pond** (! 人工のものが多い); (小さな) **a pool** (! 特に自然のもの). ●池で泳ぐ swim *in a pond*. ●池でスケートをする skate *on a pond*. ●池をさらう[干す; 埋め立てる] drag [drain; fill up] *a pond*.

いけい 畏敬 awe. ▶畏敬の念を抱く hold ⟨him⟩ in *awe*. ▶畏敬の念に打たれる be struck with *awe*. ▶畏敬の念を起こさせる眺め an *awe-inspiring* view.

いけいれん 胃痙攣 [医学] (**get**) **stomach cramps.**

いけうお 活魚, 活け魚 a live fish or shellfish (*in* a restaurant's tank).

いけがき 生け垣 a hedge. ●生け垣を作る[刈り込む] plant [trim] a *hedge*. ●庭を生け垣で囲う *hedge* (*in*) a garden.

いけす 生け簀 a fish preserve [**tank**]; (養魚池) a fishpond; (漁船の) a live well; (浅瀬の) a crawl.

いけず 〖いじわる〗 (性質) **spitefulness, nastiness**; (人) **a nasty** [**a spiteful**] **person**, 〖話〗**a meanie.**

いけすかない いけ好かない disgusting, detestable; extremely nasty (**disagreeable**). ▶ほんとにいけ好かない奴だ What a *nasty* [*a disgusting*] guy!

いけづくり 生け作り, 活け作り ikezukuri, (説明的に) *sashimi* arranged with the head and tail, served in the shape of a whole fish.

いけどり 生け捕り —— 生け捕りにする 動 (動物などを) **catch*** [**capture**] 《**it**》 **alive.** (⇨捕まえる)

いけどる 生け捕る ⇨生け捕り

*いけない **❶ [悪い]** (間違った) **wrong;** (わんぱくな) **naughty.** (⇨悪い ❶) ▶彼の感情を害するのはいけないことだ It is *bad* to hurt his feelings. ▶ねえ, 何かいけないことした? What have I done *wrong* now? ▶いけない子だね, つばを吐くのはやめなさい You *naughty* [*bad*] boy, stop spitting. ▶この事故については君がいけないのだ(=責任を負うべきである) You are *to blame* [You are *responsible*] *for* this accident. ▶あっ, いけない! 彼女にあの本を渡すのを忘れた Oh, *no!* I forgot to give her that book. (!Oh, no! は「ああ, どうしよう」と困ったことが起きたときに発する口語的慣用表現)

会話 「歯が痛いんです」「それはいけませんね」"I have a toothache." "That's too *bad.*/That's *a shame.*/I'm sorry to hear that."

❷ [禁止] (...するな) **Don't ...;** (...してはいけない) **must not;** (...すべきではない) **should not;** (当然...すべきではない) **ought not to** 《**do**》. (!禁止の意は must not, ought not to, should not の順に弱くなる) ▶怠けてはいけない *Don't* be idle [lazy]./You *mustn't* be idle. (! must は話し手の権威を含意し, 目上の者が目下の者に, 親が子に命令するような場合に用いられる) ▶時間をむだに遣ってはいけない You *shouldn't* [*oughtn't to*] waste your time. (!《話》では oughtn't to の to は時に省略される) ▶曲り角に駐車してはいけない *Don't* park your car at the corner./You *are not permitted* [*allowed*] *to* park your car at the corner. (!permit の方が堅い語で正式な許可を表す) ▶廊下を走ってはいけないことになっています We *are not supposed to* run along the corridor. (!実際は守られていないことを暗示する) ▶もう少し早くそちらの事務所におうかがいしてはいけませんでしょうか Do you think I could come [×go] to your office earlier? (! 丁寧に許可を求める言い方)

会話 「この本, 持ち出してもよろしいですか」「いいえ, いけません」"May I take out this book?" "No, you *must* [*may*] *not.*" (! must not は強い禁止, may not は不許可を表す)

❸ [必要, 当然] (...しなければならない) **must, have*** (**got**) **to** 《**do**》 (⇨ならない), (...すべきだ) **should, ought to** 《**do**》 (⇨べき). ▶あすの朝はいつもより早く起きなければいけない I *must* [*have to*] get up earlier than usual tomorrow morning. ▶なぜ彼に謝らなければいけないのか Why *should* I apologize to him? ▶風邪が悪化していると医者にかからなければいけない You *should* see a doctor if your cold gets worse. ▶彼女は当然 3 時までにはその仕事を終えていなければいけない She *ought to* finish the work by three (o'clock). ▶今朝仕事で彼のところに行かなければいけなかった(のに忘れていた) I *should* [*ought to*] have gone to him on business this morning. (! should [ought to]+完了不定詞は過去において当然なすべき行為をしなかったことに後悔・非難などの気持ちを表す)

❹ [用心] (...しないように) **so** (**that**) **... can't*** [**won't***, 《書》**may*** **not**]**...;** 《主に米》**lest ...** (**should**); (...を恐れて) (**for fear** *of*; *that* 節); (...の場合に備えて) **in case** (節). ▶彼女は太るといけないから毎朝運動をした She exercised every morning *so that* she *would not* put on weight./She got exercise every morning *lest* she (*should*) [*for fear that* she would, *so as not to*] put on weight. (! lest 節内の should は《主に英》で, 《米》では would も用いられる) ▶気分が悪くなるといけないので彼に薬を飲ませなさい Give

いけにえ 生け贄 a sacrifice. ● いけにえとしてささげる offer (it) as a *sacrifice*. (**!** 「いけにえをささげる」は offer a *sacrifice to* God))

いけばな 生け花 〖華道〗 flower arranging; (説明的に) the art of flower arrangement; *ikebana*; 〖生けた花〗 a flower arrangement; (説明的に) flowers arranged in a vase. ● 生け花を習う learn *flower arrangement*; *learn how to arrange flowers*.

いける 生ける ● 花びんにバラを生ける arrange [set] roses *in* a vase.
● 生ける屍(しかばね) a living corpse.

いける 行ける 〖味などがよい〗 be good; (飲み物が) drink* well; 〖酒がたくさん飲める〗 can* drink a lot; 〖行くことができる〗 can go (⇨行く). ▶このスープはなかないけます This soup *tastes* really *good* [*nice*]./This soup *is very good*.
会話 「トラベラーズチェックしか持ってないわ」「十分だよ.それでいけるよ」"All I have is traveler's checks." "Oh, good. That'll *work* [*That will do*]." (**!** work [使える], will do は「用が足りる」の意)

いける 埋ける (⇨埋める). ● 炭火を灰の中にいける *cover* charcoal fire with ash (to keep it going for a long time).

:いけん 意見 图 ❶〖考え〗(an) opinion 《*about*, *on*, *of*》; a view 《*about*, *on*》(**!** しばしば複数形で); a point of view, a viewpoint; an idea 《*about*, *on*, *of*》; (a) comment 《*about*, *on*》.

┌─ **使い分け** ─────────────────┐
│ **opinion** 自分の判断に基づく考え. │
│ **view** 個人的感情・偏見を含んだ考え方. │
│ **point of view, viewpoint** 特定の物事を考えるときの観点. │
│ **idea** 心の中に浮かぶ考え. │
│ **comment** 書面または口頭の論評. │
└─────────────────────────────┘

①【〜意見】● 少数[多数]意見 a minority [a majority] *opinion*. ● 賛成意見 a positive (↔a negative, an opposing) *opinion* [*view*]. ● 率直な[強硬な; 過激な; 穏健な; 個人的な]意見 a frank [a strong; an extreme; a moderate; a personal] *opinion*. ● 参考意見 (示唆に富む意見) a suggestive *comment*; (根拠のある意見) a well-founded *opinion*; a well-grounded *opinion*. ▶そこに行くべきではないというのが一致した意見だ The consensus of *opinion* is [We all agree] that we shouldn't go there. ▶新しい学校図書館の建設に彼は賛成[反対]意見を述べた He *made the case for* [*against*] a new school library.

②【意見が】● その問題について我々の意見が分かれた Our *opinions* were divided [We were divided (in *opinion*)] *on* the problem./We differed in *opinion* [We disagreed] *on* the problem. ▶我々はその点に関しては意見が一致した We agreed [We were in agreement] (with each other) on that point./We reached an agreement [a consensus] on that point./We were of the same *opinion* on that point. ▶この計画については賛否両論の意見がある There are *opinions* for and against [There are pros and cons about] this plan. ▶その事について意見が乱れ飛んだ There was a wide variety of *opinions* (expressed) on the matter.

③【意見は[では, には]】▶この企画に関するあなたの意見はどうですか What is your *opinion about* [*on*, *of*] this project?/(どう思いますか) What do you think about [of] this project? ▶このレポートについて何かご意見はありませんか Do you have any *comment* [*anything to say*] *about* this report? ▶他にご意見はありますか Does anyone have anything further (they wish) to add? ▶anyone (is there) who wishes to add? ▶anyone (by you) ▶私の意見では, 彼は間違っている In my opinion [In my view(s), ×According to my opinion], he is wrong. (**!** (1) 自分の意見についてう From my point of view, ... は《話》を除いて避けられる. (2) according to はその内容が他の人や本などに由来するときに用い, opinion や view とはいっしょに用いない. (3) I think [believe, feel, 《米》guess] he is wrong. の方が口語的)/《書》I am *of the opinion that* he is wrong./(私に言わせるかぎり) As far as I'm concerned, he is wrong./(言わせてもらえば) If you ask me, he is wrong.

┌─ **DISCOURSE** ─────────────┐
│ 利益のためなら企業は何をしてもよいという意見には反対せ │
│ ざるを得ない **I have to disagree with** the *opinion* │
│ that companies can do anything to make a │
│ profit. ●I have to disagree [cannot agree] │
│ with... (...には反対せざるを得ない)は不賛成を表すディ │
│ スコースマーカー. I disagree よりも丁寧で, 論文に適して │
│ いる. │
└─────────────────────────────┘

❹【意見の】● 意見の衝突 a conflict of *opinion*. ▶我々はそのことで意見の相違があった We had a difference of *opinion about* [*on*] it./(違った見方をした) We had a different *view about* it./(意見が合わなかった) (⇨②)

❺【意見を】● ...という意見を述べる give [express, state, ×say, ×tell] one's *opinion that*.... ● 他人に意見を押しつける force one's *opinions* [*ideas*] on others. ● 意見を交換する exchange *views* [*opinions*] 《*with*》. ● 彼はその番組については何も意見を言わなかった He made no *comments on* [*about*] the program. ▶この原稿に目を通して君の意見を聞かせてほしい Look over this manuscript and tell me *what you think* [and let me hear your *opinion*]. ▶私たちは専門家の意見を求めた We asked for expert *opinions* 《*on* the matter》. ▶私の意見をということですので思うところをお話しします Now you've asked for my *opinion*, I'll tell you how I feel about it. (**!** 第2例の what you think に対しての how I feel は「主観的な意見(=感想)」の意) ▶中村先生, この件で意見を言っていいですか Mr. Nakamura, could I say something here, please? (**!** Excuse me, Mr. Nakamura, may I...?. の方が改まった言い方)/Mr. Nakamura, could I just make a point about this?

❷〖忠告〗(a piece of) advice /ədváis/; (目上の人からの穏やかな) 《書》(an) admonition. ● 両親の意見に従う follow [take, act on, ×obey] one's parents' *advice*. ● 彼に意見を求める ask him for *advice*; ask his *advice*. ▶どうしたらよいかご意見を聞かせてくださいませんか Could you give me your *advice* about [Could you *advise* me] what to do?

── **意見する** 動 〖忠告する〗 advise /ədváiz/; 〖さとす〗《書》admonish. ● 息子に意見する *admonish* one's son 《*for*》; (道理を説く) *reason with* one's son. ▶先生は彼にもっと勉強するように意見した The teacher *advised* him to work harder [*that he* 《《主に英》*should*》work harder].

いけん 異見 ● 異見を述べる advance a *different view*

いけん [opinion] 《from him》.

いけん 違憲 (a) violation of the constitution. ●違憲である be *unconstitutional*.

いげん 威厳 (great) dignity. (!重々しさを強調して great ということがある) ●威厳がある have [possess] *dignity*. ●威厳のない *undignified*. ●威厳をもって with *dignity*; in a *dignified* manner. ●威厳のある人 a person of *dignity*; a *dignified* person. (!高徳を含意) ●威厳を保つ maintain [keep] one's *dignity*.

いけんこうこく 意見広告 opinion advertising; (特集記事形式の広告) advertorial.

いげんびょう 医原病 [医学] an iatrogenic disease.

いご 以後 ❶ [以後] (ある時より後) after ...; (ある時から) from ...; (以今以来で) since .... (⇨以来) ●それ以後の事件 later [《やや書》*subsequent*] events. ●それ以後今日まで from that time down to this day. ●今日以後酒をやめる give up drinking *from* this day *on*. ▶2時以後においでください Please come *after* two (o'clock). ▶彼は5月3日以後消息なし He's not been heard of *since* May 3. ❷ [今後] (これ以後) after this; (これからずっと) from now on [*onward*], from this time on [*onward*]. (⇨今後) ●以後もっと注意します I'll be more careful *from now on* [(今までと違ってこれからは) *in the future*]. ●以後（二度と）そんなことをしてはならない You must never do such a thing *again*.

いこい 憩い (a) rest. (⇨休憩, 休息) ●憩いのひととき a moment of *rest*. ●憩いの場 a place of *recreation and relaxation*.

いこう 以降 ▶7月3日以降 (*on and*) *after* July 3; *from* July 3 *on* [*onward*]. (⇨以来)

いこう 衣桁 a kimono [clothes, dress] rack.

いこう 威光 [影響力] influence; [権威] authority; [権力] power. ●おやじの威光で through the *influence* [×*authority*] of one's father.

いこう 移行 図 (転換) a changeover; (推移) (a) transition. ●農業から工業への移行 the *transition* from agriculture to industry. ●移行措置 (take) *transitional* [*transition*] measures.
── 移行する 動 change over 《*to*》; be changed 《*to*》.

いこう 移項 図 transposition. ── 移項する 動 transpose.

いこう 意向 (意思) (an) intention (⇨意思); (意見) (an) opinion; (考え方) a view (!しばしば複数形で) (⇨意見). ●彼の意向を打診する sound him out 《*on*, *about*》. ●父の意向に従う [逆らう] obey [disobey] one's father's *wishes*. ●辞任の意向をほのめかす [明らかにする] hint at [announce, declare] one's *intention* to resign one's post.

いこう 遺構 (遺跡) 《preserve》 the remains; (廃墟) the remains 《*of* an old building》.

いこう 遺稿 one's posthumous /pástʃəməs/ manuscripts. ●Aの遺稿集 a collection of A's *posthumous works*.

いこう 憩う rest, take [have] a rest. (⇨休憩する, 休息する)

イコール (...と等しい) equal, be (equal to). ▶5プラス4イコール9 Five plus four *equals* [*is*, *makes*] nine. (!equal は正式な読み方) ▶7−4=3 Seven minus four *equals* [*is*, *leaves*] three. ▶3×4=12 Three times four *equals* [*is*, *makes*] twelve. ▶12÷3=4 Twelve divided by three *equals* [*is*, *gives*] four.

いこく 異国 (外国) a foreign country; (見知らぬ国) 《古》 a strange land. ▶この町には異国情緒がある This town has an *exotic atmosphere*.

いごこち 居心地 ●居心地がよい comfortable; (暖かくて) cozy, snug. ●居心地の悪い 《人が主語》 feel *uncomfortable*; don't feel *at home* [*at ease*]. ▶この部屋は居心地がすごくいい This room is very *comfortable*./I feel very *comfortable* in this room.

いこじ 意固地 [かたくなな] óbstinate; [強情な] stubborn; [頑迷な] [軽蔑的な] pig-headed. (⇨頑固, 意地)

いこつ 遺骨 ashes. ●遺骨を骨つぼに納める put 《his》 *ashes* in an urn.

いこん 遺恨 (恨み) a grudge; (敵意) enmity. (⇨恨み) ●遺恨を抱く have [hold] a *grudge* 《*against*》. ●遺恨を晴らす revenge oneself 《*on*》; take revenge 《*on*》.

いざ いざ行かん Let us start *now*.
❶ [いざという時] ●いざという時に (＝最悪の場合に) 備える prepare for the worst; (まさかの時に) provide for [《古》 *against*] a rainy day [the *unexpected*]. ●いざという時 (＝非常時の) にはあの人たちは助けてくれるでしょう They will help us *in case of emergency* [*in an emergency*]. ▶いざという時 (＝困った時) には息子が頼りだ *When I need* I rely on my son for help.
❷ [いざと[...する段に]なると] ▶いざ彼女と話す段になるとあがってしまう I get nervous when it comes to talking [×talk] to her. (!前の to は前置詞) ▶彼は彼女にプロポーズしようと思っていたがいざとなると勇気が出なかった He was going to propose to her, but *at the last minute* [*moment*] he got cold feet. (!get cold feet は《話》で「しりごみする」の意)
❸ [いざとなれば] ▶いざとなれば (＝せっぱつまれば) 辞職する覚悟だ《話》When it comes to the crunch, I'm ready to quit my job. ▶いざとなれば私が引き受けます I'll take it *when I have to* [(必要ならば) *if (it is) necessary*].
●いざ知らず ●その事はいざ知らず apart from that. ●人はいざ知らず私は as for me; for my part; as far as I am concerned.

いさい 委細 [詳細] details, particulars (⇨詳細); [事情のすべて] the whole circumstances [story]. ●委細構わず (＝結果を気にせず) 実行に移す carry (it) out regardless of the *consequences*. ▶委細面談 Particulars to be arranged personally.

いさい 異才 [才能] genius, (an) exceptional talent; [人物] genius, (神童) a prodigy. ●音楽の異才 a *highly* [an *extraordinarily*] *talented* [*gifted*] musician.

いさい 異彩 ●異彩を放つ ▶彼女は若手ピアニストの中で異彩を放っている (＝目立つ) She *stands out* [*is conspicuous*] among the young pianists./She *outshines* the other young pianists.

いさかい 諍い (口論) a quarrel; an argument. ●いさかいをする have a *quarrel* [*an argument*] 《*with*》; quarrel [argue] 《*with*》.

いざかや 居酒屋 a bar; 《英》 a pub. (⇨バー)

いさき [魚介] a grunt.

いさぎよい 潔い [男らしい] manly. ●潔く (あっさりと) with 《*a*》 *good* (↔*bad*) *grace*; (男らしく) in a *manly* manner. (!通例 manlily は使わない) ●潔い態度 a *manly* attitude. ▶彼は自分のあやまちを潔く認めた He admitted his fault *with* 《*a*》 *good grace*./He *had the grace to* admit his fault. ▶やったことを潔く (＝すっかり) 白状しろ Make a *clean breast of* your crime. ▶彼は困ったときでも援助を求めるのを潔くしない He *is above* asking [(軽蔑して拒絶する) He *scorns* to ask] for help even in time of need.

いさく 遺作 one's posthumous /pɑ́stʃəməs/ work [works].

いざこざ [もめごと] (a) trouble; [口論] a quarrel.
●いざこざを起こす make [cause] *trouble*.

いささか 些か, 少し, 少しも(=少なからず)(=少なからず)《書》*not a little*; very《disappointed》. ●その結果にいささか(=少し)失望した I was *a little*《話》[*a bit*,《いくぶん》《やや噸》*somewhat*] *disappointed* at the result. ●彼はその知らせにいささかも動揺しなかった He was *not at all* upset by the news.

いさましい 勇ましい (勇敢な) brave; (勇気のある) courageous (**!**前の語は行動上の勇気を、後の語は精神的面での勇気を強調する); (鼓舞する) stirring.
●彼の勇ましい行為をほめた We praised his *brave* [*courageous*] act.
— 勇ましく 圖 bravely; courageously. ●彼らは敵と勇ましく戦った They fought the enemy *bravely*.

いさみあし 勇み足 ●勇み足をする (相撲で) step out of the ring accidentally; (張り切りすぎて失敗する) overplay one's hand; go too far.

いさみたつ 勇み立つ be [feel] encouraged; be high-spirited.

いさみはだ 勇み肌 ●勇み肌の男 a chivalrous(-spirited) man; a gallant(-spirited) man.

いさめる 諫める tell*〔him to do〕; (抗議する, 文句を言う) remonstrate《with him about…》.

いざよい 十六夜 ●十六夜の月 the moon on the sixteenth night of the lunar month.

いざよいにっき 『十六夜日記』 *Izayoi Nikki*. 《参考》鎌倉時代の紀行文

いさりび 漁り火 a fishing fire; a fire for luring fish (on a fishing boat).

いざる 躄る (ひざがしらを使って) move slowly on one's knees.

いさん 胃散 powdered stomach medicine.

いさん 胃酸 acid in the stomach; stomock acid.
●胃酸過多(症) [医学] (gastric) hyperacidity.

いさん 遺産 [相続財産] an inheritance; [遺言による] a legacy; [先祖伝来の] a heritage; [古代の遺物] antiquities. ●遺産を相続する come into a *legacy* [an *inheritance*]. ●1億円の遺産を受け取る receive a *legacy* of one hundred million yen.
●彼は息子にばく大な遺産を残した He left a vast *legacy* to his son. ●彼の財産は遺産相続によるものだった His fortune came to him *by inheritance*. ●この古い建物は国民的遺産である This old building is a national *heritage*.
●遺産争い a quarrel over the inheritance.

:いし 石 ❶[石ころ] a stone (「石material」の意では U); [米] a rock (「小石」にも用いる); (丸い小石) a pebble (**!**大きなboulderという); (砂利) (集合的) gravel /ɡrǽvl/.
①【石(の)～】 ● 石の(=石造りの)建物 a *stone* building. ● 石だらけの道 a *stony* road. ● 石のように冷たい心 a *stony* heart. ● 石頭, 石けり, 石橋 (⇨)
❷【石が】 ● この土地は石が多くて農業に向かない These fields are too *rocky* for farming.
③【石に[を, で]】 ▶石を投げるな Don't throw *stones* [*rocks*]. ●彼らの家は石でできている Their houses are built of *stone* [×*stones*].
❷[宝石] a jewel, a precious stone; [時計の] a jewel, a ruby (⇨一石(⾊)); [ライターの] a flint.
❸[碁石] a (go) stone, a *go* piece.
❹[じゃんけんの] a stone, a fist.
❺[結石] a stone. (⇨胆石, 腎臓(⾊)) [腎臓結石].
●石にかじりついても ▶石にかじりついても(=どんな犠牲を払ってでも)やる I will do it *at all costs*《書》*whatever the cost*.
●石の上にも3年 'Even a stone will get warm if one sits on it for three years.' (ことわざ) Patience wins [Perseverance will win] (out) in the end. (**!**「忍耐すれば最後には勝利を得る」の意)

*****いし** 意志 (a) will《to do》,《書》volition. ●意志決定 decision-making. ●意志薄弱のため失敗する fail for want of *will*. ●意志の力で勝つ win by *willpower* [the strength of *will*]. ●生きる意志を失う lose the *will* to live. ●意志を曲げる [押し通す] give up [stick to] one's *will*. ▶うちの社長は意志の強い人だ Our boss is a man of strong (↔weak) *will*./Our boss has a strong *will* (↔weak) an iron *will*)./Our boss is strong-willed (↔weak-willed). ▶彼は自分の(自由)意志でそれをやった He did it *of his own* (free) *will* [*of his own volition*]./(自発的に) He did it *voluntarily*. ▶彼は意志に反してそこへ行かなければならなかった He had to go there *against* his *will*. ▶どの野球団に入るかは彼の意志で決めることだ It is *up to* him to decide which baseball team he will join. ▶私たちは意思統一にやっと成功した We managed to *share the same opinion*.

*****いし** 意思 (意向) (an) intention《of doing; to do》; (希望) a wish《to do》(**!**しばしば複数形で); (考え) a mind.
①【意思(の)～】 ▶意思表示をする express one's *intention*(s), make one's *intention*(s) clear; (…したいと言う) express a *wish*《to do》. ●意思決定をする make a decision《about, on; to do》. (**!**「意思決定」は decision-making.) ▶彼らはお互いの意思疎通を欠いている They don't *communicate with* each other [*aren't communicating*]. (⇨疎通)
②【意思は】 ▶彼にはそれをする意思はない He has no *intention* of doing it./He doesn't *intend* to do it./(それをするつもりはない) He's not *going to* [He's not *planning to*] do it. (⇨つもり ❶③)
③【意思に[を]】 ●意思を変える change one's *mind*. ●意思を達成する fulfill one's *wish* [(目的) *purpose*]. ●英語で自分の意思を(彼らに)伝える make oneself understood (to them) in English. ▶彼は留学の意思を表明した He announced his *intention to* study [*of studying*] abroad. ▶彼は父親の意思に反して[に添って]結婚した He married *against* [*to*] his father's *wishes*. ▶彼らはそこへ行くという彼女の意思を尊重した[無視した] They respected [disregarded] her *wish* [*intention*] that she (《主に英》*should*) go there.

いし a doctor. (⇨医者)
●医師会 a medical association. ●医師国家試験 the National Examination for Medical Practitioners.

いし 遺志 ●父の遺志(=生前の願い)により according to the *wish* of my deceased father.

いし 縊死 [書] death [suicide] by hanging.
— 縊死する 動 hang oneself.

*****いじ** 意地 ❶[意志] will; [根性] spirit,《話》guts; [強情] obstinacy, stubbornness. ●意地を貫く carry out one's *will*. ●日本人の意地を見せる display the Japanese *spirit*. ●意地が汚い (⇨意地汚い)(=自説を歪め譲らない) [話] stick to one's guns. ●意地を通せば窮屈だ (⇨『草枕』) ▶あんなつまらないことで意地を張るんじゃなかったよ I shouldn't have been too *stubborn* about little things like that. (⇨意地っ張り) ▶彼は意地になって(=かたくなに)申し出を拒んだ He refused the offer *obstinately*. ▶彼にあんな質問をするなんて君も意地悪

悪いね It is wicked of you to ask him a question like that. 〖⇨意地悪〗●先生の冗談はおもしろくない 意地でも笑いたくない The teacher's jokes are not funny at all. I won't laugh at them under any circumstance. (〖!〗won't... under any circumstance は「絶対に[意地でも]...しない」の意)
❷〖面目〗face, honor; 〖自尊心〗self-respect.
●横綱は面目を破って勝を示した[=面目を保った] The yokozuna saved face by beating him.

*いじ 維持 maintenance; 〖建物・庭・車などをよい状態に保つこと〗upkeep (〖!〗「維持費」にもなる); 〖保管〗preservation. ●治安の維持 the maintenance [preservation] of order. ●この車の維持費は高くつく The cost of maintenance [Maintenance cost] for this car is high./The upkeep of this car costs a lot [is expensive]./This car costs a lot in upkeep. ●この家の維持費はどのくらいだろう I wonder how much the upkeep is on this house. ●政府は現状維持に努めているだけだ The government is simply trying to keep things as they are.
── 維持する 動 〖現状を〗maintain, 〖一定の状態で〗keep*; 〖奪われないように〗retain; 〖害・破壊などから〗preserve; 〖生命を〗support, sustain. (⇨保つ) ●健康を維持する maintain [preserve] one's health; 〖体調を整えておく〗keep fit. ●友好関係を維持する maintain friendly relations 《with》. ●大きな家を維持する maintain [〖よい状態に〗keep up] a large house. ●ランナーはその速いペースを維持できなかった The runner could not maintain the fast pace.

いじ 医事 medical matters.
●医事訴訟 a medical suit.

いじ 遺児 〖両親を失った子〗an orphan; 〖あとに遺(の)された子〗a bereaved child (〖!〗children). ●岡氏の遺児たち the children of the late Mr. Oka. (〖!〗late は「先ごろ亡くなった (recently deceased)」の意) ●交通遺児 children orphaned in road accidents.

いしあたま 石頭 ●彼とこれ以上話し合ってもむだだ。まったく石頭なんだから It's no use talking to him any longer. He's really stubborn [really hardhead, as stubborn as a mule]. (〖!〗物理的に「石のように固い頭」をいう場合は His head is (as) hard as a stone.)

いじいじ ●いじいじした子 a nervous [a timid] child.
●いじいじと答える answer nervously [timidly].

いしうす 石臼 〖ひきうす〗a stone mill, a millstone; 〖つきうす〗a stone mortar. (⇨臼)

いしがき 石垣 a stone wall [fence].

いしがめ 石亀 〖動物〗a Japanese pond turtle.

:いしき 意識 名 consciousness (〖!〗事実・真実・状態などを内心で自覚すること); awareness (〖!〗見たり、聞いたり、感じたりなどして五感で気づくこと); (one's) senses (〖!〗五官による体の感覚。この意味では複数形).
●意識不明の unconscious.
①〖~の意識〗●民族[政治; 階級]意識 ethnic [political; class] consciousness. ●強い共同体[対抗; 危機]意識 a strong sense of community [rivalry; crisis]. ●被害者意識をつのらせる heighten one's fears of being victimized. ●彼には罪の意識がない He has no consciousness of sin [guilt]./He is unconscious of it [guilt]. (〖!〗sin は道徳上・宗教上の罪) ●彼を動乱のイラクに駆り立てたのはジャーナリストとしてのプロ意識であった What drove him to go to strife-torn Iraq was his journalistic professionalism. ●彼は私に激しい競争意識を抱いているようだ He seems to have an intense sense of rivalry with me.

②〖意識が〗●その患者は最後まで意識があった The patient was conscious to the last. ●その国では女性の間で人権意識が高まっていた In the country there has been a growing consciousness of human rights among women.

③〖意識を〗●意識を失う lose consciousness [one's senses], fall [become] unconscious,《米》pass out. ●意識を回復する recover consciousness [one's senses]; come to one's senses; come to oneself; còme tó [aróund]. ●環境問題に対する意識を高める raise one's consciousness [awareness] of environmental issues. ●彼女は数分間意識を失って横になっていた She lay unconscious for several minutes.
── 意識する 動 be conscious; be aware. ●自分の短所を意識する be conscious of one's faults. ●彼女はあの男がうっとり見つめていることを意識していた She was conscious [aware] of being admiringly gazed at by the man./She was conscious [aware] that the man was gazing in admiration at her. ●順調にいっているときは自分ではそれを意識しない人もいる Some people don't know when they're well off.
── 意識的に 副 〖わざと〗on purpose, 〖故意に〗deliberately; 〖意図的に〗intentionally. (⇨わざと) ●意識的にその犬を殺そうとする attempt to kill the dog deliberately; make a deliberate attempt to kill the dog. ●彼は意識的に私を避けていると思う I think he's avoiding me on purpose [intentionally].

いじきたない 意地汚い 〖食欲(ぶ)な, 食い意地のはった〗greedy; 〖食いしんぼうの〗gluttonous (〖!〗glátnəs). ●彼は金に意地汚い He is greedy for money. ●皿に残ったソースをなめるのはやめなさい。本当に意地汚い子ね Stop licking the leftover sauce in your dish, dear. What a glutton you are!

いじくる ●時計の鎖をいじくる(=もてあそぶ) play [toy] with one's watch chain. ●電気回路をいじくる(=いじり回す) tamper with electrical circuits. (⇨いじる)

いしくれ 石塊 〖⇨石ころ〗.

いしけり 石けり ●石けり(遊び)をする play (×the) hopscotch /hápskɑ̀t∫/.

いじける 〖しりごみする〗shrink*; 〖ものおじする〗become* timid; 〖内に向かう〗become withdrawn; 〖ひねくれる〗become warped 〖〖書〗perverse〗. ●いじけた少年 a timid [a warped] boy. ●いじけた筆跡 one's cramped [constrained] handwriting.

いしころ 石ころ a stone. (⇨石)

いしずえ 礎 〖土台石〗a foundation stone, 〖隅石〗a cornerstone; 〖基礎〗〖比喩的に〗a foundation, a cornerstone. ●彼が国立公園の礎を築いた He laid the foundation of the national park.

いじずく 意地尽く ●意地ずくで obstinately, stubbornly.

いしずり 石摺り a rubbing; a rubbed copy 《of》.

いしだい 石鯛 〖魚介〗a striped beak-perch, a parrot fish.

いしだたみ 石畳 a stone pavement [floor].

いしだん 石段 stone steps.

いしつ 異質 heterogeneity.
── 異質の 形 heterógeneous; 〖違った〗different. ●異質な文化に触れる experience a different culture.

いしづき 石突き ❶〖雨傘やステッキの〗a ferrule 〖férəl〗; 〖槍(や)の〗a butt (end). ❷〖キノコの〗a hard tip.

いじっぱり 意地っ張り 〖強情な人〗an obstinate [a

いしつぶつ 遺失物 a lost [a missing] article;《集合的》lost property.
- 遺失物取扱所《米》the lost and found (department);《英》a lost property office.

いしのらいれき 『石の来歴』 *The Stones Cry Out*. (参考) 奥泉光の小説

いしばし 石橋 a stòne brídge. (⇨橋)
- 石橋をたたいて渡る ▶彼は石橋をたたいて渡るような人だ (非常に用心深い) He is extremely cautious./ (決して危険を冒さない) He never runs a risk.

いしべきんきち 石部金吉 a person of very strict morality; an extremely inflexible person.

いじましい (けちくさい) stingy, mean, tight-fisted; (心が狭い) narrow-minded.

いしむろ 石室 a stone hut (for climbers).

いじめ 苛め bullying. ●学校でいじめに遭うbe bullied at school.

いじめっこ 苛めっ子 (主に暴力で) a bully, (口でからかって)《話》a tease.《会話》

*****いじめる** 苛める (虐待して) mistreat; (つらく当たって) be hard on ..., 《話》pick on ...; (からかい半分に) tease, bait; (弱い者を) bully /búli/. ●いじめられっ子 a bullied child. ▶小さい動物をいじめるな Don't *mistreat* small animals [*treat* small animals *badly*]. (! *little* animals では話し手の価値判断が入る。ここでは一般的な場合なので不適)/Don't be *cruel to* little animals. ▶妹をいじめるのはよせ Stop *bullying* [*teasing, picking on*] your sister! ▶なぜ上司が私をいじめるのか分からない I don't understand why my boss *is hard on* [*picks on*] me.《会話》「ほら，クモ」「いじめなさんなよ」 "Look. A spider." "Don't *hurt* it." (! *hurt* は「傷つける」)

いしもち 『魚介』 a white croaker, a silver jewfish.

*****いしゃ** 医者 a doctor,《話》a doc,《話》a medical man [×woman] (!女性は a woman doctor),《米やや書・英古》a physician; (内科医)《米》an internist; (外科医) a surgeon; (一般開業医) a general practitioner (略 GP); (専門医) a 〈skin〉 specialist.

> 解説 doctor は《米》では歯科医 (dentist), 獣医 (veterinarian) など広く医者を表す一般的な語だが，《英》では通例内科医を指す。

① 【医者(に)～】 ●医者になる become a *doctor*. ●医者に見てもらう see [《やや書》consult] a [one's, the] *doctor* (!《米》では「かかりつけの」, 《英》では「かかりつけの」または「特定の」医者をさす); go to see a *doctor* (!《話》では go (and) see a doctor とも言う。and のない方がさらにくだけた言い方); take *doctor*'s advice ●医者任せにする rely entirely on the *doctor*. ▶先月から医者にかかっています I have been seeing a *doctor* [under a *doctor*'s care, 《やや書》under medical treatment] since last month. ▶彼は息子を医者にした (⇨する④[最終例])

② 【医者を】 ●医者を(開業)する practice medicine. ●医者を呼ぶ call in [get] a *doctor*. ●医者を呼びにやる send for a [the, one's] *doctor*. ▶彼女はしょっちゅうあちこちの医者を渡り歩いている She is always going *from doctor to doctor*.

③ 【医者へ】《会話》「ときどきめまいがするんだ」「まあ，だったら医者へ行った方がいいんじゃない」 "I sometimes feel dizzy." "Ah, then you'd better go to the *doctor's*, hadn't you?"

いしやき 石焼き (磁器) porcelain.
- 石焼き芋 a sweet potato baked in hot pebbles. ●石焼きビビンバ a dolsot [a stone bowl] bibimbap.

いじゃく 胃弱 indigestion,《書》【医学】dyspepsia. ▶胃弱である have [suffer from] *indigestion*.

いしゃりょう 慰謝料 (精神的苦痛に対する補償[見舞]金)《米》【法律】solatium. (! 肉体的・財産的損害に対する補償〈金〉は compensation) ●慰謝料を請求する[支払う] demand [pay] *solatium*《to+人, for+事》.

いしゅ 異種 a different kind [species, 変種] variety]《of》. ●異種交配する crossbreed.
- 異種交配種 a crossbreed, a hybrid.

いしゅ 意趣 a grudge. (⇨恨み) ●意趣返しをする repay an injury.

いしゅう 異臭 ●異臭を放つ give off a *bad* [(いやな) a *nasty*] *smell*.

いじゅう 移住 图 emigration; immigration; migration.
── 移住する 動 [転居する] move; [(遠くの)他国へ移り住む] emigrate 《from, to》; [(遠くの)他国から移り住む] immigrate 《to, into》; [場所から場所へ] migrate 《from, to》 (! emigrate, immigrate は人が市民権を得て永住のため移住すること。migrate は人・動物が集団で，特に一時的に転住する場合に用いられる); [移住して定住する] settle 《in》. ●日本からブラジルへ移住する *emigrate* [*migrate*] *from* Japan *to* Brazil. ●日本に移住してくる *immigrate into* Japan. ▶彼は職を求めて転々と移住した He *moved from* place *to* place to find a job.
- 移住者 an emigrant; an immigrant.

いしゅく 畏縮 ── 畏縮する 動 ●恐怖で畏縮する(＝縮み上がる) shrink [(すくむ) cower] in horror.

いしゅく 萎縮 ── 萎縮する 動 wither; (栄養不良などで) atrophy. ●じろりと見て萎縮させる *wither* 〈him〉 with a stare.
- 萎縮症 【医学】atrophy.

いじゅつ 医術 medicine; the medical art.

いしゆみ 石弓, 弩 (中世の) a crossbow; (古代の) catapult.

いしょ 医書 a medical book, a book on medicine.

いしょ 遺書 (遺言書) a will, one's last will and testament (! 後の方が正式); (自殺者の) a suicide note. ●遺書を書く make [draw up] one's [a] *will*.

いしょう 衣装 (ある特定の職業・国民などに特有の; 舞台用の) (a) costume, 【衣類一般】clothes, 《集合的》clothing; 【服装】(a) dress. (⇨服) ▶インドの民族衣装 the national *costume* of India. ▶花嫁衣装 a wedding *dress*. ▶スペインの衣装をつけて踊るdance *in* a Spanish *costume*. ▶彼女は衣装持ちだ She has a lot of *clothes* [a large *wardrobe*]. ▶馬子(まご)にも衣装 'Even a packhorse driver looks better in an expensive *kimono*.'/(ことわざ) The tailor makes the man./(多く女性に対して) Fine feathers make fine birds.
- 衣装だんす a wardrobe.

いしょう 異称 (⇨別名)

いしょう 意匠 (a) design. (⇨デザイン)
- 意匠登録 registration of designs. 〈関連〉登録済みの意匠は a registered design という)

いじょう 以上 (上記のこと) the above. (! 単・複両扱い) ●以上はこれを立証する *The above* justifies this. ▶以上です (一連の伝達を終える時に) *That's all*. ▶以上で今日の討議は終わります *That's all* for today's discussion. 《話》*That* wraps up the discussion for today.
① 【以上の】 (上にあげた) above, above-mentioned; (前述の) foregoing, preceding (⇔ following). (! 以上はすべて堅い言い方) ●以上の例 *the above* [*above-mentioned*] example; the ex-

ample *above*; the example (which I *have*) mentioned [*stated*] *above* (┃後の二つの above は副詞). ▶以上の言葉 the *foregoing* [*preceding*] words.

② 【…する以上】 (一度したからには) once …; (…だから) since …; (…となった今) now (that)…; (┃that はしばしば省略される); (いやしくも…するのならば) if … at all; (…する限りは) as [so] long as …. ▶始めた以上, 目的を達成しなくてはならない *Once* you start, you must attain your goal. ▶援助すると口に出した以上, 後には退けぬ *Now that* I've said I'll help you, I won't back out. ▶戦う以上はあくまで戦え *If* you do fight *at all*, fight to the (very [bitter]) end. (┃very, bitter は最後の最後までを強調する) ▶家が台風で全壊した. こうなった以上は(=その結果)引っ越さざるをえない Our house has been completely destroyed by the typhoon. *As a result*, we have to move.

③ 【…以上】 (数量・程度が) more than…; over …; above …; (範囲・限界が) beyond ….

解説 (1) more than, over はほぼ同意だが, more than の方が普通の言い方. above は一般に最小限度や基準値などを上回る場合に用いられる. (2) more than, over, above … は日本語の「…以上」と異なり, 厳密には…の数を含まない. 例えば more than [*over*, ×above] ten apples は, 11 個以上のリンゴを意味する. 10 個以上のリンゴは, 正確に言うなら *not less than* [*at least*] ten apples; ten *or more* apples; ten apples *and over* となる. しかし, 日常的には more than, over で十分間に合う.

●10 歳以上の子供 children *more than* [*over*, *above*] ten (years old) (┃厳密には 10 歳ちょうどは含まない (⇨解説)); children *of* ten (years) *and over* [*above*]; children *not less than* ten (years old). ▶25 歳以上 30 歳までの人 people *from* 25 *to* 30 (years of age); people *between* (the ages of) 25 *and* 30. ▶平均以上な *above* average. ●収入以上の暮らしをする live *beyond* (↔*within*) one's income. ▶私は彼を 2 時間以上待った I waited for him (*for*) *more than* [*over*] two hours. (┃for を省略する方が普通) ▶このトンネルは 10 キロ以上の長さがあります This tunnel is *more than* 10 kilometers long. (┃… is longer than 10 kilometers. は避ける) ▶その絵は 10 億円ぐらいするかな. ひょっとするとそれ以上かもしれない The painting may be worth a billion yen; it might even be worth *more*. ▶その飛行機墜落事故は私の想像以上にひどいものだった The air crash was *more dreadful than* I (had) imagined. ▶船は定員以上乗せていた The ship *was overloaded*. ▶これ以上豊かにも便利にもならなくていい We don't have to be *more affluent* or possess *more convenient things*. I wish for neither *more* affluence nor *more* convenience. 会話 「でもまだ今井君の協力が必要なんだよ」「今まで以上にね」 "But we still need Imai's help." "*More than* ever before, don't we?"

④ 【これ以上…(でき)ない】 ▶これ以上申し上げることはありません I have nothing *more* [*further*] to say./This is *all* I have to say. ▶これ以上待てない I can't wait *any longer*./I can wait *no longer* [*no more*]. ▶これ以上私にはできません This is *the best* (that) I can do./I can't do this *any better*.

‡**いじょう** 異状 【ふだんと違うこと】; 【故障】 something wrong. ▶巡回中異状はなかった *Nothing unusual* happened during my patrol. ▶機械に異状がある[ない] Something [Nothing] is *wrong with* the machine./(故障している[調子がよい]) The machine is *out of* [*in good*] *order*. ▶彼は体の異状を訴えた He complained that *something* was *wrong with* him.

‡**いじょう** 異常 (an) abnormality. ●このところ彼女の行動は確かに異常だ Her behavior is certainly *abnormal* [*out of the ordinary*] these days.
—— 異常な 形 【正常でない】 abnormal; 【普通でない】 unusual; 【並外れた】 extraordinary; 【めったにない】 uncommon. ●異常な行動 abnormal [*extraordinary*] behavior. ●異常な物音 an *unusual* [(奇妙な) a *strange*] noise.
—— 異常に 副 abnormally; unusually; extraordinarily; (書) uncommonly. ▶この時期にしては異常に暑い It is *unusually* [*abnormally*] hot for this time of (the) year.
●異常気象 extraordinary [abnormal] weather. ●異常心理 abnormal mentality.

いじょう 委譲 名 (a). tránsfer.
—— 委譲する 動 transfér (A *to* B).

いじょうふ 偉丈夫 【体格のよい男】 a well-built man, (話) a (real) hunk; (堂々たる風采の男) a man of commanding appearance (⇨体格); 【すぐれた男】 a great man.

いしょく 衣食 food and clothing (┃語順に注意); (日常の生活) living. ●衣食足りて礼節を知る (ことわざ) Well fed, well bred.

いしょく 委嘱 a commission.
—— 委嘱する 動 commission 《him *to do*》; (任命する) appoint. (⇨任命) ▶首相の肖像画の作成を委嘱された I got a *commission* [be commissioned] to paint a portrait of the prime minister.

いしょく 異色 — 異色の 形 ●異色の(=特別な)顔合わせな *special* combination. ●彼は文壇では異色の存在だ He is a *unique* figure in the literary world.
●異色作 (珍しい) a rare [(目新しい) a novel] work.

いしょく 移植 名 transplantation; (臓器・皮膚などの) a tránsplant. ●心臓移植患者[手術] a heart *transplant* patient [operation]. ●腎臓(ジン)移植手術を受ける [行う; 待つ] have [do; wait for] a kidney *transplant*. ▶心臓移植はうまくいった[拒絶反応が出た] The heart *transplant* has been accepted [been rejected].
—— 移植する 動 【植物・器官などを】 transplánt; 【皮膚・骨などを】 graft. ●野生の花を庭に移植する *transplant* the wild flowers to the garden. ●心臓を移植する *transplant* a heart 《*into* a boy》. ●やけどした手に新しい皮膚を移植する *graft* new skin *onto* [*on*] the burnt hand.

いしょくじゅう 衣食住 food, clothing(,) and housing [shelter]. (┃語順に注意) ●人に衣食住を与える provide people with *food, clothing and housing*; feed, clothe and house /háuz/ [*shelter*] people.

いしょくどうげん 医食同源 Medicine and diet are closely connected.

いじらしい 【感動させる】 moving, touching; 【哀れな】 pitiful. ●助けてという彼女のいじらしい嘆願に耳を傾ける listen to her *moving* plea for help.

いじる 【指で】 finger; (無器用に) fumble 《*with*》; 【さわる】 touch; 【もてあそぶ】 play 《*with*》. ●人形をいじる *touch* [*play with*] a doll. ▶彼女は落ち着きなくハンカチをいじり回した She nervously *fumbled with* her handkerchief./She *was playing with* a handkerchief because she was nervous. ▶机の上の書類をいじるな Don't *touch* the papers on

いしわた 石綿 《アスベスト》 asbestos /æsbéstəs/.

いじわる 意地悪 ── 意地悪な, 意地悪い 形 《人を困らせてやろうとする》spiteful;《不愉快な, 不親切な》nasty, mean;《根性の悪い》ill-natured;《悪意のある》vicious. ● 意地悪ばあさん *a nasty [a mean] old woman*. ● あの生徒はよく意地悪な質問をする That student often asks *nasty [embarrassing]* questions. ● 意地悪い言葉 *a vicious [spiteful] remark*. ● そんなに彼女に意地悪をするな Don't be so *mean [unkind]* to her. ● 意地悪で言ったのではありません I didn't tell you *out of spite*.
会話「今日の体育の授業は代返してくれる?」「冗談でしょう」「いじわる」"Can you answer the roll-call for me in today's gym class?" "Are you kidding?" "You're such a *tease*." (**!** *tease* は「(からかって)いじめる人」の意 (⇨ 苛(t)めっ子))

いしん 威信 《声望》prestige;《威厳》dignity;《権威》authority. ● 国の威信の失墜 loss of national *prestige [dignity]*. ● 威信を失墜させる(保つ; 高める)lower [maintain; raise] the *prestige (of)*. ▶ その事はこの学校の威信を危うくするだろう That would jeopardize the *prestige* of this school./That would put the *prestige* of this school at stake.

いしん 維新 ● 明治維新 the Meiji Restoration.

いじん 異人 a foreigner. (⇨ 外人)

いじん 偉人 a great person.

いしんでんしん 以心伝心 ● 以心伝心でお互いの気持ちが分かる《テレパシー》understand each other by *telepathy*;《心が読める》can read each other's mind.

*****いす** 椅子 ❶【腰掛け】a chair; an armchair; a sofa /sóufə/, a settee /setí:/; a couch /káutʃ/; a stool; a bench; a seat.

> (使い分け) chair 4本足の背もたれ付きいす. ひじ掛けの付いているものもある. 通例1人用.
> armchair 休息用のひじ掛けいす. 通例クッションがついており sofa や settee と組み合わせて用いることが多い. 1人用.
> sofa 居間などに置かれる背もたれ・ひじ掛け・クッション付きの休息用長いす. 2人以上用.
> settee 小型・中型の sofa.
> couch 中型の sofa. 特に片ひじの長いす. 通例2-4人用.
> stool ひじ掛け・背もたれのない, 持ち運び可能な小型丸いす. 通例1人用.
> bench 特に公園・庭園などの屋外に置かれた長いす. 2人以上用.
> seat いすの形状は問わず「座る場所」を表す総称.

chair | sofa, settee | armchair
stool
bench | couch

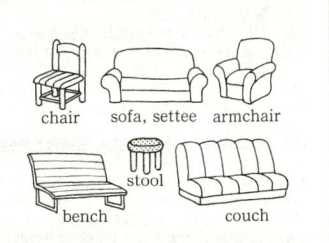

● いす取りゲーム 《play》 musical chairs.
❶【一椅子】● 安楽いす an easy *chair*. ● 回転いす a swivel *chair*. ● 座り心地のよい[悪い]いす a comfortable [an uncomfortable] *chair*. ● 小児用(の)食卓いす a high *chair*. ● 車いす a wheelchair.
❷【椅子に】● いすに座る sit down on [in] a *chair*. (**!** *on* は普通に腰をかける場合は, *in* は深々と[ゆったりした]場合に用いる) ● いすに深く腰掛ける sit back in a *chair*. ● 長いすに横になる lie (down) on a *couch* [a *sofa*, a *bench*]. (**!** *down* は横になる動作を強調する. *lie* だけでは「横になっている」の意)▶ どうぞいすにおかけください Have [Take] a *seat* [a *chair*], / *please*./Please be seated. (**!** この順に Please sit down. の「軽い言い方」) ● 彼はその箱をいす(代わり)に使った He used the box as a *seat*.
❸【椅子を】● いすを前に引き寄せる pull [draw] up a *chair*. ● (テーブルの)いすを引き抜け出す pull [draw] out a *chair*. ● いすを引いて立ち上がる push one's *chair* back and get up. ▶ マイクは由佳にいすを勧めた Mike offered a *chair* to Yuka.
❷【地位】a post, a position;《教授の》a chair;《議員の》a seat (⇨ 議席). ● いすをねらう have an eye on the *post (of)*. ● いすを失う《=免職される》lose one's *post*; be dismissed. ▶ 彼は20年間R大学で教授のいすを占めている He has held a professor's *chair [post]* at R University for 20 years./He has been in the *professorship* at [in] R University for twenty years. ▶ 議長のいすが空いた[空いている] The chairman's *post* has become vacant [is vacant]. ▶ 首相のいすに座るのはだれだろう Who is it that would get the *post* of the Prime Minister [become Prime Minister]?

いすか 《鳥》a crossbill.

いすくまる 居竦まる ● 恐ろしさに居すくまった I *stood there petrified [transfixed]* with terror.

いすくめる 射竦める ● 彼の鋭い目で射すくめられた I *was overawed by* his piercing [penetrating] eyes [gaze].

イスタンブール〖トルコの都市〗Istanbul /ístɑːnbùːl/.

いずのおどりこ『伊豆の踊り子』*The Izu Dancer*; *The Dancing Girl of Izu*. (参考) 川端康成の小説

イスパニア《スペイン》Spain.《詩》Hispania.

いずまい 居住まい ● 居住まいを正す sit up straight; straighten (oneself) up; sit oneself upright.

いずみ 泉 a spring;《詩》a fountain. ▶ トレビの泉 the Trevi *Fountain*.

いずみしきぶにっき『和泉式部日記』*The Izumi Shikibu Diary*. (参考) 平安時代の日記

いずみねつ 泉熱《医学》Izumi fever.

イスラエル〖国名〗Israel /ízriəl/;《公式名》the State of Israel;《首都 Jerusalem》● イスラエル人《現代の》an Israeli /izréili/,《集合的》Israeli people, the Israelis;《古代の》an Israelite /ízriəlàit/,《集合的》Israel (**!** 複数扱い). ● イスラエル(人)の Israeli.

イスラマバード〖パキスタンの首都〗Islamabad /islá:məbà:d/.

イスラム Islam. ● イスラム教 (⇨ イスラム教)● イスラム原理主義 Islamic fundametalism. ● イスラム暦 the Islamic calender.

イスラムきょう イスラム教 图 Islam /íslɑːm/. (参考) 神は Allah, 始祖 Mohammed, 経典は the Koran, 礼拝堂は a mosque という）
── イスラム教の 形 Muslim, Islamic /islǽmik/;《countries》.
● イスラム教徒 a Muslim /mázləm/. (**!** *Moslem* は古いつづり字);《集合的》Islam, the Muslims.

*****いずれ** 何れ 副 ❶【そのうち】《間もなく》soon, before long;《近いうちに》one of these days;《いつか》

someday; (適当な時期に) in due course; (遅かれ早かれ) sooner or later; (結局) after all; (最後には) eventually; (長い目で見れば) in the long run. ▶いずれ彼は来るだろう He'll come soon [before long]. ▶いずれ彼とのことを相談いたします We'll talk it over with him one of these days [someday, in due course]. ▶彼はいずれ逮捕されるでしょう He will be arrested sooner or later [eventually]. ▶仕事に精を出せばいずれ報われる時がくるだろう You'll be rewarded for your hard work in the long run./It will pay you in the long run if you work 〖精を出し続ける〗 keep working hard.
❷ 〖とにかく〗 (いずれにせよ) anyway, anyhow (!(米) は anyway の方が好まれる); (どんな割合[速度]でも) at ány ràte (!at àny ráte では「どんな割合[速度]でも」の意); (どんな事情にせよ) in ány câse. ▶いずれにせよもう一度電話します Anyway [At any rate, In any case], I'll call you (up) again. ▶いずれにせよパーティーにまいります I'll come to the party anyway.

── いずれ 代形 〖どちら(の)〗 which (!疑問詞); 〖2者について〗 (どちらか一方の) either; (両方(の)) both; 〖3者以上について〗 〖肯定文…でも〗 any; (全て(の)) all. ▶ which, either, any は単数扱い, both, all は複数扱い (⇨どちら, どの, どれ, すべて) ▶いずれの道を選ぶか教えてください Tell me which way to choose. ▶それらのいずれでも結構です Any [Either] of them will do. (!否定文は None [Neither] of them will do. で, ×Any [Either] of them won't do. は不可) ▶君たちのいずれかがそれをやらなくてはならないだろう One of you will have to do it. (!3人以上の場合。2人の代わりに either (one) を用いる) ▶彼らはいずれも学生だ All [Both] of them are students. (!(1) both は2人の場合。(2) ×all [both] them は不可)/They are all [both] students./Every one [×Everyone] of them is 〖(話)〗are] a student.

 • いずれ劣らぬ ▶2人はいずれ劣らぬ(=等しく)美人だ The two are equally beautiful.

いすわる 居座る 〖居続ける〗 stay 〖なかなか去らない〗 linger] on; (公的な地位に) remain in office. ▶冬が居座っている Winter lingers (on).

いせい 威勢 ── 威勢のいい 形 (人が勇ましい) dashing (!主に男性について用いる); (精力旺盛(ﾋﾞﾝ)の) vigorous; (精力的で) energetic; (活発な) lively; (元気な) spirited (!通例限定的に). (⇨元気) ● 威勢のいい若者 a dashing [a lively, a high-spirited] young man. ● 威勢のいい声が聞こえた I heard a lively call. ── 威勢よく 副 dashingly; vigorously.

いせい 異性 the opposite [other] sex. ▶彼女は異性に興味を持ち始めている He is beginning to be interested in the opposite sex. ▶彼女は異性(=男性)を意識しすぎる She's too conscious [aware] of men [boys].

─いせい ─以西 ● 以西の[に] in and (to) the west of ...; at [in] 〖(the place)〗 and westward. (⇨以北)

いせいしゃ 為政者 〖統治者〗 a ruler; 〖行政官〗 an administrator; 〖政治家〗 a statesman (-men).

いせいじん 異星人 an alien. ●⇨宇宙〖宇宙人〗

いせえび 伊勢海老 〖動物〗 a (spiny) lobster. (!その肉は Ⓤ)

いせき 移籍 图 (a) transfer. ● 移籍を申し込む 〖サッカー〗 offer.
── 移籍する 動 (登録を移す) transfer one's registration 〖to〗. ▶その選手はジャイアンツへ移籍した The outfielder was traded to the Giants.
● 移籍金 a transfer fee.

いせき 遺跡 remains; (遺物) 《やや書》 a relic; (廃墟) ruins. ▶ローマの遺跡 the remains [relics, ruins] of Rome.

いせつ 異説 ● その問題について異説(=異なった意見)を述べる give a different opinion on the subject. ▶その学説には異説がある(=意見が分かれている) Opinion is [Opinions are] divided on the theory.

いせつ 移設 ── 移設する 動 ▶その工場を堺から宇部に移設された They transferred the factory from Sakai to Ube.

いせまいり 伊勢参り a visit [a pilgrimage] to (the) Ise Shrine.

いせものがたり 伊勢物語 The Tales of Ise. 〖参考〗平安時代の歌物語

*いぜん 以前 副 (現在・過去のある時より前に) before (!現在[過去]完了形とともに用いられる); (今より…前に) ... ago; 〖かつて〗 once (!前に置く); 〖昔は〗 formerly, in former times; (今はそうではないが昔は…だった) used to 《do》 /júːsta/ (!「かつてはよく…したものだ」の意でも用いる〈⇨昔 動〉. ▶彼女には前にそれ以前にも数回会っていた I had seen her several times before [previously]. ▶以前にそのことを聞いたことがない I (have) never heard of it before. ▶そのことはずっと以前に起こった That happened a long time ago [way back in the past]. (!「ずっと以前, まだ子供だったころに」なら … way back when I was a child. となる) ▶彼は以前この町に住んでいた He lived in this town before./He once [formerly] lived in this town./He used to live in this town. ▶彼は以前よりよく勉強する He studies harder than (he did) before [he used to, 《書》 he once did]. ▶彼は以前ほど暮らしが楽でない He is not as well off as he used to be [×used to]. (! be は省略不可)/He is not as well off as (he was) before [he (once) was]. ▶以前はよく山登りをしたものだ I (often) used to [would often] go mountain climbing. (!前の方は長い期間繰り返して, 後の方は比較的短い期間しばしば行ったことを暗示する) ▶以前ここには病院はなかった There never used to be 〖(米・英語)〗 There didn't use(d) to be] a hospital here. (!Here didn't use(d) to be a hospital here. は避ける)/In former days there was not a hospital here. ▶彼の名前はずっと以前から知っている I have known him by name for a long time [since a long time ago]. ▶彼は彼女以前にもまして好きになった He loved her more than ever.

── 以前の 形 〖昔の〗 former; (もとの) old; 〖時間・順序的に前の〗 previous. ● 以前の日本 former Japan. ●彼の以前の住所 his old [former] address. ● 以前の状態に戻る a return to the previous condition. ● ずっと以前の[からの]知り合い a long-ago [a long-time] acquaintance. ▶彼以前の彼ではない He is not what he used to be./He is not his former self./(すっかり変わった) He's changed a lot. (!最後が最も口語的)

いぜん 依然 (今も) still; (相変わらず) as ever; 〖以前と同様に〗 as before. (⇨まだ) ●依然として怠け者だ (as) lazy as ever. ▶彼の身元は依然分かっていない His identity is still unknown [remains unknown]. ▶彼は依然として行方不明だ He is still missing.

DISCOURSE
上記の欠点にもかかわらず, この計画には依然として多くの利点がある Despite such shortcomings, there are still many advantages to this plan. (! Despite は 〖…にかかわらず〗 は逆接を表すディスコースマーカー. still と組み合わせることで主張をより強調できる)

いせんこう 胃穿孔 〖医学〗a gastric perforation.
いせんじょう 胃洗浄 〖医学〗gastric lavage.
いそ 磯 (*on, at*) a (rocky) beach. (⇨海岸)
いそいそ 〖〘ばずんだ心で〗 lightheartedly, cheerfully, happily; (熱心に) eagerly. ▶子供たちはいそいそとピクニックに行った Children went *happily* on a picnic.
いそいで 急いで in a hurry. (⇨急ぐ[急いで])
いそう 位相 〖天文・物理〗a phase;〖数学〗topology.
● 位相が一致して[異なって] in [out of] *phase*. ● 位相空間 phase space. ● 位相差 a phase difference. ● 位相差顕微鏡 a phase microscope. ● 位相速度 phase velocity. ● 位相変調 phase modulation.
いそう 移送 图 transport. ▶貨物の空輸移送は高くつく The *transport* of freight by air is expensive.
── 移送する 動 transport, convey; take [carry] 《people [goods]》 from one place to another (in a vehicle).
いそう 遺贈 图 devise, bequest; (遺贈物) a legacy, a bequest.
── 遺贈する 動 (A を B に)《書》bequeath /bikwíːð/ 《A *to* B; B A》in one's will; leave 《A *to* B》in one's will. ▶彼は娘に200万ドル遺贈した He *bequeathed* his daughter the sum of two million dollars.
● 遺贈者 a devisor, a testator.
いそうろう 居候 图《話》a freeloader; (寄生虫のような人)《軽蔑的》a parasite.
── 居候する 動 ▶彼は兄のところに居候している He *lives off* [《米話》*freeloads on*] his brother.
いそがしい 忙しい 〖手が空いていない〗be busy 《doing; with》; (手がふさがっている) be occupied 《*in* doing, with》,《やや話》be tied up. (⇨多忙)
● 忙しそうに[忙しく]働く work *busily* /《懸命に》*hard*》. ● 忙しそうにその部屋を出入りしている be *busily* getting [急ぎ足で] be hurrying] in and out of the room. ▶今忙しくて手が離せません I'm *busy* [I'm *occupied*,《やや話》I'm *tied up*] at the moment./(相手の要求を断わるとき) Since I'm *busy* now, I can't help you. /(! If I weren't *busy* now, I could help you. の方が丁寧な言い方) /私は忙しすぎて新聞を読む暇もない I'm too *busy* to read the (news)paper. ▶もし明晩お忙しくなければ遊びに来てください Please come to see me if you are free [not *busy*] tomorrow evening.
① 〖忙しい〜〗 形 ▶忙しい男 a *busy* man. ▶忙しい(=差し迫った)仕事 *pressing* work; *urgent* business. (! 事柄の場合は busy は用いない) ● 忙しい日程 a heavy [a tight, a *full*] schedule. ▶忙しい生活を送る lead a *busy* [an *active*] life. ▶お忙しいところおじゃまして申し訳ありません 《日本人的発想》I'm sorry to interrupt your *tight schedule*./《米英人的発想》Thank you very much for taking time out of your *tight schedule*.
② 〖…で[に]忙しい〗 ▶彼は仕事でとても忙しい He is very *busy with* [*at*] his work./He *is* fully [ᵡ*very*] *occupied with* his work./(する仕事がたくさんある) He has a lot of work to do. ▶彼は旅行の準備に忙しかった He was *busy* [He *busied himself* 《*with*》] getting ready for his trip./He *was occupied in* [*occupied himself with*] getting ready for his trip. ▶この仕事で君もまた当分忙しくなるね This work [job] will keep you *busy* for a while.
── 忙しがる 動 ▶彼は忙しがっている He *looks busy*.
いそがせる 急がせる hurry 《him》(up). (⇨急ぐ[急いで])

いそぎ 急ぎ (あわただしい) hurried; (十分な時間をかけない) hasty; (せかせる) rush; (緊急の) urgent;《すばやい》quick. ● 急ぎの注文 a *rush* [an *urgent*] order. ● 大急ぎで in a great [a big] *hurry*. (⇨急ぐ[急いで])
いそぎんちゃく 磯巾着 〖動物〗a sea anemone /sɪˈænəməni/.
いそぐ 急ぐ hurry; rush;《書》hasten /héisn/,《古》make* haste.

> **使い分け** **hurry** 最も一般的な日常語で、人があわてて移動・行動することを表す。一定の時間に遅れまいとする混乱した精神状態を暗示する。
> **rush** hurry より差し迫った状況で移動・行動するときのすばやさや激しさを強調するが、しばしば軽率さや無謀さを暗示する。

● 道を急ぐ (道中を急ぐ) *hurry on* one's way; (どんどん進む) *press* on. ● 結論を急ぐ(=結論に飛びつく) *rush* [*jump*] *to* a conclusion. ▶彼は病院へと急いだ He *hurried* [*rushed*] *to* the hospital. (! hurry は通例人が主語の場合に限られる) (⇨図) ▶彼はそのバスに乗ろうと急いでいた He *was hurrying* to catch the bus./He *was in a hurry for* [to catch] the bus. ▶急げ *Hurry* (*up*)! (! 命令文や要請を表す文ではしばしば強意の up を伴う (⇨[第3文例])) /*Be quick*! (! 話 では しばしば *Quick*! となる)/《古》*Make haste*! /(遅れないようにさっさと行動に移せ)《話》*Get a move on*! ● 急ぐことはない *Don't hurry*. (! hurry は否定文では通例 up は伴わない)/*Don't be in a hurry*./*There's no hurry*. (ゆっくりやれ) *Take your time*. ▶なぜそんなに急ぐのですか What's the *hurry*?/Why all this *hurry*?
会話「それをお返ししなくてすみません」「ちっともかまいませんよ、特に急いでいるわけではないのですから」"Sorry I haven't returned it." "That's quite all right. I'm in no particular *hurry* for it."
── 急いで 副 〖あわてて〗in a hurry, hurriedly;《やや書》in haste, hastily;《すばやく》quickly. (⇨急ぎ)
● 仕事を急いでする *hurry* (*up*) a job; *rush* a job (*through*). ● 急いで病院へ行かせる *hurry* [*rush*] 《him》 *to* the hospital. ● 急いで結論を出させる *hurry* 《him》 *into* (making) a decision. ▶我々は急いで昼食をとった We had lunch *in a hurry*./We had a *quick* [a *hurried*,《やや書》a *hasty*] lunch. (! hurry lunch は「昼食の準備を急ぐ」の意) ● 急いで準備しなさい *Get ready quickly*!/*Hurry and get ready*. (!《話》では hurry and (*do*) (急いで…する) の形でよく用いる) ▶本は急いで返してくれなくていいよ There's no *hurry about giving* the book back to me. ▶急いで行かなくちゃ。約束の時間に遅れているのだ I really have to *run* [*dash*]. I'm late for an appointment. ▶空港までお願いします。急いでね (タクシーの運転手に) The airport, please, and *quickly*.
● 急がば回れ 'If you are in a hurry, go around.'/(ことわざ) Slow and steady wins the race./(急ぐ時はゆっくりと) *More haste, less speed*./(ゆっくり急げ) *Make haste slowly*. (! ラテン語からの英訳)
いぞく 遺族《書》the bereaved (! 単・複両用い). ▶a bereaved family. ▶戦死者の遺族 the war *bereaved*.
● 遺族年金 a survivor's pension.
いそしぎ 磯鴫 〖鳥〗a common sandpiper.
イソップ 〖ギリシャの寓話作家〗Aesop /íːsəp/.
イソップものがたり イソップ物語 *Aesop's Fables*. 〖参考〗イソップの寓話集
いそづり 磯釣り beach fishing; surf-casting. ● 磯釣りをする surf-cast.

いぞん 依存 图 (頼ること) dependence; (当てにすること) reliance.
—**依存する** 動 ●外国に石油を依存する depend [rely] on foreign countries for oil.

いぞん 異存 (an) objection (to). ●私は彼を雇うことに異存はない I have no objection to hiring him.

いた 板 a board, a plank (❗plank は厚さが約 5-15 cm で幅が 20cm 以上の厚板); 〖金属・ガラスなの〗a plate (❗通例厚さ 0.5cm 以上); (薄い) a sheet; 〖石・木材・金属などの幅の広い厚板〗a slab. ●厚さ 2 センチの板 a board two centimeters thick.
①【板~】●板張りの床 a boarded floor.
②【板を】●板を切る［削る］saw [plane] a board. ●床に板を張る board the floor; lay boards on the floor. ●窓に板を打ちつける board the windows up [in].
●板につく ▶彼の警察官ぶりも板についている(=すっかり慣れている) He is [looks] quite at home as a policeman. ●制服が板についてきた(=よく似合う) He came to look good in uniform. ●彼はまだ先生という仕事が板についていない(=未熟である) He is still green at his teaching profession.
●板石 a stone slab. ●板金 a (metal) plate; (薄い) a sheet metal. ●板ガラス plate glass; (薄い) sheet glass; (窓の) a (window)pane. ●板飛び込み〖水泳競技〗springboard diving. ●板塀 a board fence.

いたい 痛い ❶【痛みのある】sore, (傷・体の部分が) painful; (人が痛がる) have* a pain (in + one's [the]+身体部分), have a headache [toothache, stomachache, backache]; (体の部分が痛く) hurt*, 《書》pain (him) (❗主語には痛みの原因となるものもくる); (人・体の部分が) ache. (⇨痛む)

> [使い分け] **painful** 肉体的・精神的な痛みをいうが, 主に肉体的な痛みに用いる.
> **sore** 外部表面的な炎症・筋肉痛などの痛み.

●痛い傷 a sore [a painful] wound. (❗sore の方が口語的) ●ほこりでのどが痛い have a sore throat from dust. ●痛くて泣く cry with pain. ●頭ががんがん[ずきずき]痛い I have a splitting [a throbbing] headache./My head aches terribly [throbs]. ▶目が痛くて開けていられません My eyes hurt so much [are so painful] that I can't keep them open. ▶目が覚めたらのどが痛かった I had a sore throat when I woke up./I woke with soreness in my throat. ●体中が痛い I have pains all over./I ache [I'm aching] all over./《やや書》I'm sore all over. ▶痛いですか Do you have [feel] any pain?/Are you in pain [×painful]?/Does it hurt?/(医師が腹部を押さえて患者に) Is it tender here? ▶「痛い, そこだ」と彼は叫んだ "Ouch!" That's where the pain is [where it hurts]," he cried.
会話「痛そう」「大丈夫. 痛くはしないから」"It's going to be painful." "No, I won't hurt you." (❗It はこれから行う治療を漠然とさす)
会話「足が痛くてたまらないよ」「ちょっと休んでいこう」"My feet are killing me./My feet are all aching (from walking)." "Let's stop and rest for a while." (❗いずれも進行形に注意)

❷ (つらい) painful; (不快な) 《話》sore. ●痛い損失 a painful loss. ●痛い目にあう(⇨痛い目) ●彼女は彼の痛い所を突いた She touched him on a sore point./She touched [hit] a raw nerve of his sensitivity [his sensitive nerve]./《英》He was caught [touched] on the raw by her question. ▶1 億の損失はその会社にはひどく痛かった(=大打撃だった) The loss of one hundred million yen was a big [a great, a serious] blow to the firm. ●その知らせを聞いて胸が痛い I feel very sad [touched, 《やや書》feel grieved] to hear the news./The news makes me very sad. ●耳の痛いことを言う What you say sounds harsh [disagreeable] to my ear. ●彼女の悔しさは電話ごしにも痛いほど伝わってきた I was painfully aware even over the phone (line) that she was very much frustrated. (❗line を入れると「実際には見えないが(電話を通じて)感じることができる」の意を強調する)
●痛くもかゆくもない ▶そんなことをしても痛くもかゆくもない That doesn't matter [make any difference] to me at all./That's nothing to me.
●痛くもない腹を探られる ▶私は痛くもない腹を探られた(=あらぬ疑いをかけられた) I've been wrongly suspected.

いたい 遺体 a (dead) body; 〖死骸〗a corpse (⇨死体); 〖なきがら〗《書》remains (❗複数扱い. a (dead) body の婉曲語). ●彼の遺体は火葬された His remains were cremated.
●遺体安置所 a mortuary.

***いだい 偉大** 图 greatness. ●チャーチルの偉大さ the greatness of Churchill; Churchill's greatness.
—**偉大な** 形 great. ●偉大な政治家 a great statesman. ▶彼は科学の分野で偉大な業績をあげた He produced great achievements in the field of science.

いだい 医大 a medical college [school].
●医大生 a medical student.

イタイイタイびょう イタイイタイ病 〖医学〗itai-itai disease; (説明的に) a bone disease related to cadmium pollution caused by waste water from mines.

いたいけ(ない) (かわいい) sweet; (無邪気な) innocent; (いじらしい) touching, pathetic.

いたいたしい 痛々しい 〖苦痛を与える〗painful; 〖哀れをもよおす〗pitiful, pathetic; 〖悲惨な〗tragic.
●痛々しいまでやせている be painfully [pitifully] thin. ▶その飢えた子供は見るも痛々しかった It was painful [pitiful] to see the starved child.

いたいめ 痛い目 ●痛い目にあう(=ひどい経験をする) have a terrible 〖苦い〗a bitter) experience. ●痛い目にあわせる make 〖him〗suffer; (訓戒される) teach 《him》a lesson. ●彼は横柄なため痛い目にあった(=罰を受けた) He paid a lot for his insolence.

いたがゆい 痛痒い sore [painful] and itchy.

いたがる 痛がる (⇨-がる)

***いたく 委託** 图 trust; (任務などの) (a) commission; (商品の) consignment.
—**委託する** 動 (物・事を) 《やや書》entrust (⇨託す); (問題などを) refer; (商品に) consign. ●彼にその任務を委託する entrust the duty to him 〖him with the duty〗. ●その件を役員会に委託する refer the matter to the board of directors.
●委託学生 (奨学生) a scholarship student. ●委託金 a trust fund; money in trust. ●委託販売 consignment (sale [selling]), a sale [a selling] on consignment. ●委託販売で売る sell goods on commission.

いだく 抱く 〖心の中に〗have*; (悪意などを) bear*; (望みなどを) cherish; 〖両腕に〗hold* 〖nestle〗... in one's arms (⇨抱く). ●彼に悪意を抱く bear ill will toward him; (恨みを) bear [have] a grudge against him, bear him a grudge. ●密かな望みを抱く have [cherish] a secret hope. ●関心を抱く get interested [take an interest] 《in》. ●山に抱

いたけだか 居丈高 ● 居丈高になる(=威圧的な態度をとる) take a *threatening* attitude 《*toward*》; draw oneself up.

かれた静かな町 a quiet town *nestling* [×nestled] among the hills. ▶あなたは将来に何か不安を抱いていますか Do you *have* any anxiety about the future?

いたご 板子 a (deck) plank. ●板子一枚下は地獄 A sailor has only a plank between him and Hell.

いたさ 痛さ (a) pain. (⇒痛み)

いたしかたない 致し方無い (⇒仕方(が)無い)

いたしかゆし 痛し痒し ● 痛しかゆしの(=微妙な)立場 a *delicate* [《かたやかに》 an *awkward*] situation. ● 痛しかゆしである(=どちらを選ぶにしても少し問題がある) be in a bit of a dilemma [a quandary /kwándəri/] 《*about, over*》.

いたじき 板敷き ● a wood(en) [board] floor; (板の間) a room with a wood(en) [board] floor.

いたす 致す do*. (⇒する)

いたずら 悪戯 图 (子供のちょっとした悪さ) mischief /místʃif/; (❗数えるときは a piece [two pieces] of 〜 で, ×two mischiefs のような複数形はない); (悪ふざけ) a trick; (悪意のない/やや古) a prank; (受けたからって) a practical joke; (人をかつぐ行為) a hoax (❗通例公共施設[機関]に対するもの). ▶彼女はいたずらっぽい目でちらっと彼を見た She gave him a *mischievous* [*playful*] glance.

① 【いたずらな】 ● いたずらっ子 [小僧] (⇒形) ● いたずら盛り(=最もふざけたがる年頃)の男の子 a boy of *the most playful age*. ▶彼はそれをほんのいたずら半分でやった He did it just *in* [*for*] *fun* [*only out of mischief*].

② 【いたずらが】 ▶男の子はいたずらが好きだ Boys like *mischief* [*playing tricks*]./(男の子のいたずらしたがない) Boys will be boys. ▶あなたはいたずらがすぎますよ You're too *mischievous*. (⇒形)

③ 【いたずらを】 (⇒動) ▶いたずらをたくらんでいる be up to *mischief*. ▶子供たちにいたずらをさせないでおくのは難しい It's hard to keep the children out of *mischief*.

── 悪戯な 形 mischievous /místʃivəs/; (腕白な) naughty. (❗前の方は時にかわいげのあるものを含むが, 後の方は行儀の悪さを暗示する) ● いたずらな子供 a *mischievous* [a *naughty*] child; (わんぱく小僧) an elf (履 elves).

── 悪戯(を)する 動 play a trick [a joke, a prank, a hoax] 《*on* +人》; (始める) get* into mischief (❗以上いずれもこの意には do は用いない) (⇒图③); (女性・子供にいたずら行為をする) molést 《a woman》. ● カメラをいたずらする(=いじくる) *play* [《話》 *monkey* 《*around*》] *with a camera*. ▶彼は私にひどいいたずらをした He *played* a nasty *trick on me*. ▶あの子はいつもいたずらをしている That boy is always *up to* 《*some*》 *mischief*./That boy *is* always *getting into mischief*.

● いたずら書き (考え事・話をしながらの) a doodle; (落書き) a scribble; (壁などの) graffiti (❗単・複両扱い).

● いたずら電話 a prank [a hoax] phone call.

*** いたずらに** 徒らに [無益に] uselessly; in vain; [むだに] to no purpose; [のらくらして] idly. ▶いたずらに金を遣う *waste* one's *money*. ▶いたずらに努力を重ねた All his efforts were *in vain* [《話》 *went down the drain*] (❗ go down the drain は「下水道へ流れて, まったくむだになる」の意).

いただき 頂 ❶ [山の] the top, the summit (❗後の方が堅い語); (とがった所) the peak. (⇒頂上)

❷ [もらうこと] ● いただきだ(= 確実に手に入る) be

sure [certain] to get.... ▶この試合はいただきだ We are sure to win this game. (❗《話》 This game is *in the bag*. (❗この成句は「獲物が袋に入って」の意) ▶ごちそうさまでした. 申し訳ありませんがお立ち(=ごちそうになってすぐに辞去)させてください I really enjoyed the meal, but excuse me for *leaving so soon*.

● いただき物 a present 《*from*》.

いただきます 頂きます (❗米英では日本語のような決まり文句はないが, 食事を始めるときに May I start? (頂いていいですか) とかすわれた, Go ahead and start! (さあさあ召し上がれ) とうながしたり, 家庭によっては神に食前の祈りをする (say grace) こともある: 主よ今私たちが頂くこの糧に感謝させ給え, アーメン For what we are about to receive, may the Lord make us truly thankful, Amen /éimén/.)

いただく 頂く ❶ [もらう] (受け取る) get*; (手に入れる) have*; (選び取る) take*; (支払われる) be paid. ▶母から誕生日のプレゼントを頂いた I *got* [*received*] a birthday present from my mother. ▶これをいただくわ (店で) I'll *take* this one. ▶鉛筆1本につき100円頂きます(=請求します) I *charge* (you) 100 yen for each pencil. ▶本の代金はまだ頂いておりません(=支払われていません) The book hasn't *been paid for* yet. (❗文頭または文尾に I'm afraid をつければ丁寧な言い方になる)

會話「この本を頂いてもよろしいですか」「いいですよ」"Could I *have* [*keep*] this book?" "Sure." (❗許可を求める言い方と断る言い方は (⇒いい⑭ 解説 II》)

❷ [飲食する] have*, (食べる) eat*; (飲む) drink*.

會話「もう少しステーキをいかがですか」「ありがとう. もう十分頂きました」"Would you like some more steak?" "No, thanks. I've *had enough*. (❗「ええ, 頂きます」なら Yes, thank you./Yes, please. という. ❷ OK. は無作法な言い方)

會話「紅茶とコーヒーとどちらがよろしいですか」「コーヒーを頂きたい」"Which would you like, tea or coffee?" "*I'd like* coffee, please." (❗would like は《話》 'd like は want の丁寧表現)

會話「(お酒)一杯いかが」「頂きます」"Will you have a drink?" "I'd like one."

❸ [.... してもらう] ▶窓を閉めていただけませんか Would [Could] you (please) close the window? (❗(1) Will you...? より丁寧, また could より would の方が丁寧. (2) please をつけるとより丁寧になる)/Would you mind closing [×to close] the window? (❗(1) 前の文より丁寧. would の他にも可能だが丁寧さは劣る. (2)「ええ, いいですよ」という肯定の返答は No, not at all. が普通だが, 《話》では Yes, certainly./Sure. なども言う. 否定の返答は通例理由を添えて I'm sorry I can't, because .... などという) ▶ご予約いただいていますか Do you *have* a reservation? ▶妻にお会いいただければと思います I'd like you [《米話》 for you] *to meet* my wife. I *want* you *to meet*.... や *Please meet*.... は命令的になるので注意)/(目上の人に) I *hoped* [*was hoping*] you would meet my wife. (❗ I hope [I'm hoping] you will .... より控え目で丁寧ないい方)

❹ [その他の表現] ▶雪をいただいた山 a snow-*capped* [《文》 a snow-*crowned*] mountain. (❗snow-covered は「全体が雪でおおわれた」の意) ▶君のヘアスタイルはまったくいただけない Your hairstyle is totally *unacceptable*./I don't *like* [《我慢できない》 I *can't stand*] your hairstyle.

いたたまれない 居たたまれない ▶彼の態度が恥ずかしくていたたまれなかった I was so ashamed of his attitude that I *couldn't stay* there *any longer*.

いたち 鼬 【動物】a weasel.
● いたちごっこ (悪循環) a vicious circle; (きりのない競争) a rat race.

いたチョコ 板チョコ a bar of chocolate, a chocolate bar.

いたって 至って very; quite; extremely. ● 至って質素な食事 a *very* simple meal. ▶彼女は至って健康だ She is in *very* good health./She is in the pink (of health).

いたで 痛手 (大きな損失) a heavy loss; (大きな損害) serious damage; (大きな打撃) a great blow. ▶我が社は不況で大きな痛手を受けた Our company suffered a *heavy loss* [*serious damage*] during the recession. ● 母親の死は彼女には大きな痛手だった Her mother's death was a *great blow* [(衝撃) *a great shock*] to her.

いだてん 韋駄天 a swift [a very fast] runner. ● 韋駄天走りに走る run like (greased) lightning; (危険なほど速く) run at breakneck speed.

いたどり 【植物】a Japanese knotweed.

いたのま 板の間 (床) a wooden floor; (部屋) a room with a wooden floor.
● 板の間稼ぎ a bathhouse thief; (行為) (a) bathhouse theft. ● 板の間稼ぎをする steal (money) from a bathhouse.

いたばさみ 板挟み 【ジレンマ】a dilemma. ●そのことで板挟みになっている (選択に悩んでいる) be in [on the horns of] *a dilemma* about it; (窮地に立っている) (話)be in *a fix* about it. ●「板挟みになる」の場合、前方を含めて代わりに、後の方は get oneself into a fix となる。● 義理と人情の板挟みになる be torn [*get oneself into a bad fix*] between duty and sentiment.

いたぶる 【ゆする】extort (money *from* him); 【いじめ、痛めつける】 (⇨いじめる、痛めつける)

いたまえ 板前 an *itamae*; (説明的に) an expert cook who prepares Japanese cuisine in a restaurant or a hotel.

いたましい 痛ましい 【人を悲しませる】sad; 【哀れな】pitiful, pathetic; 【哀れみの心を起こさせるような】touching; 【悲劇的な】tragic; 【みじめな】miserable. ● 痛ましい事故で死ぬ be killed in a *sad* [a *tragic*] accident. ● 痛ましい光景 a *pitiful* [a *pathetic*] sight. ● 痛ましい死 a *miserable* [a *tragic*] death.

いたみ 痛み, 傷み ❶ [苦痛] (a) pain; an ache; (an) agony, 《やや書》anguish; a pang.

> 使い分け
> **pain** 「痛み」を表す最も一般的な語. 慢性的な痛みは複数形で用いることが多い.
> **ache** 継続的な鈍い痛み. しばしば痛む場所を示す語とともに複合語として用いる. (⇨腹痛, 胃痛, 頭痛, 歯痛)
> **agony** 身を引き裂かれるような心身のひどい苦痛.
> **anguish** 主に精神的な心身のひどい苦痛.
> **pang** 突然の激痛, 鋭い痛み.

①【〜痛み】● 軽い[ひどい]痛み a slight [a bad, a terrible, a violent] *pain*. ● 鈍い[鋭い]痛み a dull [a sharp, a severe, an acute] *pain*. ● 刺し込み[締めつける; 焼けるような]痛み a stabbing [a pressing; a burning] *pain*. ● ちくちく[ひりひり]する痛み a prick, a sting.

②【痛みが[は]】 ▶痛みが増した[ひどくなった; ましになった; 治まった; とれた] The *pain* increased [got worse; eased off, lessened; stopped; went away]. ▶そのとき突然腕に激しい痛みが走った Then suddenly a sharp *pain* shot through my arm. ▶その薬で痛みはいくらか楽になった The medicine gave me some relief from the *pain*./The medicine has somewhat eased the *pain*. ▶痛みが残るようだったら医者に診てもらいなさい If the *pain* persists, see your doctor. (❗ your doctor は「あなたのかかりつけの医者」の意)

会話「痛みはいくらかとれてきていますか」「ええ, お陰さまで」 "Are the *pains* easing off a bit?" "Yes, they are."

③【痛みを】● 薬で痛みを止める[軽くする; 除く] kill [ease; remove] the *pain* with drugs. ▶背中に痛みを感じた I had [felt] a *pain* in my [the] back. ▶(次例より上品な言い方)/I had a backache [a back *pain*].

④【痛みで】● 痛みでゆがんだ顔 a face distorted in *pain* [*agony*]. ▶傷のずきずきした痛みで彼は一晩中眠れなかった The throbbing *pain* of his wound kept him awake all night.

❷ [損傷] damage; (破損) (a) breakage; (果実などの当たり傷) a bruise /brúːz/. ▶地震で壁のいたみがひどい The walls (of the room) *have been* badly *damaged* by the earthquake.
● 痛み止め (inject) a painkiller.

いたみわけ 痛み分け [相撲] a draw in a *sumo* match (because one of the opponents suffered an injury).

***いたむ** 痛む, 傷む ❶ [体が] 《人が主語》have* [feel*] a pain (*in*); 《体の部分が主語》hurt*, 《書》pain (*him*) 《受身不可》; (鈍く持続して) ache; (ひりひりと) burn, sting*; (ちくちくと) prick; (きりきりと) tingle; (ずきずきと) throb (-bb-), kill. (⇨痛み) ▶耳がひどく痛んだ I *had* a bad *pain* in my [the] ears./I had a severe earache./My ears *hurt* [*ached*] very much. ▶少し痛むかもしれません (医者が患者に) I'm afraid this may *hurt* a little. ▶(医者が腹部を押さえて)ここ痛みますか Is it *tender* here? ❗ tender は「さわると痛い」の意) ▶塩水で彼の目はひりひり痛んだ His eyes *stung* from [with] the salt water. (❗ from は「塩水にふれたこと」が原因で, with は「塩水にふれていて」の意) ▶そのことを考えただけでも胃が痛む My stomach *hurts* just to think of it.

会話「どこが痛みますか」「ここです」"Where does it *hurt* (you) [*pain* you]?" (❗ it は問題になっている(痛い)箇所を漠然とさす)/ Whereabouts are the *pains*?" "Just here, doctor."

会話「で, 今も痛みますか」「ええ」「ひどいですか」 "Well, are the *pains* there now?" "Yes." "Are they bad?"

❷ [心が] ache; (心痛を与える)《書》pain; (悩ます) bother. ▶そのニュースを聞いて私は心が痛んだ My heart *ached* to hear the news./(心を痛めた) The news *made* my heart *ache*./It *was* painful [*pained* me] to hear the news./I *was* touched by the news. ▶良心が痛む My conscience *bothers* [(ちりちりと) *stings*, *pricks*] me./I feel the pricks [pangs] of conscience./(心がやましい) I had a bad [a guilty] conscience.

❸ [品物などが] (損なわれる) damage; (腐る) go* bad; (当たり傷をつくる) bruise /brúːz/. ▶日光に当たると商品が傷みますよ It will *damage* the goods if they are exposed to the sun. ▶夏場は卵が傷みやすい Eggs *spoil* easily [easily *go bad*, *are perishable*] in summer. (❗ ×Eggs are easy to spoil [go bad]. は不可) ● ナシは傷まないように注意して扱いなさい Treat the pears carefully so that they do not *get bruised*.

いたむ 悼む 【死などを】mourn, (嘆く)《やや書》lament, (深く悲しむ) grieve 《*over*》; (残念に思う)

いためつける regret (-tt-); 〘死者を〙mourn (for...); lament ⟨for⟩; grieve ⟨for⟩. ▶彼の死を悼む *mourn* [*lament, grieve over*] his death.

いためつける 痛めつける (懲らしめる) punish; (ひどく苦しめる) torment; (いびる)《話》pick on..., get* at .... ▶彼を痛めつけて本当の事をしゃべらせよう I'll *punish* him and make him tell the truth.

いため(もの) 炒め(物) fried [sautéd] dishes. ▶野菜炒め fried vegetables.

いためる 炒める fry; (こげ目がつくまで) brown. (⇨料理) ▶野菜をさっと炒める *stir-fry* vegetables. (!) stir-fry は形容詞用法にもあるので「さっと炒めた野菜」の意にもなる) ▶タマネギのみじん切りを薄く色がつくまで炒める *fry* chopped onions until they are golden brown.

いためる 痛める 〘体の部分を〙injure; hurt*; (くじく) sprain; (使い過ぎる) strain; 〘心を〙be worried ⟨*about*⟩. ▶足を痛めている *have trouble with* one's foot; have foot *trouble*. ▶本の読み過ぎで目を痛める *strain* one's eyes by reading too much. ▶この石鹸ではお肌を痛めません This soap won't *hurt* [*irritate*] your skin. ▶テニスをしていて手首を痛めた I *sprained* my wrist playing tennis. ▶風邪でのどを痛めている(=のどが痛い) I have a *sore* throat from a cold. ▶彼は息子のことでたいへん心を痛めている He *is* very (much) *worried about* his son.

いためる 傷める damage. ▶車を傷める *damage* a car.

いたらない 至らない 〘行き届かない〙incompetent; 〘不注意な〙careless; 〘未熟な〙inexperienced. ▶私が至らないばかりにあなたに大変なご迷惑をかけてすみません I'm sorry to have troubled you so much—I ought to have done it more carefully [(私の過失でした) That was my *fault*]. ▶至らない者ですがよろしく I am *inexperienced*, but I hope I'll try (my best) to do a good job.

いたり 至り (⇨極み)

イタリア 〘国名〙Italy /ítəli/; (公式名) the Republic of Italy. (首都 Rome) ▶イタリア人 an Italian;《集合的》Italian people, the Italians. ▶イタリア語 Italian. ▶イタリア(人[語])の Italian /itǽljən/.

イタリック italics. (!) 時に単数扱い) ▶イタリック体の italic《words》. ▶イタリック体で印刷する print 《words》in *italics*. ▶イタリック体にする italicize《words》.

いたる 至る ❶〘通じる〙lead* ⟨*to, into*⟩. ▶山頂に至る道 the path to the top of the mountain. ▶この道は大津を経て京都に至る This road *leads to* Kyoto via [by way of] Otsu.
❷〘ある結果になる〙result ⟨*in*⟩; (結局...になる) lead* ⟨*to*⟩ (!) to に続く名詞・動名詞は通例好ましくない事態を示す); (...するようになる) come* [get*] to ⟨do⟩; 〘引き起こす〙(原因となる) cause, (結果として もたらす) bring*... about; 〘結論に達する〙reach. ▶その実験でがんの治療法を発見するに至った The experiment *resulted* [*ended*] *in* the discovery of a cure for cancer. ▶その国境紛争は戦争には至らなかった The border conflict did not *lead to* [(発展する) *develop into*] war. ▶どうして君はそんなことをするに至ったのか How did you *come* [×*become*] *to* be so foolish?/What *made* you [*caused* you *to*; (こういう気にさせる) *led* you *to*] do such a foolish thing? (!) make を用いるのが最も口語的) ▶その問題はまだ解決に至っていない The problem has not been solved [resolved] *yet*. ▶決定には至らなかった No decision *was reached*.
❸〘及ぶ〙▶社長から用務員に至るまで from the president *down to* the janitors. ▶今に至るまで *up to* now [the present]; (今日まで) to this day.

いたるところ 至る所 everywhere. ▶世界の至る所から *from all parts* [*every corner*] *of the world*. ▶至る所でそれを耳にした I heard it *everywhere*. ▶至る所で(=どこへ行っても)彼は好意を持って迎えられた He was warmly received *wherever* he went.

> 翻訳のこころ そういえばヨーロッパでもアメリカでも、町の広場には至る所にみごとな噴水があった(山崎正和『水の東西』) For that matter, [That reminds me that] there are *many* fine fountains in *every* town center in Europe and the US. (!) (1) that matter や That はこの文の前で述べたことをさす。(2)「至る所」はここでは every town center と表す

いたれりつくせり 至れり尽くせり ▶あのホテルのサービスは至れり尽くせりだった(=完ぺきだった) The service at [×of] that hotel was *perfect*./The service was *perfect* at that hotel./I got *very good* service at that hotel.

いたわさ 板わさ *itawasa*, (説明的に) slices of *kamaboko* served with *wasabi* and soy sauce.

いたわり 労り kindness. ▶いたわりの心がない have no kindness ⟨*to*⟩; be not kind(-hearted). ▶いたわりの言葉をかける say some *kind* words [(慰めの言葉) some words of *comfort*] ⟨*to*⟩.

***いたわる 労わる** (親切にする) treat ⟨him⟩ kindly, be kind ⟨*to*⟩; (大事にする) take* (good) care of ...; (思いやる) be considerate ⟨*of, to, toward*⟩ (!) of は永続的な, to [toward] は一時的な態度に用いる); (励まし慰める) comfort. ▶病人を労わる *take care of* a sick person. ▶老人をもっといたわるべきだ You should *be more considerate of* [*be kinder to*] elderly people.

いたん 異端 图 (a) heresy /hérəsi/. ▶異端視する regard ⟨it⟩ as *heresy*.
— 異端の 形 heretical /hərétikl/.
— 異端者 a heretic /hérətik/.

***いち 一** ❶〘数〙one; 〘第1番め〙the first; 〘トランプの1〙an ace. ▶(単なる)一読者として as *a* (mere) reader. ▶一に健康が大切だ The *first* thing is your health./Your health comes *first*.
❷〘最初, 首位〙▶一から出直す make a *new start*.《話》start again *from scratch*. ▶私はこの会社を一から作り上げた I built this company up *from nothing*. ▶彼女は日本で一二を争う名優である (⇨一二)
▶一から十まで ▶彼はそれについては一から十まで知っていた He knew *everything* about it./He knew it *from A to Z*.
▶一にも二にも ▶強い力士になるには一にも二にも(=もっぱら)けいこを積むことだ You need *nothing but* a lot of practice to be a strong sumo wrestler.
▶一を聞いて十を知る ▶彼は一を聞いて十を知る人である(理解が早い) He is *very quick to understand*./(聡明(:)である) He *is very intelligent*.

***いち 位置** 图 (他との相対的な) a position; (ある場所の特定の) a place; (物があるのに適当な) a location (!) 前の2語より堅い語); 〘地位, 身分〙(⇨地位, 立場) ▶この地図で我々の学校の位置が分かりますか Can you find the *position* [*location*] of our school on this map? ▶その本を元の位置にもどしなさい You must put the book back where it was [in its (proper) *place*]./The book must be replaced where it belongs. ▶位置について, 用意, どん!(競走で)《米》*Get ready, get set, go*!/《英》*Ready, steady, go*!/*On your marks, get set, go*!
— 位置する 動 ▶そこは県の南西に位置している It *is situated* [*is located, lies*] in the southwestern

いち 市 (定期的な) a market; (博覧会) a fair. ●青物[青空;魚]市 a vegetable [an open-air; a flea] market. ●国際見本市 an international trade fair. ▶毎月曜日に市が立つ Markets are held every Monday. (!市の立つ日は a market day)

いちあくのすな『一握の砂』 A Handful of Sand. (参考 石川啄木の歌集)

いちい 一位 (順位) first place; (賞) (the) first prize. (⇨一等) ●1位のタイガース the first-place Tigers. ▶彼は100メートルレースで1位になった He took first place [《英》got a first place] in the 100-meter dash./He finished [came (in)] first in the 100-meter dash./He won first prize in the 100-meter dash. ▶彼はパリーグで盗塁数1位だ He leads the Pacific League in stolen bases.

いちい 櫟, 一位〖植物〗a yew (tree).

いちだいすい 一衣帯水 a very narrow river [strait].

いちいち 一々 〖一つ一つ〗one by one; 〖詳しく〗in detail. ●製品をいちいち点検する check the products one by one. ▶いちいち(=何もかも)私に相談する必要はない You don't have to talk about everything with me.

いちいん 一因 a cause. ●家庭不和の一因 one of the causes of family trouble.

いちいん 一員 a member. (⇨メンバー, 会員) ●私たちのチーム[家族]の一員 a member of our team [family].

いちいんせい 一院制 the single-chamber [unicameral] system.

いちえん 一円 ●関西一円に throughout [all over] the Kansai district.

*__いちおう 一応__ 〖ともかく〗anyway, at ány ràte; 〖念のために〗just to make sure; 〖万一のため〗just in case; 〖さしあたり〗for the present, for the time being; 〖仮に〗tentatively; 〖いくぶん〗(まあまあ) fairly; (いくぶんとも) more or less. ▶一応そこへ行ってみよう Let's go there anyway. ▶一応その書類に目を通しておこう I'll look through the papers just to make [be] sure. ▶一応この本で間に合う This book will do for the present. ▶私たちは一応(=仮の)合意に達した We came to a tentative agreement. ▶君の言うことは一応もっともだ I more or less [〖話〗kind of] agree with you./What you are saying is fairly [《英》quite] reasonable.

いちおし 一推し ●先生の一推しの(=強く推薦する)辞書 a dictionary that my teacher strongly recommends. ●これは一推し(=必読)の書です This book is a must-read /-rìːd/./This is a must book.

いちがいに 一概に 〖必ずしも〗necessarily (!この意では否定語を伴う); 〖無差別に〗indiscriminately. ▶彼が正しいとは一概にいえない He isn't necessarily [always] right.

:__いちがつ 一月__ January (略 Jan.). (⇨1月に in January of 2008; in January(,) 2008. (! in January in 2008 という形は書き言葉では避けられる) ●2008年1月17日に on the 17th of January, 2008; 《米》on January 17, 2008 《略記 1/17/08》; 《英》on 17(th) January(,) 2008 《略記 17/1/08》. (!後の二つは on January seventeen [(the) seventeenth], two thousand eight; on January the seventeenth (the seventeenth of January], two thousand eight と読む。日付の後の st, nd, rd, th は年に続く場合《米》ではつけないのが普通)

いちかばちか 一か八か ▶一か八かやってみよう I will take a chance (on it)./I will run risks [a risk]./ Sink or swim, I'll try it.

いちがん 一丸 ●我々が一丸となってこれに当たらないと成功しない If we don't do this all together [in unison, as a group], we can't succeed. (参考 United we stand or we fall. がある)

いちがんレフ 一眼レフ ●一眼レフのカメラ a single-lens reflex camera.

いちぎ 一義 ●一義的な[一義的でない]表現 an unequivocal [an equivocal] expression. ●一義的な(=最も重要な)機能 a primary function.

いちぐう 一隅 ●一隅に at [in] one [a] corner. ●広間の一隅に in the corner of the hall. ●広場の一隅に at the corner of the square.

いちぐん 一群 (⇨群れ) ●一群の星 a group of stars.

いちげい 一芸 ●一芸に秀でている人 a master of an art. ●一芸をきわめる master an art.

いちげき 一撃 (こぶしなどによる) a blow; (武器などによる) a stroke. ●頭に強烈な一撃をくらわす strike (him) a hard blow on the head.

いちげん 一元 ●一元的な 形 unified. ●一元一次方程式 a simple equation with one unknown. ●(⇨一元化, 一元論)

いちげん 一見 ●一見の客 a new [an unfamiliar] customer.

いちげんか 一元化 名 unification; (集中) centralization. ── 一元化する 動 unify; (集中させる) centralize.

いちげんこじ 一言居士 ▶彼は一言居士だ He has something to say about everything.

いちげんろん 一元論 名 monism. ── 一元論の 形 monistic(al).
●一元論者 a monist.

いちご 苺 〖植物〗a strawberry. ●イチゴを摘む pick strawberries.
●苺畑 a strawberry patch.

いちごいちえ 一期一会 the only chance in a lifetime; (説明的に) One meeting, One opportunity—the concept in the Way of Tea of regarding every encounter as a unique opportunity of a lifetime, or in general, of treasuring each passing moment in order to live meaningfully.

いちごん 一言 a (single) word. ●一言のもとに(=きっぱりと)断わる refuse flatly.
●一言一句 ▶私は彼女の言うことを一言一句(=すべての言葉を)聞き漏らすまいとした I listened to every single word she said.
●一言半句 ▶これについては一言半句も(=少しも)(他の人に)漏らすな Keep mum about this. (!成句表現) ▶彼女は演説するときに一言一句もおろそかにしない She weighs her words when she makes a speech.
●一言もない ▶一言もありません(=弁解の余地もない) I have no excuse./I have nothing to say.

いちざ 一座 ●一座の人々(=そこに居た人々) all those present; everyone there. ●俳優の一座 a company [a troupe /trúːp/] of players.

*__いちじ 一時__ ❶ 〖ひとときは〗at one time; (かつて) once (!通例肯定文国, be 動詞・助動詞の後、一般助動詞の前で); (以前に) before. (⇨以前, かつて) ●一時有名だった歌手 a once-famous singer. ▶私は一時京都に住んでいたことがある At one time I lived [used to live, ×have lived] in Kyoto. (! at one time は過去時制に用いる。used to live を用いる場合は今はもう住んでいないことを含意して, at one time は省略可)/I once lived [×have once lived] in Kyoto. (! once は過去時制と用いる)/I have lived [lived] in Kyoto *before.* ▶大阪の空気は一時ほど汚れていない The air in Osaka is not so dirty as it *used* to be [as it (*once*) *wás, as* (it was) *before*]. (❗ *once* は無勢で、このように be 動詞(や助動詞)が強勢を受ける位置にくる場合は前に置くのが普通)

❷ [しばらく] for a while, for a time; (一時的に) temporarily; (さしあたり) for the time being, for the present [moment]. ▶明日から一時休業します We will be closed *for a while* from tomorrow. ▶彼は昨年一時帰国をした He *temporarily* went back home last year. ▶政府が一時(的に)その政策を棚上げした The government shelved the policy *temporarily*.

①【一時～】(からの箱を一時しのぎにテーブルの代わりに使う use an empty box as a *makeshift* for a table [as a *makeshift* table]. ●一時逃れの言い訳をする make a *makeshift* excuse; (言い訳をして時間を稼ぐ) make an excuse to buy [play for] time. ●交差点で一時停止する *stop* [*come to a halt*] before entering a crossing. (❗ 掲示などの「一時停止」は Stop/Halt)

②【一時の】(一時の間に合わせの) temporary (⇨一時的); (一瞬の) momentary; (すぐ移り変わる) transient; (束の間の) passing. ●一時の感情 *transient* emotion. ●一時の気まぐれ a *passing* [(長続きしない) *a short-lived* /-láivd/] fancy. ●一時の出来心(=衝動)で on a *momentary* impulse; on the impulse [spur] of *the moment*.

❸ [一回で] (現金での) full cash payment. ●一時預かり所 (ホテル・劇場などの) a cloakroom; 《米》 a checkroom; (駅などの手荷物の) 《米》 a checkroom, a baggage room; 《英》 a left-luggage office. ●一時預かり証 a claim check. ●一時解雇[帰休] a (temporary) layoff. ●従業員を一時解雇する[帰休させる] lay off the workers, lay the workers *off* (*from*). ●一時金 (1回限りの手当) a one-time allowance; (一括払い金額) a lump sum; (ボーナス) a bonus.

いちじ 一次 (最初の) the first; (予備の) preliminary; 【数学】 linear. ●第一次中東戦争 the *First* Middle East War. ●一次関数 a linear function. ●一次産業 primary industry. ●一次産品 primary products. ●一次試験 a preliminary (exam); 《話》 prelims. ●一次方程式 a linear equation.

いちじいっく 一字一句 every (single) word and phrase. ▶詩を一字一句間違いなく覚える memorize a poem *word for word*; memorize a poem (until 《he》 is) *letter-perfect* 《米》 [*word-perfect* 《英》]. ▶これを一字一句翻訳(=逐語訳)することは不可能に近い It is almost impossible to translate this *word for word* [*literally*] into another language.

いちじがばんじ 一事が万事 ▶彼は一事が万事あの調子だ He does *everything* that way.

いちじく 無花果 〖植物〗 (実) a fig; (木) a fig (tree).

いちじせんきん 一字千金 great writing. ▶シェイクスピアは偉大な詩人で、作品には一字千金の重みがある Shakespeare is such a great poet that his works are worth *a million dollars a word*.

いちじつ 一日 (⇨一日(いちにち)) ●一日の長 ▶車の運転では真理は私より一日の長がある Mari is *a little more experienced than* I in driving a car./Mari is *a little ahead of* me *as* a driver.

いちじてき 一時的 ――一時的な 形 [一時の間に合わせの] temporary (↔permanent). ●一時的な快楽 *temporary* [(はかない) *passing*] pleasures. (❗ pleasure は「楽しい事」で ⓒ) ▶不況は一時的なもので景気は間もなく回復した The recession was *temporary* and the economy soon recovered.

―― 一時的に 副 temporarily. (⇨一時(いちじ)❷)

いちじゅういっさい 一汁一菜 'a bowl of soup and one dish (besides rice)'; a very simple meal.

いちじゅん 一巡 ――一巡する 動 ●九州を一巡(=周遊)する make a (circular) *tour* of Kyushu; *tour around* Kyushu. (❗ around の代わりに in を用いると、あちこち旅行したことを示すが一巡ではない) ●公園を一巡する(=一回りする) *walk around* the park. ●巨人は初回に打順が一巡した The Giants *batted around* in the first inning.

いちじょ 一助 a help. ●一助となる be a help (*to*); be helpful (*to*); be of some help (*to*).

*****いちじるしい 著しい** 形 (注目に値する) remarkable (↔unremarkable); (際立った) marked /má:rkidl/, noticeable (❗ marked の方が強意的); (印象的な) striking. ●著しい類似点 *striking* similarities. ▶これとそれとでは著しい相違がある There is a *remarkable* [a *marked*] difference between this and that./This is *remarkably* [*markedly*] different from that. ▶その視覚効果は著しかった The visual effect was *striking*.

―― 著しく 副 remarkably (❗ 通例形容詞・副詞を修飾する); (はっきりと) markedly /má:rkidli/, noticeably; (目立つと) strikingly /má:rkiŋli/ (❗ 形)テニスが著しく上達する make 《a》 *remarkable* [*marked*] progress in tennis. ▶彼女の健康は著しく改善した Her health has improved *markedly* [*noticeably*, (大いに) *greatly*].

いちじん 一陣 ❶ [ひとしきりの風] ●一陣の風 a gust of wind. ❷ [先陣] (軍隊の) the vanguard; (最初の一行) the first party [group].

いちず 一途 ――一途な 形 [人が] single-minded; [表情などが] intent.

―― 一途に 副 intently; (心から) wholeheartedly. ▶私はあの人を一途に愛した I loved him *with* all my *heart and soul*.

いちせいめん 一生面 a newly developed field.

いちぜんめし 一膳飯 a bowl of rice. ●一膳飯屋 a cheap restaurant; 《米》 a diner.

いちぞく 一族 one's (whole) family (⇨一家); (氏族) a clan. ●平家一族 the Heike *clan*.

いちぞん 一存 ▶私の一存(=個人的な判断だけ)では決めかねます I can't decide it by *my judgment alone*./I have no discretion over this matter. (❗ discretion は「決定する権限・自由」の意)

いちだい 一代 〖1世代〗 one [a] generation (⇨代, 世代); 〖一生〗 one's lifetime (⇨一生, 代). ●一代前に *a generation* ago. ▶関口氏は一代で大きな財産を築いた Mr.Sekiguchi made a large fortune *in* his *lifetime*. ●一代記 a biography; a life. (⇨伝記) ●出世一代記 a success story. ●一代雑種 the first filial generation; F1.

いちたいいち 一対一 ●一対一の話し合いを持つ have a *one-to-one* discussion [talk] 《*with*》.

いちだいじ 一大事 ●お家の一大事 a *matter of serious concern* to the family. ▶そりゃ一大事だ (Good) heavens! That's *serious*.

いちだん 一団 (移動中の) a troop (⇨集団); a body ●行動をともにする団体) 《団》 ●旅行者の一団 *a group* [*a party*] of tourists. ●一団となって *a group*.

いちだん(と) 一段(と) 〖なお一層〗 much, far, even, still (❗ 比較級を強める); 〖今までにないくらい一層〗 more than ever (⇨一層) [さらに進んで] further.

いちだんらく

▶彼女は今日は一段と美しく見える She looks *much* [*still*] *more* beautiful today. ▶彼は英語が上達した He has made *further* progress [*progressed further*] in English. ▶経済は一段と悪化してきている The economy has been going *from bad to worse*.

いちだんらく 一段落 ── 一段落する 動 ▶仕事が一段落した The work *has come to the end of the first stage*./We *have completed the first stage* of the work.

いちづけ 位置付け ranking.

いちづける 位置付け rank ... (*above, as, among*). ▶彼の長編小説は英文学史上どう位置づければよいでしょうか Where should we *rank* his long novel in the history of English literature?

いちてんき 一転機 a turning(-)point. (⇨転機)

***いちど** 一度 ❶ once; one time. (◎後の方が強意的) ●一度ならず(=再三) more than once; again [once] and again; time and (time) again. (**!** 後の言い方は time を反復する方が強意的) ▶それは一度や二度やってみる価値があるかもしれない It might be worth trying *once* or twice. ▶これが起きたのは一度や二度ではない。This happened not *once* or twice./(何度か起きた) This happened several times. (⇨何度 ❷) ●一生に一度でいいからパリへ行ってみたい I want to go to Paris just *once* in my life(time). ●一度(=かつて)犬を飼ったことがある *Once* we had a dog./We *once* had a dog./We had a dog *once*. (**!** いずれも過去のある時を表し, 完了形には用いない) (⇨飼う) ●一度(=いずれ)お立ち寄りください Drop in *sometime* [*one day*, ×*once*]. (**!** 未来のある時を表す) ▶一度見れば[言えば]十分だ *One* look [*A* word] is enough.

会話 「どのくらいの割で美容院へ行くの」「月に[3か月に]一度さ」 "How often do you go to a beauty salon?" "*Once a month* [*in three months*]."

会話 「そこへ何回行ったことがあるの」「一度だけだよ」 "How many times have you been there?" "*Only once*."

① 【もう一度】 once more, again. (⇨もう ❸ ②)
② 【一度の】 ●年に一度の祭の *annual* festival.
③ 【一度に】 (同時に) at the same time; at one time; (all) at once; (いっしょに) all together; (一回に) at a time (⇨一時). ▶みんな一度に話すな Don't everybody talk *at the same time* [*at once*]. ▶みんな一度にやって来た They came *all together*. ▶一度に二つのことをするな Don't do two things *at a time*.

④ 【一度も(...ない)】 never. ▶一度も彼とテニスをしたことがない I've *never* [*まれ*に I haven't *ever*] played tennis with him before. (**!**(1) I never have played ... の語順は強意的. (2) Have you ever played ...? に対する応答では No, I never have [×I have never]. となる) ▶その老人は一度も(=一度たりとも)不平を言ったことはない The old man *never once* complained. (**!** once は never, not を強調する)

会話 「田舎にいたころよく釣りに行きましたか」「いや一度も」 "Did you often go fishing while you were in the country?" "Nót *\once*." (**!** Did you *once*...? に対して Nót ⌣*once*. の音調で発音すれば「一度どころではない」の意)

いちどう 一同 all (of us). (⇨みな) ●出席者一同 *all* those present. ●関係者一同 *all* concerned (*in* it). ▶我々一同はその知らせに喜んだ *All* of us were glad at the news./We were all glad to hear the news. ▶家族一同, お二人をお迎えしたいと願っております〈招待状〉My family join me in wishing to have both of you with us.

いちどう 一堂 ●一堂に会(かい)する meet together; assemble (*in* a hall).

いちどきに 一時に (⇨一度 ③)

いちどく 一読 图 ▶その本は一読の価値がある The book is worth *reading*./It is worth while *reading* [*to read*] the book.

── 一読する 動 read (a book). ▶一読しただけではその作品のよさはわかりません You will not be able to appreciate the masterpiece in *one reading*.

いちなん 一難 ●一難去ってまた一難 'One misfortune is generally followed closely by another.'/(ことわざ) Misfortunes never come singly. (**!**「悪いことは続けざまに起こる」の意)

いちに 一二 ●一二年 a year or two; one or two years. ●一二回 once or twice. ●「一二, 一二」と掛け声を掛ける call out, "*One-two, one-two*." ▶富士山は世界で一二を争う美しい姿をしている Mt. Fuji is one of the most beautiful mountains in the world. ▶彼女は日本で一二を争う名優である She ranks among just *the few greatest actors* in Japan.

***いちにち** 一日 ❶ 【24時間】 a [one] day. (**!** one は特に「1日」を強調する場合) ●1日半 *a day* and a half. (**!** one and a half days より普通) ●1日おきに every other [second] *day*; every two *days*. ●1日休みを取る take *a day* off. ●1日一善を行う do one good deed *every day*. ●1日いくらで働く work *by the day* [*by a day*]. ●日一日と day by day. ▶彼女は普通1日に8時間働く She usually works (for) eight hours *a day*. ●**/a** は per の意で「...につき」) ▶1日や2日でできることではない You can't do it in *a day* or two. ▶昨日は1日中病気の母の看病をしていた I spent *the whole day* [はとんど *most of the day*] looking after my sick mother yesterday./Yesterday I looked after my sick mother *all day* (*long*). ▶私は朝刊を読まないと1日のリズムが狂う My *whole day* is [*goes*] *awry* /əráɪ/ if I don't read the morning paper. ▶朝食は1日のエネルギーの源だ Breakfast is the source of energy for the [×a] *day*. ▶彼は1日たりとも彼女のことを思わない日はなかった Never *a day* went by when he didn't think of her [without his thinking of her]. (**!** not (even) *a day*, not a single day に対する口語的な言い方. 否定語が文頭にあっても倒置は起こらない) ▶私は1日も早く(=できるだけ早く)彼に会いたかった I wanted to see him *as soon as possible*.

❷ 【ある日】 one day. ▶秋の1日, 私たちは京都を訪ねた *One day* in the autumn we visited Kyoto.

❸ 【ついたち】 (⇨一日(ついたち))

いちにちせんしゅう 一日千秋 ▶一日千秋の思いでその日が来るのを待った I waited *impatiently* for the day to come.

いちにょ 一如 (不可分であること) inseparability. ▶物心一如 Matter and mind *are inseparably related*.

いちにん 一任 ── 一任する 動 ▶これは君に一任しよう(=いっさい任せよう) I'll *leave* this entirely *to* you. (⇨任せる)

いちにんしょう 一人称 〖文法〗the first person. ●一人称小説 a first-person novel.

いちにんまえ 一人前 ❶ 【1人分の食事】 ▶ご飯一人前 *one helping* [*serving, portion*] of rice. ●一人前1,000円 a thousand yen *a head* [*for one person*]. ▶フライドポテトの大盛り一人前お願いします〈レストランで〉A large *order* of French fries, please. (**!** *order* は「注文料理の一品」)/(日常的に

いちねん

は) French fries, large, please.
❷ 〖成人〗 an adult, 《話》 a grown-up (！子供が[に対して]用いる). ●一人前の (成人した) grown-up 《men [women]》; (立派な) full-fledged 《米》fully-fledged 《英》 (carpenters). ●一人前になる (成人する) grow up; (成人に達する) come of age (！《米》では21歳(一部の州では18歳)、《英》では18歳); (独立する) become independent. ●年齢にふさわしい行動をしろ。君はもう一人前なんだから Act your age. You're an *adult* now. ●彼は年だけは一人前だがすることは子供だ He is a *man* in years, but a child in his actions. ●君を一人前の男にしてやる I'll make a *man* of you!

*いちねん 一年 ❶ 〖年数〗a [one] year. (！one は特に「1年」を強調する) ●1年おきに every other [second] *year*; every two *years*. ●1年半 a *year* and a half. (！(1) one and a half years より普通. (2) これぐらいまでの時の長さは月数で表すことも多い: 1年半して彼は死んだ After *eighteen months* he died.) ●1年は365日あるA *year* has 365 days. ●当地では1年中泳げるWe can swim here *all (the) year around [throughout the year]*. ●だれでも1年1年歳をとる Everyone gets older *year by year*.
❷ 〖学年〗(⇨一年生) ●一年坊主 (⇨一年生)

いちねん 一念 〖願望〗a great [an ardent, a strong] desire, a very fervent [a strong] wish; 〖熱意〗zeal; 〖決意〗(firm [great]) determination, (firm) resolution. ●彼に会いたい一念で (⇨一心) ●一念発起する make a firm resolution 《*to* do》.

いちねんせい 一年生 ❶ 〖生徒・学生〗a first-year student [pupil] (《米》では小学生、《英》では中学生以下は pupil の方が普通); (《米》(大学・高校の) a freshperson, a freshman 《機 -men》, (短大の) a junior, (小[中;高]の) a first [a seventh; a tenth] grader; (新入生) a newcomer. (⇨一年生, 学年) ●高校1年生 a first-year student of 〖*in*《英》〗high school (！固有名詞の校名の前では米英ともに at: at Kobe High School); 《米》a high school freshperson [freshman].
❷ 〖植物〗●一年生の annual. ●一年生植物 an annual [a yearly] plant.

いちねんそう 一年草 (一年生植物) an annual [a yearly] plant.

いちば 市場 a market. ●魚市場 a fish *market*. ●卸売市場 a wholesale *market*. ●市場に行く go to (the) *market* (！買い物に行く場合 《英》では通例無冠詞); (買い物に行く)《米》go marketing.

いちはつ 〖一八, 鳶尾〗〖植物〗an iris.

いちはやく 逸早く ●いち早く(=素早く)現場に駆けつける hurry to the scene *quickly* [(ただちに) *at once*]; (真っ先に) be *the first* to rush to the scene.

‡**いちばん 一番** ❶ 〖番号〗(番号・順位・実力などが1位) number one, No. 1 (！無冠詞・単数形で用いる). ●君が一番だ You are *No. 1*.
❷ 〖順位〗最初の[に] first; (一番の位置) first place; (首席で) at the top [head] of ….
①【一番(の)〜】●彼は現場に一番乗りをした He was *the first* (person) to arrive [that arrived] at the spot. ●中田氏は知事候補の一番手だ Mr. Nakata is the *most prospective* candidate for governor.
②【一番に】●彼女はこの前の試験で一番になった She took 〖《英》got a〗 *first place* in the last exam. / (最高得点を取った) She had the best score on the last exam. ●彼は毎朝一番にラジオのニュースを聞く He listens to the news on the radio *first thing* in the morning.
③【一番】●彼女のクラスで一番だ He is *at the top* [*head*] *of* the class. / He stands [ranks] *first* in the class. ●彼女は100メートル競走で一番だった She took *first place* in the 100-meter dash. / She finished [came in] *first* in the 100-meter dash. / (優勝した) She won the 100-meter dash.
❸ 〖最も〗(！通例形容詞・副詞の最上級を用いて表す) ●いちばん右の家 the *first* house on the [your] right; the *rightmost* house. ●いちばん北の港 the port *farthest* to the north; the *northernmost* port. ●洞穴のいちばん奥に *farthest* inside a cave; in the *innermost* [*inmost*] depth of a cave. ▶健康がいちばん(大切)だ Health is *the most important thing [is everything]*. / (やや書) *Nothing is more important than* health. ▶休養と気分転換をお望みならば海が一番(いい) If you want a rest and a change, then the sea is (the) best. (！叙述用法では the を省略する方が普通) ●彼はクラスでいちばんよく勉強する He is *the most* hard-working [*works* (*the*) *hardest*] of all the students in the class. (！後の方は最後の例のように比較級で表す方が普通) / He is (*the*) *most* hard-working [*works* (*the*) *hardest*] in the class. / He is *the most* hard-working student in the class. / He is *more* hard-working [*works harder*] *than* any other student in the class. ●彼は彼女がそれまでに出会った中でいちばん厳しい先生だった He was the *strictest* teacher (that) she had ever met. ▶春がいちばん好きだ I like spring (*the*) *best* [*most*]. ▶京都は秋がいちばん美しい Kyoto is (×the) *most beautiful in the fall.* (！一部の人や物の中で比べる場合通例 the をつけない cf. Kyoto is *the most beautiful in Japan.*) ▶いろいろある中でこの辞書がいちばん安かった This dictionary was *the cheapest* [*least expensive*] *of all.* (！後の方が婉曲的な言い方で、そこにあった辞書は話し手の判断ではすべて値段が高かったことを暗示. most は *the most inexpensive* のように否定の接頭辞を持つ語と用いることは避けられる)
❹ 〖最善〗 ▶こういう問題は専門家に任せるのがいちばんだ Problems of this kind are *best* left to the experts. (！この best は 圃 well (適切に)の最上級) ▶彼は医者にみてもらうのがいちばんだ He *should [had better,* 《やや古》*had best] see* a doctor. (！ should より had better の方が緊迫感を暗示)／*It is best* for him to see [that he (《主に英》*should*) see, that he sees] a doctor.
❺ 〖一勝負〗●碁を一番打つ have a *game of* go. ●相撲を一番取る wrestle one *bout of* sumo.

いちひめにたろう 一姫二太郎 'first a girl, then a boy'; (説明的に) It's ideal to have a daughter first and then a son.

いちびょうそくさい 一病息災 (説明的に) People with a slight illness are more careful about their health and often live longer (than those with none).

***いちぶ 一部** ❶ 〖一部分〗(a) part 《*of*》(！a は省略することが多い); (全部ではなく) some /sʌm/; (区切られた一部) a section. (⇨一部分) ●第一部 Part I [One]. ●彼の財産の一部 (a) part [a portion] of his property. ●彼はその仕事のほんの一部しかしなかった He did only (《話》*the only*) *part of* the work. ●一部のお客様はお帰りになりました *Part of* the guests [*Some* (*of* the) guests] have gone home. (！複数名詞のときは some を用いるのが普通) ●彼のことをよく思っていない人も一部にはいる *Some* people have a bad opinion of him. ▶鯨を捕って食べることは日本文化の不可分の一部だ Hunting

and eating whales is *part and parcel* of Japanese culture. (❗*part and parcel* は part の強調形)
❷ [一冊] (書物・新聞などの) a copy. ▶その本を一部ください Give me *a copy* of the book.
── 一部(は) 副 [部分的に] partially; [一部は] partly, 《やや書》in part. (⇨部分的に) ▶この法案は一部修正しなければならない This bill should be *partially* amended./We should make a *partial* amendment of this bill. ▶この事故の責任の一部は彼にある He is *partly* responsible for this accident./This accident is *in part* due to his fault [×him]. (❗due to の後には「人」でなくその原因となるものがくる)

いちぶしじゅう 一部始終 ▶その一部始終を知っている know *everything* about it; know *all the details*. ▶このことの一部始終聞かせてくれ Tell me *all* about it./Tell me *the whole story*.

いちふじにたかさんなすび 一富士二鷹三茄子 (説明的に)(富士山か鷹かナスを初夢に見ると縁起がいい) It is considered a good omen to see *Mt. Fuji*, *a hawk* or *an eggplant* in the first dream of the New Year.

いちぶぶん 一部分 (a) part (*of*). (⇨部分)

いちべつ 一瞥 a glance. ▶一瞥して at a *glance*. ▶男女の後ろ姿に一瞥をくれた The man *glanced* [*cast a glance*] after her.

いちぼう 一望 ▶この家から町を一望できる You can see [get] *a whole view* of the town from this house./This house *enjoys* [《書》*commands*] *a whole view* of the city. (⇨見渡す)

*いちまい 一枚 ❶ [板状の] (紙・板・ガラスなど) a piece [a sheet] (*of* paper) (❗ piece は形や大きさが一定でないことを暗示することがある); (パン・チーズ・肉など) a slice (*of* toast); (ノートなどの) a leaf. ▶皿 1 枚 a [one] dish. ▶one は特に「1枚」を強調するので、可算名詞の場合は単に a, one を添える ▶(板)チョコレート 1 枚 a *bar* of chocolate. ▶ガム 1 枚 *a stick of* gum. ▶紙をもう 1 枚いただいてよろしいですか May I have another *piece* [*sheet*] of paper? ▶彼はノートを 1 枚ちぎった He tore *a leaf* from the notebook.
❷ [その他の表現] ▶君の計画に私も一枚加えてくれ *Count me in* on your plans. ▶新しい社長は前の社長より一枚上手だ《やや話》The new president is *a cut above* the last one.
●一枚噛む ▶その計画には彼が一枚かんでいる He is *involved in* the plan.

いちまいいわ 一枚岩 a monolith. ▶私たちの組合は一枚岩的団結(=強い団結)を誇っている We are proud of the *strong solidarity* of our union. (❗monolithic unity (一枚岩的団結)は完全に統制された団結を意味し、しばしば軽蔑的な含みを持つためここでは不適)

いちまいかんばん 一枚看板 (花形役者など) a star; (花形女性オペラ歌手) a prima donna; (団体などの中心人物) a leader, a leading figure.

いちまつ 一抹 ▶その結果に一抹の(=少しではあるが)不安がある feel *a little* uneasy about the results.

いちまつもよう 市松模様 图 a checked pattern; check. ▶市松模様の 形 checked.

いちみ 一味 (悪者の一団) a gang (❗一人の場合は a gangster); (私利などを得るための一団) a ring. ▶スパイの一味 a spy ring.

いちみゃく 一脈 ▶一脈通ずる(=何か共通する)ものがある have something in common 《*with*》; (類似する) have some analogy (*to*).

いちめい 一名 ❶ [一人] a [one] person. (⇨一人) ▶1名につき 500円 500 yen *a* [*per, each*] *person*.
❷ [別名] another name. (⇨別名) ▶ジョンソン、一名ジョーンズ Johnson, *alias* /éilias/ Jones.

いちめい 一命 one's life. ▶危うく一命を取り留める have a narrow escape from death; narrowly escape (×from) death. ▶彼の一命に関わる be fatal to him; cost him his *life*.

*いちめん 一面 ❶ [一方の面] one side [aspect]. ▶君は物事の一面しか見ていない You're just looking at *one side* [*aspect*] of the matter. ▶私は彼の性格の新しい一面を発見した I discovered *a new side* [*aspect*] of his character. ▶君の言うことに一面の真理がある(=一理ある)かもしれない (⇨一理)
❷ [そのあたり全体] ▶あたり一面を見渡す look *all around*. ▶一面のススキ a *sea* of pampas grass. ▶一面星空だった(=星が空一面に輝いていた) The stars were twinkling *all over* the sky./The sky was full of stars. ▶湖は一面水でおおわれていた The lake was covered *all over* with ice./(一面凍っていた) The lake was frozen [froze] *over*. ▶一面緑のじゅうたんだった There was a *carpet* of green grass. (❗carpet は「草花などの一面の広がり」)
❸ [新聞の第一面] the front page. ▶その殺人事件は新聞の第一面で報じられた That murder case was reported *on the front page* of the newspapers./The murder case made *front page news*.
── 一面的な 形 ▶一面的な議論 a *one-sided* argument. ▶彼は自分の一面的な考え方を他人に押しつける He forces his *one-sided* point of view on others.

いちもうさく 一毛作 a single crop (farming).

いちもうだじん 一網打尽 ▶ギャングどもを一網打尽にする(=いっせいに逮捕する) *round up* the gang.

いちもく 一目 ▶一目置く[置いている] take [raise] one's hat off (*to* him); tip one's hat (*to* him).

いちもくさん 一目散 ▶一目散に 副 ▶一目散に逃げる(必死に) run away *for dear* [*one's*] *life*; (全速力で) run away *at full speed*; (ただちに)《書》take to one's heels.

いちもくりょうぜん 一目瞭然 ▶それは一目瞭然だ(まったく明白だ) It is quite obvious [《as》 clear as day]./(一目でわかる) You can see it *at a glance*.

いちもつ 逸物 (優れた人) a superb [a first-class, a first-rate] person; (優れたもの) an excellent [a superb, a first-class, a first-rate] thing.

いちもにもなく 一も二もなく ▶彼は一も二もなく(=すぐに)その計画に賛成した He *readily* agreed to the plan. ▶彼は一も二もなく(=きっぱりと)我々の申し出を断わった He *flatly* refused our offer./He gave a *flat* refusal to our offer.

いちもん 一門 [一家・一族] a family; (氏族) a clan; [流派] a school; [宗教上の分派] a sect. ▶平家一門 the Heike *clan*.

いちもんいっとう 一問一答 ▶その本の巻末には一問一答の欄がある The book has *a Q and A section* at its end [back].
── 一問一答する 動 hold a Q and A session.

いちもんじ 一文字 ── 一文字に 副 in a straight line; in a beeline; staright. ▶彼は口を一文字に結んでいた He closed his lips *tight*(*ly*).

いちもんなし 一文無し penniless. (⇨文無し)

いちや 一夜 one [a (single)] night. (❗single は特に「一」を強調する) ▶一夜の宿をとる stay [put up] 《*at* a hotel》 *for the night*; stay *overnight* 《*at* a hotel》. ▶一夜にして in a (single) night; overnight. ▶不安な一夜を過ごす spend [pass] *an uneasy night*. ▶一夜を明かす sit [stay] up *all night*. ▶彼は一夜にして(=突然)作家として有名にな

いっさくじつ 一昨日 (⇨一昨日(ﾋｾﾞﾝ))
いっさくねん 一昨年 (⇨一昨年(ﾋｾﾞﾝ))
いっさくばん 一昨晩 the evening [night] before last; two nights ago.
いっさんかたんそ 一酸化炭素 [化学] carbon monoxide /mənάksaid/. ●一酸化炭素中毒にかかる be poisoned by carbon monoxide.
いっし 一矢 ●一矢を報いる (怒って言い返す) retort; (反撃・反論する) strike back 《at, against》.
いっし 一糸 ●一糸乱れず (順序) in perfect order; (隊形) in a straight line.
 ●一糸もまとわず completely [stark] naked /néikid/; without clothes on. (⇨裸)
いっし 一指 ▶私に一指(=一指一本)でも触れたら警察を呼ぶぞ If you lay a finger on me, I'll call the police.
いつしか ▶いつしか(=知らないうちに)夏休みも終わりに近づいた The summer vacation was nearly over before I was aware of it [I knew it].
いっしき 一式 [ひとそろい] a set 《of》; [用具, 衣装] an outfit; [家具] a suite /swi:t/ 《of》. (!set, outfit さらに complete で修飾されることもある) ●茶器一式 a tea set. ●釣り道具一式 a fishing outfit. ●花嫁衣装一式 an outfit for a bride; a bride's outfit.
 ●家具一式 a suite of furniture.
いっしそうでん 一子相伝 a secret art handed down from a father to one of his sons.
いっしつりえき 逸失利益 lost profits.
いっしゃせんり 一瀉千里 —一瀉千里に 副 rapidly; with alarming [great] rapidity; at high [top] speed.
いっしゅ 一首 ●一首詠む compose [write] a tanka [poem].
いっしゅ 一種 [種類] a kind; a sort; [種] a species (!単・複同形); [変種] a variety. ●一種のおもちゃ a kind of toy. (!おもちゃみたいなもの(で実はそうでないもの)、の意であることもある) ▶それはチョウの一種だ It is a kind [a species, a variety] of butterfly. (!ofのあとの名詞は単数形で無冠詞に注意) ▶このお盆は一種のプラスチックでできている This tray is made of a [some] sort of plastic. ▶この花は一種独特のかおりがある This flower has a peculiar sort of smell.
いっしゅう 一周 图 a circuit; a round; (競走路の) a lap. ●一周400メートルのトラック a (running) track 400 meters around. ▶彼女は最後の一周で3人抜いた She passed three runners on [in] the final lap. ▶彼は小さなヨットで単独無寄港世界一周を達成した He sailed his small yacht around the world, alone and non-stop.
— 一周する 動 go* (a)round.... (!(1)[米] では around が普通. (2) 表す意味によって go の代わりに walk, run*, travel (〔英〕 -ll-), fly*, drive*, sail などを用いる) ●グランドを走って一周する run around [run one circuit of] a playground. ●ゴルフのコースを一周する play a round of golf. ▶地球は1年で太陽を一周する The earth revolves [moves, goes] around the sun once a year.
いっしゅう 一蹴 —一蹴する 動 (軽く負かす) beat easily. ●プロポーズを一蹴する(=はねつける) turn down [reject] one's proposal.
*いっしゅうかん 一週間 (for) a [one] week. (!one は「一」を強調する) (⇨週) ●(今から)1週間で[以内に]完成する complete (it) in [within] a week.
 ●この1週間 [1週間] で [during] the last [past] week. (!× ... the last [past] one week としない) ●1週間ずっと all week (long). ●1週間休暇をとる take a vacation for a week; take a week's vacation. ●京都に1週間滞在する stay (for) a week in Kyoto. ▶お父さんは1週間出張しています My father is away on business for a week. ▶1週間のうちで私が最も忙しいのは土曜日だ Saturday is the day when I'm busiest [Saturday is the busiest day for me] of all the days in the [xa] week.
いっしゅうき 一周忌 the first anniversary of 《his》 death.
いっしゅうねん 一周年 ●結婚一周年記念日 (one's) first wedding anniversary; the first anniversary of 《one's》 wedding.
いっしゅつ 逸出 — 逸出する 動 [逃れ出る] get out 《of》 (⇨逃れる ❶, 逃げる ❶); [傑出する] stand out 《from, among》 (⇨傑出する).
いっしゅん 一瞬 a moment; an instant. (!後の方が緊急性瞬間的の); [話] a minute. ●一瞬のためらい a momentary [a moment's] hesitation. ●一瞬しんとなった There was a moment of [a moment's] silence. ▶彼は一瞬口がきけなかった He lost his tongue momentarily. ▶それは一瞬の出来事だった It happened in an instant. ▶一瞬あなたを他の人かと思った For a moment [an instant] I thought (that) you were somebody else.
*いっしょ 一緒 图 (同じ) the same. ▶この帽子は私のと一緒だ This hat is the same as mine./This is the same hat as mine. ▶彼はこじきと一緒だ(=同然だ) He is no [little] better than a beggar. (⇨同じ, 同然, 同然) ▶若い人と一緒だと楽しい I enjoy being with young people./Young people are good company to have around. (!company は単独では「ともに居る人たち」の意)
会話 「お一人でご旅行ですか」「いいえ、息子夫婦が一緒です」 "Are you traveling on your own?" "No. My son and his wife are with me."
— 一緒に 副 [ともに] together; (...とともに) (together [along] with ...; [いっせいに] all together; (声をそろえて) in chorus. (⇨一斉) ▶一緒に遊ぼうよ Let's play together./(仲よくして) Be my friend. ▶さあ、みんな一緒に歌いましょう Now, let's sing (all) together [in chorus, in unison]. ▶先生は生徒と一緒にあすまることになっている The teacher, together [along] with his pupils, is coming tomorrow. (!together [along] with ...は挿入的に用いられることが多い)/The teacher is coming with his pupils tomorrow. (!×The teacher with his pupils is .... は不可) ▶私とピザを一緒に食べない [部屋を一緒に使わない]？ Would you like to share the pizza [room] with me? (!一つのものを他人と分け合う場合には share を用いる)
会話 「一緒にコーヒーを飲みませんか［ゲームをしませんか］」「遠慮しておくわ. 急ぎの用があるの. お二人でどうぞ」 "Will you join us for a cup of coffee [in a game]?" "No, ⁄thank you. I have urgent business. You two go ahead." (!join は「人の仲間に入る」こと)
— 一緒にする 動 [ひとまとめにする] (結合する) join 《them》 (together); (集める) put* 《them》 together; (混ぜる) mix 《A with [and] B》; [同一視する] identify; (混同する) confuse. ●個人主義を利己主義と一緒にする identify [confuse] individualism with egoism. ▶私とこあなたと私の家を一緒にしたくらいの大きさだ His house is as large as your house and mine put together. (!put は過去分詞) ▶他の女の子と一緒にしないでちょうだい I'm not one of other girls.
— 一緒になる 動 [一つにまとまる] join; [結婚する] get* married (to). ▶二つの村が一緒になって新しい町

いっしょう が生まれた The two villages *joined to* form a new town. ●彼らは1年ほど付き合って一緒になった They *got married* after going together for a year or so.

*****いっしょう** 〚生涯〛one's [a] life (⇨ lives);〚存命期間〛one's [a] lifetime. ▶彼は一生独身で通した He remained single *all* [*throughout*] *his life*. (⚠×He didn't get married until he died. は不可) ▶その辞書を作るには一生かかるだろう It would take your (*whole*) *lifetime* to make the dictionary. ▶君たちそんなことをしたら一生(＝残りの生涯)悔やむことになるよ If you do so, you'll regret it *for the rest of* your *lives*.

① 【一生は】 ●彼の一生は不幸の連続だった His *life* was a series of misfortunes.

② 【一生の】 ●一生の友 a *lifelong* friend. ●一生の仕事 one's *life* [*lifetime*] career; (一生をかけた大仕事) one's lifework [*life's* work]. ▶一生のお願いです. パリに留学させてください Let me go to Paris for study. This is *the only favor I will ever ask of you*./For heaven's *sake, please* let me study in Paris.

③ 【一生に】 ●そんなことは一生に一度しか起こらない Something like that happens only once in a *lifetime*./(一生にまたとないチャンスだ) That's the chance of a *lifetime*.

④ 【一生を】 ●幸せな一生を送る lead [live] a happy *life*. ●その町で一生を過ごす spend all one's *life* [*the whole of* one's life, one's *whole life*, one's *entire lifetime*] in the town; live in the town *all* [*throughout*] one's *life*. (⇨生涯) ●教育に一生を捧げる give [devote] (*all*) one's *life* to education. ▶彼はかけ事で一生を棒に振った Gambles ruined his *life* 〚経歴〛 *career*]. ▶彼はその町で一生を終えた He *ended his life* in the town.

いっしょう 一将 ●一将成り(て)万骨(ばんこつ)枯る Tens of thousands die to make one hero.; One general's success is built on the sacrifice of tens of thousands of soldiers.

いっしょう 一笑 ●一笑に付す (笑い飛ばす) laugh … away [off]; (あざ笑う) laugh … to scorn.

いっしょうがい 一生涯 all one's life. (⇨一生, 生涯)

*****いっしょうけんめい** 一生懸命 very hard; 〚力一杯〛with all one's might; 〚熱心に〛eagerly; 〚必死で〛desperately; (命がけで) for one's [dear] life (⇨必死). ●一生懸命働く work *very hard*; work *as hard as possible* [one *can*]; work *with all* one's *might*. ▶彼の言うことに一生懸命耳を傾ける listen *eagerly* to what he says. ●一生懸命命に戦う fight *desperately*. ●一生懸命努力をする make *every possible* effort (*to do*). ▶すべてのことに一生懸命やりなさい(＝最善をつくせ) *Try* [*Do*] your *best* in everything. ▶何事も一生懸命になれば(＝専念すれば)なしとげられないものはない If you *put* your *mind to* it, you can accomplish anything. (⚠is anythingをさす) ▶少女たちはクリスマスキャロルを一生懸命歌った The girls sang Chirstmas carols *for all* they were *worth*. (⚠成句表現)

会話「残念ながら彼は落第したよ」「当たり前でしょ. 一生懸命勉強しなかったんだもの」 "He's failed, I'm afraid." "I'm not a bit surprised. He didn't work *hard* enough."

いっしょく 一色 ●白一色に塗る(＝一面白に塗る) paint (it) *white all over* [*all over* in white]. ▶スタンドは白一色でうまっていた The stands *are crowded to capacity with* white-shirted fans. ▶町は金メダリスト歓迎の一色に包まれていた The town *was filled*

with a festive mood to welcome the gold medalist. ▶ …の人たちで結成された組織は必ず間違いを犯す An organization with [made up of] *like-minded* members is bound to make mistakes.

いっしょくそくはつ 一触即発 ●一触即発の(＝爆発寸前の)状態だ The situation is *very explosive* [*volatile*]. ▶現在両国間は一触即発の関係にある The relationship between the two countries is *touch-and-go* at this point.

いっしょくた 一緒くた (⇨ごちゃ混ぜ)

いっしん 一心 図 ●彼に会いたい一心で from a *sheer desire* to see him. ●マイクは一心不乱に読書していて, あたりが暗くなっていることにも気づかなかった Mike was *totally absorbed in* reading and didn't notice it had become too dark for it.

── 一心に 副 (心から) wholeheartedly; (真剣に) earnestly; (熱烈に) fervently; (敬虔(けいけん)に) (やや書) devoutly. ●一心に祈りをささげる pray *earnestly* [*fervently, devoutly*]; offer an *earnest* [a *fervent*, a *devout*] prayer. ▶私はその仕事に一心に取り組んだ(＝専念した) I *concentrated on* the work.

●一心同体 togetherness; one flesh. ▶我々は一心同体だ We are *one flesh*.

いっしん 一身 ●仕事に一身を捧げる *devote oneself to* one's work; (熱心に) *be intent on* one's work. ●…の責任を一身に引き受ける take the responsibility for … *upon oneself*. ●一身上の理由で辞職する resign for *personal* reasons.

いっしん 一新 ──一新する 動 ●生活を一新する turn over a new leaf; begin [start] a new life. ●気分が一新する(＝まったくさわやかになる) be [feel] quite refreshed.

いっしん 一審 ▶彼は一審で無罪を宣告された He was declared not guilty *in the first trial*.

いっしんいったい 一進一退 ●一進一退の試合 a seesaw game. ▶彼の病状は一進一退だ His condition is uncertain: it is the repetition of getting better or worse. ▶我が国の経済は一進一退だ The economy of our country is *taking one step back for each step forward*.

いっしんきょう 一神教 mónotheism.
●一神教信者 a monotheist.

いっすい 一睡 ●一睡もしないで夜を明かす spend a *sleepless* night. ▶昨夜は一睡もしなかった I *had no sleep* [*didn't sleep at all*] last night./I *didn't get a wink of sleep* [*sleep a wink*] last night. (⚠ a winkも日本語の「一睡」と同様に否定文で用いる)

いっする 逸する miss. (⇨逃がす) ●好機を逸する miss [*失う*] *lose*] a chance. ●完全試合を逸する miss [*loss*] a perfect game. ●入賞を逸する *miss winning* a prize. ▶彼の行動はまったく常軌を逸している(＝異常だ) His conduct *is very eccentric* [*abnormal*].

いっすん 一寸 ▶一寸先も見えなかった We couldn't see *an inch* ahead (of us).
●一寸先は闇(やみ) (明日はどうなるかはだれにも分からない) Who knows what tomorrow will bring?
●一寸の光陰(こういん)軽んずべからず 《ことわざ》 Nothing is more precious than time.
●一寸の虫にも五分の魂 《ことわざ》 Even a worm will turn. (⚠「(踏めば)向き直って抵抗する」の意)
●一寸法師 (小人) a dwarf (⇨〜s); (おとぎ話の) Inch-high *samurai*; (英国の話の) Tom Thumb.

*****いっせい** 一斉 〚そろって〛all together [×altogether]; (声をそろえて) in chorus; 〚同時に〛(all) at once, at the same time. ●一斉射撃をする fire a volley.

▶一斉にしゃべるな Don't speak *at once* [*at the same time*, *in chorus*, *in unison*]. ●一斉に拍手が起こった There was a *round* [*a burst*] of applause.
●一斉検挙 a wholesale arrest; 《話》a roundup.

いっせい 一世 ❶[日系米人] an Issei (複 ～(s)), a first-generation Japanese American (🔁「二世」の意でも用いられる (⇨二世, 三世)).
❷[一代目] ●エリザベス一世 Elizabeth Ⅰ. (🔁 the First と読む)
●一世を風靡(ふうび)する ●彼は一世を風靡した歌手だった He was a *dominant* singer in his time.

いっせいいちだい 一世一代 ●一世一代の大ばくちを打つ take the chance of *one's life*.

いっせき 一石 ●一石を投じる (問題を提起する) bring up a problem; (論議を引き起こす) stir up [cause] a controversy (*in* the present situation).
●一石二鳥 ●それは一石二鳥だ That will kill two birds with *one stone*.

いっせき 一席 ●一席（=第一位）となる win *first place* [*prize*] (*in* the race).
●一席ぶつ make [give, deliver] a speech.
●一席設ける give [have, hold, 《話》throw] a party.

いっせつ 一説 ●一説によれば... It is said [reported] that....

いっせん 一戦 ［戦い］a battle; a fight; ［勝負］a game; (ボクシングなどの) a bout /báut/. ●一戦を交える fight [engage in] *a battle*; have *a game* [*a bout*].

いっせん 一線 ●一線級の投手陣 *front-line* pitching staff. ●第一線 (⇨第一線)
●一線を画(かく)す draw the [a (clear)] line (*between*). (⇨けじめ)

いっそ (⇨むしろ ❶) ▶降参するぐらいならいっそ死んだ方がましだ I *would rather* [*sooner*] die *than* give in./ I would die before giving in [I give in].

いっそう 一双 ●一双の手袋 *a pair of* gloves.

いっそう 一掃 名 eradication; a sweep; a cleanup.
●春物一掃セール《米》a *close-out* (sale) [a clearance sale] of spring wear;《広告》*selling out* of spring wear! ●走者一掃の二塁打を打つ《野球》hit a bases-*clearing* double.
——一掃する 動［根絶する］root ... out,《書》eradicate; ［破壊する, 殺す］wipe ... out; ［掃くように］sweep*... out; ［取り除いてきれいにする］clear ... (away); ［売りつくす］sell* out (*of*). ●社会の弊害を一掃する *sweep away* [*root out*, *eradicate*] social evils; (浄化する) clean up society. ●敵を一掃する *wipe out* an enemy. ●走者を一掃する《野球》*clear* [*clean*] the bases.

いっそう 一層 ［なお一層］much*, far*, even, still (🔁 比較級を強める。比較変化については (⇨もっと 解説)); ［今までにないくらい一層］more than ever; ［それだけますます］all the more. ●いっそう熱心に働く work *much* [*far*, *still*, *even*] *harder*; work *harder than ever*. ●彼女は美しいが姉の方がいっそう美しい She is beautiful, but her sister is *much* [*still*, *even*] *more* beautiful. ▶彼女は息子の体が弱かったのでいっそう彼を甘やかした She spoiled her son *all the more for* his physical weakness [*because* he was physically weak].

いっそくとび 一足飛び ●一足飛びに at a single bound [leap]; in one leap [jump].

いつぞや sometime ago; the other day. (⇨いつか ❷)

*いったい 一体 副 ［いったいぜんたい］《一般疑問文で》at all, ever; ［疑問詞を強めて］《話》on earth, in the world, ever (🔁 the hell や, 時に the devil なども用いられるが, 下品で乱暴な感じを伴う。ever は主に女性語). ▶いったいその人を知っているのかい Do you know the man *at all*? ▶いったいどこであんなドレスを買ったの Where *on earth* [*in the world*] did you buy that dress?/Where *ever* [*Wherever*] did you buy that dress? (🔁 (1) where ever と 2語につづる方が普通。(2) ever は you の直後の位置も可) ▶いったいそれはどういう意味なのか *Just* what does that mean? (🔁 just はいらだちを示す) ▶いったいそれは本当なのか *Can* it be true? ▶いったいに(=全般的に)私は和食が苦手だ *In general*, I'm not fond of [don't care for] Japanese dishes. (🔁「苦手である」を *don't* で表現する表現となり, I'm weak とすると「和食には弱い=和食が好きである」の意になるので注意)
会話 「いったい彼は手伝うことがあるのかい」「時にはね」 "Does he *ever* lend a hand?" "*Sometimes*."
会話 「行かれないだろうな」「いったいどうして」 "I won't be able to go." "Why not?/《話》Why not, *for heaven's sake*?" (🔁 ×Whyever はつうらない. for heaven's sake はいらだちの気持ちを示す)
——一体 名 ［同体］one body, unity. ●一体となって in a body; united. ▶我々は自然と一体となっている《米英人的発想》Nature is *part of* us./《日本人的発想》We are *part of* nature. (🔁 発想の違いに注意)
●一体感 a sense of unity [oneness].

いったい 一帯 ●このあたり一帯（の地域）一帯で in the *whole* neighborhood [area]. (⇨付近, 全体) ●近畿地方一帯に *all over* the Kinki district. ▶一万年前はこの地域一帯は海の底だった This *whole* region was under water ten thousands years ago.

いったいいち 一対一 one-to-one, one-on-one.
いったいか 一体化 名 unification; (和合) unity; (統合) integration.
——一体化する 動 unify; integrate.

いったいぜんたい 一体全体 ●一体全体君は何を言っているんだ What *on earth* [*the hell*] are you talking about? (⇨一体 副)

いつだつ 逸脱 名 (a) deviation. ●諸規則からの逸脱 *deviation*(*s*) *from* the rules.
——逸脱する 動 deviate (*from*).

いったん 一旦 (一度) once; (一時は) for a time; (一時的に) temporarily; (当分の間) for the time being. ●踏切りでいったん停止する stop at a (railroad) crossing. (🔁「いったん」は文脈で表される) ●いったんコツを覚えたらその仕事は決して難しくありません *Once* you get the knack of [for] (doing) the work, it isn't difficult at all. (🔁 once の接続詞用法) ●いったんはたばこをやめた I quit smoking *for a time*.

いったん 一端 (片端) one end; (一部) some, to some extent. ●ロープの一端 *one end* of a rope. ●感想の一端を述べる give *some* of one's impression (*of*).

*いっち 一致 名 ［合致, 同意］agreement; ［適合］《書》accord; ［意見の一致］(a) consensus; ［符合］《書》coincidence; ［対応］correspondence; ［調和］harmony.
①【～(の)一致】 ●言行一致 the *correspondence* of one's words *with* one's actions. (⇨言行) ●意見の一致をみる reach a *consensus* (*on*); (同意に達する) reach [arrive at, come to] an *agreement* (*about*, *on*). ●偶然の一致なら What a *coincidence*! (🔁 この coincidence は「(時間・場所などの) 偶然の一致」の意)
②【一致〜】 ●一致団結して努力する make a

united [a concerted] effort 《to do》. ● 一致点(=共通点)を見いだす find common ground. ▶私たちは彼らと一致協力してその計画を遂行した We cooperated with them in carrying out the plan./We carried out the plan in cooperation with them.
—— **一致する** 動 agree 《with》; 《やや書》accord 《with》; coincide 《with》; correspond 《with》; harmonize 《with》; [一致している] be in agreement [accord, harmony, line] 《with》.

> 使い分け agree 意見や事柄などに食い違いがなく合致していること.
> accord 性質・精神などが完全に適合していること.
> coincide 意見・利益などが完全に一致すること. 偶然の一致を暗示することもある.
> correspond 二つの事柄の相違や類似にかかわらず、お互いがうまく対応して調和していること.
> harmonize はっきりした相違があるにもかかわらず二つの事柄がうまく調和がとれていること.

▶あなたの話は彼の話と一致していない Your story doesn't agree [accord, coincide, correspond] with what he says. ▶ただちに出発することで意見が一致した We agreed to start [on starting] at once. (! agree on を用いるときは主語は通例複数形)/We agreed that we should start at once. ▶我々の利害は一致する Our interests coincide. ▶君は考えを現実と一致させた方がいい You had better make your ideas correspond with reality. ▶彼とあらゆる点で意見が一致している I am in agreement [accord] with him on all points. ▶私たちは一致した(=同意された)政策に従って行動しないといけない We must act according to the agreed-on policy.

いっちゃく 一着 ❶[競走などで] the first (to come). (⇨一等, 一位) ●一着になる come in first; take first place.
❷[衣類の] a suit 《of clothes》.

いっちゅうや 一昼夜 the whole day and night, all day and all night. (! 始まりが夜から night を先に持ってくる) ●まる一昼夜眠る sleep the whole day and night; sleep around the clock.

いっちょう 一丁 ●豆腐一丁 a cake [a piece] of tofu [bean curd]. ▶さあ, 一丁(=ひとつ元気を出すか Let's get down to business, shall we?/(掛け声) Here we go! ▶一丁上がり(料理人の言葉) Ready to go.

いっちょう 一聴 ▶このレコードは一聴に値する This record is worth listening to.

いっちょういっせき 一朝一夕 ▶一朝一夕に(=短期間で)外国語を習得することはできない You cannot master a foreign language in a very short time.

いっちょういったん 一長一短 ▶その方法には一長一短(=長所と短所)がある That method has both good points and bad points [merits and demerits /di:mérits/]. (! 対照を示すためのアクセントの移動に注意)

いっちょうまえ 一丁前 (⇨一人前 ❷)

いっちょうら 一張羅 ●一張羅を着込んで (dressed in) one's (Sunday) best. (! best は単・複同形 (⇨晴れ着))

いっちょくせん 一直線 (⇨直線) ●ゴールへ向かって一直線に飛ぶ fly straight to the goal; fly to the goal in a straight line.

いつつ 五つ five. (⇨三つ) ●五つ子(1人) a quintuplet; (全員) quintuplets /kwíntʌplɪts/; (米話) quints; (英話) quins. ●五つ目の角 the fifth corner.

いっつい 一対 (同一のものの) a pair 《of》; (同種のものの) a couple 《of》. ●一対のオール a pair of oars. ●一対の花びん a couple of flower vases. ●ソックスを一対にする pair socks.

いつづける 居続ける stay on 《at a place; with him》.

いって 一手 ❶[自分だけですること] ●責任を一手に(=全部)引き受ける take full responsibility for it; (一身に) take responsibility for it upon oneself. ●一手販売人 a sole agent. ●一手販売権を得る(握っている) get [hold] the exclusive sales rights.
❷[何かをする方法] a way. ●(チェスなどの)うまい一手 a good move. ▶彼女をものにするにはその一手しかない That's the only way to win her heart.

いってい 一定 ●一定の 形 [固定した] fixed; [規則的な] regular; [一様の] uniform; [不変の] constant. ●一定の日に on a fixed [(既定の) a given, (ある一定の) a certain] day. ●一定の間隔で at regular [uniform] intervals. ●一定の収入 a regular [a fixed] income. ●一定のスピードで車を走らせる drive at a uniform [a constant] speed. ●温度を一定に保つ keep a constant temperature. ▶田中氏はそのことは一定限(=ある程度)の知識がある Mr. Tanaka has some knowledge of it./Mr. Tanaka knows about it to some extent.

いってき 一滴 a drop. ▶彼は酒を一滴も(=決して)飲まない He never drinks (alcohol)./He doesn't drink at all./He never touches a drop (of alcohol).

いってきます 行ってきます I'm leaving [going] now. (! あいさつとして特に決まった英語はない. ほかに ✓Bye. とか See you ✓later. (じゃあね)とか, I'll be back after 9 (o'clock). (9時過ぎに帰るよ)のように帰宅時間を言うことも多い)

いってつ 一徹 ●一徹な 形 ●一徹な(=生来頑固な)老人 a stubborn [(自説を曲げない) an obstinate] old man.

いってみれば 言ってみれば so to speak. (⇨言わば)

*いつでも the time; [常に] always, 《書》at all times; [始終] all the time; [どんなときでも] 《主に米》anytime, 《英》(at) any time; [...のときはいつ] whenever (+節). ▶午後ならいつでもお目にかかれます I can always see you in the afternoon. ●身分証明書はいつでも身につけていなさい Always carry your identification card with you. ▶(命令文の場合の文頭が可)/Carry your identification card with you at all times. ▶いつでも好きなときにお電話ください You can call me anytime [any time you like, whenever you like]. (! 接続詞用法では《米》でも any time と 2 語につづるのが普通. whenever より口語的) ▶いつでもよろしい ✓Any time will do. ▶いつでも出発できますよ(=準備ができている) I'm ready to leave. ▶どこでもいつでも勉強するようにしなさい (⇨どこでも[第 4 文例])

会話 「さて, いつ始めましょうか」「いつでもあなたのご都合のよい時に」 "Well, when shall we start?" "(At) any time that suíts you."

■ **DISCOURSE**

人がＥメールを使うのは, いつでも人に連絡できるからである. ...また, Ｅメールは電話で話すより安い People use e-mail because they can communicate with people anytime. ... Besides, e-mail is cheaper than the telephone. (! besides (その上)は追加するときに用いるディスコースマーカー. 後から付け足すようなニュアンスで用いられる)

いってらっしゃい 行ってらっしゃい Bye. (**!** あいさつとして特に決まった英語はない。ほかに See you (later). (じゃあ(また))などの別れのあいさつや Have a nice day [trip; party]!(楽しい1日[ご旅行; パーティー]を), 学校へ行く子供には Come straight home!(寄り道しないで帰ってらっしゃい), 旅立つ夫には Take care!(気をつけてね)など, さまざまな表現が用いられる)

いってん 一天 (空全体) the whole sky. ▶一天にわかにかき曇った All of a sudden *the whole sky* became overcast.

いってん 一点 (⇨点) ▶私には一点のやましいところもない I have a clear conscience. ▶彼の潔白については一点の疑惑もない There *isn't a shadow of* doubt [There's *no* doubt *at all*] that he is innocent. (**!** 前の方は凝った言い方)

● 一点豪華主義 the idea of having one extravagant feature in an event; the idea of possessing one expensive item.

いってん 一転 ―― 一転する 動 [回転する] (向きをぐるりと変える) turn around; (とんぼ返りをする) do a flipflap; [いっぺんに変わる] change completely (⇨一変). ▶その時以来形勢が一転した(=逆転した) The situation *has been reversed* since that time.

いってんばり 一点張り ●実用一点張りの(=もっぱら実用向きの)家具 a very utilitarian furniture; furniture *exclusively (designed) for* practical use. ▶彼はそのことは知らぬ存ぜぬの一点張りだった(=あくまで主張した) He *persisted in* saying that he did not know anything about it./He *insisted* that he had no knowledge of it.

いっと 一途 ▶破滅の一途をたどっている(=どんどん破滅に向かっている) be *steadily* going [on the way] to ruin. (**!** ruin は名詞)

*****いっとう 一等 图** [競技などの一等賞] (the) first prize; [順位が1位] first place; [乗り物などの一等] (the) first class. ▶一等で旅行する travel *first-class* [by *first class*]. (**!** 前の副詞用法の方が普通) ▶彼はそのレースで1等になった He got [won] (the) *first prize* in the race./He took *first place* in 《英》 got a *first place*] in the race./He *finished [came (in)] first* in the race./(勝利した) He *won* the race.

―― 一等(の) 形 (第一の) first; (一流の) first-class; (第一級の) first-rate.

● 一等機関士 a first engineer. ● 一等航海士 a first officer. ● 一等車 a first-class carriage. ● 一等乗客 first-class passenger. ● 一等寝台 a first-class berth. ● 一等星 a star of the first magnitude. ● 一等地 (場所) an excellent location; (土地) an excellent piece of land.

いっとう 一刀 ● 一刀両断 ▶一刀両断にする cut 《an enemy》 in two with a single stroke of a sword; (思い切った方策をとる) take *drastic measures*; (敏速果敢に解決する) cut the Gordian knot.

いっとう 一党 (党派) a party; (派閥) (しばしば軽蔑的に) a clique; (仲間) a group. ● 一党一派にかたよらない be not partial to specific political *party*; nonpartisan.

いっとう 一頭 ●一頭立ての one-horse.

● 一頭地を抜く tower 《above, over》; excel 《at, in》; be exceptionally good 《at》; be by far the best.

いっとき 一時 (⇨一時(いち), 一度 ③)

いっとくいっしつ 一得一失 (⇨一長一短, 一利)

いっと(は)なく before one knows it. (⇨いつの間にか)

いつなんどき 何時何時 (at) any moment [time].

▶いつなんどき交通事故にあうかしれない You may be involved in a car accident *at any moment* [*any time*]. ▶いつなんどきだれが起きるか分からなかった Avalanches could happen at *any time of the night or day*.

いつに ―に (⇨または, ひとえに)

いつにない ▶今日はこの時期としてはいつになくいい天気だ It's *unusually* nice weather today for this time of (the) year. (**!** 簡単には It's *unseasonably* nice weather today. でも表せる) ▶彼女は今日はいつになく(=特に)魅力的だ She is looking attractive, *particularly* today. (**!** この進行形は一時的状態を表す) いつになく(=今までになく)気分がよい I feel better *than ever*.

いつのまにか いつの間にか (あっという間に) before one knows it (**!** 速さを強調); (気づかないうちに) without one's noticing it. ▶いつの間にかパーティーは終わっていた The party was over *before we knew it [all too soon]*. (**!** 後の方は心残りがあることを暗示) ▶いつの間にか夜もふけた The night has far advanced *unnoticed [without our noticing it]*. ▶いつの間にか(=ふと気づくと)我々は敵に囲まれていた We *suddenly found* ourselves surrounded by the enemy.

いっぱ 一波 one wave. ▶一波, 万波を呼ぶように, 1人の少女の抗議の手紙が全国的な抗議運動を引き起こした Just as *one wave* creates tens of thousands of waves, so a girl's letter of protest triggered off a nationwide protest movement. ▶空爆の第一波は夜明けに始まった They launched the first *wave* of bombing at dawn.

いっぱ 一派 [党派] a party; [分派] a faction; [流派] a school; [分派] a group; [宗派] a sect; (sect より大きい宗派) a denomination.

*****いっぱい 一杯** ❶ [a] [分量] (お茶の茶わん1杯) a cup 《of》; (コップ[グラス] 1杯) a glass 《of》; (ボウル[ご飯の茶わん] 1杯) a bowl 《of》; (さじ1杯) a spoon(ful) 《of》. ●さじ1杯の砂糖 a spoon(ful) *of* sugar. ●2杯は two spoon(ful)s of sugar という) ●ご飯1杯 a bowl *of* rice. ●かご1杯の果物[リンゴ] 1杯 a cup *of* hot coffee; a hot cùp *of* cóffee. 会話「ビールをもう1杯いただけますか」「承知いたしました」 "Could I have *another glass of* beer?" "Certainly." 会話「今お茶を飲んでいる. あなたも1杯いかが」「ええ, いただくわ」 "We're just having some tea. Would you like *a cup*?" "Yes, please." (**!** a cup a cup of tea の略)

(b) [酒類などのひと飲み] a drink. ▶ワインを1杯飲む have [take] *a drink* of wine. ▶今晩一杯やろう Let's have *a drink* tonight./Would you like (to have) *a drink* tonight? (**!** 前の方は積極的な提案. 後の方は「よかったら...しませんか」という控え目な提案) ▶我々は一杯やりながら政治の話をした We talked about politics over *a drink*. (**!** over は「...しながら」の意)

❷ [充満] ① [～いっぱい] ▶新鮮な空気を胸いっぱい吸い込む draw in *a lungful of* fresh air. ▶食物を口いっぱい入れたままでしゃべるな Don't speak with your mouth *full* [×filled]. ▶腹いっぱい食べた I ate until I was *full (up)*./(書) I ate *my fill*./(満腹です) I'm *full (up)*. ▶リンゴの木には実がいっぱいなっている The apple trees are *heavy* with fruit [a lot of apples].

② [いっぱいの] (満ちた) full; (込み合った) crowded; (ぎっしり詰まった) packed. ●いっぱい(=満杯)のびん a *full* bottle. ●買い物客でいっぱいの店 a store *full of* [*crowded with*] shoppers.

③ [いっぱい(に)＋動] ●いっぱいにする (人・物がAをBで満たす) fill A (場所・人(の心)・物) with B (物・

いっぱい 人・事); (AにBを詰め込む) crowd A (場所) with B (人・物); (AにBをぎっしり詰め込む) pack A (容器・場所) with B (物・人). ▶そのびんに水をいっぱい入れる fill the bottle (up) with water. ▶牛乳がいっぱい入ったコップ a glass full of [filled with] milk. ▶コップ1杯の牛乳は a glass of milk, コップ1杯の量の牛乳は a glassful of milk) ▶衣類をかばんにいっぱい詰め込む pack one's bag with one's clothes; pack one's clothes into one's bag. ▶夕方の6時ともなるとバーはいっぱいになってきた The bar was filling up [getting full] at six o'clock in the evening.
❹《いっぱいである》 be full of ..., be filled with ...; (混雑している) be crowded with ...; (ぎっしり詰まっている) be packed with .... ▶この本は誤植がいっぱいだ This book is full of misprints./There are a lot of [a great number of] misprints in this book. (⇨❸) ▶駅は観光客でいっぱいだった The station was crowded [was packed, was filled] with tourists./There was a large [a lot of] crowd of tourists at the station. ▶そのことでは感謝の気持ちでいっぱいです I'm full of [I'm filled with] gratitude for that. ▶私は胸がいっぱいで彼にうまくお礼が言えなかった I was so choked up (that) I couldn't thank him properly. (【!】《話》ではしばしば that を省略する)

翻訳のこころ デュークが死んだ。わたしのデュークが死んでしまった。わたしは悲しみでいっぱいだった (江國香織『デューク』) Duke died. My dear Duke is dead. I was filled with saddness. (died は「死んだ（動作）」、is dead は「死んでいる（状態）」の意)

❸《たくさん》 a lot of .... (⇨たくさん) ▶髪の毛がいっぱいついているヘアブラシ a hairbrush thick with hairs. ▶宿題がいっぱいある I have a lot of [《話》heaps of] homework [✗homeworks] to do. ▶あなたに話したいことがいっぱいある I've got so much [a hundred things] to tell you.
❹《全部》 all. ▶力いっぱい押す push with all one's strength. ▶音量をいっぱいに上げる (=最大に) turn up the volume full. ▶野原いっぱいに(=一面に)花が咲いている Flowers are in bloom all over the field.
●一杯食わせる ▶私はその男に一杯食わされて(=だまされて)金を取られた I was cheated [was tricked] out of my money by the man.

いっぱい 一敗 ── 一敗する 動 lose one game.
●一敗地にまみれる suffer [meet] a crushing [a complete] defeat; be completely defeated [beaten].

─いっぱい (...の末まで) till the end of ...; (すべて) 丸. ▶今週いっぱい(=の間ずっと)忙しい I'll be busy all [throughout] this week./(今週の終わりまで) I'll be busy till the end of this week.

いっぱいいっぱい 一杯一杯 ▶この値段がいっぱいいっぱいです (商人が客に) This is our lowest possible price. ▶これがいっぱいいっぱいだ(=これ以上はできない) I can't do better than this.

いっぱいきげん 一杯機嫌 ── 一杯機嫌の老人 a tipsy old man. ●一杯機嫌になる get tipsy.

いっぱく 一泊 图 an overnight stay. ● 一泊1万円のホテル a 10,000-yen-a-night hotel. (⇨−泊) ▶そのホテルは一泊2食で15,000万円だった The hotel charges were [The hotel charged (me)] fifteen thousand yen a night, including two meals.
── 一泊する 動 ▶ ロンドン [YMCA] で一泊する stay overnight in London [at YMCA].
会話「ご宿泊でいらっしゃいますか」「ええ、そうです。一泊したいのですが」"Are you checking in, Sir [Madam]?" "Yes, I am. I need a room for one night."
●一泊客 an overnight guest. ●一泊旅行 an overnight trip.

いっぱし 一端 ── 一端の 形 《有能な, 一人前の》(有能な) competent; (一人前の)《米》full-fledged [《英》fully-fledged]. ●一端の(=腕のいい)大工 a skilled carpenter. ●一端の(=一人前の)俳優 a full-fledged actor. ●一端の大人のような口を利く talk like an adult.

いっぱつ 一発 ●鳥をめがけて一発撃つ fire a shot at the bird. ●一発で仕留める drop 《the animal》 with a [one, a single] shot. (【!】この順に「一発」であることが強調される) ●彼のあごに一発お見舞いする give him a blow to the chin; punch him on the chin. ●(試合で)一発勝負を決する play a single-game [a single-bout] match. (【!】bout はボクシングなど) ▶ピストルには(弾は)一発しか残っていなかった There was only one charge left in the gun.

いっぱつや 一発屋 ●《一度の勝負にすべてを賭ける人》(説明的に) a person who puts all one's eggs in one basket; 《一度だけ活躍して消え去る芸能人など》 a flash in the pan. ●彼は一発屋だ (野球で) He is a home-run hitter [threat].

＊いっぱん 一般 ●この庭は一般(=一般の人)に公開されている This garden is open (↔closed) to the (general) public. ●この雑誌は一般(=一般読者)向きだ This magazine is made [is edited] for general readers.
── 一般(の) 形 《世間一般の, 特大でなく一般的な》general; 《普遍的な》universal; 《普通の》ordinary; 《平均的な》average; 《普通によく見られる》common; 《大衆向けの》popular. ●一般の学生 average [ordinary] students.
── 一般的(な) 形 《一般(の)》●一般的真理 (a) universal truth. ●この習慣はこの地方では一般的だ This custom is common in this district.
── 一般(的)に 副 generally, in general; 《普通に》commonly; 《普遍的に》universally. ●一般的に言うと generally speaking. ●その計画は広く一般に受け入れられた The plan was generally [widely] accepted. ▶当時, 地球は平らだと一般に信じられていた In those days it was generally believed that the earth was flat. ●一般にこの地方では雪が多い Generally (speaking) [In general], we have a lot of snow in this district.
●一般教育 a general (↔a special) education; (大学の) a liberal education. ●一般教養 general culture. ●一般職 《公務員の》regular civil service; 《企業の》(事務職) clerical work; (総合職に対する) the general track. ●一般大衆 the (general) public; the public (at large) (【!】以上二つは単・複両扱い); people in general; ordinary people. ●一般投票 (a) popular vote. ●一般論 a generalization.

いっぴき 一匹 ── 犬1匹 a dog.
●一匹狼 a lone wolf (複 wolves),《話》 a loner; (批判を気にせず独自の行動をする人) a maverick.

いっぴつ 一筆 ●一筆したためる(= 短い手紙を書く) write 《him》 a note; 《話》 drop 《him》 a line. ▶どうしているかと思って一筆にします Just a note to see how you're doing. ●一筆啓上 I am writing this note [letter] to tell you that ....

いっぴん 逸品 《珍品》●《すぐれた品》an excellent article; 《珠玉》 a gem; 《傑作》 a masterpiece.

いっぴんりょうり 一品料理 (お好み料理) an à la carte

いっぷいっぷ(せい) /à: la: ká:rt/ dish. (❗定食は a table d'hôte /tá:bl dóut/)

いっぷいっぷ(せい) 一夫一婦(制) monogamy. ● 一夫一婦(制)主義者 a monogamist.

いっぷうかわった 一風変わった strange, odd; peculiar (❗「独特の」の意を含む). ● 一風変わった味 a *strange* [*a peculiar*] taste. ▶彼には一風変わったところがある There is something *strange* about him.

いっぷく 一服 ❶ 【休憩】(a) rest; a break. (⇨休憩)
❷ 【たばこの】a smoke, a puff. ● 一服吸う have *a smoke*; take *a puff*.
❸ 【薬の】a dose; 【抹茶の】a cup. ● 薬を一服のむ take *a dose* of medicine. ● 一服盛る poison 《him》. ▶〈茶席などで〉もう一服いかがですか Would you like another *cup*? (❗これに対して I've had enough, thank you. (もう十分いただきました) などと返答する)
── 一服する 動 ● 仕事を一服する take [have] *a break* from (one's) work.
● 一服の清涼剤 小川氏の歌は私にとって一服の清涼剤になった I *felt refreshed* by the way Mr. Ogawa sang.

いっぷく 一幅 ● 一幅の掛け軸 a hanging scroll. ▶山頂からの眺めは一幅の絵のようだった The view from the top of the hill looked just like *a picture scroll*.

いっぷす 鋳潰す melt 《coins》 down.

いっぷたさい(せい) 一夫多妻(制) 图 polygamy (↔polyandry). ── 一夫多妻(制)の 形 polygamous.

いっぺん 一片 ❶ 【断片, 小片】a piece 《of》. ● 一片の肉 *a piece of* meat. ● 一片の花びら a petal.
❷ 【ほんの少し】● 一片の良心も持ち合わせていない do not have *a trace* of conscience; have *no* conscience *at all*.

いっぺん 一変 ── 一変する 動 ▶この道路ができて私たちの生活が一変した Our life *has changed completely* [*greatly*,《話》*a lot, dramatically*] since this road was built. (❗There have been *complete* [*great, a lot of, dramatic*] *changes* in our life since…. ともいえる)/(この道路が私たちの生活を一変させた) This road *brought about a lot of changes* in our life.

いっぺん 一遍 图 ❶ 【ひととおり】(⇨通り一遍)
❷ 【一度】(⇨一度) ❸ 【純粋にそれだけの】● 正直いっぺんの extremely honest; honesty itself.
── 一遍に 副 【たちまち】at once (⇨忽ち); 【同時に】at the same time (⇨同時に).

いっぺんとう 一辺倒 ● あの人はアメリカ一辺倒だ〈徹底的な支持者だ〉He is an *out-and-out supporter* of America./〈心底からアメリカびいきだ〉He is *pro*-American *through and through*./〈もっぱら日本酒だけを飲む〉He drinks *only* [*nothing but*] *sake*.

いっぽ 一歩 ❶ 【歩み】a [one] step. ● 一歩ごとに at every *step*. ● 一歩前に出る〈後ろにさがる〉take *a step* forward [*back(ward)*]. ● 研究をさらに一歩進めるなら *a step* further in one's study. ● 第一歩 (⇨第一歩) ▶疲れてもう一歩も歩けない I am so tired (that) I can't take another *step* [can't move a *step* further, (もうこれ以上歩けない) can't walk any further]. ● 一歩一歩知識を身につけることが必要だ It's necessary to get knowledge *step by step*.
❷ 【ほんの少し】▶この会社は倒産一歩手前だ(=今にも倒産しそうだ) This company is *on the verge of* bankruptcy [*is about to go bankrupt*]. ● on the verge of は通例好ましくないときに用いる) ▶彼はその点については一歩も譲らなかった He did*n't budge an inch* [*never budged*] on that point. (❗budge は通例否定文で用いる)

いっぽう 一方 图 ❶ 【片方】(初めの一つ) one; (残りの一つ) the other; (どちらか一つ) either. ● 通りのもう一方側に on *the other* side of the street. ● 一方[もう一方]の言い分を聞く let *one* [*the other*] party have his say. ▶ここに 2 冊の本がある. 一方は辞書でもう一方は小説である Here are two books. *One* is a dictionary, and *the other* is a novel. ● 二つの道のどちらか一方が駅に通じている *Either* of the two roads leads to the station. (❗either は単数扱い)
[会話]「これいただいてもいいですか」「どうしてもというのならいいよ. でももう一方の方がいいんだけどね」"Can I take this one?" "You can if you insist. But *the other one's* better."

① 【〈一方では〉…もう一方では〉】 on the one hand ... on the other hand (❗二つの対立する見方を示す. 会話では一方を省略することが多い) ▶彼は一方では私にへつらい, もう一方では陰口を言っている *On the one hand* he flatters me [He flatters me *on the one hand*], and *on the other* (*hand*) he talks behind my back. (❗(1) on the one hand の位置は会話では文末の方が普通. (2) on the other hand の hand は on the one hand が前にある場合には省略可)

② 【…である一方で】▶飢えている人がいる一方で, 食物をむだにしている人もいる Some people are starving, (but) *on the other hand* others [but others, *on the other hand*,] are wasting food. (❗後の位置の方が主語の対照が明示れ好まれる)/*While* some people are starving, others are wasting food./Some people are starving, *while* [*but*] others are wasting food. (❗while 節を用いるのは書き言葉. while 節が主節の後にくる場合は比較対照の意味が薄れ弱い逆説を示す. but は対立関係を強調する) ▶彼は英語を教える一方で研究もしている *Besides* [*While*] teaching English, he studies [×is studying] it. (❗besides は「その上, さらに」という意)

❷ 【…の傾向が著しい】▶人口は増える一方だ(=着実に増えている) The population is *steadily* increasing. ▶天気は悪くなる一方だ The weather is getting *worse and worse*. (❗比較級+比較級の形で「ますます…」の意)
── 一方的な 形 ● 一方的な試合 a *one-sided* [×a oneside] game. ● 一方的な決定 a *unilateral* decision.
── 一方的に 副 ● 一方的に勝つ win a *runaway* victory. ● 一方的に話を聞かされる人 (うるさい車内放送を聞かされている人など) a *captive* audience.

いっぽう 一報 图 ▶彼が死んだという第一報 the *first report* [*news*] of his death.
── 一報する 動 ▶ご到着の時刻を電話でご一報ください Please *let me know* by phone what time you will arrive./Please give me a (telephone) call [call me (up),《英》ring me (up)] and let me know when you'll arrive.

いっぽうつうこう 一方通行 one-way traffic. (❗両面通行は two-way traffic);《標識》One way.

いっぽうつうこうろ 一方通行路 a one-way street.

*__いっぽん__ 一本 ❶ 【長い物1個】a, an; one. (❗可算名詞の場合は a, an で表されるが, 特に「一」を強調する場合は one を用いる. 不可算名詞の場合は表すものによって a piece of, a bottle of などが用いられる) ● 鉛筆 1 本 *a pencil*. ● たばこ 1 本 *a cigarette*. ● チョーク 1 本 *a piece of chalk*. ● カラーフィルム 1 本 *a roll of*

いっぽんか

color film. ●牛乳を1本飲む drink *a bottle of milk*.
❷［柔道など で］ ●一本取る gain [score] an *ippon*. ●議論で一本取る win *a point* in an argument. ●こいつは一本参った（＝やられた）よ You win./別義（⇨勝ち）/You've gót [háve] me there.（【】この have got, have は〈話〉で「打ち負かす (defeat)」の意）
❸［統一］●候補者を一本に絞る put candidates into *one*.

いっぽんか 一本化 图 ［統一］unification；［集中化］centralization. ── 一本化する 動 unify; centralize.

いっぽんぎ 一本気 ●一本気な人 a *single-minded* person.

いっぽんだち 一本立ち ── 一本立ちする 動 become *independently*.

いっぽんちょうし 一本調子 ●一本調子の話し方 a *monótonous* way of speaking. ▶彼は作品は多いが，いかんせん一本調子だ He has written a lot of books, but they lack *diversity*.（【】diversity は「多様性」の意）

いっぽんづり 一本釣り ▶細川氏は一本釣りが得意だ Mr. Hosokawa is good at *hooking-and-line fishing*. ▶彼らは一本釣りにあって，その議案に賛成させられた They *were individually persuaded* to support the bill.

いっぽんやり 一本槍 ▶彼は若いころ勉強一本槍だった He *was entirely devoted to* his studies when young. ▶豊は京大一本槍だった Yutaka *tried hard* for Kyoto University *only*.

いつまで（⇨いつ❷）

いつまでも ［永久に］forever,《英》for ever；［終わりなく］endlessly；［無期限に］indefinitely. ●いつまでも続く説教 an *endless* sermon. ▶いつまでもあなたを愛していますI'll love you *forever*. ▶こんなことがいつまでも続くはずはない This can't last *forever* [*endlessly*]. ▶ご親切はいつまでも（＝決して）忘れません I shall *never* forget your kindness (*all my life* [*for the rest of my life*]).（【】この shall は will より強い意志を表す）

:いつも 動 ［常に］always,《書》at all times；［始終］all the time；［通常］usually; ordinarily; commonly；［習慣的に］《書》customarily；《書》habitually.

解説 (1) **always, usually** は主に文中に用いる．位置は原則として一般動詞の前，助動詞・be 動詞の後．
(2) 頻度を表す副詞のその度合いはおよそ次のとおり：always (100%)/usually (80%)/often, not always (60%)/sometimes (50%)/occasionally, not often (40%)/rarely, seldom (20%)/never (0%).

●いつもより早く起きる get up earlier than *usual*. ▶彼はいつも我々を支持してくれた He *always* supported us./He supported us *always*.（【】×Always he supported us. は不可．命令文以外では文頭に用いない）▶彼はいつも何か不平ばかり言っている He is *always* [*forever*] complaining about something./He is complaining about something *all the time*.（【】進行形とともに用いると通例非難の気持ちを表す）▶君はいつも早いね．本当に早いよ You're ＼*always* éarly. You *always* ＼are (early)./You're *always* early, indeed. ▶我々は健康にいつも注意を払わねばならない We must *always* [*always have to*] be careful of our health.（【】always の位置に注意）▶父は大体いつも7時に帰ってくる My father *usually* [*nearly always, almost always*] comes home at seven. ▶いつもながら［いつもどおり］彼は30分遅れてやって来た He arrived, as is *usual with him* [*as usual*], half an hour late. ▶彼はいつも時間どおりに来ない He *never* comes on time.（【】(1) always は否定語の前にはおけない．したがって ×He always does not come. は不可．(2) He does *not* always come on time. は「彼はいつも時間どおりではない」という部分否定になる）▶彼は来るときはいつも何かみやげ物を持ってきてくれる When he comes, he *always* brings me some present./（来るたびに）*Whenever* [*Every time, Each time*] he comes, he brings me some present.（【】後の二つの方が口語的）/《書》He *never* comes *without* bringing me some present.

会話 「でも日曜日はいつも暇がないんじゃないの」「いつもはそうなんだけど今週は暇なんだよ」"But you *usually* [*normally*] aren't free on Sundays." "＼*Usually* [＼*Normally*] I'm ＼not. But ＼this week, I ＼am." （【】他の副詞と対照させる場合は文頭にくることが多い）

── **いつもの** 形 usual；［定期的な，一定の］regular. ▶彼はいつもの通り遅れてきた He came late *as usual*.（【】×as usually とはいわない／As *always*, he came late. ▶じゃ，いつもの所で At the *usual* place, then. ▶彼はいつもの席についた He took his *regular* [*usual*] seat.

いつらく 逸楽 ●逸楽にふける abandon oneself to *pleasure*; give oneself up to *pleasure*; be addicted to the pursuit of *pleasure*.

いつわ 逸話 (著名な人・事件の) an ánecdòte；［話］a story.（⇨エピソード）

いつわり 偽り ［うそ］a lie,《書》(a) falsehood；［作り事］fiction.（⇨嘘(ｳｿ)）

*****いつわる** 偽る ［うそを言う］lie (*about*), tell＊ a lie；［装う］pretend,《書》feign；［だます］deceive. ●経歴を偽る *lie about* one's career. ●名前を偽る use a false name. ●事実を偽って伝える give a false report of the fact; *falsify* the fact. ●病気と偽る *pretend* sickness [*to be sick*]. ▶あの仕事をやめてほっとしたというのが偽らざる（＝正直な）気持ちです *Honestly, I* feel released after quitting the job.（【】To tell (you) the truth も可）

イディオム ［熟語，成句］an idiom. ●よく使われるイディオム a common idiom.

イデオロギー ［観念形態］an ideology /àidiáləd͡ʒi/. ●イデオロギーの相違 a difference in *ideology*.（【】ここでは無冠詞）●イデオロギーの対立 an *ideological* conflict.

いてざ 射手座 ［占星・天文］Sagittarius /sæd͡ʒitéəriəs/（【】the はつかない）; (人馬宮)【占星】the Archer.（⇨乙女座）●射手座(生まれ)の人 a Sagittarius, a Sagittarian. ▶後の方は形容詞としても用いる）

いでたち 出で立ち（⇨身支度，支度❷, 装い）

いてつく 凍て付く freeze＊.（⇨凍る）●凍てついた地面 the *frozen* ground. ▶昨夜は凍てついた It *froze hard* last night. ▶凍てつくように寒い It's *freezing* cold.

いてもたっても 居ても立っても ▶彼女が病院に運ばれたと聞いて居ても立ってもいられなかった I *couldn't sit still* after hearing she had been taken to the hospital.

いでゆ 出で湯 a hot spring.（⇨温泉）

いてん 移転 图 ［引っ越し］a move,《英書》(a) removal.（⇨引っ越し）

── **移転する** 動 move,《英書》remove (*to*).（⇨移る❶）▶本社が大阪から東京に移転した The head office *has moved* [*has been transferred*] from

Osaka *to* Tokyo. (❗後の方は「移転させられた」の意)
- 移転先 (新しい住所) one's new address. ● 移転通知 a notice of a change of address; a removal [×a move] notice. ● 移転費用 relocation expenses.

いでん 遺伝 图 heredity;［資質などを受け継ぐこと］inheritance. ● 遺伝性の病気 a *hereditary* [*genetic*] disease. ● 遺伝の法則 the laws of *heredity*. ▶彼の縮れ毛は遺伝です His curly hair is *hereditary*.
— 遺伝する 動 inherit. ▶頑健な体質は父から遺伝した I *have inherited* my strong constitution *from* my father.
● 遺伝学 genetics. (❗単数扱い)

いでんし 遺伝子 a gene. ● 遺伝子組み換えトマト[食品] *genetically* modified [engineered] tomatoes [food(s)]. (❗「食品」については GM(F) と略す)

DISCOURSE
遺伝子組み換え食品は体に悪い影響を与えるかもしれない. ...さらに悪いことに, そうした影響は何十年も先になって現れるかもしれないのだ *Genetically* modified food may have harmful effects on the body. ... **What is more**, the results of these effects may show up decades later. (❗what is more (さらに)には用いるディスコースマーカー。what is more に続けて, より強調したい要素を述べる)

● 遺伝子組み換え genetic recombination. ● 遺伝子工学 genétic enginéering. ● 遺伝子障害 genetic defects. ● 遺伝子操作 gene manipulation. ● 遺伝子治療 géne thèrapy.

:**いと** 糸 (a) thread /θréd/;［縫い糸などに用いる細い糸］(a) string (❗thread より太い糸);［紡ぎ糸］yarn;［ラケット・外科用の］gut;［釣り糸］a line (⇨釣り ②).
①【〜糸】● 1本の糸 a (piece of) *thread* [*string*]. ● 一巻きの糸 a spool《米》[a reel《英》] of *thread*. ● 細い糸 fine [thin] *thread*. ● 太い木綿糸 thick [heavy, coarse] cotton *thread*.
②【糸に[で]】● ビーズを糸に通す string beads (*on thread*); thread beads. ● 糸で縫う sew *with thread*. ● 糸で結ぶ tie it with (a piece of) string. ▶この人形は糸であやつります We manipulate these puppets *by strings*.
③【糸を】● 糸を通した針 a needle and /(ə)n/ *thread*. (❗単数扱い.「針と糸」の意では and /ænd/ と発音し, 複数扱い) ● 糸を紡ぐ spin *yarn*. ● 針に糸を通す thread a needle; pass a *thread* through a needle. ● (手術の)糸を抜く take out the *stitches*.
● もつれた糸を解く unravel [unloose] tangled *thread*.
● 糸を引く ▶彼が陰で糸を引いていた He was pulling [×pulled] the *strings* behind the scenes.
● 糸くず waste thread.

いと 意図 图 (an) intention, intent (❗後の方が堅い語);（目的）(a) purpose. (⇨つもり) ▶彼の真の意図 his true *intention* (*to do*). ▶彼にはあなたを欺く意図はない He *has* no *intention of* cheating you./He does not *intend* to cheat you. (❗後の方が一般的)
— 意図的に 副 intentionally;（わざと）on purpose, purposely;（故意に）deliberately.

*いど 井戸 a well. ● 深い[浅い]井戸 a deep [a shallow] *well*. ● 井戸の水をくむ draw water from a *well*. ● (飲料水として)井戸の水を飲んでいるは get one's water from a *well*). ● 井戸がかれている[かれてしまった]. 新しいのを掘らなくては This *well* has gone [run] dry. We have to dig [bore] a new one. ▶この井戸水は飲めない The water from this *well* is not good to drink.
● 井戸水 well water.

いど 緯度 latitude. (⇨北緯) ▶パリの緯度は何度ですか What is the *latitude* of Paris?

いとう 厭う ❶［嫌う］(⇨嫌心, 嫌う) ▶待つのは少しもいといません I don't *mind* waiting at all.
❷［いたわる］▶お体をおいといください Take (good) *care* of yourself.

-いとう -以東 ● 以東の[に] in and (to) the east of ...; at [in]《the place》and eastward. (⇨-以北)

*いどう 移動 图 (a) movement; (a) tránsfer. ● 難民の移動 the *movement* of refugees.
— 移動する 動 (動く, 動かす) move;（別の場所へ移る, 移し)transfér (-rr-). ● 核物質を安全な場所に移動する transfer nuclear materials *to* a safe place. ▶車を移動させてください Can you *move* your car?
● 移動診療所 a mobile clinic. ● 移動性高気圧 a moving high pressure system; a migratory anticyclone. ● 移動性低気圧 a migratory cyclone. ● 移動日《野球》a travel day.

いどう 異同 (a) difference. (⇨相違, 違い)

いどう 異動 a change. ● 人事異動 personnel *changes*;（閣僚などの大異動）a (Cabinet) reshuffle ［《話》shakeup］. ● 教員の異動を行う make personnel *changes* in the teaching staff. ▶彼は大阪支店へ異動(= 転動)となった He *was transferred to* the Osaka branch.

いとおしい 愛おしい (⇨可愛(かわい)い)
いとおしむ 愛おしむ (⇨可愛(かわい)がる)
いときりば 糸切り歯 an eyetooth; a canine (tooth); a cuspid.

いとく 遺徳 the (high) virtue of the deceased.
いとぐち 糸口 ❶［発端］a beginning. ▶それが成功の糸口になった That was the *first step* to success.
❷［手がかり］a clue. ● 糸口を得る get a *clue*. ▶その事件の解決への糸口がない We have no *clue* to solving the case [the solution of the case].

いとけない 幼けない young. (⇨幼い)
いとこ a (first, full) cousin /kÁzn/. ● またいとこ(=はとこ) a second *cousin*. ● いとこの子[孫] a *first cousin* once [twice] removed. ● いとこの太郎 my *cousin*(,) Taro. (⇨友達) ▶ぼくと彼とはいとこ同士だ He and I [×I and he] are *cousins*.

いどころ 居所 ［所在］one's whereabouts (❗単・複両扱い);［住所］one's address. ● 行方不明の男の居所を突きとめる locate a missing man. ▶彼女の居所はまだ不明だ Her *whereabouts* are [is] still unknown. (❗単・複両扱い) ▶君の居所がいつでも分かるようにしておいてほしい I want your *whereabouts* at all times.

いとこんにゃく 糸蒟蒻 *itokonnyaku*; strings of *konnyaku*. (⇨蒟蒻)
いとしい 愛しい ● いとしい妹 my *dear* [*beloved*] sister. (❗beloved /bilÁvid/ は much loved の意) ● いとしく思う think *tenderly* (*of* him). ▶彼女は子供をいとしく思っている She loves her children *dearly*./Her children *are* very *precious* to her.

いとすぎ 糸杉 《植物》a cypress (tree).
いとづくり 糸作り *itozukuri*,（説明的に）thin strips of fresh squid and raw fish.
いととんぼ 糸蜻蛉《昆虫》a damselfly.
いとなみ 営み ［仕事］work;［営業］business;［活動］(an) activity;［準備］preparation(s)《*for*》.

*いとなむ 営む ❶［生活などを行う］● 多忙な生活を営む lead ［《やや古》live］ a busy life.
❷［経営する］● 事業を営む do [conduct] busi-

いとのこ 糸のこ (電動の) a saber saw.
いどばたかいぎ 井戸端会議 housewives' gossip [《話》chit-chat]. ◆井戸端会議をする gossip (about); 《話》chit-chat.
いとま 暇 〔辞去〕leaving; 〔休暇〕leave; 〔閑暇〕leisure (time); 〔(あいた)時間〕time (to spare). (⇨暇) ◆枚挙にいとまがない be too many to list [enumerate]. ▶もうおいとましなければなりません I think I must *be leaving* [*be going*] now. (❗ leave, go は進行形の方が柔らかな言い方)/I must *be off* now. ◆彼は私にいとまごいをした(＝別れを告げた) He *said good-by* [《書》*bid farewell*] to me./He *took* (his) *leave* of me.
いとまき 糸巻き 《米》a spool;《英》a reel.
いとみみず 糸みみず 〔生物〕a tubifex.
いどむ 挑む 〔挑戦する〕challenge; 〔公然と反対する〕defy; 〔試みる〕try. (⇨挑戦する) ◆決闘を挑む *challenge* 《him》 to a dual. ◆世界新記録に挑む *try* [*challenge*] to make a new world record. ◆彼にけんかを挑む *pick* a fight [a quarrel] with him. ▶彼にテニスの試合を挑んだ I *challenged* him to a game of tennis./I gave him *a challenge* to a game of tennis.
いとめ 糸目 ◆金に糸目をつけない (⇨金[成句])
いとめる 射止める ❶〔射殺する〕shoot* 《a bird》 dead.
❷〔獲得する〕win*; get*. ◆少女の心を射止める *win* the heart of a girl 《a young woman》.
いとも ▶彼女はいとも(＝非常に)簡単にその問題を解いた She solved the problem *very* easily [*with great ease*].
いとやなぎ 糸柳 〔植物〕a weeping willow.
いな 否 no. ◆否と言う say *no* (to); deny. ◆否と答える answer *in the negative* (↔affirmative).
いな 鯔 〔ボラの幼魚〕《魚介》a gray mullet.
*いない 以内 within …,《話》inside (of)…; 〔…未満〕less than …; 〔多くて…ぐらい〕not more than …. ◆収入以内の生活をする live *within* (↔*beyond*) one's income [means]. ▶レポートを2,000語以内で書いてください Write your report *within* [*in less than*] 2,000 words. ◆後の方は厳密には2,000を含まないので，*in* 2,000 words *or less* とする (⇨以下) ▶学校は駅から歩いて30分以内のところにあります The school is *within* half an hour's walk of [×*from*] the station./The school is *not more than* [*less than*] half an hour's walk *from* the station. ▶10分以内に戻ってきます I'll be back *within* [*in, less than*] ten minutes. (❗ in は「今料…の時間がたてば」の意。《米》語では未来時制に用いて、しばしば *within* と同義に用いることがあるが、誤解を招くことがあるので避ける方がよい) ▶今週以内にやりなさい Do it (×*within*) this week. (❗ 日本語につられて *within* を使わないこと)
《会話》「彼女はいつ退院するの」「医者は10日以内には って考えてるようだ」"When will she be out of the hospital?" "The doctor thinks *in ten days* [*in ten days' time*]." (❗ 後の方は堅い言い方)
いない 居ない (⇨居る)
いないいないばあ ◆いないいないばあをする play peeka-boo.
いなおりごうとう 居直り強盗 a thief [a burglar] turned a robber on being detected.
いなおる 居直る 〔開き直る〕take* a threatening [a defiant] attitude; 〔座り直す〕sit* up.
*いなか 田舎 図 ❶〔都会に対して〕the country, the countryside, a rural area;《話》the sticks.

《使い分け》**country** 都心から離れた地方都市・農業地域.
countryside 特に郊外に広がる静かで美しい田園・農村.
rural area 都会との対照で田舎をさす場合に用いる.
sticks 都心から遠く離れ、現代生活からかけ離れた地域。口語的な語で、しばしば軽蔑的に用いる.

◆イギリスの田舎 the English *countryside*. ◆大阪の田舎 a *rural area* of Osaka. ◆田舎に行く go into [to] *the country*. (❗ go to the country は「その国へ行く」の意にもなる) ◆彼は都会より田舎が好きだ He prefers *the country* to the city [the town] (❗ country と対比させる場合は city の方が好まれる: country life↔city life). ▶田舎は春がきれいだ The *countryside* is beautiful in 《米》 the spring. ◆彼が住んでいるところは田舎だ He lives *in the country* [*in a rural area*,《話》*out in the sticks*].
❷〔故郷〕(one's) home (❗ home は副詞としても用いる); 〔生まれた・子供時代を過ごした町〕one's hometown (❗ one's native place は通例いわない; where one was born [grew up]. ◆田舎の母から手紙がくる get a letter from my mother *back home*. ▶夏は田舎に帰りたい I'd like to go *home* [go (back) to my *hometown*] in summer.
《会話》「田舎は何ですか」"Where is your *home* [*hometown*, ×*country*]?" "Hakata./My *home* is in Hakata. (❗「博多に住む家がある」の意にもなる)/My *hometown* is Hakata." ◆家・建物が集まっている市街地をさすので国・県・農村・山間部の場合は不適。「福岡県です」というときは My *hometown* is *in* Fukuoka Prefecture (×is Fukuoka Prefecture.) / (出身地はどこですか) "Where do you come [are you] *from*?" "I come [I'm] from Hakata." (⇨出身)

━ 田舎(の) 形 country (↔*town*) (❗ 通例限定的に); rural (↔*urban*), 〔純朴な、または粗野で下品な〕rustic (〔田舎臭い、または偏狭な〕provincial. ◆田舎の小学校 a *country* elementary school; an elementary school in the *country*(side). ◆田舎の人 a *countryman* (❗ 女性形は a *countrywoman*); 〔集合的〕*country* people. ◆田舎の生活 *country* [*rural*] life (↔*city* [*urban*] life). ◆田舎じみた風習 *country* manners. ▶彼は田舎なまりで話した He spoke with [in] a *rural* [a *provincial*] accent.
◆田舎町 a country town. ◆田舎道 a country road. ◆田舎者 a rustic, a provincial,《話》a (country) bumpkin. (❗ いずれも軽蔑的に) ◆田舎料理 country cooking [food].
いなかきょうし『田舎教師』*Country Teacher*. (《参考》 田山花袋の小説)
いながらに 居ながらに ▶新聞のおかげで居ながらにして(＝国内にいて)国際情勢がわかる Thanks to the newspapers, we know the international situation *at home* [在《間》の] in the living room]. (❗ 後の方はニュース番組でよく用いられる) ▶居ながらにして部屋から富士山が眺められる I can see [enjoy a view of] Mt. Fuji from my room. (❗ この場合「居ながらにして」は from my room に含まれているから訳出しなくてもよい)
いなご〔昆虫〕a grasshopper;〔大群をなし、作物に害を与える種類〕a locust.
いなさく 稲作 rice growing. (⇨米作)
いなす 往なす ◆質問[一撃]をいなす(＝かわす) *parry* a question [a blow].
いなずま 稲妻 lightning. ◆稲妻に打たれる be struck

いなせ dashing, gallant.

 古今ことばの系譜『草枕』
「失礼ですが、旦那はやっぱり東京ですか」
「東京と見えるかい」
「見えるかいって、一目見りゃあ、一第一⁽ⁿ⁾言葉でわかりまさあ」(略)
「こう見えて私も江戸っ子だからね」
「道理でいなせだと思ったよ」
"Excuse me, but are you from Tokyo?"
"Is it so obvious?"
"Yes. You can tell at a glance… Well, anyway, I can tell from your accent."
"I may not look it, but I'm from Tokyo too."
"That's why you're so smart-looking."
(!「いなせ」は「侠気があって威勢がよいこと」. smart-looking は「かっこよくて、きびきびしていること」. 少し違うかもしれないが、相手を調子よくほめている文脈上の意味は出る (⇨草枕))

いなだ 〘ブリの幼魚〙〚魚介〛a young yellowtail.

いなだ 稲田 a paddy [a rice] field, a paddy. (⇨田んぼ)

いななく 嘶く (馬・ロバが) neigh /néɪ/; (ロバが大きく) bray.

イナバウアー 〘フィギュアスケート〙an Ina Bauer. 〘参考〙この技を開発した旧西ドイツの選手の名から

いなばのしろうさぎ 因幡の白兎 The White Hare and the Crocodiles. 〘参考〙古事記にみえる神話

いなびかり 稲光 lightning. (⇨稲妻)

いなほ 稲穂 an ear of rice.

いなめない 否めない undeniable. ●否めない証拠 (×an) undeniable evidence. ▶その責任が君にあることは否めない There is no denying [You can't deny] that you are responsible for it.

***-いなや** -否や (…するとすぐ) as soon as …. (⇨すぐ❶ 解説) ●彼が家を出るや否や雨が降りだした As soon as [The moment, Immediately after, 《英語》Immediately] he left home, it started to rain./《書》No sooner had he left home than it started to rain./《書》Hardly [Scarcely] had he left home when [before] it started to rain. (!no sooner, hardly [scarcely] 節では元はこのように過去完了形が普通であったが、今は No sooner did he leave …. などの過去形も用いられるようになった)

いならぶ 居並ぶ sit in a row 《on the stage》.

いなり 稲荷 the god of the harvest.
●稲荷神社 an Inari shrine. ●稲荷寿司 inari-zushi; (説明的に) sushi stuffed in a pouch of fried bean curd.

-いなん -以南 ●以南の[に] south of and (to the) south of …; at [in] 《the place》 and southward. (⇨以北)

イニシアチブ 〘主導権〙the initiative. ●イニシアチブを取る take the initiative 《in doing》.

イニシャル an initial; (姓名の略記) initials. ●イニシャル入りのハンカチ an initialed handkerchief.

いにん 委任 ⓐ commission. ●白紙委任状 a carte blanche /kɑ́ːrt blɑ́ːnʃ/.
── 委任する 動 ▶総理大臣は彼に条約交渉の全権を委任した The Prime Minister gave him the commission of [entrusted him with] full powers to negotiate the treaty.
●委任状 a commission; 〘法律〙a power [a letter] of attorney.

イニング 〘野球〙an inning. (!(1) 裏表を含めた回も、投手が投げる回(アウト 3 つで 1 回)の両方がある. (2) クリケットでは打撃側の回を innings という; 第 2 打撃回 the second innings) ●イニングの表[裏] the top [bottom] of an inning. ●序盤[中盤; 終盤]のイニング the early [middle; late] innings. ●ビッグイニング (3 点以上得点するイニング) a big inning. ●6 イニングを投げる pitch six innings.

***いぬ** 犬 ❶ 〚動物〛 a dog (狭義では雄犬をさす); (雌犬) a bitch; (子犬) a puppy; (猟犬) a hound.
①【〜犬, 犬(の)〜】●野良犬 a stray dog. ●愛玩用の犬 a pet dog. ●犬まで泳ぐ swim the dog paddle; dog-paddle. ●犬の飼い主 a dog owner.
②【犬が】●犬が見知らぬ人にほえて[うなって]いた The dog was barking [growling] at a stranger.
③【犬を】●犬を飼う have [keep] a dog. (!ペットを飼う場合《米》では通例 have) ●犬を散歩させる walk a dog.
❷ 〘スパイ〙a spy; (警官)《軽蔑的》a pig. ●警察の犬 a police spy.
❸ 〘その他の表現〙●負け犬(=敗北者) a loser. ●犬死にする (⇨犬死に)
●犬も歩けば棒に当たる 〘ことわざ〙(しゃばるのは災いのもと) Forwardness causes trouble.; (幸運にあう) The dog that trots about finds a bone. ●犬小屋 a kennel; 《主に米》a doghouse.

いぬ 戌 the Dog.
●戌年 〘十二支〙the year of the Dog. (⇨干支⁽ᵉ⁾ 関連)

イヌイット an Inuit [Innuit] /ínuət/; (複) 〜s, (集合的に) 〜). ●イヌイット語 Inuit. ●イヌイット(語)の Inuit.

いぬき 居抜き ●居抜きで買う buy 《a house》 with furnishings and all; buy 《a house》 lock, stock(,) and barrel.

いぬじに 犬死に ●犬死にする 動 die in vain [to no purpose]; die a useless death. (! die like a dog は「悲惨な最期を遂げる」の意)

いぬちくしょう 犬畜生 ●犬畜生のような bestial; inhuman. ●犬畜生同然のやつ a brute.

いぬねこびょういん 犬猫病院 a pet [an animal] hospital [clinic].

いぬのふぐり 犬のふぐり 〘植物〙 a wayside speedwell.

いぬわし 犬鷲 〘鳥〙 a golden eagle.

***いね** 稲 rice (!米・ご飯・稲・もみなどすべてに用いる); (植物) a rice plant. ●稲を刈る reap [harvest] rice. ▶稲が実り始めた The rice plants have begun to seed.
●稲刈り rice reaping.

いねむり 居眠り ⓐ a doze; (快い) a drowse /dráʊz/.
── 居眠り(を)する 動 (浅く短く) doze, drowse; (うっかり) fall into a doze [a drowse], doze 〚話〛drop] off; (こっくりこっくりと) nod (off) (! off を伴う方が普通. ●会議中に(うっかり)居眠りする doze [nod] off during the meeting. ▶彼は疲れていたので運転中居眠りをしてしまった He was tired, so he fell into a doze [dozed off] while (he was) driving.

いいちばん いの一番 (ほかの何よりも先に) first of all, before anything else; (真っ先に) first thing; (最も重要なことを最初に) first things first; (第一番に) the first 《to come》. ▶明日いの一番にお電話します I'll phone you first thing tomorrow.

いのう 異能 (人より優れた才能) an exceptional [an extraordinary, an incomparable, an unequaled] talent; (特異な才能) a unique talent.

いのこる 居残る stay [remain] behind; (残業する) work overtime [extra hours].

いのしし 猪 〚動物〛a wild boar.

イノシンさん イノシン酸 〚生化学〛inosinic acid.

いのち 命 (a) life (⑬ lives). (❶人の一命は [C]) (⇨生命)

① 【命~】 ▶ 命ある[なき]もの a *living* [a *lifeless*] thing. ▶ 命づいをする beg for one's *life*. ▶ 命知らず(=無鉄砲な人) a *reckless* person; a daredevil. ▶ 命知らずのドライバー a *reckless* [a *daredevil*] driver. ▶ 命取りの(=致命的な)病気 a *fatal* [〚書〛a *deadly*, a *mortal*] disease. ● (⇨命懸け, 命綱) ▶ その汚職事件が内閣の命取りになった The corruption case proved (to be) *fatal to the* Cabinet.

② 【命が[は]】 ▶ あの子の命が危ない The child's *life* is in danger. ▶ だれしも命は惜しい Nobody wants to be killed. ▶ 母は老衰のため100歳で命尽きた My mother *died* of old age when she was 100 years old.

〖会話〗「彼の命はあとどのくらいもつと思いますか」「3か月もたないでしょうね」"How long do you think he will last?" "He won't last (for) three months, I'm afraid."

③ 【命の】 ● 命の糧 the staff *of life*. ● 命のある限りご親切は忘れません I will never forget your kindness *as long as* I *live* (〖生涯〗*all my life*). ▶ 彼は命の恩人だ(=命あるのは彼のおかげだ) I owe my *life* to him. ▶ ×I owe him my life. は不可/(彼が私の命を救ってくれた) He saved my *life*.

④ 【命に】 ● 命にかけて誓う swear on one's *life* (*that*...). ▶ 彼はまるでそれが命(=生死)にかかることであるかのように話した He spoke as if it were a matter of *life or* [*and*] *death*. ▶ 彼は重傷だが, 命に別状はありません He is seriously injured, but his *life* is in no danger (死なないだろう) but he won't die.

⑤ 【命を】 ● 命を犠牲にして at the cost [sacrifice] of (one's) *life*. ● 命を大切にする value one's *life*. ● 命を救う save (his) *life*. ● 自分の命を絶つ take *one's own life*. (自殺する) kill oneself. ▶ その自動車事故で5人が命を落とした Five people lost their *lives* [死んだ] were killed] in the car accident. (❶their life と単数形にはしない)/Five *lives* were lost in the car accident./(自動車事故が命を奪った) The car accident took the *lives* of five people [*five lives*]. ▶ こんな下らないことで命をかけるなんてばかげている It's foolish to risk your *life* [*neck*] over such a trifling matter. ▶ 彼らはパンと水で命をつないだ They sustained themselves [生き続けた] kept themselves alive] on bread and water.

⑥ 【命に】 ▶ 音楽は彼女の命(=生きがい)です Music is her *life*./(すべてである) Music is *everything* to her.

● 命あっての物種 Life is everything to us.; 《ことわざ》While there is life, there is hope.

● 命拾いをする ▶ (野球で)命拾いをする have a (new) life. (〖参考〗やさしいファウルフライを落球してもらった場合) ▶ 彼らは飛行機事故で危うく命拾いをした(=死をまぬがれた) They had a narrow escape (from death) [narrowly escaped (×from) death] in the plane crash.

● 命を縮める ▶ 私は命が縮まる思いをした I felt as if my *life* had been shortened.

いのちがけ 命懸け ● 命がけで闘う fight for one's *life*. ● 命がけの(=必死の)努力をする make *desperate* efforts (*to do*). (⇨必死) ▶ 彼は命がけで(=自分の命を危険にさらして)彼女の命を救った He saved her life *at the risk of* his *life*.

いのちからがら 命からがら ● 命からがら逃げる run away for one's life [for dear life]; (危うく命拾いする) have a narrow (a hairbreadth) escape; 〖話〗escape by the skin of one's teeth.

いのちづな 命綱 a lifeline; (生活を託す) one's only means of living.

いのなかのかわず 井の中の蛙
● 井の中の蛙大海を知らず《ことわざ》The frog in the well does not know the ocean.

いのぶた 猪豚 〚動物〛an *inobuta*; a hybrid of a wild boar and a pig.

イノベーション 〚技術革新〛innovation.

いのり 祈り (a) prayer /ˈpreɪər/ (❶「祈りの言葉」の意ではしばしば複数形); 〚食前・食後の感謝の祈り〛(a) grace. ● 朝の祈り morning *prayers*. ● お祈りの言葉を唱える say one's *prayers*; say (a) *grace*. ▶ 彼は平和の祈りをささげた He offered a *prayer* [prayed] for peace.

いのる 祈る pray, offer a prayer, (お祈りを言う) say one's prayers; 〚食前・食後に〛say (a) grace; 〚願う〛wish. ● 神に助けてくださいと祈った I *prayed to* God *to* help me [*for* help]. ▶ 彼は妻が回復するようにと一心に祈った He *prayed* very hard (*to* God) *that* his wife would recover. ▶ ご健康を祈ります I *wish* [×pray] you good health./I *pray for* your good health. ▶ ご家族のご多幸を祈ります May you and your family be happy./I *hope* you and your family will be happy. (❶前の文は堅い言い方) ▶ 飛行機が緊急着陸するとき私はうまくいくようにと祈った I *kept* my *fingers crossed* as the plane made an emergency landing. (❶cross one's fingers は願いがかなうように祈るしぐさで立てた人指し指の形を表す) ▶ 私は祈るように空を見上げた I looked up *prayerfully* at the sky.

いはい 位牌 a Buddhist memorial tablet; (説明的に) a black wooden tablet with his or her posthumous Buddhist name inscribed in gold in the front, and secular name, the date of death, and the age at death on the back.

いばしょ 居場所 one's whereabouts. (⇨所在, 居所)

いはつ 衣鉢 a secret handed down from a master to his disciple. ● 衣鉢を継ぐ assume [inherit, take on, wear] the *mantle of* one's *master*.

いはつ 遺髪 the hair of a dead person.

いばら 茨 (とげ) a thorn; (とげのある低木) a thorn, a bramble. ▶ 彼の思想家としての過去はいばらの(=困難な)道であった He had followed a *difficult* [a *thorny*] path as a thinker. ▶ 君の前途にはいばらの道があるだろう You will face a *rocky road* ahead.

いばる 威張る 動 〚横柄にふるまう〛act big; 〚偉ぶる〛put* on airs; 〚なにかと命令する〛〚話〛be bossy; 〚自慢する〛be proud (*of*); 〚豪語する〛boast (*of*, *about*). ▶ 彼は奥さんの前ではいつもいばっている He always *acts big* in front of his wife./He always *lords it over* his wife. ▶ 彼は会社ではいつもいばり散らしている He *is* always really *bossy* in the office./He *is* always *throwing* his *weight around* [*about*] in the office. ▶ 彼はいばって(=もったいぶって)座っていた He sat *with an air of importance*.

— **威張った** 形 〚傲慢(ごうまん)な〛; (傍若無人で) arrogant; (地位などを鼻にかけて) haughty; 〚見下す〛overbearing. ● いばった人 an *arrogant* [a *haughty*] person.

*いはん 違反 名 〚法律・規則などの〛(a) violation; (不法行為) an *offense*; (約束・法律などの) (a) *breach*; 〚命令などにそむくこと〛disobedience. ● 交通違反をする commit a traffic *violation*; violate

traffic regulations. ●スピード違反でつかまる be caught for *speeding*. ●契約違反で彼を訴えるsue him for *breach* of contract. ▶サッカーでは手でボールに触れるのはルール違反だ It's *against* the rules to touch a ball with hands in soccer.
── 違反する 動 violate; offénd (*against*); break* (■ 口語的な語); (従わない) disobey. ●法律に違反する violate [break] the law; offend [commit an *offense*] *against* the law; act in *violation* [*breach*] of the law. ●彼の命令に違反する *disobey* his orders.
●違反者 a violator; an offender.

いびき 鼾 a snore. ●いびきのひどい人 a terrible *snorer*; (寝言うるさい人も含む). ●大きないびきをかく give loud *snores*; *snore* loudly. ●彼のいびきで私は眠れなかった His *snores* kept me awake.

いびつ 图 distortion. ── いびつな 形 distorted.
いひょう 意表 ▶彼はよく人の意表をつくようなことをする (= 我々を驚かせる) He often *takes* us *by surprise* [(まったく予期せぬ事をする)] does something *quite unexpected*].
いびょう 胃病 stomach trouble.
いびる (つらくあたる) be hard (*on him*); (あら探しをして) pick on ... (■ 受け身で); (からかう) tease.
いひん 遺品 ●父の遺品はan article of my deceased father's; an article left by my father.
いふ 畏怖 (畏怖の念) awe /ɔː/; (恐れ) fear. ●畏怖の念に打たれる feel *awed*; be struck with *awe*.
── 畏怖する 動 ●神を畏怖する stand *in awe of* God; *fear* God.
いぶ 慰撫 ── 慰撫する 動 (慰める) soothe, console; (なだめる) appease, pacify.
イブ ❶ [旧約聖書の中の女性の名] Eve /iːv/.
❷ [祭日などの前夜] Eve. ●クリスマスイブに on Christmas *Eve*.
いふう 威風 majesty. ▶軍隊は威風堂々と行進して市内に入った The army marched *majestically* into the city.
いぶかしい 訝しい (確信が持てない) doubtful; (半信半疑の) dubious; (あやしい) suspicious. ●いぶかしげなまなざし a *suspicious* [*doubtful*, *dubious*] look. ●いぶかしげに私を見る look at me *suspiciously*.
いぶかしがる 訝しがる (不審に思う) doubt, suspect. (⇨疑う) ●彼の行動をいぶかしがる suspect [*be suspicious of*] his movements.
いぶかる 訝る ●...かどうかいぶかる (...かしらと思う) I wonder if ...; (...でないかと思う) I suspect that ....
いぶき 息吹 [微かなしるし] (a) breath. ▶春の息吹が感じられる We feel a *breath* [感触] a *touch*] of spring in the air. ▶There is a breath ... も可)
***いふく** 衣服 clothes /klouz/, 《集合的》 clothing /klóuðiŋ/; [書] a garment (■ メーカーが好んで用いる語); (服装) a dress; (衣装) a costume; (...着 wear; (一そろいの) a suit; an outfit. (⇨服)
いぶくろ 胃袋 a stomach. ●胃袋を満たす fill one's *stomach* (*with*); eat one's fill.
いぶしぎん 燻し銀 oxidized silver. ●いぶし銀の演技 a restrained but superb performance.
いぶす 燻す (魚・肉などを薫製にするため, また害虫などを追い出すため) smoke; (消毒のため) (やや書) fumigate. ●台所からゴキブリをいぶし出す smoke cockroaches *out of* the kitchen. ●衣服すべてをいぶして消毒する *fumigate* all one's clothes.
いぶつ 異物 a foreign substance [body, object]; foreign matter. ●異物の混じった食品 food containing *foreign matter*. ●胃の中の異物(=飲み込んだもの)を取り出す take the *foreign* [*ingested*]

object out of one's stomach.
いぶつ 遺物 (やや書) a relic; (遺跡) the remains. ●過去の遺物 a *relic* of the past.
イブニングドレス (an) evening dress [gown]. (■ 通例丈が長く胸や背中が出たもの)
いぶる 燻る [[煙る]] smoke; [[くすぶる]] smolder. ▶たき木がひどくいぶっている The firewood *is smoldering* badly.
いぶん 異聞 a strange rumor.
いぶんか 異文化 a different culture. ●異文化接触 contacts of different cultures; crosscultural [intercultural] contacts. (■ 後の語は人と人との関係に意味の重点がある) ●異文化間コミュニケーション crosscultural [intercultural] communication.
いぶんし 異分子 a foreign element; (局外者) an outsider.
いへき 胃壁 [解剖] the stomach lining.
イベリア ●イベリア半島 Iberia /aibíəriə/, the Ibèrian Peninsula.
イベリコぶた イベリコ豚 (肉) Iberico pork.
いへん 異変 ●暖冬異変 *unusually* warm winter. ▶今年は天候異変だった We had *unusual* weather this year. ▶彼の身辺に異変(=変わったこと)が起こった Something *unusual* happened to him.
イベント an evènt. ●メーンイベント [[主要試合]] a main *event*. ●大きなイベントを催す hold a big *event*.
いぼ 疣 a wart. ▶足にいぼができた I have a *wart* (grown) [A *wart* has grown] on my foot.
いぼ 異母 ●異母兄弟 a half-brother. ●異母姉妹 a half-sister.
いほう 違法 图 illegality. ●違法行為を犯す commit an *illegality* [an *illegal* act]. (⇨違反する) ●ここでの駐車は違法だ It is *illegal* [*against the law*] to park here./Parking here is *against* [《書》] weather a *violation of*] *the law*.
── 違法の 形 illegal; unlawful.
いほうじん 異邦人 a foreigner, an alien. (⇨外人)
いぼがえる 疣蛙 [動物] a toad.
-いほく -以北 ●東京以北の[に] in and (to) the north of Tokyo; at [in] Tokyo and northward. ▶新潟以北は大雪だ It's snowing heavily *in and* (to) *the north of* Niigata. (■ in and がないと新潟は含まない)
いぼく 遺墨 one's posthumous writing [letter].
いぼじ 疣痔 [医学] (blind) piles; hemorrhoids.
・**いま** 今 ❶ [現在] now; (目下) at present, at the present time; (ちょうど今, 今のところ) at the moment; (こんにち) today; (現代) at the present day. (■ 日本語の「今」は now より期間が短く at the moment に当たることが多い)
① [今(が[は])] ▶今何時ですか What time is it (×now)? (■ is という現在形でわかるので now は通例不要) ▶彼は今パリに滞在中です He is (now) staying in Paris. (■「今」は特に now で示されないこともある) ▶彼は「今暇ですか」と言った He said, "Are you free *now*?"/He asked if I was free *then*. (■ 間接話法で時制の一致が行われたとき now は通例 then になる) ▶私は今とても忙しい I'm very busy *at present* [*at the moment*, (ちょうど今) *just now*, (話) *just now*, right now は現在の状況を表す文脈で用いる (⇨❷❸) ▶ブログが今(= 最近)流行だ Blogs are popular *these days* [*nowadays*, ×recently]. (■ recently は完了形または過去形とともに用いる) ▶今がそれをするまたとない好機だ *Now* is the best time to do [for doing] it. ▶今は原子力の時代だ *This* is the age of atomic

energy. ▶今思えば彼が辞職を決意したのはあの瞬間だった *Looking back now*, we see it was at that mement that he decided to resign.
会話「ところでそれまであとどれくらいしたら要るの？」「今だよ．まさに今の今」"Well how soon do you want it?" "*Now. This very minute*."
②【今の】(現在の) present; (現在ある) existing; (現時点の，現行の) current (《やや堅い語》; (今日の) ... of today. ●今の校長 the *present* principal. ●今の政府 the *present* [*existing*] government. ●今の気温 the *current* temperature. ●今の(はやり)のファッションを追う follow the *current* fashions. ●今のところ (⇨今のところ) ●今の世の中 (⇨現代) ▶今の学生はあまり本を読まない The students of *today* [Students *today*, *Today's* students] don't read many books. ▶今のうちに(＝手遅れにならないうちに)医者に診てもらいなさい You'd better see a doctor *before it is too late*. ▶今の私があるのも，敏子のおかげです I owe what I am to Toshiko.
③【今から】▶今から始めれば今日中に宿題は終わるよ If you start *now* [×from now], you will finish your homework today. (! from now は単独で用いない．次の3例参照) ▶彼は今から4年後に大学を卒業します He will graduate from college four years *from now* [*in* four years]. ▶今から(＝今後)酒とたばこをやめよう I'll quit drinking and smoking *from now on*. ▶今から1年以内に英語がぺらぺらになる You'll be speaking fluent English in less than a year *from now*. ▶今から6時までの間はだれが来ても会いません I won't see anyone between *now* and six. ▶今から5年前に彼女は死んだ She died five years *ago*. (! ago は過去時制で期間を表す名詞(句)とともに用いる) /She has been dead for five years./It's been 《主に米》 [It's《主に英》] five years since she died.
④【今より】▶彼らは今より幸福になるだろう They'll be happier *than they are now* [×than now].
⑤【今まで】(これまでに，過去のいつか) ever (! 通例疑問・否定文で); (今まで一度も...ない) never, (今までずっと) until [till] now (! 通例継続を表す動詞とともに). ▶今までに2度行ったことがある I've been [×I've ever been] there twice./I've twice been there. ▶その人には今まで一度も会ったことがない I've *never* met him. (! I *never* have met him. の語順は強意的. *Never* have I met him. は堅い言い方. I haven't *ever* met him. ははずれ) ▶今まで何をしていたんですか What have you been doing *till now* (この間ずっと) *all this while*)? ▶高山は今まで見た中で最も美しい町です Takayama is the most beautiful city (that) I've *ever* seen [I *ever* saw]. (!《話》では通例 that を省略する) ▶私は今までよりも熱心に勉強します I'll study harder than *before* [*ever*]. (! before は「前より」, ever は「前も熱心だったからさらに」の意) ▶その事故については今の今まで知らなかった I knew nothing at all about the accident *up to right now*. ▶彼らは今までにない(＝先例のない)悲惨な事故にあった They met with an *unprecedented* tragic accident. ▶彼の今までの生活には多くの浮き沈みがあった His life has had many ups and downs *until now*. ▶今までの怠惰な生活を改めて再出発します I'm going to break with *my idle life* and make a fresh start.
会話「今までに京都を訪れたことがありますか」「いいえ，ありません」"Have you (*ever*) been to Kyoto?/Have you been to Kyoto *before*?" "No, never [I haven't, ×I have never]." (! *ever* がある方が強意的)
⑥【今までのところ】(今後は変わるだろうがこれまでのところは) so far, up to now (! ともに通例現在完了形とともに用いる); (今後はわからないが今のところは) as yet (! 通例否定文で). ▶今までのところ何も困ったことはない I've had no trouble *so far* [*up to now*, *until now*, 《話》 *up until now*]. ▶今までのところ何も起こっていない As yet nothing has happened. (! 文頭・文中・文尾で用いる)
会話「大学生になってどう？」「今までのところうまくいってるよ」「試験期間になると大変だよ．範囲が広いから」"How does it feel like to be a college student?" "*So far*, so good." "Wait till the exam week(s). You have so much to cover."
⑦【今になると】会話「やらないってあなた言ったでしょ」「だけど今になったらやりたいんだよ」"You said you wouldn't play." "Well I ▾want to, /*now*." (⇨今に)

❷【ほんの少し前】just (! 通例完了形と用いる．過去形と用いるのは《米話》); just now (! 通例文尾で過去形と用いる．現在時制では「ただ今」「今のところ」の意となる (⇨❶, ③, ❸)) ▶彼は今ここに来たばかりです He has *just* [*only just*] come here. (! *only just* は「ちょうど今の今」という強意形になる)/《米話》He *just* came here./He came here *just now* [*just a moment ago*].
❸【ただちに】at once; immediately (! 後の方はやや堅い語だが，会話でもしばしば強意的に用いる); 《話》right away; (少ししてすぐ)《話》in a minute; just (! 通例文中で進行形や be going to などとともに); (just) now (! 通例文尾に置き，未来の状況を表す文脈で用いる (⇨❷,❸)). ▶私は今すぐパリに出発します I'm leaving for Paris *at once* [*immediately*]. ▶今すぐ行きます I am (*just*) coming [going]. (! 相手の方へ行くときは come. 相手から離れていくときは go)/I'll be there *right away* [*just now*, *right now*, *in a minute*]./I'll be right there. ▶音楽会は今始まるところです The concert is *just going to* [*is about to*] start. ▶今すぐカタログをご請求ください《広告文》Write for our catalogue *today*.
❹【さらに】▶この問題の解決には今少しの時間が必要です We need a little *more* time to solve the problem. ▶今しばらくお待ちください Please wait a little *longer*. ▶今一度やってみよう Let's try it *again* [*once more*].
❺【その他の表現】▶もう今となっては手遅れだ By now it's too late. ▶彼は今をときめく(＝今も最大る)政界の大物です He is *now the biggest* [(最も勢力のある) *the most influential*] figure in politics. ▶今こそ行動の時だ Now is the time for action./The time for action is *now*.
会話「どうして今朝はだめなの？」「時間がないからよ．今だってもう(＝すでに)10分遅れてるのよ」"Why not this morning?" "Because there isn't time. We're ten minutes late *as it is*./We're *already* ten minutes late."
●今か今かと ▶母は息子の来るのを今か今かと(＝絶えず)待っていた The mother was expecting her son *every moment*./(うずうずして) The mother was waiting *impatiently* [(ひたむきに) *eagerly*] for her son to come.
●今は昔 once upon a time. (⇨昔)

いま 居間 a living [《米》a family, 《主に英》a sitting] room; (茶の間)《米》a den (for a family) (! den は「隠れ場所」から広くはないがくつろげる暖かい感じを伴う).
いまいち 今いち (⇨もう一つ 圖❷)
いまいましい 忌ま忌ましい 形 [(いらいらさせる] irritating; [(腹だたしい)] annoying; [(胸が悪くなるような)] disgusting. ●いまいましい騒音 an *irritating* [an

いまごろ

annoying] noise. ●いまいましい天気 disgusting [(嫌な) nasty, (ひどく嫌な) hateful] weather. ●いまいしいことには to one's disgust [vexation]. ▶こんな雨の日に出かけなくてはならないとはいまいましい（＝ひどく嫌だ）I detest [very much hate] having to go out on such a rainy day.

── 忌ま忌ましそうに 副 disgustedly; in disgust [vexation].

*いまごろ 今頃 （今）now; （この時）about [at] this time. ●（1日のうち［夜］の）今ごろになって at this time of day [night]. ●明日の今ごろ about this time tomorrow. ▶京都を訪れるには今ごろがいちばんいい時だ Now is the best time to visit Kyoto./It is best to visit Kyoto at this time of (the) year. ▶去年の今ごろ大雪が降った We had a heavy snow (about) this time last year. ▶今ごろ彼はその手紙を受け取っているだろう He must have gotten the letter by now [by this time]. ▶今ごろまで（＝こんな時刻まで）何をしていたのだ What have you been doing till now [till this hour, この間ずっと all this while]?

いまさら 今更 ❶ [今になって] now. ▶いまさら発言を取り消してもむだだ It is no use [good] taking back your remarks now./(手遅れだ) It is too late (for you) to take back your remarks.
❷ [今あらためて] again. ▶いまさら言うまでもありませんが、遅れないでください I don't have to tell you again [言う必要はまずない] It is hardly necessary to say], but please don't be late. ▶いまさらながら（＝それだけいっそう）彼の努力に感心した I was all the more impressed by his efforts.

いましがた 今しがた just; just now. (⇨今❷)

イマジネーション [想像力] an imagination.

いまじぶん 今時分 about this time; (1日 [1年] の中の) at this time of day [(the) year (1日)].

いましめ 戒め (叱責) [書] (an) admonition (！ この意で lesson を使うのは口語的); (教訓) a lesson; (警告) a warning; (禁止) (a) prohibition. ▶それは彼たちに戒めとなった That was a lesson [a warning] to us.

いましめる 戒める (諭す) [書] admonish; scold; (懲らしめる) punish; (警告する) warn, (注意する) caution; (禁じる) forbid. ●彼の無礼を戒める admonish him for being rude [for his rudeness]; ●彼に2度と遅れないよう戒める warn [caution] him not to be late again. ▶彼は自らの行動を厳しく戒めていた He was trying hard to control his actions. ▶ただ酒をご馳走になる（＝飲食の接待を受けること）を自ら戒める Refrain from being treated to free drinks [sake].

いまだ(に) 未だ(に) (依然として) still; (今でも) even now; (まだ…ない) not (…) yet, still (…) not; (今までに) ever (！最上級を強調して); (今までに一度も…ない) never. (⇨今❶) ▶その家はいまだに空き家だ The house is still vacant [is vacant even now]. ▶私はいまだにその真相がわからない I still don't know the truth. (！ still は否定語より前に置く) ▶いまだに彼女のお父さんに会ったことがない I haven't seen her father yet./I have never seen her father. ▶その迷信はいまだに（＝今日まで）残っている The superstition persists to this day.
●いまだかって こんな美しい光景を見たことがない I have never seen such a beautiful sight as this (before)./This is the most beautiful sight (that) I have ever [×never] seen.

いまどき 今時 [このごろは] (×in) these days, 《主に書》 nowadays (⇨この頃に); [こんな時刻に] at this time (⇨今頃に). ●今時の若者 the young people of today; young people today [these days]; today's young people. ▶今時そんなことを言う者はだれもいない No one says such things these days [nowadays].

いまに 今に ❶ [間もなく] soon, before long; (やがて) in time; (いつか) someday; (そのうちに) one of these days; (将来) in the (near) future. ▶今に真実が分かるだろう The truth will come out soon [in time, someday]. ▶彼は今に有名になるだろう He will be famous someday [one of these days, in the future].

[会話]「博多行きの列車はいつ着きますか」「もう今に（＝今すぐにも）到着しますよ」"When will the train for Hakata arrive?" "It should arrive any minute now." (！ should は「…するはずだ」の意)

❷ [その他の表現] ●今に見ていろ, いつか大物になってみせる Just you wait and see. One day I'll be a great man. (！単に Just you wait. では「覚えていろよ」の脅し文句になる) ▶彼の外泊は今に始まったことではない（＝何も目しいことではない）It's nothing new that he stays out overnight.

いまにして 今にして now. ▶今にして思えば彼女は彼を愛していたのだ We now know that she loved him.

いまにも 今にも [いつなんどき] (at) any moment (！通例 may を伴う); [今にも…しそうだ] be just going to 《do》, be about to 《do》; be on the point of 《doing》. (！この順に切迫の度合いが強くなる) ▶彼は今にも泣き出しそうな顔をしている He looks as if he might cry at any moment. ▶今にも雨が降りそうだ It's just going to [It's about to] rain.

いまのところ 今のところ [当分の間] for the present, for the time being, for the moment; [現在は] at present, at this moment; [今までのところは] so far (⇨今❶❺). ▶今のところこの辞書で間に合います This dictionary will do for the present [《話》 for now]. ▶今のところ暇です I am free at present.

いまひとつ 今ひとつ (⇨もう一つ 形, 副 ❷)

いまふう 今風 形 modern, present; (最新の) up-to-date. ●今風のファッション the present [up-to-date] fashion.

いままで 今まで (⇨今❶❺)

いまもって 今以て still. (⇨未だ(に))

いまや 今や ●今やそれをする絶好の時だ Now is the best time to do [for doing] it. ▶彼は今や日本の総理大臣である He is now the Prime Minister of Japan. ▶君は今や大学生なんだから何でも自分でしなくちゃだめだ Now (that) you are a college student, you must do everything by yourself. (《話》では that はしばしば省略される)
●今や遅しと 今や遅しと（＝うずうずして）待つ wait impatiently [for him].

いまよう 今様 (⇨今風)

いまわしい 忌まわしい ●忌まわしい＝胸が悪くなるような ふるまい disgusting [detestable, loathsome] behavior.

*いみ 意味 ❶ [意義, わけ] (言葉の) (a) meaning; (定義された個々の) a sense; (言外の) (an) implication; (単語の含み) a connotation (！しばしば複数形で).

① [～意味] ●表面的な (隠れた; 文字どおりの; 比喩的な) 意味 an apparent [a hidden; a literal; a figurative] meaning. ▶このことわざには深い意味がある This proverb has a deep [a profound] meaning.

② [意味が] ▶この語句は意味がはっきりしない The meaning of this phrase isn't clear./This phrase isn't clear in meaning. ▶あなたのおっしゃる意味が分かりません I don't understand what you

mean [what you're getting at]./(話についていけない) I can't follow you. ▶君の言っているのと、言おうとのは意味が違う The *implication* of your words differs from that of mine. ▶彼の言うことにはいつでも言外の意味が含まれている What he says *always* has an implicit *meaning* of his words. ▶あの標識の意味が理解できません I can't make out of that sign.
③【意味を】 ▶この単語はいくつかの意味を持っている This word has several *meanings* [*senses*]. ▶その表現は意味をなさない The expression doesn't *make (any) sense*. ▶彼女のいう意味をはっきり理解した I grasped her *meaning* clearly.
④【意味で】 ▶彼の言ったことはある意味では正しい What he said is right *in a sense* [*way*]. ▶彼女はあらゆる意味ですばらしい女性です She is a magnificent woman *in every sense*. ▶いい意味でも悪い意味でもあの人は商売人だ In *a good sense or a bad sense* he's a merchant at spirit.
⑤【意味だ】 ▶この単語はどういう意味ですか What does this word *mean*?/What is the *meaning* of this word? ▶'CA'はカリフォルニアの意味だ(=を表す) 'CA' *stands for* 'California.'
会話 「ああうるさいなあ」「うるさいって？ ちょっと、それどういう意味よ」"Oh, you're a nuisance!" "I'm a nuisance? Just what do you mean (by that)?" (!) just は疑問詞につけて話し手のいらだちを表す
❷【目的, 意図】(目的) (a) purpose; (意図) (an) intention; (ねらった効果) point; (意義) (a) significance. ▶彼は意味もなくそんなことをするはずがない I'm sure he doesn't do that without any special *purpose* [*reason*]. ▶彼は私に意味ありげに微笑んだ He smiled at me *meaningfully* [*with meaning*]./He gave me a *meaningful* [心得顔の] a *knowing*] smile. ▶横flexionは言語発達上重要な意味を持つ Imitation has (a) great *significance* [*an important meaning*] in the development of language. ▶また同じ手を使っても意味がない There is not much *point in* playing the same trick again. ▶社会に出て役に立める事を学校で講義するところに教育の(真の)意味がある The true [real] *meaning* of education lies in lecturing about matters that will serve no practical purpose [has no practical use] outside the classroom.
── 意味する 動 mean*; (暗に) imply; [表す] (書) signify; (略語が) stand for ... (⇨❶⑤). ▶日本語の「花」は flower を意味する 'Hana' in Japanese *means* [書] *signifies* 'flower.' ▶彼の言葉は私たちといっしょに行きたいということを意味していた His words *implied* that he would like to come with us.
いみきらう 忌み嫌う hate (intensely) 《*to* do, doing》; abhor 《doing》; detest 《doing》; loathe 《doing》. (!) (1) いずれも進行形は不可. (2) 最後の語が最も意味が強い
いみことば 忌み言葉 taboo words.
いみしん 意味深 (⇨意味深長)
いみしんちょう 意味深長 ── 意味深長な 形 ●意味深長な(=意味ありげな)目つきをする 《*him*》 a *meaningful* look; look 《*at him*》 *meaningfully*.
いみづける 意味付ける give significance 《*to*》.
イミテーション 『模造品』 an imitation. ●イミテーションの真珠 an *imitation* pearl.
いみょう 異名 a nickname. ▶彼は「けんか太郎」の異名を持つ男だ His *nickname* was 'Fighting Taro.' / He earned a *nickname* 'Fighting Taro.' / He *was* once *nicknamed* 'Fighting Taro.'

いみん 移民 〖移住〗(遠い外国への) emigration; (遠い外国からの) immigration; 〖人〗(遠い外国への) an émigrant; (遠い外国からの) an immigrant. ●米国在住の日本からの移民 Japanese *immigrants* in the U.S.; *immigrants* [*into*] America *from* Japan. ▶その船はブラジルからの移民を大勢運んだ The ship carried a lot of *emigrants from* Japan *to* Brazil.
●移民局 the Immigration Office.
いむしつ 医務室 (学校・工場などの) 〖米〗an infirmary; 〖英〗a sick [a first-aid] room ▶看護師が常勤しているので、「医務室へ行く」ことを go to a nurse ということもある); 〖主に米〗a dispensary.
*イメージ 〖心象, 印象〗 an image; 〖外観〗 a look. (印象) ▶田園のイメージが浮かんだ An *image* of the countryside came into my mind. ●…のイメージをふくらませる hold up an *image* of ... in one's mind. ▶その製品は我が社のイメージアップ [ダウン] になるだろう That product will improve [hurt] the *image* of our company. ▶その議員の発言はイメージダウンにつながった The remark harmed [damaged] the *image* of the Diet member.
●イメージキャラクター a poster child [boy, girl].
イメージスキャナー 『コンピュータ』an image scanner.
イメージチェンジ ●建物のイメージチェンジ the *makeover* of a building. ▶彼女は最近髪を切ってイメージチェンジをした She has recently changed her *look* [given herself a new *look*] by having a haircut. (!) (1) did her *makeover* ともいう. (2) change one's *image* は人や会社などを完全に中身まで変えてしまうことをいい、単に外見を変えてしまう意味では用いない
イメージトレーニング an imagery rehearsal; 《和製語》an image training.
*いも 芋 (ジャガイモ) a potato (複 ~es); (サツマイモ) a sweet potato; (タロイモ) (a) taro (複 ~s).
●芋を洗うよう ▶暮れの商店街は芋を洗うような(=たいへんな) 人ごみだった The shopping streets *were very crowded with* year-end shoppers.
*いもうと 妹 a (younger [little, 《米話》kid]) sister. (⇨兄 解説), 弟)
いもがゆ 芋粥 rice and sweet potato porridge.
いもがゆ 『芋粥』Yam Gruel. (参考) 芥川龍之介の小説)
いもがら 芋幹 dried stems of a taro plant.
いもちびょう 稲熱病 rice blast.
いもづる 芋蔓 ●泥棒の一味を芋をもつる式に(=次々に)逮捕する arrest a gang of thieves *one after another*.
いもの 鋳物 a casting, a molding.
●鋳物工場 a foundry.
いもほり 芋掘り potato digging.
いもむし 芋虫 〖昆虫〗a green caterpillar.
いもようかん 芋羊羹 imoyokan; (説明的に) (a bar of) sweet potato paste.
いもり 井守 a newt.
いもん 慰問 名 (慰め) consolation; comfort.
── 慰問する 動 console; comfort; (見舞いに行く) visit.
●慰問品 a comfort (article).
*いや ❶ [否定の返事] no, 《主に米話》uh-uh /ʌʔʌ/; (否定疑問文に対する肯定文に対する反応) yes. (⇨いいえ 囲) ▶いやとは言わせないぞ I won't let you say *no*./I won't take *no* for an answer. (!) take no refusal はあまり一般的でない
会話 「これ以上話し合う必要はない」「いや、そうじゃない」 "We don't have to talk any more." "Yes, we must."

❷ [驚き・嘆息など] oh; well; oh dear. (⇨まあ) ▶いや, 驚いた *Oh* [*Well*], *what a surprise!* ▶いやかではない *Well, I am not sure.* (⇨ためらい) ▶いやいや彼には困ったものだわ *Dear, dear! What shall I do with him?* (❗主に女性の言葉) (⇨いやぁや)

会話 「いや! 忘れずに犬にえさをやった?」「いや, やらなかった. 君がやると思ってたもの」 "*Uh-oh!* Did you remember to feed the dog?" "*No,* I didn't. I thought you were going to feed him." (❗ *uh-oh* /ʌ́ou/ は好ましくないことが生じたのではないかと疑ったときに用いられる)

❸ [言い直し] well; (強意を) no; (それどころか) even; (いや正確に言えば) (or) rather. ▶彼は88歳で死んだんだ, いやたぶん90だった He died at (the age of) 88 —*well* 90 perhaps. ▶それは100円, いや10円の値打ちもない *It's not worth 100 yen, no,* not even 10 yen. ▶彼は日本, いや世界一流の作家だ He is one of the best writers of Japan, *even* [*no, yes*], of the world. (❗より強意的な語に訂正するときには yes も用いる) ▶彼は同意した, いやむしろ反対したというわけではなかった He agreed, *or rather* he didn't oppose.

いや 嫌 (嫌う) don't like (*to do*; *doing*), (ひどく嫌う) hate (*to do*; *doing*) (❗ *to do* でも *doing* でもほぼ同意だが, 通例「今その行為が嫌」の意では *to do*,「いつでもその行為が嫌」の意では *doing* を用いる), (うんざりする) be (sick and) tired (*of*); (気が進まない) be unwilling [reluctant] (*to do*). ▶彼はその日勉強するのがいやだった He *didn't like* [*hated*] *to* study that day. ▶毎日同じことばかりするのはいやだ *I don't like* [*hate*] *doing* the same thing every day. / (話) Doing the same thing every day is a real *drag*. (❗ *drag* は (退屈で) うんざりすること」の意) ▶彼に口出しされるのはいやだ *I don't like* [*hate*] him *to* interfere in it. ▶私は生きるのがいやになった *I'm* (*sick and*) *tired of* [(話) *am fed up with*] *life.* / (興味を失った) *I've lost interest in life.* ▶その件について話すのはいやです *I'm unwilling* [*not willing*] *to* talk about the matter. ▶いやなら話してくれなくていい You need not tell me if you *don't want to.* ▶何もかもいやになった(=うんざりした) *I'm disgusted with* the whole thing. ▶ああいやだ, また故障だ! *Oh no,* it's out of order again!

会話 「自分の仕事は気に入っていますか」「時々いやになります」 "Do you like your job?" "Sometimes I *hate* it."

会話 「給料日まで1万円貸してくれ」「いやだよ」 "Can you let me have 10,000 yen till payday?" "*No.*"

——**嫌な** 形 nasty (❗最も意味の広い語); [むかつくような] disgusting, offensive; [不快な] unpleasant, disagreeable; [身の毛のよだつような] horrible; [ありがたくない] unwelcome; [望ましくない] undesirable. ▶いやな天気 *nasty* [*bad, unpleasant*] weather. ▶いやなにおい a *nasty* [an *unpleasant,* a *bad,* a *disgusting*] smell; a stink. ▶そっとするよいやな光景 a *horrible* sight. ▶いやなお客 an *unwelcome* guest. ▶いやなやつ a *disagreeable* [a *disgusting*] fellow. (❗後の方が強意的) ▶何ていやな日だ What a *nasty* cold day! ▶彼は彼女の無作法にいやな顔をした He looked *displeased* [*unpleasant*] at her rude manners. (まゆをひそめた) He *frowned* [*made a wry* /ráI/ *face*] at her rude manners. ▶彼はいやな顔(=迷惑という表情)ひとつせずに私を助けてくれた He helped me *without* the slightest look of *annoyance.* / (まったく喜んで) He helped me quite *willingly.*

——**嫌というほど** 副 ▶嫌というほど(=ひどく)しかられる be *really told off.* ▶去年の冬は嫌というほど(=うんざりするほど多く)雪が降った We had *more than enough* of snow last winter.

イヤーブック [年鑑] a yearbook. (⇨年鑑)

いやいや 会話 「ご親切さま」「いやいや」 "It's very kind of you." "Oh, *not at all.*"/"You're welcome." "*Don't mention it.*"

会話 「何と言った?」「いやいや, 何でもないよ」 "Beg your pardon?" "*Oh, nothing.* Just forget it."

いやいや 嫌々 [気の進まぬまま] reluctantly, grudgingly; [不本意に] unwillingly; [心ならずも] against one's will. (⇨しぶしぶ) ▶いやいやその決定に同意する *reluctantly* agree to the decision; agree *unwillingly* to the decision.

いやおうなしに 否応なしに by force. (⇨否)(が応でも, 無理やり) ▶物不足のため物価はいや応なしに上がった Shortages *forced* the price of goods *up.*

いやがうえにも いやが上にも (なおさら) even [still] more; (ますます) all the more. ▶パリへ転勤することになっていたのでいやが上にもフランス語の勉強に力が入った I was being transferred to Paris, and I tried *even harder* to learn French.

いやがおうでも 否が応でも ▶いやがおうでも親の言うことには従わねばならなかった I had to obey my parents *whether I liked it or not.*

いやがらせ 嫌がらせ harassment. ▶職場での女性に対する性的嫌がらせ sexual *harassment* of [against] women at work. ▶嫌がらせ電話 a *harassing* [a *nuisance,* a *hate*] (phone) call. ▶嫌がらせの手紙 *hate* mail. (❗ a hate letter は (まれ)) ▶彼らは私の靴や傘を隠して嫌がらせをした They *did nasty things to* [*harassed*] me by hiding my shoes or umbrella.

いやがる 嫌がる [気が進まない] be unwilling [reluctant] (*to do*); [嫌う] don't like, dislike; hate; detest. (⇨嫌う) ▶急に行ったら嫌がられるかもしれないよ You might *not be welcome* if you drop in on him [her].

いやく 医薬 ▶医薬品 (a) medicine. ▶医薬部外品 quasi-medicine. ▶医薬分業 the separation of pharmacy and clinic.

いやく 意訳 (a) free translation.
——**意訳する** 動 translate (...) freely [for the meaning], make [give] a free translation (*of*).

いやく 違約 (a) breach of contract [agreement, promise].
——**違約する** 動 break a contract [an agreement, an appointment]; break one's promise.
▶違約金 (pay) the penalty (*of*+金額; *for*+事).
▶違約条項 (契約の) a penalty clause (in a contract).

いやけ 嫌気・嫌気さす ▶自分に嫌気がさす(=嫌になる) be disgusted with oneself. ▶彼女はパリの生活に嫌気がさして帰国することにした She *got tired of* her life in Paris and decided to go home.

いやし 癒し healing. ▶いやし系 a healer. ▶いやしブーム a *healing* boom. ▶いやし系の女性 a *healing* [a *stress-relief*] woman.

いやしい 卑しい ❶ [どん欲な] greedy. ▶彼は食べ物に大変卑しい He is very *greedy for* food.
❷ [下品な] (野卑な) vulgar; (粗野の) coarse; (下劣な) low. ▶卑しい言葉遣い *vulgar* [*coarse, low*] language.
❸ [外見のみすぼらしい] shabby. ▶卑しい身なりの男 a *shabby* man. ▶人品いやしからぬ老婦人 a *noble-looking* old woman.
❹ [身分の低い] humble; low.

いやしくも 《条件節で》at all. ▶いやしくも戦うからには最後まで戦えIf you do fight *at all*, fight it out. ▶いやしくも(=その名にふさわしい)教育者ならそんな態度は取るべきではない An educator *worthy of the name* should not take [assume] such an attitude. ▶それはいやしくも良識ある人のできることでない No person of sound judgment could do it. (🅘 could は仮定法を表し「良識のある人なら…できないだろう」の意)

いやしむ 卑しむ despise. (⇨軽蔑) ▶卑しむべき行動 déspicable conduct.

いやしんぼう 卑しん坊 a glutton. (⇨食いしん坊)

いやす 癒す 《病気などを》cure;《傷などを》heal;《空腹などを》satisfy. ▶病をいやす *cure* a disease. ▶彼むちひしがれた心をいやす *heal* his broken heart. ▶空腹をいやす *satisfy* one's hunger《with》. ▶のどの渇きをいやす *quench* one's thirst.

いやでもおうでも 否でも応でも (⇨否が応でも)

いやに [[ひどく]] terribly, 《話》awfully; [[妙に]] strangely; [[鼻持ちならないほど]] intolerably, unbearably; [[不快なほど]] unpleasantly. ▶いやに暑いですね It's *terribly* [*awfully*] hot, isn't it? ▶この地下室はいやに(=不快なほど)じめじめしている This cellar is *unpleasantly* damp.

いやはや ▶いやはや驚いた Oh, what a surprise!

イヤホーン an earphone, 《イヤピース》an earpiece. ▶一対を表して a pair [a set] of earphones [earpieces] ●イヤホーンで聞く use *earphones* to listen《to music》; listen《to music》on [with, through] *earphones*.

いやみ 嫌味 图 ●嫌味を言う speak sarcastically; make *sarcastic* remarks; say *nasty* things. ●嫌味たっぷりに言う be full of *irony* [*sarcasm*]. ●嫌味を並べる list [make a series of] *nasty* remarks. ●嫌味のない態度では an *agreeable* [気取らない] an *unaffected* manner. ●彼女の嫌味らしいばか丁寧なあいさつ *obnoxious* politeness of her greetings.

——嫌味な 形 [[皮肉な]] sarcastic, ironical; [[気にくわない]] disagreeable (⇔agreeable); [[不愉快な]] unpleasant. ●嫌味な人 a *sarcastic* [an *offensive*] person.

いやらしい 嫌らしい [[不愉快な]] unpleasant; [[嫌な]] disgusting; [[けがらわしい]] dirty; [[みだらな]] lecherous; indecent, improper (🅘前の方が意味が強い); (わいせつな) obscene. ▶いやらしい奴 an *unpleasant* [a *disgusting*] fellow. ▶いやらしい言葉をつかう use *indecent* [*improper*, *obscene*] language. ●(性的な)いやらしいことを言う make an *improper* suggestion; make a *suggestive* comment. ▶いやらしい(=助平)じじい a *dirty* [a *lecherous*] old man. ●いやらしい目付きで女を見る look at a woman *with sexual interest*; eye up a woman. ▶彼女にいやらしいふるまいをする behave *indecently* toward her.

イヤリング 《a pair of》earrings. ●イヤリングをつける[つけている] put on [wear] *earrings*. (⇨ピアス)

いゆう 長友 one's honorable [highly esteemed, greatly respected] friend.

いよいよ ❶ [[ますます]] more and more (🅘 more に限らず他の形容詞・副詞の比較級も用いる); (それだけいっそう) all the more [better]《for; because 節》. ▶その問題を解決するのがいよいよ難しくなった We have found it *more and more* difficult to solve the problem. ▶雨がいよいよ激しくなった It rained *harder and harder*. ▶彼は控えめなのでいよいよ好きだ I like him *all the better* for his modesty [*because of* his modesty, *because* he is modest]. (🅘(1) like の場合は通例 more でなく better を用いる. (2) 後の二つは彼が控えめである点が好きな理由となり、「控えめでなければ好きでない」ことを暗示する) ▶彼女に会えば会うほどいよいよ嫌いになる The more I see her, the less I like her. (🅘 the＋比較級, the＋比較級は「…すればするほどますます…」の意) /As I see her *more* (often) [see *more of* her], I like her *less*. (🅘前の例より口語的)

❷ [[確かに]] certainly; (疑問の余地なく) undoubtedly; (本当に) really. ▶彼が言っていることはいよいよ間違いない What he says is *certainly* true [には違いない) *must* be true].

❸ [[ついに]] at last, 《書》at length; (やっと) finally; (さあ) now. ▶いよいよ休みがやってきた The vacation has come *at last* [has *finally* come]. ▶いよいよよくの番だ *Now*, it's my turn. ▶いよいよあしたから大学生だ I am a college [a university] student tomorrow [✕from tomorrow] *at last*. ▶いよいよレースが始まるぞ The race *is about* [*is just going*] to start. (🅘まさに)

❹ [土壇場・正念場] (⇨いざ) ▶彼はいよいよというときに(=いちばん大事なときに)病気になった He got [became] sick *at the most important time* [*at the last moment*]. ▶彼はいよいよというときまで(=時間にせき立てられるまで)何もしない He doesn't do anything *until* [*till*] he is pressed for time. /(ぎりぎりになってからする) He always does things *at the last moment*. ▶いよいよとなれば(=その時がくれば)彼も一生懸命やるだろう He will work hard *when the time comes* [✕*will come*].

会話 「用意はいいかい」「さあいよいよ(出発)だ、行こう」"Are you ready?" "*This is* ⤴ *it*. Let's go." (🅘 出発, 別れ, 開始の直前に用いられる)

いよう 威容, 偉容 (堂々たる様子) magnificent [堂々とし, かつ優美な] stately, (威厳のある) dignified appearance. ▶ハイドパークの東側にヒルトンホテルがその威容を誇っている The Hilton Hotel rises *stately* to the east of Hyde Park.

いよう 異様 —— **異様な** 形 (不思議な) strange; (変わった) odd, 《話》weird /wiərd/; (風変わりな) 《やや古》queer; (不可解な) mysterious. (⇨変な) ▶異様なドレスを a *strange* [a *queer*, a *funny*] dress. ▶彼の態度は異様な気がする I feel (that) his manner is *strange* [*odd*, *queer*]. /His manner strikes me as *strange* [*odd*, *queer*].

*****いよく 意欲** 图 [[意志]] (a) will; [[欲望]] (a) desire; [[積極性]] drive; [[熱意]] eagerness, enthusiasm; [[やる気]] motivation. ▶彼に意欲を起こさせる arouse his *desire*《for; to do》. ●意欲をそぐ dampen one's *enthusiasm*《about; for》; spoil one's *appetite*《for》. ▶彼は働く意欲がない He has no *will* [*desire*, *inclination*] to work. ▶彼は意欲満々だ He has plenty [lots] of *drive*. ▶この本を読めば勉強する意欲がわくよ If you read this book, you will *want to study*. /This book will *motivate* you to study.

——意欲的な 形 ●意欲的な学生 an *eager* student; a *highly motivated* student. ●意欲的な(=野心的な)作品 an *ambitious* work.

——意欲的に 副 ▶彼は意欲的に仕事に取り組んだ He got down to work *enthusiastically* [*with enthusiasm*].

:いらい 以来 [[過去のある時から]] (今までずっと) since (…). (🅘通例完了時制で); (…から) from … (on) (🅘通例過去時制で). ▶それ以来 20 世紀の初頭まで *from* that time *up to* the early twentieth century. ▶彼は火曜日以来ずっと病気で寝ている He's been sick in bed *since* [✕from] Tuesday. ▶彼

いらい

は1970年に来日し，それ以来ずっと日本に住んでいます He came to Japan in 1970 and has lived here (*ever*) *since* [*since* then]. (**!** ever is since を強める) ▶それ以来彼らは愛し合うようになった *From* that time *on* [*From* then *on*, *After* that], they came to love each other. ▶彼の死以来5年がたった It's been《主に米》[It's《主に英》] five years *since* he died.(**!** (1) 主節が現在(完了)形では since 節は通例過去形, 主節が過去形では since 節内は過去(完了)形を用いる. (2) 次例はより堅い言い方)/Five years have [ˣhas] passed *since* he died./He *has been* dead [ˣhas died] *for* five years. (**!** He died five years ago. ともいえる) ▶20年以来の大雪だ This is the heaviest snowfall (that) we *have had for the past*《主に米》*in*] twenty years./We *haven't had* a heavy snowfall like this in《主に米》[for《主に英》] twenty years. (**!** in は否定文も最上級, first, only などの後に用いる)

:いらい 依頼 名 [要請] (a) request (⇨頼み); [依存] dependence. ●彼の友人の依頼で at his friend's *request*; at the *request* of his friend. ▶彼女は依頼心が強い She is too *dependent* on others./(すべてに自主性を欠く) She lacks self-motivation [independence] in everything.
— **依頼する** 動 ❶[要請する] ask, 《やや書》request. (⇨頼む) ▶[彼に]援助を依頼する ask (him) *for* help; *make* a request (*to* him) *for* help. ▶加藤教授に講演を依頼した I *asked* [*requested*] Prof. Kato to give a lecture./《書》I *requested* of Prof. Kato *that* he ((主に英)) *should*) give a lecture.
❷[委託する]《やや書》entrust (*with*). ●弁護士にその件を依頼する *entrust* a lawyer *with* the matter; *entrust* [*leave*] the matter *to* a lawyer. ●[*leave* の口語的]
●依頼状 a letter of request. ●依頼人 (弁護士などの) a client.

いらいら — **いらいらする** 動 get irritated; get [annoyed]《*at*+事; *with*+人》(**!** 前の方が意味が強い); (我慢できなくなる) get impatient. ●ウエーターのいらいらするほどのろい反応 the *irritatingly* slow response of the waiter. ▶何をそんなにいらいらしているの What *are* you so *irritated at*? ▶隣の犬がわんわんほえるのにはいらいらする The neighbor's noisy dogs *irritate* me [*are irritating*, *get on* my *nerves*]. ▶彼はいらいらしてバスを待っていた He was waiting *impatiently* for the bus.

いらか 甍 (屋根) a tiled roof; (かわら) a roofing tile.
イラク [国名] Iraq /iræk, irɑːk/; (公式名) the Republic of Iraq. (首都 Baghdad) ●イラク人 an Iraqi. ●イラク(人)の Iraqi. ▶ショックなこともたくさんあるけど, イラク人のことを嫌いになれない I had lots of shocking experiences. But I am still fond of Iraqis. (**!** like より強く, 溺愛(ほう)している場合に用いる fond of を用いていることに注意)

いらくさ 刺草 [植物] a nettle.
イラスト（レーション） [挿し絵] an illustration.
●イラストマップ a pictorial map.
イラストレーター an illustrator.
いらだたしい 苛立たしい irritating (⇨いらだつ); [うるさい] annoying.
いらだち 苛立ち (an) irritation. ●いらだちを隠す hide [《やや書》conceal] one's *irritation*.
いらだつ 苛立つ [立腹する] get* angry; [我慢できなくなる] get impatient; lose* (one's) patience; [神経質になる] get nervous. ●いらだたせる irritate; (神経にさわる) get on (his) nerves. (⇨いらいら)

いらつく 苛つく get irritated. (⇨いらいら)
***いらっしゃい** ❶ [お入りください] Come in. ; [話] Come on in. (**!** come in の強調形); [ようこそ] Welcome!; Glad to see you! ▶いつか遊びにいらっしゃい *Come* (*and*) *see* [*Come to see*] us sometime, will you? (**!** 前の方がくだけた言い方. 特に and を省略するのは《米話》) ▶いらっしゃいませ [店員が客に] May [Can] I help you, sir [ma'am]? (**!** (1) may の方が丁寧. How may [can] I help you? ともいう. (2) 男性には sir, 女性には ma'am を用いる. (3) 客の方は Yes, I'd like to see that necktie. (そのネクタイを見たいのですが) とか No, thank you. I'm just looking. (いや, ちょっと見ているだけですの)ように答える)/What can I do for you, sir [ma'am]? ▶さあ, いらっしゃい (客寄せの言葉) *Step right up*, ladies and gentlemen.
❷ [ある場所へ一緒に行く] come.
会話「あなたもいらっしゃいますか」「ええ, ぜひお供します」"Are you *coming*, too?" "Yes, I'm glad to."

いらっしゃる (**!** 英語では上下関係に基づく敬語は特に用いない) ❶ [行く] go*. (⇨行く) ▶京都へは奥様といらっしゃったのですか Did you *go to* [*visit*] Kyoto with your wife?
❷ [来る] come*. (⇨来る) ▶あす何時にここへいらっしゃる予定ですか What time *are* you *coming* here tomorrow?
❸ [居る] be. (⇨居る) ▶倉敷にいらっしゃる間にそこへ行かれるといいですよ You might as well go there while you *are* [*are staying*] in Kurashiki.
❹ [...している] be doing. (⇨-ている) ▶あの方は新聞を読んでいらっしゃいます That gentleman *is reading* the newspaper.

いられない (⇨居(¹)る) ❺
イラン [国名] Iran /irǽn, irɑːn/; (公式名) the Islamic Republic of Iran. (首都 Teheran) ●イラン人 an Iranian. ●イラン(人)の Iranian.
いり 入り ❶ [入ること] entering; [入場者数] an attendance. ●日の入り (=日没) までに by [before] *sunset*; by the time [before] *the sun sets*. ●寒[土用]の入り (=始まる) *the beginning* (最初の日) *the first day*] of midwinter [midsummer]. ▶その日の公演は入りがよかった There was a large *attendance* [*audience*] at the performance./The performance *was* well *attended*. ▶芝居は八分の入りだった We played to eighty percent *audience*.
❷ [含まれていること] ●フッ素化合物入りの歯みがき toothpaste *with* fluoride /flúərəid/. ●絵入りの本 an *illustrated* book.
いりあい 入会 ●入会権 common. ●入会地 common land; a common.
いりうみ 入り海 an inlet; (閉ざされた小湾) a cove. (⇨湾)
いりえ 入り江 an inlet. (⇨湾)
***いりぐち 入り口** an entrance, 《英》a way in; [戸口] a door, a doorway. [玄関, 戸口] ▶ホテルの入り口 the *entrance* of [*to*] a hotel. (**!** of は建物自体の, to はそこへ通じる入り口を表す) ●銀座の地下鉄の入り口 the Ginza subway *entrance*. ●正面から入り口から家に入る enter the house through the front *entrance* [*door*]. ▶公園の入り口に電話ボックスがあります There is a telephone booth *at the entrance of* the park. ▶1957年人類は宇宙時代の入り口に立った In 1957, mankind stood *on the threshold of* the space age.
いりくむ 入り組む [複雑になる] get* complicated [complex]. ●入り組んだ問題 a *complicated* [a *complex*] problem.

イリジウム 〖化学〗iridium 《元素記号 Ir》.

いりしお 入り潮 (⇨引き潮)

いりたまご 炒り卵 scrambled egg(s). (🔎複数形でも単数扱い) ●いり卵 2 人前 *scrambled eggs* for two. (🔎 two *scrambled egg* は「2 人前のいり卵」で two *scrambled eggs* (卵 2 個分のいり卵)とまぎらわしい) ▶私は普通朝食にいり卵を食べる I usually eat *scrambled egg(s)* for breakfast.

いりつける 炒り付ける (煮詰める) boil(...) down; (豆・穀類を) parch.

イリノイ 〖米国の州〗Illinois /íləˈnɔɪ/《略 Ill. 郵便略 IL》.

いりひ 入り日 (the light of) the setting sun.

いりびたる 入り浸る 碁会所に入りびたる (=絶えず行っている) *frequent* the go club. ●正義は彼女のアパートに入りびたっている (=いつもそこにいて時間を過ごす) Masayoshi *spends all his time* at her apartment.

いりまじる 入り交じる mix, mingle《with》. (⇨交じる) ●彼女は喜びと悲しみの入り交じった複雑な気持ちだった She had *mixed* feelings of joy and sorrow.

いりみだれる 入り乱れる ●入り乱れて in confusion [disorder]. ●入り乱れて戦う fight *riotously* in *confusion*; fight *in a melee* /méɪleɪ/.

いりむこ 入り婿 ●入り婿となる marry into one's wife's family.

いりもや 入母屋 〖建築〗a gabled, hipped roof.

いりゅう 慰留 ―慰留する 🔷 ●部長を慰留する (職に留まるように説得する) *persuade* the manager *to stay* in office; (辞職しないように) *persuade* the manager *not* to resign. ●いずれも相手がその気になったことを示している. 単に慰留の努力をすることは try to persuade... で表す)

いりゅうひん 遺留品 (あとに残された物) things left behind. ●多くの遺留品が犯行現場に残されていた A lot of *things were left behind* at the scene of the crime.

いりゅうぶん 遺留分 a portion [a share] of the legacy.

いりょう 衣料 clothing (🔎集合的に衣類全体をさす); clothes (🔎個々の衣類全体をいう); garments (🔎 clothes より上品な語. 特に製造・販売する人が用いる); wardrobe (🔎集合的に個人・団体の所有する衣料全部をさす); wear (🔎集合的に複合語として用いることが多い: レジャー用衣料 sports*wear*). ●婦人用衣料品 ladies' *clothing* [*garments*]. ●衣料品 2 点今日は二ピース [articles] of *clothing*. ●冬物衣料を買う buy winter *clothes*; buy *clothes* for the winter.
●衣料費 clothing expenses. ●衣料品店 a clothing store.

いりょう 医療 🔷 〖治療〗medical treatment [care]; 〖医療活動全般〗medical service(s). ▶日本の医療は向上した *Medical treatment* [*care, service*] has improved in Japan.
―医療の 🔷 medical.
●医療過誤 [ミス] medical malpractice. ●医療機関 a medical institute. ●医療器械 a medical instrument [appliance]; medical equipment. ●医療従事者 medical workers. ●医療費 (治療費) a fee for medical treatment; (医療関係の出費) medical expenses. ●医療費控除 deduction for medical expenses. ●医療品 (補給医療物資) medical supplies. ●医療法人 a medical corporation. ●医療保険 medical insurance.

*****いりょく 威力** 🔷 power; 〖権力〗authority; 〖勢力〗influence. ●威力を振るう exercise one's *power*

《*over*》. ▶彼のパンチには威力がなかった His punch lacked *power* [was not *powerful*].
―威力のある 🔷 powerful; influential.

:いる 居る ❶ 〖存在する〗there is [are], be (⇨在る); exist; (捜せば見つかる) be found. ▶広場には多くの若者がいる [いた] There are [were] many young people in the square. ▶それを好きな人はあまりいない Lots of people don't like it. / *There are* many (people) who don't like it. ▶幽霊がいると思いますか Do you believe (that) ghosts *exist*?/Do you believe in ghosts? (🔎 believe in は「...の存在を信じる」の意) ▶今どき親と同居している若い夫婦はあまりいない You won't *find* many young couples living with their parents these days. ▶その夫婦には子供がいない (=その夫婦は子供を持っていない) The couple *have* no children [(1 人もいない) no child]. ▶若死にする人もいれば長生きする人もいる *Some* die young, *others* live long.

会話「だれかその仕事に適任者はいるかい」「そうだね, 田中さんとか鈴木さんがいるじゃないか」"*Is there* anyone good for the job?" "Let's see. *There's* Mr. Tanaka and Mr. Suzuki." (🔎 (1)《話》では複数主語でもしばしば単数で there's とする. (2) 下の構文で主語は不定の名詞であるが, このように列挙する場合は固有名詞など特定の名詞も主語に用いられる (⇨ ❷ 会話[第 1 例]))

❷ 〖場所にいる〗 be; (とどまる) stay, (後に居残る) remain; (捜した結果見つけ出される) be found. ▶彼は日曜日はたいてい家にいる He usually *stays* [*is* usually] (at) home on Sunday(s). (⇨家 ❶ 🔷) ▶(これまで)どのくらい日本にいるのですか How long *have* you *been* (*staying*) in Japan? (🔎社交上の会話では Have you been in Japan for a long time? が普通で, 応答も Yes, about twenty years now./No, just about ten months. などとなる) ▶ああ, あなたがここにいてくれたならな How I wish you *were* here!(あなたがいなくて本当に寂しい) I really miss you. ▶彼は他の者が出て行った後も部屋にいた He *stayed* [*remained*] in the room after the others went out. ▶捜していた子猫はお隣りの物置小屋にいた The kitten I was looking for has *been found* in the neighbor's shed. ▶彼は私がいること [いないこと]に気づかなかったようだった He seemed unconscious (unaware) of *my presence* [*absence*]. ▶そのことは彼女のいる所 (=面前)では話さないでください Please don't speak of it *in her presence* [(彼女の周辺で) *around* her].

会話「ほら, あそこに淳と令子がいるわ. ちょっとあいさつに行きましょう」「そうだね」"*There's* Jun and Reiko. Let's go (and) say hello." "OK." (🔎 (1) there は文頭に置いて相手の注意を喚起する. (2)《米話》では and を省いて go say ともいう (⇨❶ 会話))

会話「やあ里美」「あら, そこにいたの淳」"Hello, Satomi." "Oh 、*there* you ↗ *are*, Jún." (🔎主語が代名詞の場合はこの語順)

会話「もう少しいてもいいか」「もちろん. いていただきたいよ」"Can I *stay* a bit longer?" "Why not? *Stay* as long as you wish."

❸ 〖居住する〗live; (種族・民族が) 〖書〗inhabit; (滞在する) stay. ▶私はおばのところに [am *living*, am *staying*] with my aunt [at my aunt's]. (🔎進行形は一時的にいることを含意) ▶その規則はこの地域にいる外国人には適用されない The rule cannot be applied [does not apply] to foreigners *living* in this district. ▶この魚は海にいる These fish *live in* [*inhabit*, ×are *inhabiting*] the sea.

❹ 〖...している〗(⇨(し)ている, (し)ていた

いる ❺ [...せずにはいられない] can't [《書》cannot] help 《doing》,《話》can't help but 《do》,《書》cannot but 《do》; [...なしでいる] do without.... ▶ その光景を見て笑わずにはいられなかった I *couldn't help* [《慎む》*keep from*] *laughing* at the sight. ▶ 1 週間たばこなしでいることができますか Can you *do without* cigarettes for a week?

いる 要る ❶ [必要とする] need, 《やや書》require; [欲する] want; [必要がある] be necessary [needed, required] 《*for, to*》. (⚠この順に堅い表現) (⇨必要)
● 要らない物 (不必要な物) what you do not *need*; *unnecessary* things;《不要品》*useless* articles. ▶この本は要りますか Do you *need* [*want*] this book?/Is this book *necessary for* you? ▶英語の学習にはずいぶん根気が要ります Learning English *needs* [*requires*,《書》*demands*] a lot of patience. ▶彼にはもう医者は要らない(=医者なしですませる) He can *do without* a doctor's care now. ▶おつりは要りません(=とっておけ) Keep the change. ▶要らぬ世話をやくな Mind your own business.
❷[時間・金・労力などが] take*; cost*. (⚠cost は行為に伴う努力や負担の大きいことを含意する) ▶コート 1 着作るのにどのくらい布が要りますか How much cloth does it *take* [do you use] to make a coat? ▶この家を建てるのにたくさんの時間と金が要った It *took* (us) a lot of time and money to build this house./This house *took* (us) a lot of time and money to build. (⇨掛かる)

いる 射る [矢・動物を] shoot*; [標的を] hit*. ▶ 矢で鳥[的]を射る *shoot* an arrow *at* a bird [*into* a target]. ▶ 弓は的を射た The arrow *hit* the target.

いる 煎る, 炒る roast 《beans》. ▶コーヒー豆はもう煎ったよ We've *roasted* coffee beans.

いる 鋳る 《像・鐘などを》cast 《a bell *in* bronze》; 《貨幣を》mint, coin.

いるい 衣類 clothes; 《集合的》clothing;《書》garments; dress. (⇨衣料, 服) ● 衣類の虫干しをする air the *clothes* [*clothing*].

いるか 海豚 〔動物〕a dolphin; (ネズミイルカ) a porpoise /pɔ́ːrpəs/ (優~s,《集合的》~).

いるす 居留守 ● 居留守を使う pretend to be out; pretend not to be in.

イルミネーション 〔照明〕illumination. ▶橋にイルミネーションを施す *illuminate* a bridge.

-いれ -入れ (ケース, 箱) a case; (差し入れるもの) a holder. ● 鉛筆入れ a pencil *case*. ● 名刺入れ a card *case* [*holder*]. ● 定期券入れ a commutation [《主に英》a season] ticket *holder*.

いれあげる 入れ揚げる lavish money [spend money lavishly] 《*on* a woman [a thing]》.

いれい 威令 authoritative orders; a peremptory command.

いれい 異例 ── 異例の 形 (例外的な) exceptional; (前例のない) unprecedented. ●異例の記者会見 an *unprecedented* press conference. ▶彼の欠勤は異例のことだ(=普通でない) It is *unusual* for him to stay away from the office.

いれい 慰霊 ● 慰霊祭 a memorial service 《*for*》. ● 慰霊碑 a memorial monument;《英》a cenotaph.

いれかえ 入れ替え [物の] a change; replacement; 〔人事の〕 a change, a reshuffle (⚠トランプの切り返しのイメージ). ● 古い車と新しい車の入れ替え the *replacement* of one's old car *with* a new one. ● 大臣の入れ替え a *reshuffle* of some Cabinet ministers; a partial Cabinet *reshuffle*. ● 人員の大幅な入れ替えを行う make major *changes* in personnel.

いれかえる 入れ替える 〔AをBと取り替える〕replace A with B, change A for B; 〔Bの代わりにAを用いる〕substitute A for B. ● 部屋の空気を入れ替える *air* [*ventilate*] a room; (新鮮な空気を入れる) *let* some fresh air *into* a room. ● 心を入れ替える(=改心する) reform (oneself);《やや書》mend one's ways [manners];《やや話》turn over a new leaf. ● 敷き物を新しいものにする(=新しいものにする) *renew* carpets. ▶彼は切れた電池を新しいものと入れ替えた He *replaced* a dead battery *with* a new one [*changed* a dead battery *for* a new one]./He *substituted* a new battery *for* a dead one. ●お茶を入れ替える(=新しいお茶を入れ)ましょうか Would you like me to make some fresh tea?

いれかわり 入れ替わり ● 入れ替わり立ち替わり ● 入れ替わり立ち替わり(=次から次へと)来客がある have *one* visitor *after another*; have visitors *one after another*.

いれかわる 入れ替わる 〔場所などを〕change [exchange] 《places》(交換する); [前任者などと] take* 《his》place. (⇨変わる)

イレギュラー irregular. ▶ボールはショートの前でイレギュラーバウンドした The ball took a *bad* bounce [*hop*] in front of the shortstop.

いれこ 入れ子 ● 入れ子式テーブル a *nest of* tables. ● ...を入れ子にする nest.

いれこむ 入れ込む ❶〔盛り込む〕▶君の提案を今回の企画に入れ込んだ We *incorporated* your suggestion *into* our plans. ❷〔熱中する〕 be enthusiastic [《話》crazy, mad] 《*about*》; be into 《jazz》.

いれずみ 入れ墨 a tattoo /tætúː/ (優~s). ● 背中に竜の入れ墨をしてもらう[してもらう] have a dragon *tattooed* on one's back.

いれぢえ 入れ知恵 ── 入れ知恵(を)する 動 put an idea into 《his》head; prime 《him》with an idea; 〔ちょっとのめかす〕give 《him》a hint. ▶だれが彼にそんな入れ知恵をしたんだ Who *put* it *into* his *head*?

いれちがい 入れ違い ▶彼と入れ違いに彼女がやってきた She came *just as* he went out [*left*]. ▶ どうも私の手紙は彼との入れ違いになったようだ I am afraid my letter *crossed* his in the mail.

いれば 入れ歯 a false [an artificial] tooth (優 teeth),《やや書》dentures (⚠しばしば総入れ歯をさす。正式には a set of dentures. a full set of false teeth ともいう). ● 入れ歯を 1 本入れてもらう have a *false tooth* put in. ● 入れ歯をはめる[はめている; はずす] put in [wear; take out] one's *false teeth*.

いれもの 入れ物 a container; (箱・ケースなど) a case; (液体用の)《やや古》a vessel. (⇨器)

いれる 入れる, 容れる

INDEX
❶ 器に入れる　　❷ 物に加える
❸ 入らせる　　　❹ 収容できる
❺ 仲間に加える
❻ 要求・提案などを受け入れる
❼ 含める　　　　❽ 納入する
❾ スイッチなどを　❿ 精力を注ぐ
⓫ その他の表現

❶ [器に入れる] put*... 《*in, into*》; (注ぎ込む) pour... 《*into*》; (流し込む) run* ...《*into*》; (入れておく) keep*... 《*in*》. ● 水を手おけに入れる *pour* [*run*] water *into* a pail. ● カメラに新しいフィルムを入れる *load* a new film *into* a camera; *load* a camera *with* a new film. ▶車を車庫に入れよ *Put* the car *in* [*into*] the garage, will you? (⚠単に「中に入

れ」」put the car in [×into]. このように前置詞の目的語は文脈上明らかな場合は省略される) ▶彼は私にコーヒーを1杯いれてくれた He *poured* [*made*, *got*] me a cup of coffee./He *poured* [*made*, *got*] me a cup of coffee *for* me. (❗ pour は「注ぐ」動作をいい、make と get は小一れて出すまでの行為をいう.「いれたての紅茶1杯」は a cup of freshly-*made* tea) ▶動物をたいていおりに入れておかれるのをいやがる Most animals don't like *being kept in* cages. ▶ポケットに両手を入れたまま歩いてはいけない Don't walk with your hands *in* your pockets.

会話 「花子、コーヒーを入れてくれない？」「今手がはなせないの、自分で入れたら」 "Can you *get* a cup of coffee *for* me, Hanako?" "I've got my hands tied [full]. Why don't you *get* it yourself?"

❷ 【物に加える】(差し込む) put*... 《*in*, *into*》,《やや書》insert ... 《*in*, *into*》; (機械などに) feed*. ● その二つの文章の間にコロンを入れる *put* [*insert*] a colon between the two sentences. ▶硬貨を駐車メーターに入れる *put* [*insert*] coins *into* [*in*] the parking meter; *feed* coins *to* the parking meter. ▶コンピュータにデータを入れる *feed* data *into* a computer. (❗ ×*feed* a computer with data. とは通例いわない) ▶歯を1本入れてもらう (⇨入れ歯) ▶卵と小麦粉とどっちを先に入れるの Which *goes in* first, the eggs or the flour?

会話 「このココアあんまり甘くないよ」「砂糖をもう一つ入れなさい」 "This cocoa's not very sweet." "*Put* another lump of sugar *in* it./Have another lump of sugar."

会話 「紅茶はどのようにして召し上がりますか」「砂糖とミルクを入れてください」 "How would you like your tea?" "*With* sugar and milk, please."

会話 「クリームをどうぞ」「私はコーヒーにクリームを入れないんだよ」 "Have some cream." "I don't *take* [×*put*] cream in my coffee." (❗ take は「取り入れる」の意)

❸ 【入らせる】let*・《*it* [*him*] *into* ...》; (許可を与えて)《やや書》admit (-tt-); (送り込む) send*. ● 彼を私の傘の中に入れてやる *let* him *in* under my umbrella. ▶息子を大学に入れる *send* one's son *to* college [*university*]. ▶新鮮な空気を入れなさい You'd better *let in* some fresh air [*let* some fresh air *in*]. ▶猫を(家の)中に入れるな Don't *let* [*get*] the cat *in*./(外に出しておきなさい) Keep the cat *out*. (❗ 場所を明示する場合はたとえば in [into] the kitchen; out of the kitchen のように) ▶彼はその学校に入れてもらった(= 入学を許可された) He *was admitted to* [*was allowed to get into*] the school. (❗ 後の方が口語的). get into の代わりに enter も可)/The school *accepted* him. ▶あなたはどこの幼稚園に入れるか決めましたか Have you decided what kindergarten to *send* your son *to*? (❗ 文尾の to に注意)

❹ 【収容できる】(施設などが)《やや書》(can) accommodate; (座席をもつ) seat; (入れる余地がある)《やや書》admit (-tt-). (⇨入る❹) ▶この会館は1,000人の人を入れることができる This hall *can accommodate* [*seats*, *admits*] one thousand people.

❺ 【仲間に加える】《やや書》receive ...《*into*》; (受け入れる) accept; [雇う] employ,《米》hire; (臨時に)《英》hire. ▶彼を私たちのクラブに入れることはできない We can't *receive* [*accept*] him *into* our club [*as* a *member of our club*]./We can't *let* him *join* our club. ▶その会社は彼女を秘書として入れた The company *employed* her as a secretary. ▶この会社は多くのパートタイマーを入れている This firm *hires* a lot of part-timers.

❻ 【要求・提案などを受け入れる】(容認する) accept; (応じる)《書》comply《*with*》; (耳を傾ける) listen《*to*》. ▶彼の忠告を入れる take [*follow*, *listen to*] his advice. ▶彼女の要請をいれる *comply with* her request. ▶彼はなかなか他人の説をいれようとしない He will not *accept* [*listen to*] other people's opinions./(自分の考えに固執する) He *sticks to* his own opinion(s).

❼ 【含める】include. ▶消費税を入れて10ドル Price $10, consumption tax *included* [*including* consumption tax]. ▶あなたを入れて7人の少年が招待された Seven boys were invited, *including* [*counting*] you. ▶それを計算(= 考慮)に入れましたか Did you *think* it over [*consider* it]? (❗ 次例より口語的)/Did you *take* it *into account* [*consideration*]?

会話 「クラス会に来る？」「行けそうにないわ．だから私は数に入れないで」 "Are you coming to the class reunion?" "Not likely, so *count* me *out* (↔*in*)."

❽ 【納入する】(物を) supply; (お金を) pay*. ● 図書館に新刊本を10冊入れる *supply* ten new books *to* the library; *supply* the library *with* ten new books. ▶彼は家賃をふた月も入れていない He *has* not *paid* his rent for two months.

❾ 【スイッチなどを】▶エアコンを入れる *turn on* the air conditioner; *turn* the air conditioner *on*. ▶アイロンのスイッチを入れる *switch on* the iron.

❿ 【精力を注ぐ】▶仕事に身を入れる *put* one's *heart into* one's work; (集中する) *concéntrate on* one's work. ▶あの辞書は特に文法と語法に力を入れている(= 重点を置いている) That dictionary *puts* [*lays*, *places*] a special *emphasis on* grammar and usage.

⓫ 【その他の表現】▶ちょっとお耳に入れておきたいことがあります I *have something to tell* you./Let me *have a word with* you. ▶だれに入れましたか(= 投票しましたか) Who did you *vote for*?

:いろ 色 ❶ 【色彩】(a) color; (a) hue; (色合い) a tint, a tinge; (色彩の濃淡) a shade.

> 使い分け color 「色」を表す最も一般的な語. 主に原色をさす.
> hue color の詩的な語. 混色で生じた淡く微妙な色調をさす.
> tint ほのかに明るい色合い.
> tinge tint より濃く色づけられ通例全体に広がっている色合い.
> shade ある色の濃淡や明暗の度合い.

① 【~色】● 感じのよい色 a pleasant [a delightful] *color*. ● 濃い[薄い]色 a dark [a light] *color*. ● はでな[落ち着いた]色 a bright [a quiet] *color*. ● 虹(!`)のあらゆる色 all the *colors* [*hues*] of the rainbow. ● もっと薄い[明るい]緑色 a lighter [a brighter] *shade* of green. ▶赤は彼女の好きな色です Red [×The red] is her favorite *color*. (❗ 一口に赤といってもさまざまな色合いの赤があり、その中の特定の色をさす場合には the をつける: 彼女にはその赤は似合わない *The* red doesn't suit her.) ▶秋の色が深くなった There are fall *colors* everywhere./It has become more like fall.

会話 「君の車は何色？」「赤だ」 "What *color* is your car?/What is the *color* of your car?" "It's red [×red color, ×red in color]."

② 【色~】● 色もののワイシャツ a *colored* shirt. ● やわらかな色合い a soft *color* tone. (⇨色調)

③ 【色は[が]】▶この色はあせやすい The color *fades* easily. (❗ ×The color is easy to fade. とはいわない) ▶それは色が桃の花に似ている It resembles a

peach blossom *in color*. ▶犬は色が識別できない Dogs can't see [perceive] *colors*.
会話「このバッグの黄色はありますか」「黄色はないですね. 緑だけだと思います」"Do you have this bag in yellow?" "We don't have it in yellow. Apparently, it only comes in green."
❹[色を] ▶その動物は居る場所に合わせて色を変える The animal changes its *color* to match its surroundings. ▶その子は絵に色を塗っていた The child *was coloring* a picture. (! paint a picture は「絵の具で絵を描く」の意)
❷[顔色] (a) complexion;〔健康な顔色〕(a) color;〔表情〕a look. ●目の色を変えて怒る(=怒りで赤くなる) turn red with anger. ●色白の (⇔色白) ▶彼は色が白い[黒い](顔色の) He has a fair [a dark] *complexion*./He is fair-*complexioned* [dark-*complexioned*]./(皮膚が) He has (a) fair [(a) dark] skin./He is fair-skinned [dark-skinned]. ▶失望の色が彼の顔に現れた A *look* of disappointment came to [over] his face.
❸[恋愛, 情事] 色っぽい(=色気がある) have sex appeal. (⇔色気) ●色っぽい声[女性] an alluring voice [woman]. ●色(=官能的快楽)におぼれる give oneself up to [indulge in] *sensual pleasures*. ●色目を使う (⇔色目)
●色を失う ▶彼はその知らせを聞いて色を失った He lost *color* [turned pale] at the news.
●色を好む ●色を好む(=好色な)老人 an *amorous* old man. ●英雄を好む(⇔英雄[成句])
●色をつける ●話に色をつける(=潤色する) *color* [*embellish*] one's story.
●色刷り (a) color printing. ●色づかい a color scheme. (⇔彩り❶)

いろあい 色合い (⇔色調)
いろあげ 色揚げ 图 redyeing. ── 色揚げする 動 redye.
いろあせる 色褪せる fade. (⇔褪(ぁ)せる)
:いろいろ 色々 ── いろいろな 形 various, a variety of ...;〔違った〕different, diverse /daivə́ːrs/;〔寄せ集めの〕miscellaneous. (⇔雑多)

> 使い分け ▶ various 物事が多種多様で数が多いこと.
> different 複数の物が互いに異なっていて多種多様であること. しばしば前に a lot of, many, several などを伴う. 日本語の「いろいろな」はこれに相当することも多い.
> diverse 物事が多種多様で, 特に互いに顕著な差異を示すこと.

●その問題をいろいろな角度から調べる investigate the matter from *various* [*different*] angles. ▶彼はいろいろな本を読んでいる He reads *several* [*a lot of*,《やや書》*many*] *different* (*kinds of*) books. ▶そのネクタイはいろいろな柄がそろっています The tie comes in a (wide) *variety of* patterns. ▶仕事上いろいろな人と会います I have to meet *all kinds of* people on business. (! *various* people より自然)
── いろいろ(と) ▶いろいろ=ずいぶん)考えあぐむ I thought *hard* [《話》*a lot*] and finally ...; after *a great deal of* thinking. ▶いろいろ(=ずいぶん)ご面倒をかけすみません I'm sorry to have troubled you *so much*./I'm afraid I'm being *too much* trouble. ▶いろいろお世話になりました Thank you very much for *everything* [*all you've done*]. ▶辞書にもいろいろある There are good dictionaries and bad dictionaries./There are dictionaries and dictionaries.
いろう 慰労 ── 慰労する 動 ▶彼を慰労する acknowledge [recognize] his services; express one's thanks for his services.
●慰労会 a party given in appreciation of《his》services. ●慰労金 a (special) bonus.
いろう 遺漏〔手抜かり〕(an) omission;〔見落とし〕(an) oversight. ●万に遺漏なきを期す take the utmost care not to leave any unwanted *omission*.
いろえんぴつ 色鉛筆 a colored pencil.
いろおち 色落ち ── 色落ちする 動 ▶色落ちしない靴下 *colorfast* socks. ▶この靴下は洗ったらひどく色落ちした The dye came out terribly when I washed these socks. ▶この生地だと色落ちしない This cloth *holds dye well*./The color doesn't run from this cloth.
いろおとこ 色男〔女好きのする男〕a sexy man (⇔men);《! a lady-killer はいわゆる「女たらし」;〔美男子〕a handsome guy;《話》a hunk (! 大柄で強く, 魅力がある男).
いろか 色香〔花の〕color and fragrance [scent];〔女性の〕charms, beauty. ▶私は彼女の色香に迷った I was captivated [infatuated, smitten] by her *charms* [*beauty*].
いろがみ 色紙 colored paper.
いろけ 色気 ❶[性的魅力] sex appeal; sexiness.
●色気のある sexy; sexually attractive [exciting]. ●色気づく become sexually awakened; begin to think of love.
❷[愛想] ●色気のない(=そっけない)返事をする give《him》a *blunt* [*a curt*] answer.
❸[興味] (an) interest. ●政治に色気を示す show (an) *interest* in politics. ▶父はもうけ話には色気をだした(=関心を示した)ことはない My father has not had any *interest* in money making. ▶彼は色気(=野心)を出しすぎて事業に失敗した He was so *ambitious* that he failed in his business.
いろこい 色恋〔情事〕love; a love affair. (⇔恋愛)
●色恋さた a love affair.
いろごと 色事 a love affair,《古》an amour.
●色事師 a seducer;《話》a Don Juan, a lady-killer.
いろごのみ 色好み sensuality. (⇔好色)
いろじかけ 色仕掛け ▶メアリーは色仕掛けでジョンから情報を得ようとした Mary tried to *seduce* John *to* get some information.
いろじろ 色白 色白の 形〔皮膚が〕fair(-skinned);〔顔が〕fair-complexioned. ●色白の美人 a beautiful woman with (a) *fair* skin. ▶彼女は色白の顔をしている She has a *fair* (↔*dark*) complexion.
いろちがい 色違い ▶同じ形で色違いのものはありますか Do you have the same style in *different* [*other*] colors?
いろづく 色付く〔赤く[黄色く]なる〕turn [《主に米》become,《主に英》grow] red [yellow];〔変色する〕color, change color. ▶美しく色づいた森 woods of beautiful *colors*. ▶木の葉が色づき始めた The leaves of the trees have begun to *color* [*turn*].
いろつや 色艶〔顔色〕a complexion;〔色と光沢〕color and luster [gloss]. (⇔艶(つや)) ●色つやのいいりんご a *glossy* [*a shiny*] apple. ▶彼女は若く色つやがいい(=輝くような肌をしている) She is young and has a *glowing* [*透きとおるような*] *clear*] complexion.
いろどり 彩り ❶[彩色] coloring;〔配色〕a color scheme. ●この部屋の彩りが気に入っている be pleased with the *color scheme* of this room.
❷[面白味] spice. ▶彼のギター演奏がパーティーに彩りを添えた His performance on the guitar gave

いろとりどり 色とりどり ● 色とりどりの花 flowers of various colors; (種々さまざまな) a wide variety [all kinds] of flowers.

いろどる 彩る (彩色する) color; (薄く色付けする) tinge; (飾る) decorate. ● 雲は朝日で金色に彩られものThe clouds *are colored* gold by the rising sun.

翻訳のこころ 普通の家の普通の生活を彩る花屋になりたいと思った (吉本ばなな『みどりのゆび』) I wanted to become a florist who *decorates* an ordinary life in an ordinary home. (**!** an ordinary life には部屋や家具だけでなく人間の活動も含まれるので、「家」は house でなく home とする)

いろは ❶ 〖文字〗いろは順に並べる arrange in (Japanese) *alphabetical* order.
❷ 〖初歩〗(米) the ABC's 《of》;(英) ABC 《of》; the first thing 《about》 (**!** 通例否定文で用いる). (⇒初歩)
● いろはガルタ 《a pack of》 Japanese alphabet cards.

いろまち 色町 a red-light district.

いろめ 色目 ● 色目を使う cast an *amorous glance* 《at》,《話》make eyes 《at》.

いろめがね 色眼鏡 〖サングラス〗sunglasses, dark glasses; (淡い色の) tinted glasses; 〖偏見〗(a) prejudice; (a) bias.
● 色眼鏡で見る ● 物事を色眼鏡で見る look at things *through colored spectacles* [with a prejudiced eye, (偏した見方で) from a biased viewpoint].

いろめく 色めく 〖活気づく〗enliven, liven /láivn/ (...) up (⇒活気づける〖うく〗); 〖動揺する〗be shaken (up) 動揺する; 〖なまめかしくなる〗be sexy; 〖書〗become amorous 《coquettish》.

いろやけ 色焼け (⇒日焼け, 変色)

いろよい 色よい ● 色よい返事をする give a *favorable* [a *good*] answer.

いろり 囲炉裏 〖暖炉〗a fireplace; a hearth. (⇒暖炉) ● 囲炉裏を囲んで歌う sing around the *fireplace* [*fireside*].

いろわけ 色分け ● 色分けする 動 (分類する) categorize; sort 《classify》... into categories.

いろん 異論 〖異なった意見〗a different opinion; 〖反対意見〗(an) objection 《to》. (⇒異議)

いろんな (⇒いろいろな)

*****いわ 岩** (a) rock. ● 個々の岩石は〖C〗, 岩壁は〖U〗 ● 岩の多い [でできた; のように固い] rocky. ● 巨大な岩 a huge *rock*. ● 固い岩 solid *rock*. ● その家は岩の上に建てられた The house was built on the *rock*.

*****いわい 祝い** 〖祝賀〗celebration; 〖祝いの行事〗(祝賀式) a celebration, (祝祭) a festival, (祝宴) a feast, (記念祭) a commemoration; 〖祝いの言葉〗congratulations; 〖祝いの品〗a gift, a present.
● 結婚祝いに wedding *gift* [*present*]. ● 祝いの酒 celebratory *sake* [drink]. ● 新年のお祝いをする *celebrate* New Year's Day. ▶ ご成功に心からお祝い申し上げます Please accept [I'd like to offer you] my sincere *congratulations on* your success. ▶ 君の卒業の祝いに酒を飲もう Let's drink *in celebration of* [*to celebrate*, ×*to congratulate*] your graduation. ▶ 私は誕生日のお祝いに時計をもらった I received a watch as [for] a birthday *present*.
会話「木村先生の名前が叙勲者名簿に出ていたよ」「じゃお祝いしなくてはね」"I've found Professor Kimura on the honors list." "This calls for a *celebration*." (**!** call for ... は「...を必要とする」の意)

● 祝い箸 (a pair of) celebratory chopsticks.

*****いわう 祝う** 〖式などを挙げて〗célebrate 《an event》; 〖言葉で〗congrátulate 《him *on* an event》; 〖行事・祝日などを慣行に従って〗observe; 〖記念日などを公式行事を行って〗commemorate. ● 彼の60歳の誕生日を祝ってパーティーを開く have a party *in honor of* his 60th birthday. ▶ 多くの家庭ではクリスマスを祝う Many families *celebrate* Christmas. (**!** celebrate の目的語には人ではなく誕生日 (one's birthday), 勝利 (a victory), 結婚記念日 (one's wedding anniversary) などがくる) ▶ 彼らは私の昇進を祝ってくれた They *congratulated* [×*celebrated*] me *on* my promotion./They *celebrated* [×*congratulated*] my promotion. ▶ 彼らは成功を祝って乾杯した They drank to [toasted] their success.

いわかん 違和感 the sense of incongruity. ● 違和感のある 〖書〗incongruous 《with, to》; (なじみのない) strange. ● 札幌の町並みにはひどく違和感のある寺院 a temple quite *incongruous with* the streets of Sapporo. ▶ 新しい入れ歯は一向に違和感が解消しない The new set of false teeth still remains *strange* in my mouth. ▶ 彼らといっしょにいるとどうも違和感を感じる Somehow I feel *out of place* [I *don't* feel I can *fit in*] *with* them.

いわく 曰く ❶ 〖訳〗(a) reason (⇒訳 ❶, 理由); 〖歴歴〗a history, a past. ● この絵についてのいわく話をお話ししましょう Let me tell you *how that has come about*. ❷ 〖言う〗● ことわざにいわく A proverb says....
● 曰く言い難し ▶ 事情はいわく言い難しだ The situation is *too complicated to explain* in a few words.
● 曰く付き ● いわくつきの女 a woman *with a past* [*a history*]. (**!** past では不倫などの, history では犯罪などの前歴をさすことが多い) ● いわくつきの刀 a sword /sɔːrd/ *with a story behind it*.

いわし 鰯 〖魚介〗a sardine /sɑːrdíːn/; 《集合的》 sardine. ● イワシの缶詰 a can of *sardines*. ● イワシの群れ a shoal of *sardine*.
● いわし雲 fleecy clouds. (**!** (1) 羊のやわらかい毛を連想する。(2) a mackerel sky は青い空にはいわし雲でおおわれている空をいう: いわし雲は雨の降る前兆だ The *mackerel sky* is a sign of rain to come.)

いわずかたらず 言わず語らず ● 言わず語らずのうちに tacitly, implicitly. (⇒暗黙)

いわずとしれた 言わずと知れた ● 言わずと知れたアルカポネ best-know [well-known] Al Capone.

いわずもがな 言わずもがな 〖言うまでもない〗● そんなことは言わずもがなだ (言わない方がよい) It would be better to leave it *unsaid*./(言うべきでない) You should not [ought not to] say it.

いわだたみ 岩畳 a heaps of rocks.

いわだな 岩棚 a (rock) ledge. ● 岩棚のある絶壁 a *ledged* cliff.

いわな 岩魚 〖魚介〗a char (⇨ ～, ～s).

いわのぼり 岩登り rock-climbing.

いわば 岩場 a rocky tract; (岩壁) a wall.

いわば 言わば 〖たとえて言えば〗so to speak; as it were/(日常的には ... in a way (ある意味では) などと言うことも多い) 〖実質的には〗virtually. ▶ 彼女は言わばお姫様だ She is, *so to speak* [*as it were*], a princess. ▶ 彼女は a princess, *so to speak* [*as it were*]. ▶ 言わば (= 事実上) 彼がその本の著者です He is the *virtual* writer of the book.

いわはだ 岩肌 the rock surface; bare rock.

いわぶろ 岩風呂 a rock-bound bath.

いわゆる what is called, what we [you, they] call;

いわれ so-called (⚠軽蔑的に「その名に値しない」を含意することが多い). ▶いわゆる知識人 a *so-called* intellectual. ▶彼らはいわゆる過激派学生です They are *what is called* [*what we call*] radical students./ They are "radical students." (⚠このように引用符で包んでも表現できる)

いわれ 謂れ ❶〖理由〗a reason, a cause. (⇨理由)
● 何のいわれもなく解雇される be dismissed *without any reason* [*cause*]. ● いわれのない怒り *causeless* anger; anger without a cause. ● いわれのない(=根拠のない)うわさ a *groundless* [*an unfounded*] rumor. ▶彼が辞職しなければならないいわれはない There is no *reason why* he should resign his post. ▶ぼくは君から軽蔑されるいわれはない I don't *deserve* your contempt.
❷〖由来〗(歴史) a history; (起源) (an) origin; (言い伝え) a story. ● この習慣のいわれ the *origin* of this custom. ● あの古い家には面白いいわれがある That old house has an interesting *history*.

いわれる 言われる ▶そう言われてみればおかしいね Now that you mention it, it's strange. (⇨言う)

いわんや〖まして…でない〗much less, let alone (⚠否定文の後に);〖言うまでもなく〗not to mention. (⇨まして❶)

いん 印〖印章〗a seal;〖スタンプ〗a stamp. ● ゴム印 a rubber *stamp*. ● 印をおす put a *seal* [a *stamp*] (*to* a document); stamp.

いん 院 ❶〖法皇・上皇などの尊称〗崇徳院 the retired Emperor *Sutoku*.
❷〖官庁・機関など〗衆議院 the House of Representatives. ● 会計検査院 the *Board* of Audit.
❸〖建物・施設名〗正倉院 (the) *Shosoin* (Building). ● 美容院 a beauty *parlor* [*salon*].

いん 陰 ● 陰にこもる 陰にこもった顔つき a *gloomy* outlook [face].
● 陰に陽に in public and in private; publicly and privately; (あらゆる機会に) at every available opportunity; whenever possible.

いん 韻 (a) rhyme /ráim/. ● 韻を踏んで in *rhyme*. ● 韻を踏んだ詩 *rhymed* verse. ▶"long" と "song" とは韻を踏む "Long" and "song" *rhyme*./"Long" *rhymes with* "song."

イン〖ゴルフ〗the back nine. (参考 後半の9ホール)

いんあつ 陰圧 negative pressure.

いんイオン 陰イオン〖化学〗a negative ion.

いんいん 殷殷 ● 殷殷たる砲声 the *bloom* [*roar*] of guns.

いんうつ 陰鬱 图 gloom. (⇨陰気, 憂鬱)
― 陰鬱な 形 ● 陰鬱な天気 *gloomy* weather.

いんえい 印影 an imprint of a seal.

いんえい 陰影 (影) a shadow; (日陰) a shade. ● 絵に陰影をつける *shade* a painting. ● 言葉の陰影(=微妙な違い) subtle /sÁtl/ *shades* [*nuances*] of meaning.

いんえいらいさん『陰翳礼讃』*In Praise of Shadows*. (参考) 谷崎潤一郎の評論)

いんか 引火 图 ignition. (⇨点火, 発火)
― 引火する 動 catch fire; ignite.
● 引火点 a flash point.

インカ Inca. ● インカ人 an Incan. ● インカ人〖帝国; 文明〗の Incan.
● インカ帝国 the Inca Empire. ● インカ文明 the Inca civilization.

いんが 因果 (運命, 宿命) fate,《やや書》destiny. ● 因果は君から軽蔑されるいわれはない resigned to one's *fate*.
● 因果な(=不幸な[いやな])稼業 an *unlucky* [a *rotten*, a *nasty*] business. ● 因果応報 ● 因果応報) ▶何の因果でこんなことをしなくてはならないのか What irony of *fate* makes me do such a thing?
● 因果を含める ● 彼に二度とそこへ行かないよう因果を含める(=説得してあきらめさせる) *persuade* him not *to go* [《やや書》*dissuade* him *from going*] there again.

いんがい 院外 ― 院外の 形 outside Congress [the Diet, Parliament]; nonparliamental.
● 院外活動 lobbying. ● 院外団〖集合的〗a lobby; (個人) a lobbyist.

いんがおうほう 因果応報 (当然の報い) retribution. (⚠「神や運命による罰」の意) ● 因果応報だ(=罰せられて当然だ) It *serves you right*. (⚠ It を省略して Serves you right. ともいう)

いんがかんけい 因果関係 a relation between cause and effect; a causal relationship 《*between*》. ▶両者の間に因果関係を見出すことは難しい It is difficult to find a *causal relationship* between the two.

いんかく 陰核〖解剖〗a clitoris.

いんがし 印画紙 photographic paper.

いんかしょくぶつ 隠花植物 a cryptogam. (対 顕花植物)

いんがりつ 因果律 causality.

インカレ〖大学間の〗intercollegiate; (大学間対抗競技大会) intercollegiate (soccer) games.

いんかん 印鑑〖印章〗a seal. (事情 米英では公文書など以外には通例署名ですます)
● 印鑑証明 an official certificate of one's registered seal impression. ● 印鑑届 the registration of one's seal. (⇨実印)

いんき 陰気 ● 陰気な〖憂うつな〗gloomy; morose;〖元気のない〗cheerless. ● 陰気な性格をしている have a *gloomy* disposition. ▶彼女はいつも陰気な顔をしている She always looks *gloomy*./ She always has a *gloomy* expression.

インキ ink. (⇨インク)

インキュベーション〖起業支援〗incubation.

いんきょ 隠居 图 retirement; (人) a retired person. ― 隠居する 動 retire [be retired]《*from work*》; go into retirement.
● 隠居所 a retreat.

いんきょく 陰極 a cathode (↔an anode); the negative pole.
● 陰極線 a cathode ray. ● 陰極線管 a cathode-ray tube.

いんきん 陰金 (⇨陰金田虫)

いんぎん 慇懃 ― 慇懃に 副 (丁寧に) politely; (丁重に) courteously.
● 慇懃無礼 ▶あの男は慇懃無礼だ(=礼儀正しさを装っているだけで, 腹では人を人とも思わぬ男だ) He feigns politeness. He's an insolent man at heart.

いんきんたむし 陰金田虫〖医学〗tinea (cruris); (症状から一般的に) crotch rot.

***インク** ink. ● インクのしみ an ink *stain* [*spot*, *blot*].
● インクがきれる [きれている] run [be] out of *ink*.
● 万年筆に赤インクを入れる fill a pen with red *ink*.
● 万年筆にインクを入れる *ink* a fountain pen. ● インクをこぼす spill *ink*. ● ペンにインクをつける *ink* a pen. ▶インクで書きなさい You should write in [with] *ink*.
● インク消し an ink eraser. ● インクスタンド an ink-stand. ● インクびん an ink bottle; a bottle of ink.

インクジェット ink-jet.
● インクジェットプリンター an ink-jet printer.

イングランド England. (⇨イギリス)

インクリボン a ribbon;《和製語》an ink ribbon.

いんけい 陰茎 a penis /píːnɪs/ (複 penes /píːniːz/).

いんけん 引見 图 an audience. ▶彼は大統領との引見を許された He was granted an *audience with* the president.
— 引見する 動 have an audience 《with》.
いんけん 陰険 图 slyness.
— 陰険な 形 〖悪質な〗sly /slái/; 〖邪悪な〗wicked /wíkid/. ●陰険なやつ a *sly* fellow; a snake. ●陰険な目つき a *wicked* [a *sly*] look. ▶それをぼくに話してくれないとは彼は陰険なやつだ It is *sly* of him not to tell it to me.
いんげん 隠元 〖植物〗(サヤインゲン) a green [《英》a French] bean.
いんこ 〖鳥〗a parakeet. ●セキセイインコ a búdgerigàr; 〖話〗a budgie.
いんご 隠語 (犯罪者などが使う俗語) (an) argot (/サッ, スケの類)/, cant. ●泥棒仲間の隠語 thieves' *cant* [*slang*].
いんこう 引航 (⇨曳航(ホ))
いんこう 咽喉 (のど) a throat. (⇨喉(½)①)
●咽喉を扼(*)する (要所をおさえる) hold [maintain] the key 《to》.
●咽喉炎 a sore throat.
いんごう 因業 — 因業な 形 (無情な) heartless, harsh, cold-hearted; (苛酷な) merciless, cruel, harsh; (頑固な) obstinate, hard-hearted.
インコース 〖陸上〗the inside track; 〖野球〗the inside (corner), 〖和製語〗in course.
インコーナー 〖野球〗an inside (corner), 〖和製語〗an inner corner. ▶インコーナーへ投げる pitch *inside*. ▶インコーナーへ速球を投げる throw a fastball on the *inside*.
インサイダー 〖〖内部関係者〗〗an insider.
●インサイダー取引 insider trading [dealing].
●インサイダー情報 insider information.
インサイド 〖〖内角の〗〗〖野球〗inside. ▶インサイドのカーブ an *inside* curve. ▶インサイドへ投げる throw 《on the》*inside*.
●インサイドワーク 〖野球〗inside work [baseball].
***いんさつ** 印刷 图 〖印刷すること〗printing (✍ 「印刷術」の意もある); 〖印刷された状態〗print; 〖印刷技術・業務〗press.
① 【~印刷】 ●カラー印刷 colored [color] *printing*.
② 【印刷(の)~】 ●印刷の誤り (⇨誤植) ●印刷術の発明 the invention of *printing*. ●印刷業を営む engage in *printing* business. ●印刷用紙 *printing* paper. ▶この辞書の初版の印刷部数は5万冊だった This dictionary had a first *printing* of 50,000 copies.
③ 【印刷に】 ●原稿を印刷に回す send a manuscript to the *press*. ●校正刷りは印刷に回った The proofs have gone to *press*.
— 印刷する 動 print, put*...into print. ●台本を印刷する *print* a script; *put* a script *into print*. ●そのページに大きな活字で表を印刷する *print* a list in large type on the page. ●パンフレットを100部印刷する *print* (*off*) 100 copies of the pamphlet.
▶このちらしはうまく[きれいに]印刷されていない This leaflet *hasn't been* properly [clearly] *printed*.
▶その本は今日印刷されている The book *is being printed* now./The book *is in* [*at*] (the) *press* now.
●そのニュースは印刷に回された The news *was rushed into print*.
●印刷機 a (printing) press; 《英》a printing machine. ●印刷所 a printing house [office].
●印刷物 (郵便物としての) (xa) printed matter; (手渡し用の) a handout. ●印刷屋 a printer.
いんさん 陰惨 — 陰惨な 形 陰鬱な(=陰気な)ニュース *dismal* [(ぞっとする) *ghastly, horrible*] news.
いんし 印紙 a stamp. ●収入印紙 a revenue *stamp*.
●印紙税 the stamp duty.
いんし 因子 a factor. ●遺伝因子 a gene.
インジケーター 〖表示計器〗an indicator.
いんしつ 陰湿 — 陰湿な 形 〖暗くて湿った〗gloomy and damp, shady and damp; 〖陰険な〗sly; wicked (⇨陰険).
いんじゃ 隠者 a recluse, a hermit.
いんしゅ 飲酒 drinking.

> **DISCOURSE**
>
> 若いころからの飲酒はさまざまな問題を引き起こす。 第一に、飲酒の習慣は、生活の乱れにつながる可能性がある。 ... さらに、若い年齢での飲酒は肉体にダメージを与える *Drinking alcohol* from an early age may lead to various problems. First of all, drinking habits are likely to cause a lack of discipline. ... **Moreover**, under-age drinking is harmful to their health. (✍ moreover (さらに) は追加に用いるディスコースマーカー。 前の内容をさらに強調する内容を述べるときに用いる)

●飲酒運転 《米》drunk-driving; 《英》drink-driving. ●飲酒運転する drink and drive. ▶彼は飲酒運転で逮捕された He was arrested for *drinking and driving*. ●飲酒運転者 《米》a drunk-driver; 《英》a drink-driver. ●飲酒癖 a drinking habit.
いんしゅう 因習 (古い慣習) an old custom, tradition; (過去) the past. ●因習を打ち破る break *old customs* [*tradition, the past*]. ●因習にとらわれる stick to [《やや書》be a slave to] *old customs*.
インシュリン 〖生化学〗insulin. ●インシュリンの注射を受ける have an *insulin* injection.
***いんしょう** 印象 图 (an) impression. ●先生に悪い印象を与える(人・物事が) make [×give] a bad [an unfavorable] *impression on* one's teacher; (人が) *impress* a teacher unfavorably. ●第一印象で人を判断する judge people by first *impressions*. ▶彼の印象はどうでしたか What was your *impression of* him?/How did he *impress* you?/What *impression* did he make *on* you?/How did you *find* him? (✍ 最後の文が最も口語的の) ▶彼女はとても上品だという印象を受けた I *got* [*had, was under*] *the impression* (*that*) she was very elegant./She *impressed* me *as* a very elegant woman [*as* (being) very elegant]. ▶彼の最後の言葉が強烈に印象に残っている His last words *have left* a strong *impression on* my mind.
— 印象的(な) 形 impressive. ●卒業式はとても印象的だった The graduation ceremony *was very impressive to* me./The graduation ceremony *made* a great *impression on* me./I *was very impressed with* [*by*] the graduation ceremony./(心を打たれた) I *was struck by* [*with*] the graduation ceremony.
いんしょう 印章 a seal, a stamp. (⇨印)
いんしょうは 印象派 Impressionism. ●印象派の画家 an impressionist painter.
いんしょく 飲食 图 eating and drinking. (✍ 語順に注意) — 飲食する 動 eat and drink.
●飲食店 a restaurant, an eating place.
●飲食物 food and drink; (軽い) refreshments.
いんしん 殷賑 殷賑通り a crowded [a busy, a bustling] street.
いんすう 因数 〖数学〗a factor.
いんずう 員数 (⇨数(½))
いんすうぶんかい 因数分解 图 〖数学〗factorization.

——因数分解する 動 factorize;《米》factor《an integral expression》.
インスタント • インスタントカメラ an instant camera. • インスタントコーヒー instant coffee. • インスタント食品 instant food(s). (⇨食品) • インスタントラーメン instant noodles.
インストーラー〖インストール用プログラム〗〘コンピュータ〙an installer.
インストール 图〖ソフトを使えるように設定すること〗〘コンピュータ〙installation.
——インストールする 動 install.
『インストール』 *Install*. (参考) 綿矢りさの小説)
インストラクター an instructor. • ジャズダンスのインストラクター a jazz dancing *instructor*.
インスピレーション〖霊感〗(an) inspiration.
いんする 淫する〖度が過ぎる〗go to excess, go to extremes;〖…にふける〗be addicted 《to》, indulge 《in》;〖みだらなことをする〗molest 《a young girl》.
いんせい 院生〖主に米〗a graduate〖主に英〗a postgraduate》student. (⇨大学院)
いんせい 院政 rule by a retired emperor.
いんせい 陰性 **——陰性の** 形〖反応が〗negative (↔ positive; (⇨陽性); 〖気質が〗gloomy (⇨陰気).
いんぜい 印税 a royalty 《on, for》. (!しばしば複数形で) ▶ 彼は小説の印税を100万円受け取った He has received a million yen in *royalties* [a *royalty* of a million yen] *on* his novel.
いんせき 引責 (take) responsibility 《for》. (⇨責任)
いんせき 姻戚 〖姻戚関係にある〗be related 《to her》 by marriage.
いんせき 隕石 a meteorite /míːtiəràit/.
いんぜんたる 隠然たる • 隠然たる勢力(=隠れた影響力)を保つ still exercise influence behind the scenes.
インセンティブ〖意欲刺激〗(an) incéntive.
いんそつ 引率 **——引率する** 動 ▶ 学生たちを引率して博物館に行った I led [took] a group of students *to* the museum. (!lead は先に立って案内する, take は単に連れて行くこと)
• 引率者 a leader; (観光団などの) a tour conductor [guide].
インターカレッジ (⇨インカレ)
インターセプト 图〖サッカーなど〗an interception.
——インターセプトする 動 intercept 《a pass [a ball]》.
インターチェンジ an interchange 《on the Tomei Highway》.
インターナショナル〖国際的な〗international.
インターネット the Internet; the Net. • インターネットに接続する access *the Internet*. • インターネットで交信する communicate 《with him》 on *the Internet*. • インターネットエクスプローラー (商標) Internet Explorer (略 IE). • インターネットカフェ an Internet cafe; a cybercafe. • インターネットショッピング Internet shopping. • インターネットバンキング Internet banking.
インターハイ〖学校対抗体育競技〗an inter-high school athletic competition;《米》an interscholastic athletic meet.
インターバル an interval. ▶ 彼はインターバルを取った He took a *break*.
インターフェア〖スポーツ〗(an) interference. • インターフェアをする interfere.
インターフェース〖二つの装置をつなぐ機器・手段〗〘コンピュータ〙an interface.
インターフェロン〖生化学〗interferon.
インターポール〖国際刑事警察機構〗Ìnterpòl. (!単複両扱い). the *International Criminal Police Organization*《略 ICPO》が正式名称)
インターホン an intercòm 《intercommùnicátion system の略》;《米》an interphone. • インターホンで話す talk on [over] the *intercom*.
インターン (人) 《主に米》an intern /íntəːrn/,《英》a houseman (複 -men); (地位・期間) internship. • 神戸の病院でインターンをする work as an *intern* at a hospital in Kobe.
インターンシップ〖就業体験〗internship.
いんたい 引退 图 (a) retirement. • 引退を発表する announce one's *retirement* 《from》.
——引退する 動 • 65歳で政界〖現役〗を引退する retire *from* politics [one's job, (軍隊の) active service] at (the age of) 65. ▶ 新庄選手は今シーズン限りで現役を引退すると発表した Shinjo announced his *retirement* as an active player at the end of the season. ▶ 病気のため彼は舞台を引退せざるをえなかった Illness forced him to quit the stage.
• 引退試合 a farewell game.
いんたい 隠退 图 retirement. **——隠退する** 動 retire.
インダス • インダス川 the Indus. • インダス文明〖歴史〗the Indus (valley) civilization.
インダストリアル〖工業[産業]の〗industrial. • インダストリアルエンジニアリング〖経営工学〗industrial engineering. • インダストリアルデザイン〖工業デザイン〗industrial design.
インタビュー 图 an interview. (⇨面会, 面接) • (独占)インタビューに応じる agree to give an (exclusive) *interview* 《to a newspaper》. • テレビのインタビューで言う say 《it》 at [in] the TV *interview*. ▶ その問題に責任のあるイギリスの大臣がインタビューを受けていた The British Minister responsible for these matters *was being interviewed*.
——インタビュー(を)する 動 • 空港で彼にインタビューをする *interview* him at the airport. • インタビューをする[される]人 an ínterviewer [an ínterviewée, an interview subject].
インタホン (⇨インターホン)
インタラクティブ〖双方向的〗interactive.
インチ an inch. (参考) 2.54cm • 5フィート4インチ five feet four *inches*; 5 ft. 4 *in.*; 5′4″. • 26インチの自転車 a 26-*inch* bicycle. ▶ 1インチは何センチですか How many centimeters are there in an *inch*?
いんちき 图〖ごまかすこと〗cheating;〖詐欺〗fraud;〖にせもの〗a fake, a counterfeit (後の方が堅い語). ▶ 彼の話はいんちきくさい (話) His story sounds *fishy*./There's something *fishy* about his story.
——いんちき(な) 形 (にせの) fake, counterfeit; bogus. • いんちきな署名 a *fake* [a *counterfeit*] signature. • いんちきな医者 a *quack* [a *bogus*] doctor; a quack. • いんちき(な)療法 quackery.
——いんちき(を)する cheat; (偽造する) fake. • トランプでいんちきをする *cheat* at cards.
いんちょう 院長〖病院の〗the director of a hospital;〖学校の〗the president [principal, director] of a school.
インチョン 仁川〖韓国の都市〗Inchon /intʃán/.
インディアナ〖米国の州〗Indiana /ìndiǽnə/《略 Ind. 郵便協定》
インディアペーパー〖辞書・聖書などの印刷用薄紙〗Índia pàper.
インディアン a Native American (!今はこの語が最もよく用いられる). 《やや古》an (American) Indian (!軽蔑的な響きはなく, インディアン自身も使うが, a Native American が普及した今では, やや古い感じの

インディカまい 語); an Amerindian.

インディカまい インディカ米 indica.

いんてつ 印鉄 siderite.

インデックス 〘索引〙an index.

インテリ 〈ロシア語〉 an intelléctual, an intellect; 《話》(時に軽蔑的な) a high-brow.
• インテリ階級 the intellect(s); the intelligéntsia. (⚠いずれも集合的にも用い, 前の方は複数扱い, 後の方は単･複両扱い)

インテリア • インテリアデザイナー an interior designer [decorator]. • インテリアデザイン interior design [decoration].

インテリジェント • インテリジェントビル a computerized office building.

インテルサット 〘国際電気通信衛星機構〙 Intelsat 《*International Telecommucation Satellite Organization* の略》. • この通信衛星は ∼)

いんてん 院展 the Japanese Art Institute Exhibition.

いんでんき 陰電気 negative electricity.

インデント 〘字下げ〙an indent.

インド 〘国名〙India (⚠公式名も同じ). (首都 New Delhi) • インド人 an Indian. • インド(人)の Indian.
• インド洋 the Indian Ocean.

インドア 〘屋内の〙indoor. (⚠限定的) (⇔アウトドア)
• インドアスポーツ indoor sports.

いんとう 咽頭 〘解剖〙a pharynx (複 ∼es).
• 咽頭炎 〘医学〙pharyngitis.

いんとう 淫蕩 〘みだら〙lewdness; 〘酒色にふけること〙debauchery; 〘放蕩〙dissipation.
— 淫蕩な 形 • 淫蕩な生活にふける lead [live] a life of *debauchery*; lead [live] a *dissipated* life.

いんどう 引導
• 引導を渡す (死者のためにミサを唱える) say a requiem for the deceased; (最終的な言い渡しをする) give 〈him〉 one's last word 〈*on* the matter〉.

いんとく 陰徳 • 陰徳を施す do good deeds [conduct] secretly.

いんとく 隠匿 名 concealment; secretion.
— 隠匿する 動 conceal; hide; 《話》stash ... 〈away〉. • 犯人を隠匿する *shelter* [*harbor*] a criminal.
• 隠匿物資 《米話》a stash.

インドシナ 〘半島名〙Indochina /ìndou-tʃáinə/. • インドシナ(地域)の Indochinese. • インドシナ(地域)の人 an Indochinese. (⚠単･複両形)

イントネーション (an) intonation. • 上昇[下降]調のイントネーションで発音する pronounce 〈a sentence〉 with a rising [a falling] *intonation*.

インドネシア Indonesia /ìndənɪ́ːʒə/; (公式名) the Republic of Indonesia. (首都 Jakarta) • インドネシア人 an Indonesian. • インドネシア語 Indonesian. • インドネシア(人[語])の Indonesian.

インドヨーロッパご(ぞく) インドヨーロッパ語(族) the Indo-European (languages).

イントラネット 〘組織内通信情報網〙〘コンピュータ〙an intranet.

イントロダクション 〘序文･曲の前奏部〙an introduction 〈*to*〉.

いんとん 隠遁 名 seclusion. • 隠遁生活をする lead [live] a *secluded* life; live [dwell, rest] in *seclusion*.
— 隠遁する 動 seclude oneself 〈*from* the (outer) world〉.

いんない 院内 — 院内の 形 (病院内の) in-hospital; (国会の) inside Congress [the Diet, Parliament], parliamentary.
• 院内感染 (a) hospital(-acquired) infection.

(⚠症例は C) • 院内総務《米》the floor leader (⚠与党) the majority leader, (野党) the minority leader に分かれる); 《英》the party whip.

いんにく 印肉 an ink pad; a stamp pad; seal ink.

いんにん 隠忍 名 endurance, patience. • 隠忍自重して行動する act *patiently* and *prudently*.
— 隠忍する 動 endure, be patient.

いんねん 因縁 〘運命〙one's [the] fate; 〘関係〙(a) connection 〈*with, between*〉. ▶前世(から)の因縁とあきらめた I resigned myself to my *fate*. ▶我々がここで会ったのも何かの因縁だろう(=たぶんここで会うよう運命づけられていた) We were possibly *destined* 〘書〙*predestined*〙to meet here.
• 因縁をつける (けんかを吹っかける) pick a quarrel 〈*with*〉; (けんかの口実を見つける) find a pretext for a quarrel 〈*with*〉.

いんのう 陰嚢 〘解剖〙a scrotum (複 ∼s, scrota).

インバーター 〘逆変換装置〙〘電気〙an inverter.
• インバーターエアコン an air conditioner with an inverter.

インハイ 〘野球〙high and inside; up and in. (⚠日本語とは語順が逆)

いんばい 淫売 (⇒売春)

インパクト 〘衝撃〙an impact. ▶その報道は彼女に大きなインパクトを与えた The news made [had] a big *impact* on her.

インパラ 〘動物〙an impala.

インバランス imbalance. (⇒アンバランス)

いんぶ 陰部 the pubic region; 《婉曲的》the private parts.

インフィールドフライ 〘野球〙an infield fly. (⚠「内野フライ」の意にもなる) • インフィールドフライを宣する declare an *infield fly*.

インフォーマル — インフォーマルな 形 (正式でない) informal; (くだけた) casual. • インフォーマルなパーティー an *informal* party. • インフォーマルな服装の *informally* [*casually*] dressed.

インフォーマント 〘言語資料提供者〙〘言語〙an informant.

インフォームドコンセント 〘納得診療〙(ask for) an infòrmed consént.

インフォメーション 〘情報〙information (⇒情報); 〘案内所, 受付〙an information (desk); 〘案内業務〙information service.
• インフォメーションセンター an information center.
• インフォメーションテクノロジー 〘情報技術〙information technology 《略 IT》.

インプット 名 input. (↔output).
— インプットする 動 input. • コンピュータにインプットされたデータ data *input*(*ted*) *into* a computer.

インフラ 〘水道･ガスなどが社会基盤〙infrastructure.

インフルエンザ 〘医学〙influenza; 《話》(the) flu.
• 鳥インフルエンザ bird *flu*. • インフルエンザにかかっている [かかる] have [catch, get] (the) *flu*. • インフルエンザで寝込む come down [be down, be in bed] with (the) *flu*. ▶インフルエンザがはやっている *Influenza* is raging./*The flu* [*Flu*] is spreading.

*****インフレ(ーション)** inflation. (↔deflation). • 悪性インフレ vicious [spiral] *inflation*; an *inflationary* spiral. • インフレ率の上昇[低下] a rise [a drop] in the *inflation* rate; rising [easing] in *inflation*. • インフレ対策を取る take anti-*inflation* measures. • インフレを抑え[抑制する] cause [control, 《やや書》curb] *inflation*. • インフレの時代に in *inflationary* times. ▶物価は多少下がったがインフレはまだ続いている Prices have dropped to a

certain extent, but the *inflation* continues.
●インフレ傾向 an inflationary tendency [trend]. ●インフレ懸念 worries [fears] of inflation. ●インフレ政策 an inflationary policy.

インプレー in play. ▶ボールはインプレーだ The ball is in play [alive].

いんぶん 韻文 (散文に対して) verse; (詩)《集合的》poetry (❗1 編は a poem, a piece of poetry という、×a poetry とはいわない). ●韻文で書かれた詩 a poem written *in verse* (↔prose).

いんぺい 隠蔽 🅰 concealment; a cóver-ùp.
── 隠蔽する 🅥 conceal; hide. (⇨隠す)

インポ (⇨インポテンツ)

インボイス 〘送り状〙〘商業〙 an invoice. (⇨送り状)

いんぼう 陰謀 a plot (*to do*; *against*), (an) intrigue (*against*) (❗plot より複雑で、策謀に満ちたもの); 〖共同謀議〗 (a) conspiracy (*to do*; *against*). ●王に対する陰謀を企む *plot* [*intrigue*, *conspire*] *against* the king; form a *plot* [a *conspiracy*] *against* the king. (⇨企む) ▶彼は政府転覆の陰謀にかかわっていた He was involved in the *conspiracy to* overthrow the government.

インポテンツ [＜ドイツ語] 〖医学〗 (ペニスの) ejaculatory impotence; (勃起障害) erectile dysfunction 《略 ED》.

いんもう 陰毛 pubic /pjúːbik/ hair.

いんゆ 隠喩 (a) metaphor. (⇔ 直喩)

いんよう 引用 🅰 (a) quotation; (a) citation. ●聖書からの引用 a *quotation from* the Bible. ●引用符付きの文 a sentence *in quotation* marks [《話》quotes]. (❗いずれも複数形で用いることに注意) ▶この本は他の作品からの引用が多い This book has a lot of *citations* from other works.
── 引用する 🅥 quote, make* a quotation 《*from*》; (例として引用する) cite. (❗quote は言葉をそのまま引用することで、cite は quote ほど正確な引用ではない) ●ミルトンを引用する *quote* 《*from*》 Milton.

(❗*from* は出所を強調する) ●バイロンから一節を引用する *quote* a passage *from* Byron. ▶大統領はリンカーンの言葉を引用して演説を締めくくった The President finished his speech with a *quotation from* Lincoln.
●引用句[文] a quotation; 《話》a quote; a citation. ●引用書 reference books; the books referred to.

いんよう 陰陽 (明暗) light and shade; (中国の易学) yin and yang.

いんよう 飲用 ── 飲用の 🅵 drinking, for drinking.
●飲用水 drinking water,《書》potable water.

いんよく 淫欲 (a) lust; sexual desire.

いんらん 淫乱 🅰 lechery. ── 淫乱な 🅵 lecherous.

いんりつ 韻律 (詩の) (a) meter; (リズム) (a) rhythm.

いんりょう 飲料 〖飲み物〗 (a) drink (❗種類をいうときは Ⓒ);《書》a beverage (❗水・薬以外のあらゆる飲料をいう). ●アルコール[清涼]飲料 alcoholic [soft] *drinks*; alcoholic [cooling] *beverages*. ●かん[びん]詰飲料 canned [bottled] *drinks*. ▶この水は飲料に適する This water is fit [good] to *drink*.
●飲料水 drinking [(飲める) drinkable] water; water fit to drink.

いんりょく 引力 (一般に) 〖物理〗 gravitation; (地球・その他惑星の) gravity; (磁気の) magnetism; 〖物体間の〗 attraction. ●万有引力の法則 the law of *gravity* [*gravitation*].
●引力圏 the sphere of gravity; the gravitational field.

いんれき 陰暦 陰暦の 1 月 1 日 January 1 by the *lunar calendar*.

いんろう 印籠 a small portable pillbox.

インロー 〘野球〙 low and inside; down and away. (❗日本語とは語順が逆)

いんわい 淫猥 obscenity. (⇨猥褻(わいせつ))

う

う 卯 the Rabbit.
- 卯年〚十二支〛the year of the Rabbit. (⇨干支(し) 関連)

う 鵜 a cormorant. (⇨鵜飼い, 鵜匠(しょう))
- 鵜の目鷹(たか)の目 with sharp [eager] eyes be on the lookout《for something new》.

ウイークエンド 〚週末〛a weekend.

ウイークデー a weekday (❗1 週間のうちで日曜日と(だいたい)土曜日を除く日);《週末を除く 1 週間》the week. ▶彼と会うのはウイークデーだけですか Do you meet him only *on weekdays*? ▶彼らはウイークデーは精一杯働きます They work hard *during the week*.

ウイークポイント 〚弱点〛a weak point, a weakness. ▶彼の最大のウイークポイントはまだどこへ行ったことがないということだ His *weakest point* [His greatest *weakness*] is that he's never been there.

ウイークリー 〚週刊誌〛a weekly (magazine).
- ウイークリーマンション an apartment (hotel) rented by the week.

ウィーン 〚オーストリアの首都〛Vienna /viénə/; (ドイツ語名) Wien /víːn/.

ういういしい 初々しい《純真そのもの》pure and innocent;《若くて世間ずれしていない》young and innocent.

ういきょう 茴香 〚植物〛a fennel.

ウィザード 〚ソフトのガイド機能〛〖コンピュータ〗a wizard.

ういざん 初産 one's first childbirth.

ういじん 初陣 《初めての戦闘》one's first campaign 《個別の戦い》battle;《試合》game, match;《初陣を飾る》win one's *first battle* [*game*].

ウイスキー 《米》whiskey;《英》whisky. (❗(1)《米》でもスコッチは通例 whisky とつづる. (2) 種類や 1 杯, 2 杯と数えるときは 〖C〗) ▶ブレンド[バーボン]ウイスキー blended [bourbon] *whiskey*. ▶水[ソーダ]割りウイスキー 2 杯 two *whiskeys* and waters [*sodas*]. (❗注文するときなどに用いる. 複数 s の置き方に注意)
- ウイスキーをストレートで飲む drink (one's) *whiskey* straight [neat]. ▶ウイスキーの水割りをください. 水は少なめにね I'll have [Bring me] *whiskey* and water, please. Light on water.
- ウイスキーボンボン《菓子》a whiskey-filled bonbon;《和製語》a whiskey bonbon.

ウィスコンシン 〚米国の州〛Wisconsin /wiskánsn/ (略 Wis., Wisc. 郵便略 WI).

ういた 浮いた《浮気性の》flirtatious;《うわついた》frivolous, light. ▶彼には浮いた話のひとつもない There's never been a rumor of his (love) affair going around.

ウイット 〚機知〛wit.

ういてんぺん 有為転変《人生の浮き沈み》the ups and downs of life,《書》the vicissitudes of life;《この世の変わりやすさ》the mutability of this world.

ウイニング winning.
- ウイニングショット 〚野球〛one's best 《話》money pitch;《和製語》winning shot.
- ウイニングボール a game ball;《和製語》winning ball. ▶ウイニングラン《米》a victory lap,《英》a lap of honor. (❗a winning run は「《野球の》勝利得点[決勝点]」の意).

ウイルス a virus /váirəs/ (複 viruses). ▶エイズウイルス the AIDS *virus*; HIV. (⇨エイチアイブイ) ▶ウイルスによる感染症 a *virus* [*viral*] infection. ▶抗ウイルス製剤 an anti-*viral* medicine. ▶コンピュータウイルス a (computer) *virus*. ▶私のパソコンはウイルスに感染している My computer is infected with a virus.

ウインカー 〚方向指示器〛《米》a turn signal, an indicator;《話》a blinker. (❗いずれも通例複数形で)
- 右にウインカーを出す hit the right-*turn* signal.

ウインガー 〚サッカー〛a winger, a wing player.

ウインク 图 a wink.
── **ウインクする** 動 wink《at him》; give《him》a wink.

ウイング 〚サッカー〛the wing. (❗ピッチ上の両タッチラインに近いエリア)
- ウイングバック a wingback. (参考 特に 3 バックの陣形を敷く場合には中盤 5 人の両サイドにつく, いわゆる winger と *side back* を兼ね備えたプレーヤー)
- ウイングプレーヤー a wing player, a winger.

ウインザー 〚英国の都市〛Windsor.

ウインター 〚冬〛(a) winter.
- ウインターコート an overcoat, a winter coat.
- ウインタースポーツ a winter sport [game].

ウインドウズ 〚パソコンの基本ソフトの 1 つ〛〖コンピュータ〗《商標》Windows.

ウインドー 《窓》a window;《陳列窓》a (show [《米》store,《英》shop]) window. ▶ウインドーの飾り付け *window* dressing. ▶ウインドーに(飾って)あるバッグを見せてください Please show me the bag in the *window*.

ウインドーショッピング 图 window-shopping.
── **ウインドーショッピング(を)する** 動 window-shop, go window-shopping. ▶五番街をウインドーショッピングして歩いた We went *window-shopping* along Fifth Avenue.

ウインドサーフィン 图 windsurfing.
── **ウインドサーフィンをする** 動 go windsurfing; windsurf. (❗前の方が普通)

ウインドブレーカー 《米》a windbreaker;《英・やや古》an windcheater. (❗いずれも商品名 W‐から)

ウインナコーヒー 《a cup of》Viennese /×Vienna》coffee;《和製語》wiener coffee.

ウインナソーセージ 《a》Vienna sáusage,《米》(a) wiener /wíːnər/,《米話》(a) wienie /《和製語》wiener sausage.

ウインブルドン 〚ロンドンの地区〛Wimbledon /wímbldən/.

ウースターソース (⇨ウスターソース)

ウーマンリブ 〚女性解放運動〛women's movement, women's liberation,《話》women's lib. (❗今は最初の言い方が普通)

ウール wool. ▶ウールのセーター a wool [a woolen] sweater. (❗(1) 後の方が普通. (2)「冬物セーター」を winter woolens ともいう) ▶ウール 100 パーセントのセーター a pure-*wool* [an all-*wool*] sweater.
- ウールマーク Woolmark. (参考 羊毛の国際商品質証マーク)

ウーロンちゃ ウーロン茶 oolong /úːlɔŋ/ tea.

ううん《苦しい時や力を入れた時の》ungh /ʌnh/;《言葉につまった時の》h'm, hm;《感心して》Mmm. ▶ううん, うまい！ *Mmm*, yummy!

うえ 上

INDEX
❶ 上部
❷ 最上部
❸ 年長
❹ 上位
❺ 追加
❻ 前述, 前記
❼ …の後・結果

❶〖上部〗the upper part; 〖表面〗the surface; (テーブルなどの) the top; 〖上の階〗the upstairs (❗単数扱い (⇨❸)).

①〖上(は[の])～〗〖上部の〗upper (↔lower) (❗通例二つに分けたもののうちの「上の方の」の意); 〖階上の〗upstairs (↔downstairs); 〖上方への〗upward (↔downward). ●机の右上の引き出し the *upper* right-hand drawer of a desk. (❗引き出しが二つの場合 (⇨❷)) ●上の寝室へ行く go to the bedroom *upstairs* [*above*] (❗... the *upstairs* bedroom より普通). go *upstairs* to the bedroom. ▶山の上の方は雪でおおわれている The *upper* part of the mountain is covered with snow. ▶その家の上の階はまだ完成していない The *upstairs* floor of the house hasn't been completed yet. ▶彼の死体は腰から上は傷だらけであった From the waist *upward* his body was a mass of scars.

②〖…(の)上の[に, を, へ, で]〗〖場所, 位置〗(…の表面に接触・付着して) on, upon, on top of; (…の表面をおおって) over; (…より高い位置に) above (↔below); (…から離れた真上に, の上をおおって) over (↔under); (…から離れて) off; 〖移動〗(…の上に[へ]) on, upon, onto (↔off); 〖方向〗(…の上方へ) up (↔down). (…を越えて) over.

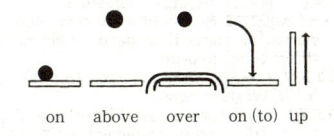

<image: 図 — 球と矢印で on, above, over, on (to), up の位置関係を示す>

on　above　over　on (to)　up

解説 (1) on と upon: upon は堅い響きを持つので,《話》では on が普通. ただし文のリズムや慣用上 upon を用いることもある: れんがを上へ上へと積み重ねる pile brick *upon* brick.
(2) on と on top of: 後の方は通例, 強調的に「…のてっぺんに」の意で用いられる: 私の頭のてっぺんに *on top of* my head. /夜中にテントが彼の上に落ちてきた The tent fell *on top of* him in the night.
(3) on と over: on は単なる接触を表すが, over には全体をおおう感じが加わる: 床の上の敷物 a rug *on* the floor; a carpet *over* the floor. また over は「…の上に重ねて」の意も表す. この意味は *on top of* も用いられる: 彼女はセーターの上にジャケットをはおっていた She wore a jacket *over* [*on top of*] her sweater.
(4) above と over: (a)「…から離れて上に」の意では同様に用いられることが多い: 暖炉の上にかけられた絵 a picture *above* [*over*] the fireplace. しかし, over は特に真上 (directly above) を暗示する, その強意形として right over も用いられる: 彼の部屋は私の部屋の真上[真上]にある His room is *above* [*right*) *over*] mine. (b) over に「…をおおって」の意が加わることがある: 両手を頭の上に上げる hold one's hands *above* [*over*] one's head ❗above は両手を肩からまっすぐ上げるのに対し, over は頭上で手を組んで頭をおおう姿勢): 川の上にかかる橋 a bridge *over* the river. また「…の上に張り出して」の意にも用いられる: バルコニーは庭の上に突き出て

いる The balcony projects *over* the garden. ただし上下関係だけを示すときは above を用いる: 雲の上に見える峰 a peak seen *above* the clouds.
(5) on と upon と onto: 「…の上に(へ)」という移動・運動を表すが, 特に強調的に upon を用いることがある,《話》では onto が多く,《英》ではしばしば on をとつぐ: 彼は馬の上に飛び乗った He jumped *on* [*upon, onto*] the horse.
(6) up と over: up は上方へ向かう動作・運動を, over は越えて向こうへ移動することを表す: 牛の群れは山の上へ移動し始めた Herds of cows began to move *up* the hill. /飛行機が山の上を飛んで行った A plane flew *over* the mountain.

❸〖上に[を, へ, で, から]〗〖上方・頭上に〗above, over, overhead; 〖階上に〗ùpstáirs (❗1階から2階に」の場合だけでなく, 現在いる階より上の階から何階でもよい. 米英では建物の構造上, go *upstairs* は自分の部屋[寝室]に行くことを暗示する), above; 〖上(方)に向かって〗up, upward. ▶上から見ると人々がアリのように小さく見えた Seen from *above*, people looked as small as ants. ▶私の寝室はすぐ上にある My bedroom is just *above*. (❗**解説** (4) (a)) ▶彼は私の部屋の 3 階上に住んでいる He lives three floors *up* (from my room). (❗通例 from my room は省略する) ▶我々の事務所は上(の階)にある Our office is *upstairs*./We have an office *upstairs* [*above*]. ▶このエレベーターは上へまいります This elevator is going *up*. ▶もっと上へ登ろう Let's climb farther *upward*.

❷〖最上部〗(上部) the top (❗「山の頂上」の意では summit の方が堅い語. 先のとがった山の頂上は peak); the head (❗上下の位置関係より機能・形状の違いを強調する). ●ページの一番上に at *the top* [*head*] of the page. ●上から 5 行目に on the fifth line from *the top*. ●机の左の一番上の引き出し the left-hand *top* drawer of a desk. ▶山の上はとても寒い It is very cold on *the top* of the mountain. ▶彼は私を上から下まで見た He looked at me from *top* to toe [《やや話》from *head* to foot]. ▶彼は上から下まで白ずくめの服装であった He was dressed *all* in white.

❸〖年長〗(…より年上の) older《*than*》, senior《*to*》(❗叙述的に); (年齢が…を越えて) over, above; (年上の[一番上の]) older [oldest],《主に英》elder [eldest] (❗限定的に).

解説 elder, eldest は older, oldest より堅い語で主に《英》で好まれる兄弟姉妹間での年長という場合に限って用いる. ただし, 英語では兄弟, 姉妹の区別はせず, 単に brother, sister ということが多い. (⇨兄)

●6 歳より上の(=以上の)子供たち children of six (years) and *over* [*above*]. (❗(1) 6 歳を含む. children *over* [*above*] six とすると「6 歳をこえる子供たち」で 6 歳児は *over* にも *above* にも含まない. (2) children aged six and over [above] ともいえる) ▶彼は年が私より 10 歳上だ He is ten years *older* [×elder] *than* I am [《話》*than* me,《書》*than* I]./He is ten years my *senior* [ten years *senior to* me]. (❗年齢差を強調して He is *older than* I am [He is my *senior*, He is *senior to* me] by ten years. などの表現も可能だが, いずれの場合も *older* を用いる文が最も一般的. my *senior* は *senior to* me より普通) ▶私の 2 人の息子のうち上は 8 歳です The *older* of my two sons is eight./Of my two sons, the *older* one is eight. ▶これは一番上[上から二番目]の姉です This is my *oldest* [*second oldest*] sister. (❗

うえ

《話》では one's *oldest* だけで「1 番上の姉[兄]」の意に用いる)
❹ [上位] (能力などがよりすぐれた) superior 《to》; (よりよい) better 《than》; (地位が上の) above ..., over ..., (**!** *above* では上下関係が、*over* では対等関係に加えて直接の支配が含意される); (上級の) advanced, upper; (質などが高い) higher 《than》; (程度が以上の) more than ..., above ....

① [(...より)上の(だ)] ▶上のクラス an *advanced* [an *upper*] class. ▶上(=上司)(から)の命令 an order from one's *superior* [*boss*]. ▶彼は能力では私よりはるかに上だ He is far [much, ×very] *superior to* [×*than*] me in ability. ▶ピアニストとしては彼女の方が私よりはるかに上だ As a pianist, she is far *above* me. ▶彼の学校の成績は平均より少し上だ His school work is a little *above* [*better than*] (the) average. ▶英語の会話力では君がクラスで一番上だ You're the *best* [×the most *superior*] speaker of English in our class. (**!** *superior* は比較級で、限定的には用いない) ▶経験では私たちの方が上だ You have *more* experience *than* I do 《《話》*than* me》. ▶彼女は私より 1 学年上だった She was a year *ahead* of me in school.

② [上を(に)] ▶上を目指す (よりよい学校を) aim to attend a better school [(上級クラス) an advanced class]. ▶上(=高い地位[階級])を目指して仕事に励む work hard aiming to go up to a higher [an upper] position. ▶上(=山の頂上)を目指して登る climb aiming for the top [summit]. ▶人の上に立つのは非常に難しい It is very difficult to *lead* others.

❺ [追加] (...のほかに) besides ..., in addition to ..., 《やや話》on top of .... (⇨その上) ▶彼は政治家である上に音楽家でもある *Besides* being a statesman, he is a musician. ▶彼は歌を歌うに(=歌を歌うだけではなくピアノも弾いた He played the piano *as well as* sang.

❻ [前述、前記] the above. (**!** 単・複両扱い) ▶上に述べたように as we have said *above*; as stated [mentioned] *above*. (**!** 後の方が堅い言い方) ▶上の図表を見よ See the table *above*. (**!** the *above* table ともいう)

❼ [...の後・結果] ▶よく考えた上で *after* careful consideration; *on* second thought(s). ▶面接の上採用する employ a person *after* an interview.
● 上には上がある (優秀さには限界がない) There is no limit to *excellence*.; (上限がない) The sky's the limit. (**!** 口語的慣用句) ▶(自分たちよりよい仕事をする者は常にいるものだ) There's always someone able to do better than we are.
● 上を下への大騒ぎ ▶その部屋では子供たちが泣き叫び、上を下への大騒ぎであった The room was in an uproar, with children crying and shouting. ▶夜中に突然火災報知機が鳴り響きホテルは上を下への大騒ぎとなった Suddenly the fire alarm sounded during the night and they were all thrown into a panic and confusion at the hotel.

うえ 飢え [飢餓] starvation; [空腹] hunger (⇨空腹). ▶飢えに苦しむ suffer from *starvation* [*hunger*]. ▶木の実を食べて飢えをしのぐ(=空腹を満たす) satisfy [stave off, 《書》appease] one's *hunger* by eating nuts. ▶飢えで死ぬ(=飢え死にする).

ウエーター a waiter; (男女共用) a waitperson, a server. (**!** 呼ぶときは Waiter! などとは通例いわない (⇨ああ 圖 ❺))

ウエーティングサークル [野球] an on-deck circle; 《和製語》a waiting circle.

ウエート [重量・重点] weight /wéit/; [重要性] importance. ● 内容より形式にウエートを置く give [attach] more *weight* to its form than to its substance.

ウエートトレーニング 《do》weight training.
ウエートリフティング [重量挙げ] weight lifting.
ウエートレス a waitress; (男女共用) a waitperson, a server. (**!** 呼びかけは Miss! (⇨ああ 圖 ❺)) ▶彼女は駅前のレストランでウエートレスの仕事をすることになった She got a job as a *waitress* [a job of waitressing].

ウエーバー [ドイツの作曲家] Weber /véːbər/ (Friedrich Ernst von ~).
ウエーブ 图 ❶ [頭髪の] a wave. (⇨パーマ) ▶生まれつきのウエーブ a natural *wave*. ▶ウエーブした髪 *wavy* hair. ❷ [競技場などでの] a wave.
── ウエーブする 動 ● 指示通りにウエーブする do the *wave* as per instruction. (**!** as per は「...に従って」の意)

ウェールズ [英国の地域名] Wales.
うえかえる 植え替える transplant 《flowers *to* a garden》.
うえき 植木 [庭木] a garden plant [tree]; [鉢植えの] a pot [a potted] plant. ▶植木に水をやる water a *plant*.
● 植木ばさみ (大きな刃と長い柄の) 《a pair of》gárden(ing) shèars; (短い刃と短い柄の) 《米》a prúning shèars, 《英》a secateurs. ● 植木鉢 a flowerpot; a (plant) pot. ● 植木屋 a gardener.

うえこみ 植え込み (灌木(かんぼく)の) a shrubbery, shrubs.
うえこむ 植え込む plant 《a tree》.
うえじに 飢え死に [餓死] starvation.
── 飢え死にする 動 die of starvation [hunger]; starve [be starved] to death. ▶飢え死にさせる starve 《him》to death.
ウエスタン (映画の西部劇) a Western (movie); (西部の音楽) Western music.
ウエスト a waist /wéist/; 《話》(胴) one's middle; (ウエストの寸法) waist measurement. ▶ウエストが細い [太い] have a slim [a thick] *waist*. ▶ドレスのウエストを詰める take in the *waist* of a dress. ▶彼女のウエストは 60 センチだ Her *waist* measurement is 60 centimeters./She measures [is] 60 centimeters around the *waist*.
ウエストバージニア [米国の州名] West Virginia /wést vərdʒinjə/ (略 W.Va. 郵便略 WV).
ウエストボール [野球] a waste ball [pitch]. ▶ウエストボールを投げる *waste* a pitch; *waste* one.
ウェストミンスター ● ウェストミンスター寺院 [英国の寺院] Westminster Abbey.
うえつけ 植え付け planting.
うえつける 植え付ける plant, (種イモなどを) sow (⇨植える); [思想などを] implant. ▶若い人たちの心に相互信頼の気持ちを植え付ける *implant* [*plant*] mutual trust *in* the minds of young people.
ウエット ── ウエットな 形 tender-hearted; sentimental.
● ウエットスーツ a wet suit. ● ウエットティッシュ a wet tissue.
ウェディング [結婚] a wedding.
● ウェディングケーキ a wedding cake. ● ウェディングドレス a wedding dress. ● ウェディングベル a wedding bell. ● ウェディングマーチ a wedding march. ● ウェディングリング a wedding ring [band].
ウエハー (⇨ウエーバー)
ウエハース (菓子) a wafar.
ウェブ [インターネットの大規模ネットワーク] [コンピュータ] the Web, the World Wide Web.

- ウェブサーバー a Web server. ●ウェブサイト a Website. ●ウェブデザイナー a Web designer. ●ウェブブラウザー a Web browser. ウェブページ a Web page. ●ウェブマスター a Webmaster.

ウエファ 〖ヨーロッパサッカー連盟〗the UEFA 《the Union of European Football Associations の略》.
- UEFAカップ the UEFA Cup.

ウェリントン 〖ニュージーランドの首都〗Wellington.

*うえる **植える** 〖木・草花・種などを〗plant; (植え替える) transplant. (⇨植え付ける) ●庭にチューリップを植える plant tulips in a garden; plant a garden with tulips. (*!* 後の方は「庭一面に植える」という含みがある) ▶校庭には[塀にそって]花が植えてある Flowers are planted in the schoolyard [along the fence]. ▶私たちは来年はトウモロコシを植えます We are going to plant [栽培する] grow, raise] corn next year.

うえる 飢える starve, be starved; (空腹である) be hungry. ●飢えて死ぬ (⇨飢え死に) ●愛情に飢える starve for [be starved of, be hungry for] affection. ●知識に飢える have a thirst [a hunger] for knowledge; be thirsty [hungry] for knowledge.

ウェルターきゅう ウェルター級 the welterweight.
- ウェルター級の選手 a welterweight; a welter.

ウェルダン (ステーキの) well-done.

うお 魚 a fish. (⇨魚(ｻｶﾅ))
- 魚心あれば水心 (ことわざ) Scratch my back and I'll scratch yours./Roll my log and I'll roll yours.
- 魚市場 a fish market.

うおうさおう 右往左往 —— **右往左往する** 動 move around [about] in confusion; (比喩的に) be confused [upset, flurried]. ▶新米ホステス(=女主人)の私は片言の英語とフランス語で招待客の間を右往左往するばかりであった As a hostess I was totally inexperienced, and all I could do was to move around the guests talking awkwardly with a little French and English I knew. ▶敵は右往左往して逃げ出した The enemy troops got [were thrown] into a muddle and ran away. ▶私自身が右往左往したら(=パニックになってまともに考えられない状態だったら)、命令できなかったし報告も受けられなかった If I had become [been] panic-stricken, I wouldn't have been able to give [issue] orders or receive reports.

ウォーキング 《do》(exercise) walking, brisk walking. ●公園へウォーキングに行く go walking in [×to] the park.
- ウォーキングシューズ wálking shòes. (*!* くるぶしまである丈のものはウォーキングブーツ wálking bòots という)

ウォークインクローゼット 〖衣服収納のための納戸(ﾅﾝﾄﾞ)〗a walk-in closet.

ウォークマン 《商標》a Walkman 《@~s》. ●ウォークマンでCDを聴こうに listen to a CD on one's Walkman.

ウォークラリー (説明的に) a sport (similar to orienteering) in which people walk from one place to another with the help of a map, solving the problems at the checkpoints on the route.

ウォーターシュート a water chute.

ウォータープルーフ 〖防水の〗waterproof. (⇨防水)
- ウォータープルーフの日焼け止め (a) waterproof sunscreen. ●ウォータープルーフの時計 a waterproof watch. ●ウォータープルーフの布 waterproof cloth.

ウォーターフロント a waterfront.

ウォーターベッド a waterbed.

ウォーターポロ 〖水球〗(play) water polo.

ウォーニングゾーン 〖野球〗the wárning tràck [pàth]; (和製語) the warning zone. ●ウォーニングゾーンに達するフライを打つ hit a fly ball to the warning track.

ウォーミングアップ 图 a warm-up.
—— **ウォーミングアップをする** 動 warm up (for the game); have [go through] a warm-up. ●(キャッチャーが)ピッチャーにウォーミングアップさせる warm up a pitcher.

ウォームビズ the "Warm Biz" campaign. (⑳ クールビズ)

ウォールがい ウォール街 〖ニューヨークの証券街〗Wall Street.

うおがし 魚河岸 a fish màrket.

うおざ 魚座 〖占星・天文〗Pisces /páisi:z/ (*!* the はつけない); (双魚宮) 〖占星〗the Fishes. (⇨乙女座)
- 魚座(生まれ)の人 a Pisces, a Piscean. (*!* 後の方は形容詞にも用いる)

ウォシュレット 《商標》a Washlet; (説明的に) a toilet that washes the user automatically.

ウオッカ 〖<ロシア語〗vodka /vádkə/.

ウォッチャー watcher. (*!* 通例複合語で) ●ホエールウォッチャー(クジラの観察者) a whale watcher. ●アラブウォッチャー(アラブ情報分析家) Arab watcher.

ウォッチング 〖観察〗watching. (*!* 通例複合語で)
- オーロラウォッチングツアー an aurora-watching trip. ●夏の浜辺で波ウォッチングをする enjoy wave-watching on the summer beach.

うおつり 魚釣り fishing. (⇨釣り)

うおのめ 魚の目 (足の)(have) a corn (on).

ウォンサン 元山 〖韓国の都市〗Wŏnsan.

うか 羽化 图 emergence, eclosion. —— **羽化する** 動 emerge, enclose.

*うかい **迂回** —— **迂回する** 動 ▶私たちは工事現場を迂回して行った We made [took] a detour around the construction area.
- 迂回路 a detour /dí:tuər/; a roundabout way [route]; (バイパス) a bypass.

うかい 鵜飼い cormorant fishing, fishing with cormorants; 〖鵜匠(ｳｼｮｳ)〗 a cormorant fisher (man). ●鵜飼いをする a fish using cormorants.

うがい 含嗽
—— **うがい(を)する** 動 ●塩水でうがいをする gargle [(口をゆすぐ) rinse out] one's mouth] with salt water.
- うがい薬 (a) gargle; (a) mouthwash.

うかうか ❶ 〖不注意に〗carelessly, negligently; (ぼんやりして) absent-mindedly. (⇨うっかり) ●うかうかと秘密をしゃべる tell《him》the secret carelessly [inadvertently].

❷ 〖何もせずに〗idly; (目的なく) purposelessly. ▶彼はうかうかと人生を送り、気がついたら50歳になっていた He spent his life idly only to find himself fifty years old.

—— **うかうかする** 動 ▶うかうかしていると(=気をつけないと)車にはねられるよ Take care or you'll be hit by a car. ▶学生の中には教師がうかうかしていられないほど英語がよくできるのがいる Some students know English so well that they give teachers stiff competition. (*!* 「手強い競争相手になる」の意)

うかがい 伺い 〖訪問〗a visit, a call; 〖意見を求めること〗(an) inquiry, a question. ●お伺いを立てる(=指示を求める) ask for 《his》instructions.

うかがいしる 窺い知る grasp [understand] the situation by guessing.

:**うかがう 伺う** ❶ 〖訪れる〗visit; 《主に英》(ちょっと立ち寄る) call 《on+人, at+場所》. (⇨訪ねる) ●あとであ

なたの事務所に伺います I'll *visit* [《主に英》*call at*] your office later. ▶あすお伺いします I'll *come to see* [*come (and) see*] you tomorrow. (❗《話》ではしばしば and を省略して come see という)

❷【尋ねる】ask, 《書》inquire. (⇨尋ねる)

❸【聞く】be told, hear*. (⇨聞く) ●犬を欲しがっていらっしゃると伺いました I *hear* [*I've heard*] (*that*) you want a dog. ▶ご用件を伺っていますか Are you *being served* [*helped, waited on,* 《書》*attended to*]?/*Is anyone serving* [*helping, taking care of*] *you*?

:うかがう 窺う ❶【のぞく】(⇨のぞく) ●鍵(穴)穴から中をうかがう *peep through* a keyhole. ●部屋の中をうかがう *peep into* a room.

❷【観察する】(⇨観察する) ●顔色をうかがう *study* 《his》 face. ●形勢をじっとうかがう *wait and see how things go* [《慣用句》*how the wind blows*].

❸【待つ】●機会をうかがう *watch for* a chance.

❹【察知する】(⇨推測する) ●彼が無罪であることはその証拠からうかがえる I *gather* from the evidence [The evidence shows] *that* he is innocent. ▶彼女の顔付きから本心がうかがわれた (暴露した) Her face *betrayed* her real feelings./(顔に出ていた) Her true feelings *showed on* her face.

うかされる 浮かされる ●(夢中になる) be crazy [mad] 《about》; be carried away 《with》(⇨夢中に), (高熱に) be delirious (with fever). ▶彼はサッカー熱に浮かされている He *has been carried away with* soccer fever./He has been in the grip of soccer fever. (❗ in the grip of は「…につかまれられて, 支配されて」

うかす 浮かす ❶【腰を】▶彼は彼女が部屋に入ってきたとき, ちょっと腰を浮かした (=いすから半ば立ち上がった) He momentarily *half stood up* [《やや書》*rose*] *from* his *chair* when she entered the room.

❷【水面に】float. (⇨浮かべる ❶) ●ボートを海面に浮かす *float* a boat on the sea.

❸【費用を】save. (⇨浮く ❷)

うかせる 浮かせる (⇨浮かす)

うかつ 迂闊 ── 迂闊な (不注意な) careless; (思慮のない) thoughtless; (愚かな) stupid. ●うかつなふるまい *careless* [*thoughtless, stupid*] behavior.

── 迂闊に carelessly. (⇨うっかり) ●うかつにもそれを彼に話してしまった It *was careless of* me [I *was careless*] *to* tell it to him.

うがった 穿った ●うがった (= 洞察力のある) 見方 a *penetrating* insight. ●うがった (=鋭敏な) 推測をする make a *shrewd* guess.

うかぬかお 浮かぬ顔 ●うかぬ顔をしている (=憂うつそうな) look gloomy [depressed]; pull a long face (❗成句であるが主語が複数のときは pull long faces も可).

うかばれる 浮かばれる ❶【成仏できる】be able to rest in peace.

❷【面目が立つ】▶その失敗が元で彼は一生浮かばれなかった (その失敗を乗り越えられなかった) He couldn't *get over* the failure as long as he lived./(破滅させられた) He *was ruined* by the failure. ▶それじゃおれは浮かばれない (面目を失わせる) That would *make me lose face*./(立つ瀬がない) That'll *put me in a fix*./(もうおしまいだ) I'm *done for* if it's like that.

うかびあがる 浮かび上がる ●【水面に出る】come* up [rise*] to the surface, 《水中などから現れる, 事実などが判明する》emerge 《from》. ●徹底的な調査の結果新事実が浮かび上がった A new fact *emerged from* the thorough investigation.

翻訳のこころ 階段の下から楽しげな音楽が, 蒸気のように廊下に浮かびあがってきた (村上春樹『レキシントンの幽霊』) Merry [Pleasant] music floated up to the hall upstairs from the hallway like steam. (❗ 「浮かびあがる」は float (水や空気中に)漂う). (2) merry は「踊りだしたくなるような」, pleasant は「心地よくさせるような」の意. (3) 「階段の下から」は float up を修飾するので, 動詞の近くに置く. 日本語の語順との違いに注意. (4) アメリカの家の「階段の下」は通例玄関広間 (hallway) になっている.

うかぶ 浮かぶ ❶【水・空に】(浮く) float; (浮遊する) swim; (浮いている) be afloat [floating]. ●あお向けで水に浮かぶ *float* on one's back. ●氷は水に浮かぶ Ice *floats* [*swims*] on water. ▶綿のような雲が空に浮かんでいた Fleecy clouds *were* [There were fleecy clouds] *floating* in the sky. ▶それは南太平洋に浮かぶ(=位置する)小島である It is a small island *located* [*situated*] in the South Pacific.

❷【心に】(考えなどが) occur (-rr-) 《to ...》; come* to mind; (人がふと思いつく) hit* on [upon]…. ▶ふと名案が浮かんだ A good idea *occurred to* me./A good idea *came to mind* [*came into my mind*]./I *hit on* a good idea. ▶自分が間違っているかもしれないという考えが私の心に浮かんだ It *occurred to* me that I might be wrong. ▶その時何も言葉が浮かばなかった (=思いつかなかった) I couldn't *think of* anything to say at that moment. ▶その名前がなかなか浮かばない (=思い出せない) I just can't *remember* the name. (❗ just の位置に注意) ▶今でもその光景が目に浮かぶ I can still *picture* the scene./(心から離れない) The scene still *sticks to* my mind.

❸【現れる】appear; (ぼんやり大きく現れる) loom (up); (光・徴笑などがちらつく) play. ▶彼の顔に不快の色が浮かんだ A look of displeasure *appeared on* his face. ▶霧の中から船の姿が大きく浮かんで来た A ship *loomed (up)* out of the fog. ▶彼女の口元に徴笑が浮かんだ A smile *played on* [*about*] her lips. ▶彼女の目には涙が浮かんだ Tears *came to* [《こみあげた》*welled up in*] her eyes./(浮かんでいた) There were tears in her eyes. ▶この証拠から何人かの男が容疑者として浮かんできた Several men *have been picked up* as possible suspects from this evidence.

●浮かぶ瀬 ●浮かぶ瀬がない be hopeless. ▶身を捨ててこそ浮かぶ瀬もあれ Fortune favors the bold.

*うかべる 浮かべる ❶【水に】(浮かせる) float; (船などを走らせる) sail. ●ヨットを浮かべる *sail* a yacht. ●子供たちは池にいろいろな船を浮かべた The children *floated* [*put*] some toy boats on the pond.

❷【表面に表す】(顔つきをしている) look; (表情などを示す) show*, express; (微笑・表情などを表している) wear* (状態を示す). ●笑み[目に涙]を浮かべて話す speak *with* a smile [tears in one's eyes]. ▶彼は顔に不満の色を浮かべていた He *looked* dissatisfied./His face *showed* dissatisfaction. ▶彼女はいつもほほえみを浮かべている She always *wears* a smile. ●一時性を強調するときは She *is wearing* a smile. と進行形を用いる) ▶彼女は目に涙をいっぱい浮かべていた Her eyes *filled with* tears./Tears *filled* her eyes.

❸【心に】(想像する) imagine, (鮮やかに) picture; (思い出す) remember, recall. (⇨思い出す, 思い浮かべる)

うかる 受かる pass. (⇨合格) ●運転免許試験に受かる *pass* [《英》*get through*] one's driving test.

うかれる 浮かれる [上機嫌だ] be in high spirits; [浮

うがん 右岸 the right bank (of a river).

ウガンダ [国名] Uganda /ju(:)ɡǽndə/, 《公式名》the Republic of Uganda. (首都 Kampala) ●ウガンダ人 a Ugandan. ●ウガンダ(人)の Ugandan.

うき 浮き [釣りの] a float; [浮き袋] 浮き袋.

うき 雨季 the rainy season. ▶雨季に入った The *rainy season* has set in. ⚠ set in は「好ましくないことが始まり、定着する」の意. 無色の表現では has come)

うきあがる 浮き上がる ❶ [浮上する] come* up [rise*] to the surface, surface. ▶鯨は再び水面に浮き上がった The whale *came up to the surface [surfaced]* again.
❷ [遠ざける] alienate /éiliənèit/. ▶彼は横柄な態度のため友人から浮き上がった His arrogance *alienated* his friends./He *alienated* his friends by his arrogance.(=支持を失った) He lost the support of his friends because of his arrogant behavior.

うきあしだつ 浮き足立つ (落ち着きを失う) be upsét; (動揺する) be agitated; be disturbed; (逃げ腰になる) be ready to run away.

うきうき 浮き浮き ― 浮き浮きと 副 happily, buoyantly /bɔ́iəntli/, merrily, cheerfully, gaily.
―― 浮き浮きする 動 feel [be] happy; feel [be] buoyant. ▶彼女は仕事が見つかってうきうきしていた She got a job. She was in *a buoyant mood* [*was over the moon*] (*about it*). (⚠ over the moon (《英話》天にものぼる心地で)

うきくさ 浮き草 a floating weed; [植物] a duckweed. ●浮き草のような生活を送る lead *a precarious* life.
●浮き草稼業 a precarious trade.

うきぐも 浮き雲 a floating [a drifting] cloud.

うきぐも 『浮雲』 *The Drifting Cloud*. [参考] 二葉亭四迷の小説)

うきさんばし 浮き桟橋 a landing stage.

うきしずみ 浮き沈み 〖人生の浮き沈み the *úps and dówns* [〖書〗the *vicissitudes*] of life. ●賭け事などの成績に〗浮き沈みがある have *wins and losses*.

うきしま 浮島 [水草の群れ] a floating island; [浮いているように見える島] an island that appears afloat.

うきだす 浮き出す (⇨浮き出る)

うきたつ 浮き立つ ▶そのニュースを聞いて浮き立つ(=元気づく) *cheer up* at the news. ▶その音楽を聞くと心が浮き立った The music *cheered* me *up*.

うきでる 浮き出る 〖表面に出る〗(水面などに) rise* to the surface (⇨浮き上がる❶); (汗などが) break* out (*on*); (血管などが) protrude; [模様などがはっきり見える] stand* out. ●静脈の浮き出た手 a veined hand; a hand with veins *standing out prominently*.

うきドック 浮きドック a floating (dry) dock.

うきな 浮き名 ●浮き名を流す A rumor about one's love affair [romance] circulates [flies, spreads].

うきはし 浮き橋 a floating bridge; a pontoon bridge.

うきぶくろ 浮き袋 (水泳用の) a float, a rubber ring; (救命用の) a life buoy /búːi, bɔ́i/; (魚の) an air bladder. ●浮き袋をして泳ぐ swim with a *rubber ring*.

うきぼり 浮き彫り (技法) relief /rilíːf/; (作品) a relief (徽 ~s). (⇨レリーフ) ●国王の横顔が浮き彫りにされたメダル a medal with a profile of the king (carved) *in relief*.
●浮き彫りにする ▶闇の中で白い仮面がくっきりと浮き彫りにされた The white mask *stood out in bold relief* in the dark. ▶これで疑獄の深刻さが浮き彫りにされた This threw the seriousness of the scandal into *relief*.

うきみ 憂き身 ●憂き身をやつす devote oneself in ...; indulge in ....

うきめ 憂き目 ●憂き目を見る (つらい経験をする) suffer greatly; have a bitter experience. ●落選の憂き目を見る experience the *misery* of losing the election.

うきよ 浮き世 the floating world; (この世) the [this] world, this life; (はかない世) the [this] fleeting world; (つらい世) the world of hardships. ●浮き世のしがらみ all that binds your life. ▶それが浮き世の習いだ It is the way of *the world*.
●浮き世離れ ▶彼はその山村で浮き世離れした生活をしている (世俗にまみれずに) He keeps himself aloof from the world [(物欲にとらわれずに) He is leading an *unworldly* life] in the mountain village.

うきよえ 浮き世絵 (an) *ukiyoe*; (説明的に) genre pictures (woodblock prints and paintings) flourished in the Edo period, depicting the life and interests of common people.

うきわ 浮き輪 a float (ring); (救命浮き輪) a life ring.

うく 浮く ❶ [水・空中に] (浮かぶ) float; (浮遊する) swim*. ▶浮き上がる❶ ●スープに浮いている油 grease *floating [swimming]* on the soup. ▶木は水に浮くが石は沈む Wood *floats* on water, but stone sinks in water.
❷ [余る] (節約になる) be saved; (残される) be left over. ▶それで1万円浮く You can *save* ten thousand yen that way.

うぐい [魚介] a Japanese dace.

うぐいす 鶯 [鳥] a bush warbler.
●鶯色 greenish brown. ●鶯嬢 (野球場などの) a sweet-voiced woman public-address announcer (at a ball park). ●鶯張り singing floorboards. ●鶯餅 [菓子] *uguisumochi*; (説明的に) a bean-jam rice cake covered with greenish soybean flour.

ウクライナ [国名] (the) Ukraine /juː(ː)kréin/ (⚠ 公式名も同じ). (首都 Kiev) ●ウクライナ人 a Ukrainian. ●ウクライナ語 Ukrainian. ●ウクライナ(人[語])の Ukrainian.

ウクレレ [<ハワイ語] a ukulele /jùːkəléili/.

うけ 受け (評判) (a) reputation; (人気) popularity; (受け入れ) (a) reception. ●受けを狙った演技 one's performance that tries to *appeal to* the audience. ▶彼は同僚の受けがよい[よくない] He *is* [*is not*] *popular with* [*among*] his colleagues. ▶「上司の受けがとてもよい」など上下関係のある場合には be high in his superior's favor ともいえる) ▶彼の新作は批評家の受けがよかった His new work *was* well *received* by the critics. (⇨好評)

うけ 有卦 ●有卦に入(い)る have (a streak of) good luck; have good fortune; be in luck.

うけあう 請け合う [保証する] guarantee /gæ̀rəntíː/; [確言・確約する] assure ▶その映画は絶対におもしろいと請け合う answer for .... ▶その映画は絶対におもしろいと請け合う I (can) *assure* you (*that*) you will enjoy the movie./You'll enjoy the movie, I (can) *assure* you. (⚠ can を加えるとより強調的)

うけい 右傾 ―― 右傾する 動 lean to the right; (思想的に) turn rightist. (㊦ 左傾)

うけいれる 受け入れる [[受諾する]] accept; [[願いなどをかなえる]] grant; [[依頼などに応じる]] [[書]] comply 《with》; [[同意する]] agree 《to+事, with+人・意見》, 《話》buy. ●彼をクラブの一員として受け入れる accept him *as* a member of the club. ●彼の要求を受け入れる grant [comply with] his request. ●彼の案を受け入れる accept [agree to] his plan. (❗彼が積極的に同意して受け入れることを示す) ▶私の提案は受け入れられなかった My proposal *was* not *accepted* [(拒絶された) *was rejected*]. ▶その学校は帰国子女を受け入れている The school *admits* [*accepts*] returnee students. (❗admit は「入学を許す」の意) ▶彼らは賃金が低いというが、それは一般の人たちには受け入れられないだろう The public will not *buy* their claim that they are underpaid.

うけうり 受け売り ▶彼は私の受け売りをしているだけです He's just *repeating* [*mouthing*, *parroting*] what I said. (❗後の動詞ほど軽蔑の度が強い)

うけおい 請負 (a) contract. ●請負で橋をかける build a bridge *by* [*on*] *contract*. ●仕事を請負に出す put the work out to the *contract*.
●請負価格 a contract price. ●請負制度 a contract system. ●請負人 a contractor.

うけおう 請け負う [[契約する]] contract; [[仕事などを引き受ける]] take*... on, 《書》undertake* (➪引き受ける). ●その会社に仕事を請け負わせる give the company a *contract for* the job. ▶その会社は新しい仕事[彼の家の建築]を請け負った The company *contracted* new business [*to* build his house].

うけぐち 受け口 (物の受け入れ口) a recéiving wíndow [hòle]. ▶彼女の受け口(=下唇が上唇より突き出た口)が妙に魅力的だった He found her slightly *sticking-out lower lip* attractive.

うけごし 受け腰 ●受け腰になる act passively [reluctantly].

うけこたえ 受け答え an answer, a reply. (➪答え、返事)

うけざら 受け皿 a saucer. ●受け皿つきのカップ a cup and /(ə)n/ *saucer*. (❗単数扱い) ▶彼には部長退任後にこうかな受け皿が用意されている There is a good *position* he will *fill* after his retirement as manager.

うけだす 請け出す ▶質屋から指輪を請け出した I *redeemed* my ring *from* the pawn shop.

うけたまわる 承る (➪承知する) ▶ご用命たしかに承りました We will *attend to* your request, sir [madam]. (❗attend to は「世話をする」に近く、受けた用件を敏速に処理することが暗示される) ▶奥様、ご用は承っておりますでしょうか[店員が] *Are* you *being attended to* [*helped*], madam? ▶きょうは遅れてご出席と承っていました(=知らされていた) I *heard* [*was told*] that you'd be late for the meeting [party].

うけつぐ 受け継ぐ [[地位・職務・財産などを]] succeed 《to》; [[仕事・責任などを]] take* ... over (➪継ぐ); [[性質などを]] inherit. ▶彼の事業を受け継ぐ succeed *to* [*take over*] his business.

__うけつけ 受付__ [[受け入れ]] acceptance; [[受付所]] an information 《英》a reception] desk, a desk; [[受付係]] a receptionist, a reception [an information] clerk. ●受付で尋ねる ask at *information* 《英》*reception*] (❗無冠詞に注意); ask at the (*information* [*reception*]) *desk*.
●受付期間 (申し込みの) the application period. ●受付番号 a receipt number.

__うけつける 受け付ける__ [[受理する]] accept; [[受け取る]] receive (❗accept と異なり「受諾する」の意はない). ●提案を受け付ける *accept* [*receive*] a proposal.

●電話による注文を受け付ける *accept* telephone orders. ●要求を受け付けない *refuse* [*reject*, *turn down*] 《his》request. (❗reject が最も意味が強い. turn down は婉曲的で口語的) ▶願書は11月5日まで受け付けます Applications will *be accepted* until November 5. ▶彼は他人の忠告を受け付け(=聞き入れ)ない He won't *listen to* [(耳を貸さない) always turns a deaf ear to] others' advice. ▶その患者は食事をまったく受け付けない The patient can't *take* any food. ▶私は体質的に卵を受け付けない(=合わない) I'm allergic to eggs.

うげつものがたり 『雨月物語』 Ugetsu Monogatari: *Tales of Moonlight and Rain*. ([参考] 上田秋成の読本(ょ_{ほん}))

うけてたつ 受けて立つ accept. ▶我々は彼らの雪辱戦の申し入れを受けて立った We *accepted* their challenge to (play) a return (match). ▶けんかを売るなら受けて立とうじゃないか(=失望させない) If you mean to fight me, I will *not disappoint* you.

うけとめる 受け止める [[意見などを]] [[解する]] take*; [[反応する]] react 《to》; [[ボールなどを]] catch* (➪捕まえる). ●批判をまじめに受け止める *take* the criticism seriously. ●その悲報を冷静に受け止める *take* the sad news calmly; *react* calmly *to* the sad news. ●彼の提案をどう受け止めますか What is your *reaction to* his suggestion?

うけとり 受け取り (a) receipt /risíːt/. (❗「受領証」の意では C). ●お金[商品]の受け取り *receipt* of money [the goods]. ●その受け取りを書いて[をもらう]サインする] make out [get; sign] a *receipt for* it. ▶彼は自分の友人を受取人として小切手を振り出した He drew a check *in favor of* his friend.
●受取人 a receiver; (年金・遺産などの) a bèneficiary; (手形などの) a pàyee.

__うけとる 受け取る__ **❶** [[受領する]] receive, get* (❗get の方が口語的. receive は差し出されたものを「受け取る」ことをいう; get は過程にかかわりなく「受け取る」ことをいう; (贈り物などを) accept (❗receive と異なり、納得してあるいは喜んで受け入れる意); (取る) take*.
▶あなたからの手紙を受け取りました I *have got* [*received*] a letter from you. ▶彼はその贈り物を受け取る気になれなかった He was unwilling to *accept* the present. ▶彼は中古の自転車の代金として5,000円受け取った He *took* 5,000 yen for the second-hand bicycle.
[会話]「ロープを投げてくれ」「さあ、いくぞ。しっかり受け取って(=つかんで)」"Throw me a rope." "Here you go. *Catch* a good *hold* of this one."
❷ [[解釈する]] (取る) take*; (理解する) interpret; (了解する) understand*. ●彼の申し出をそう深刻に受け取ってはいけない You shouldn't *take* his offer so seriously. ●彼女は私の言葉を軽蔑と受け取った She *took* [*interpreted*] my words *as* an insult. ●彼は私が黙っているのを拒絶したと受け取った He *understood* my silence *to be* [*as*] a refusal. (❗to be の方が多い)

うけながす 受け流す ●攻撃を受け流す *ward* /wɔːrd/ *off* [*parry*, (実に巧みに) *dodge*] an attack. ●質問を受け流す *parry* [*dodge*] a question.

うけみ 受(け)身 **❶** [[文法]] the passive (voice).
❷ [[消極的な態度]] a passive attitude. ●受け身に回る take a *passive attitude*; (聞き役をする) take the part of the listener.
❸ [柔道の] *ukemi*; the art of falling safely.
── 受け身の [⑱] passive.

うけもち 受け持ち (担当) charge. ●私のクラスの受け持ちの先生 the teacher *in charge of* my class. (❗多くの場合 my teacher だけでこの意味を表すことがで

きる）(⇨受け持つ) ◆彼の受け持ちの仕事 his assignment. ◆私の受け持ちの生徒 a pupil in my charge, my pupil.

うけもつ 受け持つ take* charge 《of》. ◆そのクラス[会計]を受け持つ[受け持っている] take [be in] charge of the class [accounting]. ◆私は化学を受け持っている I teach chemistry./I'm a chemistry teacher.

うける 受ける ❶[得る] (一般的に) get*; (差し出されて受け取る) receive (🔲 get より堅い語); (与えられる) be given (🔲 英語ではこの意は受身で表現されることも多い: 知らせを受ける be informed/影響を受ける be influenced). ◆よい教育を受ける get [receive, be given] a good education. ◆賞を受ける be awarded a prize. ◆ここに駐車するには許可を受けなければいけない You must get permission to park your car here. ◆彼は町の人々から暖かい歓迎を受けた He received a warm 《↔a cold》 welcome from the people of the town./(暖かく迎えられた) He was welcomed warmly [was given a warm welcome] by the people of the town. ◆私は彼の死に衝撃を受けた I was shocked at [by] his death./His death was [came as] a shock to me. /(📕 I got [received] a shock at his death. というより，上のようにいう方が普通)

❷[受け止める] catch*. ◆(捕手が)投手の球を受ける catch a pitcher; receive a pitcher's pitches. ◆雨水を受けるバケツ a bucket to catch the rain.

❸[受け入れる] (申し出・挑戦などを) accept 《to 立つ》; (客なども) take*... (in). ◆結婚の申し込みを受ける accept a proposal of marriage. ◆この条件でお受けいただけますか Could you accept this term?/Would this term be acceptable? ◆(レストランの予約で) 10名様ですか，あいにく大勢様はお受けしかねるのですが Ten! I'm sorry but we don't usually take large parties.

❹[試験などを] take*; (英) sit* (for...). ◆大学の入学試験を受ける take [sit (for)] the entrance examination for a university. ◆フランス語の講習を受けている I am taking a course in French.

❺[検査などを] have*; undergo*. (🔲 前の方が口語的) ◆胃がんの手術を受ける have [undergo] an operation on one's stomach for cancer; be operated on for stomach cancer. ◆私たちは年1回の健康診断を受ける方がよい We'd better have [undergo] an annual checkup. ◆彼が受け取り調べは厳しいものでした The investigation he underwent was tough.

❻[損害などを] (被る) suffer. ◆会社はこの取り引きで多大な損害を受けた The company suffered [(出した) made] heavy losses on that deal. ◆あらしで農作物が大きな被害を受けた The crops suffered a lot of damage because of the storm./The crops were severely damaged by the storm./(被害を及ぼした[引き起こした]) The storm did [caused] a lot of damage to the crops. ◆投手は打球を受けた The pitcher was hit by a batted ball. ◆打者は球技を受けた The batter was hit by (a) pitch.

❼[罰などを] take*; (償う) pay*. ◆報いを受ける pay the penalty 《for》. ◆金を盗んだら罰を受けるだろう If you steal money, you will be punished [take punishment].

❽[言葉などを] (受け取る) take*. ◆彼の言ったことを真(*)に受けるな (本気にとるな) Don't take what he said too seriously./(言葉どおりにとるな) Don't take him at his word.

❾[電話などを] (答える) answer. ◆たいてい私が電話を受ける I usually answer the phone.

❿[人気を得る] win* popularity; (人気がある) be popular 《with》; (気に入られる) appeal 《to》. ◆その劇はお客に受けた The play won popularity [(話) clicked] with the audience. ◆その広告は女性客に受けた The advertisement appealed to female buyers. ◆彼女の演奏は大いに受けた Her performance was a great success. ◆彼の冗談は受けなかった His joke fell flat [didn't go over].

うける 請ける (⇨請け出す, 引き受ける❶)

うけわたし 受け渡し 图 (配達) delivery. ◆商品の受け渡し delivery of goods.

—— 受け渡しする 動 deliver.
◆受け渡し条件 the terms of delivery.

うげん 右舷 (海軍) starboard. ◆右舷に to starboard.

うご 雨後 ◆**雨後の竹の子** ◆新しい基地の周辺には歓楽街が雨後の竹の子のようにできた Entertainment districts have mushroomed [have sprung up like mushrooms] around the new military base.

うごうのしゅう 烏合の衆 (暴徒) a mob; (無秩序な群衆) a disorderly crowd.

うごかす 動かす ❶[物を動かす] (a) [物を] move; remove (🔲 move は最も意味の広い語。remove は堅い語で定位置から離すことを強調する (⇨取り除く)); (移す) (話) shift (🔲 方向・位置の変化を強調); (ちょっと動かす) (話) budge (🔲 通例否定文で). ◆軍隊を前線に動かす move the troops to the front. ◆そのテーブルをもう少し右に動かしてください Please move the table a little further to the right. ◆その岩は大きくてだれも動かすことができなかった The rock was so big that no one could move [(🔲) remove, (ちょっとでも) budge] it. ◆このピアノは動かせますか Is this piano movable?

(b) [固定・静止したものを] (位置を変える) move (🔲 動かし方については特に制限はない); (そっと動かす) stir (-rr-); [揺らす] (上下前後左右に速く) shake*; (振り子のように) swing*, (大きく) sway; (ぴくぴくいわれさせる) twitch; [運動させる] exercise. ◆手足を動かす move [exercise] one's arms and legs. ◆腕をぶらぶら動かす swing one's arms. ◆左右に腰を振り動かす sway one's hips. ◆耳をぴくぴく動かす twitch one's ears. ◆まぶた一つ動かさない(=平然としている) do not bat an eye [an eyelid]. ◆このレバーでクレーンを前後に動かすことができる This lever moves the crane back and forth. ◆そよ風が木の葉を動かした A breeze stirred the leaves. ◆爆発が民家を揺り動かした The explosion shook the houses. ◆もっと体を動かさなければ(=運動しないと)太りますよ If you don't get [(英) take] more exercise, you'll get fat. ◆ほんのちょっと体を動かすだけで暑くて疲れた The smallest movement made me hot and tired.

❷[運転する] (正常に動かす) work; (操作から) operate; (継続的に動かす) run*; (始動させる) start; (車などを, 動力の機械を) drive*. ◆その機械を動かす work [operate, run] the machine; (始動させる) set the machine going [running, working]; put [set] the machine in motion. ◆車を動かす drive [run] a car; (始動させる) start (up) a car. ◆ゆっくりと自転車を動かし始めながら,「こちらですか」と彼女は言った "This way?" she said, gently getting her bicycle into motion. ◆水が水車を動かす Water drives [runs] the waterwheel.

会話「それが動かせないんだ」「やらせてみて」"I can't make it work." "Let me try [(話) have a go at it]."

❸[心を動かす] (感動させる) move, (感傷的に) touch (=感動する); (影響を与える) influence; (誘惑

うごかぬ

する) tempt. ● 彼の心を動かす move him [his heart]; touch him [his heart]. ▶ 彼は彼女の言葉に大変心を動かされた He *was* very [deeply] *moved by* her words./What she said really *touched* him [his heart]. ● 彼は簡単に金で動かされる He *is* easily *moved* [*influenced*] *by* money./(買収されやすい) He can easily *be bribed* with money.

❹ [人・組織などを動かす] (支配する) control (-ll-); (指図する) direct; (経営する) manage. ● 株式市場を陰で動かす *control* the stock market behind the scenes; 《話》*pull the strings* [*wires*] in the stock market. ▶ 彼は息子を意のままに動かした He *made* his sons *do* as he wanted them to.

❺ [変更する] change, alter (⇨変える); [信念などを動揺させる] shake*; [人・意見などを揺さぶる] sway. ● 予定を動かす *change* the schedule. ● 動かしがたい ● 彼の決心を動かす *change* his mind; *shake* his resolution. ● 彼の演説は世論を動かした His speech *swayed* public opinion.

うごかぬ 動かぬ ● 動かぬ決意 an *immovable* [(固い) a *firm*, (揺るがない) an *unshakable*] resolution. ● 動かぬ証拠をつかむ get [obtain] *hard* [(決定的な) *conclusive*, (争えない) *incontestable*, (否認できない) *indisputable*] evidence. ▶ これは動かぬ事実だ This is a *certain* [an *unshakable*, (否定できない) an *undeniable*, (確立された) an *established*] fact.

うごぎ 五加 〖植物〗an aralia.

*****うごき 動き** ❶ [運動] (抽象的・具体的な運動の様子・過程) 〖運動〗motion; (一定の方向・規則性をもった具体的な運動) (a) movement; (特に目的をもった動き) a move. ● 動きの速い*fast* sports. 〖❶ サッカー、アイスホッケーなど〗● ゆっくりした動きで in slow motion. ● 彼の動きをつぶさに(=一挙一動を)見守る watch his every move. ● 警察の動きを(=行動)を見守る watch the *movements* [*activities*] of the police. ● 子供の心の動き(=働き) the *workings* of a child's mind. ● バレエダンサーは体の動きやしぐさで感情を表現する Ballet dancers express emotions through their (body) *movements* and gestures. ● それはアメーバによく似た動きをする It moves much like an amoeba. ● 私の車は交通渋滞で動きがとれなかった My car *was stuck* [*was tied up*] in a traffic jam. ● 彼は仕事がいっぱいで動きがとれない He *is hedged in* by all his duties.

❷ [動向] (時代などの) a movement; (風潮) a trend; (変化) a change. ● 世論の動きは the *movement* [*trend, drift*] of public opinion. ● 物価の動き *changes* in prices.

⁑うごく 動く ❶ [移動する] move (最も一般的な語); (車などが走る) run*; (かすかにそっと動く) stir (-rr-); (ちょっと動く) budge (● 通例否定文で); (移る)《話》shift (● 方向・位置の変化を強調する); (別の場所・所属へ移る) transfer (-rr-). ● 動く標的に命中させる hit a *moving* target. ● 交通渋滞で動けない [立ち往生する] *be stuck* in a traffic jam. ▶ 車がゆっくり動き始めた The car slowly began to *move* [*run*]./The car *started* slowly. ▶ くたくたに疲れてもう一歩も動けない I'm exhausted, so I can't *move* another step. ● その市には地下鉄がないのであちこち動き回るのがちょっと大変だ They don't have a subway in that city, so it's a little difficult to *move* [*get*] *around*. ▶ 彼は今はよくなって元気に動き回っている He's *up and around* [*about*] now. ▶ 京都・大阪間は洪水のため列車が動いていない Trains *are* not *running* between Kyoto and Osaka because of the flood. ● (運転する) 彼はドアを開けようとしたが、どうしても動かなかった He tried to open the door, but it wouldn't *budge*. ▶ 積み荷が左の方に動いた The load *shifted* to the left. ▶ 私が戻るまでここを動いてはいけません(=ここにずっといなさい) Stay (right) here till I come back.

❷ [固定・静止している人・物が動く] move; (少し動く) stir (-rr-); [揺れ動く] (上下前後左右に速く) shake*; (振り子のように) swing*, (大きく) sway. ▶ 動いたら撃つぞ If you *move* [*make a move*], I'll shoot you./(そこを動くな、さもないと) *Stay there* [*Freeze*], or I'll shoot you. ▶ ネクタイを直してあげるからちょっと動かないで(=じっとしていて) *Hold still* a moment while I fix your tie. ● この家はトラックが通り過ぎるたびに揺れ動く Every time a truck passes, this house *shakes*. ● 木々の枝が風で揺れていた The branches of the trees *were swaying* in the wind. ▶ この人形の足は動く(=動かせる) This doll has *movable* legs.

会話「ここ君の席だったの」「いいよ、いいよ、動かないで」"Have I taken your seat?" "No, no, don't *stir* [立ち上がる] *get up*]."

❸ [機械が作動する] (正常に動く) work; (動き続ける) run*; (順調に動く) go*; (効果的に動く) act. (⇨動かす) ● そのモーターは電気で動く The motor *works* [*runs, goes*] *on* electricity./The motor is run [is powered] by electricity. ▶ この印刷機は一晩中動いている This printing machine is kept *going* all night.

会話「この古い時計動くの?」「もちろん、ちゃんと動くさ」"Does this old clock *work* [*run*]?" "Sure, it *works* [*runs*] fine."

会話「このコンピュータ動かないよ」「コンセント入れてあるの?」"I can't get this computer to *work*." "Is it plugged in?"

❹ [心が動く] (感動する) be moved; (傷感的に) be touched (⇨感動する); (影響される) be influenced. ▶ 彼のことばで心が動いた I *was moved* by his words./His words *moved* me [my heart]. ▶ 彼は簡単に金で動く He *is* easily *moved* [*influenced*] *by* money./(買収されやすい) He can easily *be bribed* with money. ▶ 条件がよかったので思わず心が動いた(=受け入れたいと思った) The terms were so favorable that I *felt inclined to* accept them.

❺ [変化する] change; (いろいろ変わる) vary; (上下に変動する) fluctuate; (人・意見などが傾く) sway. ▶ 世界は絶えず動いている The world *is* constantly *changing* [*moving*]. ● 穀物の値段は天候によって動く The price of grain *varies* [《書》*fluctuates*] according to the weather. ● 世論は改革をよしとする方向に動き始めた Public opinion has begun to *sway* in favor of the reforms. ● 失業率は4.5パーセントから動かない The jobless rate *holds steady* at 4.5 percent. ● 彼の優勝はまず動くまい(=確実だ) He *is* almost *sure to* win the championship./I'm almost *sure* [*It's* almost *certain that*] he will win the championship. (⇨動かぬ)

❻ [行動する] act. ● 彼の命令で動く *act on* his order. [〖この命は「…に従って」の意〗] ● 騒ぎを阻止するため直ちに動く(=行動する)べきだ You must *take* immediate *action* to prevent trouble. ▶ 警察は証拠がないとなかなか動いてくれない The police won't be very happy about doing anything without proof.

うごさべん 右顧左眄 ── 右顧左眄する **動** waver, vacillate, hesitate.

うごめく 蠢く (虫が) wriggle. ▶ 裏通りには麻薬の売人がうごめいていた Drug dealers were *hanging around* the back street. ● 彼女たち得意の鼻をうごめかせてたよ I saw the elation [triumph] in her

うこん 鬱金 〖植物〗(a) turmeric; 〖うこん色〗bright yellow.

うさぎ 兎 〖動物〗(飼育用の) a rabbit; (野ウサギ) a hare. ▶ウサギが人参を食べていた The *rabbit* was nibbling the carrot.
● 兎小屋 a rabbit hútch. (!) hutch は〘話〙でバラック(粗末な家)をさすこともある. ● 兎跳び hopping along in a squatting position.

うざったい (うっとうしい) annoying; (吐き気がするほど不快な) be disgusting. ▶あんなうざったい仕事вы れないよ I don't like to do such an *annoying* job. ▶うさくさく言ってうざったい奴だと思われるのがいやなんでしょう You're afraid of being thought (to *be*) *a pain* if you say this odd and that end persistently.

うさばらし 憂さ晴らし (気分を転換させるもの[こと]) (a) diversion; (a) distraction. ▶うさ晴らしに酒を飲んだ I drank sake *for a diversion* [(心配事を忘れるために) *to forget* my *care*]. ▶彼は弱い者に暴力を振ってうさ晴らしをした He *blew off steam* by turning violently on weak people. (!) blow off《米》[let off《英》] steam は、「うっ積した気持ちを吐き出す」の意)

うさんくさい 胡散臭い ▶うさん臭い人物〘話〙a *shady*-looking person; a *shady* character. ▶彼の話はどうもうさん臭い There's something *fishy* about his story./〘話〙His story smells *fishy*.

うし 丑 the Ox.
● 丑年 〖十二支〗the year of the Ox. (⇨干支) 関連 ● 丑の日 the Day of the Ox. ● 丑三つ時 in the dead of night; in the middle of the night.

うし 牛 〖動物〗(雄) a bull, an ox (複 oxen); (!) ox は特に労役用・食用の去勢した雄牛で、牛の学問的総称; (雌) a cow ▶乳牛を連想させるときは bull や ox より日常的だ; (子牛) a calf (複 calves); (総称) cattle (!) 集合的に用い複数扱い. ● 50頭の牛 (have) fifty (head [×heads) of) cattle [×cattles]. (!) 端数のない通例大きな数については、少数の牛については、例えば ×two cattle とはいわない ● 乳牛 a (milk) cow. ▶この牛は今年子牛[2頭の子牛]を産んだ This cow calved [gave birth to two *calves*] this year.
● 牛にひかれて善光寺参り be led to do something good [into doing something good] without knowing it.
● 牛の歩みのごとく at a snail's pace. (!) snail は「かたつむり」(⇨牛歩)
● 牛を馬に乗り換える (形勢を見て旗色のいい方につく) come down on the right side of the fence.
● 牛飼い a cattleman; a cattle rancher. (!) 米国、オーストラリアなどの大規模な肉牛畜産業者な) ● 牛小屋 a cowshed; a cowhouse.

うじ 氏 (名字) a family name. ● 氏素性 (⇨氏素性)
● 氏より育ち 'Breeding is more important than birth.'/(ことわざ) Birth is much, but breeding is more. (!) この場合の birth は「生まれ、家柄」)

うじ 蛆 a maggot. ▶この魚はウジがわいている This fish is infested with *maggots*. ▶男やもめにウジがわく The widowers tend to get grubby. ● ウジの一種. その形容詞の grubby には「ウジのわいた」と「汚ない」の意がある)

うじうじ ▶うじうじした (=ちゅうちょする) 態度 a *hesitant* [(決断力のない) an *indecisive*, (煮えきらない)《話》a *wishy-washy*) attitude. ▶父親は息子が何につけてうじうじするのが大嫌いだった The father hated his son to be *indecisive* all the time.

うしお 潮 (⇨海水, 潮(シオ)) ▶潮のごとく押し寄せるsurge 〈*into* the stadium, *through* the gate〉.

● 潮汁 consommé with fish in it, flavored with salt.

うじがみ 氏神 a tutelary [a tutelar] deity [guardian, god].

うじこ 氏子 people under the protection of the local tutelary deity.

うじしゅういものがたり『宇治拾遺物語』 *Uji Shui Monogatari; A collection of Tales from Uji*. [参考] 鎌倉時代の説話集

うじすじょう 氏素性 one's family background, one's birth.

:うしなう 失う lose*; miss.

> 使い分け **lose** 一般的な語で、所有物をなくしたり、能力・信頼などを維持できなくなる場合に用いられる.
> **miss** 機会などを失ったり、友人と別れて寂しく感じる. ある特定の語とともにしか用いられない: 機会を失う *miss* a chance [an opportunity]. この場合 lose も用いられるが、miss が「一時的に失う」のに対し lose は「永久に失う」の意を暗示する.「友人を失う」は *lose* one's friend で、miss を用いれば「友人がいなくて寂しい」の意になる.

▶財産[人気; 名声; 記憶]を失う *lose* one's fortune [popularity; fame; memory]. ▶ 職を失う *lose* one's job. (⇨解雇) ▶すっかり希望を失う *lose* [*give up*] all (one's) hope. ▶誇りを失わない(=保つ) retain one's pride. ▶彼はその事故で親友を失った He *lost* [(奪われた)〘書〙*was bereaved of*] his best friend in the accident. ▶彼は大衆の支持を失った He *lost* the support of the public. ▶今回の事件で私が失ったものは大きい I *lost* a great deal in this incident. ▶失われた青春は二度と帰らない *Lost youth never returns* [will never come back again]. ▶全国民が彼を失ったことを嘆き悲しんでいる The entire nation weeps [laments] at his *loss*. (!) weep は涙を流して、lament は惜しんで悲しむ) ▶彼は一目見て彼女が美貌をすっかり失ったのが分かった He noticed at a glance the total *loss of* her beauty. ▶多くの人々が洪水で家を失った A lot of people *were made homeless* by the flood.

うじむし 蛆虫 (⇨蛆)

うじゃうじゃ ▶葉っぱには毛虫がうじゃうじゃいた There were swarms of hairy caterpillars all over the leaves. ▶昔しこの池には魚がうじゃうじゃいた This pond used to be *alive with* fish.

うしょう 鵜匠 a cormorant fisher(man).

:うしろ 後ろ [〘後部, 背面〙the back (↔the front); (車・部屋などの後部) 〘やや書〙the rear.
①〘後ろ(の)～〙●ズボンの後ろポケット a back [a *rear*] pocket of the pants. ▶彼を後ろ手に縛る bind [tie] him with his hands behind his *back*. ▶後ろの車がスピードを上げてきた The car *behind* (us) is gaining speed. ▶私は車の後ろの座席に座った I sat *on the back* [*rear*] seat of the car./I sat *in the back* [*rear*] of the car. (!) 多数の席のある部屋や乗り物の場合は *at the back* [(*of the theater* [*airplane*]) が普通) ▶彼らは後ろ合わせに(=背中合わせに)座っている They are sitting *back to back*.
②〘～の後ろに〙[へ, から] 〖順序〗after ...; 〖位置, 場所〙(背面・後方に) behind ..., at the back of ..., 《米》in back of ... (!) at は位置関係を強調する(⇨①)). ▶彼の後ろについて行こう I'll go *after* [*follow*] him. ▶私たちは車の後ろから押した We got *behind* the car and pushed. ▶学校の後ろに小山がある There is a hill *behind* [*at the back of, (in) back of*] our school. ▶老人は首の後ろにしわが寄っていた The

うしろがみ

old(er) man had wrinkles *on* [*in*] *the back of his neck.* (**!** on は表面を、in はめり込んだ深いしわを示す)▶「危ない」と彼は私の後ろから叫んだ "Watch out!" he shouted *after* [*behind*] me. (**!** after は「遠ざかる背に向かって」、behind は「後方向きで」の意)▶「独裁政治打倒!」群衆の後ろから声があがった "Down with despotism!" A voice shouted *from the back* of the crowd.

❸【後ろを[へ, から, で]】(後方へ) back, backward; (後方の位置に) behind. ●後ろを振り向く look *back*; (肩越しに見る) look over one's shoulder; (背後を見る) look *behind*. ●バスの中を後ろへ移動する move *back* in a bus; move *to the back* [*rear*] of a bus. ●髪を後ろで束ねてリボンで結んでいる have one's hair tied *back* with a ribbon. ▶このブラウスは後ろで留めるようになっている This blouse fastens *at* [*down*] *the back.* ▶後ろから押すな Don't push me *from behind*. ▶敵に後ろを見せるな Don't turn tail to your enemy.
● 後ろ足 a back leg; a hind leg.

うしろがみ 後ろ髪 ●後ろ髪を引かれる思い ▶パリへ帰る娘を見送ると私はいつも後ろ髪を引かれる思いがする It's always a *wrench* parting [to part] with my daughter who returns to Paris. (**!** wrench は単数形で用い、離別の苦痛などを表す. It always gives me great pain..../I always feel very sad.... などともいえる)

うしろきず 後ろ傷 a cut on one's back.

うしろぐらい 後ろ暗い (やましい) (いかがわしい) shady; (内密の) clandestine; (不正な) underhand. ●後ろ暗い取引 a *shady* [an *underhand*] deal. ●心に後ろ暗いところがある have a *guilty* conscience.

うしろすがた 後ろ姿 one's back view. ●後ろ姿を見送る watch 《him》 go away; (じっと) gaze after 《him》.

うしろだて 後ろ盾 〘支持〙support; (後援) backing; 〘支持者〙a supporter; (芸術家などの) a patron. ●妻の莫大な財産を後ろ盾として政界に打って出る launch into the political world *backed* [*supported*] by his wife's enormous wealth.

うしろまえ 後ろ前 ●シャツを後ろ前に着る put on one's shirt *backward(s)* [*back to front*].

うしろむき[むけ] 後ろ向き[向け] 〘向いて〙backward [▶forward]. ●後ろ向きになる[歩く] turn [walk] *backward*. ●帽子を後ろ向きにかぶっている wear a hat *backward* ●後ろ向きの政策[考え方] a *backward-looking* policy [way of thinking].

うしろめたい 後ろめたい ●後ろめたそうな顔つき a *guilty* look. ●後ろめたい思いをする feel *guilty* [*guilt*]; have a *guilty* conscience; have a *sense* of guilt.

うしろゆび 後ろ指 ●後ろ指をさされる ▶人に後ろ指をさされる(=人の話のタネになる)ようなことはするな Don't do anything that will *make* people *talk about you* [〘陰で非難される〙*be criticized behind* your *back*].

うす 臼 (つき臼) a mortar; (ひき臼) a millstone. ●臼でつく pound 《boiled rice》 in a *mortar*.

うす- 薄-

*****うず** 渦 〘風・水などの〙a swirl; (勢いよく回る) a whirl; (小さい) an eddy; 〘水流の〙a whirlpool; 〘大渦巻き〙《書》a maelstrom. ●煙の渦 a *whirl* [a *swirl*] of smoke. ●渦を巻く swirl [whirl] (around). ●興奮の渦を巻き起こす arouse a wild excitement. ●争いの渦に巻き込まれる be drawn into a *whirlpool* of dispute.

うすあかり 薄明かり (微光) (×a) dim [faint, scanty] light; (朝夕の) twilight. ▶たそがれ時の薄明か

うずき

りの中で in the *twilight*; (薄暗がりの中で) in the dim [faint] light of dusk.

うすあかるい 薄明るい dim; fairly dark. ●薄明るい部屋 a *dimly lit* room.

うすあじ 薄味 ▶我が家の料理は薄味だ We have only *lightly seasoned* dishes at home. ▶スープは薄味にしてください Would you make the soup on the *thin side*, please?

:**うすい** 薄い ❶【厚さが】thin (-nn-). (⇨厚い❶) ●薄い水[紙; 唇] *thin* ice [paper; lips]. ●生地の薄いドレス[カーテン] a *thin* dress [curtain]. ●パンにジャムを薄く塗る spread the jam *thin* [*thinly*] on the bread. ▶ハムは薄く切ってあった The ham was *thinly* sliced. (**!**「薄く切ったハム」は *thinly-sliced ham*、その一切れは *a thin slice of ham*) ▶ここは表土が薄い(=浅い) The soil is *shallow* here.

❷【色・髪などが】(色が淡い) light; (髪が) thin (-nn-). ●薄い青 light [*pale*] blue. ▶彼は髪の毛が薄い He has *thin* hair. ▶髪が薄くなってきた My hair *is thinning* [is getting *thin*]./I am losing my hair./I'm getting *thin* on top.

❸【濃度・密度などが】(牛乳・霧などが) thin (-nn-); (酒・茶などが) weak (↔strong). ●薄いスープ[牛乳] *thin* soup [milk]. ●薄い霧 a *thin* [a *light*] mist. ●コーヒーは薄くしてください I'd like my coffee *weak*. ▶コーヒーは薄いのが好きです I like *weak* coffee.

〘会話〙「このお吸物の味, 薄すぎるかしら」「おいしい. お吸物は薄い味の方が好きなの」"Is this soup too *bland* for you?" "(It) tastes good. I prefer soup *lightly* (↔*strongly*) seasoned." (**!** bland は「味がきいてなくてまずい」という含みを持つ)

❹【可能性】▶彼の成功の望みは薄い (ほとんどない) There is *very little* [There is *not much*] hope of his success. ▶彼の成功はまだ遠い His success is still *a long way off*. ▶彼と衝突するな. 勝ち目は薄い(=まず勝てない) Don't clash with him; you *can't possibly* win. (**!** possibly は can't を強める)

うすいた 薄板 a thin board; (鋼板) a thin sheet of steel.

うすうす 薄々 (定かではなく) vaguely /véigli/; (わずかに) slightly. ▶彼女は彼のことをうすうす聞いていた She has *vaguely* heard of him. ▶父親は息子の問題にうすうす気づいていた The father was *vaguely* [*dimly*] aware of his son's trouble.

うずうず ― うずうずする 動 (何かしてくてたまらない) be itching 《to do; for》; have an itch 《to do; for》; be anxious [impatient, 〘話〙 dying] 《to do; for》. ▶彼は海へ行きたくてうずうずしている He *is itching* to go down to the sea. (待てない) He *just can't wait to* go down to the sea. (**!** just は「まったく」の意) ▶うずうずしちゃう(=興奮を抑えられない)なあ I *can hardly contain* my *excitement*. ▶彼はけんかをしたくてうずうずしていた He was *spoiling* for a fight. (**!** けんかに関しての成句表現)

うすがみ 薄紙 a flimsy, thin paper; (薄葉紙(うすようし)) tissue paper.
● 薄紙をはぐよう ▶彼は薄紙をはぐように(=少しずつ)病気がよくなっている He is getting better *little by little*.

うすかわ 薄皮 (動植物の) a thin skin; (薄い膜) a film; (薄い層) a thin layer, a coating.
● 薄皮まんじゅう a thin-skinned bun stuffed with sweet bean paste.

うすぎ 薄着 ●薄着している be lightly dressed; wear light clothes.

うずき 疼き (鈍い痛み) an ache; (ずきずきした痛み) a throb.

うすぎたない 薄汚い ●薄汚い(=どことなく汚れた)シャツ a bit dirty [a *dirty-looking*] shirt. ●薄汚い(=くすんだ)壁紙 *dingy* wallpaper.

うすきみわるい 薄気味悪い weird /wíərd/; eerie /íəri/. (⇨薄気味[成句])

うすぎり 薄切り a (thin) slice (*of* bread). ▶しゃぶしゃぶ用にサーロインを極薄切りにしてください Please cut sirloin into paper-*thin slices* for *shabu-shabu*.

うずく 疼く (鈍く痛む) ache; (ずきずき痛む) throb (-bb-). (⇨痛む❶, ❷)

うすくち 薄口 ●薄口しょうゆ light-colored soy sauce.

うずくまる 蹲る (前かがみになる) crouch /kráutʃ/ (down); (しゃがむ) squat (down) (-tt-). ▶うずくまって犬はクマにとびかかろうと身構えてうずくまった The dog *crouched*, ready to spring at the bear.

うすぐもり 薄曇り slightly cloudy weather. ▶今日は薄曇りで少し寒い It's *slightly cloudy* and a little cold today.

うすぐらい 薄暗い (ぼんやり見える程度の) dim (!照明が弱くて薄暗い場合は dimly-lit がよい); (薄暗くて陰気な) gloomy; (陰が多くて薄暗い)《書》dusky. ●朝の薄暗いうちに出発する start *in* the morning *twilight*; start before it gets light. ●薄暗い森では本を読む Don't read in *dim* light. ▶薄暗いところで本を読むな Don't read in *dim* light.

うすげしょう 薄化粧 — 薄化粧する 動 put on a little makeup. ▶彼女は薄化粧している She [Her face] *was lightly* (↔heavily) *made up*. ▶富士山頂は初雪で薄化粧している The top of Mt. Fuji *is lightly covered with* the first snow of the year.

うすごおり 薄氷 thin ice. ▶池に薄氷が張っている The pond is covered with *thin ice* [is *thinly* coated with *ice*]. (⇨薄氷)

うすじ 薄地 thin cloth. ●薄地のジャケット a *thin* jacket.

うすじお 薄塩 ●薄塩の肉 *lightly salted* meat.

うずしお 渦潮 an eddying current.

うすずみ 薄墨 thin Chinese [《米》India, 《英》Indian] ink. ●薄墨色 dull gray, dark gray.

ウスターソース Worcester(shire) /wústər(ʃər)/ sauce.

うずたかい 堆い ▶うずたかく積まれたいすの山 a huge pile of chairs; chairs piled high. ▶流しには洗ってない食器がうずたかく積んであった The sink was piled high with unwashed dishes./There were piles [heaps] of unwashed dishes in the sink.

うすちゃ 薄茶 [薄くたてた抹茶]weak (powdered) tea; [薄茶色]light brown.

うすっぺら 薄っぺら — 薄っぺらな 形 (薄い) thin; (浅薄な) shallow, 《やや書》superficial. ▶私の英文法の知識なんてほんの薄っぺらなものです I've got only a *shallow* [a *superficial*] knowledge of English grammar.

うすで 薄手 — 薄手の 形 thin. ●薄手の生地 *thin* cloth. ●薄手のコート a *thin* [a *light*] coat. (!light は通例「薄地で軽い」の意)

うすのろ 薄のろ ▶ a fool; (お人よし) a simpleton; (間抜け) a half-wit.
— **薄のろの** 形 foolish; stupid; half-witted.

うすば 薄刃 a thin-bladed knife.

うすばかげろう 羽羽蜉蝣 [昆虫] an ant lion. (⇨蟻地獄)

うすび 薄日 soft beams of sunlight. ▶薄日が差した The sun came through the thin layer of clouds.

ウズベキスタン [国名]Uzbekistan /uzbékəstæn/; (公式名) the Republic of Uzbekistan. (首都 Tashkent) ●ウズベキスタン人 a Uzbek. ●ウズベク語 Uzbek. ●ウズベキスタン(人[語])の Uzbek.

うすべり 薄縁 a bordered rush mat.

うずまき 渦巻き [[水流の]] a whirlpool, a vortex (複 ~es, vortices) [らせん形] a spiral. (⇨らせん) ●渦巻き状星雲 [天文] a spiral nebula. ●渦巻き模様 a whirling [a spiral] pattern.

うずまく 渦巻く (水・空気などが) whirl (around);《やや書》eddy. (⇨渦)

*うずまる 埋まる be buried. (⇨埋(う)まる)

うすめ 薄目 图 ❶[少し開いた目] ●薄目を開ける open one's eyes slightly. ●薄目で見る look (*at him*) *with* one's *eyes slightly open* [*through* one's *slightly-opened eyes*]. (!前の open は形容詞)
❷[やや薄いこと] ▶朝の紅茶は薄目がいい I prefer my morning cup of tea *rather weak*.
— 薄目の 形 (色・味などが) not strong; light; pale; (厚みが) not thick; rather thin.

うすめる 薄める ●ウイスキーを水で薄める *water down* whiskey; *dilute* [*thin*] whiskey *with* water. ●水を加えてスープを薄める add water to *thin down* the soup; *thin down* the soup by adding water. ●薄めたスープ *weakened* [*dilute*(*d*)] soup.

*うずめる 埋める (⇨埋(う)める) ●母親のひざに顔を埋める *bury* one's face *in* one's mother's lap. ●スタンドを埋める *fill* [(ぎっしりと)] *pack into*] the stands.

うすもの 薄物 light cloth [fabric, material].

うすもや 薄もや a thin haze [mist].

うずもれる 埋もれる be buried. (⇨埋(う)もれる)

うすやき 薄焼き ●薄焼き卵 a thin fried egg.

うすよごれる 薄汚れる (薄汚い) ▶彼のコートは薄汚れている His coat is *slightly stained*.

うずら 鶉 [鳥]a quail;《集合的》quail.

うすらぐ 薄らぐ (光・記憶など) become* dim (-mm-) [faint]; (不安・苦痛など) ease, 《書》abate; (情など) cool (down); (熱意・やる気など) flag (-gg-); (記憶など) fade (away). ▶痛みが少し薄らいだ The pain *eased* a little.

うすらさむい 薄ら寒い (a bit) chilly; slightly cold.

うずらまめ 鶉豆 [植物] a pinto bean.

うすれる 薄れる (色・記憶など) fade (away). ●薄れゆく午後の光 the *thinning* afternoon light. ▶やがて一般の人の関心は薄れるだろう Public interest will *fade* [*wear off*] soon.

うすわらい 薄笑い 图 ▶「君もずいぶんおめでたいね」と彼は薄笑いを浮かべて言った "You're such a naive boy!" he said with a *smirk* on his face.
— **薄笑いをする** 動 give a faint smile; (人をばかにしたようにやや笑う) give a smirk.

うせつ 右折 图 a right turn. ●右折禁止 [標識]No *right turn*.
— **右折する** 動 turn (to the) right; make a right (turn). (!右折地点は「次の信号で」at the next light(s), 「並木通りを」on Namiki (Lane) などで表す)

うせる 失せる ❶[なくなる](⇨無くなる❶, 消える❶, 紛失する) ❷[行く, 去る] ▶とっとと失せろ Get out!/Get lost!

*うそ 嘘

WORD CHOICE うそ

lie 相手をだまそうとして人がつく悪意のうそ. 日本語より強い意味で, 相手への痛烈な非難を含意. ▶うそをつくな Don't tell a *lie*.

falsehood 真実に反する誤った内容・発言. 相手をだまそうとする悪意は前提としない. ●真偽判定 judgment of truth and *falsehood*.

頻度チャート

lie ██████████████████████
falsehood ██

20　40　60　80　100 (%)

── **嘘** 图 a lie;《書》(a) falsehood;《書》an untruth (❗lie の婉曲語としても用いられる);《話》an fib;（ささいな罪のないうそ）《婉曲的》a fiction.

① 【～うそ】 ●真っ赤なうそ a downright [an out-and-out, ×a red] *lie*. ●（相手を傷つけないための）罪[悪意]のないうそ a white *lie*. ●もっともらしい[見えすいた]うそ a plausible [a transparent, (明白な) an obvious] *lie*. ●広告のうそほんとの truth and *lies* of advertising. (❗語順に注意) ▶うそには三つある。いいうそと悪いうそ、それから数字のうそです There are three kinds of lies: white *lies*, black *lies* and *lies* by the number. (❗white lie は「便宜上の，罪のないうそ」の意で，単独でも用いられる。black lie は「悪意のあるうそ」の意で，white lie と併用されることはあるが，単独ではあまり用いられない)

② 【うそ～】 ●うそ発見器にかける have《him》take a *lie* detector. ●うそ泣きをする pretend to cry. ▶彼女は泣いてなんかいないよ。ただうそ泣きをしているだけなんだ She's not crying—she's just pretending.

③ 【うそを】 ●うそを見抜く see through a *lie*. ▶彼女はそのことで私にうそをついた She *lied* [told a *lie*, *told lies*] to me about it. (❗特定の1回のうそにもしばしば lies を用いる. ×speak [×say] a lie は不可) ●うそをつけ(=言うな) Don't be silly [talk nonsense]! (⇨⑤) ●人間はうそをつく動物である A human being is an animal that tells *lies*. ▶彼女を励ますためにちょっとしたうそをついちゃった To cheer her up, I told her a little *fib*.

●うそから出たまこと A lie can turn out (to be) true./(冗談でいったことが本当になることが多い)《ことわざ》Many a true word is spoken in jest.

●うそで固める ▶彼女の話はうそで固められていた(=完全なでっち上げだ) Her story was a *total fabrication* [*was totally fabricated*].

●うそ八百を並べる tell all sorts of [a pack of, a web of] lies.

●うそも方便《ことわざ》It is sometimes necessary to stretch the truth. (❗stretch the truth は「真実を曲げて大げさにいう」の意)/(真実を語るのも時による) All truth is not always to be told.

── **嘘の** 形 false, untrue. ●うそのような(=信じられない)話 an *incredible* story. ●うその(=偽りの)証言をする give *false* witness. ▶彼の言うことはうそだ What he says is *false* [*isn't true*, is a *lie*]. ▶うそでしょう（本気で言ってるんじゃないでしょうね）You don't mean [*that*, *do you?*]/(本当か) Are you sure of that?/(からかっているんでしょう) You're kidding (me)!/You must be joking./(信じられない) I can hardly believe it!/I doubt it./(そうは思わない) I don't think so. ●Don't tell a lie. (うそをつくな) とか You are telling a lie. (うそをついている), You're a liar. (お前はうそつきだ) などというと強い非難を表すので不適当)(⇨まさか)

── **嘘!** 圖 Really?/You're kidding./I can't believe it. /《婉曲的》I don't think so./I doubt it. (❗(1) You're lying. とか That's a lie. などは不適当. (2) Are you serious? とか I can't believe you. などともあまりいわない) ▶彼女は「うそ！」と叫んだ She cried, "Really? [You're kidding!]"

うそ『嘘』lies. (⬛参考 太宰治の小説)

古今ことばの系譜 『嘘』

戦争が終ったら、こんどはまた急に何々主義だの、何々主義だの、あさましく騒ぎまわって、演説なんかしているけれども、私は何一つ信用できない気持です。主義も、思想も、へったくれも要らない。男は嘘をつく事をやめて、女は欲を捨てたら、それでもう日本の新しい建設が出来ると思う Now that the war is over, many people are talking about loudly and brazenly about various isms. I don't believe in any of them. Such slogans and thoughts are not necessary. I think we can rebuild our country if men would stop telling lies and women would stop being greedy. (❗(1) isms は否定的なニュアンスでいう「主義」。(2)「信用できない」は「…が正しいと信じることはできない」という意味だから I don't believe in… とする。I have no trust in… も可)

うそ 图 〔鳥〕a bullfinch.

うぞうむぞう 有象無象 〔たくさん集まった無価値な人〕〔集合的〕a rabble.

うそくつうこう 右側通行 《掲示》Keep (to the) right.

うそつき 嘘つき a liar (❗(1) 強い非難を含意する語で, You're a *liar*. は相手をののしる言い方. (⇨うそ) (2) ×lier とつづらないよう注意);（軽いうそをつく人) a fibber. ▶ぼくがうそつきだとでもいうのか Are you calling me a *liar*?

うそぶく 嘯く 〔とぼける〕pretend not to know;〔偉そうなに言う〕talk big; (ほらを吹く) brag (-gg-).

うた 歌 a song;（歌うこと）singing;〔詩〕a poem;（短歌）a tanka (poem). (⇨うたう) ●英語の歌 an English *song*. ●歌の先生 a *singing* [a *voice*] teacher. ●歌の本 a songbook. ●歌を習う take *singing* [*voice*] lessons. ●歌を歌う sing (a *song*). (❗歌より歌うことに重点がある場合は通例 a song をつけない) ●歌を演奏する play a *song*. ▶それは私の好きな[ビートルズの]歌です That's my favorite [a Beatles] *song*. ▶私の趣味は歌を詠むの(=作る)ことだ My hobby is writing [composing] *poems* [*tanka*(s)].

うたい 謡 a *No(h)* chant [song].

うたいあげる 歌い上げる 〔声を張り上げて歌う〕sing out, sing loudly [in a loud voice];〔表現する〕express.

うたいて 歌い手 a singer. (⇨歌手)

うたいもんく 謳い文句 a catchphrase.

***うたう** 歌う sing*;（鼻歌を）hum (-mm-);〔詩などを暗唱する〕recite. (⇨歌) ●大きな声で歌う *sing* in a loud voice;《話》*sing* out. ●正しい旋律で[調子はずれに] *sing* in [out of] tune. ●ピアノに合わせて歌う *sing* to the piano. ●歌を歌って赤ん坊を寝かす *sing* a baby to sleep. (❗sleep は名詞) ●いっしょに歌う *sing* together [along];（合唱する) *sing* in chorus. ●料理をしながら鼻歌を歌う *hum* (a song) while cooking. ▶彼女は私にその歌を歌ってくれた She *sang* me the song./She *sang* the song *to* me. ▶彼女は歌を歌うのがうまい She is a good singer [good at *singing*]. (❗singer は「プロ歌手」だけでなく単に「歌う人」の意でも用いる)/She *sings* very well.

***うたう** 謳う 〔はっきりと示す〕express, state … clearly;〔大いにほめる〕praise … highly,《書》extol (-ll-);〔評判である〕be reputed. ▶「オリンピックは選手間の競争であり，国家間の競争ではない」と五輪憲章には謳っている The Olympic Charter *proclaims* [*that*] the Olympic games are competitions between athletes, not between countries [na-

うたかい 歌会 a *tanka* [a *poetry*] party [contest]. ●歌会始め an annual New Year's *Tanka* [*Poetry*] Party at the Imperial Palace.

うたがい 疑い ❶[疑念](真実性を疑うこと, 確信が持てないこと) (a) doubt; (疑問) (a) question. ●疑いのない事実 an unquestionable [(否定できない) an un-deniable] fact. ●疑いの念を抱く have *doubts* [be *doubtful*]《about》; doubt. (⇨疑う❶) ▶彼の説明を聞いて私の疑いはすべて晴れた His explanation has removed all my *doubts*. ▶君の成功は疑いない I have no *doubt about* your success./I have no *doubt*《that》you will succeed. ▶(成功を確信している) I am sure of your success [(that) you will succeed]. (⇨確か) ▶彼が当選することに疑いの余地はない There is no *doubt* [*question*] that he will be elected. (⇨図; 疑問) ▶父は心臓発作の疑いで入院した My father was taken to (the) hospital with a *suspected* heart attack.
会話「彼がそれを盗んだって確かなの？」「まったく疑いの余地なしさ」"Are you *certain* (that) he stole them?" "Quite *certain*."
❷[嫌疑] (a) suspicion《about, against, of》. (❗ doubt と異なり悪事などをしたのではないかという疑い) ▶彼に疑いをかける throw *suspicion* on him;(疑う)suspect him. ▶疑いの目でじっと私を見る gaze at me *suspiciously* [with *suspicion*]. ▶彼の行動は彼女に疑いの念を起こさせた His behavior aroused her *suspicion*(s) [aroused *suspicion*(s) in her mind]./His behavior made her *suspicious*. ▶彼に濃い疑いがかかっている There is a strong *suspicion against* him. ▶彼に窃盗の疑いがかかった *Suspicion* of theft fell on him./He fell under *suspicion* of theft. ▶彼はその証言をした疑いがある I *suspect* [*have a suspicion*] (*that*) he gave false evidence [testimony]. (⇨疑う❷) ▶彼は盗みの疑いをかけられている He *is suspected* [*is under suspicion*] of stealing. ▶彼は殺人の疑いで逮捕された He was arrested *on suspicion of* [(容疑で) *on a charge of, for*] murder.
── 疑いなく 副 undoubtedly, without (a) doubt; beyond question. ▶それは疑いなく最善の解決法だ It is *undoubtedly* [*without doubt*] the best solution./*Undoubtedly* it is the best solution. (❗ undoubtedly, without (a) doubt は no doubt よりも意味がずっと強い. 次の訳の no doubt は I think [agree] ぐらいの意味)/There is *no doubt* [*No doubt*] that it is the best solution.

うたがいぶかい 疑い深い[人・性質などが] suspicious;[懐疑的な] skeptical;[人を信用しない] distrustful. ▶彼は疑い深い男だ He is a *skeptical* [a *distrustful*] man. ▶(疑い深い性質だ) He has a *suspicious* nature. ▶彼は私を疑い深い目でちらりと見た He gave me a *suspicious* glance./He glanced at me *suspiciously* [with *suspicion*]. ▶彼は政治家に対し疑い深い He is *suspicious* of politicians./He has a *distrust* of politicians.

うたがう 疑う ❶[怪しいと思う] doubt /dáut/, be doubtful《about》; suspect, be suspicious《of》.
使い分け doubt 確信が持てないことや信頼していないことをいい, 「…ではないと思う」という否定的意味を表わのに用いる.
suspect 信ぴょう性や価値に疑問を感じていることをいい, 「…であると思う」という肯定的意味を表わす.
▶彼はその話が本当かどうかを疑っている He *doubts* [*sus-*

pects] the story. (❗いずれも通例進行形不可)/He *doubts* [He's *doubtful*, ̽He suspects] *if* [*whether, that*] the story is true. (❗(1) whether より if の方が口語的. (2) that を用いると「本当のはずがない」といった強い不信感を表す) ▶彼の成功を信じて疑わない I don't *doubt* [*have no doubt*] *that* he will succeed. (❗否定文・疑問文の場合は, doubt(ful)に続く接続詞は通例 that を用いる)/(成功を強く信じる) I do believe (that) he will succeed. (❗ do は believe を強調) ▶彼は私の能力を疑っている He *is doubtful* [(懐疑的な) *skeptical*] *about* my ability. ▶警察はその男を疑っている The police *are suspicious of* [*suspect*] the man. ▶それについては疑う余地がない There is no (room for) *doubt about* it. (⇨疑問) ▶彼は新しい者は何でも疑ってみる癖がある He is apt to adopt a *suspicious* attitude to anything new. ▶私は自分の目[耳]を疑った I *could not believe* my own eyes [ears]. ▶何も知らないものは何も疑うことができない Those who don't know anything [know nothing] can't question anything. (❗この文脈での「疑う」は「疑問を感じる[投げかける]」の意なので doubt は不適切)
❷[そうではないかと思う] suspect. ▶彼は息子がうそをついているのではないかと疑った He *suspected* his son *of telling* a lie [(*that*) his son told a lie]. (❗後の方が口語的) ▶私は彼は胃がんなのではないかと内心疑っていた I *had* a sneaking *suspicion that* he might have stomach cancer. (❗ sneaking は「ひそかな」の意)
❸[信用しない] distrust,《ややまれ》mistrust (❗前の方が不信の程度が強い);(懐疑的になる)《やや書》be skeptical《about, of》. ▶彼は夫の言葉を疑っていた She *distrusted* [*had a distrust of, was distrustful of*] her husband's words./She *didn't believe* her husband('s words). (❗後の方が口語的)

うたかた ❶[泡] foam. (⇨泡(あわ))
❷[はかないこと] ●うたかたの恋 a short-lived love. ●うたかたの夢と消える vanish like a dream.

*****うたがわしい** 疑わしい[確信が持てない]doubtful; [半信半疑の] dúbious;[疑問がある] questionable;[怪しい] suspícious;[疑い深い] skeptical.
使い分け **doubtful** 事の信ぴょう性・正しさなどに確信が持てない気持ちを表す.
dubious doubtful より意味が弱く, 単に怪しく思ったり, ためらったりすることを表す.
suspicious 行動・行為が疑いを招いたり, 人が何かに疑念を抱いていること.
questionable 物事の真実性・価値などに疑いを抱く余地があることを表す.
skeptical 人が懐疑的で疑い深い性質であることを表す. (⇨疑う)
●疑わしい陳述 a *questionable* statement. ●疑わしい挙動 (×a) *suspicious* behavior. ▶その報道の信ぴょう性は疑わしい I'm *doubtful* [I have (my) *doubts*] *about* the truth of the report. ▶…とはいえない/It's *doubtful* [*questionable*] *whether* the report is true. ▶疑う❶ ▶彼に助ける能力があるかどうか疑わしい I'm *dubious* [*skeptical*] *about* his ability to help.

うたぐち 歌口 the mouthpiece《of a *shakuhachi*》.
うたぐりぶかい 疑り深い suspícious. (⇨疑い深い)
うたぐる 疑る doubt. (⇨疑う)
うたげ 宴 a party. (⇨宴会)
うたごえ 歌声 a singing voice. ●歌声が悪い[よい] have a poor [a good, a fine] *singing voice*. ▶若者の歌声が森に響いた Young people's *singing*

うたごえよおこれ『歌声よおこれ』 Let There Be Singing! (参考 宮本百合子の小説)

うたごころ 歌心 〖和歌の意味〗 the meaning of a *waka* [a poem]; 〖和歌の素養〗《have》 a taste for poetry.

うたたね うたた寝 图 (知らぬうちにうとうとと眠ること) a doze; (昼寝) a nap (! 時に *doze* と同じ意で用いる). (⇨居眠り)

── うたた寝をする 動 doze; (こっくりこっくり) nod (off), drop (off) (! 眠りに落ちるの意で夜の本式の睡眠にも用いる); nap; fall into a doze.

うだつ ●うだつが上がらない ▶彼はうだつが上がらない男だ (出世しない) He is a man who *never gets ahead*./(まったく成功したことがない) He *has not made anything* at all *of himself*.

うたひめ 歌姫 a female singer, a songstress; a diva.

うたよみにあたうるしょ『歌よみに与うる書』 Letters to the Tanka Poets. (参考 正岡子規の歌論書)

うだる(ゆだる) be boiled. ●うだるような暑さ the sweltering heat. ▶今日はうだるように暑かった It was *sweltering* [《話》*boiling*] hot today.

うたれる 打たれる ❶〖感動する〗 be touched, be moved; (感銘を受ける) be impressed 《with》《+動詞》; 〖突然, 恐怖・美しさなどに〗 be struck. ▶その光景を見て畏怖(いふ)の念に打たれる *be struck with* [*by*] awe at the sight. ❷〖たたかれる〗▶頭を打たれる *be struck on the head*.

ːうち 内 ❶〖内部〗 the inside. ●内(=屋内)に閉じこもる stay *indóors* [*insíde*, *in*, 《米・英古》 *within* (the house)]. ●内ポケット (⇨内ポケット)
❷〖時間内〗① 〖…うちに〗 (経過した時点で) in … (! 現在・過去から見た未来についていう); (以内に) within …; (前に) *before* …; (間に) *during* …, while 《+節》. ▶私たちの家は2, 3か月のうちに完成するでしょう Our house will be completed *in* [*within*] a few months. ▶1時間もたないうちに帰って来ます I'll be back *within* [*in less than*, 《話》*inside* (*of*)] an hour./It won't be an hour *before* I come [×*will come*] back. ▶報告書はその日のうちに送られた The report was sent *within* the same day (その日が終わる前に) *before* the day's out). ▶暗くならない[忘れない]うちに洗濯物を取り込んでおきなさい Take in the wash(ing) *before* (it gets) dark [you forget it]. ▶若いうちにいろいろ経験をしておきなさい Try to do various things *while* (you are) *young* (年を取りすぎないうちに) *before* you're too old]. (! while 節の主語が主節の主語と同じ場合には, while 節の「主語+be 動詞」は省略可)

> **翻訳のこころ** 三日のうちに, わたしは村で結婚式を挙げさせ, 必ず, ここへ帰ってきます(太宰治『走れメロス』) In the village, I'll get my sister married and surely be back in three days. ▶ in three days (三日のうちに)は「(すぐに)帰ってくる」を強調しているので, be back の後におく. 日本語との語順の違いに注意

②〖…うちは〗 (…までずっと) until …; (…のかぎり) as long as 《+節》. ▶この仕事が済まないうちは遊んでいるひまはありません I have no time to enjoy myself *until* this job is finished.

❸〖範囲内〗 of …, in … (! of は複数概念の, in は単数概念の語句の前で用いる); (2 者の間に) between …; (3 者以上の間に) among …. ▶我々のうち 2 人が彼を待っているようにと言われた Two of us were told to wait for him. (! *the* two of us は「我々 2 人」の意) ▶彼がみんなのうちでいちばん年上だ He is the oldest *of* all. ▶2 人のうちどちらが背が高いですか Which is the taller *of the two*? (! 2 者の間で比較するときは比較級でも *the* taller と the をつける) ▶あなたのクラスのうちで走るのはだれがいちばん速いですか Who is the fastest runner [can run (the) fastest] *in* your class?/Who is the fastest runner *among* your classmates? (! *Which* is … *of* your classmates? のようにもいえる) ▶これは私が今まで読んだうちで最もおもしろい本です This is the most interesting book (that) I have ever read. ▶5 冊の本のうちから 1 冊だけ選びなさい Choose only one *among* [*from*, *out of*, *from among*] the five books. ▶私は彼らを友達のうちに入れていません I don't count them among my friends.

❹〖内心〗 ●内なる声に耳を傾ける (⇨内なる) ▶彼女は胸の内を明かしてくれなかった She never told me *what was on her mind*. (悩み・心配事を暗示) /She never expressed her *feelings* to me. ▶彼は激しい情熱を内に秘めていた He had a strong passion *inside him*.

❺〖自分の(団体)〗●うちの社長 the president of *our company*;《話》*our boss*. ▶うちではその商品を扱っていません We don't [*Our store* doesn't] deal in that article. ▶うちの課には女性がいない There are no women *in our section*.

ːうち 家 ❶〖自分の家〗(a) home; a house (複 houses /-ziz, 《米》 -siz/). (⇨家(い)) ▶長女は結婚したが, 下の 2 人はまだ家にいる My oldest daughter is married, but the two younger ones are still *at home* [*haven't left home yet*]. ▶いつうちに泊まりに来るの When are you coming to stay with us [at our *home*]?

❷〖自分の家族〗●うちの者(家族) *my family* (! 通例自分自身は含まない (⇨家族)); (妻) *my wife*; (私たち) we. ▶うちの宗教 *my family's* religion. ●うちの子 *our child(ren)*. ●うちの仕事 (家庭生活上の) household affairs; (掃除・料理などの) housework. ▶うちはみな早起きです All *my family* are early risers. ▶うちは 4 人家族です We are a family of four./There are four in *my family*. ▶彼のうちは(親は金持ちだったので, 彼にたっぷり仕送りをしてもらっていた His *parents* were rich and sent him a handsome allowance.

うちあい 撃ち合い (銃撃戦) a gunfight. (⇨銃撃)

うちあげ 打ち上げ ❶〖空高く上げること〗(ロケットの) a launch; (花火の) a 《fireworks》 display. ●人工衛星の打ち上げ the *launch* [*launching*] of a satellite.

❷〖終了〗(興行の) the close; (仕事の) the successful completion of a project. ●「キャッツ」の打ち上げ the *close* [(最終日の公演) the *final performance*] of 'The Cats'. ▶打ち上げはパァーッとやろうぜ Let's whoop it up together at the *celebration party*. (! whoop it up は口語で「(飲めや歌えの大騒ぎをして)とことん楽しむ」の意)
●打ち上げ台 (ロケットなどの) a láunch(ing) pàd.
●打ち上げ花火 a rocket firework; a skyrocket.

うちあけばなし 打ち明け話 a confidéntial talk; a cónfidence; 〖率直な話〗a frank talk. ●打ち明け話をする talk confidentially [frankly] 《*to*》; be frank 《*with*》; (互いに) exchange *confidences* 《*with*》.

うちあける 打ち明ける 〖信用して話す〗confide; 〖語る〗tell*; 〖白状する〗confess. ▶私は彼に秘密を打ち明けた I *confided* [*told*, 《形式》 *revealed*] the secret to him. ▶彼は彼に心の中を打ち明けた I *confided in* him. ▶私は彼に高価な花びんを壊したことを

うちあげる 打ち上げる ❶ [空に] (ロケットなどを) send* ... up, launch ▶ [前の方が口語的に] (花火を) shoot* ... off, set* ... off; (ボールを) hit*. ●人工衛星を打ち上げる *launch* an artificial satellite /sǽtəlàit/. ▶花火を打ち上げる *shoot off* [*set off*, *display*] fireworks. (**!** display では「花火大会 (a fireworks display) をする」の意) ●内野フライを打ち上げる *hit* an infield fly.

❷ [波が岸に運ぶ] wash ... up. ▶彼女の死体は 2 日後に浜に打ち上げられた Her body *was washed up* [*was washed ashore*] two days later.

❸ [興行などを] (終える) finish. ●長期興行を打ち上げる *finish* a long run.

うちあわせ 打ち合わせ (取り決め) an arrangement; (会議) a meeting. ●打ち合わせどおりに as *arranged*; according to the *arrangements*. ▶彼たちは旅行の打ち合わせをわいわいやっていた They were busy *arranging* to go on a trip.
[会話] 「確か打ち合わせは 2 時でしたね」「ええ, そうです」 "The *meeting*'s for two o'clock, right?" "Yes."

__うちあわせる 打ち合わせる__ arrange, make arrangements (*with* him *about* [*for*] a trip). ▶今度いつ会うのか打ち合わせておこう Let's *arrange* a time to meet. ▶彼と詳細を打ち合わせた I *have arranged* the details with him.

うちいり 討ち入り 图 a raid.
—— **討ち入りする** 動 make [launch] a raid 《*on*》, raid.

うちいわい 内祝い (an) *uchiiwai*; (説明的に) [祝いの集い] 《hold》 a family celebration; [祝いの品] a present given to one's close relatives or friends on the occasion of the happy event in the family.

うちうち 内々 —— **内々の** 形 (私的な) private; (個人的な) personal. ▶その問題は内々で(=自分たちの間で)解決しよう Let's settle the question *among ourselves*. ▶結婚式は内々でやりましょう(=近親者だけを招待することにする) We will invite (only) close members of our families to our wedding.

うちうみ 内海 an inland sea.

うちおとす 撃ち落とす, 打ち落とす [銃などで] shoot* ... (down); [狩猟で鳥などを] shoot《a bird》; [ハエなどを] swat (-tt-) ... off [down]; [枝・首などを] cut* ... off. ▶「首を打ち落とす」 は behead ともいう ●敵機を撃ち落とす *shoot down* an enemy plane.

うちかぎ 内鍵 a key locked from inside the house. ▶裏口は内鍵になっている The backdoor locks only from (the) inside.

うちかけ 打ち掛け a long outer garment (worn by brides).

うちかつ 打ち勝つ (克服する) overcome*; (破る) beat*, defeat; [野球] outslug (-gg-). ▶あらゆる困難に打ち勝った She *has overcome* [*got over*] all (the) difficulties. ▶タイガースは相手チームに打ち勝った The Tigers *outslugged* the opponent.

うちがま 内釜 a built-in bath boiler; an inside-the-bathroom boiler.

うちがわ 内側 the inside. ▶通りの内側を歩く walk on *the inside* of a street. ▶箱の内側は赤色に, 外側は白色に塗ってある The *inside* of the box is painted red, the outside white. ▶コートの内側は毛皮になっている Her coat is fur *on the inside* [has a fur lining]./The *inside* of her coat is lined with fur. ▶トラックの内側のコースを走りなさい Run in the *inside* lane on the track [《米》 inside track]. ▶ドアは普通内側に開くようになってます Doors are usually fixed to open *inward(s)* [*to the inside*]. [**語法**] 米英ではこの開き方が普通 ▶忘れないように ドアには内側から鍵(ぎ)をかけておきなさい Don't forget to lock the door from (the) inside [on the inside].

うちき 打ち気 ▶打ち気にはやる be impatient [very eager] to hit a ball.

うちき 内気 图 shyness; bashfulness; timidity.
—— **内気な** 形 (引っ込み思案の) shy; (はにかみ屋で態度がぎこちない) bashful; (おどおどした) timid. ▶彼女は大変内気な子 She is a very *shy* [*bashful*, *timid*] girl. ▶彼は内気すぎて女の子にデートも申し込めない He is too *shy* [*bashful*] to ask a girl for a date.

うちきず 打ち傷 a bruise /brúːz/. ●腕に打ち傷をつくる get a *bruise* on one's arm. (⇨打ち身)

うちきり 打ち切り ▶その連載まんがは [ミュージカルの公演] は人気がなかったので打ち切りになった That cartoon series [The running of that musical] was cut short because of its unpopularity [because it didn't catch on; because it did poorly].

__うちきる 打ち切る__ (交渉などを) break ... off; (援助などを) stop (-pp-), cut* ... off; (やめる) drop (-pp-). ▶彼の捜索は打ち切られた The search for him *has been dropped* [(断念された) *been given up*]. ▶私の奨学金は打ち切られた My scholarship *got canceled*.

うちきん 内金 [内金払い] part payment; [頭金] a down payment; [手付金] a deposit. ●車に 200 ドルの内金を払う make a *down payment* of 200 dollars *on* the car.

うちくだく 打ち砕く ❶ [砕く] smash; (非常に細かく砕く) shatter.
❷ [だめにする] (希望などを) crush, 《話》 shatter; (計画などを) frustrate. ▶その事故でピアニストになる望みは打ち砕かれた The accident *crushed* [*shattered*] my hopes of becoming a pianist.

うちくび 打ち首 (a) decapitation. ●打ち首にする behead, decapitate.

うちけし 打ち消し 图 【文法】 negation; (否定語) a negative. (⇨否定) —— **打ち消しの** 形 negative.

*__うちけす 打ち消す__ deny. (⇨否定する)

うちゲバ 内ゲバ infighting, a violent intra-group [internal] strife.

うちげんかん 内玄関 the back [side] door.

うちこむ 打ち込む ❶ [くぎなどを] drive* ... (*into*); (金づちで) hammer ... 《*into*》. ●金づちで板にくぎを打ち込む *drive* a nail *into* a plank with a hammer; *hammer* a nail *into* a plank.

❷ [ボールなどを] hit*; (強く) smash; (激しく) slam (-mm-). ●相手コート [ベースラインぎりぎり] にボールを打ち込む *smash* a ball *into* the opponent's court [just *inside* the baseline]. ▶左翼外野席にホームランを打ち込む *hit* [*slam*] a home run *into* the left field bleachers. ▶(投手が)打ち込まれる get hit. ▶新人投手を打ち込む get to a rookie pitcher.

❸ [データを] input*. ●コンピュータにデータを打ち込む *input* [*feed*] data *into* a computer.

❹ [一生懸命になる] ●研究に打ち込む *apply oneself* [one's *mind*] *to* the study [research]; *put* one's *heart and soul into* the study; (身をささげる) *devote oneself to* the study.

うちころす 打ち殺す, 撃ち殺す (打ち殺す) beat* [(こん棒で) club (-bb-)]《him》 to death; (射殺す) shoot* 《him》 dead [to death]. ▶その象は撃ち殺された The elephant *was shot dead* [*was shot*

うちしおれる 打ち萎れる (⇨しおれる)
うちじに 討死に ― 討死にする 動 die [be killed] in battle. ▶この仕事と討死にするなどまっぴらだ I'll never die for this job.
うちじゅう 家中 ❶ [家族全員] all the family, the whole [entire] family; all the members of the family. (⇨家族) ❷ [家の中全体] ・家中を探す look over the house [everywhere in the house].
うちすえる 打ち据える [しっかり据える] put [place, set]《a thing》firmly《in a place》(⇨据える ❶; [強くたたく] strike [hit, knock, beat]《him》hard (⇨叩く ❶).
うちぜい 内税 tax included. ▶価格はすべて内税で表示されています All prices are displayed with *tax included*.
うちそと 内外 (⇨内外(ないがい))
うちだす 打ち出す [模様などを] emboss; [計画・方針などを] work [strike*, hammer] out《a positive plan》; [データを] output*; [紙に] print out《on》.
うちたてる 打ち立てる ・新国家を打ち立てる *establish* a new nation. ・新記録を打ち立てる *establish* [*set*] a new record.
うちつける 打ち付ける ❶ [くぎで固定させる] ・板をドアに打ち付ける *nail* a board *on* [*to*] a door; *board up* a door.
❷ [強くぶつける] ・壁に頭を打ち付ける *hit*, [(ごつんと) *knock*,(どんと) *bump*] one's head *against* [*on*] a wall. ▶雨が窓に打ち付けている The rain *is beating against* [*on*] the windows.
うちつづく 打ち続く [長く続く] (⇨続く ❶)
うちづら 内面 ・内面がよい be nice [agreeable] at home. ・内面が悪い be disagreeable [surly] at home.
うちでし 内弟子 a pupil boarding with《his》master; (徒弟) an apprentice.
うちでのこづち 打ち出の小槌 a magic mallet; [どんな願いでもかなえてくれるもの] the Aladdin's lamp.
うちとける 打ち解ける [親しい] become friendly [frank, open]《with》; [気持ちが和らぐ] feel* at ease [at home]《with》; [気楽に話す] open up《to》; [自分の殻から出る] come out of oneself. ▶彼女は同僚となかなか打ち解けない She hardly becomes *friendly* [*frank*] *with* her fellow workers./(遠慮がちである) She is somehow *reserved* among her fellow workers. ▶どうして打ち解けて話してくれないのか Why don't you *open up to* me? ▶彼女は私にかなり打ち解けた様子だった She seemed rather *comfortable* [*free and easy*] *with* me. ▶彼女はようきみなことを言ったのでパーティーは打ち解けた雰囲気になった (話) At the party he *broke the ice* saying funny things.
うちどころ 打ち所 ・打ち所が悪くて(=急所を打たれて)死ぬ die from being hit in a vital spot [part].
うちどめ 打ち止め the close; the finish; the end. ▶この一番にて本日の打ち止め(相撲で) This is the *last* bout for today [the day]. ▶この論争は打ち止めにしよう Let's *close* our debate.
うちとる 打ち取る ・三振に打ち取る [野球] strike《him》out; fan《him》.
うちとる 討ち取る [武器を使って殺す] kill《with a weapon》; [殺す] ・3人の打者を討ち取る retire three batters; set three batters down. ・四番打者を三塁ゴロに打ち取る get the cleanup on a grounder to third.
うちなる 内なる ・内なる闘志 *hidden* fighting spirit. ・内なる声に耳を傾ける listen to one's *inner* voice [(静かな細い)(良心の)声]《やや書》the still small

うちみ 打ち身
voice (of conscience)].
うちにわ 内庭 [中庭] a court, a courtyard; (校舎で囲まれた方形の) a quadrangle, 《話》a quad.
うちぬく 打ち抜く, 打ち貫く ❶ [穴を開ける] punch. ・金属板に穴を打ち抜く *punch* a hole in a sheet of metal. ❷ [やり通す] ・ストライキを打ち抜く carry a strike *out*.
うちぬかれる 打ち抜かれる shoot* through.... ▶彼は心臓を撃ち抜かれていた He was found [I found him] *shot through* the heart.
うちのめす 打ちのめす 《人をなぐり倒す》knock [strike*]... down; [徹底的にやっつける] beat*... up; [精神的にまいらせる] depress; [感情で圧倒する] overwhelm, overcome*. ・その男を一撃で打ちのめす *knock* [*strike*] the man *down* with one blow. ▶再度の失敗で彼はすっかり打ちのめされた He was deeply *depressed* [*discouraged, disheartened*] by the repeated failure.
うちのり 内法 the inside measurement(s).
うちばらい 内払い (⇨払う)
うちはらう 打ち払う [ほこりなどを] (⇨払う ❷, 払い落とす); [敵などを] drive... back [away], push... back [away], repel [追撃退する, 追い払う]
うちひしがれる 打ちひしがれる be overcome; be overwhelmed. ▶葬式で未亡人は悲しみに打ちひしがれていた The widow *was overcome by* grief at the funeral.
うちびらき 内開き ・内開きのドア a door which *opens inward*.
うちぶろ 内風呂 a bath at home, a bath in a house [an inn, a hotel].
うちべんけい 内弁慶 ・内弁慶である(=家ではいばっているが外では人の言いなりである) be bossy at home but submissive elsewhere.
うちポケット 内ポケット ・上着の内ポケット an *inside* [*inner*] pocket of a jacket; (胸部の) an *inner breast pocket* of a jacket.
うちぼり 内堀 an inner moat.
うちほろぼす 打ち滅ぼす (⇨滅ぼす)
うちまかす 打ち負かす [「負かす」の強調] defeat. (⇨負かす)
うちまく 内幕 inside information [knowledge, facts]. ・内幕に通じている have *inside knowledge* 《of》; know the *inside story* 《of》; be familiar with the *inside of*. ・内幕を(=舞台裏を)のぞく see [peep] *behind the scenes*. ・内幕(=秘密)を暴露する expose a *secret*.
うちまくる 打ちまくる (野球で) get a lot of hits; (ボクシングで) punch《one's opponent》repeatedly; (太鼓を) beat a drum away, drum... away.
うちまける 打ち負ける (野球・ボクシングで) lose a slugfest.
うちまご 内孫 a child of one's heir; a child of one's son.
うちまた 内股 (うちもも) the inside of the thigh /θái/. ・内股で歩く walk *pigeon-toed* [*with* one's *feet pointing inward*]. ▶彼女の内股だ She is rather *pigeon-toed*.
うちまたごうやく 内股膏薬 [日和見主義] fence-sitting, opportunism; [日和見主義者] a fence-sitter, an opportunist. ・内股膏薬をやる(=日和見する) sit [stand, be] on the fence; 《やや古》run [hold] with the hares and hunt with the hounds.
うちまわり 内回り [環状線の] the inside track (↔ the outer track).
うちみ 打ち身 a bruise /brúː/. ▶彼女は転んでひじに打ち身をつくった She fell and *bruised* [*got a bruise*

うちみず 打ち水 ── 打ち水(を)する 動 ・庭に打ち水をする water the garden; sprinkle the garden with water.

うちやぶる 打ち破る 〖たたきこわす〗break*... down; 〖粉々に割る〗smash, shatter (！後の方が強意的); 〖打ち負かす〗beat*, defeat (！beat より堅い語). ・壁を打ち破る break down a wall. ・窓を打ち破る smash [shatter] a window. ・選挙で対立候補を打ち破る beat [defeat] one's opponent in the election. ・敵の防御を打ち破る break through the enemy's defenses.

うちゆ 内湯 a bathhouse in the hotel [inn].

:うちゅう 宇宙 the universe; 〖宇宙空間〗space, outer space; the cosmos /kázməs/.

> 使い分け universe 地球・太陽・星など, 存在するものすべてをさす.
> space 地球の大気圏外の無限の空間としての宇宙で, 厳密には outer space という.
> cosmos 「chaos (混沌)」に対して秩序整然たる体系としての宇宙. 詩的で大げさな語.

・宇宙にロケットを打ち上げる launch a rocket into space. ・彼らは月まで宇宙(空間)を旅行した They traveled through space to the moon. ・ソ連が最初に人間を宇宙に送った The Soviet Union sent a man into space first.
── 宇宙の 形 cosmic; space. (！universal は主に「普遍的な」の意で用いられる) ・我々の世界は宇宙の小さな一部分にすぎない Our world is only a small part of the universe.
・宇宙衛星 a space satellite. ・宇宙開発 space development. ・宇宙科学 space science. ・宇宙科学者 a space scientist. ・宇宙工学 space engineering [technology]. ・宇宙時代 the space age. (！しばしば S- A-) ・宇宙食 space foods. ・宇宙人 (地球人に対しての) a celestial alien 〔an alien だけでも可能だが地球上の「外国人」の意にもなりあいまいなことがある〕; (空想科学の中の) a space creature, a spaceman, an extraterrestrial (略 ET). ・宇宙塵 cosmic dust. ・宇宙ステーション a space station. (！特に有人の) ・宇宙船 a spaceship, a spacecraft (！人工衛星なども含めた総称的な語). ・宇宙線 cosmic rays. ・宇宙探査機 a space probe. ・宇宙通信工学 space communication engineering. ・宇宙飛行 (a) space flight. ・「有人[無人]宇宙飛行」a manned [an unmanned] space flight〕 ・宇宙飛行士 (アメリカの) an astronaut, (ロシアの) a cosmonaut /kázmənò:t/, 《話》 a spaceman, a spacewoman. ・宇宙服 a spacesuit. ・宇宙兵器 a space weapon. ・宇宙遊泳 a spacewalk. ・宇宙遊泳をする walk [take a walk] in space. ・宇宙旅行 space travel; (個々の旅行) a space journey [trip]. ・宇宙連絡船 a space shuttle. ・宇宙ロケット a space rocket.

うちゅう 雨中 in the rain. (⇨雨④)

うちゅうかん 右中間 〖野球〗right center (field); alley (！「左中間」もさす). ・右中間へ二塁打を打つ hit a double to right center.

うちょうてん 有頂天 (an) ecstasy. ・有頂天になる go into ecstasies 《over》. ・有頂天にさせる throw 《him》 into ecstasies. ・有頂天になっている be in ecstasy; be beside oneself with joy;《話》be on cloud nine. ・思い焦がれている男の子からデートに誘われて彼女は有頂天になっている She is ecstatically happy [is on cloud nine] because the boy she secretly loves asked her out.

うちよせる 打ち寄せる 〖波が激しく〗beat*, dash 《against》; 〖さざ波が〗(ひたひたと) lap (-pp-) 《against [on]...》, (洗うように) wash 《against...》. ・波が断崖(がけ)に打ち寄せた The waves beat against [washed against] the cliff. ・大きな波が浜に打ち寄せていた Huge waves were rolling up on the beach [breaking against the shore].

うちわ 内輪 〖家族内の人たち〗the [one's] family circle.
── 内輪の 形 ❶〖家族内の〗family; (私的な, 内密の) private. ・内輪の結婚式 a family [a private] wedding; a wedding within one's family circle. ・内輪の事柄 a family matter; private affairs. ・これは内輪の話だよ(＝秘密にしておこう) Let's just keep this private [between ourselves,]./This is just among ourselves.
❷〖控えめな〗moderate. ・内輪に見積もる make a moderate estimate 《of》. ・建築費は内輪に見積もって 5,000 万円になるだろう A moderate [A conservative] estimate for the building expenses would amount to fifty million yen.
・内輪もめ (親子・兄弟などの) a family quarrel [squabble]; (会社などの) an internal trouble. ・もし内輪もめしたらうまく行かないよ If we quarrel among ourselves, we won't get anywhere. (！not get anywhere は「いい結果が得られない」の意)

うちわ 団扇 a (Japanese) fan. ・うちわを使う 〔であおぐ〕use a fan; fan oneself.

うちわく 内枠 ❶〖内側の〗an inner frame; (競馬で) an inside racetrack 〔《英》racecourse〕. ❷〖範囲内〗・予算の内枠で within one's budget.

うちわけ 内訳 (明細の) the details.
・旅行費用の内訳 a breakdown of traveling expenses.

うちわたし 内渡し ⇨内金(うちきん)

:うつ 打つ, 討つ ❶〖打撃を与える〗hit*; strike*; knock; beat*; punch; slap (-pp-), smack; pat (-tt-), tap (-pp-); pound; bang; clap (-pp-).

> 使い分け strike 「打つ」の意を表す最も意味の広い語だが, 堅い語で今はやや廃れ. 日常は以下の語で代用されるのが普通.
> hit ねらいを定め, 力を込めて一撃を加えること.
> knock こぶしや固い物で人や物を打つこと. 数度にわたって連打する場合が多い.
> beat 続けさまに打つこと.
> punch こぶしで強打すること.
> slap, smack 平手でぴしゃりと打つこと. smack は主に子供に対して用いる.
> pat 手のひらなどでやさしくぽんとたたくこと.
> tap 指先などで軽くたたくこと.
> pound どんどんと連打すること.
> bang どん(どん)と強打すること.
> clap 拍手するように手を打つこと.

・金づちでくぎを打つ hit [strike] a nail with a hammer; use a hammer to hit [strike] a nail; hammer in [down] a nail. ・壁にくぎを打つ(＝打ち込む) knock [drive, hammer] a nail into the wall. ・太鼓を打つ beat a drum. ・私は背中を棒でひどく打たれた I was hit [was struck] hard on the back with a stick./I had my back hit [struck] hard with a stick. (！後の文は被害を経験として述べる言い方で hit [struck] に強勢を置く (⇨-れる ❶)) ▶打ったボールは塀を越えて飛んでいった I hit [knocked] the ball over the fence. (！hit はねらい打ち, knock は力を入れて打ち飛ばす感じ. hit at the ball は球を目がけて打つことで, 球に当たったかどうかは不明 (⇨殴る)) ・転んで壁に頭を打った I fell and knocked [hit, struck, (ごつんと) bumped] my head on [against] the wall. (!) この knock, hit, strike は「偶然にぶつける」の意) ▶彼は箱をこなごなに打ちこわした They knocked the box to pieces. ▶彼女は彼の顔をぴしゃりと打った She slapped him across the face./She slapped his face. (⇨叩(たた)く ❶)

❷ [野球で] (ボールを[打席で]打つ) bat (-tt-), hit*; [塁打で] (打球を打つ) hit. (!) テニスなどでは smash (強烈に打ち下ろすを用いる). ●高めのボールを打つ bat a high ball. ●ゴロを打つ hit a grounder. ●2割8分を打つ hit [bat] (at) .280. .280 は two eighty と読む) ●5番を打つ bat fifth. ▶だれの打つ番当い Who's at bat now? ▶彼は二塁打[三塁打; ホームラン]を打った He hit a double [a triple; a home run]. ▶彼は今日の試合で3安打を打った He got [had, made] three hits in today's game.

❸ [時計が時を打つ] strike*. ▶時計はちょうど2時を打った The clock has just struck two. (!) × ... struck two o'clock とは通例いわない)/ Two o'clock has just struck.

❹ [心を打つ] (感動させる) move, (感傷的に) touch; (感銘を与える) impress. (⇨感動する) ▶彼女の話に私は心を打たれた I was moved [touched] by her story./Her story moved [touched] me [my heart]./(胸にじんときた)《話》Her story really got me. (!) 文脈によっては「かんにさわった、むっとした」という逆の意味にもなる)

❺ [討つ] (仇(かたき)を討つ) take* [get*] (one's) revenge (on him for it) (⇨復讐(ふくしゅう)); (打ち負かす) defeat, beat*. ●敵を討つ defeat the enemy. ▶彼は亡き父のかたきである彼らを討った He took [got] (his) revenge on [revenged himself on] them for his father's death. (!) 後の方は堅い言い方)/《書》He avenged his father's death.

●打てば響く ▶打てば響くような答えがその学生から返ってきた I got a quick response from the student./The student answered promptly./The student gave me a snap reaction.

:うつ 撃つ shoot*; (発砲する) fire. ●ピストルを撃つ shoot [fire] a pistol (at). ●10発撃つ fire ten shots (at). ▶鳥を撃つ shoot at a bird (!) 必ずしも命中を意味しない. 「撃ってけがをさせる [殺す]」は shoot a bird); fire at (×fire) a bird. (⇨撃ち落とす, 撃ち殺す) ▶我々は武装していない Don't shoot—we're not armed. ▶彼は自宅で撃たれて死んだ He was shot dead in his home. ▶彼は足を3発撃たれた He was shot three times in the leg. (!) in は「の内部に」の意) ●撃て! (号令) Shoot!/Fire! ●撃てるものなら撃ってみろ(=引き金を引いてみろ) I dare you to pull the trigger.

うつ 鬱 (⇨鬱病) ●うつ状態にある be in a depressive state.

うつ [恐怖・嫌悪・軽蔑などの声] ugh /úːx, ʌx, ʌɡ/.

うつうつ 鬱々 ●自分の将来のことを考えるとうつうつとした(=意気消沈した)気持ちになる I feel depressed [gloomy] when I think about my future.

うっかり 副 (不注意に) carelessly; (故意にではなく) by accident; (軽率に) thoughtlessly; (ぼんやりして) absent-mindedly; (責任ある立場の人が) negligently. ●うっかり猫のしっぽを踏む accidentally step on the cat's tail; step on the cat's tail by accident. ▶私はうっかり違う電車に乗ってしまった I carelessly took the wrong train./It was careless of me [I was careless] to take the wrong train. ▶うっかりしてコーヒーをこぼしてしまった I spilled coffee by accident [accidentally]. ▶そのキツネは家人にもよく慣れ、うっかりすると食事のおねだりまでした(=えさを求めた) The fox became quite tame with the family members. Sometimes it even dared to beg to be fed.

——うっかりする 動 ▶彼女の誕生日を忘れるなんて私もうっかりしていた It was thoughtless of me to forget her birthday.

会話 「彼女どうしたの?」「さあ、でもどうして?」「最近うっかりしていて仕事のミスが多いんだ」"What's up with her?" "I don't know, but why?" "She's getting so absent-minded these days and often makes mistakes at work."

うつぎ 空木 【植物】a deutzia.

うづき 卯月 [4月] April; (陰暦の) the fourth month of the lunar calendar.

:うつくしい 美しい 形

WORD CHOICE 美しい

beautiful 人(の顔[声])・絵画・服・景色などが美麗であること. 人をさす場合は女性が多いが、時に(若い)男性にも用いる. ●美しい女性 a beautiful woman.

pretty 人・物が小さく、こぎれいで、かわいらしいこと. 人をさす場合は、通例女性. ●若くて美しい淑女 a pretty young lady.

lovely 人(の顔)・景色・服・季節・建物などが人目をひきつける魅力を持っていること. 人をさす場合は、通例女性. ●彼の姉の美しい顔 his sister's lovely face.

頻度チャート

beautiful ████████████
pretty ██████
lovely ███

20 40 60 80 100 (%)

beautiful; pretty; lovely (⇨[類語]); (器量の良い) good-looking; handsome (!) 男性の顔立ちのよい美しさに用いる. 女性に用いると堂々とした健康的な美しさをいう); (絵のように美しい) picturesque, (魅力のある) charming; [声が] sweet; [清い] pure; [高潔な] noble. ●美しい声で話す speak in a beautiful [a lovely, a sweet, a charming] voice. ●心の美しい(=優しい)少女 a kind [a kind-hearted] girl; (心の清い) a girl pure in heart. ▶姉は美しい女性だった My sister was a beautiful [a pretty, a lovely, a good-looking] girl. ▶私はその美しい景色に魅せられてしまった I was charmed with [by] the beautiful [lovely, picturesque] scenery.

会話 「見事なバラだわね」「絵のように美しいじゃないの」 "What glorious roses!" "Aren't they a picture!"

——美しく 副 ●美しく着飾っている be beautifully dressed. ●美しく(=上品に)老いる age with grace.

うつくしさ 美しさ beauty. ●自然の美しさに打たれる be struck by the beauty [beauties] of nature; be struck by natural beauty. ●彼女の心の美しさ (=清らかさ)に深い感銘を受ける be deeply impressed with the purity of her heart.

うつけ (⇨ぼんやり, 間抜け)

うっけつ 鬱血 名 【医学】engorgement; congestion (of blood).

——鬱血する 動 ▶右ももの傷口がうっ血している The wound on my right thigh is congested.

うつし 写し a copy, a duplicate (!) duplicate は複写機による写し (exact copy), copy は手書きの写しなども含む. なお原本は the original); [複製] a reproduction. ●彼の手紙の写しを2通作る make two duplicates [copies] of his letter. ●住民票の写し a certified copy of one's resident card. (!) a certified copy は「役所などの公式の判が押してある写

うつしとる 写し取る ❶[正確に書き写す] copy, make a copy《of》; transcribe;(トレーシングペーパーを使って) trace. ●彼の講義内容をノートに写し取る copy the content of his lecture *into* a notebook. ●地図を写し取る *trace* the map. ●古文書の一節を正確に写し取る *transcribe* a passage of the ancient document accurately.

❷[写真などに写し取る] ●当時の新聞をマイクロフィルムに写し取る microfilm the newspapers of those days. ▶カメラは画家よりも実物を忠実に写し取ることができる A camera can *reflect* real life more accurately than a painter.

うつす 写す, 映す ❶[文書・絵などを写しとる](複写する), (模写する) imitate, (模写する) reproduce.
●文書を写す copy 《make a copy *of*》 a document; (そっくり写す) *copy out* a document. ●美術品を写す *reproduce* a work of art.

❷[写真をとる] take*. ●写真を写してもらう hável one's picture *taken*. ▶ここで私たち5人の写真を写しましょう Let's *take* a picture of the five of us here.

❸[描写する] describe; (表現する) express. ▶その小説には絶望感が生々しく写し出されている The sense of despair *is* vividly *expressed* [*described*] in the novel.

❹[反射する](鏡・水面などが像を映す) reflect; (鏡のように映す) mirror. ●桜の木が静かな水面(みなも)に影を映していた The cherry trees *were reflected* [*were mirrored*] *in* [×on] the still water./The still water *reflected* [*mirrored*, *illustrated*] the cherry trees. ▶彼女は鏡に自分の姿を映して見た She looked at herself [her reflection] *in* [×on] the mirror.

❺[投影する](影・映像などを) project. ▶光の影を壁に映した The light *projected* his shadow *onto* [*on*, ×*in*] the wall. ▶映画が大きなスクリーンに映し出された The film *was projected on* [×*in*] a big screen.

❻[その他の表現] ▶個人の病理は社会の病理を映す(=反映する) The illness of individual citizens often *mirrors* the illness of society as a whole.

うつす 移す ❶[移動させる] move;《英書》remove; shift; transfer (-rr-).

使い分け move 移動を表す最も一般的な語.
remove 物・人をよそに移し, 元の場所から取り除くこと.
shift 方向・位置を変化させること.
transfer ある場所から別の場所へ物事を移すこと.

●事務所を東京に移す move [《英書》 remove, *transfer*] the office *to* Tokyo. ●テーブルを窓際に移す *move* the table (*over*) *to* the window. (**!** over は障害物や距離があったりして「えっちらおっちら」移動させる感じを伝える) ●体重を右足から左足へ移す *shift* one's weight *from* the right foot *to* the left (foot). ▶彼は大阪の支店に移された He *was transferred to* a branch office in Osaka. ▶私はそのお金を金庫から書類かばんに移した I *transferred* the money *from* the safe *to* the briefcase./I took the money out of the safe and put it into the briefcase.

❷[病気を感染させる] infect; (与える) give*. ▶その種類の蚊が彼にマラリアをうつした Those kind of mosquitoes *infected* him *with* malaria. ▶君が私に風邪をうつした You *gave* me your cold [×your cold to me]. (**!** You *infected* me *with* your cold. より口語的)/(君に風邪をうつされた) I *got* [*caught*] (a) cold *from* you.

うっすら (わずかに) slightly, lightly; (薄く) thinly; (ぼんやりと) faintly, dimly. ▶富士山には雲がうっすらかかっていた Mt. Fuji was *slightly* covered with clouds. (⇨薄化粧) ▶彼の頭にはうっすらとしか毛がなかった He had *little* hair on the head./His head was *thinly* haired. (**!** 前の方が普通) ▶そのことはうっすらとしか覚えていない I remember it only *faintly* [*dimly*]./I have only a *faint* [a *dim*] recollection of it.

うっせきした 鬱積した pent-up [bottled-up] (feelings). (⇨うっぷん)

うっそう [[茂った] thick, dense (**!** thick より密度が高い). ●うっそうとした大森林 a *dense* forest. ●うっそうと樹木の生い茂っている谷間 a *thickly*-wooded valley.

うったえ 訴え ❶[訴訟] a suit, 《やや書》a lawsuit, an action (⇨訴訟); (民事訴訟の告訴) a complaint. ●訴えを起こす (⇨訴える ❶, 訴訟)
❷[不平不満など] a complaint《about》;(懇願) an appeal 《*for*+事, *to*+人》. ●彼の訴えを聞いてやる listen to their *complaint* [*appeal*].

うったえる 訴える ❶[告訴する] charge《人+*with*+行為》, accuse《人+*of*+行為》; sue /s(j)úː/, file [bring*] a suit against...; report. (⇨告訴する)

使い分け charge 特に犯罪・違法行為を犯した人を裁判所に告訴すること.
accuse 法的・倫理的に許容しがたい行為を行った人を強く非難すること. 必ずしも法的手続きをとるとは限らない.
sue 公式に損害賠償訴訟などを起こすこと.
report 事件・事故を警察などに通告すること.

●その会社を損害賠償を求めて[契約違反で]訴える *sue* the company *for* damages [*for* breach of contract]. ●彼を無謀運転のかどで警察に訴える *report* him *to* the police *for* reckless driving. ▶彼は窃盗罪で訴えられた He *was charged with* [*was accused of*] theft.
❷[不平や痛みを] complain《of》. ●頭痛[のどの痛み]を訴える *complain of* a headache [a sore throat].
❸[心・感覚に] appeal《to》. ●理性[世論; 視覚]に訴える *appeal to* reason [public opinion; the eye]. ▶彼の絵は私に強く訴えるものがあった His painting strongly *appealed to* me.
❹[(好ましくない)手段などに] resort《to》. ●暴力[戦争]に訴える *resort to* violence [war].
❺[懇願する] appeal, make* an appeal《*to*+人, *for*+事》; (感情的なやり方で) plead*《for》. ▶私は彼らに援助を訴えた I *appealed to* them *for* help [to help me]. ▶彼女は訴えるような目で私を見た She gave me an *appealing* [a *pleading*] look./She looked appealingly [*pleadingly*] at me. ▶彼女は誘拐犯に息子を殺さないでと泣いて訴えた She wept and *pleaded with* the kidnapper *for* her son's life [not to kill her son]. ▶彼は無実を訴えた(=申し立てた) (法廷に) He *pleaded* not guilty. (**!** 法廷では innocent でなく not guilty を用いる)

うっちゃり 打っちゃり [(相撲》*utchari*, (説明的に) the technique of leaning back at the edge of the ring and throwing one's opponent backward (by pivoting on one's heels).

うっちゃる 打っちゃる ❶[投げ捨てる] ⇨投げ捨てる
❷[放っておく] leave*; (すべきことを放っておく) let*... slide. ▶彼は宿題をぎりぎりまでうっちゃっておいた He let

his homework *slide* until the last moment.
❸ [相撲で] (⇨ひっちゃり)

うつつ 現 ▶この幸せは夢かうつつ(=現実)か Is this happiness a dream or *reality*?
● うつつを抜かす ▶彼はマージャンにうつつを抜かしている He *is lost in* mahjong. ▶何であんな女にうつつを抜かしているのかねえ I can't think why he's *crazy* [*mad*] *about* the girl.

うってかわる 打って変わる ▶彼女は私にまったく打って変わったような態度を取り始めた She began to take a *completely different* attitude toward me. ▶彼は以前とは打って変わって明るくなった He *completely changed* to become a cheerful person./He became a very cheerful person completely different from his former self.

うってつけ 打ってつけ ― 打ってつけの 形 (最適の) just right; (最も好ましい) best; (最も必要条件を満たした) most suitable. (⇨読(ﾖﾐ)え向き) ●うってつけの (=理想的な)場所 an *ideal* place 《*for*》. ▶彼はその仕事にうってつけだ He's *just right* for the job./He's *perfectly suited* to the job. (**!**「営業部にうってつけの人だ」なら He's *just* what our sales department needs. などのようにも言える)

うってでる 打って出る ❶ [城外へ] sally out 《*against*》. ❷ [活動の場を求めて] (選挙に) run* 《米》 [stand* 《英》] for …; (新事業などに) launch (out) into …; make* one's debut 《*as*》. ●市長選[国政]に打って出る run *for* mayor [for the Diet]. ▶政界に打って出る *launch* (oneself) *into* politics; *make* one's political *debut* 《*as* mayor》.

ウッド ❶ [木材] (a) wood. ❷ [ゴルフのクラブ] a wood.
●ウッドデッキ a wood [a wooden] deck. ●ウッドベース 《コントラバス》 a contrabass; a double bass.

うっとうしい [陰気な] gloomy; [気がめいるような] depressing. (⇨重苦しい) ●うっとうしい天気 gloomy [*depressing*, (どんよりした) *dull*] weather. ●うっとうしい(=うるさい)ハエ an *annoying* fly.

うっとり ― うっとりする 動 (魅せられる) be charmed, be enchanted, be entranced 《*by*, *with*》. (**!**後ほど意味が強くなる) ▶観客はみなその美しいメロディーにうっとりした The whole audience *was charmed* [*enchanted*, *entranced*] *by* [*with*] the sweet melody.
― **うっとりした** 形 ▶ワインを 2, 3 杯飲むと彼はうっとりした気持ちになった After a few glasses of wine, he felt *mellow* [*pleasantly intoxicated*].
― **うっとりと** 副 ▶彼女はうっとりと婚約指輪を見つめた She gazed *in* [*with*] *rapture* at the engagement ring.

うつびょう 鬱病 《医学》mèlanchólia; depression. (⇨躁(ｿｳ)病) ▶躁うつ病患者 a manic-depressive.

うつぶせ 俯せ ▶うつ伏せに倒れる fall on one's *face*. ▶彼女はベッドにうつぶせになった She laid herself *face down* upon the bed. ▶赤ちゃんをうつぶせに寝かせるのは危険です It's dangerous to lay your baby in the *prone* position. (**!**堅い表現. to 以下を *put* your baby *down* on its *stomach* ともいえる)

うつぶせる 俯せる ❶ [体を下向きに伏せる] lie on one's face [stomach]; lie face down [downward].
❷ [物を下向きに置く] ▶つぼをうつぶせる(=上下逆さまにする) turn the pot *upside down* [(底を上にして) *bottom up*].

うっぷん 鬱憤 [うっ積した怒り] pent-up anger; [欲求不満] frustration. (⇨鬱積する) ●うっぷんを晴らす vent one's *pent-up* anger 《*on*》; [話] let [work]

off (one's) steam 《*on*》.

うつぼ [魚介] a moray (eel).

うつぼかずら 靫蔓 [植物] a nepenthes; a pitcher plant.

うつほものがたり『宇津保物語』 *The Tale of the Cavern*. (⇨参考) 平安時代の物語

うつむく 俯く [下を見る] look down; [頭をたれる] hang* [(力なく)(ややまれ) droop] one's head. ●うつむいて歩く walk *with* one's *head* hanging [*drooping*, (伏し目がちに) *with downcast eyes*].

うつむける 俯ける ▶顔をうつむける(=頭をたれる) *hang* [*bend*] one's head.

うつらうつら ― うつらうつらする 動 doze (off); (こっくりこっくりする) nod (off); (半分眠っている) be half asleep; drowse /dráuz/ (off). (⇨うとうと)

うつり 映り, 写り ▶このテレビはうつりがいい[悪い] This television has a (very) clear [a blurred] *picture*. (⇨画像) ▶こちらのブラウスの方があなたにはずっとうつりがいいわ This blouse *looks much better on* you. (**!**on は「…が着用すると」の意) ▶彼は写真うつりがよい (⇨写真 ②)

うつりが 移り香 a lingering (faint) fragrance [scent].

うつりかわり 移り変わり [変化] (a) change; [推移] (a) transition (**!**change より堅い語). ●季節の移り変わり the *change* of (the) seasons (四季)をさす); seasonal *changes*. ▶ある政体から他の政体への移り変わり a *transition from* one form of government *to* another. ●運命の移り変わり (= 浮き沈み) the *ups and downs* of fortune.

うつりかわる 移り変わる (変化する) change. ●時代とともに移り変わる *change* [*move*] with the times.

うつりぎ 移り気 ― 移り気な 形 [浮気な] fickle; [気まぐれな] capricious, (ややまれ) whimsical. (⇨気まぐれ) ●移り気な女 a *fickle* [a *capricious*] woman.

うつりばし 移り箸 (説明的に) eating from one accompanying dish to another without eating rice between.

うつる 写る, 映る ❶ [写真などに] come* out. (**!**通例, 様態の副詞(句)を伴う) ●この写真に写っている少年 a boy in this picture. ▶あなたよく写っていますね You've come out (well) in the photo [*picture*]./You look nice in the photo. (⇨写真) ▶この写真では彼が走っているところが写っている This photograph *shows* him running. ▶この写真では彼女は実物以上に写っている This picture *flatters* her./This picture makes her look better [more beautiful, more attractive]. ▶テレビに映ると彼は若く見えます He looks young on TV.
❷ [調和する] match, go* (well) 《*with*》; (服装・色などが似合う) suit. ▶この帽子はあなたのドレスに映らない This hat doesn't *go with* [*match*] your dress. ▶その色は彼によく映る The color *suits* him well. (**!** ×The color matches [goes (well) with] him. とはいわない (⇨似合う)
❸ [反射・投影される] (反射する) reflect; (投影する) project. (⇨写る ❹ ❺) ▶窓のガラスに彼の顔が映っていた His face *was reflected* [*was mirrored*] *in* [*on*] the glass of the window. ▶美しい絵がスクリーンに映った A beautiful picture *was projected* on the screen.

うつる 移る ❶ [移動・移転する] [引っ越す] move 《*to, into*》 (⇨引っ越す); (転任・転校する) transfer (-rr-) 《*to*》. ▶大阪から東京に移る *move from* Osaka *to* Tokyo. ▶新居へ移る *move into* a new house; 《英》*move* house. ▶家を移る *move out* (of one's house). ▶息子夫婦が近々こちらに移ってきます Our son and his wife *are moving in* here [私たちのところに] with us] soon. ▶彼は他校へ移った He *transferred* to another school. (❗He *was transferred* to another school. はだれかほかの人の決定で転校[転勤]させられたという含意がある)

❷ 【変化する】 change; (位置・方向が) shift. (⇨変化する) ▶時代が移るにつれ人の考え方も変わる The way of thinking *changes* with the times.

❸ 【話題などが】(転じる) turn, go* 《*to*》; (知らぬ間に移る) drift 《*into*》; (次に進む) go on 《*to*》. ▶話が政治に移った Our talk *turned* [*went*] *to* politics. ▶次の項目に移ろう Let's *go on* [*move on*, *pass on*] *to* the next item.

❹ 【病気が】 infect; (伝染性である) be contágious [inféctious]; (❗前の方は接触感染, 後の方は空気感染); (伝染しやすい)《話》be catching; [人が] (病気に感染する) catch*, become* infected 《*with*》. (❗前の方が口語的) ▶うつる病気 a contagious [an *infectious*, ×a catching] disease. (❗catching は叙述用法) ▶君の風邪がうつった I *caught* a cold from you. (⇨移す ❷) ▶気をつけてね. 私の風邪がうつるから Be careful or you'll *catch* [I'll *give* you] my cold.

❺ 【燃え移る】 catch*; (広がる) spread*. ▶火が私の家に移った The fire *spread to* my house./The flames *caught* my house.

うつろ 虚ろ 图 a hollow.
——虚ろな 形 (心・笑いなどが) vacant; (音・声が) hollow; (表情が) blank. ▶うつろな声で話す speak in a *hollow* voice. ▶うつろな目で私を見る give me a *vacant* [a *blank*] look; look *vacantly* [*blankly*] at me; look at me with *blank* [*empty*] eyes.

うつわ 器 ❶ 【容器】 a container, 《書》 a receptacle; (皿) a dish; (はち) a bowl, a basin (❗後の方が浅い).

❷ 【才能】 (a) capacity, 《やや書》 (a) caliber (❗後の方は通例単数形で); (将来...になる人材) material. ▶器が大きい[なる人物ではない] He has a big *caliber*. (❗caliber は通例才能などがすぐれていることを表す) ▶彼は偉大な指導者となる器である He has the *capacity to* be a great leader./He is great leader *material*. (❗無冠詞に注意)

‡うで 腕 ❶ 【身体の】 an arm. (❗肩から先全体をさすが, 通例手首までの部分で hand を含まない. 肩から上は upper arm (上腕), ひじから手首までが forearm (前腕))

① 【~腕】 ●きき腕 one's better *arm*; one's dominant hand. ▶バランスをとるために両腕を広げる spread out one's *arms* for balance. ▶彼は長い[太い; ほっそりした; 筋骨たくましい] 腕をしている He has long [big; slender; thick; brawny /brɔ́:ni/] *arms*.

●腕いっぱいの花 an *armful* of flowers. ●腕まくりして with one's *sleeves* rolled up. (⇨相撲, 腕立て伏せ) ▶彼は腕組みをした He folded his *arms* (across his chest). (❗女性の場合は通例 She crossed her *arms* on her breast. のように one's *arms* folded [with folded *arms*]. (3) 米英人には反抗・抵抗を示す態度なので, 対話するときなどは注意が必要) ▶彼は腕っぷしが強い He has strong *arms*.

③ 【腕が】 ▶腕が痛い I have a pain in the [my] *arm*. ▶その投手は腕が長い The pitcher has long *arms*.

④ 【腕に】 ●彼の腕にすがって歩く walk *on* his *arm*. (❗on は「...を支えとして」の意) ●赤ん坊を腕に抱く hold a baby *in* [×*on*] one's *arms*. ●上着を腕にかけて持ち歩く carry one's jacket *over* one's *arm*. ▶少女は腕に買い物かごをかけていた The girl had a shopping basket *on* her *arm*. ▶彼女は本を腕に抱えた She tucked a book *under* her *arm*.

⑤ 【腕を】 ●(つかまりなさいと) 女性に腕を差し出す give [offer] one's *arm* to a woman. ●彼の腕をつかむ[とらえる] take [catch] him by the [×*his*] *arm*. ●彼の腕を振りほどく get his *arm* free. ●腕(=そで)をまくる pull up [roll up] one's *sleeves* 《*to* him》. ▶彼らは腕を組んで通りを歩いていた They were walking along the street *arm in arm*. ▶彼は私の肩に腕を回して私を抱き寄せた He moved [(急に) flung] his *arm* around my shoulders and hugged me. ●両足を開いて立って. そうです. 腕を大きく伸ばして. そして体を左に曲げなさい Stand your feet apart. OK. Stretch your arms. Now, lean to the left. ▶彼は棚の上の本を取ろうとして腕を伸ばした He reached for the book on the shelf.

❷ 【手腕】 (習得した知的または技術的能力) ability 《*in*; *to do*》; (特に生まれつきの芸術的才能) (a) talent 《*for*》; (技量, 腕前) (a) skill 《*at*, *in*》.

① 【~(の)腕】 ●プロ級の腕 professional *skill*; the *skill* of a professional. ●ダンス[碁]の腕 one's *skill in* dancing [(playing) go]. ▶彼は私たちにピアノの腕(=腕前)を披露した He showed us his *skill at* the piano [*in* playing the piano].

② 【腕~】 ●腕一本でたたき上げた人(=独立独行の人) a *self-made* person. ●腕試しする (⇨腕試し) ▶それは君の腕次第だ It depends on your *ability*.

③ 【腕が[は]】 ●腕が鈍らないようにしておく keep one's hand *in*. ●腕が鈍る(⇨鈍る) get one's hand *out*》 ▶水泳の腕が上がった I've got better [more skillful] *at* swimming./I have improved my *skill in* swimming. ▶君のクラリネットの腕はずいぶん上がってきたね You're coming on so well with the clarinet. ▶テニスの腕が落ちてきましたね(=さびついてきた) You're getting rusty in tennis, aren't you? ▶ぼくはゴルフの腕はあまり大したことはない I'm *not much of* a [*not a very good*] golf player./I'm *not very good at* (playing) golf.

④ 【腕の~】 ●腕のいいコック a *good* [an *excellent*] cook. ●非常に腕のある外科医 a very *skillful* [a highly *skillful*] surgeon; a surgeon of great *skill*. ●ここが君の腕の見せどころだ Now is the time [This is your chance] to show your *ability* [《話》*stuff*]. ●腕 ⇨「素質, 才能」の項

⑤ 【腕を】 ●英語の腕を上げる (上達する) improve one's English; (勉強し直す) polish [brush] up 《on》 one's English. ●音楽コンクールで腕を競う *compete* 《*with* him》 in the musical contest.

●腕が立つ ▶あの弁護士は腕が立つ(=有能だ) He is an *able* [a *competent*] lawyer.

●腕が鳴る can't wait to show one's skill [ability]; be itching to show one's skill. ▶アジア卓球選手権で, 大勢の観客を前にして得意のスマッシュを決めようと腕が鳴った I couldn't wait to show off my smash shot before a lot of spectators in the Asian Table Tennis Tournament. ▶その板前はお客を前に包丁さばきを披露しようと腕が鳴った The Japanese cook was itching to show off his great skill with a knife before the customers.

●腕に覚えがある (自信がある) be confident of one's *ability* [*skill*].

●腕をこまぬく can do nothing with one's arms folded (in front of one's chest). ▶私たちは大水害を目の前にして腕をこまねいて見ているよりほかに仕方がなかった We couldn't do anything but watch the

うでおし

great flood disaster before us.
- 腕を振るう 芸能界で腕をふるう show one's *talent* [*ability*] in the world of entertainment.
- 腕を磨く develop [improve] one's skill. ▶ 彼はひそかに料理の腕を磨いている He is making a secret effort to improve his cooking skill.
- 腕利き (⇨腕利き) ● 腕くらべ (競技) a contest.
- 腕時計 a wristwatch. (❗単に watch ということも多い) ● 腕輪 a bracelet /bréislət/; (留め金のない) a bangle.

うでおし 腕押し ▶ のれんに腕押し ⇨暖簾 [成句]
うてき 雨滴 a raindrop, a drop of rain.
うできき 腕利き ── 腕利きの 形 (熟達した) skillful, (熟練した) skilled; (有能な) able, competent. ▶ 腕利きの大工 a *skillful* [a *skilled*] carpenter. (❗前の方は生まれつきの器用さを, 後の方は経験の深さを暗示する) ▶ すごぶる腕利きの弁護士 a very *able* [*competent*] lawyer. (❗後の方は物事を適切に処理する能力に重点がある)
うでずく 腕ずく ▶ 腕ずくで彼の金を取る take his money *by force*.
うでずもう 腕相撲 arm wrestling. ▶ 腕相撲をする arm-wrestle 《*with* him》.
うでたてふせ 腕立て伏せ ▶ 腕立て伏せを10回する do 10 *push-ups* 《米》 [*press-ups* 《英》].
うでだめし 腕試し ── 腕試し(を)する 動 try one's skill; test one's ability.
うでっぷし 腕っ節 (⇨腕力) ▶ 彼は腕っぷしが強い He has great *strength* in his arms./He is a man of *muscle*.
うでまえ 腕前 (a) skill. (⇨腕 ❷) ▶ 彼の料理の腕前は大したものだ He is very *skillful* [shows great *skill*] *at* cooking./He is a very good cook.
うでまくら 腕枕 ▶ 彼は腕枕をして寝そべっている He is lying down, with his head (resting) on his arm.
うでる 茹でる boil. (⇨茹(ゆ)でる)
うてん 雨天 rainy [wet] weather; a rainy [wet] day. (⇨晴れ) ▶ 雨天(=屋内)体操場 a gymnasium; 《話》 a gym. ▶ 運動会は雨天順延になります In case of *rain*, the athletic meet 《米》 [meeting 《英》] will be put off till the next [first] fine day. ▶ その試合は雨天で流れた[中止になった] The game was canceled [was called off] because of (the) *rain*./The game was *rained out* [《英》*off*]. ▶ ラグビーは雨天決行です Rugby is played *rain or shine* [*even if it rains*]. (❗前の方は他のあらゆる天候(どんな天候であっても)の意が強い)
うど 〖植物〗 (an) udo (⑳ ~s). ▶ 山うど (a) wild *udo*.
- うどの大木 ▶ あいつはうどの大木だ He is a *big*, *good-for-nothing guy*.
うとい 疎い (知識のない) not well-informed 《*about*》, (なじみの薄い) unfamiliar 《*with*》; (無知の) ignorant 《*of*, *about*》. ▶ 彼は時事問題に疎い He doesn't know *about* [*is not well-informed*] *about* current topics. ▶ 彼はこの町の地理に疎い He doesn't know the geography of this town. (❗例えば, 劇場あるある地理的知識をいう)/He is a stranger in this town. (❗上に加え, その劇場の優劣など文化的側面を含むこともある)
うとうと ── うとうとする 動 doze (off), 《話》 drop (-pp-) off; (眠くて頭がこっくりとなる) nod off. ▶ 彼女はねむたそうにしていた She was *dozing* in the sun. ▶ 疲れていたので, 私は何回か授業中にうとうとした I was so tired that I *nodded off* a few times during class. ▶ おじいちゃんは安楽椅子に座ってテレビを見ながらうとうとしていた Grandpa was *dropping*

166

うなる

off [*was having forty winks*] in an easy chair while watching TV.
うとましい 疎ましい ▶ 彼が疎ましい(=いやでたまらない) I find him *unpleasant* [*offensive*].
うとむ 疎む (⇨疎んじる)
うどん udon noodles; thick wheat noodles. (⇨そば) ● きつねうどん (説明的に) (a bowl of) *noodles* in hot soup with fried bean curd on top.
- うどん粉 (wheat) flour /fláuər/. ● うどん粉病 mildew. ● うどん屋 a noodle shop.
うとんじる 疎んじる (遠ざける) keep 《him》 away; put 《him》 off; (近寄らない) avoid; (よそよそしい態度をみせる)《話》give 《him》 the cold shoulder.
*うながす 促す 〖催促する〗 urge, (しつこく求める) press (❗後の方が強意的); 〖刺激する〗 stimulate, 〖促進する〗 promote. ▶ 彼に返事を促す *urge* [*press*] him to answer; *press* him *for* an answer. ▶ そこに彼の注意を促す(=喚起する) *call* his attention *to* it. ▶ その経験が彼の英語への興味を促した The experience *stimulated* [*stirred up*] his interest in English.
うなぎ 鰻 〖魚介〗 an eel. (❗切り身は ⓤ) ▶ ウナギのかば焼き broiled *eels*; spítchcòck. ▶ ウナギ丼 (⇨鰻丼(どん))
- うなぎの寝床 ▶ うなぎの寝床のような家[部屋] a long, narrow house [room].
- うなぎ登り ▶ 物価はうなぎ登りだ Prices *are going up rapidly* [*soaring*, 《話》*skyrocketing*].
うなされる 魘される ▶ (悪夢を見る) have* *a nightmare*. ▶ 悪夢に悩まされる *suffer a nightmare*. ▶ 熱でうなされている be *delirious* with fever.
うなじ 項 the nape of the [one's] neck.
うなじゅう 鰻重 (説明的に) broiled [grilled] eel on rice served in a lacquered box.
うなずく 頷く nod (-dd-) 《*at*, *to*》. (❗nod は承認・あいさつ・合図などの動作) ▶ うなずいて同意するを nod 《one's》 consent 《*to* him》; nod 《*to* him》 in agreement [approval]. (❗(1) もっと具体的に one's head in agreement などともいえる. (2) 話し合いの場では, 同意以外に 1 回うなずいて「話し続けよ」の意を, 連続して速くうなずくことで,「発言したい」の意向を伝えることもある) ▶ うなずいてお休みと言う nod a good night. ▶ 彼が心配するのもうなずける(=理解できる) It is *understandable* that he is nervous./He is *understandably* nervous. (❗*Understandably* he ....のように文頭で用いることも可)
うなだれる 項垂れる hang* one's head. ▶ 時計の万引を見つかれた彼は(恥ずかしそうに)うなだれた When he was discovered shoplifting a watch, he *hung* his *head* (in shame). ▶ 彼女はうなだれて立っていた She stood there with her head *hanging*.
うなどん 鰻丼 (説明的に) a bowl of rice and [with] broiled [grilled] eel.
うなばら 海原 the ocean, the sea. ▶ 大海原 a wide [a vast] expanse of ocean.
うなり 唸り 〖人の〗(苦痛などの) a groan, (悲しげな) a moan; 〖猛獣などの〗a roar, (怒った) a growl, (オオカミなどの遠ぼえ) a howl, 〖ハチなどのぶんぶんという〗 a buzz. ▶ うなり声をたてる give a groan [a moan].
- 風のうなり the *roar* [*moan*] of the wind.
うなる 唸る ❶ 〖動物が〗 growl /grául/《*at*》; (歯をむき出して) snarl 《*at*》; 〖猛獣の〗(怒り狂った) howl /hául/; (ごうごうと) roar. ▶ 犬が彼に向かってうなった A dog *growled at* him. ▶ 木々をたたる風がうなっていた The wind *howled* [*roared*] in the trees.
❷ 〖うめく〗 moan; groan (❗moan より苦痛も声も大きい). ▶ 痛くうなる *moan* [*groan*] with pain. ▶ 「救急車をたのむ」とその男はうなるように言った "(Call

うに 【動物】a sea urchin; an urchin;〖食品〗seasoned urchin eggs.

うぬぼれ 自惚れ　conceit /kənsíːt/;〖虚栄心〗vanity;〖誇り〗pride,《⇨自負》. ▶うぬぼれの強い人 a *conceited* person. ▶彼はうぬぼれが強い He is very conceited./He is full of *conceit*./He *thinks too highly of* himself.

うぬぼれる 自惚れる　be conceited,《話》be puffed up,《話》be big-headed;(…と勝手に思い込んでいる) fancy oneself 《as; to be》. ▶うぬぼれるな Don't be *conceited*. ▶彼は成功してうぬぼれている He *is conceited about* [*is puffed up with*] his success. ▶彼女は演説が上手だとうぬぼれている She *fancies herself* (*as* [*to be*]) an orator./She *flatters* [×fancies] *herself* (*that*) she is an orator. ▶彼は1位になったうぬぼれている He *has had a big head* [*has been big-headed*] since he took first place.

うね 畝　〖畑の〗a ridge;〖織物・編み物の〗a rib.

うねうね 副　▶うねうねと山腹を上がっている小道 a path *winding* [*zigzagging*] up the hillside. ▶その川は関東平野をうねうねと流れている The river *winds* [*zigzags*] through the Kanto Plain(s).

—— **うねうねする** 動　(道・川などが曲がりくねる) wind /wáind/;(ジグザグになっている) zigzag.

うねり 〖波の〗a swell;(急激な)《書》a surge;〖地表の〗《書》undulation;〖曲折の〗winding /wáindiŋ/. ▶海のうねり the *surge* of the sea.

うねる 〖道・川が〗(左右に) wind*/wáind/, (上下に) roll;〖波が〗roll, swell*.

うのう 右脳　the right hemisphere, the right side of the brain.

うのはな 卯の花　❶〖植物〗a deutzia.
❷〖おから〗soy bean pulp; by-products of *tofu*-making.

うのみ 鵜呑み　—— 鵜呑みにする 動　swallow《food, a story》. ▶彼女の言うことをうのみにするな Don't *swallow* her story (*whole*[《話》*hook, line and sinker*])./(言葉どおりにとる) Don't *take* her *at her word*.《⇨丸飲み》

うのめたかのめ 鵜の目鷹の目　(⇨鵜[成句])

うは 右派　图　(人) a rightist;《集合的》the right (wing) (❗単・複両扱い), (政党内部の) the right faction. ▶彼はその政党の右派に属している He belongs to [is a member of, is on] *the right wing* of the party.
—— **右派の** 形　rightist; right-wing.

うば 乳母　a nurse;(授乳をする)《古》a wet nurse;(授乳しないで世話だけをする) a dry nurse.

うばいあう 奪い合う　scramble《for》. ▶その空いている席を奪い合う *scramble for* the vacant seat.

うばいかえす 奪い返す　take*《it》back《from》.

うばいとる 奪い取る　(⇨奪う)

:**うばう** 奪う　❶〖盗み取る〗rob (-bb-)《him [a place]》;〖強奪〗(盗む) steal*;(ひったくる) snatch. ▶彼は暗い通りでお金を奪われた He *was robbed of* his money on a dark street. ▶私はバッグを奪われた(=ひったくられた) I had my bag *snatched*./My bag *was snatched*. ▶中田はトッティからボールを奪った Nakata *robbed* the ball *from* Totti.
❷〖取り上げる〗take*… (away)《from him》;(権力などを) deprive《him *of* it》;(財産などを) dispossess《him *of* it》. ▶その少年からナイフを奪う *take away* the knife *from* the boy. ▶視力を奪われる be deprived *of* one's eyesight. ▶彼の生命を奪う *take* his life; *kill* him. ▶コンピュータのおかげで彼らは仕事を奪われてしまった Computers *have taken away* their business./They *lost* their business to computers. ▶彼は会員資格を奪われた He *was deprived of* his membership. ▶そのストライキで何百万人もの通勤客が足を奪われた(=不便な目にあった) Millions of commuters *were inconvenienced* by the strike.
❸〖心などを〗(魅了する) fascinate /fǽsəneit/;(熱中させる) absorb. ▶目を奪う draw《his》eyes;(注意を引きつける) attract《his》attention. ▶彼女の演技に心を奪われた I *was fascinated* [《書》*was enchanted*] *by* her performance. ▶私はパーティーの計画に心を奪われていた I *was absorbed in* planning the party. ▶彼女はでなドレスは人目を奪った(目をくらませた) Her showy dress *dazzled* us all./(お株を奪った) She *upstaged* all the other girls with her showy dress.
❹〖野球で〗▶(外野手が)ホームラン(ボール)を奪い取る *rob* a batter of a home run; take a home run from a batter. ▶その投手から10安打を奪う make ten hits off the pitcher; *tag* the pitcher for ten hits.

うはうは ▶今月はお小遣いがあがって子供たちはうはうは(=大喜び)だ《話》The children *are tickled pink* [*are all smiles*] because they've got more allowance this month.

うばぐるま 乳母車《米》a (baby) carriage [buggy],《英》a pram,《英書》a perambulator;(折りたたみ式の)《米》a stroller,《英》a pushchair,《和製語》a baby car.

うばざくら 姥桜　〖若くはないが魅力のある女性〗an elderly attractive woman.

うばすてやま 姥捨て山　*ubasuteyama*;(説明的に) the mountain in central Japan where, according to legend, elderly people were believed to have been left to die during the old times.

うぶ 初　—— 初な 形　(単純で世間知らずの) naive /naːíːv/;(無邪気な) innocent;(教養や経験の乏しい) unsophisticated;(経験がない) inexperienced, green. ▶あいつはまったくうぶだ He is as *innocent* as a newborn baby./He is very *green*.

うぶぎ 産着　baby clòthes; clothes for a newborn baby.

うぶげ 産毛　down; fine soft hair〖鳥の〗feathers]. ▶産毛の生えた額 a *downy* forehead.

うぶごえ 産声　the first cry of a newborn baby. ▶産声を上げる give one's *first cry*;(産まれる) be born.

うふふ (くすくす笑う) chuckle, giggle, titter.

うぶゆ 産湯　a (newborn) baby's first bath. ▶産湯を使わせる bathe a newborn baby for the first time.

うへん 右辺　(不)等式の) the right side. ▶右辺の項 the *right side* of a mathematical equation.

*****うま** 馬　❶〖動物〗a horse (❗馬の一般的総称. 狭義では成長した雄馬をさす);(雌馬) a mare;(雄の子馬) a colt, (雌の子馬) a filly (❗両者とも4歳未満までをいう);(1歳未満の子馬) a foal;(種馬) a stallion;(去勢馬) a gelding;(小形の馬) a pony.
①《馬が》▶馬がいななく *Horses* neigh [(うれしそうに) whinny]. ▶馬がぱかぱか音を立てて歩いている *Horses* are clopping [clop-clopping].
②《馬に》▶(子供などに)馬になってやる give《him》a ride on one's back; ride《him》on one's back.

うま

解説 「馬に乗る」は「馬にまたがる」動作をいう場合は get on 《やや書》 mount (on) a *horse*, get in(to) the saddle. 「馬を乗りこなす」は ride a *horse*. 「馬に乗って行く」は ride ((on) a *horse*) + 場所の副詞 (**!** on はないことが多い); ride *on horseback* [《主に米》 ride *horseback*]. 「馬に乗っている」状態の場合は be on *horseback*, be on a *horse* という.

❸【馬を】▶馬を飼う keep a *horse*. ▶馬を疾走させる gallop a *horse*. ▶馬を馴らす break (in) a *horse*. ▶馬をつなぐ hitch a *horse* 《*to* a post》. ▶(手綱を引いて)馬を止める pull [rein] up a *horse*; rein back a *horse*.

❹【馬から】▶馬から落ちる fall off [from] a *horse*; (投げ飛ばされて) be thrown off a *horse*. ▶馬から降りる get off [down from] a *horse*; 《やや書》dismount (from) a *horse*.

❷【競馬】(競走) horse racing; (馬) a racehorse. (⇨競馬) ▶今でも馬をやっている(=馬に賭けている)のですか Are you still backing *horses*? / **!**「負け[勝ち]馬に賭ける」は back the wrong *horse* [a winner]

▶**馬が合う** ▶私は彼と馬が合う I *get on very well with* him. / 《話》I *hit it off with* him.

▶**馬の耳に念仏** ▶いくら注意しても彼らには馬の耳に念仏だった They *turned a deaf ear to* my warnings. / I gave them warnings but it was (*like*) *water off a duck's back*.

▶**馬市** a horse fair.

うま 午 the Horse.
▶午年 『十二支』 the year of the Horse. (⇨干支) 関連

:**うまい 旨い** 形 ❶【上手な】good* 《*at, in, with*》; skillful 《*at, in, with*》; expert /ékspə:rt/ 《*at, in, on*》(**!** 叙述用法でも今は通例 × /ikspə́:rt/ とは発音しない); 《主に英》clever 《*at, with*》. (**!** 通例 at は活動, in, on は分野・学科, with は扱い方を示すが, 動名詞が続くときは at が好まれる (⇨上手(『ダ)))

使い分け good ある特定の分野・活動において優れていることを表す最も一般的な語.
skillful 熟練による技術の優秀さをいう.
expert 訓練・経験によって専門的知識・技術に優れていること.
clever skillful とほぼ同意で, 手先の器用さや巧妙さを表す.

● うまい答え (give) a *good* [a *clever*, (適切な)《やや書》an *appropriate*] answer. ● うまいことを言う say *clever* things. ▶彼はトランプがうまい He is *expert at* (play*ing*) cards. ▶彼はスペイン語がうまい He is a *good* [(流暢(ﾘｭｳ)な) a *fluent*] speaker of Spanish. / He is *good at* (speak*ing*) Spanish. /「あまりうまくない」は He's *not very good at* Spanish.)/ He speaks Spanish (*very*) *well* [*good* Spanish, *fluent* Spanish]. ▶彼はかんなの使い方がとてもうまい He is very *skillful* [《主に英》*clever*] at using a plane./ He is very *skillful* [*has great skill*,《主に英》*is very clever*] *with* a plane. He uses a plane very *skillfully* [*with great skill*]. ▶彼女は子供の扱いがうまい She has a way with kids.

解説 「…がうまい」の表現として "good+ある動作をする人" の形がしばしば用いられるが, 動作をする人が「職業として…する人」と単に「…する人」の両方の意味を持つ場合, 文脈によってどちらの意味が判断される: あのレストランには料理がうまい(=腕のよい)コックがいる There's a *good cook* at that restau-

うまい

rant./ 私の夫はとても料理がうまい My husband is a very *good cook*. 同様の表現には a good singer (うまい歌手/歌のうまい人), a good carpenter (腕のいい大工/大工仕事のうまい人) などがある.

会話 「君が田中と試合するんだってね」「彼はどのくらいうまいの?」 "I see you're playing Tanaka." "How *good* is he?"

❷【おいしい】good*, nice; delicious /dilíʃəs/; tasty; appetizing. (⇨おいしい)

使い分け good, nice 食べ物の味がよいことを表す最も一般的な語.
delicious 食べ物の味・香りが非常に良いこと. 強意的な語で, very などをつけることはまれ.
tasty 食べ物の風味が良いこと. 通例, 塩味の料理に用い, 甘いデザートには用いない.
appetizing 食べ物などが人の食欲をそそること.

● うまいシチュー (a) *good* [(a) *delicious*, (a) *tasty*] stew. ● うまそうな料理 [におい] an *appetizing* meal [smell]. ● 季節ごとのうまいもの(=珍味)を食べる eat the *délicacies* [*dainty food*] of the seasons. ▶これはなかなかうまい This is very [really] *good*./I really like this./ This tastes very *good* [*nice*]./ This is *delicious*. (**!** *delicious* は否定文・疑問文, 比較級・最上級などでは通例 *good* を代わりに用いる. 通例 very などの修飾を受けない (⇨類語)) ▶これはうまそうなにおいがする This smells *good* [*delicious*]! ▶彼はその料理をうまそうに食べた He *enjoyed* the food./ (よく味わって) He ate the food *with great relish*. ▶ここは空気がうまい The air is *sweet* here.

❸【好都合の】(よい) good*; (もうかる) profitable; (好運の) lucky. ● うまい仕事 a *profitable* [《話》a *juicy*, (心をそそる) a *tempting*] job. ▶それは話がうますぎる It's too *good* to be true. ▶それはうまい考えだ That's a *great* [a *good*] idea! ▶うまく(=お見事) *Well* done! ▶うまいことに彼がその場に居合わせた *Fortunately* [*Luckily*], he happened to be there. (⇨副❷)/It was *fortunate* [*lucky*] *that* he happened to be there.

— **旨く** 副 ❶【上手に】well*; (巧みに) skillfully (⇨うまい❶); (巧妙に) neatly, nicely. ● うまくだまされる be *neatly* [*nicely*] taken in. ▶自分の考えを英語でうまく言えない I can't express myself in English *well*. ▶練習するうちにスキーはうまくなる(=上達する) You will *improve* your skiing with practice. 会話「あの絵はあんまりうまくないね」「君はもっとうまくかけるのかい」"That picture isn't very *good*." "Could you paint any *better*?"

❷【好都合に】well*; (首尾よく) successfully; (運よく) fortunately, luckily (⇨うまい❸). ▶私たちの計画はうまくいった Our plan went *well* [*worked out*]. (**!**「うまくいかなかった」は Our plan went wrong [(失敗に終わった) fell through].) ▶彼はうまく新しい仕事を見つけることができた He managed to [was able to, ✗could] find a new job *successfully*. (⇨できる)/He *succeeded* [*was successful*] *in* finding a new job. ▶彼女は学業がうまくなかったので 16 歳で学校をやめて美容師の修業をすることにした She was not so *successful* in school that she left at the age of sixteen to train as a hairdresser. ▶うまくいけば彼とまた会えるかもしれない If you *are lucky*, you may see him again./ *With luck*, you may see him again. ▶クラスの人たちとうまくやっていますか Do you *get along* [*on*] *with* the other students in your class? ▶ボールは転がって

まく(=正確に)ホールに入った The ball rolled *right* into the hole.

会話「明日会議で発表するので落ち着かないんだ」「心配するな. うまくいくよ. とにかく睡眠をよく取ることだ」"I must make a presentation at the meeting tomorrow. So I'm very nervous." "Don't worry. It will *go well* [(話) *work out fine*]. You only need a good night's sleep."

会話「勉強はうまくいっていますか」「順調です. ただし化学はあまりうまくいかないんですよ」"How *are* you *getting along* [(話) *making out*] *with* your study?" "Okay, except *I'm* not *doing* very *well* in chemistry class." (! Okay は I'm doing okay. の省略した言い方)

うまく [まんまと] completely. ●うまうまだまされる be *completely* taken in (*by* his excuse).

うまかた 馬方 a packhorse driver, a wagon driver, a wagoner.

うまざけ 美酒 delicious [excellent, good] *sake* [*wine*].

うまずたゆまず 倦まずたゆまず tirelessly, untiringly, unflaggingly. ▶彼は世界平和のためにうまずたゆまず働いた He worked *tirelessly* for world peace.

うまづら 馬面 a (very) long face. ●馬面の horse-faced.

うまとび 馬跳び leapfrog; (遊び) a leapfrog game. ●馬跳びをする leapfrog; play leapfrog.

うまのあし 馬の足 [下手な役者] a bad [a poor, a ham] actor, (話) a ham; [下級の役者] an inferior [a petty, a minor] actor.

うまのほね 馬の骨 ●どこの馬の骨か分からんやつ a nobody from nowhere.

うまのり 馬乗り ▶馬乗りになる sit astride (him). (! astride はまたがった状態をいう. 例: stand astride a bicycle (自転車にまたがって立つ))

うまみ 旨味 [味] (a good) taste; (風味) (a) flavor, relish; (魅力) (a) charm; [利益] (a) profit; [利点] an advantage. ▶とろ火で2～3時間煮込みなさい Boil [Cook] the stew gently for a couple of hours to bring out the *taste* of beef. ▶彼の文章には独特のうまみがある His writing has a peculiar *charm*. ▶この仕事にはうまみがある This job has its *advantages*./(もうかる仕事だ) This is a *profitable* job.

うまや 馬屋 a stable. (⇒小屋)

うまる 埋まる ❶[埋もれる] be buried /bérid/. ▶家々は山崩れで埋まってしまった The houses were *buried in* [*under*] a landslide. (! in は「...の中に」, under は「...の下に」の意)

❷[いっぱいになる] be filled (*with*). ●若者で埋まった広場 a square *filled with* [*full of*, *crowded with*] young people. ▶席はもうみんな埋まっていた All the seats *had* already *been occupied* [*been taken*, *been filled*].

*うまれ 生まれ [出生, 家柄] birth; [家系] descent. ●アメリカ生まれの日本人 an American-*born* Japanese. ▶彼の生まれは日本だ He *was born* in Japan./He is Japanese *by birth*./He is of Japanese *birth*. ▶彼女はいいところの生まれだ She is well-*born*./She is (a woman) *of* good *birth* [*descent*]./She *comes from* a good [a noble] family./(育ちがよい) She is a woman of (good) *breeding*.

会話「生まれ(=出身)はどちらですか」「青森です」 "Where are you *from*?/Where do [xdid] you *come from*?" "I'm from Aomori." (! Where were you born? と相手に直接尋ねることは通例しない)

●生まれもつかぬ ▶自動車事故にあって彼は生まれもつかぬ姿になってしまった The car accident made him look quite different from what he used to be.

うまれあわせる 生まれ合わせる happen to be born. ▶私は第二次世界大戦が勃発した年に生まれ合わせた I *happened to be born* in the year when the World War II broke out.

うまれいづるなやみ『生れ出づる悩み』*The Agony of Coming into the World*. ([参考] 有島武郎の小説)

うまれおちる 生まれ落ちる ▶生まれ落ちてこのかた UFO を見たことがありません I have never seen a UFO since I *was born*.

うまれかわる 生まれ変わる (再び生まれる) be born again, 《書》 be reborn; (別人になる) be quite another person, a changed person (! 良い方または悪い方へ人がすっかり変わったときにいう); (生活を一新する) make* a fresh start in life; (やや話) turn over a new leaf. ▶生まれ変わったら科学者になりたい If I *were born again*, I would like to be a scientist.

うまれこきょう 生まれ故郷 [出生地] one's birthplace; [故郷] one's hometown. (⇒故郷) ●生まれ故郷の岐阜に帰る a return to one's *native* Gifu.

うまれそだつ 生まれ育つ ▶彼女は京都で生まれ育った She *was born and brought up* [*raised*, *grew up*, 《書》 *bred*, 《やや古》 *reared*] in Kyoto.

うまれつき 生まれつき by nature, naturally. (⇒生まれながら) ▶怒りっぽいのは生まれつきだ I am short-tempered *by nature*./I am *naturally* short-tempered. ▶彼は生まれつき目が見えない He is blind *from birth*./He *was born* blind. ▶彼は生まれつき音楽の才能があった He had a *natural* [an *innate*] talent for music./He had a *good ear* for music.

うまれながら 生まれながら by nature, naturally. (⇒生まれつき) ▶彼は生まれながらの詩人だ He is a *born* poet [a poet *by birth*]./He was born a poet.

‡**うまれる** 生まれる, 産まれる

WORD CHOICE 生まれる

be born 赤ん坊などが自然に生まれること. しばしば「on + 日付」「in + 場所・年号」が後に続く. 時に born and raised (生み育てられた) などの形でも用いる. ▶王族の一員として彼は生まれた He *was born* into the royal family.

be formed 主に基準・個性・関係性・組織・集団など抽象的なものが自然に生み出されること. ▶その集団は戦後に生まれた The group *was formed* after the war.

be produced 製品・作品・報告書・論文などが, かなりの努力・苦労の結果として生み出されること. ▶その作曲家によってすばらしい音楽が生み出された Wonderful music *was produced* by the composer.

頻度チャート

be born
be formed
be produced

20　　40　　60　　80　　100 (%)

❶[人・動物などが] be born. (! (1) この born は形容詞化していて by を伴わない. (2) bear の受身形は borne by ... は今はまれ) ●金持ち(の家)に生まれる *be born rich*; *be born into* [xin] a rich family; *be* born with a silver spoon in one's mouth. (参考) 金持ちの家に生まれた子供は銀のスプーンで育てられるから) ●最初の妻との間に生まれた赤ちゃん a newborn baby. ●最初の妻との間に生まれた子供 a child (he had) by his first wife. ●彼が生まれた土地 the land of his birth; the land where he was born. ▶私は1990年4月17日東京で生まれた I was born in Tokyo on April 17, 1990. ▶スミス夫妻に男の子が産まれた Mr. and Mrs. Smith had a son./A son was born to Mr. and Mrs. Smith. (やや改まった言い方) ●5月に彼女に子供が産まれます She is having [going to have] a baby in May. (確実な将来の予定を表すので ×She'll have.... とは通例いわない) /She's expecting (a baby [a child]) in May. (婉曲的な言い方。進行形で用いる。しばしば a baby [a child] は省略される) ●彼はイタリア人ピアニストを母として生まれた His mother was [is] an Italian pianist. (!was は母親が亡くなっているか、または今はもうピアノを弾いていないことを意味する)/(...から生まれた) He was born of [×from] an Italian pianist. (!後の文はだれの子かという改まったいい方) ●彼は詩人になるように生まれついていた He was born (to be) a poet. ×He was born as a poet. とはいわない (⇨生まれながら) ●彼は生まれたときから病弱だ He has been delicate from (his) birth [since he was born]. (!後の方が口語的) ●その赤ん坊は産まれたときは死んでいた The baby was dead at birth [when it was born]. (!後の方が口語的)/(死んで産まれた) The baby was born dead [was stillborn]. ●生まれて初めて東京タワーにのぼった I went up (the) Tokyo Tower for the first time in my life. ●私たちは生まれたときからずっとここに住んでいる We have lived here all our lives. ●子犬は生まれて数時間しかたっていない The puppies were a few hours old.

❷ [物事が] (生じる) come* into existence [being]; be born (of); (形成される) be formed; (設立される) be established, be founded; (産み出される) be produced; (問題などが起こる) 《やや書》 arise*. (⇨生じる) ▶戦後新しい国家が数多く生まれた A lot of new nations came into existence [were born] after the war. ▶彼らの間に親交が生まれた A close friendship was formed [was established, has developed] between them. ▶努力したが何の成果も生まれなかった My efforts produced [brought about] no results. ▶事故は不注意から生まれることがある Accidents can arise from carelessness. (!この場合の can は通例好ましくないことに用いる)(!「時に...することもある」の意)

■ DISCOURSE ■
確かに、生徒間に競争を持ち込むと多少のあつれきが生まれるかもしない。しかし私は、健全な競争は生徒間のやる気を高めると思う Competition between students may lead to some tension. However, I would say that healthy competition gives them heightened motivation. (!however (しかし) は逆接を表すディスコースマーカー)

:うみ 海
■ WORD CHOICE ■ 海
sea 海を表す最も一般的な語。●海から吹く強い風 a strong wind from the sea. ●海上の嵐 a storm at sea.
ocean 太平洋 (Pacific Ocean)・大西洋 (Atlantic Ocean) のように、特に広漠たる大海を表す。《米》では普通の sea の意でも用いる。●大海に沈む plunge [plummet] in the ocean.
waters 大海の中の一定の水域・領域を表す。●日本の領海 the Japanese (territorial) waters.

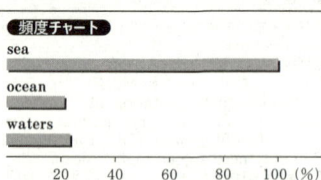

■ 頻度チャート ■
sea
ocean
waters
20 40 60 80 100 (%)

❶ [地理上の] the sea, 《主に米》 the ocean; (大洋) the ocean; (水域) waters; (ある状態の海・波) a (...) sea (!しばしば複数形で).
① [海(の)~] ●海の家 (海水浴用の) a seaside cottage. ●海の男 (船員) a seaman; a sailor. ●海の景色 a scene at sea; (絵や写真の) a seascape. ●海の幸 seafood; marine products. ●海の水 water from the sea; (海水) sea water. ●海のそばで育った He grew up [was raised] by the sea. (!前の方が自然) ▶静かな海の上をヨットがすべって行くのが見えた I saw yachts sailing on a calm sea.
② [海が[は]~] ▶私は沖縄あたりの暖かい海が好きだ I like the warm sea(s) around Okinawa. ▶飛行機から太平洋の青い海が見えた From the plane we saw the blue waters of the Pacific. ▶海は荒れていた [穏やかだった] The sea [ocean] was rough [calm, quiet, still]./There was a rough [a calm, a quiet, a still] sea.
③ [海を[に、へ、で]~] ●海を渡る cross the sea [ocean]. ●海に泳ぎに行く go swimming in [×to] the sea [ocean]. ●(海水浴・避暑・保養などで)海(=海辺)に行く go to the beach [the sea, 《英》 the seaside]. ●海に生きる make a living (by) working at sea. ▶彼は子供たちを海へ連れて行った He took the children to the beach [the sea, (海岸) the coast]. ▶地球の大部分は海におおわれている Most of the earth is covered by (the) sea. ▶サケは淡水で産まれつけられるが海で生息する A salmon spawns in fresh water, but it lives in the ocean. ▶彼はこのあたりの海で子供のころから漁をしていた He has been fishing these waters since he was a boy. ▶このあたりの海は魚がたくさんとれる We can catch a lot of fish(es) in these waters.

❷ [一面に広がったもの] a sea (of). ●血の海 a sea of blood, seas of blood; (血だまり) a pool of blood. ▶彼は赤ん坊を救うために火の海に飛び込んで行った He ran into the sea of flames to rescue the baby.

●海の藻くずとなる ▶津波がその町を襲い、多くの人々が海の藻くずとなって消えた(=海で多くの人命が失われた) A tsunami struck the town and a lot of lives were lost at sea. ▶2隻のフェリーが衝突事故を起こし2隻とも海の藻くずとなった(=海底に沈んだ) Two ferries crashed into each other and both sank to the bottom of the sea.
●海の物とも山の物ともつかない ▶彼はまだ海のものとも山のものともつかない We don't know yet how he's going to turn out.
●海亀 a sea turtle. ●海鳥 a sea bird. ●海の日 Marine Day. (⇨祝日 関連)

うみ 膿 pus /pʌs/. ●うみがたまる Pus forms [gathers] (in the wound). ●うみを持っている傷 a pus-filled wound. ●うみを出す (押して) press the pus out of the wound. ●歯ぐきからうみが出た I had a discharge of pus from the gum.
●膿を出す ▶政界のうみを出す(=害となるものを一掃する) stamp [root] out the evils in the political

うみうし 海牛 〔動物〕a nudibranch; a sea slug.
うみおとす 生み落とす have. (⇨生む❶)
うみすずめ 海雀 〔鳥〕an ancient auk; a murrelet.
うみせんやません 海千山千 ▶海千山千の人 (したたか者) an old fox.
うみだす 生み出す ▶これが好結果を生み出した This *produced* [(もたらした) *brought about*, ×*gave rise to*] good results. (❗*give rise to* は好ましくない結果を引き起こすときに用いる)
うみつける 生み付ける (鳥・昆虫が) lay ⟨eggs⟩; (魚・カエルが) spawn ⟨eggs⟩.
うみとどやく『海と毒薬』 *The Sea and Poison*. 〔参考〕遠藤周作の小説
うみなり 海鳴り the roar of the sea. ▶海鳴りがしている The sea *roars*.
うみねこ 海猫 〔鳥〕a black-tailed gull.
うみのおや 生みの親 one's natural [real, biological] parent; (創始者) the founder, the father ⟨of⟩.
• 生みの親より育ての親 We are more grateful to our foster parents than to our *natural parents*.
うみのくるしみ 産みの苦しみ the labor of childbirth; labor pains. (❗後の方は比喩的にも用いる)
うみびらき 海開き the beginning of a sea-bathing season.
うみべ 海辺 〔波打ち際〕a beach; 〔海のすぐ近くの砂地〕the seashore; 〔保養地としての海辺〕the seaside; 〔海岸〕a shore, a coast. (❗shore は海から見た海岸, coast は陸から見たもの) (⇨海岸, 浜辺)
▶海辺で遊ぶ play on the *beach*. • 海辺を歩く walk along the *seashore*].
うみべのカフカ『海辺のカフカ』 *Kafka on the Shore*. 〔参考〕村上春樹の小説
うみへび 海蛇 〔動物〕a sea snake.
うみぼうず 海坊主 〔海の怪物〕a round-headed sea monster; 〔アオウミガメ〕〔動物〕a green turtle.
うみほおずき 海酸漿 a whelk egg case.
うみわける 産み分ける ▶彼らは一姫二太郎と産み分けようとした They tried to have a daughter first and then a son as they hope.
‡うむ 生む, 産む ❶ 〔出産する〕(人・動物が) have* (❗最も一般的な語), give* birth to ..., 〈書〉bear* (❗生まれる); (分娩⟨ぶんべん⟩する) 〈書〉be delivered of ...; (動物が) breed*; (魚・カエルなどが) spawn; (卵を) lay*. ▶生みたての卵 a fresh [a new-*laid*] egg.
▶彼女は先月女の子を産んだ She had [*gave birth to*, 〈書〉*bore*, 〈書〉*was delivered of*] a (baby) girl last month. (❗日本語のように能動形で用いることは少ない (⇨[次例])) ▶私が洋子を産んだとき(=洋子が産まれたとき), 主人は仕事でニューヨークにいました When Yoko *was born*, my husband was in New York on business trip. ▶あなたの犬は何匹子を産みましたか How many puppies did your dog *have*? ▶ウサギはたくさん子供を産む Rabbits *breed* in large numbers. ▶うちのめんどりは毎日卵を産む Our hens *lay* eggs every day.
❷ 〔生ずる〕(産出する) prodúce; (引き起こす) cause; (主に悪いことを) give* rise to ...; (至る) lead* ⟨*to*⟩.
• 11 パーセントの利子を生む *yield* [*bear*] eleven percent interest. ▶彼は日本が生んだ最大の科学者である He is the greatest scientist that Japan *has* ever *had* [*produced*]. ▶不衛生は病気を生む Unhygienic conditions *cause* [*give rise to*, *lead to*] disease. ▶こういう行動は疑惑を生む Such conduct *gives rise to* [(呼び起こす)*arouses*] suspicion. ▶金が金を生む (ことわざ) Money begets money.

うむ 有無 ▶ご出席の有無を知らせてください Please let me know *whether* you will attend [be present] *or not*.
• 有無を言わせず 有無を言わせず(=力ずくで)彼を連れ出す take him out *by force*. • 有無を言わせず彼女にそれをやらせる *force* her *to* do [*into* doing] it. ▶彼の口調には有無を言わせぬところがあった There was *finality* in his tone.
• 有相(う)通じる ▶彼らには有無相通じるものがある They are complementary to each other./ They meet [satisfy] each other's needs.

うむ 倦む 〔飽きる〕get tired ⟨*of*⟩. • うまずたゆまず (倦まずたゆまず)
うむ 膿む fester. ▶脚の傷がうんだ The wound on my leg *has festered*./(膿(うみ)が生じた) *Pus has formed* in the wound on my leg.
ウムラウト 〔言語〕an umlaut.
うめ 梅 〔植物〕(木) an *ume* tree; a Japanese apricot tree; (実) an *ume* (❗単・複同形), a Japanese apricot; (花) *ume* blossoms.
うめあわせ 埋め合わせ • 損金の埋め合わせに in compensation for a loss. • 埋め合わせとして支払う pay as a compensation ⟨*for*⟩. (⇨埋め合わせる) ▶遅刻の埋め合わせにお昼をおごるよ I'll buy you lunch to *make up for* being late.
うめあわせる 埋め合わせる make* up, compensate ⟨*for*⟩ (⇨補う); (償いをする) make amends ⟨*for* + 事, *to* + 人⟩ (⇨償う).
うめきごえ 呻き声 ▶うめき声を出す give a groan [a moan]. (⇨うなる❷)
うめく 呻く moan; groan. (⇨うなる❷) • 苦痛でうめく *moan* [*groan*] with pain.
うめくさ 埋め草 (新聞・雑誌の) a filler.
うめこむ 埋め込む bury ⟨*in*⟩. (⇨埋める❶)
うめしゅ 梅酒 *ume* [plum] liqueur /líkə:r/.
うめず 梅酢 *ume* [plum] vinegar.
うめたて 埋め立て reclamation.
• 埋め立て工事 reclamation work. • 埋め立て地 reclaimed land; (ごみによる) (a) lándfill.
うめたてる 埋め立てる recláim; (湖・池などを) fill ... in. ▶空港建設のため湖の一部を埋め立てる *reclaim* part of the lake to build an airport. • 農地拡張のために海を埋め立てる *reclaim* farmland from the sea.
うめぼし 梅干し (an) *umeboshi*. (❗単・複同形) • 梅干しを漬ける make *umeboshi*.
*うめる 埋める ❶ 〔土の中に〕bury /béri/ ... ⟨*in*⟩. • 死んだ小鳥を庭に埋める *bury* a dead bird *in* the yard. • 地面にパイプを埋める(=敷設する) *lay* [*sink*] a pipe *in* the ground. ▶世界には 1 億 1,000 万個の地雷が埋められている, 1 日 70 人が死傷しているという One hundred ten million landmines are buried around the world, killing or wounding 70 people a day. (❗一般に認められている事実を語るときは it is said は不要)
❷ 〔空間・穴などを満たす〕fill ... (in). • 通りを埋める *fill* [(群れをなして)*throng*] a street. • 穴をアスファルトで埋める *fill* in a hole *with* asphalt. ▶空所を(適語で)埋めよ *Fill in* the blanks (*with* proper words).
❸ 〔補う〕fill; (埋め合わせる) make*... up. • 欠員[ギャップ]を埋める *fill* a vacancy [a gap]. • 赤字を埋める *make up* (*for*) a deficit.
❹ 〔水を入れてぬるくする〕▶ふろが熱かったのでうめた The bath was too hot, so I *added* some *cold water* to it.
うもう 羽毛 a feather; 《集合的》plumage; (鳥の綿

うもれぎ 埋れ木 bogwood, bog oak.
- 埋もれ木に花が咲く Good luck has come to a person who was unsuccessful [unfortunate] for a long time. ▶彼女も新作でついに芥川賞を取り、埋れ木に花を咲かせた She finally won the Akutagawa Prize for her new novel, which made her *rise from obscurity to center stage*.
- 埋れ木細工 bogwood work.

うもれる 埋もれる ❶〖埋まる〗be buried /bérid/ 《under, in》. ▶手紙は書類の下に埋もれていた The letter *was buried under* [*was hidden under*] papers.
❷〖知られないでいる〗埋もれた人材を見つける（隠れた）find [unearth] *hidden* talent;（新しい）discover *new* talent. (!) talent は「才能のある人々」の意) ▶彼の作品は長年世に埋もれていた His works *remained unrecognized* [*unknown to the public*] for many years.

うやうやしい 恭しい〖敬意を表する〗respectful;〖礼儀正しい〗polite.（⇨丁寧な）

うやまう 敬う 〖尊敬する〗respect;（敬意を払う）honor;〖崇拝する〗worship（-pp-）.（⇨尊敬する）●神を敬う *worship* God. ▶年上の人を敬いなさい You should *respect* [*show respect for*] your elders.

うやむや 有耶無耶 ── **うやむやな** 形 ●うやむやな（=気乗りしない）返事をする give a *halfhearted*〖明確でない〗an *indefinite*,〖vague〗answer.
── **うやむやに** 副 ●その問題をうやむや（=未解決）にしておく leave the matter *unsettled*〖未決定〗*undecided*. ●スキャンダルをうやむやに葬り去る（=もみ消す）*hush up* the scandal.

うゆう 烏有 ●烏有に帰する〖火事で何もかも失う〗be burned to ashes; be burned down; be completely destroyed by fire.

うようよ 副 ▶アリが砂糖にうようよたかっていた The sugar *was swarming with* ants.
── **うようよする** 動 ▶池にはぼうふらがうようよしている Mosquito larvas *are wriggling* in the pond./The pond *is alive with* mosquito larvas.（⇨群がる）

うよきょくせつ 紆余曲折 ▶彼の人生は紆余曲折を経て今日に至った There have been a lot of *twists and turns* in his life.

うよく 右翼 ❶〖政治上の〗（派）the right（wing）(!) 集合的、単・複両扱い),（人）a rightist, a right winger (!) 以上は、しばしば R-（W-）; R- と書く) ●右翼的な思想 right-wing [rightist] ideas.
❷〖野球〗right field.（⇨ライト）
❸〖飛行機・隊列などの〗the right wing.
●右翼手〖野球〗a right fielder. ●右翼団体 a right-wing [a rightist] organization〖この rightist は形容詞（⇨右派）. ●右翼分子 right-wing elements.

うら 裏 ❶〖裏側〗(背後）the back;（反対側の）the reverse（side）, the other-side;（意図したのと逆の側）the wrong side（⇨裏返し）;（内側）the inside;（裏張り）(a) lining.（⇨表 ❶） ●紙の裏に書く write on the *back* of paper. ●レコードの裏をかける play the *reverse* [*other*] *side* of a record. ●足の裏の sole. ▶私のコートは毛皮の裏がついている My coat *is*（fully）*lined with* fur./My coat has a fur *lining*. (!)「総」「半]両面のコート」は a fully-[half-]lined coat)
❷〖後ろ〗the back,《やぎ書》the rear. ●裏の小川 a stream *out back*. (!) out は「(家から)離れて」の意で back を修飾する副詞) ▶劇場の裏に駐車場がある There is a parking lot *at the back of* [《米》*in back of, behind, at the rear of*] the theater.
❸〖隠されて見えない面〗▶彼の言葉の裏を読み取る read the *hidden* meaning of his words;（心を読み取る）read his mind. ▶この事件には裏があるに違いない There must be something *behind* this matter. ▶物事には裏と表がある There are *two sides* to everything. ▶彼は裏で何が行われているのか知らない He doesn't know what is going on *behind the scenes*.
❹〖野球〗the bottom（↔ the top）. ● 7 回裏の the *bottom（half）* [the *second half*] of the seventh inning.
●裏を返せば ▶彼は慎重だと言われるが裏を返せば（=実は）臆病（病）なのだ He is said to be prudent, but *the truth is that* [*in reality*,] he is cowardly.
●裏をかく ●打者の裏をかく fool a batter. ●強盗は警察の裏をかいて逃げた The burglar *outwitted* [《くや話》*outsmarted*] the police and escaped.
●裏を取る ▶我々は彼が被告人の陳述の裏を取る（=裏付ける）ために新しい証拠を入手した We got new evidence to *corroborate* the defendant's story.

うら 浦（湾）a bay;（入江）an inlet,《英》a creek;（海岸）a beach.

うらうち 裏打ち 名〖衣服の〗lining;〖衣服・絵などの〗backing.
── **裏打ちする** 動 ●レースの襟を薄手の綿布で裏打ちする *line* a lace collar *with* thin cotton. ▶彼の自信は長年の経験に裏打ちされている（=裏付けられている）His confidence *is backed up with* [*comes from*] his long experience.

うらおもて 裏表〖両側〗both sides. ●肉の裏表を中火で焼く roast meat on *both sides* over medium heat. ●(人が)裏表がある have *two faces*; be *two-faced*. ●裏表のない（= 正直な）人 an honest person. ●裏表のある人 a *two-faced* person, a double-dealer. ▶彼はこの業界の裏表に通じている He knows *the ins and outs* of this trade./He has a thorough knowledge of the *nooks and crannies* of this trade.

うらかいどう 裏街道〖裏通り〗a back street;〖まともでない生き方〗the seamy side of life;〖日の当たらない人生〗the dark [shady] side of life.

うらがえし 裏返し ▶シャツが裏返しだよ Your shirt is *inside* [*wrong side*] *out*./You're wearing a shirt *inside* [*wrong side*] *out*.

うらがえす 裏返す〖上面を下へ〗turn ... over;（表側を裏へ）lay* [put*]（a picture）face down(ward);（内側を外へ）turn ... inside out. ▶ワイシャツを裏返す turn a shirt *inside out*. ▶原版をガラス板の上に裏返して置く（コピーするとき）place the original *face down* on the glass.

うらがえる 裏返る ❶〖裏が表になる〗▶声が裏返る go falsetto. ▶風でシャツが裏返ってしまった The shirt *was turned inside out* in the wind.
❷〖裏切る〗betray.

うらがき 裏書き 名 (an) endorsement.
── **裏書きする** 動 ●小切手に裏書きする *endorse* a check. ●その陳述を裏書きする証拠 evidence to *prove* the statement.（⇨裏付け）
●裏書手形 an endosed bill [note]. ●裏書人 an endorser.

うらかた 裏方〖劇場の舞台係〗a stagehand (!) 集合的にはa stage crew);（芝居の道具方）a scene-shifter;〖陰の功労者〗a person who remains behind the scenes.

うらがなしい うら悲しい ▶どういうわけかうら悲しい Somehow I *feel sad* [*sorrowful*].

うらがね 裏金 ●裏金を使う[受け取る] offer [accept] a bribe. (⇨賄賂)

うらがわ 裏側 the back; the reverse (side). (⇨裏)

うらぎり 裏切り (a) betrayal, (a) treachery. (■いずれも具体的な行為は[C]) ●彼の裏切り行為 his act of betrayal [treachery].
●裏切り者 (密告者) a betrayer; (反逆者) a traitor.

***うらぎる 裏切る** ❶[人などを] betráy, (やや話) go* back on...; (恋人・配偶者を)[話] cheat ((on)). ●彼の信頼を裏切る betray his trust. ▶友達を裏切るような男は信頼できない We cannot trust a man who betrays [goes back on] his friends.
❷[予想・期待を] disappoint ((him, his expectations)). ●その映画は私たちの期待を裏切った The movie disappointed us [our expectations]. (⇨期待) ●惨敗の予想を裏切り(て=にもかかわらず)、彼はゆうゆう当選を果たした In spite of [《書》Despite] the dire predictions, he easily won the election.

うらぐち 裏口 a back door. ●裏口へ回る go around to the back door. ●裏口から入る enter at [by, through] the back door. ●裏口からこっそり出る sneak out (of [through]) the back door. ▶学生の中には裏口入学する者もいた Some students bought their way [×ways] into school [college].

うらげい 裏芸 (⇨隠し芸)

うらこうさく 裏工作 — 裏工作(を)する 動 (裏で策略をめぐらす) (やや話) maneuver behind the scenes; (陰で糸を引く)[話] pull the strings [wires].

うらごえ 裏声 (a) falsetto /fɔːlsétou/. ●裏声で歌う sing (in) falsetto. ■「澄んだ裏声で」なら in a clear falsetto.

うらごし 裏漉し [名] straining; (道具) a strainer.
— 裏漉しする 動 ●ジャガイモを裏漉しする strain boiled potatoes.

うらさく 裏作 a secondary crop.

うらさみしい うら寂しい lonely. (⇨寂しい)

うらじ 裏地 (a) lining. (⇨裏 ❶)

ウラジオストック [ロシアの都市] Vladivostok /vlædəvástɑk/.

うらしまたろう 浦島太郎 *The Story of Urashima Taro, The Fisher Lad*. (参考) 日本の昔話.

うらじろ 裏白 [裏が白い紙] blank reverse-sided paper;[植物] a fern with white-backed leaves.

うらづけ 裏付け (⇨裏付ける) ●事実の裏付けのない議論 an argument not based on [supported by] facts. ▶私にはその申し立ての裏付けがある(=証明する)十分な証拠がある I have enough evidence to prove that statement.

うらづける 裏付ける back (... up) (with, by); (支持する) support; (補強する)《書》corroborate; (証明する) prove*. ●彼の理論を裏付ける資料 the data to back up [support] his theory.

うらて 裏手 ●私たちの学校の裏手にある丘 a hill at the back of our school. (⇨裏 ❶)

うらどおり 裏通り a back street. (■「本通り」は the main street); (路地) a back alley. (⇨道 ❶)

うらない 占い [行為] fórtunetèlling; [人] (占い師) a fortuneteller; (手相見) a palmist. ●星占いをする tell fortunes with cards. ●占いに行って相談する consult [see] a fortuneteller.

***うらなう 占う** [運勢を] tell* ((his)) fortune. ●易者に結婚を占ってもらう have a fortuneteller tell about one's marriage; (相談する) consult a fortuneteller about one's marriage.

うらなり 末生り ❶[つるの先になること] (a cucumber) grown near the top end of the vine. ❷[青白い顔をした人] a pale-faced person, a person with a pale, sickly complexion.

ウラニウム [化学] uranium /juəréiniəm/. (通 ウラン).

うらにわ 裏庭 a backyard. (■《米》では単に yard ともいう. 芝生が植えてあることが多い. 《英》では舗装してある狭い空間をさすことが多いが, 普通の広い庭をさすこともある) ●裏庭で遊ぶ play in the backyard.

うらばなし 裏話 an inside story.

うらはら 裏腹 ▶彼女は言うこととすることが裏腹だ(=正反対だ) Her actions are contrary to [(一致しない) inconsistent with] her words. (⇨言行)

うらばん 裏番 a behind-the-scenes leader (of a school gang).

うらばんぐみ 裏番組 a (competing) program broadcast on the same hour on a different channel.

うらびょうし 裏表紙 a back cover.

うらぶれた (みすぼらしくなってきた) shabby, seedy. ●うらぶれた身なりの老人 a shabbily dressed old man [woman]. ●うらぶれた劇場 a seedy [a shabby, 荒れるにまかせた] a run-down] theater.

うらぼん(え) 盂蘭盆(会) the Bon Festival. (⇨盆)

うらまち 裏町 a backstreet area [district].

うらみ 恨み a grudge; [深い恨み]《書》a rancor; [悪感情] bad [ill] feeling; [憎悪] hatred /héitrid/; [敵意]《書》enmity. ●彼に恨みを抱く have [hold, bear] a grudge against him; bear him a grudge. ●父の恨みを晴らす(=仇(かたき)を討つ) revenge [avenge] one's father. ■前の方は自分の恨み, 後の方は他人の恨みの場合に用いる) ●恨み言を言う(不平を言う) complain ((to him of it)); (非難する) blame ((him for it)). ●恨み重なる(=不倶戴天(ふぐたいてん)の)敵 one's mortal [sworn] enemy. ▶彼の不注意な発言が彼女の恨みを買った His careless remarks incurred him her ill feeling [her hatred].

うらみがましい 恨みがましい reproachful. (⇨恨めしい)

うらみち 裏道 [裏通り] a back street [alley]. (⇨裏通り)

うらみっこ 恨みっこ ●恨みっこなし ▶どういう結果になっても恨みっこなし(=お互いに相手を責めないこと)だぜ, いいかい We won't blame each other no matter what happens, right? ▶さあこれで恨みっこなしだ Let's call it quits. ■ quits は「対等の」の意の形容詞. ただし名詞の前には用いない)

うらみつらみ 恨みつらみ (a large number of) grudges.

***うらむ 恨む** [恨みを持つ] have* [hold*, bear*] a grudge ((against)); [責める] blame; [のろう] curse. ●天を恨む curse heaven. ▶なぜか分からないが彼は私を恨んでいる He has a grudge against [《話》has it in for] me, though I don't know why. ▶人を恨むな Don't blame others [other people]. ●彼は並外れた芸術的才能の持ち主であった. 恨むらくは健康に恵まれていなかった He was an exceptionally talented artist, but to our regret, he wasn't in good health.

うらめ 裏目 ●裏目に出る ▶彼の善意が裏目に出て相手の激しいうらみを買うはめになった His goodwill backfired (on him) [worked against him] and it incurred him their intense hatred.

うらめしい 恨めしい ●恨めしそうな(=非難するような)目つきで私を見る give me a reproachful look; look at me reproachfully. ●恨めしそうな(=残念そうな)表情 a regretful expression. ▶若いころ一生懸命勉強しなかったことが恨めしい(=残念だ) I regret [am sorry] that I didn't study hard when I was young.

うらやま 裏山 a hill [a mountain] at the back of [behind] a house.

うらやましい 羨ましい 〖うらやましがる〗 énvious; 〖人をうらやましがらせるような〗 enviable. ● うらやましいほど美しい女性 an *enviably* beautiful woman. ● うらやましそうな顔をするlook *envious*. ● うらやましそうに彼女を見る look *enviously* at her; look at her *with envy* [*envious eyes*]; give her an *envious* look. ▶ 君の幸運がうらやましい I *am envious of* [*envy you*], *envy you for*] your good fortune./Your good fortune makes me *envious* [*is enviable to me*]. ▶ 彼は私の今度の仕事をうらやましがった He was *envious of* my new job.
〖会話〗「新婚旅行はどちらへ」「ヨーロッパに3週間よ」「うらやましい」"Where are you going on your honeymoon?" "To Europe, and for three weeks." "You're so *lucky./Lucky* you." (↓ How I *envy* you!/I *feel* [*am*] so *envious of* you. より「悔いしいなあ」という不満を込めた場合によく用いられる)

うらやむ 羨む envy, be envious 《of》. ● 人がうらやむような(=人をうらやましがらせるような)女性 an *enviable* woman. ▶ 彼は私の成功をうらやんだ He *envied* 《me》 [*envied me for*] my success./He was *envious of* my success.

うららか うららかな春の日 a *mild* [a *beautiful*, a *balmy*] spring day.

うらわかい うら若い 《quite [very]》 young. (⇨若い)

ウラン 〖化学〗 uranium [juəréiniəm/ 〖元素記号 U〗. ● 天然［濃縮］ウラン natural [*enriched*] *uranium*. ● ウラン鉱 *uranium* ore.

うらんかな 売らんかな ● 売らんかな主義 commercialism.

ウランバートル 〖モンゴルの首都〗 Ulan Bator /úːlɑːn báːtɔːr/.

うり 売り ● 売りに出す put 《a house》 up for sale; put 《a house》 on the market. ▶ 彼らの家は売りに出ている Their house is 《up》 *for sale*.

うり 瓜 〖植物〗(マクワウリ) a melon.
● 瓜のつるに茄子(なすび)はならぬ We cannot expect a brilliant child from ordinary parents./〖ことわざ〗 Like father [mother, parent], like son [daughter, child].
● 瓜二つ ▶ あの兄弟は瓜二つ Those brothers are *exactly* [*very much*] *alike*./〖話〗 Those brothers are *as like as two peas* 《*in a pod*》 [*are like two peas in a pod*]. ▶ 彼は兄に瓜二つ He's a *carbon copy* [the *double*, the *very image*] of his brother.

うりあげ 売り上げ (売上高) sales, takings, a turnover; (売上金) prōceeds. ● 総売上高 gross *sales*. ● 年間売上高 annual *sales*. ● バザーの売り上げ the *proceeds* from a bazaar. ● 売り上げの増加[減少] a rise [a fall] in *sales*. ● 売り上げを伸ばす increase [boost] *sales*. ● 売り上げ目標に達する[達しない] meet [miss] one's sales target. ▶ 今月はテレビの売り上げが3パーセント増えた[減った] *Sales* of televisions are up [down] three percent this month.
● 売上税 sales tax. ● 売上帳 a sales book. ● 売上伝票 a sales slip [voucher]. ● 売上元帳 a sales ledger.

うりあげる 売り上げる 〖売り切る〗 sell out; 〖売る〗 sell.

うりあるく 売り歩く (行商する) peddle, vend; (売り声を上げて) hawk.

うりおしむ 売り惜しむ be not willing to sell; hold* [keep*] back one's goods.

うりかい 売り買い buying and selling, trade. (⇨売買, 商い)

うりかけ 売り掛け 图 credit, trust, 《英》tick.
—— 売り掛けする 動 grant 《him》 credit.
● 売掛勘定 an account, 《米》 a charge account, 《英》 a credit account, a tick. ● 売掛金 account(s) receivable, trade receivable. ● 売掛販売 a credit sale.

うりきる 売り切る sell out 《of the goods》.

うりきれる 売り切れる be sold out; (在庫がない) be out of stock. ▶ そのサイズの靴は売り切れました The shoes in that size *are sold out* [*are out of stock*]./We *are sold out of* the shoes in that size./We *don't have* the shoes in that size any more. ▶ 本日は売り切れ 〖掲示〗 *Sold out* today. ▶ 座席は売り切れました(=全部予約されました) The seats *were all reserved*./〖掲示〗 *All seats reserved*.

うりぐい 売り食い —— 売り食いする 動 live by selling one's property [belongings].

うりこ 売り子 〖店の〗《米》 a salesclerk, 《英》 a shop assistant; (女店員) a salesgirl, a saleswoman (働 -women); 〖駅などの〗(売り歩く人) a vendor.

うりごえ 売り声 a hawker's [a peddler's, a seller's] cry.

うりことば 売り言葉 ● 売り言葉に買い言葉 (しっぺ返し) the verbal exchange of tit for tat (↓もとは tit も tat も叫ぶ)こと. 不愉快な言葉のやりとりの意; 〖話〗 《give》 tit for tat verbally. ● 彼に売り言葉に買い言葉で応酬する give him *tit for tat*; return *tit for tat* to him.

うりこみ 売り込み ▶ 新しいCDの売り込みをする conduct a *sales campaign* for a new CD; push [promote] a new CD. (⇨売り込む)
● 売り込み合戦 a sales battle.

うりこむ 売り込む ❶ 〖広く販売する〗 sell*; (積極的に) push; (宣伝販売を促進する) promote; (販路を見つける) find* a market [an outlet] 《*for*》. ● 新車を彼らに売り込む sell 《them》 a car to them. ● ビールをテレビで宣伝して売り込む *promote* the beer on television. ▶ 彼は商品を売り込むのがとてもうまい He shows great skill in *selling* goods. ▶ ようやくこの新製品を中国に売り込んだ We managed to *find a market for* these new products in China.
❷ 〖名前や信用を広める〗 become* popular; (マスコミなどで知名度を得る) get* 《〖やや書〗 gain》 publicity. ▶ 彼は自分を売り込もうと努力した He tried to *get* [*gain*] *publicity*. (自己宣伝をした) He tried to *advertise* [〖話〗 *sell*] *himself*.
❸ 〖アイデアなどを納得させる〗〖話〗 sell*. ● 彼は上司に自分の新しいアイデアを売り込んだ He *sold* his new idea to the boss./He *sold* the boss his new idea.

うりざねがお 瓜実顔 an oval fair-skinned face.

うりさばく 売り捌く ● 古いビデオテープを売りさばく(=安く売り払う) *sell off* old video tapes (at bargain prices).

うりだし 売り出し (⇨大売り出し)

うりだす 売り出す ❶ 〖品物を〗 put* 〖やや書〗 place] ... on the market, market; put ... up for sale; (新製品などを) bring* ... out. ● 家を売り出す put one's house *on the market*; put one's house *up for sale*. ▶ 券は本日売り出します Tickets *are on sale* today. ▶ 当社はウラヌスの新型車をこの3月に売り出します We will *bring out* a new model of Uranus this March.

うりつける ❷[名を](世の中に広く知らせる) win* a reputation; (マスコミなどで知名度を得る) get* [《やや書》gain] publicity; (人気が出る) become* popular. ▶彼女は今народ手として売り出している She *is* now *gaining popularity* as a singer./(人気が出た) She *has become popular* as a singer. ▶その小説で彼は売り出した The novel *won* him *a reputation*./He *got* [*gained*] *publicity* by the novel.

うりつける 売り付ける ●客にせダイヤを売り付ける(買わせる) *get* a customer *to buy* a fake diamond; (くどいて買わせる) *talk* a customer *into buying* a fake diamond; (押しつける)《やや書》*impose* a fake diamond *on* a customer; (だまして) *fob* [《話》*palm*] *off* a fake diamond *on* a customer.

うりて 売り手 a seller (↔a buyer).
● 売り手市場 a the [the] sellers' market.

うりとばす 売り飛ばす (安く売る) sell*... off. (❗ very cheaply,《話》for a song,《話》dirt-cheap (いずれも「ただ同然の値段で」の意)などを加えて「飛ばす」の感じを出すこともできる) ●自転車をリサイクルショップに売り飛ばす *sell* one's bicycle *very cheaply* to a secondhand shop.

うりにげ 売り逃げ ─ 売り逃げする 動 (株などを) run and sell 〘one's stocks〙.

うりぬし 売り主 a seller; (土地・家屋の)【法律】a vendor.

うりね 売り値 a sále [a sélling] príce; 〖小売り値〗a retail price.

うりば 売り場 (カウンター) a counter; (百貨店などの) a shop, a department (❗ 前の方が小さくて専門的). ● おもちゃ売り場 a toy shop [*department*]. ● スーパーの野菜売り場(=部門) the vegetable [(農産物) *produce*] *section* of a supermarket. ● 切符売り場(=窓口) a girl behind the *counter*. ● 化粧品売り場で働く work at a cosmetics sales *counter*.

うりはらう 売り払う ●古い家を売り払う(=処分する) *dispose of* [(安く売る) *sell off*] one's old house.

うりもの 売り物 an article for [on] sale; 〖掲示〗FOR [ON] SALE. (❗いずれも for は通例個人の場合, on は店の場合に用いる) ●売り物の車 a car *for* [*on*] *sale*. ●売り物に出す put (it) up [offer (it)] *for sale*. ●売り物になる[ならない] be *salable* /séiləbl/ [*unsalable*]; be fit [unfit] *for sale*. ▶ 彼女は美貌を売り物にしている She makes her beauty her *selling* [×*sales*] *point*./(軽蔑的) She trades on her beauty. ▶ あの店はスープが売り物(=自慢料理)だ That restaurant's *specialty* [《米話》*special*] is soup./Soup is the *specialty* of that restaurant. ▶ 私小説の作者は, 自分で自分の生活を演技して, それを売り物にするのだ Those writers of the "I" novels are making a play out of their own life (experiences), and offering it as merchandise. (❗実際にその場で演技する場合は act out と表せるが, ここでは「演技しそれを文に書いている」ので make a play とする)

うりもんく 売り文句 sales talk.

うりや 売り家 a house for sale.

うりょう 雨量 〖降雨量〗(a) rainfall; 〖降雨〗rain.
● 年間 60 インチの雨量 an annual *rainfall* [*precipitation*] of 60 inches. ●この地方は雨量が多い There is a lot of *rainfall* in this district. ▶ 昨夜の雨量は 20 ミリだった The *rainfall* last night was twenty millimeters./We had twenty millimeters of *rain* last night.
● 雨量計 a rain gauge /géidʒ/.

うりわたす 売り渡す ●自分の家を彼に 5,000 万円で売り渡す *sell* one's house *to* him for fifty million yen.

うる 売る ● [品物などを] sell*.

〖解説〗sell は「売る」という活動に重点のある語。品物を「取り扱う (buy and sell)」という意では **deal in**, 《話》**handle** が用いられる。この sell は習慣的販売行為を表し, 進行形は不可 この店はワインを売っている This store *deals in* [《米》*trades in*, 《話》*handle*] imported wines. また「置いている」という意で日常語として **have** もよく用いられる: アメリカ製のゴルフクラブを売っていますか Do you *have* American golf clubs?

▶ あの古い型はまだ売っていますか Is the old model still *on sale* [(市場に出て) *on the market*]?

❶【...を売る】 ▶当店では卵を売っています We *sell* eggs at this store./This store *sells* eggs. (❗人を主語とする前の文のほうが普通。この sell は習慣的販売行為を表し, 進行形は不可) ▶ 自分を安く売るな Don't *sell* yourself short. (❗sell ... short は「人を低く評価する」の意)

❷【A に B を売る】 sell* A (人)·B (物); sell B (物) +to A (人). ▶彼はトムにその中古車を売った He *sold* Tom the used car./He *sold* the used car *to* Tom. (❗前の方は「何を売ったか」を, 後の方は「だれに売ったか」を問題にする言い方 (❗❗ 《会話》))
《会話》「彼はだれに自分の自転車を売りましたか」「正夫に売りました」"Who did he *sell* his bike *to*?" "He *sold* it *to* Masao." × He sold Masao it. とはいわない (⇒与える)

❸【(場所)で売る】 ▶ 米はスーパーで売っている Rice *is sold at* a supermarket. ▶ あのコンサートのチケットはどこで売っています(=手にはいる)か Where can I *get* a ticket for the concert?

❹【(価格)で売る】 (❗一般に金額には for, 単価や price のような語には at を用いる) ▶ 家を 3,000 万円で売る *sell* a house *for* 30 million yen. ▶ 彼らはジャガイモを安い[高い]値段で売った They *sold* potatoes *at* a low [a high] price./They *sold* potatoes cheap [dear]. (❗cheaply, dearly とはあまりいわない) ▶ 小麦は 1 キロいくらで売られています Wheat *is sold* by the kilogram. ▶ よし, 当店, 3 万円でいいよ Okay! It's *yours, for* 30,000 yen.

❷[裏切る] betray. ▶ 彼は祖国を売った He *betrayed* his country./《話》He *sold* his country *down the river*.

うるうどし 閏年 (a) leap (↔common) year. ▶ 閏年は 4 年ごとにめぐってくる A *leap year* comes around [*occurs*] every four years./There is a *leap year* every four years.

うるおい 潤い 〖適度な湿り気〗moisture. ●潤いのある肌 *moist* skin. ●潤いのある声 (have) a *charming* [a *sweet*] voice. ●潤いのある[ない]生活 (lead) a *full* [a *dull*] life. ●生活に潤いを与える(=を豊かにする) *enrich* one's life.

うるおう 潤う ●【湿る】(適度に) be moistened; (ぬれる) get wet.
❷[恵みや利益を受ける] benefit from [by]... (❗ from の方が普通); become* prosperous. ▶ 町は新しい工場によって潤うだろう The town will *benefit from* [*become prosperous* because of] the new factory./The new factory will *benefit* the town [*make* the town *prosperous*].

うるおす 潤す ❶[湿らせる] (適度に軽く) moisten /mɔ́isn/; (湿らす) wet*. ●のどを潤す *satisfy* [《やや書》*quench*] one's thirst (*with*).
❷[恵みや利益を与える] bénefit; make* (it) prosperous. (⇒潤う ❷)

ウルグアイ 〖国名〗Uruguay /jʊ́ərəgwaɪ/; (公式名) the

うるさい

Oriental Republic of Uruguay. (首都 Montevideo) ●ウルグアイ人 a Uruguayan. ●ウルグアイの Uruguayan.

うるさい 形　〖騒々しい〗noisy;〖迷惑な〗annoying;〖面倒な〗troublesome;〖しつこい〗persistent;〖口やかましい〗nagging. (⇨やかましい, 悩む) ●うるさい音 an annoying〖(音量の大きい) a loud〗noise. ▶あの子はうるさい子 noisy chirping [chirring] of crickets. 〖参考〗英米では虫の鳴き声を騒音ともとる ●うるさいセールスマン a persistent salesman [saleswoman,《主に米》salesperson]. ●うるさい(=執拗じつような)要求 an insistent demand. ●うるさい(=迷惑な)こと[物,人] a nuisance /n(j)úːsəns/; an annoyance. ▶あの子はうるさいやつだ He's a very noisy child. ●もう,うるさいわね Oh, you're a nuisance!/(じゃまをして困らせないでくれ) Stop bothering [annoying] me./(放っておいてくれ) Leave me alone./(がたがた口出しするな)《話》Just get off my back./(がみがみ言うな) Stop nagging《at me》./(黙れ) Stop talking./《話》Just shut up. ●うるさい言い方/(静かに) Be quiet./(騒ぐな) Don't be noisy [make a noise]. (❗ 単に×Noisy! とはいわない)/(大げさに騒ぎ立てるな) Don't make a fuss [be fussy]. ▶ハエはうるさい Flies annoy [bother] me./Flies are annoying [bothersome]./Flies are a nuisance. (❗ 主語が複数では ×nuisances とはしない) ▶あの守衛はふだんはうるさいことを言わずに通してくれた Usually, the doorkeeper let us enter without (much) fuss [difficulty]. ▶彼女は着る物にうるさい(=気難しい) She is particular [《軽蔑的に》fussy /fʌ́si/] about her clothes. ●世間の口はうるさい《ことわざ》People will talk. (❗ will は習性を表す)

— うるさく　副　〖しつこく〗persistently;〖騒々しく〗noisily. ●チョコレートをくれと母親にうるさくせがむ bother [nag,《話》pester] one's mother for some chocolate. (❗ この順に度合いが強くなる) ▶通りの騒音がうるさくて眠れない There is so much noise from the street that I can't sleep./The street is so noisy that I can't sleep. ●あんなにうるさくては何事にも没頭(=集中)できない I can't concentrate on [apply my mind to] anything with all that noise. ▶彼女は私にいっしょに来いとうるさく言ってきかなかった(=強く要求した) She insisted on my [《話》me] coming with her./She insisted that I (should) come with her. (❗ should を用いるのは《主に英》)

うるさがた　うるさ型　《話》a fussy [a picky] person. ▶妹はほんとうにうるさ型でいやになる My sister is really fussy [picky] and I'm fed up with her.

うるさがる　●くだらない質問をしてうるさがられる(him) with stupid questions. ●あの先生は生徒の質問をうるさがる That teacher finds his students' questions annoying [《いずわしい》troublesome]. ▶彼女は車内で大声で話しているうるさがられた(=やっかいだと見なされ) She was regarded as a nuisance [《迷惑をかけた》 She made a nuisance of herself] by talking loudly in the train.

うるし　漆 〖植物〗lacquer /lǽkər/; japan (❗ 日本産のうるしをいう). ●うるしの木 a Japanese sumac(h) /súːmæk/; a lacquer tree. ●うるしでかぶれる be poisoned by lacquer. ●うるしを塗る lacquer. ●うるし細工 lacquer ware.

うるち　粳　non-glutinous rice.

ウルトラ　ultra /ʌ́ltrə/. ●ウルトラ C の技に挑戦する try to perform an ultra-difficult [an extremely difficult] feat.

ウルトラマリン〖群青〗ultramarine /ʌ̀ltrəmərɪ́ːn/.

うるむ　潤む　▶彼女の目は涙で潤んでいる Her eyes are

うれしい

wet [moist, misty] with tears.

うるわしい　麗しい　❶〖美しい〗(elegant and) beautiful. ●うるわしい声で in a beautiful voice.
❷〖晴れやかな〗▶夫人はけさはことのほか機嫌がうるわしい The madam looks to be in her best mood this morning.
❸〖心が暖まる〗heart-warming. ●うるわしい友情 a warm friendship.

うれあし　売れ足　demand. (⇨売れ行き)

うれい　憂い, 愁い　〖懸念〗anxiety;〖恐れ〗fear;〖心配〗worry;〖悲しみ〗sorrow;(深い) grief. ●…の憂いがある there is some fear of ….

うれえる　憂える　(心配する) be anxious [concerned]《about》; worry《about》. ●憂えるべき(=嘆かわしい) 行為 deplorable conduct.

うれくち　売れ口　a market. ●売れ口がない cannot find a market《for》; there is no market《for》.

:うれしい　嬉しい

▌WORD CHOICE▐　うれしい

happy 喜び・うれしさ・楽しさ・幸福などの気持ちを幅広く表す. 意味を強調する場合は very, so, perfectly などの副詞をつける. ●心うれしい日々 happy days. ●この仕事が出来て嬉しい I'm happy about this job.
glad 特定の原因により強い喜びを感じることを表す. しばしば happy より強い含意を持つ. ●再びここに戻れてうれしい I'm glad to come back here again.
joyful 物が人を喜ばせること, 人が何かに喜ぶことの両方を表す. 強い歓喜というより心情の快さ・気持ちよさを含意する. ●うれしい心持ちになる have a joyful heart.

▌頻度チャート▐

happy ████████████████████████
glad ████████████
joyful ██
　　　　20　　40　　60　　80　　100 (%)

glad (-dd-)《at, about, of; to do; that 節》; happy (❗ glad の方が強意的);(ややオーバーに) thrilled (⇨喜ぶ);(有頂天になるように)《書》joyful. (⇨〖類語〗)

①《うれしい〜》●今日は生涯でいちばんうれしい日だ This is the happiest day in my life. ●今日はうれしい知らせを聞きました I heard (x a) joyful [《よい》good] news today. ●こんなうれしいことはありません Nothing would give me greater pleasure [joy] than this./I couldn't be happier. (❗ than this は通例省略される) ●大変うれしいことに母の病気が治った To my delight [great joy], my mother has recovered from her illness. (❗ To my joy, … は《不自然》)/I'm very glad to say my mother has recovered from her illness. ●花はいつもらってもうれしいものだ Flowers are always (most) acceptable. ●それはうれしい息抜きだ That's a welcome relief. ●結婚後 7 年で双子が授かり, 以来うれしい悲鳴をあげる毎日です(=てんてこまいの毎日を楽しんでいる) We were blessed with twin babies seven years after marriage and have been enjoying a hectic daily life since.

②《(…して)うれしい》●あなたにまたお会いできてとてもうれしい I'm very glad [happy, pleased] to see you again. (❗ pleased は丁寧な言い方)/It's very nice [It really ＼is great] to see you again. (❗ 後者の例は It's really ＼great …. より強意的) ●パーティーにご出席いただきましてうれしく思います I'm glad [happy, pleased, delighted] that you have

うれしがらせる please; make (him) happy. (⇨嬉しがる)

うれしがる 嬉しがる be glad [happy, pleased]. (⇨喜ぶ)

うれしさ 嬉しさ joy; delight. ●うれしさのあまり跳び上がる jump *for* [*with, in*] *joy*. ▶彼はうれしさ(=幸せな気持ち)で胸がいっぱいになった His heart swelled with *happiness*.

うれしなき 嬉し泣き ── 嬉し泣きする 動 cry [《書》weep] *for joy*.

うれしなみだ 嬉し涙 ●うれし涙を流す《書》shed *tears of joy*; (うれしくて泣く) weep for joy. ▶彼は礼を述べる声もれし泣き乱れた He expressed his thanks between sobs.

うれすじ 売れ筋 a good [a big] seller; marketable [merchantable] goods. ●上位10位の売れ筋商品 the top ten *sellers*.

ウレタン《化学》urethane /júərəθèin/.
●ウレタンフォーム urethane foam.

うれっこ 売れっ子《人気のある》a popular person;《やや書》(引っ張りだこの人) a sought-after person. ▶あの歌手は超売れっ子だ He [She] is one of the most *sought-after singers*./He [She] is one of the *busiest singers* now.

うれのこり 売れ残り《売れ残った品物》goods left unsold.

うれのこる 売れ残る be left unsold;《比喩的》《話》be left on the shelf.

うれゆき 売れ行き (a) sale;《需要》demand. ▶彼女の新しいアルバムの売れ行きはどうですか How is her new album *selling*? ▶エアコンの売れ行き(=売上高)が伸びた[落ちた] *Sales* of air-conditioners have increased [fallen off]. ▶ここのところ経済書の売れ行きがいい Books about economy *are selling well* [*are in great demand*].

うれる 売れる ❶《商品が》sell*《通例様態および値段などの副詞(句)を伴うか、否定形で用いる》●50ドルで売れる sell for [fetch] fifty dollars. ▶その本はすぐに売れた(本自体の特質が原因で) The book *sold* [×could sell] quickly./(積極的な販売活動によって) The book *was sold* quickly. ▶そのネクタイはよく売れている The tie sells [*is selling*] well./(飛ぶように売れている) The tie *is selling* [*going*] like hot cakes [《話》like crazy]. ▶以上いずれもThose ties...のように複数主語も可. また The tie is a good [a big] seller. ともいえる》▶これは当社が過去5年間に発売したものの中で最もよく売れている商品です This is the best-*selling* product we have launched in the past five years. ▶遅すぎたわ、もう売れちゃってたのよ I was too late. They *had sold it* [売り切れた]. It (*was*) *sold out*]. ▶彼の家は思ったほどの高値では売れなかった His house did not *sell at* [*fetch*] a price as high as he hoped it would.
❷《広く知られる》● 名の広く(=有名な)人 a *famous* person. ●売れている(=人気のある)作家 a *popular* writer. ▶その女優は近ごろよく売れている The actress is very much *in the public eye* these days. (⇨売れっ子)

うれる 熟れる《熟する》ripen; become* ripe (⇨熟す).
●熟れた果実 *ripe* fruit.

うろうろ 副 ▶彼女は部屋の中を落ち着きなくうろうろ歩き回りながらその知らせを待っていた She walked restlessly *up and down* her room [paced the room (restlessly)], waiting for the news.

── **うろうろする** 動《当てもなく動きまわる》(立ち止まっても当てもなく) hang around *《英》about》(...), 《やや書》loiter 《*about* the station》; (同じ所を行ったり来たりする) walk up and down 《the room [street]》; (大勢の人が) mill around [《英》about]; 《うろたえる》be confused [upset] (⇨うろたえる).
▶銀行のあたりをうろうろしていると怪しまれるよ If you *are hanging around* the bank, people will get suspicious.

うろおぼえ うろ覚え ●うろ覚えである have a dim [vague, 《かすかな》faint] memory《*of*》; remember ... dimly [vaguely, faintly]. ▶ホテルのある場所はうろ覚えだし(=はっきりとは思い出せないし)、電話番号も分からない I don't *remember exactly* the location of the hotel, and I don't know the phone number.

うろこ 鱗 a scale. ▶魚や爬虫(は）類などの ●うろこのある魚 a *scaly* fish. ●魚のうろこを取る remove the *scales* from a fish; *scale* a fish.
●鱗雲《気象》a cirrocumulus /sìroukjú:mjəles/ (《複》-li /-ai/) (cloud).

うろたえる《気が動転する》be upset;《とまどう》be confused. (⇨慌てる❶,《まごつく》) ▶時間があまりなかったのでうろたえてしまった I didn't have much time, so I *got confused*.

うろちょろ ── **うろちょろする** 動 ▶君にこの辺をうろちょろしてもらいたくない I don't want you to *be* [*hang*] *around* here.

うろつく ●スーパーのあたりをうろつく(=ぶらぶら歩く)

wander around the supermarket. ● 通りをうろつく(立ち止まったりして) *hang around* 《英》*about*] the streets; (泥棒が様子をうかがって) *prowl* the streets.

うわあご 上顎 the upper jaw. (⇨顎)

うわがき 上書き ❶ 〔郵便物・書類など〕superscription. ❷ 〔コンピュータの〕● 上書き保存する *overwrite, save*.

うわがけ 上掛け (羽布団などの) a quilt cover, 《英》a duvet /d(j)u:véɪ/ *cover*; (ベッドの) a bedcover, a bedspread; (衣服の) ● 上っ張り.

うわき 浮気 图 an affair, unfaithfulness. ● 浮気の相手 (女性) the other woman, (男性) the other man. ● その封筒から彼女のと浮気していることがばれた The envelope brought it to light that he *had an affair* [《話》*a fling*] *with* that woman.
―― **浮気な** 形 〔移り気な〕fickle; ● 浮気な女 a flirt; a *fickle* [an *unfaithful*] woman. ● 浮気の虫 the desire for a love affair.
―― **浮気する** 動 〔婚姻外関係をもつ〕have* an affair [《話》a fling] (*with*); be unfaithful (*to*); (異性と遊び回る) play around 《英》about] (*with*). ● 絶対に浮気しないでね Be true [faithful] to me./《欧く》《話》Don't *cheat on* me.

*****うわぎ 上着** 〔〔そでつきの短い〕a jacket, a coat (❕通例 coat は防寒性のまたは長いコートに用いる); a top (シャツ、スカートに対して); (総称) outerwear (❕下着 (underwear) に対する語). ● 上着を着る[脱ぐ] put on [take off] one's *jacket*. ● 上着を着て[脱いで] with one's *jacket* on [off]. ● 女性はロングスカートに胸のあいた上着を着ていた The women wore long skirts with low-cut *tops*.

うわぐすり 釉薬 (陶磁器などの) (a) glaze; (ほうろう) enamel. ● うわ薬をかけた陶器[磁器] *glazed* pottery (陶器).

うわくちびる 上唇 the upper (⇔lower) lip.

うわごと うわ言 ● うわ言を言う rave; talk in one's delirium; (たわ言を言う) talk nonsense.

*****うわさ 噂** 图 (a) rumor (*about, of; that* 節); 《書》(a) report; (特定の場所の) the talk (*of*); (私生活に関する) gossip; (未確認の) héarsày.
①【うわさが[は、も]】● 彼が昇進するといううわさが広まった The *rumor* went around [spread, circulated] that he would get a promotion.
● 彼が死んだという世間のうわさは間違いだった The common *rumor* [*report*] *that* he had died proved (to be) false. ● 彼女はうわさ話が好きだ She is fond of *gossip*. ● おうわさはかねがね伺っております I've heard a lot about you. (❕この場合に ×I've heard of your rumors. とすると「よくない風評」の意となり不適切) ● 毎日のように新しいうわさが流れる Almost every day a new *rumor* is started [makes the rounds]. (❕make the rounds はくだけた言い方) ● 人のうわさも75日 (ことわざ) A wonder lasts but nine days.
②【うわさの】● うわさの人物 a man [a woman] (who [whom]) people are *talking about*.
③【うわさに】● うわさによると…(=…というのうわさだ) (⇨⑥) ● 彼の奇妙な行動は近所のうわさの種になった His strange behavior became the *talk of* the neighborhood./His strange behavior *was talked* [*was gossiped*] about in his neighborhood. (❕「…が近所中のうわさになっている」なら …is *the talk of* the whole neighborhood./The whole neighborhood is *talking about*…. という言える) ● いっしょのところを見られなうが がいい. うわさになるから We'd better not be seen together. People might *talk*. ● その件のうわさに聞いている I

know it *by* [*from*] *hearsay*. ● それはうわさにすぎない It's just a [a mere] *rumor*./It's just *gossip*./It's only *hearsay*.
④【うわさを】● うわさを立てる start [spread] a *rumor*. ● 彼が学校はやめるといううわさを聞いた I've heard a *rumor that* he will leave school [*about his leaving school*].
⑤【うわさで】● 彼は会社中彼のうわさで持ち切りだ He is the only topic of conversation at the company.
⑥【うわさだ】● 彼が辞職したといううわさだ There is a *rumor that* [*Rumor has it* (*that*)] he resigned./〈やや書〉He *is rumored* to have resigned. (❕能動形で ×They rumored him to have resigned. とはいわない) (言われている) *I hear*(*d*) [*People say, They say, The story goes*] (*that*) he resigned. (❕that はしばしば省略される) ● それは根も葉もないうわさだ It's an idle [a groundless, an unfounded] *rumor*.
〈会話〉「あの人たち別居中なんだって」「そういううわさだわ」"They're líving ↘separately [They're ↘separated], ↗aren't they?" "So *they say*./So *I hear*."
―― **噂(を)する** 動 ● 近所の人と彼のうわさをする *gossip about* him with one's neighbors.
● 噂をすれば影 うわさをすれば影だ ほら、彼が来た (ことわざ) Speak [《英話》Talk] *of the devil*. Hére he ↘comes.

うわじき 上敷き (じゅうたん) a carpet, a rug; (ござ) a mat; (敷布) a sheet; (うすべり) a bordered mat.

うわすべり 上滑り ―― **上滑りな** 形 (表面的な) superficial; (浅薄な) frivolous; shallow. ● 上滑りな男 a *frivolous* fellow.
―― **上滑りする** 動 ● 議論が上滑りした The argument stayed at a *superficial* level./(深まらなかった) Their argument did not go any deeper.

うわずみ 上澄み ● 上澄みをすくい取る scoop the *clear layer at the top* (*of* the soup).

うわずる 上擦る (うつろに聞こえる) sound hollow; (落ち着かなくなる) become* restless; (興奮状態になる) get* [be] delirious [very excited]. ● うわずった声で話す speak in a *high-pitched and excited* voice.

うわせい 上背 height. (⇨背 ❸, 身長)

うわちょうし 上調子 ―― **上調子な** 形 frivolous /frívələs/; flippant. (⇨浮つく)

うわつく 浮つく ● 浮ついた(=落ち着きのない)生活 a *restless* [〈軽薄な〉a *frivolous*] life. ● 浮ついた(=気まぐれな)女 a *flighty* woman. ● 浮ついた(=軽々しい)返事をする make a *flippant* reply.

うわつら 上っ面 (外観) an appearance; (表面) a surface. (⇨上辺(うわべ)) ● ボールの上っ面を打つ top a ball; hit the top of a ball.

うわっぱり 上っ張り (子供・女性・画家の) a smock; 《主に英》an overall.

うわに 上荷 图 〔上の積み荷〕the upper load; the goods loaded at the top.
―― **上積みする** 動 ● その額に2,000円上積み(=加算)する *add* two thousand yen *to* that amount of money.

うわて 上手 ● 料理となると彼女は私より一枚上手だ《話》She is a cut above me when it comes to cooking./She's a better cook than me [I (am)]. (優れる) ● 警察は上手に出て(=高圧的な態度で)彼に自白をせまった The police tried *high-handedly* to force him confess his crime.
● **上手投げ** 〔野球〕an overhand throw [pitch] (❕pitch は投球, throw は投球と送球をさす); 〔相撲〕

うわぬり 上塗り 图 ▶そんなことをしたら恥の上塗りだ That will *add to* your shame.
— **する** 動 ▶ドアにペンキ[ニス]の上塗りをする give the door a *last* [*a final*] *coat* of paint [*varnish*].

うわね 上値 ▶ a higher price.

うわのせ 上乗せ — **上乗せする** 動 add (A *to* B).

うわのそら 上の空 ▶[ぼんやりした] absent-minded; [不注意な] inattentive (*to*). ▶上の空で返事をする give an *absent-minded* answer; answer *absent-mindedly*. ▶私は彼の話を上の空で聞いていた (ほとんど聞いていなかった) I *hardly* listened [paid any attention] to him. (!) listen to に注意力を含む語なので absent-mindedly, inattentively など注意力を欠く意味をもつ副詞とともには用いない(心ここにあらずで) My mind was somewhere else while he was talking.

うわばき 上履き slippers; indoor shoes. (⇒スリッパ)

うわばみ ❶ [大蛇] a giant snake. ❷ [大酒飲み] a heavy drinker.

うわべ 上辺 (表面) a surface /sə́ːrfəs/. ▶うわべと違って(＝一皮むけば) under the skin. ▶うわべだけの親切 *surface* [《やや書》 *superficial*] kindness. ▶彼はうわべは親切だが内心は冷淡だ He is kind *on the surface* but cold inside [《やや書》 *underneath*]. ▶彼女はうわべは正直そうに見える She is *seemingly* honest. /(正直そうに見えるがうわべだけだ) She seems to be honest, but it's just a *facade* /fəsάːd/ [《やや話》 she's just a *fake*]. (!) facade は「正面、外観」、fake は「にせ物」の意)

うわまえ 上前 [ピンはね] 《話》 a kickback. (⇒リベート) ●儲けの上前をはねる(＝手数料を取る) take [pocket] a *percentage* from 《his》 earnings.

うわまわる 上回る [⋯以上である] be more than ..., be above ...; (数量を) be over ...; [超える] exceed (⇒超過する); [優れる] be better than ..., surpass. ●100人を上回る人々 *over* [*more than*] a hundred people. ▶彼は過去の記録を2秒上回る世界新記録を打ち立てた He set the new world record which *exceeded* [*was better than*] the past record by two seconds. ▶そのコンサートは予想をはるかに上回る観客を集めた The concert attracted a much *larger* audience [×*many more audiences*] *than* (we had) expected.

うわむき 上向き ▶株式市場は上向きだ The stock market *is going up*.

うわむく 上向く ▶景気が上向いている(＝よくなっている) Business *is looking up* [*picking up, improving, getting better*].

うわめづかい 上目遣い ▶上目遣いに彼を見る look at him *with upturned eyes*; cast an *upward glance* at him.

うわや 上屋 [屋根だけの簡単な建物] a shelter; [貨物用倉庫] a goods shed.

うわやく 上役 one's boss [*superior*].

うわる 植わる be planted. ▶庭には多くのバラが植わっている Lots of roses *are planted* in the garden.

うわん 右腕 ●右腕投手 a right-hand(ed) pitcher. (!) a right hander, a righty には「右打者」の意も)

*****うん 運** (その場限りの) luck; (人生を左右するような) fortune; (偶然) (a) chance. (⇒幸運, 不運)
① [～運] ▶勝負は時の運だ It's a matter of *luck* whether we (will) win or not./Whether we (will) win or not depends on *luck*.
② [運が] ▶運がよい[悪い] be *lucky* [*unlucky*]; have (×a) good [bad] *luck*; be in [out of] *luck*; be *fortunate* [*unfortunate*]. ▶運が悪かったね Bad [Hard, Tough] *luck!* ▶ここで会えるとはなんて運がいいのだろう How *lucky* [What a stroke of *luck*] to meet you here! ▶(事故・戦争などで)死ななくて彼は運がよかった He was *lucky* [*fortunate*] (enough) not to be killed. (!) enough がつくと強調が)/He was *lucky* [*fortunate*] that he wasn't killed./(彼が死ななかったのは運がよかった) It was *lucky* [*fortunate*] (that) he wasn't killed. (!) 「幸運だった」のは通例「彼」であるが、それが他の人にとって「幸運だった」のであれば It was *lucky for us* (that) ..., 《話》 We are *lucky* (that) ..., *Luckily for us*, ... (⇒（のように言う）) ▶彼女は亭主運が悪い She was very *unfortunate* in her choice of husbands. ▶昨年から運がよかったのに、彼女に会って運が尽きてしまった I had been lucky in everything since last year, but I ran out of luck [my luck ran out] when I met her.
③ [運の] ▶運の悪い出来事 an *unfortunate* incident. ▶サラ金に手を出したのが彼の運の尽きだった Borrowing money from a loan shark was the beginning of his terrible *luck*.
④ [運に] ▶何事も運に任せるな Don't leave anything to *luck* [*chance*]. ▶運に恵まれて私たちは勝った *Luck* favored us, and we won./We won only by a stroke of *luck*. ▶全然ついていない。とうとう運に見放されたようだ I am absolutely unlucky. I'm afraid I have been abandoned by *good luck* [*fortune*].
⑤ [運を] ▶運をためす try one's *luck* [*fortune*] (*at* the game). ▶運を天に任せる leave one's fate to Heaven; (一か八かの冒険をする) take a *chance* [*chances*] 《*on*》; (最善を期待する) hope for the best. ▶彼はもう少しで運を逃すところだった He almost lost the good *chance*. ▶通りの角で老女が運を占っていた。足を止めて自分の結婚運を占ってもらった An elderly woman was telling *fortunes* on the street corner. I stopped to have her tell my marriage *fortune*.
⑥ [運よく[悪く]] fortunately [*unfortunately*]; luckily [*unluckily*]. ▶運よく彼は1等が当たった *Fortunately* [*Luckily*, 《やや書》 *Happily*] he won first prize. (!) happily には話し手の感情が入る) ▶先日久しぶりに太郎を訪ねたが、運悪く彼は外出していた The other day I visited Taro for the first time in ages, but *unfortunately* he was out [not in].
●運が向く ▶運が向いてきた *Luck* is coming my way.

うん [返答] (肯定) yes, 《話》 yeah, 《話》 uh-/huh /mhm, (鼻にかかって) ʌ̃hʌ̃/ (!) no の意の)uh-uh (鼻にかかって) ʌ̃ʌ̃) との違いに注意); (同意、承諾) yes, all right, 《話》 OK [O.K., okay] (⇒ええ、よろしい); [ふうん] hum, h'm. (⇒はい) ●うんと言う (肯定する) say yes, 《書》 answer in the affirmative; (同意する) say yes, agree, 《やや書》 give one's consent 《*to*, *to do*》; (承諾する) approve. ●うんとうなずく nod one's *consent*; nod *in agreement*. ▶うん、そうかもしれないね *Well*, it might be true. (!) 消極的な同意) ▶ご両親がうんとおっしゃったら泊まっていきなさいよ If you get your parents' *approval* [the *OK* from your parents], you can stay with me overnight [tonight]. ▶うん、これはうまい 《米話》 *Say*, this is really good! (!) 喜び・賞賛などを表す)

会話「行こうか」「うん、行こう」"Let's go." "Yes, let's."/**会話**「All right.」《話》OK.

会話「忘れずに投函してね」「うん、そうするよ」"Don't forget to mail it." "No, I won't." "うん、そうするよ" "Remember to mail [×mailing] it." "Yes, I will." (**!** 日本語につられて yes ということばに注意)

● **うんともすんとも** ● うんともすんとも言わない say neither yes nor no; give no answer; keep silent. ▶彼はその後うんともすんとも言ってこない I haven't heard a word [I've heard nothing at all] from him since.

うんうん ❶ 「「うん」の強調表現」 ● うんうんとうなずく nod in agreement.

会話「私がいま言ったこと、聞こえたの」「うんうん」"Did you hear what I said?" "Uh-huh."

❷ 『うなり声』 ▶トムは床に横たわってうんうんなっていた Tom lay on the floor moaning.

*****うんえい 運営** 图 (管理) management; (動かすこと) operation. ▶運営を誤る mismanage.
— **運営する 動** manage; operate, run.
● **運営委員会** a stéering commíttee. ● **運営費** óperàting [òperátional, rúnning] còsts.

うんか 雲霞 ▶雲霞のごとく人々が町に押し寄せた An enormous swarm [Enormous swarms] of people came to the town.

うんか 浮塵子 〖昆虫〗 a leafhopper.

うんが 運河 a canal. ▶スエズ運河 the Suez Canal.
● 水平[水門]運河 a level [a lock] canal. ● 運河を造る build [construct, (掘る) dig] a canal.
● **運河地帯** a canal zone. ● **運河通過料** a canal toll.

うんかい 雲海 a sea of clouds.

うんきゅう 運休 图 (運行一時中止) the suspension of a bus [train] service; (便の取りやめ) the cancellation of a bus [train].
— **運休する 動** (一時中止する) suspend; (取りやめる) cancel. ▶事故のため7時20分発の電車は運休した The 7:20 train was canceled because of the accident.

うんこ (⇨うんち)

うんこう 運行, 運航 图 ❶ 『乗り物の』(a) service; 〖列車などの便〗a run; 〖飛行機の便〗a flight. ▶運航の船 a ship in service. ▶台風のためすべての飛行機の運航は中止された All flights were canceled [Air transportation services were completely halted] because of the typhoon.

❷ 『天体の』(公転) (a) revolution; (運動) (a) movement. (⇨回る, 回転する)

— **運行[運航]する 動** ▶列車は10分ごとに運行している There is a train service every ten minutes./The trains run [×are running] every ten minutes.

うんざり — **うんざりする 動** 《話》get fed up 《with》; get sick (and tired) 《of》; (退屈する) get bored 《with》; (十分である) have had enough 《of》. ▶うんざりした表情 his bored expression. ▶私は彼女の愚痴にはうんざりしている I am fed up with her complaints./I'm sick and tired of her complaints. ▶私は田舎の生活にうんざりした I got bored with the country life. ▶お前のばかな話にはうんざりした I've had enough of your nonsense.

うんさんむしょう 雲散霧消 — **雲散霧消する** 〖消えてなくなる〗 vanish. ▶母の声を聞くと恐怖の念は雲散霧消した My fear vanished when I heard my mother's voice.

うんじょうびと 雲上人 (貴族) a nobleman.

うんしん 運針 the handling of a needle.

うんすい 雲水 an unsui; (説明的に) a wandering Buddhist priest, especially one who belongs to the Zen sect and leads a life of severe self-discipline.

うんせい 運勢 〖将来の運〗a fortune; 〖星占い〗a horoscope; 〖星回り〗a star (**!** しばしば複数形で). (⇨運, 幸運, 占う) ▶運勢を占う tell [read] 《his》 fortune. ▶易者に運勢を見てもらう have one's fortune told by a fortune-teller. ▶今月のあなたの運勢はいい[悪い] Your fortune [horoscope] for this month will be good [bad].

うんそう 運送 图 〖輸送〗《米》transportation, 《英》tránsport; 〖書〗conveyance. (⇨輸送)
— **運送する 動** transport. ▶家具をトラックで運送する transport the furniture by truck.
● **運送業** the transportation industry. ● **運送業者** (引っ越しの) a mover; (主に航空の) a carrier. ● **運送店** a fórwarding àgency. ● **運送料** transportation.

うんだめし 運試し ▶大リーグで運試しをしようとする日本人野球選手が増えている Growing [Increasing] number of Japanese baseball players are trying their luck (playing) in the US Major Leagues. (**!** There are increasing... としないことに注意)

うんち number two, No. 2; 《幼児語》caca, kaka /káːkàː/, (特に犬などの) poo. ● **うんちをする** caca; do number two; poo.

うんちく 蘊蓄 (知識・学問の貯え) a great [a vast] stock of knowledge [learning]. ▶うんちくを傾ける draw on one's profound knowledge 《of》.

うんちん 運賃 〖旅客の〗a fare; 〖貨物の〗freight (rates), carriage. ▶航空運賃 an air fare. ▶運賃精算 fare adjustment. ▶大人の運賃 adult fare, (1人前の) full fare. ▶子供の運賃 child(ren)'s fare, (半人前の) half fare. ▶往復運賃 a round-trip fare; 《英》a return fare. ▶割り増し運賃をとる[払う] charge [pay] an extra fare. ▶長距離バスの運賃は電車の運賃より安い Coach fares are cheaper than railroad fares. ▶バスの運賃がまた上がった Bus fares went up [were raised] again. ▶京都から東京まで運賃はいくらですか What's [How much is] the fare (from Kyoto) to Tokyo? (**!** fare の代わりに it を用いて How much is it...? のようにもいえる) ▶学生時代は割引運賃で旅行できた When I was a student, I could travel at a reduced fare.

うんでいのさ 雲泥の差 ▶2人の技量には雲泥の差がある There is a great [a considerable] difference in skill between the two./Their skills are quite [completely] different (from) each other.

うんてん 運転 图 〖自動車などの〗driving; 〖交通機関の運行〗a run; 〖機械の操作〗operation; 〖資金などの運用〗working.

① 〖～(の)運転〗 ▶酔っ払い運転 drunken [《話》drunk] driving. ▶無謀[安全, 無免許]運転 reckless [safe; unlicensed] driving. ▶機械の運転 the operation of a machine. ▶彼は居眠り運転で(=運転中に居眠りして)事故を起こした He dozed off at [behind] the wheel and caused an accident. (**!** at [behind] the wheel は「ハンドルを握って[の後ろに座って]運転している時に」の意の慣用表現)

② 〖運転(の)～〗 ▶運転中の機械 a machine in operation. ▶運転の教習を受ける take driving lessons. ▶このエレベーターは運転休止になっています This elevator isn't working [is out of operation]. ▶アメリカのほとんどの車の運転席は左側にあります The driver's seat is on the left in most cars in America.

> **DISCOURSE**
> 交通事故の数を減らすには、運転中の携帯電話の使用を禁止すべきである **In order to** decrease the number of traffic accidents, the use of cellular phones while *driving* should be prohibited. (⚠ in order to ... (...するには)は因果関係を述べるときに用いるディスコースマーカー)

③【運転を】● 運転を開始する (機械が) go into *operation*; start *operating*; (機械を) *set* a machine *going* [*running*, *working*]. (⇨動かす❷) ● 私の運転を信用してください Please trust the way I *drive*. (⚠ ×Please trust my driving. は不可) ● 彼は車の運転を誤って溝に落ちた He lost *control* of the car and it ended up in the ditch. ● あのころは君はひどい運転をしていたね You *were a* reckless [a wild] *driver* in those days.

—— 運転する 動 『車などを』drive*; 『車などを走らせる、列車などを運行させる、機械を動かす』run*; 『機械などを』(動かす) work, (操作する) operate. ● 気をつけてもっとゆっくり運転しなさい Be careful and *drive* more slowly. ● 彼は車の運転するのがうまい He is good at *driving* (a car). /He is a good *driver*. ● 彼らは車を運転して坂を下って行った They *drove* down the hill./They *drove* [*ran*] the car *down* the hill. ● 9 時 20 分の電車は今日は運転されていません The 9:20 train *is not running* [(取り消された)] *was canceled*] today. ● ラッシュアワーには臨時列車は運転される They *run* [×are running] extra trains during the rush hours. (⚠ 定期的に運行される文脈では進行形は用いない)/Extra trains *run* [(走らされる) *are run*] during the rush hours.

● 運転資金 wórking càpital; wórking fùnds.

うんてんしゅ 運転手 『自動車の』a driver; (おかかえの) a chauffeur /ʃóufər/; (タクシーの) a taxi [《米》a cab] driver, (話) (バスの) a bus driver, 《英》a busman (働 -men); (トラックの) a truck [《英》a lorry] driver; 『電車などの』a motorman (働 -men); 《男女共用》a (streetcar) driver; 《米》an engineer. ● そのトラックの運転手は事故で死亡した The *driver* of the truck was killed in the accident. ● ねえ、運転手さん、飛ばしてくれ Hey, *driver*! Step on it. (⚠ it は「アクセル」をさす)

うんと ● うんと働く work *very hard*; work *as hard as possible*. ● うんと(=思う存分)食べる[飲む] eat [drink] *one's fill*; eat [drink] *as much as* one *likes*. ● うんと(=ひどく)しかられる be *severely* scolded; get a *good* scolding. ● 高校の時には野球をうんとやった I played *a lot of* baseball at high school.

:**うんどう** 運動 图 ❶ 『身体の』exercise (⚠「体操」の意では Ⓒ); a sport. (⇨体操, スポーツ)

> **使い分け** exercise 健康を維持または増進するために身体を動かすこと.
> **sport** 楽しみのため主に野外で行われる運動. 魚釣り・狩猟・競馬なども含まれる.

①【〜運動, 運動〜】● 屈伸運動をする do bending and stretching *exercises*. ● 運動好きな人 a lover of *sport*(*s*). ● 運動神経(=反射神経)が発達している [鈍い] have quick [slow] reflexes. ● 彼は運動不足であり食欲がない He has little appetite for lack [want] of *exercise*. ● 水泳は運動量の多い(=体力を消耗する)スポーツである Swimming is an energy-consuming sport.
②【運動は[が]】● 適度な運動は健康によい A little [Some, 《書》Moderate] *exercise* is good for you [your health, the health]. /Moderate *exercise* will do you good. ● 彼は運動が得意だ He is good at *sports*. /(なかなかのスポーツマンである) He's quite an athlete. (⚠「運動神経が発達している」の意にもなる) ● 私はもっと運動が必要だ. 太ってきた I need more *exercise*. I'm getting fat [(婉曲的) gaining weight].
③【運動の】● 彼はいつも運動のために学校へ歩いて行く He always walks to school for *exercise*.
④【運動に】● 1 日に少なくとも 2 時間は運動に当てるべきだ Not less than two hours a day should be spent on *exercise*. /You should take not less than two hours' daily *exercise*. ● 水泳はぜい肉を落とすよい運動になる Swimming is (《主に米》a) good *exercise* to get rid of flab.
⑤【運動の】● (⇨動) 食後すぐ激しい運動をしないようにしない Try not to get [(《英》take] hard (↔ light) *exercise* soon after meals. ● 運動をした後の温かいシャワーほどいいものはない There's nothing like a good hot shower after *exercising*.

> **DISCOURSE**
> 少しの運動を毎日加えるようにしよう. 例えば, 車を使ったり, 車で送ってもらったりする代わりに徒歩で駅まで行くのでも有益だろう Try to add a small amount of *physical exercise* every day. **For instance**, walking instead of driving or being driven to the train station will be helpful. (⚠ for instance (例えば)は具体例に用いるディスコースマーカー)

❷ 『社会的・政治的な』(やや書) a campaign; a movement; a drive. (⇨活動)

> **使い分け** campaign 政治的・社会的・商業的目標に到達するための組織的運動.
> **movement** ある共通の政治的・社会的目的を達成しようとする一群の人々またはその活動.
> **drive** 募金などある目的達成のためにグループで行う(宣伝)活動.

①【〜運動】● 禁煙運動 a *campaign against* smoking; an anti-smoking *campaign*. ● 交通安全運動 a *campaign for* traffic safety; a traffic safety *campaign*. ● 政治運動 a political *campaign* [*movement*]. ● 選挙運動 an election *campaign*. ● 学生運動 a student *movement*. ● 公害追放の市民運動 an antipollution civic *movement*, a civic *movement against* environmental pollution. ● 世界平和運動 a world peace *campaign*; a *movement for* world peace. ● 草の根運動 a grass-roots *movement*.
②【運動は[が]】● 大統領選挙運動は 1 週間前に始まった The presidential *campaign* began a week ago. ● ごみを捨てない運動は十分成果を上げつつある Anti-litter *campaigns* are having a good effect. ● 麻薬の販売をやめさせるために運動が始められた A *movement* was begun to stop selling drugs.
③【運動の】● 運動の組織者 a *campaign* organizer. ● その運動の発起人たちへ to the initiators of the *movement*. ● 彼はその運動のために(=運動を支えるために)喜んで金を出した He willingly gave money to support the *movement*.
④【運動を】● 彼はその資金集めの運動をした He *campaigned* [carried on a *campaign*] *for* the funds. /He had a *drive* to raise the funds [a fund-raising *drive*]. (⚠ had の代わりに made も可) ● 私たちは市議会を浄化する運動を起こした We have started a *movement to* clean up the city council.

❸ 『物理的な』motion; movement. ● 運動の原理 [法則] the principle [laws] of *motion*.

うんどうかい

— **運動する** ❶ [身体を動かす] get* [《英》take*] exercise; exercise. (⇨⓫❺; する) ▶もっと運動しなさい Get [《英》Take] more exercise./Exercise more. ❷ [社会的・政治的に] campaign 《for, against》. (⇨❷④) ❸ [物体が] move.
- 運動競技 athletic /æθlétik/ sports; athletics (🛈 通例複数扱い). ● 運動靴 sports shoes; (スニーカー)《主に米》sneakers,《英》plimsolls. ● 運動選手 an athlete /æθli:t/. ● 運動部 (学校の) an athletic club. ● 運動服 sportswear. ● 運動量 [物理] momentum.

うんどうかい 運動会 《米》an athletic meet,《英》an athletic meeting. (🛈 以上は「陸上競技会」の意。日本の「運動会」に当たるものは通例英米ではa field《米》[a sports《英》] day) ▶私たちの学校では毎年秋に運動会がある An *athletic meet* is held at our school in fall every year [every fall]. (🛈 後の方は単に「毎年」という意だが、前の方は春でなく秋が強調され、より自然)

うんどうじょう 運動場 [学校の] a playground, (校庭) a schoolyard; [競技場] a sports ground [field]; an athletic field; [室内の] a gymnasium, (話) a gym. ● 運動場でソフトボールをする play softball *in* [*on*] the *playground*. (🛈 in は塀などで囲まれた中で、on は広い表面での感じを意識したときに用いられる)

うんどんこん 運鈍根 ▶運鈍根が成功への必要条件だ *Luck, tenacity and patience* are requirements for success.

うんぬん 云々 图 and so on; etc. (⇨など)
— **うんぬんする** 動 comment 《on》; (批判する) criticize.

うんのう 蘊奥 (奥義、極意) the mysteries, the secrets.

*****うんぱん** 運搬 图 《米》transportation,《英》tránsport;《書》convéyance (⇨輸送). ● 商品の運搬 the *transportation* [《書》*conveyance*] of goods.
— **運搬する** 動 (運ぶ) carry; (輸送する) transport,《書》. (⇨運ぶ) ▶品物をトラックで運搬するのに丸１日かかった It took all day to *transport* the goods by truck.
- 運搬車 (引っ越し用の) a móving [(大型の) fúrniture, 《英》a remóval] ván. ● 運搬人 a carrier;《書》a conveyer.

うんぴつ 運筆 the use of a brush [a pen].

うんまかせ 運任せ ▶運任せにする leave [it] to chance [the luck of the draw]; try one's luck. ▶彼は何事も運任せだ He *leaves* everything *to chance*.

：うんめい 運命 (a) fate; 《やや書》(a) destiny; (a) fortune (🛈 女神の意では F-); (a) doom;《書》(a) lot (🛈 単数形で).

> **使い分け** destiny 神から与えられた宿命、天命。
> fate 個人の力ではどうにもできない成り行き。通例、死・破滅・敗北などの否定的な結末を示す。
> fortune 偶然で決定される人生の運・運勢・運命。幸運・不運の両方を含意。
> doom 不幸で悲惨な運命。しばしば死亡・破滅を含意。
> lot 偶然に与えられた身分・境遇。

① 【運命が[は]】 ● 彼にどんな運命が待ち構えているかはだれにも分からない No one knows what *fate* [*destiny*] is in store for him./No one can tell what *fate* [*destiny*] awaits him. ▶兵士の運命は苛酷(こく)だ A soldier's *lot* (in life) is a hard one.
② 【運命(の)】 ● 運命の時 [決断] a *fateful* moment [decision]. (🛈 fateful は「運命を決する」、fatal は「致命的な」の意) ● 運命の皮肉 [いたずら] によって by the irony [a quirk, a twist] of *fate*. ● 運命の巡り合わせで by a stroke of *fate*. ▶医者になりたかったが運命の定めによりそうならなかった I wanted to be a doctor, but *fate* had decided otherwise. (🛈 その作用を支配できず結果が不幸であった場合で ×destiny は不可) ▶運命の女神が彼にほほえんだ [味方した] *Fortune* smiled on [favored] him. ● 運命の瞬間がとうとうやってきた At last the moment came when my *destiny* would be determined. ▶それが彼女との運命的な出会いだった That was a [my] *fateful* meeting with her.
③ 【運命に】 ● 運命に反抗する rebel against 《one's》*destiny*. (🛈 このように自由意志の可能性がある場合 fate は不適当) ▶我々はみな同じ運命(=困難な状況)にあるのだ We are all in the same boat. ▶彼は若死にする運命にあった He was (fated [doomed,《やや書》destined]) to die young. (🛈 be to do は堅い言い方)/It was fated that he would die young./It was his *fate* to die young./He was *doomed* to an early death. ▶彼の死後、彼の家族は運命にほんろうされることとなった After his death, his family was to become a victim of the fickle finger of *fate*.
④ 【運命を】 ● 運命を切り開く work [carve] out 《one's》*destiny*. ● 運命を受け入れる accept 《one's》*fate*; (身をゆだねる) be resigned [resign oneself] to one's *fate*. (🛈 ここでは自由意志は入らず destiny は不適当) ● 運命を左右する affect the *fate* [*destiny*] 《of》. ● 運命を決する decide [《話》seal] 《his》*fate*. ● 運命をともにする share 《his》*fate*; throw in one's *lot* 《with him》. ▶彼と結婚した後、彼女は数奇な運命(=人生)をたどった After marrying him, she led a checkered life.
⑤ 【運命と】 ● 運命と戦う struggle against one's *destiny*.
⑥ 【運命から】 ▶私たちは自分の運命から逃れられない We cannot escape our *destiny* [*fate*].

うんめいきょうどうたい 運命共同体 a community with a common destiny. ▶このプロジェクトを推進している我々は運命共同体だ Since we are carrying out this project, we belong to a community with a common destiny.

うんめいろん 運命論 fatalism.
- 運命論者 a fatalist.

うんも 雲母 [地学] mica /máikə/. ● 黒雲母 biotite.

うんゆ 運輸 《米》transportation,《英》transport;《書》conveyance. (⇨運搬)
- 運輸会社 a transportation company. ● 運輸機関 a transportation system; a means of transportation. ● 運輸局 the District Transport Bureau;《米国の》the Department of Motor Vehicles.

うんよう 運用 ● 資金の正しい運用(=使い方) the proper *use* of funds. ▶英語の運用能力(=役に立つ知識)を高めたい I want to improve my *working knowledge* of English.

うんりょう 雲量 [気象] cloud cover.

え

え 絵

WORD CHOICE 絵

painting 絵の具を塗って仕上げた絵画作品を幅広くさす. ●古い教会を描いた油絵 the oil *painting* of the old church.

drawing ペン・インク・鉛筆などを用い, 主として単色で仕上げられた絵画作品. ●フェルトペンで描いたきれいな絵 the lovely *drawing* with felt pens.

sketch 事物などを大まかに写生した絵. 芸術作品というより日常的な記録目的の素描なども含む. ●その山を大まかにスケッチする draw [do, make] a rough *sketch* of the mountain.

頻度チャート

painting ▬▬▬▬▬▬▬▬▬▬
drawing ▬▬▬▬▬
sketch ▬▬

20 40 60 80 100 (%)

a picture; (絵具による) a painting; (鉛筆・ペンなどによる画線) a drawing; 〚素描, 下絵〛a sketch; 〚挿し絵〛an illustration (⇨挿し絵); 〚絵をかくこと〛painting.

関連 いろいろな絵: 油絵 an oil painting/水彩画 a watercolor/写生画 a sketch/肖像画 a portrait/静物画 a still life/風景画 a landscape.

① 【~の絵, 絵の~】 ● 私の母の(=をかいた)絵 a *picture* of my mother; my mother's *picture*. (❗後の方は「母がかいた[所有する]絵」の意にもなる) ● モネの(=がかいた)絵 a *picture* (a *painting*, a *drawing*) by Monet; a Monet. ● パリで絵の勉強をする study *painting* in Paris. ▶それは軍服姿の男の絵だった The *picture* was of a man in army uniform.

② 【絵を[が]】 ● 花の絵をかく (絵の具で) paint (a *picture* of) flowers; (油[水彩]絵の具で) paint (a *picture* of) flowers in oils [watercolors]; (線画を) draw (a *picture* of) flowers. (❗ ✗ write a picture [a drawing] は不可) ● 彼の部屋の大まかな絵をかく sketch his room; make [draw] a *sketch* of his room. ▶彼は絵(をかくの)がうまい He is good at *painting* [*drawing*]./He is a good painter (この意で a good drawer とはあまりいわない). ▶壁に美しい絵が1枚かかっていた There was a beautiful *picture* [*painting*] on the wall.

③ 【絵のように】 ● 絵のように美しい眺め a *picturesque* [(とても美しい) a very beautiful] view.

会話 「見事なバラだこと!」「絵のよう」"What glorious roses!" "Aren't they a ↘ *picture*!" (❗単数形に注意)

● 絵になる ▶この景色は絵になる This scenery will make a good *picture*. ▶あの2人はまるで絵から抜け出たようだ Those two (people) look as if they stepped out of a *picture*.

● 絵に描いた餅 (実現の見込みのないもの) pie in the sky; (実際の役に立たないもの) something that is of no practical use.

● 絵に描いたような ▶彼は健康を絵に描いたような人間だ He is the *picture* of health. (❗ the picture of ... は「...の典型」の意)

え 柄 〚道具の〛a handle, a grip; 〚刀などの〛a hilt; 〚やり・おの・ゴルフクラブなどの〛a shaft; 〚L字形の〛a crank. ●金属製の柄のラケット a racket with a metal *shaft*. ▶フォークの柄をこんなふうに持ってごらん Hold your fork *by the handle* [the *handle* of your fork] this way. (❗前の方が一般的)

エア 〚空気〛air.

エアーズロック Ayers /éərz/ Rock. (参考) オーストラリアにある世界最大の岩石)

エアカーテン an air curtain.

エアガン an air gun. ●エアガンを撃つ shoot [fire] an *air gun*.

エアクリーナー 〚空気洗浄器〛an air purifier.

エアコン 〚空調装置〛an air-conditioner; 〚豪話〛the aircon (units); 〚空調〛air-conditioning. ●エアコンのきいている部屋[車] an *air-conditioned* room [car].

エアコンプレッサー 〚空気圧縮器〛an air compressor.

エアゾール 〚噴射式薬剤〛(an) aerosol.

エアターミナル an air [an airport] terminal.

エアバス an airbus.

エアバッグ an air bag.

エアフォースワン 〚米国大統領専用機〛Air Force One.

エアブレーキ an air brake.

エアポート 〚空港〛an airport.

エアポケット an air pocket, a pocket. ●エアポケットに入る be trapped in a [an *air*] *pocket*.

エアメール 〚航空便〛airmail, air mail.

エアライン 〚航空路, 航空会社〛an airline.

エアロビクス aerobics /eəróubiks/ (❗単・複数扱い); aerobic exercise 〚複数形にしない〛●エアロビクスをする do *aerobics*.

えい 〚魚介〛a ray.

えい (えいくそっ) Damn [Darn] it! (⇨くそ) ●えいと叫ぶ give a cry [a yell]. ▶えいとばかりに彼はそれを投げた He threw it away *with a cry*.

えい 嬰 〚音楽〛a sharp. 〚記号 #〛●嬰ハ[=]短調 C [D] *sharp* minor.

えいい 鋭意 ●鋭意努力する make *great* (精力的に) *strenuous*, (全力をあげて) *all-out* efforts 《*to do*》; *concentrate* one's efforts [energy] 《*on*》. ▶鋭意努力いたす所存であります I'll try to do my very best.

えいいん 影印 ●影印本(複製本) a facsimile edition.

えいえい 英英 ●英英辞典 an English(-English) dictionary.

えいえい 営々 ●営々と働く work *very hard*.

えいえん 永遠 图 eternity; pérmanence.

—**永遠の** 形 (始めも終わりもなく続く) eternal; (変化なく続く) pérmanent; 〚書〛(果てしなく続く) everlasting. (⇨永久) ●永遠の未来 the *eternal* future. ●永遠の平和 a *permanent* [an *everlasting*] peace. ▶私は彼女に永遠の愛を誓った I pledged her my *eternal* [*everlasting*] love./I pledged to love her *forever* [*eternally*].

—**永遠に** 副 (これから先いつまでも) forever, 〚英〛for

えいが 映画 《主に米》a movie, 《書》a motion picture, 《主に英》a film (🛈《米》でも新聞などでは普通); 《集合的》the movies, 《主に英》the cinema [×cinemas], the pictures (🛈 the cinema の古風な言い方).
① 【～映画】▶ギャング [恐怖; 戦争; 無声] 映画 a gangster [a horror; a war; a silent] movie. ●記録映画 a documentary (film). ●2本立て映画 a double feature (program). ●モンロー主演の映画 a movie starring Monroe. ●テレビ用映画 a TV movie. ●新着映画 a newly released film [movie].
② 【映画が [は]】▶私は映画が好きです I like [am fond of] movies. (🛈 通例 the をつけない) ▶この映画は最近封切られた This movie was recently released. (⇨封切り) ▶その映画おもしろかった? Did you enjoy the movie?/(どうだった?) How was the movie? ▶テレビが発達して映画は衰退した Movies declined when television was developed.
③ 【映画に】▶彼はタクシーの運転手としてその映画に出演した He appears as [plays] a cabdriver in the movie. (🛈 後の方が普通) ▶彼はその小説を映画に(=映画化)した He made [turned] the novel into a movie [a film]./He filmed the novel. (🛈 映画化したものは a movie [a film] version of the novel という)
④ 【映画を】●映画を見る see [watch] a movie [a film]. ▶今映画を見ているときは watch を用いる ●映画を上映する show [present] a movie. ●映画を撮る [封切る] shoot [release] a movie [a film]. ●映画を製作する produce [make] a movie [a film]. ▶今夜映画を見に行こう Let's go to the movies [a movie, 《英》 the cinema] tonight. (🛈 (1) ×go to see the movies [cinema] とはいわない. go to see [×watch] a movie [a film] は可. (2) go to a movie は「映画館に行く」の意にもなる. go to the movie は「特定の映画を見に行く」の意)
【会話】「その映画館では今どんな映画をやっていますか」「町の西部劇です」"What (kind of) movie is on at the movie theater?" "There's a new western (on)."
●映画音楽 film music. ●映画界 the movie [motion picture, film] world; the movies [films, 《英》cinema]. ●映画館 a movie theater; a movie house (🛈 単に a movie ともいう); 《英》a cinema. ●映画鑑賞 (一般的な) movie viewing; (学科の) cinema appreciation; appreciation of the cinema. ●映画狂 a film addict. ●映画祭 a film festival; a movie festival. ●映画撮影所 a (movie) studio. ●映画産業 the movie [film] industry. ●映画女優 a movie [a film, a screen] actress. ●映画スター a movie [a film] star. ●映画制作 moviemaking, filmmaking. 🛈 制作者は a movie [film] maker. producer は制作上の経済的責任を負う. 監督は director) ●映画俳優 a movie [a film, a screen] actor. ●映画評論家 a film critic. ●映画ファン a movie fan; 《主に米話》a moviegoer.

えいが 栄華 (繁栄) prosperity; (栄光) glory. ●栄華を極める be in one's glory; (栄華に暮らす) live in (great) splendor.

えいかいわ 英会話 English conversation. ●英会話の練習をする practice conversational English; (英語を話すことを) practice speaking English. ▶彼女は英会話が上手だ She speaks English (very) well./She speaks good English.
●英会話学校 an English language [conversation] school.

えいかく 鋭角 〖数学〗an acute angle. ●…と鋭角をなす make [form] an acute angle with ….
—鋭角の 形 sharp-pointed. ●鋭角的な才能 a keen talent. ●鋭角的なデザイン a spiky design. ●鋭角三角形 an acute-angled triangle.

えいがものがたり 映画物語 Eiga Monogatari; A Tale of Flowering Fortunes. (参考) 平安時代の歴史物語)

えいかん 栄冠 the crown; laurels. ●勝利の栄冠を得く win [gain] laurels; be crowned with victory. ●ミスユニバースの栄冠に輝く be crowned Miss Universe.

えいき 英気 ●英気を養う build up strength. ▶たっぷり飯を食っていい湯に入ってあすの試合のために英気を養おう Let's have a big dinner and a nice hot bath to build ourselves up for tomorrow's game.

えいき 鋭気 spirit. ●鋭気をくじく break one's spirit. ●鋭気を蓄える store up one's energy.

えいきごう 嬰記号 (⇨記号)

えいきゅう 永久 名 permanence; eternity.
—永久の 形 (同じ状態で変化なく続く) permanent; (始めも終わりもなく時を超越して続く) eternal; (絶えまなく繰り返される) perpetual; 《書》(未来へ果てしなく続く) everlasting. ●永久不変の真理 eternal truths.
—永久に 副 forever, 《英》for ever; (これを最後に) for good (and all); permanently; eternally. ▶永久に変わらない remain unchanged forever [permanently]. ▶君のことは永久に忘れない I will remember you forever./I'll never forget you all my life. (🛈 全面否定では forever を用いないので ×I will not forget you forever. は不可)
【会話】「たばこやめたんだ」「永久に?」"I've given up smoking." "For good?"
●永久欠番 a retired (uniform) number. ●背番号をある永久欠番にする retire one's uniform number; have one's number retired. ●永久歯 a permanent tooth. ●永久磁石 a permanent magnet.

えいきょう 影響 (an) influence 《on》; (及ぼす影響を与える人・ものの意では常に ⓒ); (効果) (an) effect 《on》; (衝撃) (an) impact 《on》.
① 【影響～】▶中央省庁の強い影響下にある民間企業 a private company under the strong influence of the central government. ▶彼は文学界に大きな影響力を持っている He has [wields] a great influence on the literary world./(影響力の大きい作家だ) He is a very influential writer [a writer of great influence]. (🛈 後の方が堅い言い方)
② 【影響が】▶円高で日本経済に対する影響が深刻になってきている The influence [impact] of the strong yen on the Japanese economy has become very serious.
③ 【影響を】▶親の離婚が子供に悪い影響を与えることが多い Parents' divorce often has [×gives] (a) bad influence on their children./Parents' divorce often affects their children in bad ways [poisons their children's minds]. ▶家庭環境は人の性格にどのような影響を及ぼすのでしょうか How will a home environment influence [affect] personality? (🛈 influence は間接的に, affect は直接的に影響することを表す) ▶彼は先生から大きな影響を受けた He was greatly influenced by his teacher. ▶ファーブルは私の生涯に影響を与えた重要な人物だ

えいぎょう

Jean Henri Fabre is an important person who *influenced* my life [had a great *impact on* my life]. ▶喫煙は健康に悪い影響を及ぼす Smoking has a bad *effect on* the health. ▶コンピュータはビジネスのすべての分野に大きな影響を与えている Computers are having a great *impact on* all fields of business.

<u>DISCOURSE</u>
上記の例が示すように，外国語を学ぶことはものの考え方に大きな影響を及ぼす As these examples sug*gest, studying a foreign language has a significant *impact* on one's way of thinking. (❗As these examples suggest, (上記の例が示すように)は結論に用いるディスコースマーカー)

④【影響で】 ▶彼は先生の影響で英語に興味を持つようになった He has become interested in English *under the influence of* his teacher. ▶台風の影響で(=のために)列車が 2 時間遅れた *Because of* [*Owing to*] the typhoon, the train was delayed (for) two hours.

―― 影響する 動 influence, have* an influence (*on*); (直接的でしばしば不利に) affect; (衝撃的に，強く) impact (*on*), have an impact (*on*). (⇨図 ③)

*えいぎょう 営業 图 [営利を目的とした業務] business; [販売] sales. ●営業成績がよい(会社や人が) do good *business*, have a good *track record* (in sales) (⇨業績); (人が) do well [a good job] in *sales*, make a good job of *sales*. ▶彼は我が社の営業部員だ He's on [a member of] the *sales* staff of our firm./He works in the *sales* department of our firm. ▶営業中[掲示] Open./Open for *business*.

―― 営業する 動 [開店している] be open (⇔be closed); [開店する] open (⇔close) [いずれも人も主語になれる]; [業務を行う] do* business; [店を営む] run* (a liquor store). ▶私どもは月曜日は営業していません(店の場合) We don't *open* [aren't *open*, are closed] on Mondays./(会社・事務所などの場合) We don't *do business* on Mondays. (❗店が主語のときにも do business を用いる)
会話 (店で)「土曜は何時まで営業していますか」「10時まで営業しています」"How late *are* you *open* on Saturdays?" "We *are open* until 10."
●営業時間 business [office] hours. ●営業所(会社などの) an office; (店などの) a branch. ●営業日 a business day. ●営業部 a sales department. ●営業部長 a sales manager. ●営業利益 an operating profit.

えいぎょうりょく 影響力 influence. (⇨影響 ①)
えいけん 英検 [『英語検定試験』の略] an English proficiency examination; [実用英語技能試験] the STEP Test《Society for *T*esting *E*nglish *P*roficiency の略》.

*えいご 英語 English, the English language (❗後の方は堅い言い方); (学科) English (language) (❗学科名には the をつけない).

① 【～英語】●アメリカ[イギリス]英語 American [British] *English*. ●標準英語 standard *English*. ●時事[商業; 実用]英語 current [business; practical] *English*. ▶でたらめな[生きた(=日常)]英語 broken [everyday] *English*. ▶17 世紀の英語 the *English* of the seventeenth [17th] century. (❗特定時期の英語をさす場合 the が必要)

② 【英語(の)～】 ▶英語の講師。 a lecturer *in English*); an *English* teacher (❗ an *English* teacher は「英国人の先生」の意). ●英語の本 an *English* book (❗「英語に関する本」の意にもなるが，それを明示するときは a *book* about [on, of] *English*); a book (written) *in English*.

<u>DISCOURSE</u>
英語力が重要なのは，多くのグローバル企業では英語で業務を行っているからである．…さらに，インターネット上の情報の多くは英語だ *English ability* is important because many international companies conduct business in English. … **Furthermore**, the majority of information on the Internet is in English. (❗furthermore (さらに)は追加に用いるディスコースマーカー)

③ 【英語が】 ▶彼は英語がうまい[へただ] He speaks good [poor] *English*./He is a good [a poor] speaker of *English*./(書) He has a good [a poor] command of *English*. ▶どの科目よりも英語が好きです I like *English* best of all subjects. ▶あなたは英語が話せますか Do [Can] you speak *English*? (❗can は露骨に能力を問う言い方) ▶カナダでは英語が話されている *English* is spoken in Canada./They speak *English* in Canada. ▶仕事で英語が必要なんです I have to use [×need] *English* in my work./My job requires *English*.

④ 【英語に[から]】 ▶「桜」は英語で何といいますか What [×How] do you call [×say] "sakura" *in English*? (❗「それは英語ではどう表現するのか」のように具体的の対応関係に触れるときは How do you say it *in English*? といえる)/What is the *English for* "sakura"? (❗特定の語句をさす場合は the が必要) ▶私は英語で十分に足せば I can make myself understood *in English*. ▶この本は英語からの翻訳だ This book is translated from the *English*. (❗「英語で書かれたもの」の意では the が必要)

⑤ 【英語を】 ▶英語をどの程度話せますか How well can you speak *English*?
●英語学 English linguistics. ●英語教育 the teaching [×education] of English; English language teaching. ●英語圏 the English-speaking world. ●英語国 an English-speaking country. ●英語国民 an English-speaking people.

えいこう 栄光 glory. ▶彼は栄光の道をたどった He followed the paths of *glory*. ▶勝利の栄光は我がチームに輝いた Our team won a *glorious* victory.

えいこう 曳航 ―― 曳航する 動 tow《a ship》, take 《a ship》in tow.

えいごう 永劫 (永遠)(書) eternity. ●未来永劫(に)(⇨永久) ●永劫不変の eternal, (書) everlasting. For the BBC).

えいこうだん 曳光弾 a tracer (bullet).

*えいこく 英国 图 Britain, England; (公式名) the United Kingdom (of Great Britain and Northern Ireland)《略 the U.K.》. (⇨ イギリス)

―― 英国の 形 British, English. (❗政治的文脈では British が ふつう)
●英国航空 British Airways《略 BA》. ●英国放送協会 the British Broadcasting Corporation《略 the BBC》.

えいせいすい 栄枯盛衰 ▶文明の栄枯盛衰 the *rise and fall* of civilizations. ▶栄枯盛衰は世の習い(=人生には浮き沈みがある) Every life has its *ups and downs*. [(書) vicissitudes].

えいさいきょういく 英才教育 special education for brilliant [gifted] children.

えいさく(ぶん) 英作(文) English composition (❗その 1 編は ⓒ); (和文英訳) translation from Japanese into English.

えいし 衛視 a Diet guard. (⇨守衛)
えいし 英字 an English letter; (ローマ字) a Roman letter. ●英字新聞 an English (language) newspaper; a newspaper in English.
えいじ 嬰児 (生まれたばかりの子) a newborn baby; (乳児) a baby; (幼児) an infant.
えいしゃ 泳者 a swimmer.
えいしゃ 映写 ——映写する 動 ▶スライドをスクリーンに映写する *project* slides on the screen.
●映写機 a (movie) projector. ●映写室 a projection booth [room].
えいじゅう 永住 permanent residence.
——永住する 動 ▶パリに永住する *live* in Paris *forever* [*permanently*]; (永住の地と定める) *make* Paris one's *permanent home*.
●永住者 a permanent resident.
えいしょう 詠唱 a chant; (オペラの) an aria /ɑ́ːriə/.
——詠唱する 動 chant (a prayer).
えいじる 映じる ❶［反映する］be reflected 《in a mirror》. ❷［印象を与える］▶その晩の光景は私には奇妙に映じた The sight *looked* funny [strange] to me.
えいしん 栄進 图 (a) promotion. ——栄進する 動 be promoted to a higher rank [position].
エイズ ［後天性免疫不全症候群］AIDS 《*A*cquired *I*mmune *D*eficiency *S*yndrome の略》. ●エイズにかかっている[かかる] have [get, 《書》 contract] *AIDS*.
●エイズ患者 an AIDS patient; a person (living) with AIDS. (■(1) 略して P(L)WA ともいう. (2) an AIDS victim は避ける) ●エイズ感染 HIV infection. (■HIV は Human Immunodeficiency Virus の略) ●エイズ感染者 an *HIV* carrier; an *HIV* infected [positive] person.
えいせい 衛生 图 (公衆衛生, 衛生設備) sanitation; (衛生学, 衛生状態) hygiene /háidʒiːn/. ●精神[公衆]衛生 mental [public] *hygiene*. ●環境衛生 environmental *sanitation*. ●歯科衛生士 a dental *hygienist*. ●病院の衛生状態 *sanitary* [*hygienic*] conditions in the hospital. ●衛生に気をつける be careful about *sanitation*.
——衛生的な 形 (きれいで汚れたもののない) sanitary (↔unsanitary); (健康に関わる) hygiénic (↔unhygienic); (衛生の方が意味の広い) ▶その調理場はあまり衛生的でない The kitchen is not very *sanitary* [*hygienic*]. ●衛生的な包装 *sanitary* wrapping.
——衛生上 副 hygiénically.
●衛生技術 sanitary engineering. ●衛生用品 sanitary goods.
えいせい 衛星 a sátellite. ●人工衛星 an artificial [a man-made] *satellite*. (■単に a satellite ともいう) ●気象[通信; 放送]衛星 a weather [a communications; a broadcast(ing)] *satellite*.
●衛星国 a satellite (state [nation, country]). ●衛星中継 satellite relay. ▶この番組はローマから衛星中継されている This program is being relayed [broadcast] live via *satellite* from Rome./This program *is being satellited* live from Rome. (■単に /láiv/ と発音する) ●衛星都市 a satellite city [town]. ●衛星放送 satellite broadcasting.
えいせいちゅうりつ 永世中立 permanent neutrality. ●永世中立国 a permanently neutral nation [country].
えいぜん 営繕 (公共物の建築と修繕) building and repairs.
●営繕課 a building and repairs section. ●営繕費 building and repairing expenses.

えいそう 営巣 图 (鳥などの巣作り) nest building; nesting. ——営巣する 動 build a nest; nest.
えいぞう 映像 (テレビ・映画の) a picture; (反射した) a reflection. ▶このテレビの映像は鮮明だ We get a clear (↔ blurred) *picture* on this TV screen.
えいぞうぶつ 営造物 a building; (公共物) public works.
えいぞく 永続 ——永続的な 形 (長続きする) lasting; (永久不変の) permanent. ▶私たちは永続的な平和を望んでいる We hope for a *lasting* [an *everlasting*] peace.
——永続する 動 last long, last forever. (⇨長続きする)
えいだい 永代 (永遠) (書) eternity; (永続) permanence.
●永代供養 (説明的に) a memorial service promised to be perpetually performed at a Buddhist temple upon the donation of money by the bereaved family. ●永代所有権 perpetual ownership.
えいたつ 栄達 (立身出世) success in life; (昇進) a promotion. (⇨出世)
えいたん 詠嘆 (賞賛) admiration; (驚嘆) wonder.
——詠嘆する 動 admire; (驚嘆する) marvel 《at》.
えいだん 英断 ▶英断を下す (決定的な処置をとる) take decisive [drastic] measures; (賢明な決断を下す) make a wise decision [judgment].
えいち 英知 wisdom. ▶多くの人の英知を集める seek the *wisdom* of many people.
エイチアイブイ ［ヒト免疫不全ウイルス］HIV (*h*uman *i*mmunodeficiency *v*irus の略). (⇨エイズ)
えいてん 栄典 ❶［儀式］a ceremony. ❷［勲章など］a honor. (■通例 ~s) ●栄典を授与する honor 《him》 (for his work).
えいてん 栄転 ——栄転する 動 be transferred on promotion 《to》. ▶彼は大阪支店長に栄転した He *was* [*has been*] *promoted to* (the position of) manager of the Osaka branch. (■昇進した地位を表す場合に promote to を用いる) ▶ご栄転おめでとうございます. 実力のしからしめるところですね Congratulations on your *promotion*. You certainly deserve it.
えいねん 永年 for many years; (長い間) for a long time.
——永年の 形 long-time; (長期の) long-term.
えいびん 鋭敏 ——鋭敏な 形 (感覚・才知の) sharp (↔ dull); keen; acute. ●鋭敏な観察者 an *acute* [明敏な] a *shrewd*] observer. ●耳が鋭敏で have *sharp* [*keen*] ears; be *keen* of hearing. ▶犬の嗅覚(*きゅう*)は鋭敏だ Dogs have an *acute* [a *sharp*] sense of smell./Dogs have a *keen* nose.
えいぶん 英文 (英語) English; (学科) English literature; (英語の文章) English writing, (英語の 1 文) an English sentence. ●英文の標識 an *English* sign; a sign (written) *in English*. ●英文に直す translate [put] 《it》 into *English*. ▶英文で友達に手紙を書いた I wrote to my friend *in English*.
●英文科 (学部) the Department of English; the English Department (■後の方がくだけた言い方); (科目) the English literature course. ●英文和訳 translation from English into Japanese; English-Japanese translation.
えいぶんがく 英文学 English literature. ●英文学を研究する study *English literature*.
●英文学者 a scholar of English literature.
えいへい 衛兵 a guard. ●衛兵に立つ (見張る) stand guard.
●衛兵所 a guardhouse.

えいべい 英米 Britain and America. ●英米人 British and American people; the British and Americans.（後の方は固定観念化された「米米人」を暗示）▶彼は最近の英米事情に通じている He knows a lot about [He is updated on] recent *British and American* affairs.

えいほう 泳法 a swimming fórm [stýle].

えいほう 鋭峰（とがった山頂）a peak.

●敵の鋭峰をくじく break the *brunt* of an enemy.

えいまい 英邁 ── 英邁な 形 ▶英邁な君主 a *sage* monarch.

えいみん 永眠 ── 永眠する 動 die,《婉曲的》pass away;《書》rest in peace.（⇨死ぬ）

えいやく 英訳 名 translation into English; (an) English translation. ●その小説を英訳《本》で読む read the novel in an *English translation*.
── 英訳する 動 ●その詩を英訳する *translate* the poem *into English*.（やや話）do an *English translation* of the poem.
●英訳者 a translator into English《*of a book*》.

*えいゆう **英雄** a hero /híːərou/（複 ~es）.（❗ベートーベンの「英雄」は *Eroica* という）●国民的英雄 a national *hero*. ●英雄的行為 *heroic* deeds; an act of heroism.
会話「英雄のいない国は不幸だ」「英雄を必要とする国こそ不幸なんだ」"A nation without a *hero* is an unfortunate nation." "On the contrary, a nation in need of a *hero* is unfortunate."
●英雄色を好む Great men are often too fond of women./Heroes enjoy playing around with women.
●英雄譚(たん)a heróic tale.

えいよ 栄誉 glory, honor.（⇨名誉, 栄光）●国民栄誉賞 the People's *Honor* Award. ▶みんなが我が校の優勝の栄誉をたたえた Everybody praised the *glorious* victory of our school.

‡**えいよう 栄養**（栄養のある物）nourishment /nə́ːrɪʃmənt/（栄養（摂取））nutrition /n(j)uːtrɪ́ʃən/;（栄養分）a nutrient /n(j)úːtriənt/.（❗後の2語はいずれも専門的で堅い語）●栄養のある nutritious; nourishing. ●栄養が十分な赤ん坊 a well-*nourished* baby. ●栄養の片寄らない食事を取る have a *nutritionally* balanced diet. ●栄養をとる take *nourishment*.（栄養のある食物を食べる）have *nutritious* [*nourishing*] food. ▶この果実は栄養満点だ This fruit is full of [rich in] *nourishment*. ▶この果実は栄養のある This fruit is very *nutritious* [*nourishing*]. ▶コーヒーに栄養はない Coffee has no *nourishment*. ▶十分な栄養をとることは健康の基本だ Good *nutrition* is the basis of good health.
●栄養価 nutritional [nutritive] value.（❗前の方が一般的）●栄養学 nutrition. ●栄養過多 overnutrition. ●栄養士 a nutrient. ●栄養士 a dietician. ●栄養状態 nutritional [nutritive] conditions. ●栄養摂取量（カロリー）(a) caloric intake. ●栄養素 a nutrient. ●栄養不良[障害] undernourishment.

えいようえいが 栄耀栄華 luxury. ●栄耀栄華に暮らす live in *luxury*; lead a life of *luxury*.

えいようしっちょう 栄養失調 màlnutrítion. ●栄養失調である be *undernourished*; be *badly nourished*; be suffering from *malnutrition*.

えいり 営利（利益）a profit; (a) gain;（金もうけ）moneymaking. ●営利を目的とした[=非営利]団体 a *non-profit* [a *not-for-profit*] organization. ▶あのやり方はあまりにも営利的だと思いませんか Don't you think that's much too *commercial*?

●営利事業 a profit-making [a for-profit, a moneymaking, a commercial] enterprise.

えいり 鋭利 ── 鋭利な 形 sharp.（⇨鋭い）●鋭利な刃物[かみそりの刃] a *sharp* knife [razor blade].

えいりん 映倫『映倫管理委員会』の略』the Administration Commission of Motion Picture Code of Ethics.

えいりん 営林（林業）forestry.
●営林署 a local forestry office.

えいれい 英霊（戦死者の霊）the souls of the war dead.

えいれんぽう 英連邦 the Commonwealth (of Nations).

えいわ 英和 ●英和辞典 an English-Japanese dictionary.

ええ ❶ [質問に対して] yes;《話》yeah /jéə/, uh- huh /ʌ́hʌ́/, mhm/（❗uh-huh は、口は開けていても閉じていてもよいが、鼻にかかった音ととることに注意）;（否定疑問文に対して）no.（⇨はい）▶ええ、そうですとも *Yes*, that's right. ▶とてもそうは思えません、ええ I really don't believe that, *no*.
会話「最近は商売ももうからないでしょ」「ええ、さっぱりです」"Your business doesn't pay these days, does it?" "*No*, it doesn't at all."
❷ [承諾して] yes, certainly, of course;《話》all right, OK, O.K., sure.
会話「じゃ、体に気をつけてね」「ええ」"Well, take care of yourself." "Ah, *yes*."
会話「これを戻してくれる？」「ええ、いいわ」"Will you put it back?" "*OK* [*Sure*]."
❸ [ためらい] well, let me see; er.

エーエム『電波の』AM《amplitude *modulation* の略》.（略 エフエム）
●エーエム放送 AM broadcasting.

エーエム『午前』a.m., A.M.（❗ラテン語 ante meridiem（=before noon）の略。用法は（⇨午前）

エーオーにゅうし AO入試（説明的に）an entrance exam in which great importance is attached to an interview held by the admissions office.

エーカー『面積の単位』an acre《略 a., A.》.

エーゲ ●エーゲ海 the Aegean / Sea.

エージェンシー『代理店』an agency.

エージェント『代理人』an agent.

エース ❶『トランプなどの』an ace. ❷『第一人者』an ace. ●リリーフエース an *ace* reliever; a bullpen ace. ❸『テニスなどの』●サービスエース an ace; a service *ace*.
●エースピッチャー『野球』an ace (pitcher).

ええっ（⇨えっ）

ええっと well; (well,) let me [let's] see;『さて、ところで』well;『言葉につまったとき』er. ▶ええっと、説明するのは難しいですね *Well*, it's difficult to explain. ▶ええっと、鍵(かぎ)をどこに置いたかな *Let me* [*Let's*] *see*. Where did I put the key? ▶それは―ええっと―10か月ほど前のでした It was about, *er*, 10 months ago.（❗文法上の違いに注意）

エーディー A.D.（❗(1) ラテン語 Anno Domini の略。(2) A.D. 1878 のように数字の前に置くのが正しいが B.C. の類推で from 300 B.C. to 1300 A.D. のように後に置くことも多い

エーディーエスエル『非対称デジタル加入者線』ADSL《*Asymmetrical Digital Subscriber Line* の略》.

エーティーエム『現金自動預け払い機』an ATM《an *Automated* [an *Automatic*] *Teller Machine* の略》.

エーティーしゃ『自動変速式自動車』an automatic transmission car.（❗an AT car とはいわないが日

エーテル 〖化学〗 ether /íːθər/.
エーデルワイス 〖植物〗 an edelweiss /éidlvàis, -wàis/.
エーブイ ❶ [視聴覚の] audio(-)visual, AV. (⇨視聴覚) ❷ [アダルトビデオ] (a) porn video. (⇨アダルト)
 ・AV 教育 audio(-)visual [AV] education.
 ・AV 教室 audio(-)visual [an AV] classroom. ・AV 機器 audio(-)visual [AV] equipment.
エープリルフール 〖日〗 April [All] Fools' Day; [かつがれた人] an April fool. ▶4月1日はエープリルフールだ April 1st is *April Fools' Day* [×April Fool].
エーペック 〖アジア太平洋経済協力〗 APEC 《the *A*sia-*P*acific *E*conomic *C*ooperation の略》.
エール ❶ [応援の声] 〖米〗 a yell. ・エールを交換する exchange *yells*. ❷ [ビールの一種] ale.
えがお 笑顔 a smiling face; [微笑] a smile. (⇨笑い)
 ・彼を笑顔で迎える welcome him *with a smile* [*smilingly*]. ▶彼らは明るい笑顔を見せた They gave a bright *smile*./They smiled brightly [*beamingly*]. ▶赤ちゃんの笑顔がかわいい The baby has a sweet *smile*.
えかき 絵描き a painter. (⇨画家)
*****えがく** 描く ❶ [絵などをかく] [鉛筆などを使って線で] draw*; [絵の具で] paint; [略図を] sketch. ▶彼はペンで紙に円を描いた He *drew* [×wrote, ×painted] a circle on the paper with a pen. (❗write は字を「書く」という) ▶彼女は母親を油絵の具で描いた She *painted* [×drew, ×wrote] her mother in oils. ▶彼は地面に地図を描いた He *sketched* a map in the ground.
❷ [描写する] [人が] describe, [絵などが] represent. ▶彼は随筆の中で戦争体験を描いている He *describes* [×is describing] his war experiences in his essay. ▶この絵は当時の校舎を描いている This painting *represents* [This is a *painting* of] the school building of those days.
❸ [思い描く] imagine; [生き生きと] picture. ▶彼女は都会の生活を心に描いた She *pictured* (*to herself*) [*imagined*] city life.
❹ [形づくる] 弧を描いて飛ぶ fly *in an arc*.
えがたい 得難い [手に入れにくい] hard to get [obtain]; [まれな] rare; [貴重な] precious, valuable. ・得がたい機会 a *golden* [a *rare*] opportunity. ▶当地では塩は得難い品だ Salt is very *hard to get* here./Salt is a *rare* [a *precious*] thing here.
えがら 絵柄 [図案] a design; [模様] a pattern. ・花の絵柄 a flower *design* [*pattern*].
えがらっぽい (⇨いがらっぽい)
:えき 駅 a station (❗「局・署」などの意味とまぎらわしいときは a train 〖米〗 a railroad, 〖英〗 a railway station とする), 〖米〗 a depot /díːpou/; [地下鉄の] a subway 〖米〗 [a tube, an underground 〖英〗] station. ・始発駅 the *starting station*. ・乗り換え駅 (⇨乗り換え). ・六甲駅から電車に乗る take a train at [×from] Rokko *Station*. (❗駅名は無冠詞.「六甲駅から梅田まで」というときは from Rokko (*Station*) to Umeda (*Station*) と Station を省略もよい) ▶彼は次の駅で降りた He got off at the next station.
 会話「新大阪はいくつ目の駅ですか」「ここから五つ目です」"How many *stops* is it to Shin-Osaka?" "(It's) five stops from here." (⇨目)
えき 役 a war, a battle. ・西南の役 〖歴史〗 the *Battle* of Seinan.

えき 易 [占い] divination, fortune-telling; [陰陽] the principles of Yin and Yang. ・易を立てる read one's *fortune*.
えき 益 图 [効用] use, good; [有利] advantage; [恩恵] (a) benefit; [利益] (a) profit. ▶そんなことをして何の益か(=得)があるのか What's the *use* [*good*] of doing such a thing? (⇨得①) ▶それは益どころか害になる(=有害無益だ) It does more harm than *good*./It's worse than useless. ▶寝る時間を過ぎてまで勉強しても何の益もない There is no *advantage in* studying past your bedtime.
 ── 益する 働 benefit; [役立つ] be useful 《*to, for*》. ▶その本は生徒を益するところ大である The book *benefits* students greatly./Students *benefit* greatly *from* the book. ・書物を益にするは(=まれ) /The book *is* very *useful* [*of great use*] to students.
えき 液 [液体] (a) liquid 〖固体 (solid) に対する語〗; [流動体] (a) fluid 〖液体と気体 (gas) の総称〗; [果汁, 肉汁, 体液] (a) juice; [溶液] (a) solution; [樹液] sap.
えきいん 駅員 a station attendant [employee].
えきか 液化 图 liquefaction.
 ── 液化する 働 liquefy.
 ・液化ガス liquefied gas. ・液化石油ガス liquefied petroleum gas (略 LPG). ・液化天然ガス liquefied natural gas (略 LNG).
えきがく 疫学 epidemiology.
えきざい 液剤 〖薬学〗 liquid medicine.
エキサイト ── エキサイトする 働 get (very) excited.
 ・エキサイトゲーム [エキサイティングな試合] an *exciting* [はらはらさせる] a *thrilling* game.
エキジビション an exhibition /èksəbíʃən/ game.
えきしゃ 易者 a fortune-teller.
えきしゃ 駅舎 a station building.
えきしょう 液晶 liquid crystal.
 ・液晶ディスプレー a liquid crystal display. 《略 LCD》 ・液晶テレビ a liquid crystal (display) television.
えきじょう 液状 ── 液状の 形 liquid, fluid.
 ・液状化 liquefaction. ・土壌の液状化 soil *liquefaction*. ・液状化現象 a liquefaction phenomenon.
エキス (an) éxtract; essence. ・牛肉エキス beef *extract* [*essence*].
エキストラ an extra, 〖話〗 a super 《supernumerary actor (端役) の略》. ・エキストラをやる play as an *extra*.
エキスパート [専門家] an éxpert. ▶彼は機械修理のエキスパートだ He is (an) *expert at* [*in*] repairing machines. (❗不定冠詞を伴わない形容詞状況用法の場合でも, 強勢は今は éxpert が普通) ▶彼は政治問題に関してはエキスパートだが, 経済に関してはアマチュアだ He's an *expert* about [on] political topics [matters], but an amateur about economic topics [matters]./He's an *expert* on politics but he knows nothing about economics.
エキスパンダー [トレーニング用具の一種] an expander.
エキスポ [〖万国〗博覧会] an expo (複 ～s). (❗(*inter*national) exposition の短縮形 (⇨博覧会, 万博))
エキゾチック ── エキゾチックな 形 [異国風の] exotic /igzátik/. ▶熱帯の国を暗示することもある) ▶この町のエキゾチックな雰囲気が好きだ I like the *exotic* atmosphere in this town.
*****えきたい** 液体 [名] (a) liquid; (a) fluid 〖厳密には気体も含むが日常的には liquid に同じ〗. (⇨液)
 ・液体酸素 liquid oxygen. ・液体洗剤 liquid de-

えきだん 易断 (占い) divination, fortune-telling.
えきちく 役畜 an animal used for labor.
えきちゅう 益虫 a useful insect.
えきちょう 益鳥 a useful bird.
えきちょう 駅長 a station manager, a stationmaster; (小さな駅) a station agent.
● 駅長室 the station manager's [stationmaster's] office.
えきでん 駅伝 [駅伝競走] a long-distance relay road race; a road relay, an *ekiden*.
えきとう 駅頭 ▶駅頭で (駅の前で) in front of a station; (駅で) at a station.
えきどめ 駅留め ▶この荷物を駅留めにしてもらいたい I want to have this baggage *held at the station*.
えきばしゃ 駅馬車 a stagecoach; [映画名] *Stagecoach*.
えきびょう 疫病 (悪性の伝染病) a plague /pléig/. ●疫病にかかる catch a *plague*. ●コレラという疫病 a cholera *plague*.
えきビル 駅ビル a train [《米》a railroad, 《英》a railway] station building.
えきべん 駅弁 (説明的に) a box lunch sold at a railroad [train] station.
えきまえ 駅前 ●駅前広場 a station plaza [square]. ●駅前旅館 an inn in front of a station.
えきむ 役務 labor; (サービス) (a) service.
● 役務賠償 a service indemnity.
えきり 疫痢 children's dysentery /dísəntèri/. (!dysentery は「赤痢」)
エクアドル [国名] Ecuador /ékwədɔːr/; (公式名) the Republic of Ecuador. (首都 Quito) ●エクアドル人 an Ecuadorian. ●エクアドル(人)の Ecuadorian.
えぐい (味の) bitter, acrid.
エクスタシー (an) écstasy.
エクステリア [外構] an exterior.
● エクステリアデザイン exterior design.
エクストラホール an extra hole. (!ゴルフでは追加ホール,ボウリングではバランスのために球にあける追加の穴.ボウリングの場合は a balance hole ともいう)
エグゼクティブ [幹部] an executive /igzékjətiv/.
エクソシスト [悪魔払いの祈祷師] an éxorcist.
えくぼ 笑窪 a dimple. [語法] 米英でもチャームポイントの一つ) ●彼女は笑うとえくぼができる She has *dimples* when she smiles./A smile dimples her face. (!「片えくぼ」なら She has a *dimple* in her right cheek. などという)
えぐみ (味の) bitterness, acridity.
***えぐる** 抉る ❶[地面・木などを] (くり抜く) hollow ... out; (丸のみなどでくり抜く) gouge /gáudʒ/ ... (out). ●目玉をえぐり出す gouge out 《his》 eyes. ▶川岸が流水でえぐられた The river banks *were hollowed out by water*.
❷[胸・問題などを] ●心をえぐるような(=痛切な)悲しみ acute [胸の張り裂けそうな] *heartbreaking*] grief. ●問題の核心をえぐる [鋭く突く] *get to the heart [core, point] of the matter.* ▶彼女は愛犬の死に胸をえぐられる思いだった He *was heartbroken over the death of his pet dog* [when his pet dog died].
エクレア [<フランス語] an éclair /eikléər/.
えげつない (無礼かつ下品な) rude, vulgar; (心くばりのない) insensitive; (いやらしい) nasty; dirty.
エコ [名] [生態(学)] ecology.
── エコの [形] (生態系を損ねない) ecological; (生態系にやさしい) eco-friendly.
● エコグッズ ecological goods. ●エコツアー an eco tour. (参考 エコツーリズムの考え方に基づいた旅) ●エコツーリズム ecotourism. (参考 環境保護と観光業・地域振興の融合をめざす観光の考え方) ●エコラベル, (日本の) an Eco Mark. (参考 環境保全型商品に付けられるマーク)
エゴ [利己心] selfishness, [哲学] egoism /í:gouizm/; [自己中心性] egotism. (!egoism を日常用いる場合, egotism の意で用いることが多い. ego は哲学用語で「自我」の意) ●彼はエゴのかたまりだ He is *selfishness* itself./He is the (very) personification [incarnation] of *selfishness*.
エゴイスト [利己主義者] an egoist; (自分勝手な人) a selfish person.
エゴイズム [利己主義] egoism /í:gouizm/. (⇨エゴ)
エコー [こだま] (an) echo (-es); [医療用超音波] echoes, supersonic waves; (超音波検査器) an echograph; (その図) an echogram. ●エコー心拍記録(法) echo cardiography. ●エコーをかける use the *echo effect* (on the microphone).
えごころ 絵心 (絵を描く才能) a talent for painting [drawing]; (絵を見る能力) an eye for paintings. ●絵心がわく want to paint [draw] a picture. ●絵心がある have *an eye for painting*.
えこじ 依怙地 ⇨意固地
エコノミー ●エコノミー(クラス)で行く go [travel] *economy* (class).
● エコノミークラス症候群 economy class syndrome; [医学] (深部静脈血栓症) deep vein thrombosis (略 DVT).
エコノミスト [経済学者] an economist; [雑誌名] *The Economist*.
エコノミックアニマル [経済上の利害だけで行動する人間] an economic animal.
えこひいき 依怙贔屓 [名] [偏愛] favoritism; [不公平] partiality.
── 依怙贔屓の [形] unfair (↔fair); partial.
── 依怙贔屓する [動] ●どの生徒もえこひいきしない(=公平に扱う) give each pupil 《a》 *fair treatment*. ▶私たちの先生は山田君をえこひいきしている Our teacher *favors* Yamada./Our teacher *is partial to* [toward] Yamada.
エコロジー [生態(学)] ecology. (⇨エコ)
***えさ** 餌 [飼料] feed (!「1回分のえさ」の意では Ⓒ), food; [釣り・わな用の] bait /béit/; [人を誘惑するための] (a) bait, a lure. ●家畜のえさ *feed* [*food*] *for cattle*; (飼い葉) fodder. ●小鳥のえさ birdseed. ●小鳥のえさ台 a bird table. ●〈魚が〉えさをつく[食う] nibble at [take] the bait. ●釣り針にえさのミミズをつける bait a hook *with* angleworms. ●小エビをえさに使う use shrimps for *bait*. ●カラス麦をえさに馬を飼う 《米》*feed* oats *to* horses; 《英》*feed* horses *on* oats. ●彼をえさで釣る lure him with a *bait*. ▶犬に1日に2回えさをやります I *feed* my dog twice a day./I give my dog two *feeds* [*feedings*] a day. (!《米》ではしばしば後の方を使う)
えざら 絵皿 a decorated [a picture] plate. ●四角いスイレンの絵皿 a square waterlilies *picture plate*.
えし 絵師 a painter, an artist.
えし 壊死 [名] [医学] necrosis /nəkróusis/ (複 necroses /-si:z/).
── 壊死する [動] become necrotic.
えじき 餌食 [犠牲] a victim. ●ネズミは猫のえじきになる Mice are the *prey* of cats./(捕食される) Cats prey on [upon] mice. ▶彼らは暴力団のえじきとなった They *fell prey [victim] to* a gang./They became [×*fell*] the *prey [victim]* of a gang.
エジソン [米国の発明家] Edison /édisn/ (Thomas

エジプト [国名] Egypt /íːdʒɪpt/; (公式名) the Arab Republic of Egypt. (首都 Cairo) ●エジプト人 an Egyptian /ɪdʒípʃən/. ●エジプト(人)の Egyptian.

えしゃく 会釈 [图][軽いおじぎ] a slight bow /báu/; [うなずき] a nod. ●会釈を交わす exchange nods.
—— **会釈(を)する** [動] ●先生に軽く会釈する make a slight bow [bow slightly] to the teacher; nod (a greeting) to the teacher. ▶私たちは彼らとは会えばちょっと会釈をする程度の知り合いです We have only a *nodding* acquaintance with them.

エシャロット [<フランス語] [植物] a shallot.

エス S ●エスサイズの靴 shoes of size *S* [*small size*]; *small-sized* shoes.

えず 絵図 a picture; [平面図] a plan.

エスイー SE [システムエンジニア] a system(s) engineer; [システム工学] system(s) engineering; [放送劇などの音響効果] sound effects.

エスエフ [空想科学小説] (集合的) science fiction (略 SF, sf), [話] sci-fi /sáifái/; (個々の) a science fiction [話] a sci-fi] novel.

エスエル [蒸気機関車] a steam locomotive; 《和製語》SL.

エスオーエス SOS ●エスオーエスを送信[受信]する send [receive] an *SOS* (*call*).

エスカルゴ [<フランス語] [食用のカタツムリ] an escargot.

*****エスカレーター** an escalator. ●上り[下り]のエスカレーター an [a down] *escalator*. ●エスカレーターに乗る step [get] on (↔off) an *escalator*; (利用する) take an *escalator*. (⇔エレベーター) ▶エスカレーターで3階に上った I rode [took] an *escalator* to the third floor./I went up to the third floor *by* [*on an*, 《in an*] *escalator*. ▶この中学校へ入れば、あとはエスカレーター式で大学まで行ける Once you enter this junior high school, you can get to college automatically like you are carried up to the high floors by escalator.

エスカレート —— **エスカレートする** [動] escalate. ▶小さな衝突が核戦争にエスカレートするかもしれない A minor conflict might *escalate into* [*to*] a nuclear war.

エスキモー an Éskimò (略 ~(s)). [!] カナダエスキモーは自らを Innuit, Innuit と呼ぶ

エスケープ —— **エスケープする** [動] ●授業をエスケープする cut a class. (⇒サボる)
●エスケープキー (キーボードの) an escape key.

エスコート [付き添いの男] an escort. ●彼がパーティーで彼女のエスコートをした He was her *escort to* the party./He *escorted* her to the party.

エスタブリッシュメント [支配体制] the Establishment.

エステ (⇒エステティック)

エステティシャン an esthetician; a beautician; a beauty therapist; a cosmetologist.

エステティック [<フランス語] (美容) 'esthétique'. (!] この日本語に対応する英語はない)
●エステティックサロン a day [a beauty] salon [parlor, shop].

エステル [<ドイツ語] [酸とアルコールの化合物] [化学] an ester.

エストニア [国名] Estonia /estóuniə/. (首都 Tallinn) ●エストニア人 an Estonian. ●エストニア語 Estonian. ●エストニア(人[語])の Estonian.

エストロゲン [発情ホルモン] [生化学] estrogen.

エスニック ethnic (foods, dishes, fabrics).

エスプリ [<フランス語] [機知, 才気] esprit /esprí/.

エスプレッソ [<イタリア語] espresso.

エスペラント Esperanto /èspərɑ́ːntou/.
●エスペラント学者[使用者] an Esperantist.

えせ 似非 (似て非なる) pseudo- /s(j)úːdou-/, false. ●えせ学者 a *pseudo*-scholar.

えそ 壊疽 [医学] gángrene.

えぞ 蝦夷 ❶ [アイヌ族] an Ainu. ❷ [北海道の古称] Yezo.

えぞうし 絵双紙, 絵草紙 an *ezoshi*; an Edo-style illustrated story book.

えぞぎく 蝦夷菊 [植物] a China aster.

えぞまつ 蝦夷松 [植物] a (Japanese) spruce.

えそらごと 絵空事 (夢想) a pipe dream; 《build》 castles in the air.

*****えだ 枝** a branch ([!] あらゆる枝を意味する最も一般的な語); [大枝] a main branch, [書] a bough /báu/; [小枝] a twig, (葉・花・実などのついた) a spray, (葉のついた) a sprig; [若枝] a shoot. ●枝ぶりのよい松 a pine tree with graceful [shapely] *branches*. ●枝に分かれる spread [divide] into *branches*. ●枝を切る cut off *branches*; (刈り込む) trim *branches*.

えたい 得体 ●得体の知れない男 a *mysterious* [(変な) a *strange*] man.

> **翻訳のこころ** えたいの知れない不吉な塊が私の心を始終おさえつけていた(梶井基次郎「檸檬」) An unidentifiable ominous feeling [dark cloud] has been heavily hanging on my mind. ([!] (1)「えたいの知れない」は unidentifiable (正体がわからない)と表す. (2)「塊」は feeling (気持ち)と表す. lump は不適切. (3) dark cloud は「暗い, 不安な思い」の慣用表現. (4)「始終」は現在完了進行形で表す. (5)「おさえつける」は heavily hang on ((心配が心に)重くのしかかる)と表す)

えだげ 枝毛 a split end (of one's hair).

エタノール [化学] ethanol.

えだは 枝葉 ❶ [木の枝と葉] leaves and branches. ❷ [物事の重要でない部分] insignificant details. ●事実に枝葉をつける add *minor technicalities* to the fact.

えだぶり 枝振り the shape of a tree. ●枝ぶりのよい松 a gracefully *shaped* pine tree.

えだまめ 枝豆 green soybeans.

えたり 得たり ●得たりとばかり...する seize the opportunity 《*to do*》.

エチオピア [国名] Ethiopia /iːθióupiə/; (公式名) the Federal Democratic Republic of Ethiopia. (首都 Addis Ababa) ●エチオピア人 an Ethiopian. ●エチオピア(人)の Ethiopian.

*****エチケット** [<フランス語] étiquette; manners. ([!] 後の方が一般的) 《礼儀, 義 ③》 ●エチケットを守る observe the rules of *etiquette*.

エチュード [<フランス語] [練習曲] an étude; (習作) a study.

エチルアルコール [化学] ethyl alcohol /éθl ǽlkəhɔ̀(ː)l/.

エチレン [化学] ethylene /éθəliːn/.

えつ 悦 ●悦に入る be very pleased [happy] 《*with*》. (⇒喜ぶ) ●ひとりで悦に入っている be [look] pleased with oneself.

えっ [驚き, 反応] oh /óu/; well (⇒まあ 图); [聞き返し] eh /éi/, huh /hʌ́/. ▶えっ, 本当ですか *Oh*, *really*? (⇒ああ 图 ❷) ／えっ, 何ですって ／*Eh*? ／*Huh*? ／*What*? ／*What did you sáy*? ([!] 以上はぶっきらぼうな言い方) ／*Párdon*　[主に英] ／*Sórry*? ([!] 以上いずれも大幅な上昇調にすると「聞こえたが信じられない」の意となる)

會話「屋根がまた雨もりしている」「えっ, またか」 "The

えっきょう 越境 ・有名校に越境入学する get into a prestigious [a famous] school outside one's school zone [district]. ・prestigious は「レベルの高い」, famous では「何かで有名な」の意もある
— **越境する** 動 (国境を越える) cross [(不法に) transgress] the border. ・越境しては(=国境を越えて)逃げる escape over [across] the border.

えづく 餌付く (鳥などが) begin to feed.

エックスきゃく エックス脚 名 knock-knee(s).
— **エックス脚の** 形 knock-kneed. ・x-shaped legs は家具の脚に用いる

エックスせん X線 X rays. (⇒レントゲン)

エックスデー [何か重大な事が起こると想定される日] D-day; (和製語) X-day.

えつけ 絵付け painting on china.

えづけ 餌付け feeding.
— **餌付けする** 動 feed; get (the wild deer) to eat [feed] the food one gives it.

えっけん 越権 ・そんなことを言うなんて越権行為だよ You're *exceeding* your *authority* in saying that./(君にはその権利がない) You *have no right* to say that.

えっけん 謁見 ・謁見を許す grant (him) an *audience*; grant an *audience* (to him).

エッセー [随筆] an essay.

エッセンス ❶ [物事の本質] essence.
❷ [エキス, 香料] (an) essence.

エッチ ・エッチな話 a *dirty* story; (わいせつな冗談) a *dirty* [an *obscene*, a *blue*] joke. ・…にエッチなことをする get fresh with…. ・…とエッチをする have sex with…; make love with…. ・エッチな人 (好色な人) a lustful person; (変態者) a (sexual) pervert. ・あの人はエッチだ He is a *dirty* old man. (!話)で慣用的な言い方. 若い男性にも用いる

えっちらおっちら ・えっちらおっちらと山道を登る drag one's *feet* along a mountain pass.

エッチング (技法) etching; (作品) an etching.

えっとう 越冬 — **越冬する** 動 ・南極で越冬する(=冬を過ごす) spend [pass] the winter on the Antarctic Continent. (!動詞 winter は通例「避寒する」の意で用いられる: winter in a warmer country (暖かい国で冬を過ごす)
・越冬パーティー a wintering pàrty [tèam].

えつどく 閲読 — **閲読する** 動 pore (over a book).

えつねん 越年 — **越年する** 動 see the old year out; (新年を迎える) greet the New Year.

エッフェルとう エッフェル塔 the Eiffel /áifl/ Tower.

えっぺい 閲兵 — **閲兵する** 動 review troops; (行進を) take the parade.

えつらく 悦楽 (快楽) (a) pleasure; (大きな喜び) (a) delight.

えつらん 閲覧 名 (careful) reading. ・それらの希覯(きこう)本を一般の閲覧に供する(=読めるよう提供する) offer those rare books for public *reading*; (利用できるようにする) make those rare books available to the public.

DISCOURSE
子供のインターネット閲覧を禁止すべきだろうか. 異論もあろうが, 私は子供のインターネットへのアクセスにも制限があるべきだと考える Should we prohibit young children from *accessing* the Internet? Although there may be some oppositions, I am of the opinion that children should have limited access to the Internet. (!「疑問文→答え」のパターン. 序論でよく用いられる)

— **閲覧する** 動 (読む) read (carefully); (調べる) look … through; (参照する) consult. ・インターネットでその商品の情報を閲覧した(=探した) I *searched* for the information of the article on the Internet.
・閲覧室 a réading ròom. ・閲覧者 a reader.

えて 得手 (⇒得意 ❷) one's strong and weak points.
・得手に帆をあげる be in one's element.

エディター [編集者, 編集プログラム] an editor. ・テキストエディタ [コンピュータ] a text *editor*.

エディプスコンプレックス [精神分析] an Oedipus /édəpəs/ complex. (男児が父親を憎み母親を思慕する傾向)

エディンバラ [スコットランドの首都] Edinburgh /édnbə:rə, -bàrə/.

えてかって 得手勝手 — **得手勝手な** 形 selfish, self-seeking.

えてがみ 絵手紙 a drawing postcard.

えてして 得てして [とかく…しがちだ] be apt [(やや書) liable] (to do); [たぶん…する傾向がある] tend (to do). (⇒とかく) ・うぬぼれるとえてして失敗するものだ We *are apt to* fail when we are conceited.

エデン Eden /íːdn/.
・エデンの園 the Garden of *Eden*.

エデンのひがし [エデンの東] *East of Eden*. (参考 スタインベックの小説)

えと 干支 (十二支) the twelve zodiac signs in Chinese astrology; (十干十二支) the sexagenary /seksǽdʒənəri/ cycle. ・今年の干支はいのししだ This is the year of the Boar in *Chinese astrology*.

> **関連 十二支**: ね(子) the Rat/うし(丑) the Ox/とら(寅) the Tiger/う(卯) the Rabbit/たつ(辰) the Dragon/み(巳) the Snake/うま(午) the Horse/ひつじ(未) the Sheep/さる(申) the Monkey/とり(酉) the Cock/いぬ(戌) the Dog/い(亥) the Boar.

えとき 絵解き (絵の説明) an explanation of a picture; (絵による説明) an illustration with pictures.

えとく 会得 — **会得する** 動 [習得する] learn, (話) pick … up; (完全に) master; [理解する] understand, (書) comprehend; [把握する] grasp. ・こつを会得している[する] have [get, learn] the knack (of it). ・普通の子供ならこんなに素早く物事を会得できないだろう No ordinary child could *pick things up* as quickly as this.

えどっこ 江戸っ子 a native Tokyoite /tóukiouàit/ (! a Tokyoite は新聞用語); a native of Tokyo.

えどまえ 江戸前 ・江戸前の魚 (fresh) fish *from Tokyo Bay*.
・江戸前寿司 Tokyo-style sushi.

えなが 柄長 [鳥] a long-tailed tit.

エナメル (塗料) enamel /inǽml/; (エナメル革) enameled leather; (くつ, ハンドバッグなどのエナメル革) patent leather. ・黒[赤]のエナメルの靴 black [red] *patent* [✕enameled] *leather* shoes.

エニシダ [植物] a genista, a broom.

えにっき 絵日記 a picture [(挿し絵入りの) an illustrated] diary.

エヌエッチケー [日本放送協会] NHK; Japan Broadcasting Corporation.
・NHK 教育テレビ NHK Educational TV. ・NHK 総合テレビ NHK General TV.

エヌジー NG (*No Good* の略). ・エヌジーを出す *spoil* [*ruin*] a sequence.

エヌジーオー [非政府組織] an NGO (*nongovernmental organization* の略).

エヌピーオー [民間非営利組織] an NPO (*nonprofit*

エネルギー [<ドイツ語] energy /énərdʒi/. (⇨精力)
• 太陽[核]エネルギー solar [nuclear] energy. • 省エネ(ルギー)の energy-saving [energy-conserving] (technology). • エネルギーを節約する save [conserve] energy. • エネルギーを消費する consume energy.
• エネルギー危機 an energy crisis. • エネルギー源 an energy source; a source of energy. • エネルギー資源 energy resources.

エネルギッシュ [<ドイツ語] • エネルギッシュ(=精力的)な実業家 an energetic businessperson. ▶彼はエネルギッシュだ He's full of energy. (⇨精力)

えのき 榎(植物の) a (Chinese) hackberry.

えのきだけ 榎茸 (植物) an enokidake mushroom; a velvet shank.

えのぐ 絵の具 colors, paints. • 油絵の具 oil colors; oils. • 水彩絵の具 watercolors. • 絵の具で絵を描く paint [color, ×draw] a picture. (❗draw は鉛筆・ペンで描くこと．「油絵の具で描く」は paint in oils)
• 絵の具チューブ a tube of color [paint]. • 絵の具箱 a paint [a color] box.

えはがき 絵葉書 a postcard, 《書》a picture postcard. (⇨葉書)

エバミルク [無糖練乳] evaporated milk.

えび 海老 (動物) (大エビ) a lobster; (伊勢エビ) a (spiny) lobster; (車エビ) a prawn; (小エビ) a shrimp. • アマエビ a sweet shrimp.
• えびでたいを釣る (ジャコをまいてサバ[クジラ; ニシン]を獲) throw (out) a sprat to catch a mackerel [a whale; a herring].
• エビフライ a fried prawn.

えびがに 海老蟹 (⇨ざりがに)

エピグラム [警句] an epigram.

えびす 恵比寿 Ebisu; (説明的に) the god of wealth, one of the seven gods of good luck.

エピソード [逸話] an anecdòte (about); [挿話] an episode. • その政治家にまつわる数々のエピソード a lot of anecdotes about the politician.

えびちゃ えび茶 maroon; reddish brown. • えび茶の背広 a maroon suit.

えびてん 海老天 shrimp tempura.

エピローグ [結末] an epilogue (↔a prologue), 《米》 an epilog (↔a prolog).

エフエー [自由契約] (人) a free agent 《略 FA》; (資格) free agency. • FA の資格がある be eligible for free agency. • FA 宣言する declare for free agency.
• FA 制 the free agent [FA] system.

エフエム FM 《frequency modulation の略》. (⇨エーエム)
• FM放送 FM broadcasting. (⇨放送)

エフオービー [本船渡し] FOB 《free on board の略》.

えふで 絵筆 a paintbrush.

エフビーアイ [連邦捜査局] the FBI 《the Federal Bureau of Investigation の略》.

エプロン an apron /éɪprən/. • エプロンをかける[かけている] put on [wear] an apron.
• エプロンステージ an apron (stage).

エフワン F1 《Formula One の略》. • F1 チーム an F1 team; a Formula 1 [One] team.

エベレスト Mount Everest. (❗チベット語名はチョモランマ (Chomolungma), ネパール語名はサガルマタ (Sagarmatha) など)

えへん (せき払いの音) hem, ahem! /əhém/. (❗相手の注意を促す)

えぼし 烏帽子 an eboshi; (説明的に) a brimless headgear worn by court nobles.

エポック [新しい時代・転機] an epoch. ▶彼の理論は科学にエポックを築いた His theory made [formed, marked] an epoch in science.

エポックメーキング ── エポックメーキングな 形 epoch-making.

エボナイト [硬質ゴム] ebonite.

エホバ [<ヘブライ語] Jehovah /dʒɪhóʊvə/.

エボラしゅっけつねつ エボラ出血熱 (医学) Ebola /ɪbóʊlə/ hemorrhagic fever.

えほん 絵本 (子供用の) a picture book; (挿し絵入りの本) an illustrated book; (飛び出す絵本) a pop-out book. • 子供に絵本を読み聞かせる read a picture book to a child.

えま 絵馬 an ema; (説明的に) a picture tablet of a horse offered to one's guardian deity for the realization of one's wish(es).

えまき(もの) 絵巻(物) a picture scroll (with interspersed narrative accounts).

えみ 笑み a smile. ▶彼女は満面笑みをたたえて私たちを迎えてくれた She welcomed us with a broad smile on her face./She was all smiles when she welcomed us. (⇨笑い)

エミーしょう エミー賞 the Emmy Awards. (参考) 米国のテレビ芸術アカデミーが授与する賞)

エミュレーション [他のコンピュータ用プログラムを実行すること] emulation.

エミュレーター [エミュレーションに用いるプログラム] [コンピュータ] an emulator.

えむ 笑む [微笑する] smile; [花が咲く] bloom; [栗の実などが熟して裂ける] split open.

エム M • エムサイズの服 clothes of size M [medium size]; medium-sized clothes.

エムアールアイ [磁気共鳴映像法] the MRI 《magnetic resonance imaging の略》.

エムアンドエー [企業の合併・買収] M&A 《merge and acquisition の略》.

エムエー M.A., MA 《Master of Arts の略》.

エムビーエー [経営管理学修士] an MBA 《Master of Business Administration の略》.

エムピースリー [音声データ圧縮の規格の一つ] (an) MP3 《MPEG-1 Audio Layer 3 の略》.
• MP3 プレーヤー an MP3 player.

エムブイピー the MVP 《most valuable player の略》. ▶彼は選手権試合のMVPに選ばれた He was selected [chosen] the MVP of the championship games.

エメラルド [宝石] (an) emerald; [色] emerald.
• エメラルド(色)の emerald. • エメラルドグリーン emerald green.

えもいわれぬ 得も言われぬ 得も言われぬ(=言語に絶する)苦しみ indescribable [inexpressible, unspeakable] sufferings. • 得も言われぬ美しさ indescribable [×unspeakable] beauty. (❗unspeakable はマイナスイメージの語とともに用いるのでここでは不可)

えもじ 絵文字 a pictorial symbol; picture writing; (メールなどで用いる) emoticons.

えもの 獲物 (狩猟などの) [集合的] game; (1回の狩猟の獲物数) a bag (❗通例単数形で); (漁獲高) a catch. ▶獲物が多い have lots of [×big] game (❗ big game にはクマ, トラなどの大きな獲物のこと); have a good (↔a poor) bag [catch] (of). • 10 頭の獲物を仕留める shoot [bring down] ten head [×heads] of game. ▶彼はいい獲物だ He is easy match 《米》[easy game 《英》], a good catch (話). (❗前の二つは組みしやすいこと・だましやすいこと, 最後のはうま味があること)

えもんかけ 衣紋掛 a kimono [coat] hanger.

えら 鰓 gills /gɪlz/.

エラー an error. (⇨間違い) ●読み込み[書き込み]エラー a read-in [a write-in] error. ●何でもないゴロをエラーする misplay [make an error on] an easy grounder. ●ショートのエラーで1点入る score a run *on* the shortstop's *error* [*misplay*]. ●送球エラーをする make a throwing *error*.
●エラーメッセージ an error message.

えらい 偉い (偉大な) great; (すぐれた) distinguished; (重要な) important; (立派な) honorable /ánərəbl/; (地位の高い) high.

使い分け	great 最も一般的な語で，能力・価値・重要性・影響力などの点でとくに優れていて偉大であること．
	distinguished 特定分野において他より抜きん出て優秀・著名であること．
	important 社会的な地位などが高くて影響力の強いこと．
	honorable 人・行為などが尊敬に値すること．
	high 地位・身分などが高いこと．

▶その子は将来偉い人物になるだろう The child will be a *great* figure [(大物) somebody] in the future. ▶彼は大変偉い科学者になった He became a *great* [a most *distinguished*] scientist. (!great には通例 very はつけない) ▶彼は日本で最も偉い政治家の1人だ He is one of the *greatest* [most *important*, most *honorable*] statesmen in Japan. ▶彼は会社で偉くなっている(=高い地位についている) He has risen to a *high* position [(大物になった) (話) has become a *big shot*] in his company. ▶あの男は自分をすごく偉いと思っている He thinks he's really *somebody* [(話) quite a *big shot*]. 会話「たばこやめたんだ」「偉い！」"I've given up smoking." "*Sensible* fellow!"

●**偉そうな[に]** ●偉そうな顔をする look *big*. ●偉そうな口をきく talk big. (!「ほらを吹く」の意にもなる) ●偉そうにする act very *important*; (親分気取りである) (話) lord it (*over him*).

えらい (つらい) hard; (ひどい) terrible; (大きな) great; (数・量・程度áかなりの多い) tremendous; (深刻な) serious. ▶きのうはえらい目にあった I had a *hard* [*terrible*] time yesterday. ▶外はえらい暑い It's *terribly* hot outside. ▶えらい損をしてしまった I've suffered a *great* [a *big*, a *heavy*, a *tremendous*] loss. ▶これはえらいことになった Now we're in *big* [*serious*] trouble. 会話「彼，足を折ったのよ」「それはえらいことだわ．どうしてそんなことになったの？」"He broke his leg." "That's *terrible*. How did he do that?"

えらぶ 選ぶ choose*; select, pick ... (out); elect; prefér (-rr-); take*.

使い分け	**choose** 最も一般的な語で，二つ以上の中から選ぶこと．
	select 三つ以上の多数の中から比較して，最良のものを選考すること．
	pick (**out**) 大勢から一つを選び出すこと．select より口語的．
	elect 公正な選挙・投票によって人を重要な職に選ぶこと．
	prefer 二つのうちの一つを話者の個人的嗜好・判断で選ぶこと．
	take 選び取ること．

①**《副+選ぶ》** ●上手に[自分で]選ぶ *choose* well [*by oneself*]. ●好きで[自分で]選んだ職業 one's *chosen* career; the career of one's choice. ●言葉を慎重に選ぶ *choose* [*select*, *pick*, (よく考える)

weigh] one's words carefully; *make a* careful *choice* [*selection*] of one's words.
②**《...を選ぶ》** ●選手を選ぶ *select* players. ●人柄で夫を選ぶ *choose* one's husband *for* his (good) personality. (!for は「理由」を表す) ●教育を生涯の仕事に選ぶ *choose* education *for* one's career. (!for は「目的」を表す) ●彼にあげるネクタイを選ぶ *choose* [*select*, *pick out*] a tie *for* him; *choose* [×select] him a tie. (!「彼にネクタイを選ぶのを手伝ってあげる」の意にもなるが，その場合には help him *choose* [*select*, *pick out*] a tie. とすると明確になる (⇨買う❶)) ▶好きなのを選びなさい *Choose* [*Pick* (*out*), *Take*] the one you like./*Take* your *choice* [*pick*]. ▶結婚式にどの日を選びますか Which day do you *choose* [*select*] for your wedding? 会話「どういう行き方を[が]選べるの」「午前の列車で行くか，午後のバスに乗るかだよ」"What are the *alternatives*?" "Go by the morning train or catch the afternoon bus." (!altérnative は「(二つ以上のうちから)選べるもの」の意)
③**《...を～から選ぶ》** ▶この本の中から2冊選びなさい *Choose* [*Select*] two *from* [*from among*] these books. (!choose では前置詞は among, out of も可) ▶その二つの学校のうちからどちらかを選びなさい *Choose* [*Make a choice*, ×Select] *between* the two schools. (!このような二者択一の場合には select は用いない)/*Choose* one (*or the other*) *of* [×between] the two schools. (!「A校かB校かどちらかを選びなさい」は *Choose* (*between*) A School *or* B School. という) 会話「チキン，ポーク，ビーフのうちから一つをお選びいただけます」「ビーフにします(=を選びます)」"You have a *choice* of [×among] chicken, pork or beef." "I'll *take* beef."
④**《...を(役職に)選ぶ》** ▶彼らはジョンを自分たちの代表に選んだ They *chose* John *as* [*to be*] their representative./(選挙で) They *elected* John *as* [*to be*] their representative. (!以上いずれも受身形では as, to be は通例省略される (⇨「次例」)) ▶だれが大統領に選ばれると思いますか Who do you think will *be elected* President To (*the Presidency*)?
⑤**《～より(も)...を選ぶ》** ●仕事より家庭を選ぶ *choose* one's family *over* one's career. ●勝つためには手段を選ばない use any means to win. ●あなたと暮らすよりも1人で暮らす方を選びます I would *prefer* living alone *to* living with you./I *would rather* live alone *than* (live) with you.

●**選ぶ所がない** ●殺すために人を派遣することは，自分で人を殺すことと選ぶところがない(=同じである) There's no difference between one's killing and sending others to kill.

えらぶつ 偉物 a great man.
えらぶる 偉ぶる act superior; put* on airs. (⇨いばる)

***えり 襟** 〖首，首元〗a neck; 〖洋服・ワイシャツ・ブラウスの〗a collar; 〖上着の襟の折り返し〗a lapel; 〖和服の〗a neckband. ●丸[角]襟 a round [a square] *neck*. ●V型の襟 a V-*neck*. ●開いた襟の(=開襟)シャツ an open-*neck* shirt. ●コートの襟を立てる turn up one's coat *collar*. ●襟首(=首筋)をつかまえる catch (him) by the back of his *neck*.
●**襟に付く** ●金持ちの襟に付く(=こびへつらう) curry favor with wealthy people.
●**襟を正す** straighten up, (やや話) shape up.
▶我々は先生の言葉を襟を正して聞いた We listened *attentively* to what our teacher said.
●襟ぐり a neckline.

エリア 〖地域，範囲〗an area. ●研究のエリアを広げる

えりあし 襟足 (かみの毛の生えぎわ) the hairline along the neck; (襟首) the nape (of the [one's] neck).

『エリーゼのために』 For Elise /íliːz/. (参考 ベートーベンのピアノ曲)

エリート the elite /ilíːt/. (🔲 集合的. しばしば軽蔑的、またしばしば複数扱い) ▶その国では限られた少数のエリートが政治を支配していた In that country, only the small *elite* controlled the government. ▶彼はエリート (=選ばれた少数の一人)だ He is *one of the chosen few*.
- エリート意識[主義] elitism. ● エリート校 an elite [an elitist] school. (🔲 前の方はエリートにふさわしい学校、後の方はエリート主義が鼻につく学校のことで、けなして用いられる) ● エリート社員 an elite employee.

えりぐり 襟ぐり a neckline. ● 胸の見えるローカットの襟ぐり a low [a plunging] *neckline*.

えりごのみ 選り好み ── 選り好みする 動 be particular [(話) choosy, (米話) (けなして) picky] (*about*). (⇨好み) ● 選り好みする客 a *choosy* customer.

エリザベス Elizabeth. (🔲 時に Elisabeth とつづる人名もあるので注意) ● エリザベス女王 Queen *Elizabeth* II. (🔲 IIは the second と読む)

えりすぐる 選りすぐる select, pick ... out. (⇨選ぶ)

エリトリア [国名] Eritrea /ɛritríːə/; (公式名) State of Eritrea. (首都 Asmara) ● エリトリア人 Eritrean. ● エリトリア(人)の Eritrean.

えりぬき 選り抜き (⇨選(⁽¹⁾)り抜き) ● 選り抜きのワイン a fine *choice* of wine. ● 選り抜きの品 *select* goods. ● クラスの選り抜きの選手 the (*very*) *best* players in our class.

えりまき 襟巻き a scarf ● ~s, scarves; (古) a muffler.

えりもと 襟元 ● 襟元が寒い feel cold *around the neck*.

えりわける 選り分ける (⇨分ける❹) ● (もみがらから)小麦を選り分ける *sort out* [*separate*] the wheat (from the chaff).

*****える** ❶ [手に入れる] get*; (やや書) obtain; (書) secure; acquire; (やや書) gain; learn*; earn; win*.

> 使い分け **get** 物を入手することを表す一般的な語. 特に口語では.
> **obtain** 一定の努力を払って所有すること.
> **secure** 入手困難なものを確保して自分のものにすること.
> **acquire** 時間をかけ手を尽くしてやっと手に入れること.
> **gain** 入手困難なものや特別な権利などを努力して獲得すること.
> **learn** 学習または慣れによって態度・習慣などを身につけること.
> **earn** 資格・賞・名声などを手に入れること.
> **win** 名声・賞・承認などを競争によって勝ち取ること.

● その大学から修士号を得る(=取得する) *get* [*obtain*] an M.A. *from* the college. ● 書物から知識を得る *acquire* [*gain*] knowledge through books. ● 賞を得る *win* [*get*, *receive*] a prize. ● 教訓を得る *learn* a lesson. ● 本を読んで多くのことを得た I *got* [*learned*] a lot *from* the book. (🔲 get は「学ぶ」の意)/I *learned* [*gained*] a lot of things by reading the book. ● 彼は懸命に働いてでなく、ギャンブルでその金を得た He didn't *earn* the money by working hard but *won* it by gambling. (🔲 この文脈では earn と win の交換および gain の使用は不可) ● 勉強して得るところがありましたか Have you *gained* profit [anything profitable] from your studies?
❷ [受ける] (得る) get*; (名声などを博する) earn; (勝ち取る) win*. ▶支持を得る [*gain*, *win*] support (*from*). ▶彼はその小説で悪評を得た He *earned* a bad reputation by the novel./The novel *earned* him a bad reputation. ▶彼女は彼の全幅の信頼を得た[得ている] She *has won* [*enjoys*] his fullest confidence.
❸ [...できる] can. (⇨できる)

エル L ● エルサイズのドレス a dress of size *L* [*large* size]; a *large*-sized dress.

エルイーディー 〖発光ダイオード〗 LED 《*light-emitting diode* の略》.

エルエスアイ 〖大規模集積回路〗 LSI 《*large scale integrated (circuit)* の略》.

エルエヌジー 〖液化天然ガス〗 LNG 《*liquefied natural gas* の略》.

エルエル ❶ 〖超大型の〗 extra-large 《略 XL》. (⇨エル, 特大) ❷ 〖語学実習室〗, LL 教室〗 a language laboratory [(話) lab]; (和製語) LL.

エルケー LK a living room and a kitchen. (⇨エルディーケー)

エルサルバドル 〖国名〗 El Salvador /el sǽlvədɑːr/; (公式名) the Republic of El Salvador. (首都 San Salvador) ● エルサルバドル人 a Salvadoran. ● エルサルバドルの Salvadoran.

エルサレム 〖イスラエルの首都〗 Jerusalem /dʒərúːsələm/.

エルシー 〖信用状〗an L/C 《*letter of credit* の略》.

エルディー LD 〖学習障害〗a learning disability. ❷ [レーザーディスク] a laser disc.

エルディーケー LDK ● 3LDK のマンション a *three-bedroom* apartment *with a living-cum-dining room plus kitchen*. (⇨ディーケー)

エルニーニョ [<スペイン語] El Niño /el níːnjou/. ● エルニーニョ現象 an El Niño phenomenon.

エルバとう エルバ島 〖イタリアの島〗 Elba.

エルピー (⇨エルピーレコード)

エルピーガス LPガス 〖液化石油ガス〗LPG 《*liquefied petroleum gas* の略》, LP-gas.

エルピーレコード an LP 《*long-playing (record)* の略》.

エレガント elegant (↔inelegant). ● エレガントな服装の淑女 an *elegantly* dressed lady; a lady in an *elegant* dress.

エレキギター an electric guitar.

エレクトーン 〖電子オルガン〗 an eléctrónic [an eléctric] órgan; (商標) Electone.

エレクトロニクス electrónics. (🔲 単数扱い)

エレジー 〖哀歌〗an elegy.

*****エレベーター** 《主に米》 an élevator; 《英》 a lift.
①〖エレベーター~〗 ● エレベーター付きの建物 an *elevator* building. ● エレベーターのない建物 《主に米》 a walkup (building).
②〖エレベーターを[に, から, で]〗 ● エレベーターを運転する 《米》 operate an *elevator*; 《英》 run a *lift*. ● 3階でエレベーターから降りる get out of (↔into) an *elevator at* [ˣon] the third [3rd] floor. ● エレベーターで3階まで上がって[下りて]行く take an *elevator up* [*down*] to the third floor (🔲 take は「利用する」の意); go up [down] to the third floor *by* [*in an*, ˣ*on an*] *elevator*. (🔲 by は「手段」を表し、in は「乗って」の意. 「上り[下り]のエレベーター」は an up [a down] *elevator*)
● エレベーターガール 《米》 an elevator operator [ˣgirl] 〖事情〗 英米には日本の百貨店などの「エレベー

エロ ターガール」は普通いない); 《英》 a lift attendant (車掌);《英》では地下鉄の駅への上り下りに lift を用いる駅がかなりある).

エロ (扇情的な) erotic, 《軽蔑的》 porno(graphic) (⇨ポルノ); (官能主義) eroticism.
● エロ文学 erotic literature. ● エロ本 (わいせつな雑誌) a dirty [《話》a porno] magazine.

エログロ erotic and grotesque.
● エログロ雑誌 a pulp (magazine).

エロス Eros /íːrɑs, érɑs/.

エロチック ― **エロチックな** 形 erótic; (官能的な) sensual. (❗ sexy の婉曲語).

*__えん__ 円 ❶ [円形] a circle.

circumference (円周)
center (中心)
radius (半径)
diameter (直径)

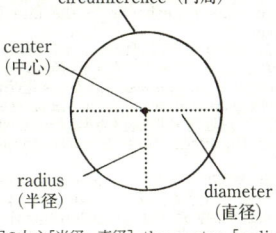

● 円の中心 [半径; 直径] the center [radius; diameter] of a *circle*. ● 円を描く draw [《書》describe] a *circle*, (鳥・機体などが) form a *circle*, circle. (⇨旋回する) ● 大きな円を描いて次第に降りてくる come lower and lower *in* wide *circles*.
❷ [貨幣の単位] a yen (記号 ¥) (❗単・複同長);〚円価〛the (value of) yen (*against* the dollar).
● 1,000 円札 2 枚 two one-thousand-*yen* bills 《米》 [notes 《英》]. ● 50 円玉 [硬貨] 2 個 two fifty-*yen* coins. ● 日本円で支払う pay *in* Japanese *yen*.
● 円運動 circular motion.

*__えん__ 縁 〚関係〛(a) relation; (つながり) (a) connection (⇨関係);〚宿縁〛fortune; fate 《⇨運命》;〚きずな〛a bond;〚結婚〛marriage.
①【縁が[の]】・縁の深い be deeply affiliated 《*with*》. ▶ 縁あって 2 人は夫婦になった *Fortune* [*Fate*] made them man and wife. ▶ *Fate* を信じていると不本意な結果を暗示する) ▶ 彼と縁が切れてせいせいしている I'm glad to *be rid of* him. ▶ 私はお金に縁がない Money and I are strangers. ▶ 私は本に縁のない人間です I'm never one for books. ▶ 縁があったらまたお会いしましょう I hope we shall meet again.
②【縁で】・不思議な縁で by a strange *coincidence*. ▶ 本を貸したのが縁で彼らと知り合いになった The loan of a book led (me) to their acquaintance. ▶ これも何かの縁だ This is a good chance [opportunity] for us.
● 縁は異なもの味なもの Amorous relations between a man and a woman are funnily unpredictable.
● 縁もゆかりもない ▶ 私は彼とは縁もゆかりもない I *have no connection* [*relation*] *whatever* [(何の関係もない) *have nothing to do*] *with* him. /(まったく知らない人だ) He is a *perfect* [a *total*] *stranger* to me.
● 縁を切る (関係を絶つ) break off relations 《*with* + 人・事》; break off 《*with* + 人》; (離婚する) divorce; (勘当する) disown 《one's son》. ▶ 私はああいう生活とは縁を切った I *have* [*am*] *done with* that sort of life.
● 縁を結ぶ form a connection 《*with* + 人》; (結婚する) get married 《*to*》.

えん 宴 (祝宴) a feast; (正式の) a banquet. ● A 氏のために宴を催す give a *feast* [a *banquet*] in honor of Mr. A. ● 宴もたけなわだった The *feast* was in full swing.

えん 塩 (塩素) 【化学】 chlorine.

えん 艶 (魅惑) (seductive) allure; (魅力) charm.

えんいん 延引 (遅れ) a delay.

えんいん 遠因 (遠い原因) a distant cause; (間接的な原因) an indirect cause; (底流にある原因) an underlying cause.

えんえい 遠泳 ― **遠泳する** 名 have a long-distance swim.

えんえき 演繹 名 deduction (↔induction).
―― **演繹する** 動 deduce.
● 演繹的推論 deductive (↔inductive) inference. ● 演繹法 the deductive method.

えんえん 延々 ● 延々と (=終わりのない) 議論 *endless* discussions. ● 延々と (=切れ目なく) 続く車の列 a *continuous* line of traffic. ▶ 私は延々 3 時間も彼女を待った I waited for her *as long as* three hours [for three *long* hours]. ▶ 会議はいつものように延々と続いた The meeting went *on and on* [went *on endlessly*] as usual. (❗ この on は継続の意を表す副詞)

えんえん 炎々 ● 炎々と燃えている be burning *furiously*.

えんか 円貨 the yen.

えんか 塩化 【化学】 chloridization.
● 塩化ナトリウム sodium chloride. ● 塩化ビニール vinyl /váinil/ chloride. (⇨ビニール) ● 塩化物 a chloride.

えんか 演歌 an *enka* ballad [song]; (説明的に) a kind of Japanese popular song, a short narrative ballad which deals with sad love, old-type duty (*giri*) or sentiment (*ninjo*) and is sung in a tone peculiar to *enka*.

えんかい 沿海 (海に沿った陸) a coast.
● 沿海漁業 coastal [(近海の) inshore] fishery.

えんかい 宴会 a party; (晩餐(ばん)会) a dinner (party); (午餐会) a luncheon (party); (祝宴) a feast, a banquet (後の方はより正式で盛大な会). ● 宴会を催す hold a *party* [a *dinner*, a *banquet*].
● 宴会場 a banquet hall.

えんがい 円蓋 【建築】 (半球形の屋根) a dome; (丸いふた) a round lid.

えんがい 塩害 damage from sea water [spray, breeze]; salt damage.

えんがい 煙害 smoke pollution; damage from 《industrial [volcanic]》 smoke.

えんかく 沿革 a history 《*of* a school》.

えんかく 遠隔 remoteness.
● 遠隔診療 【医学】 telediagnosis. ● 遠隔操作 remote control. ● 遠隔地 a remote [distant] place.

えんかつ 円滑 ― **円滑な** 形 smooth. ▶ 万事円滑に運んだ Everything went *smoothly* [(うまく) *well*]. ▶ 2 人の仲は円滑にいっている (=仲よくやっている) They are *getting along* [*on*] *well* together [with each other].

えんがわ 縁側 an *engawa*; (説明的に) a Japanese-style loggia /lóudʒiə/, a wooden-floored corridor that cuts off direct contact of a room [rooms] with the garden.

えんかん 円環 a circle; a ring.

えんかん 鉛管 a lead pipe.

*__えんがん__ 沿岸 (大洋の) the coast; (海・湖・大河の) (a) shore. ● 琵琶湖沿岸の都市 cities *on* Lake Biwa.

えんき 延期 图 (a) postponement; (会議などの) (an) adjournment.
— **延期する** 動 put*... off, postpone;《やや書》defer (-rr-); delay; hold*... off; adjourn.

> [使い分け] **put off, postpone** 何らかの事由により、特定の時期まで催事・行為などを遅らせること。put off の方が口語的。
> **defer** 意図的に行為・行事などを延期すること。
> **delay** 主に事故・悪天候などにより、当初の予定を遅らせてしまうこと。
> **hold off** (法律上の)決定などを先送りすること。
> **adjourn** 会議などを次回まで中断させること。

●出発を月曜日まで[1 週間]延期する *put off* [*postpone, delay*] one's departure till Monday [for a week]; *put off* [*postpone, delay*] leaving [×to leave] till Monday [for a week]. ●勘定の支払いを延期する *defer* payment of [*paying*, ×*to pay*] one's bills. ●雨天の場合は延期 (掲示) *Postponed* In Case Of Rain. ▶試合は雨のため延期された The game *was put off* [*was postponed*, ×was delayed] because of (the) rain. (!was delayed は「予定より遅れて続いたとの意」)(हिन्दी で流れた《話》The game *was rained* out《米》[*off*《英》]. ▶その件に関する決定は来週に延期された The decision on the matter *was put off* [*was postponed, was held off*] until next week.

えんき 塩基 图 【化学】a base. — **塩基性の** 形 basic.
●塩基性酸化物 basic oxide.

***えんぎ 演技** (劇や体操競技などの) a performance.
●演技派(の性格)俳優 a character actor. ▶彼女の演技はすばらしかった Her *performance* was excellent./She gave an excellent [(感動的な) a moving] *performance*. ▶(感銘を受けた) I was very impressed with her *performance*. ▶彼女は演技がうまい[へただ] She is a good [a poor] actress. ▶その劇は演技はよかったが、背景がもう一つだった The play *was* well *acted*, but the scenery wasn't very good. ▶それはただの演技(= 見せかけ)だった That was only a *gesture* [a *fake*,《話》an *act*].

えんぎ 縁起 (運) luck; (前兆) an omen /óumən/. ●縁起の悪いことを言う say something unlucky. ▶縁起直しの儀式 a ritual to change bad luck into good circumstances. ▶縁起直しに彼らは飲んだ They drank to forget the bad things. ▶彼らは縁起がよい[悪い] It is a *good* [a *bad*, an *ill*] *omen*./It is *lucky* [*unlucky*]./(幸運をもたらすだろう) That will bring you (*good*) *luck*. ▶アメリカではしごの下をくぐるのは縁起が悪いとされている Walking under a ladder is considered to be *bad luck* [*unlucky*] in the U.S. ▶縁起でもないことを言わないよ Stop it. That might bring me *bad luck*.

●縁起をかつぐ be superstitious; believe in omens.
●縁起物 a lucky charm; a mascot. (!マスコットは幸運をもたらすと考えられている)

えんきょく 婉曲 图 ▶「亡くなる」は「死ぬ」の婉曲語だ "Pass away" is a *euphemism* [a *euphemistic* term] *for* "die."
— **婉曲的に** 副 euphemistically; (遠回しに) in a roundabout way. (⇒遠回し)
●婉曲語法[表現] (やや書) (a) euphemism.

えんきょり 遠距離 a long distance. (⇒長距離) ●遠距離通学する walk a *long distance* to school. ▶遠距離から撃たれる be shot *at long range* [×*distance*].

えんきり 縁切り dissolution of a relationship; (離婚) a divorce; dissolution of marriage.
●縁切り寺 (説明的に) a temple which provided refuge for married women and helped them divorce their husbands in the Edo period Japan.

えんきん 遠近 ●遠近両用の眼鏡 (a pair of) bifocals /báifóuklz/. ▶遠近を問わず(= 至る所から)やって来る come *from far and near* [*wide*]. ●遠近(画)法で絵をかく paint [draw] a picture *in perspective*. ▶彼女は遠近両用の眼鏡をかけるようになった She wears the *bifocals* now./She went to the *bifocals*.

えんぐみ 縁組み 【結婚】(a) marriage; (婚約) an engagement;〘養子の〙(an) adoption. ▶ボブとメリーの縁組みが整った［= 婚約した］Bob and Mary *got engaged*. ▶その孤児と養子縁組みは We *adopted* the orphan.

えんグラフ 円グラフ a circle graph, a pie chart.

えんぐん 援軍 (send) reinforcements (*to*).

えんけい 円形 图 a round shape; a circle. ●円形に座る sit *in a circle*.
— **円形の** 形 circular; round.
●円形劇場 an amphitheater. ●円形脱毛症 [医学] alopecia areata.

えんけい 遠景 a distant view;〘背景〙a background. (⇔近景)

***えんげい 園芸** 〘庭造り〙gardening;〘園芸学〙horticulture. ▶彼は園芸の才がある He has green fingers [〘主に米〙a green thumb].
●園芸家 a gardener; a horticulturist. ●園芸植物 a garden plant. ●園芸用具 a gárdening tòol.

***えんげい 演芸** 《総称》(an) entertainment; (演技) a performance.
●演芸会 an entertainment; (寄席演芸) a variety show;《米》(×a) vaudeville. ▶演芸は歌・踊り・漫才・寸劇などを織り交ぜたもの. ●演芸場 a variety hall;《米》a vaudeville theater.

エンゲージリング 〘婚約指輪〙an engágement rìng;〘和製語〙an engage ring.

***えんげき 演劇** a drama (! 文学としての演劇の場合はしばしば the ～); the theater; 〘芝居〙a play. ▶英国演劇 (the) English *drama*. ▶彼は演劇部です He belongs [×is belonging] to the *drama* club. ▶彼は大学で演劇を研究した He studied *drama* [*the theater*] at college. ▶ブロードウェーはアメリカの演劇の中心である Broadway is the *theatrical* center of the U.S.
●演劇学校 a drama school. ●演劇欄 (新聞などの) the theater [theatrical] page.

エンゲル 〘ドイツの統計学者〙Engel (Ernst ～).
●エンゲル係数 Engel's coefficient. ●エンゲルの法則 Engel's law.

エンゲルス 〘ドイツの社会主義者〙Engels /éŋglz/ (Friedrich ～).

えんこ — えんこする 動 (エンジン・車が止まる) stall; (故障で動かなくなる) break down.

えんこ 円弧 〖数学〗an arc.
えんこ 縁故 〖有力な知人〗connections, a contact (しばしば複数形で); 〖引き〗《話》pull. (!時に a 〜) (⇨コネ) ●縁故の多い人 a man with many *contacts*. ▶彼女は友人の縁故でその職についた She got the job through her friend's *connections* [*pull*].
●縁故採用 employment through personal or business connections.

えんご 援護 图 (援助) support; (助け) help. ●援護の手を差し伸べる lend a *helping* hand. ●援護射撃をする give *protective covering* fire.
── 援護する 動 support; help. ▶守備陣が投手を援護した The defense backed up [supported] the pitcher.

エンコーダー 〖データを符号化する装置〗〖コンピュータ〗an encoder.
えんこん 怨恨 (have [bear]) a grudge. (⇨恨み)
えんさ 怨嗟 a grudge; resentment.
えんざ 円座 图 (敷物) a round carpet.
── 円座する 動 sit in a circle.
えんざい 冤罪 a false accusation [charge]. ●冤罪をこうむる be falsely accused. ●冤罪を晴らす prove that one is falsely charged; prove one's innocence.
エンサイクロペディア 〖百科事典〗an encyclopedia.
えんさん 塩酸 〖化学〗hydrochloric acid (記号 HCl).
えんざん 演算 〖数学〗operation.
えんし 遠視 图 《米》farsightedness, 《英》long-sightedness; 〖医学〗hyperopia /hàipəróupiə/.
── 遠視の 形 farsighted; longsighted.
えんじ 園児 (幼稚園の) a kindergarten child (参考 米国では 4-5 歳児); (保育園の) a nursery school child (参考 米国では 3 歳児. 英国では小学校就学前の 2-4 歳児).
えんじ 臙脂 dark red. ●えんじの帽子 a *dark red* hat.
エンジェル (⇨エンゼル)
エンジニア an engineer. (⇨技師)
えんじゃ 縁者 a relative, a relation. (⇨親類)
えんしゃっかん 円借款 a yen credit [loan].
えんしゅう 円周 (a) circumference. (⇨周囲)
●円周率 the ratio of the circumference of a circle to its diameter (記号 π).
えんしゅう 演習 图 〖ゼミナール〗a seminar; 〖練習(問題)〗(an) exercise (⇨練習); 〖訓練〗(a) training; 〖軍隊の大演習〗maneuvers. ●文学〖ハムレット〗の演習をとる take a *seminar* in literature [*on Hamlet*]. ●軍事演習を行う hold [conduct] military maneuvers. ●予行演習 a rehearsal. (⇨予行演習)
── 演習する 動 ●文法の演習をする do *exercises in* [×*of*] grammar.
えんじゅく 円熟 图 maturity; mellowness. ▶彼は年とともに円熟味が出てきた As he gets older, he has become *mellower*./He has *mellowed* with age.
── 円熟した 形 mature; mellow; ripe. ●円熟したピアニスト a *mature* pianist.
── 円熟する 動 mature; mellow; ripen.
えんしゅつ 演出 图 direction.
── 演出する 動 ●その劇を演出する *direct* the play. ●うまく [へたに] 演出されている *be* well [poorly] *directed*.
●演出家 a (stage) director. ●演出効果 stage effects.
えんしょ 炎暑 intense heat. (⇨猛暑)
***えんじょ** 援助 图 help; (公的なもの) aid (!*help* より堅い語); (補助) assistance; 〖支援〗support. (⇨助け)

●海外援助 foreign [overseas] *aid*. ●食糧援助 food *aid*. ●精神的援助 moral *support* [×*help*]. ●アフリカ諸国に経済援助を与える give economic *aid* to African nations. ●地震被災者へ援助を申し出る offer *help* [*aid*] *to* the victims of the earthquake. ●彼に援助を求める ask (正式は文書で) apply to) him for *help* [*assistance*, *support*]. ●彼に援助の手を差し伸べる give [lend] him a *helping* hand. ●生きる道は公的援助, それのみです Government *aid* [Public *assistance*] is the only hope for our survival. ●政府による公的援助は government aid, その他の公共団体によるものは public assistance.
── 援助する 動 help; aid (⇨助ける❶); 〖支援する〗support. ●発展途上国を援助する *aid* [*give aid to*] developing countries.
●援助交際 compensated dating.

エンジョイ ── エンジョイする 動 enjoy. ●学生生活をエンジョイする *enjoy* (one's) student life.
えんしょう 延焼 the spread of a fire. (⇨類焼)
●延焼を食い止める check *the spread of a fire*.
── 延焼する 動 (火が) spread (*to*) (建物などが) catch fire.
えんしょう 炎症 (an) inflammation. ●炎症を起こした傷 an *inflamed* wound. ▶傷口にばい菌が入って炎症を起こした The wound was [became] *inflamed* by infection.
えんしょう 艶笑 a humorous story with erotic content.
●艶笑文学 humorous, erotic literature.
えんじょう 炎上 ●建物全体が炎上していた The whole building was (*going up*) *in flames*.
***えんじる** 演じる (役・人などを) play, act (!*act* は演技を強調する); (観衆の前で役・人・劇などを) perform.
●ハムレットの役を演じる *play* [*act*, *perform*] (the role [part] of) Hamlet. ●意志決定に重要な役割を演じる *play* [×*act*] an important role [part] in making decisions. ●失態を演じる make [*commit*] a blunder. ▶彼の演じるハムレットなんか見られたもんじゃないと思うよ He will be terrible *as* Hamlet.
えんしん 延伸 extension; (時間の) prolongation.
●滑走路延伸 runway *extension*.
***エンジン** an engine. ●エンジンをかける start [turn on] an *engine*. ●エンジンを止める[切る] stop [cut, turn off] an *engine*. ●エンジンをかけっぱなしにしておく leave the *engine* going [running]. ▶エンジンがかかった The *engine* has started (up) [has caught]. ▶ぼくは夜型だから, 朝のうちはエンジンがかからない I'm a night person, so I can't get myself going [get down to my work] in the morning. (!*get down to ...* は「本気で...にとりかかる」の意)
●エンジンオイル engine oil. ●エンジンキー an ignition key; 〖和製語〗an engine key. ●エンジンブレーキ engine braking; 《和製語》an engine brake.
えんじん 円陣 a circle. ●円陣を作る[組む] form a *circle*; stand [座って) sit] in a *circle*.
えんじん 猿人 an ape-man (複 -men); 〖人類学〗a pithecanthropus (複 -pi).
えんしんぶんりき 遠心分離器 a céntrifùge.
えんしんりょく 遠心力 〖物理〗centrifugal force (⇔ centripetal force).
えんすい 円錐 a cone. ●円錐形の conic(al).
えんずい 延髄 〖解剖〗the bulb; the medulla oblongata.
えんすいこ 塩水湖 a saltwater [a salt] lake.
エンスト engine trouble, an engine stall; 《和製語》

えんせい 遠征 图 an expedition.
— **遠征する** 動 make [go on] an expedition (*to*).
● 遠征試合 an away (↔a home) game [match].
● 遠征隊 (軍の) an expeditionary force [army]; (探検の) an expedition (party); (スポーツの) a visiting team (**!** その 1 人は a visitor.

えんせい 厭世 — 厭世的な 形 pessimistic. (**!** pessimistic は常に物事をマイナス面にとらえる心の働きをいう。(↔optimistic)) ▶彼女は厭世的になっている She is sick of life./She thinks life isn't worth living./She is *pessimistic* about life.
● 厭世主義 pessimism.

えんせき 宴席 (宴会場) a banquet hall. ● 宴席を設ける hold [have] a banquet.

えんせき 縁戚 a relative by marriage, 《話》in-laws.

えんせきがいせん 遠赤外線 【物理】a far infrared radiation.

*__えんぜつ__ 演説 图 a speech (*about, on*); an addréss (特によく準備された公式の重要な演説)。 ● 就任演説 an inaugural *speech* [*address*]. ▶佐々木氏の演説会が今日ここである Mr. Sasaki *is speaking* here today. ▶彼は演説がうまい[へただ] He's a good [a poor] *speaker*.
— **演説する** 動 make [give,《書》deliver] a speech [an address]; speak. ● その問題について会合で[聴衆に; 聴衆の前で]演説する *speak on* the subject *at* a meeting [*to* an audience; *before* an audience]. ▶大統領はテレビを通じて国民に演説した The President *gave* a *speech* [an *address*] *to* the nation on television./The President *addressed* the nation on television. (**!** ニュース番組では後の形が多い)
● 演説会 a speech meeting. ● 演説者 a speaker.

エンゼル 【天使】an angel /éindʒəl/.
エンゼルフィッシュ 【魚介】an angelfish.

えんせん 沿線 ● その(総武線)沿線の住民 people living *along the railroad* (*line*) [*the* Sobu *Line*].

えんそ 塩素 chlorine /klɔ́ːriːn/《元素記号 Cl》.

*__えんそう__ 演奏 图 a (musical) performance. ● 彼のギター演奏を聴く hear him *play* [*perform on*] the guitar. ▶彼女のソナタの演奏はすばらしかった He gave an excellent *performance* of the sonata./He *played* [*performed*] the sonata excellently.
— **演奏する** 動【楽器・曲を】play;(《や書》perform《＋曲, *on*＋楽器》;【楽団が演奏を始める】strike* up. (⇨図;弾く) ▶彼らはベートーベンの第九を演奏した They *played* Beethoven's Ninth Symphony. ▶オーケストラが序曲を演奏し始めた The orchestra *struck up* the overture.
● 演奏曲目 a (musical) program. ● 演奏者 a player; a performer. ● 演奏旅行 a concert tour.

えんそうかい 演奏会 (give [hold]) a concert;(主に独奏会) a recital. ● オーケストラの演奏会 an orchestral *concert*.

*__えんそく__ 遠足 (通例日帰りの団体旅行)《やや書》an excursion, an outing;(ピクニック) a picnic. ▶彼らの遠足で奈良に行った We went on a school *trip* [*excursion, outing, picnic*] to Nara.

エンターテイナー an èntertáiner. ▶彼は世界的に有名なエンターテイナーになった He became a world famous *entertainer*.

えんたい 延滞 图 late payment.
— **延滞する** 動 be in arrears. ▶彼は家賃を 2 か月延滞している He is two months *behind* in his rent. / His rent is two months *overdue* [*in arrears*].
● 延滞金 arrears. ● 延滞利子 interest for arrears; overdue [default] interest.

えんだい 遠大 — 遠大な 形 ●遠大な(=広範囲に及ぶ)計画 a *far-reaching* [(長期にわたる) a *long-range*] plan. ●遠大な目的 a *far-reaching* aim.

えんだい 演題 the subject [(テーマ) theme] (of a speech [a lecture]). ●「戦争と平和」という演題で話す speak on the *subject* of "War and Peace".

えんだい 縁台 an outdoor bench.

エンタイトルツーベース 【野球】a ground-rule double;《和製語》an entitled two-base hit.

えんだか 円高 appreciation of the yen; the strong(er) yen; a rise in the yen. (⇨円安) ●急激な円高 sharp [rapid] *appreciation of the yen*. ●円高差益を還元する return a profit from *the strong yen*. ●円高ドル安に歯止めをかける put a brake on *the strong yen* against the dollar. ▶ここ 1 週間円高が進んでいる The yen has been *gaining strength* [*increasing in value*] during the past week. ▶円は現在前日の 111 円より 2 円円高の 1 ドル 109 円で取り引きされている The yen is currently trading at 109 yen to the doller, *up* 2 yen from 111 yen the previous day. ▶円高で海外旅行に安く行ける Since *the yen is strong* [*has strengthened*], it is inexpensive to travel overseas.
● 円高景気 the strong yen-caused boom. ● 円高不況 the strong yen-caused recession; the high-yen slump.

えんたく 円卓 a round table.
● 円卓会議 a round-table conference.

えんだて 円建て 图 a yen basis. ▶今回のロシアとの貿易は円建てで行われた This trade with Russia was done *on the yen basis*.
— **円建ての** 形 yen-based.
● 円建て債 a yen-denominated bond.

えんだん 演壇 a (speaker's) platform. ●演壇に立つ(＝登る) mount a *platform* [a *podium*].

えんだん 縁談 [結婚の申し込み] a proposal [an offer] of marriage; (a marriage) proposal (**!** proposal は結婚の申し込み、《縁組み》は a match. ●たくさん縁談がある have lots of *proposals* [*offers*] *of marriage*. ●縁談をまとめる arrange a *marriage*. ●[見合い結婚] は an arranged marriage) ▶その縁談はこわれた The *match* has been broken off [(取り消しになった) has been canceled].

えんちゃく 延着 图 delayed arrival.
— **延着する** 動 ▶列車は 2 時間延着した The train *arrived* two hours *late* [*after a delay of* two hours, [(定刻より遅れて) two hours *behind schedule*]./(遅れた) The train *was delayed* (for) two hours.

えんちゅう 円柱 a column;【数学】a cylinder.

*__えんちょう__ 延長 图 (an) extension. (**!** 延長期間を表す場合は C) ●鉄道の隣町への延長 the *extension* of the railroad to the next town. ●彼に 3 日間の休暇の延長を認める give [allow,《書》grant] him a three-day *extension* to his holidays. ●民主主義を徹底させれば、その延長には(＝最後には)平和がある Only when democracy prevails to the fullest extent, do we see *peace* at its end. (**!** if (もし…すれば)より when (…したあかつきには)の方が強意的) ▶大ニュースは日常の延長で起こっている(＝今日の出来事から生じる) Major news in this day and age

originates in our ordinary daily lives.
── **延長する** 動 ［長さ・幅・期間を］ extend; (特に時間を) prolong; (特に長さを) lengthen, make*(it) longer. (⇨延ばす) ▶道路をその村まで延長する *extend* the road to the village. (❗*lengthen* a road は可能だが到達点を示す場合は extend のほうが強い) ▶国会の会期が15日間延長された The Diet session *was extended* [*prolonged*] another 15 days. (❗prolong は「予定を超えて」というニュアンスが強い)
• 延長コード an extension cord. • 延長戦 (⇨延長戦)

えんちょう 園長 ▶幼稚園［動物園］の園長 the head of a kindergarten [a zoo].

えんちょうせん 延長戦 an extended game;［野球］an extra innings game;（フットボールなどの延長時間）《米》overtime,《英》extra time. ▶(サッカーで)延長戦に入る go into *extra time*. ▶野球の試合は延長戦に入った The baseball game went [ran] into *extra innings*. (❗「試合を延長戦に持ち込む」は be led [put] a game into *extra innings* [*overtime*])

えんちょうせん 延長線 ▶延長線を引く《draw》an extension (line). ▶(鉄道の)延長線を作る build an extension. ▶当方の食事の宅配サービスは在宅介護支援の延長線上にあります Our meal delivery service is an *extension* of our home care support.

えんづく 縁付く get married《to》.

えんつづき 縁続き ▶私は彼と縁続き（＝親類）です I am a *relative* of his [one of his *relatives*]./ (親戚(ｼﾝｾｷ)関係にある) I *am related to* him.

えんてい 堰堤 （ダム）a dam.

えんてい 園丁 a gardener.

エンディング (an) ending. ▶マトリックス3部作はエンディングが弱い The Matrix trilogy has a weak *ending*.
• エンディングテーマ a clósing thème sòng [tùne].

エンデバー ［米国のスペースシャトル］Endeavour. (❗英国つづりに注意)

えんてん 炎天 ▶炎天下で働く work under the *blazing sun* [in the *scorching heat*]. (❗前の方は「ぎらぎら燃える太陽」, 後の方は「焼けつくような暑さ」の意)

えんでん 塩田 a salt pan.

エンド ［サッカー］an end. (❗(1) ピッチを半分に分けた一方の側. (2) 両ゴール裏のスタンド席)

えんとう 円筒 图 a cýlinder. ── 円筒(形)の 形 cylíndrical.

えんとう 遠投 a long throw;［野球］a long toss.
• 遠投キャッチボールをする play long catch.

えんどう 沿道 ▶沿道の並木 trees *along the route* [*road*]. (⇨沿道)

えんどう 豌豆 ［植物］a pea. ▶青［サヤ］エンドウ a green [a garden] *pea*.

えんどおい 縁遠い ［関係が薄い］not closely related 《to》;［結婚の機会に恵まれない］have a poor marriage prospect.

えんどく 煙毒 smoke pollution.

えんどく 鉛毒 lead poisoning.

*__えんとつ__ 煙突 a chimney; (工場などの高い煙突) a smokestack;［機関車・汽船の］a funnel;［ストーブの］a stovepipe. ▶立ち並ぶ工場の煙突から煙がもうもうと出ていた A forest of factory *chimneys* were giving off a lot of smoke.

エンドユーザー ［最終消費［利用］者］an end user, an end consumer.

エンドライン ［競技］an end line.

エントリー 图 ［競技などへの参加登録］an entry《for》.
── **エントリーする** 動 enter《in, for》.

エンドレス ［終わりのない］endless.
• エンドレステープ an endless tape.

エントロピー ［物理］entropy.

えんにち 縁日 (社寺の祭り) a temple [a shrine] festival; (祝祭) a fete /feit/. ▶八幡神社の縁日 the *festival* of [at] the Hachiman Shrine.

えんねつ 炎熱 scorching heat. ▶炎熱下のマラソン a marathon in the *scorching* [*blazing*] *heat*.

えんのう 延納 deferred [delayed] payment.
── **延納する** 動 defer the payment (of ...).

えんのした 縁の下 the space under the floor [porch].
• 縁の下の力持ち (陰で一生懸命働く) work hard in the background; (表立って報われない仕事をする) do a thankless job;《口》 be an unsung hero (男) [heroine (女)].

えんばく 燕麦 ［植物］oats.

エンパワーメント ［能力開発・権限付与］empówerment.

えんばん 円盤 a disk, a disc;［円盤投げの］a discus.
• 空飛ぶ円盤 a flying saucer.
• 円盤投げ the discus (throw).

*__えんぴつ__ 鉛筆 a pencil.
① (〜鉛筆) ▶色[赤]鉛筆 a colored [a red] *pencil*. ▶HB [2B] の鉛筆 an HB [a 2B] *pencil*. (参考) 米国式の硬度の表示: number one (B, 2B, 3B)/number two (F, HB)/number three (H, 2H)/number four (3H, 4H) ▶消しゴム付きの鉛筆 a *pencil* with an eraser tip. ▶先が丸くなった[とがった]鉛筆 a blunt [a *sharp-pointed*] *pencil*. ▶芯(ｼﾝ)の堅い鉛筆 a hárd-lead /léd/ *péncil*. ▶短くなった鉛筆 a *pencil* stub.
② (鉛筆(の)〜) ▶鉛筆の書き込み penciled notes.
• 鉛筆の芯(ｼﾝ) the lead of a *pencil*. ▶鉛筆の先はとがっていた The *pencil* had a sharp point.
③【鉛筆が[を, で]】▶鉛筆を削る sharpen a *pencil*. ▶鉛筆をなめる suck one's *pencil*. ▶鉛筆で書く write *with a* [*in*] *pencil*. (⇨書く❶③) ▶鉛筆(の先)が折れた I've broken the point of the *pencil* [The *pencil* point].
• 鉛筆画 a pencil drawing. • 鉛筆削り a pencil (-)sharpener. • 鉛筆立て a pencil stand.

えんぴふく 燕尾服 (上着) a tailcoat, tails.

エンフォースメント ［法執行］enforcement. • ピースエンフォースメント peace *enforcement*.

えんぶきょく 円舞曲 a waltz. (⇨ワルツ)

えんぷくか 艶福家 a ladies' [a lady's] man.

エンブレム ［紋章］an emblem. ▶学校のエンブレム（＝校章）がポケットについているブレザー a blazer with a school *emblem* on the pocket.

えんぶん 塩分 salt. • 塩分のある salty. • 塩分を控えたみそ low-*salt* miso. ▶医師に塩分を減らすように言われた The doctor told me to reduce the amount of *salt* I use.

えんぶん 艶聞 a rumor about《his》love affair.

えんぺい 掩蔽 ── **掩蔽する** 動 cover up《a crime》.

えんぺい 援兵 reinforcements.

えんぼう 遠望 a distant view. ▶セントポール寺院の遠望 St. Paul's Cathedral *seen from a distance*.

えんぼう 遠謀 a foresighted plan.

えんぽう 遠方 (a) distance (❗視野に入るものから遠隔地に至るまで広い意味の語);［遠い地］a distant [《やや書》a faraway, 《a far》] place.
① [遠方に[を]] in the ［xa］ distance (❗at a distance は「ある距離をおいて」の意); a long way off, far away [off]. ▶遠方に住む《口》の親戚(ｼﾝｾｷ) a relative living *a long way off* [*in a distant place*]. (❗*a distant* relative は「遠縁の親*

戚］）▶遠方をじっと見つめる stare into the *distance*. ▶はるか遠方に湖が見えた We saw a lake in ［×at］ the far *distance*. ▶その町はここからずっと遠方にある The town is *a long way* (*off*) [*a great distance*, ×far, ×distant] from here. (❗(1) a long way は肯定文で, far は too, so, as などに続く場合を除き否定文・疑問文で用いる. (2) distant は「容易にたどりつけないほど遠い」の意なので, この文脈では不可 (⇨高))
② 【遠方から】 from a (long) distance, from a long way off; (ずっと遠くから) from far away. ▶かなり遠方から矢を放つ shoot an arrow from *a considerable distance*. ▶遠方から(=長い道のりを)やって来る come *a long way*.

エンボス 〘浮き彫り加工〙 embossment. ▶エンボス加工した embossed.
えんま 閻魔 the king of Hell.
えんまく 煙幕 a smoke screen. (❗比喩的に用いることが多い) ▶煙幕を張る throw [put] up a *smoke screen* 《*to do*》.
えんまこおろぎ 閻魔蟋蟀 〘昆虫〙 an emma field cricket; Teleogryllus emma
えんまちょう 閻魔帳 a teacher's grade 《主に米》 [mark 《主に英》] book; (ブラックリスト) a blacklist.
***えんまん** 円満 ── 円満な形 〘幸福な, 満足な〙 happy; 〘調和した〙 harmonious; 〘平和的な〙 peaceful; 〘友好的な〙 amicable. ▶円満な家庭 a *happy* home. ▶円満な夫婦 a *harmonious* couple. ▶円満な性格 a *peaceful* [a *well-rounded*] character.
── 円満に副 ▶紛争を円満に解決する settle a dispute *peacefully* [*amicably*]. ▶2人の間は円満に行かなかった They didn't *get on* [*along*] *well together*.
● 円満解決 a happy [a satisfactory] compromise; an amicable settlement.
えんむ 煙霧 〘濃霧〙 (a) thick [(a) dense] fog; 〘煙と霧〙 smoke and fog; 〘スモッグ〙 (a) smog.
えんむすび 縁結び matchmaking; (縁組) (a) marriage.
えんめい 延命 ── 延命する動 prolong one's life; (生命を維持する) sustain one's life.
● 延命治療 life-prolonging treatment.
えんもく 演目 a number, a program.
えんやす 円安 depreciation of the yen; the weak(er) yen; a fall [a slump] in the yen. (⇨円高) ▶急激な円安 a sharp *depreciation of the yen*. ▶ここ数週間円安ドル高が続いている *The yen has been weak* against the dollar for the past several weeks. ▶円安により日本製品の海外市場における競争力が高まっている *The weak yen* has made Japanese products more competitive in overseas markets.
えんゆうかい 園遊会 《hold [give]》 a garden party.
えんよう 遠洋 ● 遠洋漁業 deep-sea fishing. ● 遠洋航海 《go on》 an ocean voyage. ● 遠洋航路 an ocean lane. ● 遠洋航路の船 an ocean liner.
えんらい 遠来 ▶遠来の客 a visitor *from afar*.

えんらい 遠雷 a distant roll of thunder.
***えんりょ** 遠慮 名 (控えめ) reserve; (謙虚) modesty; (自制) restraint.
① 【遠慮して[は]】 ▶遠慮があってそんなことは言えなかった I was not able to say that *out of reserve*. ▶彼は酔うと遠慮がなくなる When he gets drunk, he breaks loose from *restraint*. ▶ここでは遠慮はいりません(=気楽になさい) Please make yourself at home here.
② 【遠慮がちに】 ▶彼は遠慮がちに(=ちゅうちょして)私のところに近づいてきた He *hesitantly* came near to [approached] me. ▶彼は遠慮がちに話す人だ He is *modest* [*reserved*] *in* speech./He speaks *modestly* [*with reserve, reservedly* /-vɪdli/].
③ 【遠慮のない】 ▶遠慮のない態度 an *unreserved* attitude. ▶遠慮のない(=率直な)意見を述べる give one's *frank* [*candid*] opinion. ▶彼らとは遠慮のない(=親しい)間柄です I am on *friendly* terms with them.
④ 【遠慮なく】 ▶その計画について遠慮なく話す talk *freely* about the plan; talk about the plan *without reserve*. (❗後の方は堅い表現) ▶子供たちは母親がいないときは家中を遠慮なく暴れまわった The children romped around the house *without restraint* when their mother was gone. ▶遠慮なく言わせてもらえば(=率直に言えば)彼の判断は間違っている *To be frank with you* [*Frankly* (*speaking*)], his judgment is wrong. ▶彼は遠慮会釈なく(=容赦なく)同僚を攻撃した He attacked his colleagues *ruthlessly* [*mercilessly*].
会話 「ワインをいただいていいですか」「ええ, ご遠慮なく」 "Can I drink some wine?" "Yes, *help yourself*." (● help oneself は「自由に取って食べる」の意)
── 遠慮する動 ❶ (差し控える) hold* back 《*from*》, reserve; (欲望を一時的に抑える) refrain 《*from*》; (ちゅうちょする) hesitate. ▶女性に年齢を尋ねるのは遠慮すべきです You should *hold back from* [*避ける*) *avoid*] asking a woman her age. ▶この部屋ではお酒[タバコ]はご遠慮ください Please *refrain from* drinking [smoking] in this room./Would you mind not drinking [smoking] in this room? ▶欲しいものがあったら遠慮しないで言いなさい *Don't hesitate* [*Feel free*] *to* ask if you want anything. ▶彼に遠慮して(=敬意を表して)最初に話してもらった I let him speak first *out of respect for* [〘書〙 *in deference to*] him.
❷ (断わる) (丁寧に) decline. ▶彼の招待は遠慮したい I'd like to *decline* his invitation.
会話 「今コーヒーを飲んでおしゃべりしているのよ. あなたも入らない?」「せっかくだけど今回は遠慮させていただくわ」 "We're just having coffee and a chat. Can't you join us?" "Thanks, but *I'd like to pass* this time."
えんれい 艶麗 ── 艶麗な形 fascinating.
えんろ 遠路 ▶遠路ははるばるおいでいただきありがとうございました Thank you very much for coming such *a long way*.

お

*お 尾 a tail; [キツネ・リスなどのふさふさした] a brush; [クジャクなどの長い] a train. (⇨尻尾) ●尾の長い猿 a long-*tailed* monkey. ●尾を垂れる droop one's *tail*; (垂らしている) keep one's *tail* low. ●尾をぴんと立てる raise [erect] one's *tail*. ●彗星(賽)の尾 a comet's *tail* [*trail*, ×*train*]. ▶犬は尾を振った The dog wagged its *tail*. ▶その事件はあとまで尾を引いた(=影響を残した) The matter *has had a lasting effect*.

お 雄, 牡 mare. (⇨雄(赟))

お‐ 御‐ (!英語では丁寧さ・尊敬を表す日本語の接頭辞「お」に直接あたる表現はない。丁寧な依頼の気持ちを表す「お」は please や助動詞を用いて表せる) ▶どうぞお座りください *Would you* like to take a seat? ●相手が座るのをちゅうちょしているような場合は, *Please* take a seat. といってもよいが, それ以外では please を用いると軽い強制と受けとられることがある (⇨どうぞ ❶). ▶お荷物お持ちします *Let me* carry your baggage.

おあいそ お愛想 [お世辞] flattery; [勘定書き] a check. ●お愛想を言う flatter 〔him〕. ●お愛想をお願いします I'd like to pay the *check* [*bill*]. ▶何のお愛想(=もてなし)もありませんで Help yourself. (! please になじまない)

おあいにくさま お生憎様 Tough luck!

オアシス an oasis /ouéisis/ (複 oases /-si:z/).

おあずけ お預け ●おあずけ (犬に) Stay! ●結婚は当分おあずけにしよう(=延期しよう) Let's *put off* [*postpone*] our marriage for a while. ●父さん, 今は感傷にひたっている場合じゃない。ここから逃げ出すまでおあずけ(=とっておいて) Don't get sentimental now, Dad. *Save* it until we get out of here.

おあつらえむき お誂え向き ●誂え向き

オアフ ●オアフ島 Oahu /ouá:hu:/.

おい (呼びかけて) hey (!主に男性語), hello; 《口語》say; (説得・挑戦などを表し) come on; (怒り・いらだちの気持ちで) look (here). ▶おい君 *Hey*, you. ▶おい, どこかで一杯飲まないか *Say*, how about a drink somewhere? ▶おい, やめろよ *Come on*, stop it. ▶おい, どうして言われたとおりにできないんだよ *Look!* Why can't you ever do as you're told?

おい 老い [老齢] old age; [老人] an old man [woman] (複 -)men). (⇨老いる) ●老いの一徹で with the stubbornness of *old age*.

おい 甥 a nephew /néfju:/. ▶彼は私の医師の甥です He is a *nephew* [×*to*] the doctor.

おいあげる 追い上げる ●彼の車は追い上げてきて, ついに彼女の車を追い越した His car *caught up with* hers and then got ahead of it at last. (⇨追い付く) ▶選挙の終盤に他の候補者も激しく追い上げてきた(=最後のがんばりをした) In the last days of the election campaign, the other candidates *made a final push* for the race [(力強く前進した) *moved up strongly*].

おいうち 追い打ち ●敵に追い打ちをかける attack the enemy in flight.

おいえげい お家芸 [家伝の技芸] a family speciality; [得意技] one's forte /fɔ́ːrt/ (⇨十八番(賦)).

おいえそうどう お家騒動 [家族内の争い] family strife; [権力抗争] a power struggle. (!派閥(賦)間の争いは an interfactional [a factional] power struggle などとなる) (⇨争い ❷)

おいおい ❶ [そのうちに] soon, before long; (しかるべきうちに) in due course. ▶おいおい返事があるでしょう You will get the answer *in due course*.
❷ [泣くさま] ●おいおい泣く cry *hard* [*bitterly*]. ▶少女はおいおい泣いてやがて眠った The little girl *cried herself bitterly* to sleep.

おいおとし 追い落とし ●社長の追い落としを計る conspire to *drive away* the president *from his position*; make an attempt to *unseat* the president.

おいかえす 追い返す turn [send*, drive*]... back 〔to〕; [追い払う] turn [send, drive]... away. ●入り口で追い返される be turned back at the entrance.

おいかける 追い掛ける [追跡する] chase (after...), 《書》pursúe; (あとを追う) run* after.... (⇨追う ❶, 追い回す) ●強盗を追いかける *chase* (*after*) [*pursue, run after*] a robber.

おいかぜ 追い風 a fair [a favorable, a following] wind. ●追い風を受けて帆走する sail *before* [*off, with*] *the wind*.

おいかぶさる 覆い被さる (⇨覆(鑾)い被さる)

おいこし 追い越し ●追い越し禁止 《標識》《米》No passing.; 《英》No overtaking. ●追い越し車線 《米》the pássing làne; 《英》the overtáking làne.

おいこす 追い越す ❶ [通り越す] (追いつき追い抜く) overtake*; (通り過ぎる) pass; (より先に出る) get* ahead of...; (競走で) outstrip (-pp-); (走って) outrun*. ●左から[カーブで]追い越してはいけない Don't *pass* on the left [on a curve]. ▶私の乗ったタクシーがバスを追い越した My taxi *overtook* [*passed, got ahead of*] a bus.
❷ [上回る] (追い抜く) overtake*; (まさる) surpass; (先んじる) outstrip (-pp-), get* ahead of .... ●工業生産において他のあらゆる国を追い越す *overtake* [*outstrip*] all other nations in industrial production. ▶彼は数学で兄を追い越した He *got ahead of* his brother in math(ematics).

おいこみ 追い込み ▶彼は競走の終盤で追い込みをかけた He put on a *spurt* toward the end of the race. ▶選挙戦は追い込み(=最後の段階)に入った The election campaign has gone into [has reached, is in] its *final* [*last*] *stage*.

おいこむ 老い込む age (a lot); (歳をとって衰える) become old and weak. (⇨老(賦)い込む)

おいこむ 追い込む [追いやる] drive*. (⇨追い詰める) ●羊を囲いに追い込む *drive* the sheep *into* an enclosure. ●彼を窮地に追い込む *drive* [*force, put*] him *into* a corner; *corner* him. ●打者[投手]を追い込む get [put] a batter [a pitcher] in the [a] hole. ▶その投手は追い込まれた The pitcher got behind the batter. ▶その問題で田中氏は辞職に追い込まれた Mr.Tanaka *was forced to* resign over the issue.

おいコン 追いコン [「追い出しコンパ」の略] a send-off party.

おいさき 老い先 ●老い先が短い do not have many years to live.

おいさらばえる 老いさらばえる grow weak with age.

*おいしい

WORD CHOICE おいしい

delicious 食べ物の味や香りが飛び抜けて良いこと。それ自身で強い意味を持つため、very などで強調することはまれ。●非常においしい食べ物[食事] *delicious* foods [meals].

tasty 食べ物の風味が良いこと。通例、塩味の料理に用い、甘いデザートには用いない。●おいしく簡単に作れる料理レシピ the recipe that is *tasty* and easy to prepare.

頻度チャート

delicious
tasty
20 40 60 80 100 (%)

❶ [味が] good*, nice (**!** いずれも delicious より口語的); [[大変おいしい]] delicious; [[味のよい]] tasty. ●おいしそうな料理 a *delicious*-looking [a *tasty*-looking] dish; (よだれの出そうな) a *mouth-watering* dish. ▶このパイはとてもおいしい This pie *is* very *good* [very *nice*, *delicious*]. (**!** (1) very delicious とはあまりいわない。(2) really [absolutely] delicious とはいえる)/This pie *tastes* very good [*nice*, ×*well*]./This pie *has* a very good [*nice*] *taste*. (**!** 日常会話では I really like this pie. などということが多い) ▶あのホテルの料理はとてもおいしい That hotel serves very *good* food./I like the food in that hotel very much. ▶その食べ物はとてもおいしそうな(=食欲をそそる)においがする The food smells very *appetizing*.

会話 (レストランで)「料理はどう?」「ええ、とってもおいしいわ。あなたのは?」「まあね」"How's your food?" "Mm, (×very) *delicious* [*tastes great*]. And yours?" "It's OK." (**!** おいしくない場合は婉曲的に)「おもしろい[変わった]味だ」Um /ʌm/, it's interesting [different]. (などとどう)

❷ [魅力的な、都合がいい] ▶「ハムレット」で墓掘り人の役をゲットしました。これはかなりおいしい役です I got to play the grave digger in 'Hamlet.' I've been very lucky [This is what I'd wanted].

会話「編み物教室のアルバイトはまだ続けているの?」「ええ、こんなにおいしいアルバイトはなかなかやめられないよ」"Are you still working parttime at the knitting school?" "Yes. I can't easily give up such a 'tasty' job." (**!** tasty を強く読む)

おいしげる 生い茂る (⇨茂る) ▶バラが生い茂っていた(=密集して育っていた) The roses *grew thick* (**!** thick は株の状態を表す). ▶小道には雑草が生い茂っていた(=一面に生えていた) The path *was overgrown* [*thick*, *rank*] *with* weeds.

おいしさ 美味しさ (a good) taste. (⇨旨味)

おいすがる 追いすがる run* after ⟨him⟩ closely; (すぐあとについて行く) follow at ⟨his⟩ heels; (しつこく追う) hound ⟨him⟩.

オイスター [カキ] [魚介] an oyster.
●オイスターソース oyster sauce.

おいせん 追い銭 money paid in addition. ▶盗人に追い銭 ⟨盗人に⟩[成句]

おいそれと(は) [たやすく] easily, readily; [[直ちに]] at once, immediately; [[即席に]] offhand; [[考えなく]] thoughtlessly. ●おいそれと承知しない do not give a *ready* consent; do not consent *readily*. ●おいそれとは彼らから返事が来ない can't answer offhand [*at once*]. ▶おいそれとはその仕事を引き受けられない I can't undertake the task *easily*. ▶おいそれと人に金を貸すな Don't lend your money to others *thoughtlessly* [(ただ相手が頼んだからといって) *just for the asking*].

おいた (⇨悪戯(いたずら)) ▶これこれ、おいたをするんじゃありません Come, come, don't be such a *mischief*. (**!** mischief は「いたずらっ子」)

おいだき 追い焚き reheating the bath (water).

おいだし 追い出し (追放) expulsion; (立ち退き)《書》eviction. ●追い出しコンパ a send-off party.

おいだす 追い出す get* (駆り立てるように) drive*, (無理やり) turn, (ほうり投げるように) throw*] ... out; [[追放する]] expel (-ll-); [[地位などから]]《書》oust ⟨*from*⟩. ●ハエを部屋から追い出す *drive* [*get*] a fly *out of* the room. ▶国から敵軍を追い出す(追放する) *expel* the enemy *from* the country; (追い払う) *drive* the enemy *out of* the country. ▶けんかをしておやじに追い出された We had a fight and my old man *turned* [*threw*, 《話》*kicked*] me *out* (*of* the house).

おいたち 生い立ち [[背景]] one's background; [[経歴]] one's personal history; [[子供時代]] one's childhood. ▶彼は不幸な生い立ちだった(=恵まれない境遇で育った) He *was brought up* in unfavorable circumstances./His *early life* was unhappy.

おいたて 追い立て (立ち退き) (an) eviction. ●アパートから追い立てを食う *face eviction from* one's apartment; *be evicted from* one's apartment; *be forced to move out of* one's apartment.

おいたてる 追い立てる ▶子供を学校へと追い立てる(=せき立てる) *hurry* [《話》*pack*] a child *off to* school. ●家賃滞納の借家人を追い立てる(=立ち退かせる) *evict* a tenant who doesn't pay his rent.

おいちらす 追い散らす drive*... away; (ちりぢりに)《やや書》disperse.

おいつく 追い付く catch* up ⟨*with*⟩; (追いつき追い越す) overtake*. ▶先に行ってくれ、すぐに追いつくから Go ahead. I'll *catch up* [I'll *be with* you] in a minute. ▶私は彼らに追いつこうと一生懸命走った I ran like mad to *catch up with* them [*catch* them *up*]. ▶彼は一生懸命勉強してクラスのみんなに追いついた He worked very hard and *caught up with* the rest of the class. ▶1 回ぐらい授業を休んでも後で追いつけるよ(=埋め合わせができる) If you miss a lesson, you can *make it up* later. ▶生産が需要に追いつかない Production does not *keep up with* demand. (**!** keep up with ... は「...に遅れずについてゆく」の意)

おいつめる 追い詰める [[窮地に]] drive*... into a corner; corner. ●その犬を袋小路に追い詰める *corner* the dog *in* [*into*] a dead-end alley. ●犯人を追い詰めて捕える *track* a criminal *down*. ▶彼は窮地に追い詰められている He *is trapped* [*driven into a corner*]./《話》He *is in a* (real) *fix*. ▶追いつめられたとき、人は真の姿が出る When *driven into a corner*, humans show [*reveal*] what they really are. / When *driven into a corner*, humans betray themselves. (**!**(1) 隠していたものを現すときは show より reveal が適切。(2) betray oneself は「本心を表す」の意で堅い言い方)

おいて 措いて ▶彼をおいてその地位に適任者はいない He is the only one for the position.

おいて 於て ❶[[場所]] at...; in.... (**!** 原則として at は点としての場所、in はある程度のある場所だを表す(⇨-で、-に) ❷[[時、場合]] at...; in.... (**!** at は時の一点、in は期間を表す)(⇨-で、-に) ❸[[関して]] about.... (⇨について)

おいで お出で ●おいでおいで beckoning. (⇨手招き) ▶よくお出で(=来て)くださいました I am glad (that)

おいてきぼり 置いてきぼり ● 置いてきぼりにする leave 《him》 behind. ▶彼はクラスメートに置いてきぼりを食った He *was left behind by* his classmates.

おいとま お暇 ⇨暇(いとま).

おいぬく 追い抜く (追いつき追い越す) overtake*; (通り過ぎる) pass. ⇨追い越す.

おいのこぶみ『笈の小文』 *The Knapsack Notebook*; *The Records of A Travel-Worn Satchel*. 〖参考〗松尾芭蕉の俳諧紀行文.

おいはぎ 追い剥ぎ a highwayman (複 -men) (!) 昔, 街道に出た馬に乗った強盗); 〖強盗〗 a robber.

おいはらう 追い払う drive* [send]... away; 〖いやなものを取り除く〗 get* rid of ...; 〖地位などから〗 expel (-ll-) 《from》, 《書》 oust 《from》. ⇨追い出す
 ● 犬を(門から)追い払う drive [send, turn] a dog away (from the gate). ● 心配事を追い払う drive away [get rid of] one's cares. ● しっしっと言って鳥を追い払う shoo [hiss] a bird away. ● 彼の悪霊を追い払う (=追い出す) drive [exorcize] evil spirits out of him. ▶警察は群衆を追い払った The police drove off [《四方に散らした》dispersed] the crowd.

おいぼれ 老いぼれ 〖人〗 (ぼけた) a senile /síːnail/ person; 〖人生の時期〗 dotage /dóutidʒ/. ● 老いぼれる get [go] senile. ● 老いぼれている be senile; be in one's *dotage*.

おいまくる 追い捲る chase 《him》 to the ends of the earth. ▶彼はいつも仕事に追いまくられている He is always [*kept*] *extremely busy with* his work./ His work *keeps* him *very busy* all the time.

おいまわす 追い回す (あちこちと追いかける) chase (after)..., run* after ...; (つきまとう) follow 《him》 around. ● 女の尻を追い回す chase (after) girls. ▶仕事に追い回されて(=仕事でとても忙しくて)本を読む余裕なんかないよ I'm *very busy with* work, so I've no time to read./Who has the time to read? I'm *pressed* [I'm *swamped*] with work.

おいめ 負い目 〖恩義, 借金〗 (a) debt /dét/. ▶私は彼に負い目がある *I am in debt to* him. (!)「借金がある」の意もある/(恩を受けている) 《やや書》 I *am indebted to* him [《《書》in his *debt*]*.

おいもとめる 追い求める 《書》 pursue. ⇨追求

おいやる 追いやる (⇨追い払う) ● 彼を自殺に追いやる drive him *to* (commit) suicide.

おいらく 老いらく (老年) old age; 《婉曲的》 golden years. ● 老いらくの恋 love [(情事) a romance] in one's golden years.

おいらん 花魁 a courtesan.

おいる 老いる grow* [become*, get*] old; (ふける) age. ● 年老いた父 my *old* [*elderly*, 《書》*aged* /éidʒid/] father. ▶彼は老いてますます盛んだ He is still healthy and active *in his old age*./《話》 He's still going strong *in his old age*.
 ● 老いては子に従え You should trust your children and listen to what they say when you grow old.

オイル (油) oil (!)種類を表すときは ⒞]; (石油) oil, petroleum; (ガソリン) 《米》 gasoline, 《米話》 gas, 《英》 petrol; (潤滑油) motor oil; (日焼け用の) suntan lotion. ● サラダオイル salad *oil*.
 ● オイルクロス oilcloth. ● オイルショック an oil [an energy] crisis (!) an oil shock も可) ● オイルダラー oil dollars. ● オイルフェンス 《place》 oil booms 《around》. (!) boom は「防材」のこと) ● オイルマネー oil money.

おいろなおし お色直し a bride's change of costume.

***おう** 追う ❶ 〖追いかける〗 (つかまえようとスピードを出して) chase (after ...); (つかまえたり殺したりするために執よに) hunt, 《書》 pursue; (痕跡(ミɛ)をたどって) track; (あとを追う) run* after ...; (あとについて行く[来る]) follow. ● 野戦の跡を追う track [trail] a wild animal. ● 目で彼を追う follow him with one's eyes. ▶警察は犯人の跡を追っている The police *are* [×is] *chasing* [*hunting*, (捜索にあたる) *searching for*] the criminal./The police *are* [×is] *in pursuit* [*on the track, in search*] *of* the criminal./ The police *are after* the criminal. ▶その子は母親のあとを追った The child *ran after* his mother.
❷ 〖追い求める〗 《書》 pursue /pərs(j)úː/. ● 快楽[理想]を追う pursue pleasure [an ideal]. ● 最新の流行を追う follow the latest fashions; (遅れないでついてゆく) keep up with the latest fashions.
❸ 〖順番に従う〗 ● 出来事の順を追う follow the order of events. ● 順を追ってそれを説明する explain it *in order*. ▶日を追って暖かくなってきた It's getting warmer *day by day* [*from day to day*].
❹ 〖追いやる〗 drive*. ● ハエを追う (=追い払う) drive [(あおいで) fan, (はたいて) flap] flies *away*. ● 家畜を野原へ追う (=追って行く) drive the cattle *to* the fields.
 ● 追いつ追われつ ▶それは追いつ追われつの接戦だった It was a *seesaw* [a *close*] game.

***おう** 王 a king; 〖君主〗 a monarch /mánərk/, 《書》 a sovereign /sávərən/; 〖実業界の〗 a tycoon.

> 〖使い分け〗 **king** 男性の「王」を表す最も一般的な語. 動物界・植物界の王者も含む.
> **monarch**, **sovereign** 世襲によって国を治める王. 女王や皇帝も含む.

● 英国王ジョージ6世 George VI, *King* of Great Britain. (!) George the Sixth と読む) ● 石油王 an oil tycoon [*magnate* /mǽgneit/]. ● ライオンは百獣の王だ The lion is the *king* of beasts. (!) *The* lion は総称の the) ▶彼は今季のホームラン王になった He became the (home-)run *king* for this season.

***おう** 負う ❶ 〖引き受ける〗 (責任などを) take*, accept, 《書》 undertake*. ▶これについては私がすべて責任を負います I will *take* [*accept, assume*] full responsibility for this. ▶私たちは納税の義務を負っている We *have* an obligation to [*are under* an obligation to] pay taxes.
❷ 〖こうむる〗 ▶そのバス事故では多くの人が重傷を負った A lot of people *got* seriously *injured* in the bus accident. (!)戦争などで傷を負う場合は get wounded)
❸ 〖恩恵を受ける〗 ▶今の私の成功はあなたに負っている I *owe* my present success *to* you. ● 親に負うところが大きい I *owe* my parents a great deal [a lot]./《書》 I *am* deeply [*greatly*] *indebted to* my parents.
❹ 〖背負う〗 carry ... on one's back.
 ● 負うた子に教えられる 《ことわざ》 A mouse may help a lion./A fool may give a wise man counsel.

おう 凹 (凹面) (a) concavity. ● 凹面の concave.

おう 翁 an old [an aged] man (複 men). ● 大隈翁 the (revered) *old* Mr. Okuma.

おうい　王位 the throne; the crown. ●王位を継承する succeed to *the throne* [*crown*]. ●王子は10歳のとき王位についた The prince *came to* [*ascended, mounted*] *the throne* at the age of ten.

おういつ　横溢 ●活気横溢しているbe full of life (and energy); be bursting with energy.

おういん　押印 sealing. (⇨捺印)

おういん　押韻［名］rhyming. (⇨韻) ── **押韻する**［動］rhyme.

‡おうえん　応援［名］［声援］cheering, a cheer;［支持］support;［助力］help. ●応援を求める ask for *support* [*help*]. ●彼の応援演説をする speak [《やや書》make a campaign speech] *for* him. (**!** for は「…のために」の意)

── **応援する**［動］［声援する］cheer,《主に米話》root for …;［支持する］support, back … (up); (昇進・就職などに)《話》pull for …;［助力する］help. ●声をからして応援する *cheer* oneself hoarse. ●候補者を応援する *support* a candidate. ▶観客はそのチームを応援した The spectators *cheered* the team (*on*). (**!** on をつけると「励ます」の意が加わる)

[会話]「どのサッカーチームを応援してるの?」「ぼくはガンバだ」"Which soccer team do you *support*?" "I'm a Gamba supporter."

●応援歌 a rooter's《米》[a supporter's《英》] song. ●応援団 a chéer(ing) gròup,《主に米話》rooters; (サッカーの) country supporters; (団員) a rooter. (**!** (1) 応援を指揮するは主に女子学生. (2) ×a cheer girl は和製英語. ●応援団席 a chéering sèction. ●応援団長 a head cheerleader [《米俗》rooter].

おうおう　往々 (度々, 時々) ●我々は往々にして(=しばしば)人の助けを当てにする We *often* [*frequently*] count on other people's [others'] help. ●若者には往々あることだ It is *often* the case with young people. ▶そういうことは往々にしてある(=珍しくない) That sort of thing is *not uncommon*.

おうか　欧化 Europeanization. ── **欧化する**［動］Europeanize. ●欧化主義 Europeanism.

おうか　謳歌 ── **謳歌する**［動］(楽しむ) enjoy; (喜びを歌う) sing* the joys [*praises*] of …. ●青春を謳歌する *sing the joys of* youth.

おうが　横臥 ── **横臥する**［動］lie on one's side.

おうかくまく　横隔膜〖解剖〗a diaphragm /dáiəfræm/.

おうかん　王冠 a (royal) crown,《書》a diadem;［びんの］a (crown) cap. ●王冠をかぶる wear a *crown*; (王位につく) be crowned king [queen]. (⇨王位)

おうぎ　扇 a (folding) fan. ●扇を使う use a fan; fan oneself.

おうぎ　奥義 (核心) the heart; (真髄) the essence, 《書》the quintessence; (秘伝) the secret.

おうきゅう　王宮 a royal palace.

おうきゅう　応急 ── **応急(の)**［形］［緊急の］emergency;［一時的な］temporary;［間に合わせの］make-shift. ●歯がずきずき痛みます. 応急処置をしていただけませんか I have a throbbing pain in the tooth. Could you give first aid to me [do a *temporary* job on it]?

●応急修理《make》 temporary repairs. ●応急措置《take》emergency [(間に合わせの) makeshift] measures.

おうぎょく　黄玉〖地学〗(トパーズ) (a) topaz.

おうけ　王家 ●王家の出だ be from a *royal family*.

おうけん　王権 sovereignty /sávərənti/; sovereign power [authority].

おうこう　横行 ── **横行する**［動］(はびこる) be rámpant.

▶その町は犯罪が横行している Crime *is rampant* in the town.

おうこうきぞく　王侯貴族《集合的に》the royalty and nobility; (王子と貴族たち) princes and nobles.

おうこく　王国 a kingdom;［君主国］a monarchy. ●神の王国は人の中にある The *kingdom* of God is within man.

おうごん　黄金 gold. (⇨金) ── **黄金の**［形］golden. ●黄金時代 (芸術・文化などの)《in》a golden [xgold] age; (全盛期)《at》the height [zenith] (of one's prosperity). ●黄金週間 ゴールデンウィーク. ●黄金分割 the golden section [mean]. ●黄金律 the golden rule.

おうざ　王座〖王の位〗the throne (⇨王位);［首位］championship, (the) first place. (⇨首位) ●王座決定戦 the *championship* match [game]. ●大学対抗戦の王座につく(を保つ; を譲る) win [retain; lose] the intercollegiate *championship*.

おうさつ　応札 ── **応札する**［動］enter [make] a bid《for, 《米》on》.

おうさま　王様 a king. (⇨王) ●喜劇の王様チャップリン Charlie Chaplin, the *king* of comedy.

おうし　牡牛［食用・労役用の去勢した］an ox《寒 oxen》;［去勢しない］a bull.

おうし　横死 (不慮の死) an accidental death.

おうじ　王子 a (royal) prince, a prince of the blood royal [royal blood]. ●ウィリアム王子 *Prince* William.

おうじ　往時 (昔) a long time ago. (⇨昔)

おうじ　皇子 an Imperial prince.

おうしざ　牡牛座〖占星・天文〗Taurus (**!** the はつけない); (牡牛宮)〖占星〗the Bull. (⇨乙女座) ●牡牛座(生まれ)の人 a Taurus, a Taurean. (**!** 後の方は形容詞にも用いる)

おうしつ　王室 the royal family.

おうしゃ　応射 a counterattack. ── **応射する**［動］counterattack《on, against》; fire back《on》.

おうじゃ　王者［王］a king (⇨王);［優勝者］a champion. ●王者の風格(=王らしい威厳)がある have a *kingly* presence [a *regal* dignity].

おうじる　応需 ── **応需する**［動］comply with《his》request.

おうしゅう　応酬［名］［反ばく］a retort;［やりとり］an exchange. ●野次［強打; 反論］の応酬 an *exchange* of heckling [blows; refutations].

── **応酬する**［動］retort, make a retort. (⇨言い返す)

おうしゅう　押収［名］(a) seizure /síːʒər/; (没収)《a》 confiscation.

── **押収する**［動］seize /síːz/; confiscate. ●調査員はその会社の帳簿を押収した The investigators *seized* the firm's books.

おうしゅう　欧州［名］Europe. ── **欧州の**［形］European.

●欧州委員会 the European Commission. ●欧州議会 the European Parliament. ●欧州中央銀行 the European Central Bank. ●欧州理事会 the Council of the European Union. ●欧州連合 the European Union 《略 EU》.

おうじゅほうしょう　黄綬褒章 a Medal with Yellow Ribbon. (⇨褒章 関連)

おうじょ　王女 a (royal) princess, a princess of the blood royal [royal blood];［皇女］an Imperial princess. ●アン王女 *Princess* Ann.

おうじょう　王城 the king.

おうじょう　応召 ── **応召する**［動］muster; be conscripted [《米》drafted] into the army.

おうじょう　王城 (王宮) the king's castle; a royal

おうじょう 往生 图 ❶ [死ぬこと] death. ▶大往生を遂げる(=安らかに死ぬ) *die a* peaceful *death*; *die peacefully*. ❷ [困ること] ▶あいつは往生際(=思い切り)が悪い He's *a bad loser*.
— **往生する** 動 ❶ [死ぬ] die; (婉曲的) pass away. ❷ [困る] (話) be in a fix. ▶金策のめどがつかなくて往生した I *was in a fix* [(途方に暮れた) *at my wits' end*] for money.

おうしょくじんしゅ 黄色人種 the yellow race(s). (! 侮蔑(ﾍﾞﾂ)的な言葉で禁句の一つ. Mongoloid people とか Asians で置き換えることもある)

*__おうじる 応じる__ ❶ [答える] answer, reply to ..., respond to ... (!この順に堅い語); (行動・動作で) respond to ... ▶先生は質問に簡単に応じた The teacher *answered* [*replied*] the question briefly./The teacher *responded* briefly to the question. ▶彼は聴衆の拍手に会釈で応じた He *responded to* the spectators' applause with a bow [by bowing]./He bowed *in response to* the spectators' applause.
❷ [承諾する] (同意する) agree 《*to*》, consent 《*to*》 (! agree より堅い語で通例重要なことについて積極的に同意すること); (受け入れる) accept; (依頼などに従う) (書) comply 《*with*》. ▶招待[彼の挑戦]に応じる *accept* an invitation [his challenge]. (! 後の方は respond to, take up も可) ▶彼女の要求[希望]に応じる *comply with* her request [wishes]. ▶奨学資金に応じる(=申し込む) *apply for* a scholarship. ▶彼はその提案に快く応じてくれた He was willing to *agree* [*consent*] *to* the proposal. ▶経営者側は賃金の引き上げに応じた Management *agreed to* raise the wages. ▶彼は頑として説得に応じなかった He *refused* [xdeclined, xdid not agree] *to* be persuaded.
❸ [見合うようにする] (要求などを満たす) meet*; (希望・必要などを十分に満足させる) satisfy. ▶その場の要求に応ずる *meet* [*satisfy*] the requirements of the situation. ▶収入に応じた生活をする(=収入の範囲内で暮らす) live *within* one's *income* [(資力) *means*]. ▶業績に応じて給料が支払われる be paid *according to* one's achievements. ▶注文はたえる一方でそれに応じられない The [xOur] orders are piling up and we aren't able to *meet* them. (! our orders は「私たちがする注文」の意) ▶物価が上がっているのにもかかわらず, 給料はそれに応じて引き上げられていない Though prices are going up, we haven't gotten a pay raise 《米》 [*rise* 《英》] *accordingly*. ▶成功は努力に応じて決まる(=…に依存する) Your success *depends on* how much effort you make. ▶あの先生は必要に応じて我々を助けてくれるでしょう The teacher will help us *as the need arises* [(時に応じて) *as the occasion demands*].

おうしん 往診 make a house [a home] visit 《(主に米) call》 (from a doctor).
— **往診する** 動 make a house [a home] visit 《*to*》; visit. ▶医者に往診をしてもらった I had a (house [home]) *visit from* the doctor./I *got the doctor to visit* me.
● 往診料 a doctor's visiting fee.

おうせい 王制 (王室の政治) royal government [rule]. ▶王制を廃止する abolish [put an end to] *royal government*.

おうせい 王政 (皇帝の支配) Imperial rule; (君主政治) monarchy.
▶王政復古 (英国の) the Restoration.

おうせい 旺盛 ▶食欲が旺盛だ have a *good* [an excellent] appetite; eat *a lot*. ▶知識欲が旺盛だ have a strong desire to learn; have a thirst for knowledge; be eager to learn [for knowledge]. ▶元気旺盛だ be *full of* energy [vigor].

おうせつ 応接 (⇨応対) ▶応接3点セット a three-piece *living-room* suite /swíːt/.
● 応接にいとまない ▶千客万来で応接にいとまがない Visitors come one after another, and I am very busy *receiving* [*seeing*] each of them.
● 応接室 (会社などの) a recéption ròom. 応接間 (家庭の) a líving ròom; 《主に英》 a sítting ròom 《!居間のこと. 米英の一般家庭では居間を広く作り客間も兼ねる》; (本式の) a drawing ròom.

おうせん 応戦 — **応戦する** 動 ▶敵と応戦する *fight back* with; (挑戦を受ける) *take up* [*accept*] *the challenge of* the enemy; (砲火で) *return* the enemy's *fire*.

おうせんこぎって 横線小切手 a crossed check.

おうぞく 王族 《集合的》 royalty; (王室の) the royal family; (王家) the blood royal [royal blood].

おうだ 殴打 图 (a) strike; (強打) a blow.
— 殴打する 動 (⇨殴る)

おうたい 応対 图 (⇨応接) ▶応対に出る *answer* the door. ▶彼女は(電話の)応対が上手だ She *handles* [*deals with*] people very well (on the phone).
— **応対(を)する** 動 (面会する) see; (迎える) receive; (取り扱う) handle; (店・人に) serve, 《書》 attend 《*to*》. ▶就職希望者の応対をする see job applicants; (面談する) give a job *interview*. ▶客の応対をする receive visitors; (店で) serve [《書》 *attend to*] customers.

おうたい 横隊 a rank. (⇨縦隊) ▶2列横隊の兵隊 two *ranks* of soldiers.

おうたいホルモン 黄体ホルモン 【生化学】 progesterone.

おうだく 応諾 — **応諾する** 動 assent [give one's assent] 《*to*》.

*__おうだん 横断__ 图 (a) crossing. ▶大陸横断鉄道 a transcontinental railroad. ▶道路に横断幕を張る stretch a *banner across* a street.
— **横断する** 動 cross. (⇨横切る, 渡る) ▶太平洋を飛行機で横断する fly *across* the Pacific; make a transpacific flight. ▶道路を横断する前に左右を確かめなさい Look both ways before you *cross* the street.
● 横断面 a cross section. 横断歩道 (⇨横断歩道)

おうだん 黄疸 【医学】 jaundice /dʒɔ́ːndɪs/. ▶彼は黄疸の症状が出てきた He's started to develop the symptoms of *jaundice*.

おうだんほどう 横断歩道 a pedestrian /pədéstriən/ crossing, 《米》 a crosswalk; 《英》 a zebra crossing (参考) 道路が白のしま模様に塗ってあることから); (信号つきの) a light-controlled crosswalk; (押しボタン式の) 《英》 a pelican crossing. ▶横断歩道の所(道路)を渡る cross at a *crosswalk*.
● 横断歩道橋 a pedestrian bridge. (参考) 欧米ではあまり見られない)

おうちゃく 横着 — **横着(な)** 形 [怠惰な] lazy; [厚かましい] impudent. ▶彼はすっかり横着になって自分のふとんも敷かない He has become very *lazy* and doesn't even make his bed.
● 横着者 a lazy person, 《話》 a lazybones (複 ～).

おうちょう 王朝 a dynasty /dáinəsti, dí-/. ▶明王朝 the Ming *dynasty*.

おうて 王手 check. ▶王手をかける *check* the king. ▶王手だ *Check!* ▶王手がかかっている The king is *in* (↔*out*) *of check*.

おうてん　横転 图 óverturn.（❗「ひっくり返ること」の意で，必ずしも横転とはかぎらない）
— **横転する** 動 overtúrn; turn on its side. ▶その車は橋のそばで横転しているのが発見された The car was found lying *on its side* by the bridge.

おうと　嘔吐 图 vomiting.（⇨吐き気）
— **嘔吐する** 動 vomit.（⇨吐く❶）

おうど　黄土 fine yellow earth;（ローム質の）loess /lóuəs/.

おうどいろ　黄土色 ocher /óukər/. ●黄土色のocherous, ocher;（髪の色が）sandy.

おうとう　応答 图 a response; an answer.（⇨答え，返事）
— **応答する** 動 respond（*to*); answer（*to*).（⇨答える）▶クック船長，応答願います。どうぞ（無線で）Captain Cook, come in, please. Over.

おうとう　桜桃 图〖植物〗(サクランボ) a cherry.

おうどう　王道 ▶学問に王道なし〖ことわざ〗There is no *royal road* to learning.

おうどう　黄銅 图〖『真鍮』の別名〗(⇨真鍮)
● **黄銅鉱** copper pyrites /paráitiːz/.

おうとつ　凹凸 unevenness.（⇨でこぼこ）▶路面の凹凸が激しい The road is very *rough* [*bumpy*,（ごつごつした）*rugged*] /rǎgid/.

おうなつ　押捺 stamping;（押印）sealing. ●指紋の押捺を拒否するrefuse to be fingerprinted.

おうねつびょう　黄熱病〖医学〗yellow fever.

おうねん　往年 ▶往年の名映画監督 a *once* [*a formerly*] famous movie director.

おうのう　懊悩 图 mental anguish;（苦悩）agony.
— **懊悩する** 動 be stricken with grief.

おうはん　凹版 an intaglio /intǽgliou/（複～s). ●凹版印刷 intaglio;（写真凹版印刷）photogravure /fòutougrəvjúər/.

おうひ　王妃 a queen;（皇后）an empress.

おうふう　欧風 ●欧風の形 European(-style).

‡**おうふく　往復** 图 ▶往復のバス代 a bus fare *both ways* [*for a round trip*]. ▶通学に往復どのくらいの時間がかかりますか How long does it take（you）to *go to and from* school [*go to school and back*, ×*go to school and from it*]? ▶往復ともタクシーに乗りなさい Take a taxi *both ways* [*there and back*].

— **往復する** 動 go* to and come* back [return]《*from*》; get* to〈a place〉and back; go back and forth《*between*》;〖米〗make* a round trip《*to*, *between*》. ▶そこへ列車で往復するには 4 時間近くかかった It took almost four hours to *get there and back* by train. ▶私は毎日東京大阪間を往復している I *go back and forth* [*make a round trip*] *between* Tokyo and Osaka every day. ▶このバスは空港とホテルの間を定期的に往復している（＝折り返し運転している）This bus *shuttles* between the airport and the hotel.（❗shuttleは乗り物・人が近距離を定期的に往復すること）

● **往復運賃**〖米〗a round-trip fare;〖英〗a return fare.（❗〖米〗で return (ticket)は「帰りの切符」の意）▶シカゴまでの往復運賃はいくらですか What is the *round-trip* fare to Chicago?／How much will it cost to *go to Chicago and back*? ● **往復切符**〖米〗a round-trip (ticket);〖英〗a return (ticket). ▶大阪までの往復切符を 2 枚ください Two *round-trip* tickets to Osaka, please.

おうぶん　応分 ●応分の＝(資力[能力]に応じて)寄付[貢献]する contribute *according to* one's *means* [one's *ability*].

おうぶん　欧文 European writing, writing in a European language;（ローマ字）Roman letters.

おうへい　横柄 图 árrogance;〖お高くまって下の者を見下すこと〗haughtiness;〖傲慢〗insolence.（❗傲慢）●彼の横柄さに我慢できない I can't put up with his *arrogance* [*haughtiness*, *insolence*].
— **横柄な** 形 árrogant; haughty; insolent. ▶横柄な態度で in an *arrogant*（高飛車な）a *high-handed*] manner. ▶彼は自分より貧しい者に対して非常に横柄だ He is very *haughty to* [*toward*] people poorer than himself.

おうべい　欧米 Europe and America; the West,〖書〗the Occident.（❗後の 2 語は西洋全体をさすが，通例欧米の意で用いられる）●欧米の European and American; Western;〖書〗Occidental. ●欧米人 Europeans and Americans; Westerners;〖書〗Occidentals.
● **欧米諸国** European and American countries.

おうへん　応変 ⇨臨機応変する 動 yellow; turn yellow.

おうぼ　応募 图（申し込み）(an) application. ▶その職に 40 名の応募があった We had forty *applicants* for the job.／Forty people *applied for* the job. ▶絵画コンクールに 25 名の[多くの]応募があった There were 25 *entries* [were many *entries*, was a large *entry*] *for* the painting contest.
— **応募する** 動 apply《*for*》;（競技などに）enter《*for*》. ●就職口に応募する apply [*make an application*] *for* a job《*with* a company》. ●懸賞論文に応募する enter《*for*》[*enter oneself for*] an essay contest.
● **応募者** an applicant;（競技などへの）an entry（❗「応募作品」の意でも用いる）. ● **応募用紙** an application (fòrm [blànk]); an éntry fòrm.

おうぼう　応報（罰）punishment.（⇨因果応報）

おうぼう　横暴 ●横暴な形（暴君的な）tyrannical /tirǽnikl/;（圧制的な）oppressive;（不当な）unreasonable. ▶何て横暴なんだろう What a *tyrant* /táiərənt/ (he is)!/He múst get [have] his own way.（❗「何かにつけ我を通す」の意）

おうむ　鸚鵡 图〖鳥〗a parrot. ●おうむ返しに言う parrot [repeat]〈his words〉.（❗parrot は通例軽蔑的な）
● **鸚鵡病**〖医学〗psittacosis /sitəkóusis/; parrot fever.

おうめんきょう　凹面鏡 a concave mirror.

おうもんきん　横紋筋〖解剖〗(a) striated muscle.

‡**おうよう　応用** 图;〖実用〗practical use. ●科学知識の産業への応用 the *application* of scientific knowledge *to* industry. ▶この定理は応用範囲が広い This theorem has wide *application*./This proposition *applies* [*can be applied*] widely.
— **応用する** 動 apply /əplái/;〖実用的に使う〗make* (×a) practical use of...; put*... to practical use. ●その現象を説明するのに彼の理論を応用する *apply* his theory *to* explaining [×explain] the phenomenon. ●技術を実地に応用する put one's skills *to practical use*.
● **応用言語学** applied linguistics. ● **応用物理学** applied physics. ● **応用問題** an applied question.

おうよう　鷹揚 ●鷹揚な形（大まかで寛大な）generous;（度量の広い）liberal.

おうらい　往来 图〖人・車の通行〗traffic;〖通り〗a street. ●往来を止める block *traffic*. ●往来をふさぐ hold [tie] up *traffic*; block the *street* [*road*]. ▶この道路は車の往来が激しい There is very heavy [a lot of] *traffic* on this road./*Traffic* is very heavy on this road.（❗The road is busy. も可）▶このあたりは往来が少ない There is little [light] *traffic* around here. ▶暗くなるとこの通りは往来がと

だえる(=人けがなくなる) This street *is deserted* after dark.
━━ 往来する 動 come and go.
おうりつ 王立 ━王立の 形 royal. ●英国王立美術院 the *Royal* Academy (of Arts).
おうりょう 横領 名 (an) embezzlement;《書》[法律] (a) misappropriation. ●公金横領で告訴されることになった be accused of *embezzling* the public funds.
━━ 横領する 動 embezzle;《書》[法律] misappropriate.
おうりん 黄燐〔化学〕yellow phosphorus.
おうレンズ 凹レンズ a concave lens (⇔a convex lens).
おうろ 往路 the way (*to*). (⇔ 復路)
オウンゴール〔サッカー〕an own goal.
おえかき お絵描き〈絵を描くこと〉painting.
おえつ 嗚咽 名〈すすり泣き〉sobbing;〈すすり泣く声〉a sob. ━━ 嗚咽する 動 sob.
おえらがた お偉方《話》a big shot (🔒 しばしば軽蔑的);〈高官〉a dignitary;〈上役〉(British) a higher-up (🔒 通例複数形で);〈要人〉a VIP /víːaipíː/ (🔊 ～s)《*very important person* の略》;〈権威者〉an authority. ●政界のお偉方の一人 one of the *big shots* in political circles.
***おえる 終える** ❶[終了する] end;〈演説などを〉close;〖仕上げる〗finish;〈完璧〈ぺき〉に〉complete;〈努力して〉get* through.... ●手続きを全部終える *go through* all the procedures. ▶彼は感謝の言葉を述べて演説を終えた He *ended up* [*closed*] his speech *by* expressing his thanks. (🔒 *up* は強意語. *by* 句の代わりに *with* a word of thanks も可) ▶今日中にその仕事を全部終えなければいけない I have to *finish* [*complete*, *get through* (*with*)] all the work today. (🔒 *with* を用いるのは〈主に米〉) ▶私はやっとこの長い手紙を書き終えた At last I *finished writing* [×*to write*] this long letter.
❷[修了する]〈課程を〉finish, complete,〖卒業する〗graduate from ... (🔒〈英〉では大学以外は通例 leave を用いる). ●大学で英文学の課程を終える *finish* [*complete*] an English literature course at college.
おお 大- ❶[大きさ・数量・程度などが大きい] big, large, great. (⇔大きい) ●大広間 a *large* [a *big*] hall. ●大人数 a *great* [a *large*] number of people. ●大火事〔地震〕a *big* fire [earthquake]. ●大急ぎで in a *great* hurry. ●大おじ a *great*-uncle; a *grand*uncle. ●それはご親切にどうも 大助かりですわ Oh, that's very kind of you. That will be a *great* [*big*] help.
おおあじ 大味 ━大味な 形 ●大味な(=おいしくない)トマト a *tasteless* [a *bland*] tomato.
おおあたり 大当たり〈芝居などの中〉a big [a great, a tremendous] hit;〈大成功〉a great success. ▶彼女のリサイタルは大当たりだった Her recital was a *great hit* [*success*]./She made a *big* [a *great*] *hit* in her recital.
おおあな 大穴 ❶[大きな損失]a big loss. ▶彼は会社の帳簿に大穴をあけた(=彼のせいで会社は大損をした) The company made *big losses* because of him. ❷[競馬などで] ●大穴を当てる hit on a *long shot*; make a *big hit*;《話》have *clean-up* [make a *killing*] (at the races). ●大穴をねらう bet on a *long shot*; try to make a *big hit*.
おおあめ 大雨 (a) heavy [(a) torrential] rain;〖土砂降り〗a downpour. (⇔土砂降り) ●大雨洪水警報を発令する issue a warning of *heavy rain* and flooding. ▶午後は大雨になった We had [There was] *heavy rain* in the afternoon./It *rained*

very hard in the afternoon.
おおあらし 大嵐 a heavy [a severe, a terrible] storm;《書》a tempest.
おおあり 大有り 会話「そんなことが本当にあるのか」「あぁ,おおありだ」"Is there any chance of that?" "Yes, *certainly there is*./*Absolutely*./*With no doubt*."
おおあれ 大荒れ 名 ❶[ひどい暴風雨]〈暴風雨〉a heavy storm,〈荒海〉a rough [a heavy, a stormy] sea.
❷[激高] ●大荒れに荒れる be in a raging [wild] temper;《話》be raving mad.
❸[紛糾] confusion. ●大荒れになる be thrown into *confusion*〖やや書〗*disorder*〗.
━━ 大荒れの 形 stormy; rough. ▶一晩中海は大荒れだった The sea was really *rough* all night.
おおあわて 大慌て ❶〈慌てる〉●大慌てで in a panic; 〈大急ぎで〉in a great hurry.
‡**おおい 多い** ❶[数が] a lot of ...,《話》lots of ...; many*; large (+集合名詞). (⇔たくさん ❶) ▶そう思っている人は多い A *lot of* [《書》*Many*] people think so./There are a *lot of* [《書》*many*] people who think so. (🔒 肯定文で many を用いるのは《書》. Those who think so are *many* [a *lot*]. のような叙述用法は〖まれ〗) ▶ここは人が多すぎる There are *too* [*so*] *many* people here. ▶〈いすが〉一つ多い[多すぎる] There is one too *many* (chairs). (🔒 肯定文でも too, as, so などの後では many を用いる) ▶本校は女子の方が男子より多い There are *more* girls than boys in this school. (🔒 (1) 最も口語的な言い方. (2) ×Girls are more than boys in this school. とはいわない. (3) 「50 名[ずっと]多い」なら There're fifty [many] *more* .... となる) /The number of (×the) girls is *larger* [×more] than that of boys in this school. /〈数で勝る〉The girls *outnumber* the boys in this school. ▶この池には魚が多い There are a *lot of* fish in this pond. 〈豊富だ〉/This pond is *rich* [*abundant*] in fish. /Fish are *abundant* in this pond. /This pond *teems with* fish. ▶彼は家族が多い He has a *large* [×*many*] family. (🔒 family, population などの集合名詞は large を用いる. many families は「多くの世帯」の意)/His family is *large* [×*many*]. ▶その学生が読んだ本は多くはなかった The student *didn't read many* books. /《受身》*Not many* [×Not most] books were read by the student. (🔒 いずれも not(...) many の語順に注意. 通例 not は many にかかり「多くはないがいくらか読んだ」ことを暗示. 受身を *Many* books *weren't* read by the student. のように many ... not の語順にすると通例「読んでいない本がたくさんあった」の意で「読んだ本もたくさんあったかもしれない」ことを暗示) ▶そこにいたのは多くて 20 人ほどだった There were *at* (*the*) *most* [*not more than*] 20 people there. (🔒 at (the) most は文頭・文尾でも可)/〈わずか〉There were *only* [*no more than*] 20 people there. (🔒 後の方は There weren't *any more than* 20 people there. も可)
会話「ぼくのクラスには 20 人も眼鏡をかけている人がいるんだ」「多いね. 何人のクラスなの」"There are twenty people with glasses in my class." "That's *a lot*. How many are there in your class?"
❷[量が] a lot of ...,《話》lots of ...; much*; 〈量が大きい〉large. (⇔たくさん ❶) ▶6 月は雨が多い We have *a lot of* [《書》*much*] rain in June. (🔒 肯定文で much を用いるのは比較的に限られる. ただし, too, as, so などの後では肯定文でも much を用いる) ▶彼の収入は私より多い His income is *larger* than

おおい mine./He earns *more* than I (do). ▶先月はビールの消費量が多かった *A large quantity of* beer was consumed last month./Beer was consumed *in large quantities* last month. ▶10ドルは多すぎる Ten dollars is *too much*.
❸【頻度が】(やや書) frequent. ▶日本は地震が多い We *often* [*frequently*] have earthquakes in Japan. ●oftenの方が口語的なもの. We have [There are] a lot of earthquakes in Japan. ともいる/Earthquakes are *frequent* in Japan. ▶私は日曜日は家にいることが多い(=たいていは家にいる) I *usually* stay (at) home [《米》I'm *usually* home] on Sundays.

おおい hello! (!)遠くの人の注意を引くための呼びかけ ▶おおい,君 Hello, there!
おおい 覆い a cover, a covering. ●覆いをする[とる] cover [uncover]. (⇨カバー, 覆う)
オーイーエム〖相手先ブランド製品製造〗OEM(*Original equipment manufacture* の略).
オーイーシーディー〖経済協力開発機構〗OECD 《the *Organisation for Economic Co-operation and Development* の略》.
おおいかくす 覆い隠す ●両手で顔を覆い隠す *cover* one's face with one's hands. ●その秘密を覆い隠す *conceal* [*hide*,《話》*cover up*] the secret.
おおいかぶさる 覆い被さる cover; (隠し) hide ... from view.
おおいかぶせる 覆い被せる cover up.
おおいそぎ 大急ぎ ●大急ぎの用事で(=急用で) on *urgent* business. ●大急ぎでその仕事をする do the work *hurriedly* [*in a great hurry, as quickly as one can*,《あわただしく》*in a rush*]; *rush* the work. ●大急ぎで駅に行く *hurry* [*rush*] to the station.
おおいちばん 大一番 a decisive game.
おおいなる 大いなる great, (注目に値する) noteworthy. ●大いなる業績 *great* achievements; (尊敬に値する)achievements worhty of respect.
おおいに 大いに a great deal, (やや書) greatly;〖非常に〗very, very much (⇨非常に);〖相当に〗considerably (!)通例動詞・比較級を修飾. ●大いに違うbe *very* [*far, much*,《まったく》*completely, entirely*] different 《*from*》. (!) different は原級だが比較の意を含むので far, much などの副詞を取ることもある ▶彼は大いに尊敬されている He is *highly* [*greatly*] respected. ▶私はパーティーで大いに楽しんだ I *very much* [*really, greatly*] enjoyed the party./I enjoyed myself *very much* [*a great deal*] at the party./I had a *very good* [*a great*] time at the party. ▶彼は大いに勉強する He studies 《*very hard*》. ▶我々は大いに彼の助力が必要です We *badly* need his help. (!) need, want など特定の語に用いる) ▶そのことを大いに(=深く)後悔しています I *deeply* regret it. /I am *very* sorry for it. ▶彼を大いに信用しています I trust him *to a great extent*./(全面的に)I trust him *absolutely*.
おおいばり 大威張り —— 大威張りする 動 be proud as a peacock.
おおいり 大入り (劇場)a full [a packed] (↔a thin) house; (観客)a large audience. ●大入り満員になる be packed [filled] to capacity; have a full house. ●大入りで Full house.)
●大入り袋 a fúll-hòuse bónus.
:**おおう 覆う** ❶【被せる】cover ...《*with, by, in*》; (上に置く)*put*... 《*over, on*》(!)*cover* は暗示. ▶彼はテーブルを白い布で覆った He *covered* the table *with* a white cloth./He *put* a white cloth *over* the table. ▶大地は一面雪で覆われていた

The ground *was covered* all over *with* [*in*] snow. (!)*with* では地面が隠れて見えないことが, *in* では地面が積雪で白一色であることが強調される)
❷【隠す】cover;(ベールで)veil. ●ベールで顔を覆う *veil* one's face;*cover* one's face *with* a veil. ▶彼女は両手で顔を覆ってすすり泣き始めた She *covered* her face *with* her hands [(うずめて) *buried* her face *in* her hands] and began to sob. ▶私はオーバーで耳まですっぽり覆っていた I *was muffled up* to my ears in my overcoat.
❸【包む】(すっぽり)envélop. (⇨包む)
おおうけ 大受け a (big) hit; a good reception. ▶そのショーは大受けだった The show was a *great* [a *smashing*] *success*. (⇨受ける⓾)
おおうちがり 大内刈り〖柔道〗an *ouchigari*, a major inner reap.
おおうつし 大写し a close-up (picture). ●大写しの顔 a *close-up* face; a face *in close-up*. ●花を大写しにする take a *close-up* of a flower.
おおうなばら 大海原 a wide [a vast] expanse of ocean.
おおうりだし 大売り出し a (bargain) sale (!)通例bargain は大売り出される);〖正мя一掃セール〗a clearance (sale). (⇨特売) ▶冬物大売り出し a winter *sale*. ▶あのデパートで大売り出しをやっている They are having [holding,《話》running] a *sale* at that department store.
オーエイチピー an OHP 《*overhead projector* の略》.
オーエー office automation,《和製語》OA.
●OA機器 the office automation equipment.
オーエル〖女子事務員〗a woman office worker (通例 women office workers). (!) ×OL は ×an office lady の略. いずれも和製語) ▶彼女は作家になる前はオーエルでした She worked at an office before she became a writer.
おおおく 大奥 the inner palace of Edo Castle for the court ladies.
おおおくさま 大奥様 the old [great] mistress;《呼びかけ》madam,《米話》ma'am.
おおおじ 大伯父, 大叔父 a great-uncle;《まれ》a granduncle.
おおおとこ 大男 a tall [a big, a large] man (通例 men); (巨人)a giant.
おおおば 大伯母, 大叔母 a great-aunt;《まれ》a grandaunt.
おおかがみ『大鏡』 *Okagami, The Great Mirror*.(參考) 平安時代の歴史物語
おおがかり 大掛かり ●大掛かりな(=大規模の)公共事業 *large-scale* public works; public works *on a large scale*.
おおかぜ 大風 a gale. (⇨強風)
おおかた 大方 ❶【ほとんど】almost, nearly.(⇨ほとんど) ▶図書館は大方完成した The library is *almost* [*nearly*] completed. ▶カリフォルニア州は大方日本と同じ大きさです California is *almost* as large as Japan. ▶卵は大方腐ってしまった *Most of* [*Almost all (of)*] the eggs have gone bad.
❷【世間一般に】generally. ●大方の読者 readers *in general*. ●大方に受け入れられている be *generally* accepted.
❸【おそらく】(十中八九)probably; (ひょっとしたら)perhaps, maybe. (⇨多分)
おおがた 大型, 大形 —— 大型 [大形](の)圏 large (-sized), large-scale. ●大型タンカー a *large* (-sized) tanker. ●大型の台風 a *large-scale* typhoon. ●最近冷蔵庫は大型化している Refrigerators are made *bigger* these days.
オーガナイザー〖まとめ役〗an organizer.

おおさわぎ ポートは大ざっぱすぎる(= 詳しく述べていない) Your report isn't *detailed* enough.
　── **大雑把に** 副 ●大ざっぱに言って *roughly* speaking.

おおさわぎ 大騒ぎ 名 〖ささいなことでの〗a fuss; 〖けんか/ごうの〗(an) uproar; 〖大評判〗a sensation. ▶彼の発言で議場は大騒ぎになった The meeting was thrown into (an) *uproar* [〖大混乱〗into *great confusion*] over his statement. ▶彼女の結婚で社内は大騒ぎになった Her marriage caused a *sensation* [〖興奮〗(✕a) *great excitement*] in the office.
　── **大騒ぎする** 動 ●そんなつまらないことで大騒ぎするな Don't make a (great) *fuss about* [*over*] such little things.

おおさんしょううお 大山椒魚 〖動物〗a great salamander.

おおしい 雄々しい 形 〖勇敢な〗brave; heroic /hə́roɪk/; 〖男らしい〗manly. ── **雄々しく** 副 bravely; heroically.

オージー 〖女性の卒業生〗a (woman) graduate, 《主に米》an alumna (複 alumnae), 《英》an old girl; 《和製語》an OG.

オージー 〖オーストラリア(人)の〗Aussie /ɔ́ːsi/, ɔ́ːzi/. ●オージービーフ Aussie beef.

オーシーアール 〖光学式文字読み取り装置〗an OCR (optical character reader の略).

オージェーティー 〖職場内訓練〗OJT (on-the-job training の略).

おおしお 大潮 a spring tide.

おおじかけ 大仕掛け ── **大仕掛けな** 形 ●大仕掛けな計画 a *large-scale* plan; a plan on a *large* scale.

おおすじ 大筋 〖概略〗an outline (*of*). ●大筋において(= だいたい)賛成です We agree *in general* [〖原則として〗*in principle*, 〖概して〗*on the whole*]./〖大部分〗*For the most part*, we agree.

オーストラリア 〖国名〗Australia /ɔːstréɪljə/; (公式名)the Commonwealth of Australia. (首都 Canberra) ●オーストラリア人 an Australian; 《話》an Aussie. ●オーストラリア(人)の Australian; 《話》Aussie /ɔ́ːsi/, 《英》/ɔ́ːzi/.

オーストリア 〖国名〗Austria; (公式名) the Republic of Austria. (首都 Vienna) ●オーストリア人 an Austrian. ●オーストリア(人)の Austrian.

おおずもう 大相撲 a grand *sumo* tournament.

おおせ 仰せ 〖上司の命令〗an order from one's superior. ●仰せのとおりにする do according to (his) wishes.

__おおぜい 大勢__ 〖群を成した人々〗a crowd (of people) 〖単・複両扱い (⇒群れ)〗; 〖多数の人々〗a lot of [a large number of, 《やや書》a great many] people. ●大勢の家族 a *large* [a *big*] family. ●大勢の聴衆 a *large* audience. 〖通例単数扱い (⇒聴衆)〗 ●大勢で(= 群がって)やって来る come *in crowds* [〖多数で〗*in great numbers*]. ▶公園には大勢の学生がいた There were *a lot of* [*a large number of*, *a good many*, *crowds of*] students in the park ▶その神社には観光客が大勢訪れる The shrine is visited by *large numbers of* tourists.
　[会話] 「ハイキングには私も行っていい？」「ええ，大勢なほど楽しいわ」"May I go hiking with you?" "Of course. *The more, the merrier*."

おおぜき 大関 an *ozeki*; (説明的に) a sumo wrestler of the second highest rank.

おおせつかる 仰せつかる ●彼は社長に来客を空港で出迎えに行くよう仰せつかった(= 命令された) He was *ordered* to go to meet the visitors at the airport by his boss.

-おおせる -果せる ●やりおおせる(= やり遂げる) carry (it) through. ●逃げおおせる(= 逃げ切る) get clear away; make a clean escape.

オーセンティック 〖正真正銘の〗authentic.

おおそうじ 大掃除 ── **大掃除(を)する** 動 clean the whole house 〖事情〗米国では春に行うことが多く，これを the spring cleaning という); 〖邪魔者を一掃する〗make a clean sweep (in the company).

オーソドックス ── **オーソドックスな** ●オーソドックスな(= 正統的な，無難だが新味のない)考え órthodòx ideas, an orthodoxy.

おおぞら 大空 the sky (⇒空); 〖主に書〗the heavens.

オーソリティー 〖権威〗an authority. ●英文学のオーソリティー an *authority on* English literature.

おおぞん 大損 ── **大損(を)する** 動 suffer heavy [big] losses; 〖話〗lose out (*on*). ▶我々はその取引きで大損をした We *had big losses* [*lost out*] *on* the deal.

オーダー 〖注文〗(an) order; 〖野球の打順〗the batting order [lineup] (⇒打順). ▶ラストオーダーは11時30分です Last *orders* are at 11:30. (〖at に注意〗)

オーダーストップ 《米》last call; 《英》last orders; 《和製語》order stop. ▶〖パブやバーで〗まもなくオーダーストップになります *Last orders*, please!

オーダーメード ●オーダーメードの服 a *made-to-order* [a *custom-made*, a *tailor-made*, 《英語》a *made-to-measure*] suit; 《和製語》an order-made. ▶私の背広はすべてオーダーメードだ I have all my suits *made to order*.

おおだい 大台 〖到達の水準〗a level; a mark. ●100万ドルの大台に達する touch the *level* [*mark*] of one million dollars. ▶世界の人口は60億の大台を越えた The world's population has exceeded [passed] the six billion *mark*.

おおだいこ 大太鼓 a bass drum.

おおだすかり 大助かり ●大助かりである be very helpful; be a great help; be of great help. (⇒助かる ❷)

おおたちまわり 大立ち回り ●大立ち回りを演じる 〖芝居で〗act out a showy sword fight; 〖派手にけんかする〗scuffle (with).

おおだての 大立者 a prominent figure. ●政界の大立者 a political *figure*; a *big figure in* politics.

おおだんな 大旦那 the old [great] master; 〖呼びかけ〗sir.

おおちがい 大違い (大きな違い) a big [a great] difference. ●見ると聞くとは大違いだった When I actually saw it, it was *completely* [*totally*] *different from* what I had heard about it. ▶結婚に関して東洋人とヨーロッパ人の考えは大違いだ There is a *big difference* between Oriental and European ideas about marriage. ▶市長であることと知事であることは大違いだ Being mayor *is a far cry from* being governor.

おおづかみ 大掴み (⇒大雑把)

おおつづみ 大鼓 a large *tsuzumi*, (説明的に) a larger-sized hand drum used in a *Noh* or *Kabuki* play.

おおっぴら 大っぴら ── **大っぴらに** 副 〖公然と〗openly; publicly; 〖自由に〗freely; 〖遠慮なく〗unhesitatingly, without hesitation. ▶それは大っぴらにはできない(= 公表できない) We cannot *make* it *public*./It cannot *be made public*.

おおつぶ 大粒 ●大粒の雨 *big drops* of rain. ▶大粒の汗が彼の額ににじみ出た *Great beads* of sweat stood

おおづめ 大詰め ❶【終わり】an end. ▶大詰めに近づく draw to an *end* [*a close*]. ▶大詰め(=追い込み)に入る enter [go into] the *homestretch*. ▶交渉は大詰めの段階に入った The negotiations have come to *the final stage*.
❷【劇の】the final act; a finale /finá:li/; (特に悲劇の) a catastrophe.

おおて 大手 〖主要な会社〗a major company; 〖大企業〗a big enterprise. ●観光産業の最大手 the *biggest* [*largest*] company in the tourist industry. ●準大手医薬品メーカー a semi-major pharmaceutical company.

おおて 大手 ●大手を広げる spend one's arms wide. ●大手を振って ▶大手を振って歩く(意気揚々と) walk *triumphantly*; (悪人が我が物顔にふるまう) have one's own way; (疑いが晴れて) have nothing more to be ashamed of.

オーディーエー 〖政府開発援助〗ODA 《official development *assistance* の略》.

オーディオ 〖装置〗an audio [a stereo] system.
●オーディオマニア an audiophile; an audio fan.

オーディション an audition. ●オーディションを行う give an *audition* 《*to*》; audition. ●オーディションを受ける have an *audition* 《*for*》; audition 《*for*》.

オーデコロン 〖<フランス語〗(eau de) Cologne /(ou da) kəlóun/. ●オーデコロンをつける put on (*eau de*) *Cologne*.

オート 〖自動装置の〗automatic. (⇨自動の)

おおどうぐ 大道具 a (stage) setting.
●大道具方 a sceneshifter.

おおどおり 大通り 〖主〗〖英〗a high] street; an avenue; a boulevard; a thoroughfare. (⇨道 1)
●大通りに面した建物 a building facing the *main street*.

オートキャンプ 《米》auto-camping; 《英》caravanning.
●オートキャンプ場 《米》a trailer camp [park]; 《英》a caravan site [park].

オートクチュール [<フランス語] haute couture /òut ku:t(j)ú:r/ 《高級婦人服を作り流行をリードする一流の洋装店. そこで作られる服》; (最新のデザイン) high fashion.

おおどころ 大所 〖資産家の家〗a wealthy household; 〖有力者[会社]〗an influential person [company].

オートバイ a motorcycle, 《話》a motorbike (❗《米》では小型の). (⇨バイク)

オートパイロット 〖自動操縦装置〗an automatic pilot, an autopilot.

オートフォーカス 〖自動焦点〗an autofocus. ●オートフォーカスのカメラ an *autofocus* camera.

オードブル [<フランス語] 〖前菜〗an hors d'oeuvre /ɔ:rdɔ́:rv/ (複 ~, ~s).

オートマチック automatic. (⇨自動の) ●オートマ(チック)車 an *automatic*.

オートミール (粉) oatmeal; (かゆ) 《主に米》oatmeal, 《主に英》(oatmeal) porridge.

オートメ(ーション) automation. ●オートメ(ーション)化する automate. ●オートメ(ーション)工場 an *automated* plant [factory].

オートリバース 〖カセットテープなどのオートリバース機能〗auto-reverse.

オートレース (自動車の) a car race; (オートバイの) a motorcycle race.

オートローン 〖自動車ローン〗a car loan; 《和製語》an auto loan.

オートロック ━━ オートロックの 形 self-locking 《doors》; 《和製語》autolock.

オーナー 〖持ち主〗an owner. ▶この店のオーナー the *owner* of this store. ▶オーナードライバーだ He is a *car owner*. (❗He is an owner-driver. より普通)/ He has a car.
●オーナーシップ 〖所有権〗ownership.

おおなた 大鉈 a big hatchet.
●大なたをふるう ▶来年度の予算に大なたをふるう(=思い切って削減する) *make a drastic cut in* the budget of the next fiscal year. (❗《話》では *slash* the budget...とも)

おおにゅうどう 大入道 a giant of a monster with a close-cropped head.

オーバー ❶〖外套〗an overcoat, a coat (❗後の方はレインコートなども含む); (軍隊用などの厚地の)《主に英》a greatcoat; 〖そでのない〗a cloak. ●厚い[薄い]オーバー a heavy [a light] *overcoat*. ●オーバーを着る[脱ぐ] put on [take off] one's *coat*. ●オーバー掛け an *overcoat* rack. ●彼にオーバーを着せて[脱がせて] help him on [off] with his *overcoat*.
❷〖誇張した〗▶オーバーだなあ You exaggerate! (❗英語の *over* には単独で「大げさな」の意はない)/You are stretching the truth.
❸〖越えて〗▶レフトオーバーの二塁打を打つ hit a double *over* the left fielder. ●レフトオーバーのホームランを打つ hit a home run *over* the left-field fence. ●制限速度をオーバーする(=超える) *exceed* the speed limit.

オーバーアクション 〖大げさな演技〗《軽蔑的》overacting. ▶君は少々オーバーアクションだ You're *overacting* a bit.

オーバーウエート overweight (⇔underweight).
●オーバーウエートの手荷物 overweight baggage.
▶メアリーは5ポンドオーバーウエートなので減量が必要だ Mary is five pounds *overweight* and needs to lose her weight.

オーバーオール 《a pair of》overalls.

オーバーコート an overcoat. (⇨オーバー ❶)

オーバースロー 〖野球〗an óverhánd thrów [pítch]. (❗野球では overthrow 《the first baseman》は「暴投する, 高い悪送球をする」の意;⇨アンダースロー, 上手) ●オーバースローで投げる throw overhand.
●オーバースローの投手 an overhand pitcher.

オーバータイム ▶オーバータイムをとられる (バレーボールで) be penalized for touching the ball four times; (バスケットボールで) be penalized for violating the three-second rule.

オーバードクター 〖博士浪人〗an unemployed PhD.

オーバーハンド ━━ オーバーハンドの 形 overhand. ●オーバーハンドの投球 *overhand* pitches.
━━ オーバーハンドで 副 overhand. ●オーバーハンドで投げる throw *overhand*.

オーバーヒート óverhéating. ▶この車のエンジンはよくオーバーヒートする This car's engine often *overheats*.

オーバーブッキング 〖予約の取り過ぎ〗overbooking.
▶オーバーブッキングのせいでそのホテルに泊まれなかった The hotel had *been* (*heavily*) *overbooked*, so there was no room for me.

オーバーフロー 〖コンピュータ〗〖上位桁のあふれ〗an overflow.

オーバーペース ▶彼女はスタートからオーバーペースだったので中間点を過ぎると急にペースが落ちてしまった As she went at *too rapid a pace* from the start, her pace suddenly fell off after the halfway point.

オーバーヘッド 〖コンピュータ〗overhead.

オーバーヘッドキック 〖サッカー〗an overhead kick; a

bicycle kick.
オーバーヘッドプロジェクター ⇨オーエイチピー
オーバーホール ― **オーバーホールする** 動 give 《a car》 an óverhàul; òverhául 《a car》.
オーバーライト ― **オーバーライトする** 動 『上書きする』 『コンピュータ』 overwrite.
 ● オーバーライトモード the overwrite mode.
オーバーラップ 名 『サッカー』 overlapping.
 ― **オーバーラップする** 動 overlap (-pp-) /òuvərlǽp/. ▸ 今日の授業は前回の授業とオーバーラップしているところがあった Today's lesson *overlapped with* the last one (to some extent)./There were some *óverlaps between* today's lesson and the last one.
オーバーラン 名 an óverrùn 《*of* 100 meters》.
 ― **オーバーランする** 動 òverrún*. ▸ 二塁をオーバーランする『野球』*overrun* second base. ▸ 飛行機が滑走路をオーバーランした The plane *overran* the runway.
オーバーワーク 『過労』 óverwòrk. ▸ オーバーワークにならないように気をつけなさい Take care not to *work too hard* 《òverwórk》.
おおはくちょう 大白鳥 『鳥』 a whooper swan.
おおばこ 車前草 『植物』 a plantain.
おおはば 大幅 ― **大幅な** 形 (大きい) big (-gg-), large; (急激な) sharp; (抜本的な) drastic; (程度なども) substantial; (かなりの) considerable. ▸ 大幅な賃上げ a *big* [*a substantial*] raise 《米》 [rise 《英》] in pay. ▸ 物価の大幅な上昇 a *sharp* rise in prices. ● 計画に大幅な変更をする make a *drastic* [*a great*, *a substantial*] change in the plan; (大幅に変える) change the plan *drastically* [*greatly*]. ▸ 会社は我々の要求に対して大幅な譲歩をする The company made a *substantial* [*a great*] concession to our demand.
 ― **大幅に** 副 ▸ 列車は大幅に遅れた The train was delayed *considerably*./The train was *long overdue*.
おおばん 大判 『広い紙面』 large-sized paper; 『昔の大型金貨』 a large(-sized) oval gold coin formerly used in Japan.
おおばんぶるまい 大盤振る舞い ― **大盤振る舞いする** 動 (豪華な宴を開いてもてなす) give a sumptuous feast. ▸ ボーナスを大盤振る舞いする *generously give* a *large bonus* 《to》.
オービー 『卒業生』 a graduate, 《主に米》 an alumnus 『女性』 an alumna 《米》 alumni /əlʌ́mnaɪ/》, 《英》 an old boy; 《和製語》 an OB. ▸ 彼は京大のオービーです He is a *graduate* of Kyoto University. ▸ 彼はこのクラブのオービーです He is a *former member* of this club. ▸ 私は就職活動でオービー訪問をします I'm visit [going to see] an *alumnus* in the company I'm applying to (work for).
オービー 『ゴルフの』 an out-of-bounds shot. ● オービーを出す hit the ball out of bounds.
おおびけ 大引け (株取引でその日の最終の相場) the closing price.
おおひろま 大広間 a hall.
オープニング an opening 《night》. (! 通例 *opening* の後に night, day などが続く)
 ● オープニングゲーム 『開幕試合』 the ópening gàme [màtch], the opener. ● オープニングセレモニー an ópening cèremony. ● オープニングナンバー 『演奏会などの最初の曲』 the ópening [first] nùmber 《*on a 《米》 an opener.
おおぶね 大船 ● **大船に乗ったような気持ち** ▸ 大船に乗ったような気持ちでいる I feel I can always depend on you./I have confidence in you.

おおぶり 大振り (野球で) a big [a long] swing; (形が) ⇨大きめ. ● 大ぶりの茶わん *a little larger* rice bowl.
おおぶろしき 大風呂敷 ● **大風呂敷を広げる** (大言壮語する) talk big 《*about*》; (大げさに自慢する) brag 《*about*》.
オーブン an oven /ʌ́vn/. ● 電気[ガス]オーブン an electric [a gas] *oven*. ● オーブンで焼く bake 《it》 in an *oven*.
 ● オーブントースター a toaster oven. (! 語順に注意)
オープン 名 『公開競技』 the Open. ● 全米オープン the U.S. *Open*.
 ― **オープンな** 形 (公開の, プロ・アマの区別のない) open; (航空券が) open 《tickets》; (価格が) open 《prices》; (性格が) open, friendly.
 ― **オープンに** 副 ● オープンに(=率直に)話す talk *frankly* [*openly*].
 ― **オープンする** 動 open. (⇨開店, 開業)
 ● オープンエア 『屋外』 《*in*》 the òpen áir. ● オープンエアの òpen-àir. ● オープンカー 《米》 a convertible; a soft-top; an open car. (! 最後の方は, 屋根をたたんだ状態のオープンカーをさす) ● オープン価格 an open [an unfixed] price. ● オープンゲーム (プロ野球の開幕戦) an opening game; 《和製語》 open game. ● オープンコース (陸上競技などの) an open lane. ● オープンサンド(イッチ) an open(-faced) sandwich. ● オープンシステム 『コンピュータ』 an open system. ● オープンシャツ an open-neck(ed) shirt. ● オープンショップ (労働組合の) an open (↔ a closed [a union]) shop. ● オープンスタンス 『野球・ゴルフ』 《take》 an open stance. ● オープンスペース 『建物がない場所』 an open space. ● オープンセット 『撮影用の』 an open-air set. (! この意では ✗an open set とはいわない) ● オープン戦 (野球の) an exhibition game; 《和製語》 an open game. (! 野球で開幕試合は 「開幕戦」) ● オープンハウス 『建売住宅』 an open house. ● オープンリール open-reel [reel-to-reel] 《tape recorders》.
オーペア 《英》 an au pair. (参考 英語学習のために住み込みで家事を手伝う女子留学生)
おおべや 大部屋 『大きな部屋』 a large room; 『撮影所・劇場などの』 a common (dressing) room; 『病院の』 a ward.
 ● 大部屋俳優 a bit actor.
オーボエ an oboe /óubou/. ● オーボエを吹く[演奏する] play [✗blow] the oboe. ● オーボエ奏者 an oboist.
おおぼら 大ぼら ● 大ぼらを吹く talk big 《*about*》; (自慢する) brag 《*about*》.
おおまか 大まか ― **大まかな** 形 rough.
 ― **大まかに** 副 roughly. (⇨大雑把)
おおまた 大股 a long stride [step]. ● 大股で歩く walk with *long strides*; stride. ● 大股で通りを横切る *stride* across the street.
おおまちがい 大間違い a big [a great, ✗a large] mistake.
おおまわり 大回り 『曲がり角などを』 《take》 a wide turn; 『遠回り』 《take》 the long way around; 《make》 a detour.
おおみえ 大見得 ● **大見得を切る** (歌舞伎で) strike a very impressive pose; (一般に) put on a big display of confidence.
おおみず 大水 a flood. (⇨洪水)
おおみずなぎどり 大水凪鳥 『鳥』 a streaked shearwater.
おおみそか 大晦日 New Year's Eve; (最後の日) the last day of the year. ▸ 大晦日にたいていの人は除夜の鐘を聞く Most people listen to the tolling of

オーム ❶[ドイツの物理学者] Ohm /óum/ (Georg Simon ～). ●オームの法則 Ohm's law. ❷[電気抵抗の単位] an ohm (記号 Ω).

おおむかし 大昔 (古い昔) ancient times [days]; (原始時代) primitive ages; (先史時代) prehistoric times. ●大昔の人々 people *in ancient times*; *ancient* people. ●大昔から from *ancient* [*very early*, *prehistoric*] *times*; (太古から) from [since] *time immemorial*. ▶*immemorial* の位置に注意》 ●大昔人間は洞窟(ﾄﾞｳｸﾂ)に住んでいた People lived in caves *long, long ago*.

おおむぎ 大麦 barley. (▮1 粒 a grain of ...)

おおむこう 大向こう the gallery. ●大向こうをうならせる deeply impress *the gallery* [*the audience*]; (一般の人に大いに受ける) win great popularity with *the public*.

おおむね 概ね (⇨大筋, ほとんど) ●彼の成績はおおむね(=全般的に見て)良好だ *On the whole* his grades are good.

■ **DISCOURSE**
人を外見で判断してはならないとよく言われる。この発言にはおおむね賛成だが、しかし外見が重要なケースもあることは事実である It is often said that a person should not be judged by their personal appearance. I basically agree with this statement, but there are some cases where appearance really does matter. ●It is often said that ... (...と言われる) は譲歩を表すディスコースマーカー。but 以下に力点がある

おおむらさき 大紫 [昆虫] a giant purple emperor.
おおめ 大目 ●大目に見る [見逃す] òverlóok; [規則を曲げる] bend the rules (*for* him); [我慢する] tolerate; [許す] excuse. ●今回は大目に見てやろう We'll *excuse* you [《米話》*give you a break*] this time.
おおめ 多目 ●多めに買う buy ... enough and to spare.
おおめだま 大目玉 (ひどくしかること) a good scolding, 《話》 a good telling-off (❶ tellings-). ●大目玉をくらう get a *good scolding*; be severely scolded. ●息子に大目玉をくぎれる give one's son a *good scolding* [*telling-off*] (*for*).
おおめつけ 大目付 an inspector general (of the Tokugawa shogunate).
おおもうけ 大儲け ── **大儲けする** 〔動〕 make a large profit (*on*, *from*); (くま手でかき寄せるほどしこたま)《話》rake in (a lot of money), rake it in. 《進行形で用いることが多い》
おおもじ 大文字 a capital, a capital letter. ●表題を大文字で書く write a title *in capitals* [*capital letters*]. ●文頭を大文字で書く begin a sentence *with a capital*.
おおもて 大持て ●大もてである be extremely popular (*with*, *among*).
おおもと 大本 (根底) the root; (土台) a foundation. (⇨根本, 根源)
おおもの 大物 [重要人物] an important person; 《話》 a big shot; (特に政界・財界などの) a VIP /víːaɪpíː/ (❶ ～s) (*very important person* の略); (有名人) a big name (in the movie, in politics) (芸能界などの) a personality; [大きな獲物] big game (❶主に猟の動物). ●大物政治家 a *big-time* politician. ●大物を釣り上げる land a *big fish*. ▶あんなことするとは大物だ He is really *something* to do such a thing.
●大物食い a giant killer.

おおもり 大盛り ▶マッシュポテトを大盛りにしてください I'll have a *big helping* [*serving*] of mashed potatoes, please. / (大目の一人前に) Please make my mashed potatoes a *generous portion*.
おおや 大家 (所有者) an owner (of a house [an apartment]), 《書》 a proprietor; (下宿屋などの) (男性) a landlord, (女性) a landlady.
おおやいし 大谷石 *Oyaishi*; (説明的に) a soft and greenish volcanic rock used in building.

***おおやけ 公** ── **公の** 〔形〕 (公衆の) public; (公式の) official; (公開の) open. ●公の事 *public* [《ﾌｫｰﾏﾙ》*private*] matters [affairs]. ●公の声明 an *official* statement. ●公の席で(=人前で)演説をする make a speech *in public*. ▶この図書館は公のもので(=一般に公開されている) This library is open to *the public*./This is a *public* library. ▶彼は公の場ではいつも愛想がよいが家では気難しい He's always so agreeable *in public* but he's so disagreeable at home.
── **公に** 〔副〕 in public, publicly; (公式に) officially. ●公にする make 《the news》 *public* [*known* (*to the public*)]. (⇨公表する) ●公になる be made public [known (to the public)]. ▶2 人は公には結婚していない They are not married *officially*.

おおやすうり 大安売り a (bargain) sale. (⇨特売)
▶大安売りをしている be having a (*big*) *sale*.
おおやまねこ 大山猫 [動物] a lynx.
おおゆき 大雪 a heavy snow(fall). ▶これは 20 年来の大雪です This is the *heaviest snowfall* (that) we have had in twenty years.
おおよう 大様 (⇨〖雅〗 鷹揚(ｵｳﾖｳ))
おおよそ (⇨およそ)
オーラ [人の発する霊気] an aura /ɔ́ːrə/.
オーライ all right; 《話》 OK, O.K. (▮ okay ともつづる) (⇨オーケー) ●発車オーライ All right. Now, start.
おおらか 大らか ── **大らかな** 〔形〕 (心の広い) broad-minded; (寛大な) generous. ●何とも大らかな娘 a girl *generous* to a fault.
オーラル oral.
●オーラルコミュニケーション the oral communication. ●オーラルセックス an oral sex; 《俗》 a blowjob. (⇨フェラチオ) ●オーラルメソッド [口頭教授法] the oral method.
オール [ボートの] an oar. (⇨漕(ｺ)ぐ)
オール [全部] all. ●オール5をとる get straight A's. 《関連》 そのような生徒は a straight-A student という

オールインワン ── **オールインワンの** 〔形〕 [一体型の] all-in-one.
オールウェザー ●オールウェザー(=全天候用の)テニスコート an *all-weather* tennis court.
オールオアナッシング ●オールオアナッシング式の決着 an *all-or-nothing* decision.
オールシーズン ●オールシーズン着用可能なコート an all-weather coat; a coat for *all reasons*. ▶このコートはオールシーズン用だ You can wear this kind of coat *at all seasons*.
オールスター ── **オールスターの** 〔形〕 all-star.
●オールスターキャスト (スター総出演) an all-star cast. ●オールスターゲーム an all-star game.
オールスパイス (木) an allspice tree; (香辛料) allspice.
オールドタイマー [時代おくれの人] an old-timer.
オールドパワー [老人パワー] gray [ˣold] power; 《和製語》 old power. (⇨老人)
オールドファッション ●オールドファッション(=流行おくれ)の水着 an old-fashioned swimsuit. ●オールドファッション(=時代おくれ)の考え an old-fashioned

オールドファン (昔[かつて]のファン) a once fan; (長年のファン) an old fan.

オールドミス 《和製語》an old miss, a high miss. (❗(1) これに当たる適切な英語はない。「彼女はオールドミスだ」という場合は、たとえば次のようにいう: She is still single./She is not yet married. (2) 中年[年配]の未婚の女性をさす an old maid, a spinster は、日本語の「オールドミス」「ハイミス」と同様に軽蔑的なので用いない方がよい)

オールナイト ━━ オールナイトの 形 all-night (restaurants).

オールバック ▶髪をオールバックにしている wear one's hair *straight back*. (❗《和製語》all back.

オールマイティ ❶ [全能の] almighty. ❷ [トランプの] an unbeatable card. (❗たとえば the ace of the spades (スペードのエース)

オールラウンド 《米》all-around, 《英》all-round. ●オールラウンドプレーヤー an all-around player; [野球] a utility player; an all-purpose player.

おおるり 大瑠璃 [鳥] a blue-and-white flycatcher.

オーロラ [極光] an aurora /ərɔ́ːrə/.

おおわざ 大技 (相撲・柔道などの) a bold [a daring] technique. (㊥ 小技)

おおわし 大鷲 [鳥] a Steller's sea eagle.

おおわらい 大笑い ━━ 大笑いする 動 give a good [a hearty, 《腹からの》《話》a belly] laugh; laugh heartily; roar with laughter. (⇨笑う ❶)

おおわらわ ▶おおわらわで働く work *busily* [*hard*, *desperately*]. ▶今週は開店の準備でおおわらわだった We had a *hectic* week preparing for the opening of the shop. (❗hectic は「忙しくて仕事が立て込んだ」の意. We had to work desperately this week preparing .... ともいう)

***おか** 丘 (小山) a hill; (日本語の丘より高い); (高台)(ややまれ) a height (しばしば複数形で). ●丘の多い地域 *hilly* areas. ▶その城は丘の上[斜面]に立っている The castle stands on (top of) a *hill* [on the side of a *hill*, on a *hillside*].

おか 陸 land; the shore. (⇨陸(?))
●陸に上がったカッパ ▶新しい職場では彼は陸に上がったカッパも同然だ(=場違いで本領が発揮できない) He seems to *be out of* his *element* in the new place of work [workplace]. (❗like a fish out of water は「勝手が違って居心地が悪い」の意で、不適切)

***おかあさん お母さん** a mother; 《米話》a mom, 《米話》a mommy, 《英話》a mum, 《英話》a mummy (❗mommy, mummy は小児語); 《話・まれ》a mama.

> [解説] (1) 子供が母親に呼びかける場合は Mom, Mommy, Mum, Mummy が普通. ハイティーンぐらいになると、改まった場合は Mother を用いる. 《米》では Mamma, Mama /máːmə/, Ma /máː/ を幼児が使う家庭もあるが、《英》で Mamma, Mama /məmáː/ は《古》. 他人に母親のことをいう場合は my mother といえば上品に聞こえる. (⇨お父さん)
> (2) 結婚相手の母親 (one's mother-in-law) に呼びかける場合、日本語同様に Mom, Mum が普通. また子供を持つ母親を Mom, Mum を中心として Grandma, Granny (おばあちゃん) と呼ぶこともある. ただし Mrs. Miller, Maggy など姓や名で呼ばれることを望む人も珍しくないので、最初に「どうお呼びしましょうか」(What should I call you?) と尋ねるのが無難.

▶彼女のお母さんは医者です Her *mother* is a doctor.
▶お母さん、おはよう Good morning, *Mom* [*Mother*]. (❗呼びかけ語はあいさつの後に置く) ▶あちらがお母さんですか Is that your *mother*?

おかえし お返し [返礼] return; [返礼の贈り物] a return gift; [釣り銭] change; [しっぺ返し]《話》tit for tat. ●彼のもてなしへのお返しに何か贈り物をする send him some gift *in return for* his hospitality. ▶30円のお返しです Here's your thirty yen *change*.

***おかえりなさい お帰りなさい** Hello!/Oh, you're back!/(❗以上は日常使う)/Welcome home [back]./We're all so happy to see you again. (❗以上は帰国時の出迎えなど改まったときに用いる)
[会話]「お母さん、ただいま」「あら、お帰りなさい」 "＼Hello, ／Mom! I'm home!" "Oh, ＼hello, ／dear. How was your day? [Did you have a nice day?]"

おかかえ お抱え ●お抱えの運転手 a chauffeur /ʃóufər/.

おがくず 大鋸屑 sawdust.

***おかげ お陰** ━━ お陰(様)で (...のために) thanks to ...(❗皮肉をいう場合にも用いられる (⇨[第2文例])); (...が原因で) because of .... ▶あなた[その機械]のおかげで予定どおりに全部の仕事を終えることができました *Thanks to* you [the machine], I finished the whole job on schedule. ▶君の不注意のおかげで仕事はやり直しだ *Thanks to* [*Because of*] your carelessness, we have to repeat the work. ▶私が成功したのはひとえに先生のご指導のおかげです I *owe* [˟am owing] my success entirely *to* your teaching. (❗˟I owe you teaching my success. の語順は不可)/My success *is* entirely *due to* [*because of*, ˟owed to] your teaching. ▶危機を切り抜けられたのは彼のおかげです I *owe* it *to* him *that* I was able to [˟could] overcome my difficulties. (❗過去の1回限りの行為には通例 could は用いない) ▶ジェット機のおかげで10時間かからずに太平洋を横断できるようになった(=ジェット機が横断を可能にした) Jet planes *have enabled* us *to* cross the Pacific in less than ten hours. ▶彼のおかげでとても安心した He made me feel so at ease. ▶おかげさまで(=幸いなことに)病気は全快しました *Fortunately*, I've completely recovered.
[会話]「ご家族の皆様はお元気ですか」「はい、おかげさまで皆元気にやっています」 "How's your family?" "They're all fine, *thank you*." (❗thank you は相手が主治医などでない限り通例 *Thanks to* you, they're all fine. とはいわない)
[会話]「パーティーはうまくいった?」「おかげさまで大成功だったわ」 "How did your party go off?" "Very well, *I'm glad* [*pleased*] *to say*." (❗Very well, *thank you* [*thanks*]. といってもこの意は表わる)
[会話]「あなたなまりがないね」「小さいときは東京で育ったの. そのおかげだよ(=それが役立っている)」 "You don't have an accent." "I lived in Tokyo when I was small [(very) young]. That *helps*."

おかざり お飾り a New Year's twisted straw decoration.

おがさわらりゅう 小笠原流 (礼法) (the) Ogasawara school of etiquette.

***おかしい** ❶ [おもしろい] amusing; funny; laughable; ridiculous; comic, comical.

> [使い分け] **amusing** 人を心から楽しませ、笑わせるようなおかしさ.
> **funny** こっけい・風変わりで人を笑わせるようなおかしさ. 話・芝居・声・名前など主に耳で聞く物に用いる.
> **laughable** あきれかえって軽蔑するほかないような、ばかげたおかしさ.
> **ridiculous** 現実や常識から乖離(?)しており、ばかげ

> てくだらないおかしさ。非現実的であり得ないという話者の気持ちを前提とする。
> **comic** 喜劇・漫画に見られるような意図して人を笑わせようとするおかしさ。
> **comical** こっけいで喜劇的であること。主に目で見る物に対して用いる。

- おかしい話 an *amusing* story. ● おかしな奴 a *funny* fellow. ● おかしな間違いをする make a *laughable* [a *ridiculous*] mistake. ● おかしな顔をする make a *funny* [(ひょうきんな)] *comical*] face. ▶ その冗談はおかしくない That joke isn't *funny*./That joke doesn't *amuse* me. ● 何がそんなにおかしいの What's so *funny* [*amusing*]?/I don't see what's so *funny* [*amusing*]. ● 君のそのだぶだぶのズボンをはいた格好はおかしい In your baggy pants (米) [trousers (英)] you look *funny* [*ridiculous, comic(al)*]. ● 彼の誤りがおかしかった(=笑いたくなった) I *was amused at* [*by*] his mistake./(話) I *was tickled by* his mistake.

❷ **[奇妙な]** (不思議な) strange; (わけの分からない) funny; (変わった) odd, 《話》weird /wíərd/; (風変りな) 《やや古》queer; (異常な) unusual. (⇨変な) ▶ 彼のおかしなふるまいは私たちをひどくいらいらさせた His *strange* [*odd*] behavior fretted us terribly. ▶ 彼が欠席するなんておかしい It *is strange* [*funny, unusual*] *for* him to stay away from school./It *is strange* [*funny, unusual*] (that) he stays away from school. (■話し手の驚き・意外さを表す場合は …(that) he *should* stay …. のように *should* が用いられる) ▶ おかしなことに, 私たちの先生はそれを聞いていない *Strange to say* [*Strangely* (*enough*)], our teacher has not heard it. ▶ 彼女は少し頭がおかしい She is a bit *crazy* [*funny*]. (■ *funny* は婉曲的)/She is a little *queer* in the head. ▶ この機械はどこかおかしい(=故障している) Something is *wrong* [*the matter*] with this machine. ▶ 何が起こってもおかしくない状態だ Anything *could* happen. (■ *could* は仮定法過去形で現在の可能性を表す)

❸ **[不適切な]** improper; not right; 《書》unbecoming. ▶ 君が口答えするのはおかしい It *is improper* [*not right*] *for* you *to* answer back./It *is improper* [*not right*] *that* you (*should*) *answer back*. (■ *improper* の場合《主に米》では *should* の省略可)

❹ **[怪しい]** suspicious. ▶ 彼の行動はおかしい His conduct is *suspicious*.

おかしがたい 犯し難い dignified.
おかしがる be amused 《*at, by, with*》. (⇨面白がる)
おかしさ [こっけいさ] humor, comicality; [奇妙さ] strangeness, abnormality.
おかしな ⇨おかしい
おかしらつき 尾頭付き ● タイの尾頭付き a whole sea bream; (姿焼き) a sea bream grilled whole.

*おかす 犯す [[法律上の]] commit a crime [a sin]. (■ crime は法律上の, sin は道徳・宗教上の罪) ● 法律を犯す(=破る) break [《書》*violate*] a law. ● 女性を犯す(=婦女暴行する) rape [《婉曲語》*attack, assault*] a woman.

*おかす 侵す [[他国などを]] invade; [[権利などを]]《書》violate, 《書》infringe 《*on*》. ● 国境を侵す invade the boundaries of a country. ● 彼の所有権を侵す *violate* [x*invade*] his ownership. ● 彼のプライバシーを侵す violate [x*invade*] his privacy.

*おかす 冒す ❶ **[危険などを]** run*. ● 危険を冒す *run* a *risk* [*risks*]; *take* a *risk* [*risks*]. ▶ 彼らは自らの生命の危険を冒してダム建設工事を続けた They continued to build a dam *at the risk of* their lives.
❷ **[病気などが]** affect; (急に) attack. ▶ 彼の胃[彼]はがんに冒されていた His stomach [He] *was affected by* cancer.

*おかず (食べ物) food; (個々の料理) a dish (■ a side dish, 《米》a side order は主料理(a main dish)の肉や魚とともに食べる別皿の野菜類のこと。(⇨主食) ▶ 朝食はあまりおかずがなかった There weren't many kinds of *food* for breakfast. ▶ 今晩のおかずは何ですか(=何を食べますか) What are we having for dinner this evening?

おかちめんこ [[醜い女性の俗語表現]] (⇨ぶす)
おかっぱ (ショートカットにした髪) bobbed hair. ● おかっぱの女の子 a *bobbed* girl. ● おかっぱにしている wear [have] one's hair *bobbed*; wear [have] one's hair *in a bob*.
おかっぴき 岡っ引き a private investigator in the Edo period.
おかづり 陸釣り fishing from the shore [bank].
おかどちがい お門違い (間違っている) be wrong; (違う人を非難している) be barking at a wrong tree. ▶ 彼を恨むのはお門違いです It's *wrong* for you to feel bitter toward him.
おかぶ お株 one's forte /fɔ́ːrt/. ● お株を奪われる《話》be beaten at one's own game.
おかぼ 陸稲 rice cultivated on dry land.
おかぼれ 岡惚れ (横恋慕) illicit love; (片思い) one-sided love.
おかま お釜 (男色) a gay, a homosexual. ● お金を掘る have homesex(uality) 《*with*》.
おかまい お構い ▶ 何のおかまいもできませんが夕食を食べていかれませんか Why don't you stay to [for] dinner, though our dinner is nothing special? ▶ 何のおかまいもできませんで (来客との別れ際に) I'm glad you could come./(食事の礼に対して) I'm glad [hope] you enjoyed it. 事情 米英には I'm sorry I had nothing better to offer you. などと接待の不備を顧る習慣はない
> 会話 「コーヒーでも取りましょうか」「いいえ, どうぞおかまいなく」"Shall I get you some coffee?" "No, thanks. Please *don't bother* for me."

おかまいなし お構いなし ─ お構いなしに (かまわずに) (⇨構う ❶, ❹) ▶ 彼は彼女の気持ちなどおかまいなしだ(=気にしない) He *doesn't care* how she feels.
おかみ(さん) 女将(さん) [旅館の] an *okami*, a landlady; (説明的に) a woman owner-manager of a traditional Japanese-style hotel or restaurant; [店の] mistress; 《話》ma'am; [妻] one's wife 《《話》better half》.
おがみたおす 拝み倒す beg [entreat] 《*him for* [*to do*]》.
おがみどり 拝み捕り ● フライを拝み捕りする [野球] make a *clamshell* catch of a fly.
おがむ 拝む [神仏を] pray; [見る] see*; [あがめる] worship (-pp-). ● 合掌して[低頭して, ひざまずいて]神を拝む *pray* to God with one's hands put together [with a bow, on one's knees]. ● ご来光を拝む *see* the sunrise. ▶ 彼は拝むようにして援助を求めた He *begged* [*prayed, implored*] me for help [*to* help him]. (■ beg はへり下って, pray は熱心に, implore は泣くようにして哀願すること)
おかめ お亀 a plump-cheeked, flat-nosed girl; (不細工な女) a plain(-looking) [《米》a homely] woman. (⇨ おたふく)
● おかめうどん[そば] *okame-udon* [*-soba*]; (説明的に) *udon* [*soba*] with *kamaboko*, a mushroom and a bit of green vegetables.
おかめはちもく 岡目八目 《ことわざ》Lookers-on see

おから *okara* (説明的に) a byproduct of *tofu*-making. (⇨卯の花)

オカリナ [<イタリア語] 【楽器】an ocarina /ɑkərinə/.

オカルト the occult.

おがわ 小川 a brook;《米》a creek; a stream. (⬛ この順で大きくなる) ●小川のせせらぎ the murmur of a *brook*; the babble of a *stream*. ●さらさら流れている小川 a babbling [a murmuring] *stream*.

おかわり お代わり 图 another [a second] helping,《話》seconds; a refill. ▶コーヒーのお代わり(=もう１杯)いかがですか Would you like *another cup of* coffee? (⬛ 親しい間では Another cup of coffee?/More coffee?のようにもいう) ▶スープのお代わりをください I'd like *a second helping of* soup(, please).
—— お代わりする 動 ▶彼はカレーライスを３度お代わりした He had [(求めた) asked for] three *helpings* of curry and rice.

おかん 悪寒 《catch [get, take]》a chill. (⇨寒気(ᄒ))

おかんむり ●おかんむりである be in a bad mood; be angry《with [《米》at]＋人, at [about, over]＋事・物》; be peevish,《主に英語》be cross. ▶社長は今日はおかんむりだ. あることないこと八つ当たりというわけだ Our boss is *in a bad mood* [very *angry*, ×bad-tempered] today. He is complaining about everything. (⬛ bad-tempered は人の性格を表すので一時的な気分には用いない)

***おき** 沖 ●神戸の油井 an *offshore* oil well. ●神戸沖に[で] off Kobe. ●沖に出る[出ている] put [be] out to sea. ●１マイル沖に停泊する drop anchor a mile *offshore* [*off the shore*].

-おき -置き《ごとに》every;《間隔》an interval. (⬛ いずれも時間にも距離にも用いる) ●5,6 分おきに *every* 5 or 6 minutes. ●４メートルおきに木を植える plant trees *every* four meters [*at intervals of* four meters, *at* four-meter *intervals*, (４メートル離して) four meters *apart*]. ●１日おきにジョギングする jog *every* other day [on alternate days, (２日ごとに) *every* two days, (２日目ごとに) *every* second day]. (⬛ 後の二つは数が一つ大きくなることに注意) ▶バスは１時間おきに出ている The buses run [The bus runs] *every* hour./The buses run *hourly*./There is an *hourly* bus service. (⬛ 「２時間おきに」なら two-hourly)

おぎ 荻 【植物】a common reed.

おきあい 沖合 (⇨沖)
●沖合漁業 offshore fishing.

おきあがりこぼし 起き上がり小法師 a self-righting (dharma) doll.

おきあがる 起き上がる [[座席・地面などから]] get* up,《書》rise*《from》; (転んだ人が) pick [(やっと) pull] oneself up; [[寝ていて上半身を起こす]] sit* up (*in* bed). ▶１週間で起き上がって歩けるようになるでしょう You will be *up and around* [*about*] in a week.

おきあみ 沖醤蝦 【動物】a krill. (⬛ 単・複同形)

おきいし 置き石 【庭石】a garden rock; [【碁】の]《two-stone》handicap (in *go*). ▶線路に置き石をしてはいけません Do not leave stones with malicious intent on train tracks.

おきかえる 置き換える [[配置し直す]] rearrange; [[移動とは]] move《*to*, *into*》;〔取り替える〕(A を B に) replace《A with B》, substitute《B for A》. (⇨代える) ●部屋の家具を置き換える *rearrange* (the furniture in) the room; *switch* the furniture in the room. (⬛ switch は「交換する (exchange)」の意) ●テレビと本箱を置き換える *switch* the TV and the bookcase *around*.

おきがさ 置き傘 (学校・職場などに置く) a spare umbrella; (客に貸す) an umbrella for customer's use.

おきぐすり 置き薬 *okigusuri*, (説明的に) a medicine chest left behind by a salesman who collects for only the amount used.

おきご 置き碁 (ハンディキャップを与えた碁の勝負) a *go* game with a handicap.

おきざり 置き去り ——置き去りにする 動 leave ... behind. ▶彼らは皆傷ついた友を置き去りにして逃げ去った All of them ran away, *leaving* their wounded friend *behind* [(見捨てて) *deserting* their wounded friend].

オキシダント [【強酸化性物質】【化学】an oxidant /áksidnt/.

オキシドール [<ドイツ語] 【化学】(hydrogen) peroxide /(h)áidrədʒən/ pəráksaid/.

オキシフル [オキシドールの商標名] Oxyfull.

おきだま 置き球 【野球】a cripple (pitch).

おきっぱなし 置きっぱなし ●花見客が大量のごみをそこらじゅうに置きっぱなしにして帰った The people who came to see the cherry blossoms went home *leaving* a lot of litter (lying) *around* [*about*]. (⬛ この around, about は「あちこちに」の意)

おきづり 沖釣り offshore fishing.

おきて 掟 (ご法度, 法律) a law; (約束事, 決まり) a rule; (公の統制規則) a regulation. (⇨法律, 規則)

おきてがみ 置き手紙 [メモ] a note; [ことづけ] a (written) message. ●彼女は置き手紙をする leave a *note* [a *message*] for her.

おきどけい 置き時計 a (table) clock. (⇨時計)

おきどころ 置き所 (余地に) room; (⇨場所)

おきな 翁 【年老いた男性】a male senior citizen; [能の面] a *No(h)* mask of an old man.

***おぎなう** 補う (金・時間などが不足を) make* ... up; (損失・欠点などを) make up for ... (⬛ 受け身はまれ), compensate for ... (⬛ 前の方より堅い言い方); (欠員などを) fill; (補足する) supplement. (⇨償う) ●欠員を補う fill a vacant post [a vacancy]. ●アルバイトをして給料の不足分を補う *make up* [*supplement*] one's salary *with* [*by doing*] a part-time job. ●経験不足を勤勉で補う *compensate for* one's lack of experience *with* diligence. ●食事にビタミンを補う *supplement* one's meal with vitamins. ▶その損失を補わねばならない We must *make up* (*for*) [*compensate for*] the loss. (⬛ make up for は受身では通例 for をつけない: The loss must *be made up.*) ▶彼のやさしさは彼の小さな欠点を補って余りある His kindness more than *makes up* [*compensates*] *for* his small weaknesses.

おきにいり お気に入り a favorite; (子供)《軽蔑的》a pet. ●彼女のお気に入り (=大好きな) 帽子 her *favorite* hat. ▶吉田はあの先生のお気に入りだ Yoshida is a *favorite with* the teacher [a *favorite of* the teacher('s), the teacher's *favorite*, the teacher's *pet*].

おきぬけ 起き抜け ▶私は起き抜けに(=起きたらすぐ)軽い運動をする I take light exercise *as soon as* I *get up*. ▶起き抜けには(=朝まず第一に)それをしよう I'll do it (*the*) *first thing* in the morning.

おきば 置き場 [【置き場所】] a place《*for*》. ●自転車置き場 a parking *place for* bicycles; (屋根つきの) a bicycle *shed*. ▶私の部屋は狭くてベッドの置き場がない There is no *place* [*room*] *for* a bed in my small room. ▶身の置き場がない I don't know what to do with myself.

おきびき 置き引き (人) a baggage thief (⬛ thieves);

おきまり (行為) a baggage stealing. ▶私はドゴール空港で置き引きにあって以来フランは嫌いだ I *had* my baggage *stolen* [Someone *walked off with* my baggage] at de Gaulle airport, and I don't like France after that.

おきまり お決まり ●お決まりの(=いつもの)料理 a *usual* dish. ●お決まりの(=習慣の)就寝時間 *customary* bedtime. ●お決まりの(=型にはまった)返事 a *stereo-typed* answer. ▶ハワイは近ごろ新婚旅行のお決まりの(=いつもの)コースになっている Hawaii is the *usual* [*common*] place for a honeymoon these days.

おきみやげ 置き土産 (別れの際の贈り物) a *parting present* [*gift*]; (死後に残すもの) a *remembrance left by the deceased*. ▶社長は退職する定年年制を置き土産とした Our president left a new retirement system as a (sort of) *parting present*.

おきもの 置き物 〚飾り物〛an ornament. ●床の間の置き物 an *ornament* in the alcove.

おきや 置屋 a *geisha house*.

おぎゃあ 赤ちゃんがおぎゃあおぎゃあと大声で泣いていた A baby *was bawling* [*crying loudly*].

おきゃん a *tomboy*.

おきゅう お灸

:**おきる 起きる** ❶〚起床する〛get* up, get out of bed, 《書》rise*. ▶彼は毎朝早く[遅く]起きる He *gets up* early [late] every morning./He is an early [a late] riser. ▶6時の目覚めたが起きたのは8時過ぎだった I woke up at six, but I didn't *get up* [*get out of bed*, *rise*] until after eight. (⇨❷) ▶あしたは6時に起きなくてはならないので、もう寝ます I must *be up* at six tomorrow morning, so I'm going to bed.

❷〚目覚める〛wake* (up), awake*; (起こされる) be awakened [wakened]《by》.

> **解説** wake (up), awake, awaken, waken (up) の違い
> (1)「起きる」も「起こす」も wake (up) が最も一般的で、他の三つは文語または堅い表現。受け身文では be waked はまれで be woken が用いられる。
> (2) awake は「起きる」に、awaken と waken (up) とは「起こす」の意で好まれる傾向がある。
> (3) awake と awaken はよく比喩的に用いられる。罪の意識に目覚める awake to a sense of sin.

▶もと子、起きなさい。7時ですよ。今起きないと学校に遅れますよ Wake up, Motoko. It's seven. If you don't *get up* now, [Get up now, or] you'll be late for school. (❗後の方が普通) ▶静かにしないと赤ん坊が起きるよ Be quiet, or the baby will *wake up* [you'll *wake* the baby (*up*)]. ▶変な音で私は起きた I *was awakened* [*was wakened*] (*from* sleep) by a strange noise.

❸〚寝ずに起きる〛(目を覚ましている) be [stay] awake (❗be waking は「目覚めかけている」の意); (夜遅くまで) stay [sit*] up (late). ▶赤ん坊は起きていますか Is the baby *awake* or asleep? ▶父から何か言ってくるのを待って夜遅く[夜12時]まで寝ないでいた We *stayed up* late [*until midnight*] waiting for some words from our father. (❗till [until] late はまれ) ▶まだ起きているの？もう2時よ Are you still *up*? It's already 2 a.m. ▶彼は起きている時間のほとんどは勉強にあてられていた Most of his *waking* hours were devoted to study. (❗この study は名詞)

❹〚起き上がる〛(立ち上がる) get* up, 《書》rise*; (上半身を起こして座る) sit* up《in bed》, (転んだ後) pick oneself up. (⇨起き上がる)

❺〚生じる〛happen; occur (-rr-). (⇨起こる) ▶どうしても英語を勉強する気が起きない I don't *feel like* study*ing* English at all./I can't *bring myself to* study English.

おきわすれる 置き忘れる mislay*, misplace; (置いてくる) leave*…(behind). (⇨起る) ▶彼は本をどこかへ置き忘れた He *mislaid* [*misplaced*] his books. ▶彼はバスの中に傘を置き忘れたに違いない He must *have left* his umbrella in [on] the bus. (❗具体的な場所を伴う場合は forget は用いない)

:**おく 奥** (内部) the *inner part*; (奥深い所) the *depth*(*s*); (深く隠れた内部) 《書》the *recesses*; (中心部) the *heart*; (背後、裏) the *back*. ▶森の奥へ入る go into *the depths* [*heart*] of the forest; go deep into the forest. ▶洞窟(悠)の奥には何もなかった There was nothing in *the inner part* [*recesses*] of the cave. ▶奥へ行ってカウンターの所で聞いてください Go *in* and ask someone behind the counter. ▶寝室は家の奥[廊下を奥に行った所]にある Our bedroom is *at the back* of the house [is *up* the hall]. (❗up は「奥また所の方へ」の意で、「2階に上がって」の意ではない) ▶彼女は彼を奥の部屋へ通した She showed him into the *back* [*inner*] room. ▶彼は私の心の奥まで見抜いた He *saw through* me soon./I soon found out *what I was really thinking*. (⇨底❷) ▶のどの奥が少しはれていますね You're a little swollen *at the back of* the throat./The *back* of your throat is a little swollen. ▶彼の住まいは市街地からだいぶ奥です(=離れている) He lives *a long way* (*off* [*away*]) *from* the town.

:**おく 置く**

▣ **WORD CHOICE** 置く

put 物をある場所に置くことをさす最も一般的な語。時に圧力・強調・優先・停止・終結などの抽象的な概念を目的語に取る。●箱を床に置く *put* a box on the floor. ●その問題に強調を置く *put* an emphasis on the problem.
place 物・人をある目的で特定の場所・状態に置くこと。put より堅い語。●グラスを注意深くテーブルに置く *place* the glass carefully on the table.
set 物などを特定の場所・状態に据えること。put より堅い語で、時に比喩的に用いて、制限・基準などを設けることを含意する。●速度に制限を置く *set* a limit on the speed.

▣ **頻度チャート**
put ██████████████
place ██████████
set ██████

20 40 60 80 100 (%)

❶〚すえて置く〛put*; place; set* (⇨類語); (横にして) lay*. ●テーブルに本を置く *put* [*place*, *lay*] a book *on* the table. ●荷物を(下に)置く *put* [*set*] *down* one's pack. ●頭をまくらに置く *lay* one's head *on* the pillow. ●受話器を置く *put back* the receiver; (電話を切る) *hang up* the phone. ▶彼女はナプキンを広げてひざに置いた She unfolded the napkin and *put* it *on* [*in*] her lap. ▶彼はペンを置いて私を見た He *laid down* his pen and looked at me. ▶彼は微妙な立場に置かれている He *is placed* [*is put*] in a delicate position.

❷〚置いていく〛(放置する) leave*; (置き忘れる) leave…(behind); (ある状態にしておく) keep*. ●ドアを開けておく *leave* [*keep*] the door open. (❗leave は

「ドアを開けたまま放置しておく」. keep は「ドアを意図的に開けたままにしておく」の意) ▶ それを言わないでおく *leave* [×*keep*] it unsaid; *keep* silent about it; (秘密にしておく) *keep* it secret. ▶ 彼は郷里に家族を置いて上京した He went to Tokyo, *leaving* his family *at home*. ▶ 急がないと置いて行くよ I'm going to *leave* you *behind* if you don't hurry./Hurry up or you'll *get left behind*. ▶ ブランデーは我が家には置いてません We don't *keep* brandy at home.
❸ [設置する] set*... up, establish (⚠ 前の方が口語的); (雇う) employ. ● 図書館を置く *set up* [*establish*] a library. ● 召し使いを置いている [置く] *keep* [*employ*] a servant. ● 下宿人を置いている [置く] *keep* [*take in*] a lodger. ● その会社京都に支店を置いている(=持っている) The company *has* a branch (office) in Kyoto.
❹ [店に置く] carry; (売る) sell*; (在庫として置く) stock. ▶ あの本屋には洋書は置いていない That bookstore does not *carry* [*sell*] foreign books. ▶ その店では冷凍野菜を置いていた The store *stocked* frozen vegetables.
会話 「ブラジルコーヒーはどこで手に入るかな」「そうねえ、あのスーパーマーケットには新しいのが最入てあるわよ」"Where can I get Brazilian coffee?" "Well, that supermarket *has* a fresh supply."
❺ [隔てる] ● 等間隔の(間)を置いて立つ stand *at equal spaces*. ● 1日置いて次の日 the day after next. ▶ 山田さんのお宅から1軒おいて隣です Mr. Yamada lives next door *but* one [two doors away].
おく 億 a [one] hundred million. ● 10億 a [one] billion;《英》a [one] thousand million. (⚠ 1 million と同じく billion も数の場合、複数形 〜s はとらない: a few billion. (2) a billion=1 兆 は《英古》)
おく 措く 〔差し置く〕(⇨措く)
おくがい 屋外 the outdoors. (⚠ 単数扱い) ● 屋外で働く work *òutdóors*. (⇨屋 ❶)
● 屋外プール an outdoor (swimming) pool.
おくがた 奥方 《古》the lady of the house.
おくぎ 奥義 (⇨奥義 (ぎ))
おくざしき 奥座敷 the inner parlor.
おくさま 奥様 ❶ [妻] one's wife (⚠ wives); Mrs. (+姓に). (⇨夫人) ● 奥様はおいでですか Is Mrs. (Tanaka) in [at home]? ▶ 奥様はお元気ですか How is your *wife*? (⚠ 親しい間柄では本人の名前を用いるが、目上の人に対しては How is *Mrs*. Hori? のようにもいう)
❷ [一家の女主人] a mistress; (呼びかけ) madam, 《米話》ma'am. (⚠ 現代では ladies が普通) ▶ かしこまりました、奥様 (店員・召し使いなど) \Certainly, /*madam* [/*ma'am*].
おくさん 奥さん (⇨奥様) ▶ 彼女ならきっと彼のいい奥さんになりますよ I'm sure she'll make him a good *wife* [make a good *wife* for him].
おくし 御髪 (a) hair. (⇨髪)
おくじょう 屋上 〔屋根〕the roof (⚠ 〜s); (特にビルなどの平たい屋根) the rooftop.
● 屋上屋を架(か)す ▶ 屋上屋を架すような(=無駄な)ことはするな Don't try to *carry* [*take*] *coals to Newcastle*. (《参考》Newcastle が英国の石炭の積み出し港として有名であることから)
● 屋上庭園 a roof garden. ● 屋上レストラン a rooftop restaurant; (屋上庭園ふうの)《米》a roof garden.
おくする 臆する (尻込みする) shrink* [flinch] 《*from*》; (ためらう) be hesitant. ● (なんら)臆することなく without (the slightest) *hesitation*; fearlessly. ▶ いいことをまねるのに臆する必要はない(=恐れることは何もない) There's nothing to *be afraid of* in [about] *copying* [*imitating*] something good.
おくせつ 憶説 a guess; a conjecture; (仮説) hypothesis.
おくそく 憶測 图 a guess; (a) speculation.
―― 憶測する 動 guess (*at*...); speculate 《*on, about*》.
おくそこ 奥底 (一番深い所) the depths; (底) the bottom. (⇨底)
オクターブ [8度音程]『音楽』an octave /áktiv/. ● 1 オクターブ下げて歌う sing *an octave* lower.
オクタン 〖化学〗octane /áktein/. ● ハイオクタンの high-*octane*.
● オクタン価 octane number; octane rating.
おくだん 憶断 a wild conjecture; a random guess.
おくち 奥地 (海岸から遠く離れた) the interior; (海・大河川の背後にある) the hinterland.
おくちよごし お口汚し (⇨口汚し)
おくづけ 奥付 an imprint.
おくて 奥手 (人) a late bloomer [developer].
会話 「健ちゃんに彼女いるの?」「あの子はそっちの方はちょっと奥手だ[ね]」"Does Ken have a girlfriend?" "No, he's a bit of a *late bloomer* in that department."

おくない 屋内 ―― 屋内で[に] 副 indoors. (⇨室内)
● 屋内スポーツ indoor sports. ● 屋内競技場 a gymnasium,《話》a gym. ● 屋内プール an indoor (swimming) pool.
おくに 御国 (相手の国) your native country; (故郷) your hometown. ● お国自慢をする boast [talk proudly] about one's *hometown*. ● お国なまりで話す speak with a regional accent. ▶ お国はどちらですか Where are you from?/Where [Which country] do you come from? (⚠ この意で Where *did* you come from? と動詞を過去形で用いることはない). (2) ×Where is your country? は地理上の位置をたずねる言い方で不適切)(⇨出身)
おくにぶり お国振り characteristic customs of a nation.
おくのいん 奥の院 the inner shrine; the inner depths. ● 科学の奥の院(=到達しがたい地域) farthest reaches of science.
おくのて 奥の手 ● 奥の手を出す[使う] play one's *last* [*trump, best, strongest*] *card*.
おくのほそみち 『奥の細道』 *Narrow Road to the Interior*; *Narrow Road to the Deep North*. (《参考》松尾芭蕉の俳諧紀行)

古今ことばの系譜 「奥の細道」
月日は百代(はくたい)の過客(かかく)にして、行きかふ年も又旅人也. (略) 古人も多く旅に死せるあり. 余りというより、片雲の風にさそはれて、漂白の思いやまず (略) Days and months are travellers of eternity. So are the years that pass by. There are great number of ancients, too, who died on the road. I myself have been tempted for a long time by the cloud-moving wind ― filled with a strong desire to wander. (Yuasa Nobuyuki) (⚠ (1)「月日」は「(年月) years, (時) time」だが、この場合は次の文の「年」と対比させているので、文字どおり days and months としている. (2)「古人」は、単に「古代の人」「昔の人」というのでなく、過去の世の、芭蕉の尊敬する詩人や歌人(杜甫・宗祇・西行ら)をさしているとも思われる. その意味をはっきりさせて There were not a few poets of the past ages whose life ended on a journey. とすることもできよう)

おくば 奥歯 a back tooth (複 back teeth); [医学] a molar tooth.
- **奥歯に物が挟まる** ▶彼は奥歯に物がはさまったような言い方をする(率直に言わない) He doesn't talk frankly./(遠回しに言う) He beats around [(英) about] the bush./(軽蔑的) He is mealy-mouthed.

おくび (げっぷ) a belch. (⇨げっぷ)
- **おくびにも出さない** ▶彼女の前では彼は彼女に夢中であることをおくびにも出さなかった In her presence, he said nothing at all about [(そぶりも見せなかった) gave no sign of] having her around.

おくびょう 臆病 图 cowardice; timidity. (❗ 前の方は勇気に欠けていること,後の方は勇気・自信に欠け,内気で用心深いことをいう)
—— **臆病な** 形 cowardly; timid. ▶シカは臆病な動物だ Deer are timid animals. (❗ deer は単・複同形) ▶彼は臆病にもあんなふるまいをした It was cowardly [×coward] of him to behave like that.
- **臆病風をふかす** get frightened. (⇨おじけつく)
- **臆病者** a coward; (話) a chicken.

おくふかい 奥深い deep. ▶奥深い森 a deep forest.
- **奥深い意味** a deep [a profound] meaning. ▶彼の顔には奥深い人間性を感じさせるものがあった I detected some profound human nature [(話) humanness] in his face.

おくまる 奥まる ▶奥まった座敷に通される be shown into a fine back room. ▶通りからずっと奥まった2階家 a two-story house far back from the road.

おくまん 億万 ▶何億万年も昔 billions [millions] of years ago.
- **億万長者** a billionaire.

おくめん 臆面・**臆面もなく** ▶若い女性が臆面もなく(=恥ずかしげもなく)人前で化粧直しをするのを見てこっちが恥ずかしくなった I was embarrassed to see a young woman touching up her makeup in public without (a trace of) shame. (⇨図々しく)

おくやみ お悔やみ [哀悼] condolence. (❗ [哀悼の言葉」の意では複数形で) ▶吉本氏のご遺族に対し心からお悔やみ申し上げます I'd like to offer [extend] my heartfelt condolences to Mr. Yoshimoto's family. ▶お父様のご逝去に対し心からお悔やみ申し上げます Please accept my sincere condolences [my deepest sympathy] on the passing of your father./I'm so sorry to hear about (the death of) your father. (❗ この文にだけ言う言い方) ▶父が死んだとき,たくさんの人がお悔やみに来てくれた When my father died, lots of people came to see me. (⇨弔問する)
- **お悔やみ状** a letter of condolence.

おくゆかしい 奥床しい [洗練された] refined; [上品で優雅な] elegant, graceful (and beautiful); [遠慮深い] reserved; [慎み深い] modest.

*__おくゆき 奥行__ ▶奥行き20フィートの舞台 a stage twenty feet deep [in depth]. (⇨幅❶) ▶この棚はけっこう奥行きがある These shelves are fairly deep. ▶彼の学問には奥行きがない His learning is not deep.

> 翻訳のこころ ひさしに,漠然とながら人生の奥行きのようなものを感じさせた (竹西寛子『蘭』)That made Hisashi become aware of the depth of life, as vague as it was. (❗ (1) That はこの文の前に述べられたことをさす.(2) 「奥行き」は depth (深さ)と表す.(3) 「…に感じさせる」は make ... become aware of (...に気づかせる)と表す)

おくら お蔵・**お蔵入りする** be put on a shelf; (原稿など) be unpublished. ▶これまでも多くの企画がお蔵入りになるのを見てきた I've seen many projects put on the shelf. (❗ この put は過去分詞)

オクラ [植物] (木) an okra; (集合的) (さや) okra. (❗ さやは lady's fingers ともいう)

おぐらあん 小倉餡 Ogura-an; (説明的に) sweetened bean paste with whole beans stirred in.

おくらせる 遅らせる,後らせる delay, (《会議》) postpone, (話) put*... off [back]. (❗ 延期する,遅れる) ▶時計を10分遅らせる put [set] one's watch back ten minutes. ▶約束の時間を少し遅らせてもらえませんか Could you make our appointment a bit later? ▶その戦争は開発の発展を20年遅らせた The war has delayed [held back] national development (by) 20 years.

おぐらひゃくにんいっしゅ 小倉百人一首 (⇨百人一首)

オクラホマ [米国の州] Oklahoma /ˌoʊkləˈhoʊmə/ (略 Okla. 郵便略 OK).

おくりおおかみ 送り狼 'a (lustful) wolf in sheep's clothing [skin].' ▶家に送ってくれる途中の男突然送り狼の本性を現しんですって She says he suddenly turned a 'lustful wolf' when he was seeing her home.

おくりかえす 送り返す ▶小包を送り主に送り返す send a parcel back [return a parcel] to the sender.

おくりがな 送り仮名 kana added to a Chinese character to form a word.

おくりこむ 送り込む ▶彼を系列会社に送り込む send him to a subsidiary company.

おくりさき 送り先 (受け取り人) a receiver; (運送先) a destination. ▶送り先の住所 the address of the receiver.

おくりじょう 送り状 an invoice. (参考 invoice は納品書と請求書を兼ねたもの)

おくりだす 送り出す ❶[もの・人を送る] [手紙・小荷物などを] send*... off; [人を] send [get*]... off, [玄関まで] see*... out. (⇨送る❶❷) ▶子供たちを学校に送り出す send one's children off to school. ▶この港から世界中に商品を送り出して(=出荷しています) We ship goods all over the world from this port. (⇨送る) ❷[相撲・レスリングなどで] push ... out (of the ring) from behind.

おくりな 贈り名 a posthumous /pástfəməs/ title [name].

おくりぬし 送り主 a sender; (荷物の) a consignor.

おくりバント 送りバント [野球] a sacrifice bunt. (⇨バント)

おくりび 送り火 okuribi; (説明的に) the bonfire lit to speed the spirits of one's ancestors. (闥 迎え火)

おくりぼん 送り盆 okuribon; (説明的に) the last day of the Bon Festival. (闥 迎え盆)

おくりむかえ 送り迎え —— **送り迎えする** 動 take [(車で) drive] ⟨him⟩ to ⟨school [the station]⟩ and back.

*__おくりもの 贈り物__ a present; a gift (❗ present よりやや形式ばった上品な感じを与える語). ▶結婚の贈り物をする[もらう] give [get, be given] a wedding present [gift]. (事情 米英でもナイフ・フォーク類は結婚祝いには避ける傾向があるが,相手に少し使い賃を出してそれを買ってあげたことにする人もいる) ▶彼女の誕生日の贈り物にルビーの指輪を買ってやった I bought her a ruby ring as [for] a birthday present [gift]. ▶これはあなたへの[彼からの]贈り物です Here is a present for you [from him]. (❗ 贈り物を渡すときの言い方は他に Here you are./This is for you./Here's a little something for you. などがある) ▶すばらしいクリスマスの贈り物ありがとうございます

おくる 送る

ました Thank you for the wonderful [lovely, (話) beautiful] Christmas *present* [*gift*]. 会話「これを贈り物用に包装してください」「かしこまりました」 "Please *gift-wrap* this." "Sure, sir [ma'am]."

おくる 送る ❶[発送する] send* (■最も一般的な語.以下の語と交換できる場合が多い); (手紙・使者などを急送する) dispatch; (船・列車・トラックなどで遠距離輸送する) ship (-pp-); (郵送する) (米) mail, (英) post; (支払い金を郵送する) remit (-tt-); (信号を) signal. ●手紙を航空便では *send* a letter by airmail; *airmail* a letter. ●その国へ使節を送る(=派遣する) *dispatch* [*send*] an envoy *to* the country. ●遭難信号を[通信を信号で]送る *signal* an SOS [a message]. ●彼女はその人[島]に食糧を送った She *sent* food *to* the man [island]./She *sent* the man [×island] food. (■(1) 前の文は man [island], 後の文は food に重点がある. (2) 目的語が場所のときは後の方の文型は不可) ●その工場は製品を列車[飛行機]で送る The factory *ships* its products by rail [air]. ●この請求書を受領したら残金をお送りください Please *remit* the balance (due) upon receipt of this bill.
❷[送り届ける] send*; (見届ける) see*; (車で) drive*; (付き添って) escort; [見送る] see ... off (⇨見送る). ●客を玄関まで送る *see* one's guest *to* the door; *see* one's guest *out*. ●走者を(二塁へ)送る *move* a runner up (to second). ●私は彼女を家まで送った I *took* [*saw*, (歩いて) *walked*, (車で) *drove*, ×*sent*] her home. ●送り届けよ send her home [by taxi] は「自分でなく他の人がタクシーなどを使って送り届ける」の意) ●車で駅まで送ってくれない? Will you *drive* me to the station?/Will you *give* me *a ride* [(米)[*a lift* (英)] to the station?/(話) Will you *drop* me *off* at the station? ●(家まで)車で送ってくださってありがとう Thank you for the *lift* home. ●私は成田空港に妹を送りに行った I went to Narita Airport *to see* my sister *off*.
❸[過ごす] spend*, pass (■ pass は単に「時を過ごす」のに対し, spend は「特定の目的を持って時間を使うこと」を含意する); (生活をする) live, lead*. ●故郷で余生を送る *spend* the rest of one's life in one's hometown. ●青春時代をむだに送る *idle away* one's youth. ●幸福な人生を送った He *led* [*lived*] a happy life./He *lived* happily.

おくる 贈る [与える] give*; (公式に贈呈する) present /prizént/; (授与する, (書) confer (-rr-). (⇨与える) ●彼の誕生日に何を贈ろうか What should I *give* him for his birthday [as a birthday present]? (■このような場合動詞の present を用いるのは不自然) ●彼は勝者に金時計を贈った He *presented* the winner *with* a gold watch [a gold watch *to* the winner]. (■前の方が口語的. (主に米) では *with* が省略されることがある) ●文化勲章がその画家に贈られた The Order of Culture *was conferred on* [*awarded to*] the artist./The artist *was awarded* [×*conferred*] the Order of Culture. (■人が主語の場合は confer は不可)

おくるみ 産着, 襁褓 a báby blànket.

おくれ 遅れ, 後れ (a) delay. ●配達の遅れ a *delay* in delivery. ●仕事[勉強]の後れを取り戻す catch up on one's work [studies]. ●遅れないで来る come without *delay*. ●バスは 5 分遅れて来た The bus came five minutes *late*./The bus came after a *delay* of 5 minutes. ●最初の交渉で遅れを取る(=遅れる) ●脱線事故で 2 時間の遅れが出た The derailment caused a *delay* of two hours. ●列車は遅れを取り戻すことができなかった The train could not

make up for the *lost* time.
●後れを取る 仕事や(人に)後れを取っている[取る] *be* [*lag*, *fall*] *behind* (the others) in one's work.

おくれげ 後れ毛 loose hair. (⇨ほつれ)

おくればせながら 遅ればせながら though it is a little too late. ●遅ればせながらご返事申し上げます I'm very sorry that I'm *late in* answering your letter.

おくれる 遅れる, 後れる ❶[定刻・期限に] be late (*for*; (*in*) *doing*); (避けられない理由で) be delayed; (遅れている) be behind schedule (■やや遅れている) time]. ●電車に遅れる *be late for* [乗りそこなう] *miss* the train. (⇨乗り遅れる) ●私は約束に遅れた I *was late for* [*came late to*] my appointment. ●今日は昼食をおごれた I *was late with* [(*in*) *having*] lunch today. (■動名詞が続く場合, (話) では通例 *in* を省略する) ●I had a *late* lunch today. ●霧のため飛行機の出発が遅れた The plane's departure *was delayed* by the fog. ●どのくらい遅れるんでしょうか How long will the *delay* be? ●事故のため列車は 10 分遅れた Because of the accident, the train *was delayed* (for) ten minutes [*was* ten minutes *late*, *was* ten minutes *behind schedule*, arrived ten minutes *late*]./There was ten minutes' *delay* [a *delay* of ten minutes] because of the accident. ●家賃の支払いが 1 か月遅れていますよ You're a month *behind with* [*in*] your rent. (⇨滞る)
❷[後れを取る] 仕事などが be [fall*, lag (-gg-), get*] behind (*with*, *in*); (他のものより) be [fall, lag] behind .... (■いずれも be は状態を表す) ●他の走者[時代]に後れないようにする *keep up with* the other runners [the times]. ●(期限のある)仕事を遅れないようにする *catch up on* the work. ●彼はかなり勉強が後れている He *is* well [far, (話) *way*] *behind with* his studies. ●far より way の方が程度が大きい) ●この地域は 10 年くらい時勢に後れている This area *is* about ten years *behind* the times. ●彼は他の走者からだんだん後れていった He gradually *fell* [*lagged*, ×*ot*] *behind* the other runners. (■通例 get behind は具体的距離は表さない) ●2 位の走者は 1 位の走者よりずっと [10 メートル]後れて入ってきた The second runner came in much *later* than [ten meters *behind*] the first.
❸[時計が] lose*; (後れている) be slow. ●ずっと以前は時計が 1 日に 10 秒後れるぐらいは普通だった Years ago it was usual for a watch to *lose* ten seconds a day. ●君の時計は 1 分後れている Your watch *is one* minute *slow* [×*behind*, ×*late*]. (■ behind はスコットランド英語で用いられる)

おけ 桶 a tub; (バケツ) a bucket, (主に米) a pail. ●すし桶 a sushi *tub*. ●洗い桶 a wash*tub*. ●桶 1 杯の水 a *tub* [a *bucket*(*ful*), a *pail*(*ful*)] of water.

おけら 螻蛄 [昆虫] a mole cricket. ●おけらになる(一文なしになる) become penniless.

おける [位置, 観点] in ...; [所属] of ... ●外交における重大問題 a serious problem *in* diplomacy. ●教育における基本問題 the fundamental problems *of* education. ●A の B における(=対する)関係は C の D におけるがごとし(=関係と同じだ) A is to B what C is to D./What C is to D, A is to B.

おこえがかり お声掛かり ●お声かかりで (推薦で) on [at] the *recommendation* of ...; (命令で) under the *order*(*s*) of ....

おこがましい [さしでがましい] presumptuous /prizʌ́mptʃuəs/; [身の程知らずな] impudent; [思い上がっている] conceited, (話) stuck-up. ●自分

言うのもおこがましいのだが, 私は歌がうまい I don't wish to sound *conceited*, but I'm a good singer.

おこさまランチ お子様ランチ a special dish for children; a kiddie special lunch.

おこし (粔籹) *okoshi*; (説明的に) a sweetened cake made of rice, sesame and beans.

おこし お越し ▶お越しいただいてうれしく存じます I'm very pleased to have you here. ▶またのお越しをお待ちしております Please come again./(ホテルなどで) Please stay with us again. (関連) これに対する応答は(きっと来るわ)I will./Definitely./(来れたらいいなあ) I hope so. など

おこしいれ お輿入れ [『嫁入り』の尊敬語] (⇒嫁入り)

:**おこす 起こす** ❶[目を覚めさせる] wake*…(up), waken …(up), awaken (⇒起きる[類語]); [起床させる] get*… up. (⇒叩き起こす, 揺り起こす) ▶6 時に起こしてください Please *wake* me (*up*) at six./(ホテルのフロントへ) I want a call at six, please. ▶眠っている赤ちゃんを起こさないで Don't *wake* (*up*) [《書》 *arouse*] the sleeping baby. ▶電話の音で起こされた I *was woken* (*up*) by the ring(ing) of the telephone./The ring(ing) of the telephone *woke* me (*up*). ▶子供を遅くまで起こしておかないように Don't *keep* your children *up* too late.
❷[倒れたものを] raise (*up*). ●体を起こして座った姿勢になる raise oneself *up* to a sitting position. ▶彼は転んだ子を助け起こした He *raised* [(手を貸して) *helped*] the fallen child *to his feet*./He *helped* the fallen child (*to*) *stand up* (**!** to のない方は直接「手を貸して」, ある方は励ますなどの間接的援助を含意する).
❸[発生させる] cause; (…に通じる) lead*to…; (もたらす) bring*… about; (生み出す) create; (熱・電気などを発生させる) generate. ●電気を起こす *generate* electricity. ●火を起こす *make* [*build*] a fire. ●飲酒運転は事故を起こすことである Drunk(en) driving *causes* [*leads to*] accidents. ▶いつその事故を起こしたのですか When did you *cause* [*have*] the accident? ▶面倒を起こさないでくれ Don't *cause* [*give*] (us) any trouble. (**!** 後の方が口語的) ▶彼は食べすぎて腹痛を起こした He ate too much and *had* a stomachache.
❹[始める] start, begin*; (活動などを) launch; (設立する) set*… up, establish, found (**!** 後の 2 語の方が堅い語). ●事業を起こす *start* [*launch*] an enterprise. ●新しい会社を起こす *set up* [*establish*] a new firm.
❺[感情を生じる] arouse /əráuz/. ●やる気を起こす *get up* one's drive (*to do*). ●短気を起こす *lose* one's temper.
❻[耕す] ●土を起こす plow [break*] the ground.

おこす 熾す ●火を熾す make [build] a fire.
おこす 興す ●産業を興す build up [set up, promote] industries. ●新しい国を興す build a new nation.
おこぜ (魚津) a stonefish; a scorpion fish (参考) 背びれのとげに毒があることから.
おごそか 厳か ── 厳かな 形 solemn. (⇒厳粛(だ゚゚゚))
おこた (炬燵) (⇒炬燵)
*:**おこたる 怠る** [怠(な)ける] be lazy; be idle (⇒怠ける); [任務などを] neglect, be neglectful (*of*). ●職務を怠る *neglect* [*be neglectful of*] one's duties. ●注意を怠る be careless [negligent]. ●監視を怠っている *be off* one's guard. ●手紙の返事を怠る *neglect* answering [*to answer*] a letter. (放っておく) leave a letter unanswered.

おことば お言葉 (⇒言葉 ❸)
*:**おこない 行い** an act; (an) action; (主に書) a deed

; (書) conduct; behavior.

> (使い分け) **act** 一回限りの行為.
> **action** 一定期間に反復して行われる行為の総体.
> **deed** 人が特定の意図に基づいて行う行為. 特に顕著な善行ないし悪行のいずれかをさす.
> **conduct** 人や組織などが意図をもって行う行為. しばしば行儀や道徳性を含意する.
> **behavior** 人間の態度・振る舞い. 表面的に目に見える行為をさし, 礼儀・行儀などの意味も持つ.

▶彼は勇気ある行いをした He did a courageous *act*./He did an *act* of courage. ▶身障者に手を貸してあげるのは親切な行いです Giving a helping hand to a handicapped person is a kind *act* [*action*]. (**!** *an act* of kindness ともいえる. ×an action of kindness とはいわない) ▶彼の日ごろの行いはとても悪い His everyday *conduct* [*behavior*] is very bad. ▶行いを改めなさい Improve your *behavior*./Mend your ways.

:**おこなう 行う** [行為を行う] do*; [役を務める] act (*as*); [会などを開く] hold*, give*; [為(な)す] ❷ (a) (b) (f); [式などをとり行う] perform; [実行する] carry… out. ●準備を行う (＝準備(を)する) ＝為(な)す ❷ (a). ●実験を行う carry out [*perform*, 《書》 *conduct*] an experiment. ▶入学式は 10 時から行います (＝行われます) The entrance ceremony will *be held* [*take place*, *be performed*] at 10 o'clock. ▶調査は内密に行われた The investigation *was carried out* in secret. ▶その仕事は彼によって行われた (＝なされた) The task *was done* [《やや書》 *was performed*] by him. ▶ストが行われている (＝続行している) A strike *is* (*going*) *on*. ▶言うは易く行うは難し Saying [To say] is easy, but *doing* [*to do*] is difficult./(ことわざ) Easier said than done.

おこなわれる 行われる (⇒行う)
おこのみやき お好み焼き *okonomiyaki*; (説明的に) a thin and flat pancake fried on a hot plate with bits of meat, vegetables and seafood.
おこぼれ お零れ (分け前) one's share; (副産物) a spin-off; (残り物) leftovers.
おこらせる 怒らせる make* 《him》 angry; (感情を害す) offend. (**!** 前置詞その他の連語関係については (⇒怒る)) ●冗談のつもりで言った一言が彼女をすっかり怒らせてしまった What I said for a joke *made* her very *angry* [*offended* her terribly, 《話》 *drove* her *mad*].
おこり 起こり [原因] (a) cause; [起源] (an) origin. (⇒起源) ●祭りの起こり the *origin* of the festival. ▶事の起こりは何でしたか What was the *cause*?/What started it?/How did it happen [*start*]?
おごり 奢り ❶[ぜいたく] luxury /lʌ́gʒəri/. ●おごりをきわめる live in the lap of *luxury*; enjoy the greatest *luxury*.
❷[人にごちそうすること] treat. (⇒奢る) ▶これは私のおごりです This is my *treat*./(話) This is *on* me. (**!** *on* は「…の負担で」の意)
おごり 驕り (うぬぼれ) pride; (高慢) arrogance.
おこりじょうご 怒り上戸 a person who usually loses his temper when he drinks.
おこりっぽい 怒りっぽい [気が短い] quick-[short-, hot-]tempered (⇒怒る); [いらいらした] irritable, testy; [気分を害しやすい] touchy. ▶今晩の彼はなぜ怒りっぽい. どうして? He's a bit *short-tempered* tonight. Why?
おこりんぼう 怒りん坊 a hot-tempered [a quick-tempered] person. (⇒癇癪(だ゚゚゚)) [癇癪持ち])

おこる 起こる

WORD CHOICE 起こる, 起きる

happen 物事が偶然に起こることをさす最も一般的な語. 主語は what や something などが多く, to+人や in+場所などが多く後続する. ▶彼らに何が起こったのか What *happened* to them?

occur happen よりやや堅い語で, in+場所, to+人, when S+V などが多く後続する. ●その地域で起こりがちな犯罪 the crimes that tend to *occur* in those areas.

take place 特に会議・選挙・変革など, あらかじめ想定された通りに起こること. ●過去に起こった様々な出来事 various events that *took place* in the past.

頻度チャート

happen	▰▰▰▰▰▰▰▰▰▰
occur	▰▰▰▰▰▰
take place	▰▰▰
	20 40 60 80 100 (%)

❶ [発生する] happen; occur (-rr-); take* place (⇨[類語]); (戦争・火事・革命・伝染病などが突然発生する) break* out (❗ 事故には用いない). ●何が起ころうとも no matter what *happens*; whatever *happens*; whatever may *happen*. (❗ 後の方ほど堅い表現になる) ●もし何かが起こったら if anything *happens*. ●おもしろい出来事が起こった An amusing incident *happened* [*occurred*, *took place*]. ▶自宅の前で交通事故が起こった A traffic accident *happened* [*occurred*, ×*broke out*] in front of my house./There was a traffic accident in front of my house. ▶火事は台所から起こった The fire *broke out* [*occurred*, ×*took place*, ×*happened*] *in* [×*from*] the kitchen./The fire *started in* [*from*] the kitchen. ▶昨夜東海地方で地震が起こった An earthquake *occurred* [*happened*, ×*broke out*] in the Tokai district last night. (❗ took place はまれ)/There was an earthquake in the Tokai district last night./An earthquake *hit* [*struck*] the Tokai district last night. ▶日米間で戦争が起こった A war *broke out* [*started*, ×*happened*] between Japan and America. (❗ took place, occurred はまれ) ▶彼 (の身) に何が起こったのか What *has happened* to him? (❗ occurred to him なら「何を思いついたのか」の意) ▶そこでは何が起こっているのだ What's *going on* there? ▶その問題は 2, 3 年ごとに起こっている The issue *comes up* every few years. (❗ come up は「問題などが生じる」)

❷ [起因する] (生じる) arise* (*from*); (結果として生じる) result (*from*); (引き起こされる) be caused (*by*); (...に源を発する) originate (*in*, *from*). ▶そのけんかは 2 人のちょっとした感情の行き違いが原因で起こった The fight *resulted from* [*arose from*, *was caused by*] some misunderstanding between the two. ▶その習慣は中国から起こった The custom *originated in* China./(...に由来する) The custom *comes* [×*came*] *from* China. (❗ 後の方が口語的)

おこる 怒る

WORD CHOICE 怒る

get angry 腹を立てることを意味する最も一般的な表現. get のほかに become, feel なども用いる. 「怒っている」状態をさす場合には be を用いる. 時に very, so, really などで意味を強調する. ●僕に怒らないで Don't *get angry* with me.

lose one's temper 原義は「平静 (temper) を失う」. 「怒る」のほか, 気持ちの動揺や取り乱しなども含意する. ●そのとき私は本当に怒った Then, I really *lost my temper*.

頻度チャート

get angry	▰▰▰▰▰▰▰▰▰▰
lose one's temper	▰▰▰
	20 40 60 80 100 (%)

[腹を立てる] get* angry ⟨*at* [*about*, *over*]+事 [*doing*], *with* [*at*, *about*]+人; *that* 節; *to do*⟩; (話) get mad ⟨*at* [*with*]+人, *about* [*at*]+事⟩; [感情を害する] be offended; [心の平穏を失う] lose* one's temper; [しかる] tell* (*him*) off. (叱(しか)る) ●怒らせる make (*him*) angry [mad]; offend; (話) get [take] a rise out of (*him*). ▶彼はすぐ怒る He *gets angry* [*gets offended*] easily./He *loses* his *temper* easily./(気が短い) He has a short temper. ▶彼女は彼の言ったことに怒った She *got angry* [*offended*] *at* (hearing) his remarks [*to* hear his remarks]./(事が主語) His remarks *made* her *angry* [*offended* her]. ▶何をそんなに怒っているのですか What *are* you so *angry* [⟨話⟩*cross*] *about*? (❗ about は省略不可) ▶彼女は彼が彼女の誕生日を忘れていたことを怒っていた She *was angry* [*offended*, ×*mad*] *that* he had forgotten [forgot] her birthday. (❗ She *was angry* [*mad*] *because* he had forgotten [forgot] her birthday. の方が口語的)/She *was angry* [*mad*] *about* [*at*] his forgetting her birthday. (❗ 目的語が事の場合, about は怒りの間接的な理由を, at は (直接的な)原因を表す)/She *was angry* [*mad*] *with* [*at*] him *for* forgetting her birthday. (❗ with では怒りは彼自身に向けられ, その理由が for 句で二次的に示されるが, at では彼の言動に対する怒りが含意されるため for 以下に直接的な怒りがぶつけられる) ▶彼はまだ娘のことを怒っている He's still *angry at* [*about*, *with*] his daughter. (❗ 目的語が人の場合, at, about では怒りの気持ちに重点があり, at では直接的な, about では間接的な怒りのぶつけ方が含意される. 一方 with では怒りの対象が強調される) ▶彼はそれを知ればかんかんになって怒るだろう He'll *be furious* [*very angry*] to know it [if he knows it].

—— 怒った 形 ●怒った顔をする look *angry* [*mad*, ⟨話⟩*cross*]; have an *angry* [⟨話⟩a *cross*, ×a *mad*] look. (❗ この意での mad は限定166的には用いない) ▶怒った群衆が建物の外に集まった An *angry* crowd gathered outside the building.

—— 怒って 副 in anger; (激怒に) in a rage. ●怒ってわめく shout in *anger* [*angrily*]. (❗ angrily は形相・声の調子などに怒りが表れた様子をいう)

おこる 熾る ▶湿っためきはなかなか火がおこらない Wet wood won't *catch fire* [*start burning*] so easily.

おこる 興る rise*, (突然) spring* up; [栄える] flourish /flə́ːrɪʃ/. ●新しい産業が興った A new industry *sprang up*.

おごる 奢る [ごちそうする] treat, give* (*him*) a treat; buy*. (⇨奢(おご)り) ▶君にステーキをおごろう I'll *treat* you to a (beef) steak./I'll *buy* you a (beef) steak. (❗ 後の方は日常会話では親しい人にのみ用いる)

会話「夕食はぼくがおごるよ」「私にも払わせてくれない?」「とんでもない. ぼくがおごるって」「ごちそうさま. 次は私が払うわね」"Let me pay for the dinner."

"Can't I help pay?" "Don't be silly. It's *on me*. I insist." (❗*on* は負担の意を表す) "Thank you. I'll pay next time."
❷ [ぜいたくする] live in luxury. ●おごった生活をする lead [live] a *luxurious* life. ●口がおごっている have a *pampered* taste. (❗*pamper* は「甘やかす」の意)

おごる 驕る 〖高ぶる〗be proud 《*of*》; 〖ご慢な〗be arrogant; 〖思い上がる〗be conceited. (⇨自惚(ﾞﾚ)れる) ▶おごる者久しからず《ことわざ》Pride will have a fall. (❗*will* は強く発音され、続く言葉の内容が習慣的に実現されることを示す.「上を向いて歩くとつまずいて倒れることになる」の意)/Pride goes before a fall.

おこわ お強 (こわめし) steamed rice; (赤飯) ⇨赤飯).
●山菜おこわ *steamed rice* with lightly seasoned edible wild plants.

おさえ (おもし) a weight.

おさえ 抑え 〖制御、統制〗control; 〖救援投手〗〖野球〗a closer; a stopper. ●部下に抑えがきかない cannot control one's men.

おさえこむ 押さえ込む (動けないように) hold ... down. (⇨抑える)

おさえこむ 抑え込む (反乱・暴動などを) suppress; (試合の相手を) 《米》shut ... out, 《米》blank, 《英話》whitewash. (⇨抑える)

おさえつける 押さえ付ける (⇨押さえる) ●あばれる犬を押さえつけて予防接種をしてもらう hold one's struggling dog *down* to have it vaccinated. ●はしごを壁に押さえつける *press* a ladder *against* the wall.

おさえつける 抑え付ける (⇨抑える) ●暴徒を抑えつける *put down* [*suppress*] a riot.

__おさえる 押さえる__ ❶ [動かぬように押さえる] hold; (固定した状態に保つ) hold 《it》steady; (おおう) cover.
●傷口をハンカチで押さえる [《置く》*put*, (押し当てて) *press*] a handkerchief *to* one's wound. ●ドアが閉まらないように押さえておく *hold* the door open. (❗*open* は形容詞) ●首筋をしっかりと押さえる *hold* 《him》tightly by the neck. ●はしごを両手でしっかり押さえる *hold* a ladder *steady* with one's hands; *steady* a ladder with one's hands. ●耳を押さえる *cover* [*hold*] one's ears. (❗... with one's hands と明示しなくても「手でおおう」ことが含意される) ▶彼らは強盗が動かないように押さえていた They *held* the robber *from* moving [*so that* he *couldn't* move].
❷ [捕らえる] catch*; (逮捕する) arrest; (つかむ) grasp; (手に入れる) get* hold of ...; (差し押さえる) seize, 〖法律〗attach. ●警官に取り押さえられる *be caught* [*be arrested*] by a policeman. ●物的証拠を押さえる *get hold of* 《書》*secure*》 material evidence. ●要点を押さえる *grasp* [*seize*] the point; (外さない) *keep* to the point. ▶彼らは彼が金を盗む現場を押さえた They *caught* him (in the act of) steal*ing* [just as he was steal*ing*] the money. (❗*catch* him do*ing* は「...しているところを見つける」の意) ▶彼の財産は債権者に(差し)押さえられた His property *was seized* [*was attached*] by his creditors.
❸ [その他の表現]

> **翻訳のこころ** 胸のポケットからハンカチーフを取り出して額の汗を押さえた (竹西寛子 『蘭』) Taking a handkerchief out of a shirt [a breast] pocket, he pressed it to his sweaty forehead. (❗(1)「胸のポケット」は通例 breast pocket. 男性の胸ポケットは shirt pocket ともいう.
(2)「額の汗を押さえた」は pressed it to a sweaty forehead (汗をかいている額を押さえた)と表す)

__おさえる 抑える__ ❶ [反乱などを] (鎮圧する) suppress, put ... down (❗後の方が口語的); (取り締まる) control (-ll-). ●暴動を抑える *put down* [*suppress*] a riot; *bring* a riot *under control*. ●敵の進撃を抑える(=妨げる) *prevent* [阻止する) *check*] the advance of the enemy.
❷ [数量・程度を] keep* [hold*] ... down; (抑制する) control (-ll-); (制限する) limit; (減らす) reduce.
●生活費を抑える *keep down* [*hold down*, (切り詰める) *cut down* (*on*)] living expenses. ●インフレを抑える *control* [*bring down*] inflation. ●輸出を抑える *limit* [*restrict*] exports. ▶政府は物価を抑えるにあらゆる努力を払っている The government makes every possible effort to *keep* [*hold*] prices *down*. ▶彼は相手のチームを2安打 [2点] に抑えた He *held* [*limited*] the opposing team *to* two hits [runs].
❸ [感情をこらえる] (抑制する) control (-ll-), keep* ... down (❗後の方が口語的); (控える) restrain, keep ... back (❗後の方が口語的); (抑圧する) suppress. ●怒りを抑える *control* [*hold back*, 《書》*contain*, *repress*, *restrain*] one's anger; *bring* one's anger *under control*. ●涙を抑える *keep back* [*restrain*, *control*] one's tears. ●あくびを抑える *suppress* a yawn. ●自分の気持ちを抑える *control* [*restrain*] oneself.

おさおさ 準備はおさおさ怠りない(=完ぺきである) be *perfectly* prepared. ●おさおさ劣らぬ(=少しも劣っていない) be *not at all* inferior 《*to*》.

おさがり お下がり 〖兄・姉などのお下がりの服〗hand-me-downs; (着なくなったもの) cast-offs. (❗二つとも複数形で) ●兄のお下がりを着る wear one's big brother's *hand-me-downs*. ●母のお下がりのセーター one's mother's *hand-me-down* sweater; a sweater *handed down from* one's mother.

おさき お先 ❶ [順番] ●お先に失礼します Excuse me, but I must be leaving [going] now. (⇨失礼) ❷) ●どうぞお先に Go ahead 《, please》./After you 《×, please》. (❗(1) 後の方が丁寧な言い方で, after の方を強く発音し, 通例 please はつけない. (2) 次のような文脈では After you は用いない: (料理が温かいうちに)どうぞお先に. お待ちにならないで You go ahead. Don't wait for me.)
❷ [見通し] ●お先真っ暗だ Our future is bleak./There's no hope (for the future).

おさきぼう お先棒 ●お先棒をかつぐ (人の手先となって働く) act as 《his》cat's paw.

おさげ お下げ 《米》a braid, 《主に英》a plait; (短いもの) a pigtail. (❗以上いずれも複数形で用いることが多い) ●彼女は髪をお下げにしている She wears her hair *in braids* [*in a braid*].

おざしき お座敷 (⇨座敷) ●お座敷がかかる (指名を受ける) be called to entertain the customer(s) at a drinking party.

おさつ お札 paper money; 《米》a bill, 《英》a note. (⇨紙幣, 札(ﾆ))

おさと お里 one's origin.
●お里が知れる (正体を暴露する) give 《him》away. (❗そんな下品な言葉づかいはやめなさい. お里が知れますよ Don't use such vulgar language. That will *give you away*.

*__おさない 幼い__ 〖年が少ない〗little, very young; 〖幼稚な〗childish (❗childlike (子供らしい, 純真な)と異なり軽蔑的に用いる); (未熟な) immature /ɪmətjʊər/.
●幼い男[女]の子 a *little* boy [girl] (❗通例 2-6 歳くらいをさす); a *very young* boy [girl] (❗a *young* boy [girl] では通例 10 代の若者をさす. ただし a *young* boy [girl] *of three* (3 歳の幼い男[女]の

おさなご
子)は可). ▶幼いころよく彼女と遊んだものだ I used to play with her when I was a *child* [when I was *small*, when I was *very young*]./I used to play with her *in* my *childhood* [*in* (my) *infancy*]. (⦅堅い言い方は⦆《書》. さらに年少であることを強調するときは ... in my *early* childhood [*in* (my) *early* infancy]. とする) ▶彼の考え方はとても幼い His way of thinking is very *childish* [*immature*]. ▶そんなことを言うなんて彼は本当に幼い It's really *childish of* [xfor] him *to* say something like that.

おさなご 幼子 an infant.

おさなごころ 幼心 (one's) childish mind. ▶祖母の死は幼心にとても悲しかった Though I was a small child, I felt very sad about my grandmother's death.

おさななじみ 幼なじみ a childhood friend. ▶私たちは幼なじみだ We have been friends since we were small children./We are *childhood friends*./We grew up together.

おざなり 御座成り ●おざなりを言う make perfunctory remarks; (その場限りのことを言う) say things just to suit the occasion.
— おざなりの 形 ⦅書⦆perfunctory.
— おざなりに 副 perfunctorily. ●おざなりに視察する make a *perfunctory* inspection ⟨*of*⟩.

:おさまる 治まる ❶ [安定した状態になる] (解決する) be settled; (終わる) end; (制御される) be brought under control. ▶口論ははるく治まった The argument *was settled* [*ended*] peacefully. ▶暴動[火事]はやっと治まった The riot [The fire] *was* finally *brought under control*.

❷ [静まる] (風・気持ちなどが) die (〜d; dying) down, ⦅書⦆subside; (痛みが和らぐ) ease (off), wear* off. ▶風は夜になって治まった The wind *died down* [⦅書⦆*subsided*, ⦅書⦆*abated*, (急に衰えて) *fell*] in the evening. ▶彼に対する怒りは治まらなかった My anger toward him didn't *die down* [⦅書⦆*subside*]./I couldn't *control* my anger toward him. ▶この薬を飲むと痛みは治まった The pain *eased* (*off*) [*wore off*, ⦅書⦆*subsided*] after I took this medicine./This medicine *removed* [*eased*, (消した) *killed*] the pain. ▶にわか雨でほこりがおさまった A shower *has laid* the dust.

*おさまる 収まる ❶ [きちんと中に入る] fit (-tt-) ⟨*into*⟩. ▶その服は全部この箱に収まるでしょう All (of) those clothes will *fit into* this box./This box will *hold* [*be big enough for*] all (of) those clothes. ▶この記事は20行では収まらない(=20行で書く[に減らす]ことができない) I can't *write* this article [*cut* this article *down*] *within* 20 lines.

❷ [解決がつく] be settled. ▶ストはまだ収まっていない The strike is still not *settled*.

*おさまる 納まる ❶ [地位などに] ▶重役に納まり返っている *be settled* and content in one's position as director.

❷ [納得する] (得心がいく) be satisfied ⟨*with*⟩; (承知する) consent ⟨*to*⟩; understand*. ▶その回答では彼らは納得しないだろう They will not *be satisfied with* that answer. ▶四方八方丸く納まるというわけにもいかないだろう It would be impossible to *satisfy* everybody concerned./I don't think everybody will be happy after all.

おさまる 修まる ▶彼の素行はいっこうに修まらない He hasn't *improved* his conduct at all.

おさむい お寒い (貧弱な) poor; (満足するには程遠い) far from satisfactory. ●お寒い福祉の予算 a *poor* welfare budget. ●あの大学の教授陣はお寒いかぎりだ The teaching staff at the college is *far from satisfactory* [*in a sorry state*]. (⦅直接 *very bad*, *worst* などといっていないことに注意)

:おさめる 収める ❶ [得る] ▶権力を手中に収める(合法的に) *come into* power; (非合法的に) *take* [*seize*] power. ▶勝利を収める *win* ⦅書⦆*gain*) a victory ⟨*over*⟩. ▶学校で優秀な成績を収める *achieve* [*have*, *get*] brilliant results at school. ▶ばく大な利益を収める *make* a huge profit ⟨*from*⟩. ▶実験は大成功を収めた They [We] *achieved* (a) great success in the experiment./The experiment was a great success. (⦅前方は a がついてもつかなくてもよいが, 後の方は具体的な事例なので a が必ずつく⦆)

❷ [しまう] (入れる) put*... ⟨*into*⟩; (戻す) put*... back ⟨*in*⟩; (片付ける) put*... away ⟨*in*⟩; (保管する) keep*... ⟨*in*⟩. ●リンゴを全部箱に収める *put* all the apples *into* boxes. ●道具箱を元の場所に収める *put* a tool box *back in* its place. ●絵を額ぶちに収める *set* a picture *in* a frame. ▶宝石類は金庫の中に厳重に収められていた The jewels *were kept* secure in a safe.

❸ [収録する] (一部として含む) include; (全体として含む) contain; (発表する) publish. ▶彼の論文がその雑誌に収められている His treatise /tríːtis/ *is included* [*is published*, *is printed*] in the journal.

❹ [範囲を越えさせない] ▶彼女は毎月の出費を15万円以内に収めるようにしている She tries to *keep* her monthly expenses *under* [*less than*, *within*] 150,000 yen.

*おさめる 治める ❶ [統治する] rule ⟨over ...⟩ (⦅権力を行使して専制的に支配する⦆), govern (⦅国家その他会社・家庭などの管理運営を行う⦆); (君臨する) reign ⟨*over*⟩. ▶国を治める *rule* ⟨*over*⟩ a country.

❷ [鎮静する] (力ずくで) suppress, put*... down (⦅後の方が口語的⦆); (話し合いなどで) settle. ▶暴動を治める *suppress* [*put down*] a riot; *bring* a riot *under control*. ▶紛争を治める *settle* a dispute. ▶彼女はけんかを丸く治めた She *settled* the quarrel peacefully.

おさめる 納める ❶ [納入する] (支払う) pay; (配達する) deliver; (供給する) supply. ●税金[授業料]を納める *pay* (one's) taxes [school fees]. ●小売店に商品を納める *supply* [*deliver*] goods *to* retail stores.

❷ [受け取る] accept. ▶これは感謝の印です, どうぞお納めください This is just a token of my thanks. Please *accept* [x*take*] it.

❸ [終える] finish. ▶彼らは歌い納めに大ヒット曲を歌った They *finished* (*up*) *with* [*by singing*] their biggest hit.

❹ [しまう] (元の場所へ戻す) put*... back; (片付ける) put*... away. (⇨収める)

おさめる 修める ❶ [課程などを修了する] complete; [技能・知識を習得する] acquire, master. ●2年間の修士課程を修める *complete* the two-year MA course. (⇨履修する) ❷ [修養する] (⇨修養)

おさらい [復習] a review; [劇・音楽などの下げいこ] (a) rehearsal. ▶前の授業のおさらいをする *do* a *review* of the last lesson; *review* [*go over*] the last lesson.

おさん お産 [出産] childbirth; (過程) a delivery; [分娩 (ぶんべん)] (a) labor. ●お産をする give birth to a baby [a child]; have a baby. ●お産で死ぬ die in *childbirth* [*giving* (*him*) *birth*]. ●お産が楽である have an easy (↔a difficult) *delivery* [*labor*]. ▶花子の時も陽平の時もお産が楽だった I had *easy births* with Hanako and Yohei.

おさんどん 〘台所仕事〙〈人〉a kitchen maid; 〈仕事〉(do) kitchen work.

おし 押し ❶〘押すこと〙a push; 〈重し〉a weight. ▶ひと押しでドアを開ける open the door *with* [〘まれ〙*at*] one *push*. ▶机をひと押しで与える *give* the desk *a push*. (❗×give a *push* to the desk とはいわない) ❷〘強引なこと〙aggressiveness, 〘話〙push. ▶押しの強いセールスマン an *aggressive* [a *pushing*, 〘押しつけがましい〙a *pushy*] salesman.

おじ 叔父, 伯父 an uncle. ▶おじ夫婦が今日訪ねてくる My *uncle* and aunt are coming to see us today. ▶太郎おじさんはどこ？ Where is *Uncle* Taro? 〘❗Uncle（Taro）は呼びかけにも用いる. Uncle は姓の前には用いない. (⇨おじさん)〙

おしあいへしあい 押し合いへし合い 〘名〙▶バスひとつ乗るのにも押し合いへし合いだからいやになる I don't like having to *push and shove* in order to get on the bus.
── 押し合いへし合いする 〘動〙push and shove /ʃʌv/.

おしあける 押し開ける push (the door) open; push open 《the door》. (❗前の方が普通)

おしあげる 押し上げる ▶ハッチを押し上げる *push* the hatch *up*. ▶彼を押し上げて塀を越えさせる *boost* him *over* the fence.

おしあてる 押し当てる ▶窓ガラスに顔を押し当てる *press* one's face *against* the windowpane. ▶手を顔に押し当てて泣く *sob into* one's hands.

***おしい** 惜しい 〘形〙❶〘残念な〙regrettable. ▶惜しい！ What a *shame* [a *pity*]!/How *regrettable*! ▶1点差で試合に負けたのは惜しい It's a *shame* [a *pity*, 〘不運だ〙*too bad*] 〘that〙 we lost the game by one point. ▶後の方は *Too bad* (×that) we lost the game by one point. ともいえる/What a *shame* [a *pity*] 〘that〙 we lost the game by one point! ▶惜しいことに好機を逸した *Unfortunately* I missed a good chance. ▶試合は惜しいところで雨になった It began to rain just in the heat of the game. ❷〘もったいない〙be too good 《to do》. ▶このバッグは捨てるには惜しい This bag *is too good to* throw away. ▶この部屋を子供の遊び場にしておくのは惜しい This room *is too good for* children to play in. (❗in に注意) ▶お前に金をやるのは惜しい I *grudge* 《giving》 [×to give] you my money. ❸〘貴重な〙precious, dear. ▶だれでも命は惜しい Life is *dear* [*precious*, everything] to everybody. ▶everything は「最も大切なもの」の意/〘ずっと生きていたい〙Anybody wants to stay alive. ▶まったく惜しい人を亡くした（= 彼の死は我々にとって大きな損失だ）His death is a *great loss* to us. ▶時間が惜しい（= ぐずぐずしている暇はない）の意で急ごう There's [We have] no time to lose. We'd better hurry.
── 惜しそうに 〘副〙〘物惜しみして〙grudgingly; 〘いやいや〙unwillingly.

おじいさん ❶〘祖父〙a grandfather; 〘話〙a grandpa, 〘話〙a gran(d)dad, 〘米話〙a gran(d)daddy. (❗ いずれも呼びかけるときは、無冠詞で通例大文字で、Grandpa が最も普通) ❷〘老人〙an old man 〘殿-men〙. (⇨おばあさん❷)

おしいただく 押し頂く hold 《it》 up to one's head.

おしいる 押し入る 〘無理に入る〙force one's way 《into》; 〘強盗などが〙break* 《into》. ▶留守中に泥棒が押し入った A thief *broke in* [*into* our house] while we were away. (❗「押し入り強盗事件」は a break-in, その強盗は a housebreaker という)

おしいれ 押し入れ a closet with Japanese sliding doors. (❗単に closet では衣類・食糧品などの収納室〘庫〙を表し、日本の押し入れとは少し異なる. タオル類だけの収納であれば linen closet, 立ったまま入れるほどの大きい物置であれば a walk-in closet という)

おしうり 押し売り 〘名〙〘行為〙a forced sale, the hard sell; 〘人〙a high-pressure [a pushy] (door-to-door) salesman 〘殿-men〙. ▶押し売り無用 〘掲示〙〘米〙No *solicitors*.
── 押し売りする 〘動〙▶金〘㈲〙を押し売りする force [pressure, 〘主に米〙pressurize] 《him》 to buy [into buying] gold.

おしえ 教え 〘道徳的・宗教的な教え〙teaching(s) (❗しばしば複数形で); 〘実学・学問上の指導〙〘やや書〙instruction. (⇨教訓) ▶キリストの教えに従う follow Christ's *teachings* [the *teachings* of Christ]. ▶ラテン語の教えを受ける（= 体系的に教わる） receive *instruction* in Latin 《from》.

おしえご 教え子 〘学生〙one's student; 〘生徒〙one's pupil 〘❗個人レッスンの場合も含む〙.

おしえこむ 教え込む teach*; 〘訓練する〙train; 〘習慣・思想などをたたき込む〙〘書〙inculcate. ▶犬に芸を教え込む *teach* [*train*] a dog to do some tricks; *teach* [×train] some tricks *to* a dog. ▶子供たちに行儀作法を教え込む *inculcate* good manners *in* children; *inculcate* children *with* good manners. ▶子供に健全な道徳を教え込む（= 植えつける）*implant* sound virtues *in* one's child.

:おしえる 教える

WORD CHOICE 教える

teach 学科・技能などを教授すること. ▶子供に英語を教える *teach* the kids English; *teach* English *to* the kids.

educate 主に高等教育制度のもとで、高度な学問・知識を体系的に教授すること. しばしば過去分詞で用いる. ▶ケンブリッジ大学で教えを受けた I *was educated* at Cambridge.

instruct 実践的に、機器の操作法や技能・技術などを指導すること. ▶子供にパソコンの使い方を教える *instruct* the kids how to use computers.

頻度チャート

teach ████████████████████
educate ██████
instruct ███

20　40　60　80　100 (%)

❶〘教授する〙teach* (❗単に情報を伝えるだけの場合には用いないことに注意. (⇨❷)); 〘特定分野を体系的に〙〘やや書〙instruct; 〘能力を引き出す〙educate; 〘指導する〙coach.
①〘...を教える〙▶子供たちを教える *teach* children. (❗×teach *to* children とはいわない) ▶ピアノを教える *teach* piano; *give lessons in* piano; *give piano lessons*. ▶第1学年を教える *teach* in [×at] the first grade. ▶彼は英語を教えている（= 英語の先生だ）He *teaches* [×is teaching] English. (❗習慣的行為を表すので is teaching とはいわない)/He *is a teacher of* English [an *English teacher*]. (❗an English teacher は「英国人教師」の意) ▶話術を教えることはできない The art of conversation cannot *be taught* [*learnt*] only through practice].
②〘...に～を[だと]教える〙▶彼らに英語を教える *teach* them English; *teach* English *to* them; *coach* them *in* English. ▶あるクラスに物理学を教える *instruct* [*give instruction to*] a class *in* physics. ▶彼に車の運転を教える *teach* him to drive

[how to drive] (a car). (!過去形の場合, to の方は「教えた…できるようにした」, how to の方は「仕方を教えた」の意となる) ▶彼は生徒たちにうそをついてはならないと教えた He *taught* his pupils *that* they *should not tell lies.*/He *taught* his pupils not *to* tell lies.

③《…で教える》(a) 《場所》● 高校で教える *teach at high school*;《米》*teach high school*.

(b) 《道具》● 視聴覚教材[日本語]で英語を教える *teach* English *with* audio-visual aids [*in* Japanese].

❷《表示する》(口頭で) tell*; (実際に示して) show*; (知らせる) let*《him》know,《書》inform.(⇨通知する) ▶彼にその機械の使い方を教える *show* him how to use the machine. ▶お名前を教えていただけませんか Could you *tell* [×*teach*] me your name(, please)? / May I have [*ask*] your name(, please)? ▶何か変わったことがあったらすぐ教えてください *Let* me *know* at once if anything happens./ Please *inform* me at once of any change.(!後の方は堅い言い方) ▶彼の電話番号を教えてくださいませんか Could you *give* me his phone number? ▶アメリカの大学への入学について教えていただきたいのですが I'd like (you to *give* me) some *information on* how to get into an American university.

会話「ちょっと教えていただきたい(= 不思議なので知りたい)のですが, どうしたらそんなにお元気でいられるのですか」「ただ規則正しい生活をしているだけです」"I'm just *curious*. How do you keep yourself in such good shape?" "Just by keeping regular hours."

会話「すみませんが, ここの電話のかけ方を教えてくださいませんか」「いいですとも. こちらは初めてですか」「ええ, 今着いたばかりです」"Excuse me. Could you show [×*teach*] me how to make a phone call here?" "Sure. Are you new to this country?" "Yes. I've just arrived."

おしおき お仕置き 图 (a) punishment.
— **お仕置きする** 動 punish.
おしかえす 押し返す push [press]... back.
おしかける 押し掛ける ❶《訪れる》(招待もされないのに) invite oneself《*to* a party》, come* [go*] uninvited《*to* a party》, gatecrash. ● 押しかけ客 an *uninvited* guest;《話》a (gate)crasher.

❷《押し寄せる》(群がる) crowd《in, into》,《やや書》throng《*to*》. (⇨押し寄せる) ▶彼の話を聞こうと押しかける *crowd* in to hear him speak.

おじぎ お辞儀 图 a bow /báu/.(!bow はあいさつとしてのおじぎというより, 尊敬・崇拝・感謝・服従を表す動作. ただし女性が男性に, または女性同士の場合には握手をせずに軽くおじぎをすることも多い)

— **お辞儀(を)する** 動 bow, make* a bow《*to*》. ▶私たちはお互いに別れのおじぎをした We said goodbye, *bowing* low to each other. ▶彼は私たちに丁寧に[軽く]おじぎをした He *bowed* politely [slightly] *to* us. /He *made* a polite [a slight] *bow to* us. ▶彼女はおじぎをして感謝の気持ちを表した She *bowed* her thanks.

おしきせ お仕着せ 图 (制服) (a)《company》uniform. ● お仕着せの和服姿のホテル従業員 hotel workers in kimono *uniform*. ▶この行事はお仕着せ(= 上から強制されたもの)だと彼らは言った They said that this event had *been forced on* them.

おじぎそう おじぎ草 《植物》a sensitive plant.《参考》mimosa (ミモザ)は本来は「眠り草」の総称)

おしきる 押し切る ▶数で押し切る *force* one's *way by numbers.* ▶彼女は親の反対を押し切って(= 反対にもかかわらず)結婚した She got married *in spite of* (制して) *over*] her parents' opposition.

おしくも 惜しくも ❶《残念ながら》to one's regret, regrettably (⇨惜しい ❶);《失望したことに》to one's disappointment;《小差で》by a narrow margin. ▶惜しくも入選を逃がした To our regret [*disappointment*], he could not win a prize. ▶彼は惜しくも落選した He was defeated in the election *by a narrow margin.*

おしくらまんじゅう 押し競饅頭 《play》push and shove /ʃʌ́v/.

おじける 怖じける 怖気付く 《怖くなる》be [*get**] frightened [scared]; (こわくなってやめる)《話》《軽蔑的に》chicken out《*of*》; 《度胸を失う》lose* one's nerve; 《おどおどする》become* timid [nervous]. (⇨怖気付く [気後れがする])

会話「せっかく段取りしてあげたのにどうしてブラインドデートに行かなかったの」「きっとなってしまったの」「本当に臆病者ね」"Why didn't you go on the blind date I had fixed up for you?" "Well, I *got cold feet* at the last minute." "What a coward!"

おしげなく 惜しげなく generously, freely. ● 惜しげなく慈善事業に寄付する give《one's money》*generously [freely]* to charity.

おしこみ 押し込み ▶押し込み強盗 (行為) a break-in; (人) a housebreaker. (⇨強盗)

おしこむ 押し込む ❶《押して入れる》● (ビデオに)カセットを押し込む push [*press*] a cassette *in* [*in(to)*] a video]. ● (ズボンの中に)ワイシャツの裾を押し込む *tuck* one's shirt *in* [*into* one's pants]. ● かばんに本を押し込む *push* [*press*, (乱暴に) *shove* /ʃʌ́v/, (ぐいっと) *thrust*, *force*] one's books into one's bag. (⇨詰め込む) ▶ゴール前の混戦からドログバがこぼれ球をきっちり押し込んだ 《サッカー》Drogba picked up the ball in goal-front fracas and *pushed* home neatly.

❷《強盗に入る》break* in. (⇨押し入る)

おしこめる 押し込める ❶《押し込む》▶彼らは私たち全員を1台のバスの中に押し込めた They *jammed* us all *into* one bus. (⇨押し込む) ❷《閉じ込める》shut* [lock]... (up)《*in*》. (⇨閉じ込める)

おしころす 押し殺す ▶笑いを押し殺す *suppress* [*stifle*] a laughter. ● 押し殺した声で in a *subdued* voice.

おしさげる 押し下げる push [press, (無理やり) force, (余儀なく) drive*]... down. ▶輸入野菜が国産野菜の値段を押し下げた Imported vegetables *drove down* the prices of home-grown ones.

おじさん 小父さん 《大人の男》a man (⑳ men); 《呼びかけ》sir, Mister. (⇨伯父) ▶よそのおじさん a stranger. ▶おじさんの仕事は何ですか What do you do, Sir [*Uncle*]? (!前の方は丁寧な, 後の方は子供が用いる呼びかけ方. いずれも時に大文字で用いる)

おしずし 押し寿司 《a cut of》pressed *sushi* (topped with a variety of ingredients).

おしすすめる 推し進める ▶その計画を推し進める go [(強引に) *push*] ahead with the plan; (助長する) *further* the progress of the plan.

おしせまる 押し迫る draw* near. (⇨迫る ❶)

おしたおす 押し倒す ▶彼を後ろから押し倒す *push* him *down* [*over*] from behind.

おしだし 押し出し ▶押し出しで1点入れる 《野球》score a run on a bases-loaded walk. ● 押し出しで1点与える 《野球》walk [force] in one run. ● 押し出しの立派な男 a gentleman of fine (dignified, imposing, stately) *presence*.

おしだす 押し出す push... out. ▶リングの外に相手を押し出す *push* [(強引に) *force*, (乱暴に) *shove* /ʃʌ́v/,

おしたてる one's opponent *out of* the ring. ● 練り歯みがきを チューブから押し出す (=しぼり出す) *squeeze* toothpaste *out of* the tube.

おしたてる 押し立てる 〚看板・旗などを〛set ... up, (高く) put... up;〚人を前面に〛bring [push] *him* forward (*as* captain). ● 土俵際で押し立てる (=押し返す) *push and push* (*him*) *to the edge of* the ring.

おしだまる 押し黙る become* 〚(無言で)つらぬく〛 keep*, remain〛 silent;〚(貝のように)(話)〛clam (-mm-) up.

おしちや お七夜 the seventh night after birth.

おしつけがましい 押し付けがましい 《話》pushy. ▶ 彼にはどこか押しつけがましいところがある He has something *pushy* around him. /自分の思いどおりに人を動かすところがある) He sometimes forces his own way on other people.

おしつける 押し付ける push [press, pin (-nn-)] ... (*against*).〚❗pin は「くぎうけにする」の意〛; (受け入れるよう強制する) force [impose] ... (*on*)〚❗後の方が堅い語〛. ● 彼を壁に押しつける push [press, pin] him *against* the wall. ● 自分の意見を他人に押しつける force [impose] one's opinion(s) *on* [*to*] others. ● 誤りの責任を彼女に押しつける (=彼女のせいにする) put [place] the blame for the mistake *on her*; blame the mistake *on her*. ● やっかいな仕事を押しつけられる *be left with* a difficult job. ▶ しつこいセールスの女性に高い化粧品を押しつけられた I *was forced to* buy expensive cosmetics by a pushy saleswoman. ▶ 最近のテレビは, とかく一つの視点を押しつけてくる These days [Today] television programs tend (to try) to *force* a certain point of view on viewers [*us*].

おしっこ 《話》(a) pee /píː/, 《主に英語》(a) wee /wíː/, No. 1 [one]〚❗時に動詞にも用いる〛● おしっこをする do [have] a *pee* [a *wee*]; pee, wee. ● おしっこに行く go for a *pee* [a *wee*]. ▶ 夜中におしっこに起きますか Do you get up at night to pass (your) *urine*? ● おしっこ(に行きたい)! I want to *pee* [*wee*]!/I want (to do [have]) a *pee* [a *wee*]!

おしつぶす 押し潰す crush, (ぐしゃぐしゃに) squash. ● 帽子をしりで (=しりに) 敷いて押し潰す I *crushed* [*squash*] a hat by sitting on it. ▶ 彼の自転車はトラックの下敷きになってぺちゃんこに押し潰された His bicycle *was crushed flat* under the truck. ▶ 家は雪の重みで押し潰された The house *collapsed* under the weight of the snow.

おしつまる 押し詰まる ● 押し詰まってきた (=切迫している) 情勢 an *urgent* situation. ▶ 今年もいよいよ押し詰まってきた It's almost [(very) nearly] *the end of the year*. /(近づいてくる) The end of the year *is getting close* [*near*].

おして 押して ▶ 彼は病を押して (=病気をおして) 出勤した Though [Although] he was sick, he went to the office. /He went to the office *in spite of* his sickness. 〚❗前の方が口語的〛

おして 推して ● 推して知るべし ● 結果は推して知るべし (=結果を容易に想像できる) You can easily *imagine* the result.

おしとおす 押し通す 〚無理に通す〛push [force] ... through;〚言い張る〛insist (*on*; *that* 節);〚固執する〛persist (*in*). ● 我がままを押し通す get [*have*] one's *own way*. ● 自分の計画を押し通す (=遂行する) *carry* out one's plan *through*. ▶ 彼は自分の正当性を押し通した He *insisted on* his being correct. /He *insisted that* he was correct. ▶ 田舎に引っ越した後も彼は都会の暮らしぶりを押し通そうとした He tried to *persist in* his urban lifestyle even after he moved to the country.

おしとどめる 押し止める hold* back. ▶ 涙を押しとどめる *a hold back* one's tears. ▶ 警官は何十人もの侵入者を押しとどめるために, 空へ向けて発砲した The police fired in the air to *hold* [*keep*] *back* dozens of trespassers. ▶ 私には彼女が妻子ある人と駆け落ちしようとするのを押しとどめることができない I can't *stop* her *from* running away with a married man with a family.

おしどり 〚鳥〛a mandarin duck. ▶ 麻生夫妻は彫刻部門でおしどり入選を果たした Mr. and Mrs. Aso both won the prize in the sculpture division. ● おしどり夫婦 a happily married couple; a loving couple, 《話》love birds (❗おどけた用法).

おしながす 押し流す ▶ 洪水で橋は押し流された The flood *washed* the bridge *away*. /The bridge *was washed away* 〚(運び去られた)was carried *away*〛by the flood. ▶ 船は下流へ押し流された The boat *was washed* [*was carried*] down the river.

おしなべて 押し並べて 〚概して〛generally (⇨一般(的)に);〚すべて一様に〛all (⇨すべて).

おしのける 押し退ける push 〚(乱暴に)〛shove /ʃʌ́v/, (強く) thrust ... aside, 〚ひじで〛elbow ... aside, 〚肩で〛shoulder ... aside. ▶ 彼を押しのける *push him aside* 〚(じゃまにならないように)out of the way〛. ● 肩で力づくで, 乱暴に〛人ごみを押しのけて進む *shoulder* [*force*; *shove*] one's *way through* the crowd.

おしのび お忍び ● お忍びの女王 a queen *incognito* /ɪnkɑːɡníːtoʊ/. ● お忍びで旅行する travel *incognito*.

おしば 押し葉 a pressed leave.
おしはかる 押し量る guess. (⇨推測)
おしばな 押し花 a pressed flower. ▶ 本にはさんで押し花をつくる *press* a flower *in* [*between*] the pages of] a book.

おしひろげる 押し広げる spread ... out (by force).
おしひろめる 押し広める (⇨広める)
おしべ 雄蕊 〚植物〛a stamen /stéɪmən/.
おしボタン 押しボタン a púsh bùtton.
おしぼり お絞り an *oshibori*; (説明的に) a moist hand towel (used for cleaning your hands usually before you eat and drink at restaurants or outdoors).

おしまい 御仕舞い ● 卵はおしまいです (=売り切れです) Eggs are sold out. ▶ これでおしまいだ. 殺されてしまう *This is it*. They're going to kill me.

おしみない 惜しみない ● 惜しみない賞賛 *lavish* [*unstinting*] praise.

＊**おしむ** 惜しむ ❶〚出し惜しむ〛(労力・費用などを) spare 〚❗通例否定文で〛; (物を与えるのを) grudge; (倹約する) be frugal (*of*); (けちをきる) be stingy (*of*). ● 骨身を惜しまず働く work without *sparing oneself*; *spare* no pains over one's work. ● 金を惜しむ *be frugal of* one's money; (気前がよくない) *be not generous* [*free*] *with* one's money. ● 着る物に金を惜しまず遣う spend money *freely* [*generously*] *on* one's dress. ▶ 彼は我々を援助するための努力[骨身; 費用]を惜しまなかった He *spared* no effort [pains; expense] to help us. ▶ 彼は自分の犬に食べさせる物すら惜しんだ He *grudged* (giving) his dog even its food. ▶ 君のためならどんな協力も惜しまない (=いつでも喜んで協力する) I'm always *willing to* help you.

❷〚残念に思う〛regret (-tt-); (嘆く)《やや書》lament; (気が進まない) be reluctant [unwilling] (*to*). ● その青年の死を惜しむ *lament* [*regret*] the young man's death. ▶ 友との別れを惜しむ *be reluctant* to leave 〚《書》 part from〛one's friend.

おしめ

▶彼女は彼が好機を何回も逸したことを惜しんだ She *regretted* his having missed [*that* he had missed] his good chances. (❗後の方が口語的)
▶これは彼の非常に惜しむべき失態です This is a most *regrettable* [*lámentable*] mistake on his side.
▶惜しむらくは、彼は才ありながら若死にした *It is a pity* [*It is to be regretted*, *It is regrettable*] that he (should have) died young, though he was talented.

❸ [尊重する] value. ●命より名を惜しむ I *value* honor *above* life. ●彼は寸暇を惜しんで英文学を研究した (あらゆる暇な時間を利用して) He *made use of every spare moment* to study English literature./(暇な時間すべて使った) He *spent all his spare time* (*in*) *studying* English literature. (❗in は省略する方が普通)

おしめ (米) a diaper. (⇨おむつ)

おしめり お湿り ▶いいお湿りですね It's a *welcome rain*. (❗晴天の続いたあとに降る, 適度の雨のこと)

おしもおされもしない ●押しも押されもしない (=揺るぎのない) 大スター an *unchallenged* [(一流の) *a leading*] superstar. ●押しも押されもしない (=名声が定まった) 偉大な学者 a great scholar of *established* reputation. ▶彼は今や押しも押されもしない (=定評のある) 作家です He is now a *fully established* writer [a writer *with an established reputation*].

おしもんどう 押し問答 ⓝ a hot argument 《*about*》; (口論) a wrangle. ── **押し問答する** ⓥ wrangle 《*about*》; bandy words 《*with*》.

おじや (⇨雑炊)

おしゃか お釈迦 ●おしゃかになる (失敗に終わる) come to nothing; (台なしになる) be ruined.

おしゃく お酌 (⇨酌)

おしゃぶり (口さびしい赤ん坊用の) a pacifier; (歯の生えかけた赤ん坊用の) a teething ring.

おしゃべり ⓝ a talk (❗打ち解けた話から会談, 講演まで幅広い意味の語); (社交的な言い方) a chatter (❗騒がしさを暗示); (うわさ, 世間話に) a gossip. ●おしゃべりな人 (話し好きな人) a talkative [(話した) a chatty] person; (ぺちゃくちゃ話す人) a chatterbox (主に子供に); (うわさ話をする人) a gossip. ●おしゃべりである (話) have a big mouth. ▶「おしゃべりはやめなさい」と先生は言った "Stop all that *chattering*," said the teacher.

── **おしゃべり(を)する** ⓥ ▶彼とおしゃべりする *chat* [*have a chat*] *with* him. ▶彼女たちはベンチに座って長い間おしゃべりをした They sat on the bench and *talked* for a long time. ▶週末にはよく友達同士で簡単な夕食を用意してはおしゃべりして夜を過ごした On weekends I often arranged little dinners with my friends and *chatted* the night away.

おしゃま [ませていること] ⓝ (⇨ませる) ▶おしゃまな子 a pre*cócious* child. ▶あの子まだ 5 つなんだぞ. おしゃまだけど The girl is only five years old, but she talks just *like a grown-up*.

*****おじゃま お邪魔** ▶あすお邪魔したいと思っています I'd like to *visit* [*come to see*] you tomorrow. (❗後の方がくだけた言い方) ▶長々とお邪魔しました (日本人的発想) (多く時間を取ってすみません) I am sorry to *have taken up so much of your time*/(米英人的発想) (時間を割いてくださって本当にありがとうございました) I really appreciate the time you've taken to talk with me/(お時間を割いてくださってありがとう) Thank you for your time/(そろそろおいとまします) I think I must be going now. ▶お邪魔してすみませんが緊急の伝言があります Sorry to *disturb* [*interrupt*] you, but there's an urgent message.

会話 「ようこそおいでくださいました」「こちらこそ、お邪魔します」"Thank you for coming." "Don't mention it; *thanks for having us*."

会話 「あら、もうお帰りになるの?」「これ以上いたらお邪魔虫になりそうだからね」"Oh, are you leaving so soon?" "If I stay any longer, I'm afraid I'll *be a third wheel* 《米》[*play gooseberry*《英》]." (❗恋人同士など 2 人より 2 人以上いたい人たちに対して用いる)

おしゃれ お洒落 ── **おしゃれな** ⓟ ●おしゃれな (=流行の先端をゆく) 街 a (*trendy and*) *fashionable* street. ●おしゃれな (=気[成句], 素敵な) 包装紙 *tasteful* wrapping paper. (⇨気[成句], 素敵な) ●彼女はおしゃれだ She *is always careful about* her appearance./(着こなしがよい) She is a *good* [*a smart*] *dresser*. ▶絹のスカーフは首に巻くと暖かいし, おしゃれにもなる (=見ばえがよくなる) If you wear a silk scarf around your neck, it will keep you warm and *make you look attractive* as well.

── **おしゃれする** ⓥ (正装する[している]) dress up; (女性がめかす) (話) doll up.

おじゃん ●おじゃんになる fall through; be ruined; (中止させられる) be canceled. (⇨駄目になる)

おしゅう 汚臭 (悪臭) a bad [an unpleasant, a nasty] smell; (むかつくような) a stink.

おしょう 和尚 [僧] a Buddhist priest; [住職] the chief priest of a temple.

おじょうさん お嬢さん [他人の娘] your [his, her, their] daughter; [呼びかけ] Miss (❗気さくな呼びかけで、店員やウェートレスなどに対してよく用いる. 無作法と受けとられることも多い) young lady; madam; (米話) ma'am (↔sir) (❗(米)では「奥様」の意にもなる. (英)では ma'am は女王などの高位の女性に用いる) ▶お嬢さん育ち (⇨坊ちゃん) ▶ちょっとお嬢さん, そこいてHey, *Miss*. Get out of the way./Excuse me, *ma'am*. Make way, please. (❗後の方は丁寧な言い方. いずれも複数の場合は young ladies) ▶お嬢さんが 9 月に結婚されるそうですね I hear *your daughter* is getting married in September.

会話 (ポーターが客に) 「お嬢さん, 荷物をお持ちしましょうか」「ええ, お願いします」"Can I help you with your baggage, *young lady*?" "Oh, yes. Thank you."

おしょく 汚職 ⓝ corruption;《主に米》graft (❗政府高官などが関与する大がかりな汚職 (⇨疑獄)).

── **汚職(を)する** ⓥ practice corruption; (わいろを受け取る) take [accept] a bribe.

●汚職事件 a corruption [a graft] case. ●汚職役人 a corrupt official (❗この corrupt は形容詞);《主に米》a grafter.

おじょく 汚辱 (恥) (a) shame; (辱め) (an) insult; (屈辱) (a) humiliation.

おしよせる 押し寄せる [群がる] crowd; (押し合って) throng; (大挙して) flock; (うようよと) swarm. ▶週末に田舎へ押し寄せる (=群れをなして行く) *flock to* [(どっと流れ込む) *pour into*] the country for the weekend. ▶サインを求めて歌手の周りに押し寄せた (=群がる) *crowd* [*swarm*, *throng*] *around* the singer for his [her] autograph. ▶若い女の子たちが大勢劇場へ押し寄せた Young girls *crowded* [*thronged*] the theater./The theater *was crowded* [*thronged*] *with* young girls. ▶高波が沿岸に押し寄せた High waves *swept* [*hit*] the coast.

おしろい 白粉 (face) powder. ●おしろいをつけている wear powder (化粧) (powder). ●おしろいをそこそこに [薄く] 塗る *powder* one's face heavily [lightly]. ▶このおしろいつきが悪い This *powder* won't stay on [x*in*] my face.

おしろいばな 白粉花 〚植物〛 a four-o'clock; a marvel-of-Peru (⑱ marvels-of-Peru).

オシログラフ 〚電気〛 an oscillograph.

オシロスコープ 〚電気〛 an oscilloscope.

おじろわし 尾白鷲 〚鳥〛 a white-tailed eagle.

おしわける 押し分ける ▶人ごみを押し分けて進む push [force; 乱暴に] shove /ʃʌv/; (肩で) shoulder; (ひじで) elbow] one's way through the crowd. ▶彼らは人を押し分けて最前列に出た They *pushed* their *way* [×ways] *to* the front row.

おじん an old guy.

おしんこ お新香 (⇨漬物)

:おす 押す ❶〚力を加える〛push;《俗話》shove /ʃʌv/; 《やや書》thrust*; press.

使い分け push 特定の意図をもって, 力を入れて何かを自分の反対側に押し動かすこと.
shove 人や物を一定方向に乱暴に押すこと.
thrust 人や物を強く突くように押すこと.
press 一定の圧力を加えて物・人を押すこと.

●ボタンを押す push [press] the button. (❗カメラのシャッターを押す場合は press [×push] the shutter. 軽く触れる感じのときは touch the button) ●テーブルをすみへ押しやる push [press, (ぐいと) thrust] a table *into* a corner. ●窓を押して開ける[閉める] *push* the window open [shut]. ●そんなに強く押さないでください Please don't *push* (me) so hard. (❗目的語が明らかなときは省略可) ▶彼は肩でドアを押した He *pushed* the door with his shoulder./He gave the door *a push* with his shoulder./He *pushed* his shoulder *against* the door. (❗against は不動詞なのに用いられ, …, but it didn't open. (しかし開かなかった)のような表現が続く) ▶彼は皿をぐいと押してわきにやった[テーブルから落とした] He *shoved* the dish *aside* [*off* the table]. ▶それは重すぎて持ち上げられない, 押して運ばなければならない It's too heavy to lift, we'll have to *walk* it. (❗walk は「押して歩く」の意)

❷〚印形を押す〛stamp; (公式に) seal. ●封筒に住所を印で押す *stamp* an envelope *with* one's address; *stamp* one's address on an envelope.

❸〚その他の表現〛▶彼は今や押しも押されもしない作家だ (⇨押しも押されもしない) ▶駅は押すな押すなの混雑だった The station *was jammed with* people. ▶わが社はライバル会社に押されている We're *losing ground to* our rival company. ▶彼は病を押して(=病気にかかわらず)出勤した (⇨押して) ▶私立の高校に押されっぱなしで(=追い越されるばかりで), 年々この学校も進学率は悪くなる一方だ Overtaken by several private high schools, we [they] are falling further behind with the success rate of our [their] students' college entrance exams. (❗主語は this school でなく we [they] となることに注意)

> **翻訳のこころ** メロスは, 待つことはできぬ, どうか明日にしてくれたまえ, とさらに押して頼んだ (太宰治『走れメロス』) Melos *pressed* [*pushed*] further *and entreated*, "Please do it tomorrow, for I can't wait any longer." (❗「押して頼む」は press [push] and entreat ((意見などを)強く訴え説得しようとする)と表す)

*****おす 雄** a male, (話) a he; (鳥の) a cock; (牛・象など大形動物の) a bull; (羊・鹿・ウサギなど小形動物の) a buck. ●雄の象 an elephant *bull*, a *bull* elephant.
●雄牛 a bull. ●雄猫 a male cat; a he-cat; a tomcat.

おす Howdy! (⇨おっす)

おす 推す ❶[推薦する] recommend. (⇨推薦する)
❷[推量する] (⇨察する) ▶結果は推して知るべし (⇨推して [成句])

オズ Oz; the Land of Oz. (参考)「オズの魔法使い」に出てくる魔法の国

おすい 汚水 〚汚れた水〛filthy water; 〚汚染された水〛polluted water; 〚廃水〛waste water; 〚下水〛sewage.
●汚水処理 sewage disposal.

おずおず (びくびくして) timidly; (ためらって) hesitantly, hesitatingly; (内気で) shyly. ▶彼女は遅刻したのでおずおずと教室に入った She entered the classroom *timidly* because she was late for school.

オスカー an Oscar /ɑ́skər/. (参考) アカデミー賞受賞者に与えられる小型黄金像)
●オスカー賞 the Oscar Awards (of the American Academy of Motion Picture Arts and Sciences), the Academy Awards.

おすそわけ お裾分け ▶卵をたくさんもらったので近所の人にお裾分けした I got [received] too many eggs, so I *shared* them *with* one of my neighbors [*asked* one of my neighbors *to* have some].

オズのまほうつかい『オズの魔法使い』the Wizard of Oz. (参考) ボームの童話)

おすまし お澄まし ❶[すました態度] (⇨澄ます❷)
❷[すまし汁] clear soup.

おすみつき お墨付き (正式な許可) an official go-ahead, authorization (❗前の方は口語的); (正式な保証) an official guarantee. ▶大阪府からお墨付きをもらう get a *stamp of approval* [《話》the go-ahead] 《for it》*from* Osaka Prefectural Government. ▶その戦争は国連のお墨付きなしで始められた The war was started without UN *authorization*.

オスロ 〚ノルウェーの首都〛Oslo /ázlou, ás-/.

オセアニア Oceania /òuʃiǽniə/.

おせいぼ お歳暮 a year-end gift [present]. (⇨歳暮, お中元)

おせおせ 押せ押せ ❶[押しまくる] keep* on pushing. ▶第8ラウンドからはチャンピオン側の押せ押せムードになった After the seventh round, the champion got strength and *was always on the offensive*. (❗「攻勢の状態にあった」の意)
❷[しわ寄せされている] ▶夏休みの大半はバイトをしていたので宿題が押せ押せになってしまった I spent most of my summer working part-time, so I've *been pressed with* a lot of homework.

おせじ お世辞 (大げさ, 心にもない) (a) flattery; (社交上の) a compliment (❗「ほめ言葉」の意で, flattery の持つ含みはない). ●心にもないお世辞を言う pay [make] an insincere [an empty] *compliment* ((to him)). ▶彼は歌が上手だと彼女にお世辞を言った He *flattered* her *about* [*on*] her singing./He said in [as] a *compliment* that she is a good singer./He *complimented* her *on* singing beautifully. ▶私にお世辞を言ってもだめだよ *Flattery* will get you nowhere with me. ▶彼はお世辞がうまい He has a *flattering* tongue./He's a *flatterer*./ (軽蔑で) He's a smooth talker. ▶彼女にお世辞にも歌が上手だとはいえない(= 上手な歌手にはほど遠い) She is far from (being) a good singer. (❗《話》では being は通例省略される)

会話 「まあ, お世辞のうまいこと」「いいえ, 本当にそう思うわ」"Oh, ↘come ↗on! You *flatter* me!/(口先だけでしょ) Don't you saying that!" "No, I mean it./I'm being honest with you." (❗いずれもほめてもらったときに謙遜していう言い方. being honest に注意)

おせち 会話「すばらしい出来の作品だ」「それ本心？ それともお世辞を言っているだけなの」"It's an excellent piece of work." "Do you réally ˎmean that, or *are* you júst *being* ˎnice about it?" (❗通例ほめてもらったときは Thank you for your *compliment* [×*flattery*]. (お世辞でもうれしいわ)とか，さらにならなおに Thanks for saying so. とか I'm glad you like it. などと答えるのがよい)

おせち 御節 ●御節料理 (special) dishes for the New Year's Day.

おせっかい お節介 ━━ **お節介な** 形 meddlesome; (世話好きな／やや書) officious; (せんさく好きな)〔話〕nosy, nosey. ▶よけいなお節介だ(=お前の知ったことではない) That's none of your business./Mind your own business! ▶彼はお節介な男だ He is a *nosy* person [a *busybody*].

━━ **お節介をする[やく]** 動 (干渉する) interfere, meddle 《*in, with*》; (鼻を突っ込む) 〔話〕poke one's nose 《*into*》. ▶彼のことにお節介をやくのはよしなさい You shouldn't *interfere* [*meddle*] *in* his affairs./〔話〕Keep your nose out of [Stop *poking* your nose *into*] his affairs. (❗最後の言い方はすでにお節介をしている行為を制止する場合)

おせっきょう お説教 (⇨説教)

オセロ [日本で誕生したゲーム]〔商標〕othello. ●オセロをする play *othello*; have a game of *othello*.

***おせん 汚染** 图 [主に化学物質による] pollution; [主に病原菌・毒物などによる] contamination. ●環境汚染 environmental *pollution*. ●大気[水質]汚染 air [water] *pollution*. ●食品の放射能汚染 radioactive *contamination* of the food. ●海岸の汚染を防ぐ protect beaches from *pollution*; control the *pollution* of beaches.

━━ **汚染する** 動 pollute; contaminate. ▶この川はその工場廃液で汚染された This river *was polluted* [*was contaminated, was poisoned*] *with* waste from the factory. (❗with の代わりに by も可) ●**汚染源** a pollution source. ●**汚染物質** a pollutant; a contaminant. ●**汚染防止** pollution control.

おぜんだて お膳立て ━━ **お膳立て(を)する** 動 ●朝食のお膳立てをする *set the table* for breakfast; *prepare* breakfast. ●パーティーのお膳立てをする(=準備をする) *make preparations* [*arrangements*] *for* the party. ●彼と憲子のデートのお膳立てする *fix* him *up* with Noriko; *arrange* his date with Noriko. ●(一塁を詰めて)ダブルプレーのお膳立てをする(up) [*set the stage* for] a double play. ▶彼が平和条約のお膳立てをした(=舞台を設けた) He *set the stage* [*paved the way*] *for* the peace treaty.

おそ 悪阻 [医学] hyperemesis. (⇨) つわり

***おそい 遅い** 形 ❶[時間が] late (↔*early*).

> 解説 late の比較級・最上級は，later, latest と latter, last の２種類があるが，前の方は時間に関して，後の方は順序に関して用いる。

●遅い(=もっとあとの)列車に乗る take a *later* train. ●遅い朝食をとる have a *late* breakfast; have breakfast *late*. (⇨ 動❶) ●花子は遅いなあ，どうしたのだろう Hanako is *late*. What's the matter with her? ▶彼は毎晩会社の帰りが遅い He comes home *late* from the office every night [evening]. ▶この地方は春が来るのが遅い Spring comes *late* in this district./Spring is *late* (*in*) coming in this part of the country. (❗〔話〕では late の後の in を省略する) ▶彼は着くのがほんの数分遅かった He got there only a few minutes *late*. ▶今から行ってももう遅い[遅いんじゃない] It is [would be] too *late* to go now. ▶やってしまったことを後悔してももう遅い 'It's too *late* for regret.'/《ことわざ》It is no use crying over spilt milk./《ことわざ》What's done cannot be undone.

❷[速さ] (動きののろい) slow (↔*fast*); (...するのに時間がかかる) be slow to do [*at* do*ing*, (*in*) do*ing*]. ●遅い列車 a *slow* train. (❗「各駅停車の」の意もある) ●仕事が遅い be slow at (do*ing*) one's job. ▶彼は理解が遅い He *is slow to* understand./He *is slow in* understand*ing*. ▶彼は歩くのが遅い He walks *slowly* [*slow*]. (⇨ 動❷)/He is a *slow* walker. (❗後の方は ×He was a slow walker when he came over to me. のような特定場面の描写には用いない)

━━ **遅く** 副 ❶[時間が] late. (❗×lately は「近ごろ」の意) ●午後遅く *late* in the afternoon; in the *late* afternoon. ●夜遅く寝る go to bed *late* at night [at a *late* hour]. ●夜遅くまで働く work (till) *late* at night; work *late* [*far*] into the night; work *late* hours. ▶遅くなってすみません (I'm) sorry I'm *late*. (❗)I'm sorry to be late [for being late]. ともいうが(まれ)／(お待たせしてすみません) I'm sorry that I have kept you waiting. (❗) I'm sorry to have kept you waiting. はより改まった言い方)▶だいぶ遅くなってきましたので，そろそろおいとまします It's getting rather *late*. I must be going now. ▶帰りは遅くなるので起きていなくていいよ Don't wait up (for me). I won't be home until *late*. ▶遅くなってもやらないよりはまし 'It is better to be done *late* rather than (to be) left undone.'/《ことわざ》Better *late* than never. ▶列車が30分遅く着いた The train arrived thirty minutes *late* (=予定より遅れて) *behind schedule*. (❗×later と比較級にしない) ▶彼はいつもより遅く家を出た He left his house *later* than usual. ▶私は家中でいちばん遅く起きます I get up《主に米》the *latest* of my family./I'm the last to get up in my home. ▶どうして今日は遅くなったの What made you *late* today?/(何があなたを引き留めたのか) What kept you today? ▶遅くならないでね(=長くかからないでね) Don't be *long*. (❗使いを頼んだときなど) ▶君のために出発が遅くなった You *delayed* our departure.

❷[速度が] slow(ly). (❗slow は slowly よりくだけた語で動詞や直接の用い，きびきびした文体で好まれる／⇨ゆっくり) ▶遅くてもよいから着実に勉強しなさい You should work *slowly* but steadily.

●遅きに失する be too late. ▶何とかそこにたどりついたが，遅きに失した I managed to get there, but it *was too late*.

***おそう 襲う** 動 ❶[人・動物が] attack, make* an attack 《*on*》; (突然激しく) assault; (強奪のために) rob (-bb-); [警察などが] (場所を突然に) raid, make a raid 《*on*》. ●その町を襲う *attack* [×attack on] the town; *make an attack* [*an assault*] *on* the town. ●銀行を襲う *rob* a bank; (侵入する) *break into* a bank. ●町を襲って占領する take a town *by assault*. ▶敵は夜明けに[夜陰に乗じて]襲ってくるだろう The enemy will *attack* (us) at dawn [under cover of darkness]. ▶彼女は暗い路地で襲われた She *was attacked* [*was* (sexually) *assaulted*, *was* (sexually) *assailed*] in a dark alley. (❗いずれも強姦の婉曲語) ▶彼らはこん棒で彼女を襲った They *came at* her with clubs. (❗come at は「威嚇(じょう)しながら襲いかかる」の意) ▶純粋な野生のサルは人間を襲わない Monkeys that are truely wild do not *attack* (=傷つける) *harm*) humans.

❷[災害・不安などが] strike*; [災害・疫病が] hit*, 〔書〕visit. (❗通例受身で); [感情・発作などが

おそうまれ 遅生まれ ● 遅生まれの(=4月2日から12月31日の間に生まれた)子供 a child born between April 2 and December 31.

おそかれはやかれ 遅かれ早かれ 〖早晩〗 sooner or later; 〖いつか〗 someday; 〖ゆくゆく, 最後には〗 eventually; 〖長い目で見れば〗 in the long run. ▶遅かれ早かれ彼の事業は失敗するでしょう Sooner or later his business will fail./His business will eventually fail.

おそく 遅く (⇨遅い [遅く])

おそくとも 遅くとも at (the) latest. ▶遅くとも10時までに帰宅しなさい I want you (to come) home by ten o'clock at the latest. (! さらに強調して at the very latest ともいう) (⇨〜まで ❶ 解説 Ⅱ) ▶遅くとも(=遅くなっても)やらないよりはまし (⇨遅い [遅く] ❶)

おそざき 遅咲き ● 遅咲きの桜 a late-blooming [a late-blossoming] cherry tree. ●遅咲きの花 late flowers. ●遅咲きの人 a late bloomer. ▶このボタンは遅咲きだ This peony blooms late.

おそじも 遅霜 a late [a spring] frost.

おそなえ お供え 〖神仏への供物〗 an offering; 〖かがみもち〗 a rice-cake offering.

おそばん 遅番 (be on) the afternoon [night] shift. (対) 早番

おそまきながら 遅まきながら ▶遅まきながら警察がその殺人事件を調査しだした The police have begun to investigate the murder, though it seems a little too late. (⇨遅ればせながら)

おそましい 〖ぞっとするような〗 horrifying; 〖話〗 creepy; 〖気味の悪い〗 weird.

おそまつ お粗末 ― お粗末な 〖形〗 ●お粗末な(=粗野な)理論 a crude theory. ●お粗末な(=まずい)言い訳をする make a poor [a shabby] excuse. (⇨粗末な) ▶この町の交通機関はお粗末だ(=ひどい) The transportation in this city is terrible.
【会話】「ごちそうさまでした」「お粗末さまでした」"Thank you very much." "You're welcome." /"Thank you for the wonderful dinner." "I'm glad you enjoyed it."

おそらく(は) 恐らく(は) probably. (⇨多分)

おそるおそる 恐る恐る 〖こわがりながら〗 fearfully; 〖用心して〗 cautiously; 〖おずおずと〗 timidly; 〖びくびくして〗 nervously. ●恐る恐るトラを見る look fearfully at the tiger. ●恐る恐る運転する drive a car cautiously. ●恐る恐る彼に許可を求める ask him for permission [ask his permission] timidly [nervously].

おそるべき 恐るべき terrifying; (恐ろしい) terrible. (⇨恐ろしい, 驚くべき) ●恐るべき戦争の実態 the terrifying [terrible] realities of war.

おそれ 恐れ ❶ 〖恐怖〗 fear; (ぎょっとさせる) (a) fright; (身をすくめる) (a) terror. (⇨恐怖) ●恐れを知らない兵士 a fearless soldier. ●恐れを感じる[抱く] (⇨恐れる)

❷ 〖心配〗 fear; 〖危険性〗 danger; (危険の可能性) (a) risk. ▶禁煙しないと君は肺がんにかかる恐れがある There's some fear that you'll get [You're in danger of getting] lung cancer unless you give up smoking. ▶その事件は戦争につながる恐れがある It is feared (that) the incident may develop into war. ▶精一杯勉強すれば落第する恐れはない If you study as hard as you can, you will be safe from failure in the exam [there is no risk that you will fail the exam].
●恐れをなす ●恐れをなして逃げる run away in terror; be frightened away 《by》. ▶彼はその大きな犬に[を見て]恐れをなした He was frightened by [at (the sight of), to see] the big dog.

おそれいる 恐れ入る ❶ 〖すまなく思う〗 ▶恐れ入りますが,銀行へ行く道を教えていただけますか Excuse me (I'm sorry to trouble you), but could you tell me the way to the bank? (⇨すみません)

❷ 〖あきれる〗 〖驚く〗 be surprised [astonished] 《at》; 〖閉口する〗 ▶彼の数学の上達の速さには恐れ入った(=驚嘆した) I was amazed at his rapid progress in mathematics. ▶彼のぶしつけな質問には恐れ入った(=当惑した) I was embarrassed by his blunt questions. ▶恐れ入りました(私の負けです) You win./(降参!) I give up./(君に脱帽するよ) I'll take my hat off to you.

❸ 〖感心する〗 ▶彼の英語をよく知っているのには恐れ入った I was greatly [deeply, very] impressed by [with] his good knowledge of English.

おそれおおい 恐れ多い 《書》august /ɔːgʌ́st/. ▶恐れ多いことながら,...と申し上げたい With all [due] respect, I would like to say ....

おそれおののく 恐れ戦く be very frightened 《of》.

おそれながら 恐れながら ▶ If I may (say) so ...; If I may be so bold to ask ....

***おそれる** 恐れる, 畏れる be afraid 《of; that節; to do》; 《書》 fear; (畏怖する) 《書》 fear; 〖怖がる〗 ▶死をも恐れぬこともない兵士たち death-defying soldiers. ●神を畏れる be in awe of God. ▶彼は死を恐れている He is afraid of death (死ぬのを) of dying, (that) he will die)./He fears death. (恐ろしくて死ねない) He is afraid to die. (⇨恐ろしい ❶ 解説) ▶質問するのを恐れては(=ちゅうちょしては)いけません Don't hesitate to ask questions. ▶彼は風邪をひくのを恐れて(=風邪をひくといけないので)泳ぎに行こうとしなかった He wouldn't go swimming for fear of catching [for fear (that) he might catch] (a) cold. ▶我々は毎日敵の襲撃を恐れながら暮らしていた We lived in daily fear of an enemy attack. ▶彼は人に恐れられている Many people are scared of him./He scares people around him. ▶恐れひるまずにわず Don't be afraid, Don't back up [Hold your ground], Don't be bound by anything.

おそろい お揃い ●お揃いで(=いっしょに)行く go together. ▶彼女は青いサテン地の服を着て,それとお揃いのハンドバッグを持っていた She was dressed in blue satin and had a matching purse in her hand. (⇨揃い)

***おそろしい** 恐ろしい 〖形〗 ❶ 〖怖い〗 fearful; (極度に) terrible; (身震いするほど) dreadful; 《書》 awful; (突然ぎょっとするような) frightful; (残虐さにぞっとするような) horrible; (怖がらせる) frightening; terrifying. ▶あのときは本当に恐ろしかった I was very frightened [very scared, really terrified] at that time. (!
(1) terrified は強意的で通例 very では修飾しない.
(2) ×I was fearful [terrible] .... とはいわない)

①〈恐ろしい〜〉 ●恐ろしい運命 a dreadful fate. ●恐ろしい映画 a horror (《話》 a scary, ×a scaring) movie. ●恐ろしい殺人事件 a horrible murder. ●恐ろしい目にあう have a (terrifying) experience. ●恐ろしい列車事故がその夜発生した A fearful [A terrible, A dreadful] railroad accident occurred that night.

②〈...は[が]恐ろしい〉 (⇨恐れる) ▶私は昆虫が恐ろしい I am afraid [scared] of insects (×an insect). ▶戦争は恐ろしい War is terrible./We're afraid of war. ▶私は飛行機に乗るのが恐ろしい I'm afraid [scared,《書》fearful] of flying (in [on] a plane)./I'm afraid [scared] to fly (in [on] a plane).

> 解説 通例 afraid, scared の後に of doing が続く場合は「...するのを恐れる」の意で, to do が続く場合は「(結果を心配して)恐れられる...できない」の意を表すが,《米》では区別なく用いることも多い.

③《...ではないかと[なので]恐ろしい》▶私は彼女が怒るのではないかと恐ろしかった I was afraid [scared,《書》fearful] that she might [would] be angry./I was afraid [scared,《書》fearful] of her anger. ▶最近地震が多いので恐ろしい It scares me that we have frequently had earthquakes lately.

④《恐ろしくて》in [with] terror. (⇨恐怖 ④, ⑤, ⑥) ●恐ろしくて逃げる run away in terror. ▶恐ろしくて動けなかった I was much too frightened [terrified] to move. (❗×...too much frightened... とはいわない. ただし much をとれば可)

⑤《恐ろしくなる》be [get] frightened [scared]; have [get] a fright.
❷［程度がはなはだしい］《話》awful;《話》terrible;《話》terrific;《米話》awesome. ▶恐ろしいスピードで at a terrific speed. ▶彼は恐ろしく〈=非常に〉頭がいい《話》He's awfully [terribly] bright.
── 恐ろしさ 图 (⇨恐怖)

おそわる 教わる be taught; (外国語・技術などを) learn*...(from.) ▶私は阿部先生にドイツ語を教わった I was taught German by [×from] Mr. Abe./I learned German from Mr. Abe. ▶やり方を教われば彼はできる He can do it if he's shown how.

おそん 汚損 ─ 汚損する 動 (汚す) make ... filthy; (傷つける) damage. (⇨汚す, 汚れる)

オゾン 图 ozone /óuzoun/. ●オゾンで処理する ozonize.
── **オゾン(性)の 形** ozonic.
●オゾン層 the ozone layer; (紫外線をさえぎる) the ozone shield. ●オゾン破壊物質 an ozone-depleting substance; an ozone-unfriendly substance. (⇨フロンガス) ●オゾンホール an ozone hole.

おだ おだを上げる (気炎を上げる) talk big about ....
おだい 御代 (値段) a price; (費用) (a) cost. (⇨代金)
おだいもく お題目 ❶［日蓮宗の］odaimoku; the Nichiren chant. ❷［内容を伴わない主張］▶彼の演説はお題目を並べたにすぎなかった His speech was nothing but empty statements.
おたいら お平ら ▶どうぞお平らに〈=楽に座ってください〉Please make yourself at home.
おたおた ●おたおたする〈=あわてうろうろする〉be in confusion;《話》be in a dither /díðər/; get flustered.
おたかい お高い ●お高くとまる (おうへいな) be haughty; (うぬぼれている) be conceited; (やたらと偉ぶる)《話》be stuck-up. ▶彼女は高くとまって人を見下すようなところがある She is stuck-up and looks down on everybody.
おたがい お互い each other, one another. (⇨互い)
おたがいさま お互い様 (⇨互い) ▶そうする時間も金もないというなら, お互いさまです〈=私も自分もそうです〉If you have neither time nor money for it, neither [×so] do I.
会話「このごろ物忘れがひどいね」「お互いさまよ〈=こっちも同じよ〉」"I'm very forgetful these days." "Same here./Me too."
会話「宿題やったのか」「まだだよ」「今日すべきことはさっさと済ませないと」「お互いさまじゃないか. きのう頼みでおいたのに直してくれたんだ」「わかったよ. こっちもやるからおまえも

やりなさい」"Did you do your homework, son?" "Not yet, Dad." "Don't put off what you should do today." "Look, who's talking? Have you fixed the chair I asked you yesterday?" (❗この Who's talking? は「どなたのお言葉かしら」とか「〈自分のことは棚に上げて〉よう言うよ」といった皮肉をこめた言い方) "OK. I'll do my thing. You'll do your own thing, too."

おたく お宅 ❶［相手の家］your home [house]; (相手) you. ●お宅のご主人 your husband.
❷［マニア］《軽蔑的》a nerd; (...にはまっている人) a fanatic; (...通) a buff.《以上はいずれも《話》) ▶彼はコンピュータおたくだ He's a computer nerd [fanatic, buff]./He's really into computers. ▶ビル・ゲイツ氏は学生時代はおたくの典型だったと言われている Mr. Bill Gates is said to have been a real nerd when he was a college student. [参考] きちんとした服装にしばしば度の強いめがねをかけた若者で,特に勉強しなくても理数系が抜群に強い半面, 対人関係やスポーツなどは全く苦手なタイプをさす)

おだく 汚濁 (⇨汚れ, 濁り) ●水質汚濁 water pollution.

おたけび 雄叫び ●雄たけびをあげる give a war [battle] cry.

おたずねもの お尋ね者 a wanted person. ▶あいつは強盗容疑で手配されているお尋ね者だ He is wanted by the police for robbery.

おたっし お達し (通達, 通知) (a) notice.

おだて flattery. ▶彼はおだてに乗りやすい「乗りにくい」He is [is not] easily flattered. ▶あの子はおだてがきかない The boy is above flattery.

おだてる 〖はめそやす〗flatter; (説得して...させる) coax.
●彼をおだてて使いに行かせる coax him into going [to go] on an errand. ●お世辞を言っておだてないでくれ Don't flatter me with compliments.

おたふく お多福 (不細工な女) a plain(-looking) [《米》a homely] woman. (⇨ おかめ)
●お多福風邪 〖医学〗(the) mumps. (❗単数扱い. the は今はつけないのが普通) ●おたふく風邪をひいている [ひく] have [get] (the) mumps. ●お多福豆 a boiled and sweetened broad bean.

おだぶつ お陀仏 ●お陀仏になる (死ぬ) be dead;《話》kick the bucket; (人が再起不能になる) be finished.

おたま お玉 a (soup) ladle. ●スープをお玉でおわんに入れる put soup into a bowl with a ladle.

おだまき 苧環 〖植物〗a columbine.

おたまじゃくし 〖カエルの子〗a tadpole;〖音符〗a (musical) note;〖しゃくし〗a ladle.

おためごかし 御為ごかし ●おためごかしを言う〈=相手のためと見せかけて実は自分の利益をねらうのをやめます〉Stop saying what is actually good for you as if it were good for me. (❗you, me を強く発音して対照性を伝える)

*かだやか 穏やか ─ 穏やか(さ) 图 (平穏) calmness; (静けさ) quietness; (適度) moderation.
── **穏やかな 形** ❶［平穏な］calm; quiet; mild; gentle; peaceful; friendly.

> 使い分け calm 自然や人の態度などが穏やかなこと.
> quiet 騒音がなく静かなこと, 動きがなく平穏であること. 喧噪状態と対比した絶対的な静寂さを含意する.
> mild 人の態度が穏やかなこと, 物事の程度がはほどよどなこと.
> gentle 人の性格が穏和なことや, 自然が穏やかなこと.
> peaceful 物や人が平穏で平和であること.
> friendly 人の性格が穏やかなこと.

●穏やかな風 a mild [a gentle] breeze. ●穏やかな気

オタワ 〖カナダの首都〗Ottawa.

候 a *mild* climate. ●穏やかな人 a *quiet* [a *gentle*] person. ▶海はとても穏やかだった The sea was very *calm*. ▶穏やかな(=静かな) 1 日だった It was a *quiet* [a *peaceful*] day. ▶武田氏は穏やかな口調で話した Mr. Takeda talked in a *quiet* [a *gentle*] tone. ▶その紛争は大変穏やかな方法で解決された The dispute was settled in a very *peaceful* [*friendly*] manner.

会話「今日は穏やかな日だったね」「いや、京都はひどく寒かったよ」"It was a *mild* day today, wasn't it?" "No, it was bitterly cold here in Kyoto."

❷〖適度な〗moderate; (穏当な) reasonable. ●穏やかな要求 *moderate* [*reasonable*] demands. ▶彼は穏やかな処置をとった He took *moderate* measures.

── 穏やかに 副 (静かに) quietly; (控えめに) moderately; (平和的に) peacefully. ▶争いを穏やかに解決する settle a conflict *peacefully*. ▶穏やかに議論しよう Let's discuss it *quietly* [*peacefully*]./Let's have a *quiet* [a *peaceful*] discussion.

オタワ 〖カナダの首都〗Ottawa.

おだわらひょうじょう 小田原評定 (いつまでも決まらない相談) an endless discussion; (会議) an endless conference.

おたんこなす ▶このおたんこなすめ! You *good-for-nothing*! (❗呼びかけなので無冠詞)

おち 落ち ❶〖抜かすこと〗(an) omission; (しくじり) a slip. ●署名の落ちの *omission* of a signature. ●書式に落ちなく書き込む fill in an application form *without omission* [*in full*].

❷〖冗談・漫画などの〗▶その冗談の落ちが分からない I don't get the *punch line* [I miss the *point*] of the joke. (❗(1) the punch line は「急所となる文句」の意. (2) おおまかに I don't see the joke. でもよい)

❸〖結末〗▶彼の計画は失敗するのが落ちだ(きっと失敗に終わる)His plan *is bound to end* [〈やや書〉 *result*] *in failure*./(運命づけられている) His plan *is doomed to fail* [*failure*]. (❗fail は動)

おちあう 落ち合う meet*. (⇨合流) ▶彼といつものホテルのロビーで 6 時に落ち合うことになっている I'm *meeting* [〈やや書〉*getting together with*] him at the hotel lobby at six.

おちあゆ 落ち鮎 (産卵で川を下るアユ) *ochiayu*; (説明的に) a sweetfish coming down the river for spawning.

おちいる 陥る be thrown into 《a panic》; fall* into 《his trick》; come* to 《a deadlock》. ●危篤に陥る *fall into* a critical condition. ▶その会社は倒産に陥った The company *was thrown into* bankruptcy /bǽŋkrʌptsi/ [《破産して》 went bankrupt]. ▶アフリカには貧困の悪循環に陥っている国が数多くある Many African countries *are trapped in* a vicious circle of poverty. (❗be trapped in ... は「…に捕らえられている」の意)

おちおち ▶状況が厳しいので, おちおちできない The situation is too hard for me to *set* my *mind at rest*. ▶昨晩は雷がひどくておちおち眠れなかった Last night it thundered so hard (that) I couldn't get a good sleep [sleep well, sleep peacefully].

おちくぼむ 落ち窪む sink (in); become hollow [sunken]. (⇨窪む, 沈む)

おちくぼものがたり『落窪物語』 *The Tale of the Lady Ochikubo*. (参考 平安時代の物語)

おちこぼれ 落ちこぼれ〖途中で学校や会社をやめた人〗a dropout; 〖他より遅れた生徒〗a student who can't keep up with the others.

おちこぼれる 落ちこぼれる (仕事・勉強などが) fall behind 《with, in》. ▶彼は勉強でかなり落ちこぼれている He *is far* [〈話〉 *way*] *behind with* his studies.

おちこみ 落ち込み a drop; (緩やかな) a decline, a downturn; (急激な) a slump. ●消費支出の落ち込み a *slide* in consumer spending.

おちこむ 落ち込む ❶〖ぼむ〗(沈下する) sink*; (陥没する) fall* in, cave in. ▶屋根がそっくり落ち込んだ The entire roof *fell* [*caved*] *in*. ▶彼の頬は病気のため落ち込んでいた His cheeks *were sunken* after the [his] long illness.

❷〖落ちはまる〗▶みぞに落ち込む *fall into* a ditch.

❸〖下がる〗drop (-pp-); fall* off. ▶今月は売り上げが 5% 落ち込んだ Sales *have dropped* [*fallen off*] (by) five percent this month.

❹〖意気消沈する〗get* depressed. (⇨塞ぎ込む) ▶彼は成績のことでひどく落ち込んでいる He *is very depressed* [*is feeling so low*] about his grades. ▶そんなことで落ち込むな Don't let that get you down.

おちつき 落ち着き ❶〖人・態度などの平静さ〗calmness; 〈やや書〉composure; (危急に際しての) presence of mind. ●落ち着きのある calm, 〈やや書〉composed; (沈着冷静な) self-possessed; (もの静かで風格のある) 〈書〉sedate. ●落ち着きの (じっとしていない) restless; (神経質な) nervous. ●落ち着きを失う (取り戻す, 欠く) lose [regain; keep] one's *calmness* [*composure*]. ▶彼女は若い娘さんにしては落ち着きがある She is *self-possessed* for such a young girl. ▶彼は危機に直面しても落ち着きを失わなかった He kept his *head* [*presence of mind*] *in* (*the*) *face of danger*. ▶彼女は年をとるにつれて落ち着きを増した She became more *sedate* as she grew older.

❷〖物の安定〗steadiness. ●落ち着きの悪い(=ぐらぐらするいす) an *unsteady* (↔a *steady*) chair.

おちつきはらう 落ち着き払う (まったく冷静にしている) be perfectly composed; keep* one's cool. ●落ち着き払って彼に話しかける speak to him *with great composure*.

***おちつく** 落ち着く ❶〖気持ちなどが静まる〗calm down; calm oneself, compose oneself; relax; feel* at ease [secure].

使い分け calm down 平静になること.
calm [compose] oneself 自分自身を静めること.
relax 緊張から解放されて安らぐこと.
feel at ease [secure] 安心して心からの落ち着きを感じること.

●落ち着いた態度で in a *calm* manner; calmly. ●落ち着け *Calm down./Pull yourself together*./(びくびくするな) *Don't be nervous*./(興奮するな) *Don't get so excited*./(気楽にやれ) *Take it easy*. ▶彼はその男に水を与えて落ち着かせた He *calmed* the man (*down*) by giving him some water. ▶彼女は非常の時も落ち着いて(=冷静に)行動した She acted *calmly* [*with calmness*] in an emergency. ▶「案外落ち着いて」のように修飾語を伴う場合は unexpectedly calmly より with unexpected calmness の方が好まれる) ▶彼女は 1 日中心が落ち着かなかった She *felt restless* [*uneasy*] all day long. ▶今日は忙しくて落ち着いて(=くつろいで)本を読む暇もない Today I am so busy that I have no time to *relax and read*. ▶ホテルでは落ち着かない(=くつろいだ気分になれない) I don't *feel relaxed* [*at home*] in a hotel. ▶小川のせせらぎの音を聞くと気分が落ち着く(=神経が静まる) The murmur of a brook *settles* [*soothes, is soothing to*] me [my nerves]. (⇨

おちつける

❸) ▶彼は落ち着かない(=神経質そうな)様子でひげをいじった He trifled *nervously* with his beard.
❷[新しい生活・職などに] settle (down). ▶新しい仕事に落ち着く *settle* [*get settled*] *into* a new job. ▶彼もそろそろ結婚して落ち着いていいころだ He's old enough to get married and *settle down*. ▶(生活が)落ち着きしだいお電話します I'll call as soon as I *get settled* [I know what I'm doing]. (❗急用で国へ帰った人の置き手紙)
会話「新居にはそろそろ落ち着かれましたか」「ええだいぶ落ち着きました」"Are you *getting settled* in your new home?" "Pretty ↘well. (↔Not ↗quite.)"
❸[安定する] settle down. ▶物価が落ち着いた Prices *have settled down* [*have come*] *stabilized*]. ▶痛みがだいぶ落ち着いた The pain *has* almost *settled down* [(薄らいだ) *has worn off*, (消えた) *has gone away*]. ▶彼の病状は落ち着いている[落ち着いている] His condition *has stabilized* [*is stable*]. ▶事態は落ち着き始めた Things began to *fall in places*.
❹[結論などに達する] come* to .... ▶遠足は延期することに落ち着いた We *came to* [*reached*] *an agreement* that the excursion would be postponed.
❺[その他の表現] ▶落ち着いた(=地味な)色 a *quiet* [《話》a *conservative*, (やや書) a *subdued*] color.

おちつける 落ち着ける (心・気持ちを) calm oneself; compose oneself. (⇨落ち着く) ▶腰を落ち着けて研究する *settle down to* study [studying]. (❗study は自動詞)

おちど 落ち度 [過失] a fault; [誤り] a mistake. (⇨過失) ▶それは私の落ち度だ It is my *fault*./I *am to blame for* it. ▶何の落ち度もない多くの人が命を奪われた Many people were killed through no *fault* of their own.

おちのびる 落ち延びる (逃げ延びる) escape safely 《*from*》.

おちば 落ち葉 [落ちている葉] fallen leaves, scattered (dead) leaves; [落ちてくる葉] falling leaves.

おちぶれる 落ちぶれる go* [come*] down in the world; go to ruin; (話) go to the dogs. ▶彼は落ちぶれてしまった He *came down in the world*./(無一文になった) He *was down and out*. ▶国民のモラルが低下し,この国は三流国家に落ちぶれようとしている This country *is going to the dogs* as a result of moral decay of the people.

おちぼ 落ち穂 gleanings.
●落ち穂拾い(をする人) a gleaner.

おちぼひろい『落穂拾い』 The Gleaners. (参考 ミレーの絵画)

おちむしゃ 落ち武者 a fugitive /fjúːdʒətɪv/ warrior after losing a battle.

おちめ 落ち目 ▶落ち目である(=つきに見放されている) be down on one's luck. ▶あの歌手の人気も落ち目だ That singer *is getting less and less popular* [*is losing popularity*]./That singer's popularity *is declining* [*waning*].

おちゃ 茶 ❶[茶] tea. (⇨茶) ●お茶を摘む pick *tea*. ●お茶を挽く(=粉にする) grind tea leaves (into powder). ●お茶を入れる[点(た)てる] make (the) *tea*《*for* him》. ●お茶をつぐ pour *tea*《*for* him》. ●お茶を1杯飲む have a cup(of) *tea*. (❗「2杯飲む」は have two cups of *tea* または have two *teas*) ●お茶を熱いうちに出す[飲む] serve [drink] the *tea* hot. ▶お茶をもう1杯いかがですか Would you like another cup of *tea*? ▶彼女は彼にお茶を入れた[出した] She made *tea* for [served *tea* to] him. ▶お茶を飲みながら話をしよう Let's talk over (a cup of) *tea*.

おちる

(❗(1) 主語が複数であっても ×cups of ... とはいわない.
(2) over は「...を飲みながら」の意の前置詞) ▶彼女は私をお茶に招いてくれた She invited me to *tea* [*a tea party*]. ▶ごいっしょにお茶でもいかが Won't you have some *tea* with me? ▶お茶も飲んでいっていただきたいところなんだけど,これから出かけるところなの I would invite you to *tea*, but I'm just going out.

❷[休憩] ●お茶にする have a coffee 《主に米》 [a tea 《英》] *break*. ▶お茶の時間ですよ It's *teatime*!
会話「お茶にしない?」「いいね」"How [What] about a *coffee* [a *tea*]?" "Good idea./That would be nice."

❸[茶道] (⇨茶道) ●お茶を習う[のけいこをする] take lessons in *tea ceremony*.

●お茶の子さいさい ▶そんなことはお茶の子さいさいだ That's quite an *easy task*./Nothing can be easier./(話) It's a piece of cake. (❗慣用表現)

●お茶を濁す ▶彼は私の質問に対していつもお茶を濁す He always *gives* an *evasive answer* to [*fudges* (his *answer* to)] my question.

おちゃうけ お茶請け (⇨ 茶菓子) ▶お茶請けには何がよろしいでしょうか What do you like with your tea?

おちゃくみ お茶汲み ▶お茶くみをする serve tea.

おちゃづけ お茶漬け *ochazuke* (説明的に) a bowl of rice, covered with some appetizing food such as salmon, *nori*, etc., immersed in green tea and eaten hot.

おちゃっぴい ▶おちゃっぴいな少女 a mischievous girl.

おちゃらかす (⇨茶化す)

おちゅうげん お中元 a midsummer [a midyear] gift. (⇨お歳暮) ●お中元大売り出し a *midsummer* sale.

おちょうしもの お調子者 ▶お調子者である (すぐにおだてに乗る) be easily flattered; (軽々しい) be frivolous, be light-minded; (口先だけで信用できない) be a glibtalker.

おちょこ a *sake* cup. (⇨杯(さかずき))
●おちょこになる ▶傘が強風でおちょこになった(=裏返しになった) My umbrella *was turned inside out* by a strong wind.

おちょぼぐち おちょぼ口 a little charming mouth.
●おちょぼ口をする pucker up one's lips. (❗ pucker up は「しわを寄せて」つぼめる」の意)

:**おちる 落ちる**
WORD CHOICE 落ちる
fall 物・人の落下を表す最も一般的な語. 比喩的に「眠り[恋]に落ちる (fall asleep [in love])」などの表現でも用いる. ▶コインが床に落ちた A coin *fell* to the floor.
drop 物・人が高い位置から勢いよく下に落ちること. 比喩的に数値の下落なども含意する. ▶崩れ落ちて膝をつく *drop* to one's knees. ▶数値は急に落ちた The figure sharply *dropped*.
collapse 建物・計画などが崩壊することや, 人が崩れ落ちるように倒れること. ▶彼はベッド[床の上]に崩れ落ちた He *collapsed* in his bed [on the floor].

頻度チャート
fall ████████████
drop ████████
collapse ███
　　　20　40　60　80　100 (%)

おちんちん

❶ [落下する、崩れる] (落下する) fall*, go* [come*] down (fall より口語的で、広い意味で用いられる); (急に落ちる) drop (-pp-); (水などがぼたぼたと) drip (-pp-); (日・月が沈む) go down, sink*, set* (!後になるほど堅い言い方); (墜落する) crash; (重みなどで崩れる) give* way, collapse; (陥没する) fall in, cave in.

① [～から[に]落ちる] ● 窓から落ちる fall off [from, out of] the window. (!off は「足をふみはずして」, from, out of は「身を乗り出しすぎて」を暗示するが広義の場合は fall over a cliff で「階段から落ちる fall down [×from] the stairs; fall downstairs. (!「ころがり落ちる」は roll down the stairs) ▶川に落ちる fall into a river. ▶深い眠りに落ちる fall into a deep sleep; fall sound [fast] asleep. ▶橋が雪の重みで落ちた The bridge gave way [collapsed] under the weight of the snow. ▶火が燃え盛って屋根が落ちた The roof collapsed [fell in] as the fire took hold. ▶彼のカーブは垂直に落ちる His curveball drops off the table.

② [A(物)がB(場所)から[に]落ちる] ▶皿は床に落ちた The plate fell on [onto] the floor. ▶本が棚から落ちた A book fell [dropped] from [off] the shelf. ▶太陽が沈み始め、木立の向こうに落ちていった The sun began to set, sinking down behind the trees. ▶飛行機が山腹に落ちた A plane crashed into the hillside. ▶雷がその塔に落ちた Lightning struck the tower. ▶100 円玉が床に落ちていた A one hundred-yen coin lay on the floor./There was a one hundred-yen coin lying on the floor. ▶彼女の目からしたたり落ちた Tears dropped [dripped, ×fell] from her eyes.

❷ [程度が下がる] go* [come*] down, fall* (!前の方が口語的); (急に下がる) drop (-pp-); (数量が減じる) fall off; (衰える) decline; fail. ●5番に落ちる go down [drop (back)] to (the) fifth place. ●5番落ちる go down [drop] five places. (!five places は by five places (5番だけ)の by の省略口語句) ▶彼は成績が落ちた His grades went down [fell, dropped]./(前より悪い成績を取った) He got worse grades (英) marks). ▶スピードが落ちた The speed dropped. ▶5月は売り上げが7パーセント落ちた Sales were off 7 percent in May. ▶彼の人気が落ちた He has lost his popularity./His popularity has declined. ▶病気で彼は食欲が落ちた His appetite failed [He lost his appetite] when he got sick. ▶話が落ちてきた(=下品になった) The talk has become vulgar. ▶その投手は球威が落ちた The pitcher has lost his stuff.

❸ [抜け落ちる] (しみなどが) come* out [off]; (取り除かれる) be taken out, be removed; (色があせる) fade; (ページなどが) miss. ▶そのしみはなかなか落ちない The stain won't come out [off]. (!「洗って落ちない」は …won't wash out [off].)/The stain won't be taken out [be removed]. ▶その生地は洗うと色が落ちた This fabric faded when it was washed./The colors washed out of this fabric. ▶この洗剤よりもこの方が汚れがよく落ちる(=よりきれいになる) This detergent gets clothes cleaner than that one does. (!get … clean は「…をきれい(な状態)にする」の意) ▶この本は数ページ落ちている Several pages are missing from this book.

❹ [失敗する] fail (in …) (!今は通例 in は省略する); (米話) flunk. ▶彼は運転免許試験に3回落ちた He failed [(米話) flunked] his driving test three times.

❺ [人の所有となる] ▶その都市は敵の手に落ちた The city fell to [fell into the hands of] the enemy. ▶入札は我が社に落ちた(=受け入れられた) Our bid was accepted.

おちんちん one's penis; one's thing. (!one's peepee は幼児語中の幼児語. one's peter ともいう)

おつ 乙 图 [順序, 等級] (2番目) the second; (前者に対する後者) the latter; (2級) (the) second (class); (成績の良) grade B, a "B". (⇒甲, 甲乙)
── **乙な** 形 ▶乙な味がする It has a good taste of its own./It tastes nice and unique [different, ×peculiar]. (!peculiar は味について用いると「不快な」を含意する)
● 乙にすます be very prim. (!be prim and proper (苦労しく上品ぶっ, すぐにショックを受けたふりをする)は女性についていう慣用句)

おつかい 御使い ⟨go on⟩ an errand. (⇒使い)

おつかいもの 御遣いもの a gift. (⇒贈り物)

おっかけ 追っかけ (アイドルなどの熱狂的なファン) a groupie.

おっかない (⇒恐ろしい)

おっかなびっくり ●おっかなびっくりで(…する) be scared ⟨and do⟩; (おそるおそる) ⟨do⟩ fearfully [(びくびくして) nervously].

おつかれさま 御疲れ様 [日常的な別れの時] Goodbye.; Bye (now).; See you.; [ちょっとしたねぎらいの時] (お世話になりました) Thank you very [so] much (for your trouble). (⇒お帰りなさい) ▶今日はお疲れさまでした。おうちでゆっくりしてください It was a busy, tiring day. You need really to relax at home.

おつき 御付き an attendant. (⇒御供)

おっくう 億劫 ▶外出するのをおっくうがる be reluctant [unwilling] to go out. ▶おっくうがらずに辞書を引きなさい Don't spare yourself the trouble of consulting your dictionary. (!spare oneself は通例否定文で用いる) ▶それを書き直すのはおっくうだ(=やっかいだ) It is troublesome [bothersome] to rewrite it.

オックスフォード [英国の都市] Oxford.
● オックスフォード英語辞典 The Oxford English Dictionary (略 OED). ● オックスフォード大学 Oxford University.

おつげ お告げ (神託) an oracle, a divine message; (啓示) (a) revelation.

オッケー (⇒オーケー)

おっさん (話) a gent; (俗) a dude; (親しみのある呼びかけ語として) (米話) a pop, a pops (圈 pops) (!(1) father の意の papa の異形 poppa より. (2) 中年男を「父さん」と呼ぶのに近い).

おっしゃる (=言う) ▶おっしゃったことがよく聞き取れませんでした I didn't quite catch what you said. ▶おっしゃること(=意味されていること)はよく分かります I see what you mean. ▶ご都合のいい場所をおっしゃってくださいませんか Can you suggest a place that's convenient to you? (!suggest は「控えめに提案する」の意) ▶何とおっしゃいましたか I bég your ⌣pardon?/⌣Pardon?/(英) ⌣Sorry?/Whát did you ╱sáy? ▶よくそんなことおっしゃいますねえ How can you dare say that! (!dare は「あえて…する」の意の動詞で、ここでは to が省略されている) ▶私にできることがありましたらおっしゃってください(=お知らせください) If there's anything I can do, you'll let me know.
会話 「ジョージはすばらしい男だ」「よくそんなことおっしゃいますわ」"I think George is a wonderful man." "Sáys ↘you [who]!"

おっす Howdy!; Hey (there)!; Hi!; ╱Morning! (!いずれも通例, 後に相手の名前をつける. 後になるほど「おっ

オッズ 〖競馬・競輪の配当予想〗odds. ●最もオッズの高い馬にかける bet on the highest-*odds* horse; bet on the longest-*odds* horse.

おっちょこちょい (不注意な人) a careless person, 《話》a scatterbrain.
会話「あらら、しまった」「拾うのを手伝ってあげましょう」「私って本当におっちょこちょいなんだから、ご親切にどうも」"Oops! Oh, no!" "Let me help you pick them up." "How *clumsy* of me! You're so kind." (!) clumsy は「所作や扱いが不器用で失敗しやすい」の意. I'm really clumsy. ともいえる.

おっつかっつ (互角の) equal; (対等の) even.

おっつけ 追っ付け ▶まもなく、やがて

おって 追手 (追跡者) a pursuer; (追跡する一団) a pursuing party.
●追っ手書き (追伸) a postscript《略 ps; PS》.

おって 追って (後ほど) later (on), afterward. ▶それは追って説明します I'll explain it to you *later (on)*. ▶追って連絡があるまで君は停学です You will be suspended *until further notice*.

‡おっと 夫 a husband. (⇔妻) ●夫に死なれる[を亡くす] lose one's *husband*; be widowed. (関連) 残った妻を widow という. 妻に死なれた夫は (a widower) ▶彼は私にとって理想の夫です He is an ideal *husband* for me.

おっと 〖呼びかけ〗oh; hey; 《米話》say, 《英話・古》I say; 〖失敗して〗《話》oops /wúəps/, whoops /hwú(:)ps/. ●おっと (危ない) (*Oh*,) look [*watch*] out! ●おっと待った Wait [Just] a minute. /(呼びかめて) *Hey!* Stop! ●おっと, 指をすりむくとこだった *Oops!* I almost [nearly] scraped my finger. ●「おっと失礼」と少女に突き当たった男が言った "*Oops!* Pardon me." said the man when he ran into the girl.

おっとせい 〖動物〗a fur seal.

おつとめ お勤め (⇔勤め) ●朝のお勤め (寺院で) morning service.

おつとめひん お勤め品 (お買い得の品) a bargain.

おっとり ●おっとりした人 (穏やかな) a *gentle* [(ものの静かな) a *quiet*; (朗らかな) a *calm*] person. ▶彼はおっとりした性格だ He has a *gentle* [a *quiet*, a *calm*] disposition.

おっとりがたな 押っ取り刀 ●押っ取り刀で (= 大急ぎで) in a big hurry.

おっぱい (乳房) the breast. ●おっぱいを飲む take [suck (at)] the *breast*. ●おっぱいを飲ませる *give* (a baby) *the breast*. ●おっぱいで育てる breastfeed.

おつまみ お摘み an hors d'oeuvre /ɔːrdɚːrv/, 《複》hors d'oeuvres. (!) 日本語のおつまみにぴったりする英語はない)

おつゆ お汁 (a) soup, (みそ汁) miso soup.

おつり お釣り change. (⇔釣り銭)▶1,000 円お預かりしましたのでお釣りは 300 円になります Your *change* from one thousand yen is three hundred yen. ▶お客様, お釣りですよ Don't forget your *change*, sir [ma'am]! ▶あのう, お釣りが足りません I'm afraid I'm short-changed. ▶あれ, お釣り多すぎませんか Oh, you've given me too much *change*.

おて お手 (犬に向かって) Shake hands!

おてあげ お手上げ ●お手上げだ I don't know what to do./It's all up with me.

おてあらい お手洗い a toilet, 《米》a bathroom. (⇔便所)

おでかけ お出かけ ▶お出かけですか *Are* you *going out*? (!) 日本語と異なり単なるあいさつには用いない) ▶いつかこちらへお出かけください (ぶらりと来てください) Please *come around* [*over*] (*and see us*) some-time. /(お立ち寄りください) Please *drop in* (*on* us) sometime.

おでき 御出来 a boil; 〖吹出物〗a rash. (⇔出来物) ●おできを切開する lance a *boil*.

おでこ (額) a forehead /fɔːrhèd, f(ː)rəd/.

おてだま お手玉 ●お手玉をする juggle with (small) *beanbags*. ●ゴロをお手玉する 〖野球〗juggle [fumble] a grounder.

おてつき お手付き ●お手つきをする pick up [touch] the wrong card.

オデッサ 〖ウクライナの都市〗Odessa.

おてつだい(さん) お手伝い(さん) (通いの) 《米》a helper, 《英》a help, (主に英話) a daily (help); (住込み込みの) a (live-in) maid 類語 米英では today's (の) が普通; (英語学習のための) 《英》an au pair (⇔オーペア).

おてなみ お手並み (技量) skill; (能力) ability; competence. ▶さて講釈は十分うけたまわった. 次はお手並み拝見といきたい (= 君がいかに上手にそれをするか見せてほしい) I've heard a lot of your theory. Could you please let me see *how well* you *do it* [(君自身の実地での技量を) your *own skill*]?

おてのもの お手の物 one's forte /fɔːrt/; one's specialty. ▶彼女はコンピュータを使う仕事ならお手の物です Working with computers is *her forte* [*specialty*]./She is *good at* [*at home*] working with computers.

おてまえ お点前 〖茶道〗the ritualized procedure of making and serving tea. ●けっこうなお点前でした I very much appreciate your skill at serving tea./(気軽に) Thank you very much for serving nice tea.

おてもと お手元 〖「箸(はし)」の丁寧語〗(⇔箸)

おてもり お手盛り ── お手盛りの 形 (自分でよしとした決めた) self-approved [self-decided] 《pay rise》▶役員たちはお手盛りの昇給を決めた The directors decided to *raise their own salary*.

おてやわらか お手柔らか ●お手柔らかにお願いします (厳しくしないように) Please *don't be hard on me.*/(ひどい目にあわさないように) I hope you *won't give me a hard time.*

おてん 汚点 〖不名誉〗a blot; (やや書) a stain. (⇔染(し)み) ●彼の名声の汚点 a *blot* [a *stain*] *on* his reputation. ▶その収賄事件は我が国の政治史上に大きな汚点を残した The bribery case left a great *blot* [*stain*] *on* the political history of our nation.

おでん oden; (説明的に) a mixture of *kon'nyaku*, *kombu* (sea kelp), several kinds of food made from fish meat, eggs, and such vegetables as radishes and potatoes, seasoned lightly with soy sauce, simmered for a long time in ample soup.

おてんきや お天気屋 a moody [a temperamental] person. ▶お隣さんはすごくお天気屋で付き合いきれない Our neighbor is so *moody* [*temperamental*] (*that*) we can hardly get along with him. (!) (1) Our neighbor has such an uncertain temper (that).... のようにもいえる. (2) 会話では that は省略される.

おてんば お転婆 a tomboy; 《やや古》a filly.

‡おと 音
WORD CHOICE 音
sound 各種の音をさす最も一般的な語. 快適な音, 不快な騒音のいずれにも用いる. ●うなりをあげるエンジン音 the growling *sound* of the engine.
noise 特に神経を苛立たせる不快な騒音をさす. ●大きな騒音を出す make loud *noises*

おとあわせ

tone 楽器の音，人の声質，各種の音調などをさす．高さ一低さ，鋭さ一柔らかさなど，音調の種類を示す形容詞を伴う． ▶彼の声のやわらかな[鋭い，甲高い，低い]音調 soft [acute, high, low] *tone* of his voice.

頻度チャート
sound ████████████████████
noise ████████
tone ████

20 40 60 80 100 (%)

(a) sound; (a) noise; a din (**!** noise よりさらに大きく長く続く音); a tone; (波やエンジンなどのとどろく音) a roar; (ばふっぶつかったり壊れたりする音) a crash. ▶音と映像 pictures and *sound* (**!** 語順に注意)

①【～音】 ▶大きな音 a loud *sound* [*noise*]. ▶小さな音 a soft [a tiny] *sound*. ▶高い[低い]音 a high [a low] *sound*. (**!** (1) 楽器の音には note を用いる. (2) かん高く鋭い音は a shrill *sound* [*noise*], 深く低い音は a deep *sound*) ▶鋭い[鈍い]音 a sharp [a dull] *sound*. ▶乾いた音 a dry [a clanking, a rustling] *sound*. (**!** dry は一般的に乾いた音. clanking は金属製のものが触れたり，打ち合ったりする時にでる音. rusltling は枯葉などの「かさかさ」という音) ▶澄んだ音 a clear [a transparent] *sound*. ▶(ハチ・機械などが)ブンブンいう音 a buzzing *sound*. ▶(鍵などが)カチッという音 a clicking *sound*. ▶何の音だ What's that *sound*?

関連 ベル[電話]の音 the ring(s) of a bell [a telephone] (**!** 鐘の音は (the) toll ともいえる)/ピストルの音 the bang(s) [〖書〗 report(s)] of a pistol/雷の音 (⇨雷鳴)/小川のせせらぎの音 the babble [murmur] of a stream/ペンの走る音 the scratch(es) of a pen/時計のかちかちいう音 the ticks of a clock/雨戸のがたがたという音 the clatter of a sliding door/ドアのぎいぎい[靴のきゅっきゅっと]きしむ音 the creaks of a door [shoes]/タイヤのきいっときしむ音 a screech of tires

②【音は[が]】 ▶その家からピアノの音がした I heard the *sound* of a piano from the house. ▶音は毎秒約 340 メートルの速さで空気中を伝わる *Sound* travels at about 340 meters per second in (the) air. ▶エンジンの音が変だ The engine is making a strange *noise*. ▶君の新しく買ったステレオは音がいいか Does your new stereo *sound* all right? ▶この靴は床を歩いても音がしません These shoes are silent on the floor. ▶ばたんという音がして戸が閉まった The door shut with a bang./The door banged shut.

③【音を】 ▶音を出す[立てる] make a *sound*; (騒音を) make a *noise*. ▶音を立てて noisily; with a *noise*. ▶音を立てないで noiselessly; (静かに) quietly; (黙って) silently. ▶そんなうるさい音を立てないでください Don't make so much *noise* [a *noisy sound*]. ▶彼はテレビの音を大きくしっぱなしにしている He keeps the TV on loud [the TV volume *up*]. ▶車がきいっと音を立てて止まった A car screeched to a stop.

会話 「ラジオの音(=音量)を小さくしてくれませんか」「はい，分かりました」"Would you mind turning down (⇔up) (the volume of) your radio?" "Sure. I'd be happy to." (**!** ( )内は省略する方が普通)

おとあわせ 音合わせ tuning (up). ▶音合わせをする tune 《a violin》 (up).

おといれ 音入れ (⇨録音)

***おとうさん** お父さん a father; 〖話〗 a dad, 〖話〗 a daddy; 〖話・まれ〗 a pa, a papa.

解説 (1) 家族内で父親に呼びかけたり，父親のことをいう場合は無冠詞・大文字で Dad, 幼い子供は Daddy が普通. Father は改まった言い方. 《米》では Papa /pɑ́ːpə/, Pa /pɑ́ː/ は主に小学校へ行くまでの幼児が用いる語. 《英》Papa /pəpɑ́ː/ は〘古〙.
(2) 他人の父親や他人に自分の父親のことをいう場合は正式には one's father のように所有代名詞を伴う. 「父は…」というのに似て，発話者の育ちの良さを示すと考えられる.

▶彼のお父さんは技師だ His *father* is an engineer. ▶お父さんはお元気ですか How is your *father*? ▶あの人は私にとってお父さんのようなものだ He is (like) a *father* to me. ▶お父さん，お母さんはどこ? *Dad*, where is Mom? ▶太郎，お父さんの言うことを聞きなさい (母親が子供に) Taro, listen to *Dad* [*Father*].

***おとうと** 弟 a (younger [little, 《米話》kid]) brother. (**!** little や kid を用いるのは自分より小さいという気持ちが入っているので，成人の弟には用いないのが普通) (⇨兄 解説) ▶彼は私の弟だ He's my *brother*. ▶私は彼を弟のように思っている I look upon him as my *little brother*. ▶彼は同じ相撲部屋の弟弟子だ He's a sumo wrestler *junior* to me in the stable [under the stable master]. ▶あいつはぼくの弟分だ (=自分にとって弟のような人だ) He's like a *younger brother*.

おとおし お通し 〖日本料理の前菜〗 an hors d'oeuvre /ɔːrdˈəːrv/ (⑩ hors d'oeuvres /-/).

おどおど timidly; (神経が張りつめて) nervously; (ためらって) hesitantly. ▶おどおどしている(ように見える) look *intimidated* [*scared*]. ▶おどおどした目つきをしている with a *timid* [a *scared*] look in one's eyes. ▶少年がおどおどしながら犬に近づいた The small boy *timidly* came closer to the dog. ▶面接のとき彼がおどおどしていたのははた目にもよく分かった He *was* visibly *nervous* when he had the interview [during the interview].

***おどかす** 脅かす ❶【ぎょっとさせる】 frighten, scare. (**!** 後の方が口語的) ▶部屋から急に飛び出して彼を脅かした I *frightened* [*scared*] him by popping out of the room.
❷【脅迫する】 threaten. (⇨脅す)

おとぎぞうし 『お伽草子』 *Otogi Zoshi*. 〖参考〗 太宰治の小説

おとぎのくに 御伽の国 a fairyland.

おとぎばなし 御伽話 a fáiry tàle [stòry] (⇨メルヘン); (子供向きの話) a children's story. (⇨童話)

おどけもの おどけ者 〖冗談を言う人〗 a joker; 〖道化師・ひょうきん者〗 a clown.

おどける 動 〖ひょうきんぶる〗 clown (around); 〖ばかなまねをする〗 play [act] the fool.
—— **おどけた** 形 ▶おどけた演技 a *clownish* [a *funny*] performance. (⇨ふざける)
—— **おどけて** 副 jokingly; as a joke.

***おとこ** 男 ❶【男性】 a man (⑩ men), 〖話〗 a guy; a gentleman (⑩ -men /-mən/); a male; 〖愛人〗 one's lover. (⇨男性, 男らしい)

使い分け **man** woman に対し成人した男性をさす最も一般的な語. 成人していない少年や赤ん坊には boy を用いる.
gentleman 敬意を表し丁寧にいう時に用いる.

male 動植物の性に重点を置いたり, 統計などに用いたりする学術的な語. 一般に人に用いると通例軽蔑的な.

① **[男~]** ●男と女 man and women; men and women. (通例この語順で用いる) ●男女の関係 a *male*-female relationship; the relationships between *men* and women. ●男同士の約束 a promise between *men* and *men*. (通例冠詞は省略される) ●お互い引かれるものはありますよ, だけど男と女の間のものではありません There's a kind of attraction but it's not a *male*-female thing.
② **[男は]** ●男はつらいよ It's tough being a *man*. ●男は度胸だ Men must not flinch from difficulties.
③ **[男の]** male; (男らしい) masculine, manly. (⇨男らしい) ●男の中の男 a *man* among *men*; a *man's man*. ●彼女は男のような声で話す She speaks in a *masculine* voice [a *manly* tone of voice]. (⇨男らしい [類語])
④ **[男に]** ●彼は立派な男になった He grew up to be [grew into] a fine *man*. ●その苦しい経験のおかげで彼は一人前の男になった The hard experience has made a *man* of [ˣfrom] him.
❷ **[やつ]** 《話》a fellow, a guy. ●彼はなかなかおもしろい男です He is quite an [ˣa quite] interesting *fellow* [*guy*]. (!quite の位置は不定冠詞の前後のいずれでもよいが, ˣa quíte interesting は ㇐㇐ と続き音調が悪いので避ける. He is a quíete unúsual man. (まったく変わった人だ)なら ㇐㇐㇐ で可.)
❸ **[名誉, 評判]** ●男を上げる raise one's *reputation*. ●そんな悪いことをすると君の男が下がるよ(=名誉を傷つける) Such bad conduct will reflect on your honor [dishonor you].
● **男親** a father. ● **男友達** a boyfriend. (!通例1人の決まった恋人をいう) ● **男物** (品物) men's things; (衣類) men's wear.

おとこいっぴき 男一匹 (一人前の男) a man in his own right.
おとこおんな 男女 (女みたいな男) an effeminate man; (男みたいな女) a masculine woman.
おとこぎ 男気 (男らしさ) manliness, chivalry.
—— **男気のある** 形 manly, chivalrous.
おとこぐせ 男癖 ●男癖の悪い女 a woman who has problems being faithful to ⟨one's husband [boyfriend]⟩. (⇨ 女癖)
おとこぐるい 男狂い a wanton woman.
おとこごころ 男心 a man's heart. ●男心と秋の空 A man is as moody as autumn weather.
おとこざか 男坂 [急な方の坂] the steeper slope. (⇔女坂)
おとこざかり 男盛り ●彼は45歳の男盛りだ He is 45 years old and *in the prime of life* [*manhood*].
おとこしゃかい 男社会 (男性優位の社会) a male-dominated society.
おとこじょたい 男所帯 a womanless household.
おとこずき 男好き ●a wanton woman, a man chaser. ●男好きのする(=男に好かれる)女 a woman who *attracts* men.
おとこだて 男伊達 (男気) manliness, chivalry; (男気のある人) a chivalrous man.
おとこっけ 男っ気 (⇨女っ気) ●男っ気抜きのパーティー a party for *women* only; (米) a bachelorette party; (英) a hen party (!特に結婚式前夜に新婦とその友人で行う宴会). ●彼女の家はまったく男っ気がない Her house is completely manless.
おとこで 男手 male help. ●男手のない家 a house *without a man*; a manless household.
おとこなき 男泣き —— **男泣きする** 動 shed a man's bitter tears.
おとこのこ 男の子 a boy; [赤ん坊] a baby boy.
おとこぶり 男振り ●男振りのいい (男前の) handsome, manly, chivalrous.
おとこまえ 男前 a handsome [a good-looking] man.
おとこまさり 男勝り ●男勝りの女性 (活動的な) a spirited woman (!a manly [a mannish] woman は性差別語としてだんだん用いられなくなっている).
おとこみょうり 男冥利 (⇨冥利) ●そのような機会を与えられたことは男冥利に尽きる *I am grateful [It is fortunate for me] to have been born a man* and have had such an opportunity.
おとこやもめ 男やもめ a widower.
おとこらしい 男らしい masculine; manly; manful.

> **使い分け** **masculine** 男性としてふさわしい資質を持っていることを意味する.
> **manly** 成熟した男性の勇気・力強さなどを意味する. masculine より気品のある語.
> **manful** manly の意に他を寄せつけない「断固とした」という意が加わる.

●男らしい行動 a *manly* (↔an unmanly) act. ●男らしさに欠ける lack in *masculinity*. ●男らしくない unmanly;《話》sissy. ●彼は強くて男らしい He is strong and *manly* [a real man]. ●ボクシングは男らしいスポーツだ Boxing is a *masculine* sport. ●男らしくしろ Be a *man*!/Act like a *man*!

おとさた 音沙汰 (消息) news. ●この3年というもの彼から何の音沙汰もない I've heard nothing *from* him for the last three years. (⇨便り)
おどし 脅し (a) threat /θrét/. ●彼に脅し文句を吐く utter *threats* [*threatening*] words] *against* him. ●脅しに屈する give in [yield, bow] to a *threat*. ●彼らは飛行機を爆破すると脅しをかけてきた They made their *threat to* blow up [*that* they would blow up] the plane. ●彼らの脅しは口先だけのものだった Their *threat* turned out to be empty [(たのはったりである) be only a bluff]. (!「口先だけの脅し」は an empty [an idle] threat)
おとしあな 落とし穴 [動物などを捕らえる] a pitfall, a pit; [人が陥る] (予期せぬ危険) a pitfall; (謀略) a trap; (誘惑) a snare; (ひっかけ) a trick,《話》a catch. (⇨ 罠) ●落とし穴にかかる fall into a *trap*; be caught in a *trap*. ●一見やさしそうな問題の落とし穴 a *catch* in an easy-looking question.
おとしいれる 落とし入れる [わなにかける] trap (-pp-),《書》entrap (-pp-); [投げ入れる] throw (*into*-); [はめる]《話》frame. ●彼を困難な状況に陥れる *trap* [*entrap*] him *into* a difficult situation. ●世界経済を混乱に陥れる *throw* the global economy *into* (a) turmoil. ●彼は窃盗の罪に陥れられた He *has been framed for* theft.
おとしご 落とし子 a child born out of wedlock. ●高度成長の落とし子(=ひずみとして生じたもの), たとえば大気汚染 unwelcome *by-products* of high economic growth, such as air pollution. ●原爆は第二次大戦の落とし子だ The atomic bomb is the *child* of World WarⅡ.
おとしだま お年玉 a New Year's present [gift] (of money). ●おじがお年玉に5,000円くれた My uncle gave me 5,000 yen as a *New Year's present*. ●お年玉付き年賀はがき a New Year's lottery postcard; a lottery postcard with New Year's greetings.
おとしどころ 落とし所 ●私たちは落とし所を見いださなくてはならない We have to find *the middle ground*.
おとしぬし 落とし主 the owner of lost article. ●こ

おとしぶた 落とし蓋 の財布の落とし主はだれだと思いますか Who do you think *lost* this wallet? ▶その本の落とし主は現れなかった Nobody *claimed* the book. (**!** claim は「自分のものだと主張する」の意。「落とし主の現れない財布」は an unclaimed wallet という)

おとしぶた 落とし蓋 an *otoshibuta*, (説明的に) a smaller lid placed directly on the top of the food in a pot.

おとしまえ 落とし前 ▶落とし前をつける pay some money to settle a problem.

おとしもの 落とし物 the thing one found [has lost] (**!** 前の方では見つけた場合、後の方では失った場合) (遺失物) a lost article. (⇨とす)

:おとす 落とす ❶【落下させる】 drop (-pp-); 〖失う〗lose*; 〖影などを投げかける〗throw*, cast*. ▶都市に爆弾を落とす *drop* bombs *on* [*over*] *a city*. ▶視線を落とす *drop* one's gaze. ▶フライを落とす *drop* a fly ball. ▶その皿を床に落としたら粉々に壊れるでしょう If you *drop* the dish on the floor, it will break into pieces. ▶財布をどこかこの辺に落としたI *lost* my wallet somewhere around here.

❷【程度を下げる】(量・価値などを) reduce; (品質・声などを) lower; (信用・人気などを失う) lose*; (音・声などを) drop (-pp-); (速力などを) slow (…) down; (品位などを) degrade, debase. ▶体重を 5 キロ落とす *reduce* [*lose*] one's weight by five kilograms. ▶曲がり角で速度を落とす *reduce* speed at a corner; *slow down* at a corner. ▶品質を落とす *lower* the quality. ▶ステレオの音量を落とす *lower* [*turn down*] the volume of a stereo set. (**!** 単に *turn down* a stereo ともいえる) ▶声を落としてささやく *drop* [*lower*] one's voice *to* a whisper. ▶医師としての信用を落とす *lose* one's credit as a doctor. ▶車の速度を落とす *slow down* a car; *slow* a car *down*. ▶金のために品位を落とすようなことをするな Don't *degrade* [*debase*] yourself for money. ▶不正なことをしたため彼は評判を落とした He *lowered* his reputation by dishonesty. ▶彼女は調子(=体調)を落としている She *isn't in good shape*./(最高の状態ではない) She *isn't at her best*.

❸【除去する】(しみなどを抜き取る) take* [get*] ... out, remove (**!** 前の方が口語的に). (洗って落とす) wash... out [off]; (そり落とす) shave* ... off. ▶ワイシャツのインクのしみを落とす *take out* the ink stains [spots] *from* the shirt. ▶口ひげを落とす *shave off* one's mustache. ▶彼はズボンの泥[しみ]を洗って落とした He *washed* the mud *off* [the spot *out of*] his trousers.

❹【落第する・させる】fail. ▶英語を落とした I *failed* 〖《米話》*flunked*〗 English. ▶試験官は口答試問で志願者の 3 分の 1 を落とした The examiners *failed* one third of the applicants on the oral examination.

❺【抜かす】 leave* [miss] ... out, (わざと) omit (-tt-); (見[聞き]落とす) miss. ▶その名簿から私の名前を落とさないでください Don't *leave out* [*omit*, *miss out*] my name *from* the list. ▶私は 1 行を読み落としていた I *have left out* [*missed*] one line in reading. ▶君の番号を書き[言い]落とさないでください (=忘れないでください) Don't *forget* to write [say] your number.

❻【手中におさめる】▶城を落とす(=攻め取る) *capture* [*seize*] a castle. ▶彼はその家具を競売で落とした(=買った) He *got* the furniture at [《英》by] auction.

❼【その他の表現】▶試合を落とす *drop* [*lose*] a game. ▶第 1 戦を 2 点差で落とす(=負ける) *lose* the first game [match] by two points. ▶データを CD-ROM に落とす(=記録する) put [record, save] data on a CD-ROM. ▶犯人を落とす(=責めて)白状させる) force a criminal to confess. ▶費用を必要経費として落とす(=控除する) *deduct* the expenses as necessary expenditure. ▶観光客はたくさんの金をその温泉地に落とす(=使う) The tourists *spend* a lot of money at the hot-spring resort.

***おどす 脅す** 〖脅迫する〗 threaten /θrétn/, 《書》menace /ménəs/; 〖怖じけさせる〗 scare, frighten, terrify. ▶彼をナイフで脅す *threaten him with a knife.* ▶彼は私を逮捕するといって脅(おど)した He *threatened* to arrest me./He *threatened* me *with* arrest. ▶彼を脅して契約条件をのませた I *frightened* [*terrified*] him *into* agreeing to the term.

おとずれ 訪れ ❶【訪問】 a visit. (⇨訪問) ❷【到来】 coming. (⇨到来) ▶今年は春の訪れが遅かった Spring *has come* late this year./Spring was late (in) *coming* this year. (**!** 前の方が普通)

***おとずれる 訪れる** ❶【訪問する】 visit; pay* a visit 《*to*》; (職務・儀礼で) call 《*on*+人, *at*+場所》. (⇨訪ねる) ❷【到来する】 come*. (⇨来る)

おととい 一昨日 the day before yesterday. (**!**(1) 《米話》では the はしばしば省略される. (2)《英》では *on* the day … ということもある. (3) 英語では曜日表現が優先され, 「おととい」が月曜日なら (last) Monday などということが多い ⇨明後日(あ)) ▶おとといの朝[夜]に (on) the morning [night] *before last*; the morning [night] 《*of*》*the day before yesterday*. (**!**(1) ×(on) the morning [night] *before yesterday* とはいわない. (2) 今日が水曜日なら具体的に on Monday morning [night] ということが多い) ▶おととい彼を訪ねた I visited him *the day before yesterday*. ▶おとといおいで(=二度と来るな) Come when two Sundays meet.

おととし 一昨年 the year before last; two years ago. ▶一昨年の春 [5 月] に (in) the spring [(in) May, (in) the May] *before last*. (**!** in をつけるのは《英》. 今が 2009 年なら具体的に (in) the spring of 2007, in May, 2007 ということも多い)

:**おとな 大人** an adult; 《話》a grown-up; (男性) a man (**複** men), (女性) a woman (**複** women /wímin/). (⇨成人) ▶大人らしいふるまい *grown-up* behavior. ▶もう大人なんだから大人らしく行動しなくては You are an *adult* and should act accordingly./You're not a child anymore, you should act more *grown up*. ▶彼女は大人になったら女優になりたいと思っている She wants to be an actress when she *grows up* [*is grown-up*, ×*grows*]. ▶彼の娘たちはもう大人である His daughters *are grown up* now./His daughters are *grown* women now. ▶彼は大人のような口のきき方をする He talks like a *grown-up*. ▶大人 2 枚, 子供 1 枚ください Two *adult* tickets and one child, please./《主に英》Two and a half, please. ▶彼女は実際の年齢より大人びていて女性という感じです She looks more *adult* [*mature*] and womanly than she really is. ▶(何を言っているの)ジョージ, もうちょっと大人になりなさい *Grow up*, George.

> **翻訳のこころ** 「けっこう, すてきだよね, 相沢くんて.」「大人っぽい気がする.」 (山田詠美 『ひよこの眼』)
> "That guy Aizawa's rather [fairly] cool, isn't he?" "Yes, he looks quite *matured*." (**!** matured は「精神的に大人である[成熟している]」の意)

おとなげない 大人気ない (子供っぽい) childish. ▶そんなささいなことで騒ぎたてるなんて大人気ないよ(=子供っぽ

おとなしい / 241 / おどろき

い) It *is childish of* you *to* fuss about such trifles.

*おとなしい 形 ❶[従順な](素直で) obedient, (気が弱くて) meek; [温和な] mild; [物静かな] quiet; [動物が狂暴でない] gentle; (なれた) tame. ● a *tame* [a *gentle*] dog. ▶彼はおとなしい子だ He's an *obedient* child. ▶彼はおとなしく内気な青年だ He is a *quiet*, shy young man. ▶彼女はおとなしくふりをしているだけです She looks *obedient* [*meek*] but she is stubborn. ▶彼は先生の前ではおとなしい He is very *quiet* [*meek*] in front of his teacher [(そばにいるときは) when his teacher is around].

❷[じみな] quiet. ●おとなしい柄 a *quiet* pattern.
― おとなしく 圖 obediently; meekly; quietly. ▶彼はおとなしく先生の忠告に従った He followed his teacher's advice *obediently*. ●おとなしく(=静かに)しなさい Be *quiet*!/(行儀よくしなさい) Behave yourself! (!強盗がいう「おとなしくしろ」は You just *take it easy*.) ▶彼女はおとなしくできないのなら出て行ってもらいます If you don't keep *quiet*, you have to leave. ▶彼はおとなしいふりをしているだけです His *meek* attitude is really only put on. (!put on は「とってつける」の意の《話》)

おとめ 乙女 a (young) girl, 《書》a maiden; [処女] a virgin.

おとめざ 乙女座 [占星・天文] Virgo (!the はつなぎない); [処女宮][占星] the Virgin. ●乙女座(生まれ)の人 a Virgo (徴 ～s), a Virgoan. (!後の方は形容詞としても用いる) ▶彼女は乙女座生まれです She's (a) *Virgo* [*Virgoan*]. ▶彼女は典型的な乙女座です She is a typical *Virgo* [*Virgoan*]./She has a typical *Virgoan* personality.
会話 「あなたは何座(生まれ)ですか」「乙女座(生まれ)です」 "Which sign of the zodiac were you born under?" "(I was born under) *Virgo*."

おとも 御供 图 (重要人物の) a retinue /rétən(j)uː/ (!集合的に用い単・複両扱い); an entourage /ɑ̀ːntərɑ́ːʒ/ (!集合的に用い単・複両扱い); (案内等) an attendant. ●王とそのお供 the king and his *retinue*.
― 御供(を)する 動 ▶駅までお供する *go* to the station *with* (him), (やや書) *accompany* (him) to the station. ▶女王のお供をする(=随行して世話をする)女性たち the ladies *attending* (*on*) [*in attendance on*] the queen.

おどらす 踊らす ▶彼女は彼にうまく踊らされている(=意のままに操られている) He *has* [*keeps*] her *on a string*.

おどらす 躍らす ▶胸を躍らせて with one's heart *leaping*; with a *leap* of one's heart. (⇒躍る)

おとり 囮 [おびき寄せる人, おとり用の鳥] a decoy. ▶おとりに使う use (him) as a *decoy*; use (a bird) for calling. ●おとり商品 a loss leader. ●おとり捜査 (an) undercover investigation; 《米話》a sting (operation). ●おとり捜査官 an undercover cop [agent of the police].

おどり 踊り a dance (!「ひと踊り」の意もある); dancing. ●踊りがうまい be good at *dancing*; be a good dancer; (女性) a *dancer*. ●踊りの師匠 a dancing màster [(女性) mìstress]. (!アクセントに注意) ●踊りを習う take *dancing* lessons; take lessons in *dancing*. (⇒踊る)

おどりあがる 躍り上がる jump [spring*] up. ●踊り上がって喜ぶ *jump* [*dance*] for joy.

おどりかかる 躍り掛かる ▶ライオンが獲物に躍りかかった A lion *fiercely jumped on* its prey.

おどりぐい 躍り食い eating (small fish or prawns) alive.

おどりこ 踊り子 a dancer (!最も一般的な語でプロ・素人を含意する); (プロの) a dáncing gìrl (!アクセントに注意. dàncing gírl は「踊っている女」の意); (ショーの) a show girl; (バレエの) a ballet /bǽleɪ/ dancer [girl].

おどりでる 躍り出る ●首位に躍り出る (先頭に立つ) take* the lead; (首位になる) come* (out) top 《*in* the exam》 (!この top は形容詞); (1 位になる) take first place.

おどりば 踊り場 (階段の) a landing.

*おとる 劣る be inferior (*to*); [下位である] be below …; [より悪い] be worse (*than*). (⇒勝る) ●品質が劣った品物 goods of *inferior* quality. ▶これはあれより品質の点ではるかに劣る This is far *below* [*inferior to*] that in quality. ▶その殺人犯は犬畜生にも劣るやつだ The murderer *is worse than* a beast. ▶正夫は身長では君に劣る Masao *is not as* [*so*] *tall as* you are. (!《米》では so を用いるのは古風で強意的に響く)/Masao is shorter than you are. ▶Masao is *less* tall *than* you are. ともいえるが (まれ) (⇒ほど) ▶彼は父に劣らず足が速い He runs *as fast as* his father. (!「同等に」の意) ▶これは 2 世紀前に劣らず今でも真実だ This is *no less* true today *than* it was two centuries ago.

*おどる 踊る dance. ●踊りを踊る have a *dance* (*with*); do [perform] a *dance*. ●ワルツを踊る *dance* a waltz; waltz. ●音楽[ピアノ]に合わせて優雅に踊る *dance* gracefully (↔awkwardly) to the music [piano]. ▶ぼくは彼女に一曲踊ってほしいと頼んだ I asked her for a *dance*. (!実際にいう場合は, Would you please have a [the next] dance with me? など)

おどる 躍る leap (up), throb (-bb-), jump. ▶喜びに胸が躍った My heart *leaped* (*up*) [*throbbed*] with joy. ▶今あこがれている彼に話しかけられたとき, 私の胸は躍った When he, my latest crush, talked to me, I felt my heart *jump*. ▶ディズニーランドへ行くことを思うと少年の心は躍った The boy *was thrilled* when he thought of going to Disneyland. (!thrill は「胸をときめかす」の意. 強調して, 《話》で *be thrilled to bits* [《米》*pieces*] ともいう)

おとろえ 衰え ●記憶力[視力]の衰え(=減退) the *failure* of one's memory [sight]. ●健康の衰え the *decline* of health.

おとろえる 衰える [弱くなる] get* [become*] weak; [あらし・風などが] die (～d; dying) down [die (away) の形で「完全になくなる状態」をさす]; 《書》subside; 《書》abate; [力・価値などが] 《やや書》decline; [健康などが] fail. (⇒弱る ❶) ▶彼は体力が衰えた He has got [grown] *weak*./His strength *has declined* [*failed*]./He has declined [failed] in strength. ▶視力が衰えてきている My eyesight *is failing*. ▶その歌手の人気は衰えてきている《事が主語》The singer's popularity *is declining* [*on the decline*]./《人が主語》The singer *is losing* popularity./The singer *is getting less and less* popular. ▶台風は次第に衰えた The typhoon gradually *died down* [*weakened*] (its *force*).

おどろかす 驚かす [びっくりさせる] surprise, amaze, astonish, startle; [こわがらせる] frighten, scare (!後の方が口語的に); [不安にさせる] alarm. (⇒驚く [類243]) ▶その大統領の暗殺は世界を驚かせた The president's assassination *surprised* the world [*took* the world *by surprise*]. ▶大地震のうわさは町中を驚かせた The rumor of a great earthquake *alarmed* the whole city.

おどろき 驚き ❶[びっくり] surprise, astonishment; [驚異, 驚嘆] wonder, amazement. (⇒驚く [類

語]). ▶彼は驚きを顔に表した His face showed his surprise./He had a *surprised* look on his face. ▶だれもが驚きの目をみはった Everybody stared *in wonder*. ▶彼女の驚きはだれの目にも明らかだった Her *astonishment* was plain to everyone. ▶彼が英語を話せることに驚きはしない I'm not *surprised (that)* he can speak English./(不思議はない) *(It is) no [little, small] wonder (that)* he can speak English. (!)《話》では( )内はしばしば省略する）

❷ 【驚くべきこと】 a surprise; a wonder. ▶そこに彼女がいたのは大きな[全くの]驚きだった It was a great [a complete] *surprise* to find her there. ▶彼があんなにもしんぼう強いとは驚きだ It's *surprising* [*amazing*] how patient he is.

:おどろく 驚く 動 ❶【びっくりする】be surprised, be amazed, be astonished 《*at; to do; that* 節》; be taken aback 《*at, by*》; be shocked 《*at; to do; that* 節》; 《やや書》wonder 《*at; to do; that* 節》, 《書》marvel 《*at; that* 節》.

【使い分け】 **be surprised** 予期せぬ事態に驚くことを意味する最も一般的な表現.
be amazed 仰天して心の底からびっくりすること.
be astonished 信じがたい事態に仰天し, 呆然とすること.
be taken aback 予期せぬ事態に面食らい, まごつくこと.
be shocked 突然の出来事によって精神的に衝撃・打撃を受けること. 不愉快な出来事を原因とする場合が多い.
marvel 主に立派な物に対し, 感動して驚くこと.
wonder 不思議に思って驚くこと.

▶驚くなかれ Don't be *surprised*, but .../(実は) In fact/(なんと) get this (【驚くようなことを言う直前に挿入的に用いる).

会話「あのう, もしかして山田先生では」「やあ田中君! 驚いたなあ」"Well, if it isn't Mr. Yamada!" "Hi, Tanaka! What a pleasant *surprise*!"(【意外な人に会ったときのうれしい驚きを表す言い方. What a surprise! という丁寧）

会話「ぼくたち結婚するんです」「こりゃ驚いた. ともかくおめでとう」"We're going to get married." "Well, I'll be damned. Anyhow, congratulations."(【意外な事実に直面したときの強い驚きを表すくだけた言い方）

会話「太郎が試験に受かったよ」「へえ驚いたね(=冗談でしょう)」"Taro has passed his exam." "You're kidding./(信じられないわ) I don't [can't] believe it./(まったく予想しなかった) Who would have thought!/I would have never guessed!"

① 【...には【驚】】 ▶先生は彼のそつのない返答に驚いた The teacher *was astonished at [by]* his clever answer. (!)(1) at では「驚いている」状態を, by では「驚かされる」という動作に重点がある. (⇨解説)
(2) 能動形では次のように表せる: His clever answer *surprised* [*was surprising to*] the teacher. (3) The teacher *was amazed* [*wondered, marveled*] *at* his clever answer. では「感心した」の意を含意)/He gave a clever answer [when he heard his clever answer]./The teacher *was surprised* to hear his clever answer. ▶彼女にそこで会ったのは驚いた I *was surprised (that)* [*It was surprising that*] (should have) met her there. (!) should を用いると話し手の感情を表して「会うなんて」の意となる)/It *surprised* me [*was a surprise* to me] *that* I met her there. ▶私は彼の無作法なふるまいに少し驚いた I was slightly *taken aback* by his rude manner. ▶彼がその事故で死んだのには驚いた I *was shocked (that)* [*to learn that*] he had died in the accident. (!)shocked の代わりに astonished, amazed は可能だが, surprised はこのような深刻な内容には不適当）

会話「敏雄には驚いたよ」「あんなことをすべきじゃなかったよね」"I'm *surprised at* Toshio." "He shouldn't have done such a thing, should he?"

【解説】surprised と修飾語
修飾語で強めるときは be *very* surprised *at*, be *very much* [《やや書》be *much*] surprised *by* となるのが普通. ただし, amazed, astonished は通例 very ではなく absolutely, quite などで修飾する.

② 【驚いて】 ▶驚いて物も言えなかった I *was so surprised that* I couldn't utter a word./I couldn't utter a word *in surprise*./I was speechless *with amazement*./I was *dumbfounded*.

③【驚くほど】surprisingly, amazingly, astonishingly. ▶試験は驚くほど簡単だった The exam was *surprisingly* easy. ▶こんな時に君は驚くほど冷静だ You are *astoningly* calm in this situation.

④【驚いたことに】 ▶驚いたことに彼は突然辞表を出した *To my surprise*, he suddenly handed in his resignation. / *Surprisingly*, he suddenly handed in his resignation./It *was surprising that* he suddenly handed in his resignation. ▶だれもが驚いたことにその子を誘拐したのは実の母親であった *To the astonishment of* everybody, it was the boy's real mother who kidnapped him.

❷ 【おびえる】 be frightened 《*at, by; to do; that* 節》; (飛び上がるほど) be startled 《*at, by; to do*》. ▶突然の物音にひどく驚いた I *was* very (much) *frightened at* [*to hear*] the sudden noise./The sudden sound *frightened* me very much.

─ **驚くべき** 形 surprising, amazing, astonishing; [驚嘆すべき] wonderful, marvelous. (!以上の語は surprising を除いて通例 very ではなく absolutely, quite などで修飾する) ▶驚くべき記録 an *amazing* record. ▶それはまったく驚くべき事実だ It is quite a *surprising* fact. ▶読み書きのできない人がたくさんいるのは驚くべきことだ It's *surprising (that)* so many people can't read or write./It's *surprising* how many people can't read or write. ▶彼は驚くべきおじいちゃんだ. また現役で働いているんだから He's a *wonderful* [a *marvelous*] old man. He still does a full day's work.

─ **驚いた** 形 surprised; [おびえた] frightened. • 驚いた表情 a *surprised* look.

おないどし 同い年 ▶彼と同い年の少女 a girl (*of*) his *age* (!《話》では通例 of を省略する. a girl *of an age* with him は《今はまれ》)/a girl *the same age as* he (is). (!is は通例省略される) ▶私は彼と同い年ですI am *as old as* he (is)./I am (*of*) his *age*./I am (*of*) *the same age as* he (is). (!いずれも of は通例省略）

おなか お腹 [腹部] (胃) a stomach; (子宮) a womb /wúːm/. (ˇ小腹) ▶お腹の中の子の命を絶つのは犯罪になることもある It can be a crime to end the life of an *unborn* child. ▶何とかうちで祐子はお腹を痛めた子ですから After all, I had carried Yuko in my *womb*. ▶だいぶお腹が出てきたんじゃない? I'm afraid you're getting a spare tire.

会話「おなかは?」「すいてないの. お昼は済ませてあるの」"Aren't you hungry?" "No. I've already eaten [had lunch]." (!空腹状態を表すときは be

おなが 尾長 〖鳥〗an azure-winged magpie.
おながどり 尾長鶏 〖鳥〗a long-tailed cock.
おながれ お流れ ●[中止される] be called off; (雨で) be rained out《米》[off《英》]. ▶お流れちょうだい(=目上の人からさがずに差してもらう酒) Let me have the honor of using your cup. 〘事情〙 米英にはこのような習慣がない)
おなぐさみ お慰み (楽しみ) amusement. ▶うまくいったらお慰み(=喜ばしい) It will be *a pleasure* if it goes well.
おなさけ お情け (⇨情け) ●お情けで彼を雇う employ him *out of compassion* [*pity, charity*]. ▶彼は先生のお情けで試験に及第した His teacher helped him pass the exam *out of pity*./Thanks to his teacher's *mercy*, he passed the exam.
おなじ 同じ 形 ❶[同一・同種の] the same; identical /aidéntikl/; similar.

> 〘使い分け〙 **same** 時間・時期・方法・性別・年齢などが完全に同一であるか、ごく類似していることを示す最も一般的な語。通例 the, 時に this, that, these, those などの限定詞とともに用いる。the same を強調すると exactly [very much] the same, the very same, one and the same の形が用いられる。
> **identical** 寸分も違わず、完全に同一であること。
> **similar** 完全に同一ではないか、種別・特性・形状などが同種似ていること。

▶君が行こうと行くまいと同じことだ(=どうでもよい) It is *all the same* [(違いはない) It *makes no difference*] whether you will go or not. (!わを忘れないよう注意) ▶でも同じことじゃない? But what difference does it make? (!But isn't it the same? としない方がよい) 〘会話〙「お茶を１杯持ってきてください」「私も同じものをお願いします」"Please bring me a cup of tea." "*Same* for me [〘話〙 *Same* here], please." 〘会話〙「どっちの月がいい?」「6月だろうが7月だろうがぼくにとってはどっちでも同じことだよ」"Which month would you prefer?" "June or July, it's *all the same* to me." 〘会話〙「かわいそうな小犬、悲しそうだわ。連れて帰ったらいけないかなあ」「私も同じことを今考えていたところだ(=まさに私が考えていたことだ)」"Poor puppy! He looks sad. Can't we take him home?" "That's just what I was thinking." 〖…と同じ〗 the same ... as [that].... ▶彼は昨年の夏着ていたのと同じ上着を着ている He is wearing *the same* jacket (*that*) he wore last summer./He is wearing *the same* jacket (*as*) he wore last summer [*as last summer*]. (!(1)一般に the same ... の後に節が続く場合、また「同種」のもの、that は「同一」のものを暗示するが、このような区別は守られないことも多い。(2)〘話〙では文脈から明らかな場合は the same の後の(主語+)動詞がしばしば省略される。that では不可。(3) the same ... の後に節が続く場合、that の方が口語的. 〘話〙では the same ... がそれに続く節の目的格にあたる場合、that や as がしばしば省略される) ●いつも同じ(列車)の電車に乗り遅れる miss *the same* train as one always takes; miss one's *usual* train. ▶彼のペンは私がきのう買ったのとそっくり同じだ His pen is exactly *the same as* [×*with*] the one I bought yesterday. (!...*the same as* I bought yesterday. より普通。「同一」でなくて「同種」であることを明確にする場合は His pen *is exactly like* the one .... とする)/His pen *is identical with* [〘話〙*to*] the one I bought yesterday. ▶彼の意見は私とだいたい同じだ His opinion is much *the same as* mine. (!much は質に関して用い、量に関しては about を用いる (⇨❷)))/I mostly *agree with* him. ▶彼が事故死したのとまったく同じ地点で車の衝突事故があった Two cars collided at the *identical* [*the very same*] place where he was killed in the accident. ▶その脱獄囚とテロリストは実は同じ人物だった The escaped prisoner and the terrorist were in fact *one and the same* (person). ▶私はあなたと同じような経験をした I had a *similar* experience [an experience *similar*] *to* yours. ▶ずいぶん変わったでしょうがこの一角は以前と同じたたずまいを見せている The town has changed a lot, but this quarter looks just *the same as* before. ❷[等しい] (数量・程度・大きさなどが) equal; (価値などが) equivalent 《*to*》; (...も同然で) as good as ...(⇨同然). ▶彼の収入は私とほぼ同じです His income is about *the same* [about *as large*] *as* mine. ▶この場合沈黙は承認と同じだ Under these conditions silence *is equivalent to* [*amounts to*] consent. ▶我が子を愛する気持ちは親なら誰でも同じだ(=共通だ) Love for their own children *is common to* all parents. ▶私は6つのレポートを同じ数の月を費やして書いた I wrote six reports *in as many months*. (!*as many* は先行する数詞を受けて「同じ数だけの」の意)
①〖…と同じくらい...〗 as+形 [+名・副] + as ....(!後の as に続く節中では、比較するうえで重要でない要素はしばしば省略される) ▶彼女は私と同じくらい速く泳げる She can swim *as fast as* I (can)./She is *as fast a swimmer* [×*as a fast swimmer*] *as* I (am). (!as の後に人称代名詞が続く場合、(助動詞を添える方が口語的。また〘話〙では as me の形が多い) ▶花子は私と同じくらい多くの本を持っている Hanako has *as many* [×*much*, ×*a lot of*] books *as* I (do). ▶仙台にはここと同じくらい多くの友人がいる *As many* of my friends are in Sendai *as* (are) in here. 〘会話〙「この前のコンサートよりよかったかい」「同じくらいかな(=ちょうど同じだよかった)」"Was it better than the last concert?" "Just *as good*." (!後の文は as the last concert が省略されている)
②〖…と同じように〗 ▶彼も君と同じようにそこへ行った He went there, *like* [×as] you. (!he と you を強調的に対照する場合は He, *like*, you, went there. の語順も可)/He went there, *as* [〘話〙*like*] you did. ▶その知らせを聞いて私も君と同じように悲しかった I was *equally* unhappy at the news.
── 同じ 副 (⇨どうせ) ▶同じ行くのなら君と行きたい I'd like to go with you if I go *at all*.
● **同じ穴のむじな** ▶連中は同じ穴のむじなだ They are all in the same gang.
● **同じ釜の飯を食う** work at the same place; live together under the same roof.
● **同じ轍(⑤)を踏む** ▶同じ轍を踏むな Don't make *the same* mistake (*that*) your predecessors made.

おなじく 同じく 〖同じやり方で〗 in the same way [manner]; 〘書〙likewise; 〖…と同様に〗like ..., as .... (⇨同じ ❷ ②)) ▶彼は彼女を無視した He ignored her, and she ignored him (*in*) *the same way* [*likewise*, (彼女もまた) *too*]. ▶彼女はお母さんと同じように料理が上手だ She cooks well *as* [〘話〙*like*] her mother does. ▶もし私があなたと同じふるまったら、笑われるだろう If I were to behave *like* [×*as*] you, I would be laughed at by all. ▶彼女と同じく彼も信仰心がなかった *Like* her, he had no religious feeling.

おなじみ お馴染み ❶[客] (商店などの) a (regular) customer. (⇨馴染む) ❷[親しんでいること] おなじみの (周知の) well-known; (見慣れた, 聞き慣れた) familiar; (好きな) favorite. ●西部劇でおなじみの光景 a *familiar* sight from Western films.

オナニー [<ドイツ語] 名 masturbation.
── **オナニー(を)する** 動 masturbate;《話》play with oneself.

おなみだちょうだい お涙ちょうだい ●お涙ちょうだいの a sob story;《話》a tearjerker.

おなら 名 (腹の中のガス)《米》gas,《英》wind;《卑》a fart. ▶サツマイモを食べるとおならが出る Eating sweet potatoes will give me *gas* [*wind*].
── **おなら(を)する** 動《米》pass gas,《英》break wind;《卑》fart.

おに 鬼 (悪霊) a demon /díːmən/; (悪魔) a devil; (鬼ごっこの鬼) a tagger (⇨鬼ごっこ). ●人食い鬼 an ogre /óuɡər/. ●鬼のような人(=男) a *devil* of a man. ●心を鬼にする(⇨心[成句]) ▶彼は仕事の鬼である He is a *demon* for work./He works like hell [《やや古・話》like the *devil*]. ●渡る世間に鬼はない (⇨渡る[成句])
● 鬼が出るか蛇(じゃ)が出るか Prepare yourself for the worst.
● 鬼が笑う ▶来年のことを言うと鬼が笑う You can't tell what will happen next.
● 鬼に金棒 ▶彼が探検隊に加われば鬼に金棒だ If he joins the expedition, it will make the party doubly powerful [it'll be a double advantage].
● 鬼のいぬ間に洗濯 (ことわざ) When the cat is away, the mice will play.
● 鬼の霍乱(かくらん) ▶彼のような元気者が病気になるなんてさに鬼の霍乱だね For a healthy guy like him to get sick is just like the devil getting sunstroke.
● 鬼の首を取ったよう ▶もし勝ったら鬼の首でも取ったような気分になるでしょう You'll be *on top of the world* if you win.
● 鬼の目にも涙 It will melt the coldest heart.
● 鬼は外、福は内 Out with devils, in with good fortune! (❗the Devil は「サタン」のことなので注意)
● 鬼も十八、番茶も出花 'A girl at eighteen looks her best.'/(慣用的に) She is sweet sixteen.
● 鬼婆 a hag.

おにあざみ 鬼薊 〖植物〗a plumed thistle.

おにがわら 鬼瓦 an *onigawara*, (説明的に) a ridge-end roofing tile with the design of a devil.

おにぎり お握り a rice ball. (⇨🍙 お結び)

おにごっこ 鬼ごっこ tag; (鬼が目隠しをする) the blind man's buff.
会話 「鬼ごっこしよう」「だれが鬼だ」「彼が鬼だ」 "Let's play *tag*." "Who is the tagger?" "He's *it*."

おにび 鬼火 a will-o'-the-wisp.

おにもつ お荷物 (重荷) a burden; (足手まとい) a drag; (役に立たない人)《話》deadwood. ▶たいていの老人は子供のお荷物になるよりは一人暮らしをするほうがましだと思っている Most older people would rather live by themselves than become a *burden* to [*a drag on*] their children. (❗主語が複数であっても ×burdens, ×drags とはいわない)

おにゆり 鬼百合 〖植物〗a tiger lily.

おね 尾根 a mountain ridge. ●尾根づたいに歩く walk along the *ridge*.

おねがい お願い ●鬼まで話を聞いて、お願いします Hear me out, I beg (of) you! ●of がある方が切実な感じが強い) ▶お願いだからちょっと静かにしていてよ *Please* [《話》*For goodness sake*, 《話》*For heaven's sake*], keep quiet a minute. (❗please には強い強調が置かれる. 後の二つの方がより強いいら立ちを表す. goodness, heaven's の代わりに God's, Christ's も用いられるが, より強意的で主に男性に好まれる) ▶コーヒーをお願いします Two coffees, *please*. (❗×Please two coffees. とはいわない)
会話 「お願いがあるんですけど」「はい、何でしょう」 "Could you do me a (little) favor?/Could I (possibly) ask you a favor?/I have a favor to ask (of) you./There is something I'd like to ask you." "Sure. What \is it?" (❗(1) I'd like … の代わりに I want … というと、直接すぎる. また Do me a favor and (do). では「お願いだから…して」といった相手に選択の余地を与えない言い方になる. (2) この代わりに「今手が空いていますか」 Are you busy (now)? (❗now は通例省略) とか Are you doing anything? と間接的にいうことも可)

おねしょ 名 bed-wetting.
── **おねしょする** 動 wet one's bed; wet oneself.
●おねしょする子 a beddy-wetty. ▶太郎はまたおねしょしたわ Taro *has wet himself* again.

おねつ お熱 (⇨熱 ❸)

おの 斧 an ax,《主に英》an axe;〖手斧〗a hatchet.
●おので丸太を割る split a log with an *ax*.

*おのおの 各** each. (⇨それぞれ)

おのずから 自ら [自然に] naturally;〖思わず知らず〗spontaneously;〖ひとりでに〗by oneself, of one's own accord. ●おのずから明らかな(=自明の)事実 a *self-evident* fact.

おのずと 自ずと ▶真実は時がたてば自ずと明らかになる In time the truth will *speak for itself*. (❗慣用表現)

おののく 戦く shiver. ●不安におののく *shiver* in one's shoes; (恐怖でひとりでに震える) *tremble* with fear.

おのぼりさん お上りさん (田舎からやってきた観光客) a tourist [a visitor] just up from the countryside. ▶パリの夏は上りさんでにぎわう Paris is filled with *tourists* in the summer. (❗このような文脈では特に「田舎から出てきた」などの形容句は不要)

オノマトペ 〖擬声語, 擬態語〗an onomatopoeia /ànəmætəpíːə/.

おのれ 己 oneself. (⇨自分) ●おのれに勝つ control [restrain] *oneself*.
●己をむなしくする (私利私欲を捨てる) empty oneself of one's own interests.

おは 尾羽 wings and tail.
●尾羽打ち枯らす ▶尾羽打ち枯らした敗軍の将 a *down-and-out* [a *shabby*] defeated general. (❗前の方は「落ちぶれた」, 後の方は「みすぼらしい身なりの」の意)

おば 叔母, 伯母 an aunt;《話》an auntie,《話》an aunty. ●花子おばさん[ちゃん] *Aunt* [*Auntie*] Hanako. (❗名前をつけずに呼びかけるときは Auntie が普通)

おばあさん ❶[祖母] a grandmother;《話》a grandma,《話・小児語》a granny. (❗いずれも呼びかけるときは, 無冠詞で通例大文字で. Grandma が最も普通 (⇨🇯🇵 お父さん)) ▶栄子おばあさん *Grandma* Eiko. ▶おばあさんから贈り物をもらう get a present from *Grandma* [*my grandma*]. (❗前の方は身内の者に, 後の方は他人に対するもの)
❷[老人] an old woman [lady] (複 old women [ladies]). (❗「おばあさん」という呼びかけはせず主に名前で, または He は madam,《米話》ma'am と呼ぶ)

オパール (an) opal /óupl/. ●宝石として個々にいうときは C

オハイオ 〖米国の州〗Ohio /ouháiou/ (略 O. 郵便略

おはぎ　お萩　an *ohagi*; (説明的に) a soft rice cake covered with sweetened bean paste. (⇨ぼた餅)

おはぐろ　お歯黒　tooth blackening; (説明的に) a traditional tooth staining custom with married women in the Edo period Japan.

おばけ　お化け　[幽霊] a ghost; [妖怪(ﾖｳｶｲ)]《小児語》a bogey (man). (⇨化け物)

おはこ　十八番　[専門] a specialty, 《英》a speciality; [気に入りのもの] a favorite; [得意] one's forte /fɔːrt/. ● …を得意で[楽しんで]する get on [ride] one's hobbyhorse. ▶その歌は彼のおはこだ That song is his *favorite*./That is his (×most) *favorite* song.

おばさん　小母さん　[よその人] a woman (women); a stranger; [呼びかけ] madam, 《米話》ma'am, (子供の) aunt. (⇨小父さん)

おはじき　(an *ohajiki* 《噯～》) (説明的に) a small glass disc used in a game played by little girls. Discs are flipped to hit and capture the other discs. ● おはじきをする play (a game of) *ohajiki*.

おはち　お鉢　❶[おひつ] a boiled rice container. ❷[順番] one's turn. (❗常に単数形で: their turn 〔×turns〕) ▶皿洗いのおはちが回ってきた My turn has come to do [wash up] the dishes.

おはつ　お初　▶お初にお目にかかります It's a great pleasure [(I'm very) pleased] to meet you.

おばな　尾花　[ススキの穂]《植物》(flowers of) Japanese pampas grass.

おばな　雄花　《植物》a staminate [a male] flower.

おはなばたけ　お花畑　a flówer gàrden; (高山植物群落) a colony of an alpine flora.

*****おはよう**　Good morning. ▶彼は私におはようと言った He said *good morning* to me.
　会話「おはようございます」「おはよう、健」"*Good morning,* sir [ma'am, miss]." "(*Good*) *morning*, Kén." (❗通例, 後に相手の名や sir, ma'am などをつける)

おはらい　御祓い　图 (罪業の) purification; (悪霊祓い) exorcism.
　── **御祓い(を)する**　動　purify; exorcise. (⇨祓う)

おはらいばこ　御払い箱　● お払い箱にする (不用品などを) throw … away; (人を) fire. ▶彼は会社をお払い箱になった He *got fired* from his office./[老齢のために引退させた]《英話》They *put* him *out to pasture*. (❗後の方は they（=会社）に対する非難の意が含まれる)

おはりこ　お針子　a seamstress.

おばん　(オールドミス)《軽蔑的》an old maid; (服装のやぼったい女性) a frump. ▶彼女はおばんくさい服装をしている She is dressed like an old woman.

*****おび　帯**　(ベルト) a belt; (和服の) an *obi*, (説明的に) a broad Japanese sash for a kimono; (装飾用) a sash. ●帯を解く[締める] undo [put on, tie, fasten] an *obi*. ●帯をきつくする[緩める] tighten [loosen] an *obi*. ●うすい帯状の雲 a thin *ribbon* of clouds.
●帯に短したすきに長し ▶あの辞書は帯に短したすきに長しで, 高校生には詳しすぎるし, 先生方にはものたりない That dictionary falls between two tools; it's too detailed for high school students but not satisfactorily enough for teachers.
●帯留め an *obi* clip; an *obi* fastener.

おびいわい　帯祝い　*obiiwai*; (説明的に) the custom of tying a cloth around one's waist as a prayer for an easy delivery in the fifth month of pregnancy.

おびえる　脅える　be frightened; be terrified. (⇨怖がる) ●おびえた犬 a *frightened* [a *terrified*] dog. ●恐怖におびえる(=震える) shake with fear. ▶彼女は何かにおびえているような目をしていた She had a *frightened* look in her eye(s).

おびがみ　帯紙　(新刊本などの) a paper band for a blurb put on a book jacket or a slipcase; (帯封の紙) a band wrapper.

おびがら　お日柄　(⇨日柄) ▶本日は大変お日柄もよい (=幸先がよい) This is an *auspicious* day.

おびきだす　おびき出す　lure … away (*from*). ▶警察は女をおとりにしてその犯人を隠れ家から誘き出した The police used the criminal's girlfriend as a decoy to *lure* him *out of* his hideout.

おびきよせる　おびき寄せる　lure (*into*). ▶そのクマをはちみつでわなにおびき寄せる *lure* the bear *into* a trap with honey. ●彼をおびき寄せる(=誘い込む) *entice* him *in*.

おひざもと　お膝元　殿様のお膝元 (住んでいる土地) the town where our lord resides; (城下町) the lord's castle town.

おひたし　御浸し　*ohitashi*; (説明的に) boiled vegetables seasoned with blended soy sauce.

おびただしい　●おびただしい量の水 a great [a large] quantity of water. ▶その通りにはおびただしい数の観光客がいた There were a *great many* [a *great number of*, an *enormous crowd of*] tourists on the street. ▶彼は頼りないことおびただしい He is *quite* [*utterly*] unreliable. (⇨全く)

おひつじざ　牡羊座　[占星・天文] Aries /éariːz/ (❗the はつけない); (白羊宮) [占星] the Ram. (⇨乙女座) ●牡羊座(生まれ)の人 an Aries, an Arian. (❗ Arian は形容詞にも用いる)

おひとよし　お人好し　[気の良い人] a good-natured person (甘い人」というニュアンスも含む); [だまされやすい人] a credulous [a gullible] person (後の方が意味が強い), a dupe /d(j)úːp/; (単純で) a simple person. ▶お人好しにも程がある Don't be so *simple*.

おびな　男雛　a doll representing the Emperor. (⇨女雛)

おひなさま　お雛様　a doll. (⇨雛(ﾋﾅ)人形)

オピニオンリーダー　[世論形成者] opinion-makers; [特定の理論的指導者] an opinion leader.

おひねり　お捻り　monetary gift wrapped and twisted in paper.

おびばんぐみ　帯番組　an across-the-board program.

おびふう　帯封　a band wrapper.

おひめさま　お姫様　a princess. (⇨姫)

おひや　お冷や　(冷たい水) (a glass of) cold water.

*****おびやかす　脅かす**　[脅迫する] threaten /θrétn/; 《書》 menace; [怖がらせる] frighten.

おひゃくど　お百度　●お百度を踏む, お百度参りをする (社寺で) walk the fixed route a hundred times and pray (to Buddha) for the realization of one's wish; (比喩的に) visit [call on] (him) again and again [many times] (*for*; *to do*).

おひょう　[魚介] a (Pacific) halibut.

おひらき　お開き　● 会をお開きにする break up a meeting; bring a meeting to a close /klóuz/. ▶パーティーがお開きになったら飲み直しに行こう Let's go for a drink after the party *is over*.

*****おびる　帯びる**　❶ [含む] (…の気味を添える) be tinged (*with*). ●赤味を帯びた空 a reddish sky. ▶彼女の口調は憂いを帯びていた Her tone *was tinged with* [*had a tinge of*] sadness./There was a tinge of sadness in her tone.
❷ [ある性質・感じを持つ] (見える) look; (聞こえる) sound 《+形》. ▶その歌は哀調を帯びている The song *sounds* sentimental./I feel a tinge of

sadness in the song.
❸ [[委任される]] be charged 《with》. ▶彼は極秘の使命を帯びていた He *was charged with* a secret mission. ▶彼は特別な任務を帯びてアメリカにたった He left for America on a special mission.
❹ [[その他の表現]] ▶彼は酒気を帯びていた He *was under the influence of* alcohol [liquor, drink]. ▶私たちの勝利が現実味を帯びてきた Our victory *is becoming* a reality.

おひれ 尾鰭 a caudal fin. ▶話に尾ひれをつける(= 誇張する) *exaggerate* [(粉飾する) *embellish*] a story.
おひれ 尾鰭 a tail fin.
おひろめ お披露目 [[「披露(ろう)」の丁寧語]](⇨披露)
オフ ▶ラジオをオフにする turn *off* (↔turn on) the radio. ▶15パーセントオフでCDを買う buy a CD at 15 percent *discount* [*off* (the price)]. ▶サッカーはこはシーズンオフだ This is the *off-season* for soccer.
オファー [[申し入れ]] an offer. ▶オファーを受諾[拒絶]する accept [reject, refuse, turn down] an *offer*.
オフィシャル 图 [[公認審判員]] an official. ▶彼はこの試合のオフィシャルです He is an *official* in this game.
―― **オフィシャル(な)** 形 official. ▶オフィシャルな(= 公の)場所での発言 speech at an *official* occasion. ▶政府の発表によるオフィシャルな(= 公式の)数字 the *official* figures announced by the government.
●オフィシャルサイト an official website. ●オフィシャルスポンサー an official sponsor [supplier]. ▶ナイキは今年のオリンピックのオフィシャルスポンサーに登録された Nike has been registered as one of the *official suppliers* of the Olympic Games this year. ●オフィシャルレコード an official record. ▶オフィシャルレコードとして認められる be recognized as an *official record*.
オフィス an office.
●オフィスオートメーション office automation. (❗通例 OA とは略さない) ●オフィスガール an office assistant [help, girl]. (❗性差別を避けるため前の二つが好まれる) ●オフィスビル an office building. ●オフィスラブ an office romance; 《話》 an interoffice fling; 《和製語》 office love. ●オフィスレディー (⇨オーエル)
おぶう 負ぶう (⇨背負(せ)う)
おふくろ お袋 《米》 one's mom, 《英》 one's mum.
▶おふくろの味 one's mom's home cooking; 《米》 Mom's apple pie (❗事情 apple pie は日本人にとってのみそ汁のように、アメリカ人にとって各家庭の味を伝える代表的な食べ物。). ▶これはおふくろの味だ This *is just like mom used to make*! ▶おふくろの味を懐かしがる人が多くいる A lot of people miss the food their mothers used to cook for them.
オブザーバー [[陪席者, 監視員]] an observer.
オフサイド [[サッカー]] offside (↔onside). ▶オフサイドの反則をする be offside; commit an *offside* penalty. ▶そのゴールはオフサイドからのもので得点にならなかった The goal was disallowed for *offside*. ▶高原はオフサイドポジションに残っていました Takahara could not get himself out of an *offside* position.
●オフサイドトラップ offside trap. ●オフサイドライン offside line.
オフサイトセンター [[原子力防災センター]] an off-site center.
オフザボール ●オフザボールの動き [[サッカー]] movement *off the ball*. ([[参考]] ボールを持っていない局面での動き)
おぶさる 負ぶさる [[おんぶしてもらう]] be carried [《話》 get a piggyback ride] on 《her》 back; [[頼る]] depend 《on》.
オブジェ [<フランス語] an objet d'art /ɔ(:)bʒei dɑ́ːr/. (❗通例複数形 objets d'art /~/ で用いられる)
オプショナル ▶グランドキャニオンへの日帰りオプショナルツアーに参加した We went on a day *optional* tour of Grand Canyon.
●オプショナルパーツ optional parts. ●オプショナルプラン an optional plan.
オプション an option. ▶オプションする(= 選択する) make one's *option*. ▶ベルサイユ宮殿見学はオプションになります A tour to Versailles /vɑːrsái/ Palace is *optional*. ▶このカーナビはオプションです This car navigation system is an *optional extra*.
おふせ お布施 an offering 《to a priest》.
オフセット ●オフセット印刷 offset (printing).
おふだ お札 a good luck charm [talisman].
オフタイム ❶ [[休憩時間, 勤務時間終了後]] one's free [break] time; one's off-time. ▶午後7時からのオフタイムはビデオを見て過ごします I spend my *free time* from 7 p.m. watching videos.
❷ [[休日]] a holiday; a day off. ▶オフタイムに着る服 clothes worn on a *holiday*.
❸ [[サッカーの試合が中止している時]] off-time.
おぶつ 汚物 (排せつ物) excretions; (汚いもの) filth; 《話》 muck. ▶本来は動物のふんや尿が泥と混ざったもの。
●汚物処理袋 a disposal bag; a poop bag.
オプティミスト [[楽天家]] an optimist.
オブラート [<オランダ語] a wafer. ▶オブラートに包んだ(= 間接的な)表現をする use an *indirect* expression.
オフライン off-line (↔on-line).
おふる お古 ▶彼女のお古を着る wear her *hand-me-down* dress [her *hand-me-downs*]. (⇨お下がり)
おふれ お触れ 《書》 a notification. (⇨通告)
オフレコ ▶オフレコの(= 非公式の)発言 an *off-the-record* remark. ▶オフレコで自分の誤りを認める admit one's mistakes *off the record*.
オフロードしゃ オフロード車 an off-road vehicle 《略 ORV》.
オペア (⇨オーペア)
おべっか flattery; 《話》 soft soap. ▶上司におべっかを使う 《話》 *flatter* [*butter up*, 《話》 *soft-soap*] the boss; (取り入る) 《話》 *play up* to the boss.
●おべっか使い a flatterer; 《話》 a soft-soaper; (ごますり) a yes-man; (口先だけの) a brown-noser (❗今は an apple-polisher はあまり用いられない).
オペック [[石油輸出国機構]] OPEC /óupek/ 《the *O*rganization of *P*etroleum *E*xporting *C*ountries の略》.
オペラ [[歌劇]] (an) opera /ɑ́pərə/.
●オペラ歌手 an opera singer. ●オペラグラス (a pair of) opera glasses. ●オペラハウス Opera House.
オベリスク [[方尖(せん)塔]] an obelisk /ɑ́bəlisk/.
オペレーション [[公開市場操作, 作戦行動]] an operation.
オペレーター [[機械の操縦者, 電話交換手]] an óperator.
オペレーティングシステム [[基本ソフト]] [[コンピュータ]] an operating system 《略 OS》.
オペレッタ [[喜歌劇]] an operetta.
オペロン [[DNA上の機能単位]] an operon.
おべんちゃら ▶おべんちゃらを言う *flatter*; 《話》 *soft-soap* 《him》; [[お世辞]] (⇨お世辞) ▶おべんちゃらを言うな You *flatter* [《話》 *soft-soap*] me.
おぼえ 覚え ❶ [[記憶]] (a) memory; [[学習]] learning (⇨物覚え, 見覚え); [[経験]] an experience. ▶うろ覚

おぼえがき 覚え書き　a memorandum (複 ～s, memoranda) [=メモ]; [外交文書] [正式の] a note; (略式の) a memorandum.

おぼえる 覚える　❶ [記憶する] (暗記する) memorize, (そらで覚える) learn* [know*]... by heart, (覚えている) remember, (心にとめる) bear* [keep*]... in mind (!remember より堅い言い方). ▶彼は1日に英単語を10語覚える He *memorized* ten English words a day./He *learned by heart* ten English words a day. ▶これは私の息子です。覚えていますか This is my son. (Do you) *remember*? ▶次郎のことはよく覚えている I *remember* [×am remembering] Jiro very well. (!進行形は不可)/I well *remember* Jiro./I *remember* much of Jiro./I *remember* a lot of things about Jiro. ▶私の誕生日を覚えていてくれてありがとう Thank you for *remembering* my birthday. ▶花に水をやるのを覚えておいてください Please *remember* to water [×watering] the flowers. (!未来のことに言及する場合には to 不定詞を用い, 動名詞は不可)/(花に水をやるのを忘れないでください) Please *don't forget to* water the flowers. ▶彼が私たちにその話をしてくれたのを覚えていますか Do you *remember* (*that*) he told us the story?/Do you *remember* his [《話》him] telling [having told, ×to have told] us the story? (!(1) having told は過去の経験を特に強調する場合に限る。(2) 過去のことに言及する場合は動名詞を用い, 完了不定詞は古風) ▶ぼくが君をとても愛していることを覚えておいてくれ *Remember* [*Keep in mind*] *that* I love you. ▶彼女の電話番号は覚えやすい [覚えにくい] Her telephone number is easy [hard] to *remember*. ▶これは覚えてやがれ I'll *remember* this! (!発想が逆であることに注意) ▶私の覚えている限りでは彼は2002年に亡くなった As far as I (can) *remember* [To the best of my *memory*], he died in 2002. ▶あのあとどのようにして家に帰りついたのか, 何も覚えていない How did I get to my place after that? I can't [don't] *remember* a thing (of it).

❷ [習得する] learn*; (聞き[見]覚える) pick ... up. ▶九九の表をむろん *learn* one's tables. ▶機械の操作をいつ覚えたのですか When did you *learn* (how) to operate the machine? (!learn how to operate は「操作の仕方を習う」, learn to operate は「操作できるようになる」の意 (⇨習う)) ▶ローマにいた時にイタリア語を多少覚えた I *learned* [*picked up*] some Italian when I was in Rome. ▶彼は見ているだけでそのゲームを覚えた He *picked up* the game just by watching.

❸ [感じる] feel*. ▶腹部に激痛を覚えた I *felt* an intense pain in the stomach. ▶私たちは彼女の話に深い感動を覚えた We *were deeply moved* [*impressed*] by her story.

オホーツク ● オホーツク海　the Sea of Okhotsk /oukátsk/, [=the Okhotsk Sea とはいわない].

おぼこ 未通女　[世間を知らずすれていない女性] an inexperienced [an innocent] girl; [処女] a virgin.

おぼしい 思しい　●犯人と思しき(=思われる)男　a man who seems [見える appears] to be a criminal.

おぼしめし 思し召し　●神の思し召し the *will* of God; God's *will*.

おぼつかない 覚束無い　❶ [見込みがない] 《事が主語》 uncertain, doubtful; 《人が主語》 be not quite sure (*of*; *that* 節), be doubtful (*of*, *about*). ▶我々の勝利はおぼつかない There *is* little chance of our victory [*that* we will win]./*It is doubtful whether* we will win./We *can hardly expect* to win.

❷ [頼りない] unreliable; (不安定な) unsteady; (揺れる) shaky. ▶おぼつかない足どりで歩く walk with *unsteady* [*uncertain*, *staggering*] steps. (!staggering は今にも倒れそうな感じ) ●おぼつかない英語で話す speak in *shaky* English.

おぼっちゃん お坊ちゃん　(⇨坊ちゃん)

おぼれる 溺れる　❶ [溺死(でき)する] drown /dráun/; be get*] drowned.

> 解説　(1) 英語の drown は「泳げないで死ぬ」という意で, 必ずしも「死ぬ」ことまでを含むが, 日本語の「おぼれる」は必ずしもそうでない。したがって, 日本語で「彼はおぼれたが幸い助かった」といえるが, 英語では ×He drowned, but was happily saved. とはいえず, He nearly [almost] *drowned, but ....* または He *was drowning, but ....* としなくてはならない.
> (2) 《米》や法律用語では通例 drown は「おぼれて死ぬ」という「事故死」, be [get] drowned は「溺死させられる」という意で「他殺」, drown oneself は自ら身を投げての「自殺」を表す。ただし《英》ではしばしば be [get] drowned を事故死に用いる.

▶助けて！あきちゃんがおぼれている Help! Aki-chan is *drowning*! ▶彼は川でおぼれて死んだ He *drowned* [《英》*was drowned*] in the river. (!*drowned* [*was drowned*] *to death* とは通例いわない (⇨解説)) ▶彼は子供がおぼれそうになるのを助けた He saved the child from *drowning*.

❷ [耽(ふけ)る] ▶彼は酒におぼれている He's *giving himself up* to drink. (!drink は名詞)/《話》He's a *slave* to the bottle. [=「酒におぼれるようになった」は He's *taken* to drink.)

●おぼれる者はわらをもつかむ 《ことわざ》 A *drowning* man will grasp [clutch, 《今はややまれ》catch] at a straw. (!×a *drowned* man は「おぼれて死んだ人」の意でここでは用いることができない)

おぼろ 朧　●そのことはおぼろに(=かすかに)しか分からない have only a *faint* idea of it. (⇨おぼろげ)
●おぼろ月夜 a night with a hazy moon.

おぼろげ 朧ろ気　●彼の死をおぼろげに(=漠然と)覚えている have a *dim* [a *vague*] memory of his death; remember his death *dimly* [*vaguely*]. ▶遠くにタワーの輪郭がおぼろげに見えた The *vague* outline of the tower was seen in the distance.

おぼん 盆　the *Bon* Festival. (⇨盆)

オマーン 〖国名〗Oman /oumάːn/; 《公式名》the Sultanate of Oman. 《首都》Muscat) ◆オマーン人 an Omani. ◆オマーン(人)の Omani.

おまいり お参り a visit. (⇨参拝)

おまえ お前 《あなた、私》

おまけ お負け 〖景品〗something thrown in; a giveaway;〖追加〗an addition;〖賞品〗a prize, a premium. ▸これはおまけです This is *free (of charge)* [*for nothing*]. ▸私が机を買ったときこの本立てをおまけにつけてくれた They *threw in* this bookstand when I bought a desk.

── **お負けする** 動 throw (it) in. (⇨負ける)

おまけに ▸おまけに(=その上)彼は留守だった *What is more* [*Besides*,《書》*Moreover*, (さらに悪いことには)*What is worse*], he was not at home [《米》wasn't home]. (❗文頭に And が添えられることがある)

おませ ▸最近の子供はおませだ(=ませている) Children these days are *beyond* their *years* [年の割には大人びている *too grown-up* their *years*].

＊**おまちどおさま お待ち遠さま** 〖日本人的発想〗(おわびの気持ちで)I'm sorry I've [to have] kept you waiting;《米英人的発想》(お礼の気持ちで)Thank you [Thanks] for waiting; (物を渡すとき)↘Here you ↗áre.

おまつり お祭り a festival. (⇨祭り) ▸お祭り気分である[になる] be [get] in (a) *festive* mood. ▸町はお祭り騒ぎだった (何かを祝って)The town was in a state of celebration./(大いに楽しみ浮かれて)There was joy and *festivity* in the town.

おまもり お守り (通例身につける) an amulet, 《魔除け》a talisman, a charm. ▸魔除けのお守りを人びとにをward off devils, a good luck *charm*. (参考)馬蹄(horseshoe)や四つ葉のクローバー (four-leaf clover)など

おまる (幼児用の)a potty; (病人用の)a bed-pan; (寝室用の)a chamber pot. ▸おまるに座る sit on a *potty*.

おまわりさん お巡りさん (男)a policeman (複 -men);《女》a policewoman (複 -women); (改まって)《男女共用》a police officer; (呼びかけ)officer. (⇨警官)

おみおつけ 御御御付け 〖「みそ汁」の丁寧語〗(⇨味噌汁)

おみき お神酒 *omiki*; (説明的に)the sacred sake which is used as a ritual libation offered to a god.

おみくじ 御神籤 a fortune slip. (❗「くじ」の意とされる lot は複数の中から何かを決めるときに用いるものをさし「おみくじ」とは違う) ▸おみくじを引く pick a *fortune slip*. ▸神社でおみくじを引いたら吉と出た At the shrine, I picked [bought, got] a *fortune slip*, which predicted good fortune for me.

おみこし お神輿 a sacred portable shrine. (⇨神輿) ▸おみこしを上げる (立ち上がる)rise to one's feet; get up; (取り掛かる)start 《*to do; doing*》;《話》get going 《*on*》; (立ち去る)leave.

おみそれ 御見逸れ── 御見逸れする ▸あれまあ、松井君じゃない。すっかりお見それしちゃったわ Matsui! Oh, my goodness! I *didn't even recognize* you. ▸大した腕だね。あなたが育てたの? 見それしました Did you grow this orchid? I *didn't know* you had such a green thumb. (❗a green thumb は《英》で「園芸の才」の意、《英》では green fingers という)

オミット ── オミットする 動 〖除外する〗leave ... out ((omit は「うっかり入れ忘れる」の意もあるので注意が必要));〖削除する〗delete. ▸最初の部分をオミットする *leave out* [*delete*] the first part.

おみなえし 女郎花 〖植物〗Patrinia scabiosaefolia.

おむかえ お迎え (⇨迎え)

おむすび お結び an *omusubi*; (説明的に)a rice ball, which sometimes contains *umeboshi*, salmon flake, etc. in its center, often wrapped with a piece of *nori* sheet.

おむつ《米》a diaper;《英》a nappy,《英書》a napkin. ▸使い捨ておむつ a disposable *diaper*. ▸おむつを[替える] put on [change] a diaper. ▸この子はもうおむつはいらない This child no longer needs (to wear) a *diaper*. (❗「おむつがとれた子」を *toilet-trained* [a *potty-trained*] *child* という) 会話「太郎のおむつを替えてやってくれた?」「うん、ぐっしょり濡れていたよ」"Have you changed Taro [Taro's *diaper*]?" "Yes. He [It] was soaking wet."

オムニバス ◆オムニバス映画 an omnibus film. (参考 いくつかの短編を一つにまとめた映画)

オムライス an *omuraisu*; (説明的に)a dish of tomato-flavored fried rice wrapped with a round thin omlet.

オムレツ an omelet(te) /άmlit/; (卵だけの)a plain omelet(te).

おめい 汚名 〖悪い評判〗a bad name [reputation];〖不名誉〗disgrace. ▸汚名を着せる ▸そのことで彼は汚名を着せられた It gave him a *bad name*. /It brought *disgrace on* [*to*] him. ▸彼は反逆者の汚名を着せられた(=レッテルをはられた)He *was labeled (as)* a traitor. ▸汚名をすすぐ clear one's name.

おめおめ ▸あんなことがあったのでおめおめと(=恥ずかしく思わずに)故郷に帰れない After all that happened, I can't ever [can never] go home *without feeling ashamed* [*without shame*].

おめかし ── おめかしする 動 〖化粧〗make (oneself) up;〖服装〗dress (oneself) up.

おめしもの お召し物 〖相手の衣服の尊敬語〗your [his, her] clothes.

おめしれっしゃ お召し列車 the train for Imperial exclusive use.

おめおくせず 怖めず臆せず (気後れせずに)without flinching; boldly and bravely.

おめだま お目玉 ◆お目玉を食う ▸父からお目玉をくう(=ひどくしかられる) be severely scolded [《話》be severely told off] by one's father (❗前の方は《英》では(やや古)); get a good *scolding* [《話》a good *telling-off*,《話》a good *talking-to*] from one's father. ▸そんなことをするとひどくお目玉をくうよ You will *get a good telling-off* [《話》*get it*] if you do that.

おめでた (祝うべきこと) a happy event. ▸めぐみがまたおめでたなんですって I hear Megumi *is expecting (a baby* [*a child*]*) again.* (❗( )内は省略されることが多い)/I hear Megumi *is expecting* another baby.

おめでたい ❶〖祝うべき〗happy. ◆おめでたいこと a *happy* event; a matter for *congratulation*. (⇨めでたい)

❷〖お人よしの〗stupid, silly; (考え方が甘い) be too optimistic. ▸彼を信じるなんて君はおめでたいね How *stupid* you are to believe him!

＊**おめでとう** ❶〖個人的な喜び事に対して〗Congratulations! (❗常に複数形で); Good for 《you》. (❗親しい間柄で用い)

解説 **Congratulations.** は本人の努力による成功を祝う表現。したがって結婚の場合、花嫁には、たとえ I wish you every happiness./I hope you will be very happy. などの表現を使う方がよいとさ

れてきたが, 最近では結婚・誕生日など一般にめでたいことがあった人にも用いられるようになっている.

▶成功[合格]おめでとう I *congratulate* you *on* your success [pass*ing* the exam]. (**!**×I congratulate your success. とはいわない)/*Congratulations on* your success [pass*ing* the exam]. (**!**応答としては Thank you. I did devote all my energy to it. (ありがとう. 全力投球したからね)などという. 日本人特有の謙遜から Oh, I was just lucky. (運がよかっただけです)などということばは文字どおり解釈されるので注意. ただし, 英国人は控えめな表現としてよく用いる)

会話 「娘に赤ん坊が生まれたのよ」「おめでとう」「ありがとう」"My daughter just had a baby." "(相手に対して) I'm so happy for you./(娘さんについて) *Good for* her." (**!**本人や身内の人には Congratulations. ともいう) "Thank you."

❷[祝祭日や特別の日に] ▶新年おめでとう (A) *Happy* New Year. (**!**I wish you a Happy New Year. は堅い言い方 (⇨新年)

会話 「お誕生日おめでとう」「覚えていてくださってありがとう」"*Happy* birthday (to you)!/*Congratulations* (on your birthday)!/(《書》Many happy returns (of the day)." "How very nice of you to remember!"

会話 「新年おめでとう」「おめでとう」 "*Happy* new year (to you)!" "(*The*) *same* to you./And you, too."

おめにかかる お目に掛かる 〖『会う』の謙譲表現〗 meet*; see*. ▶ぜひお目にかかりたいです I would very much like to *see* you. ▶お目にかかるのを楽しみにしています I'm looking forward to *seeing* [xsee] you. ▶お目にかかれてうれしく存じます I'm pleased to *meet* you. (**!**相当改まった表現 (⇨初めまして)) ▶おはようございます. 福田常務に 11 時にお目にかかる約束になっております Good morning. I have an appointment with Mr. Fukuda, the managing director, at eleven o'clock.

おめみえ お目見え ── **お目見えする** 動 (初公演する) make one's debut /dib(j)ú:/ [first appearance]; (発行[出版]される) come out.

:**おもい 重い** ❶[物が] heavy; (やや書) weighty. ● 重い小包 a *heavy* [a *weighty*] parcel. ▶この机は重すぎて(私には)持ち上げられない This desk is too *heavy* (for me) to lift./The desk is so *heavy* (that) I cannot lift it. (**!**二つの文での it の有無に注意) ▶あなたの荷物は 5 キロ重すぎる Your baggage is 5 kilos *heavier* [too *heavy*]. ▶この板はどんな重い人が乗っても大丈夫です This plank is strong enough to support the *weight* of any person.

❷[心・気分が] (ふさぎこんでいる) depressed; (憂鬱(ﾕﾂ)な) gloomy, (話) blue. (⇨憂鬱) ▶今日は気が重い I *feel depressed* [*blue*] today. ▶頭が重い (一般に) I *feel heavy in* the [xmy] head./I have a *heavy* head./My head *is heavy*.

❸[動きが] heavy (ﾉ鈍い); [口が] (遅い) slow of speech; (無口な) reserved, 《書》taciturn. ● 重い足どりで歩く walk with *heavy* steps [《書》treads]; walk heavily. ▶重い腰を上げて(＝いやいや)仕事に取りかかった He *unwillingly* started to do the work.

❹[責任が] heavy, grave; [任務が] important, (責任ある) responsible; [罪が] serious. ● 重い責任を負う assume a *heavy* [a *grave*, a *great*] responsibility (*for*). ▶重い地位にある be in an *important* [a *responsible*] position. ▶重い罪を犯す commit a *serious* crime.

❺[病気などが] serious. ▶彼は重い病気にかかってい

る He is *very* [*quite, seriously*] sick./His illness is very [quite] *serious*.

おもい 思い ❶[考えること] (a) thought. (**!**具体的な「考え」を表すときは 〖C〗) ● 思いにふける be lost [deep, absorbed, buried] in *thought*. ● 自分の思いを人に言わない(＝心にしまっておく) keep one's *thoughts* to oneself. ▶彼は故郷に思いをはせた(＝故郷のことを考えた) He *thought of* his hometown./His *thoughts* went back to his hometown.

❷[気持ち] a feeling. ▶そんなことをして恥ずかしい思いをしている I *feel* [am] ashamed of having done so. ▶心臓が止まるような思いがした I *felt* as if my heart stopped beating [xto beat]. ▶私と同じ思いの人も何人かいる There are some people who *feel* as I do.

❸[経験] an experience. ● つらい思いをする have a bitter *experience*; have a hard time (of it). ▶旅行中楽しい思いをした I had a good time [enjoyed myself] during the trip.

❹[願望, 期待] (願望) (a) wish; (夢) a dream; (期待) (an) expectation. ● やっと思いがかなった At last my *wish* [*dream*] came true./At last I had my *wish* fulfilled [realized].

❺[愛情] love; (情的な心) heart. ▶私は彼女に思いを打ち明けた I declared my *love* to her./I told her how deeply I loved her. (**!**後の方が口語的) ▶彼は年寄り思いだ(＝思いやりがある) He *is* considerate *to* elderly people.

● 思いに沈む (ある事を心配している) be worried about something.

● 思いも寄らない ● 思いもよらない出来事 an *unexpected* event. ▶こんなことが起ころうとは思いもよらなかった I *hardly expected* anything like this to happen.

● 思いを晴らす ● 彼に思い(＝うらみ)を晴らす take one's *revenge on* [xto] him.

● 思いを寄せる ▶彼は彼女に思いを寄せた He gave his *heart* to her.

おもいあがる 思い上がる 〖傲慢(ｺﾞｳ)である〗 be arrogant; 〖うぬぼれる〗 get* conceited [《話》stuck-up]. ● 思い上がっている人 an *arrogant* [a *conceited*, a *stuck-up*] person. ▶言わせてもらえば, あの男は思い上がりもはなはだしい He's very *arrogant* [《話》too *big for* his *boots*], in my opinion.

おもいあたる 思い当たる ▶その事件について何も思い当たることはない(＝全然知らない) I *don't have the slightest* [*faintest*] *idea of* the incident. (⇨分かる**❶**) ▶そう言われると思い当たる節がある(＝何かを思い出させる) That *reminds* me *of* something.

おもいあまる 思い余る do not know what to do; be at a loss what to do. ▶彼女は思い余って母親に相談した She *was at a loss what to do* and asked for her mother's advice. (**!**Not knowing what to do, she asked .... のように分詞構文にすると堅い表現になる)

おもいあわせる 思い合わせる (A と B を比べて考える) weigh A and B; consider A and B.

おもいいたる 思い至る (悟る) realize.

おもいいれ 思い入れ ● 思い入れが強い feel deeply attached (*to* one's old furniture). ▶思い入れたっぷりの(＝大げさで芝居がかった)しぐさをする make *a theatrical* gesture.

おもいうかぶ 思い浮かぶ ▶彼の名が思い浮かばない His name doesn't *come to* me [*mind*]./(思い出せない) I can't *remember* his name.

おもいうかべる 思い浮かべる ▶彼女の顔を思い浮かべる(＝思い出す) *remember* [《やや書》*recall*] her face. ● 故郷を思い浮かべる(＝心に描く) *picture* one's hometown *to oneself*.

おもいえがく 思い描く imagine; picture. ▶新居での生活を思い描いた I *imagined* [*pictured*] life in a new house.

おもいおこす 思い起こす (思い出す) remember;《やや書》recollect;《やや書》recall. (⇨思い出す)

おもいおもい 思い思い (好きなように) just as one likes [pleases]; (自分自身のやり方で) in one's own way.

おもいかえす 思い返す [[振り返る]] look back 《on》,《やや書》reflect 《on》; [[再考する]] think*... over (again), [[考え直してやめる]] think better of .... ▶私は去年の夏に起こった事件を思い返してみた I *looked back on* the incident that took place last summer.

おもいがけず 思い掛けず unexpectedly. (⇨図[はか]らずも, 思い掛け無い) ▶思いがけず母が訪ねてきた My mother visited me *unexpectedly*./My mother came *when I least expected her*.

おもいがけない 思い掛け無い [[予期しない]] unexpected; [[偶然の]] accidental; [[突然の]] sudden. ●思いがけない訪問客 an *unexpected* [a *casual*] visitor. ●思いがけない出会い an *accidental* meeting. ▶それはまったく思いがけないことだった It was quite *unexpected*./It was [came as] a great *surprise* to me.
会話「君に花を持ってきたよ」「わあ, うれしい. 思いがけないことだわ」"I've brought you some flowers." "What a pleasant [a delightful] *surprise*!"

おもいきった 思い切った [[大胆な]] daring;《やや書》drastic; [[改革・治療などが徹底的など]] radical. ●思い切った事をする do *daring* things. ●思い切った処置をする take *drastic* measures. ▶思い切った外科治療をする perform *radical* surgery on a patient.

おもいきって 思い切って [[大胆に]] boldly; [[断固として]] resolutely /rèzəlúːtli/. 【思い切って...する】 venture; dare. (❗venture は行動, dare は精神面を強調する) ▶思い切って彼の提案に反対する *venture* (*to* make) an objection to his proposal; (はっきりと反対意見を述べる) speak *boldly* [speak *out*] against his proposal. ▶彼らは思い切って話す勇気がなかった They did not *dare* (*to*) speak. (❗動詞用法. 否定文・疑問文ではしばしば to が脱落する)/They *dared* not speak. (❗助動詞用法. 肯定文には通例用いず, 動詞用法に比べて文語的)/They didn't have *enough* courage [*courage enough*] to speak. ▶(失敗など覚悟で)思い切ってやってみるつもりだ I'm going to *take a chance* [*take a risk*,《話》*chance* it].

おもいきや 思いきや expect..., (but). ▶楽に卒業試験に合格できると思いきや, できなかった I had expected to pass the graduation exam easily, but I couldn't.

おもいきり 思い切り ●思い切り(=思う存分)楽しむ enjoy 《it》 *as* much *as* one likes [《話》*all* one *wants*]. ●思い切りボールを蹴る kick a ball *as* hard *as* one *can*. ●思い切り笑う have a *good* laugh. ●思い切り安く売る sell 《it》 at *the* lowest price. ▶彼は思い切りが悪い《話》He is slow [quick] to make decisions./He is indecisive [《やや書》decisive]. (❗「...思い切りが悪い」は He lacks decision [is irresolute]. とも言える)

おもいきる 思い切る (あきらめる) give* 《...》 up. ▶彼女のことが思い切れない(=忘れられない) I *can't forget* her.

おもいこみ 思い込み one's one-sided belief [impression]; (先入観) (a) prejudice. ▶勝手な思い込みで物を言わないでください I think you are stating your *one-sided belief*. ▶彼女は思い込みが激しいから何を言ってもむだだ She's blinded by *prejudice*, so it's no use telling her anything.

おもいこむ 思い込む ▶彼は自分が成功するものと思い込んでいた(=信じ切っていた) He *was convinced of* his success [*that* he would succeed]. (⇨確信する)/(当然のことと思った) He *took it for granted that* he would succeed. ▶なぜか彼は妻が自分を殺そうとしていると思い込んでしまった《話》Somehow he *took it into his head that* his wife was trying to kill him. ▶一度思い込んだら(=心を決めたら)彼は決してあきらめない Once he *has made up* his *mind*, he never gives up.

おもいしる 思い知る (十分わかる) fully realize; (懲りる) learn* a [one's] lesson. ●思い知らせる (懲らしめる) punish 《him》; teach 《him》 a lesson.

おもいすごし 思い過ごし 思い過ごしである think [make] too much 《of》; (心配し過ぎる) worry (too much) 《about》. ▶それは君の思い過ごしだよ(=想像のすぎない) It is just your *imagination*!

おもいだしわらい 思い出し笑い a reminiscent smile [chuckle; laugh]. ▶今朝の食卓での妻の言葉が浮かんできて, 彼は思い出し笑いをした He smiled to himself, remembering what his wife said at the breakfast table this morning.

＊おもいだす 思い出す
【WORD CHOICE】 思い出す
remember 本義は「覚えている」こと. 時に人名・過去の体験などを自然に思い出すことをさす. ▶彼の名前がちっとも思い出せない I can't *remember* his name at all.
recall 意図的に思い出そうとすること. 他に比べてやや堅い語. ▶後になって, 彼女がいかに親切だったか思い出した I later *recalled* how kind she was to me.
be reminded 何らかの理由・きっかけによって, 思い出すこと. ▶彼女の親切を思い出した I *was reminded* of her kindness [how kind she was, that she was kind].

頻度チャート

remember ██████████
recall ████
be reminded █
　　　20　40　60　80　100 (%)

remember;《やや書》recall;《やや書》recollect; think* of ...; (思い出させる) remind 《A *of* B》. ▶ああ思い出したぞ Now I *remember*! (❗(1) ×Now I remembered [have remembered]. とはいわない. (2) Now I'm remembering. は「だんだん思い出してきたぞ」という意) ▶よく楽しかった学生時代のことを思い出す I often *remember* [*recollect*] my happy school days. ▶彼女の生年月日をどうしても思い出せない I can't *remember* [*think of*] the date of her birth. (❗can't の代わりに don't も可) ▶彼はだれがその場にいたかを思い出そうとした He tried to *remember* [*recall*, *recollect*] who was there. ▶彼女は突然ドアに鍵をかけていないことを思い出した She suddenly *remembered* (*that*) she had not locked the door. ▶これらの写真を見るとアメリカで過ごした日々を思い出す When I see these pictures, I always *remember* [《やや書》I'm *reminded of*] my days in the United States. ▶では普段のことを完全に忘れていることを暗示)/《やや書》These pictures *remind* me *of* my days in the United States. ▶彼の手紙を読んで本を返さなくては

らないことを思い出した When I read his letter, I *remembered* that I had to give the book back to him./His letter *reminded* me *that* I had to return the book to him. ▶たまには私のことを思い出してくれよ *Think of* me sometimes, will you? ▶それを思い出すと今でも胸が痛む It is still a painful *memory*. ▶彼は時々思い出したように仕事をした He did his work *by [in] fits (and starts)*.
会話 「それで思い出した」「何を？」"That *reminds* [×reminded] me." "*Of* what?"

おもいたつ 思い立つ (⇨思い付く) ▶彼は思い立って(=ふと思いついて)パリへ行った *Suddenly he had an idea* to go to Paris, and he went there immediately./He *had a whim* for a trip to Paris and left at once. (❗ *whim* は「思いつき」での意で必ずしもよい結果とならないこともある)
● 思い立ったが吉日(きちじつ) (ことわざ) Strike while the iron is hot.

おもいちがい 思い違い 图 〖誤解〗(a) misunderstanding,《書》misapprehension. ▶何か思い違いがあるようです There seems to be some *misunderstanding*. ▶私の思い違いでなければ、確かに彼はそこに居合わせたと思う If I *am not mistaken* [記憶が正しければ] If I *remember correctly*], I am sure (that) he was there. ▶いつでも私が力になってくれるとでも思っているのならとんだ思い違いだ 《話》If you think I'm going to help you any time, *you've got another think coming*. (❗相手の思わくを強く拒否する慣用表現)
── 思い違いをする 動 misunderstand*;(誤って A を B と考える) mistake* [take*] A for B. ▶君はぼくの(言った)ことを思い違いをしている You *misunderstand* me./(やや話) *You've got* me *wrong*. ▶私は彼のことで思い違いをしていた I *was wrong* [(やや書) *was mistaken*, ×mistook] *about* him. (⇨誤解) ▶私はその青年を中国人と思い違いをした I *took* [*mistook*] the young man *for* a Chinese.

おもいつき 思い付き an idea, a notion; 〖考え〗(a) thought. (⇨思い付く❷) ▶いい思いつき a good *idea*; a happy [×a good] *thought*. ▶思いつきで(=準備なしに)話す speak *impromptu* [《話》 *off the cuff*]. ▶それは単なる(何気ない)思いつきだ That's just a casual *idea*.

おもいつく 思い付く 〖ある考えがふと浮かぶ〗《人が主語》hit* [strike*] *on* ...,〖思いつく〗think* *of* ...;〖事が主語〗occur (-rr-) *to* .... ▶すばらしい考えをふと思いついた I *hit* [*struck*] *on* a bright idea./A bright idea *occurred to* me. ▶どうしてそんなこと思いつかなかったのかしら(私ってばかね) Now why didn't I *think of* that? ▶彼は思い付いたままをしゃべった He spoke the first words that *came* [*sprang*] *to* mind. ▶そのいい口実を思いついた(=考え出した) I *thought up* a good excuse for it.

おもいつめる 思い詰める 〖くよくよする〗brood 《about, over》; 〖心配する〗worry 《about, over》. ▶そう思い詰めるな Don't *worry about* it so much./(深刻に考えるな) Don't *take* it so *seriously* [《米話》*serious*] (←*easy*). ▶彼は彼女の言ったことを思い詰めてじっと座っていた He sat still *brooding over* [*about*] what she had said. ▶彼女は死のうと思い詰めている(=自殺の考えに取りつかれている) She *is obsessed with* [*by*] the idea of committing suicide.

*****おもいで 思い出** a memory; (追想) (a) recollection (❗ *memory* より堅い語); (回想) (a) reminiscence (❗特に楽しい経験の). ▶思い出にふける be lost in one's *memories*. ▶彼女は子供時代の[昔の]思い出話をしてくれた She told us her *memories* [*recollections*, *reminiscences*] of childhood [days

gone by]. ▶この部屋にはいろいろな思い出がある This room has (a lot of) *memories*./(人が主語) I have many fond *memories* about this room. ▶この旅行はいい思い出になるでしょう This trip will be a pleasant *memory* [something pleasant to *look back on*]. ▶彼女は青春時代の思い出(=記念となる物)として彼らのラブレターをとっておいた She kept the love letters from him as a *memento* of her youth. ▶彼女は亡夫の思い出を胸に秘めている She cherishes the *memory* of her dead [late] husband.

おもいでのき『思い出の記』 Footprints in the Snow. (参考 徳冨蘆花の小説)

おもいどおり 思い通り ▶思い通りにする have [get] one's own way; do (just) as one likes [wants to]. ▶すべてが思い通り(=望むように)うまくいった Everything went well *as I (had) expected*. ▶どんなことでも思い通りになるとは限らない You can't *have [get]* your *own way* about everything.

おもいとどまる 思いとどまる […しないように説得される] (やや書) be dissuaded 《from》; 〖考えを変える〗change one's mind; 〖あきらめる〗give* (a plan [an idea]) up. (⇨止(や)める) ▶私たちは彼女に彼との結婚を思いとどまらせることはできなかった We tried to *persuade* her *not to* marry [*dissuade* her *from* marrying] him, but we couldn't./We couldn't *stop* her *from* marrying him. ▶彼は留学を思いとどまった He *changed* his *mind about* [*gave up* the plan of] *studying abroad*. ▶私はやつに殴りかかろうとしたが思いとどまった(=自分を抑えた) I tried to hit him, but I *stopped* [*checked, controlled*] *myself*.

おもいなおす 思い直す 〖考えを変える〗change one's mind; 〖再考してやめる〗think* better of ...; 〖考え直す〗(やや書) reconsider, think 《about it》 again. ▶退職を思い直してくださいませんか Will you *change* your *mind about* quitting your job? ▶彼はその男の顔を殴ってやりたかったが思い直してやめた He was tempted to strike the man in the face, but *thought better of* (doing) it. ▶思い直して彼は外国へ行くのを取りやめた *On second thought* 《米》 [*thoughts* 《英》] he gave up (the idea of) going abroad.

おもいなし 思いなし ▶思いなしか(=そう思うからか)彼は疲れているようだ It *may be my imagination*, but he looks tired.

おもいなやむ 思い悩む (⇨悩む)

おもいのこす 思い残す ▶好きなように生きてきた、思い残す(=後悔する)ことはない I've led a life my own way and I *have no regrets*.

おもいのたけ 思いの丈 ▶思いの丈を述べる (言いたいことを全部言う) say out one's mind; (胸の内を明かす) open (up) one's mind [heart] 《to him》(❗ *mind* は「考え」, *heart* は「気持ち, 感情」の意). ▶思いの丈を述べると気持ちがすっきりした I felt at ease when I said out (what had been on) my mind.

おもいのほか 思いの外 ▶私たちは思いの外(=予想していたより早く)目的地に着いた We arrived at the destination earlier *than we (had) expected*./We got to the destination *unexpectedly* early.

おもいめぐらす 思い巡らす 〖あれこれ思案する〗turn 《it》over in one's mind; 〖よからぬことを〗plot (-tt-); 〖回顧する〗look back on .... (⇨巡らす❷)

おもいもよらない 思いも寄らない ▶思いも寄らない(=予期しない)不幸 an *unexpected* [an *unforeseen*] misfortune. ▶その申し出は私たちの思いも寄らないものだった We *never thought of* such an offer./(予想外であった) The offer *was beyond* our

おもいやられる 思いやられる ▶先のことが思いやられる I can't help worrying *about* the future. ▶「今からそんな乱暴ばかりしていると,先が思いやられます」と母は悲しそうに言った Mother told me sadly, "I *feel anxious about* your future because you are being so violent."

おもいやり 思い遣り consideration 《*for*》, thoughtfulness; [[同情]] sympathy, 《深い》compassion. (⇨同情, 情け) ●思いやりのある人 a *considerate* [a *thoughtful*] person (後の方は「思慮深い人」という意もある); (情に厚く面倒見のいい人) a *caring* person (❢しばしば warm(-hearted) [gentle] and caring の連語で用いられる). ▶彼はだれにでも思いやりがある He's *considerate* to [*toward*] everyone./He's *kind* to everyone. ▶思いやりは礼儀正しい基本的な要素である *Consideration* is a basic factor in politeness [manners]. ▶君はもっと他人の気持ちに思いやりを持つべきだ You should *have* [*show*] more *consideration for* other people's feelings./You should *be* more *considerate* [*thoughtful*] *of* other people's feelings. ▶そんなことを言うなんて彼女には思いやりがない It is *thoughtless* [*inconsiderate*] *of* her *to* say so.

おもいやる 思い遣る ❶ [[同情する]] think 《*of*》; sympathize 《*with*》. ▶彼の心境を思いやって涙があふれた Tears ran out of my eyes when I *thought of* his feelings.
❷ [[(遠く離れたところから)思いをはせる]] ▶ブラジルに渡った移民たちは,はるか日本の故郷を思いやって望郷の念にかられた The immigrants to Brazil, *thinking of* [*about*] their far-off hometown in Japan, felt homesick.
❸ [[案じる]] (⇨思いやられる)

おもいわずらう 思い煩う worry 《*about*》. (⇨悩む)

:おもう 思う   INDEX
❶ (a) 考える	❶ (b) 信じる
❶ (c) 想像する	❶ (d) 推測する
❶ (e) 感じる	❶ (f) 予期する
❶ (g) 申し上げにくいが…だと思う	
❷ 願望する	❸ 意図する
❹ みなす	❺ 気にする
❻ 疑う	❼ 恋しく思う
❽ 思い出す	

WORD CHOICE 思う
think 思考・考察を幅広く含意する最も一般的な語. ●その国のことを思う *think* of that country.
feel 原義は「感じる」. そこから派生して, 感性的判断を示し, 時に控えめに考えを述べる場合に用いる. ▶君は正しいと思うよ I *feel* that you're right.
expect 原義は「予想する」. そこから派生して「当然…すると思う」の意も持つ. 好ましい, 好ましくないことの両方に用いる. ▶君ならきっとできると思うよ I *expect* that you can do it.
suppose 曖昧な根拠のもとで自分なりに考察すること. しばしば受身で用いる. ▶利口と思われている I'm *supposed* to be clever.
imagine 原義は「空想する」. そこから派生して, 明確な根拠を伴わず, あれこれなんとなく思うこと. ▶彼らは成功するんじゃないかなと思うよ I *imagine* they will succeed.
guess 限られた根拠に基づき, 推測を行うこと. ▶これ, 何だと思う? Can you *guess* what this is?

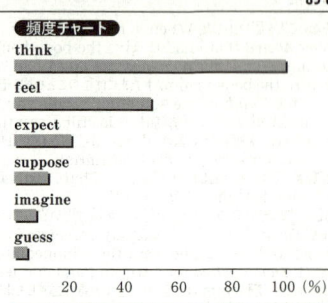

頻度チャート
think ██████████
feel ██████
expect ████
suppose ██
imagine ██
guess █
  20 40 60 80 100 (%)

❶ [[考える]] think*, (熟慮する) consider; (信じる) believe, (想像する) imagine, 《書》fancy; (推測する) suppose, guess; (感じる) feel*; (予期する) expect.

(a) [[考える]] think*; (熟慮する) consider. ●彼のことをよく[悪く]思う *think* well [badly] *of* him. ▶この計画をどう思いますか What [×How] do you *think of* [*about*] this plan? (✓文中の方が具体的な意見を求める言い方)/(気に入っているか) How [×What] do you *like* this plan?/What's your *opinion* of this plan? (❢ 応答は I think (that)…のように, 挿入的に if you ╱ask me (私に言わせれば)を文頭・文尾に, As fár as ˇI'm concérned (私に関する限り)を文頭に, など同様の位置が可) ▶彼の英語はとても上手だと思います I *think (that)* his English is very good./(文中) His English, I *think*, is very good./(文尾) His English is very good, I *think*. (❢ 文頭が最も普通. believe, imagine, suppose, guess なども同様の位置が可) ▶三郎と吉彦はどちらが年上だと思いますか Who [×Which] do you *think* is older, Saburo or Yoshihiko? (❢ (1) 人についての比較には, 通例 Which は用いない. (2) ×Do you *think* who is …? は誤り) ▶雨にはならないと思います I don't *think* it will rain. (❢ I *think* it will not rain. とは通例いわない. ただしはっきり否定することが相手に好ましい場合は可: I *think (that)* this report is not bad.) ▶私は彼女を天才だと思う I *think* [*consider*] *(that)* she is a genius. (❢ 以下の言い方より一般的)/《書》 I *think* [*consider*] her *(to be)* a genius. (❢ to be は通例省略される)/I *think of* [*consider*] her *as* a genius./(みなす) I *regard* [*look on*] her *as* a genius. ▶それをやってみる価値があると思うかい Do you *think* [*consider*] it worth trying? ▶君のやり方でいいと思う(=に賛成する) I *approve of* the way you handle things. ▶それは実際的な企画だと思うかい Would you *say* it's a practical proposition? (❢ 控えめな言い方)
会話「彼は頼りになると思いますか」「はい, そう思います[いいえ, そうは思いません]」 "Do you *think* he is reliable?" "Yes, I think so./ I don't *think* so./ No, I *think* not.]" (❢ No の答えでは後の方は語調が強い)

(b) [[信じる]] believe. (⇨信じる) ▶君の言うことは本当だと思う I *believe* you [what you say]./I *believe (that)* what you say is true./《書》 I *believe* what you say *(to be)* true. ▶彼は正直だと思われている He *is believed* [*is thought*] *(to be)* honest. ▶幽霊はいると思いますか Do you *believe in* [×believe] ghosts? (❢ 存在や価値を信じる場合, または人格を信用する場合には in が必要)
会話「彼は子供が何人いるの」「確か 6 人だと思います」

"How many children does he have?" "Six, I ↗believe."

(c) [想像する] imagine; 〘書〙 fancy; (夢想する) think* [dream*] 《*of; that* 節》 (❶ 否定文で). (⇨想像する) ▶彼は戻ってこないと思います I don't *imagine* (*that*) he will be back. (❶ 通例×I *imagine* (*that*) he won't be back. とはいわない) ▶私は君が来ているものと思っていました I *imagined* (*that*) you were here./〘書〙 I *imagined* you *to be* here. ▶何事にも成功できるなどと思うな Don't *fancy that* you can succeed in everything. ▶彼女は自分を美人だと思っている(=うぬぼれている) She *flatters herself that* she is beautiful./〘主に英語〙 She *fancies* herself (*as*) beautiful. ▶それを思っただけでも身震いした I shuddered *at the* (mere) *thought of* it. ▶私の小説がその賞をもらうとは夢にも思わなかった I *never thought* [*dreamed*] (*that*) my novel would get the prize. (❶ 否定を強調すると *Never* [*Little*] *did* I *think* [*dream*].... となる. やや堅い言い方)

会話「彼女どの列車で来るの？」「10時半のだと思います」"Which train is she coming on?" "The ten thirty, I ↗imagine."

(d) [推測する] suppose; (根拠なく) guess; (観察結果から) gather (⇨推測する); (証拠・状況から判断する) judge (⇨判断する). ▶彼はその答は正しいと思った He *supposed* [*guessed*] (*that*) the answer was right./〘書〙 He *supposed* [*guessed*] the answer (*to be*) right. ▶彼は40歳ぐらいだと思います I *judge that* [*think that*] he is about 40./〘書〙 I *judge* him (*to be*) about 40.

会話「今日タクシーの運転手に何て聞かれたと思う？」「何て聞かれたの？」"Guess [*You won't believe*] what a taxi driver asked me today!" "What did he ask you?" (❶ 聞き手の興味をそそる話題の切り出し表現. 後の方は (b) の意)

会話「どうも彼は90を越えると思うよ」「えっ, ほんと！ あの人がそんなに年をとっているとは思わなかった(=まるで分からなかったな)」"He's over ninety, I *gather*." "↗Really! I *had no idea* he was that [so] old."

(e) [感じる] feel*. (⇨感じる) ▶彼は病気だと思います I *feel* (*that*) he is sick. (❶ I *feel* him *to be* sick. とするのは〘まれ〙) ▶もう一度彼と話し合う必要があると思います I *feel* it necessary to talk with him again. ▶まるで違う世界にいるように思った I *felt* [×*thought*] *as if* I were [〘話〙 was] in a different world. (❶ as if の前に think は不可 (⇨まるで)) ▶彼女のことをどう思いますか How [×*What*] do you *feel about* [*toward*] her?

会話「何てひどいコーヒーだ！」「私にはまあまあの味に思えるけど」"What a terrible cup of coffee!" "It *seems* [*tastes*] all right to me."

(f) [予期する] expect; think* (❶ 通例否定文・疑問文で). (⇨予期する) ▶会場は思ったほど混雑していなかった The hall was not as crowded as I (had) *expected* [*thought* (it would be)]. (❶ 〘話〙 では had は省略されることが多い) ▶給料はどのくらいもらえると思うの？ What salary do you *expect* to get? ▶あんなに大勢の人がパーティーに来るなんて思っていなかった We hardly *expected* so many people to come to the party. ▶そこで彼に出くわすとは思ってもみなかった I never *thought to* run across him there./I never *thought* (*that*) I'd (=I would) run across him there.

(g) [申し上げると...だと思う] I am afraid. (❶ よくない事ををいうのに語気を和らげて) ▶あなたのおっしゃっていることは間違いだと思います I'm *afraid* you're wrong./You're ↘wrong, I'm ↗*afraid*.

❷ [願望する] want, would [should] like 《*to do*》 (❶ 通例 'd like と短縮する); wish; hope; (切望する) be anxious [eager] 《*to do*》.

使い分け want 「…したいと思う」の意の最も一般的な語.
would like want より丁寧で控えめな言い方.
wish 実現不可能, 困難なことを望むこと.
hope 常によい未来のことを望み, wish と異なり実現できると思われることについていう.

▶私は将来医者になりたいと思います I *want to* be a doctor in future. (❶ 日本語につられて×I *think* I *want*.... としない) ▶近いうちにぜひ留学したいと思っています I really *want* [*am* very *eager*] *to* study abroad one of these days. ▶あなたにいっしょにいてもらいたいと思います I *want* [*I'd like*] you *to* be with me. ▶食事は自分で作っていますが, なかなか思うような味になりません I cook my own meals but I can't get my food to taste the way I *want* it *to*. ▶そのうちお目にかかりたいと思います I'*d like to* see you soon./I *hope* to see you soon./I *hope* (*that*) I will see you soon. ▶もう10歳若かったらなあと思う I *wish* I *were* [〘話〙 *was*, ×*am*] ten years younger. (❶ 現在実現不可能な願望を表し, 節内は仮定法過去) ▶彼女は来るんじゃなかったと思った She *wished* she had not come.

会話「恵子について何か聞いてる？」「彼女, あす帰ってくるそうよ」"Any news of Keiko?" "She'll be ↘home tomórrow, I ↗*hope*."

会話「彼は元気になるでしょうか」「そう思います[そうは思いません]」"Will he get well?" "I ↘*hope* so [I'm ↘*afraid* nót]." (❶「…だと思うけど」の気持ちのときは ↘音調)

❸ [意図する] (...するつもりである) be going to 《*do*》 (❶ すでに計画済みの明確な意図を表し, 以下の言い方より強意的); (意図する) 〘やや書〙 intend 《*to do*》; (...しようかと思っている) think* 《*(that*) 節》 (❶ 意志をやわらげる表現で節内は will, would を用いる. 進行形は不可), be thinking 《*of doing*》 (❶ 進行形でまだ意志は固まっていないことを表す. (⇨つもり) ▶今年はアメリカへ行こうと思っている I'm *going to* go to the US this year./I *intend to* go to the US this year./I'm *thinking of* going to the US this year./I *think* (*that*) I'll go to the US this year. ▶この会社をやめようと思う I *intend* [*mean*] to quit this company.

会話「いいえ, 私が欲しいのはそれではありません」「ほう, ではあなたが思っていたのはこれですか」"No, that's not the one I want." "Well then, is this the one you *had in mind*?" (❶ have ... in mind は「心に決めている」の意)

❹ [みなす] (A を B とみなす) regard [look on] A as B (⇨みなす), (A を B と考える) consider [think*] A (*to be*) B, think of A as B (⇨ (a); 考える ❶ ②); (A を B と受け取る) take* A as [for, *to be*] B. ▶私を何だと思っているの一馬鹿だとでも？ What do you *take* me *for*—a fool?

❺ [気にする] mind, care 《*about*》 (❶ いずれも否定文・疑問文に用いる); (心配する) be concerned 《*about, for*》; (何とも思わない) think* nothing of .... ▶騒音なんか別に何とも思わない I *don't mind* [*care about*] the noise. ▶彼はカンニングをするのを何とも思っていない He *thinks nothing of* cheating on [in] a test.

❻ [疑う] (...でないと思う) doubt; (...であると思う) suspect (⇨疑う); (...かしらと思う) wonder (⇨かしら). ▶彼がここに来るとは思わない I *doubt if* [*whether*] he will come here. ▶彼はその秘密を知っている

のではないかと思う I *suspect (that)* he knows the secret. ◆彼は果たして時間どおりに来るのだろうかと I *wonder* if he will come on time. ◆彼は何を考えているのだろうかと, 彼女は思った "What is he *thinking (about)*?" she *wondered*.
❼[恋しく思う] *think* of* .... ◆1日たりともあなたのことを思わない日はありません I can't stop *thinking of* you even (for) a day.
❽[思い出す] remember. ◆今思えば彼は何となく様子が変だった (Now) I *remember* he looked somehow strange.

おもうぞんぶん 思う存分 ◆思う存分(=好きな[欲しい]だけ)食べる eat *as much as* one *likes* [*wants*]; 《書》eat *all* one *wants*; (心ゆくまで)(やや書) eat to one's *heart's content*; (食べられるだけ)《書》eat one's *fill*. ◆自分の能力を思う存分(=最大限に)発揮する use one's *talents and abilities to the full*. ◆思う存分泣く have a *good* cry; have a cry *out*; (胸が張り裂けるほど泣く) cry one's *heart out*.

おもうつぼ 思う壺 ◆敵は彼の思う壺にはまった(わなにかかった) The enemy *fell right into* his *trap*./(彼の利益になるように行動した) The enemy *played right into* his *hands*.

おもうに 思うに ◆思うに彼は善人だ I *think* [*I should say*] he is a good man./(私の考えでは) *In my opinion* [*To my way of thinking, As I see it*, ×*According to my opinion*] he is a good man.
会話 「じゃあ, だれのせいだ」「ぼくが思うには山田だな」 "Well, who is to blame?" "Yamada, *in my opinion*."

おもうまま 思うまま [思うとおりに] (just) *as* one *wants* [*wishes*].

おもおもしい 重々しい [深刻で厳粛な] grave; [荘厳な] solemn /sáləm/; [威厳のある] dignified; [重苦しい] oppressive. ◆重々しい雰囲気 an *oppressive* atmosphere. ◆重々しい口調で in a *grave* [*solemn*] tone. ◆重々しい態度をとる assume a *dignified* air.

*****おもかげ 面影** (顔) one's *face*; (生き写し) the *image* /ímidʒ/; (跡) a *trace*. ◆亡き母の面影をしのぶ remember one's dead mother's *face*. ◆彼女には母親の面影がある She *looks somewhat like her mother*. ◆(思い起こさせる) She *reminds me of her mother*. ◆この町には昔の面影がない This town *has* (保存する)《書》*retains*] no *traces of* the old days.

おもかじ 面舵 starboard. ◆面かじいっぱい！ Hard starboard!

おもき 重き ◆重きを置く put [lay, 《やや書》place] emphasis on .... (! emphasis の代わりに stress も可) ◆うちの学校では特に語学に重きを置いている Our school *puts* special *emphasis on* language studies. ◆うちの課ではいつも彼の意見が重きを成している His opinion always *counts* (for much) in our section./(尊重されて影響力がある) His opinion always *carries* (a lot of [great]) *weight* in our section.

おもく 重く [ずっしりと] heavily; [重大に] seriously. ◆心配事が彼の心にしかかった The worries hung [lay] *heavy* on him. ◆彼はその問題を重く見た He took the problem *seriously*. (⇨重視する)

おもくるしい 重苦しい [空・気分が] heavy; [陰気な] gloomy; [重くのしかかる] oppressive. ◆重苦しい空 a *heavy* [a *gloomy*] sky. ◆重苦しい雰囲気 a *heavy* [an *oppressive*] atmosphere. ◆重苦しい気分 (=悲しい)気分で with a *heavy* heart. ◆胃が重苦しい feel *heavy* [have a *heavy* feeling] in the stomach.

*****おもさ 重さ** weight. (⇨重量, 目方) ◆箱の重さは5キロです The box *weighs* [The *weight* of the box is] 5 kilos. (!動詞を用いる方が普通)/The box is 5 kilos in *weight*. (!×The box is 5 kilos *heavy*. とはいわない) ◆その本はどれくらいですか How much does it *weigh*?/What is the *weight*? (!×How heavy is it? とはいわない)

おもざし 面差し [顔立ち] features; [顔つき] (an) expression; a look. (⇨顔つき, 表情)

おもし 重し a weight. ◆風で書類が飛ばないように重しを置いた I put a *weight* on the papers so that they wouldn't be blown off.

*****おもしろい 面白い** ❶[楽しい, 愉快な] interesting; enjoyable; amusing; funny; entertaining; exciting.

> 使い分け **interesting** 知的興味をそそるをさす最も一般的な語.
> **enjoyable** 人を楽しませて満足させること.
> **amusing** 人を愉快にさせて笑わせること.
> **funny** こっけいではしゃげていて人を笑わせること.
> **entertaining** 人をなごませること.
> **exciting** 人を興奮させる刺激・スリルを持っていること. しばしば interesting の強意語として用いる.

◆大変おもしろい劇 a very *interesting* [*amusing*, *entertaining*] play. ◆おもしろい冗談 a *funny* joke. (!面白味のない古臭い冗談は stale joke という) ◆実におもしろい接戦 a really *exciting* close game. ◆おもしろくない(=退屈な)本 a *dull* [a *boring*] book. ◆英語がおもしろくなくなる(=興味を失う) lose *interest* in English. ◆その話は私にはとてもおもしろかった The story was very *interesting* to me./I *was greatly amused at* [*by*] the story. (⇨面白がる) ◆その本は読んでみるとおもしろかった(おもしろくなかった] I found the book *interesting* [*boring*]. ◆その話を大変おもしろく読んだ I read the story *with* great *interest*./The story was really *exciting*. ◆あの男はとてもおもしろいやつだ He's a very *funny* fellow./He is great [good] *fun*. (!×a great [a good] *fun* とはいわない) ◆鬼ごっこはとてもおもしろい Playing tag is a lot of *fun* [is really *enjoyable*, ×is really *interesting*]. ◆パーティーはとてもおもしろかった We *had* lots of *fun* [(楽しんだ] *had* a very *good time*, *enjoyed ourselves* very much] at the party. (⇨楽しい) ◆そのレスリングの試合は実におもしろかった (I found) the wrestling match was really *exciting*./I really *enjoyed* the wrestling match.
会話 「来週の土曜日バレエを見に行かないかい」「まあ, おもしろそうね」 "Would you like to go to the ballet next Saturday?" "Oh, that sounds *interesting* [*like fun*]."
❷[その他の表現] ◆あれはおもしろいですか(=心に訴えますか) Does that *appeal to* you? ◆彼のやけた態度がおもしろくない(=気にさわる) His sissy attitude *gets on* my nerves.
会話 「太郎はあいかわらずゴルフに夢中になってるよ」「あんなものどこがおもしろいのか分からないよ」 "Taro's still very keen on golf." "I can't understand *what he sees in it*."
会話 「なんとかしていらしてください. あなたがいないとあまりおもしろいパーティーにならないから」「そう言ってくれてありがとう. できるだけ行くようにするよ」 "Please try to come. It won't be *much of* a party without you." "It's nice of you to say that. I'll do my best." (!否定文に用いて「たいした...(でない)」の意. ここではパーティーがあまり盛り上がらないことをいう)

おもしろおかしい 面白おかしい 形 (こっけいな) funny;

おもしろがる (おどけた) comical; (愉快な) amusing.
— 面白おかしく 圖 (おどけて) comically; (愉快に) amusingly; (ユーモアたっぷりに) humorously. ●自分の失敗談をおもしろおかしく話す tell *comically* of the story one's own faults.

おもしろがる 面白がる be amused 《*at, by, with*》, amuse oneself 《*with, by*》. ●おもしろがって(=ふざけて)彼の弁当を隠す hide his [box] lunch (just) *for fun* [*for the fun of it*]. ●生徒たちはその冗談を大変おもしろがった The pupils *were* very much [《話》very, 《書》much] *amused at* [*to hear*] the joke. ●その子は漫画を読んでおもしろがった The child *amused* himself [*herself*] (*by*) *read*ing the comic book. (⇨*enjoyed reading* …) ●彼は手品をして子供たちをおもしろがらせた He *amused* the children *by show*ing them some magic [*with* some *magic*].

おもしろさ 面白さ fun, interest. (⇨面白味)

おもしろはんぶん 面白半分 ●おもしろ半分にそう言った I said it (*just*) *for fun* [*in fun*].

おもしろみ 面白味 (楽しみ) fun; (ユーモア) humor. ●彼はおもしろ味のない人だ He has no *sense of humor*./(退屈な人だ) He is a bore. (❗ a dull person ともいえるが,「ばか」と意味が重なるので避けたい)

おもたい 重たい (⇨重い)

おもたせ お持たせ ●お持たせ(=あなたに頂いたもの)で失礼ですが Sorry to serve you what you brought (us).

おもだち 面立ち features; looks. (⇨顔立ち)

おもだった 主立った chief; leading; important. (⇨主な)

***おもちゃ** a toy; 《書》a plaything (❗ 子供は用いない語. 比喩的に「もてあそばれる人」の意でも用いられる). ●おもちゃのピアノ a *toy* piano. ●鉛筆をおもちゃにする *toy with* a pencil. ●その子はおもちゃで遊んでいた The child was playing with its [his, her] *toys*. ●彼女のアクセサリーはみんなおもちゃのようだった Her accessories are all mere knick(-)knacks.
● おもちゃ箱 a toy box [chest]. ●おもちゃ屋 (店) a toy store 《主に米》[shop 《主に英》]; (人) a toyman.

おもて 表 ❶ [表面] the face; (前面) the front; (正しい向き) the right side. ●コインの表 *the face* (↔*back*) of a coin. ●その建物の表 *the front* (↔*back, rear*) of the building. ●トランプの表を出して置く lay the cards *face up*. (❗「表を上にして」の意. 裏を出すときは face down という) ●封筒の表に住所と名前を書く write one's name and address on *the front* (↔*back*) of an envelope. ●布地の表 *the right* (↔*wrong, reverse*) *side* of the cloth. ●警官隊が建物の表と裏から突入した The police rushed into the building from both *the front* and *rear*. ●その建物は表側が大通りに面している The building faces the main street *in front*. ●表か裏か? *Heads* or *tails*? (❗ コインを投げて勝負を決めるときの言葉)

❷ [うわべ] ●表をつくろう(=世間体をよくする) keep up *appearances*. ●表を飾る be showy [flashy]. ●感情を表に出す show one's feelings.

❸ [戸外] (屋外) *outside* [*outdoors, out of doors*]; (通りで) play *on* [*in*] *the street*. ●表に出てはいけません. ひどく雨が降っているから Don't go *outside*. It's raining hard.

❹ [野球で] the top (↔the bottom). ●7 回表に in *the top* (*half*) [*the first half*] of the seventh inning.

おもて 面 [[顔]] a face; a head (⇨顔); [[仮面]] a mask. ●面を上げる lift one's face [head].

おもてがき 表書き one's name and address.

おもてかんばん 表看板 ❶ [劇場の正面の看板] a sign over the entrance of a theater.
❷ [主な仕事や政策] the main business [policy]. ●その党の表看板はテロ対策である The major policy of the party is to take effective measures against terrorism.
❸ [表向きの仕事] a cover, 《話》a front. ●その会社は金融業を表看板としていたが, 実は麻薬の取り引きをしていた The company's financial business was just a *front* for drug trafficking.

おもてさく 表作 the primary crop (in double-cropping).

おもてざた 表沙汰 ●表ざたにする (明らかにする) bring … *to light*; (人々に知らせる) make … *public* [*known*]; (裁判に持ち込む) take … *to court*.

おもてだつ 表立つ [[人々に知れ渡る]] become* known (to the public); (人目につく) attract (one's) attention. ●今のところ新党結成の表立った(=目に見える)動きはない There is as yet no *visible* [(あからさまな) *open*] movement to set up a new political party.

おもてどおり 表通り (大通り) a main street. (❗ 通例は a street で間に合う)

おもてぶたい 表舞台 ●表舞台に立つ act as a leading person. ●彼は団十郎を襲名して歌舞伎界の表舞台に立って活躍した He succeeded to the name of Danjuro and *played an active part as a leading actor in the kabuki world*.

おもてむき 表向き (公式の) official; (公の) public; (建前の) 《書》ostensible. ●彼の名を表向きにしたくない I don't want his name made *public*. ●表向きは彼は休暇を取っているが, 実際は肝臓を悪くして入院している *Officially* he is on his vacation—actually he is in the hospital with liver trouble. ●彼が欠席した表向きの理由は病気だった 《書》His *ostensible* reason for absence was sickness. (❗ He *pretended* (*that*) he was sick and didn't go there. などのようにいう方が日常会話では普通)

おもと 万年青 [[植物]] a lily-of-China.

おもな 主な [[最も重要な]] chief, (やや重)[[中心的な]] main; [[他より大きくて重要な]] major; [[主導的な]] leading (❗ 以上 5 語はいずれも通例限定的に); [[重要な]] important. ●主な産業 the *chief* industry. ●日本の主な新聞 the *leading* [*major*] newspapers of Japan. ●この計画の主な目的は何ですか What is the *main* [*chief, principal*] purpose of this plan? ●小麦はこの地域の主な作物です Wheat is the *chief* crop in this area. ●このプロジェクトの主な部分はほぼ完成した The *major* part of this project is almost completed. ●カメラはその国の主な輸出品の一つだ Cameras are among the most *important* exports of the country.

おもなが 面長 ●面長の女 a woman with an *oval face*; an *oval-faced* woman.

おもに 重荷 ❶ [負担] a burden (*to*), a load; [重い荷物] a heavy load. (⇨荷, 荷物) ●借金の重荷 a (heavy) *burden* [*load*] of debt. ●心の重荷を下ろす take a *load* off one's mind. ●任務を重荷に感じる feel *loaded* with one's duties. ●その店の経営が彼の(=彼には)重荷になってきた Running the store is becoming a *burden to* him. ●やっと重荷を下ろした At last I am relieved of my *burden*./At last my *burden* is off my shoulders.

おもに 主に mainly; chiefly; 《大部分》mostly; [[大方は]] largely; [[典型的には]] typically. ●その事故は主に君の不注意のせいで起こった The accident happened *mainly* [*chiefly, largely*] because

おもねる you were careless./The accident is due *largely* to [*largely* due to] your carelessness. (**!** due largely to の方が普通) ●父は主に運動のためにテニスをする My father plays tennis *mainly* [*chiefly*] for exercise. ●乗船客は主に日本人だった The passengers on board were *mostly* [*for the most part*] Japanese./*Most of* the passengers on board were Japanese.

おもねる 阿ねる flatter; curry favor《*with*》. (⇨お世辞, へつらう)

おもはゆい 面映ゆい feel embarrassed. (**!** つづり字に注意) (⇨きまり(が)悪い)

おもみ 重み 〖重量〗weight; 〖威厳〗dignity; 〖重要性〗importance. ●重みに耐える[を支える] bear [support] the *weight* (*of*). ●雪の重みでつぶれる be crushed under the *weight* of the snow. ●重みのある人 a man [a woman] of *dignity*. ●非常に重みのある事実 a very *important* fact; a fact of great *importance*. ▶ウエストミンスター寺院を訪れる人々はだれしも歴史の重みを感じるだろう Those who visit Westminster Abbey will feel the *weight* of history.

おもむき 趣 〖魅力, 風情〗(a) charm, (味わい) (a) taste, (a) flavor; 〖雰囲気〗(an) atmosphere; 〖(色などの)感じ〗(an) effect. ●趣のある装飾 *tasteful* decoration. ●独特の趣がある have a *charm* of its own. ●その古い町は大変趣があった The old town was full of *atmosphere* [had a lot of *atmosphere*]. ●その小説は東洋的な趣があった The novel has an oriental *flavor*. ▶淡い青色が絵に美しい趣を添えている The light blue makes a lovely *effect* on the painting.

***おもむく** 赴く 〖行く〗go*; 〖出発する〗leave* (*for*); 〖訪問する〗visit. ●新しい任地に赴く *go to* [*leave for, set out for*] one's new post. ●感情の赴くにまかせる give free play to one's feelings. ▶私たちは美しい田園を足のおもむくままに散策した We wandered about [*walked aimlessly*] in the beautiful countryside.

おもむろに slowly (and quietly). ●おもむろに腰を上げる stand up *slowly*. ●彼はおもむろに話し始めた He began to speak *slowly and quietly*.

おももち 面持ち (⇨顔つき, 表情)

おもや 母屋 the main house in the premises.

おもやつれ 面やつれ ── 面やつれする 動 (病気で) become gaunt; (ほおがこける) become sunken-cheeked.

おもゆ 重湯 rice gruel.

おもらし お漏らし ●お漏らしをする wet one's pants.

おもり お守り ●赤ん坊のお守りをする (世話をする) take care of [*look after*] a baby; (雇われて世話をする) baby-sit. ●赤ん坊のお守り(をする人) a baby-sitter. (話) a (⇨世話)

おもり 重り (はかりの) a weight; (釣り糸などの) a sinker. ●釣り糸に重りをつける *weight* a line.

おもわく 思惑 〖予期〗expectation (**!** しばしば複数形で); 〖計算〗(a) calculation; 〖投機〗(やや書) (a) speculation. ●事業は思惑どおりには行かなかった Our business wasn't as good as we (had) *expected*./Our business didn't come up to [didn't live up to, fell short of] our *expectations*. ▶日本株が上がるだろうという思惑が外れた We speculated that Japanese stocks would rise, but we were wrong. ▶世間の思惑など気にするな Don't mind about *what* other people [*others*] *think* (*of you*).

●思惑買い[売り] speculative buying [selling].
●思惑買い[売り]をする buy [sell] (it) as a *speculation*. [〖英話〗a *spec*].

おもわしい 思わしい (満足のゆく) satisfactory; (よい) good (↔bad, poor)《condition》. ●彼の学校の成績は思わしくない His school record is not *satisfactory* [*good*]. / He is not doing well at school.

***おもわず** 思わず 〖心ならずも〗in spite of oneself; 〖思わず知らず〗involuntarily /ɪnvάləntèrili/; 〖無意識に〗unconsciously; 〖本能的に〗instinctively; (知らず知らずに) before one knows it. ●思わず目を閉じる close one's eyes *unconsciously* [*involuntarily*]. ▶彼は思わず叫び声をあげた He cried *in spite of himself*./He cried *involuntarily*./He gave an *involuntary* cry.

おもわせぶり 思わせ振り ── 思わせ振りな 形 (意味ありげな) significant; (挑発的な) suggestive (**!** obscene の婉曲語). ●思わせ振りな態度をとる (主に動作で) make a *significant* [a *suggestive*] gesture; (発言で) say something *significant* [*suggestive*].

── 思わせ振りに 副 significantly; suggestively; in a significant [a suggestive] manner.

おもわぬ 思わぬ unexpected; (予測できなかった) unforeseen. ●思わぬ客 an *unexpected* guest. ●思わぬ状況の変化のために by *unforeseen* circumstances. ●思わぬ事故にあう meet with an accident. (**!** meet with の代わりに単に ×meet は用いない) (⇨思い掛けない)

おもんじる 重んじる (高く評価する) value; (尊敬する) respect; (重要視する) make* much of ...; (尊重する) 〖書〗esteem. ●健康を何よりも重んじる *value* good health above anything else. ▶彼は学会で重んじられている He *is respected* [*is made much of*] in the learned society.

おもんぱかる 慮る give careful consideration《*to*》; consider ... carefully.

:**おや** 親 ❶〖人の〗a parent (**!** 片親を示す場合を除き通例複数形で)親は一般を表し, one's をつけて「両親, 父母」を表す); 〖父(親)〗a father; 〖母(親)〗a mother. (⇨父, 母, 両親)

①〖親〜〗●彼はとても親思いだ He is very kind [(献身的な) 〖書〗devoted] to his *parents*./He's always caring for his *parents*.

②〖親の〗●親の子への愛 *parents*' 〖書〗*parental*] love for [×to] their children. ●親のない子 a child with no *parent*(s); (孤児) an orphan. (**!** 片親の場合は a motherless [a fatherless] child という) ●親の許しを請う[得る] ask for [get] one's *parents*' permission. ●親の言うとおりにする (従う) obey one's *parents*; (従順である) be obedient to one's *parents*. ●親の手を離れる become independent of one's *parent*(s). ●親の代から since a parental time [days]. ▶子供をしつけるのは親の責任だ It's *parents*' responsibility to discipline their children.

③〖親に〗●親になる become parents (*a father, a mother*). ▶彼は親にそっくりだ He is [looks] just like his *father* [*mother*]. (**!** is は性格など, look は容姿をいう)/He resembles his *father* [*mother*] very much [*closely*]. (**!** 性格・容姿などをひっくるめた言い方)(⇨生き写し)

④〖親を〗●親を敬う respect one's *parents*. ●親をみる (経済的に) support one's *parents*; (世話する) look after [take care of] one's *parents*. ●親を親とも思わない defy one's *parents*. ●彼は幼い時に親をなくした He lost his *parents* when he was a child [very young].

❷〖動植物の〗●親犬[鳥] a *parent* dog [bird].

(❗ a mother [a father] dog の方が一般的)
❸ 中心的なもの. (⇔親会社)
❹ [トランプの] the dealer. ▶ぼくが親だよ It's my deal.

● 親の心子知らず Children never really know their parents./Children do not know how much they owe their parents.
● 親のすねをかじる be dependent on [live on,《やや話》sponge off] one's parents.
● 親の七光り Parental fame is a magnifying glass for children. (⇒七光り)
● 親の欲目 親の欲目かもしれないが, あの子は絵の才能がある I may be prejudiced in favor of my son, he seems to have a talent for painting.
● 親は無くとも子は育つ (ことわざ) Nature is a good mother.
● 親心 parents' [《書》parental] love for [×to] their children.

*おや [驚きなど] Oh! /óu/ (⇒まあ) ▶おや, そこにいたのか, 哲也 *Oh*, there you *are*, Tetsuya. ▶おやおや *Dear, dear!* (❗ 困ったり, 失望して) */ Well, well, well.* (❗ 意外な人に意外な所で出会って) ▶彼の風采(ふうさい)におやと思った(= 驚いた) I *was surprised* at his appearance. ▶エンジンをかけたとたんにおやと思った(= 何か変な感じがした) The moment I started the engine, I *felt something strange about it* [(どこか狂っている) *something wrong with it*].

おやおや (⇒まあ 😊) ▶おやおや, 座ってどうしたのか話してごらん *Dear! Dear!* [*Oh dear! Dear me!*] Just sit down and tell me what happened. (❗ 主に女性に好まれる言い方) ▶おやおや, こういう成績でよく平気でいられるよ It *surprises* [《話》*gets*] me you can remain calm at such a poor result. (❗ この get は「あきれさせる, いやにならせる」ぐらいの意)

おやがいしゃ 親会社 a parent (⇔subsidiary) company.
おやがかり 親掛かり ● 親掛かりでいる depend [be dependent] on one's parents; (親のすねをかじっている) live on one's parents' income.
おやかた 親方 [上役] a chief (~s), 《話》a boss, (職人の) a master; [相撲部屋の] a stable master. ▶大工の親方 a *master* carpenter. ▶親方日の丸 The (Japanese) Rising Sun stands behind you./Uncle Sam will foot the bill. (❗「米国政府が勘定を払ってくれる」の意)
おやがわり 親代わり ● 親代わりをする act as 《his》parents.
おやくしょしごと お役所仕事 bureaucracy; red tape [参考] 英国でかつて公文書を赤のひもでとじたことから.
おやこ 親子 parents and children. ● 親子の愛 *parents'* [《書》*parental*] affection [love]. ● 親子の縁を切る disown one's son [daughter]. ● 親子の2人は親子のようには見えない They don't look like (a) mother and daughter [(a) father and son]. ❗ 日常的には (a) parent and child より普通. 冠詞 a をつけるのは《主に米》) ▶彼は親子ほど年の違う女性と再婚した He remarried a girl (who was) young enough to be his daughter.

DISCOURSE
携帯電話は人と人との関係を変えた. 特に, 親子関係を変えた Cellular phones have changed human relationships. **Specifically**, they have changed *the relationship between parents and children*. (❗ especially; specifically (特に)は言い換えに用いるディスコースマーカー)

● 親子関係 a parent-child relationship. ● 親子心中 a parent-child suicide. ● 親子電話[回線] a party telephone [line]. ● 親子丼 a bowl of rice topped with cooked chicken, eggs and some vegetables.

おやこうこう 親孝行 filial piety /páiəti/ [duty]. (❗「親に対する子として当然の敬愛, 従順」の意) ▶親孝行しなさいよ *Be dutiful* [*good*] *to* your parents. ▶彼はとても親孝行なので, 両親は彼を誇りに思っている He is such a *good* son that his parents are proud of him./He's so *good* to his parents that they are proud of him.

おやじ 親父 one's father; 《話》one's old man.
おやしお 親潮 (千島海流) the Kurile /kúril/ Current.
おやしらず 親知らず (知恵歯) a wisdom tooth (⑧ teeth). ▶親知らずが生えてきた I'm having a *wisdom tooth* coming in [×coming out]. (❗ ×come out = fall out [抜ける]の意)
おやすい お安い ▶お安いご用です. 喜んでやります It's no trouble [No problem]. I'm happy to do it.
おやすくない お安くない ▶あの2人はお安くない仲だ They *are in love with* each other./They are lovers.

*おやすみ お休み good night. ● お休みのキスをする kiss 《him》*good night*. ● お父さんにお休みなさいを言いなさい Say *good night* to Dad. ▶ゆうべはよくお休みになれましたか Did you *sleep well* [*have a good sleep*] last night?

[会話]「ママ, お休みなさい」「はい, ぐっすりお休み」「うん」"Good night, Mom!" "Good night. Sleep tight." "I will."

おやだま 親玉 a boss; a leader; 《話》a kingpin.
おやつ 御八つ [お菓子] a snack; [間食] a snack, [菓子など] snacks. ▶おやつにドーナツを食べる eat doughnuts for *snacks*; 《主に米》snack on doughnuts. ▶太郎, おやつの時間ですよ Taro! It's *teatime*.
おやばか 親馬鹿 (むやみにかわいがる親) a doting parent. ● 親馬鹿ぶりを発揮する *dote on* [(夢中になる)《話》*be crazy about*] one's son [daughter].
おやばなれ 親離れ ● 親離れしている be independent of one's parents.
おやふこう 親不孝 (親を敬愛しないこと, 親に従順でないこと) undutifulness to one's parents. ● 親不孝な息子 an *undutiful* [《悪い》*a bad*] son.
おやぶん 親分 [指導者] a leader; [上役] a boss; [暴力団の] a gang leader. ● 親分風を吹かす《話》be very bossy; (こき使う) boss 《him》about [around]. ▶彼には親分肌の(= 太っ腹な)ところがある There's something *magnanimous* about him./(面倒見がいい) He *takes good care of* other people./(頼りがいがある) He is very *dependable*.
おやま 女形 (集合的) the *oyama*; a *kabuki* female impersonator; (説明的に) a *kabuki* actor playing a female role.
おやまあ Oh! (⇒おや)
おやまのたいしょう お山の大将 the king of a small mountain; 《話》《軽蔑的に》the [×a] cock of the walk [dunghill].
おやもと 親元 ▶彼は親元(= 親)から借金してその家を建てた He borrowed some money from his *parents* to build the house. ▶親元(= 家)を離れて10年になる It is [It's been] 10 years since I left *home*.
おやゆずり 親譲り ── 親譲りの 圏 (性格・財産が) inherited from one's parent(s) [father, mother]; (代々受け継いできた) hereditary /hərédɪtèri/. ● 親譲りの財産 one's *hereditary* property; one's property *inherited* from one's father [mother]. ▶孫

おやゆび 親指 (手の) a thumb /θʌm/; (足の) a big toe. ●親指を立てる raise one's *thumb*. ▶勝利・成功を表すしぐさ. 亭主・上司などは表さない (⇨指)

およがす 泳がす (放しておく) let ... move around freely; (助けておく) give ... line enough.

およぎ 泳ぎ swimming; (ひと泳ぎ) a swim. ●泳ぎ方を教える teach (him) how to *swim*. ▶ひと泳ぎしよう Let's have a *swim* [go for a *swim*]. ▶泳ぎが上手だ He is a good *swimmer*./He is good at *swimming*. (🅛 前の方が普通)

:およぐ 泳ぐ ❶ [水泳する] (手足・ひれ・尾などを使って) swim*. ●泳いで川を渡る swim (*across*) the river. ▶プールよりは海で泳ぐ方がいい I'd rather *swim in* the sea [*ocean*] than *in* the pool. ▶彼は毎日川へ泳ぎに行く He goes *swimming in* [*to*] the river every day./He goes to the river to *swim* [for a *swim*] every day. ▶これらの魚は群れをなして泳ぐ These fish *swim* in schools. ▶監視員は泳いでいる人から目を離さなかった The lifeguard kept an eye on the *swimmers*.

会話 「いつものように泳がなかったの?」「うん、そうなんだ、今朝はね」"Didn't you have your usual *swim*?" "No, I didn't, not this morning." (🅛 Didn't you swim, as usual? では「いつも泳がないが、今回もそうだったのか」の意になる)

❷ [その他の表現] ●(打者が)泳ぐ [泳いだスイングをする] swing far ahead of a pitch. ●打者のタイミングを外して泳がせる get a batter out in front. ▶彼は政界を巧みに泳ぎ渡った He *got* [*swam*] *along* skillfully in the political world.

***およそ 凡そ 圖 ❶** [約] about, 《米話》 around; some (🅛 数詞の前に限る). (⇨約) ●およそ20冊の本 about [*around*, *some*] twenty books. ▶およそ3時間かかるでしょう It will take *about* [*around*, *approximately*] three hours.

❷ [だいたいのところ] (ほとんど) almost; nearly; (一般に) generally; (一般的に言って) generally speaking; (大ざっぱに言って) roughly speaking. ▶仕事はおよそ終わった The work is *almost* [*nearly*] finished./《話》 I'm *almost* done with the work. ▶およそ、男の子の方が女の子より活発だ *Generally* (*speaking*) [*In general*], boys are more active than girls (are).

❸ [まったく] quite; (完全に) completely. (⇨全く) ▶そんなことをしてもよそ意味がない It is *quite* meaningless [It makes *no* sense *at all*] to do it.

— およその 形 ●およその(=概算の)距離 an *approximate* distance. ●およその(=大ざっぱな)考えを述べる give a *rough* idea (*of*). ▶それについておよその(=大ざっぱな)察しはついている I can make a *rough* guess about it.

およばずながら 及ばずながら ▶及ばずながら(=できる限り)力になりますこと I'll do all [《やや書》 *what little*] I can to help you./I'll try to do my best to help you.

およばない 及ばない (⇨及ぶ ❷❸)

およばれ お呼ばれ ▶あしたの晩は英語の先生のお宅にお呼ばれです Tomorrow evening I'm *invited to* dinner at my English teacher's house.

および お呼び ▶お呼びですか Did you call me, sir [ma'am]? ▶君はお呼びじゃない You are (completely) useless. ▶社長からゴルフのお呼び(=誘い)がかかると、彼はしぶしぶ出かけた When the boss *asked* [*invited*] him *to* play golf together, he went out reluctantly.

および 及び ▶この映画は東京及び大阪で公開されている This film is released (*both*) in Tokyo *and* in Osaka [in (*both*) Tokyo *and* Osaka]. (🅛 (1) ... *both* in Tokyo *and* Osaka の形は避けた方がよい. (2) 三つ以上の要素を列挙する場合は A, B(,) and C のように最後の要素の前に and をおく) (東京だけでなく大阪でも) This film is released in Tokyo *and* Ósaka *as well* [in Ósaka *as well as* in Tokyo]. (🅛 いずれも Osaka を強調) (⇨並びに、又 ❸、両方、共)

およびごし 及び腰 ●及び腰である (自信がなく決断できない) be indecisive; (おどおどしている) be hesitant.

およびもつかない 及びもつかない ▶彼は学者としては父には及ばない(=及ばない) He *never matches up to* his father as a scholar. (⇨及ぶ ❷) ▶現在の収入から考えると家を持つなんてことは及びもつきません Judging from my present income, owning a house is *far beyond my reach* [is an *absolutely impossible* dream].

***およぶ 及ぶ ❶** [達する] reach; (広範囲・長期間にわたって広がる) spread*; (時間・距離・範囲などが伸びる) extend; (範囲がわたる) range; (含む) cover; (続く) last (⇨亘(る)); (合計...になる) amount to ... (⇨達する❷). ▶その国の勢力は世界中に及んでいる The power of the country *reaches* [*extends*] throughout the world. ▶水害は隣村に及んだ The flood damage *spread* [*extended*] *to* the next village. ▶彼の牧場は盆地全体に及ぶ His ranch *extends* [*ranges*] *over* the whole valley. ▶話は広範囲に及んだ The conversation *covered* a wide range of subjects. ▶会議は深夜に及んだ The conference *extended* [*lasted*] till late at night. ▶実際の支出は毎週数千ドルに及んだ Actual expenses *amounted to* [*ran to*] several thousand dollars per week.

❷ [匹敵する] (力が及ぶ) be in one's power; (匹敵する) match; (等しい) equal, be equal 《*to*》. (⇨匹敵する) ▶その仕事は私の力の及ぶところではない The task *is beyond me* [*my power*, *my ability*]./I am not *equal* to the task. ▶テニスでは君にとても及ばない I *am no match for* you in tennis./I am not (*at all*) *equal* to you in tennis. ▶その映画は原作(の本)に及ばない The movie doesn't *come up to* the book. ▶彼のタイムは世界記録に2秒及ばなかった His time was two seconds *off* the world record./His time *came* [*fell*] *short of* (⇔came up to) the world record by two seconds.

❸ [するには及ばない] (する必要がない) do not have to 《*do*》; 《話》 haven't got to 《*do*》. ▶はるばる空港まで迎えにきていただくには及びません *Don't take the trouble to* [You *don't have to*] come a long way to meet me at the airport.

***およぼす 及ぼす** ▶私たちに大きな影響を及ぼす have [*exert*] a great influence *on* us; influence us greatly. ●作物に害を及ぼす do [*cause*] damage *to* the crops; damage the crops.

オランウータン 《動物》 an orangutan /əˈræŋətæn/, an orangutan(g).

オランダ 《国名》 Holland; (公式名) the Kingdom of the Netherlands. (🅛 通例単数扱い) (首都 Amsterdam) ●オランダ人 a Dutchman, a Hollander; (総称) the Dutch. ●オランダ語 Dutch. ●オランダ(人[語])の Dutch.

***おり 檻** 《獣の》 a cage; 《ウサギなどの》 a hutch; 《家畜を入れる囲い》 a pen; (特に羊用の) a fold; 《監獄》 a prison; (独房) a cell. ▶ライオンをおりに入れる put a lion into a *cage*; 《やや書》 *cage* a lion.

おり 織り (a) weave. ●あや[平]織り twill [plain]

weave. ● 手織りのじゅうたん a *handwoven* [a *homespun*] carpet.

おり 折 ❶〖機会〗an opportunity, a chance; (場合) an occasion; (…の時に) when …. (⇨おりよく) ▶こちらへおいでの折はぜひお立ち寄りください Do drop in on us *when* you happen to come this way [(近く) in the neighborhood]. ▶彼に折をみて(=彼の都合のいい時に)話そう I'll talk to him *at his convenience* [*when it's best for* him, *when it's convenient to* him].
❷〖折り箱〗a small wooden [cardboard] box.
● 折り詰め弁当 →折り詰め
❸〖折りたたむこと〗folding. ● 給料袋を二つ折りにしてポケットにしまう *fold* the pay packet *into* one's pocket.
● **折に触れて** ▶彼は折にふれて(=時々)飲み過ぎないよう注意してきた *From time to time* [(*Every*) *now and again*] I've warned him not to drink too much.
● **折も折** ▶出かけようとする折も折(=ちょうどその時)、雨が降り出した I was about to go out *just when* it began to rain.

おり 澱 (ワインなどの)the dregs 《複数扱い》; (a) sediment 《!複数形なし》; (コーヒーの) grounds. ● コーヒーをおりまで飲んでしまう drink one's coffee to *the dregs*; drink one's coffee *grounds*.

おりあい 折り合い〖合意〗an agreement, (非公式の)an understanding;〖妥協〗(a) compromise. (⇨折り合う) ● 折り合いをつける settle the matter; (妥協する) compromise 《with+人》; reach (an) *agreement* [a *compromise*] 《with+人, on+事》. ▶彼女はしゅうとめとの折り合いが悪いようだ She does not seem to *be getting along* [*on*] *with* her mother-in-law. ▶彼は職場の同僚と折り合いが悪かった He was *on bad terms with* other workers in the office.

おりあう 折り合う〖仲よくやっていく〗get* on [along] 《with》;〖意見が一致する〗agree 《with》, come* to [reach] (an) agreement 《with》;〖妥協する〗compromise 《with》. ● これらの条件で彼と折り合う *compromise with* him on these conditions. ▶値段の点で彼と折り合わなかった I couldn't *agree with* him *on* the price. ▶あなたにもうまく折り合って行けない人がいるのですか Are there any people you can't *get along with*?

おりあしく 折悪しく (あいにく) unfortunately, unluckily. (⇨あいにく)

おりいって 折り入って ▶折り入ってお願いしたいことがあるのですが Can I ask you a big favor?/I'd like to ask a *special* favor of you. (!後の方は改まった言い方)

オリーブ (木, 実) an olive /áliv/. ● オリーブ色 olive (green).
● オリーブ畑 an olive grove. ● オリーブ油 olive oil.

オリエンタル Oriental, oriental. ● オリエンタル芸術 *Oriental* [*oriental*] art.

オリエンテーション (an) orientation; (新入社員のための) a mentoring program, mentoring. ● 新入生のためのオリエンテーション the *orientation* of new students. ● オリエンテーションをする give [offer] 《him》(an) *orientation*.

オリエンテーリング orienteering /ɔ́ːriəntíəriŋ/. ● オリエンテーリング参加者 an orienteer.

オリエント the Orient of the Romans; the Ancient Near East and North Africa.
● オリエント学者 an Orientalist. (!the Orient は通例「東アジア, 東南アジア」の意。文脈がなければ an Orientalist は「東洋学者」の意)

おりおり 折々 ❶〖その時々〗▶ここでは四季折々の料理が楽しめる We can enjoy dishes of *each season* here. **❷**〖時々〗now and then. (⇨時々)

オリオン〖ギリシア神話〗Orion /əráiən/.
● オリオン座 Orion. ● オリオン座の三つ星 *Orion's* Belt.

おりかえし 折り返し (上着のえりの) a lapel /ləpél/; (ズボンのすその) (米) a cuff, 《英》a turn-up; (封筒の) a flap; (詩歌の) a refrain; (水泳の) a turn. ● (マラソンの) 折り返し地点で at the halfway point. ● 折り返し反信する answer *by return mail* [*by return* 《米》 *of post* 《英》]. ▶この件については調査の上、折り返しお電話をさしあげます (相手のクレームなどに対して) I'll investigate the matter and *get back to* you [*call* you *back*] *as soon as possible*.
● 折り返し運転 (operate, provide) a shuttle service 《between》.

おりかえす 折り返す〖紙などを〗turn [fold]… back [down]; 〖ズボンのすそなどを〗turn up 《the ends of one's trousers》; 〖引き返す〗return, turn back; (来た道を) double back; 〖向きを変える〗turn around. ● ページの隅を折り返す *turn back* [*turn down, fold back, fold down*] the corner of the page. ● えりを折り返す *turn down* [*back*] one's collar. ▶高速道路にまた乗るには折り返すより手がなかった I had to *double back* to get on the expressway again.

おりかさなる 折り重なる ▶彼らは床の上に折り重なるように倒れていた They were found lying *one upon another* [on top of one another] on the floor.

おりがみ 折紙 origami, (説明的に) (技術) the art of Japanese paper folding; (折の紙) colored paper for folding (⇨千代紙). ● 折り紙を教えてちょうだい Please show me how to do *origami*. ▶彼女は折り紙で鶴を折った She folded a piece of *colored paper* into the shape of a crane.
● **折り紙付き** ▶そのホテルは神戸で最高のホテルだとの折り紙付きです (世に知られている) The hotel is *universally known to be* [as] the best one in Kobe./(認められている) It *is admitted* that the hotel is the best in Kobe.

おりから 折から (ちょうどその時) just then. ▶折からの雨でずぶぬれになった It began to rain *just then* and I got all wet. ▶気候不順の折からご自愛ください Please take care of yourself in this unseasonable weather.

おりぐち 降り口 the way down; (列車などの出口) the way out.

オリゴとう オリゴ糖〖生化学〗oligosaccharide.

おりこみ 折り込み (新聞に入った広告) an advertising insert (in the newspaper); (雑誌のページ) an foldout, (二つ折りの)《主に米》a gatefold.

おりこむ 折り込む ● 新聞にビラを折り込む (=挿入する) *insert* bills *in* [*into*] the newspapers. ● ブラウスのすそを折り込む (=中へ押し込む) *tuck* one's blouse *in*; *tuck in* one's blouse.

おりこむ 織り込む ● その報告書に自分自身の考えを織り込む (=入れる) put one's own ideas *into* the report. ● 君の提案を計画に織り込む (=組み込れる) *incorporate* your suggestions *into* the plan.

オリジナリティー〖独創性〗originality. ▶彼の作品には人の意表をつくオリジナリティーがある He displays [shows] striking *originality* in his works.

オリジナル〖原物, 原作, 原文〗the [ˣan] original;〖独自の原曲〗an original piece of music;〖演劇などの創作脚本〗an original scenario (徧 ～s).

おりしも 折しも (ちょうどその時) just then. (⇨折から)

おりじわ 折り皺 a crease 《in》; (折り目) a fold.

おりたくしばのき 折りたく柴の記 Told Round a Brushwood Fire. 〔参考〕新井白石の自叙伝.

おりたたみ 折り畳み ●折り畳み式のいす〔傘〕a folding [a *collapsible*] chair [umbrella]. 🅘いくつにも折り畳んで小さくできるものに、fold-up《bicycles》を用いることができる）

おりたたむ 折り畳む fold;（何回かに折る）fold ... (up).（⇨畳む）●手紙を二つに折りたたんで封筒に入れる *fold* a letter in half and put it into an envelope. ●きちんと折りたたんだハンカチ a neatly *folded* handkerchief. ●このベッドは折りたたみ式だ This bed *folds away*.／(折りたたみ式ベッドだ) This is a foldaway [a folding, a fold-up] bed.

おりたつ 折り立つ、下り立つ come [go] down on one's feet.

おりづめ 折り詰め ●折り詰め弁当 a box lunch.

おりづる 折り鶴 a folded paper crane.

おりなす 織り成す さまざまな登場人物が織り成す物語 an intricate tale with many characters [a cast of thousands].

おりばこ 折り箱 a small wooden [cardboard] box.

おりひめ 織り姫〔天文〕Vega.

おりまげる 折り曲げる （まっすぐな・平らな物を）bend*. 🅘丸く曲げる場合にも、角をつけて曲げる場合にも用いる）（折りたたむ）fold;（曲げたものを折り返す）turn ... back [down];（かがむ）bend down. ●腕［針金］を折り曲げる *bend* one's arm [a piece of wire]. ●そのボール紙を二つに［四つに］折り曲げる *fold* the cardboard in half [into quarters]. ●ページの隅を折り曲げないでください Please don't *turn back* [*down*] the corners of the pages. ●彼は体を折り曲げてそれを拾った He *bent down* and picked it up.

おりめ 折り目 a fold; a crease. 🅘通例 fold は折りたたんでできたもの、crease は折り返したり曲げたりしてできたものをいう）●きちんと折り目のついたズボン well-*creased* [*neatly-pressed*] trousers. ●折り目に沿って封筒を切り開く *cut* the envelope *along the fold*. ●ズボンに折り目をつける *crease* [*press*] one's trousers.

●折り目正しい ●折り目正しい(＝礼儀正しい)紳士 a *well-mannered* gentleman; a gentleman *with good manners*.

おりもと 織り元 a textile manufacturer.

おりもの 下り物〔生理〕vaginal /vædʒáinl/ discharge.

おりもの 織物 (a) (textile) fabric, (a) textile. ●織物業 the textile industry. ●織物工場 a textile factory [mill]. ●絹織物 silk fabrics [textiles].

おりよく 折よく （運よく）fortunately, luckily;（いいタイミングで）with good timing.

:**おりる 下りる、降りる** ●【高い所から下りる】come* [go*] down, get* down,（やや書）alight,〔書〕descend (↔ascend);（伝って下りる）climb down. ●山を下りる come [go, climb] down a hill;〔書〕*descend* (*from*) a hill. ●階段を下りる *get*（歩いて）*walk*,（急いで）*hurry*] *down* the stairs. ●はしごを下りる *climb* [*get*] *down* a ladder. ●演壇から下りる *step down from* [*step off*] the platform. ●木から下りなさい *Get* [*Come, Climb*] *down* (*from*) the tree. ●幕が下りた The curtain *fell*. ●ヘリコプターがここに降りた(＝着陸した) A helicopter *landed* here. ●ブラインドが下りているから彼は寝ているのだろう The blinds *are down*. He must be asleep.

❷【乗り物などから降りる】(バス・列車などから) get* off (...), (↔get on);（車などから）get out of ... (↔get in). ●飛行機［列車］から降りる *get off* a plane [a train]. 🅘×*get* a plane [a train] *off* とはいわない）●車［エレベーター］から降りる *get out of* a car [an elevator]. ●馬を降りる *get down from* [*get off*] a horse;〔書〕*dismount* (*from*) a horse. ●彼は次の駅で降りた He *got off* at the next station. ●彼は電車から降りる時に滑ってころんだ He slipped and fell while he *was getting off* [*getting out of*] the train. ●このように中から出て行く動作を強調するときには get out of も用いられる) ●彼は自転車から飛び降りた He *jumped off* his bicycle [〔話〕bike].

会話 「三千院へ行くにはどこで降りればよろしいですか」「終点です」"Where do I *get off* for (the) Sanzenin Temple, please?" "It's the last stop."

❸【身を引く】(仕事などをやめる) quit*,（途中で）drop (-pp-) out (*of*),（共同の仕事から）bow out (*of*);（要職から）step (-pp-) down (*from*). ●ゲームを降りる *quit* [*drop out of*] the game. ●彼女がニュース番組から降りるといううわさが流れた A rumor spread she was going to *quit* [*bow out of*, *step down*] the TV news show. ●市長は収賄汚職のため降りざるを得なかった The Mayor was forced to *step* [*stand*] *down* because of the bribery scandal. ●そういう条件ならぼくは降りる(＝加わらないよ) I will *not join* you on that condition.

❹【許可・公金などが出る】●年金が下りる *receive* a pension. ●先生にその部屋を使ってもよいという許可が下りた The teacher *gave* us *permission* [*permitted us*] *to* use the room.

オリンピア〔ギリシャの古代遺跡〕Olympia. 〔参考〕オリンピック発祥の地)

オリンピック the Olympic Games, the Olympics 🅘ともに通例複数扱い);〔書〕the Olympiad. ●冬季オリンピック the *Olympic* Winter Games, the Winter *Olympic* Games. ●プレオリンピック the Pre-Olympics. ●国際オリンピック委員会 the International *Olympic* Committee（略 the IOC). ●オリンピック記録を出す set [make] an *Olympic* record. ●オリンピックに出場する take part in *the Olympics*. ●オリンピックで金メダルを獲得する win a gold medal *at the Olympic Games* [*the Olympics*]. ●オリンピックは4年ごとに開かれる *The Olympic Games* [*The Olympics*] are held every four years. ●オリンピックは勝つことより参加することに意義がある The important thing in *the Olympic Games* is not winning but taking part.

●オリンピック競技場 an Olympic stadium. ●オリンピック聖火 the Olympic torch. ●オリンピック村 an Olympic village.

:**おる 折る** ●【強く曲げて切りはなす】break* ... (off);（急にぽきんと）snap (-pp-) ... (off);（骨を）fracture. ●枝を折る *break* [*snap*] (*off*) a branch. 🅘off を伴うと「折って取る」という意が加わる) ●木［枝］を折るな Don't *break* the branches. ●彼はサッカーの練習中に右腕を折った(自分の不注意で) He *broke* [*fractured*] his right arm while practicing soccer.／(不可抗力で) He *had* his right arm *broken* while practicing soccer.

❷【曲げて重ねる】fold;（曲げる）bend*;（紙などを折り返す）turn ... back [down]. ●紙を二つに折る *fold* the paper in half [in two]. ●鶴を折る *fold* the paper *into* the shape of a crane. 🅘「折り紙」は paper folding,「折り鶴」は a folded-paper crane という) ●ひざを折る（床にひざをつく）kneel [fall] *down* on one's knees. 🅘fall は急に折る感じを伴う; 座ったり、または寝て）*bend* one's knees. ●指を折って数える count on one's fingers.（⇨数える）●その紙ナプキンは折ってあった The paper napkins *were folded*. ●ページのすみを折っておくとど

こまで読んだか分かっていいよ *Turn back* [*down*] *the corner of a page, and it will mark your place.* (⇨折り返す)
❸【中断する】interrupt; (終える) end. ● 筆を折る *end* one's literary career. ● 彼の話の腰を折る *interrupt* him while he is talking.

おる 織る weave. ● 織機で布を織る *weave* cloth on a loom. ● 亜麻糸を織り敷物を作る *weave* flax yarn *into* a rug; *weave* a rug *out of* flax yarn.

オルガズム 【性的絶頂感】(an) orgasm /ɔ́:rgæzm/. ● オルガズムに達する reach [achieve] *orgasm*; have an *orgasm*.

オルガン 【<ポルトガル語】 an organ, 《米》 a pipe organ; (足踏み式) a pedal organ. ● オルガン奏者 an organist. ● オルガンを弾く play the *organ*. (⇨ピアノ)

オルグ 【労働組合などの組織活動者】 an organizer.

オルゴール 【<オランダ語】 a music 《米》 a musical (主に英)】 box.

*おれい お礼 gratitude; thanks. (⇨礼) ● お礼奉公をする work without pay in return for what one's employer did for one. ● お礼参りをする visit a shrine [a temple] to give thanks (*for* the realization of one's wish); (やくざなどが) take revenge (*on* one's accuser).

オレガノ 【植物】oregano.

おれきれき お歴々 (著名な人たち) notables; prominent figures, 《話》VIPs.

おれこむ 折れ込む fold inside; include within.

オレゴン 【米国の州】 Oregon /ɔ́:rəɡən/ 《略 Ore., Oreg. 郵便略 OR》.

おれる 折れる ❶【曲がってはなれる】break; (急にぽきんと) snap (-pp-). ● 鉛筆が折れちゃった My pencil's *broken*. ▶ 彼は右腕が折れた (⇨折る❶)
❷【曲がる】turn; (折り重なっている) be folded. ▶ 道が右に折れている (⇨曲がる❶) ● その角を右に折れて左側の 3 軒目です *Turn* (to the) right at the corner and it's the third house on the left.
▶ ページの端が折れていた The corner of a page *was folded*.
❸【妥協する】give* in, 《書》yield. ▶ 我々の熱心な説得にとうとう彼も折れた He finally *gave in* [*yielded*] *to* our powers of persuasion.

オレンジ 【植物】(実, 木) an orange /ɔ́(:)rɪndʒ/ (📘「オレンジの木」は通例 an *órange*(-)trèe); (色) orange.
● オレンジジュース orange juice.

おろおろ (どうしていいか分からなくて) helplessly, (おびえて) frightenedly, 《話》in a dither, (心配のあまり) very worried, nervously. ▶ 人々は空襲を受けておろおろ逃げ回わった People ran about *helplessly* in the air raid. ● 彼らはただおろおろするばかりでどうすればよいのか分からなかった They just *got into a dither* and didn't know what to do. ● 彼はおろおろとへたな弁解をした He *was panicked into* making a poor excuse./*Panic-stricken*, he made a poor excuse.

おろか 愚か ── 愚かな 形 foolish; silly; stupid. (⇨馬鹿な 【類語】) ● 愚かなこと[女] a *foolish* thing [*woman*]. ▶ 愚かにも彼女の言葉を信じてしまった I was *foolish* enough to believe what she said./ I *foolishly* believed what she said. ▶ 彼は愚かにもまたそこへ行った It *was foolish of* him to go there again.

おろか 【…は言うまでもなく】not to mention …; to say nothing of …; not to speak of …; 《通例否定文で》 let alone …. ▶ 彼女はフランス語はおろか英語も話せない She can't speak English, *let alone* [*not to mention*] French.

おろし 卸 (卸売り) wholesale (↔retail). ● 卸で売る [買う] sell [buy] (at [by]) *wholesale*. (📘前置詞を用いないのが普通)
● 卸業 a wholesale business. ● 卸業者 a wholesaler; a wholesale dealer. ● 卸値 a wholesale price. ● 卸売価 wholesale prices.

おろしがね おろし金 a grater. ● おろし金で大根をおろす grate (⇨) a radish.

おろす 下ろす, 降ろす ❶【上から下へ移す】 take [bring*, put*] … down; (下に置く) put [set*] … down; (落とす) drop (-pp-); (高さ・位置を低くする) lower; (引き下ろす) pull … down; (巻き下ろす) roll … down (↔roll … up); (積み荷を) unload; (船荷を) discharge. ● 2 階から荷物を下ろす *bring down* one's things *from* the second floor [《英》the first floor]. ▶ バケツを井戸へ下ろす *put* a bucket *down into* the well; *lower* a bucket *into* the well. ● 幕を下ろす *drop* a curtain; (下げる) *lower* a curtain. ● ブラインドを下ろす *pull down* [*lower*] a shade. ● 車の窓ガラスを下ろす *roll down* a car window. ● トラックから商品を下ろす *unload* goods *from* a truck; *unload* a truck. ● なべを火から下ろす *take* a pot *off* [*from over*] the fire. ● ボートを下ろす(=下ろして水に浮かべる) *get* a boat *on the water*. ▶ その箱を本棚から下ろしてください Please *take down* the box from the shelf. ● 彼は荷物を下ろして木陰で休んだ He *put* [*set*] his load *down* and rested in the shade of a tree.
会話 「スーツケースをここに降ろすよ」「そっとね」 "I'll *dump* the suitcases here." "Gently, please." (📘 dump は「(重い荷物などを)どさっと降ろす」こと)
❷【乗り物から人を】let*… *off*, (ある場所で) drop (-pp-). ● バスから乗客を降ろす *let* passengers *off* a bus. ● そのおばあさんに手を貸してバスから降りてあげる *help* the old woman (get) *off* the bus.
▶ 次の角のところで降ろしてください Please *drop* me (*off*) [*let* me *off*, 《英》*put* me *down*] at the next corner.
❸【新品を使う】 ● 下ろしたてのワイシャツ a *brand*(-)*new* shirt. ● バスタオルを下ろす *use* a *new* bath towel; *put* a new bath towel *to use*. ● 靴を下ろす (=はく) *put on* one's *new* shoes.
会話 「このいすカバー新しいの?」「ええ, おろしたてよ」 "Are these chair covers new?" "Yes, they are just *new*."
❹【預金を】draw*… out, withdraw*. ● 銀行から預金 [5 万円] を下ろす *draw out* [*withdraw*] one's savings [50,000 yen] *from* the bank.
❺【役職・地位から】 ● 役職から降ろされる(=職を解かれる) *be relieved of* one's post. ● 彼を首相の座から降ろす *drop* him from the premiership.
❻【料理で】 ● 魚を 3 枚に下ろす *fillet* fish. ● (おろし金で) 大根を下ろす *grate* (⇨) a radish.
❼【除去する】 ● 木の枝を下ろす (切り取る) *cut off* [(切ってそろえる) *trim off*] the branches of a tree; (木を刈り込む) *prune* a tree. ● 胎児を下ろす (=中絶する) have an abortion; get rid of a baby. ● 表札を下ろす (=取り外す) *remove* [*take away*] a nameplate.
❽【その他の表現】▶ 政策の出発点に文化のよりどころがなければ根を下ろす力にはなりません Policies that are not culturally based cannot *take root*.

おろす 卸す (卸売りする) sell (goods) (at [by]) wholesale; wholesale (goods).

おろそか 疎か ── 疎かな 形 (怠慢な) négligent; (不注意な) careless.
── 疎かにする 動 (怠る) neglect; (軽んじる) make light of …. ● 勉強をおろそかにする neglect [*be neg-*

おわい 汚穢 (糞尿) stool and urine; 《書》excrement; excreta (🔈 複数扱い).

おわせる 負わせる ❶ [傷を] (刃物などで) wound. ▶犯人はその女性に重傷を負わせた The criminal *wounded* the woman seriously./The criminal *inflicted* a serious wound *on* the woman.

❷ [責任・罪・義務などを] ▶彼に責任を負わせる *put* responsibility *on* him; (転嫁する) *shift* responsibility *onto* him. ●罪を彼に負わせる *put* [*blame*] a crime *on* him. ●彼に負債を負わせる *burden* him *with* debts.

おわび 御詫び (an) apology. (⇨詫(ᵂ)び)

おわらい お笑い (ユーモラスな話) a humorous [(こっけいな) a funny] story; (冗談) a joke. ▶とんだお笑い草だ That's a *laugh*./What a *joke* [a *laugh*]!

*****おわり 終わり** [物事の最後] an end; (会などの) a close /klóuz/; [結末] (演説などの) a conclusion; (物語などの) an end, an ending.

① 【終わりが】 ▶何事にも必ず終わりがある All things must have an *end*. ▶この種の仕事には終わりがない This sort of work is *never done*./This is a never-ending work. (🔈 never-ending は Housekeeping is a never-ending work. (家事は終わりのない仕事だ)のように用いる)

② 【終わりの】 (一番最後の) the last; (決定的な) final; (締めくくりの) closing. ●プログラムの終わりの種目 the *last* event in the program. ●式などでの終わりの言葉 the *closing* (↔*opening*) remarks.

③ 【終わりに】 in conclusion. ●今世紀の終わりに at the *end* of this century. ●(演説などで) 終わりに臨んで last of all, to conclude (one's speech). (🔈 通例文頭で) (⇨最後 ❶ ②) ●終わりに[が]近づく draw [come] *to an end* [*a close*]. ●今日はこれで終わりにしよう (仕事などを) Let's *call it a day*. (🔈 Let's finish it today. は「今日中に仕上げてしまおう」の意で, ここでは用いない) /(授業などを) *That's all* for today./(もううんざりなので) *So much* for today! (⇨授業) ▶これでミーティングは終わりにしよう Let's *close* [《話》*wrap up*] the meeting.

④ 【終わりの】 ▶そのスキャンダルで彼の長い政治生活は終わりを告げた(=終止符を打った) The scandal *put an end* [*a period* 《主に米》, *a stop* 《主に英》] *to* his long political career. (🔈 主に書き言葉)

⑤ 【終わりまで】 to the end [last]; (完全に) through, out. (🔈 前の方が普通) (⇨最後 ❶ ⑤) ▶その小説を終わりまで読んだ I have read the novel *through* [*to the end*]. ▶彼は夕食の始めから終わりまで(=食事の間中)それについてしゃべっていた He talked about it *throughout* [*all through*] dinner.

⑥ 【終わりから】 ▶それは終わりから三つめの章に書いてある It is written in the third chapter from the *last* [the third *last* chapter].

おわりね 終わり値 a clósing price. (㊟ 初め値) ▶先週の終わり値は 379 円だった It *closed* last week at 379 yen.

:おわる 終わる

WORD CHOICE 終わる

end 物事の終了を含意する最も一般的な語. ▶会議は成功のうちに終わった The meeting *ended* successfully.

finish 当初の予定・計画がつつがなく完了して終わること. ▶その調査はついに終わった The investigation finally *finished*.

be over 戦争中・日・季節・不景気などがすっかり終わること. 終了によって新しい段階・状態が始まることを含意する. 口語で多く用いる. ▶戦争は終わった The war *was over*.

頻度チャート
end ████████████████████
finish ██████
be over ████
20 40 60 80 100 (%)

❶ 【終了する】 end (↔begin); (仕事などを) finish (↔start); (会などを) close (↔open); be over. ▶学校が終わると太郎はバスで家に帰ります When school *ends* [*is over*], Taro goes home by bus. ▶会議は午後 4 時に終わった The meeting *closed* [*ended*] at 4:00 p.m. ▶ショーはいつ終わりますか What time will the show *be over* [*end*]? ▶仕事がまだ終わっていない I haven't *finished* [*completed*] the work yet. (🔈 後の方が堅い語で, 仕上がりの完璧(ᴷᴬ)さを強調する) /The work hasn't *been* (*been*) *finished* [hasn't *been completed*] yet. (🔈 complete は他動詞なので常に受身形になることに注意) ▶今朝この本を読み終わった I *finished* reading [I read *through*] the book this morning. (🔈 ×... finished *to read* とはいわない) ▶宿題は終わったかい Have you *finished* [*Are you done with*] your homework?/*Is* your homework *finished* [*done, over*]? ▶夏も終わろうとしていた The summer *was* nearly *over*./It was almost the end of the summer. ▶式典は彼の演説で終わった The ceremony *ended* [*closed*] *with* his speech. ▶これで今日の放送は終わります This brings today's program *to an end* [*a close*]. ▶映画が終わったときはみんな泣いていた Everyone was in tears *at the end of* the movie. ▶ついに終わった. 試験も何もかも終わったのだ It is finally *over*. The exams and everything else is [are] *over*. (🔈 (1) 第 1 文は finally を, 第 2 文は It is を強く読む. (2) 主語の exams and everything else を一つの概念として is で受けるのが自然)

❷ [結果...になる] end [result] in .... ▶その税制改革案は失敗に終わった The plan to reform the tax system *ended* [《やや書》*resulted*] in failure.

おわれる 追われる ❶ 【追放される】 (国・団体などを) be expelled 《*from*》; (地位などを) be ousted 《*from* one's post》; (母国・故郷などを) be exiled 《*from* one's country》. (⇨追放する) ●学校を追われる *be expelled from* school; 《話》*be kicked out of* school.

❷ [せかされる] ▶時間に追われている *be pressed for* time. ▶彼は仕事に追われている He *is pressed* [(大変忙しい) *is very busy*] *with* work.

:おん 恩 (恩義) obligation, indebtedness, a debt of gratitude; 《恩恵》; (親切) kindness. ▶私の頼みを断わるとは彼は恩を知らないやつだ He is ungrateful [an *ungrateful* person] to have refused my request.

● 恩に着る ●恩に着せる *expect* something *in return*. ▶ご援助に恩に着ます I'm *grateful* [《書》*indebted*] *to* you *for* your help./I'll never forget your help.

会話 「ワールドシリーズのチケット, 何とか取れたよ」「どうも. 恩に着るよ(=一つ借りができたね)」"I managed to get you a ticket for the World Series." "Thanks. I *owe you one*." (🔈 この one は one favor のことで, この表現は謝辞の後に続けて用いる)

● 恩を仇(ᴬᵈᵃ)で返す return evil for good; repay kindness with evil. (🔈 前の方が普通)

● 恩を売る be kind to someone expecting a

good return from him [her]. ▶彼は金に困っている人を助けることで恩を売った He helped those in trouble with money expecting good returns from them.

おん 音 a sound. (⇨音(ホ))

おんいき 音域 a range; 〖音楽〗a register. ▶この高音は私の音域外だ This high note is out of my *range*.

おんいん 音韻 〖音声〗a phoneme.
● 音韻論 phonology.

オンエア on the air (↔off the air). ▶その番組は現在オンエア中です The program is now *on the air*.

おんかい 音階 a (musical) scale. ● 音階の練習をする practice the *scales*.

おんがえし 恩返し ▶彼女は彼への恩返しにと子供の世話をしている She feels morally indebted to him and takes care of his children./She takes care of his children *in return for* his *kindness*.
── 恩返し(を)する 動 ▶彼に恩返しをする repay (him for) his favor [kindness]. (⇨報いる) ▶いったいどうご恩返しの仕方か分かりません I don't know how I can ever *repay* you (for all your kindness).

*****おんがく** 音楽 music. ● 音楽一家 a *musical* family. ● 野外音楽堂 an open-air *music* hall.
①〖音楽が〗どこからともなく美しい音楽が流れてきた Beautiful *music* came floating up from nowhere. ▶私はピアノ音楽が好きです I like [am interested in, 《主に女性語》love] piano *music*. (❗ I like *music*. とはあまりいわない。副詞をかえると、I like *music* very much. または《主に米女性語・英》I'm (very) fond of *music*. はごく普通。I like symphonies. のようにいえる) ▶彼は音楽が分からない He doesn't understand *music*./He is not at all musical. (❗「音楽がきらいだ」の意にもなる)/(音楽を聞き分ける力がない) He has no ear [×ears] for *music*./He doesn't have a *musical* ear.
②〖音楽の〗彼女は音楽の先生です She is a *músic* tèacher [a teacher of *music*]. (❗ a musical teacher では「音楽好きな先生」の意) ▶彼は音楽の才能がある He has a talent for [×of] *music*./He has *musical* talent [ability].
③〖音楽に[を]〗● 音楽を聴く listen to [〖楽しむ〗enjoy] *music*. ● 音楽を演奏する play [《やや書》perform] *music*. ▶彼らは音楽に合わせて踊った They danced to (the) *music*. (❗ the がつくと特定の音楽をさす) ▶仕事中は音楽をかけておくのが好きです I like to have (the) *music* on while (I am) working [I work].
● 音楽映画 a musical film. ● 音楽家 a musician. (❗通例プロの人をさす) ● 音楽会 a (give, hold) a concert; (独奏会) a (violin) recital. (⇨コンサート, リサイタル) ● 音楽学校 a músic schòol. ● 音楽室 [教室] a music ròom. ● 音楽隊 a band.
● 音楽評論家 a músic crìtic. ● 音楽療法 a music therapy.

おんかん 音感 〖音楽を聞きとる能力〗an ear for music; 〖音程を正しく取る能力〗(sense of) pitch. ● 絶対音感 《have》perfect 〖〖音楽〗absolute〗pitch.
● 音感教育 acoustic training [education].

おんぎ 恩義 an obligation. ● 彼女に親切にしてもらった恩義を感じる feel an *obligation* to her for her kindness; 〖書〗feel *indebted* to her for her kindness. ● 彼に恩義を施す place [put] him *under an obligation*.

おんきせがましい 恩着せがましい ▶彼は恩着せがましい態度でお金を貸してくれた He lent me some money, but *his attitude showed (that) he expected something bigger from me*./(威張って) He lent me some money *patronizingly* [in a *patronizing* way].

おんきゅう 恩給 a pension. (⇨年金) ● 軍人恩給 a soldier's *pension*.

おんきょう 音響 〖音〗(a) sound, (騒音) (a) noise. (⇨音(ホ)) ● 大音響とともに爆発する explode with a loud *noise*.
● 音響効果 (放送・劇などの) sound effects; (講堂などの) acoustics /əkúːstiks/. (❗複数扱い). ▶このホールの音響効果はすばらしい The *acoustics* of [in] this hall are excellent./This hall has excellent *acoustics*./This hall is *acoustically* very good.

おんくん 音訓 the Chinese- and Japanese-style readings for *kanji*.

*****おんけい** 恩恵 (a) benefit. ▶私たちは自然から多くの恩恵を受けている We get a lot of *benefit* from nature./We *benefit* a lot *from* nature.

おんけつどうぶつ 温血動物 a warm-blooded animal.

おんけん 穏健 ── 穏健な 形 moderate. ▶彼は(思想的に)穏健な人だ He is *moderate in* his thought./He is a *moderate*.

おんげん 音源 a sound source.

おんこ 恩顧 (目上からの) favor; (商人・芸人などに対する) patronage. (⇨引き立て)

おんこう 温厚 ── 温厚な 形 (穏やかな) mild; (優しい) gentle. ● 温厚な人柄 a *mild* personality. ● 温厚な老紳士 a *mild* old gentleman.

おんこちしん 温故知新 learning history's lessons.

おんさ 音叉 a tuning fork.

オンザロック ウイスキーのオンザロック whiskey *on the rocks* [×rock]. ● スコッチをオンザロックで飲む drink Scotch *on the rocks*. (⇨スコッチ)

おんし 恩師 one's (former) teacher; (偉大な師) one's great teacher.

おんし 恩賜 ▶恩賜の時計 a watch given by the Emperor.

おんしつ 音質 (音色) tones, sound quality; (原音再生の忠実度) audio fidelity /fidéləti/.

おんしつ 温室 a greenhouse (複 -houses /-ziz, 《米》-siz/); (大型の) a hothouse; (促成栽培用の) a forcing house.
● 温室育ち ▶彼の息子は温室育ちだ(=世間の風にさらされないで育った) His son has been brought up completely protected from the hardships of the world.
● 温室効果 the greenhouse effect. ● 温室効果ガス a greenhouse gas (略 GHG). (参考) 二酸化炭素 (CO₂), メタンガス (CH₄), フロンガス類など. ● 温室植物 a hothouse [a greenhouse] plant.

おんしゃ 恩赦 an amnesty /æmnəsti/, a 《Presidential》pardon. ● 恩赦で釈放される be set free [released] under an *amnesty*; be granted an *amnesty*. ● 政治犯に対する恩赦を実施する declare an *amnesty* for political prisoners; *pardon and release* political prisoners.

おんしゅうのかなたに 『恩讐の彼方に』 *The Realm Beyond*. (参考) 菊池寛の小説

おんじゅん 温順 (⇨温和)

おんしょう 温床 ▶苗床で苗を育てる raise seedlings in a *hotbed*. ● 悪の温床 a *hotbed* of vice.

おんじょう 温情 (思いやり) consideration; (親切) kindness. ● 温情のこもった(= 心の温かい)言葉 *warm-hearted* [(同情ある) *sympathetic*] words.

おんしょく 音色 (the quality of) tone; 〖音楽〗(a) timbre /tæmbər/.

おんしらず 恩知らず (事) ingratitude; (人)《書》an ingrate. ●恩知らずの学生 an *ungrateful* student.

おんしん 音信 (消息) news. ▶彼とは昨年来音信不通です I *have* not *heard* [I *have heard* nothing] *from* him since last year. (⇨以後)

おんじん 恩人 (特に財政面での) a benefactor. ▶彼は私の恩人だ I *owe* a great deal *to* him [him a great deal]. /《書》I'm (*deeply*) *indebted to* him. ●その医者は私の命の恩人だ The doctor has saved my life./I *owe* my life *to* the doctor [×the doctor my life]. (⇨お礼)

オンス〘重さの単位〙an ounce /áuns/.《略 oz.》.

おんすい 温水 warm water.
●温水プール a heated pool; a warm swimming pool.

オンステージ on-stage. ●美空ひばり歌謡オンステージ (興行名) Misora Hibari song show *on stage*.

おんせい 音声 [声] voice; [音] a sound. ●テレビの音声を大きく[小さく]する turn up [down] the TV.
●音声学 phonetics. (❗単数扱い) ●音声学者 a phonetician. ●音声多重放送 a multiplex broadcast.

おんせつ 音節 a syllable. ●2 音節の語 a word of two *syllables*; a two-syllabled word.

*__おんせん 温泉__ a hot spring; (湯治用の) a spa;〘温泉保養地〙a hot-spring resort. ●温泉に行く go to a *hot spring*. ▶ヨーロッパの温泉はスパと呼ばれる European *hot springs* are called *spas*.
●温泉町 a hot-spring [a spa] town. ●温泉宿 《stay at》an inn [a hotel] in a hot-spring resort. ●温泉療法 a hot-spring cure; balneotherapy.

おんぞうし 御曹司 (良家の子息) a son of a noble family.

おんそく 音速 the speed [velocity] of sound; sound speed. ●超音速機 a *supersonic* transport (略 sst). ●音速の壁を破る break the *sound* [*sonic*] barrier.

おんぞん 温存 ── 温存する 動 (保つ) keep; (保持する)《書》retain; (取っておく) save. ●その古い制度を温存する *retain* the old system. ●切り札のピッチャーを温存する *save* the ace pitcher.

おんたい 温帯 the temperate zone(s). ●北半球の温帯 the northern *temperate zone*.
●温帯気候 temperate climate. ●温帯植物 temperate plants. ●温帯低気圧 an extratropical cyclone.

おんたい 御大 (親分) the boss.

おんだん 温暖 ── 温暖な 形 temperate; (穏やかな) mild; (温かい) warm. (⇨温かい) ●日本の気候は温暖だ Japan has a *temperate* [a *mild*] climate. ●ここ静岡の冬は大変温暖です The winter is very *mild* here in Shizuoka.
●温暖化 (⇨温暖化) ●温暖前線〘気象〙a warm (← a cold) front.

おんだんか 温暖化 ▶気候が温暖化して(=だんだん暖かくなって)いる The climate *is becoming warmer* [*more temperate*]. ▶地球(規模)の温暖化の原因は二酸化炭素, メタン, 亜酸化窒素といった排ガスの増加である Global *warming* is caused by increased emissions of gases such as carbon dioxide, methane and nitrogen suboxides.

DISCOURSE
地球温暖化のひとつの例として, 近年の非常に暑い夏がある. もうひとつは, 大型のハリケーンや台風の数だ One example of global *warming* is the extreme heat in summer in recent years. ... **Another is** the number of hurricanes and typhoons of larger scale and greater intensity. (❗One [Another] is ...(ひとつ[もうひとつ]には...)は列挙に用いるディスコースマーカー)

おんち 音痴 ── 音痴な 形 be tone-deaf; have no ear for music. ●方向[味]音痴である have no [a terrible] sense of direction [taste].

おんちゅう 御中 Messrs. /més*ərz*/ (❗Mr. の複数形として特に会社名の前で用いる) ●田中貿易株式会社御中 *Messrs*. Tanaka Trading Co., Inc. ●サンフランシスコ州立大学教務課御中 (*To*) The Registration Office, San Francisco State University. (❗To は通例省略される)

おんちょう 音調 (音楽の旋律) a tune; (詩の韻律) meter; (言葉の抑揚) (an) intonation.

おんちょう 恩寵 ●神の恩寵により by the *grace* of God.

おんてい 音程〘音楽〙an interval, a musical interval. ●音程が合っている be in *key* [*tune*]. ▶彼の歌声は音程がはずれている He sings *out of* [*off*] *key*.

オンデマンド〘注文対応〙on demand. (❗「注文あり次第」の意)
●オンデマンド出版 publication on demand.

おんでる 追い出る ▶こんなところからは追い出で(=自分から出ていって)やる I'm getting the hell out of here.

*__おんど 温度__ (a) temperature. ●華氏[摂氏]温度計 a Fahrenheit [a Celsius, a centigrade] thermometer /θərmάmətər/. (参考) 米英では普通華氏を用いる) ●絶対温度 the absolute *temperature*. ●摂氏−273.15度 ●室内[屋外]の温度 indoor [outdoor] *temperature*. ●温度を計る take [×measure] the *temperature* (*of*). (⇨体温) ●温度を上げる[下げる] raise [lower] the *temperature*. ●温度を調節する control [adjust] the *temperature* (後の方が多くの場合「微調節する」の意) ▶この部屋の温度は何度ですか What is the *temperature* in this room? (❗答えは It's 18℃ (in this room). 18℃ は eighteen degrees centigrade [〘気象〙Celsius] と読む) ▶温度が40度に上がった[下がった] The *temperature* rose [fell] to 40 degrees. (●「40度上[下]がった」なら rose [fell] (by) 40 degrees.) ▶温度計が氷点下[マイナス] 5度をさした The thermometer read [registered, stood at] five degrees below zero [minus five].

おんど 音頭 [先導] the lead. ●A氏の音頭とりで under *the lead* of Mr. A.
●音頭をとる take the lead (*in*). ●乾杯の音頭をとる propose [drink] a toast ((*to*) *him*).

おんとう 穏当 ── 穏当な 形 (適切な) proper; (理にかなった) reasonable; (穏健な) moderate. (⇨妥当)

おんどく 音読 ── 音読する 動 read (it) aloud [×loudly]. (❗loudly は「大声で」の意)

おんどさ 温度差 ❶[温度の差] difference in temperature; temperature difference. ▶朝晩と日中の温度差が大きいので風邪をひかないように注意してください Be careful not to catch a cold because there is a lot of *temperature difference* between the morning and night and the daytime.
❷[熱意の差] a difference in degrees of enthusiasm. ▶熟年層と若年層の間では仕事に対して温度差があるように思います The degrees of enthusiasms for jobs seem [The attitude towards jobs seems] (to be) different between the mature-aged generation and the younger generation.

おんどり 雄鳥〘雄の鳥〙a cock (bird);〘鶏の〙a cock;《主に米》a rooster.

オンドル [<朝鮮語>]〘暖房装置〙a (Korean) floor heater.
おんな 女 a woman (⚥ women /wímin/); a lady; a female /fíːmeɪl/; a girl; 〘愛人〙〘軽蔑的〙one's woman; 〘古〙mistress. (⇨女性, らしい)

> **使い分け** **woman** man に対し, 成人した女性をさす最も一般的な語.
> **lady** gentleman に対し, 本来は育ちがよくて上品な婦人を意味したが, 今は woman の単なる丁寧語として用いることが多い.
> **female** male と同様, 動植物の性についていう語で, 人に用いると軽蔑的. ただし学術や統計上の用法としては普通に用いる.
> **girl** 少女や赤ん坊から未婚の若い女性までもさす語.《話》では woman の代わりに用いられることもあるが, 成人した女性はこう呼ばれるのを好まない人も多い.

① **【～女】** ● 魅力的な女 an attractive *woman* [*girl*]; (感じのいい女) a charming *woman* [*girl*]. ● 顔のみにくい女 a plain(-looking) [《米》a homely] *woman*. (❗ an ugly woman の婉曲的な言い方)
② **【女～】** ● 女物の服 [傘] *ladies'* wear [a *ladies'* umbrella]; ● 女らしくない unlike a *woman*.
③ **【女は】** ▶ 女は男よりも長生きだ *Women* live longer than men. ▶女(=女は)3 人寄ればかしましい When three women meet, there will be noise.
④ **【女の】** ● 女の医者 a *wòman* [a *fèmale*, (ややまれ) a *làdy*] dóctor. (❗ (1) 職名の前では lady は軽蔑的な含みをもつ. ● women [lady] doctors. (2) a wóman dòctor と発音すれば「産婦人科医」となる) ● 女の権利 woman's [women's] rights. ▶ 女の声は一般に男の声よりも高い The *female* voice is generally higher than the male voice.
⑤ **【女に】** ▶ 彼女も一人前の女になった She has grown up to be [grown into] a *woman*./She has come [grown] to *womanhood*.
● 女親 a mother. ● 女友達 a female friend; (男性にとっての恋人) a girlfriend. (⇨友達)

おんなぐせ 女癖 ▶彼は女癖が悪い He can't stay away from women./He wanders from woman to woman. (⇨ 男癖)
おんなぐるい 女狂い a womanizer.
おんなごころ 女心 a woman's heart. ▶女心と秋の空 (ことわざ) A *woman's* mind and winter wind change often.
おんなざか 女坂 〘ゆるやかな方の坂〙the gentler slope. (⇨ 男坂)
おんなざかり 女盛り ▶彼女は 35 歳の女盛りだ She is 35 years old and *in the prime of life* [*womanhood*].
おんなじょたい 女所帯 a manless household.
おんなずき 女好き 〘事〙womanizing; 〘男〙a womanizer; (女のしりを追いかける男) a woman chaser. ● 女好きのする(=女に好かれる)男 a ladies' man.
おんなたらし 女たらし ▶あの男は女たらしだ He's a *womanizer* [a *Casanova*]. (❗ Casanova は女たらしの典型とされている)
おんなっけ 女っ気 (⇨男っ気) ● 女っ気抜きのパーティを a party for *men* only; 《米》a bachelor party; 《英》a stag party. (❗ 特に結婚式前夜に新郎とその友人で行う宴会) ● 彼にはまだ女っ気がない(=ガールフレンドがいない) He still has no girlfriend./He still has no luck with woman.
おんなで 女手 female help. ● 女手一つで子供を育てる bring her children up *all by herself* [*all alone*].
おんなのこ 女の子 a girl; 〘赤ん坊〙a baby girl.
おんならしい 女らしい feminine; womanly. ● 女らしい的な) 女らしい a real woman. ● とても女らしく見える look very *feminine* [*womanly*]. ● 女らしさ fèmínīty; womanhood. ▶彼女には女らしいところが少しもない There's nothing *feminine* (↔*masculine*) [*of the woman*] about [in] her. (❗ この the は「性質」を表す) /She lacks *femininity*. ▶ 彼女の womanly 表情を読み取った I read a *womanly* expression on her face. ▶彼女は小柄だが, きわめて女らしい体つきをしていた She was (rather) small [short] but she had a very *womanly* [*feminine*] figure. (❗ short でも誤りでないが露骨すぎるので人については避ける方がよい)
おんねつりょうほう 温熱療法 thermotherapy.
おんねん 怨念 a deep grudge, 〘書〙rancor.
おんのじ 御の字 ▶1日で2万円稼げたら御の字だ(=十分でありがたい) It's *quite enough* if I get 20,000 yen a day.
おんぱ 音波 a sound wave.
オンパレード 〘俳優などが勢ぞろいで〙on parade.
おんばん 音盤 〘レコード盤〙a (phonograph) record.
おんびき 音引き ● 音引きの(=発音や字音により項目が配列された)辞書 a *phonetically arranged* dictionary.
おんびん 音便 〘音声学〙euphony.
おんびん 穏便 ― 穏便に 〘副〙(平和的に) peacefully.
● 事件を穏便に解決する settle the case *peacefully* [(裁判ざたにしないで) *out of court*]; (友好的に) in a *friendly way*]; (寛大に扱う) treat the case *mercifully* [《やや書》 *leniently*].
おんぶ 負んぶ ● 赤ん坊をおんぶする carry a baby *on one's back*; give a baby a piggyback 《米》 a *pickaback*《英》(*ride*). ▶さあ, 帰ろう, おんぶしてあげるよ Let's go home. *Get on* (*me*). (⇨ 負ぶさる)
おんぷ 音符 a (musical) note.

> **関連** いろいろな音符: 全音符《米》a whole note;《英》a semibreve／二分音符《米》a half note;《英》a minim／四分音符《米》a quarter note;《英》a crotchet／八分音符《米》an eighth note;《英》a quaver／十六分音符《米》a sixteenth note;《英》a semiquaver.

おんぷう 温風 a warm current of air.
● 温風暖房機 a warm air circulator.
オンブズマン [<スウェーデン語] 〘行政監察委員〙an ombudsman (⚥-men) (❗ 性差別的表現なので mediator, a regulatory agent が好まれる);《英》a parliamentary commissioner.
おんぼろ ― おんぼろ(の) 〘形〙(衣服などが) worn-out; 〘話〙ratty; (建物・機械などが) run-down; ramshackle. ● おんぼろ車 an old, *ramshackle* car; an old wreck.
おんみ 御身 ▶御身お大切に Please take care of *yourself*.
おんみつ 隠密 隠密の計画 a *clandestine* plan.
おんやく 音訳 (a) transliteration.
おんやさい 温野菜 hot [cooked] vegetables. ● 温野菜を添えたサーモン salmon garnished with hot vegetables.
おんよく 温浴 a hot [a warm] bath. (❗ 「微温浴」は a tepid bath)
おんよみ 音読み 《use》the Chinese-style reading for *kanji*.
オンライン on-line (↔off-line). ● オンライン処理設備のある会社 a firm with *on-line* equipment. ● オンラインで結ぶ connect (*it*) *on-line*.
● オンライン辞書 an on-line dictionary. ● オンライン

システム the on-line system. ●オンラインショッピング on-line shopping. ●オンラインヘルプ an on-line help. ●オンラインマニュアル an on-line manual.

オンリー ▶仕事オンリーの毎日だった(=毎日仕事だけした) I *only* worked day after day.

おんりょう 怨霊 a vengeful spirit [ghost].

おんりょう 音量 volume. ●テレビの音量を上げる[下げる] turn up [down] the TV; turn up [down] the *volume* on the TV. (*❗*前の方が普通)(⇒ボリューム❶)

おんわ 温和 ── 温和な 形 ❶[気候が] (穏やかな) mild; (温暖な) temperate. ●温和な気候 a *mild* [a *temperate*] climate.
❷[性質が] (穏やかでやさしい) gentle; (穏やかな) mild; (物静かでおとない) quiet. ▶彼女は温和な人だ She is of a *quiet* nature./She is, by nature, a *quiet* woman.

か

か 下 (⇨下(と))

か 可 ❶ [成績] a C (!Fair, Passing, Average とも表す); a D (!Below Average とも表す). (⇨優)
❷ [よいこと] Either *will be fine [will be satisfactory, will do]*. ▶それはそれでも不可もなしというところです It is neither (very) *good* nor (very) *bad*./It's not *good* or *bad*./(まあまあだ) 《話》It's (just) *so-so*.

か 科 (大学・病院などの) a department; (課程) a course; (動植物などの) a family. ●普通科 a general *course*. ●社会科 social studies. ●ネコ科の動物 animals of the cat *family*.

か 蚊 a mosquito (徼〜(e)s). ●蚊取り線香 ⇨蚊取り線香 ●蚊がぷーんと鳴く音 the hum [humming] of *mosquitoes*. ●蚊に食われる be bitten by a *mosquito*.
●蚊の鳴くような声 蚊の鳴くような声で in a feeble [a faint] little voice.

か 課 ❶ [教科書の] a lesson. ●第3課 *Lesson* 3; the third *lesson*.
❷ [会社・官庁などの] a section. (⇨部❶) ●会計課 the accóunting sèction.

かー 過ー (過度の) over-; super-. ●過食 *over*eating. ●過飽和 *super*saturation.

*-**か** 《終助詞》 ❶ [疑問, 質問] (a) [be 動詞＋主語]
▶この本は彼女のですか Is this book hers?
会話 「失礼ですが山田さんではありませんか」「ええそうですよ」 "Excuse me. *Aren't* you Mr. [Miss, Ms., Mrs.] Yamada?" "Yes, that's right." (!否定疑問文は肯定の答えを期待した尋ね方)
(b) [do, does, did＋主語＋一般動詞] ▶彼女は毎朝早く起きますか Does she *get up* early every morning? ▶君はその理由を知っていますか *Do you know* the reason?
会話 「君が窓ガラスを割ったのか」「いいえ違います」 "*Did* you *break* the window?" "No, I \didn't." (!You broke the /window, \didn't you? のような平叙文の形をした肯定疑問文や付加疑問文は肯定の答えを期待する言い方になるので, その応答は No, I /didn't [\didn't]. の音調をとって「あなたは私だと思ったかもしれないが」の含みをもたせるのが普通. 上記のような下降調ではぶっきら棒な応答になる)
(c) [助動詞＋主語＋一般動詞] ▶君は車を運転することができますか Can you *drive* a car?/Do you know how to drive (a car)? ▶彼女はあす家にいるでしょうか Will she *stay* at home [《米》be home] tomorrow? (!《米》では stay home ともいう)
(d) [疑問詞を用いて] ▶あの少年はだれですか Who is that boy? ▶君はだれを待っているのですか Who [《書》Whom] are you waiting for? ▶昨夜彼に何が起こったのですか *What* happened to him last night?
▶君はどんな果物がいちばん好きですか *What* (kind of) fruit do you like best?
❷ [反語] (!強い主張を示すので, 音調は普通の疑問文の場合より大きな下降または上昇調をとる) ▶そんな難しいことだれができるものか *Who can* do such a \difficult thing? ▶そんなこと知らない人がいるものか *Who doesn't know* \that? (=Everybody knows that.) ▶だからその仕事は君には無理だと言ったじゃないか *Didn't* I \tell you the task would be too /much for you? (=You know I told you ....)
❸ [念を押す] (You) see; understand. (⇨いい⓱)
▶いいか, 宿題を絶対忘れてはだめだよ Never forget to do your homework. Do you understand? ▶いいか, 夜の女性の一人歩きは危険だ It is dangerous for women to go out alone after dark, *I warn you [I'm warning you]*. (!後の方が強い警告)
❹ [依頼, 勧誘, 許可] (...してくれませんか) Will [Can, Would, Could] you ...?, Do [Would] you mind 《*doing*; *if* 節》?, Would you be so kind as to 《*do*》? (!この順に丁寧な依頼になる; kind を用いる最後の言い方は今では丁寧すぎてあまり好まれない); (...しませんか) Let's ..., Shall we ...?, How [What] about ...?; (...してよろしいか) Can [Could, May] I ...? ▶夕食後公園へ散歩に出かけませんか Let's go out for a walk in [xto] the park after supper. (!文尾に shall [should] we を添えて, ..., *shall* [*should*] *we*? のように言うと丁寧さが加わる)/*Shall* we go out for a walk in the park after supper? (!shall を用いるのは《米》では堅い言い方で, 日常は通例 Should we ...? を用いる)/How [What] about going out for a walk in the park after supper?
会話 「このはがきをポストへ入れてくれませんか」「いいですよ」 "*Will* [*Can, Would, Could*] *you* (*please*) mail this postcard?" "Oh, sure." (!この順に丁寧な言い方. Do you think you can ...? や I wonder if you could ... はさらに控えめな言い方になる. will は「...する気はあるか」という意になるので親しい人以外には避けた方が無難)/"*Would* [*Do*] *you mind* mailing this postcard?" "No, not at all." (!肯定の返事は No となることに注意)
会話 「ここでたばこを吸ってよろしいですか」「ええいいですよ」 "*Can* [*Could, May*] *I* smoke in here?" "Yes, you can [may, ×could, ×might]." (!応答の may は目上の人が目下の者に許可を与える言い方で, しばしば尊大に響く)/"*Is it all right if* I smoke in here?" "Yes, of course [certainly]." (!⇨⓮)
❺ [感動, 驚き, 命令など] ▶ああ, これが月の岩石か Oh, this is the moon rock! ▶ついにやったか You've done it, *at last*. ▶静かにしないか Will you be \quiet! (!\Will you be quiet! の音調でいうと, さらに強いいらだちを表す)

―か 《副助詞》 [選択] or. ▶彼は1週間か2週間で戻って来るでしょう He will come back in a week *or* two. ▶彼が生きているのか死んでいるのかわからない I don't know whether he is dead or alive [×alive *or* dead] (!日本語との語順の違いに注意). ▶彼女は東京か横浜のどちらかにいる She is *either* in Tokyo *or* in Yokohama.
【...か〜か】[選択肢を増して丁寧に] or something. (!口語的慣用表現で, 物にも場所にも用いることができる) ▶酒かビールか何か飲みませんか Let's drink sake or beer *or something*? ▶この夏は海かどこかへいらっしゃいましたか Did you go to the sea *or something* this summer?

-か 化 [[...の状態にする(こと)]] -ize, -ization. ●植民地化する colon*ize* 《a country》. ●貿易の自由化 the liberal*ization* of trade.

-か -禍 （災難）(a) disaster. 〖災難〗● 豪雨禍 a flood [a heavy rain] *disaster*.

-か -歌 ❶ 〖短歌〗a *tanka*. 〖短歌〗
❷ 〖歌〗a *song*. ● 流行歌 a popular [《話》a pop] *song*. ● 校歌 a school *song*.

が 我 〖自己主張〗self-assertion; 〖わがまま〗self-will, selfishness; 〖自我〗ego. ● 我の強い人 a *self-assertive* person; ● 我を通す have one's own way; (自説を曲げない) refuse to change one's opinion [decision]; stick to one's guns. ● 我を殺す (＝自制する) control oneself.

[会話]「言っておくけど聞く耳もたないからね」「どうしてそんなに我を張るの」"I tell you I can't listen." "Must you *be* so *obstinate*?"

が 賀 celebration. ● 父の88歳の賀の祝いを行う *celebrate* one's father's 88th birthday.

が 蛾 〖昆虫〗a moth.

:-が INDEX

《接続助詞》
❶ しかし　　　　❷ そして
❸ 譲歩
《終助詞》
❶ 語尾の断定調をやわらげて
❷ 実現を願う気持ちを表して
《格助詞》
❶ 動作・状態の主体
❷ 能力・知識・感情などの対象
❸ その他の表現

── -が《接続助詞》❶ 〖しかし〗but; (しかしながら)《やや書》however; (それでもなお)(and) yet; (それにもかかわらず)《話》all the same,《書》nevertheless; (…だけれども) though, although (■ 後の方が堅い語); (ところが一方) on the other hand,《主に書》while,《書》whereas. ● 頭はよいが身勝手な少年 a bright *but* selfish boy. ● 両親は貧しかったが, 私たちを大学へ行かせてくれた Our parents were poor, *but* they sent us to college. (■ ... poor. But they …. のように文頭位に用いない方がよい)/*Though* [*Although*] our parents were poor, they sent us to college. (■ (1) *Though* [*Although*] poor, our parents sent us to college. とも いえる. この場合は「主節と同じ主語＋be 動詞」は省略可. (2) though 節は主節の後にも置ける. although 節は通例主節の前に置くが, くだけた会話では though 節同様に主節の後に置くこともある: Our parents sent us to college, *though* [*although*] they were poor.)/Our parents were poor, *however* [*all the same, nevertheless*], they sent us to college. ● 太郎はゴルフが好きだが花子はスキーが好きだ Taro likes golfing(,) *but* [*while*] Hanako enjoys skiing. (■ (1) 明確な対立関係を示す場合, ×Though [×Although] Taro likes golfing, Hanako enjoys skiing. とはいわない. (2) but は「太郎はゴルフが好きだが花子は嫌いだ」のような場合, Taro likes golfing(,) *but* Hanako doesn't. のように後半を省略することも可)/Taro likes golfing. *On the other hand* Hanako enjoys skiing. (■ Taro likes golfing, *on the other hand* Hanako enjoys skiing. とも書く. Taro likes golfing, *on the other hand*, enjoys skiing. の語順の方が対照の意味合いが強くなる) ● 申し訳ございませんが, 山田は今日は休みをとっております I'm sorry, (*but*) Mr. Yamada is off today. (■ (1) 前置き表現で, but はしばしば省略される. (2) 社内の人に対しても呼びすてにせず Mr. をつける) ● どういうわけかまだ分からないが左脳は右半身の営みをつかさどっている For some reason that is still not understood, the left-brain controls the right side of the body. (■補足説明部を「もっとも...だが」として主文の後に加える場合は The left-brain…, *though* the reason for it is still not understood. となる)

❷ 〖そして〗and. ▶ 彼は50歳ですが, 10歳は若く見えます He is fifty *and* [*but*] he looks ten years younger. (■ この and は「対照」を表し「それなのに」の意であるが, 相反する対立を強調するときは but も用いられる) ▶ 乗客はほとんどいなかったが, たいしたけがもなく避難した There were few ⱽpassengers, who [passengers, *and* they] escaped without serious ⱽinjury. (■ ... passengers who ... のようにコンマで⌃音調を抜くと「たいしたけがもなく避難したが乗客はほとんどいなかった」の意になる) ▶ テニスのラケットを買いたいのですが, スポーツ用品売り場はどこですか (百貨店などで) I'd like to get a (tennis) racket. Where's the sporting goods section? (■「が」が対立・対照を示さない文では, 単にピリオドかセミコロンで文を区切る方がよい場合が多い)

❸ 〖譲歩〗(…であろうとなかろうと) whether ... or not, whether or not ...; (たとえ...だとしても) even if [though]…. (■ 譲歩節中では未来のことであっても will を用いず, 通例直説法を用いる) ▶ 雨が降ろうが降るまいが, あす決行するさ *Whether* it rains *or not* [*Whether or not* it rains], we'll carry it out tomorrow. ▶ 彼が来ようが来まいが私にはどうでもよい It doesn't matter to me *whether* he comes *or not*. ▶ たとえ親に反対されようが, 僕はやるよ *Even if* [*though*] my parents object to my plan, I'll do it. ▶ 小説はとても好きですがこれは長すぎる (*As*) *much as* I like novels, this is too long.

── -が《終助詞》❶ 〖語尾の断定調をやわらげて〗▶ ジーンズを見たい[見たかった]のですが I'*d like* to see [to have seen] jeans. (■ 仮定法を用いた丁寧表現. 断定調にするとそれぞれ I *want* to see jeans./I *wanted* to see jeans, but I couldn't. となる) ▶ 京都の名所をご案内しようかと思っている [思っていた] のですが I'm thinking [I *was* thinking, I *thought*] of showing you around the sights of Kyoto. (■ 進行形を用いて「まだ決めたわけではない」, 過去形や過去進行形を用いて「今は必ずしもそう思っていない」の含みを持たせてもしつけがましさを出さない言い方) ▶ あすの朝一番でやらねばならないと考えています I think I must do it first thing tomorrow morning. (■ 特に日本語の「が」は表されないことも多い)

[会話]「7時ならいかが」「それで結構ですが」"How about 7 o'clock?" "That'*ll* be [That *sounds*] fine." (■ is という現在形に対して, 未来の助動詞や sound (…と思える) を用いる)

[会話]「無愛想な口のきき方をする人ですね」「ええ, でも根はいい人だと思いますが」"He talks bluntly to us." "Yes, *but* I think he's kind at ⱽheart." (■ 反論する場合は通例断定調の↘は避けられる)

❷ 〖実現を願う気持ちを表して〗▶ あなたのお力になれるといいのですが I *wish* I could help you. (■「残念ながら無理だ」を含意. cf. I hope) ▶ 宿題を早く済ませておけばよかったのですが I *should have finished* my homework earlier. (■「should＋have (done)」の形で実際はそうしなかったことを表す) (⇨ -のに ❹)

── -が《格助詞》❶ 〖動作・状態の主体〗《英語では主語で》

[解説] (1) 日本語の「...が」で表される主体が, 聞き手や読み手にとって新しい事柄であることを表すときは, 英語では定冠詞や他の限定詞を伴わない不特定な名詞で表すなどの工夫を要することが多い. (⇨ -は《副助詞》)

❶
(2) 日本語の「...が」で表される主体は、英語では主語で表されるのが普通だが、天候・時間・温度・距離・環境・現在の状況などを表す文脈では、通例 it を形式主語として用いる。

▶車の下から猫が1匹飛び出した *A cat* ran out from under the car. ▶どれがあなたの車は普通だ *Which is your car?* (❗which が主語) ▶学校の向かいに郵便局がある *There's a post office* opposite 《(米) across from》 the school. ▶きのうの午後、その人が急に私の事務所にやって来た *That man* suddenly came to my office yesterday afternoon. ▶この本は父が誕生日に買ってくれたんです *This book* is the one *my father* bought for my birthday. ▶あす雨が降ったら、試合は延期だ If *it* rains tomorrow, the game will be put off. (❗形式主語の it に注意 (⇨ 解説 (2)))

❷ [能力・知識・感情などの対象] 《英語では目的語で》▶まゆ子は水泳が得意だ *Mayuko* is good at swimming./*Mayuko* is a good swimmer. ▶太郎には会いたいが、住所が分からない I want to see Taro, but I don't know [have] *his address.* ▶クラシック音楽が好きだ I like *classical music*./《音楽を聴くのが好きだ》I like listening [to listen] to *classical music*.

❸ [その他の表現] ▶タクシーよりも電車の方が早く着きます《比較》You can get there earlier [sooner] by train than by taxi. ▶東京には数回行ったことがあります《頻度・経験》I've been to Tokyo several times. ▶このばか者が《ののしり》You fool [《話》idiot]! (❗無冠詞に注意)

かあ (カラスの鳴き声) a caw /kɔ́ː/. ●かあと鳴く caw. (⇨かあかあ)

カー a car. (⇨マイカー)
●カーシェアリング [車を共同で使用すること] carsharing. (❗car pooling ともいう. cf. worksharing)
●カーステレオ a cár stèreo. ●カーセックス 《have》sex in a car;《和製語》car sex. ●カーチェイス a cár chàse. ●カーナビ(ゲーションシステム) (⇨カーナビ) ●カープール [駐車場] a párking lòt, 《英》 a cár pàrk. ●(a) car pool は「自家用車の輪番相乗り方式」の意 ●カーフェリー a cár fèrry. ●カーポート a carport. ●カーマニア a cár màniac [xmania].

カーキ khaki. ●カーキ色の制服 a khaki uniform.
かあさん 母さん a mother. (⇨お母さん)
ガーシュイン [米国の作曲家] Gershwin (George ～).
カースト [インド古来の階級制度] a caste.
●カースト制度 the cáste sỳstem.
ガーゼ [<ドイツ語] gauze /ɡɔ́ːz/.
カーソル [コンピュータ] a cursor.
●カーソルキー a cúrsor kèy.
ガーター [靴下留め] 《米》 garters,《英》 suspenders.
●ガーターベルト a gárter 《米》[a suspénder 《英》] bèlt.
かあちゃん 母ちゃん 《米話》 mom(my)《英話》 mum(my). (⇨お母さん)
かあつ 加圧 ② pressurization; pressure.

— **加圧する** ⓥ pressurize; pressure; apply pressure (*to*). ●蒸気を加圧する *pressurize* steam.
ガーディアン *The Guardian*. 《参考》英国の新聞
カーディガン a cardigan (jacket [sweater]).
ガーデニング gardening. ●彼女はガーデニングが好きだ She likes [is fond of] *gardening*.

*カーテン a curtain; 《厚手の》《米》a drape. (❗)《英》でカーテンは薄手、厚手のいずれのカーテンをもさす. 区別するときには a net curtain (薄手の), a thick curtain (厚手の)という. (2) 両開きのカーテンの場合は複数形 ●カーテンをかける (the windows); hang [put up] *curtains*. ●カーテンを開ける open [draw (back)] the *curtains* (*at* [*over*] the window). ●窓のカーテンを閉める close [draw] the *curtains* over [across] the window. ●カーテンで仕切る separate [divide off] ... with a *curtain*; *curtain* ... off. ●窓にはカーテンもかかっていなかった There was no *curtain* at the window.
●カーテンレール a curtain rail. ●カーテンロッド a curtain rod.

カーテンコール a curtain call. ●5回もカーテンコールにこたえる take five *curtain calls*.
ガーデンパーティー [園遊会] (hold [have]) a garden party.
カート 《米》 a cart; 《英》a trolley. ●カート置場 a *cart* pool.

*カード ❶ [固い厚紙の] a card; (細長い紙片) a slip; (トランプの) a card, 《書》a playing card. ●会員カード a membership card. ●バースデー [クリスマス] カード a bírthday [a Chrístmas] càrd. ●英単語をカードにとる put [note] down English words on *cards*. ●(トランプの) カードを配る [切る] deal (out) [shuffle] the *cards*. ▶イギリスの友達が毎年クリスマスカードを送ってくれる My English friend sends me a *card* at Christmas time every year.
❷ [クレジットカードなど] a (credit) card. 《参考》特定店発行のカードを a charge card という: ハロッズ百貨店のカード a Harrods charge card / プリペイドカード a prepaid *card*. ●テレフォンカード a phóne càrd. 《会話》(店で) 「お支払いは現金でなさいますか、それともカードですか」「お店のカードでお願いします」「ではカードを (読み取り機に) 通してください」"How would you like to pay, cash or *credit* (*card*) [*charge*]?" "I want to put this on house *charge*." "Swipe the *card*, please."
❸ [スポーツの組み合わせ] a card. ●好カード a drawing *card*. (❗drawing は「客を引きつける」の意)
●カードキー a card key. ●カードケース a card case.
●カード公衆電話 a card phone. ●カード社会 a cashless society. ●カード犯罪 a credit card crime. ●カード目録 a card catalogue. ●カードローン a credit card loan.

ガード ❶ [護衛] (行為) guard; (人) a (secúrity) guàrd, 《和製語》a guard man. ●銀行のガードマン a bánk *guàrd*.
❷ [スポーツの] (防御の行為, 姿勢) guard; (人) a guard. ●ガードの堅い [甘い] チーム a 《basketball》 team tight [loose] at *guard*. ●ガードを固める guard tightly [closely]; keep up one's *guard*.
❸ [その他の表現] ▶以前は母親が娘たちに男性に対していつもガードを固めている(=油断しない)ように言い聞かせたものだった Mothers used to tell their daughters to *be* always *on* their *guard* against [(自分の身を守る) defend themselves from] men. (❗ their *guard* of their は daughters をさす)
— **ガードする** ⓥ guard (him).
ガード [鉄橋] a railroad 《米》[a railway 《主に英》] bridge; (陸橋) 《米》a railroad overpass, 《英》

カートリッジ a cartridge.
ガードル a girdle.
ガードレール a guardrail; (英)a crash barrier. ▶スピードで走ってきた車がガードレールを突き破った A speeding car broke [crashed] through the *guardrail*.
カートン a carton (*of cigarettes*).
ガーナ [国名]Ghana /gáːnə/; (公式名)the Republic of Ghana. (首都 Accra) ● ガーナ人 a Ghanaian. ● ガーナ(人)の Ghanaian /gáːniən/.
カーナビ a car [an auto(mobile), a vehicle] navigation system.
カーニバル a carnival. ● リオのカーニバル the *carnival* in Rio.
カーネーション [植物]a carnation.
カーネギーホール Càrnegie Háll. (参考)ニューヨークにある大演奏会場)
ガーネット a garnet. (参考)1月の誕生石
カーバイド [炭化物][化学]carbide.
カービンじゅう カービン銃 a carbine.
カーフ [子牛の皮]calfskin.
カーブ ❶[曲線, 曲がり] a curve; (道·川などの) a bend. ●ヘアピンカーブ a hairpin *curve* [(米) *turn*, (英) *bend*]. ●道の急カーブの所では at the sharp *bend* [*turn*] in the road. ●カーブの多い道 a *curving* [a winding /wáindiŋ/] road. (!)(1)前の方は限定用法のみ。(2)後の方の「曲がりくねった」の意にはカーブを曲がる go around a *curve* [a *bend*]. ▶道路は左にカーブしている The road *curves* to the left around the building. (⇒曲がる)
❷[野球の] a curve (ball). ●スローカーブ a slow (-breaking) *curve*. ●ハンガーカーブ a hanging *curve*; a hanger; [和製語]a hanger curve. ●縦に落ちるカーブ a down-breaking *curve*. ●投手がカーブを投げる throw a *curve* (ball).
●カーブ投手 a curveballer; a curve pitcher.
●カーブミラー a safety mirror at a blind spot; [和製語]a curve mirror.
カーペット (a) carpet. (⇒じゅうたん)
ガーベラ [植物]a gerbera.
カーボベルデ [国名]Cape Verde /kéip vɜ́ːrd/; (公式名)the Republic of Cape Verde. (首都 Praia) ●カーボベルデ人 a Cape Verdean. ●カーボベルデ(人)の Cape Verdean.
カーボン [炭素]a carbon.
●カーボン紙 (a) carbon (paper). ●カーボンファイバー[炭素繊維]carbon fiber. ●カーボンブラック carbon black.
カーラー [髪をカールする用具]a curler, a roller.
ガーリック garlic; (一片)a clove of garlic.
カーリング [スポーツ]curling. ●カーリングをする play *curling*.
カール (a) curl; (長い髪の)a ringlet. ●髪をカールする *curl (up)* one's hair; (してもらう) have one's hair *curled*. ▶彼女の髪はカールしている She has *curly* hair./Her hair is *curly*.
ガールスカウト the Girl Scouts; [団員]a girl scout.
ガールハント ●ガールハントする [話]pick up a girl.
ガールフレンド a girlfriend. (!)しばしば男女関係のあることを連想させる。ただの女友達は She's a friend of mine. のようにいう)
かあん (鐘などの音) a clang. (!)通例単数形で) ●教会の鐘がかあんと鳴る *clang* a church bell. ●ボールがバットに当たるかあんという音と同時にスタートを切る be off at the *crack* of the bat. ●打球でかあんという金属音を残してサードの横を抜けていった The ball shot past the third baseman leaving a *metallic sound*.

があん (衝撃音) a crash. ▶トラックとトラックががあんと正面衝突した *Clang*! A truck collided head-on into another truck. ▶ケイトの死を知らされて私は頭をがあんと殴られたような衝撃を受け When I was told of Kate's death, I felt as if I *got a severe blow* [*were hit hard*] on the head.

*:**かい 会** ❶[集まり] a meeting, (やや書)a gathering; (親しくあいだの非公式な) a get-together; (社交会) a party; (特定の目的の) (an) assembly (⇒集会); [会議] (専門的討論するための) a conference; (国·各界の代表者が集まる大規模な) a congress; [大会] (宗教·政治·社会団体などの代表者のための) a convention; (運動競技の) an athletic meet (meeting(英)). (⇒会議) ●会を開く[催す] have [hold] a *meeting*. ●会を招集する call [convene] a *meeting*.
|会話|「1度会を開かなくてはならないな」「で, いつにするの」"We must have a *meeting*." "Well, when exactly?" (!)英会話中でもよいが, 英語では exactly (厳密に)をそえていうことがある

❷[団体組織]a society, an association; (スポーツで楽しみのための同好会) a club; (社会的·教育的事業のための) an institution; (労働者·学生などの団結した会) a union. ●会に入る[をやめる] join [leave] a *society*. ●会を発足させる establish [found, set up] a *society*.

*:**かい 回** ❶[回数] a time. ●1回 once. (⇒一回, 今回, 次回) ●2回 twice; two times. (!)前の方が普通。後の方は他の回数と対照する場合によく用いられる ●4[5]回 four [five] *times*. ●1-2回 once or /ə/ twice. ●2-3回 two or /ə/ three times [z:r]; とすれば「2度または3度」の意となる); a few *times*. ●何回も many *times*; again and again, over and over (again). ●1回で試験にパスする pass the exam *at one try* [(1回目の試みで) *on one's first try*]. ▶彼は何回か彼女を訪問した He visited her several *times* [(やや書) *on several occasions*]. ▶年に何回上京しますか How many *times* [How *often*] a year [×in a year] do you go to Tokyo? ▶その会は3年に1回開かれます The meeting is held *once* in (every) three years [(once) every three years]. ▶もう1回やらせてみてください Let me try *again* [*once more*]./Let me have *another* try.

❷[競技](野球の)an inning (⇒イニング); (クリケットの)innings; (ボクシングなどの) a round; (1試合中の1勝負) a game. ●7回の表[裏]にホームランを打つ hit a home run in the first [second] half of the seventh *inning*; hit a homer in the top [bottom] of the seventh *inning*. (!)この *inning* は省略可) ●毎回得点をする score every *inning*. ●(ボクシングの)12回戦 a bout of twelve *rounds*; a twelve-*round* bout; [話] a twelve-*rounder*. ●(トーナメントの)2回戦で敗退する[に進む] be beaten in [move into] the second *round*. ●3回勝負 a match of three *games*; a three-*game* match. ▶その野球の試合は回を重ねるにおもしろくなった The baseball game got more exciting with each *inning* [(終わりに近づくにつれて) as its end drew near].

*:**かい 貝** (二枚貝) a clam; (甲殻類) a shellfish (!)単·複同形であるが種類をいうときは 〜es. 食用としては [U]); (貝殻) a (sea) shell. ●貝のように(急に)口を閉ざす shut up like a *clam*; [話] clam up.

*かい 階 a floor (!通例建物の内部の特定の階);《米》a story,《英》a storey (!建物の外部から見た階).

解説 《米》では1階をthe first floor, 2階をthe second floor となるが,《英》では1階は the ground floor と表すので, 2階が the first floor となり,《米》《英》で数え方が1階分ずれる.

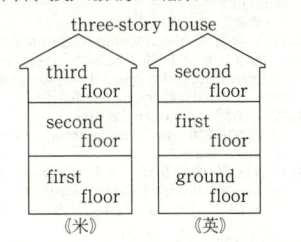

three-story house

《米》	《英》
third floor	second floor
second floor	first floor
first floor	ground floor

● 最上階 the top *floor* [*story*]. ● 30階建てのビル a thirty-*story* [a thirty-*storied*] building; a building of thirty *stories*. ● 上[下]の階に住んでいる少女 a girl who lives upstairs [downstairs]. ▶ そのビルは何階建てですか How many *floors* [*stories*] are there in that building?/How many *floors* [*stories*] does that building have? (!How high [tall] is that building? ともいえるが測定値をたずねる言い方と解されるのが普通. ▶ このデパートは10階建てです This department store is ten *stories* high [×tall]./This department store has ten *stories*. ▶ それはもう1階上です It's one *floor* up.
会話 「家具売り場は何階ですか」「7階です」 "What [Which] *floor* is the furniture department on?" "It's on the seventh《米》[sixth《英》] *floor*."

かい 買い buying (↔selling). ▶ 彼らは今大豆の買いに出ている(=強気買いをしている) They are now long on [of] soybeans.
● 買いオペレーション (bond) buying operation. ● 買い為替 buying exchange. ● 買い材料 a positive factor. ● 買い相場 a buying [a bid] rate. ● 買い注文 a buy order.

かい 快 (a) pleasure.
● 快をむさぼる enjoy pleasure.

かい 怪 (不可解な物・事) a mystery; (不思議な物・事) a wonder.
● 怪電話 a mystery phone call.

かい 解 (答え) an answer 《*to*》; (解法) a solution 《*to*》; (解釈) (an) interpretation. (⇨解答)

かい 隗 ● 隗より始めよ When you want to do something, do it first yourself.

かい 櫂 [オール用] an oar; [カヌー用] a paddle; [ともがい] a scull. ● かいをこぐ pull an *oar*. (⇨漕(こ)ぐ)

かい 下位 ● 下位にある be in a *low(er) position* [*rank*], be *low(er) in rank*; (…より劣っている) be inferior《*to*》; (次位である) be subordinate《*to*》. ● 下位打線と対戦する face the bottom of the batting order.

かい 甲斐 ● 甲斐のある(…の価値がある) worth (!叙述的に); (時間・労力をかける価値のある) worthwhile. (⇨-甲斐(がい), 価値) ▶ それは苦労のかいが十分あった It was well *worth* the trouble. ▶ その仕事はやってみるかいがある The job is *worth doing* [×*being done*]./It is *worth* (*while*) doing [*worth your while to do*] the job. (!動名詞が続く場合, while は省略されることが多い)/The job is *worthwhile* [*報*

いられる) *rewarding*]. ▶ 努力のかいがあって彼は成功した (おかげで) *Thanks* to his efforts, he succeeded. / (成功が彼の努力に報いた) Success *rewarded* him for his efforts. (!His efforts *were rewarded with* success. ともいえる) ▶ 手厚い看病のかいもなく(=にもかかわらず)弟は死んだ My brother died *in spite of* [《書》*despite*] their devoted nursing [care].

古今ことばの系譜 『草枕』
世に住むこと二十年にして, 住むに甲斐ある世と知った. 二十五年にして明暗は表裏のごとく, 日のあたる所にはきっと影がさすと悟った. 三十の今日(こんにち)はこう思っている. ― 喜びの深きとき憂(うれ)いよいよ深く, 楽(たのし)みの大いなるほど苦しみも大きい. When I grew to manhood at twenty, I found that this is a world worth living in. At twenty-five I realized that light and darkness are the opposite sides of the same thing and that all sunny places would eventually turn shady. Now at thirty, I think that joy is deepest when sorrow is deepest, and happiness is greatest when hardship is greatest. (!(1)「二十」は「成人して」という意味があると考えて grew to manhood と付け加えた. (2)「明暗は表裏の如く」は,「明暗は同じものの表裏のようなもので, 物事には表裏があり, 表が裏に転ずることも, その逆もある」と解釈した. このような例では字句を置き換えるのではなく, 自分なりの解釈をしてそれを英語で表現することが必要) (⇨『草枕』)

かいー 快● 快記録 a *fine* record. ● 快速力で at *full* [*top*] speed.

かいー 皆● 国民皆保険 the National *Full* Insurance.

-かい《終助詞》❶ [軽い感動・疑問] ▶ 試合を見に来てくれるかい *Will you* come to see our game?
❷ [反語的に強い断定] ▶ そんなこと分かるかい *Who knows* such a thing?

-かい 海● 日本海 the *Sea* of Japan. (⇨日本海) ● 北海 the North *Sea*.

-かい 界● (一般に) the world; (集団) circles; (特に動植物などの) the kingdom. ● 政界 the political *world*; political *circles*. ● 芸能界 (⇨芸能界) ● 動物界 the animal *world* [*kingdom*].

*がい 害● [損害] harm; [物への害] damage (⇨被害); [悪影響] bad [ill, harmful] effects. ● 喫煙の害 the *bad effects* of smoking. ● 害のない harmless. ● 害を被る suffer *damage*; be damaged《*by*》. ● 虫の害を防ぐ prevent *damage* from insects. ● 健康に害がある be *bad for* the [one's] health; be *harmful to* (one's) health. (⇨有害) ▶ 子供の折檻(せっかん)は益より害が多いものだ Beating a child will *do more harm than good*. ▶ 少しぐらい日光浴をしても害にはなりません A bit of sunbathing won't *do* you any *harm* [won't *harm* you]./There's no *harm* doing [×to do] a bit of sunbathing. ▶ 台風は稲作に大きな害を与えた The typhoon *did* [*caused*, ×*gave*] great *damage to* the rice crops.

DISCOURSE
率直に言って, 携帯電話は子供にとって害の方が益より大きい **Frankly speaking**, cell phones do more *harm* than good to young children. (!Frankly speaking, ... (率直に言って...)は主張を表すディスコースマーカー. 反論されそうな意見を思い切って述べるときに用いる. 誰もが納得するような内容には用いることはできない. ×Frankly speaking, nuclear war must be avoided.)

がい 我意〔わがまま〕self-will. ●我意を押し通す have one's *own way*.

-がい -外 ●時間外に働く(=残業する) work *overtime*. ●区域外に *outside* the area. ●国境外に *beyond* the border. ▶それはまったく問題外(=不可能)だ It's quite *out of* the question.

-がい -街〔通り〕a street;〔行政区〕a district;〔都市の特殊な〕a quarter;〔中心部〕a center;〔地域〕an area. ●ニューヨークの5番街 Fifth *Avenue*, New York. (❗✕*the* Fifth Avenue は誤り). ●商店街 a shopping *center* [*street*];〔歩行者専用の〕《米》a shopping *mall*. ●住宅街 a residential *area* [*district*, *quarter*]. ●サンフランシスコの中国人街 the Chinese *quarter* in San Francisco.

-がい -甲斐〔価値のある〕worth; worthwhile. (⇨甲斐(ポ)) ▶それは努力のしがいがありますか Is it *worth* the effort?

かいあく 改悪 ── **改悪する** 動 ●憲法を改悪する *revise* the constitution *for the worse*.

がいあく 害悪〔害〕harm. (⇨害) ●害, 害毒 ●世に害悪を流す do *harm* to society; have a *harmful* influ-*ence on* society.

かいあげ 買い上げ buying,《書》purchasing. ●ボストン美術館買い上げ品 a *purchase* by the Boston Museum.
●買い上げ価格 the púrchasing [púrchase] price 《*for*》.

かいあげる 買い上げる buy*;《書》purchase. (⇨買う)

かいあさる 買い漁る ●米を買い漁る *try to buy as much rice as possible*; *hunt* for rice.

がいあつ 外圧〔外国からの圧力〕foreign pressure《*on* Japan》. ●外圧に屈する〔をはねのける, に耐える〕yield to [reject; withstand] *foreign pressure*.

ガイアナ〔国名〕Guyana /gaiǽnə/;〔公式名〕the Co-operative Republic of Guyana. 〔首都 Georgetown〕●ガイアナ人 a Guyanese. ●ガイアナ〔人〕の Guyanese.

かいい 怪異 图〔化け物〕a monster.
── **怪異な** 形〔不思議な〕mysterious; strange. ●怪異な事件 a *mysterious* case.

かいい 魁偉 ●容貌魁偉な男 a man of *imposing* ap-pearance.

かいいき 海域 a sea area;〔特定の〕waters.

かいいぬ 飼い犬 a pet [a house] dog; one's (own) dog.
●飼い犬に手をかまれる be bitten by one's own dog; be double-crossed by one's trusted follower.

かいいれ 買い入れ buying,《書》purchasing. ●古書高価買い入れ〔表示〕Old Books *Bought*.

かいいれる 買い入れる buy* (⇨買う);〔仕入れる〕stock, lay* ... in.

***かいいん 会員** a member (of a society);〔会員の地位・資格〕membership;〔会員数〕a membership (❗単数扱い). ●その会の正〔終身〕会員になる become a regular [a life] *member* of the soci-ety. ●会員の資格を失う lose one's *membership*. ▶クラブの会員数はどれくらいですか How large is the club's *membership*? ●会員が500人の(多くの)会員を有している The club has 500 [a lot of] *members*./The club has a *membership* of 500 [a large *membership*]. ●会員資格は21歳以上の男女にあります *Membership* is open to men and women (who are) twenty-one years old and over. ●このホテルは会員制です This hotel is for *members* only. ●彼らは新会員を募集中である They are recruiting new *members*.
●会員証 a《Kitano Tennis Club》membership card; a membership card 《*for* Kitano Tennis Club》. (❗後の方は名称が長いときに好まれる)
●会員名簿 a mémbership list.

かいいん 改印 ●改印届をする report *a change of* one's *seal*.

かいいん 海員 a sailor;〔書〕a mariner;〔男の〕a seaman.
●海員組合 a seaman's union.

かいいん 開院 图 the opening of a hospital.
── **開院する** 動 ▶4月にこの近辺に総合病院が開院する A general hospital *opens* [*is opened*] around here in April. (❗*opens* の方が普通)

がいいん 外因 an external cause.
●外因性精神病 an exogenous /eksádʒənəs/ mental disease.

かいうける 買い受ける buy,《書》purchase. (⇨買う) ▶彼はあの車を安い値で買い受けた He *bought* that car at a low [✕cheap] price./《話》He *bought* that car cheap.

かいうん 海運 shipping; marine transportation.
●海運業 the shípping bùsiness [tràde]. ●海運業者 a shípping àgent.

かいうん 開運 cultivation [improvement] of one's fortune. ●開運のお守り a good-luck charm. ●開運を祈る pray for *better fortune*.

かいえん 海淵 the deepest part of a trench.

かいえん 開宴 the opening of a party.

かいえん 開園 图 the opening 《*of* a zoo [a kinder-garten]》. ●開園 9:00～18:00〔掲示〕Hours: (from) 9 a.m. to 6 p.m.
── **開園する** 動 ●その遊園地は午前8時に開園する The amusement park *opens* at 8 a.m.

かいえん 開演 ●午後5時開演です The *performance begins* [*starts*, *opens*] at 5 p.m./The *curtain rises* [*goes up*] at 5 p.m./The 5 p.m. *curtain* とも書く. (❗プログラムなどでは(a) 5 p.m. *curtain* とも書く)

がいえん 外苑 an outer garden. ●明治神宮外苑 the *Outer Gardens* of Meiji Shrine.

かいおうせい 海王星〔天文〕Neptune.

かいおき 買い置き 图〔蓄え〕a stock,《やや書》a re-serve. ●買い置きが少なくなる〔なくなる〕〔物が主語〕run short [run out of stock];〔人が主語〕run short [out] of《potatoes》.
── **買い置きする** 動 buy a stock of ...; lay ... in 《*for*》. ▶パーティー用に食料をたくさん買い置きしてある We have [We keep, There's, We've *laid in*] a large *stock of* food *for* the party.

かいおん 快音 a pleasure sound.

かいか 怪火〔不審火〕a mysterious fire;〔鬼火〕a will-o'-the-wisp.

かいか 開化 civilization. ●文明開化 *civilization* and enlightenment.
── **開化する** 動 be civilized [enlightened].

かいか 開花 图 ●開花中である be in flower [blos-som, (満開) (full) bloom]; be out. ●開花予報を出す predict the time for *flowering*.
── **開花する** 動〔植物の〕flower; bloom; come into flower [bloom];〔主に果樹が〕blossom (❗以上はいずれも比喩的にも用いられる);〔花が〕come out. ●こと北国では5月にいろんな花が開花する Many flowers *bloom* [*come into bloom*] in this north region in May. ▶彼のバイオリンの才能は幼くして開花した His genius for playing the violin *flowered* [*bloomed*] early.
●開花期 a flówering time.

かいか 開架 ●開架式の open-shelf, open-stack,《英》open-access.
●開架式図書館 an open-shelf library.

かいか 階下 ――階下の[へ, で, に] 形 副 downstairs. ●階下の浴室[トイレ] a downstairs bathroom. ●階下へ客を迎えに行く go downstairs to welcome one's guest. (! 玄関のある階まで下りると意味もする)

かいが 絵画 a picture;〚絵の具による〛a painting. (⇒絵)

がいか 外貨 〚貨幣〛foreign currency [money];〚外国債券〛foreign bonds;〚外国為替〛foreign exchange. ●外貨を確保する[得る] generate [access to] a foreign currency [foreign currencies]. ●外貨建ての foreign currency denominated.
●外貨獲得 acquisition of foreign currency. ●外貨準備(高) foreign currency reserves. ●外貨(建て)債 a foreign currency bond. ●外貨保有高 foreign currency holdings. ●外貨預金 foreign currency deposit.

がいか 凱歌 〚戦勝を祝う歌〛a triumphal song. ●凱歌をあげる〚戦いに勝つ〛win a victory 《over》.

ガイガーカウンター 〚放射能測定器〛a Geiger counter; (正式名) a Geiger-Muller counter.

かいかい 開会 名 the opening of a meeting. ●開会の辞を述べる give an opening (↔a closing) address.
――**開会する** 動 open 《a meeting》. ▶国会はあす開会する The Diet opens (↔closes) tomorrow. ▶ただ今よりこの会を開会します《開会宣言》Ladies and Gentlemen, I now declare this meeting open. (! この open は形容詞)
●開会式 an ópening cèremony;《米書》ópening èxercises; (国会を) be in session. ●開会日 the ópening dày.

***かいがい 海外** foreign countries, overseas countries. (! overseas は「海をへだてた外国」にしか用いない) ●海外へ行く go 《×to》 overseas [abroad]. ●海外向け放送（番組）an overseas [a foreign] broadcast. ●金(🜚)の海外流出 an outward flow of gold. ●軍隊を海外に派遣する send the army overseas [abroad]. ●海外で暮らす live overseas [abroad]. ●海外からの留学生 overseas [foreign] students (! 前の方が普通); students from overseas [abroad]. (!「海外へ行っている留学生」は students overseas [abroad] という) ●海外事業を展開する develop [expand] overseas business. ●日本代表の海外組 some members of Japanese National Team who play in foreign soccer teams. ▶そのバレエ団は海外公演中だ The ballet company is on an overseas tour. ▶彼は仕事でしょっちゅう海外に行っている He frequently goes overseas [abroad] on business. ▶彼は海外事情に詳しい He knows a lot [is well informed] about foreign affairs.
●海外移住 emigration overseas. ●海外遠征 an overseas tour [visit]. ●海外居住者 a resident abroad. ●海外拠点 an overseas base;（系列販売店）an overseas outlet. ●海外勤務 an overseas assignment. ●海外視察旅行 a tour of inspection abroad. ●海外市場 an overseas market; a foreign market. ●海外支店 overseas [×foreign] branches. ●海外出張 a business trip abroad; an overseas business trip. ●海外生活 an overseas life; a life in a foreign country. ●海外生産 overseas [foreign, offshore] production. ●海外駐在員 an overseas representative. ●海外展開 overseas business expansion; business expansion in a foreign country [abroad]. ●海外ニュース news from abroad. ●海外版 an overseas edition. ●海外赴任 staying abroad on [for] business. ●海外貿易 foreign trade. ●海外メーカー an overseas maker [manufacturer]. ●海外旅行 (⇒海外旅行)

がいかい 外海 the open sea; (公海) the high seas; (大洋) the ocean.

がいかい 外界 the outside world; (自分の周りの世界) the world around one. ●外界との接触を避ける avoid contact with the outside world.

かいがいしい 形 〚手ぎわよい〛efficient;〚勢いよい〛energetic, brisk;〚献身的な〛devoted.
――**かいがいしく** 副 efficiently, energetically, briskly; devotedly. ▶彼女は台所仕事から夫の看病までひとりかいがいしく立ち働いた She worked in the kitchen and nursed her sick husband with praiseworthy efficiency. (! praiseworthy は「賞賛に値する」の意)

かいがいりょこう 海外旅行 overseas [foreign] travel; a trip abroad. ●海外旅行をする travel abroad [overseas].
●海外旅行客 a tourist abroad.

かいかえ 買い替え a replacement purchase; a purchase for replacement. ▶この冷蔵庫は買い替え時だ This refrigerator will soon need to be replaced. ▶今はマンションの買い替え時だといわれている They say that now is a good time to get rid of an old condominium and buy a new one.

かいかく 改革 (a) reform 《in》. ●経済[社会; 税制]改革案 a plan of economic [social; tax] reform. ●宗教改革 (一般の) (a) religious reformation; (歴史上の) the Reformation. ●教育改革を進める advance educational reforms; advance reforms in education. ●抜本的な行政改革を断行する carry out drastic administrative reforms. ●改革なくして成長なし No reform, no growth.
――**改革する** 動 reform; make* [carry out] reforms 《in》. ●教育制度を改革する reform [make reforms in] the educational system.
●改革者 a reformer.

かいかく 開学 〚大学を開設すること〛(⇒創立)

がいかく 外角 〚数学〛an exterior angle;〚野球〛the outside (corner). (⇒内角) ●外角高目へ投げるpitch high and outside. (! 英語では高低を後にいう) ●外角へスライダーを投げる throw a slider on the outside. ▶カーブは外角を外れた The curve missed the outside corner.

がいかくだんたい 外郭団体 〚付属の団体〛an affiliated organization;〚政府組織外の団体〛an extra-governmental organization.

かいかけ 買い掛け ●買掛金 account(s) payable (↔ account(s) receivable).

かいかた 買い方 a buyer (↔a seller); (強気の) a bull (↔a bear).

***かいかつ 快活** 快活な 形 (陽気な) cheerful; (活発な) lively; (率直でこせこせしていない) open.

かいかつ 開豁 ――**開豁な** 開豁な(=心の広い)気性 a broad-minded a [generous] temper.

がいかつ 概括 名 (概要) a summary. ●概括的に言えば generally speaking (⇒一般(的)に); to sum up (⇒つまり❷).
――**概括する** 動 summarize; (要約する) sum up.

かいかぶる 買い被る 〚過大評価する〛overestimate, overrate. ▶買いかぶらないで Don't overestimate [overrate] my ability./Don't think better of me than I deserve. ▶あなたは彼のことを買いかぶっている You speak too highly of him.

かいがら 貝殻 a shell; (特に海の) a seashell. ●浜で貝

かいがら 殻を拾う gather [collect] *shells* on the beach. ● 貝殻細工 *shellwork*. ● 貝殻虫 a *scale* (insect).

かいかん 会館 a *hall*. ● 学生会館 a students' *hall*; 《米》a student [《英》a students'] *union*.

かいかん 快感 a pleasant [an agreeable] feeling [sensation]; pleasure. ● 快感を覚える feel *pleasure*; feel *good* [*fine*, *comfortable*, *nice*].

かいかん 開館 ▶午前9時開館 《掲示》*Open* [《まれ》*Opens*] at 9 a.m.
● 開館時間 the ópening time.

***かいがん** 海岸 (a) shore; (the) seashore; a [the] beach, 《英》the seaside; 《沿岸》the coast.

> 使い分け **shore** 最も一般的な語．特に海から見た岸
> **seashore** 特に岸の砂や岩のある部分をさす．
> **beach** 砂や小石におおわれた浜辺をさす．《米》では通例をつけ行楽地としての意味を myös持つ．
> **seaside** 《英》で行楽地としての海岸地帯をさす．
> **coast** 海と陸の境界線をさす．特に地理的・地誌的な文脈で多く用いる．

● 海岸通りのレストラン a seafront restaurant; a restaurant *on* the seafront. ● 海岸地方 *coastal* area; a *seaside* district. ● 海岸沿いのホテル a *seaside* hotel; a hotel at the *seaside*. ● 銚子の海岸沖で[に] off the *coast* of Choshi. ● 海岸を散歩する walk along the *seashore* [*beach*, ×*coast*]. ● 海岸沿いを航行する sail along the *coast*. ● 休暇で海岸(=海水浴)に行く go to the *beach* [*seaside*] on vacation. ▶子供たちは海岸で遊んでいた The children were playing on the *beach* [*seashore*]. ▶手紙の入ったびんが海岸に打ち上げられた A bottle with a message inside was washed up *on the beach* [*washed ashore*]. ▶海岸沿いにはごくわずかの漁村しかなかった There were only a few fishing villages *on* [*along*] *the coast*.
● 海岸線 a coastline. ● 海岸段丘 a marine terrace.

かいがん 開眼 ── 開眼する 動 《やり方やこつを悟る》awaken (to ...).
● 開眼手術 an operation to give《him》sight.

がいかん 外患 a foreign [an external] threat; pressure from foreign countries. ● 内憂外患 (⇨内憂 [成句])

がいかん 外観 (an) (outward [external]) appearance; a look. (⇨外見) ▶奇妙な外観を呈する present a strange *appearance*. ▶建物の外観からすると，それは教会のようだった By the *appearance* [*look*] of the building, it seemed to be a church. ▶その古い美術館は気鋭の建築家の手で現代的なガラスの外観を付与された The old museum was given a modern glass *façade* by a talented architect. (! *façade* は建築物の「正面の顔」の意)

がいかん 概観 图 a general survey; 《書》an óverview.
── 概観する 動 ● 20世紀のフランス文学を概観する *survey* [*make a súrvey of*] the 20th-century French literature. ● 本書は北アイルランド紛争の背景を概観したものである This book *outlines* the background to the conflict in Northern Ireland.

かいき 会期 《国会などの》a session; 《展覧会などの》a period. ● 国会の会期 the [a] *session* of the Diet. ▶国会は今会期中だ The Diet is now in *session*. ▶古代ペルシャ展の会期は8月1日から2週間だ The Ancient Persian Art Exhibition will open on August 1st and last two weeks.

かいき 回帰 名 (a) revolution; (a) recurrence.
── 回帰する 動 revolve; recur 《*to*》. ▶サケやマスは生まれた川へ回帰する習性がある Salmon and trout have the habit of *coming back again to* the river they were born.
● 回帰線 (⇨回帰線) ● 回帰熱 [医学] a recurrent [a relapsing] fever.

かいき 怪奇 ● 怪奇な(=異様な)姿 a *weird* [a *grotesque*, 《神秘的な》a *mysterious*] appearance. ▶この部屋で怪奇現象が起きたという話だ They say that *mysterious* things have happened in this room.
● 怪奇小説 a *mystery* (story); a thriller.

かいき 開基 (⇨開山《仏教》)

-かいき -回忌 the anniversary of one's death. ▶祖父の3[7]回忌 《*on*》the second [sixth] *anniversary* of my grandfather's death. (! 日本語と英語で数がずれることに注意)

***かいぎ** 会議 a meeting; a conference; a council; a congress; a convention; 〘議会などの会期中の〙a session.

> 使い分け **meeting** あらゆる会合に用いられる一般的な語．
> **conference** 専門的な問題について意見交換する集まり．
> **council** 特定問題の審議・諮問を行う比較的小規模な会議．
> **congress** 各派・各国の代表者が参加する大規模な会議．
> **convention** 政治・宗教・事業団体などの代表者会議．

① 〖～(の)会議〗 ▶軍縮(に関する)会議 a disarmament *conference*; a *conference on* [《やや書》*concerning*] disarmament. ● 編集会議 an editorial *meeting*. ● 国際会議 an international *conference* [*congress*]. ● 家族会議 a family *council* [*conference*]. ● 実業家の会議 a businessmen's *convention*; a *convention* of businessmen. ● 本会議(国会などの) a plenary *session*. ● 首脳会議 (⇨会談)

② 〖会議～〗 ▶社長は今会議中です(=会議しています) The boss is *in* a [the] *meeting* at the moment./The boss is *in* [×*at*] *conference* now. (! 無冠詞に注意)

③ 〖会議が[は]〗 ▶きのうの会議があった There was [We had] a *meeting* yesterday./A *meeting* was held yesterday. ▶次の会議はいつにしましょうか When shall we have the next *meeting*? (! 「…いつでしょうか」(＝When will the next meeting be?) の意にもなる)/When shall we meet next?

④ 〖会議に[で]〗 ▶会議に出席する attend a *meeting* [a *conference*]. ● 会議にかける bring up 《a proposal》 at the *meeting*. ● 環境会議で公害問題を取り上げる take up the pollution problem at the environment *conference*. ▶彼は会議で議長を務めた He chaired [took the chair at, presided over] the *meeting*./《会議を取り仕切った》 He conducted the *meeting*.

⑤ 〖会議を〗 ▶会議を招集する[開く] call [hold, have] a *conference* [a *meeting*].
● 会議室 a cónference ròom. ● 会議場 a cónference hàll.

かいぎ 懐疑 图 〖疑い〗 (a) doubt; 〖懐疑的な考え方〗 skepticism, 《英》 scepticism.
── 懐疑的な 形 skeptical; 《容易に信じない》 incredulous. ▶彼はそのニュースに懐疑的だった He was *skeptical* [*incredulous*] about the news. ▶知識の

がいき 外気 (外の空気) the outside 〖戸外の〗outdoor air. (⚠️「外」の意は outside や outdoor より文脈で表されることが多い) ◆外気に触れる be exposed to *the air*; (屋外に置かれる) be put *in the open air*.

かいきいわい 快気祝い the celebration of 《his》 recovery from 《his》 illness. ◆父の快気祝いをする celebrate my father's recovery from his illness.

かいきえん 怪気炎 ◆怪気炎をあげる talk big 《about》; exaggerate.

かいきしょく 皆既食 (皆既日[月]食)〖天文〗a total eclipse of the sun [moon].

かいきせん 回帰線 ◆南[北]回帰線 the tropic of Capricorn [Cancer].

かいぎゃく 諧謔 (冗談) a joke;(ユーモア) humor;(機知) a wit. ◆諧謔に富んだスピーチ a *witty* speech.

*****かいきゅう** 階級 class (⚠️しばしば複数形で) 〖地位〗a rank; 〖等級〗a grade. ◆上流[中流; 下層]階級 the upper [middle; lower] *class*(*es*). ◆労働者階級 the working 〖(まれ)laboring〗 *class*(*es*). ◆支配階級 the ruling *class*(*es*). ◆無産階級 the proletariat. ◆知識階級 the intellectual [educated] *class*(*es*). ◆彼は特権階級に属している He belongs to [is a member of] the privileged *classes*. ▶軍隊には多くの階級がある The army has a lot of *ranks*.
◆階級意識 class consciousness. ◆階級社会 a cláss sòciety. ◆階級制度 the cláss sỳstem. ◆階級組織 (行政官の) the hierarchy /háiərɑ̀ːrki/. ◆階級闘争 cláss strùggle 〖wàr〗.

かいきゅう 懐旧 (昔を懐かしく思い出すこと) reminiscence /rémənisns/;〖書〗retrospection.
◆懐旧談 reminiscences.

かいきょ 快挙 〖すばらしい業績〗a splendid achievement; (輝かしい功績) a brilliant feat; (賞賛されるべき行為) an admirable act. ◆金メダル獲得の快挙を成し遂げる accomplish a *splendid achievement* of winning a gold medal.

かいきょう 回教 〖「イスラム教」の別称〗Islam.

かいきょう 海峡 a strait (⚠️しばしば複数形で単数扱い); a channel 〖strait より大きい〗. ◆津軽海峡 the Tsugaru *Straits*. ◆イギリス海峡 the (English) *Channel*.

かいきょう 開胸 ◆開胸手術を受ける undergo chest surgery 〖医学〗thoracotomy /θɔ̀ːrəkάtəmi/.

かいきょう 懐郷 (⇨望郷)

かいぎょう 改行 a new line [paragraph].
—— 改行する 動 start a new line [paragraph].

かいぎょう 開業 opening. ◆店の開業 the *opening* of a store. (⚠️日本語につられて ×the open of ... とはいわない)
—— 開業する 動 (店などを) open, start; (医者などを) practice. ◆本屋を開業する open [start] a bookstore. ◆弁護士[医者]を開業している practice law [medicine].
◆開業医 a medical practitioner; a general practitioner 《略 G.P.》. ◆開業時間 (開店・始業) the ópening tìme. ◆開業中 (店などが) be open; (医師・弁護士などが) be in practice.

がいきょう 概況 a general condition. ◆天気概況 a *general weather condition*.

かいきょうのひかり 『海峡の光』Lights in the Channel. (参考) 辻仁成の小説)

かいきょく 開局 图 the opening 《of a new post office》.
—— 開局する 動 ◆FM放送局を開局する open [set up, 〖書〗establish] an FM broadcasting station.

かいきょく 外局 (中央省庁の) an extra-ministerial bureau /bjúərou/.

かいきる 買い切る 〖買い占める〗buy ... up; (バスなどを借りりる) charter 《a bus》. ◆在庫品をすべて買い切る *buy up* all the stock.

かいきん 皆勤 图 perfect attendance.
—— 皆勤する 動 go to work [school] without missing a (single) day; do not miss a (single) day of work [school].
◆皆勤賞 a prize for perfect attendance.

かいきん 開襟 ◆開襟シャツ an open-necked shirt.

かいきん 解禁 图 the lifting of the ban [embargo] 《on》; 〖書〗embargo 〖特に通商停止について〗;〖猟などで〗the opening of the hunting [fishing] season. ▶アユ漁は6月に解禁となる The *ayu* season *opens* in June./The open season on *ayu* starts in June.
—— 解禁する 動 ◆金(の輸出入)を解禁する *lift* the *embargo* on gold; *lift* the gold *embargo*.

がいきん 外勤 《on》 outside duty. (⇔内勤)
—— 外勤する 動 work outside (the office).

がいく 街区 a block.

かいぐい 買い食い —— 買い食いをする 動 spend one's money on snacks [sweets].

かいくぐる 搔い潜る 〖どうにか通過する〗manage to pass through ...; make* one's way through 《the crowd》. ◆たくみにディフェンスをかいくぐってゴールに突進する charge at the goal *passing through* the defenses deftly.

かいくん 回訓 instructions. (⇨訓令)

かいぐん 海軍 the navy (⚠️単・複両扱い); the naval forces 《複数扱い》. (⇨軍隊) ◆米国海軍 the United States [U.S.] *Navy* 《略 U.S.N.》. ◆英国海軍 the Royal [British] *Navy* 《略 R.N.》.
◆海軍軍人 a navy man; (水兵) a sailor. ◆海軍士官 a naval officer. ◆海軍兵学校 the Naval Academy. ◆海軍力 naval power.

*****かいけい** 会計 ❶〖金銭の取り引き・計算〗accounts; 〖会計学, 計算〗accounting. ◆一般[特別]会計 general [special] *accounts*. ◆一般会計予算 the general *accounting* budget. ◆会計を調べる audit [examine] the [one's] *accounts*.
❷〖勘定〗(飲食店での勘定書) 《米》a check, 《主に英》a bill. (⇨勘定) ◆会計をお願いします (レストランなどで) (Let me have the) *check* [*bill*], please.
会話「ストロベリーアイスクリームをください」「承知しました. 85セントです. 会計はレジでお願いします」"I'd like some strawberry ice cream, please." "O.K. That's [That'll be] 85 cents. Please pay the cashier." (⚠️That'll be .... の方が柔らかな表現)
◆会計課 the accóunts [accóunting] sèction. ◆会計係 an accounting clerk; an accountant; (会社・団体などの) a treasurer; (ホテルなどの) a cashier /kæfíər/. ◆会計監査 auditing. ◆会計検査院 the Board of Audit. ◆会計検査官 an auditor. ◆会計士 an accountant; (公認会計士)《米》a certified public accountant 《略 C.P.A.》;《英》a chartered accountant 《略 C.A.》. ◆会計年度 the fiscal 〖英〗financial] year. ◆2007会計年度 the 2007 *fiscal* year; *fiscal* 2007. (⚠️《米》では2007年10月1日から2008年9月30日まで) ◆会計簿 (keep) an accóunt bòok. ◆会計報告 (get [give, make]) a treasurer's [a financial] report.

がいけい 外形 an outward form.
- 外形標準課税 a tax on business size.

がいけい 外径 an outside diameter.

かいけつ 解決 图 (問題などの) (a) solution 《*to*, *of*》; (紛争などの) (a) settlement 《*of*》;《書》resolution 《*of*, *to*》. ⚠ resolution はどちらの場合にも用いる.
- その問題の二つの解決策 two *solutions to* [*of*] the problem. ▶労使紛争で円満な解決をつける reach [arrive at, come to] an amicable *settlement* of the labor dispute. ▶エネルギー問題の早急な解決が望まれる We expect a speedy *solution* [*resolution*] *to* the energy problem. ▶その紛争の解決には相当時間がかかるだろう The *settlement* of the trouble will take a long time./It will take a long time to settle the trouble. ▶それは短絡的な解決法だ That's the easy way out (of it). (⚠ way out は「(苦境・ジレンマなどの)脱出」)

— **解決する** 動 [解く] solve, clear ... up; (苦労して) work ... out;[決着をつける] settle,《書》resolve.
- ▶金では[何もしないで心配していては]問題は解決しないよ You can't *solve* [✗work out] the problem *with* money [*by* sitting and worrying]. ▶警察は指紋を見つけてその事件を解決した The police found the fingerprints and *solved* [*cleared up*] the case. ▶愚痴をこぼしても何も解決はしない Grumbling won't *solve* anything [*get you anywhere*]./Nothing will be solved by grumbling. (⚠ get [take]《you》nowhere は「何の役にも立たない」の意) ▶仲間内(その件を双方話し合って500万円で解決した They *settled* [*worked out*] (the matter) between themselves [with each other,(法廷に持ち込まないで)out of court] *for* 5 million yen. ▶両国間の紛争は武力によって[平和的に]解決された The dispute between the two countries *was settled* by force [amicably, peacefully].
- 会話「割った窓ガラスは弁償するつもりだ」「でもそれで事は解決するの(=済むの)?」"I'm going to pay for the broken window." "Will that *be the end of* it, though?"

かいけつ 怪傑 a person of exceptional talent; an exceptionally [an extraordinary] talented person.

かいけつびょう 壊血病 〖医学〗scurvy.

かいけん 会見 图 an interview, a meeting. (➪ インタビュー, 面会) ▶テレビ会見 a television [TV] *interview*. ▶会見を求める ask for an *interview*《*with*》. ●記者会見を行う hold a press *conference* (⚠ a press interview は《まれ》); meet the《foreign》press; have an *interview with* the press corps.

— **会見する** 動 meet,《米》meet with ...; (インタビューをする) have [(会見に応じる) give] an interview 《*with*》. ▶小泉総理は昨夜大統領と会見した Prime Minister Koizumi *met with* the President last night.

かいけん 改憲 〖憲法改正〗(➪ 憲法) ●改憲論議を戦わせる argue for and against the *constitutional amendment*.
- 改憲論者 an advocate of constitutional amendment.

かいげん 改元 图 the change of the name of an era.

— **改元する** 動 ▶昭和から平成に改元する *change from* the Showa *to* the Heisei era.

がいけん 外見 [全体的な外面の印象] 图 (an) appearance (⚠ しばしば「見せかけ」の意も含む); [表情] a look (⚠ 複数形で「容貌(ようぼう)」の意にも用いる ➪ 顔つき);[うわべ] (a) show. (➪ 見掛け) ▶外見は(= 見かけ) in *appearance*. ▶外見からすると彼は貧しそうだ By [From] his *appearance*, he seems poor. ▶(... のように見える) He *looks* poor. (➪ 見える) ▶人を外見で判断してはいけない Don't judge people by (their) *appearances* [by their *looks*]. ▶(... by how they *look* [*appear*]. ともいえる) ▶その傷は外見ほどひどくない The wound is not as bad as it *looks*.

かいげんれい 戒厳令 martial law. ●戒厳令を敷く[解く] proclaim [lift] *martial law*. ●戒厳令下にある be (put [placed]) under *martial law*.

かいこ 蚕 〖昆虫〗a silkworm. ●蚕を飼う raise [rear] *silkworms*.

かいこ 回顧 — **回顧する** 動 ▶学校時代を回顧する(= 振り返る) *look back on* [(想起する) *recollect*] one's school days.
- 回顧展 a retrospective exhibition. ●回顧録 memoirs; (やや書) reminiscences.

かいこ 解雇 图 (従業員の落ち度による) (a) dismissal,《書》(a) díscharge; (会社の都合による一時的な) a layoff (働 ～s). ●即刻解雇 (a) summary *dismissal*. ▶5人の従業員の不当解雇がもとでストライキが起こった The unfair *dismissal* of five workers caused a strike.

— **解雇する** 動 dismiss,《書》dischárge;《話》fire;《話》sack,《話》give* ... the sack; (特に一時的に) lay* ... off (⚠ (1) 上記とした3語のうち, 後の2語は《米》では俗語的. (2) discharge は《英》ではあまり用いられない. (3) lay ... off は最近は永久解雇の婉曲語として多用される). ▶私は3か月間一時解雇されていた I *was laid off* for three months. ▶彼は勤務状態がよくないために解雇された He *was dismissed* (from his job) for missing too much work.
- 解雇通知 a dismissal notice,《米話》a pink slip.

かいこ 懐古 图 retrospection; (懐古の情) nostalgia.
- 懐古趣味がある have a *longing* [《話》a *yen*] *for the good old days*.

— **懐古する** ▶look back on the past (with nostalgia);《やや書》reminisce《*about*》.

かいご 介護 图 nursing, care; nursing care. ●老人介護 *nursing* of the aged. ●在宅介護 home *care* [*nursing*]. ●介護休暇を申請する apply for leave to *care for* an elderly person.

— **介護する** 動 look after, care for ....
- 介護支援サービス cáre mànagement. ●介護支援専門員 a cáre mànager. (参考 今は「ケアマネージャーということが多い」) ●介護人 a care-giver. ●介護福祉士 a (certified) care worker. ●介護保険 nursing care insurance. ●介護保険制度 a nursing-care insurance system. ●介護老人福祉施設 a nursing home for the aged. ●介護老人保健施設 a health facility for the aged.

かいこう 回航 — **回航させる** 動 bring [take] a ship 《*to*》.

かいこう 改稿 — **改稿する** 動 rewrite one's manuscript.

かいこう 海港 a seaport.

かいこう 海溝 a [an ocean] deep;〖地理〗a trench. ▶日本海溝 the Japan *Deep*.

かいこう 開口 〖開口一番〗▶太郎が開口一番言ったのは, その男とは何の関係もないということだった The first thing Taro *said* was that he had nothing to do with that man. (⚠ Taro started off his speech [(答え) reply, (反論) refutation, etc.] by saying .... ともいえる. ✗open one's mouth は多くの場合不適)

かいこう 開校 图 ●開校5周年記念 the fifth anniversary of the *opening of a school*. ▶4月開校

《掲示》Open in April.
— **開校する** 動 open [start] a school. ▶あの学校はいつ開校しますか When will the school be ready? ● **開校記念日** (celebrate) the anniversary of the opening of a school. ● **開校式** the opening ceremony of a school.

かいこう 開港 — **開港する** 動 open a port 〔空港〕 an airport〕.

かいこう 開講 图 the start of a new course. ▶4月1日より開講 Classes [Lectures] start on April 1st.
— **開講する** 動 start a new course 《in French》; bring one's first lecture 《on World History》

かいこう 邂逅 ⇨巡り合う

*****かいごう** 会合 图 〔集まり〕a meeting, 《やや書》a gathering; (an) assembly (⇨会, 集会); 〔会談〕a conference. (⇨会談) ▶我々のクラブは毎週月曜日に会合を持つ Our club holds [has] a meeting every Monday.
— **会合する** 動 meet; gather; 《やや書》assemble. ● **会合場所** a méeting plàce; 《好んで利用される》《やや書》a rendezvous /rá:ndəvù:/.

がいこう 外交 图 ❶〔外国との交際・交渉〕diplómacy.
❷〔社外でのセールス〕▶彼は保険の外交をしている He is an insurance salesman./〔保険の外交で生計を立てている〕He sells insurance for a living.
— **外交(の)** 形 ❶〔外国との交際[交渉]の〕diplomátic, foreign. ▶外交関係を絶つ break off diplomatic relations [ties] 《with》. ▶加藤氏はその問題の解決に外交手腕をふるった Mr. Kato used diplomacy [showed diplomatic skill] in dealing with the issue.
❷〔その他の表現〕▶彼はなかなかの外交家だからだれとでも仲よくやっていけるよ He is so diplomatic [tactful, sociable] that he can get along with anybody. (❗diplomatic は「人扱いが上手な」, tactful は「如才ない」, sociable は「社交的な」の意) ▶そう言ったのは外交辞令だよ He said so but he was just being diplomatic./He said so just to be polite [just out of politeness].
● **外交官** a diplomàt. ● **外交官試験** the Diplomatic Service examination. ● **外交交渉** diplomatic negotiations. ● **外交筋** diplomatic sources. ● **外交政策** a foreign [ˣa diplomatic] policy. ● **外交青書** a diplomatic blue book. ● **外交団** the diplomatic corps /kɔ́ːr/ [body]. (❗単数扱い) ● **外交特権** diplomatic immunity. ● **外交文書** diplomatic documents. ● **外交問題** 〔事情〕foreign affairs; 〔課題〕a diplomatic problem.

がいこう 外港 〔主港の補助港〕an outport.

がいこうせん 外航船 an ocean liner.

がいこうてき 外向的 éxtrovérted (↔íntrovèrted). ▶彼は外向的だ (= 外向的な人だ) He is an extrovert./He is extroverted.

がいごうないじゅう 外剛内柔 ▶彼は外剛内柔だ He is tough outwardly but soft and gentle inwardly. (⇨外柔内剛)

かいこく 戒告 (a) warning; 〔公式の〕 (a) reprimand. (❗後の語は国家公務員法でいう「戒告」にも当たる)

かいこく 開国 图 〔国交開始〕the opening of a country to the world.
— **開国する** 動 open (the gate(s) of) the country to the world.

:****がいこく** 外国 图 a foreign country; 〔自国と比較して〕the rest of the world.
①〔外国～〕▶外国生まれの foreign-born. ● 外国産の foreign produced 《fruit》; 《fruit》 of foreign-growth. ● 外国製の foreign [foreign-made] 《watches》; 《watches》 of foreign make. ● 外国航路の船 a ship on an overseas route; an ocean liner.
②〔外国に[へ, を, から, で]〕▶ 外国に[へ]行く go abroad [overseas]; go to a foreign country. ● 外国へ電話をする make [place] an overseas call. ● 外国を旅行する travel abroad [overseas]. ● 外国から帰る come back [return] from abroad [overseas, a foreign country]. ● 外国からの留学生 a foreign student 《以下の言い方の方が丁寧》; an overseas student; a student from overseas. (❗a student overseas は「外国で学ぶ留学生」) ● 外国で暮らす live abroad [overseas, in a foreign country].
— **外国の** 形 foreign; 《海外の》overseas (❗限定的. foreign より口語的); alien /éiliən/. (❗alien は通例公民権のない外国人について用いる. 排他的なニュアンスがあるので一般には避ける)
● **外国為替** foreign exchange. ● **外国為替銀行** a foreign exchange bank. ● **外国為替市場** a foreign exchange market. ● **外国為替相場** the foreign exchange rate. ● **外国貿易** foreign [overseas] trade. ● **外国旅行** 《make [take]》 an overseas [a foreign] trip; 《make [take]》 a trip abroad.

がいこくご 外国語 a foreign language. ● **外国語学校** a language school. ● **東京外国語大学** Tokyo University of Foreign Studies. ▶日本語にはたくさんの外国語が入ってきている There are lots of foreign words [ˣlanguages] in Japanese. (❗日本語につられて languages とじない. a foreign language は一つの外国語全体をさす)

がいこくじん 外国人 a foreigner (❗時に「よそ者」という冷たい感じがするので国籍が分かっている場合は避ける (⇨外人)); 〔法律〕an alien; 〔在留外国人〕a foreign resident.
● **外国人観光客** a visitor from abroad [overseas]; a foreign visitor. ● **外国人登録** alien registration.

がいこつ 骸骨 a skeleton. ▶骸骨のようにやせる (= 骨と皮ばかりになる) become very thin [skinny]; 〔話〕become (all) skin and bone(s). ▶彼は骸骨みたいだ He looks like a skeleton.

かいこむ 掻い込む 〔抱え込む〕(⇨抱え込む); 〔すくい入れる〕scoop 《water》.

かいこむ 買い込む lay* ... in; 〔買いだめする〕stock up 《on, with》. ▶正月のために食料を買い込む lay a lot of food in for the New Year holidays; stock up on [with] food for the New Year holidays.

かいごろし 飼い殺し ▶飼い殺しにする (= 動物を殺さずに) 〔動物を〕keep an animal which has no apparent use for life; 〔従業員を〕keep 《him》 on the payroll without giving 《him》 proper work to do.

かいこん 悔恨 〔書〕repentance; (a) regret. (⇨後悔)

かいこん 開墾 cultivation. (⇨開拓) — **開墾する** 動 cultivate.
● **開墾地** cultivated [reclaimed] land.

かいこん 解梱 — **解梱する** 動 unpack. ▶解梱作業中である We are unpacking (from boxes) now.

かいさ 海佐 (1等) Captain; (2等) Commander; (3等) Lieutenant-Commander.

*****かいさい** 開催 图 ▶オリンピックの開催地を知っていますか Do you know the site for [of] the (next) Olympics?/〔どこで開催されるかを〕Do you know where the Olympics will be held [take place]?

かいさい

— **開催する** 動 [催す] hold*; [開会する] open. ● 会を開催する hold a meeting. ● 見本市は来週の日曜日から開催される The trade fair will be held [open, be open] 《×from》 next Sunday.
● 開催国 a host country 《for》.

かいさい 快哉 ● 快哉を叫ぶ shout for [with] joy; yell with delight.

かいさい 皆済 full payment. — **皆済する** 動 pay 《one's debt》 off.

かいざい 介在 名 (an) intervention.
— **介在する** 動 lie [exist, stand] 《between》; intervene 《in, between》. ▶我々はまず2国間に介在するあらゆる障害を取り除く必要がある First of all, it is necessary that we (英) should) clear away every obstacle lying between the two countries.

がいさい 外債 a foreign bond; a foreign debt issue. (対 内債). ● 円建外債 an yen-dominated foreign bond.

がいざい 外材 imported [foreign] timber.

かいさく 改作 名 (an) adaptation 《of》.
— **改作する** 動 adapt. ● 小説を舞台用に改作する adapt a novel for the stage.

かいさく 開削 名 (発掘) (an) excavation.
— **開削する** 動 excavate 《a tunnel》; cut 《a canal through...》

かいささえ 買い支え price support, buying support.

かいささえる 買い支える support. ▶日銀はドルを売って円を買い支えた The Bank of Japan supported the yen by selling dollars.

かいさつ 改札 名 ● 自動改札機 an automatic ticket checker; 《1人ずつ通す回転式の》 an automatic turnstile.
— **改札する** 動 《切符を調べる》 inspect tickets; 《切符にはさみを入れる》 punch tickets.
● 改札係 a ticket inspector. ● 改札口 a (ticket) wicket 《米》 gate, 《主に英》 barrier]. 補給 米国の鉄道では改札口は無人のため車内検札が多い

*__かいさん 解散__ 名 《議会・会社などの組織の》 dissolution; 《会議・群衆などの》 a breakup.
— **解散する** 動 dissolve; break up. ● 衆議院を解散する dissolve the House of Representatives.
● 会社を解散する dissolve 《やや話》 wind up] a company. ● 群衆を解散させる break up a crowd; (四方に散らう) disperse a crowd.

かいざん 改竄 名 (a) falsification.
— **改竄する** 動 ● データを改ざんする falsify data.

かいざん 開山 (寺の創立) the foundation of a temple; (寺の創立者) the founder of a temple.

がいさん 概算 名 a rough estimate. ● 概算で at a rough estimate. ▶日本の人口は概算で1億2,000万である The population of Japan is (roughly) estimated at one hundred and twenty million./It is (roughly) estimated that Japan has a population of 120,000,000./There are an estimated 120,000,000 people in Japan.
— **概算する** 動 estimate ... (roughly). (! 特に強調する場合を除いて roughly はなくてもよい); ● 建築費を概算する estimate the building cost.
● 概算要求 an (estimated budget) request. ● 概算要求基準 guidlines for budget requests.

かいさんぶつ 海産物 marine products; [海産食品] seafood.
● 海産物商 a dealer in marine products.

*__かいし 開始__ 名 a beginning, a start; an opening.

● 試合開始 the beginning [start, opening] of a game.
— **開始する** 動 begin*, start; open. (⇨始める) ● 仕事を開始する begin [start] to work; begin [start] working. ● 銀行と取り引きを開始する(=口座を開く) open an account with a bank.

かいし 怪死 a mysterious death. (⇨変死)
かいし 懐紙 pocket paper for tea ceremony.
かいじ 快事 a pleasant [a splendid] event.
かいじ 海事 名 maritime affairs [matters]. ● 国際海事機構 the International Maritime Organization 《略 IMO》.
— **海事の** 形 maritime.
● 海事衛星 a maritime satellite. ● 海事局 the Maritime Bureau.

かいじ 開示 名 disclosure 《to》; (a) release 《to》.
● 市民への情報開示 the disclosure [release] of information to the citizens.
— **開示する** 動 disclose; release. ● その件についての個人情報を開示する disclose personal information about the matter.

がいし 外史 an unofficial history.
がいし 外紙 a foreign newspaper.
がいし 外資 ● 外資を投下する invest foreign capital.
● 外資系の会社 a foreign-affiliated firm.
● 外資導入 the introduction of foreign capital.
がいし 碍子 an insulator.
がいじ 外字 [ワープロなどに未登録の文字] an external character; [外国の文字] foreign letters; [常用漢字以外の漢字] Chinese characters except the ones in everyday use.
がいじ 外耳 the external ear.
● 外耳炎 [医学] otitis externa /outáitəs ikstə́:rnə/.

がいじかく 外痔核 [医学] external hemorrhoid.
がいして 概して [一般に] generally, in general; (一般に言うと) generally speaking; (全体として) on the whole. (⇨一般(的)に) ● 概して彼はよくやった Generally [On the whole, All in all] he did well.

かいしめ 買い占め a buy-out; (株・商品の) a corner, cornering.
かいしめる 買い占める buy* ... up [out]; (株・商品を) corner [make a corner on] 《the coffee market》. ● トウモロコシを買い占める make a corner in corn. ● ワールドカップのチケットを手当たり次第買い占める buy up all available tickets for the World Cup.

*__かいしゃ 会社__ a company 《略 Co., /kóu, kʌ́mpəni/》, 《米》 a corporation 《略 Corp., corp.》; a firm 《! 以上いずれも単・複数扱い》; an office; a house 《圏 houses /-ziz, (米) -siz/》.

使い分け	
company	各種の会社を広くさす最も一般的な語.
corporation	法人組織としての会社を表すやや堅い語.《英》では「市町自治体」を表す.
firm	主に小規模な合資会社・事務所. しばしば company のくだけた言い方としても用いる.
office	仕事場としての会社.
house	主に出版・金融・衣料関係の会社.

① (〜会社, 会社〜) ● 株式[有限]会社 《米》 a corporation, an incorporated company 《略 (Co.) Inc.》; 《英》 a limited (liability) company 《略 Co. Ltd.》; a stock 《米》 [a joint-stock 《英》] company (! 社名としては用いない) (⇨解説). ● 出版会社 a publishing company [house]. ● 保険会社 an insurance company [firm]. ● 民間会社 a private company. (! 「株式非公開の会社」の意もある)

- 親[子]会社 a parent [a subsidiary] *company*.
- 関連会社 an affiliated [an associated] *company*.

解説 株式[有限]会社の社名を表すときは次のようにする．なお，日本では英式に従うのが普通．田中モータース株式会社 Tanaka Motors (*Co.*) *Ltd.* 《英》 [(*Co.*) *Inc.*; *Corp.* 《米》]

② 【会社は】 ▶その会社は何を作っているのですか What does the *company* [*firm*] produce?
③ 【会社の】 ▶会社の車 a *company* car. ▶会社の旅行 for on a *company* trip.
④ 【会社に[で]】 ▶会社に入る(= 入社する) join [《官》enter] a *company*. ▶会社で昼食をとる have lunch at the *office* [×at the company]. ▶お父さんは毎朝7時に会社に行く My father goes to work [the *office*] at seven every morning. (❗ go to the *company* はその会社に何らかの用件で出向くことに使い, 毎日の出勤には用いない) ▶父はまだ会社にいます My father is still *at* [*in*] the *office*.
会話 「どこの会社にお勤めですか」「松下です」"Who [Which *company*, ×Where company] do you work for?" "I work for [at, in] Matsushita."
⑤ 【会社を】 ▶会社を経営する run [manage] a *company*. ▶会社を設立する establish [form] a *company*. ▶会社を休む(帰宅のため) leave an *office* [a *company*]. (❗「会社をやめる」の意にもなる) ▶会社をやめる leave [quit] one's *job*; (定年で) retire from one's *job* [*company*, *office*]. ▶会社を首になる be fired from one's *job*.

関連 会社の役職名：取締役会長 Board Chairman/取締役副会長 Vice Chairman/最高経営責任者 Chief Executive Officer (略 CEO)/取締役社長 President/取締役副社長 Vice President/代表取締役 Representative Director/専務取締役 Executive [Managing] Director/常務取締役 Senior [Managing] Director/取締役 Director/取締役会 Board of Directors/監査役 Auditor/顧問 (Corporate) Adviser/部長 (General) Manager/課長 Section Manager/係長 Sub-section Manager/支店[工場]長, 店長 Branch Manager.
日本と米英では会社の組織・役職の分化が異なり，また会社によっても異なる．上記はその1つの訳例．

- 会社案内 a company brochure [guide, pamphlet]. • 会社更生法 the Company Resuscitation Law. • 会社説明会 a job fair. (⇨就職) • 会社組織 the system of a company; a company system. • 会社人間 a company-first person; an organization person. (⇨社員) • 会社法 《米》the corporation law; 《英》the company law. • 会社役員 a director; an executive; 《集合的》a board of directors.

かいしゃ 膾炙 ▶彼の冒険談は人口に膾炙している(=よく知られている) His adventure story *is well known* to everybody.

かいしゃ 外車 (外国の車) a foreign(-made) car; (輸入車) an imported car. (❗後の方が普通)

かいしゃいん 会社員 a company employee; (事務系の) an office worker. (❗英語では一般名としての「会社員」はなく, secretary (秘書), accountant (会計係)などと職種をいうか, I work for a law office. (法律事務所に勤めています)などと具体的にいうのが普通)

*かいしゃく 解釈 図 (an) interpretation; [説明] (an) explanation. ▶誤った[片寄った]解釈 put a wrong [a one-sided] *interpretation* (*on* it). ▶それは彼の解釈にすぎない That's only his *interpretation*.
—— 解釈する 動 intérpret 《A *as* B》; (理解する) make 《B *of* A》(❗B is what, nothing などで疑問文・否定文で用いられる); [受け取る] take*; [説明する] explain. ▶沈黙を否認と解釈する *interpret* [*take*] 《his》silence *as* denial. ▶ぼくの発言をそんな風に解釈しないでくれ Don't *interpret* [*take*] my words (in) that way. (❗ that [this] way では通例 in を省略する) ▶この文は二通りに解釈できる This sentence can *be interpreted* in two ways./This sentence can be given two *interpretations*./There are two possible *interpretations* of this sentence.
会話「彼のばかげた行為をどう解釈したらよいだろうか．あなたはどう解釈しますか」「あんなのは見せかけにすぎないと思います」"How can we *interpret* [*explain*] his foolish act? What do you *make of* it?" "That's only a gesture."

かいしゃく 介錯 —— 介錯する 動 assist 《him》in commiting *harakiri*.

がいじゅ 外需 foreign demand. (⇔ 内需)

かいしゅう 会衆 (参会者たち)《集合的に》an attendance, an audience; (教会の) a congregation. (❗後の2語は複数動詞で受けることもできる)

かいしゅう 回収 図 (廃品・配布物の) (a) collection; (欠陥商品・通貨の) (a) recall, 《米》(a) callback; (損失・宇宙船などの) recovery, 《やや書》retrieval.
▶廃品回収 a *collection* of waste articles. ▶ごみの回収は週2回だ There are two *collections* of garbage a week.
—— 回収する 動 (集める) collect; (声をかけて呼び戻す) recall, call ... in; (取り戻す) get*... back, recover, 《やや書》retrieve. ▶売り掛け金を回収する *collect* bills. ▶欠陥車を回収する *recall* [*call in*] defective cars. ▶ブラックボックスを回収する *recover* [*retrieve*] the plane's black box.

かいしゅう 改宗 図 (a) conversion. ▶仏教徒のキリスト教への改宗 a *conversion* of a Buddhist *to* Christianity.
—— 改宗する 動 ▶仏教に改宗する *convert to* Buddhism; (仏教徒になる) *turn* Buddhist [×a Buddhist].
• 改宗者 a convert (*to* Christianity).

かいしゅう 改修 repair. (❗「改修する箇所」の意では ©) ▶河川改修工事 river *improvement*. ▶道路[橋]の改修をする *repair* a road [a bridge].
• 改修工事 repáir [restoráton] wòrks.

かいじゅう 怪獣 a monster, a monstrous animal.
• 怪獣映画 a monster film.

かいじゅう 海獣 a sea [a marine] animal.

かいじゅう 晦渋 —— 晦渋な 形 晦渋な(= 難しい)文章 *puzzling* passages; passages which *are difficult to understand*.

かいじゅう 懐柔 —— 懐柔する 動 conciliate /kənsílièit/《him》[win《him》over] to one's side.
• 懐柔策 《take》conciliatory /kənsíliətɔːri/ measures; 《adopt》a conciliatory policy.

がいしゅう 外周 (円の周囲)《書》periphery /pərífəri/; (外側で測った周囲の長さ) the outer circumference.

がいじゅう 害獣 a harmful animal.

がいじゅうないごう 外柔内剛 ▶彼は外柔内剛だ He is soft and gentle outwardly but tough inwardly. (⇨内剛内柔)

*がいしゅつ 外出 図 ▶外出中に while one is *out* [*away*] (❗ out は比較的近くへの, away は離れた別の場所への外出を意味する); in [during] one's ab-

かいしゅん sence. ▶しばらく外出はやめて(=家に居て)ちょっと勉強しなくちゃ I must *stay in* [(*at*) *home*] and do some work for some time. ▶夜間外出禁止令が全市にしかれた A *curfew* was imposed on the whole city.
会話「どうしたらよろしいでしょうか, 先生」「当分外出を控えて(=屋内にこもっていて)ください」"What do you advise, doctor?" "*Stay indoors* for the time being."

— 外出する go* out. ▶(会社で)田中は外出していて今日は戻りません Mr. Tanaka *is out* for the day.
事情 社内の人に対して日本のように身内意識を持たない欧米では呼びすてにせず Mr. などをつける.
会話「夜はどのようにお過ごしですか」「そうですね, よく外出します—芝居, 映画, それに時には食事をしにね」"What do you do in the evenings?" "Well, we *go out* quite a lot—to the theater, cinema, sometimes to eat."
● 外出着 street clothes [wear]; (部屋着に対する) outdoor clothes.

かいしゅん 回春 (若返り)《書》rejuvenation.
● 回春剤 a rejuvenator.

かいしゅん 改悛《書》repéntance.
— 改悛する 動 彼は自分の愚行を改悛している《書》He repents [×is repenting] *of* his folly. ❶《米》用法では to repent his folly (他動詞+目的語)も多い/(改悛の情を示している) He shows *repentance for* his folly.

かいしゅん 買春 — 買春する 動 buy [《話》pick up] a prostitute.

かいしょ 会所 a méeting pláce. ● 碁会所 a go parlor [club].

かいしょ 開所 图 the opening (*of an office*).
— 開所する 動 研究所を開所する *open* an institute.

かいしょ 楷書 the printed [square] style (of Chinese character writing). ▶申込書には名前を楷書でお書きください Please *print* your name on the application.

*かいじょ 解除 图 [取り消し] (a) cancellation; [武装の] disarmament.
— 解除する 動 [契約などを] [取り消す] cancel; [終わらせる] terminate; [武装を] disarm; [禁令などを] lift; [障害を取り除く] remove; [免除する] release.
● 契約を解除する *cancel* [*terminate*] a contract. ● その本の発禁を解除する *lift* [*remove*] the ban on the book. ● 彼の武装解除する *disarm* the rebels. ● 彼の責任を解除する *release* him *from* his responsibilities; (解放する) *relieve* him *of* his responsibilities. ● ストを解除する *call off* a strike.

かいじょ 介助 图 (助け) help, 《書》assistance; (介添え) attendance.
— 介助する 動 help, assist; attend 《a sick person》.
● 介助犬 a partner [a service] dog.

かいしょう 快勝 — 快勝する 動 win a fine [(決定的な) a decisive, (かっさらっていく) a sweeping] victory.

かいしょう 改称 — 改称する 動 (AをBに) rename /riːnéim/ 《A B》; change one's name 《to》.

かいしょう 海将 a Vice Admiral.
● 海将補 a Rear Admiral.

かいしょう 解消 图 (a) cancellation; (解除) (a) dissolution. ● 彼らの婚姻関係の解消 the *dissolution* [(破局) *breakup*] of their marriage. ● ストレス解消にスポーツをする enjoy sports to *get rid of* stress.

— 解消する 動 (約束などを取り消す) cancel; (関係を急に絶つ) break ... off. ● 契約を解消する *cancel* a contract. ● 婚約を解消する [=破棄する] *break off* [*up*] one's engagement. ● 提携を解消する *dissolve* the partnership. ● 疑いがすっかり解消した All my doubts *have disappeared*.

かいしょう 甲斐性 ● 甲斐性のない人[男] a good-for-nothing; an *incompetent* man. ● 甲斐性のある人 a person *of ability*; an *able* man.

*かいじょう 海上 ● (船が)海上を行く sail on the *sea*. ● はるかな海上を眺める look across the *sea*.
— 海上の 形 marine; (海事の) maritime.
— 海上に[で] 副 on the sea; at sea.
● 海上勤務 (be on) sea duty. (↔shore) duty.
● 海上(交通)輸送路 a sea lane. ● 海上自衛隊 the Maritime Self-Defense Force. ● 海上生活 life at sea. ● 海上保安庁 the Japan Coast Guard.
● 海上保険 marine [maritime] insurance.
● 海上輸送 marine transport [transportation].

かいじょう 会場 (会合場所) a méeting pláce; (集会場) an assémbly hàll; (博覧会などの場所) grounds. ● 演奏会場 a concert [(リサイタルの) a recital] hall. ● 万博会場 the Expo grounds.
▶党大会の会場はどこですか Where is the party convention going to be held? (⇨催す)

かいじょう 回状 a circular (letter).

かいじょう 開城 图 the surrender of a castle [fortress]. — 開城する 動 surrender a castle 《to》; 《書》capitulate 《to》.

かいじょう 開場 图 ● 開場中である be *open*.
— 開場する 動 open (the doors). ▶その劇場は午前9時に開場する The theater *opens* at 9 a.m.

かいじょう 階上 — 階上の[へ, で, に] 形 upstairs. ● 階上の部屋 an *upstairs* room. ● 階上へ上がる go *upstairs*.

かいじょう 階乗 〔数学〕a factorial.

かいじょう 塊状 图 (大きなかたまり) a mass; (小さな固いかたまり) a lump; (木・石などのかたまり) a block.
— 塊状の 形 massive.

がいしょう 外相 the Minister of Foreign Affairs. (⇨外務) ● 麻生外相 *Foreign Minister* Aso.

がいしょう 外商 (外国の商人[商社]) a foreign merchant [firm].
● 外商部 (デパートの) a direct sales department.

がいしょう 外傷 an external injury; 〔医学〕(a) trauma /tráumə/. ● 心的外傷後ストレス障害 posttràumatic strèss disòrder (略 PTSD).

がいしょう 街娼 (売春婦) a prostitute; 《やや古》a streetwalker.

かいじょうたつ 下意上達 ● (官庁・会社などで)下意上達する convey the will of those who are governed to those govern.

かいしょく 会食 ● 友人たちと会食する *dine with* one's friends.

かいしょく 快食 ● 祖父は快食快眠だ My grandfather *eats* well and sleeps well.

かいしょく 海食 〔地学〕wave erosion.
● 海食崖 a sea cliff. ● 海食洞 a sea cave.

かいしょく 解職 — 解職する 動 be dismissed 《from》; 《やや書》be discharged 《from》. (⇨免職)

がいしょく 外食 — 外食する 動 eat [《書》dine] out. ▶(食べる) ● 今晩は外食しよう Let's *eat out* this evening.
● 外食産業 the food service industry.

かいしん 会心 (満足) satisfaction. ● 会心の笑み 《give》a smile of *great satisfaction*. ● 会心の作 a *very satisfactory* work; (思いどおりの作品) a work *after* one's *heart*. ● 会心のヒットを打つ get a

かいしん clean [a solid] hit.

かいしん 回心 图 〖宗教〗 conversion.
— **回心する** 動 be [get] converted 《from; to》.

かいしん 回診 图 (巡回往診) a doctor's rounds.
▶山下先生は回診中です Doctor Yamashita *is doing* [*is making, is out on*] *her rounds*.
— **回診する** 動 do [make] one's rounds; visit one's patients.

かいしん 改心 图 reformation. ▶彼は改心の見込みがない He is past *reformation*.
— **改心する** 動 reform (oneself); (素行を改める) mend one's ways [*manners*]. ● 改心させる reform 《him》.

かいしん 改新 (a) reform; (a) reformation. ● 大化の改新 the *Reformation* of the Taika era; the Taika *Reforms*.

かいじん 灰燼 图 ashes.
● 灰燼に帰す (火事で跡形もなく焼けてしまう) be reduced [burned] to ashes.

かいじん 怪人 a mysterious [a mystery] person.

かいじん 海神 the God of the Sea; 〖ローマ神話〗Neptune; 〖ギリシャ神話〗Poseidon.

がいしん 外信 foreign news.
● 外信部 the foreign news desk; the foreign news department.

がいじん 外人 a foreigner; (市民権を持たない) 〖法律〗an alien /éilién/. (❗ 前の方は対面した相手に使うと「よそ者」といった悪い響きを与えることがあるので, はっきり国籍をいうか a person from another country などという方が普通)

かいず 海図 a chart. ● 海図に載っている島々 islands (shown) on the *chart*; 《やや書》charted 《↔uncharted》 islands.

かいすい 海水 seawater (❗文脈によって単に water だけでよいこともある); (塩水) salt water 《↔fresh water》.
● 海水着 a swimsuit; a swimming [a bathing] suit. ● 海水魚 a saltwater fish. (❗単・複回形) ● 海水パンツ swimming trunks. ● 海水帽 a swimming [a bathing] cap.

かいすいよく 海水浴 swimming in the ocean 《主に米》[the sea 《主に英》], sea bathing /béiðiŋ/.
● 須磨へ海水浴に行く go to Suma for *sea bathing* [*a swim*, 《やや古》*a bathe*]; go swimming [*for a swim*, 《英・やや古》*for a bathe*] 《in 〖×to〗 Suma.
— **海水浴(を)する** 動 swim in the ocean; 《英》have [take] a bathe in the sea;《主に英》bathe in the sea.
● 海水浴客 a swimmer. ● 海水浴場 a beach [《主に英》a seaside] resort.

かいすう 回数 the number of times; 〖頻度〗a frequency. (⇨回) ● 訪問回数を増やす increase the *frequency* of one's visits.

がいすう 概数 (おおその数)an approximate number [figure]; (端数のない数) a round number [figure]. ● 概数で500です It is 500 in *round numbers* [*figures*]./It is *approximately* [*about*, *around*] 500.

かいすうけん 回数券 (1枚) a coupon (ticket); (一つづり) a book of coupons.

かいする 介する ● 通訳を介して(=通して)話す speak *through* 《通訳の助けで》with the help of 》 an interpreter. ● 友人を介して(=尽力によって)職を得る get a job *through* the influence [《書》*good offices*] of one's friend. ● 彼がなんと言ったろと意に介さない(=気にしない) I don't mind [*care*] what he says.

かいする 解する (理解する) understand*; (味わう) appreciate; have a sense of ...; (解釈する) interpret. ● 風流を解する *appreciate* unworldly elegance. ● ユーモアを解さない *have no sense of* humor. ● 字句どおりに解する *interpret* (it) literally.

がいする 害する (⇨害, 損なう) ● 健康を害する *injure* [*harm, ruin*] one's health. ● 彼女の感情を害する *hurt* [*injure*] her feelings; (怒らせ) *offend* her.

***かいせい** 改正 图 〖改訂〗(a) revision; 〖法律などの語句の〗(an) amendment 《to》. ● 条約改正 a *revision* of a treaty. ● 法律の改正 an *amendment* to [×*of*] a law. ● 憲法改正を唱える advocate constitutional *revision* [*amendment*]. ● 民法の全面改正を行う make a full-scale *revision* of the civil law. ● 電話の改正料金 the *revised* telephone rates.
— **改正する** 動 revise; (一部) amend. ● 規約を改正する *revise* the rules. ● 憲法を改正する *revise* [*amend*] the constitution.

かいせい 快晴 fair [clear] weather. (❗fair と clear の区別については ⇨晴れ) ▶今日は全国的に快晴に恵まれている The weather [It] is *fair* all over the country today.

かいせい 改姓 — **改姓する** 動 ● 彼女は斉藤から石田に改姓した(=姓を変えた) She *changed* her *surname* [*family name, last name*] from Saito *to* Ishida.

かいせき 会席 (寄り集まる場所) a meeting place; (宴会の席) a banquet seat, a party table.
● 会席膳 a dinner tray. ● 会席料理 a dinner.

かいせき 解析 图 〖数学〗analysis. (⇨分析)
— **解析する** 動 analyze.
● 解析幾何学 analytical geometry.

がいせき 外戚 (母方の親戚) a maternal relative; a relation on one's mother's side. 《働内戚》

かいせきりょうり 懐石料理 〖茶席で茶を出す前に出す簡単な料理〗(説明的に) a simple meal served before a tea ceremony;〖できた順に出す高級な懐石風の日本料理〗(説明的に) a set menu of selected food served in order.

***かいせつ** 解説 图 〖説明〗(an) explanation 《of》 (⇨説明);〖論評〗(a) comment 《on, about》(❗on は専門的なものに用いる);〖注釈(書)〗a commentary 《on》;〖スポーツ 時事問題などの(実況)解説〗(a) commentary 《on》(❗上記いずれの commentary もしばしば集合的に用いる) ● (テレビの)ニュース[スポーツ]解説 a news [a sports] *commentary* (on television). ● 野球の実況(=進行に逐一沿った)解説 a running [《米》a play-by-play] *commentary on* a baseball game.
— **解説する** 動 (説明する) explain; (論評する) comment 《on, about》. ● 選挙の結果について解説する *comment on* [*make comments on*] the election results.
● 解説者 a commentator; (ニュースの) a news commentator. (⇨説明 [説明書])

かいせつ 回折 〖物理〗diffraction.
● 回折波 diffracted wave.

かいせつ 開設 ● 幼稚園の開設 the *establishment* of a kindergarten.
— **開設する** 動 ● 研究所を開設する *establish* [*set up, open*] a laboratory.《❗後の2語の方が口語的》● 新たに事務所を神戸に開設する(=新しく設ける) *locate* a *new* office in Kobe.

がいせつ 外接 〖数学〗circumscription.

がいせつ 概説 〖概要〗an outline; 〖要約〗a summary.
— **概説する** 動 give an outline 《of》; outline 《it (to

かいせん [for] him)). ● ヨーロッパ全史を概説(=概観)する *survey* the whole of European history.

かいせん 会戦 名 (局地的戦争) a (land) battle ((with, against; between)). ● ワーテルローの会戦 the *Battle* of Waterloo /wɔ́ːtərlúː/.
— **会戦する** fight (a battle); 《やや書》battle ((with, against)).

かいせん 回船 (海上の運送船) a lighter, a barge.
● **回船問屋** a shipping agent.

かいせん 回線 (電気回路) a circuit; (電話の接続) a line. ● 回線が故障して全館が停電した A break in the *circuit* caused all the lights to go out.

かいせん 改選 名 [[再選]] reelection.
— **改選する** 動 ● 参議院議員の半数を改選する *reelect* half (of) the members of the House of Councilors.

かいせん 海戦 a naval [a sea] battle; a sea fight.

かいせん 海鮮 fresh fish and shellfish.
● **海鮮料理** fresh seafood dishes.

かいせん 疥癬 the itch; [医学] scabies /skéibiːz/ (単数扱い). ❗

かいせん 開戦 名 the opening [outbreak] of war.
— **開戦する** 動 open [begin, start] war ((against, on)); go to war ((against)); (宣戦を布告する) declare war ((against, on)).

*__かいぜん__ 改善 名 (an) improvement ((in, of)); (改正) (a) reform. ● サービスの改善 an *improvement of* service. ● 労働条件の改善を要求する demand an *improvement in* working conditions; demand *better* working conditions. ● …の改善策を講じる take measures to *improve*…. ● 彼の仕事には大いに改善の余地がある There is much room for *improvement in* his work. ● 彼は体質の改善を図った He tried to *improve* his constitution.
— **改善する** 動 improve, make (it) better. (⇔改良する) ● 日中の外交関係を改善する *improve* diplomatic relations between China and Japan. ● 新版は旧版よりも著しく改善されている The new edition is a significant *improvement over* [*on*] the previous one.

がいせん 外線 an outside line ((↔an extension)). ▶外線をおかけになるには1をダイヤルしてください Dial 1 for [to get] an *outside line*. ▶この電話で外線がかけられますか Can I make an *outside call* [Can I *call outside*] by this phone?/Can I *get outside* on this phone?

がいせん 凱旋 — **凱旋する** 動 make a triumphant return.
● **凱旋将軍** a triumphant [a victorious] general. ● **凱旋門** a triúmphal àrch; an arch of tríumph. (❗ 固有名詞はthe A- of T-)

がいせんしゃ 街宣車 an advertising van [car].

がいぜんせい 蓋然性 (見込み) (a) probability.

かいそ 改組 名 reorganization.
— **改組する** 動 reorganize ((an English literature department)).

かいそ 開祖 (宗派などの) the founder; (芸道などの) an originàtor.

かいそう 会葬 名 (葬式に参列すること) one's attendance at a funeral.
— **会葬する** 動 attend [come to] a funeral. (❗ 後の方が口語的)
● **会葬者** mourners; people who came to a funeral.

かいそう 回送 名 ● 回送のランプがついているバス a bus with [which has] an *out-of-service* light on.
● (電車の)回送車(です)[掲示] Out of service; Not in service.

— **回送する** 動 ▶ 手紙をこの住所に回送(=転送)してください Please *forward* [*send on*] the letter to this address. (❗封書に書く場合は Please forward to:〈転送先住所〉とする)

かいそう 回想 名 (追憶) (a) reminiscence; (思い出) (a) recollection.
— **回想する** 動 (遠い過去を追想する) reminísce /rèmənís/ ((*about*)); (特に楽しい経験を) (努力して思い出す) recollect; (過去を振り返る) look back ((*on*, *upon*)). ● 子供時代を回想する *reminisce about* [*recollect, look back on*] one's childhood. (❗ 後の二つの方が普通)
● **回想録** (遠い過去の思い出) reminiscences ((*of*)); (政治家などの) memoirs ((*of*)).

かいそう 快走 — **快走する** 動 (走者が) run fast; (帆・船が) fly along.

かいそう 改葬 — **改葬する** 動 reburial. — rebury ((one's remains)).

かいそう 改装 名 remodeling. (⇒改造)
— **改装する** 動 ● 店を改装する *remodel* [(特に装飾を)] 《話》*do over, redecorate*] a store. ● 新しい設備を入れたついでに台所を全面改装(=内装を一新)した They installed some new appliances and *did over* the whole kitchen.

かいそう 海藻, 海草 (a) seaweed; marine plants.

かいそう 階層 (社会の) a class, a stratum (複 strata, ~s). ● あらゆる階層の人 people of [from] all *classes* [*strata*], 《書》people from all *walks of life* [every walk of life].
● **階層社会** a stratified society.

かいぞう 改造 名 [[内閣の]] a reshuffle; [[建物などの]] (an) alteration, (a) renovation, (a) conversion.
● 内閣改造 (carry out) a cabinet *reshuffle*.
— **改造する** 動 remodel; alter; renovate; convert ((*into*)) (❗remodel は形, alter は一部の変更, convert はある物を他の物に変えてしまうこと); (作り直す) remake*; [[内閣を]] reshuffle. ● 台所を改造する *remodel* [*renovate*] a kitchen. ● 倉庫を工場に改造する *remodel* [*convert*] a storehouse *into* a factory. ● 総理は内閣を改造した The Prime Minister *reshuffled* his cabinet.

かいぞう 解像・解像度 [光学] resolution. ● 解像度の悪い[よい]テレビの画面 a television screen with low [high] *resolution*; a low-*resolution* [a high-*resolution*] TV screen. ● **解像力** [光学] resolving power; resolution.

がいそう 外装 [[建物などの外側]] the exterior ((of a building)); [[外観]] (特に, 内面と異なる) (an) extérior. ● 車の外装 a car's *exterior*. ▶家の外装はしっくいだった The *exterior* of the house was (covered with) plaster.

かいぞえ 介添え 名 [[世話する人]] a helper; (病人などの付添人) an attendant; (花嫁の) a bridesmaid; (花婿の) a best man; [[世話すること]] attendance.
— **介添えする** 動 attend ((a sick person)).

かいそく 会則 the rules [articles, constitution] of a society. ● 当クラブの会則および細則 the club's *constitution* and bylaws. ● 当会の会則を改正する amend the *rules of* our *society*.

かいそく 快足 ▶ 彼は快足だ He is a fast runner./He runs fast./He is quick on his feet.

かいそく 快速 (a) high speed. (⇒高速) ▶ この列車は大阪行快速です This is *rapid service* bound for Osaka.
● **快速艇** (モーターボート) a speedboat; (一般の船で) a fast sailing ship. ● **快速電車** a fast [a rapid] (transit) train. (関連 express train 急行列車)

かいぞく 海賊 (1人の) a pirate /páiərət/.

がいそう ●海賊版 a pirate(d) edition; (CD[DVD]など) a bootleg (CD [DVD]). ▶海賊版がインターネットで大量に出回っている A lot of *bootleg* copies are up for sale on the Internet. ●海賊船 a pirate (ship). ●海賊放送 pirate broadcast.

がいそふ 外祖父 a grandfather on one's mother's side; a maternal grandfather.

がいそぼ 外祖母 a grandmother on one's mother's side; a maternal grandmother.

かいだ 快打 〔野球〕a clean [a solid] hit.

かいたい 解体 图 (建物の) demolition; (工場・設備などの) dismantlement.
── 解体する 動 (ばらばらにする) take* (a machine) apart [to pieces]; (建物などを) demolish, knock [pull]… down; (後の二つの方が口語的); (足場などを取り壊す) take … down; (装備・設備を取り除いて) dismantle. ●古い校舎を解体してそのあとに新しい図書館を建てる *demolish* [*knock down*] the old school building and replace it with a new library. ●工場を解体する *dismantle* a factory. ●車を解体する(=くず処理) *scrap* a car. ●法人を解体(=解散)する *break up* [(やや書) *disband*] the corporation.
●解体業者 (米) a (house) wrecker, (英) a (house) breaker.

かいだい 改題 图 the change of a title.
── 改題する 動 change the title (*of* a book [a movie]).
●改題本 a retitled book.

かいだい 解題 图 (書籍解説) a bibliography; (注釈) explanatory notes (*on*).
── 解題する 動 ●不朽の名著を解題する *make explanatory notes on* eternal classics [great books].

＊かいたく 開拓 图 (耕作) cultivation; (開墾) reclamation.
── 開拓する 動 cultivate; reclaim. ●原野を開拓する *cultivate* [*reclaim*, (切り開く) *open up*, *clear*] the wilds. ●輸出市場を開拓する *open up* [(見つける) *find*, (求める) *seek*] an export market. ●いつの日か砂漠を開拓して農業に利用する日がくることであろう The desert will *be reclaimed* for agricultural use someday.
●開拓者 (先駆者) a pioneer (▶比喩的にも用いる); (植民者) a colonist; (移民) a settler. ●開拓地 (耕作地) cultivated land; (開墾地) reclaimed land.

かいだく 快諾 ready consent; willing consent. (▶後の方は異議はない程度のこともある). ▶その結婚に両親は快諾を与えた The parents were happy to give their *consent* to the marriage.

かいだし 買い出し ●スーパーへ買い出しに行く go shopping at [×to] a supermarket; go to a supermarket *to do some shopping* [×for shopping].

かいだす 掻い出す bail (water) out (of a boat); bail (a boat) out.

かいたたく 買い叩く beat* (him [the price]) down (to); ●野菜を買い叩く(=不当な安値で買う) buy the vegetables *at an unreasonably low price*. ▶彼はそのおもちゃを買い叩いて1,000円にした He *beat* the price of the toy *down to* 1,000 yen.

かいだめ 買い溜め ▶まさかの時のために食料を大量に買いだめしてある We have [We've laid in] *a large stock of* food for a rainy day.

がいため 外為 foreign exchange.

＊かいだん 会談 图 (政治上などの正式な) talks. (▶通例複数形で (⇨会議)) ●首脳会談 summit *talks*; a summit (conference [meeting]). ▶和平会談は来週始まる The peace *talks* begin [×begins] next week.
── 会談する 動 have [hold] talks (*with*); (話し合う) talk (*with*, *to*), have a talk (*with*); (会見する) (米) meet with (the President).

＊かいだん 階段 stairs; steps; a staircase; a stairway; (はしご) a ladder.

> **使い分け** stairs 通例屋内の階上へ通じる一続きの階段をさす。
> steps 通例屋外から玄関に通じる階段や, 乗り物などの昇降段などをさす。
> 階段の1段をさすときは a step, a stair. 特に一続きの階段をいうときは a flight of stairs [steps].
> staircase, stairway 手すりなど階段に付属する部分も含んだ階段全体をさす。

●非常階段 emérgency stàirs; (火災時の) a fire escape. ●らせん階段 a spiral [a circular; (曲がりくねった) a winding] *staircase*. ●急な階段 a steep flight of *stairs*. ●階段の上[下]で at the top [bottom, foot] of the *stairs*. ●スーツケースを階段の上まで運ぶ carry the suitcase up the *stairs*. ●階段を上る[下りる] go up [down] the *stairs*. ●階段から落ちる fall down the *stairs*; fall off the *staircase*. ●出世の階段を登る climb up the *ladder to* [*of*] success. ▶階段は急だ The *stairs* are steep. ▶彼は階段を駆け上がって教室へ行った He ran up the *stairs* to the classroom. (▶「階段を2段ずつ駆け上がる[下りる]」は run up [down] the *stairs* two at a time) ▶トイレは階段を上ってすぐ左側にあります The bathroom is up the *stairs*, just to the left.
●階段教室 a lecture theater.

かいだん 怪談 a ghost [a horror] story.

かいだん 解団 图 disbandment, dissolution (*of*). (⇨解散) (⇨結団) ── 解団する 動 disband [dissolve, (話) break up] (an organization).
●解団式 the ceremony of disbandment.

がいたん 慨嘆 ── 慨嘆する 動 deplore; regret; (書) lament (*over*).

かいだんじ 快男児 a nice fellow [guy].

ガイダンス 〔指導〕 guidance; (入学[社]時などの) orientation. ●新入生にガイダンスを行う give [provide] *orientation* for freshmen.

がいち 外地 〔外国の土地〕 a foreign [an overseas] land; 〔日本の旧領土〕 Japan's former overseas territories. (対 内地)

かいちく 改築 图 reconstruction. ●改築中である be *under reconstruction*.
── 改築する 動 reconstruct; (再建する) rebuild. ●校舎を改築する *reconstruct* [*rebuild*] a school building. ▶神社は創建時の図面により改築された The shrine *was rebuilt* by closely follwing the original plan.

かいちゅう 回虫 a roundworm. ●回虫がわく have [get] *roundworms*.

かいちゅう 改鋳 图 (鐘などの) recasting; (貨幣などの) reminting, recoinage.
── 改鋳する 動 recast; remint, recoin. ●古銭を改鋳して新銭を作る *remint* old coins into new ones.

かいちゅう 海中 ●海中の潮の流れ *undersea* [*under water*] currents. ●海中に落ちる fall *into the sea*; (船から) fall *overboard*. ●海中に潜る go *under the sea*.
●海中探検 undersea exploration. ●海中農場 an ocean farm.

かいちゅう 懐中 a pocket. (⇨懐(ふところ)) ●懐中に in one's *pocket*.

- 懐中電灯 (⇨懐中電灯) • 懐中時計 a (pocket) watch. • 懐中物(ミェ)〔財布〕《米》a wallet,《英》a purse. (⇨財布)

がいちゅう 外注 图 an outsourcing; an outside order.
—— **外注する** 動 outsource; contract (a job) out; place an order with an outside supplier. ▶今後はこれらの機械部品は外注しなければならない We have to *order* these machine parts *from* [×to] an *outside supplier* from now on.

がいちゅう 害虫 a harmful insect; vermin (⚠ vermin にはネズミ・カラスなどの害獣・害鳥も含まれる. 集合的. 通例複数扱い). • 害虫に荒らされる be infested by *vermin*. • 害虫を駆除する exterminate *vermin* [*harmful insects*].

かいちゅうでんとう 懐中電灯《主に米》a flash-light,《英》a torch. • 懐中電灯をつける[消す] turn on [off] a *flashlight*. ▶彼は懐中電灯で私の行く手を照らしてくれた He shone his *flashlight* on my way./His *flashlight* lighted my way.

かいちょう 会長 a president (⚠ 英国では特に株式上場クラブの代表取締役のことをさし、クラブの代表職は chairman と呼ぶのが普通); (会社などの) a chairman (of the board) (働 -men) (⚠ 男女両用. 特に女性を明示する場合は a chairwoman を用いる). • 取締役会長 a board *chairman*. • 彼をゴルフクラブの会長に選ぶ elect him (the) *president* of the golf club. (⚠ 1 人の役職名が補語になるときは通例冠詞無し)

かいちょう 回腸〔解剖〕 the ileum /íliəm/.

かいちょう 快調 • 快調である be in good [*excellent, the best*] *condition*. (⇨調子❶) • エンジンは快調に動いている The engine is running [working] *smoothly*.

かいちょう 海鳥 a seabird.

かいちょう 開帳 图〔仏像の一般公開〕a public exhibition (*of* a Buddhist image).
—— **開帳する** 動〔仏像を一般公開する〕exhibit a Buddhist image;〔賭場(ミ)を開く〕open a gambling house.

かいちょう 害鳥 a bad [harmful] bird.

かいちょく 回勅〔カトリック〕an encyclical letter.

かいちん 開陳 图〔言明〕(a) statement.
—— **開陳する** 動 state [express] (one's views) clearly.

かいつう 開通 图 opening; (やや書) (an) inauguration. • 新しい橋の開通 the *opening* of a new bridge.
—— **開通する** 動 ▶高速道路は一部開通した The expressway *was* partially *opened to* [*for*] *traffic*. ▶来月地下鉄が開通する They will *start* [《書》*inaugurate*] the subway service next month. • 開通式 an opening ceremony [an inauguration (ceremony)] (*of*).

かいづか 貝塚〔考古学〕a (kitchen) midden.

かいつけ 買い付け〔購入〕purchase.

かいつける 買い付ける buy*;《書》purchase.

かいつぶり〔鳥〕a little grebe.

かいつまむ 掻い摘む〔要約する〕sum (-mm-) ... up, summarize;〔概説する〕give* an outline (*of*). • かいつまんで言うと to sum up; (いろいろ話したが、結論は) in short [brief]. ▶かいつまんで君の計画を話してくれ Tell me briefly what your plan is./Give me a *short* [a *brief*] account of your plan.

かいて 買い手〔買う人〕a buyer,《書》a purchaser;〔お客〕a customer. • 買い手市場 a [the] buyers' market.

かいてい 改定 图 (a) revision. • 運賃改定 a *revision* of fares. —— **改定する** 動 revise.

かいてい 改訂 图 (a) revision. —— **改訂する** 動 教科書を改訂する *revise* a textbook. • 改訂(増補)版 a revised (and enlarged) edition.

かいてい 海底 the bottom [bed,〈書〉depths] of the ocean《主に米》[the sea《主に英》]; the seabed; (海底の表面) the ocean floor (⚠ 主に海底描写に用いるやや専門的な語). • 海底の岩を掘り起こす dig up the rocks *on the sea bottom*. ▶船は台湾沖の海底に沈んでいた The ship was lying *on* [*at*] *the bottom of the ocean* off Taiwan. (⇨底③)
• 海底火山 a submarine volcano. • 海底ケーブル a submarine cable. • 海底山脈 a submarine ridge. • 海底トンネル a submarine tunnel. • 海底油田 a submarine oil field.

かいてい 開廷 图 • 現在開廷中です The court *is now sitting* [*in session*].
—— **開廷する** 動 (法廷を開く) open a court; (一定時間審理する) hold a court.

***かいてき 快適** —— **快適な** 形 (体をくつろがせる) comfortable; (人を楽しませる、引きつける) pleasant, nice; (暖かく居心地のよい) cozy. • 快適な部屋 a *comfortable* [a *pleasant*, a *cozy*] room. • 快適な住環境をつくる create a *pleasant* environment to live in. ▶この車は快適な乗り心地だ This car is *comfortable* [*pleasant*] to ride in. ▶このいす[ホテル]は快適だ(= 座り心地[居心地]がいい) I am [feel] *comfortable* in this chair [at this hotel]./This is a *comfortable* chair [hotel].
—— **快適に** 副 comfortably. • 生活を快適にするものの comforts [amenities] of life. (⚠ comforts は家具・冷房設備など, amenities はプール・映画館・ショッピングセンターなど社会的なものをさす) • 快適に暮らす live *in comfort* [*comfortably*].
—— **快適さ** comfort.

がいてき 外的 ❶〔外部の〕external. ❷〔肉体面の〕physical, bodily.
• 外的圧力 external pressure • 外的条件 external conditions. • 外的欲求 bodily needs.

がいてき 外敵 a foreign enemy. • 外敵の侵入 a *foreign invasion*〔攻撃〕attack).

かいてん 回転 图 ❶〔回る[回す]こと〕a turn (⚠ 部分的回転も含む); (軸による) (a) rotation; (軸または他の物のまわりを回る) (a) revolution; (高速の) (a) spin. (⇨回る〔類語〕, 回す) ▶太陽を回る地球の回転(=公転) the *revolution of the earth around the sun*. • (大)回転競技〔スキー〕(the) (giant) *slalom* /slάːləm/. • シュート回転のボール a curveball. • フル回転 (⇨フル回転)
❷〔その他の表現〕 ▶彼は頭の回転が早い He has a quick [a nimble] mind./He is quick-witted. ▶あの店は客の回転がいい That store has a good flow of customers.
—— **回転する〔させる〕** 動 turn(...) (around); rotate; revolve; spin*. (⇨回る, 回す) • ボールを回転させる spin [put spin on] a ball; give a ball spin. ▶そのモーターは毎秒 20 回転していた The motor *was turning* [*spinning*] at 20 revolutions [rotations] a second./The motor *was making* 20 *revolutions* [*rotations*] a second. ▶落水がタービンを回転させる Falling water turns the turbine./《受身》The turbine *is run* [*is operated*, (まれ) *is turned*] by falling water. ▶その車は 2 回転して(= 2 回ひっくり返って)川へ落ちた The car *turned over* twice before falling into the river.
• 回転いす a swivel chair. • 回転運動 a rotary

かいてん motion [movement]. ● 回転儀 (ジャイロスコープ) a gýroscòpe. ● 回転資金 a revolving fund. ● 回転ずし conveyer-belt sushi; sushi served on a conveyer belt. ● 回転ドア a revolving door. ● 回転翼 (ヘリコプターの) rotor blades. (❗通例複数形で) ● 回転レシーブ『バレーボール』turning to one side after returning a ball.

かいてん 開店 图 the opening of a store. ▶本日開店 (掲示) *Opened* today. (❗「10時開店」は *Open* 10 a.m.) ▶開店中 (掲示) *Open*. (❗時に We are *open*. とも) ▶その店は開店休業だ The store is *open*, but there's no business.
── 開店する 動 ▶銀行は9時に開店します Banks *open* (↔*close*) at 9 a.m.

がいでん 外伝 (本伝以外の伝記 [逸話]) a supplementary biography [anecdote].

がいでん 外電 (海外からのニュース電報) a foreign telegram; (海外ニュース) an overseas report, news from overseas [abroad].

かいてんじく 回転軸 『力学』a rotation axis; an axis of rotation (gyration); 〖フィギュアスケートのスピンの〗a pivot; 〖地球などの〗the axis.

かいてんとびら『回転扉』*Revolving Door*. (参考 河野多恵子の小説)

かいてんもくば 回転木馬 a merry-go-round.

ガイド 〖案内人〗a guide. ● 観光ガイド a tourist *guide*. ● 旅行のガイドをする *conduct* a tour. ● ガイド付きで市内観光をする go on [make] a *guided* tour of a city.
● ガイドブック a guide [a guidebook] 《to》.

***かいとう 回答** 图 a reply; an answer; a response. (⇨ 答え)
● 回答者 an answerer; (クイズ番組の) a panelist; (アンケートの) a respondent.

***かいとう 解答** 图 an answer to a question; a solution to [of, for] a problem. (⇨答え) ● 練習問題の解答集 a *key* to exercises. ▶その問題の解答を教えてください Please tell me the (correct) *answer* to the question.
── 解答する 動 answer 《a question》; solve 《a problem》.
● 解答用紙 an ánswer shèet, 《米》an exám pàper.

かいとう 会頭 the president. ● 商工会議所会頭 the *president* of the Chamber of Commerce and Industry.

かいとう 快刀 a sharp sword.
● 快刀乱麻を断つ (見事に難問を解決する) solve a difficult problem successfully; cut the Gordian Knot.

かいとう 快投 图 〖野球〗good [nice, strong] pitching.
── 快投する 動 pitch well.

かいとう 怪盗 a mysterious thief.

かいとう 開頭 图 ● 開頭手術を受ける〖医学〗undergo a craniotomy /krèiníətəmi/.
── 開頭する 動 open one's skull; remove a part of one's skull.

かいとう 解党 the disorganization [dissolution] of a party. (⇨ 結党)
── 解党する 動 dissolve a party.

かいとう 解凍 thawing.
── 解凍する 動 ● 冷凍肉をゆっくり解凍する give enough time to *thaw* (*out*) [*defrost*] frozen meat.

かいどう 会同 图 (会合) a meeting, a gathering, an assembly.
── 会同する 動 meet, gather, assemble.

かいどう 会堂 (公会堂) a hall, an assembly hall; (教会) a church.

かいどう 海棠 〖植物〗an aronia.

かいどう 海道 〖海路〗a sea route; 〖海に沿った海道〗a coast road; a coastal highway.

かいどう 街道 a highway,《英》a highroad. ● アッピア街道 the Appian *Way*. (参考 イタリアの旧街道の一つ) ● オックスフォード街道 the Oxford *Road*. (参考 ロンドンとオックスフォードを結ぶ旧道. 現在の Oxford Street はその一部分) ● 西国街道 the Saigoku *Highway*.

がいとう 外灯 an outdoor lamp [light].

がいとう 外套 an overcoat. (⇨オーバー)

がいとう 街灯 a street light [lamp]. ▶街灯がつき始めた [まだついていた] The *street lights* were coming on [were still on].

がいとう 街頭 the street. ● 街頭でビラをまく give out handbills *on* [*in*] the street.
● 街頭インタビュー a man-in-the-street interview. ● 街頭演説 street [soapbox] oratory. ● 街頭デモ a street demonstration. ● 街頭デモをする take to the streets. ● 街頭募金 street fund-raising.

がいとう 該当 ── 該当する 動 〖項目に入る〗come 《*under*》; 〖適用される〗apply 《*to*》; 〖相当する〗correspond 《*to*》; 〖満たす〗fulfill. ▶書類などの欄に書き入れる「該当事項なし」は "None.") ▶それは刑法第5条に該当する It *comes* [*falls*] *under* Article 5 of the Criminal Code./Article 5 of the Criminal Code *applies to* it. ▶これらの条件に該当する人はだれもいない There is nobody who *fulfills* these conditions.

かいどく 買い得 ▶このコートは買い得だ This coat is a (*good*) *bargain* [*a good buy*].

かいどく 回読 ── 回読する 動 (回し読みする) read 《a book》 in turns; take turns reading 《a book》.

かいどく 解読 ── 解読する 動 (筆跡・暗号などを) decipher /disáifər/; (暗号などを) decode. ● その暗号化された通信を解読する *decipher* a message in code [a coded message]; *decode* a message.

かいどく 害毒 〖害悪〗an evil; 〖被害〗harm. ● 害毒を流す corrupt; poison; exert a bad [an evil, a harmful] influence 《on》; do harm 《to》.

ガイドライン 〖指針〗guidelines. ● 政策のガイドライン *guidelines* on policy.

かいとり 買い取り buying,《書》purchasing; (手形などの) negotiation(s).

かいとる 買い取る buy*,《書》purchase; (人・会社の営業権・株を) buy 《him, a company》out.

かいならす 飼い慣らす tame; (やや書) domesticate.

かいなん 海難 〖難破〗shipwreck; 〖海上の災難〗a sea disaster; a disaster at sea. ● 海難に遭う meet with a *sea disaster*; (難破する) be *shipwrecked*.
● 海難救助 (a) sea rescue; salvage. ● 海難救助する salvage. ● 海難審判 a marine accident inquiry. ● 海難審判庁 the Marine Accidents Inquiry Agency (略 MAIA).

かいなんとう 海南島 〖中国の島〗Hainan /háinɑ́ːn/ Island.

かいにゅう 介入 图 (an) intervention 《in》. ● 軍事介入 armed *intervention*. ● 人道的介入 an act of humanitarian *intervention*. ● 我が国の内政に対する大国の介入 *intervention in* our country's domestic affairs by a major power.
── 介入する 動 ● 内戦に介入する intervene in a civil war. ▶他人のことに介入するな (＝お節介をやくな) Don't *meddle* [*interfere*] *in* other people's affairs. ▶ゼネストを中止させるために政府が介入した

The government *stepped in* to prevent a general strike.

かいにん 解任 名 dismissal; 《書》discharge.
— 解任する 動 dismiss; 《書》dischárge; remove (him) from the post.

かいにん 懐妊 名 pregnancy; (a) conception. (⇨妊娠) ● ご懐妊の兆し signs of *pregnancy*.
— 懐妊する 動 get [become] pregnant; 《書》conceive (a baby).

かいぬし 買い主 a buyer, 《書》a purchaser; (主に不動産の) a vendee (↔vendor).

かいぬし 飼い主 (ペットなどの飼育者) a keeper; (牛・馬などの所有者) an owner. ● 飼い主のない猫 a stray [a homeless] cat. ● その犬は飼い主にかみついた The dog bit its *keeper* [*master*]. ● この犬の飼い主はだれか Who keeps this dog?/Whose dog is this?

かいね the búying 《書》púrchase price. ● 買値を割る drop below the *buying price*.

かいねこ 飼い猫 a pet [a house] cat; one's (own) cat.

*****がいねん** 概念 [[考え]] a concept, (a) conception, an idea. (⚠ 後の語ほど抽象度が低くなる) (⇨考え, 観念) ● 「馬」の概念 the *concept* of "horse". ● 民主主義の概念をつかむ grasp a general *concept* [*conception, idea*] of democracy. ● 概念図 a schematic diagram.

かい 会派 (政治の派閥) a faction (⇨派閥); (宗派) a denomination. ● 二つの院内会派 two *factions* in the House [Diet].

かいば 買い場 〖経済〗 the best time to buy.

かいば 飼い葉 (牛馬の飼料) feed, fodder, forage. ● 飼い葉桶 a manger.

かいはい 改廃 名 reform and abolition 《of laws [systems]》; (再編成) (a) reorganization.
— 改廃する 動 reform [abolish] 《laws [systems]》; reorganize 《a company》.

がいはく 外泊 — 外泊する 動 stay out [be away] overnight. ● 2 日間外泊する *stay out* [*be away*] for two nights.

がいはく 該博 — 該博な 形 ● 該博な(=広い)知識 an *extensive* knowledge 《of》.

かいはくしょく 灰白色 grayish white; light gray.

かいばしら 貝柱 (ホタテガイの) a scallop. (⚠ 料理を表すときは複数形で)

*****かいはつ** 開発 名 development; (資源などの利用) exploitation. ● 宇宙[経済]開発 space [economic] *development*. ● 新製品の開発 the *development* of a new product. ● 土地開発事業 a land *development* project. ● 土地開発業者 a developer. ● 開発が最も遅れている国 the least *developed* countries. ● シベリアの天然資源の開発に協力する help (to) *develop* [*exploit*] natural resources in Siberia.
— 開発する 動 develop; (やや書) exploit. ● 荒地を(宅地・工場用地として)開発する *develop* wasteland. ● 独特の絵画の手法を開発する *develop* a unique technique of painting. ● 開発途上国 a developing country. ● 開発費 start-up cost; development cost.

かいばつ 海抜 ● 海抜 2,000 メートルである be 2,000 meters *above sea level* [*above the sea*]. (⇨標高)

かいはん 改版 名 (改訂) (a) revision; (改訂版) a revision, a revised edition.
— 改版する 動 revise 《a book》.

がいはんぼし 外反母趾 〖医学〗 hallux valgus.

かいひ 会費 a membership fee; dues; 〖会合の費用〗 expenses. ● 毎月会費を払う pay one's *dues* every month. ● 当クラブの年会費は5,000 円です The annual *membership fee* for this club is 5,000 yen. (⚠「5,000 円の年会費」は an annual *membership fee* of 5,000 yen という)

かいひ 回避 — 回避する 動 〖避ける〗 avoid, avert; (怠けて) shirk; (策などを用いて) evade. ● その危機を回避する *avoid* [*avert*] the crisis. ● 責任を回避する *avoid* [*shirk, evade*] one's responsibility. ● 経営側の譲歩でストはどたん場で回避された The concessions made by the management *averted* the strike at the last minute.

かいびかえ 買い控え 名 (控えめの購入) restrained purchasing.
— 買い控えする 動 restrain oneself from purchasing.

かいびゃく 開闢 (世界の始まり) the beginning [creation] of the world. ● 開闢以来のできごと an *unprecedented* event.

かいひょう 開票 名 vote [ballot] counting. ● 開票の結果を公表する publish the results of *vote counting*; publish the election results.
— 開票する 動 count the votes [ballots].
● 開票速報 early returns. ● 開票率 the rate of vote counting.

かいひょう 解氷 名 a thaw. — 解氷する 動 thaw. ● 解氷期 the tháwing sèason.

がいひょう 概評 a general comment 《on》.

かいひん 海浜 a beach; (a) shore; (the) seashore. (⇨海岸, 浜辺)

かいふ 回付 — 回付する 動 circularize 《the letter》.

がいぶ 外部 〖外側〗 the outside, the exterior; 〖組織の外側〗 the outside. ● 建物の外部 the *outside* [*exterior*] of a building. ● 外部からの影響 *exterior* [*external*] influences. ● 外部の者 people on the *outside*; outsiders. ● 外部の意見を聞く obtain an *óutside* opinion. ● この情報が外部に漏れないように十分注意してくれ Be very careful not to let this information leak *out*.

かいふう 海風 a sea breeze 《wind》.

かいふう 開封 ● クリスマスカードを開封で出す send a Christmas card *unsealed*.
— 開封する 動 open 《a letter》; (厳重に封印された文書を) break the seal 《of his will》. ● 彼の手紙を開封せずに送り返す send his letter back *unopened*.

かいふうそう『懐風藻』 Fond Collections of Poetry. 〖参考〗 奈良時代の漢詩集)

*****かいふく** 回復 名 ❶(病気などの) (a) recovery 《from》(⚠ 複数形なし); (もとの状態への) restoration 《to》; (改善) (an) improvement 《in》.
① [~回復] ● 疲労(の)回復 recovery from tiredness [exhaustion, fatigue]. ● 健康の回復 one's *restoration* to health. ● 天候の回復 an *improvement* in the weather.
② [回復が] ● その患者は回復が早い[遅い] The patient is making a quick [a slow] *recovery*.
③ [回復の] ● 回復の見込みのない病気 a desperate [a hopeless] illness. ● 回復の見込みなみない He is beyond [past] *recovery*./There is no hope of his *recovery*. ● 患者の病状に回復のきざしがみえる The patient shows some signs of *recovery*./The patient's condition shows some *improvement*.
④ [回復を] ● 早いご回復をお祈りしています I'm expecting your quick [speedy] *recovery*.
❷ [平和・関係などの復活] restoration; 〖失ったものを取り戻すこと〗 (a) recovery. ● 外交の回復 the *restoration* of diplomatic relations. ● 失地の回復 the *recovery* of lost territory. ● 信頼回

restoration of trust. (⇨信頼)
── 回復する 動 ❶ [病気から、天候・景気などが] recover ((from)); (改善する; よくなる) get* better. ▶彼は回復してきている(=回復に向かっている) He *is recovering from* his illness./He *is getting better*./He *is improving* in health./His health *is improving*. ▶彼は健康を回復した He *recovered* [*regained*] his health./He *was restored to* health. (⇨recover, regain は自力による回復で、regain の方が意味が強い. restore は他の力による回復) ▶彼女は数日すれば回復するでしょう She will be quite well [*all right*] *in* a few days. /(回復に数日かかる) It will take her a few days *to get over* [*recover from*] her illness. ▶天気が回復した The weather *has improved* [*got better*; (上向いた)《話》*picked up*]. ▶不況は一時的なもので経済はまもなく回復した The recession proved temporary and the economy soon *recovered*.
❷ [失ったものを取り戻す] recover, regain; [復活させる] restore. ●視力[聴力]を回復する *recover* [*regain*] one's sight [hearing]. ●意識を回復する *recover* [*regain*] consciousness; *come to* one's senses [oneself]. ●平和[法と秩序]を回復する *restore* peace [*law and order*].

かいふく 開腹 ──開腹手術を受ける undergo a laparotomy /lǽpərətɑ̀mi/.
── 開腹する 動 make an incision through the abdominal wall; [医学] perform a laparotomy.

かいぶつ 怪物 a monster.
●怪物映画 a monster movie.

かいぶん 回文 [回状] a circular notice [letter]; [どちらから読んでも同じになる語句・文] a palindrome 《参考》Madam, I'm Adam. など).

かいぶん 灰分 ash; (食品中の) a mineral.

がいぶん 外聞 [世評] reputation, publicity; [体裁] decency. ●外聞にかかわる(=を傷つける) damage [compromise] one's *reputation*. ●恥も外聞もない do not care what other people (×will) think. ●構う❶ [第1文例]. ●外聞が悪い (不評の) disreputable; (恥ずべき) shameful; (不面目な) scandalous. ●外聞を重んじる think much of one's *reputation*.

かいぶんしょ 怪文書 a mysterious [a dubious] document; (人を中傷する文書) a libelous [a defamatory] document.

がいぶんぴつ 外分泌 external secretion.
●外分泌腺 [生理] an exocrine gland.

かいへい 皆兵 ●国民皆兵制 the system of universal conscription.

かいへい 開閉 图 opening and shutting [closing].
── 開閉する 動 ●ドアを開閉する *open and shut* [*close*] a door.
●開閉器 a switch. ●開閉機 (遮断機) a (crossing) gate (barrier). ●開閉橋 a swing bridge; a drawbridge.

かいへいたい 海兵隊 《米》the Marine Corps /mərí:n kɔ̀ːr/, the Marines, 《英》the Royal Marines.

がいへき 外壁 an outer wall.

かいへん 改変 图 (a) change, (an) alteration. ●制度の改変 a *change* of a system.
── 改変する 動 ●教育内容を改変する *change* [*alter*] the contents of education.

かいへん 改編 图 a reorganization; (再編集) reedition. ── 改編する 動 reorganize (a system)*; reedit (a book).

かいべん 快便 regular bowel movements.

かいへんのこうけい 『海辺の光景』 *A View by the Sea*. 《参考》安岡章太郎の小説)

*かいほう 開放 ── 開放的な 形 (広々した) open; (人が率直な) frank, 《ざっくばらんな》outspoken.
── 開放する 動 open. ●庭園を一般に開放する *open* one's garden *to* the public. (⇨公開) ●開放厳禁《ドアの掲示》Don't *leave the door open*./(Please) close the door after you.

*かいほう 解放 图 [束縛・義務などからの] (a) release ((from)); [自由にすること] liberation; [奴隷からの] emancipation. ●仕事[苦痛]からの解放 a *release from* duty [suffering]. ●女性解放 the *liberation* [*emancipation*] of women. (⇨「女性解放運動」は women's lib(eration) [W-L]. しかし、今では the women's movement の方が普通) ▶彼女は解放感を思う存分味わった She felt an enormous sense of *release*. ▶グライダー飛行は私にすごく解放感を与えてくれる Gliding gives me a terrific feeling of *freedom*.
── 解放する 動 release, free, set* ... free (!後の方ほど口語的); emancipate; [書] liberate. ●人質を解放する *release* hostages. ▶彼を仕事[責任]から解放する *release* him *from* the responsibility [*job*]. ●奴隷を解放する *emancipate* [*liberate*, *free*] slaves; *set* slaves *free*. ●オートメーションで人間は重労働から解放された Automation *freed* men *from* doing laborious jobs.
会話 「四六時中仕事をしてるんでしょう」「平日はね. でも日曜日は仕事から解放されてるよ」"I suppose you're working all the time." "On weekdays. But on Sundays, I'm *free*."

かいほう 介抱 图 [病人やけが人の世話をすること] (⇨世話)
── 介抱する 動 ●酔っ払いを介抱する *look after* [*take care of*] a drunken man.

かいほう 会報 (学会の報告) a bulletin /búlitn/; (報告) a report.

かいほう 回報 (返事) a reply; (回覧状) a circular (letter).

かいほう 快方 ▶患者は快方に向かっている The patient *is getting better* [(回復する) *is recovering*,《話》*is on the mend*]./(病状が好転している) The patient's condition is *taking a turn for the better*.

かいほう 解法 a method [(例) an instance] of solving; (説明) an explanation; (答え) an answer. ●その問題の解法を教えてください Please show me *how to solve* the problem.

かいぼう 解剖 图 [人体・動植物の] (a) dissection; [人の死体の] an autopsy ((on)), a post(-)mortem (examination). ●ネズミの解剖 a *dissection* of a mouse. ▶解剖の結果彼は毒殺されたことが分かった The *autopsy* [*postmortem*] showed that he had been poisoned.
── 解剖(を)する 動 ●殺された男の解剖をする carry out [do, perform] an *autopsy* [a *postmortem*] on the murdered man. ●カエルを解剖する *dissect* a frog.
●解剖学 anatomy. ●解剖学者 an anatomist. ●解剖教室 a dissection laboratory. ●解剖図 an anatomy chart.

がいぼう 外貌 an [one's] (outward) appearance; one's looks.

かいぼつ 海没 图 sinking in the sea. ── 海没する 動 sink in the sea; (船が沈没する) founder.

かいぼり 掻い掘り 图 (排水) drainage.
── 掻い掘りする 動 drain ((a pond)).

かいまく 開幕 图 (開始の) the opening. (⇨開演) ●午後6時開幕 The *curtain rises* [*goes up*] at 6 p.m. ── 開幕する 動 open.
●開幕時間 the cúrtain time. ●開幕戦 an open-

かいまくる 買いまくる buy* (gold) as much as one can*; (話) go* on a buying binge.

かいまみる 垣間見る (ちらりと見る) catch* [get*, have*] a glimpse 《of》; (のぞき見る) peep 《at, over》. ●(…を)カーテンの間から垣間見る peep 《at …》 through the curtains.

かいみょう 戒名 a posthumous /pástʃəməs/ Buddhist name.

かいみん 快眠 图 a sound sleep. ── **快眠する** 動 sleep soundly [very well].

かいむ 会務 (会の事務) business of a club [society].

かいむ 海霧 a sea fog.

かいむ 皆無 (何もないこと) nothing. ▶欠席者は皆無だった Nobody was absent. ▶それについて私たちでできることはほとんどない、いや皆無だ There is little or nothing we can do about it.

がいむ 外務 foreign affairs.
●**外務省** the Ministry of Foreign Affairs; the Foreign Ministry. ●**外務大臣** the Minister for Foreign Affairs; the Foreign Minister. (❗(1) 米国の国務長官[省] (the Secretary [Department] of State), 英国の Foreign Secretary [Office] に相当. (2)「麻生外務大臣」は Foreign Minister Aso)

かいめい 改名 图 ●改名届を出す(=登記する) register one's change of name. (❗この場合, name は通例無冠詞)
── **改名する** 動 change one's name 《from A to B》.

かいめい 解明 图 〖解決〗(a) solution 《to, of》.
── **解明する** 動 ●問題を解明する(解決する) solve a problem; (細かく調べて解く) unravel a problem; (真相を突き止める) get to the bottom of a problem. ▶マヤ人の初期の歴史は依然として解明されていない(=不明なままである) The early history of the Mayans remains obscure [in the dark].

かいめつ 壊滅 图 〖完全なる破壊〗complete [utter] destruction; 〖全滅〗annihilation /ənàɪəléɪʃən/. ●核戦争による世界の壊滅 the annihilation of the world by (a) nuclear war. ●壊滅的打撃を受ける[与える] suffer [give] a crushing blow. ▶壊滅的な地震が兵庫県南部を襲った A devastating [(話) A killer] earthquake hit the Southern Hyogo Prefecture. (❗killer は形容詞的用法で「致命的な」の意)
── **壊滅させる** 動 destroy (it) completely; annihilate /ənáɪəleɪt/.

かいめん 海面 sea level (❗海抜などを測る基準); the surface of the sea. ●海面下 1,000 メートル one thousand meters below sea(-)level [the surface of the sea].

かいめん 海綿 (a) sponge /spándʒ/.
●**海綿動物** a sponge; 〖動物〗a poriferan.

がいめん 外面 (表面, うわべ) a surface. ●(見掛け, 外見) ── **外面的な** 形 surface [superficial] 《kindness》.

かいめんかっせいざい 界面活性剤 〖化学〗a surface-active agent; surfactant.

かいもく 皆目 (not …) at all. (⇨全く).

かいもどし 買い戻し buyback, repurchase. ●**株式の買い戻し** stock buyback [repurchase].

かいもどす 買い戻す buy* … back. ▶彼に売ったバイクは買い戻したい I want to buy back the motorbike I sold him.

かいもとめる 買い求める buy, purchase. (⇨買う). ▶もうすぐお買い求めいただけるようになります It is just about to become available.

***かいもの 買い物** ●〖行為〗shopping. ●**買い物上手な人** a smart [a good] shopper. ▶私は今日たくさん[ちょっと]買い物がある I have a lot of [some] shopping to do today. ▶彼らは大阪[デパート]へ買い物に行った They went shopping in Osaka [at a department store]. (❗×… went shopping to Osaka [to a department store] とはいわない)(=買い物をするために) They went to Osaka [a department store] to shop. ▶買い物に[=店に]行くのならパンを買って来てくださる? If you go (out) to the stores, can you get me some bread, please? ▶買い物はみんな済ませた(=欲しいものはみな買った) I've bought everything I wanted.
❷〖購入した物〗《書》a purchase (❗計画的で大量に買われた物. しばしば複数形で用いる), 《集合的》shopping; 〖安い買い物〗a bargain, a buy. ▶買い物に行ったとき、高価な買い物をしないように注意する必要がある When we go shopping, we should be cautious about making expensive purchases. ▶彼女は買い物袋を 2 袋持ってエレベーターを待っていた She had two bags of shopping and was waiting for the elevator. ▶買い物してきた? Did you get the shopping? ▶これはよい買い物だ This is a good bargain [buy].
── **買い物(を)する** 動 do the [one's] shopping; shop. ▶彼女はその店で 1 週間分の買い物をした She did her shopping for the [a] week at that store. (❗(1) … did the week's shopping … ともいえる. (2) go shopping が本格的な買い物を暗示するのに対して, do shopping はちょっとした買い物をいう)
●**買い物客** a shopper; (売り手にとっての) a customer. ●**買い物袋** a shópping《米》[a cárrier《英》] bàg.

かいもん 開門 the opening of the gate.
── **開門する** 動 ▶城は 9 時に開門する The castle opens the gate at 9:00.

がいや 外野 the outfield. ●**外野を守る** play (in the) outfield. ●**外野フライで 1 点取る** score a run on a fly to the outfield. ●**前進の外野を越す二塁打を打つ** hit a double over the drawn-in outfield. ▶外野へ飛んだ打球は一つもなかった Not a ball was hit out of the infield.
●**外野手** an outfielder. ●**外野手を右に寄せる** shift the outfielders to right. ●**外野席** the outfield stands [(屋根なしの) bleachers].

かいやく 改訳 图 a revision of a translation.
── **改訳する** 動 revise a translation; retranslate.

かいやく 解約 图 (a) cancellation.
── **解約する** 動 ●**契約を解約する** cancel [dissolve] a contract. ●**銀行口座を解約する**(=閉じる) close a bank account.

かいゆ 快癒 a complete [a full] recovery 《from illness》. (⇨ 全快)

かいゆう 会友 a (fellow) member of a society [an association].

かいゆう 回遊 图 (周遊) an excursion; (魚の) (a) migration.
── **回遊する** 動 make an excursion 《to the seashore, into the country, around Kyoto》.
●**回遊券** 《米》an excursion ticket, 《英》a round-trip ticket. ●**回遊魚** a migratory fish.

がいゆう 外遊 图 a trip abroad. (❗×an abroad trip は不可) ●**外遊中** be abroad.
── **外遊する** 動 go [travel] abroad.

かいよう 海洋 the sea; the ocean. (⇨ 海) ▶廃油の海洋投棄は地球環境を破壊している Dumping of waste oil at sea has damaged the global envi-

かいよう ronment. ● 海洋学 oceanography. ● 海洋学者 an oceanographer. ● 海洋気候 an oceanic climate; a maritime climate. ● 海洋気象台 a marine meteorological observatory. ● 海洋投棄規制条約 the Sea Dumping Regulation Treaty.

かいよう 潰瘍 an ulcer /ʌlsər/. ● 胃[十二指腸]潰瘍ができている[できる] have [get, develop] a stomach [a duodenal] ulcer.
── 潰瘍性の 形 ulcerative 《diseases》.

がいよう 外洋 the open sea. (⇨外海) ● 外洋生物 the oceanic living things. ● 外洋船 an ocean liner.

がいよう 概要 an outline 《of, for》. (⇨概略, 要約)

がいようやく 外用薬 (a) medicine for external use [application].

かいらい 傀儡 《操り人形》a puppet; 《手先》《やや書》a tool.
● 傀儡政権 a puppet government.

がいらい 外来 ── 外来の 形 《外国の》foreign; 《輸入された》imported. ● 外来の思想 an idea of foreign origin; an imported idea.
● 外来患者 an óutpàtient 《↔ínpàtient》. ● 外来語 (借用語) a loanword 《from French》. ● 外来種 a foreign species. (🔒 単複同形)

かいらく 快楽 《満足からくる》pleasure; 《楽しむこと》enjoyment. (🔒 ともに具体的な事柄を表すときは ⓒ) ● 快楽主義者 an epicurean /èpikjuərí(ː)ən/. ● 快楽を求める xa《a》pleasure.

かいらん 回覧 circulation.
── 回覧する 動 ● その手紙を彼らに回覧する circulate the letter 《pass the letter around》 to them (🔒 後の方が口語的); 《次々に回す》pass the letter on to them. (⇨回す)
● 回覧板 a notice for circulation; a circular notice.

かいらん 壊乱 (道徳的堕落) corruption.
── 壊乱する 動 corrupt. ▶ この種の映画は風俗を壊乱する恐れがある It is feared that this kind of movie corrupts public morals.

かいり 乖離 图 (疎遠) (an) estrangement 《from》; alienation 《from》.
── 乖離する 動 become estranged [alienated] 《from》. ▶ 残念ながら現実の政治は世論から乖離している Regrettably, realistic politics is estranged [alienated] from public opinion.

かいり 海里 a nautical [a sea] mile.

かいりき 怪力 superhuman (ヘラクレスのような) 《書》 Herculean /hɚːrkjəliːən/ strength.

かいりつ 戒律 《宗教的教え》《やや書》religious precepts. (🔒 precept は /príːsept/ と読む) ● 戒律を守る[破る] follow [break, violate] the precepts of one's religion.

がいりゃく 概略 an outline 《of, for》; 〖要約〗a summary 《of》. ● 概略を述べる give 《him》 an outline [a summary]. ● 論文の概略を書く write an outline for one's thesis. ● 彼は私たちに販売計画の概略を説明した He outlined a sales campaign to us. ● 概略すると, この小説は悲恋物語だ Roughly 《speaking》, the novel is a tale of tragic love.

かいりゅう 海流 an ocean [a sea] current. ▶ 千島海流の Chishima Current. ● 彼は幸運にも海流にのって大洗海岸に流れついた He was lucky and was carried along by the sea current to the Oarai Coast.

***かいりょう** 改良 图 (an) improvement 《of, in, on》; 〖改革〗(a) reform. ● 輸送の改良 the improvement of the transportation system. ● 国字の改良 the reform of the Japanese script. ● (家畜の) 改良種 an improved [a select] breed. ● 新しい車は古い型の改良型だ The new car is an improvement on [xof, xin] the old one. (🔒 「…より改良したもの」の意では on をとる) ● その計画には改良の余地がある[ない; 大いにある] There is some [no; much] room for improvement in the plan. (🔒 「改良[善]の余地」の意では常に Ⓤ) ● 彼は機械にいくらかの改良を加えた He made several improvements on the machine.
── 改良する 動 improve; 《方法などにさらに改良を加える》improve on [upon].... ● 機械を改良する improve a machine. ● 従来のやり方を改良する improve on [upon] the traditional method.

がいりん 外輪 《外側の輪》an outer ring; 《車輪の》a rim.
● 外輪山 the outer rim of a volcanic crater. ● 外輪船 a paddle wheeler [steamer]; 《米》a side-wheeler.

かいれい 回礼 《礼に回ること》a round of complimentary visits [calls]. ● 年始の回礼をする make [pay] New Year's calls.

かいろ 回路 《電気》a circuit. ● 集積回路 an integrated circuit 《略 I.C.》.

かいろ 海路 ▶ 海路別府へ行く go to Beppu by sea 《船で》 by boat, by ship]. ● 船 [類語], ③) ● 海路ハワイに向かう sail for Hawaii.

かいろ 懐炉 a (pocket) body warmer. ● 使い捨てかいろ a disposable body warmer. ● かいろを腰に当てている carry a body warmer against one's lower back.

カイロ 〖エジプトの首都〗Cairo /káiərou/.

がいろ 街路 a street; an avenue. (⇨道 ❶)
● 街路樹 a street [a roadside] tree. ● 街路樹のある通り a tree-lined street; a street lined with trees.

かいろう 回廊 〖廊下〗a corridor, 《米》a hall (🔒《米》では後の方が普通); 〖建物の外側の屋根のついた歩廊〗a gallery.

かいろうどうけつ 偕老同穴 ▶ 偕老同穴の契りを結ぶ《夫婦として長く連れ添う約束をする》promise to live together harmoniously until death parts them.

カイロプラクティック 〖脊椎指圧療法〗chiropractic /káiərəpræktik/ treatment. (🔒 関連) その療法師 a chiropractor)

がいろん 概論 〖概観〗a survey 《of》; 〖概説〗an outline 《of》; 〖入門〗an introduction 《to》. ● 英文学概論 an introduction to English literature.

***かいわ** 会話 图 (a) conversation; (a) talk. (🔒 conversation は話のやりとりを強調する語. talk が方一般的に. ⇨話 ❶) ● 会話体 a conversational style. ● 会話文 coversational 《English》 sentences. ● 英会話集 a book of English conversations [dialogues]. ● 英会話を学ぶ learn English conversation [conversational English]; learn how to speak English. ● 英会話が得意である be good at speaking English. (🔒 be good at English conversation では「会話の駆け引き・会話術にすぐれている」の意) ● 私は会話を通してその言葉を覚えた I have conversationally learned the language. / I picked up the language through conversation.
── 会話する 動 talk [speak] 《with, to》 (⇨話す ⑥); have a conversation [a talk] 《with》.

かいわい 界隈 (近所) a neighborhood, 《書》vicinity. ▶ この界隈では in this neighborhood; around here. ● 道頓堀界隈を案内する show 《him》 around the Dotonbori area.

かいわれだいこん 貝割れ大根 〖植物〗white radish

かいわん 怪腕 ●彼はコンピュータの販売競争の分野で怪腕を振るった He displayed his *marvelous* [*remarkable*] *skill* in the field of sales competition for computers.

かいん 下院 the Lower House; (米国の) the House (of Representatives); (英国の) the (House of) Commons. ●後の二つは単・複両扱い
●**下院議員** a member of the Lower House; (米国の) a Representative, a Congressman [(女性) a Congresswoman]; (英国の) a member of the House of Commons, a Member of Parliament 《略 an M.P.》.

:かう 買う

WORD CHOICE 買う

buy 主に安価な商品・物品を買うこと．通例くだけた文脈で用い，しばしば [want, would like] を伴続する．●切符を買うお金を持っていない We don't have the money to *buy* the ticket.

purchase 主に高価な商品を正式の手続きをふまえて購入すること．●その土地を買う *purchase* the land.

頻度チャート

buy ████████████████
purchase ███
    20 40 60 80 100 (%)

❶【購入する】buy*; 〖話〗get* ●くだけた会話の文脈から明らかな場合に，しばしば buy の代わりに用いる; purchase /pɚ́rtʃəs/．●父が買った時計 a watch *bought* by my father．(● a watch which was bought by my father の略)

① 《…を買う》●たばこ屋にたばこを買いに行かせる send *(him)* to the tobacco shop *for* some cigarettes. ●私はあまり高いものは(=を)買えない I *can't afford* anything very expensive.（● afford は「買う余裕がある」という意で通例否定文・疑問文で can, could, be able to とともに用いる）●ぼくは電車の切符を買うお金も持っていないんだ．それで電話したってわけ I'm phoning because I have no money *for* the train ticket.

会話「彼は新車を買ったばかりなんだよ」「どこのメーカーのを買ったの」"He's just *bought* a new car." "What make *has* he *got*?"

② 《人に B 〖物〗を買う》buy* 〖get*〗A B; buy* 〖get*〗B for A. (● 前方の語順はBに，後の方の語順はAに重点を置いた言い方) ●美津子はお母さんに新しいスーツを買ってもらった《受身》Mitsuko *was bought* a new suit by her mother.(●(1) 「美津子」に重点を置いた言い方．×A new suit was bought Mitsuko by her mother. とはいえない．(2) このような受身文はぎこちないのであまり用いられない．次例も同様) ●次郎は新しい辞書を父に買ってもらった《受身》A new dictionary was bought *for* Jiro by his father. (● 「新しい辞書」に重点を置いた言い方．for の省略は不可) ●自分のが(=に)スカーフを1枚買っただけで I only *bought* a scarf *for myself*.

会話「息子さんに何を買ってあげましたか」「時計を買ってやりました」"What did you *buy* your son?" "I *bought* him a watch."(●(1) watch を特に強めて A watch, I *bought* him. (時計をね，買ってやったんだよ)ともいえる．(2) ×I bought a watch for him. は不適．

会話「だれにこの靴を買ってあげたのですか」「トムに買ってやりました」"Who did you *buy* these shoes *for*?" "I *bought* them [the shoes] *for* Tom."(●(1) こ

の答えとして ×I bought Tom them [the shoes]. は不適．(2) Tom を強めて, For Tom, I *bought* them [the shoes]. (トムにね，買ってやったんですよ)ともいえる)

③《A 〖物〗にB 〖物〗を買う》buy* A for B. ●この部屋に新しいカーテンを買わなくてはならない We must *buy* a new curtain *for* this room. (● この場合 ×We must buy this room a new curtain. の構文は不可)

④《(購入先) 〖から〗買う》●自動販売機でコーヒーを買う *get* coffee *from* [*out of*] a (vending) machine. ●彼女は食料品店で米を買った She *bought* rice *from* the grocer [*at* the grocer's]. (● buy に続く購入先が店の場合は前置詞は at，人・会社の場合は from を用いる) ●その店で何か買ってくるものある? Do you *need* anything *from* the store?

会話「ツアーのチケットはどこで買えますか」「ホテルか観光案内所で買えます」"Where can I *get* tickets *for* tours *(from)*?" "You can *get* them *in* hotels or information centers." (● from を省略する方が口語的)

⑤《(価格)で買う》●彼はトマトを安い[高い]値段で買った He *bought* [*got*] tomatoes *at* a low [a high] price. (● 次例より普通)/He *bought* [*got*] tomatoes cheap [dear]. (● cheaply [dearly] とはあまりいわない) ●彼は鉛筆を1ダース1ドルで買った He *bought* pencils *at* [*for*] a dollar a dozen.(● at は割合, for は交換を示す) ●私はこの機械を20ドルで買った I *bought* this machine *for* [×*at*] twenty dollars. (● 価格の後に「…につき」という単位が示されていない場合は for のみ可)/I paid twenty dollars *for* this machine. ●それいくらで買ったの? How much did you *give* [*pay*] *for* it? ●彼はその指輪を100万円で買うと言った He *offered* one million yen *for* the ring.

⑥《(手段・道具)で買う》●金で何でも買える You can *buy* anything *with* money./《(物が主語)》Money can *buy* anything. ●50ドルで(=出せば)あのブラウスが買えるでしょう Fifty dollars will *buy* that blouse.

❷【評価する】●私は君の友情をとても高く買っている(=評価している) I *value* your friendship very much. ●私は彼を高く買っている I *think highly* [*well*, ×*much*] *of* him. (● much は通例否定文で: 彼をあまり高く買っていない I *don't think much of* him.)/I *have a good* [*a high*] *opinion of* him.

かう 支う ●つっかい棒をかう prop 《a wall》; support 《a wall》with a prop. ●支える

かう 飼う ●(ペットなどを) have*, (ペットや家畜などを) keep*; (家畜を大きくなるまで育てる) raise, rear; (繁殖させる目的で) breed*. ●豚を飼う *raise* [*rear*, *breed*, *keep*] pigs. ●彼は犬を飼っている He *has* [*keeps*] a dog. ●彼女はかごの中でカナリアを2羽飼っている She *keeps* two canaries in a cage. (● 場所を示すときは keep を用いる)

ガウス 〖電磁単位〗a gauss 《記号 G》.

カウチポテト 〖スナックを食べながらテレビばかり見ている人〗《話・軽蔑的》a couch potato.

カウボーイ a cowboy.
●カウボーイハット a cówboy hàt.

かうん 家運 the fortunes of a family. ●家運が隆盛に向かいますように I hope the *fortunes of* my *family* will change for the better.

ガウン a gown; (部屋着，化粧着) 《米》a (bath)robe, 《英》a dressing gown.

カウンセラー a counselor.

カウンセリング counseling. ●児童相談所でカウンセリングを受ける receive [*get*] *counseling* at the Consultation [Counseling] Center for Children.

カウンター 〖テーブル、台〗a counter; 〖ボクシングの〗a cóunterpunch; a counter. ▶カウンターで支払う pay at the *counter*.
- カウンターアタック 〖スポーツ〗a counter-attack.
- カウンターカルチャー cóuntercùlture.

カウンターオファー 〖貿易での修正申し込み〗a counter offer.

カウンターテナー 〖音楽〗a countertenor.

カウンターパート 〖対応相手〗a counterpart.

カウント ❶〖野球〗a count. 〖参考〗(1) 英語ではボールを先にストライクを後にいう。(2) 日本語で「ボールカウント」ということもあるが英語では単に count という。▶フルカウント a full *count*. ●カウントを不利にする fall [get] behind (in) the *count*. ●若いカウントで打つ swing early in the *count*. ●(投手が)カウントをツーワンに持ち込む run the *count* to one and two. ●ワンツーのカウントで走る run on the count of two balls and one strike. ▶カウントはツーストライクワンボールだ One ball and two strikes is the *count*./ The *count* is one and two. ▶カウントはツーツーの五分になった The *count* leveled at two and two.
❷〖ボクシング〗a count. ●カウントアウトする count 《him》 out.

カウントダウン a countdown. ▶あと10分でロケット打ち上げのカウントダウンが始まる The *countdown to [for]* the rocket launch will begin in ten minutes./They will begin *counting down to* rocket blast-off in ten minutes.

かえ 替え 〖取り替え、着替え〗a change; 〖代わりをする物[人]〗a substitute 《*for*》. ●替えズボン (予備の) *spare* pants; an *extra* pair of pants. ●肌着の替えを持って行く take a *change* of underwear (with one).
● 替え芯(しん) (ボールペンなどの) a refill.

かえうた 替え歌 (もじった歌) a parody. ●その歌の替え歌を作る make a *parody* of the song; parody the song.

かえぎ 替え着 ⇒着替え

かえし 返し ❶〖返すこと〗return. (⇒お返し)
❷〖波・風・地震などの〗an aftershock.

かえしぬい 返し縫い a backstitch.

かえしわざ 返し技 〖柔道〗《use》a counter technique.

:かえす 返す ❶〖返却する〗return, give* ... back (〖後の方が口語的の〗, (返しに行く〖来る〗) take* 〖bring*〗... back; 〖金銭を〗repay*, pay* ... back (〖後の方が口語的の〗; 〖元の位置に〗put* ... back, 〖書〗replace, 〖やや書〗restore. ▶その本を図書館に返す *return [take back]* the book to the library. (〖図書館側から言う場合は return 〖bring back〗... となる〗 ▶拾い物を持ち主に返す *give back [restore]* what is found *to* its owner. ▶鍵(かぎ)を返してくれ *Give [Bring]* the key *back* to me. ▶*Give [Bring] back* the key to me. ともいえるが (まれ)// *Give [Bring]* me *back* the key. (〖*Give [Bring]* me the key *back*. ともいえる〗/*Return* the key (*back*) *to* me 〖〖英〗 me the key〗. (〖返してほしい〗I want the key *back*. ▶彼は銀行に借金を返した He *paid* his loan *back* to the bank./He *paid* the bank *back* his loan. (〖銀行側からは借金には his debt とはしない〗 ▶そのお金は返します I'll *repay* you the money [the money *to* you] tomorrow./I'll *let* you *have* the money *back* tomorrow./(〖You can have the money *back* tomorrow. ともいえる〗 ▶コップを棚に返しなさい *Put* the glass *back* 〖*Return* the glass〗 on its shelf. ▶借金を全部返すのに10年かかった It took ten years to *pay off* all my debts. ▶ちちを

かえせ、ははをかえせ Give back my father, give back my mother. (〖参考〗峠三吉「平和への誓い」中の言葉)
〖会話〗「カメラをいつ〖いつまでに〗返していただけますか」「あす〖あと2,3日したら〗お返しします」 "When 〖How soon〗 can I *have* my camera *back*?" "(You can *have* it *back*) tomorrow 〖in a couple of days〗."
❷〖報いる〗repay*; return. ▶恩をあだで返す *return* evil for good. (⇒恩 〖成句〗) ▶私はあなたにお返しできないほどのご恩を受けています I owe you more than I can *repay* 〖×*pay*〗. ▶彼が彼女にほほえみかけたので彼女はほほえみ返した He smiled and she smiled *back*./She *returned* his smile. ▶彼の言うことには返す言葉もない I don't know how to *answer* his words.

かえす 反す (裏返す) turn 《one's pocket》 inside out; (ひっくり返す) turn ... over. ●オムレツをかえす *turn* 〖*flip*〗 an omelet *over*.

かえす 帰す、還す make*, let*... go back 《*to*》(〖 make は無理やり帰す、let は許可して帰してやること)〗; get*... back 《*to*》. ▶その子供たちを家に帰らせる *let* the children *go home*; (送り届ける) *send* the children *home*. ▶走者を還す bring in [home] a runner; bring a runner across; drive in a runner. ▶6時までに帰してくれますか Can you *get* us *back* by six o'clock?

かえす 孵す hatch. ●ひな〖卵〗をかえす *hatch* a chick 〖an egg〗.

かえすがえす 返す返す ▶あの時に軽率な約束をしたことがかえすがえす(=非常に)悔やまれる How I regret making such a rash promise at that time. ▶〖!〗 It is much to be regretted that I made such .... (〖ともいえる. 前の方が口語的〗)

かえだま 替え玉 (代わりをする人) a substitute; (ラーメンなどの) a ball of cooked noodles without soup.
● 替え玉をする substitute (oneself) 《*for*》; act as a *substitute* 《*for*》. ▶彼の替え玉として受験する take the exam for him as a *substitute*.

かえち 替え地 (土地を取り替えること) exchanging land; (取り替えた土地) exchanged land.

かえって 却って ❶〖反対に〗(それどころか) on the contrary; (...しないで) instead of 《*doing*》; far from 《*doing*》. (⇒反対) ▶雨はやむどころかかえって強くなった *Instead of* stopping, the rain got heavier 〖increased〗. ▶私が彼を助けようと思ってしたことがかえって(=皮肉にも)彼を窮地に立たせるはめになった My attempt to help him *ironically* ended by putting him in a difficult position.
〖会話〗「ジョギングは健康にいいんじゃないんですか」「とんでもない、かえって疲れるだけですよ」 "Isn't jogging good for the health?" "On the ＼*contrary!* It only makes you tired."
〖会話〗「この包装は省かせていただいてよろしいでしょうか」「ええ、かえってありがたいです」 "Would you mind if I saved 〖《話》save〗 wrapping this?" "No. *In* ＼*fact*, I appreciate it." (〖!〗 no と答えたあとで、前の否定の内容をさらに強調するためのつなぎ語 (⇒それどころか))
❷〖むしろ〗rather than ... (⇒むしろ); 〖なおさら〗all 〖so much〗 the+比較級 《*for*, *because*》. ▶私の方こそおわびしなければなりません It is for me *rather than* for you to apologize. ▶転地がかえって彼には悪かった A change of air did him more harm than good./He was so much *the worse for* a change of air. ▶彼女には欠点があるのでかえって気に入っている I like her *all the better for* her faults 〖*because* she has faults〗.

かえで 楓 〖植物〗(木) a maple (tree); (材木) maple; (葉) a maple leaf (覆 leaves).

かえば 替え刃 a spare razor blade.

かえらぬ 帰らぬ (⇨帰る〖成句〗)

かえり 返り ❶〖物が返ってくること〗return.
❷〖元の状態[地位]に戻ること〗coming back to one's former situation [post].
❸〖返事〗an answer, a reply.

かえり 帰り (a) return. (⇨帰る) ▶帰りの旅[切符] a return trip [ticket]. (!〖英〗では往復旅行[切符]を意味する)(⇨往復) ▶夫の帰りを待つ wait for one's husband to return [come home]. ▶帰りを急ぐ hurry back [home]. ▶学校からの帰りに彼らをちょっと訪ねた I dropped in on him on my way home [back] from school. ▶父は昨夜帰りが遅かった My father came home late [was late (coming) home] last night. ▶今日は帰りが早いのね You're home early today. ▶帰りはバスにしよう I'll go home [back] by bus.
●帰り新参 a person who works again at a place where he used to.

かえりうち 返り討ち ●返り討ちにあう be beaten by a person on whom one seeks to revenge oneself.

かえりがけ 帰り掛け ▶帰りがけに(=ちょうど帰ろうとしていたとき)校門で校長先生に会って話しかけられた Just as I was leaving school, I met the principal at the school gate and was spoken to by him. ▶帰りがけに(=帰る途中で)必ずクリーニング屋さんに寄って洗濯物を取ってきてね Don't forget to drop in at the laundry and pick up the clothes on your way home.

かえりぎわ 帰り際 ▶帰り際(=帰りがけ)に校門で校長先生に会って話しかけられた (⇨帰り掛け)

かえりざき 返り咲き ❶〖二度咲き〗a second bloom.
❷〖復活〗a comeback. ▶彼は政界への返り咲きをねらっている He is planning his comeback to the political world.

かえりざく 返り咲く make* a comeback; 〖取り戻す〗regain. ▶舞台に返り咲く make a stage comeback. 〖stage a comeback (=再び咲くことを目指して舞台に立つ)の意)▶前ヘビー級チャンピオンは見事に返り咲いた The former heavyweight champion has made a successful comeback. ▶彼は大関に返り咲いた He regained the rank of ozeki.

かえりじたく 帰り支度 ▶帰り支度をしている時に彼が話しかけてきた He spoke to me when I was preparing to go home. ▶帰り支度をしなさい Get ready to go home [to leave].

かえりち 返り血 ▶返り血を浴びる be stained with the blood rushing from another person's wound.

***かえりみる 顧みる, 省みる** ▶〖振り返る〗(⇨振り返る❶);〖回顧する〗look back on ...;〖反省する〗reflect (on);〖気にかける〗take* notice of .... ▶身の危険を顧みずに regardless of the danger. ▶家族を顧みない neglect one's family. ▶彼らは私の忠告を顧みなかった They took no notice of my advice./(無視された) My advice was ignored by them. ▶彼は人の気持ちを顧みない He has [shows] no regard for the feelings of others. ▶我が学生時代を顧みると隔世の感がある Looking back on our school days, it seems as if they were a century ago.

:かえる 代える, 換える, 替える ❶〖交換する〗change; exchange; 〖古い物などを取り替える〗replace. (⇨交換する, 取り替える) ▶指輪を金に換える exchange a ring for money. (!この意では ×change, ×turn は不可) ●1,000円札を100円硬貨10枚に[と]替える change a 1,000-yen bill into [for] ten 100-yen coins; exchange a 1,000-yen bill for ten 100-yen coins. ●かみそりの刃を替える change [×exchange] a razor blade; replace the razor blade (with [by] a new one). ▶彼女は服を替えに部屋へ入った She went into her room to change (her dress). ▶彼はよく職業を換える He often changes [shifts] jobs. (!複数形に注意) ▶部屋を替えてください I'd like to change my room. ▶このソファーはベッドにも替えられる This sofa is convertible into a bed.
❷〖代用する〗súbstitute; 〖代わりをする〗replace, take* the place of .... ▶バターをマーガリンに代える substitute margarine for butter; replace butter with [by] margarine. ▶どんな大金も人命には換えられない A man's life cannot be bought with any amount of money.

:かえる 変える 〖変化させる〗change; alter; (物の構造などを少し) modify; (別の物に) turn; 〖改正する〗reform.

> **使い分け** change 規則・外観・内容などを全面的に変えること。
> alter 作法・様式・方法などを部分的に変えること。
> reform 見かけが変わるぐらい大幅に改変すること。しばしば, 政治改革・制度改革などを含意する。

●計画を変える change [alter] a plan. ●名前を太郎と変える change [×alter] one's name to Taro. ●水を蒸気に変える change [turn] water into steam. (⇨変わる) ●教育制度を変える reform the system of education. ▶あなたは私の人生を大きく変えた You've made a big change [difference] in my life. ▶彼は表情を変えなかった His face remained unchanged. ▶飛行機は南に向きを変えた The airplane turned (its course to) the south. ▶信念を変えるな(=貫き通せ) Stick to your principle.

:かえる 返る 〖もとに戻る〗return 《to》; 〖戻される〗be returned 《to》. ▶我に返る come to oneself. ▶盗まれた自転車が持ち主に返った The stolen bicycle was returned to its owner. (!この場合 return to とはしない) ▶落とした財布はまず返って(=取り戻せない)でしょう You will hardly be able to get back the wallet you've lost.

:かえる 帰る

> **WORD CHOICE** 帰る, 戻る
> **go back** 話し手・聞き手のいない場所に戻ることを含意する。
> **come back** 話し手・聞き手のいずれかがいる場所に戻ることを含意する。
> **get back** 戻る行為, 特にたどり着いた瞬間を強調する。
> **be back** 戻るべき場所にすでにいることを含意する。
> **return** 主に書き言葉で用いる。back の意味が含まれているので, ×return back とはいわない。

頻度チャート

go back					
come back					
get back					
be back					
return					
20	40	60	80	100 (%)	

【もとの場所へ】come* [go*, get*, be] back; return (⇨類語); (帰宅する) come [go, get, be] return] home; [去る] leave*, go away. (⇨行く)
●走って家に帰る run back to the house. ●家今に帰る途中 on one's [the] way home. ●英国へ帰ろう go home to England. (❗go back to に比べて自分の属している場所という意識が強い) ▶彼はまたすぐに日本に帰ってくるだろう He will come back to Japan soon. ▶私はホテルへ帰る道が分からなくなった I couldn't find my way back to my hotel. ▶彼女は昨夜英国から帰って来た She returned from England last night. ▶10時までに帰って来なさい Be [Come] (back) home by ten. (❗back がある方が強意的)/Be [Come] back by ten. ▶彼は夜中の2時まで帰らなかった He didn't get home [get in] until two o'clock in the morning. (❗get in は「着く (arrive)」の意) ▶東京に住んでいる息子が夏休みで帰っています My son who lives in Tokyo is now home on a visit during [for] the summer vacation. (❗(1) on a visit は「滞在中で」の意で「…を過ごすため」の意. (2) 「東京に住んでいる息子が…」は My son is now home from Tokyo on a visit…. ともいえる) ▶そろそろ帰らなくてはなりません I think I must be going now. ●帰る際のあいさつ言葉. I will go now. (もう帰ります)などとは言わず, このように進行形を用いて表現を和らげる)/I must say good-by now. (失礼 ❷) ▶君はもう帰ってよい You can leave [go] now. (❗You may leave [go]. は目上の者が目下の者に許可を与える言い方でしばしば尊大に響く) ▶彼は2日間家に帰っていない He hasn't been home for two days. ▶さっさと帰れ Go home!/(出て行け) Get out! ▶タクシーに乗って帰ろうよ Let's take a taxi home. ▶陽子, 帰ったわよ(=ただいま). (陽子)な の? I'm home, Yoko. Are you in?

会話 「あの人はどこ」「彼なら帰りました」"Where is he?" "He went back [went away, left]." (❗go back はどこに帰ったか分かっていることを, 後の二つは分からないことを暗示)

会話 「散歩に行ってくるよ」「早くお帰りなさいね」"I'm going for a walk." "Don't be long."

会話 「いつ京都から帰ってくるの」「あすの朝そちらを立って夕方の6時ごろ帰れると思うよ」「よかった. あなたが帰ってくる(=帰ってきてくれる)のを楽しみにしてるわ」"When can you come [When are you coming] back from Kyoto?" "I'll be leaving here tomorrow morning, so I should be [come] back around six o'clock in the evening." "Good! I'm looking forward to having you back."

● 帰らぬ旅に出る (死ぬ) die; go on one's last journey; go to Heaven; leave this world; go to the other world; pass to the other shore. (❗2例目以下はいずれも「死ぬ」の意の婉曲表現)

かえる 蛙 【動物】 a frog. ●食用ガエル an edible frog. (⇨参考) a bullfrog など ●ヒキガエル a toad.
●カエル飛び(をする) (play) leapfrog; leapfrog. ●春になるとカエルが鳴きだす Frogs begin to croak in (the) spring. (⇨関連) カエルの鳴き声 the croaking of a frog

● かえるの子はかえる 《ことわざ》 (この父にしてこの子あり) Like father, like son.

● かえるの面(?)に水 ▶あんな連中と関わらないよう何度も注意したが彼にはかえるの面に水 I've told him to stay away from those guys over and over again but it's like water off a duck's back.

かえる 反る ●上着のすそが反っている(=裏返しになっている) The hem of your coat is inside [wrong side] out.

かえる 孵る hatch (out). ▶ひよこが3羽[卵が三つ]かえった Three chicks [eggs] hatched (out).

かえんびん 火炎瓶 a Molotov cocktail; 《英》 a petrol bomb.

かえんほうしゃき 火炎放射器 a flámethròwer.

:かお 顔

◆WORD CHOICE◆ 顔

face 人の顔・顔面を指す最も一般的な語. ▶私は青ざめた彼女の顔をじっと見た I watched her pale face closely.

look 外見的に表れた顔つきや表情のこと. この意で用いる場合は, しばしば形容詞を伴う. ▶彼女は悲しそうな顔つきをしていた She had a sad look (on her face).

◆頻度チャート◆

face ▬▬▬▬▬▬▬▬▬▬▬▬▬▬▬▬▬
look ▬▬▬▬▬▬▬▬▬▬▬
    20   40   60   80   100 (%)

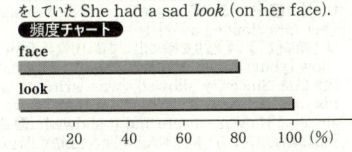

❶ 【顔面】 a face; [首から上部全体] a head. (⇨頭)
① 【～顔】 ●うりざね顔 an oval face. ●美しい[みにくい]顔 a beautiful [an ugly] face. ●やつれた顔 a haggard [a pinched] face. ●角ばった[丸い; ふっくらした, 骨ばった; やせた; 血色の悪い]顔 a square [a round; a plump, a bony; a lean; a sallow] face. ▶彼女は色白の[色の黒い, 浅黒い]顔をしている She has a fair [a dark] complexion./She is fair- [dark-, darkish-] complexioned.
② 【顔が[は]】 ▶私は恥ずかしくて顔が赤くなった I blushed for [with] shame. (❗blushed with embarrassment ともいえる) ▶怒りで彼の顔は真っ赤になった He turned red [(赤味の強い紫) purple] with rage. ▶自分の顔が青ざめていく(=顔から血の気がさっとひいてゆく)のが分かった I felt the blood was rushing from my face. ▶彼の顔は知っている(=顔見知りである) I know him by sight. (❗(I think) I know his face. は「(どうも)あの顔には見覚えがある」の意)
③ 【顔を】 ●顔を上げる lift one's face [head] 《from》; look up 《from》; (はっと) shoot [fling] up one's face. ●花に顔を近づけてにおいをかぐ bring one's face [head] close to a flower and sniff at it. ▶彼は急いで顔を洗って服を着た He washed and dressed in a hurry. (❗文脈があれば wash his face としなくてよい) ▶顔(=あごを)をしゃんと上げて (元気なくうつむいた人に) Keep your chin [xface] up! ▶彼は窓から顔を出した He put [stuck] his head [xface, xneck] out of the window./(身を乗り出した) He leaned out of the window. ▶彼らは顔を見合わせた They looked at each other [each other's faces]. ▶目が合うと彼女は顔をそむけた When our eyes met, she turned her face away [(視線をそらした)] looked away. ▶彼女が私の方に顔を向けたときに私は彼女に手を振った When she turned her face to me, I waved to her.
▶恥ずかしくて彼にまともに顔を向けられない I am so ashamed that I can't look him (straight) in the face [eye]. ▶今も彼の顔を覚えている I (xcan) still recognize [remember] him. (❗(1) どちらも「覚えている」の意で can はつかない. (2) him の代わりに通例 his face とはいわない. 次の例も同様) ▶私は彼の顔を見るのもいやだ I hate to see him./I hate [I'm sick of] the sight of him. ▶彼は顔を近づけて(=新聞に顔をうずめるようにして)新聞を読んでいた He was reading the newspaper with his face buried in it.

❷ 【顔つき】 a face; (表情) a look, (an) expres-

sion; 〔感情の表れた顔つき〕《書》a countenance.
① 〖～顔〗 ● 楽しそうな顔 a happy face 〔look, countenance〕. ● 笑い顔 smiling faces. (!複数形はいろいろな表情を含意) ● 失望した顔で私を見る give me a disappointed *look*; 《書》look at me with an *expression* of disappointment. ▶彼女はもったいぶった顔(=真顔)をしてよく冗談を言います She often jokes with a straight *face*.
② 〖顔が〗 ▶その知らせを聞くと彼女の顔が急に明るくなった When she heard the news, she suddenly looked happy 〔her *face* suddenly brightened (up)〕. (!逆に「顔が曇った」なら … she looked sad 〔her *face* clouded over〕.)
③ 〖顔に〔で〕〗 ▶怒りを顔に出してはいけない Don't show (your) anger. ▶誠実な人であることが彼の顔に表れていた Sincerity showed 〔was written〕 *on* his *face*./He was sincere and it showed. (!最後は口語的な言い方) ▶日本人と中国人を顔だけで見分けるのは難しい It's hard to tell a Japanese from a Chinese just by their 〔his〕 *looks*.
④ 〖顔を〗 ● 顔をしかめる make 〖《英》pull〗 *faces* 〔*at* him〕; 《書》make 〔give〕 a grimace. ▶彼はいつものまじめくさった顔をした He put on his usual serious *face*. ▶彼はおもしろくなさそうな顔をしている He does not *look* pleased./《やや書》He wears a displeased *expression*. ▶「顔」(face) にとらわれず、この例や以下の例を参考に工夫するのがよい ▶どうしてそんなに情けない顔をしているの？ Why are you *looking* so miserable? ▶彼はそのことは何も知らないような顔をしている He *looks* 〔*acts*〕 as if he knew nothing about that. ▶けげんな顔をした He narrowed his eyes in suspicion. ▶うちの娘は手伝いを頼むといつもいやな顔をする(=顔をしかめる) My daughter always *scowls* 〔*frowns*〕 when I ask her to help.
❸ 〖その他の表現〗 ● 大きな顔をする look proud 〔haughty〕; act important 〔《話》big〕. ● こんなことして彼に合わせる顔がない How can I see him after all this! (!反語的表現) ▶反対運動のリーダーとしてマスコミに顔が出たせいで、とんだ嫌がらせを受けた I've been unreasonably harrassed, because I appeared in the media as a leader of the opposition campaign. (!マスコミは顔だけでなく人物像として出たので my face ではなく I とする) ▶日本外交はよく顔がないといわれる It is often said that Japan has a faceless diplomacy. (!主語が Japanese diplomacy でなく Japan となることに注意)
● 顔が売れる, 顔が広い ▶彼は世界で顔が売れている He *is well-known*. 〔知り合いが多い〕 He *has a large* 〔*a wide*〕 *circle of acquaintances*〕 in the financial world.
● 顔がきく ▶彼は政治家に顔がきく(=交際が広い) He *has extensive* 〔*many*〕 *contacts with* politicians.
● 顔から火が出る ▶恥ずかしさで顔から火が出る思いだった I flushed 〔blushed〕 *with shame*./My face was burning with shame.
● 顔に泥を塗る ▶親の顔に泥を塗る (面目を失わせる) *make one's parents lose face*; 〔辱める〕 *disgrace* 〔*bring disgrace on*〕 one's parents.
● 顔を合わせる ▶私たちは通りでよく顔を合わせる (=出会う) We often *meet* in the street. ▶彼は極力彼女とは顔を合わせないようにしていた Mostly he kept out of her way.
● 顔を売る make oneself known to the public; gain publicity.
● 顔を貸す ▶ちょっと顔を貸して(=話をさせてくれない)？ I'd like to *have a few words with* you.
● 顔を出す ▶彼はその事務所にはよく顔を出す(=姿を現す) He often shows 〔turns〕 *up* at the office./He often looks 〔(ひょっこり) drops〕 *in* at the office. ▶二度と顔を出すな Don't *show your face*. (!歓迎しない場合に用いる)
● 顔を立てる ▶彼の顔を立ててその仕事を引き受けた I took the job to save his *face*.
● 顔をつぶす ⇨❸ 〖顔に泥を塗る〗

かおあわせ 顔合わせ 〔会合〕 a meeting; 〔相撲の取組〕 a bout; 〔試合〕 a match. ● 初顔合わせ the first *bout* 〔会合 *meeting*〕.

かおいろ 顔色 〔顔の皮膚の色〕 a complexion; 〖表情〗 (an) expression; 〔顔〕 a face; 〖血色〗 (a) color. ● 顔色を変える change *color*; 〔青く〔赤く〕なる〕turn pale 〔red〕. ● 彼の顔色をうかがう look into his *face*; study the *expression* on his face; 〔彼の気分に敏感だ〕 be sensitive to his mood. ● 顔色がよい She has a good (⇔a pale, a poor) *complexion*. /〔健康そうに見える〕 She looks *well* 〔*healthy*〕 (⇔*pale, off color*). ▶彼は顔色ひとつ変えなかった His *face* remained unchanged./〔まったく平然としていた〕 He remained completely calm 〔didn't turn a hair〕./He seemed almost nonchalant /nὰnʃəláːnt/.

かおう 花押 〔書き判〕 a written seal; a signature.

かおかたち 顔形 ⇨顔立ち, 容貌

かおく 家屋 〔家〕 a house (圏 houses /-ziz, 《米》-siz/); 〔建築物〕 a building; 〔家屋敷〕 premises. (⇨家)

かおじゃしん 顔写真 〔上半身写真〕 a head-and-shoulders photo (⇨上半身); 〔警察の〕 a múgshòt 〔a múg shòt〕 (of a person).

カオス 〔<ギリシア語〕〖混沌〗 chaos /kéiɑs/.

かおだし 顔出し 〔短い訪問〕 a short visit, a call; 〔短時間の出席〕 one's brief presence. (⇨出席) ▶たまには顔出しくらいしなさい *Visit* 〔*Call on*〕 us from time to time.

かおだち 顔立ち features; 《やや話》looks. ● 整った〔はっきりした〕顔立ち regular 〔clear-cut〕 *features*. ● いかつい顔立ちの男 a rugged-*looking* man; a man with rugged *features*. ● 似通った顔立ち facial resemblance. ▶彼女は母親似の顔立ちだ She has her mother's *looks*./She *takes after* her mother. ▶後の言い方は日本語の「母親似だ」と同じで, 性格などの類似もさすことがある

かおつき 顔つき 〖表情〗 (an) expression, a look; 〖容貌〕 looks. (⇨顔, 表情) ● 顔つきで人を判断する a judge a person by his *looks*. ▶彼女は悲しそうな顔つきをしていた She had a sad *expression*./She looked sad. ▶彼は怒った顔つきで私を見た He gave me an angry *look*.

かおつなぎ 顔つなぎ 〔知り合いになること〕 getting acquainted 《*with* one another》; 〔接触を保つこと〕 keeping in contact 《*with*》. ● 彼らと顔つなぎをしておくために同窓会に出る attend the alumni association to *keep in contact with* them. ● 政治家に顔つなぎをしてもらう(=紹介してもらう) *be introduced* 《*to* him》 by a politician.

かおなじみ 顔馴染み a familiar face. (⇨顔見知り, 知り合い) ▶彼とは顔なじみです〔になった〕 I *know* him *very well* 〔*got acquainted with* him〕.

かおパス 顔パス ▶おれは K 劇場なら顔パスで入れるんだ I use my influence to enter the K Theater free of charge./I can get in K theater free, because they know me. (!「コネを使ってただで入場する」の意)

かおぶれ 顔ぶれ 〔人員〕 the members 《*of*》; 〔陣容〕 a lineup. ● 新内閣の顔ぶれ the *members* of the new

かおまけ 顔負け ▶数学では大学生もあの子供には顔負けだ(あの子供は大学生でさえ恥じ入らせる) That child *puts* even college students *to shame* in mathematics./(打ち負かす) That child *beats* even college students in math. ▶彼はチャップリン顔負けの(=をしのぐほどの)喜劇俳優だ He's *such* a comic genius (*that*) he *can outdo* Chaplin.

かおみしり 顔見知り (知人) an acquaintance. ▶私は彼とはただの顔見知りだ I only *know* him *by sight*./He is only an *acquaintance*, not a friend. ▶パーティーで彼女と顔見知りになった I *made* her *acquaintance* [*got to know* her, *got acquainted with* her] at the party.

かおみせ 顔見せ (役者の)one's (stage) debut /deibjúː/.

かおむけ 顔向け ▶家族に顔向けができない I *can't look* my family *in the face*. (⇨顔❶)/(会う勇気がない) I *don't have the courage* to meet my family.

かおやく 顔役 (大物) a big man [《話》shot]; (影響力の強い人) an influential man; (ギャングなどの) a boss. ▶彼はその土地の顔役だ He is *the big shot* there./(暗黒街のボス) He is a *boss* in that territory./(暗黒街のボス) He runs that territory. ともいう)

*__かおり 香り, 薫り__　　[花などの] (a) fragrance /fréigrəns/, (a) perfume (❗️前の方は新鮮な後の方は強い香り), [コーヒーや香料の]《書》 an aroma; [かすかな] (a) scent; [におい] (a) smell. (⇨におい) ▶バラの香り the *scent* of roses. ●コーヒー[ブランデー]の香り the *aroma* of coffee [brandy]. ●香りのよい花 a *fragrant* [*sweet-smelling*] flower. ●バラの香りのする石けん soap *scented with* roses; *rose-scented* soap. ●香水[香]の香りをきく test the quality of perfume [incense] by smelling its scent. ▶花の香りがミツバチを引きつけた The *fragrance* [*scent*] of the flowers attracted the bees. ▶この茶は香りがよい This tea *smells* good [*nice*].

かおる 香る, 薫る (いいにおいがする) smell* sweet; be fragrant. (⇨におい) ▶庭にはライラックが薫っていた The lilacs *smelled sweet* [*were fragrant*] in the garden. (❗️×were smelling は不可)

かか 呵呵 (あはは) ha! ha! ●呵呵大笑する (大声で笑う) laugh hard [loud(ly)].

がか 画家 a 《landscape [portrait]》painter. (❗️品位のある言い方に an artist がある) ●日本画家 a Japanese-style *painter*.

がか 雅歌 (旧約聖書のソロモンの雅歌) The Song of Solomon.

がが 峨峨 ●峨峨たる(=険しくそびえ立つ)連峰 a steep, towering range of mountains.

かかあでんか かかあ天下 ▶彼の家はかかあ天下だ His *wife is the boss* in his house./(しばしば軽蔑的) His wife *wears the pants* [*the trousers* 《英》] in his family. (❗️He wears.... とすれば「亭主関白」の意になる(⇨亭主))/(彼は妻の尻(㋐)に敷かれている) He is a *henpecked* husband. (⇨尻)

かがい 課外 (正課以外の) extracurricular; (補習の) supplementary.
●課外活動 extracurricular activities (❗️スポーツ・音楽その他の活動をさすので常に複数形). ●課外活動のスポーツ *extracurricular* sports.

がかい 瓦解 (崩落) (a) collapse. (⇨崩壊)
—— 瓦解する 動 fall; collapse. ▶連立内閣は瓦解した The coalition government *fell* [*collapsed*].

かがいしゃ 加害者 (暴行などの)an assailant; (殺人者) a murderer. ▶彼がその事故の加害者だ He caused the accident.

-かかえ -抱え [両手で抱えるほどの大きさ・量] ●ひと抱えの花 an *armful* of flowers. ●3抱えもある杉の木 a Japanese cedar measuring three *stretched* [*spans*] of one's *arms*.

かかえこむ 抱え込む (持つ)have*; (引き受ける) take* ... on. ▶彼はこなしきれないほどの仕事を抱え込んでいる He *has* too much work to do./He *has taken on* too much work.

__かかえる 抱える__ ❶[持つ](両腕で) hold ... in one's arms [小わきに] under one's arm; (両手で) hold* ... in one's hands. ●ひざを抱えて座っている sit *hugging* one's knees. ▶彼女は大きな箱を両腕で抱えていた She *was holding* [*had*, ×was having] a large box *in her arms*. ▶彼は本をわきにかかえてやって来た He came *with* some books *under* his *arm*. ▶彼は両手で頭を抱えた He *held* his head *in* his *hands*.

❷[引き受ける] have*. ●大家族を抱える *have a large family to support*. ●難問を抱える *have a difficult problem to solve*. ●たくさん仕事を抱える *have a lot of* work *to do*.

カカオ (木・実) a cacao /kəká:ou/.
●カカオバター cacao butter.

*__かかく 価格__ (値段) a price; (値打ち) (a) value. (⇨値段)
①【〜価格】●住宅価格 house *prices*. ●仕入れ価格 a púrchase [an ínput] *price*. ●販売価格 a sélling [a sáles] *price*. ●希望小売価格 a recommended retail *price*. ●オープン価格 an open *price*. ●額面価格 a fáce *válue*. ●生産者[消費者]価格 the producer('s) [consumer('s)] *price*. ●市場価格 a márket *price* [*válue*]. ●最低価格 the lowest *price*; (底値) a rock-bottom *price*. ●法定価格 legal *value*. ●協定価格 a contracted [an agreed] *price*. ●適正[法外な]価格で売る sell at the right [an exorbitant] *price*.
▶大量注文の場合は通常価格より値引きいたします We can offer a discount on our regular [ordinary] *price* for bulk orders.
②【価格が[は]】▶価格が急激に下落した *Prices* fell [declined, were down] rapidly./*Prices* collapsed. ▶土地価格は毎年上昇している Land *prices* [*values*] are going up [are rising] every year. ▶この古後の本当の価格はどれくらいでしょか What is the real *value* of these old coins?
③【価格を】▶オペックは原油価格を引き下げる予定だ OPEC will reduce the *price* of crude oil. ▶そのモデルの価格を5万ドルに設定した The model *was priced* at 50,000 dollars.
●価格安定 price stability. ●価格競争 price competition [war]. ●価格協定 an agreement on prices. ●価格設定 pricing. ●価格統制 price control. ●価格破壊 price slashing; price destruction; pricing revolution. ●価格表 a price list. ●価格票 a príce tàg. ●価格変動 price fluctuation.

*__かがく 化学__ 图 chemistry. ●有機[無機; 応用; 物理]化学 organic [inorganic; applied; physical] *chemistry*.
—— 化学の, 化学的の 形 chemical.
—— 化学的に 副 chemically.
●化学記号 a chemical symbol. ●化学工業 chemical industry. ●化学工場 a chemical factory. ●化学式 a chemical formula. ●化学実験 a chemical experiment. ●化学実験室 a chemical laboratory. ●化学者 a chemist. ●化学製品 chemicals; chemical products. (❗️前の方は化学薬品の意にも用いる) ●化学戦 chemical warfare.

かがく ●化学繊維 (a) chemical [(合成) (a) synthetic] fiber. ●化学調味料 (a) chemical seasoning. ●化学反応 (a) chemical reaction. ●化学反応式 a reaction formula. ●化学肥料 chemical fertilizer. ●化学物質 a chemical. ●化学物質過敏症 chemical sensitivity 《略 CS》. ●化学兵器 a chemical weapon. ●化学変化 (a) chemical change. ●化学方程式 a reáction fòrmula. ●化学療法 chemotherapy.

*かがく **科学** 图 science. (!通例「自然科学」の意で用いられることが多い) ●自然[社会; 応用]科学 natural [social; applied] *science*. ●人文科学 the humanities 《複数扱い》. ●近代[先端]科学 modern [advanced] science. ▶科学の発展は必ずしも人間を幸福にしない The progress of *science* does not always make man happy. ▶科学とは、人間の問題なんです *Science* is in fact [actually] a human issue. (!一般に知られている事実でなく、個人の意見の場合は in fact や actually を挿入する)
── 科学的な 形 scientific. ●科学的なやり方で in a *scientific* way.
── 科学的に 副 scientifically.
●科学衛星 a science satellite. ●科学技術 technology. ▶コンピュータは科学技術の発達に新しい展望を開いてきた Computers have opened up new vistas in *technological* developments [advances]. ●科学者 a scientist. ●科学小説 science fiction; (話) sci-fi /sáifái/《略 SF》. ●科学博物館 a scíence muséum.

かがく 下顎 the lower jaw; 〖解剖〗 the mandible, the submaxilla.

かがく 価格 (評価額) (a) valuation, (a) value; (値段) a price; (総額) amount.

がかく 雅楽 ancient Japanese court music.

がかくせい 画学生 an art student.

*かかげる **掲げる** 〖高く上げる〗 put* ... up; 〖旗を〗 fly*, hoist; 〖主義・主張などを〗 hold* ... up; 〖掲載する〗 carry; (印刷を) print. ●旗を掲げる put up [fly] a flag. ●「安全第一」をスローガンに掲げる hold up [use, (採り上げる) adopt] "Safety First" as one's slogan. ●「安全第一」をスローガンに掲げて *under* the slogan of "Safety First". ●壁に掲示を掲げる put [(つるして) hang] up a notice on the wall. ●第一面に掲げられた記事 an article (*carried* [*printed*, *appearing*]) on the front page.

かかし 案山子 (説明的に) a scarecrow (put up in a rice paddy field to frighten birds—sparrows in particular—away).

かかす 欠かす ●欠かせないもの (必需品) a necessity;《やや話》a must (!単数形で). ▶彼はその会合には欠かさず(=規則正しく)出席する He attends the meeting regularly. (!どんなことがあっても) whatever happens, (必ず) without fail. (!without fail は命令・約束などを強めるときに用いることが多い) ▶コンピュータは私たちの仕事には欠かせない Computers are essential [indispensable] to our job. (⇒必要な/Computers are a *must* for our job [when we do our job]./We can't do our job without computers. ▶コンビニは日本の街には欠かせないものになった Convenience stores have become something (that) people [×Japanese cities] cannot do without in Japan.

かかずらう (係わりをもつ) be concerned, concern oneself 《in, with》; (こだわる) be particular 《about》; (執着する) stick to.... ●事件にかかずらう be *concerned* in the affair. ●小事にかかずらう *stick to* trivial matters.

かかって 掛かって (もっぱら) entirely; (全面的に) wholly. ▶未来はかかって若者の双肩にある The future falls [rests] *entirely* on young people's shoulders.

かかと 踵 a heel. ●かかとの高い[低い]靴 high-*heeled* [low-*heeled*] shoes; shoes with high [low] *heels*. ●靴下のかかと部分 the *heel* of a sock.

*かがみ **鏡** a mirror. (!最も一般的な語で、あらゆる種類の鏡に用いられる); (姿見) a full-length mirror (!等身大のもの), 《主に英語》a glass (!特に女性用. a looking glass というが《古》); (手鏡) a hand mirror. ●鏡(の中の自分の姿)を見る look (at oneself) in [×at] a *mirror*. ●鏡に向かってネクタイを結ぶ tie one's tie at [×to] a *mirror*; look in the *mirror* to tie one's tie. ●海は鏡のように静かだった The sea was as smooth as *glass* [a *mirror*]. ▶子は親の鏡 (ことわざ) As parents are, so are their children. (!Children are a *mirror* of their parents. などと普通の英語でいえる)

> **翻訳のこころ** そのわきに鏡がかかって、その下には長い柄のついたブラシが置いてあったのです(宮沢賢治『注文の多い料理店』) Next to it was a *mirror* on the wall. Under the mirror was a brush with the long handle. (!「(壁に)かかっている鏡」は a mirror on the wall)

●鏡板 (戸・天井などの平たい板) a pane, a panel; (能舞台の) a backdrop scene panel on the Noh stage. ●鏡開き kagamibiraki, (説明的に) the cutting of the New Year's rice cakes (on January 11th). ●鏡文字 mirror writing. ●鏡餅 kagamimochi, (説明的に) round mirror-shaped rice cakes (offered on the household altar at the New Year).

かがみ 鑑 a paragon.

かがむ 〖前に曲げる〗〖上体を〗 bend* down, lean forward [down, over]; (頭と肩のあたりを) stoop; 〖うずくまる〗 crouch; 〖しゃがむ〗 squat (-tt-). ●かがんで靴をはく *bend* [*stoop*] *down* to put on one's shoes.

かがめる 〖前に曲げる〗(上体を) bend* (down [over]); (傾ける) lean (down [over]); (腰を) bow; (頭と肩のあたりを) stoop (down [over]); 〖(打撃を受けて)体をひょいと下げる〗 duck (down). ●身をかがめて少女にキスをする bend [stoop] over the little girl to kiss her (!上からかがみこむ感じ); bend forward to kiss the little girl. ●身をかがめて門をくぐる lean (one's body) through the gate. ▶彼は腰をかがめて消しゴムを拾った He bent [leaned, stooped, crouched] *down* to pick up the eraser. (!crouch はしゃがみこむ感じ)/He *bent* at his waist and picked up the eraser. ▶石が飛んできたので思わず身をかがめた A stone came hurtling toward me, so I *ducked* (*down*) to avoid it.

*かがやかしい **輝かしい** (明るい) bright; (光り輝く) brilliant; (はなばなしい) glorious, 《やや書》illustrious. ●輝かしい未来 a bright [a brilliant, a glorious] future. ●輝かしい勝利 a brilliant [a glorious] victory. ●輝かしい業績 a glorious [a brilliant, an illustrious] achievement.

かがやかす 輝かす brighten. ●目を輝かして見る look at (it) with bright [sparkling] eyes.

かがやき 輝き (きらめき) brightness; (まぶしい明るさ) brilliance; (きらめき) glitter; (燃えるきらめき) sparkle. ●目[ダイヤモンド]の輝き the sparkle of one's eyes [a diamond]. ▶彼女が喜んでいるときの目の輝きが好きだ I like the brightness in her eyes when she's happy.

*かがやく **輝く** (光り輝く) shine*; (闇(%)の中でぴかぴか光る) twinkle; (反射してきらきら光る) glitter; (ぬれたように光る) glisten; (ぱっと光る) flash; (きらめく) sparkle; (ぎらぎら光る) glare. (⇨光る[類語])

> 使い分け **shine** 物が輝くことや、喜び・希望などで人・目・顔が輝くことをさす.
> **twinkle** 目などが輝くこと. 興奮・茶目っ気・かわいしさなどを含意する.
> **glisten, glitter** 目が特定の感情を表してきらりと光ること.
> **flash** 喜び・怒りなどの強い感情によって人・目・顔などが輝くこと.
> **sparkle** 目・人・事などが活気・才能などで輝くこと.
> **lighten**（**up**）顔・表情が明るくくつろいだものになること.
> **brighten**（**up**）顔・人などがうれしそうに明るくなること.

▶月[太陽]が明るく輝いている The moon [sun] *is shining* bright(ly). (❗*bright* は結果の状態に重点がある)▶夜空に星がきらきら輝いている Stars *were twinkling* [*glittering*] in the sky. ▶海が日の光で輝いていた The ocean *shone* [*glittered, sparkled*] in the sun. ▶彼女の顔はうれしさで輝いた Her face *shone* [*lit up, lightened* (*up*), *brightened* (*up*)] with happiness. (❗「輝いていた」という状態の意では ... *was bright* with happiness.) ▶彼女は健康美で輝いて見える She's *shining* [*beaming*] with good health. ▶彼は目を輝かせて(=輝いた目をして)その話をした He talked about it with *shining* [*sparkling*] eyes./He talked about it with a *twinkle* in his eyes.

*__かかり 係__ (担当) charge; (担当者) a person in charge (*of*); (部署) a department; (公共施設などの案内係) an attendant. ●受付係 a receptionist. ●遺失物係のところへ行く go to the Lost and Found (*department*). ▶彼女は何の係ですか What is she *in charge of*?
●係員 [[担当の人]] a person (職員) a clerk, (下級公務員) an official) in charge. ●係長 (広い意味で) a manager, (役職名) sub-section manager.

かかり 掛かり ❶ [[動き出すこと]] ▶車のエンジンのかかりが悪い The engine of my car is slow to *start*.
❷ [[必要な費用]] expenses. (❗「(必要)経費」の意で通例複数形で) ▶かかりがかさむ *Expenses* are piling [*running*] up.

-がかり [時間・人手がかかる]] take*; [費やす]] spend*.
▶親がかりである（=親に依存している）be *dependent* [*depend*] *on* one's parents. ▶彼は2日がかりで部屋の掃除をした It *took* him [He *took*] two days *to* clean the room./He *spent* two days (*in*) clean*ing* the room. ▶5人がかりでピアノを持ち上げた It *took* [*required*] five people *to* lift the piano./The piano was lifted *by* five people.

かかりあう 掛かり合う [[関係がある]] have* ... to do 《*with*》; (取り引きなどの) have relations (communications] [*with*]; [巻き込まれる] be involved [(やや書) entangled] (*in*). (⇨係り合う)

かかりきり 掛かり切り ▶彼は歴史の研究に掛かりきりだった(=専念していた) He *was devoted to* [全時間を捧げた] *gave his whole time to*, (ふけっていた) *was given up to*] the study of history. (⇨専念)

かかりつけ 掛かり付け ▶掛かりつけの医者に行く go to one's *family* [x*home*] doctor; go to one's (*regular* [*personal*]) doctor. (❗(1) *one's* [*the*] *doctor* が「掛かりつけの医者」の意になる. (2) (英) では one's (general) practitioner が普通.

かかりび かかり火 (祝賀などの) a bónfire; (キャンプの) a campfire. ▶かかり火をたく make [build] a bonfire [a campfire].

かかりゆ 掛かり湯 (⇨@) 上がり湯)

➤**かかる 掛かる, 架かる**   INDEX
❶ 垂れ下がる   ❷ ふりかかる
❸ わななどに   ❹ しっかり留まる
❺ 渡される   ❻ 作動する
❼ 負う, 被る   ❽ 電話などが
❾ 費やされる   ❿ 取り掛かる
⓫ 依存する   ⓬ 医者に
⓭ その他の表現

❶ [[垂れ下がる]] hang*; (覆い被さる) hang over ....
▶絵が壁に掛かっている A picture *hangs* [*is hanging*] on the wall. (❗後の方は一時的状況を強調する)/There *is* a picture (*hanging*) on the wall./The wall has a picture (*hung*) on it. (❗最後の文は絵で飾るという感じを伴う) ▶雲は山に低くかかっていた The clouds *hung* [(静止していた) *rested*] low *over* the mountains.

❷ [[ふりかかる]] (はねる) splash 《*on, over*》; (上に落ちる) fall* 《*on*》. ▶水が私の上着にかかった The water *splashed* (*on*) my coat./My coat *was splashed with* the water.

❸ [[わななどに]] (動物が) be caught 《*in* a trap》; (人が) fall* 《*into* a trap》. ▶わなにかかったキツネ a *trapped* fox. ▶彼が木の間に仕かけておいた網に鳥が数羽かかった Several birds *were trapped* [*caught*] *in* the nets he had set in the trees. ▶彼は我々の計略にかかった He *fell into* our trap [snare].

❹ [[しっかり留まる]] (鍵(ﾞ)がかかる) lock; (ボタンがかかる)button (*up*). ▶このドアは鍵がかかっている[自動的に鍵がかかる] This door *is locked* [*locks* automatically]. ▶このワイシャツは第一ボタンがうまくかからない This shirt doesn't *button* (*up*) easily at the top.

❺ [[渡される]] (橋が) span (-nn-); (虹が) appear 《*in* the sky》; span 《a valley [a lake]》. ▶この川に2本の橋がかかっている Two bridges *span* this river./There *are* two bridges *across* [*over*] this river. ▶この川にこの橋がかかった(=建設された)のは5年前でした It was five years ago that this bridge *was built* [*was constructed*] over [across] this river. ▶はしごが屋根にかかっていた A ladder *stood* [*rested*] *against* the roof. ▶こんろになべがかかっている There is a pan *on* the stove./A pan is *on* the stove. ▶箱にひもがかかっていた(=縛られていた) The box *was tied up* with string.

❻ [[作動する]] work; (動き出す) start. ▶ブレーキがかからない The brake doesn't *work*. ▶大きな音をたてて エンジンがかかった The engine *started* (*up*) with a loud roar. ▶エンジンがかかっている The engine *is on* [*is running*].

❼ [[負う, 被る]] ▶すべての品に税金がかかる All goods *are taxed* [*are subject to* taxation]./Taxes are imposed on all goods. ▶彼らにわいろを使った疑いがかかった They *were suspected* [×*were doubted*] *of* bribery./Suspicion of bribery *fell upon* them.

❽ [[電話などが]] ▶君に電話がかかっているよ There is a phone [a telephone] call *for* you./You *are wanted on* the phone [telephone]. (❗×*on a* phone [*a* telephone] とはいわない) ▶彼から電話がかかってきた I had a phone call *from* him. ▶どこから電話がかかってきたの？ Who's *calling*?

❾ [[費やされる]] (時間・労力などが) take*; (費用が) cost*. ▶その実験は時間と金がかかる The experiment *takes* time and money. ▶その仕事は大変手数がかかる It *takes* a lot of trouble to do the work./The work *takes* [*requires*] a lot of trouble to do. ▶彼が全快するまでに2週間はかかるだろう It will be [xtake] two weeks before he gets well. ▶10分とかからずに彼女はその問題を解いた She solved the problem in less than ten minutes.

【会話】「ここから駅までどのくらいかかりますか」「歩いて[バスで]10分です」 "How long [How many minutes] does it take (you) to go from here to the station?" "It takes ten minutes on foot [by bus]." (❗xHow long [How many minutes] does it take from here to the station? とはいわない)

【会話】「あとどのくらいかかるんだい」「今行くよ」 "How much longer [How soon] are you going to be?" "Coming (right now)."

【会話】「この本を航空便で送るといくらかかりますか」「1,000円かかります」 (郵便局で) "How much does it cost (me) to send this book by airmail?" "That'll cost (you) [That'll be] 1,000 yen." (❗That costs [is].... より柔らかな言い方)

❿ [取り掛かる] (始める) start, begin*; (着手する) set* about..., go* about...; (従事する) be engaged in..., be occupied with.... ● 本気で仕事に取り掛かる start [begin, set about] one's work in earnest. ▶世間話はやめて仕事にかかろう Let's skip the small talk and get down to business, shall we? ▶彼は今辞典の編集に取り掛かっている He is now engaged in [occupied with] compiling a dictionary. ▶彼女は新しい著作にかかっている She is working [at work] on a new book. ▶彼女は子供の世話にかかりっきりだ(=非常に多忙だ) She is very busy looking after her children. ▶(時間をすべてとられている) Her time is fully taken up with looking after her children.

⓫ [依存する] depend on [upon]...; (責任・決定などが) rest with...; [賭けられている] be at stake. ▶私たちが成功するかどうかはみなさんの努力にかかっている Our success depends on everyone working hard [your efforts]. ▶その国の存立は大統領[彼の外交手腕]にかかっていた The fate of the nation rested with the President [on his diplomacy]. ▶これは軽々しく決められる問題ではない。何百万人もの運命がかかっている This is not a matter to be decided lightly; the fate of millions is at stake.

⓬ [医者に] ● 医者にかかる see [go to (see), go and see, consult] a doctor. ● consult a doctor (ややかたい言い方) ▶彼は風邪で医者にかかっている He is under the care of the doctor with a cold.

⓭ [その他の表現] ▶静かな音楽がかかっていた Music was playing softly. ▶さあ、かかってこい Come on! ▶気にかかることが2,3ある There are a few things which are on my mind [worry me]. ▶君にかかったらだめだ(=君にはとてもかなわない) I am no match for you.

かかる 罹る (病気に) get, (病気・災難に) fall*; (感染する) catch*; (冒される) be affected (by); (経験する) have*; (苦しむ) suffer from.... ▶がんにかかった[かかっている] those affected [with] cancer. ● 病気にかかりやすい be liable [susceptible] to disease. ▶彼は病気にかかって1週間学校を休んだ He got [became, fell] sick and was absent from school for a week. ▶彼ははしかにかかった He has caught [has come down with] (the) measles. ▶彼女はチフスにかかっている She has [is suffering from] typhoid (fever).

かかる 懸かる ❶ [空高く浮かぶ] ▶夕月が東の空にかかる The evening moon is high in the eastern sky.

❷ [賞金などが渡される] ▶最優秀作文には100万円の賞金がかかっている A prize of one million yen is awarded for the best composition.

−かかる (⇨−かける)

かがる (繕う) mend, (主に英) repair; [縫い合わせる] sew*... up; [編んだ衣類・穴などを繕う] darn. ● スカートの穴をかがる mend [sew up] the hole in one's skirt; darn (the hole in) one's skirt.

−かかる (...の様子を帯びる) be tinged (with); (...に似ている、近い感じがする) look like.... ▶芝居がかったふるまい dramatic [theatrical] behavior. ● 緑がかった色のセーター a greenish sweater.

*かかわらず ❶ [...だけれども] though, although (❗後の方が堅い語); [...にもかかわらず] in spite of ..., despite ..., (❗最近は in spite of より短いこの語が好まれる傾向にある); (それにもかかわらず)《話》all [just] the same (《文頭または文尾で》); 《書》nevertheless; (しくし) but; 《やや書》however. ▶彼女は病気にもかかわらず入学試験を受けた Though [Although] she was sick, she took the entrance exam./ She took the entrance exam in spite of [despite] her sickness./She was sick; however [all the same, nevertheless], she took the entrance exam. (❗最後の二つは She was sick, but she took the exam all the same [nevertheless]. のようにも用いられる) ▶あれほど苦労があるにもかかわらず彼はいつも陽気だ He has such trouble, but he is cheerful all the time./For [With] all his trouble, he is cheerful all the time. (⇨けれども)

❷ [関係なく] (...に構わずに) 《やや書》regardless of ...; (...にかかわりなく) 《やや書》irrespective of .... ▶年齢性別にかかわらず regardless of [irrespective of] age or sex. ▶結果のいかんにかかわらず最善を尽くせ Do your best regardless of the consequences [no matter what the consequences are]. (❗後の方が口語的) ▶晴雨にかかわらずラグビーの試合は行われる Whether it rains [xwill rain] or not, the rugby match will take place./The rugby match will take place, rain or shine. (❗慣用的な言い方)

かかわり 係わり (つながり) (a) connection; (やっかいな関係) (an) involvement. (⇨関係) ● 自然と人間のかかわり(=関係) the relationship between nature and human beings [people]. ▶それとは何の係わりもない I don't have any connection with it./I have nothing to do with it./(知ったことでない) It's none of my business.

かかわりあう 係わり合う ▶そんな事に係わり合ってはいけない Don't get involved in [have anything to do with] such a matter. (⇨係わる)

かかわる 係わる ❶ [関与する] get mixed up 《with＋人, in＋事》, be concerned 《with, in》; (巻き込まれる) be involved 《in》; (干渉する) have*... to do 《with》; (干渉する) interfere 《in》. (⇨関係する) ▶あんな連中とかかわるな Don't get mixed up [have anything to do] with such people./(離れておけ) Keep away from such people. ▶彼はその犯罪にかかわった He was concerned [was involved] in the crime.

❷ [影響する] affect; (関係する) concern. ● 名誉にかかわる affect one's honor. ▶その問題は我々全員にかかわる The matter concerns us all.

❸ [こだわる] ▶つまらないことにかかわっている暇はない I have no time to bother [be concerned] about trifles.

❹ [その他の表現] ● 命にかかわる endanger one's life. ● 命にかかわる病気 a fatal disease.

かかん 果敢 ― 果敢な 形 (恐れを知らぬ) dauntless; (大胆な) daring, bold; (確固とした) resolute. ●果敢な勇気 *dauntless* courage. (! *undaunted* は叙述的に用いるのが普通)
―果敢に 副 ●果敢に立ち向かう fight *resolutely* 《*against*》.

かがん 河岸 a (river) bank.
●河岸段丘 a river terrace.

かがんぼ 大蚊 〖昆虫〗 a crane fly. (参考 吸血はしない)

かき 柿 〖植物〗 a (Japanese) persimmon /pərsímən/.

かき 下記 ― 下記の 形 the following. ●下記の項目 *the following* items; the items *mentioned below*. ▶彼らの名前は下記のとおりです Their names are *as follows*: .... (! 主語の単・複にかかわらず常に follows とする)

かき 火気 ▶火気厳禁 〖掲示〗 No fire./(注意: 可燃物) Caution: Flammables.

かき 火器 a firearm. (! 通例複数形で)

かき 牡蠣 〖魚介〗 an oyster. 語法 (1) 米英では精力のつく食べ物と考えられている。(2) the R months (つづりに r のつく September から April まで)がカキのシーズン) ●生カキ a raw *oyster*.
●牡蠣フライ a fried oyster. ●牡蠣養殖業者 an óyster fàrmer. ●牡蠣養殖場 an óyster fàrm.

かき 花卉 (花を観賞する植物) a flowering plant; (観賞植物) an ornamental plant.

かき 花期 the flowering season.

かき 花器 (花瓶) a (flower) vase; (水盤) a flower bowl.

かき 夏期, 夏季 summer, summertime. (⇨夏)
●夏期休暇 (⇨夏休み) ●夏期講座 a summer course.

かぎ 鍵 ❶ 〖ドアなどの〗a key; 〖錠〗a lock (! 日本語の鍵は錠の意でも用いられるが, 英語の key は stricly に区別される); (南京錠) a padlock. ●ドアの鍵 a door *key*; a *key* to [*for*] a door. (! the *key of* a door も可) ●鍵のかかったドア a *locked* door.
①〖鍵が〗 ▶かちっと音がして鍵がかかった The *lock* closed with a snap. ▶この戸はどうしても鍵(=錠)がかからない This door won't *lock*. ▶スーツケースに鍵がかかっている[いない] The suitcase is *locked* [is not *locked*, (開いている) is *unlocked*]./The suitcase is *on* [*off*] the lock.
②〖鍵を〗 ●鍵を錠前に差し込む put [insert] a *key* in the lock; fit a *key* to the lock [〖鍵穴〗 keyhole). ●鍵をかける(=錠を下ろす) lock (〖a door〗; fasten [set] a *lock*; (かかっている) have the *lock* on. ●鍵(=錠)を開ける(=はずす) unlock (〖a door, a car〗; turn [open] a *lock*; (開けてある) have the *lock* off. ●鍵(=錠)をかけてしまっておく keep (〖a diamond〗 *under lock and key*. ●鍵(=錠)をこじ開ける pick a *lock*. ●家を出る前にしっかりと鍵(=錠)をかけて戸締まりをする *lock* (a house) *up* before leaving home. ▶842号室の鍵をお願いします(フロントで) May I have the *key for* room 842, please? ▶引き出しの鍵をかけ忘れた I forgot to *lock* the drawer./(鍵を開けたままにしていた) I left the drawer *unlocked*. ▶彼女は鍵を中に置き忘れて(=閉じ込めて)しまったために車に乗ることができなかった She locked the *key* in the car and couldn't get in.
❷〖問題解決の〗 a key, a clue (*to*). ●なぞを解く鍵を握っている hold the *key* [*clue*] *to* the mystery.
●鍵穴 a keyhole. ●鍵束 a bunch of keys.

かぎ 鉤 /kúk/. ▶池に落ちていた靴をかぎで釣ってとてくる *hook* a shoe out of the pond. ▶雁(ﾁ)がかぎになって飛んで行く A group of wild geese are flying away in V-formation.

●かぎホック a hook and eye. (範 hooks and eyes).

がき 餓鬼 ❶ 〖仏教の〗 the starving dead; (説明的に) the dead who, because of their bad conduct in life, are made to always suffer from acute hunger in hell. ❷〖子供〗(軽蔑的に) a brat; 《俗》 a snotnose kid.
●がき大将 餓鬼大将

かきあげ 掻き揚げ *kakiage*; (説明的に) a variation of *tempura*; a deep-fried mixture of vegetable chips and shrimp [scallop].

かきあげる 書き上げる finish writing [xto write]; (書き込んで完成する) fill ... out 《主に米》 [in 《英》]. ▶パスポートの申請書を書き上げるのに少々手こずった I had some difficulty *filling out* the application form for my passport. ▶彼は5年間の研究の成果を論文に書き上げる(=完成する)のに半年を費やした He spent six months *completing* his thesis after five years' research.

かきあげる 掻き上げる push back 《one's hair》 from one's forehead. ▶ほつれた髪をくしでかきあげる *comb up* one's loose hair.

かきあじ 書き味 ▶ボールペンの書き味を試す try to see how *well* a ball-point pen *writes*.

かきあつめる 掻き集める ●落ち葉をかき集める (寄せ集める) gather (*up*) fallen leaves; (くま手で) rake *up* [*together*] fallen leaves. ●金をかき集める scrape money *together* [*up*].

かぎあてる 嗅ぎ当てる smell [scent, 《話》sniff] ... out. ▶その警察犬はバッグの中のコカインを嗅ぎ当てた The police dog *sniffed out* cocaine in a bag.

かきあらためる 書き改める rewrite* /ríːràit/. ▶その物語をやさしい英語に書き改める (=書き直す) *rewrite* the story in easy English.

かきあらわす 書き表す put* [express] 《one's feelings》 in writing [words]; 〖描写する〗 describe.

かきあらわす 書き著す write 《a book》; (出版する) publish. ●回想録を書き著す *write* [*publish*] one's memoirs.

かきあわせる 掻き合わせる ●シャツの襟元をかき合わせる *adjust* the neck of a shirt.

かきいだく 掻き抱く hug. ▶娘をしっかりと[強く]かき抱いた I *hugged* my daughter [*hard*].

かきいれ 書き入れ a note. (⇨〖⇨〗書き込み)

かきいれどき 書き入れ時 a rush. ▶冬はスキー場の書き入れ時だ(=最高の稼ぎ時) Winter is *the best* [最も忙しい *busiest*] *season* for ski resorts.

かきいれる 書き入れる (名前・金額などを日記・帳簿などに) put* ... (*in*), 〖書〗 enter; (書류または必要事項を記入する) fill ... out 《主に米》 [in 《英》]. ●空欄に住所氏名を書き入れる *put* one's name and address *in* the blanks; *fill out* the blanks with one's name and address. ●単に「住所氏名を書き入れる」は *fill in* one's name and address) ●支出を出納簿に書き入れる *enter* [*make an entry of*] expenses *in* the account book. ▶この用紙に必要事項を書き入れてください *Fill out* [*in*] this form, please.

かきうつす 書き写す copy. ●彼の言ったことを手帳に書き写す *copy* (*down*) what he said *in* one's small notebook. ▶その本の1節をノートに書き写した I *copied* a passage from the book *into* my notebook.

かきおき 書き置き (置き手紙) a note [a letter] left behind (! note は短い手紙); (書面による伝言) a written message; (自殺者の) a súicide nòte; (遺言書) a will. ●書き置きを残す leave a *note* [a

かきおこす　書き起こす　[最初の部分が書く] write the first part 《*of*》. ●入学の思い出から書き起こす *start* [*begin*] *writing* the memoirs of entrance.

かきおこす　掻き起こす　●消えかけた火を棒きれでかき起こす *stir* (*up*) the dying fire with a stick.

●記念切手 ●郵便番号を書き落とす(忘れる) *forget to write* the zip code; (抜かす) *omit* the zip code *by mistake*.

かきおろし　書き下ろし　—— 書き下ろしの 形 newly-written.

かきかえ　書き換え　(書き改めること) rewriting; (契約などの更新) (a) renewal; (株式などの名義の) (a) transfer. ●免許の書き換え the *renewal* of one's license.

かきかえる　書き換える　[書き改める]rewrite*/ri:ráit/; [やさしく言い換える]《やや書》paraphrase; [物語などを]retell*/ri:tél/, adapt; [契約・手紙などを更新する] renew; [財産などの譲渡をする] transfer (-rr-). ●子供用に書き換えられた物語 a story *retold* for children. ●その伝記を子供向けに書き換える *adapt* the biography for children. ●手形[免許証]を書き換える *renew* a bill [one's license]. ●土地を息子名義に書き換える *transfer* one's estate *to* one's son. ●次の文章をよりやさしい言葉で書き換えよ *Paraphrase* the following passage in easier words.

かきかた　書き方　●手紙の書き方 *how to write a letter*; a *way* [a *manner*] *of writing* a letter. ▶この用紙は書き方(=記入の仕方)が間違っている This form is incorrectly filled out 《主に米》[in《英》].

かぎかっこ　鉤括弧　((日本語文の)引用符) quotation marks, 《話》quotes 「『」, 『』」.

かききず　掻き傷　a scratch. ▶彼は有刺鉄線で額にかき傷を作った He scratched his forehead on a barbed wire.

かききる　掻き切る　●ナイフで喉をかき切る *cut* [*slit*] one's throat with a knife.

かきくだす　書き下す　(上から下へ書く) write 《a letter》 from top to bottom; (筆にまかせて一気に書く) write off 《an essay》at a stretch. ▶10 枚の原稿を一気に書き下した I *wrote off* ten pages of manuscript *at a stretch*.

かきくどく　掻き口説く　(繰り返し説得する) urge ... repeatedly 《*to* do》. ●彼は私に辞職するようかきくどいた He *urged* me *repeatedly* to resign.

かきくもる　掻き曇る　▶一天にわかに書き曇った Suddenly the sky *became overcast*.

かきくれる　掻き暮れる　（目が曇って見えなくなる）be misted [clouded]; (空が暗くなる) be overcast.
▶父の死で彼女は終日涙にかき暮れていた She *did nothing but cry* all day [*spent* the whole day *crying*] because of her father's death.

かきけす　掻き消す　drown /dráun/ ... out. ●(声などが)騒音にかき消される be drowned (out) by the noise. ▶彼の声は作業場の騒音にかき消されてほとんど聞こえなかった I could hardly hear his voice *over* [*above*] the noise in the factory./His voice *was almost lost in* the noise of the factory.

かきごおり　かき氷　(a dish of) a shaved ice with syrup on the top; (ぶっかき氷) chipped ice.

かきことば　書き言葉　(the) written (↔spoken) language.

かきこみ　書き込み　[注記]a (handwritten) note; (メモ的なもの) a jotting; (乱雑なメモ) a scribbles (!後の 2 語は通例複数形で); [記入] an entry. (⇨書き入れる) ●欄外の書き込み(=傍注) marginal *notes*. ▶彼の教科書にはほとんど書き込みがない He has entered [written] very few *notes* in his textbook./(開けてみたら) We found very few *jottings* in his textbook.

かきこむ　書き込む　〖書く〗write*; 〖書類・空白などに〗fill ... out 《主に米》[in《英》]; 〖帳簿などに〗enter. (⇨記載する) ●本に注を書き込む *write* notes in a book. ●申込書に必要事項を書き込む *fill out* [*in*] an application (form). ●名簿に名前を書き込む *fill in* [*write*, 《書》*enter*] one's name on a list.

かきこむ　掻き込む　●かきこむように食べる bolt (*down*) one's food; *shovel* one's food *into* one's mouth. ●朝食をかきこむ(=急いで食べる) have a quick breakfast.

かぎざき　鉤裂き　a tear /téǝr/. ●上着の大きなかぎ裂き(=裂け目) a big *tear* in a coat. ●スカートをくぎに引っ掛けてかぎ裂きを作る *tear* one's skirt *on* a nail.

かきしるす　書き記す　(書き留める) write* [*put*, *take*] ... down. ●観察結果をノートに書き記す *write down* [*record*] one's observations in one's notebook.

かきぞめ　書き初め　the first calligraphy of the New Year. ●書き初めをする practice artistic writing using a brush for the first time in the New Year.

がきだいしょう　餓鬼大将　the boss of the kids; (お山の大将) (the) cock of the walk (!大人にも用いる).

かきだし　書き出し　●小説の書き出し(=始まりの文) opening sentence; [一節] paragraph》 of a novel. ▶その物語は大金持ちの事故死の書き出しで始まっている The story begins with the accidental death of a millionaire.

かきだす　書き出す　●小説を書き出す(=書き始める) *begin to write* a novel. ●本からある一節を書き出す(=抜粋する) *extract* a passage *from* a book. ●候補者を書き出す(=一覧表を作る) *make a list of* candidates.

かきだす　掻き出す　（くま手などで）rake 《the ashes》out; (排水する) drain 《water》 off.

かきだす　嗅ぎ出す　●荷物中の麻薬を嗅ぎ出す smell [*scent*, (においを嗅ぎ回って) *sniff*] *out* drugs in 《his》 luggage. ●秘密を嗅ぎ出す(=探り当てる) *detect* [*smell out*] 《his》 secret. (⇨嗅ぎ付ける)

かきたてる　書き立てる　〖大々的に扱う〗(興味本位に) write* sensationally; 《話》splash 《a scandal》; (突出させて大きく) play ... up; 〖書き並べる〗make* a list of ..., list, 《書》enumerate. ●彼は新聞に新作の劇のことを書き立てた(=ほめてあれこれ書いた) He *wrote up* the new play in the newspaper. ●その醜聞は第一面に大いに書き立てられた The scandal *was splashed across* the front page. ▶彼は私の欠点を手紙の中で書き立てた He *gave a list of* my faults in his letter.

かきたてる　掻き立てる　(感情などを) stir (-rr-) ... up, fire, arouse /ǝráuz/, provoke, 《書》excite. ●想像力をかき立てる excite [stir up] 《his》 imagination. ▶彼らは反日感情をかき立てようとした They tried to *stir up* anti-Japanese feeling. ●その話は私の想像力をかき立てた The story *fired* my imagination [me with imagination].

かきたまご　掻き卵　beaten-egg soup.

かきつけ　書き付け　a note, a memo (複 ~s); (勘定書) a bill.

かきつける　書き付ける　❶〖メモする〗 make* a note

かぎつける 《of》; (書き留める) write* [put*] ... down. ▶彼女はカレンダーにスケジュールを書き付けておく習慣がある She has a habit of *writing* her schedule on the calendar.

❷[書き慣れる] ▶恋愛物は書き付けると簡単だ Love stories are easy to write once you *get used to doing* them. (❗*doing* は直前の write の代動詞で writing に同じ)

かぎつける 嗅ぎ付ける (それとなく)《話》get* [have*] wind 《of》,《話》get wise 《to》; (薄々) scent; (いろいろ調べて) smell* ... out; (見つけ出す) find* ... out. ▶彼は危険を嗅ぎつけた He could *smell* danger (coming). (❗could については (⇨出来る 解説 (5))) ▶その記者にはニュースをかぎ分ける鼻がある That reporter *has a* (good) *nose for* news.

かぎっこ 鍵っ子 a latch-key [a door-key] child [kid].

かぎって 限って ●今日に限って today of all days [times]. ▶その日に限って家に財布を忘れてきた I left my wallet at home on that *particular* day. (❗数ある中で特に「この[その]...」という場合に this [that] *particular*... が用いられる) ▶あの人に限って(=彼は決して)そんなことはしない He'll *never* do that./(最もそんなことをしそうにない人だ) He would be [is] *the last* person to do that./He is *the last* person who would [×will] do that. (❗the last ... に続く内容が非現実的なものである場合, 不定詞が続くときは主節の, 関係詞が続くときは関係詞節を通例仮定法にする. 前者の場合, is を用いると last が「最後の」の意にもなる) ▶急いでいるときに限ってバスが遅れる Our bus comes late *particularly* when we are in a hurry.

会話 「ひょっとしてあの子ホームシックになっているんじゃないかしら」「花子に限ってそんなことはない. すぐ友達のできるタイプなんだから」"Possibly she may be homesick." "*Not* Hanako. She's the type who makes friends quickly." (❗not は Other people may be, but に節して省略したもの)

かぎつばた 杜若 〖植物〗an iris /áiəris/ (圈 〜es, irides /írədi:z/).

かぎつらねる 書き連ねる ●買う物を書き連ねる list [make a list of] things to buy. ▶うらみつらみを日記に書き連ねる《書》*enumerate* one's complaints in one's diary.

かきて 書き手 (書く人) a writer; (文章家) an author (図 読み手); (書家) a penman, a calligrapher; (画家) a painter. ▶筆の立つ書き手 a good *writer*. ▶書き手の興奮が読み手にも伝わってくる A *writer*'s excitement communicates itself to the reader.

かきとめ 書留 registered mail 《米》[post 《英》]. ●書留にする register. ●書留の小包 a *registered* parcel. ▶この手紙を書留でお願いします I'd like to send this letter *by registered mail*./I'd like to have this letter *registered*.

●書留速達 registered special [《英》express] delivery. ●書留料金《米》a régistry fèe;《英》a regiştrátion fèe.

かきとめる 書き留める write* [put*, take*] ... down. ▶彼の住所を書き留める *write* [put] down his address; (メモする) *make a note of* [take notes of] his address. (⇨書き取る) ▶彼女の秘書は私たちの話をすべて書き留めた Her secretary *took down* everything we said.

かきとり 書き取り dictation. (❗「書き取るべきもの」の意では ⓒ) ▶書き取りテスト a *dictátion* tèst. ●国語の時間にある *dictation* [have a kanji test] in Japanese class. ▶先生は私たちに英語の書き取りをさせた Our teacher gave us an English *dictation*.

かきとる 書き取る 〖書き留める〗write* [put*, take*] ... down; (その場で即座に) jot (-tt-) ... down; 〖メモとして書く〗make* a note of ..., take* notes of ..., (大事な点を) note ... down. ▶警官は私の一言一句を手帳に書き取った The policeman *wrote* [put] *down* every word I said in his notebook./The policeman *took notes of* [《米》*on*] every word I said in his notebook. ▶先生は英詩をクラスに書き取らせた The teacher *dictated* an English poem to the class.

かぎとる 嗅ぎ取る ●政治的陰謀をかぎ取る smell [《話》sniff] out a political plot.

かきなおす 書き直す (内容を改める) rewrite* /ri:ráit/; (再び書く) write* again. ●記事を書き直す *rewrite* an article; 《米話》do an article *over*.

かきながす 書き流す (すらすらと書く) write off; (急いで書く) dash off. ▶彼は10分で手紙を2通書き流した He *wrote* [*dashed*] *off* two letters in ten minutes.

かきなぐる 書きなぐる scribble (down)《a note *on* a piece of paper》.

かきならす 掻き鳴らす strum (-mm-), thrum (-mm-). ●ギターをかき鳴らす *strum* (*on*) a guitar. (❗下手であることを含意)

かきぬく 書き抜く ●その本から気に入った一節を書き抜く extract [excerpt] one's favorite passage from the book.

かきね 垣根 〖生け垣〗a hedge;〖さく〗a fence. ●高い垣根 a high *hedge*. ▶その家の周りが垣根がめぐらされている The house *is fenced around* [*about*]. ▶垣根越しに隣の奥さんと話をする have a chat with the neighbor's wife *over the hedge*.

かきねつ 夏季熱 〖暑い時期の乳児の熱病〗summer fever.

かきのける 掻き退ける ●人をかきのけて前に出る push one's *way through* the crowd in order to move forward.

かきのこす 書き残す ❶〖書いて残す〗leave* 《a note [a written message]》(behind). ●遺言を書き残す *leave* a will *behind*.

❷〖書き忘れる〗forget* to write; (書きもらす) leave ... out.

❸〖書き終わらずに残す〗leave (one's writing) unfinished [incomplete].

かぎので 鉤の手 ▶廊下がかぎの手に(=直角に)曲がっている The passage bends at a *right angle*.

かぎばな 鉤鼻 a hooked [an aquiline] nose.

かぎばり 鉤針 a hook; (編み物用) a crochet /króuʃei/ (hook [needle]).

かきまぜる 掻き混ぜる (飲み物などをスプーンなどで) stir (-rr-) ...; (卵・クリームなどを) beat*, whisk. ●スープに塩を少々入れてかき混ぜる *stir* a little salt *into* the soup; add a little salt to the soup and *stir*.

かきまゆ 描き眉 painted [penciled] eyebrows.

かきまわす 掻き回す 〖かきまぜる〗(液体を) stir (-rr-) ... (up); (炭火を) poke ... (up); 〖秩序・平静を乱す〗disturb; put* ... out of order. ●スプーンでコーヒーをかき回す *stir* coffee with a spoon. ●会議をかき回す (=混乱させる) *throw* the conference *into confusion*.

かきみだす 掻き乱す disturb. (⇨乱す) ▶心の平静をかき乱す(=動揺させる) *disturb* the peace of one's mind. ▶彼の言葉が彼女の心をひどくかき乱した His remarks *upset* her greatly.

かきむしる 掻きむしる 〖つめで〗scratch (⇨掻(ク)く).

かきもじ [髪を] tear* /téər/. ●絶望のあまり髪の毛をかきむしる tear [引き抜く] pull out] one's hair in despair. (!) tear one's hair (out) は具体的な動作から通例比喩的な意味で「(髪をかきむしらんばかりに)深く悲しむ，激しく怒る」

かきもじ 書き文字 (手書きの文字) a handwritten letter.

かきもち 掻き餅 thin-sliced and dried rice cake.

かきもの 書き物 (a piece of) writing; [書類] (⇨書類,文書). ●書き物机 a writing dèsk. ●書き物をする write.

かぎゃく 加虐 (いじめること) bullying, tormenting (いじめ); (虐待を加えること) ill-treatment, cruelty (虐待).

かぎゃく 可逆 ●可逆機関 a reversible engine. ●可逆性 reversibility. ●可逆電池 a reversible cell. ●可逆反応 [化学] a reversible reaction. ●可逆変化 [物理] a reversible change.

かきゃくせん 貨客船 a cárgo-pàssenger ship [bòat]; a pássenger-càrgo ship [bòat].

かきゅう 下級 ●下級の [形] lower; [[昇進の] junior; [[階級が]] inferior. (⇨上級)
●下級裁判所 a lower court. ●下級将校 a junior officer. ●下級生 (米) an underclassman; (英) a junior (pupil [student]).

かきゅう 火急 [名] (緊急) urgency.
── 火急の [形] urgent; pressing; (切迫した) imminent. ●火急の問題 an urgent [a pressing] matter.

かきゅう 加給 (増給) an increase in pay; a raise.
●加給年金 a supplementary pension.

かぎゅう 蝸牛 [かたつむり] [動物] a snail; [蝸牛殻の] [解剖] a cochlea /kákliə/ 〜s, cochleae /-liː/).
●蝸牛角上の争い (米) a tempest in a teapot; (英) a storm in a teacup.

かきゅうてき 可及的 ●可及的すみやかに (できるだけ早く) as soon as possible; (できるだけ早い機会に) at the earliest opportunity.

かきょう 佳境 ●話は佳境に入った(=最も面白い部分に達した) We reached *the most interesting part* of the story./(よい所に達した) We got to *the best part* of the story./(最高潮に達した) The story reached its *climax*.

かきょう 架橋 bridge-building.
── 架橋する [動] ●本州と四国の間に架橋する build [construct] *a bridge* between Honshu and Shikoku.
●架橋工事 brídge wòrks.

かきょう 華僑 a Chinese merchant abroad.

かぎょう 家業 one's family business. ●家業を継ぐ [に携わる] take over [work for] one's *family business*.

かぎょう 稼業 one's business; one's occupation; one's job. ●商売

かきょう 課業 (学科) a lesson; (学業) schoolwork.

かきょく 歌曲 (ドイツの) a lied (複 lieder); (フランスの) a chanson /ʃɑːnsɔːn/; (イタリアの) a canzone /kænzóuni/ (複 canzoni /-ni/).

かきよせる 掻き寄せる sweep*... together. (⇨掻き集める)

かぎらない 限らない [[必ずしも...とは]] be [do*] not always [necessarily]...; [[すべてが...とは]] not all .... (!)いずれも部分否定) ●政治家が賢明だとは限らない Politicians *are not always [necessarily]* wise./Not all politicians are ˅wise./Áll politicians are nót ˅wise. ●最後の文で ... not ˅wise. と下降調にすると全否定で「すべての政治家が賢明である」の意味になりあいまいで，部分否定の場合は通例 not を all の直前に置く ●君が勝つとは限らない You will *not always* win./(=勝つかもしれないし勝たないかもしれない) You *may or may not* win.

かぎられた 限られた ●限られた(=狭い)場所 a *limited* space. ●限られた理解力 a limited [a *restricted*] intelligence. (!)後の方が意味が強い

*かぎり **限り** ❶ [限界] (限度) a limit; (終わり) an end.
●限りない(=永遠に続く)喜び an *everlasting* [an *eternal*] joy. ●人間の力には限りがある There is a *limit to* man's power./Man's power *is limited*. ●宇宙に限りはない There is *no limit to* the universe./The universe is *boundless*. ●討論は限りなく続いた There was *no end* to the discussion./The discussion was *endless*.
❷ [範囲・限度いっぱい] ●声を限りに叫ぶ shout *at the top of* one's voice; (できうる限り大声で) shout *as loudly as possible* [*as loudly as one can*]. ●私に関する限りでは *as* [*so*] *far as* I am concerned. ●彼は母親のためにできる限りのことをしたがよくならなかった He did *all* [*everything*, *as much as*] he could for his mother, but she didn't get well. ●生きている限りご親切は忘れません I'll never forget your kindness *as long as* I live [am alive]. ●もっと勉強しない限り落第しますよ You will fail *unless* you work harder. (!*as long as* you don't work harder のように否定文を含む言い方はあまり用いられない)

[会話]「この町に映画館はありますか」「私の知っている限りではありません」 "Are there any movie theaters in this town?" "Nót *that I* ˅*know of* [Nót *as far as* I ˅*know*]."

❸ [制限, 限定] ●今回に限り彼を許す forgive him *just this once* [*this time only*]. ●学生に限り入場可 Admission to students *only*. ●申し込みは今月10日までに限り受け付けます Applications will be accepted (*only*) until the eleventh of this month. (!)(1) *until* は通例その日を含まない。日本語の「まで」はその日を含むことに注意。(2) *only* のないほうが英語としては普通)/(11 日以後は受け取れません) Applications will *not* be accepted *on or after* the eleventh of this month. (!)日常英語では *on* または省略されることが多い) ●今日限り(=以降は永久に)たばこをやめる I'll stop smoking *forever* [*for good*] *after* today.

かぎりなくとうめいにちかいブルー 『限りなく透明に近いブルー』 *Almost Transparent Blue*. [参考] 村上龍の小説

*かぎる **限る** ❶ [制限する] (限界を設ける) limit; (制限・条件をつける) restrict. (⇨制限) ●1日の仕事を8時間に限る *limit* a day's work *to* eight hours. ●...とは限らない (⇨限らない) ●会員は大人に限る Membership *is limited to* adults. ●彼の権限は狭い範囲に限られている His power *is restricted* within narrow limits. ●日本では天然資源が非常に限られている Natural resources *are* very *limited* [*scarce*] in Japan./There is only a *limited* amount of natural resources in Japan. ●お支払いは現金に限ります(掲示) Cash *only*./Payment is *only* accepted in cash. ●おいでになる方はどなたに限らず歓迎します Whoever comes will be welcome.
❷ [最もよい] ●その手に限る That's *the best* way. ●ハイキングは秋に限る Autumn is *the best* season for going on hikes. ●暑い日は冷たいビールに限る There is *nothing like* cold beer on a hot day.

かきわける 掻き分ける plow /pláu/. ●人込みをかき分けて進む plow [push, (ひじでかき分けて) elbow] one's way through the crowd.

かぎわける 嗅ぎ分ける smell*; (嗅いで発見する) smell ... out. ▶この二つの石鹸を嗅ぎ分けるのは難しい It's hard to *smell* the difference between those two cakes of soap. (🛈 smell ... を tell ... by smelling ともいえる) ▶この犬は麻薬を嗅ぎ分けることができる This dog can *smell out* drugs.

かぎわり 書き割り 〖演劇〗(舞台背景) a stáge sètting; (背景画) a backdrop, 《英》a backcloth.

かきん 家禽 a fowl /fául/; 《集合的》(食用としての) poultry (🛈 複数扱い).

かきん 瑕瑾 (きず) a flaw, a crack; (欠点) a fault, a defect.

かきん 課金 charging. (🛈 その料金 a charge).

＊かく 書く, 描く

WORD CHOICE 書く

write 文字・本・論文・手紙などを書くこと。●本〖物語〗を書く *write* the book [story]

spell 単語のつづりを書くこと。つづりを省略せず、すべて書くことを強調する場合は spell out. ▶その単語のつづりはどんなふうに書けばいいんですか How can I *spell* (*out*) that word?

compose 断片的なアイデア・発想などを頭の中でさまざまに組み合わせ、秩序だった文章などを書くこと。▶彼女は初の文芸作品を書いた. She has *composed* her first literary work.

〖頻度チャート〗

write ████████
spell ████
compose ██

20 40 60 80 100 (%)

❶〖文などを〗write*; (書類・小切手などを) make* ... out; (詩歌・楽曲などを) compose; (つづる) spell*.
①《...を書く》●字を上手に[はっきり]書く *write* well [clearly]. ●自伝を書く *write* an autobiography; *write about* one's own life. ●返事を書く *write back* (*to him*). (⇨返事) ▶フランスについて本を書く[のことを本に書く] *write* a book about France [about France in a book]. ●国際情勢について論文を書く *write* a thesis on international situation. (🛈 on は専門的内容を暗示. cf. about) ●薬の処方箋を書く *write* [*make*] *out* a prescription. ▶彼は脚本を書いている(職業として) He *writes* for the stage./He is a _playwright_./(執筆中) He's *writing* [*working on*] a play. ▶Eメールをもらってその日の夜に返事を書くようにしています I try to send an *answer* to an e-mail on the day I receive it.
会話「それでは皆さん答えを書きなさい(=書き留めなさい)」「鉛筆でいいですか」"Now *write* [*put*, *take*] *down* your answers." "Will pencils do?"
会話「ダンさん、お名前(=姓)はどう書くのですか」「D-O-N-N-E です」"How do you *spell* your last name, Mr. Donne?" "It's D-O-N-N-E."
②《...に～を書く》●雑誌[新聞]に原稿を書く(=寄稿する) *write for* a magazine [a newspaper]. ▶彼に長い手紙を書いた I *wrote* a long letter *to him*. (🛈 (1) 単に a letter であれば a letter は通例省略して I *wrote to* 《英式・米》*wrote* him. という. (2) I *wrote* (a long letter) *for him*. は「彼の代わりに(長い)手紙を書いた」の意)/I *wrote* him a long letter. ▶受身は A long letter *was written to* [×*written*] *him*./《主に米》He *was written* a long letter.)
③《...で書く》●ペンで書く *write with* a pen [*in* pen]. (🛈 with は書く道具を, in は書かれた状態や書く動作に焦点を当てた言い方) ●インク[墨]で書く *write in* [*with*] ink [India ink]. ●手で[左手で; 大文字で]書く *write* (it) *by* hand [*with* one's left hand; *in* capitals]. ●英語で書く *write* in English.
④《...と(書いてある)》say*; (....と読める) read*. ▶新聞に関西で大地震があったと書いてある The newspaper *says* [話] It *says* in the newspaper] that there was a great earthquake in the Kansai district. (🛈 ×It is said [is written] in .... とはいわない)/*According to* the newspaper, there was a great earthquake in the Kansai district. ▶彼は日曜日に来ると書いてよこした He *wrote* (me) *that* he would be coming on Sunday. ▶標識には「一方通行」と書いてある The sign *reads* [*says*], "One Way." ▶彼は「事務所」と書いてあるドアのところへ行ってノックをした He went over to a door *marked* "Office," and knocked on it.
会話「ガイドブックには宿泊施設のことについて何か[ビザが要るかどうか]書いてありますか」「一番安いのは 35 ドルほどだ[ビザは要らない]と書いてあります」"Does the guidebook *say* anything about accommodations [*say if* we need a visa]?" "It *says* (*that*) the cheapest is around thirty five dollars [(*that*) you don't need one]."

❷〖絵などを〗(線画を) draw*; (彩色して) paint. (⇨描く❶) ●地図[下絵; 円]をかく *draw* a map [a sketch; a circle]. ●油絵をかく *paint* in oils.

＊かく 欠く ❶ 〖一部をこわす〗chip (-pp-), nick. ●刀の刃を欠く *nick* the blade of a sword. ▶だれかがぼくの湯飲みを欠いた Someone *has chipped* my cup.
❷〖足りない〗lack. (⇨欠ける❷) ●集中力を欠く *lack* [*be lacking in*] concentration. ●義理を欠く *neglect* one's duty (*to him*). ▶幸福な生活には経済的安定を欠くことができない Economic security *is indispensable* [*essential*] *to* a happy life. ▶君は行動に慎重さを欠いていた You were *careless* [*imprudent*] in your action.

＊かく 掻く scratch. ●(照れて)頭をかく *scratch* one's head shyly [in embarrassment]. 事情 米英では scratch one's head というのは, 困ったとき, ものを考えるときなどの仕草なので, shyly などを添えないと日本語での意味が違って伝わる必要が生じる) ●蚊にさされたところをかく *scratch* mosquito bites. ▶体をかいてはいけません Don't *scratch* yourself.

かく 各 〖すべての〗every; 〖それぞれの〗each. (⇨それぞれ) ●各部屋 *every* room. ●本とノートが各 1 冊 a book and a notebook. (🛈 英語では数詞で明らかなので「各」の訳の入る余地はない) ●アジア各国を歴訪する make a *circular* tour of Asian countries.

かく 角 an angle (⇨角度); 〖四角〗a square; 〖将棋の〗a bishop. ●鈍[鋭]角 an obtuse [an acute] *angle*.

かく 画, 劃 (字画) a stroke. ●5 画の漢字 a five-stroke character.

かく 格 ❶〖格式〗(地位) (a) status; (階級) a rank. ▶彼の方が社会的には格が上だ He is higher in social *status* [*rank*] than I am 〖話〗*rank*]. ▶彼は私より格が上である I am below him in social *status* [*rank*]. ▶我が社と NHK では格が違う(=比べられない, NHK より劣っている) Our company *is not comparable with* NHK./Our company *is not in the same league as* NHK.
❷〖文法〗(a) case. ●主格 the nominative *case*.

かく 核 〖原子・細胞などの〗a nucleus (🔊 nuclei) (🛈 比喩的にも用いる); 〖物事の核心〗a core. ●原子核 an atomic *nucleus*. ●非核三原則 three nonnuclear principles. ●その国に核攻撃を加える make a *nuclear* attack on the country. ●細胞の核が傷つけられた The *nucleus* of the cell was damaged. ▶核を, 持たず, つくらず, 持ち込ませず, が日本の政策である Not to own *nuclear* weapons, neither to produce nor to allow them into the country, this is the policy of Japan.

── 核の *nuclear*. ●核の傘 a *nuclear* umbrella. ●核の冬 *nuclear* winter. ●日本への核(=核兵器)の持ち込みを禁ずる ban the introduction of *nuclear* weapons into Japan.

●核開発 nuclear development. ●核拡散防止条約 the nuclear nonproliferation treaty 《略》(N)NPT》. ●核家族 a nuclear (↔an extended) family. ●核軍縮 nuclear disarmament. ●核実験 《carry out》a nuclear test. ●核戦争 (a) nuclear war. ●核弾頭 a nuclear warhead. ●核燃料 nuclear fuel. ●核爆弾 a nuclear bomb. ●核爆発 a nuclear explosion. ●核武装 nuclear armament. ●核武装する go nuclear; arm with nuclear weapons. ●核分裂 nuclear fission. ●核兵器 (⇨核兵器) ●核保有国 a nuclear power. ●核融合 nuclear fusion. ●核抑止力 a nuclear deterrent.

かく 斯く ●かくなる上は now that...; since it has come to this. ●かく言う (このように言う) say this way.
●かくのごとし like this; such. ▶彼はかくのごとく語った He spoke *like this* [*in*] *this way*,《書》*thus*].

*かく 家具 furniture, furnishings. (❗ともに集合的に家具類を表す)

┌─────────────────────────────┐
│ 使い分け furniture table, chair, cupboard │
│ (食器棚), bed など, 一般にかなり大きなもので含めた │
│ 移動可能な家具類をさすが, 日本語の「家具」よりか │
│ なり適用範囲が広く, clock, (clothes) dryer (乾 │
│ 燥機), dishwasher (食器洗い機), refrigerator │
│ (冷蔵庫), washing machine (洗濯機), air con- │
│ ditioner (エアコン)などにも用いる. 不加算名詞で, 数 │
│ えるときは a piece [an article] of *furniture* の │
│ ようにいう. │
│   │
│ furnishings furniture よりさらに広義で, sink, │
│ bath, toilet などの設備のほか, picture や mat, │
│ rug (敷物), carpet, curtain, seat cover などの │
│ 装飾品も含み, 複数扱い.《主で英》では, 上の mat │
│ 以降の室内装飾用品を soft furnishings と呼ぶ. │
└─────────────────────────────┘

●家具付きの貸家 a *furnished* house for rent 《米》[to let 《英》]. (事情) 米英ではアパート・貸家には家具調度品(furniture and fittings)が備わっている場合が多い●彼女に家具を入れる *furnish*《主に英》[fit up] a room; put *furniture* into a room. ▶その部屋には多くの家具があった There was a lot of *furniture* [×were a lot of furnitures] in the room. ▶家具類は高価ではあるが, 趣味の悪いものだった The *furnishings* were expensive, but tasteless.
●家具一式 a set [a suite /swi:t/] of furniture.
●家具屋[店] a fúrniture stòre.

かく 嗅ぐ smell (at...), have* [take*] a smell 《of》; (鼻を鳴らして) sniff (at...). ●香水のにおいを嗅ぐ *smell* 《at》[*have a smell of*] the perfume.
▶犬は地面をくんくん嗅いだ The dog *sniffed* 《at》the ground.

がく 学 〖学問〗(学識) learning;〖教育〗(an) education;〖知識〗knowledge. ●学をつける(=教育を授ける)《give》him》a good *education*. ▶彼は非常に学がある He is a man of great *learning*./He is very learned /lɔ́:rnid/.

がく 萼 〖植物〗a calyx /kéiliks/《複》-lyxes, -lyces /-ləsi:z/》, a cup.

がく 額 ❶〖金額〗a sum;(量) an amount. (⇨幾ら)
❶ ●生産額 the *amount* of production. ▶それをするにはかなりの額の金が必要だ You need a large *sum* (*of* money) [a large *amount of* money, a lot of money] to do it. (❗ *much sum [amount] は不可)* ▶損失額は全部で 400 万円以上に達している The total loss *amounts* [*sums up*] *to* more than four million yen.

❷〖額縁〗a frame;(絵の) a picture fràme;(書の) a framed piece of calligraphy. ●絵を額に入れる put a picture in a *frame*; frame a picture;(人に頼んで) have a picture *framed*. ●壁に額を掛ける hang a (*framed*) *picture* on the wall.

かくあげ 格上げ 図 (階級が上がること) a rise in rank,《書》an elevation in rank;(昇進) (a) promotion.《⇔格下げ》▶彼は大尉に格上げになった He was *promoted* to captain. (❗ 役職名は通例無冠詞)
── 格上げする 動 (昇進させる) promote; raise 《him》to a higher rank.

かくい 各位 (皆さん) everyone, all;(手紙で) Dear Sirs. ●関係者各位 To whom it may concern. (❗ 相手の宛名が不明のときの公式な手紙の書き出しの文言) ●出席者各位 *all those* present.

かくい 隔意 (⇨ 遠慮). ●隔意なく(=率直に)話し合う talk *frankly* 《with》; have a *heart-to-heart* talk 《with》;(遠慮なく) talk 《with him》*without reserve*.

がくい 学位 a degree. ▶彼は東京大学で法学修士[博士]の学位を取った He took a master's [a doctor's] *degree in* law at Tokyo University. ▶彼女は博士の学位を持っている She has a Ph.D. [the *degree* of Ph.D.] ▶彼はシェイクスピアについての学位論文(=博士論文)を書いた He wrote a *doctoral* dissertation《主に米》[*thesis*《主に英》] on Shakespeare. (⇨論文)

かくいつ 画一 ―〖一様であること〗uniformity;〖規格化〗standardization. ●画一化[主義] standardization. ●自動車の部品を画一にする *standardize* the parts of an automobile. ▶いろいろな問題を画一的に扱うわけにはいきません We can't deal with various sorts of problems *in the same way*《書》*uniformly*].

がくいん 学院 an academy. (❗日本の学校名では通例 Gakuin を用いる)

がくいん 楽員 a bandsman;(男女共用) a member of the band, a band player.

かくう 架空 ── 架空(の) 形 (想像上の) imaginary;(創作上の) fictional;(事実と違う) fictitious, unreal. ●架空の動物 an *imaginary* animal. ●架空の人物 a *fictitious* person;(小説の中の) a *fictional* character. ●架空名義で under a *fictitious* 〖虚偽の〗a *false*》name.

かくうえ 格上 a higher position [status]. (⇨ 格下) ▶会社では私より彼の方が格上だ In the office he holds a *higher position* than I〖話〗*me*].

かくえきていしゃ 各駅停車 《列車》a local train《for Kyoto》. ▶この列車は明石から先は各駅停車になる This train *stops at every station* from Akashi on.

がくえん 学園 (学校) a school;(大学構内) (a) campus. (❗日本の学校名では Gakuen を用いる)
●学園祭 a cámpus [a schóol] fèstival. ●学園生活 cámpus lífe. ●学園都市 a cóllege [a univérsity] tòwn. ●学園紛争 a cámpus dispùte;〖暴動〗rìot.

がくおん 学恩 academic indebtedness 《to; for》.

かくか 角化 ── 角化する 動 keratinize.

- 角化症 〖医学〗keratosis.
- **かくかい 各界** ・各界の名士 eminent people from *various fields* [*circles*].
- **かくがい 閣外** ・与党に閣外協力する support the ruling party from *outside the Cabinet*. (⇨閣内)
- **がくがい 学外** outside the university [campus]. (⇨学内) ・学外より教授を招く invite a professor from *outside the university*.
- **かくかく** 〖話〗such and such. (⇨これこれ)
- **がくがく** 動 ▶あまりの寒さで私の歯はがくがく鳴った It was so cold that my teeth *chattered*.
- ── **がくがくする** 動 (体が震えて) shake*, tremble; (歯が震えて) chatter; (歯がゆるんで) wobble, be loose (⇨ぐらぐら❶). ▶緊張のあまり膝(ひざ)ががくがくした My knees *were shaking badly* because I was so nervous. (▪「がくがくする膝」は shaky knees) ▶彼は恐怖でがくがくした He *trembled* with fear.
- **かくかぞく 核家族** a nuclear family.
- **かくがり 角刈り** 〖米話〗a flattop.
- ・角刈りにする [している] get [wear, have] a crew cut.
- ── **角刈りの** 形 crew-cut.
- **かくぎ 閣議** a cabinet meeting. (▪しばしば C-) ・定例 [臨時] 閣議 a regular [an extraordinary] cabinet meeting.
- **かくぎょう 学業** schoolwork; studies. ・学業にはげむ study hard. ・学業を終える finish one's *studies*.
- ・学業成績 a school record; grades. (⇨成績)
- **かくぐんしゅく 核軍縮** nuclear disarmament.
- **がくげい 学芸** arts and sciences.
- ・学芸員 a specialist in a museum. (▪curator は「館長 (所蔵品の管理責任者)」) ・学芸会 (hold) the school plays. ・学芸欄 (新聞の) an arts-and-sciences page.
- **がくげき 楽劇** a musical drama.
- **かくげつ 隔月** ・隔月刊行の雑誌 a *bimonthly* (magazine). ▶この雑誌は隔月に出版される This magazine is published *every other* [*second*] *month*.
- **かくげん 格言** a proverb; (言いならわし) a saying; (処生訓) a maxim. (⇨諺(ことわざ))
- **かくげん 確言** 图 (an) assertion, (an) affirmation. (⇨断言) ・責任者の確言を得る get the *assertion* [*affirmation*] of a responsible person.
- ── **確言する** 動 say definitely; assert, affirm.
- *かくご 覚悟** 图 (用意, 心構え) readiness, preparedness; 〖決心〗(a) resolution, determination. ▶私は地位を捨てる覚悟をしている I *am ready* [*determined*] *to* give up my position. ▶万一 (=最悪) の覚悟をしておけ *Prepare* for *the worst*./You should *be prepared for* [*get ready for*] *the worst*. ▶*Prepare yourself for the worst*. は文語的な表現) ▶私は最後まで戦う覚悟を決めた I've *made up my mind to* fight it out. ▶危険は覚悟 (=十分承知) の上でやってます I *am fully aware of* the danger but I will try. ▶こうなると覚悟はしていたもののやはりショックでした I *was ready for* this, but it still shook [shocked, was still a shock to] me. (▪shake は「動揺させる」の意)
- ── **覚悟する** 動 prepare (*for*; *to do*), (心構えができている) be ready [prepared] (*for*; *to do*); (気を引き締める) brace oneself (*for*); 〖決心する〗make* up one's mind (*to do*); (堅く決心している) be determined (*to do*), be resolved (*to do*); (あきらめる) resign oneself, be resigned (*to*+图, *to doing*).
- 会話 「これから数年は経済状態は悪化するだろう」「厳しい時期に向けて覚悟してかからないといけないね」"Economic situation will worsen in a few years to come." "We've got to *brace ourselves for* a hard time."
- **かくさ 格差** 〖隔たり〗a (wide [large]) gap; 〖違い〗(a) difference; 〖釣り合い〗(a) disparity. ・賃金格差 a *difference* in wages; 〖英〗a wage *differential*. ・格差社会 a classed society. ・格差のない社会 a classless society.
- **かくさ 較差** (変動幅) a range. ・年間の気温較差 the annual *range* of temperature.
- **かくざい 角材** (切り口の四角な木材) squared lumber 《主に米》 [timber 《英》]; (小角材) a scantling. (⇨材木)
- **かくさい 学才** (学問上の才能) academic [scholastic] ability.
- **がくさい 学債** (issue) a school bónd.
- **がくさいてき 学際的** ・学際的協力 interdisciplinary collaboration.
- **かくさく 画策** 图 (計画) a plan; a scheme /skiːm/; (策略) a maneuver /mənúːvər/.
- ── **画策する** 動 ・その教授を大学から追い出そうと画策する *plan* [*scheme*, *maneuver*] to expel the professor from the university. ・陰で画策する *maneuver* behind closed doors [the scenes]; 〖話〗pull strings.
- **かくさげ 格下げ** 图 (地位・階級を下げること) 《やや書》 degradation; 《やや書》demotion. (⇨格上げ)
- ── **格下げする** 動 ・支配人は職務怠慢のため格下げされた The manager *was degraded* [*was demoted*, *was reduced to a lower position*] for neglecting his duties.
- **かくざとう 角砂糖** lump [cube] sugar; (1個) a (lump [cube] of) sugar. (⇨砂糖)
- **かくざら 額皿** (hang) a framed picture plate.
- **かくさん 拡散** 图 (広がること) spread; 〖液体・気体の〗diffusion; 〖増殖〗(a) proliferation. ・核兵器の拡散をふせぐ prevent nuclear *proliferation* [*diffusion*]; stop the *spread* [*proliferation*] of nuclear arms.
- ── **拡散する** 動 ・ガスを拡散する 《やや書》*diffuse* gas. ▶有毒ガスがたちまち空気中に拡散した The poisonous gas *spread* through the air quickly.
- **かくさん 核酸** nucleic acid. ・リボ核酸 ribonucleic /ràibounjuːklíːik/ acid (略 RNA).
- **がくさん 学参** (「学習参考書」の略) (⇨学習)
- **かくし 隠し** ❶〖隠すこと〗・収入隠し the *concealment* of one's income. ❷〖ポケット〗a pocket.
- ・隠し絵 a picture puzzle. ・隠しカメラ a hidden [a candid] camera. ・隠し子 a secret love child. ・隠しマイク a hidden microphone [〖話〗mike]; 〖話〗a bug.
- **かくし 客死** ・客死する 動 (外国で死ぬ) die abroad [in a foreign land].
- **かくじ 各自** each (person) (⇨それぞれ); だれもみな everyone. (▪前の方が個別的な) ▶だれもが各自の意見を持っている *Each* (*person*) [*Everyone*] has his own opinion. ▶彼らは各自, 自分の席についた They sat in their *respective* seats [×each seat].
- **がくし 学士** a bachelor; (大卒者) a college [a university] graduate. ・文学士 a *Bachelor* of Arts 《略 B.A., A.B.》 ・理学士 a *Bachelor* of Science 《略 B.S(c)., S(c).B.》 ・日本学士院 the Japan Academy. ・K 大学で学士号を取る take a *bachelor*'s degree [〖まれ〗a *bachelor*('s)] at K University.
- **がくし 学資** schóol expénses. (⇨学費)
- **がくし 楽士** a musician.
- **がくじ 学事** (学校に関する事柄) school [education-

かくしあじ 隠し味 (説明的に) a small amount of seasoning just to enrich the taste.

かくしき 格式 〖格式ばること〗(a) formality; 〖儀礼〗ceremony; 〖社会的なしきたり〗a social rule; 〖社会的階層〗a social class [status, level]. ●格式ばった手紙 a *formal* letter. ●格式ばらずに without *formality* [*ceremony*]; informally. ●格式にこだわる stick to *formality* [*ceremony*]; (通例否定文で) stand on *ceremony*. ●格式が高い be high *in social status*. ●格式を重んじる stick to *social rules* [*formalities*].

がくしき 学識 〖学問〗learning; 〖研究などによって得た深い知識〗scholarship. ●深い学識 profound *scholarship*. ●学識のある人 a person of *learning*; a learned /lˈɜːrnɪd/ person; (学者) a scholar. ●学識経験者 people of learning and experience.

かくしげい 隠し芸 (説明的に) amateur singing, mimicry, conjuring tricks, and so on displayed at a party just for fun.

かくしごと 隠し事 a secret. ●私に何か隠し事をしているね [be hiding] something *from* me. ▶隠し事がとうとう明るみに出た The *secret* came to light at last.

かくした 格下 a lower position [status]. (⇨格上) ▶彼女は相手が格下でも全力でプレーする She plays for all she is worth even against a *lower-ranking* opponent.

かくしだて 隠し立て ── 隠し立て(を)する 動 (その必要がないのに[わざと]隠す) be secretive (*about*). ▶そんなことなら何も隠し立てすることもなかったのに If that's what you say, you didn't have to *keep it away from* us [you didn't have to *be secretive* about it].

かくしだま 隠し球 〖野球〗a hidden-ball trick. ●タイガースに対して隠し球を行う play [pull] a *hidden-ball trick* on the Tigers.

かくしつ 角質 名 horny [scaly] substance; keratin.
── 角質の 形 horny; keratinous.
── 角質化する 動 keratinize.
●角質層 a horny [a scaly] layer.

かくしつ 確執 a deep-rooted discord [strife].

*****かくじつ 確実** 〖確かなこと〗certainty; sureness; 〖信頼性〗reliability.
── 確実な 形 certain, sure; (絶対確実な) positive (⇨確か); (疑いのない) undoubted, unquestionable; (信頼できる) reliable; (安全な) safe; (勝利が保証された) secure. ●確実な証拠 *certain* [*positive*, *undoubted*] evidence. ●確実な方法 a *sure* method. ●確実な情報 (xa) *reliable* information. ●確実な投資 a *safe* [*secure*] investment. ●(理論などが)確実な根拠に基づいている be based on *firm* [*solid*] ground. ▶彼が落第するのは確実だ He is *certain* [is *sure*] to fail./*It is certain* [*a certainty*] *that* he will fail./*There is no doubt that* he will fail. ▶彼が再選されるだろう His reelection seems *sure*. ▶この馬は絶対確実だ。負けっこない This horse is a *sure* thing, he can't lose. ▶我々の勝利は確実だ Our victory is *secure*.
会話 「確かかい？」「確かさ」 "Are you *sure?*" "*Certain*."
── 確実に 副 certainly, surely, for certain [sure]; (間違いなく) without fail (⇨必ず); (疑いなく) undoubtedly, without doubt (⇨確かに).

かくじつ 隔日 ●隔日に医院に通う go to the doctor [doctor's (office)] *every other* [*second*] *day*.

かくしどり 隠し撮り 《take》a sneak [a candid] shot (*of*).

かくしどり 隠し録り 《make》a secret recording (*of*).

*****がくしゃ 学者** 名 (人文系の) a scholar, 〖書〗a learned /lˈɜːrnɪd/ man (複 men); (理科系の) a scientist. ●英語学者 an Énglish *schólar*. (❗ an English *schólar* は「英国人の学者」の意) ●学者ぶる set oneself as a *scholar*; be pedantic. ▶彼には学者肌のところがある(くない) He has something [nothing] of a *scholar* about him. ▶彼は古代史の著名な学者だ He is a distinguished *scholar* (in the field) of ancient history.
── 学者的な 形 scholarly; academic.

がくしゃ 学舎 a schóol building.

かくしゃく 矍鑠 ●かくしゃくとしている (=元気はつらつとしている) be vigorous; 〖書〗be hale and hearty.

かくしゅ 各種 ── 各種の 形 〖あらゆる〗〖多くの種類の〗all [many] kinds [sorts] of ...; 〖さまざまな種類の〗a large [wide] variety of .... ▶当店には各種の楽器が取り揃(そろ)えてあります We have *all* [*many*] *kinds* of musical instruments./We have musical instruments *of all* [*many*] *kinds*./We have *a large* [*wide*] *variety of* musical instruments. (⇨種類)
●各種学校 (職業訓練学校) a vocational school.

かくしゅ 鶴首 ▶彼は結婚の申し込みに対する彼女の返事を鶴首して(=首を長くして)待っている He is expectantly [anxiously] waiting for her reply to his marriage proposal.

かくしゅう 隔週 ── 隔週の 形 (米) biweekly, (英) fortnightly. ●隔週発行の雑誌 a *biweekly* /〖英〗a *fortnightly*] (magazine). ●隔週にそこへ行く go there *every other week* [*every second week*, (once) *every two weeks*, *once in two weeks*, *biweekly*, *fortnightly*]. ●隔週火曜日に発行する publish (it) *every other* [*second*] Tuesday. (⇨一置き, 一毎(ごと)に)

かくじゅう 拡充 名 expansion. ── 拡充する 動 expand; enlarge. (⇨拡張する)

*****がくしゅう 学習** (学科の) study; (技能などの) learning. (⇨勉強) ▶英語の学習にアメリカに行きたい I want to go to the U.S. to *learn* [*study*] English.
●学習参考書 a stúdy áid. ●学習辞典 a learner's [a learners'] dictionary. ●学習指導要領 a course of study (*for 7th grade science*). ●学習者 a learner. ●学習塾 (⇨塾) ●学習障害 léarning disability (difficulty) (略 LD).

がくじゅつ 学術 (科学) science; (学問) learning.
●日本学術会議 the *Science* Council of Japan. ●学術雑誌 a scientific [a technical] journal. ●学術書 a scientific [a technical] book. ●学術調査団 a scientific investigation commission. ●学術論文 《write》a treatise (*on*).

かくしょう 確証 (決定的な証拠) conclusive [(明確な) positive, (十分な) sufficient] evidence [proof] (*of*, *for*; *that* 節). (⇨証拠) ●彼の無実の確証を得る get [〖やや書〗obtain] *conclusive evidence* of his innocence. ●確証を提出する give [produce, (持ち出す) bring forward] *conclusive evidence*. ▶共謀の確証は(=信頼するに足る証拠)はあがっていない We have found no *reliable evidence* of conspiracy./We did not find *sufficient evidence* for a charge of conspiracy.

がくしょう 楽章 〖音楽〗a movement. ●第3楽章 the third *movement*.

がくしょく 学食 a schóol cafetéria.

がくじゅ 学殖 《⇨⓪ 学識》●学殖の深い人 a person of *profound learning*; a *very learned* /lə́ːrnid/ person.

かくじょし 格助詞 〖文法〗a case particle.

***かくしん 革新** 图 〖技術の〗(an) innovation;〖制度などの〗(a) reform. (⇨改革) ●技術革新 technological [technical] *innovations*.

―革新的な 形 ●革新的な考え(進歩的な) *progressive* ideas;(革命的な) *revolutionary* ideas.

―革新する innovate 《*in, on*》; reform. ●革新政権 a refórmist góvernment. ●革新政党 a refórmist párty.

かくしん 核心 the core, the heart;〖要点〗the point. ●その問題の核心に触れる get to *the core* [*heart*, (根本) *root*] *of* the problem. ▶ 彼の話はするどく核心を突いたものだった His speech was very much *to the point*.

かくしん 確信 图 〖堅い信念〗a firm [a strong] belief, (a) conviction 《前の方がより口語的》;〖自信〗confidence. ●確信を持って言う say *with confidence* [*conviction, certainty*]. ▶ 彼女の証言で彼が犯人だという確信を持った Her testimony confirmed my *conviction* of his guilt [*that* he was guilty]./Her testimony *convinced* me *that* he was guilty. 《convince は「確信させる」の意》▶ それが本当かどうか確信が持てない I am not *sure if* [×*that*] it is true.

―確信する be sure 《certain, positive, convinced》《*of; that* 節》, 《堅く信じる》firmly believe, 《自信を持つ》be confident 《*of; that* 節》.

> **使い分け** **sure** 主に主観的判断により確信すること.
> **certain** 主に客観的証拠に基づき確信すること.
> **positive** 独断的なほど強く確信すること.
> **convinced** 事実に基づき,揺るぎのないほど強く確信すること.

▶ 私は彼の成功を確信している I *am sure* [*certain, positive, convinced, confident*] *of* his success./ I *am sure* [*certain, positive, convinced, confident*] *that* he will succeed. (⇨きっと) ▶ 私は君の潔白を確信している I *am convinced of* your innocence [*that* you are innocent]. / I *firmly* [*strongly*] *believe* your innocence [*that* you are innocent]./It is my *firm* [*strong*] *belief that* you are innocent.

●確信犯 (人) a prisoner of conscience.

かくじん 各人 each 《person》. (⇨各自, それぞれ) ▶ その楽団は解散になり, メンバーは各人各様の第二の人生に踏み出した The orchestra was dissolved and each of the members started a new life *of their* [《書》*his or her*] *own*.

***かくす 隠す** ● 〖姿·物を〗hide*, 《やや書》conceal. ●押し入れに[カーテンの後ろに; 警察から]身を隠す *hide* 《*oneself*》 *in* the closet [*behind* the curtain; *from* the police]. ●両手で顔を隠す *hide* [*conceal*] one's face *in* [*behind*] one's hands. (❗in では「包み込むように」, behind では「陰に隠すように」を含意する) ▶ 彼はピストルをベッドの下に隠した He *hid* [*concealed*] a pistol under his bed. ▶ 背の高い草が彼の姿を隠していた The tall grass *hid* him 《*from view*》/He *was hidden* 《*from view*》 by the tall grass. (❗このような主語が意図的に隠すのではない文脈では ×conceal は不可) ▶ 先生がやって来ると相太は漫画本をそっと隠した As the teacher approached, Sota *slid* the comic *out of sight*. ❷ 〖悪事·感情などを〗hide*,《やや書》conceal;《覆い隠す》cover, cover … up (❗主に前の方は当惑など, 後の方は失敗·悪事など);《秘密にしておく》keep* 《it》 secret [back] 《*from* him》(⇨秘密). ●その事実を隠す *hide* [*conceal*] the fact. ●隠さずに without *concealing*; (率直に) frankly. ●何を隠そう(正直に言えば) to be frank 《*with* you》. ●自分の失敗を隠す *cover up* one's mistake. ▶ 彼は内心の当惑をにっこり笑って隠そうとした He tried to *hide* [*cover*] his confusion by smiling [with a smile]./He tried to smile to *hide* [*cover*] his confusion. ▶ 私はあなたに何も隠したりしていません I'm not *hiding* [I don't *hide*] anything *from* you. (❗進行形は現時点で, 現在形では「いつも」を強調する)/(何でも隠さず話している) I *keep* nothing [(何も秘密はない) have no secrets] *from* you. ▶ 彼女はもう年を隠せない年齢になった She has reached an age where the years tell. ▶ 名前は隠しておいてください I want to remain anonymous. (⇨匿名)

かくす 画す, 劃す ❶〖(線を)引く〗draw 《a line》; 《区別する》make a distinction 《*between*》. ▶ 善悪の間に明確な一線を画すことは難しい It is difficult to *draw* a clear *line* [*make a clear distinction*] between right and wrong. ❷〖計画する〗(⇨計画する)

かくすい 角錐 〖数学〗a pyramid. ●六角錐 a six-sided *pyramid*.

かくすう 画数 漢字の画数 the *number of strokes* in a Chinese character.

かくせい 覚醒 图 an awakening.

―覚醒する wake (up); awake. (⇨覚める❶❷) ●昏睡状態から覚醒する *wake* (*up*) from a coma.

かくせい 隔世 ●当時のことを思うと隔世の感がある When I recall those days, I feel as if we were [《話》are] living in *another age*. (⇨顧みる [最後の文例])

●隔世遺伝 atavism.

***がくせい 学生** a student.

> **解説** 《米》では student を原則として中·高·大にわたって用いるため, はっきりと大学生を示したいときには a college [a university] student とする.《英》では student は大学生のみに用いるので, 日本語とほぼ一致する. (⇨生徒)

●よい[熱心な; 優秀な; 全優の]学生 a good [a diligent; an earnest; an all-A] *student*. ●大学学部生 an undergraduate 《*student*》. (❗a graduate 《student》(大学院生) に対して用いる) ●貧乏学生 a poor *student*. ●学生時代 in one's *student* days [×age, ×times] (❗以下の方が口語的); when one is a *student*; when one is in school [college]. ▶ 彼は医学[歴史学](専攻)の学生だ He is a medical [a history] *student*./He is a *student of* medicine [history]. (⇨専攻) ▶ どこの学校の学生ですか What school do you go to? ▶ 私は京都大学の学生です I am a *student at* Kyoto University [《やや書》 the University of Kyoto]. [《話》 I am a Kyoto University *student*. (❗(1) at の代わりに of を用いるのは正式でない. (2) 後の方は「京大生」といった感じ. (3) 上の代わりに動詞を用いて I *study at* [*go to*] the University of Kyoto./I *go to* Kyoto University. ともいえる) ▶ 2人は学生結婚だ They got married while (they were) in school [college].

●学生運動 a stúdent móvement. ●学生課 the student affairs office. ●学生自治会 a stúdent cóuncil. ●学生証 a stúdent's ID (card). ●学生食堂 a schóol cafetéria. ●学生新聞 a stúdent néwspaper. ●学生生活 stúdent [cóllege, univérsity, schóol, cámpus] life.

●学生大会 a stúdent ràlly. ●学生野球 stúdent báseball.

がくせい 学制 an educátion(al) [a schóol] sýstem. ●抜本的な学制改革に着手する start on a drastic reform of the *education(al)* [*school*] *system*.

がくせい 楽聖 a master musician. ●楽聖ベートーベン Beethoven, the *great master of music*.

かくせいき 拡声器 a (loud) speaker; (携帯用の) a megaphone; (電気メガホン)《米》a bullhorn,《主に英》a loudhailer.

かくせいざい 覚醒剤 a stimulant (drug), stimulating drug,《書》amphetamine /æmfétəmi:n/. (⚠俗に speed という).

がくせき 学籍 a schóol règister. ●学籍に学生全員を登録する enroll all the students on the *school register*.

かくぜつ 隔絶 图 〖孤立〗isolation /àisəléiʃən/; 〖離れること〗separation.
—— 隔絶する ●社会から隔絶して暮らす live *in isolation*; live apart from the world. ▶その島は文明社会から隔絶している The island *is isolated* [*is separated*] *from* civilization.

がくせつ 学説 a theory. (⇨説)

かくぜん 画然 ●画然たる違い a *clear* [a *decided*] difference. ●それらの間には画然とした区別がある There is a *clear* [a *sharp*] distinction between them.

がくぜん 愕然 ●愕然とする be amazed, be astonished; be shocked. (⇨驚く) ●愕然として in amazement [astonishment].

がくそう 額装 ●額装する ● frame; put (a picture) in a frame.

がくそく 学則 a school rule [regulation] (⚠後の方は堅い言い方。いずれもしばしば複数形で); (服装についての) dress code. (⇨校則) ●新しい学則を設ける make [lay down] new *school rules*.

がくそつ 学卒 a college [a university] graduate.

*かくだい 拡大 图 〖範囲・勢力などの〗(an) expansion; (an) extension;〖規模・面積などの〗enlargement. ●貿易の急速な拡大 a rapid *expansion* [*extension*] of trade.
—— 拡大する ● 〖広げる〗〖四方八方に〗expand; (ある点で、またはそれを越えて) extend; (大きくする) enlarge (⇨拡張する);〖形を大きく見せる〗《やや書》magnify;〖戦争などを段階的に〗escalate. ●生産性を拡大する expand productivity. ●市場をアジアまで拡大する extend the market *to* Asia. ●3倍に拡大する *magnify* [*enlarge*] (it) (*by*) *three times.* (⚠ magnify は顕微鏡などで、enlarge は複写機などで) ●彼らの事業は拡大している Their business *is expanding.* ▶戦火が拡大した The war (*was*) *escalated* [*was expanded*]. ▶彼はその法律を可能な限り拡大解釈した He *stretched* the law to its full extent.
●拡大鏡 a mágnifying glàss. ●拡大再生産 extended reproduction.

がくたい 楽隊 《form》a band; (吹奏楽の) a brass band; (管弦楽の) an órchestra.

かくたる 確たる (確か) A. ●確たる証拠 *positive* [*definite*] proof.

かくたん 喀痰 (たんを吐くこと)〖医学〗expectoration; (たん) phlegm /flém/, sputum /spú:təm/.
●喀痰検査 an examination of sputum.

かくだん 格段 ●格段に(=断然)はるか *by far* the best. (⚠ by far は通例最上級を修飾する) ●英語が格段に(=著しく)進歩する make *remarkable* progress in English. ▶両者の間には格段の(=顕著な)相違がある

There is a *marked* [(明瞭な) a *distinct*, (目立った) a *striking*] difference between the two.

がくだん 楽団 an orchestra; (吹奏楽・ジャズ・ロックなどの) a band.
●楽団員 (オーケストラの) a member of an orchestra; (ジャズなどの) a member of a band; a bandsman.

がくだん 楽壇 the musical world; musical circles.

かくち 各地 each [every] place (地方) district; 〖いろいろな場所〗various places [districts]. ●各地の今日の温度 today's temperature *in each district*. ●世界各地から来る come from *various* [*all*] *parts* of the world; come from *all over* the world.

かくちゅう 角柱 〖数学〗a prism; (切面が四角な柱) a square pillar. ●三角[五角]柱 a triangular [pentagonal] *prism*.

かくちょう 拡張 图 (an) expansion (⚠四方八方にわたる拡張); (an) extension (⚠ある1点までの、あるいはそれを越えての拡張). (⇨拡大) ●領土拡張 the *expansion* [*extension*] of one's territory. ●軍備拡張 the *expansion* of armaments; military *expansion*. ●彼らは校舎の拡張を計画している They plan to *extend* the school building.
—— 拡張する ● 〖容積・範囲などを〗expand; 〖長さ・勢力などを〗extend; 〖規模・面積などを〗enlarge; (幅を) widen. ●事業を拡張する expand [extend, enlarge] one's business. (⚠ expand は販売域を広げ、売り上げを伸ばすこと、extend は支店や扱う品目、業務を増やすこと、enlarge は単に規模を大きくすること) ●道路を駅まで拡張する extend [×widen] the road *to* the station. (⚠ widen は「幅を広げる」ことなのでこの文脈では用いない) ●空港を拡張する enlarge an airport.
●拡張子 〖コンピュータ〗an extension.

かくちょう 格調 ●格調高い(=高尚な)文体で書く write in an *elegant* [(やや書) a *lofty*,《書》an *elevated*] style.

がくちょう 学長 (大学の) a president,《主に英》a principal, a chancellor (⚠いずれもしばしば大文字で. chancellor は《英》では名目上の学長で実務は vice-chancellor がとる.《米》では president の方が一般的). ●彼をT大学の学長に任命する appoint him (the) *president of* T University.

がくちょう 楽長 〖音楽〗a bandmaster; a conductor (of a band).

かくづけ 格付け ●年間優秀映画の格付け(=評価) the *rating* [(順位) *ranking*] of the year's best movies.
—— 格付けする ● ●彼は最高級の職人と格付けされている He *rates* [*ranks*] *as* the best craftman./He *is rated* [*ranked*] (*as*) the best craftman.

がくっと (がくんと、がっくり) ●近くにスーパーができてから店の客足ががくっと(=急激に)落ちてしまった The number of our customers has dropped *sharply* since a supermarket opened in the neighborhood.

*かくてい 確定 图 (決定) (a) decision.
—— 確定的な ● (最終的な) final; (明確な) definite; (確実な) certain. ●彼が昇進することはほぼ確定的だ It is almost *definite* [*certain*] that he will be promoted./His promotion is almost *definite* [*certain*].
—— 確定する ● (決定される) be decided; (日取りなどが) 動きの堅い語. ●会合の日を確定する *fix* [*settle*] the date of the meeting. (⇨決定する) ▶新しい校舎を建てることが確定した It *has been decided* that a new school building

カクテル a cocktail /kákteil/. ●カキのカクテル an óyster còcktail. ●フルーツカクテル a frúit còcktail. ●カクテルグラス a cócktail glàss. ●カクテル光線 artificial daylight lighting. ●カクテルドレス a cócktail drèss. ●カクテルパーティー a cócktail pàrty. ●カクテルラウンジ a cócktail lòunge.

がくてん 楽典 musical grammar. ●(本) a book of musical grammar.

***かくど** 角度 an angle. ●角度を測る take [measure] the angle. ●はしごを壁に対して30度の角度でたてかける set a ladder at an angle of 30° [a 30° angle] to the wall. ●30°は thirty degrees と読む) ●別の[異なった; いろいろな]角度から眺めよう look at 〈it〉 from another angle [a different angle; various angles]. ●あらゆる角度から論じる discuss 〈it〉 in all its aspects [from all sides].

かくど 確度 (正確さ) accuracy; (信頼性) reliability. ●確度の高い情報を得る get accurate [reliable] information.

がくと 学徒 (学生) a student; (学者) a scholar. ●学徒出陣 the departure of students to the front. ●学徒動員 students' mobilization [call-up]. ●学徒兵 a stúdent sòldier.

がくと 学都 a college [a university] town; a campus city.

かくとう 格闘 图 (打ち合いの) a fight; (取っ組み合いの) a grapple, (乱闘) a scuffle, (奪い合いの) 《話》 a tussle.
— 格闘する 動 fight [grapple, tussle]《with》. (!いずれの語も比喩的に用いることができる) ●格闘技 a combative sport.

かくとう 確答 图 ●確答を避ける avoid giving a definite answer, (言質を与えるのを避ける) avoid committing oneself; (どっちつかずの[責任逃れの]答えをする) give a noncommittal [an evasive] answer.
— 確答する 動 answer definitely; give a definite answer.

がくどう 学童 a schoolchild (徳 -children). (⇒小学生) ●学童保育を行う take care of latch-key children after school hours. ●その施設は an after-school-care center)

***かくとく** 獲得 图 acquisition. ●版権の獲得 the acquisition of copyright.
— 獲得する 動 〖得る〗 get*, obtain, acquire; 〖確保する〗 secure; 〖競って〗 win*. (⇒得る) ●英国国籍を獲得する get [acquire, receive] British citizenship. ●金メダルを獲得する win a gold medal. ▶新党は400議席中30議席を獲得した The new political party won 30 of 400 seats.

かくない 閣内 within the Cabinet. (◎ 閣外) ▶閣内にはさまざまな意見がある There is much diversity of opinion within the Cabinet.

がくない 学内 (学校の構内) a campus; school premises. (◎ 学外) ●学内で on (the) campus [the school premises]. ●学内新聞 a schóol [a cóllege] nèwspaper.

かくに 角煮 ●豚肉の角煮 cubed pork stewed in soy-sauce and sugar.

かくにん 確認 图 (間違いないことの) confirmation; (真実・正確であることの) verification, (同一であることの) identification. ▶確認のため復唱いたします Let me repeat your words for confirmation: ..../Just to make sure I've got it right: .... (!...で復唱内容を伝える)
— 確認する 動 confirm; verify; identify. (⇒確かめる) ●電話でホテルの予約を確認する confirm [make sure of] one's hotel reservation by telephone. ●指紋によって死体の身元を確認する identify [make identification of] a body by his fingerprint.

かくねん 隔年 ●隔年の行事 a biennial /baiéniəl/ event. (!biennial はやや堅い語) (⇒隔週)

***がくねん** 学年 ❶ [同一学齢の生徒の] a year (!「第...番目の学年」の意は「the [one's] +序数+year」で表す. 以下も同様); (小・中・高等学校の) 《米》 a grade (!6・3・3制の場合は通例第12学年まで通算して数えるか(この場合, 「...学年の生徒」には grader を用いる), または高校の3学年の学生をそれぞれ freshman, junior (時に) sophomore, senior という. 小・中学校8, 高校4の制度では第8学年まで通算で数え, 下6年を下から(大学と同じく)freshman, sophomore, junior, senior という);《英》a form (!小学校・中学校のいずれも第6学年まで. この場合,「...学年の生徒」には - former を用いる). (⇒年年) ●中学校第2学年の生徒《米》an eighth grader,《英》a second former (at secondary school) (!《英》では小学校か通算して a year eight student のようにもいう. 担当の先生は an eighth grade《米》[a second form《英》]《math》teacher となる) ▶大学で彼は私より1学年上でした He was one year ahead of me [in the year just above mine] in college. ▶彼女は高校第1学年を終えてアメリカから帰国したとき, K 高校の2学年に入れてもらった. そこでは1学年からフランス語が必修であった When she returned home from the US after the end of her 10th grade, she was accepted as a second-year student at K High School, where French language classes were required from the first year on.
❷ [学校年度] a school [an academic] year (●** 米英では通例9月から翌年の6月まで.) ●K 大学1991年度卒業の学年《米》the class of (19)91 at K University. ▶日本では1学年はふつう3学期に分かれている A school [an academic] year is usually divided into three terms in Japan. ●学年末試験 a year-end exam; the [one's] finals (!通例複数形で期間中の一連の試験をさす.《英》では大学に限る).

がくのうきん 学納金 schóol expènses; schóol fèes. ▶学納金が毎年高くなる一方だ School expenses are increasing [piling up] every year.

がくのうこ 格納庫 a hangar. (!つづり字に注意) ●飛行機を格納庫に入れる put an airplane in a hangar.

かくのごとし 斯くの如し (⇒斯く [成句])

がくは 学派 a school. ●エピクロス学派 the school of Epicurus /epikjúərəs/.

がくばつ 学閥 (出身校による)《軽蔑的》an academic clique /klíːk/. ●学閥の弊害 the evils of an academic clique. ●学閥を打ち破る[作る] break down [form] academic cliques.

かくばった 角張った (四角い感じの) square; (骨ばった) angular. ●角ばったあごの男 a man with a square jaw; a square-jawed man.

かくばる 角張る ❶ [角がある] angular; (四角い) square. ●角ばった顔 an angular face.
❷ [四角ばる] (⇒四角 [四角ばる])

かくはん 攪拌 — 攪拌する 動 stir. (⇒掻(か)き混ぜる) ●攪拌器 a mixer; (卵・クリームなどの泡立て器) a whisk.

がくひ 学費 schóol expènses (!種々の費用を含めて); 〖授業料〗 schóol fèes;《主に米》tuition. ●ア

バイトをして学費をかせぐ earn one's *school expenses* by working part time. ▶おじが私の大学の学費を出してくれた My uncle paid my college *fees* [my *tuition* at college]. (⚠正確にはこれでよいが，単に ... paid my college. という方が普通)

かくひつ 擱筆 ── 擱筆する 動 (書き終える) finish writing.

がくふ 岳父 (妻の父) one's father-in-law; one's wife's father.

がくふ 楽譜 a (musical) score;《総称》music; (1枚の) a músic shèet. ● ピアノの楽譜 a piáno scòre. ● 楽譜を読む read *music* [a (musical) *score*]. ● 楽譜なしで演奏する play without *music* [(聞き覚えで) by ear, (暗譜で) from memory].

がくぶ 学部 (一般教養を終えてから入る専門学部) (a) school; (総合大学の) (a) college, a department (⚠単·複両扱い), 《主に英》a faculty. (⚠下位区分としての学科いずれも department.《米》では faculty は大学の教授陣を集合的に表すことが多い) 法[医]学部 the *School* of *Law* [*Medicine*], the *Law* [*Medical*] *School*. 語順 米国で学部を終えてから進学する) ▶ニューヨーク大学医学部 New York University Medical *College*. ● 学部学生 an undergraduate,《話》an undergrad. ● 学部長 a dean.

がくふう 学風 [学問の伝統] an academic tradition; (研究の方法) a method of study;[大学の校風] school traditions. ▶あの 2 人の学者は学風が違う Those two scholars have different *academic traditions*.

かくふく 拡幅 图 ● 道路の拡幅工事 the widening construction of the road.
── 拡幅する 動 widen [broaden] (a road).

がくぶち 額縁 a (picture) frame. (⇒額❷)

かくへいき 核兵器 (個々の) a nuclear weapon,《話》a nuke; (全体) nuclear arms [weapons]. (⇒核 ❷) ▶核兵器反対! No (more) *nukes*!

かくべえじし 角兵衛獅子 *kakubejishi*; the street performance of young boys who wear lion headdresses and perform acrobatic stunts.

かくへき 隔壁 (飛行機·船の) a bulkhead; (建物の) a wall, a partition. (⚠ partition は「簡単な間仕切り」)

かくべつ 格別 ── 格別の 形 particular;[特別の] special;[例外的な] exceptional;[著しい] remarkable;[普通でない] unusual. ▶格別の(=心から)お引き立てありがとうございます Thank you very much for your *kind* patronage.
── 格別(に) 副 particularly, especially;(例外的に) exceptionally. (⇒特に) ▶その映画を格別見たいわけではない I don't *particularly* [*especially*] want to see the movie. ▶今日は格別寒い It is *exceptionally* [*unusually*] cold today./(今日の寒さは格別だ) Today's cold is *exceptional* [*unusual*]. ▶神戸の夜景は格別だ(=格別に美しい) The night view of Kobe is *especially* beautiful. ▶格別これといったことはなかった Nothing *remarkable* [*particular*] happened.

*かくほ 確保 ── 確保する 動 [物を] (苦労して) secure;(努力·計画して) obtain;[人を]line ... up. ● 彼女のために席をかくほする *secure* her a seat; *secure* a seat *for* her. ● 必要な人員を確保する *obtain* the required number of people. ▶私は席を確保するために新聞をシートに置いた I put a newspaper on my chair to *keep* my place. ▶(選挙で)彼が何票確保できると思いますか How many votes do you think he can *line up*? (⚠

「票」は「人」に同じ)

かくほう 確報 a reliable [a confirmed, a correct] report (*on*). ● この事件に関する確報を待つ wait for a *reliable report* on this incident.

かくほう 角帽 (square) college cap; (大学の儀礼用の帽子) a mortar board.

がくほう 学報 (学術上の報告雑誌) a bulletin /búlətn/;(学校の) a schóol nèwspaper.

がくぼう 学帽 a schóol càp.

かくまう [保護する] harbor (⚠食料·隠れ場所を与えることを含意);[隠れ場所を提供する] shelter. ● 逃亡者をかくまう *harbor* [*shelter*] a runaway; *give harbor* [*shelter, refuge*] *to* a runaway.

かくまく 角膜 【医】 a cornea /kɔ́:rniə/. ● 角膜の corneal. ● 角膜移植を行う perform a *corneal* transplant; transplant a *cornea*.

かくまく 隔膜 【生物】 the septum. ● 横隔膜 (⇒横隔膜)

がくむ 学務 school [educational] affairs. ● 学務委員 a member of the Board of Education. ● 学務課 the school [educational] affairs section.

*かくめい 革命 图 (a) revolution.
① [~革命] ● 武力[無血]革命 an armed [a bloodless] *revolution*. ● 反革命 a counter-*revolution*. ● 産業[フランス]革命 the Industrial [the French] *Revolution*. ● IT 革命 an IT *revolution*.
② [革命が[を]] ● 母国で革命が起こった A *revolution* broke out [×happened] in my home country. ▶軍隊が革命を起こした The army started the *revolution*. ▶車社会生活に革命をおこした Automobiles *revolutionized* [brought about a *revolution* in] social life.
── 革命的な 形 revolutionary. ▶それは革命的な(=画期的な)考えだ That's a *revolutionary* [(斬新な)a *novel*] idea. ● 革命運動 a revolutionary movement. ● 革命家 a revolutionary; a revolutionist. ● 革命軍 a revolutionary army. ● 革命思想 a revolutionary [(過激な) a radical] idea. ● 革命政府 a revolutionary government.

かくめい 『革命』 *Revolutionary*. (参考 ショパン作曲のエチュード)

がくめい 学名 a scientific [(俗に) a Latin] name.

がくめん 額面 face (value),【金融】par (value). ● 額面で[以下で]株を買う buy stocks *at* [*below* (⇔*above*)] *par*. ● 彼のことばを額面どおりに受け取る take him *at face value*; take his words *literally*.
● 額面価格 face value [amount]; par value.
● 額面株式 a par (value) stock; a stock at par; a stock with par value. ● 額面発行 a par issue; an issue at par. ● 額面割れ drop under [below] par.

*がくもん 学問 (読書·研究による知識(習得)) learning; (学業，研究) study [しばしば複数形で];(学識) scholarship;(教育) education.
① [学問が[は]] ▶彼はとても学問がある人だ He is a man of great *learning*./He is a very *learned* /lə́:rnɪd/ man. ▶彼には学問がない(=教育を受けていない) He is uneducated./He had no schooling. (⇒教育) ▶学問は結局世のため人のためでなくてはならない *Learning*, after all, must serve the world and the people.
② [学問の] ● 学問の世界 the *scholarly* [*academic*] world. ● 学問の自由 *academic* freedom. ● 学問の一分野 a branch of *learning*. ● 学問の

がくもんのすすめ 歩によって多くのことが明らかになった The advancement of *learning* has made a lot of things clear.
③【学問に[を]】●学問を修める acquire [gain] *learning*. (⇨勉強する) ▶彼は学問に励んだ(＝熱心に研究した) He *studied* hard./《書》He attended diligently to his *studies*.
④【学問だ】●哲学は高尚な学問だ Philosophy is a noble *study*.
⑤【学問的】●学問的方法を使う use a *scholarly* [(科学的)] [*scientific*] method. ●学問的に扱う treat (it) *in a scholarly way* [*academically*, (科学的に) *scientifically*].
●学問に王道なし (ことわざ) There is no royal road to *learning*.

がくもんのすすめ『学問のすゝめ』 *An Encouragement of Learning*. [参考]福沢諭吉の論文集

かくや 斯くや ●極楽もかくやと思われる別世界 another world which *seems like* a Paradise.

がくや 楽屋 (劇場などの) a dréssing ròom, (俳優の休憩室) a greenroom. ●楽屋裏の private; (内部の) inside; (裏面の) behind-the-scenes. ●楽屋裏へ行く[にいる] go [be] *backstage*. (!この backstage は副詞)
●楽屋落ち an in-joke; a private joke. ●楽屋雀 (内部の事情に詳しい人) an insider, (話) a person in the know; (芝居通) (話) a theater buff.

かくやく 確約 ⓖ a definite promise. (⇨約束)
―**確約する** 動 give (him) a definite promise (*to* do; *that* 節); give (him) one's word (*to* do; *that* 節).

かくやす 格安 ●私はそれを格安の値段で買った I bought it at a *special* [*a bargain*] *price*. ▶このラジオは本当に格安[=格安の品]だ This radio is a *real bargain* [*a good buy*].

かぐやひめ かぐや姫 the Shining [Moon] Princess.

がくゆう 学友 a school friend.

かくよう 各様 ●各人各様 So many men, so many ways.

がくようひん 学用品 school supplies [things].

かぐら 神楽 *kagura*, (説明的に) sacred dances and music performed at shrines.

かくらん 攪乱 ⓖ (a) disturbance; (混乱状態) (a) confusion.
―**攪乱する** 動 disturb; throw ... into confusion.

がくラン 学ラン (つめえりの) a school uniform with a stand-up collar; (長い上着とだぶだぶのズボンの) a school uniform of a long jacket and baggy pants.

かくり 隔離 ⓖ isolation (⇨孤立); (伝染病予防のための) quarantine /kwɔ́(ː)rəntiːn/.
―**隔離する** 動 isolate; quarantine. ●その患者を隔離しておく keep the patient *in quarantine* [*isolation*].
●隔離病院 an isolation [a quarantine] hospital.

がくり 学理 ⓖ (学問での理論) a theory.
―**学理的な** 形 theoretical.

*****かくりつ** 確率 (見込み) probability. ▶彼の成功の確率はほとんどない There is little *probability* of his success [that he will succeed]./The *probability* of his success [that he will succeed] is very small. (! possibility, probability, certainty の順で確率が高くなる) ▶2個のさいころをころがしてどちらも6が出る確率は 36分の1である There is a 1 in 36 *probability* of throwing two sixes with two dice.
●確率論『数学』 probability theory.

かくりつ 確立 ⓖ (しっかりさせること) establishment. ▶方針の確立 the *establishment* of a policy.
―**確立する** 動 ●婦人の地位を確立する *establish* women's status. ▶その作品で彼の画家としての名声が確立した The work *established* his reputation as an artist.

かくりょう 閣僚 a member of the Cabinet, a Cabinet member [minister];《集合的》ministry (!しばしば M-). (! minister, ministry は英国・日本の場合) ●閣僚級の会談 a *ministerial* level conference; talks at the *ministerial* level. ●閣僚の1人である hold a seat in the Cabinet. ▶全閣僚が抗議のため辞職すると言っている The entire *Ministry* has threatened to resign in protest.

がくりょう 学寮 (大学などの)《米》a dormitory,《米話》a dorm; a residence hall;《英》a hall (of residence). (⇨寮)

*****がくりょく** 学力 académic [《書》scholástic] ability; (学識) scholarship. ●学生の学力を高める enhance [《改善する》improve] students' *academic ability*. ▶彼は大卒以上の学力がある He is superior to a college graduate in *academic ability*. ▶彼女の英語の学力(＝知識)は大したものだ[低い] Her *knowledge* of English is great [poor].
●学力試験[考査] an achíevement tèst.

がくれい 学齢 school age. ●学齢に達する reach *school age*. ●学齢に達していない子 a child under *school age*;《書》a preschooler (!日本でいえば幼稚園児).

かくれが 隠れ家 [場] a híding plàce; (犯罪者などの) a hide-out; (避難所)《やや書》a réfuge, (隠遁所)《話》a hideaway. ●隠れ家を捜す[つきとめる] search for [locate] (his) *hideout*.

がくれき 学歴 one's educational [academic] background; (学校教育) one's schooling. ▶日本は学歴社会だ Japan is a society in which an *educational background* counts./Japan is an *academic-background*-oriented [a *schooling*-conscious] society. ▶彼はほとんど学歴がない He's had very little *schooling* [*school education*]./(学歴が低い) He is not well-educated.

DISCOURSE
出生率の低下は，高学歴の女性が増えていることに一因がある The decrease in the birth rate **is** partly **attributable to** the increase in the number of women with a *higher education*. (!〜 is attributable to ... (〜は...に起因する)は理由に用いるディスコースマーカー)

かくれキリシタン 隠れキリシタン (徳川時代の)『歴史』a hidden [a separated] Christian,《書》a crypto-Christian. (⇨キリシタン)

かくれみの 隠れ蓑 (衣服) an invisible cloak; (手段) a cover (*for*).

かくれもない 隠れもない (よく知られている) well-known, widely-known; known to everybody.

*****かくれる** 隠れる ❶ [身を隠す] hide*;《やや書》conceal] (oneself) (!oneself は省略する方が普通); [遮蔽する] take* refuge (*with*＋人, *in*＋場所), (砲撃などを避けて) take cover (*in*); (待ち伏せる)《軽蔑的》lurk. ▶彼が出てゆくまで奥の部屋[ベッドの下; カーテンの後ろ]に隠れています I'll *hide in* the back room [*under* the bed; *behind* the curtain] until he leaves. ▶私の家族はみな教会に隠れた All my family *took* [*sought*] *refuge* in the church. ▶その強盗はドアの後ろらにピストルを構えて隠れていた The robber *lurked* behind the door with his gun at [to] the ready.

かくれんぼう

❷ [見えなくなる] disappear, go* out of sight; be lost (to sight); be hidden from view, (おおわれて) be covered. ▶慈善の美名に隠れて *under* (×the) *cover* [*the veil*] *of* charity. ▶飛行機は雲に隠れて見えなくなった The plane *disappeared* [*was lost*] *in* the clouds./The plane *was hidden by* [*in*] the clouds. (🔔 by では雲の方が覆いかぶさって見えなくなるのに対して, in では雲の中にすっぽり機体が埋まってしまう感じを伴う) ▶雲が出て来て月が隠れた Clouds moved in and *hid* the moon *from view*. ▶潮が満ちて岩が隠れた The tide came in and *covered* the rocks.

❸ [潜在する] lurk. (⇨潜む❶) ●隠れた意味 a *hidden* meaning; a meaning *between lines*. ●隠れた才能を引き出す draw out a *potential* [《書》a *latent*] talent. (🔔 potential は将来の可能性を, latent は表に出ないで隠れていることを強調":する)

❹ [人に知られないようにする] ー (俗世間から)隠れて暮らす live *in seclusion*. ▶親に隠れてアルバイトをする work part time without one's parents knowing (it). (⇨内緒) ▶彼女は私に隠れて(=私の背後で)それをした She did it *behind my back*. (🔔 慣用表現)

かくれんぼう 隠れん坊 《play》 hide-and-seek. (事情 米英のこの遊びでは鬼は1人または複数いて, 鬼は it, 「見つけた」は "Caught!" という)

かくろん 各論 [詳細な討論] a detailed discussion; [詳細] detail. ●各論に入る go into *detail* [*particulars*]. ●総論から各論へ進む proceed from a general discussion to a *detailed one*; descend from generals to *particulars*.

かぐわしい 香しい sweet; sweet-scented; fragrant. ▶これらの花はかぐわしい香りがする These flowers smell *sweet*.

がくわり 学割 a (special) discount for students, a stúdent('s) discount. ▶あの店は学割がきく That store gives a (*special*) *discount for* [*special publics*] *to*] *students*.
●学料料金 a stúdent fàre; a stúdent ràte.

かくん 家訓 one's family motto [《書》precept]. ▶我が家の家訓は「よく学びよく遊べ」だ Our *family motto* is "All work and no play makes Jack a dull boy."

かくんと ▶人形の首がかくんと折れてしまった The doll's neck *broke suddenly*.

がくんと [ぐいと] with a jerk; [急に] suddenly. ▶バスがくんと止まった The bus stopped *with a jerk*./The bus *jerked* to a stop. ▶彼は成績ががくんと下がった His grades *suddenly* [*sharply*] fell. ▶バスはがくんがくんと揺れながら田舎道を進んで行った The bus *jolted* (*along*) over the country road. ▶その老人はがくんとひざをついた The old man *dropped to* his knees. ▶追突された拍子に首がかくんとなった My neck *snapped* when my car was hit from behind.

かけ 欠け ❶ [月の] ▶月の満ち欠け the waxing and *waning* of the moon. ❷ [かけら] (⇨かけら)

かけ 掛け credit. (⇨付け) ▶掛け売りお断わり (⇨掛け売り)

かけ 賭け [賭け事] (一般に) a bet 《*on*》, betting; (ゲームなどの) gambling, a gamble 《*on*》 (⇨賭ける); [危険] a risk. ▶大きな賭けをする make a big *bet*; (high stakes for *big* [*high*] *stakes*) 《大きな危険を冒す》run [take] great *risks*. ●賭けに勝つ[負ける] win [lose] a *bet*. ●賭けが好きだ (⇨賭博) ▶彼は賭け事が好きだ He likes *gambling*. ▶その事で彼と賭けしたい I bet him [*made a bet with* him] *on* it. ▶人生は賭け(=運まかせの勝負)だ Life is a game of chance.

かげ

●賭け金 a bet; stakes.

―かけ ―掛け ▶私は書きかけの本の筆を執り直した I started to work again on the book (that) I *was writing*. ▶彼は宿題をやりかけたままにして遊びに出かけた He went out to play, *leaving* his homework *unfinished* [*half done*].

かげ 陰 ❶ [日陰] shade (🔔 しばしば the 〜); shadow(s). (🔔 shade は太陽の熱から逃れられて好ましいこと, shadow は光が当たらず暗いことを強調する) ●陰干しする dry (it) in the *shade*. ▶とても暑かったので陰に入って休んだ It was so hot that I got into the *shade* [×*shadow*] and took a rest. ▶大きな木が公園のあちこちに陰[すてきな陰]を作っていた Big trees gave *shade* [a pleasant *shade*] here and there in the park. (🔔 形容詞を伴う場合は a がつく) ▶彼の家はいつも陰に[あの建物の陰に]なっている His house is always *in shadow* [*in the shadow of* that building]. ▶ちょっと, そこのいてくれませんか. 陰になるんですよ Excuse me, will you please step aside? You're blocking the sun. (🔔 block は「さえぎる」の意)

❷ [背後] ▶彼はカーテンの陰に隠れた He hid (himself) *behind* the curtain. (🔔 himself を省略する方が普通) ▶彼がドアの陰から中をのぞいていた He was looking in from *behind* the door.

❸ [目の届かないところ] ▶本人の前ではいいことを言っておいて陰で悪口を言うような人は嫌いです I don't like the kind of person who will be nice to someone's face but say bad things about them *behind* their *backs*. (🔔 someone を them, their で受けるのは《話》) ▶彼らは陰で上からぬこをたくらんでいる《話》They are plotting something *behind the scenes*.

●陰で糸を引く ▶彼が陰で糸を引いていたのだ He *was pulling strings*.

●陰になりひなたになって ▶次夫は今まで陰になりひなたになって私を支えてくれた Tsuguo supported me *both publicly and privately*.

かげ 影 (影法師) a shadow (🔔 光がさえぎられてできる輪郭のはっきりした暗い部分をいう); (人などの姿) a figure; (物などの姿) (a) shape; (人・物の輪郭) a silhouette /sɪluˈɛt/; (鏡・水などに映った影) a reflection, an image. ▶夕方になると影が長くなる *Shadows* lengthen [grow longer] in the evening. ▶暗がりの中でゆっくりと動く人の影が見えた I could see someone [a *figure*] moving slowly in the dark. ▶山々の影が水に映っていた The *reflection* of the mountains was in the water./The mountains *were reflected in* [《まれ》*on*] the water. ▶彼は水に映った自分の影を見た He looked at his shadow [*reflection*] in the water. ▶かつての大スターであった彼女も今では見る影もなかった(=昔の面影はなかった) Once a great star, now she is only a *shadow of her former self*. ▶昔は三歩下がって亭主の影を踏まず、だったのである It used to be that a wife walked three steps behind her husband, so not to step on his *shadow*. (🔔「下に」は down でなく behind (後ろ)を用いる)

●影が薄い ▶彼が偉すぎて兄の影が薄い(=目立たなさすぎる) He is so great that he [His greatness] *puts* his brother *in* [*into*] *the shade* [×*shadow*].

●影がさす ▶都合がよいことにはその木の下には影がさしている The tree gives [offers] welcome *shade*. ▶一家に暗い影がさし始めていた(=不吉な兆候が現れる) A *shadow* was beginning to fall over the family. ▶うわさをすれば影(がさす) Speak of the devil (and he will appear). (🔔 ( )内は通例省略

- **影も形もない** ▶島は影も形もなく(=跡形もなく)消えた The island has disappeared *without (a) trace*. ▶その娘の影も形もなかった。湖に突き落とされたのかもしれない There was *no sign* [*nothing to be seen*] of the girl. She might have been pushed into the lake.
- **影を落とす** ▶ビルが地面に影を落としていた The building *cast* [⌧*dropped*] *a shadow on* the ground. ▶父親の死が我々に暗い影を落とした Our father's death cast *a* [*the*] *dark*] *shadow over* us.
- **影をひそめる** ▶最近ではそのような犯罪も影をひそめている(=犯罪はない) There have recently been no such crimes.

*がけ 崖 (絶壁) a cliff (⊕~s), (断崖) a precipice (❢ 特に, 海に面した崖), (川・海などに面した幅の広い崖) a bluff (⊕~s 注意, 海から見た六甲山系の急な斜面). ▶切り立った崖をよじ登る climb (up) a sheer *cliff*. ▶崖から海に落ちる fall over [off] *a cliff* into the sea. ▶日本経済は崖っぷちに立っていた Japan's economy was on the edge of the [a] *precipice*.
- 崖崩れ a landslide.

-がけ 掛け ❶ [身につけた状態] ▶ゆかた掛けで外出する go out *in a yukata*.
❷ [途中] ▶帰り掛けにスーパーで買い物をする do the shopping *on* one's *way* home. ▶出掛けに客が来た I had a visitor *just when* [*as*] I was leaving home.
❸ [割] ▶彼は8掛けで(=定価の8割で)新車を買った He got a new car at a 20 *percent discount*.
❹ [...人掛け] ▶5人掛けのベンチ a bench *for* five. ▓翻訳のこころ▓ 広い居間には大きな暖炉があり, 座り心地の良い三人掛けのソファがあった (村上春樹「レキシントンの幽霊」) In the large living room, there was a big fireplace and a comfortable couch [sofa] *for* three. (❢(1)「三人掛け」は *for* three. (2) 米国では「ソファ」は couch と呼ぶことが多い. 通例三人掛けの大きさなので, for three を特に入れる必要がない場合もある)

かけあい 掛け合い ❶ [水などの] splashing 《water》 on each other. ❷ [交渉] a negotiation. (❢ 通例複数形で) ❸ [台詞・歌などの] a dialogue.
- 掛け合い漫才 a comic dialogue.

かけあう 掛け合う ❶ [互いに掛ける] ▶水を掛け合う *splash* water on each other. ▶声を掛け合う *call* out to each other.
❷ [交渉する] negotiate 《with; about》. (⇨交渉する) ▶労働組合は現在賃上げについて会社側と掛け合っている The labor union *is* currently *negotiating with* the company *about* a wage increase.

かけあがる 駆け上がる run* up...; (急いで) rush up .... ▶階段を駆け上がる run [rush] *up* the stairs. ▶2階へ駆け上がる run upstairs.

かけあし 駆け足 a run; [馬の] a gallop. (❢ gallop は最大速度の駆け足, 他より駆け足は canter. 以下 trot, amble, walk の順に遅くなる) ▶2日間の駆け足旅行 a *whirlwind* two-day tour. ▶駆け足で来る come running; come at a *run*; (兵隊が) come at [on] the *double*. ▶駆け足になる break into a *run* (馬が) a *gallop*]. (❢「急に駆け出す」の意もある)

かけあわせる 掛け合わせる ▶3と4を掛け合わせる(=乗じる) *multiply* 3 *by* 4. ▶雌馬と雄のロバを掛け合わせる(=交配する) *cross* a mare *with* [*and*] a male donkey.

かけい 火刑 the stake. (⇨火炙(ぁぶ)り)
かけい 花茎 [植物] a flower stalk; a scape.
かけい 家系 a family line, 《書》 lineage /líniɪdʒ/. (⇨家柄)
- 家系図 a family tree. (⇨系図)

かけい 家計 [家庭の予算] a fámily [a hóusehold] bùdget; [家庭の財政状態] fámily finances; [家計費] hóusehold expènses; (生活費) living expenses. ▶家計簿をつける keep a *household account book*. ▶家計を切り詰める cut down (on) one's *living expenses*. (❢ on をつけると「必要に迫られて」という意味合いが加わる) ▶我が家の家計は赤[黒]字 Our *household budget* is in the red [black]. ▶彼女は家計を助けるためにアルバイトをしている She works part time to help (to) support her family.

かけうどん 掛けうどん *kakeudon*; (説明的に) *udon* noodles in hot soup.

かけうり 掛け売り 图 sale on credit; a credit sale. ▶掛け売りお断り〔掲示〕No *credit* given [allowed]./Cash only./No *credit sale*.
── 掛け売りする 動 sell 《goods》 on credit.

かけえ 影絵 a silhouette /sìluˈɛt/; (作品) 〔集合的に〕 silhouette art.

かけえり 掛け襟 (説明的に) a protective collar sewn on the neck of a kimono.

かけおち 駆け落ち 图 (an) elopement.
── 駆け落ちする 動 ▶愛人と駆け落ちする (女性が) *run away* [*elope*] *with* one's lover (後の方が堅い語); (男性が) (やや古) *run away* [*elope*] *with* one's love. ▶2人は駆け落ちした They *ran away together*./They *eloped*.

かけおりる 駆け下りる run* down...; (急いで) rush down.... ▶坂を駆け下りる run [rush] *down* the slope; run [rush] downhill.

かけがい 掛け買い 图 buying 《書》 purchasing) on credit; a credit purchase.
── 掛け買いする 動 buy 《goods》 on credit.

かけがえのない 掛けがえのない (取り替えられない) irreplaceable; (貴重な) precious; (ただ一つの) the only 《Earth》. ▶かけがえのない命 one's *precious life*. ▶かけがえのない(=最愛の)子 one's *dearest child*. ▶彼女は彼にとってかけがえのない人だ She is [means] *all the world* to him.

かけがね 掛け金 (ドア・窓などの) a latch; (ネックレス・ベルトなどの) a clasp. ▶戸に掛け金をかける [はずす] *latch* [*unlatch*] the door. ▶戸に掛け金がかけてある The door *is on the latch* (⇔*off the latch*)./The door *is latched* (⇔*unlatched*).

かげき 過激 ── 過激な 形 [過度の] excessive; [極端な] extreme; [急進的な] radical; [暴力的な] violent. ▶過激な運動 *excessive* [*激しい*] *strenuous*] exercise. ▶過激な思想 *radical* [*extreme*] ideas. ▶若者は過激に走りやすい Young people tend to *go to extremes*.
- 過激派 (the) radicals; (the) extremists.

かげき 歌劇 (an) opera. (❢ 演劇の一部門では無冠詞) ▶喜歌劇 a comic *opera*; an operetta. ▶歌劇を見に行く go to the *opera*.
- 歌劇場 an ópera hòuse [《まれ》thèater].
- 歌劇団 an ópera còmpany [tròupe].

かけきん 掛け金 premium(s).

がけくずれ 崖崩れ 图 a landslide, (小規模な) a landslip. ▶崖崩れで3名が生き埋めになった Three people were buried in a *landslide*. ▶大雨で崖崩れが起きた A heavy rainfall caused [set off] the *landslide*./The *landslip* occurred when the rain fell heavily.

かげぐち 陰口 backbiting. ▶彼の陰口をきく[たたく] talk [speak] about him behind his back; backbite him.

かけごえ 掛け声 〚叫び声〛a shout /ʃáut/; 〚呼び声〛a call; 〚かっさい〛a cheer. ▶私たちは「よいしょ」と声をかけてピアノを持ち上げた We lifted the piano with the *shout*, "Yō-hó!" /改革案はかけ声だけに終わった(=先細りになった) The reform plan *fizzled out*.

かけごと 賭け事 gambling. (⇨賭け) ●賭け事で財産を失う lose one's fortune by *gambling*; gamble away one's fortune.

かけことば 掛け言葉 a pun; a play on words; 〚修辞〛paronomasia /pæ̀rənouméiʒiə/.

かけこみ 駆け込み ●駆け込み乗車する *dash onto* a train *just before* the doors close. ▶税率引き上げ直前に異常な駆け込み需要(=需要の急増)が発生した There was an extraordinary *rush* for cars just before they put up the tax on them. (❗これは「当局」, them は cars) ●駆け込み寺 a women's shelter; (説明的に) a shelter for a woman fleeing from violence by her husband.

かけこむ 駆け込む ●家の中に駆け込む *run* [*rush*] *into* a house. ▶彼らは大使館に駆け込んだ(=保護を求めた) They *took* [*sought*] *refuge in* the embassy./They *rushed into* the embassy *seeking refuge*.

かけざん 掛け算 图 multiplication (↔division).
── 掛け算をする 動 multiply, do multiplication. (⇨掛ける)

かけじく 掛け軸 a hanging scroll.

かけす 懸巣 〚鳥〛a joy.

かけず 掛け図 (図表) a wáll chàrt; (地図) a wáll màp.

かけすて 掛け捨て ●掛け捨ての地震保険 earthquake insurance with no premium at the end of the term.

かけずりまわる 駆けずり回る (走り回る) run around [〚主に英〛about]. (⇨駆け回る)

かけそば 掛け蕎麦 *kakesoba*; (説明的に) buckwheat noodles in hot soup.

かけだし 駆け出し (新米) a novice; (初心者) a beginner. ▶駆け出しの新聞記者 a *cub* reporter.

かけだす 駆け出す ❶〚走り出る〛run* out. ▶庭へ[部屋から]駆け出す *run out* into the garden [from the room].
❷〚走り出す〛●急に駆け出す *start running* suddenly; *break into a run* (馬が) *a gallop*].

かけちがえる 掛け違える (行き違える) cross (each other); 〚電話を〛have the wrong number. ▶シャツのボタンをかけ違えていますよ Your shirt's *buttoned wrong*.

かけつ 可決 图 〚承認〛appróval; 〚採択〛adoption.
── 可決する 動 (承認する) approve; (法案を通す) pass; (特に動議を通過させる) carry; (採択する) adopt; (投票で) vote ⟨a bill into law⟩. ▶その法案は圧倒的多数で可決された The bill *was passed* [*was approved*] by an overwhelming majority. ▶その動議は 3 対 1 の票決で可決された The motion *was carried* by a three-to-one vote. (❗議長の発言の場合は is [has been] carried と現在または現在完了を用いる)

かけつけさんばい 駆けつけ三杯 (説明的に) making a latecomer drink three cups of sake [three glasses of beer] as a punishment.

かけつける 駆けつける (走って行く[来る]) run* (*to*); (突進して行く) rush (*to*); (急いで行く) hurry (*to*). ●彼の救助に駆けつける *run to* his aid. ▶犯行現場に急いで駆けつける *rush* [*hurry*] *to* the scene of the crime.

かけっこ 駆けっこ 图 a race. (❗正確にはfootrace)
── 駆けっこする 動 have [run] a race ⟨*with*⟩. ▶あそこの木まで駆けっこしよう I'll *race* you to the tree over there.

かけて ❶〚わたって〛●月曜から木曜にかけて *from Monday to* 〚(米) *through*〛 Thursday. (⇨ーまで❶) ●週末にかけて *over* the weekend. (⇨亘〘ⓢ〙る❷) ▶首から腰にかけて痛い I have a pain *from* the neck down to the back.
❷〚関して〛 ▶テニスにかけては彼はだれにも負けない *When it comes to* tennis, he is second to none. (❗No one can beat him *in* tennis. (テニスではだれも彼を負かせない)といっても意味は同じ)

かけどけい 掛け時計 a wáll clock.

かけなおす 掛け直す 〚軸などを〛rehang*; 〚目方を〛reweigh; 〚電話を〛call ⟨him⟩ again; (折り返し) call ⟨him⟩ back.

かげながら 陰ながら ●陰ながら成功をお祈りします I do hope and pray that you will be successful./I do hope and pray for your success. (❗do を強く読み「ぜひとも」の気持ちを伝える。日本語にひかれて ×secretly pray のようにいわない)

かけぬける 駆け抜ける (…の間を) run* through…; (走って…を追い越す) run past… from behind. ▶そのニュースはものの 1 時間もしないうちに全世界を駆け抜けた(=伝わった) The news *traveled around* [〚急速に広まった〛*spread rapidly all over*] the world in less than an hour.

かけね 掛け値 〚つり上げられた値段〛an inflated [〚法外な〛a fancy] price; 〚不当な値段〛an overcharge; 〚誇張〛(an) exaggeration. ●掛け値なしの値段 a *net* price. ●掛け値なしに 10 ドルで売る sell ⟨it⟩ at 10 dollars *net*. ●30 パーセント掛け値をする overcharge ⟨him⟩ (by) 30 percent. ●掛け値のないことを言う talk frankly [honestly] ⟨*about*⟩; give one's *frank* [*honest*] opinion ⟨*about*⟩.

かげのすみか 『蔭の棲みか』 *A Dwelling in the Shade*. 〚参考〛玄月の小説

かけのぼる 駆け登る, 駆け上る run* up ⟨a hill [the stairs]⟩.

かけはぎ 掛け接ぎ invisible mending.

かけはし 架け橋 ❶〚仮の橋〛a temporary bridge. ●にじのかけ橋 a rainbow *bridge* (*that spans the sky*).
❷〚仲介者〛a gó-bètween; an intermediary. ●両国間のかけ橋となる act as an *intermediary* [a *bridge*] *between* the two countries.

かけはなれる 掛け離れる 〚距離が〛be a long way (off) ⟨*from*⟩; 〚まったく異なる〛be quite different ⟨*from*⟩. ▶その結果は私たちが期待したこととまったくかけ離れている The result *is quite* [*completely, entirely*] *different from* what we expected. ▶君の考えは現実からかけ離れている Your ideas *are far from* (being) realistic. ▶その報告は真相からかけ離れている The report *is a long way from* the truth [being true]./〚やや書〛The report *is far from* (being) true [the truth].

かけひ 筧 (懸け樋) a waterspout; a flume.

かけひき 駆け引き 图 〚策略〛tactics (複数形); 〚取り引き〛bargain. ▶彼は駆け引きがうまい He is a good *bargainer*./(人の扱いがうまい) He is skillful [is skilled] *in dealing with* other people./(巧みな策略家である) He is a shrewd tactician.
── 駆け引きする 動 ●彼との値段のことで駆け引きする *bargain with* him *about* the price.

かげひなた 陰日向 ●陰日向のある(=表裏二心のある)人 a *two-faced* [a *double-faced*, (不正直な) a *dishonest*] person. ●陰日向のない(=正直な)人 an

かけぶとん　　　　　　　　　　　　　　　315　　　　　　　　　　　　　　　かける

honest [(良心的な) a conscientious] person. ●陰日向なく働く work honestly [conscientiously].
かけぶとん 掛け布団 a quilt. (⇨布団)
かけへだてる 懸け隔てる (⇨掛け離れる)
かげぼうし 影法師
かげぼし 陰干し ━陰干しする 動 ▶濡れた靴を陰干しする dry wet shoes in the shade.
かけまわる 駆け回る ❶ [走り回る] run* around [back and forth, to and fro]. (❢ run の代わりに rush を用いる方が迅速な動きを表す) ▶子供たちは庭を駆け回って遊んでいる The children are running around [(主に英) about] in the garden.
❷ [奔走する] (忙しい) be busy 《doing; with》; (忙しく動き回っている) 《話》 be on the run. ▶彼は資金集めに駆け回っている He is running around [(主に英) about] raising funds./He is busy raising funds. ▶うちのお父さんはいつも忙しく駆け回っている My father's always on the run.
かげむしゃ 影武者 ❶ [(大将などの)身代わり] a dummy.
❷ [黒幕] 《米話》a wirepuller; 《話》a fixer. (⇨黒幕) ▶彼は芸能界の影武者として有名だ He is well-known as a wirepuller [fixer] in the world of entertainment.
かけめぐる 駆け巡る (走り回る) run* around; (仕事で駆け回る) 《話》 be on the run. (⇨駆け回る) ▶そのうわさはまたたく間に町中を駆け巡った The rumor went quickly throughout the town. (⇨駆け抜ける)
かけもち 掛け持ち ▶彼女は三つの高校をかけ持ちで(=異なった学校)教えている She teaches at three different high schools.
かけもの 掛け物 a hanging scroll with painting or calligraphy (or both) on it.
かけよる 駆け寄る run* up (to).
かけら [破片] a fragment, a broken piece; (木・ガラスなどのかけら) a splinter. ▶建設現場から多くの土器のかけらが出て来た A lot of fragments [shards] of earthenware were dug up in the construction site.
●…のかけらもない ▶あいつには良心のかけらもない He doesn't have an ounce [a hint] of conscience./He has no conscience (at all). ▶それはまったくの作り話だ. 真実のかけらもない It's a pure invention. There isn't a fragment [a scrap, an atom, a crumb] of truth in it.
かげり 陰り ❶ [陰] a shadow; shade. (⇨陰)
❷ [表情などの] ▶彼女の表情に陰りが現れた A cloud came over her expression. ▶その事故で彼らの友情に陰りが生じた The accident cast a shadow on their friendship.
❸ [よくない兆候] ▶最近景気に陰りが見え始めた In recent years business has begun to decline.

:かける 掛ける, 架ける　　　　　　　　　　　　**INDEX**

❶ つり下げる	❷ 上に置く
❸ 立てかける	❹ ふりかける
❺ わななどに	❻ ひも・留め具などを
❼ 橋を	❽ 作動させる
❾ 身につける	❿ 腰かける
⓫ 負担・苦労などを	⓬ 電話・声などを
⓭ 費やす	⓮ 掛け算をする
⓯ その他の表現	

(WORD CHOICE) 掛ける
hang 物を壁から少し高いところに吊り下げて, ぶらぶらさすこと. hook に比べると, 物をがっしり固定するという含意は弱い. ▶彼は壁[フック, 木]に帽子を掛けた He hung his cap on the wall [hook, tree].

hook 物をかぎ・フック・釣り針などに引っ掛けてしっかり固定すること. ▶彼女は彼の腕に自分の手を掛けてまきつけた She hooked her hand through his arm.

(頻度チャート)

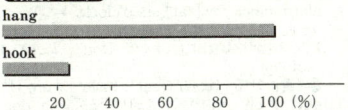

hang ▬▬▬▬▬▬▬▬▬▬▬▬▬▬▬

hook ▬▬▬▬

20　　40　　60　　80　　100 (%)

❶ [つり下げる] hang*. ▶壁[掛けくぎ; 床の間に]に軸を掛ける hang (up) a scroll on the wall [on the hook; in the alcove]. ▶窓[居間]に新しいカーテンをかけた We hung new curtains at the windows [in the living room]. (❢ at の代わりに on, over も可) ▶彼女はカーディガンを肩から掛けた She put her cardigan across her shoulders. ▶ハンドバッグをそんなふうに肩から掛けていてはいけません You shouldn't wear your handbag on your shoulder like that.
❷ [上に置く] (置く) put*, place (❢ put より堅い語); (横たえる) lay* [類語]; (覆う) cover.
●こんろにやかんをかける put a kettle on the stove. ●彼の肩に手をかける lay [put, place] one's hand on his shoulder. ●彼に毛布を肩から掛けてやった I covered him with a blanket./I put [laid] a blanket on [over] him. ▶とても寒いからふとんをちゃんと掛けて寝なさい It's very cold, so you must cover yourself up well.
❸ [立てかける] (立てる, 掲げる) put*... up; (立たせる) stand*. ▶看板を壁に立てかける put up [set up] a signboard against the wall. ▶彼は屋根にはしごをかけた He stood [put up, set up] a ladder against the roof.
❹ [ふりかける] (水をかける) water; (注ぐ) pour; (まき散らす) sprinkle; (吹きかける) spray; (はね散らす) splash. ●庭の花に水をかける water [pour water on, sprinkle water on] the flowers in the garden. ●ホットケーキにシロップをかける pour syrup over a pancake [《米》a hot cake]. ●ハンバーガーにマヨネーズをかける put mayonnaise on a hamburger. ●料理に塩を振りかける sprinkle salt on the dish; sprinkle the dish with salt. (❢ 後の言い方は一面に掛けることを暗示. 次の2例も同様) ●ハンカチに香水をかける spray perfume on [upon] a handkerchief; spray a handkerchief with perfume. ▶その車が私の上着にどろをはねかけた The car splashed mud on [over] my coat./The car splashed my coat with mud.
❺ [わななどに] ●キツネをわなにかける trap a fox; catch a fox in a trap. ●魚を網にかける catch a fish in a net; net a fish. ●彼をぺてんにかけて金を巻き上げる cheat [trick] him out of his money.
❻ [ひも・留め具などを] tie (〜d; tying) ... 《with》, bind*... 《with》. (〜縛る) ●まきになわをかけて bind [fasten] the sticks together with (a) rope. ●シャツのボタンをかける button (up) a shirt. ●ドアに鍵(ᡘ)をかける lock (↔unlock) a door. ▶この荷物にはひもを十分かけてください Please tie (up) this package with much string. ▶私はスーツケースに革ひもをかけた I put a strap around the suitcase./I strapped up the suitcase.
❼ [橋を] (やや書) span (-nn-) ... 《with》. ▶村人らは川に橋をかけた The villagers spanned the river with a bridge./(建設した) The villagers built a bridge over [across] the river.
❽ [作動させる] (エンジンなどを) start; (スイッチを) turn

かける

[switch]... on; [レコードなどを] play. ●エンジンをかける start (up) an engine; get an engine going. ●ラジオをかける turn [switch] on (↔off) the radio. ●6時に目覚まし時計をかける(=合わせる) set an alarm clock for [×at] six o'clock. ●このテープ[レコード]をかけよう Let's play this tape [record]. ▶ラジオをかけっぱなしにしておくな Don't leave the radio on.

❾ [身につける] (状態) wear*, have*... on; (動作) put*... on. ●白いマスクをかけている医者 a doctor with a white mask on. ●彼は眼鏡をかけている He wears [is wearing] glasses. (❗進行形は一時的状態をさす)/He has glasses on. ●先生は眼鏡をかけたがすぐはずした The teacher put on his glasses, but took them off soon after that.

❿ [腰掛ける] sit* (in, on). (⇨座る) ●おかけになりませんか Would you like to sit down? ●かけたまえ Have [Take] a seat, won't you?

⓫ [負担・苦労などを] ●彼に負担をかける put a burden on him; burden him. ●大変ご面倒をおかけしてすみませんでした I'm sorry to have given you [put you to] a lot of trouble. ●彼は他人に迷惑をかけて(=他人を犠牲にして)自己の利益を守ろうとする He looks after his own interests at the cost of others.

⓬ [電話・声などを] ●彼に電話をかける call [《英》ring] him (up); give him a call [《英》a ring]; phone [telephone] him. ●922番に電話をかける dial [《パッシュホンで》punch] 922. ●声もかけずに通り過ぎる pass by (him) without even saying hello. ●どこから電話をかけているの? Where are you calling from? ●交換手さん、その番号にもう一度かけてくれませんか Could you call [try] that number again, operator?

⓭ [費やす] spend*; (要する) take*. ●本に多くの金をかける spend [《話》lay out] a lot of money on books. ●教育に金をかける put money into (his) education. ●彼は車を洗うのに2時間かけた He spent two hours (in) washing his car. (❗《話》では通例 in を省略する)/He took two hours to wash his car./(かかった) It took him two hours [took two hours for him] to wash his car. (⇨掛かる❾) ●彼はいつも十分時間をかけて決める He always takes his time about making a decision. ●つまらないことに時間をかけるな(=浪費するな) Don't waste your time on trifles.

⓮ [掛け算をする] ●5掛ける4は20 Five times four is [are, make(s)] twenty./Five multiplied by four is [equal(s)] twenty. (❗だけで Five fours are twenty. のようにもいう) ●3にいくつを掛けると21になるか What must you multiply 3 by to get 21?

⓯ [その他の表現] ●彼はほんの子供だということを心にかけていて(=心に留めていて)ください Keep [Bear] in mind that he is only a child. ●私たちは彼に期待をかけている We place [rest] our hopes on him./Our hopes rest on him. ●その案を会議にかけよう(=提案しよう) Let's put the plan before [submit the plan to] the conference. ●彼はいつも私たちの案に水をかける He's always throwing cold water on our plan. (❗成句表現)

かける 欠ける ❶ [一部がこわれる] (陶器などの縁や表面が欠ける) chip (-pp-), be chipped; (折れて取れる) break off. ●コップ(の縁)が欠けた The cup (was) chipped./(欠けさせた) I chipped the cup./I chipped a piece off [out of] the cup. ●この皿は縁が欠けている There is a chip in the edge of this plate./This plate has a chip on the edge. ●前歯が半分欠けてしまった I've lost half a front tooth.

❷ [不足する] (必要なものを欠いている) lack, be lacking in..., (書) be wanting in.... (⇨欠く❷) ●彼には知性が欠けている He is lacking in [lacks (×in)] intelligence. (❗lacks の方が普通) He has no intelligence. ●我々の生活には何かが欠けている There is something lacking in [missing from] our lives. ●この本は数ページ欠けている There are a few pages missing [wanting] in this book./This book has a few missing pages. ●メンバーが1人欠けている We are one member short. ●彼の説明は説得力に欠ける His explanation is unconvincing.

❸ [月が] wane. ●月が欠けた The moon waned.

かける 駆ける run (⇨走る); [馬が] gallop. (⇨駆け足)
かける 賭ける [金を馬・チームなどに] bet (money) (on); [金・財産などを賭事などに] venture; [賭け事をする] gamble (on, at); [命・財産などを] risk, stake (on). ●競馬に賭ける bet [make a bet, gamble] on a horse race. ●金を賭けてトランプをする(=賭けトランプをする) play cards for money; gamble at cards. ●命を賭けてその仕事をする risk one's life to do the work; do the work at the risk of one's life. ●会談の結果に政治生命を賭ける stake one's political future on the outcome of the talks. ●アメリカでの新生活に賭ける take a chance on a new life in America. ●トムが勝つ[負ける]方に10ドル賭けよう I'll bet (you) 10 dollars (that) Tom will win [lose]. (❗I bet (that) Tom will win. は「きっとトムは勝つだろう」の意)/I'll bet 10 dollars on [against] Tom's winning. ●彼は全財産を新しい事業計画に賭けた He ventured his whole fortune on [upon] the new business project.
会話 「ぼくの作文は今回はノーミスだよ」「じゃ、賭けてみるかい」 "There's no mistake in my composition this time." "You want to bet?" (❗相手の主張が間違っていると確信を持ったときの応答表現)

かける 書ける write*. ●このペンはよく書ける[もう書けない] This pen writes well [doesn't write any more]. ●その小説はよく書けている(=なかなか読ませる) The novel reads well./The novel is a good read./The novel is well written.

かける 描ける paint. (⇨書く, 描く) ●この筆はよく描けている This brush paints well.

かける 懸ける (⇨掛ける, 賭ける)

かける 翔る (空高く飛ぶ) soar. ●大空を翔る鷲(わし) an eagle soaring [flying] high in the sky.

-かける [し始める] begin*, start (to do; doing); [まもなく...する] be (doing) (❗do は arrive, leave (出発する), die, stop, set (沈む)など瞬時の変化を含意する動詞); [ちょうどしようとしている] be about [just going] to (do). (❗). ●be about to は be going to より時間的に近接している ●泣きかけている be beginning [be starting] to cry (×crying). (❗進行形に続くときは音調をよくするため to do とするのが普通) ●彼は何か言いかけたが二言三言で止めた He began [started] to say something but stopped after a few words. (❗) (1) この例のように行為が中断されるときは to do が好まれる. 逆に継続されるときは doing が好まれる. (2) 行為の前段階での中断は通例 begin は不可: He started [×began] to say something but didn't say a word. (何か言おうとしたが一言も話さなかった)) ●ちょうど出かけようとしていたときに電話が鳴った I was about [just going] to leave when the telephone rang./I was on the point [verge] of leaving when the telephone rang. ●彼は死にかけていた He almost died. (❗もう少しで死ぬところだっ

かげる

たが, 死ななかったことを含意)/He *was* dying./He *was on the brink* [*verge*] *of* death. (⚠以上の2文は回復の見込みがない場合)

かげる 陰る ▶さっと日が陰った(=太陽が雲の背後に隠れた) Suddenly *the sun went behind the clouds*. ▶日が陰る(=太陽が沈む)と風が強くなった When *the sun set* [*went down*], *the wind became strong*. ▶景気が陰り(=悪くなり)始めた *Economic conditions began to get worse*.

かげろう 陽炎 a heat haze. ▶かげろうが立つ[立っている] The *heat haze arises* [*is shimmering*].

かげろう 蜉蝣〖昆虫〗 a mayfly; a dayfly. ●かげろうの(ようにはかない)命 *ephemeral life*.

かげろうにっき 蜻蛉日記 *The Gossamer Years*; *The Kagero Diary*. (参考 藤原道綱母の日記)

かけわたす 掛け渡す ●川に橋を掛け渡す *build a bridge over a river*.

★かげん 加減 图 ❶ 〖程度〗 an extent, a degree; 〖具合〗 (a) condition. (⇨具合) ●暑さ加減 the *extent of heat*. ●体の加減が悪い be in bad [*poor*] *condition*; feel sick 〖《主に》ill〗. ●スープの味加減を見る *taste* the soup. ●湯加減を見る *see how hot the bath is*. ●うつむき加減に *bending slightly forward; with one's head slightly bent*. ▶田中さん, 今朝はお加減いかがですか How *are you* [*we*] *feeling this morning, Mr. Tanaka?* (⚠医師などが患者に聞くときは you の代わりに親しみをこめて we を用いることもある) ▶いい加減にしろ(=やめろ)〖話〗 *Cut it* [*that*] *out*!/(もうたくさん) *That's enough!*
〖会話〗「ふろの湯加減はどうですか」「ちょうどよい加減です」"How is the bath (water)?" "It's warm enough [*just right, OK*]."

❷ 〖調節, 斟酌(にん)〗 ●塩加減をする *salt*; *season* 〖it〗 *with salt*.

❸ 〖影響〗 ●陽気の加減で病気が重くなった My *illness was affected* [×*was influenced*] *by the weather*. (⚠直接の影響の場合は affect を用いる)/My *condition grew worse because of the weather*.

❹ 〖足し算と引き算〗 addition and subtraction. ●加減乗除 *addition, subtraction, multiplication and division*; (算術の四則) *the four rules of* [*in*] *arithmetic*.

── **加減する** 動 (調節する) adjust; (適度にする) moderate; (斟酌する) allow for...; make* allowance(s) for...; (味つけする) season. ●冷房を加減する *adjust* the air-conditioning. ●声の大きさを加減する *moderate* one's voice. ▶塩加減して使ってね. 塩分の取り過ぎは心臓によくないのよ *Go easy on* [*with*] *salt. Too much salt is bad for your heart*. (⚠口語的な表現)

かげん 下弦 ●下弦の月 a *waning* (↔*waxing*) *moon*.

かげん 下限 (下の方の限界) the lower limit; (最低値) the minimum; (底値) the bottom.

★かこ 過去 图 the past; (人・国などの) a [one's] past. (⚠人については通例隠された暗い過去をいう)

① 〖過去に[は]〗 ▶日本には長い *past* と古い歴史がある *Japan has a long past and an ancient history*. ▶彼女にはいかがわしい過去がある *She has a past*./*She is a woman with a past*. ▶過去は水に流せ *Let us forgive and forget past quarrels*./〖ことわざ〗 *Let bygones be bygones*.

② 〖過去に[を]〗 ●過去を振り返る *look back on the past*. ●彼の過去を問題にする *hold his past against him*. ●私は過去に1度そこへ行ったことがある *I've been there once* (*in the past* [*以前before*]). (⚠ともに現在[過去]完了形・過去形で用い

るが, ここではつけない方が普通) ▶過去をもとに戻すことはできない *We can't undo the past*./〖ことわざ〗 *What is done can't be undone*.

■ **DISCOURSE** ■
将来何をすべきかを知るためにも, この国の過去について学ぶべきだ *We should all learn about our country's past* so as to *know how we should act in the future*. (⚠so as to ... (...するために)は因果関係などを述べるときに用いるディスコースマーカー. 主節に続けて用いる)

── **過去の** 形 past. ●過去の出来事 a *past event*. ●過去の遺物 a thing of *the past*; 〖話〗 a has-been (⚠ともに人・物事のいずれにも用いる); (時代遅れの人[もの]) an *out-of-date* person [thing]. ●過去の栄光 the *past* [the *former*] glory. ●過去5年間彼から何の便りもない *I haven't heard from him for the past* [*last*] *five years*. ●現在完了形とともに用いる.「過去1年間」は ×for the past [last] one year とせずに *for the past* [*last*] *year* とする)/*I haven't heard from him these past* [*last*] *five years*. (⚠...*these five years* は〖古〗)

●過去完了 〖文法〗 the past perfect. ●過去時制 〖文法〗 the past tense. ●過去分詞 〖文法〗 the past participle.

★かご 籠 (編みかご) a basket; (鳥かご) a (bird) cage. ●買い物かご a shópping bàsket. ●くずかご 〖《米》〗 a wástebàsket, 〖《英》〗 a wástepaper bàsket. ●自転車の前につけたかご a *basket on the front of one's bicycle*; a bícycle bàsket. ●かご1杯の果物 a *basket*(*ful*) *of fruit*. ●かごの鳥 a *bird in a cage*; a *caged bird*. (⚠比喩的な意味でも用いる) ●かごを編む *make a basket*.

かご 加護 (divine) providence (⚠しばしば (Divine) Providence); divine protection. ●神のご加護で *by* (*divine*) *providence*. ●神のご加護がありますように *God bless you*. ●我々は神の加護のもとにある *We are in the care of Providence*.

かご 過誤 (誤り) a mistake, an error; (失敗) a failure. (⇨誤り)

かご 駕籠 a *kago*; a palanquin; (西洋のいすかご) a sedan (chair). ●かごかき a *palanquin bearer*.

がご 雅語 (上品なことば) elegant [refined] words.

かこい 囲い an enclosure; 〖さく〗 a fence; 〖家畜などを入れる〗 a pen. ●土地を囲いをする *put a fence around the land; fence the land*.

かこう 下降 图 a descent /dìsént/; (徐々に) a decline; (落下) a fall. ●飛行機の下降 the *descent of a plane*. ●景気の下降 a *decline* [a *downturn*] *in business*. ▶景気は下降線をたどった *The business took a down trend*.

── **下降する** 動 descend; decline; fall. ▶飛行機は大きく旋回して下降した *The plane descended in a wide turn*. ▶出生率が下降している *The birthrate is going down* [*is falling, is declining, is on the decline*]. (⇨下がる)

●下降気流 a downdraft; a descending air current. (対 上昇気流)

かこう 火口 a crater. ●火口丘 a *volcanic cone*. ●火口原 an *atrio*. ●火口湖 a *crater lake*.

かこう 加工 图 (食品・農産物の) processing; (機械による) manufacturing.

── **加工する** 動 ●チーズを加工する *process cheese*. ▶ミルクは加工されてバターやチーズになる *Milk is made into butter and cheese*.

●加工食品 *processed foods*.

かこう 河口 the mouth of a river, a river mouth;

かこう 〚潮のさす大河の〛an estuary. ●ナイル河口にある町 a town *at* the Nile *estuary* [*the estuary of the* Nile, *the* delta *of the* Nile]. ●東京は隅田川の河口にある Tokyo is *at the* mouth *of the* Sumida.

かこう 河港 a river port.

かこう 囲う (⇨囲む) ▶庭をさくで囲った I *enclosed* [*surrounded*] the garden *with* a fence. / I *fenced* (*in*) the garden.

かごう 化合 (chemical) combination. (⇨混合) ▶酸素は水素と化合して水になる Oxygen *combines with* hydrogen *to form* water. ●化合物 a (chemical) compound.

がごう 雅号 a pen name, a pseudonym /s(j)úːdə-nim/. (⇨ペンネーム)

かこうがん 花崗岩 granite /grǽnit/.

かこうそう 鵞口瘡 〚医学〛thrush.

かこきゅう 過呼吸 ●過呼吸になる hyperventilate. ●過呼吸症候群〚医学〛hyperventilation syndrome.

かこく 苛酷 ━ 苛酷な 形 ●苛酷な(=残酷な)運命 a *cruel* fate. (⇨残酷な)

かこく 過酷 ━ 過酷な 形 ●過酷な(=厳しい)労働条件 *severe* working conditions. (⇨残酷な)

かこつ 託つ (不平を言う) complain (*about, of*); (嘆く) 《書》 lament (over…). ●病弱の身をかこつ *complain about* one's ill health.

かこつける 託つける (口実とする) make* a pretext 《*of*》. ●何とかかこつけて on some pretext or other. ▶彼は病気にかこつけて学校を休んだ He didn't go to school *on* [*under*] *the pretext of* being sick./ He didn't go to school *by pretending* to be sick. ●かこつけて as a pretext 《*for*》; under the guise of; on the excuse of. ●…にかこつけて(=口実にして) on the excuse of; on [under] the pretext of.

かごぬけ 籠抜け ▶籠抜け詐欺を働く swindle 《him》 out of money and escape *by the back door*.

かこみ 囲み ; 〚包囲〛a siege; 〚囲い〛an enclosure; (新聞・雑誌の) a box, a column. ●囲みを解く raise [lift] a *siege*. ●囲み記事 a boxed article, a column.

:**かこむ** 囲む ❶ [取り囲む] (四方を) surround; (囲う物で) enclose, (さくで) fence (in), (丸で) circle. ●高い塀に囲まれた大きな家 a big house with a high wall *around* it. ●学校は高い生け垣で囲まれている The school *is surrounded* [*is enclosed*] *by* a high hedge. (▶my の代わりに with も可能だがまれ) ●記者たちが彼を取り囲んだ The reporters *gathered around* [*surrounded*] him. ▶日本は四方が海に囲まれている Japan *is surrounded by* the sea./Japan *is bounded by* the sea on all sides. ▶正解の番号を丸で囲みなさい *Circle* the number of the correct answer. ▶彼らはテーブルを囲んで(=の周りに)座った They sat *around* the table. ▶彼は友達に囲まれてくつろいでいた He was at ease *among* his friends.
❷[包囲する] surround; (包囲攻撃する) besiege. (⇨包囲)

かこん 禍根 (災いの元) the source of trouble; (悪の生ずるところ) the root of evil. ●禍根を絶つ cut off 〚書〛eradicate the *root of evil*. ●将来に禍根を残す be the *source of trouble* in the future.

かごん 過言 ▶彼は天才だといっても過言(=言い過ぎ)ではない It is not too much [no exaggeration] to say he is a genius.

***かさ** 笠 ; [頭にかぶる] (竹笠) a bamboo hat, (すげ笠) a sedge hat; [電灯の] a (lamp) shade; [キノコの] a cap. ●人の権力を笠に着る *take advantage of* 《his》power [*influence*]; *make* (*wrong*) *use of* 《his》power [authority].

***かさ** 傘 ; [雨傘] an umbrella, [日傘] a parasol, a sunshade. (▶ umbrella は男性用も女性用もあるが, parasol, sunshade は通例女性用) ●折りたたみ傘 a folding *umbrella*. ●傘の柄 the handle of an *umbrella*. ●傘をさす[広げる] put up [open] an *umbrella*. ●傘をたたむ close [fold] an *umbrella*. ●傘の水を切って巻く shake one's *umbrella* and roll it. ●核の傘 a nuclear *umbrella*. ▶傘を持って行きなさい Take an [your] *umbrella* with you. ●雨の中を傘をささずに歩いた I walked in the rain with no *umbrella*. (▶「傘をさして歩く」は walk with one's *umbrella* up) ▶傘に入れていただけますか Will you let me in under [May I share] your *umbrella*? (▶後の方が普通.「私の傘にお入りなさい」なら Why don't you share [get under] my *umbrella*? のようにいう) ●傘立て an umbréllastànd.

かさ 嵩 ; (大きいこと) bulk; (容積) volume; (量) quantity. ●ごみのかさ the quantity [amount] of garbage. ●かさはあるが軽い箱 a *bulky* but light box. ●かさにかかった[=横柄な]言い方をする speak *arrogantly* [高圧的な] high-handedly, (いばりちらした) bossily]. ●かさにかかって相手を攻撃する make full use of the chance of beating the opponent.

かさ 暈 ; 〚太陽・月の光の輪〛a ring; a halo; a corona. ●月のかさ a halo [ring] around the moon.

かさあげ 嵩上げ 名 ●堤防のかさ上げ工事 *raising* of riverbanks [levees].
━ 嵩上げする 動 (高さを) raise; (数・量を) increase. ●治療費がかさ上げされた Doctor's fees *have been increased*.

かざあな 風穴 ; a windhole; an air hole; (通気口) a ventilator. ●風穴を開ける ▶政府は停滞している経済活動に風穴を開ける(=新風を吹き込む)よう国民から強く迫られている The Government is under heavy pressure from the people to *mark a new phase in* staggering economic conditions.

***かさい** 火災 (a) fire. (⇨火事) ▶その船は火災を起こしていた The Ship *was on fire* [*was burning*]. ▶そのビルで火災が発生した A *fire* started [broke out, occurred] in the building./There was a *fire* in the building. ●火災訓練 (have) a fíre drìll. ●火災警報 a fíre wàrning. ●火災報知機 a fíre alàrm. ●火災保険 《take out [《米》buy, get]》 fíre insùrance.

かさい 花菜 〚花の部分を食べる野菜〛flower vegetables.

かさい 果菜 〚実の部分を食べる野菜〛fruit vegetables.

かさい 家裁 〚「家庭裁判所」の略〛(⇨家庭)

がざい 画材 〚絵になる題材〛subject matter for a painting; (絵の材料) artist's materials.

かざい(どうぐ) 家財(道具) 〚家財類〛household goods [〚書〛effects]; 〚家具類〛furniture. (⇨家具)

かさいりゅう 火砕流 〚地学〛(a) pyroclastic /pàiroukl'æstikə/ flow.

かさかさ ; (枯れ葉・紙などがこすれ合って音を出す) rustle; (肌が乾いた) dry. ●風で葉がかさかさ鳴った The breeze *rustled* the leaves./ The leaves *rustled* in the wind./(かさかさ鳴る音を聞いた) I heard the *rustle* of the leaves in the wind. ▶冬になると肌がかさかさになる I have *dry* (*and scaly*) skin in winter.

がさがさ ; (物がこすれ合って音を出す) rustle; (手・壁などがざらざらした) rough. ●かさかさ音をたてる▶新聞をがさがさいわせるな Don't *rustle* the paper. ●木の葉が風がさがさ音をたてた The tree leaves *rustled* in the wind.

▶私は冬になると肌ががさがさする I have rough (↔ smooth) skin in winter.

かざかみ 風上 [海army] windward (↔leeward). ●風上へ航行する sail (to) windward; (風に向かって) sail against the wind. ●火の風上の方に座る sit (to) windward of the fire.
●風上にも置けない ▶彼は教師の風上にも置けぬやつだ He doesn't deserve to be called a teacher.

かさく 佳作 a fine work.

かさく 家作 [家] a house; [貸家] a house for rent [《英》to let].

かさく 寡作 — 寡作な [形] 寡作な(=作品を少ししか作らない)作家 an unprolific composer.

かざぐるま 風車 (おもちゃの)《米》a pinwheel, 《英》a windmill.

かさご 笠子 [魚介] a scorpion fish.

かぜごえ 風邪声 (鼻声) a nasal) voice.

がさごそ ▶ネズミが納屋の中でがさごそ動いていた I heard mice rustling in the barn.

かささぎ 鵲 [鳥] a (Korean) magpie /mǽɡpài/.

かざしも 風下 leeward (↔windward), downwind. (⇒風上) ▶風下になるときには, 高速道路を走る車の騒音が聞こえる When we are downwind of the expressway, we can hear the booming noise of passing cars.

かざす 翳す ❶ [手に持って掲げる] ●優勝旗をかざす hold a pennant aloft; hold up a pennant.
❷ [手などを覆うように差し出す] ▶彼は火に手をかざして温めた He warmed his hands over the fire.
❸ [光を遮る] ●手を目にかざす shade one's eyes with one's hand.

かさだか 嵩高・嵩高な [形] (かさばる) bulky; (横柄な) arrogant, 《書》haughty. ●かさ高なマットレス a bulky mattress.

がさつ — がさつな [形] (粗野で無作法な) unrefined, rough and unpolished; 《やや書》ill-mannered. (⚠️ rude は「意識的に無礼である」の意で不適)

がさつく ❶ [がさがさ音がする] rustle. ▶落ち葉が風でがさついている Fallen leaves are rustling in the breeze.
❷ [言動ががさつである] ●がさついたやつ a rough guy.

かさなり 重なり (重複) (an) overlap. ●メンバーの重なりをチェックする check an overlap of members.

かさなる 重なる ❶ [物が上に乗る] (積み重なる) be piled up; be [lie] on top of one another. (⇒重ね) ●折り重なって倒れる fall on top of one another. ●重なり合って寝ている子犬 puppies sleeping in a heap. ●机の上に 10 冊の本が重なって置いてある There are ten books piled up on the desk. ▶遠くに山々が重なって見えた The mountains piled up in the distance.
❷ [かち合う] (ある日に当たる) fall* on …; (部分的に重複する) overlap (-pp-). ▶今年は文化の日が日曜日に重なる Culture Day falls on (a) Sunday this year. ▶彼と私の休暇が重なった His vacation and mine overlapped./His vacation overlapped with mine.
❸ [さらに加わる] ▶不幸は重なるものだ(=次々やって来る) Misfortunes come one after another [in succession]. ● [ことわざ] Misfortunes never come single [singly].

かさね 重ね ❶ [積み重ねる] a pile.
❷ [層] a tier. ● 3 段重ね three tiers. ● 3 段重ねのケーキ a three-tiered cake.

かさねあわせる 重ね合わせる ▶屋根がわらをもう少し重ね合わせる必要がある I think the roof tiles need to overlap a little more. ▶その工場では薄板を重ね合わせて丈夫な合板を作っている In that factory they laminate layers of wood to make strong plywood.

かさねがさね 重ね重ね ●重ね重ねの失敗のあげく after repeated mistakes. ●重ね重ねの不幸 a succession [a series] of misfortunes. ●重ね重ねのご親切 (so) many kindnesses. ●重ね重ねお礼申し上げます Thank you very [《話》so very] much. (⚠️この 《話》の用法はこの文脈で用いられることが多い) I don't know how to thank you enough.

かさねぎ 重ね着 layering.
— 重ね着する [動] ●白のシャツの上に青のセーターを重ね着する wear a blue sweater over a white shirt.

かさねる 重ねる ❶ [積む] (積み上げる) pile [(山のように) heap]… (up) (⇒積む ❶); (上に者の上に置く) put (one thing) on (top of) (another). ●れんがを重ねる pile up bricks; (1 枚ずつ) put bricks one on top of another (⚠️この言い方は 3 枚以上のときに用いる。2 枚重ねるときは put two bricks one on top of the other [each other] という). ●シャツを 3 枚重ねて着る wear three undershirts one over another.
❷ [繰り返す] repeat. ●同じ間違いを重ねる repeat the same mistake; make the same mistake repeatedly. ●苦労を重ねる go through a lot of hardships; (次から次へと体験する) go through one hardship after another. ●悪事を重ねる commit a series of crimes. ●重ねて言いますが彼は頼りになりません I repeat [I tell you once again] that you can't depend on him. ▶私たちは協議を重ねた上決定をした We held some consultations, then made our decision. (⚠️ some (何回かの)によって「重ねる」の意を表せることもある)

カサノバ [イタリアの冒険家・作家] Casanova /kæzənóuvə/ (Giovanni Giacomo 〜).

かさばる 嵩張る ●かさばった包み a bulky package. ▶これはかさばって郵便で送れない This is too bulky [《書》voluminous] to send by mail.

カザフスタン [国名] Kazakhstan /kɑːzɑːkstɑːn/; (公式名) the Republic of Kazakhstan. (首都 Astana) ●カザフ(スタン)人 a Kazakh. ●カザフ(スタン)語 Kazakh. ●カザフ(スタン)(人[語])の Kazakh.

かさぶた a scab. ●傷口にかさぶたができた A scab has formed over the wound. ▶かさぶたがはがれた [取れた] The scab fell off [came off].

かさぶたしきぶこう『かさぶた式部考』 Our Lady of the Scabs. (参考) 秋本松代の戯曲

カサブランカ [モロッコの都市] Casablanca.

かざみ 風見 a weather vane.

かざみどり 風見鶏 [おんどりの形をした風見] a weathercock. ▶あいつは風見鶏だ。いつも勝った方についている 《比喩的》He is a weathercock—always on the side of the winner.

かさむ 嵩む (増える) increase, 《やや書》mount up; (山のようにたまる) pile up. ▶彼の借金はかさんでいた His debts increased [mounted up, piled up]. ▶事故で予想以上に出費がかさんだ The accident increased our expenses more than we expected. ▶近ごろは出費がかさむ Expenses are high these days.

かざむき 風向き ❶ [風の方向] the wind direction, the direction of the wind. ●風向きを調べる see the wind direction; see which way the wind is blowing. ▶風向きが南に変わった The wind has changed [shifted] to the south./(風向きが変わって今は南に吹いている) The wind came around and is now blowing south. ▶風向きがよかったので帆走に出かけた As the wind was favorable, we went for a sail.
❷ [形勢] the situation. ▶風向きが悪くなってきた

The situation has become unfavorable to us./ *Things* are turning against us (↔in our favor). ❸【機嫌】●彼は今風向きが悪い He is *in a bad temper* [*mood*] now.

かざり 飾り【飾る物】a decoration (⚠しばしば複数形で);(実用品に対する) an ornament.(⇨装飾)●新年[クリスマス]の飾り物 New Year's [Christmas] *decorations*.●床の間の飾り an *ornament* in an alcove.●飾りのない(=質素な)服 *simple* [*plain*] clothes.●クリスマスツリーに飾りをつるす hang *ornaments* on a Christmas tree; *decorate* [*trim*] a tree.▶部屋の飾りは質素だった The room *was* plainly *decorated*.
●飾り棚 a display shelf;(ガラス戸つきの) a cabinet.●飾りボタン an ornamental button; a fancy button.●飾り窓 a show window.

かざりけ 飾り気●飾り気のない(=率直な)人 a *frank* [*candid*] person.●飾り気のない(=気取らない)態度を取る take an *unaffected* attitude.

かざりたてる 飾り立てる●部屋を飾り立てる *decorate* a room *gaudily* [*strikingly*].(⚠前の方は「はでに」,後の方は「目立つように」の意)

かざりつけ 飾り付け●店[クリスマス]の飾り付け shop [Christmas] *decorations*.●クリスマスツリーに照明をつけて飾り付けをする *decorate* [*dress*] a Christmas tree *with lights*.▶その通りにはクリスマスの飾り付けがしてあった There were Christmas *decorations* all along the street./The street was *decked out* for Christmas.

かざりつける 飾り付ける decorate.(⇨飾る)

*かざる 飾る ❶【美しくする】(はでに飾る) decorate;(場所・物に装飾をほどこす) ornament;(人・服装を飾っていっそう美しくする) adorn;(晴れ着で着飾っている) be decked in one's best.●宝石で身を飾る *adorn* oneself with jewels.●劇場の入り口には花で飾ってあった The theater entry *was decorated* [*decked*] *with* flowers.▶彼女の帽子はバラで飾られていた Her hat *was ornamented with* roses.
❷【陳列する】display;(展示する) exhibit /iɡzíbit/.●彼の絵を美術館に飾る *exhibit* his paintings in the gallery.●新刊本がショーウインドーに飾られている New books *are displayed* [*are on display*] in the (show) window.
❸【気取る】●うわべを飾る人 a *showy* [《書》 *ostentatious*] person.●飾った文体で書く write in a *showy* style.

かさん 加算图(加えること) adding;(足し算) addition.
──**加算する** 動(加える) add;(算入する) include.●臨時収入を加算する *include* one's extra income.●加算税 an additional tax.

かざん 火山 a volcano (圏 〜(e)s.●海底火山 a submarine *volcano*.(⇨活火山,休火山,死火山)●その火山は現在活動しているのでいつ何どき噴火するかもしれない As the *volcano* is now active, it may [×can] erupt at any time.
●火山活動 volcanic activity.●火山岩 volcanic rock.●火山帯 a volcanic zone.●火山弾 a volcanic bomb.●火山灰 volcanic ash(es).●火山爆発 a volcanic eruption [×explosion].●火山礫(れき)【地学】a lapillus /ləpíləs/ (圏 -li /-laɪ/).

かさんかすいそ 過酸化水素【化学】hydrogen peroxide /pəráksaɪd/.

*かし 貸し【貸し付けられた物・金】a loan;【売掛金】a bill;【賃貸し】rent,《英》hire (⇨貸す❷).●貸しを取り立てる collect *bills*.●彼には5万円の貸しがある He owes me 50,000 yen./He is in my debt for 50,000 yen.
●貸し衣装 costumes for rent [《英》 hire].

●貸し自転車 a rental《米》[a hire《英》] bicycle [《話》 bike;《英》《話》cycle].●貸し切りキャンパス内移動用.(掲示) Bikes For Hire.●貸しビル a building with office space for rent《米》[to let《英》].●貸しボート a boat for rent [《英》 hire].●貸し本 a book for rent [《英》 hire].

*かし 菓子【ケーキ類】(a) cake (⇨ケーキ);【キャンデー・チョコレート類】(a) candy,《英》a sweet;【パイ・タルト類】a pastry;【クッキー類】《米》a cookie,《英》a biscuit;【総称】confectionery (⚠つづり字に注意.やや堅い語で,他の具体的種類を示す語を用いる方が日常的).●お菓子を召し上がりますか Would you like (to have) some *cake* [*candy*]?
●菓子折り a box of cake; a box of candy.●菓子屋《米》a cándy stòre,《英》a swéet shòp; a pástry shòp; a confectionery (shop).

かし 樫【植物】an oak (tree).(参考 カシワ・ナラ・カシなどの総称)●樫の実 an acorn.

かし 下肢 the lower limbs; the legs.

かし 可視 visibility.
●可視宇宙 a visible universe.●可視圏 (the range of) visibility.●可視光線【物理】radiant rays.

かし 仮死●仮死状態にある be in (a state of) *suspended animation*.

かし 河岸【魚市場】a fish market;【川岸】a riverbank.

かし 華氏 Fahrenheit /fǽrənhàɪt/ (略 F, Fah., Fahr.).(事情 米英では日常生活には通例華氏を用いる)●気温は華氏32度だ It's 32°*F*.(1) thirty-two degrees Fahrenheit と読む.(2) 摂氏0度に相当)

かし 歌詞 words, the words to [of] a song;(ポップソングなどの) lyrics /lírɪk/.●この歌詞に曲をつける set these *words* [*lyrics*] to music.

*かじ 舵【船のかじ板, 飛行機の方向舵(だ)】a rudder;【舵柄】a helm,【船舵】a tiller;【舵輪】a helm.●かじ取り(の)●かじを取る steer (a boat).●be at the *helm* [*wheel*, *tiller*];(あやつる) manage (a business), handle.▶かじいっぱい Full *rudder*.▶かじを中央に戻す Ease the *rudder*.●取りかじ[おもかじ] Left [Right] *rudder*.

*かじ 火事(a) fire.●大火事 a big *fire*.●山火事 a forest *fire*.●隣の家が火事だ(=燃えている) The house next door *is on fire* [*is burning*]!●火事だ!火事だ!*Fire! Fire!*(⚠この場合は無冠詞)
①【火事が[を]】●彼の家の近くのスーパーマーケットで火事があった There was a *fire* [A *fire* broke out, ×A fire happened, ×A fire took place] at the supermarket near his house.▶昨年このあたりでは火事が多かった[6件あった] We had a lot of *fires* [six cases of *fire*] in this neighborhood last year.▶空気が乾燥していると火事はすぐ広がる When the air is dry, a *fire* spreads quickly.▶火事はおさまった The *fire* was brought under control./(消し止められた) The *fire* was put out [《書》was extinguished].
②【火事の】▶火事の増加の主な原因は天候異変だ The main reason for the increase in *fires* is the abnormal climate.
③【火事に】●火事にあう suffer a *fire*.▶もしあなたの家が万一火事になったらどうしますか What (would you do) if your house should catch [be on ×become] *fire*.
④【火事で】▶多くの人が火事で焼け出された A lot of people lost their houses in [×by] the *fire*.
●火事場 (⇨火事場)

かじ 家事 housework (!掃除・料理・洗濯など);(家庭の雑用) household chores; (家庭の切り盛り) housekeeping. ●家事に追われる be busy with *housework*. ●家事をする keep house; do the [one's] *housework*. ●家事を分担する share the *housework* (*with* him). ●母親について家事見習いをする learn *housekeeping* under one's mother. ▶彼女は家事の切り盛りがうまい She is an efficient housewife.

かじ 加持 〘呪文〙an incantation; 〘祈祷〙a prayer. ●加持祈祷 incantations and prayers. ●加持祈祷を行う perform *incantations*.

かじ 鍛冶 (⇨鍛冶屋)

がし 餓死 starvation; death from hunger.
── 餓死する starve to death; die of starvation [hunger].

カシオペアざ カシオペア座 〘天文〙Cassiopeia /kæsiəpíːə/.

かじか 鰍 〘魚介〙a bullhead.

かじか 河鹿 〘動物〙a *kajika* frog; a Japanese river frog.

かしかた 貸し方 〘簿記〙a credit. (⇨借り方)

かじかむ 寒さで手がかじかんだ My hands *were* [*felt*] *numb* /nʌ́m/ with cold.

かしかり 貸し借り ▶彼は金の貸し借りはしない He neither *lends* nor *borrows*. ▶これで貸し借りなしとなった(=対等になった) We are *even* [(*all*) *square*,《話》*quits*] *now*./This has made us [Let's call it] (*all*) *square*.

かしかん 下士官 〘陸軍〙a noncommissioned officer; 〘海軍〙a petty officer.

かじき(まぐろ) 梶木(鮪) 〘魚介〙(マカジキ) a marlin, a spearfish; (メカジキ) a swordfish.

かしきり 貸し切り ●貸し切りバス a *chartered* bus. ▶このホールは団体のために貸し切りになっている This hall *is reserved* [*is chartered*] for a group. (!charter は公共の乗り物に用いる)

かしきる 貸し切る ❶ 〘一定期間その人専用に貸す〙(劇場などを) reserve, (!) book; (乗り物を) charter. ●劇場の席を40人分貸し切る *reserve* [ˣcharter] forty seats at the theater. ●観光バスを3台貸し切る *charter* three sightseeing buses.
❷ 〘残らず全部貸す〙▶彼に有り金を貸し切った I *lent all the money* I had.

かしきんこ 貸し金庫 a safe(ty)-deposit box.

かしげる ●小首をかしげる *lean* [*tilt*] one's head *to one side*; (疑いを表して) doubt. ▶ⁿcock one's head は「真剣に聞く・考える」ときのしぐさを表す

かしこ (手紙の結語) (⇨敬具)

かしこい 賢い wise; clever, (主に米) smart; intelligent; bright, brilliant, 《話》brainy.

> **使い分け** **wise** 知識・経験が豊富で正しい判断ができること。通例年配の人に用いる。日常会話では wise の代わりに sensible がよく用いられる。
> **clever** 聡明で洗練されていること。時にずるがしこさを含意する。
> **smart** clever のくだけた語。
> **intelligent** 生まれつき知能が高いこと。
> **bright, brilliant** ともに頭のよさをいうが, 特に brilliant は並はずれて頭がよいこと。また bright は子供についていうことが多い。
> **brainy** 通例生徒が頭のよい子をうらやんでいう語。

▶君がそれを断わったのは賢かった *It was wise of you* [You *were* (*enough*)] *to refuse it*. (!相手を前にしていう場合は前の言い方が普通) ●彼はクラスの中で最も賢い少年だった He was the *brightest* boy in the class. ▶人間は動物よりもはるかに賢い Humans are much more *intelligent* than animals. ▶彼はこの前会ったときよりも多少賢くなった (=知恵がついた) He's gained some *wisdom* since I saw him last.

かしこさ 賢さ (⇨賢い)

かしこし 貸し越し an overdraft. ●当座貸し越し bank *overdraft*.

かしこまる 〘正座する〙sit* straight [upright]. ▶彼は教授の前でかしこまっていた He *sat* upright [(堅くなっていた) *was stiff*] before the professor. ●そうかしこまらないでください (気楽にしてください) Make yourself at home [comfortable]./《話》Take it easy./Just relax./(堅苦しくしないでください) Don't *stand on ceremony*.
会話 「そこのコップ見せてください」「かしこまりました」"Could you show me those glasses?" "*Certainly* [*Very good*], sir [ma'am 《米》, madam 《英》]."

かししつ 貸し室 《米》a room for rent, 《英》a room to let. ●貸し室あり 〘掲示〙For Rent./To Let.

かししぶり 貸し渋り a credit crunch; restricted [tight] lending. ●貸し渋りが原因の倒産 a bankruptcy caused by *restricted* lending. ▶銀行は株主資本比率を高めるために貸し渋りを続けている Banks *are clamping down on their lending* to hike their capital-to-assets ratios.

カシス 〘植物〙(クロスグリ) a cassis; a black currant; 〘リキュール酒〙(crème de) cassis.

かしずく 〘書〙attend (on) 《the king》.

かしせき 貸席 a room for hire.

かしだおれ 貸し倒れ a bad debt. ●貸し倒れ倒産 bad debt bankruptcy. ●貸し倒れ引当(禁)金 a bad debt allowance.

かしだし 貸し出し 図 ❶ 〘金銭の〙a loan; (前貸し) an advance.
❷ 〘本やビデオなどの〙▶そのビデオは貸し出し中です The videotapes *are out on loan* [*have been lent out*].
── 貸し出し(を)する 動 lend; loan; advance. (⇨貸す). ●本の貸し出しをする *lend* [*loan*, 《米》*check out*] a book.
●貸し出しカウンター《米》a chéckout còunter.

かしだす 貸し出す 〘無料で〙lend*... out, (図書などを借り出す)《米》check... out; (その窓口はa checkout counter (⇨借りる❶)); 〘有料で〙rent 《米》[let* 《英》]...(out). (⇨貸す)

かしちん 貸し賃 〘土地・家屋などの〙(a) rent; 〘乗り物などの〙hire, a hire charge.

かしつ 過失 〘不完全な結果をもたらす落度〙a fault (!one's fault は過失責任を暗示する); 〘誤った判断や規則の無視による誤り〙a mistake; 〘意図せず正しい行動からはずれること〙an error; 〘不慮の事故〙an accident; 〘必要な注意を怠ること〙negligence. (⇨間違い) ●重大な過失を犯す make a serious *mistake*; commit a serious *error*. ▶彼女は過失が自分にあることを認めた She admitted her *fault*./She admitted that it was her *fault*. ▶彼はそれを過失でなく故意にやった He did not do it *by accident*, but on purpose.
●過失傷害(罪) accidental [unintentional] infliction of injury. ●過失致死(罪) an accidental killing [homicide, 〘後の方が堅い語〙; 〘法律〙(involuntary) manslaughter]. ▶彼は業務上過失致死(罪)で起訴された He was accused of [ˣfor] manslaughter through professional *negligence*.

かじつ 佳日 a lucky [an auspicious] day.

かじつ 果実 (a) fruit. (⇨果物)

かじつ

翻訳のこころ 芸術や教養は「果実よりは花」なのであり、そのもたらす結果よりも花に価値があるというわけです（丸山真男『「である」ことと「する」こと』）The art and cultural education are "the flowers rather than the fruits." Their value resides not in the results they produce but resides in and of themselves. (!fruit (果実)は「成果」などの抽象的な意も含む)

• 果実酒 fruit liquor;《apple》wine.

かじつ 過日 (先日) the other day. (⇨先日)

がしつ 画質 picture quality. • 高画質 a high [superior] *picture quality*. ▶このテレビは画質がいい[悪い] This TV has a good [poor] *picture quality*.

かしつき 加湿器 a humidifier.

かしつけ 貸し付け lending;《貸付金》a loan;《前貸金》an advance. • 銀行貸し付け a (commercial) bank *loan*.
• 貸し付け係 a loan tèller. • 貸付信託 a lóan trùst.

かしつける 貸し付ける lend*, loan; (前貸しする) advance. (⇨貸す)

かして 貸し手 a lender (↔a borrower).

かじとり 舵取り (行為) steering; (舵手) a steersman; a helmsman. • 経済のかじ取りに失敗する *mishandle* the economy.

かしぬし 貸し主 a lender; (債権者) a creditor; (土地・建物の) a lessor; (アパートなどの) (女) a landlady; (男) a landlord (!landlady, landlord はアパートの家主であるだけでなく、土地の賃貸も行う場合が多い)

カジノ 〖公営の賭博(とばく)場〗a casino /kəsí:nou/ (複 ~s).

かじば 火事場 the scene of a fire. ▶私の母は火事場(=難しい状況)になるほど落ち着くタイプなんだろうか I wondered if Mom's the kind (of person) who gets calmer as the situation gets worse. (!この文脈での「火事場」に当たる表現は英語にはない)
• 火事場のばか力 adrenaline rush, wired [superhuman] power [strength]; (説明的に) an enormous power [strength] one exerts in the case of emergency, such as when one is caught in a fire.
• 火事場泥棒 a thief at a fire.

かしパン 菓子パン a sweet roll; a bun;《米話》a Danish (pastry).

かしほんや 貸し本屋 a lénding [《米》a réntal] library.

かしま 貸し間 a room for rent《米》[to let《英》]. ▶貸し間あり《掲示》Rooms for rent [to let].

かしましい 姦しい (やかましい) noisy; clamorous. ▶女 3 人よればかしましい(ことわざ) Many women *many words*./Three women (and a goose) *make a market*.

カシミール 〖インド北部からパキスタン北東部にひろがる山岳地域〗Kashmir /kǽʃmiər/.

カシミヤ cashmere. • カシミヤのセーター a *cashmere* sweater.

かしもと 貸元 〖お金を貸す人〗a financial backer [supporter]; 〖ばくち打ちの親分〗a boss gambler.

かしや 貸し家 a house for rent《米》[to let《英》]. (!《掲示》などでは単に For rent, To let とも書かれる) • 貸し家を捜す look [hunt] for a *house to rent*. (⇨借家)

かしゃ 『火車』*All She Was Worth*.〖参考〗宮部みゆきの小説

かしゃ 貨車《米》a freight /fréit/ car,《英》a (goods) wagon; (有蓋(ゆうがい)の)《米》a boxcar,《英》a (goods) van; (無蓋の)《米》a gondola (car),《英》an (open) wagon (!wagon は通例無蓋)

かしょう

かじや 鍛冶屋 〖人〗a smith, a blacksmith (!この語は黒人に侮蔑的な a smith または a farrier (蹄鉄工)を用いる). 〖店〗a smithy, a smith's shop.

かしゃく 仮借 (許すこと) (a) pardon《for》; an excuse《for》(⇨仮借ない).
― **仮借ない** 形 merciless; ruthless; unsparing. ▶彼は仮借なく(=容赦なく)私の無作法を責めたてた He criticized me *mercilessly* [*without mercy*] for my bad manners.
― **仮借する** 動 pardon; excuse.

かしゃく 呵責 • 良心の呵責を感じる feel guilty《about》(!最も一般的な言い方); be [feel] conscience-stricken《about》; (良心の痛みを感じる) feel a pang [a twinge, a prick] of conscience《about》(!比喩的な言い方で主に書き言葉. conscience の代わりに guilt も可). (⇨良心②) ▶田中氏はその計画に賛成することに良心の呵責は感じなかった Mr. Tanaka didn't *feel guilty about* agreeing to that plan.

かしゃっ ▶かしゃっとカメラのシャッターを切る音聞こえた I heard the shutter of the camera *click*. ▶ドアがかしゃっと音を立てて閉まった the door *clicked* shut.

がしゅん 賀春(がしゅん)

かしゅ 歌手 a singer; (バンド演奏で歌う) a vocalist.
• 流行歌手 a pop [a popular song] *singer*. • オペラ歌手 an opera *singer*.

かじゅ 果樹 a fruit tree.
• 果樹園 an orchard. • 果樹栽培 fruit growing [cultivation].

がしゅ 雅趣 elegance. • 雅趣に富んだ庭 a garden full of *elegance*.

カジュアル (カジュアルウェア) casual wear [clothes], casuals. • カジュアルな服装で出かける go out in *casual clothes*.

かしゅう 歌集 〖歌唱集〗a songbook; a collection of songs; 〖短歌集〗a collection of *tanka* poems.

かじゅう 加重 (重さ) weighting; (刑・負担などの) aggravation. ― **加重する** 動 weight; (刑などを) aggravate.
• 加重平均 a weighted average.

かじゅう 果汁 fruit juice.

かじゅう 荷重 〖機械〗a load. • 固定荷重〖工学〗a dead [a deadweight] *load*. • 積載荷重〖工学〗a live *load*.
• 荷重試験 a lóad tèst.

かじゅう 過重 overweight. • 過重な負担を負う be overburdened《with》.
• 過重積載 overload. • 過重労働 overwork.

がしゅう 画集 a book of paintings (デッサン) drawings]; (特定の画家などの) a collection of paintings [pictures].

カシューナッツ a cashew (nut).

ガジュマル 〖植物〗a banyan [a banian] (tree).

かしょ 箇所 〖場所・物の表面の特定の部分, 書物などの箇所〗a place; 〖地点〗a spot; (1 点) a point; 〖文章の 1 節〗a passage; 〖部分〗a part. • 脚の痛む箇所 a sore *place* [*part*] on one's leg. • 読みかけていた箇所を見失う[忘れないようにしておく] lose [keep] one's *place*. ▶同じ箇所で事故があった There was an accident in the same *place* [*spot*]. ▶市内数箇所で道路が不通になった Roads were blocked at several *points* in the city. ▶先生は聖書から数箇所引用した The teacher quoted several *passages* from the Bible.

かしょう 仮称 图 a tentative [a temporary] name.
― **仮称する** 動 call [name]《a thing》tentatively [temporarily]. ▶この会は「コンピュータクラブ」と仮称

かしょう されている This club *is tentatively named* [*called*] the 'Computer Club.'

かしょう 河床 a riverbed.

かしょう 過少, 過小 〖数が過少の〗too few; 〖量が過少の〗too little.

かしょう 歌唱 (歌を歌うこと) singing; (歌) a song.
● 歌唱力のある have a talent for singing.
● 歌唱指導 the teaching of singing.

かじょう 箇条 〖項目〗an item; 〖条項〗an article, a clause. ● 10 箇条より成る consist of ten *articles*. ● 箇条書き items. ● 箇条書きにする itemize.

かじょう 下情 ● 下情は庶民の生活事情によく通じている know well *how the common people are living*.

かじょう 渦状 (⇨渦巻き)
● 渦状銀河〖天文〗a spiral galaxy. ● 渦状星雲〖天文〗a spiral nebula /nébjələ/.

かじょう 過剰 图 〖過多〗(an) excess; 〖余剰〗(a) surplus. ● 生産過剰 excess [surplus] production; overproduction. ● 人口過剰 overpopulation.

── 過剰(な) 形 too much [many]; excessive; surplus. ● 過剰報道から彼女を守る protect her from press *intrusion*. ● 彼女は自意識過剰です She is *too* self-conscious. ● 過剰包装ではありませんか Doesn't it have *too many* layers of wrapping? ● 科学はしばしば人間を自信過剰にさせる Science often makes people overconfident.
● 過剰生産 overproduction. ● 過剰投資 over-investment. ● 過剰防衛 excessive self-defense.

がしょう 画商 a picture [an art] dealer.

がしょう 賀正 I wish you a happy New Year. (!「よい年をお迎えください」の意にもなる)

がじょう 牙城 (守りの堅い本拠) a stronghold. ● 資本主義の牙城 a *stronghold* of capitalism; a capitalist *stronghold*.

がじょう 賀状 (年賀状) a New Year's card.

かしょうひょうか 過小評価 图 underestimation; an underestimate.

── 過小評価する 動 underestimate [underrate] (it, him).

かしょく 過食 图 overeating. ── 過食する 動 eat too much; overeat.
● 過食症〖医学〗compulsive eating disorder, bulimia (nervosa) /bjuːlíːmiə (nəːrvóusə)/.

かしょくのてん 華燭の典 ● 華燭の典(=結婚式)を挙げる hold a *wedding* [a *marriage*] *ceremony*; celebrate a *wedding*.

かしょぶんしょとく 可処分所得 disposable income.

かしら 頭 ❶〖あたま〗a head. ● かしら右[左]〖号令〗*Eyes right* [*left*]!
❷〖長〗a chief (爥 ～s), a head. ● 給仕頭 a *head* waiter. ● インディアンの頭(=酋長) the *chief* [*head*] of an Indian tribe.

*-**かしら** 〖終助詞〗❶〖自問〗I wonder (if 節, whether 節, wh-節); 〖疑心〗I doubt (if 節, whether 節).
● あしたは雨かしら I wonder if [whether] it will rain tomorrow. ● 1,000 円で足りるかしら I doubt whether a thousand yen will be enough (or not). (!if の方が口語的であるが, ×… if … or not. は不可)
会話 「彼仙台にいたことがあるって言ってたよ」「いつのことかしら」"He told me he'd been in Sendai." "When was that, *I wonder*? (=*I wonder when* it was.)"
❷〖依頼〗● 少しお金を貸していただけないかしら Will [Can, Could, Would] you lend me some money? (! 後ほど丁寧な言い方)/*I wonder if* you could [would] lend me some money. (! if 節内は仮定法)/*Would you mind* lending me some money?
❸〖希望〗● 早く夏休みが来ないかな I hope [✕wish] the summer vacation will come soon.
❹〖その他の表現〗会話「彼は何歳かしらいじゃないかしら」「30 歳くらいかな」"How old *do you think* he is?" "I'd say about thirty."

かしらもじ 頭文字 an initial (letter) (!姓名の頭文字は通例 initials); 〖文頭の大文字〗a capital (letter). ● 私の名前の頭文字 the *initials* of my name; my *initials*.

かじりつく 〖ぱくつく〗bite* (*into, at*); 〖すがりつく, 執着する〗cling* (*to*); 〖あくまで続ける〗stick (*to*). ● ナシにかじりつく *bite into* [*at*] a pear. ● 旧習にかじりつく *cling to* an old custom. ● 机にかじりつく study hard. ● テレビにかじりついている be glued to the TV. ● その子は母親にかじりついていた The child *clung* to his mother. ● 石にかじりついても目標は達成してみせる I'll *stick to* it until the goal is reached.

かじる ❶〖かむ〗bite*; (少しずつ) nibble; (固い物を繰り返し) gnaw /nɔː/. ● リンゴをかじる *bite* an apple. ● ビスケットを一口かじる have [take] *a bite* of a biscuit. ● 骨をかじる *gnaw (at*) a bone. ● チーズをかじる *nibble* (*at*) a piece of cheese. ● ネズミが壁をかじって穴をあけた The mice *nibbled* [*gnawed*] a hole in the wall.
❷〖少し知る〗know* a little of.... ● ドイツ語は少しかじりましたが, しゃべるのは苦手です I've *learned a little of* German, but I can't speak it well.

かしわ 柏〖植物〗an oak (tree).
● 柏餅 *kashiwamochi*, (説明的に) a soft rice cake stuffed with sweetened bean paste and wrapped in an oak leaf.

かしわで 柏手 ● 柏手を打つ clap one's hands 《in prayer before a shrine》.

かしん 過信 ── 過信する 動 ● 自己の能力を過信する (=自信過剰である) put [have] *too much confidence in* one's ability; *be too confident of* one's ability; (過大評価する) *overestimate* one's ability.

かしん 家臣 a retainer; (封建時代の) a vassal, a man (爥 men).

かじん 佳人 (美人) a beauty; a beautiful woman.
● 佳人薄命 (ことわざ) Whom the gods love die young.

かじん 家人 (家族) one's family; a member of the family. ● 彼はよく家人に無断で外出する He often goes out without telling *anyone* in his *family*.

かじん 歌人 a *tanka* poet. (⇨詩人)

がしんしょうたん 臥薪嘗胆 ● 臥薪嘗胆すること 5 年, 彼はついに外交官試験に合格した After five years of *great perseverance*, he finally passed the examination for a diplomat.

:かす 貸す ❶〖金品などを〗lend*; loan.

> 使い分け lend 一定期間, 物を貸与すること. 家のように移動できないものには用いない.
> loan 高価なものを長期間正式に貸すこと. lend と同意にも用いるのは〖英書・米〗.

① 〖…を貸す〗● 20 ポンド(を)貸してくれという ask for a *loan* of 20 pounds. ● 金融会社は高い利子で金を貸す Finance companies *lend* [*loan*] money at high interest (rate). ● 余分な水泳パンツがあるから貸してあげられる I have an extra pair of trunks, so I can *loan* you a pair [you can

have a pair].
❷【A(人)にB(物・金)を貸す】 lend A B; lend B to A ▶太郎は私にこの辞書を貸してくれた Taro lent [《主に米》*loaned*] me this dictionary./Taro *lent* [《主に米》*loaned*] this dictionary to me. (❗(1) 前の文は this dictionary を, 後の文は me を強調した言い方 ⇨与える. (2) 反義語 borrow を用いて表現すると: I *borrowed* this dictionary *from* [×to] Taro. (⇨借りる❶) (3) 受身は次の二つが可: This dictionary *was lent* (*to*) me by Taro./I *was lent* this dictionary by Taro.)(少々改まった言い方) Taro let me use this dictionary. ▶彼女は妹にはよく金を貸してやる She often *lends* (money) *to* her sister.
会話「(私に)お金を少し貸していただけませんか」「いいですよ. いかほどですか」"Would [Could, Can, Will] you lend me some money, please?"(丁寧さは劣る)/Would you mind [《話》Would it be OK] if I borrow(ed) some money (from you)? (❗borrowed (仮定法過去形)を用いるといっそう改まった言い方) "Sure. How much do you need?"
❷【賃貸しする】rent ... (out), 《英》let*... (out), 《英》hire ... (out).

使い分け 《米》では一般に一定の金額で物を貸すときには rent (out) を用いる. 《英》では通例設備・建物・土地などの不動産を貸す場合には let (out) を, 移動できる物を長期間貸す場合(車など)は rent (out) を, 特定の目的に短期間貸す場合(建物・車・衣装などは hire (out) を用いる.

▶私は夏休みの間, 部屋を学生に貸した I *rented* [《英》*let*] my room *to* a student during the summer vacation. ▶彼は時間制でボートを貸し出している He *rents* [《英》*hires*] *out* boats by the hour. (❗rent は「賃借りする」の意もあるので out を使った方が明確) ▶この家は月5万円で貸している This house *rents at* 50,000 yen a month.
❸【その他の表現】 ▶彼に手を貸してやる help him; lend him a (helping) hand. (⇨助ける, 手伝う) ▶その計画に名前を貸す lend one's name *to* the project. ▶彼に知恵を貸す give advice to him. ▶耳を貸して. そっと言いたい[大きな声で言えない]ことがある *Give me your ear*. I want to whisper something in it. ▶電話を貸してください(=使用してもよろしいですか) Can I *use* your telephone? (⇨借りる①)
会話「火を貸していただけませんか」「いいですとも. はいどうぞ」"Could you *give* me a light, please?" "Okay. ↘Here it ∕ is [×Yes, please]." (❗Do you have a light? はくだけた直接的な言い方)

*かす 滓 〖液体の底に沈んだ〗dregs, lees; 〖コーヒーなどの〗grounds; 〖浮きかす〗(a) scum.
かす 粕, 糟 〖酒かす〗sake lees; 〖説明的に〗edible meal-like residue from *sake* production.
● 粕汁 sake lees soup. ● 粕漬け vegetables [fish] pickled in *sake* lees.
かす 化す change. (⇨化する)
かす 科す impose. (⇨科する)
かす 課す impose. (⇨課する)
*かず 数 (a) number. (⇨多い, 少ない)
①【~数】 ▶大きな[小さな]数(=数字) a high [low] *number*. (❗a large [a small] *number* とすれば「多[少]数」の意 (⇨解説))
❷【数が[は]】 ▶観客の数はおよそ5,000人だった There were about 5,000 spectators./The *number* of spectators was [×were] about 5,000./The spectators were about 5,000 *in number*. (❗最初の言い方が最も普通) ▶この会社は女性の数の方が男性より多い There are *more* women than men [women exceed men *in number*, women outnumber men] in this company. (❗最初の言い方が最も口語的) ▶この学校の生徒の数はどのぐらいですか *How many* students are there in this school?/What [×How many] is the *number* of students in this school? (❗前の方がり堅い言い方) ▶最近海外旅行者の数が増えてきている *More and more* people travel [are traveling] abroad these days./The *number* of people who travel abroad is [×are] increasing these days. (❗前の方が口語的)

解説 the number of ... は特定の数を表し, 単数扱い, of の後には無冠詞の複数名詞が続き, number の前の the は話しことばでは省略される. a (large) number [a small number] of ... は数が多い[少ない]ことを表し, 複数扱い: 観客の数は多かった[少なかった] There were *a large* [*a small*] *number of* spectators. (❗There were *a lot of* [*a few*] spectators. より堅い言い方)/The *number of* spectators was large [small]. なお, 一般に the number of ... を使うと文が回りくどくなるので, 他の数量表現を用いる方が自然な言い方となる (❹以下の例を参照).

❸【数の[に]】 ▶彼を数の中に入れる[入れない] *count* him *in* [*out*]; *include* [*do not include*] him. (❗前の方が口語的) ▶数にものを言わせて勝つ win *by* (*force of*) *numbers*. (❗numbers は「数の上での勢」の意) ▶数の上で優勢なる be *numerically* superior (*to*). (⇨❺) ▶1クラスの生徒の数の多いのに(=何と多くの生徒がいることかと)驚いた I was surprised *how many* [*what a lot of*] students there were in one class. (❗口語では後の方が自然) ▶公立病院は住民の数に応じて建設すべきだ Public hospitals should be built in proportion to *how many* people live there.
❹【数を】 ▶本の数をかぞえる count the (*number of*) books. ▶数を増やす[減らす] increase [decrease, reduce] the *number* (*of*). ▶数をこなす(=何度もやってみれば)こつが分かってくるよ You'll be getting the hang of it if you try often enough. ▶数をかぞえまちがえる *count* wrong(ly).
❺【数で】 ▶数ではまさっている *outnumber* 《the enemy》; be *numerically superior* (*to*). ▶数でこなす(=大量に売って利益を得る) make profits by selling in large quantities.
❻【その他の表現】 ▶数知れない countless; 《書》 innumerable. (⇨無数の) ▶数ある彼の小説の中でこれこそ最高傑作だ This is the very best among *many* of his novels. ▶私の作品などの数ではない(=大したことはない) My work doesn't count [counts for nothing].

かず 下図 the lower chart. ▶下図参照 See the *chart below*.

*ガス ❶【気体】gas /gǽs/ 《複-es, 《時に米》-ses》. ▶ガス(状)の gaseous.
①【~ガス】 ▶天然ガス natural *gas*. ▶石炭ガス coal *gas*. ▶毒ガス poison *gas*. ▶催涙ガス tear *gas*. ▶都市ガス town [municipal] *gas*. ▶プロパンガス propane (*gas*). ▶ガス自殺をする kill oneself with *gas*; *gas* oneself. ▶ガス中毒を起こす get *gas* poisoning(ガスにやられる) be *gassed*.
②【ガスが】 ▶彼の家にはガスが引いてある His house has *gas* laid on. ▶ガスがついている[消えている] The *gas* is on [off]. ▶ガスがこんろから漏れている The *gas* is leaking [escaping] from the stove.
③【ガスの[を, に]】 ▶ガスの火を強く[弱く]する turn

the *gas* **up** [**down, low**]． ●ガスの元栓をしめる close the *gas* valve． ●ガスの混合物を作る[消す] a mixture of *gases*． ●(栓をひねって)ガスをつける[消す] turn on [off] the *gas*． ●ガスにかける put 《a pot》on the *gas*．

❷ [濃霧] a (dense [thick]) fog． ▶ガスが発生する A *fog* rises．

❸ [ガソリン] 《米》gasoline,《米話》gas;《英》petrol． ●ガス欠になる[である] run [be] out of *gas*．

❹ [胃・腸内の] gas． ●腹にガスがたまる have gas in the bowels．

●ガスオーブン a gas oven /ʌvn/． ●ガス会社 a gas company． ●ガス管 a gas pipe;(本管) a gas main． ●ガスストーブ a gas heater [《英》fire]． ●ガスタービン a gas turbine． ●ガス代 gas rates [charge(s)]． ●ガスタンク (⇨ガスタンク) ●ガス灯 a gas lamp, a gaslight． ●ガスバーナー a gas burner． ●ガス爆発 a gas explosion． ●ガスボイラー a gas-fired boiler． ●ガスボンベ a gas cylinder;(卓上コンロ) a cooking-gas canister． ●ガスマスク a gas mask． ●ガスメーター a gas meter． ●ガス漏れ a gas leak． ●ガス屋(職員, 検針人, 集金人) a gasman;(工事人) a gasman; a gasfitter． ●ガス湯わかし器 a gas water heater;《英》a geyser． ●ガスライター a gas lighter． ●ガスレンジ 《米》a gas range [stove];《英》a gas cooker．

かすい 仮睡 (⇨㊥ うたたね, 仮眠)

かすいぶんかい 加水分解 図 [化学] hydrolysis /haɪdrǽləsɪs/． ●加水分解する hydrolyze．

***かすか** 微か ── 微かな 形 (光・音・希望などが弱い) faint; (光・形・記憶などがぼんやりした) dim; (はっきりしない) vague; (わずかな) slight． ▶タマネギのかすかなにおい a *faint* smell of onions． ●回復のかすかな望み a *faint* [*slight*] hope of recovery． ●ろうそくのかすかな明りで読書する read by the *dim* [*faint*] light of a candle．

── 微かに 副 faintly; dimly; vaguely; slightly． ▶その音は壁を通してかすかに私の耳に届いた The sound came to me *faintly* through the wall． ▶私は死んだ父をかすかに覚えている I *dimly* [*vaguely*] remember my [dead] father． (❗文脈で分からない時に dead はなくてもよい場合が多い) ▶葉が風にかすかに揺れていた The leaves were trembling *slightly* in the wind．

かすがい 鎹 ❶ [両端の曲がった大釘] a cramp (iron); an iron clamp．

❷ [つなぎとめるもの] ▶子はかすがい A child is a *bond* between husband and wife．

かずかぎりない 数限り無い (⇨無数の)

かすかに [やっとのことで] barely (⇨すれすれ); [水分が少なく味のない] dry and tasteless．

かずかず 数々 many; much. (⇨たくさん)

DISCOURSE
上記から判断するに, インターネットは高齢者にとって数々のメリットがあるといえよう Judging from the above, I would say that the Internet has *numerous* benefits for elderly people． (❗ Judging from the above, I would say that ... (上記から判断して, 私は...と考える)は結論に用いるディスコースマーカー.   間接的な理由を受けて結論を述べるときに用いる)

カスタード (a) custard．
●カスタードクリーム custard． (❗custard cream は甘いビスケットの一種) ●カスタードパイ a custard pie． ●カスタードプリン custard pudding．

カスタネット 《a pair of》castanets．

カスタマー [顧客] a customer．

●カスタマーサービス a customer service．

カスタマイズ ── カスタマイズする 動 (ソフトの設定などを) customize．

カスタムメード ── カスタムメードの 形 (特注生産, あつらえ品) custom-made; custom-built．

ガスタンク a gas tank;《英》a gasholder, a gasometer．

カステラ [<ポルトガル語] sponge /spʌ́ndʒ/ cake,《話》sponge．

かずとり 数取り [数を数えること] counting; [計数器] a counter, a tally; [計数係] a tallyman, a tally keeper (❗性差を避けるために後の方が好まれる)．

●数取りゲーム a counting game．

ガスぬき ガス抜き ●乱痴気騒ぎをしてガス抜きをする(= うっぷんを晴らす) have a drinking spree to *let off some steam*; *vent* one's *frustration* in a drinking spree．

かずのこ 数の子 (a) herring roe．

カスピ ●カスピ海 the Caspian Sea．

かすみ 霞 ❶ [薄い霧] (a) mist; (a) haze． (参考) 日本語では春の薄い霧を霞といい, 英語でこの差を厳密に表現すると, spring light haze となる (⇨霧 ❶)． ●霞を食べて生きる live on *air*． ▶森には薄く霞がかかっていた A thin *mist* [*haze*] hung over the woods./There was a thin *mist* [*haze*] (hanging) over the woods．

❷ [目のくもり] dimness; a mist．

かすみそう 霞草 [植物] a babies' [a baby's] breath．

かすみめ 霞目 bleary [blurred, blurry] eyes．

***かすむ** 霞む ❶ [かすみがかかる] be hazy [misty]． (⇨霞)． ▶かすんだ空[景色] a hazy sky [view]． ▶山の頂上が遠く(の方に)かすんで見える The top of the mountain can be seen *dimly* [is *dimly visible*] in the distance．

❷ [はっきり見えなくなる] (目がかすむ) dim (-mm-); be blurred． ▶彼女の目は涙でかすんだ Her eyes *were dimmed* [*were blurred*] *with* tears． ▶「かすんでいた」では ... were *dim* [*blurry*] *with* tears． となる/Tears *dimmed* her eyes．

❸ [人の関心を失う] [話] be upstaged． (❗ upstage は「他人に向けられている関心を自分に引き寄せる」の意) ▶女の子が生まれると兄の一郎の存在は一時かすんでしまった The new-born baby girl *upstaged* her brother Ichiro for a while．

かすめとる 掠め取る (奪い取る) snatch 《A *from* B》; (油断しているすきに盗み取る) steal 《A *from* B》． ▶ぼんやりしている間に手付金をかすめ取られた I *had* the deposit *stolen* while I was absent-minded．

かすめる 掠める ❶ [盗む] steal*; [ごまかす] cheat; [着服する] pocket． ●彼から金をかすめる *steal* money *from* him; *cheat* him *out of* his money． ●売上金をかすめる *pocket* the proceeds． ●人の目をかすめて(=こっそりと)たばこを吸う smoke *on the sly*．

❷ [かすって通る] graze; (鳥などがかすって飛ぶ) skim (-mm-) 《over ...》． ●弾丸が彼をかすめた A bullet *grazed* [(ひゅっと) *whistled past*] him． ▶ツバメが川面[軒下]をかすめた A swallow *skimmed* (over) the river [underneath the eaves]． ▶ナイフが彼の右の耳元をかすめた The knife *almost touched* his right ear． ●不安が心をかすめた A fear *came across* [*into*] my mind．

かずら 葛 [植物] a vine, a creeper, a climber．

かすりきず 掠り傷 (かすった傷) a scratch; (すりむいた傷) a scrape; (軽い打ち身) a minor [light] injury． ●ほんの小傷だ It's just [only] a *scratch*． ●転んでひざに少しかすり傷ができた I fell and got a few *scratches* [*scrapes*] on my knee． ●大破した車な

かする ら赤ん坊がかすり傷ひとつせずに救出された A baby was saved from the wrecked car without a *scratch*.

かする 化する [[変化する]] change [turn] 《*into, to*》; [[感化する]] influence. ▶戦場は血の海と化した The battle field *was turned into* a sea [a river] of blood. ▶競技場は興奮のるつぼと化した The whole stadium *was thrown into* extreme excitement. ▶その町は焦土と化した The town *was burned to* ashes.

かする 科する impose 《a fine (*up*)*on* him》; inflict 《punishment (*up*)*on* him》.

かする 課する [[税・義務などを]] impose, lay* (🔔前の方が堅い語); [[問題・仕事などを]] (割り当てる) assign. ▶たばこに税を課する impose [lay, (徴収する) levy] a tax *on* tobacco; tax tobacco. ▶多くの宿題を課する *assign* [*give*] them a lot of homework; *assign* [*give*] a lot of homework *to* them.

かする 掠る ❶ [[かすって通る]] graze. (⇨掠(かす)める) ▶車で門を出るとき門柱をかすってしまった I *scratched* my car against the gate post [My car *grazed* the gate post] as I was driving through the gate. ▶弾丸が彼の頭をかすった A bullet *almost grazed* his head. (🔔 *almost* を省略することもある)
❷ [[上前をはねる]] ▶手間賃をかする pocket a kickback from the wages [pay].

かすれる 掠れる (声が) get* hoarse [husky] (⇨嗄(か)れる); (字などが) get blurred. ▶かすれた字 a blurred character.

かせ 枷 ❶ [[昔の刑罰の道具]] shackles; (足かせ) fetters; (手かせ) handcuffs. ▶足かせをはずす remove the *fetters*.
❷ [[障害物]] an obstacle; a hindrance.

:かぜ 風

📕 WORD CHOICE 風

wind 「風」の意を表す最も一般的な語. 自然の風や扇風機・エアコンなどによる人工の風をさす. ▶風速 the *wind* speed.
blast 物を吹き飛ばすほどの特に強い勢いで吹き付ける突風・強風・爆風. 扇風機やエアコンの「強風」は strong wind で, 通例 blast は用いない. ▶爆風 a bomb *blast*.
breeze やさしく吹く自然の微風やそよ風. 通例, 快適さ・やさしさなどの肯定的意味合いを含意する. ▶朝のそよ風 the morning *breeze*.

📊 頻度チャート

wind ████████████████████
blast ███
breeze ██
         20   40   60   80 100 (%)

❶ [[空気の動き]] (a) wind; (そよ風) (a) breeze; (強風) a gale; (突風) a gust, a blast; (すきま風) 《米》 (a) draft, 《英》 (a) draught /drǽft/.
① 〜風, 風〜 ▶身を切るような風 a cutting [a biting] *wind*. ▶さわやかな [心地よい] 風 a refreshing [a pleasant] *breeze*. ▶北からの冷たい風 cold *winds* from the north; cold north *winds*. (🔔複数形で大風, 強風を表す) ▶風のある [ない] 日 a *windy* [a *windless*] day. ▶風任せにする be at the mercy of the *wind*.
② 【風が】 ▶今日は風が強い The *wind* is strong today./It is *windy* today./There is a strong *wind* blowing today./There is a lot of *wind* today. ▶今日はまったく [ほとんど] 風がない There is no [not much, almost no] *wind* today. ▶西風が吹くと雨になる The west *wind* brings rain. ▶風が出てきた [収まってきた] The *wind* is rising [falling, dying down]./(主に英) We have the *wind* rising [falling]. ▶強い風が北から吹いている It [The *wind*] is blowing hard from the north./There is a strong *wind* blowing from the north [blowing south]. (🔔 ... blowing south は「南から北へ吹いている」の意では今は用いないのが普通) ▶風が強いときは外へ出たくない I don't like to go out in *windy* weather. ▶あしたはあしたの風が吹く 'Tomorrow tomorrow's *wind* will blow.'/(ことわざ) Tomorrow is another day./Tomorrow will take care of itself.
③ 【風を [に, で]】 ▶部屋に風を通す let in fresh *air* into a room; air [ventilate] a room. ▶風に逆らって走る run against (↔before) the *wind*. ▶風に乗った [運ばれた] ホームラン a wind-blown home run. ▶木の枝が風で揺れている The branches are shaking in the *wind*. ▶私は帽子を風に吹き飛ばされた I had my hat blown off [×I was blown off my hat] by the *wind*./The *wind* blew off my hat./My hat was blown off by the *wind*. (🔔後の2文は客観的な表現で被害の気持ちはあまりない) ▶ドアが風でぱっと開いた The door blew open./The *wind* blew the door open. ▶どこからともなく美しい調べが風に乗って流れてきた A sweet melody came floating *on the wind* from nowhere. ▶落ち葉が風に吹かれて舞っていた There were fallen leaves dancing in the *wind*. ▶高く上がった打球は風に押し戻された The wind worked against the high drive.
❷ [[その他の表現]] ▶彼は先生のおしかりにどこ吹く風という顔をしていた He looked (quite) *indifferent to* his teacher's telling-off.

● **風の便り** ▶風の便りに彼が結婚したことを聞いた I hear [People say, (古) I hear tell] (that) he has got married. (🔔 that は通例省略する)
🗣 会話 「だれから聞いたの?」「風の便りさ」 "Who told you that?" "A little bird." 🔔 A little bird (told me). は「風の便りに聞いた」の意

● **風の吹き回し** 🗣 会話 「それでフレッドがアイスクリームの代金を払ったのさ」「フレッドが払ったって! どういう風の吹き回しだい?」 "And Fred paid for the ice cream." "Fred paid for it! What's come over him?"

● **風を切る** ▶スポーツカーが風を切って通り越して行った A sports car whizzed past.

*かぜ 風邪 (普通の風邪) (a) cold; (インフルエンザ) influenza, 《話》(the) flu.
① 〜風邪 ▶せきの出る [鼻] 風邪 《have》 a *cold* on [in] the chest [in the head]; a chest [a head] *cold*. ▶夏風邪 a summer *cold*. ▶ひどい [しつこい] 風邪 a bad [a slight; a stubborn] *cold*.
② 【風邪〜】 ▶風邪気味である have a slight [a touch of a] *cold*.
③ 【風邪が [は]】 ▶風邪は万病のもと (⇨万病) ▶風邪が学校ではやっている (The) *flu* is [*Colds* are] going around in our school. ▶彼の風邪がうつった I got a cold [caught (a) *cold*] from him./He gave me his *cold* [×his cold to me]. ▶ちっとも風邪が治らない I just can't get over [(取り除く) get rid of, (振り払う) shake off] my *cold*. ▶風邪はだいぶよくなりました [ひどくなってきました] My *cold* is much better now [is getting worse]. ▶患者は快方に向かっているようだったが, 突然風邪がぶりかえした

かぜあたり

The patient seemed to be recovering from his *cold*, but suddenly he suffered [had] a relapse.
④【風邪を[で]】● 風邪を引いている have a *cold*; be sick [《英》ill] with a *cold*. ● 風邪を引きかけている be getting [《米》coming down] a *cold*. ● 風邪を引きやすい catch (a) *cold* easily; be subject [susceptible] to *colds*. ● 風邪を引いて熱がある have a fever with a *cold*. ● 風邪をこじらせる make one's *cold* worse. ● 風邪を引かないように気をつけなさい Take care [Be careful] not to catch (a) *cold*. ● 今日は風邪を引いちゃった I've got a bit of a *cold*. ● 彼は今日は風邪を引いて寝ている He is in bed with a *cold* today. ● 風邪で胃(の調子)が変になっている My *cold* is affecting my stomach.
● 風邪薬 (take) medicine for a cold; a cóld mèdicine (錠剤) pill].

かぜあたり 風当たり ● 風当たりが強い 《風が主語》blow hard 《against》; (場所が主語) be windy.
● 風当たりが強い山腹 a windy [a windswept] mountainside. ● 警察に対する世間の風当たりが強い (=警察は世間から厳しく批判されている) The police *are being* severely [*sharply*] *criticized by* the public. / The police *are under* severe [*sharp*] *criticism from* the public.

かせい 火星 〖天文〗Mars. ● 火星(人)の Martian.
● 火星人 a Martian.

かせい 火勢 the force of a fire; the fire. ● 火勢を抑える control *the fire*. ● 火勢が衰えた *The fire* has gone down [died down].

かせい 加勢 〖助けること〗help; aid;《書》assistance;〖支持〗support; backup;〖援軍〗reinforcements. ● 加勢に来る come to (his) aid [assistance].

かせい 仮性 ● 仮性近視《米》false nearsightedness,《英》false short-sightedness;〖医学〗pseudomyopia /s(j)u:doumaióupiə/.

かぜい 課税 图 taxation. ● 累進課税 progressive *taxation*. ● 非課税所得 *tax-free* income. ● その国では教会の土地は課税対象[非課税]になっている Church lands are subject [not subject] to *taxation* in the country. ● このウイスキーは課税対象になります(税関で) There will be *duty on* the whiskey.
— 動 tax《alcohol》; impose [lay] a tax 《on alcohol》.
● 課税商品 taxable [dutiable] goods. (🈁 後の方は 通例輸入品について言う) ● 課税所得 taxable income. ● 課税標準 a standard of assessment.

かせいか 家政科 a course in home economics; (家政学科) the department of home economics.

かせいがん 火成岩 〖地学〗igneous /ígniəs/ rock.

かせいソーダ 苛性ソーダ caustic soda; (水酸化ナトリウム)〖化学〗sodium hydroxide.

かせいふ 家政婦 a housekeeper; (介護ヘルパー)《英》a home help [×helper]; (通いの)《英》a daily (help).

かせき 化石 a fossil /fásl/. ● 生きた化石 a living *fossil*. ● 動物の化石 a *fossil* animal. ● 化石になる [にする] fossilize.
● 化石燃料 (a) fóssil fùel.

かせぎ 稼ぎ (所得) earnings; (収入) (an) income. (⇒儲け) ● 稼ぎが多い[少ない] make [do not make] much money; have a big [a small] *income*. ● 小遣い稼ぎに随筆を書く write essays *for* pocket money. ● うちの亭主は稼ぎが悪い My husband doesn't *earn* much money [is a poor *provider*]. ● 歯医者さんの多くは稼ぎがいい(=金をよくもうける) Many dentists *make* good *money* [*earn* a lot of *money*]. ● 老夫婦は息子の稼ぎに頼って生活している The old couple live on *the money* their son *earns*.
● 稼ぎ手 (家族を養う人) a provider; (大黒柱) the breadwinner 《in one's family》.

かせぐ 稼ぐ ❶【金を】make*; (働いて) earn; (賭け事で) win*. ● (稼ぐ) ● 生活費を稼ぐ earn [make] one's living (a living)l. ● パートタイムをして1日に6,000円稼ぐ make [earn] 6,000 yen a day by working part-time. (⇒儲ける) ● 妻の方が私よりよく稼ぎます My wife *makes* [*earns*, *gets*] more *money* than I do.
❷【時間を】(相手の進行を妨害したりなどして) gain, buy*; (実行や決断の先送りを図る) play for 《time》. ● 彼は聞こえないふりをして時間を稼ごうとした He tried to *gain* [*buy*] time by pretending that he didn't hear it.

かぜけ 風邪気 ● 風邪気である I have *a touch of a cold* [(軽い風邪) a *slight cold*].

かせげる 稼げる (⇒稼ぐ) ● 車の輸入で金が稼げる Car imports *make money*. ● コンピュータで時間と労力がともに稼げる(=節約される) The computer *saves* both time and labor.

かぜたちぬ 『風立ちぬ』 The Wind Has Risen. 〖参考〗堀辰雄の小説

〖古今ことばの系譜〗**『風立ちぬ』**
私が何んということもなしに口ずさむことを好んでいた、
　　　　　風立ちぬ、いざ生きめやも。
という詩句が、それをきりきっと忘れていたのに、又ひょっくりと私達に蘇ってきた(略)。
　　The wind is rising: we must endeavor to live.
I liked to recite this phrase from time to time, and then forgot it for some time. But then again, it revived to us. (🈁 (1) この詩句はポール・ヴァレリーの詩の一節の和訳。「さあ生きよう」という意味なので「生きざらめやも」とあるべきところ、ここでは、ヴァレリーの詩句の意味を訳した。(2)「立ちぬ」は完了形だが「吹き終わって今は吹いていない」のではなく、「今も吹いている」あるいは「秋風の吹く季節になっている」から、そのような思いをかきたてられると解釈して、進行形に訳した。

かせつ 仮設 ● 仮設の 圏 temporary 《houses》, provisional.
● 仮設住宅《集合的》temporary housing; (一戸の) a temporary dwelling.

かせつ 仮説 a hypothesis /haipáθəsis/ 《複 hypotheses /-si:z/》. ● (…である)仮説を立てる form a *hypothesis* (that …); hypothesize (that …).
● (…という)仮説に基づいて on the *hypothesis* (that …).

かせつ 架設 图 (電話の) installation; (橋の) construction. ── 架設する install; construct.

カセット a cassètte. ● カセットにとる record (it) on a *cassette tape*; tape (it) on a *cassette*. ● カセットをデッキに入れる insert a slot a *cassette*.
● カセットテープ a cassétte tàpe. ● このテキストにはカセットテープ2巻がついている This textbook is accompanied by two *cassettes* [×two volumes of cassettes] of recorded tapes. ● カセットテープレコーダー a cassétte (recòrder). ● カセットブック an audio book. (🈁 a cassette book より普通)

かぜとおし 風通し ventilation. (⇒換気) ● 風通しがいい[悪い]部屋 an *airy* [a *stuffy*, a *close*] room. ● 風通しを入れる ventilate. (🈁 比喩的にも用いる) ● この部屋は風通しがよい This room is *airy* [is *well-ventilated*].

かぜとともにさりぬ 『風と共に去りぬ』 *Gone with the Wind*. (参考) マーガレット・ミッチェルの小説)

がせねた ●がせねた(=にせものの情報)をつかまされる be given *false information*.

かぜのうたをきけ 『風の歌を聴け』 *Hear The Wind Sing*. (参考) 村上春樹の小説)

かぜのこ 風の子 ▶子供は風の子 Children like to play outdoors [out of doors] in all weathers.

かぜのなかのこども 『風の中の子供』 *Children in the Wind*. (参考) 坪田譲治の小説)

かぜのまたさぶろう 『風の又三郎』 *Matasaburo the Wind Imp*. (参考) 宮沢賢治の童話)

かぜむき 風向き (⇨風(が)向き)

かぜよけ 風除け ▶a windbreak; a shelter from the wind. ▶これらの垣根は校舎の風よけになっている These fences *protect* the schoolhouse *from the wind*.

かせん 下線 an underline. (⇨アンダーライン)

かせん 化繊 chemical [[合成繊維] synthetic] fiber.
● 化繊製品 synthetics.

かせん 河川 a river.
● 河川工事 river construction work. ● 河川敷 a riverbed (terrace).

かせん 架線 [[線] a [an overhead] wire; [[工事] wiring. ▶架線事故で電車は1時間遅れで着いた The train arrived an hour late owing to the damage done to the *overhead wires*.
● 架線工事 wiring works.

かせん 寡占 [独占] [経済] oligopoly; a monopoly. (⇨独占) ●寡占する monopolize (a market).
●寡占価格 an oligopoly price; a monopoly price. ●寡占経済 an oligopolistic economy; a monopolistic economy. ●寡占市場 an oligopolistic market; a monopolistic market.

かせん 歌仙 a great [a master, a major] poet.
● 六歌仙 the six *major poets*.

かせん 果然 (⇨⑩ 果たして)

がぜん 俄然 suddenly. ▶彼はがぜん張り切り出した He *suddenly* became enthusiastic about it.

がせんし 画仙紙 Chinese drawing paper.

かそ 可塑 ● 可塑性 plasticity. ● 可塑性の 形 plastic. ── 可塑化する 動 plasticize.
● 可塑剤 a plasticizer. ● 可塑物 plastics; plastic materials.

かそ 過疎 depopulation. ● 過疎になる become *underpopulated*.
● 過疎化 depopulation. ● 過疎地域 a depopulated area; an underpopulated area.

がそ 画素 [コンピュータ] a picture element; a pixel; a pel.

かそう 下層 [[地層の] a lower layer, an underlying layer; [[階級の] the lower class(es).
● 下層社会 the lower strata of society.

かそう 火葬 图 cremation. ── 火葬する 動 cremate; burn.
● 火葬場 a crematórium (複 ~s, -toria); (米) a crématory.

かそう 仮装 (a) disguise.
── 仮装する 動 disguise oneself (*as*). (⇨変装する)
● 仮装行列 a fancy dress parade. ● 仮装舞踏会 (いろんな人・物に扮した) a fancy dress [a costume] ball (▶前の方が普通。(仮面なら) a masked ball.

かそう 仮想 [[想像] (an) imagination; [[仮定] (a) supposition.
── 仮想(上)の 形 imaginary.
── 仮想する 動 imagine; suppose.

● 仮想敵国 an imaginary [(将来敵になりうる) a potential] enemy.

かそう 家相 the (physical) aspect of a house. ▶この家は家相が悪い This house has an *unlucky aspect*.

がぞう 画像 a picture. ▶テレビの画像がぼやけている The *picture* on the TV screen is out of focus [is blurred]. ▶逆に「とてもきれい」なら ... is nice and /ənd/ cléar. のようにいう)/The TV has a blurred (↔a nice clear) *picture*.

かぞえあげる 数え上げる (列挙する) list, [書] enumerate. ▶数え上げたらきりがない be too many (to *list*); [書] be too numerous to *enumerate*.

かぞえうた 数え歌 a counting sòng.

かぞえたてる 数え立てる (⇨数え上げる) ● 他人の失敗を数え立てる *count up* [[書] *enumerate*] others' failures.

かぞえどし 数え年 *kazoedoshi*; (説明的に) one's age counted faithfully by the calendar year, that is, a baby born on the 31st December becomes two years old when the new year comes in. ▶私は数え年16歳だ I am in my sixteenth (*calendar*) *year*.

かぞえる 数える ❶ [勘定する] count. ▶票数を数える *count* the votes. ▶指で1から10まで数えてごらん *Count* from one to ten on your fingers. (事情) 米英人は、日本人のように指を折りながら数えるのではなく、こぶしを握り、順に指を起こしていったり、開いた指をもう一方の手の人さし指の腹で順にふれてゆくのが普通）
▶鳥が多くて数え切れなかった There were so many birds that we *lost count* of them. (! *lose count* of は人が主語)/There were more birds than we can *count*. ▶行方不明者は50を数えた The missing *numbered* 50. ▶正解は数えるほどしかなかった Only a few answers were correct. ▶その会合は数えるほどの人しか出席しなかった *Only a handful* of people came to the meeting.
会話 「お宅の坊ちゃはいくつまで数えられますか」「まだ10まで数えられません」 "How high [×many, ×much] can your boy *count* (*to*)?" "He can't *count* [*count* (*up*) *to*] ten."
❷ [その他の表現] ▶彼は日本で最もすぐれた詩人の一人に数えられている(= とみなされている) He *is counted* [*is reckoned, is numbered*] among the best poets in Japan. ▶私はあなたに会えるのを指折り数えて待っています(=とても楽しみにしています) I *am* so much *looking forward* to seeing [×to see] you.

かそく 加速 acceleration. (!「加速度」の意にもなる) ● 加速のよい車 a car with good *acceleration* [(米) *pick-up*]. ● 加速度運動 an *accelerated* motion. ● 加速度がつく gather [gain, pick up] *speed*; gather *momentum* (!学術的な言い方).
── 加速する 動 ▶車は加速した The car *speeded up* [*increased speed*]. (! *speed* の過去・過去分詞は (米) では *sped* も用いられる)/The car [driver] *accelerated*.

かぞく 家族 图 a family; (主に米話) (one's) folks.

解説 (1) family は通例親子で構成されるが、時には祖父母、おじ、おばを含めることもある。使用人など血縁のない同居人を含めれば household が普通。
(2) family は単数扱いが原則であるが、《英》では通例家族の個々の成員を考える場合には複数扱いとなる: その家族はこのあたりでは評判がいい That *family is* popular around here. /うちの家族は(皆)早起きだ My *family is* [《英》*are*] (all) early risers./(All) my *family gets* [《英》*get*] up early. (! ただし all をつけると《米》でも複数扱いが

普通．また前の言い方で early risers という複数形があるので《米》でも all がなくても are となることが多い: Everyone in my *family* is an early riser.)

① 【〜家族】 ●大家族 a large [a big] *family*. (ℹ️ a great family は「名門」の意．I have a *large family*. は通例「私は子供が多い」の意（⇨［次例］）)
●核家族 a nuclear *family*. ▶うちは大[小]家族です My *family* is large [small]./There are many [a few] people in my *family*. (ℹ️ ×I have many [a few] *families*. とはいわない（⇨［上例 注］）) ▶初めは 2-3 家族だけздесь住んでいた At first only a few *families* [×family] lived here.

②【家族〜】 ●家族連れで出かける go (to a place) with one's *family*. ●家族団らんを楽しむ have a good time with one's *family*.

③【家族は】 ▶ご家族は何人ですか How many (people) are there in your *family*? (ℹ️ ×How many (people) are your *family*? とはいわない)/How large is your *family*? ▶私の家族は 5 人です There are five (people) [five of us] in my *family*./We are a *family* of five./We are five (in my *family*)./《書》My *family* consists of five people. (ℹ️ ×My *family* has [is, are] five people. とはいわない．また My *family* is five. は通例「私には 5 人の子供がいる」の意) ▶私の家族は今大阪に住んでいます My *family* now lives [《主に英》live] in Osaka.

|会話| 「ご家族はいかがですか」「皆元気です」"How *is* [《英》*are*] your *family*?" "They [×We] are all fine [《米》very well《主に英》]." (ℹ️ your family に you は含まれないので，応答文でこれをさす代名詞として we は用いない)

④【家族の】 ●家族の一員 a *family* member; a member of a *family*. ▶うちの犬は家族の一員です Our dog is one [a member] of the *family*. ▶ご家族の皆様によろしく Give my love [《話》Say hello] to all your *family*./《書》Please give my best regards [wishes] to all your *family*. (⇨よろしく)

⑤【家族を】 ▶彼は家族(=妻子)を日本に置いてパリに赴任した He took his *wife and children* to Japan for his new post in Paris. ▶一緒に暮らすために家族を福岡に呼び寄せた I brought my *family* to live together in Fukuoka.

— **家族的な** 形 homelike, 《米話》homey. ●家族的な雰囲気 a *homelike* [a *homey*] atmosphere. (⇨家庭的な)
●家族構成 a family make-up. ●家族数 the size of a family. ●家族計画 family planning. ●家族旅行 a family trip.

かぞく 華族 a noble; (男) a nobleman; (女) a noblewoman; 《集合的に》the nobility; the peerage. (⇨貴族)

がぞく 雅俗 『上品なことと通俗的なこと』refinement and vulgarism; 『文語体と口語体』literary styles and colloquial styles.

カソリック （信者）a Catholic. (⇨カトリック)

***ガソリン** 《米》gasoline, 《米話》gas, 《英》petrol. ▶ガソリンが切れそうだ We are [The car is] running out of *gas*./We are [The car is] almost out of *gas*. ▶この車はガソリンを食いすぎる This car uses [consumes] too much *gas*. ▶将来の車はガソリンでなく別の燃料で走ることになろう Cars will move not *on gasoline* but on some other fuel in the future.
●ガソリン車 gasolin-powered car. ●ガソリンスタンド a filling [《米》a gas, 《英》a petrol, a service] station; 《英》a garage; 《和製語》a gasoline stand. (ℹ️ a service station, a garage では修理・点検も行う)

***かた 肩** ❶ 『人体の』one's shoulder(s). (ℹ️ (1) 上背部を含み日本語の「肩」より広い．(2) 肩全体を指すときは複数) ▶肩越しに見る look over one's *shoulder* (at him).

①【〜肩】 ●がっしりした(= 広い)肩 broad (↔ narrow) *shoulders*. ●五十[四十]肩 (suffer from) a frozen *shoulder*. ▶彼はなで[いかり]肩をしている He has sloping [square] *shoulders*. ▶あの外野手は鉄砲肩だ The outfielder has [has] a rifle *arm*.

②【肩が】 ▶肩がこっている I have stiff *shoulders*. (ℹ️ 片方なら a stiff shoulder)/My *shoulders* are stiff. (事情) 米英人は shoulder ではなく neck や back を用い，「肩がこる」は I have a stiff *neck* [*back*]./My *neck* [*back*] is stiff. ということが多い ▶あのキャッチャーは肩が強い The catcher has a strong *arm* [×shoulder].

③【肩の】 ●肩の骨をはずす dislocate [put out] one's *shoulder*. ●肩の力を抜く(=肩の筋肉をゆるめる) relax one's muscles in the *shoulders*.

④【肩に】 ●釣りざお[荷物]を肩にかつぐ carry a fishing rod over [a package on] one's *shoulder*. (ℹ️ over は「渡して」, on は「のせて」の意)

⑤【肩を】 ●肩を落とす[すぼめる] droop [hunch] one's *shoulders*. ●肩をいからせて with one's *shoulders* squared [held back]. ●肩を並べて歩く walk *side by side* [×shoulder to shoulder] (with him). (ℹ️ 後の方は「協調し合って」の意) ●肩をもんでやる give (him) a massage on the *shoulders*. (ℹ️ 米英では rub the back of (his) *neck* ということが多い) ●(投手が)肩をつくる get heated. ▶息子のことを尋ねられると彼女は肩をすくめるだけだった She just shrugged her *shoulders* when asked about her son. 事情 米英では「知らない」「勝手にしてくれ」「困ったもんだ」「どうしようもない」といった意を表す身振りで，肩をすくめると同時に両手を上に向けて広げる) ▶彼は肩のこりをほぐすため母の肩をたたいてあげた He gave pats to his mother on the *shoulders* to relieve stiffness there.

⑥【肩で】 ●(人を)肩で押しのける *shoulder* (him) aside. ●走者はゴールに着くとひざをついて肩で息をした(=息を切らしてあえいだ) When he reached the goal, the runner dropped to his knees and panted [gasped] (for breath). (ℹ️「肩で息をした」は文字通りに breathed *at his shoulders* も可)

❷ 『衣服などの』a shoulder. ●上着の肩の部分 the *shoulders* of a coat. ●スーツの肩をつめてもらう have one's suit taken in at the *shoulders*.

●肩がこる ●肩のこる(=堅い)書物 demanding [serious] reading. ●肩のこらない読み物 light reading. ▶おじさんと話すといつも肩がこる(=落ち着かない) I feel ill at ease [feel uncomfortable, feel nervous] when I speak with my uncle.
●肩で風を切る ●肩で風を切って歩く(=いばって歩く) walk with a swagger; swagger [《気どって歩く》strut] along. ▶スポーツカーが風を切って(=ふんぞり返って)通り越して行った He *was swaggering* along in his brand-new suit.
●肩にかかる ●家族の生活をよくすることがあなたの肩にかかっている(=責任だ) *It's up to* you not to let your family go hungry.
●肩の荷を下ろす ●息子が入試に合格して肩の荷が下りた It *took a load off our minds* [ほっとした] It *put us at ease*, We *felt relieved*] when our son passed the entrance exam. (ℹ️ 日本語的に A

huge burden was lifted from *my shoulders* when my son passed .... も可》
- **肩を入れる**（⇨肩入れ）
- **肩を貸す**（手伝う） help 《him》《to do》.
- **肩をたたく** ▶肩をたたかれる（=退職勧告をされる） be advised to resign.
- **肩を持つ**（味方する） take sides 《*with* him》; take 《his》 side; side 《*with* him》;（支持する） support 《him》; be in 《his》 favor.
- **肩を並べる** ▶彼は学識では先生と肩を並べている（=同等だ） He *is on the same level as* [*on a par with, equal to*] his teacher in scholarship. ▶雄弁では彼と肩を並べる者はいない He *has no equal* [*rival*] *in* eloquence.

***かた** 型, 形 ❶ [原型]（ひな型） a model;（鋳型）《米》a mold,《英》a mould;（型紙） a pattern;（鋳型） an impression. ● 鉛を型に流し込む pour lead into a *mold*. ● 洋服の型を取る cut [make] a (paper) *pattern* for a dress. ● 石膏(ﾞゥ)で胸像の型を作った I made a *model* for a bust in plaster.
❷ [スポーツにおける動作の形式] a form. ▶レスリングの型を覚える learn *forms* of wrestling [wrestling *forms*].
❸ [様式]（タイプ） a type;（スタイル） a style;（パターン） a pattern;（自動車などの年式） a model. ● 1987年型の車 a 1987 *model* (of a) car. ● その時計は新しい型だ The watch is (of) a new *type*. (❗ be の後では of はしばしば省略する) ▶帽子の最新の型はどんなものですか What are the latest hat *styles* [*styles* in hats]? ▶彼女の考え方には一定の型がある There's a *pattern* in her way of thinking.
❹ [慣例] a convention;［定型] a stereotype.
● 型を破る （=慣例を無視する） disregard the *convention*. ● 型にはまった言い方 a stereotyped [a conventional] expression. (⇨型破り, 型破り)
❺ [形状] a shape. ● V 字形の指輪 a V-*shaped* ring; a ring in the *shape* of a letter V. ● 卵形の顔 an egg-*shaped* face. ● 形がくずれる (⇨型くずれ)
❻ [大きさ] ▶大きな型の冷蔵庫がほしい I want to buy a large-*sized* refrigerator.

かた 片（⇨片方, 片を付ける） ▶その殺人事件はなかなか片がつかないだろう The murder case will not *be easily solved* [*settled*].

かた 潟（入り江; 干潟） tideland(s).

かた 過多 (an) excess. ● 供給過多 an *excess* supply 《*of*》; an *excessive* supply; oversupply.
● 情報過多の社会 society *glutted* with information; information *glutted* society. (❗ glut は「過度に供給する」の意) ● 愛情過多 *too much* affection.

-**かた** -方 ❶ [仕方] a way; a manner (❗ way より堅い語);［...する方法] how to 《do》. ● 彼の歌い方 his *way* [*manner*] of singing; the *way* (that) he sings. ● 彼にその問題の解き方を教える show him the *way* to [*how to*] solve the problem.
▶私と同じようにやり方でやりなさい Do it just *as* I do. (❗ just は as を強める。なくても可)/Do it (in) the same *way* as I do. (❗《話》では通例 in を省略し副詞的に使う) ▶彼はいつもそんなしゃべり方をする He always talks *like* that.
| 会話 | 「彼の家にはどうやって行ったらいいの」「歩いて行くのがいちばん簡単な行き方だよ」 "How can we get to his house?" "Walking's the easiest *way*."
| 会話 | 「ぼくのやり方どう思う」「のろいよ」 "How am I doing?" "You are slow."
❷ [人] ▶田中さん, ご面会の方が下においでになってます Mr. Tanaka, there's a *gentleman* [*a lady*] downstairs who wants to see you. ▶編集部の

方につないでください. どなたでもかまいません Please connect me with *someone* in the editorial department. Anyone will do. ▶警察の方ですか Are you from the police? (❗ Are you a police officer? に比べて間接的で丁寧な言い方になる)
❸ [血縁] a side. ▶母[父]方のおじ an uncle on one's mother's [father's] *side*;《書》one's maternal [paternal] uncle.
❹ [気付] care of ...;《米》in care of .... (❗ あて名では通例 ％ /siːóu/ と略す) ● 山田様方田中様 Mr. Tanaka, ％ Mr. Yamada.

がた がたのきた （使いすぎて調子の悪くなった） decrepit, worn-out;（ぐらぐらする）《話》shaky,《話》rickety. ● がたのきたテーブル a shaky [a rickety] table.
● 体にがたのきた老人 a decrepit old man.

がた -方 ❶ [複数人の尊称] ▶あなた方 3 人は今までどこにいましたか Where have *you three* been all this time? ▶あそこにいるご婦人方のことを話題にしているのですか Are you talking about the *ladies* over there?
❷ [おおよそ] about. ▶給料はここ 5 年間で 2 割方減少している My salary has decreased by *about* 20 percent during the past five years.
❸ [...ごろ, ...近く] toward. ▶夕方 *toward* evening. ▶明け方彼は出張でパリに向けて出発した *Toward* daybreak he left for Paris on business.
❹ [一方の側] a side; a party. ▶敵方は都市に向かって前進した The *enemy* [The hostile *party*] was advancing on the city.

かたあがり 肩上がり ▶肩上がりの文字 characters *written with an upward stroke from left to right*. (⇨肩下がり)

かたあし 片足 one leg. ● 片足で立つ stand on *one leg*.

かたあて 肩当て a shóulder pàd.

カタール [国名] Qatar /káːtər, kətáːr/;（公式名） the State of Qatar. （首都 Doha）● カタール人 a Qatari. ● カタール(人)の Qatari.

:**かたい** 固い, 硬い, 堅い ❶ [物などが] hard（↔soft）; firm（↔loose）; solid（↔fluid）; tough /tʌ́f/（↔tender）; stiff（↔flexible）,（文）rigid.

> 使い分け hard へこませたり突き通すのが困難なほど表面が硬いこと: 硬い岩 a *hard* rock.
> firm 曲げてもねじっても引っ張っても形がくずれない弾力性のある緻密(ﾞ)さ: 彼の筋肉は硬い His muscles are *firm*.
> solid あらゆる圧力や力に耐えるほど強くて緻密で固いこと: 家は固い地盤に建てられる We build houses on *solid* ground.
> tough 肉などが固いこと.
> stiff 容易に曲がり形の変わらない堅さ.
> rigid 無理に曲げようとすると壊れるほど堅いこと.

● 硬いベッド a *hard* [(しっかりしている) a *firm*] bed.
● この辺の地盤は固い The ground is *firm* [*solid*] around here. (⇨[類語]) ▶彼女は髪が硬い She has *wiry* hair.
❷ [まじめな] [正直な] honest;（生まじめな） serious;（信頼できる） reliable;（頑固な） óbstinate, stubborn /stʌ́bərn/;（厳格な） strict;（融通がきかない） inflexible,《やや書》rigid. ● 硬い表情 a *serious* [(こわばった) a *stiff*] expression. ● 堅い内容の本[話] a *serious* book [talk]. ● 口の固い男 a *tight-lipped* [a *close-mouthed*] man; a man who keeps a secret. ● 堅い人 an *honest* [(良心的な) a *conscientious*,（公正な） an *upright*] person;（誠実で信頼できる） a *sincere and reliable* [*trustworthy*]

かたい person. ●堅い文体(形式ばった) a *formal* style; (ぎこちない) a *stiff* style; (文語調の) a *bookish* style. ●堅い(=堅実な)商売 a *safe* [a *solid*, a *sound*] business. ▶そう堅いことは言わないで You shouldn't be so *strict* [*rigid*]. ▶彼は昔は実に堅い人だったが、今はずいぶん柔らかくなった He was just *upright* then, but he's much softer now.

❸『確固とした』 固い意志[信念] a *firm* will [belief]; a *strong* will [belief]. ●堅い約束を結ぶ make a *firm* promise.

❹『きつい』 tight. ●固い結び目 a *tight* knot. (🛈「結び目を固くする」 to tighten a knot)

❺『その他の表現』 ●固い握手をする have a *firm* handshake. ●堅い守備 *tight* defense. ●彼の成功は固い(=確かだ) *It is* [I'm] *certain that* he will succeed. (🛈He *is certain to* succeed./I'm *certain of* his success. ともいえる)/I'm [×It is] *sure that* he will succeed. (🛈He *is sure to* succeed. ともいえる)/He will *surely* [*certainly*] succeed.

かたい 難い (難しい) difficult; hard. ●守るに易く、攻めるに難い It is easy to defend but *hard* to attack.

かだい 仮題 a tentative title. ●新しい本に仮題をつける give a *tentative title* to a new book.

かだい 過大 ●過大な要求をする make excessive [(法外な) unreasonable] demands. ●過大な期待を寄せる expect *too much* (*of* him). ●彼の能力を過大評価する overestimate [overrate] his ability. ▶円の価値は実質とかけ離れて過大に評価されている The yen is wildly *overvalued*.

●過大評価 overestimation; an overestimate.

かだい 課題 ❶『解決を要する問題』a problem; (論争の) a question; (差し迫った) an issue; (練習用の) an exercise; (宿題) an assignment. ●当面の(=緊急課題 an urgent *problem* [*question*]; (問題になっている) a *problem* at issue. ●学習課題 a study *assignment*; a (school) *project*. ●今後に課題を残す leave a *problem* to be solved.

❷『主題』a subject; (作文などの) a theme. ●論文の課題 the *subject* of a thesis; a thesis *subject*. ●課題曲 a set piece.

-がたい -難い …しにくい、…するのが難しい (to do). (⇨難しい) ●得難い *hard* to get; (まれな) rare. ●結果がどうなるか断言し難い It's *difficult* [*hard*] *to* say what the outcome may be.

がだい 画題 [題目] the title of a painting; [題材] the subject of a painting.

かたいじ 片意地 ― 片意地な 彫 [強情な] obstinate (⇨頑固); [偏屈な] perverse.

かたいっぽう 片一方 ●片一方の手袋は1日で編み終えたけれど、もう一方は3日かかった I finished knitting *one of* the gloves in a day, but it took three days to finish the other one.

かたいなか 片田舎 a remote rural area; a remote village.

かたいれ 肩入れ ●候補者の肩入れをする(=応援する) support [back (up)] a candidate.

かたうで 片腕 ●片腕の男 a man with *one arm*; a *one-armed* man. ▶彼は私の片腕(=一番頼りにしている人)だ He is my *right-hand* man.

がたおち がた落ち ― がた落ちする 動 (生産などが) drop [fall, decrease] sharply; (品質などが) decline sharply.

かたおもい 片思い one-sided [(報われない) 《書》unrequited] love. ▶彼の片思いだった He came to love [fell in love with] her, but she didn't love him [it was his *one-sided love*]./(恋が報われない) His love was not returned.

かたおや 片親 a single [《主に英》a lone] parent; (両親のうちの1人) one of one's parents. ●片親の家庭 a *single-parent* [a lone-parent] family. (🛈《米》では離婚などによる崩壊家庭(a broken home)の婉曲語として用いる) ●大多数の片親家庭の戸主は母親である Most *single-parent* families are headed by mothers.

かたがき 肩書き (a) title (🛈Lord, Doctor, Professor, Mr. などの称号のこと); [学位] a degree; [役職] one's position (in the company). ●貴族の肩書き a *title* of nobility. ●博士の肩書き a doctor's *degree*; a Ph.D. ▶この世の中で物をいうのは容姿や肩書きではない。いかにいい仕事をやるかだけなのだ What counts in this world isn't what you look like or *what you are*. It all comes down to how well you do at your job. (🛈what title you have といえる)

かたかけ 肩掛け a shawl; (長い) a stole. ●肩掛けをする[している] put on [wear] a *shawl*.

かたかた (⇨がたがた) ●かたかた音がする clatter; rattle. (⇨がたがた) ●げたをはいて飛び石伝いにかたかたと行く *clatter* along the stepping stones in one's *geta*. ▶台所で母が食事の用意をしているかたかたという音が聞こえる I hear *clattering* noises of my mother preparing the meal in the kitchen. ●古い家の窓が風でかたかた鳴った The windows of the old house *rattled* in the wind.

かたがた 方々 ●ご来場の方々 《呼び掛け》ladies and gentlemen /-mən/. ●次の方々が新しい委員になられました The following *people* are new committee members.

かたがた 旁 (⇨-がてら) ●お礼かたがた(=直接会ってお礼を言いたいので)日曜日の午後にお宅にかたがたでしょうか May I visit 《主に英》call on] you on Sunday afternoon? I'd very much like to see you to express my gratitude. (🛈「かたがた」はわざわざ礼を言いに行くのではないと述べて相手の気持ちの負担をやわらげる日本的な表現)

がたがた ❶『かたがた音がする[を立てる]』(短い、強い、速い音) rattle; (長い、持続的な、響く音) clatter. ▶窓が強風でがたがたいていた The windows *were rattling* in the gale./The gale *was rattling* the windows. ●馬車ががたがた通り過ぎていった A wagon *rattled* past. ▶そのいたずらっ子がいすをがたがたいわせた The naughty boy *rattled* his chair. ●台所で食器類ががたがた音が聞こえた I heard the *clatter* of dishes in the kitchen.

❷『寒さ・恐怖などで震える; 物が揺れる』 tremble, shiver, shake*, quake. ▶非常に寒かったので子供たちはみんながたがた震えていた It was so cold that all the children *were trembling* [*shivering*]. ▶地震はとても強く町中の建物をがたがた震わせた The earthquake was so strong that it *shook* all the buildings in the town.

❸『文句をうるさく言う』make* a loud complaint, complain noisily. ▶彼はその決定にがたがた言っていた He *was making a loud complaint against* the decision. ●がたがた(=泣き言を)言うな! Stop *whining*!

― **がたがたの** 彫 (組み立てがひどくゆるんだ) 《話》shaky, 《話》rickety; (ぐらぐらの) wobbly. ●がたがたの机 a *shaky* [a *rickety*, a *wobbly*] desk.

かたかな 片仮名 (a) katakana.

かたがわ 片側 one side. ●片側3車線の目抜き通り the main road with three lanes of traffic going *each way*.

かたがわり 肩代わり ― 肩代わりする 動 (引き継ぐ) take ... over. ●彼の借金の肩代わりを *take over* his debts; (代わりに払う) pay his debts *for* him.

かたき 敵 an enemy; (対抗者) a rival. ●恋[商売]敵 a *rival* in love [business]. ●友人の敵を討つ *avenge* [*revenge*] one's friend.

かたぎ 気質 ●学生かたぎ(=学生のものの考え方) students' *way of thinking*; a *characteristic feature* of students. ●職人かたぎ craftsmanship. ▶彼は芸術家かたぎだ He is an artistic *type* of person./He is a person of artistic *temperament.*/He has an artistic *temperament.*

かたぎ 堅気 ●堅気の商売 an *honest* business. ●堅気なら start on a *decent* life. ●堅気に暮らす lead an *honest* life.

-がたき -敵 (競争相手) a rival; a competitor. (⇨敵(かたき)) ●恋敵 a *rival* in love. ●商売敵 a *rival* in business [trade]; a business *rival*.

*****かたく 固く, 硬く, 堅く ❶** [物体が] hard; (こわばって) stiffly; (すき間のないようにぴったりと) tight, tightly; (固く, しっかりと) fast. ●卵を固くゆでる boil an egg *hard*. ●固くてかみ切れない肉 tough [×hard] meat. ●堅くのりづけたシーツ a *stiffly* starched sheet. ●目を固く閉じる close one's eyes *tight*[*ly*]. ▶このベッドは堅くて寝られない This bed is too *hard* to sleep in. ▶このふたは堅くて取れない This lid is so *tight* (that) I can't open it. ▶窓は固く閉められていた The windows were *fast* [*tightly*] shut. (❗過去分詞の前の than ではなく till よりも tightly が好まれる) ▶粘土が固くなるまでさわらないでください Don't touch the clay until it *gets hard* [*hardens*].
❷ [考えなど] (しっかりと) firmly; (きっぱりと) flatly; (厳重に) strictly; (強く) strongly; (きまじめに) seriously. ●固く約束する make a *firm* [(まじめな) a *solemn*] promise. ●固く考える take (it) *seriously*. ▶彼は辞職しようと固く決心していた He was *firmly* resolved to resign. ▶彼女は固くそれを断わった She *flatly* [(断固として) *firmly*] [(話) *positively*] refused it to./She gave a *flat* [a *positive*] refusal to it. ▶この部屋での喫煙は固く禁じられている Smoking in this room is *strictly* forbidden. ▶人間は年を取ると頭がだんだん固くなるものだ People [We] will get more *stubborn* [(融通がきかない) *inflexible*, *rigid*] as they [we] grow older.
❸ [緊張して] tensely. ▶まあそう硬くならないで Don't be so *tense*. [神経質に] *nervously*./(気楽にしてください) [話] Take it easy./(くつろいでください) Please make yourself at home [*comfortable*].

かたくずれ 型くずれ ●型くずれしない素材 a material that *keeps* its *shape*. ●型くずれする lose one's *shape*; get out of shape.

かたくそうさく 家宅捜索 a domiciliary /dàməsíliəri/ search. ▶彼は家宅捜索を受けた His *house was searched.*

かたぐち 肩口 the shoulder. ▶彼は子供の肩口をつかまえた He took hold of [seized] the child's *shoulder*. ▶肩口が寒い I feel cold around the *shoulders*.

かたくちいわし 片口鰯 [魚介] a (Japanese) anchovy.

かたくな 頑な ── 頑なな [形] (強情な) obstinate. (⇨頑固) ●頑なに口を閉ざす refuse to say anything (*about* it).

かたくない 難くない ▶コンピュータが我々の日常生活に影響を与える想像に難くない *It is not hard* for us to imagine [We *can easily imagine*] what a great influence computers have on our daily lives.

かたくり 片栗 [植物] a dogtooth violet. ●片栗粉 potato starch. [[参考]] 今はジャガイモのでんぷんから作ることが多い)

かたくるしい 堅苦しい (形式的な) formal (⇔informal); (ぎこちない) stiff; (きちょうめんな) [書] punctilious. ●堅苦しい表現 a *formal* expression. ●堅苦しい雰囲気 a *formal* [a *stiff*] atmosphere. ▶ホワイト博士なんて堅苦しすぎるよ. ジョンと呼んでくれ Dr. White sounds too *formal*. Call me John. ▶彼の態度[文体]にはかなり堅苦しいところがあった His manner [His style of writing] was rather *stiff*. ●堅苦しく考えすぎるな(=そんなにまじめにとるな) Don't take it so *seriously*.
[会話] 「本日はお招きにあずかりありがとうございます」「堅苦しいことはいいから, さあ上がって」 "Thank you for inviting me today." "Don't mind the *formalities*. Come on in."

かたぐるま 肩車 ●息子を肩車する(=肩に乗せる) carry one's son *on* one's *shoulders*. ●肩車をしてもらって *be sitting on* one's *back*.

かたごし 肩越し ●肩越しに彼女を見る look at her *over* one's *shoulder*.

かたこと 片言 ●片言の英語を話す speak *broken* English; speak a *smattering* of English. (❗前の方はひどい, 後の方はなまかじりの英語をさす) ▶娘はまだ片言しか話せない My daughter still *babbles* [speaks *baby talk*].

かたこり 肩凝り 《have》a stiff neck; 《have》stiff shoulders. (❗前の方が普通) (⇨肩 ❶ ❷)

かたさ 固さ, 硬さ, 堅さ [物体の] hardness; [信念などの] firmness; [態度などの] stiffness; [頑固さ] stubbornness. ●信念[決意]の固さ the *firmness* of one's belief [resolution]. ●彼の頭の固さに驚く be surprised at his *hard-headedness*.

かたさがり 肩下がり ●肩下がりの文字 characters *written with a downward stroke from left to right*. (御 肩上がり)

かたさき 肩先 (⇨肩口)

かたじけない 忝い (ありがたい) grateful; (親切で寛大な) gracious. (⇨ありがたい) ●かたじけないお言葉 *gracious* words. ▶我々にいろいろと親切にしていただいて本当にかたじけない I am really *grateful to* you for your kindnesses.

かたず 固唾 ●固唾を飲む hold one's breath. ●かたずを飲むような(=はらはらさせる) 自動車レース a *breathtaking* [(スリル満点の) a *thrilling*] car race. ●かたずを飲んで事態の推移を見守る *hold* one's *breath* to see how things will develop.

かたすかし 肩透かし ●肩透かしを食う [当てが外れる] be disappointed; [むだになる] be wasted. ●肩透かしを食わせる dodge; sidestep; skillfully evade 《the question》.

かたすみ 片隅 a corner; (目立たない隅) an obscure corner. ●部屋の片隅に in the *corner* of a room. ●大都会の片隅にひっそりと暮らす live *obscurely* in a big city.

かたそでづくえ 片袖机 a desk with drawers on one side.

かたたたき 肩叩き [名] pounding on one's shoulders to remove the stiffness. ▶彼は肩たたき(=退職勧告)を受けた He *was tapped for retirement*.
── 肩叩きする [動] pound on one's shoulders.

:かたち 形
WORD CHOICE 形
form 個々の部分から成り立った全体の形状のこと. 個々の具体的事実の形状だけでなく, 比喩的に, 政治形態・組織形態・芸術的形態などをさす場合が多い. ●さまざまな指導の形式 various *forms* of teaching.
shape 個々の具体的事物に関する, 立体的で具体的な形のこと. しばしば人間の姿形をさす. ●その動物の大きさと形 the size and *shape* of the animal.

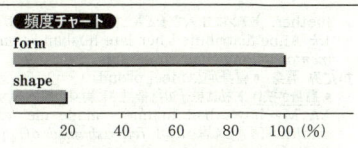

頻度チャート
form ▇▇▇▇▇▇▇▇
shape ▇▇▇▇
0 20 40 60 80 100 (%)

かたち 形 ❶ [外形] (a) shape; (a) form (⇨[類語]); a figure (▮線で囲まれた図形など輪郭に重点を置く語). ●リンゴのような形をした物 an object in the *shape* [*form*] of an apple; an object *shaped* like an apple; an apple-*shaped* object. ▶このクッキーは魚の形をしている These cookies have the *shape* of fish. ▶この松の木は形がよい This pine tree has a good (↔a bad, a poor) *shape* [*form*]./This pine tree is well-*shaped* (↔ill-shaped). ▶それらは形は似ているが大きさが違う They are similar in *shape* but different in size. ▶ボールは形が丸い A ball is round (in *shape*). ▶形がくずれないように上着をハンガーに掛けなさい Put your jacket on a hanger to hold its *shape* [to keep it in *shape*]./Put your jacket on a hanger, or it will lose its *shape* [get out of *shape*]. ▶いろいろな形をした石を集めた We gathered stones of different *shapes* [in every *shape* and *form*]. [会話]「そのお皿はどんな形ですか」「木の葉のような形です」"What *shape* is the plate?" "It is in the *shape* of a leaf./It *is shaped* like a leaf./It is like a leaf in *shape*."

❷ [形式] form. ●形だけのあいさつ a *formal* greeting. ▶いかなる形にせよわいろを受け取ってはいけない Don't accept bribes *in any shape or form*. (▮通例否定文で) ▶彼は形ばかりの(=名ばかりの)社長だ He is a *nominal* president./He is a president in name only. ▶形ばかりの(=単なる)お礼のしるしにこの品をお受け取りください Please accept this present as a *mere* [a *small*] token of my gratitude. ▶彼は形ばかりの(=形式上の)抗議をした He made some protests as a mere *formality*. ▶さまざまなカップルがあり、そしてさまざまな愛の形がある There are various kinds of couples and various *forms* of love.

❸ [まとまった形] form, shape. ▶彼の考えはようやく形をなしてきた His thoughts are finally beginning to take *shape* [*form*].

かたちづくる 形作る (形成する) form; (作る) make*. (⇨作る)

かたづく 片付く ❶ [部屋などが整理される] be put in order; [取り除かれる] be cleared away. ▶彼女の部屋はいつもきちんと片付いている Her room *is* always (*kept*) *neat and tidy*.

❷ [終了する] finish; be finished. ▶宿題がやっと片付いた At last I have *finished* [*done*] my homework./At last my homework *has been finished* [*done*].

❸ [解決される] be settled. ▶例の件はうまく片付いた The matter in question *was settled* [*was disposed of*] successfully.

❹ [結婚する] get* married. ▶娘が今年やっと医者のところに片付きました My daughter *got married to* [×*with*] a doctor this year.

がたつく be shaky. (⇨ぐらつく)

***かたづける 片付ける** ❶ [整理・整とんする] clear [clean]... up, 《主に英》tidy... (up); put* 《a room》 in order; tidy [clean] 《a room》 up; (取り去る) clear [《英》tidy]... away; [しまう] put... away; (元に戻す) put... back. ●食卓を片付ける clear [×clean] the table. ▶彼女は自分の部屋を片付けた She *cleared up* [《主に英》*tidied* (*up*)] her room./She *put* her room *in* (*good*) *order*. (▮「片付けた状態にしておいた」は She *kept* her room *clean* [*tidy*].) ▶父は食器を片付けてテーブルをきれいにふいた My father *removed* [*cleared away*] the dishes and wiped the table clean. ▶お遊びが終わったらおもちゃを片付けなさい *Clear* [*Put*] your toys *away* when you finish playing. ▶彼は本を棚に片付けた He *put* the books *back* on the shelf.

❷ [解決する] settle; (解く) solve; [うまく処理する] dispose of.... ▶まず最初にこの件から片付けるつもりだ I'll *settle* the matter first. ▶やっと難問を片付けた At last I *solved* [*worked out*] the difficult problem.

❸ [終了させる] finish; get* through... (⇨終える ❶); (いやなことを) get... over with. ▶さっさと雑用を片付けよう Let's *finish* the chores [*get* the chores *over with*] quickly. ▶今週の仕事は今日全部片付けた I *finished* [*completed*] the week's work today./《主に米》I *got* the week's work *done* today.

❹ [娘を結婚させる] marry 《her》 (off).

かたっぱし 片っ端 ▶彼は図書館の辞書を片っ端から調べた He saw *all the* dictionaries in the library *one by one* [*one after another*]./He consulted *every* dictionary in the library.

かたつむり 蝸牛 [動物] a snail.

かたて 片手 one hand. ●片手でボールをつかむ catch a ball with *one hand* [*one-handed*]. ▶彼は片手に本、もう一方の手には傘を持っていた He had a book *in one hand*, and an umbrella in the other.

かたておち 片手落ち (不公平) one-sidedness; unfairness; partiality. ●片手落ちの処分 a *one-sided* [an *unfair*] punishment.

かたてま 片手間 ▶片手間の(=臨時の)仕事 an *odd* [(本業以外の) a *side*] job. ▶片手間に(=暇な時に)仕事をする do a job *in* one's *free* [*spare*] *time*.

かたどおり 型通り ●型通りの 厖 [因習的な] conventional; [類型的な] stereotyped. ●型通りの生活 a *conventional* life. ●型通りの表現 a *stereotyped* [(陳腐な) a *hackneyed*] expression; (陳腐な決まり文句) a cliché /klíːʃéɪ/.

かたとき 片時 (ちょっとの間) a moment. ▶私は母の言葉を片時も忘れることはありません I *never* forget my mother's words.

かたどる 象る ▶城をかたどった(=城の形をした)ケーキを作る make a cake *in the shape of* a castle.

***かたな 刀** a sword /sɔːrd/; (軍刀) a saber. ●刀のさやa sheath. ●刀の刃 the edge of a *sword*. ●刀を腰に差す[差している] put on [wear] a *sword* at one's side. ●刀を抜く draw a *sword*. ●刀をさやに納める sheathe a *sword*.
●刀傷 a sword cut; a sword wound.

かたながれ 片流れ ●片流れ屋根 a lean-to roof; a lean-to.

かたなし 形無し ●形無しだ[になる] (台なしだ) be ruined; (面目を潰す) lose (×one's) face.

かたならし 肩慣らし 图 warming-up; a warm-up.
—— 肩慣らしをする 動 warm up (*for* the game).
▶彼は試合前に入念に肩慣らしをした He *warmed up* carefully before the game.

かたば 片刃 a single edge. ●片刃の安全かみそり a *single-edged* safety razor.

かたはい 片肺 one lung.
●片肺飛行 flying on only one engine.

かたはだ 片肌 ●片肌(を)脱ぐ (力を貸す) help 《him》 (out); give [lend] 《him》 a helping hand. (⇨一

肌)

かたはば 肩幅 ●肩幅が広い have *broad* (↔*narrow*) *shoulders*; be *broad-shouldered*, be *broad across the shoulders*. ▶両足を肩幅(=腰の幅)くらいに開いて立ってください Stand with your feet *hip-distance* apart.

かたばみ 酢漿草 〖植物〗a creeping lady's-sorrel; a wood sorrel.

かたはらいたい 片腹痛い (こっけいな) ridiculous; (ばかげた) absurd.

かたひざ 片膝 one knee. ●片膝立ち sitting with *one knee* up.

かたひじ 片肘 shoulders and elbows. ●肩ひじ張る (横柄にふるまう) act big; (堅苦しい) be formal.

がたぴし ■ a rattle; a rattling sound. ▶雨戸をがたぴしと開ける open a sliding shutter *with a rattling noise*.
—— **がたぴしする** 動 rattle; make a rattling sound.

かたびらき 片開き ●片開きのドア a single swing [swinging] door.

かたぶつ 堅物 (軽蔑的に) a strait-laced person.

かたぶとり 固太り —— **固太りの** 形 (a young person) of solid [firm] build. (⇨がっしり)

がたべり がた減り 图 (急に減ること) a marked [a sharp] decrease (*in number*).
—— **がた減りする** 動 decrease markedly [rapidly]. ▶ここ数年工場生産ががた減りしている Factory production *has been markedly [rapidly] decreasing* in recent years.

かたほう 片方 (2者のうちの) one (⇨一方, 片一方); (一対の物の) the mate; 〖片側〗one side (⇨片側). ●片方の目が見えない be blind in *one eye*. ▶この手袋の片方が見当たらない I can't find the *mate to* [(まぁof)] this glove./(もう片方) I can't find *the other glove*.

かたぼう 片棒 ●片棒を担ぐ (…の共犯者である) be (a) party *(to)*; (加担する) take part (*in*).

かたぼうえき 片貿易 one-way [one-sided, unilateral, imbalanced] trade.

*****かたまり 塊** (固まった物) (固くて小さい) a lump; (大きな) a mass; 〖土の〗a clod; (平らな面をもつ木・石の) a block; (肉・チーズなどの) (やや話) a chunk; 〖血などの〗a clot; 〖人・物の集まり〗a group (*of*), (多数の) a body (*of*) (⇨一団); (密な) a cluster. ●粘土の塊 a *lump* [a *clod*] of clay. ●うその塊 a *pack* [a *crop*] of lies. ▶彼は欲の塊だ He is full of greed./(心底欲が深い) He is greedy to the core. (❗×He is a lump of greed. とはいわない) ▶空に巨大な黒雲の塊がある There is a huge *mass* of dark clouds in the sky. ▶子犬たちはひとかたまりになって眠っていた The puppies were sleeping in a *cluster*.

*****かたまる 固まる** ❶〖物が固くなる〗harden; become* hard; (ゼリー・セメントなどが) set*. ▶雪が固まって氷になった The snow *hardened* into ice. ▶ゼリーは冷えると固まる Jelly *sets* as it cools.
❷〖ひとまとまりに集まる〗gather; crowd. ▶子供たちは部屋の隅に固まっていた The children *gathered* [*crowded*] in the corner of a room. ▶3,4人ずつ固まって帰ってきなさい Come home *in groups of* three or four.
❸〖しっかり定まる〗 ▶彼の頭の中でその考えが固まった The idea *took shape* [*crystallized*] in his head.

かたみ 片身 one-side. ●タイの片身 *one side* of a bream.

かたみ 形見 (思い出の品) a keepsake, a memento. ●母の形見の指輪 a ring as a *keepsake* of my mother. ▶アンは3人の子どもたちに亡夫の形見分けをした Anne distributed her late husband's *mementos* among their three kids.

かたみ 肩身 ●肩身が広い feel proud.
●**肩身が狭い** ▶私は息子の行儀悪さに肩身の狭い思いをした My boy's bad manners made me *feel small*./(恥ずかしく思った) I *felt ashamed of* my boy's bad manners.

かたみち 片道 one way; (距離) the distance to the destination. ▶大阪までは片道5,000円だ The fare to Osaka is 5,000 yen *one way*./The *one-way* fare to Osaka is 5,000 yen. ▶ガソリンは片道分がやっとだ The gas is barely enough for *one-way trip*.
●**片道切符** 〖米〗a one-way (ticket); 〖英〗a single (ticket).

かたむき 傾き ❶〖水平・垂直に対する傾き〗a slant; (端が持ち上がって傾くこと) a tilt; (勾配) an inclination. ●塔の奇妙な傾き a peculiar *tilt* of the tower. ●ネクタイの傾きを直す(=まっすぐにする) straighten one's tie.
❷〖傾向〗a tendency; (流れの方向) a trend.

*****かたむく 傾く** ❶〖傾斜する〗(ある方向に) lean*, (やや書) incline (*to, toward*); (左右などに) slant; (坂になる) slope; (一方が持ち上がって) tilt, tip (-pp-) (❗tip は tilt より瞬間的, 突発的). ●左側[家の方]へ傾く *lean* [*incline, slant*] *to the left* [*toward the house*]. ●その塔は3度傾いていた The tower *leaned* [*inclined*] *at a three degree angle*. (=at an angle of 3 degrees ともいう) ●この床は少し傾いている This floor *slants* [*slopes*, ×*leans*] a little. ●右の翼が上へ上がると, 機体は左側へ大きく傾いた The left wing *tipped up* and the plane *tilted* violently. ▶ヨットは風で傾いた The sailboat *tipped* (*to one side*) in the wind.
❷〖傾向を帯びる〗(人の心が) lean*, (やや書) incline (*to, toward*); (傾向がある) tend (*to, toward*); (…する傾向がある, したい気がする) be inclined (*to do*). ●彼の意見に傾く *lean* [*incline*] *toward his opinion*. ▶彼は共産主義に傾いている He *leans* [*tends*] *toward communism*. ▶私はあなたに同意する方に傾いている I *am inclined to agree* [*toward agreeing*] to it. (❗自分の意見を控えめにいう表現)
❸〖日・月が沈む〗set*, go* down, sink*. ●傾く月 a *setting* [a *sinking*] moon. ▶日はゆっくりと西に傾いていった The sun *was going down* [*setting, sinking*] slowly in the west. (❗go down が最も口語的)
❹〖衰える〗decline. ▶彼の運勢も傾いてきた His fortune *is declining* [*on the decline*]. ▶彼が死ぬと事業は傾き始めた With his death, the business began to *fail*.

*****かたむける 傾ける** ❶〖物を〗(ある方向に) lean*; (左右などに) slant; (一方を持ち上げて) tilt, tip (-pp-). (⇨傾く) ●頭を前に傾ける *lean* [*tilt*] one's head forward. ●テーブルを傾ける *tip* [*tilt*] the table.
❷〖心を〗(専念する) devote oneself [all one's energies] (*to*); (注意を集中する) concentrate (one's attention) (*on*). ●耳を傾ける listen to 《him, what he says》(carefully); (耳を向ける) bend [incline] one's ear (*to him*). ▶彼はその仕事に全力を傾けた He *devoted* [*applied*] *all his energies* to the work./He *put a great deal of effort into* the work.

かたむすび 片結び a tight knot.

かため 固め ❶〖誓い〗a pledge; an oath; a vow. (⇨誓い) ●夫婦固めの盃を交わす (書) exchange *nuptial cups*.

かため ❷ [防備] defense; (警備) guard. ◆国の固めを強化する strengthen the national *defense*.

かため 片目 one eye. (⇨目 ❷) ◆片目で見る look 《*at it*》with *one eye*. ◆片目が見えない be blind in *one eye*. ◆片目をつぶる close *one eye*.
◆片目が開(*)く (やっと1勝する) win for the first time.

かため 固目 ◆卵を固めにゆでる boil an egg *rather hard*.

かためうち 固め打ち ◆彼は5安打固め打ちをした 『野球』He *made five hits* in a game.

:**かためる 固める** ❶ [固くする] harden, make*…hard; (液体・糊(%)状のものを) set*. (⇨固まる) ◆熱で粘土を固める *harden* clay by heat. ◆家を建てる前に彼らは地面を固めた They *hardened* the ground before building a house. ◆ゼリーを氷で冷やして固めなさい *Set* the jelly by cooling it with ice.
❷ [強固にする] strengthen; (意見・信念などを) be confirmed 《*in*》; (地位などを) 《書》consolidate. ◆組織を固める *strengthen* the organization. ◆信念を固める *strengthen* one's belief. ◆地位を固める *consolidate* one's position. ◆守備を固める *strengthen* the defense. ◆国境の守りを固めねばならない We must *strengthen* our defenses on 《×of》the border. ◆彼の手紙を読んで留学の決意を固めた His letter *confirmed* (me *in*) my decision to study abroad.
❸ [身を固める] settle down. ◆彼はどうして結婚して身を固めないのか Why doesn't he marry and *settle down*?

かためわざ 固め技 『柔道』a gráppling technìque.

かためん 片面 one side. (⊕ 両面) ◆テープの片面 *one side* of a tape. ◆それぞれの用紙の片面だけに委員会報告を書きなさい Write a committee report on only *one side* of each sheet of paper. ◆君は事実の片面しか見ていない You look at only *one side* of the facts.

かたやぶり 型破り ── 型破りな 形 (枠にはまらない) unconventional; (並はずれた) unusual; (とっぴな) 《話》offbeat. ◆型破りな衣装 an *unconventional* [an *unusual*, an *offbeat*] costume.

かたゆで 固茹で ◆固めで卵 a *hard-boiled* (⇔a soft-boiled) egg.

かたより 片寄り, 偏り 『偏見』a bias. (⇨片寄る) ◆当時彼は平和主義への片寄り(=傾向)が強かった He had a strong *leaning toward* pacifism in those days. ◆政府は来年度の予算の片寄り(=不均衡)を是正すべきだ The Government should correct the *imbalance* in the budget for next year.

*__かたよる 片寄る, 偏る__ 『公平でない』be partial 《*to*》; 『偏見がある』be prejudiced 《*biased*》; 『一面的な』be one-sided; 『記事などがゆがめられている』be slanted. ◆片寄らない意見 an *impartial* [an *unprejudiced*, an *unbiased*] opinion. ◆彼の判断は片寄っている His judgment *is partial* [*is prejudiced*, *is one-sided*]. ◆食事が片寄らない(=バランスのとれた食事を)ようにしよう Try to have a (*well-*)*balanced* diet.

かたらう 語らう ❶ [話し合う] talk 《*about*》. ◆友人と野球について楽しく語らう *talk* happily *about* baseball with one's friends.
❷ [仲間に引き入れる] win 《him》over to one's side.

かたり 語り (a) narration. ◆その物語の語りの部分 the *narrative* part of the story.
──語り手 a narrator. ──語り部 (語り伝える人) a storyteller.

かたり 騙り (⇨詐欺(%))

かたりあう 語り合う (話す) talk 《*with*》. ◆私たちは昨夜趣味について語り合った We *talked* [*had a talk*] about our hobbies last night.

かたりぐさ 語り草 (話の種) a topic of conversation. ◆その不可解な出来事は後々までの語り草となるだろう The mysterious happening *will be talked about* for generations to come.

かたりくち 語り口 the way one talks.

かたりつぐ 語り継ぐ ◆戦争体験を語り継ぐ *hand down* one's war experiences *from generation to generation*.

かたりつたえる 語り伝える pass … down [on]. (!しばしば受身で) ◆親から子へ語り伝えられてきた戦争体験 war experience which has been *passed down* [*on*] from parents to their offspring.

:**かたる 語る** 『物語などを』tell*, (物語る) narrate; 『話す』talk, speak*; 『吟唱する』recite; chant. (⇨話す) ◆真実を語る *tell* [*speak*] the truth. ◆子供たちに民話を語って聞かせる *tell* folk tales *to* the children. ◆彼らの結婚について語る *talk* [*speak*] *about* their marriage. ◆聴衆に語りかける *talk* [*speak*] *to* the audience. ◆その伝説は何百年にもわたって語りつがれている The legend *has been handed down* over many centuries.
◆語るに落ちる (うっかり本当のことをいう) reveal 《a secret》by mistake; let 《a secret》slip.

かたる 騙る ❶ 『詐欺を働く』swindle; cheat. (⇨詐欺) ◆彼は彼女から宝石類をかたった He *swindled* [*cheated*] her out of her jewelry.
❷ 『名をいつわる』assume a person's name. ◆彼はテレビタレントの名をかたっていた He *assumed* a TV star's name.

カタル 『医学』catarrh /kətáːr/. ◆腸カタル intestinal *catarrh*.

カタルシス [<ギリシャ語] catharsis /kəθáːrsɪs/.

カタログ a catalog; (パンフレット) a brochure. (⇨目録) ◆カタログを見て買う buy 《it》from a *catalog*. ◆カタログショッピング mail-order shopping. ◆カタログショッピングをする buy 《a dress》by *mail order*.

かたわく 型枠 a mold.

かたわら ❶ [わき, 横] the [one's] side. ◆彼のかたわらに立つ stand *at* [*by*] his *side*; stand *beside* [*by*] him (! by him は「彼のそばに」の意で必ずしも横とは限らない). (⇨横, one's) ◆スーパーのかたわら(=横, 並び)に住む live *alongside* 《*of*》a supermarket. ◆彼らが通れるようかたわらに寄る step [stand] *aside* to let them pass.
❷ […する一方で] ◆鷗外は医者として働くかたわら小説を書いていた *Besides* [*While* (he was)] working as a doctor, Ogai was writing novels.

かたわれ 片割れ ◆強盗の片割れを追う (2人のうちの1人) chase the *other* robber [(3人以上のうちの1人) *one* of the robbers].

かたをつける 片を付ける (解決する) settle; (話し合いで) have* it [things] out 《*with* him》.

かたん 加担, 荷担 图 (力を貸すこと) help, assistance; (支持) support.
──加担[荷担]する 動 (力を貸す) help, assist; (支える) support; (関与する) take part 《*in*》. ◆彼はその陰謀に加担していた He *is involved in* the plot./He *is* (a) *party to* the plot.

かだん 花壇 a flower bed.

かだん 果断 ── 果断な 形 ◆果断な(=思い切った)行動を取る take *decisive* [*drastic*, (迅速な) *prompt*, (断固たる) *resolute*] action.

かだん 歌壇 the world of *tanka* poets.

がだん 画壇 the árt wòrld, páinting cìrcles.

がたん(と) ❶ [音] ◆がたんと音がする (すさまじい) crash;

かち (大きな) bang; (重いにぶい) thud; (急に揺れて) jerk; (激しく揺れて) jolt. ▶がたんと音を立てて with a bang [a *thud*, a *jerk*, a *jolt*]. ●自動車はがたんと大きな音を立ててガードレールに衝突した The car *crashed* into the guardrail. ●列車はがたんと止まった The train *jolted* to a stop./The train stopped with a *jolt*.
❷ [急激に] (突然) suddenly; (激しく) sharply. ▶生産量ががたんと落ちた The output fell *suddenly* [*sharply*].

‡**かち** 価値 worth; value. (⚠ worth はそのもの自体にある絶対的な価値を, value は人の決める相対的な価値値・重要性をいうことが多い)

① 【～(の)価値】 ●利用価値 utility *value*. ●存在価値 the significance of existence. ▶人間の価値はその人格にある Man's *worth* [×value] consists in what he is. ●その時まで私は音楽の価値を理解していなかった Until that time I didn't realize the *value* of music. ●その調子はずれのピアノは商品価値がない The off-key piano has no commercial *value*.

② 【価値観～】 ▶人はそれぞれ価値観が違う Everyone has his own (sense [×view] of) *values*. (⚠通例複数形で)

③ 【価値が[は]～】 ▶この仕事はやるだけの価値が十分ある This job is well *worth doing* [×to do, ×to be done, ×being done]./This job is well *worthy of being* [to be] done.

> **解説** worth は前置詞 (⚠ 形容詞とする説もある). 上例はやや堅い言い方だが形式主語を用いて *It is worth (while) doing* [*worth while to do*] this job. とすることも可 (⚠ while は「時間」の意). 今日では動名詞が続く場合, while は省略されることが多い. なお, This job is *worth while* [*worth the time*]. のような言い方も可能だが, This job is *worth while to do* [*doing*]. の形は避けた方がよい

▶そのルビーはどのくらいの価値がありますか How much [What] is the ruby *worth*? (⚠ how much は値段は, what は一般的な価値を尋ねる言い方)/What is the *value* of the ruby? ▶これは 100 万円の価値がある This is *worth* one million yen./This has a *value* of one million yen. ▶これは高いがそれだけの価値はある This is expensive, but it's *worth* it [the money, ×its money]. ▶彼の持っている古書はほとんど価値がない The old books he has have almost no *value*./(書) The old books he has are *of little value*. ▶この人の絵は近い将来必ず価値が上がりますよ I'm sure his paintings will appreciate *in value* in near future. ▶彼はその賞をもらうだけの価値がある(=ふさわしい) He *deserves* (to get) the award.

【会話】 「ロンドンは行ってみる価値がありますか」「大ありですよ」 "Is London *worth* a visit?" "Very much so."

【会話】 「それ彼に話しましょうか」「話すだけの価値があると思う?」 "Shall I mention it to him?" "Is it *worth while* [*worthwhile*], do you think?"

④ 【価値のある】 ●大変価値のある絵 a painting of great *value* (⇔of no value); (高価な) a *valuable* (⇔a valueless) painting. ●それは価値ある(=時間・注意を払う価値)のある)発言だ That is a *worthwhile* (⇔a worthless) remark. ●金もうけは私にとって何の価値もないことです Making money is [means] nothing to me.

●価値判断 (make) a value judgment.

かち 勝ち (勝利) (a) victory. (⇨勝つ) ▶3 対 2 でうちのチームの勝ちだ Our team *won* the game [*beat them*] (by [with] a score of) 3-2. (⚠ 3-2 は three to two と読む) ▶君の勝ちだ(やられた) You beat me. (⚠ beat は現在形)/(まいった) You *win*. (⚠ won とはしない (⇨-た❷))/(君の勝ちだ) You've *won*. (⚠ You win. は口頭語で争いや言い争いの末しぶしぶ相手の意向にそうことを表す: いいだろう, 分かった OK [Very well], *you win*.) ▶大切なのは勝ち負けではない It's not important whether you *won* (the *victory*) or not. ▶私たちは勝ちパターンを使うべきだった We should have followed our (usual) *winning* game plan [*winning* strategy]. ▶早い者勝ち《ことわざ》 First come, first served.

●勝ちを拾う win an unexpected victory; have an unexpected win.

-がち -勝ち [傾向がある] tend 《*to* do; *to*》; 《通例けなして》be apt 《*to* do》; 《書》 (好ましくない) be liable 《*to* do; *to*》; (傾向に); [しばしば] often. ▶彼は最近怠けがちだ He *tends* [is apt, is liable, is inclined] to be lazy these days./He *tends* [is liable] to laziness these days. ▶学生は理想に走りがちだ Students are *often* idealists [very idealistic].

かちあう かち合う (運悪くぶつかる) clash 《with》; (利害などがぶつかる) conflict 《with》. (⇨ぶつかる❸) ▶彼女に向けたばくら 2 人の視線がかち合った Our gaze at her met momentarily.

かちあがる 勝ち上がる (⇨勝ち進む)

かちあげる 搗ち上げる 【相撲】 (説明的に) push up [raise up] 《the opponent's chest》 with one's elbow.

かちいくさ 勝ち戦 (戦いに勝つこと) a victory; (勝った戦い)(つまり) a victorious battle. (⇔負け戦)

かちうま 勝ち馬 a winning horse; (勝つと予想される馬) a probable winner. ●勝ち馬を当てる choose [pick] a *winner*.
●勝ち馬投票券 ⇨馬券

かちえる 勝ち得る ・信頼を勝ちえる win [gain] 《his》 trust.

かちかち ❶ [音] ● (時計や機械などが)かちかち音を立てる tick. ▶静かな部屋で時計のかちかちいう音が聞こえた I could hear the clock *ticking* [the *ticktock* of the clock] in the quiet room.
❷ [固い] hard; (こわばった) stiff; (石のように固い) stone-hard; (氷のように固い) hard-frozen. ▶道路はかちかちに凍っていた The roads were frozen *hard*. ▶あの人の頭はかちかちだ(=柔軟性がない) He *doesn't have a flexible* [別の考えを受け入れられる) *a receptive*] *mind*.

がちがち ❶ [歯などがふれあう音] ▶彼は寒さに震えて歯をがちがち鳴らしていた ●He was trembling with cold and his teeth *chattered*.
❷ [堅い様子] ●がちがちに凍る be frozen *solid*. ▶彼は初舞台でがちがちになった(=あがってしまった) He has *got extremely nervous* as he made his debut. (⇨かちんかちん)
❸ 【欲の深い様子】 ●がちがちの守銭奴 a real miser.

かちき 勝ち気 ── 勝ち気な 形 (競争心の強い) competitive; (屈しない) unyielding; (断固とした) strong-minded. ●勝ち気な女 a *competitive* [a *strong-minded*] woman.

*かち 家畜 a domestic animal; 《集合的》livestock; (特に畜牛) cattle (⚠以上 2 語は通例複数扱い). (⇨牛) ▶家畜を飼う keep *livestock*.

かちぐり 勝ち栗, 搗ち栗 a dried chestnut.

かちこし 勝ち越し ── 勝ち越し点 the go-ahead [tie-breaking] run [goal]. (⚠ run は野球の, goal はサッカーなどの得点)

かちこす 勝ち越す (勝った回数が負けた回数より多くなる)

かちすすむ 勝ち進む ●決勝に勝ち進む get through to the finals.

かちっ ▶宝石箱はかちっと音がして開いた The jewel box opened with *a click*./The jewel box *clicked* open.

がちっ ▶2人の警察官が泥棒をがちっと押さえつけていた Two police officers held down the thief *tight*. ▶振り下ろしたつるはしががちっと(=激しく)石に当たった The pick I swang down hit *hard* against a rock.

かちっぱなし 勝ちっ放し straight [successive] victories; a series of victories. ▶そのチームは6戦勝ちっ放した The team has *six straight victories* [*six victories in succession*; *six victories in a row*].

かちてん 勝ち点 a point. ●勝ち点3 points, full points. (!)(1) 通例 three points とはいわない (2) 引き分けの場合の「勝ち点1」は (a point) ●勝ち点3 獲得を逃す fail to collect *full points*. ●勝ち点で並ぶ level with *points*.

かちどき 勝ち鬨 (⇨⑱ 凱歌(がいか)) ●勝ちどきをあげる give a triumphant shout [a shout of victory]; cry triumphantly.

かちとる 勝ち取る 〘勝利・賞品などを〙win*; (大きな努力をして得る) gain. ●勝利を勝ち取る win [gain] a victory 《over one's opponent》. ▶自由は与えられるものではなく、勝ち取るものである Freedom is not given but (it) *is won*.

かちなのり 勝ち名乗り ●勝ち名乗りをあげる declare the winner.

かちぬき 勝ち抜き ●勝ち抜き戦 a tournament.

かちぬく 勝ち抜く ●予選を勝ち抜く get through a preliminary (heat [match]); (決勝に勝ち進む) get through to the finals.

かちのこる 勝ち残る survive. ●激戦に勝ち残る survive a fierce battle. ▶選手がオリンピックで決勝に勝ち残るのは並大抵ではない It is no easy task for the players to *win their way to the finals* in the Olympic Games.

かちほこる 勝ち誇る be triumphant 《over》. ●勝ち誇って triumphantly, in triumph.

かちぼし 勝ち星 a win, a victory. ●勝ち星をあげる have a *win*; win a *victory*.

かちまけ 勝ち負け victory or defeat; (結果) the outcome (of a game). ▶勝ち負けはたいした問題ではない *Victory or defeat* is a matter of little importance.

かちみ 勝ち味 (⇨⑱ 勝ち目)

かちめ 勝ち目 (勝つ可能性) a chance of winning; (勝算) the odds. ▶彼には勝ち目がない [十分あり] He has no [*a good*, x*a strong*] *chance of winning*./The *odds* are against him [strongly in his favor]. ▶勝ち目は五分五分です There is *an even chance* of my *winning* [*for me to win, that I will win*]./The *odds* are even [fifty-fifty] against me.
〖会話〗 「ところで勝ち目はどれくらいあると思う？」「あの連中相手ではこちらに勝ち目はないよ」 "So what *chance* do you think we have?" "We don't have a *chance* against them."

かちゃかちゃ ●かちゃかちゃ音がする click; clank; clink; jingle (!)どの語も名詞(かちゃかちゃという音)に用いてもよい) (!)どの語も名詞(かちゃかちゃという音)にも用いてよい) ▶彼女錠前の鍵を何度もかちゃかちゃ回し戸を開けようとした He tried to open the door by turning the key in the lock and it made a *clicking noise* [*sound*].

がちゃがちゃ ●がちゃがちゃ音がする[音を立てる] clatter; clank, jangle. (!)どの語も名詞(がちゃがちゃという音)にも用いてよい) ▶大きな鍵束をがちゃがちゃいわせる *jangle* a big bunch of keys. ▶彼女は銀食器をがちゃがちゃさせずに注意深く洗った She washed her silverware carefully without *clattering*.

がちゃつかせる rattle; clatter; clank. ▶彼は鍵の束をがちゃつかせながら歩いていた He was walking *rattling* a bunch of keys.

がちゃん ❶〖ガラス・金属の衝突音〗●がちゃんと音を立てる(金属などが当たって響いて) clang, clank (!)前の方が大きい音); (物が落ちたり、衝突して) crash. ▶グラスは全部がちゃんと床に落ちてこなごなに割れた All the glasses *crashed* to pieces on the floor [fell to pieces on the floor *with a loud crash*]. (!)上の動詞はいずれもこの例のように名詞に用いることができる)
❷〖物を乱暴に置いたり、戸を激しく閉める様子〗slam (-mm-), bang. ▶彼は受話器をがちゃんと置いた He *slammed* [*banged*] *down* the receiver./He put the telephone down *with a bang*.

かちゅう 火中 ●(救助や自殺などで)火中に身を投じる plunge [throw oneself] *into the fire* [*flames*]. ●火中の栗を拾う pull 《his》 chestnuts out of the fire 〖参考〗西洋の寓話から); take a big risk 《for him》.

かちゅう 渦中 ●事件の渦中に巻き込まれる get caught up in the scandal.

かちょう 家長 the head of a family; (男性) a patriarch; (女性) a matriarch.

かちょう 課長 a section manager, the manager of a section. (!)呼び掛けには Mr. ~ などと名前を呼ぶ) ●課長補佐 an assistant section manager; an assistant manager of a section. ●課長代理 an acting [a deputy] section manager.

がちょう 画帳 a sketchbook; a sketchpad.

がちょう 画調 the tone [mood] of a picture. ▶あの絵のやわらかい画調が気に入っている I like the soft *tones* of that picture.

がちょう 鵞鳥 〘鳥〙 a goose (複 geese) (!)狭義では雌をさす); (雄) a gander; (ひな) a gosling.

かちょうきん 課徴金 a surcharge 《on》. ●輸入 [輸出] 課徴金 an import [an export] *surcharge*. ●輸入品に課徴金を課す impose [levy] a *surcharge* on imported goods.

かちょうふうげつ 花鳥風月 ●花鳥風月に親しんで余生を送りたい I'd like to spend the rest of my life communing with *nature* [enjoying the *beauties of nature*].

かちり ▶彼はピストルの撃鉄をかちりと上げた He *cocked* the hammer of his pistol. ▶彼女はスーツケースにかちりと鍵(かぎ)をかけた She locked her suitcase *with a click*.

かちわり 搗ち割り (ぶっかき氷) cracked [crushed, chipped] ice.

かちん ❶〖金属やガラスなどが軽く当たる音〗●かちんと音を立てる clink. ●かちんといって with *a clink*. ▶彼らはグラスをかちんと合わせて、未来のために盃を上げた They *clinked* their glasses and drank to their future.
❷〖立腹する様子〗▶彼女は彼の言葉にかちんときた She *got mad at* his words./His words *got her mad*.

かちんかちん ▶池がかちんかちんに凍っていた The pond was frozen *solid*. ▶あの人はかちんかちんの石頭だ He is (as) *stubborn as a mule*.

かちんこ (映画) clapperboards; clapboards.

かつ 勝つ ❶ [勝利する] (試合・戦いなどに勝つ) win* (↔ lose); 敵・敵などを負かす) beat*; defeat. (beatの方がくだけた語で主に競技に, defeatは主に戦いに用いる) ▶戦い[試合；賭(か)け；選挙]に勝つ win a battle (a game; a bet; an election). ▶テニス[チェス]に勝つ win at tennis (chess). (×win tennis (chess) とはしない) ▶どちらのチームが勝っていますか Which team's *winning* [*leading*]? ▶敵に勝ったぞ We've *defeated* the opponent!/(勝利を勝ち取った) We've *won a victory* over the opponent! ▶阪神は巨人に 2 対 1 で [1 点差で] 勝った The Tigers *beat* [*won over*] the Giants (by a score of) 2-1 [*by* one run]. (❗(1) ×won the Giants としない. (2) 2-1 is two-to-one と読む) ▶私は妻とテニスをして勝った I *beat* [×won] my wife at tennis. ▶彼らのチームに 3 点差で勝っている We are three points *ahead of* their team. ▶我がチームは相手に打ち勝った We outslugged the opposition. ▶山田(投手)は伊東(投手)に投げ勝った Yamada outpitched Ito.
会話「レースはどうだった」「例の馬が鼻の差で勝ったよ」"How was the race?" "That horse *won* [*was a winner*] by a nose."
❷ [打ち勝つ] ▶彼はその誘惑に勝った He *resisted* [《やや書》*overcame*] the temptation.
❸ [その他の表現] ▶パチンコで 1,000 円勝った(=得た) I *won* 1,000 yen at pachinko. ▶おまえ[お上(か)]には勝てないよ I can't *fight* you [the City Hall].
● **勝ってかぶとの緒を締めよ** 'Tighten your helmet strings after victory.'/(ことわざ)(森を完全に出てしまうまでは安心して喜ぶな) Do not halloo till you are out of the wood(s).
● **勝てば官軍** (ことわざ) Might is [《英》makes] right./(負ければ賊軍) Losers are always in the wrong.
かつ 活 ● **活を入れる** ▶彼に活を入れてやらねばならぬ I've got to shake [*wake*] him *up*. (shake ... up, buck ... up はともに 《話》で「(人)を元気づける」の意)
かつ 渇 (のどの渇き) thirst. (⇨渇き)
かつ 且つ ▶画家でかつ弁護士 an artist *and* /ən/ lawyer. ▶この魚はおいしいし, かつ(=その上)栄養もある This fish is delicious, *and besides* [*what is more*, 《英》*moreover*], it is nourishing. (⇨その上)/(おいしいと同時に栄養がある) This fish is *both* delicious *and* nourishing./(おいしいだけでなく栄養もある) This fish is nourishing *as well as* delicious [*is not only* delicious *but* (*also*) nourishing]. (❗いずれも nourishing を強調するが, 後の方が強意的) ▶我々は驚き, かつ(=同時に)喜んだ We were surprised *and* delighted *at the same time*.

カツ a cutlet. (❗英語ではフライまたはあぶり焼きのこと) ▶ひと口カツ a pork nugget. ▶カツを揚げる deep-fry a 《pork [veal]》 *cutlet*.

-がつ -月 a month. ● 5月 May.
会話「今何月だっけ」「9月だよ」"What *month* are we in?/What *month* is it?" "September."
かつあい 割愛 ● **割愛する** 動 omit. (⇨省略する)
かつお 鰹 《魚介》 a bonito. ● 通例単・複同形. 肉は ⓤ)
かつおぶし 鰹節 《a piece of》 dried bonito /bənitou/. (❗複数形は two pieces of ... のようにする) (削った) dried bonito shavings. ● 鰹節を削る shave *dried bonito*.
かっか 圖 [熱・光などが激しい様子] hotly, burningly, intensely, fiercely; (色や興奮がたかまって) aglow. ● かっかと照る真夏の太陽 the *burning* midsummer sun. ▶熱帯の島では金属類はかっかと熱くなる Metal pieces get *burningly* [《話》*burning*] hot on a tropical island.
— **かっかする** 動 ❶ [興奮する] get excited (❗気持ちの高ぶりを示し, 怒りにも喜びにも用いる); (怒る) get angry [mad, indignant, furious]. ▶まあそうかっかするな(興奮するな) Don't be so *excited*./(かんしゃくを起こすな) Don't *be so hot-tempered*./(落ち着け) Calm down. ▶何をそんなにかっかしているの What are you so *mad about*? ▶あんな男にかっかするな. 無視すればいいんだ Don't *be so angry* [《話》*mad*] *with* [*at*] that man; just ignore him. ▶父親は息子が期待どおりではなかったので(怒って)かっかした The father *got indignant* because his son failed him.
❷ [ほてる] blush, flush. ▶恥ずかしくて顔がかっかした(=ぽっと赤くなった) My cheeks *blushed* [*flushed*] with embarrassment./My face *was aglow* with shame. ▶彼の額は熱でかっかしていた His forehead *felt hot* with a fever.
かっか 閣下 〖大臣・大使・総督・知事などへの敬称〗 His Excellency; [判事・市長などへの敬称] His Honor, 《英》 His Lordship. (❗以上いずれも呼びかけのときや you の代わりに用いるときは His を Your にする. すべて三人称単数扱い) ▶フランス大使閣下 *His Excellency* the French Ambassador. ▶大統領閣下 *Mr. President*. ▶閣下にはご機嫌いかがでいらっしゃいますか How is [×are] *Your Excellency*?
がっか 学科 (科目) a subject; (科) a department. ● 英語学科 the English *Department*; the *Department* of English. (❗後の方が堅い言い方) ▶あなたの好きな学科は何ですか What is your favorite *subject*? ▶君は何学科ですか What *department* are you in?
がっか 学課 a lesson; schoolwork. ▶いろいろな学課を予習[復習]する prepare [review] different *lessons*.
かっかい 各界 (⇨各界(かく))
がっかい 学会 a (learned /lˈɚːnɪd/) society; 〖学会の会合〗 an academic meeting. ● 第65回日本英文学会 the 65th general meeting of the English Literary *Society* of Japan. ● 日本医学[癌(がん)]学会に出席する attend the meeting of the Medical [Cancer] *Society* of Japan.
がっかい 学界 the academic world; academic circles.
かっかく 赫々 — **赫々たる** 形 ▶赫々たる(=輝かしい)戦果をあげる achieve *brilliant* [*glorious*] military results.
かっかざん 活火山 an active volcano (⸺~(e)s).
かっかそうよう 隔靴掻痒 ▶隔靴掻痒の感がある(=もどかしい) feel *irritated*; feel *impatient*.
かつかつ (やっとのことで) barely, (only) just. ▶かつかつ時間に間に合う be *barely* in time. ▶月10万円でかつかつの生活をする *just manage to live* [*survive*] *on* 100,000 yen a month; *scrape along on* 100,000 yen a month. ▶典子は小柄で 150 センチかつかつしかない(=以上であることはまずない) Noriko is small, and *hardly* more than one and a half meters tall.
がつがつ devouringly; hungrily, greedily. ▶がつがつ食べる devour; eat hungrily; munch (❗リンゴなどを音を立て, 口を大きく動かして食べるときに用いる). ▶がつがつ勉強する study *like mad*. (⇨むやみ勉) ▶あの少年たちは昼食をいつもがつがつ食べる Those boys always eat their lunch *devouringly* [*devour their lunch*]. ▶犬は肉をがつがつ食べた The dog ate the meat *greedily*.

がっかり

がっかり ── がっかりする 動 〚失望する〛be disappointed (⇨失望する), 〚落胆する〛be discouraged; lose heart (⇨落胆する). ● がっかりさせる disappoint; discourage; let 《him》 down. ●《ご期待くださったのにがっかりなさったでしょう》I've disappointed you. (❗ 口語的慣用表現) ●私はその知らせを聞いてがっかりした I was disappointed at [to hear] the news. ●あなたがパーティーに来てくれなかったのでとてもがっかりしました We were very disappointed that you didn't come to our party.

会話「また試験に落ちたんだ」「ほんとにがっかりだね」"I failed [《米話》flunked] the exam again." "What a ＼disappóintment (fór you)!/＼Very [How] disappóinting ＼indeed!" (❗ この形容詞 for you はしばしば相手の注意を引くために文尾にそえる)

会話「おい、落ち込んだ顔をして何かあったのかい」「彼女に振られてしまったんだ」「そんなことでがっかりするな、女なんていくらでもいるんだから」"Hey, what's up? You look so depressed." "She's dumped me." "Don't let it get you down. There are plenty more fish in the sea." ●最後の言い方は失恋した好機を逃した人を慰める常套(じょうとう)句で, 女性に対して「男なんて...」という場合にも用いられる

かつがん 活眼 piercing [penetrating] eyes 《for》; 〚眼識〛insight 《into》.

がくかん 学監 a schóol superintèndent; 《大学の》a dean.

かっき 活気 名 〚活力〛vigor; 〚精力〛energy; 〚活発さ〛liveliness; 〚生気〛life. ●彼は将来のことを語ると活気に満ちあふれていた He was full of life 《and energy》 when he talked about his future. ●東京は活気あふれる都市だ Tokyo is a city teeming with life.

── **活気のある** 形 〚元気のある〛lively; vigorous; spirited; 〚精動的な〛active; energetic. ●活気のある若者 a young person full of vigor [energy, life]; a vigorous [energetic, lively] young person. ●活気のある討論 a lively [a spirited, an animated] debate. ●活気のある市場 an active market. ●活気のない生活 a dull life. ●毎年夏に音楽祭週間が始まると, その静かな湖畔の保養地は大変活気のある町になる Every summer when the week of music festivals starts, the quiet lakeside resort becomes a very lively town.

── **活気づける[づく]** 動 enliven, liven /láɪvn/ 《...》up. ●パーティーを活気づける enliven [liven up] the party. ●夜明けとともに町は活気づいてきた The town came to life [began to liven up] at dawn.

***がっき 学期** (3学期制の) a term, 《米》a trimester; (2学期制の) a semester. ●学期中[末]に during [at the end of] (the) term. ●第1[春]の学期に in the first [spring] term. ●学期末試験 a term [《英》an end-of-term, 《まれ》a terminal] examination; (大学の最終試験) the [one's] finals (❗ 通例複数形). ●4月から新学期が始まる The new term starts in [×from] April.

***がっき 楽器** a musical instrument. (❗ 文脈上明らかな場合は単に an instrument でよい) ●弦楽器 a stringed instrument. ●楽器を演奏する play a musical instrument.

● **楽器店** a musical instruments shop; a music shop.

かつぎあげる 担ぎ上げる ● 肩に担ぎ上げる lift 《it》onto one's shoulder. ●重いいすを2階に担ぎ上げて carry a heavy chair upstairs. ●彼女を生徒会の会長に担ぎ上げる (=押し立てる) make her (the) president of the student council.

かつぎこむ 担ぎ込む ●彼は交通事故にあって病院に担ぎ込まれた He had a car accident and was brought [was carried] into a hospital. (❗ was taken to a ... ともいう)

かつぎだす 担ぎ出す ●彼は燃えている家の中から女の子を担ぎ出した He carried a girl out of the burning house. ●我々は彼を新会社の社長に担ぎ出した We persuaded him to be the president of the new company./We coaxed him to be the president of the new company 《and he agreed》. (❗ coax は persuade と異なり, お世辞などでだめすかすことを強調し, 説得の成功を含意しないので, あいまいな場合は and he agreed などを添える)

かっきてき 画期的 ── 画期的な 形 epoch-making. ● 画期的な発明 an epoch-making invention. ●その発明は語学教育の分野で画期的なものだ The invention is a landmark [×an epoch-making] in language teaching. (❗ epoch-making は形容詞)

がっきゅう 学究 〚学者〛a scholar. (⇨学者) ●学究生活 a scholarly [an academic] life. ●学究的な人 a scholarly person; (学究肌の人) an academic-looking person [type].

がっきゅう 学級 a class. ●集合的に. 学級の個々の構成員を考えるときは複数扱い 《⇨クラス》 ●流感のため10クラスが1週間学級閉鎖になった Ten homerooms were suspended from school for a week due to the flu.

● **学級委員** a cláss represèntative, 《話》a class rep. ● **学級委員長** a cláss prèsident. ● **学級新聞** a cláss nèwspaper. ● **学級担任** a cláss [《米》a hómeroom] teacher. 《任》●**学級日誌** a cláss diary. ● **学級崩壊** classroom breakdown; the breakdown of order in classes.

かっきょ 割拠 ── 割拠する 動 defend one's own territory. (⇨群雄(ぐんゆう)割拠)

かつぎょ 活魚 live fish. ●活魚輸送 live fish transportation.

● **活魚料理** fresh fish cuisine.

かっきょう 活況 (商況などの) activity. ●株式市場は活況を呈してきた The stock market is getting active [is picking up].

がっきょく 楽曲 a musical piece [composition]; an instrumental piece.

かっきり exactly, precisely, just. (⇨くっきり, はっきり) ●かっきり9時に right at nine (o'clock); at nine sharp; precisely at nine. ●その袋はかっきり5キロある The bag weighs exactly five kilos. ●お代はかっきり3,000円でございます It's exactly three thousand yen, please.

かつぐ 担ぐ ❶ 〚肩で〛shoulder; (かついで運ぶ) carry* ... on one's shoulder(s). ●荷をかつぐ shoulder a pack. ●彼は子供を肩にかついでいた He was carrying his child on his shoulders. (❗ 両肩に乗せる場合は shoulder は複数となる)

❷ 〚だます〛deceive, 《やや話》take* ... in, 《話》kid (-dd-); 《米話》put*... on; (いたずらをする) play a trick 《on》. ●彼は彼女の話にまんまとかつがれた He was easily taken in by her stories. ●本気じゃないね. さてはぼくをかつごうとしているな You can't be serious! You must be putting me on! (❗ 通例進行形で) ●彼は彼女をかついで警官だと思い込ませた He deceived [kidded] her into believing that he was a policeman.

がっく 学区 a school district.

かっくう 滑空 ── 滑空する 動 glide.

がっくり ❶ 〚落胆するさま〛●彼は試験の結果にがっくりき

た He *was very* [*bitterly*] *disappointed* at the result of the examination.
❷【下向きの動き】▶がっくりとひざをつく *fall down on one's knees.* ▶「ぼくがやりました」と少年はがっくりと頭を下げて言った "I did it," said the boy with his head *drooped.*
❸【急に, 目立って】 suddenly; (いちじるしく) markedly, strikingly. ▶彼女の顔ががっくりやせて見えた Her face looked *unexpectedly* gaunt.

── がっくりする 動 be very disappointed [dejected].

かっけ 脚気 【医学】beriberi /béribèri/. ▶脚気にかかる suffer from *beriberi.*

かつげき 活劇 (格闘) a fight, a scuffle; (映画) an action film; (演劇) an action drama. ●活劇を演じる play a *fighting scene.*

かっけつ 喀血 【医学】hemoptysis /himáptəsis/.
── 喀血する 動 spit [cough up] blood.

かっこ 各戸 ▶町内の各戸に新聞を配る deliver newspaper *from door to door* in town.

かっこ 各個 (⇨それぞれ)

かっこ 括弧 〖丸かっこ〗 a parénthesis (⑱ parentheses) (( ));〖角かっこ〗a bracket ([ ]);〖大かっこ〗a brace ({ }). (❗以上いずれも対をなすので通例複数形で用いる) ●かっこ内の語 a word *in parentheses* [*brackets*]. ▶句をかっこに入れる *parenthesize* [*bracket*] a phrase; *put* a phrase *in parentheses* [*brackets*].

かっこ 確固 ─ 確固たる 形 (ゆるぎない) firm. ●確固たる信念 a *firm* [a *strong*] belief. ●確固たる(=決然とした)態度で in a *determined* manner. ▶彼は人生に確固たる目的を持っていた He had a *firm* [*明確な*] *definite*] aim in life.

── 確固として 副 firmly.

かっこいい 格好いい cool. ●かっこいい車 a *classy* [《米》a *neat*] car. ●すごくかっこいいジーンズ really [《米話》real] *cool* jeans. ▶彼かっこいいでしょ Isn't he a knockout (a *cool* guy)? (❗knockout is cool より強い語で女性にも用いる)

***かっこう** 格好 ⑬ ❶【外形】(a) shape; (a) form. (⇨形 ❶) ▶そのつぼは格好がいい The pot has a good *shape* [*form*]./The pot is well-*shaped.* ▶彼は背が高くて格好が(=スタイル)がよい He is tall and has a nice *build.* (❗女性の場合は *figure* [an attractive *shape*]. などという) ▶あなたのドレスは格好(=仕立て)がよい Your dress is *well-cut.* (❗ファッション性がある) Your dress is *fashionable* [*stylish*].
❷【姿勢】(a) posture; (一時的な) a position; (意識的な) a pose. (⇨姿勢 ❶) ▶字を書くのに一番よい格好です This is the best *posture* for writing. ▶彼は堅苦しい格好で座っていた He sat in a stiff *position* [*pose*]. ▶彼は踊り子たちのいろいろな格好をスケッチした He sketched the dancers' various *poses.*
❸【外見】(an) appearance; (服装) (a) dress. ▶人を格好で判断する人たちもいる Some people judge others by *appearances.* ▶新しい家具を入れたら部屋らしい格好がついた The room has *improved in appearance* [*形が整った*] has taken shape] with new pieces of furniture. ▶彼女は地味な格好をしていた She *was* plainly *dressed*./She wore [*was wearing*] a plain *dress.* (❗進行形は「見たその時は」という一時的状態を表す) ▶UFOってどんな格好をしているの(=何に似ているの) What does a UFO *look like*? ▶ひどい格好しているから写真を撮られるのはいやだな I'm a *mess.* I don't like to have my picture taken. ▶そんな格好で外出するのはやめて You're not going out (*dressed*) like that.
❹【その他の表現】▶彼は競走でビリになって格好が悪かった(=少し恥ずかしかった) He *felt a bit ashamed* because he came last in the race. ▶彼は会議に遅れて格好がつかなかった(=面目を失った) He *was late for the meeting and lost* (*his*) *face.* ▶彼はパーティーにガールフレンドが来ていたのでいい格好をした(=気取ってかっこよくふるまった) He *put on airs* [いいところを見せようとした] *tried to look good*], because his girlfriend was present at the party.

── 格好の 形 (ちょうどよい) suitable, fit; (ほどよい) reasonable. ▶ここは本を読むのに格好の場所だ This is a *suitable* [a *fit*, a *good*] place for reading. ▶彼は格好の値段でその車を買った He bought the car at a *reasonable* price.

かっこう 郭公 【鳥】a cuckoo /kúːkuː/ (⑱ ~s).

かっこう 滑降 ⑬ 〖スキー〗a descent. ●斜滑降 a traverse.

── 滑降する 動 ▶ゲレンデを滑降する *glide* [(スキーで) *ski*] *down* a slope.
●滑降競技 a downhill race.

かつごう 渇仰 (⇨崇拝)

:がっこう 学校 a school; (軍事・音楽などの特殊科目の) an academy.

解説 (1) school は《米》では大学・幼稚園も含むことがあるが, 通例小・中・高校をさす.
(2) school が建物ではなく学校教育・授業などの機能を表す場合は通例無冠詞. したがって, 一般に生徒が授業を受けたり, 先生が学校で授業をしたりで「学校へ行く」go to《やや書》attend] *school* という. ただし, 修飾語を伴ったり特定・不特定の学校を表す場合は冠詞がつく: 【よい】学校へ行く go *to the* [*a good*] *school*./仙台の学校へ行く go *to* (*a*) *school* in Sendai.

①【～学校, 学校～】▶私立[公立]学校 a private [《米》a public,《英》a council, a county] *school.* (❗public school は《英》では一部の有名私立学校をさすことがある) ●私の学校時代の友達 a *school* friend of mine; my friend *at* [*from*] *school.* ▶学校時代に北海道へ行った I went to Hokkaido *in my school days* [《学生のときに》when I was a student]. (❗後の方が口語的で普通)

②【学校が[は]】▶学校が終わってから公園で遊ぼう Let's play in the park *after school* (is over). ▶学校は 4 月 8 日から始まります *School* [×*The school*] *begins* [*starts*] *on April 8.* (❗(1) ×*from April 8* は不可. (2) *April 8* は *April* (*the*) *eighth* と読む) ▶あさっては学校はありません We have [There will be] *no school* [*classes*] *(the) day after tomorrow.* ▶学校は駅の隣です *The school* [×*School*] *is next to the station.* (❗この school は「建物」をさす)

③【学校を[に]】▶学校に入る(入学する) *get into* [《やや書》*enter*] (*a*) *school*; (出席して勉強を始める) *begin* [*start*] *school.* ●学校に遅れる be late for *school.* ●学校に行く日 fall on *a school day.* (❗「学校のある日の朝」なら on *a school morning.*) ▶彼は学校の先生です He is a schoolteacher./He teaches *school*./He teaches *at* [*in*] (*a*) *school.* ▶親は子供を学校にやらなければならない Parents must send their children to *school.* ▶弟はまだ学校に通って(=在学して)います My brother *is still in* [《主に米》*at* (《主に英》)] *school.* (❗(1) *be in* [*at*] *the school* は「学校内にいる」の意.《米》では *be at school* をこの意に用いることがある. (2) 固有名詞の学校

かっこく 各国 〚各々の国〛every [each] country; 〚諸国〛various countries; 〚万国〛all countries. (⇨国)

かっさい 喝采 〘声による〙a cheer; 〘拍手による〙applause; 〘声と拍手による〙《tremendous》cheers and applause. ●熱狂的なかっさいを送る cheer [applaud] 《him》enthusiastically. ●かっさいを博すbe (loudly) cheered [applauded]; win [get, receive] applause. ●手を振ってかっさいに答える acknowledge the cheers 《of the crowd》by the wave of one's hand(s). ●拍手かっさいで迎えられるbe greeted with applause. ▶割れるようなかっさいの中を指揮者は退場した The conductor left the stage amid [xamong] thunderous [great, loud] applause [cheers]. (❗通例 among は抽象的なものには用いられない)

がっさく 合作 图 a collaboration.
— **合作する** 動 collaborate 《with; on, in》; work together 《with》.

かっさつ 活殺 〘生かすか殺すか〙life or death. ●活殺自在に人を操る manage a person at will [freely].

がっさつ 合冊 (⇨❸ 合本(がっぽん))

かっさらう 〘さらう〙carry ... off.

がっさん 合算 〘合計〙(⇨❸)

*__かつじ 活字__ ❶〚1 個の〛a (printing) type. (❗印刷された活字を集合的に扱う場合は Ⓤ); 〚活字の字体〛print. ●活字を組む set (up) type. ●活字を拾う pick (out) type(s). ●活字になる print [put] 《an article》in type. ●活字体で書く print 《one's name》; write 《one's name》in print [block letters]. (❗block letter は通例大文字の活字体) ●大きい[小さい]活字の本 a book in large [small] print; a book printed in large [small] print. ●彼女の本は活字になって(=印刷[出版]されて)いない Her book hasn't been printed [in print] yet. ▶このごろ,若い人の活字離れがはなはだしいのは遺憾なことだ It is regrettable that young people today do not read many books.

かつじ 活写 〘生き生きと表すこと〙a vivid description.
— **活写する** 動 ●世相を活写する describe social conditions vividly; give a vivid description of social conditions.

かっしゃ 滑車 a pulley.

がっしゅうこく 合衆国 the United States (of America) 〘略〙(the) U.S.(A.); (the) US(A). (❗(1) 略記の場合も正式には the をつける。(2) 通例アメリカ人は母国のことを the US, the United States, 《話》the States と呼ぶ)

がっしゅく 合宿 — **合宿する** 動 lodge [board] together; 〘練習等に〙stay in [have] a camp for training [for practice].
●合宿所 (スポーツの) a tráining càmp.

かつじょう 割譲 图 《書》cession.
— **割譲する** 動 《書》cede 《to》. ▶メキシコは 1848 年にニューメキシコをアメリカに割譲した Mexico ceded New Mexico to the United States in 1848.

がっしょう 合唱 图 a chorus. (❗参考 ベートーベンの交響曲第 9 番の「合唱」は Choral (賛美歌))) ●混声合唱 a mixed chorus. ●二部合唱 a chorus in two parts; a two-part chorus. ●男声[女声]合唱曲 a chorus of male [female] voice. ▶最後に大合唱が行われた There was a great chorus at the end.
— **合唱する** 動 ▶彼らはその歌を合唱した They sang the song in chorus [all together]./They chorused the song.
●合唱団 the chorus. (❗(1) 単・複両扱い。一員は a member of the chorus. (2) 特に教会の聖歌隊は the choir /kwáiər/)

がっしょう 合掌 图 〚建築〛a principal rafter. ●合掌造りの家 a wooden house with a huge, steep-sloping roof.
— **合掌する** 動 〘両方の手のひらを合わせて拝む〙put [place] one's hands together in prayer.

かっしょく 褐色 brown. (⇨茶色)

がっしり ❶〚体つきとがしっかりしている〙be solidly built; 〘丈夫な〙sturdy; 〘肉付きのよい〙substantial. ●がっしりしたいす a sturdy chair. ●母のがっしりした肩 my mother's substantial shoulders. ▶彼はがっしりした体格をしていた He was solidly built./He had a sturdy build. (背は低いが) He was stocky.
❷〚しっかりと〛firmly, tight(ly). ▶父親は赤子をがっしり両腕に抱いた The father held the baby firmly in his arms.

かっすい 渇水 a shortage of water, a water shortage; 〚かんばつ〛(a) drought /dráut/.
●渇水期 (乾期) the dry season.

がっする 合する ❶〚結合する〛join; 〘合う〙meet; 〘一になる〙become one. ●二つの川が合する場所 the place where the two rivers join [meet].

❷ [一つに合わせる] ▶これらの数字を合計する add up these figures.

かっせい 活性 ▸活性酸素 active oxygen. ▸活性炭 activated charcoal.

かっせいか 活性化 activation; (再活性化) revitalization. ▸経済の再活性化 economic *revitalization*.

——活性化する 動 activate; revitalize.

かつぜつ 滑舌 articulation.

かっせん 合戦 [戦い] a fight; (大規模な) a battle; [競演] a contest.

かっそう 滑走 ——滑走する 動 slide, glide 《*on, over*》; (飛行機が) run 《*on the ground*》. (❗離陸の前、着陸後にゆっくり移動するのは taxi) ▶彼女は体を後ろにそらせて滑走するイナバウアーを含めて完璧な演技をした She performed flawlessly, including an Ina Bauer in which she *glided* 《in a backbend position.
▸滑走路 a runway; (仮設の) an airstrip.

がっそう 合奏 an ensemble /ɑːnsάːmbl/. (❗「合奏曲」の意にもなる)

——合奏する 動 ▶彼らは合奏した They *joined in the ensemble*./They *played* [*performed*] *all together*.

カッター ❶ [刃物の] a cutter;《和製語》a cutter knife.《野球の》a cutter; a cut fastball.

カッターシャツ a shirt, a long-sleeved (sport(s)) shirt.

カッターナイフ (⇒カッター)

がったい 合体 名 union; (結合) combination.

——合体する 動 unite《*with*》; combine《*with*》; (組み入れる) incorporate. ▶2チームが合体して新チームができた The two teams *united* to make a new one.

かったつ 闊達 ——闊達な 形 ▸闊達な (=度量が広い) 気性 a broad-minded [(寛大な) *generous*] temper.

かったるい (⇒だるい) ▶日曜日に学校へ行くのはかったるい I *don't feel like going to* school on Sunday.

かつだんそう 活断層 [地学] an active fault.

がっち 合致 ——合致する 動 (符号する) coincide /kòuinsάid/《*with*》; (一致する)《やや書》be consistent《*with*》; (かなう)《書》answer 《one's purpose》. (⇒一致)

かっちゅう 甲冑 《a suit of》armor. (⇒よろい)

かっちり (⇒ぴったり)

がっちり ❶ [造りなどが] ▶がっちりしている be solidly built; (丈夫な) sturdy. (⇒がんじょう) ▶この建物はがっちりできている This building *is solidly built*.
❷ [しっかりと] firmly, tight(ly). ▶彼は彼女をがっちり抱いた He held her *tight(ly)*.
❸ [計算高い] (けちな)《話》tightfisted; (打算的な) calculating. ▶財布のひもをがっちり握っている hold the purse strings. ▶彼はお金の事になるとがっちりしている He is *tightfisted* when it comes to money.

ガッツ [根性] guts. ▸ガッツのある男 a man *with* [*who has*] *a lot of guts*. ▶彼はガッツがない He has no *guts* [*spirit*]. ▶勝った選手はガッツポーズを取りながらグランドを1周した The winner ran around the ground, striking a *victory* pose [raising his fist(s) over his head in triumph; punching the air]. (参考) (1) これを a victory sign という。単に celebrate (喜びを全身で表す)ということも多い。ｘa guts pose は和製英語。後の言い方は説明的な。(2) なお、このように走ることを a victory lap または a lap of honor という。ｘa winning run は和製英語 (⇒勝ち越し [勝ち越し点]))

がっつく be greedy [《話》grabby]. (⇒がつがつ) ▶がっ

ついて勉強する study like mad; (ガリ勉する)《米話》grind away. ▶がつついて食う eat greedily; devour;《話》gobble (down).

***かつて** (過去のある時に) once (❗通例過去時制で); (過去のいつか) ever (❗通例現在完了形・過去時制の疑問文で); (以前) formerly, in former times (❗通例過去時制、時に現在完了時制で); (現在・過去のある時より) before (❗通例現在・過去完了形で).

| 解説 | ▸「(今と違って)かつては...だった」という状態は **used to**、「かつてはよく...したものだ」という動作は **used to, would** などでも表せる。(⇒昔 解説) |

▶私たちはかつて京都に住んでいたことがある We *once* [*formerly*, ×*ever*] *lived* in Kyoto. (❗We have *once lived* in Kyoto./We have *lived* in Kyoto *once*. のように現在完了形で用いると「一度住んだことがある」の意)/We *lived* in Kyoto *before*./We *used to* [×*would*] *live* in Kyoto./《やや書》*There was a time when* we *lived* in Kyoto. ▶かつては彼は6人雇っていたんだ。今では1人で仕事してるんだよ *Once* he employed six men. Now, he works on his own. (❗対比による前置詞に注意) ▶かつて (=ひところ) はよく蔵王ヘスキーに行ったものだった (*At one time*) I often *used to* [*would often*] go skiing at Zao. (❗*would* は主に書き言葉) ▶過去半世紀、かつてない経済発展があった The last [past] half-century has seen unprecedented economic development.

【会話】「かつてパリへ行ったことがありますか」「いいえ、ありません」"Have you (*ever*) been to Paris? (❗*ever* はある方が強意的)/Have you been to Paris *before*?" "No, I haven't./No, never [×No, I have never]."

① [かつての] former; one-time. ▸かつての歌手 a *former* [a *one-time*] singer. ▶彼はかつての夫で He is my *former* husband [my *ex*-husband,《話》my *ex* /éks/]./He was *formerly* my husband. ▶彼はかつてのように裕福ではない He is not as well off as he *used to* be [as he (*once*) *was*, as (he was) *before*,《書》as *once he was*]. (⇒昔 ①)
② [かつて (こ)] (これ [それ] までに一度も...ない) never. (❗通例現在 [過去] 完了形で) ▶こんな美しい景色をいまだかつて見たことがない I have *never* seen such a beautiful sight (as this). (❗強意的に I *never* have seen .... の語順をとることも。*Never* have I seen .... は堅い表現. I *haven't ever* seen .... の形はまれ)/(これはこれまでに見た最も美しい景色が) This is the most beautiful sight (that) I have *ever* [×*never*] seen. (❗この用法の *ever* は最上級を強調する) ▶彼女はかつてないほど泣いた She cried as she had *never cried before*.

***かって** 勝手 ❶ [台所] a kitchen. (⇒台所)
❷ [様子] ▸勝手を知っている (物事の) know how to do; 《話》know the ropes. ▸勝手の分からない国 a *strange* country. ▶私はこの辺の勝手を知っている I'm *familiar* with this neighborhood. ▶カラスの勝手でしょう Crows are *free* to do as they please./(カラスの視点で) Leave us crows alone as we do as we please.

•勝手が違う ▶左ハンドルの車は勝手が違うよ I'm *not used to* (driving) a left-hand-drive car.

——勝手な 形 (自分本位の) selfish. ▶彼は勝手なやつだ He is a *selfish* man./(自分のこと [便宜] しか考えない) He thinks only of himself [his own convenience]. ▶人の勝手でしょう Don't be so *selfish*. ▶行くもとどまるも君の勝手だ (自由だ) You are *free* to go or stay./(君次第) It's *up to* you whether you go or stay. ▶私が何をしようと勝手

かってでる しょう(=あなたの知ったことではない) It's *none of your business* what I do./That's my business. (❗ my を強く読む) ▶彼女は息子に勝手気ままなことは許さない She never lets her son *have his own way*.

—— **勝手に** 副 〖自由に〗as one likes [pleases]; 〖無断で〗without permission, 〖書〗leave]; 〖独断で〗at one's own discretion. ▶勝手にしなさい Do *as you like* [*please*]./Have it *your own way*./Please yourself. (❗「ご勝手に」「勝手にすればいいだろう」など皮肉や怒りなどを含む失礼な言い方)/(怒りを込めて) Go to Hell [the Devil]! (❗一種ののろしい表現) ▶彼に勝手にやらせておきなさい Let him *have his own way*. ▶勝手にこの機械を動かしてはいけない You shouldn't operate this machine *without permission*./(やや書) Don't *take the liberty of operating* [(まれ) *to operate*] this machine. ▶規則を自分たちに都合のいいように(=自分たちの利益になるように)勝手に解釈する選手がいる Some players *arbitrarily* interpret the rules to [*for*] their advantage.

● 勝手口 a kitchen door; (裏口) a backdoor.

かってでる 買って出る volunteér 《*for, to do*》; (まったくの親切心から) go out of one's way 《*to do*》. ▶私はパーティーの幹事役を買って出た I *volunteered* [*offered*] *my services* as the organizer of the party. ▶ぼくたちの疲れきっているのを見て若い農夫は川から水を汲んでくる仕事を買って出てくれた When the young farmer saw we were extremely tired, he *went out of his way* to fetch water from the river for us.

がってん 合点 图 (うなずくこと) a nod; (了解) understanding; (同意) (an) agreement.

—— **合点する** 動 (同意してうなずく) nod in approval, nod one's consent; (了解する) understand; (同意する) agree.
〘会話〙「さあ、行くぞ」「合点だ」"Here we go!" "*All right*./(話) *OK*."

かっと 副 〖強さ激しく〗intensely; fiercely; furiously. ▶夏の太陽がかっと照りつけた The summer sun shone down *intensely*.

—— **かっとなる** 動 〖急に怒る〗get angry 〖(話) mad, furious]; fly into a rage; lose one's temper. ▶彼はその言葉にかっとなった He *got angry* [*mad, furious*] *at* the words. (❗ furious が最も意味が強い)/He *flew into a rage* *at* the words.

—— **かっとなって** 副 in a fit of anger [rage] (❗ rage は抑えようのない激しい怒り) ▶彼はかっとなって彼女を殴った He hit her *in a fit of anger*.

カット 图 ❶〖切断〗a cut; (ヘアカット) a haircut. ▶白のローカットの服 a white dress of low cut. ▶髪を短くカットしてもらう have [get] one's hair *cut* short. 〘会話〙「今日はどのようにカットいたしましょうか」「ちょっと整える程度でお願いします」"How would you like your hair *cut* today?" "Just a trim, please." (❗ cut は過去分詞、like のあとに to have が省略された言い方)
❷〖さし絵〗an illustration.

—— **カットする** 動 cut. ▶論文を 10 ページにカットする(=縮小する) *cut* the essay *to* ten pages. ▶その文をカットする *cross out* the sentence. ▶残酷なシーンをカットする *cut* brutal scenes.
● 余剰人員をカットする(=余剰) (打者が)投球をカットする cut foul off a pitch; fight it off. ▶三塁手はショートの前でゴロをカットした The third baseman cut off the grounder in front of the shortstop. ▶給料が 5 パーセントカットされた My salary *has been cut* by 5 percent.

ガット 〖ラケットやバイオリンの弦などに用いる糸〗gut. ▶堅く張ったガット tightly-strung *gut*. ●テニスラケットにガットを張る *string* a tennis racket.

ガット 〖関税と貿易に関する一般協定〗GATT 《the General *A*greement on *T*ariffs and *T*rade の略》.

カットアンドペースト 图 〖パソコン画面上での切り貼り〗cut and paste.
—— **カットアンドペーストする** 動 cut and paste.

カットイン 〖挿入画面〗(映画・テレビ) a cút-in (shot).

かっとう 葛藤 a conflict. ●心の葛藤に苦しむ go through a psychological *conflict*.

かつどう 活動 图 (an) activity 〖ある特定の活動に C、またはしばしば複数形で〗; 〖人の行動〗action; 〖作業〗an operation. ▶火山活動 volcanic *activity*; the *activity* of a volcano. ▶課外活動 an extracurricular *activity*. ▶学級〖クラブ〗活動を行う(=参加する) take part in classroom [club] *activities*. ▶救援活動を行う carry out a rescue *operation*. ▶彼は昔政治活動をしていた He was once involved in political *activities* (運動) campaign, movement]. ▶火山が再び活動を始めた The volcano has become *active* again. ▶彼は就職活動で忙しい He is busy hunting for a job. (●就職)

—— **活動的な** 形 (積極的な) active; (精力的な) energetic. ▶活動的な男 an *active* man. ▶あの教師は非常に活動的だ That teacher is very *energetic* [*full of energy*, very *active*].

—— **活動する** 動 〖活躍している〗be active; 〖積極的な役割をはたす〗play an active part 《*in*》. (●活躍) ▶その組織はもう何年も活動していない The organization has been *inactive* for years.

● 活動家 a man of action (政界などに対して政治家、事業家など); (政治的信条を持つ運動家) an activist. ● 活動計画 an áction prògram. ● 活動範囲 a scope of activity [action]. ● 活動方針 an áction pòlicy; an áction prògram.

カットグラス cut glass. ●カットグラスの鉢 a *cut-glass bowl*.

カットシート 〖1 枚ごとに切り離された印刷用紙〗a cut sheet.
● カットシートフィーダー a cut-sheet feeder, a sheet feeder.

カットソー cùt-and-séwn.

かっとばす かっ飛ばす ▶彼はホームランをかっ飛ばした He hit [*slugged, belted*] a home run. (❗ slug, belt は「強打する」の意)

カットバック (映画・小説・劇・アメフト・サーフィンの) a cutback.

カットプレー 〖野球〗a cútoff play.
カットボール 〖野球〗a cut fastball; (和製語) a cut ball (❗ この英語は「故意に傷をつけた反則球」の意).

カットワーク 〖刺繡(ししゅう)〗cútwòrk.

かつどん カツ丼 katsudon; (説明的に) a rice dish (served) in a bowl topped with a breaded, deep-fried pork cutlet and sauteed onions cooked in an egg sauce.

かっぱ 河童 a kappa; (水の小悪魔) a water imp; (水の妖精(ようせい)) a water spirit. ●陸(おか)に上がったかっぱ(⇒陸(おか))
● かっぱの川流れ Even Homer sometimes nods.
● かっぱ巻き a cucumber (*sushi*) roll.

かっぱ 『河童』 Kappa. (参考) 芥川龍之介の小説

かっぱ 喝破 —— **喝破する** 動 ▶彼は日本美術の優秀性を喝破した(=鋭く指摘した) He *keenly* indicated the excellence of the Japanese arts.

かっぱつ 活発 —— **活発な** 形 (活動的な) active; (元気のよい) lively; (生気のある) animated; (きびきびした) brisk; (精力的な) vigorous. ●活発な議論をする

かっぱらい have a *lively* [an *animated*] discussion. ● 活発な市況 a *brisk* market. ● 動作が活発だ be *brisk* [*quick*] in one's movements; move *briskly* [*quickly*]. ▶彼は活発な少年だ He is an *active* [a *lively*, a *brisk*] boy.
— 活発に 副 *actively*; *lively*; *briskly*; *vigorously*. ▶彼は活発に仕事をしていた He was working *vigorously* [*energetically*].

かっぱらい (行為) snatching; (人) a snatcher.

かっぱらう [[引ったくる]] snatch; [[盗む]] steal*, 《話》 rip (-pp-) ... off. ● 彼女のハンドバッグをかっぱらう *snatch* her purse.

かっぱん 活版印刷 metal type printing. ● 活版で印刷する print with type. (⚠ type は「活字」の意)

がっぴ 月日 the date.

がっぴょう 合評 图 a joint review 《of》.
— 合評する 動 review 《a book》 jointly.
● 合評会 a joint review meeting 《for a novel》.

かっぷ 割賦 [[分割払い]] 《米》 the installment plan, 《英》 the hire purchase.
● 割賦販売 sales in installments.

カップ [[茶わん]] (紅茶・コーヒー用の) a cup; (計量カップ1杯の量) a cup(ful) (参考 約 250cc); [[賞杯]] (優勝杯) a trophy. ● コーヒーカップ a cóffee cùp. ● ティーカップ a teacup. ● カップと受け皿(の一組) a cup and saucer /kǽpənsɔ́ːsər/. (⚠ a saucer ではないことに注意) ● 計量カップ a méasuring cùp. ● 砂糖2カップ two *cups* [*cupfuls*] of sugar. ● 優勝カップを獲得する win the *cup*. ● ボールはカップインした [ゴルフ] The (golf) ball went into the *hole* [*cup*]. ● カップケーキ a cúpcàke. ● カップボード (食器棚) a cupboard /kʌ́bərd/. ● カップラーメン instant noodles in a (plastic) bowl*; (1個) a cup of noodles.

かっぷく 恰幅 ● 恰幅のいい (=でっぷりした体格の)男 a man *of stout* [(しっかりした) *heavy*] *build*; a stout man.

かっぷく 割腹 (⇨切腹)

がっぷり ● がっぷり四つに組む come to grips 《with》; grapple 《with》.

カップル (夫婦または恋人同士) a couple. (⚠ 単・複両扱い) ▶あのカップル that [✗those] *couple*. ▶なんてすてきなカップルでしょう What a nice *couple*!

*__がっぺい__ 合併 图 [[会社などの]] (a) merger, [[書]] (an) amalgamation; [[吸収による]] absorption. ● 3社の合併 the *merger* of three companies.
— 合併する 動 merge, [[書]] amalgamate; (吸収する) absorb. ▶その2社は合併した The two companies *merged* [*were joined in a merger*]. ▶三つの銀行は合併して世界最大の銀行になった The three banks *were merged into* the biggest bank in the world. ▶近接の村々が市に合併された The neighboring villages *were absorbed into* the city.
● 合併症 [[医学]] complications.

かっぽ 闊歩 — 闊歩する 動 (大きく歩く) stride; (いばった感じで) stalk; (いばって) 《通例軽蔑的》 swagger; (気取って) 《通例軽蔑的》 strut. ● 往来を闊歩する *stalk* along the street.

かつぼう 渇望 图 an eager desire 《for》, thirst 《for》. (⇨熱望)
— 渇望する 動 ● 名声を渇望する have a great *desire* [a *great thirst*] *for* fame; *thirst* [*be thirsty*] *for* fame.

かっぽう 割烹 [[料理]] Japanese-style cooking; (日本料理専門店) a traditional Japanese restaurant.
● 割烹着 a Japanese-style apron with sleeves.

がっぽがっぽ ● がっぽがっぽもうける make [earn] *a large amount of* money; 《話》 *rake in* money.

かっぽじる 搔っぽじる pick 《one's nose [teeth]》; clean 《one's ears》. ▶耳の穴をかっぽじってよく聞け Listen to me carefully [*attentively*, *without missing a single word*].

がっぽり ● 株でがっぽりもうける 《話》 make *a pile* (of money) on the stock market.

がっぽん 合本 图 copies bound together in one volume [in book form]. — 合本する 動 bind 《magazines》 in one volume [in book form].

かつもく 刮目 图 ▶このディズニー映画は刮目(=注意して見る)に値する This Disney film deserves [*is worthy of*] *close attention*.
— 刮目する 動 (注意して見る) watch closely [*attentively*, *keenly*].

*__かつやく__ 活躍 图 ● 活躍(を)する 動 ● 実業界で活躍する be active [*play an active part*] in business circles. ● その試合で大活躍する do a very good job [*do extremely well*] in the game. ▶彼はその法案の通過を促進するのに活躍した He *was active* in helping that bill get passed [(道具の役をする) *instrumental* in getting the bill passed].

かつやくきん 括約筋 [[解剖]] a sphincter (muscle).

*__かつよう__ 活用 图 ❶[[利用]] use; (応用) application. ❷[[動詞の語形変化]] a. conjugation. ● 規則[不規則]活用 regular [irregular] *conjugation*.
— 活用する 動 ❶[[利用する]] make use of ...; (うまく) take advantage of ...; (実用的に) put ... to practical use. ● 機会を十分に活用する *make full use* [*take full advantage*] *of* the opportunity. ● 能力を最大限に活用する *make* the best *use* [*make the most*] *of* one's talents. ● 資料を活用する *use* the data *well*; *put* the data *to practical use*. ▶彼女はこれからは時間をもっとうまく活用しようと決心した She determined to *make better use of* her time from now on.
❷[[動詞が語形変化する]] cónjugate.

かつら 桂 [[植物]] a katsura tree.
● 桂むき (料理) (説明的に) a technique of peeling in a continuous paper-thin sheet of *daikon*, cucumbers or carrots.

かつら 鬘 (扮装etc)・はげ隠し用) a wig; (はげ隠し用, 美容用) a hairpiece (⚠ 入れ毛 (switch) も含む); (はげた部分をぴったり覆う) a toupee /tuːpéɪ/ (⚠ 通例男性用). ● かつらをつけている wear a *wig*. ▶髪をふっくらさせるのなどを着用する人もいる Some women wear a *hairpiece* that makes their hair look full.

かつらく 滑落 ● 滑落事故 a *slip* accident.
— 滑落する 動 slip [slide, slither] down 《a slope》. ▶彼は足を滑らせて山の斜面を滑落した He slipped and *slid* [*slithered*] *down* the mountain slope.

かつりょく 活力 energy; vitality. ● 経済に活力を与える *vitalize* [*energize*] the economy. ▶その少年は活力にあふれていた The boy was very *energetic* [*full of energy*].

カツレツ a cutlet. (⇨カツ)

かつろ 活路 (方法) a way; (手段) a means. ● 活路を見いだす find *a way* out of the difficulty; find *a means* of survival.

がつん ● ドアに頭をがつんとぶつける *bump* one's head *against* [*on*] the door. ● あいつは態度がでかいよ。一度がつんと言ってやれば (=ずけずけ文句を言うほうがいい) He acts too big, indeed. You should give him a piece of your mind.

かて 糧 [[食物]] food; [[生計]] bread. ● 心の糧 mental *food*; *food for the mind*. ● 日々の糧を得

る earn [win] one's daily *bread*.

かてい 家庭 图 a home; a family;〔所帯〕a household.

使い分け home 家族とともに暮らす場としての家をさす。暖かい家庭的雰囲気を含意する。
family 社会単位としての家族をさす。
household 使用人や下宿人なども含む、所帯の全員をさす。

①【〜家庭】● 楽しい家庭 a happy [a sweet] *home*. ● 裕福な家庭 a well-to-do [a wealthy] *family*. ● 崩壊家庭 a broken *family* [*home*]. ● 母[父]子家庭 a *home* of (a) mother [(a) father] and child; a fatherless [a motherless, a single-parent] *home*. ● 上流[中流]家庭 an upper- [a middle-]class *family*. ● あそこ[お隣り]は新婚家庭だ They [Our next-door neighbors] have just married. ● 幸福な家庭はみな同じように似ているが、不幸な家庭は不幸なさまもそれぞれ違うものだ All happy *families* resemble one another; every unhappy *family* is unhappy in its own way. (❗「幸福な家庭」は all happy families と複数形で,「不幸な家庭」は every unhappy family と個々を強調するために単数形になっていることに注意)

②【家庭(の)〜】● 家庭(の)事情 *domestic* affairs; *family* circumstances. ● 家庭の事情で for *family* reasons. ● 家庭の幸福[不和] *domestic* happiness [discord].

DISCOURSE
家庭ゴミの量に関しては、変化はない Regarding *household* garbage, the amount has remained constant. (❗ regarding ... (...に関しては)は関連を表すディスコースマーカー)

③【家庭に[を]】● 家庭に入る(=結婚する[している]) get [be] married. (⇨所帯 [第１文例]) ● 家庭を破壊する break up a *family*. ▶ 彼は政治家の家庭に生まれた He was born into a political *family*. ▶ どうか幸せなご家庭を築いてください I do hope you will have a happy *family* [*home*] life. ▶ 私たちは宮崎で家庭を築いた We made our *home* in Miyazaki. ▶ 妻は家庭を切り盛りするのがうまい My wife is good at housekeeping./My wife is a good housekeeper. ▶ 仕事のために家庭を犠牲にした He sacrificed his *family* [*family* life] for his career.

④【家庭で】● at home; in the home. ● 家庭で礼儀作法を教える teach good manners *in the home*. ● 貧しい[厳格な]家庭で育つ be brought up in a poor [a strict] *family*.

— **家庭的な** 形 《米》homey,《英》homely; (我が家のような) homelike; (家庭を愛する) home-loving, domestic. ● 家庭的な雰囲気 a *homey* [a *homely*, a *homelike*] atmosphere. ● 家庭的な男性 a *family*(-oriented) [(しばしばおどけて) a *domesticated*] man. (❗ domesticated は《英》では「所帯の切り盛りの上手な」の意) ● 家庭的な女 a *home-loving* [a *home-minded*] woman; a *domestic* woman. (❗《米》「器量の悪い人」の意) ▶ この旅館はこの前泊まったときはもっと家庭的だった This hotel had a *homelier* atmosphere [gave us *homier* service] the last time we stayed here.

● 家庭科 home economics (❗ 単数扱い); domestic science. ● 家庭環境 a *home* [xa house] environment. ● 家庭菜園 a végetable [《主に英》a kítchen] gàrden. ● 家庭裁判所 a family court; a court of domestic relations. ● 家庭生活 one's home life. ● 家庭争議 a family dispute; family troubles [strifes]. ● 家庭内暴力 domestic [family] violence. (❗ しばしば DV という) ● 家庭訪問 a call at a student's home; a home visit. ● 家庭訪問をする visit [call at] a student's home. 〔事情〕米国には a home-visiting teacher がいる) ● 家庭用品 (主に台所用品) household utensils; (備品) home appliances.

*かてい 仮定 图 《書》(a) supposition; (憶測) (an) assumption. ● ...という仮定のもとに on the *assumption* [*supposition*] that ....

— 仮定する 動 suppose; assume. ▶ 彼が職を失うと仮定しよう (*Let's*) *suppose* [*assume*] (*that*) he loses his job. (❗ that はしばしば省略される。節内が未来のことであっても通例現在形となる) ▶ その仕事を勧められたと仮定して、あなたは引き受けますか *Suppose* [*Supposing*, *Assuming*] (*that*) you're offered the job, will you accept it?

● 仮定法〔文法〕the subjunctive mood.

*かてい 過程 图 (a) process. ● 成長の過程(で) (in) the *process* of (one's) growth.

かてい 課程 a course;〔教科課程〕a curriculum (複 curricula, 〜s), a program. ● 教育課程 a *course* of study. ● 高校の課程を終了する finish a *course* in high school [a high school *course*]. ▶ 君はその過程を終了しなかったので卒業は無理だ You didn't complete the *course*, so you can't graduate.

かていきょうし 家庭教師 a tutor; a private teacher. ▶ 家庭教師を雇う employ [hire] a *tutor*. ● 英語の家庭教師についている take *private* lessons [be *tutored*] in English. ● 英語の家庭教師をする teach 《a boy》English at 《his》home; tutor 《a boy》 in English. ● 家庭教師をして学費を払う meet one's university expenses by *tutoring*.

カテーテル [<ドイツ語]〔医学〕a catheter /kǽθətər/.

カテキン〔化学〕catechin /kǽtətʃɪn/.

カテゴリー a cátegòry. (❗ class より堅い語)

かてくわえて かてて加えて (❗ その上、おまけに)

—がてら ● 散歩がてら(=の途中で)本屋に寄った I stopped by a bookstore *while* (I was) taking a walk. ● 京都での仕事がてら(=の仕事のついでに)金閣寺に行ってきた *When* I went to [was in] Kyoto on business, I visited the Kinkakuji Temple.

かでん 家伝 ● 家伝の名刀 a celebrated sword handed down from generation to generation [from father to son].

かでん 家電 ● 家電製品 home [household] electrical appliances. ● 家電メーカー a home electrical appliance manufacturer.

がてん 合点 ● 合点がいかない cannot understand (it). (⇨納得, 理解)

がでんいんすい 我田引水 (...を自分の都合のいいようにする) turn ... in one's (own) favor.

かと 過渡 图 (移り変わり) (a) transition. (⇨過渡期)

— **過渡的な** 形 transitional. ● 過渡現象 a *transitional* phenomenon.

*かど 角 ❶【物の】a corner;〔出っ張った〕an angle;〔端〕an edge. ● 木片の角を取る round off the *corners* of a piece of wood. ● 角のある[ない]石 an angular [a round] stone. ▶ 彼はピアノの角に頭をつけた He hit [struck] his head against [on] the *corner* [*edge*] of the piano.

❷【道の曲がり角】(街角) a corner; (道の曲がり目) a turn, a turning. ● 銀行の角を曲がって３軒目の家 the third house around the *corner* of the bank. ● 角の店 a store on [at] the *corner* (❗ on が普通. at は場所規定を強調); a *corner* store. ▶ 最初の角を左へ曲がりなさい Turn (to the) left at the

かど first *corner*./Turn [Go round] the first *corner* to the [your] left./Take the first *turn* [*turning*] to the [your] left. (🔔 もっと簡略化して、たとえば「最初の角は左へ、次は右へ曲がれ」は (Take the) first left, second right. ともいえる)
- 角が立つ 智に働けば角が立つ (⇨『草枕』) ● そんなことを言うと角が立つよ It will sound too *harsh* if you say that.
- 角がとれる become mellow; mellow.

かど 門 [出入り口] a door; [門] a gate; [家] a house. (⇨門(も)) ● 門(=1 軒)ごとに at every *house*. ● 笑う門には福きたる (ことわざ) Laugh and grow fat. (⇨笑う [成句])

かど 廉 (罪科) a charge; (容疑) a suspicion. ● 殺人のかどで手配中だ be wanted *for* murder. ▶警察は彼を殺人のかどで逮捕した The police arrested him *on a charge of* murder [*on a murder charge*].

かど 過度 ― 過度の 形 ● 過度の飲酒 excessive (↔moderate) drinking; *too much* drinking. (🔔 後の方が口語的) ● 過度の(=法外な)要求 an *unreasonable* [*an excessive*] demand.
― 過度に 副 ● 過度に働く work excessively [*to excess*]; overwrite.

かといって かと言って ●海外旅行もしたいが、かと言って貯金もしなくちゃならないし I'd like to take a trip abroad, *but on the other hand* I should try to save money.

かとう 下等 ― 下等な 形 [低級な] low(er), (より劣った) inferior, [品性の劣った] mean; (教養のない) vulgar. ●下等な人間 a *mean* fellow; a person of *mean* character.
- 下等動物 the lower (↔higher) animals.

かとう 果糖 fruit sugar; 〖化学〗 fructose, levulose.

かどう 可動 名 mobility; movability. ― 可動な 形 mobile; movable.
- 可動橋(きょう) a movable bridge. ●可動コイル計器 a moving-coil meter. ●可動堰(ぜき) a movable dam.

かどう 華道 (the art of) flower arrangement. (⇨生け花)
- 華道部 a flower arranging club.

かどう 稼働 動 (操業) operation. ●その工場の稼働時間 the plant's *running* time.
― 稼働する 動 (機械などが) run. ▶その工場は 24 時間体制で稼働している The factory *is working* twenty-four hours a day.
- 稼働率 the rate of operation.

-かどうか whether (*or not*), if ....

> 解説 whether が普通. if は whether より口語的で ask, see, know, doubt, wonder, tell, be not sure, find out, remember などの目的節となる場合に用いられる. (discuss は不可)

▶そこへ行くべきかどうか分からない I don't know *whether* [*if*] I should go there (*or not*). (🔔 I don't know *whether* [×*if*] *or not* I should go there. のように or not を直後に置く場合は if は不可) I don't know *whether* [×*if*] to go there (*or not*). (🔔 不定詞を従える場合は if は不可)/*Whether* [×*If*] I should go there (*or not*), I don't know. (🔔 目的節が文頭にある場合は if は不可) ●ご出席いただけるかどうかお知らせください Please let us know *whether* you can attend. (🔔 この場合 if では「もし出席できるなら...」の意ともなるので避けた方がよい) ●それは彼が来るかどうかにかかっている It depends on *whether* [×*if*] he comes (*or not*). (🔔 前置詞の後では if は不可)
▶問題は我々が君を助けられるかどうかだ The question is *whether* [×*if*] we can help you (*or not*). (🔔 be 動詞の補語の場合 if は不可. 主語の場合も同様: *Whether* [×*If*] we can help you (*or not*) is a difficult question.)

かとうきょうそう 過当競争 ●過当競争を始める come [enter] into excessive competition (*with*).

かとうせいじ 寡頭政治 (少数者による独裁的政治) oligarchy /ɑ́ləgɑ̀ːrki/.

かとき 過渡期 a period [a stage] of transition, a transition(al) period [stage]. ●子供から大人になる過渡期 the transition (period) from child (hood) to adult(hood); the period of adolescence. ▶我々は過渡期にある We are *in transition* [*a transition period*]. (🔔 今は前の方が普通)

かとく 家督 [跡継ぎ] (男) an heir, (女) an heiress; 〖家長の地位〗 the headship of a family; 〖遺産〗 (an) estate. ●家督を相続する inherit an *estate*.
- 家督相続 succession to a house.

かどぐち 門口 the door, the entrance; 〖門〗 the gate.

かどち 角地 a corner lot. ●南向きの角地 the *corner lot* facing south.

かどで 門出 (出発) a start. ●新しい人生の門出を祝う celebrate the *start* of (his) new life.

かとてき 過渡的 ― 過渡的な 形 (やや書) transitional.

かどばる 角張る 〖角のある〗 be angular; 〖堅苦しい〗 be formal [stiff, ceremonious]. ●角ばったあいさつを交わす exchange *formal* greetings.

かどばん 角番 〖勝敗を決する試合〗 a do-or-die game; a desperate game for survival. ▶大関は角番に追い込まれた The Ozeki champion was driven to *the brink of demotion*.

かどまつ 門松 a *kadomatsu*; (説明的に) New Year decorations made with pine branches, bamboo sticks, and plum tree sprigs, (which are) set up on either side of the front door [gate].

カトマンズ [ネパールの首都] Katmandu /kɑ̀ːtmɑːndúː/.

カドミウム 〖化学〗 cádmium (元素記号 Cd).
- カドミウム汚染 cadmium pollution [contamination].

かとりせんこう 蚊取り線香 (burn) a pyrethrum /paiˈriːθrəm/ coil (蚊よけ香) mosquito-repellent (incense).

カトリック (信者) a Catholic; (宗教) Catholicism.
- (ローマ)カトリック教会 the (Roman) *Catholic* Church.

カトレア 〖植物〗 a cattleya /kǽtliə/.

かどわかす 勾かす kidnap (a child). (⇨誘拐する)

かとんぼ 蚊蜻蛉 〖昆虫〗 a crane fly, (英) a daddy longlegs.

*****かな 仮名** *kana* (🔔 個々の字は C で単・複同形); (説明的に) a Japanese system of syllabic writing; 〖仮名表〗 the Japanese syllabary. ●歴史的[現代]仮名づかい the old [current] use of *kana*. ●仮名で書く write in 〚×with〛 *kana*. ●漢字に仮名を振る(=ルビを振る) (⇨ルビ)

-かな ▶そうかな Is that so?

かなあみ 金網 a wire net; (総称) wire netting; [囲い] a wire fence. ●金網を張る(=でおおう[仕切る]) cover [screen] (it) with *wire netting*; put up *wire netting* over [around] (it).

かない 家内 [(自分の)妻] my wife ((敬) wives) (⇨妻); 〖家族〗 a family. (⇨家族) ●家内安全を祈る pray for the well-being of one's *family*.
- 家内工業 a household [a cottage] industry.
- 家内労働 household labor.

*****かなう 叶う** [願望などが実現する] be realized

かなう

[fulfilled]. (夢などが本当になる) come* true. ●かなわぬ願い[夢; 恋] an *impossible* wish [dream; love]. ●(=できる)ことなら if *possible*. ▶ぼくの望みがかなった My wish *was realized* [*was fulfilled*, 《書》*was granted*]. (!夢 (dream) の場合は〈be granted《文書けない》/I *got* [*had*] my wish. ▶私の長年の夢がかなった My long-cherished dream *has come true* [*has been realized*]. (!前の方が口語的的)

かなう 適う 〖適する〗suit; (役立つ) serve; (要求などを満たす) meet, 《書》answer. ●彼の要求にかなう(=必要を満たす) *suit* [*serve, meet, answer*] his needs. ●建築規準[構想]にかなう(=従う) *conform to* the building code [one's idea]. ●理にかなった判断 a *reasonable* decision. ▶その車は君の目的にぴったりかなうだろう The car will *suit* [*serve*] your purpose nicely. ▶彼は私の理想にかなった男性です He *is* [*represents, measures up to*] my ideal.

*かなう 敵う ▶ゴルフでは彼にかなう[=匹敵する]者はいない No one can *match* him in golf./He *has no equal* in golf./(彼は他人にも劣らない) He *is second to none* in golf. (⇨敵わない)

かなえ 鼎 (3本足の鉄かま) a tripod kettle.
●鼎の軽重を問う (政治治の権威や実力を疑う) doubt the ruler's ability [prestige].

かなえる 叶える 〖実現させる〗realize; 〖聞き入れる〗《書》grant. (⇨叶う) ●神さま, どうか私の願いをかなえてください Oh God, please *answer* my prayer [《書》*grant* my wish].

かなか 哀(かな)か

かなきりごえ 金切り声 a shrill voice [cry]; (興奮・恐怖・苦痛などによる) a scream; a shriek (! scream より甲高い). (⇨叫び声, 叫ぶ) ●恐怖で金切り声を出す *scream* [*shriek*] in horror.

*かなぐ 金具 (金属製付属物) metal fittings.

かなくぎりゅう 金釘流 (なぐり書き) a scrawl; (乱雑な筆跡) crabbed handwriting.

かなぐりすてる かなぐり捨てる 〖脱ぎ捨てる〗throw* [fling*]... off. ●私は恥も外聞も(=いっさいの体面を)かなぐり捨てて一家を養うためにあらゆる職について働いた I *cast off* my dignity and did all sorts of jobs in order to feed my family.

かなけ 金気 (鉄分) a metallic taste.

*かなしい 悲しい 形

WORD CHOICE 悲しい

sad 悲嘆・悲痛をあらわす最も一般的な語. ●とても悲しく感じる feel very *sad*. ▶それを聞いて悲しく[気の毒に]思います I'm *sad* to hear that.

unhappy 不幸・悲しみ・不満などを表す. ●悲しい経験 *unhappy* experiences.

pathetic 哀れみや同情を誘うような悲しみを表す. ●その映画の一番悲しいシーン the most *pathetic* scene of the film.

頻度チャート

sad ████████████████████
unhappy ████████
pathetic ██
  20 40 60 80 100 (%)

sad (-dd-); sorrowful (!sad より強い感じの語); 〖不幸な〗unhappy; 〖(死などを)嘆き悲しむ〗mournful; 〖哀れな〗a *pathetic* story. ●悲しい顔つきをする look *sad* [*sorrowful, unhappy, mournful*]. (! have a

かなづち

sad face のようにもいう. 「悲しい顔つきをした人」は a sad-looking[-faced] person) ●悲しい気持ちになる, 悲しい思いをする feel *sad* [*sorrowful, unhappy*]. (⇨悲しむ) ●何度も悲しい目にあう have a lot of *sorrows* [*sad things*]. ●悲しいことには(=残念ながら) *sad* [*sorry*] to say; to my *sorrow* [*regret*]. (!文修飾語) ●なぜそんなに悲しいの Why are you so *sad* [*unhappy*]?/What makes you so *sad* [*unhappy*]? ●彼がいなくなると思うと悲しい It is *sad* [It makes me *sad*] to think that he won't be here any more. (!I am *sad* to think that..., また I am *sad* (that)... ともいえる) ●彼のもとを去るのが悲しかった I was *sad* to leave him.

——悲しげな, 悲しそうな 形 (悲しげな) sorrowful; mournful; unhappy; (悲しい) sad (-dd-). ●悲しそうな顔をする look *sad* [*sorrowful*].

——悲しそうに 副 sadly; sorrowfully; unhappily; mournfully. ●悲しそうに泣く weep *sorrowfully* [*mournfully*]. ▶彼は悲しそうに私を見た He looked *sadly* at me./He gave me a sad look.

かなしきがんく『悲しき玩具』*Sad Toys*. (参考)石川啄木の歌集)

かなしばり 金縛り ●金縛りにする 〖強く縛りつける〗be fast bound hand and foot; 〖金で自由を束縛する〗be tied down with money; 〖恐怖などで身動きができない〗be rooted to the spot [ground] 《in horror》.

*かなしみ 悲しみ 〖悲しい気持ち〗sadness; 〖死・不幸などに対する〗 (a) sorrow; 〖強烈で短期間の〗《書》 (a) grief. (! 通例, grief は「悲しみの種」の意では〖C〗で扱う ⇨ s. sorrow はしばしば複数形で) ●息子を失った悲しみ one's *sorrow* [*grief*] at the loss of one's son. ●悲しみに打ちひしがれた人 a *grief-stricken* person. ●悲しみに沈んでいる be in deep *grief*; be deep in *grief*. ▶彼の死は我々にとって大きな悲しみだ His loss is a great *sorrow* to us. ▶彼は悲しみで気も狂わんばかりであった He was nearly mad with *grief*. ▶彼は彼女が死んだという知らせを聞いて悲しみに打ちひしがれた He was overcome [overwhelmed] by [with] *grief* when he heard the news of her death./(悲しみでいっぱいにした) The news of her death filled him with *grief* [*sorrow*]. (⇨悲しむ)

かなしむ 悲しむ feel [be] sad; feel sorrow; 〖深く悲しむ〗grieve. ●人の死を悲しむ feel *sad* about a person's death; *grieve for* a dead person; *grieve about* [*at, over*] a person's death. ▶ は悲しみの原因を示す. over は後ろにめぐらうよくよく悲しむ気持ちを示す. ●悲しむべき (悲しい) sad; sorrowful; (嘆かわしい)《書》deplorable; (遺憾な)《書》regrettable. ▶彼らはその知らせを聞いて深く悲しんだ They *grieved* deeply [*felt* very *sad*] *at* [*to* hear] the news./The news *grieved* them deeply [*made* them very *sad*]./They *felt* great *sorrow* when they heard the news.

かなた 彼方 ●海上はるかかなたに *far out* at sea. ●海のかなた(=向こう)から *from beyond* [(越えて) *across*] the sea. ●はるかかなたに(=遠くに明かりが見える) see a light *far in the distance* [*far away*]. ▶太陽は水平線のかなたに沈んだ The sun went down *below* the horizon.

カナダ 〖国名〗Canada (!公式名も同じ). (首都Ottawa) ●カナダ人 a Canadian; (全体に) the Canadians. ●カナダ(人)の Canadian /kənéidiən/.

かなだらい 金盥 a metal basin; (洗面器) a washbasin.

かなづかい 仮名遣い (⇨仮名)

かなづち 金槌 a hammer. ●くぎ抜き付き金づち a

claw *hammer*. ●金うちでくぎを打つ *hammer in a nail*; *hammer a nail (into a board)*; *drive [hit] a nail (into a board) with a hammer*. ▶私は金うちなし(=ひとかきも泳げない) I can't swim a stroke.
●金槌頭 (⇨石頭)
カナッペ [<フランス語] a canapé /kǽnəpéɪ/.
かなてこ 鉄梃 a crowbar.
かなでる 奏でる (演奏する) play.
かなぶん 金ぶん 【昆虫】 a scarab beetle.
かなへび 金蛇 【動物】 a Japanese grass lizard.
かなぼう 金棒 an iron rod. ●鬼に金棒 (⇨鬼 [成句])
●金棒引き (人のうわさをあちこち話して歩く人) a rumormonger; a scandalmonger.
カナマイシン 【薬学】 (抗生物質) kanamycin.
かなめ 要 ❶ [扇の] a pivot (比喩的にも用いる); 【大切な点】 the point. ▶そこが議論の要だ That's the *point [pivot]* of our argument.
かなもじ 仮名文字 (⇨⑳ 仮名).
***かなもの** 金物 (集合的) hardware, 《英》 ironmongery; 【金具】 metal fittings.
●金物屋 (店) a hárdware stòre; 《英》 an ironmonger's (shop); (人) a hárdware dèaler, 《英》 an ironmonger. ▶金物店でくぎを買う buy nails at a *hardware store*.
***かならず** 必ず ❶ [きっと] surely, certainly; (きっと…する) be sure [certain] to do; [間違いなく] without fail (⚠通例約束・命令などを強調する); [間違いなく…する) not fail to do; [何としても] at all costs.

> 解説 surely は通例主観的判断を交えて「確かな」ことを述べるのに対し, certainly はある距離をおいて客観的にいう場合に用いる. したがって surely より certainly の方が確信の度が強い. なお, 《米》 では certainly の意で surely を用いる傾向がある. surely, certainly とも通例助動詞の後か動詞の前に置かれる.
> (2) surely は主観的判断を表すことから話し手の強い希望や信念を表すことがある. このときは通例文頭か文尾に置かれる: 君は必ずそこへ行くんだね *Surely* you are to go there.

▶彼は必ず来るでしょう He will *surely [certainly]* come./He *is sure [certain] to* come. (⚠以上2例では主語 He でなら話し手の確信を表す. したがって話し手を主語にして *I'm sure [certain] (that)* he will come. ともいえる)/*It is certain (that)* he will come. (⚠ It は形式的に立てた客観的な言い方. ×It is sure that …. は通例不可)/He *won't fail [×never fails] to* come. (⚠ never fail to do は 1 回限りのことには用いない (⇨❷))▶必ずこの手紙を出してください *Be sure to* [《話》 *and*] mail this letter. (⚠答えとして「ええ必ずそうするわ」は I *sure* will.)/*Don't fail* [×*Never fail*] *to* mail this letter. (⚠ Mail this letter *without fail*. はやや堅い言い方)/*Remember [Don't forget] to* mail this letter./*Make sure (that)* you mail this letter. (⚠通例 that 節中に未来を表す助動詞を用いない)

❷ [常に] always, without fail (⚠後の方が強意的で堅い語); (いつも…する) never fail to do; [必然的に] necessarily. ▶必ずと言っていいほど *always*. ▶彼は必ず遅刻してくる He is *always [always comes] late.* (⚠ always の位置については (⇨いつも))/He *never fails to* be [come] late. ▶軍拡競争は必ず戦争を引き起こす An arms race *necessarily* leads to war. (⚠ … causes war は不自然)

❸ [必ず…することにしている] make a point of 《*doing*》. ▶私は必ず早く寝ることにしている I *make a point of going* [*make it a rule to go*] to bed early. (⚠(1) make it a rule to do は非常に堅い言い方で, 今は特別の場合を除いて用いられない. 日常では代わりに always, every, never などを用いる: I *always* go to bed early./I go to bed early *every* night./I *never* go to bed late (at night). (2) habit, custom を用いて, It is my *habit [custom]* to go to bed early./I am in the habit [have a habit] of going to bed early. のようにもいう)

❷ [必ずしも…とは限らない] (頻度的に) not always; (論理的に) not necessarily; (数量的に) not all [every]; (厳密に) not exactly. ▶がんは必ずしも不治の病ではない Cancer is *not always [necessarily]* a fatal disease. ▶すべての人が必ずしも幸せとは限らない *Nót all* people are [*Nót éveryone is*] ╱*háppy.*/*Áll* people are [*Éveryone is*] *nót* ╲*háppy.* (⚠ happy を下げ調子(╲)に読むと「すべての人が幸せではない」のように全否定の意にもとれるため避けられる)

会話 「あの講演どう思った」「必ずしもよかったとはいえないよ」 "What did you think of the lecture?" "It *wasn't exactly* good."

❸ [...すれば必ず~する] cannot [never]… without~; whenever…, ~. ▶このセーターを見ると必ず姉のことを思い出します *Whenever [Every time]* I see this sweater, I *(always)* think of my sister. (⚠ always を添える方が強意的)/(やや書) I *never* see [*can't look at*] this sweater *without* thinking of my sister. (⚠前の例よりさらに強意的. 以上の例で think of の代わりに remember を用いると普段は姉のことを忘れていることを暗示する)/This sweater *always* reminds me of my sister.

***かなり** rather; 《主に英》 quite; fairly; 《話》 pretty; considerably (⚠通例比較級・動詞を修飾); well* (⚠通例前置詞句の前で).

> 解説 rather, quite, fairly の順で意味が弱くなる. rather は本来は「ある程度」の意が控えめに言ってかえって意味を強める. quite は 「けっこう」, fairly は 「まあまあ」に近い. この用法の quite は通例程度を表す形容詞・動詞を修飾し, 《主に英》で用いられる. 《米》では通例 「まったく」の意で用いる. ただし極限状態を表す語を修飾するときは米英ともに 「まったく」の意となることに注意. また好ましくない意味の語を, fairly は好ましい意味の語を修飾することが多いが, この区別は絶対的なものではない. なお, fairly を好ましい意味の語に用いても意味が弱く, たいていは通例誉め言葉とはならない: あの映画は部分的にはかなりおもしろかったが, 長すぎる Parts of the film were *fairly* interesting, but it was too long.

▶今朝はかなり暑いですね It's *pretty [rather, fairly, quite]* hot this morning. (⚠ rather は暑くて困る, fairly は心地よく暑いことを含意する. pretty にはこのような含みはない) ▶彼女は水泳がかなりうまい She is *rather [quite]* a good swimmer. (⚠(1) rather がよい意味の語を修飾するときは話し手の驚きを暗示する. (2) 「a+形+ერ可算名詞」を修飾する場合は She is a *rather [a quite]* good swimmer. の語順も可能だが quite の場合はあまり一般的ではない)/She swims *rather [pretty, fairly, quite]* well. ▶彼はかなり努力した He made *rather [quite, ×pretty, ×fairly]* an effort. (⚠ rather, quite は 「a+程度を表す名詞 (effort, fool, nuisance, failure) 」を修飾可. ただし, ×…a rather [a quite] effort の語順不可) ▶その患者はかなりよくなった The patient has gotten *rather [considerably]* better. (⚠通例 quite, fairly は比較級の前では用いない)/The patient has *rather [quite, considerably]* improved in health. (!rather, quite はにかに enjoy, like など程度を表す動詞の前で使用可) ▶彼は60をかなり超えているに違いない He must be *well past [over] sixty*.

──かなりの 形 (数量・大きさ・程度などが) considerable, a good...; (以外れた) (主に米) quite a... (!よい意味で用いることが多いが、悪い意味にも用いる). ▶かなりの(=かなり多くの)人 a *considerable number* of [*a good many*] people; *quite a few* [*a good few*, 《書》*not a few*] people. ▶彼はかなりの(=かなり優れた)学者だ He is *quite* [《話》*something of*] *a scholar*.

カナリア 〖鳥〗a canary /kənéəri/.
● カナリア諸島 【大西洋にある諸島】 the Canaries, the Canàry Íslands.

がなる (大声で言う) shout 《*at*》. (⇨わめく)

かなわない 敵わない 〖匹敵しない〗be no match 《*for*》; 〖堪えられない〗can't stand [bear, put up with] (!bear より stand の方が口語的); 〖ひどすぎる〗《話》be too much 《*for*》. ▶料理ではお母さんにはかなわない *I'm no match for* my mother in cooking. ▶こう暑くてはかなわない *I can't stand [put up with]* such hot weather./Such hot weather *is too much for* me [*is more than I can bear*, *is unbearable to me*]. ▶将棋にかけてはクラスでだれも彼にはかなわない When it comes to *shogi*, he *has no equal* in our class [no one in our class can beat him]./He is the best player of *shogi* in our class. ▶また小遣いかい。かなわないな Pócket money *again! You're impossible.*

かなん 火難 (a) fire; a fire disaster. (⇨火災, 火事)
● 火難除け a charm [《書》a talisman] against fire.

かなん 河南 ● 河南省 Henan /hánɑːn/ Province.

かに 蟹 a crab. ● カニの身 crab (meat). ● カニのはさみ 《a pair of》 claws. ● カニの甲 a *crab* shell; a carapace. ● カニにはさまれる be nipped [pinched] by a *crab*. ▶カニは横にしか動けない *Crabs* move [walk] only sideways.
● 蟹缶 canned crab. ● 蟹工船 a crab factory ship. ● 蟹玉 (説明的に) a Chinese-style omelet containing sautéed /soutéid/ crab meat and vegetables.

かにく 果肉 ■ (動) flesh; (柔らかい) (the) pulp. ▶食物繊維の多い果肉 the *pulp* (which is) high in fiber.

かにこうせん 『蟹工船』*The Factory Ship*. (参考) 小林多喜二の小説

かにざ 蟹座 〖占星・天文〗Cancer (!the はつけない); (巨蟹(きょ)宮) 〖占星〗the Crab. (⇨乙女座) ● 蟹座 (生まれ)の人 a Cancer, a Cancerian. (!後の方は形容詞としても用いる)

がにまた がに股 bandy legs, bowlegs. ▶彼はがに股だ He has *bandy legs* [*bowlegs*]./He is *bandy-legged* [*bow-legged*].

かにゅう 加入 图 (仲間に加わること) joining, entry; (承認されて入ること) admission; (電話などの) subscription. ● 電話加入者 a telephone *subscriber*. ● 日本の国連加入 Japan's *admission* to [*into*] the United Nations.

──加入する 動 join; be admitted 《*to, into*》; subscribe 《*for*》; (会員になる) become* a member 《*of*》. (⇨加盟する, 入会する) ▶そのクラブに加入する join [become a member of] the club. ▶生命保険に加入する *take out [buy]* life insurance.

カヌー a canóe. ● カヌーをこぐ paddle a *canoe*. ▶カヌーで川下りをする go down a river by [in a] *canoe*; canoe down a river.

⇨かね 金 money, 《話》cash. (⇨金銭)

解説 (1) 通例単数形で a をつけないが、通貨の種類を表すときは Ⓒ: different *moneys* of different countries (諸国のいろいろなお金). (2) *moneys*, 時に *monies* と複数形にすると「(政府などの)財源, 基金」の意: tax *moneys* (税収入), foreign aid *monies* (外国援助資金).

① 【~金】 ● 偽金 counterfeit [bogus, fake] money. ● 不正な金 dirty [《やや書》ill-gotten] *money*. ● 莫大な[わずかな]金 a huge [a small] sum *of money*. ▶(一万円札を出されて)もっと細かいお金はございませんか Have 〔‾ Got〕 anything smaller? (!それぞれ Do you have ... [《話》Have you got ...] の最初の部分が省略されたもの)

② 【金が[は]】 ● 私の自由にできる金が10万円あった I had 100,000 yen at my disposal. (!*at one's disposal* は「...の自由になる」の意) ▶飛行機でハワイまで行くのにどれくらいお金がかかりますか How much does it *cost* us to fly to Hawaii? ▶このアパートは1人で住むには金がかかりすぎる This apartment is too *expensive* for one person.
会話 「ねえ, パパ, 新しいアンプが欲しいんだ」「それは無理だ。そんなの買うだけの金はない〔そんな金がどこにある〕」"Hey, Dad, I want a new amp." "That's impossible. We don't have enough *money* to buy one (with). [《話》そんな余裕がない] How can we afford to buy one?]"(!《話》では通例 with は省略される)

③ 【金の】 ● 金の亡者 a *money*-mad. ● 金のために働く work *for money*. ▶今お金の持ち合わせがない I have no *money* [《話》*cash*] *on* [*with*, 《英》*about*] me. (!金なとが小切手に普通) ▶金で金の貸し借りをしないのが私の主義だ It is my principle never to lend or borrow *money*. ▶万事金の世の中だという考え方もいる Some people think that *money* is everything [almighty] in this world. ▶それは金の問題だ It's a matter of *money* [金銭上の問題] a *financial* problem].

④ 【金を】 ● 金を引き出す draw (out) [withdraw] *money* 《*from* a bank》. ● 金を預ける deposit *money* 《*in* a bank》. ▶お金を少し貸してくださいませんか Will you lend me some [✗*any*] *money*? (!間接的に Do you have some [✗*any*] *money*? ともいう) ▶車を買うために金をためている I am saving *money* to buy a car./I'm saving (up) for a car. ▶彼女は推理小説を書いて金をもうけている She makes [earns] *money* by writing detective stories. ▶そのかわいそうな子供たちのためにお金を集めた We raised *money* for the poor children. ▶彼女は書物にたくさん金を使う She spends a lot of [《書》*much*, ✗*many*] *money* on books./She spends a lot of *money* (in) buying books. (!in のない方が普通) ▶借りていた金を返した I paid back the *money* I had borrowed. ▶なけなしの金をはたいて彼にプレゼントを買った I spent what little *money* I had to buy a present for him.
会話 「新しい服が欲しいわ」「だれがその金を払うんだい」"I'd like to buy a new dress." "Who's going to *pay for* it?" (!「...の代金を払う」の意)

⑤ 【金で】 ● 私はその本を自分の金で買った I bought the book *with* [✗*by*] my own *money*. ▶それはアメリカの金で100ドルする It costs 100 dollars in U.S. *currency*. ▶彼は金で釣られるような人ではない He is not a man who can be seduced *by* [*with*] *money*.

● 金が物を言う《ことわざ》Money talks.
● 金に飽(あ)かす ▶彼は金に飽かせて(=金をふんだんに使って)骨とう品を買った He spent a huge sum of

money on antiques.
- 金に糸目をつけない be free [generous] with one's money.
- 金になる ●金になる(=儲かる)取り引き a *profitable* [*a lucrative*] (↔*an unprofitable*) *deal*. ▶彼は金にならないことは決してやろうとしない He will never do any job that does not *pay*. (❗ *pay* は「引き合う」▶生易しい仕事ではないけれど金になる(=ペイがいいんだ It's not easy work, but *I'm well paid for it* [but the *money's good*].
- 金の切れ目が縁の切れ目 The end of *money* is the end of *love*; 《ことわざ》When poverty comes in at the door, love flies out of the window.
- 金のなる木 the money tree; (イソップ物語の) the goose that lays the golden egg.
- 金は天下の回りもの Money comes and goes. (⇨行き来)/《ことわざ》Money is a great traveler in the world.

*かね 鐘 a bell; (どら) a gong; [鐘の音](音楽的な調子の) a chime (of bells); (大きく長い) a peal. ●鐘を鳴らす ring [toll] a *bell* (❗ *toll* は「晩鐘・弔鐘などを長い間(″)をおいて鳴らす」の意); (突いて) strike a *bell*; (たたいて) beat a *gong*. ●誰(″)がために鐘は鳴る[書名]*For Whom the Bell Tolls*. ▶教会の鐘ががらんがらんと鳴った The church *bells* rang ding-dong. ▶寺の鐘がごーん、ごーんと鳴り響いた There sounded the peals of a temple *bell*. ▶時計台の鐘が3時を告げた The *bells* of the clock tower chimed three (o'clock) [struck three (o'clock), (3回) struck three times].

かね 鉦 a handy gong (shaped like a basin). ●鉦や太鼓で(=やっきになって)捜す search [hunt, look] high and low 《for》.

かねあい 兼ね合い balance. ▶両者[輸入額と輸入額]の兼ね合いが難しい It's hard to *balance* both of them [exports *with* imports]. ▶予算の兼ね合いで(=予算のことを考慮して)その計画を中止した *Taking* the budget *into consideration*, we canceled the plan.

かねあまり 金余り having more money than can be spent. (⇨ 金詰まり)

かねかし 金貸し a moneylender; (高利貸し) a usurer; 《話》a loan shark.

かねて (長い間) for a long time; (すでに) already; (何度も) several times. (⇨かねて) ▶おうわさはかねより伺っております I've heard *a lot* about you.

かねくいむし 金食い虫 ●大型車はまったく金食い虫だ 《話》A big car just *eats up* money.

かねぐり 金繰り ●金繰りがつかない can't raise (enough) money.

かねじゃく 曲尺, 矩尺 a carpenter's square; a metal measure.

かねずく 金尽く ●何でも金ずくで解決しようとする try to settle everything *with* [*by force of*] *money*.

かねそなえる 兼ね備える ●知力と勇気を兼ね備えている(=同時に持っている) *have both* intellect *and* courage.

かねたたき 鉦叩き[昆虫]a bush cricket.

かねつ 加熱 图 heating. ── 加熱する 動 heat ... (up). ●加熱器 a heater. ▶「ストーブ」の意にもなる

かねつ 過熱 图 overheating. ▶過熱気味の論議 a rather heated argument.
── 過熱する 動 モーターが過熱した The motor *overheated*.

かねづかい 金遣い ▶彼は金遣いが荒い(=惜しげもなく使う) He *spends* his *money* too *freely* [*wastefully*]./(乱費する) He is *extravagant*./He is a *spendthrift*.

かねづまり 金詰まり ●金詰まり(=金の不足)のため because of the *shortage* [*scarcity*] *of money*. ▶そのころは金詰まりだった(= 金融がひっぱくしていた) *Money was tight* then. (⇨ 金余り)

かねづる 金蔓 [お金を出してくれる人]《look for [find]》a (financial) backer [supporter] 《for》; (頼まれるとすぐお金などを出す人)《話》a soft [easy] touch; [金もうけになるもの] a moneymaker 《for》; 《話》a (real) goldmine 《for》(❗ 後の方は通例単数形で).

かねて (以前に) before, previously; (前もって) beforehand, in advance; (すでに) already. ▶かねてお知らせしたとおり、4月1日に会議を行います We are having a meeting on April 1, as we have informed you *before* [*previously*, *beforehand*]./We are having a meeting on April 1, as we have *already* informed you. ▶我々はかねてから(=長い間)懸案となっていた問題について議論した We discussed the problem that had been unsettled *for a long time*. ▶おうわさはかねてからうかがっております I've heard *a lot* about you./I've *already* heard about you./(何回も) I've been told about you *several times*.

-かねない -兼ねない be likely to 《do》; [できる] be capable of 《doing》(❗ 皮肉にも用いる). ▶彼ならそれくらいのことはやりかねない(=するだろう[かもしれない]) He *would* [*could*, *may*] do that. (❗ He に強勢を置く. would, could は仮定法)/(しそうである) He *is likely to* do that./*It's likely that* he will do that./(する可能性がある) He *is capable of doing* that./(するのをためらわないだろう) He *wouldn't hesitate to* [(しさえするだろう) *would go so far as to*] do that./(やったのも不思議ではない) *It's no* [*little*, *small*] *wonder* (*that*) he did that himself./(しないとは思わない) I *don't think* he *is above* (doing) that.

かねばなれ 金離れ ●金離れがいい[悪い] be generous [stingy] with (one's) money.

かねまわり 金回り ●金回りがいい be well off; be in funds. ●金回りが悪い be badly off; be short of money. ▶彼はここのところは(以前よりも)金回りがいいようだ He seems (to be) *better off* now.

かねめ 金目 monetary value. ●金目の物 an article *of value*; (金・宝石などの貴重品) valuables.

かねもうけ 金儲け moneymaking. ●金儲けのためにランを栽培する cultivate orchids *for profit*. ▶彼は金儲けのためなら何でもする He will do anything to *make money*. ▶彼は金儲け(をするの)がうまい He is good at *making money*.

*かねもち 金持ち a rich [a wealthy] person. (❗ wealthy の方が堅い語. rich が資産の面だけをいうのに対し、wealthy は地位や生活の安定さと富裕層に重点がある) ●金持ちの人々 *rich* [*wealthy*] people; 《書》the *rich* [*wealthy*] (複数扱い). ●金持ちの娘 a *rich* man's daughter. (❗ ✗ a rich daughter ではない) ●金持ちになる get [become] *rich*. (❗ 一夜にして[突然]金持ちになるの意の慣用表現は strike it *rich* がある) ●金持ちの家に生まれる be born into a *rich* [a *wealthy*] family; be born *rich*; 《書》be born with a silver spoon in one's mouth. ▶あの男は金持ちだ He is *rich* [*wealthy*]. (❗ 前の方は露骨な感じの語)/He's *well-off* 《話》*well-to-do*)./(資産家だ)《書》He is *a man of means*. ▶金持ちも貧乏人も政府を支持している Both *rich* and *poor* support the government. (❗ 対句的に用いるときは通例 the を省略する)
- 金持ち喧嘩(")せず The rich never quarrel./《ことわざ》Agree, for the law is costly.

かねる 兼ねる 〖両方の役目をする〗serve both as A and (as) B; 〖兼務する, 兼用される〗double as ...; 〖結合する〗combine 《A with B》. ▶この部屋は書斎と居間を兼ねている This room *serves both as a* study *and as a* living room. (⇨兼) ▶物理の先生は水泳のコーチも兼ねていた The physics teacher *doubled as a* swimming coach. ▶この映画は教育と娯楽を兼ねている This is a movie which *combines* education *with [and]* recreation. (!*and* は対等の関係を示す) ▶大も小も兼ねる The greater *serves for* the lesser as well. ▶彼は商用と観光を兼ねてアメリカに行った He went to America *both* on business *and* for pleasure.

-かねる -兼ねる 〖できない〗cannot《do》; be unable to《do》; 〖ためらう〗hesitate《*to* do》; 〖立場にない〗be not in a position to《do》. ▶君の案には承服しかねる I *cannot [am unable to, hesitate to]* agree to your plan. ▶それは私には何とも申し上げかねます I'm afraid I *can't [am not in a position to]* say anything about it. ▶彼女にはどうもその話はしかねます(=する気にはなれない) I *can't bring myself to* tell her the story. (!否定文・疑問文で用いる)
〘会話〙「あのう, 郵便局はどっちでしょうか」「ちょっと分かりかねますが」"Excuse me. Which way is the post office?" "Sorry, I'*m not really sure*."

かねんせい 可燃性 图 combustibility.
—— **可燃性の** 形 combustible (↔incombustible), inflammable, 《主に米》flammable (↔nonflammable).

かのう 可能 —— **可能な** 形 possible; (実行可能な) practicable. ▶可能な仕事 a *possible* task. ▶実行可能な計画 a *practicable* plan. ▶これは返品可能ですか Is it *possible* (for me) to return this? (!不定詞の目的語を主語にして ×Is this possible to return? とはいえない (⇨不可能). また人を主語にして ×Am I possible to return this? ともいえない)/Can I return this?/*Can [Do]* you take it back? ▶彼がその川を泳いで渡るのは可能だ It is *possible* for him to swim across the river. (!(1)「能力」を表す場合、主語を置くとすれば for him の後. (2)「可能性」を表す場合と異なり ×It is possible that he swims across the river. は不可 (⇨図))/He *can [is able to,* ×*is* possible to] swim across the river. ▶仕様の変更が可能か検討してみます We'll discuss a *possible* change in specifications.
—— **可能にする** 動 enable 《him *to* do》, make* it possible 《*for* him *to* do》. ▶文字の発明が後世に記録を残すことを人類に可能にした The invention of writing *enabled [made it possible for]* man *to* hand down records./Man *became able to* hand down records thanks to [because of] the invention of writing. (!後の文の方が口語的)

かのう 化膿 图 〖医学〗suppuration.
—— **化膿する** 動 suppurate; fester. (!前の方は堅い語/〘膿〙かき傷が化膿した The scratch *has festered.*

かのうせい 可能性 图 a possibility; (特に好ましい) a chance. ▶彼が成功する可能性はない[少しある; 大いにある] There is no [some; every] *possibility of* his succeed*ing* [that he will succeed, ×*for* him *to* succeed]./There is no [a small; a good] *chance of* his success [that he will succeed, ×*for* him *to* succeed]. ▶今夜は雪になる可能性は高い] There is a [quite a] *possibility that* it will snow tonight./There is a [strong] *pos-sibility of* snow tonight./It's *possible* [quite possible, probable] (that) it'll snow tonight. (!いずれも quite より ×highly, ×very は不可. 《話》ではしばしば that は省略される)/*Possibly [Probably]* it will snow tonight. (⇨たぶん)
〘会話〙「彼が仕事につける可能性はどれぐらいですか」「かなり高いと思うよ」"What are his *chances of getting* a job?" "I think they're pretty good."/"What's the *possibility of* his getting a job?" "I think it's pretty good." (!いずれも good の代わりに ×high は不可)

かのこ 鹿の子 —— **鹿の子の** 形 (まだらの) white-spotted; dappled.

:かのじょ 彼女 代 (彼女が[は]) she (徳 they); (彼女の) her (their); (彼女に[を]) her (them); (彼女のもの) hers; theirs; (彼女自身) herself (them-selves). (⇨私(⌒))
—— **彼女** 图 (恋人) a girlfriend; a love. ▶かわいい彼女 (one's) pretty *girlfriend* [*love*]. ▶こちらはぼくの彼女で田中恵美さん This is my *girlfriend,* Emi Tanaka.

カノン 〖音楽〗(追復曲) a canon /kǽnən/.
—— **カノン砲** (兵器) a cannon /kǽnən/.

かば 樺 〖植物〗a birch (tree).

かば 河馬 〖動物〗a hippopotamus /hìpəpɑ́təməs/ (徳 ~es, hippopotami), 《話》a hippo (徳 ~s), a river horse.

***カバー** 图 〖覆い〗(特に上に被せて保護するもの) a cover ▶日本語の「本のカバー」は a (book [dust]) jacket, 《英》は a book's wrapper という. cover は本の表紙のこと; (一般に上に被せられる) a *covering*; (ベッドの) a bedspread; (まくらの) a pillowcase. ▶いすにカバー(=覆い)をかける put a *cover* over [on] the chair; cover a chair. ▶カバーを取る take off a *cover* 《*from*》. ▶カバーをつけないとぬれてしまうよ *Cover* it or it'll get wet.
—— **カバーする** 動 ❶〖埋め合わせる〗cover. ▶彼女がいない分をカバーする *cover for* her. ▶損失をカバーする *make up for* [*compensate*] the losses.
❷〖塁を守る〗▶二塁をカバーする *cover* second base. ▶三塁がカバーされていない Third base is un*covered* (undefended).
● **カバーガール** 〖雑誌の表紙を飾る女性〗a cover girl. ● **カバーガラス** cover glass. (参考) 顕微鏡のスライドに載せる標本をおおうガラス. ● **カバーストーリー** a cover story. (参考) 雑誌の表紙写真に関する特集記事 ● **カバーチャージ** (テーブルチャージ) a cóver chàrge.

カバーリング 〖サッカー〗covering.

かばいだて 庇い立て ▶かばいだてする(=必要以上にかばうのは未成年のためにならない *Being overprotective of* minors isn't good for them.

かばいろ 蒲色 (赤みを帯びた黄色) reddish yellow.
かばいろ 樺色 (やや明るい茶色) light [pale] brown.

***かばう 庇う** 〖保護する〗protect 《*from*》; 〖気をつける〗take* care 《*of*》; 〖弁護する〗stand* up [stick* up] 《*for*》, speak* up 《*for*》. ▶傷ついた腕をかばう *take care of* one's injured arm. ▶弱い者をかばってやりなさい You should *protect* the weak. ▶彼は彼女をかばって(=のために)うそをついている He's lying *on* her *account*. ▶母はいつも私をかばってくれる My mother always *stands up* [*sticks up, speaks up*] *for* me.

〘翻訳のこころ〙少年はずっとわたしのそばにいて, 満員電車の雑踏から, さりげなくわたしをかばってくれていた (江國香織『デューク』) The boy stayed close to me and somewhat (unpretentiously) *pro-tected* me from the crush on the crowded train. (!(1)「かばう」は protect で表す. (2) un-pretentiously (わざとらしくなく) は堅い表現)

がはく 画伯 a (great) painter [artist]. ▶渡辺画伯と対談する have a talk with *Painter* Watanabe.

かばしら 蚊柱 ▶蚊柱が立っていた There was a *mosquito pillar* floating in the air.

がばっと ▶がばっと(=大量に)本を買い込む buy *a large number of* books [*a large amount of* gold]. ▶がばっと起き直る sit up *with a jerk*. ▶彼はがばっと起きた He *jumped* out of bed.

ガバナンス [統治] governance.

かばね 屍 a (dead) body. (⇨屍(しかばね))

かばやき 蒲焼き ウナギの蒲焼きを broiled [grilled, (米) barbecued] eel with (soy) sauce.

かばらい 過払い 名 overpaying. ── **過払いする** 動 pay 《him》 too much 《for》; overpay 《him *for*》.

かばり 蚊鉤 a [an artificial] fly.
● 蚊ばり釣り fly-fishing.

かはん 河畔 the riverside. ●河畔に by [on] the *riverside*. ●河畔の宿 a *riverside* hotel. ●利根川河畔に *on* the Tone (River).

:かばん 鞄 a bag 〘最も一般的な語で, school, traveling などの修飾語を伴って各種のかばんを表す〙; 〘通学かばん〙 a satchel; 〘書類用〙 (革製の) a briefcase; (小型で折りたたみ式の) a portfolio 《愈~s》; (角型の) an attaché case; 〘旅行用〙 (大型の) a trunk; (小型の) a suitcase; (さらに小型の) a grip.

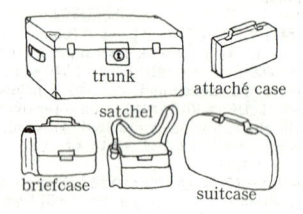

trunk
attaché case
satchel
briefcase
suitcase

● かばんを開ける[閉める] open [close] a *bag*. ▶子供たちは肩からかばんを下げて学校から帰ってきた Children came back from school with their *school bags* [*satchels*] over their shoulders.

〘古今ことばの系譜〙『どんぐりと山猫』
こんなのです. 字はまるでへたで, 墨もがわって指にけくっくいでした. けれども一郎はうれしくてうれしくてたまりませんでした. はがきをそっと学校のかばんにしまって, うちじゅうとんだりはねたりしました. That was all. The writing was terrible, and the ink so blobby it almost stuck to his fingers. But Ichiro was quite delighted. He put the card in his satchel when no one was looking and took it to school, and all day long he was bouncing up and down with joy. (John Bester) ※はがきは学校のかばんに入れたのだが, それを学校に持って行ったわけではない. and took it to school を取りたい 〘『どんぐりと山猫』〙

● かばん持ち (上役のお供) (a) private secretary 《to Mr. A》(⇨秘書); (有力者の腰ぎんちゃく) 《軽蔑的》 a hanger-on.

がばん 画板 a drawing board; a panel.

かはんしん 下半身 the lower half of the body. ●下半身(の性的意味合いで) below the navel. ●下半身が麻痺(まひ)している *The lower part* of his *body* is paralyzed./He is paralyzed *below the waist* [*from the waist down*].

かはんすう 過半数 a [the] majority. ●過半数を獲得する[占める; に達していない] gain [hold, have; lack, be short of] a *majority*. ●過半数を占めてい be in (the) majority. ●過半数の得票で選ばれる be elected by *a* (large) *majority* of votes.

かひ 可否 the pros and cons. ●その計画の実行の可否について話し合った We discussed all *the pros and cons* of the plan before carrying it out./(実行できるかどうか) We discussed *whether* [*if*, ×*that*] we *could* carry out the plan.

かひ 歌碑 a monument inscribed with a (*tanka*) poem. ●啄木の歌碑を建てる build [erect] *a monument* with Ishikawa Takuboku's *tanka*.

*かび 黴 mold; (白っぽいかび) mildew. ●青かび blue [green] *mold*. ●かびが生える go moldy; *Mold* grows. ●かびのはえたチーズ *moldy* cheese. ●かび臭い物置部屋 a *musty* storeroom. ●ぼくの革のジャケットに一面にかびが生えている There's *mold* all over my leather jacket.

かび 華美 名 (はで) showiness. ── **華美な** 形 《通例軽蔑的》 showy; 《華やかな》 《話》 gorgeous.

かひつ 加筆 名 (改善) (an) improvement; (修正) (a) revision 《of》; (仕上げの一筆) a touch. (⇨仕上げ)
── **加筆する** 動 (訂正してよくする) correct and improve 《a manuscript》; (修正する) revise; (絵などに手を加える) retouch, touch 《a painting》 up.

がひつ 画筆 a paintbrush.

がびょう 画鋲 (米) a thumbtack, (英) a drawing pin. ●壁に画びょうでとめる *pin up* 《a notice》 on [to] the wall; put 《a notice》 on the wall with *thumbtacks*.

かびる 黴びる go* moldy. (⇨黴(かび))

かひん 佳品 (すぐれた作品) an excellent work; (すぐれた食品)《xan》 excellent food.

*かびん 花瓶 (a flower) vase; (花の入った) a vase of flowers. ●花びんに花をさす[生ける] put [arrange] flowers in a *vase*.

かびん 過敏 名 化学物質過敏症 chemical *sensitivity*. ●食物過敏症 food *allergy* [*intolerance*].
── **過敏な** 形 sensitive 《to》; (過敏症の) intólerant, 〘医学〙 hypersensitive. ●過敏な肌 *sensitive skin*. ●彼は寒さに過敏だ He is *too sensitive to* cold. ●彼女はそのことで神経過敏になっている She is *too nervous* about it.

かふ 寡夫 a widower. (⇨やもめ)

かふ 寡婦 a widow. (⇨やもめ, 未亡人)

*かぶ 株 ❶ 〘株式〙 (a) stock (❢ 会社が発行する株全体); a share (❢ stock を分割した個々の株). ●成長株 growth *stocks*; (比喩的の) an up-and-coming person. ●優良株 a blue chip. ●上場株 a listed (↔an unlisted) *stock*. ●株でもうける make (↔lose) money on the *stock* market. ●株に手を出す dabble in *stocks*. ▶彼はこの会社の株を5,000 株 [約45パーセント] 所有している He owns [holds] five thousand *shares* (of stock) *in* the company [some forty-five percent of the company's *stock*]. ▶最近石油株が上がり続けている Oil *stocks* have been going up in recent years.
❷ 〘植物の根〙 a root. ●つつじ 5 株 five azaleas with roots. ●ランを株分けする separate the *roots* of orchids.
❸ 〘切り株〙 a stump. (⇨切り株)
● 株が上がる ▶彼は社内での株(=評価)が上がっている His reputation is rising in the office. (⇨お株)

かぶ 蕪 〘植物〙 a turnip.

かぶ 下部 the lower part. (⇨上部)
● 下部構造 (橋脚などの) a substructure. ● 下部組織 (従属組織) a subordinate organization; a lower branch of the organization.

がふ 画布 《paint on》 (a) canvas.

かふう 家風 the family tradition. ●山田家の家風 the Yamada family tradition. ●家風に合わない do not fit in with the *family tradition* [*the ways of the family*].

かふう 歌風 a style of poetry. ●これらの短歌はいかにも啄木らしい歌風だ These *tanka* poems are typical of Takuboku's *style*.

がふう 画風 a style of painting [drawing]; (画家の筆遣い) one's brushwork; (特質) a ... touch. (❗単数形で. ...は形容詞)

カブール 〖アフガニスタンの首都〗Kabul /kɑ́ːbul/.

カフェ [<フランス語] a café, a coffee house (複 houses /-ziz, 《米》-siz/).
● カフェカーテン a café curtain.

カフェイン caffein(e) /kǽfiːn, ˈ-ˈ/. ●カフェイン抜きの caffeinless [càffein-frée, decaffeinated /diːkǽfənèitid/ (coffee). (❗《話》では decaf(f) で カフェイン抜きのコーヒー[コーラ]をさす. また decaf(f) coffee [cola] ともいう)

カフェー [<フランス語] (⇨カフェ)

カフェオレ [<フランス語] (a cup of) cafe [café] au lait /kɑ́ːfei ou léi/; (a cup of) coffee with milk.

カフェテラス a sidewalk café; (和製語) café terrasse. (参考 フランス語の café と terrasse を組み合わせた和製語)

カフェテリア [<スペイン語] a cafeteria /kæ̀fətíəriə/.

カフェラテ [<イタリア語] (a) latte; (a) caffè latte.

かぶか 株価 《米》a stock price, 《英》a share price.
●株価の下落 a rise [a fall] in *stock prices*. ●株価の急騰[急落] a surge [a sharp decline] in *stock prices*. ●株価の安定[低迷] stability [depression] of *stock prices*. ●株価の平均 an average *stock price*. ●株価を上げる[下げる] drive *stock prices* up [down]. ●株価を操作する manipulate *stock prices*. ▶先月以来株価は15パーセント上昇[下落]した The *stock price* has increased [dipped] by 15 percent since last month.
●株価指数 a stock price index. ●株価収益率 price-earnings ratio 《略 PER》. ●株価操作 stock price manipulation. ●株価動向 stock price movement.

がぶがぶ ●がぶがぶ飲む swill, guzzle. (❗guzzle は食べることも含む) ▶彼は夜通し酒をがぶがぶ飲んだ He swilled [guzzled] sake all night.

かぶき 歌舞伎 *kabuki*; a *kabuki* drama [play]; (説明的に) a traditional Japanese drama performed in a highly stylized manner by males only.
●歌舞伎十八番 the *kabuki* repertoire of the 18 most successful plays (handed down in the Ichikawa family). ●歌舞伎役者 a *kabuki* actor.

かふく 禍福 ●禍福はあざなえる縄のごとし Good and bad periods of life come following one another./Life is full of ups and downs. (❗後の方が普通)

かふくぶ 下腹部 a belly, 〖解剖〗a (lower) abdomen /ǽbdəmən/; (陰部) the pubic region.

かぶけん 株券 a stock [《英》a share] certificate.

かぶさる 被さる (重なる) overlap (-pp-); (負担がかかる) 《話》be saddled (with). ▶(打者がホームベースにかぶさる) crouch over [crowd] the plate.

かぶしき 株式 (a) stock; (1株) a share. (⇨株)
●株式会社 a corporation; a joint-stock [《米》a stock] company. ●株式市場 the stóck màrket. ●東京株式市場の株が下がった[暴落した] Stocks fell [crashed] on the Tokyo *stock market*. ●株式証券 (⇨株券)

カフス(ボタン) (a pair of) cuff links; (縫い付けの) sleeve buttons.

かぶせる 被せる (覆う) cover ... (with); (上に置く) put*... (over, on). ●彼に責任を被せる put [place, lay] the blame *on* him; (転嫁する) shift the blame to him. ▶燃えている土に砂をかぶせた I *covered* the burning wood *with* earth./I *put* earth *over* the burning wood. ▶お母さんは髪にネットをかぶせている Mother *wears* a net *over* her hair.

カプセル a capsule /kǽpsl/.
●カプセルホテル a capsule hotel.

かぶそく 過不足 ●過不足なしである(=ちょうど足りている) be just enough. ●お金を過不足なく(=等分に)分配する divide the money *equally*.

カプチーノ [<イタリア語] cappuccino.

かふちょうせい 家父長制 patriarchy /péitriɑ̀ːrki/.

かぶと 兜 a helmet (worn by feudal lords). ▶勝ってかぶとの緒を締めよ(⇨勝つ)
● かぶとを脱ぐ (降参する) admit oneself beaten; throw one's hands in (❗手札を場にさらけて負けを認めるの意); (脱帽する) 《話》take one's hat off (to him).

かぶとがに 兜蟹 〖動物〗a horseshoe crab.

かぶとむし 甲虫 〖昆虫〗a beetle. (❗カブトムシを含む甲虫類の虫の総称)

かぶぬし 株主 a stockholder, 《英》a shareholder.
●法人[個人]株主 an institutional [an individual] *stockholder*. ●筆頭[大]株主 the largest [a majority] *stockholder*.
●株主資本 stockholders' equity [funds]. ●株主資本配当率 a dividend rate for stockholders' equity. ●株主総会 a stockholders' meeting; a general meeting of stockholders. ●株主配当 a dividend to stockholders. ●株主割当 share allotment; an offering to shareholders.

がぶのみ がぶ飲み ── がぶ飲みする 動 (貪欲に飲む) drink greedily; (ぐいぐい飲む) gulp (酒類を) 《話》swig (-gg-)... down; (やたらと飲む) 《話》guzzle.

かぶら 蕪 (⇨蕪(蕪))

かぶり 頭 one's head.
●かぶりを振る shake one's head (in denial).
●かぶり ●足にかぶりとかみつく bite 《him》*hard* in the leg. (⇨かみつく)

かぶりつき 齧り付き (劇場の最前列) (in) the front row; (ボクシング・サーカスなどの) (at) the ringside (❗単数形で).

かぶりつく 齧り付く bite* (into). ▶彼女はパイにかぶりついた She *bit into* the pie.

かぶりもの 冠り物 (集合的) headgear; (装飾的な) a ...

***かぶる 被る** ❶ [身に付ける] put*... on; wear*, have*... on.

> 使い分け put on 「かぶる」という1回の動作を表す.
> wear, have on 「かぶっている」という状態を表す. put on と異なり *Wear* your hat *during the day*. のように期間を示す副詞句[節]を伴う場合以外は命令文に用いない.

▶彼女は鏡を見ながら新しい帽子をかぶった She *put on* her new hat while looking in the mirror. ▶彼女はかわいい帽子をかぶっていた She *wore* [*was wearing*] a pretty hat. (❗進行形は一時的状態を強調)/She *had on* a pretty hat [*had a pretty hat on*]. (❗have on は進行形では用いない) ▶帽子をかぶるのは好きじゃない I don't like to *wear* a hat. ▶その女の子は帽子をかぶったまま部屋に入ってきた The girl came into the room *with* her hat *on*. ▶この帽子

をかぶってみてもいいですか May I *try* this hat (*on*)? ▶翻訳のこころ スニーカーをはいて、Tシャツの上からセーターをかぶった（村上春樹『レキシントンの幽霊』）Putting on [Wearing] sneakers, I pulled a sweater over the T-shirt. (1)「かぶる」はpull … over（〈何かを引っ張るようにして〉上に着る）と表す。(2)「Tシャツ」はすでに着ているものなので the をつける）

❷［頭をすっぽり覆う］pull … over one's head. ● 水泳帽をかぶる *pull* a bathing cap *over* one's *head*. ▶彼はふとんを頭からかぶって寝ていた He was sleeping with the quilt *over his head*.

❸［覆われる］be covered [coated]《with》. ● 本はほこりをかぶっていた The books *were covered* [*coated*] *with* [*in*] dust. (⇨覆う)

❹［浴びる］dash … over oneself;（船が波を）ship (-pp-) water. ▶彼は水をバケツに2杯かぶった He *dashed* two buckets of water *over himself*. ▶船は波をかぶって傾いた The boat *shipped water* and listed.

❺［引き受ける］take*. ▶そのことの責め［責任］は私がかぶります I will *take* [*assume*] the blame [responsibility] for that.

かぶれ ❶［皮膚の］a rash.（!種類をいうとき以外は単数形で）● おむつかぶれ a diaper《米》[a nappy《英》] *rash*.
❷［異常な感化を受けること］● 西洋かぶれ(事) excessive Europeanization;（人）an excessively Europeanized [westernized] person.

かぶれる ❶［うるしなどに］（発疹〔ほっしん〕ができる）get* a rash 〈*from*〉, come* out in a rash 〈*from*〉. ▶私はうるしにかぶれた *I got a rash from* lacquer poisoning./*I was poisoned by* [*with*] lacquer./（皮膚が炎症を起こした）My skin *was irritated by* lacquer.
❷［感化される］▶彼女はフランス風の生活にかぶれている（=大いに影響を受けている）She *is greatly influenced by* [*with*]《主に米》*is big on* [the] French way of life. ▶彼は共産主義にかぶれている He *is under the influence of* communism./（感染している）He is *infected with* communism.

かぶわけ 株分け 图《園芸》(a) division.
── 株分けする 動 divide … into segments for replanting.

かふん 花粉 pollen. ● 杉花粉アレルギーを起こす develop an allergy to cedar *pollen*.
● 花粉症《医学》a pollinosis /pɑ̀linóusis/《複-noses》; háy fèver.

かぶん 過分 ── 過分な 形（過度の）excessive;（不相応な）undeserved. ▶過分なおほめをいただき恐縮しております《日本人的発想》Thank you very much for your compliment. It's *more than I deserve*./《米英人的発想》I'm very much flattered by your words of *lavish* praise.
── 過分に 副 excessively; undeservedly.

かぶん 寡聞 ▶その役者のことは寡聞にして存じません I'm sorry to say that I've heard [I know] nothing about the actor.

かぶんすう 仮分数《数学》an improper fraction.

*かべ **壁** a wall（!単に建物の壁だけでなく、防御のために敷地などを囲む、石・れんがでできた塀の意も含む）;［障害］a barrier. ● 高い壁 a high [ˣa tall] *wall*. ● 壁のひび割れ a crack in the *wall*. ● 壁のコンセント an outlet in [on] the *wall*.（!on は外に出ている場合に限り用いる）● 壁ぎわに立てかけて lean the ladder against the *wall*. ● 壁ぎわにすを並べて place the chairs next to the *wall*. ● 部屋の壁を（塗料〔しりょう〕で）塗る paint [plaster] the *walls*

of the room. ● 居間を壁で仕切る *wall off* the living room. ● 音速の壁を破る break a sound *barrier*. ● 彼の絵［写真］が壁に掛かっている His picture hangs on [ˣin] the *wall*. ● 彼は修士論文を書こうとして壁にぶつかった He hit a brick *wall* when he tried to write his master('s) thesis.（!修士号は a master's degree）▶言語の壁が多くの誤解を生む Language *barriers* cause a lot of misunderstandings. ● 壁はキッカーから10ヤード離れなければならない The *wall* should be 10 yards away from the kicker.

── 壁の 形 mural.
● 壁に耳あり（ことわざ）Walls have ears.
● 壁掛け a wall decoration [ornament];（大型の布）wall hangings. ● 壁掛けテレビ a wall TV; a wall-mounted TV. ● 壁紙 (⇨壁紙) ● 壁新聞 a wall newspaper. ● 壁パス a wall pass.

かべ『壁』 The Wall ── The Crime of Mr S. Karuma. （参考）安部公房の小説.

*かへい **貨幣**［金(幣)］money;［紙幣］《米》a bill;《英》a note;［通貨］a currency;［硬貨］a coin. ● 補助貨幣 a subsidiary *coin*.
● 貨幣価値 the value of *money* [*currency*].
● 貨幣経済 a monetary economy. ● 貨幣制度（通貨制度）a monetary system; a currency system. ● 貨幣単位 a monetary unit.

がべい 画餅 ● 画餅に帰す（徒労に終わる）come to nothing [《書》naught].

かべがみ 壁紙《米・モニター用の》a wallpaper. ▶私は自分の部屋には淡いグリーンの壁紙を張ってほしかった I wanted my room *papered* in light green.

かへん 可変 形 variability. ── 可変の 形 variable.
● 可変資本 variable capital. ● 可変棚 an adjustable shelf《of a refrigerator》. ● 可変抵抗器 a rheostat; a variable resistor. ● 可変翼 variable wings.

かべん 花弁 a petal /pétl/. ● バラの花弁 a rose *petal*.

かほう ● 下方 ● 下方を見る look down [*below*]; look *downward*. ● 経済成長率予測(値)を下方修正する revise *down* the forecast of economic growth. ▶はるか下方に谷が見える We can see a valley far *below*.

かほう 加法《数学》addition.
● 加法定理 an addition theorem.

かほう 果報（幸運）good luck.
● 果報は寝て待て（ことわざ）Everything comes to those who wait.
● 果報者 a very lucky [fortunate] person.

かほう 家宝（伝来の）a family heirloom. ▶この刀は我が家の家宝だ This sword is our *family heirloom*.

がほう 画法 the art of drawing;（a）drawing technique.

がほう 画報 an illustrated [a graphic] magazine; a pictorial.

がぼがぼ ● 水を飲みすぎておなかがぼがぼだ I drank too much water and my stomach *is gurgling*. ● この手の商売は今はがぼがぼ儲かっている In this line of business, they are making money *hand over fist* [they are raking it in].

かほく 河北 ● 河北省 Hebei /hʌ́béi/ Province.

かぼく 花木 a flowering tree.

かほご 過保護 overprotection, overprotectiveness. ● 過保護の子供 an overprotected [甘やかされた] a *pampered* child; the child *of overprotective parents*. ▶彼女は息子に過保護である She *takes too much care of*《主に米》*overprotects* her son./She *is very overprotective* [*too protective*] *toward* her son.（!toward の代わりに of も

カポジにくしゅ　カポジ肉腫〖医学〗a Kaposi's sarcoma.

かぼす〖植物〗a kabosu (orange).

かぼそい　か細い(細い)thin (-nn-), (ほっそりした)slender; (弱々しい)weak, feeble. (⇨細い) ●か細い腕 *thin* arms. ●か細い声で in a *feeble* [a *weak*, a *thin*] voice.

かぼちゃ　南瓜〖植物〗a pumpkin; (西洋かぼちゃ)a squash. (🛈果肉は Ⓤ)

ガボン　〖国名〗Gabon /gæbóun/; (公式名) the Gabonese Republic. (首都 Libreville) ●ガボン人 a Gabonese. ●ガボン(人)の Gabonese.

***かま　釜**　an iron pot (for boiling rice [water]). ●蒸気釜 a steam boiler. ●同じ釜の飯を食う break bread 《*with*》(🛈大げさな言い方); live under the same roof.

***かま　窯**　a kiln.

かま　鎌　❶〖農具〗(片手用) a sickle /síkl/; (両手用大型) a scythe /sáið/. ●稲を鎌で刈る cut rice plants with a *sickle*.
❷〖策略〗a trick.
●鎌を掛ける trick 〈him〉into telling the truth.

かま　蒲〖植物〗《米》a cattail,《英》a bulrush.

がま　蝦蟇（ヒキガエル）〖動物〗a toad.

かまあげ(うどん)　釜揚げ(饂飩)　*kamaage*(-*udon*); (説明的に) noodles served boiled and hot from an iron pot with dipping sauce.

かまいたち　鎌鼬　'a weasel's cut'; (説明的に) a sharp slash in the skin caused probably by exposure to a vacuum in the whirlwind.

***かまう　構う**　❶〖気にかける〗mind, care 《*about*》(🛈いずれも通例否定文・疑問文で用いる); (わざわざ…する)bother [trouble] oneself 《*to* do; *about*》; (配慮する) show* consideration 《*for*》; (注意する) pay* attention 《*to*》. (⇨お構い,お構いなし) ●世間が何と言おうとかまわない I don't *mind* [*care* 《*about*》] what other people say. (🛈次に wh- 節が来ると前置詞は通例省略する. 節の中は未来時制にしない) ●彼は身なりのことはかまわない He doesn't *care about* his appearance./He doesn't *care* 《*about*》how he looks./(無関心だ) He *is indifferent to* his appearance.

〖会話〗「本をお返ししなくてすみません」「ちっともかまいません よ. 特に急いでいるわけではないですから」"Sorry I haven't returned the book." "That's quite *all right* [It does*n't matter*, I don't *mind*]. I'm in no particular hurry for it."

〖会話〗「彼は断わってきたよ」「かまうもんか」"He's refused." "*Does* that *matter*?"(🛈反語的用法. That does*n't matter*. より語調が強い) What (does it) *matter*? もよく用いる)

〖会話〗「友達をつれてきてもかまいませんか」「ええ,どうぞ, ご遠慮なく」"Do you *mind if* I bring a friend?" "No, not at all." (🛈*mind* 文に対する応答にも, 文法的には正しくないが Yes, certainly [sure]. とか Sure. ともいう)/"Is it *all right* [OK] if I bring a friend?" "Yes, that's fine."/"May [Can] I bring a friend?" "Yes, you can [may]." (🛈 may は尊大に響くので目上の人から目下の人に許可を与えるときにのみ用いる)

❷〖干渉する〗interfere《*in*, *with*》; meddle《*in*》. ●私にかまわないでくれ Don't *interfere with* me./Don't *interfere* [*meddle*] *in* my affairs./(放っておいて)Leave me alone./(君の知ったことではない) That's none of your business [no business of yours]./(大きなお世話だ) Mind your own business. ●あの男にかまわない方がよい (遠ざかっておけ) You should *keep away from* him./(何の関係も持たない) You should *have nothing to do with* him.

❸〖世話する, かまうつ〗look after..., take* care of ...; (からかう) tease. ●だれもその子をかまってやらなかった No one *looked after* [*took care of*, (やや書) *cared for*] the child./(無視した) Everyone *neglected* the child. ●彼女は弟をかまってうれしそうでいる She *is teasing* her brother for fun.

❹〖その他の表現〗●おもしろければどんな本でもかまいません Any book's *fine* [*will do*] as long as it's amusing. ●彼らは経費のことなどかまわずに(=熟慮せずに)計画を立てた They made a plan *without thinking over* [(無視して)《書》 *regardless of*,《書》 *without regard to*] the expenses.

***かまえ　構え**　〖作り〗a structure;〖姿勢〗(やや書) a posture; (態度) an attitude;〖用意〗preparation(s)《*for*》.

***かまえる　構える**　●さあこいと構える take a fighting stance; take a defiant attitude. ●打席で構える take one's stance in the batter's box. ●銃を構えて立つ stand up with one's gun *at the ready*. ●一家を構える *set up* house. ●店を構える *set up* 《as a florist》; open a《flower》shop;（構えている）*run* [*keep*] a《flower》shop. ●どの写真も自然な感じではなく構えた感じだ All the photos seem *posed* rather than natural.

がまがえる　蝦蟇蛙　(⇨蝦蟇⁽⁾)

かまきり　蟷螂〖昆虫〗a mantis 《⁀》 ~es, mantes.

がまぐち　蝦蟇口　a coin purse,《英》a purse.

かまくび　鎌首　●鎌首をもたげる (蛇が) raise its head; (襲いかかろうとして身構える) be ready to attack; (考えなどが) grow (develop) (in one's mind).

かまくら　a *kamakura*; (説明的に) a hut made of hardened snow (in which children play).

かまける　busy [occupy] oneself《*with*, in doing》; busy oneself [be busy]《*with*, in doing》; occupy oneself [be occupied]《*with*, doing》. ●雑事にかまけてそのことをすっかり忘れておりました I had forgotten all about it because I had *been* so *occupied with* other things.

-がましい　●押しつけがましい be pushy [pushing]. ●差し出がましいことを言うようですが I hesitate to say, but.... (⇨差し出がましい)

かます〖魚介〗a barracuda. (🛈通例単・複同形. 肉は Ⓤ. a pike は「カワカマス」で川魚なので当てはまらない)

かます　噛ます　❶〖差し込む〗(くさびを) wedge; (さるぐつわを) gag (-gg-); put a gag in 《his》mouth. ●ドアにくさびをかませて開けておく *wedge* a door open; *push a wedge* under a door and keep it open.
❷〖攻撃などを与える〗give*; deal*. ●1発かませ give [deal] 《him》a blow. ●つっぱりをかます〖相撲〗*give* a frontal thrust.

かまち　框〖枠〗a frame;〖化粧横木〗a horizontal wood.

かまど　竈　a (cooking) stove, (レンジ) a (cooking) range,《英》a cooker.

かまとと　●かまととぶる play the innocent; feign innocence.

かまびすしい　囂しい〖「やかましい」の文語的表現〗(⇨やかましい)

かまぼこ　蒲鉾　*kamaboko*; (説明的に)《a piece of》steamed fish paste [sausage]. ●かまぼこ形の体育館の屋根 the *semicylindrical* roof of a gym.

かまめし　釜飯　*kamameshi*; (説明的に) a small pot of rice cooked with vegetables and chicken or seafood, and served hot individually.

かまもと　窯元　(場所) a potter's workshop, a pottery; (人) a potter.

かまゆで 釜茹で ― 釜茹でする 動 boil ... specially in a large iron pot.

かまわない 構わない do* not mind. 《⇨構う》

***がまん 我慢** 名 〔忍耐〕patience /péiʃəns/ 《with》;〔長期間の苦難に対する〕endurance 《of》.《⇨忍耐, 辛抱》[事情] 英語でもそのまま gaman を用いることがある ▶ここが我慢のしどころだ This is when [where] your *patience* is required [needed].

― **我慢する** 動 ❶〔耐える〕〔苦痛・悲しみなど重みに〕bear*;〔ひるまず〕stand*;〔長い間忍耐強く〕《やや書》endure;〔大目にみる〕《やや書》tolerate;〔ちょっとしたことに耐える〕《話》put* up with ...〔耐えることよりあきらめを含意する〕(❗以上の語句には can を伴い, 否定文・疑問文で用いることが多い);〔差し控える〕《書》hold* back; hold oneself back 《from doing》;《書》refrain 《from doing》.《⇨控える, 慎む》 ▶もう我慢できない I'm beginning to lose my *patience*./My *patience* has run out./My *patience* was exhausted.〔誘惑などに抗しきれない〕I just can't resist./〔もうたくさん, やめてくれ〕I have had enough (of it). 〔Enough of that./Enough is enough. などともいう〕 ▶あの教師には我慢できない I can't bear [stand, endure, put up with] that teacher./I have no *patience* with that teacher. ▶彼女は他人が部屋に入るのが我慢できない She can't stand [〔話〕take] it when other people go into the room.〔(1) 最も日常的な言い方; (2) it は漠然と when 以下の状況をさす〕/She can't bear [stand, endure] other people('s) *going* into the room./She can't bear other people to go into the room./She can't endure [《米》stand] *that* other people *should* go into the room.〔可能だが上例の方が普通〕 ▶彼のふるまいは我慢するより仕方がない His behavior must be endured [〔まれ〕be put up with, ×be stood, ×be borne].〔stand, bear は受身不可〕 ▶その痛さは我慢できないほどだった The pain was almost unbearable./The pain was almost more than I could bear [stand, endure]. ▶彼女はアル中の夫に我慢できなくなった She became impatient [lost (all) *patience*] with her alcoholic husband./She's had enough of 〔(うんざりしている)〕《話》She's had it with her alcoholic husband. ▶彼が話し終わるまで我慢して聞いていなさい Be patient with him until he finishes talking. ▶彼は電車の中でたばこを吸いたいのを我慢できない He can't hold back a smoke in the train. ▶笑いたいのを我慢しようとしたがだめだった I tried to hold myself back from laughing but couldn't.

[会話]「お父さんごめんなさい. お父さんの車を使ってボディをへこませてしまったんだ」「もう我慢ならない. この前はタイヤをパンクさせるし」"Sorry, Dad. I drove your car and made a big dent on the side." "That's *the last straw*. You had a flat tire last time."[❗最後の麦わら1本で限界重量を超えて背骨を折ったらくだのことわざから]

[会話]「夜行で行ったらどう」「列車の中で寝るなんてとても我慢できないんだよ」"Why not travel overnight?" "Sleeping on a train I *find impossible*."[❗find の目的語が強調のため文頭に置かれている]

❷〔間に合わせる〕make* do with ...; do* with ....(❗前の方が口語的)《⇨済ます❷》 ▶後でもっといいのを送ろう. 当分はこれで我慢してくれ I'll send you a better one later. In the meantime, *make do with* [〔何とか乗り切る〕*make the best of*] this one. ▶すごく大学に行きたいのだけど, 短大で我慢しているわ I really want to go to a (four-year) college, but I'd *settle for* a junior college. (❗settle for は「〔不本意だが〕...で手を打つ」の意)

― **我慢強い** 形 patient《with+人, of+事》;〔頑張り通す〕persevering.《⇨根気》 ▶我慢強い母親 a *patient* mother.

― **我慢強く** 副 patiently, with patience. ▶私は彼女が来るのを我慢強く待った I waited *patiently* for her to come.

カマンベール〔<フランス語〕(a) Camembert /kǽməbèər/ (cheese).

***かみ 髪** (a) hair.

[解説] 頭髪全体をさすときは集合的に [U] だが, 1本1本の髪の毛をさすときは [C] となる. たとえば, He has gray hair [hairs]. では hair は全体の印象として白髪まじりであることを, hairs は白髪が何本かあることを意味する.

① 〔~髪〕 ▶硬い [柔らかい] 髪 bristly [soft] *hair*.(❗×hard hair は不可) ▶赤い [長い] 髪の男 a red-haired [a long-haired] man; a man with red [long] *hair*.《⇨長髪》 ▶もじゃもじゃの髪 a shock of *hair*; woolly *hair*. ▶ちりちりの〔波打っている〕髪 curly [wavy] *hair*. ▶乱れた髪 untidy *hair*. ▶もつれた髪 tousled *hair*. ▶1房の髪 a strand [a wisp, a lock] of *hair*.(❗strand はひもぐらいの太さの, 髪は細い, 丈は比較的長い)

② 〔髪が[は]〕 ▶彼は髪が多い [少ない] He has thick [thin] *hair*./His *hair* is thick [thin]. ▶髪が薄くなってきた I am losing my *hair*./My *hair* is getting thin. ▶彼女の黒っぽい髪が白くなった Her dark *hair* went white.

[会話]「彼の髪は何色ですか」「茶色です」"What color is his *hair*?" "It's brown./He has brown *hair*."

[会話]〔理髪店で〕「髪はどのようにいたしましょうか」「横と後ろを少し切って〔短く刈り込んで〕ください」"How would you like your *hair*?" "Trimmed [Short-cropped] back and sides, please."(❗応答文は I'd like my hair の省略した言い方)

③ 〔髪を〕 ▶髪を〔短く〕刈ってもらう have one's *hair* cut (short); have [get] a (short) haircut.(❗主に男性が用いる表現. 自分で刈る場合は cut one's *hair*) ▶髪を結ってもらう have one's *hair* done [dressed].(❗主に女性が用いる表現. 自分で髪を結う場合は do [dress] one's *hair*) ▶髪を長く [短く] している have [×a] long [×a short] *hair*; wear one's *hair* long [short, close-cut].(❗wear long [short, close-cut] hair では, hair は通例「かつら」の意となる) ▶髪を三つ編みにしている have pigtails [《米》braids]; wear one's *hair* in pigtails [《米》braids,《英》plaits]. ▶髪を長く伸ばす grow one's *hair* long; let one's *hair* grow long. ▶髪を編む《米》braid [《英》plait] one's *hair*. ▶髪をとかす comb /kóum/ [let down] one's *hair*. ▶髪を真ん中で分ける part one's *hair* in the middle. ▶髪を後ろで結ぶ bind one's *hair* at the back. ▶髪をおろす〔僧侶[尼僧]になる〕become a priest [a nun];〔結っていた髪を解く〕undo [let down] one's *hair*.

[会話]「彼女はどんな髪(の毛)をしているの」「長くてまっすぐだ [短くてカールした, 中ぐらいの長さでウェーブがかかっている] よ」"What kind of *hair* does she have?" "It's long and straight [short and curly; medium length and wavy]."

▶髪油〔液体の〕háir òil;〔クリーム状の〕háir crèam;〔固形の〕pomade. ▶髪油を塗る apply hair oil to one's *hair*;〔べっとりとなでつける〕plaster one's *hair* down with pomade. ▶髪飾り a háir òrnament.

― **髪結い**《⇨髪結い》

***かみ 神** 〔キリスト教など一神教の〕God, the Lord, the

Almighty, the Creator; 〖多神教の〗(男神) a god; (女神) a goddess. ●神をたたえる〖崇拝する〗praise [worship] *God*. ●彼は神を信じていますか Does he believe in *God*? ●それは神の恩寵(おんちょう)だった It was the grace of *God*. ●彼女は彼の無事を神に祈った She prayed (to) *God* for his safety. ●ポセイドンは古代ギリシアの海の神です Poseidon is the ancient Greek god of the sea.
● 神ならぬ身〖戦場では明日は何が起こるかは神ならぬ身の知るよしもない(=人知の及ぶところではない) It's beyond the ken of a mere mortal [(神の知っている) God only knows] what will happen to me tomorrow in the battlefield.
● 神に召される〖神に呼ばれる〗be called by God; (死ぬ) be called home to Heaven.
● 神も仏もない〖この世には神も仏もない It's a *merciless* world.

*かみ 紙 paper (❗(1) 数えるときは a sheet [a piece] of *paper*, two sheets [pieces] of *paper* などという. (2) sheet は一定の規格のもの, piece は紙切れから規格に合ったものまでその形状を問わない (⇨切れ)).〖(白紙) blank [white] paper (❗前の方は用紙などの所定の箇所に何も書かれていないことを暗示 ⇨白紙));〖(メモ用紙) mémo pàper (❗束ねた1つづりは a notepad, a memopad (⇨メモ)),《米》scratch [《主に英》scrap] paper (❗通例ぼでで表を使ったり, とじて裏を使う); (便箋) wríting pàper, notepaper (❗1つづりは a wríting pàd); (包装紙) wrapping (《英》(茶色の) brown] paper; (包装用薄葉紙) tissue (paper); (ちり紙) a tissue (❗束ねた1箱 is a box of tissues, 商標の (a) Kleenex を用いることが多い); (トイレ用) (a roll of) toilet paper [tissue]. ●折り紙 *paper* folding, origami. ●紙をすく make *paper*. ●紙を丸めてぽいっと捨てる make a wad of *paper* and throw it away. ●プレゼントを紙に包む wrap up the present in some *paper*.
● 紙と鉛筆 a pencil and *paper*. (❗この語順が普通)
▶紙は中国人によって発明された *Paper* [×The paper] was invented by the Chinese.

┌──────────────────────────────────────┐
│ 関連 いろいろな紙: 和紙[日本紙] (artistic) Japa-│
│ nese hand-made *paper*/(西)洋紙 machine-│
│ made *paper*/半紙 Japanese *paper* often used │
│ for calligraphy/ザラ(半)紙 rough [cheap] │
│ (Japanese) writing *paper*. (事典 日本独特のもので決まった英語はない) │
└──────────────────────────────────────┘

● 紙入れ a wallet,《米》a billfold. ● 紙細工 paper craft. ● 紙包み a paper package(《主に米》) [parcel《主に英》]. ● 紙鉄砲 a popgun (that fires paper pellets). ● 紙粘土 paper-mâché (pèipəmə́ʃéi). ● 紙パック (掃除機の) a vacuum cleaner dust bag; (牛乳などの) a (milk) carton. ● 紙雛 a paper *hina* doll. ● 紙表紙 a paper cover. ● 紙袋 a paper bag. ● 紙巻たばこ a cigarette. ● 紙やすり sandpaper, emery paper.

かみ 上(の方)〖(上流) the upper part; (上流) the upper river; (最初の方) the first part.
かみ 加味 ── 加味する 動 〖味をつける〗season(*with*),《ハーブ・スパイスなどで》flavor (*with*)(❗塩・砂糖による味付けには用いない); 〖少し付け加える〗add; (含める) include. ●出席状況を加味して(=含めて)成績をつける mark《米》grade] *including* the students' class attendance.
かみあう 噛み合う〖歯車などで〗mesh (*with*) (❗比喩的な意味にも使える);〖書〗engage (*with*). ▶歯車[意見]がお互いにかみ合わない The cogs [Our opinions] don't *mesh* (*with* each other).
かみあわせ 噛み合わせ 〖歯車などの〗engagement;

〖歯の〗occlusion /əklúːʒən/. ▶入れ歯のかみ合わせが悪い My false teeth don't *meet* well [*come together* right].

かみあわせる 噛み合わせる〖歯車などを〗engage《(the gears》;〖歯を〗clench《one's teeth》.
かみがかる 神憑る〖何かに取り付かれる〗《やや書》become [be] possessed. ●神がかっている人(やや書)(狂信的な人) a *fanatical* person; a fanatic.
かみかくし 神隠し ●神隠しにあう vanish mysteriously; be spirited away.
かみかぜ 神風 a providential wind.
● 神風タクシー a *kamikaze* taxi; a taxi with a *kamikaze* [a reckless] driver. ● 神風特攻隊員 a *kamikaze* [a suicidal] pilot.
かみがた 上方 the Kyoto-Osaka district.
● 上方言葉 (speak with) a Kansai accent;《(speak in》) Kansai dialect. ● 上方漫才 a comic dialogue developed in Osaka.
かみがた 髪形, 髪型〖(特に男性の) a haircut; (特に女性の) a hairdo (優 ~s) ●特異な髪型をさすことが多い. ●違った髪形にする do one's *hair* differently.
がみがみ ●がみがみ言う nag (at...), snap (at...), bawl... out; (いやになるほど長々と)《話》be [go, keep] on (at...). ▶彼女はそのことで一晩中私にがみがみ言った She *nagged* [*went on*] (*at*) me about it all night.
かみき 上期 (⇨上半期)
かみきず 噛み傷 a bite.
かみきりむし〖昆虫〗a long-horned beetle.
かみきる 噛み切る bite*... off. ●舌をかみ切る *bite off* one's tongue. ▶この肉はかみ切れない(=かみ砕けない). 堅くてだめだ I can't *chew* this meat *up*. It's too tough.
かみきれ 紙切れ (a piece [a scrap, (細長い切れ) a slip, a strip] of) paper.
かみくず 紙屑 wastepaper;〖道路などに散らかった〗litter (❗紙くず以外に空きびん・空き缶なども含む).
● 紙くず入れ《米》a wastebasket,《英》a wastepaper basket. ●紙くずを拾う pick up *wastepaper*. ●紙くず同然だ be as good as *wastepaper*; be a mere *scrap* of *paper*. ▶紙くず捨てるべからず《掲示》No littering, fine or thrown.
かみくだく 噛み砕く (ばりばりと) crunch. ●かみ砕いて(=やさしく)説明する explain *simply* [*plainly*].
かみころす 噛み殺す〖かんで殺す〗bite*... to death;〖抑える〗stifle,《やや書》suppress. ●あくびをかみ殺す *stifle* [*suppress*] a yawn. ▶家の猫がネズミをかみ殺した Our cat *bit* a rat *to death*.
かみざ 上座 ●上座に座る(部屋で) take a seat *at the back of* a room; (食卓で) sit *at the head of* a table.
かみさま 神様 a god;〖不世出の名人〗a genius. ●打撃の神様 a batting *genius* [*wizard*]. ●チェロの神様 the *king* of cellists. ▶お客様は神様です The customer is the *king*. (参考 英国のデパート Selfridge の合言葉に The customer is always right. がある)
かみさん (妻) one's wife [better half].
かみしばい 紙芝居 a picture-story show (which has a series of colored pictures depicting the content of the tales).
● 紙芝居屋 a picture-story showman.
かみしめる 噛み締める bite*, chew (⇨噛む); 〖味わう〗enjoy, taste;〖熟考する〗contemplate. ●唇をかみしめる *bite* one's lip. ●自由の喜びをかみしめる *enjoy* one's freedom.

かみしも 裃 a *kamishimo*; (説明的に) official attire of samurai, consisting of a stiff sleeveless jacket pointed at the shoulder, and a long pleated shirt.
- 裃を脱ぐ (くつろぐ、打ち解ける) throw away all formalities; relax; let one's hair down.

かみそり 剃刀 a razor. ●電気かみそり an electric *razor*. ●よく切れる[切れない]かみそり a sharp [a dull] *razor*. ●かみそりのような頭脳 a brain like a *razor*, *razor-sharp* intelligence. ●かみそりの刃 a *razor*(-)edge, a *razor*'s edge; (替刃) a *razor* blade. ●安全かみそりの刃を替える put a new blade in one's safety *razor*. ●かみそり負けをする get a *razor* rash. ●かみそりをとぐ sharpen a *razor*. ●かみそりでひげをそる shave one's face with a *razor*.

かみだな 神棚 a household *Shinto* altar [shelf] (on which a miniature *Shinto* shrine is placed).

かみだのみ 神頼み ●苦しいときの神頼み 'We pray to God to help us when (we are) in danger.'/(ことわざ) Danger past, God forgotten.'/Once on shore, we pray no more. (⇒呪(のろ))

かみつ 過密 ●人口過密 overpopulation.
- 過密スケジュール (ぎっしり詰まった) a tight [a full, a heavy, a busy, ˣa hard] schedule. ●過密ダイヤ a crammed [《やや書》a congested] train schedule. ●過密地帯 an overcrowded [《やや書》a congested] area. ●過密都市 an overpopulated [an overcrowded] city.

かみつく 噛み付く bite*; (ぱくりと) snap (-pp-) (at ...). (🅛 比喩的には = は省略しない) ●上司にかみつく (= 激しく意見を言う) *snap* [*snarl*] at one's boss. ●犬が私の足にかみついた A dog *bit* me in the leg./ A dog *bit* [*snapped* (at)] my leg. 「さわらないでよ」と彼は(私に)かみつくように言った "Don't touch me," she *snapped* (at me).

かみつぶす 噛み潰す (かみこなす) chew. ●苦虫をかみつぶしたような顔をする make a sour face.

かみて 上手 (観客席から見て舞台の右側) the left (side of the stage). (🅛 英語は日本語と異なり舞台から見ていう) ●上手から登場する appear from the *left*.

かみなり 雷 [雷鳴] thunder; [雷電, 落雷] a thunderbolt; [稲光] (a flash of) lightning. ●雷の音におびえる show fright at a roll [a rumble, a clap, a peal, a roar] of *thunder*. (🅛 前の2語はごろごろ鳴る遠雷の音, 後の3語はそれぞれどかん、がーん、低いごうごうという轟音(ごうおん)) ●(雷雨) rain with *thunder* and *lightning*; (雷雨) a thunderstorm. ●雷が鳴っている It is thundering./The *thunder* is roaring [rumbling, rolling]. (🅛 その順に音の勢い/減少する) ●彼の家に雷が落ちた Lightning [ˣA thunder] hit [struck] his house./His house was hit [struck] by *lightning*. (🅛 は用いるが口が目的的) ●彼は雷に打たれて死んだ He was hit dead [was struck dead, was killed] by (a stroke of) *lightning*./He was hit by *lightning* and died. ▶宿題をしていかなかったので先生の雷が落ちた(=先生は私をひどく叱り飛ばした) 《話》The teacher *bawled me out* for not doing my homework.
- 雷雲 a thundercloud.

かみのけ 髪の毛 (a) hair. (⇒髪)

かみばさみ 紙挟み (紙ばさみ入れ) a paper holder [file]; a folder; (クリップなど) a clip.

かみはんき 上半期 the first (↔second [latter]) half (of the year).

かみひとえ 紙一重 ▶ばかと天才は紙一重だ(=ほんのわずかの差だ) There's *only a slight difference* between a fool and a genius. ▶君がしたことは詐欺と紙一重だ What you've done *borders on* cheating.

かみふぶき 紙吹雪 confetti /kənféti/. (🅛 単数扱い)

かみゆい 髪結い (結うこと) hairdressing; (人) a hairdresser, a hairstylist; (店) a hairdresser's (shop).
- 髪結いの亭主 ●彼は髪結いの亭主だ(=妻に食わせてもらって自分はふらふらしている) He does nothing useful and live's on his wife's earnings.

かみよ 神代 ●神代の昔から since the age of gods; since the mythological age.

かみわける 噛み分ける ●彼女は酸(す)いも甘いもかみ分けた人だ She is well experienced in the way of the world. ●酸い [成句]

かみわざ 神業 (奇跡) a miracle; (超人的な行い) a superhuman act.

かみん 仮眠 图 a doze; (特に昼間の) a nap.
- 仮眠する 動 take [have] a doze [have] a nap.

かむ 噛む bite; (口の中でかみ砕く) chew; (固いものを繰り返し強くかむ) gnaw /nɔ́ː/. ●唇をかむ *bite* one's lip. (🅛 感情を抑える動作) ●つめをかむ *gnaw* [*bite*] one's (finger)nails. ●寝ている間に蚊にかまれた I *was bitten* by a mosquito while sleeping. ●小さな女の子が犬に手をかまれた A little girl *was bitten* on the hand by a dog./A dog *bit* the little girl on the hand. ▶食べ物をよくかみなさい You must *chew* your food well. ▶マギー(=犬の名)を中へ入れないで, 敷物をかんでぐちゃぐちゃにしてしまったのよ Keep Maggy out. She *chewed up* the rug.

かむ ●ティッシュで強く鼻をかむ *blow* one's nose hard *into* [*on, with*] a tissue.

ガム 《a piece of [a stick of]》(chewing) gum. ●ガムをかむ chew *gum*. ●ペーパーミントガム (pepper)mintflavored (chewing) *gum*.

がむしゃら — がむしゃらな 形 ●彼のやったことはがむしゃらで思慮がなかった What he did was *reckless* and thoughtless [without thought].
— がむしゃらに 副 (無謀に) recklessly; (必死に) desperately; (狂ったように) frantically; 《話》like mad. ●がむしゃらにその計画を実行する carry out the plan *recklessly*. ●がむしゃらに働く work *like mad* [*crazy*].

ガムテープ gummed tape; (粘着テープ) sticky tape; (包装用テープ) packing tape. ●やつらはぼくの口にガムテープを貼った They stuck *sticky tape* over my mouth.

カムバック 图 a comeback.
— カムバックする 動 ●奇跡のカムバックをする make [have, do] a miraculous *comeback*.

カムフラージュ [<フランス語] (a) camouflage /kǽməflɑ̀ːʒ/.
— カムフラージュする 動 ●木の枝でカムフラージュする *camouflage*... with branches.

ガムラン [<インドネシア語] [音楽] a gamelan.

かめ 瓶 (陶器の) an earthenware pot.

かめ 亀 [動物] (陸ガメ) a tortoise /tɔ́ːrtəs/; (海ガメ) a turtle. ●亀の甲 a *tortoise* shell. (🅛「べっこう」の意もある)
- 亀の甲より年の功 'Age and experience are better than tortoise shells.'/(ことわざ) Wisdom [Sense] comes with years./Years bring wisdom [sense].

かめい 下命 (命令[注文]を出すこと) giving orders. ●ご命令を賜る be ordered 《to do》; receive a command 《from》.

かめい 加盟 图 (加入) joining; (連合) affiliation 《with》.

かめい — **加盟する** 動 (加入する) join; (承認されて) be admitted 《to, into》; (会員になる) become* a member 《of》; (団体などがより大きな組織へ) affiliate 《with, 《英》to》. ‣ 国連に加盟する join [be admitted to, become a member of] the United Nations.
• 加盟国 a member nation. • 加盟店 a member store.

かめい 仮名 a pseudonym /s(j)úːdənɪm/; (でっち上げた) a made-up name.

かめい 家名 〖家の名〗the family name; 〖家の名誉〗the reputation of one's family. • 家名を上げる raise [enhance] *the reputation of one's family*.
• 家名を汚す disgrace [bring disgrace on] one's *family name*; blacken [smear, damage] one's *family reputation*.

カメオ a cameo (複 ~s).

がめつい 〖=貪欲(どんよく)な〗人 a greedy [a grasping] person.

かめのこたわし 亀の子束子 (説明的に) a scrubbing brush shaped like a baby tortoise.

かめむし 椿象 〖昆虫〗a stinkbug.

***カメラ** a camera; (映画用の) 〖米〗a movie [a motion-picture] camera, 〖英〗a cinecamera.
① 〘~カメラ〙 • 一眼[二眼]レフカメラ a single-lens [a twin-lens] reflex *camera*. • ビデオ[インスタント]カメラ a video [an instant] *camera*. • テレビカメラ a TV [a television] *camera*. • 自動焦点 35 ミリカメラ an autofocus 35-millimeter *camera*. • デジタルカメラ a digital *camera*. • 監視カメラ (街に設置されている) a surveillance *camera*; (防犯用に) (home) security *camera*; (システム全体) a security *camera* system.
② 〘カメラに[を]〙 • カメラに収める take a picture [a photograph, 《話》one] 《of》; photograph 《him》. • カメラにフィルムを入れる load a *camera* 《with a film》; load a film into a *camera*. • カメラを向ける point [aim] one's *camera* 《at him》. • カメラを回す turn a *camera* 《on him》; (作動させる) run a *camera*; (撮影する) shoot 《a movie》.
• カメラアイ the camera(-)eye. • カメラ付き携帯 a camera phone; a camera-equipped cell(ular) (tele)phone. • カメラマン (写真家) a photographer 〖関連〗新聞[スポーツ]カメラマン a newspaper [a sports] photographer/タイム誌のカメラマン a photographer for *Time* magazine; (映画・テレビの) a cameraman 《with NHK-TV》. 〖-man を避けて〗cameraperson, camera operator (のようにもいう) • カメラワーク camerawork.

カメリア 〖ツバキ〗〖植物〗a camellia /kəmíːliə/.

がめる (ちょろまかす) pilfer. (⇨盗む)

カメルーン 〖国名〗Cameroon /kæmərúːn/; (公式名) the Republic of Cameroon; (首都) Yaoundé.
• カメルーン人 a Cameroonian. • カメルーン(人)の Cameroonian.

カメレオン 〖動物〗a chameleon /kəmíːliən/; 〖主義主張を簡単に変える人〗a chameleon, a fickle person.

かめん 仮面 a mask. • 仮面をかぶる[かぶっている] put on [wear] a *mask*; (偽善の) play the hypocrite.
• (…の)仮面をかぶる (比喩的) under the *mask* 《of friendship》. • 仮面を下ろす lower [take off] one's *mask*. • 仮面をはぐ unmask; take off the *mask* 《of》. • 仮面を脱ぐ (=正体を現す) throw off [drop, pull off] one's *mask*.
• 仮面舞踏会 a masked ball.

がめん 画面 〖映像が映る面〗a screen; 〖テレビ・映画の映像〗a picture (⇨画像). • 29 インチのテレビの画面 a 29-inch television *screen*.

かめんのこくはく 『仮面の告白』 *Confessions of a Mask*. 〖参考〗三島由紀夫の小説

かも 鴨 〖鳥〗(wild) duck (複 ~s; 〖集合的〗~); (狭義では雌をさす); (雄) a drake; 〖だまされやすい人〗a dupe, an easy mark [victim], 《話》a sucker.
• かもにする make a sucker 《of him》. • いいかもになる fall *easy* victim [prey] 《to》.
• 鴨がねぎを背負(しょ)ってくる It is all the more convenient.

-かも 〖副助詞〗may. (⇨-かもしれない) ‣ あの人はその秘密をもう知っているかもね He *may* know the secret already./*Perhaps* [*Maybe*] he already knows the secret.
〖会話〗「だれが優勝すると思う?」「丸山かもね」 "Who do you think will win?" "Maruyama *might*."

かもい 鴨居 〖建築〗a lintel.

***かもく** 科目, 課目 a subject (of study). • 試験科目 an examination *subject*; a *subject* for examination. • 必修[選択]科目 a required [an elective] *subject*, 《英》a compulsory [an optional] *subject*. ‣ 得意科目は物理です Physics is [×are] my favorite [strong (↔ weak)] *subject*. ‣ どの科目を取っていますか What *subjects* are you taking?

かもく 寡黙 taciturnity; (話したがらないこと) reticence.

—— **寡黙な** 形 taciturn; reticent. • 寡黙な人 a *taciturn* (↔talkative) person. (❗ 人づきあいの悪さを含意); a man [a woman] *of few words*. ‣ 話が自らの過去に及ぶと、彼は急に寡黙になった When our conversation drifted to his past, he became suddenly *reticent about* it.

かもじ 髢 (put on, wear) a hairpiece.

かもしか 〖動物〗(日本カモシカ) a Japanese serow; (俗に、レイヨウ) an antelope (複 ~, ~s). • カモシカのようにすらりとのびた足 long graceful [beautiful] legs.

かもしだす 醸し出す • くつろいだ雰囲気を醸し出す *produce* [*create*] a relaxed atmosphere.

***-かもしれない** 〖助動詞を用いて〗(現在または未来についての推量) may (❗ この意の否定は may not で mayn't とは縮約しない); might (❗ この義の過去形の意味はない); (過去についての推量) may [might] have 《done》; 〖副詞を用いて〗(あるいは) perhaps, maybe (❗ perhaps より口語的. may be と 2 語につづらない); (ことによると) possibly.

〖解説〗(1) **may** は話し手が約 5 割の可能性があると思っている場合. **might** は may より可能性が低い場合に用いられるが、may とほぼ同意のこともある. 副詞 3 語の可能性の高さはおよそ **perhaps** 5 割以下, **maybe** 5 割程度, **possibly** 1-3 割である. ちなみに probably は 8-9 割である.
(2) **perhaps** は文中・文尾も可だが文頭に置くのが一般的. **maybe** は通例文頭に, **possibly** は文頭・文中に置く.

‣ 彼は家にいるかもしれない He *may* [*might*] be at home./*Perhaps* [*Maybe, Possibly*] he is at home./He is *perhaps* [*possibly*, ×*maybe*] at home./*It is possible that* he is at home. (❗ いると推測する) I guess (that) he is at home. (❗ 最初の文に possibly を入れて He *may* [*might*] *possibly* be …. とすると、possibly 単独より可能性が低くなる) ‣ 母は雨が降るかもしれないと言った 〖直接話法〗Mother said, "It *may* rain."/〖間接話法〗Mother said that it *might* rain. (❗ may → might に注意

(⇨よろしい ❶ [第1文例])) ▶彼はクラブに入るかもしれないし入らないかもしれない He *may* or *may not* [×mayn't] join the club./*Maybe* he'll join the club, and *maybe* he won't. ▶きのう彼は彼女に会ったかもしれない He *may* [*might*] *have met* her yesterday./*Perhaps* [*Maybe*, *Possibly*] he met her yesterday. ▶もっと熱心に勉強していた試験に通ったかもしれないのに If I had studied harder, I *might* [×may] *have passed* the exam. (!仮定法の帰結文で)
[会話]「彼はそれいらないのよね？」「ええ、いらないの。でも彼の弟がほしがるかもしれないわ」"He doesn't want it, does he?" "No, he doesn't. But his brother *may*."
[会話]「彼に電話すべきだと思う？」「待つよりはいいかもしれない」"Do you think I should call him?" "It *might* be better than to wait."
[会話]「玄関にだれか来たんだろう」「郵便屋さんかもしれないよ」"Who's at the door?" "It *could* be the mailman." (!(1) It の漠然と人をさす用法に注意. (2) could は might, may より確信度が高い)

*かもつ 貨物 freight /fréit/; (a) cargo (働 〜(e)s) (!以上は海・陸・空のいずれの輸送法にも用いるが, (英)では陸運貨物は goods の方が普通。 (海)) 鉄道貨物 rail *freight* [*cargo*]. ●航空貨物 air *freight* [*cargo*]. ▶貨物はトラックから船へ積み換えられた The *freight* was transferred from trucks to ships. ●貨物集積所 a fréight tèrminal. ●貨物船 a freighter; a cargo boat. ●貨物列車 《米》 a fréight tràin; 《英》 a goods train.

かものはし 鴨の嘴 [動物] a duckbill, a (duckbill) platypus /plǽtipəs/.

カモフラージュ a camouflage. (⇨カムフラージュ)

カモミール [植物] a chamomile, 《主に英》 camomile /kǽməmàil/.

かもめ 鴎 [鳥] a seagull, a gull.

かもん 下問 图 an inquiry; a question.
―下問する 動 inquire ⟨*about*⟩, make an inquiry ⟨*about*⟩; ask a question.

かもん 家門 a family; (一族) relatives; [[家柄] family; [[その家の歴史] lineage /líniidʒ/.

かもん 家紋 a family emblem [crest].

かや 榧 [植物] a torreya.

かや 蚊帳 a mosquito net. ●蚊帳をつる[はずす] put up [take down] a *mosquito net*.

がやがや noisily, clamorously. ▶子供たちの一団ががやがや階段を登って行った A troop of children went up the stairs *noisily*. ▶A troop of *noisy* children ... stairs. も可) ▶隣の部屋でがやがや言うのが聞こえた I heard *noisy voices* in the next room. (!日本語の「がやがや」は人の声についてだが, 英語には人の声を抜き出している単語はない) ▶人々は増税に反対してがやがや言っている(=騒ぎ立てている) People *are clamoring* against tax increases.

かやく 火薬 (gun)powder. ●大砲に火薬をつめる load a gun (*with powder*). ●火薬庫 a (powder) magazine.

かやく 加薬 ●かやく御飯 (説明的に) boiled rice mixed with vegetables, fish, meet or other ingredients.

カヤック [[カヌーの一種] a Kayak.

かやつりぐさ 蚊帳吊草 [植物] an umbrella plant.

かやぶき 茅葺き (屋根) a thatched roof (働 〜s); (家) a thatched house, a house with a thatched roof.

かやり 蚊遣り ●蚊やりをたく burn mosquito-repellent (incense); keep off mosquitoes by smoke.

かゆ 粥 rice-porridge. ●七草がゆ (a) seven-herb *porridge*. ●かゆをすする eat [(音を立てて) slurp] *rice-porridge*.

*かゆい 痒い itchy. ●かゆい所をかく scratch an *itchy* place. ▶背中がかゆい My back *feels* [*feels itchy*]./I *feel itchy* on my back./I *have an itch* on my back. ▶彼は蚊にかまれた所がかゆかった His mosquito bite *itched*.
●痒い所に手が届く ▶あのホテルはかゆい所に手が届くほどサービスが行き届いている The service is *excellent* at that hotel.

かゆがる 痒がる (かゆみを訴える) complain of an itch. ▶あの子供は背中の発疹(ほっしん)をかゆがっている That child *complains of* the *itchy* rash on the back.

かゆみ 痒み an itch. ●かゆみ止め anti-itch medicine; antipruritic /ǽntipruːritik/.

かよい 通い ●通いのお手伝いさん a *live-out* [↔a *live-in*] maid; a *daily* help [maid]. ●通い婚 (平安時代の) a marriage system in the Heian period Japan in which a husband visits his wife or one of his wives at her home only in the nighttime.

かよいつめる 通い詰める frequent 《the theater》; go* 《to the theater》 frequently. ▶彼があのバーに通いつめているのには訳がある He has good reason to *go to* the bar *very often*.

かよう 通う ❶ [往復する] go to and from 《a place》; (電車,バスなどが) run* 《船が》《やや書》ply. ▶新潟・佐渡間を通う汽船 a steamboat *plying* between Niigata and Sado [*from Niigata to Sado*]. ▶その村へは1日1本しかバスが通っていない The bus runs to the village only once a day./There is only one bus service to the village a day.
❷ [通学・通勤する] (通学する) go* to [attend] school (! go to school の方が口語的); (出勤する) go to one's [the] office, (定期券で通う) commute 《*to*》. ●歩いて学校に通う walk to school; *go to school on foot*. (!後の言い方は他の手段と対比して用いる以外はあまり用いない) ▶どちらの学校に通っていますか Where do you go to school?/What school do you go to? (!前の方の言い方は校名・所在地のいずれも問える) ▶彼はバスで会社に通っている He *goes* [*commutes*] to his office by bus./He *takes* a bus to (and from) his office.
❸ [たびたび行く] go* to [visit] ... frequently [(定期的に) regularly]. ▶図書館に通う go to [visit] the library *frequently*; 《やや書》 *pay frequent visits to* the library. ▶医師は彼に週に2回病院に通うように言った The doctor told him to *come to* the hospital twice a week.
❹ [心が通う] (気持ちを理解する) understand*; (意思を通じ合う) communicate 《*with*》. ▶私たちの学校では先生と生徒の心が通い合っている All the teachers and pupils of our school *understand one another* well./Teacher-student *communication is good* at our school./(調和がうまくとれて) There is a *good rapport* between teachers and students at our school.
❺ [血液・電流などが通う] ▶血が体内に通う(=流れる) Blood runs [*flows*, (循環する) *circulates*] *through* the body. ▶この線は電流が通っている(=帯びている) This wire *is charged with* electricity./An electric current is running [*flowing*] *through* this wire./This is a live /láiv/ *wire*./This wire *is alive*. ▶彼にはフランス人の血が通っている(=流れている) He *has* French blood *in him* [*in*

かようきょく his veins).

かようきょく 歌謡曲 a popular song.

がようし 画用紙　drawing paper; (画用紙風) a drawing pad.

かようせい 可溶性 ── 可溶性の 形 soluble; (金属が) fusible.

***かよう(び)** 火曜(日)　Tuesday 《略 Tues.》. (⇒日曜(日))

がよく 我欲 self-interest. (⇨私欲, 私利) ●我欲の強い selfish, 《書》self-seeking.

かよわい か弱い weak, feeble. (⇨弱い)

かよわす 通わす (⇨通う ❷ ❹) ●息子を大学に通わせる send one's son to college. ▶彼らは身振りで意思を通わせることができる They can *communicate* (*with* each other) by gestures.

***から** 空 名 emptiness.
── 空の 形 empty. ●バケツ(の水)を空にする *empty* the water out of a bucket; *empty* a bucket. ▶彼女の部屋は空だった I found her room *empty*./I found no one in her room. ▶三塁が空になった Third base was uncovered [undefended].
●空タッチ 《野球》a phantom tag. ●空見出し a dummy entry; (説明的に) a headword in a dictionary the meaning of which is written under another synonymous headword.
●空約束 an empty [a false, 《書》a vain] promise.

***から** 殻 〖貝・卵・果実などの〗a shell; 〖穀類の〗a husk; 〖種・豆類などの〗a hull; 〖抜けがら〗(セミの)a cast-off shell; (蛇の) a slough /slʌf/. ●木の実の殻 a nutshell. ●卵の殻 an eggshell. ●殻つきのカキ an oyster in the *shell*. ●麦の殻を取る remove *the husks* from wheat; husk wheat. ●自分の殻を出る(＝打ちとける)《話》come out of one's *shell*.
●自分の殻に閉じこもる(＝打ちとけない) go [retire] into one's *shell*; retire [withdraw] into oneself.

***-から** 〖格助詞・接続助詞〗

INDEX

❶ 場所の起点　　　　❷ 時間の起点
❸ 原因, 理由　　　　❹ 原料, 材料
❺ 根拠, 観点
❻ 動作の起こるもとになる人
❼ 数量の初め　　　　❽ その他の表現

❶ [場所の起点] from …; out of …; off …; at …; through …; in …. (⇨-より)

解説 **from** 運動の起点を示し到達点を表す (↔to).
out of 「…の(中から)外へ」という動きを表す (↔into).
off 「…から離れて」の意 (↔on).
at 出入りの地点を示す.
through 「…を通って」という貫通の意を示す.
in 「…に」という広がりを持つ空間の範囲を示す.

▶彼は成田からパリへ向けて出発した He left Narita for Paris./He started *from* Narita for Paris. ▶犬がテーブルの下[戸の後ろ]から現れた A dog appeared *from* under the table [behind the door]. (❗*from* の後には場所を表す前置詞が続くことがある) ▶彼女は店から出てきた She came *out of* [*from*] the shop. (❗out of は店の「中から外へ」の運動を表し, from は店を単に動作の起点としてとらえる) ▶私は芝生からタンポポを引き抜いた I weeded the dandelions *out of* the lawn. ▶本が2冊机から落ちた Two books fell *off* [*from*] the desk. (❗*off* は「机から離れ落ちる」ことに, from は「落ちる起点」に重点がある) ▶その事務所は駅から車で[歩いて] 20 分以内のところにある The office is (situated) within a twenty-minute travel [walk] *of* the station. (❗within の後に of の代わりに from を用いることはまれ) ▶正面玄関からの家に入った I came into the house *at* [*from*] the front door. (❗出口, 入り口といった通過点を示す「から」は by, through も用いられるが, from は通例用いない) ▶85 ページから始めましょう Let's begin *on* [《英》*at*, *from*] page 85. ▶何から始めようか What should we begin *with*? ▶窓から光がさし込む The light comes in *through* the window. ▶太陽は東から昇って西に沈む The sun rises *in* [*from*] the east and sets in the west. ▶中年は普通 40 歳ぐらいから 60 歳ぐらいまでとされている Middle age is usually considered to be *from* around age 40 *to* around age 60./Middle age is usually between about 40 and about 60 years of age.

会話 「そのホテルから駅までどのくらい距離がありますか」「4 キロあります」"How far is it *from* the hotel to the station?" "It's four kilometers."

会話 「どこから列車に乗りましたか」「静岡からです」"Where did you get on the train?" "*At* [*From*] Shizuoka."

❷ [時間の起点] from …; since …; (…の後) after …. (⇨これから, それから, 今 ❶ ③)

解説 **from** 時の起点を示す.
since 過去のある時点から現在[過去のある時点]まで継続している動作の出発点を示し現在[過去]完了形とともに用いる.
after 過去または未来からある期間が「経過した後で」の意を表す.

▶農民は朝から晩まで熱心に働く Farmers work hard *from* morning till [to] night. ▶朝からずっとテレビを見ています I have been watching television *since* [*from*] morning. ▶この前会ってから何年にもなりますね It's been 《主に米》[It is 《主に英》] many years *since* I last saw you. (❗It's＝It has) ▶3 時から会合に出席します I'll be at the meeting *from* three o'clock (*on*) [*after* three o'clock]. (❗*on* は「ずっと(出席している)」という状態の継続を強調する)/I'll go to the meeting *after* [*from*] three o'clock. (❗from は go to (…に出席する)といったよう, 持続性を含まない動詞とともに用いられない) ▶彼に電話をしてから出かけた I went out *after* I (had) called him. (❗after 節では時間の前後関係が明らかなので, 過去形で表すことが多い) ▶I called him, *and* (*then*) (I) went out.

会話 「学校は何時[いつ]から始まりますか」「8 時 30 分[火曜日, 4 月]からです」"*What time* [*When*] does school begin?" "*At* eight thirty [*On* Tuesday; *In* April]." (❗「…から始まる」は ×begin *from* としない. 時間は at, 日は on, 月・年・季節などは in を用いる) ❸ [原因, 理由] from …, through …; (…であるから) because, 《やや書》since, 《主に英・書》as; (というのは) 《書》for. (⇨-ので, -て ❹)

解説 **from** ある結果を引き起こす直接の原因を示し, 成句を構成する場合が多い: 働きすぎから過労になる get too tired *from* overwork.
through ある結果を引き起こす直接の原因を示し, 通例抽象名詞が続く.
節で原因・理由を表すのは because, since, as, for.
because 直接の理由・原因を表し, 一般に主節の後, 強調する場合は主節の前に置く.
since 周囲の状況から明白な理由・原因を表す.
as 軽く付帯状況的な理由を表す.

since と as は通例主節より前に置く. 以上の3語は この順に意味が弱くなる.
for 前に述べた内容に対し, 補足的に理由を付け加える場合に用い, 主節の後に置く.

▶彼は飲みすぎから病気になった He became sick *from* too much drinking [*because* he drank too much]. (!)後の方が口語的) ▶つらい経験からそのことを知った I realized it *from* [*through*, *by*] my bitter experience. ▶その事故は運転手の不注意から起こった The accident happened *through* [*because of*] the driver's carelessness. (!)節を用いて…*because* the driver was careless. の方が口語的)/《やや書》The accident resulted *from* the driver's carelessness./The driver's carelessness caused [《やや書》resulted in] the accident. ▶彼は好奇心から吸い始めた He began to smoke *out of* [×*from*] curiosity. (!)*out of* curiosity は慣用句) ▶彼は一番上だったから, みなの面倒をみなければならなかった *Since* [*As*] he was the oldest, he had to look after all the others. ▶彼女が来なかったのはただお父さんが許さなかったからだ She didn't ╱come, símply [ónly] *because* her fáther wóuldn't ╲let her. (!)*simply*, *only*, *chiefly*, *partly* などの副詞の後に *because* のみ可. このように副詞の修飾を受けたり, 強調構文で強調部分になれる節は *because* 節に限られる) The simple [only] reason she didn't come was *that* [《話》*because*] his father wouldn't let her. ▶お待ちください. 彼を呼んで来ますから Wait a minute, please. I'll call for him. (!)《話》では, 補足的に理由を添える場合 *because* を用いずに原因を続けて言うことが多い. 特に主節で依頼・要求を示す場合, 「から」に対して ×Please wait a minute, because … because は用いない)

会話「本当に召し上がりませんか」「そうですね. そんなにおっしゃってくださるからにはいただくわ」"Won't you really want one?" "Well, *since* you insist, I think I will."

会話「どうして行ってはいけないの」「まだ小さいからよ」"Why can't I go?" "*Because* [×*Since*, ×*As*, ×*For*] you are too young." (!)*because* 節を単独で用いるのは why に対する応答の場合に限る: 行ってはだめ. まだ小さいのだから You can't go, *because* [×*You can't go. Because*] you're too young.)

会話「どうしてそれを選んだの」「ただ欲しかったからよ」"What made you take it?" "*For* the simple *reason* I wanted to."

❹ [原料, 材料] *from* …; *of* …; *out of* …. (⇨ ❺)

解説 原料・材料の質的変化を伴う場合は **from**, 伴わない場合は **of** を用いるのが原則. 動詞と *of* が離れるときには **out of** が普通.

▶チーズは牛乳から作る Cheese is made *from* milk. (!)milk を主語にすると Milk is made into cheese. となる)/We make cheese *from* milk. ▶ワインはブドウから作る Wine is made *from* [*of*] grapes./We make wine *from* [*of*] grapes. ▶私たちは紙から多くの有用なものを作る We make a lot of useful things *out of* paper./We make a lot of useful things *out of* paper. (!)受身の文は Lot of useful things are made (*out*) *of* paper. となり, *out of* でも可) ▶人間は精神と肉体から成っている Man *is made up* [*consists*, 《やや書》*is composed*] *of* soul and body. (!)× … *is consisting* は不可)

❺ [根拠, 観点] *from* …; (…に基づいて) *on* …. ▶彼の言うことからするとそれはありうることだ *From* [*Judging from*] what he says, it is possible. ▶いろいろの資料から火山の噴火は判断した *From* [*On*] various data we concluded that there would be no volcanic eruption. ▶彼らの暮らしぶりから見ると相当に裕福らしい *From* the way they live, they seem to be quite well off.

❻ [動作の起こるもとになる人] *from* …; *by* …. ▶これは友人からの贈り物です This is a present *from* a friend of mine. ▶先生から不注意だとしかられた I was told off [was scolded] for being careless *by* the teacher. (!)*scold* は《英》では古風)

❼ [数量の初め] (…ほど多くない) no less [fewer] than …. (!)原則として less は量に, fewer は数に用いるが, 金額・距離・期間・重量などについては less を用いる方が普通); (少なくとも) at least, not less than; (…を超える) more than …; over …. ▶この本は 5,000 円からする This book costs *no less than* [*at least*, *not less than*] 5,000 yen. ▶そのマラソンには 3 万人からの人が参加した *No fewer than* [*More than*, *Over*] 30,000 people took part in the marathon race.

❽ [その他の表現] ▶親から独立する become *independent of* one's parents. ▶寝ても覚めても彼のことは彼女の心から去らなかった Awake or asleep, he was never *out of* her thoughts. ▶どんなことがあってもやめないから No matter what happens, I'll *never* [*won't ever*] give it up. (!)後の方が強意)

*から 柄 ❶ [権利] a right; [立場] a position; [資質] (a) quality. ▶君はそんなことを言える柄ではない You have no *right* [are not in a *position*] to say so. ▶彼は教師らしい柄ではない He doesn't have the *qualities* of a teacher. ▶彼は柄にもないことをした It was quite *unlike* him to do that./What he did was quite *out of character* for [*with*] him.

❷ [態度, 品] ●柄の悪い (下品な) low; (粗野な) coarse /kɔːrs/; (野卑な) vulgar. ●柄の悪い態度 *low* [*coarse*, *vulgar*] behavior. ●柄の悪い連中とつき合う keep *low* company.

❸ [体格] (a) build. ●大柄[小柄]な男 a man of large [small] *build*; (背の高い[低い]) a tall [a short] man.

❹ [模様] a pattern, a design. (⇨模様) ●はでな柄 a loud *pattern* [*design*]. ●セーターを柄編みにする knit a *pattern* into a sweater.

から 殻 ●鶏(ミネ)がら chicken bones 《for soup》.

カラー ❶ [色] a color. (⇨色) ●学校のカラー (校色) the *colors* of a school; the school *colors*; (特色) the *character* [雰囲気] the *atmosphere* of a school. ▶ワインカラーのジャケット a wine *colored* jacket. ▶その映画はカラーです The film is *in color* (↔in black and white).

❷ [えり] a collar. ●ぼくの新しいワイシャツにはボタン留めのカラーがついている My new shirt has a button-down *collar*.

❸ [植物] a calla /kǽlə/; (花) a calla lily.

●カラーコーディネーター a color coordinator. ●カラー写真 a color(ed) photo; a color(ed) picture. ●カラーテレビ(放送) color television [TV]; (受像機) a color television [TV] (set).

がらあき がら空き ── がら空きの 形 almost empty. ▶バスはがら空きだった The bus was *almost empty.*/There were very few passengers on [in] the bus.

からあげ 空揚げ 图 ●魚[若鶏]の空揚げ *deep-fried fish* [*chicken*].

── 空揚げする 動 deep-fry, French-fry.

カラーリング coloring; (髪の) hair coloring.

からい 辛い (味が) (ひりひりと) hot (-tt-), spicy; (塩辛い) (ぴりっと) sharp, pungent; (酒が) dry; (点数などに) strict (*in*) (⇨甘い❸). ● 辛いカレー a *hot* (↔*mild*) curry. 辛いソースは a *sharp* [a *pungent*] sauce. 辛い点をつける grade (*them*) *strictly*. ● 点の辛い先生 (米) a *hard* grader.

からいばり 空威張り 图 bluster. —**空威張りする** 動 bluster.

からいり 空炒り —**空炒りする** 動 roast [parch] (beans brown).

からうり 空売り 图 【株式】 a short sale, short selling.
—**空売りする** 動 ● 先物を空売りする *short* the futures.

からおくり 空送り —**空送りする** 動 forward a tape without playing (recording); (早送りする) fast-forward a tape, forward a tape rapidly.

カラオケ [< 日本語「空(から)」+ *orchestra* (+ *box*)] keraoke /kærάouki/; (説明的に) singing to the accompaniment of orchestrated music on video. ● カラオケで歌う sing to *karaoke*. ● カラオケに行く go *karaoke*-singing. ● カラオケ大会をする give a *karaoke* party (競技会) contest).
● カラオケ装置 a *karaoke* machine; a *karaoke* kit. ● カラオケバー a *karaoke* bar. ● カラオケボックス a *karaoke* box.

からかう (冗談を言って) kid (-dd-), joke [play a joke] on ...; (だまして) (話) pull one's leg; (いたずらをして) play a trick on ...; (軽くいじめて) tease; (ばかにして) make* fun of ..., poke fun at .... ▶ 気にするな。彼はちょっとからかっているだけだよ Don't worry. He's only *kidding* you [*teasing* you]. ▶ 彼らは彼の田舎なまりをからかった They *made fun of* his provincial accent.

からかさ 傘, 唐傘 an oil-papered umbrella with a bamboo frame.

カラカス [ベネズエラの首都] Caracas /kərά:kəs/.

からかみ 唐紙 [紙] (a sheet of) *karakami*, (説明的に) thick printed paper of Chinese origin; [ふすま] (⇨ふすま).

からから ❶ (水気がまったくない様子) completely dry.
● からから天気 *dry* weather. ▶ 干ばつで川がからからになった The river *dried up completely* because of the drought. ▶ The river was *completely dry* [(*as*) *dry as a bone*] because of the drought. ▶ 緊張のあまり、口がからからになった I was so nervous (that) my mouth felt (*as*) *dry as a bone*. ▶ 私はのどがからからだ I've got a *very dry* throat./(のどが渇いて) I'm *very* [(話) *dead*] *thirsty*.
❷ [音] ● からからと音を出す clatter; (戸などが) rattle. (⇨がらがら) ● から笑い出す break [burst] into *peals* of laughter. ▶ 空き缶が道路をからから転がった An empty can *clattered* down the road.

がらがら ❶ [おもちゃ] a rattle.
❷ [がらがら音を出す] rattle. ▶ 荷馬車ががらがら通り過ぎた A cart *rattled* past (us).
❸ [(物が)がらがら崩れる] rattle. ▶ 山腹の小石ががらがら落ちてきた Small stones *rattled down* the mountainside.
❹ [内にほとんど何もない様子] empty. ▶ 駐車場はがらがらだった The parking lot was *almost empty*./Very few cars were seen in the parking lot.

がらがらへび 蛇がらがら蛇 [動物] a rattlesnake.

からきし (少しも...でない) not ... at all; (まったく) quite. (⇨まるっきり, 全く, まるで) ▶ 人の名前を覚えるのはからきしだめなんです I'm *no good* [*not any good*] at remembering names./I'm *terrible* about names.

からくさ 唐草・唐草模様 an arabesque (design).

からくじ 空くじ a blank (ticket). ● 宝くじで空くじを引く draw a *blank* in a public lottery.

がらくた useless [worthless] things, (話) junk; (寄せ集めの) odds and ends; [くず] (米) trash, (英) rubbish.

からくち 辛口 ● 辛口の酒 *dry* (↔*sweet*) *sake*. (⇨辛党). ● 辛口の(=手厳しい)批評 *severe* [*bitter*] criticism.

からくも 辛くも (⇨辛(から)うじて)

からくり (仕掛け) a device; (計略) a trick.
● からくり人形 a mechanical doll.

からげいき 空景気 a show of prosperity.

からげる 絡げる [束ねる] bind* [bundle] up; [すそなどをたくし上げる] tuck up, hitch up, (巻き上げる) roll up.

からげんき 空元気 (空威張り) false courage; (酒で) (話) Dutch courage.

カラコルム ● カラコルム山脈 Karakoram /kὰ:rəkó:rəm/.

からころ ▶ 誰かがからころと下駄の音を立てて通りを歩いていく I can hear someone *clattering* along the street in *geta* [clogs]./I can hear the *clatter* of *geta* going down the street.

からさわぎ 空騒ぎ (やや話) (make [kick up]) a fuss about nothing.

からし 辛子 mustard. ▶ ホットドッグに辛子をぬる put *mustard* on a hot dog.
● 辛子入れ a mustard pot. ● 辛子漬け pickles in mustard. ● 辛子明太子 cod roe salted and flavored with chili pepper.

からじし 唐獅子 a lion; (中国的イメージの獅子) an artistically designed Chinese lion.

-からして ❶ [例を挙げて] ▶ あの男は顔つきからして気に入らない For example [(まず第一に) First of all], I don't like his looks.
❷ [「-から」の強調形] ▶ 好況であるからしてなおいっそう商売には慎重さが求められる We must conduct business all the more carefully because we are in good times.

からしな 芥子菜 mustard (greens). ▶ このサラダはからし菜を入れすぎている There's too much *mustard* in this salad.

からしゅっちょう 空出張 a made-up [a fictitious] business trip.

からす 烏 [鳥] a crow /króu/; (渡りガラス) a raven (参考) raven は不吉の鳥とされる). ▶ カラスが鳴いている A *crow* is cawing./A *raven* is croaking.
● からすの行水 (take) a hurried bath.
● からすの足跡 [目じりにできるしわ] crow's feet (at the ends of one's eyes).
● 烏口 a dráwing pèn; a rúling pèn.

からす 枯らす kill; (霜や虫害で) blight; (しおれさせる) wither; (木材を) season. (木枯れる) ● よく枯らした木材 well-*seasoned* timber. ▶ 夏の炎暑で花を枯らしてしまった The flowers *died* in the summer heat./The summer heat *killed* the flowers.

からす 涸らす ● 井戸を涸らす *dry up* the well. ● 資源を涸らす *exhaust* the resources. ● 才能を涸らす *use up* one's talent (*for*).

からす 嗄らす (⇨嗄れる) ● 声をからして in a *hoarse* voice; hoarsely. ▶ 私は歌いすぎて声をからしてしまった My voice has become [got] *hoarse* from singing too much.

:ガラス [<オランダ語] (a sheet of) glass. (!ガラス製品をさすときは C)

① 【～ガラス】 ● 網入りガラス wire *glass*. ● 色ガラス colored *glass*. ● ガラス戸付きの木櫃 a *glass-fronted bookcase*. ● 透明[半透明]ガラス transparent [translucent] *glass*. ● 板[窓]ガラス (⇨板①) ● クリスタルガラス (*glass*). ● 強化安全ガラス safety *glass*. ● 1枚の窓ガラス a pane (of *glass*).

② 【ガラス(の)～】 ● ガラスの破片 a piece of broken *glass*; a *glass* splinter. ● ガラス張りの本棚 a *glass-fronted bookcase*. ● それはガラス製だ It is (made of) *glass*. ▶彼とガラス越しに面会した I met him with a sheet of glass between us. (⇨越し) ▶ガラスの天井が働く女性の昇進を阻んでいる The *glass* ceiling blocks women from promotion in their workplaces. (❗ *glass* ceiling は女性は上級職になかなか就けないという目に見えない壁をさす)

③ 【ガラスは[が]】 ▶ ガラスはこわれやすい *Glass* breaks easily. ▶ガラスが彼女の息で曇った The glass clouded over with her breath.

④ 【ガラスを】 ● ガラスを割る break (a piece of) glass. ● 窓にガラスをはめる glaze [glass] a window.
● ガラス器(製品)《集合的》 glassware. ● ガラス切り a glass cutter. ● ガラス工場 a glass factory; a glassworks. ● ガラス細工《集合的》 glasswork. ● ガラス職人 a glassworker; (ガラス製品を細長い管で吹いて作る) a glass blower. ● ガラス繊維 fiberglass; glass fiber. ● ガラス窓 a glass window. ● ガラス屋 (店) a glass shop; (人) a glazier.

からすうり 烏瓜【植物】 a snake gourd.
からすがい 烏貝【魚介】 a freshwater mussel.
からすのし 『鴉の死』*The Death of a Crow*. 《参考》金石範の小説)
からすばと 烏鳩【鳥】 a Japanese wood pigeon.
ガラスばり ガラス張り ▶ ガラス張りの *glazed* [a *glassed-in*] showroom. ▶ガラス張りの外交 diplomacy *in a fishbowl*. (❗ fishbowl は「金魚鉢」の意) ▶市政はガラス張りであるべきだ The city administration should *be open to the public* [*for all to see*].
からすみ dried mullet roe.
からすむぎ 烏麦【植物】 oats.
からせき 空咳 ● 空咳をする have a dry [a hacking] cough. (❗後の方は絶え間なく出る短い咳); (わざと) give a *mock cough*. (⇨咳)
からせじ 空世辞 an empty compliment; flattery. (⇨お世辞)

からだ 体 ❶ 【身体】(肉体) a body. (❗(1) 広い意味では体全体、狭い意味では手・足・首を除いた胴体を意味する。 (2) しばしば精神 (mind), 魂 (soul) と対比して用い、セックスの対象としての肉体の意にも用いる) ● 体の bodily; physical. (❗bodily の方が直接的に肉体をさす) ● 心も体も健全な人 a man of sound mind and *body*. ● 体の欠陥 a *bodily* [a *physical*] defect. ● 体の発達 *physical* (↔*mental*) development. ● 体を洗う[暖める] wash [warm] oneself. (❗oneself の代わりに one's body を用いることはまれ) ▶彼は強く健康な体をしている He has a strong and healthy *body*. ▶若いうちに体を鍛えなさい Build up your *body* while (you are) young. ▶精神は体を左右する The spirit controls the *body*. ▶運動の後は体中が痛い I ache *all over* [My whole body aches] after the exercises. ▶彼は芝生の上に寝て思い切り体を伸ばした He stretched *himself* out on the lawn. ▶体の自由がきかなくなった He was unable to move a muscle.

❷ 【体格】(造り) (a) build (❗男女とも用いられる); (主に男性の) (a) physique; (主に女性の体型の) a figure; (体型, 骨格) (a) frame; (体格, 体質) (a) constitution. ● 体のがっしりした男 a man of [with a] sturdy *build* [with を用いる方が口語的に) a sturdy man. ▶彼は頑丈な体をしている He has a strong *build* [*physique*, *constitution*]./He is (a man) of strong *build* [*physique*, *constitution*]. ▶彼の体はフットボールをするには小さすぎる His *build* [*physique*] is too small for playing football. ▶あの婦人はほっそりとした体(の線) [骨ばった体つき]をしている That lady has a slender *figure* [an angular *frame*]. ▶彼女のきゃしゃな体はその重労働には向いていなかった Her tender *frame* was not suited to the heavy work. ▶彼は相撲の力士のような体つきをしている He *is built* like a sumo wrestler. ▶このドレスは彼女の体に合わない This dress doesn't fit *her*.

❸ 【健康】 体(の調子)『話』 shape (❗通例形容詞を伴う). ● 体の丈夫な[弱い]子供 a *healthy* [虚弱な] a delicate, [病弱な] a sickly] child. ● 体の具合が ― I am in good [×bad, poor] *health*./I am *healthy*. (❗×My body is healthy. とはいわない) ▶私は忙しい時が体の調子が最もよい My *health* is at its best when I am busy. ▶適度の運動をすることは体によい Getting some exercise is good for the [our, your] *health*. (❗単に ... good for *you*. ともいえる) ▶彼は過労で体をこわした He ruined [damaged, injured] his *health* from overwork./(病気にした)《主に米》 Overwork made him sick. ▶マラソンに備えて体の調子をよくしておきたい I want to *get into* good *shape* for the marathon race. ▶彼は生まれつき体が弱い(=病弱だ) He has been *sickly* [*in delicate health*] from birth. ▶事故以来彼はずっと体の具合が悪い He's not *been (feeling) well* since the accident. ▶1日も早く体をよくしたい(=回復したい) I want to *get better* [*recover my health*] as soon as possible. ▶お体を大切に Please take care of *yourself* [your *health*, xyour body]. (❗病人などにいう言葉。親しい間柄では単に Take care. ともいう)
● 体があく ▶今日から3日間は体をあけて(=約束・予約を入れないで)自由な状態でおいてくれ Keep yourself free for the next three days. (❗one's body は用いるのは不適切)
● 体が言うことを聞かない ▶気は若いつもりなのだが体が言うことを聞かない I think I am young at spirit but my *body* doesn't work as I want it to.
● 体を売る (売春する) sell one's body [oneself].
● 体を張る (一身を投げうつ) devote oneself (*to the work*); (自分の命を危険にさらす) risk one's life [《話》lay one's life on the line] (*to do*); (自分の体を盾にして) shield (him) with one's own *body*.

からだき 空焚き ―― 空焚きする 動 ▶風呂を空だきする heat an empty bathtub.
からたち 枳殻 【植物】 a trifoliate /traifóuliit/ orange.
からだのみ 空頼み (⇨空頼み)
カラチ 『パキスタンの都市』Karachi /kərάːtʃi/.
からちゃ 空茶 ▶空茶ですが、いかが？ Won't you have some tea? ❗あえて Nothing to have with it, though. (お茶以外は何もありませんけど) などととつけ加える必要はない)
からっかぜ 空っ風 a strong dry wind.
からっきし (⇨からきし)
からっけつ 空っ穴 (absolutely) penniless; 《話》(flat) broke. (❗no の語を加えるほうが強調的) ▶競馬ですってからっけつだ I've lost all the money at the races. I'm *flat broke*.
からっと ❶ 【全体に及んで】 ● 風を通すために窓をからっと

(=大きく)開けておく keep the window *wide* open to let in fresh air. ▶天気ががらっと晴れた It [The weather] *cleared up*./(空が晴れ渡った) The sky turned *all* [*perfectly*] clear.
❷[[性格が]] ▶からっとした (率直な) frank, straightforward; (心が開いた) open-hearted. ▶彼はからっとしていて何事も根にもたない He is *straightforward* and bears no grudge.
❸[[べとべとしないで]] ▶(揚げ物が) からっとあがっている be fried *nice and crisp*. ▶空気がからっとしている The air is *pleasantly dry*. (!nice and は /náisənd/ と1語のように読み,「申し分なく」の意. 限定的に用いる場合は and なしで nice crisp *tempura*, nice dry air のようにいう)

カラット [<ギリシャ語] (金) (米) a karat (略 k., kt.), (英) a carat (略 c., ct.); (宝石) a carat (略 c., ct.). ▶24 カラットの金 24-*karat* gold. ▶(純金)1 カラットのダイヤモンド a one-*carat* diamond. [[参考]] 1 カラットは 0.2 グラム.

がらっと (⇨からりと) ▶窓をがらっと開ける *throw* a window *wide*. ▶彼女はがらっと変わった She has become a *completely* different person./She has changed *a lot*.

がらっぱち a noisy and coarse (guy).

からっぽ 空っぽ empty. (⇨空) ▶スーツケースの中は空っぽだった There was *nothing* in the suitcase. ▶あいつの頭は空っぽさ He has *no brains*./He's *empty*-headed. ▶財布がすっかり空っぽになってしまった I've spent all my money.

からつゆ 空梅雨 a dry rainy season. ▶去年は空梅雨だった It didn't much rain during the rainy season last year.

からて 空手 [[競技]] *karate* /kərάːti/, (説明的に) a Japanese martial art of (unarmed) self-defense using kicks and openhand blows. ▶彼は空手の有段者だ He's a *karate* black belt.

からて 空手 [手に何も持っていない状態] (⇨素手, 手ぶら) ▶お客に呼ばれて空手で行くわけはいかない You cannot *go without taking a present* when you are asked to tea [dinner].

からてがた 空手形 [[融通手形]] a fictitious bill; [[空約束]] an empty promise (⇨空). ▶空手形を振り出す issue a fictitious bill; fly a kite.

からとう 辛党 (酒が辛党だ(=酒好きだ) He is a drinker./He likes to drink.

-からに ▶見るからに(=ただ見るだけでも)はきやすそうな靴ですね These shoes *look* very comfortable (to walk in)./*One look tells* these shoes are comfortable.

-からには ▶やると決めたからには(=以上は)完璧にやりたい *Once* I've decided to do it, I'll do it perfectly. ▶こうなったからには最後まで頑張ろう *Now that* it has come to this, we'll do our best to the end. (!この now that は次に来る事実をしっかりと受け止めることを表す) ▶ここで働くからには(=限りにおいて), 私の命令に従ってもらう You'll have to obey me *so* [*as*] *long as* you work here.

-からぬ ▶彼しらぬぬ(=彼らしくない)発言で一同がとまどいを隠せなかった They were all bewildered at his remarks which *were quite unlike* him. ▶その事故で少なからぬ(=多くの)死者が出た *Not a few* people died in the accident.

からねんぶつ 空念仏 ❶[[口先だけの念仏]] ▶空念仏を唱える do *not* chant a *prayer from the heart*; pray a *perfunctory* [an *empty*] *prayer*.
❷[[口先だけの主張]] ▶ほとんどの選挙公約は空念仏に終わる Most campaign promises will not be fulfilled [be carried out].

ガラパゴス ▶ガラパゴス諸島 the Galapagos /gəlάːpəgòus/ Islands; (公式名) Archipiélago de Colón.

からぶかし 空吹かし idling. ▶エンジンの空吹かしをする *leave* one's car engine *idling*. (!この idling は動詞).

からぶき 乾拭き ―― 乾拭きする 動 wipe [polish] 《(a table) with a dry (⇔damp) cloth. (!関連) a dustcloth (主にちり払い用の)ぞうきん.

からふと 樺太 (サハリン) Sakhalin /sǽkəliːn/. ▶樺太犬 a Sakhalin dog.

からぶり 空振り 图 [[野球]] a swing and a miss. ▶空振りのストライク a *swing-and-miss* strike; a *swinging* strike. ▶空振りの三振 a swinging strike-out.

―― 空振りする 動 [[野球]] swing (at the ball) and miss; fan. ▶その打者は空振りに三振した The batter (got) struck out *swinging*.

カラフル colorful 《shirts》.

からませる 絡ませる [[巻きつける]] twist, twine 《*around*》. ▶彼女の腰に両腕をからませる *twine* one's arms *around* her waist.

からまつ 唐松 [[植物]] a larch. (!材木は U))

からまる 絡まる [[もつれる]] tangle; (動けない) get* tangled [entangled]; [[巻きつく]] twist, twine 《*around*》. ▶ツタが絡まった壁 an *ivied* wall. ▶細い糸はからまりやすい Fine threads *tangle* easily. ▶ツタが木にからまった The ivy *twisted* [*twined*] *around* the tree. ▶複雑な事情がその汚職事件にからまっている(=関係している) There are complicated circumstances *involved in* that corruption case.

からまわり 空回り ―― 空回りする 動 (高速で) race; (低速で) idle, run idle. ▶モーターは空回りした The motor *idled*. ▶議論は空回りした The argument went round (and round) in circles and got nowhere.

からみ 絡み complicated relations [[状況]] situations, (経過, 手続き) processes. ▶…とのからみで in (close) relation to …; linked with …; (巻き込んで) involving …. (⇨絡む ❷) ▶出会い系サイトがらみの犯罪が急増している Crimes originating [stemming] from 'Encounter Sites' ['Meeting Sites'] of the cell phone are snowballing. (! (1) 日本の出会い系サイトは米国ではインターネット上の Meeting Sites, Encounter Sites とするとロマンチックな出会いの意味を含む. (2) snowball は「急増する」の意の慣用表現)

からみ 辛味 (辛い味) a hot taste; (塩味) a salty taste.

-がらみ -搦み ❶[…くらい] (近接) nearly; (周辺, 前後) around, about. ▶五十がらみの立派な紳士 a fine gentleman *about* [*around*] fifty; a fine fifty*ish* gentleman. ❷[…に関係した] (⇨絡み)

からみあう 絡み合う get* tangled [twisted], get into a tangle. ▶糸がからみ合っていた The thread *was tangled* [*was twisted*] (together)./The thread *was in a tangle*. ▶この事件は複雑な事情がからみ合って(=関係し合って)いる In this case, some complicated situations *are connected to each other*.

からみつく 絡み付く twist (oneself)《*around*》, get* tangled (up) 《*in*》, get entangled [entangle oneself] 《*in*, *with*, *among*》, 《やや書》entwine (oneself) 《*around*, *in*, *with*》. ▶ひもがプロペラにからみついている A piece of string *has twisted* (*itself*) *around* the propeller. ▶私の足につるがからみついた My feet *got tangled* [(ひっかかった) *got caught*] in

からむ 絡む ❶【言いがかりをつけて困らせる】▶彼は酔うといつも人にからむ Whenever he gets drunk, he picks a quarrel with someone [gives someone a hard time]. ❷【関係する】▶この件には金がからんでいる Money is involved in this matter. ❸【巻き付く】▶ツタが木のまわりにからまっていた Ivy twined [twisted] around the tree. ▶彼が投げるたびに釣り糸がからんだ(＝もつれた) The line tangled every time he cast. ❹【引っ掛かる】▶たんがのどにからんだ Phlegm /flém/ stuck in my throat. ▶きれがからんでファスナーが動かない The zipper caught the cloth and it won't move.

からめ 辛目 ❶【味が】(いつも[思っていた]より辛い) hotter [spicier, (塩辛い) saltier] than usual [I expected]; (いくぶん辛い) rather hot [spicy, salty]. ▶この料理は少し辛めだ This food is a little too hot. ❷【判定・評価が】severer than usual; rahter severe. ▶採点は少し辛目にしました I've graded a little severely. (＠ 甘目)

からめて 搦め手 ❶【城の裏門】the back entrance [gate] to the castle; 《古》a postern. ❷【守りの薄いところ】● からめ手から取り入る approach 〈him〉from the back door.

からめとる 搦め捕る catch* and tie up; arrest.

からめる 搦める, 絡める ❶【巻きつける】● 柱につるをからめる entwine creepers around the posts. ❷【和える, まぶす】● 薄切りのレモンにハチミツをからめる toss lemon slices in honey. ❸【関係づける】▶事件を外交問題にからめる link an event to a diplomatic issue. ❹【合わせる, 一緒にする】● 二つの四球とヒット 1 本をからめて 1 点取る put together two walks and a single to score a run.

カラメル caramel /kǽrəml/. ● カラメルソース cáramel sáuce.

がらもの 柄もの patterned material.

からやくそく 空約束 《make》an empty [a false, (書) a vain] promise.

カラヤン [オーストリアの指揮者] Karajan /kǽrəjən/ (Herbert von 〜).

からりと (⇨からっと) ▶最近からりと晴れた日がない We haven't had any perfectly fine days recently.

がらりと ❶【音】▶彼はノックもせずにがらりと戸を開けた He rattled open the door without knocking. ❷【まったく変わってしまう様子】▶その後彼の態度はがらりと変わった His attitude toward us changed completely [dramatically] after that.

かられる 駆られる (ある状態に追いやられる) be driven 〈to do; into〉; (取りつかれる) be seized 〈with〉; (急に...したいという気になる) have an impulse 〈to do〉. ▶彼は嫉妬にかられて妻を殺した Jealousy drove him to kill his wife. ▶あの大地震のとき私は死の恐怖にかられた I was seized with the fear of death when the earth shook hard. ▶彼はその男をなぐり倒したい衝動にかられた He had an impulse to knock the man down./He impulsively wanted to knock the man down. ▶パンドラは好奇心にかられてその箱を開けた Pandora opened the box out of curiosity./Curiosity drove Pandora to open the box. (！「好奇心がパンドラに...をさせた」の意)

がらん 伽藍 a grand Buddhist temple.

がらんと ❶【音】● がらんという音 (やや大きめの響く音) clang; (響きは低いが衝撃音) bang; (低音から高音までの幅広い鐘の連続音) ding-dong. ▶少年がバケツをけったので, バケツがからがらんと転がっていった The boy kicked the bucket so it rolled away clanging. ❷【広々として何もない様子】・(建物の内部などが)がらんとしている empty; deserted. (！ (1) 後の方がさびれた感じを強調する。(2) almost, very, completely などで修飾可) ● がらんとしたホール an empty hall. ▶私の部屋は, 家具は小さな勉強机が一つあるだけでがらんとしている My room is very empty because I have no furniture except a small desk. ▶町は人々が休暇でいなくなりがらんとしていた The town was deserted with its people gone on vacation [holiday].

がらんどう ▶宴会場はがらんどうになっていた The banquet room looked empty [looked deserted, was completely bare]. (！ bare はその部屋に期待される家具がないことで, ここでは宴席がすっかり片付けられてただの空間のみが広がっている様子を表す) ▶その仏像はがらんどうだ The statue of Buddha is hollow.

***かり 仮** ━ 仮の 形 ❶【臨時の】temporary; (暫定的な) provisional; (間に合わせの) makeshift; (一時の) transient; [試験的な] tentative. (⇨仮に) ● 仮の住まい a temporary home. ▶彼は仮採用になった He was hired on a tentative basis [on trial, on probation]. (！ probation は「試用期間」の意)

❷【偽りの】false.
● 仮契約 a tentative [a provisional] agreement. ● 仮条約 a provisional treaty. ● 仮免許 (⇨仮免許)

かり 狩り (狩猟) a hunt, hunting; (銃猟) shooting. (⇨狩猟) ● キツネ [猛獣] 狩り fox [big game] hunting. ● イチゴ狩り strawberry picking 〈xhunting〉. ● カモ狩り duck shooting. ▶シカ狩りに森へ行く go deer hunting [go on a deer hunt] in the woods; go to the woods to hunt deer.

かり 借り [借金] a debt /dét/; [代金] a bill; [人からの恩義] a debt of gratitude. ▶あなたにいくら借りがありますか How much do I owe you? (！ 買い物をして「おいくらですか」と聞く時にもいう) ▶私は彼に 1 万円の借りがある I'm in debt to him for 10,000 yen./I owe him 10,000 yen. (⇨借りる ❸) ▶あなたにはご好意にあずかった借りがある I owe you a debt of gratitude for your favor. (！ 改まった感謝の表現. 日常的には I owe you dinner. (ごちそうになった借りがある) など簡略して用いられる) ▶いつか借りを返す I'll repay you someday. (！ 文脈によって借金の返済の意と返礼の意のいずれにもなる)/(法違の埋め合わせをする) I'll make it up to you some day. (！ with you とすると「(君と)仲直りする」意となる)/(仕返しする) 《話》I'll get back at you some day or other.

かり 雁 [鳥] a wild goose (傻 wild geese). (⇨ 雁(ガン))

かりあげ 刈り上げ [髪型が] 《have [get]》close [cropped] hair at the back. (！ close は非常に短く, cropped は五分刈り)

かりあげ 借り上げ (賃貸借契約) (a) lease. ● 借り上げ条件 the terms of lease. ● 10 年間の借り上げ契約 a ten-year lease.

かりあげる 刈り上げる 《髪を》have* one's back hair cut very short.

かりあげる 借り上げる lease; take* out a lease 《on the whole apartment building》.

かりあつめる 駆り集める gather together, round up 《several volunteers》.

かりいれ 刈り入れ [収穫] (a) harvest. ● 刈り入れ時 harvest(time). ▶早い刈り入れ an early harvest. ● 小麦の刈り入れをする harvest [reap, gather in] wheat. ▶稲はもう刈り入れできる The rice is ready for harvest.

かりいれ 借り入れ ●企業[消費者; 銀行]借り入れ corporate [consumer; bank] *borrowing*. ●借り入れ金 borrowed money; a loan (「貸し出し金」の意にもなる); a debt. ●長期[短期]の借り入れ金 a long-term [a short-term] *loan*.

かりいれる 刈り入れる reap [gather, harvest] 《a crop》. (⇨刈る ❶)

かりいれる 借り入れる borrow [loan] 《ten million yen *from* a bank》.

かりうける 借り受ける (⇨借りる)

かりうど 狩人 (⇨狩人(かりゅうど))

カリウム [<ドイツ語]〖化学〗potássium (元素記号 K).

ガリウム 〖化学〗gallium (元素記号 Ga).

カリエス [<ドイツ語]〖骨結核〗(結核性脊椎炎) tuberculous spondylitis /t(j)uːbə̀ːrkjələs spondiláitis/; 〖虫歯〗(dental) caries /kέəris/.

かりかえる 借り換える (前の借りを返して新たに借りる) renew. ●借金[図書館の本]を借り換える *renew* a loan [a library book].

かりかた 借り方 (簿記) a debit. (⇦ 貸し方)

かりかぶ 刈り株 stubble.

かりかり ❶〖怒っているさま・神経質な様子〗▶彼は相手の理不尽な要求にかりかりしている He is *mad at* their unreasonable demand. ▶そんなささいなことでかりかりするな Don't *get worked up* [*work yourself up*] about such a trifling matter.
❷〖硬質のものが砕ける音・歯ごたえのよい様子〗●ベーコンをかりかりに焼く grill bacon *crisply* [*crisp*]. ●かりかり梅を食べる eat *crunchy* plums. ●かりかりに凍る (⇨かちかち ❷) ▶ネズミが何かをかりかりかじっている A rat's *nibbling at* something.

がりがり ❶〖がりがりひっかく〗scratch (hard); (へらなどで) scrape. ▶そんなにがりがりかいたらだめ Don't *scratch* so hard. ▶彼は古い壁紙をがりがりかき落とした He *scraped* down the old wallpaper.
❷〖大変やせている〗▶その子はがりがりだった The child was *extremely thin* [〖話〗*all skin and bone*].
❸〖猛烈に〗●がりがり勉強する work *like mad* [*crazy*]; 〖話〗keep one's nose to the grindstone. (⇨がり勉)

がりがり 我利我利 ●名誉欲でがりがりになっている男 a man who *has a blind* [〖あくことなき〗*an insatiable*] *desire for* fame; a man *blinded by* a desire for fame.
●がりがり亡者(もうじゃ) (利己主義者) a selfish and greedy person; a grasping person.

かりぎ 借り着 图 borrowed clothes.
— 借り着する 動 wear borrowed clothes; (貸衣装を) wear a rented [a hired 〖英〗] clothes.

カリキュラム a curriculum (圀 curricula, ~s); 〖1科目の〗a course of study.

かりきる 借り切る rent; (バスなど) charter.

かりこし 借り越し an overdraft. ●当座借り越し bank *overdraft*.

かりこみ 刈り込み cutting; shearing; trimming; pruning; mowing. (⇨刈り込む)

かりこむ 刈り込む cut*; (羊・羊の毛を) shear; (切ってそろえる) trim (-mm-); (木・余分な枝を) prune; (芝を) mow. (⇨刈る) ●街路樹を刈り込む trim [*prune*, *cut*] branches *off* street trees.

かりしゃくほう 仮釈放 release on parole [parole. — 仮釈放する 動 release [put] 《him》 on parole; give 《him》 parole; parole.

かりしゅっしょ 仮出所 (⇨仮釈放)

かりじゅよう 仮需要 imaginary [speculative] demand (↔actual demand).

かりしょぶん 仮処分 〖一時的差し止め命令〗a temporary [a provisional] injunction 《*to do*, *that* 節, *against*》; 〖暫定的な処分〗(make) a provisional disposition 《*of* land [property]》. ●販売差し止めの仮処分 an *injunction* [*a temporary injunction*] to stop 《them》 from selling the goods.

カリスマ [<ギリシャ語] 《have》charisma /kərízmə/. ▶ヒトラーはカリスマ的なリーダーだった Hitler was a *charismatic* leader.

かりずまい 仮住まい 图 one's temporary residence. — 仮住まい(を)する 動 live temporarily 《*at* a hotel, *in* Kobe》.

かりせいほん 仮製本 〖印刷〗temporal binding. (関連 本製本 permanent binding)

かりそめ 仮初め — 仮初めの 形 ●かりそめの(=はかない)恋 a *temporal* [a *transient*] love. ●かりそめの(=ちょっとした)病 a *slight* illness.
— 仮初めにも 副 (何があろうと決して...してはならない) Whatever happens, you should never 《do》[must not 《do》]. ; 〖話〗Whatever you do, don't 《do》. ▶かりそめにも(=いやしくも)教師たるものは常に言動に十分留意すべきだ Teachers worthy of the name should always pay special attention to what they say and do.

かりたおす 借り倒す (借金を) borrow money and never return it; fail to pay one's debt; (勘定を) jump 《the bill》. (⇨踏み倒す)

かりだす 狩り出す hunt ... out; force ... into the open place; beat 《the bush》 for ....

かりだす 借り出す borrow; (特に本を) 《米》check ... out. ●図書館から本を借り出す *borrow* [*check out*, *take out*] a book from the library. ●書籍を 1 か月以上借り出すことは認められない Books may not *be kept* (*out*) [*be borrowed*, *be checked out*] over a month.

かりだす 駆り出す get* [bring*] 《him》 out 《*to*; *to do*》. ●有権者を投票所へ駆り出す *get* the voters *out* [*bring out* the voters] *to* the polls. ▶私たちが結局彼の引っ越しに駆り出された After all, it was we who helped him move out. (! 強調構文にすることで「ほかのだれでもないおれたちがやることになった」とはやくさまを表す)

かりたてる 駆り立てる 〖馬・人などを追い立てる〗drive* ... 《*to*, *into*; *to do*》. ●馬を駆り立てる drive (拍車を加え進ませる) *spur* a horse *on*. ●国民を戦争に駆り立てる drive [*urge*] the nation *to* war. ▶貧困が彼をその犯罪に駆り立てた Poverty drove him *to* commit the crime.

かりちん 借り賃 a rent; a rental. ▶この車の借り賃はいくらですか How much is the *rent* [*rental*] *for* this car?

かりっぱなし 借りっ放し 会話「例の本借りっぱなしでごめん」「気にしないで. 当分必要無いから」"Sorry I haven't returned the book yet." "Never mind. I won't use it for some time." (! 現在完了形で「今現在返した状態にしていない」の意)

かりて 借り手 〖一般の物の〗a borrower; 〖家屋・土地などの〗a tenant.

かりとじ 仮綴じ (⇨仮製本)

かりとる 刈り取る (草を) cut*, mow; (芝を) mow, clip (-pp-); (作物を) reap. ●小麦をかまで刈り取る reap 《a》 wheat with a sickle. (⇨刈る ❶)

*かりに 仮に ❶〖もし...だとしたら〗 if, suppose [supposing] 《that》(⇨もし); (万一) if ... should [were to] .... (⇨もし) ❷〖たとえ...だとしても〗even if [though] .... (⇨たとえ)

かりぬい 仮縫い 图 a fitting. ●仮縫いに洋服店へ行く go to a tailor's for a *fitting* [*to be fitted*].

かりぬい —— 仮縫いする 動 ●上着を仮縫いする *fit* ⟨him⟩ with a coat; (仮に縫う, しつけをする) *tack* [*baste*] a coat.

かりぬし 借り主 a *borrower*; (債務者) a *debtor* /détər/; (土地・家屋の) a *ténant*.

かりね 仮寝 (⇨うたたね, 仮眠)

ガリバーりょこうき 『ガリバー旅行記』 *Gulliver's Travels*. (参考 スウィフトの小説)

かりばら 借り腹 (代理母の子宮) a *surrogate* /sə́rəgeit/ *womb*. ●借り腹する (代理母になってもらう) *get* ⟨her⟩ *to act as a surrogate mother for his wife*.

かりばらい 仮払い *temporary payment*.

がりばん がり版 a *mimeograph*. ●がり版刷りの *mimeograph* (*copies*).

カリブ ●カリブ海 the *Caribbean* /kǽrəbìːən/ (*Sea*).

カリブー 〖動物〗a *caribou*.

カリフォルニア 〖米国の州〗*California* /kǽlifɔ́ːrnjə/ (略 Cal., Calif. 郵便略号 CA).

カリフラワー 〖植物〗a *cauliflower* /kɔ́ːliflàuər/.

がりべん がり勉 (人) 《米話》a *grind* /gráind/;《英話》a *swot*. (⇨勉強) ●彼はがり勉タイプではない He's not the *grind* type.

—— がり勉する 動. 《話》*bone up* ⟨*on* English; *for* an exam⟩. 《米話》*grind away* ⟨*at* English⟩.《英話》*swot* (*up*) ⟨*on* English; *for* an exam⟩.

かりめんきょ 仮免許 a *temporary* (*driver's*) *license*;《米》a *learner's permit*;《英》a *provisional* (*driver's*) *licence*.

かりもの 借り物 图 a *borrowed thing*. —— 借り物の 形 *borrowed* ⟨*from*⟩; *on loan* ⟨*from*⟩.

かりゅう 下流 the *lower reaches* (of a river). (⇨上流) ●下流へ行く *go down the river*; *go downstream*. ●橋から2マイル下流にダムがある *There is a dam two miles below* [*down the river from*] *the bridge*.
●下流階級 the *lower* [*welfare*] *class*.

かりゅう 顆粒 a *granule* /grǽnjuːl/. ●インスタントコーヒーの顆粒 *instant coffee granules*.

がりゅう 我流 (⇨自己流)

かりゅうかい 花柳界 the *world of geisha*; the *geisha house quarters*.

がりゅうてんせい 画竜点睛 (⇨画竜(がりょう)点睛)

かりゅうど 狩人 (⇨猟師)

かりょう 加療 图 ●加療中である *be under medical treatment*. —— 加療する 動 *give* ⟨him⟩ *medical treatment*.

かりょう 科料 a *fine*. ●科料に処せられる *be fined* ⟨*for* speeding⟩. (⇨罰金)

かりょう 過料 an *administrative fine*. (⇨罰金)

がりょう 雅量 ●雅量がある (心の広い) *broad-minded*; (寛容な) *generous* ●あんな雅量のない男は人の上に立つ資格はない *Such a narrow-minded fellow isn't good enough for a leader*.

がりょうてんせい 画竜点睛 ●画竜点睛を欠く *lack the finishing touches to make... perfect*.

かりょく 火力 (ガスなどの) *caloric force*. ●火力が強い *have strong* (↔*weak*) *caloric force*; (ガスコンロなどが) *have a strong flame*.
●火力発電所 a *thermal power station* [*plant*].

カリヨン 〖教会の鐘楼の組み鐘〗a *carillon* /kǽrəlɑ̀n/.

かりる 借りる ❶ 〖無料で借りる〗*borrow* (↔*lend*); *use* (⇨使用する); (手元に持ち続ける) *keep*.

〖使い分け〗 **borrow** 通例借りた物を他の場所へ持って行って使う場合に用い, 移動できない物には用いない. **use** 「ちょっと使わせてもらう」の意で, 移動できない物にも用いることができる.

❶ 【...を借りる】 ●家を担保に金をいくらか借りる *borrow* [⟨銀行から⟩ *get a loan of*] *some money on a house*. ●ちょっと鉛筆をお借りしてもいいですか *Can I borrow* [*use*] *your pencil for a moment*? (⚠ 疑問文でなく I'd like you to *lend me* your pencil for a while. ともいえる (⇨貸す ❶ ❷))) ●ちょっと電話を借りていいですか *Can* [*May*] *I use your telephone*? 〖会話〗「どのくらいお借りして(＝持って)いいですか」「ご随意に, いつまでもどうぞ」"*How long can I have it* (*for*)?" "*Keep it for as long as you like*." 〖会話〗「この雑誌借りられますか」「残念ですがだめです. 雑誌は図書館から持ち出せないことになっていますので」"*Can I check this magazine out*?" "*I'm afraid not. Magazines are supposed to stay in the library*."

❷ 【...に[から]借りる】 ●図書館から借りた本 a *book* (*I borrowed*) *from the library*. (⚠ 文脈によって( )内は省略される) ●きのう彼に金を借りたがまだ返していない *I borrowed some money from* [*x to*] *him yesterday, but I haven't paid him back yet*.

❷ 【金を出して借りる】 *rent*,《英》*hire*, *charter*.

〖使い分け〗《米》では一般に一定の金額で物を借りるときには, **rent** を用いるが,《英》では短期間借りる場合(車・衣装など)には **hire** を, 長期間借りる場合(家, 土地など)には **rent** を用いる. **charter** はバスなどの公共的な乗り物を団体のために契約で借りるの意. いずれの語も borrow, use とは異なり賃借りするという点に注意.

●九州へ行ったとき車を借りた *I rented* [《英》*hired*, ×*borrowed*] *a car when I visited Kyushu*. ●月2万円で佐藤さんから部屋を借りた *I rented the room from Mr. Sato at* [*for*] *20,000 yen a* [*per*] *month*. ●ホールを時間ぎめで借りられます *You can rent* [《英》*hire*] *a hall by the hour*. (⚠ rent には「賃貸しする」の意もある(⇨貸す)) ●バスを1台借りて京都へ行った *We chartered a bus* (*for our trip*) *to Kyoto*.

❸ 〖借金を負うている〗 *owe*. ●私は彼に5,000円借りている *I owe* [*xam owing*] *him 5,000 yen*. ●彼に5,000 yen *to him*. (⚠ 前の方は金額に, 後の方は人に重点を置いた言い方. したがって, 「彼にいくら借りているの」は *How much do you owe him*?, 「だれに5,000円借りているの」は *Who do you owe 5,000 yen to*? となる)

❹ 〖助けなどを〗 ●言葉を借りて言えば *to use* [*borrow*] ⟨his⟩ *words*; *in* ⟨his⟩ *words*. (⚠ この直後にその言葉を引用符("　")付きで続ける) ●彼に知恵を借りたい *Ask for his advice*./*Ask him for some advice*. ●ぼくは君の力を借りたくない *I want to do it without your help*./*I don't want to rely on your help* [*on you to help me*]. ●身元保証人(＝紹介先)としてお名前をお借りしたいのですが *May* [*Could*] *I use* [×*borrow*] *your name as a reference*? (⚠ reference は就職の履歴書などに書き入れる. 推薦状は a *letter of reference* という)

ガリレオ 〖イタリアの天文・数学・物理学者〗*Galileo* /gælíliːou/ (～ *Galilei*).

かりん 花梨 〖植物〗a *Chinese quince*.

かりんさんせっかい 過燐酸石灰 〖化学〗(*calcium*) *superphosphate*.

かりんとう 花林糖 *fried dough cake*.

かる 刈る ❶ 〖切りはらう〗*cut*;(草・芝を) *mow*;(はさみで) *clip* (-*pp*-);(芝・植木などを手入れする) *trim* (-*mm*-);(作物を刈り入れる) *reap*, *gather*. ●芝を刈る *mow* [*clip*, ×*cut*] *the lawn*; *cut the grass*. ●稲を刈る *cut* [*reap*, *harvest*] *rice*. ●生け垣を刈る

trim [clip] a hedge. ● 羊の毛を刈る shear a sheep. ❷ 〖髪の毛などを〗cut*; (そろえる) trim (-mm-); (刈り込む) clip (-pp-). ● ペットの犬の毛を刈ってもらう have the hair of one's pet dog cut [trimmed, clipped]. ● 頭を刈ってもらった I got [had] a haircut./I got [had] my hair [×head] cut. (!後の方は「刈られた」の意もある) ● 彼は髪を短く刈っている He has his hair cut very short./(短い角刈り) He has a crew cut.

かる 狩る hunt. (⇨狩り)
かる 駆る (追い立てる) drive. ● 牛を牧草地へかる drive cattle to the pasture.
ーがる 〖感じる〗feel*; 〖…したい〗want 《to do》; (強く) be anxious 《to do》 ● 希望どおりにならない不安を含意) 〖好む〗like 《to do》; 〖ふりをする〗pretend 《to do》. ● さみしがる feel lonely. ● 足を痛がる feel 《(the)》 pain in the [one's] leg. ● 彼に会いたがる want [be anxious] to see him. ● 強がる pretend to be strong; (からいばりする) bluff. ▶ 年をとると人は昔の思い出話をしたがるものだ Older [Elderly] people like to talk about their young days.

‡**かるい** 軽い ❶ 〖物が〗light. ● 軽いスーツケース a light suitcase. ▶ このかばんは軽いので私でも持てる This bag is light enough for me to carry.
❷ 〖負担・罰・食事・気持ちなどが〗light. ● 軽い負担 [税; 読み物; 仕事] light burdens [taxes; reading; work]. ● 軽い刑罰 a light [a mild] punishment. ● 軽い食事を取る have a light meal; (話) grab a bite. ● 軽い気持ちで(何気なく) casually; (うきうきと) with a light heart; (よく考えずに) without thinking. ● 軽い運動をする get [《英》take] light exercise. ● 軽いたばこを吸う smoke mild cigarettes.
❸ 〖病気などが〗slight. ● 軽いけがをする be slightly injured; receive a slight [a minor] injury. ● 軽い心臓発作を起こす have a mild heart attack. ▶ 軽い風邪を引いている[頭痛がする] I have a slight cold [headache].
❹ 〖動きが〗light. (⇨軽快, 軽やか) ▶ 彼女は足が軽かった She was light on her feet.

—— 軽く 圓 lightly; 〖静かに〗softly; 〖やさしく〗gently; 〖容易やすと〗easily; 〖かなり〗much. ● 軽く見る(軽視する) take 《it》 lightly (!通例否定文で); make light of 《it》; (いい加減にあしらう) trifle with 《him》. ● ドアを軽くノックする knock softly [lightly] on the door. ● 彼女の肩に軽く触れる touch her gently [lightly] on the [×her] shoulder; touch her shoulder gently [lightly]. ● 彼は読書の中でその問題をかなり軽く扱っている He treats the subject rather lightly in his book. ▶ それを聞いて心が軽くなった I'm relieved [It's a relief] to hear that./It's a load off my mind. ● 私の車だと140キロは軽くでる My car does 140 kilometers per hour easily. ▶ 彼の身長は6フィートを軽く越えている He is well over six feet tall.

かるいし 軽石 pumice; pumice stone. ● 軽石2個 two pieces of pumice [stone].
カルカッタ 〖インドの都市〗Calcutta /kælkʌtə/. (参考 コルカタ(Kolkata) の旧称)
かるがも 軽鴨 〖鳥〗a spot-billed duck.
かるかや 刈萱 〖植物〗a beardgrass, a broom sedge.
かるがる 軽々 —— 軽々と (たやすく) easily, (軽く) lightly. ● 軽々と持ち上げる lift 《it》 easily [with ease].
かるがるしい 軽々しい 圈 (不注意な) careless, (思慮に欠ける) thoughtless; (分別のない) 《やや書》 imprudent.

—— 軽々しく (軽率に) lightly; (思慮なく) thoughtlessly. ▶ そう軽々しく(=なれなれしく)話しかけないでくれ Don't speak to me in too friendly a manner.

カルキ [<オランダ語] 〖塩化石灰〗化学) chlorinated lime; 〖さらし粉〗chloride of lime, bleaching powder. ▶ 水がカルキ(=塩基)臭い The water smells of chlorine.
かるく 軽く (⇨かるい)
かるくち 軽口 an irresponsible talk; (軽薄な) a facetious remark; (冗談) a joke. ● 軽口をたたく crack a joke.
カルシウム 〖化学〗calcium /kǽlsiəm/; (元素記号 Ca). ● カルシウム欠乏症 calcium deficiency.
カルスト [<ドイツ語] 〖地学〗Karst /kάːrst/. ● カルスト地形 Karst topography.
カルタ [<ポルトガル語] karuta; (説明的に) the card game of the Japanese alphabet. ● カルタ会 a karuta party. ● カルタ1組 a pack 《主に米》 a deck] of karuta. ● カルタをする play karuta. ● カルタを配る deal cards.
カルチャー culture. ● カルチャーショックを受ける suffer from 《a》 culture shock.
● カルチャーセンター 〖和製語〗a culture center. (! (1) たとえば「料理学校」なら a cooking school. のように施設の種類を具体的にいう。(2) a culture center は文化中心地の意)
カルテ [<ドイツ語] a medical [a patient's, 〖医学〗a clinical] record (! 単に one's record(s) ともいう) a (medical) chart, a (medical) file.
カルテット 〖音楽〗a quartet(te).
カルデラ [<スペイン語] 〖地学〗a caldera /kældéərə/. ● カルデラ湖 a crater lake. (! 通例 a caldera lake とはいわない)
カルテル [<ドイツ語] a cartel.
カルト 〖少数派新興宗教〗a cult.
かるはずみ 軽はずみ —— 軽はずみな 圈 (思慮のない) thoughtless; (不注意な) careless; (性急な) hasty, rash; (無分別な) imprudent. ● 軽はずみなふるまい thoughtless [imprudent] behavior. ● 軽はずみな結論を下す form a hasty [a rash] conclusion. ▶ 軽はずみなことを言うな Don't say anything careless [imprudent]. ● 彼女にその秘密をしゃべるとて彼女も軽はずみだ It is thoughtless [careless, imprudent] of 《×for》 her to tell him the secret.
かるみ 軽み lightness.
かるめ 軽め ● 軽めの服装 (薄手の) light clothes; (カジュアルな) casual clothes. ▶ 〈お代わりは〉軽めにしてください A small helping, please.
『カルメン』 Carmen /kάːrmən/. (参考 (1) メリメの小説。 (2) ビゼー作曲の歌劇)
かるわざ 軽業 àcrobátics. (! 「軽業術」の意では単数扱い、「一連の軽業の芸当、離れ業」の意では複数扱い)
● 軽業をする do [perform] acrobatics.
● 軽業師 an ácrobàt.

‡**かれ** 彼 ㈹ (彼は[が]) he (彼ら) they; (彼の) his (彼らの) their); (彼に[を]) him (彼らに) them); (彼のもの) his (彼らのもの) theirs); (彼自身) himself (彼ら自身) themselves. (⇨私) ▶ 太郎を紹介するよ。彼は神戸大学の学生なんだ I'd like to introduce Taro (to you). Taro [×He] is a student at Kobe University. (! 当人を前にしているときや目上の人のことをさすときは代名詞は用いない方がよい)

—— 彼 图 〖恋人〗a boyfriend; 《やや古》a sweetheart; (愛人) a lover. ● やさしい彼 《one's》 gentle

boyfriend [lover]. ▶私の彼は大学生です My *boyfriend* is a college student.
がれ 〘登山〙scree.
-がれ -枯れ ❶〘草木が枯れること〙• 霜枯れの野原 a grassy field *nipped by* frost. ❷〘ほとんどなくなること〙• 資金枯れ *lack* of funds.
かれい 鰈 〘魚介〙a flatfish (〖通例単・複同形. 肉は Ⓤ〗).
かれい 加齢 图 ageing, aging.
—— 加齢する 動 grow old, become older. • 加齢臭 'aging odour', (especially) body odor increasing as a person gets older. (〖「加齢臭」という語や概念は日本で生まれたもの〗) • 加齢現象 (老化現象) a symptom of aging.
かれい 華麗
—— 華麗な 形 splendid; 〈話〉gorgeous. • 華麗な演技 a *splendid* [a *brilliant*] performance.
カレー 〘料理〙(a) curry /kɔ́ːri/; (カレーライス) curry and [with] rice (〖通例単数扱え. 単に curry という方が普通. ×curry rice, ×rice and [with] curry とはいわない〗). • エビカレー a (plate of) shrimp *curry* with rice. • ドライカレー *curried* rice. • お昼にカレーを食べる have *curry* for lunch.
• カレー粉 curry (powder). • カレー南蛮 curry noodles with (Welsh) onion in them. • カレー料理 (a) curry; curried food.
カレー 〘フランスの都市〙Calais /kǽleɪ/.
ガレージ a garage /gərɑ́ːdʒ/. (〖英語の garage には「自動車修理工場」の意もある〗) (⇨車庫) • 2 台用のガレージ a double *garage*. • 車をガレージに入れる put a car in a *garage*.
• ガレージセール a garage sale.
かれえだ 枯れ枝 a dead branch.
かれおばな 枯れ尾花 (枯れススキ) withered (plumes of) pampas grass.
かれき 枯れ木 a dead tree; (葉の落ちた) a leafless [a bare] tree.
• 枯れ木に花 blossoms on a dead tree. ▶チンパンジーが人間の言葉を話せるようなら枯れ木に花が咲くよ You might as well expect *a dead tree to blossom* as expect an chimpanzee to speak human language. (〖might as well A as B は「B は A も同然である」の意〗)
• 枯れ木も山のにぎわい 'Even a mountain with leafless trees looks better than a mountain without any trees.'/〈ことわざ〉Something is better than nothing.
がれき 瓦礫 (破壊された物の破片) debris /dəbríː/; (瓦・れんがなどの破片) rubble. • 瓦礫の山 a heap of *debris*.
かれきなだ 〘枯木灘〙*Karekinada*. (〖参考〗中上健次の小説)
かれくさ 枯(れ)草 dead grass.
• 枯草剤 (a) herbicide.
かれこれ ❶〘およそ〙(約) about, 〈米話〉around, some; (ほとんど) almost, nearly. ▶かれこれ 10 年間 for *about* [*some, almost*] ten years. ▶かれこれ 10 時 It is *nearly* [*almost*] ten o'clock./(近づいている) It *is getting on toward* [〈主に英〉*for*] ten o'clock.
❷〘あれやこれや〙this and (or) that, 〈話〉one thing and another. • かれこれ話す talk about this and that. ▶かれこれしているうちに戦争が起こった *In the meantime* [*Meanwhile*] the war broke out.
かれさんすい 枯山水 *karesansui*; a Japanese rock garden. (⇨石庭)
かれし 彼氏 one's boyfriend.
かれつ 苛烈 —— 苛烈な 形 (戦闘が) bitter, fierce,

hard; (競争が) bitter, fierce, cutthroat, tough.
カレッジ 〘単科大学〙a college. (⇨大学)
かれの 枯れ野 a desolate, winter field; a wintry field.
かれは 枯れ葉 a dead [a dry] leaf (〖榎〗 leaves).
• 枯れ葉剤 (a) defoliant.
:かれら 彼ら (彼らは[が]) they; (彼らの) their; (彼らに[を]) them; (彼らのもの) theirs; (彼ら自身) themselves. (⇨私〔〗)
:かれる 枯れる 〘死ぬ〙die (〜d; dying); 〖しおれる〗wither. ▶庭の花が霜で枯れた The flowers in the garden *died* from [*were killed* by] frost. ▶リンゴの木が枯れてきた[枯れている] The apple trees *are dying* [*dead*].
かれる 涸れる 〘川などが〙dry up, run* [go*] dry.
• 涙がかれるまで泣く cry until *there are no tears left*. ▶井戸がかれていた The well *dried up completely*. (〖かれた井戸〗は a *dried-up* well) ▶ぼくはアイデアがかれてしまった I'm *out of* ideas.
かれる 嗄れる 〘声が〙get* [go*, grow*] hoarse; get [go, grow] husky. ▶彼は風邪を引いて声がかれている His voice *is hoarse* [*husky*] *from* a cold. ▶学生たちは声がかれるまで叫んだ The students *shouted* themselves *hoarse*./The students shouted till they were *hoarse*.
かれん 可憐 —— 可憐な 形 • 可憐な少女 a *dainty little girl*. (⇨可愛い)
★カレンダー a calendar. (⇨暦)
かれんちゅうきゅう 苛斂誅求 exaction of tax.
カレント 〘時事的〙current.
• カレントトピックス current topics; topics of current interest.
かろう 家老 the chief retainer 《of a *daimyo*》.
かろう 過労 (働きすぎ) overwork; (極度の疲労) extreme fatigue. ▶過労で倒れた He collapsed from [with] *extreme fatigue*. ▶彼は過労のため病気になった He got sick from [because of, through] *overwork*. ▶... from *working too hard*. ともいえる)/*Overwork* made him sick.
• 過労死 (⇨過労死)
がろう 画廊 an art [a picture] gallery.
かろうし 過労死 图 death from overwork.
—— 過労死する 動 die from overwork.
かろうじて 辛うじて 〘やっと〙(危ういところで) narrowly; 〖苦労して〗with difficulty. • 辛うじて試験にパスする pass the examination *with difficulty*. ▶辛うじて生計を立てる (= 細々と暮らす) (⇨暮らす) ▶その法案は辛うじて過半数を得て通過した The bill passed with a *bare* majority. ▶辛うじて列車に間に合った I *barely* caught the train. ▶辛うじて列車に間に合った I *managed to catch* the train./(もう少しで乗り遅れるところだった) I *almost* [*nearly*] missed the train. ▶辛うじておぼれ死にせずにすんだ I *narrowly* escaped [had a *narrow escape* from] drowning.
〖会話〗「最終電車に間に合ったの?」「辛うじてね」 "Did you catch the last train?" "*Just*." (〖この場面で just の代わりに barely を用いるのはまれ〗)
カロチン (⇨カロテン)
カロテン 〘<ラテン語〙carotene /kǽrətiːn/.
かろとうせん 夏炉冬扇 (時節にあわないで役に立たないもの) 'a fireplace in summer and a fan in winter'; useless things (persons, people).
かろやか 軽やか —— 軽やかな 形 light. (⇨軽快)
—— 軽やかに 副 • 軽やかに舞う dance *lightly* [〖優雅に〗*gracefully*].
カロリー 〘<ラテン語〙a calorie, a calory (略 cal.).
• 低カロリーの[カロリー制限をした]食事 a low-*calorie* [a *calorie*-controlled] diet. • 1 日 2,500 カロリー

を取る eat [医学] take] 2,500 *calories* a day. ▶この料理はカロリーが高い This dish is high in *calories* [has a high *calorific* value]. ▶このビフテキは何カロリーくらいだと思いますか How many *calories* do you think there are in this beefsteak? ●カロリー計算 calorie counting. ●カロリーメーター 〘熱量計〙 a calorimeter /kǽlərimitər/.

かろん 歌論　an essay on *tanka* poetry.

がろん 画論　an essay on pictures [painting].

ガロン　a gallon.（参考）《米》約 3.8 リットル，《英》約 4.5 リットル

かろんじる 軽んじる (軽く扱う) make* light of ...; (あまり評価しない) think* little [poorly] of ...; (無視する) neglect. ▶彼の警告を軽んじてはいけない Don't *make light of* his warning.（!）人を目的語にとって、×Don't make light of him. のようにはいえない) ▶君は自分の義務を軽んじがちだ You are apt to *neglect* your duty.

:**かわ** 川, 河

WORD CHOICE 川

river「川」の意を表す最も一般的な語．大小いずれの川にも用いるが，他の語と比べると大きな川をさす場合が多い．●テムズ川越しに向こうを見つめる stare across the *river* Thames.

stream river よりいくぶん小さい川のこと．比喩的に「物事の流れ」を表すことも多い．●近くの川に有毒物質を流す dispose of toxic chemicals into the nearby *stream*.

●頻度チャート
river ████████████████
stream ██████
　　　20　40　60　80　100（%）

a river; a stream（⇒[類語]）;《書》a brook.（!）この順で小さくなる. jump over a *stream*〚a river〛)
❶〚～(の)川〛●流れの早い[ゆるやかな]川 a fast-flowing [a slow-moving] *river*. ●幅が 100 メートルの川 a *river* 100 meters wide [in width]; a 100-meter-wide *river*. ●隅田川 the Sumida (*River*); the (*River*) Sumida.（!）《米》では前の方が普通．2 つ以上の川をいう場合は通例小文字で the Sumida and Yodo rivers)
❷〚川は〛●大部分の川は海に流れ込む Most *rivers* flow into the ocean.《米》[sea《英》].
❸〚川に[を]〛●川に臨んだ都市 a city on a *river*; a *river* city. ●川を上る[下る] go up [down] the *river*.（⇒上る，下る）●川を渡る cross a *stream* [*river*].
❹〚川へ〛●私たちは川へ魚釣りに[ボートをこぎに]行った We went fishing in [boating on] the *river*./We went (down) to the *river* to fish [boat].
●川床[川底] a riverbed. ●川開き a river festival. ●川岸（=川岸）

*かわ 皮　❶〚動物の〛(a) skin（!）動物の体をおおう皮．または体からはいだ皮のことで，なめした皮は leather という（⇒革); (特に大きな動物からはいだ堅い皮) (a) hide; (羊など毛を生やした動物からはいだ毛皮) (a) pelt. ●牛の皮 (a) cowskin; (a) cowhide. ●ビーバーの皮 a beaver *pelt*. ●ウサギの皮をはぐ *skin* a rabbit. ▶壁には 2 枚の大きな虎の皮が掛けられてあった There were two large tiger-*skins* on the wall. ▶彼女は日焼けで(=日焼けして)皮がむけた Her *skin* peeled from sunburn. ●わかした牛乳の上に皮ができた A *skin* formed on the top of the milk I boiled.
❷〚果物・野菜などの〛(a) skin（!）通例薄い皮に用いる);（メロン・レモン・オレンジなどの厚い皮）(a) rind /ráind/; (果物のむいた皮) (a) peel; (穀物の皮，パンの) (a) crust. ●オレンジの皮 an orange *skin* [*rind*, (むいた皮) *peel*]. ●リンゴの皮 an apple *skin* [*peel*]. ●バナナの皮 a banana *skin* [*peel*]. ●トマトの皮 a tomato *skin* [×*peel*]. ●皮むき器 a peeler. ●皮をむく (指・刃物などで) peel (an orange); (特に刃物で) pare (an apple). ●皮ごと食べる eat (an apple) *skin* and all; eat (an apple) with the *skin* on. ▶リンゴを食べる前に皮をむきなさい Take the *skin* off before you eat the apple./Peel the apple before you eat it. ▶このオレンジは皮がむきやすい This orange *peels* easily.
❸〚樹皮〛bark. ●木の皮をはぐ take [peel] the *bark* off a tree; bark a tree.
❹〚その他の表現〛●化けの皮をはぐ make known 〚his〛 true nature [character, identity]; unmask 〚him〛. ▶彼は面の皮が厚い（厚かましい）He is thick-skinned./He has a thick *hide*./He is *brazen* [*brazen-faced*]. /（面の皮に焦点を置いて）His *skin* is *thick*. ▶彼も一皮むけばただの高校生だ Scratch him and you will find him an ordinary high school boy.

かわ 革　〚なめし革〛leather, tanned hide. ●革のジャケット[いす] a *leather* jacket [chair]. ▶この手袋は革製です These gloves are made of *leather*.
●革製品 leather goods; leather products.

:**かわ** 側　a side; 〚論争・交渉などの一方〛a part. ●紙の表[裏]側 the right [wrong] *side* of paper. ●川のこちら[向こう]側に on this [the other] *side* of a river. ●太平洋[日本海]側 on the Pacific [the Sea of Japan] *side*. ●家の東側の窓 a window at [on] the east *side* of the house. ●反対側[右側]のページの写真 a photograph on the opposite [the right-hand] page. ●電話の相手側 the person (who is) on the other end of the line. ▶彼は議論で山田の側についた He took Yamada's *side* [*part*] in the argument. ▶責任は彼の[会社]側にある The fault is on his *part* [the *part* of the company]. ▶日本はドイツの側について参戦した Japan entered the war on the *side* of Germany. ▶君はどちらの側かたい Which *side* are you on?（!）on の位置に注意)

かわあいさ 川秋沙 〚鳥〛a common merganser; a goosander.

かわあかり 川明かり　the gleaming surface of a river in the darkness.

:**かわいい** 可愛い　❶〚愛らしい〛(美しくかわいい) pretty （!）通例女性・子供・小さな物やドレス・花など女性的なものに用いる); (小さくて，幼くて) cute; (感じのよい) (すてきに) lovely. ●かわいい花 a *pretty* [a *lovely*] flower. ●かわいい赤ちゃん a *cute* baby.（!）pretty より普通) ●かわいい声で話す speak in a *sweet* [a *pretty*] voice. ●かわいくて魅力的な女性 a very *attractive* and charming woman.（!）pretty には「小さい」，cute には「子供っぽい」という響きがある) ▶彼女はその服を着ると可かわいく見える She looks *pretty* [*lovely*] in that dress. ▶彼女の弟はとてもかわいい（=美男子だ）Her brother is very *good-looking* [*handsome*].

会話「こちらは私の妹です」「まあかわいい」"This is my little sister." "Oh, how *cute*!"
❷〚いとしい〛dear. ●私のかわいい坊や my *dear* boy. ▶孫娘は目に入れても痛くないほどかわいい My little granddaughter is the apple of my eye.
❸〚小さい〛little*; (ごく小さい) tiny. ●息子のかわいいいたずら my son's *little* tricks. ●かわいい時計 a *tiny* watch.

かわいい子には旅をさせよ 'Let your dear son go traveling and see the world.'/《ことわざ》Spare the rod and spoil the child.

かわいがる 可愛がる 〖愛する〗love; 〖腕に抱きしめて〗cuddle; 〖手で触れたりさわしたりして〗caress; 〖愛玩〈誤〉する〗pet (-tt-); 〖盲愛する〗dote 《on》. ▶私は彼を弟のようにかわいがっている I *love* him like my brother. ▶彼は孫をかわいがっている He *made a pet of* his grandson. ▶彼は長男をいちばんかわいがった(=長男がお気に入りだった) His oldest son was his *favorite*.

かわいげ 可愛気 ●かわいげのない(従順でない) disobedient; (ませた) precocious. ▶あの子供はまったくかわいげがない The child *has nothing endearing* in her]./The child *doesn't have the charm* (most) boys [girls] usually have.

かわいこちゃん, かわい子ちゃん (女の子)a pretty girl, (話)a cutie, (米話)a baby. (!後の2語はしばしば呼び掛けに用いる)

かわいさ 可愛さ ●可愛さ余って憎さ百倍《ことわざ》Love too hot turns hate.; No hatred is greater than that which proceeds from love.

＊かわいそう 可哀相 ― 同 **哀相な** 〖形〗〖哀れな〗poor; 〖悲しい〗sad (-dd-); 〖みじめな〗miserable; 〖残酷な〗cruel (-ll-). ●かわいそうな罪人たち poor [*miserable*] sinners. ●かわいそうな身の上 a pitiful [a *sad*, (感動的な)a *touching*] story. ●その孤児をかわいそうに思う feel pity [*sorry*] for the orphan; *pity* [take pity on] the orphan. ●かわいそうに思って(=同情心から)彼を助けてやる help him *out of pity*. ▶かわいそうにその子[太郎]はまたしかられた The *poor boy* [*Poor Taro*] was told off again. ▶子猫にそんなかわいそうなことをしてはいけません Don't *be so cruel* [*unkind*] to the kitten. ▶まあ, かわいそうに Oh, *poor* you [*you* fellow, (little) *thing*]! (!you は相手に対して用いる)/What a *pity*!

かわいらしい 可愛らしい pretty. (⇨可愛い)

かわうお 川魚 a river fish (複 ~, ~s) (⇔a sea fish); a freshwater fish (⇔a saltwater fish).

●**川魚料理** freshwater fish cuisine.

かわうそ 川獺 〖動物〗an otter.

＊かわかす 乾かす dry. (⇨乾く) ●体を乾かす *dry* oneself. ▶ぬれた靴を日なたで乾かすな Don't *dry* (your) wet shoes in the sun.

かわかぜ 川風 a breeze blowing from a river.

かわかみ 川上 the upper reaches (of a river). (⇨上流)

かわき 渇き (a) thirst. ●1杯の水で渇きをいやす satisfy [quench] one's *thirst* with a glass of water.

かわぎし 川岸 a riverbank, the bank of a river; the riverside. ●川岸を散歩する walk along a *riverbank*.

かわきり 皮切り ●この事件を皮切りに... With this incident *as a starter*, ... ; This incident happened *first of all*, and then .... ●彼は講演の皮切りに冗談を言って聴衆を引きつけた He *began* his speech *with* a joke to attract the audience.

かわぎり 川霧 a river mist [fog].

＊かわく 乾く; become* dry. ▶洗濯物はもう(すっかり)乾いていると思う I hope the clothes *have dried* (out) [*are* (well) *dried*] now. ▶気をつけて, ペンキはまだ乾いていない Be careful. The paint *is not dry* yet [is still wet].

＊かわく 渇く (のどが) be [feel*] thirsty. (⇨からから) ▶のどがからからに渇いている I'm terribly *thirsty*. ▶歌を歌うといつものどが渇く I always *get thirsty* when I sing.

かわくだり 川下り a cruise going down a river.

●**川下りを楽しむ** cruise [go] down the river in a (pleasure) boat.

かわざかな 川魚 (⇨川魚〈シェ〉)

かわさきびょう 川崎病 〖医学〗Kawasaki disease. 〖警〗正式名は「皮膚粘膜リンパ節症候群」(mucocutaneous lymph node syndrome)

かわざんよう 皮算用 ▶捕らぬたぬきの皮算用 (⇨捕る)

かわしも 川下 the lower reaches (of a river). (⇨下流)

かわジャン 革ジャン a leather jacket. (⇨ジャンパー)

かわじり 川尻 (河口) the mouth of a river.

かわす 交わす ●彼とあいさつ[二言三言ことば]を交わす exchange greetings (a few words) *with* him. ●酒を飲みかわす drink together. ●彼と言葉を交わしたことがない I've never *talked to* him. (!exchange words with ... は通例「言い争う」の意)

かわす 躱す dodge. ●殴られまいと身をかわす dodge [ward off] a blow. ●ディフェンダーをかわす dodge the defender. ●マーカーを楽にかわす easily round the marker. ●タッチをかわす elude a tag. ●打者をチェンジアップでかわす pitch around a batter with a changeup. ●微妙な質問をかわす evade [dodge] a delicate question.

かわすじ 川筋 〖川の流れる道筋〗the course of a river; 〖川に沿った土地〗the land along a river.

＊かわせ 為替 〖外国通貨の交換〗exchange; 〖郵便・銀行などの〗a money order. ●外国為替市場 the foreign *exchange* market. ●外国為替管理法 the Foreign *Exchange* Control Law. ▶今日の円の対米ドルの為替レートはいくらですか What is the *exchange rate* for today between the yen and the U.S. dollar? ▶私は彼に郵便為替で1万円送った I sent him 10,000 yen by *postal money order* [(米) *money order*, (英) *postal order*]./I sent him a *money order* for 10,000 yen.

●**為替相場** the exchánge ràte, the rate of exchange 《for the dollar》. ●**為替手形** a bill of exchange.

かわせ 川瀬 (川の早瀬) the rapids.

かわせみ 〖鳥〗a kingfisher.

かわぞい 川沿い ●川沿いの村 a village *along* the river; a village that lies *parallel to* [*with*] the river.

かわそう 革装 ●革装本 a leather-bound book.

かわった 変わった 〖奇妙な〗strange, odd, 《話》weird, (やや古)queer, (風変わりな)eccentric; (一種独特な)peculiar; 〖いつもと異なった〗unusual; 〖違った〗different; 〖珍しい〗rare; 〖目新しい〗new. ●変わった名前 a *strange* 〖話〗a *funny*, (めったにない) an *uncommon*] name. ●一風変わった老人 a *strange* [an *odd*, an *eccentric*] old man. (!queer を用いると青年男性の同性愛者を連想することが多い) ●何か変わったことがあれば if anything (*unusual*) happens; (重大な展開があれば) if there are any developments. ●変わった宣伝のやり方 a *different* [a *peculiar*] way of advertising. ●変わった事件 a *rare* [an *unusual*] event. ▶彼は小さい頃からいろいろ変わったところがある He has been *strange* [a *strange* person] in many ways since he was a child. (! person の代わりに man を用いるのは大人の男性をさすので不可) ●最後に建物を見回ったときは何も変わったことはなかった I couldn't find anything *unusual* the last time I went around the building. ▶最近あの人にはあまり会わないけれど, 別に変わったことはないようです I haven't seen much of him lately, but he seems just *as usual*. ▶この店ではいろいろ変わった品物が売られている Various *rare*

[new] articles are sold in this store.
会話「あなたのお兄さんに会ったよ」「そうなの？ 変わった人でしょ？」"I met your brother." "You did? Isn't he a *character*?" (❗ここでは「変わり者」というけなした言い方であるが，文脈によっては「たいした奴」とほめて用いられる．いずれも口語的)
会話「やあ，太郎，何か変わったことない？」「いや，別に」"Oh, hi, Taro. What's *new* [*up*] (with you)?" "Nothing [Not] much." (❗親しい仲間同士のあいさつの言葉)

かわと 革砥 a strap, a strop.
かわながれ 川流れ 〖川の水に流されること〗being carried away by the stream; 〖水死〗being drowned in the river; (水死者) a drowned person. ▶かっぱの川流れ (⇨河童 [成句])
かわのじ 川の字 ▶私たち夫婦は子どもと川の字に(＝子どもを真ん中にして)寝ている My husband and I sleep together with our child between us.
かわはぎ 皮剥ぎ 〖魚介〗a filefish, a leatherjacket.
かわばた 川端 the riverside; 〖川の土手〗a riverbank. ●川端の (a tree [trees]) by a river, 《trees》 along a river; riverside 《tree(s)》; on [along] the bank(s) of a river.
かわべ 川辺 (⇨川端)
かわべり 川べり (⇨川端)
かわます 河鱒 a brook trout (～, ～s).
かわむこう 川向こう ▶川向こうに on the other [opposite] side of the river; across the river.
かわも 川面 the surface of a river. ▶川面を渡る涼風 a cool breeze blowing across a river.
かわや 厠 〖「便所」の古い言い方〗(⇨便所)
かわやなぎ 川柳 〖植物〗a purple willow.
***かわら** 瓦 a tile. ●屋根瓦 a roofing *tile*. ●瓦ぶきの家 a *tile*-roofed house. ●瓦で屋根をふく roof 《a house》 with *tiles*; tile a roof. ●家は赤い瓦屋根です The house has a red *tile* roof.
●瓦煎餅(ﾍﾟﾝ) a tile-shaped rice cracker. ●瓦版〖歴史〗*kawaraban*, (説明的に) a commercial block-printed newssheet in the Edo period Japan. ●瓦屋(店) a tile shop; (商人) a tile dealer; (焼く人) a tile maker, a tiler; (ふく人) a tiler.
かわら 河原 a dry riverbed.
かわらけ 土器 〖集合的〗unglazed earthenware; (かずき) an unglazed earthen [earthenware] *sake* cup.
かわらない 変わらない (一定の) steady; (不変の) constant; (永遠の) eternal. ▶いつも変わらない愛 *constant* [*eternal*] love. ▶永遠に変わらない真理 *eternal* truths. ▶長年付き合っているが，彼は少しも(人柄が)変わらない I have been friends with him for a long time and found that he is *consistent* in character. ▶この靴は新品と変わらない (＝同然だ) These shoes are *as good as* new.
会話「体重の方はどうですか」「ずっと変わっていません」"What about your weight?" "It's *steady*."
かわらひわ 河原鶸 〖鳥〗an Oriental greenfinch.
***かわり** 代わり 图 〖代用品，代理人〗a substitute 《for》; (取り替え品，交代者) a replacement 《for》(⇨お代わり); 〖代理人〗a deputy. ▶彼の代わりはいない There is no *substitute* [*replacement*] for him./There's no one to *replace* 《a substitute, sit in for》 him. ▶いかなるコンピュータも脳の代わりにはならないだろう No computer would be a *substitute* for brains. /No computer would *substitute* [*serve*, *do*] for brains. (❗ ... serve *instead of* brains ともいえる) ▶あの子は父親を恋しがっていて僕がその代わりになっている The boy misses his

dad. I'm just a *fill-in*. (❗ fill-in は 口語で「代役」の意)
── **代わりに** 副 前 ❶〖代理・代用として〗instead of ..., in place of ...; 〖...を代表して，のために〗for ..., 〖...に〗on behalf of .... (❗後の方が堅い言い方).
▶彼の代わりに私が行きます I will go *instead of* [*in place of*] him./I will go *in his place*. ▶人工甘味料は砂糖の代わりに使われる Sweetener is used *instead of* [*as a substitute for*] sugar. ▶彼に手紙を書く代わりに，彼の事務所にちょっと顔を出したらどうだい *Instead of* writing to him, why not drop in at his office? (❗ Why not ...? は Why don't you ...? ともに，提案を示すときによく用いる) ▶この箱をいすの代わりに(＝として)使いなさい Use this box *for* [*as*, ×*instead of*] a chair. ▶社長の代わりに電話しています I'm calling *on behalf of* the president [*on the president's behalf*]. (❗ (1) 代名詞との関係は常に on *his* behalf の形で用いる．(2) on 《...》 behalf の代わりに《米》ではしばしば in 《...》 behalf も用いられる) ▶紅茶がなかったので，その代わりにコーヒーを飲んだ We had no tea, so we drank coffee *instead*. (⇨その代わり)
会話「あなたの代わりに私が彼に頼んであげる」「私が自分で頼むわ」"I'll ask him *for* you." "I'll ask him myself."

❷〖代償として〗(交換に) in exchange 《for》; (お返しに) in return 《for》. ▶あなたにコンピュータを教えてもらう代わりにテニスを教えてあげます *In return* [*exchange*] *for* the computer lessons you'll give me, I'll teach you how to play tennis./If you give me computer lessons, I'll teach you how to play tennis *in return* [*exchange*]. ▶この間の日曜出勤の代わりに(＝埋め合わせるために)今週1日休みを取ってください You can take a day off this week to *make up for* last Sunday you spent at work.

── **代わりをする** 動 〖代用・代理になる〗substitute 《for》; 〖取って代わる〗replace, take* the place of ...; (代理を務める) act for .... (⇨代わる) ▶彼女は休暇をとって休んでいる秘書の代わりをした She *substituted for* [*replaced*, *took the place of*, *acted for*] the secretary who was away on holiday.

かわり 変わり ❶〖変化〗(a) change. ▶計画に変わりはない There is no *change* in the plan./(そのままである) The plan remains unchanged. ▶すべては以前と変わりなかった Everything was *the same as* before.

❷〖相違〗a difference. ▶その二つの物は品質においてほとんど変わりがない There is very little *difference* in quality between the two things./(ほぼ同じだ) The two things are almost *the same in* quality. ▶お前が出かけようと家にいようとたいして変わりはないよ It doesn't make much *difference* whether you go out or stay 《at》 home.

❸〖異常〗▶変わりなく(＝元気に)暮らす get along well [*all right*]. ▶お変わりありませんか How are you?/How are you doing [getting along]? (❗ I'm quite well, thank you. などと答える)/《親しい人に》 What's new [up]? (❗ Nothing special [much]! (いべつに) などと答える)

かわりだね 変わり種 〖異色の人〗a unique figure; an exceptional person; (変わった経歴の持ち主) a person with an unusual career; 〖動植物の変種〗a variety.

かわりばえ 代わり映え ▶彼女の新調の服もあまり代わり映えしない Her new dress is no great *improvement on* her last one./Her new dress doesn't *look much better* on her than the old one.

かわりはてる　変わり果てる change completely; (元の状態が分からなくなる) change out of recognition. ▶夜が明けてみると地震のあとの神戸の街は変わり果てて(＝ぞっとするほど外観が損なわれて)いた When it was day, we saw Kobe lying *horribly disfigured* after the earthquake. ▶母親は担架に乗せられて変わり果てた(＝死んで冷たくなった)息子の姿を見た The mother saw her son, now *dead and cold*, on a stretcher.

かわりばんこ　代わりばんこ ― 代わりばんこに 🔁 by turns; (順番に) in turn; (次々に) one after another (❗いずれも 3 者以上に用いる); (2者が) one after the other, alternately /ɔ́ːltərnɪtli/. ▶彼らは代わりばんこにそのコンピュータを使った They used the computer *by turns* [*one after another*]./They took turns using 〔《主に英》took it in turns to〕use] the computer. (❗単に「彼らは代わりばんこにした」というときは They *took turns* 〔《主に英》*took it in turns*〕.) ▶ぼくは弟とその一つのリンゴを代わりばんこにかじった My brother and I ate the apple *alternately*./I ate the apple *alternately* with my brother.

かわりびな　変わり雛 (説明的に) an unconventional type of *hina* doll made to reflect the current topics.

かわりみ　変わり身 ●変わり身が早い be quick to adapt (oneself) to a new situation; adapt (oneself) quickly to a new situation.

かわりめ　変わり目 ▶季節の変わり目 the *change* of seasons. ▶我が国の歴史の変わり目(＝転換点) a *turning point* in our history. ▶世紀の変わり目に at the *turn* of the century. ▶学年[学期]の変わり目に(＝終わりに) at the *end* of the school year [term].

かわりもの　変わり者 a strange [an eccentric, an odd, 《話》a weird /wɪərd/] person.

★かわる　代わる, 替わる, 換わる ❶【代わりをする】 take* (his [its]) place, replace, (代理のる) substitute ⟨*for*⟩; (順番に) take a turn. (⇨代わり) ▶彼は負傷した選手と代わった He *took the place of* [*substituted for*, *replaced*] the injured player. (❗受身は The injured player *was taken the place of* [*was substituted*, *was replaced*] by him.)/(代行した) He *filled in for* the injured player. ▶芝刈り機をかける仕事を代わってあげよう Let me *take a turn with* the mower.

❷【替わる, 換わる】 take* (his, its) place, replace (⇨取って代わる); (席などを) change. ▶席を換える *change seats* ⟨*with* him⟩. (⇨交換する) ▶彼に替わるチームの後任監督はだれですか Who will *replace* him [*take his place*] as team manager? (❗as の後の唯一の地位を示す名詞は通例無冠詞) ▶彼と替わります(電話で) I'll get him on the phone. ▶市長が替わった We have a *new* mayor. (❗Our mayor *has changed*. は「市長が(外観・性格などが)変わった」の意) ▶あの建物はこの 1 年間に数回持ち主が替わった That building *has changed* hands several times in the past [last] year. ▶年が替わった The new year *has come around*.

★かわる　変わる

WORD CHOICE 変わる

change 変化を表すもっとも一般的な語。しばしば全面的・本質的な変化をさす。▶彼はすっかり変わってしまったように見える He seems to have *changed* a lot.

vary 物事が、根拠が部分的には保ちながら表面的・部分的にいくぶん変化すること。▶サイズと量が変わる *vary* in size and quantity. ▶習慣は国によって変わる The custom *varies* from country to country.

turn 形勢・状態・色合い・職業などが変化すること。change のような本質的な変化ではなく、同一の枠組みの中での変化をさす。▶葉の色は黄色く変わった Leaves *turned* yellow.

❶【変化する】 change ⟨*into*, *to*⟩ (❗通例 into は別の物への質的変化, to は同一物内での程度・度合いの変化を含意する); vary; turn (⇨【類語】); (方向・位置などが変わる) shift ⟨*to*⟩. ● 気が変わる *change* one's mind. ▶事態はいい[悪い]方向に変わった The situation *has changed for the better* [*worse*]. ▶君はこの前会ったときずいぶん変わったね[ちっともお変わりになりませんね] You've *changed* a lot [You *haven't changed* a bit] since I last saw you. ▶この町はあまり変わっていない This town *hasn't changed* much [*greatly*]./(以前とほぼ同じだ) This town is almost the same as before. ▶雪が氷雨(ひさめ)に変わった The snow *changed* [*turned*] (*in*)*to* icy rain. ▶信号が赤に変わった The lights *turned* [×*changed*] *to* red. (❗「黄色から赤に変わった」は…*turned* [*changed*] *from* yellow *to* red.) ▶愛が憎しみに変わることがある Love can *turn to* hate./(反って代わられる) Love can *give way to* hate. ▶価格は需要によって変わる The price *varies* with demand. ▶風は西から南に変わった The wind *has shifted* from west to south. ▶このごろ天気が変わりやすい The weather *is changeable* [*unsettled*] these days.

会話 「今年はどこに行こうか」「信州のどこかなんて気が変わっていいでしょう」"Where should we go this year?" "Somewhere in Shinshu would *make* a pleasant *change*." (❗応答は述部を省略して "Somewhere [Some place] in Shinshu *for a change*." でもよい)

❷【移動する】 move ⟨*to*⟩. ▶住所が変わる *move to* a new address. ▶彼は名古屋支店に変わった(＝転任になった) He *was transferred to* the Nagoya branch.

❸【異なる】 be different ⟨*from*⟩. ▶事態は以前と少しも変わっていない The situation *is no different from* what it used to be. (❗used to be の方が現在との対比が強調される) ▶彼は権力を握ったら口のきき方まで変わってきた He speaks *differently* now that he's got power. (❗彼は言うことがころころ変わる He says *one thing and then another*. ▶彼はすっかり人が変わって(＝別人となって)帰国した He returned home quite another [*a different*] man. ▶所変われば品変わる(＝国の数だけ慣習の数がある)《ことわざ》So many countries, so many customs./Different people have different customs.

かわるがわる　代わる代わる (3者以上が) by turns (❗繰り返しを暗示); (順番に) in turn; (2者が) one after the other, alternately. (⇨代わりばんこ) ▶3人は代わる代わる車を運転した The three men drove the car *by turns*./The three men *took turns* (*at*) driving the car. ▶私は 2 台の車を毎日代わる代わる使っている I use two cars, *alternating* them each day.

かわれる　買われる (評価される) be thought highly of. (⇨買う❷)

かわん　下腕 the lower (⟷upper) arm.

★かん　勘 〖直観〗(an) intuition,《やや話》a hunch; (本能) instincts; 〖芸術・スポーツなどの〗a sense; 〖かぎつける能力〗a nose. ▶勘を働かす use one's *intuition* [*head*],《やや話》play one's *hunch*. ▶勘による trust one's *intuition* [*instincts*]. ▶言語[ゲーム]に対する勘がいい have a good language

[game] *sense*. ●ニュースをかぎつける勘がある have a nose *for* news. ●彼は勘がいい(=理解が早い) He *is quick* (↔*slow*) *to understand* [《話》*catch on*]. ▶私は勘で彼女が来ないことが分かった I knew *by intuition* that she wouldn't come./I *sensed* [I had an *intuition*, Intuition told me] that she wouldn't come. ▶勘で行ったが道に迷わなかった《話》I just *followed* my *nose* and didn't get lost. ▶彼女は来なかった，ぼくの勘があたった She didn't come. My *hunch* was [proved] right. ▶彼女はとても勘の鋭い(=敏感な)人で，心の中を見すかされているような気がすることもある She is a very *sensitive* person. Sometimes I feel she can read my thoughts.

*かん 間 ❶ [期間] (特定の期間の間) during ...; (不特定な期間の間) for ...; (...の期間内で) in .... (⇨間(ﾏ)) ●その3日間 *during* [×*for*] the three days. (❗*during* の後には the, those などの限定詞がくる) ●3日間 *for* [×*during*] three days. ●過去10年間 *for* [*during, in*] the past ten years. (❗*for* の後にはのがくるのは for the past [last]... の場合のみ) ●2週間でその本を読み終える read through the book *in* two weeks. ❷ [場所・人の間] (2 者の) between ...; (3 者以上の) among .... ●3 国間の条約 a treaty *between* three nations. (❗相互の関係を個々に表すときは三つ以上でも使う) ●山間の村 a village *among* the mountains. ●ロンドン-ニューヨーク間の空の便 an air service *between* London *and* New York. ●右中間に高々と二塁打を打つ loft a double *into* rightcenter.

かん 刊 ▶この本は 1980 年刊である This book *was published* [*was printed*] in 1980.

かん 缶 a can;《英》a tin (❗飲料以外の缶詰の缶). ●缶切り a can [a tin] opener. ●缶ビール a canned beer.

かん 完 〖終わり〗the end;〖書物で〗finis /fínis/;〖全部そろっていること〗completion. ●上巻完 *the end* [*finis*] *of* the first volume. ●全 20 冊完(結) *complete* in twenty volumes. ●冷暖房完(備)《揭示》Air-conditioned.

かん 官 〖支配する者〗(役人) a government official; (政府) the government;〖朝廷〗the Imperial Court. ●官と民 the *government* and the people; (公営企業と私企業) the *public sector* and the private sector.

かん 冠 (かんむり) a crown; (第 1 位) the top. (⇨冠(ﾑﾘ))

かん 巻 〖書物の〗a volume (略 vol., 働 vols.); a book (❗volume は外形から, book は外見的に見た場合に); 〖映画の〗a reel. ●20 巻からなる百科事典 an encyclopedia *in* [×*of*] 20 *volumes* [*vols*.]; a twenty-*volume* encyclopedia. ●ポー全集の第 4 巻 *Volume* [*Vol*.] 4 of Poe's Complete Works. ●「クラウン英語読本」第 1 巻 the Crown English Readers *Book* 1 /búkwʌn/. ●6 巻ものの映画 a six-*reel* film [picture]. ▶その辞書は (上下) 2 巻のものです The dictionary comes [is] in two *volumes*.

かん 疳 〖子供の神経質で興奮しやすい性質〗nervousness; 〖過敏〗sensitiveness; 〖ひきつけ〗convulsions; 〖腹を立てやすい性質〗irritability(ɪ̀ɚ). ●疳の虫を起こす have [起こしている] be in] convulsive fit.

かん 貫 〖重量の単位〗a *kan* (働 ～). 〖参考〗3.75kg)

かん 寒 〖真冬〗midwinter; 〖最も寒い季節〗the coldest season [days] (of the year). ●寒の入り [明け] the beginning [end] of *the coldest season*.

かん 棺 a coffin,《米》a casket. (❗後の方は婉曲語) ●棺に納める lay (a corpse) in a *coffin*.

かん 閑 leisure /líːʒɚ/; spare time; time to spare. ▶忙中閑あり (⇨忙中 [成句])

かん 感 〖主観的な感情〗a feeling; 〖感覚〗a sense (❗feeling より客観的な語. sensation より精神的意識に重点を置く); 〖肉体的感覚〗a sensation; 〖喜怒哀楽の感情〗(an) emotion. ●疲労感 a tired [a fatigue] *feeling*. (❗後の方が語調が強い) ●快 [不快; 空腹; 満足] 感 a *feeling* of pleasure [discomfort; hunger; satisfaction]. ●優越 [劣等] 感 a *sense of* superiority [inferiority]; superiority [inferiority] complex. ●危機感 a *sense* [(意識) an *awareness*] *of* crisis. ●恐怖感を持つ have a *sensation of* fear.
●感極まる be filled with emotion; (感動する) be moved [be touched] (*by*). ●感極まって涙を流す weep *with emotion*; be moved to tears.
●感に堪えない ▶今昔の感に堪えない be struck with [by] the change of times.

かん 漢 ❶ [中国の王朝名] Han. ●漢民族 the *Han* race. ❷ [男] a man (働 men). ●熱血漢 a hot-blooded [a passionate] *man*.

かん 管 a tube; (比較的太い) a pipe. ●真空管《米》a tube,《英》a valve. ●水道管 a water *pipe*. ●ゴム管 a rubber *tube*. ●ブラウン管 a picture *tube*, a cathode-ray *tube*《略 CRT》.

かん 歓 ●歓を尽くす (十分に楽しむ) have a very good time.

かん 燗 warming sake ▶酒は熱燗 [ぬる燗] にしてください I'd like my sake to be heated until it's just *warm enough* [*lukewarm*].

かん 環 a ring. ●環をなす form a *ring*.

かん 癇 ●癇にさわる ▶彼のやることすべてが癇にさわる《話》Everything he does *irritates* me [*annoys* me,《話》*gets on* my *nerves*].

かん 簡 〖簡単〗simplicity; 〖簡潔〗brevity. ▶簡にして要を得た説明がなされた The explanation was *brief* and to the point.

かん 鐶 a ring; (鎖の) a link; (引き出しの) a handle, a pull.

-かん -観 a view; an outlook. ●人生観 one's *view of* [*outlook on*] life.

がん 眼 an eye.
●ガンをつける ▶連中はガンをつけてきたといってけんかを吹っかけてきた They tried to pick a quarrel with me saying I had *given* them *a dirty look*. (❗a dirty look は「非難するような目つき」の意)

がん 雁 〖鳥〗a wild goose (働 wild geese).

がん 『雁』 The Wild Goose. (参考) 森鷗外の小説)

がん 癌 ❶ [病気] (a) cancer; (悪性腫瘍(ﾖｳ)) a malignant tumor,〖医学〗carcinoma. ●胃腕部の the Big C, a tumor ともいう) ●胃[肺]がん stomach [lung] *cancer*. ●進行がん advanced *cancer*. ●初期 [末期] がん early [terminal] *cancer*. ●末期がん患者 a person (living) with terminal *cancer*, a terminal *cancer* patient. ●のどにがんができる[できている] have [have] *cancer* in one's throat; get [have] *cancer* of the throat. ●がんの検診を受ける undergo an examination [a test] for *cancer*. ▶がんは彼の体中に広がった [肝臓に転移した] The *cancer* spread throughout his body [to his liver].
❷ [障害] (社会などの) a cancer. ●社会のがん a *cancer* of [in] society.
●癌細胞 cancer cells. ●癌死 death of [from] cancer. ●癌腫〖医学〗a cancerous tumor.

がん願 願をかける ●夫の病気平癒の願をかける(=祈り願う) *pray for* one's husband's recovery from illness.

ガン 〖銃, 鉄砲〗 a gun. (⇨銃)

がんあつ 眼圧 the pressure within the eye; 〖医学〗 intraocular pressure.

かんあつし 感圧紙 carbonless duplicating paper.

かんあん 勘案 ── 勘案する 動 take into consideration [account]. ●諸要素を勘案して計画を立案する *take* many factors *into consideration* before drawing up a plan.

かんい 官位 (官職と位階) office and rank; (官等) an official rank. ●官位を剥奪(はくだつ)される be dismissed from one's *office*; be stripped of one's *rank*.

かんい 簡易 ── 簡易な 形 (簡単な) simple; (容易な) easy; (分かりやすい) plain.
●簡易書留 simplified registered mail 〖《米》post〗. ●簡易裁判所 a summary court. ●簡易食堂 (カフェテリア) a cafeteria; (軽食堂) a snack bar; (自食式食堂) a buffet /bəféi/. ●簡易保険 postal [post-office] life insurance.

かんいっぱつ 間一髪 (⇨かろうじて) ●間一髪のところで死を免れる *narrowly* escape death; have a *narrow* [a *hairbreadth*, a *hair's-breadth*] escape from death; escape death *by a hairbreadth* [*hair's-breadth*].

かんいん 姦淫 (an) adultery.
── 姦淫する 動 commit adultery. ▶汝(なんじ)姦淫するなかれ Thou shalt not *commit adultery*. ▶〖参考〗聖書『出エジプト記』にある言葉

かんいん 館員 a member of the 《embassy》 staff; 《集合的》 the staff 《of the art museum》. ●図書館員になる be employed by a library; become a librarian; become *a member of* the library *staff*.

かんえつしき 観閲式 《hold》 a military review.

かんえん 肝炎 〖医学〗 hepatitis /hèpətáitəs/. ●血清肝炎 serum /síərəm/ *hepatitis*. ●A型[B型; C型]肝炎 *hepatitis* A [B; C]. ●A型[B型; C型]肝炎ウイルス (virus) をその頭文字を取って HAV [HBV; HCV], その感染者を an HA [HB; HC] carrier という

がんえん 岩塩 róck sált; 〖鉱物〗 hálite.

かんおう 観桜 ●観桜会 a cherry blossom viewing party.

かんおけ 棺桶 a coffin, 《米》《婉曲的》 a casket.
●棺桶に片足を突っ込んでいる have one foot in the grave. (▶ 日本語に似た表現だが英語は幅が広い)

かんおん 漢音 (説明的に) the Japanese version of Han pronunciation of a Chinese character.

かんか 干戈 'a shield and a pike'; 《武器》 arms.
●干戈を交える (開戦する) go to [start] war 《against, with》; (交戦する) fight 《against, with》. (⇨開戦, 交戦)

かんか 看過 ── 看過する 動 ●看過できない(=見逃せない)悪行 bad behavior that cannot *be overlooked*.

かんか 感化 图 (an) influence. ●…の感化を受けて under the *influence* of 《a person, a thing》. ▶その本は少年たちによい[悪い]感化を与えた The book *had* a good [a bad] *influence* (up)on the boys.
── 感化する 動 influence; have* an influence 《on, upon》. ●環境に感化されやすい *be* easily *influenced* [*affected*] by the environment.

かんか 眼下 ●眼下に 副 below one's eyes. ●我が家から眼下に港が見える We *overlook* the port from our house./From our house we can see a port *below*.

がんか 眼科 (眼科学) ophthalmology /ɑfθəlmɑ́lədʒi/. ●(病院の) the department of ophthalmology. ●眼科医 an eye doctor [specialist]; 《やや古》 an oculist; an ophthalmologist.

がんか 眼窩 图 an eye socket; an orbit.
── 眼窩の 形 orbital.

がんか 癌化 图 canceration.
── 癌化する 動 ●癌化した細胞組織 cancerous [cancerated] cell tissues.

かんかい 官界 the circle of government officials. ●官界に入る enter into government service.

かんかい 感懐 (⇨感慨)

かんがい 旱害 drought /draut/ damage. ●旱害をこうむる suffer damage from a *drought*; be affected by drought.

かんがい 寒害 damage caused by cold weather; cold weather damage.

かんがい 感慨 (⇨感動) ▶感慨無量だ My heart is filled with *deep emotion*. ▶その本を感慨深く読んだ I am deeply impressed with the book./I thought about a lot of things as I read the book.

かんがい 灌漑 图 irrigation. ── 灌漑する 動 irrigate 《paddy fields》.
●灌漑用水 irrigation water.

がんかい 眼界 (⇨視野)

***かんがえ** 考え ❶ 〖思考〗 (a) thought (▶「思考(力), 思想」の意では Ⓤ, 具体的な「考え, 思いつき」の意では Ⓒ); an idea; a notion; a concept; thinking.

> 〖使い分け〗 **thought** 熟考の結果としての何らかの考え.
> **idea** 心に浮かぶ考え.
> **notion** idea より漠然とした考え.
> **concept** 整然と構築された概念・観念.
> **thinking** 思考作用.

●考えにふける be lost [deep] in thought. ●その件について考えをまとめる collect one's *thoughts* on [shape one's *ideas* about] the matter. ●後の方がより口語的な ●急進的な考え(=思想)の持ち主 a person with radical *ideas* [*thought*]. ●他人に自分の考えを押しつける force one's *ideas* [*views*] on other people. ▶彼の演説には注目すべき考えがたくさんあった His speech was full of striking *thoughts* [*ideas*]. ▶女性は結婚したら仕事をやめるべきだという彼の考えは時代遅れだ His *idea that* women should quit their jobs after marriage is out of date [outdated]. ▶人はそれぞれ幸せについて違った考えを持っている Everyone has his own *concept* of happiness. ▶それはいかにもアメリカ的な考え(=考え方)だ That's a typical American *way of thinking*. ▶私には君の考え(ていること)が分からない I don't understand *what you are thinking*. ▶…understand your thoughts [thinking] は不自然

❷ 〖思いつき〗 an idea, a notion; (考え) a thought. ▶そいつはいい考えだ That's a good *idea*. (▶単に That's an *idea*. ともいう) ▶私にいい考えがある I have [I've got] a good *idea* (for it). ▶I've got an idea. だけでも「よい考え」は十分に表される) ▶新しい考えが浮かんだ A new *idea* occurred to [struck, came to] me./I hit on [got, struck on] a new *idea*. ▶彼の考えはかなり空想的で実行不可能だ His *ideas* are rather airy and impossible to carry out. ▶突然彼女に花を贈ろうという考えが浮かんだ I suddenly had the *idea of giving* [I had a sudden *notion to give*] her some flowers. ▶彼

は考えをノートに書き留めた He put down his *thoughts* in the notebook.
❸ [[意見]] an opinion; (見解) a view (通例複数形で); (考え) (a) thought (通例複数形で); (判断) (a) judgment. ●考えを述べる express one's *opinion* [*views*]; express oneself; speak one's mind. ●考えを変える change one's mind (*about*). ▶その政治情勢についてあなたの考えはどうですか What's your *opinion* of the political situation?/What [×How] do you *think of* [*about*] the political situation?/Where do you *come down* on the political situation? (米国のニュース番組のキャスターが専門家の意見を求めるときによく用いる) ▶そのことについてあなたのお考えをぜひうかがいたい I'd very much like to hear your *opinion* [*what you think*] about it. ▶私の考えでは, 彼は無実だ In my *opinion* [*view, judgment*], he is innocent./To my (*way of*) *thinking*, he is innocent./(書) I *am of the opinion that* he is innocent.

❹ [[意図]] (an) intention (*of doing, to do*); an idea; (目的) a purpose. (⇨つもり) ▶彼はまだ結婚する考えは全然ない He *has* no *intention* [*idea*] *of getting* married or not./(やや書) He doesn't *intend* to get married yet. ▶彼は音楽を勉強しようという考えでイタリアへ行った He went to Italy *with the intention of* [*with the idea of*, (目的で) *for the purpose of*, 《書》*with a view to*] studying music. (日常会話では He went to Italy *to* study music. の方が普通 ため)) ▶父は私を教師にする考えです My father is *thinking of* making me a teacher. (*...intends to* make ... より口語的)/(主に英・やや書) My father *intends* (for) me to be a teacher. (米) ではしばしば for を入れる)

❺ [[思慮]] (用心深さ) prudence; (思慮分別) discretion; 配慮 consideration. ▶そのことを考えに入れる[入れない] take it *into* [*leave it out of*] *consideration* (前の方は consider it ともいえる); take it into [*leave it out of*] *account* (後の方は比較的まれ). (⇨考慮) ▶彼はまだ若いから考えが足りない He lacks *prudence* because he is still young. ▶そんなばかなことをするとは彼は考えのない人だ It is *thoughtless* [*imprudent, indiscreet*] of him to do such a foolish thing.

❻ [[期待]] (an) expectation (しばしば複数形で); (希望) a hope; (願望) (a) wish. ▶その結果は私の考えとはまるっきり違っていた The result was quite contrary to my *expectations* [*what I expected*]. ▶物事は必ずしも考えどおりにはいかないものだ Things don't always go *as you wish*.

❼ [[想像]] (an) imagination; (見当) an idea. ▶それがどんなに難しいか君には考えつかないでしょう You can't *imagine* [*have no idea*] how difficult it is.

かんがえあわせる 考え合わせる (...も考慮に入れる) take*... into consideration. (⇨考慮する)

かんがえかた 考え方 one's (way of) thinking; [[見地]] one's point of view, one's viewpoint. ▶それが日本人の考え方です That's the Japanese *way of thinking*. ▶君の考え方が気に食わない I don't like *the way you're thinking*. ▶君の考え方は正しい[間違っている] You are right [wrong]. ▶母と私は考え方が違う My mother and I think differently [have different *opinions*]. ▶なるほど, そういう考え方もあるのですね. 思いつきませんでした Well, that seems a good *idea*. It didn't occur to me. ▶違った考え方をせよ Think differently [《米話》different]. (「考え方を変えよ」にも相当し, 助言的・訓示的によく用いられる)

かんがえかんがえ 考え考え ●考え考えしゃべる speak with carefully selected words; speak thoughtfully.

かんがえごと 考え事 [[考える事柄]] something to think about; [[心配事]] a worry. ●考え事をする think (*about*). ●考え事にふける be in deep *thought*; be lost [absorbed] in *thought*; think hard (*about*).

かんがえこむ 考え込む [[じっくり考える]] brood /brúːd/ (*over, about*), reflect (*on upon, over*); [[沈思する]] meditate (*on*); [[考えにふける]] be lost [absorbed, deep] in thought. ●自分の不幸についてじっと考え込む *brood over* [*meditate on, think deeply about*] one's misfortunes. ●考え込むようにじっと遠くを見つめる look into the distance meditatively [*thoughtfully*]. ▶彼がそう言ったので私は考え込んだ When he said that, I began to *think about* it./(やや書) His remarks set me *thinking*.

かんがえだす 考え出す think*... up; (考案する) devise, invent. (⇨考え付く) ▶だれがオセロゲームを考え出したの? Who *invented* Othello game? ▶そのことを考え出したら(=考え始めたら)きりがない Once you *begin to think* about it, there will be no end to it.

かんがえちがい 考え違い (⇨思い違い) ▶ぼくのことを考え違いしないでくれ Don't *misunderstand* [(誤って解釈する) *misinterpret*] me.

かんがえつく 考え付く think*of...; (考え出す) think... up. ▶よい案を考えつく *hit on* [*get*] a good idea. ▶あのときそのことは考えつかなかった I didn't *think of* it at the time. ▶あれは気の利いた考えだった. だれが考えついたの? That was a clever idea. Who *thought it up*?

かんがえなおす 考え直す [[再考する]] think* about ... again, rethink* /riːθíŋk/, 《米》have a second thought, 《英》have second thoughts, 《やや書》 reconsider; [[熟考する]] think ... over; [[考え直してやめる]] think better of .... ▶計画全体を考え直す *rethink* [*reconsider*] the whole plan. ▶決定する前にもう一度考え直してごらん *Think* it *over* once again before you decide./*Think twice* about it before you decide. ▶辞表を提出しようと思ったが考え直してやめた I was going to hand in my resignation, but I *thought better of* (*doing*) it./*On second thought* (米) [*thoughts* (英)] I gave up the idea of handing in my resignation. (成句では(米)でも a をつけない)

かんがえぬく 考え抜く think*... out [《米》through]; [[頭をしぼる]] rack one's brains (*over*). ●よく考え抜いた計画 a well-thought-out plan. ●問題点をよく考え抜く *think out* the problems. ▶そのことをとことん考え抜いたか Did you *think* it *out* to the end?

かんがえぶかい 考え深い thoughtful; [[思慮深い]] 《やや書》prudent.

かんがえもの 考え物 ▶それをするのは考えものですね(=あまりおすすめできません) I *don't think it's advisable* (for you) to do that. ▶安ければ安いほどというのは考えものだ(=どうかと思われる) I *doubt* [*question*] *the wisdom* of "the cheaper, the better."

かんがえる 考える INDEX
❶ 思考する ❷ 考慮する
❸ 反省する ❹ 想像する
❺ 予期する ❻ 意図する
❼ 見なす

WORD CHOICE 考える

think 思考や考察をさす最も一般的な語．特に深い熟考をさす場合は think over の形も用いる．▶それよりすごいものなんて考えつかない I can't *think* of anything greater than that.

consider 物事をじっくりと熟慮・深慮すること．時に政府・機関・組織などによる公式の検討も含意する．need, have to, should など，義務や必要を表す表現と共起することが多い．▶現在の状況をじっくり考える必要がある We have to *consider* the current situation.

contemplate 物事を静かに熟慮すること．しばしば公的・社会的な文脈で用いる．▶我が国としてその申し出を考える用意は整っている．Our country is ready to *contemplate* the offer.

頻度チャート

think ▉▉▉▉▉▉▉▉▉▉
consider ▉▉▉
contemplate ▏

0 20 40 60 80 100 (%)

❶ [思考する] think 《*of, about*》; (熟慮する) think ... over, consider (❗前の方が口語的); contemplate. (⇨[類語])

> 解説 (1) 日本語の「考える」は思考活動を行うときに用い,「思う」と区別されるが，英語の think は両方の意に用いられる．(⇨思う [類語])
> (2) 米英人は考え事をするとき習慣的に頭をかく (scratch one's head) 動作をする．

● 英語で考える *think* in English. ▶人間は考える動物であるといわれる Man is said to be a *thinking* animal. ▶よく考えてから返事をしなさい *Consider* [*Think* carefully] before you reply. ▶彼にじっくり考える時間を与えた I gave him time to *think*./ I left him to his thoughts. ▶長い間いろいろと考えた末，パリで勉強することにした After I *thought* it *over* for a long time [After long *consideration*], I decided to study in Paris. ▶よく考えてみると，私が悪かった *Thinking* it *over* [(考え直して) On second *thought*(*s*), (熟考の上) On *reflection*], I found I was wrong. (❗(1) when 節を用いて When I stop to *think* [come to *think* of it, give a second *thought* to it], ... のようにもいえる．この方が口語的．(2) 逆に「よく考えもしないで」は without *thinking* twice) ▶あまり考えすぎないでね(=あまり深刻にとるな) Don't take it too seriously.

① 【...(のこと)を[について]考える】 ● 将来を考える think about the [one's] future. ● その問題を考える think of [*about*] the matter. (❗ of では「頭に思い浮かべる」, about では「いろいろとくわしく考える」の意が暗示される) ● その問題についてずいぶん考える *think* hard [a great deal, 《話》a lot] *about* the matter. ● 人生の意義についてじっくり考える *think* deeply *about* [*reflect on,* (めい想する) 《やや書》 *meditate on*] the meaning of life. ● 一晩寝て考える(=決定を翌日まで延ばす) *sleep on* it.
● ごみをあさるカラス対策を考える devise [work out] a countermeasure against crows scavenging through garbage. ● それについてどうお考えですか What [×How] do you *think of* [*about*] it?/ What's your *opinion of* [*about*] it? ▶今何を考えているのですか What *are* you *thinking* (*about*)? (❗ 文法的には about が必要だが，会話は省略されることが多い)/What do you *have in mind*?/(何をたくらんでいるのか) What *are* you *up to*? ▶今すぐ返事をしなくてもいい．考えておいてくれ You don't have to give me an answer right away. *Think about* [*Give some thought to*] it. ▶金のことか，考えておこう．大した金は出せないが Money? I'll *see*. It won't be a big sum, though. ▶I'll have to see. なら拒絶の婉曲表現) ▶彼は自分のことしか考えていない He never *thinks of* anyone but himself. /He *thinks* only *of* himself. ▶この問題をもっと注意深く考えなければならない We have to *consider* this problem more carefully./We have to *give* this problem more careful *consideration*. ▶何てばかなことを考えているのかしら What a stupid *idea*! ▶彼はあまり深くものを考えない He doesn't *think* deeply./He is not a very deep *thinker*. ▶考えてみると，次郎は昨日も来ていませんでした (Now (that) I) come to *think* of it, Jiro was absent yesterday. (❗ (Now (that) I) come to think of it は よく使う口語的慣用表現)

② 【A を B と考える】 consider [think*] A (to be) B (❗B は名詞・形容詞); think of A as B (❗B は名詞・分詞). ● ピカソは20世紀最大の芸術家だと考えられている Picasso *is considered* (*to be* [*as*]) the greatest artist in the 20th century. (❗ to be は通例省略されるが，as (は受身では用いられることも多い)/Picasso *is thought* (*to be*) [*is thought of as*] the greatest artist in the 20th century. (見なされている)/Picasso *is regarded* [*is looked on*] *as* the greatest artist in the 20th century. (❗ 日常会話では以上の表現の代わりに People *think* (*that*) Picasso is the greatest artist in the 20th century. ということが多い (⇨③)) ▶私はいかなる場合でもうそをつくのはよくないと考える I *consider* [*think*] it wrong to tell a lie in any situation [under any circumstance]. (❗ 形式目的語の it の後には to be は通例入れない)

③ 【...であると考える】 ▶私はこんな制度は廃止すべきだと考える I *think* [*consider*] (*that*) such a system should be abolished./《書》I *am of the opinion that* they should abolish such a system.

④ 【...であるか考える】 ▶彼はその時何をすべきか考えられなかった He couldn't *think what* to do [*what* he should do] then. (❗ 後の方が口語的) ▶我々は行くべきかどうかよく考えなければならない We must *consider whether* we should go.

❷ [考慮する] consider; (しんしゃくする) allow for .... (⇨考慮する) ▶彼の年齢を考えてやらなければならない You should *consider* his age [《やや書》*take* his age *into consideration*]. (❗ *take ... into account* ともいう) ▶若いということを考えれば，彼はよくやった *Considering* (*that*) he is young [*Considering* his youth] he's done well [《話》a good job]. ▶すべての状況を考えてみると私が責任を取らざるを得ない *In view of* all the circumstances, I have to take the responsibility.

❸ [反省する] 《やや書》 reflect 《*on*》; (追想する) look back 《*on*》. ● 昔のことを考える *look back on* old times. ● 自分のしたことをよく考えなさい *Reflect on* what you have done.

❹ [想像する] (あれこれ思いつく) think* 《*of*》; (心の中に描く) imagine; (空想する) fancy; (夢想する) dream 《*of*》. (⇨想像する) ● 考えてみろ．国中で一番の金持ちになるんだぞ (Just) *think of* it. You'll be the richest man in the country. ● そのことを考えただけでわくわくする I feel excited just to *think of* it [*at the mere thought of* it]. ● きっと君は考えているほど遠くはないよ It's not as far as you *imagine*. ● 彼のいない生活なんて考えられない I can't *imagine* [*fancy*] what life would be like without him.

▶彼らがその秘密を知っているとは考えられない I can't *imagine that* they know the secret./I can't *imagine them* [their] *knowing* the secret. (!) them の方が口語的) ▶彼にそれをしてくれと頼むなんて考えられないことだ It is *unthinkable* to ask him to do that./(問題外だ) Asking him to do that is *out of the question*. ▶彼は考えられないほど正直だった He was the most honest man *imaginable*./(信じられないほど) He was *unbelievably* honest. ▶他の惑星に生命が存在することは考えられることです It is *conceivable* that there is life on other planets.

❺ [予期する](思う) think*; (予期する) expect; (懸念する) fear. (⇨予期する) ▶その数学の試験は考えていたより難しかった The math exam was more difficult than I (had) *expected* [*thought* (it would be)]. ▶彼の病気は私が考えていたほど重くない His sickness is not as serious as I *feared*. ▶考えられないことが彼女に起こった Something *unexpected* has happened to her.

❻ [意図する](…しようかと考える) think* 《*of doing*》; (…するつもりである) be going to, 《やがて》intend 《*to do*》; (つもり) ▶結婚を考える think of marrying 《him》. ▶私たちは来年家を買おうと考えている We *are thinking of buying* [*are going to buy*, *intend to buy*] a house next year.

❼ [見なす] regard 《A *as* B》; (⇨①②); (受け取る) take*; (⇨言う) ▶ (a) view. ▶物事をまじめに[軽く]考えすぎる *take* things too seriously [lightly]. ▶その問題をあらゆる角度から考える *view* the problem from every angle. ▶事態を悲観的に考える *take* a pessimistic *view* of the situation.

かんがえるひと『考える人』*The Thinker*. (参考 ロダンの彫刻)

:**かんかく 感覚** 图 (外的な刺激による) feeling, (a) sensation; (内的に備わっている) a sense; (芸術・道徳的感性)《書》sensibility (!通例は複数形で). ▶ユーモアの[方向; 距離]感覚がある have a (good) *sense* of humor [direction; distance]. ▶彼の指はすっかり感覚を失ってしまった He couldn't *feel* his fingers./He lost all *feeling* [*sensation*] in his fingers./(感覚がなかった) There was no *feeling* [*sensation*] in his fingers. ▶(しびれてしまった) His fingers *got numb*[話]*went to sleep*]. ▶彼は音楽に対してすぐれた感覚を持っている He has a good *ear* [has fine *sensibility*] for music. (!前の方は「音感」を意味する)

— 感覚的に 副 ▶感覚的に分かる know *by intuition* [*instinctively*] 《*that* 節》.

● 感覚器官 a sense [a sensory] organ. ● 感覚神経 a sensory nerve.

*かんかく 間隔 [時間・場所の] an interval; [何もない空間] (a) space. ▶一定の間隔をおいて *at* regular *intervals*. ▶10フィートの間隔をあける leave a *space* of ten feet 《*between*》. ▶8メートル間隔に木が植えてある There are trees [Trees are planted] at *intervals* of eight meters.

会話「どのくらいの間隔でバスは出ていますか」「30分間隔です」"How often do buses leave?" "They leave *at* thirty-minute *intervals* [(30分ごとに) 《×at》*every* thirty minutes]."

かんがく 漢学 the study of the Chinese classics [classical literature].

● 漢学者 a scholar of the Chinese classics.

がんかけ 願掛け offering prayers to the god to achieve one's wishes. (⇨願)

かんかつ 管轄 图 [法的権限による管理(権)] jurisdiction; [管理, 支配] control. ▶この件は財務省の管轄下にある This matter comes [falls] under 《 outside》 the *jurisdiction* of the Ministry of Finance.

— 管轄する 動 have jurisdiction [control] 《*over*》.

● 管轄地 a jurisdiction.

かんがっき 管楽器 a wind instrument; the wind (!集合的に用い単・複両扱い).

かんがみる 鑑みる (手本にする) take example 《*by*》; model 《*after*, *on*》. ▶その教訓に鑑みて自己を律する *model* oneself *on* the moral. ▶時局に鑑みて *in view* [*in the light*] *of* the current state of affairs.

カンガルー [動物] a kangaroo /kǽŋɡərúː/ (𝗣 ~s; (集合的)).

かんかん ❶ (とても怒っている様子) very angry [《米話》mad], (really) furious. ▶彼はその言葉にかんかんになった He was *furious* at the words.

❷ [日光や熱などが強い様子] ▶外はかんかん照りだ The sun *is blazing* outside./(焼けつくように暑い) It's *scorching* outside.

❸ [かんかんと鳴る] toll; clang. ▶火事の警鐘がかんかん鳴っている The firebell *is clanging*.

かんがん 汗顔 ▶汗顔の至り (= 非常に恥ずかしい) be thoroughly [deeply] ashamed of oneself 《*for doing*》.

かんがん 宦官 a eunuch /júːnək/.

がんがん ❶ [がんがん音を立てる] (金属がぶつかり合う) clang; (強く音を立てて打つ) bang. ▶どらをがんがん打ち鳴らす hit a gong *hard*. ▶彼はハンマーでがんがん車をたたいた He banged the car with a hammer.

❷ [強い調子で] (活発に) vigorously; (激しく, 懸命に) hard. ▶彼は仕事をがんがんやる He works *vigorously* [*hard*, 《狂ったように》*like mad*].

❸ [ひどい頭痛] ▶頭ががんがんする have a *splitting* headache.

かんかんがくがく 侃侃諤諤 ▶彼らは侃々諤々の議論を戦わせた They argued *furiously*./They had a furious [a heated, a loud] argument.

かんかんしき 観艦式 (hold) a naval review.

かんかんぼう かんかん帽 a boater; a stiff flat-topped straw hat.

かんき 官紀 official discipline [regulations]. (! regulations が組織運営上の規律の意であるのに対し, discipline はそれにモラルの観点が強く含まれる)

かんき 乾季 the dry season.

かんき 勘気 ▶勘気をこうむる (勘当される) be disinherited; (縁を切られる) be disowned.

かんき 喚起 — 喚起する 動 ▶彼の注意を喚起する call [draw] his attention 《*to*》. ▶世論を喚起する arouse /əráuz/ public opinion.

かんき 寒気 (the) cold. ▶2月の寒気 the Feburary cold.

● 寒気団 [気象] a cold air mass.

かんき 換気 图 ventilation (通風) airing. ▶あの部屋は換気が悪くなばこ臭い The room *is* poorly *ventilated* and smells of tobacco.

— 換気する 動 ventilate; air. ▶寝室をよく換気する *ventilate* [*air*] the bedroom well; give the bedroom a good *airing*.

● 換気扇 a véntilating [an exháust] fàn. ● 換気装置 a ventilator.

かんき 歓喜 (great) joy; delight. ▶青春の歓喜 the *great joy* of life one feels in one's youth. ▶歓喜のあまり跳び上がる jump *for* [*with*] *joy*.

かんぎく 観菊 chrysanthemum viewing.

● 観菊会 a chrysanthemum viewing party.

かんきつるい 柑橘類 citrus /sítrəs/ fruits.

かんきのう 肝機能 líver fùnction.

かんきのうた 肝機能障害 impaired liver function.

かんきのうた 歓喜の歌 *Ode to joy*. 〖参考〗ベートーベンの交響曲第9番の「合唱」中のシラーの詩)

かんきゃく 観客 (スポーツ・催し物などの) a spectator; (劇場などの) an audience (⦅集合名詞で通例複数扱い⦆(⇨観衆 解説)). ●満員の観客 a sell-out crowd. ●観客による守備妨害〖野球〗spectator [fan] interference. ●その試合に5,000人[多く]の観客が集まった The game drew 5,000 *spectators* [a large *crowd*]. ●観客席 the seats; (スポーツの) the stands (⚠通例単数扱い). ●観客席にファウルを打ち込む hit a foul into the stands.

かんきゃく 閑却 图 negligence.
— 閑却する 動 neglect; be not serious 《*about*》; (無視する) disregard.

かんきゅう 感泣 — 感泣する 動 be moved to tears.

かんきゅう 緩急 ❶【調子の変化】(スピードのあるなし) fast and slow movement; (ゆるやかさと険しさ) lenience and severity. ▶あのピッチャーは投球の緩急自在 The pitcher can throw *fast and slow balls* as he wants./The pitcher makes a good combination of fast and slow pitches.
❷【差し迫った状態】●いったん緩急あれば in an emergency.

がんきゅう 眼球 an eyeball. ●眼球銀行⇨アイバンク

かんぎゅうじゅうとう 汗牛充棟 ●あの学者の家はまさに汗牛充棟の趣がある(=至る所に本が置かれている) There are books and books and books all over the scholar's house. (⚠同一の複数名詞を3度反復すると「…わあわあわあ」的な表現になる)

かんきょ 閑居 图 〖静かな生活〗a quiet life 《in the country》; 〖することもないひまな生活〗an idle life.
— 閑居する 動 〖小人閑居して不善をなす (⇨小人(ビル))〖成句〗〗

かんきょう 環境 (an) environment (⚠人の成長・思考などに影響を及ぼすあらゆる環境．自然環境の意では the をつける); surroundings (⚠周囲の物理的状況).
●生活[社会]環境 a living [a social] *environment*. ●環境にやさしい製品 an *environment*-friendly [an eco-friendly, a green] product. ●環境を汚染する pollute the *environment*. ●自然環境を保護[保全]する protect [preserve] the natural *environment*. ●悪い[幸福な; 恵まれた]家庭環境で育つ be brought up in a bad [a happy; a favorable] home *environment*. ●環境の変化に適応する adjust (oneself) to changes in *environment*. ▶その青年の人格は彼が置かれた環境によって形成された The young man's character was formed by his *environment*. ▶子供は環境から学ぶものである Children learn from its *surroundings*. ▶彼の家は理想的な環境にある His house has ideal *surroundings* [an ideal *environment*]. ▶私たちには環境があると同時に環境保全義務もある Not only do we have the right to live in a good *environment*, but we have the responsibility to protect this *environment* as well.
●環境アセスメント environmental (impact) assessment. ●環境汚染 the pollution of the environment; environmental pollution. ●環境省 the Ministry of Environment. ●環境大臣 the Environment Minister. ●環境破壊 the destruction of the environment; environmental destruction. ●環境ホルモン an environmental hormone; (内分泌かく乱物質)〖医学〗an endocrine disrupter.

かんきょう 感興 ●感興がわく take an *interest* 《in》. ▶夕日に映えるからすうりを見て私は感興のおもむくままに一句を口ずさんだ The red snake gourds in the setting sun excited my *interest* and a *haiku* poem was on my lips spontaneously.

かんきょう 艦橋 the bridge 《of a warship》.

かんぎょう 官業 (官営事業) (a) government enterprise. (⚠国をさすときは ⓤ, 企業体をさすときは ⓒ).

がんきょう 頑強 — 頑強な (断固とした) stubborn /stʌ́bərn/; (頑健な) sturdy.
— 頑強に 圖 stubbornly.

かんきり 缶切り a cán [⦅英⦆a tín] òpener.

かんきん 桿菌 a bacillus (⦅複⦆bacilli); a rod-shaped bacterium (⦅複⦆bacteria).

かんきん 換金 cashing; conversion into money.
— 換金する 動 convert into money; (小切手を) cash a check. ●商品券を換金する *cash* a gift certificate.

かんきん 監禁 图 confinement.
— 監禁する 動 ▶彼はその部屋に1週間監禁された He was confined to [in] the room for a week.

がんきん 元金 〖金融〗(a [the]) principal. ●元金に利息をつけて repay *principal* and interest.

かんぎんしゅう 閑吟集 *The Song in the Dream of the Hermit: Selections from the Kanginshu*. 〖参考〗室町時代の歌謡集

かんく 管区 a district (under jurisdiction).
●管区気象台 a district meteorological observatory.

かんく 艱苦 〖書〗adversity, hardships, troubles. ▶我々は幾多の艱苦を耐え抜いてきた We have come through much *adversity* in our lives.

がんぐ 玩具 a toy; 〖書〗a plaything.

かんくう 関空 〖関西国際空港の略〗⇨関西

がんくつ 岩窟 a cave; (大きな洞窟) a cavern.

がんくび 雁首 〖キセルの頭の部分〗the bowl 《of a Japanese-style pipe》; 〖人の首〗one's head.
●雁首をそろえる (全員がそろう) get together.

かんぐる 勘ぐる (疑う) ▶彼女は彼がうそをついているのではないかと勘ぐった She suspected (that) he was lying. ▶あまり勘ぐりすぎないで．嫌だなんて言ってないわ Don't *read* too much *into* what I'm saying. I didn't say I hated it.

かんぐん 官軍 (朝廷方の軍) the Imperial army; (政府軍) the government army. ●勝てば官軍〖ことわざ〗Might is [⦅英⦆makes] *right*. (⇨勝つ 〖成句〗)

かんけい 関係 图 ❶〖関連〗(a) relationship; (a) relation; (つながり) (a) connection; 〖利害関係〗an interest.

解説 relationship と relation(s)
relationship の方が意味用法が広く漠然とした語で, 血縁関係は relation より普通. また relationship は血縁関係以外の人に使うと強い感情を伴う緊密な関係を暗示する. 人・国・団体などの公的関係には relations (複数形に注意), relationship を用い, 類似性・依存性などがいう場合には relation, relationship を用いる.

①〖〜の関係〗●国際関係 international *relations*. ●家族関係 family *relationships* [*connections*]. ●男女関係 *relations* between the sexes. ●利害関係者 an *interested* party. ●親子の関係 a parent-child *relationship*; the *relationship between* parents *and* children; the *relationship* of parents to children. 〖⦅米⦆では相互間の関係だが, to では親が子にかかわる一方向性の関係が強調される〗 ●喫煙と肺がんとの間の因果関係 a cause-effect *relation(ship)* [a causal *connection*] be-

tween smoking *and* lung cancer. ▶当社はその会社と取り引き関係にない Our firm has no business *relations* [*connection*] *with* that firm. ▶健と私の関係は何でもないのよ There's nothing between Ken and me.
②【関係〜】▶関係者以外立ち入り禁止《掲示》Private. Please do not enter./Staff only.
③【関係の】●テレビ関係の人々 TV people. ●IT 関係の本[仕事] a book on [work in the field of] information technology. ●関係がある be connected (*with*); be related (*to*), relate (*to*); have ... to do (*with*) (❗...is something, nothing, much など). ▶その二つの事件には互いに密接な関係がある The two incidents *are closely connected with* [*related to*] each other. /There is a close *connection* [*relation*] *between* the two incidents. ▶それとこれとはどんな関係があるのですか What does that *have to do with* this? ▶君の答えはその問題と何の関係もない Your answer *has no relation to* [*has no connection with*, *has nothing to do with*] the question. /Your answer *is irrelevant to* the question. ▶私はその会社と関係がある I *have* some *connection* [*contacts*] *with* the company. /(株主などとして) I *have* an *interest in* the company. ▶彼はあの娘と関係がある He *has* (*sexual*) *relations with* the girl. (❗ 堂々形には注意. sexual がなくても性関係を含意する) ▶学校を出たら音楽に関係のあることをしたい When I leave school, I'd like to do something *with* music.
④【関係に】▶その国はアメリカと敵対関係にある The country *is on* hostile (↔friendly) *relations with* America. ▶彼女とどういう関係にあるか (親族関係) How *are* you *related to* [×*with*] her?/What's your *relationship* [What *relation* are you] *to* her?/(交友関係) How *are* you *connected with* [*are* you *related to*] her?/(どういう知り合いか) How do you *know* her?
⑤【関係を】●外交関係を絶つ break off [(書) sever] diplomatic *relations*. ●日中間の通商関係を促進する[保つ; 改善する] promote [maintain; improve] the trade *relations between* Japan and China. ●外国と友好関係を結ぶ[築く] form [build, establish] friendly *relations with* foreign nations.
❷【その他の表現】▶それは私には関係のないことです I've *nothing to do with* it./That's *none of my business*./It doesn't *concern* me. ▶読書の精神に対する関係は食物の身体に対する関係のようなものである Reading is *to* the mind *what* [*as*] food is *to* the body. ▶私は結果に関係なくそれはやるつもりだ I'll do it *regardless of* the consequences. ▶どういった関係のお仕事ですか What kind of job do you have?/What does your job involve?
●関係修復 (外国などの) fence-mending. ●関係当局 the authorities concerned. ●関係当事者 the parties [the people] concerned; (利害関係者) an interested party [person]. ●関係法規 the related laws and regulations.
── 関係する 動 【関係がある】(⇨③)
❷【関与する】(参加する) take* part (*in*), (やや書) participate (*in*), (巻き込まれる) be involved (*in*), (かかわりある) be concerned (*with*, *in*). ▶その事業に関係した人たちはひと財産を作った Those who *took part* [*who were*] *concerned*] *in* the enterprise made a fortune. ▶全世界が戦争に関係した The whole world *was involved in* the war. ▶彼はその犯罪[その件]に関係していない He *is not concerned in* the crime [*with* the matter]. (❗ 犯罪・企てなどに関係する場合は通例 in. 後の方は「その件に関心を持っていない」の意にもなる)
❸【影響する】have* (an) influence 《*on*》; affect. ▶潮流は日本の気候に大いに関係する The current *has a great influence* [*effect*] *on* the climate [×*weather*] of Japan. (❗ weather は特定の日の天候)

── 関係づける 動 relate; connect. ●この結果を考えられる原因と関係づける *relate* this result *to* [*with*] possible causes. (❗ to は結果からの一方的な関係づけ, with は結果と原因との相互照合によるという関係づけを意味する. 対等に関係づける場合は *relate* this result *and* possible causes)

かんけい 奸計 (悪だくみ) a wicked /wíkid/ design; an evil plot. ●奸計をめぐらす devise *an evil plot*.

:**かんげい** 歓迎 图 a welcome; a reception. ●あたたかい歓迎を受ける receive [get] a warm *welcome*; get a warm *reception*. ●彼の歓迎会を開く give a *welcoming* [(話) a *welcome*] *party* for him; (正式で盛大に) hold a *reception* for [to welcome] him. 《事情》米英では社会的地位の高い人を除いて歓迎会を開く習慣はあまりない ●私は彼に歓迎の言葉[辞]を述べた I said a few words of *welcome* to him./I gave a *welcoming* address to him./I made an address [a speech] of *welcome in honor of* him. (やや堅い表現). ●歓迎シカゴ交響楽団《掲示》 *Welcome*: Chicago Symphony Orchestra. ●投稿歓迎 Contributions are cordially received.

── 歓迎する 動 welcome; give* (*him*) a welcome (❗ 後の方は通例 welcome の前に warm, kind, friendly などの形容詞がつく); make* (*him*) welcome (❗ この welcome は形容詞). ●新入生[新入社員]を歓迎する *welcome* newcomers. ●忠告[提案]を歓迎する *welcome* advice [a suggestion]. ▶私たちは彼らを心から歓迎した We *welcomed* [*received*] them heartily [cordially]./We *gave* them *a hearty* [*a cordial*] *welcome*. ▶彼はどこへ行っても歓迎された He *was* (*made*) *welcome* [*was welcomed*] wherever he went. ●前の方が普通

かんげいこ 寒稽古 mid-winter training (in *kendo*).

*****かんげき** 感激 图 【感動】(deep) emotion; 【感銘】impression. (⇨感動)

── 感激する 動 ●人を感激させる演説 a *moving* [a *touching*] speech. ●感激して涙を流す be *moved* [be *touched*] to tears. (❗ 前の方が普通) ▶彼の誠実さにひどく感激した His sincerity *impressed* [*moved*] me deeply./I was deeply *impressed* [*moved*] by his sincerity.

かんげき 間隙 【すき間】(物と物の間の) a gap, an opening; (時間と時間の) a short while; (人と人との関係の) distance, unfriendliness; (心の) unguarded moments, carelessness.
●間隙を突く ▶すりは人の心の間隙(=すき)を突く A pickpocket takes advantage of people's *unguarded moments*./A pickpocket does his quick job when people *are off their guard*.
●間隙を縫う ▶群集の間隙を縫うように (=間を進んで) 行く thread one's way *through* the crowd. ▶忙しい仕事の間隙を縫って (=合間を見て) 数日京都へ旅行した We went on a few days' trip to Kyoto taking advantage of [when there was] *a short lull* in our busy work.

かんげき 観劇 theater-going. ●観劇に出かける go to the theater; go to see a play.

かんげざい 緩下剤 a (mild) laxative. (⇨下剤)

かんけつ 完結 图 【完了】completion; 【結び】con-

かんけつ 完結 — ▶(連載物などの)本号完結 Concluded./The End. ▶次号完結 To be concluded.
— **完結する** (終える) complete, conclude; (終る) be completed, be concluded.
かんけつ 簡潔 conciseness. (⇨簡単)
— **簡潔な** 形 concise; (手短な) brief; (語・文章などが簡潔で要を得ている) brief and to the point. ●簡潔な報告 a brief report.
— **簡潔に** 副 concisely; (手短に) briefly. ▶この報告書はくどい. もっと簡潔にできませんか This report is too wordy; can't you be more *concise*? ▶君の計画を簡潔に言ってください Tell me your plan *briefly*.
かんげつ 観月 moon-viewing.
●観月会 a moon-viewing party.
かんけつせん 間欠泉 a geyser /gáizər/.
かんけん 官憲 (警察) the police (authorities); (当局) the (government) authorities.
かんけん 管見 ●管見によれば in my (poor) opinion.
かんげん 甘言 flattery; sweet [(巧みな) smooth] talk. ●甘言につられて...した be *flattered* [*cajoled*] into do*ing*....
かんげん 換言 ●換言すれば in other words; that is (to say); (具体的に言えば)《書》namely. (⇨言い替える, すなわち)
かんげん 諫言 名《書》(a) remonstration, (an) admonition.
— **諫言する** 動《書》remonstrate (*with* him *about* [*on*] it; (*with* him) *that* both); 《書》admonish (*for* what he has done; *against* what he intends to do).
かんげん 還元 【化学】(a) reduction.
— **還元する** 動【化学】reduce; (比喩的に)(戻す) return. ●利益を社会に還元する *return* one's profits to society.
がんけん 眼瞼 [まぶた] an eyelid.
がんけん 頑健 — **頑健な** 形 (強い) strong; (たくましい) robust; [[体格が強い]] sturdy.
かんげんがく 管弦楽 orchestral music.
●管弦楽団 an orchestra. ●管弦楽器 wind and stringed instruments.
かんこ 歓呼 a cheer. (⇨歓声)
かんご 看護 名 nursing. (⇨看病) ▶彼は手厚い看護を受けた He *was* well *looked after*.
— **看護する** 動 nurse; (世話をする) look after...; (付き添う)《やや書》attend (to...).
●看護学校 nursing [a nurses'] school. ●看護協会 a nursing association. ●看護師 (⇨看護婦) ●看護実習生 a student nurse. ●看護大学 nursing [a nurses'] university. ●看護人 an attendant (*on, for*).
かんご 漢語 (中国起源の) a Japanese word of Chinese origin; (日本起源の) a word of Japanese origin written in Chinese characters.
かんご 監護 — **監護する** 動 ▶親には子供を監護する義務がある Parents have a duty [It is parents' duty] to *supervise and protect* their children.
***がんこ** 頑固 名 (頑固さ) obstinacy; stubbornness.
— **頑固な** 形 (頑固さ) obstinate [a stubborn] father.

> **使い分け** **obstinate** 他人の意見などに耳を貸さず, 自説を押し通す悪い意味での強情さ.
> **stubborn** 自分の考え・意見をなかなか変えない意志の強さ. しばしば生まれながらの頑固さを暗示.

●頑固なおやじ an *obstinate* [a *stubborn*] father. ●頑固な(=治りにくい)皮膚病 an *obstinate* [a *stubborn*] skin disease. ▶彼はとても頑固です He is very *stubborn* [《話》(as) *stubborn* as a mule, 《主に米》*hard-headed*].
— **頑固に** 副 obstinately; stubbornly. ▶彼は頑固にその受け取りを拒否した He *obstinately* [*stubbornly*] refused to accept it. ▶彼は自分の意見を頑固に主張した(=固執した) He *persisted in* his opinion. (**!**He expressed his opinion *obstinately* [*stubbornly*]. より普通)

***かんこう** 観光 sightseeing (**!**観光+名 の場合 tourist がよく用いられる); [[観光事業]] tourism. ▶観光(業)はその国の大きな産業です *Tourism* is a big industry in the country. ▶彼は観光でハワイに行った He went to Hawaii to *do some sightseeing* [to *see the sights*]./He went to Hawaii *for sightseeing* [*for pleasure*]./(観光旅行で) He went on a *sightseeing* [a *pleasure*] *trip* to Hawaii./(観光旅行した) He *made a sightseeing tour of* Hawaii./(観光に行った) He went *sightseeing in* [xto] Hawaii.

● **DISCOURSE**
京都観光は秋が一番良いと思う I would say that autumn is the best season for *sightseeing* in Kyoto. (**!**I would say that...(...だと思う)は主張を表すディスコースマーカー)

●観光客 a tourist, a sightseer. ●観光客相手の店 a *tourist* shop. ▶北海道の夏はたいてい観光客でいっぱいです Hokkaido is usually full of *tourists* [*sightseers*] in 《主に米》the summer. ●観光シーズン the tóurist séason. ●観光団 a tóurist párty [gróup]. ●観光地 a tóurist síte [área]; a place for sightseeing; (保養地) a (holiday) resort; (見るべき所) the sights; a tourist attraction. ▶日光は日本の観光地の一つです Nikko is one of the *sights* of Japan. ●観光バス a sightseeing bùs. ●観光ホテル a tóurist hòtel. ●観光ルート a tóurist ròute.

かんこう 刊行 名 publication. (⇨出版) ●定期刊行物 a periodical (publication).
— **刊行する** 動 publish; issue.
かんこう 完工 名 completion (of construction work). (⇨竣工(しゅんこう))
— **完工する** 動 be completed.
かんこう 敢行 — **敢行する** 動 dare (*to do*); (遂行する) carry out. (⇨決行) ▶彼らは3日間のストを敢行した They *went on* [*carried out*] a three-day strike.
かんこう 感光 exposure (to light). ▶このフィルムの感光度はどれくらいですか What is the *speed* of this film? ▶初期のころの乾板は感光が鈍かったので, 被写体になる人は長い時間動かないでいなければならなかった The primitive plate was not very *sensitive to light*, so people had to remain motionless before the camera for a long time.
— **感光させる** 動 expose (to light).
●感光紙 photosensitive paper.
かんこう 慣行 (社会的な) custom; (商売・法律上の) (a) practice. (⇨習慣) ●社会の慣行に従う follow social *customs*. ●時代遅れの規制やむだな慣行 outdated regulations and useless [wasteful] *customs and practices*.
がんこう 眼光 ●眼光鋭い男 a man with piercing eyes; a sharp-eyed man. (**!**eagle-eyed や sharp-sighted は「視力が非常によい」の意)
●眼光炯炯(けいけい)として人を射る (目つきが鋭い) have strong, piercing eyes. (**!**eagle eye は決して見逃さない鋭い視力や観察力をいう)
●眼光紙背(しはい)に徹する (内容を深く読み取る) (have power to) read between the lines.

がんこう 雁行 ── **雁行する** 動 fly [go] together slantwise; fly [go] side by side.

がんこうしゅてい 眼高手低 ▶ほとんどの批評家は眼高手低である Most critics are clever at finding fault with other people's works, but they fail to be good writers.

かんこうちょう 官公庁 government and municipal [public] offices.

かんこうへん 肝硬変 〖医学〗cirrhosis /sərɔ́usis/ (of the liver).

かんこうり 官公吏 government officials, 《集合的》 officialdom.

かんこうれい 箝口令 (米) a gag order. (!本来は裁判中の事件についての口外禁止命令)
● 箝口令をしく gag 《about》; order 《him》 not to talk 《about》. ▶あの汚職事件について一切の報道はされないところをみると外務省で箝口令がしかれているのだろ The officials of the Foreign Ministry must have been gagged about the scandal because nothing has been reported.

*かんこく 勧告 图 (official) advice /ədváis/, counsel (⇨助言, 忠告); 〖勧め〗(a) recommendation; 〖提言〗(a) suggestion. ●医師の勧告で静養する take a rest on one's doctor's advice. ▶多くの会社が政府の週休2日制実施勧告を受け入れた Many companies accepted the government's advice [suggestion, recommendation] that they (should) be on a five-day week. (!should を用いるのは《主に英》)
── **勧告する** 動 ●人に辞職を勧告する advise /ədváiz/ him to resign.

かんこく 韓国 〖国名〗South Korea; (公式名)《大韓民国》the Republic of Korea (略 ROK). (首都 Seoul) ●韓国人 a Korean. ●韓国語 Korean, the Korean language. ●韓国(人[語])の (South) Korean.

かんごく 監獄 a prison; a jail. (⇨刑務所)

*かんごし 看護師 ● a nurse (!呼びかけるときは無冠詞でときに大文字); a sick-nurse (!a (dry) nurse (保母), a (wet) nurse (乳母)と区別し). ●正看護師《米》a registered nurse (略 R.N.); (英) a state registered nurse (略 S.R.N.). ●准看護師《米》a (licensed) practical nurse (略 L.P.N.). ●看護師の仕事 nursing. ▶彼女は病院で看護師として働いている She works as a nurse at a hospital./She is a hospital nurse. ●外科の看護師 a surgical nurse.
●看護師長(=婦長) ●看護師養成所 a training school for nurses; a nurses' training school. (⇨看護[看護学校])

かんこつだったい 換骨奪胎 ── **換骨奪胎する** 動 'make a new work of art by adapting the ideas and expressions in old literary works'; (焼き直し版を作る) make a slightly changed edition 《of》; adapt 《from》; (けなして) rehash.

かんこどり 閑古鳥 a cuckoo /kúːkuː/ (複 〜s). ▶やがて店は閑古鳥が鳴くようになった The store has become very slack before long./Business has become very slack at the store after a while. (⇨閑散)

かんごふ 看護婦 a nurse. (⇨看護師)

かんこんそうさい 冠婚葬祭 (説明的に) ceremonial occasions such as a coming-of-age ceremony, a marriage ceremony or a funeral.

かんさ 監査 图 〖検査〗(an) inspection; 〖会社や会計などの〗an audit.
── **監査する** 動 ●鉱山を監査する inspect a mine. ●会計を監査する audit accounts.

●監査役 an auditor.

かんさい 完済 图 full payment.
── **完済する** 動 pay ... in full; (借金を) pay [clear] off 《one's debt》.

かんさい 関西 the Kansai district [area].
●関西(国際)空港 Kansai (International) Airport. ●関西弁 Kansai Japanese; (方言) the Kansai dialect; (なまり) a Kansai accent.

かんさいき 艦載機 a carrier-based [a shipborne] plane.

かんざいにん 管財人 (倒産会社の) a receiver. ●破産管財人 a trustee in bankruptcy. ▶その会社は管財人の管理下にある The company is in the hands of the receiver./The company is now in receivership.

かんさく 奸策 (⇨奸計(然))

かんさく 間作 图 〖うねとうね、株と株の間の〗(栽培) intercropping; (作物) an intercrop, a catch crop; 〖時間的に二つの作物の間の〗(栽培) catch crop growing; (作物) a catch crop.
── **間作する** 動 intercrop; grow a catch crop.

がんさく 贋作 a fake; a counterfeit. (!前の方は「本物」でないことを、後の方は「にせ物」であることを強調) ●正宗の贋作 a fake of a Masamune sword.
── **贋作する** 動 fake; counterfeit.

かんざけ 燗酒 warmed sake. (⇨燗)

かんざし (wear) an ornamental hairpin.

カンザス 〖米国の州〗Kansas /kǽnzəs/《略 Kan., Kans. 郵略 KS》.

*:**かんさつ 観察** 图 (an) observation.
①【〜観察】●野鳥観察 bird watching. ●自然の観察(=を観察すること)は科学において大切なことだ The observation of nature is important in science.
②【観察〜】●観察記録をとる keep a record of (his) observations 《on》. ●鋭い観察眼 a keen, observant eye. ●彼は観察力が鋭い He has sharp [keen] powers of observation./He has a sharp eye./He is a man of observation.
── **観察する** 動 (科学的に) observe; (動きに注目して) watch. ●イヌワシの生態を注意深く観察する watch [observe the life of] golden eagles carefully; make a careful observation of the life of golden eagles. ●その花をよく観察して(=見て)ごらん Have a close look at the flower.

かんさつ 監察 (an) inspection. ●行政監察 administrative inspection.
●監察医《米》a medical examiner. ●監察官 an inspector.

かんさつ 鑑札 a license. ●犬の鑑札 a dog license.
●無鑑札の犬 an unlicensed dog. ●鑑札を受ける get [take out] a license.

かんざらし 寒晒し exposure to the dry and cold air [soaking in icy cold] in the winter; 〖寒ざらし粉〗(⇨白玉).

かんさん 甘酸 ●世の甘酸をなめる experience the joys and sorrows of life; taste the sweets and bitters.

かんさん 換算 图 conversion 《of A into B》.
── **換算する** 動 ●ドルを円に換算する convert [change] dollars into yen. ●円[ポンド]に換算して in yen [pounds].
●換算表 a conversion table. ●換算率 the exchange rate 《between》.

かんさん 閑散 ── **閑散とした** 形 (静かな) (very) quiet; (人がいない) deserted; (あいている) empty; (出席者などがまばらな) thin (-nn-). ▶今日はお客さんも少ない店は閑散としている It's very quiet at the store

かんし 監視 图 [[行為]] (a) watch;《やや書》observation;《書》surveillance;[[人]] a guard; a lookout;(海水浴場などの) a lifeguard. (⇨見張り) ▶休戦は国連の監視の下で実現した The truce was effected under U.N. *surveillance*.
── 監視する 動 watch, keep watch 《on》;《やや書》observe. (⇨見張る) ▶過激派グループを監視する *watch [keep watch on]* a radical group; *keep a radical group under observation*.
● 監視所 a lookout (post);[[軍事]] an observation post.

かんし 冠詞 [[文法]] an article. ● 定冠詞 the definite *article*. (!英語では the) ● 不定冠詞 the indefinite *article*(s). (!英語では a または an. 特に両方の形をさすときは複数形で)

かんし 看視 图 a watch. ── 看視する 動 watch.

かんし 漢詩 a Chinese poem; (集合的) Chinese poetry. ● 漢詩を読む[作る] read [write] *Chinese poems*.

かんし 鉗子 《a pair of》forceps. ● 鉗子分娩(ぶんべん)を行う have a *forceps* delivery.

かんし 諫止 图 dissuasion. ── 諫止する 動 dissuade. (⇨思いとどまる)

かんし 環視 (⇨衆人環視)

かんじ 感じ ❶ [[感覚]] feeling, a sense; [[感触]] a [the] feel; (手触り) a [the] touch. ● 痛みの感じ a *sense* of pain. ● セリフの感じをつかむ get the *feel* of [*a feel for*] one's lines. ● その絵はその場所の感じをよくとらえていた The drawing really captured the *feeling* of the place. ● その皮はさらさらとした感じがする The skin *has* a rough *touch* [*feel*]./The skin *feels* rough./The skin is rough *to the touch* [*feel*]. ● 寒くて手の感じがまるでない My hands *are numb from* the cold./I have no *feeling* in my hands *from* the cold. ● まるで左足が折れているような感じがする I *feel as if* my left leg *were* [[[話]] *was*, [[話]] *is*] broken. ● だれかが後ろにいるような感じがした I *sensed that* someone was behind me. ● 彼の声にはユーモアの感じがあった There was just *a touch* of humor in his voice.

❷ [[印象]] an impression (⇨印象), (予感, 心持ち) a feeling. ● 感じのよい[悪い]人 a *pleasant* [an *unpleasant*] person; an *agreeable* [a *disagreeable*] person. ● 感じやすい年ごろの少女 a girl (who is) at an *impressionable* [a *sensitive*] age. ● 彼がすぐに戻ってくるような感じがする I *feel* [*have a feeling*] (*that*) he will come back soon./I have [*am under*] *the impression that* he will come back soon. ● 初めて彼に会ってどんな感じを受けましたか How [×What] did you *feel* when you first met him? ● 彼女は優しい感じの人です My (general) *impression* is that she is a kind person./(のように見える) She *looks like* a kind person. ● 君はいつも仕事仕事って感じだね You always *seem to be* working.

*かんじ** 漢字 (a) *kanji*; a Chinese character (!×a Chinese letter は不可 ●字). ● 常用漢字 *Chinese characters* for daily [everyday] use. ● 漢字で書く write in *kanji* [*Chinese characters*]. ▶漢字には通例二つの違った読みがある There are usually two different readings for each *kanji*.

かんじ 莞爾 ● 莞爾としてほほえむ smile contentedly [complacently].

かんじ 幹事 a manager, a secretary; (会合などの) an organizer; (パーティー・宴会などの司会・進行係) a master of ceremonies (略 M.C.).
● 幹事長 a chief secretary; a secretary-general. (!しばしば大文字で) ● 自民党(副)幹事長 the (Deputy) *Secretary-General* of the LDP.

かんじ 監事 (監査役) an auditor.

ガンジー [[インドの政治家]] Gandhi /gάːndi(ː)/ (Mohandas Karamchand 〜, 通称 Mahatma 〜).

かんじいる 感じ入る be deeply [profoundly] impressed 《by, with》.

がんじがらめ ● 規則でがんじがらめになっている(=束縛されている) *be bound* [*be tied down*] by rules. ● 借金でがんじがらめになっている(=手も足も縛られている) *be bound hand and foot* by one's debt; *be bound head and foot* in debt (!慣用句). ● 彼女は学があるために内面ではその学にがんじがらめにされている She, who has had education, *is fastened up* on the inside.

かんしき 乾式 ● 乾式の 形 dry 《copies》. (⇨湿式)
かんしき 鑑識 [[鑑定]] (a) judgment; [[犯罪確認]] criminal identification.
● 鑑識課 the section of criminal identification.

かんじき 《a pair of》(oval-shaped) snowshoes. ● かんじきをはく wear *snowshoes*; *snowshoe*.

ガンジス ● ガンジス川 the Ganges /ɡǽndʒiːz/.

カンジダしょう カンジダ症 [[医学]] candidiasis /kændidάiəsis/.

がんじつ 元日 New Year's Day. (⇨元旦(がん))

かんきゅうりょうしつどけい 乾湿球湿度計 a psychrometer /saikrάmətər/.

*かんして** 関して about...; on...; [[関する限り]] as far as... concerned. (⇨ついて, 関する).

かんじとる 感じ取る (情況などを) grasp; (見て感じる) perceive; (五感で察知する) sense.

*かんしゃ** 感謝 图 thanks; (感謝の念) gratitude. ● 神に感謝を捧げる give *thanks* to God. ▶これは私たちのほんの感謝のしるしです This is only a token of our *gratitude*. ▶彼らは彼に時計を贈って感謝の意を表した They showed their *gratitude* [*appreciation*] by giving him a watch. ▶ご援助に対し感謝の言葉もありません I have no words to *thank* you *for* your help. ▶(どのように感謝したらよいか分からない) I don't know how to *thank* you *for* your help./(いくら感謝しても足りない) I cannot *thank* you enough *for* your help.

── 感謝する 動 thank 《人+*for*+事》; be grateful [thankful] 《*to*+人+*for*+事》; 感謝する(自然・神などへの場合も用いる); (好意などに) appreciate (!人を目的語にとらない). ▶ご親切に心より感謝します *Thank* you very much *for* your kindness./I'm most *grateful* (to you) *for* your kindness./I very much *appreciate* [×thank] your kindness./I wish to *express* my deep *gratitude* [*appreciation*] *to* you *for* your kindness. (!この順に丁寧な言い方となる) ▶彼は私たちの贈り物に感謝してにっこり笑った He smiled *in appreciation of* our gift. ▶あなたに感謝しなければならないことがたくさんあります I've got a lot to *thank* you *for*.
● 感謝感激雨霰(あめあられ) ▶いろいろお世話いただき感謝感激雨あられです I can't thank you enough for everything you've done for me.
● 感謝祭 (米国の) Thànksgíving Dày. (⇨参) 11

かんじゃ 患者 a patient; (特定の病状の) a case; (特定の病状で苦しんでいる) a sufferer (⚠ a victim (犠牲者)は避ける). ●重症患者 a seriously ill *patient*; a serious *case*; a person with a serious disease. ●エイズ患者 an AIDS *sufferer*. ●入院患者 an ínpatient. (⚠ impátient と混同しないこと) ●通院[外来]患者 an óutpatient. ●初期のがん患者 a cancer *patient* in the early stages; an early *case* of cancer. ▶医者は患者に禁煙するように勧めた The doctor advised the *patient* to stop smoking. ▶医者は同一の患者を診る場合も、毎日新しい患者を診る気持ちで観察していかなければならない Even when a doctor deals with [sees] the same *patient* every day, the doctor should observe him or her with the attitude of examining a new *patient*.

かんしゃく 癇癪 a temper; a fit of anger. ●かんしゃく持ち a *hot-tempered* [a *quick-tempered*] person. ●かんしゃくを起こす lose one's *temper* (⚠ この temper は「心の平静」の意); get impatient 《with》; fly into a rage [a temper]; 《話》blow up 《at》. ●かんしゃくを起こして in a *temper* [a *fit of anger*].

●癇癪玉 a fit of rage; (爆竹) a firecracker. ▶この言葉に彼女のかんしゃく玉が破裂し彼の横っ面を張り飛ばした At this she burst into *a fit of rage* and slapped him on the cheek.

かんじやすい 感じ易い (敏感な) sensitive 《to》; (感受性が強く、かつ影響を受けやすい) susceptible 《to》; (単純に影響を受けやすい) (けなして) impressionable 《boys》. ▶十代は最も感じやすい年頃です The teens are the most *sensitive* time of life.

かんしゅ 看守 a (prison) guard; 《英》a warder.

かんしゅ 看取 — **看取する 動** (感じ取る) realize; (察知する) sense; (見抜く) see through .... ●先方の意向を看取する *find out* what he wants.

かんしゅ 館主 《書》a proprietor /prəpráiətər/ 《of a hotel [a restaurant]》; an owner.

かんしゅ 艦首 the bow(s) /báu(z)/ of a warship.

かんじゅ 甘受 — **甘受する 動** どんな運命も甘受する (=服従する) submit to [(受け入れる) accept] any fate. ●侮辱を甘受する (我慢する) *put up with* [《話》*swallow*] an insult; (屈服する) *submit* (oneself) *to* an insult.

かんじゅ 官需 the official demand; the demand of the government (and municipal) offices [agencies]. (⇔民需)

かんじゅ 貫首, 貫主 the superintendent Buddhist priest; the head [chief] Buddhist priest.

かんしゅう 慣習 (a) custom; (しきたり) (a) convention. (⇨習慣) ●慣習により by *convention*. ●慣習を守る observe a *custom*. ●その土地の慣習を破る break the local *customs* [*conventions*]. ●社会の慣習に従う follow social *customs* [*conventions*].

DISCOURSE
新しく住む国の慣習に従うことで、環境により早く慣れるだろう。...また、その国についてより理解することができるはずだ By following the *customs* of the new country you live in, you will get used to the environment more quickly. ... **In addition**(,) you will come to understand it better. (In addition (to ...) ((...に)加えて)は追加に用いるディスコースマーカー)

かんしゅう 監修 (editorial) supervision. ▶この辞書はK教授が監修だ This dictionary was compiled *under the supervision of* [*was supervised by*] Professor K.
●監修者 an (editorial) supervisor.

かんしゅう 観衆 (スポーツ・催し物などの) a spectator; (劇場などの) an audience ((⚠ 集合名詞で通例単数扱い (⇨聴衆 解説))); (通りすがりの) an onlooker, a spectator. ●大観衆 crowds of *spectators*. ▶競技場は3万人の観衆で埋まった The stadium was filled with 30,000 *spectators*. ▶このスタジアムは5万人の観衆を収容できる This stadium seats 50,000 *spectators*.

かんじゅく 完熟 — **完熟の 形** fully-ripened [fully ripe] 《tomatoes》.
— **完熟する 動** be fully ripened (by the sun). (⚠ mature は形容詞・動詞ともに肉体や精神について用いるのが普通)

かんじゅせい 感受性 (受感性) sensibility (⚠ しばしば複数形で); (受容力) receptivity. ●詩人の感受性 the *sensibility* of a poet. ●感受性のすぐれた人 a person of refined *sensibilities*. ▶彼女は感受性が強い She has a *sensitive* [a *receptive*] mind. ▶彼は色に対する感受性が鋭い He *is sensitive* to color./He has a fine *feeling* [has fine *sensibility*] *for* color.

かんしょ 甘蔗 〖「サトウキビ」の異称〗〖植物〗a sugar cane.

かんしょ 甘藷 〖「サツマイモ」の異称〗〖植物〗a sweet potato (⚠ ~es).

かんしょ 寒暑 heat and cold. ●寒暑の差の著しい国 a country with great differences of *temperature between seasons*.

かんじょ 官女 (女王・皇后・内親王に仕える女性) a lady-in-waiting 《ladies-》.

がんしょ 願書 an application (form). ●大学入学願書を提出する send in [file] an *application for* admission to a university.

*****かんしょう 干渉 图** interference 《in, with》; (内政への)《書》(an) intervention 《in》. ●政治に対する干渉 *interference* in politics. ●武力干渉 armed *intervention*. ▶私生活への干渉は我慢できないと彼女は言う She says she won't tolerate *interference* in her private life.

— **干渉する 動** interfere [meddle] 《in, with》, 《話》poke one's nose in [into ...], butt in 《on》[into ...]. ●夫婦のことに干渉(=口出し)する *interfere with* [*between*] a husband and wife. ●他国の内政に干渉する *interfere*《書》*intervene*] *in* the domestic affairs of another country. ▶ぼくらの事に干渉するのはやめて、そっとしておいてほしいんだ Stop *interfering in* [*meddling in, poking your nose into*] our affairs, and leave us alone. ▶男は家庭のこまごましたことに干渉すべきでない A man shouldn't *interfere with* domestic details.

*****かんしょう 鑑賞 图** (an) appreciation. (⚠ 「鑑賞力」の意味では ⓒ) ●美術の鑑賞力がある have an *appreciation* of art; have an eye for art. ▶趣味は絵画[音楽]鑑賞です My hobby is looking at pictures [listening to music].

— **鑑賞する 動** (価値を認めて味わう) appreciate; (楽しむ) enjoy. ●英詩を鑑賞する *appreciate* English poetry.

かんしょう 完勝 图 a complete [a crushing] victory.
— **完勝する 動** 敵に完勝する have [get, win] a *complete victory over* the enemy.

かんしょう 冠省 ⇨前略

かんしょう 勧奨 图 (推奨) recommendation; (奨励) encouragement; (勧告) advice; (提案) suggestion.
— **勧奨する** 動 recommend; encourage; advise; suggest. ● 退職を勧奨する *suggest* that (he) (should) retire. (!*should* を用いるのは《主に英》で, 省く傾向は弱まってきている)

かんしょう 感傷 图 sentiment.
— **感傷的な** 形 sentimental. ● 感傷的になる get *sentimental* 《*about*》.

かんしょう 管掌 — **管掌する** 動 take charge of; (管理する) manage. ● 人事業務を管掌する take charge of the personnel. ● 政府管掌保険 insurance *under government management*.

かんしょう 緩衝 ● 緩衝器 (鉄道車両の) a bumper, 《英》a buffer; (自動車の) (⇨バンパー). ● 緩衝国 a buffer state. ● 緩衝地帯 a buffer zone.

かんしょう 環礁 an atoll /ǽto(ː)l/. ● ビキニ環礁 the Bikini *atoll* [*Atoll*].

かんしょう 観照 — **観照する** 動 ● 自然[人生]を観照する contemplate nature [life].

かんしょう 観賞 — **観賞する** 動 ● 朝顔を観賞する (= 楽しむ) *enjoy seeing* morning glories.
● 観賞(用)植物 ornamental plants.

* **かんしょう 感情** feeling(s) (!「理性」に対する語で,「感情」を示す最も一般的な語); (an) emotion (!愛情・悲しみ・喜びなどの強い感情); (a) passion (!理性的な判断を圧倒してしまうほどの激しい愛情や怒りなど); (a) sentiment (!感情的要素を含んだ見解).

❶【～感情】● 国民感情 public *feeling* [*sentiment*]. ● 恋愛感情 the feeling of love. ● 宗教的感情 religious *emotions* [*feelings*]. ● 強い反日感情 strong anti-Japanese *sentiment*(s) [*feeling*].

❷【感情が】● 感情が高ぶる (= 興奮する) get excited. ● 感情が薄らぐ get over one's *emotions*.

❸【感情(の)】● 感情の問題 a matter of *sentiment* [*feeling*]. ● 感情の激しい人 a person of strong *emotion*(s). ● 人間は感情の(=感情的な)動物だ Man is an *emotional* creature./Humans [Human beings, We] are creatures of *emotion*. (!性差別を意識する人は後の方を好む)

❹【感情に】● 感情に負ける (= 流される) give way to one's *feelings*. ● 一時の感情に駆られてそれをする do it *on* [×*with*] *the spur of the moment*. ● 理性よりもむしろ感情に訴える appeal to one's *feelings* [*emotions*] rather than to one's reason. ▶裁判官は感情に動かされるべきではない A judge should not be guided by *sentiment*.

❺【感情を】● 感情を抑える control one's *feelings*; control oneself. ● 感情を隠す hide [《やや書》conceal] one's *feelings* [*emotions*]. ● 感情を顔に表す show one's *feelings* [*emotions*] on one's face. ● 人の感情を汲み取る enter into another's *feelings*. ● 彼に対して特別な感情[悪感情]を持つ have *feelings* for [ill *feeling* toward, bad *feeling* toward] him. ● 感情を込めて歌う sing with great *feeling* [deep *emotion*]. ▶彼の感情を害さないように注意しなさい Be careful not to hurt [injure] his *feelings*. ● 特に無神経な言動によって人の感情を害するときに, 成句で tread /tréd/ on 《his》 toes [corns] という) ▶日本人は感情を食っている人間だ Japanese are people feeding on their *sentiment*. (! feed on を食べ物以外について用いるときは「利用する, よいところだけを取る」(taking advantage) の意を含む)

— **感情的な** 形 emotional. (⇨图 ❸)

— **感情的に** 副 ● 感情的に不安定だ be *emotionally* unstable. ▶あまり感情的にならないでくれ Don't get so *emotional*.
● 感情指数 an emotional quotient 《略 EQ》. (≫ IQ に対し心の知能指数といわれる) ● 感情論 an emotional argument.

* **かんじょう 勘定** ❶【計算】calculation; (数えた数) a count. ● 勘定する時に間違いをする make mistakes in *calculation*; miscalculate. ● 勘定高い人 a *calculating* person. ▶私を勘定に入れて10人いた There were ten people present, *including* me [*counting* me *in*]. (!前の方が普通)

❷【支払い】(請求書) a bill; (レストランなどの)《米》a check; (清算(書), 掛け勘定) an account. ● 5,000円の勘定を払う pay a *bill for* [×*of*] 5,000 yen. ● 勘定をためる run up *bills*. ▶勘定をお願いします(レストランなどで) (Let me have the) *check* [*bill*], please./I'd like to pay the *check* [*bill*]. ▶勘定は別々にしてください (We'd like) separate *checks* [*bills*], please. (!*separate* /séparət/ の発音に注意. 動 は /séparèit/) ▶勘定は別々に払いましょう Let's separate the *bill*. ● split the bill なら「各自が同じ金額を払う」の意)/(話) Let's go Dutch. (!オランダ人の前では避ける) ▶勘定はいくらになりますか How much is my *bill*?/How much do I owe you?/(おとけて) What are the *damages* [What's the *damage*]? ▶食事の勘定は私が持ちます The meal is *on* me. I'll *treat* you this time. (≫奢(ポッ)る) ▶上司があなたを昼食に誘ったら, 彼がおそらくあなたの勘定を払うだろう When your boss invites you to lunch, he is likely to pay the *check* [《話》pick up the *tab*] (*for* it). ▶この靴を私の勘定につけておいてください Please put these shoes on my *account*. (⇨付け)

❸【考慮】consideration, account. (⇨考慮) ● 彼の援助を勘定に入れる (= 当てにする) *count on* his help [him *to* help].

— **勘定する** 動 calculate; (一つずつ数えて) count. ● 財布の中の金を勘定する *count* the money in one's wallet.

かんじょう 冠状 — **冠状の** 形 coronary.
● 冠状静脈『解剖』a coronary vein. ● 冠状動脈『解剖』a coronary artery. ● 冠状動脈血栓『医学』(a) coronary thrombosis.

かんじょう 環状 — **環状の** 形 circular.
● 環状線 (道路) a circular road;《米》a beltway, a belt highway,《英》a ring road; (鉄道) a loop [a belt] line. ● 大阪環状線外回り Osaka Outer Loop Line.

がんじょう 岩床『地学』a sheet.

がんじょう 岩礁 a (shore) reef (複 ～s); a rock (!しばしば複数形で). ● 岩礁にぶつかる[乗り上げる] strike [go on] *rocks*.

がんじょう 頑丈 — **頑丈な** 形 [強い] strong; [体がたくましい, 物が頑丈な] sturdy; [堅固にできた] strongly-built. ● 頑丈な体 a *strong* [a *sturdy*] body. ● 頑丈な土台 a *strong* [a *solid*, しっかり固定した] a *firm*] foundation.

— **頑丈に** 副 ● この家は頑丈にできている This is a *strongly-built* house./This house is *strongly* built.

かんじょういにゅう 感情移入 图《やや書》empathy.
— **感情移入する** 動 empathize《*with*》.

かんしょく 官職 a government office [rank]. ● 官職についている be in government *service*; have a *post* [a *position*] *in a government office*.

かんしょく 寒色 a cool color (↔a warm color).

かんしょく 間色『中間色』(⇨中間)

かんしょく　間食 图 a snack. ●間食を控える eat less between meals; eat less.
——**間食する** 動 eat between meals; snack.
かんしょく　閑職 a sinecure /sáinikjʊər/. (!)(あまり働かなくても収入と地位のある職) ●閑職に移される be transferred to a position with few duties to do.
かんしょく　感触 ❶[触れた感じ] a [the] touch; a [the] feel. ●感触が柔らかい毛布 blankets soft to the *touch* [*feel*]; blankets with a soft *touch* [*feel*]. ●私はウールが肌に当たる感触が嫌いだ I don't like the *feel* of wool against my skin. (⇨手触り, 感じ)
❷[相手の話や様子から受ける感じ] a feeling. ●彼は我々の提案に好意的だとの感触を得た We had a *feeling* that he was in favor of our proposal.

がんしょく　顔色 complexion. ●顔色を失う lose color; turn pale. ●本職も顔色なし(=圧倒される) put a professional to shame.

かんじる　感じる ❶[ある感覚を生じる] feel* (!)最も一般的な語); (感うく) sense; (印象を受ける) be impressed 《by, with》; [実感する] realize; [気づいている] be aware 《of》; [自覚している] be conscious 《of》; [よさをしみじみ味わう] appreciate; [感動する] be touched [be moved] 《by》. ●腹立たしく[わくわくするのを]感じる *feel* angry [thrilled]; *feel* anger [a thrill]. ●危険を感じる *sense* danger. ●背中に痛みを感じる I (can) *feel* some pain in the back./(背中が痛い) I have a pain in the back. ●私は何かが私の足に触れている[触れた]のを感じた I *felt* something touching [touch, against] my foot. ●私はこの平和があまり長くは続かないと感じていた I had a *feeling* that this peace would not last much longer. ●1時間が100年のように感じられた An hour *felt* like a century. (!)feel like は「物事が…のような感触がある」の意) ●部屋に足を踏み入れたとたん何か妙なものを感じた The moment I stepped into the room, I *sensed* [*felt*] something wrong. (!)…sensed [*felt*] (that) something was wrong. ともいえる) ●私は自分の無知を痛いほど感じています I keenly *realize* [I am fully *aware of*] my ignorance. (!)×I'm keenly realizing.... とはしない)/I keenly *realize* [I am fully *aware* (*of*)] how ignorant I am. (!)wh- 節の前では it が省略されることが多い) ●私は尾行されているのを感じていた I *was aware* [*conscious*] of being followed./I *was aware* [*conscious*] that I was being followed. ●何か月も一生懸命働いた後なので，私たちは休暇のありがたさをしみじみ感じた We *appreciated* [*realized* the blessing of] a holiday after months of hard work. ●彼の深い友情を身にしみて感じた I *was* immensely *touched* [*moved*] by his deep friendship.

会話「彼の講演を聞いてどのように感じましたか」「説得力があると感じました」"How did you *feel* about his speech?" "I *felt* (that) it was persuasive./(書) I *felt* it (to be) persuasive."/"How did his speech *impress* you?" "It *impressed* me as (being) persuasive." (⇨印象)

❷[その他の表現] ●猫の目は光を感じやすい Cats' eyes *are sensitive* to light. ●君の親切には恩義を感じています I *owe* you a *debt of gratitude* for your kindness.

かんしん　感心 图 admiration. ●感心して彼を見る look on [at] him *with admiration* [*admiringly*]. (!)「ある感情を持って見る」場合は look on の方が普通
——**感心な** 形 [立派な] good*; (感嘆すべき) admirable /ǽdmərəbl/; (賞賛に値する) (やや書) praiseworthy. ●感心な行い an *admirable* act [《書》deed]. ●なんて感心な子なのだろう What a *good boy* (he is)! (!)he is を省略する方が普通
——**感心する** 動 (気に入る) like; (感嘆する) admire; (印象づけする) be impressed 《by, with》. ●そのような考えはあまり感心しない I don't *like* [*care for*] such an idea very much. (!)care for は否定文・疑問文・条件文で用いる) ●それにはあまり感心できない That's not very good. ●彼の勤勉ぶりに私はすっかり感心した I *was* deeply [*greatly*] *impressed* by his diligence./I (very) much *admired* (him for) his diligence. (!)for は理由を表す)/I *had* [*felt*] great *admiration* for his diligence. (!)for は対象を表す

:**かんしん　関心** ❶[興味] (an) interest 《in》 (!)形容詞を伴うときは通例 a(n) を付ける); [気がかり] concern. (!)いずれも「関心事」 (a matter of *interest* [*concern*]) の意では Ⓒ) ●関心を呼ぶ[引く] attract *interest*. ●音楽に関心を示す[持つ] show [take, have] (an) *interest* in music. ●私はコンピュータに大変関心がある I *am* very [*greatly*,《書》much] *interested* in learning [to learn] computers./I *have* a great *interest* in learning computers. ●その問題は私の関心事ではない The matter is not my *concern* [no *concern* of mine]. ●彼の方が私には「どうでもよい」という含みがある) ●彼の最大の関心は金と名声だ His greatest *interest* is (in) money and fame. (!)in のある方が正確) ●彼らは環境問題には関心がない(=無関心だ) They are *indifferent* to environmental issues.

かんしん　奸臣 a wicked /wikid/ [a treacherous, a scheming] vassal [retainer,《従者》follower].

かんしん　寒心 ●…は寒心に堪えない (たいへん心配だ) I am deeply anxious [seriously concerned] about…; (恐ろしさにぞっとする) I shudder [I am horrified] at… [to do…].

かんしん　歓心 (愛顧) favor. ●彼女の歓心を買う win her *favor*; (機嫌をとる) (軽蔑的) curry *favor* with her.

かんじん　肝心 —— **肝心な** 形 [重要な] important, vital; [必要な] essential; [決定的な] crucial. (⇨大切) ●肝心かなめ the most important. ●約束の時間に遅れないようにすることが肝心だ It is *important* not to be late for the appointment. ●そこが肝心だ That's *the point*./That's where *the point* lies. ●肝心なのは彼にそれをする気があるかどうかだ The thing is whether he feels like doing it. ●彼は肝心なとき(=最も必要なとき)にいなかった He wasn't there when he *was needed most*.

かんじん　閑人 (ひまな時間がたくさんある人) a leisured person; (することがなくてぶらぶらしている人) an idle person.

かんじん　勧進 educational missionary work in Buddhism.
●勧進相撲 a fund-raising *sumo* tournament held in aid of a temple or a shrine. ●勧進帳 a subscription list. ●勧進元 a promoter.

かんすい　完遂 《書》accomplishment. (⇨遂行)
かんすい　冠水 —— **冠水する** 動 be flooded; (完全に水中に没した)《やや書》be submerged.
●冠水地帯 a flooded area.
かんすい　灌水 —— **灌水する** 動 water; sprinkle water. ●畑に灌水する *water* the field.
●灌水装置 a wátering device; (畑などにある散水装置) a sprinkler.
かんすい　鹹水 (⇨回 塩水)
がんすいたんそ　含水炭素 (a) cárbohýdrate.

かんすう 関数 a function. ・一次[二次]関数 a linear [a quadratic] *function*. ▶y は x の関数である Y equals f of x.

かんすうじ 漢数字 Chinese numerals.

かんする 関する ❶《関係する》be connected (*with*). ・動物に関する本 a book *about* [*on, concerning*] animals. (!) about では動物についての「一般的」な本、on では「専門的」な計画には反対しないに関することでやって来ました I've come to you about the matter *connected with* your daughter.
会話「彼女は何か悩んでいるようでした」「その何かとは職場に関することかしら」"She seemed to be worried *about* something." "Something at work?"
❷《その他の表現》・彼女は我関せずという態度で私のそばを通り過ぎた She passed by me *with an air of indifference*. ・私に関する限りその計画には反対しないよ As [So] far as I'm *concerned*, I have no objection to the plan.

かんする 冠する give ... at the top 《*of*》; (称号を) confer(-rr-) the title 《*of*》. ・「新」を冠した社名 the name of a company with a prefix "new" [beginning with "new"].

かんする 緘する《封をする》seal.

かんせい 完成 图 completion; perfection. ・劇場はもうすぐ完成です The theater is near *completion*./The theater is nearing *completion*./The theater *is* almost [nearly] *completed*.

――完成する 動《人が主語》《完全に仕上げる》complete; 《終える》finish (!) complete より口語的); 《完璧なものにする》perfect《やや堅い語》; 《物が主語》be completed, be finished; be perfected.
・技法を完成する perfect one's technique; *make* one's technique *perfect*. ・完成された美しさ perfect beauty. ・完成の域に達したバイオリン奏者 an *accomplished* violinist. ・彼は 2 日で仕事を完成した He *completed* [*finished*] the job in two days. ・橋はまだ完成していない The bridge *is not completed* yet./(建設中である) The bridge is still *under construction*.
・完成品 finished products [goods].

かんせい 官制 a system [an organization] of government; a government system [organization].

かんせい 官製 官製の 形 government-manufactured; (政府発行の) government-issued《postcards》.

かんせい 陥穽《落とし穴》a trap; (わな) a snare; (策略) a trick, wiles. ・陥穽に落ちる fall into [be caught in] a *trap*; be trapped.

かんせい 乾性 ――乾性の 形 dry.
・乾性塗料 dry paints. ・乾性肌 dry skin. ・乾性油 drying oil. ・乾性肋膜炎《医学》dry pleurisy /plíʊ(ə)rəsi/.

かんせい 喚声 an excited cry. ・喚声を上げる cry excitedly《*at, over*》.

かんせい 喊声《⇨ 鬨（とき）の声》

かんせい 閑静 ――閑静な 形 quiet. ・閑静な住宅街 a *quiet* residential quarter [area].

かんせい 感性《感受性》《書》sensibility, sensibilities; (感じやすさ) sensitivity. ・豊かな感性の人 a man of great *sensibilities*. ・芸術的感性がない have no [lack] artistic *sensibility*.

かんせい 慣性《物理》inertia. ・慣性の法則 the law of *inertia*.
・慣性飛行 inertial navigation. ・慣性モーメント the moment of inertia. ・慣性誘導（航法）inertial guidance.

かんせい 管制 contról; (検閲) censorship. ・灯火管制 a bláckòut. ・航空管制官 an air-traffic [an air] controller.

――管制する 動 contról; censor.
・管制塔 a control tòwer.

かんせい 歓声〔かっせい〕〔喜びの叫び声〕a cheer; 〔喜びの叫び声〕a shout of joy. ・歓声をあげる cheer; shout for joy; give a *shout of joy*. ・選手たちが到着すると群衆から大歓声があがった A great *cheer* went up [There was a great *cheer*] from the crowd when the players arrived./The crowd *cheered* loudly [*gave a great cheer*] when the players arrived. ・勝利の知らせは大歓声で迎えられた The news of the victory was received with [was greeted by] loud *cheers*.

かんぜい 関税 customs (!) 単・複両扱い), customs duty [duties] (!) しばしば複数形で単数扱い); (特に輸入品にかかる) a tariff (靏 ～s). ・関税のかからない (= 免税の) ワイン *duty-free* wines. ▶100 ドルのスイス時計に 5 ドルの関税がかかった (=を払った) I paid 5 dollars *customs on* the 100 dollars Swiss watch. ▶輸入宝石の関税は非常に高い There is a very high *tariff on* imported jewelry. ・国内生産を刺激するために関税が引き上げられた *Tariffs* were raised in order to stimulate domestic production.
・関税障壁 a tariff barrier [wall]. ・関税率 a tariff rate.

がんせいひろう 眼精疲労 eyestrain; 《医学》asthenopia /æsθəˈnoʊpiə/.

かんぜおん（ぼさつ）観世音（菩薩）《⇨ 魁 観音（かんのん）》

かんせき 漢籍 a Chinese book; a book written in Chinese.

がんせき 岩石《a》rock.

かんせつ 間接 間接の 形 indirect. ・間接の原因 an *indirect* cause. ・間接的影響 an *indirect* influence 《*on*》.

――間接（的）に 副 indirectly; （遠まわしに）in a roundabout way; （また聞きで）secondhand, at second hand. ・彼は私の質問に間接的に答えた He gave an *indirect* answer to my question. / He answered my question *indirectly*. ▶彼から間接的にそれを聞いた I heard it *secondhand* [*at second hand*] from him.
・間接照明 indirect lighting. ・間接税 an indirect tax. ・間接選挙 an indirect election. ・間接喫煙 inhaling secondary [sidestream] smoke. ・間接費 an indirect [an overhead] cost. ・間接話法《文法》indirect speech; reported speech.

かんせつ 冠雪 a snowfall on the top 《of a mountain》. ・冠雪の山々 snow-capped mountains; mountains with snow-covered peaks. ▶富士山頂に昨日初冠雪があった The first *snow* of the year *fell* on the top of [《書》crowned] Mt. Fuji yesterday.

かんせつ 関節 a joint. ・はずれた腕の関節を直す set the arm in *joint*. ・あご[肩]の関節をはずす put one's jaw [shoulder] out of *joint*; dislocate one's jaw [shoulder]. ・指を第一関節から切断する cut off one's finger at the first *joint*.
・関節炎《医学》arthritis /ɑːrˈθraɪtɪs/. ・関節リューマチ《医学》articular rheumatism.

がんぜない 頑是無い ・がんぜない子供 a *naughty* child.; （幼くて聞き分けのない）a child *too young to listen to reason*.

かんせん 感染 图 (空気・水・虫などを介した) infection; (接触による) contagion. ・コレラの二次感染 second-

かんせん ary *infection* of cholera. ●感染力が強い be highly infectious; have high infectivity.
── **感染する** 動 (病気が人に) infect; (人が病気に) catch. ▶彼は非加熱血液製剤を通してHIVに感染した He caught an HIV *infectious disease* [*was infected with HIV*] through unheated blood products. (⇨感染症) ▶この病気は感染しません This disease is not *contagious* [*catching*]. ▶エイズはキスをしても感染しない《話》You can't even *get* AIDS by kissing./(蔓延(まん)しない) AIDS *is not spread* even by kissing.
●**感染経路** the route of infection. ●**感染源** the source of infection.

かんせん 汗腺 〖解剖〗sweat glands.

かんせん 官選 ●かつての官選の知事 a prefectural governor formerly *appointed by the central government*; a *government-appointed* prefectural governor in the past.

かんせん 幹線 a trunk [a main] line. (⇨新幹線)
●**幹線道路** a main road;《主に米》a highway,《英》a trunk road.

かんせん 観戦 ── **観戦する** 動 watch《a baseball game》. (⇨見る)
●**観戦記** a report on the match [game].

かんせん 艦船 warships and other vessels.

*:**かんぜん** 完全 completeness. ●完全を目ざす aim at *perfection*. ▶彼の作品は完全にはほど遠い His work is far from *perfection*. ▶彼は完全主義者だ He tries to *be perfect* in everything./He's a perfectionist. ▶自分は完全無欠だとでも思っているの？ そうでなければ他人のあら探しはよしなさい Do you think you're *absolutely perfect* [*you have no fault at all*]? If not, you should not pick holes in other people.
── **完全な** 形 〖欠けるところがない〗complete; full; (全部そろっている) entire;〖完璧(かんぺき)な〗perfect;〖損なわれていない〗intact. ●完全な勝利［敗北］a *complete* victory [defeat]. ●切手の完全な収集 a *complete* [an *entire*] collection of stamps. ●完全な円 a *perfect* circle. ●イギリスからの完全な独立を求める seek *full* [*complete*] independence from Great Britain. ▶彼は完全な英語を話す He speaks *perfect* English./His English is *perfect*. ▶地球は完全な球体ではない The earth is not *perfectly* round. ▶その化石は完全な姿で発見された The fossil was found *intact*.
── **完全に[は]** completely; fully; entirely; perfectly; (まったく) quite. (⇨全く❶) ●完全に満足している be *completely* [*entirely, perfectly, fully*] satisfied. ●そのことを完全に忘れていた I *completely* [*entirely, utterly, totally,*《話》*clean*] forgot about it. ●その仕事はまだ完全には出来上がっていない The work is not *quite* [*completely, entirely*] finished yet. (❗部分否定) ●今言ったこと完全には理解できなかったよ I didn't *quite* catch that.
会話「確かかい」「確かかだって？ じゃ(= 絶対に)確信を持っているよ」"Are you sure?" "Am I sure? I'm *absolutely* positive." (❗sure と positive の対比に注意)
── **完全にする** 動 make*... perfect; complete; perfect.
●**完全雇用** full employment. ●**完全試合** (⇨完全試合) ●**完全失業者** a completely unemployed person;《集合的に》the completely unemployed. ●**完全主義** perfectionism. ●**完全燃焼** complete [full] combustion. ●**完全犯罪** a perfect crime.

かんぜん 間然 ●間然する所がない (完璧である) be perfect; (非難する点がない) be impeccable.

かんぜん 敢然 ── **敢然と** 副 (勇敢に) bravely; (断固として) resolutely.

かんぜん 眼前 (⇨目の前)

かんぜんしあい 完全試合 〖野球〗a perfect game.
●完全試合を達成する throw [pitch, toss] a *perfect game*. ●完全試合を阻止する break up a *perfect game*. ▶彼は9回に完全試合を逃した He lost a *perfect game* in the ninth inning.

かんせんしょう 感染症 〖空気感染などによる〗an infectious disease, an infection;〖接触感染による〗a contagious disease, a *contagion*;〖古〗(しばしば両者は区別なく用いられる);〖短期間に広い地域に広がる〗an epidemic. ●感染症にかかる catch an *infectious* [a *contagious*] *disease*. ●サーズ感染症は発生してまもなく町中に広がった The SARS *epidemic* spread all over the town soon after it broke out [its outbreak].
●**感染症患者** an infectious [a contagious, an epidemic] case.

かんぜんちょうあく 勧善懲悪 rewarding good conduct and punishing bad conduct.
●**勧善懲悪劇** a morality play. (参考) キリスト教的視点による道徳劇) ●**勧善懲悪小説** a didactic novel.

かんそ 簡素 名 simplicity. ●その手続きを簡素化する *simplify* [*streamline*] the procedure.
── **簡素な** 形 (単純で素朴な) simple; (飾り気のない) plain. ●簡素な食事 a *simple* [a *plain*] meal; *simple* [*plain*] food. ●簡素＝質素に生活する live a (*plain and*) *simple* life (a life of *simplicity*]. ▶彼女は簡素な衣服を着ている She is (dressed) in *simple* [*plain*] clothes./She is *simply* [*plainly*] dressed.

がんそ 元祖 (創始者) the originator《*of*》.

*:**かんそう** 乾燥 名 〖状態〗dryness;〖作用〗drying.
── **乾燥した** 形 dry, dried; (からからに) parched. ▶空気が大変乾燥している The air is very *dry*.
── **乾燥する[させる]** 動 dry (wet clothes).
●**乾燥機** (工業用の) a drying machine; (洗濯機などの) a dryer. ●**乾燥気候** a dry [an arid] climate. ●**乾燥剤** a desiccant; a desiccating agent.

*:**かんそう** 感想 〖印象〗(an) impression;〖意見〗an opinion;〖批評〗a comment. ●全般的な感想 one's general [overall] *impression*《*on*》. ●その小説について感想を述べる give one's *impressions of*《×*about*》the novel; *comment on*《×*about*》the novel. ▶この件についてあなたのご感想は(=意見)は？ What's your *opinion* [What are your *views*] on this matter?/What [×How] do you *think* of this matter?
会話「自転車で日本列島を縦断したご感想は」「そうですね、すばらしいこともあったし、中には苦しかったり、恐いこともありました」"Tell me, *what was it like*, riding a bicycle through Japan?" "Well, some of the time it was great and some of the time it was just hard work or really scary."
●**感想文** a description of one's impression(s).

かんそう 完走 ── **完走する** 動 finish《a race》.
●**完走者** a finisher.

かんそう 間奏 an interlude.
●**間奏曲** an interlude; an intermezzo (複 ~s) (参考) 幕間に演奏される曲または独立の小曲); an entr'acte /a:ntrǽkt/ (参考) 幕間のダンスなどをさすことも多い).

かんそう 観相 physiognomic judgement of character.
●**観相家** a physiognomist. ●**観相術** physiog-

かんぞう 甘草 〖植物〗 licorice /líkəris/.
・甘草エキス licorice extract.
かんぞう 肝臓 〖解剖〗 a liver.
・肝臓移植 (手術) a liver transplant. ・肝臓がん liver cancer, 〖医学〗 hepatoma. ・肝臓病 liver trouble.
がんそう 顔相 facial features or expression.
がんぞう 贋造 名 (貨幣などの) counterfeit /káuntərfit/; forgery. (⇨偽造)
— 贋造する counterfeit; forge.
かんそうかい 歓送会 a good-by [《話》a send-off, 《やや書》a farewell] party. ・彼の歓送会を行う give a good-by [a farewell] party for him.
*カ**んそく** 観測 名 ❶ (観察) (an) observation. ・天体観測 (make) an astronomical *observation*. ❷ (考え, 意見) thinking, an opinion. ・希望的観測 wishful *thinking*. ・私の観測では彼は正しい In my *opinion* [*estimation*], he is right./As I *see* it, he is right.
— 観測する 動 observe; (見つける) sight. ・毎夜星を観測する observe [make observations of] the stars every night. ・その彗星はコロラド州の上空で観測された The comet *was sighted* over Colorado.
・観測者 an observer. ・観測所 an observatory.
かんそん 寒村 a désolate village. ・山あいの寒村 a *desolate* mountain *village*.
かんそんみんぴ 官尊民卑 ・官尊民卑の風潮はいまだにすたれていない The custom of *putting officialdom above the people* dies hard./There is still a tendency to *give more importance to officialdom than the people*.
カンタータ 〈イタリア語〉 〖音楽〗 a cantata /kəntɑ́:tə/.
かんたい 寒帯 the frigid zone(s).
・寒帯植物 polar plants. ・寒帯地方 (極地方) the polar regions.
かんたい 歓待 名 〖温かい・心からの歓迎〗 a warm [《やや書》a cordial] welcome; a warm [a cordial] reception.
— 歓待する 動 ・招待客を歓待する give a warm welcome [reception] to one's guests; welcome [《やや書》receive, (もてなす) entertain] one's guests *warmly*.
かんたい 艦隊 a fleet. ・小艦隊 a squadron. ・連合艦隊 a combined *fleet*.
かんだい 寛大 〖度量が広いこと〗generosity; 〖心が広いこと〗broad-mindedness; 〖慈悲深くて処罰などが厳しくないこと〗leniency; 〖他人の言動などに寛容なこと〗tolerance. ・裁判官の寛大さに感銘を受ける be impressed by the judge's *generosity* [*broad-mindedness*, *leniency*].
— 寛大な 形 generous; broad-minded; lenient; tolerant. ・寛大な言葉 *generous* remarks. ・寛大な判決 a *lenient* sentence. ・寛大な〖人を許す〗a *forgiving* person. ▶彼はその違反者に[の処遇に]寛大だった He was *generous to* [*in* his treatment] *of* the offender. ▶彼は他人の意見に寛大だ He is *tolerant of* other people's [others'] opinions. (❗前の方が普通) ▶彼女は子供に寛大だった She was *tolerant toward* [*to*] her children. (❗「理解がある」という意味では She was *understanding with* her children.)
がんたい 眼帯 an eye bandage, an (eye)patch.
・眼帯をとる[する] take off [put on, apply] an *eye bandage*. ▶彼女は左目に眼帯をしていた She was wearing a *bandage* [a *patch*] over her left eye.
かんたいじ 簡体字 a simplified Chinese character.
かんたいへいよう 環太平洋 the Pacific Rim.
・環太平洋合同演習 RIMPAC (*Rim of the Pacific Exercise* の略). ・環太平洋地震帯 the Pacific rim earthquake zone [belt].
かんだかい 甲高い high-pitched; (金切り声の) shrill.
・甲高い声 a *high-pitched* [a *shrill*] voice. ・甲高い悲鳴をあげる give a *shrill* [a *sharp*] cry.
かんたく 干拓 名 land reclamation by drainage.
— 干拓する 動 ▶この土地は海を干拓したものだ This land *was reclaimed from* the ocean *by draining*.
・干拓工事 reclamation works. ・干拓地 reclaimed land.
カンタベリー 〖英国の都市〗Canterbury /kǽntərbèri/.
・カンタベリー大聖堂 Canterbury Cathedral.
カンタベリーものがたり 『カンタベリー物語』 *The Canterbury Tales*. (〖参考〗チョーサーの叙事詩)
かんたる 冠たる ・世界に冠たる技術国家 the *most technologically advanced country in the world*; *a country that boasts its highest standards of technology in the world*.
‡**かんたん** 簡単 名 〖単純〗simplicity; 〖(表現の)簡潔さ〗《書》brevity.
— 簡単な 形 〖易しい〗(単純な) simple; (明解な) straightforward, clear-cut; (骨の折れない) easy; 〖短い〗short; 〖簡潔な〗brief. ・簡単な手紙 a *short* [a *brief*] letter. ❗ brief はそっけなさを含意 ・簡単な (= 軽い) 食事をする have a *light* [(簡素な) a *simple*] meal. ・簡単な英語で書く write in *easy* [*simple*, (分かりやすい) *plain*] English. ・それの方が簡単な問題だ That is a *simpler* [an *easier*] question./(解答のに易しい) The question is *easier* [*simpler*] to answer. ▶英語を身につけるのは簡単ではない It's not *easy* to master English./English is not *easy* to master [*to be mastered*]. (⇨口頭) ▶口で言うのはよりも簡単だ《ことわざ》It's *easier* said than done.
— 簡単に 副 simply; easily; briefly. ・簡単な (= 分かりやすく) 言えば to put it *simply*, quite *simply* (❗いずれも文頭で用いる). ・(手短に) in brief, to be *brief*; (要約して) in short. ・簡単に試験に通る pass one's exam easily [with ease]. ・その事件を簡単に説明する explain the case *briefly*; give a *brief* account of the case. ▶彼はその問題をいとも簡単に解いた He solved the problem quite *easily* [(何ら苦労せずに) *without any difficulty*]./He had *no trouble* at all solving the problem. ▶どんなことでもそう簡単ではいかない Nothing comes so [《話》that] *easy*. ▶事は簡単に (= 順調に) 運ばれた Things went on *smoothly*. ▶彼は簡単に (= すぐに) 謝った He apologized *readily*.
かんたん 肝胆 ・肝胆相照らす ▶彼とは肝胆相照らす仲だ He is a very close friend of mine./We are the best of friends.
かんたん 邯鄲 ・邯鄲の夢 〖栄枯盛衰のはかないことのたとえ〗The glory in this world is but a fleeting dream.
かんたん 感嘆 名 〖賛美〗admiration; 〖驚嘆〗wonder. (⇨感心) ・感嘆すべき (賞賛すべき) admirable; (驚嘆すべき) marvelous; (すばらしい) wonderful. ・感嘆して絵を見る take a look at a picture *in* [*with*] *admiration* [*wonder*].
— 感嘆する 動 〖賞賛する〗admire; 〖驚嘆する〗marvel 〈at〉. ・そのすばらしい光景に感嘆する *marvel at* the fantastic sight.
・感嘆詞 〖文法〗an exclamation; an interjec-

かんだん 寒暖 ▶砂漠では1日の中での寒暖の差が大きい In a desert there is a great difference of *temperature* in a day.

かんだん 間断 ── **間断なく** 形 without a break; (継続を強調して) continuously; (ばらつきがないことを強調して) constantly; (しつこさも含めて) incessantly. ●間断なくしゃべり続ける go on talking *without a break*. ▶黒い雨が間断なく降り注いだ Black rain continued to fall *without a break [a letup]*./Black rain fell on us *continuously*.

かんだん 閑談 (気楽なおしゃべり) a chat; (とりとめのない会話) a rambling conversation.

かんだん 歓談 ── **歓談する** 動 chat *(with)*. ▶私たちは酒を汲みかわし夜遅くまで歓談した We had a *pleasant chat* over cups of *sake* till late at night.

がんたん 元旦 New Year's Day; the *first day of the year*. ●元旦に on *New Year's Day*. ▶1年の計は元旦にあり *New Year's Day* is the key of the year.

かんだんけい 寒暖計 a thermómeter. ▶寒暖計は摂氏30度を示している The *thermometer* reads [stands at] 30℃. (!) 30℃は thirty degrees centigrade と読む.

かんち 奸知, 奸智 奸知にたけた crafty; cunning; sly. (⇨悪知恵)

かんち 完治 名 (a) complete [(a) full] recovery. ── **完治する** 動 recover completely; fully recover *(from)*; make a *complete recovery*.

かんち 寒地 a cold place [district, region]; (寒帯地帯)the frigid regions.

かんち 感知 ── **感知する** 動 sense; (気づく) become aware *(of)*; (悟る) realize. ●危険を感知する *sense* [*be aware of*] danger.
●感知器 a sensor.

かんち 関知 ── **関知する** 動 ▶その事件は我々の関知するところではない We *have nothing to do with* [*are not concerned with*] the case.

かんちがい 勘違い 名 a mistake; an error. (⇨間違う **1**, **2**) ●どめんなさい．私の勘違い(=取り違い)でした I'm sorry I *was confused* [*was mixed up*].
── **勘違いする** 動 ▶君は何か勘違いしているのだ You *are mistaken* [have some misunderstanding]./You are *under the wrong impression*.

がんちく 含蓄 (含み, 示唆) (an) implication; (意味の深さ) (a) significance. ▶彼の演説には含蓄に富んでいた His speech was full of *significance* [*suggestive ideas*].

かんちゅう 寒中 the coldest wintertime; (真冬) midwinter. ●寒中水泳をする swim in the *midwinter cold*. ●寒中水泳大会 a *midwinter* swimming meet. ●寒中見舞いを出す send a *midwinter* greeting [(英) greetings] card.

がんちゅう 眼中 ●眼中にない (無視する) ignore; (注目しない) take no notice *(of)*; (まったく意に介さない) don't care, (話) couldn't care less *(about)*. ▶彼は金のことしか眼中にない(=関心があるのは金だけだ) The only thing he cares about is money./(金だけに関心を抱いている) He takes (an) interest in nothing but money.

*かんちょう 官庁 a government office.
●官庁街 a government office quarter [area].

かんちょう 干潮 (a) low tide. (⇨満潮) ▶干潮時に at *low tide*; when the tide is *low* [*out*].

かんちょう 完調 the best [perfect] condition.

かんちょう 浣腸 名 an enema /énəmə/.
── (浣腸を)する 動 give (him) an enema.
●浣腸器 an enema (syringe).

かんちょう 間諜 間課の. (⇒スパイ)

かんちょう 管長 the superintendent priest.

かんちょう 館長 〖管理者〗a director; 〖博物館・美術館の〗a curator; 〖図書館の〗a chief [a head] librarian.

かんちょう 観潮 観潮をする watch the whirlpools of (sea) current.

かんちょう 艦長 a captain. (! 呼びかけにも用いる)

かんつう 姦通 名 adultery. ── **姦通する** 動 commit *adultery (with)*; have an adulterous relationship *(with)*.

かんつう 貫通 ── **貫通する** 動 pénetràte; (通り抜ける) go through .... (⇨貫く) ▶その銃弾が私の腕を貫通した The bullet *went through* my arm. ▶トンネルが貫通した(=完成した) The tunnel *was completed* [*was penetrated*].

カンツォーネ [<イタリア語] 〖イタリアの叙情的歌曲〗a canzone /kænzóuni/ (複 ~s, -ni).

かんづく 感づく (気づく) sense, become* [be] aware *(of)*; (臭いと感じる)《話》smell a rat. ▶私はだれかが後をつけているのに感づいた I *sensed* [*had a feeling, just knew*] that someone was following me. ▶彼女は我々の陰謀に感づいているようだ She seemed to *be aware of* our plot.

かんつばき 寒椿 a winter camellia.

かんづめ 缶詰 (缶詰食品) canned [〖英〗tinned] foods; (一つの缶詰) a can, 《英》a tin. ●缶詰にする can; 《英》tin. ▶彼女はイワシの缶詰をあけた She opened a *can* of sardines. ●缶詰になる(=閉じ込められる)作家はよほどの売れっ子で, 今では少なくなった Those writers who get themselves locked up in a hotel room till they finish writing are very popular ones. We have only a few of them these days. (事情) 英語圏では, 作家と出版社とは契約を結んでおり, 作品が締め切りに間に合わなければ契約が破棄されるので, このように出版社が作家を閉じ込めるような状況は生じない
●缶詰業者 a canner; a packer. ●缶詰工場 a cannery.

かんてい 官邸 ●首相官邸 the Prime Minister's office.

かんてい 艦艇 naval vessels; warships.

かんてい 鑑定 〖判定〗(a) judgement; 〖評価〗(an) appraisal. ●専門家に絵の鑑定を依頼する ask an expert to *judge* [*appraise*] a painting; ask an expert for his *judgment* [*appraisal*] of a painting.
── **鑑定する** 動 ▶それが本物かどうか鑑定する *judge* whether it is genuine or not. ▶筆跡を彼のものと鑑定する(=認定する) *identify* the handwriting *as* his [belonging to him].
●鑑定家 (美術品などの) a judge, a connoisseur /kònəsá:r/; (筆跡の) a handwriting analyst.

がんてい 眼底 〖解剖〗the fundus of the eye.
●眼底検査 a funduscopic examination. ●眼底出血 〖医学〗fundus bleeding.

かんてつ 貫徹 ── **貫徹する** 動 ●初志を貫徹する *carry out* [*accomplish*] one's original plan. ●賃上げ要求を貫徹する *carry through* a demand for higher wages. (! carry out より「困難を排して」の感が強い)

かんでふくめる 噛んで含める ●彼に噛んで含めるように話す talk to him so that he can understand easily.

カンテラ [<オランダ語] a kerosene 《米》[a paraffin 《英》] hand lamp.

カンデラ 〚光度の単位〛a candela 《略 cd》.
かんてん 干天 dry weather.
● 干天の慈雨 a welcome [a merciful] rain after a long spell of dry weather.
かんてん 寒天 agar /ɑ:gɑr/.
かんてん 観点 〚見地〛a point of view, a viewpoint; 〚立場〛a standpoint. ● 別の観点からその問題を見る look at the problem from a different *point of view* 〚角度〛*angle*. ● 経済的な観点から見るとその計画には長所がある From an economic *point of view* [*viewpoint*] the plan has some merits. ▶ その問題を社会学的観点から考えてごらん Think about the matter *in terms of* sociology./View the matter from a sociological *standpoint*.
かんでん 乾田 a dry rice-field.
かんでん 感電 图 an electric shock. ● 感電死する be killed by an *electric shock*; be [get] electrocuted.
―― 感電する 動 get a [an electric] shock.
かんでんち 乾電池 a (dry) battery. (⇨電池)
カント 〚ドイツの哲学者〛Kant /kænt/ (Immanuel ～).
かんど 感度 〚フィルム・計器などの〛sensitivity; 〚ラジオなどの〛reception. ● 高感度の地震計 a *sensitive* seismograph. ● 超高感度のテレビカメラ an *ultra-sensitive* TV camera. ● 高感度フィルム a fast (↔ a slow) film. ● このラジオは感度がいい This radio has [gets] good (↔poor) *reception*.
かんとう 完投 ―― 完投する 動 pitch a complete game; 《話》 go the distance [route].
かんとう 巻頭 the opening (of a book).
● 巻頭言 a preface /préfəs/, a fóreword. 巻頭論文 the opening article.
かんとう 敢闘 ―― 敢闘する 動 (勇敢に) fight bravely [courageously] 《*against*》; (善戦する) make [put up] a good fight 《*against*》.
● 敢闘賞 a fighting spirit award.
かんとう 関東 the Kanto district [area].
● 関東平野 the Kanto plain(s).
かんとう 関頭 (⇨瀬戸際, 分かれ目)
:かんどう 感動 图 〚感激〛(deep) emotion; 〚感銘〛(an) impression. ● 感動をもって音楽を聴く listen to the music *with* (deep) *emotion*. ● 彼の演説は聴衆に深い [大きな] 感動を与えた His speech *made* [ˣgave] *a deep* [*a great, quite an*] *impression on* the audience. (⇨動)
―― 感動的な (深く心をゆさぶる) moving; (感傷的な気持ちにさせる) touching; 〚感銘を与える〛impressive; 〚感情に訴える〛emotional. ● 感動的な光景 a *moving* [*a touching*, *an impressive*] sight. ● その芝居の感動的な場面 an *emotional* scene in the play. ● 彼の感動的な話に集まった人たちはみな涙した His speech moved the whole gathering to tears. ● 彼らは感動的な再会をした Their reunion was filled with *emotion*.
―― 感動する 動 be moved 《*by*》; (感傷的に) be touched 《*by, with*》; 〚感銘を受ける〛be impressed 《*with, by*》. ● 彼の話に感動して涙を流した I *was so moved by* his story that I shed tears./ His story *moved* me to tears. (⚠この場合 be touched はあまり用いられない) ● 彼の言葉にとても [深く] 感動した I *was very* [*deeply*] *impressed with* his words. (この場合 impressed は形容詞化している)/His words *impressed* me very much [*deeply*].
かんとう 勘当 ―― 勘当する 動 disown. ▶ おまえは勘当だ I'll *disown* you!
かんどう 間道 a byway. (⇨抜け道, 脇道)
かんとうし 間投詞 (⇨感動詞)

かんどうし 感動詞 〚文法〛an interjection; an exclamation.
かんどうみゃく 冠動脈 〚解剖〛the coronary arteries.
:かんとく 監督 图 〚事〛(権限・責任などを持った) supervision; (指揮) direction; (管理) control; 〚人〛a supervisor; (仕事・労働者の) an overseer; (映画などの) a director; (職場・野球の) a manager; (スポーツの) a coach.

> 参考 サッカーの監督: 通例 coach, 特に head coach と呼ばれる。チームの采配以外にも権限を持つ場合は manager. 代表監督のように主にチーム構成に携わる場合, selector とよばれることもある。

①〚～監督〛● 映画〚音楽〛監督 a movie [a music] *director*. ● 現場監督 a site [a field] *overseer*; a supervisor. ● 試験監督《米》a proctor; 《英》an invigilator. ● 舞台 [野球] の監督 a stage [a baseball] *manager*. ● 暫定監督 interim *manager* [*coach*]. ● 共同監督 joint *manager* [*coach*]. ● 黒沢監督の映画 a movie *directed* by Kurosawa. (⇨動)
②〚監督(の)～〛● A氏の監督のもとに under the *supervision* [*direction, control*] of Mr. A. ▶ 彼がそんなことをしたのは君の監督不行き届きだ He did that because you didn't *take* proper *care of* him. (⇨動)
―― 監督(を)する 動 (人・事・場所などの) supervise, 《書》superintend; oversee*; (指導する) direct; (世話をする) look after …, take* care of …; (チームなどの) manage. ● 試験の監督をする supervise [《米》proctor, 《英》invigilate] an examination. ● タイガースの監督をする *manage* the Tigers. ● 1,000 試合以上の監督をする *manage* over a thousand games. ▶ 君は仕事をしなくてよい。従業員の監督だけをしてくれ I don't want you to work. Only *supervise* [*superintend, oversee*] the workers. ● 監督官庁 the competent authorities. ● 監督兼任選手 a player-manager; a playing manager.
かんとく 感得 ―― 感得する 動 be (spiritually) awakened 《*to* the ultimate truths》; get 《the truth of life》. (⇨悟る)
かんどころ 勘所 〚最も大切なところ〛the (vital) point; (最重要点) the crux; 〚弦楽器の〛a fingerboard. ● 彼女の話は短かったが勘どころはちゃんと押さえていた Her speech was brief but *to the point*. (⚠but の代わりに and を用いると「話が簡潔だった点もよかった」の意になる)
がんとして 頑として 〚頑固に〛stubbornly; 〚断固として〛firmly. ● 頑として自説を主張する maintain one's opinion *stubbornly*. ● (固執する) stick to one's opinion. ● 彼女は私の頼みを頑として聞き入れない (どうしても聞こうとしない) She will *nót* listen to my request./(断固断わる) She *refuses* my request *stubbornly*./(耳を貸さない) She *turns a deaf ear* to my request.
カントリー ● カントリークラブ a country club. ● カントリーミュージック country music; country and western《略 C&W》
カントン 広東 Guangdong /gwáːŋdáŋ/.
● 広東語 Cantonese. ● 広東省 Guangdong Province.
かんな 鉋 a plane. ● 鉋くず (wood) shavings. ● 板に鉋をかける *plane* a board.
カンナ 〚植物〛a canna.
かんない 管内 ● 神田警察署の管内で in [within] the *jurisdiction* of Kanda Police Station.

かんない 館内 ●館内に[で] in the building [house]; ●館内放送で over the PA system. (⇨校内［校内放送］)

かんなづき 神無月 〖10月〗October; (陰暦の) the tenth month of the luna calendar.

かんなん 艱難 (困難) difficulties; (困難にあうこと) hardships; sufferings. ●かん難辛苦(ﾅ)を乗り越え overcome all (the) difficulties.
●艱難汝(ﾅ)を玉にす(ことわざ) Adversity makes a man wise.

かんにん 堪忍 图 (忍耐) patience; (勘弁) forgiveness.
── **堪忍する** 動 (我慢する) be patient 《with》;(話) put up with …; (許す) forgive.
●堪忍袋の緒がついに切れた●堪忍袋の緒がついに切れた My patience has snapped [has run out]./I came to the end of my patience./I've lost (my) patience [run out of patience] (with it)./I can't put up with it any more.

カンニング 图 cheating. (❗cunning は「ずるい」の意)
── **カンニングする** 動 ●彼は歴史の試験でカンニングしているところを見つかった He was caught cheating [《話》cribbing] on [《英》in] the history exam.
●カンニングペーパー《話》a crib [a cheat] sheet.

カンヌ 〖フランスの都市〗Cannes /kæn/.
●カンヌ国際映画祭 Cannes International Film Festival.

かんぬき a bolt, a bar. ●かんぬきをかける[はずす] bolt [unbolt] 《a gate》; bar [unbar] 《a gate》.

かんぬし 神主 a Shinto priest.

かんねつし 感熱紙 thermal [thermosensitive] paper.

かんねん 観念 图 (考え) an idea, a notion (❗notion は idea とほぼ同義だが、しばしば漠然とした また気まぐれな考えを含意する); a concept (❗個人の物事に対する特定の考え方); 〖意識〗sense (❗複数形にはしない). (⇨考え, 概念). ● 固定観念 a fixed idea 《about》; a stereotype 《about》. ● 時間の観念がない have no notion of punctuality. ▶彼は結婚について誤った観念を抱いている He has a mistaken idea [notion, concept] of marriage. ▶あなたにはプライバシーの観念がない You have no sense of privacy.
── **観念的な** 形 (現実ばなれした) ideal; (非現実的な) unrealistic.
── **観念する** 動 〖運命に身を任す〗resign oneself to one's fate, accept one's fate with resignation; 〖あきらめる〗give* up; 〖覚悟する〗be prepared 《for》. (⇨覚悟する, 諦(ﾗ)める) ▶彼はもはやこれまでと観念した He resigned himself to his fate [was resigned to his fate], thinking that it was all over with him. ▶もう一度やってみてもむだだよ。観念しろよ It's no use trying it again. Give up.
●観念論 idealism.

がんねん 元年 the first year 《of Heisei》.

かんのう 完納 图 full payment.
── **完納する** 動 pay … in full; complete the payment 《of》.

かんのう 官能 ── **官能的(な)** 形 sensual. ●官能的快楽 sensual (↔spiritual) pleasure(s).
●官能主義 sensualism.

かんのう 間脳 〖解剖〗the diencephalon.

かんのう 感応 图 a response.
── **感応する** 動 respond 《to》; be responsive 《to》.
●感応コイル〖電気〗an induction coil.

かんのん 観音 the Kannon, the Goddess of mercy. ●観音開き (扉) double [swing, swinging] doors.

かんぱ 看破 ── **看破する** 動 see through; detect.

かんぱ 寒波 〖気象〗a cold wave; (厳寒) the [a] freeze. ●寒波に見舞われる be hit by a cold wave.

カンパ [<ロシア語] 图 〖資金集め〗a fund-raising campaign.
── **カンパする** 動 ●1,000円カンパする give [contribute] 1,000 yen 《to》.

かんばい 完売 ▶チケット完売 Tickets [All of the tickets] are sold out.

かんばい 寒梅 (花) early ume blossoms; (木) an early blooming ume tree.

かんばい 観梅 ume-blossom viewing.

かんぱい 完敗 图 (完全な) a complete [(徹底的な) a thorough, (壊滅的な) a crushing] defeat.
── **完敗する** 動 suffer a complete defeat; (完全に負かされる) be completely beaten [defeated].

かんぱい 乾杯 图 a toast. ●乾杯の音頭をとる propose a toast 《to》.
── **乾杯する** 動 drink (a toast) to …; toast. ▶ご親切な主催者の方々のために乾杯したいと思います。乾杯！ I'd like to propose a toast to our very gracious hosts. Toast! [(主に英) Cheers!, (話) Bottoms up!] ▶彼の健康を祝して乾杯しよう Let's drink to [toast] his health./(話) (To) his health! (❗Here's to his health! の省略表現)

かんぱく 関白 〖関白太政大臣〗the Chief Adviser to the Emperor. ●亭主関白 (⇨亭主)

かんばしい 芳しい 〖いいにおいの〗sweet-smelling, (花などが) fragrant (⇨香り, におい); 〖よい〗good. ●バラの芳しいにおい the fragrance [sweet smell] of roses. ▶彼の評判はあまり芳しくない He doesn't have a very good [great] reputation. ▶彼は頑張って勉強したが、結果は芳しくなかった He worked hard, but the results were poor.

かんばしる 甲走る ●甲走った女性の声 a woman's shrill [sharp and high-pitched] voice.

カンバス (a piece of) canvas. (⇨キャンバス)

かんぱち 間八 〖魚介〗an amberjack.

かんばつ 干ばつ (a) drought /dráʊt/. (⇨日照り)

かんばつ 間伐 图 (森林の) thinning.
── **間伐する** 動 ▶この森は間伐する必要がある It is necessary to thin out this forest.
●間伐材 lumber from thinning.

かんぱつ 間髪 ●間髪を入れず ▶彼は強烈な張り手でひるんだ相手を間髪を入れずに押し出した He pushed his opponent out of the ring immediately when [the moment] the opponent flinched under a hard slap.

かんぱつ 煥発 ●才気煥発 (⇨才気)

カンパニー 〖会社〗a company.
●カンパニー制 a company system. (参考 ひとつの企業を各事業分野の独立性を高めて複数の企業の集合体のように組織する制度)

がんばり 頑張り hard work; 〖努力〗(an) effort; 〖やる気〗drive; 〖闘志〗〖話〗guts; 〖粘り〗〖米話〗stick-to-itiveness; 〖押し〗(a) push; 〖持続できる体力〗(やや書) stamina. ▶彼は頑張り屋だ He is a hard worker./He has a lot of drive.

*****がんばる 頑張る** ❶〖精を出す〗work hard 《to do》; 〖全力を尽くす〗do* [try] one's best 《to do》; 〖懸命にやってみる〗try hard 《to do》; 〖努力する〗make* an effort [efforts] 《to do》(❗より堅い言い方). ▶彼は宿題を9時までに終えようと頑張っている He is working [trying] hard to finish his homework by nine./He is making an effort to finish his homework by nine.
❷〖頑張り通す〗persevere /pə̀ːrsəvíər/ 《with》;(も

かんばん ちこたえる) hold* on [out] (**!** out では「もちこたえて切り抜ける」の意).(⇨辛抱, 根気) ▶君は頑張ればきっと成功すると思うよ If you persevere, you'll succeed, I'm sure. ▶彼は長い不況の年月を頑張って切り抜けた He *held out* until the years of depression were over.

❸ [言い張る] insist 〈*on*; *that* 節〉. (⇨主張) ▶彼はもう1割まけても頑張った He *insisted on* [*that* he (should) be given] another 10 percent reduction.

❹ [じっと動かずに] ▶戸口には大きな犬が頑張っていた There was a big dog blocking the doorway.

❺ [その他の表現] ▶頑張れ! (元気を出せ) "Come on!"/"Cheer up!"/(固執せよ) "Stick to it!"/(耐え抜け) "Hold out!"/(目標に向かって進め) "Go for it!"/(その調子で) "Keep at it."/(マラソンで競走している人に) "Keep going."/《米話》"Hang in there!"/(仕事で何か困難な状況にある人に) "Stick with it!"/(幸運を祈る) "Good luck (to you, with your work)!"/(全力を尽くせ) "Do [Try] your best!" (**!** (1) 後の二つは受験者・競技参加者などに対して. (2) Let's work harder. などはまだまだしっかりやっていないという含みを持つので不適切) 〖事情〗米英では日本のようにこのような励ましを言うことは少なく Take it easy. (気楽に構えて)/Don't work too hard.(あまり無理をしないでね)のようにリラックスさせることの方が普通.

〖会話〗「いつか舞台に立ちたいと思ってるのよ」「そうなるといいね, 頑張って」「ええ, 頑張るわ」"Someday I want to go on the stage." "That would be nice, wouldn't it? I *wish you luck.*" "OK! *Wish me luck!"*

*かんばん 看板 ❶ [店頭に掛ける] a signboard; a sign. ●本屋の看板を出す put up a bookstore's *signboard* [*sign*]. (**!** 医師・弁護士が看板を出す は《米話》hang [put] out one's *shingle*) ▶そのレストランには看板が出ていない There's not a *sign* up on that restaurant./That restaurant doesn't have a *sign up* [*out*].

❷ [外見・評判] ▶あの科学博は看板倒れだ The science exposition *is not as good as it looks* [《やや書》it *is reputed to be*]. ▶彼女はあの店の看板娘だ She is the *draw* at that store.

❸ [閉店時間] ▶看板までねばる do not leave until *closing time*.

〖会話〗「あれ, もう看板だ」「本当だ, それじゃこれを空けなくっちゃ」"It's just on *closing time*!" "So it is. We'll have to drink up."

●看板が泣く ▶いい加減な仕事をしたら老舗(しにせ)の看板が泣くよ(=老舗としての評判が台無しになるよ) If you don't do your work properly, the *reputation* as a long-established shop will be ruined.

●看板を下ろす (1日の営業を終える) close for the day; (廃業する) give up one's business; (免許を返上する) give up one's license.

●看板屋 a sign painter.

かんぱん 甲板 a deck. ●正[上; 下]甲板 the main [upper; lower] *deck*. ●前[後]甲板 the forecastle [quarter] *deck*. ●甲板に出る go (up) on *deck*. ▶甲板にはだれもいない There's nobody on *deck*.

かんばん 乾板 a dry plate.
かんパン 乾パン a hard-baked biscuit.
がんばん 岩盤 bedrock.
かんばんほうしき かんばん方式 a *kamban* system; a just-in-time production system. 〖参考〗必要なものを必要な時に必要な量だけ生産し, できるだけ在庫を持たないようにする生産管理方式)
かんび 甘美 ▶甘美なメロディー a *sweet* melody.

かんび 完備 ●設備の完備した体育館 a well-equipped gymnasium. ●家具の完備した部屋 a *fully-furnished* room. ●このホテルは冷暖房完備です This hotel is *fully air-conditioned*.

かんび 艦尾 the stern (of a warship).
かんぴ 官費 (政府の費用[支出]) government expense [expenditure]; (政府の資金) government funds. ●官費で視察旅行をする go on a tour of inspection *at government expense* [*financed by the government*].

ガンビア 〖国名〗the Gambia; (公式名) the Republic of the Gambia. (首都 Banjul) ●ガンビア人 a Gambian. ●ガンビア(人)の Gambian.
がんぴし 雁皮紙 *gampi* paper; (説明的に) lustrous thin Japanese paper.

*かんびょう 看病 图 nursing; (介護) care; (付き添い) attendance 〈*on*〉.
── 看病する 動 nurse; 〖世話する〗look after ..., take* care of ...; 〖付き添う〗(やや書) attend 〈on ...〉. ●病人(=患者)を手厚く看病する *nurse* a patient with great care; give a patient careful *nursing*.

かんぴょう 干瓢 dried shavings of gourd.
がんびょう 眼病 ▶眼病を患う suffer from an *eye disease*; have *eye trouble*.

*かんぶ 幹部 〖団体の〗(指導者) a leader; (指導的なメンバー) a leading member; 〖会社の〗(役員) an executive /ɪɡzékjutɪv/; (経営陣) 〖集合的〗the management (**!** 単・複両扱い).

かんぶ 患部 ●患部を冷やす cool (↔warm) the *affected* [*diseased*] part.
かんぶ 完膚 ●完膚なきまでに 完膚なきまでに(=徹底的に)打ちのめす *beat* (him) *thoroughly* [*completely*]; (話) beat (him) (*all*) *hollow*.
かんぷ 還付 ──還付する 動 return; (金銭を) pay ... back; refund.
●還付金 (税金の) a (tax) refund.
カンフー [<中国語]〖中国拳法〗kung fu.
かんぷう 完封 图 (試合) a shutout. ●3安打完封 a three-hit *shutout*. ●完封負け a whitewash.
──完封する 動 shut ... out; 《話》blank; whitewash.
かんぷう 寒風 a cold [an icy] wind. ●寒風吹きさぶ荒野 the wild land swept by *cold winds*.
かんぷく 感服 图 deep [great] admiration.
──感服する 動 feel deep [great] admiration 〈*for*〉; admire ... deeply [greatly].
かんふぜん 肝不全 〖医学〗hepatic insufficiency; hepatic [liver] failure.
かんぶつ 乾物 dried goods.
●乾物屋 (店) a dried goods store; a grocery (**!** 後の方は乾物など食料のほか日用品も扱う); (人) a grocer.
かんぷまさつ 乾布摩擦 《have》a rubdown with a dry towel.
かんぶり 寒鰤 (a) winter yellowtail.
カンフル [<オランダ語] ●カンフル注射をする give a *catecholamines* /kætʃóːləmiːnz/ injection. 〖参考〗今日では強心剤として camphor は用いられない) ●公定歩合の引き下げは経済成長のためのカンフル剤(=刺激剤)になる The lowerings of discount rates will act as a *stimulant* [〖話〗a *shot in the arm*] to the economic growth.
かんぶん 漢文 classical Chinese (writing); (科目名) Chinese classics (**!** 単数扱い).
かんぺき 完璧 perfection. (⇨完全) ▶彼の英語は完璧だ His English *is perfect* [*flawless*]./(自由にあやつる) He *has a good* [*a perfect*] *command of*

がんぺき 岩壁 a rock face; the face of a cliff.
がんぺき 岸壁 a quay /kiː/; (波止場) a wharf (働 wharves) (⇨波止場); (海岸のがけ) a cliff (働 〜s).
かんべつ 鑑別 (差を認め区別すること) discrimination; (評価し決定を下すこと) judgment. ● 少年鑑別所 the juvenile *classification* home.
— **鑑別する** 動 discriminate (distinguish) 《A from B, between A and B》; judge 《that B》. ▶ ひよこの雌雄を鑑別する *distinguish* the sex of chicks; *sex* chicks.
かんべん 勘弁 — 勘弁する 動 〔許す〕forgive, pardon, excuse (⇨許す❷);〔我慢する〕bear. ▶ どうかご勘弁ください Please *forgive* me. ▶ 今日のけいこは勘弁していただけますか Can I *be excused from* today's lesson? ▶ 彼の乱暴にはもう勘弁ならない I can't *bear* [*stand*,《話》*put up with*] his violence any longer.
会話 「コーヒー入れてくれる?」「もう勘弁してよ(＝いいかげんにして)。自分で入れたら。雑用だらけでいっぱいいっぱいなんだから」 "Would you make coffee for me?" "*Give me a break*. Do it yourself. I'm tied up with chores."（ℓ命令文で用いられる慣用表現）
かんべん 簡便 — 簡便な 形 〔簡単な〕simple, easy;〔持ち運びが〕portable,〔取り扱いが〕handy;〔便利な〕convenient.
かんぼう 官房 the secretariat /sèkrətɛ́əriət/. ● 大臣官房 the Minister's *secretariat*.
● 官房長官 the Chief Cabinet Secretary.
かんぼう 感冒 (⇨風邪(ｶｾﾞ))
かんぼう 監房 a ward; (独房) a cell.
かんぽう 官報 an official gazette;《英》a gazette.
かんぽう 漢方 Chinese medicine. ● 漢方医 a 《米》an hérb dòctor.
● 漢方薬 Chinese medicine; (薬草剤) a [《米》an] herbal medicine.
かんぽう 艦砲 ● 艦砲射撃 bombardment from a warship; a naval bombardment.
がんぼう 願望 (a) wish, (a) desire. (⇨望み, 願い).
かんぼく 灌木 a shrub, a bush. ● かん木の茂みa clump of *bushes*; a shrubbery.
カンボジア 国名 Cambodia /kæmbóudiə/; (公式名) the Kingdom of Cambodia. (首都 Phnom Penh) ● カンボジア人 a Cambodian. ● カンボジア語 Cambodian. ● カンボジア(人[語])の Cambodian.
かんぼつ 陥没 名 (土地の) subsidence /səbsáidns/, a cave-in.
— **陥没する** 動 subside; cave in.
かんぽん 完本 (完全な本) a complete copy 《of》; (揃いの全集) a complete [a full] set 《of Natsume Soseki's works》; (無削除本) an unexpurgated edition [copy, book] 《of》
がんぽん 元本 principal. ● 元本を返済する repay *principal*.
ガンマせん ガンマ線 物理 gamma rays.
かんまつ 巻末 ● 巻末に at *the end* [*back*] *of the book*.
かんまん 干満 the ebb and flow (of the tide). (⇨潮)
かんまん 緩慢 ● 緩慢な流れ a *slow* [動きの少ない] *sluggish*] stream. ▶ 彼の動作は緩慢だ He is *slow in* (his) movements.
ガンマン a gunman (働 -men).
がんみ 玩味 — 玩味する 動 (味を) taste, savor; (文の意味内容を) appreciate. (⇨味わう).
かんみりょう 甘味料 (a) sweetener. ● 人工甘味料 an artificial *sweetener*.
かんみん 官民 (政府と国民) the government and the people; (官庁と民間) the government and the private sector. ● 官民一致協力して with the united efforts of *government and people*.
● 官民格差 a government-private gap 《*in* wages》; a《wage》difference between the government and the private sector.
かんむり 冠 [王冠] a crown; [書] a diadem. ● 冠をかぶる[かぶっている] put on [wear] a *crown*. ● おかむりである (⇨おかんむり)
かんめ 貫目 (⇨貫)
かんめい 感銘 (an) impression. (⇨感動) ▶ 彼の勇気は私たちに深い感銘を与えた His courage *made a* deep *impression on* us./His courage *impressed* us deeply./We *were* deeply *impressed by* [*with*] his courage.
かんめい 簡明 — 簡明な 形 (簡単明瞭な) simple and clear; (簡潔な) concise.
— **簡明に** 副 簡明に言えば to put it *simply and clearly*.
がんめい 頑迷 — 頑迷な 形 bigoted; stubborn. (⇨頑固) ▶ 彼は頑迷な男だ He is *stubborn as a mule*./(自分の考えに凝り固まっている) He's such a *bigot* [*so begoted*] that he is set in his ways.
かんめん 乾麺 dried noodles.
がんめん 顔面 the face. ● 顔面蒼白(ｿｳﾊｸ)になる turn pale.
● 顔面神経痛 [医学] facial neurálgia.
がんもく 眼目 (いちばん大事な点) the most important point; the main object. ▶ 教育の眼目は人間形成にある *The main object* of education is to build good character.
がんもどき 雁擬き fried *tofu* mixed with chopped vegetables.
かんもん 喚問 名 a summons (働 -es). ● 喚問に応じる answer (↔ignore) the *summons*.
— **喚問する** 動 summon. ● 証人として法廷に喚問される *be summoned* to appear in court as a witness.
かんもん 関門 a hurdle. ● 関門を突破する overcome [get over] the *hurdle*《of》.
かんやく 完訳 名 a complete translation 《of Shakespeare's sonnets》.
— **完訳する** 動 make a complete translation.
かんやく 漢訳 名 a Chinese translation 《of》.
— **漢訳する** 動 梵語の仏典を漢訳する *translate* the Buddhist scriptures *from* Sanskrit *into* Chinese.
かんやく 監訳 名 ● 山田太一監訳 *Translation under the supervision* of Taichi Yamada.
— **監訳する** 動 supervise a translation.
かんやく 丸薬 a pill.
かんゆ 肝油 cod-liver oil.
かんゆ 換喩 [修辞] metonymy.
かんゆう 官有 government [federal, state] ownership.
● 官有地 state (owned) [national] land.
かんゆう 勧誘 名 〔誘い〕(an) invitation. ▶ 保険の勧誘員 an insurance salesperson. ▶ 我々もその運動に加わるよう勧誘を受けた We *were asked to* join in the movement [campaign].
— **勧誘する** 動 (彼に)寄付を勧誘する(＝求める) *ask* (him) *for* a contribution.
がんゆう 含有 名 (量) cóntent. (ℓ contént と読むと「満足(して)」の意になるので, 特に注意) ● 脂肪含有量が多い have a high fat *content*; *contain* a lot of fat. ▶ 強いウイスキーはアルコールの含有率が高い Strong whiskey *contains* a high [a large] percentage of alcohol.
— **含有する** 動 contain.

かんよ 関与 图 《参加》participation.
— **する** 動 participate 《in》, take part 《in》;《関係する》be involved 《in》. ●国政に関与する *participate in* the (national) government. ●その強盗事件に関与する *be involved in* the robbery. ▶私はその問題に一切関与していない I have nothing *to do with* the matter./I have no *connection with* the matter.

かんよう 肝要 图 importance.
— **肝要な** 形 (very) important;《不可欠な》vital, essential.（⇨重要な）

かんよう 涵養 cultivation. ●日々徳性の涵養に努める make efforts everyday to *cultivate* one's moral character.

かんよう 寛容 图 tolerance;〖寛大〗generosity.（⇨寛大）— **寛容な** 形 tolerant; generous;《理解のある》understanding.

かんよう 慣用 ●現代英語の慣用語法 modern English *usage*.
●**慣用句** an idiom. ●**慣用表現** an idiomatic expression.

かんよう 簡要 ●このハンドブックは簡要にして便利だ This handbook is *concise* and very useful.

かんようしょくぶつ 観葉植物 a foliage [an ornamental] plant.

がんらい 元来 图〖もともと〗from the beginning [start];〖生まれつき〗by nature, naturally;〖本質的に〗essentially.（⇨本来）●新潟は元来港町である Niigata *has grown as* a seaport. ●《現在完了形で「昔から今まで」の意を示す》●彼は元来楽天家だ He is an optimist *by nature*.

かんらく 陥落 图〖陣地などの〗a fall;〖降伏〗surrender. ●トロイの陥落 the *fall* of Troy.
— **陥落する** 動 ●大阪から陥落する drop [降格される] be demoted] from the *ozeki* rank. ●要塞(ﾖｳｻｲ)がついに陥落した The enemy fort *fell to us* at last./《敵が明け渡した》The enemy *surrendered* the fort to us at last.

かんらく 歓楽 图《喜び》(a) pleasure. ●歓楽におぼれる indulge oneself in *pleasures*. ●歓楽を求める seek *pleasures*.
●**歓楽街** an entertainment district [area];《赤線(地帯)》a red-light district.

かんらん 観覧 — **観覧する** 動 watch 《a baseball game》; see 《a play》.
●**観覧券** a ticket 《for [to, ×of] a show》. ●**観覧者** 《観客, 見物人》a spectator;《参観者》a visitor. ●**観覧車**《米》a Ferris [a ferris] wheel;《英》a big wheel. ●**観覧席**《劇場・球場などの》a seat;《競技場などの》《集合的に》the stands（⇨スタンド).

*かんり 管理** 图〖運営, 経営〗management,《国や行政などによる》administration;〖支配〗《統制, 取り締まり》control,《指導, 指図》direction;〖監督〗《仕事・労働者・組織などの》supervision;〖管理責任〗《一時的保管》care 《of》〖日常語〗.
①【〜(の)管理】●工場の管理 the *control* [*management, supervision*] of a factory. ●生産〖労務〗管理 production [labor] *management*. ●品質管理 quality *control*《略 QC》. ●健康管理（⇨健康）●安全管理（⇨安全）●情報管理（⇨情報）●お金の管理 the *management* of money. ●国家管理下にある be under state *control*. ●中間〖上級〗管理職《職責》the middle [senior] *management*《集合的に》, a middle [senior] *manager*. ●その国は国連平和維持軍の管理下に置かれている The country is *under* [*in*] *the control of* the United Nations Peacekeeping Force.
②【管理が[を]】●その古い建物は管理が行き届いている The old building is well *kept* [*taken care of*]. 《!「管理の行き届いた建物」は a well-kept building》▶戻ってくるまで事務所の管理をお願いします I want you to *take* [*have*] *charge of* the office until I come back.
— **管理する** 動《事業などを運営する》manage;《治める》administer;《統制する》control;《監督する》supervise.（⇨图 ③）●彼は会社のお金を管理している He *manages* the company's money. ▶彼の財産はおじが管理している His property is *in the charge of* his uncle./His property is *under* his uncle's *charge*./His uncle is *in charge of* his property. ●私はこの仕事を管理するよう頼まれた I was asked to *supervise* this job. ●その財宝は大英博物館で管理されている The treasures *are looked after* in the British Museum.
●**管理栄養士** a règistered dietícian. ●**管理事務所** a superintendent's [a control] office. ●**管理者** a manager, an administrator. ●**管理社会** a controlled society. ●**管理職**《地位》a managerial [an administrative] position [post];《人》a managerial(-level) staff. ●**管理通貨** managed currency. ●**管理通貨制度** the managed currency system; the planned monetary system. ●**管理人**《ビルやアパートなどの》a superintendent,《米》a janitor,《米》《婉曲の》a custodian,《英》a caretaker;〖財産〗a property custodian;〖遺言者から任された》《公的に任命された》an administrator,《遺言者から任された》an executor. ●**管理費** mánagement chàrge [expènses]; admìnistrátion cósts.

かんり 官吏 a public servant.（⇨公務員, 役人）

かんり 監理 图《監督, 管理》management;《統制》control, regulation.
— **監理する** 動 manage; control, regulate.

がんりき 眼力《洞察力》(an) insight;《観察力》observation. ●眼力の鋭い人 a person of great *insight* [keen *observation*].

*かんりゃく 簡略** — **簡略な**《簡素・単純な》simple;《簡潔な》concise;《短い》brief.（⇨簡潔）
— **簡略化する** 動《単純化する》simplify, make (it) simple;《合理化する》streamline, improve the efficiency 《of》. ●運転免許証の更新手続を簡略化する必要がある It is necessary to *simplify* the procedure for renewing a driver's license.

かんりゅう 貫流 — **貫流する** 動 flow [run] through…. ●淀川は大阪を貫流している The Yodo (River) *flows* [×*is flowing*] *through* Osaka.

かんりゅう 寒流 a cold current.

かんりゅう 還流 图 a back flow; a return current. ●資金の還流〖経済〗the *reflux* of capital.
— **還流する** 動 flow back; return.

かんりょう 完了 图 completion. ●現在[過去]完了形〖文法〗the present [past] *perfect*. ●その仕事の完了 the *completion* of the work. ▶準備完了 (We're) all set!
— **完了する** 動 ●在外《海外での》研究を完了する *finish* [*complete*] one's studies abroad. 《!前の方は「終了」を、後の方は「完全に」を強調する》●首脳会談の準備は完了した Preparations for the summit meeting *have been completed*.

かんりょう 官僚 a bureaucrat /bjúərəkræt/.《!日常会話では a government official ということも多い》;《集合的に》the bureaucracy /bjuərɑ́krəsi/.《!いずれも通例軽蔑的》●彼にはどこか官僚的なところがある There is something *bureaucratic* about him.
●**官僚主義** búreaucràtism;《官僚的形式主義》a

がんりょう 官僚政治 bùreaucrátic government; bureaucracy.

がんりょう 含量 (⇨含有)

がんりょう 顔料 pigment (!種類をいうときは C); (絵の具) colors; paints.

がんりょく 眼力 (⇨眼力(がんりき))

かんるい 感涙 ●感涙にむせぶ (感謝の涙を流す)《書》shed *tears of gratitude*; (感動して涙を流す) be moved to tears.

かんれい 寒冷 cold, coldness; chilliness.
●寒冷紗 cheesecloth. (参考)昔チーズを包んだ布だったことから。今は目の荒い綿布一般をさす)●寒冷前線 (⇨寒冷前線)●寒冷地手当 a cold district allowance.

かんれい 慣例 图 (社会的習慣) (a) custom; (商売・法律上の) (a) practice (!悪習も含む); (因習) (a) convention; (先例) a precedent /présidənt/ ⟪for⟫. ●古い慣例を守る[破る] keep up [break] old *customs*. ●社会の慣例に従う follow [observe] social *customs*. ●そうするのが我々の慣例だ It is our *custom* to do so./It is the *custom* for us to do so./It is *customary* for us to do so.

── 慣例の 形 customary; (因習的な) conventional; (いつもの) usual.

かんれいぜんせん 寒冷前線 a cold (↔a warm) front. ●寒冷前線が日本海を通過した A *cold front* passed over the Sea of Japan.

かんれき 還暦 ●還暦を祝う celebrate one's *60th birthday*. ●還暦を迎える(=数え年61歳に達する) reach one's 61st calendar *year*; reach *the age of 60*.

***かんれん** 関連 图 [関係] (⇨関係); [関連性] relevance. ▶肺がんと喫煙の間には密接な関連がある There is a close *connection* [*correlation*] *between* smoking and lung cancer. ▶その証拠はその事件に関連がある[ない] The evidence *is relevant* [*irrelevant*] *to* the case.

── 関連する 動 be connected ⟪with⟫; be related ⟪to⟫. ●関連した事実 *related* facts. ●その事件に関連した問題 matters *connected with* the incident. ▶彼はこの点[その問題]に関連していくつか質問した He asked me some questions *in* this *connection* [*in connection with* the matter]. (⇨関して)
●関連会社 an affiliated company.

かんろ 甘露 ●フナの甘露煮 caramelized small crucian. ●ああ、甘露、甘露 How delicious! (!飲み物についていう)

がんろう 玩弄 ── 玩弄する 動 toy [play] ⟪with⟫. (⇨玩(もてあそ)ぶ)

かんろく 貫禄 〚立派な風采〛 presence; 〚威厳〛 dignity; 〚自信〛 confidence. ●貫禄がつく gain an air of *confidence* [*dignity, presence*] ⟪as⟫. ●貫録勝ち[負け] an expected win [loss]. ▶彼は貫禄がない He does not have (great) *presence* [*dignity*]./He lacks (stately) *presence* [*dignity*]. ▶彼は最上級生としての貫禄を示した He showed what a senior could do [was made of, was supposed to be]. (!could do は行為、後の二つは資質についていう)

かんわ 漢和 ●漢和辞典 a dictionary of Chinese characters explained in Japanese.

かんわ 緩和 图 relaxation; relief. ●規制緩和 deregulation. ●国際間の緊張緩和 the *relaxation* of international tension(s); (a) détente /deitɑːnt/, -é- (!は本来のつづり字). ●金融の量的緩和 quantitative monetary *easing*. ●金融市場の規制緩和を行う *deregulate* the financial markets.

── 緩和する 動 (苦痛・緊張などを和らげる) ease; (苦痛などを軽減する) relieve, soothe; (緊張・規則などをゆるめる) relax; (規制を) deregulate. ●輸入制限を緩和する *relax* [*ease*] restrictions on import. ●交通難を緩和する *ease* a traffic jam; *relieve* traffic congestion.
●緩和ケア palliative care.

かんわきゅうだい 閑話休題 Let's leave it at that. (!「この件についてはこのあたりで話をやめておきましょう」の意); Well, putting this aside, ….

き

き 木

WORD CHOICE 木
tree 樹木を表す最も一般的な語. 大木にも小振りの木にも用いる. ●熟した実がたくさんついたリンゴの木 an apple *tree* full of ripe fruits.
wood 材質としての木材・材木. ●木製のおもちゃ a toy made of *wood*.

頻度チャート

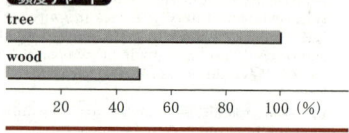

tree ████████████████████
wood ██████████
20 40 60 80 100 (%)

〖樹木〗a tree; 〖低木〗a bush, a shrub; 〖木材〗wood, 《主に米》lumber, 《英》timber; 〖板〗a board.

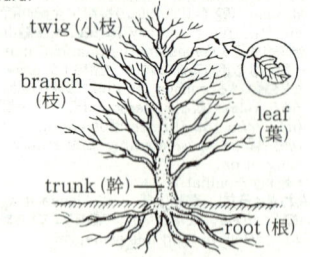

twig (小枝)
branch (枝)
leaf (葉)
trunk (幹)
root (根)

① 【〜(の)木】 ●リンゴ[カシ]の木 an ápple [an óak] trèe. ●バラの木 a rose bush. ●枯れ木 a dead tree. ●葉の落ちた木 a bare tree.
② 【木が[の]】 ●木の机 a wooden [a wood] desk; a desk made of wood. ●木の枝 one's name. ●木の茂った山 a hill covered with trees; a woody [《やや書》a tree-covered, a wooded] hill. ▶木の葉が紅葉した The leaves of trees turned red and yellow. ▶そこにはいろいろな木が生えていた All kinds of trees grew there./There were all kinds of trees growing there.
③ 【木に】 ●木に登る climb a tree. ●木にとまっている鳥 a bird on [in] the tree. (❗ in は枝葉でおおわれた内側にいる感じ) ●木に名前を刻む carve one's name on [xin] a tree. (❗「木(幹)の表面に」の意なので in は通例不可) ●果実は木になる Fruit grows on trees.
④ 【木を】 ●木を切り倒す cut down [fell] a tree. ●木を植える plant a tree. ●木をかんなで削る plane a board.
●木で鼻をくくる ▶彼は木で鼻をくくったような返事をした He gave me a blunt [a curt] answer./He answered me bluntly [curtly].
●木を見て森を見ず can't see the wood for the trees; be too busy looking at trees to discern the shape of the forest.

き 気 ❶【心の働き，傾向】(a) mind; (a) heart; (a) spirit; a mood; (気持ち, 感じ) feelings (⇨心); (意識) consciousness.

使い分け **mind** 理性・精神・知力などを表す. 時に冷静・冷徹などを含意する.
heart 感情的な気分を表す. 時に勇気・熱意などを含意する.
spirit 精神活動の全般を表す. 時に情熱・熱意などを含意する.
mood 一時的な「気分」を表す. (⇨心)

① 【気が[は]】 ●気が変わる change one's mind. ▶たび重なる失敗に彼は気がくじけてしまった He was discouraged [《やや書》was disheartened] by so many failures./So many failures discouraged [《やや書》disheartened] him./He failed so many times that [After so many failures] he lost his drive [《やや書》lost heart]. ▶今朝食事をとる気がしない I don't feel like eating this morning. ▶彼は本当のことを言っていないという気がした(=直感した) I had a feeling [《話》a hunch] that he was not telling the truth. (❗My gut told me that ... ともいえるが, 男性がよく用いる表現) ▶あの人, 気は確かなのか Do you think he is in his right mind?/Is he all right? ▶そのいい知らせを聞いて気が楽に[軽く]なった(=ほっとした) I felt relieved at [to hear] the good news./(気が晴れた) The good news brightened me up. (⇨晴れる) ▶携帯電話を買う気が起こらない I don't feel inclined to buy a cellphone.
② 【気の】 ●気の変わりやすい(=気まぐれな)女 a capricious [《軽蔑的》a fickle] woman. ▶それは気の持ちようだ It depends (on) how you think of [look at] it.
③ 【気に】 ▶先生の話を聞いて勉強する気になった I felt inclined to study after hearing the teacher's talk./The teacher's talk inclined me to study. ▶私はどうしてもその動物を殺す気になれなかった I couldn't bring myself to kill the animal./《やや書》I couldn't find it in my heart to kill the animal. (❗以上いずれも can を伴い, 通例否定文・疑問文で用いる)
④ 【気を】 ●生きようという気(=気力)を失う lose the will to live. ▶彼はショックに備えて気を引き締めた He prepared himself [braced himself (up)] for the shock.
❷ 【性質】(a) nature; (性癖) (a) disposition; (気質) (a) temper. ●気の弱い男 a weak-willed [《やや書》a faint-hearted] man. ●気の荒い船員 a hot-tempered sailor. ▶彼は気が大きい He has a generous nature. ▶彼女は気がやさしい She is kind at heart./(人がよい) She is good-natured.
❸ 【意向, 意図】(意思) intention; (向こう) mind; (意志) will. (⇨つもり ❶) ●やる気のある学生 a well-motivated student. ▶(誘った気) 私はパーティーに出席する気はない I'm not going [I'm not planning, 《やや書》I don't intend] to go to the party. (❗次の例より普通. intend to do は会話で用いると強意的に響く)/I have no intention of going to the party. ▶それを我慢する気はありません I wouldn't tolerate [put up with] it.
(❗intention は no, any, などを冠するときは of ＋動名詞を伴い, 無冠詞または one's を冠するときは to do を伴うのが普通) ▶これからどうする気だ What are you going to do in the future?

(❗ tolerate は堅い語で「容赦する」, put up with は「しょうがないとあきらめる」意のくだけた語)(耐えることができない) I *can't bear* [*endure, stand*] it. (❗ stand は前の2語より口語的) ▶彼女は(本気で)行く気でいたが, 気が変わって行かないことにした She *meant to* [*was going to*] go, but she changed her mind. (❗ mean to do は本来の意図を実際の結果と対比する場合に用いることが多い) ▶彼は私たちを助ける気がないようだ It seems (that) he does not *want to* help us. ▶彼女がどういう気なのか全然分からない I can't understand at all what she *means*./(話) I can't figure her out at all.

❹ [注意, 配慮, 心配] (注意) care, attention; (配慮) consideration; (心配) (a) worry.

❺ [香り, 味] (風味) (a) savor. ● 気が抜ける (炭酸飲料などが) go *flat* [*stale*]. ● 気の抜けたビール *flat* [*stale*] beer. ● 気の抜けたコーラ [サイダー] にがつまらない The coke [soda pop] has lost its *flavor* [*freshness*].

● **気が合う** ▶私たちは気が合う《やや書》We are very *congenial*./(仲よくやっている) We *are getting on well* (*together* [*with each other*])./(話) We *hit it off* (*with* each other).

● **気がある** ▶彼, それを貸してくれる気があるかしら I wonder if he will *be willing to* lend it. ▶彼は彼女に気がある(=好意を持っているらしい He seems to *like* [*be fond of*, (関心がある) *be interested in*] her. (❗ be fond of は like より強意的. 米国の男性はあまり用いない)

● **気が多い** ● 気が多い人 a person of many *interests* [*moods*]. (❗ 前の方は「いろいろなことに関心を持つ」, 後の方は「むら気の」の意)

● **気が利く** be clever [smart]《*to* do》(❗ 当人を前にして言う場合は It is clever [smart] of you《*to* do》. の方が普通)(いつでも手助けしてくれる) be always ready to help. (⇨気が付く ❷, ❸)

● **気が気でない** ▶私は息子のことで気が気でない I *am* very *anxious* [*very uneasy, worried, greatly concerned*] *about* my son.

● **気が狂う** ▶彼はその知らせを聞いて気が狂いそうになった He almost *went mad* [*out of mind*, 《話》*crazy*》at the news./The news almost *drove* him *mad* [《話》*crazy*》.

● **気が進まない** ▶彼は彼女との結婚に気が進まなかった He *was unwilling* [*reluctant*] to marry her.

● **気が済む** (満足している) be satisfied. ▶気の済むまで(=満足するまで)何度でもやってごらん Try it over and over again *until* you *are satisfied* (心ゆくまで) *to* your *heart's content*./(好きなだけ) Try *as many times as* you *like*.

● **気が立つ** ▶彼らはみなその知らせで気が立っていた They *were* all *excited by* [*at*] the news./(神経がぴりぴりしていた) They *were* all *on edge* because of the news.

● **気が散る** ▶騒音のために気が散って読書ができなかった The noise *distracted* me *from* my reading./I *got distracted* by the noise and couldn't concentrate on reading.

● **気がつく** (意識が戻る) become conscious. (⇨気が付く ❶)

● **気が強い** ● 気が強い男 a *strong-willed* [a *strong-hearted*, a *brave*, a *bold*] man.

● **気が遠くなる** ▶彼は暑さで気が遠くなった He *fainted* [*lost consciousness*, 《やや話》*passed out*] because of the heat.

● **気がとがめる** ▶彼のことを先生に告げ口したことでがめる I *feel sorry* [*guilty*] *for* having told on him to our teacher.

● **気が長い** ▶彼は気が長い(=忍耐強い) He is *patient*.

● **気が抜ける** ▶先生が試験を延期したので気が抜けてしまった The teacher *let me down* by postponing the exam.

● **気が乗らない** ▶この仕事には気が乗ら[向か]ない I don't *feel inclined to* do 〔(興味がない) *feel interested in*〕 this work.

● **気が張る** ▶試験の前の夜は非常に気が張って(=緊張して)よく眠れなかった I *was so tense* [*nervous*] the night before my exams that I couldn't sleep well.

● **気が引ける** ▶夫にダイヤの指輪をねだるのは気が引ける I *feel hesitant* about asking my husband to buy a diamond ring. (⇨気後れ)

会話 「彼らって何て食欲なんでしょう!」「私だったらあんなに食べるの気が引けちゃうわ(=恥ずかしくあんなに食べられない)」"What an appetite he's got!" "I'd *be ashamed to* eat as much as that."

● **気がふさぐ** feel [get] depressed;《話》feel blue. (⇨塞(ふさ)ぎ込み)

● **気が回る** ● 気が回る店員 an *attentive* [an *observant*] salesclerk. ▶忙しくてそこまで気が回らなかった I was so busy that I didn't *think of* [*pay any attention to*] that. (❗ think of は「思いつく」, pay attention to は「注意を行き届く」の意)

● **気が短い** ▶彼は気が短い He is *quick-tempered* [*short-tempered*]./He has a *quick temper*./He easily loses his temper.

● **気が向く** ▶私は気の向くままに(=目的もなく)森の中を歩いた I walked [wandered] in the woods *aimlessly*.

● **気がめいる** ▶彼女の歌を聞くと気がめいるわ《話》Her song *makes me feel blue* [*gets me down*].

● **気が若い** ▶彼はまだ気が若い He is still young *at* [*in*] *heart*./He is still young *in mind* [*spirit*]. (❗ He feels young. は彼自身が勝手に「自分は若い」と思っている意)

● **気にかかる** ▶何が気にかかっているのですか What *are you worrying about*?/What's *on* your *mind*?/What *is bothering* you?

● **気に食わない** ▶あいつのものの言い方が気に食わない I *don't like* the way he speaks.

● **気に障(さわ)る** ▶何かが気にさわりましたか Is there something that *gets on* your *nerves* [*offends you*]? ▶少し太ったみたいね. こんなこと言ってお気にさわったかしら You've put on weight a bit. You don't *mind* my saying so.

● **気にする** (⇨気にする)

● **気の置けない** ▶彼は気の置けない(=気楽な)友だ He is a friend I *can feel at ease with*./(とても親しい) He is a *very close* friend [《書》a *bosom* friend] of mine.

● **気の利いた** ● 気の利かぬ男 a *dull* [an *awkward*] man. ● 気の利いた贈り物 a *well-chosen* gift. ▶彼は時々気の利いたことを言う He sometimes says nice things.

● **気のせい** ▶彼があなたを疑っているなんてあなたの気のせいよ It's just your *imagination* [《書》*fancy*] that he is suspicious of you.

● **気のない** ● 気のない返事をする give a *half-hearted* answer.

● **気を失う** faint;《やや話》pass out. (⇨失神)

● **気を落とす** be disappointed《*at*; *to* do》. (⇨失望する)

● **気を利かせる** ▶彼女は気を利かせて部屋から出て行った(思慮分別をきかせて) She *was sensible enough* [*had enough sense*] to go out of the room./(そ

れと気付いて)《やや話》She took the hint and went out of the room.
●気を配る ▶ その少年に気を配る be attentive to the boy. (⇨配る, 気配り)
●気を静める calm oneself; calm down.
●気を遣う ▶ ありがとう. でも本当に気を遣わないでね. うちにみな(用意して)あるから. ただ来てくださればいいの(人を招待して) That's very nice of you, but really don't *bother*. We've got everything here. Just bring yourselves.
●気をつける ⇨気を付ける
●気を取られる ▶ 本にすっかり気をとられていて(=夢中になっていて)あなたの呼ぶ声が聞こえなかった I *was absorbed in* reading and didn't hear you call me.
●気を取り直す ▶ 彼女は気を取り直しまた話し始めた She *pulled herself together* and started to talk again.
●気を引く attract [draw]《his》attention.
●気を紛らす ▶ 彼女は映画に行って気を紛らせた She went to the movies *for a change* [*to cheer* herself *up*]./《書》She *diverted herself by* going to the movies.
●気を回す get the wrong idea [《話》get it wrong]《about》.
●気をゆるめる relax [become lax with] one's attention [mind].
●気を良くする ▶ 彼女は全優の成績をもらって気をよくしてるんだ She's got straight A's and *is feeling very good*. (!A's は A の複数形)
●気を悪くする take offense [get offended, 《主に米話》get sore]《at》.

き 生 ❶ [まじりけのない] straight [neat]《brandy, whiskey》; pure《liquor, soy sauce, vinegar》; undiluted《wine》. ●ウイスキーを生で飲む drink whiskey *straight* [*neat*].
❷ [精製していない] ●生糸 raw silk.

き 希, 稀《液体が薄い》dilute(d), [まれな] rare.

き 忌《命日》(一周忌, 三回忌); [忌中] mourning, a mourning period ●喪, 喪中.

き 奇《奇異》strangeness; [風変わり] eccentricity. ●事実は小説より奇なり《ことわざ》Truth 《時に》Fact] is stranger than fiction.
●奇をてらう ▶ 彼は奇をてらってあんなことをしたのだ He did such a thing just *to be different* [*to attract attention*].

き 軌 ●軌を一にする ▶ 彼は何事をするにも父親と軌を一にした He *did* anything and everything *in the same way as* his father did.

き 黄 yellow. (⇨黄色)

き 機《機会》a chance, an opportunity;《時機》the time. ●機を失する miss a *chance*.
●機が熟す ▶ 反乱の機が熟した *The time* was ripe for revolt.
●機を見るに敏 ▶ 機を見るに敏である never miss a *chance*.

-き 紀 [[地学]] a period. ●白亜紀 the Cretaceous *period*.

-き 期 [[時代]] an age; [[期間]] a period; (期限つきの) a term; [[会期]] a session; [[段階]] a stage. ●米河期 the ice *age*. ●市長を3期勤める serve three *terms* as mayor. ▶ 彼は公職を2期勤めた He was in office for two *terms*. ▶ この法案は今期は国会に通わない We cannot introduce this bill during the *session*.

ぎ 擬《見せかけの》pseudo-. ●擬古典主義 *pseudo*-classicism.

ギア a gear. (⇨ギヤ)

きあい 気合い [叫び] a yell, a shout; [やる気] spirit;

(闘志) fight. ●気合いもろとも敵へ突撃する charge at the enemy with a *yell*. ●気合いの入った議論 a spirited discussion. ●気合いを入れる fire [《話》pep]《him》up《for》. ●彼に気合い負けする(=威圧される) *be overawed by* him. ▶ 仕事にもっと気合いを入れろ Put more *spirit* into your work.

ぎあく 偽悪 ●偽悪ぶる pretend [make believe,《書》feign, affect] to be bad.

きあけ 忌明け the end of mourning. ●忌明けになる go out of mourning.

きあつ 気圧 [[気象]] atmospheric [air] pressure; [[物理]] an atmosphere (略 atm). ●気圧の谷 a low *pressure* trough /trɔ(ː)f/. ●10気圧の圧力 the pressure of 10 *atmospheres*. ▶ 高い山の上では気圧は低くなる The *atmospheric* [*air*] *pressure* becomes [gets] low on high mountains. ▶ 中心気圧は 950 ヘクトパスカルである The central *barometric reading* is 950 hectopascals [hPas].
●気圧計 a barometer. ●気圧配置 the distribution of atmospheric pressure.

ギアナ ●ギアナ高地 Guiana /ɡiǽnə/ Highlands.

きあん 起案 — 起案する 動《起草する》draft《a bill [a contract]》, make*《a rough》draft;《文書などを作成する》draw*《a document》up.

ぎあん 議案 a bill. ●議案を国会に提出する introduce [submit] a *bill* to the Diet;《書》lay a *bill* before the Diet. ●議案を採択[否決]する adopt [reject, vote down] a *bill*.
●議案書 an agenda.

きい 忌諱 ●忌諱に触れる incur《his》displeasure; offend《him》.

きい 奇異な — 奇異な 形 ●奇異な風習 strange [odd, peculiar] manners. ●奇異に映る look [seem] *strange*. (⇨異様, 奇妙, 変な)

きい 貴意 your wishes [opinion].

キー a key. (⇨鍵) ●車のキー a car *key*; a *key* to one's car. ●ピアノのキーをがんがん[軽く]たたく pound [touch] the *keys* of a piano. ●キー(=音の調子)が高すぎる be pitched too high.
●キーステーション [放送網の中心局] a key station. ●キーパーソン [鍵を握る人] a key person. ●キーポイント a [the] (main [key]) point. ▶ それがキーポイントだ That's *the point*. ●キーボード (⇨キーボード) ●キーホルダー (輪の) a key ring;《ケース状の》a key case;《和製語》a key holder. ●キーマン a key person, a key man. ●キーワード a key word.

キーウィーフルーツ ⇨キウイ❶

きいきい ●きいきい音を立てる squeak, squeal (! squeal は squeak より長めで, 強い音);《きしる》creak. ▶ 彼女はきいきい声で話す He speaks in a *squeaking* [*squeaky*] voice. ▶ このドアは開ける時きいきいいう This door *creaks* [*squeaks*] as it opens.

ぎいぎい ●ぎいぎい音を立てる《きしむ音など》creak, squeak;《金属片などでこする音》rasp. ▶ 階段がぎいぎいいきしんだ The stairs *creaked*.

きいちご 木苺 [[植物]] a raspberry.

きい(っ)と ▶ 自転車がきいっと止まった The bike *squeaked* to a stop. (⇨きいきい)

ぎいっと ぎいっと鳴る[音を立てる] creak; squeak. (⇨ぎいぎい)

きいっぽん 生一本 ❶ [交じり気のない(もの)] pure [ˣgenuine]. ●灘の生一本 pure Nada sake.
❷ [一本気な] straightforward and honest; single-minded. ▶ 彼は生一本な男だ He is a *single-minded* man *and hates anything wrong*. (! 人について straight もこの意味で用いられるが, 今は「(麻)薬を用いない」「ゲイ (gay) でない」の意の方が一般的なの

きいてまわる 聞いて回る ask around.

きいと 生糸 (raw) silk.

キーパー 《競技》a goalkeeper, 《話》a keeper, a goalie.
● キーパーチャージ charging the goalkeeper.

キープ ── **キープする 動** ●ボールをキープする *keep* the ball; retain possession.

キーボード ❶［コンピュータ・ピアノなどの］a keyboard. ▶彼女はキーボードを打つのが速い She keyboards [types] fast./She is a fast keyboarder [typist]. (⚠この意味では type, typist の方が普通). ❷［楽器］a keyboard (instrument), keyboards. ▶彼はキーボード奏者である He is a keyboardist [a *keyboard* player]./He plays the keyboard.

きいろ 黄色 图 (a) yellow. (⚠種類をいうときは〖C〗) 《事柄》英語では yellow は「臆病（#%&）」、「卑劣」などのイメージを伴う）●黄色がかった緑 *yellowish* green. ▶木の葉が黄色に変わりつつある Leaves are turning *yellow* [are yellowing].
── 黄色い［の］ 形 yellow. ●黄色い帽子 a *yellow* hat. ●黄色のペンキ *yellow* paint. ●黄色い（＝かん高い）声で in a shrill voice.

きいん 起因 ── **起因する 動** arise* 《*from*》; be caused 《*by*》. (⇨原因) ▶国連の弱さは冷戦後に超大国が一つしかないことに起因する(＝結果として生じている) The weakness of the United Nations *stems from* the fact that the post-Cold War world has only one [a sole] superpower.

ぎいん 議員 ❶［国会の］(日本の) a Diet member, a member of the Diet, (男性) a Dietman (*第* -men), (女性) a Dietwoman (*第* -women); (米国の) a member of Congress (*略* M.C.), (男性) a Congressman (*第* -men), (女性) a Congresswoman (*第* -women)「以上 2 語は「下院議員」の意になることが多いが、これは正式には a *member* of the House (of Representatives), a Representativeと訳す。上院議員は a Senator」, (英国の) a member of Parliament (*略* M.P.). ❷［地方議会の］a member of an assembly. ●都[県; 市; 町; 村]議会議員 a *member* of the Metropolitan [prefecture; city; town; village] *assembly*. ▶彼は府会議員です He is [sits] on [×in] the prefecture council.
● 議員立法 legislation by House members.

ぎいん 議院 the House; (国会) (⇨国会) ●衆議院 the *House* of Representatives. (⇨衆議院) ●参議院 the *House* of Councilors. (⇨参議院)
● 議院制度 the parliamentary system. ●議院内閣 a parliamentary cabinet system.

キウイ ❶［果物］(a) kiwi /kiːwiː/ (fruit [berry]), a Chinese gooseberry. ❷［鳥］a kiwi.

きうつり 気移り ── **気移りする 動** ●気移りする（＝関心の対象が次々と変わる）性格で、何をしても長続きしない He *gets interested in one thing after another* and can't stick to anything. ●一般大衆は気移りする（＝気まぐれな）傾向がある The public tends to be *fickle*.

きうん 気運 a tendency 《*to, toward*; *to do*》; a trend 《*toward*》. ▶生活の質を向上させようという気運が高まっている There is a growing *tendency* [*expectation*] (among people) *to* improve the quality of life.

きうん 機運 the (right) time. ●機運が熟する（＝そのような時期になる） The *time* is ripe 《*for*; *to do*》.

きえ 帰依 ── **帰依する 動** ●仏教に帰依する（信者になる） become a believer in Buddhism; become a Buddhist; （受け入れる）《*書*》embrace Buddhist faith.

きえい 気鋭 ●新進気鋭の若い学者 an *up-and-coming* young scholar.

きえいる 消え入る (⇨消える) ●消え入るような（＝かすかな）声で in a *faint* [*weak, feeble*] voice. ▶ズボンの前が開いていると言われて恥ずかしくて消え入る思いだった（＝死ぬほど恥ずかしかった） I *nearly died of* embarrassment when someone told me my fly was undone.

きえうせる 消え失せる disappear; （突然に、不思議にも）vanish. ▶とっとと消え失せろ！ *Get lost* right now!/*Get out of* my *sight* this instant! ▶トイレから戻ってみるとバッグが消え失せていた When I came back from the toilet, I found my bag *had disappeared* [*vanished*].

きえのこる 消え残る （雪が） remain unmelted; （火が） remain unextinguished.

キエフ ［ウクライナの首都］Kiev /kiːef/.

きえる 消える ❶ (a)［見えなくなる、存在しなくなる］disappear; （突然に、不思議にも） vanish; （徐々に） fade (away); ［見えなくなる］go* out of sight; ［消え去る］be [have*] gone. (⇨無くなる ❶) ●消えた宝石 *missing* [×disappeared, ×gone] jewels; jewels that *have disappeared* [*are gone, have gone*, 行方不明である] *are missing* (⚠be gone は単に「(人・物が)もうそこに存在しない」ことを表すが、have gone は移動方向を強調する：その宝石はどこへ消えたか Where have [×were] the jewels *gone*?). ▶その山の雪がすっかり消えた All the snow on [×of] the mountain *has disappeared* [*has gone*, 溶けてなくなった] *has melted away*. ▶すりは人ごみの中に消えた The pickpocket *disappeared into* [姿を消した] *was lost in, lost himself in*] the crowd. ▶船は霧の中に消えていった The ship *faded into* the fog. ▶ジェット機はあっという間に視界から消えた The jet plane *shot out of sight*. ▶この部屋代に収入の大半が消えた These rooms *took* most of my money.
(b)［感覚・感情などが］（痛み・においなどが消え去る）go*; （過ぎ去る） pass; （感情・思い出などが消滅する） die （-d; dying）; ［音・興奮などが次第になくなる］die away. ▶痛みがなかなか消えない The pain won't *disappear* [*go* (*away*), *pass* (*away*)]. ▶その知らせを聞いて私の怒りは消えた My anger *vanished* [*died*] at the news. ▶足音が遠のいて消えていった The footsteps *died* [*faded*] away into the distance.
❷［火が］go* [die ─d; dying] out; ［電灯・ガスなどが］go out [off]. ▶マッチをお持ちですか。葉巻の火が消えてしまったのですから Do you have a match? My cigar *has gone* [*died*] *out*. ▶ろうそくが消えかかっている The candle *is dying out* [*down*]. (⚠out は「完全に」、down は「次第に」の意) ▶明かりが消えている The light *is out* [*off*]. ▶その火事はまもなく消えた（＝消し止められた） The fire *was put out* [《*書*》*was extinguished*] soon. ▶パーティーの後の部屋は火が消えたようだった After the party everything seemed *dead* in the room. ▶希望の灯は突然消えた All hope suddenly *vanished* [《*書*》*was suddenly extinguished*].
❸［跡・しみなどが取れる］（こすって） rub (-bb-) off; （すり減って） wear* away [off]. ▶このペンキはなかなか消えない This paint won't *rub off* [はがれる] *come off*] easily. ▶印刷の文字が消えてしまった The printing *has worn away* [*off*].

きえん 気炎 (be in) good [high] spirits.
● 気炎を上げる （大言壮語する）《*話*》talk big; （激論する） argue hotly [have a hot argument]

きえん 奇縁 [めぐり合わせ] a strange [a curious] chance; [因縁] a strange [a curious] fate. (⇨ 合縁奇縁)

きえん 機縁 (⇨⑪ 機会)

ぎえんきん 義援金, 義捐金 ▶阪神大震災の被災者のために義援金を集め始めた We started a *relief fund* for the victims of the Great Hanshin Earthquake.

きえんさん 希塩酸 【化学】 diluted hydrochloric acid.

きおい 気負い great eagerness; enthusiasm; excitement.

きおう 気負う ●気負っている be very keen [very eager, very enthusiastic]. (⇨張り切る)

きおうしょう 既往症 a previous illness; (病歴) one's medical history.

‡**きおく** 記憶 [名] [覚えておくこと[力]] (a) memory (!「(個人の)記憶力」の意では [C]); [覚えている状態] remembrance; [思い出すこと] recollection. ●記憶すべき出来事 a *memorable* event.

① 【～記憶】 ●かすかな記憶 a dim *memory*. ●なまなましい記憶 a vivid *memory*.

② 【記憶～】 ●650 メガバイトの記憶容量を持つ CD-ROM a CD-ROM with a storage capacity of 650 megabytes. ▶母は数字の記憶力がいい[悪い] Mother has a good [a bad, a poor] *memory for figures*. ▶君, すごい記憶力(の持ち主)だね You've got a wonderful *memory*./What a *memory* you have! ▶私は記憶力がだんだん衰えている My *memory* is failing./My ability to remember is declining./(ますます忘れっぽくなってきた) I'm getting more and more forgetful. ▶すみません. 私の記憶違いでした I'm sorry. I was mistaken in [(やや書) had a lapse of] *memory*.

③ 【記憶が[は]】 ●私の記憶が正しければその事件は 1980 年の秋に起こった The incident happened in the fall of 1980, if my *memory* serves me (well [correctly, right]) [(正しく記憶していれば) if I *remember* correctly]. (!(1) この if 節は主文の内容に対する直接効果がないので, 主文の後に置かれる. (2) 後の言い方のほうが普通) ●さまざまな記憶が心によみがえってきた All kinds of *memories* came back to [in] my mind. ●私は彼にどこかで会った記憶がある I *remember* seeing him somewhere. (⇨覚える) ▶その事件の記憶はまったく[ぼんやりとしか]ない I have no [only a vague] *memory* of the incident. ▶その写真を見て子どもの頃の遠い記憶がよみがえった The picture revived *distant memories* of my childhood. ▶その記憶がいまだに心に残っている The *memories* still *linger* (on) in me.

④ 【記憶に】 ●記憶に新しい be fresh *in* one's *memory* [*mind*]. ●その光景は私の記憶にいまだに生々しく残っている[深く刻まれている] The scene still remains vivid *in* my *memory* [is deeply engraved *on* my *memory*]. ▶君の言葉は記憶に留めておこう I'll *keep* [*bear*] your words *in mind*./I'll *remember* your words. (!remember を用いる方が口語的) ▶これほど笑ったことってちょっと記憶にないなあ I don't *know* when I've laughed so much. ▶それは記憶にございません. I have no *memory* of that./(やや書) (帰化して日本人になった方)

⑤ 【記憶を】 ●記憶を新たにする[失う; 取り戻す] refresh [lose; restore] one's *memory*. ●記憶をたよりに書く write from *memory*. ▶アルバムを見ながら子どもの頃の記憶を呼びさました The album brought back [awakened] my earliest childhood *memories*.

⑥ 【記憶では】 ▶私の記憶では彼は 60 歳で死んでいる As I remember [As far as I can remember], he died at the age of 60.

― 記憶する [動] [暗記する] memorize; (そらで覚える) learn* ... by heart; [心に留める] keep* [bear*] ... in mind; [覚えている, 思い出す] remember. ●覚える❶ ▶私の記憶している限りではその男の人は黒い口ひげをたくわえて(=はやして)いた As far as I (can) *remember* [To the best of my *memory*], the man had a black mustache /mʌstǽ(:)ʃ/. ▶私は彼大変頭のいい生徒だったと記憶している I *remember* him *as* a very bright student [(that) he was a very bright student]. (!後の方が口語的)

●記憶喪失 loss of memory; 【医学】amnesia /æmníːʒə/. ●記憶装置 【コンピュータ】a memory; a storage (device).

きおくれ 気後れ ― 気後れする [動] (度胸を失う) lose* one's nerve; (ためらう) hesitate, feel* hesitant; (自信がない) (やや書) feel diffident; (舞台などで上がる) get* stage fright.

キオスク [<トルコ語] a kiosk /kíːɑsk, kiɑ́sk/.

きおち 気落ち ― 気落ちする [動] (がっかりする) be discouraged, lose* heart; (意気消沈している) be depressed; (落ち込む) feel* down. (⇨失望) ●すっかり気落ちする be completely *discouraged*. ▶そんなに気落ちするな Don't be so *discouraged*.

きおも 重気 ― 気重な [形] (feel*) dispirited and depressed.

‡**きおん** 気温 (a) temperature. (⇨温度) ●最高[最低]気温 the maximum [minimum] *temperature*; the highest [lowest] *temperature*; (天気予報などで) (today's) high [low]. ●(年)平均気温 the average *temperature* (for the year). ●気温の急激な変化[上昇; 低下] a sudden change [rise; drop] in *temperature*.

会話 「今気温は何度ですか」「25 度です」"What's the *temperature* now?" "It's 25℃." (!twenty-five degrees centigrade と読む)

会話 「明日の気温は予想では 34 度まで上がるそうよ」「本当かい, ここ数日はずーっと最高気温 30 度台が続いているね」"Tomorrow's temperature is expected to reach a *high* of 34℃." "Oh, yeah? The *highs* have been in the thirties for the last several days." (!この high は「(...の)最高記録」の意の名詞)

ぎおん 擬音 an imitation sound.
●擬音語 an onomatopoeia /ɑ̀nəmæ̀təpíːə/. ●擬音効果 sound effects.

きか 気化 [名] vaporization.
― 気化する [動] vaporize.
●気化熱 the heat of vaporization.

きか 奇貨 ●奇貨居(*)くべし Don't miss a golden opportunity; (ことわざ) Make hay while the sun shines; Strike while the iron is hot.

きか 帰化 [名] naturalization. ●帰化日本人 a *naturalized* Japanese.
― 帰化する [動] ▶彼は日本に帰化した He *was naturalized* in Japan [as a Japanese (citizen)]./(帰化して日本人になった) He became a Japanese citizen through *naturalization*.
●帰化植物 a naturalized plant.

きか 幾何 [名] geómetry.
― 幾何学的(な) [形] gèométric; geometrical. ●幾何学的模様の壁紙 wallpaper with a *geometric(al)* pattern (on it).
― 幾何学的に [副] geometrically.
●幾何級数 【数学】a geometric(al) progression [series].

きが 起臥 ●起臥を共にする live together 《with him》; live under the same roof.

きが 飢餓 starvation, hunger. (!後の方は単なる「空腹」も表す意味の広い語) ●飢餓に瀕している人々 *starving* people. ▶凶作だった. 人々は飢餓に瀕していた The crops failed. The people were suffering from *starvation* [There was much *hunger* among the people].

ぎが 戯画 (人物の特徴・欠点を誇張した) a caricature; (政治・時事を風刺した) a cartoon; (文学作品を茶化するという意味を含む) a burlesque.

きかい 機会 (an) oppórtunity 《for+图; to do; of [for] doing》, a chance 《of [for]+图; to do; of doing》; (an) occasion 《for+图; to do》.

> **使い分け** **opportunity** 望ましい状態に至るためのよい機会を表す.
> **chance** 偶然に訪れた機会・可能性を表す. くだけた文脈で多く用いる.
> **occasion** 原義は「時, 場合」だが, 時に特別な場合としての好機を表す.

① 【～機会】 ●絶好の機会 a golden *opportunity*; an excellent *chance*. ●教育[就職]の機会 an *opportunity for* education [employment]; an education [a job] *opportunity*. ●海外旅行は視野を広げるよい機会だ Traveling abroad is a good *opportunity for* widening your horizons [(*for* you) *to* widen your horizons]. ▶今こそ絶好の機会だ Now is the [your, my, our] *time* (*to* do).
② 【機会～】 ●女性に対する機会均等 equal *opportunities for* women.
③ 【機会が[は]】 ●機会がある[できる] have [get] a *chance* [an *opportunity*]. ●彼に会う機会がない have no *chance* [*opportunity*, ×*occasion*] *to* see him. ●機会では「必要[理由]がない」の意となる) ●機会があり次第 at the earliest [first] *opportunity*; on the first *occasion*. (!いずれも堅い言い方. 日常的には as soon as possible (できるだけ早く)が普通) ●機会があればその博物館に行ってごらんなさい If there is a *chance*, you should visit the museum./You should visit the museum if the *occasion* arises. (!後は堅い言い方) ▶克哉に会う機会があったらよろしく言ってください Say hello to Katsuya for me if you have [get] a *chance to* see him. ▶今やらなければ2度と機会はない Either we do it now or never. ▶よい音楽を聞く機会がほとんどなかった I haven't had very few *opportunities* [(あまり) I haven't had much *opportunity*] *to* listen to good music./(めったに) I've rarely had a *chance* [(書) I have seldom had an *occasion*] *to* hear good music. ▶外国へ行く機会が増えている We *are having more and more opportunities* to go abroad. ▶彼は機会(が)あるごとに英語を話した He never missed any *opportunity* [*chance*] *to* speak English./He spoke English *at every opportunity* [whenever he got a *chance*]. ▶彼は生け花を教えているので和服を着る機会が多い He is an *ikebana* master and *has a lot of occasions to* wear a kimono.
会話 「ここにはよく来るの?」「機会(が)あるたびにね」"Do you come here often?" "Every *chance* I get."
④ 【機会に】 ●この機会に on this *occasion*. ●できるだけ早い機会に on the first possible *occasion*. ●次の機会に回す reserve it for another *occasion*. ●費用の安いパック旅行の機会に飛びつく jump at the [×a] *chance* of a cheap package tour. ▶またの機会にしましょう Let's make it some other *time*./Maybe another *time*. ▶機会にめぐまれる have a great *opportunity* 《*to* visit Paris》.
⑤ 【機会を】 ●機会をとらえる take [seize] an *opportunity*. ●機会を待つ wait for an *opportunity*. ●機会をねらう watch one's *opportunity*. ●機会を逃す[ふいにする] miss 〔見送る〕 blow; 〔話〕 pass up [a one's] *chance*. ▶そのうち機会を作って1杯やろう Let's *have* [*find*] *an opportunity* to have a drink soon. ▶政府は彼に留学の機会を与えた The government gave him an [the] *opportunity to* study abroad. (! an ではたくさんある機会の一つ, the では留学というその機会を示す) ▶この機会をお借りして皆さんにお礼を申し上げたいと思います I'd like to take this *opportunity to* thank [*of* thanking] you all./I'd like to take this *occasion to* thank [(英) *of* thanking] you all.

●機会均等計画 an equal-opportunity [equal opportunities] program.

きかい 機械 a machine; (集合的) machinery (!単数扱い. 数える場合は a piece [two pieces] of ～のように)); (家庭用電気器具) an appliance; (仕掛け) a mechanism; (集合的) machinery; (時計などの) works.

① 【～機械】 ●工作機械 a *machine* tòol. ●時計の機械装置 the *mechanism* [*machinery*, *works*] of a watch. ●精密機械メーカー a precision instrument manufacturer.
② 【機械～】 ▶その工場は来年までに完全に機械化される The plant will *be fully mechanized* by next year. ●機械製品は手製の品より安い The *machine*-made [*manufactured*] goods are cheaper than handmade ones.
③ 【機械は】 ▶この機械は調子よく動く[動かない] This *machine* runs smoothly [doesn't work well, ×doesn't move well]. ▶機械は多大の労力を省いてくれる *Machines* save (us) a lot of labor [(やや書) dispense with much labor]. (!*Machinery* saves… [dispenses…]. も可)
④ 【機械の[に]】 ●機械の運転時間 *machine* hours. ●機械のように正確に like clockwork. ▶機械に手を触れるな《掲示》Hands off the *machinery*./Keep away from the *machines*. ▶単純な作業を機械にやらせた We had simple work done by *machine*. (! háve…dòne のように have に強勢を置く. done の方に強勢を置くと「機械に単純作業を奪われた」といった被害の受身表現と解される)
⑤ 【機械を】 ●工場に機械を据え付ける install a *machine* in a factory. ●機械を組み立てる put together [(やや書) assemble] a *machine*. ●この機械を操作するのは難しい It is difficult to operate [use, work, run] this *machine*.

— **機械的な** 形 mechanical; (習慣的な) automatic. (!前の語はしばしば非人間性を暗示し軽蔑的に用いる) ●機械的な返事 a *mechanical* [an *automatic*] answer. ▶それは機械的な仕事なので精神的な満足は得られない The work is very *mechanical* and not very satisfying mentally.

— **機械的に** 副 mechanically; automatically. (⇨形) ●何事も機械的にやる do everything *mechanically* [*in a mechanical way*]. ●機械的に(=そらで)文の1節を覚える learn a passage *by rote*. (! by rote は「機械的に(棒暗記する)」の意)

●機械油 machíne òil. ●機械化 mechanization. ●機械科 (学校の) a mechanical course; a course in mechanical engineering. ●機械技術 machine [mechanical] technology. ●機械語 〔コンピュータ〕(a) machíne lànguage. ●機械工 a mechanic; a mechanical engineer. ●機械工学 mechanical engineering. ●機械工業 the machinery industry. ●機械工場 a machine shop [factory]. ●機械文明 (a) machine civilization. ●機械翻訳 machine translation. ●機械力 mechanical power.

きかい 『機械』 *The Machine*. (参考) 横光利一の小説

きかい 奇怪 ― 奇怪な 形 ●奇怪な(=不可解な)事件 a *mysterious* incident. ●奇怪な(=奇妙な)行動 *strange*〔(わけの分からない) *funny*〕conduct.

きかい 棋界 the *go* world; the *shogi* world.

きかい 器械 〔器具〕 an instrument; 〔器具一式〕 apparatus. ●医療器械 medical *instruments*. (関連) 器械または徒手体操 gymnastics with or without apparatus.

きがい 危害 ●危害を加える hurt [harm, injure, wound]《him》; do《him》(bodily) harm. (⇨怪我(%)) ●危害のない=無害な harmless. ▶静かにしてろ, そうしたら危害は加えない Be quiet and you won't *get hurt* [*get harmed, get wounded, get injured*].

きがい 気概 〔気骨〕 spirit; (根性) backbone; 《話》 guts; 〔勇気〕 courage; (強い意志) strong will. ●気概のある人 a man of *spirit* [*backbone*]. ●気概のある兵士 a soldier with a lot of *courage* [*guts*]. ▶彼には困難に打ち勝つ気概がない He has no *spirit* [*backbone*] to get over difficulties.

*****ぎかい** 議会 an assembly; 〔国会〕(日本の)the Diet; (米国の) Congress; (英国・カナダの) Parliament /pάːrləmənt/. (⇨国会) ●県[市; 町]議会 a prefectural [a municipal; a town] *assembly*. ▶日本の国会は英国議会にならって作られた The Japanese Diet was modeled after the British *parliament*.
●議会主義 parliamentarism. ●議会政治 parliamentary government. ●議会制度 parliamentary system. ●議会制民主主義 parliamentary democracy.

きがえ 着替え 〔着替えること, 着替えの服〕 a change of clothes; (余分の衣服) spare clothes. ▶着替えを2着持っていきなさい Take two *changes of clothes* with you.
●着替え室 a changing room.

きがえる 着替える change one's clothes;〔…に着替える〕change 《into a dress》. ●上着を脱いでセーターに着替える *change out of* [*from*] the jacket *into* a sweater; *change* the jacket *for* a sweater. ▶夕食のために着替えた I *changed* for dinner. ▶シャツを着替えなさい *Change* your shirt.

きかがく 幾何学 geometry. (⇨幾何)

きがかり 気掛かり (an) anxiety; (a) worry; (a) care. (⇨心配) ▶私のただ一つの気がかりは息子の体のことだ My only *worry* [*care*] is the health of my son.

*****きかく** 企画 名 〔計画〕 a plan; (大がかりな) a project; 〔計画すること〕 planning;〔手はず〕arrangements. (⇨計画, 手はず)
―― 企画する 動 ●旅行を企画する *plan* a trip; *make plans for* a trip; *arrange* [*make arrangements for*] a trip.

きかく 規格 a standard. ●自動車の部品を規格化する *standardize* the parts of cars. ▶この品は規格に合っている This article meets [satisfies, is up to] the *standard*.
●規格化 standardization. ●規格外商品 nonstandardized goods. ●規格商品 standardized goods.

きがく 器楽 instrumental music. ●器楽曲 an instrumental piece.

ぎがく 伎楽 *gigaku*;(説明的に) an ancient masked dance.

きかざる 着飾る dress (oneself) up. ▶彼らはみんな結婚式のために着飾っていた They *were* all *dressed up* for the wedding./《話》They *were* all (*dressed*) *in* their *Sunday best* for the wedding.

きかす 利かす (⇨利かせる)
きかす 聞かす (⇨聞かせる)

きかせる 利かせる ●スープに塩を利かせる(=味付けする) *season* the soup *with* salt; *put* salt *in* the soup. ▶すごみを利かせて(=おどして)小切手に署名させる *frighten*《him》*into* signing the check. ●機転を利かせる show tact; be tactful. ●ボールにスナップを利かせる (⇨スナップ ③)

きかせる 聞かせる ●子供に本を読んで聞かせる *read* a book *for* [*to*] a child. ▶さあひとつ私たちに歌を歌って[演奏して]聞かせてください Come and *sing* [*play*] *for us*. ▶どうしてそれが嫌いなのか私に聞かせて(=言って)ください *Tell* me why you don't like it.

きづつく 気が付く ❶〔意識を回復する〕●3分後に彼女は気がついた She *became conscious* [*came to* her *senses*] after three minutes. (⇨意識)
❷〔目覚ます〕(見て, 感じて) notice; (知る) find*; (思いつく) think* *of* ...; (実感する) realize. (⇨気付く) ▶いつ時計がないのに気がつきましたか When did you *notice* [*find*] (*that*) your watch was missing?/When did you *find* your watch missing?/When did you miss your watch? ▶私たちは話に夢中になっていて, ふと気がつくと他の人はだれもいなくなっていた We were absorbed in talking and *found ourselves* left alone there 〔(いつの間にか) and everyone else was gone *before we knew* (*it*)〕. ▶11時半だわ. もうこんなに遅い時間だなんて気がつかなかったわ It's half past eleven. I didn't *realize* how late it was.
会話「彼女に花束か何か要るよ」「うん, それはいいことに気がついたわ」"We're going to need a bouquet or something for her." "Hmm ... You've got a good point there."
会話「テレビの音を落としていただけないでしょうか. とやかく言うつもりはないのですが, 近所のみなさんが迷惑しているのです」「まあ, そんなことにはちっとも気がつきません. すみませんでした」"Could I possibly ask you to turn down the volume on your TV? I don't mean to be critical, but you're keeping all the neighbors up." "Oh! I *had no idea* I was keeping them up. I appologize."
❸〔注意が行き届いている〕●彼はよく気がつく人だ He *is* very *observant*./〔気が回って面倒見のいいと〕 He's a very *sensitive and caring* man.

きがね 気兼ね ▶気兼ねせずに(=自由に)ご質問ください Ask any question *freely*./Please *feel free to* ask questions. ▶欲しいものがあれば気兼ねなく言ってくれ (ちゅうちょせずに) Don't *hesitate to* tell me if you want anything./〔遠慮をしないで〕《書》Please tell me *without reserve* if you want anything. ▶彼女の前では少し気兼ねした(=窮屈に感じた) I *felt* a little *constraint* [*ill at ease*] in her presence.

きがまえ 気構え 〔心構え〕 preparation (*for*);〔決心〕determination (*to do*). ●気構えができている be prepared [ready] (*for; to do*).

きがる 気軽 形 〔喜んで〕 readily; (遠慮せずに) freely; (親しく) in a friendly manner. (⇨気さく, 気楽) ●仕事を気軽に引き受ける *readily* take the job. ●気軽に読める本を推せんする recommend a book for *light reading*. ▶何なりと気軽におたずねください Please *feel free to* ask me anything.

*****きかん** 機関 ❶〔エンジン〕an engine. ●蒸気[ディーゼ

ル] 機関 a steam [a diesel] *engine*.

❷ [機構, 手段] (政府などの) an organ, 《米》 an agency; (社会・教育・福祉施設の) an institution; (便宜をはかるための) facilities; (手段) means (⚠ 単・複両扱い) ● 政府機関 a government *agency*. ● 教育[公共]機関 an educational [a public] *institution*. ● 金融機関 financial *institutions*. ● 交通機関 *means* of transportation 《米》 [transport 《英》]; transport *facilities*. ● 報道機関 the (mass) media. (⚠ 単・複両扱い)
● 機関士 (船の) an engineer; (列車の) 《米》 an engineer, 《英》 an engine driver. ● 機関誌[紙] (会報などの) a bulletin; (政党などの) an organ. ● 機関室 an engine room. ● 機関長 a chief engineer. ● 機関投資家 an institutional investor [buyer, player]. ● 機関砲 a heavy machine gun.

*きかん 期間 a period; (契約・任期などの) a term 《of》. ● 契約期間 the *term* of contract. ● 休暇期間中に *during* the holidays. ● 短期間で英語をマスターする master English in a short *period* (of time) [*time*, ×*term*]. ▶ そこでの私たちの滞在期間は 1 週間です The *length* of our stay there will be one week. ● 彼は長期間入院していた He was in 《米》 the) hospital for a long (*period* of) *time*. ▶ この時計の保証期間は 1 年です This watch is guaranteed *for* one year.

*きかん 器官 an organ. ● 生殖器官 the reproductive *organs*. ● 発声器官 the *organs* of speech; the vocal *organs*.

きかん 気管 图 a windpipe; [解剖] a trachea /tréikiə/ (德 ~s, tracheae).
━ 気管の 形 tracheal. ● 気管支 (⇨気管支)

きかん 奇観 a spectacular [a wonderful] sight; (自然が造った) a natural wonder.

きかん 季刊 ━ 季刊の 形 quarterly.
● 季刊誌 a quarterly (magazine).

きかん 帰還 (a) return; (本国送還) (a) repatriation.
● 帰還者 a returnee; a repatriate. ● 帰還兵 a returned soldier.

きかん 既刊 ━ 既刊(の) 形 previously published [issued].
● 既刊書目録 a backlist. ● 既刊号 a back issue; a back number; a back copy.

きかん 基幹 (土台) a foundation. (⇨元 ❸)
● 基幹産業 a key [a basic] industry.

きがん 祈願 图 (a) prayer /préər/. ━ 祈願する 動 pray 《for》. (⇨祈る)

ぎかん 技官 a technical officer [official].

ぎがん 義眼 an artificial [a false, a glass] eye.

きかんき 利かん気 ━ 利かん気の 形 (負けん気の) competitive; (手に負えない) unruly; (言うことを聞かない) disobedient.

きかんし 気管支 [解剖] a bronchus /bráŋkəs/ (德 bronchi /bráŋkai/); bronchial /bráŋkiəl/ tubes.
● 気管支炎 [医学] bronchitis /braŋkáitis/; bronchial /bráŋkiəl/ infection. ● 気管支ぜんそく [医学] bronchial asthma /ǽzmə/.

きかんしゃ 機関車 a railroad 《米》 [a railway 《英》] engine (⚠ an engine とも しない) ● ディーゼル機関車 a diesel locomotive (engine). ● 蒸気[ディーゼル; 電気]機関車 a steam [a diesel; an electric] locomotive. (⚠ ×SL と略すのは和製英語)

きかんじゅう 機関銃 a machine gun. ● 軽機関銃 a submachine gun, 《話》 a sub. ● 機関銃で撃つ machine-gun; shoot 《at the enemy》 with a *machine gun*.

きかんぼう 利かん坊 (勝ち気な) a competitive [an unbending, an unyielding] child; (やんちゃな) a naughty child.

*きき 危機 (重大な時点, 岐路) a crisis /kráisis/ (德 crises); (緊急事態) (an) emergency. (⚠ 政治・経済・社会・心の危機が続く状態は unrest)
① 《~(の)危機》 ● 食糧[エネルギー]危機 a food [energy] *crisis*. ● 政府[財政]の危機 a governmental [a financial] *crisis*. ● 経済危機 (⇨経済)
● 差し迫った[深刻な]危機 an impending [a serious, a grave] *crisis*. ● 戦争の危機 a war crisis.
▶ それは彼女の人生の危機であった It was a *crisis* in her life.
② 《危機~》 ▶ 彼らの間に危機感があった They felt [had] a sense of *crisis*.
③ 《危機に》 ● 危機に直面する face a *crisis* [an emergency]; arrive at [reach] the *critical moment*. ● 危機に臨んで at a *crisis*; in an *emergency*. ● 危機に立ち向かう confront a crisis. ● 当時我が社は危機的状況にあった [陥った] Our company was in [fell into] *crisis* then.
④ 《危機を》 ● 会社の危機を脱して help a company out of the *crisis*. ● 患者[会社]は危機を脱した (乗り切った) The patient [company] has got over [has overcome] a *crisis*. /(峠を越した) The patient [company] *has turned the corner*.
● 危機一髪 (⇨危機一髪) ● 危機管理 (経営上の) risk management; 《米》 (国家的な) crisis management. ● 危機的な状況 a critical situation.

きき 鬼気 ● 鬼気迫る bloodcurdling; ghastly; horrible; very frightening. ● 鬼気迫る場面 a *frightening* situation.

きき 嬉々 ● 嬉々として merrily; joyfully; cheerfully; happily.

きき 機器 (機械) machinery (⚠ 集合的に用い単数扱い); (精密器具) an instrument; (家庭用器具) an appliance; (特定の目的の器具) an apparatus (⚠ 集合的にも用いる (⇨器具)). ● 医療機器 medical *instruments*. ● 事務機器 business *machines*.

-きき -利き (...の手を使う) - handed. ● 右利きの right-*handed*.

ききあきる 聞き飽きる be tired [sick] of hearing .... (⇨飽きる) ▶ (きみのお説教は) もう聞き飽きた (＝十二分に聞いた) I've heard enough (of your lecture).

ききあし 利き足 one's dominant leg [foot].

ききいっぱつ 危機一髪 ● 危機一髪で助かる have a narrow escape 《*from* death》; narrowly escape 《death》; escape 《death》 by a hair's breadth (《話》 by the skin of one's teeth). ▶ 「危機一髪だった」 は That was *close*. /That was a *close* call [*shave*].)

ききいる 聞き入る listen attentively 《to》. ● ラジオに聞き入る *listen attentively to* the radio. ▶ 彼女は熱心に聞き入った She was *all ears*.

ききいれる 聞き入れる [要求などを] (同意する) agree 《to》, 《書》 grant; [忠告を] take*; [提案などを] accept. ● 彼の願いを聞き入れる [聞き入れない] *agree to* [*refuse, turn down*] his request. ● 彼の忠告を聞き入れない refuse to *take* his advice.

ききうで 利き腕 one's dominant hand. ▶ ぼくは左が利き腕だ I'm left-handed.

ききおく 聞き置く only [just] listen to ... (without giving any answers or expressing one's opinions).

ききおとす 聞き落とす (⇨聞き漏らす) ▶ 1 語たりとも聞き落とさないように注意しなさい Be careful not to *miss* a single word.

ききおぼえ 聞き覚え ● 聞き覚えのある (＝聞いたことのある) 声 a *familiar* (↔a strange) voice. ● 聞き覚えで

演奏する play 《it》 by ear. ▶彼の名前は聞き覚えがあるが顔が思い出せない I've heard his name 《話》 His name *rings a bell*, but I can't remember his face.

ききおよぶ 聞き及ぶ hear* of [about]...; 《書》learn* of [about].... (⇨習得 ❶) ●お聞き及びのとおり as you know. ●私の聞き及ぶところでは as far as I know.

ききかいかい 奇々怪々 ━━奇々怪々な形 extremely strange [fantastic]. (⇨奇怪な)

ききかえす 聞き返す 〔値段を聞き返す(=もう１度尋ねる)〕ask the price *again*. ●テープを何回も聞き返す(=何回も聞く) *listen* to the tape *many times* [*again and again*]. ▶警官はその男に何度も何度も聞き返していた(=質問し続けた) The police officer kept (on) *throwing questions* at the man. ▶「それできみは何をしたのだ?」私は思わず聞き返した "What did you do then?" I *asked back* automatically.

ききがき 聞き書き (行為) writing down exactly what one hears; (書き取った記録) a verbatim /vəːrbéitəm/ account [report] (of their conversation)

ききかじる 聞きかじる 〔浅薄な知識を身につける〕get* [(聞きかじっている) have] a smattering [a superficial knowledge] (of).

ききくるしい 聞き苦しい ❶〔聞いて不愉快である〕be unpleasant to hear; sound unpleasant, be offensive to the ear. ❷〔聞こえにくい〕(⇨聞きづらい ❶)

ききごたえ 聞き応え ●聞き応えのある演説 a speech *worth listening to.*

ききこみ 聞き込み an interview; (捜査) 《話》legwork. ●聞き込み(捜査)をする interview 《witnesses》; do 《a lot of》 *legwork*.

ききこむ 聞き込む get* [obtain] information 《from+人; on [about] +事》; get a line 《on》.

ききざけ 利き酒, 聞き酒 (行為) wine [sake] tasting; (酒) wine [sake] for tasting.
━━利き酒(を)する動 taste wine [sake]; judge the quality of wine [sake] by tasting it. 《関連》「利き酒をする人」を a 《wine [sake]》 taster)

ききじょうず 聞き上手 ▶彼女は聞き上手で, 自分からはあまりしゃべらない She's *a good listener*, but she doesn't say much herself.

ききすごす 聞き過ごす (⇨聞き捨て, 聞き漏らす)

ききずて 聞き捨て ●聞き捨てにする ignore, 《大目に見る》pass 《it》 over. ●彼の会議での発言は聞き捨てならない I *can't ignore* [*pass over*] his remarks at the meeting./(許せないと思う) I think his remarks at the meeting *are inexcusable*.

ききそこなう 聞き損なう 〔聞き漏らす〕fail to hear; (聞きのがす) miss a chance to ask 《about》; 〔聞き間違って聞く〕misunderstand*.

ききだす 聞き出す ●ラジオで英語を聞き出す(=聞き始める) begin to listen to English on the radio. ▶警察は事件について彼から情報を聞き出した(=得た) The police got [引き出した](*drew*) some information about the case *out of* him.

ききちがい 聞き違い ━━聞き違いをする動 mishear*.

ききちがえる 聞き違える mishear*, hear* wrongly [mistakenly].

ききつける 聞き付ける 〔耳にする〕hear*. ●彼について妙なうわさを聞き付けた hear queer rumors about him. ●聞き付けた(=聞き慣れた)声で in a *familiar* voice. ●昨夜彼の重病を聞き付けた(=偶然聞いた) Last night I *happened to hear* [聞き知る](*learn*) of his being very sick.

ききづらい 聞きづらい ❶〔明瞭に聞こえない〕▶(電話で)声がちょっと聞きづらいんだけど, 大きな声で話してくれる I *can't hear* you *well*. Please speak up. ❷〔書〕●彼女にそんなこと聞きづらいよ. 君が聞いたらどう I *just can't ask* her things like that. You try.

ききて 利き手 one's dominant hand. (⇨利き腕)

ききて 聞き手 (会話などの) a hearer; (ラジオ聴取者) a listener; (会見などの) an interviewer; (聴衆) an audience (⇨聴衆)

ききどころ 聞き所 (最もよい[重要な]箇所) the best [most important] part.

ききとどける 聞き届ける (同意する) agree to ...; (受け入れる) accept; (聞き入れる) 《書》grant.

ききとり 聞き取り hearing.
●聞き取りテスト a listening comprehension test. (**!** hearing test は通例「聴力検査」の意)

ききとる 聞き取る catch*, follow, 《話》get*; 〔聞こえる〕(can*) hear*. ●彼の言うことがきまった聞き取れなかった I couldn't *catch* what he said. ▶すみません, よく聞き取れませんでした Excuse me, I didn't *hear* you well [I didn't quite *follow* you]. (**!** 前の方は声が小さい, 雑音のために聞こえない, 後の方は早口などで内容についていけないこと)

翻訳のこころ 話し声も聞こえた. 話の内容は聞き取れないが, いかにも華やいだ声であることはわかった (村上春樹『レキシントンの幽霊』) I heard them talking. Although I couldn't tell what they were talking about, I sensed the cheerfulness of their voices [that their voices were cheerful]. (**!** (1) 「話の内容は)聞き取れない」は cannot tell ((自分の言葉で)述べたり説明したりすることができない)と表す. (2) 「わかった」は sensed (感覚的に[聞いて])わかったと表す. understood (理性的に)わかったはここでは不適切)

ききなおす 聞き直す 〔もう１度尋ねる〕ask again; 〔もう１度聞く〕listen again.

ききながす 聞き流す 〔無視する〕ignore, turn a deaf ear 《to》; 〔まじめに考えない〕pay* no serious attention 《to》.

ききなれる 聞き慣れる ●聞き慣れた(=よく知っている)電話の声 a *familiar* voice on [xof] the phone. ▶彼の講義は聞き慣れないうちは分かりにくい His lectures are hard to understand before you *get used to* them.

ききにくい 聞きにくい 〔聞きづらい〕be difficult [hard] to hear; 〔尋ねにくい〕hesitate to ask. ▶女性に年齢のことは聞きにくい I *hesitate to* ask a woman about her age.

ききほれる 聞き惚れる (うっとりする) be entranced [《やや書》enchanted] 《by》.

ききみみ 聞き耳 ●聞き耳を立てる listen carefully 《to》; 《話》prick (up) one's ears. ▶彼女のうわさ話になると彼は聞き耳を立てた 《話》He *was all ears* when other people began to talk about her.

ききめ 効き目 (効果) (an) effect 《on》; (有効性) effectiveness, 《書》efficacy. (⇨効果)

ききもらす 聞き漏らす fail to catch [hear, 《話》get]. ●聞き漏らすまいと聞く listen closely 《to》. ▶彼の名前を聞き漏らした I *failed to catch* his name.

ききやく 聞き役 (役目) the part of a listener; (人) the listener. ●聞き役に回る take [play] the *part of a listener*.

ききゃく 棄却 图 (a) rejection; (却下) (a) dismissal.
━━棄却する動 reject; dismiss. ●控訴を棄却する

reject [dismiss] the appeal.
ききゅう 危急 (緊急事態) (an) emergency; (重大局面) an impending crisis. ●危急の場合に in an *emergency*; in case of (an) *emergency* (⚠通例文頭に); (in times of *crisis*; in a time of *crisis*. ●危急存亡のときに at a critical moment; in a crisis; in an emergency.
ききゅう 気球 A balloon. ●熱気球 a fire [a hot air] *balloon*. ●観測気球 an observation *balloon*. ●気象観測気球 a weather *balloon*. ●気球を上げる fly [launch] *a balloon*. ●気球に乗る ride in *a balloon*.
ききゅう 希求 图 (a) longing 《for》; a great desire 《for》.
—**希求する** 動 ●平和を希求する long for *peace*; have a strong *desire for* peace.
ききゅう 帰休 图 (特に軍隊などの) leave; (特に海外勤務の公務員・軍人などは) (a) furlough; (一時解雇) a lay-off. ●帰休中の兵士 a soldier home *on furlough*.
—**帰休させる** 動 lay* (employees) off 《for three months during the recession》.
ききょう 奇矯 图 —**奇矯な** 形 (普通と違って奇妙な) odd; (とっぴな) eccentric.
ききょう 帰京 图 —**帰京する** 動 come* [go*] back to Tokyo.
ききょう 帰郷 图 a homecoming, coming home.
—**帰郷する** 動 go* [come*, return] home; return [go back, come back] to one's hometown (⚠a hometown は「生まれた(育った)所; 主たる住所」の意).
ききょう 桔梗 〖植物〗a Chinese bellflower.
*ききょう 企業** a business; an enterprise (⚠専門用語に); (会社) a company, a corporation (⚠後の語は特に法人の. 形容詞は córporate). (⇨会社) ●大[零細]企業 a big [(a) small] *business* [*enterprise*] (⚠総称する場合には Ⓤ); a big [a small] *company*. ●多国籍企業 a multinational *corporation* [*enterprise*]. ●民間[公営]企業 a private [a public] *enterprise*. ●上場企業 a listed company.
●企業イメージ a corporate image. ●企業家 an industrialist. ●企業会計 corporate [business] accounting; accounting for business enterprises. ●企業活動 business activity. ●企業経営 corporate control [decision(-)making]; business administration. ●企業合同 a trust. ●企業再生 corporate revitalization. ●企業収益 corporate earnings (performance); corporate profits [bottom lines]. ●企業提携 a business tie-up. ●企業年金 a corporate pension (plan). ●企業買収 purchase [acquisition] of business. ●企業秘密 a company [a business, an industrial] secret. ●企業文化 corporate culture; cultures of the companies. ●企業別組合 a company union. ●企業利潤 corporate [business] profit(s). ●企業理念 corporate philosophy. ●企業連合 a cartel, a syndicate.
ききょう 起業 —**起業する** 動 start new venture [business]; go* into [set* up] business.
●起業家 an entrepreneur. ●起業家精神 entrepreneur spirit; entrepreneurship.
ききょう 義侠 图 chivalry. ▶彼には義侠心がある He is *chivalrous*.
—**義侠的(な)** 形 chivalrous.
ききょうだい 義兄弟 (婚姻による) a brother-in-law (圈 brothers-in-law, (主に英) ～s); (盟友) a sworn brother; (血盟の) a blood brother.
ききょく 戯曲 a drama; (劇) a play. ●小説を戯曲化する dramatize a novel.
ききわける 聞き分ける ❶ [聞いて区別する] ●人の声を聞き分ける tell one voice *from* another; (聞いてそれと分かる) recognize 《his》 voice. ▶小鳥の声を聞き分けることができますか Can you *tell* [《やや書》 *distinguish*] one bird *from* another *by hearing* [*listening to*] them?
❷ [納得する] understand*; (道理が分かる) listen to [hear*] reason. ●あいつは聞き分けがなくて困る He won't *listen to reason*./He is unreasonable.
*ききん 飢饉** (a) famine /fǽmin/. ●水飢饉 (水不足) a water *shortage*; (干ばつ) a drought /dráut/. ●飢饉で[飢饉の間に]死ぬ die of *famine* [*during a famine*]. ▶その国はたえず飢饉に苦しんでいる The country regularly suffers *famines*.
ききん 基金 a fund; a foundation. ●国際交流基金 the Japan *Foundation*. ●国連児童基金 the United Nations Children's *Fund* (略 UNICEF /júːnɪsef/ (旧称から)). ●救済基金を募る [設ける] raise [found, establish] a relief *fund*. (⇨資金)
ききんぞく 貴金属 noble metals; (noble であるから) 貴重な) (a) precious metal.
●貴金属商 (人) a dealer in precious metals (⚠加工した貴金属や宝石を扱う商人は a jeweler); (店) a jéwelry shòp.
*きく 聞く、聴く**

WORD CHOICE 聞く

hear 音・声・話などが無意識のうちに耳に入ること. ●2発の銃声が聞こえる *hear* the sound of two shots. ●彼が「やあ」というのを聞く *hear* him say 'hi'.
listen 人・人の声・人の話・要求・TV・ラジオ・音楽などを意識して聞くこと. ●ラジオを聞く *listen to* the radio. ●彼の話を聞く *listen to* him.

頻度チャート

hear ▬▬▬▬▬▬▬▬▬▬
listen ▬▬
　　　20　40　60　80　100 (%)

❶ [聞こえる] hear*; [聞き知る] hear, 《書》 learn*; be told, 《書》 be informed. (⚠いずれもの意味では命令文や進行形で用いない) ●その知らせを聞く *hear* the news 《from him》. ▶昨晩遅く隣の犬がうるさく吠える声を聞いた I *heard* the neighbor's dog bark [barking] noisily late last night. (⚠原形 bark では始めから終わりまでを聞くこと、進行形 barking では一部分を聞くことを暗示. 受身は The neighbor's dog *was heard to* bark [barking]....) ▶私の父はその知らせを聞いて喜びました My father was delighted *by* [*at, to hear*] the news. ▶彼は病気だと聞いている(=聞くところによれば彼は病気だそうだ) I *hear*(d) [*People say, I'm told*] (*that*) he is sick. ▶彼らが無事に着いたことを聞いた I *heard* [*learned, was told*] (*that*) they had arrived safely./I *learned* [*heard*] *of* their safe arrival. (⚠hear of は通例否定文・疑問文や完了形で用いる (⇨[次例], 会話 第1例]) ▶そういう通りの名は聞いたことがありません I've never *heard of* any street by that name. ▶奥様、何か苦情がおありと聞いて(=了解して)おりますが I *understand* you have a complaint, ma'am.
会話 「田中さんのこと聞いた?」「いいえ、聞いてないわ. 何かあったの?」"*Have* you *heard about* [*of*] Mr. Tanaka?" "No, I haven't. What happened?"

きく

(!*hear about* him 彼のことについて詳しく聞く. *hear of* him 彼のうわさ・消息などを聞くの意)

会話「『竹下通り』って聞いたことがある？」「聞いたような気がする. 東京の若者に人気のある通りじゃない？」"*Have* you ever *heard* a street name called Takeshita-dori?" "*That rings a bell*. Isn't that a street popular among young people in Tokyo?"

会話「どこへ行ったらその人に会えるの」「これが彼の電話番号よ. でも私から聞いたことは内緒にしておいてね」"Where can I find him?" "Here's his phone number. But you didn't *hear it from me*." (!事実に反することを相手に念押しする言い方に注意)

❷ [耳を傾ける] listen to ...;(講演・コンサートなどを) hear*, (古) give* ear to ...; [注意して聞く] pay* attention to .... ● 音楽を聴く listen to music. (!特定の音楽を聴くときは ...*the* music) ▶ 説教を聞く *hear* [*listen to*] a sermon. (!listen to は声が小さいとか騒音とかで聞こえにくい状況を暗示する) ▶ 昨夜ラジオでそのニュースを聞きましたか Did you *listen to* [*hear*] the news on the radio last night? (!hear ではニュースを聞いて(ある出来事について)知っているかどうかを問う文となる(⇨❶)) ▶ 彼の話をよく聞きなさい *Listen* carefully *to* him [what he says]./*Pay attention to* him [what he says]. (!「[だれであれ]人の話を...」ともいえるよ Be a good listener. ▶ さあ彼がバッハを弾くのを聞きましょう Now, let's *listen to* him play Bach. (!「弾いているのを聞く」の意では listen to him play*ing*) ▶ 聞いているの？ Do [×Can] you hear me? (⇨聞こえる❶ 会話 注) /Are you still there? ▶ 最後まで聞いてください *Hear me out*, please. ▶ 私が言ったのを聞いたでしょ. すぐやめなさい You *heard* me. Stop that right now. (!親や先生がよく用いる注意表現) ▶ この騒音では私の話を十分に聞いてもらうことができまいと思った I thought I couldn't *make myself heard* enough in this din. ▶ 今の話は聞かなかったことにしてください Just forget what I've said.

会話「来週のゴルフはつきあってくれるよね」「ジョン, よく聞いて. 歩くのは大嫌いなの. それに寒くなってきたし. 行かないわ」"You're coming with us to play golf next week, aren't you?" "*Read my lips*, John. I hate walking, and it's getting cold. I'm not going." (!慣用表現. 遠くから話しかける声が届きにくい場合にも用いられる)

❸ [従う] obey, follow; [耳を貸す] listen to ...; [願いをかなえる] (書) grant. ● 親の言うことを聞く *obey* [*mind*, (いつも は) *be obedient to*] one's parents. ● 言うことを聞かない子供 a (*very*) *disobedient* child. ▶ 医者の言うことを聞いて, おとなしく寝ていなさい *Take* [*Follow*, ×*Listen* to] the doctor's advice and stay in bed. ▶ 私は彼の願いをかなってやった I did what he asked me to do./(書) I *granted* his request. ▶ 彼に何度も頼んだが聞いてもらえなかった I asked him again and again, but he *didn't listen to* [無視した] he *ignored*, (注意を払わなかった) he *didn't pay attention to*] me. ▶ ... but he *turned a deaf ear to* me. は (主に書) ▶ 私は子供たちにおばさんの言うことをよく聞くように言った I told my children to *be obedient to* [*good with*] their aunt. ▶ 彼は私といっしょに行くと言って聞かない He *insists on going* [*that* he ((主に英) should) *go*] with me.

❹ [尋ねる] ask, (ややぶ) inquire (⇨尋ねる); (尋ねて情報を得る) find*... out. ● 駅へ行く道を聞く *ask* [*inquire*] the way to the station. ● 案内所で聞く *ask* at the information. ▶ その問題について彼に聞く *ask* him about the question. ▶ 私は彼がどこに住んでいるのか聞いた I *asked* him where he lived. ▶ 一つ二つ聞きたいのですが I'd like to *ask* you one or two questions. ▶ 彼に住所を聞いておいてください *Ask* him his address./(書) *Inquire* his address of him. (!×*Ask* his address of him. は不可(⇨尋ねる❶③).) ▶ 聞くんじゃなかった I shouldn't *have asked*./I should have known better than to *ask*. (!尋ねた内容や相手が不適切であったことを後悔する気持ちを表す) ▶ よく聞いてくれた Good question!/I'm glad you *asked*. ▶ 聞かないでおくれ(返事をしたくないときに) Don't *ask*! (!*Don't ask me*! は「知らないね」と質問を突っぱねる言い方. どちらもよく使う口語的慣用表現) ▶ 何のために大学に行くのか, もう一度自分自身に聞いてみた方がいい You should *ask yourself once again why* [(書) for what purpose] you want to go to college [university]. (!「大学レベルの教育を受ける」の意では, (米)では university でなく college が一般的)

会話「その値段はいくら」「電話して聞いてみたら」"What's the price?" "Why don't you call and *find out*?"

● 聞いて極楽見て地獄(聞くと見るとでは大違い) There is a big difference between what we see and what we hear; (ことわざ) Fame is a liar.

● 聞く耳を持たない ▶ そんなことを聞く耳は持たない I won't listen to that kind of thing.

*きく 効く, 利く ❶ [効き目がある](作用する) work ⟨*on*⟩;(効果が出る) take* effect; (効果がある) be effective ⟨*against*⟩, have* (an) effect ⟨*on*⟩; (...によい) be good ⟨*for*⟩. ▶ この薬には私には効かない This medicine doesn't *work* [*act*] *on* me./This medicine has no effect on me. ▶ 逆に「驚くほど効く」なら This medicine works wonders for me.) ▶ この温泉はリューマチに効く This hot spring *is effective against* [*good for*] rheumatism. (!後の方が口語的) ▶ この薬は君の風邪[頭痛]に効く(=を楽にする)だろう This medicine will *help* your cold [headache].

会話「この薬はどのぐらいで効いてきますか」「飲んでから 2-3時間ですね」"How soon will this medicine *take* ⟨xan⟩ *effect*?" "In two or three [(話) a couple of] hours."

❷ [機能する] (!多くの場合意訳が必要) ▶ ブレーキがよくきかなかった The brakes didn't *work* [*act*] well. ▶ 彼は左手がきかなくなった(=左手を使用する力を失った) He *has lost the use* of his left hand. ▶ 犬は鼻が(よく)きく(= 鋭い嗅覚を持っている) Dogs *have a sharp sense* of smell. ▶ この部屋は冷房がきいていない(=弱すぎる) The air conditioning *is too weak* in this room. ▶ このスープはコショウがきき過ぎている(=多すぎる) This soup *has too much* pepper in it.

❸ [可能である] ● 修理がきかない *be not* repairable; *be beyond* repair. ▶ この服は洗濯がきく This dress *is* wash*able*.

きく 菊 [植物] a chrysanthemum /krɪsǽnθəməm/. 【語源】米英では菊(特に白菊)は葬式の花として嫌う人が多い)

● 菊人形 a chrysanthemum figure; (説明的に) a life-sized doll covered with chrysanthemum flowers (displayed at chrysanthemum festivals). ● 菊日和 a beautiful [fine] fall weather.

*きぐ 器具 (家庭用電気・ガス器具など) an appliance; (精密な) an instrument; (調理・掃除用) a utensil; (構造の単純な) (書) an implement; (特定の目的を持った) (集合的) apparatus (!特定の種類をさすときは不定冠詞を伴うが, 複数形 〜 (es) はまれ). (⇨道具)

● 電気器具 electric *appliances*; ⟨a piece of⟩

electric *apparatus*. ● 外科手術用器具 surgical *instruments*. ● 調理器具 cóoking *utènsils*. ● 医療用器具 medical *implements*.

きぐ 危惧 (将来に対する不安) an apprehension 《*of, about*》． しばしば ～ s), fear 《*for*; *of doing*》． ● 危惧の念を抱く have an *apprehension* 《*of*》; feel *fear*《*about*》．

きぐ 機具〖書〗an implement.（⇨器具）● 農機具 fárming *implements*.

きぐいむし 木食い虫 a borer.

きぐう 奇遇 ここで君に会うなんて奇遇だ What a *coincidence* to meet you here!（!文脈によっては This is *a coincidence*! も可)/《主に英》 *Fancy* meeting you here!

ぎくしゃく — ぎくしゃくした 形 ● ロボットのぎくしゃくした（＝ぎこちない）動き the *awkward* movements of a robot. ● 日米間のぎくしゃくした（＝荒れた）関係 *troubled* [*uneasy*] relations between Japan and the United States.

きぐすり 生薬 a raw drug; a [《米》an] herbal medicine.

きぐずれ 着崩れ — 着崩れする 動 come* loose; get* untidy.

ぎくっと (⇨ぎくりと)

きくばり 気配り 名〖配慮〗attention, consideration;〖注意〗care. ● あの男は気配りのない（＝無神経な）やつだ What an *insensitive* fellow he is!
— **気配り(を)する** 動 ● 老人に気配りするbe *attentive* [*helpful, kind*] *to* older people. ● 仕事には十分気配りをしなさい You should *be* very *careful about* your work.

きぐみ 木組み〖建築〗timberwork, timbering.

きぐらい 気位〖自尊心〗pride;〖うぬぼれ〗conceit. ● 気位が高い proud; conceited.

きくらげ 木耳〖植物〗(a) Jew's-ear;（説明的に）a kind of mushroom which looks like a man's ear.

ぎくりと ❶〖驚く様子〗● ぎくりとする (大変驚く) be startled;（不意をつかれて驚く) be taken aback. ● 名前を呼ばれて彼はぎくりとした He *was startled* when his name was called./He showed a *startled* look when he was called.
❷〖体が〗creak. ● 肩がぎくっと鳴った I heard the bones in my shoulder *creak*.〖関連〗倒れたとき足首がぎくっとなった My ankle twisted audibly when I fell./腰がぎくっとなった One's back *slipped* [*went*] *out*.（⇨ぎっくり腰）

きぐろう 気苦労〖悩み〗(a) worry;〖気がかり〗(a) care.（⇨心配）● 気苦労が多い have a lot of *worries*. ● 気苦労のない生活 a carefree life; a life free from *care*.

きけい 奇形 名 deformity. — **奇形の** 形 deformed.
● 奇形児 a deformed child.

ぎけい 義兄〖義理の兄〗a brother-in-law (複 ～s, brothers-).（⇨兄弟 ❶ ①）

ぎげい 技芸 (美術工芸) arts and crafts; (手工業) handicrafts.

きげき 喜劇 (a) comedy (⇔(a) tragedy).（!演劇の部門を表すのは無冠詞)
— **喜劇的な** 形 comical.
● 喜劇映画《主に米》a comic movie,《主に英》a comic film. ● 喜劇作家 a comic [(a tragic) dramatist [writer]. ● 喜劇俳優 a comic actor [（女優）actress]; a comedian（!女性形は comedienne).

きけつ 帰結 (成り行き) a cónsequènce; (結果) a resúlt; (結末) a conclúsion.（⇨結果）● 当然の帰

結 a [the] natural *consequence*《*of*》．

きけつ 既決 — 既決の 形 decided; (処理済みの) settled. ● 既決囚 a convict,《話》a con.

ぎけつ 議決 名 (決議)《やや書》a resolution; (票決) a vote.
— **議決する** 動 resolve; pass a resolution.
● 議決権《have》a vote (in a meeting)（! the vote は「投票権」の意;《株》の vóting rights.

『きけわだつみのこえ』 *Hear the Voices from the Sea*.〖参考〗第二次大戦の出陣学徒兵 75 名の遺稿集）

＊きけん 危険 名 (a) danger (⇔safety)（!「危険なもの」の意では C. 以下の語についても同様)，《主に書》(a) peril; (a) risk; (a) hazard.

〖使い分け〗**danger** 「危険」の意を表す最も一般的な語．
peril 差し迫った，予測できない大きな危険．
risk 不利・不幸などをこうむる危険性．しばしば自らそれを冒すことを含意する．
hazard 偶然の，または避けることのできない危険．

▶ 危険！〖掲示〗*Danger!!*/(注意) *Caution!* もし地震が起これば住民は何もかも失う危険度が高い If an earthquake occurs, they will *be in great danger of* losing everything. ▶ 危険度は増大している The *danger* is increasing [growing].
① 〖危険は[が]〗● 噴火の危険があるはない) There is a *danger* [no *danger*] of an eruption. ▶ 彼が山で遭難する危険(性)は大いにあった[あまりなかった] There was (a) great [not much] *risk* of his getting lost in the mountains. ▶ この手術には危険はまずありません[多くの危険が伴う] There is hardly any *risk* [There are a lot of *risks*] (involved) in this operation.（! involved は「付随的に伴う」の意で，ここではこの語を入れなくてもその意は表される）● この都市は攻撃を受ける危険しはない This city is *safe from* attack. ▶ 危険が迫ったらどこへ避難すればいいのですか Where should we take refuge if the *danger threatens us*.
② 〖危険に〗● 危険に直面する face (a) *danger* [a *risk*]. ● 危険に陥る get into *danger*. ● 危険にさらす [陥れる] put... in *danger*,《やや書》endanger; risk, put... at risk. ● 多くの危険にさらされている be exposed to a lot of *danger*. ▶ 消防士や警官は常に生命の危険にさらされている Fire fighters and police are regularly *in danger of* (losing) their lives./Fire fighters and police regularly put their lives *in danger*〖《話》*on the line*〗. ▶ その船は火に包まれ乗客は死の危険にさらされた The burning ship *put* the passengers *in danger* [*peril*] of death.（! peril の方が差し迫った状況を示す）
③ 〖危険を〗● 危険を冒す run [take] a *risk* [*risks*]. ● 危険を脱する get *out of danger*. ● 危険を避ける avoid danger. ● どんな危険を冒しても（＝ぜひとも) at any *risk*.（! ×at all risks は不可）● 私は身の危険を感じた I felt *danger* [×dangerous].（! dangerous は「危険・危害を及ぼす」の意（⇨形)) ● 患者はもう危険(な状態)を脱している The patient is now out of *danger*. ▶ 彼らは大きな危険を冒して封鎖線を突破した They ran [took] a big *risk* (in) running the blockade. ▶ 私は全財産を失うという危険は冒したくない I don't want to *risk* [run the *risk* of] *losing* all my fortune. ● ×*risk* to lose は不可）● 彼は生命の危険を冒してその子を助けた He *risked* his life to rescue the child./(命がけで) He rescued the child *at the risk of* his life. ● 危険を冒さないで引き返しましょう Should [Shall] we *play safe* and turn back?
〖会話〗「たいした危険じゃないさ」「いくらかでも危険を冒す

のは賢明なのかい」"It's not much of a *risk.*" "Is it wise to take any *risk*?"（❗much of a ... は「ひどい…」「すごい…」の意で否定文・疑問文で用いる）

── 危険な 形 dangerous (↔safe),《主に書》perilous; risky;《やや書》hazardous; (安全でない) unsafe.（⇨危ない）●危険な(=危険性の高い)手術 a *risky* operation. ●危険な(=危険を伴う)旅 a *hazardous* [危険に満ちた *a perilous*] journey. ●危険(な)区域 a *danger* [a *dangerous*] zone. ●危険(な)思想 *dangerous* ideas [thoughts]. ▶スキンダイビングは危険なスポーツだ Skindiving is a *dangerous* sport. ▶クマはキャンプする人にとって危険だ Bears are *dangerous* [a *danger*, ×*dangers*] *to* campers.（❗前の方が口語的）●彼は危険な人物だ(=危険を与える恐れがある) He is *dangerous* [a *dangerous* person, (社会にとって) a *danger to* society, (国家機密をもらす恐れのある) a security risk].（❗He is *in danger.* は「危険な状態にある」の意）▶この通りは女性が夜 1 人で歩くのは危険だ This street is *dangerous* [*not safe*] *for* a woman *to* walk alone at night./It is *dangerous* [*not safe*] *for* a woman *to* walk on this street alone at night.（❗×A woman is *dangerous* [*not safe*] to walk…. や ×It is *dangerous* that…. とはいわない）●彼は(体力が)弱ってきて危険な状態です He's getting *dangerously* weak.

●危険球〖野球〗a beanball; a knockdown pitch. ●危険信号 a dánger signal. ●危険水域 dangerous waters.

きけん 棄権 名 〖投票での〗(an) abstention (from voting);〖権利などの放棄〗abandonment; (正式の) renunciation (*of* one's right);〖競技への不出場〗(a) withdrawal (*from* a race), default. ●棄権が 2 票 [棄権者が 2 名] あった There were two *abstentions.*

── 棄権する 動 abstain (from voting);〖権利を〗abandon, renounce;〖競技を〗withdraw* (*from*), default. ●権利を棄権する *abandon* [*renounce, give up*] one's right(s).（❗give up が最も口語的）●競技を棄権する(=競技への出場を取り消す) *withdraw* one's entry into a race; *default* (*in*) a race. ●競技の途中で棄権する(=落伍(らくご)する) *drop out of* a race. ▶有権者の半数以上が棄権した More than half of the voters *abstained* [*stayed away*].

*きげん 起源 (an) origin, (発端) (a) beginning.（❗通例複数形で）●生命の起源 the *origin*(s) of life. ▶その建築様式は中国が起源です That style of architecture has its *origin* [has its *beginnings*, (始まる) *originates*, (始まった) *originated*] *in* China.（❗他の過去の出来事より古い場合にも可）

*きげん 期限 (指定期間) a time limit; (契約などの) a term; (期間) a period; (締め切りの時) a deadline.（⇨締め切り）

① 【~期限, 期限~】 ● 期限付きの with a *time limit*; limited(-)life. ▶この切符の有効期限は 2 日だ This ticket is good [《書》valid] for two days.（❗「有効期限二日の切符」は a ticket with a 2-day *time limit* [a *time limit* of two days]）▶納税期限まであと 10 日しかない We only have ten days to go before the tax *deadline*.

② 【期限が[は]~】 ● 契約の期限が切れた The *term* of the contract has run out [《やや書》expired]. ▶期限は 5 月 19 日に来る The bill is [*falls, becomes*] *due* on May 19.

会話「その請求書の支払い期限はいつですか」「5 月 10 日です」"When is the *time limit* [the *deadline*] for (paying) the bill?" "It's May 10."/"When is the bill *due*?" "It's *due* on May 10."

③ 【期限に[を]】 ● 期限に間に合う [合わない] meet [miss] the *deadline*. ●期限を延ばす [決める] extend [set,《やや話》fix *up*] a *time limit* [a *term*, a *period*, a *deadline*] (*for*). ▶図書館から借りた本は返却期限を 3 日間過ぎている My library books are three days *overdue*.（❗「返却期限切れの本」は an *overdue* book）

*きげん 機嫌 ❶ 【気分】 a mood; (a) humor; (a) temper; feelings.

使い分け mood「気分」を表す一般的な語.
humor 気まぐれで一時的な気分を表す.
temper 強い感情, 特に怒っている心の状態を表す.
feelings 人の感情や気持ちを表す.

●機嫌がよい [悪い] be in a good [a bad,《話》a rotten] *mood*; be in high [low] *spirits*; be in a good [a bad] *humor*; be in a good [a bad] *temper*. ●彼の機嫌をそこねる (怒らせる) *offend* [*give offense to*] him; (感情を害する) *hurt* his feelings,《話》get on his bad [wrong] side. ▶母は私より遅れて来たので機嫌が悪い My mother *is angry* [《話》*cross*] *with* me because I was late./My mother *is displeased with* me for being late. ▶彼はじきに機嫌が直るだろう He will come round [*become cheerful*] in time./He will soon be back to his bright self again. ▶彼は私を機嫌よく(=暖かく)迎えてくれた He welcomed me *warmly*. ▶今日は朝からご機嫌が悪いですね You must have gotten up on the wrong side of the bed《米》[have got out of bed on the wrong side《英》] this morning.（❗成句表現）

❷ 【安否】 ● 彼のご機嫌を伺う (元気かと尋ねる) ask [《書》inquire] *after* his health（❗inquire after は「第三者を通して尋ねる」》; (あいさつに行く)《書》pay one's respects *to* him. ▶ご機嫌いかがですか How are you?/(病人に) How do you feel [do you feel] today? ▶ ではご機嫌よう Good-by!/Take care./See you soon [later]./Have a nice day.

会話「ご機嫌伺いにちょっと立ち寄ってみようと思いまして」「それはご親切に」"I just thought that I'd call in and *see how you are*." "How kind."

●機嫌をとる (…の気に入るようにする) humor; please;《話》get on the good [right] side of…; (…にへつらう) curry favor with…;《話》play up to…; (女をくどく) play court to …. ▶父は機嫌がとりにくい [とりやすい] My father is hard [easy] to *please*.

きげん 紀元 (時代) an era; (新紀元) an epoch.（⇨時代）●紀元前 264 年 264 *B.C.*（❗*B.C.* は Before Christ の略で年号の後に置く）●紀元後 375 年 375 *A.D.*; *A.D.* 375.（❗(1) ラテン語 Anno Domini の略.（2) 紀元前との区別を明確にするときにつける.（3) 後の方が正式な言い方）（⇨西暦）

きげんそ 希元素 a rare element.
きげんとり 機嫌取り（⇨機嫌 [成句]）
きご 季語 〖俳句〗a seasonal word; (説明的に) a seasonal indicator in a haiku, such as the moon for autumn and wild ducks for winter.

*きこう 気候 (a) climate; (×a) weather.（⇨天気, 天候）

使い分け climate ある地方・国の長期間にわたる総合的な天候: 熱帯性気候 a tropical *climate*.
weather 特定の時・場所における一時(いちじ)の天候や天気: 変わりやすい秋の気候 changeable autumn *weather*.

▶ここはとても温暖な気候だ We have a very temperate *climate* here. ▶日本の気候はイギリスより一般に温和である The *climate* of Japan is generally milder than that of England. (‼ 主語は Japan's *climate* も可。本文 The climate in Japan ... that *in* England. も可。この場合比較の対照は「気候」なので日本語に引かれて × ... than England としないこと)/Generally (speaking), Japan has a milder *climate* than England. ▶最近気候が不順だ The *weather* has been unsettled [unseasonable] recently. (‼ 主語に用いた weather には通例 the がつく。ただし mild weather (温暖な気候)のように形容詞がつく場合は無冠詞) ▶アフリカの乾燥した気候は彼女には合わなかった The dry *climate* in [×of] Africa did not agree with her. (‼ 場所につきまとう客観的な気候 (⇒[第 2 文例]) と異なり、その場所で体験される気候をいうときは用いる in を用いる) ▶その木は気候条件次第でいろいろな高さになる The trees may reach various heights depending upon *climatic* conditions.
  ● 気候帯 a climátic zòne.

きこう 気孔 a pore; (植物の) a stoma (⨯ stomata, ~s); (岩石の) a vesicle.

きこう 気功 《practice》qigong /tʃiːgúŋ/; (説明的に) a system of deep breathing exercises.

きこう 奇行 (an) eccentricity; eccentric behavior.
  ● 奇行の多い人 an *eccentric* (person).

きこう 季候 a season. ▶季候がよくなってきた It's getting warm(er) [cool(er)].

きこう 紀行 an account of one's trip [journey]; (短い) a travel sketch [note].

きこう 起工 the commencement of construction (work). (⇔竣工) ▶トンネル工事は来月起工の予定だ *Construction* on the tunnel [The tunnel's *construction*] begins next month.
— 起工する 動 begin* the work of constructing 《new roads, a dam》; start [begin] to build 《a railroad》.
  ● 起工式 a commencement ceremony.

きこう 起稿 — 起稿する 動 begin* [start] writing. (⇔脱稿)

きこう 寄港 图 a call 《at a port》.
— 寄港する 動 ▶この船は神戸に寄港する This ship calls [stops] at Kobe.
  ● 寄港地 a port of call (⨯ ports of call).

きこう 寄稿 图 contribution.
— 寄稿する 動 ▶(短編小説を)雑誌に寄稿する *contribute* (a short story) *to* a magazine; *write* (a short story) *for* a magazine.
  ● 寄稿家 a contributor.

きこう 機構 [全体の仕組み] a mechanism; (構造) a structure; (骨組み) a framework; [組織] (体系) a system; (組織体) (an) organization. ▶近代政治機構 the *mechanism* [*framework*] of modern government. ● 石油輸出国機構 the Organization of Petroleum Exporting Countries 《略 OPEC /óʊpɛk/》.
  ● 機構改革 a structural reform.

‡**きごう** 記号 图 a symbol; [印] a mark. (⇒印) ▶プラス [マイナス] 記号 a plus [a minus] (*sign*). ● フラットの記号 a flat *sign*. ▶ト音記号 [音楽] a G (a treble) clef (♪). ▶∞記号は無限を表す The *sign* ∞ represents infinity. ▶"H" は水素を表す記号です "H" is the *symbol for* [×of] hydrogen.
  ● 記号化する 動 symbolize.
  ● 記号化 symbolization.

きごう 揮毫 图 (書) calligraphy, writing; (画) painting, drawing.
— 揮毫する 動 (書) write*; (画) paint, draw*.

ぎこう 技工 《人》a craftsman, an artisan, a skilled (manual) worker; (技術) a craft. ● 歯科技工士 a dental technician.

ぎこう 技巧 图 (熟練による) (a) (technical) skill; (専門的技術による) (a) technique; (職人の) craftsmanship. (⇒技術) ▶技巧を凝らす make full use of one's *skill* [*technique*]. ▶ボクサーとしての彼の強みは筋力よりも技巧だ His strength as a boxer is *technique* rather than muscle.
— 技巧的な 形 (洗練された) polished; (手の込んだ) elaborate.
  ● 技巧派 (文章の) a stylist; (音楽・絵画などの) a technician.

きこうし 貴公子 a young nobleman (⨯ -men).
きこうしき 起工式 a ground-breaking ceremony.
きこうしょ 希覯書, 稀覯書 (貴重書) a rare book.
きこうぶん 紀行文 (⇒紀行)
きこうほう 気功法 (⇒気功)

きこえ 聞こえ [聴力] hearing; [ラジオ・テレビの感度] reception; [評判] (a) reputation. ▶ラジオの聞こえがとても悪い Radio *reception* is very bad [poor]. ▶代表販売人というと聞こえがよい A sales representative *sounds* good [all right, (偉そうに) big]. (‼ a traveling salesman の美称)

きこえよがし 聞こえよがし — 聞こえよがしに 副 《say》loud enough for 《him》to hear. ▶聞こえよがしに言うわざと聞こえるところで私の悪口を言うな Don't say bad things about me *while I'm around*./Do not criticize me (deliberately) *within* [*in*] *my hearing.*

‡**きこえる** 聞こえる ❶ [耳に入る] 《人が主語》(can*) hear* (‼ 進行形不可); 《物が主語》be heard, (書) be audible; reach one's ears. (⇒聞く ❶) ▶足音が聞こえた I *heard* footsteps [someone walking]. ▶耳をすましたが何も聞こえなかった I listened, but I couldn't [didn't] *hear* anything. (‼ ..., but I *heard* nothing. ともいえる) ▶彼は耳がよく聞こえない He can't *hear* very well./He is hard of *hearing*. (‼ 彼は(片方の)耳が聞こえない は He is deaf /déf/ (in one ear).) ▶彼女の声は聞こえなかった Her voice could not *be heard* [*was not audible, was inaudible*]./I couldn't *hear* her. ▶遠くの鐘の音が私の耳に聞こえてきた A distant bell sound *came up to* [*reached*] *my ears*.
(会話) (電話などで)「聞こえますか」「はい、よく聞こえてますよ」"Can [×Do] you *hear* me?" "Yes, I *can hear* you clearly." (‼ (1) Do you ...? はぼんやりしている人に「聞いているのか」と注意する言い方でここでは不適当 (⇒聞く ❷[第 4 文例]). (2) can hear の can は進行形の代用形で聞こえている状態を示す。進行形は不可)

❷ [響く] sound 《+形容詞(句・節)》. ▶奇妙に聞こえる *sound* strange. ▶それは冗談に聞こえるかもしれないが本当の話です It may *sound like* a joke but it is a true story. ▶君の声はまるで風邪でも引いたように聞こえる Your voice *sounds as if* you had a cold.

❸ [有名である] be well known, be famous. ▶彼は文学者として[その著作で]世に聞こえている He is *well known as* a literary man [*for* his works].

❹ [その他の表現] ▶呼べば聞こえる所にいてくれ Stay *within call* [*hearing, calling distance*]. ▶その車の音はしだいに聞こえなくなった The sound of the car *died* [*faded*] *away*.

きこく 帰国 图 a homecoming. ● 帰国の途につく leave *for* home.
— 帰国する 動 return [go*, come*] (back)

きこく 帰国 〖帰る〗 return [go back, come back] to one's country. (! return はやや改まった語. go, come の区別は (⇨行く)
- 帰国子女 a returnee (student [child]). ●帰国者 a returnee.

きこく 鬼哭 ・鬼哭啾々(しゅうしゅう)々たる古戦場 an *extremely horrible* old battlefield.

ぎごく 疑獄 〖贈収賄〗 a bribery [a corruption,《話》a payoff] scandal,《主に米》graft case. ●疑獄事件に発展する develop into a *payoff scandal*.

きごこち 着心地 ・このドレスは着心地のよい[悪い] This dress is *comfortable* [*uncomfortable*] to wear.

きごころ 気心 ・気心の知れた(=信頼のおける)友 a *reliable* [*close*] *friend*. ・私たちはお互いに気心の知れた仲だ We *know* each other *well*./We are *close* friends. ・あの男はどうも気心が知れない(=何を考えているか分からない) I don't know how he thinks./He still remains a stranger to me.

ぎこちない awkward, clumsy (! 後の方が強意的);〖堅苦しい〗stiff. ・ぎこちない表現 an *awkward* [a *clumsy*] expression. ・ぎこちない態度で in an *awkward* manner; awkwardly; stiffly. ▶彼の動きはぎこちなかった His movements were *awkward*./He was *awkward in* his movements. ▶彼女の話し方はかなりぎこちなかった She spoke rather *stiffly*.

きこつ 気骨 ・気骨のある人 a man [a woman] of *spirit* [*backbone*]. ・…する気骨に欠ける have no *spirit* [*backbone*] to do…; lack the *spirit* [*backbone*] to do….

きこなす 着こなす wear* a dress well. ・黒を上手に着こなす wear black clothes *very well*.

ぎこぶん 擬古文 an archaism; a pseudo-classical style.

きこむ 着込む (上着の下に) wear* (a sweater) under《a coat》;(重ねて) pile on one's clothes;(コートなどに身をくるむ) wrap (-pp-) up.

きこり 木こり a woodcutter,《米》a lumberjack.

きこん 気根 〖植物〗 an aerial root;〖根気〗(⇨根気).

きこん 既婚 ・既婚男性[女性] a *married* man [*woman*].
- 既婚者 a married person;《総称》the married, married people.

きざ 気障 図 (気取り) (an) affectation.
— **きざな** 形 (気取った, いやみな) affected, disagreeable;(うぬぼれの強い) pretentious, smug;《俗物的で》snobbish. ・きざな男 an *affected* man. ▶彼のあごひげはきざだ His beard is an *affectation*.

きさい 奇才 〖才能〗genius,(an) unusual ability, a rare talent;(人) a person of unusual ability, a genius.

きさい 記載 図 〖言及〗mention;〖日記・帳簿などの記入〗(an) entry. ・この問題について何の記載もない There is no *mention* [No *mention* is made] of this matter.
— **記載する** 動 ・会計簿に記載する *make an entry of* [《書》*enter*] (it) in an account book.
- 記載事項 items mentioned. (! ×mentioned items とはしない) ●記載漏れ an omission.

きさい 鬼才 〖才能〗genius, (a) remarkable [(an) exceptional] ability, a remarkable talent;(人) a person of exceptional [great] ability, a genius.

きさい 起債 図 (発行) an issue of bonds; (募集) flotation of bonds.
— **起債する** 動 (発行) issue bonds; (募集する) float [raise] a loan.
- 起債市場 a bond issuing market.

きざい 器材 (器具と材料) instruments and materials. (⇨器具)

きざい 機材 (機具と材料) machinery and materials. (⇨機具)

きさき 妃, 后 ❶〖皇后〗an empress. ❷〖国王の妻〗a queen.

ぎざぎざ ・ぎざぎざした (のこぎり歯状の) serrated; (不ぞろいな) jagged. ・ぎざぎざとした cut [make] notches. (! notch は V 字形の切り込み. 一つであれば a notch でいいが, ぎざぎざとはいえない) ▶100 円玉の側面にはぎざぎざがついている 100 yen coins have *serrated* [*milled*] edges. ▶その棒にはぎざぎざがついている The bar *is notched*. ▶海岸線はぎざぎざがついたように入り組んでいる The coastline *is indented*. (! indent は「歯でちぎったようなぎざをつける」の意)

きさく 気さく — 気さくな 形 (友好的な) friendly; (率直な) frank, candid. ・彼はとても気さくな人 He's very *friendly*./(気取らない) He never puts on airs./(付き合いやすい) He's easy to get along [on] with. ・彼女は良家のお嬢様にしては気さくな人だ(=お高くとまっていない) She's *not* as *proud* [*haughty*] as a lady from a good family would be.

きさく 奇策 a cunning plan; a smart strategy; an ingenious idea. ▶彼は奇策縦横の人物だ He is very *ingenious*.

きざけ 生酒 pure [undiluted] sake.

きざし 兆し 〖兆候〗a sign,《やや書》an indication;(悪い)a symptom;〖前兆〗an omen. ・春のきざし a *sign* of spring. ・来たるべき変革のきざし a *symptom* of the coming change. ▶インフレが収まるきざしはまったくない The inflation still shows no *signs* of remitting.

きざす 兆す show signs [《やや書》indications; symptoms] of…. (⇨兆し)

きざっぽい 気障っぽい affected. (⇨気障)

きざみ 刻み (切り込み) a notch. ・樹液を採るために木に刻みを入れる notch [cut some *notches* on] a tree to collect sap from it. ・刻み目つきの棒物差し *notched* measuring rod.

-きざみ -刻み (間隔) an interval. ▶首相の分刻みのスケジュール the Prime Minister's schedule *arranged to the minute*. ▶電車は2分刻みで入って来る The train comes in [arrives] *at* two-minute *intervals* [*at intervals*] of two minutes; (2分ごとに)《×at》every two minutes].

きざみたばこ 刻み煙草 図 tobacco.

きざみつける 刻みつける engrave…(on). (⇨刻む)

*   **きざむ** 刻む ❶〖細かく切る〗cut* [chop (-pp-)]…into small pieces; cut [chop]…up; (特に肉をミンチにする) mince*; 〖ずたずたに〗shred*. ・タマネギを刻む *chop (up)* [*shred, mince*] an onion. ・鳥肉を刻む *mince* [*hash*] chicken.
❷〖彫る〗carve,(表面に名前などを記す)《書》inscribe;(光景・言葉を心に) engrave…(on). (⇨彫る) ・自分のイニシャルを木に刻む *carve* one's initials *on* [×in] a tree. ・彼の命日を墓石に刻む *inscribe* the date of his death *on* a tombstone; *inscribe* a tombstone *with* the date of his death. ▶彼女の言葉は彼の心に刻みつけられた Her words *were engraved on* [*in*] his mind./《やや書》Her words *were implanted in* his heart.
❸〖時を〗・正確に時を刻む keep good time. ▶時計が時を刻む音だけが聞こえた I could hear no sound except the clock *ticking*. (⇨かちかち)

きざわり 気障り — 気障りな 形 (気に食わない) disagreeable.

きさん 起算 — 起算する 動 ▶使用料は到着の日から起

算される The hire charge *is reckoned from* the date of delivery.
きさんじ 気散じ (⇨気晴らし, 気楽)
***きし 岸** 〈海・湖・大河の〉(a) shore (❗最も一般的な語で海から見た岸); 〈大洋に面した〉(a) coast (❗特に陸から見た海岸); 〈川岸〉a bank; 〈浜〉a beach (❗大きな湖の岸にも用いる); 〈池などの〉a border, a margin. (⇨海岸) ▶我々の船は岸に到達した Our ship reached the *shore*. ▶岸からずっと遠く離れた所に船が見えた I saw a ship a long way from [off] the *shore*. ▶その劇場は淀川河岸にある The theater is *on the bank* of the Yodo River. ▶その死体は岸に打ち上げられた The body was washed *ashore*.
きし 棋士 〈囲碁の〉a *go* player; 〈将棋の〉a *shogi* player.
きし 騎士 a knight /náit/.
　●騎士道 chivalry /ʃívlri/.
*** きじ 生地 ❶** 〈服などの〉(a) material; 〈布地〉cloth (⇨服地), 〈ある目的・種類の布地〉(a) fabric (❗店・業界で cloth より一般的だ); 〈パン・めん類の〉dough /dóu/.
　●コートの生地 coat *material*; *material* for a coat.
　●伸縮性のあるポリエステルの生地 stretch polyester fabric [*material*]. ▶背広 3 着分の生地はありますか Is there enough *material* for three suits? ▶この生地はざらざらしている This cloth is rough in texture [has a rough texture]. ▶生地は「織り方」の意) ▶できるだけいろいろなカーテン用の生地を見せていただきたい I'd like to view as many types of curtain fabric(s) as possible.
❷ [**本質**] one's true colors. ▶生地のままの plain, undisguised. ▶生地のままふるまいなさい Just be yourself.
　●生地屋 a fabric store.
*** きじ 記事** a story; 〈ニュース〉news (❗単数扱い. 個々を数えるときは a piece [two pieces] of news などという), a news story; 〈解説的な〉an article; 〈詳細な説明・報告〉an account; 〈報告〉a report; 〈1 項目の〉an item. ▶特集記事 a feature 〈story [*article*]〉; 〈雑誌の表紙の説明記事〉a cover *story*. ▶囲み記事 a boxed *item*; a box. ▶記事を書く write a *story* [an *article*, a *report*] 〈*about* [*on*] politics; *for* a newspaper〉. ▶新聞のその記事によると according to the *story* [*article*] in the newspaper. ▶どの新聞もその殺人事件の記事を載せている All newspapers carry the *story* of the murder case. ▶それを取材して記事にしたい I want to do a *story* about it. ▶今日の新聞で児童書についてのよい記事を読んだ I read a good *article on* [*about*] children's books in today's paper.
きじ 雉 [鳥] a pheasant (❗〜s; 〈集合的〉〜).
　●雉も鳴かずば撃たれまい 〈ことわざ〉(黙っていれば被害なし) Silence seldom does harm.
*** ぎし 技師** an engineer. ▶土木[電気, 機械]技師 a civil [an electrical, a mechanical] *engineer*.
ぎし 義士 a loyal *samurai* [*warrior*].
ぎし 義姉 [[義理の姉]] one's sister-in-law (❗〜s, sisters-). (⇨兄弟 ❶)
ぎし 義肢 an artificial [〈人工的補充の〉a prosthetic] limb /lím/.
　●義肢装具士 an artificial limb maker.
ぎし 義歯 a false tooth. (⇨入れ歯)
ぎじ 擬似 [[擬似科学]] pseudoscience. ▶擬似コレラ paracholera. ▶擬似症状 a suspected case.
ぎじ 議事 proceedings. ▶議事を急ぐ[妨害する] 《書》expedite [《書》obstruct] the *proceedings*. ▶議事に入る[を閉じる] start [close] the *proceedings*. ▶円滑な議事進行に協力する cooperate with the smooth *proceedings* of the meeting. ▶これにて

本日の議事日程を終了します (閉会宣言) That concludes our *business* for today. Thank you.
　●議事進行 the progress of the proceedings; 〈議事規則どおりにやれ〉Order! Order! ▶議事日程 an agenda. ●議事録 〈会議の完全記録〉the proceedings; 〈会議の要約〉the minutes /mínəts/《*of* the last meeting》.
きしかいせい 起死回生 ●起死回生させる bring 《him》 back to life; revitalize. ▶起死回生の策を講ずる try to *revitalize* 《him》; give 《him》 the kiss of life. ▶彼は起死回生のホームランを打った His home run [homer] *pulled* the game *out of the fire*.
きしかん 既視感 (a feeling of) déjà vu /dèiʒɑː-v(j)úː/.
*** ぎしき 儀式** a ceremony; 〈宗教的な〉a rite (❗しばしば複数形で). ●儀式を行う hold a *ceremony* [a *rite*]. ●儀式に参列する attend a *ceremony*. ●儀式ばる stand on *ceremony* [*formality*]. ●儀式ばったあいさつを交わす exchange ceremonious greetings.
ぎしぎし ▶馬車が積み上げた荷をぎしぎしいわせて進んだ The wagon, piled up with its shaky cargo *squeaking*, went along the road. ▶箱にはリンゴがぎしぎしに詰まっている The box is *densely* [*tightly*] packed with apples. ▶歩くと床がぎしぎし鳴る The floor makes *creaking noises* as you walk.
きじく 基軸 a base; a basis; a foundation.
　●基軸通貨 a key currency.
きじく 機軸 〈活動の中心〉the center of 《politics, the movement, learning》; 〈方式・やり方〉(⇨新機軸).
きしつ 気質 nature; (a) disposition; (a) temperament. (⇨気性)
*** きじつ 期日** 〈定められた日〉a 〈fixed〉 date; 〈約束の日〉an appointed day; 〈締切日〉a time limit 《*for*》, a deadline. (⇨期限) ●期日を定める fix [set] the *date* 《*for*》. ●期日に間に合わす meet the *deadline* 《*for*》. ●約束の期日までに仕事を仕上げた I finished the work by the *appointed day*.
ぎじどう 議事堂 an assembly hall; [[国会]] 〈日本〉the Diet Building, 〈米国〉the Capitol, 〈英国〉the Houses of Parliament.
きじばと 雉鳩 [鳥] a turtledove.
ぎじばり 擬餌鉤 a lure; an artificial fly.
きしべ 岸辺 〈海・湖・大河の〉(a) shore; 〈大洋に面した〉(a) coast; 〈川・湖・水路などの〉(a) bank; 〈浜〉a beach. (⇨海岸, 岸)
きしむ 軋む 〈油切れで, 重さでぎいぎいと〉creak; 〈こすれて〉grate; 〈短く高い音で〉squeak; 〈ブレーキなどの鋭い音で〉screech. ▶ドアのちょうつがいがきしむ The door *creaks* on its hinges. ▶車はブレーキをきしませて急停車した The car *screeched* to a sudden stop./ The car stopped suddenly *with a screech of brakes*.
きしめん 碁子麺 *kishimen* noodles; flat noodles.
*** きしゃ 汽車** a train. (⇨列車, バス)
きしゃ 記者 [[報道記者]] a reporter; [[ジャーナリスト]] a journalist (❗reporter の仕事は新聞・雑誌・テレビ・ラジオなどでニュースを伝えることだが, journalist はそれ以外に編集, 出版, 放送など広く報道界の仕事に携わっている人についていう); [[特派員]] a correspondent. ●新聞記者 a newspaper; 〈特に男性〉a newspaperman; a néwspaper repòrter; 〈英話〉a pressman. ●雑誌記者 a magazíne repòrter. ●スポーツ記者 a spórts repòrter. ●女性記者 a newsperson; a woman reporter. (❗今は特に「女性」といわなくても a journalist, a reporter だけで男

きしゃ

女共通で用いられる). ●担当記者 a *reporter* in charge 《*of*》. ●科学担当記者 a *science reporter*.
▶彼はタイムズの記者です He *reports for* [is a *reporter on*, works as a *journalist on*] *The Times*.
● 記者会見 (hold) a préss [a néws] cònference; (have) an interview with the press corps. ●記者クラブ a préss clùb. ●記者席 (スポーツの) a préss bòx; (議会の) a préss gàllery. ●記者団 a press corps /kɔ́ːr, kɔ́ːrz/. (🖉集合的に用い、単・複両扱い)

きしゃ 喜捨 图 寄進

きしゃく 希釈 图 dilution /dailúːʃən/.
—— 希釈する 動 dilute 《whiskey *with* water》.
● 希釈液 a dilution; a diluted solution.

きじゃく 着尺 (説明的に) the standard length and width of cloth for one *kimono*.

きしゃぽっぽ 汽車ぽっぽ a choo-choo, 《英》a puff-puff.

きしゅ 気腫 〔医学〕emphysema /émfəsíːmə/. ●肺気腫 pulmonary emphysema.

きしゅ 奇手 ●奇手を用いる take *novel measures* 《*against*; *to do*》.

きしゅ 鬼手 ●鬼手を打つ (碁・将棋などで) make a *surprisingly daring move*.

きしゅ 旗手 (競技などの) a flág bèarer; (軍隊などの) a standard bearer. (🖉後の方は比喩的に「(政党・運動などの)指導者」の意でも用いられる)

きしゅ 機首 the nose (of an airplane). ●機首を上げ[下げ]て lift [lower] the *nose*. ▶飛行機は機首を下げて着陸態勢に入った The plane turned [lowered] its *nose* to land.

きしゅ 機種 a model [a type] 《*of* a computer》.

きしゅ 騎手 (競馬の) a jockey; (一般に) a rider, a horseman (🖉 -men), a horsewoman (🖉 -women). ▶後の2語は上手な乗り手をさすことが多い: a fine [an excellent] *horseman*.

きじゅ 喜寿 one's 77th 《*calendar*》 year. (⇨還暦)

ぎしゅ 技手 an assistant engineer. ●土木[電気; 機械]技手 a civil [an electrical; a mechanical] *assistant engineer*.

ぎしゅ 義手 a prosthetic [an artificial] arm [hand].

きしゅう 奇習 a strange custom.

きしゅう 奇襲 (make) a surprise [《やや話》a sneak] attack 《*on*》.

きしゅう 既習 ●既習単語 a word one has already learned [studied]. (🖉 未習)

きじゅう 機銃 a machine gun.
●機銃掃射 machine-gun fire.

きじゅうき 起重機 a crane; (船の) a derrick (crane). (⇨クレーン)
●起重機船 a floating crane.

きしゅく 寄宿 lodging; (食事付き)《米》room and board, 《英》board and lodging; (三食付き) full board (and lodging); (朝食と昼食[夕食]付き) half board.
—— 寄宿する 動 lodge; (食事付き) board. ▶私はおじのところに寄宿しています I'm *lodging at* my uncle's (house) [*with* my uncle].
●寄宿学校 a boarding school. ●寄宿舎 a dormitory, 《話》a dorm. (⇨寮), 寄宿人 a lodger, 《米》a roomer; (食事付きの) a boarder.

きしゅつ 既出 ●既出 (試験) 問題集 a collection of previously-posed (exam) questions.

きじゅつ 奇術 magic, conjuring. (⇨手品)

きじゅつ 既述 —— 既述の 形 above-mentioned.
●既述の通り as mentioned above.

きじゅつ 記述 图 (a) description; an account.

きしょう

—— 記述的 (な) 形 descriptive.
—— 記述する 動 describe; give* an account 《*of*》.

:ぎじゅつ 技術 图 (芸術・文筆・競技・科学などの専門的技術) (a) technique /tekníːk/; (訓練などによって得られた特殊技能) (a) skill; (知識よりも経験などから得た要領・こつ) (an) art (🖉 しばしば science (理論的知識)と対照的に用いられる); (手先を使う職業などの技術) (a) craft; (科学的応用の) (a) technology. ●心臓移植の技術 the *technique* of a heart transplant. ●会話の技術 the *art* of conversation. ●技術畑の人間である私は on the *technical* side. ▶私は彫像を彫る技術を学んだ I have learned the *technique* [×*technic*] *of* carving a statue. ▶その先生は教授法にすぐれた技術(=技量)を持っている The teacher has great *skill* in teaching. ▶傷口に包帯をするのには技術がいる Bandaging injuries requires *skill*./It takes [requires] *skill* to bandage injuries. ▶日本の科学技術はすばらしい進歩をとげた Japan has made remarkable progress in 《*science and*》 *technology*.
—— 技術的な, 技術上の 形 (専門的技術の) technical (🖉 通例限定的に); (科学技術の) technological.
—— 技術的に 副 ▶それは技術的に不可能だ That is *technically* impossible.
●技術革新 (a) technical [(a) technological] innovation. ●技術協力 technical cooperation. ●技術者 a technical expert; a technician; (技師) an engineer. ●技術提携 a technical tie-up. ●技術屋 a technician; (話) a techie.

:きじゅん 基準 a standard; (判断の基準) a criterion (🖉 criteria); (比較評価の) a benchmark; 〔根拠〕a basis (🖉 bases). ●基準 (基準内) 賃金 standard [fixed; extra] wages. ●判断の基準 a *criterion for* judgment. ●あらゆる基準に照らして by any *standard*(*s*). ●安全基準に合う meet safety *standards*. ●大学への入学の基準を定める set *standards for* admission to college. ▶この計画は必要な基準を満たしていない This plan does not meet the required *standard*(*s*). ▶人気は成功を計る基準ではない Popularity is not a *criterion* of success. ▶彼の見事なプレーは他の選手たちに新しい基準を与えた His fine play set a new *benchmark for* the other players.

きしょ 希書, 稀書 a rare book. (🖉 希覯(きこう)書)

きしょ 奇書 a rare [an unusual] book.

きじょ 鬼女 an ogress; a she-devil.

ぎしょ 偽書 a forgery; a forged document [letter].

＊きしょう 気象 weather (conditions). ●異常気象 abnormal *weather*. ●気象の変化 a change in the *weather*. ●天気図で気象を調べる check the *weather* (*conditions*) by reading the weather map. ●いろいろな気象状態でのヨットの操縦法を学ぶ learn how to handle a yacht in different *weather conditions*.
●気象衛星 a weather [a meteorological] satellite. ●気象学者 a meteorologist. ●気象観測 weather [meteorological] observation. ●気象台 a meteorological observatory; a weather station. ●気象庁 the Meteorological Agency; 《米》the National Weather Service. ●気象予報士 a weather forecaster; (テレビ・ラジオの) (男) a weatherman, (女) a weatherwoman (🖉 -men).

きしょう 気性 (特徴的な性質) a disposition; (感情面に重点を置いた性質) a temper, (形式) a temperament (🖉 後の方が生来のものであることを強く暗示する). (⇨性質) ●さっぱりした気性 an open *disposiiton*. ●負けん気の強い気性 an unyielding *dis-*

きしょう position [temper]. ● 激しい気性 a violent [a fiery] temper [temperament]. ▶彼は怒りっぽい性分の人だった He had a quick temper./He was quick-tempered./He was a man of [with a] quick temper.

きしょう 希少 ● 希少価値がある have scarcity /skéərsəti/ [rarity /réərəti/] value.

きしょう 奇勝 [いい景色] exceptionally beautiful scenery; [思いがけない勝利] an unexpected victory. ● 奇勝の地 a beauty spot; a place famous for its scenic beauty.

きしょう 記章 (wear) a badge.

きしょう 起床 ― 起床する 動《書》rise*, get* up. (⇨起きる) ▶起床(する)時間ですよ It's time to get up.

きじょう 机上 ● 机上版の辞書 a desk dictionary. ● 机上の空論 a mere theory. (⇨空論)

きじょう 気丈 ― 気丈な 形 (気の強い) strong-minded.

きじょう 軌条 [レール] a rail.

きじょう 機上 ● 機上の人となる board the airplane; go on board the airplane.

きしょう 騎乗 ― 騎乗する 動 ride* (on a horse).

ぎしょう 偽称 ― 偽称する 動 (名前を偽る) give* a false name [職業]; career; (国籍) nationality; (身分を) social status); ▶弁護士だと偽称する pretend to be a lawyer.

ぎしょう 偽証 名 (罪)《法律》pérjury.
― 偽証する 動《法律》pérjure oneself, commit perjury.

ぎじょう 議場 an assembly hall;[議会の議員席]the floor. ▶議場を混乱させる throw the floor into confusion [《やや書》disorder].

きしょうてんけつ 起承転結 (説明的に) the four-part structure (of Chinese poetry): introduction, development, turn, and conclusion.

ぎじょうへい 儀仗兵 《米》an honor guard, 《英》a guard of honor.

きしょうゆ 生醤油 pure [×genuine] soy sauce.

きしょく 気色 ● 気色の悪い (むかつくような) sickening, disgusting; (嫌悪感をもよおす) repulsive; (見て不愉快な) ugly. ● (何かを見ると気色が悪い (人が主語)) feel sick (at the sight of ...);《物が主語》make (him) feel sick. ▶あのピンクは気色が悪い That pink makes me feel sick./That pink is disgusting.

きしょく 喜色 a joyful [a jubilant] look. ▶彼は喜色満面である He is all smiles./He is beaming with pleasure [with joy].

キシリトール [化学] xylitol /záilətɔ:l/. (参考 甘味料)

きしる 軋る (⇨軋む)

きしん 寄進 (a) contribution 《to》. (⇨寄付)

きじん 奇人 An eccentric person, 《話》an oddball.

ぎじん 擬人 ― 擬人化 名 personification.
― 擬人化する 動《やや書》personify.
● 擬人法 personification; prosopop(o)eia.

ぎしんあんき 疑心暗鬼 (疑い) a suspicion. ● 疑心暗鬼になる be suspicious of everything.
● 疑心暗鬼を生(ばう)ず (ことわざ) Suspicion breeds phantoms.

きす 鱚 〖魚介〗a sillago.

きす 帰す ① come* to ...; (...に終わる) 《やや書》 result in ...; (負わせる) put*... down 《to him》(⇨所為(せい)). ▶水泡に帰す come to nothing.

きす 期す ①[期待する] expect; hope for .... ▶彼の回復は期しがたい There is hardly any hope of [《米》for] his recovery.
②[約束する] promise. ▶再会を期して彼らは別れた They separated, promising to meet again.
③[決意する]《やや書》determine, resolve;[覚悟している] be prepared 《for; to do》. ▶我々は必勝を期している We are determined [resolved] to win.
④[期日を定める] fix. ▶来月 1 日を期して大会を開催することになった We fixed the conference for the first of next month.

キス 名 a kiss.
― キス(を)する 動 kiss, give* (her) a kiss. (通例 ×give a kiss to her とはいわない) ▶投げキスをする throw [blow] a kiss 《to》. ▶彼女の額にちゅっとキスをする give her a smack on the forehead; smack a kiss on her forehead. ▶おやすみ[さよなら]のキスをする kiss (him) good night [good-by]. ▶彼女は息子のほおにキスした She kissed her son on the cheek./She kissed her son's cheek. (前の方は人に焦点を置いた言い方)
● キスマーク a love bite, 《米》a hickey; (口紅の跡) a lipstick mark; 《和製語》a kiss mark.

きず 傷 ❶[負傷] (事故などによるのは) an ínjury, a hurt; [injury の方がひどい例]; (刃物・弾丸などによる傷) a wound /wúːnd/.

〖関連〗傷の種類: 刺し[突き]傷 a stab/切り傷 (短い) a cut; (長い) a slash; (深くて長い) a gash/引っかき傷 [かすり傷] a scratch/すり傷 a scrape;〖医学〗an abrasion/打撲傷 a bruise /brúːz/.

①【～傷】● 大きな傷 a major [a severe, a fatal, a mortal] injury [wound]. ▶心の傷はなかなか治らない Emotional [Psychological] wounds take a long time to heal.
②【傷～】● 傷口を縫う stitch [sew] up a wound. ▶傷口が完全にふさがった The wound has completely closed. ▶傷口をアルコールで消毒しきないない You'd better disinfect a cut with alcohol. ▶彼は傷だらけだった He was covered with injuries./He was injured all over.
③【傷が】▶傷がまたうずき始めた The wound started to smart again. ▶交通事故の傷が時々痛む The injury in [×by] the traffic accident sometimes hurts (me). ▶傷がすっかりいえるまでには 3 か月以上かかるでしょう It will be more than three months before the wound heals up.
④【傷を】▶母が足の傷を手当てしてくれた Mother treated me for the wound in [injury to, hurt on] the leg. (前置詞に注意) ▶彼は弾に当たって頭に深い傷を負った He got [received, suffered] a deep bullet wound in the head./He was badly [×deeply] wounded in the head by a bullet. (deeply は「精神的な傷」に用いる) ▶彼の言葉は彼女の心に傷を残した His remarks left emotional [mental] scars on her mind.

❷[品物の傷](損傷) damage; (ひび、傷) a flaw; (ひび) a crack; (引っかき傷) a scratch; (こすり傷) a scrape; (果物のいたみ) a bruise /brúːz/. ● 皿の傷 a flaw [a crack] in the plate. ▶テーブルには傷が少しある There are some scratches [scrapes] on the table.

会話 「車に傷がついた?」「どこにもかすり傷ひとつないよ」"Was the car damaged?" "Not a scratch anywhere."

❸[欠点, 汚点] a flaw, a defect. ▶会社の名前に傷をつける damage [injure, hurt] the company's reputation. ▶彼は短気なのが玉にきずだ A short temper is his only flaw [defect]. ▶彼の経歴には一点の傷もなかった His record was without a scratch.
● 傷跡 (⇨傷跡) ● 傷薬 (軟膏(なんこう)) ointment.

きずあと 傷跡 (皮膚・心・災害などの) a scar. ●ほおの傷跡 a scar across one's cheek. ●戦争の傷跡のある市 a war-scarred city. ▶彼の場合、おそらく額に傷跡が残るだろう Probably a scar will stay on his forehead. ▶その経験は彼の心に傷跡(＝精神的外傷)を残した The experience scarred him [his mind]./The experience left him traumatized.

きずいせん 黄水仙 [植物] a jonquil.

きすう 奇数 an odd [an uneven] number.

きすう 基数 a cardinal (↔an ordinal) number.

きずきあげる 築き上げる build* ... (up). (⇨築く)

ぎすぎす ❶[肉体が] ●彼女はぎすぎすした体つきをしている She looks unhealthily thin.
❷[人間関係が] ▶私は秘書のぎすぎすした応待に腹が立った I was angry at the secretary's unfriendly reception. ▶あのことがあって以来彼らの関係はぎすぎすしている(＝うまくいっていない) They just can't get along together after that trouble./(よそよそしく冷たい) They are distant and cold with each other after that incident. ▶世の中がぎすぎすしているのは金に重きが置かれすぎているからだ It's because people think too much of money that the world is not running comfortably [the world is a hard place to live in].

*きずく 築く** (建物などを) build*; construct. ●堤防を築く build [construct] a bank. ●財産を築く make a fortune.

きずぐち 傷口 (傷) a wound. (⇨傷)

きずつく 傷つく (事故などで) be [get*] injured, be [get] hurt (❗後の方が軽い); (刃物・弾丸などで) be [get] wounded. (⇨傷). ●傷ついた心 injured [wounded] feelings. ▶私は信頼を裏切られてひどく傷ついた I felt so hurt when my confidence was betrayed. ▶そのうわさで彼女はひどく傷ついた She was deeply [×badly, ×seriously] hurt [×injured, wounded] by the rumor. (❗badly, seriously は「肉体的な傷」に用う) ▶彼女はとても傷つきやすい人、ほんのちょっと注意されても傷つくんだもの She's too sensitive; she feels hurt at the slightest criticism.

*きずつける 傷つける** (けがをさせる) injure, hurt*; wound (❗いずれも感情などを害する意にも用いられる); [損害を与える] damage; (表面をこすって) scrape; (ひびを入れる) crack. ●彼の頭を傷つける wound him in the head. ●商品を傷つける damage the goods. ●彼の名誉を傷つける injure [hurt, wound, damage] his reputation. ▶彼はそのひと言で彼女の心を深く傷つけた He deeply [×badly, ×seriously] hurt [injured, wounded] her feelings with that remark./That remark of his was a great hurt [injury, wound] to her feelings. ▶テーブルの表面を傷つけないように気をつけなさい Be careful not to scrape the table-top.

きずな 絆 ties; (強い) a bond (❗しばしば複数形で). ●家族のきずな family ties; a family bond. ●親子のきずな the bond between parent and child. ●友情のきずな the bonds [ties] of friendship. ▶私たちは強い友情のきずなで結ばれている We are tied to each other by great friendship.

きずもの 傷物 (やや書) a defective article. ●(娘が)傷物にされる be ruined.

きする 帰する come* to .... (⇨帰す) ●帰する所 (つまり、結局)

きする 期する expect. (⇨期す)

*きせい 規制** [名] [規則による取り締まり] (a) regulation; [管理, 抑制] (a) control; [制限] (a) restriction. ●交通規制 control [regulation] of traffic; traffic control [restriction].
— **規制する** [動] regulate; control. ●大気汚染を規制する regulate air pollution. ●輸出を規制する control [put restrictions on] exports.
●**規制緩和** deregulation. ●規制緩和をする deregulate [ease restrictions on] 《the banking industry》. ●**規制撤廃** deregulation; removal [abolition] of regulation.

きせい 気勢 spirits. ●気勢をそぐ 《事が主語》dampen [break] 《his》 spirits; discourage 《him》 (a lot).
●気勢を上げる lift [raise, boost] one's spirits.
●気勢が上がっている be in high spirits.

きせい 奇声 ●奇声を発する give [raise] a queer, shrill voice.

きせい 帰省 [名] a homecoming.
— **帰省する** [動] go* [come*, return] home. (❗return はやや改まった語. go, come の区別は ⇨行く) ●休暇で帰省している be home for the vacation [on vacation]. (⇨休暇)

きせい 既成 — **既成の** [確立した] established; [現存の] existing. ●既成の事実 an established fact; (今さら変更のきかない事実) a fáit accomplí /féitæko(:)mplí:/ (複) faits accomplis /féizæko(:)mplí:z/) (＝an accomplished fact).
●既成概念 (やや書) a stereotype; (先入観)(やや書) a preconceived idea. ●既成政党 the existing [established] political parties.

きせい 既製 — **既製の** [形] (できあいの) réady-màde. (❗限定的のみ)
●既製品 ready-made goods [articles]; a ready-made. ●既製服 ready-made clothes; 《米》off-the-rack clothes; 《英》off-the-peg clothes; 《古》ready-to-wear clothes.

きせい 寄生 [名] párasìtism.
— **寄生する** [動] parasitize 《animals》.
●寄生植物 a parasitic plant. ●寄生虫 (⇨寄生虫)
●寄生動物 a parasitic animal.

きせい 期成同盟 an association 《for》.

きせい 棋聖 a champion go [shogi] player.

*きせい 犠牲** (a) sacrifice /sækrəfàis/; (被害者) a victim.
① [犠牲に] ●スポーツのために勉学を犠牲にする sacrifice [make a sacrifice of] studies for sports.
●健康を犠牲にして仕事を成し遂げる complete one's work at the sacrifice [cost, expense] of one's health. ▶彼女は子供のために自分を犠牲にした She sacrificed herself for her children. ▶多くの人が阪神大震災の犠牲になった A lot of people lost [×sacrificed] their lives in [were victims of] the Great Hanshin Earthquake. (❗sacrificed は「他人のために自分の命を犠牲にする」で不可) ▶彼はその病気の犠牲になった He fell victim to [×of] the disease.
② [犠牲を] ●多大の犠牲を払って得た勝利 a costly victory. ▶親は子供の教育のためには多くの犠牲を払うものだ Parents make a lot of sacrifices to educate [for the education of] their children.
▶我々はどんな犠牲を払っても行方不明の少女を捜さねばならない We must find the missing girl at all costs [whatever the cost]. ▶彼は多大の犠牲を払ってやっと成功した He paid dearly for his success. ▶私たちはその若者の払った多くの犠牲に報いなければならない We have to reward the young man for many sacrifices he made.
●**犠牲者** a sacrificer; 被害者. ●**犠牲的精神** the spirit of self-sacrifice. ●**犠牲バント** [野球] a sacrifice bunt. (⇨犠打) ●**犠牲フライ** [野球] a sacrifice fly. (⇨犠打)

ぎせい 擬制 (a) (legal) fiction.
- 擬制資本 fictitious capital.

ぎせいご 擬声語 onomatopoeia /ὰnəmǽtəpíːə/; an onomatopoeic word.

ぎせいしゃ 犠牲者 (被害者) a victim; (事故などの死傷者) a casualty 《しばしば複数形で》. ● 戦争犠牲者 a *victim* of war; a war *victim*. ▶ 自動車事故の犠牲者が増えている The number of *victims* in automobile accidents is increasing. ▶ その事故では多くの犠牲者が出た The accident caused a lot of *casualties.*／There were a lot of *casualties* in the accident.

きせいちゅう 寄生虫 a párasite, 《やや書》a parasitic worm. ● 人間[社会]の寄生虫 a *parasite* on human beings [society].
- 寄生虫学 parasitology. ● 寄生虫駆除剤 a parasiticide.

きせかえ 着せ替え a change of clothes.
- 着せ替え人形 a dress-up doll; a doll with several changes [sets] of clothes.

きせかえる 着せ替える change clothes 《on a doll》, change 《a doll's》 clothes.

きせかける 着せ掛ける put* (a coat) on [over] 《him》 from behind.

きせき 奇跡 图 a miracle. ● 奇跡を起こす work [perform] a *miracle*. ▶ 奇跡が起こった A *miracle* happened [occurred].
— **奇跡的な 形** miraculous. ▶ その患者は奇跡的な回復をみせた The patient showed a *miraculous* improvement.
— **奇跡的に 副** miraculously. ▶ 奇跡的に助かる be saved by a *miracle*; be saved *miraculously*. ▶ 彼らは奇跡的に洪水を逃れた They made a *miraculous* escape from the flood./It's a *miracle* (that) they escaped from the flood. (⚠ that は通例省略する)

きせき 軌跡 〖数学〗a locus (⚠ loci /lóusai/); (たどった跡) a track. ● 軌跡を求める derive [find] a *locus*.

きせき 鬼籍 ● 鬼籍に入(い°)る die; (婉曲的)《亡き人々の数に入る》join the majority.

ぎせき 議席 a seat. ● 議席を失う lose one's *seat*.
● 選挙で10議席を得る win ten *seats* in the election.

きせずして 期せずして (意外にも) unexpectedly; (偶然に) accidentally, by chance. ▶ 我々は期せずして(=偶然に)再会した We *happened to* meet again.

＊きせつ 季節期 图 a season ▶ 四季の一つ, または物事の最盛期》; (時期) time. ● 季節感が薄れる lose the sense of (the) *seasons*. ● 季節の変わり目に at the change of (the) *seasons*. ● この季節には at this *time* of (the) year. ● 季節の野菜を食べる eat vegetables *in season*. ▶ 秋はスポーツに最良の季節だ Fall [《主に英》Autumn] is the best *season* for sports. ▶ スキーの季節となった[が近づいて来た] The skiing *season* has come [is coming]. ▶ 景色の中に季節の移り変わりを感じとった We noted the *seasonal* changes [the change of the *seasons*] in the scenery. ▶ ブドウは今季節はずれでとても高い Grapes are *out of season* now and very expensive. ▶ 季節はずれの大雪に見舞われた We had an *unseasonably* heavy snowfall. ▶ 夏はなによりも, 死者の霊が帰ってくる季節なのである More than anything else, summer is the *season* for the homecoming of the souls of the dead [the departed soul].
— **季節の 形** seasonal.
- 季節商品 seasonal goods [merchandise].
- 季節調整 seasonal adjustment. (⚠参考) 経済統計の原計数から季節要因による変動を除くこと) ● 季節風 a seasonal wind; (インド洋・南アジアのモンスーン) the monsóon. ● 季節変動 (a) seasonal variation.
- 季節労働者 a seasonal [a migrant] worker.

きせつ 既設 —— 既設の 形 ● 既設の(=稼動中の)原子力発電所 a nuclear power station *in operation*.

きぜつ 気絶 图 a faint.
— **気絶する 動** faint; get* stunned. (⇨失神) ● 気絶して倒れる fall (down) in a *faint*; (意識を失う) fall unconscious [senseless].

きせる 着せる ❶ [衣類を] dress; clothe (⚠ dress のように着給る感じはない); (無理やりに) get* (him) into 《a suit》. ● 赤ちゃんに服を着せる *dress* a baby. ● 彼女にコートを(手伝って)着せる *help* her *on with* her coat; *help* her (to) *put* her coat *on*.
❷ [かぶせる] (⇨かぶせる)
❸ [負わせる] ● 彼に罪(=責任)を着せる lay [put, place] the blame (for it) on him. ▶ 彼は私に恩を着せたがっているようだった He expected me to feel indebted to him.

キセル [<カンボジア語] a (tobacco) pipe. ● キセル(乗車)をする cheat on the fare.

きぜわしい 気ぜわしい (せきたてられるよう) feel* rushed; (落ち着かない) feel restless.

きせん 汽船 〖小型で川・湖・内海用の〗a steamboat; 〖大型外洋船〗a steamship (⚠略 S.S.), a steamer; (定期船) a [an ocean] liner. (⇨船) ● 汽船成臨丸 the *S.S.* Kanrin Maru. (⚠ 船名には定冠詞がつく)

きせん 基線 (測量) a báse line.

きせん 貴賤 ● 貴賤の別なく irrespective of [regardless of] rank. ▶ 職業に貴賤なし Each and every occupation is honorable.

きせん 輝線 ● 輝線スペクトル an emission line spectrum.

きせん 機先 ● 機先を制する (先手を打つ) beat 《one's rival》 to the punch; 《やや書》 forestall 《one's rival》. (⇨先手)

きぜん 毅然 —— 毅然とした (=断固とした)態度を取る take a *resolute* [きっぱりした] a *firm* attitude 《toward》. ▶ 彼は非難に対しても毅然としていた He stood firm against [stood tall under] criticism.

ぎぜん 偽善 图 (a) hýpocrisy. — **偽善的な 形** hypocrit(al).
- 偽善者 a hýpocrite; a wolf in sheep's clothing. (⚠聖書より)

＊きそ 基礎 〖土台〗a foundation; (基部) a base (⚠前の語の方がしっかりした堅い土台を暗示する); 〖基本〗a basis (⚠ bases); (下地) groundwork; (基本事項) the fundamentals; the basics. (⚠後の2語は通例複数形で) ● 英語の基礎的な知識 a *fundamental* [a *basic*, (初歩の) an *elementary*] knowledge of English. ▶ その建物は基礎がしっかりしている The building has a solid *foundation* [*base*]. ▶ 彼はまだ英語の基礎が出来ていない He has not yet mastered the *fundamentals* [*basics*] of English. ▶ 彼は現代言語学の基礎を築いた He laid the *foundation* [*basis*, *groundwork*] *for* modern linguistics. ▶ 彼はフランス語の基礎知識が十分ある He has a good *grounding* in French./He *is well grounded* in French. ▶ 君は数学を基礎から(=最初から)やり直した方がいい You'd better study mathematics again from the (very) *beginning*.
- 基礎語彙(い) the basic vocabulary. ● 基礎工事 the foundátion wòrk. ● 基礎控除 basic deduction. ● 基礎代謝 〖生理〗basal metabolism.

きそ 起訴 图 (告訴) prosecution; (陪審制での) indictment /indáitmənt/.

きそう
── 起訴する 動 …のかどで起訴されている be under *indictment* for …; be on charges of …. ▶彼は殺人罪で起訴された He *was prosecuted* [*was indicted*] *for* murder.
● 起訴状 an indictment. ● 起訴猶予 (⇨起訴猶予)
きそう 帰巣 ── 帰巣本能 the homing instinct.
きそう 起草 ── 起草する 動 draft.
● 起草委員会 a dráfting commíttee.
きそう 基層 a substratum (複 -ta).
きそう 競う (競争相手を倒すべく争う) compete; (相手と力で競い合う) 《やや書》 contend; (勝利や賞をめざして争う) contest. ▶賞をめざして互いに競い合った We *competed* [*contested*] *with* each other *for* the prize.
きそう 寄贈 donation.
── 寄贈する 動 donate; (贈る) present; (与える) give*. ▶彼は蔵書を母校に寄贈した He *has donated* [*presented*] his library *to* his school.
きそう 偽装 (カムフラージュ) camouflage /kǽməflàːʒ/; 具体的には C; (変装) (a) disguise. (⇨カムフラージュ, 変装)
── 偽装する camouflage 《*as*》; disguise 《*as*》.
ぎぞう 偽造 (文書などの) forgery; (通貨などの) counterfeit; (にせ物) fake. (⇨偽) ● 文書偽造 *forgery* of documents.
── 偽造する 動 forge; counterfeit; fake. ● 小切手 [証明書] を偽造する *forge* a check [a certificate]. ● 偽造紙幣 a counterfeit [a fake] bill. ● 偽造文書 a forged document.
きそうきょく 奇想曲 《音楽》 a capriccio /kəprítʃioʊ/ (複 -os), a capricci /kəprítʃi/; a caprice (⇨カプリス)
きそうてんがい 奇想天外 形動 (現実離れした) fantastic; (まったく予期しない) totally unexpected.

:きそく 規則 (個々の成員に視点を置く決まり) a rule; (権威者によって与えられる公の規定) a regulation. (いずれもしばしば複数形で) 《法律》・交通規則 (公の交通法規) traffic *regulations*; (一般常識) traffic *rules*. ● 規則を守る observe the *rules* [*regulations*]. ● 規則を破る break the *rules* [*regulations*]. ● 規則を曲げる (= 拡大解釈をする) bend [stretch] the *rules*. ● 厳しい規則を設ける make strict *rules* [*regulations*] 《*about*》. ● 規則にがんじがらめに縛られる be tangled up in *rules and regulations*. (細かくつまらないという含みがある. 語順に注意) ● 規則正しい (⇨規則正しい) ▶1人でそこへ行くことは規則違反だ It's against the *rule*(*s*) to go there alone. ▶学校は男子は丸刈りにするという規則を設けている The school has a *rule* that the boys (《主に英》should) wear their hair close-cropped. ▶私は規則どおりにそれをやった I did it according to the *rules* [*regulations*]. ▶例外のない規則はない There is no *rule* without 《古》[but] some exceptions./Every *rule* has some exceptions. ● 規則的に便通がありますか Are your bowels [stools] regular? / Do you have a bowel movement *regularly* [a *regular* bowel movement]? ▶漫画には規則など存在しない There is no *rule* for creating comics. (comic には「お笑いの喜劇役者」の意もあるので,「漫画」を明確にするには comics とする)

きそく 気息 (a) breath. (⇨息)
● 気息奄々 (えんえん) be dying; be breathing very feebly [weakly].
● 気息音 《音声》 an aspirate /ǽspərət/.
きぞく 帰属 belonging. ── 帰属する 動 belong to ….
● 帰属意識 a sense of belonging.

きぞく 貴族 a nobleman (女性形は noblewoman. 複 はともに (- men)), an aristocrat, 《英》a peer (女性形は peeress); 《集合的に》the aristocracy, the nobility, the peerage (いずれも単・複両扱い). ▶彼は貴族の生まれだ He is of *noble* birth.
── 貴族的な 形 aristocrátic.

【解説】 peer は次の5階級: (上から順に) duke (公爵), marquess (侯爵), earl (伯爵), viscount /váikàunt/ (子爵), baron (男爵). これ以下の baronet (準男爵), knight (ナイト) は peer ではない.

ぎぞく 義足 an artificial leg; (木製の) a wooden [《話》a peg] leg. ● 義足をしている wear an *artificial leg*.
ぎぞく 義賊 a Robin Hood; a chivalrous robber.
きそくただしい 規則正しい 形 regular. ▶彼は規則正しい生活をしている He leads a *regular* life./He is *regular* in his life. ● keep regular hours は,通例「早寝早起きの習慣がある」の意)
── 規則正しく 副 regularly. ▶規則正しく食事をするよう医師に言われた The doctor advised me to have *regular* meals [to eat *regularly*].
きそつ 既卒 ── 既卒者 a graduate.
きそゆうよ 起訴猶予 ── 起訴猶予にする drop charges 《*against*》; decide not to prosecute. ▶証拠不十分のため彼女は起訴猶予となった The police have *dropped charges against* her due to lack of evidence.
きぞん 既存 ── 既存の 形 (将来はともかく, 今ある) existing; (今も)ある) 《書》existent. ● 既存の施設 the *existing* institutions.
きそん 毀損 名 ・名誉毀損 defamation (of character); (文書・写真による) (a) libel; (口頭による) (a) slander.
── 毀損する 動 damage 《a car [furniture]》; (名誉を) defame 《him》, injure 《his reputation》.

:きた 北 north, North. ● 通例 the ～》東, 南. ── 北(の) north; northern; northerly. (⇨北国, 北風)
── 北に 副 (北方に) (to the) north; (北部に) in the north; (北側に接して) on the north (side); [北へ(向かって)] north; to [toward] the north; northward.

ぎだ 犠打 《野球》a sacrifice (hit). (sacrifice bunt (犠牲バント)と sacrifice fly (犠牲フライ)をまとめていう) ● 犠打を打つ make a *sacrifice*. ● 犠打で走者を三塁に進める *sacrifice* a runner to third; move a runner to third on a *sacrifice*. (この場合の犠打はふつう. 外野フライは使われない)

ギター a guitar /gitɑ́ːr/. ● ギター奏者 a guitarist. ● ギターを弾く[かき鳴らす] play [pluck, 《米》pick] (the) *guitar*. (⇨ピアノ)
きたアイルランド 北アイルランド Northern Ireland.
きたアメリカ 北アメリカ North America.

:きたい 期待 (an) expectation (しばしば複数形で); 《希望》 (a) hope; 《見込み》 (a) prospect; 《予期》anticipation.
①《期待~》 ▶その映画の期待はずれだった The movie wasn't up to [fell short of] my *expectations*./The movie was disappointing [a disappointment, ×disappointed] (to me). ▶彼は親の期待どおりには勉強しなかった He didn't study as hard as his parents (had) *expected*. (as 節内は通例過去完了形だが, 口語ではしばしば過去を用いる) ▶試験の結果は期待以上だった The results of the exam exceeded [were beyond] my *expectations*. (前の方は堅い言い方)

② [期待が[は]] ▶彼の生存はあまり期待が持てない [期待薄だ] There isn't much hope of [《米》for] his survival. ▶私の期待ははずれた My hopes were destroyed. ▶そのことを知ると息子に対する期待が高まった His expectations for his son have risen [soared] at it.

③ [期待に] ▶彼は我々の期待にこたえてくれた He came up to [lived up to, met] (←fell short of) our expectations. ▶私の期待に反して彼は失敗した Contrary to [Against] my expectation(s), he failed. ▶私たちは期待にわくわくした[胸を躍らせた] We were excited with expectation. ▶新しい世界に第一歩を踏み出したとき, 彼女は期待に胸をふくらませていた When she took the first step into a new world, her heart swelled [was filled] with hope.

④ [期待を] ▶両親は私に期待をかけすぎる My parents expect too much from [［書］of] me. (!×...expect me too much. は不可) ▶信じてくれ, 今度は君の期待を裏切る(=がっかりさせる)ようなことはしないよ Trust me. I'll never let you down [fail you] this time.

会話「例のパーティーではスーパーマンの扮装をするつもりなんだ. 君はどうするの」「乞うご期待」"For that party, I'm going to disguise myself as Superman. How about you?" "Wait and see."

―― 期待する 動 expect, (今に起こると) anticipate; [希望する] hope; [楽しみにする] look forward to ...; [しばしば進行形で] [当てにする] count on ...

使い分け expect 根拠に基づく確かな予想を表す. よいことへの期待だけでなく, 悪いことの予測も含意する.
hope 現実的な根拠に基づく可能性のある希望を表す.
anticipate 差し迫った事柄を予則し, 心構えをすることを表す. 歓迎・不安の両方の文脈で用いる.

▶あなたが手伝ってくれると期待しています I hope [expect] (that) you will help me. (!口語では通例 that 節を省略する. expect の方が相手に強く気持ちが強い)/I expect [×hope] you to help me. (!that 節を従える場合より期待の度合いが強い)/I count on your help [you to help me]. ▶彼が勝つものと期待された He was expected to win./We [They, 《書》It was] hoped that he would win. ▶この本は期待していたよりずっといい That book is much better than I (had) expected. (!expect は主節が現在形であっても ×have expected とはならない. (⇨図①) ▶彼は昇給を期待して新車を買った In expectation of a pay raise, he bought a new car. ▶その歌手はアンコールを3回受けることを期待していた The singer anticipated getting [×to get] three encores./The singer anticipated that he would get three encores. ▶あなたからの便りを期待しています I'm looking forward to hearing [×hear] from you./I'm expecting [hoping for] a letter from you.

● 期待感 a feeling of hope.

*きたい 気体 图 (a) gas; (蒸気) vapor. ―― 気体の 形 gaseous, (空気の) aerial.

きたい 奇態 ―― 奇態な 形 strange.

きたい 機体 the body (of an airplane); an airframe (!エンジンを除いた機体).

きたい 希代 ―― 希代の 形 (無類の) matchless; (特別に優れた) exceptional.

きだい 季題 图 (⇨ 季語).

ぎたい 擬態 图 [生物] mimicry, [書] simulation.
―― 擬態する 動 ●葉の形に擬態する mimic [simulate] a leaf.

● 擬態語 a mimetic word.

ぎだい 議題 a subject [a topic] (for discussion); (議事日程) an agenda (!通例単数扱い). (⇨話題)
●議題にのぼる come up (for discussion); be placed [be brought up] on the agenda. ▶今日の議題は何ですか What would we discuss today? ▶次の議題に移ろう Let's go [move, pass] on to the next subject for discussion [item on the agenda].

きたえあげる 鍛え上げる ●鍛え上げた技術 well-trained skills. ●鍛え上げた身体 a well-exercised body. ▶彼は足腰を鍛え上げた He built up his leg strength to the full. ▶彼はワールドカップに備えて日本代表チームを鍛え上げた He trained the Japanese national 《soccer》 team very hard for the World Cup.

きたえる 鍛える (訓練する) train; (増強する) build ... up; (しつける) discipline, (鉄などを) forge. ●体を鍛える train [build up] one's body. ●腕の筋肉を鍛える(=つける) develop one's arm muscles. ●精神を鍛える discipline [train] one's mind. ●マラソンに備え体[彼]を鍛える train oneself [him] for the marathon. ●鉄を鍛えて鋼鉄にする forge iron into steel. ▶英語は若いうち本気で鍛えないとだめだ(=真にマスターできない) We can't truly master English, unless we really put our minds to studying it [training ourselves] when we're young.

きだおれ 着倒れ ▶京の着倒れ大阪の食い倒れ Kyoto people are too extravagant with clothing and Osaka people with food.

きたかぜ 北風 a north wind. (⇨北, 東風) ▶北風が吹いている The wind is blowing south [from the north, northerly, ×north]. (!south は「南の方へ」の意の副詞.「南から」の意では今は用いない. northerly では南風の意にもとれる)/It's a north [a northerly] wind. (!northerly は north より漠然とした方向をさす)

きたきりすずめ 着たきり雀 (説明的に) a person who has no spare clothes to wear.

きたく 帰宅 图 ●帰宅の途中で on one's [the] way home [back]. ●帰宅が遅い come home late; be late (coming) home. (⇨動)
―― 帰宅する 動 go* [come*] home (!go, come の区別は 《行く》; 《家に戻る》 return home (!やや改まった言い方); 《帰り着く》 get* home. ▶母はまもなく帰宅すると思います I think my mother will come [be] (back) home soon. (!(1) この be は come と同義. (2) come (back) to our home で可だが ×come (back) to home は不可) ▶帰宅してみると父から手紙が届いていた I got home to find a letter from my father. (!When I returned (home) [《書》 On my return] I found .... のようにもいえる) ▶彼は今日はもう帰宅しました He's gone home for the day.

きたく 寄託 图 deposition, [法] bailment.
―― 寄託する 動 deposit (it with him); entrust 《him with it; it to him》.
●寄託者 a depositor, [法] a bailor. ●寄託証書 a deposit certificate. ●寄託物 a trust.

きたぐに 北国 (国) a northern country; (地方) northern country (!無冠詞に注意) (⇨山国), a northern province [district].

きたたいせいようじょうやくきこう 北大西洋条約機構 the North Atlantic Treaty Organization 《略 NATO /néitou/》.

きたちょうせん 北朝鮮 [国名] North Korea; (公式名) the Democratic People's Republic of Korea (朝鮮民主主義人民共和国). (首都 Pyongyang)

●北朝鮮人 a North Korean. ●北朝鮮(人)の North Korean.

きたて 来たて ── 来たての 形 newly-arrived; new. ●田舎から来たての若者 a young man *fresh from* the country.

きたて 気立て ●気立てのいい娘 a *good-natured* [*sweet-tempered*, a *kind-hearted*] girl; a girl with a sweet *temper*. ▶気立てのいい娘だが、しつけがすぎる She's a *good-natured* girl [She's *good-natured*, She's *kind and helpful*], but she talks too much.

:きたない 汚い ❶ [よごれた] dirty (↔*clean*); filthy; foul /fául/; [乱雑な] untidy.

> **使い分け** **dirty** 皿・仕事・部屋・言葉などが汚いことを表す。
> **foul** 悪臭を放つほどの強烈な汚さ・不潔さを表す。
> **filthy** 胸が悪くなるほどのひどい汚さ・不潔さを表す。

●汚い手 a *dirty* hand. ●汚い台所 a *filthy* kitchen. ●汚い(=散らかった)部屋 an *untidy* [a *messy*] room. ▶その沼の水は汚い The water in [of] the swamp is *dirty* [*foul*]. ▶彼の作業服は汗と油で汚くなっていた His working clothes were *dirty* with sweat and oil. ●白い靴はすぐ汚くなる White shoes get *dirty* quickly.

❷ [卑劣な] mean; (不正な) unfair, dirty; (けちな) [話・けなして] stingy. (⇨卑劣) ●汚い金 *dirty* money. ▶彼は権力の地位を得るため汚い手段を使った He used *unfair* means to obtain his position of power. ▶彼を汚い手でだますのはよくない It is not good to play a *mean* [a *dirty*] trick on him. ▶彼は金には大変汚い He's very *stingy* [*mean*] *with* his money.

❸ [下品な] (上品でない) indécent; (みだらな) dirty; (低俗な) vulgar. ▶そんな汚い言葉を遣ってはいけません Don't use such *dirty* [*vulgar*] words. /(汚い言葉遣いをやめろ) Stop [Quit] swearing!

きたまくら 北枕 ●北枕で寝る sleep with one's pillow [head] (toward the) north.

ぎだゆう 義太夫 *gidayu* (reciting); (説明的に) a dramatic recitation accompanied on the *samisen*.

ギタリスト a guitarist.

きたる 来たる(べき) 形 [次の] next; [来たるべき] coming. ●来たる日曜(日に) this *coming* Sunday; *next* Sunday. (⚠ 後の方は「来週の」の意味もある (⇨次に)) ●来たる選挙 the *coming* [*forthcoming*, (間近にせまった) *upcoming*] election.

きたん 忌憚 ●忌憚(=遠慮)のない(=率直な)意見 a *frank* [a *candid*] opinion. ●忌憚なく(=歯に衣着せぬ)批評 *outspoken* [*frank*, (遠慮のない) *honest*] criticism. ●忌憚なく(=腹蔵(ぞう)なく)話す speak *without reserve* [*frankly*, *candidly*].

きだん 気団 [気象] an air mass. ●寒[暖]気団 a cold [a warm] *air mass*.

きだん 奇談 a strange story [tale].

*****きち 基地** a base, (海軍の) a station. ●軍事[海軍, 空軍, 燃料補給]基地 a military [a naval; an air; a fueling] *base*. ●普天間基地 *Futemma Air Station* [*Base*].

きち 吉 *kichi*; good luck [fortune]. (⇨御神籤(おみくじ))

きち 危地 a dangerous place; a critical situation; danger. ●危地に陥っている be in *danger*. ●危地を脱する get out of *danger*.

きち 既知 ── 既知の 形 (already) known. ●既知数 [数学] a known quantity; a known.

きち 機知 wit. ●機知に富む言葉 a *witty* remark [*comment*]. ▶彼は機知に富んだ人だ He is a man *of wit*./He is very *witty* [*full of wit*].

きちがい 気違い [『精神障害』の差別語] ●精神 気違い沙汰 (⇨狂気)

きちく 鬼畜 a brute; a fiend. ●鬼畜のように残忍な brutal; fiendish.

きちじつ 吉日 a lucky [(書) an auspicious] day.

きちじょう 吉祥 ●吉祥天 *Kichijoten*, the goddess of happiness and wealth.

きちっと(した) (⇨きちんと)

きちゃく 帰着 ── 帰着する 動 [『帰り着く』] return (home) (⇨帰る); [『議論が行き着く』] arrive at (an agreement [a decision]); (つまるところ...になる) boil down to .... ▶結局金の問題に帰着した It all *boiled down to* money matters in the end.

きちゅう 忌中 (in) mourning. (⇨喪(も))

きちゅう 機中 ⇨機内

きちょう 帰朝 ── 帰朝する 動 return from abroad. (⇨⚤ 帰国)

きちょう 記帳 名 [帳簿などに記載] (an) entry; [名前・出来事などの記録(表)] a register; [署名] a signature.

── 記帳する 動 ●支出を会計簿に記帳する *make an entry of* [(書) *enter*] expenses in the account book. ●宿帳に記帳する *register* [*write* one's *name*] at a hotel; *sign* a hotel register.

きちょう 基調 [基本的な傾向] the keynote; the basic tone [theme]. ▶...の基調をなす form the *keynote* [*basis*] of .... ●基調演説 (give) a keynote speech [address].

きちょう 貴重 ── 貴重な 形 (価値があり失いたくない) precious; (価値があり有益な) valuable; (非常に貴重な) invaluable. ▶私のことで貴重なお時間を無駄にしていただきたくありません Please don't waste your *precious* [*valuable*] time on my account. ▶平和ほど貴重なものはない There's nothing more *precious* than [nothing as *precious* as] peace. ▶彼の忠告は私たちの研究にきわめて貴重なものであった His advice was *invaluable* [*most valuable*] to our research.

●貴重品 valuable things; valuables. ●貴重品保管ボックス a safe [a safety] deposit box.

きちょう 機長 a (flight) captain. (⚠ 呼びかけにも用いる。また肩書では *Captain* Aoyama のようにいう)

ぎちょう 議長 a chair, a chairperson, a chairman (複 -men). (⚠ 男女兼用。特に女性をさすときは chairwoman (複 -women), 以前は男女差を解消するchairpersonが好まれたが、今は単に chair が好まれる。呼びかけは(男性)Mr. Chairman, (女性) Ms. [Madam] Chairperson; (衆議院・英米下院の) the Speaker; (参議院・英米上院の) the President. ●議長を務める be in [take] the *chair* (*at* a meeting); chair [(書) preside at] (a meeting); act as *chairman* [*chairwoman*]. ●彼を議長に選ぶ elect him (as [to be]) *chairman*; choose him as [for, to be] *chairman*. (⚠ chairman は無冠詞) ●議長のお許しを得てべさせていただきます With the *Chair(man)*'s permission, let me make a point here.

きちょうめん 几帳面 ── 几帳面な 形 (整然とした) methodical; (細かい点まで徹底した) thorough /θɑ́rə/; (*in*, *about*); (正確無比の) precise; (厳密な) exact; (時間厳守の) punctual. ●几帳面な人 a person *of method*; a *methodical* person. ●几帳面にセリフを覚える memorize one's lines *exactly*.

*****きちんと** ❶ [物事が整然として] (小ぎれいに) neatly, tidily; (整然と) orderly; (正しく) properly. ●きちんとした服装をしている be *neatly* dressed. ●きちんと(=背筋を伸ばして)座る sit up *straight*. ▶彼らは本を棚に

きちんと並べた They *neatly* arranged the books on the shelves. ▶彼女は机をきちんとしておくのがだった She liked to keep her desk *neat* [*tidy, in order*]. ▶彼女は部屋を元のとおりにきちんと整理した She *cleared up* [《英》*tidied* (*up*)] the room as it had been. ▶この窓はきちんと閉まらない This window doesn't shut *properly*.

❷【定まって】regularly; 〈変わることなく〉invariably;〈必ず〉without fail. (⇨必ず) ▶猫はきちんと夕方ねこをもらいに来る The cat comes for food *regularly* in the evening. ▶彼は決まれきちんと朝8時に家を出る He *invariably* [〈常に〉*always*] leaves home at eight in the morning.

❸【正確に】exactly, precisely. ▶彼は何日かはきちんと言わなかった He didn't say *exactly* what day it was. ▶彼は言葉をきちんと遣う He likes to use his words *precisely*.

❹【まともに】decently. ▶今きちんとしていないので、入って来ないで Don't come in as I am not *decently* dressed. ▶きちんとした格好(今人前に出られる様子をしていない)も決まり文句}

❺【その他の表現】▶あの人は非常にきちんとした人だ He [She] is a highly *organized* person.

きちんやど 木賃宿 a cheap inn;《米話》a flop-house,《英話》a dosshouse.

*****きつい** 厖 【強烈な】strong; intense;【厳しい】hard; severe;〈非情な〉harsh;【厳格な】stern; strict;【窮屈な】tight; close;【鋭い】sharp.

① 【きつい〜】▶きつい酒 *strong* [*hard*] liquor. ▶きつい仕事 *hard* [*tough, exhausting*] work. ▶きついスケジュール a *tight* [a *heavy, a full, a busy,* ×a *hard*] schedule. ▶〈気のきつい女 a *strong-minded* woman. ▶きつい顔をする look *stern*. ▶きついことを言う say *harsh* things 《*about*》. ▶彼はきつい調子で話した He spoke in a *harsh* tone.

② 【…が[は]きつい】▶目つきがきつい have *sharp* eyes. ▶この靴はきつい These shoes *pinch* [*are too tight*, 〈小さすぎる〉*are too small*]. ▶今日は日差しがきつい There is *too much* sun today. ▶何ときついつ言葉だ What a *cutting* remark! ▶この辺は川の流れがきつい The current is *rapid* around here. ▶山の北斜面は勾配がきつい The hill is a *steep* [a *sharp*] slope on the north side. 【会話】「このズボンはウエストが少しきついです」「それでは一つ上のサイズをお持ちします」"These pants are a bit too *tight* around the waist." "OK, I'll get you one size larger."

—**きつく** 副 〈激しく〉hard; severely;〈しっかりと〉tight(ly); hard;〈厳しく〉strictly. ▶きつく叱る tell 《him》off *severely* [*bitterly*]; give 《him》a *good telling-off*. ▶きつく握る grip 《it》*tightly* [*hard*]. ▶そんなきつく当たるなよ Don't be so *hard* on me.

きつえん 喫煙 图 smoking. ▶間接喫煙 passive [involuntary, second-hand] smoking. ▶喫煙は健康に悪い *Smoking* is bad for your [the] health. ▶喫煙席と禁煙席とどちらになさいますか Would you like *smoking* or non-*smoking*?

—**喫煙する** 動 smoke.
▶喫煙コーナー a smóking àrea. ▶喫煙室 a smóking ròom. ▶喫煙車 a smóking càr.

きつおん 吃音 a stammer, a stutter.

きっかい 奇怪 (⇨奇怪)

きづかい 気遣い (⇨心配) ▶無用の気遣い needless *worry*. ▶気遣いをする show *concern* 《*for* his health》. ▶私のことは気遣い無用です There's no need to [You don't have to] *worry about* me.

きづかう 気遣う worry 《*about*》, be worried 《*about*》, be concerned 《*about, for*》. (⇨心配する) ▶我々はその子の安否を気遣った We *were concerned for* the safety of the child.

きっかけ 【手始め】a start, a beginning;〈誘因〉a trigger;【好機】a chance, (an) opportunity;【手掛かり】a clue. ▶ふとしたきっかけで by mere [pure, sheer] *chance*. ▶本当のことを言うきっかけを失う miss a *chance to* tell the truth. ▶問題解決のきっかけがつかめない get [find] a *clue to* the problem [*for solving the problem*]. ▶それがきっかけで彼らは親友になった That *started* a firm friendship between them. ▶その事故が大規模なデモのきっかけとなった(=誘発した) The incident *triggered* a large demonstration.

きっかり 〈正確に〉precisely, exactly. ▶彼はきっかり6時に帰ってくる He comes home *precisely* [*exactly*] at six./He gets home at six *sharp* [《話》*on the dot*].

きつかれ 気疲れ 图 mental fatigue /fəti:g/.
—**気疲れする** 動 be mentally tired [《書》fatigued].

きっきょう 吉凶 good or bad luck; good or bad [ill] fortune. ▶吉凶を占う tell a person's *fortune*.

キック a kick.

> 関連 いろいろなキック: インステップキック instep kick/オーバーヘッドキック overhead kick; bicycle kick/スポットキック spot kick (= penalty)/ドロップキック drop kick/パントキック punt/ヒールキック heel kick/プレースキック place kick.

*****きづく** 気付く 〖見て、感じて〗notice, become* aware 《*of*》;〈秘密・企みなどに〉get* wise 《*to*》;〈じっくり観察して〉observe;〖自覚して〗become conscious 《*of*》;〖知る〗find* … (out);〖発見する〗discover;〖実感する・分かる〗realize;〖感じつく〗sense;〖思いつく〗think* of …. ▶すでにお気づきのとおり as you *have noticed*, as you already *know*. ▶彼は交通標識に気づかなかった He didn't *notice* the traffic signs. ▶私は彼がにっこりする[している]のに気づいた I *noticed* him smile [smiling]. (❗ notice の対象となる原形動詞は持続性のものに限る: I noticed him taking [×take] a nap.) ▶彼女は自分の誤りに十分気づいています She *is* well *aware of* [fully *realizes*] her mistake./She *is* well *aware* [fully *realizes*] that she is mistaken. ▶警察はそのグループの襲撃計画に気づいてアジトを手入れした The police *became aware of* [《話》*got wise to*] the group's assault plot and made a raid on their hideout. ▶私は隣の部屋にだれかいるのに気づいていた I *was conscious* that somebody was in the next room. ▶私は財布がなくなっているのに気づいた I *found* my wallet gone [missing]./I *found* [*discovered*] that my wallet was gone [missing]. ▶彼は危険に気づき逃げた He *sensed* [*suspected*] danger and ran away. ▶だれにも気づかれずに高志は立ち去った Takashi left *unnoticed*./Takashi *was* not *noticed* walking off. (❗ 一般の感覚動詞と異なり、受身の場合 ×to walk off は通例不可)

キックオフ 图 a kíckòff;〔サッカー・ホッケー〕《話》a bully-off.
—**キックオフする** 動 kick off. (❗ イベントの開始などにも用いる: The rock festival *kicked off* on Friday. (ロックフェスティバルは金曜日に始まった))

キックターン 〔スキー〕a kick turn.

キックバック (a) kickback. ▶彼は市職員に10パーセントのキックバックを渡した He gave a 10 percent *kickback* to city officials. (⇨リベート)

キックボクシング 〖競技〗kickboxing.

ぎっくりごし ぎっくり腰 〘get〙 a strained back, a slipped disk. ▶彼はまたぎっくり腰をやった He has got a strained back [put his back out] again.

きつけ 気付け 〖正気づけること〗recovering [regaining] consciousness; coming to [regaining] one's senses; 〖薬〗(アルコール飲料) a restorative, a pick-me-up; (かぎ薬) smelling salts; (興奮剤) a stimulant, a tonic.

きつけ 着付け 图 dressing.
— **着付け(を)する** 動 ▶花嫁の着付けをする *help* a bride (to) *dress up* for the wedding ceremony.
● **着付け教室** (説明的に) a *kimono* (Japanese clothes) school that teaches how to wear a kimono properly.

きづけ 気付 care of ...; 《米》in care of ... (略 %). (❗略記号の読み方は /kɑːrə́v/ または /síːóu/) (⇨一方 ❹)
▶それを会社気付けで彼に送る send it to him (in) *care of* his office.

きつご 吃語 (⇨吃音)

きっこう 拮抗 — **拮抗する** 動 compete (*against* [*with*]+人); vie (*with*+人; *for*+物). ▶数社が契約を取ろうと拮抗していた Several companies *were competing against* [*vying with*] each other *for* [*to*] win] the contract.
● **拮抗筋** 〖解剖〗antagonists. ● **拮抗作用** antagonism.

きっこう 亀甲 tortoiseshell; the carapace of a tortoise. (⇨亀)
● **亀甲模様** a honeycomb pattern; a hexagon-shaped pattern.

きっさき 切っ先 the point (*of* a sword [a knife]).
● 切っ先をかわす parry [ward off] the *point* (*of* a sword).

きっさてん 喫茶店 a tearoom, 《主に米》a cóffee shòp, 《英》a cóffee bàr. (❗事情 いずれも日本の喫茶店と異なり,主に軽食をとる所)

ぎっしゃ 牛車 an ox-drawn carriage.

ぎっしり (密集して) densely; (きつく) tightly; (密に) closely. ▶文字をぎっしり書く write letters *closely*. ▶香港には人がぎっしり住んでいる Hong Kong is *densely* populated. ▶今週は予定がぎっしりだ I have a *tight* [a *heavy*, a *very crowded*] schedule this week. /The schedule is *filled up* this week. ▶箱にはリンゴがぎっしり入っていた The box *was very full of* apples. ▶彼女のかばんには本がぎっしり入っている Her bag *is packed with* books. ▶ホールにはぎっしり人がいた The hall *was very crowded* [*was jam-packed*] *with* people.

キッズ 〖子どもたち〗kids; children. ▶最新のキッズファッション the latest *kids* [*children's*] fashion/ the latest fashions for children.

きっすい 生っ粋 《主に》 純粋》 ▶生っ粋の江戸っ子 a *native* [a *trueborn*, a *one hundred percent*] *Tokyoite* /tóukiouàit/.

きっすい 喫水 《略》draft, 《主に英》draught. ● 喫水の浅い[深い]船 a ship of shallow [deep] *draft*.
● **喫水線** the waterline.

きっする 喫する suffer. ● 惨敗を喫する *suffer* a crushing [complete, thorough] defeat. ● 三振を喫する strike out; get struck out. ● ホームランを喫する give up [allow] a home run.

きつぜん 屹然 ● 屹然(として) toweringly. ● 屹然そびえ立つ高峰 a *towering* mountain.

きっそう 吉相 (人相) a good physiognomy /fizi-ágnəmi/; (前兆) (⇨吉兆).

きったはった 切った張った ▶テレビで切った張ったの場面が多い There is lots of *violence* on TV. ▶口論が高じて切った張ったのけんかになった The quarrel escalated into *a violent brawl*.

ぎっちょ (⇨囫 左利き)

きっちょう 吉兆 a good [a lucky] omen; 〖書〗a good [a lucky] augury.

きっちり (しっかりと) tight(ly); (正確に) precisely, exactly; (正しく) properly. (⇨きちんと, きっちり) ▶戸をきっちり閉めてください Close the door *tightly*. The cold air will come in. ▶彼は仕事をきっちり(=正しく)しないと満足しない He is never satisfied with his work unless it is *properly* done. ▶私の父はきっちり7時に帰ってきます My father comes home *exactly* [*precisely*] at seven./My father gets home at seven *sharp* [〘話〙 *on the dot*]. ▶彼はきっちり時間を守る He is *very punctual*. ▶この箱にきっちり靴が3足はいる(=箱の大きさが3足の靴にちょうどよい) This box is *just* large enough for three pairs of shoes.

ぎっちり (⇨ぎっしり)

キッチン 〖台所〗a kitchen.
● **キッチンキャビネット** 〖台所用食器棚〗a kitchen cabinet. ● **キッチンドリンカー** an alcoholic housewife. ● **キッチンペーパー** (a roll of) kitchen paper; a kitchen roll. ● その1枚は a piece of kitchen paper [roll] という. ● **キッチンユニット** a kitchen unit.

『**キッチン**』 *Kitchen*. (〖参考〗吉本ばななの小説)

きつつき 啄木鳥 〖鳥〗a wóodpècker.

きって 切手 a (postage) stamp. ● 記念切手 a commemorative (postage) stamp. ● 切手をはった封筒 a *stamped* envelope. ▶切手を収集することが私の唯一の趣味です Collecting *stamps* is my only hobby. ▶手紙に切手をはり忘れてはいけません Don't forget to *stamp* your letter./Remember to put [stick] a *stamp* on your letter. ▶80 円切手を10枚ください I'd like (to get) ten 80-yen *stamps*, please. (❗単に Ten 80-yen stamps, please. ともいえる) ▶この手紙は切手不足です This letter is insufficiently *stamped*. ▶日本への(手紙の)切手代はいくらですか What's the *postage* (for a letter) *to* Japan?
● **切手シート** a sheet of stamps. ● **切手収集** stamp(-)collecting. ● **切手収集家** a stamp collector. ● **切手帳** a stamp album.

−きっての −切っての ▶クラス切っての美人 the *most beautiful* girl in the class.

きっと 〖確かに〗surely, certainly; (きっと...する) be sure [certain] to (do); 〖間違いなく〗without fail (⇨必ず❶); [...に違いない] must (do) (❗do は通例状態を表す動詞); 〖十中八九〗probably (⇨多分).
▶あしたはきっと晴れるだろう I'm sure 〘話〙 I bet] (that) it will be nice weather tomorrow. (❗that は省略されることが多い)/It will *surely* [〘X It must〙] be nice weather tomorrow. (❗must は話し手の現在の確信を表し,純粋な未来の判断に用いるのは不自然)/It is *sure* [*certain*] to be nice weather tomorrow. ▶きっと彼は知っているに違いない *Surely* he *must* know. (❗surely と must を併用することによって話し手の確信を表す) (⇨会話 〖第2例〗)
〘会話〙 「彼は申し訳ないという気持ちでいっぱいなのです」「きっとそうでしょうね」"He's full of apologies." "He *certainly* [*surely*, 〘話〙 *sure*] is./I [*I'll*] *bet* (疑いなく) *No doubt*] he is./*Probably* (so)."
〘会話〙 「友子は眠そうな顔をしてるね」「きっと疲れているよ[きのうの晩夜ふかしをしたのよ]」 "Tomoko looks

きっと sleepy." "She *múst* be tired [have stayed up late last night]." (⚠この意のmustには通例強勢を置く)
会話「出かけるときにはガスを止めてね」「うん、分かった」「本当に？止めにしていいのね」「もちろん、きっと止めてくったら」"Will you turn off the gas when you leave?" "Yes, I will." "Really? Can I rely on you?" "Absolutely! *I promise* I'll turn it off." (⚠I'll turn it off, (I) promise. のように文尾にも用いる。また、独立して I promise that. ということもある。強い言い回しを与えて相手を安心させる言い方)

きっと [鋭く] *sharply*; [きびしく] *sternly*. ●彼をきっとにらむ look *sharply* [*sternly*, *hard*] at him; give him a *sharp* [a *stern*, a *hard*] look. ●彼の言葉に彼女はきっとなった(=表情が硬くなった) Her face *hardened* at his words.

キット a kit. ●裁縫[救急]キット a séwing [a first-aid] *kit*. ●模型帆船組み立てキット a model sail-boat *kit*.

キッド [子ヤギの革] kid (leather).

きつね 狐 〖動物〗(特に、雄)a fox (愛〜es; 〖集合的〗〜); (雌)a vixen; (子)a cub. ●きつねの(毛皮の)襟巻き a *fox*-fur muffler.
● きつねにつままれる ●彼はきつねにつままれたような(=困った)顔をしていた He had a *puzzled* expression on his face./He looked *puzzled*.
● 狐色 (light) brown. ●きつね色になるまで炒める fry it until it is golden brown. ●狐蕎麦 ⦅ǎ⦆(a bowl of) buckwheat noodles with deep-fried *tofu*.
● 狐付き, 狐憑き〔事〕 fox possession; (人) a person possessed by a fox. ●狐の嫁入り 'the fox's wedding', a monkey's birthday; (雨がふるのに) a shower in the sunshine. 狐火 (鬼火) a will-o'-the-wisp; (菌類の燐光⦅ǎ⦆) foxfire.

きっぱり *flatly*; (明確に) *definitely*; (決定的に) *decisively*; (断固として) *firmly, resolutely*; (最終的に) *once and for all*. ▶彼女は彼の申し込みをきっぱり断わった She *flatly* rejected [turned down] his proposal. ▶「ええ、間違いありません」と彼はきっぱり言った "Yes, I'm sure," he said *definitely* [*firmly*]. ▶彼女はきっぱりと彼と別れることを決めた She made up her mind to part with him *once and for all*.

きっぷ 切符 a ticket; (切り取り式の) a coupon. ●片道切符 (米) a one-way *ticket*, (英) a single *ticket*. ●往復切符 (主に米) a round-trip *ticket*, (主に英) a return *ticket*. (⚠return *ticket*は米英ともに「帰りの切符」の意でも用いる)●音楽会[試合]の切符 a concert [a game] *ticket*; a *ticket* for a concert [*to* a game]. (⚠これらの「前売りの切符」(=前売券)」は an advance *ticket*) ●交通[スピード; 駐車]違反切符 (get) a tráffic [a spéeding; a párking] *ticket*. ●後の二つは *a ticket for speeding* [*parking*] も可. ●割引切符 a cheap ticket; a discount [a cut-price] ticket. ●切符を切る punch [clip] a *ticket*. ●東京までの切符を買う buy a *ticket to* [*for*] Tokyo. ▶6時30分のショーの切符を2枚ください Two *tickets for* [×to, ×of] the 6:30 show, please. ▶切符を拝見します Can I just see your *ticket*?
● 切符売り場 (駅の) (米) a tícket óffice, (英) a bóoking óffice; (駅の窓口の) a tícket window; (空港などのカウンター式の) a tícket cóunter; (劇場やスタジアムなどの) a bóx óffice. ●切符販売機 a tícket machine.

きっぷ 気っ風 ●きっぷがいい be generous (with). (⇨気前) ▶貧しい人たちにそんな大金を寄付するとは君はきっぷがいいね It is *generous* of you to make a huge donation to poor people.

きっぽう 吉報 ●吉報をもたらす bring ⦅him⦆ *good* ⦅*happy, glad*⦆ *news*.

きづまり 気詰まり ▶彼女といると何となく気詰まりだ I feel a little *ill at ease* with her./I feel somewhat *awkward* when I'm with her.

きつもん 詰問 图 close questioning; (a) cross-examination. ●詰問調で言う say in a *cross-questioning* tone.
──**詰問する** 動 question ⦅him⦆ closely; demand an explanation ⦅*from* [*of*] him⦆; cross-examine. ▶「それはルール違反です。お分かりですか」彼はキャディに詰問した "It's against the rules. You know that, don't you?" He *demanded* of the caddy. (⚠demand (an answer) of him の ( ) 内を省略したもの)

きづよい 気強い (安心な) secure; (意志の強い) strong-minded.

きつりんしょう 吉林省 〖中国の省〗 Jilin /dʒiːlín/ Province.

きてい 規定 图 〖規則〗a rule; (公の) a regulation (⇨規比); 〖条規〗〖法律〗a provision; (契約などの) 〖書〗 a stipulation. ●そのクラブの会員規定 the club's *rules for* membership. ●第9条の規定に触れる政策 a policy which contradicts the *provisions* of Article 9 [what Article 9 *prescribes*]. ●それを禁止する政府の規定がある There is a government *regulation* which prohibits it.
──**規定する** 動 provide; (契約などで) 〖書〗 stipu-late; 〖命ずる〗〖書〗 require; 〖指示する〗〖書〗 pre-scribe. ▶規約には会長がそれをしなければならないと規定されている The rule *provides* [*requires*] *that* the president (*should*) do it. (⚠should を用いるのは ⦅主に英⦆. that は通例省略不可)
● 規定種目 ⦅米⦆ required exercises, ⦅英⦆ com-pulsory exercises. ●規定打席数 〖野球〗 the required number of plate appearances.
● 規定料金 the regulation [明示された] stated] charge.

きてい 既定 ── 既定の 形 established. ●既定の方針 an *established* policy.

きてい 基底 a base; a foundation.

ぎてい 義弟 〖義理の弟〗 a brother-in-law (愛〜s, brothers-). (⇨兄弟 ❶ ①)

ぎていしょ 議定書 a protocol.

きてき 汽笛 a whistle; (船の) a siren. ●汽車の汽笛 the *whistle* of a locomótive. ●汽笛を鳴らす blow a *whistle*; whistle; sound a *siren*. ▶汽笛が鳴った The *whistle* blew./The *siren* sounded.

きてれつ 奇天烈 ── 奇天烈な 形 ●奇妙きてれつな日本語 *extremely strange* [*funny*] Japanese.

きてん 起点 the stárting pòint.

きてん 基点 a cardinal [a basic, a fundamental] point. ●方位基点 the cardinal points of the compass.

きてん 機転 wit (「理解力, 思考力」の意では複数形で); 〖人の気をそらさない如才なさ〗 tact. ●機転がきく have a ready [a quick] *wit*; be tactful. ●機転のきいた返事をする give a *witty* [a *tactful*] reply.
● 機転をきかせてその問題を切り抜ける use one's *wits* [頭脳] brain(s), head] to get around the prob-lem.

ぎてん 儀典 the rules of a ceremony.

きと 企図 (⇨計画, 企て)

きと 帰途 ●帰途につく start on one's way back ⦅*to* Japan⦆; start back ⦅*for*⦆. ●香港から帰途につく leave Hong Kong *for home*.

きどあいらく 喜怒哀楽 feelings; an emotion (⚠前

きとう の語より強い感情を表す). ▶喜怒哀楽を表す show one's *feelings* [*emotions*]. ▶彼女は喜怒哀楽がとても激しい She is a very *emotional* woman.

きとう 気筒 a cylinder. ▶6気筒のエンジン[車] a six-*cylinder* engine [car].

きとう 祈祷 图 prayer /préər/; 〖食前食後の〗(a) grace. (⇨祈り)
― **祈祷する 動** pray; say* one's prayers.
▶祈祷師 (原始宗教の) a shaman; (悪魔払いの) an exorcist; (信仰療法の) a faith healer. ▶祈祷書 a práyer bòok.

きどう 軌道 ❶ 〖線路〗 a track. (⇨線路) ▶軌道を敷く lay a *track*.
❷ 〖天体・人工衛星の〗(an) orbit. ▶月の軌道 the *orbit* of the moon. ▶軌道修正をする make an *orbit* [a *course*] correction. ▶気象衛星を地球を回る軌道に乗せる [*launch*] a weather satellite *in* [*into*] *orbit* around the earth.
▶軌道に乗る ▶計画を軌道に乗せる put a plan on *track*. ▶私たちの計画は軌道に乗っている Our plans *are running smoothly* [*well under way*]./Our plans *have got into gear* [〖話〗*got into the swing of things*, (うまくいき始める)(話) *been taking off*]./We *have got* our plans *in gear*. (❗後の二つの例のように get(...) into gear は物も人も主語にできる)

きどう 起動 图 starting.
― **起動する 動** start〖a car [an engine]〗(up);〖コンピュータ〗boot up. ▶再起動する reboot.
▶起動装置 a starter. ▶起動力 motive power.

きどうしゃ 気動車 an internal combustion railcar.

きどうたい 機動隊 the riot police (❗複数扱い); a riot squad (❗単・複両扱い).

きどうらく 着道楽 〖事〗love of (fine) clothes; 〖人〗a lover of (fine) clothes.

きどうりょく 機動力 〖軍隊〗mobility. ▶機動力のある mobile /móubl/. ▶機動力のあるチーム a team well-organized for quick and efficient action; (野球の) a track team. ▶うちのチームは機動力を重視している We think it important to *do our job quickly* [*effectively*].

きとく 危篤 ▶危篤に陥る fall into (a) *critical condition*. ▶彼は危篤だ He is in (a) *critical condition*./His *condition* is *critical*./He is *critically sick*./ 《話》He's *on* (↔*off*) *the danger list*. ▶熱が下がって彼の病状はようやく危篤状態を脱した His fever had gone and his illness was just past *the critical stage* (*where he might die*).

きとく 奇特 ― **奇特な 形** (賞賛に値する) (やや書) praiseworthy, (書) commendable. ▶なかなか奇特なことをする人だ What he has done is very *praiseworthy*.

きとくけん 既得権 a vested right [interest]. ▶既得権を守る[侵す] protect [violate] *vested rights*.

きどぐち 木戸口 an entrance. (⇨入り口)

きどる 気取る be affected; 〖もったいぶる〗put* on airs, give* oneself airs; 〖見せかけてふるまう〗pose 《as》, act 《*as if* 節》. ▶気取った態度で in an *affected* manner. ▶そんなに気取るな Don't *be so affected*./Don't *put on airs* like that. ▶彼は気取ったものの言い方をする He speaks *in an affected way* [*affectedly*]. (⇨気障(毳)) ▶彼は学者気取りでいる He *poses as* a scholar. ▶He *acts as if* he were 〖話〗*was*] a scholar. ▶まあ、急にいっぱしの作家気取りか Oh, so suddenly you're the expert writer. (❗文脈に依存し、対応する訳語を示さなくてよいこともある)

きどるい 希土類 〖化学〗(元素) a rare-earth element; (金属) a rare-earth metal.

きない 機内 ▶機内に on [in] an airplane. ▶申し訳ありませんが、そのかばんは機内へお持ち込みができません I'm sorry but you aren't allowed to carry the bag *on* [*into*] *the plane*.
▶機内食 an in-flight meal. ▶機内持ち込み手荷物 carry-on luggage; 《米》a carry-on.

きなが 気長 ― **気長に 副** 〖忍耐強く〗patiently; 〖急がずに〗without hurry [haste]; 〖のんびりと〗at leisure; 〖ゆっくり〗slowly. ▶気長に待つ wait *patiently* [*with patience*].

きながし 着流し ▶着流しで 〖go out〗 in casual [in an informal] *kimono*; casually dressed; with no *hakama* on.

きなくさい きな臭い ▶きな臭いにおいがする *smell* something *burning*; 《比喩的》It looks as if war is imminent [*impending*]. (❗名詞の前につけて impending war(さし迫っている戦争)は可)

きなこ 黄な粉 soybean flour.

きなり 生成り unbleached [undyed] cotton [hemp].

きなん 危難 (a) danger; (a) peril. (⇨危険)

ギニア 〖国名〗Guinea /gíni/; (公式名) the Republic of Guinea. (首都 Conakry) ▶ギニア人 a Guinean. ▶ギニア(人)の Guinean.

ギニアビサウ 〖国名〗Guinea-Bissau /gìni-bisáu/; (公式名) the Republic of Guinea-Bissau. (首都 Bissau) ▶ギニアビサウ人 a Guinea-Bissauan. ▶ギニアビサウ(人)の Guinea-Bissauan.

キニーネ 〖薬学〗quinine /kwáinain/.

きにいり 気に入り (⇨お気に入り)

きにいる 気に入る (好きである) like; (満足する) be pleased 《*with*》; (非常に満足する) be delighted 《*with*》. ▶こんなこと言うと気に入らないでしょうが、ぼくは今はだれとも結婚する気にはなれないのです I know you won't *like* me saying so, but I'm not up to marrying anyone at the moment.

会話 「うーん、このケーキは最高」「気に入っていただいてよかった」 "Mmm! This cake is superb!" "I'm glad you *like it*." (❗Did you really like it?(本当に気に入っていただけたか)では控えめで丁寧な応答になる)

会話 「いいお宅ですね」「ありがとう. 私どもも気に入っているんですよ」 "You have a very lovely house." "Thank you. We *like it*, too."

会話 「新しい仕事が気に入っていますか」「それはもう」 "*Are* you *pleased* [*happy*, *satisfied*] *with* your new job?" "Very."

きにする 気にする (気にかける) care 《*about*》(❗通例否定文・疑問文で); mind (❗通例否定文・疑問文で); (心配する) worry 《*about*》. ▶私のすることなどだれも全然気にしてないもの. おかげで気楽な No one *cares* a bit [〖話〗*could care less*] what I do [×will do]. That makes me feel at ease. ▶彼は身なりを気にする[気にしない] He is particular about [doesn't *care about*, *is careless about*] his appearance. ▶人はあなたが思うほどあなたのことを気にしていない(=注目していない)ものです Nobody *takes* as much *notice of* you as you think.

会話 (相手の服をよごしてしまって)「キャー、どうしよう! ごめん、あなたのブラウス台無しにしちゃった」「いいのよ、気にしないで. どうせクリーニングしなくちゃならなかったの」 "Oops! Oh, no. I'm so sorry, I've just ruined your blouse." "That's all right. Never *mind*. It needed to be cleaned anyway." (❗×Don't mind. とはいわない)

会話 「彼女がパーティーに行かないと言っていたけど気にしないでね」「全然、大丈夫よ」 "I hope this won't *upset* you, she said she was not coming to your party." "No, not a bit."

きにゅう 記入 图 (an) entry. (⇨記載)
● 記入済み 《表示》 Entered.
― **記入する** 動 ● ペンで申し込み用紙に記入する *fill in [out]* an application form in pen. ● 空欄に氏名を記入する *fill in [out]* the blank with one's name; *fill in* one's name; write one's name in the blank (space).

きにん 帰任 ― **帰任する** 動 《任地に帰る》 return to [resume] one's place of work 《(公務に) official duties》.

きぬ 絹 silk; 《絹地》 silk cloth. ● 絹のドレス a *silk* dress. ● 絹のような髪 *silky* hair. ● 絹の服を着ていること be dressed in *silk*(s).
● **絹を裂くよう** ▶女は絹を裂くような声をあげた She gave [let out] *a piercing shriek*.
● 絹糸 silk thread; 《織物用》 silk yarn. ● 絹織物 silk fabrics, silk goods, silks.

きぬけ 気抜け ― **気抜けする** 動 《人が》 feel* deflated; 《話》 lose* one's steam; 《飲料が》 go* flat. (⇨気 ❺)

きぬごし(どうふ) 絹漉し(豆腐) silk bean curd; (説明的に) the smooth bean curd formed directly from soy milk.

きぬずれ 衣擦れ 《音》 the rustle [the rustling] 《of silk》. ▶絹のロングドレスを着たメアリーが歩くと衣擦れの音がした Mary's long silk dress *rustled* as she moved.

きね 杵 a mallet. ● 杵で餅をつく pound steamed rice into rice cake with a *mallet*.

『ギネスブック』 *The Guinness Book of Records*. 《参考》英国のビール会社が毎年発行する, さまざまな世界一の記録を集めた本。

きねずみ 木鼠 《『リス』の別称》《動物》 a squirrel.

きねづか 杵柄 ● 昔取った杵柄で, 今もテニスくらいできるよ Although I'm out of practice, I still can play tennis. ▶さすが, 昔取った杵柄だね You never lose your touch!

きねん 記念 图 commemoration; 《覚えておくこと》 memory; remembrance. (⚠通例 in memory [remembrance] of ... の熟語で用いる) ▶旅行の記念にこの航空券をとっておこう I'll keep this air ticket as a *souvenir* of my trip. ▶永年勤続の記念として彼は金時計を授与された He was awarded a gold watch *in token of* his long years of service.
― **記念の** 形 commemorative; memorial; 《記念すべき》 memorable.
― **記念する** 動 《式などを挙げて祝う》 celebrate. ▶オリンピックを記念して新しい硬貨が発行された They issued new coins to *commemorate [in commemoration of*, 《祝って》 *in celebration of*] the Olympic Games.
● 記念館 a memorial hall. ● 記念切手 a commemorative stamp. ● 記念行事 a memorial event. ● 記念硬貨 a commemorative coin. ● 記念祭 a commemoration; a memorial (festival). ● 記念写真 a souvenir picture [phòto]. ● 記念乗車券 a commemorative ticket. ● 記念碑 a monument; a memorial. (⚠例えば a monument to (the memory of) [in memory of] Shakespeare, the Washington Monument のように用いる) ● 記念日 a memorial day; 《例年の》 an anniversary. (⚠「結婚記念日」は one's wedding anniversary) ● 記念品 《旅などの》 a souvenir (⇨土産); 《記念のしるし》 a token; 《友や出来事などの思い出となるちょっとしたもの》 a memento; 《古》 a remembrance.

きねん 祈念 图 (a) prayer. (⇨祈り) ― **祈念する** 動 pray. (⇨祈る)

ぎねん 疑念 图 (a) doubt. ● 疑念をいだく have *doubts* 《*about*》. (⇨疑う ❶)

:きのう 昨日 yesterday. ▶昨日の晩 *yesterday* evening; last evening; last [Xyesterday] night. (⚠後になるほど口語的) ▶昨日は日曜だった *Yesterday* was Sunday. は Sunday *yesterday*. より普通。 ▶昨日の新聞でそれを読んだ I read it in *yesterday*'s paper. ▶彼女は「昨日公園でばったり彼に会いました」と言った She said, "I ran into him in the park *yesterday*." (⚠ yesterday を強調する場合はしばしば文頭に置かれる: Yesterday I ran ....) / She said that she had run into him in the park *the day before* [*the previous day*]. (⚠間接話法で時制の一致が行われたとき通例 yesterday は the day before か the previous day になる (⇨言う ❶ 解説)) ▶昨日の今ごろは何をしていましたか What were you doing about this time *yesterday*? ▶昨日は1日中家でごろごろしていた I was lazing around all day *yesterday*. (⚠Xall yesterday とはいわない) ▶よくいっしょにテニスをしたのがまるで昨日のようだ It seems like *yesterday* that we used to play tennis together. ▶昨日の敵は今日の友 (標語的に) Yesterday's foe is today's friend.
● **昨日今日** quite [only] recently. ▶昨日今日の話ではない It's *nothing new*. / It's *the same old story*.

:きのう 機能 图 a function. ● 肝(臓)の機能 the *function* of the liver; liver *function*.
― **機能的な** 形 functional.
― **機能的に** 副 ● 機能的に設備された台所 a *functionally* equipped kitchen.
― **機能する** 動 ● この装置はちゃんと機能している This system *is functioning* [*working*] well.
● 機能障害 a functional disorder. ● 機能性食品 functional food 《略 FF》; nutraceuticals.

きのう 気嚢 《鳥の》 an air sac; 《魚の》 an air bladder.

きのう 帰納 ― **帰納的な** 形 帰納的な推論 inductive reasoning.
― **帰納的に** 副 inductively. ● 帰納的に導き出す induce.
● 帰納法 induction (⇔deduction).

きのう 帰農 ― **帰農する** 動 return [go* back] to farming.
● 帰農運動 a "back-to-the-land [back-to-farming]" movement [campaign].

ぎのう 技能 《技術》 (a) (technical) skill; 《能力》 ability. (⇨技術, 能力, 技)
● 技能士 《男性》 a certified skilled craftsman; 《女性》 a certified skilled craftswoman; 《男女共用》 a certified skilled worker. ● 技能賞 the technical award [prize].

きのえ 甲 甲子(ᵏ⁽ᴺ⁾) *kinoene*, the first year of the sexagenary cycle.

きのか 木の香 the smell of (new) wood. ● 木の香も新しい家 a brand-new wooden house.

きのこ 茸 《植物》 a mushroom; (通例毒の) a toadstool. ● 森へキノコ狩りに行く go *mushrooming* [go to pick *mushrooms*] in [Xto] the woods.

きのさきにて 『城の崎にて』 *At Kinosaki*. 《参考》 志賀直哉の小説。

*****きのどく** 気の毒 图 ● その病気の老人を気の毒 (= かわいそう) に思う feel *sorry* [*pity*] *for* that sick old man. ● 気の毒に思って彼に金を貸す lend him some money *out of pity* [*sympathy*]. (⇨同情) ▶彼が両親を事故で亡くしたなんて本当に気の毒に I am very *sorry* [*残念だ*] It's a real *pity*, It's a real *shame*,

きのぼり

(話) It's really too *bad*! (*that*) he lost his parents in the accident. ■ shame is pity と口語的) ●誠にお気の毒に存じますが(=遺憾ながら),あなたの本校への入学は認められないことになりました I am truly *sorry to* inform you that we are not offering you admission to our school. (■I regret to... より普通).

会話 「ひどい風邪を引いているんです」「それはお気の毒に」 "I've caught a bad cold." "That's *too bad*./ I'm *sorry to* hear that./What a *pity* [a *shame*]"

会話 「昨ész車のキーをなくしたので家まで歩いて帰るはめになったんだ」「まあ,お気の毒に.家に着いたのは何時だったの」 "Last night I lost the car key and had to walk home." "Oh, *poor you*. What time did you get home?"

―― 気の毒な形 [かわいそうな] poor; [不幸な] unfortunate; [みじめな] miserable, 《やや古・書》wretched /rétʃid/; [哀れな] pitiful. ●気の毒な人 a *poor* [an *unfortunate*] person. ●気の毒な状況 an *unfortunate* [a *pitiful*] situation. ●気の毒な生活を送る lead a *miserable* [a *wretched*] life.

翻訳のこころ いろいろ注文が多くてうるさかったでしょう.お気の毒でした (宮沢賢治『注文の多い料理店』) You must have been quite fed up with so many requests [demands]. We apologize (for it). (■(1)「お気の毒でした」は apologize (申しありませんと言って許してこう)を表す. 「...でした」につられて apologized と過去形にしないことに注意. (2) ここでの「注文」は,この文の前後の状況から「客からの注文」でなく「店の方が客に求めた注文,要求」なので order でなく request とする)

きのぼり 木登り 图 tree climbing.
―― 木登り(を)する 動 climb (up) a tree.

きのぼりうお 木登り魚 [魚介] a climbing perch; an anabas. (参考 木には登らない)

きのみきのまま 着のみ着のまま ●着のみ着のままその場所から避難する get out of the place *with nothing but* (his) *clothes* (he wears).

きのめ 木の芽 a bud. (⇨芽)
●木の芽あえ [山椒の若芽あえ] (説明的に) a dish of vegetables or meat dressed with the mixed sauce made of *miso* and *Japanese pepper herb*.
●木の芽時 early spring when new leaves come out.

きのやまい 気の病 a (nervous) breakdown; [医学] neurosis /njʊəróusis/.

きのり 気乗り (an) inclination. (⇨乗り気) ●気乗りしない返事 a *half-hearted* answer. ●気乗りがしない feel no *inclination* (to do).

会話 「私たちは毎週日曜日にテニスをしているのよ.そのうちあなたもいっしょにいかが」「そうね,テニスはあまり気乗りしないわ」 "We play tennis every Sunday. Won't you join us sometime?" "Well, I'm not so *keen on* playing tennis."

きば 牙 [象・イノシシなどの] a tusk; [犬・狼などの] a fang. ●牙をたてる strike its *tusks* [*fangs*] 《into》. ●牙を研(と)ぐ get ready for an attack; prepare for an attack.
●牙をむく ●その犬は見知らぬ人に牙をむきだしてうなった The dog *snarled* [*growled*] *at* the stranger.

きば 木場 [米] a lumberyard, [英] a timberyard.

きば 騎馬 horseback riding; horse-riding.
●騎馬警官 a mounted policeman; (集合的) the mounted police. ●騎馬行進 a cavalcade. ●騎馬戦 a cavalry battle. ●騎馬隊員 a ranger. ●騎馬民族 a nomadic people.

きばえ 着映え ●このドレスは着映えがする This dress will *look nice* [*good*] (on you).

きはく 気迫 [気力] spirit; [やる気] drive; [決意] determination; [魂] (a) soul. (⇨気力) ●気迫のこもった顔つき a *spirited* [a *determined*] look. ●彼らには気迫がない They lack *determination and drive*.

きはく 希薄 ―― 希薄な 形 (空気などが) rare; (液体・気体が) thin (-nn-); (熱意・意識などが) little. ●高山の希薄な空気 the *rare* [*thin*] air on high mountains. ●エベレストの山頂あたりは空気が希薄である The air is *very thin* near the top of Mt. Everest. ●その問題について彼らの誠意が希薄である They are *not very sincere about* the problem.

きばく 起爆 ―― 起爆剤 priming. ●起爆剤になる (引き金になる) trigger. ●起爆装置 a trigger device.

きばさみ 木鉄 (a pair of) pruning shears.

きはずかしい 気恥ずかしい be ashamed.

きはだ 木肌 a bark.

きはだまぐろ 黄肌鮪 [魚介] a yellowfin (tuna).

きばたらき 気働き a quick and efficient.

きはつ 揮発 ―― 揮発性 图 volatility.
―― 揮発性の 形 volatile /válətl/.
●揮発油 (ナフサ) naphtha; (ガソリン) benzine; [米] gasoline, [英] petrol.

きばつ 奇抜 ―― 奇抜な 形 ●奇抜な着想 [趣向] (新考) a *novel* idea; (独創的な) an *original* idea. ●奇抜な(=風変わりな)服 *eccentric* clothes.

きばむ 黄ばむ ●その写真は年とともに黄ばんできた The picture *has yellowed* [*has been yellowed, has become yellow*] with age.

きばらし 気晴らし (娯楽) a pastime; (気分転換) 《やや書》 a diversion; (休養) (a) recreation; (息抜き) (a) relaxation. ●気晴らしに for recreation [*relaxation*]; (気分転換) for a change. ●ゴルフは父の唯一の気晴らしだ Golf is my father's only *pastime*. ●私たちは気晴らしにドライブに出かけた We went for a drive just *for a change*.

きばる 気張る ❶ [張り切る] exert oneself; make* a great effort. ❷ [気前よくお金を出す] be generous [liberal] with one's money.

* **きはん 規範** 《やや書》a norm; (目安) a standard. ●社会的規範 a social *norm*. ●道徳規範 a moral *standard*.
●規範文法 prescriptive [normative] grammar.

* **きばん 基盤** a base; a basis (趣 bases /béisi:z/); a foundation. (⇨基礎) ●基盤をなす form the *basis* [*foundation*] (*of*). ●(選挙の)支持基盤を広げる broaden one's *base* of support.

きはん 基板 [コンピュータ] (回路基板) a (printed) circuit board; (主回路) a motherboard.

きはんせん 機帆船 a motor sailer.

きひ 忌避 avoidance, (an) evasion. ●徴兵忌避 the *avoidance* of draft (主に米); [英]. ●徴兵忌避者 a draft dodger.
―― 忌避する 動 avoid, 《やや書》evade.

きび 黍 [植物] millet.
●きび団子 a millet dumpling.

きび 機微 ●人情の機微に通じている know the *subtleties* /sʌ́ltiz/ of human nature.

きびき 忌引き 图 absence oneself of mourning.
―― 忌引きする 動 absent oneself [be absent] (*from* school [*work*]) on account of a death in one's family.

きびきび (活発に) briskly; (精力的に) energetically; (能率よく) efficiently. ●きびきびした動作 a *brisk* movement. ●彼女は質問にきびきび答えた She answered the questions *energetically* [*crisp-*

ly)]. ▶その店では人々がいつもきびきび働いている They always work *briskly* [*efficiently*] in the shop.
きびしい 厳しい 形 [[厳格な]] strict; severe; stern; 《やや書》rigid; [[人・表情などが冷たく厳しい]]《やや書》austere; [[人・罰などが無情な]] harsh, hard; [[強烈な]] intense; [[緊迫した]] tense.

> **使い分け strict** 規律・規準などの厳正さ・厳守ぶりを表す.
> **severe** 裁量・情状酌量の余地を残さないような厳しさ・厳格さ・厳正さを表す.
> **stern** 厳格で容赦なく服従を求めることを表す.
> **rigid** 規則・基準などの厳格さ・厳正さを表す.

● 厳しい裁判官 a *strict* [a *severe*, a *stern*] judge. ● 厳しい規律 *rigid* [*severe*, *stern*, *rigorous*] discipline. ● 厳しい罰 a *harsh* [a *severe*] punishment. ● 冬の厳しい寒さ the *intense* [*severe*] cold of winter. ● 厳しい訓練 *hard* training. ● 厳しい経済状況 a *tense* economic situation. ▶彼は子供に厳しい He is *strict* [*severe*, *stern*, (きつい) *harsh*] with his children. (🔴厳格さの程度は severe が strict より強い)/(つらく当たる) He is *hard on* his children. ▶あなたは自分に対して厳しすぎる You're too *hard on* yourself. ▶あの先生は文法には厳しい That teacher is *strict about* [*on*] grammar. ▶今年の冬は大変厳しかった We had a very *severe* [*hard*, *harsh*] winter this year./Winter was very *severe* this year. ▶厳しい世界ですね，ビジネスの世界は It's a *hard* [*not an easy*] world, the world of business. (🔴後の方が普通) ▶厳しい顔をしていた He looked *stern* [*austere*].

—— 厳しく 副 strictly; severely; sternly; rigidly; harshly; intensely; (綿密に) closely. ● 厳しく子供を育てる bring up one's child *strictly* [*with strict discipline*]. ● 囚人を厳しく扱う deal *harshly* with a prisoner. ● 規則を厳しくする *tighten* a rule. ▶彼は不正を働いて厳しく処罰された He was *severely* [*harshly*] punished for cheating.
会話 「作品の審査はどの程度厳しくすべきでしょうか」「最高のもの以外はどれも受けつけないでください」 "How *critical* should I be in judging the works?" "Don't accept anything but the best."

きびす 踵 ● きびすを返す (引き返す) go [turn] back. ● きびすを接して very close together; one after another.
きびたき 黄鶲 [[鳥]] a narcissus flycatcher.
ぎひつ 偽筆 名 forged handwriting; (絵画) a forged [a counterfeit] picture.
—— 偽筆の 形 forged; counterfeit.
—— 偽筆する 動 forge; counterfeit.
きびなご 黍魚子 [[魚介]] a *kibinago*; a banded blue sprat
きひょう 起票 —— 起票する 動 write* a slip out.
きびょう 奇病 a rare disease.
ぎひょう 戯評 名 (漫画) a satiric(al) cartoon, a caricature; (風刺文) a lampoon, a satire, a caricature. —— 戯評する 動 satirize; lampoon.
きひん 気品 (上品) elegance; (優美) grace. ▶彼女にはどことなく気品がある There's something *elegant* [*graceful*] about her.
きびん 機敏 —— 機敏な 形 [[動作が速い]] quick; [[反応が早い]] prompt; [[動きがきびきびした]] brisk. ● 機敏に行動する act *promptly* [*take prompt action*]. ● 機敏に立ち回る (てきぱきと) be *quick* [*prompt*] in action, 《話》be on the ball; (抜け目なく) act *smartly*.
きひんせき 貴賓席 seats (reserved) for honored guests; [[皇族の]] a royal box.

*__きふ 寄付__ 名 (a) contribution ((to)); (公共福祉のための) a donation ((to)). (🔴いずれも「寄付金」の意では C) ● 寄付を募る raise *contributions*. ▶寄付は今のところあまり集まっていない The *donation* doesn't amount to much.
—— 寄付する 動 contribute; donate; (与える) give* (🔴前の 2 語より口語的). ● 難民に衣料品を寄付する *contribute* [*send*] clothing *to* [*for*] the refugees. (🔴to は直接, for は仲介者を通して) ▶彼はその慈善事業に 100 万円寄付した He *contributed* [*made a contribution of*, *donated*, *made a donation of*, *gave*] one million yen to the charity.
▶集まったお金は赤十字に寄付いたします Money received will *go to* the Red Cross.
● 寄付者 a contributor; a donor.
きふ 棋譜 a record of a game of *go* [*shogi*].
きふ 貴腐 ● 貴腐ワイン pourriture noble.
きぶ 基部 (柱などの) the base; (建物の) the foundations.
ぎふ 義父 [[配偶者の父]] a father-in-law (🈴 ～s, fathers-); [[継父]] a stepfather; [[養父]] a foster-father.
ギブアップ —— ギブアップする 動 give* (...) up; admit defeat.
ギブアンドテーク ● ギブアンドテークで on a *give-and-take* principle; by cooperation; by mutual concessions.
きふう 気風 [[全体の調子, 風潮]] a tone; [[精神]] spirit; [[性格]] (a) character, (特性)《書》a trait /tréit, (英) tréi/. ● 当時の自由な気風 the liberal *tone* [*spirit*] of the times.
きふう 棋風 one's way [one's style] of playing *go* [*shogi*].
きふく 帰服 —— 帰服する 動 submit [surrender] (oneself) ((to)). ▶ハイジャッカーは警察に帰服した The hijacker *surrendered* (*himself*) *to* the police.
きふく 起伏 [[地形の]]《やや書》undulation(s); (ゆるやかな) rolling; [[人生などの]] ups and downs. ● 起伏のある平野 a *rolling* [《やや書》an *undulating*] plain. ● 起伏に富んだ (= 丘陵の多い) 田園地方 a *hilly* countryside. ▶彼は感情の起伏が激しい He has a lot of emotional *ups and downs*.
きぶくれ 着ぶくれ —— 着ぶくれる 動 look fat with layers of clothes; be bundled up ((*in* heavy clothes)).
きふじん 貴婦人 a (noble) lady.
ギプス [＜ドイツ語] a cast; [[ギプス包帯]] a plaster cast. ● 足にギプスをはめる put a *cast* on one's leg. ▶彼は腕にギプスをはめている He has [wears] a *cast* on his arm./His arm is in a *cast*.
きぶつそん 器物破損 property damage; damage to property.
ギフト a gift, a present.
● ギフトカード [券] 《米》a gíft certíficate, 《英》a gíft tòken [còupon, vòucher]. ● ギフトショップ a gift shop.
きぶとり 着太り —— 着太りする 動 ▶彼女は着太りする (= 服を着ると太って見える) 体つきだ She has the type of figure that makes her *look plumper* (than she actually is) *when dressed*. (🔴着膨れ)
きふるす 着古す wear* out. ● 着古した old (clothes); used; (すり切れたほど古た) worn-out.
キプロス [[国名]] Cyprus /sáiprəs/; (公式名) the Republic of Cyprus. (首都 Nicosia) ● キプロス人 a Cypriot. ● キプロスの 形 Cypriot.
*__きぶん 気分__ 名 [[一時的な気分]] a mood; [[気持ち]] a ... frame [state] of mind (🔴...は形容詞); [[感情]] feeling(s); [[雰囲気]] an atmosphere. (⇨気持ち)

ぎふん

①【~気分】● 妙な気分である feel strange [funny]; be in a strange [a funny] mood. ▶金持ちになった気分だ I *feel* rich. ▶町中戦勝気分だった The whole town *was in victorious mood*.

②【気分~】▶ 気分転換に川へ泳ぎに行きましょう Let's go swimming in [x to] the river *for a change*.

③【気分に】▶ 今は勉強する気分になれない I am in no *mood* [am not *in the mood*] *to* study now./I don't *feel like* studying now. ▶これでやっと正月らしい気分になった This makes me *feel* that we are in the New Year. ▶不安な気分に襲われた A *feeling* of fear *gripped* me./I *was seized* by fear./I *had* an anxiety *attack*.

会話「音楽はどんなのがいちばん好きなの」「そのときの気分によるわ(=気分次第です)」"What do you like most about music?" "It depends on the *mood* I'm *in*."

④【気分を】● 気分を変える change one's *mood*. ● 祭りの気分を壊す[出す] destroy [create] an *atmosphere* of festivity. ● 人の気分を害してはいけません Don't *offend* other people's [others'] *feelings*./Don't *offend* other people.

会話「彼らはどうして気分を害していたんだい」「そうだな、あんなに長いこと待たなくちゃならないのが気に入らなかったんだろう」"What *upset* them?" "Well, they didn't like having to wait such a long time."

── 気分がよい[悪い] 形 〖気持ちが〗《物・事が主語》be pleasant [unpleasant] (⇨気持ちがいい); 〖体調が〗《人が主語》feel* well [sick]; feel all right [fine]. ▶風邪を引いて気分がよくない I've got a cold, and I *don't feel well* [I'm *feeling a little sick*]. ▶私は船酔いしやすいたちなの. だから船に乗るとすぐ気分が悪くなってしまうのよ I'm not a good sailor, so I'm easily *upset* [I get *sick* easily] on boats. (!upset は「気分的に混乱する」の意にもとれる)

会話「今日は気分はいかがですか」「おかげさまであの薬を飲んでからだいぶよくなりました」"How do you *feel* [How *are* you *feeling*] today?" "I've been *feeling* much *better* since I took that medicine, thank you." (!better は well の比較級)

会話「気分はいいですか」「あまりよくありません[最悪です]」"*Are* you *feeling all right*?" "No, not quite [I couldn't be worse]."

● 気分屋 a person of moods.

ぎふん 義憤 righteous indignation. ▶彼らの弱者への仕打ちに彼は強い義憤を感じた He felt really *indignant at [about]* what they had done to weak people (《やや書》).

きへい 騎兵 a cavalryman (複 -men); 《集合的》the cavalry (!「騎兵隊」の意でも用いる. 通例複数扱い).

きへき 奇癖 an eccentricity; a peculiarity; a quirk; a strange [an odd] habit.

きべん 詭弁 《書》a sophistry, a sophism. (!「詭弁をろうすること」の意では U) ● 詭弁を使って talk *sophistry*. ● 詭弁をろうする use *sophistry*; quibble.

● 詭弁家 a sophist; (屁(へ)理屈をこねる人) a quibbler.

*きぼ **規模** (a) scale; 〖大きさ〗(a) size. (⇨大規模) ● 大[小]規模に on a large [a small] *scale*. ▶その会社はどれくらいの規模ですか How big is the company? ▶会社は事業の規模を拡大[縮小]した The company enlarged [reduced] the *scale* [*size*] of its business./The company scaled up [down] its business.

ぎぼ 義母 〖配偶者の母〗a mother-in-law (複 ~s, mothers-); 〖継母〗a stepmother; 〖養母〗a foster-mother.

きほう 気泡 ▶ (!通例複数形で) ▶シャンペンをグラスに注ぐと気泡が生じ, やがて消える When champagne is poured in a glass, *bubbles* form and they break soon.

きほう 気胞 《魚の》an air bladder.

きほう 既報 ● 既報の通り as previously announced [reported].

*きぼう **希望** 名 〖望み〗(a) hope 《*of, for; that* 節》; 〖願望〗(強い) (a) desire; (実現不可能[困難]な) (a) wish 《*for; to do*》; 〖期待, 見込み〗(an) expectation 《*of*》; 〖夢〗a dream; 〖要求〗(a) request. (⇨望み) ● 第一希望 one's first *preference*. (!preference は「好み」の意) ▶大学に行くことが彼の希望です It is his *wish* [*desire*] *to* go to college. (!日常会話では以下のように言う方が普通)/He *hopes* [*wants*] *to* go to college./He *hopes* [×*wants*] (*that*) he will go [he goes] to college. (!《話》では通例 that を省略する)

①【希望~】● (クラブの)入会希望者 a person who *wants to* join (a club); an applicant for membership (in a club). ● 希望的観測 one's *wishful* thinking. ▶私は希望どおり A 大学に入れた I was able to go to A University as I (*had*) *wanted* (*to*) [*hoped*, 《書》*wished*]. (!口語ではしばしば had を省略する)

②【希望が[は]】▶ 彼の回復は希望が持てる There is a *hope* of his recovery [*that* he will recover]. (!「希望の持てる程度は hope の前に every, some, not much, no などをつけて表す) ▶この勝利で希望がわいた This victory gave me *hope* [私を勇気づけた] *encouraged* me]. ▶とうとう私の長年の希望がかなった What I had wanted *to do* for a long time [《やや書》My long-cherished *hope*] finally came true. (!finally の代わりに at last を用いれば通例文尾に置く) ▶私の希望は打ち砕かれた My *hopes* were destroyed [were shattered]. ▶そのニュースを聞いて彼女の希望が高まった My *hope ran high* [*rose*] on hearing the news.

会話「座席にご希望はございますか」「はい, 禁煙席にしていただけますか」"Do you have any seat *preferences*, sir?" "Yes, could you put me in the non-smoking section?"

③【希望の】▶ 彼は希望のない人生を送った He led a *hopeless* life. ▶最後の希望の光が彼女の心の中で消えた The last flicker of *hope* died in her. ▶マイクは我が校の希望の星だ Mike is the *hope* [a *rising star*] of our school.

④【希望に】▶ 彼は希望に胸をふくらませて上京した He went to Tokyo, full of [(燃えて) *burning with*] *hope*. ▶ご希望に添えなくて残念です I'm sorry I can't fulfill your *wishes*. ▶彼女は親の希望に反して法学部に進学した She went on to study law against her parents' *wishes*. ▶多数のファンの希望により劇は再演された They again put on the play because a lot of fans *asked for* it./《書》The play was staged again *at the request of* many fans. ▶希望に生きる者は常に若い Those who live in *hope* are always young.

⑤【希望を】● 希望をふくらませる develop *hope*. ▶彼は試験に失敗してすっかり希望を失った He failed the exam and lost all his *hopes*. ▶みんなの希望を聞いてください Please listen to everyone's *wishes* [what everyone *wants* (to do)].

会話「留学する希望を捨てるなよ」「ありがとう, 希望は持ち続けないとね」"Don't give up [*your*] *hope* of studying abroad." "Thanks. I just have to keep (my) *hope* alive, you know."

ぎほう ― **きまる**

— **希望する** 動 hope 《*for*; *to do*; *that* 節》; wish 《*to do*; *that* 節》(! that は通例省略される); expect 《*to do*; *that* 節》; want 《*to do*》(⇨図; 望む, 欲しい)

DISCOURSE
日本が国連安保理の常任理事国入りを希望するのは、ひとつは国家の威信、もうひとつは世界情勢に影響を及ぼしたいという欲求による Japan's *desire* to become a permanent member of the United Nations Security Council is based *partly* on national pride and *partly* on a desire to influence world events. (! *partly* ... and *partly* ~ 〈ひとつには…, またひとつには~〉は列挙に用いるディスコースマーカー)

● 希望小売価格 a recommended retail price《略 RRP》; a manufacturer's recommended price《略 MRP》.

ぎほう 技法 (a) technique. (⇨技術)
ぎぼうし 擬宝珠 (⇨擬宝珠(ぎ,))
きぼうほう 喜望峰 〖南アフリカ共和国の岬〗the Cape of Good Hope.
ぎぼし 擬宝珠 ❶〖欄干の柱の頭〗an ornamental top of a railing. ❷〖植物〗(ネギの花) a leek [a green onion] flower; (ユリ科の花) a plantain lily.
きぼね 気骨 • 気骨が折れる(気疲れする) get [become] mentally tired.
きぼり 木彫り wood carving. • 木彫りの人形 a doll *carved out of wood*.

*: **きほん** 基本 (基礎) a basis《動 bases》; (根本事項) the fundamentals; (基礎事項) the basics; (初歩) the elements. (! 後の3語は通例複数形で) ▶ 英語の基本をマスターしてますか Have you mastered the *fundamentals* [*basics*, *elements*] of English?

— **基本の** 形 basic; fundamental. ▶ この公式は数学の基本だ This formula is *basic* [*fundamental*] *to* mathematics.

— **基本的に** 副 ▶ 基本的には君が正しいと思う I think you're *fundamentally* [*basically*] right.

● 基本給 basic [base] pay. • 基本計画 a master plan. • 基本契約 a master agreement. • 基本原理 a fundamental [a basic] principle. • 基本的人権 fundamental [basic] human rights. • 基本料金 a basic charge [(タクシーなどの) fare].

ぎまい 義妹 〖義理の妹〗one's sister-in-law《動 ~s, sisters-》. (⇨兄弟 ❶)
きまえ 気前 generosity. • 慈善事業に気前よく金を出す人 a *generous* giver of one's money to charities. • 気前よく金を遣う be *generous* [*free*,《やや書》*lavish*] *with* one's money; (やたらと) *lavish* one's money 《*on*》. ▶ 彼は困った人に気前よく物を与える He is *generous* to [*toward*] people in need./He gives *generously* to people in need.

きまぐれ 気まぐれ 名《やや書》(a) caprice /kəprís/; (でき心) (a) whim, 〖一時的な思いつき〗a fancy. • 気まぐれから from [out of] *caprice* [*whim*]. • 一時の気まぐれ a passing *fancy* [*whim*]. • 気まぐれで時計を買う buy a watch *on a whim* [*at whim*].

— **気まぐれな** 形 〖移り気な〗fickle, capricious; 〖変わりやすい〗changeable; 〖思いつきで行動する〗《やや書》whimsical; 〖空想好きの〗fanciful; 〖感情の起伏が激しい〗temperamental. • 気まぐれな天気 *changeable* [書・比喩的] *capricious*] weather. ▶ 彼女は非常に気まぐれだ She's very *fickle* [*capricious*, *whimsical*].

きまじめ 生真面目 — **生真面目な** 形 very serious, dead earnest; (道徳的に堅い) strait-laced. (⇨真面目) ▶ 淳二は生真面目すぎる Junji is too *earnest*.

— **生真面目に** 副 • 生真面目に働く work *earnestly*.
きまずい 気まずい (ばつの悪い) awkward; (緊張した) strained. • 気まずい沈黙(の時間) an *awkward* [an *uncomfortable*] silence. • 金が足りなくて気まずい思いをする feel *embarrassed* for lack of money. ▶ あれ以来私たちの関係は気まずいものになった Our relationship got *strained* after that incident.
きまつ 季末 the end of the season. • 季末大バーゲン an *end-of-the-season* sale; a *season-end* sale.
きまつ 期末 • 期末に at *the end of the term*. • 期末のレポート a *term* [《英》an *end-of-term*] report. • 期末試験 a term [《英》an end-of-term,《まれ》a terminal] exam; (大学の最終試験) the [one's] finals (! 通例複数形で).
きまま 気まま (⇨動 我が儘(まま)) • 気ままに(=人の気に)暮らす live an *easy* [a *carefree*] life. • 子供を気ままに(=好きなように)させておく allow children to *have their own way*; let children *do whatever they like*.
きまよい 気迷い 〖迷うこと〗(a) hesitation. (⇨躊躇(ちゅう,), 迷い)

*: **きまり** 決まり ❶〖規則〗a rule; (公的な) a regulation. (⇨規則) ▶ 学校の決まりは守らないといけない You must observe school *rules* [*regulations*]. ▶ 彼らは共同生活をするためにいくつか決まりを作った They made several *rules* to live together.

❷〖区切り〗(解決・決着) (a) settlement; (合意) an agreement; (終わり) an end. • 決まりをつける (解決する) settle; reach a settlement [an *agreement*]《*with*+人, *on* [*about*]+事》; (終わらせる)《やや書》put an end 《*to*》. ▶ その件はまもなく決まり(=決着)がつくだろう The matter will *be settled* soon./We will *put an end to* the matter before long. ▶ それで話は決まりだ(=決まった)(今交渉している相手に対して) That *settles* the matter [it]. (! しばしば受身で Then it's settled. ともいう。単純現在形に注意)/(それで手を打とう) 《話》It's a deal./《話》You've got a deal./《話》That's that.
[会話] 「彼なら許可してくれないだろう」「そうするとこれで決まりだな。その計画はあきらめなくちゃならない」"He won't give us permission." "So *that's that*." We must abandon the idea.

❸〖習慣〗(個人的な) (a) habit; (社会的な) (a) custom. ▶ 早朝のジョギングが彼の決まりになっている He *is in the habit of* jogging early in the morning./He *makes a point of* jogging early in the morning./He *always* [*usually*] jogs early in the morning. (! 最後の言い方が最も口語的)

きまり(が)わるい きまり(が)悪い be [feel*] embarrassed; feel awkward. • 息子の行儀が悪くてきまりが悪い be *embarrassed by* [*at*, *about*] one's son's bad behavior. ▶ 彼は人前に出るときまり悪がる He feels *awkward* [*embarrassed*] in front of other people.
きまりきった 決まりきった 〖一定の〗fixed; 〖明白な〗plain; (自明の) self-evident; (当たり前の) obvious. • 決まりきった(=型にはまった)言葉 *stereotyped* [(使い古された) *hackneyed*] expressions. • 決まりきった日常の仕事 *routine* work; one's daily routine.
きまりて 決まり手 〖相撲〗a winning technique.
きまりもんく 決まり文句 a fixed [a set, (ありふれた) a stock] phrase; a stereotype; (陳腐な) a cliché /kli:ʃéi/.

*: **きまる** 決まる 動 ❶〖決定される〗(一般的に) be decided; (日取り・価格などがはっきりと) be fixed, be set-

tled (🔁 be fixed より堅い言い方); (取り決められる) be arranged. ▶会議はあすまで延期されることに決まった It has been decided that the meeting ((主に英) should) be postponed till tomorrow. ▶結婚式の日取りは11月10日に決まった The date of the wedding was fixed [was arranged, was set] for [×on] November 10. (🔁 10は(米)では ten, (英)では the tenth と読む) ▶それで話は決まった(⇨決まり❷) [第2文例]) ▶彼はまだ就職が決まっていない(＝見つけていない) He has not found [got] a job yet. ▶ごめんね、もっと早く言えばよかったんだけど、実は私はもう(結婚の)相手が決まっているの(＝予約済であるよ) I'm sorry I didn't tell you this sooner. But to tell you the truth, I'm already spoken for.
会話「金曜日はいかがですか」「申し訳ないけれど無理です。今は1週間ずっとスーパーで働いていて予定の変更はできないの。何か月も前から決まっていることなのでね」"How about Friday?" "Sorry I can't. I'm working at a supermarket all week. And I can't change that, because we fixed it up months ago."(🔁 we は自分と雇用主をさす)
会話「本社を東京に移すことにしたのですか」「いや、まだはっきり決まっていません」"Are you going to move your head office to Tokyo?" "Well, that is still an open question."

❷〖確実である〗be sure [certain] (to do). (🔁 後の方が客観的な理由があることを含む) ▶彼が勝つに決まっている He is sure [certain] to win./(確信している) I am sure [certain] (that) he will win./It is certain [×sure] that he will win./He will win. I promise you that. (🔁 最後は会話体で, that は先行文の内容をさし「さうに決まっているよ」の意. 軽く, He will win, (I) promise. ともいう)
会話「うそなんかついてないよ」「うそに決まってるじゃないか」"I'm not telling lies." "Of course, you ˇare."

❸〖その他の表現〗▶昔は詩人というものは貧乏なものと決まっていた(＝運命づけられていた) In those days, poets were bound to be poor. ▶今日のそのスーツは決まってるね You look smart [sharp] in that suit today. (🔁女性には You look gorgeous…. (目を見はるほど美しい)などを用いる)

── **決まった** 形 (一定の) fixed; (いつもの) regular; (単調で同じことのくり返しの) routine /ru:tí:n/. (⇨決まりきった) ●決まった席につく take one's regular seat; (指定された) sit in one's designated place. ▶彼は決まった仕事がない He has no regular job./He doesn't have a regular job.

── **決まって** 副 ▶彼は土曜になると決まって釣りに行く He always goes fishing on Saturday(s). ▶彼はそこへ行くと決まってコーヒーを注文する Whenever [Every time] he goes there, he orders coffee. (🔁every time を用いる方が口語的)/(や古書) He never goes there without ordering coffee. (⇨必ず❷)

きまわし 着回し ●着回しがきくスーツ an all-purpose suit.

ぎまん 欺瞞 (a) deceit, (a) deception. ●自己欺瞞 self-deceit, self-deception. ●欺瞞に満ちた deceitful. ▶彼は欺瞞の名人だ He is a master of deception.

きみ 君 you. (⇨あなた, 私)
会話「やあ, 健」「太郎, 君か」"Hi, Ken." "Taro, is that you?"

きみ 気味 ●いい気味だ(＝当然の報いだ) It serves you right!/(話) Serve(s) you right. (🔁第三者についていうときは you の代わりに him, them などを用いる)
●気味(の)悪い, 気味が悪い (不気味な) weird /wíərd/-

(不可解な) uncanny; (ぞっとする) creepy. ●気味悪げな give a weird old house. ●気味の悪い笑みを浮かべる give a weird [(不吉な感じのする) an evil, a sinister] grin. (⇨不気味) ▶その音を聞いて気味が悪くなった The sound gave me a creepy feeling./(ぞくぞくぞっとした) The sound made my flesh creep [gave me the creeps]. ▶この古い家は夜になると気味が悪い (話) This old house feels creepy at night.

きみ 黄身 yolk (of an egg). (🔁白身と対照するときは ˇ) ●黄身が二つ入っている卵 an egg with two yolks in it.

きみ 黄味 ●黄味を帯びた yellowish; slightly yellow.

-ぎみ -気味 〖傾向がある〗tend (to do); 〖少し〗 a little; 〖わずかな〗 slight; 〖…の気味〗 a touch of …. ●少し疲れ気味である be a little [(話) a bit, a little bit] tired; (話) be on the tired side. ▶ちょっと風邪気味です I have a slight [a touch of (a)] cold. ▶彼女の体重は増え気味です She tends [is showing a tendency] to increase in weight. ▶物価は上がり気味だ Prices are slowly going up.

きみがよ 君が代 Kimigayo; the Japanese national anthem.

きみじか 気短 ── **気短の** 形 (怒りっぽい) quick-[hot-, short-]tempered; (我慢強くない) impatient. ▶彼は気短だ He is quick-tempered [hot-tempered]./He has a quick [a hot] temper./He easily gets angry.

きみつ 気密 airtightness. ●気密性の高い áirtight, áirproof.

きみつ 機密 ── **機密の** 形 (秘密の) secret; (国家・軍事など機密扱いの) classified. ●機密を守る keep a secret. ●機密を暴露する[漏らす] disclose [let out] a secret.
●機密事項 a secret; (秘密の情報) (a piece of) secret information. ●機密文書 secret [classified] documents.

きみどり 黄緑 yellowish green.

きみゃく 気脈 ●気脈を通じる (ひそかに了解し合っている) have a secret understanding (with); (ひそかに連絡を取り合う) communicate tacitly (with); (違法行為の計画などに) conspire (with).

きみょう 奇妙 ── **奇妙な** 形 (不思議な) strange; (わけの分からない) funny; (変わった) odd, (話) weird /wíərd/; (風変わりな) (や古) queer; (好奇心をそそる) curious; (一種独特な) peculiar; (風変わりで変人的な) eccentric. (⇨変な, 妙な) ●奇妙な癖 a strange [an odd, a peculiar, an eccentric] habit. ●奇妙なふるまい strange [odd, queer, funny, peculiar, eccentric] behavior. ●奇妙なふるまいをする behave strangely [oddly, curiously]. ▶だれも彼女が部屋に入ってくるのに気づかなかったのは奇妙だ(＝変だ) It is strange [funny, odd] that nobody noticed her coming into the room. ▶彼には何となく奇妙なところがある There is something strange [unusual] about him.

きみわるい 気味悪い (⇨気味 [成句])

きみん 棄民 a displaced person (略 DP).

ぎむ 義務 (a) duty ●良心や道徳上当然しなければならない一般的な義務); (an) obligation (🔁法律・慣習・契約などにより生ずる義務). (⇨任務) ●義務を果たす do [(や書) perform, (書) fulfill] one's duty. ●義務を怠る neglect [fail in] one's duty. ●義務を負わせる impose an obligation (on him). ▶すべての人は親に対する義務を負っている Every person has a duty to [toward] their [his] parents. (🔁口語では their を用いる) ▶納税は国民の

義務だ Paying taxes is every citizen's *obligation*. ▶君には借金を払う義務がある You *have* an [You *are under* (*an*)] *obligation to* pay the debt. (❗(1) under の後では《米》では無冠詞が多い. (2)「借金を払う義務はない」は You have [You are under] no *obligation* to pay the debt.) ▶ドライバーはシートベルトを締めることを義務づけられている Drivers *are obliged* (*by law*) *to* fasten their seat belts. ▶すべての会員に出席が義務づけられている Every member *must* attend./Attendance is *compulsory* for all members.
● **義務感** a sense of duty. ● **義務教育** compulsory education.

きむずかしい 気難しい (扱いにくい) difficult; (怒りっぽい) bad-tempered. ● 気難しい老人 a *bad-tempered* [《話》a *crabby*] old man. (❗後の方は「文句が多く扱いにくい」の意で年寄りに用いることが多い) ▶彼はいつも気難しい(=むっつりした)顔をしている He always looks *sullen*.

きむすめ 生娘 (処女) a virgin. (❗「世間知らずでうぶな(=naive)人」の意でも用いる)

キムチ kimchi; kimchee.

きめ 木目, 肌理 〖木材の〗grain; 〖皮膚・木材などの〗texture.
● きめが細か ● きめの細かい [粗い] 木材 wood of fine [coarse] *grain*; *fine-grained* [*coarse-grained*] wood. ▶彼女の肌はきめが細かい She has *smooth* skin./Her skin has a fine *texture*./Her skin is *smooth*. ● きめの細かい(=繊細な)人 a *delicate* [(よく気のつく) an *attentive*] person. ● きめの細かい注意をする pay *minute* [〖注意深い〗*careful*, (細心の) *close*] attention (*to*). ● きめの細かい指導をする give 《him》*careful* instructions.

きめい 記名 图 (署名) a signature.
── **記名する** 動 (署名する) sign (one's name); (名前を書く) write* one's name 《*on*》.
● **記名投票** an open [a signed] (↔a secret) vote.

きめい 偽名 an assumed [a false, 《やや書》a fictitious] name; (犯罪者などの使う) an alias /éiliəs/. ● 偽名を使う sign [assume] a *false name*. ● 偽名で生活する live under a *false name* 《of Curtis》.

きめこむ 決め込む 〖当然のことと思う〗take* (it) for granted 〖《口》は that, 時に it も省略する〗; 〖証拠なしに決めてかかる〗 assume 《*that* 節》; 〖早合点する〗 jump to the conclusion 《*that* 節》; 〖ふりをする〗 pretend 《*to do*; *that* 節》; 〖心を決める〗 make* up one's mind, decide 《*to do*》. ▶居留守を決め込む *pretend to* be out. ▶なぜ君は失敗すると自分で決め込んでいるのか Why do you *take it for granted* [Why *are* you *so sure*] (*that*) you will fail?

きめだま 決め球 〖野球〗a finishing pitch; a money pitch.

きめつける 決めつける conclude; (軽率に) jump to the conclusion. ▶彼が犯人だと決めつけないでください Don't *conclude* [*jump to the conclusion*] *that* he is the culprit.

きめて 決め手 〖決定的な証拠〗《a piece of》conclusive evidence; 〖成否を決めるもの〗a decisive factor. ● 決め手を欠く find no *conclusive evidence*. ▶彼を味方につけられるかどうかが決め手になる We'll succeed if we can win him over [around].

きめどころ 決め所 ▶今がこの問題の決め所だ Now is the *time* to settle the matter. ▶決め所を逸した I missed the *best chance* to solve [to settle] the problem.

きめる 決める

┌─── **WORD CHOICE** ─── **決める** ───┐

decide 熟慮の結果としてきっぱりと決断すること. to 不定詞, または that 節が後続することが多い. ▶戦争を止めようと決めた I *decided* to try to stop the war.
determine decide 以上に強い意志をもって決断すること. to 不定詞, that 節, whether 節が後続することが多い. ▶彼に資格があるかどうか決めるのは重要[困難]なことだ It is important [difficult] to *determine* whether he is qualified or not.
resolve 困難な課題などをやり抜く決断をすること. 主に改まった文脈で用いる. ▶容易には決められない問題 the issue that cannot be easily *resolved*.

頻度チャート

decide ████████████████████
determine █████████
resolve ████

20　40　60　80　100 (%)

❶ 〖決定する〗(一般的に) decide 《*that* 節, *wh-* 節》; (確定する) 《書》 detérmine 《*wh-* 節》; (選んで) choose* 《*to do*; *wh-* 節》; 〖規則などを制定する〗lay* ... down; make*; 〖投票で〗vote 《*to do*; *that* 節》. ● 校則を決める lay down [make] school rules. ● 決められている(⇒決まる❶) ▶あなたは今後の進路を決めておかないといけない You must *decide* on your future course./You must *decide* [*determine*] what to do in the future. ▶それらのどちらにするか決めかねています I'm having difficulty trying to *decide* [*choose*] between them. ▶ぼくにとって何を優先すべきかはぼくが決める I shall decide what I should place first. (❗この shall は強く発音され,「是が非でも」という強い意志を表す)/(判断する) Let me be the judge of what I should give priority to. (❗開き直ったときなどに用いる堅い表現) ▶それは君の決めることだ You *decide*./You *tell me*./You're the boss [doctor]. (❗いずれも口語的慣用表現) ▶それはあなたが決めることではありません That's not *your decision*. (❗「私が決める」をやわらかく言う表現) 会話「2時か 2時半に来いよ」「あまり自由に決めさせてくれないんだね」"Come at two or two thirty." "You don't *give* me much *choice*, do you?"

❷ 〖決心する〗 decide, make* up one's mind; 《書》detérmine; 《やや書》resolve. (❗この順に固い決意を表す. 以上いずれも通例 to do, that 節を伴う) ▶彼は来年はヨーロッパに行かないと決めた He *decided* [*determined*] not to go to Europe next year. (❗時に ... decided [determined] *against* 《↔on》 going ともいう)/He *decided* [*determined*] that he would not go to Europe next year. ▶家を買うかどうか決めましたか Have you *decided* [*made up your mind*] *whether* to buy a house? ▶彼は教師になろうと決めている He *is determined* [*is resolved*] *to* become a teacher. (❗He has decided to ... とすると通例「今決めた」という動的な意味を表す) 会話「この上着はいかがですか」「まだはっきりとは決めかねるよ」"How about this jacket?" "I can't quite *make up* my *mind* about it."

❸ 〖取り決める〗 (日時・場所などを) set*; (指定する) appoint; (はっきりと決める) fix, settle (❗fix より堅い語); (手はずを整える) arrange. ▶時間と場所を決めよ. そこへ行くから Just *appoint* [*name*] the time and place and I'll be there. ▶会の日取りを土曜日に(=と)決めた We *have fixed* [*settled*, *set*] the date of the meeting *for* [×*on*] Saturday. ▶今日の午後彼らと駅で会うことに決めた We *have arranged* [*decided*] *to* meet them at the station this afternoon.

❹ [必ず...する] (信条として) make* a point of 《*doing*》; (習慣としている) be in the habit of 《*doing*》; (いつも...する) *always*. (⇨必ず❷) ▶彼は早起きをすることに決めている He *makes a point of getting* [《まれ》*makes it a rule to get*] up early./He *always* [*usually*] gets up early. (❗最後の言い方が最も口語的)

❺ [思い込む] (当然...と思う) take* (it) for granted 《*that*節》; assume 《*that*節》. (⇨決め込む) ▶子供だからといってその子の言うことは当てにならないと決めてかかるのはおかしいと思う I think it's wrong of you to *assume that* you can't rely upon his words just because he is too young.

❻ [成功させる] ▶試合を決めるホームラン a (game-)deciding home run. ●リーグ優勝を決める clinch the pennant. ●(投球を)外角に決める hit the outside corner. ▶3メートルのパットを決めた He *sank* a ten-foot *putt*. 事情 米英ではフィートで表すのが普通

❼ [服装を整える] ▶その決めに決めた姿(=詳細にわたって配慮して選んだ服装)は、率直なところマフィアのボスにしか見えなかった In his *meticulously well-chosen* attire [《完璧に着飾った》*Impeccably dressed*], he looked nothing but a Mafia boss, to be honest with you.

きめん 鬼面 a mask of an ogre /óʊɡər/.
● 鬼面人を驚かす frighten a person with [making] an empty threat. (❗empty threatは「口先だけの脅し」)

きも 肝 ❶ [肝臓] a liver.
❷ [度胸] courage, 《話・まれ》pluck; 《根性》《話》guts. ●肝の太い [小さい] 男 a *bold* [a *timid*] man. ●肝試しをする (⇨肝試し)
● 肝が据わっている ▶次夫は肝が据わっている Tsugio *has nerves of steel* [*steady nerves*]./Tsugio *is as steady* [*solid*] *as a rock*.
● 肝に銘じる ▶彼の忠告を肝に銘じる *take* his advice *to heart*.
● 肝をつぶす ▶そのニュースを聞いて肝をつぶす(=非常に驚く) *be astounded* [*stunned*] at the news.
● 肝を冷やす be frightened, be terrified 《*at*, *by*》. (❗後の方が強意的)

きもいり 肝煎り ▶ ...の肝煎りで through the good offices of .... (⇨幹旋(ボ),世話❷)

きもだめし 肝試し a test of one's courage. ●肝試しをする(=一度胸を試す) test one's *courage* [*nerve*]. (⇨度胸)

:**きもち** 気持ち 图

WORD CHOICE 気持ち
feeling 主観的な感情・感覚・感興を表す. ▶私の本当の気持ち my true *feeling*.
mood 一時的な気分を表す. ▶彼は遊びたいというような気持ちではなかった He was not in the *mood* to [*for*] play.

頻度チャート
feeling
▬▬▬▬▬▬▬
mood
▬▬▬
0 20 40 60 80 100 (%)

〚感じ〛a feeling; (外的な刺激に対し) a sensation; 〚感情〛feelings, 〚気分〛a mood, a frame [state] of mind.

① [〜の気持ち] ▶不安な気持ち an uneasy *feeling*; a *feeling* of uneasiness. ●素直な気持ち (⇨素直) ●感謝の気持ちでいっぱいである be filled with (a *feeling* of) gratitude. ●悲しい気持ちで歌を歌う sing in a sad *mood*. ▶まるで夢を見ているような気持ちです I *feel* as if I were [《話》was, 《話》am] dreaming. ▶日記では自分の気持ちを素直に表現すべきだ A Diary should be an open expression of *your feelings*. ▶これはほんの気持ちですが、お礼の印にどうぞ This is [Here's] a small token of thanks to you.

② [気持ちは] ▶彼女に対する君の気持ちはどうなのだ What are *your feelings* toward her?/How do you *feel* toward her? ▶お気持ちは大変うれしいのですが、お金をいただくわけにはいきません I'm very touched, but I couldn't take your money. (❗ *be touched* は「感激している」の意) ▶家を出ようかなという気持ちはある 《話》I've half *a mind* to *leave home*.

会話「まったくがっかりさせられるよ」「お気持ち(は)よく分かります」"It's all so discouraging." "I know exactly [《お察しします》] I can just imagine] *how you feel*."

③ [気持ちの] ●気持ちの(=気味)悪い (⇨気味 [成句]) ●気持ちのよい(=感じのよい)人 a *pleasant* [an *agreeable*] person. ●気持ちのよい(=居心地のよい)部屋 a *comfortable* room. ●気持ちのよいそよ風 a *pleasant* [a *refreshing*] breeze.

会話「気持ちのよい日ですね」「本当ですね」"It is a *nice* [a *beautiful*, a *lovely*] day, isn't it?" "It sure ↘is."

④ [気持ちに] ▶そのニュースを聞いて泣きたいような気持ちになった I *felt like* crying at the news./I *felt inclined to* cry at the news. ▶どうしてもその仕事を引き受ける気持ちになれなかった I *couldn't bring myself to* take the job. (❗*can*を伴って否定文で用いることが多い) ▶彼女は彼と結婚する気持ちになれない She *is in no mood to marry* [*for marrying*] him.

⑤ [気持ちを] ●気持ちを落ち着かせる (自分の気持ちを) calm [《やや書》compose] oneself; (人の気持ちを) calm 《*him*》(down). ●気持ちを取り直す pull oneself together. ●自分の気持ちを言葉で言い表す put one's *feelings* into words. ●彼の気持ちをくみ取る (⇨汲む❷) ●人の気持ちを害してはいけない Don't hurt other people's [others'] *feelings*. ▶彼はその言葉で気持ちを害された He *was hurt* by the words./The words *offended* him. ▶由香は大いに気持ちを込めて歌った Yuka sang *with great feeling*. ▶言葉にもっと気持ちを込めなさい Put more *feelings* into what you say [your word]. ▶散歩して気持ちを切り替えた I took a walk *for a change* (*of pace*).

── 気持ちがいい 動 (快適な気分である) feel* good [《大変楽しい》great]; (心地よく思う) feel comfortable; (物事が心地よい) be pleasant. ▶風呂あがりは気持ちがいい I *feel good* [《さわやかだ》*feel refreshed*] after a hot bath. ▶このベッドはとても気持ちがいい I *feel* very *comfortable* in this bed./This bed is very *comfortable* to sleep in. ▶風はひんやりして気持ちがよかった The breeze was *comfortably* cool. ▶朝早く海辺を散歩するのは気持ちがいい It's nice [*pleasant*] to walk along the beach early in the morning.

── 気持ちが悪い 動 (吐き気がする) feel* sick (to one's stomach) (❗( )内を用いるのは《米》); (心地が悪い) feel [be] uncomfortable. ▶赤ちゃんが泣き

きもったま

だした. きっとおむつがぬれて気持ちが悪いんだわ The baby has begun to cry. He [She] must be wet and *uncomfortable*. ▶クモを見ただけで気持ちが悪くなる The mere sight of spiders *makes* me *(feel) sick*./(ぞっとする)〔話〕Just looking at spiders *gives* me *the creeps* [✗*makes me creepy*].

── 気持ちよく 副 ●気持ちよく働く work *pleasantly* [(楽しく) *happily*. ▶気持ちよく(=愉快に)彼女と話す talk to [with] her *pleasantly* [*cheerfully*]; have a *pleasant* talk with her. ▶頼めば彼はいつも気持ちよく(=喜んで)手伝ってくれた He was always *ready* [*willing*] *to* help me when I asked him./He helped me *readily* [*willingly*] whenever I asked him. ▶猫は毛をなでてやると気持ちよさそうにゴロゴロのどを鳴らした The cat purred *comfortably* [(満足げに) *with satisfaction*] as I stroked its fur.

きもったま 肝っ玉 ●肝っ玉の太い(=大胆な)男 a *bold* [a *daring*, (度量の大きい) a *large-minded*] man. ●肝っ玉の小さい(=臆病な)人 a *cowardly* [(やや書) a *timid*] person; a coward; (弱虫)〔話〕a wimp, a chicken.

*きもの 着物 ❶[衣服] clothes /klóuz/; (集合的) clothing /klóuðiŋ/; (書) a garment (!メーカーが好んで用いる語); (服装) (a) dress. (⇨服)
❷[和服] a *kimono* (働〜s). (!衣類であることを明確にして a kimono dress ともいう) ▶着物を着た婦人 a woman in a *kimono*; (書) a *kimono*-clad woman. ▶彼女の着物姿はすてきだ She is very attractive [(よく似合う) looks very nice] in a *kimono* (*dress*). ▶着物は母に着せてもらいます My mother helps me on with my *kimono*.
●着物地 kimono material [fabric].

きもん 鬼門 (縁起の悪い方角・場所) the unlucky quarter; (説明的に) the northeast quarter which is believed to be the entrance gate of demons in Chinese folklore. ▶数学は鬼門だ(苦手だ) I'm poor at math./(嫌いだ) I hate mathematics. (⇨苦手)

きもん 奇問 ●奇問を発する ask a trick question.

*ぎもん 疑問 〖疑念〗(a) doubt, (a) question; 〖質問〗a question.

> 使い分け **doubt** 漠然とした理由のない疑い.
> **question** 理由のある疑いを示し, doubt の方が疑いの念が強い. 「質問」の意では ⓒ 扱い. (⇨疑い ❶)

● 疑問(=質問)を出す put up [present] a *question*. ● その可能性を疑問視する *doubt* the possibility; cast *doubt* on the possibility. ▶私自身そのことには疑問を持っている I have [entertain] *doubts about* it myself. ▶疑問点(=質問)があったらおたずねください Please ask me if you have any *question*(s) [✗doubt(s)]. ▶彼が正直なことは疑問の余地がない There is no *doubt* [*question*] *about* [*of*] his honesty./There is no *doubt* [*question*] that he is honest. ▶疑問では(「彼が正直であることはありえない」という逆の意もある)/His honesty is beyond *question*. ▶彼が成功するかどうかは疑問だ I *doubt* [*question*] *if* [*whether*] he will succeed. (!(1) if の方が口語的. (2) doubt では that 節も可)/It *is doubtful* [*questionable*] *whether* he will succeed./I am *doubtful* [✗*questionable*] *of* his success. (⇨疑わしい)
● 疑問詞 an interrogative. ● 疑問符 a question mark. ⇨巻末[句読法] ● 疑問文 an interrogative sentence.

ギヤ (a) gear. ● トップギヤ high [《英》top] *gear*. ● ローギヤ low [《英》bottom] *gear*. ● リバースギヤ

きゃく

reverse *gear*. ● ギヤがかかっている[いない] be in *gear* [out of *gear*]. ● ギヤをローに入れる put (a car) into low *gear*;《主に米》shift to low *gear*. ● ギヤを切り替える《米》change [shift] *gears*;《英》change *gear*.

きゃー (女性の) eek /i:k/.

ぎゃあぎゃあ ●ぎゃあぎゃあ言う scream; shriek. (!scream よりかん高い) ▶子供たちはぎゃあぎゃあわめきながら家中を走り回った The children ran through the house *yelling and screaming*. ▶少女たちが観光バスの中できゃあきゃあ騒いでいた Girls *were* merrily *talking and shouting* on a sightseeing bus. (!英語には適切な対応語がないので, 動詞を重ねたり, 副詞で工夫する方がよい)

ぎゃあぎゃあ ▶赤ん坊がぎゃあぎゃあ泣き始めた The baby started *crying noisily* [*screaming*, *squalling*]. ▶そんなことでぎゃあぎゃあ言うな(=騒ぎ立てる) Don't *make a fuss over* [*about*] it.

きゃいん ●犬がきゃいんと鳴く yelp.

きやく 規約 〖規則〗a rule; (公の) a regulation; 〖協約〗an agreement; 〖細々としたつまらない〗rules and regulations. (!語順に注意) (⇨規則)

*きゃく 客 ❶[訪問客] a visitor; (短時間の) a caller; (招待客) a guest; company (!1 人または 2 人以上の客に用いる).

①[〜の客] ●招かれざる[不意の]客 an uninvited [an unexpected] *guest*. ●見物客(名所の) a sightseer; (試合・ショーの) a spectator. ●アメリカからの日本への客 a *visitor* from America to Japan.

②【客が】 ▶きのうは大勢客があった We had a lot of *visitors* [*guests*, *company*] yesterday. (!✗a lot of *companies* は不可) ▶客が食事に来ることになっている We are expecting [having] *guests* [*company*] for dinner. ▶I expect は通例目上の人には用いない ▶外出中にどなたかお客様が見えましたか Did anyone visit me while I was out?/Were there any *callers* while I was out? ▶お客様がお越しですが Someone wants to see you. ▶そろそろお客様が見える時間だ It's almost time for the *guest*(s) to arrive. ▶その客が帰ったのは何時でしたか What time was it that the *guest* left?

③【客を】 ●客を招く[迎える; もてなす] invite [receive; entertain] a *guest*. ●来た客を応接室へ通す show the *visitor* into the drawing room.

❷[顧客] (商店などの) a customer; (買い物客) a shopper; (弁護士など専門職の) a client; (銀行の大口の客にも用いる) a (ホテルなどの宿泊客) a guest; (乗り物の) a passenger (⇨乗客); (劇場の) an audience (!集合的だに用い単・複両扱い) (⇨聴衆); (観光客) a visitor; a tourist; a sightseer. ▶お客様, ご用はお伺いしておりますか Are you being served [being waited on], *sir* [*madam*,《米》*ma'am*]? (!sir は男性, madam [ma'am] は女性に用い, customer は呼びかけには用いない)

①[〜の(の)客] ●婦人客 a woman *customer*. ●通りいっぺんの[昔からの; なじみの]客 a casual [an old; a regular] *customer*. ●利用客(乗客) a passenger; (宿泊客) a guest; (商店の) a customer; (買い物客) a shopper; (弁護士の依頼人) a client; (消費者) a user.

②[客を(は)] ▶その店は客が多い The store has [They have] a lot of *customers*. ▶お客様は神様です *Customers* are always right. ▶その日以来商店街に客が途絶えた The shopping streets have been deserted since that day.

③【客を】 ●客を失う lose *customers*. ●客を引きつける attract *shoppers*. ●客をとる(売春する) prostitute [sell] oneself. ▶新しい店に客を取られた The new shop has taken away some of our *customers*. ▶お客様を大切に, ただし採算は度外視しないように Worship your *customers*, but don't give away the store.

ぎゃく 逆 图 (方向や順序が反対) the revérse; (位置・行動・傾向などが正反対) the ópposite; (内容などが反対) the cóntrary; (命題などが反対) the convérse. (⇔反対) ▶逆もまた真なり The *converse* is equally true. ▶彼は親切どころかその逆です He is *the reverse* of kind. (❗ of の次に形容詞がくることに注意. 堅い言い方では日常会話では He's *not* kind *at all*. の方が普通) ▶君の意見と私の意見はまったく逆だ Your opinion and mine are completely *opposite*. ▶私が彼を援助してきたとお思いかもしれませんが, 実はその逆なのです You may think I have been helping him. In fact *the reverse* is true.
会話「新聞記者のいるところ常に事件ありだ」「それは逆だと思うけど」"Where there's a news-person, there's always trouble." "I think it's *the other way around*."
── 逆の 形 revérse 《to》; ópposite 《to》; cóntrary 《to》. ●逆の順序で in *reverse* order. ▶彼はときどき本心とは逆のことを言う He sometimes says *the opposite* [*reverse*] of his real intention./What he says is sometimes *contrary* to what he really means. ▶彼は逆の方向に歩いて行った He walked *the other way*. ▶(次の語句は口語的)/He walked in [×to] *the opposite* direction.
会話「このふたしまらないよ」「逆の方向に回してみてごらん」"This lid doesn't fit." "Try turning it *the other way* (*around*)."
── 逆に (⇔反対に) ▶彼は私の手を逆にねじった He twisted my hand *the wrong way*.
── 逆にする 動 (順序を) revérse; (方向を) turn ... the other way; (表裏を) turn ... inside out; (上下を) turn ... upside down. ▶アルファベットの順を逆にしない *Reverse* the order of the alphabet.
●逆光線 backlight. (⇔逆光)

ギャグ 《話》 a (funny) gag, a joke (❗ 日本語のギャグはこれに近いこともある). ▶ギャグを飛ばす tell [make] a *gag*. ▶あのコメディアンのギャグは大したものだ That comedian tells a good *gag*.

きゃくあし 客足 (客) customers. ▶客足が遠のく lose *costomers*. ▶あそこは客足がついてきた They are getting more and more *customers*. (❗ 口語的な表現)/They are getting an increasing number of *customers*.

きゃくあしらい 客あしらい (来客に対して) hospitality; (ホテル・レストランで) service. ▶彼女は客あしらいがうまい[下手だ] She is a *good* [a *poor*] hostess. ▶あのホテルは客あしらいがいい[悪い] The service is good [poor] at that hotel./That hotel gives good [poor] *service*.

きゃくいん 客員 a guest (member).
●客員教授 a guest [a visiting] professor.

きゃくいん 脚韻 a rhyme. ▶脚韻を踏む rhyme 《with》.

きゃくうけ 客受け ▶あの店員は客受けがいい That clerk *is popular with customers*.

きゃくうん 客運 advérse [bad, ill] fortune.

きゃくえん 客演 ── 客演する 動 make* a guest appearance 《on television [(the) stage]》; give* a guest performance; appear [perform, play] as (a) guest.
●客演指揮者 a guest conductor.

きゃくこうか 逆効果 a contrary [an opposite, an adverse, a reverse] effect. ▶彼の発言は逆効果になった His remarks had *the contrary effect*./The effect of his remarks was *contrary to what he expected*.

ぎゃくさつ 虐殺 图 slaughter; (大虐殺) a massacre, a holocaust. ▶ドイツのナチ政権下で行われたユダヤ人の大量虐殺を特に the Holocaust と表記する The mass murder of Jews under the German Nazi regime is specifically written as the Holocaust.
── 虐殺する 動 slaughter; massacre.

ぎゃくざや 逆鞘 back spread; adverse spread; negative spread.

ぎゃくさん 逆算 ── 逆算する 動 count [calculate] backward 《to》. (❗ 後の方が堅い言い方)

ぎゃくさん 逆産 《have》a breech birth [delivery].

きゃくし 客死 (⇔客死(かっ))

きゃくしつ 客室 〘個人宅またはホテルの客用寝室〙 a guest room; 〘船・飛行機の〙 a cabin.
●客室係 (ホテルの) a room clerk; 客室乗務員 (飛行機の) a flight attendant; (集合的に) a cabin crew.

きゃくしゃ 客車 《米》 a (passenger) car, 《英》 a (railway) carriage; a coach (❗ coach は《米》では食堂車などと区別して普通客車をさす. また寝台車と区別して a day coach という).

ぎゃくしゅう 逆襲 a counterattack. (⇔反撃)

ぎゃくじょう 逆上 ▶逆上した男 a *frenzied* man. ▶彼はその知らせを聞いて逆上した He got *furious* [*really mad*] at the news./The news drove him *into a frenzy*.

きゃくしょうばい 客商売 the hospitality industry; a service industry.

きゃくしょく 脚色 图 (劇化) (a) dramatization; (改作) (an) adaptation.
── 脚色する 動 ▶小説をテレビ用に脚色する *dramatize* [*adapt*] a novel *for* television. ▶『マイフェアレディ』はバーナード・ショーの『ピグマリオン』を舞台用に脚色したものである *My Fair Lady* is a stage *adaptation* of Bernard Shaw's *Pygmalion*.

ぎゃくしん 逆進 ── 逆進性の 形 regressive.
●逆進税 a regressive tax.

ぎゃくシングル 逆シングル 【野球】 a backhand(ed) catch. ▶逆シングルで捕球する make a *backhand catch* 《of a liner》.

ぎゃくすう 逆数 〘数学〙 a reciprocal; a multiplicative inverse. ▶2の逆数は 1/2 である The *reciprocal* of two is one half.

きゃくすじ 客筋 (a) clientele /klàiantél/ (❗ 単・複両扱い); customers. ▶この店は客筋がいい(=地位の高い常連を持っている) This store has a high-class *clientele*./This store is patronized by well-to-do people 《customers》.

ぎゃくせい 虐政 (暴政) tyranny; (専制政治) despotism.

ぎゃくせいせっけん 逆性石鹸 a cationic soap.

きゃくせき 客席 a seat.

ぎゃくせつ 逆説 图 a paradox. ▶逆説めくが, 我々はその町を救うために破壊したのだ *Paradoxically*, we destroyed the town in order to save it.
── 逆説的な 形 paradoxical.

きゃくせん 客船 a passenger boat [ship]; (海洋航路の大型定期船) a passenger liner.

きゃくぜん 客膳 (客用の食事) a meal for a guest; (客用の膳) a small tray with legs on which a meal is arranged (for a guest).

ぎゃくせんでん 逆宣伝 《spread》counterpropaganda.

キャピタルレター 〚大文字〛a capital letter (↔a small letter).
キャピタルロス 〚資本売却差損〛capital loss.
キャビネット a cabinet.
キャビン 〚船室〛a cabin.
キャプテン 〚主将, 船長, 機長〛a captain.
キャブレター 〚気化器〛〚機械〛a carburetor /kɑ́ːrbəreɪtɑr/.
ぎゃふん ・ぎゃふんと参る be beaten (all) hollow.
・ぎゃふんと言わせる beat 《him》(all) hollow.
キャベツ 〚植物〛a cabbage /kǽbɪdʒ/. (!)料理した葉は U) ・キャベツ1玉 a head of [《話》a] cabbage. ・ロールキャベツ a stuffed cabbage roll.
・キャベツ畑 a cabbage patch.
キャミソール a camisole.
きゃら 伽羅 〚沈香〛aloes, agalloch; 〚伽羅木〛a Japanese yew.
・伽羅蕗(ぶき) (説明的に) butterbur boiled out in soy sauce.
ギャラ 〚最低保証出演料〛a guarantee; 〚出演・講演料〛a performer's fee. ▶彼の講演のギャラは20万円だった He got [We paid him] 200,000 yen for his lecture. (!)必ずしも a 200,000 yen *fee* という必要はない)
キャラウェー 〚ヒメウイキョウ〛〚植物〛a caraway.
キャラクター a character. ・キャラクターグッズ 〚商品〛goods featuring popular cartoon *characters*. ▶キティーちゃんのキャラクターグッズは若い女性にとても人気がある Goods *with the picture of Kitty on* them are very popular among young women.
ギャラップ ・ギャラップ調査 〚商標〛〚米国の世論調査〛Gallup poll.
キャラバン 〚隊商〛a caravan; 〚遠征隊〛an expedition (party).
・キャラバンシューズ hiking boots.
キャラメル 《eat》a caramel /kǽrəml/.
ギャラリー 〚画廊〛a gallery; 〚ゴルフ競技の観客〛the gallery (!)単数形で複数扱いも可)
キャリア 〚職歴〛a career /kəríər/. ・外務省のキャリア[ノンキャリア]組 *elite* [*non-elite*] *officers* in the Foreign Ministry. ▶彼は教師としてのキャリアが長い He has a long *career* as a teacher [*in* teaching]./(経験が豊かだ) He has a lot of experience in teaching./He has been a teacher for a long time. ▶彼女はキャリアアップを目指して努力した She worked hard to get a more favorable *position* [*job*].
キャリア 〚保菌者〛a carrier. ・エイズウイルスのキャリア a *carrier* of the AIDS virus; an HIV *carrier*.
キャリーバッグ 〚大型スーツケース〛a carryall, 《英》a holdall; 《和製語》a carry bag.
ギャル 《話》a gal, a girl.
ギャロップ 〚馬の早駆け〛a gallop.
キャロル 〚祝歌〛a 《Christmas》carol.
きゃんきゃん ・きゃんきゃん鳴く《犬が》yap. ▶しっぽを踏まれたときなどの悲鳴を yelp (⇨きゃん) ▶小犬がきゃんきゃん鳴いている The puppies *are yapping*.
ギャング 〚集団〛a gang; (一員) a gangster.
・ギャング映画 a gangster movie.
キャンセル 图 〚取り消し〛(a) cancellation. ・キャンセル待ちの旅客 a *standby* (passenger). ▶504便のキャンセル待ちをしています I'm *on standby* for Flight 504.
── **キャンセルする** 動 〚取り消す〛cancel 《one's reservation》.
・キャンセル料 a cancellation fee.
キャンデー 《主に米》(a) candy (!)種類をいうときは C). 米英ともにチョコレート, フルーツキャンデーなども含める); 《英》a sweet; (棒つきのあめ)《口》a lollipop, 《米話》a sucker. ・ミックスキャンデー mixed *candies*.
きゃんきゃん ・きゃんと鳴く yelp. ▶犬はしっぽを踏まれてきゃんと悲鳴を上げた The dog *yelped* when he was trod on his tail.
キャンドル a candle.
・キャンドルサービス a candlelight service. (参考)(1)クリスマスなどにろうそくに火をともして行う礼拝のこと. (2)結婚式の披露宴で行う「キャンドルサービス」は含まない. candle service という英語もない)
キャンバス 〚帆布, テント〛(a piece of) canvas; 〚画布〛(a) canvas. ・キャンバスシューズ (a pair of) *canvas* shoes. ・一塁キャンバス first base; a first-base bag. (!)canvas は base の材料)
キャンパス ・キャンパスで on (the) *campus*. ・キャンパス外で off (the) *campus*. ▶その大学のキャンパスは広くて美しい The university has a large, beautiful *campus*.
キャンピングカー 《主に米》a camper (van), a motor home, 《英》a motor caravan; 《和製語》a camping car.
キャンプ 图 a camp. ・(登山の)ベースキャンプをはる set up [make] a base *camp*. ・子供たちをキャンプに連れて行く take one's children *camping*. ・(野球チームなどが)キャンプインする start pre-season [spring] training. (!)a spring training camp は「キャンプ地」の意) ▶毎年山にキャンプに行きます We go *camping* in [×to] the mountains every year. (!)×go for [to] camping は不可)
── **キャンプする** 動 ▶その湖の近くで1週間キャンプした[していた] We camped (out) [*were in camp*] by the lake for a week.
・キャンプ場《主に米》a campground,《主に英》a campsite. ・キャンプファイアー《make》a campfire.
・キャンプ村 a cámping village. ・キャンプ用品[用具] 〚集合的〛a cámping òutfit, cámping equipment.
ギャンブル 〚賭け, 賭け事〛gambling.
キャンペーン 〚運動〛a campaign. ・教育改革推進[反対]のキャンペーンを始める start a *campaign for* [*against*] the educational reform.
・キャンペーンガール a promotion girl;《和製語》a campaign girl. ・キャンペーンセール (販売促進のための) a sales drive [campaign]; (売り出し) a sale.
キャンベラ 〚オーストラリアの首都〛Canberra /kǽnbərə/.
きゅう 杞憂 〚無用な心配〛needless fears. ▶あなたの心配事は杞憂にすぎない Your *worries* are *needless* (根拠がない) *groundless*].
∶**きゅう 急** 图 ❶ 〚急ぎ〛(緊急) urgency. ▶これは急を要する問題だ This is an *urgent* [(差し迫った) a *pressing*] problem.
❷ 〚突然〛suddenness. ・急ブレーキをかける brake *suddenly* [(激しく) *hard*]. ・急停車 (⇨急停車)
❸ 〚速いこと〛rapidity. ▶広告業は急成長事業の一つである Advertising is one of the *fastest* growing businesses.
❹ 〚傾斜が大きいこと〛▶道路の急カーブ a *sharp* turn [bend, curve] in the road.
❺ 〚非常事態〛(an) emergency; (危機) a crisis (複 crises). ・急に備えるprepare for an *emergency* [(最悪の場合) *the worst*]. ▶彼の財政の急を救う get him out of his financial *crisis* [困窮) difficulties].
── **急な** 形 ❶ 〚急ぎの〛(緊急の) urgent; (即座の) immediate. ・急な用事で外出する go out on *urgent* business.

きゅう ❷【突然の】▶出発の日程の急な変更は可能ですか Can I change the date of my departure *at short notice*?
❸【速い】(動きが) rapid; (速度が) fast; (すばやい) quick, (やや書) swift. ▶この川の流れは急だ The current of this river is *rapid* [*swift*].
❹【傾斜が大きい】(急角度の) sharp; (険しい) steep. ●急な階段[登り] a steep staircase [climb]. ▶あの道は急なので自転車では登れない That path is so *steep* that I can't go up by bike.

── **急に** 圖 ❶【急ぎで】immediately; at once.
❷【突然に】suddenly, all of a sudden; (思いがけなく) unexpectedly; (不意に) abruptly. (⇨突然 [類語]) ●急に泣き[笑い]出す burst out crying [laughing]; break into tears [laughter, a laugh]. ▶急に明かりが全部消えた *Suddenly* [*All of a sudden*], all the lights went out. ▶そんなに急に言われても無理よ That's a bit too *sudden*.
❸【傾斜が大きく】▶山は急に上り坂になり岩だらけの頂上へと続いていた The mountain ascended *sharply* to a craggy peak.

***きゅう** 九 nine; 〖9番目の〗the ninth. (⇨三)
***きゅう** 級 ❶【等級】a class; (段階) a grade; (階級) a rank; 〖水準〗a level. ●外相級の会談 talks at the *level* of foreign ministers; talks at foreign minister *level*. ●3,000メートル級の山 a mountain *in* the 3,000 meter *class*. ▶彼女は日本で第一級のピアニストだ She is a first-[top-]*class* pianist in Japan./She is one of the best pianists in Japan.
❷【学級】a class; 〖学年〗a year; 《米》(小・中・高校の) a grade; 《英》(中等学校の) a form. ▶彼は大学では私より1級上だ He is one *year* senior to [ahead of] me at college.
❸【将棋などの】a class, a degree. ●1級の first *class*. ●(ボクシングなどの) 重[軽]量級 the heavyweight [lightweight] *division*.
きゅう 旧 ●旧思想 *old* ideas. ●旧住所 one's *old* [*former*] address. ●旧市街地 the *old* part of a city. ●旧正月 (⇨旧正月)
きゅう 灸 a moxa cautery, a moxibustion. ●灸をすえる *cauterize* (*him*) with moxa.
きゅう 宮 ❶【宮殿】a palace. ●バッキンガム宮殿 Buckingham *Palace*.
❷【天文】a sign, a star sign. ●十二宮 the *signs* of the zodiac.
きゅう 球 图〖球体〗a globe; 〖幾何〗a sphere; (たま) a ball; 〖電球〗a bulb; 〖投球〗a pitch. ●三球三振をくらう be struck out [strike out] on three *pitches*.

── **球(形)の** 圏 global; spherical; ball-shaped 《+图》; ... in the shape of a ball.
キュー (ビリヤードの) a cue.
ぎゅう 義勇 ●義勇軍 a voluntary army.
きゅうあい 求愛 图 (a) courtship.
── **求愛する** 働 (やや古) court; woo.
きゅうあく 旧悪 past misdeeds; (犯罪行為) a past crime. ▶旧悪が露見した His *past crime* came to light [was brought to light].
キュウアンドエー〖質疑応答〗Q & A; question(s) and answer(s).
きゅうい 球威 stuff. ●球威のある投球 a pitch with plenty of *stuff*. ●球威がある have good [a lot of] *stuff*.
きゅういん 吸引 图 (力) suction. ●吸引力が強い have great *suction*.
── **吸引する** 働 suck.
ぎゅういんばしょく 牛飲馬食 ── **牛飲馬食する** 働

eat* like a horse and drink* like a fish; eat and drink very heavily.
きゅううん 球運 one's (base)ball luck. ▶私たちは球運に恵まれた *Fortune* smiled on us [*Luck* was with us] in the ball game. ▶私たちは9回に球運に恵まれた We got a break in the ninth inning.
きゅうえん 休園 ▶本日は休園です (幼稚園が) The kindergarten *is closed* today./(遊園地が) This amusement park *is closed* today./(掲示)*No Business* Today.
きゅうえん 休演 ── **休演する** 働 (劇場が) cancel an appearance; cancel a performance; (俳優が) be absent [absent oneself] from the stage; do* not appear on the stage.
きゅうえん 求縁 seeking [looking for] a match [a marriage partner].
●求縁広告 an advertisement for a match.
きゅうえん 救援 图 〖貧者などの〗relief; 〖救助〗rescue; 〖助力〗help. ●難民に救援物資[基金]を送る send *relief* goods [a *relief* fund] to the refugees. (❗send relief なら救援物資・救援金のどちらでも表せる) ●災害のとき救援活動をする give *help* in time of disaster. ●救援登板をする make a relief appearance; pitch [work] in relief.

── **救援する** 働 〖書〗relieve, rescue. (⇨助ける ❶)
●先発投手を救援する *relieve* a starting pitcher.
●救援隊 a relief [a rescue] party [team].
●救援投手 a relief pitcher; a reliever.
きゅうえん 球宴 an all-star game; the summer classic.
キューオーエル〖生活の質、精神的満足度〗QOL 《quality of life の略》.
きゅうおん 旧恩 ●旧恩に報いる return [repay] 《his》 *old favor* [*kindness*].
きゅうおん 吸音 absorption of sound.
●吸音材 acoustical material. ●吸音処理 acoustic treatment. ●吸音タイル acoustical tile.
***きゅうか** 休暇 vacation, a holiday; leave.

> **使い分け** vacation《主に米》では通例一定期間の休暇をさし、短期・長期ともに用いるが、《英》では大学の休暇などに用いられる。
> holiday 《米》では通例法定の祝祭日の意。《主に英》では通例週末(weekend)を除く一定期間の休暇をいうが、公休日の場合は1日のときもある。複数形の holidays は通例長期の休暇を表す。
> なお、何らかの理由で仕事から解放される一定期間の休暇は「期間+off」で表されることも多い。
> leave は公務員・軍隊などの休暇(の許可)を意味する。

①【～休暇】●夏期休暇 the summer *vacation* [《英》*holiday*(s)]. (⇨夏休み) ●有給休暇 a paid *vacation* [《英》*holiday*]; a vacation [《英》a *holiday*] with pay. ●特別休暇 a special [an extra] *vacation* [《英》*holiday*]. ●出産休暇中で[に] on maternity *leave*. ▶彼らは年に12日間の病気休暇がもらえます They earn [receive] twelve days of *sick leave* in a year.
②【休暇～】●休暇届を出す give [hand in] *a leave notice*. ▶休暇中に彼女に会いましたか Did you see her during [in, ✗for] the *vacation*《米》[the *holiday*(s)《英》]? ●生徒は今休暇中だ The students are *on vacation*《米》[*holiday*《米》, ✗*holidays*》 now. (❗on の後では無冠詞。以下同様)
③【休暇は】●休暇は来週からです Our *vacation* begins《米》[*holidays* begin《英》] next week. ▶休暇は2週間ある The *vacation* is《米》[*holidays* are《英》] two weeks long.
④【休暇を】●2週間の休暇を取る take two

きゅうか weeks *off*; take two weeks' [a two-week] *vacation*《米》[*holiday*(*s*)《英》]. ▶休暇を願い出るask for time *off* [*leave* (*of absence*)]. ▶1日休暇をもらう *get* a day *off*; *get* a day's *holiday*. ▶今日は休暇を取っております Mr. Yamada is having a day *off* [is on *leave* (*of absence*)] today. ▶彼らは今ハワイで休暇を過ごしている They are now spending their *vacation*《米》[*holiday*(*s*)《英》] in Hawaii./They are now *vacationing*《米》[*holidaying*《英》] in Hawaii.

⑤[休暇で] ▶休暇でカナダヘスキーに出かける go to Canada *for* one's skiing *vacation*《米》[*holidays*《英》] (![] for は「…を過ごすために」の意); go skiing in Canada *on vacation*《米》[*holiday*《英》]. ▶下宿生たちは今休暇で不在です[帰省している] The boarders are away [*away home*] *on vacation* now.

きゅうか 旧家 an old family. ▶旧家の出である come from an old family.

きゅうかい 休会 图 (一時的な休み) (an) adjournment; (休会期間) (a) recess. ▶国会は休会中です The Diet is *in recess*.

── **休会する** 動 ▶会議をあす午前10時まで[次の月曜まで]休会します We will *adjourn* the meeting till tomorrow at 10 a.m. [to the following Monday].

きゅうかく 嗅覚 (a sense of) smell. ▶犬の嗅覚は鋭い Dogs have a keen *sense of smell*.

きゅうがく 休学 图 absence from school.

── **休学する** 動 ▶彼は病気で3か月休学した He stayed away [《やや書》was absent] *from school* for three months because he was sick [because of sickness].

きゅうかざん 休火山 a dormant volcano《英》~(e)s.
きゅうがた 旧型 ── 旧型の 形 old-fashioned. (⇨古い❸)
きゅうかなづかい 旧仮名遣い old *kana* orthography.
きゅうかん 旧観 (状態) the former state; (光景) the former sight. ▶新しい礼拝堂は旧観をとどめていない There remains no trace of the *former appearance* in the new chapel.

きゅうかん 休刊 图 (雑誌・新聞などの) no issue [(news)paper]. ── **休刊する** 動 stop [(一時的に) suspend] publication.
●休刊日 (新聞の) a newspaper [a press] holiday.

きゅうかん 休館 ▶この図書館はあすは休館です This library *is* [*will be*] *closed* tomorrow. (▶決まった休館日をさす場合、will be は臨時の休みを含意する) ▶月曜は休館 (掲示) Closed Monday(s).

きゅうかん 急患 [救急患者] an emergency patient [case]. (⇨救急)
きゅうかんちょう 九官鳥 [鳥] a myna(h) /máinə/.
きゅうかんび 休肝日 a nonalcoholic day.
きゅうき 吸気 (an) inhalation; (an) inspiration.
きゅうぎ 球技 a ball game. (![]特に野球)
きゅうぎ 球戯 a ball game. [ビリヤード] billiards.
きゅうきゅう ▶真新しい靴がきゅうきゅう鳴った My brand-new shoes *squeaked*. ▶金がなくてきゅうきゅうとしていた I lived *hand to mouth*./I *was* very *pressed for money*.

きゅうきゅう 汲々 be intent 〈*on*〉. ▶彼は出世[金もうけ]にきゅうとしている He *is intent on* getting promoted [making money].

きゅうきゅう 救急 ●救急患者 an emergency patient [case]. ●救急救命士 a paramedic. ●救急車 (⇨救急車). ●救急処置 first aid. ●救急隊員 an ambulance attendant [《(米)》driver] (![]an ambulanceman, an ambulancewoman ともいう);《集合的》an ambulance crew (![]複数扱い).
●救急箱 a first-aid kit [box]. ●救急病院 an emergency hospital.

ぎゅうぎゅう ▶彼女はかばんに服をぎゅうぎゅう詰め込んだ She *stuffed* her bag with her clothes./《張り裂けそうなほど》She *packed* [*squeezed*] her clothes into her bag *till it almost burst*. ▶列車はぎゅうぎゅう詰めだった The train *was packed full*./The train *was extremely crowded*. ▶通勤客はぎゅうぎゅう詰めのまま東京駅まで行く Commuters stay *packed in like sardines* until the train gets to Tokyo Station.
▶私は後ろからぎゅうぎゅう押された I *was pushed* [*was pressed*] *hard* from behind.

きゅうきゅうしゃ 救急車 an ambulance. ●救急車で運ばれる be taken [*rushed*] to hospital by *ambulance* [in an *ambulance*]. ▶救急車を呼んでくれ Call (me) [Ask for] an *ambulance*. (![]米国ではDial nine-one-one. と呼んでもよい. ただし「警察を呼んで」の意にもなる) ▶もしもし、こちらはメイプル街のマクドナルドです. 救急車を至急お願いします Hello. I'm at McDonald's on Maple Avenue. We need an *ambulance* right away.

きゅうぎゅうのいちもう 九牛の一毛 (only) a drop in the bucket《米》[ocean《英》].
きゅうきょ 旧居 one's old house; one's former residence.
きゅうきょ 急遽 in a hurry;《やや書》hastily, in haste. ▶きゅうきょ帰国する return home in haste.
きゅうきょう 旧教 (Roman) Catholicism (↔Protestantism). ●旧教徒 a (Roman) Catholic (↔Protestant).
きゅうきょう 窮境 (⇨窮地)
きゅうぎょう 休業 图 ▶臨時休業日 a special holiday. ▶本日休業 (掲示) Closed today.
── **休業する** 動 close a store. (⇨休む) ▶あす当店は休業します This store will *be closed* tomorrow.
(⇨休館 [第1文例])

きゅうきょく 喜遊曲 [音楽] a divertimento /divə́ːrtəméntou/ (![]-ti /-tiː/).
きゅうきょく 究極 ── **究極の** 形 ultimate; final.
●人生の究極の目標 the *ultimate* [*final*] goal in one's life.

── **究極的に** ultimately.
きゅうきん 球菌 a coccus /kákəs/;《複》cocci /káksai/.
●ブドウ球菌 a staphylococcus.

***きゅうくつ** 窮屈 ── **窮屈な** 形 ❶ [狭苦しい] cramped; (衣類・靴がきつい) tight. ▶この部屋は窮屈だ This room is *cramped* [*confining*]. ▶ズボンのウエストが窮屈だ[になってきた] The waist of the pants is [has gotten] *too tight* (for me). ▶この靴は窮屈で足が痛い These shoes *pinch me* [*my feet*].

❷ [堅苦しい] (儀式ばった) formal; (きびしい)《やや書》rigid; (心地よくない) uncomfortable. ▶窮屈な規則をゆるる get rid of *rigid* [*restrictive*] rules. ▶あの学校はあまりにも窮屈だ There is too much *formality* in that school. ▶窮屈に[≒深刻に]考えないでください Don't take it *seriously*. ▶僕は理数系ではない. 答えは一つしかないという窮屈な[≒柔軟性のない考え方]がいやなんだ I'm not a math-and-science type [《米》I'm a liberal arts major]. I can't agree with that *rigid thinking* that there's only one right answer [≒one answer]. (![]「理数」の日本語と英語の語順に注意)

きゅうけい 休憩 图 (a) rest; (仕事・勉強などの合間の) a break (from work); (授業間の) a break, 《米》(a) recess; (音楽会などの) an intermission, 《英》 an interval; (バス旅行での) a comfort [a rest] stop.
- 休憩なしで3時間勉強する study for three hours without a *break*. ▶だれでも時々休憩が必要だ Everyone needs *rest* from time to time. ▶休憩時間のベルが鳴った The bell rang for a *break*. ▶劇には2回の休憩がある There were two *intermissions* in the play. ▶彼女は昼の休憩で学校の食堂に行っているということだった I was told she was on her lunch *break* [xin the lunch break] in the lunchroom [(セルフサービスの) cafeteria].

── **休憩する** 動 rest, take* [have*] a rest; take [have] a break. ▶授業の合間で10分間休憩する *take* a ten-minute *break* [《米》*recess*] between classes. ▶あの木陰で休憩しよう Let's *take a rest* under that tree.

- 休憩室 a résting [xa rest] ròom (**!** a rest room は「(ホテルなどの) 洗面所」の意); (ホテル・船などの) a lounge. ● 休憩所 a résting plàce; (ホテル・劇場などの) a lobby.

きゅうけい 求刑 ── **求刑する** 動 ▶検事は被告人に死刑を求刑した The prosecutor *demanded* the death penalty for the accused.

きゅうけい 球形 a global; 《書》a spherical shape. ● 球形の 形 global; 《書》spherical.

きゅうけい 球茎 a corm; (鱗茎(ラボ)) a bulb.
- 球茎植物 a cormous plant.

きゅうけいしゃ 急傾斜 图 a steep slope; (上り) a steep ascent. (下り) a steep descent.

── **急傾斜の** 形 (坂などが) steep; (屋根などが) high-pitched.

きゅうげき 急激 ── **急激な** 形 [突然の] sudden, abrupt; [急速な] rapid (⇒突然 [類語]); [下降・旋回などが] sharp. ▶気温の急激な変化 a *sudden* [a *quick*] change in temperature.

── **急激に** 副 suddenly, abruptly; rapidly; sharply. ▶人口が急激に増加した The population has *rapidly* increased. ▶株価が急激に下落した Stock prices fell *sharply*.

きゅうけつき 吸血鬼 a vampire, a bloodsucker.

きゅうげん 急減 图 a rapid [(突然の) a sudden] decrease. (対 急増). ▶人口の急減 a *rapid decrease* in population.

── **急減する** 動 decrease rapidly [suddenly].

きゅうご 救護 图 (⇒救助)

── **救護する** 動 ▶けが人を救護する *help* the injured; (応急手当てをする) *give first aid to* injured people [《やや書》the injured].

- 救護所 a first-aid center [station]. ● 救護班 a relief pàrty.

***きゅうこう 急行** 图 [列車] an express (train). ●特別急行 a limited [a special] *express* (train).
- 8時30分発東京行き急行 the 8:30 *express* for [to] Tokyo. (**!** to は到着点, for は方向を示す) ▶彼は東京行きの急行に乗って行った He took the *express* (*train*) for Tokyo. / (急行で東京へ行った) He went to Tokyo by *express* [on an *express*]. ▶京都への急行は10分ごとにあります The *express* runs every ten minutes to Kyoto.

── **急行する** 動 hurry; rush; hasten [hurry より堅い語]. (⇒急ぐ) ▶消防士は火事現場に急行した The firemen *hurried* [*rushed*] *to* the scene of the fire.

- 急行便 (貨物などの) an express; (郵便の) 《英》express (delivery) (⇒速達). ● 急行料金 express charges.

きゅうこう 旧交 《renew one's》old friendship.
- 旧交を暖める ▶クラス会は旧交を暖めることができてとても楽しかった We much enjoyed knitting up *old friendship* at the class reunion.

きゅうこう 休校 ▶あしたは休校です We'll have [There will be] *no school* tomorrow. / School will *be closed* tomorrow. ▶たくさんの学校が流感 [大雪] のため休校に入っている Many schools are facing flu [snow] days.

きゅうこう 休航 (⇒欠航) ▶結氷のためすべての船舶は休航している All navigation has *been suspended* by ice.

きゅうこう 休講 图 ▶1時間目は休講です We have *no class* in the first period. ▶本日休講《掲示》*No lectures* [*classes*] today. / *Lectures* [*Classes*] *canceled* today.

── **休講する** 動 cancel a lecture.

きゅうごう 糾合 ── **糾合する** 動 muster; rally. ● 同士を糾合する *muster* like-minded people.

きゅうこうか 急降下 图 [飛行機・鳥の] a swoop; [飛行機の] a nosedive. ● 急降下爆撃をする dive-bomb.

── **急降下する** 動 swoop (down) (on); nosedive. ▶飛行機は精油所めがけて急降下し機関砲で攻撃した The planes *dived in* on the oil refinery with their fire guns. ▶気温が急降下した (=急に下がった) There was a *sudden drop in* [xof] temperature. / Temperature *dropped suddenly*.

きゅうこうばい 急勾配 (⇒急傾斜)

きゅうこく 急告 an urgent notice.

きゅうこく 救国 saving one's country; the salvation of one's country.
- 救国者 a savior of the country.

きゅうごしらえ 急ごしらえ ── **急ごしらえの** 形 built in a hurry, hastily constructed; (一時しのぎの) makeshift.

きゅうこん 求婚 图 《receive [accept, refuse]》a proposal of marriage [a marriage proposal] 《from him》.

── **求婚する** 動 ▶彼は真由美に求婚した He *asked* Mayumi *to marry* him. / He *proposed* [*made a proposal*] *to* Mayumi.

きゅうこん 球根 (チューリップ・ユリなどの) a bulb; (ダリアなどの) a tuber. ● チューリップの球根《plant》a tulip *bulb*.
- 球根植物 『植物』 a bulbous plant.

きゅうさい 休載 ── **休載する** 動 ▶第一面の連載中の記事は本日休載します The story *does not appear* on the front page of the paper. ▶本紙の漫画は休載中です The paper *is not carrying* the comic strip.

きゅうさい 救済 图 relief; [助力] help; [魂の] salvation. ● 飢饉(ﾟﾁ)からの救済 famine *relief*. ● 救済資金 a *relief* fùnd 《for the poor》. ● 貧しい人々の救済 the *relief of* the poor. ● 救済策を講ずる take *relief* measures 《for》.

── **救済する** 動 (⇒助ける ❶). ▶洪水の被災者を救済するために食料を送る send food to *relieve* the flood victims.

- 救済融資 a relief loan.

きゅうし 九死 ●九死に一生を得る have a narrow escape from death; narrowly escape death.

きゅうし 旧師 one's former teacher.

きゅうし 休止 图 (一時的な) suspension; (休み) (a) rest. ● 小休止をとる take [have] a short *rest*.

── **休止する** 動 suspend; (一時的に休む) pause.

- 休止符『音楽』a rest. (**関連**「全音 [2分; 4分; 8分] 休止符」a whole [a half; a quarter; an

きゅうし 臼歯 (大臼歯) a mólar (tooth (複 teeth)); (小臼歯) a premólar (tooth).

きゅうし 急死 图 a sudden death. ━急死する 動 die suddenly.

きゅうし 急使 a swift messnger.

きゅうし 球史 baseball history; the history of baseball.

きゅうし 給紙 (プリンターなどの) paper feed. ●給紙する feed paper.

きゅうじ 球児 (高校野球の) a high school baseball player.

きゅうじ 給仕 图 a server; (ウエーター) a waiter, (ウエートレス) a waitress;《男女共用》waitperson.
━給仕する 動 wait at the table《米》[at table《英》](!職業として); serve (at table). ●客に給仕する wait on a guest. ▶母が食卓でお給仕をしてくれる Mother serves at table.

ぎゅうじ 牛耳 ●牛耳を執る ⇨牛耳る.

きゅうしき 旧式 ━旧式の 形 (⇨古い❸)

きゅうしつ 吸湿 ━吸湿性(の) 形 absorbent; hygroscopic.

*きゅうじつ 休日 a holiday; (一日の休暇) a day off. (⇨休暇)

きゅうしゃ 厩舎 a stable.

きゅうしゃ 鳩舎 a dovecot(e).

ぎゅうしゃ 牛舎 a cowshed.

きゅうしゅ 球種 ●いろいろな球種 (throw) a large [a wide] variety of pitches.

きゅうしゅ 鳩首 鳩首凝議(髭ぢ)する put one's heads together in earnest; discuss a difficult problem together seriously.

*きゅうしゅう 吸収 图 absorption《of》. ●ミネラルの吸収 mineral absorption; absorption of mineral.
━吸収する 動 [液体・音・光などを] absorb; [主に液体を] soak ... up; (口で吸い込む) suck ... in. ●大企業に吸収される be swallowed up by a big business. ▶スポンジは水を吸収する A sponge absorbs water. ▶彼は新しい思想を吸収した He absorbed [soaked up] new ideas.

きゅうしゅう 九州 (地方) the Kyushu district; (島) Kyushu Island, the island of Kyushu.

きゅうしゅう 旧習 an old custom;《ほめて》a time-honored custom.

きゅうしゅう 急襲 图 a sudden, surprise attack; a storm; a raid.
━急襲する 動 make* a sudden, surprise attack《on》; (軍・警察が) make [carry out] a raid《on》. ▶警察はギャングの隠れ家を明け方に急襲した The police made a dawn raid on the gang's hide-out.

*きゅうじゅう 九十 ninety;〚90番目の〛the ninetieth. (⇨二十, 五十)

きゅうしゅつ 救出 (a) rescue. (⇨救助, 助ける❷)

きゅうじゅつ 弓術 archery.

きゅうしゅん 急峻 ━急峻な 形 steep; precipitous.

きゅうしょ 急所 〚生命にかかわる所〛a vital spot [part, organ]; (股間) the groin, the crotch;〚大切な点〛the point, a key [a vital] point;〚弱点〛a weak point. ●急所をついた〈言を得た〉質問 a question that is to the point [touches on a vital point]. ●急所をける kick〈him〉in the groin [crotch]. ▶彼は彼女の急所(=弱み)を握っている He has something on〈米〉[some evidence against〈英〉] her./He knows her weak point(s).

*きゅうじょ 救助 图 (a) rescue (!特に差し迫った危険からの救助); help. (⇨助け) ●救助を求める ask for help. ●遭難した登山者の救助に向かう go to the rescue of [set out to rescue] the climbers in distress. (⇨助ける❷) ▶救助が来るまで私たちは何時間も待った We waited for hours before help arrived./We waited for rescue for hours.
━救助する 動 save; rescue; help. (⇨助ける❷) ●人命を救助する save〈his〉life《from》. ▶船客は全員沈没する船から救助された All the passengers were rescued from the sinking ship.
●救助活動 a rescue operátion. ●救助機 a réscue pláne. ●救助信号 a distress sìgnal [càll]; an SOS (call); (船舶・航空機の) a mayday. ●救助船 (救難船) a sálvage bòat; (救命艇) a lifeboat. ●救助隊 a rescue párty [tèam]; (隊員) a rescue wòrker. ●救助袋 an escápe chùte.

きゅうしょう 旧称 an old name; a former title.

きゅうじょう 弓状 ━弓状の 形 arched; bow-shaped.

きゅうじょう 休場 ━休場する 動 (劇場などが) be closed; (力士が) stay away from the ring, sit* out. ▶彼はけがのため(途中から)休場した He was injured and had to sit out (the rest of) the tournament.

きゅうじょう 球場 a báseball gròund [fìeld],《米》a ballpark.〚参考〛米国の球場名には通例 ... Field, ... Park, ... Stadium が用いられる. ●甲子園球場 the Koshien Stádium.

きゅうじょう 窮状 〚ひどい状態〛a terrible [a miserable] condition; a plight (!単数形で);〚困窮〛《やや書》distress. ●窮状を訴える complain about one's miserable condition [one's plight]. ●貧民の窮状を救う save poor people from distress; help poor people in distress.

きゅうしょうがつ 旧正月 the lunar New Year; New Year's Day by the old [lunar] calendar.

きゅうじょうしょう 急上昇 图 a sharp [a sudden] rise《in》; (物価・株価などの) a boost《in》.
━急上昇する 動 rise* sharply [suddenly]. ▶そのニュースによってフランスの株が急上昇した The news has given an especially big boost to French stocks.

きゅうしょく 求職 图 job hunting. ●求職の申し込みをする apply for a job.
━求職する 動 (職を探す) look [hunt] for a job;《書》seek employment.
●求職広告欄 the "Situations Vacant [Wanted]" column. ●求職者 a job hunter [seeker]; (申し込み者) a job applicant.

きゅうしょく 休職 leave of absence (from work [employment, duty]). (!文脈により leave のみも可) ●休職を許可する give leave of absence. ●休職中である be on〈sick, maternity〉leave;have〈three months'〉leave of absence.

きゅうしょく 給食 图 ●学校給食 a school lunch.
━給食する 動 (生徒に) provide lunch for schoolchildren; (労働者に) provide meals for workers. ●給食費 the charge for a school lunch.

ぎゅうじる 牛耳る (支配する) control (-ll-), dóminate. ▶彼が会社を牛耳っている He controls [is in control of] the company./The company is under his control.〚話〛thumb;〚口〛control 图 を firm (断固とした)で強めることができる. thumb はそれ自体で firm control というイメージである.

きゅうしん 休診 ●本日休診《掲示》Closed Today.

きゅうしん 急伸 图 a sudden [a sharp] increase; a

きゅうしん 急伸 rapid [a sharp] rise 《in sales》.
— **急伸する** 動 rise* sharply. ▶最近数週間で物価が急伸した Prices have *risen sharply* over the last few weeks.

きゅうしん 急進 急進的な 形 radical; extreme. ●急進思想 radical ideas. ●急進主義 radicalism. ●急進主義者 a radical. ●急進派 a radical faction [group].

きゅうしん 球審 the plate úmpire; a ball-and-strike umpire.

きゅうじん 九仞 ●九仞の功を一簣(ﾂｷ)に欠く (ことわざ) There's many a slip between the cup and the lip./One hour's cold will spoil seven years' warming.

きゅうじん 吸塵 sucking in [up] dirt and dust.

きゅうじん 求人 a job offer. ●求人難 a labor shortage; a shortage of labor. ●秘書の求人広告を新聞に出す put a *want ad* [an ad] *for* a secretary in the newspaper ▶求人《広告ビラ》Help wanted. ▶今年は求人が少ない There are not many *job offers* this year.

きゅうしんりょく 求心力 〖物理〗centripetal /séntripítl/ (↔centrifugal) force.

きゅうす 急須 a small teapot.

きゅうす 休す (休止する) take* a rest. ●万事休す(ﾏﾝｼﾞ).

きゅうすい 吸水 — 吸水性の(ある) 形 absorbent (paper).
— **吸水する** 動 suck (up) moisture 《*from* the soil》; absorb water.
●吸水管 a siphon. ●吸水ポンプ a suction pump.

きゅうすい 給水 图 water supply, the supply of water. ●給水を制限する[止める] restrict [turn off] the *water supply*.
— **給水する** 動 ●船に給水する *water* a ship. ▶その町は琵琶湖から給水されている The town *is supplied with water* from Lake Biwa./Lake Biwa *supplies water to* [*for*] the town [the town *with water*].
●給水車 a wáter wàgon [《英》càrt]. ●給水塔 a wáter tòwer.

きゅうすう 級数 〖数学〗a series; a progression. ●等差[算術]級数 an arithmetic(al) *progression*. ●等比[幾何]級数 a geometric(al) *progression*.

きゅうする 窮する (途方に暮れる) (やや堅) be at a loss; 《話》be at one's wit's end; (窮地に立っている)《話》be in a fix; (板ばさみになっている) be in a dilemma. ●返答に窮する *be at a loss for* an answer [*what to answer*]; (知らない) *don't know* [*be not sure*] *what to answer*.
●窮すれば通ず There's always a way out.

きゅうする 給する pay*. (⇨支給する)

きゅうせい 旧制 ●旧制の中学校 a high school under the *old system*.

きゅうせい 旧姓 (女性の結婚前の姓) one's maiden [birth] name. (**!** (1) 性差別を意識する人は後の方を好む. (2) 結婚後の姓は one's married name) ●井上夫人, 旧姓秋吉 Mrs. Inoue, née /néi/ Akiyoshi; Mrs. Inoue, Akiyoshi *that was*. ▶旧姓を秋吉と申します I was an Akiyoshi before my marriage.

きゅうせい 急性 — 急性の 形 acute (↔chronic). ●急性肺炎 *acute* pneumonia /n(j)uːmóunjə/.

きゅうせい 急逝 〖「急死」の丁寧な言い方〗a sudden death.

きゅうせいぐん 救世軍 the Salvation Army. 〖参考〗国際的なキリスト教社会福祉団体)

きゅうせいしゅ 救世主 the [our] Saviour /séivjər/ (《米》でも Savior とつづりより普通); the Messiah /misáiə/. ●救世主イエス・キリストを賛美する praise Jesus Christ, our *Saviour* [*Messiah*].

きゅうせいちょう 急成長 图 fast [rapid, (爆発的な) explosive] growth.
— **急成長する** 動 grow* rapidly; (一気に) shoot* up. ▶その国は急成長(=発展)している The country *is developing rapidly*.
●急成長市場 a fast-growing [a rapidly-growing] market. ●急成長分野 a fast-growth area.

きゅうせいど 旧制度 《*under*》the old system. (⇨旧制)

きゅうせかい 旧世界 the Old World.

きゅうせき 旧跡 a historic [a historical] spot. (**!** historic は「歴史上有名な」, historical は単に「歴史に関する」の意) ●名所旧跡を訪ねる visit the places of scenic beauty and *historical interest*.

きゅうせっきじだい 旧石器時代 the Old Stone Age, the Paleolithic /pèiliouliθik/ (period).

きゅうせん 休戦 图 (通例一時的な) a truce, an ármistice. ●クリスマス休戦 a Christmas *truce*. ●休戦協定に調印する sign an *armistice* (agreement).
— **休戦する** 動 call [declare] a truce; (一時的に戦いをやめる) stop fighting temporarily.

きゅうせんぽう 急先鋒 (先頭) the vanguard. ●改革運動の急先鋒となる be in the *vanguard* of the reform movement.

きゅうそ 窮鼠 ●窮鼠猫をかむ (追い詰められた動物は危険な敵) A cornered animal is a dangerous foe.

きゅうぞう 窮造 — **急造する** 動 build* [construct] in haste [in a hurry]; throw* ... up. ▶1晩で急造した家 a house *thrown up* overnight.

きゅうぞう 急増 a rapid [(突然の) a sudden] increase; a surge. (↔ 急減) ●人口の急増 a rapid *increase in* population; (爆発的な) a population explosion. ●利益[売上高; 需要]の急増 a *surge* [*a sharp increase*] *in* profits [sales; demand].
— **急増する** 動 increase rapidly [suddenly]; surge. ▶外国人旅行者数がすでに急増している The number of foreign tourists has already *jumped sharply*. ▶そのコマーシャルのおかげで売り上げが急増した The commercial gave sales a *real boost*.

きゅうそく 休息 (a) rest. (⇨休憩)
— **休息する** 動 ●ちょっと[十分]休息する take [have] a short [a good] rest.

きゅうそく 急速 — 急速な 形 fast; (動作が) rapid; (対応が遅れのない) prompt. ●急速な進歩をとげる make rapid [fast] prógress 《*in*》. (**!** 通例 ×make progress *rapidly* とはいわない; prógress *rapidly* 《*in*》.
— **急速に** 副 fast; rapidly; promptly. ●急速に変化しているコンピュタ技術の世界 a *rapidly* changing world of computer technology. ▶すでにどこの畑には数百戸の住宅ができ, 村は急速に変貌(ﾍﾝ)している Already there were hundreds of houses in the field. The village is changing *very fast*.

きゅうそく 球速 〖野球〗the speed [velocity] of a pitched ball. ●その投手の球速は速い The pitcher throws with *velocity* [has great *velocity*].

きゅうたい 旧態 ●旧態を脱する depart from the old habit 《*of doing*》. ●旧態依然としている(=元のままである) remain unchanged.

きゅうたい 球体 a sphere; a globe. — 球体の 形 spherical; global.

きゅうだい 及第 ▶彼は英語で及第点をとった He got a *passing* (↔a *failing*) grade [mark] in English. (⚠通例成績の「可」は C, D,「不可」は F で表示 (⇨点, 成績))
── **及第する** 自 ▶試験に及第する *pass* the exam.
きゅうだん 糾弾 名 《書》censure.
── **糾弾する** 他 《書》censure. ▶賄賂(わいろ)受領で彼を糾弾する *censure* him *for* taking bribes.
きゅうだん 球団 名 a ball club; an organization. (⚠アマのチームにも使える) ▶球団のオーナー the owner of a *ball club*.
きゅうち 旧知 ▶真紀とは旧知の間柄だ Maki is an *old acquaintance* of mine./I have *known* Maki *for years*.
きゅうち 窮地 an awkward [a difficult, a serious] position,《話》a mess,(やや話) a (tight) corner,〖板ばさみ〗a dilemma. (⇨難局) ▶窮地に陥る[立つ; 追い込まれる; 陥っている] get into [find oneself in; be forced into; be in] a *difficult position*. ▶その会社は窮地を脱した The company went [came, got] *through* a *tight squeeze*. (⇨難局)
きゅうちゃく 吸着 名 adhesion;〖化学〗adsorption.
── **吸着性の** 形 adsorbent;〖化学〗adsorptive.
── **吸着する** 自 adhere [stick]《*to*》(⚠前の方が堅い語で強意的);〖化学〗adsorb.
●**吸着剤** (an) adsorbent. ●**吸着盤** a sucker.
きゅうちゅう 吸虫〖動物〗a fluke; a flukeworm.
きゅうちゅう 宮中 the (Imperial) Court. ▶宮中の儀式 a ceremony at *Court*.
きゅうちょう 窮鳥 ●窮鳥懐に入(い)れば猟師も殺さず《ことわざ》The lion spares the suppliant.
きゅうつい 急追 ── **急追する** 他 pursue《the bank robber》hotly. ▶...を急追した in *hot pursuit* of ...
きゅうてい 休廷 名 (a) recess. ▶休廷中である The court is *in recess*.
── **休廷する** 自 adjourn.
きゅうてい 宮廷 (a) court. (⚠しばしば C-) ▶宮廷で at *court*.
●**宮廷詩人** a court poet.
きゅうていしゃ 急停車 名 (不意の) a sudden [an abrupt] stop; (すばやい) a quick stop.
── **急停車する** 自 ▶バスは通りの真ん中で急停車した The bus *stopped suddenly* [*came to a sudden stop*] in the middle of the street. ▶車を急停車させるな Don't *stop* the car *suddenly*. /(急にブレーキを踏むな)《話》Don't *jam* [*slam*] *on the brakes*.
きゅうてき 仇敵 ⇨(🚩 敵(かたき))
きゅうてん 急転 名〖突然の変化〗a sudden change [turn].
●**急転直下** suddenly, all of a sudden; all at once. ▶急転直下その問題は解決した The problem has *suddenly* been solved./*All at once* we found a solution to the problem.
── **急転する** 自 ▶情勢が急転した There was a *sudden change* in the situation./The situation *changed suddenly* [took a *sudden turn*].
きゅうでん 宮殿 a palace /pǽləs/. (⚠御殿) ▶バッキンガム宮殿 Buckingham /bǽkiŋəm/ Palace.
きゅうと 旧都 an old [a former] capital.
キュート ▶キュートな(=とてもかわいい)赤ちゃん a *cute* baby. (⚠大人に対して用いると,《米》で「セクシーな」「頭のよく働く」などの意が加わる)
きゅうとう 急騰 名 a sudden [a rapid, a sharp] rise, a jump《*in*》. (⚠暴騰) ▶価格の急騰 a *jump in* prices.
── **急騰する** 自 ▶rise* suddenly [rapidly, sharply]; jump. ▶土地の価格が急騰した The price of land has *jumped up*. ▶同社の株は53パーセントも急騰し

た The company's stock *rocketed* 53 percent.
きゅうとう 給湯 ── **給湯する** 他 supply hot water.
●**給湯設備** hot-water supply equipment; a hot-water (supply) system.
きゅうどう 弓道 *kyudo*; Japanese archery.
きゅうどう 旧道 an old road [highway].
きゅうどう 求道 the search for (the) truth.
●**求道者** a seeker after truth.
きゅうとう 牛刀 a cleaver; a butcher knife.
●牛刀をもって鶏(にわとり)を割(さ)く take a stone to break an egg, when you can do it with the back of your knife.
ぎゅうどん 牛丼 a beef bowl.
きゅうなん 急難 ●急難にさらされている be in imminent danger [peril]《*of* collapse》.
きゅうなん 救難 rescue. ▶救難作業 *rescue* work.
ぎゅうにく 牛肉 (a slice of) beef.
きゅうにゅう 吸入 ▶患者に酸素吸入を行う give a patient oxygen. ── **吸入する** 他 inhale.
●**吸入器** an inhaler.
*****ぎゅうにゅう 牛乳** (cow's) milk. ●牛乳1杯[1パック; 1びん] a glass [a carton; a bottle] of *milk*.
●牛乳を配達する deliver *milk*. ●牛乳を搾る *milk* a cow. ●コーヒーにたっぷり牛乳を入れる take much *milk* in one's coffee.
●**牛乳びん** a milk bòttle. ●**牛乳屋** (配達人) a milk delìverer, (男性の) a milkman; (販売者) a milk dèaler, (店) a milk shòp, a dairy.
きゅうねん 旧年 last year. ▶旧年中はお世話になりました Thank you for everything you did for me *last year*.
きゅうは 旧派 the old school [style].
きゅうは 急派 名 dispatch.
── **急派する** 他 dispatch; rush. ▶現場へ警官を急派した Policemen *were dispatched* to the scene.
きゅうば 急場〖危機〗a crisis (⚠ crises);〖非常の場合〗an emergency. ▶彼の急場を救う help him out of a *crisis* [難事) a *difficulty*]. ▶彼から借金をして急場をしのぐ borrow some money from him to tide oneself over the *crisis*. ●急場の間に合わせ(=一時しのぎ)として as a *makeshift*. ●急場の間に合わせる(=当面の必要を満たす) meet *immediate needs*;《やや書》devise a *makeshift*. ▶この金で私は急場をしのげるだろう This money will be a temporary help to me [will help me temporarily]./This money will tide me over the *crisis*.
キューバ〖国名〗Cuba;(公式名) the Republic of Cuba. (首都 Havana) ●キューバ人 a Cuban.
●**キューバ(人)の** Cuban.
ぎゅうば 牛馬 ▶牛馬のようにこき使う work [drive]《him》very hard [like a *beast of burden*].
きゅうはい 休配 ── **休配する** 他 do* not deliver《mail [milk]》.
きゅうはいすい 給排水 water supply and drainage. (⇨給水, 排水)
きゅうはく 急迫 名 (切迫) urgency.
── **急迫する** 自 urgent; pressing. ▶試合は急迫した(=緊迫した)してきた The game was getting very *tense*.
きゅうはく 窮迫 (live in) extreme poverty. ●窮迫している家族[地域] *poverty-stricken* families [areas]. ▶府の財政は窮迫している The prefecture's finances *are in a tight corner*./The prefecture *is under* financial *pressure*.
きゅうはん 急坂 a steep slope [hill].
きゅうばん 吸盤 (タコなどの) a sucker.
きゅうひ 厩肥 cattle manure; manure made of cattle excreta and litter.
ぎゅうひ 牛皮 (a) cowhide.

キューピー〖商標〗a Kewpie [a kewpie]〘doll〙.

キュービズム〖立体派[主義]〗cubism, Cubism.

きゅうひせい 給費生〘奨学金受給生〙a student on [×of] a scholarship; a scholarship student.

きゅうひつ 休筆 ▶彼は若い頃休筆したことがあった He stopped [gave up] *writing for a while* when (he was) young.

キューピッド〖ローマ神話〗Cupid;〖ギリシャ神話〗Eros.

きゅうびょう 急病 a sudden sickness [illness]. (⇨病気) ●急病人が出た場合には in case of medical emergency. ●急病人を病院へ運ぶ take an *emergency patient* [case] to a hospital. ●急病にかかる fall [get, become] *suddenly sick*.

きゅうふ 休符〘休止符〙〖音楽〗a rest. (⇨休止)

きゅうふ 給付〘金〙a bénefit. (👉しばしば複数形で)

きゅうぶ 休部 — 休部する 動〘部活動を停止する〙stop [suspend]《one's activities》; 〘部員が休む〙do [×] not attend [do not take part in]《one's activities》.

きゅうぶん 旧聞 old [stale] news. ▶旧聞に属するが…… It's an *old story*, but....

ぎゅうふん 牛糞 cow dung [manure].

きゅうへい 旧弊 ●旧弊(=昔からの弊害)を一掃する sweep away *old social evils*. ●旧弊に(=因習にとらわれている)人々 people *sticking to old customs*.

きゅうへん 急変 — 急変する 動〘病状などが急に悪化する〙take* a sudden turn for the worse. ▶情勢が急変した There was a *sudden* [(予期しない) an *unexpected*] *change* in the situation./The situation *changed suddenly*.

きゅうぼ 急募 名 ●従業員急募〘掲示〙Employees Urgently Wanted.
— 急募する 動 recruit 《employees》hurriedly.

ぎゅうほ 牛歩〘話〙(at) a snail's pace. ●牛歩戦術 snail's pace tactics.

きゅうほう 急報 an urgent message.

きゅうぼう 窮乏 extreme poverty. ▶窮乏生活をする live in *extreme poverty*.

キューポラ〖溶鉄(ようてつ)炉〗a cupola.

きゅうぼん 旧盆 the lunar Bon Festival.

きゅうみん 休眠 名〘生物・活動・書〙dormancy,《書》torpor.
— 休眠する 動 ▶この植物の種は山火事が起こるまでずっと休眠している The seeds of this plant *lie dormant* [*keep resting*] until a forest fire breaks out.

きゅうみん 窮民 poor people. (⇨貧民)

きゅうむ 急務 a matter of great urgency.

きゅうむいん 厩務員《男女共用》a stable attendant;《男》a stableman《複 -men》.

きゅうめい 究明 — 究明する 動 investigate; inquire《into》; find* ... out; make*《the cause》clear.

きゅうめい 糾明 — 糾明する 動 make* an investigation [a thorough inquiry, a probe]《into the scandal》.

きゅうめい 救命 ●救命具《主に米》a life presèrver (👉救命胴衣〘ベルト; 浮き輪〙a life jacket [belt; buoy]《の個々をさす》; a lifesaving apparatus. ●救命士 (⇨救命〘救急救命士〙) ●救命艇 a lifeboat.

きゅうめん 球面 a spherical surface. ●球面幾何学 spherical geometry. ●球面計 a spherometer.

きゅうもん 糾問 名 (a) cross-examination; a grilling. — 糾問する 動 cross-examine《a witness》; question《him》closely, grill.

きゅうやくせいしょ 旧約聖書 the Old Testament (略 O.T.).

きゅうゆ 給油 名〖燃料補給〗refueling. ▶飛行機は給油のためシカゴ[フランス]に立ち寄った The plane stopped at Chicago [in France] for *refueling* [給油を受けるために] to *refuel*.
— 給油する 動 refuel《a plane》.
●給油所 a filling [a gas,《英》a petrol] station.

きゅうゆう 旧友 an old friend《of mine》.

きゅうゆう 級友 a classmate. (👉《米》では a boy [a girl]《who is》in the same (homeroom) class as me などという方が普通)

きゅうよ 給与《a》pay (👉一般的な語で以下の語を含む); a salary; 〘賃金〙wages. (⇨給料) ●給与所得 earned [employment] income. ●給与水準 a pay [a wage] level. ●給与体系 a pay [a wage] structure.

きゅうよ 窮余 ●窮余の一策 a last-ditch measure.

*きゅうよう 休養 名(a) rest. (⇨静養) ▶君はとても疲れているようだから十分な休養が必要だ You look very tired, so you need [should get] a good *rest*.
— 休養する 動 rest; take* [have*] a rest.

きゅうよう 急用 urgent business. (⇨用) ●急用で on *urgent business*. ▶私は急用のためそこへ行けなかった I couldn't go there because I had [because of] *urgent business*. (👉前の方が口語的) ▶急用でもないかぎり会社へは電話をしないでくれ Don't call me up at the office unless you need me *urgently*.

きゅうらい 旧来 — 旧来の 形 old; traditional. (⇨《動》従来)

きゅうらく 及落 success or failure《in an examination》. ●及落を発表する announce the *results*《of an examination》.

きゅうらく 急落 名 a sudden [a rapid, a sharp] drop [fall]; a slump. ●需要[失業率; 金利]の急落 a *sharp drop in* demand [unemployment; interest rates].
— 急落する 動 fall* steeply [rapidly; suddenly]; slump. ▶そのニュースで同社の株が急落した The news *sent* the company's stock *sharply lower*.

きゅうり 胡瓜〖植物〗(a) cucumber. (👉料理したものは Ⓤ)

きゅうりゅう 急流 a rapid stream [current]. ▶いかだで急流を下る shoot [run] the *rapids* on a raft. (👉「急流下り」は *rapids* shooting)

*きゅうりょう 給料《a》pay; (a) salary; wages.

> 使い分け **pay** 給与・給料・賃金を表す最も一般的な語。
> **salary** 固定給制の月給・年俸などを表す。
> **wage** 肉体労働等に対する日給・週給を表す。また, 広義で各種の労働の対価としての賃金を表す。

① **給料の** ●給料のいい仕事 a well-*paid* job. ▶給料の前借りを頼んだ I asked for an advance on my *salary*. (👉前借り) ▶いやな仕事だがこれも給料のうちだと思ってがまんする I don't like this work. But I am trying to be patient, because I'm getting *paid* for this(, too). (👉最後に too を入れると「他の仕事もあるがこれも仕事の一部である」という意味になり, 「給料のうち」というニュアンスが出る)

② **給料が[は]** ●給料が安いとぼやく mutter about one's small *salary*. ▶あの会社は給料がいい That company pays good [high] (↔poor, low) *salaries*./The company pays well. ▶今年給料が1万円上がった I have got a *pay* [a *wage*, ×wages] raise《米》[rise《英》] of 10,000 yen

this year./My *pay* has been raised by 10,000 yen this year. (⇨昇給) ▶我々の給料は安い(= 薄給だ) We get low [small, ×cheap] *salaries*./Our *salaries* are very low [small, bad, ×cheap]./ We *are poorly* [*badly*] *paid*. ▶看護師の給料はもっと高くあるべきだ Nurses should *be paid* more. ▶給料はどのくらいお望みですか What *salary* do you expect to get?
会話「給料はいくらですか」「月 20 万円です」"What [×How much] is your *salary*?" "It's 200,000 yen a month." (⇨月給)
③【給料を】 ●給料を払う pay him his salary. ●給料を家に入れる《話》bring home the bacon; earn money to support the family. ▶彼は金曜日に給料をもらう He gets his *pay* on Friday(s). (⇨給料日 事例) ▶私は何とかやっていける程度の給料をもらっています I *get paid* enough to keep my head above water.
④【給料で】 ▶この給料で私たちは十分な暮らしをしている We get along very well *on* this *salary*. ▶この給料では生計を立てるのに不十分です(= やっていけない) This *salary* isn't enough to live on.
●給料日 payday. (!通例無冠詞) 事例 米英では週給制が一般的で通例金曜日. (米) では通例給料支払い小切手 (paycheck) で支払われる ●給料袋 a páy énvelope [《英》pàcket). ●給料明細(書) a pay slip.

きゅうりょう 丘陵 hills. ●起伏する丘陵 rolling *hills*. ●千里丘陵で開かれた万博 the exposition in [×on] the Senri *Hills*. (!単に「丘の上で」は *on* the hill) ●丘陵地帯 hilly areas [districts].

きゅうりょう 休猟 ― 休猟する 動 stop hunting. ●休猟期 the off season (for hunting). ●休猟日 a non(-)hunting day.

きゅうりょう 休漁 ― 休漁する 動 stop fishing. ●休漁期 the off season (for fishing). ●休漁日 a non(-)fishing day.

きゅうれい 急冷 名 rapid cooling. ― 急冷する 動 cool rapidly.

きゅうれき 旧暦 the lunar (⇔solar) calendar. (!the old calendar は大陰暦もさすが, あいまいなことがある)

きゅっきゅっ ●きゅっきゅっという squeak. ●きゅっきゅっという音 a squeak. ●きゅっきゅっと鳴る床 a squeaky floor.

きゅっと ●子供のほっぺたをきゅっとつねる *pinch* the child's cheek; *give* the child *a pinch* on the cheek. ▶彼はきゅっと(=一気に)盃を飲み干した He emptied his glass *at one* [*a*] *gulp*.

ぎゅっと ●ぎゅっと握る hold *tight*(*ly*); (握りしめる) squeeze; (つかむ) grab. ●ぎゅっと抱きしめる hold 《him》tight(ly). (!命令形では tight を用い, 意味を強めるのが普通) ; hug 《him》; give 《him》a hug. (! ×give a hug to 《him》とはいわない) ●ブレーキをぎゅっと踏む brake *hard*; *jam* [*slam*] *on* the brakes. ●彼はロープをぎゅっと縛った He tied the rope *tightly*. ●彼は彼女の手をぎゅっと握った He held her hand *tightly*./He *squeezed* her hand. ▶彼はロープをぎゅっと締めた He tightened the rope *fast*.

キュリー ●キュリー夫人『フランスの物理・化学者』Madam Curie /kjúri, kjuri:/.

キュロット(スカート) 《a pair of》culottes /k(j)u:láts/. (!複数扱い)

きゅん ▶彼の悲惨な生活ぶりを聞いて胸がきゅんとなった(= 胸が痛んだ) The story of his miserable life *wrung my heart*.

きよ 寄与 名 (a) contribution 《*to*》. (⇨貢献)

― 寄与する 動 contribute 《*to*》.

きょ 居 ●居を構える settle 《*in*》; (書) take up residence; set up one's home [house].

きょ 虚 ●虚をつかれる be caught (completely) unawares [unprepared].

きょあく 巨悪 a great [a grave, a serious, a vast] evil.

きよい 清い [[清潔な]] clean; [[澄みきった]] clear; [[清純な]] pure; [けがれのない] innocent. (⇨清らか)

ぎょい 御意 ●御意のまま as you like. ▶御意に召しますか Would you like it?/Are you pleased with it?
●御意を得る ●御意を得たく存じます (指図を承りたい) I'd like to *ask* you *for directions*./I'd like to お目にかかりたい) I'd like to *have the honor of meeting* you.

きよう 紀要 (大会・学会などの会報) a bulletin; (年次会報) annuals; (学会論文集) memoirs /mémwa:rz/; (学会の年次大会の記録) proceedings.

きよう 起用 ― 起用する 動 ●(野球で) 彼を先発に起用する put him in the (starting) lineup; start him. ●ピンチヒッターを起用する put in a pitch hitter; send a pitch hitter up to bat.

きよう 器用 ― 器用な 形 ●道具を扱う器用さ, 手先などを使う器用さをいう; (熟練した) skillful; (上手な) good; (扱うのがうまい) handy; (手先の) 《やや書》dexterous. ●器用な人 a *clever* [a *dexterous*] person; (器用貧乏な男性) a jack-of-all-trades. (⇨多芸) ●器用な(=多芸の) 役者 a *versatile* actor. (! actor は女性も含む) ●手先がとても器用だ be very *clever* [*skillful*, *good*, *dexterous*] *with* one's *hands*.
― 器用に 副 ●器用に編み物をする be *skillful* [*good*] *at* knitting; knit *skillfully*. ●道具を器用に使う be *handy with* tools; handle tools *dexterously* [*with dexterity*].

*:**きょう** 今日 today; (この日) this day. (!現在(完了)・過去・未来のいずれの時制にも用いる) ●今日の朝 *this* [×today's] morning. ●今日の新聞 *today's* (news)paper [▶the newspaper [paper] (of) *today* は「こんにちの新聞」の意). ●今日まで till [up to] today; to this day. (!通例現在完了形, 時に現在形と用いる) ●5年前の今日 five years ago *today*; *this day* five years ago. ●今日この頃 (⇨今日この頃)

解説「先週の今日」にあたる英語は (i) a week ago *today*, (ii)《米》*today* [*this day*] last week, (iii)《英》*today* [*this day*] week, (iv)《英》(a) week *today* などが可. (iii)(iv) は文脈によって「来週の今日」の意にもなる.「来週の今日」はこの他 a week from [later] *today*, *today* next week としうる.

▶今日は何の日か知っているかい.君のお父さんの誕生日だよ Do you know what day *this* is? It's your father's birthday. ▶今日中に彼と会わなければならない I must meet him *today* [今日中のうちに] sometime *today*, (今夜までに) by tonight, by the end of the day, before the day's out]. (! ×within today [this day] は不可) ▶その店今日の午後は開いているでしょうか Will the store be open *this* afternoon? ▶今日の君はいつもとちがう. 何かあったのですか You're different *today*. What happened? ▶彼は「今日彼女に会いました」と言った He said, "I met her *today*."/He said that he had met her *that day*. (!間接話法で時制の一致が行われたとき today は通例 that day になる) ●今日という今日は彼に愛想がつきた I've run out of patience with him *this very day*. (! *very* は day を強める) ▶今日はこ

れでおしまい That's all [it] for *today*. (**!**) 授業の終わりなどに教師がいう. この意味では So much for today. とはいわない)/Let's call it a *day*. (**!**) 仕事などを終えるとき) ▶我々は君が来るのを今日あすかすかと待っていた We have been expecting you every day.
会話「今日は何日ですか」「5月5日です」 "What's the date *today* [*today*'s date]?/What day of the month is it *today*?" "It's [*Today*'s] May 5 [the fifth of May]." (**!**) May 5 は《米》May five [(the) fifth], 《英》May the fifth と読む)
会話「今日は何曜日ですか」「日曜日です」 "What day (of the week) is it *today*?" "It's [*Today*'s] Sunday."

きょう 凶 kyo; bad [ill] luck [fortune]. (⇨御神籤(みくじ))

きょう 京 (首都) the capital; the metropolis; (京都) Kyoto. ●京へ上る go (up) to *the capital* [*Kyoto*].
●京の着倒れ People in Kyoto spend too much money on clothes./Kyoto people are very extravagant with clothes. (⇨着倒れ)

きょう 卿 Lord (**!**) 侯[伯, 子, 男]爵の姓(名)の前につける); Sir (**!**) ナイト[準男]爵の姓(名)の前につける). ●(アルフレッド・)テニスン卿 *Lord* (Alfred) Tennyson; (Alfred), *Lord* Tennyson. ●フランシス・ドレーク卿 *Sir* Francis (Drake). (**!**) ×*Sir* Drake. と姓だけにつけるのは不可)

きょう 経 a sutra; (仏教経典) the Buddhist scriptures. ●経を読む read [(吟唱する) recite, (詠唱する) chant] *a sutra*.

きょう 境 ●無我の境(=境地) (*in*) *a spiritual state of* selflessness. ●無人の境(=境地) *an uninhabited* area.

きょう 興 interest; fun. ●興が乗る get [become] more and more *interested* (*in*). ●興をさます[ぐ] (話) put a damper on (the party); dampen one's *enthusiasm* [*excitement*]. (⇨興醒め) ●興をそそる arouse [stir up], excite one's *interest*. ●興を添える add to [increase] one's *interest*.
●興に入(い)る ▶彼はスリラー小説を読んで興に入っていた He *amused himself* by reading a thriller. (⇨面白がる)

ーきょう 狂 (軽度的) a maniac /méiniæk/; (愛好家) a fan, (話) a buff. ●マニア (fan) ●自動車狂 a car *maniac*. ●カメラ狂 a camera *fan* [*buff*].

ーきょう 強 [...より少し多い] a little more than ..., a little over .... ▶このペンは 10 ドル強だった This pen cost *a little more than* ten dollars./This pen cost ten dollars *odd* [ten-*odd* dollars].

ぎょう 行 ❶【文章・文字の】 a line (略 l., ⓟ ll. /láinz/); [詩の] a verse. ●30 ページの 10 行目は *at line* 10 on [×*in*] page 30. (⇨ページ) ●1 行おきに書く write on every other *line*. ●3 ページの下[上から] 3 行目から読む read from the third *line* from the bottom [top] of the third page. ●行をかえる(=改める) begin a new *line* [(段落) *paragraph*]. ●行間 (行間) ▶10 ページの 3 行目を見よ See page 10, *line* 3.
❷【宗教的】 (苦行) (religious) austerities; (勤行) (a) service. ●行をする practice (*religious*) *austerities*.

ぎょう 業 (家業) one's family business; (学業) studies, schoolwork.

ーぎょう ー業 (産業) industry; (営利を目的とした商業) business; (専門的技能と訓練を必要とする職業) profession; (手による熟練を必要とする職業) trade; (規則的に従事しているか, そのための訓練を受けた職業) occupation. ●製造業 the manufacturing *industry*. ●サービス業 the service *business*. ●弁護士業 the lawyer's *profession*.

きょうあい 狭隘 ── 狭隘な 形 narrow. (⇨狭い)

きょうあく 凶悪 ── 凶悪な 形 (獣のように残忍な) brutal; (ぞっとするような) atrocious; (憎むべき) (書) heinous /héinəs/.
●凶悪犯罪 a brutal [an atrocious] crime.

きょうあすあさって 今日明日明後日 ▶今日明日のうちに in a couple of days; in a day or two; very soon.

きょうあつ 強圧 ── 強圧的な 形 ●強圧的なやり方[人] a *high-handed* manner [person].

きょうい 胸囲 ●胸囲を測る take one's *chest* [(女性の) *bust*] *measurement*. ▶君の胸囲はどれくらいですか What is your *chest measurement* [*size*]?

きょうい 脅威 ●(書) (a) menace (*to*); (**!**) threat より強意的); (a) threat /θrét/ (*to*). ●戦争の脅威にさらされている be exposed to the *menace* [*threat*] of war; be under (the) *menace* [*threat*] of war. ▶その国は周辺諸国にとって重大な脅威である The nation is a serious *menace* [*threat*] *to* the surrounding countries.

きょうい 強意 名 (an) emphasis. (**!**) 具体例では Ⓒ)
── 強意の 形 ●強意の副詞 an *intensive* adverb. ●強意語 [文法] an intensive; an intensifier.

きょうい 驚異 名 (不思議) (a) wonder; (驚嘆) a marvel. ●自然の驚異 the *wonders* [*marvels*] of nature. ●驚異の目をみはる stare *in wonder* 《*at*》. ▶人工衛星は科学の驚異だ An artificial satellite is a scientific *wonder*.
── 驚異的な 形 (驚嘆すべき) amazing, marvelous. ▶彼は驚異的なスキージャンプの記録を作った He set a *marvelous* ski-jumping record.

きょういき 境域 (境界) a boundary, a border; (領域) an area.

:きょういく 教育 education (**!**) 時に an ～); (学校教育) schooling; (教授) instruction; (訓練) training; (教養) culture.
①【～の(教育)】 ●同和教育 anti-discrimination *education*. ●英語教育 (⇨英語) ●情操教育 *culture* [*cultivation*] of aesthetic sentiments. ●学校[家庭, 社会]教育 school [home; social] *education* [*training*]. ●基礎教育 basic *education*. ●義務教育 compulsory *education*. ●専門教育 professional [specialized] *education*. ●職業教育 vocational *education*. ●幼児[初等; 中等; 高等]教育 infantile [elementary; secondary; higher] *education*. ●大学教育 a college [a university] *education*. ●成人[生涯]教育 adult [lifelong, (一生継続している) on-going] *education*. ●若者の教育 the *education* of young people. ●特別教育活動 extracurricular activities. ●詰め込み教育 (⇨詰め込み)
②【教育(の)～】 ●教育のある人 an educated [a cultured] person; (やや書) a person of *education* [*culture*]. ●教育のない人 an uneducated [an uncultured] person. ●教育方法を工夫する devise [improve] *teaching* methods. ●父の教育論 my father's theory on *education*. ▶私は教育現場をよく知っている I'm experienced in the actual work of *teachers*. ●陽子は教育熱心な教師 Yoko is a *dedicated* teacher.
③【教育を】 ●十分な教育を受けた[受けていない]人 a well-[a half-]*educated* person. ●医学教育を受ける receive [get, have] a medical *education*; be educated in medicine. ●子供たちに必要となる教育を与える give children a good *education*. ▶私のおじは正規の教育をほとんど[まったく]受けていなかった My uncle had very little [no] formal *education*.

④ [教育は]
DISCOURSE
教育はもっと実用的であるべきだと主張する人もいれば、視野を広げることを重視すべきだという人もいる Some argue that *education* should be more practical; **others** say that education should focus on broadening one's views. (!some...; others〜 (...な人もいれば、〜な人もいる)は対比を表すディスコースマーカー。対照的な内容を述べるのに使う)

── **教育的な** 形 [教育に関する]; [教育上有益な] educational; [ためになる] instructive. ▶教育的な経験 an *educational* experience. ▶その映画はおもしろくもあり教育的でもある The film is both interesting and *instructive*.

── **教育する** 動 educate, give* 〈him〉 education; [教授する] instruct; [訓練する] train (!特に専門職・技能などを身につけさせること). ▶外国で[イギリスで;大学で]教育される(=教育を受ける) be educated abroad [in England; at college]. ▶私は法律家になるように教育された I *was educated* [*was trained*] to be a lawyer.

●**教育委員会** a board of education. ●**教育映画** an educational movie. ●**教育家** an educator; (教育理論家) (やや書) an education(al)ist (!《米》では通例軽蔑的に); (教育熱心な人) an education-minded person. ●**教育改革** an educational reform. ●**教育学** pedagogy; pedagogics (!単数扱い). ●**教育学部** the college of education. (⇨学部) ●**教育課程** a curriculum (複 curricula, 〜s); (高校・大学の) a course of study. ●**教育漢字** the basic *kanji*; the 1,006 Chinese Characters. ●**教育機関** educational institutions. ●**教育基本法** the Fundamentals of Education Law. ●**教育行政** educational administration. ●**教育施設** educational facilities. ●**教育者** (教師) a teacher, an educator. (!後の方が上品な語) ●**教育水準** a standard of education; educational standards. ●**教育制度** an education(al) system. ●**教育大学** 《米》a teacher's college, 《英》a teacher-training college, 《豪》a teachers college. ●**教育長** 《米》a superintendent (of school); 《英》chief education officer [director]. ●**教育勅語** the Imperial Rescript on Education. ●**教育テレビ** educational television [TV]; (チャンネル) the educational channel. ●**教育番組** an educational program. ●**教育費** educational [school] expenses. ●**教育法** a method of education; a teaching method. ●**教育ママ** an education-minded [《米》a grade-conscious] mother.

きょういん 教員 a teacher; [全体] the teaching staff. (⇨先生) ▶私は大学の教員です I'm a university [a college] *teacher*. (⇨教授)

●**教員組合** a teachers' union. ●**教員室** a teachers' room [office]. ●**教員免許状** (申請して文部省から与えられる) a teacher's certificate; (教職についてから与えられる) a teacher's license; (出身大学から与えられる) a teacher's diploma. ●**教員養成大学** 《米》a téachers còllege, 《英》a teacher-training college (!単に a training college ともいう).

きょううん 強運 good luck. ●**強運の人** a very *lucky* person.

きょうえい 共栄 co-prosperity. ●**共栄共存** coexistence and *co-prosperity*.

きょうえい 競泳 图 a swimming race.
── **競泳(を)する** 動 swim* (in) a race.

きょうえきひ 共益費 'a fee for common service'; a management fee [charge].
きょうえつ 恐悦 delight, pleasure. ▶恐悦至極に存じます I *am exceedingly pleased* 《to do》.
きょうえん 共演 ── 共演する 動 co-star 《with》. ●**共演者** a co-star.
きょうえん 協演 ▶歌舞伎俳優と狂言師が博多座で協演した A *kabuki* actor *co-starred with* a *kyogen* actor at the Hakata Theatre.
きょうえん 競演 ── 競演する 動 ▶二大名優が競演した The two great actors *rivaled each other* 《on the stage》.
きょうえん 饗宴 a feast; (正式の) a banquet. ●饗宴を催す hold a *banquet*.
きょうおう 供応 ── 供応する 動 (接待する) do* 《a lot of》entertaining; entertain 〈him to [at] dinner〉; (おごる) treat 〈him to dinner〉.

****きょうか** 強化 图 strengthening.
── **強化する** 動 strengthen, (規則などを厳しくする) tighten ... up; (補強''する) 《やや書》reinforce; (増強する) build* ... up. ▶壁を強化する *strengthen* [*reinforce*] a wall. ▶法律を強化する *tighten up* 〈on〉 the law. ▶体力を強化する *build up* one's (physical) strength.

●**強化合宿** a camp training. ●**強化ガラス** tempered glass. ●**強化食品** enriched food(s). ●**強化プラスチック** reinforced plastics.

きょうか 狂歌 (compose [write]) a comic *tanka*.
きょうか 供花 (send) a floral tribute 《to》;《make》 a floral offering 《to》.
きょうか 教化 图 enlightenment; civilization.
── **教化する** 動 (啓発する) enlighten; (開化する) civilize; (福音により) evangelize.
きょうか 教科 (科目) a subject. ▶英語の教科主任 the head of the English section [teaching staff].
●**教科課程** a curriculum (複 curricula, 〜s); a course of study.

****きょうかい** 教会 a church; a chapel; a synagogue /sínəgòg/.

| 使い分け | **church** キリスト教の教会をさす一般的な語。《英》では国教会の教会をさす。
chapel 学校・病院などに付設された教会や非国教会の教会をいう。
synagogue ユダヤ教の教会. |

●(ローマ)カトリック教会 the (Roman) Catholic *Church*. (!宗派としての「教会」は大文字) ▶私は教会で結婚式を挙げたい I'd like to have a *church* wedding./I'd like to hold my wedding in 《xa》[at a] *church*. (!at a church は単に式場を示すが, in church は「キリスト教式で」に近い意) ▶彼は毎日曜日に教会へ行きます He goes to *church* [×the church] every Sunday. (!church が「(教会での)礼拝」の意のときは無冠詞)
●**教会堂** a church; (礼拝堂) a chapel.

****きょうかい** 境界 [地図上の] a boundary; [山・川などの地理的特徴による] a border. (!両語を区別なく用いることも多い) ●境界を接する border 《on》. ●境界を決める fix the *boundary*. ▶それらの木が我々の地所と彼の地所の境界になっている Those trees form a *boundary between* our estate and his. ▶私たちは境界の内側に柵(?)をめぐらした We made a fence within our *borders*.
●**境界線** a boundary line; a borderline; a border line; a demarcation line.

きょうかい 協会 an association, a society. (⇨組合) ●**交通安全協会** the Traffic Safety *Associa-*

きょうがい 境涯 (⇨⓪ 境遇)

ぎょうかい 業界 〚特定の産業〛the industry; 〚実業界〛the business world; business circles. ●鉄鋼[自動車]業界 the steel [car] industry. ●出版業界 the publishing business [world].
●業界紙 a business [a trade] paper.

きょうかく 侠客 (人) a chivalrous person; (気質) a chivalrous spirit.

きょうかく 胸郭 〚解剖〛the thorax.

きょうかく 共学 co-education. ●共学の学校 a co-educational [《話》a có-ed] school.

きょうがく 驚愕 名 astonishment; amazement.
── 驚愕する 動 be astonished [amazed] 《at, by》.

ぎょうかく 仰角 an angle of elevation; an elevation.

ぎょうかく 行革 〚「行政改革」の略〛(⇨行政)

きょうかしょ 教科書 a (school) textbook, a schoolbook; (技術習得用の) a manual. ●英語[歴史]の教科書 an English [a history] textbook. ●文法[作文]の教科書 a textbook on grammar [of composition, in composition]. (❗通例 in は理論を, of, in は実践を扱うものに用いる). ●高校用の教科書 a textbook for high school students [for use in high school]. ●コンピュータの教科書 a computer manual. ▶ 万事教科書どおりに行くとは限らない Everything does not go in a textbook way.
●教科書検定 screening of school textbooks (by the Ministry of Education). ●教科書検定制度 the textbook screening system. ●教科書体 (in) boldface [fullface] type.

きょうかたびら 経帷子 a shroud, a winding sheet.

きょうかつ 恐喝 名 blackmail.
── 恐喝する 動 ●金を巻き上げようと彼を恐喝する blackmail him for money. ●彼を恐喝して盗みをさせる blackmail him into stealing; make him steal by blackmail.

きょうかん 凶漢 a ruffian; a thug; (暗殺者) an assassin.

きょうかん 共感 名 sympathy; (反響) (a) response. ●読者の共感を得る win [get, 《やや堅》 gain] the sympathy of the readers. ▶ その記事は広く世間の共感を呼んだ The article excited public response [sympathy].
── 共感する 動 ▶ 彼の意見に共感する I sympathize with his opinions./I have sympathy for [with] his opinions./(同意する) I agree with him.

きょうかん 教官 (国立大学の) a teacher (at a national university). ●自動車学校の教官 a driving instructor.

ぎょうかん 行間 space between the lines. ●行間をあける[つめる] leave more [less] space between the lines.
●行間を読む read between the lines.

きょうき 凶器 (殺人事件の) a murder weapon. ●走る凶器 a weapon on vehicle [wheels].

きょうき 狂気 名 madness; insanity /ínsǽnəti/.
── 狂気の沙汰 mad; (《やや古・話》insane /ɪnséɪn/. ▶ こヘ行くのは狂気の沙汰だ It would be sheer madness /《話》You must be absolutely crazy/ to go there.

きょうき 狂喜 名 raptures. (❗通例複数形で)
── 狂喜する 動 go* into raptures 《at, about, over》.

きょうき 侠気 侠気に富む chivalrous; gallant.

きょうき 狭軌 〚鉄道〛a narrow gauge. (⇔ 広軌)

きょうぎ 競技 〚試合〛a game; a match; 〚賞をめざす〛a contest; a competition; 〚種目〛an event. ●運動競技 athletic sports; sporting events. ●室内[屋外]競技 an indoor [an outdoor] sport. ●水泳競技 a swimming contest. ●陸上競技 track and field events. ●スキージャンプ競技会 a ski jumping meet. ●五種競技 the pentathlon. (❗その選手は a pentathlete) ●十種競技 the decathlon. (❗その選手は a decathlete) ▶ 2004年のオリンピック競技はアテネで開かれた The 2004 Olympic Games were held in Athens. ▶ フットボールはアメリカでは人気のある競技です Football is a popular game in America.
●競技場 (観覧席のある) a stadium; (特定競技の) a field (❗an athletics field, a football field のように用いる).

きょうぎ 協議 名 〚討議〛(a) discussion; 〚相談〛(a) consultation (しばしば複数形); (意見交換) a conference. ●協議がまとまる reach [arrive at, come to] an agreement. ●協議中である (問題が) be under discussion; be being discussed; (人が) be in consultation [conference] 《with》. ▶ 我々は当局と緊密な協議を行った We held [had] (a) close consultation with the authorities. ▶ 私たちは何度も協議を重ねた上で決定を下した We held several consultations, (and) then made our decision./We decided after several consultations.
── 協議する 動 (話し合う) talk 《about, over》; (議論する) discuss; (相談する) consult 《with》. ▶ 日本はその問題についてアメリカ政府と協議した Japan consulted [held a consultation] with the U.S. Government about the matter.
●協議会 a conference; a council. (⇨会議) ●協議事項 (議事日程) the agenda (❗その一つは an item on the agenda); (議論の主題) a subject of discussion. ●協議離婚 (a) divorce by agreement.

きょうぎ 狭義 〚狭い意味〛a narrow (↔ a broad) sense. ●その語を狭義に用いる use the word in a narrow sense.

きょうぎ 教義 (宗教上の) (a) doctrine; (教会が下す) 〚しばしば軽蔑的〛(a) dogma.

きょうぎ 経木 a paper-thin sheet of wood (for wrapping food).

ぎょうぎ 行儀 manners. (⇨礼儀) ●行儀よくする behave (oneself). ●行儀がよい[悪い] have good [bad] manners; be well[ill]-mannered. ●行儀を身につける learn good manners; learn how to behave. ▶ お行儀よくしなさい Behave yourself. ▶ お行儀に気をつけてね Remember [Don't forget] your manners. ▶ そんな座り方は行儀が悪い It's bad manners to sit like that. ▶ その子は客の前で行儀が悪かった The child behaved badly in front of the guest. ▶ 他人行儀はやめにしよう Let's stop standing on formality [ceremony].

きょうきゃく 橋脚 (橋桁の) a pillar; a (bridge) pier (❗a pier では「桟橋」の意の方が強い).

きょうきゅう 供給 supply (↔ demand). (⇨需要)
●電力の供給 the supply of electricity. ▶ アメリカが小麦の主な供給地となっている The United States is the chief source of supply for wheat. ▶ 近ごろ石油の供給が少ない[過剰だ] Oil is in short [excessive] supply these days./There is a short [an excessive] supply of oil these days. ▶ 供給過剰で物価が急落した Prices dropped sharply in response to the oversupply.
── 供給する 動 (足りない物を) supply; (あらかじめ準備して) provide; (必需品を) 《書》furnish. ▶ 農家が都会の人に食料を供給してくれる The farmers supply

きょうぎゅうびょう 狂牛病 mad cow disease;〔牛海綿状脳症〕〖医学〗bovine spongiform encephalopathy〈略 BSE〉.

ぎょうきょう 業況 business conditions.
● 業況判断指数 business conditions DI.(⦿ DI は Diffusion Index〈景気動向指数〉の略)

ぎょうぎょうしい 仰々しい〈大げさの〉/ìgzǽgəreitid/;〔芝居じみた〉dramatic,《やや書》histrionic,〔これ見よがしの〕ostentatious, showy. ● 仰々しく身を飾り立てて in a *showy* dress; be showily dressed. ● 彼の仰々しいふるまいにはうんざりである be disgusted by his *exaggerated* behavior.

きょうきん 胸襟 ● **胸襟を開く** そのことについて彼と胸襟を開いて語り合う have a *heart-to-heart*〔a *frank*〕talk with him about the matter.

きょうく 狂句 a comic *haiku*.

きょうく 教区 a parish.(参考) 教会があり牧師がいる)
● 教区の教会〔牧師〕a *parish* church [priest, pastor].

*****きょうぐう 境遇**〔回りの状況〕circumstances;〔生活の条件〕condition(s),〔環境〕an environment. ● 〔経済的に〕恵まれた〔楽な; 苦しい〕境遇にある be in good [easy; bad] *circumstances*. ● 今の境遇に甘んじる content oneself with [be content with] the present *circumstances* [*condition(s)*].

きょうくん 教訓图〔戒め〕a lesson;〔寓意(✽)的な〕a moral;〖教え〗teaching(s);〔道徳的な〕《やや書》(a) precept;〖教えること〗instruction.(⇨教え)
①【～教訓】 ● いい教訓 a good lesson. ● にがい教訓 a bitter *lesson*. ● 自然の教訓 the *lesson(s)* of nature. ● その物語の教訓は「正直は最善の策」である The *moral* of the story is "Honesty is the best policy."
②【教訓を】 ● イソップ物語から教訓を得る(= 引き出す) draw some *morals* from Aesop's Fables.
▶ 私はこの経験から貴重な教訓を得た I learned a valuable *lesson* from the experience./The experience taught [gave] me a valuable *lesson*./The experience was a valuable *lesson* to me. ▶ この教訓をむだにするな(= 心に留めておけ) Bear [Keep] this *lesson* in mind.
── 教訓的な 形 instructive.

きょうげき 京劇 a classical Chinese opera.

きょうけつ 供血 (a) blood donation. (⇨㊙献血)

ぎょうけつ 凝血 clotted [coagulated] blood. ● 凝血剤 a coagulant.

きょうけん 狂犬 a mad [a rabid] dog.
● 狂犬病 rabies /réibiːz/;〖医学〗hydrophobia.

きょうけん 教権〔宗教上の〕ecclesiastical authority;〔教育上の〕educational authority.

きょうけん 強肩 強肩の外野手 an outfielder with a *strong* arm; a *strong-armed* outfielder.

きょうけん 強健 ── **強健な** 形〔強い〕strong,〔たくましい〕robust,〔頑丈な〕sturdy.

きょうけん 強権〔国家権力〕state power. ● 強権を発動する《書》invoke *state power*.

きょうげん 狂言 ❶ [能狂言] a *kyogen* (play), a *Noh* farce,〔説明的に〕a comical play performed during the interlude of *Noh* plays.
❷ [見せかけ]〔ふり, 芝居〕a sham. ● 狂言師 a *kyogen* actor. ● 狂言自殺 a sham suicide. ● 狂言回し *kyogenmawashi*,〔説明的に〕a supporting role necessary for a *kyogen*.

きょうこ 強固 ── **強固な** 形〔堅い〕firm;〔強い〕strong. ● 強固な意志 a *strong* [an *iron*] will.
── **強固に** 副 ● その計画に強固に反対する *strongly* oppose the plan. ● 強固にする strengthen; make 〈it〉 *firm*.

ぎょうこ 凝固 图 coàgulátion.
── 凝固する 動 coagulate /kouǽgəleit/.

きょうごいん 教護院〈米〉a reformatory, a reform school;〈英〉a community home.

きょうこう 凶行〔暴力行為〕an act of violence;〖犯罪〗a crime;〖殺人〗(a) murder. ● 凶行におよぶ 〈an *act* of〉*violence* 〈to him〉; commit *murder* [a *crime*]. ● 凶行の現場に居合わせる be at the scene of the *crime* [*murder*].

きょうこう 恐慌 (a) panic. ● 金融〈大〉恐慌 a〈great〉financial *panic*. ● 恐慌をきたす〈人が主語〉be panicked〈into〉; get into a *panic*,〈事が主語〉panic〈at〉; cause a *panic*.

きょうこう 教皇 a pope, the Pope. ● 教皇ベネディクト 16 世 *Pope* Benedict XVI.

きょうこう 強行 ── **強行する** 動 ● 採決を強行する *force* a vote〈on the bill〉. ● 戦線を強行突破する *force* one's *way through* the〈enemy's〉line.

きょうこう 強硬 ── **強硬な** 形〔堅い〕firm;〔強い〕strong;〔断固とした〕《ほめて》《書》resolute. ● 強硬な手段をとる take *strong* measures.
── **強硬に** 副 ● 彼はその法案に強硬に反対している He is *strongly* [*firmly*] opposed to the bill.
● 強硬派 a hard-liner. ● 強硬路線〈take〉a hard line〈against〉.

きょうごう 強豪 強豪と対戦する compete with a *powerful*〔(すぐれた) an *excellent*〕team (チーム) play against a *powerful* [a *strong*] team.

きょうごう 競合图〖競争〗(a) competition;〖衝突〗a cónflict.
── 競合する 動 ● その 2 大商社はお互いに競合している The two big trading companies *are competing* [*are in competition*] with each other.

ぎょうこう 行幸 the emperor's visit [attendance, presence].

ぎょうこう 僥倖 luck; good fortune. (⇨幸運)

きょうこうぐん 強行軍 〈make〉a forced march.
● 強行軍で旅行する go on [make] a *heavily-scheduled* tour〈of France〉.

きょうこく 峡谷 a gorge, a ravine /rəvíːn/;〔大きな〕a canyon. (⇨谷)

きょうこく 強国 a strong [a powerful] country, a 〈great〉power. ● 西欧の強国(= 列強) the Western *powers*.

きょうこのごろ 今日この頃 ▶ 家事に追われる今日このごろです I'm very busy with my housework *these days* [*nowadays*].

きょうさ 教唆 instigation; abetment.
── 教唆する 動 instigate〈him *to do*〉; abet〈a crime〉.
● 教唆者 an instigator; an abettor.

ぎょうざ 餃子 (⇨ギョーザ)

きょうさい 共済 mutual-aid.
● 共済貸付金 a mutual-aid loan. ● 共済組合 a benefit [a benevolent] society,〈英〉a friendly society. ● 共済事業 a mutual-aid project. ● 共済年金 a mutual-aid pension. ● 共済保険 fraternal insurance.

きょうさい 共催 ▶ スピーチコンテストは市当局と新聞社の共催で開かれた The speech contest *was held under the*〈*joint*〉*sponsorship* [《書》*auspices*] of the city government and a newspaper company.

きょうざい 教材 téaching matérials. ●補助教材 téaching aíds.

きょうさいか 恐妻家 a henpecked husband.

きょうさく 凶作 a bad crop [harvest]. (⇨不作)

きょうさく 狭窄 〚医学〛a stricture. ●幽門狭窄 a *stricture* of the pylorus /paɪlɔ́ːrəs/.

きょうさく 競作 ── 競作する 動 compete 《against, with》; vie 《with》. ●その 2 人の作曲家は賞を competing している The two composers are *competing with* each other *for* the prize.

きょうさつ 挾殺 〚野球〛a rundown. ●走者を挾殺する get a runner out in a *rundown*; run down [up] a runner.
●挾殺プレー a rundown play.

きょうざつぶつ 夾雑物 impurities; foreign matter.

きょうざめ 興醒め ●彼女のへたな歌には興ざめした Her poor singing *spoiled our fun*.

きょうさん 協賛 (協力) coòperátion. ●婦人会協賛バザー a bazaar *in cooperation with* the women's association.

きょうさんしゅぎ 共産主義 图 cómmunism. (!マルクス・レーニン主義をさすときは通例 C-)
──共産主義(者)の 形 cómmunist(ic).
●共産主義国家 a communist country [nation]. ●共産主義者 a communist; 《話》a red (!後の語はしばしば R- と書き軽蔑的).

きょうさんとう 共産党 the Communist Party. ●日本共産党 the Japanese *Communist Party* 《略 JCP》.

***きょうし 教師** 〚先生〛a téacher; 〚専門分野の指導員〛an instrúctor. (⇨先生) ●女教師 a woman *teacher*. ●(特に性の区別を必要とする場合を除いては)このようにはいわない ●ダンス教師 a dáncing màster.
●教師用指導書 a *teacher*'s manual. ●教師になる become a (school) *teacher*; go into teaching. ●教師をやめる give up teaching. ▶彼女はこの学校の教師です She *teaches at* [*in*] this school./She is a *teacher at* [*in*, ×*of*] this school. (! *in* よりも *at* の方が普通) ▶経験は最上の教師である Experience is the best *teacher*.

DISCOURSE
教師が生徒による評価を受けるべきだとする意見に賛成する。一つの理由は、教師を評価することで教える技術が増す可能性が高いからだ I *support* the opinion that teachers should be evaluated by their students. **One reason is that** such an evaluation will encourage teachers to improve their teaching skills. (!One [Another] reason is that ... (ひとつの[もうひとつの]理由は...)は理由に用いるディスコースマーカー)

きょうし 狂死 ── 狂死する 動 die from madness; go* mad and die.

きょうし 狂詩 ●狂詩曲 〚音楽〛a rhapsody /rǽpsədi/.

きょうじ 凶事 (不幸) a misfortune; (災害) a disaster; (大災害) a calamity.

きょうじ 矜持 pride. (⇨⊕ 誇り) ●自分の仕事に矜持を持て Take *pride* in your job.

きょうじ 教示 图 instruction.
──教示する 動 instruct; teach*. ●先生は生徒たちに応急手当を教示した The teacher *instructed* his students *in* first aid./The teacher *taught* his students how to give first aid.

ぎょうし 凝視 图 a (steady) gaze; a (fixed) stare; an intent look.
──凝視する 動 gaze [stare] 《at》; look hard [intently] 《at》; fix one's eyes 《on》.

ぎょうじ 行事 〚催し物〛an event, an occasion 《for》; 〚公的な式典〛a function (!口語では単に大きな集会・宴会などにも用いる). ●年中[学校]行事 an annual [a school] *event*. ●...を記念する公式行事に出席する attend an official *occasion* [*function*] *for* commemorating....

ぎょうじ 行司 a *sumo* referee. ●立て行司 the head *sumo* referee.

きょうしきこきゅう 胸式呼吸 thoracic respiration.

きょうじせい 強磁性 图 〚物理〛ferromagnetism.
──強磁性の 形 ferromagnetic.
●強磁性体 a ferromagnet.

***きょうしつ 教室** ❶〚部屋〛a clássroom, a schóolroom; (講義室) a lecture room; (階段の一つ) a (lecture) theater. ▶教室[音楽教室; 10 番教室]にはだれもいなかった There was nobody in the *classroom* (the music room; *Room* 10). (!麺麮 米英では教室は教室番号 (room number) で呼ぶことが多い)
❷〚講習〛(集団的) (a) class. ●料理教室を開く[に通う] give [go to,《やや書》attend] a cooking *class*.

きょうじつ 凶日 an unlucky day.

きょうじゅ 香車 〚将棋〛a spear, a lance.

きょうじゃ 強者 the strong. (!複数扱い)

きょうじゃ 経師屋 (表具師) a paperhanger; a paperer.

ぎょうじゃ 業者 (販売人) a dealer, a trader; (製造業者) a maker, a manufacturer; (同業者) a fellow dealer [trader]; people in the same trade. ●出入りの業者 a *dealer* who regularly comes around to take orders.

ぎょうじゃ 行者 (苦行者) an ascetic /əsétɪk/; (イスラム教・ヒンズー教の) a fakir /fɑːkɪr/.

きょうじゃく 強弱 〚強さと弱さ〛strength and weakness; 〚音声の〛a stress.

きょうしゅ 凶手 (人) an assassin; (手段) (an) assassination. ●凶手に倒れる be assassinated.

きょうしゅ 拱手 拱手傍観する simply look on with one's arms folded; just stand by.

きょうしゅ 教主 (教祖) the founder of a religious sect; (代表者) the head of a religious sect.

きょうじゅ 享受 ── 享受する 動《書》enjoy. ●自由[人間らしい生活]を享受する[している] *enjoy* freedom [a life worth living].

きょうじゅ 教授 ❶〚大学の教員〛a proféssor,《俗》a prof (略 ~s); 〚教授陣〛the fáculty (!《米》では全学の,《英》では各学部の教授陣をさす), the téaching staff (!いずれも単・複両扱い).

解説 (1)《米》では大学の教授に限らず助教授, 講師を含めて大学の先生すべてに, あるいは中学・高校の教師にも professor を用いることがある.《英》では professor は学科や講座の主任教授の意で用いられる. (2) 呼びかけには Professor ~, 日常的には Mr. [Mrs., Miss, Ms.] ~, またはファースト・ネームで呼ぶことも多い.

●名誉教授 an emeritus *professor*. (!しばしば a *professor* emeritus) ●(ロナルド・)スミス教授 *Professor* (Ronald) Smith; *Prof*. Ronald [R.] Smith. (!(1) この肩書きは助教授などにも用いる. (2) 略語 Prof. には通例姓のほかに名(のイニシャル)をつけ, 姓だけにつけて ×*Prof*. Smith とはしない) ●京都大学の歴史の教授 a *professor* of history *at* [×*of*] Kyoto University. (!ただし第 1, 第 2 例のように役職の意味を人名が加わる場合は of Kyoto University が普通. 「京都大学の医学部の教授」は a professor *at* the medical department of Kyoto University または a professor *in* the medical department at

Kyoto University の両方が可) ▶教授会は月1回開かれる The *faculty* meeting is held once a month.

[関連] **大学の教員名**:《米》教授 (full) professor/準教授 (日本の助教授に近い) associate professor, (大学によっては) adjunct professor/助教授 assistant professor/講師 instructor.
《英》教授 professor/助教授 reader/講師 lecturer.

❷ [教えること] teaching, instruction. (⇨教える)
● 英語の個人教授を受ける take private *lessons in* English.
● 教授法 a téaching mèthod; a method of teaching.

ぎょうしゅ 業種 a type of industry [(職業)] trade].

きょうしゅう 強襲 an assault; a violent attack.
— **強襲する** 動 assault; attack violently. ● 敵の前線を強襲する *make an assault on* the enemy lines. ▶打球は一塁手を強襲してライトへ達した The ball caromed off the first baseman into right field.

きょうしゅう 郷愁 [故郷に対する] homesickness; [過去のものに対する]《やや書》nostalgia. ● 郷愁を感じる be [feel, get] *homesick* [*nostalgic*] (*for*).

ぎょうしゅう 凝集 图 cohesion. — **凝集する** 動 cohere.
● 凝集力 cohesive force.

きょうしゅうじょ 教習所 a school. ● 自動車教習所 a dríving schòol.

きょうしゅく 恐縮 — **恐縮する** 動 ❶ [深く感謝する] ▶ご援助をいただき恐縮しております I'm *very grateful* [*very*] *much obliged*] (*to* you) *for* your help. [!]後の方は丁寧すぎてかえって無礼にひびくこともあり, 今はあまり用いない) *I deeply appreciate* your help.
❷ [すまなく思う] ● 恐縮ですが Excuse me, but ...; I'm sorry to trouble you, but .... ● お待たせして恐縮です《日本人的発想》I'm sorry *to* have kept you waiting./《米英人的発想》Thank you (very much) for your waiting.
❸ [恥じる] be ashamed (*of*); (肩身が狭い) feel* small. ▶彼は自分の行儀の悪さに恐縮している He *is ashamed of* his bad manners./His bad manners make him *feel small*.

ぎょうしゅく 凝縮 图[化学] condensation. ● 蒸気が凝縮して水滴になること the *condensation* of vapor *to* [*into*] droplets.
— **凝縮する** 動 ● ガスを液体に凝縮する *condense* a gas *into* a liquid.

きょうしゅつ 供出 图 (a) delivery 《*of* rice *to* the government》.
— **供出する** 動 deliver 《rice *to* the government》.
● 供出割り当て a quota.

きょうじゅつ 供述 图 [宣誓供述書による証言][法律] (a) deposition; [法廷で行う証言][法律] (a) testimony.
— **供述する** 動 depose; testify. ▶彼女は彼が彼の家から走り去るのを見たと供述した She *testified* that she had seen him run out of the house.
● 供述書 [法律] a deposition.

きょうじゅん 恭順 (an) allegiance. ▶彼らは新国王に恭順の意を表した They swore (an oath of) *allegiance* to the new king.

きょうしょ 教書 (大統領の) a message. ● 大統領教書 the President's *message*. ● 一般[年頭]教書《米》the State of the Union *Message* [*Address*]. [!] state は「状況」の意)

ぎょうしょ 行書 the semi-cursive style (of Chinese character writing).

きょうしょう 協商 entente /ɑːntɑːnt/. [!] 条約ほど正式なものではない) ● 和親協商 *entente* cordiale /kɔːrdiɑːl/.

きょうじょう 凶状 a crime. (⇨罪状, 犯罪)
● 凶状持ち (前科者) an ex-convict.

きょうじょう 教条 图 (a) dogma. — **教条的(な)** 形 dogmatic.
● 教条主義 dogmatism.

ぎょうしょう 行商 图 peddling.
— **行商する** 動 ● 野菜を行商する *peddle* vegetables.
● 行商人《主に米》a peddler;《英》a pedlar.

きょうしょく 教職 the téaching proféssion. ● 教職につく become a teacher;《やや書》enter the *teaching profession*. ▶彼は教職についている He is engaged in *teaching*.
● 教職課程 a teacher-training course.

きょうしょくいん 教職員 [ある学校の教職員全体] the staff of a school; [主に大学の教員陣]《主に米》the faculty,《主に英》the (teaching) staff. [!] 以上はすべて単・複両形扱い) ▶私はこの学校の教員員です I am *on the staff* of this school. [!]✗I am a staff [one of the staffs].... とはいわない)

きょうじる 興じる amuse oneself. (⇨楽しむ)

きょうしん 狂信《やや書》fanaticism. [!] 狂信的言動は [C])
● 狂信者 a fanatic; a fanatical believer《*in*》.

きょうしん 強振 [野球] a mighty swing [cut].
— **強振する** 動 take* a mighty cut.

きょうしん 強震 a severe earthquake.

きょうじん 凶刃 ● 凶刃に倒れる fall victim to《his》dagger [knife], (刺殺される) be stabbed to death with《his》dagger.

きょうじん 強靱 — **強靱な** 形 (頑強な) tough; (不屈の)《やや書》tenacious /tənéiʃəs/.

きょうしんかい 共進会 《hold》a fair. ● 農作物[家畜]共進会 an agricultural [a cattle] *fair*.

きょうしんざい 強心剤 a heart stimulant.

きょうしんしょう 狭心症 [医学] angina /ændʒáinə/ (pectoris).

ぎょうずい 行水 ● 行水を使う take a *bath in a washtub*. ● カラスの行水 (⇨烏)

きょうすいびょう 恐水病 [[「狂犬病」の別称]] (⇨狂犬)

きょうする 供する (差し出す) serve; (提供する) offer.
● 珍本を閲覧に供する *offer* the rare book for reading.

*** きょうせい** 強制 图《やや書》compulsion; [権力や脅しによる]《書》coercion /kouə́ːrʃən/. ● 強制処分を行う take [carry out] cumulsory measures. ▶その自白は任意によるもので強制によるものではない The confession was voluntary and *not forced* [*unforced*]. ● 出席は望ましいが強制はされない(＝義務的ではない) Attendance is expected but not *obligatory*.
— **強制的に** 副 by compulsion; (力ずくで) by force; forcibly. ▶彼女の両親は強制的にその男と結婚させた Her parents *forced* [*compelled*] her *to* marry the man.
— **強制する** 動 [無理やり...させる] force; (余儀なく)《やや書》compel (-ll-) ([!] force より強制力が弱い); (強要する)《書》coerce. ● 強制されて署名する sign under *compulsion* [*coercion*]. ▶彼の意志に反して強制することはできない You can't *force* him against his will.
● 強制執行 compulsory execution. ● 強制送還 forced [enforced] repatriation. ● 強制着陸 (a) forced landing. ● 強制労働 compulsory

[forced] labor.

きょうせい 共生 〖生物〗 symbiosis /simbióusis/; (一般に) coexistence. —— **共生する** 働 〖生物〗 live symbiotically; (一般に) coexist, live together.
● 共生関係 a symbiotic relation.

きょうせい 強勢 〖音声〗 (a) stress; (特に単語の) an accent. ● 語[文]強勢 word [sentence] *stress*. ● 最初の音節に強勢を置く put [(やや格)place] the *stress* [*accent*] on the first syllable.

きょうせい 強請 —— **強請する** 働 make* a high-handed [a strong, a coercive] demand 《for him *to do*》; demand 《it *of* him》 forcibly.

きょうせい 教生 〖教育実習生〗 a student [a practice] teacher. ● 教生に行く do one's *teaching practice*.

きょうせい 嬌声 ● 嬌声を発する[あげる] utter a coquettish voice.

きょうせい 矯正 图 〖誤りなどを正すこと〗 (a) correction; 〖悪・欠点などの改善(法)〗 (a) remedy; 〖品行などを改めさせること〗 (a) reform.
—— **矯正する** 働 correct; remedy; reform. ● 悪い癖[どもり]を矯正する *correct* a bad habit [one's stuttering]. ● 彼の非行を矯正する *reform* his misconduct. ● 歯列を矯正する *straighten* teeth. ▶彼女は今歯列を矯正してもらっている She's *wearing braces* [*a brace*] for her crooked teeth./She is *having* her teeth *straightened*.
● 矯正視力 corrected eyesight [vision].

ぎょうせい 行政 图 administration; (政治) government. ● 地方行政 local [municipal] *administration* [*government*]. ▶彼には行政的手腕がある He has *administrative* ability.
● 行政改革 an administrative reform 《for, to do》. ● 行政官 an administrator. ● 行政機関 an administrative organ; (政府の) a government (agency). ● 行政区 an administrative ward. ● 行政権 administrative rights [authority]. ● 行政指導 administrative guidance. ● 行政書士 an administrative scrivener. ● 行政処分 an administrative measure [disposition]. ● 行政訴訟 administrative litigation.

ぎょうせい 擬陽性 ● 擬陽性反応 a pseudopositive reaction. (⇨陽性)

*****ぎょうせき 業績** an achievement; 〖会社などの過去の実績〗 a track record. ▶彼は科学の分野ですばらしい業績をあげた He *produced* remarkable [wonderful] *achievements* in the scientific field. ▶今期の業績(=営業成績)は今までのところ不振だ Our *track record* has been poor so far this term.

ぎょうせい 行動 everyday behavior.

きょうせん 教宣 education and its public relations.

きょうそ 教祖 the founder of a religion [a religious sect]. ● 教祖的指導力 charisma /kərízmə/.

:きょうそう 競争 图 còmpetition, (a) rivalry 《with, between, among, for》(前の方は圧倒、後の方は対抗意識を強調); (争い) a struggle 《for》.
① 【~競争】 ● 生存競争 a *struggle for* existence [survival]. ● 軍拡競争 an arms *race*. ● 国際競争 international competition. ● 価格競争 a price war. ● 女子200メートル自由形競争 the women's 200-meter freestyle *competition*. ● 日本の大学入試の激しい競争 cutthroat [fierce] *competition* in Japan's college entrance exams. ● これらの店の間では激しい客の獲得競争が行われている There's intense [keen] *competition between* these stores to get customers.
② 【競争~】 ● 競争入札をする make [put in] a *competitive tender* [*bid*] 《*for*》. (⇨入札) ▶これらの製品は国際市場で競争力を失っている[十分な競争力がある] These products have lost their *competitiveness* [are *competitive* enough] in the international market. ▶彼は競争心が強い He has a *competitive* spirit. ▶あの子の今度のボーイフレンドは太郎にとってはてごわい競争相手だなあと思う I think her new boyfriend is a formidable *rival* to Taro. ▶衣料品は競争激化で値段が下がってきた The prices of clothes have been going down because of growing *competition*. ▶K大学の競争率は例年非常に高く20倍前後だ The admission rate of K University is usually very low and it stands at about 5 percent. (日admission rate は「入学できる率」の意なので日本語の倍率の高低や数値は逆になる)
③ 【競争に[を]】 ● その競争に勝つ win (↔lose) the *competition*. ● 競争を始める enter into *competition* [*rivalry*] 《*with*》. ▶水泳では幸子とでは競争にならない I am no match for Sachiko in swimming./Sachiko is *more than a match for* me in swimming.
—— **競争する** 働 compete 《with, against, for, in》. ▶彼とどちらが速く計算できるか競争する compete with him as to who can calculate faster. ▶その契約をめぐって2社が互いに競争した Two companies *competed* [*were in competition*, *vied*] *with* each other *for* the contract. ▶この分野で日本と互して勝てる(=日本に匹敵する)国はない No countries can *compete* successfully *with* [*against*] Japan in this field. (日この意のcompete は通例否定文で用いる)
● 競争相手 a competitor, (the) competition (日通例集合的に); (対抗者) a rival (日日本語と異なり、よい意味で用いることはなく通例enemy (敵)に近い対抗意識を含意); (好敵手) a match 《for》. ● 競争原理 the principle of competition; a competitive principle. ● 競争社会 a competitive society.

*****きょうそう 競走** 图 a race; a ... run (日...は距離); (短距離) a dash. ● 100メートル競走 the 100-meter *dash*; the 100 meters. ● 競走に勝つ[負ける] win [lose] a *race*. ● 競走に出場する take part in a *race*. ▶5キロ競走では3等だった I finished third [took third place] in the 5-kilometer *race* [*run*]. (日(話)では ... in the 5 kilometers. とも言う)
—— **競走する** 働 race 《against, with》, have* [run*] a race 《against, with》. ● 時間と競走する (⇨時間) ▶あの木まで競走しよう Let's *race* [*have a race*] to that tree./I'll *race* you up to that tree.
● 競走者 a racer. ● 競走路 a track; a rácing còurse. ● 競走馬 a ráce hòrse.

きょうそう 強壮 —— **強壮な** 形 strong; (強健な) robust; (体格が頑丈な) sturdy.
● 強壮剤 a tonic.

きょうそう 胸像 a bust.

ぎょうそう 形相 a look. ● ものすごい形相 a fierce [a furious] *look*. ▶彼女の形相はすさまじかった She looked *furious*.

きょうそうきょく 狂想曲 〖音楽〗 (奇想曲) a capriccio. (⇨奇想曲)

きょうそうきょく 協奏曲 〖音楽〗 a concerto /kəntʃéərtou/ (複 ~s). ● バイオリン[ピアノ]協奏曲 a violin [a piano] *concerto*.

きょうそく 脇息 (lean on) an armrest.

きょうそくほん 教則本 a manual. ● ギター教則本 a guitár mànual.

きょうそん 共存 图 coexistence.

きょうだ **共存する** 動 coexist; live [exist] together.
・平和共存していく *coexist* in peace; live in peaceful *coexistence*.

きょうだ **強打** 图 a hard [a heavy] blow;〖野球〗a hard hit, a drive. ・頭に強打を受ける get [receive] *a hard blow* on the head. ・強打のタイガース the hard-hitting Tigers.

—— **強打する** 動 ・彼のあごを強打する give [〖主に書・古〗deal] him *a hard blow* on the chin. ・(打者が)レフトに強打する *hit a hard drive* to left.
・強打者〖野球〗a hard [a power] hitter; a slugger.（**!**「強打の外野手」は a *slugging* outfielder）

きょうたい **狂態** disgraceful behavior; shameful conduct. ・狂態を演じる behave *disgraceful*.

きょうたい **嬌態** coquetry. ▶彼女は若い男であればだれにでも嬌態を示した She *coquetted with* every young man she saw.

:**きょうだい** **兄弟** ❶〔兄, 弟〕a brother;〖姉, 妹〗a sister.

> 解説 (1) 話し言葉での日本語の「きょうだい」は男女の区別なく使うことが多い. これに当たる英語は a sibling でもとは堅い語であったが今日では日常的にも用いられるようになってきた.（〖話〗a sib）: 私は 4 人きょうだいで, 男のきょうだいが 2 人, 女のきょうだいが 1 人です I have three *siblings*: two brothers and a sister. (2) brother(s) and sister(s) の語順はこの順が普通だが, 絶対的なものではない. （⇨父母 (⚤)）

❶【～兄弟】・ケネディ兄弟 the Kennedy *brothers*. ・下の兄弟 a younger *sibling* [〖話〗sib]. ・双子の兄弟 twin *brothers* [*sisters*].（**!** 双子の一方をさすときは単数形）・親兄弟 one's *parents and siblings*;〔家族〕one's *family*. ・義理の兄弟 one's *brother-in-law*.（**!** 複数形は brothers-in-law,〖英語〗brother-in-laws）・腹違いの兄弟 one's half *brother* [*sister*]. ▶うちは 4 人兄弟だ I have three *siblings*./（兄 1 人, 妹 2 人なら）I have *a brother* and *two sisters*.（**!** 自分は数えないことに注意）▶ぼくは 3 人兄弟で, 兄と弟がいます I have two [×three] *brothers*. One's younger and one's older. ▶one's は one is の短縮形/（3 人兄弟の真ん中だ）I am the second oldest of three *brothers*.（**!** 自分も数に入る）▶太郎と花子は(実の)兄弟です Taro and Hanako are (full) *siblings* [*brother and sister*].（**!** 関係を表すときは無冠詞）

❷【兄弟は】▶兄弟は何人ですか How many brothers and sisters do you have? ▶ご兄弟はおありですか Do you have (any) *brothers* and [or] *sisters*?（**!** 通例 ×Do you have (any) *brothers*? とはいわない）▶兄弟はありません I have no *brothers* or [×and] *sisters*.

❷〔同胞, 仲間〕brothers. ▶人間はみな兄弟だ All men are (our) *brothers*. ▶彼と私は宮崎で兄弟同然に育てられた He and I were raised together in Miyazaki *just like two brothers* [*as if we were two brothers*].

・兄弟は他人の始まり Ties between brothers are very fragile.
・兄弟愛 *brotherly* [*sisterly*] affection [*love*].
・兄弟げんか (男同士) a quarrel between brothers [(女同士) sisters, (男と女) brother(s) and sister(s)]; (a) sibling rivalry. ▶私は兄[弟]と兄弟げんかをした I had a quarrel [an argument, a row] with my brother.（⇨けんか）・兄弟分 a sworn brother. ・兄弟力士 a fellow *rikishi*; a fellow *sumo* wrestler.

きょうだい **強大** —— **強大な** 形 （強い）powerful; strong;〖書〗mighty;（大きな）great. ・強大な敵 a *powerful* enemy. ・強大な権力[軍事力] *great* power [military strength].

きょうだい **鏡台** a dréssing táble, a dresser, a vanity (table). ・鏡台の上には化粧品が散らばっていた The top of the *vanity* was littered with cosmetics.

ぎょうたい **業態** （分野）a business category;（形態）a business form;（状態）business conditions.
・業態を予報する forecast *business conditions*.
・業態調査をする make a survey of *business conditions*（*in* Japan）.

きょうたく **供託** —— **供託する** 動 deposit.
・供託金 a deposit; deposit money. ・供託金を没収される have one's *deposit* forfeited /fɪˈɔːrfɪtɪd/; lose one's *deposit*. ・供託所 a depository.

きょうたく **教卓** the teacher's desk (in a classroom).

きょうたん **驚嘆** 图 ▶彼のピアノの演奏技術は驚嘆に値する His skill on the piano is well worth *admiration* [is quite *amazing*].

—— **驚嘆する** 動 wonder 《at》;〖書〗marvel 《at》（**!** 後の方が強意的）;〔感嘆する〕admire;（びっくりする）be amazed 《at》; be struck with wonder. ・驚嘆すべき amazing; wonderful;（信じられないほどすばらしい）marvelous. ▶私はその少年の才能に驚嘆した I *wondered* [*marveled*] at the boy's talent.

きょうだん **凶弾** ▶彼は凶弾に倒れた He *was shot down by an assássin*.（**!** *assassin* は「暗殺者」, shoot down は「(丸腰の人を)撃ち殺す」の意）

きょうだん **教団** a religious organization.

きょうだん **教壇** a (teacher's) platform. ・教壇に立つ teach a class; teach at [in] a school; 〖米〗teach school; （教師になる）become a teacher.

きょうち **境地** （状態）a state. ・無我の境地に達する attain the *state* of selflessness. ・独自の境地を開く find one's own way.

きょうちくとう **夾竹桃** 〖植物〗an oleander; a rosebay.

きょうちゅう **胸中** （心）one's heart. ・彼に胸中をあかす unburden one's *heart* to him. ・彼の胸中を察する(同情する) sympathize with him; feel for him.

ぎょうちゅう **蟯虫** a threadworm; a pinworm.

きょうちょ **共著** （共同著作物）a joint work;（共同制作）collaboration. ▶彼は私と共著で数冊の本を書いた He *wrote* several books (*in collaboration*) *with* me./He and I *collaborated* on several books.
・共著者 a coauthor, a joint author; a collaborator.

きょうちょう **協調** 图 〔協力〕cooperation;〔調和〕harmony. ・労使間の協調 *cooperation* between labor and management. ・協調性を欠く lack *co-operation*. ・…と協調して in *cooperation* [*harmony*] with …. ▶戦争を防止するには国際協調がぜひ必要です International *cooperation* is essential to prevent war. ▶彼は非常に協調的だ He is very *cooperative*.

—— **協調する** 動 cooperate 《with》; go* along 《with》.

きょうちょう **強調** 图 (an) emphasis; stress.

—— **強調する** 動 emphasize; stress; put* [lay*] emphasis [stress] 《on》. ▶彼は時間厳守を強調した He *emphasized* [*stressed*] the need to be punctual./He *emphasized* [*stressed*] that we must be punctual.

:**きょうつう** **共通** 图 ・共通点を見いだす find *common* ground. ▶彼と私には共通点が何もない[たくさんある];

きょうつう 多少ある】I have nothing [a lot; something] *in common* with him./He and I have nothing [a lot; something] *in common*.
── 共通の 形 common;〖お互いの〗mutual. ● 共通の場に立って on common ground. ● 私たちにはガーデニングという共通の趣味がある We have a *common* hobby of gardening. ▶彼らは共通の利害で結ばれていた They were united by *common* interests. ▶彼は私たちの共通の友人だ He is our *mutual* [×common] friend.
── 共通する 動 ▶これらの文法上の誤りは学生に共通している These grammatical mistakes are *common to* students./These are *common* grammatical mistakes of [×to] students.
● 共通語 a common language.

きょうつう 胸痛 ● 胸痛がする have a *pain in* one's *chest*.

きょうてい 協定 〖同意・合意したもの〗an agreement;〖取り決め〗an arrangement;〖国家間の〗a treaty; a pact 〖!〗新聞の見出し語などに好まれる〗(⇨条約). ● 紳士協定 a gentleman's *agreement*. ● 協定を結ぶ make an *agreement* [an *arrangement*]《with him about it》. ● 協定が成立する come to [arrive at, conclude, reach] an *agreement* [an *arrangement*]. ● 協定を破棄する break an *agreement*. ● 5年間の穀物[価格]に調印する sign a five-year grain [price] *agreement*. ● 新しい貿易協定が調印された The new trade *agreement* was signed.
● 協定違反 a breach of an agreement. ● 協定価格 an agreed price.

きょうてい 教程 〖課程〗a course;〖教本〗a textbook ● フランス語教程 a French *course*. ▶彼はジャーナリズム1年教程をとっている He is taking a one-year journalism *course* [a one-year *course in* journalism].

きょうてい 競艇 mótorboat [spéedboat] rácing;(1回の)a mótorboat [a spéedboat] ráce.

きょうてき 強敵 〖戦争の〗a powerful [〖やや書〗formidable] enemy;〖試合の〗opponent;〖競争相手〗a strong [a powerful] rival.

きょうてん 教典 scriptures. (〖!〗通例複数形で)

ぎょうてん 仰天 ── 仰天する動 be astounded 《at; to do》;(口で)be flabbergasted 《at, by》. ● 暗がりの後ろから肩をたたかれてびっくり仰天した I *was frightened out of my wits* when someone tapped me on the shoulder from behind in the dark.

ぎょうてん 暁天 dawn. ▶清廉潔白な政治家は暁天の星のごとくまれである An honest stateman is as rare as a black swan [a white crow].

きょうてんどうち 驚天動地 ── 驚天動地の形 absolutely astounding; astonishing.

きょうと 凶徒 〖悪人〗a villain, a thug;〖暴徒〗a mob, a rioter.

きょうと 教徒 a believer, a follower. ● モルモン教徒 a *believer in* Mormonism. ● イスラム教徒 a Muslim. ● キリスト教徒 a Christian. ● 仏教徒 a Buddhist.

きょうど 匈奴 (フン族) Huns.

きょうど 強度 〖光[熱]の強度〗the intensity of light [heat]. ●橋の強度 the strength of a bridge. ● 強度の近眼鏡 *strong* [*powerful*] glasses for a near-sighted person.

きょうど 郷土 ● one's home. (⇨故郷) ● 郷土色豊かな rich in *local* color.
── 郷土の形 local.
● 郷土愛 love for [of] one's home [hometown]; local patriotism. ● 郷土玩具 a folk toy. ● 郷土芸能 (集合的) local performing arts. (〖!〗「この地方の郷土芸能」は a performing art peculiar to this district) ● 郷土史 (a) local history. ● 郷土史家 a local historian. ● 郷土料理 local [country] dishes.

きょうとう 共闘 名 a joint struggle.
── 共闘する動 ▶彼らは政府の政策に反対して共闘した They *struggled jointly* [共同戦線を張った] *presented a united front*] *against* the Government's policy.
● 共闘委員会 a joint struggle committee.

きょうとう 教頭 (副校長) a vice-principal,(英)a deputy headteacher.

きょうとう 驚倒 ── 驚倒する動 ● 世間を驚倒させる *amaze* [*astonish*, *astound*] the world.

＊**きょうどう** 共同 名 〖力を合わせること〗cooperation;〖文芸・科学などにおける共同制作〗collaboration;〖共有〗community.
── 共同の形 (合同の)joint. ▶(団結した)united. ▶私は妻と共同名義の預金口座を開いた My wife and I opened a *joint* bank account. ▶この寮では台所は共同で使っている Everyone *shares* the kitchen in this dorm.
── 共同する動 coóperàte; collàboràte;(手を組む)team up《with》. (⇨協力する) ▶彼は友人と共同でその仕事をした He *cooperated* [*collaborated*] *with* his friend *in* doing the work./He did the work *in cooperation* [*collaboration*] *with* his friend. ▶我々は共同でその新製品を開発した We have *jointly* developed [We *have teamed up to* develop] the new product.
● 共同開催 joint hosting. ● 共同企業体 a joint enterprise. ● 共同記者会見 a joint press [news] conference. ● 共同経営 joint management; partnership. ● 共同研究 (×a) joint research (*in* linguistics). ● 共同コミュニケ (issue) a joint communiqué. ● 共同社会 a community. ● 共同生活 (⇨共同生活) ● 共同正犯 〖共犯行為〗complicity. ●〖共犯者〗an accomplice /əkάmplis/. ● 共同声明 (issue) a joint statement. ● 共同責任 a joint responsibility 《for》. ● 共同戦線 (present [form]) a united front 《against》. ● 共同体 a community. ● 共同テレビアンテナ a communal [a shared] television antenna. ● 共同謀議 〖法律〗conspiracy. ● 共同募金 a community chest. ● 共同墓地 a cemetery.

きょうどう 協同 〖協力〗cooperation. (⇨協力)
ぎょうとう 行頭 the beginning of a line. (⇨行末)
きょうどうくみあい 協同組合 (生協)a cooperative (society), a co-op /kóu-àp/.
きょうどうせいかつ 共同生活 communal life. ▶彼らは2年間共同生活をした They *lived together* [共同で部屋を借りて生活した] *shared a room*] for two years. 〖事情〗後の方は学生などが経費節約のためによくやる)

きょうとうほ 橋頭堡 (陣地) (establish) a bridgehead; (上陸拠点) (establish [hold, secure]) a beachhead.

きょうねん 凶年 〖不作の年〗a lean year, a year of poor harvest;〖災いのある年〗a bad year.
きょうねん 享年 ● 享年80歳 died at (the age of) eighty.
きょうばい 競売 名 (an) auction. ● 競売で中古車を買う buy a used car *at auction*.

きょうはく

— 競売する 動 ・その家具を競売する sell the furniture at [《英》by] auction; auction off the furniture; (競売に付す) put the furniture up at [for, 《英》to] auction.
・競売場 an áuction ròom. ・競売人 an auctioneer.

*きょうはく 脅迫 名 (a) threat /θrét/;《書》(a) ménace (❗ threat より強意的). (⇨脅し) ▶下劣な脅迫に屈しなかった He didn't give in to dirty threats.

— 脅迫する 動 threaten;《書》menace. ▶私を脅迫するのか Are you threatening me? ▶彼らは秘密を漏らしたら殺すぞと彼を脅迫した They threatened him with death [threatened to kill him] if he revealed the secret. (⇨脅す)
・脅迫状 a thréatening càll. ・脅迫電話 a thréatening (phòne) càll.

きょうはく 強迫〖強制〗《やや書》compulsion;〖抑圧, 威圧〗《書》coércion. (⇨強制)
・強迫観念 an obsession. ▶彼女は彼に殺されるのではないかという強迫観念にとりつかれている She is obsessed by [with] the idea that she will be killed by him. ・強迫神経症〖医学〗(an) obsèssive-compúlsive neurósis (略 OCN).

きょうはん 共犯〖書〗complicity. ▶彼女は彼との共犯(関係)を否定した She denied having taken part [denied complicity] in his crime./She denied (that) she had taken part in his crime.
・共犯者 an accomplice, a partner in crime.

きょうふ 恐怖 (a) fear (❗ 最も一般的な語. しばしば臆病(おく)さを意含する); (ぎょっとさせる) (a) fright; (身をすくませる) (a) terror; (ぞっとさせる) (a) horror; (差し迫った危険などを予期したときの) (a) dread; (差し迫った危険の察知による) alarm; (動転させる) (a) panic, (恐怖症) a phobia 《about》.
①【～(の)恐怖, 恐怖～】・死の恐怖 the fear of death. ・戦争の恐怖 the horror(s) [terror(s)] of war. ・～s は「種々の惨事」の意) ・閉所恐怖である have a fear of [a phobia about] closed-in places; be a clàustrophóbe. ・恐怖心を抱かせる scare [frighten, make] (him) afraid. ・恐怖心から out of fear, (恐怖心で(ために)) with fear.
②【恐怖が】・突然恐怖が彼を襲った A sudden fear came over him./Suddenly he was filled with fear.
③【恐怖の】・恐怖のあまり悲鳴を上げる scream with [in] terror.
④【恐怖に】・恐怖におののいて逃げる run away in terror. ・恐怖に襲われる (ひどくおびえる) be terrified 《by, at》; be struck by [seized with] terror; be terror-stricken 《at》; (ぎょっとする) take fright 《at》. ・恐怖にかられて悲鳴をあげた Terror-stricken, I screamed.
⑤【恐怖を[で]】・恐怖で震える shake with fear [fright, horror]. ▶私は暗やみにいると大きな恐怖を感じる I feel great fear in the dark.
・恐怖映画〘主に米〙a horror movie,《主に英》a horror film. ・恐怖政治 terrorism.

きょうふ 教父〖カトリックの高僧の敬称〗Father;〖洗礼の名付け親〗a godfather.

きょうぶ 胸部 the chest. ▶胸部に痛みがある have a pain in one's chest.
・胸部外科 chest [thoracic] surgery. ・胸部レントゲン検査 a chest X-ray examination.

きょうふう 強風 a strong wind;〖気象〗a gale (参考) 風速 13.9-28.5m/秒). ▶強風が吹いている [吹くのっている] It is blowing hard [harder]./The gale [A strong wind] is blowing./There is a gale [a strong wind] blowing.

きょうふうき 『狂風記』 Tales of Crazy Winds. (参考) 石川淳の小説

きょうへい 強兵 (強い兵隊) a powerful army; (軍事力強化) a military buildup.

きょうへき 胸壁〖軍隊〗a breastwork, a parapet;〖胸部〗walls of the chest.

きょうへん 共編 coéditorship.
・共編者 a coéditor.

きょうべん 強弁 — 強弁する 動 insist without good reason 《that 節; on, upon》.

きょうべん 教鞭 teaching.
・教鞭を執(と)る go into teaching. ・教鞭をとっている be a teacher at [in] a high school;《米》teach 《high》school.

きょうほ 競歩 race walking;〖陸上〗the walk. ・20キロメートル競歩 the 20-kilometer walk.

きょうほう 凶報 (悪い知らせ) bad news; (死亡の知らせ) sad news.

きょうぼう 凶暴 名 (獰猛(どうもう)) ferocity; (残忍) brutality.
— 凶暴な 形 (残忍な) fierce; (獰猛な) ferocious; (凶暴な) violent; (獣のように残酷な) brutal.

きょうぼう 共謀 (a) conspiracy. (⇨陰謀)
— 共謀する 動 ・彼と共謀する conspire [plot] with him. (❗ 悪の方が口語的) ▶彼らは共謀して銀行強盗をした They conspired together to rob the bank.
・共謀者 a conspirator.

きょうぼう 狂暴 — 狂暴な 形 frenzied; (暴力的な) violent; (激怒した) berserk ▶通例 go [run] berserk 「狂暴になる」の連語で用いられる). ・その犬の狂暴な吠え声 the dog's frenzied barks.

きょうほん 狂奔 — 狂奔する 動 make* every effort [desperate efforts, frantic efforts] 《to do》. ▶彼は金策[職探し]に狂奔していた He was very busy raising money [hunting for a job].

きょうほん 教本 a textbook; a manual. (⇨教則本)

ぎょうまつ 行末 the end of a line. (㋐ 行頭) ・行末をそろえる justify margins.

きょうまん 驕慢 — 驕慢な 形 arrogant; haughty. (⇨傲慢(ごうまん))

:きょうみ 興味 (関心) (an) interest 《in》 (❗「関心事」の意では ⓒ); (人を引きつける魅力) appeal.

> 解説 interest は動詞としては「(人)に興味を持たせる」という意の他動詞. interested は「(人が)興味を持たせられた[持った]」, interesting (=of interest) は「(人・物事)の興味を持たせるような, 興味深い」の意の形容詞として用いる.

①【興味(の)～】・興味のある話 an interesting [(わくわくさせる) an exciting] story. ・興味本位の(=扇情的な)週刊誌 a sensational weekly magazine.
・興味本位で (好奇心から) out of curiosity; (おもしろ半分に) just for fun. ・興味深く [興味深げに] 彼の話を聞く listen to him with (great) interest [with an interested look]. ・興味津々である (=非常に興味深い) 《人が主語》be very [deeply, greatly] interested; 《事が主語》deeply [greatly] interest (him).
②【興味が】・興味がある be interested, have (an) interest 《in》 (❗ 状態を表す); (興味を持つ) get interested, take an interest 《in》 (❗ 動作を表す). ▶彼はスポーツに大変興味がある He is very [greatly] interested in sports./He has a great interest in sports. ▶私は音楽に興味がない I'm not interested [I have no interest] in music./Music is of no interest to [doesn't interest] me./Music has [holds] no appeal for me. ▶さ

きょうむ 教務 (学校の) school affairs; educational affairs.
- 教務課 the department of school affairs; the registration office; the educational affairs department.
- 教務主任 the head of the educational affairs department.

ぎょうむ 業務 〖職業上の仕事〗business; 〖遊びに対して〗work; 〖職務〗a duty (⚠通例複数形で). ● 業務に励む attend to one's *business* [*duties*]; (専念する) apply oneself to one's *work*. ● 業務を拡張する expand [extend] one's *business*. ● 業務用の車 a car for *business* use. ● 業務の海外委託 business outsourcing offshore (↔onshore).
- 業務委託企業 an *outsourcer*. 業務受託企業 an *outsourcee*.
- 業務上過失致死傷 professional negligence resulting in injury or death.
- 業務上災害 an on-the-job accident. 業務提携 a business tie-up; business collaboration.
- 業務命令 a business order.

きょうめい 共鳴 〖共感〗sympathy 《with, for》; 〖音の〗resonance.
── 共鳴する 動 sympathize 《with》; 《やや書》resonate. ▶その計画に共鳴している *be in sympathy with* [(支持している) *be in favor of*] the plan. ▶先生は学生の意見に共鳴した The teacher *sympathized* [*expressed*] his *sympathy*] *with* his student's opinion(s).
- 共鳴者 a sympathizer.

きょうもん 経文 〖仏教〗a sutra. (⇨経)

きょうやく 共訳 (a) joint translation. ▶この本は A, B 両氏の共訳による This book *was translated by* Messrs. A and B.
- 共訳者 a joint translator.

きょうやく 協約 (a) cóntract. ● 労働協約 a labor *contract*.

きょうゆ 教諭 a teacher. (⇨先生, 教師)

きょうゆう 共有 图 joint [dual] ownership.
── 共有する 動 own (it) jointly 《with him》; have* (own) (it) in common 《with him》; (共同使用する) share (it) 《with him》.
- 共有財産 joint property; (公共の財産) common property. 共有者 a joint owner.

きょうゆう 享有 ── 享有する 動 ▶彼女は音楽の才能を享有していた She *was gifted with* a talent for music.

きょうよ 供与 图 (供給) (a) provision. ● 技術供与 the *provision* of technology.
── 供与する 動 ▶武器を供与する *provide* weapons 《for the country》; *supply* weapons 《to the country》.

*きょうよう 教養 culture (⚠長い間に養われた芸術・思想に対する高度な理解や好みをいう); (主に教育による知識) (an) education (⚠複数形はまれ). ● 教養のある educated; (知的に洗練された) sophisticated; cultured; (知識や作法を身につけた) cultivated; (学識のある) literate. ● 教養のない uneducated; 《話》illiterate. ● 教養を身につける acquire *culture*. ● 教養を高めるために外国語を習う learn a foreign language for *cultural* enrichment [to cultivate oneself]. ▶彼は大変教養のある人だ He is a highly *cultured* man. ▶《書》cultured は通例叙述的でも使い) 《書》He is a man of high [rich] *culture*./He is a well-*educated* [a highly *educated*] man.
- 教養学部 a liberal arts college. 教養課程 a liberal arts course. 教養科目 (集合的) the liberal arts (and sciences); a subject for general education. 教養小説 a bildungsroman /bíldungzrouma:n/ (⑱ -s). 教養番組 an educational program.

きょうよう 共用 图 ● 共用の庭 a garden (which is) for *common use*.
── 共用する 動 ▶私は同級生のエミーとこの部屋を共用している I *share* this room *with* Emmy, my classmate.

きょうよう 供用 ── 供用する 動 ▶この運動場は一般に供用させている This playground *is open to* the public.

きょうよう 強要 图 《書》coercion /kouə́ːrʃən/. ● 強要されて under *coercion*.
── 強要する 動 ▶彼に自白を強要する *force* him *to* confess; 《やや書》*coerce* him *into* confessing.

きょうらく 享楽 图 (a) pleasure. ── 享楽的(な) 形 pleasure-seeking; 《書》hedonistic.
- 享楽主義 hedonism. 享楽主義者 a pleasure-seeker; a hedonist.

きょうらん 狂乱 ● 半狂乱(狂乱状態)になる become frantic; go mad. ● 半狂乱で frantically; in a frenzy; 《話》like mad.

きょうらん 供覧 图 (a) display. ── 供覧する 動 display 《goods for sale》.

*きょうり 郷里 one's hometown; one's (old) home; 〖出生地〗one's birthplace. (⇨故郷) ● 郷里の金沢で in one's *native* Kanazawa. ● 郷里の両親に手紙を出す write *home* to one's parents; write (to) one's parents *at home*.

きょうり 胸裏, 胸裡 one's heart. ● 胸裏で in one's heart (of hearts). (⇨心中)

きょうり 教理 (a) doctrine. (⑱ 教義)

きょうりきこ 強力粉 hard-wheat [strong-wheat] flour.

きょうりゅう 恐竜 a dinosaur /dáinəsɔ̀ːr/.

きょうりょう 狭量 narrow-mindedness; intolerance. ── 狭量な narrow-minded; intolerant.

きょうりょう 橋梁 a bridge. (⇨橋)
- 橋梁工事 the construction [building] of a (new) bridge.

‡きょうりょく 協力 图 coöperátion; (助力) help; (支援) support; 〖文芸・科学などにおける共同制作〗colláborátion. ● 経済協力 economic *cooperation*.
① 【協力が】 ▶この計画にはあなたの協力が必要です I need your *cooperation* [*help*, *support*, 《やや書》*assistance*] in this plan. ▶あなたのご協力がなければこのことはできなかったでしょう Without your *cooperation*, this would not have been possible.
② 【協力に(を)】 ▶ご協力に感謝します I'm grateful for [*xto*] your *cooperation*./Thank you for your *help*. ● 後の方が普通の言い方. Thank you for your *cooperation*. は「ご協力はほどよろしくお願いします」の意で, 依頼文書の結びとしてはよく用いられる) ▶彼は私に協力を惜しまなかった He was very willing to *cooperate with* [*help*] me./He spared no efforts in *cooperating with* me. ▶高校生の協力に

より献血運動は成功した The blood donation campaign was successful *through the cooperation* of high school students. ▶資料収集のことで友人に協力を求めよう We will ask our friends to *cooperate in* collecting data.

— **協力的な** 形 coöperative (↔uncooperative).
●協力的な態度 a *cooperative* attitude. ●彼だけがこの計画に協力的だった He alone was *cooperative* in this plan.

— **協力する** 動 coöpèrate; collàborate《with＋人, in [on]＋事; *to* do》; (提携する) team up《with》; work [pull] together.(＊共同する》宇宙開発には多くの国が協力している Many nations *cooperate on* [*pull together for*] space development. ▶子供たちは先生と協力してテントを張った The children *cooperated with* their teachers [The children and their teachers *cooperated*] *in setting* up a tent./The children set up a tent *in cooperation with* [*with the cooperation of*] their teachers. ▶この病院では内科と外科が緊密に協力し合っている The medical and surgical divisions *work* closely *together* at [in] this hospital. ▶私どもはいつでも全面的に協力いたします You can always count on our full *cooperation*.

●協力者 a cooperator; a collaborator; (支持者) a supporter.

*きょうりょく 強力 — 強力な 形 powerful; strong.
●強力な指導者 a *powerful* [a *strong*] leader; a leader of *great power*. ●強力なエンジン a *powerful* [a *high-powered*, ✗a *strong*] engine. ●強力な薬 a *strong* [a *powerful*] medicine.

— **強力に** 副 ▶彼女を強力に推せんします I recommend her *strongly* [*highly*].

きょうれつ 強烈 — 強烈な 形 intense; strong.
●強烈な光 *intense* light. ●強烈な味のインドカレー *strong* Indian curry with rice. ●強烈な印象[個性] a *strong* impression [personality]. ●強烈な一撃 a *heavy* [a *powerful*] blow.

*ぎょうれつ 行列 ❶[行進する列] a procession; (見せるための) a parade; [順番待ちの列] a line, (英) a queue /kjúː/ (⇨列). ●仮装行列 a masquerade *parade*. ▶行列をつくってバスを待つ wait for a bus in a *line* [a *queue*]; *line up* [《英》*queue* (up)] for a bus. ▶兵隊の行列は大通りを通って町の広場まで進んで行った The *procession* of soldiers marched [Soldiers marched *in procession*] down the avenue to the town square.
❷[数学] matrix /méitriks/. (複 matrices /-siːz/).

きょうれん 教練 military drill [training].
きょうわおん 協和音 《音楽》(a) consonance. (↔不協和音)
きょうわこく 共和国 a republic.
きょうわせいじ 共和政治 (a) republican government.
きょうわとう 共和党 (米国の) the Repúblican (↔Democratic) Party, the Grand Old Party. ●共和党員 a Republican (↔a Democrat).
きょうわん 峡湾 [フィヨルド] a fiord, a fjord.
きょえいしん 虚栄心 vanity. (⇨見え) ●虚栄心の強い女 a *vain* woman. ●彼女の虚栄心を満たす[くすぐる; 傷つける] satisfy [tickle; hurt] her *vanity*.
ぎょえん 御苑 an Imperial garden. ●吹上御苑 the Fukiage *Imperial Garden*.
きょおく 巨億 billions 《of》. ●巨億の富 fabulous wealth.
ギョーザ 餃子 ▶焼き[水]餃子 a baked [a boiled] *Chinese dumpling*.
*きょか 許可 名 [許すこと] (✗a) permission, 《書》 leave; [認可] (法律による) (a) license; (権威による) authority; [承認] approval; [入場・入会などの] admission. ●当局の許可を受ける get *permission* [《話》an *OK*] from the authorities. ●許可なく外泊するstay out *without permission*. ●大統領の許可を得て by (the) *authority* of the President. ▶パレードをするには警察の許可が必要だ You can't hold a parade without the *permission of* [an *authorization from*] the police./Police *permission* is necessary to hold a parade. ▶彼は先生に早退の許可を願い出た He asked his teacher for *permission* [asked his teacher's *permission*] to leave school early. ▶その店はたばこの販売許可を与えられた The store *was given a license* [*was licensed*] to sell tobacco. ▶彼は東北大学への入学許可を得た He *got* [《書》*was granted*] *admission* to Tohoku University./(やや書) He *was admitted* to Tohoku University.

— **許可する** 動 (積極的に) permit (-tt-); (消極的に) allow, let* (↑後の語はど口語的 (⇨許す)); (公式に) authorize. ▶父は私が父の車を使うのを許可した My father *permitted* me *to* [*allowed* me *to*, *let* me] use his car./(やや書) My father *gave* me *permission* to use his car. ▶ここでは喫煙は許可されていない Smoking *is* not *permitted* [*allowed*] in here./It *is* not *permitted* [✗allowed] to smoke in here. ▶知事はその金の支払いを正式に許可した The governor *authorized* the payment of the money.

●許可証 a 《work》 pérmit; a 《driver's》 license.
●通行[居住]許可証 a pass.

ぎょかいるい 魚介類, 魚貝類 fish and shellfish (❗複数扱い); (海産食品) seafood.
きょがく 巨額 a huge [a vast, an enormous, 《話》 a colossal] amount 《of》. ●巨額の負債で苦しむ suffer from [groan under] a *huge* debt. ●美術館を建てるのには巨額の金がかかるだろう It will cost a *huge amount* of money to build a museum.
ぎょかくだか 漁獲高 (量) a catch. ●今年最高のマグロの漁獲高 the largest *catch* of tuna this year.
きょかん 巨漢 a giant. (⇨巨人)
ぎょがんレンズ 魚眼レンズ a fish-eye lens.
きょぎ 虚偽 (偽り)《書》falsehood; [婉曲的] misinformation. ●虚偽の証言をする give *false* testimony.
ぎょき 漁期 a físhing sèason. (⇨漁(りょう)期)
きょぎょう 虚業 a risky [a high-risk] business [venture].
*ぎょぎょう 漁業 [漁獲] fishing; the fishing industry; [魚介・海草類の捕獲・採取および加工] fishery; (❗通例複数形で). ●日本の漁業 Japan's [the Japanese] *fishing industry*. ●沿岸[沖合, 遠洋]漁業 coastal [offshore; deep-sea] *fishing* [*fisheries*]. ●漁業が盛んである be active in *fishing*.

●漁業協同組合 a fishermen's cooperative (association). ●漁業権 físhing ríghts. ●漁業国 a físhing nàtion. ●漁業資源 fishery resources.

きょきょじつじつ 虚々実々 ▶虚々実々の(＝巧みな)駆け引き *shrewd* tactics.
きょきん 拠金 名 a collection 《for charity》; (make) a contribution 《for the fund》; a subscription 《to the charity》.

— **拠金する** 動 collect 《for a local charity》; contribute 《five pounds》; subscribe 《to a society》.

*きょく 曲 (楽曲) music (❗「一つの曲」 = a piece of music); (旋律) a tune, 《書》a melody (⇨節)

きょく ❸;(聞き覚えのある)《古》an air; (歌) a song; (小曲) a piece. ●バイオリン曲 violin *music*. ●合唱曲 choral *music*. ●詩に曲をつける《慣用表現》set [put] a poem to *music*. ▶フルートで1曲聞かせてください Play us a tune on [×with] your flute.

きょく 局 ❶〖官庁などの〗an office, 《米》a bureau /bjúərou/ ～s, bureaux /-z/,《英》a department; (官庁・会社などの) a division. (⇨部 ❶) ●電話局 a telephone *office*. (交換局) *exchange*]. ●放送局 a broadcasting *station*. ●連邦捜査局 the Federal *Bureau* of Investigation; the FBI. **❷**〖囲碁・将棋などの〗a game. ●将棋を1局打つ play a *game* of shogi.

きょく 極 ❶〖地球・磁気の〗a pole. ●北[南]極 the North [South] *Pole*. ●陽[陰]極 the positive [negative] *pole*.
❷〖極限〗the extreme, the extremity; (最高潮) the height. ●疲労の極に達する be *extremely* exhausted [tired]. ▶彼女のその発言で民衆の怒りは極に達した That remark of hers drove people to *extreme* indignation [made people's rage reach its *height*].

ぎょく 玉 〖宝石〗a gem, (翡翠(ﾋｽ)) jade (⇨宝石) 〖信用取引で〗stocks, shares; 〖将棋で〗a king; 〖飲食店などで〗an egg.

ぎょく 漁区 fishing grounds; a fishery (⚠通例複数形). ●漁場

ぎょく 漁具 fishing tàckle; fishing gèar.

きょくいん 局員 (一員) a staff member,《集合的》a staff. (職員) ●郵便局員 a postal clerk; (全体) the *staff* of a post office.

きょくう 極右 the extreme [far] right (↔left). (⚠単・複両扱い)

ぎょくおん 玉音 the Emperor's voice.
●玉音放送 the broadcast by the Emperor.

きょくがいしゃ 局外者 an outsider; 〖第三者〗a third party.

きょくげい 曲技 acrobatics. (⇨曲芸, 軽業)

きょくげい 曲芸 a feat, a stunt (⇨芸当); acrobatics (⚠通例単数扱い. 一連の演技をさす場合は複数扱い); (動物の) a trick. ●サーカスで曲芸をする perform *acrobatics* in a circus.
●曲芸師 an acrobat. ●曲芸飛行 stunt flying; (aerial) acrobatics.

きょくげん 局限 ── 局限する 動 limit ... (to); set* a limit to .... ▶その津波の被災地は島の南岸の2村に局限されている The tsunami-hit area *is limited to* two villages on the southern coast of the island.

きょくげん 極言 ── 極言する 動 go* so far as to say 《that 節》. ▶彼は私が不正直だと極言した He *went so far as to say* that I was dishonest.

きょくげん 極限 〖限度〗a limit. ●忍耐の極限に達する reach the *limit* of one's patience. ●能力の極限まで努力を尽す exert oneself to the *utmost limit* of one's ability.
●極限状態 an extreme situation.

きょくさ 極左 the extreme [far] left (↔right). (⚠単・複両扱い)

ぎょくざ 玉座 the (Imperial) throne; the Emperor's seat.

ぎょくさい 玉砕 ── 玉砕する 動 die an honorable death; die a hero's [a heroic] death.
●玉砕攻撃 a banzai attack (by Japanese troops).

きょくじつ 旭日 the rising sun.
●旭日昇天の勢い ▶彼は旭日昇天の勢いである He is *in the ascendant*.

●旭日章 the Order of the Rising Sun.

きょくしょ 局所 a part. (⇨局部, 局所的)

きょくしょう 極小 〖数学〗a minimum (⚠ minima, ～s) (↔a maximum).

ぎょくしょう 玉将 〖将棋〗a king.

ぎょくせきこんこう 玉石混交 a mixture of wheat and chaff.

きょくせつ 曲折 曲折した (複雑な) complicated; (曲がりくねった) twisted, distorted. ●幾多の曲折を経て through *twists and turns*. (⇨紆余(ｳﾖ)曲折)

きょくせん 曲線 a curve, a curved [a curving] line. ●曲線を描く draw a *curved line*; (カーブがる) curve (to the left). ●曲線を描いて飛ぶ fly in a *curve*. ●曲線美の curvy [shapely]《women》.

きょくそう 曲想 曲想を練る work hard on *a motif of a piece of music*.

きょくだい 極大 〖数学〗a maximum (⚠ ～s, maxima) (↔a minimum). ●極大の量刑 the *maximum* penalty.

きょくたん 極端 名〖極度〗(an) extreme. (⚠「極端な状態・行為・手段」の意では通例複数形で) ●極端から極端へと走る go from one *extreme* to the other. ▶若者は極端に走りがちだ Young people are apt to *go to extremes*. 〖慣用表現〗
── 極端な 形〖極度の〗extreme; 〖過度の〗excessive (↔moderate). ●極端な例を挙げる give an *extreme* example. ●極端な言い方をすれば to put it in an *extreme* way. ●極端な甘やかし *excessive* indulgence.
── 極端に 副 extremely; excessively. ●極端に用心深い be *extremely* [*excessively*] cautious;《書》be cautious *in the extreme*.

きょくち 極地 the pole; the polar regions.
●極地探検 a polar exploration. ●極地探検家 a polar explorer.

きょくち 極致 〖書〗the acme /ǽkmi/, the peak. ●美の極致 the *acme* of beauty; (理想の) *ideal* beauty; (完璧(ｶﾝﾍﾟｷ)な) *perfect* beauty. ●円熟の極致(=頂点)に達する reach the *acme* of maturity.

きょくちてき 局地的 ── 局地的な 形 local. ▶昨夜局地的な豪雨があった There was a *local* downpour last night./Last night's downpour was limited to a small area.
── 局地的に 副 locally.

きょくちょう 曲調 a tune; a melody.

きょくちょう 局長 〖部の上の組織の長〗the chief [director] of a division [(官庁の) a bureau]; 〖郵便局長〗a postmaster.

きょくてん 極点 the North [South] Pole.

きょくど 極度 名 (an) extreme.
── 極度の 形 ●極度の貧困にあえいでいる人たち people living in *extreme* poverty. ●極度の疲労で倒れる collapse from *extreme* fatigue.
── 極度に 副 ●極度に用心深い be *extremely* cautious;《書》be cautious *in the extreme*.

きょくとう 極東 the Far East. (⚠語源 米英では時に東南アジアを含めることがある) ●極東問題 *Far Eastern* problems.

きょくどめ 局留め 《表示》《米》general delivery, 《英》poste restante /pòust restáːnt/.

きょくのり 曲乗り 名 (馬の) stunt riding; (飛行機の) stunt flying.
── 曲乗り(を)する 動 ●自転車[バイク]の曲乗りをする do *stunt cycling* [*riding*].

きょくば 曲馬 an equestrian feat.
●曲馬団 a circus; a circus troupe.

きょくばん 局番 a télephone còde. ●市外局番《米》an área còde,《英》a díalling [an STD] còde 《subscriber *trunk* dialling code の略》.

きょうふ 曲譜 a note, 《集合的》music; 《総譜》a score.

きょくぶ 局部 [一部] a part; [患部] the affected part; [陰部] one's private parts, 《話》one's privates. ● 局部的苦痛を訴える complain of a *local* pain.
● 局部麻酔 local anesthesia /ænisθíːʒə/.

きょくめん 局面 [段階] a stage, a phase; [情勢] the situation; [碁や将棋の] the position. (⇨情勢)
● 局面(=行き詰まり)を打開する break the *deadlock*; get out of the *deadlock*. ● 重大な局面を迎える[に差しかかる, に立たされる] enter [reach; be in] a serious *phase*. ● その報告書はその問題のあらゆる局面を網羅している The report takes in all *aspects* of the problem.

きょくもく 曲目 [曲の名前] the name of a tune; [演奏、種目表] a program; [歌・演奏などの1曲] a piece (of music); (ポピュラー・ジャズなどの) a number. ▶ 今夜の音楽会の曲目はどうなっていますか What's on the *program* for tonight's concert? ▶ 彼の好きな曲目はビートルズの「イエスタデー」です His favorite *number* is "Yesterday" by Beatles.

きょくりょく 極力 [力の限り] to the best of one's ability; [できるだけ] as ... as possible [one can]; [最後まで] to the last (!むくわれない結末を暗示する); [全力で] with all one's might; [すべての方法で] in every way. ● 極力治安の回復に努める do [try] *one's best* to restore public peace. ● 極力それに反対する oppose it *to the last* [*in every way*].

ぎょくろ 玉露 green tea of the best quality.

きょくろん 極論 —— 極論する 動 (突き詰めて論ずる) argue ... out; (極端な論を立てる) go* *too far in one's argument*.

ぎょぐん 魚群 a school [a shoal] of fish.
● 魚群探知機 a fish detèctor [fínder].

きょけつ 虚血 [医学] ischaemia, ischemia.
● 虚血性心疾患 ischemic heart disease.

きょげん 虚言 a lie. (⇨嘘)

きょこう 挙行 —— 挙行する 動 hold* 《a meeting》; perform 《a ceremony》. ● 挙行される be held; be performed; take place.

きょこう 虚構 名 (a) fiction. —— 虚構の 形 fictional.

ぎょこう 漁港 a fishing pòrt [hàrbor].

きょこく 挙国 the whole nation [country]. ▶ 私たちは挙国一致して国難を克服した We were all united to overcome our national crisis.

きょざい 巨財 ● 巨財を築く make [amass] *an enormous* [*a large, a vast*] *fortune*.

きょしき 挙式 (結婚式) a wedding (ceremony). ▶ 挙式はいつですか When is your *wedding ceremony*? ▶ 教会で挙式の予定です Our *wedding* will be held in church.

きょしつ 居室 (居間) a lìving ròom (⇨居間); (個室) one's (own) room.

きょじつ 虚実 truth [fact] and fiction. ● 虚実を尽くす employ [use] *wily* tactics.

きょしてき 巨視的 ● 巨視的に見る take a *macroscopic* [(全体を一つの有機的な構成物として見た) *holistic* /houlístik/] view 《of》. ● 巨視的立場に立っての環境問題の解決 a *holistic* solution to the environmental problem.

ぎょしゃ 御者 a driver; (4輪大型の馬車の) a coachman (複 -men /-mən/).
● 御者座 [天文] the Charioteer, Auriga.

きょじゃく 虚弱 —— 虚弱な 形 weak; delicate. ● 虚弱な体質の人 a person with a *weak* [*a sickly*] constitution; a person (who is) in *delicate* health.

きょしゅ 挙手 名 挙手で決をとる decide by a show of hands.
—— 挙手する 動 raise [put* up] one's hand.

きょしゅう 去就 one's course of action. (⇨進退 ❷)
● 去就を明らかにする decide on *one's course of action*.

きょじゅう 居住 —— 居住する 動 live, 《書》reside /rizáid/.
● 居住空間 lívíng spàce. ● 居住権 the right of residence. ● 居住者 a resident. ● 居住性 habitability; (住みやすさ) comfort. ● 居住性の高い家屋 a house *comfortable* to live in. ● 居住地 one's place of residence.

きょしゅつ 拠出 —— 拠出する 動 contribute, donate.
● 拠出金 (a) contribution, (a) donation. (!donation は慈善的な意味合いが強い)

きょしょ 居所 one's abode; one's whereabouts. (!単・複両扱い) (⇨居所(いどころ))

きょしょう 巨匠 a (great) master. (⇨名人, 大家)
● 音楽の巨匠 a *great master* of music, a maestro. ● 巨匠の作品 a work by a *master*.

きょじょう 居城 one's castle.

ぎょしょう 漁礁 a breeding ground for fish.

ぎょじょう 漁場 fishing grounds, fisheries. ● 我々の漁場を荒らす damage our *fishing grounds*. ● 津島沖の漁場 *fisheries* off Tsushima.

きょしょく 虚飾 《書》ostentation. ● 虚飾に満ちた生活 《書》an *ostentatious* lifestyle.

ぎょしょく 漁色 lechery.
● 漁色家 a womanizer; a lecher.

きょしょくしょう 拒食症 [医学] anorexia /ænəréksiə/. ● 拒食症で苦しむ suffer from anorexia.

きょじん 巨人 a giant; [偉人] a great man [woman] (!複数形は men, women); [野球] (巨人軍) the Giants (!巨人軍の選手の1人は a Giant).

きょじん 『巨人』 *Titan* /táitn/ (参考 マーラー作の交響曲の名でギリシア神話の巨人族の1人).

ぎょしん 魚信 a bite, a strike.

きょしんたんかい 虚心坦懐 虚心坦懐に 副 虚心坦懐に話し合う talk *frankly* 《with》; have a *heart-to-heart* talk 《with》.

キヨスク (⇨キオスク)

ぎょする 御する (馬を) drive*, manage; (人を) manage, control, handle. ● 御しやすい easy to *manage*; manageable; tractable. ● 御しにくい hard to *manage*; unmanageable; intractable.
● 御しやすい客 a customer easy to *deal with* [*to please*].

きょせい 巨星 ❶ [天体] A giant star.
❷ [人物] a great person.
● 巨星墜(お)つ A great man [woman] is lost. (!日本語のような定型表現はない. The mighty oak has fallen. も一例)

きょせい 去勢 名 castration. —— 去勢する 動 cástrate.

きょせい 虚勢 [はったり] (a) bluff; (強がり) bravádo; [大胆な態度では] a bold [a brave] front.
● 虚勢を張る bluff; make [pull, put on] a bluff; put on [show] a bold front. ● 虚勢を張る人 a bluff; a bluffer.

きょせき 巨石 a huge stone; [考古] a megalith.
● 巨石記念物 a megalith monument.

きょせつ 虚説 a groundless [a false, a baseless] rumor.

きょぜつ 拒絶 图 (a) refusal; (a) rejection (⚠️後の方が強意的); (要求などの) 《やや書》 (a) denial.
— **拒絶する** 動 ▶要求をきっぱりと拒絶する give a flat refusal [denial] to a request; refuse [reject, deny] a request flatly. (⇨断わる❶) ▶彼の転勤願いは拒絶された His transfer request was rejected [was turned down].
● **拒絶反応** 〖医学〗 (a) rejection. ▶移植臓器の拒絶反応を抑える stop rejection of transplanted organs.

ぎょせん 漁船 a fishing boat [vessel].
きょぞう 巨像 a colossus (圈 colossi /-sai/, ~es); a gigantic statue.
きょぞう 虚像 〖物理〗 a virtual image (↔a real image).
ぎょそん 漁村 a fishing village.
きょたい 巨体 (人の) (a) heavy build; (人・物の) (a) huge [great] bulk. ▶巨体の男 a man of [with a] heavy build. ▶オイルタンカーの巨体 a huge bulk of an oil tanker. ▶巨体をいすに沈める lower one's bulk into a chair.
きょだい 巨大 — **巨大な** huge, gigantic; (並はずれて大きい) enormous. ▶巨大なタンカー a huge [a gigantic] tanker.
● **巨大都市** a megalopolis.
きょだく 許諾 consent; assent. (⇨承諾)
ぎょたく 魚拓 (make) a fish print.
きょだつ 虚脱 ▶虚脱状態になる be in a state of (mental) collapse ▶(酒・麻薬による)《やや書》stupor].
きょっかい 曲解 — **曲解する** 動 ▶彼の言葉を曲解する twist 《やや書》distort, pervert] his words.
きょっかん 極冠 a pole cap.
きょっけい 極刑 capital punishment. (⇨死刑) ▶極刑に処する mete out capital punishment (to).
きょっこう 極光 an aurora /ɔːrɔːrə/. ▶北[南]極光 the aurora borealis [australis]; the northern [southern] lights.
ぎょっ(と) ▶彼女は彼を見てぎょっとして後ずさりした She drew back [recoiled] in fright from him. ▶彼はぎょっとして立ちすくんだ Shocked, he stood motionless.
きょてん 拠点 (足がかり) a foothold, a footing; (根拠地) a base. ▶拠点を築く establish a foothold.
きょとう 巨頭 a leader; a magnate; a tycoon. ▶実業界の巨頭 a business tycoon.
● **巨頭会談** summit talks; a top-level conference.
きょとう 挙党 the whole party. ▶挙党一致で行革に取り組んだ The whole party united to reform the administrative structure.
きょどう 挙動 ▶挙動不審の男 a man who is acting suspiciously; a suspicious-looking man.
きょときょと — **きょときょとする** 動 ▶look around restlessly.
きょとんと ▶きょとんとして with a blank look. ▶きょとんとした顔をしている look blank.
きょにんか 許認可 (a) license; (許可) permission; (認可) authorization.
*****きょねん 去年** last year. ▶去年の5月に last May (⚠️同じ年の7-8月以後使うと「今年の5月」の意味にもなる); in May last year. ▶前の方は「5月」, 後の方は「去年」に重点のある言い方 ▶去年の優勝者 last year's champion. ▶去年の夏北海道一周旅行をした I took a trip around Hokkaido last summer [×in last summer]. (⚠️通例「この前の夏」の意ではない)
ぎょばん 魚板 a fish-shaped wooden disk.

きょひ 拒否 图 (きっぱりした) (a) refusal; (断固とした) (a) rejection (⇔拒絶); (否定) (a) denial; 〖拒否権〗 (a) veto (圈 ~es). ▶きっぱりした拒否 a flat refusal [rejection, denial]. ▶拒否権を行使する exercise one's veto (over); veto (a bill).
— **拒否する** 動 ▶ refuse; (断固として) reject (⚠️refuse より強意的); (丁寧に) (話) turn down, (要求などを) 《やや書》decline, (要求などを) 《やや書》deny (⇨断わる❶); (議案などを) veto (a bill). ▶私の申し出を拒否する refuse [reject, turn down, decline] my offer. ▶彼はこの問題をそれ以上議論するのは拒否した He refused to discuss the matter further. ▶彼はビザの発給を拒否された He was refused a visa.
● **拒否反応** 〖医学〗 rejection.
きょひ 巨費 (an) enormous expenditure; (a) huge cost. ▶巨費を投じて at (a) huge cost.
ぎょふ 漁夫 a fisher; a fisherman (圈 -men).
● **漁夫の利** ▶彼は競争相手同士を戦わせてまんまと漁夫の利を得た He played the competitors off against each other to get much profit. (⚠️play A off against B で「AとBを戦わせて漁夫の利を得る」の意)
ぎょぶつ 御物 (所有物) Imperial property; (宝物) Imperial treasures.
ぎょふん 魚粉 fish meal.
きょへい 挙兵 — **挙兵する** 動 rise* (up) 《in revolt; against the invaders》; take* up arms 《against》; raise an army.
きょほう 虚報 a canard; a false report; false news.
ぎょほう 漁法 a fishing method. ▶延縄(はえなわ)漁法 long-lining.
きょほうへん 毀誉褒貶 praise and [or] blame [censure].
きょまん 巨万 ▶巨万の富を築く build (up) [amass] huge [immense, enormous, (信じがたい)《書》fabulous] wealth. (⚠️wealth に代わる fortune は 𝐂 に扱う)
きよみず 清水 ▶清水の舞台から飛び降りる (暴挙に出る) take a leap in the dark; (決定的な挙に出る) cross the Rubicon.
きよみずやき 清水焼き Kiyomizuyaki chinaware.
ぎょみん 漁民 fishermen, fishing people.
きょむ 虚無 图 (無) emptiness. — **虚無的な** 形 nihilistic.
● **虚無主義** nihilism /náiəlizm/.
きょめい 虚名 《やや書》a false reputation. ▶虚名を博する acquire a false reputation.
きよめる 清める purify. ▶塩で身を清める purify [《書》cleanse] /klénz/ oneself with salt. ▶彼の罪を洗い清める purify [《書》purge, 《書》cleanse] him of [from] sin.
きょもう 虚妄 a lie. (⇨嘘, 偽り)
ぎょもう 漁網 a fishing net.
きよもと 清元 kiyomoto; a school of joruri.
きょよう 許容 ▶許容できる permissible; (法規上) allowable. ▶許容範囲 a permissible range. ▶許容量を超える exceed permissible [allowable] amount.
きょらい 去来 — **去来する** 動 (雲などが) come* and go*; (考えなどが) fit through 《one's mind》; recur 《to one's mind》.
ぎょらい 魚雷 (fire, launch) a torpedo (圈 ~es).
● **魚雷艇** a torpedo boat; (小型高速哨(しょう)戒艇) a PT boat (patrol torpedo boat の略).
きよらか 清らか ▶ (澄みきった) clear; (清純な) pure. ▶清らかな泉 a clear fountain. ▶心身ともに清らかに

ある be *pure* in body and mind [mind and body].

:**きょり 距離 ❶**[隔たり] (a) distance; (間隔) an interval.
①[~(の)距離] ●長[短]距離 a long [a short] *distance*. ●東京大阪間の距離 the *distance* between Tokyo and Osaka. ●鳥類の移動距離 migrating *distance* of birds. ●10 メートルの距離をおいて柱を立てる put up posts *at intervals of* 10 meters [33 feet]. (*事情*米英ではメートル法よりヤード法が日常的) ●その村はここから 45 キロの距離です The village is 45 kilometers [28 miles] (*in distance* [《話》*away*]) from here./The village is *at a distance* of 45 kilometers from here. It's *a distance* of 45 km to the village. ▶駅まで歩いて[車で]10 分の距離だ It is ten minutes' [a ten-minute] walk [drive] to the station.
②[距離が] ●(競技などで)相手と距離が開く(リードする) get a good [a long] lead over one's opponent(s). (遅れる) lag behind one's opponent(s). ●ここからその町まではかなりの距離がある It is *a long way* [*quite a way*, ×*distant*, ×*far*] from here to the town. (⇨遠い)/It is *a great distance* from here to the town. ▶先頭ランナーとの距離が縮まっている The *distance from* the front-runner *is getting shorter*.
《会話》「ここから東京までの距離はどのくらいですか」「約 200 キロです」"*How far* is it [*What is the distance*] from here to Tokyo?" "It's about 200 kilometers [120 miles]."
③[距離を] ●彼と少し距離を保つ keep a little *distance* from him; keep him at a *distance*. (!比喩的に「敬遠する」の意もある) ●前を行く車との間に安全な距離を保つ keep a safe *distance* from a car ahead. ●スーパーは私の家から歩いて[車で;簡単に]行ける距離にある The supermarket is within walking [driving; easy] *distance of* [×*from*] my house.
❷[違い] a difference; (断絶) a gap. (⇨隔たり) ▶訴えたいことと文章のあいだに距離があったら それは失敗なんです When [×If] there's a *gap* [×*distance*] between what you really wanted to say and what you've written down, you've failed [×it's a failure].
●距離感 a sense of distance. ●距離競技 a distance race. (スキーの) a crosscountry race.

きょり 巨利 ●巨利を博する make [earn] an *enormous* [a *large*, a *huge*] *profit*.

きょりゅう 居留 — 居留する 動 live 《*at, in*》; reside 《*abroad*》;《書》dwell.
●居留地 a settlement. ●居留外国人 an alien; a foreign resident 《*in* Japan》.

ぎょりん 魚鱗 the scales of a fish.
●魚鱗癬(*)《医学》fishskin disease.

ぎょるい 魚類 fish(es).
●魚類学 ichthyology.

きょれい 虚礼 a [an unnecessary] formality. ●虚礼は廃止する do away with *formalities*.

ぎょろう 漁労 fishery; fishing.
●漁労長 a chief fisherman.

きょろきょろ ●きょろきょろ見る (落ち着きなく) look around *restlessly* [*nervously*]; (物めずらしく) look *curiously*, goggle 《*at*》. ●いかにもお上りさんらしい人がきょろきょろ街を見ていた People who looked as if they had just come from the country *were goggling around* the city streets.

ぎょろぎょろ ●ぎょろぎょろ目を goggle 《*at*》. ▶彼は目をぎょろぎょろさせて私を見た He *goggled at* me. (!近語に glare (こわい顔つきをして), stare (凝視する)があるが,視線をじっと定めるので「ぎょろぎょろ」とはやや違う)
▶彼はぎょろぎょろした目つきをしている He is *goggle-eyed*.

ぎょろっ[ぎょろり]と ●ぎょろっとにらむ (怒って) glare 《*at*》; (じっと) stare 《*at*》(!威圧的に見ることに限らず,恐れたり,考え事でじっと見ることも含む). ▶父親は黙って息子をぎょろりと見た The father *glared* silently at his son.

きよわい 気弱い(気の弱い) timid; (弱腰の)《話》weak-kneed.

キョンジュ 慶州 〖韓国の都市〗Kyŏngju, Kyongju.

キラー a killer. ●マダムキラー an extremely sexy man;《俗古》a lady-*killer*.
●キラーショット a killer shot. (*参考*テニスなどで相手が打ち返せない強烈な一打) ●キラーパス a killer pass. (*例* スルーパス)

:**きらい 嫌い ❶**[好きでないこと] a dislike 《*for, of*》; (嫌悪)《やや書》(a) distaste 《*for*》; (憎悪)《やや書》(a) hatred 《*for*》;《やや書》(強い嫌悪) (an) aversion 《*to*》; (毛嫌い)《やや書》an antipathy 《*to, toward, against*》(⇨嫌う, 大嫌い) ▶猫が嫌いだ I *don't like* [*dislike*, *hate*, *detest*] cats. (!この順に嫌悪感が強くなる)/I have *a dislike* [*a hatred*, *a distaste*] *for* cats./(婉曲的) I *don't care for* cats *very much*. ▶読書が嫌いになったら 私は読書を *dislike* reading. (!*to* read は《まれ》) ▶朝早く起きるのが嫌いなんだ I *hate getting* [*to get*] up early in the morning. (!不定詞は「今…したくない」の意でも用いられる)
❷[傾向] (a) tendency; (気味) a touch, a smack. ▶彼は時々ばかなことを言うきらいがある He *tends* [*has a tendency*] to talk nonsense once in a while.

きらい 機雷 a mine; an underwater mine. ●浮遊機雷に触れる hit a surface [a floating] *mine*.

:**きらう 嫌う**[好きでない] don't like (!*dislike* より口語的), dislike; [ひどく嫌う] hate, detest,《やや書》loathe (!この順に意味が強くなる); [憎悪する]《やや書》abhor (-rr-). ●暴力を嫌う *abhor* violence. ▶彼女は人に嫌われている People *dislike* [*don't like*] her. (!*hate* はこの場合強く響きすぎる) ▶彼は皿洗いをひどく嫌っている He *hates* [*detests*, *loathes*] [*doing* [*washing*] the dishes. (⇨嫌い❶)

キラウエア ●キラウエア火山 Kilauea 《/kiːlauéiə/》; Mount Kilauea volcano.

きらきら ●きらきら光る (宝石などが) glitter, sparkle (!前の方が明るい); (まぼゆく) dazzle; (闇の中で) twinkle, shine. ●きらきらと dazzlingly, brilliantly. ●目をきらきら輝かせて with *sparkling* [*shining*] eyes. ▶彼女の指にはダイヤの指輪がきらきら光っていた A diamond ring *glittered* [*sparkled*] on her finger. ▶海が太陽の光できらきらまぶしかった The sea *was dazzling* in the sunshine.
▶たくさんの星が夜空にきらきら光っている A lot of stars *are twinkling* [*brightly*] in the night sky.

ぎらぎら ●ぎらぎら光る glare. ●脂ぎらぎら浮いているオックステールのスープ very greasy ox-tail soup. ▶彼はぎらぎらする目で相手を見た He looked at his opponent with *glaring eyes*. ▶太陽がぎらぎら照りつけた The sun *glared* down.

きらく 気楽 — 気楽な 形 easy, (あくせくしない) easygoing; (心配のない) carefree. ●気楽なやつ an *easygoing* fellow. ●気楽な生活をする lead a *carefree* [an *easy*] life; (安楽に暮らす) live *comfortably* [*in comfort*]. ▶彼を気楽な気分にさせる (緊張をほぐして) put him [make him feel] *at ease*; (気がねさせない) make him feel *at home*.

— **気楽に** ▶そんなに心配するな。気楽にやれよ《慣用表現》Don't get so nervous about it. *Take it easy.*

きらす 切らす (品物を) run* out 《*of*》; (在庫がない) be out of stock; (息を) get* out of breath. ▶その品は今切らしています We *don't have* the articles *in stock* at present./The articles *are out of stock* at present. ▶彼は息を切らして飛び込んできた He *was breathless* [*out of breath, short of breath*] when he rushed in./He rushed in *breathlessly* [*out of breath*].
会話「牛乳はおいてますか」「あいにく切らしています」"Do you have milk?" "I'm sorry, but we've *run out* (of it) [we're *out of it* at the moment]."

ぎらつく glare. ●ぎらついた glaring 《lights [eyes]》. ▶彼は目をぎらつかせて無言のまま私を見た He *glared at* me silently.

きらびやか 名 (きらびやかさ) gorgeousness.
— **きらびやかな** 形 ●きらびやかな装い a *gorgeous* dress.

きらぼし きら星 a shining [a twinkling, a glittering] star. ▶式には映画スターがきら星のごとく居並んでいた There was *a galaxy* [*a dazzling array*] of movie stars at the ceremony.

*きらめく (きらきら光る) glitter; (闇(ಜ)の中で) twinkle; (無数の小さな光が) sparkle. ●光る) ▶日の光が波にきらめいた The sun [Sunlight] *glittered* on the waves.

きらら 雲母(ウ{ん})

きらり ●きらりと光る (水滴などが) glisten; (金属などが) sparkle. ●涙できらりと光る目 eyes *glistening* with tears. ▶砂金が強い太陽の光線を浴びてきらりと光った Gold dust *sparkled* under the fiery sun.

ぎらり ●ぎらりと光る (まぶしく) glare; (瞬間的に) flash. ▶男の目が闇の中で一瞬ぎらりと光った The man's eyes *flashed* momentarily in the dark.

*きり 霧 ❶【気象上の】(a) fog; (a) mist; (a) haze. (⓵ (1) fog は濃い霧のことで、mist (=thin fog), haze (=thin mist) の順に薄くなる (⇨靄(ಜ), 霞(ガ{す})) いずれも視界をさえぎるやっかいな存在で、日本語の持つロマンチックなイメージはない)

①【～霧】●濃い [深い] 霧 (a) thick [(a) dense, (a) heavy] *fog* [*mist*]. ×《a *deep fog* [*mist*] とはいわない》●白い霧 a white mist. ●朝(⏝) [夕] 霧 (an) morning [(an) evening] *mist*. ●冷たい霧 a chilly [a cold, (とても冷たい) an icy] *mist*.

②【霧が】●あたり一面霧が立ちこめている It's *foggy* [*misty*] all around./*Fog* [*Mist*] is everywhere. (⏝ この例に対し A mist is rising from the marsh. (沼から霧が立っている) のように視界の一部に霧が出ている状態や、1 回 1 回の発生を意識する場合は可算名詞になる) ▶濃い霧が町にかかっている A *fog* lies thick over the town./There's a thick *fog* over the town. ▶霧が濃くて何も見えなかった The *fog* [*mist*] was so thick that I could not see anything. ▶霧が晴れた The *fog* [*mist*] has cleared (up [away])./The *fog* [*mist*] has lifted [let up]. ▶霧がしだいに薄らいだ The *mist* has gradually thinned (↔thickened). ▶この地方はひどい霧がよく出る We often have bad *fogs* in this district./Bad *fogs* often come down [fall] in this area. ▶今日は霧がでている It's *foggy* [*misty, hazy*] today. (⏝「出てきた」なら It's getting *foggy* [*misty, hazy*].)

③【霧の】●霧の深い夜 a *foggy* night. ●霧のような雨 a fine [a misty] rain. ●霧のかかった朝 a *misty* morning. ▶彼女は霧の中で迷子になった She got lost in the fog. ▶濃い霧のために飛行機は着陸できなかった A dense *fog* stopped the plane from landing.

④【霧に】●霧に煙る谷 a *misty* valley. ●霧にぬれる get wet in the mist. ▶霧になりだした It began to *mist*. ▶町は霧に包まれている The town is covered [is enveloped, is wrapped] in *fog* [*mist*].

❷【噴霧】(a) spray. ●服に霧を吹く *spray* water *on* the clothes. ●霧吹き *霧吹き*

きり 切り (終わり) an end; (限界) a bound, a limit (⏝ 通例複数形で). ●きりをつける (=やめる) stop, 《やや書》put an end 《*to*》. ●ピンからキリまで (⇨ピン) ●これきり (⇨これきり) ▶きりがないのでここでやめよう This is a good place to *leave off*. So let's stop here. (⏝ leave off は「切り上げる」の意)

●きりがない (際限がない) boundless; limitless; without bounds [limits]. ▶お金に対する欲望にはきりがない There are no *bounds* [*limits*] to our love [lust] of money. ▶ある月に成績がよければ、次の月にはそれ以上を期待される。きりがないのです If you do well one month, they expect you to do better the next. It *never stops* [*ends*]. ▶家事にはきりがない Housework *is never done* [*ending*]. ▶心配すればきりがない The list of worries is a long one.

きり 桐【植物】a paulownia [pɔːlóuniə].
●桐たんす a chest of drawers made of paulownia wood.

きり 錐【もみきり】a gimlet;【靴の皮などをうがつ】an awl;【木工きり】an auger;【ドリル】a drill;【氷割り用の】an ice pick. ▶きりで穴を開ける bore a hole with a *gimlet*; drill a hole (*in* a metal plate).

-きり きり ❶【だけ】only. (⇨-だけ) ▶そこへ行ったのは 1 回きりです I have been there *only* once. ▶今度だけはやってあげるがこれっきりだよ I'll do it for you this time but *never again* [(これを最後にきっぱりと) *once* (*and*) *for all*]! ▶それっきりか Is that all?

❷【以来】since. (⇨以来) ▶彼は散歩に出かけたきりまだ帰ってこない He has not come home yet *since* he went out for a walk.

❸【その他の表現】寝たきりの老人 a *bedridden* old man [woman].

*ぎり 義理 ❶【交際上のおきて】(義務) (a) duty; (恩義) (an) obligation (⏝「当然相手に返すべき恩義」と考え、a binding obligation ともいう). **事情** 米英人にはこの概念はないか、または薄いといわれる) ▶彼に義理を立てる do one's *duty to* him. ▶義理がたい have a strong sense of *duty*; (きちょうめんに恩義を果たす) scrupulously fulfill one's *obligations*. ▶私はあなたに義理がある I feel an [I am under (an)] *obligation to* you. (⏝ 後の an は《米》ではしばしば省略される)/(それはあなたのおかげです) I *owe it to* you. ▶それでは彼に義理が立たない (= 恩知らずになる) That would be *ungrateful to* him. ▶どうも義理を欠いたようだ I'm afraid I failed in my *duty* [*obligation*]. ▶私は義理で彼の演奏会に行った I went to his recital out of a sense of *obligation*.

❷【姻戚(⏝)関係】in-law. (⏝ 通例複合語で) ●義理の弟(たち) one's brother(s)-*in-law* (《英話》brother-in-law(s)). ●義理の両親 one's parents-*in-law*; (話) one's in-laws.

❸【その他の表現】▶今さら私に借金を頼むのは義理ではない (=立場にない) You are *not in a position* to ask me to loan you money.

会話「君の欠点は怠け者だっていうことだな」「そんなこと言えた義理かよ」"The trouble with you is you're lazy." "You're a fine one to talk. (⏝ 皮肉として) ●義理チョコ 'obligation chocolates'; (説明的に) chocolates given to someone out of a sense of obligation.

きりあげる 切り上げる ❶ [終わりにする] (会合などを) close, 《米話》wrap ... up; (仕事などを) stop (-pp-), leave*... off, 《話》knock ... off; (中途で終わらせる) cut*... short. ▶早々に仕事を切り上げる *leave* (*off*) *work early*. ▶滞在を切り上げる *cut* one's stay *short*. ▶今日はこの辺で仕事を切り上げよう Let's *stop* [*knock off*] *work today*. (/今日はここまでにしよう)《話》Let's call it a day. (!慣用的表現) ▶家から悪い知らせがあったので旅行を途中で切り上げた The bad news from home *cut* my trip *short*.
❷ [端数・平価などを] ●小数点以下などを切り上げる (=1 位の数まで上げる) *raise* [*round up*] the decimals to a unit (最も近い整数) the nearest whole number. ●平価 [ドル] を切り上げる *revalue* the currency [the dollar].

きりうり 切り売り — 切り売り(を)する 動 (ちびちび) sell* bit by bit; (部分的に) sell in parts. ●布地を1メートルいくらで切り売りする *sell* cloth by the [*a]meter. ●土地を切り売りする *cut up* land *for sale*; *divide* the land *into plots* and *sell* them. ▶その俳優は多くのコマーシャルに出演して演技力の切り売りをした The actor *wasted away* his acting opportunities by appearing on many TV commercials.

きりえ 切り絵 (⇨切り紙)

きりおとす 切り落とす cut* ... off; (枝などを) prune ... away [off]. ●古枝を切り落とす *cut* [*prune*] *off* old branches.

きりかえし 切り返し 〖映画〗a cutback; 〖鉄道〗a switchback; 〖相撲〗 *kirikaeshi*, twisting backward knee trip.

きりかえす 切り返す ❶ [反撃する] strike* back (*at*); make* a counterattack (*against*), counterattack. ▶部下にちょっと文句を言ったらぱっと切り返して (=言い返して) きた When I complained to my man about his work, he *made an* immediate *retort*.
❷ [ハンドルを] turn (the wheel) quickly to the other way; (急に) swerve (one's car). ▶私はその犬をひくまいと夢中でハンドルを切り返した I instinctively *swerved* (my car) to avoid hitting [xto hit] the dog.

きりかえる 切り替える 〖変える〗change; (方法・制度などを) change 〖(やや話)switch〗over (*to*); (受信局を) switch over; 〖更新する〗renew. ●頭を切り替える(=発想を転換する) *change* one's way of thinking. (⇨転換) ●(灯油から)電気に切り替える *change* [*switch*] *over* (*from* kerosene) *to* electricity. ●チャンネルを切り替える *switch over* (to another channel); *turn* [*change*] channels. ●運転免許証を切り替える *renew* one's driver's license. ●ギアを切り替える *shift* [*change*] gears.

きりかかる 切りかかる 〖切りつける〗slash 〖cut*〗《*at*》; 〖切り始める〗begin* to cut 《cloth》.

きりかぶ 切り株 〖樹木の〗a (tree) stump; 〖稲などの〗stubble. ●麦の切り株が残っている畑 a field of wheat *stubble*.

きりがみ 切り紙 *kirigami*, a paper cutout.

きりかわる 切り替わる 〖変わる〗change; (転じる) switch 《*to*》; (取って替わられる) be replaced 《*by*》; 〖更新される〗be renewed 《*by*》. ▶ポイントが切り替わらなかったので事故が起こった The switches did not *work* and so the accident happened.

きりきざむ 切り刻む cut* ... into small pieces; cut [chop (-pp-)] ... up; (肉・タマネギみじん切りにする) mince. (⇨刻む, 刻む)

きりきず 切り傷 (短い) a cut; (長い) a slash; (長く深い) a gash. ●足に切り傷ができる *get a cut on* [*in*] one's foot. (! in の方が深い傷) ●木の幹に切り傷をつけて樹液を集める *cut a gash* on [in] the tree trunk and collect the sap.

きりきり ❶ 〖きしむ音〗▶ドリルが板に穴を開けていくときときりきり音を立てた The drill *squealed* as it drove into the wood.
❷ 〖さしこむ痛むさま〗●私は胃がきりきり刺し痛む I have a *griping* stomachache [pain in my stomach]. (!gripe /gráip/ は「(お腹などが)しぼるように痛む」の意. きりきりする頭痛のときは a *splitting* headache にする. splitting は「割れるような」の意)
❸ 〖てきぱき動くさま〗●こまめにきりきりと立ち働く work *briskly* [*furiously*] without a break. (⇨きりきり舞い)

ぎりぎり ●ぎりぎり(=かろうじて)間に合う (⇨かろうじて) ●もうぎりぎりだ. 出かけなければいけない It's *high time* we started. ▶ぎりぎりの生活をしている I *barely manage* to live within my income./My income *only just* keeps me alive. ▶これが譲れるぎりぎりの線です This is all I could do./I can't do better than this. ▶ぎりぎりになって OK をもらった We got an OK *at the last minute* [*just in time*].

きりきりじん 『吉里吉里人』 *The People of Kirikiri*. (〖参考〗井上ひさしの小説)

きりぎりす 〖昆虫〗a grásshòpper.

きりきりまい きりきり舞い (とても忙しい) be very [extremely] busy; have* a hectic time. ▶今週はきりきり舞いだったね We've had a *hectic* week. ▶彼は借金できりきり舞いしている《話》He *is up to his neck* [*over his head*] *in debt*.

きりくずす 切り崩す (平らにする) level; (分裂させる) split*. ●丘を切り崩して道を作る *cut* a road *through* a hill.

きりくち 切り口 (切った端) a cut end; (立体の切断面) a section; (開ける所) 〖表示〗Open here. ●その問題を新しい切り口で(=角度から)論ずる approach the problem from a new *angle*.

きりこ 切り子 a facet.
●切り子ガラス cut glass.

きりこうじょう 切り口上 ●切り口上で言う speak *in a stiff* [*a starchy*] *manner*; use *formal language*.

きりこみ 切り込み (切れ目) a cut; a nick. ●布の端に切り込みを入れる make a *cut* [a *nick*] in the edge of the cloth.

きりこむ 切り込む (深く切る) cut* deeply, gash; (議論などで) attack; question 《him》sharply.

きりさいなむ 切り苛む hack ... to pieces cruelly.

きりさく 切り裂く slit*; (さっと切る) slash; (切り取る) rip (-pp-) 《... up》.

きりさげ 切り下げ (為替の) devaluation; depreciation. ●通貨の切り下げ *devaluation* of the currency.

きりさげる 切り下げる (給料・費用・物価などを) cut* 《... down》; 〖平価を〗devalue. ●ドルを20パーセント切り下げる *devalue* the dollar by 20 percent.

きりさめ 霧雨 (a) drizzle (!霧状形なし), (a) drizzling rain. ▶霧雨が降っている It's *drizzling*.

キリシタン [<ポルトガル語] (キリスト教) (early) Christianity; (キリスト教徒, 特に1603–1868の徳川幕府によるキリスト教禁止下の) a hidden [separated] Christian. (!米英では「かくれキリシタン」が普通. 後の方は「はなれキリシタン」でフランス語の les séparés の英訳 (⇨隠れキリシタン))

ギリシャ 〖国名〗Greece; (公式名) the Hellenic Republic. (首都 Athens) ●ギリシャ人 a Greek. ●ギリシャ語 Greek. ●ギリシャ(人[語])の Greek.
●ギリシャ神話 a Greek myth; (集合的) Greek mythology. ●ギリシャ正教 the Greek (Ortho-

dox) Church. ●ギリシャ文字 the Greek alphabet.
きりすて 切り捨て 〖端数の〗 rounding ... down 《to》.
●切り捨て御免 the right to cut 《him》 down unpunished 〖with impunity〗.
きりすてる 切り捨てる 〖『切って捨てる』〗 cut* ... away 《from》; 〖除外する〗 omit (-tt-), leave* ....
●1,000 未満の端数を切り捨てる *omit* 〖*無視する*〗 *ignore*〗 fractions under one thousand. ●小数第3位以下を切り捨てる *omit* the figures below the third decimal place. ●少数意見を切り捨てる *ignore* 〖*disregard*, 〈話〉 *cut*〗 the minority opinion.
キリスト (Jesus) Christ /dʒíːzəs) kráist/, the Lord, the Messiah /məsáiə/, the Saviour /séivjər/.
●キリスト教 Christianity. ●キリスト教会 a Christian church. ●キリスト教国 a Christian country; 〖総称〗〖古〗 Christendom /krísndəm/.
●キリスト教女子青年会 the Young Women's Christian Association 〖略 YWCA, 〖今はまれ〗 Y.W.C.A.〗 では Y と略すこともある〕.
●キリスト教青年会 〖プロテスタント系の〗 the Young Men's Christian Association 〖略 YMCA, 〖今はまれ〕 Y.M.C.A.〕〖〖米話〗〕 では Y と略すこともある〕.
●キリスト教徒 a Christian. ●キリスト降誕祭 Christmas 〖略 Xmas〗.
きりそろえる 切り揃える cut* even; 〖刈り込んできれいにする〗 trim (-mm-).
きりたおす 切り倒す ●木を切り倒す *cut* 〖おのなどで〗 *chop* (-pp-)〗 *down* a tree; *fell* a tree.
きりだし 切り出し 〖小刀〗 a pointed knife; 〖木材の〗 logging; 〖言い出し〗 starting to talk 《about》.
きりだす 切り出す 〖木などを〗 cut* ... down; 〖石を〗 quarry /kwɔ́(ː)ri/; 〖話を〗 start to talk 《about》, 〖やや書〗 broach.. ●結婚話を切り出す *start to talk about* the subject of marriage. ●積もる話が山ほどあって何から切り出したものか迷ってしまうわ I've got a million things to talk to you, but I don't know where to *start*.
***きりつ** 規律 〖秩序〗 order; 〖集団の〗 discipline; 〖規定〗〖個々に関する〗 a rule; 〖権威者による公の〗 a regulation. 〖秩序, 規則〗 ●規律正しい生活を送る lead an *ordered* life. ●規律正しく行動する act in an *orderly* manner. ●学生間の規律を維持する keep *order* 〖*discipline*〗 among the students. ●規律を乱す(=規則を破る) (⇨規則) ●あの学校は規律がやかましい〖乱れている〗 *Discipline* is strict 〖loose〗 in that school. (〖*Discipline in that school*... でも文法的には誤りではないが頭っかちな感じがするのでしては避けられる)/That school has firm 〖lax〗 *discipline*.
きりつ 起立 ── 起立する 動 stand* up; 〖書〗 rise* (to one's feet). ●ご起立願います *Stand up* 〖*All stand*〗, please./Please *rise*. (❗ all は「全員, みなさん」の意)
きりっと 〖きりりと〗 neat and smart, 〖やや書〗 spruce; 〖輪郭のはっきりした〗 clear-cut. ●きりっとした顔立ち *clear-cut* features. ●背広にネクタイといういでたちをしている look *spruce* in coat and tie.
きりづま 切り妻 〖建築〗 a gable.
●切り妻窓 a gable(d) window. ●切り妻屋根 a gable(d) roof; a span roof.
きりつめる 切り詰める 〖出費などを〗 cut* ... down 〖back〗; 〖長さ・時間を短くする〗 shorten, cut ... short (⇨短縮する). ●経費を切り詰める *cut down* 〖*on*〗〖*reduce*〗 expenses. ●生活を切り詰める *cut down* 〖*on*〗 one's living expenses; 〖倹約して暮らす〗〖やや書〗 live *frugally*, lead 〖live〗 a *frugal* life.
きりど 切り戸 a wicket gate; a small side gate
きりどおし 切り通し 〖*railroad*〗 cutting.
きりとりせん 切り取り線 perforations; a perforated line; 〖指示〗 Cut Here.
きりとる 切り取る cut*... (off) 《from》. ●パイナップルの芯(ː)を切り取る *cut off* the pineapple core. ●新聞からその記事を切り取る *cut* the article *from* 〖*out of*〗 the paper; *cut out* the article *from* 〖*out of*〗 the paper. (❗ *cut off* his clip も可) ●ドーム球場の屋根が冷たく澄んだ空を切り取っている(=空の世界をさえぎっている) The roof of the domed baseball stadium has *blocked out* 〖*cut out*〗〖was sharply defined against〗 the crisp, clear sky.
きりぬき 切り抜き 〖新聞・雑誌などの〗 〖主に米〗 a clipping, 〖英〗 a cutting.
きりぬく 切り抜く cut* 〖clip (-pp-)〗 ... 《out of, from》. (⇨切り取る) ●新聞の写真を切り抜く *cut* 〖*clip*〗 a picture *out of* the newspaper.
きりぬける 切り抜ける 〖『危機などをくぐり抜ける』〗 get* through ...; 〖『困難などを乗り越える』〗 get over ...; 〖『うまく対処する』〗 manage. ●はったりでその場を切り抜けるbluff it out. ▶彼はついにその困難を切り抜けた He finally *got over* 〖*overcame*〗 the difficulties. ●家族全員が戦争を切り抜けてきた All my family *has* 〖〖英〗*have*〗 *come through* the war./〖生き返る〕 All my family *has* 〖〖英〗*have*〗 *survived* the war. ●心配するな何とか切り抜けるさ Don't worry, I'll *muddle through* 〖*along*〗 somehow. ▶その投手は満塁のピンチを切り抜けた The pitcher got 〖pitched〗 out of the bases-loaded jam.
〖会話〗 「いったいどうやって切り抜けたのさ」「運よく予備のを二つ持っていたんだよ」 "How on earth did you *manage* 〖*get through*〗 that?" "Fortunately, I had a couple of spare ones."
キリバス 〖国名〗 Kiribati /kiribáːti/; 〖公式名〗 the Republic of Kiribati. (首都 Tarawa) ●キリバス人 a Kiribati. ●キリバス(人)の Kiribati.
きりばな 切り花 a cut flower.
きりはなす 切り離す ❶ 〖切って離す〗 cut* ... off.
●ボートを係留してあるロープから切り離す *cut* the boat *off* the moorings.
❷ 〖分離する〗 separate; (取りはずす) detach. ●添付のクーポンを切り離す *separate* the attached coupon. ●経済を政治と切り離す *separate* economics *from* politics. ●この問題をそれと切り離して(=別にして)論ずる discuss this problem *apart* 〖〖主に米〗 *aside*〗 *from* that one.
きりはらう 切り払う ❶ 〖枝などを〗 cut* ... away 《from》; (余分な枝を) prune.
❷ 〖攻め込んで追い払う〗 ●彼は敵を切り払った He *cut* 〖*fought*〗 *his way* into the enemy troops and *drove* them *away*.
きりばり 切り張り ── 切り張りする 動 ●古いジーンズに切り張りする(=継ぎを当てる) *patch* an old pair of jeans *up*. ●新聞記事をノートに切り張りする *clip* an article *out of* 〖*from*〗 the newspaper and *paste* it in a notebook.
きりひとは 桐一葉 ●桐一葉落ちて天下の秋を知る 〖ことわざ〗 A straw shows which way the wind blows. (「むら一本ほどのわずかな兆しで世論の動向が分かる」の意)
きりひらく 切り開く ●封筒を切り開く *cut open* an envelope. ●山を切り開いて道を作る cut 〖open〗 a road *through* a hill. ●荒れ地を切り開く(=開拓する

きりふき 霧吹き a sprayer; (香水の) an atomizer.

きりふせる 切り伏せる (切り倒す) cut* ... down; (征服する) conquer.

きりふだ 切り札 (トランプの) a trump (card); (⇨奥の手) ▶切り札を出す play a trump (card); (奥の手を出す) play one's trump card. ▶最後の切り札(=手段)として as a [in the] last resort; 《米話》as an ace in the hole.

きりぼし(だいこん) 切り干し(大根) dried strips of white radish.

きりまわす 切り回す 〖管理する〗manage; 〖処理する〗handle. ▶家庭を切り回す manage [handle] one's household. ▶店を切り回す manage [run] a store.

キリマンジャロ 〖タンザニア北東部の山〗Mount Kilimanjaro /kìlɪməndʒɑ́ːrou/.

きりみ 切り身 (薄い) a slice; (骨のない) a fillet; (厚い) a steak; 〖肉の〗a cut; (豚(子羊)の) a pork [a lamb] chop. ▶タラの切り身3枚 three slices [steaks] of cod. ▶赤身の豚肉の切り身 a slice [a steak, a cut] of lean pork. ▶サケを三枚におろして切り身にする fillet a salmon and cut it in slices.

きりめ 切り目 (切れた跡) (V字型の) a notch; (表面につけた浅い) a small cut; (筋状の) a score; 〖区切り〗an end, a stop (⇨区切り). ▶切り目をつける cut [make] a notch; notch; make a nick [a small cut]; score.

きりもみ 錐揉み (きりもみ降下) a spin, a tailspin. ▶きりもみ降下する go into a spin; fall in a spin.

きりもり 切り盛り 〖事業・家などの管理〗management. ▶彼女は家事の切り盛りがうまい She keeps house well. (❗keep house で「家事を切り盛りする」の慣用表現)/She is a good housekeeper [《米》homemaker].

きりゃく 機略 resource. ▶機略に富む人 a person of great resource; a very resourceful person.

きりゅう 気流 an air current, an airflow. ▶上昇気流 an ascending current. ▶乱気流 turbulent air. ▶気流に乗って飛んでいるグライダー a glider sailing on air currents.

きりゅう 寄留 图 temporary residence.
— 寄留する 動 live [stay; 《書》reside] temporarily 《at+場所; with+人》.
▶寄留地 a place of one's temporary residence.

きりゅうさん 希硫酸 〖化学〗dilute(d) sulfuric acid.

きりょう 器量 ❶(容貌) She is good-looking. (⇨美しい, 奇麗(ﾟ)). ▶あの子は器量は十人並みだ《婉曲的》She is a plain(-looking) [《米》a homely] girl. ▶彼には社長の器量がある He is equal to the task of a president./He is good enough to be a president.
▶器量を下げる (面目を失う) lose face. (⇨面目)

ぎりょう 技量 〖技能〗(a) skill; 〖能力〗(an) ability. ▶スキーの技量を発揮する〖磨く〗show [improve] one's skill [ability] in skiing. ▶技量のある外科医 a skillful surgeon. ▶彼女の教師としての技量はよく知られている Her skill as a teacher is widely known.

きりょく 気力 spirit; 〖元気〗vigor; 〖精力〗energy; 〖活気〗vitality; 〖やる気〗drive. ▶彼は気力旺盛(ﾟ)だ be full of spirit [vigor, energy, vitality]; be vigorous [energetic]. ▶気力が衰える lose one's vigor [energy]. ▶気力を回復する recover one's vigor [vitality]. ▶彼の成功は才能より気力によるものだ He has succeeded more [rather] by spirit than by talent./His success has been not so much by talent than by spirit.

きりわける 切り分ける (特に肉を) carve. ▶客にケーキを切り分ける cut and serve the cake to the guests.

きりん 麒麟 ▶きりんも老いては駑馬(ﾟ)に劣る Even a genius can be no match for ordinary people when he grows old.

きりん 麒麟 〖動物〗a giraffe /dʒəræf/ (圈 ~s, ~).
▶麒麟児 a child prodigy [genius].

●**きる** 切る ❶〖切断する〗cut* (❗刃物で切る意の最も一般的な語); (たたき切る) chop (-pp-) (❗cut と異なり反復動作を含意); (薄く切る) slice; (さっと切る) slash; (肉を切り分ける) carve; (のこぎりで) saw*; (はさみで) snip (-pp-), clip (-pp-). ▶薄く切ったベーコン slices of bacon. ▶のこぎりで木を切る cut the wood with a saw; saw the wood. ▶枝を切る cut [chop] (off) a branch. ▶切符を切る punch [《英》clip] a ticket. ▶つめを切る cut [trim, pare] one's nails. (❗trim は「こぎれいにそろえる」, pare は「ナイフでそろえるように切る」) ▶手紙の封を切る open a letter; cut [(ちぎって) rip] a letter open. ▶パンを1枚切る cut (off) [slice (off)] a piece of bread. ▶パンを薄く[6枚に]切る cut bread thin [in six, into six slices]; slice bread thin [in six]. ▶パイを四つに切る cut a pie in [into] four pieces [quarters].
▶ガラスの破片で指を切った I cut my finger on [with] the broken glass. (❗with では故意に切る含意を伴うことがある) ▶おっ, 切っちゃった Oh, I cut myself. ▶彼はひげをそっていて(顔を)切ってしまった He cut himself while (he was) shaving. (❗さらに while の he も省略可) ▶肉を少し切ってください Cut [Slice, Carve] me some meat./Cut [Slice, Carve] some meat for me.
[会話]「この箱どうしましょうか」「小さく切ってたきぎにしてちょうだい」"What do you want me to do with the box?" "Chop it up for firewood."
❷〖切って止める〗cut* ... off; (電話を) hang* up; (電気・テレビなどを) turn ... off, switch ... off; (人との関係を) break* ... off《with》. ▶エンジンを切る cut (off) the engine. ▶期限を切る fix a deadline.
▶水道料金を払わなかったので給水を切られてしまった My water has been cut off because I didn't pay my bill. ▶彼は怒って電話を切ってしまった He hung up on me in anger. (❗on を伴うと話の途中で一方的に切るの意を表す) ▶「じゃ, これで切るよ」なら I'll hang up. または I'll get off the line. のようにいえる.「このまま(電話を切らないで)待っててくれる?」は Can you hold (on)?) ▶テレビを切ってください Turn [Switch] off the television, please. ▶彼女とは手を切った I've broken (off [up]) with her./I'm through with her. ▶(会うことをやめた) I stopped seeing her. ▶彼は父親から親子の縁を切られた(=勘当された) His father has cut him off 《《やや書》disowned him》.
❸〖切断するような動作を表す〗▶お皿の水を切る drain the dishes dry. ▶トランプを切る(=まぜる) shuffle the cards; (二つに分ける) cut the cards. ▶ハンドルを(右に)切る turn the steering wheel (right). ▶肩で風を切る walk in a triumphant air [with a swagger]. ▶料理する前にエビの水をよく切りなさい Let the shrimp drain thoroughly before cooking. ▶高速艇は波を切って進んだ The fast ship sliced through the water.
❹〖新しく始める〗▶口を切る(=話し始める) start [begin] to talk; (特に初対面の者同士で) 《話》break the ice. ▶そこして議論の火ぶたを切る start to argue about it; start the argument about it.
❺〖金額・数量に達しない〗▶100メートルで10秒を切る run 100 meters in under [less than] 10

きる ●(ゴルフで) 110 を切る *break* one-ten. ❻[最後まで(…する)] ●売り切る *sell* (it) *out*. ●所持金を遣い切る *use up* [《書》*consume*] all the money 《he》 has. ●本を読み切る *read through* a book; *read a book from cover to cover*. ●長い距離を走り切る *complete* one's long run.

きる 着る ❶[衣類を] (a) [動作] *put*... *on* (↔*take* ... *off*); (身支度する) *get* *dressed* [《やや書》*dress* (oneself)] 《*in*》(!(子供などが)自分で服を着る」の意以外では oneself は省略する方が普通); (苦労して) *get into*...; (試着する) *try* ... *on*; [状態] *wear**, (一時的に) *have**... *on*, *be* (*dressed*) *in*...; (習慣的に) *dress in* .... ●黒い帽子に黒いコートを着ている紳士 a gentleman *wearing* [*dressed in*] a black coat and a black hat. (!(1) 名詞の後では通例 *dressed* は省略される。(2) 二つの物 (A, B) の着用を表現する場合、両者の「一対」の感じを伴うときは in an A and B と後の冠詞が省略される。また「〜姿の」の意味合いでは in A and B のように無冠詞となる) ●彼は服を着た He *put* ón his ⇘clothes [*pút his* ⇘*clothes on*]. (!his clothes を代名詞で表す場合 He *pút* them ⇘*on*. の語順と音調となる) /(パーティー・外出などのために) He *got dressed* [*dressed*, ×*dressed his clothes*]. ●彼はチョッキを着ていた He *wore* [*was wearing*] a vest. (!進行形は一時的状態を強調する)/He *had* a vest *on* [*had on* a vest]. ●彼女はいつも赤い服を着ている She always *wears* [always *dresses in*, is always *dressed in*] red. (!服の色を問題にするときは通例色を表す語のみを用いる) ●彼は貧しいので着るものが買えなかった He was so poor that he couldn't buy anything to *wear* [×*put on*]. ●彼女は青いドレスを着てパーティーに行った She went to the party in a blue dress./ She *wore* a blue dress *to* the party. ●メアリーはまだ自分で上手に服が着られないのです Mary still can't *dress herself* very well. ●この服を着て(=試着して)みたらどう? Why don't you *try* these clothes *on*? ●彼はひどく酔っていて服を着たままベッドに潜り込んだ He was dead drunk and got into his bed *with* his clothes on [*in* his clothes]. ●彼女はかなり太ったので以前の服が着られない She can't *get into* her old dress, because she has become very fat.
❷[負う] ●罪を着る(=引き受ける) *take* [*assume*, *bear*] the blame 《*for*》. ●君には大変恩に着ています I *feel* [*am*] deeply *indebted to* you./I *owe* you a great deal to you./I *owe* you a great deal.

きるい 帰塁 ●かろうじて二塁に帰塁をする make it [*get*] back in time to second.

キルギス [国名] Kyrgyz /kıərgíːz/; (公式名) the Kyrgyz Republic. (首都 Bishkek) ●キルギス人 a Kyrgyz. ●キルギス語 Kyrgyz. ●キルギス(人[語])の Kyrgyz.

キルティング [刺し子縫い] quilting /kwíltɪŋ/.

キルト [スコットランド特有のスカート状の男性用衣裳] a kilt; [刺し子縫い掛けぶとん] a quilt /kwɪlt/.

ギルド [中世の同業組合] a (blacksmiths') guild.

***きれ** 切れ ❶[布] cloth; (ぼろ切れ) (a) rag; (端切れ) a remnant of cloth. (⇒布)
❷[切れ味] sharpness. (⇒切れ味) ●彼は切れがいいカーブを投げる He throws *sharp* [*sharply*] breaking] curves.

-きれ 切れ [小片] a piece, [a slice] (of cake). (!個々の名詞の項目を参照 ⇒紙切れ)

きれあがる 切れ上がる ●小股の切れ上がった(=粋ですらりとした)女性 a stylish and slender woman.

きれあじ 切れ味 (鋭さ) sharpness. ●切れ味がいい(鋭い) be sharp; (よく切れる) cut well. ●ナイフの切れ味を試す test the *sharpness* [[刃]*edge*] of a knife. ●切れ味のよい[悪い]ナイフ a *sharp* [a *blunt*, a *dull*] knife.

‡**きれい** 奇麗 ── 奇麗な 圏 ❶[美しい] beautiful; (小さくてかわいい) pretty; (愛くるしい) lovely; (器量のよい) good-looking; (男性の顔立ちの整った) handsome. (⇒美しい) ●きれいな少女 a *beautiful* [a *pretty*, a *lovely*, a *good-looking*] girl. ●きれいな花 a *pretty* [a *beautiful*, a *lovely*] flower. ●きれいな顔立ちの若い男 a *handsome* [a *good-looking*] young man. ●きれいな声で歌う sing in a *beautiful* [a *lovely*, a *sweet*] voice. (!a clear voice は「よく通る声」) ●きれいな花にはとげがある No rose without a thorn./Every rose has its thorn.
❷[清潔な] clean (↔*dirty*); (澄んだ) clear; (清く汚れのない) pure; [きちんとした] tidy, neat. (⇒潔) ●きれいな水 *clean* [*pure*] water. (!clear water は「透き通った水」の意) ●きれいなタオル a *clean* towel. ●きれいな空 a *clear* sky. ●きれいな部屋 a *tidy* [a *neat*] room. ●きれい好きな (⇒奇麗好き) ●彼の机はいつもきれいだった His desk was always *tidy* [*neat*]. ▶彼女はきれいな(=見事な)字を書く He has *beautiful* handwriting./(彼の字はきちんとしている) His (hand)writing is *neat*.
会話「台所をいつもきれいにしていらっしゃるわね」「そのように心掛けてるのよ」"You always keep your kitchen *neat and clean*." "I try."
❸[公正な] fair; (汚れのない) clean. ●きれいな勝負 *fair* play. ●きれいな選挙を行う hold [conduct] a *fair* [a *clean*] election. ●彼の履歴はきれいだ He has a *clean* record./(汚点がない) There is *no stain* on his record.

── 奇麗に 圐 ❶[美しく] ●きれいに装う dress oneself *beautifully*; (装っている) be *beautifully* dressed. ▶あなたはきれいに写っていますね You look *beautiful* [*nice*] in the picture.
会話「あたしこれでいいかしら」「とってもきれいに見えるよ」"Will I do?" "You look *lovely*, my dear."
❷[清潔に] cleanly /klíːnli/ (!形容詞は /klénli/ と読む); [きちんと] neatly, tidily. ●もっときれいに皿を洗う wash the dishes more *cleanly*. ●車を(洗って)きれいにする wash a car *clean*; *clean* a car. ●部屋をきれいにする(=片づける) make a room *tidy* [*neat*]; *clear up* [《英》*tidy* (*up*)] a room; *put* a room *in order*; (掃除する) *clean up* a room. (!「きれいにしておく」は keep a room *tidy* [*neat*]) ▶いつも歯をきれいにしておきなさい Always *keep* your teeth *clean*. ▶ごしごしこすったけど床はきれいにならなかった I scrubbed hard, but the floor would not be [become] *clean*. ●彼女はきれいに髪を整えた She arranged her hair *neatly*.
❸[すっかり] completely, entirely; (すべて) all. ▶そのことはきれいに忘れていた I *completely* [《話》*clean*] forgot about it./I forgot *all* about it. ●彼は借金をきれいに返した He *paid* [*cleared*, *wiped*] *off* his debts. (!「きれいに返す」は pay back, 《書》 discharge ともいう)
❹[その他の表現] ●彼女ときれいに別れる(=縁を切る) *cut loose from* her. ●きれいに戦ってきれいに負けよう Let's play *fair* and be *good losers*.
●奇麗所 (美しい女性) a beautiful woman; (芸者) a geisha (⇒芸者).

ぎれい 儀礼 (礼儀正しさ) courtesy /kɑ́ːrtəsi/; (礼儀作法) etiquette. ●儀礼的な訪問をする pay a *courtesy* call 《*on*+人》. ●儀礼的なものだった The party was a (mere) *formality*.

きれいごと 奇麗事 ●きれい事を言う give a high-sounding talk. ●人種問題をきれい事ですませる(=う

まく取り繕う) whitewash [gloss over] the racial problems.

きれいずき 奇麗好き — 奇麗好きな 形 (neat and) tidy; 《書》cleanly /klénli/. ●彼女はきれい好きだ She likes everything neat and tidy. (●「きれい好きな主婦」は a tidy housewife, 《英》a house-proud wife など).

きれぎれ 切れ切れ — 切れ切れの 形 (とぎれとぎれの) broken (sleep); (断片的な) fragmentary (memories).
—— **きれぎれに** 副 《tear a letter》to shreds [to pieces]. ●切れ切れに話が聞こえる hear only *fragments* of the conversation.
『**きれぎれ**』 *Shreds*. (参考) 町田康の小説

きれこみ 切れ込み a cut; (細長い) a slit; (V字型の) a notch; (外科手術の) an incision. ●切れ込みを入れる cut [make] a *notch*; notch; make a *slit* [a *cut*]; slit.

きれじ 切れ地 (織物) cloth, (a) fabric; (織物の切れ端) a remnant (■通例複数形で); a small piece of cloth.

きれじ 切れ痔 [医学] bleeding hemorrhoids.

きれつ 亀裂 a crack (■比喩的にも用いる (ひびみ)); [平面上の細長い] (やや書) a fissure; [岩や山の斜面の] a crevice. ●壁に入っている1本の長い亀裂 a long *crack* across [on, in] the wall. (■in は深い亀裂を示す). ●(人間関係の)亀裂を深める deepen [widen] the *split* [*between* them, *in* the group].

きれなが 切れ長 ●切れ長の(美しい)目 (beautiful) eyes with long tapering slits.

きれはし 切れ端 ●布の切れ端 *remnants* of cloth. ●紙の切れ端 a *scrap* of paper.

きれま 切れ間 (間) (途絶え間) ●雲の切れ間から through a *break* [《やや書》a *rift*] in the clouds.

きれめ 切れ目 [すき間] a gap; [中断] a break; [休止] a pause; [刃物で作った] a cut. ●切れ目なく without a *break* [a *pause*]. ●雲の切れ目 a *break* [《やや書》a *rift*] in the clouds.

きれもの 切れ者 a sharp [a shrewd, a bright and able] person.

*****きれる** 切れる 動 ❶【切断される】break*; (ぷつんと) snap (-pp-); (刃物などで) cut*. ●手の切れるような(=新券の)1万円札 a brand-new [a *crisp*] 10,000-yen bill. ●魚の重みで釣り糸が切れた The (fish) line *broke* [*snapped* (*off*)] under the weight of the fish. ●最近の輪ゴムは切れやすい Rubber bands of today *break* easily. ●堤防が切れた The dike [《主に英》dyke] *broke* [*gave way, collapsed*]. (■dike には「男役のレズビアン」の意があるので, このつづり字を避ける人もいる). ●この木はなかなか[全然]切れない This tree doesn't *cut* easily [won't *cut* at all]. (■can't cut は不可) ●ヒューズが切れた(=飛んだ) The fuse *has blown*.
❷【とぎれる】(電話が) be cut (off). ●走って息が切れる[切れた] *get* [*be*] *out of breath* from running. ▶話している最中に突然電話が切れた While talking, we *were* suddenly *cut off*./While we were talking, the phone suddenly *went dead*. ●雲が切れて眼下に陸地が見えた The clouds *broke* and we could see land below. ▶あの男とはもう手が切れた(=関係を絶った) I *have* now *broken* (*off*) *with* him. (⇨切る ❷)
❸【使わなくなる】(人が在庫品・時間などを使い切る) run* out of ...; (在庫品・時間などが切れる) run out; (電池などが) go* dead; (電球などが) burn* out; (有効期限が) run out, 《やや書》expire. ▶ガソリンが切れた[ている] We've run [We're] *out of gas*./

The gas *has run* [*is*] *out*./Our car *has run dry*. ▶今在庫が切れています We are *out of stock* now. ▶この本の著作権はあと3年で切れる This book *runs out of* copyright in three years./The copyright on this book *runs out* [*expires*] in three years. (■確実な期限を暗示する文脈では通例 will は用いない) ▶この本は貸出期限が切れている This book *is overdue*.
❹【するどい】(刃物や人が) be sharp [keen]. ●頭の切れる男 a *sharp* (↔a dull) [《主に米》(賢くて抜け目のない) a *smart*] man. ●切れないかみそり a razor that won't *shave* [×cut]. ▶この包丁はよく切れる[あまり切れない] This knife *is* very *sharp* [is rather dull, is not very sharp]./This knife *cuts* well [badly].
❺【方向がそれる】curve. ●打球は大きく左に切れた The ball *curved* [*hooked*] greatly to the left.
❻【完全には(...できない)】 ▶全部食べ切れないよ. 残してもいい? I can't *eat* them *all* [*eat* them *up*]. Can I leave some untouched? (■them は文脈によっても可)
❼【その他の表現】

■ DISCOURSE
これらの化学物質は身体に重大な影響を及ぼす可能性がある. 例えば脳に作用して「キレる」子供につながる可能性がある These chemicals may give some serious effects to our body: they may affect the brain of children and cause them to become "*short-tempered*". (■コロン(:)は具体例に用いるディスコースマーカー)

きろ 岐路 (十字路) a crossroads. (■複数形だが単数扱いに注意) ●人生の岐路に立つ come to a *crossroads* [the turning point] in one's life.

きろ 帰路 ●帰路を急ぐ hurry *back* [《家に向かって》*home*]. ●帰路に着く start [leave] *for home*. ▶帰路(=帰る途中で)彼女に会った I saw her on my *way back*.

キロ [キログラム] a kilogràm, 《話》a kilo (複 ~s)(略 kg); [キロメートル] a kilómeter (略 km)(■通例 x a kilo と略さない); [キロリットル] a kilòliter (略 kl) (語法) ■以上のような長さ・重さ・容積などは米英ではメートル法よりヤード・ポンド法の方が日常的だ); [キロワット] a kilowatt (略 kw). ●1キロ600円 600 yen per [a] *kilo*. ●時速40キロで運転する drive at a speed of 40 *kilometers* [×kilos] per hour [40 kph].
●**キロワット時** kikowatt-hour (記号 kWh; kwh; KWH).

*****きろく** 記録 名 ❶【書き留めること】(a) récord; (文書) a document; (議事録) the proceedings; (the) minutes /mínɪts/; (メモ) a note. ●公式記録 an official *record*. ●交通事故記録 a *record* of road accidents. ●人生記録 the *record* of a person's life; (伝記) a biography. ●会議の記録をとる keep the *records* for [take *notes* of] the meeting. ●体験を記録に残す leave one's *experience*(s) *on record*. ●記録に残る大地震 the greatest earthquake *on record*. ●旅の記録写真を作る make *a photographic record* of one's journey. ●あの男について何か記録がないかを警察に問い合わせる ask the police if they have anything about the man *on their files*. ▶大英博物館には中世の生活に関する記録が多くある The British Museum is full of *records* of medieval life. ▶彼の偉大な業績は記録に残っている His greatest achievement *is on record* [*is recorded*].
❷【競技の成績】a record. ●通算記録 a career [a

ギロチン

lifetime] *record*. ●新記録 (⇨新記録) ●自己の記録を更新する renew [better] one's own *record*. ●40 セーブを記録する set [log] forty saves. ●ホームラン記録を作る set the *record* for home runs. ▶君の 400 メートルの最高記録はいくらだ What is your best *record* in [for] the 400-meter race? ▶走り幅跳びの世界記録が今日破られた The world *record* for the running broad jump was broken [was beaten] today. ▶彼は走り高跳びの日本記録を保持している He holds a Japan *record* [is a Japan-*record* holder] for the high jump. ▶世界記録が出た A new world *record* (*in* speed skating) was set. ▶彼女は 200 メートル自由形で 1 分 58 秒の世界新記録を出した She swam the 200-meter freestyle in a new world *record* of 1 minute 58 seconds. ▶彼は 100 メートルを 10 秒 3 の記録(=時間)で優勝した He won the 100-meter dash *with a time of* 10.3 seconds. ▶きみの努力に記録(達成)がかかっている Setting a (new) *record* depends [rests] on your efforts. ▶記録は破られるためにある (Sports) *records* are made to be broken.

— 記録的(な) 形 récord. ●記録的短時間で in *record* time. ▶記録的な大雪が東北地方に降った A *record* snow fell in the Tohoku district. ▶公園は記録的な人出だった There was a *record* number of people in the park.

— 記録する 動 récord, put*... on récord; (書き留める) write* [put*, take*]... down. ●事件を記録する *record* an event; *put* an event *on record*; *write down* an event. ▶彼は日々の出費を細大もらさず記録している He keeps a *record* [keeps track] of all his daily expenses. (⚠ ×is keeping と進行形にはしない)

●記録映画《主に米》a documentary movie, 《主に英》a documentary film. ●記録係 a recorder; a record keeper; (競技の) a scorer. ●記録管理 records management. ●記録装置 a recording device; a recorder. ●記録保持者 a record holder.

ギロチン [断頭台] a guillotine /ɡíləti:n/. ▶彼はギロチンで処刑された He was sent to the *guillotine*.

※ぎろん 議論 名 (検討をして合意するための) (a) discussion; (論理を尽くし説得するための) (an) argument; (賛否対立の正式な) (a) debate (⇨討論); [論争] (感情的で激しい) (a) dispute; (紙上などでの公的な)《やや書》(a) controversy. (⇨論争)

① 【～議論】 ●白熱した議論 a hot [a heated] *argument*. ●激論 ●活発な議論 an animated [a lively, an intense] *discussion*. ▶その計画について は反対[賛成]の議論はなかった There was no *argument* against [for, in favor of] the plan. ▶私たちは教育について建設的な議論をした We had a constructive *discussion* about education.

② 【議論～】 ●議論好きな (理屈っぽい) argumentative; (けんか好きな) quarrelsome. ▶その計画論議論百出した There was *lots of argument* about the project.

③ 【議論が】 ▶新しい高速道路についてさまざまな議論がある There is a lot of *discussion* about the new expressway. ▶議論がなかなかかみ合わなかった They *talked past each other*, with the arguments only rarely meshing. ▶民主主義には議論が必要だ *Discussion* is indispensable for democracy.

④ 【議論の】 ●議論のための議論をする argue for *argument*'s sake. ●それを議論のたたき台とする use it as a springboard [(試案) a tentative plan]

きわまる

for *discussion*. ▶このことについては議論の余地がない There is no (⇨plenty of) room for *argument* [*dispute*, *controversy*] *about* this./This is beyond *argument* [*dispute*, *controversy*]. ▶活発な議論の末, 私たちは計画を実行に移した We put the plan into action after a lively *discussion*.

⑤ 【議論に】 ●議論に勝つ win an *argument*. ●その事で彼と議論になる get into an *argument* with him *about* the matter.

⑥ 【議論を】 ●議論を重ねた末 after plenty of *discussion*. ●大いに議論を呼んでいる[呼びそうな]本 a very controversial book; a book of much *controversy*. ●議論を深めよう Let's *discuss* it further. ▶彼が私に議論を仕掛けてきた He challenged me to a *debate*.

— 議論する 動 discuss (⚠ talk about ... の堅い言い方); argue; debate (⇨討論する); dispute (⇨論争する). ●彼とその問題について議論する *discuss* [×*discuss about*] the matter with him; *have a discussion* with him *about* [*on*] the matter; *argue* (*about*, *over*) the matter with him; *argue* [*have an argument*] with him *about* [*over*] the matter. ▶我々は店を売るべきかどうか議論した We *discussed* [*argued about*] *whether* to sell the shop [*whether* we should sell the shop]. (⚠ ×discuss+that 節, ×argue+wh- 節は不可) ▶私たちは長時間激しく議論した We *argued* [*discussed*] heatedly for a long time./We had a long heated *argument* [*discussion*].

きわ 際 [そば] the side (⇨側(ミラ)); [端] an edge (⇨端). ●窓際の席に座る take a seat *by* [*beside*] a window. ●いまわの際に《やや書》on one's deathbed. ▶別れ際に「じゃ, また」と彼は言った "See you again," he said to me *when* we parted.

ぎわく 疑惑 [嫌疑] (a) suspicion; [疑い] (a) doubt. (⇨疑い, 疑う) ●世間の疑惑を招く arouse [raise, cause, create] public *suspicion*. ●...の疑惑を受けている be under *suspicion* of .... ●殺人の疑惑で逮捕される be arrested *on suspicion of* murder.

きわだつ 際立つ 動 [目立つ] stand* out; [対照によって引き立つ] contrást (*with*).

— 際立った 形 outstanding; (注目すべき) remarkable; (人目を引く) striking. ●際立った業績 an *outstanding* achievement. ●際立った美人 a *striking* [an *outstanding*] beauty. ▶彼女の美貌(ぼう)は際立っていた Her beauty made her *stand out* from the others. ▶際立った変化はない There is no *remarkable* [*striking*] change.

きわどい ●きわどい(=危険な)仕事をする do a *risky* [a *dangerous*] business. ●きわどい(=微妙な)質問をする ask a *delicate* question. ●きわどい(=みだらすれすれの)冗談を言う make a *suggestive* [《話》a *naughty*] joke. ●きわどい(=接戦の)試合に勝つ win a *close* game [contest]. ●きわどいところで事故にあわずにすむ have a *narrow escape from* an accident; *narrowly* escape an accident. ▶きわどいところで最終列車に間に合った I was *just* in time for the last train.

きわまりない 極まりない, 窮まりない ●無礼[危険]極まりない *extremely* impolite [dangerous].

きわまる 極まる, 窮まる [終わる] end, come* to an end. ●危険極まる be *most* [*extremely*] dangerous. ●進退窮まる be driven into a corner; (絶体絶命である)《話》have one's back to the wall. ▶彼の欲望は極まるところを知らない《やや書》There are *no bounds* to his desire./His desire knows *no bounds*. ●感極まって言葉が出なかった My heart

きわみ 極み（極致）the height.（⇨極）・愚かさの極みthe *height* of folly. ・…は遺憾の極みである It is *most regrettable that* .... ・悲惨の極みにある be in extreme misery; *No life can be* more miserable《than his life》.（!主語に否定の言葉をもってくる意味を強調する）

きわめつき 極め付き ── 極め付きの 形（保証された）gùarántéed;（最高の）the best;（名うての）notórious.

きわめて 極めて〚非常に〛very;（並はずれて）exceedingly;（極度に）extremely;〚実に〛really. ・きわめて難解な本 an *extremely* [an *exceedingly*;（実に）a *really*] difficult book. ▶きわめて遺憾です I am *very* [*terribly, extremely*] sorry.

きわめる 究める,極める,窮める〚徹底的に研究する〛study, invéstigate《it》thoroughly;（精通する）master. ・芸をきわめる *master* an art. ・事の真相をきわめる *get at* the truth of the matter; *get to the bottom of* the matter. ・ぜいたく〚多忙〛をきわめる be *most* [*extremely*] extravagant [busy]. ・頂上をきわめる *reach* the summit《of a mountain》.

きわもの 際物 ❶〚季節商品〛seasonal goods. ❷〚一時的興味のもの〛・きわもの小説 'a novel of passing [temporary] interest'; a claptrap [a sensational] novel.

きをつけ 気をつけ ・気をつけの姿勢をとる come to [（さっと）snap to,（立つ）stand at] *attention*. ▶気をつけ〚号令〛*Attention! /*(ə)tenʃən/.（!口語ではさらに縮約して *'shun!* /ʃʌn/ ともなる）

きをつける 気を付ける（用心する）take* care《of》, be careful《of》;（警戒する）look [watch] out《for》. ・健康に気をつける *take care of* one's health [oneself]; *be careful of* [*about*] one's health. ▶暗いから道に迷わないように気をつけなさい *Be careful* [*Take care*] not to lose your way in the dark./*Be careful* [*Take care*]《that》you don't [✗won't] lose your way in the dark.（!that 節内は現在形で未来形は不可. 最後の例の see to it that 節と比較）▶車に気をつけなさいよ *Watch* [*Look*] *out* for cars. ・気をつけて *Careful!* [*Be careful* より語調がやわらかく，日常よく用いられる]/（危ない）*Look* [*Watch*] *out!* ・足下に気をつけなさい *Watch* [（主に英）*Mind*] your step [✗steps]. ▶だれもこの部屋に入らないよう気をつけなさい *See to it that* nobody enters [will enter] this room.（!(1) see to it that は確認・徹底của を表す．やや堅い言い方. (2) that 節内は現在形が普通であるが，最近未来形も用いられるようになってきた．第 1 例の be careful [take care] that 節と比較）

会話「ではまた」「お体に気をつけてね」"Good-by for now." "*Take care*《of》yourself./*Look after* yourself."　▶別れのあいさつ）

*きん **金** 图（鉱物）gold《元素記号 Au》.
── 金の 形（金製の）gold;（金色の）golden. ・18 金の指輪 an 18-karat *gold* ring. ・金の延べ棒 a *gold* bar.
・金時計 a *gold* watch. ・金ボタン（真鍮(しんちゅう)の）a brass button. ・金本位制 the gold standard. ・金メダル《win》a *gold* medal. ・金めっき gílding.

きん 斤（食パンの 1 塊）a loaf《@ loaves》.

きん 菌〚ばい菌,病原菌〛a germ;（バクテリア）a bacterium《@ bactéria》（!単数形となることはまれ）; a bacillus《@ bacilli》（!バクテリアの一種．桿(かん)菌）;〚キノコ・カビなどの〛a fungus《@ fungi /fʌŋɡai/》.
・病院などの無菌室 a *germ*free room. ・赤痢菌 a dysentery bacillus. ▶ばらの菌による病気にかかりや

すい Roses are prone to *fungal* disease.

きん 禁 prohibition; a ban. ・禁を犯す violate the *prohibition* [the *ban*].

*ぎん **銀** 图（鉱物）silver《元素記号 Ag》. ▶湖は月光で銀色に輝いていた The lake was shining like *silver* [*was silvering*] in the moonlight.（!後の言い方は文語的）
── 銀の 形（銀製の）silver;（銀のような）silvery.（⇨銀製）・銀のブローチ a silver brooch.
・銀器（集合的）silverware. ・銀本位制 the silver standard. ・銀メダル《win》a silver medal. ・銀めっき silver gilt.

きんあつ 禁圧 ── 禁圧する 動（鎮圧する）suppress;（禁止する）prohibit;（法律などで禁止する）ban.

きんいしゅくしょう 筋萎縮症〚医学〛muscular atrophy.

きんいつ 均一 uniformity.
── 均一の[な] 形（やや書）úniform;（料金・価格などが）flat;（均等の）equal /íːkwəl/. ・均一値段 a *uniform* price. ・均一料金 a *flat* rate;（電車などの）a *uniform* fare. ・大きさと色が均一な花 flowers *uniform* [*equal*] *in* size and color; flowers of *uniform* [*equal*] size and color. ▶そのおもちゃは 100 円均一です It's=すべて 100 円です] The toys are all 100 yen./The toys are 100 yen *apiece* [*each*].（! all と apiece を重ねて用いるのは冗語. いずれか一方だけにする）

きんいっぷう 金一封（receive [get]）a gift of money.

きんうん 金運 ・金運がよい be financially lucky [fortunate]. ・金運が悪い be unlucky [unfortunate] with money.

きんえい 近影 one's latest [recent] photograph [（話）photo].

ぎんえい 吟詠 ── 吟詠する 動（歌う）recite [sing, chant]《a poem》;（作る）compose《a poem》.

きんえん 近縁 ── 近縁の 形 closely-related. ▶メアリーは私の近縁です Mary *is closely related* to me./（近親者である）Mary is one of my *close relatives*.
・近縁種 related species.

きんえん 禁煙 ▶禁煙《掲示》*No smoking*/（やわらかく）Thank you for *not smoking*. ▶車内は禁煙だ *Smoking is prohibited* [*is not permitted*] in this car./It *is not permitted to smoke* in this car./（話）There's *no*（cigarette）*smoking* in the car. ・医者は彼に禁煙をすすめた The doctor advised him to *give up* [*stop*,《話》*quit*] smoking.
・禁煙車 a nonsmoking car. ・禁煙席 a nonsmoking seat.

きんか 近火 a fire in one's neighborhood.

きんか 金貨 a gold coin;《集合的》gold. ・金貨で支払う pay in *gold*.

ぎんか 銀貨 a silver coin;《集合的》silver.

ぎんが 銀河 the Milky Way; the Galaxy.

ぎんがけい 銀河系 the galactic system.

きんかい 近海（沿海水域）coastal [inshore] waters. ・日本近海で in Japanese *waters*.

きんかい 金塊（自然の）a gold nugget;（レンガ型の）a gold ingot;（延べ棒の）gold bullion.

きんかいわかしゅう『金槐和歌集』 *Golden Pagoda* ── *Tree of Japanese Poetry*.《参考》源実朝の歌集）

きんかぎょくじょう 金科玉条 a golden rule.《参考》これを冠するキリストの山上の説教中の名文句に「黄金律」（Matthew 7:12）, 特に(欽定訳（1611）)Do to others as you would be done by./(American Bible Society 訳(1966)) Do for others what you want them to do for you.

(自分のしてもらいたいように人にもしなさい)をさす)

きんがく 金額 a sum (of money); an amount of money. (⇨幾ら❶) ▶費用はかなりの金額にのぼる The expenses come (up) [amount] to a large [˟much]sum. ▶この絵は金額にすると100万円ほどのものだ This picture *is worth* one million yen.

きんかくし 金隠し a front screen of a lavatory bowl.

きんかくじ『金閣寺』 *The Temple of the Golden Pavilion*. 《参考》三島由紀夫の小説.

きんがしんねん 謹賀新年 (I wish you a) Happy New Year. (■英語の方は「どうかよいお年を」という意で年末でも用いることができる)

ぎんがてつどうのよる『銀河鉄道の夜』 *Milky Way Railroad*; *Night of the Milky Way Railway*. 《参考》宮沢賢治の童話.

ぎんがみ 銀紙 silver paper [foil]; aluminum foil.

きんかん 近刊 ── 近刊の 形 [[近日出版予定の]] forthcoming [[主に米]] upcoming [[books]]; [[books]] in preparation; [[最近出版された]] recently published. (⇨新刊)

きんかん 金冠 a gold crown. ●歯に金冠をかぶせる put [cap] a *gold crown* [*top*] on a tooth.

きんかん 金柑 [[植物]] a kumquat, a cumquat.

きんかん 近眼 nearsightedness. (⇨近視)

きんかんがっき 金管楽器 a brass instrument;《集合的》the brass. ▶オーケストラ中の人・楽器の集団をいい単・複両扱い.

きんかんしょく 金環食 [[天文]] an annular /ˈænjələr/ eclipse. ●金環食は「リング状の」という形.

きんかんばん 金看板 [[金色の看板]] a signboard with gilt lettering; [[世間に誇示する特徴]] a feature. ●金看板の教授[プレーヤー] a *star* professor [player].

きんき 近畿 (地方) the Kinki district.

きんき 欣喜 ── 欣喜雀躍(じゃく) ▶彼は欣喜雀躍した He *jumped* [*danced*] *for joy* (*at the news*).

きんき 禁忌 [[タブー]] (a) taboo; [[医学]] a contraindication.

***きんきゅう** 緊急 图 (an) emergency; urgency. ▶その患者の手術は緊急を要する It is *urgent* that the patient (should) be operated on. (■should を用いるのは《主に英》)(緊急に必要である)The patient *urgently* needs to be operated on.

── 緊急の 形 urgent, pressing (■前の方が強意的); (緊急事態の) emergency. ●緊急の必要 an *urgent* [a *pressing*, 《話》a *crying*] need (*for*). ●緊急の場合[際, 時]には in an *emergency*, in the event of an *emergency* (■前の方が口語的); 《主に米》in case of (an) *emergency*. (■通例文頭に置く. 文尾に置くと「緊急事態に備えて」の意) ●緊急の用件 an [upon] *urgent* business.

●緊急会議 an urgent [an emergency] conference. ●緊急事態 《provide for》emergencies. ●緊急措置《take》emergency measures. ●緊急逮捕《make》an emergency arrest without (a) warrant. ●緊急着陸《make》an emergency landing. ●緊急動議 an urgent motion. ●緊急避難 emergency evacuation.

きんぎょ 金魚 [[魚介]] a goldfish (複 ~, ~es).
●金魚の糞(ふん) ▶姉妹は母親の後を金魚のふんについて歩いた The two sisters always *tagged along after* [*behind*] their mother wherever she went.
●金魚すくい goldfish-scooping. ●金魚草 a snapdragon. ●金魚鉢 a goldfish bowl.

きんきょう 近況 the present [recent] state. (⇨現状) ▶近況をお知らせください Please let us know

how you*'re getting along*. ▶近況といってもさして話しますことはありません There is not much to say about my life.

きんきょり 近距離 a short distance.
●近距離列車 a local train.

きんきらきん ── きんきらきんの 形 (やたらとはでな) gaudy; (高価だが品のない) flashy. ▶彼女はきんきらきんの服を着ている She wears *flashy* clothes./She is *flashily* dressed.

きんきん 近近 soon; 《書》before long; (近い将来に) in the near future.

きんきんごえ きんきん声 ●きんきん声で in a *shrill* [a *highpitched*] *voice*.

きんく 禁句 taboo words. ▶それはここでは禁句です That's *taboo* here.

キング [王] a king. ●スペードのキング the *king* of spades.
●キングサーモン a king salmon; a Chinook /ʃənʊk/ sálmon. ●キングダム [王国] a kingdom. ●キングメーカー [要職の人選を左右する政界の実力者] a kingmaker.

キングサイズ ●キングサイズのたばこ a *king-size*(*d*) cigarette.

きんけい 近景 the foreground. (対 遠景) ●その絵の近景の人物 a figure in the *foreground* of the painting.

きんけい 謹啓 [手紙の冒頭] Dear Sir [Madam]. (■通例, 会社・団体などに対しては Dear Sirs, Gentlemen を用いる)

きんけつ 金欠 poverty; a lack of money. ●金欠にかかっている 《話》be (a bit, really) strapped (for cash); 《話》be (flat, completely) broke.

きんけん 近県 neighboring [nearby] prefectures.

きんけん 金券 (金貨兌換紙幣) a gold note; (金銭の代わりに通用する券) a note; a certificate.

きんけん 金権 the power of money.
●金権(政治)家 a plutocrat. ●金権政治 plutocracy; money politics.

きんけん 勤倹 diligence and thrift.
●勤倹貯蓄 diligence, thrift and saving.

きんげん 金言 a wise saying; (有名な) a maxim; (古くからの) an adage; (短い) an aphorism.

きんげん 謹厳 图 (まじめで気軽には笑わないさま) seriousness.
── 謹厳な 形 serious. ▶あの方は謹厳実直な方でいらっしゃいます He's *quite* a *serious* person.

きんこ 金庫 a safe, a strongbox; [銀行などの金庫室] a strong room; [巨大金庫] a vault. ●貸し金庫 a safe-[a safety-]deposit box. ●夜間金庫 a night *depository*. ●金を金庫に入れる[しまっておく] put [keep] money in the *safe*.
●金庫破り (人)《主に米》a safecracker,《英》a safebreaker. ●金庫破りをする break into [break open, crack] a *safe*.

きんこ 禁固 imprisonment. ▶彼は5年の禁固刑の宣告を受けた He's been sentenced to five years' *imprisonment*.

***きんこう** 均衡 bálance (⇔imbalance); [力などの均衡状態] equilibrium. (釣り合い, バランス) a bálance. ●力の均衡 the *balance* of power. ●均衡を破る[回復する] upset [restore] the *balance*. ●同点の均衡を破る break a *tie*. ●均衡を破る1点をあげる [野球] score a *tie*-breaking run. ●両大国間の勢力均衡を保つ maintain the *balance* of the two powers. ▶二つの軍隊は勢力が均衡していた The two armies *balanced* each other.

きんこう 近郊 (都市の周辺部) the environs /ɪnˈvaɪərənz/; (■後の2語より堅い語); (郊外)《in》

きんこう suburbs; 《on》the outskirts. (⇨郊外) ●東京とその近郊 Tokyo and its *environs*; (東京近郊の) the *environs* of Tokyo. ●ワルシャワ近郊の小さな村 a small village *outside* Warsaw /wɔ́:rsɔ:/.

きんこう 金工 (工芸) metalwork, metakworking; (工芸品) 《a piece of》 metalwork; (人) a metalsmith, a metalworker, (金細工職人) a goldsmith.

きんこう 金鉱 (鉱山) a gold mine.
● 金鉱石 gold ore.

きんごう 近郷 the surrounding countryside.

:きんこう 銀行 a bank.
① 【～銀行】 ● 都市[地方; 信託]銀行 a city [a regional; a trust] *bank*. ●大手銀行 a big [a large, a major] bank. ●日本銀行 the *Bank* of Japan. ●世界銀行 the World *Bank*. [参考] 国際復興開発銀行の略称) ●血液銀行 a blood *bank*. ▶おたくの取り引き銀行はどちらですか What are you banking with?/Who are your *bankers*?
② 【銀行(の)～】 ● 給料を銀行振り込みにする transfer one's salary to one's *bank* account. ▶彼は銀行員です He is a *bank* clerk [employee]. [!] banker は「銀行家[経営者]」/He works for [at, in] a *bank* (勤める). ●銀行の営業時間は午前 9 時から午後 3 時までです *Banking* hours are from 9 a.m. to 3 p.m.
③ 【銀行に～】 ● 銀行に口座を持つ[開く] have [open (⇔close)] an account with [at] a *bank*. ▶彼女は給料の半分を銀行に預けた She put [deposited] half her salary in [xto] the *bank*. ▶私は銀行に 100 万円の預金がある I have a million yen in the *bank* [my (*bank*) account]./I have a *bank* account [deposit] of a million yen.
④ 【銀行から】 ● 銀行から融資を受ける borrow (money) from a *bank*; get [take out] a *bank* loan 《*of*》. ▶彼女は銀行から 5 万円おろした She withdrew 50,000 yen from the *bank* [her (*bank*) account].
● 銀行カード a bank card. ●銀行貸し出し bank lending [financing]. ●銀行借り入れ a bank loan; bank borrowing. ●銀行業界 the bánking industry. ●銀行業務 banking. ●銀行券 a bank note; 《米》bill]. ●銀行口座 a bank account. ●銀行強盗 (行為) a bank robbery; (犯人) a bank robber. ●「銀行強盗をする」は rob a bank) ●銀行小切手 a bank check. ●銀行手数料 bank charge. ●銀行預金 bank deposits.

ぎんこう 吟行 ── 吟行する 動 ▶彼は郊外や名所を吟行した(=詩歌作りに出かけた) He *went out to compose a poem* [*a tanka*] in the suburbs or in a noted place.

きんこく 謹告 ── 謹告する 動 inform with respect 《*that* 節》; respectfully announce 《*that* 節》.

きんこつ 筋骨 ● 筋骨たくましい (very) muscular; brawny; 《やや書》sinewy.

きんこん 緊褌 ● 緊褌一番 ▶緊褌一番(=気持ちを引き締めて)この難局に対処しよう Let's *brace* ourselves [*gird* (*up*) *our loins*] *for* this difficult situation.

きんこんしき 金婚式 (celebrate) a [one's] golden wedding (anniversary); 《米》 a [one's] golden anniversary.

ぎんこんしき 銀婚式 《celebrate》 a [one's] silver wedding (anniversary); 《米》 a [one's] silver anniversary.

きんさ 僅差 a narrow margin. ●僅差で勝つ[負ける] win [lose] by a *narrow margin*; win [lose] a close game. ▶彼は僅差で議長に選ばれた He was elected chairperson by a *narrow* [a *small*, a *slim*] majority.

きんざい 近在 (⇨ 近郷)
きんさく 近作 a [one's] recent [latest] work.
きんさく 金策 ● 金策に迫られている be busy *raising money*; (金に詰まっている) be financially pressed. ▶やっと金策がついた I succeeded in *raising funds* [*getting a loan*] at last.
── 金策する 動 raise money [funds].

きんざん 金山 a gold mine.
ぎんざん 銀山 a silver mine.

:きんし 禁止 名 【法律・法令などによる公的な】《やや書》prohibition (!「禁止令」の意では C に《書》); 【道徳上非難されることに対する禁止(令)】 a ban 《*on*》; 【通商・出入港などの禁止(令)】 an embargo (複 ～es) 《*on*》. ●賭博の禁止令を発する a *prohibition against* gambling. ●その肥料を使用禁止にする put [place, lay] a *ban on* (the use of) the fertilizer; put [place] (the use of) the fertilizer under a *ban*. ●金輸出の禁止を解く lift a *ban* [an *embargo*] *on* the export of gold. ▶この道路は通行禁止となっている Traffic *is prohibited* [*No traffic is allowed*] on this street. ▶その劇は検閲により上演禁止となった The play *was banned* by the censor. ▶駐車禁止《揭示》*No* parking/(やわらかに) Thank you for *no* [*not*] parking./You *are not supposed to* park here. ▶立入禁止《揭示》Keep off./(区域名) 《米》Off limits, 《英》Out of boundary. ▶関係者以外立入禁止《揭示》the Authorized Only./Private.
── 禁止する 動 《書》 prohibit; ban (-nn-); forbid*. (⇨禁じる❶)

きんし 近視 名 《米》 nearsightedness, 《英》 shortsightedness; [医学] myopia /maióupiə/.
── 近視の, 近視眼的な 形 ● 非常に近視眼的な判断 very *shortsighted* judgment. ▶彼は近視だ He is *nearsighted* [*shortsighted*].

きんし 菌糸 a hypha (複 hyphae /háifi:/); (キノコの) a spawn.

きんし 錦糸 ● 錦糸卵 thin fried-egg strips.
きんジストロフィー 筋ジストロフィー [医学] muscular dystrophy. ●進行性筋ジストロフィー progressive *muscular dystrophy*.

きんじち 近似値 [数学] an approximation.
きんしつ 均質 名 homogeneity /hòuməɗʒəníːəti/.
── 均質の 形 《やや書》homogéneous (↔heterogéneous).

きんしつ 琴瑟 ● 琴瑟相和(す) 服部夫妻は琴瑟相和している Mr. and Mrs. Hattori *are extremely happily married*./Mr. and Mrs. Hattori *live like Darby and Joan*. (! Darby and Joan は「仲のよい老夫婦」の意).

きんじつ 近日 ● 近日中に (間もなく) soon (⇨間もなく); (2,3 日中に) in a few days; (近いうちに) one of these days. ▶近日発売 (広告で) Coming *soon*./ (近日発行) *Near* publication.

きんじつてん 近日点 [天文] a perihelion (複 perihelia).

きんじて 禁じ手 ● 禁じ手を使う use a *prohibited technique* 《*at* wrestling》.

きんじとう 金字塔 (不朽の業績) a monument; a monumental achievement.

きんしゃ 金紗, 錦紗 silk crepe [crêpe] /kréip/.
きんしゅ 金主 a financier; a financial backer.
きんしゅ 金種 denominations of money. ▶金種はどのようにいたしましょうか (両替所などで) How would you like your money?

きんしゅ 筋腫 [医学] a myoma /maióumə/ (複

myomata, ~s). ●子宮筋腫を切除する remove the *myoma* of the uterus /júːtərəs/.

きんしゅ 禁酒 图 《酒を断つこと》《やや書》abstinence (from alcohol);《やや書》temperance (**!**「節酒」の意もある).▶彼は禁酒を誓った He promised to give up drinking [*never* to drink *alcohol* again]./《話》He swore off *drinking*.

── 禁酒する 動 (酒をやめる) give* up [stop] drinking.
● 禁酒会 a temperance society.

きんしゅく 緊縮 austérity,《やや書》retrenchment.
● 緊縮予算 an austerity budget.

きんしょ 禁書 a banned book.

*きんじょ 近所 a neighborhood (**!**暖かさ・親しさのある語);《やや書》vicinity (**!**前の語より広いような地点を囲む地域);[近所の人] a neighbor;《集合的》the neighborhood (**!**単・複両扱い).

①【近所〜】 ●近所うきあいのよい[悪い]人 a good [a bad] *neighbor*.●近所うきあいを mix with one's *neighbors*.▶近所中あちこちでもちきりだ The whole *neighborhood* [ˣ*vicinity*] is [are] talking about the story.(**!**neighborhood は集合的に「近所の人々」の意で, 単・複両扱い)

②【近所の】●近所の公園 a park *nearby*; a *nearby* park; a *neighborhood* park; a park in the *neighborhood*.●近所の女の人 a woman *neighbor*.●近所の家 a neighboring [a nearby] house.

③【近所に[で, まで]】●この近所で[に] (⇨付近 ②) ●お寺の近所に in the *neighborhood* [*vicinity*] of the temple; *near* [*around*] the temple.▶次夫君は私たちの近所に住んでいる Tsugio lives *in our neighborhood*.▶この近所まで来たものですからちょっとごあいさつまでに寄らせていただきました I happened to be in this *neighborhood* [(通りがかったので) I was just passing by], so I dropped in to say hello.
● 近所迷惑 a neighborhood nuisance.●近所迷惑なことをする bother the *neighbors*.

きんしょう 金賞 a gold (award [(メダル) medal]). (⇨銅賞)

きんじょう 今上 ●今上天皇 His Majesty the Emperor; the (present) Emperor [Tenno].

きんじょう 金城 ●熊本城は金城湯池(=難攻不落の要塞)で有名だ Kumamoto Castle is famous for its *impregnable fortress*.▶この地域は自民党の金城湯池(=ゆるぎない支持地盤)です This area is an *impregnable stronghold* of the Liberal Democratic Party.

きんじょう 錦上 ●錦上(さらに)花を添える 錦上花を添えるために to add beauty to beauty.

ぎんしょう 銀賞 a silver (award [(メダル) medal]). (⇨銅賞)

ぎんしょう 吟唱, 吟誦 图 (a) recitation.
── 吟唱する 動 recite《a poem》.

ぎんじょうしゅ 吟醸酒 *ginjoshu*;《説明的に》quality *sake* brewed from thoroughly polished rice fermented under low temperature.

きんじられたあそび 『禁じられた遊び』 *Forbidden Games*.[参考] フランスの映画. フランス語名は *Jeux interdits*.

きんじる 禁じる ❶[禁止する] forbid; ban (-nn-);《書》prohibit;(...するなと命じる) order [tell*]《him》not to do.(⇨禁止)

> 使い分け forbid 主に私的・個人的に禁じること.
> ban 道徳上などの理由から法的に禁止すること.
> prohibit 法律・法令によって公的に禁止すること.

●禁じられた恋 a *forbidden* love.●全面的に禁じる *ban* (it) completely.▶列車内での喫煙は禁じられている Smoking *is forbidden* [*is prohibited*] on [《英》in] the train./There is a *ban on* smoking on [《英》in] the train./(許されていない) You *are not permitted* [*allowed*] to smoke on [《英》in] the train./It *is not permitted* [ˣ*allowed*] to smoke on [《英》in] the train.▶両親はぼくがフットボールをするのを禁じている My parents *forbid* me *to* play [me play*ing*, my play*ing*] football./(許さない) My parents *don't allow* [*permit*] me *to* play football.▶医者は彼にアルコールを禁じた The doctor *forbade* him alcohol./The doctor *told* [*advised*] him *not to* touch alcohol.▶警察はこの道路に駐車するのを禁じている The police *ban* [*have a ban on*] parking cars on this street.

❷[抑える] *keep*... back.▶涙を禁じえなかった I couldn't *keep* [*fight*] *back* my tears./(泣かずにいられなかった) I *couldn't help* crying./《主に米話》I *couldn't help but* cry.

ぎんじる 吟じる (詩歌を歌う) recite《a poem》;(詩を作る) compose《a poem》.

きんしん 近親 a near [a close, (肉親の) an immediate] relative [relation]. (⇨親戚(読), 肉親)▶葬儀は近親者だけで行われた The funeral was held by the *immediate family* [*families*] only.
● 近親結婚 marriage between near relations; intermarriage《*between*, *with*》.(**!**後の方は異人種間の結婚などの意もあり厳密さに欠ける)●近親相姦(読) (commit) incest《*with*》.

きんしん 謹慎 good [best] behavior.●謹慎を命じる put [place]《him》on his *good behavior*;《やや書》place《him》in disciplinary confinement.▶彼は謹慎中です(=行儀よくしている) He *is on his good behavior*./He *is behaving himself*.

きんせい 均斉 [左右の対称] symmetry; [バランス・釣り合い] balance.▶その寺院の均斉 the *symmetry* of the temple.●均斉のとれた体 a *well-balanced* body.▶その手紙は均斉のとれた字で書いてあった The letter was written in a *well-balanced* hand.

きんせい 近世 (early) modern ages [times]. (**!**日本史の近世は「近代」の一つ前の時代である江戸時代をさすので early が必要. 西洋史では「近代」と同意なので不要(⇨近代))

きんせい 金星 Venus.

きんせい 金製 ●金製の時計 a *gold* watch; a watch *made of gold*. (⇨金)

きんせい 禁制 ── 禁制の 形 (禁じられた) forbidden; (排他的な) closed.●女人禁制の霊峰 a sacred mountain *closed to* women.

きんせい 謹製 Most Carefully Produced [Made]《*by*》.

ぎんせい 銀製 ●銀製の盆 a *silver* tray; a tray *made of silver*. (⇨銀)

ぎんせかい 銀世界 the white world.▶一面銀世界だった There was *snow everywhere* [*all around*].

きんせき 金石 ●金石文 an epigraph.

きんせつ 近接 图 nearness,《書》proximity.
── 近接した 形 (隣接の) near, nearby; (隣接する) neighboring;《書》adjacent /ədʒéɪsnt/. (⇨近く).

きんせん 金銭 money; [現金] cash. (⇨金(念))●金銭上の問題 a *money* question [matter].●金銭的な損失 loss of *money*;《書》pecuniary loss.▶彼らは金銭上の問題でいつももめている They are always having trouble over *money*.▶彼は何でも金銭ずくだ He thinks about everything in terms of *money*./He is very *mercenary*.▶彼女には金銭感覚がない She's insensitive to the *value of money*.

- **きんせん** 金銭出納簿 a cashbook. ● 金銭的援助 financial help. ● 金銭欲 the love of money.
- **きんせん** 琴線 heartstrings. ● 心の琴線に触れる (=感情を深く揺り動かす) pull at 《his》 *heartstrings*; move 《him》 emotionally.
- **きんぜん** 欣然 ── 欣然と 副 willingly; gladly.
- **きんせんか** 金盞花〖植物〗a pot [a common] marigold. (● 単にa marigold というと別の花になる)
- **きんそく** 禁足 confinement. ● 禁足をくう be confined to one's house; be ordered to stay in [not to go out of] one's house.
- **きんそく** 禁則 a prohibition. ● 禁則処理をする (ワープロで) make a program of a word processor to place punctuation marks, etc. properly.
- ***きんぞく** 金属 图 (a) metal /métl/. (! 種類を表すときは 〖C〗) ● 貴[重]金属 precious [light; heavy] *metals*. ▶ このテーブルは金属製だ This table is made of *metal*. ▶ 金は非常に有用な金属だ Gold is a very useful *metal*.
  ── 金属の 形 metal; (金属性の) metallic.
  ● 金属音 a metallic sound. ● 金属工業 the metal industry. ● 金属製品 metal goods (⇨商品). ;《集合的》hardware. ● 金属バット a metal (baseball) bat. ● 金属疲労 metal fatigue. ● 金属片 a piece of metal.
- **きんぞく** 勤続 图 continuous [long] service. ● その学校での 30 年の勤続により表彰を受ける 《書》be commended for one's thirty years' *service with* the school.
  ── 勤続する 動 ● その会社に長年勤続する *serve* in the company for many years.
  ● 勤続年数 the length of one's service.
- ***きんだい** 近代 modern times [ages] (! 前の方は「現代」の意にもなる); recent times. ● 近代における最大の発見 the greatest discovery in *modern* [*recent*] *times*.
  ── 近代の, 近代的(な) 形 modern. ● 近代的思想 *modern* ideas.
  ── 近代化する modernize. ● 日本[産業]を近代化する *modernize* Japan [industries]. ● 完全に近代化された工場 a fully *modernized* factory.
  ● 近代化 modernization. ● 近代建築 modern architecture. ● 近代国家 a modern state. ● 近代五種競技 the modern pentathlon. ● 近代産業 a modern industry. ● 近代史 modern history. (〖参考〗西洋史ではルネサンス以後) ● 近代詩 modern poetry.
- **きんたま** 金玉〖解剖〗testicles;《卑》balls;《米卑》nuts.
- **ぎんだら** 銀鱈〖魚介〗a sablefish; a black cod.
- **きんたろう** 『金太郎』 *The Adventures of Kintaro, the Golden Boy*. (〖参考〗日本の昔話)
- **きんたろうあめ** 金太郎飴 *kintaro-ame*; (説明的に) a hard candy bar with *kintaro*'s face seen in any slice of it.
- **きんだん** 禁断〖法的な禁止〗prohibition. (⇨禁止). ● 禁断の木(の)実 (the) forbidden fruit. ● 禁断症状が出る suffer from 《drug》 *withdrawal* (symptoms).
- **きんちさん** 禁治産 〖法律〗incompetence, incompetency. ▶ 彼は禁治産の宣告を受けた He was adjudged *incompetent*.
  ● 禁治産者 an incompetent.
- **きんちゃく** 巾着 a purse; a money pouch.
  ● 巾着切(すり) a pickpocket.
- **きんちゃく** 近着 ── 近着の 形 just [newly] arrived 《book》.
  ● 近着品 new [latest] arrivals.
- **きんちょ** 近著 one's recent [latest, newest] book [work].
- ***きんちょう** 緊張 图 (a) tension, (a) strain.

  〖使い分け〗**tension** 精神的な緊張・不安感や, 対人関係における緊張状態を表す.
  strain 心身に対する重圧や過労などによる緊張状態を表す.

  ① 〖～緊張〗● 国際間の緊張 international *tension*(s). ● 2 国間の緊張 the *tension*(s) [*strained*] relations] between the two countries. ▶ 私は極度の緊張に悩んでいた I felt [suffered from] excessive *tension* [*strain*].
  ② 〖緊張が〗● 労使間の緊張が高まっている *Tension* is building up [increasing, high, 《やや書》mounting] between labor and management. ▶ 音楽を聞くと緊張がほぐれる Music makes me *relax* [*relaxes* me]. ▶ 彼の冗談で室内の緊張がほぐれた His joke eased [relieved] the *tension* in the room.
  ③ 〖緊張〗● 緊張のあまり手が震えていた I was so *nervous* (that) my hands were shaking. ▶ リスニングテストが終わったとたん, 緊張の糸が切れた They felt extremely relieved [The *tension* 《in the classroom》 *was all gone*] the instant the listening comprehension test was over. ▶ 当時の私は毎日が緊張の連続でした I was under constant *stresses* of daily life.
  ④ 〖緊張を〗● 緊張を緩和する ease [(弱める) reduce, (ゆるめる) relax, (取り除く) relieve] the *tension*.
  ── 緊張した 形 tense; strained. ● 緊張した雰囲気 a *tense* atmosphere.
  ── 緊張する 動 be [get*, feel*] nervous [self-conscious, tense] (! nervous は神経質になって, self-conscious は人目が気になって, tense はぴんと張りつめて緊張すること. tense は人だけでなく顔など体の一部にも使う); tense (up); (聴衆の前などで) get stage fright. ● 筋肉を緊張させる tense one's muscles. ● 緊張して耳を傾ける (=耳を澄ませる) *strain* to hear. ▶ 彼が入って来ると私はかちかちに緊張した I *tensed up* [*got tense and nervous*] when he came in. ▶ その証人は非常に緊張していた The witness was very *nervous* [extremely tense, under extreme *tension*]. ▶ 彼がせりふをとちるなんてよっぽど緊張しているのだわ He must *have* intense *stage fright* because he's made a slip in his lines.

  〖翻訳のこころ〗私は埃っぽい丸善の中の空気が, その檸檬の周囲だけ変に緊張しているような気がした (梶井基次郎『檸檬』) I felt that the dusty air in Maruzen was unnaturally tense (particularly) around that lemon. (! (1)「状況・雰囲気が」緊張している」は tense. nervous は「(人が)緊張する」の意で, ここでは不適切. (2)「変に」は unnaturally (不自然に)と表す)

- **きんちょう** 謹聴 ── 謹聴する 動 listen attentively 《to》.
- **きんちょく** 謹直 ── 謹直な 形 (誠実な) conscientious; (正直な) upright; (慎重な) scrupulous.
- **きんてい** 欽定 ● 欽定憲法 the Imperial Constitution; a constitution granted by the Emperor [King]. ● 欽定訳聖書 the Authorized Version (of the Bible)(略 A.V.); the King James Version; the King James Bible.
- **きんてい** 謹呈 图〖表示〗With the compliment of the author. ; With good wishes.
  ── 謹呈する 動 present 《him *with* a book》.
  ● 謹呈本 a complimentary copy. (! a presen-

きんてき 金的 a bull's-eye.
●金的を射止める hit [score] a bull's-eye.
きんてんさい 禁転載 All rights reserved.
きんでんず 筋電図 an electromyogram /ilèktrou-máiougræm/ (略 EMG).
きんとう 均等 equality. (⇨平等) ●教育の機会均等 *equal* opportunity for education; *equality* of educational opportunity. (!) oppotunities と複数形も可) ●雇用機会均等法 *Equal* Employment Opportunities Law. ●利益を均等に分ける divide the profits *equally*; divide the profits into *equal* [*even*] shares.
●均等割り(税) a per capita tax. ●均等割りで課税する impose [put, levy] taxes *per capita* [*on a per capita basis*].
きんとう 近東 the Near East. ●近東の Near Eastern. ●近東諸国 the countries of *the Near East*; *Near Eastern* countries. (⇨極東)
ぎんなん 銀杏 a ginkgo nut.
*きんにく 筋肉 名 (a) muscle /mʌ́sl/. (!) 個々の筋肉は C); (特に腕・脚のたくましい)筋肉 /brɔ́:n/. ●筋肉たくましい腕 a *muscular* [a *brawny*] arm. ●腕の筋肉の発達 the development of arm *muscles*. ●筋肉を収縮させる contract one's *muscles*. ●筋肉をゆるめる[引き締める] relax [tighten] one's *muscles*. ▶毎日重い荷物を扱っているので筋肉がついてきた I'm getting *muscles*, handling heavy baggage every day. ▶その運動選手はたくましい筋肉をしている The athlete is very *muscular* [has well-developed *muscles*]. ▶筋肉は使えば使うほど発達する The more you use your *muscle*, the more it develops.
— 筋肉の 形 muscular; (筋骨たくましい) brawny.
●筋肉運動 muscular movement. ●筋肉質 muscularity. ●筋肉組織 the muscular tissue [system]. ●筋肉注射 an intramuscular injection. ●筋肉痛 muscular pain; (使い過ぎて痛い筋肉) sore muscles. ●筋肉労働 manual [physical] labor. ●筋肉労働者 a manual laborer [worker].
ぎんねず 銀鼠 (a) silver-gray.
きんねん 近年 in recent years; (最近) recently, lately. (⇨最近) ●近年にない暑い夏だ This is the hottest summer we've had *in recent years*. ▶近年急激な政治の変革が見られる *In recent years* [*Recently*] there have been radical changes in politics.
きんのう 金納 名 a cash payment. —— 金納する 動 pay*.
きんのう 勤王, 勤皇 loyalism; loyalty to the Emperor.
●勤王の志士 a loyalist.
ぎんのさじ 『銀の匙』 The Silver Spoon. (参考)中勘助の小説)
きんのたまご 金の卵 a very small number of promising young people; golden boys [girls] (, who are so talented and few that it is hard to employ them).
きんば 金歯 a gold tooth; (かぶせた) a tooth with a gold crown.
きんばえ 金蝿 『昆虫』a greenbottle fly.
きんぱく 金箔 (a sheet of) gold leaf [foil]. (!) foil は通常は薄くのばした金属. ●金箔をかぶせる[置く, はる] gild (it) with *gold leaf*.
きんぱく 緊迫 (a) tension. ●両国間の緊迫した関係 *tense* [*strained*] relations between the two countries. ▶国際情勢が緊迫してきた The interna-

tional situation has become *tense*.
きんぱつ 金髪 blond [fair, golden] hair. ●金髪の女[男] a *blond-haired* woman [man]; a *blond(e)* woman [a *blond* man]; a blonde [a blond]. (!) (1) 形容詞では男女とも blond を用いる傾向があるが, 名詞では男性に blond, 女性に blonde を用いる傾向がある. ただし発音はいずれも /blάnd/. (2) 金髪のほかに白い肌, 青い目の人であることも含意する.
ぎんぱつ 銀髪 silver hair. ●銀髪の紳士 a *silver-haired* gentleman.
ぎんばん 銀盤 『スケートリンク』an ice(-skating) rink.
●銀盤の女王 the queen on *the ice*.
きんぴ 金肥 (a) chemical fertilizer.
きんぴか 金ぴか (金色の輝き) gilded splendor; (クリスマスツリー用の) tinsel. ●金ぴかのライター a *glittering* lighter. ●金ぴかの衣装 *gaudy* clothes.
きんぴらごぼう 金平牛蒡 *kimpira(gobo)*; (説明的に) strings or thin-shavings of burdock root, fried and boiled down in sugar and soy sauce.
きんぴん 金品 money and (valuable) goods. ●金品を贈与する present (him) with *money* and *other valuables*. ●金品を奪う rob (him) of (his) *money and goods*.
きんぶち 金縁 ●金縁の本 a *gilt-edged* book; a book with *gilt edges*. ●金縁の眼鏡をかけている wear *gold-rimmed* glasses.
きんぶん 均分 名 (an) equal division.
—— 均分する 動 divide (...) equally 《among》.
●均分相続 an equal division of an inheritance.
*きんべん 勤勉 名 diligence; 《やや書》industry. ●勤勉と倹約 *industry* and thrift.
—— 勤勉な 形 hardworking; (特定のことに) diligent; (性格的に) industrious. ▶日本人は勤勉です The Japanese are a *hardworking* [an *industrious*] people./Japanese people work very hard. ▶彼は職務に勤勉だ He is *diligent* in his duties.
きんぺん 近辺 名 the neighborhood. (⇨近く, 辺(た)り❶) ●駅の近辺に住む live *in the neighborhood* of the station; live *near* the railroad (米) [railway (英)] station.
—— 近辺の 形 neighboring.
きんぽうげ 金鳳花 『植物』a buttercup.
きんぼし 金星 ●金星をあげる『相撲』gain [score] a *victory* over a *yokozuna* by a *maegashira*; (大きな勝利) win a *glorious* victory.
ぎんまく 銀幕 (スクリーン) a screen; (映画) a movie, a film. ●銀幕のスター a star of *screen* [the *silver screen*]; a movie [a film] star.
ぎんまんか 銀満家 a rich person. (⇨金持ち)
ぎんみ 吟味 名 (よく調べること) (a) close examination; (精選) careful selection.
—— 吟味する 動 examine (it) closely; select (it) carefully. ●吟味した品 a *choice* [a *carefully selected*] article. ●言葉を吟味する *weigh* one's words.
きんみつ 緊密 —— 緊密な 形 close. (⇨密接) ▶日米の間には緊密な関係がある There is a *close* connection between the U.S. and Japan.
きんみゃく 金脈 a vein of gold; (資金を出してくれる人) a financial supporter [backer].
きんみらい 近未来 《in》the near [immediate] future.
きんむ 勤務 名 『仕事』work; 『公務』service; 『職場』duties. (⇨勤め, 務め)
① 【～勤務】●夜間勤務 night *duty*. (⇨夜勤) ●ロンドン支店勤務を命ぜられる be told to *work* in [《やや書》be assigned to (*work* in)] the London

branch office.
② 【勤務〜】・勤務成績がよい show good *work* performance. ・勤務中である be *at work* [*on duty, on the job*]. (⇨仕事)［第1文例］・勤務時間外である be *off duty*. ・積極的な勤務態度であるhave a positive attitude to one's work. ・私は会社勤務より在宅勤務の方がいいなと思います I'd prefer to *telecommute* [*telework*] rather than *work at an office*. ・吉田氏は勤務熱心であった Mr. Yoshida was diligent in［献身的で］devoted to］*his work*.
会話「勤務時間について教えていただけますか」「はい，1日の勤務時間は9時から5時までで，12時から昼休みが1時間あります」"Could you tell me about the *work* schedule?" "Yes. The *working hours* (for the day) are from 9 to 5, with a one-hour lunch break at noon."
③【勤務を[に, を]】・勤務を怠る neglect one's *duties*. ・勤務につく［つける］come [put《him》] *on duty*. ・今日は勤務がない I'm not working today./(非番である) I'm *off duty* today. ・美穂は出産後勤務に戻った Miho *resumed her work* after the baby was born.
── 勤務する 動 work.（⇨勤める）・1日8時間勤務する *work* (for) eight hours a day; *work* [*have*] an eight-hour *day*. ・彼はその会社に30年間勤務した He *has worked for* the company for thirty years./He *has completed* his thirty years' *service with* the company. (! 後の言い方は「勤め上げた」ぐらいの意)
・勤務医 a hospital doctor. ・勤務先 one's office; one's place of work. ・勤務時間 working [office, business] hours. (! 後の2つは「営業時間」の意) ・勤務条件 working conditions.
・勤務日数 working days. ・勤務表（任務当番表）［軍隊］a duty roster;（勤務記録）a work log;（出勤簿）an attendance. ・勤務評定 an [the] efficiency rating.

きんむく 金無垢 （純金）a pure [solid] gold.

きんむりょくしょう 筋無力症 〖医学〗myasthenia /màiəsθíːniə/.

きんめだい 金目鯛〖魚介〗an alfonsino;（説明的に）a bright-red fish with golden goggle eyes.

きんもくせい 金木犀 〖植物〗a fragrant orange-colored olive.

きんもつ 禁物 （してはならないとされている言動）(a) taboo《*against*》(! ⓒのとき 複 〜s). ・食事中にそういう話は禁物だ That kind of topic is (a) *taboo* [a *taboo subject*] at (the) table./You should never talk about that subject during a meal. ・この部屋ではたばこは禁物です Smoking *is forbidden* [*is prohibited*;（許可されていない）*is not permitted*] in this room. ・あの男には油断禁物だ（注意をしろ）Be careful of that man./（厳重に警戒しろ）Keep a close watch [eye] on that man.

きんもんきょう 金門橋 the Golden Gate Bridge.

きんゆ 禁輸 图 an embargo. ・石油禁輸 an oil *embargo*.
── 禁輸(に)する 動 ・小麦を禁輸にする *embargo* [put an *embargo on*] wheat exports. ・彼らは石油を禁輸した They *embargoed* oil shipments to the country.

＊**きんゆう** 金融 （財務, 財政）finance;（金）money.
・住宅金融公庫 the Housing *Loan* Corporation. ・金融引き締め［緩和］政策 a *tight-money* [an *easy-money*] policy. ・金融(=金融市場)を引き締め[緩め]る tighten [ease] the *money* market.
▶ 金融がひっぱくしている *Money* is tight (↔slack). ▶ 金融市場が徐々に引き締まって［緩んで］きた The *money market* has gradually tightened [eased] up.
・金融界 the financial world; financial circles. ・金融機関 a financial [a banking] institution;（会社）a financial company. ・金融業者（金貸し）a moneylender (! 時にけなして「高利貸し」の意にもなる);（大金を扱う）a financier. ・金融恐慌 a financial panic [crisis]. ・金融市場 the money [financial] market. ・金融資本 financial [banking] capital. ・金融庁 the Financial Services Agency.

ぎんゆうしじん 吟遊詩人 a minstrel; a troubadour /trúːbədɔːr/.

＊**きんよう(び)** 金曜(日) Friday《略 Fri.》. (⇨日曜(日))
［参考］イスラム教はモスクへ礼拝に行く日」

きんよく 禁欲 abstinence, （特に, 性欲の）《書》continence;〖宗教的立場からの〗asceticism. ・禁欲生活をする practice *abstinence* [*asceticism*]; lead an *ascetic*〖書〗a *continent*] life.
・禁欲主義 asceticism. ・禁欲主義者 an ascetic /əsétik/, （やや書）a stoic.

きんらい 近来 （最近）recently, lately (⇨最近);（このごろ）these days, nowadays. (⇨この頃(3)) ・近年まれにみる豊作だ It's the richest harvest (that) we've had *in recent years*.

きんり 金利 （利率）the rate of interest, the interest rate;（利子）interest. ・高[低]金利 high [low] *interest rates*. ・金利を上[下]げる raise [lower] *interest rates*. ・5パーセントの金利で銀行から金を借りる borrow money from a bank at 5 percent *interest*. ▶ このローンの金利は年5パーセントです The *(rate of) interest on* [x*in*] this loan is 5 percent a year.

きんりょう 禁猟 the prohibition of hunting.
・禁猟区 a preserve. ・禁猟期 the closed [《英》close] season in hunting.

きんりょう 禁漁 the prohibition of fishing.
・禁漁区 a preserve; fishing grounds closed to fishermen. ・禁漁期 the closed [《英》close] season in fishing.

きんりょく 筋力 muscular strength. ・筋力トレーニングをする(=筋肉を発達させる運動をする) get [《主に英》take] exercise to develop one's *muscles* /mʌ́slz/.

きんりん 近隣 图 neighborhood;《書》(a) vicinity.
── 近隣(の) 形 neighboring. ・秋田市とその近隣地域 Akita City and its *neighboring areas* [*its vicinities*].
・近隣諸国 neighboring countries.

ぎんりん 銀輪 （自転車）a bicycle.

ぎんりん 銀鱗 （銀色のうろこ）a silvery scale;（魚）a fish.

きんるい 菌類 fungus（複 fungi /fʌ́ŋɡai/, 〜es）.
・菌学 mycology.

きんれい 禁令 a prohibition; a ban;《書》an interdict. (⇨禁止) ・日曜営業禁令 a *prohibition on* Sunday trading.

きんれんか 金蓮花 〖植物〗a nasturtium /næstə́ːrʃəm/.

きんろう 勤労 work;〖肉体労働〗labor;〖勤め〗service. ・勤労意欲 the [one's] will to work [xof working]. ・勤労階級 the working class(es).
・勤労感謝の日 Labor Thanksgiving Day. ・勤労者 a worker. ・勤労所得 (an) earned income. ・勤労奉仕 labor service.

く

く 九 nine; 〖9番目の〗the ninth. (⇨三)

く 区 〖行政区画〗a ward; 〖特別に設けられた〗a zone; 〖選挙区〗a constituency; 〖駅伝の〗a leg. ●中央区 Chuo Ward. (❗ローマ字書きの Chuo-ku が手紙の住所などでは普通が、しばしば日常語としても用いられる) ●駐車禁止区 a no-parking zone. ●東京3区 the 3rd constituency of Tokyo. ●第3区5キロを走る run the 5 km third leg.
●区議会 the ward assembly. ●区議会議員 a member of the ward assembly. ●区役所 a ward office.

く 句 〖語の集まり〗a phrase; 〖表現〗an expression; 〖引用の1節〗a passage; 〖俳句〗a haiku 〖単・複同形〗. ●名詞句 a noun phrase. ●一句よむ compose a haiku.

く 苦 〖心配〗worry; 〖苦痛〗pain 〖「骨折り」の意では複数形で〗; 〖困難〗(a) difficulty. ▶そんなことを苦にするな Don't worry about [be anxious about] it./(のん気に構えろ) Take it easy. ▶彼は苦もなくその数学の問題を解いた He solved the math problem without (any) difficulty [(やすやすと) easily, with ease]./He had no difficulty (in) solving the math problem. (❗in は省略されるのが普通) ▶彼は雪の中を歩くのを苦にしない(=何とも思わない) He thinks nothing [little] of walking in the snow. ▶試験の結果が時々苦になる The result of the exam sometimes makes me worry [(心の重荷になる)(やや書) weighs (heavily) on my mind]. (❗後の方は単に ... weighs on me も可)
●苦あれば楽あり 《ことわざ》Every cloud has a silver lining. (❗どんな雲にも銀色の裏がある)
●苦は楽の種 《ことわざ》No pleasure without pain./《ことわざ》No pains, no gains.

ぐ 具 ❶〖手段〗a means. (⇨政争)
❷〖料理に入れる実〗ingredients. (❗ある料理に使う、調味料も含めたすべての材料) ▶みそ汁の具に大根を入れる put radish in miso soup. ▶(ご飯に具をまぜる mix in other ingredients.

ぐ 愚 stupidity; 〖書〗folly. (❗ともに「愚行」の意では Ⓒ)
●愚にもつかない absurd; ridiculous. ●愚にもつかないことを言う talk nonsense. ▶詩なくて愚にもつかない無益なものだと彼は言う He says poetry is nothing but a useless thing.
●愚の骨頂 ▶こんな嵐に出かけるなんて愚の骨頂だ It is the height of stupidity [folly] to go out in a storm like this.

ぐあい 具合 ❶〖調子, 状態〗(a) condition. (⇨調子 ❶, 加減 ❶) ●具合=(健康状態)がよい〖悪い〗 be in good [bad] condition; be in good [bad] health; feel well [unwell]. ●肉の焼け具合を見る see how well the meat is done. ▶母の具合はますます悪くなった My mother's condition got worse and worse. ▶あいにく母がひどく具合が悪いんです(=重病です) My mother's very sick [(主に英) ill], I'm afraid. ▶あなた、このごろ顔色がよくないわ。どこか具合が悪いんじゃないの You look pale these days, darling. Is there something wrong [the matter] with you? (❗疑問文・否定文・条件文では通例 anything を用いるが、このように「具合が悪そうだ」という前提で yes の答えを予想する場合は something を用い

る) ▶腹具合が悪い Something is wrong [the matter] with my stomach./My stomach is upset./I have an upset stomach. ▶バスで旅行するといつも胃の具合が悪くなるよね Bus journeys always upset my stomach. ▶この機械は具合が悪い This machine does not work [run] well. ▶どんな具合でしたか(商談など) How did it go? ▶どんな具合にいっていますか How are things going on?/How's everything? ▶万事具合よくいっている Everything is going well [moving smoothly, all right].
〖会話〗「今日は体の具合はどうですか」「ずっとよくなりました」 "How do you feel [are you feeling] today?" "I feel [I'm feeling] much better, thank you."
〖会話〗「あした試験なんだ」「どんな具合だったか教えてね」 "It's my exam tomorrow./I have an exam tomorrow." "Let me know how you get on (with it)." (❗スケジュール的に確定した事柄については現在形を用いるのが普通)
❷〖都合〗convenience. (⇨都合 ❶, ❸) ●具合のよい〖悪い〗convenient [inconvenient] 《for, to》; (運のよい〖悪い〗) fortunate [unfortunate]. ▶今日は別の約束があって具合が悪い Today is inconvenient (for me) [It is inconvenient (for me) today, ×I am inconvenient today] because I have another appointment. ▶そこへ着くとちょうどいい具合にバスが発車するところだった Fortunately, the bus was just going to leave when I got there.
❸〖方法〗a way, a manner.
〖会話〗「これはどんな具合にすればいいの」「こんな具合にさ」 "How should I do this?" "(Do it) like this [(in) this way]." (❗in も省略可 (⇨調子 ❸)

グアテマラ 〖国名〗Guatemala /gwàːtəmάːlə/; (公式名) the Republic of Guatemala; (首都 Guatemala City) ●グアテマラ人 a Guatemalan. ●グアテマラ(人)の Guatemalan.

クアハウス 〖<ドイツ語〗〖温泉利用施設〗a hot-spring (health) resort, a health spa.

グアム 〖米国領の島〗Guam /ɡwάːm/.

クアラルンプール 〖マレーシアの首都〗Kuala Lumpur /kwάːlə lumpύər/.

くい 杭 a stake; (支え・掲示用などの) a post; (建造物の基礎として打ち込む) 〖建築〗a pile, (集合的) piling. ▶杭を打つ〖抜く〗drive [pull up] a stake. ●杭を立てる put up a post. ▶出る杭は打たれる (⇨出る〖成句〗)
●杭打ち機 a pile driver. ●杭打ち〖工事〗〖建築〗piling; pile driving.

くい 悔い regrets; repentance. (⇨悔いる) ▶悔いはない I have no regrets. ▶悔いを残すよ You'll regret later. ▶悔いのない学生生活を！Get the most out of your campus life!

くいあう 食い合う ▶候補者は互いに票を食い合っている The candidates are stealing each other's votes. ▶2頭のトラが獲物を食い合っていた(=取り合ってけんかしていた) The two tigers were fighting over their prey.

くいあげ 食い上げ ▶そんなことをしたら飯の食い上げになるぞ Doing such a thing will cost you your job [(生計) living]. (⇨飯)

くいあらす 食い荒らす ●イノシシに食い荒らされた(=食べ尽くされ荒らされた)作物 the crops *eaten up* and *spoiled* by wild boars. ●腹の減った少年たちはハンバーガーを食い荒らした The hungry boys *devoured* [(がつがつ食べる) *wolfed down*] their hamburgers. ●彼は対立候補の地盤を食い荒らした He *stole* [(食い込んだ) *cut into*] his opponent's support.

くいあらためる 悔い改める (行動を改める) mend one's ways, turn over a new leaf; (深く心に記す)《書》repent《one's bad conduct, *of* one's sin》.

くいあわせ 食い合わせ ●うなぎと梅干しは食い合わせが悪い When you eat eels and pickled plums together, you will have a harmful effect./ Eating eels and pickled plums together will make you feel sick.

くいいじ 食い意地 greediness,《書》gluttony. ●食い意地の張った greedy, gluttonous.

くいいる 食い入る ●彼は彼女の顔を食い入るように(=じっと)見つめた He *stared* her *in the face*./He gazed at her face *with staring eyes*. ●その子はおりの中のトラを食い入るように見ていた The child *was looking intently* at a tiger in the cage.

クイーン a queen. (⇨女王) ●ハートのクイーン the *queen* of hearts. ●クイーンサイズのベッド[シーツ; 毛布] a *queen*-size bed. (！(1) そのベッド用日のサイズには large-sized [《婉曲的》《主に米》plus size, queen-sized] women's clothes. ●クイーンズイングリッシュ Queen's English. (！男性が王位にある時には King's English)

くいき 区域 [用途を持った] a zone; [行政上の] a district; [特定の人々が住む] a quarter; [漠然とした] an area; [大きな地域の一部] a section; [警官の担当区域] a (policeman's) beat; [郵便の配達区域] (配達人の)《米》a (delivery) route,《英》a (postman's) round; (郵便局内勤の) a postal district. ●駐車禁止区域 a no-parking *zone*. ●住宅区域 a residential *quarter* [*section, area, district*].

くいきる 食い切る [歯でかみ切る] cut (it) off with one's teeth; bite (it) off; [全部食べる] eat up. ●私の家族ではこれだけの食べ物はとても食い切れない My family simply can't *eat up* [《書》*consume*] all this food.

ぐいぐい ❶ [ぐいぐい人をひきつけるような] magnetic,《やや書》compelling; (強い力を及ぼす) forceful. ●この小説は人をぐいぐい引っ張っていく This novel is *compelling*. ●彼はぐいぐい人をひきつける (人柄を持っている) He has a *magnetic* personality.
❷ [ぐいぐい引っ張る] ●ロープをぐいぐい引っ張る *pull* a rope *quickly and forcefully*.
❸ [ぐいぐい飲む] ●彼はビールを大ジョッキでぐいぐい飲んだ He *gulped down* beer from a big mug.

くいけ 食い気 (食欲) (an) appetite.

くいこむ 食い込む [ひもなどが] cut* into ...; [事が予定時間を越えて] run* over (*into*), stretch on (*into*); [蓄えなどを消耗する] eat* into .... ●わなはわがウサギの足に食い込んでいった The snare *was cutting into* the foot of a struggling rabbit. ●彼の英語の授業はしばしば休み時間に食い込む His English class often *runs over* [*stretches on*] *into* the break time. ●彼は 100 メートル競走で 3 位までには食い込む(=入る)だろう He will *enter* one of the first three places in the 100-meter dash. ●賠償金の支払いは私の貯金を食い込んだ The compensation *has eaten into* my savings.

くいさがる 食い下がる [しがみつく] hang* [hold*] on to ...; [要求してねばる] hold out for .... ●質問をして食い下がる(=次々と質問して困らす) *harass* 《him》with (persistent) questions.

くいしばる 食いしばる ⇒歯を食いしばる(⇨歯 [成句])

くいしろ 食い代 (⇨⑩ 食費)

くいしんぼう 食いしん坊 (食い意地の張っている人) a glutton.

クイズ a quiz (劔 ~zes), a quiz game. ●クイズ番組 a quiz prógram [shów]. ●クイズ番組の司会者 a quizmaster.《英》a quéstion màster. ●クイズ番組の解答者 a contestant [a competitor] (*on a quiz show*); a panelist. ●彼はクイズ番組に出た He took part in a *quiz* show.

くいぞめ 食い初め the wéaning cèremony; (説明的に) a ceremony to celebrate a baby's eating rice for the first time and wish for its growth.

くいだおれ 食い倒れ ●食い倒れになる ruin oneself by wasting too much on [by one's extravagance in] food; (食べ過ぎて破産する) eat oneself bankrupt;《話》eat oneself out of house and home. ●京の着倒れ大阪の食い倒れ(⇨着倒れ)

くいだめ 食い溜め ── 食い溜めする 動 stuff oneself with food to keep one going for some time. (！ keep one going は「人の生活を続けさせる」の意)

くいたりない 食い足りない (十分食べていない) have* not had enough; (もの足りない) be not satisfied《with》.

くいちがい 食い違い ●彼らの間に意見の食い違いは認められなかった We couldn't see any *difference* of opinion between them. ●彼の話には 2,3 食い違い(=矛盾点)があった We found some *contradictions* [*inconsistencies*] in what he said. (！前の方は内容の対立を,後の方は一貫性の欠如を示す)

くいちがう 食い違う [異なる] be different [differ]《*from*》(！前の方が口語的); [衝突する] clash《*with*》; [矛盾する] conflict《*with*》, contradict. ●食い違う証言 *conflicting* evidence. ●私は彼と意見が食い違っている I *am different* [*differ*] *from* him in opinion./My opinion *is different from* [*clashes with*] his. ●田中さんの説明と私の説明は食い違った Mr. Tanaka's explanation *contradicted* [*conflicted with*, ×contradicted with] my explanation.

くいちぎる 食いちぎる bite* ... off [*away*].

くいちらす 食い散らす ❶ [食べ物を] ●子供たちはお菓子の果物だのを食い散らしていた The children *left* their cakes and fruits *in a mess*.
❷ [物事を] ●あの人はあれこれ食い散らすばかりでどれもものにならない He *has a go at* this and that, and nothing will be a success.

くいつく 食い付く bite* 《*at*》; (とびつく) jump 《at a chance [an offer]》. ●魚が餌(え)に食いついた A fish *bit at* the bait.

クイックモーション (a) quick motion. (！動作の意では C, 映写技法の意では U) ●クイックモーションで投球する deliver a ball with a *quick*(*-pitch*) *motion*; be quick to the plate. ●種の発芽の様子をクイックモーションで見てみましょう Let's watch the seeds sprouting in *quick* [*fast*] *motion*.

くいつなぐ 食いつなぐ [細々と暮らす] make a poor [a scanty, a meager] living, live on one's small income. ●私はパートをやってやっと食いつないでいる I *scrape a living* by working part-time. ●今ある食料であと 1 週間食いつながねばならない We'll just have to *stretch* the food *out* (for) another week.

くいつぶす 食い潰す ●財産を食いつぶす(=使い果たす) *run through* one's fortune. ●貯金を食いつぶしてい

くいつめる 食い詰める （生活に困る）be unable to make a living; (落ちぶれる) be down-and-out.

くいで 食いで (⇨食べで)

ぐいと ▶彼はぼくのネクタイをぐいっと引っ張った He *jerked* my tie./He *pulled* my tie *with a (violent) jerk.* ▶男はコップ半分の冷や酒をぐいとあおった The man *gulped down* a half glassful of cold *sake.*

くいどうらく 食い道楽 (美食主義) gourmandism /gu*a*rmǽ:ndizm/; (美食家) (軽蔑的に) a gourmánd; (食通) a gourmet /gu*a*rméi/.

くいとめる 食い止める 〖止める, 抑える〗check; 〖防ぐ〗prevent. ●防ぐ ▶敵の攻撃を食い止める *check* [(撃退する) *fight off*] the enemy. ●延焼を食い止める *check* [*stop*] the spread of a fire. ●被害[出費]を最小限に食い止める(=少なくする) *reduce* the damage (the expenses) to a minimum.

くいな 水鶏 〖鳥〗a water rail.

くいにげ 食い逃げ ― 食い逃げする 動 get away 《*from* a restaurant》, skip out 《*on* a restaurant》without paying the bill; (食事のあとすぐに帰る) eat and run.

くいのばす 食い延ばす make food last longer. ▶2日分の食料をもう 2, 3 日食い延ばす We *make* the food for two days *last* a few more days *longer*.

ぐいのみ ぐい飲み ❶〖底の深い大きめの杯〗an extra-large *sake* cup. ❷〖一息に飲むこと〗▶酒を茶碗でぐい飲みする *drink up sake* in a cup *at one gulp*.

くいはぐれる 食いはぐれる (食いそこなう) miss out on 《one's favorite ice cream》; (生活できない) be unable to make a living. ▶彼女は忙しくてよく昼飯を食いはぐれている She is often *too busy to eat* lunch./She *misses* lunch very often because she's busy. ▶彼は手に職があるから食いはぐれることはない He'll get along [by] because he've got skill. (❗get along [by] は「十分ではないが何とかやっていく」の意)

くいぶち 食い扶持 the cost of one's board. ●給料から食いぶちを入れる pay for *one's board* out of one's paycheck. ●商売をして食いぶちを稼ぐ(=生計を立てる) *earn* one's *living* by trade.

くいほうだい 食い放題 (⇨食べ放題)

くいもの 食い物 〖食べ物〗food; 〖犠牲に〗prey. ▶彼女は暴力団のやくざの食い物にされた She *fell prey* [*victim*] *to* the gangsters. ▶詐欺師は老女を食い物にした The swindler *preyed on* the old woman.

くいる 悔いる regret (-tt-); be [feel] sorry. (⇨後悔)

クインテット 〖五重奏団〗〖音楽〗a quintet(te).

くう 食う ❶〖食物などを〗eat, have*, take*. (⇨食) ●食い逃げする (⇨食い逃げ)

❷〖動物が食う〗eat*; feed* on 《grass》 (❗「...を常食とする」の意でも用いられる; (かみつく) bite*. ▶ライオンがシマウマを食った A lion *ate* [(むさぼり食う) (やや書) *devoured*] the zebra. ▶蚊に食われた I *was bitten* by a mosquito. ▶魚が(餌に)食った A fish *took* a bite. ▶犬が肉片を食った(=食いちぎった) The dog *bit off* a piece of meat.

❸〖生活する〗live 《*on*》; (生計を立てる) earn [make*] a living. ●わずかな収入で食っていく *live* [(なんとか) *get by*] *on* a small income. ●食っていけるだけの金を稼ぐ make enough money [earn enough] to *live on*. ▶彼はタクシーの運転手をして食っている He *earns* [*makes*] *a living* as a taxi driver [by driving a taxi].

❹〖消費する〗〈書〉consume /kənsjú:m/. ●時間をひどく食う仕事 a time-*consuming* job. ▶私の車はよくガソリンを食う My car *uses* [*burns*] a lot of gas./〈話〉My car *guzzles* gas like crazy. (❗My car is a gas-*guzzler*. ●食う/My car *eats up* gas. ●ぜいたくな暮らしで彼は遺産を食いつぶしている His extravagant life style *is eating up* [*squandering*] his inheritance.

❺〖好ましくないことを身にうける〗●一杯食わされる be cheated, be taken in. ●待ちぼうけを食う be kept waiting. ●一喝を食う be bawled out. ●その事件に巻きぞえを食う get involved in the case.

❻〖その他の表現〗●人を食った態度 an insolent [a haughty] attitude. ●何食わぬ顔 an innocent [(やや書) a nonchalant] look. ●その手は食わない You can't *fool* me./I won't *fall for* that. ▶彼は失業して以来、食うや食わずの生活をしている He has been living from hand to mouth since he lost his job.

● **食うか食われるか** ●食うか食われるかの企業社会 the *dog-eat-dog* world of business. ▶食うか食われるか二つに一つだった。だから彼をやっつけざるを得なかった It was him or me, so I let him have it.

くう 空 (空間) space; (空中) the air. ●空を見つめる stare into *space*. ●空を切って飛ぶ fly through *the air*.

● **空に帰する** ▶我々の計画はすべて空に帰した(=むだになった) Our plans came to naught [(役に立たなかった) went for nothing].

● 空対空ミサイル 〖軍事〗an air-to-air missile.

くう (じゃんけんの石) (show) (a) rock. (⇨じゃんけん)

くうい 空位 (a) vacancy; a vacant post (王位) throne]. ●空位になる fall *vacant*.

ぐうい 寓意 (寓意物語) an allegory, a moral; (隠された意味) a hidden meaning.

● 寓意小説 an allegorical story; an allegory; (たとえ話) a parable.

くういき 空域 airplace. ●管制空域 controlled airspace. ●羽田空域 Haneda airplace.

クウェート 〖国名〗Kuwait; (公式名) the State of Kuwait. (首都 Kuwait) ●クウェート人 a Kuwaiti. ●クウェート(人)の Kuwaiti.

*くうかん 空間 名 space; 〖人・物などの占める場所・余地〗room. ●時間と空間 time and *space*.

― 空間の, 空間的な spatial.

● 空間芸術 a plastic art; a visual art.

くうかんち 空閑地 unused [vacant] land. (⇨〖国〗空閑地)

*くうき 空気 ❶〖気体〗air; (特定の場所の) an átmosphère; (大気) the air, the atmosphere.

①《～空気, 空気～》●乾いた[湿った, よどんだ, さわやかな]空気 dry [damp; stale; crisp] *air*; a dry [a damp; a stale; a crisp] *atmosphere*. ●外の空気 the outside [outdoor] *air*. (⇨外気) ●汚染された都会の空気 the polluted *air* [*atmosphere*] of the city. ●空気中の[に] in the air.

②〖空気は[が]〗●空気は冷たい The *air* is cold. ▶山の空気はおいしい[澄んでさわやかだ] Mountain *air* smells good [is pure and crisp]. ●この部屋の空気は悪い The *air* is bad [stale] in this room./(風通しが悪い) This room is stuffy. ▶ここは空気が希薄なので息がしにくい It is difficult to breathe here because the *atmosphere* is thin. ▶タイヤの空気が抜けているよ You've got a flat tire. ▶空気は洞窟の入り口から流れ込んでくる The *air* flows in through the mouth of the cave.

③〖空気を〗●部屋の空気を入れ換える *air* the room. ●空気を吸う breathe [inhale] *air*. ●新鮮な空気を胸いっぱい吸う take a deep breath of fresh *air*. ●タイヤに空気を入れる put *air* into a tire; pump up a tire. ●気球に空気を送り込む

くうきょ

send [pump] *air* into a balloon. ▶窓を開けて空気を入れなさい Open the windows to let in some *air*.

❷［雰囲気］an átmosphère. ●重苦しい空気 a depressive *atmosphere*. ●彼は自由な空気の中で育った He was brought up in an *atmosphere* of freedom. ▶事故の第一報が入ると事務所の空気が張り詰めた The *atmosphere* of the office became tense right after the first report of the accident.

●空気圧 áir ［(タイヤの) tíre］prèssure. ▶君の左のタイヤの空気圧が少し弱いようだ Your left tire looks a little low. ●空気感染 airborne infection. ●空気銃 an áir gùn. ●空気清浄器 an áir pùrifier. ●空気伝搬音 airborne sound. ●空気調節 air conditioning. ●空気調節装置 an áir condìtioner. ●空気ポンプ an áir pùmp. ●空気枕 an áir cùshion [pillow].

くうきょ 空虚 ⦿ emptiness.
—— 空虚な ⦿ (むなしい) empty; (うつろな) vacant; (何もない) 《書》 void. ●空虚な人生 an *empty* life. ●空虚な笑い a *vacant* smile. ●空虚感を覚える feel *empty*.

|翻訳のこころ| 友達が学校へ出てしまったあとの空虚な空気の中に取り残された (梶井基次郎『檸檬』) After all my friends left for school, I found myself alone in the hollow [empty] surroundings. (❗(1)「空虚な空気」は hollow [empty] surroundings (周囲に何もない環境)と表す. (2)「ぽつねんと」のような擬態語に相当する語は英語にはない. alone は「一人ぼっち, ただ一人」の意を含む)

ぐうきょ 寓居 ⦿ a temporary abode [residence].
—— 寓居する ⦿ (割れ目) ●上野に寓居する live [reside] *temporarily* in Ueno.

くうくう ▶ハトがくうくうと鳴いている A pigeon *is cooing*.

ぐうぐう ▶彼女はぐうぐう(=ぐっすり)寝ている She is *fast* [*sound*] asleep. ▶空腹になるとぐうぐうと腹が鳴るんだ My stomach *growls* [*rumbles*] when I'm hungry. ▶彼はぐうぐういびきをかいて寝る He snores *loudly* [*noisily*, *heavily*]. (参考 漫画などでは ZZZで表すことが多い)

くうぐん 空軍 the áir fòrce. (❗単・複両扱い. 一国の空軍の総称は the A- F-)
●空軍基地 an áir bàse. ●空軍力 áir pòwer.

くうげき 空隙 (すき間) an opening, a gap; (空所) a vacant space; (割れ目) a crevice. ●政治の空隙を埋める fill up [ふさぐ) stop] a *gap* [a *vacancy*] in politics.

くうけん 空拳 (素手) bare [empty] hands. ●徒手空拳で (⇨徒手空拳)

くうげん 空言 (根拠のないうわさ) groundless rumors; 《話》 lies.

***くうこう** 空港 an airport; an airfield (❗*airport* はど設備が整っていない飛行場). ●成田空港 Narita *Airport*. (❗固有名詞の場合は無冠詞). ●空港に着陸する［から飛び立つ］ land at [take off from] an *airport*.
●空港施設 áirport fàcilities. ●空港ターミナル an áir tèrminal.

ぐうさく 偶作 (即興の) an impromptu; [偶然に作られた] an occasional] piece of work.

くうさつ 空撮 aerial photography.

くうし 空士 ●空士長 a senior airman.

ぐうじ 宮司 the chief priest of a Shinto shrine.

くうしゃ 空車 an empty taxi [《主に米》cab]. ●空車《タクシーの掲示》*Vacant*./《英》*For hire*. ▶ほら, 空車だ Look, there's an *empty taxi* coming ［、*there comes an empty ╱ cab*］.

くうしゅう 空襲 ⦿ ●空襲を受ける suffer an *air raid*; be bombed. ●空襲警報を発令する issue an *air-raid* alarm [warning].
—— 空襲する ⦿ make an air strike [bombing] 《*on*, *upon*》; bomb.

くうしょ 空所 a blank. ▶空所を適切な語で埋めなさい Fill in the *blanks* with the right words.

くうしょう 空将 a general; a lieutenant general.
●空将補 a major general.

ぐうすう 偶数 an even (↔ an odd) number. ●偶数ページ an *even* page.

グーズベリー 〖植物〗 a gooseberry.

ぐうする 遇する 〖［待遇する〗 treat; ［もてなす] entertain.

くうせき 空席 a vacant [an empty] seat; (職・地位などの) a vacancy. ▶これら二つの席が空席になっている These two seats are *vacant* [*free*, *empty*]. ▶本校には教員の空席はありません There are no *vacancies* [*openings*] for teachers at our school.

会話 「香港行きの385便の席はありますか」「はい, 一つ空席がございます」"Can you get me a seat on flight 385 to Hong Kong?" "Yes, we have a *seat available*."

くうぜん 空前 —— 空前の ⦿ (前例のない)《やや書》unprecedented; all-time (❗後の語は限定的に使い, 形容詞を伴うことがある); (比類のない) incomparable, 《書》unparalleled; (記録的な) record; (記録破りの) record-breaking. ●空前のヒット an *unprecedented* [an *all-time*] hit. ▶街は空前の人出だった There was an *incomparably* [*unprecedentedly*] large number of people on the streets./There was a *record* number of people on the streets. ▶その劇は空前の客入りだった The play drew *record* crowds.
●空前絶後 ●空前絶後の大事業 the greatest enterprise which has ever been made and probably will never be attempted.

:**ぐうぜん** 偶然 ⦿ (a) chance; 〖偶然の出来事〗 an accident; 〖偶然の一致〗 a coíncidence. ▶彼のアメリカ発見はまったく(ほんの)偶然だった His discovery of America was a sheer [a mere] *chance*./His discovery of America was quite an *accident*. (❗強調構文を用いて It was *by* sheer *chance* [*quite by chance*] that he discovered America. のようにもいえる (⇨副)) ▶2人が同じバスに乗り合わせたのは単なる偶然(の一致)だった It was just [*quite*] a *coincidence* that the two were on the same bus. (❗It was sheer [*pure*] *coincidence* that … ともいえる)/By sheer *coincidence*, the two were on the same bus.

会話 「今夜そのコンサートへ行くんだ」「私もよ. 偶然ね」"I'm going to go to the concert tonight." "So am I [《話》Me, too]. What a *coincidence*!"

—— 偶然の ⦿ àccidental; chance; casual. (❗以上3語のうち叙述的にも用いられるのは accidental のみ) ●偶然の死 *accidental* death. ●偶然の出会い an *accidental* [a *chance*, a *casual*] meeting. ▶彼らの出会いは偶然だった Their meeting was *accidental* 〖×*chance*, ×*casual*〗.

—— 偶然(に) by chance; accidentally, by accident. ▶私は京都で偶然彼女に出会った I met her in Kyoto *by chance* [*accident*]./I *happened* [《話》*chanced*] to meet her in Kyoto./《話》I *ran into* [*came across*] her in Kyoto. ▶彼は通りで偶然財布を見つけた He *found* a wallet on the street *by*

chance [*accident*]. (!)偶然性を含み持つ動詞は happen とともにしか用いないので ×He happened to find .... は不可)

くうそ 空疎 ── 空疎な 形 (実質のない) empty; of little substance; unsubstantial. ●空疎な議論 an *empty* argument; an argument of *little substance*.

＊くうそう 空想 名 [気まぐれな]〈やや書〉(a) fancy;[途方もない] (a) fantasy ((!)fancy より現実離れした空想); [夢見るような] a daydream; (想像) (an) imagination. ▶彼は空想力が豊かだ He has a lively *imagination* [*fancy*]. ▶それはまったくの空想だった It was all *imagination*. ▶彼はいつも空想にふけっていた He *was always daydreaming*.

── **空想上の** 形 (想像上の) imaginary; fanciful.

── **空想する** 動 fancy; daydream 《about》. (⇨想像する)

●**空想家** a (day)dreamer. **空想科学小説**《集合的》science fiction 《略 SF, sf》,《話》sci-fi /sáifái/ (個々の) a science fiction novel. **空想的社会主義** Utopian Socialism.

ぐうぞう 偶像 an idol /áidl/. ●偶像を崇拝する worship an *idol*.

●**偶像化する** 動 idolize《it》. **偶像崇拝** the worship of idols;〈やや書〉idolatry /aidálətri/. **偶像破壊**〈やや書〉iconoclasm /aikánəklæzm/.

ぐうたら (だらしない人)《話》a slob ((!)(1) you slob で呼びかけも可. (2) 風呂嫌い、横のものを縦にもしないなどの悪い生活習慣に染まっている人);(怠け者)《話》a loafer.

── **ぐうたらな** 形 lazy, idle. ●ぐうたら亭主 a *lazy* husband;《俗》a *slob* of a husband. ●ぐうたらな生活をする loaf around. ●ぐうたらになる turn into a *slob*. ▶あいつはろくに仕事もしないぐうたらだ He's a *loafer* on the job.

＊くうちゅう 空中 名 [空] the air; midair. ●空中に *in the air*; in *midair*. ●空中高く飛ぶ fly high (up) *in the air* [*sky*]. ●空中に跳び上がる leap *into the air*. ▶パラシュートが空中に浮かんでいた A parachute was [There was] a parachute floating *in the air* [*in midair*]. ▶魔女は空中をほうきに乗って飛ぶという Witches are said to *fly through the air* on a broom.

── **空中の** 形 aerial; in the air.

●**空中権** an air right. **空中散布**(農薬の) crop spraying [dusting]. 関連 空中散布用のヘリコプター a crop duster. **空中衝突** a collision in the air; a midair collision. **空中戦** an air fight;(特に戦闘機同士の) a dogfight. ▶多くの飛行機での空中戦は (air battle) 空中戦に競り勝つ《サッカー》win in the air battle. **空中爆発** an explosion in the air; a midair explosion. **空中ブランコ** a (flying) trapeze /trǽpiːz/. **空中分解** midair disintegration [split]. ●空中分解する break apart *in the air*; disintegrate *in midair*. ●空中楼閣 [根拠のないこと] a castle in the air; [蜃気楼] a mirage.

くうちょう 空調 air-conditioning. ●空調設備のある建物 an *air-conditioned* building.

くうてい 空挺 ── 空挺師団 an airborne division. ●空挺部隊 airborne troop; paratroops.

クーデター [＜フランス語] a coup d'état /kùː deitáː/ (複 coups /kùːˈ d'état/);《話》a coup. ●クーデターによって *by coup d'état*. ●無血クーデターを起こす carry out [stage] a bloodless *coup d'état*.

くうてん 空転 ── 空転する 動 (⇨空回り)

くうどう 空洞 名 a hollow; (虫歯の穴) a cavity. ●国内産業の空洞化 the *hollowing out* [産業基盤を失うこと] deindustrialization] of the domestic industry.

── **空洞の** 形 hollow.

ぐうのね ぐうの音 ●ぐうの音も出ない (完全にやりこめられて) be completely beaten; be beaten all hollow.

＊くうはく 空白 a blank (⇨空欄);(比喩的) a vacuum. ●記憶の空白 a *blank* [a *vacuum*, (途切れ) a *gap*] *in* one's memory. ●政治的空白を生む [埋める] create [fill] a political *vacuum*.

くうばく 空漠 ── 空漠とした 形 (広大な) vast; (果てしない) boundless; (漠然とした) vague, hazy. ●空漠とした考え a *vague* idea.

くうばく 空爆 bombing; an air strike [raid] (⇨空襲). ●空爆を行う carry out a *bombing* [an *air*] *raid* ((!)air raid は主に爆撃された側が用いる表現); bomb. ▶米空軍は敵の軍事基地に激しい空爆を繰り返した The US air force repeated heavy *bombing* [×air] *raids on* the enemy's military base.

ぐうはつ 偶発 名 (偶然) (an) áccident.

── **偶発的** 形 accidéntal; (不測の) unforeseen.

くうひ 空費 (a) waste. (⇨浪費)

── **空費する** 動 ●つまらぬ事に時間を空費する *waste* one's time *on* trifles.

＊くうふく 空腹 名 hunger. ●空腹のときに [をかかえて] on an empty stomach. ●空腹を覚える [になる] feel [get] *hungry*. ●パンで空腹を満たす [抑える] satisfy [(一時的に)《書》stay] one's *hunger* with some bread.

── **空腹な** 形 hungry. ▶ひどく空腹です I'm terribly *hungry*. /I'm *starving*.

くうぶん 空文 a dead letter; a mere scrap of paper. ▶この法案は今や空文に等しい This bill is now a *dead letter* [a *mere scrap of paper*].

クーペ [＜フランス語]《米》(自動車) a coupe /kúːp/, a coupé /kuːpéi, kúːpei/.

くうぼ 空母 [軍事] an aircraft carrier.

くうほう 空砲 a blank (dummy) cartridge; a blank. ●空砲を放つ fire a *blank cartridge* [a *blank*].

クーポン a coupon,《主に英》a voucher. ●クーポン券 a coupon (ticket).

くうゆ 空輸 名 air transportation, transportation by air [plane];[戦時や災害時の] an airlift.

── **空輸する** 動 ●郵便物を空輸する *transport* [*send*] mail *by air*. ●被災者に食料を空輸する *airlift* [*fly*] food to the sufferers.

クーラー [室内冷房用の] an air-conditioner;《和製語》a room cooler; [冷却保存用の] a cooler, a cool bag [box].

くうらん 空欄 a blank; a blank column [space]. ●空欄に住所と氏名を記入する fill in (the *blanks* with) one's name and address.

くうり 空理 an empty [an impracticable] theory. ●空理空論に走る indulge in *theoretical* [×academic] *discussion* ((!)academic は学問上の議論の意でここでは不適)

くうりく 空陸 (空中と陸上) land and air; (空軍と陸軍) the land and air forces.

クーリングオフ (期間) a《five-day》cooling-off period ((!)日本語のクーリングオフは a trial period (試用期間) に当たることが多い);(制度) a cooling-off system. ●クーリングオフ期間内に契約を解除する cancel the (signed) contract within the *cooling-off period*.

クール (冷静な) cool; cool-headed. (⇨冷静) ●クールな男 a *cool-headed* man; (a man with) a *cool*

クールダウン a cool(-)down; (a) cooling down.
●クールダウンする do a cool-down.

クールビズ the "Cool Biz" campaign. (⇨ウォームビズ)

くうれい 空冷 图 air cooling. ── 空冷式の 圏 air-cooled.
●空冷エンジン an air-cooled engine.

くうろ 空路 图 an air route [lane]. ●空路ニューヨークに飛ぶ fly to New York; leave for New York by air [airplane].

くうろん 空論 ── 空理空論に走る (⇨空理) ▶それは机上の空論だ That's a paper plan./That is an empty [an impracticable] theory.

ぐうわ 寓話 (動物を主人公にした) a fable; (観念を擬人化した) an allegory.

くえき 苦役 (主に書) toil; (単調な) drudgery.

クエスチョンマーク ●クエスチョンマークをつける put a question mark.

くえない 食えない ❶[食べられない] (⇨食う) ▶月20万円の給料では食えない(=生活できない) I cannot make a living on a salary of 200,000 yen a month. ❷[油断のならない] (悪賢い) shrewd; (抜け目のない) smart; (ずるい) cunning, crafty. ▶あいつは食えない男だ He is a crafty [a cunning] fellow./(手ごわい相手だ) He is a tough customer to deal with.

くえる 食える ❶[食べられる] (食べて安全だ) be eatable, be good [fit] to eat; (食用に適する) be edible. ❷[生計を立てられる] ▶彼女は歌で食える She can make a living out of [by, from] singing.

クエンさん クエン酸 【化学】citric /sítrik/ acid.

クォータ [割り当て(数)] a quota. ●クォータ制 a quota system. (参考) 雇用・昇進などについて女性などを一定の割合で採用する制度]

クォーター [競技で сон一時間の4分の1] a quarter. ●クォーターバック 【アメフト】a quárterbàck (略 QB, qb).

クォーツ ●クォーツ時計 a quartz watch [clock].

クォーテーション (⇨引用)
●クォーテーションマーク quotation marks; (話) quotes.

クオリティ [質, 品質] quality. ●ハイクオリティな... of high quality.
●クオリティ・オブ・ライフ [生活の質, 精神的満足度] the quality of life. ●クオリティペーパー [高級な新聞] a quality paper. ●クオリティライフ (a) good (quality) life; (和製語) quality life.

くおん 久遠 图 eternity. ── 久遠の 圏 ▶久遠の生命を願う wish for eternal life.

くかい 句会 a haiku gathering.

くかく 区画 (区切られた土地) a division (▶境界線の意にも用いる); (一片の土地) 【米】a plot, a lot; (街区) a block (▶道路で囲まれた四角形の1区画).
●区画整理をする rezone. ●行政区画 an administrative division. ●家を建てるために1区画を買う buy a lot [a piece of land] to build a house on.

くかいじょうど 苦海浄土 Paradise in the Sea of Sorrow. (参考) 石牟礼道子の小説]

くがく 苦学 ── 苦学する 動 (働いて大学を出る) work one's way through college; (学費を稼ぐ) earn one's school expenses.

***くがつ 九月** September (略 Sept., Sep.). (⇨一月)
●9月に in September.

くかん 区間 (部分) a section; (駅伝やリレー競走の) a leg. ▶その区間のバスは雪のためよく不通になる Bus services on that section are often suspended because of snow.

***き 茎** a stem; (草本の) a stalk. ●トウモロコシの茎 corn stalks.

***ぎ 釘** a nail; (枕木用の) a spike; (木の) a peg.
●釘を打つ drive [hammer] a nail (into). ●板の釘を抜く pull [draw] a nail out of a board; unnail a board. ●板にビラを釘で打ちつける nail a notice to [on] a board. ●セーターをあの釘に引っかけた I caught my sweater on [in] that nail./(セーターが引っかかった) My sweater caught on that nail. ●出る釘(=杭) は打たれる (⇨杭)
●釘をさす ▶二度とあんなばかなことをするなと彼に釘をさした(=警告した) I gave him a (strong) warning not to do such a foolish thing again.
●釘づけ (⇨釘付け) ●釘抜き (ペンチ型の) (a pair of) pincers (通例複数扱い); (L字型の) a nail puller.

くぎづけ 釘付け ❶[釘で固定すること] ●ドアを釘うけする nail up [down] a door. ❷[その場から動けない状態] ●ランナーを(塁に)釘づけにする hold (up) a runner; keep a runner close. ●彼は恐怖のあまりその場に釘つけになった He was riveted [stood rooted, froze] to the spot with terror./Terror riveted [nailed, froze] him to the spot. ●兵士たちは機銃掃射で釘うけにされた The soldiers were pinned down by machine gun fire. ●彼女はテレビに釘うけになってその試合を見ていた She was glued to the TV (set) watching the game.

くきょう 苦境 [困難な立場] a difficult situation; a plight (複数形なし); [板ばさみ] a dilemma; [難局, 財政困難に] difficulties; [面倒] trouble. ●苦境に立っているを be in a difficult situation [a predicament]; be in a dilemma; (話) be in a (real) fix.
●苦境に陥る get into a difficult situation. ●彼を苦境から救う get him out of trouble. ▶彼は財政的苦境にある He is in financial difficulties.

くぎょう 苦行 图 (宗教の) asceticism /əsétəsìzm/, mortification (of the flesh); (ざんげの) penance.
── 苦行する 動 practice asceticism [mortification]; mortify the flesh; do penance.
●苦行僧 an ascetic (Buddhist) monk.

くぎり 区切り [終わり] an end, a stop; [句読] punctuation; [休止] a pause. ●論争に区切りをつける stop [(やや書) put an end to] an argument.
●仕事に区切りをつける (やめる) stop work; (休憩する) break off (work).
●区切り符号 a punctuation symbol.

***くぎる 区切る** [土地などを] (分割する) divide; (分離する) separate; (印で) mark ... off; (部屋を壁などで) partition (⇨仕切る). [文などを句読点で] punctuate. ●運動場を二つに区切る divide [separate] the playground into two parts. ●うちの庭は隣の庭と柵(さく)で区切られている Our garden is separated [is divided] from our neighbor's by a fence.

くく 九九 ●九九を10の段まで言う [覚える] say [learn] one's multiplication table up to the 10's. (事情) 米英の表は12×12まである。また、それぞれの段は0を掛けることから始まる] ▶9の段の九九を言ってごらん Tell me the 9 times table.

くぐもる ●くぐもった声 indistinct voices.

くぐらせる 潜らせる ●そうめんを冷水にちょっとくぐらせてから水気を切る dip thin noodles in the cold water for a short while and drain them.

くくりぞめ 括り染め (⇨絞り❷)

くくりつける 括り付ける ●自転車の荷台に荷物をくくりつける tie packages down on a bicycle's carrier. ▶彼女は棒の先にくくりつけたハンカチを振って助けを求め

くぐりど 潜り戸 (横からの小さな入口) a small side gate [door].

くぐりぬける 潜り抜ける (通り抜ける) pass through ...; (切り抜ける) come* through .... ●戦争を潜り抜ける come through the war.

くくる 括る tie ... (up) (〜d; tying); (束ねる) bind* ... (up). (⇨縛る❶) ●小荷物をひもでくくる tie (up) the parcel with string. ●その語をかっこでくくる put [enclose] the word in parentheses. ●絶望して首をくくる(=首つり自殺する) hang oneself in despair. ●彼の力は大したことないと高をくくる(=過小評価する) underestimate his strength.

くぐる 潜る ❶『通る』(中を通り抜ける) go* [pass] through ...; (下を通る) go [pass] under ...; (水中をもぐる) dive*. ●トンネルをくぐる go through a tunnel. ●鳥居をくぐって参拝する visit a shrine through a torii. ●敵の砲火をくぐって前進する advance under the enemy's fire. ▶私たちは有刺鉄線の柵の下を這いくぐって脱出した We escaped by crawling under a barbed-wire fence.
❷『法の網などを』 get* around ..., (やや書・軽蔑的) evade. ●法の網をくぐる evade the law; escape from the clutches of the law.

くげ 公家 a court noble.
くけい 矩形 a réctangle. (⇨長方形) ●矩形の建物 a rectangular building.
くける 絎ける (隠し縫いをする) blind-stitch 《a hem》; (へり・縫い目をかがる) whip (-pp-).
くげん 苦言 ●苦言を呈する give 《him》 candid [frank] advice. (❗いずれも「率直に忠告する」の意だが，前の方はどんな不快な真実をも隠さないことを強調する)
ぐげん 具現 图《やや書》embodiment.
— **具現する** 動 ●彼は思想を作品に具現した《書》He embodied his idea in his work.
くこ 枸杞 〖植物〗a boxthorn, a matrimony vine.
ぐこう 愚行 an act of folly; a foolish act.

くさ 草 〖牧草，芝草〗grass ●集合的に用いるが種類を表す場合は〔C〕; 〖雑草〗weeds; 〖薬用・風味用の〗a herb.
①【〜(の)草】●1本の草 a blade of grass. ●各種の草 various grasses. ●夏草 summer grass(es). ▶あたり一面緑の草が生えていた Green grass grew all around.
②【草〜】▶その広大な野は草1本生えていなかった The vast field was bare of any grass [growth]. (❗growth は「生えたもの」の意)
③【草が】●草が枯れた The grass withered. ●花壇に草が生えないように管理する keep the flowerbeds free of weeds. ▶運動場には草が生い茂っていた The playground was covered [was overrun, was overgrown] with weeds./Weeds were growing thick(ly) in the playground.
④【草の】●草の中の(に) in the grass. ●草の葉 a leaf [a blade] of grass. ●草の生い茂った土地 grassy [grass-grown, (雑草だらけの) weedy] land. ●草の上に寝ころぶ lie down on [in] the grass. (❗in は草の丈が高い場合) ●草の根 (⇨草の根)
⑤【草を】●草を取る weed 《a garden》; (引き抜く) pull the weeds (out). ●草を刈る (芝・牧草を) cut the grass; mow (the grass). ●草を踏む tread [step] on the grass. ▶羊は草を食べている〔常食とする〕Sheep are grazing [feed on grass].
●草サッカー sandlot soccer. ●草地 (芝生) a grass plot; (草原) gráss lànd(s). ●複数形は広大な感を伴う

くさ 瘡 〖医学〗(湿疹) eczema; (発疹) a rash.
くさい 臭い ❶(いやなにおいの) bad- [nasty-] smelling, (話) smelly; (むかつくように) stinking, foul (⇨におい). ●臭い液体 a bad-smelling [a nasty-smelling] liquid. ▶彼は臭い息をしている He has bad [stinking, foul, smelly] breath./(息曲的に)His breath smells (bad) 〖婉曲的〗has a rather strong smell〗. ●臭い(=何のにおいだ) What stinks? ▶ガス臭いぞ I smell gas! ●その部屋はたばこ臭かった The room smelled of tobacco.
❷『疑わしい』suspicious; (うさん臭い) dubious, (話) fishy. ●インチキ臭い商売 a dubious [a fishy] business. ▶この事件では彼がいちばん臭い He is the most suspicious man [the leading suspect] in this affair. ▶警察はその男を臭いとにらんでいる The police suspect [are suspicious of] the man.
❸『気味がある』●彼の話し方には少しも学者臭いところがない His words don't have the slightest savor of pedantry.
●臭い飯を食う《話》do [serve] time《for robbery》.
●臭いものにふたをする ▶彼らは臭いものにふたをするようなやり方で事件をもみ消した They covered up [put a lid on] the scandal.
くさいきれ 草いきれ a sickening smell of grass. ▶森はむっとするような草いきれがした The woods gave off a very sickening smell of grass.
くさいろ 草色 green.
くさかげろう 草蜻蛉 〖昆虫〗a lacewing (fly).
くさかり 草刈り mowing. ●草刈りをする mow (the grass). (⇨草⑤〖草を刈る〗)
●草刈り鎌 (長い柄の) a scythe; (短い柄の) a sickle. ●草刈り機 a láwn mòwer. ●草刈り場 (干し草畑) a háyfield; (選挙の乱戦地) a free-for-all.
くさき 草木 plants; 〖集合的〗vegetation.
●草木もゆらぐ sway 《toward》. ●草木も眠る ●草木も眠る丑(氵)三つ時に in the small hours of the morning.
●草木染め vegetable dyeing.
ぐさく 愚作 a poor work; poor stuff; (がらくた) rubbish; (自分の作品を謙遜して) one of my (poor) works.
ぐさく 愚策 a stupid plan [(はかりごと) plot]. ●愚策を弄(ś)する use a stupid plot.
くさくさ ●くさくさする 動 feel blue [(気分がすぐれない) out of sorts, (憂うつである) depressed]. ●気分がくさくさするような天気 depressing [(陰うつな) gloomy] weather.
くさけいば 草競馬 a local horse race.
くさしぎ 草鴫 〖鳥〗a green sandpiper.
くさす 腐す run 《him》 down. (⇨けなす)
くさずもう 草相撲 amateur sumo wrestling.
くさたけ 草丈 the height of a plant.
くさだんご 草団子 a kusadango; (説明的に) a rice-flour dumpling flavored with mugwort.
くさち 草地 grassland.
くさった 腐った rotten. (⇨腐る〖腐った〗)
くさとり 草取り weeding.
くさのね 草の根 the gràss róots.
●草の根を分けても捜す ●草の根を分けても犯人を捜す (徹底的に) search for the criminal thoroughly; (あらゆる努力をする) make every possible effort to find the criminal.
●草の根運動 the gráss-ròots móvement. ●草の根民主主義 gráss-ròots democracy.
くさば 草葉 ●草葉の陰 ●草葉の陰で in one's grave; 《書》under the sod. ●草葉の陰から従業員の安全を見守る watch over the safety of one's workers

くさばな 草花 a flower, 《花の咲く植物》a flowering plant. (⇨花)

くさはら 草原 a field (of grass). (⇨草原(ｿｳｹﾞﾝ)) ● 草原に寝ころぶ lie down on the *grass*.

*__くさび__ 楔 (a) wedge; 《止め木》a chock. ● くさび形の葉 a *wedge*-shaped leaf. ● くさび形に切ったパイ a *wedge* of pie.
 ● **くさびを打ち込む** drive a wedge 《*into* the rock》. (❗比喩的にも用いる)
 ● **くさび形文字** cuneiform /kjuːníːəfɔːrm/ characters.

くさひばり 草雲雀 〖昆虫〗a grass cricket.

くさぶかい 草深い grassy; 《へんぴな》remote. ● 草深いいなかに住む live in the *remote* countryside 〘《話》the sticks〙.

くさぶき 草葺き ● 草葺きの小屋 a *thatched* hut.
 ● **草葺き屋根** a thatched roof.

くさまくら〖草枕〗 *The Three Cornered World*.
〘参考〙 夏目漱石の小説

　古今ことばの系譜〖草枕〗
　山路を登りながら，こう考えた．智に働けば角が立つ．情に棹させば流される．意地を通せば窮屈だ．とかくに人の世は住みにくい．While I climbed up a mountain road, I thought: if we rely on intellect and logic, we will sound harsh, and if we are guided solely by sentiment and emotion, we will lose ourselves. If we insist on ego, we feel cramped. This world is indeed a difficult place to live in. (❗(1) 原文は「自分の行動基準を「智」「情」「意地」のどれか一つに偏って置くと円滑に進まない」という趣旨であろう．それが分かりやすくなるように訳した．(2) 訳文末の in is to live と place を結ぶ前置詞であるが，語法的には省略可) (⇨甲斐)

くさみ 臭み 《悪臭》a (bad) smell; 《臭気》《やや書》an odor. ● 臭みをとる remove the *smell* 《of》.

くさむしり 草毟り 图 weeding. ── 草むしりする 動 weed 《the garden》.

くさむら 草むら a grassy place; the grass; 《茂み》a bush. ▶草むらで虫がすだき始めた Insects have started to chirp in *the grass*.

くさもち 草餅 a *kusamochi*; 《説明的に》a mugwort-flavored rice cake (stuffed with sweetened bean paste).

くさもみじ 草紅葉 red or yellow leaves of grass.

くさや *kusaya*, 《説明的に》a dried horse mackerel which has a very characteristic, strong smell.

くさやきゅう 草野球 《米》sandlot baseball; 《試合》a pickup baseball game.

*__くさり__ 鎖 (a) chain; 《時計の》a watch chain. ● ドアに鎖をかける put the *chain* on the door; *chain* the door. ● 鎖をはずす unchain 《*it*》; undo the *chain*.
 ● 犬を柱に鎖でつなぐ chain a dog to a post. ▶その犬はつながれていた The dog was on a *chain* [was chained (up)]. (❗on の使い方に注意)
 ● **鎖編み** (a) chain stitch. ● **鎖帷子** (ｶﾀﾋﾞﾗ) 《a coat of》 (chain) mail. ● **鎖鎌**(ｶﾞﾏ) a sickle and chain; 《説明的に》a sickle with a chain and a weight attached.

ぐさり ▶彼は太ももをぐさりと刺された He *was stabbed deep* in the thigh. ▶少年はカボチャをナイフでぐさりと刺した The boy *stabbed* a pumpkin *hard* with his knife./The boy *stuck* [*thrust*] his knife 《*deep*》 into a pumpkin.

__くさる__ 腐る ❶〖腐敗する〗go bad; rot (-tt-); decay; spoil*.

使い分け go bad 「食物が悪くなる」の意の最も口語的な表現．
rot 特に野菜や肉に細菌やかびがついて腐ること．
decay 一般に物質が徐々に変質して腐ること．rot より堅く専門的な語．
spoil 「食物の質が損なわれる」の意の日常語．

● 腐りやすい食品 *périshable* foods; perishables. (❗×foods easy to go bad は不可) ▶肉が腐ってしまった The meat *has gone bad* [*has spoiled*]. ▶そのリンゴは腐りかけている The apple *is rotting* [*decaying*]. ▶暑いとき牛乳はすぐに腐る Milk will *spoil* [*go bad*, *turn sour*] easily in hot weather.

❷〖堕落する〗corrupt, rot (-tt-). ▶彼は根性が腐っている He's *corrupt* [*corrupted*] at heart. (❗前の方は形容詞) ▶あの男は芯まで腐りきっている That man is *rotten* to the core. ▶私の眼は幸いまだ腐ってはいないLuckily, I haven't gone mentally blind yet [×my eyes haven't rotten]. (❗(1) rotten は「(眼の内部が肉体的に)腐る」という意になるのでこの文脈には不適切．(2) 眼の精神的な能力について語っているので mentally を加える)

❸〖気持ちが沈む〗▶彼女は今とても腐っている (落胆している) She's very *depressed* now./She's *feeling rotten* now./(元気がない) She's *in low spirits* [《話》(*down*) *in the dumps*] now.

● **腐っても鯛**(ﾀｲ) A diamond in a dunghill is still a diamond. (❗dunghill は「家畜のふんの山」); A good horse never becomes a jade. (❗jade は「やくざ馬」)
● **腐る程** ▶私は腐る程(=勘定しきれないほど)金を持っている I have more money than I can [you could] count. (❗後の言い方は仮定法)
── 腐った 形 bad*; rotten; decayed; spoiled. ● 腐った魚[リンゴ] *bad* fish [apples]. ● 腐った卵[野菜，木] *rotten* eggs [vegetables; wood]. ● 腐ったミルク *sour* [*bad*] milk. (❗sour /sáuər/ は「腐敗してすっぱくなった」の意)

会話「このミカン腐ってるよ」「どうりでだれも欲しがらなかったわけだ」"This orange is *bad* [*rotten*, *no good*]." "No wonder nobody wanted it!"

くされえん 腐れ縁 《絶ち切れない》inseparable relation; 《芳しくない》an unsavory relation. ▶あの男と今では腐れ縁でつながっている I can't seem to get rid of him [free myself from him].

くさわけ 草分け 《先駆者》a pioneer, 《米》a trailblazer (❗荒野に道を切りひらいた初期開拓者から). ▶彼は辞書出版の草分けの存在だった He *poineered* the publication of dictionaries.

*__くし__ 串 《料理用の長い》a skewer; 《焼き肉用の細い》a spit. ● 肉を串に刺す put a piece of meat on a *skewer* [a *spit*]; *skewer* a piece of meat. ● 竹串に刺しただんごを(ひと串)むしゃむしゃ食べる gobble dumplings off a bamboo *skewer* [*stick*].

くし 櫛 a comb /kóum/. ● くしの歯 the teeth of a *comb*. ● くしを入れる comb 《one's hair》; pass [dash, run] a *comb* 《through one's hair》. ● くしを入れていない髪 unkempt [uncombed] hair.
 ● **くしの歯が欠けるように** as if some important parts were missing.

くし 駆使 ── 駆使する 動 《十分に[最大限に]利用する》make full [the best] use of 《the latest technology》 (⇨使う, 利用); 《言語を使いこなす》have a good command of 《English》.

*__くじ__ 籤 《何かを決めるための》a lot; 〖宝くじ〗a lottery.
 ● くじ付きのはがき a *lottery* postcard. ▶彼はくじ運が強い He is *lucky* (↔*unlucky*) *in drawing lots* [in

くしがた 櫛形 ― 櫛形の 形 arch-shaped. ●櫛形切りにする cut into wedges.

くしカツ 串カツ a *kushikatsu*; (説明的に) crumb-covered pork cutlets (and onion slices) deep-fried on a skewer.

くしき 奇しき strange. ●奇しきめぐり合い a *strange* chance meeting.

くじく 挫く 〘手首などをねんざする〙twist, sprain; 〘粉砕する〙crush; 〘計画・希望などを挫折(ざっ)させる〙frustrate; 〘人を落胆させる〙discourage. ●足首をくじく *twist* [*sprain, wrench*] one's ankle [*xfoot*]. (▪後になるほど程度が小さい) ●予期せぬ問題で出鼻をくじかれる *be discouraged* [*frustrated*] by an unexpected problem at the start.

くしくも 奇しくも strangely enough; miraculously. ●奇しくも一命をとりとめた *Miraculously* [(うれしい運命のいたずらで) *By a happy quirk of fate*], I escaped death.

くしけずる 梳る comb. ●髪をくしけずる comb one's hair.

くじける 挫ける 〘落胆する〙be discouraged [《やや書》disheartened]; 〘気力をくじく〙《やや書》be daunted; 〘勇気を失う〙lose* heart [courage]. ●そんなことでくじけてはいけない Don't let it *discourage* you./Don't *be discouraged* [《やや書》*be disheartened*] by a thing like that.

くしぬい 串縫い (説明的に) the common way of sewing, in which one neatly sews the seam of the right and wrong sides of cloth.

くじびき 籤引き 〘行為〙drawing lots; 〘富くじ〙a lottery. (⇨籤(くじ), 抽選)

くしめ 櫛目 ●櫛目の通った髪 *well-combed* hair. ●黒髪に櫛目を入れる *comb* one's black hair.

ぐしゃ 愚者 ●愚者にも一得 Even a fool sometimes comes up with a good idea. (▪愚か者でもときには良い考えを思いつくことがある)

くしやき 串焼き *kushiyaki*; (説明的に) grilled seafood, meat, or vegetables on skewers.

くじゃく 孔雀 〘鳥〙a peacock 〘狭義では雄をさす〙; (雌) a peahen; (雄, 雌) a peafowl (複peafowl(s)). ●孔雀石 〘鉱物〙malachite /mǽləkàit/.

くじゃくサボテン 孔雀サボテン 〘植物〙an orchid cactus.

くしゃくしゃ ❶〘しわの状態〙●くしゃくしゃにする[なる] crumple; rumple; (しわになる) wrinkle, crease. ●くしゃくしゃになったシーツ a *crumpled* [a *rumpled*, a *creased*] bed sheet. ●くしゃくしゃの髪 *messy* [*disheveled*] hair. ●彼は紙をくしゃくしゃに丸めて捨てた He *crumpled* up the paper and threw it away. ●風が強くて私の髪はくしゃくしゃになった The strong wind *tousled* my hair [*made* my hair *messy*]. ●あの人の顔はしわでくしゃくしゃだった The old man's face *was all wrinkled*. ●おばあちゃんは顔をくしゃくしゃにして笑った Grandma's face *wrinkled up* in a smile.
❷〘気持ちの状態〙●くしゃくしゃする be upset, be irritated, be annoyed. (⇨むしゃくしゃ) ●けさおやじとけんかをしたので気持ちがくしゃくしゃする I *feel* greatly [*very*] *upset* because I quarreled with my father this morning.
❸〘噛(か)む音〙《chew》unappetizingly. (⇨くちゃくちゃ❷)

ぐしゃぐしゃ ●ぐしゃぐしゃになる (つぶれたりしてしわだらけになる) crumple; (ぬれて) get wet, soak; (広い意味で乱れる) get messy. ●アイロンをかけたシャツがかばんの中でぐしゃぐしゃになった His ironed shirts *crumpled* in his bag. ●車は衝突してぐしゃぐしゃになった The car crashed and *got out of shape* [*and was completely wrecked*]. ●女優の化粧が涙でぐしゃぐしゃになった The makeup on the actress *got messy with* her tears.

ぐしゃっと ●ダンボール箱は彼が座った拍子にぐしゃっとつぶれた When he sat on a cardboard box, it *crushed* under his weight. (⇨押し潰す)

くしゃみ a sneeze. (⇨はくしょん) ●大きなくしゃみをする give a loud *sneeze*; sneeze loudly. ●その人はくしゃみをしたり咳をしたりしていた The man *was sneezing* and coughing.

くしゅう 句集 the collected works of haiku.

くじゅう 苦汁 ●苦汁をなめる, 苦汁を飲む have a hard time (of it); have a bitter experience.

くじゅう 苦渋 ●苦渋に満ちた表情をする wear a *deeply-troubled* look [*a look of distress*].

くじょ 駆除 图 (an) extermination.
― **駆除する** 動 ●害虫を駆除する(=根絶する)《やや書》exterminate harmful insects. ●倉庫からネズミを駆除する(=取り除く)*get rid of* all the rats in the warehouse; 《やや書》*rid* the warehouse *of* rats.

くしょう 苦笑 a wry/rái/; smile. (⇨苦笑い)

くじょう 苦情 a complaint; (不当な扱い・不正に対する) a grievance. ●苦情を処理する deal with [handle] *complaints*; (トラブル処理に当たる) troubleshoot (▪その任に当たる人は a troubleshooter). ●弁護士に苦情を持ち込む take one's *complaints* to a lawyer. ●彼らの苦情の調査に乗り出す start looking into their *complaints* [*grievances*]. ●彼は(支配人に)料理のことで[料理が冷めていると]苦情を言った He *complained* (*to* the manager) *about* the food [*about* the food being cold, *that* the food was cold]. (▪*complained* の代わりに made a complaint も可)
●苦情処理 complaint procedure. ●苦情処理係 a complaint officer.

ぐしょう 具象 ― **具象的な** 形 cóncrete (⇔抽象的).
●具象画 a representational painting.

ぐしょぐしょ ●ぐしょぐしょに(=水がしたたるほどに)ぬれる get *soaking* [*dripping*] wet; (雨などで) get *drenched* to the skin. (▪「ぬれている」という状態の意のときは be を用いる (⇨びしょ濡れ)) ●涙でハンカチがぐしょぐしょになった The handkerchief *got soaking wet* with tears.

ぐしょぬれ ●彼女は雨にあってぐしょぬれになった She *got dripping wet* [*got drenched to the skin*] in the rain. (⇨びしょ濡れ)

*くじら** 鯨 〘動物〙a whale; (雄) a bull whale, (雌) a cow whale. ●長須(ながす)[抹香(まっこう)], 白長須]鯨 a finback [a sperm; a blue] *whale*. ●ザトウクジラ a humpback (whale). ●鯨の子 a *whale* calf. ●鯨の肉 *whale* meat. ●鯨のひげ whalebone. ●鯨が潮を吹いているのを見物する watch a *whale* blowing [spouting].
●鯨尺 a measuring stick used in kimono making. ●鯨幕 a black and white striped drape.

*くしん** 苦心 图 〘骨折り〙《やや書》pains; 〘努力〙(an) effort (▪しばしば複数形で); 〘労力〙labor. (⇨苦労)
●苦心談 an account of one's *bitter* [*painstaking, hard*] experiences. ●苦心の跡が見える bear

ぐしん

traces of one's great *pains* [*efforts, labor*].
 ── **苦心する** 動 《やや書》 take* [be at] pains (*to do*); 《やや書》 take [go* to great] pains 《*with* + 事》; work hard. ▶彼は苦心してそれを完成した He *took* (great) *pains* [*was at* (great) *pains*] to complete it./He completed it *with* great [much, ×many] *pains*. ▶彼はその仕事には苦心した He *took* (great) [*went to great*] *pains with* that work. (🔔 ...*to* finish that work. ともいえる)/He *worked hard* to finish that work.

ぐしん 具申 ── **具申する** 動 report (*to* one's superior *on* a matter); ▶上司に意見を具申する *give* [*offer*] one's opinion to one's superior.
● 具申書 a full report.

くす 樟 (⇨ 🔖 樟(しょう))

***くず 屑** 《主に乾いたごみ》《主に米》 trash, 《主に英》 rubbish; 《捨ててある空き缶や紙》 litter. ● パンくず bread *crumbs*. ● 鉄くず *scrap* iron. ● 紙くず a *scrap* of paper; wastepaper. ● 糸くず *waste* thread. ● くずダイヤ *chip* diamonds. ● 星くず *stardust*. ● 人間のくず 《集合的》 the *scum* of the earth, the *dregs* of society; 《役立たずの人》 a *good-for-nothing*.
● くずかご (⇨ 屑籠) ● くず屋 (廃品回収業者) a junk [a scrap] dealer.

くず 葛 〚植物〛 a kudzu [a Japanese arrowroot] (vine).
● 葛あん kudzu (starch) sauce. ● 葛切り strings of kudzu starch jelly. ● 葛粉 kudzu starch. ● 葛まんじゅう a ball of sweetened bean paste glazed with kudzu starch. ● 葛餅 a kudzu starch cake. ● 葛湯 kudzu starch gruel.

ぐず 図 (のろまな) a laggard; a dawdler; (意志の弱い) a feeble-minded person; (決断力に乏しい) an irresolute person.
── **ぐずな** 形 dull; slow; 《話》 logy; poky. ● ぐずなドライバー a poky driver.

くずおれる 崩折れる (崩れるように) fall* [sink*] down; (ばったり) drop (-pp-) (to the floor); (どしんと) flop (-pp-) down.

くずかご 屑籠 (室内の) 《米》 a wastebasket, 《英》 a wastepaper basket; (駅・公園の) 《米》 a trash basket, 《英》 a litter basket, 《英》 a litterbin.
● 紙くずをくずかごに入れる put wastepaper into a *wastebasket*.

くすくす ● くすくす笑い a giggle, a titter, a chuckle. (🔔 giggle は抑えられない笑い, titter は声を立てまいとする笑い. chuckle は1人でおもしろがっている笑い) ● くすくす笑う laugh quietly; giggle; titter; chuckle. ▶若い娘は何にでもすぐくすくす笑ってしまう Young girls are ready to *giggle* [*titter*] at anything. ▶若い男が漫画雑誌を読んでくすくす笑っていた I saw a young man *chuckling* (*to himself*) over a comic magazine.

ぐずぐず ❶ 〖行動がてきぱきしない様子〛 ● ぐずぐずする [している] be slow; 《話》 dilly-dally; 《やや書》 linger on; dawdle. ▶彼は何をするにもぐずぐずしている He is *slow* in everything he does. ▶彼女は授業が終わってもぐずぐず残っていた She *lingers on* even after class is over. ▶ぐずぐずしている場合ではない There is no [isn't any] time to lose. (🔔 no の方が強意的) ▶支配人は部下がぐずぐずのをいやがる The manager dislikes to see his men work *inefficiently*.
❷ 〖不平を言う様子〛 ● ぐずぐず言う complain, grumble. ▶彼は何をするにもぐずぐず言う He never does anything without *complaining*.

くすぐったい ▶背中がくすぐったい My back *tickles*./I've got a *tickle* in my back. ▶彼女はくすぐったがり屋だ She is *ticklish*. ▶知らぬ女性にお世辞を言われてくすぐったかった (=照れくさかった) I *felt embarrassed* by her compliments.

くすぐる tickle. ▶彼は草の葉で私[私の足]をくすぐった He *tickled* me [my feet] with a blade of grass.

くずしがき 崩し書き cursive [(草書の) running] writing.

くずじ 崩し字 a Chinese character written in a simplified way [a cursive or semicursive style]. (🔔 前の方は「字画を省略して」, 後の方は「草書または行書で」の意)

***くずす 崩す** 〚壊す〛(取り壊す) pull [tear*/téar] ... down; 〚原則などを〛change; 〚列などを乱す〛fall* out of line; 〚姿勢などを〛(ひざを崩す) sit* at (one's) ease; (バランスを) lose* one's balance; 〚字を崩す〛(筆記体で) write* in the cursive [running] style; 〚お金を細かくする〛break*, (両替する) change; 〚体調を〛get* out of shape. ▶石垣を崩す pull down the stone wall. ▶基本方針を崩す *change* the basic policy. ▶1万円札を(千円札に) くずしてくれませんか Could you *change* [*break*] this 10,000-yen bill (*into* 1,000-yen bills)?

くすだま 薬玉 a decorative paper ball (for festive occasion).

ぐずつく 〚天気が〛be unsettled; 〚ぐずぐずする〛be slow (⇨ ぐずぐず). ▶このごろ天気がぐずついている The weather is *unsettled* these days.

くすっと ▶彼女はくすっと笑って向こうへ歩いていった She *gave a short smile* and walked away./She walked away *with a quick smile*. (🔔 giggle や chuckle は繰り返しを含むので, くすっと (一度きり) 笑うには不適)

くすねる 《やや話》 pilfer, filch. (⇨ 盗む)

くすのき 樟, 楠 〚植物〛〚木〛 a camphor tree; 〚材〛 camphorwood.

くすぶる ❶ 〚煙を出す様子〛smoke; (煙だけで炎は出さずに) 《米》 smolder, 《英》 smoulder. ▶暖炉がひどくくすぶっている The fireplace *is smoking* badly. ▶彼に対する怒りが何年もくすぶり続けた 《やや書》 My anger at him went on *smoldering* for years.
❷ 〚活動の少ない様子〛 ● 家の中でくすぶっている stay indoors [sit around the house] doing nothing. ● いなかにくすぶっている lead an obscure life in the country.

くすむ ● くすんだ色 a *dark* [a *dull*, a *drab*] color. ● 色がくすんでいる be *dull* in color. ● くすんだ (= 退屈でおもしろくない) 生活 a *dull* life.

くすり 薬 ❶ 〚薬剤〛(内服薬) (a) medicine (*for*), a drug; (治療薬) a cure (*for*); (粉薬) (a) powder; (錠剤) a tablet; (丸薬) a pill (🔔 the pill は経口避妊薬); (水薬) a liquid medicine; (カプセルに入った) a capsule; (塗り薬) (an) ointment.

> **使い分け** **medicine** 通例調合した内服薬をさし, 外用薬は含めない. 通例無冠詞で用いるが, 修飾語を伴うと a がつくことが多い: 風邪薬 a *medicine* for a cold; a cóld mèdicine. ただし製品化された薬や種類に言及する場合は ⓒ 扱い.
> **drug** 薬一般または調合前の薬をいうが, 今では主に麻薬の意で用いられる. 医師の処方箋 (a prescription) なしで買える薬を特に over-the-counter drugs 《略 OTC》という.

① 〚〜(の)薬〛 ● せき薬 (a) *medicine for* a cough; (a) cóugh mèdicine. ● 痛み止めの薬 páin killer médicine; a páinkiller. ▶風邪には睡眠が最良の薬です Sleep is the best *medicine for* a cold. ▶この薬 (= 錠剤) は頭痛によく効く薬です You'll find these

くすりゆび

tablets pretty good for your headache./These *tablets* are a sure *cure* for your headache. ▶ばかにつける薬はない 'There is no *medicine* for curing a fool.'
② 【薬～】 ●薬1服 a dose of *medicine*. ▶彼は薬漬けになっている He is loaded up with *medicine*.
③ 【薬は】 ●あの薬はよく効いた That *medicine* worked [acted] well on me.
会話 「この薬は何に効きますか」「頭痛に効きます」 "What is this *medicine* good for?" "It is good for a headache."
④ 【薬を】 ●薬を飲む take *medicine*. (❗ 粉状の薬の場合は take の代わりに drink を用いることもある) ●薬を飲み過ぎる use *medicine* [*drug*]. ●薬を飲みすぎる overdose oneself; take an overdose (*of*). ●薬を出す（=調合[処方]する）dispense [prescribe] *medicine*. ●傷に薬をつける put *ointment* on a wound; apply *ointment* to a wound. ●薬をせんじる decoct *medicine*. ●この薬を2錠ずつ食間[食後]に飲みなさい Take two tablets of this *medicine* [処方薬] *prescription*] between meals [after each meal]. ▶この薬を飲むと痛みがとれます This *medicine* will relieve [kill] the pain. ▶まだ咳が出ますので、お薬をもう1回分いただきたいのですが I still have a cough. Can I get a refill? (❗ refill は「詰め替え分」の意)
❷ 【ためになるもの】 ▶その失敗は彼にはいい薬になった〈比喩的〉 The failure was *good medicine* for him./The failure was a *good lesson* for him.
●薬九層倍（くすりくそうばい）Medicine is very profitable because its cost is very low [one tenth of its price].
●薬にしたくもない ▶彼女には道徳心など薬にしたくもない（=少しもない）She has *no* morality *whatsover*.
●薬売り（人）a patent-medicine seller;（行為）patent-medicine selling. ●薬代 medication cost. ●薬箱 a médicine chèst. ●薬瓶 médicine bòttle. ●薬屋（店）《書》a pharmacy;《米》a drugstore（事情 薬以外に化粧品・新聞・飲み物なども売る）;《英》a chemist's (shop)（事情 化粧品なども売る）;（人）《書》a pharmacist,《米》a druggist;《英》a chemist. ●薬湯 a medicine (herbal) bath. ●薬指（⇨薬指）

くすりゆび 薬指 the third finger;（特に左手の）the ring finger.

ぐずる 愚図る ●【むずかる】fret (-tt-);【だだをこねる】get* peevish;【文句を言う】grumble (*at*). ●赤ん坊は眠くなるとぐずる Babies *fret*［《米話》*get cranky*］when they are sleepy.

くずれ 崩れ ●化粧の崩れを直す touch up one's makeup.

-くずれ -崩れ（身を持ち崩した...）ruined ...,《話》... gone to the dogs;（成功できなかった...）failed .... ▶あの男はボクサー崩れだ He is a *ruined* boxer./He hasn't quite made it as a boxer.

くずれおちる 崩れ落ちる（屋根のなどが）cave in;（崩れ）fall* down［内側に] in];（崩壊する）collapse.

*****くずれる** 崩れる ❶ 【建造物などが崩壊する】collapse;（腐ってぼろぼろと）crumble;（壊れ）fall* down;（大きな音を立てて倒れる）crash down;（壊れる）break* down;（床・足場が重みで）give* way. ▶地震で壁が崩れた The walls *collapsed* [*fell down*] in the earthquake./The earthquake *destroyed* the walls. ▶川の水位が上がって橋が崩れた The bridge *gave way* as the river rose higher.
❷ 【形が】lose* one's shape; get* out of shape. ▶タンカーからの油漏れは美しい海岸線を崩した（=損なった）The tanker spills *have spoiled* the beautiful

くせん

coastlines.
❸ 【天気が】 ▶天気は午後から崩れるでしょう The weather will *break* in the afternoon.
❹ 【その他の表現】 ●泣き崩れる *break down* and cry. ▶涙で彼女の化粧が崩れた（=台なしになった）Her makeup *was ruined* by her tears./Her tears *ruined* her makeup. ▶1万円札くずれますか Do you *have change* for a 10,000-yen bill?（⇨change）●先発投手は3回に崩れた The starting pitcher was in trouble [was roughed up] in the third inning.

くすん ●鼻をくすんとやる[する] sniff. ●くすんと笑う《米》snicker,《英》snigger.

***くせ ❶ 【習慣】（個人の）a habit;（妙な癖）a peculiarity,（やや悪い）a trick;（やり方）a [one's] way. ▶彼のいつもの癖で=やり方で It's always the *way with* him. ▶自分の失敗をごまかすのが彼の癖だ It is his *habit* to laugh off his mistake.
① 【癖か】 ●悪い癖がつく get into a bad *habit*; pick up [《書》develop] a bad *habit*. ●悪い癖が直る get out of a bad *habit*. ▶彼女は本を読んでいるときに髪をいじくる癖があった She was in [She had] the *habit of* playing [×*to play*] with her hair when she was reading. ▶だれにでも癖がある（=なくて七癖）Everyone has his own *habits* [*peculiarities*].
② 【癖に】 ●それは癖になりそうだ It may get to be [become] a *habit*. (❗ 前の方は口語的) ●喫煙は私には抜き難い癖になっているのです Smoking is a *habit* I just can't break. (❗ just は否定語の前に置いて、否定を強調する)/Smoking is my hard-to-break *habit*.
③ 【癖を】 ●耳をつまむ癖を直した I broke [got rid of] the *habit of* pinching my ear. ▶彼女は子供の指をしゃぶる癖を直した She got her boy out of the *habit of* sucking his fingers.
④ 【癖で】 ▶彼はいつもの癖で頭をかいた He scratched his head *out of* [*from*] habit.
❷ 【独特な性質】 ●癖がある（=特異な歩き方）a *peculiar* way of walking. ●癖が強い have a distinctive character. ●癖がない have no distinctive character. ▶彼女の髪の毛は癖がある（=縮れた）kinky). (❗次例の方が普通)/She has *curly* [*kinky*] hair.（⇨癖毛）

くせげ 癖毛（縮れた毛）curly [frizzy, kinky] hair;（手に負えない毛）unruly hair. ●癖毛を直す take out kinks in one's hair; make one's hair straight.

くせだま 癖球【野球】a junk ball. ▶彼はくせ球を投げる（野球の）He throws *junk balls*./（一般に）He says and does unexpected things.

くせつ 苦節 ●苦節10年、うちの会社も軌道に乗ってきた After ten years of *unremitting efforts* [（一途の忠誠）*unswerving loyalty*], our firm is now a going concern. (❗ a going concern は「もうかっている会社」の意)

くせに ●彼は金もないくせに外車を買いたがる Though [*Although*] he doesn't have enough money, he wants to buy a foreign-made car. ▶大きな口をきいたくせに（=にもかかわらず）君は何もやっていない You're not doing anything, *for all* your big talk. ▶知ってる[知らない]くせに As if you didn't know [you knew]! ▶知ってるくせに黙ってるなんてずるい It's not fair to keep it from me *when* you know it.

くせもの 曲者（不審な者）a suspicious person;（油断のならない人）a tricky person [《話》customer].

くせん 苦戦 図（厳しくつらい戦い）a hard [a severe, a

くそ 糞 图 ❶[大便]《卑》shit. 糞をする《卑》shit. (⇨大便, 糞③)
❷[その他の表現] ▶彼はくそまじめだ He is *too serious*.
会話「奥さん出産で入院だ, 早く帰れ」「しかし」「しかしも糞もあるものか(= 躊躇(ちゅうちょ)している時間はない)」"Your wife's having a baby. She's going to the hospital. Go home now." "Well, but…" "There's no time to lose [to say, 'Well, but …']."

── **くそ** 圃 [[怒り・失望・困惑などを表して]]《卑》shit, 《米俗・婉曲的》shoot;《俗》damn (!damn /dǽm/ ではばかられて d— /díː, dǽm, dǽm/ のように伏せ字にされることがある), 《俗・婉曲的》darn;《俗》Jesus (Christ) /dʒíːzəs (kráist)/, Christ (事柄) 特にキリスト教信者の中ではこの表現を嫌う人がある;《俗》hell, heck. ▶くそ, あいつめ *Damn* (and blast him)!
● **くそ食らえ** お前なんかくそ(でも)くらえ (*God*) *damn* you!/You *damned*!/Go to *hell*! ▶近所の人たちが何と思おうとそんなことくそくらえだ To [The] *hell* with what the neighbors think. ▶To [The] hell with は俗語で文頭に用いて「…なんかくそくらえだ」の意の慣用表現 ▶数学なんかくそくらえだ Math *be hanged*!

くそぢから 糞力 brute force.
くそったれ 糞っ垂れ ▶このくそったれめが You *bastard* [*wretch*, 《古》*swine*]!
くそどきょう 糞度胸 daredevil courage. ●くそ度胸がある be recklessly daring; be foolhardy.
くそみそ 糞味噌 ●くそみそに言う(ひどくこきおろす)《話》run [put] (*him*) down. ▶みんなのいる所でくそみそに言うなんてひどいじゃないか Why did you *put* me *down* in front of everybody? It was cruel.

****くだ** 管 (細い)a tube; [[導管]]a pipe.
● **管を巻く** (酔ってくどくどしゃべる)be drunk and rave.

****ぐたいか** 具体化 ── **具体化する** 動 (具体的な形をとる)take form; take (concrete) shape; (実現する)《やや書》materialize. ▶その計画は具体化された The plan *took shape* [《書》(*was*) *materialized*]. ▶彼の理論はこの本の中で具体化されている His theory *takes form* [*is embodied*] in this book.

ぐたいせい 具体性 concreteness.

****ぐたいてき** 具体的 ── **具体的な** 形 《やや書》concrete (↔abstract); [[明確な]]specific (↔vague). (飜) 抽象的な ●具体的な例をあげる give a *specific* example.
── **具体的に** 圃 ●具体的に説明する give a *concrete* explanation (*for* it); explain (it) concretely. ▶それはおもしろそうですね. もう少し具体的にお話しいただけますか It sounds interesting. Could you be a little more *specific*?
会話「貿易会社に勤めています」「具体的にはどういうお仕事を?」「営業部にいます」"I work for a trading company." "What do you do there *exactly*?" "I'm in the Sales Department."

****くだく** 砕く [[壊す]]break*…(into pieces); (破片が飛び散るように)shatter; (激しく打ち砕く)smash; (押しつぶす)crush; (すっでつぶす)grind*; (ついてつぶす)pound. (破砕する)●石を粉々に砕く break a stone *into pieces*. ●砕いて(=分かりやすく)説明する explain *plainly* [*in simple terms*]. ●心を(千々に)砕く(=非常に心配する) worry a great deal 《*about*》.

▶彼の野望は打ち砕かれた His ambition *was shattered* [*was crushed, was destroyed*].

くたくた ❶[ひどく疲れる] ●くたくたになる be exhausted; 《話》be dead tired; be tired [worn] out. ▶1日中歩き回って私はくたくただ I'm (*completely*) *exhausted* from walking all day. (! completely または absolutely を添えるとさらに意味が強まる)
❷[張りがなくなる] be worn out. ▶このシャツはくたくただ This shirt *is worn out*.
❸[物が弱い火で煮える] simmer. (⇨ぐつぐつ) ●いもがくたくたになるまで煮る boil up till potatoes are *shapelessly soft* [are *mushy*].

くだくだ 砕々と (⇨㊤ くどく)
くだくだしい (⇨㊤ くどい)

くだけた 砕けた [[親しい]]friendly; [[打ち解けた]]familiar; [[形式ばっていない]]informal; [[文などが分かりやすい]] plain; [[簡単な]]simple, plain; [[愛想のよい]]affable. ●くだけた態度で in a *friendly* [a *familiar*, an *informal*] manner. ●くだけた説明 a *simple* explanation. ●くだけた若者 an *affable* young person; a young person *pleasant and easy to talk to*. ●くだけた言葉を遣う use *informal* [(日常の)*everyday*] language. ●くだけた服装で in *casual* clothes; (be) *casually* dressed. ▶やがて座もくだけ宴もたけなわとなった Gradually we were *relaxed* and the party got into full swing.

くだける 砕ける [[壊れる]]break*, be broken; (粉々になる) smash, shatter, crash; (押しつぶされる)crush. (!smash は受ける衝撃の強さに, shatter は飛び散る砕け方に, crash はすさまじい音に重点がある《砕く》) ●岩に砕ける波 waves *breaking* [*crashing*] against the rocks. ▶花びんが落ちて粉々に砕けた The vase dropped and *smashed to pieces*. (!*broke* into pieces では上記ほど細かく割れた感じがしない)

****ください** 下さい ❶[与えてくれ](⇨与える) ▶風邪薬をください *Give* me some cóld mèdicine, please. (!店員などに対しては間接的に I'd like some cold medicine (, please). などのようにいう. please をつけるとより丁寧) ▶コーヒーを二つください Two coffees, *please*. (!×please two coffees. は不可(⇨二つ)) ▶ええ, この靴ならぴったりです. じゃ, これをください(=これにします) Yes, these shoes fit perfectly. I'll *take* them, *please*. [I think I'll *take* them.]
❷[指示, 依頼] (!語尾を上げ調子にした命令文や(付加)疑問文で聞き手に選択の余地を与えたり, please を添えて丁寧な依頼を表す)
(**a**) [[[下げ調子＋]上げ調子で]] ▶気をつけてください Be ˇcareful.
(**b**) [[please を用いて]] ▶窓を開けてください *Pléase* open the ↗window. (!このように語尾を上げ調子にいうといっそう丁寧. 否定文は *Please* don't [×*Don't please*] open the window.)/Open the ↘window, ↗*please*.

解説 please は通例話し手の利益になる場合に用い, 聞き手の利益や singing を表す場合は不自然なことが多い: この錠剤を食後に飲んでください Take [×*Please* take] this pill after meals [(まれ) meal].

(**c**) [[will, would, can, could を用いて]] (!will, can より would, could を用いる方が丁寧. 次の例では順に丁寧な言い方になる) ▶この手紙をタイプしてくださいませんか *Will* [*Can*] *you* type this letter (, *please*)? (!please を添えると一層丁寧)/*Could* [*Would*] *you* type this letter?/*Do* [*Would*, ×*Will*] *you* mind typing this letter?/*Could you possibly* type

くださる ▶この手紙をタイプしてくださいませんか Would you type this letter?/Would you be so kind as] to type this letter? (⚠かなり丁寧な言い方なので親しい間柄ではかえって皮肉を表すことにもなるので注意)
会話「この本を貸してください」「ええ、いいですよ」"Can [Could, May] I borrow this book?" "Yes, certainly." (⚠この順に丁寧な要求となる)
(d)〖過去時制・進行形などを用いて〗 ▶またいらしてください Will you be visiting us again? (⚠未来進行形を用いることによって唐突さを避け、丁寧な依頼を表す) ▶手伝ってくだされはうれしいのですが I wonder [am wondering, wondered, was wondering] if you could help me. (⚠(1)後の方ほど丁寧さを増す。(2)主に女性に好まれる表現)
(e)〖付加疑問文を用いて〗(⚠親しい間柄の場合を除いてあまり丁寧な言い方ではない) ▶戸を閉めてください Shut the door, /will [/won't, /would] you? (⚠下げ調子にすると命令的) ▶遅れないでください Don't be late, /will [×won't] you?

くださる 下さる 〖「くれる」の尊敬語〗(⇨頂(`いただ`)く,下さい,どうぞ) ●先生の下さった御本 a book my teacher gave me. ●いろいろご親切にして下さってありがとうございます Thank you for your many kindnesses.

くだされもの 下され物 ▶この金時計は社長からの下され物です This gold watch is a gift (I got) from the president of my company.

くだす 下す ❶〖命令などを〗 order, give orders [the order] (to do; that 節). ●隊長は私たちに進軍を続けよと命令を下した The captain ordered [〖軍隊〗commanded] us to march on./The captain ordered [〖軍隊〗commanded] that we should march on./The commander gave us orders [gave orders for us] to march on. (⇨命令)
❷〖判決・結論などを〗(判決を)pass; (結論を)draw*. ●被告に判決を下す pass [〖やや書〗pronounce] sentence on the defendant; pass judgment on the defendant. ●経験から推して結論を下す draw [form] conclusions from experience. ●その件に早急な結論を下す(=結論に達する)come to [reach] a hasty conclusion on that matter.
❸〖負かす〗beat. ●テニスで兄を下す beat [defeat] one's brother at tennis.

くたばる (死ぬ)《話》kick the bucket (⚠die の意のおどけた表現); (疲れ果てる)《話》be dead tired, be pooped (out). ▶ああ働きづめではいつかくたばるかしれない He could drop dead if he goes on working like this. ▶くたばってしまえ Go to hell!

くたびれもうけ くたびれ儲け ●骨折り損のくたびれもうけ (⇨骨折り)

くたびれる 〖疲れる〗get* tired 《from》(⇨疲れる); 〖服などが〗wear* out, get worn-out. ●くたびれた(=着古した)コート a worn-out coat. ●彼を待ちくたびれる(=待つことにうんざりする)get tired of waiting for him; 《話》get fed up (with) waiting for him.

*くだもの 果物 ①fruit (⚝ ~, ~s)(⚠果物を表す一般的な語。通例単数形で、集合名詞扱い。料理として出されるものは Ⓤ、種類をいうときは Ⓒ だが、複数形は fruit の方が普通) ●いろいろな果物 various fruits; various kinds of fruit. (⚠後の方が普通) ●新鮮な果物や野菜は健康によい Fresh fruit and vegetables are good for your health. ▶果物をもう少しいかがですか Would you like some more fruit? ▶その土地はオレンジやレモンのようなかんきつ類の果物に向いています The soil is very good for citrus fruits, such as oranges and lemons. ▶トマトは果物ではなく野菜だ The tomato is a vegetable, not a fruit. (⚠冠詞に注意)

●果物屋 (店) a frúit stòre 《主に米》 [shòp 《主に英》], 《主に英》a fruiterer's; (人)《主に英》a fruiterer.

くだらない ❶〖価値のない〗worthless; (くず同様の) trashy; (取るに足りない) trivial; (役に立たない) useless. ●くだらない物 a worthless [a trashy] thing; (がらくた) rubbish. ▶くだらない事を心配するな Don't worry about trifles [trivial matters]. ▶そんなくだらない本は読むな Don't read such a useless [《話》rubbish] book. ▶大学を出ていないからって,おれのことをくだらないやつと思っているのだろう Just because I didn't go to college, you think I'm nothing.
❷〖ばかげた〗foolish; stupid. ●くだらない質問 a stupid question. ▶くだらない事を言うな Don't talk nonsense [〖話〗rubbish]./Don't be foolish. ▶彼の提案はくだらないと片づけられた His suggestion was treated as nonsense. ▶最近はくだらないテレビ番組がちょっと多すぎる There's a bit too much rubbish on TV these days.

くだり 下り (下ること)going [coming] down, 〖やや書〗(a) descent (↔(an) ascent). (⇨上り) ●下り坂(⇨下り坂) ▶下り列車に乗る take a down train. ▶そこで道は下りになる The road goes downward [goes down, slopes down, 〖やや書〗descends, (急に) drops down] from there.

くだり 件 〖文章の箇所〗(条文) a clause; (条項) an article; (節) a passage; (段落) a paragraph. ●このくだりを変更する変更します alter the clause.

くだりざか 下り坂 ❶〖道の〗 a downhill (↔uphill) road, a downward (↔an upward) slope, a downhill, 〖書〗a descent (↔an ascent). ●急な〖ゆるやかな〗下り坂 a steep [a gentle, a gradual] downward slope. ▶下り坂をおりる go down a slope. ▶道はここからずっとだらだらの下り坂になっている The road is downhill [goes downhill, slopes downward, goes down] gently (↔steeply) all the way from here.
❷〖衰退・悪化してゆくこと〗〖やや書〗(a) decline. ●人生の下り坂 the downhill of life. ▶彼の人気は下り坂だ He's losing (↔gaining) popularity./《やや書》His popularity is on the decline [is declining]. ▶天気は午後から下り坂になった(=くずれた) The nice (spell of) weather broke [changed (for the worse)] in the afternoon.

くだりばら 下り腹 (⇨下痢)

くだる 下る ❶〖降りる〗go [come*, get*] down ..., 〖書〗descend (↔ascend). ●急いで山を下る go down [climb down, descend] a hill in a hurry; hurry down a hill. ▶私たちは川をボートで10 キロ[1 時間]下った We went ten kilometers [one hour] down the river by boat (in a boat). ▶郵便局はこの通りを1キロほど南に下ったところです The post office is about one kilometer (to the) south along this street [《主に米》about one kilometer down this street]. ▶山を下ったところに学校がある There is a school down [(ふもとに) at the foot of] the hill.
❷〖命令・判決などが〗 be ordered; (判決が下される) be sentenced. ●進軍せよと命令が下った We were ordered [〖書〗were commanded] to march. ●被告に死刑の判決が下った The defendant was sentenced to death.
❸〖下痢する〗 ●私は腹が下っている I have diarrhea /dàiərí:ə/ [have the runs]. (⚠今は have loose bowels とはあまり言わない)
❹〖その他の表現〗 ●敵の軍門に下る surrender to the enemy. ▶その着物は 100 万円に下らない The kimono can't be under a million yen. ▶100人

を下らない野次馬が事故現場に押しかけた *No less than* 100 onlookers rushed to the scene of the accident.

くだんの 件の ▶くだんの(=問題の)人 a person *in question*. ▶くだんの(=いつもの)話 one's *usual story*. ▶くだんの(=前述の)用件で参上します I'll come and see you on the *above-mentioned* business.

＊くち 口   INDEX

❶ 器官   ❷ 器物などの口
❸ 入り口，穴   ❹ 言葉を発する口
❺ 飲食する口   ❻ 就職口
❼ 割り当て

❶ [器官] (人・動物の) a mouth; (唇) a lip (⇨唇). ●口一杯食物をほうばる take a *mouthful* of food. ●杯を3口で飲み干す drink up a cup of *sake* in three *mouthfuls*.

①【口が】 ▶赤トウガラシを食べたら口(=舌)がひりひりした I burned my *tongue* on [with] these red peppers. (❗with は故意にしたことを含意する) ▶彼は口(=息)が臭い He has bad [foul] *breath*. ▶眠っている間に口が乾いて目が覚めた I woke up because my *mouth* dried up while I was asleep.

②【口に】 ▶食べ物を口に運ぶ bring food to one's *mouth*. ▶彼はパイプを口にくわえている He has a pipe in his *mouth*. ▶その赤ちゃんは何でも口に入れる The baby puts [stuffs] everything into his *mouth*. ▶その子は人指し指を口にくわえた The child put [(曲げてひっかける)] hooked] a forefinger to his *lower lip*. ●口に食物を入れたまましゃべるな Don't talk with your mouth full.

③【口を】 ▶口を大きく開ける open one's *mouth* wide [×large]. ●口を閉じる close [shut] one's *mouth*. ●口をゆがめる twist one's *mouth*; (冷笑して) curl one's *lips* (❗軽蔑を示す); (×の字に) pull down the corners of one's *mouth*. ●グラスに口をつける set one's *lips* to a glass; put one's *lips* to a glass. ▶彼は驚いて口をぽかんと開けた His *mouth* fell open in [×with] surprise./He dropped his *jaw* in surprise. (⇨ぽかんと) ▶彼女は口を丸めてろうそくを吹き消した She rounded her *mouth* to blow out the candles.

❷ [器物などの口] (びん・袋などの) a mouth; (楽器などの吹き口) a mouthpiece; (やかんなどの) a spout; (ホースなどの) a nozzle. ●口の広いびん a wide-mouthed bottle. ●びんの口を開ける *open* (↔close) a bottle; (ふたを取る) take off a top; (コルクの栓をとる) *uncork* (↔cork) a bottle. ●(…に)口をつける set one's *lips* (*to* a glass); put one's mouth (*to*). ●ビール樽の口を開ける *tap* (↔stopper) a barrel of beer.

❸ [入り口, 穴] (入り口) an entrance; (穴) a hole. ●駅の南口で at the south *entrance* [(改札口) gate, (出口) exit] of the railroad station. ●階段の上がり口で(=下のところ)で at the *bottom* (↔top) of the stairs. ▶壁に大きな口がぽっかり開いていた There was [I saw] a gaping *hole* in [×on] the wall. ▶富士山の登山口は数か所あります There are several *routes* [近うく道) *approaches*] you can climb Mt. Fuji from.

❹ [言葉を発する口] (しゃべること) speech; tongue. (⇨話す) ▶心配するな. あれは口だけだ Don't worry, that's just *big talk*. ▶母さんはいつも僕を悪く言うんだ. もっとも口だけだけど(= 本気ではないけど) Mother always calls me names. She doesn't mean it though. (❗副詞の though は文末または

文中で用いる) ▶あの人は口ばっかりで行動しない《話》He's all *mouth* [all *talk* (and no action)].

① 【口が[は]】 ▶彼は口がうまい(=口先だけだ) He can be a slick [a smooth] *talker*; have a smooth [(お世辞のうまい) a flattering] *tongue*. ▶彼は口達者だ(舌がよく回る) have a ready [a fluent] *tongue*; (雄弁だ) be eloquent. ▶彼の常識のなさに開いた口がふさがらなかった(=物も言えないほど驚いた) I *was completely dumb-founded by* his lack of common sense.

② 【口の】 ▶口のうまい奴 a smooth-[a honey-]tongued fellow. (⇨4①) ▶目上の人にそんな口のきき方をするものではありません That's no *way to talk* to your elders./Don't speak to your elders *like that*. ▶権力を握ったら彼は口のきき方で変わってきた He speaks differently now that he's got power.

③ 【口に】 ▶彼は一言もわびの言葉を口に出さなかった He didn't *say* [(書) *utter*] a word of apology. ▶彼の名前ですか．ええっと，口に出かかっているんだけど His name? Well, well. It's on the tip of my *tongue*.

④ 【口を[で]】 ▶口をすぼめる[ゆがめる] purse up [curl] one's *lips* [×mouth]. ●口をふさぐ (開口部を閉じる) close an opening; (話せないようにする) block 《his》 mouth; make 《him》 silent. ●耳元に口を寄せてささやく put one's mouth close to 《his》 ear and whisper. (⇨ささやく) ▶あいつとは二度と口をきかないぞ I shall [will] never *speak to* him again. (❗shall が話し手の決意の度合いが強い) ▶口を慎め Watch *your tongue* [*mouth*]./Be careful what *you say*. ▶彼女は私には[会議中]一言も口をきかなかった She didn't *say* a (single) word to me [(黙っていた) kept silent during the meeting]. ▶その時どんなに悲しかったかは口では言えません *I can't tell you* how sad I was then.

⑤ 【口から】 ▶そのニュースは口から口へ伝わった The news passed *from mouth to mouth* [*by word of mouth*, (口頭で) orally]. ▶これは彼の口から聞いた話です This is a story I heard from his own *lips*. ▶いいか，私の口から言いたくないけど，彼には妻も子供もいるのだよ Listen, I hate to be the one to tell you, but he has a wife and children.

❺ [飲食する口] (味覚) taste, a palate /pǽlit/. (⇨口当たり) ▶良薬は口に苦し《ことわざ》Good medicine is bitter *in* [*tastes* bitter *to*] the *mouth*.

❻ [就職口] (勤め口) a job; (仕事) work; (仕事の空き) a vacancy, 《やや書》an opening. ●勤め口を探し look for [seek] a *job* [*work*, (職業) *employment*]. ▶彼はバス運転手の口を見つけた He got [found] a *job* [(書) a *position*] as a bus driver. ▶ウエートレスの口があった There was a *vacancy* [an *opening*] *for* a waitress.

❼ [割り当て] a share. ●赤十字に3口寄付する contribute three *shares* to the Red Cross.

●口が重い ▶彼女は口が重い(=口数が少ない) She *says very little*./《やや書》She is a *reticent* woman [a woman of *few words*]. (⇨口下手)

●口が堅い be tight-lipped [closemouthed /klóusmàuðd/]. ▶彼女は今度の恋人についてはいつも口が堅い She is being *secretive* about her new boyfriend. (❗進行形に注意. 単純形より秘密を漏らすまいとする気持ちが強い) (⇨口堅い)

●口が軽い ▶彼に言ってはだめよ. 口が軽いんだから Don't tell it to him. He has a big *mouth* [a loose tongue]. (⇨口軽い)

●口が腐っても, 口が裂けても ▶口が裂けても(=何があろうと)本当のことは言えない I can't tell the truth, *no matter what*.

- 口が肥える ▶彼は口が肥えている He has a refined *palate* [a refined *taste in* food]./(食べ物にやかましい) He *is particular about* his food.
- 口が滑る ▶口をすべらしてその秘密を漏らす *let slip* the secret; let the secret *slip* [*out*]. ▶彼はよく口をすべらせる(＝失言する) He often *makes a slip of the tongue* [*lets* his *tongue slip*].
- 口が減らない ▶口の減らない奴だ He is never *at a loss for words*.
- 口が曲がる ▶ご先祖さまに無礼なことを言うと口が曲がりますよ(＝罰が当たるよ) You'll *pay for it* if you say something rude to your ancestors.
- 口から生まれる ▶彼は口から先に生まれたような人だ He is a natural born talker.
- 口が悪い have a sharp [a bitter, a nasty] tongue (いやなことを言う) always say a lot of offensive things.
- 口に合う ▶このワインが私の口にはいちばん合っています This wine is the most *agreeable* for me. ▶イタリア料理は口に合わない Italian food *does not suit* [*please*] *my palate*./Italian food *is not to my taste* [*liking*]./I don't like Italian food.
- 口にする ▶彼の前でそのことを口にする(＝しゃべる) Don't *talk about* [*say*, *speak of*] it in front of him. ▶彼は酒を全然口にしない He never *touches* liquor.
- 口に上る ▶彼の名はよく我々の口にのぼる His name is often *on our lips*./(言及する) We often *refer to* [*mention*] his name.
- 口にはできない (言えない) cannot say (openly); (食べられない) can't eat. ▶神戸牛は高いのでめったに口にできない You can rarely eat Kobe beef because it is very expensive.
- 口は災いのもと (ことわざ)(悪事は口から生まれる) Out of the mouth comes evil.
- 口を利く ▶彼は恐怖で口がきけなかった He was speechless [lost his *tongue*] with fear./He was too scared [was terrified] to speak. ▶(驚きなどで言えなくなったが)彼は再び口がきけるようになった He has found his *speech* [*tongue*] again. ▶先生が私のために口をきいて(＝口添えして)くださって私は就職できた My teacher *said* [*put in*] a (good) *word for* me and I got a job. (⇨口利き, 口添え)
- 口をすっぱくして ▶口がすっぱくなるほど(＝何度も何度も)そのことを彼に言ったが, 聞こうとしなかった I told him about it *over and over again* [*again and again*], but he wouldn't listen to me. (⇨口酸っぱく)
- 口をそろえて ▶口をそろえて(＝一斉に)抗議する protest in chorus.
- 口を出す ▶他人のことに口を出すな Don't *interfere in* [(話) *poke your nose into*] other people's affairs./(大きなお世話だ) Mind your own business. (⇨口出し)
- 口を叩く ▶大きな口をきく talk big; boast. (❗前の方は口語的に)
- 口を突いて出る ▶すばらしいアイデアが彼の口をついて出てきた Marvelous ideas flowed out of his *lips*.
- 口をとがらせる (息を吹こうとして) purse one's lips; (子供が不満・不快のために) pout, have a pout.
- 口を濁す say ambiguous things on purpose; speak ambiguously on purpose.
- 口をぬぐう (汚れを取る) wipe one's mouth 《*on* one's sleeve》; (無関係のふりをする) pretend not to have anything to do 《*with*》.
- 口を開けば ▶母は口を開けばダメと言う Mother always begins with "Don't."/Mother never opens her *mouth* without saying "Don't."
- 口を割る ▶彼は拷問にかけられたがどうしても口を割らなかった He was tortured, but he wouldn't talk [confess].

ぐち 愚痴 图 a grumble (❗ぶつぶつ文句をいうこと); (useless) complaint. (⇨不平) ▶仕事の愚痴をこぼす *grumble* [*complain* 《*about*》] one's work.
── 愚痴っぽい 形 grumbling; (泣き言を言う) whining /hwáinɪŋ/. ▶愚痴っぽい人 a grumbler.

くちあけ 口開け ❶【びんなどの】▶このワインは口開けです This wine bottle has just been opened.
❷【物事の初め】▶慈善興業の口開けの日 on the *opening* [*first*] day of a charity performance.

くちあたり 口当たり ▶口当たりがよい [悪い] taste nice [bad]; be pleasant [unpleasant] to the taste.
- 口当たりのよいワイン soft [mild] wine; wine *pleasant* [*agreeable*] *to the taste*.

くちいれ 口入れ 图 (仲介) agency; (あっせん, 尽力) good [kind] offices. ▶先生の口入れで through the good offices of one's teacher.
── 口入れする 動 act as an agent; use 《his》 good offices.
- 口入れ屋 an agent, a broker.

くちうつし 口写し ▶先生の説を口写しする(＝受け売りする)(軽蔑的) *parrot* one's teacher; *repeat* what oen's teacher says.

くちうつし 口移し ▶口移しの mouth-to-mouth.
- 口移しに[で](口から) from one's mouth; (じかに口で言って) by word of mouth.
- 口移し人工呼吸 mouth-to-mouth respiration.

くちうら 口裏 ▶口裏を合わせる ▶我々はその問題について口裏を合わせることにした We decided to *agree on a story* about the problem./We decided to *rearrange a story* so as not to contradict each other about the problem.

くちうるさい 口うるさい (⇨口喧(やか)しい)

くちえ 口絵 a frontispiece.

くちおも 口重 ── 口重い 形 quiet, 《書》 taciturn. (⇨口 [口が重い]) (砂 口軽)

くちかず 口数 ▶彼は口数が多い He *talks a lot*./He is talkative [a talkative man]. (❗「よくしゃべる」の意で特に軽蔑的な含みはない) ▶彼女は口数が少ない She *says very little*./《やや書》 She is a reticent woman [a woman of *few words*].

くちがたい 口堅い tight-lipped. (⇨口 [口が堅い])

くちがね 口金 (びんの王冠) a cap (❗代わりに a top (ふた)を用いることも多い); (かばん・ベルトなどの) a clasp.
- 銀石口金のついたかばん a bag with a silver *clasp*.

くちがる 口軽 ── 口軽い 形 talkative, 《書》 voluble. (⇨口 [口が軽い]) (砂 口重) ▶ばかげたことを口軽にしゃべる(＝ぺちゃくちゃしゃべる) *prattle on* about nonsense; *chatter away* about nonsense.

くちき 朽木 (立ち木) a dead [a decayed] tree; 《木材》 dead [decayed] wood.

くちきき 口利き (尽力)《書》 good offices; (援助) help. (⇨口 [口を利く]) ▶...の口利きで through the *good offices* 《*of*》; with the *help* 《*of*》.

くちぎたない 口汚い abusive; [汚らわしい] foul. ▶彼を口汚くののしる(＝ばかやろうと悪態をつく) *call* him (*bad*) *names*; 《やや古》 *abuse* him. ▶彼はよく口汚い言葉を遣う He often uses *abusive* [*foul*] language./He often *swears*.

くちきり 口切り ❶【物の始め】▶その話の口切りをする (話を切り出す) *broach* the subject 《*to* him》; *break the ice* of the subject.
❷【びんなどの口開け】opening.

くちく 駆逐 ── 駆逐する 動 (追い払う) drive*... away* [*off*]; (追い出す) drive *... out*. ▶敵を駆逐

くちぐせ　口癖 [［…と言う癖］the habit of saying …; ［お気に入りの文句］a pet [a favorite] phrase. ▶「気をつけて(= 安全第一)」が母の口癖です My mother *has the habit of saying* [*always says*] "Safety first."

くちぐちに　口々に (異口同音に) in únison, in chorus. ▶彼らは口々に「だめだ」と叫んだ "No!" they shouted *in unison*.

くちぐるま　口車 (甘い言葉) one's sweet [sugar-coated,《書》honeyed] words.
● 口車に乗せられる be deceived by [《やや話》be taken in by, fall for] one's sweet words.

くちげんか　口喧嘩 图 an argument, a quarrel; [［激しい口論］《話》a row /ráu/; (公衆の面前での) a brawl /bró:l/.
── 口喧嘩する 動 ▶彼は妻とつまらぬことで口喧嘩した He *had an argument* [*had a quarrel*, *quarrelled*] *with* his wife about little things./《やや話》He *had words with* his wife about little things.

くちごたえ　口答え 图 《米話》back talk,《英話》backchat.
── 口答え(を)する 動 talk back (*to him*); answer 《him》back. ▶口答えするな None of your *back talk*./Don't *talk back*. ▶彼女は子供が口答えしたのでしかった She told her child off for *talking back*.

くちコミ　口コミ ▶そのことを口コミで知る hear about it *by word of mouth*. (⇨ろて)
● 口コミ宣伝　word-of-mouth advertising, mouth-to-mouth advertising.

くちごもる　口ごもる [［とぎれとぎれに言う］falter; [［もぐもぐ言う］mumble; [［話すのをためらう］hesitate, hem 《米話》[hum《英話》] and haw (**!**) hem, hum の変化形は (-mm-). (2)「言葉にのごす」の意でも用いる。目的語はとらない）. ● 口ごもりながら言い訳を言う *falter* (*out*) an excuse.

くちさがない　口さがない ● 口さがない人たち gossipy people; people *who like gossip*; gossip-mongers.

くちさき　口先 [［唇］a lip. ● 口先だけの(= 誠意のない)約束 an *insincere* promise. ● 口先だけのことを言う pay [give] *lip service* (*to him*). ▶彼は口先だけの男だ《話》He is all talk (and no action)./(誠意がない) His talk is cheap. (⇨口 ❹ ①)

くちさびしい　口寂しい ▶禁煙すると口寂しい When we give up smoking, we *feel the need for* [*have to have*] *something to put in our mouth*.

くちざわり　口触り (⇨《俗》口当たり)

くちしのぎ　口凌ぎ ● 口しのぎをする(= どうにか暮らす) live from hand to mouth; eke out a living. ● 口しのぎに(= 一時しのぎに)ひと切れのパンとコップ1杯の水を飲む have a slice of bread and glass of water to *tide me over*.

くちじゃみせん　口三味線 ● 口三味線を入れる hum a samisen tune. ● 口三味線に乗る(= 口車に乗る) be taken in by one's *sweet words*. (⇨口車)

くちずさむ　口ずさむ (歌を) croon; (詩などを) recite 《it》to oneself. ● 小声で子守歌を口ずさむ *croon* a lullaby in a low voice.

くちずっぱく　口酸っぱく ● 口ずっぱく言う tell 《him》 *over and over again*. (⇨口 [口をすっぱくして])

くちぞえ　口添え 图 ［推薦］recommendation; ［世話］《書》good [kind] offices. ▶彼女の口添えで就職できました I got the job *on her recommendation* [*through her good offices*].
── 口添えする 動 ▶彼が社長に口添えしてくれました He *recommended* me to the boss./He *put in* [*said*] *a good word* for me with the boss.

くちだし　口出し 图 (⇨干渉)
── 口出し(を)する 動 ● 彼らの話に口出しする(= 口をはさむ) *cut* [《話》*butt*] *in on* their conversation; (じゃまをする) *interrupt* their conversation. ▶私のことに口出しするな Don't *interfere* [*meddle*] *in* my affairs. ● よけいな口出しをするな Mind your own business. ▶私の口出しすることではないのでしょうが、そんなことなさらなければよかったのにと思います Perhaps *it's none of my business* [*I'm out of place saying so*, *it's sticking my nose where it doesn't belong*], but you really shouldn't have done that. (**!**最後の言い方がより口語的(⇨口　[口を出す]))

くちだっしゃ　口達者 图 a glib talker.
── 口達者な 形 (口先の上手な) glib, (おしゃべりな) talkative.

くちつき　口付き (口の形) the shape of one's mouth. ▶彼の口つき(= 話し方)には好感が持てない I don't like *the way he speaks*.

くちづけ　口づけ a kiss. (⇨キス)

くちづて　口づて ▶そのうわさは口づてに広まった The rumor spread *by word of mouth* [*from mouth to mouth*].

くちどめ　口止め ── 口止めする 動 make 《him》 promise to keep quiet [not to tell anything] 《about》; tell 《him》 to hush 《the fact》 up; (人に話させない)《話》stop [shut] 《his》 mouth.
● 口止め料 hush money. ● 口止め料として5万円もらう get [be paid] 50,000 yen for hush money.

くちとり　口取り *kuchitori*; (説明的に) a dish of assorted delicacies like mashed sweet potatoes, and boiled fish paste, and so on.

くちなおし　口直し ▶てんぷらを食べた後、口直しに緑茶を飲んだ I drank green tea *to kill* [*take off*] *the taste* after eating *tempura*.

くちなし　梔子 [［植物］a gardenia /ɡɑːrdíːnjə/ (**!**この種の木の総称); a Cape jasmine (参考 中国産).

くちならし　口慣らし ── 口慣らし(を)する 動 ● 声を出して読んで口慣らしをする learn to speak 《it》 well [(下や唇を働かせる) *exercise* one's *tongue and lips*] by reading aloud.

くちのは　口の端 (うわさ話) gossip.
● 口の端に上る ● 世人の口の端にのぼる(うわさされる) be talked by people; (町のうわさの種となる) be the talk of the town.

くちばし　嘴 (細く平たい) a bill; (鋭く曲がった) a beak.
● くちばしで種をつつく *peck at* the seeds. ● くちばしでついて木に穴を開ける *peck a hole* in [*on*] a tree.
● くちばしが黄色い ［未熟だ］be wet behind the ears; be young and inexperienced.
● くちばしを入れる ▶お前の関係ないことにくちばしを入れるな Don't *interfere in* [*poke your nose into*] what doesn't concern you.

くちばしる　口走る ● 秘密を口走る(= うっかり言う) let *slip* a secret; *let* a secret *slip* [*out*]; *blurt out* a secret.

くちはっちょう　口八丁 ● 口八丁手八丁 ▶彼は口八丁手八丁だ He is efficient as well as eloquent.

くちはてる　朽ち果てる (すっかり腐る) rot (-tt-) away; (世に知られずに死ぬ) die (〜d; dying) in obscurity.
● 朽ち果てたお堂 a temple *in ruin*; a *ruined* temple.

くちはばったい　口幅ったい ▶口幅ったい(= 生意気な)ようですが、あなたの意見には同意しかねます I may sound *impertinent*, but I can't agree with your opin-

くちばや ion. (!) 英語の表現としては、With all due respect, I disagree with you. (敬意は十分払いながらも賛成いたしかねます)などの方がふさわしい

くちばや 口早 (⇨⑱ 早口)

くちび 口火 ❶【火薬などに点火するための】(導火線) a fuse;《ガス湯沸かし器などの》a pilot light [burner]. ❷【比喩的に】▶彼の発言が激しい論争の口火となった His remarks *touched off* [*led to*] a heated argument.
• **口火を切る** ▶市長攻撃の口火を切る(＝開始する) *start* [*begin*] to attack the mayor.

くちひげ 口ひげ a mustache. (⇨ひげ)

* **くちびる** 唇 a lip. (!)《上下の唇をさすときは複数形》厚い[薄い] 唇 thick [thin] *lips*. ▶上唇を舌でなめる lick [moisten] one's upper *lip* by running one's tongue along it. ▶(ふくれて)下唇を突き出す push one's *underlip* [*lower lip*] out. (!) 子供がふくれて「唇をとがらせる」は pout》▶彼女は唇に指を当て て「しっ」と言った She raised [put] a finger on [to] her *lips* and said "Sshhh ...." (!) to の方が、すばやく勢いのある動作》
• **唇をかむ** bite one's (lower) lip. (!) しばしばいらだち・立腹・笑い・苦痛などをこらえる動作として》
• **唇を盗む** steal a kiss from 《her》 lips; steal 《her》 lips in a kiss.

くちふうじ 口封じ ▶口封じをする (脅して) threaten 《him》 into keeping silent 《about, on》; (金で) buy 《him》 silence.

くちぶえ 口笛 a whistle. ▶曲を口笛で吹く *whistle* a tune. ▶彼は仕事をしながらよく口笛を吹く He often *whistles* as he works.

くちふさぎ 口塞ぎ (⇨⑱ 口止め, 口汚し)

くちぶちょうほう 口不調法 (⇨⑱ 口下手)

くちぶり 口ぶり 【話し方】 the way 《he》 talks; the way of 《his》 talking. ▶彼の口ぶりから判断して judging from *the way* he *talks*. ▶彼女は結婚するような口ぶりだった She *talked as if* [(ほのめかした) *hinted that*] she would get married.

くちべた 口下手 (⇨⑱ 口下手) ▶彼は口下手だ He is a *poor talker* [*speaker*]./He is *poor* [*not very good*] at expressing himself.

くちべに 口紅 [棒口紅] lipstick (!) 具体的な化粧道具としては ⓒ]; [（粉） rouge. ▶口紅をつける put on *lipstick*. ▶新しい口紅を 3 本持っている I have three new *lipsticks*. ▶彼女は口紅が濃すぎる She wears [uses] too much *lipstick*.

くちべらし 口減らし ▶彼は口減らしのために娘を女中奉公に出した In order to *cut down* [*reduce*] *the number of mouths to feed*, they sent their daughter into domestic service.

くちまね 口真似 ⓝ mimicry. ▶彼は口真似がうまい He is a good *mimic*. (!) この mimic は「物真似をする人」の意で、しぐさの真似まで含む。正確には He is good at mimicking [copying, imitating] other people's way of speaking. などとする》
— **口真似(を)する** 動 mimic 《his》 way of speaking.

くちもと 口元 [口] a mouth; [唇] lips. ▶しまりのない口元 a slack *mouth*. ▶口元を引きしめる tighten one's *lips*. ▶口元に笑みを浮かべて話す talk with a smile on one's *lips*.

くちやかましい 口喧しい (うるさく小言を言う) nagging. ▶口やかましい母親 a *nagging* mother. ▶父は門限のことでいつも私に口やかましく言う My father *is always nagging* (*at*) me about how late I am allowed to get home [I may stay out] in the evening. (!) always を進行形とともに用いると非難の気持ちが強まる》 (⇨がみがみ)

くちゃくそく 口約束 ⓝ ▶彼からは単なる口約束でなく書いたものを必ずもらいなさい Be sure to get not a mere *verbal promise* but a written one from him.
— **口約束(を)する** 動 make a verbal promise [agreement]; give one's word 《to do》.

くちゃくちゃ ❶ [紙や布などが] ▶くちゃくちゃにする crumple, crease. ▶くちゃくちゃになる be [get, become] crumpled. ▶包装紙をくちゃくちゃにしてくず箱に捨てた He *crumpled* the wrapping paper and threw it into the wastebasket.
❷ [かむ音など] ▶ガムをくちゃかむ chew [eat] *noisily*; chew [eat] *with a noise*; munch. ▶泥をくちゃくちゃこねる *squish* mud. ▶子供たちはくちゃくちゃ音を立てて食べてはいけないと言われた The children were told not to *munch* [*eat noisily*].

ぐちゃぐちゃ ▶ぐちゃぐちゃにつぶす (押して) squash, crush; (打ち砕く) smash. ▶礼子はソースを作るためにトマトをぐちゃぐちゃにつぶした Reiko *squashed* tomatoes to make some sauce. ▶ケーキが箱の中でぐちゃぐちゃになっていた The cake *was squashed* in the box. ▶爆発でその建物はぐちゃぐちゃになってしまった The building *was wrecked* by the explosion. ▶部屋の中はぐちゃぐちゃで何がどこにあるのか分からない The room is *in such a mess* that I can't find where things are.

くちゅう 苦衷 (苦しい立場) a difficult position; a predicament; (困難な) agony.

くちゅう 駆虫 ▶駆虫薬[剤] (殺虫剤) (an) insecticide; (a) pesticide.

くちょう 口調 a tone. (⇨調子 ❷) ▶命令口調で in a *tone* of command. ▶穏やかな[激しい]口調で in a gentle [a sharp] *tone*. (!) しばしば複数形で》 ▶演説口調で(＝まるで演説をしているように)話す speak as if 《he》 were [《話》 was] making a speech. ▶口調を和らげる soften one's *tone*; tone down one's voice. ▶彼の口調からすると試験の出来はよくなかったらしい Judging by *the way* he *spoke* he didn't do well in his exam. ▶この方が口調がよい This *sounds* better.

くちょう 区長 the chief 《⑱ chiefs》 of a ward.

ぐちょく 愚直 — **愚直な** 形 (正直すぎる) too honest, 《やや軽》honest to a fault.

ぐちょごし 口汚し ▶ほんのお口汚しでございますが Won't you *just try some of* this cake?

くちよせ 口寄せ [巫女(?)が霊魂の言葉を伝えること] spiritism, spiritualism; [霊魂の言葉を伝える巫女] a female shaman, a medium.

くちる 朽ちる (腐る) rot (-tt-) 《away》, decay; (ひっそりと死ぬ) die 《〜d; dying》 in obscurity.

ぐちる 愚痴る 《話》 gripe 《about》. (⇨愚痴)

* **くつ** 靴 [短靴] shoes; [長靴] 《米》 boots, 《英》 high boots. (!) いずれも複数扱い》

> **使い分け** shoe 《米》では通例くるぶしより少し上までの靴にもそれより下までの靴にも用いられ、特に両者を区別する場合は high shoe, low shoe で表すが、《英》では通例くるぶしより下までの靴にのみ用いる。
> boot 《米》では high shoe よりさらに高い靴を表すのに対し、《英》では《米》の high shoe と同じ高さかそれ以上の靴をいう。

> **解説** shoe, boot とも特に片方を表すとき以外は複数形で用い、数えるときは a pair [two pairs] of shoes のようにいう。その場合単・複の扱いは pair の数に一致する。

① [〜靴] ▶運動靴 《米》 sneakers, 《英》 plimsolls, 《英》 trainers. ▶革[ゴム]靴 leather [rubber] *shoes*. ▶紳士[婦人]靴 men's [ladies']

くつ

shoes. ●雨靴 rain *boots*. ●新しい靴 1 足 a new pair of *shoes*. (❗new の位置と注意。ただし「白い靴 1 足」は a pair of white shoes). ●すり減った靴 worn-out *shoes*. ●ゴム底の靴 *shoes* with rubber soles; rubber-soled *shoes*.

② 〖靴は〗 ▶この靴は窮屈だ These [×This] *shoes* pinch (me)./These *shoes* are [This pair of *shoes* is] too tight for me.

③ 〖靴の〗 ●靴の中 the inside of shoes. (❗inside of the shoes は「靴の中へ」の意) ●靴の裏 the sole of a shoe. ●靴の右と左を逆にはく put one's *shoes* on the wrong feet. ●靴のひもを結ぶ tie [lace (up)] one's *shoes*. ●靴のかかとを張り替える resole [reheel] one's *shoes*.

④ 〖靴を〗 ●靴をはく [脱ぐ] put on [take off] one's *shoes*; pull on [pull off] one's *boots*. (❗はいている状態を表すときは wear one's *shoes* [*boots*]; have (got) one's *shoes* [*boots*] on) ●靴をはいたままで [はかずに, 脱いで] with (one's) *shoes* on [off]. ●(自分で)靴をみがく shine [polish] one's *shoes*. ●靴をみがいてもらう get one's *shoes* shined [polished]. ●靴を直す(=直してもらう) have one's *shoes* repaired [《英》 mended]. ▶マットで靴をぬぐう wipe one's *shoes* on the mat. ▶靴を買いにデパートへ行った I went to the department store to buy some *shoes*. (❗漠然と「靴」を表す場合や何足かの不明の場合は通例 some をそえる) ▶靴を引きずって歩くな, 靴底がすぐすり減ってしまうよ Don't drag your *shoes* as you walk. Otherwise, the soles will be worn thin quickly.

●靴跡 a shoe imprint. ●靴墨 shoe [boot] polish [×cream]. ●靴ぬぐい a doormat. ●靴べら a shoehorn. ●靴屋 《店》《米》a shóe stòre; 《英》a shóe shòp; 《人》a shoemaker.

* **くつう** 苦痛 〖心身の痛み〗(a) pain (❗身体の局部の痛みには C (⇨痛み)); (激しく発作的な) a pang; (持続的な) (a) torment; (a) torture; 〖心身の苦悩〗suffering; distress. (⇨苦しみ) ●肉体的 [精神的] 苦痛 physical [mental] *pain*. ●痛みを感じる feel *pain*. ▶何時間も座っているのは苦痛だ It's *painful* to keep sitting [remain seated] for hours. ▶私の息子は苦痛の種だ My son is a real *pain* (in the neck).

くつがえす 覆す 〖ひっくり返す〗overturn (❗以下の語と交換できる); (権威・権力を) òverthrów*; (決定・方針などを) reverse; (判決などを)《やや書》overrule. ●定説をくつがえす *overturn* [*discredit*] an established theory.

クッキー 《米》a cookie, a cooky; 《英》a biscuit.

くっきょう 屈強 ●屈強な 形 (たくましい) sturdy; (強健な) robúst; (強い) strong.

くっきょく 屈曲 图 a bend; (曲がり)a curve; (曲がりくねること) winding.

— 屈曲した 形 bendy; crooked; winding.

— 屈曲する 動 bend; be crooked; curve; wind; (ジグザグに曲がる) zigzag.

くっきり (はっきりと) clearly; (紛れなく) distinctly. ●富士山が冬空にくっきり見える We can see Mt. Fuji *clearly* against the winter sky./Mt. Fuji stands out *starkly* against the winter sky. ▶彼女が正直であることは顔にくっきり出ていた Her honesty was *distinct* [showed *distinctly*] on her face./She looked honesty itself.

クッキング 〖料理〗cooking.
●クッキングスクール a cóokery [a cóoking] schòol. (❗前の方が普通) ●クッキングホイル cóoking fòil. ●クッキングワイン a cóoking wine.

ぐつぐつ ●ぐつぐつ煮る simmer. ▶それを沸騰させて, 15 分ぐつぐつ煮なさい Bring it to the [a] boil and *simmer* (it) for fifteen minutes.

くっさく 掘削 图 (an) excavation; digging.
— 掘削する 動 excavate; dig. ●山にトンネルを掘削する *dig* a tuunel *through* the mountain.
●掘削機 an excavator.

くっし 屈指 ●日本屈指のピアニスト one of *the best* [*greatest*] pianists in Japan. ●この町屈指の大金持ち one of *the richest* men in this city.

* **くつした** 靴下 (短い) socks; (女性用のひざまで・ひざより上の) stockings (❗いずれも片方だけをいう場合は単数形で); (パンティストッキング)《米》pantyhose (❗複数扱い), 《英》tights. ●靴下 1 足 a pair of *socks* [*stockings*], (ナイロンの) nylon *stockings*. ●靴下をはく [脱ぐ] put on [take off] one's *socks*. (⇨穿(は)く) ●靴下をはいて [はいたままで] with one's *socks* on. ▶あなたの靴下伝線しているわよ Your *stocking* has a run (in it).
●靴下留め (女性用の)《a pair of》garters 《米》[suspenders 《英》].

くつじゅう 屈従 图 submission [subservience] 《to》; (隷属) subjection 《to》. ●…に屈従して in *submission* [*subjection*] to ….
— 屈従的な 形 submissive [subservient] 《to》.
— 屈従する 動 submit 《to》.

くつじょく 屈辱 图 (a) humiliation; 〖不名誉〗(a) disgrace; 〖侮辱〗an insult. ●屈辱を与える humiliate, disgrace, insult. ●屈辱を受ける be humiliated [disgraced, insulted]. ●屈辱(感)を味わう feel *humiliated* [*disgraced, insulted*]. ●屈辱に耐える put up with [bear] an *insult*.
— 屈辱的な 形 humiliating, insulting.

ぐっしょり ●ぐっしょりぬれている be soaking [dripping] wet; be drenched to the skin. (⇨びしょ濡れ) ▶猫がぐっしょりぬれて帰ってきた The cat came back *soaking* [*dripping*] *wet*.

クッション a cushion, 《米》a pillow. ●クッションのいいソファ a well-*cushioned* sofa.

クッションボール 〖野球〗a carom. ▶松井はクッションボールの処理を誤った Matsui mishandled a *carom* [a ball rebounded from [off] the wall].

くっしん 屈伸 bending and stretching. ●屈伸運動をする do *bending and stretching* exercises.

グッズ goods. (❗複数扱い。数詞や many はつけずに使うのが普通) ●スポーツグッズ sporting *goods*.

ぐっすり ▶彼女は毎日ぐっすり眠る She sleeps *well* [*soundly*] every day. ▶ジョンはぐっすり眠っています John is *fast* [*sound, deeply,* ×*very*] asleep.

* **くっする** 屈する 〖書〗yield 《to》; give* way [in] 《to》. ●彼女の要求に屈する *yield to* [*give way to, give in to*] her demand. ●権力に屈する a *bow* before authority.

くつずれ 靴ずれ a shoe sore; (まめ) a blister. ●靴ずれができる get a *shoe sore*; get a *sore from a shoe*.

くっせつ 屈折 图 (光・音の) refraction.
— 屈折する 動 be refracted. ●屈折させる refract. ●屈折した(=複雑な)心理 one's *complicated* state of mind; (ひねくれた) a *warped* [a *twisted*] mind.
●屈折語 〖言語〗an inflectional [inflective] language. ●屈折率 the index of refraction; the refractive index.

くったく 屈託 ●屈託のない (気苦労のない) carefree; (こせこせしない) easygoing. ▶彼は何の屈託もない様子だった He looked quite *carefree* [*free from worry*].

ぐったり 图 ❶〖ぐにゃっとなった〗limp. ●ぐったりいすに腰をおろす *sink* [*collapse*] into a chair.
❷〖疲れて動かない〗be exhausted; 《話》be dead

くっつく 〖粘着する〗stick* 《to》; 〖しっかりと〗〖やや書〗adhere 《to》; (ぴったりと, すがりついて) 〖やや書〗cling* 《to》. ● 壁にぴったりくっついて立っている stand *close to* the wall. ▶ ガムが靴底にくっついた Chewing gum *stuck* [*adhered*, *clung*] *to* the bottom of my shoes. ▶ 子供は甘えて母親にくっつく Small children *cling to* their mothers for affection. ▶ 彼の折れた骨は完全にくっついた His broken bones *knitted* perfectly. ▶ 家々はくっつくようにして立ち並んでいた The houses *were crowded close* together.

くっつける 〖結合する〗join ...（together); 〖寄せ集める〗put* ...together; 〖取りつける〗attach; 〖据え付ける〗fix; 〖張り付ける〗stick*; (接着剤で) glue ...(together), (のりで) paste ...(together). ● 2枚の厚板を接着剤でくっつける *join* [(ぺたりと張り付ける) *stick*] two planks *with glue*; *glue* two planks *together*. ● 花びんの破片をくっつけて元通りにする *put* [*glue*] the broken pieces of a vase *back together*. ● 小包に札をくっつける *attach* a label *to* a parcel; (のりで) *paste* a label *on* a parcel, *paste* a parcel *with* a label. ● 果物型マグネットを冷蔵庫のドアにくっつける *stick* some fruit-shaped magnets on the door of a refrigerator. ▶ そのベッドをもっと壁にくっつけなさい (=接近させなさい) *Put* the bed *closer to* the wall.

くってかかる 食ってかかる 〖敵意を示す〗turn 《on》; 〖激しく非難する〗lash out 《at》. ● 彼に食ってかかる *lash out at* him; *fly* [*let fly*] *at* him. ▶ 彼はこぶしを固めて私に食ってかかってきた He *turned on* [×to] me with clenched fist. (❗ to では単に「...の方を向く」だけで敵意は含まれないからここでは不適)

ぐっと ❶〖一段と〗〖比較級を強調して〗much, even, 〖話〗a lot; 〖著しく〗remarkably; 〖鋭く〗sharply; 〖大いに〗greatly. (⇨ずっと) ▶ 彼女はピンクの服を着るとぐっと若く見える She looks *much* younger in pink. ▶ 彼はテニスがぐっと上達した He has made *remarkable* progress in tennis.
❷〖一息に〗● ぐっとウイスキーを飲む *gulp* (down) whiskey; drink whiskey *at a* [*one*] *gulp*. ● ぐっと息を吸う take a deep breath.
❸〖力を入れて〗(ぐっと…する) jerk. (❗ 引く, 押す, 突く, ねじることなどを表す) ● ぐっとロープを引く *jerk* the rope; *give* the rope *a jerk*. ▶ 彼は頭をぐっと引いた He *jerked* his head back. ▶ 車はぐっとなって止まった The car stopped *with a jerk* [*jerked* to a stop].
❹〖感情などを強く抑える様子を〗● 怒りをぐっと抑える *repress* one's anger; (飲み込む) *swallow* one's anger.

グッド good. (⇨いい) ▶ グッドアイデアだ What a *good* idea!
● グッドタイミング perfect [good] timing. ● グッドデザインマーク the Good Design Mark.

グッド）バイ Good-by.; See you. (⇨さよなら)
グッドラック Good [Best of] luck 《with the exam》!（「うまくいきますように」「頑張って」などの励ましの声掛け. 応答は Thanks!, Wish me luck! など）

くぬぎいし 沓脱ぎ石 a stépping stòne; (説明的に) a stone on which you take off your shoes before going into a house.

グッピー 〖魚介〗a guppy.

くつひも 靴紐 a shoelace, a lace, 《主に米》a shoestring. ● 靴ひもを結ぶ tie (up) [do up, 《米話》fix] (↔untie) one's *shoelaces*. ▶ 靴ひもがほどけた[ほどけている] My *shoelace* has come undone [is undone].

くっぷく 屈服 名 〖降参〗(a) surrender 《to》; 〖服従的〗submission 《to》.
―― 屈服する 動 〖降参する〗surrender 《to》; (服従する)〖やや書〗submit 《to》; (譲歩する) give way 《to》. ● 世論の圧力に屈服する *surrender* [*give way*] *to* the pressure of public opinion.

くつみがき 靴磨き 〖事〗shoeshine, shoe polishing [cleaning]. ● 靴磨きをする clean [(ブラシをかける) brush, (磨く) polish] one's shoes.

くつろぎ 寛ぎ relaxation. ● くつろぎの午後 a *relaxing* afternoon. ● くつろぎのために for *relaxation*.

くつろぐ 寛ぐ 〖緊張をほぐす〗relax; (気が楽である) feel* at home [at ease, comfortable]. ● くつろいで話す have a *relaxed* conversation. ▶ どうぞおくつろぎください Please *make yourself at home* [*comfortable*]./Please *relax*. ▶ 彼女は父親のいるところではくつろげなかった She didn't *feel at ease* [couldn't *relax*] in the presence of her father. ▶ バロック音楽を聴くと私は心身がくつろぐ I feel *relaxed* while (I'm) listening to Baroque music./Baroque music *relaxes* me.

くつわ 轡 a bit. ● くつわをはめる put a *bit* in a horse's mouth; bit a horse. ● くつわを並べて進む ride abreast; ride one's horses side by side. ● くつわを並べて落選する be defeated *all together* in the election.

くつわむし 轡虫 〖昆虫〗*Kutsuwa-mushi*; a giant katydid /kéitidid/.

くてん 句点 (ピリオド)《米》a period, 《英》a full stop. (⇨句読点)

くでん 口伝 〖口授〗oral instruction; (口碑) oral tradition; (奥義) the mysteries.

ぐでんぐでん ▶ 彼は昨夜ぐでんぐでんに酔っ払った 《話》He was *dead* drunk last night. (⇨べろべろ ❷)

くどい ❶〖言葉が〗(繰り返しの多い)〖やや書〗repetitious; (言葉数が多い) wordy; (長たらしい) lengthy; 〖人がしつこい〗〖やや書〗insistent. ● くどい演説 a *repetitious* [(a *wordy*, a *lengthy*)] speech. ▶ くどいようですが, 必ず時間どおりに来てください This may sound *repetitious* [I may *be repeating myself*, Excuse me for *repeating myself*], but be sure to come on time. ▶ くどいぞ Don't be so *wordy* [*insistent*].
❷〖味などが〗● くどい味の(=しつこすぎる)料理 *too rich* food.

くとう 苦闘 名 a struggle. ―― 苦闘する 動 struggle 《to do; for》.

くどう 駆動 〖駆動装置〗(a) drive. ● 前輪[後輪]駆動の車 a car with (a) front-wheel [rear-wheel] *drive*.

くとうてん 句読点 a punctuation mark. (⇨巻末〖句読法〗) ● 文に句読点をつける put *punctuation marks in* a sentence; *punctuate* a sentence.

くとうほう 句読法 (a method of) punctuation.

くどき 口説き ● 口説き falling ＝ persuade (him *to do*) (⇨口説く); (異性を) win 《her》over; win 《her》heart.
● 口説き文句〖話〗(説得するための) a clincher; (異性に対する) a pickup line.

くどく 功徳 〖仏教〗a virtuous [pious, charitable] deed. ● 功徳を積む do good deeds.

くどく 口説く 〚言い寄る〛make* advances 《to》; (肉体関係を求めて) seduce, 《話》make a pass 《at》; (結婚を求めて) 《古》court 《her》; 〚説得する〛persuade 《him to do》; (うまい言葉で) coax 《him into doing》. ▶彼を口説いて市長に立候補してもらうことにした I *persuaded* him to run [*talked* him *into* running] for mayor.

くどくど (言い張って) insistently; (執拗(ょぅ)に) persistently; (繰り返し) repeatedly, over and over again; (絶えず) continually; (うんざりするほど) tediously. ▶彼はくどくどと時間を守る大事さを強調した He *insistently* stressed the importance of punctuality. ▶彼女にくどくどと(＝何度も)言い訳をした He made an excuse to me for being late *over and over again*. ▶彼女は夫の欠点をくどくど話した She went on complaining about her husband's faults *at tedious length*. (⚠ *at length* (長々と)を聞き手の気持ちを表す tedious で修飾したもの)

ぐどん 愚鈍 ── 愚鈍な 形 stupid; silly. (⇨愚か)

くないちょう 宮内庁 the Imperial Household Agency.
● 宮内庁長官 the Director General of the Imperial Household Agency.

くなん 苦難 〚困難な状態〛(a) hardship (⚠しばしば複数形で); 〚苦しみ〛suffering(s). ● 幾多の苦難を経験する[に打ち勝つ] go through [get over] many *hardships* [*sufferings*]. ▶彼女は人生の苦難に耐え切れなかった Life was too hard on her.

くに 国

WORD CHOICE 国

country 国家を指す最も一般的な語. 特に国土を含意する. ● 発展途上国 developing *countries*. ● 国中で across [around, throughout, all over] the *country*.

nation 民族集団としての国家のこと. 特に国民・民族を含意する. ● 国連 the United *Nations*.

state 国際法上の統一的政治体としての国家のこと. 特に国政を含意する. ● 独立国 an independent *state*.

❶ 〚国土, 国家〛a country; a nation; a state (⚠しばしば5); a land 《country の文語で, 土地とその住民をさす》. ● この国 this *country*, our *country* (⚠前の方は自国にいる人が自分のことをいう場合に用いる. 後の方は我が祖国[母国]という感じを含む) ● 世界の国々 the *countries* of the world. ● おとぎの国 a fairyland. ● 国中を旅行する travel all over the *country*. ● 国(＝国庫)に納める税金 tax to pay to the *government* [《米》(国税庁) the *Internal Revenue Service*]. ● 国柄 (⇨国柄) ● 二つの国は漁業協定を結んだ The two *nations* entered into an agreement concerning fishing rights. ▶失礼ですがどこの国のお方ですか Excuse me, but what *country* are you from [but what's your *nationality*]? (⚠前の方は出身を, 後の方は国籍を尋ねる言い方) ▶そのことで国中がひっくり返るような騒ぎになった The whole *nation* got upset by it. ▶食習慣は国により異なる Eating habits differ *from country to country*. (⚠無冠詞に注意)

❷ 〚故郷〛one's hometown (⇨故郷); 〚故国〛one's home country (⇨本国). ● 東北のお国なまりで話す speak with a Tohoku accent.

❸ 〚国の一地方〛a province, (a) county (⚠通例無冠詞), 《地方》. ● 大和の国 Yamato *province*; the *province* of Yamato. (⚠日本の昔の「国」は province)

くにがら 国柄 〚国の性格〛national character; 〚国の特質〛national characteristics; 〚背景〛backgrounds]. ▶それぞれの国には独特のお国柄がある Each country has a unique *national character*.

くにくのさく 苦肉の策 ▶彼が車を売ったのは苦肉の策(＝最後の手段)だった As a last resort he sold his car.

くにざかい 国境 the border, the boundary 《between》. ● 国境を越える cross *the border*.

くになまり 国訛り a provincial accent. (⇨御国(〔)

くにもと 国元, 国許 one's home; one's hometown [home village]; (生まれ故郷) one's native place.

くにゃくにゃ ● くにゃくにゃしている soft; (力や張りがなくて) limp; (たるんで) flabby. ● くにゃくにゃに曲げる[する] bend (out of shape), twist; wriggle, wiggle. ▶熱でタールがくにゃくにゃになった Heat made the tar *soft* [*limp*]. ▶彼女は体をくにゃくにゃ曲げて踊った She danced *twisting* her limbs.

ぐにゃぐにゃ ❶ 〚力が抜けたさま〛(張りがなくして) limp; (垂れ下がって) flabby, soft. ● ぐにゃぐにゃになる become [get] *limp* [*flabby*, *soft*]; (ぺしゃんこになる) go *flat*. ▶あまりの暑さに線路がぐにゃぐにゃになった The intensive heat has melted train rails.
❷ 〚言うことがはっきりしないさま〛● ぐにゃぐにゃ言う mumble, mutter. (⇨むにゃむにゃ)

ぬぎ 椚 〚植物〛an oak; a kind of oak.

くねくね ● くねくね曲がる (山道や流れなど) wind /wáind/, meander /miǽndər/; (左右に繰り返すように) wriggle, wiggle; (波打つように) wave. ● (体などを) くねくね曲げる twist; turn and wriggle. ▶くねくねと流れる川が見えた I saw a long and *winding* [*meandering*] river. ▶踊り子たちは音楽に合わせて体をくねくねさせた The dancers *twisted* their bodies to the music. ▶みみずが身をくねくねとよじらせた The earthworm *turned* and *wriggled* [*twisted about*].

くねる twist; (道などが) wind* /wáind/. ▶その道はくねって森を抜けている The path *winds* [*twists*] (its way) through the forest. ▶踊り子は体をくねらせて舞台を踊り回った The dancer *twisted around* on the stage.

くのう 苦悩 图 (an) agony, 《やや書》distress; 《やや書》anguish. ▶苦悩に満ちた叫び声を上げる give an *anguished* cry.
── 苦悩する 動 be in anguish [agony] 《over》; 《やや書》be distressed 《about》.

くはい 苦杯 ● 苦杯をなめる (人生で苦い経験をする) drink a bitter cup (⚠『聖書』からの句); (スポーツで負ける) be beaten, be defeated.

くばりもの 配り物 ▶隣近所へ配り物をする give [(配布する) distribute] *presents* [*gifts*] to one's neighbors.

くばる 配る ❶ 〚物などを〛(分配する) distribute; (渡す) give*... out; (手渡す) hand... out; (特にトランプの札などを) deal*... (out); (配達する) deliver. ▶貧しい人に食物を配る *distribute* [*hand out*] food *among* the poor. ▶新聞を配達する *deliver* newspapers. ▶彼は生徒に答案用紙を配った He *distributed* [*gave out*, *handed out*] the examination papers *to* the students. (⚠ ×...*distributed* [*gave out*, ...] the students the examination papers. の語順は不可) ▶案内係が入口に立ってプログラムを配っていた An usher stood at the door *giving out* the programs. ▶彼は彼女に 4 枚のエースの札を配った He *dealt* her four aces [four aces *to* her].
❷ 〚気を〛be attentive 《to》; (目を) keep* watch 《on》. ● その老女に気を配る be *attentive to* the old woman.

くひ 句碑 (石銘板) a stone tablet [(石碑) a stone

monument] inscribed with a *haiku*.

くび 首 ❶ [身体の] a neck; (首から頭部全体) a head.

解説 日本語の「首」は頭部全体をさすことがあるので「頭」も「首」ということがあるが,英語の neck は頭部 (head) と肩 (shoulder) をつなぐ部分をいい,前を throat (のど),後を nape (うなじ)という.したがって「首なし死体」は a *headless* body.

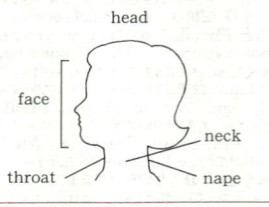

(図: head, face, neck, throat, nape)

① [首が] ▶彼は首が短い He has a short *neck*./(太く短い) He *is bull-necked*. ▶「細長い首」は a long, skinny [(ほっそりとした) a slender] neck,「太い首」は a heavy [(男性の) a thick] neck)
② [首の[に]] ▶首のあたり the neck area. ▶首の付け根 the root of the [one's] neck. ▶事故で首の骨を折る break one's *neck* [suffer a broken *neck*] in an accident. ▶首のない死体 a *headless* body. ▶彼女は首にスカーフを巻いている She wears a scarf around her *neck*. ▶彼女は彼の首に抱きついた She threw [flung] her arms around his *neck*.
③ [首を] ▶首をすくめる[ひっこめる] duck one's *head*; draw [pull] one's *head* in. 事情 恐縮して首をすくめる動作に米英人はしない ▶首を前後[左右]に曲げる bend one's *neck* back and forth [right and left]. ▶首を縮める shorten one's *neck*. (❗亀 (のような)動作) ▶コードで首を絞めて殺す strangle ⟨him⟩ with a cord; kill ⟨him⟩ by tightening a cord around ⟨his⟩ *neck*. ▶彼はそれを見ようと首を伸ばした He craned his *neck* [made a long *neck*] to see that. ▶彼は首をつって自殺した He committed suicide by hanging *himself*./(首つり自殺した) He hanged *himself*. (⇨首吊り) ▶彼は首をはねられた He had his *head* [×neck] cut off. (罰として) He was beheaded.

❷ [びん・服などの] a neck. ▶びん[ギター]の首 the *neck* of a bottle [a guitar]. ▶首の長い花びん a tall-*necked* vase. ▶丸首 (⇨丸首) ▶シャツの首回りはいくらですか What's the *neck* size of your shirt? ▶私は首回り13号のシャツを着ている I wear shirts with a size 13 *neck*.

❸ [解雇] (a) dismissal. ▶首が危ない be in danger of being fired; (今にも首になりそうである) be on the verge of being fired. ▶3人の労働者に対する不当な首切り the unfair *dismissal* of three workers. ▶君は首だ You're *fired*./(首にするぞ) I'll *fire* you.

❹ [その他の表現] ▶(ピッチャーが)キャッチャーのサインに首を振る give the catcher the shake-off; shake off the catcher's sigh. ▶彼がそれを知っていたら首をやる I'll *be* [*I am*] *hanged if* he knows it. (❗I'll be hanged if は⟨話⟩で,「...なら首をやる,絶対...なんかではない」といった強い否定を表す慣用表現)

● 首が飛ぶ ▶そんなにしょっちゅう残業を断っていたらしまいに首が飛ぶよ If you refuse to work overtime so often, you're going to *get the boot*. (❗be [get] *fired* の口語表現 (⇨首になる))
● 首が回らない ▶肩が凝って首が回らない I can't turn my *head* [×neck] because of a stiff neck. (❗

肩を neck ということに注意 (⇨肩)) ▶彼は借金で首が回らない He is *deeply* in debt./⟨話⟩ He is *up to* his *neck* [*ears*] *in* debt.
● 首にする ⟨話⟩ fire; (主に英語) sack, give ⟨him⟩ the sack; (解雇する) ⟨書⟩ dismiss.
● 首になる ▶彼女は怠けたので仕事を首になった She *was fired* [*was sacked*] *from* her job for being lazy./She *got fired* [*got sacked*, *got the sack*] because she was lazy.
● 首の差で勝つ ⟨やや書⟩ win (↔lose) *by* a neck. (❗競馬以外にも「辛勝する」の意で用いる)
● 首をかしげる tilt [incline] one's head to one side; (はてなと思って) cock one's head; (懐疑的である) be skeptical ⟨*about*, *of*⟩.
● 首を縦に振る ▶彼は同意のしるしに首を縦に振った He nodded his *head* in assent./He *nodded* his assent./He showed his assent *by nodding*.
● 首を突っ込む ▶机の下に首を突っ込む thrust one's *head* in under the desk. ▶他人の事に首をつっこむな ⟨話⟩ Don't poke [stick] your *nose* into other people's affairs.
● 首を長くする ▶彼が東京に来るのを首を長くして待っている I *am* very much *looking forward to* him coming to Tokyo./I *am* eagerly [*impatiently*] *waiting for* him to come to Tokyo.
● 首をひねる (一心に考える) rack one's brains [think hard] ⟨*over*, *at*⟩.
● 首を横に振る ▶彼は信じられないというように[不賛成の気持ちを表して]首を横に振った He shook his *head* in disbelief [*disapproval*]. (事情 英語国民の場合, 横に振るのは否定を表すほかに「ひどい」「信じられない」「悲しい」「同情・感心」などの気持ちを表しぐさ)
● 首飾り a necklace. ▶首かせ (刑具) a pillory; (重荷) a burden. ● 首筋 the nape of the neck. ● 首巻き (⇨❨ 襟巻き

ぐび 具備 ── 具備する 動 (備わっている) be furnished ⟨*with*⟩; (持っている) have, possess. ▶必要条件を具備する have [(満たしている) *fulfill*] a necessary condition.

くびきり 首切り [斬殺] beheading, decapitation; [解雇] (a) dismissal.
● 首切り台 a guillotine; a scaffold.

ぐびぐび ▶ぐびぐび(と)酒を飲む *gulp* [⟨米俗⟩ *chug*] *down* a drink of *sake*.

くびじっけん 首実検 图 [本人確認] identification ⟨*of* a suspect⟩.
── 首実検(を)する 動 ▶殺人犯の首実検をする *identify* the murderer; (身元を確かめる) *establish* [(調べる) *check*] the murderer's *identity*.

ぐびじんそう 虞美人草 ⇨ぐびじんそう(❨)

くびったけ 首ったけ ▶彼は彼女に首ったけだ ⟨話⟩ He *is crazy about* her./⟨話⟩ He *has a crush on* her./⟨話⟩ He's *madly in love with* her.

くびっぴき 首っ引き ▶英語の本を辞書と首っ引きで読む read an English book by *constantly using* [⟨主に書⟩ *consulting*] a dictionary [*with* a dictionary *at* one's *side*].

くびつり 首吊り ── 首吊り(を)する 動 (自殺をする) commit suicide by hanging oneself; hang oneself. (⇨首「首を吊る」)

くびなげ 首投げ [相撲] *kubinage*; a headlock throw.

くびねっこ 首根っこ the scruff of the [one's] neck; (横首) one's shirtcollar. ▶首根っこをつかむ hold ⟨him⟩ by the *scruff* of his *neck*.
● 首根っこをおさえる take [⟨やや書⟩ *seige*] ⟨him⟩ by the scruff of the neck; [人を思い通りにできる] have [get] ⟨him⟩ by the short hairs; (人をあご

くびれる 括れる ● 彼女のくびれたウエスト her *slender* waist. ● 赤ん坊の手首のくびれ a *crease* in a baby's wrist. ● そのびんは真ん中がくびれている The bottle is *narrow* in the middle.

くびわ 首輪 (犬などの) a (dog) collar. ● 首輪のない犬 a dog without a *collar*. ● 犬に首輪をつける put a *collar* on a dog; *collar* a dog.

***くふう** 工夫 图 ［方案, 仕掛け］a device /diváis/; ［着想］an idea; ［考案］(an) contrivance (**!** 「考案品」の意では ⓒ); ［発明］(an) invention (**!** 「発明品」の意では ⓒ). ● 工夫に富んだ人 an *ingenious* [《やや書》a *resourceful*] person. ● 工夫を凝らした計画案 a fully *worked-out* plan. ▶ この機械にはいろいろ工夫がしてある(=装置がある) There are various *devices* in this machine.
—— **工夫(を)する** 動 ［方法を見つける］find* a way (*of doing*; *to do*); ［方法などを］(苦労して) work ... out; (上手に)《やや書》devise /diváiz/; ［何とか考え出す］《書》contrive /kantráiv/; ［発明する］invent; ［考え出す］come* up with ...;《話》think* ... up. ● 料理を温かくしておく工夫をする *find* [*work out, devise*] a way of *keeping* the dishes warm. ▶ これらは私の工夫したものです These are the things I *invented* [(自分で作った) *made by myself*]./These are my *inventions* [*contrivances*]. ▶ 何とか工夫してみましょう I'll see if I can *come up with* something.

くぶくりん 九分九厘 ［十中八九］ten to one; in all probability; nine cases out of ten. ● 彼は試験に九分九厘合格するでしょう *Ten to one* [*In all probability, Nine cases out of ten*] he will pass the exam./(ほぼ確実に合格する) It is *almost certain* that he will pass the exam. (**!** It is sure that ... の文型はまれ)

くぶどおり 九分通り ▶ 体育館は九分どおり(=ほとんど)完成した The gymnasium has *almost* [*nearly*] been completed. (**!** nearly は完了が間近いこと, almost は間近だが完了していないことを含意) ▶ 私たちの計画は九分どおりうまくいくでしょう Our plan is *90 percent* sure to work well./It is *almost certain* that our plan will work well.

くぶん 区分 图 ［分けること］division; ［分類］classification, sorting. —— **区分する** 動 divide, partition ... (off); classify, sort. (➪分ける, 分類する)

:**くべつ** 区別 图《やや書》(a) distinction; discrimination. ● 性・年齢の区別なく regardless [*irrespective*] *of* sex or age.
—— **区別する** 動 tell* ［know*］《A *from* B》, tell [know] (them) apart (**!** 通例 tell は can を伴い, know は否定文・疑問文・条件文で用いる); ［特徴によって］《やや書》distinguish (**!** 通例進行形にしない); ［価値評価を伴って］《やや書》discriminate. ▶ 彼は正邪を区別できない He can't *tell* right *from* wrong [*the difference between* right *and* wrong]./He can't *distinguish* right *from* wrong./He can't *distinguish* [*make a distinction*] *between* right *and* wrong. ▶ 私はどっちがどっちか区別できない I can't *tell* [don't *know*] who is who [which is which]. (**!** who は人, which は物の場合) ▶ 彼らは目の色で区別できます You can *tell* them *apart* [*distinguish* them] *by* the color of their eyes./They can *be distinguished* [*are distinguishable*] (*from* each other) *by* the color of their eyes.

くべる ● 石炭を炉にくべる put coal *into* [*in*] a furnace; *feed* a furnace *with* coal. (**!** 「火にくべる」は *put* coal *on* the fire)

くぼち 窪地 a hollow;《やや書》a depression; ［周囲より下がった所］a hollow, 《やや書》a depressed] place; ［盆地］a basin.

くぼみ 窪み ［空洞］a hollow; ［地面の］a dip, (くぼ地)《やや書》a depression; ［打撃による］a dent. ● 彼女のほおのくぼみ *hollows* in her cheeks. ▶ ジープは地面のくぼみに突っ込んで大きくバウンドした The jeep hit a *dip* in [×on] the ground and bounced high.

***くぼむ** 窪む sink* (in); become* hollow [sunken]; (陥没する) cave in. (➪へこむ) ● 目のくぼんだ男 a *hollow*-eyed man; a man with *hollow* [疲労などで *sunken*, (生まれつきで) *deep-set*] eyes. ● くぼんだ道路 a *hollow* [a *sunken*] road.

くま 隈 ● 目の縁にくまができる get *dark circles* [*rings*] under one's eyes.

くま 熊 ［動物］a bear. ● 白熊 a white [a polar] bear. ● 子熊 a (*bear*) cub.
● 熊の胆(ｲ) dried bear's gall-bladder (used as a stomach medicine).

ぐまい 愚昧 图 stupidity; ignorance.
—— **愚昧の** 形 愚昧の人 a *stupid* [an *ignorant*] person.

くまげら 熊啄木鳥 ［鳥］a black woodpecker.

くまざさ 熊笹 ［植物］striped bamboo grass.

くまで 熊手 ● a rake. ● くま手でかき集める [かきのける] rake 《fallen leaves》together [off]. ● くま手でかく rake (a lawn).

くまどり 隈取り ❶ ［絵画の］color gradation; (濃淡) shading. ❷ ［歌舞伎の］*kumadori*; *kabuki* make-up.

くまなく 隈なく ● それをくまなく(=至る所を)探す look [search] *everywhere* for it; (すみずみまで)《話》search *every nook and cranny* for it. ● その時計がないか部屋をくまなく探す search the room *thoroughly* for the watch; search *everywhere* in the room for the watch; 《話》*comb* the room for the watch (**!** comb /kóum/ は「(場所を)徹底的に捜査する」の意). ● その国をくまなく旅行する travel *all* over [*throughout*] the country.

くまんばち 熊蜂 ［昆虫］(スズメバチ) a hornet; (クマバチ) a carpenter bee.

***くみ** 組 ❶ ［グループ］a group; ［仲間］company; ［チーム］a team. ● 5 人 1 組で in *groups* of five. ● 3 人ずつ 5 組ずつ 組からなる form five *groups* of three. ● 50 人を 5 つの組に分ける divide the 50 people into five *groups* [*teams*]. ● 男子 100 メートル一次予選第 8 組に出場する compete in the men's 100-meter preliminary, Round 1, *Heat* 8.
❷ ［一対］a pair, a couple (**!** pair の方が結びつきが強い. couple は主に成人男女のペアをさす); ［一そろい］a set. ● 2 人 1 組で in *pairs*. ● 2 人組の強盗 a *pair* of burglars. ● 3 組の新婚夫婦 three newly-married *couples*. ● 10 点 1 組の茶器 a ten-piece tea *set*. ● 彼と組になる (➪ペア, コンビ)
❸ ［学級］a class. (➪クラス) ● 1 年 1 組 *Class* 1 [one] of the first grade. ● この組はよく勉強する The students of this *class* study hard./The students work hard in this *class*./This *class* is《米》[are《英》] hardworking. (**!** この class は「クラスの人たち」の意)

ぐみ 茱萸 ［植物］a gumi; (北米産) a silverberry.

グミ ［<ドイツ語］a gummy candy.

***くみあい** 組合 ❶ ［(生活)協同組合］a cooperative (society) [(店) store]; (略 coop.); a co-op /kóuɑp/; ［協会］an association, a society (**!** 後の方が活動目的が限定され, 構成員の結びつきが強い).
● 農業協同組合 an agricultural *cooperative* (*association*); a farmers' *cooperative*. ● 共済組合 a

benefit 《米》[a friendly 《英》] society; 《英》a benefit *club*.
❷[[労働組合]] a union. (**!**(1) 正式には 《米》a labor union, 《英》a trade(s) union という. (2) 単・複の扱いについては (⇒団体 [解説])) ● 組合に加入する become a *union* member. ● 組合を作る[解散する] form [dissolve] a *union*. ● 工場労働者を組織して組合を作る organize the factory-workers into a *union*.
● 組合活動 únion activities. ● 組合活動家 únion àctivist. ● 組合費 únion dùes.

くみあう 組み合う [[組み合わせる]] link; (結びつく) join (together); [[とっくみ合う]] wrestle. ● 腕を組み合って歩く walk arm in arm [with one's arms *linked*].

くみあげる 汲み上げる [[くみ出す]] draw*; (ポンプで) pump ... up; (バケツやひしゃくで) dip (-pp-). ● 井戸から水をくみ上げる *draw* water [*pump* water *up*] from a well. ● かまから湯をくみ上げる *dip* hot water *out of* a boiler.

***くみあわせ 組み合わせ** ● いい色の組み合わせ(=配色)になる[である] make [be] a good color *combination*. ● 試合の組み合わせを抽選で決める decide the *matching* [*who plays who*(*m*)] for the tournament by lot. ▶そのコートと靴は絶妙な組み合わせだ The coat and the shoes are a perfect *match*.

くみあわせる 組み合わせる [[くっつける]] put*... together; [[結合させる]] combine; [[釣り合わせる]] match. ● バッグと靴を組み合わせる *match* one's bag *and* shoes; *match* one's bag *with* one's shoes. ● 両手をしっかり組み合わせる *fold* [*clasp*] one's hands tight *together*.

くみいれる 組み入れる (加え入れる) incórporàte. (⇒組み込む) ● 彼の提案を計画に組み入れる *incorporate* his suggestion *into* the plan.

くみいん 組員 a member of a gang; a gangster.

くみおき 汲み置き ● 汲み置きの水 (いつでも使える水) some water *ready for use* (*when needed*).

くみかえ 組み替え (計画・予定などの変更) rearrangement [recomposition] (*of* a plan); [[活字の]] recomposition (*of* printing type); [[遺伝子などの再結合]] recombination (*of* linked genes); [[予算などの修正]] revision (*of* the national budget).

くみがえ 組替え (クラス替え) reorganization of classes [(米) homerooms].

くみかえる 組み替える [[再整理する]] rearrange; [[作り直す, 改造する]] recompose; [[遺伝子などの再結合をする]] recombine; [[修正する]] revise; [[新しくグループ分けする]] regroup. ● 計画を組み替える *rearrange* [*recompose*] a plan. ● 遺伝子を組み替える *recombine* genes. ● 社会福祉の予算を組み替える *revise* the budget for social welfare.

くみかわす 酌み交わす (杯を交わす) exchange cups of *sake* (*with*); (いっしょに飲む) drink* together (*with*).

くみきょく 組曲 [[音楽]] a suite /swíːt/.

くみこむ 組み込む ● タイマーを組み込んだストーブ a heater with a *built-in* timer. ● 奈良見物を旅行計画に組み込む *include* a visit to Nara *in* the itinerary /aitínərèri/.

くみしく 組み敷く hold [get, pin]《him》down. (⇒組み伏せる)

くみしやすい 与し易い ▶彼はくみしやすい相手だ He *is easy to deal with*.

くみする 与する [[味方する]] take sides with, side with; [[賛成する]] approve of. ▶私はその議論では彼にくみして彼らに反論した I *took sides with* him *against* them in the argument. ▶どちらにもくみし

ません I won't *side with* either party./I'll maintain neutrality.

くみだす 汲み出す (ひしゃくなどで) dip out, ladle out; (ポンプで) pump out; (すくって) scoop out; (船の水を) bail out. ● ボートから水をくみ出す *bail out* a boat; *bail* water *out of* a boat.

くみたて 組み立て [[機械などの]] assembly; [[構造]] structure; [[文・語句の]]《やや書》construction. ● 組み立て式洋服ダンス a *knockdown* [(やや書) a *sectional*] wardrobe. ● 小説の組み立て the *structure* of a novel.
● 組み立て工 an assembler. ● 組み立て工場 an assémbly shòp (plànt).

***くみたてる 組み立てる** [[つなぎ合わせて]] put*... together; [[積みονあて]] build*, construct; [[部品を集めて機械などを]] assemble. ● 積み木を組み立てる *put* blocks *together*; *build* blocks. ● 文を組み立てる *construct* a sentence. ● 模型飛行機を組み立てる *build* a model airplane. ● エンジンを組み立てる *assemble* an engine.

くみちがい 組違い ❶[[組が違うこと]]● 組違いの同番号 the same number for a ticket with *the right number but the wrong letter*.
❷[[間違って組むこと]] putting up [constructing] (scaffolding) in a wrong way.

くみちょう 組長 (職工の) a foreman; (暴力団の) a gang leader, the boss of a gang; (級長) a class monitor.

くみつく 組み付く tackle. ● 泥棒に組みつく *tackle* a thief.

くみとる 汲み取る draw*. (⇒汲(´)む)

くみはん 組み版 (活字に組むこと) typesetting, composition; (印刷の版) 《米》a form, 《英》a forme.
● 組み版する set [compose] type; set up 《a manuscript》; put 《a manuscript》 in type; make into a form.

くみひも 組み紐 a braid; a braided [(編んで作った) a plaited] cord.

くみふせる 組み伏せる (押さえつける) hold* [get*] 《him》down; (格闘して) wrestle 《him》down; (地面[床]に) pin (-nn-) 《him》to the ground [floor].

くみほす 汲み干す empty (out); drain (out); pump out, bail out.

くみわけ 組み分け (学級編成) class organization.

***くむ 汲む** ❶[[くみ出す]] draw*; (ポンプで) pump; (ひしゃくやコップなどで) ladle; (すくって) scoop ... up. ▶彼はバケツで井戸から水をくんだ He *drew* water from the well with a bucket.

❷[[推し量る]] consider. (⇒思い遣り) ● 彼の気持ちをくむ *consider* his feelings; (やや書) *take* his feelings *into consideration*; (思いやる) *enter into* his feelings; *sympathize with* him. ● 言外の意味をくむ *catch* the connotative [implied] meaning; (文章の) *read* between the lines.

***くむ 組む** ❶[[協同する]] (いっしょに仕事をする) work together; (協力する) cooperate /kouɑ́pərèit/ 《with》; (団結する) unite 《with》; (話) (チームを組む, 協力する) team (up) 《with》; (力を結集する) join forces; (共謀する) 《やや書》 conspire 《with》. ▶私は彼と組んでその事業を始めた I *worked with* him [He and I *worked together*] to start the business. (**!**後の方より口語的)/I started the business *in cooperation* [*partnership*] *with* him. ▶警察と市民が結んで暴力防止に当たった Police and citizens *united* [*joined forces*] to prevent violence. ▶私は彼とテニスの試合でペアを組んだ I *was paired with* him in the tennis match./He was my partner in

[of] the tennis match. ▶彼らはペアを組んで(＝2人1組になって) walked *in pairs*. ▶彼らは手を組んで政府を倒そうと企てた They *conspired* (*with* each other) *to* overthrow the government.

❷【交差させる】cross; (両手・両腕を) fold. ●脚を組む *cross* one's legs. ●腕を組む *fold* one's arms. ●脚を組んでいすに座る sit on the chair *with* one's legs *crossed* [×crossing]. (⚠「あぐらをかいて」は (sit) *cross-legged* (⇨あぐら)) ▶私は彼が女の子と腕を組んで歩いているのを見た I saw him walking *arm in arm with* a girl.

❸【組み立てる】(つなぎ合わせる) put*... together; (部品を) (やや書) assemble; (建てる) put... up, erect; (建設する) construct; (活字を) set*... (up), (印刷) compose. ●建築の足場を組む *put up* [*erect*] a scaffold for the construction. ●見出し[活字]を組む *set* (*up*) [*compose*] a headline [the type]. ●プログラムを組む *write* a program.

くむ 酌む (注ぐ) pour 《*sake for* him》 (酒を飲む) drink.

くめん 工面 ── 工面する 動 ●金を工面する (用意する) *get* money *ready*; (調達する) *raise* money. ●なんとか工面して借金を払う *manage to* pay one's debt(s). ●どうにかしてその金を工面する *find* the money *somehow*.

:**くも** 雲 (a) cloud. ●物質としての雲、または形状のはっきりしない雲 ⓊⒸ, 雲片・雲塊は Ⓒ

①【~(の)雲】 ●きのこ雲 a mushroom *cloud*. ●黒い雲 black [dark] *clouds*. ●薄い雲 a thin cloud; a thin layer of cloud. ●飛行機雲 a vapor trail. ●雲ひとつない cloudless; unclouded. ▶空には一点の雲もなかった There wasn't a speck of *cloud* [were no *clouds*] (to be seen) in the sky.

> 関連 いろいろな雲: 絹雲 a cirrus/絹積雲 a cirrocumulus/絹層雲 a cirrostratus/高積雲 an altocumulus/高層雲 an altostratus/積乱雲 a cumulonimbus (⚠この雲の中には入道雲 a thunderhead, 雷雲 a thundercloud なども含む)/積雲 a cumulus/層雲 a stratus/層積雲 a stratocumulus/乱層雲 a nimbostratus.

②【雲(の)~】 ●雲間に[から] among [through] the *clouds*. ●雲のない[雲の多い]空 a *cloudless* [a *cloudy*] sky. ●雲のかかった月 the *clouded* moon. ●雲の切れ目(＝雲間)から飛行機が見えた We could see a plane through a break in the *clouds*. ▶太陽が雲間から顔を出した The sun came out from behind the *clouds*.

③【雲が】 ●雲が流れていくのを眺める watch a cloud floating by. ▶雲がある There's a cloud (in the sky). ▶雲が出てきたようだ *Clouds* seem to be gathering [forming]. ▶雲が切れて青空がのぞいた The *clouds* broke and the skies became blue. ●綿のような雲が空に浮かんでいる A fleecy *cloud* is floating [drifting, sailing] in the sky. ▶雲が低く垂れている The *clouds* are hanging low.

④【雲を】 ●山々は雲にそびえている The mountains rise [×is rising] above the *clouds*. ▶山々の頂上は厚い雲におおわれていた The mountain tops were covered in [with] thick *clouds*. ▶彼の乗った飛行機が上昇して雲に隠れるまで見送った I gazed after his plane until it went up and disappeared behind the *clouds*.

> 会話 「月が見えるかい」「雲にさえぎられて見えないよ」"Can you see the moon?" "No. It's blocked (out) by a *cloud*."

> 翻訳のこころ わたしたちは, 本当によい友と友であったのだ. 一度だって, 暗い疑惑の雲を, お互い胸に宿したことはなかった (太宰治『走れメロス』) We were truly good friends. Not once did we hold a dark cloud of suspicion in our hearts toward [against] each other. (⚠dark cloud は心の中などにある漠然とした不安・心配・懸念などを意味する慣用表現)

●雲突くばかり ●雲突くばかりの大男 a man of towering height.

●雲をつかむような ▶それは雲をつかむような(＝実現不可能な)計画だ It is a *visionary* [a *fantastic*, an *unfeasible*] plan.

くも 蜘蛛 【動物】a spider. ●くもの糸 a *spider*'s thread. ●くもの巣 a *spider*'s web; a cobweb. ▶小屋はほこりっぽくてくもの巣だらけだった The hut was dusty and full of *cobwebs*. ▶くもが巣を作っているのを見ていた I watched the *spider* spinning [making] a web.

●くもの子を散らすように ●くもの子を散らすように(＝四方八方に)逃げる run away *in all directions*.

くもあし 雲脚 the movements of the clouds. ▶雲脚が速い The clouds are moving fast./(空を飛ぶようによぎる) The clouds are driving across the sky.

くもがくれ 雲隠れ ── 雲隠れする 動 (姿をくらます) disappear 《*from*》; (逃げる) escape 《*from*》.

くもすけ 雲助 (悪質なかご担ぎ) a rascally palanquin bearer; (無頼者) a ruffian, a rascal; (暴漢) a thug.

くもつ 供物 a votive offering; an offering. ●亡母の仏前に供物を捧げる put [place] *offerings* before the memorial tablet of one's deceased mother.

くものいと『蜘蛛の糸』The Spider's Thread. (参考 芥川龍之介の小説)

くものうえ 雲の上 (宮中) the Imperial Court. ●雲の上人 (宮廷貴族) a court nobleman [noblewoman]; (皇族) an Imperial prince [princess].

くもま 雲間 ▶太陽が雲間から現れた The sun appeared *from behind the clouds*. ▶日光が雲間からもれた The sunlight broke [got] *through the clouds*.

くもまく くも膜 【解剖】arachnoid membrane. ●くも膜下出血 【医学】subarachnoid hemorrhage /hémərɪdʒ/.

くもゆき 雲行き ●雲行きを見る see which direction the clouds are moving; (形勢を) see how the wind blows; see how the situation develops. ●雲行きの荒い午後 under an afternoon sky of driving cloud. ▶雲行きが怪しい (悪天候になりそうだ) The weather would break./(形勢が怪しい) The situation is [Things are] getting worse.

くもらす 曇らす ●ガラスに息を吹きかけて曇らす breathe on the glass and *make* it *dim* [(不透明に) *opaque*]. ●目を涙で曇らせて with one's eyes *dimmed* [*clouded*] *with* tears. ▶彼はニュースを聞いて顔を曇らせた His face *clouded over* [His face took on a troubled look] when he heard the news./He *frowned* at the news.

*****くもり** 曇り ●【曇天】cloudy weather. ●曇り空 a *cloudy* [an *overcast*] sky. ●きのうは曇りだった It was *cloudy* [*overcast*] yesterday./We had (×a) *cloudy* weather yesterday.

❷【物の表面の汚れ・傷】(水滴・涙などによる) mist; (大理石などの) a cloud; (鏡などの) a blur. ●外を見ようと窓ガラスの曇りをぬぐう wipe the *mist* from the

windowpane to look out.
● 曇りガラス (⇨回 擦りガラス)

くもる 曇る ❶ [空が] get [become*] cloudy; (一面に) cloud over; get [become] overcast. (⇨曇り) ▶曇った空 a *cloudy* sky. ▶空が曇ってきた It's *getting cloudy*./The sky *is getting overcast*./The sky *is clouding over*. ▶スモッグで空が曇った The smog *clouded* the sky.

❷ [ガラスなどが] cloud up; (主に米) fog (-gg-) up, 《主に英》 mist. ▶紅茶の湯気で眼鏡が曇った My glasses *were misted* by the steam rising from my tea. ▶彼女の部屋の曇った窓ガラスに彼の伝言を書き残されていた His message was left on the *clouded* window of her room. ▶彼女の目は涙で曇っていた[曇った] Her eyes *were clouded with* tears (*misted over*). (⇨霞(㊥)む)

❸ [心・顔が] cloud (over). ▶彼女の心[顔]は悲しみで曇った Her mind [face] *clouded over* [*was clouded*] *with* grief.

くもん 苦悶 (心の) (やや書) ánguish; (心身の) (an) ágony. (⇨苦悩) ▶苦悶の表情 an *agonized* [an *anguished*] expression.

ぐもん 愚問 ▶愚問を発する ask a *stupid* [a *silly*, a *foolish*] *question*.

*くやしい 悔しい 〖人が〗 be frustrated 《at》; 《やや古》 be vexed 《at》; 〖出来事が〗 frustrating; 《やや古》 vexing; 《婉曲的》 regrettable. ▶悔しまぎれに(=悔しさから) out of *frustration* [《書》 *vexation*]. ▶悔し涙を流す (⇨悔し涙) ▶ああ悔しい How *frustrating* [*vexating*, *regrettable*]! (■ frustrating と vexing はいらだちを、frustrating は後悔を表す)(ああ残念) What a *shame*!/(ああがっかり) How *disappointing*! ▶私は試験に落ちて悔しかった I was [*felt*] *frustrated* [*upset*] when I failed the exam./(やや話) I was *sick at* having failed the exam. ▶悔しいことにその提案は却下された To my *disappointment* [《書》 *chagrin*], the proposal was turned down.

くやしがる 悔しがる be frustrated; 《やや古》 be vexed 《at》. ▶彼は失敗して[試合に負けて]悔しがった He *was frustrated* [*was upset*] *at* his failure [when he lost the game].

くやしさ 悔しさ (挫折(㊥)感) frustration; (いらだち) 《書》 vexation; (残念) regret. ▶悔しさがこみあげてきた My *frustration* mounted.

くやしなき 悔し泣き ▶悔し泣きする 動 cry with frustration; (悔し涙を流す) 《やや書》 shed bitter tears

くやしなみだ 悔し涙 ●悔し涙を流す shed tears of regret [frustration, mortification]. ▶試合に負けて彼女は悔し涙を流した She *was mortified* and *cried* [*shed bitter tears* (*of disappointment*)] when she lost the game.

くやしまぎれ 悔し紛れ ▶彼女は悔し紛れにコップを私に投げつけた She was so *upset* [*frustrated*] that she threw a glass at me.

くやみ 悔やみ ❶ [後悔] regret. (⇨後悔)
❷ [弔い] condolence. (⇨お悔やみ)
●悔やみ状 a letter of condolence.

*くやむ 悔やむ ❶ [後悔する] be sorry; regret (-tt-) (⇨後悔); [死を悼む] mourn. ▶その子供の死を悔やむ *mourn* (*over*) [*grieve over*] the child's death; *mourn* [*grieve*] *for* the dead child.

くゆらす 燻らす smoke. ▶葉巻をくゆらす *smoke* a cigar (leisurely).

くよう 供養 (hold) a memorial service.

くよくよ ── くよくよする 動 ▶そんなにくよくよするな Don't *worry* [*bother*]./Don't be so *pessimistic*. (■ pessimistic は「物事をマイナス方向に考える」という含意)/(元気を出せ) Cheer up. ▶何をくよくよしているのだ What *are you worried about*?/What's *eating you*? ▶過ぎた事をくよくよしてもしようがない(ことわざ) There is no use crying over *spilt milk*. (■ spilt は spill (こぼす) の過去分詞. spilt milk は「こぼしたミルク」の意)

くら 鞍 a saddle. ▶鞍を置く[はずす] saddle [unsaddle] 《a horse》.

くら 倉, 蔵 (⇨倉庫) ▶倉が建つ become rich.
●蔵払い (在庫一掃セール) a cléarance sàle.

*くらい 暗い

WORD CHOICE 暗い

dark 光がなくて見通しがきかないこと. しばしば色が黒みがかっていることをさす. また, 比喩的に用いて, 秘密・邪悪なども含意する. ●暗い青色 *dark* blue.

dim 光が不十分で物がぼんやりとしか見えないこと. ●薄暗い明かり *dim* light.

gloomy 部屋・空模様などが陰気で薄暗いこと. ●ある薄暗い日に on a *gloomy* day.

▶頻度チャート

dark
████████████████████████
dim
███
gloomy
██

20 40 60 80 100 (%)

❶ [明暗] dark (↔light); dim (-mm-); gloomy; dusky (■ 文語的で場所・光・特定の時間帯がたそがれのように陰が多く薄暗いこと). ●暗い=濃い赤 *dark* (↔light) red. ●暗い空 *dark* [*gloomy*] skies. ●暗い冬の夕方 a *gloomy* [a *dusky*] winter evening. ▶この部屋は暗い This room is *dark*./It's *dark* in this room. (■ it は明暗を表す主語)/This is a *dark* [a *dim*, (照明が不十分な) a *dimly lighted*, a *dimly lit*] room. (■ 限定用法の過去分詞としては lighted が普通だが, 前に副詞を伴うときは lit も可) ▶暗くて本が読めない It's too *dark* to read./The light is too *dim* to read by. ▶彼らは暗くならないまだ暗い)うちにそこを去っていた They got there before (it got) *dark* [while it was still *dark*, (夜明け前に) before daybreak]. (■「暗くなる」は It gets dark. のほかに It grows [turns] dark. が可) ▶舞台の照明はだんだん暗くなった The stage lights slowly *darkened*. ▶彼は暗いところで何か捜し物をしていた He was looking for something *in the dark*. ▶暗い所で本を読むのは目に悪い Reading in a *dim* [a *poor*] *light* is bad for the eyes.

❷ [前歴, 未来] (光明のない) dark; (憂うつな, 悲観的な) gloomy; (気をめいらせるような) depressing; (気のめいった) depressed; (後ろ暗い) shady. ▶戦時中の暗い日々 *dark* days during the war. ●暗い絵 a *gloomy* [a *depressing*, ×a *depressed*] picture.

▶暗い過去のある人 a man with a *shady* past. (■ 単に a man with a past ともいえる) ▶暗い気持ちになる feel *gloomy* [*depressed*, ×*depressing*]. ▶彼女は性格が暗い She has a very *gloomy* character. ▶その話を聞くと彼の表情は暗くなった His face grew *dark* when he heard the story. ▶私の前途は暗い I have a *dark* future (before me)./My future is *gloomy*./(将来を悲観する) I feel *gloomy* about my future. ▶人質釈放の見通しは今のところ暗い The outlook for the release of the hostages is *gloomy* [*bleak*] now.

❸ [知らない] not know 《it》; very well; (無知だ) be ignorant 《of》. (⇨明るい ❹) ▶彼は仕事に

He *knows nothing of* the world. ▶私はこの辺りの[この街の]地理に暗い(＝土地柄に不案内だ) I am a *stranger* here [in this town].

くらい 位 ❶[階級] (a) rank; [地位] (social) standing. (⇨地位)〔位の高い[低い]人〕a person of high [low] *rank*; a high-*ranking* [a low-*ranking*] person. ●位が上がる[下がる] rise [come down] in *rank*. ▶彼は私より位が上[下]だ He is above [below] me in *rank*./He *ranks* higher [lower] than I do [《話》than me,《書》than I]. ▶彼は大佐の位に昇進した He was promoted to the *rank* of (full) colonel./《英》He was promoted (to be) (full) colonel. (⚠ 2 例とも (full) colonel の無冠詞に注意)

❷[王位] the throne. ▶王は息子に位を譲った The king abdicated and passed his *throne* to [onto] his son.

❸[数字の] the position of a figure;〔小数以下の〕a place. ●位どりを間違える mistake *the position of a figure*. ●100 分の 1 の位まで計算する calculate to the second decimal *place* [two decimal *places*].

●位人臣(じん)を極める rise to the highest position as a civil servant.

*ーぐらい -位 (副助詞) ❶[およそ] about,《やや話》around; some [⚠数詞の前に限る]; ... or so. (⇨ほど❹) ▶そこには 50 人ぐらいの人がいた There were *about* [*around*, *some*] fifty people there. (⚠いずれも 32 などの端数の前では用いない) ▶駅まで歩いて 10 分ぐらいかかる It is *about* a ten-minute walk [It takes (us) ten minutes *or so* to walk] to the station. ▶それは卵ぐらいの大きさです It is *about* the size of an egg./It is *almost as big as* an egg. ▶昼食時ぐらいには帰ってきます I'll be back *about* [*around*] lunchtime. ▶彼らは 30 代前半ぐらいだった They were *somewhere* in their early thirties.

会話 「さて出かけなくちゃ」「何時ぐらいに帰るの」"I have to go out now." "When do you think you will be back?"

会話 「それはいつになりそう」「今月末ぐらい(＝近く)だと思うよ」"When do you think that'll be?" "(Sometime) *toward* the end of this month, I imagine."

❷[程度] so ... that; enough to (do); (どのぐらい) how many [much, long, old]. ▶この問題は中学生でもできるぐらいやさしい This question is *so easy that* even junior high school students can solve it./This question is easy *enough for* even junior high school students *to* solve. ▶その高さ[深さ，幅，厚さ，大きさ]はどれぐらいありますか *How high* [*deep*, *wide*; *thick*; *large*] is it? ▶君のお父さんはいくつぐらいですか *How old* is your father? ▶体重はどのぐらいですか *How much* do you weigh?/*What* is your weight? ▶ここから学校までどのくらいありますか *How far* is it from here to your school? ▶1 か月に何回ぐらい図書館に行きますか *How often* [*How many times*] do you go to the library a month? ▶あとどのぐらいでこの列車は出発しますか *How soon* will this train start?

❸[軽く見る気持ちを表す] ▶私にもそれぐらいのことならできますよ I could do *that much* [*things like that*]. (⚠ could は仮定法. 前の方は仕事量, 後の方は仕事の種類が話題) ▶そんなぐらい何でもない *That's* no trouble at all. ▶おばかさんぐらいかわいいものはない *How foolish* [*What a fool*] you are!/No one is as [《やや書》*so*] stupid *as* you are. ▶ぼくだって英語ぐらい話せるよ Even I can speak English *at* *least*. ▶彼はきっとだめとは言わないだろうが, 一応聞いてみるぐらいのことはしてもよかろう I'm sure he won't object to it, but it wouldn't hurt just to ask.

❹[...するくらいなら(むしろ)] ▶みじめな生活を送るぐらいなら死んだ方がましだ I *would rather* die *than* lead a miserable life./I *might as well* die *as* live a miserable life.

クライアント[顧客] a client.
くらいえ『暗い絵』*Dark Pictures*. (参考) 野間宏の小説)
くらいこむ 食らい込む[刑務所に入れられる] be thrown in jail;《話》be locked up;《話》be put away;《話》be sent up. ●他人の借金を食らい込む(＝背負い込む) *be saddled* [*burdened*] *with* other people's debts.
クライストチャーチ[ニュージーランドの都市] Christchurch.
くらいする 位する ❶[地位を占める] ▶その会社は建築業界でも上位に位する That company *ranks as* one of the larger of the building trade.
❷[位置する] ▶日本はアジアの東北に位する Japan *is located* [*is situated*; *lies*] to the northeast of Asia.
グライダー a glider. (長距離用) a sailplane.
くらいつく 食らい付く ▶犬は肉に食らいついた The dog *snapped* [*bit*] *at* the meat./(しっかりとくわえて放さなかった) The dog *latched onto* the meat.
くらいまけ 位負け ─ 位負けする 動 ▶彼は位負けしている(自分の地位に) He cannot live up to his position [title]./(相手に) He is outranked [《やや書》is overawed] by his opponent.
クライマックス[最高潮] a climax. ▶ここでその話はクライマックスに達する Here the story reaches [comes to] its *climax*.
くらう 食らう[食べる] eat*;〔むさぼり食う〕《やや書》devour /dɪváʊər/;〔飲む〕drink*;〔受ける〕get*. ●大酒を食らう drink heavily. ●致命的な一撃を食らう *get* a fatal blow.
クラウチング ●クラウチングスタート a crouch(ing) start. ●クラウチングスタイル a crouching style.
クラウン[王冠, 帽子の山] a crown.
グラウンド[学校の運動場] a playground;[競技場] a ground; an athletic field;〔観覧席つきの〕a stadium. ●野球のグラウンド a baseball *ground* [*field*].
●グラウンドキーパー a groundsman;《英》a ground(s)man;[野球] (a member of) ground crew ▼groundkeeper はその主任. ●グラウンドストローク [テニス] a ground stroke. ●グラウンドゼロ (ゼロ地点) ground zero,《しばしば大文字で》Ground Zero (参考) アメリカ同時多発テロ事件による世界貿易センタービル崩壊跡地). ●グラウンドボーイ a batboy (⚠日本語は ball boy も含む);[男女共用] a batkeeper. ●グラウンドマナー pláying mànners.
くらがえ 鞍替え ─ 鞍替えする 動(変える) change;(切り換える) switch. (後の方が口語的) ●新しい仕事にくら替えする *change* jobs [one's job]; *switch to* another job; get a new job. ●教職からもの書きにくら替えする *switch (over) from* teaching *to* writing (stories).
くらがり 暗がり the dark;〔暗い所〕a dark place. (⇨暗闇(くらやみ)) ▶暗がりでつまずかないように注意しなさい Be careful not to trip in *the dark*.
くらく 苦楽 joys and sorrows. ●苦楽をともにする stick together [help each other] through thick and thin; share one's lot (*with*).
クラクション a (car) horn. ●クラクションを鳴らす

くらくら

sound [honk] a *horn*.

くらくら 副 ❶【湯のわくさま】(⇨ぐらぐら❷)
❷【情念の燃えるさま】▶嫉妬の炎が彼女の中でくらくらと燃えた Jealousy *burned* [*boiled*] in her breast./She *was consumed with* jealousy.
—**くらくらする** 動 feel *dizzy* [*giddy*]; have a dizzy [a giddy] feeling [spell]. ●くらくらする高さ a *dizzy* [a *giddy*] height. ▶強い酒を飲んで頭がくらくらした The strong drink made me feel *dizzy* [*giddy*]. ▶頭がくらくらする I feel my head *spin*./My head *is reeling*.

ぐらぐら 副 ❶【不安定な様子】▶地震で家がぐらぐら揺れた Our house *was jolted* with the earthquake./The earthquake *shook* our house violently.
❷【煮え立つ様子】▶湯がぐらぐら煮えている The water *is boiling hard* [is *at a full boil*]. (❗ hardやfullを除くと「くらくら」ぐらいのわき方)
—**ぐらぐらする** 動 shake, tremble. ●ぐらぐらしている be unsteady, (やや話) be wobbly, (話) be shaky. ●ぐらぐらする歯 a *loose* [*wobbly*] tooth. ▶この机はぐらぐらしている This desk is *unsteady* [《話》 *rickety*]. ▶彼女の考えはよくぐらぐらしている Her thoughts are often *shaky* [*unstable*].

くらげ 水母【動物】a jellyfish (複 ~, ~es).

*くらし 暮らし【生活】life (複 lives /láivz/)(⇨生活); 【生計】(a) living; (a) livelihood (⇨生計). ●田舎(の)暮らし country *life*; *life* in the country. ●貧乏暮らし *living* in poverty. ●暮らし向きがよい[悪い] be well [badly] off. ●収入内[以上]の暮らしをする live within [beyond] one's income. ●その日暮らしをする(将来を考えず) *live* from hand to mouth; (細々と) *scrape* a living day by day. ●一人暮らしをする a *live* alone.

■ **DISCOURSE**
情報技術は暮らしを楽にした一方で,多くの点で生活を大変にもした **While** information technology has made *life* easier, in many ways it has made life more difficult, too. (❗ While ..., や Too (...である一方,また~でもある)は対比を表すディスコースマーカー. 対照的な内容を述べるのに使う)

グラジオラス【植物】a gladiolus (複 gladioli, ~es).
くらしきりょう 倉敷料 warehouse charges; storage (charges).
クラシック【古典音楽】classical [ˣclassic] music.
●クラシックカー a classic car; (特に1920年代の) a vintage car. ●クラシックレース【競馬】(五つの重賞レースをまとめて) the classic races; (その一つ) a classic race.

‡**くらす 暮らす**【生活する】live (⇨生活する);【何とかうまくやってゆく】get* on [along];【生計を立てる】make* a [one's] living (⇨生計). ●ぜいたくに[何不自由なく]暮らす *live* in luxury [comfort]; *lead a* luxurious [a comfortable] *life*. ●仲よく暮らす *live* in peace [harmony] 《with》. ●安月給でどうにか暮らしています I'm *managing* (to live) [《細々と》 *scraping along*, 《四苦八苦して》 *struggling along*] on a small salary. ▶彼の収入があなくても何とか暮らせると思います I'm sure I can *get on* [*along*] without his salary.

*クラス ❶【学級】a class; 《米》(ホームルーム) a homeroom. (語法) 米英では授業ごとに学生が教室を移動するのが普通なので, 日本の中学・高校の「クラス」はむしろ homeroom に当たる)【学級】英語のクラス an English *class*. ●40人のクラス a *class* of 40 pupils [students]. ●少人数のクラス a small *class*. ▶このクラスの生徒は勉強好きではからかだ This

グラニューとう

class is 《米》[are《英》] studious and cheerful. (❗ 通例《米》では単数扱い,《英》では複数扱い) クラスは意見が分かれている The *class* are [ˣis] divided in their opinion. (❗ この場合, 個々の構成員を問題にするため複数扱いになる)
❷【等級】a rate, a class;【質】quality. ● A クラスのホテル a first-*rate*[-*class*] hotel. ●トップクラスの新聞 a top-*quality* newspaper. ●トップクラスの学者たち top-*class* scholars.

●クラス会 a class meeting; (同窓会) a class reunion. ●クラス担任 one's homeroom [class] teacher. (⇨担任) ●クラスメート a classmate.

グラス【コップ】a glass (⇨コップ);【ガラス】glass. ●ステンドグラス stained *glass*. ●グラスをかちんと当てて...の乾杯をする clink one's *glasses* together and drink to ....

●グラスウール【ガラス綿】glass wool. ●グラスファイバー【ガラス繊維】glass fiber, fíberglàss. ●グラス(ボトム)ボート【船底がガラス張りの遊覧船】a glass-bottom boat.

グラス【芝生】grass.
●グラスコート a grass court. ●グラススキー grass [turf] skiing.

グラスゴー【スコットランドの都市】Glasgow.
クラスター【ディスク装置の記憶領域の単位】【コンピュータ】a cluster.
●クラスター爆弾【軍事】a cluster bomb.

グラスノスチ【<ロシア語】【情報公開】glasnost /glǽznəst/.

くらだし 蔵出し delivery 《of goods》 out of the warehouse. ●蔵出しの酒 *sake* direct from the warehouse.

グラタン【<フランス語】gratin /grǽtn,《英》grǽtæŋ/.
●マカロニグラタン macaroni *au gratin* /òu grǽtn/.

クラッカー【菓子】a cracker;【爆竹】a (fire)cracker.
●クラッカーを鳴らす set off a *cracker*.

クラック【亀裂】a crack.

ぐらつく【揺れる】shake*;（ぐらぐらする）《やや話》wobble;（ゆるくなる）get* loose;（人・物が今にも倒れそうになる）totter;【動揺する】（人・信念などが）be shaken, waver. ▶いすがぐらついている The chair is *unsteady* [*wobbly*, 《話》 *shaky*]. ▶その患者はまだ足がぐらついていた The patient was still *unsteady* on his feet./The patient's legs were still feeling *wobbly*. ▶彼の決心がぐらついた His decision *was shaken*./He *wavered in* his decision.

クラッシュ 名【衝突, コンピュータの故障】a crash. ●ディスククラッシュ a disk crash.
—**クラッシュする** 動 crash. ▶ハードディスクがクラッシュしてデータが失われたかもしれない The hard disk has *crashed* and the data may have been lost.
●クラッシュ症候群【医学】《suffer *from*》crush syndrome.

クラッチ ❶【自動車の】a clutch. ●クラッチを入れる[切る] let in [release, let out] the *clutch*. ●ノークラッチ (機能) (an) automatic transmission; (車) an automatic.
❷【ピンチ・チャンス】a clutch, a pinch.
❸【握りかかえること】a clutch.
❹【ボートの】a crutch.
●クラッチバッグ a clutch (bag). ●クラッチヒッター【チャンスに強いバッター】【野球】a clutch hitter.

グラデーション【色彩, 色調や明暗のぼかし】(a) gradation /greidéiʃən/. ●色の微妙なグラデーション subtle *gradation* in [of] color.

グラナダ【スペインの都市】Granada /grənɑ́ːdə/.

グラニューとう グラニュー糖 granulated sugar; (白砂糖) table sugar.

グラビア ●グラビア印刷 photogravure, gravure /ɡrəvjúər/. ●グラビア写真 a photogravure.

クラブ ❶[団体] a club; [その建物] a club, (特にスポーツクラブなどの) a clubhouse (圈 -houses /-ziz, (米) -siz/). ●クラブ活動をする attend *club* activities [(学校の教科外活動) extracurricular activities]. ●クラブに入る join a *club*; become a member of a *club*.
会話「学校でどんなクラブに入っているの」「テニスクラブに入っています」 "*What club* are you in at school?" "I'm in [I belong to, I'm a member of] the tennis *club*."
❷[ゴルフの打棒] a (golf) club. ▶それはグリーンに乗せるのに十分な番手のクラブじゃないだろうと彼は言った He said it wouldn't be enough *club* to make the green. (!*club*の無冠詞に注意)
❸[トランプの] clubs. (!単・複両扱い. クラブのカードの1枚は a club) ●クラブの5 the five of *clubs*.
●クラブ員 a club member; a member of a club. ●クラブ顧問 a club adviser. クラブハウス a clubhouse (圈 -houses /-ziz, (米) -siz/).

****グラフ** a graph; [図表] a diagram. (⇨図) ●棒[折れ線]グラフ a bar [a line] *graph*. ●円グラフ a circle *graph*, a pie *chart*. ●グラフをかく make [draw] a *graph* (*of*). ●出欠をグラフにして記録する make a *graphic* record of school attendance.

グラブ a 《baseball [boxing]》glove /ɡlʌ́v/. (⇨グローブ)

グラフィック graphics (!画像は複数扱い, 処理法は単数扱い); graphic arts (!複数扱い). ●コンピュータグラフィックス computer *graphics*.
●グラフィックデザイナー a graphic designer. ●グラフィックデザイン (作業) graphic design; (作品) a graphic design.

クラフトし クラフト紙 《a sheet of》kraft paper.

-くらべ -比べ ●力[腕]比べ a *contest* of (physical) strength [skill]. ●力[知恵; 腕; 背]比べをする *measure* one's strength [wits; skill; height] 《*against* [*with*] him》.

くらべもの 比べもの (⇨比較)
●比べものにならない ▶これはあれとは比べものにならないほどいい This is incomparably [(はるかに) *much*, *far*, (話) *a lot*] better than that. ▶それも悪くはないが良質のフランスワインと比べものにならない That's drinkable, but not to be *compared with* good French wine. ▶頭のよさでは私は彼とは比べものにならない I'm *no match for* him *in* intelligence.

くらべる 比べる

WORD CHOICE 比べる
compare 複数の物や人を比較し, 相違点・類似点などを多面的に明らかにすること. ●オーストラリアと比べた場合 when *compared* with Australia
contrast 複数の物や人を比較し, 相違点をくっきりと浮き立たせること. ●兄弟を対照的に比べる *contrast* the brothers.

頻度チャート

compare	████████████
contrast	████
	20 40 60 80 100 (%)

compare 《A *with* [*to*] B》; [対比・対照する] contrast 《A *with* [*and*] B》; [優劣を試す] measure 《A *against* [*with*] B》. (⇨比較する) ●その二つの時計を比べる *compare* the two watches; *make a comparison between* the two watches. ▶父はいつも私を兄と比べる My father always *compares* me *with* my brother./My father always *measures* me *against* my brother. ▶彼女の悩みに比べたら君の悩みなど何でもない (*As*) *compared with* [*to*] her trouble, yours is nothing. (!*as*は通例省略される. 前置詞句を用いて *In* [*By*] *comparison with* her trouble, …. ともいえる)/Your trouble is nothing *to* hers. (!「…に比べて」の意) ▶彼と競走してどちらが速いか比べた(=確かめた) I ran a race with him to *see* [*find* (*out*)] which of us could run faster. ▶5月は4月に比べ(=よりも)消費者物価が0.2パーセント上昇した In May, consumer prices were 0.2 percent *higher than* (those) in April. (!than の代わりに文字通りに *higher* [*high*] *compared with* those in April としてもよい. この構文では high の方が正しいとされるが慣用的には higher が多く用いられる. (2) 0.2 は point two と読む) ▶彼は心の中で二つの考えを比べて(=天秤にかけて)みた He *balanced* the two ideas in his mind.

グラマー ——グラマーな 形《やや書》voluptuous /vəlʌ́ptʃuəs/; (曲線美の) 《話》curvaceous /kərvéiʃəs/. (!*glamorous* は必ずしも肉体的魅力を意味しない) ▶彼女はグラマーです She is *voluptuous*. (!胸だけに言及して She is top heavy. とか胸とヒップに注目して She's got a fantastic [a great, a well-rounded] body. などという. 直接的に She has big breasts. などというのは下品)

くらます 晦ます disappear; (隠れる) hide* (oneself); (人の目を) deceive.

グラミー [最優秀レコード賞] a Grammy (Award).

くらむ 眩む (一時的に目が見えなくなる) be blinded (!比喩的な意味でも用いられる); (特に, まぶしくて) be dazzled. ●目もくらむようなダイヤのネックレス a necklace of *dazzling* diamonds. ●目がくらむような高さ a *dizzy* [a *giddy*] height. ●欲に目がくらむ *be blinded* by one's own desire. ▶ヘッドライトの光で目がくらんだ The headlights *dazzled* [*blinded*] me.

グラム 《略 g, gm, gr.》 a gram. (!事情 米英ではヤード・ポンド法が日常的) ▶牛肉500グラムください Give me 500 *grams* of beef.

くらもと 蔵元 a sake brewery [brewhouse].

****くらやみ 暗闇** the dark; (暗さ) darkness. (⇨真っ暗)
●暗闇が怖い be afraid of *the dark*. ●暗闇に紛れて逃げる run away *under* (*the*) *cover of darkness*. ▶暗闇で何も見えなかった I couldn't see anything *in the dark* [*darkness*].

クラリネット [楽器] a clarinét. ●クラリネット奏者 a clarinet(*t*)ist; (楽団の一パートとして) a clarinet. ●クラリネットを吹く play the *clarinet*.

くらわす 食らわす (パンチを) punch; (殴る) hit*. ●彼にげんこつを1発食らわす *punch* him (*on the jaw*), *give* him *a punch* (*on the jaw*); *give* him *a hard blow* (*to* the jaw). (!*blow* ではこん棒などでなぐる場合もある)

クランク ▶その映画はパリでクランクイン[クランクアップ]した They have *started* [*finished*] *shooting* the movie in Paris. (!The movie cranked up は「映画の上映が始まった」の意)
●クランクシャフト a crankshaft.

グランド [学校の運動場] a playground. (⇨グラウンド)

グランド [規模の大きな] grand.
●グランドオペラ (a) grand opera. ●グランドスラム a grand slam. (参考 ゴルフ・テニスで主要な大会すべてに優勝すること. 野球では満塁本塁打を指す) ●グランドデザイン [全体構想] grand design. ●グランドピアノ a grand piano.

グランドキャニオン [米国の渓谷] the Grand Can-

yon.
グランプリ [＜フランス語] 『大賞』a grand prix (⑱ grands prix) / ⑲ grá:n prí:/; (the) first prize. (⇨賞)
くり 栗 『植物』(実) a chestnut /tʃésnʌt/; (木) a chestnut tree. ●栗のいが a chestnut prickle. ●栗を拾う[拾い集める] pick up [gather] chestnuts. ●栗色の髪 chestnut [nut-brown] hair.
●栗きんとん kurikinton; (説明的に) chestnut paste or sweet potato paste with sweetened chestnuts mixed in.
くり 庫裏 (寺の台所) the kitchen of a Buddhist temple; (住職とその家族の居間) a Buddhist priest's and his family's living room.
クリア ── クリアする 動 (跳び越える) clear; (難関を突破する) pass; (達成する) achieve, attain; (乗り越える) get over..., overcome; (解決する) settle, solve; 『サッカー』clear the ball.
●クリアボール 『サッカー』a cleared ball.
くりあがる 繰り上がる ▶(選手が) 3位に繰り上がる move up into third place. ▶出発の日時が繰り上がった The time and date of our departure has been moved up.
くりあげ 繰り上げ ▶次点者が彼の代わりに繰り上げ当選した The runner-up was declared elected in place of him.
くりあげる 繰り上げる ▶彼は予定を繰り上げて帰って来た He came back earlier than scheduled. ▶彼らは結婚式(の日取り)を6月5日から5月5日に[1か月]繰り上げた They advanced [moved up] (the date of) the wedding from June 5 to May 5 [(by) one month]. (❶ move up の方が口語的)
クリアビジョン an extended definition television [TV] (system)《略 EDTV》. (❶ (1) Clear Vision はこの規格の日本名. (2) ワイドクリアビジョン《EDTV II》は TV in a wide-screen format.)
クリアランスセール a cléarance sàle.
クリアリング 『決算, 決済』『経済』clearing.
くりあわせる 繰り合わせる ▶何とか時間を繰り合わせて入院中の先生を見舞った I managed to make the time to visit my teacher in the hospital. ▶万障繰り合わせのうえご出席ください Your attendance is earnestly requested.
グリー ●グリークラブ 『男声合唱団』a glee club. (関連) その合唱団 a glee)
グリーグ 『ノルウェーの作曲家』Grieg (Edvard ～).
グリース grease.
グリーティングカード 『お祝い状』a gréeting càrd.
クリーナー (道具) a cleaner; (洗剤) cleaner. (⇨クレンザー) ●窓拭き用クリーナー window cleaner.
クリーニング 『ドライクリーニング』cleaning; (水洗い) laundering. ●ドライクリーニング dry cleaning. ●ドライクリーニングをする dry-clean (a suit); have (a suit) dry-cleaned. ●クリーニングに(＝洗濯屋)出して送る (one's suit) to the laundry [cleaner's, cleaners]. (⇨洗濯①) ●クリーニング代を節約する save the cleaner's expense.
*****クリーム** 『クリーム一般』cream; 『アイスクリーム』íce crèam; 『化粧用の』cream (❶ a face cream, a hand cream など). ●コールドクリーム cold cream. ●シュークリーム a cream puff. ●生クリーム fresh cream. ●クリーム色の cream-colored. ●顔にクリームを塗る apply cream to one's face. ▶クリームを入れますか Do you take cream?
●クリームスープ crèam sòup. ●クリームソーダ an ice cream float. ●(米) a cream soda はバニラ風味のソーダ水) ●クリームチーズ créam chèese.
くりいれる 繰り入れる (加える) add; (繰り送す) carry ... forward [over]. ●利子を元本に繰り入れる add interest to the capital.

クリーン ── クリーンな 形 『きれいな, 清潔な』clean.
●クリーンエネルギー clean energy. (参考) 太陽熱・風力など) ●クリーンヒット 『野球』a clean hit.
●クリーンルーム 『無塵室』a clean room.
グリーン 『緑色』green (⇨緑); 『ゴルフの』a (putting) green; (ゴルフ場) a golf course. ●2打でグリーンに乗せる《人が主語》get to [make] the green in two strokes. ●グリーンを左にはずす miss the green to the left. ●グリーンを読む read the green(s).
●グリーンカード 『外国人永住[就労]許可証』(米) a green card. ●グリーンサラダ (盛り合わせ) (a) (mixed) green salad. ●グリーン車 (一等車) a first-class car. ●グリーンティー green tea. ●グリーンピース 『植物』green peas; 『団体名』Greenpeace.
●グリーンベルト (道路の植え込みのある中央分離帯) (米) a planted median strip; (英) a planted central reservation; (都市の環境保全用緑地帯) a gréen bèlt.
クリーンナップ 『野球』(3-5番) the heart of the (batting) order; (野球) the 3-4-5 hitters (❶ the three, four, five hitters と読む; 《和製語》clean-up trio. (❶ the cleanup (hitter) は 4番打者 (the fourth hitter, 《話》the number-four hitter)のこと)
グリーンランド 『デンマーク領の島』Greenland. ●グリーンランドの Greenlandic.
クリエーティブ ── クリエーティブな 形 『創造的な』creative.
クリエート ── クリエートする 動 『創造する』create.
クリオネ 『魚介』a clione.
くりかえし 繰り返し (やや書) (a) repetition; (歌の) a refrain. ●繰り返しの多い話 (やや書) a repetitious speech. ●同じ歌を繰り返し繰り返し歌う sing the same song over and over (again) [again and again, repeatedly].
●繰り返し符号 (語句の) a ditto mark (記号 〃); (楽譜の) a repeat sign [mark].
*****くりかえす 繰り返す** 『もう一度言う[行う]』repeat; 『もう一度...する』動+(over) again; 『何度も言う[起こる]』repeat oneself [itself]. ▶彼はその質問を繰り返した He repeated the question. ▶同じ間違いを繰り返すな Don't make the same mistake again. (❶ repeat はすでに「同じことをもう一度」という意味を含んでおり ×Don't repeat the mistake again. は不可. また Don't repeat the same mistake. のような言い方も避けた方がよい) ▶歴史は繰り返す History repeats itself. (❶ ×History repeats. は不可) ▶その患者は入退院を繰り返していた The patient had been in and out of ((主に米) the) hospital.
くりくり ●くりくり太ったかわいい赤ちゃん a cute, chubby baby. ●くりくりした目 cute, round eyes. ●くりくりしたお尻 small, firm buttocks. ▶彼は頭をくりくりにした He had his head shaved [shaven] clean./ (短く刈った) He had his hair cropped short.
●くりくり坊主 (頭) a clean-shaven head, a close haircut; (子供) a kid with a close haircut.
ぐりぐり ●首にぐりぐりができている I have a lump on the neck. (❶ lump は「しこり」から「ぐりぐり」まで触感に幅がある) ●ぐりぐりした目 rude-looking big eyes.
●目をぐりぐりする rub one's eye(s) hard.
くりげ 栗毛 ●栗毛の馬 a chestnut (horse); a bay (horse); a sorrel.
クリケット 『競技』(play) cricket.
グリコーゲン 『生化学』glycogen /ɡláikədʒən/.
くりこし 繰り越し ●繰越金 (次期への) the balance carried forward; (前期からの) the balance

くりこす brought forward.
くりこす 繰り越す transfér (-rr-) 《*to, from*》; (次へ) carry 《it》 forward 《*over*》 《*to*》; (前から) bring* 《it》 forward 《*from*》. ●その金額を翌月に繰り越す *carry* the money *forward* to the next month.
くりごと 繰り言 ●繰り言を言う tell the same story (over and) over again; harp on the same string; (不平を言う) grumble 《*over, about*》; complain.
くりこむ 繰り込む [ぞろぞろ入る] march [swarm] 《*in; into*》; [繰り入れる] [繰り返す] transfer (-rr-) …《*to*》; (加える) add…《*to*》; [たぐり寄せる] pull [haul] in 《the rope》.
くりさがる 繰り下がる (繰り下げられる) be moved back; (延期される) be postponed, be put off. ▶音楽会の日程が繰り下がった The schedule for the concert *has been moved back*.
くりさげる 繰り下げる (延期する) postpone, put*…off. (後の方が口語的の) ●コンサートを2か月(だけ)繰り下げる *postpone* the concert for two months.
クリスタル crystal 《glass》.
クリスチャン a Christian. ●敬けんなクリスチャン a devout *Christian*.
●クリスチャンネーム a Christian name; a baptismal name. ([米]ではキリスト教徒でない名前の多いので given name, first name が好まれる。[英]では forename がよく用いられる)
*クリスマス** Christmas ([!] 12月25日をさす場合と、24日から元日([英]では1月6日)までをさす場合とがある。前の方は明確にいう場合は Christmas Day. 後の方なら Christmastime; [[略]] [話] Xmas は[掲示などに用いる。X'mas は誤り) ●クリスマスの贈り物 a Chrístmas prèsent [gìft]. ●クリスマスに (12月25日) on *Christmas* (Day); (クリスマスの季節に) at *Christmas* [*Christmastime*]. ●クリスマス(の贈り物)に彼に時計を買ってやる buy him a watch for *Christmas*. ●クリスマスはハワイで過ごした We stayed in Hawaii over *Christmas*. ([!] over は「…の間ずっと」の意)
[会話] 「クリスマスおめでとう」「おめでとう」"(I wish you a) merry *Christmas*!/(A) Merry *Christmas* (to you)!" "The) same to you/Best wishes to you, too." ([!] [英] ではしばしば merry のほかに happy も用いる)
●クリスマスイブ (on) Christmas Éve. ●クリスマスカード a Chrístmas càrd. ●クリスマスキャロル a Chrístmas cárol. ●クリスマス休暇 the Chrístmas vacátion [hólidays]. ●クリスマスケーキ a Chrístmas càke. [参考] 米英の Christmas cake は日本のものとは異なりフルーツケーキの一種。またケーキでなくクッキーを焼く人が多い) ●クリスマスツリー a Chrístmas trèe. ●クリスマスリース a Chrístmas wrèath.
グリセリン [化学] glycerin(e) /glísərin/, glycerol.
●ニトログリセリン nitroglycerine /nàitrou-/.
くりだす 繰り出す (出かける) go*; (送り出す) send*. ●街へ繰り出す *go* downtown. ●大軍を繰り出す *send* a large army. ●ロープを(少しずつ)繰り出す *pay out* a rope. ●釣り糸を繰り出す *reel* [*let*] *out* a line.
クリック [名] [コンピュータ] a click.
── **クリックする** [動] click. ▶開きたいファイルのアイコンをダブルクリックしてください Double-*click* on the icon for the file you want to open.
クリップ [紙はさみ] a (paper) clip; [髪の] a hairpin; (カール用) a curling pin, a curler. ●クリップで留める *clip* 《documents》 together.
●クリップボード [コンピュータ] a clipboard. ([参考] データを一時保存しておく場所)

グリップ a grip; [野球] (バットの) a handle.
グリップエンド [野球] a knob. ●バットをグリップエンドぎりぎりに握る hold a bat at the *knob*.
くりど 繰り戸 a sliding door.
クリトリス [陰核] [解剖] a clitoris.
クリニック [診療所] a clinic. ●マタニティクリニック an antenatal [×maternity] *clinic*.
くりぬく 刳り貫く (ものを中空にする) hollow … out; (山などを掘り抜く) dig* through …; (ドリルなどで穴を開ける) bore. ●丸太をくりぬいてカヌーを作る *hollow out* a tree trunk to make a canoe; *hollow* a canoe *out of* a tree trunk. ●山にトンネルをくりぬく *cut* a tunnel *through* a mountain. ●リンゴの芯(し)をくりぬく *cut* the core *out of* an apple [*core* an apple]; *take out* an apple core.
くりのべ 繰り延べ (延期) postponement; (据え置き) deferment.
●繰り延べ勘定 a deferred account. ●繰り延べ資産 a deferred asset. ●繰り延べ利益 a deferred income.
くりのべる 繰り延べる (延期する) postpóne, put*…off.
くりひろげる 繰り広げる ●熱戦を繰り広げる *play* an exciting game. ●絵巻物を繰り広げる *unroll* [*spread, unfold*] a picture scroll.
クリミア ●クリミア半島 the Crimea /kraimí:ə, kri-/.
グリム ●グリム兄弟 the brothers Grimm. ([参考] 兄は Jakob, 弟は Wilhelm. 共に言語学者でグリム童話の編者)
クリムト [オーストリアの画家] Klimt 《Gustav ~》.
くりょ 苦慮 ──**苦慮する** [動] worry oneself 《*about, over*》.
グリル ❶ [ホテルの中の軽食堂] a grill, a grillroom.
❷ [焼き網] a grill, a gridiron /grídàiərn/.
❸ [格子付き放熱口] a grill.
クリンチ [名] [ボクシング] a clinch. ●クリンチして in a *clinch*. ── **クリンチする** [動] clinch.
:**くる 来る** ❶ [やって来る] come* 《⇔go》; [到着する] arrive 《*at, in*》, get* 《*to*》; (予定どおりを指す) turn [話] show* up; [訪問する] visit; (ちょっと訪ねる) call 《*on*+人, *at*+場所》. ▶私たちは今夜映画へ行くことにしているんですが、来ますか We're going to the movies tonight. Would you like to *come* 《*with* us》? ▶さあバスが来ましたよ Here *comes* [×came] our bus. ([!] 副詞が文頭に来る場合、主語が代名詞なら Here *he comes*. のように「主語＋動詞」の語順になる) ▶ここへ来なさい *Come* (over) here./(私のところへ) *Come* (over) to me. ▶さあ、来い(けんかのときなど) *Come* on! ▶何でも来いで I'm up for anything. ([!]「心の準備はできている」の意の慣用表現) ▶彼はすぐ来ます He *is coming* soon. ([!] この進行形はすでに来ることが取り決められていることを表す) ▶彼は午前10時にここへ来ることになっている He will *come* [*be, get*] here at 10:00 a.m. ([!] 未来を表す助動詞なしで be か come が用いられることがある) ▶どこから来たのですか Where did you *come* [*have* you *come*] *from*? ([!] (1) 後の方は相手がここにかなりの間いると想定している。(2) Where do you come from? は状況によって「出身地はどこですか」ということにもなるので注意) ▶彼は走ってやって来た He *came* running. ▶彼はアメリカから日本に来たばかりです He *has* just *come* to [*has*] just *arrived* in] Japan from America. ▶招待した人はみな来ました(=姿を現しました)か Did everyone we invited *turn* [[話] *show*] *up*? ▶私は以前ここへ来たことがある I *have been* [*have visited*] here before. ([!] ×have come は通例完了形を表すので不可) ▶何の用でここへ来たのですか What *are* you here for?/What *has* brought

you here? (⇨①) ▶ここはあなたのような若いお嬢さんの来るところじゃないよ This is no place *for* a young lady like you.
会話「パリに来てどのくらいになりますか」「約3か月です」"How long *have* you *been* in Paris?" "(I've *been* here) for about three months."/"How long has it been 《主に米》[is it 《主に英》] since you *came to* Paris?" "It's been 《主に米》[It's 《主に英》] about three months."

① 【…しに来る】 come to 《do》; 《話》come and 《do》, 《米話》come 《do》. (⇨②) ▶以上二つは主に命令文で). ▶見に[取りに; 呼びに; 挨拶に]来る *come* to see 《it》 [pick 《it》 up; call 《me》; greet 《me》]. ▶彼らは空港に出迎えに来てくれた They *came* to meet me at the airport. ▶都合のよいときにはいつでも遊びに来てください Please *come and* see 《come* see》 me whenever it's convenient. (**!** (1) 日常会話では *come* to see より普通. ただし, *come* が活用変化するときは come (and)… の形に不可. (2) 日本語にひかれて ×come to play とはしない)/Please *come over* whenever it's convenient. ▶何しに来たの What has brought [brings] you here? (**!** 現在形で聞いた後の方は「やあ, 今日はまた何のご用?」といった生き生きした臨場感のある表現)
会話「田中さんとおっしゃる方が会いに来ておられます」「お通ししてください」"A Mr. Tanaka wants to see you./There's a Mr. Tanaka here to see you." "Send him in, please." (**!**「a+Mr. [Mrs., etc.]＋姓(名)」は「…という(名)の人」の意)

② 【(行って)…して来る】 《話》go and 《do》, 《米話》go 《do》. (⇨❶①) ▶急いで医者を呼んで来てちょうだい *Go* (*and*) *get* a doctor quickly./Just *run* (*and*) *get* a doctor. ▶友人を見送りに駅へ行って来たところです I *have been* to the station to see my friend off.
会話「あら, 朝食のパンが足りないわ」「じゃ, ちょっと買って来るよ」"Oh, no! We don't have enough bread for breakfast." "Then I'll *go* (*and*) *get* some."

❷ [[時・季節などが(巡って)くる]] come*. ▶出発すべき時が来た The time *has come* when we should start. (**!** The time when we should start. の語順より普通) ▶もうじきクリスマスがやって来る Christmas will *come* [*be* with us] *soon*./Christmas *is coming* [*drawing*] *near* (*at*) *hand*)./Christmas *is just around the corner*. ▶今月の20日に家賃の支払日が来る The rent *is due* on the twentieth of this month. ▶今年は梅雨がいつもより早く来るだろう The rainy [wet] season will *set in* [*begin*] earlier than usual this year. ▶その週は来る日も来る日も雨だった It rained *day after day* [*day in, day out*] throughout the week.

❸ [[(ある状態)になってくる]] get*, 《やや書》become*; (しだいに) grow*; (変化して別の状態に) turn; (するようになる) come* to 《do》. (⇨為(°)る) ▶日ごとに寒くなってきた It *is getting* [*becoming*] colder day by day. ▶彼は年を取ってきた He *is growing* [*getting, becoming*] *old*. ▶モミジが紅葉してきた Maples *are turning* [《話》*going*] red. ▶彼がますます好きになってきた I *have come* [×become] *to* like him more and more ([**!** *come* to の後には通例 like, know などの感情・意識を表す動詞がくる) ▶この橋を渡ると交差点が見えてくるはずです After you cross the bridge, you should [would] *see* [*come to, ×come to see*] a crossroads. (**!** would の方が話し手の確信の度合いが強い)

❹ [[起因する]] come* from …; be caused by …; [[言葉が由来する]] 《やや書》derive [be derived] from …. ▶彼の病気は過労から来ている His sickness *comes from* [*is caused by*] overwork./He *has gotten* sick through overwork. ▶bribe という言葉はフランス語から来ている The word "bribe" *comes* [*derives, is derived*] *from* French./"Bribe" is a word of French *origin*.

❺ [[到達する]] reach, get* 《to》. ▶舗装道路は私の家まで来ていない The paved road doesn't *reach* as far as my house. ▶今日彼から手紙が来た His letter *reached* me [*got* here] today./(手紙を受け取った) I *got* [*received*] a letter from him today. (**!** いずれも get の方が口語的) ▶あなたに彼女から手紙が来ています Here's a letter from her for you.

くる 刳る (穴を開ける[掘る]) bore [scoop out] 《a hole》; (くりぬく) gouge out 《a hole》; hollow out.

くる 繰る ▶ページを繰る(＝順にめくる) *turn over* the pages (*one by one*). ▶雨戸を繰る *pull in* [*out*] the shutters. ▶釣り糸を繰る(＝巻き取る) *reel in* (⇨繰り出す)

ぐる ▶ハイジャックの犯人は乗務員の1人とぐるだったことが分かった It turned out that the hijacker *was in league* [《話》*cahoots*] *with* a member of the crew.

くるい 狂い [[手順の]] confusion; 《やや書》disorder; [[ひずみ]] a warp (**!** 通例複数形にしない). ▶狂いのある羅針盤 a compass *out of order*. ▶彼の不注意で手順に狂いが生じた His carelessness caused some *confusion* in the procedure. ▶このドアは狂いがある This door doesn't open and shut *properly*./(そったりして) This door *is warped*. ▶彼の目に狂いはなかった (観察は正しいことが分かった) His observation proved *right*./(判断が正しかった) He was *right* in his judgment.

-ぐるい -狂い (⇨-狂, マニア)

くるいざき 狂い咲き ── 狂い咲きする 動 (季節外に咲く) bloom out of season.

くるいじに 狂い死に 名 death from madness.
── 狂い死にする 動 die mad (with grief).

くるう 狂う ❶ [[人が]] go* mad [《話》crazy, 《話》nuts, 《やや書》insane]; 《話》go out of one's mind; 《話》go off one's head. ▶気が狂っている *be mad* [*crazy, insane, out of one's drawing*]. (**!** いずれも精神異常の意だけではなく, 単に「愚か」「常識はずれ」の意でも用いる) ●狂ったような叫び声 a *wild* cry. ▶彼女は悲しみのあまり気が狂った She *went mad* [*went out of her mind*] with grief. ▶そんなことをするなんて気でも狂ったのか You are *mad* [*crazy*, 《話》*off your head*] *to* do such a thing./It *is mad* [*crazy*] *of* [×*for*] *you to do* a thing of that kind. ▶その音で気が狂いそうだ The noise *is driving me mad* [*crazy*, 《話》*nuts*]. ▶彼は狂ったように逃げ去った 《話》He ran off as if mad. (**!** like mad は「死に物狂いで」)

❷ [[機械などが]] go* wrong; get* out of order. (⇨故障する) ▶機械の調子が狂った The machine *has gone wrong* [*has gotten out of order*]. ▶ぼくの時計は狂っている [3分遅っている; よく狂う] My watch *is wrong* [*is three minutes off*, 《英》*is three minutes out*; *doesn't keep good time*]. ▶ピアノの調子が狂っている The piano *is out of tune*. ▶どこで計算が狂ってしまったんだろう Where did I *go wrong* [*make a mistake*] in that sum?

❸ [[計画・予定などが]] (めちゃめちゃにされる) be upset; (うまく行かない) go* wrong. ▶天候が急に変わって計画が狂ってしまった Our plans *were upset* by the sudden change in the weather. ▶台風のため列車のダイヤが狂っている The typhoon *has upset* the train schedule [*caused* some *irregularities* in the schedule].

クルー a crew. (**!** 単・複両扱い) ●(ボートレースの)早稲田クルー the Waseda *crew*.
● クルーネック a crew neck.

クルーザー 〖遊覧用の大型ヨット・モーターボート〗a cruiser.

クルージング 名 〖遊覧航海〗a cruise.
── クルージングする 動 take [go on] a cruise 《*to*, *around*》.

クルーズ 〖遊覧航海〗a cruise. ●ディナークルーズ a dinner *cruise*.

*****グループ** a group. (⇨集団) ●フォークグループ a folk *group*. ●密輸グループ a *gang* of smugglers. ●グループで in *groups* [a *group*].
● グループ学習 cooperative (group) learning. ● グループ行動 group activity. ● グループサウンズ a pop group. ● グループホーム a group home.

グルーミング ── グルーミングをする 動 〖毛づくろいをする〗groom. ▶サルが赤ん坊のグルーミングをしている A monkey *is grooming* its baby.

くるおしい 狂おしい ▶彼はジェーンを狂おしいばかりに愛していた He was *madly* [*head over heels*] in love with Jane.

くるくる ●くるくる回す[回る] (⇨ぐるぐる) ●警棒をくるくる回す *twirl* one's club. ●予定をくるくる変える *change* the schedule *so often*. ●カーペットをくるくる巻く *roll up* a carpet. ●目をくるくるさせる *roll* one's eyes. ▶彼女は雨の中で傘をくるくる回した She *spun* her umbrella in the rain.

ぐるぐる ●ぐるぐる回す[回る] 〖軸があって早く〗spin;〖回転〗revolve;(うずのように) whirl, turn around (and around);(棒などを) twirl;〖腕などを〗wind 《*around*》(up);(円を描いて) circle. ●地図をぐるぐる巻く *roll up* a map. ●包帯をぐるぐる巻く bandage 《the cut》 heavily. ▶酔って部屋がぐるぐる回るように見える I'm drunk and the room seems to *be spinning around*. ▶ピッチャーが腕をぐるぐる回した The pitcher *wound up* his arm. ▶タカが空でぐるぐる回っていた A hawk *was circling* in the air. ▶道は山をぐるぐる回って上がって行く The road goes up *round and round* the mountain.

グルコース 〖ブドウ糖〗〖化学〗glucose /glúːkous/.

グルジア 〖国名〗Georgia /dʒɔ́ːrdʒə/. (公式名称) the Republic of Georgia. (首都 Tbilisi) ●グルジア人 a Georgian. ●グルジア語 Georgian. ●グルジア(人[語])の Georgian.

ːくるしい 苦しい 形 〖苦痛な〗painful (**!** 物事が心身を痛めること (=痛い));〖困難な〗hard, tough /tʌf/, difficult (⇨難しい). (**!** 日本語の「苦しい」はよく肉体的苦労について用いられ, 精神的苦労は「つらい」で表されることが多い ⇨辛{つら}い)

①【苦しい〜】 ●苦しい仕事 hard [tough] work. ●苦しいこと (=苦労) ●苦しい目にあう (=苦しい思いをする) have a *hard* [a *tough*] time (of it); (苦しい経験をする) have a *painful* [a *bitter*] experience; go through *hardships* [*sufferings*]; (切ない思いをする) feel *painful*. ●苦しい立場にある be in a *difficult* [気まずい: an *awkward*] position. ●苦しい(=不十分な)言い訳をする make a *feeble* [話] a *lame*] excuse. ●苦しい息の下で under labored breathing. ●苦しい時期 a difficult time. ▶戦時中は苦しい目にあった(=苦労した) We had a *hard* time [*suffered greatly*] during the war. ▶その会社はひどく苦しい状況にある The firm *is in serious trouble* [(財政的苦境にある)] in financial *difficulties*].

②【...が苦しい】 ●胸が苦しい (⇨胸{むね}が苦しい) ●息が苦しい (⇨息苦しい) ●呼吸が苦しい be hard [difficult] to breathe. ●スケジュールが苦しい have little time to spare. ●給料だけでは生活が苦しい I'm *having a hard time living* [I *find it hard to live*] on my salary alone. ▶最近彼は生活が苦しいHe's *been badly off* recently. ▶当社は経営が苦しい Our company is in financial *difficulties*.

③【苦しそうに】 ▶彼は苦しそうに息をしていた He was breathing *hard* [*with difficulty*].
●苦しい時の神頼み We pray to God only when we're in trouble. /(苦しみが消えると神も忘れる) Danger past, God forgotten./Once on shore, we pray no more.

── **苦しさ** 名 pain; suffering. (⇨苦しみ)

くるしまぎれ 苦し紛れ ▶彼女は苦しまぎれに(=何と言っていいか分からなかったので)テーブルの花が美しいと言った She complimented her on the flowers on the table, *because she didn't know what to say.* (**!** パーティーなどで初対面の人と共通の話題のないときなどに) ▶彼は苦しまぎれに(=窮地に追い込まれて)うそをついた *Driven into a (tight) corner*, he told a lie.

くるしみ 苦しみ 〖心身の苦痛〗pain (⇨苦痛);〖心身の苦悩〗suffering (苦痛・苦悩・苦労などの意では通例複数形で);(ひどい)(やや書) distress;〖苦難〗(a) hardship (⇨苦難). ●数々の苦しみを乗り越える overcome a lot of *sufferings* [*hardships*, 困難] *difficulties*]. ●地獄の苦しみ(=責め苦)を味わう go through the *tortures* of hell. ▶その患者は大した苦しみもなく死んだ The patient died without much *pain* [*suffering*]. ▶世界の苦しみの元凶は, 人々が愛されていないと感じていることだ The root cause of the woes /wóuz/ around [in] the world is that people have the feeling that they are not loved.

*****くるしむ 苦しむ** suffer 《*from*+病気など, *for*+事・人》 (**!** suffer from は長期間続く状態を表すが, 進行形で用いると一時的状態を表す. 他動詞の suffer は「(苦痛・損害などを)被る」の意で, 一時的な行為を表す);〖心配・病気などで悩む〗be troubled 《*with, by*》.(⇨悩む) ●苦しんでいる人々 (苦痛を受けている) people *in pain* [*who are suffering*] (**!** ×painful people は不可);(困っている) people *in trouble* [*difficulty*]. (**!**...in trouble は自分の悪行のため警察などにやっかいになっていることを暗示することがある)

①【〜苦しむ】 ●悩み苦しむ be troubled by anxiety. ●もがき苦しむ struggle 《*to do*; *for*》;(身もだえる) writhe in agony. ▶そのけが人はひどく苦しんだ The injured man *suffered* terribly [*terrible pain*]. (**!** ×suffer from pain とはいわない. He *suffered* terrible pain *from* his injury. は可)

②【...に苦しむ】 ●重税に苦しむ *suffer from* heavy taxes (**!** ×suffer heavy taxes とは通例いわない);(負わされている) be burdened with heavy taxes. ▶旅行の間, 彼はしょっちゅうひどい頭痛に苦しんでいた He *was constantly suffering from* [*was constantly troubled by*] severe headaches during the trip. (**!** 反復する頭痛なので複数形となる) ●判断に苦しむ have difficulty in deciding [decision making]. ●後遺症に苦しむ suffer from residuals [sequelae]. ●生活に苦しむ (苦しい生活をしている) be badly off; (生活に困っている) find it difficult to make a living. ▶彼がなぜ逃げ出したのか理解に苦しむ (理解しがたい) It is *hard to understand* [*I can't understand*] why he escaped./(頭を悩ませる) Why he escaped *puzzles* me.

③【...で苦しむ】 ●自分のしたことで苦しむ *suffer for*

くるしめる something one has done. (⇨悩む) ● 板ばさみで苦しむ suffer from a dilemma. ●農民は雨不足で大変苦しんだ The farmers *suffered* greatly *from* lack of rain./(ひどい目にあった) The farmers *had a hard* [*a terrible*] *time* because of lack of rain./(苦しみを引き起こした) Lack of rain *caused great hardship* [*suffering*] *to* the farmers.

くるしめる 苦しめる 〖苦痛を与える〗give* [cause]《him》pain [suffering]; 〖ひどく苦しめる〗torture, 《やや強》torment.

グルタミンさん〖化学〗glutamine (略 Gln).
● グルタミン酸 glutamic acid. ● グルタミン酸ソーダ〖ナトリウム〗monosodium glutamate (略 MSG).

くるっと ●くるっと回る〖回り〗turn(...) around, (回転) spin around; (旋回) circle, make a circle. ●くるっと…の方へ曲がる turn to.... ●猫はくるっと丸くなって眠ってしまった The cat *curled up* and went to sleep. ▶彼女はくるっと私の方に向いてにっこり笑った She *turned toward* me and smiled. ▶たこはくるっと1回転して落ちてきた The kite *made a circle* and fell down.

ぐるっと ●ぐるりと) ●公園の外側をぐるっとひと回りする walk *around* the park. ●得意先をぐるっと回る make《米》[do《英》] the *rounds* of one's clients.

グルテン［＜ドイツ語〗〖化学〗gluten /glúːtn/.
クルド ● クルド人 a Kurd /kə́ːrd/.
クルトン［＜フランス語〗a crouton /krúːtɑn/. (!通例複数形で) ● クルトンを浮かせたオニオンスープ onion soup with *croutons*.

くるびょう 佝僂病 〖医学〗rickets, rachitis /rəkáitəs/.

くるぶし 踝 an ankle. (⇨足首)

くるま 車

WORD CHOICE 車
car 自動車をさす最も一般的な語。ただし, バス・トラックなどは通例 car に含まない. ● 車に乗り込む[から下りる] get into [out of] the *car*.
vehicle 自動車・バス・トラック・自転車などの乗り物を広くさす. 特に自動車であることを強調する場合は motor ～. 比喩的に運搬・送達手段の意味でも用いる. ● 四輪駆動車 a 4WD *vehicle*.

頻度チャート
car ████████████████
vehicle ██████
       20   40   60   80   100 (%)

❶〖乗り物〗a vehicle /víːəkl/ (⇨車両); 〖乗用車〗a car (⇨自動車); 〖タクシー〗a taxi, a cab; 〖交通量〗traffic.

① 〖車が〗●3本のしっかりした杭で車が入れないようにしてある狭い道路 a narrow street closed to *traffic* by three solid posts. ●車が通る Cars pass by. ▶車が来る Here comes a car. ▶うちには車がある We have a car. ▶今朝は車が多かった[少なかった] There was a lot of *traffic* [not much *traffic*] this morning.

② 〖車の〗●車の中 in a car. ●車の窓 a car window; a window of a car. ●車の両輪が互いに密接に結びついている be closely connected with each other [one another]; be inseparable. ▶あなたをはねた車の型を覚えていますか Do you remember the make of the *car* that hit you?
会話「見て, あの子たち[バイクで]車の間をジグザグに走って行くわ」「命知らずもいいとこだね」"Look at the boys riding zigzag through *traffic*." "They're really asking to be killed."

③ 〖車に〖から〗〗●車に乗る(乗車する) get in [×on] a *car* (! get on a bus は可 (⇨乗る)); (乗って行く) ride in [on] a *car*; (運転する) drive (a *car*). ●車に飛び乗る jump [hop] into a car. ●車から降りる get out of [×off] a *car*. (! get off a bus は可 (⇨降りる)) ▶あなたの車に乗せてくれませんか Will you *give me a ride*《米》[*a lift*《英》](*in* your *car*)? ▶乗るように言われて彼女はいやいや彼の車に乗り込んだ When she was told to get in his *car*, she reluctantly got into it. (! *get into* (↔out of) a car は *get in* より『中へ乗り込む』の意を強調する)

④ 〖車を〗●車を拾う (⇨次例) ●車を止める (走行中に) stop a *car*; (駐車する) park a *car*; (タクシーを拾う) hail〖手を上げて〗flag down] a *taxi*. ●車を出す drive a car out of (a parking lot). ●車を修理に出す get a *car* repaired [serviced]. ▶今日は車を運転しているの?(⇨運転する) Are you driving (×a car) today? (! drive 自体が『車を運転する』の意なので, a new car のように新しい情報が加わらない単なる a car より『中へ乗り込む』の意は不要) ▶駐車場で彼は私の車の横に止めた He *pulled up* next to me in a parking lot.
会話「お父さん, 今夜車を使ってもいいかしら」「うん, いいだろう. でも母さんにも確かめておくほうがいいよ」"Can I possibly have [take] the (family) *car* tonight, Dad?" "Well, I guess so. But maybe you should also check with your mother."

翻訳のこころ その夕方父は, あのアロエは育ちすぎだ, お隣さんが駐車場から車を出す時にゆくゆくは迷惑になるんじゃないか, と言いだした (吉本ばなな 『みどりのゆび』) That evening my father said that the aloe had grown too big, and might eventually be in the way of our next door neighbor when they pulled out their car from the garage. 翻訳 (1)「…の邪魔になる」は be in the way of ... と表す. (2)「車を(駐車していたところから)出す, 動かす」は pull out the car. (3) that 以下の文が時制の一致で, 日本文とは異なり過去形になっていることに注意

⑤ 〖車で〗●車で大学へ通う go to college *by car* [*in a car*] (!in one's car の形だが ×*by* one's *car* は不可); ride to college *in a car* (! *ride ... by car* は避けられる); (自分で運転して) *drive to* college. ●車で家へ帰る途中で on the *drive* back to one's home. ▶彼を車で家[駅]まで送った I *drove* him home [*to* the station]. (! *home* は副詞) ▶彼女は週末になると車で富山の両親に会いに行く She *drives over to* Toyama to visit her parents on weekends. ▶車で迎えに来てください Please come to *pick* me *up*. ▶彼の家へは車で20分です It's a twenty-minute *drive* to his home.

❷〖車輪〗a wheel (⇨車輪); 〖足車〗a caster. ●足車のついた家具 a piece of furniture *on casters*. (⇨車椅子)

くるまいす 車椅子 〖病人・身障者用の〗 a wheelchair. ●車椅子の人 a person *in* [*confined to*] a *wheelchair*; a *wheelchair-bound* person.

くるまいど 車井戸 (説明的に) a well from which buckets are raised and lowered by means of a pulley.

くるまえび 車海老 〖魚介〗a prawn.
くるまざ 車座 ●車座に座る sit in a circle.
くるましゃかい 車社会 (*in*) the age of automobiles.
くるまだい 車代 〖交通費〗 tráveling expènses; 〖薄謝〗an honorarium.
くるまどめ 車止め (自動車の) a chock; (鉄道の)

bumping post, 《米》a bumper.
くるまひき 車引き (a) rickshaw pùller.
くるまよせ 車寄せ a porch; (屋根つきの) a porte-cochere /pɔ̀ːrtkouʃéər/.
くるまる wrap (-pp-) oneself (up). ▶彼は毛布にくるまって火の前に座っていた He *wrapped himself up* in a blanket and was sitting in front of the fire.
くるみ 胡桃 〖植物〗a walnut. ●クルミを割る crack a *walnut*.
  ●クルミ割り器 (a pair of) nutcrackers.
-ぐるみ ▶町ぐるみでその難題に取り組んだ The *whole town* tackled the difficult problem. ▶彼とは家族ぐるみの付き合いだ He is a friend of the family [a family friend].
くるみわりにんぎょう 『胡桃割り人形』 *The Nutcracker*. (参考) チャイコフスキー作曲のバレエ音楽.
くるむ 包む (おおう) cover; (wrap (-pp-) (... up). ●皮でくるんだボタン a leather-*covered* button. ▶彼女は赤ん坊を(すっぽり)毛布にくるんだ She *wrapped* her baby (*up*) in a blanket.
グルメ [＜フランス語] 〖美食家〗a gourmet /guərméi/; 《書》an epicure.
  ●グルメツアー a tour organized for gourmets. ●グルメブーム a craze for gourmet food.
くるめる (一括する) lump [put] (it) together; (総計する) total; (含める) include. ●全部くるめる all in all; all told; in total. (⇨合計)
くるりと (⇨くるっと)
ぐるりと ▶彼は土地の周りにぐるりと有刺鉄線をめぐらした He strung barbed wire *all around* the lot. ▶その温泉地はぐるりと山に囲まれている The hot-spring resort *is surrounded* by mountains. ▶彼は聴衆をぐるりと見渡した He looked *around* at the audience./He swept his eyes over the audience.
くるわ 郭, 廓 (遊郭) a red-light district.
くるわす 狂わす 〖人を〗drive* (him) mad (⇨狂う ❶); 〖機械などを〗put* (it) out of order; 〖計画などを〗upset*.
くれ 暮れ 〖年末〗the end of the year, the year-end; 〖夕暮れ〗nightfall, the close of day, twilight. ▶去年の暮れにボーナスをもらった at *the end of* last year. ●2007 年暮れに *at the end of* 2007. (！2007年の春以降では *in the winter of* 2007 ということも多い) ▶日の暮れに *at nightfall*; in the evening twilight.
クレー 〖粘土〗clay; 〖クレー射撃の的〗a clay pigeon. ●クレーコート〖テニス〗a clay court (cóurt). ●クレー射撃 trapshooting; clay pigion shooting.
グレー 〖灰色〗gray. ●グレーのコート a *gray* coat. ●グレーゾーン a gray zone. ●グレーマーケット 〖非合法すれすれのやみ市場〗a gray market.
クレーター a crater.
グレード grade. ●ハイグレードな材料 high-*grade* materials. ●グレードアップする upgrade; 《和製語》grade up.
グレートデン 〖動物〗(犬) a Great Dane.
グレーハウンド 〖犬〗a greyhound; 〖米国の長距離バス〗a Greyhound bus.
クレープ [＜フランス語] 〖薄いパンケーキ〗a crepe, crêpe; 〖縮み織りの布〗crepe, crêpe.
グレープ 〖葡萄〗)
  ●グレープジュース grape juice.
グレープフルーツ 〖植物〗(a) grápefrùit (⑧ ～, ～s).
  ●グレープフルーツジュース grapefruit juice.
クレーム 〖苦情〗a complaint. (！「(損害賠償的な)請求」の意では a claim) ●クレームをつける complain, make a *complaint* 《of [about]+物・事; to+人;

that 節).
クレーン a crane. ●クレーンで釣り上げる lift [hoist] (it) with a *crane* [by *crane*].
  ●クレーン車 a crane truck.
クレオソート 〖化学〗creosote. (参考) 木材の防腐剤)
クレオパトラ 〖古代エジプトの女王〗Cleopatra /klìːəpǽtrə/.
くれがた 暮れ方 (an) evening. (⇨⑱ 夕方) (⑱ 明け方)
くれぐれも ▶くれぐれもお大事に Take ⟨Ⓧa⟩ *good* [*great*] care of yourself.
グレコローマン 〖レスリング〗Greco-Roman (wrestling).
  ●グレコローマンスタイル the Greco-Roman style (of wrestling).
クレジット a credit. ●クレジットで買う buy *on credit*. ▶お支払いは現金でしょうか, クレジットでしょうか (Will it be) cash or *charge*?
  ●クレジットカード a crédit càrd; (銀行発行の) a bank (credit) card; (店発行の) a chárge càrd. (！以上いずれも文脈により単に card ともいう) ▶クレジットカードが使えますか(＝で支払いができますか) Do you accept [take] a (*credit*) *card*? ●クレジットクランチ 〖貸し渋り〗a credit crunch. (⇨貸し渋り) ●クレジットタイトル 〖映画・テレビの〗crédit títles. ●クレジットライン 〖貸出最高限度額〗a crédit line; a line of credit. ●クレジットローン a loan with one's credit card; 《和製語》a credit loan.
グレシャム ●グレシャムの法則 Gresham's law. (参考) 「悪貨は良貨を駆逐する」という経済学の法則 (⇨悪貨)
クレゾール [＜ドイツ語] 〖化学〗cresol /kríːsɔːl/.
  ●クレゾール石鹼液 a saponated cresol solution.
クレソン [＜フランス語] wátercrèss.
クレタ ●クレタ島 Crete /kríːt/.
ぐれつ 愚劣 ⊗ (愚かさ) foolishness.
 ── **愚劣な** 形 愚劣な(＝ばかげた)行為 a *foolish* [a *stupid*] act.
くれない 紅 deep red; crimson.
くれなずむ 暮れ泥む ●暮れなずむ空 the sky still somewhat light from lingering evening glow.
グレナダ 〖国名〗Grenada /grənéidə/. (！公式名も同じ) (首都 St George's) ●グレナダ人 a Grenadian. ●グレナダ(人)の Grenadian.
くれのこる 暮れ残る ●白く暮れ残る夕顔の花 a white moonflower *in the glow of the sunset*.
クレバス 〖氷河の深い裂け目〗a crevasse /krəvǽs/.
  ●クレバスに落ちる fall into [down] a *crevasse*.
クレパス (a) pastel crayon. (！クレパスは商品名で和製英語)
クレマチス 〖植物〗(a) clematis; a traveller's joy.
クレムリン [＜ロシア語] 〖宮殿〗the Kremlin.
くれゆく 暮れ行く ●暮れゆく(＝暗くなってゆく)秋の空 the *darkening* autumn sky. ▶今年も暮れゆく(＝終わりに近づく) The year *draws to a close*.
クレヨン [＜フランス語] (a) crayon. ●クレヨン画 a *crayon* (drawing); a drawing in *crayon*(s). ●クレヨンで絵を描く draw a picture *with crayons* [*in crayon*(s)].
__くれる__ 呉れる ❶ 〖与える〗give. ▶おじは私に時計をくれた My uncle *gave* me a watch [a watch *to* me]. (！前の方は「時計」, 後の方は「私」に焦点を当てた言い方. このような場合動詞の present を用いるのは不自然 (⇨贈る) ▶そんなものくれてやる You can have it.
❷ [...してくれる] (わざわざ) take* the trouble 《to do》; (親切にも) be kind enough 《to do》. ▶彼はわざわざ[親切にも]手伝ってくれた He took the trouble

[was kind enough] to help me. ▶今日来てくれますか Can [Could] you come today?(⚠依頼の表現 (⇨下さい, 頂く)) ▶ぼくの両親に会ってくれますよね I hope you won't mind meeting my parents, will you?(⚠付加疑問で …don't I? としないことに注意 (⇨ね❷❷)) ▶彼女が朝食を作ってくれました She made me breakfast./She made breakfast for [×to] me.

❸ [...してくれ] (頼む) ask; (許可する) let*, allow. ▶彼にそうしてくれるよう頼んだ I asked him to do that. ▶早く家に帰らせてくれ Let me [Allow me to] go home as soon as possible. ▶今日中にそれを仕上げられるかどうかやってみてくれ See if you can finish it before you leave today.(⚠目上の人が指示するときの比較的丁寧な言い方)

くれる 暮れる 動 ❶[暗くなる] get [grow*, become*] dark. ▶日が暮れてきた(=暗くなりつつある) It's getting [growing] dark.(⚠通例 ×It's becoming dark. とはいわない.主語は常に it) (⇨暗い ⚠[第3文例]) ▶彼は日が暮れてから [暮れないうちに] 帰って来た He came back after [before] dark.

❷ [終わる] ▶今年もあと2時間で暮れる The year comes to an end in two hours./(暮れるまで2時間残されている) Two hours are left before the year is out.

❸ [思案などに] ▶思案に暮れる be lost in thought. ●途方に暮れる (⇨途方 [成句]) ▶涙に暮れる do nothing but weep. ▶彼は悲嘆に暮れた様子だった He looked very sad [(書) sorrowful, in a deep sorrow].

❹ [その他の表現] ▶そんなことをしていたら日が暮れるよ(=時間がかかりすぎる) If you do it that way, it will take too much time./(今はそんな時間はない) You have no time to do such a thing now.

ぐれる [身を誤る] go* wrong [to the bad]; (道を踏みはずす) go astray; (悪に)fall* into evil ways. ▶その少年 [少女] は a bad boy [girl]; (犯罪を犯すほどの) a juvenile delinquent.

クレンザー (a) cleanser; (洗剤) (a) detergent.
クレンジングクリーム cléansing crèam.
ぐれんたい 愚連隊 (a gang of) hooligans; street gangsters; (⚠) hoodlums.

:くろ 黒 [色] black. ▶黒を白と言う (やや話) swear black is white; talk black into white; (⚠目的達成のためには手段を選ばないこと) ▶彼は黒 (=有罪) だ He is guilty.

クロアチア [国名] Croatia /króuéɪʃə/; (公式名) the Republic of Croatia. (首都 Zagreb) ●クロアチア人 a Croatian. ●クロアチア語 Croatian. ●クロアチア (⚠) の Croatian.

:くろい 黒い black; [髪・皮膚などが黒っぽい] dark; [目などが浅黒い] brown. ▶黒(い)髪 black [dark] hair. ▶黒い目 dark [brown] eyes. (⚠ a black-eyed girl は「目の周りに殴られてできた黒いあざ」ただし a black-eyed girl は「黒い目の少女」の意) ▶黒いめがね (a pair of) dark glasses. ▶仕事で真っ黒になった手 one's work-blackened hands. ▶日に焼けて黒くなる get sunburnt [tanned, brown]. ▶それを黒く染める [塗る] dye [paint] it black. ▶彼女は黒い服を着ている She wears a black dress.(⚠ black clothes では帽子や靴を含むから) /She is (dressed) in black.(⚠「喪服を着ている」の意にもなる)

会話 「ずいぶん黒くなりましたね」「ええ,一生懸命焼いてるんです」"You are very brown." "I work hard at it."

グロい (⇨グロテスク)
くろいあめ 『黒い雨』Black Rain.(参考) 井伏鱒二の小

説)

:くろう 苦労 图 ❶ [困り事] trouble; [困難] (a) difficulty; [苦難] (a) hardship.(⚠いずれも具体的には [C]) ●仕事の苦労話をする talk about the difficulty of the trouble in] (doing) one's duties. ▶彼は苦労人だ(多くの苦難を経験した) He has gone through a lot of hardships./(人生経験が豊富だ) He has a lot of experience of life. ▶君には苦労が足りない (人生経験が十分でない) You haven't seen enough of life./(まだ学ぶことがたくさんある) You've still got a lot to learn.

❷ [心配] (a) trouble; (a) worry; (a) care; (an) anxiety.(⇨心配) (⚠いずれの語も「心配事」の意では [C]) ●苦労が多い have a lot of troubles [worries, cares]. ▶彼は苦労性だ (心配しすぎる) He worries too much./(物事を深刻視する) He takes things too seriously. ▶苦労が絶えない There's no end to our troubles [worries]. ▶彼は両親に大変苦労をかけている He causes his parents a lot of trouble [great anxiety]./(心配の種だ) He is a great trouble [anxiety] to his parents.

❸ [面倒,手数] trouble. ▶ご苦労さまでした (米英人的発想) (ご苦労を感謝します) Thank you very much (for your trouble)/((日本人的発想) (ご苦労をかけてすみません) I'm sorry to have given you [put you to] so much trouble/I'm sorry to have troubled you so much.

❹ [努力] (an) effort (⚠しばしば複数形で); (苦闘) (a) struggle; [骨折り] trouble; pains. ▶長年の苦労の末,その画家はついに真価を認められた After long years of efforts, the painter finally came into his own.

── 苦労する 動 [難儀する] have* trouble [difficulty] 《with+事・人; (in) doing》 (⚠ trouble の方が口語的); [つらい目にあう] have a hard [difficult] time 《with+事; doing; to do》; (苦しむ) suffer 《for》; [苦難を経験する] experience [go* through] hardships (⇨苦); [骨折る] take* pains 《to do; with》. ●金で苦労する have [be in] financial difficulties (⚠しばしば複数形で); (話) be hard up. ▶英語ではずいぶん苦労しました I had a lot of trouble [had a very hard time] with English./I suffered a lot for English. ▶彼の家を見つけるのに少しも苦労しなかった I had no [didn't have much] trouble [difficulty] (in) finding his house. (⚠(話)では通例 in を省略する.また ×...trouble to find his house. は不可/I found his house without any [much] trouble [difficulty]. ▶彼はその仕事を終えるのに非常に苦労した He took great pains to finish the work. ▶彼は苦労して(=働いて) 学校を出た He worked his way through school.

ぐろう 愚弄 图 ridicule; mockery. ── 愚弄する 動 ridicule; mock 《at...》; make fun of ....

くろうと 玄人 [プロ] a professional (↔an amateur); [大家] a master; [専門家] an expert, a specialist. ●玄人 [玄人はだし] の芸 a professional [semiprofessional] performance.(⚠しばしばしのしは semiprofessional とは限らない; オムレツにかけてはうちの母さんは玄人はだしよ Mother is a real professional in making omelettes.) ●玄人の腕前を披露する show one's professional skill.

クローク [携帯品一時預かり所] a cloakroom, (主に米) a checkroom (a coatroom ともいう). ▶クロークにコートを預ける leave one's coat in the cloakroom.

クローザー [野球] a closer.(参考) 通例リードしている最

クローズアップ 終回に登板する)
クローズアップ 〖大写し〗《take》a close-up /klóusʌp/. ●クローズアップで撮った花 a *close-up* of a flower; a picture of a flower *in close-up*. ▶この問題が大きくクローズアップされている(=多くの注意を引いている) This problem *has attracted a lot of attention*.
クローズドエンド ── **クローズドエンド型の** 形 〖投資信託が資本額固定式の〗 closed-end.
● クローズドエンド型投資信託 a closed-end (investment) fund; a closed-end type investment trust.
クローズドキャプション 〖聴力障害者用字幕〗 a closed caption.
クローズドショップ a closed shop.
クローゼット 〖納戸〗 a closet. ●ウォークインクローゼット a walk-in *closet*.
クローバー a clover. ●四つ葉のクローバー a four-leaf *clover*.
グローバリズム globalism.
グローバリゼーション 〖地球規模化〗 globalization.
グローバル ── **グローバルな** 形 〖地球規模の〗 global.
●グローバルな問題 a *global* issue. ●グローバルな視点で考える think things *globally* [from a *global* point of view]. ●グローバルな競争の激化に巻き込まれる suffer from intensive *global* competition. ●世界経済がますますグローバル化する中にあって with the glowing [increasing] *globalization* of the world economy.
●グローバルスタンダード 〖世界標準〗 a global standard. ●グローバルマーケティング global marketing.
くろおび 黒帯 a black belt. ▶彼女は黒帯だ She is [has] a *black belt*.
グローブ (野球の) a glove /glʌ́v/. (❗通例捕手用は mitt, 一塁手用は glove または mitt, 他の野手用は glove); (ボクシングの) (boxing) gloves. (⇨手袋)
●打撃用グローブ a bátting glóve. ●グローブさばき *glove* work. ●グローブトスをする make a *glove* flip [a shovel throw]. ●グローブをはじいて off one's *glove*. ●グローブを当てる get a *glove* 《on》.
グローランプ 〖点灯管〗 a glow lamp.
クロール the crawl (stroke). ●クロールで泳ぐ swim *the crawl*.
クローン a clone. ●クローン羊 a *cloned* sheep. ●クローン人間の誕生を全面的に禁止する impose a total ban on the birth of a human *clone*. ●クローンで繁殖させる clone; produce by cloning.
くろかみ 黒髪 black hair.
くろがも 黒鴨 〖鳥〗 a common scoter.
くろぐろ 黒々 ── **黒々とした** 形 deep-[jet-]black (hair).
くろこ 黒子, 黒衣 ❶〖歌舞伎などの〗a kuroko; (説明的に) a stage assistant dressed in black; (その衣装) black clothes. ❷〖裏で人を操る人〗a person maneuvering behind the scenes; 《主に米》a wirepuller.
くろこげ 黒焦げ ●黒焦げの死体 a *charred* body. ●黒焦げにする[なる] char. ▶彼はパンを黒焦げにした He *burned* the toast *black*.
クロコダイル 〖動物〗 a crocodile.
くろさぎ 黒鷺 〖鳥〗 an eastern reef heron.
くろざとう 黒砂糖 (unrefined) brown sugar.
*****くろじ** 黒字 a surplus (⇔a deficit). ▶日本は昨年貿易が黒字だった Japan had a trade *surplus* last year. ▶その会社は黒字に[なりつつある] The company *is in* [*is going into*] *the black* (⇔the red). ▶黒字倒産する go into insolvency due to cash-flow problems.

くろじ 黒鵐 〖鳥〗 a gray bunting.
くろしお 黒潮 Kuroshio; the Japan [Japanese] Current.
くろしろ 黒白 black and white. (⇨㊉ 白黒)
クロス 〖布〗 a cloth. (❗しばしば複合語で) ●テーブルクロスを広げる spread a table*cloth*. ●クロス装の本 a *cloth*-bound book.
クロス 〖サッカーの〗a cross. (⇨センタリング) ●アーリークロス an early *cross*. ●クロスを入れる send a *cross* (in).
くろず 黒酢 dark vinegar.
クロスオーバー 〖音楽〗(a) cross over. (❗音楽のジャンルを指す場合は Ⓤ, 歌手(artist)を指す場合は Ⓒ)
クロスカウンター 〖ボクシング〗 a cross (counter).
クロスカントリー a cross-country race.
●クロスカントリースキー a cross-country skiing.
クロスゲーム 〖接戦〗 a close game.
クロスステッチ 〖十字縫い〗(a) crósssstitch.
クロスバー 〖サッカー〗 a crossbar, a bar; (ゴール枠全体) a woodwork (❗かつてはゴール枠がすべて木製だったことから).
クロスファイアー 〖野球〗 a crossfire.
クロスプレー 〖野球など〗a close play. ●ランナーをクロスプレーでアウトにする put out a runner on a *close play*.
くろずむ 黒ずむ blacken, become* [get*] black [dark]. ▶目のあたりが黒ずんでいる. 相当疲れているようだ He is *dark* [×black] around his eyes. He must be very tired. (❗ black and blue では「打撲による青あざができる」)
クロスライセンス 〖相互技術供与〗 cross license.
クロスレファランス 〖相互参照〗 a cross-reference.
クロスワード(パズル) 〖do〗 a crossword (puzzle).
くろだい 黒鯛 〖魚介〗 a black porgy. (⇨鯛)
クロッカス 〖植物〗 a crocus /króukəs/. (㊉ ~es).
グロッキー ●グロッキーである (足元がふらふらで) 〖話〗 feel groggy /grági/; (*from* the blow); (疲れ切る) be tired out 《*from*, *by*》. ●グロッキーになる (ボクサーが) become [be knocked] *groggy*. ▶今日は睡眠不足でグロッキーだ I feel *groggy* [*dazed*] from lack of sleep.
クロック 〖コンピュータ〗 a clock.
●クロック周波数 a clock frequency. ●クロック速度 a clock speed [rate].
くろつぐみ 黒鶫 〖鳥〗 a gray thrush.
くろづくり 黒作り kurozukuri; (説明的に) chopped cuttlefish salted and fermented with its own ink.
グロッサリー 〖用語解説集〗 a glossary.
くろっぽい 黒っぽい darkish; dark. (❗後の方が色が濃い) ●黒っぽい背広を着ている wear [be in] a *dark* suit.
グロテスク ── **グロテスクな** 形 〖異形(ぎょう)な〗grotesque, strange, weird /wɪərd/, bizarre /bɪzɑ́ːr/. (❗後の 2 語は異様さからくる気味・気色の悪さをいう).
くろてん 黒貂 a sable.
クロノメーター 〖天文観測・航海などに用いる高精度の携帯時計〗 a chronometer.
くろパン 黒パン (主にライ麦製の) black bread, rye bread.
くろビール 黒ビール dark beer; (英国の) porter, stout.
くろびかり 黒光り ── **黒光りする** 動 shine black; have a black luster [sheen].
くろぼし 黒星 (黒い丸) a black spot; (敗北) a defeat (⇔a victory); (失敗) a failure. ●黒星続きである be on a *losing* (⇔winning) streak.
くろほびょう 黒穂病 〖植物〗 smut.

くろまく 黒幕 《米》a wirepuller. (❗a string puller は普通でない) ● 政界の黒幕 the *wirepuller* in politics; (舞台裏から政治を支配する人) a man who *controls* politics *from behind the scenes*. (❗二重前置詞に注意) ● 黒幕になる pull strings; be [work] behind the scenes.

くろまぐろ 黒鮪 〖魚介〗a bluefin tuna.

くろまめ 黒豆 〖植物〗a black soybean.

クロム 〖化学〗chrome, chromium 《元素記号 Cr》.
● クロムテープ a chrome tape.

くろめ 黒目 the iris of the eye. ● 黒目がちの目 eyes with clearly defined dark irises.

くろもじ 黒文字 〖植物〗a spicebush; 〖つまようじ〗a toothpick.

くろやま 黒山 ▶ その店の前は黒山の人だかりだった There was *a large crowd* [There were *large crowds*] (of people) in front of the store.

クロレラ 〖植物〗(a) chlorella.

クロロキン 〖薬学〗chloroquine. (〖参考〗マラリヤの治療薬)

クロロフィル 〖葉緑素〗chlorophyl(l).

クロロホルム 〖化学・薬学〗chloroform.

クロロマイセチン 〖化学〗chloromycetin /kl5(:)roumaisi:tn/. (❗商標としては大文字で始める)

くろわく 黒枠 图 a black frame; black borders (死亡通知などの) mourning borders.
—— 黒枠の 圏 black-edged, black-framed; black-bordered. ● 黒枠の手紙 a *mourning* card. ● 黒枠の記事 (=死亡記事) an *obituary* notice.

クロワッサン [<フランス語] a croissant /kwa:sá:ŋ/. 《米》crescent (roll).

ぐろん 愚論 a foolish argument; an absurd view.

くわ 桑 〖植物〗a mulberry (tree).
● 桑畑 a mulberry field.

くわ 鍬 a hoe. ● くわを入れる(=で耕す) hoe [cultivate] (land); break ground.
● くわ入れ式 a ground-breaking ceremony.

くわい 慈姑 〖植物〗an arrowhead; (球根) an arrowhead bulb.

くわえこむ 咥え込む ▶ うちの犬は靴なら何でも犬小屋にくわえこんでくる My dog *brings* all kind of shoes *into* the kennel. ● あの女はどこからか男をくわえこんでくる She *hooked* a man from somewhere or other.

くわえたばこ 咥え煙草 ● くわえたばこで歩く walk *with a cigarette in one's mouth*.

くわえて 加えて besides(...), 《やや書》on top of ... (❗不快なことに用いることが多い) 《やや書》in addition (to ...); (含めて) including .... (⇨その上) ▶ 彼は帰宅が遅れた上に、加えて酔っていた He came home late, and *besides* [and *on top of that*], he was drunk. ● 部屋には彼女を加えて 6 人いた There were six people in the room, *including* her./*Besides* [×Beside] her, there were five people in the room. (❗人数の数え方に注意) ▶ 彼は能力があることに加えて努力家でもある *Besides* [*In addition to*] being capable, he is hardworking./He is hardworking *as well as* capable. ● 容貌(ぼう)に加えて人柄がよかったので彼は人気者になった His personality *together with* his (good) appearance made him popular.

くわえばし 咥え箸 ● くわえばしでテレビを見る watch television with chopsticks in one's mouth.

:**くわえる 加える** ❶ 〖足す〗add; 〖合計する〗add [sum (-mm-)] ... up. (⇨加えて) ▶ 2 に 6 を加える add 6 to 2. ● その数を全部加える add the figures up [together]. (⇨付け加える) ▶ 水を 2 カップ加えてかき回してください Add two cups of water and stir.

❷ 〖与える〗give*; (苦痛などを) 《やや書》inflict; (侮辱・圧力などを) give*. ● 頭に一撃を加える give [*inflict*, 《書》deal, 《話》land] 《him》a blow on the head. ● 危害を加える harm 《him》; do 《him》harm; inflict (an) injury 《on him》. ● 圧力を加える put pressure (on him).

❸ 〖含める〗include; (数には入る)count ... in (⇨含める); (仲間に加える)let* 《him》join (⇨加えて). ● 彼を仲間に加える include him *in* our group; *count* him *in* among our group. ● ぼくもゲームに加えてください Let me join in the game.

❹ 〖増す〗(数量を) incréase (⇨増やす); (速度を) gather, pick up. (⇨加速)

くわえる 咥える ● パイプをくわえる hold a pipe *in* one's mouth. ● ナイフを歯でくわえる hold a knife *between* one's teeth. ● 犬は骨をくわえて逃げた The dog ran away [made off] *with* the bone.

くわがたむし 鍬形虫 〖昆虫〗a stag beetle.

くわけ 区分け 图 (区分) division; (分類) classification.
—— 区分けする 動 divide; classify.

▶**くわしい 詳しい** ❶ 〖詳細な〗detailed; 〖十分な〗full; 〖細密な〗《書》minute /main(j)ú:t/. ● 詳しい情報を得る get *detailed* [*full*] information (*about*). ● それを詳しく説明する give a *detailed* [a *full*] explanation *of* it; explain it *in detail* [*minutely*]; go into *detail*(s) about it. ▶ 詳しい事は知りません I don't know the *details* [*particulars*]. (❗ともに通例複数形で用いる) ▶ もっと詳しく話していただけませんか Could you give me some more information about it?/Are you able to tell us any more?

❷ 〖精通している〗be familiar 《with》; (よく知っている) know*... very well; (情勢などに通じている) 《やや書》be well-informed 《about, of》. (⇨精通) ▶ 彼は韓国の情勢に詳しい He *is* familiar *with* [*well-informed about*] the Korean situation./He has a *good knowledge of* the Korean situation.

くわずぎらい 食わず嫌い ● 食わず嫌いである have a prejudice [be prejudiced] 《against》.

くわせもの 食わせ者 (ぺてん師) a humbug, deceiver, 《やや古》an impóster. ● あいつはとんだ食わせ者だった I never thought he was such a *deceiver*.

くわせる 食わせる (食べ物を与える) feed*. ● 家族を食わせる feed 〖養う〗support, provide for] a family.
● 一杯食わせる (だます) deceive, cheat, 《やや話》take ... in.

くわだて 企て 〖計画〗a plan; (たくらみ) a plot; 〖試み〗an attempt. ▶ 大統領暗殺の企てが発覚した The *plot to* assassinate the President was discovered.

▶**くわだてる 企てる** 〖計画する〗plan (-nn-); (陰謀などを) plot (-tt-); 〖試みる〗try, attempt (❗attempt は失敗を伴うこと); 〖意図する〗intend. ▶ 敵は我々を夜明けに攻撃しようと企てた The enemy *planned* [*tried*, *attempted*] *to* attack us at dawn. ▶ 彼らは大統領暗殺を企てた They *plotted to* assassinate the President. (❗計画のみ)/They made an *attempt* on the President's life. (❗実行して失敗) ▶ 彼は自殺を企てたが失敗した He *attempted* suicide but failed./He failed in an *attempt to* kill himself.

くわばら 桑原 ● 雷が落ちませんように、くわばら、くわばら Let's *keep our fingers crossed* so that we won't be struck by lightning. (〖語源〗keep one's fingers crossed は一般に願い事や災いよけのしぐさで、中指を人差し指に重ねて十字架を作る)

▶**くわわる 加わる** ❶ 〖参加する〗(一員になる) join (in ...) (❗人・団体に加わる場合は in を伴うのが普通ではない); (活動・競技に) take* part [《やや書》participate] in

....（⇨参加する）•そのチームに加わる join the team. •レースに加わる take part in the race. •ゲームに加わりませんか Will you join (us) in the game? (!文脈で明らかな場合は ... join (with) us? でよい) •私は彼らの議論に加わりたくなかったので黙っていた I didn't want to take part in their argument, so I remained silent.
❷ [増す]（速度・重量が）gain;（数量が）incréase.（⇨増す, 増える）•日増しに寒さが加わっている It is getting colder and colder day by [×after] day [(主に米話) by the day].

くん 訓 （⇨訓読み）
くん- 勲- •勲一等 the First Class Order 《of》.（⇨勲章）
-くん -君 （!「君」に当たる英語はなく, 名（特に first name）を呼び捨てて親愛を表す）（⇨-さん）
ぐん 軍 （軍隊）an army;（陸・海・空の）the forces;（軍勢）troops. •占領軍 an occupation army. •国連軍 U.N. troops.
ぐん 郡 (米) a county, (英) a district. (!(1) いずれも「州」(state (米) [county (英)]) の下位の行政区. (2) 米国ルイジアナ州では parish, アラスカ州では borough /báːrou/ を用いる) •那須郡 Nasu County. (!手紙などの住所では通例 Nasu-gun とする)
ぐん 群 a group. (⇨群れ, 集団) •一群の蜂 a swarm of bees.
•群を抜く excel all others 《in》; have no equal 《in》. (⇨抜群, 傑出)
くんい 勲位 the Order 《of》. (⇨勲章)
ぐんい 軍医 an army（海軍の）a naval surgeon;（軍隊内で）a medical officer.
•軍医総監 (米) the Surgeon General.
くんいく 訓育 education; discipline.
くんいく 薫育 moral education.
ぐんか 軍歌 a war [a martial] song.
くんかい 訓戒 图 (an) admonition.
— **訓戒する** 動 《書》admonish.
ぐんがく 軍楽 military music.
•軍楽隊 a military band. •軍楽隊長 a military bandmaster.
ぐんかん 軍艦 a warship.
ぐんき 軍紀 military discipline. •軍紀を維持する[乱す] maintain [violate] military discipline.
ぐんき 軍機 a military secret.
•軍機漏洩 disclosure [betrayal] of military secrets.
ぐんきもの 軍記物 a war tale; a military romance.
ぐんきょ 群居 — **群居する** 動 live gregariously [together, in flocks].
•群居動物 gregarious animals. •群居本能 the herd instinct.
くんくん •くんくん臭いをかぐ sniff 《at ...》. •犬がお互いをくんくんかいだ The dogs sniffed each other. •彼女は香水を買う前に何度もくんくんかいでみた She sniffed 《at》 the perfume before she bought it.
ぐんぐん •（著しく）remarkably;（急速に）rapidly;（急に）sharply. (⇨ぐいぐい) •患者はぐんぐん回復した The patient got better and better. (!「比較級＋比較級」の形で「ますます」の意) •彼は前の走者にぐんぐん追いついていった He ran at great speed to catch up with the runner ahead of him. •彼はぐんぐん英語の力が伸びた He made rapid progress in English. •気温はぐんぐん上昇した The temperature rose sharply.
くんこう 勲功 （功績）one's exploits;（殊勲）one's distinguished services. •勲功を立てる render distinguished service 《to the state》; distinguish oneself 《in》.

くんこう 薫香 （香料）incense.
ぐんこう 軍港 a naval base [port].
くんこく 訓告 图 (a) warning;《書》admonition.
— **訓告する** 動 •社員を遅刻しないように訓告する warn [admonish] one's employees against being late. •スピード違反で厳しく訓告される be given a strong warning against speeding.
ぐんこくしゅぎ 軍国主義 图 militarism.
— **軍国主義の** 形 militaristic.
•軍国主義者 a militarist.
くんし 君子 a man of virtue [noble character]; a (true) gentleman. •君子ぶる assume a virtuous air; pose as a man of virtue.
•君子危うきに近寄らず Wise men keep away from [don't court] danger.;（用心は勇気の大半）（ことわざ）Discretion is the better part of valor.
•君子は豹変す Wise men can adapt themselves to any circumstances.
くんじ 訓示 图 （指示）instruction(s).
— **訓示する** 動 （やや書）instruct.
くんじ 訓辞 an admonitory speech; an address of instructions. •校長は卒業式に訓辞を垂れる The principal addresses [speaks to] his students on a commencement day.
ぐんじ 軍事 military affairs.
— **軍事の, 軍事的(な)** 形 military. •軍事的脅威 a military [a war] threat. •軍事行動を起こす start military action [operations].
•軍事基地 a military base. •軍事教練 military drill [training]. •軍事施設 military installations. •軍事政権 a military regime [government]. •軍事大国 a military power. •軍事同盟 a military alliance. •軍事費（予算）an arms budget;（経費）military [war] expenditures. •軍事力 military strength [power].
ぐんしきん 軍資金 a war fund (!しばしば複数形で); a war chest. •選挙の軍資金 campaign funds.
くんしゅ 君主 （やや書）a monarch /mánɚk/;《書》a sovereign /sάvərin/. •どんなに強力な君主といえども, 死ななければなりません Kings are mortal no matter what power they may have.
•君主国 a monarchy. •君主制 （やや書）monarchism.
ぐんじゅ 軍需 [物資] munitions; military supplies.
•軍需工場 a munition(s) factory. •軍需産業 a munition(s) industry.
ぐんしゅう 群衆, 群集 （雑然とした人の群れ）a crowd,《やや書》a throng,（暴徒化した）《軽蔑的》a mob. (!いずれも単・複両扱い) •大群衆 a large [a big, a huge] crowd; a crowd [crowds] of people. •群衆の中に彼を見つける find him among [in] the crowd. •群衆は静まりかえっていた The crowd was [were] all silent. (!個々の成員に注目して複数扱いすることもあるが,（米）では単数扱いが普通) •大勢の群衆が広場に集まった A big [A large] crowd (of people) gathered in the square./There were [×was] crowds of people in the square. (!ただし, There were [×were] a big crowd (of people)) •群衆は鎮圧のためにやってきた警官隊に囲まれていた The crowd was surrounded by the police who came to put them 《書》it down. •群衆の心理に流されてはいけない Don't get carried away by the mob's spirit [the mob psychology].
•群集心理(学) mass psychology.
ぐんしゅく 軍縮 disarmament, arms limitation. (⇨軍備)
•軍縮会議 a disarmament conference. •軍縮会談 arms talks.

くんしょう 勲章 a decoration 《for》; (勲位を示す) an order; (コイン形の) a medal. ● 勲章をつける[つけている] put on [wear] a *decoration*. ● 彼に勲章を授ける award him a *decoration* [a *decoration* to him]; 《やや書》 decorate him with a *medal* (!) 通例 him を主語にした受身で). ▶ 芸人にとっての勲章は, お金でも肩書きでもない The *medal* of honor for an entertainer is neither money nor a title.

くんじょう 燻蒸 图 fumigation. ── **燻蒸する** 動 fumigate.
● 燻蒸剤 fumigant. ● 燻蒸消毒器 a fumigator.

ぐんしょう 群小 ── 群小の 形 minor; lesser; petty.
● 群小国 lesser nations. ● 群小作家 minor [(あまり有名でない) lesser-known] writers.

ぐんじょう(いろ) 群青(色) (a) ultramarine.

くんしらん 君子蘭 〖植物〗a scarlet Kaffir lily.

ぐんしれいかん 軍司令官 an army commander.

ぐんしれいぶ 軍司令部 the military headquarters. (! 単・複両扱い)

ぐんじん 軍人 〖兵士・下士官〗a serviceman (複 -men), (女性) a servicewoman (複 -women); (陸軍の) a soldier; (海軍の) a sailor; (空軍の) an airman (複 -men), (女性) an airwoman (複 -women); 〖将校〗an officer (! (陸軍) a military officer と (海軍) a naval officer に下位分類. (2) 下士官 (non-commissioned officer) は正式の将校には含めない). ● 職業軍人 a professional [《米》a career] *soldier*. ● 軍人精神 the military spirit. ● 軍人らしい軍人 become a *soldier*. (! a military man は「軍隊の好きな男性」の意で「軍人」の意ではない) ● 軍人を志願する wish to be a *soldier*; choose a military career.

くんずほぐれつ 組んず解れつ ● 組んずほぐれつの乱闘になる wrestle [grapple] wildly 《with》; scuffle fiercely together.

くんせい 薫製 smoked meat [fish]. ● 薫製にする smoke; smoke-dry. ● サケの薫製 *smoked* salmon.

ぐんせい 軍政 ● 軍政をしく[下にある] establish [be under] *military government*.

ぐんせい 群生 (植物の) 〖生物〗a colony, 〖生態〗a community. ── **群生する** 動 (植物が) grow in crowds.
● 群生植物 gregarious plants.

ぐんせい 群棲 图 (動物の) 〖生物〗a colony, 〖生態〗a community. ── **群棲する** 動 (動物が) live in flocks [herds]. (⇨群れ)
● 群棲動物 gregarious animals.

ぐんせい 『群棲』 Life in the Cul-De-Sac. (〖参考〗黒井千次の小説)

ぐんぜい 軍勢 an army; (部隊) a force; (兵数) the number of soldiers. ● 20万の軍勢 a 200,000-strong *army*; an *army* 200,000 strong. ● 敵の軍勢 the enemy *forces*.

ぐんせき 軍籍 ● 軍籍に入る join [《やや書》enlist in] the army [(空軍) the air force; (海軍) the navy].

ぐんそう 軍曹 a sergeant.

ぐんぞう 群像 〖美術〗a group.

くんそく 君側 ● 君側の奸(かん) a disloyal subject in a court. ● 君側の奸を除く clear the court of its *disloyal subjects*.

ぐんぞく 軍属 an army [a navy] civilian employee; a civilian attached to the army [navy].

***ぐんたい 軍隊** (陸・海・空軍を総称して) the armed forces (! 複数扱い), an army (! 単・複両扱い); (警察・市民に対して) the military (! 複数扱い); (兵員に重点を置いて) troops (! 複数扱い). ● 軍隊をやめ

る[に入る] leave [join, enlist in] the *army*. ● 軍隊を派遣する send the *army*; send in *troops*. ● 軍隊生活をする serve in the *army*. ▶ 彼は第二次大戦中軍隊にいた He was in the *army* during World War II.

-くんだり (…まで) as far as…. ● 長崎くんだりまで行く go as far as Nagasaki.

ぐんだん 軍団 a [an army] corps /kɔːr/ (複 corps /kɔːrz/)
● 軍団長 the commander of an army corps.

くんてん 訓点 (説明的に) guiding marks for reading classical Chinese (writing) in the Japanese (writing).

ぐんと (著しく) remarkably, 《比較級を強めて》much, even, 《話》a lot. ▶ 彼女はぐんと美しくなった She became *remarkably* beautiful. ● 列車はぐんと速力をあげた The train gathered speed *suddenly*. (! 「ぐんと揺れる」は jolt (badly))

くんとう 勲等 (勲章の等級) the order of merit.

くんとう 薫陶 图 (教育) education, instruction; (訓練) discipline, training. ● 小西先生の薫陶を受ける *study under* [*receive instruction from*] Mr. Konishi.
── **薫陶する** 動 educate, instruct; discipline, train.

ぐんとう 軍刀 a saber; a military sword.

ぐんとう 群島 (a group of) islands; an archipelago (複 〜(e)s). (⇨諸島)

くんどく 訓読 (⇨訓読み)

ぐんばい 軍配 『相撲』a *sumo* referee's fan.
● 軍配を上げる declare 《him》 the winner. ● 軍配があがる (勝者である) be the winner.
● 軍配を返す start a *sumo* bout with the turn of a referee's fan.
● 軍配うちわ a military fan; a *sumo* wrestling referee's fan.

ぐんぱつじしん 群発地震 an earthquake swarm.

***ぐんび 軍備** (やや書) armaments; (武器) arms. (! いずれも複数扱い) ● 再軍備 rearmament. ● 軍備を縮小[拡張; 強化]する reduce [increase; reinforce] *armaments*.
● 軍備拡大 the expansion of armaments.
● 軍備拡大競争 the arms race. ● 軍備縮小 the reduction of armaments; disarmament; arms limitation. ● 軍備制限 the limitation of armaments.

ぐんぶ 軍部 (総称) the military (! 複数扱い); 〖軍当局〗the military authorities.

ぐんぶ 群舞 group dancing.

くんぷう 薫風 a balmy breeze; a breeze in early summer.

ぐんぷく 軍服 a military uniform. (! 陸[海; 空]軍の軍服は an army [a naval; an air-force] uniform)

ぐんぽうかいぎ 軍法会議 a court-martial (複 courts-, 〜s). ● 許可を得ずにキャンプを離れたかどで軍法会議にかけられる be court-martialed for leaving the camp without asking [permission].

ぐんもう 群盲 the blind men [(大衆) masses]; the stupid.
● 群盲象を評す It's just like the blind men who touched only part of an elephant and gave the wrong description of the whole animal.

ぐんゆうかっきょ 群雄割拠 ▶ 当時は群雄割拠の世の中であった In those days *numerous* (regional) *warlords* competed [struggled] with each other for power. (! この warlord は「戦国時代の武将」をさす) ▶ 現在の IT 業界は群雄割拠の観がある It

ぐんよう　軍用 military use [purposes]. ● 軍用に供する（軍隊用）be for *military use*; (軍事用) be used for *military purposes*.
● 軍用機 a warplane.

くんよみ　訓読み 图 the Japanese-style reading for *kanji*. ── 訓読みする 動 read 《a *kanji*》 in the Japanese way.

ぐんらく　群落 （植物の）【生物】a colony; 【生態】a community. ● シダの群落 a *colony* of ferns. ● 群落をなして生育する grow *in colonies*.

ぐんりゃく　軍略 a stratagem.

くんりん　君臨 图 reign /réin/. (❗ 国王などの地位にあることをさし，支配・統治することは必ずしも含まない (⇨ 支配))
── 君臨する 動 reign 《*over*》; (支配する) rule. (❗ rule は「専制的に支配する」の意が強い) ▶ 英国女王は君臨すれども統治せず The queen *reigns* but does not rule.

くんれい　訓令 图 (指図) instructions; (命令) orders.
── 訓令する 動 give instructions [orders] 《*to*》.

● 訓令式ローマ字 the *kunrei* system of romanizing Japanese.

:くんれん　訓練 图 [[練習]] (a) training; (集団での集中的・反復的な) (a) drill (⇨練習); [[訓育]] discipline (❗「訓育法」の意では Ⓒ). ● 語学訓練 language *training*. ● 火災訓練 a fire *drill*. ● 海兵隊のスパルタ式訓練(法) a Spartan *discipline for* marines. ● 合宿訓練をする have [hold] a *training* camp.
▶ 私はコンピュータの使い方の基礎訓練を受けた I *was given* [*got*] basic *training* in the use of computers. ▶ 彼女は警察官になるための訓練を受けています She is undergoing *training for* a police officer./She is *training as* [*to be*] a police officer. (❗ She is *being trained*.... ともいえる)
── 訓練する 動 train; drill; discipline; (身体を) exercise. ● よく訓練された兵士たち well-*trained* [well-*disciplined*] soldiers. ● 新兵を厳しく訓練する *drill* recruits rigorously. ● 彼らに水泳を訓練する *drill* [*exercise*] them *in* swimming. ▶ 彼はその犬を見世物[ウサギ狩り]のために訓練した He *trained* the dog *for* a show [*to* hunt rabbits].

くんわ　訓話 a lesson; an instructive talk.

け

け 毛 ❶【体毛】(人間や動物などの) (a) hair (▶全体をさすときは U だが、1 本 1 本の毛をさすときは C);(動物の柔毛)fur;(動物の剛毛)a bristle (▶特に豚の毛で、ブラシなどによく用いられる);(動物の外被)a coat;(羽毛)a feather (⇨羽毛);(羊毛)wool (⇨羊毛). ▶うちの猫は毛が柔らかい Our cat has (*a*) soft *fur*./My cat's *fur* is soft. ▶スープに毛が入っていた I found a *hair* in my soup.
❷【植物の】•タンポポの毛 dandelion *fluff*.
❸【頭髪】(a) hair. (⇨髪) •巻き毛 curly *hair*; a curl of *hair*.
•**毛が生えたような** ▶アマチュアに毛が生えた程度の野球選手 a baseball player who is *little better than* an amateur.
•**毛を吹いて疵(きず)を求める**《ことわざ》He finds fault with others, and does worse himself.

け 気 (軽い症状・少量) a touch (*of*);(気配・兆候) a sign. •おしろい気のない(=化粧していない)顔 a face *without* (*any*) makeup. •人気のない通り a deserted street. •塩気のある水 a *slightly* salty water. •塩気の足りないスープ a soup *without enough* salt. •糖尿病の気がある show a *sign* of diabetes. ▶少し風邪気がする I have a *touch* of a cold. ▶彼女はふだんはおしろい気のない顔をしている She usually wears *little* makeup.

け 卦 a divinatory sign. •八卦 divination; fortune-telling. (⇨占い) •よい卦が出た A good *sign* has appeared.

−け −家 徳川家 the Tokugawas; the Tokugawa house [family];(名門の場合)the House [Family] of Tokugawa. •ウィンザー家 House of Windsor. [参考] 現在の英国王家)

げ 下 ❶【劣っていること】inferiority; lowness;(成績評価の)(get) a C [a D] (参考 C は 3 段階評価の最低、D は 5 段階評価の及第の最低). •中流の下 *lower* middle class. •下の下である be the worst (of all); be the lowest of the low. ▶あんなこと言うなんて下の下だ(=ありうるうちで最悪の発言)That was *the worst possible* remark./(それより悪くは言えない) *No one* could say *worse* than that.
❷【本の下巻(かん)】(2 巻本の) the second volume;(3 巻本の) the third volume. •上中下の 3 巻よりなる be [come] in three volumes.

−げ −気 [気配・感じ] (⇨−そうだ❷) •さびしげに笑う smile *sadly*; give a *sad* smile. ▶彼女はいつもさびしげな顔をしている She always *looks* sad. ▶彼女は何か言いたげに私を見た She looked at me *as if* she wanted to say something to me. •(⇨あぶなげ、大人(おとな)気ない、かわいげ)

ケア 【介護、手当て】care. •緩和ケア palliative *care*. •デイケア day *care* (services). •優しい愛のケア tender loving *care* (略 TLC).

けあがり 蹴上がり a kick. •蹴上がりをする kick (up).

けあし 毛足 ❶【織物などの】•毛足の長いじゅうたん a *thick-pile* [a *deep-pile*] carpet.
❷【毛の伸び具合】•毛足の早い(=毛が早く伸びる)人 a person whose *hair grows* fast.
❸【毛深い足】a hairy legs.

けあな 毛穴 pores (*in* the skin).

ケアマネージャー 【介護支援専門員】a nursing care manager.

ケアレスミス 《make》a careless mistake.

ケアンズ 〖オーストラリアの都市〗Cairns /kéərnz/.

けい 兄 •兄たりがたく弟(おとうと)たりがたし《ことわざ》They are much of a muchness. (⇨甲乙)

けい 刑 [刑の宣告] a sentence;[罰する[される]こと](a) punishment. •刑に服する serve (out) one's *sentence* [刑期) *term*]. •刑を宣告する give [〖法律〗pass, pronounce] (a) *sentence* [*on* him]. •軽い刑ですむ get off with a light *sentence*. ▶彼は強盗の罪で重い刑に処せられた He received a heavy [a long, a severe] *sentence* on a charge [on charges] of robbery./He *was* severely *punished* for robbery. ▶彼女は懲役 10 年の刑に処せられた She *was sentenced to* ten years in prison. (⚠「刑は懲役 10 年だった」は The *sentence* was ten years (in prison).) ▶その男はまだ刑が確定していない The *sentence* hasn't been decided for that guy [man].

けい 計 〖合計〗the sum, the total (⇨合計);〖計画〗a plan;〖計器〗a meter, a gauge /géidʒ/. ▶1 年の計は元旦にあり You should make your *plans* for the year on the New Year's Day.

けい 罫 (定規で引いた線) a rule;(線) a line. •罫を引く(罫書) rule, line. •罫紙 ruled [lined] paper.

けい− 軽− (軽い) light. •軽トラック a *light* truck.

−けい −系 ❶〖系図〗a system. •太陽系 the solar *system*. •神経系 the nervous *system*. •医科大学 a medical college. •保守系候補者 a conservative candidate. (⇨系統)
❷〖血統〗descent, stock. •日系米人 an American of Japanese *descent*; a Japanese American. (口語的な言い方)▶私は日系人です I am *of* Japanese *descent*.

****げい 芸** (技芸) (an) art;(たしなみ、芸事) an accomplishment (▶しばしば複数形で);(演技) a performance;(手品、動物の芸当) a trick. •芸をきわめる(みがく) master [cultivate] an *art*. •犬に芸を教える train a dog to do *tricks*; teach a dog some *tricks*. •われわれの仕事は一種の芸事(=技術を身につけること)で、理論や方法よりも年数なのです Our profession is about acquiring skills, so theories or techniques do not matter so much as the years we put in.
•**芸が細かい** ▶彼の仕事は念入りで芸が細かい He does things with careful attention to small details.
•**芸が無い人** •芸がない(=平凡な)人 a dull and uninteresting person;《やや書》a prosaic /prouzéiik/ person.
•**芸は身を助ける**《ことわざ》He who learns a trade [an art] has a purchase made./Any skill you've learned will help you someday.
•**芸達者** a versatile [vɚrsətl/ entertainer. •芸人(通例プロの芸人をさすが、素人にも使用可)•**芸の虫** a person who is eagerly acquiring artistic skills.

ゲイ 〖話〗a gay. (⚠女性の同性愛者は lesbian だが、時に a gay も用いられる。同性愛者自身が好んで用い、a queer のような軽蔑的な含みはない) •ゲイ解放運動 *gay* liberation. (⚠その活動家は a *gay* activist)

──ゲイ 形 gay.
● ゲイバー a gay bar. ● ゲイボーイ a gay boy.

けいあい 敬愛 love and respect; 〔書〕 reverence /révərəns/. ● 非常に敬愛されている be much *loved and respected*; be held in great *reverence*.

けいい 経緯 (細かいこと) details; (一つ一つ) 〔書〕 particulars; (経過) progress, course. ● 事件の経緯を説明する explain the *details* [*course*] of the case.

けいい 敬意 (尊敬) respect, 〔書〕 deference; (心からの) honor; (権力者に対する) 〔書〕 homage. ● …に敬意を表す pay *respect* [*homage*] to…; honor. ● 敬意を表して with *respect*; respectfully. ● …に敬意を表して out of *respect* for…; as a mark of *respect* for…; in honor of…. ▶年長者には敬意を払うべきだ You should *respect* [*show respect for, be respectful to*] your elders.

げいいき 芸域 a range of skills. ● 芸域が広い have a *wide range of skills*; (多芸だ) be very versatile.

けいいん 契印 ● 契印を押す put 〔(やや書) 〕 affix 》 *a seal overlapping* [*at the joining of*] two leaves 《of a deed》. (四 割り印)

けいいんばしょく 鯨飲馬食 ── 鯨飲馬食する 動 eat like a horse and drink like a fish.

‡**けいえい 経営** 名 〔管理〕 management (*! 所有者から任されたもので、しばしば手腕を暗示*); (公務・商売などの) administration; 〔商売〕 business. ● 経営状態がよい [ひどい] be well [badly] *-managed*. ● 手堅い 〔安定した; 健全な〕 経営 conservative [solid; sound] *management*. ● 多角経営 multilateral *management*. ● 経営の合理化 improving *management* efficiency; the streamlining of *management*. ● 経営難に陥っている be in financial difficulties. ▶彼がその会社の経営を引き継いだ He took over the *management* of the firm.
── 経営する 動 (自己資本で) run*, keep*; (所有者から任されて) manage. (*! 基本的には上の区別があるが、口語では区別なく用いられることも多い*) ▶彼はこの町でホテルを経営している He *runs* [*keeps, manages*] a hotel in this town. (*! 進行形は「(今のところ)一時的に」という意を表すのでここでは is *running* [*keeping, managing*] は不適; (所有している) He *owns* [*is the owner of*] a hotel in this town.
● 経営学 business administration [management]. ● 経営感覚 a business sense. ● 経営権 management rights. ● 経営コンサルタント a management consultant. ● 経営者 (所有者) an owner; (支配人) a manager; (経営陣) the management. (*! (1) 通例集合的に用いるが時に単数扱い. (2) labor and management (労使)のような対句や senior [top] management (経営首脳部)のように形容詞を伴う場合は無冠詞*) ● 経営手腕 managerial [administrative] ability. ● 経営情報システム a management information system. ● 経営責任 management responsibility. ● 経営戦略 business strategy. ● 経営体質 business structure. ● 経営判断 managerial judgment [choices]. ● 経営費 operating costs. ● 経営方針 a business [a management] policy. ● 経営理念 a management ideology.

けいえん 敬遠 ── 敬遠する 動 ❶ [避ける] (一般的に) avoid; (離れている) stay [keep] away 《from》, 〔話〕 give 《him, it》 a wide berth; (寄せつけない) keep 《him》 at arm's length. ▶彼は私たちを敬遠しているようだ He seems to *stay* [*keep*] *away from* me.
❷ [野球で] walk 《a batter》 intentionally; give 《a batter》 an intentional walk. ▶相手チームは》カンドにランナーを置いてイチローに敬遠の四球を与えた

They *walked* Ichiro intentionally with a runner on second base.

けいえんげき 軽演劇 a light comedy.

けいおんがく 軽音楽 light music.

*‡**けいか 経過** 名 ❶ [事の] (進行状況) progress; (進展) a development; (成り行き) course. ▶和平会談の経過 *progress* in the peace talks. ● 事の経過 the *course of things* [*events*]. ● 捜査の経過報告 a *progress* report on the investigation; a report on the *developments* in [of] the investigation. (⇨中間) ▶患者の経過は良好です The patient *is improving* [*progressing, doing*] well. ▶大したことはありません. お食べになったものが悪かったのかもしれません. 少し経過を見ましょう It's nothing serious. It could be something you've eaten. I'd like you to see *how it goes*.
❷ [時の] passage; (隔たり) a lapse. ● 時の経過につれて with the *passage* of time; as time goes by. ● 5 年経過後 after 《a lapse》 of five years. ▶父が亡くなってから 10 年が経過した It's [It's been] ten years since my father died./Ten years *have passed* since my father died.
── 経過する 動 pass (by); go by. (⇨経つ)
● 経過措置 〔⇨経過措置〕

けいが 慶賀 ── 慶賀する 動 congratulate 《him on his success》; offer one's congratulations 《to him on his success》. ● …は慶賀すべきことである It is *a matter for congratulation* that….

‡**けいかい 警戒** 名 [見張り] watch, lookout; [警備] guard; [用心] care, caution; [予防措置] a precaution. (⇨用心) ● 警戒心を解く relax 《one's, his》 *guard*. ● 警戒線 (=非常線)を張る[突破する] put a [break through the] *police* cordon. ▶水位は警戒線に達した The water rose to the danger level.
── 警戒する 動 [見張る] watch out, look out 《for》, be on the watch [lookout] 《for》; [警備する] guard 《against》, be on 《one's》 guard 《against, for》. ● 警戒して warily. ● 警戒するような目つきで見る give 《him》 a *wary* look. ▶この時期に山道を行くときには親子づれのクマにくれぐれも警戒しなさい When you go along the mountain path this time of the year, you must be careful and *watch out* for bears with their cubs. ▶警官がすべての出入り口を厳重に警戒していた The police *were* [was] *keeping* strict *guard* at all the doors./All the doors *were* strictly *guarded* by the police. ▶キツネは警戒しながら近づいて来た The fox approached *warily*.
● 警戒警報 a precautionary warning. ● 警戒色 (動物) warning coloration.

けいかい 軽快 ── 軽快な 形 (動作・服装などが) light; (リズムが) swinging. ● 軽快な足どりで [身のこなしで] with *light* steps [movements]. ● 軽快な服装をして in *light* clothes. ● 軽快な音楽 *rhythmical* music. (*! light* music は「肩のこらない音楽」)

けいがい 形骸 ● 形骸化した民主主義 democracy that *has become a dead letter*; (見せかけだけの) *a mere shell of* democracy. ▶その組織は形骸化している The organization *remains only in name*.
● 形骸をとどめない 火事の後, その建物は形骸をとどめなかった(=跡形もなかった) *Nothing remained of* the building after the fire.

けいがい 警咳 ● 警咳に接する [「会う」の謙譲表現] have the pleasure of meeting [speaking with] 《him》 personally.

‡**けいかく 計画** 名 a plan; a project; a scheme /skíːm/; a design /dizáin/; a plot; a prógram.

けいかそち

使い分け **plan** 計画・予定をさす最も一般的な語。細かい作業計画などをさす場合はしばしば複数形で用いる。
project 組織的に行われる大規模な計画。しばしば国家事業などをさす。
scheme 漠然とした空想的な計画，特に悪意を持った陰謀。《主に英》では政府事業などの意でも用いる。
design 綿密に立てた計画あるいはたくらんだ計画。
plot ひそかな計画・陰謀。
program 行事や番組などの実施計画。

①【～計画】 ▶長期計画 a long-term *plan*. ●都市計画 a city *plan* [*planning*]. ●空港建設計画 an airport construction *project*; a *project to* construct [*for* constructing] an airport. ●財政計画 a financial *program*. ●事業計画 a business *plan* [*project*, *program*]; a *project*. ●宇宙旅行の空想的計画 a visionary *scheme* for space travel. ●大統領失脚計画 a *scheme* [a *design*, a *plot*] *against* the President. ●商業地区の開発5か年計画 a five-year *project* for the development of the commercial area; a five-year development *plan* for the commercial area.

②【計画を～】 ●計画を作る draw up a *plan* [a *plan*]. ▶新しい幹線道路は今計画中です A new highway *is* now *being projected* [*planned*]. ▶計画倒れに終わるだろう The *plan* will not work out. ▶研究は計画どおりに進んでいる The study is going(on) *as planned*./The study is progressing *according to plan*. (❗この場合 plan の冠詞は省略するのが普通)

③【計画は[が]～】 ▶計画はたいへんうまくいった The *plan* worked very well (↔badly). ▶パリ訪問の計画が狂った[中止になった] The *plan for* visiting [*to* visit] Paris was upset [(延期される) suspended, called off, (取り消される) canceled]. ▶今度の連休のご計画は？ What *are* you *going to* do during the coming holidays? (❗すでに決めている相手の意志を尋ねる言い方)

④【計画を】 ●計画を実行する carry out a *plan*; put a *plan* into practice [operation]; (進行させる) get a *plan* under way. ●計画をぶちこわす[取りやめる; 中止する] spoil [stop; hold up] a *plan*. ●計画を決定する decide [settle] on a plan. ●週末の計画を立てる make plans for the weekend. ▶彼は自分の計画をだれにも話さなかった He didn't tell anyone what he *was planning*. ▶彼は家を買う計画(=考え)をあきらめた He gave up the *idea of* buying [a *plan to* buy] a house. ▶警察は違法駐車を減らすための新しい計画を発表した The police announced a new *plan for* reducing illegal parking.

—— **計画する** 動 make* plans (*for*; *to do*) (⇨图④); plan (-nn-) (*to do*); (前もって精密に) map (-pp-) ... out; [事業などを] project (❗通例受身で (⇨图②)); [たくらむ] scheme (*to do*). ●旅行を計画する plan (*out*) a trip (❗ out があると「十分に練って」の意が加わる); *make plans for* a trip; *map out* a trip. ●銀行強盗を計画する *scheme to* rob a bank. ▶海外へ留学することを計画している I'*m making plans for* study*ing* [*to* study] abroad./I'*m planning* [I have a *plan*] *to* study abroad. (留学するつもりである) I *am going* [*intend*, *mean*] *to* study abroad. ▶彼は億万長者になろうというばかげたことを計画していた He had a crazy *scheme* to become [*of* becom*ing*] a billionaire.

—— **計画的な** 形 planned; [[故意の]] 《やや書》 intentional; (熟考した) deliberate; (前もって考えた) 《やや書》 premeditated /priːméditèitid/; [[体系的な]] systematic. ●計画的(な)殺人 planned [*deliberate*, [[法律]] *premeditated*] murder.

—— **計画的に** 副 intentionally, on purpose; deliberately; premeditatedly; systematically. ▶家は偶然ではなく計画的に(=故意に)焼かれた The house was burnt down not by accident but *by design*.
●計画経済 a planned economy.

けいかそち 経過措置 ●経過措置を取る take interim [*temporary*] measures. ●経過措置として as an interim measure.

*けいかん 警官 a policeman /pəlíːsmən/ (複 -men) (❗男性で主に巡査をさす); (正式に, 婦人警官も含めて) police officer; 《話》 a cop(per); (平の)《英》 a (police) constable /kʌ́nstəbl/; (巡回の)《主に米》 a patrolman (複 -men). (⇨警察). ●婦人警官 a policewoman (複 -women). ●交通警官 a traffic *policeman*. ●私服警官 a plainclothesman, a plain-clothes *policeman* [(婦人警官も含めて) *officer*, *detective*]. ●警官を現場に急派する dispatch the *police* [*policemen*] to the scene. ▶角という角にはおびただしい数の警官が立っていた There were a lot of *policemen* [*police*] standing at every street corner.
●警官隊 the police (force). (❗集合的に用い複数扱い)

けいかん 景観 (一望の風景) a scene, (全体の) scenery; (眺め) a view. (⇨景色). ●赤城山の雄大な景観 a magnificent *view* of Mt. Akagi. ●街の景観をそこなう廃墟 the *fine* [*nice*] *view* of the town.

けいがん 慧眼 名 a keen [a quick] eye; keen insight.
—— **慧眼の** 形 keen-eyed, quick-eyed; quick sighted; perceptive. ●慧眼の士 a man of *keen insight* [*perception*].

けいかんしじん 桂冠詩人 a poet laureate /lɔ́ːriət/ (複 poets laureate, poet laureates). (❗文脈により poet を省略することも可)

:**けいき** 景気 ❶ [[商況]] business (conditions); [[経済(状態)]] economy, economic conditions; [[時勢]] times.

①【～景気】 ●好景気 prosperity. (⇨好況). ●不景気 a depression; (景気後退) a recession. (⇨不景気). ●にわか景気 a boom.

②【景気の～】 ●景気の谷[底] a bottom; a (business) trouble. ●景気の減速 a (business) slowdown. ●景気の上昇 an economic upturn. ●景気の先行きを予測する forecast the *economy's* direction. ●景気の踊り場 a temporary lull of the economy.

③【景気が[は]～】 ▶景気がよい[悪い] *Business* is brisk [dull, slack]./The *economy* is in good [poor] shape./*Times* are good [bad, hard] now. ▶景気がよく[悪く]なってきた *Economic conditions* are improving [getting worse]./*Business* is picking up [slowing down]. (❗「景気がにわかによくなってきた」は *Business* is booming.) ▶景気は停滞している(=回復の足取りが鈍い) Economic recovery has been sluggish [slow to a snail's pace]. ▶景気が底を打った The *economy* hit bottom. ▶あの会社は景気がよい That company is doing a good *business* [doing well]. ●景気はどうですか (商況の) How's (your) *business*?/(世間の) How *are the times*?/(個人の生活・暮らし向きなど) How goes it [is it going] with you?/How's everything? ▶景気は回復基調[傾向]にある The *economic conditions* are recovering [im-

けいき

proving]. ▶日本の景気はこれからどうなるだろうか How is the Japanese *economy* going to fare in the days ahead?
④【景気を】 ● 景気を刺激する stimulate the *economy* [*economic activity*]; encourage *economic growth*.
❷【活気, 威勢】 ● 景気のよい音楽 *lively* music.
● 景気よく(=気前よく)金を遣う spend money *lavishly*. ● 景気よく騒ぐ(浮かれ騒ぐ) have a spree; (豪遊する)《話》live it up. ● 景気づける(=元気づける) cheer (him) up; 《話》give (him) a lift. ▶ 景気づけに 1 杯やろう Let's have a drink to *cheer* [《話》*perk*] ourselves *up*. (🔲 Let's *take* a drink ... ともいう. Let's *drink* では「飲んで酔っ払おう」といった含みがある)
● 景気回復 (an) economic [(a) business] recovery. ● 景気拡大 (an) economic expansion. ● 景気後退 recession; an economic downturn. ● 景気指標 economic indicators. ● 景気循環 a business 《米》[a trade 《英》] cycle. ● 景気対策 (刺激策) measures to stimulate the economy; stimulative measures. ● 景気調整 (a) business adjustment. ● 景気停滞 (economic) stagnation; a slump. ● 景気低迷 a recession; an economic recession. ● 景気動向 business [economic] trends. ● 景気見通し an economic [a business] outlook.

けいき 刑期 a term of imprisonment. ● 3 年の刑期を終える *serve* three years (*in prison*)《*for robbery*》; serve out *a sentence of* three years' *imprisonment*.

けいき 契機 (機会) an **o**pportúnity; (転機) a túrning pòint; 〔哲学〕momentum. ● これを契機に with this as an opportunity [a turning point].

けいき 計器 (計量器) a meter /míːtər/; (雨量・風速などの) a gauge /géɪdʒ/; (器具) an **i**nstrument.
● 計器着陸 instrument [blind] landing. ● 計器盤 an instrument board [panel]. (🔲 自動車・航空機の計器盤は a dashboard,《主に米》a dash ともいう) ● 計器飛行 instrument [blind] flying.

けいき 継起 — 継起する 働 重大な事件が継起する(=続いて起こる) Important events *occur one after another*.

けいきかんじゅう 軽機関銃 (⇒機関銃)

けいきへい 軽騎兵 (人) a light cavalryman 《-men》; (隊) light cavalry.

けいきょ 軽挙 a rash [a reckless] action.
● 軽挙妄動 ● 軽挙妄動を戒める warn《him》against *rashness*. ● 軽挙妄動は慎まねばならない Don't *act* [*behave*] *rashly* [*recklessly*]. / Be prudent in your behavior.

けいきょう 景況 〔景気の状態〕business (conditions); (経済状態) economic conditions; 〔事態〕a state of things; a situation.
● 景況感 business expectation [(企業の) confidence].

けいきんぞく 軽金属 a light metal.

けいく 警句 an **é**pigram, an **á**phorism (🔲 後の方は必ずしも機知を含むとは限らない); 〔機知に富んだ言葉〕a witty remark. ● 警句を吐く(飛ばす) make *witty remarks*.

けいぐ 敬具 〔一般に〕《米》Sincerely yours, /《英》Yours sincerely, ∥〔面識のない場合, 商業文〕《米》Yours truly, /《英》Yours faithfully, ∥〔親しい場合〕Sincerely/Yours, (友人などに対して心をこめて) With warm regards, . (🔲 いずれの場合もコンマを打ち, 次行に自筆で署名する)

けいけん

けいぐん 鶏群 ● 鶏群の一鶴(ᴋᴋ) a Triton /tráɪtn/ among [of] the minnows /mínouz/. (🔲「雑魚(ᴋᴋ)の中の海神トリトンのような存在の人」の意)

げいげき 迎撃 图 interception; an intercept.
— 迎撃する 働 intercept.
● 迎撃戦闘機 an interceptor. ● 迎撃ミサイル an interceptor missile /mísi(ə)l/.

けいけん 経験 图 (an) experience 《*of, at, in*》. (🔲 具体的な「経験」の意では Ⓒ)
①【〜(の)経験】 ● 実務経験 business *experience*; *experience* in business. ● 海外経験 one's *experiences* abroad. ● 優勝経験 (⇒優勝[優勝経験]) ● 彼は人生経験が浅い He has little [doesn't have much] *experience* of life./He has seen little of life. (⇒③) ● 彼女は運転の経験が長いですか Does she have long [(多くの) much] driving *experience*? ▶山登りはそのときが初めての経験でした That was the first time I had climbed a mountain./That was my first time mountain climbing.
②【経験〜】 ● 経験不足 (a) lack of *experience*. ● 経験年数 years of *experience*. ● 経験上…ということが分かる know [learn] from experience. ● 海外留学の経験者 a person with [who has] *experience* of studying abroad; a person who *has studied* abroad. (⇒③) ● 経験不問《広告》No *experience* required [necessary].
③【経験が[は, の]】 ● その仕事に経験のない男を雇う hire an *inexperienced* man for the job. ● 豊富な経験の持ち主 an *experienced* person; a person with a lot of [a wealth of] experience. ▶彼は英語を教えた経験がない He has no *experience of* [*in*] teaching English. (🔲 in は特に専門分野における経験に用いる)/He *has* never *taught* English. (🔲 このように完了形を用いて経験の有無を表すこともできる) ▶彼女は看護師として 10 年の経験がある She has ten years' *experience* as a nurse. ▶この仕事では経験がものをいう *Experience* counts in this job. ▶彼はファイトはあるがまだまだ経験は不足している He shows a lot of fight [《話》*guts*], but he's still lacking in *experience*. ▶その仕事には多少の経験が必要である The job needs [requires] some *experience*.
④【経験に】 ● その失敗は私には(=にとって)よい経験になった That failure was a good *experience* [(教訓) *lesson*] for me./I learned much [a lot] from the failure.
⑤【経験を】 ● 不愉快な[楽しい; つらい]経験をする have an unpleasant [a pleasant; a bitter] *experience*. (🔲 have の代わりに make は不可) ● 幅広い経験を積む gain [get, acquire] wide *experience*. ● 経験を広める widen [broaden] one's *experience*. ● 経験を経る accumulate [build up] one's *experience*. ● 経験を振り返る look back at [on] one's *experience*. ▶彼はセールスマンとしての経験を新しい仕事に生かした He put his *experience* as a salesman to (good) use in his new job. ▶彼は経験を積んだ(=経験豊かな)英語教師だ He is an *experienced* (↔an *inexperienced*) English teacher./He is very *experienced in* [*at*] teaching English./He has a lot of [(長年の) years of] *experience* as an English teacher. ▶彼は経験を通して金の価値を学んだ His *experience* taught him the value of money. ▶彼は自分も同じような経験をしたのでその少年に同情した He felt sympathy for the boy, because he had been through a similar *experience* himself. ▶彼は自分の戦争の経験(=体験談)を戦争を知らない子供たちに語った He told

[《書》related] his war *experiences* to the children who (had) never experienced war.
⑥【経験から】● 経験から学ぶ learn by [from] *experience*; experience 《*that* 節》. ▶私の経験から言うと[である]言葉を覚えるのは女の子の方が男の子より早い From my *experience*, I'd say [*In my experience*,] girls are quicker with words than boys. ▶私の経験 shows that girls ...のようにもいえる)
⑦【経験だ】● 何事も経験だ One learns by *experience*./*Experience* teaches us everything.
── 経験的な 形 empirical; experiential. ● 経験的概念 empirical concept.
── 経験する 動 experience, (試練などを) undergo*, go* through ...; 〘遭遇する〙see*; (事故・困難などに) meet* with .... ▶こんな暑さは経験しなかった This is the hottest weather (that) I (*have*) ever *experienced*./I've never *experienced* (×a) hot weather like this. ▶彼らは厳しい試練を経験した(=くぐった) They *underwent* [*went through*] a terrible ordeal. ▶愛というのは実際に経験しなければなかなか書けないよ You can hardly write about love if you *haven*'t *lived* it.
● 経験主義 empiricism. ● 経験主義者 empiricist. ● 経験値 experience quotient /kwóuʃənt/; (ゲームの) an experience point.

けいけん 敬虔 ── 敬虔な 形 devout /diváut/; pious /páiəs/. (▶後の方は「敬虔を装った」の意にもなるので注意) ● 敬虔なクリスチャン a *devout* Christian.
── 敬虔に devoutly; piously.

けいげん 軽減 图 (a) reduction.
── 軽減する 動 reduce. ▶税負担を軽減する *reduce* taxes.

けいけんわんしょうこうぐん 頸肩腕症候群 a neck-shoulder-arm sydrome.

けいこ 稽古 图 〘練習〙(a) practice; 〘訓練〙(a) training; 〘下げい〙(a) rehearsal, a dry run. (⇨練習) ● 書道のけいこを欠かさずする do regular *practice* in [×of] calligraphy.
── 稽古(を)する 動 ● ピアノのけいこをする take [have] piano *lessons*; take *lessons* in piano. ▶その劇の舞台げいこをする have a dress *rehearsal* of the play. ▶発表の下げいこをする have a *dry run* of the presentation. ▶柔道の寒げいこをする undergo a cold-season *training* in judo.
● けいこ事 accomplishments; social graces. ● けいこ台 (けいこ用の板張りの場所) a wooden stage for practice. ▶彼は私をけいこ台(=練習相手)にして柔道の技を磨いていった He has developed skills of *judo* by practicing *judo* routines with me.

けいご 敬語 (日本語・中国語などの) an honorific /ànərífik/ (word [expression]), a word [an expression] of respect (▶特に尊敬語をさすことがある). ● 敬語をつかう use *honorifics*.

けいご 警護 图 guard /gáːrd/.
── 警護する 動 guard; (守る) protect. ● 大統領を警護する *guard* the president.

げいこ 芸子 (⇨芸者)

:けいこう 傾向 〖人・物・事の特定の方向への発展〗(やや書) a tendency 《*to, toward*; *to do*》; 〖一般的傾向, 趨勢(秋ぷ)〗a trend; 〖性向, 性癖〗(やや書) (an) inclination. ▶最近の入試の傾向 a recent *tendency* [*trend*] in entrance examinations. ● 物価の上昇傾向 the upward *trend*(*s*) in prices; the upward price *trend*(*s*). ▶著しい保守化傾向を示す show a marked *tendency to* [*toward*] conservatism. ● 世論の一般的傾向をうかがう observe the general *trend* of public opinion. ▶彼は食べ過

ぎる傾向がある He *tends* [*is apt, is inclined,* 《書》*has an inclination*] to eat too much. ▶暴力に訴える傾向が増えている The *tendency toward* violence is increasing./There is a growing *tendency* to resort to violence. ▶女性が高い教育を求める傾向は今後も引き続き強まってゆくであろう The growing *trend* for women to pursue higher education will continue in (主に米) the future.

けいこう 蛍光 ● 蛍光灯 a fluorescent /flùərésnt/ light [lamp]. (⇨明かり) ● 蛍光塗料 fluorescent paint. ● 蛍光ペン a highlighter (pen).

けいこう 携行 ── 携行する 動 carry [take] 《*it*》《*with* him》.

けいこう 鶏口 ▶鶏口となるも牛後となるなかれ 《ことわざ》 Better be the head of an ass than the trail of a horse.

げいごう 迎合 ── 迎合する 動 ● 世論に迎合する(=調子を合わせる) *accommodate* oneself *to* public opinion. ● 上司に迎合する(= 気に入るようにする) *play up to* one's boss.

けいこうかんせん 経口感染 〖医学〗oral infection.
けいこうぎょう 軽工業 the light (↔heavy) industry.
けいこうひにんやく 経口避妊薬 an oral contraceptive, a contraceptive pill; (翌朝飲んでも効く) (婉曲的) a morning-after (pill). (⇨ピル)
けいこく 渓谷 (峡谷) a gorge, a ravine /rəvíːn/; (大きな) a canyon. (⇨谷)
けいこく 警告 图 (a) warning; (a) caution. (▶前の方が強制力が強い) ● 警告なしに without *warning*. ▶警告ランプがついた The *warning* lamp has lit up. ▶警察はスピードを出さないようにと警告を出した The police have issued a *warning* against driving [not to drive] fast. ▶彼はレフェリーから警告を受けた He was given a *caution* by the referee.
── 警告する 動 warn 《him》《*of, about; against; to do*; *that* 節》; warn 《*of*》. ▶彼に危険だと警告したが、私の警告にはがんとして耳を貸さなかった I *warned* him *of* the danger, but he refused to listen to my *warning*. ▶彼女に気をつけるように警告したでしょう I *warned* you *about* her. ▶医者は患者に食べ過ぎないよう警告した The doctor *warned* the patient *not to* eat too much [*against* overeat*ing*].
けいこくしゅう 『経国集』 *Collection for Governing the Country*. (参考) 平安時代の勅撰漢詩文集)
けいこつ 脛骨 〖解剖〗a tibia; a shinbone.
けいごと 芸事 accomplishments. (⇨芸)
けいさい 掲載 ── 掲載する 動 carry, run*; (活字として印刷する) print. (⇨載せる, 載る) ▶今日の新聞はその事故の記事を大見出しで掲載している Today's paper *carries* the story of the accident in a big headline. ▶毎日新聞は新市長の写真を掲載した The *Mainichi ran* a photo of the new mayor. ▶彼の随筆が学校新聞に掲載された His essay *appeared* in the school paper.

:けいざい 経済 图 ❶〖社会・国家・家庭などの経済〗economy (▶「経済機構」の意では C でしばしば the 〜); 〖財政〗finance. (▶「財源・財政状態」の意では通例複数形で)
①【〜経済】● 家庭[国内]経済 a household [a domestic] *economy*. ● 国際[国民]経済 international [a national] *economy*. ● 資本主義[計画, 統制]経済 a capitalist [a planned; a controlled] *economy*. ● 世界[地域]経済 the world [a regional]*economy*. ● 政治経済 (⇨政治[政治経済]) ● 市場経済に参加する[移行する] participate in [convert to] a market *economy*.

②〖経済〜〗●安定した[鈍い]経済成長 stable [slow] (*economic*) growth. ●高度経済成長 high [rapid] (*economic*) growth. ●経済性を高める promote [improve] economic efficiency. ●経済制裁を加える impose *economic* sanctions 《*on*, *against*》. ▶その国は我が国に経済協力[援助]を求めてきた The country has asked for our *economic* cooperation [aid].

③〖経済は[が]〗●日本経済は安定成長の過程にある Japan's [The Japanese] *economy* is in (the) process of stable growth. ●経済は回復した[上向いてきた]ようだ The *economy* seems to have recovered [picked up]. ●そんなことはうちの経済が許さない(=する余裕がない) We *can't afford it*./(うちの資力を超えている) It is *beyond* our *means*.

④〖経済を〗●経済を活性化する[刺激する; 発展させる; 安定させる] revitalize [stimulate; develop; stabilize] an *economy*. ●経済を支える support an economy; sustain economic growth.

❷[節約] (節約, 倹約) (an) economy; (倹約) thrift (⚠*economy* より強意の ⇨節約, 倹約). ▶彼はまだ経済観念がない He still has no [lacks a] sense of *economy*.

—— 経済の 形 economic; (財政上の) financial.
—— 経済的な 形 (物・事がむだのない, 人が倹約する) economical (⚠*economic* は「経済の」「経済学上の」の意); (金や物の使い方が上手な) thrifty; (質素に暮らし節約する) frugal. ●経済的な車 an *economical* [an *economy*] car. ▶タクシーに乗るより電車を使った方が経済的だ Using trains is more *economical* than taking taxis./It's more *economical to* use trains than taking [(*to*) take] taxis. ▶彼は経済的な理由で学校をやめた He left school for *economic* reasons. ▶少々高くてもよい品物は結局経済的だ(=割に合う) Even though they are a little expensive, good articles *pay* in the long run.

●経済家 a person with a strong sense of economy; an economical [a thrifty, a frugal] person. ●経済界 economic circles; the economic world; (財界) financial [business] circles. ●経済改革 economic reform. ●経済外交 economic diplomacy. ●経済開発 economic development. ●経済学 economics (⚠単数扱い); economic science. ●経済格差 an economic differential. ●経済学者 an economist. ●経済学博士 a doctor of economics. ●経済学部 the department of economics. ●経済活動 economic activities. ●経済企画庁 the Economic Planning Agency (略 EPA). (参考 現在は内閣府に移行) ●経済危機 an economic crisis; 《米》a [the] crunch. ●経済恐慌 an economic crash. ●経済協力開発機構 the Organization for Economic Cooperation and Development (略 OECD). ●経済圏 the economic bloc. ●経済構造 an economic structure. ●経済産業省 the Ministry of Economy, Trade and Industry. ●経済産業大臣 the Minister of Economy, Trade and Industry. ●経済誌 a business magazine. (参考 *Fortune*, *Economist*, *Business Week* など) ●経済指標 economic indicators. ●経済状態 the state of the economy; the economic [financial] situation. ●経済新聞 a financial [a business] newspaper. ●経済水域 economic waters; an economic (sea) zone. ●経済政策 an economic policy. ●経済成長率 the economic growth rate; the rate of economic growth. ●経済制度 an economic system. ●経済大国 an economic power. ●経済動向 economic trends. ●経済白書 an economic white paper. ●経済封鎖 an economic blockade. ●経済摩擦 economic friction. ●経済見通し an economic forecast [outlook]. ●経済面(新聞の) the financial page. ●経済問題 an economic problem. ●経済欄 the financial columns. ●経済力 economic power [strength]. (⚠*economic power* は「経済大国」の意)

*けいさつ 警察 the police; the police force; 《話》the law.

> 使い分け **police** 「機構としての警察」「警察官たち」の両意で用いられ, いずれも the を伴い複数扱いが原則だが, 新聞英語では the を省略することもよくある. したがって,「5人の警察官」は five *police* [*policemen*, ×*polices*],「1人の警察官」は a policeman, 正式にはまた婦人警官 (a policewoman) を含めて a police officer となる.
> **police force** 特定の国・地域の機構としての警察.
> **law** 法の施行機関としての「警察(官, 官たち)」の意の口語で, 単・複両扱い.

●警察に届ける report to [(書) inform] *the police*. ●警察に突き出す hand over [deliver] 《him》to *the police*. ●警察に協力する cooperate with *the police*. ●警察に捕まる be arrested [caught] by *the police*. ●警察は彼を追っている *The police* are [×is] on his track [after him]. ▶帰らないと警察を呼ぶぞ If you don't leave, I'll call [(人に頼んで) send for] *the police*. ▶警察の手が彼に回った *The police* [*law*] caught up with him. ▶彼は警察沙汰(ざた)にしたくなかった He didn't want (to get) *the police* involved.

●警察学校 a police school [academy]. ●警察官 (⇨警官) ●警察犬 a police (tracker) dog. ●警察国家 (軽蔑的) a police state. ●警察署 (特定地域の) a police station, 《米》a station house; (本署) police headquarters (⚠単・複両扱い). ●警察署長 the chief of a police station; a police chief. ●警察庁 the National Police Agency. ●警察手帳 a police handbook. 事情▶米国では警察の身分を示すのは身分証明書とバッチ (police officer's ID [badge])であるから「(身分を示すため)警察手帳を見せた」という文脈ではこの語は使えない. その場合には He showed the woman his *police identity card*. などとなる) ●警察当局 the police authorities.

*けいさん 計算 图 ❶[算出] (a) calculation; (a) computation; (数算の) a sum. ●計算が速い[遅い; うまい; へただ] be quick [slow; good; poor] at *calculation* [*calculating*, *sum*, (数字) *figures*]. ●頭の中で計算する(=暗算する) do a *sum* in one's head. ●計算を間違える make mistakes in *calculation* [one's *sums*]; miscalculate; miscount. ▶彼の計算は正確だ[間違っている] His *calculations* [*sums*] are accurate [wrong]. ▶君の計算(=計算の結果の数字)は私のと合っている Your figures agree with mine.

❷[予測・考慮] ●それを計算(=考慮)に入れる take it *into account* [*consideration*]. (⚠この逆は leave it *out of account* [*consideration*]. (⇨考慮)) ▶この新製品は我が社の主力商品になると思ったが, それはとんだ計算違いだった I expected that this new product would be our major money-maker, which was my serious *miscalculation*.

—— 計算する 動 calculate, (書) compute, 《米やや話》figure ... out; (一つずつ数えて) count. ●旅行の費用を計算する calculate [reckon (*up*), 《米やや話》figure out] the cost of the trip; calculate [*figure out*] how much the cost of the trip will come to. ▶ページ数を計算する *count* (*up*) the number of the pages.

会話 「あの人いくつぐらいかしら」「大阪万博の年の生まれよ. 計算してごらんなさい」"How old is she?" "She was born in the year of Osaka Expo. So you *do the math*."

- 計算尺 a slide rule. ● 計算書〖経済〗a statement.

けいさんずく 計算ずく ▶計算ずくの発言 a *calculated* utterance. ▶計算ずくの人生なんてつまらない It is not enjoyable to lead a *calculating* life. ▶私は彼の計算ずくで物事をする遣り方が好きではない I don't like his *mercenary* attitude. (!*mercenary* は「欲得ずくの」の意)

けいさんだかい 計算高い ▶彼は計算高いやつだ He is a *calculating* man./He knows on which side his bread is buttered. (!「権力のある人にうまく取り入る」など自分の利益にさといの意)/He does everything for money. (!「損得勘定で動く人だ」の意)

けいさんぷ 経産婦 a woman who has given birth to a child; (出産を2回以上経験した人)〖医学〗a multipara.

けいし 刑死 ── 刑死する 動 反逆罪のかどで刑死する be *executed for treason*.

けいし 軽視 ── 軽視する 動 (低く評価する, ばかにする) make light [〖書〗little] of ....

けいし 罫紙 ruled [lined] paper.

けいし 警視 《米》(市・州警察の) a major, 《英》(市警察の) a superintendent. (!日本の「警視」は通例後の方で表される)
- 警視正《米》a lieutenant colonel; 《英》a chief superintendent. ● 警視総監 the Superintendent General (of the Metropolitan Police). ● 警視庁 the Metropolitan Police Department.

けいじ 刑事 a (police) detective. ● 部長刑事 a *detective* sergeant.
- 刑事事件 a criminal [〖法律〗a penal] case. ● 刑事訴訟 a criminal action [suit]. ● 刑事訴訟法 the Criminal Procedure Act. ● 刑事補償 criminal indemnity.

けいじ 計時 a time check. ── 計時する 動 time; clock; check time.
- 計時係 a timer; a timekeeper.

けいじ 啓示 (a) rèvelation. ● 神の啓示 divine *revelation*.

けいじ 掲示 〖公告, びら〗a notice; 〖公の通知〗a bulletin; 〖標識〗a sign. ▶禁煙の掲示 a "No smoking" *sign*; a *sign* of "No smoking". ▶掲示板に掲示を出します put up [〖書〗post] a *notice* on a *bulletin*《米》[a *notice*《英》] board. ▶入口の戸に「外出中」の掲示が出ていた The *notice* on the door said [read], "I am out."

けいじ 慶事 a happy event; (めでたいこと) a matter for congratulation. (⇨弔事)

けいじか 形而下 ── 形而下の 形 physical.

:けいしき 形式 名 〖内容に対して〗(a) form; 〖形式ばった行為〗a formality. ▶それは単に形式上のことがらないわけにはいかない It's merely a matter of *form*, but we have to do it. ▶そんなに形式ばるなよ Don't be so *formal*./Don't *stand on ceremony*. ▶彼は形式ばかりにこだわって中身がない He is all *form* and no content.
── 形式的な 形 formal. ● 形式的な儀礼 *formal* courtesy. ▶総理の演説は形式的なものにすぎない The Prime minister's speech is only a [a mere] *formality*.
- 形式主義 (宗教・芸術上の) formalism. ● 形式

主義者 a formalist. ● 形式主語 the formal subject. ● 形式目的語 the formal object.

けいしき 型式 a model. (⇨型)

けいじじょう 形而上 ── 形而上の 形 metaphysical.
- 形而上学 metaphysics.

けいしつ 形質 (遺伝上の) a character. ● 獲得形質 an acquired *character*.
- 形質細胞 a plasma cell. ● 形質転換 transformation. ● 形質導入 transduction. ● 形質発現 phenotypic expression.

けいじどうしゃ 軽自動車《米》a subcompact (car), 《英》a minicar; (日本の) a midget car.

けいじばん 掲示板 a bulletin《米》[a notice《英》] board. (⇨けいじ (掲示))

けいしゃ 傾斜 名 〖水平・垂直に対する〗a slant; 〖道路などの〗a slope; 〖船の〗a list; 〖勾配(𝑘𝑜)〗an inclination. (⇨傾き) ▶屋根の傾斜 the *slant* [*slope, inclination*] of a roof. ● 山の傾斜地 mountain *slopes*. ● 急傾斜 a steep *slope* [*inclination*]. ● 傾斜具合が大きい tilt to a great extent. ● 傾斜具合が小さい tilt slightly [to a small extent].
── 傾斜した 形 slant(ing); sloping; inclined. ▶20度に傾斜した坂 a slope with an *inclination* of 20 degrees. ▶ビー玉が傾斜した床の上を転がった The marble rolled down the *slanted* floor.
── 傾斜する〖させる〗動 slant; slope; incline. ▶雪がすべり落ちるように屋根は大きく傾斜している The roof *slants* [*is sloped*] sharply to let the snow run off. ▶道は海岸の方へ急傾斜している The road *slopes* [*slants*] steeply down to the shore. ▶建築家は屋根を40度傾斜させた The architect *inclined* the roof at a 40 degree angle.
- 傾斜角 an angle of inclination. ● 傾斜度 a gradient, 《米》a grade. ● 傾斜面 a slope; an inclined plane.

けいしゃ 鶏舎 a henhouse.

げいしゃ 芸者 a geisha (複 〜, 〜s); (説明的に) a woman who is professionally trained to provide entertainment to customers (mostly men) at a feast (by playing the *samisen*, dancing, serving food or drinks, or telling witty stories).

げいしゃ 迎車 ▶10時にホテルへ迎車を行かせます We're sending a taxi to pick you up [We'll have a taxi for you] at the hotel at 10 o'clock.

けいじゅう 軽重 (⇨軽重(𝑘𝑒𝑖𝑐ℎ𝑜̄))

けいしゅく 慶祝 ── 慶祝する 動 celebrate.
- 慶祝行事 a celebration (program).

:げいじゅつ 芸術 名 art (!部門をさすときは ⓒ); (美術) the fine arts. ● 現代芸術 modern *art*. ● 日本芸術院 the Japan *Art* Academy. ● 芸術を解する appreciate *art*; have a sense of *art*. ▶能は日本の伝統芸術です Noh is a form of Japanese traditional *art*.
── 芸術の, 芸術的な 形 artistic. ● 芸術(的)な一家 an *artistic* family. ▶彼の演奏は芸術的でした His playing was *artistic*./He gave an *artistic* performance.
- 芸術は長く人生は短し (ことわざ) Art is long, life is short.
- 芸術映画 an árt film. ● 芸術家 an artist;《書》a person of *art*. ● 芸術祭 an árt fèstival. ● 芸術作品 a work of art; (集合的) art, works of art.

げいしゅん 迎春 ▶迎春のお喜びを申し上げます I wish you a Happy New Year!

げいしゅんか 迎春花 〖植物〗(黄梅) a winter jásmine.

けいしょう 形象 a shape, a figure.
— **形象化する** give shape [form] 《to》.

けいしょう 敬称 (肩書き) a title. (■ Mr., Dr., Professor, Prince など).

けいしょう 景勝 ▶景勝の地 a *scenic* spot [area]; a place of *scenic beauty*.

けいしょう 軽少 — **軽少な** 形 ●軽少な被害 *slight* [*little, trifling*] damage. ●軽少ですがお礼のしるしです I hope you will accept this as a *small* token of my gratitude.

けいしょう 軽症 〔軽い病気〕a slight sickness; 〔軽い症状〕a mild case (■「軽症の患者」の意もある). ●軽症のハシカ(患者) a *mild case* of measles.

けいしょう 軽傷 a slight injury [wound]. (⇨負傷)
●事故で軽傷を負う be *slightly injured* [*hurt*] in the accident; get a *slight injury* in the accident.

けいしょう 継承 (地位・財産の) succession. ●王位継承(権) the *succession* to the throne.
— **継承する** 動 ●王位を継承する *succeed to* the throne.

けいしょう 警鐘 (sound) an alarm bell; (警告) a warning. ●警鐘を鳴らす give a *warning* 《to》; warn.

けいじょう 刑場 an execution ground; (絞首台) a scafford.
●刑場の露と消える die on the scaffold; be executed.

けいじょう 形状 (形) a shape; (型) a form.
●形状記憶合金 shape memory alloys.

けいじょう 計上 名 (充当) 《やや書》 appropriation. — **計上する** 動 《やや書》 appropriate 《...for》, allocate 《...to, for》.

けいじょう 経常 ▶経常黒字[赤字]が急激に拡大した The *current* account surplus [deficit] rose suddenly.
●経常収支 current account. ●経常損益 pretax [ordinary] profit and loss. ●経常損失 pretax [ordinary] loss. ●経常費 rúnning [óperating] cósts. ●経常利益 pretax [ordinary] profit.

けいじょうみゃく 頸静脈 〖解剖〗the jugular /dʒégjələr/ (vein).

けいしょく 軽食 a light meal, 《米》(a) lunch; (間食) a snack; (軽い飲食物) refreshments.
●軽食堂 (大学・工場などのセルフサービス式の) a cafeteria; a snack bar; 《主に米》(ホテルなどの) a cóffee shòp; (drugstore などの中にある) a lùncheonétte.

けいしん 敬神 respect for God and religion; piety.

けいしん 軽信 名 credulity, credulousness; (だまされやすいこと) gullibility.
— **軽信する** 動 believe (it) too readily [easily].

けいず 系図 a family tree, a genealogy. ●系図をさかのぼる trace one's *family tree* back 《to》.

けいすいろ 軽水炉 〖物理〗a light-water reactor.

けいすう 係数 〖数学・物理〗a coefficient. ●エンゲル係数 Engel's *coefficient*.

けいすう 計数 (計算) (a) calculation; (数えること) (a) count. ●ガイガー計数管 a Geiger counter. ●計数に明るい be good at [have a (good) head for] figures.

けいする 敬する ●敬して遠ざける keep 《him》 at a distance with pretended [superficial] respect. (⇨敬遠)

けいせい 形成 名 formation; making. ●よい習慣の形成 the *formation* of good habits.
— **形成する** 動 ●人格を形成する *form* [*mold, shape*] one's character.

●形成期 the formative years 《of a person》; the formative period 《of a nation》. ●形成外科 plastic surgery. ●形成外科医 a plastic surgeon.

けいせい 形勢 〖情勢〗the situation; (全体的な流れ) the tide, the current; 〖先の見込み〗prospects, an outlook; (勝ち目) chances, odds. ●戦術上の形勢 the tactical *situation*. ●形勢の逆転 the reversal of the *situation*. ●形勢を見る[読む] watch the development of the *situation*; (状況を判断する) size up the *situation* [*chances*]. ▶5ラウンドでの彼の強烈な一撃で形勢は一変した At the fifth round, his powerful blow turned the *tide* (in his favor). ▶形勢はほぼ互角[君に不利]だ The *chances* are about even [against you].

けいせい 経世 (世を治めること) administration; (政治的手腕) statesmanship.
●経世家 an administrator; a statesman. ●経世済民 national administration and relief from the people's hardships.

けいせい 警世 a warning (to the world). ●警世の書 an *admonitory* book.
●警世家 a social critic; (先の見える人) a seer.

けいせき 形跡 (痕跡) a trace, a mark (■ しばしば複数形で); (しるし) a sign (■ 通例否定文で); (証拠) (an) evidence. ▶このあたりには人が住んでいた形跡はない There is no *sign* [*trace, evidence*] that any people have lived in this neighborhood.

けいせつ 蛍雪 diligence in study; diligent study.
●蛍雪の功を積む apply oneself entirely to one's studies.

けいせん 係船 (船をつなぎとめること) mooring; (つなぎとめられた船) a boat [ship] moored 《at a buoy [a pier]》. — **係船する** 動 moor a boat [ship].

けいせん 経線 a line of longitude /lánʤət(j)ùːd/ (↔ latitude), a longitude line; (子午線) a merídian.

けいせん 罫線 a ruled line.

けいそう 係争 ●係争中である be *in dispute* [*at issue*].
●係争点 a disputed point, the point at issue.

けいそう 珪藻 〖植物〗a diatom.
●珪藻土 〖地学〗diatomaceous /dàiətəméifəs/ earth; diátomìte. ●珪藻類 diatoms.

けいそう 軽装 ●軽装である be lightly dressed [(登山する人が) equipped]. ●軽装で旅をする travel *light*.

けいそう 継走 a relay (race). (⇨リレー)

けいそく 計測 名 measurement. — **計測する** 動 measure.
●計測器 a méasuring ìnstrument.

***けいぞく 継続** 名 〖続けること〗continuation; (連続性) continuity; 〖継続期間〗duration; 〖更新〗renewal. ●友好関係の継続 the *continuation* of friendly relations 《with》. ●外交政策の継続の重要性 the importance of *continuity* in foreign policy. ●法案を継続審議にする *carry* a bill *over* to the next session.
— **継続的な** 形 continuous.
— **継続的に** 副 continuously; (中断なく) without interruption.
— **継続する** 動 ●仕事を継続する *continue* one's work [*to work, working*]; *go on working* [*with* one's work]. (⇨続ける, 続く ❶) ●雑誌の購読をもう1年継続する *renew* one's magazine subscription for another year.

けいぞく 係属 〖法律〗pendency. ●訴訟係属中 during the *pendency* of action; pendente lite.

***けいそつ 軽率** 名 (性急) hastiness; (無分別) indis-

けいそつ

cretion; (軽はずみ) rashness. ▶彼の行動は軽率のそしりをまぬがれない He cannot escape censure of his *indiscreet* behavior.
— **軽率な** 形 hasty; indiscreet /ɪndɪskríːt/; rash; (思慮がない) thoughtless; (不注意な) careless. ▶彼の判断は軽率だった He made a *hasty* judgment. ▶君がそんなことを言ったのは軽率だった It was *indiscreet* of you to say that.
— **軽率に(も)** 副 hastily; rashly; thoughtlessly; carelessly.

けいそん 恵存 ▶佐藤誠様恵存 To Mr. Makoto Sato, With the Compliments (of …). (**!**…には贈る人の名前が入る)

けいだ 軽打 ▶軽打した打球 a tap; a tapper. ●カーブを軽打して二塁ゴロを打つ tap a curveball for a grounder to second.

けいたい 形態 a form. ●政治の一形態 a *form* of government. ▶彼は酔っ払いの形態模写をして私たちを笑わせた He made us laugh a lot by *mimicking* a drunk man. (**!** mimicking の原形は mimic). ●形態模写 mimicry. ●形態論 [言語] morphology.

けいたい 携帯 图 **❶**[持ち運ぶこと] ●携帯に(=持ち歩くのに)便利な物 a handy thing to *carry about*. ▶パスポートは常時携帯のこと Make sure that you *carry* your passport at all times. (**!** 注意書で) **❷**[携帯電話の略] ▶今携帯でかけているのよ I'm on the *cell phone*. ▶知らない女の子が私の携帯に電話してきた A girl called me on my *cell*.

DISCOURSE
携帯電話を持つことで、親や友人に頼りすぎる可能性がある。…また携帯電話は時間を食うので、勉強や休息の時間に影響するかもしれない By having *a cellular phone*, children may become over-dependent on their parents and friends. … Also, the frequent use of the cellular phone takes up a lot of their time, depriving them of the time they need to study or rest. (**!** also (さらに)に追加に用いるディスコースマーカー)

●携帯電話 《米》a cellular /séljələr/ [a cell] phone, a cell; 《英》a mobile phone, a mobile. ●携帯メール an email message on a cellular 《米》 [mobile 《英》] phone. ●携帯品 one's things; one's belongings. (⇨所持品) ●携帯品預り所 a cloakroom, 《米》a checkroom. ●携帯ラジオ a portable radio.

けいだい 境内 precincts /príːsɪŋkt/. ●神社の境内で in the *precincts* of a shrine [shrine *precincts*].

げいだん 芸談 an artist's [an actor's] talk on his art.

けいだんれん 経団連 [日本経済団体連合会] Japan Business Federation.

けいちつ 啓蟄 *keichitsu*; (説明的に) the day around March 6, when insects appear from their holes in the earth.

けいちゅう 傾注 — **傾注する** 動 ●この事業に全力を傾注する *devote oneself entirely* [努力を集中する] *concentrate one's efforts*] to this undertaking.

けいちょう 軽佻 frivolity. (⇨軽薄)

けいちょう 軽重 **❶**[軽いことと重いこと] heavy and light. **❷**[重要度] ●事の軽重を計る weigh *the importance* of a matter. ●事の軽重を問わず regardless of what is important and what is not.

けいちょう 傾聴 — **傾聴する** 動 listen (attentively [intently, eagerly]) 《to》. ▶彼の演説は傾聴(する)に値する His speech is worth *listening to*. (⇨聞く

❷)

けいちょう 慶弔 congratulations or condolences. ●慶弔費 the expenditure for gifts given on happy or unhappy occasions.

けいつい 頸椎 [解剖] the cervical vertebrae /vɔ́ːrtəbriː/ (単 ~ vertebra).

けいてき 警笛 a whistle, an alarm whistle; (自動車の) a (car) horn. ●警笛を鳴らす whistle a warning; give an *alarm whistle*; (自動車の) sound [blow] a *horn*.

けいと 毛糸 [編み物用の] knitting wòol; [紡ぎ毛糸] woolen yarn. ●赤い毛糸玉 a ball of red *wool*. ●毛糸の靴下 *woolen* socks. ●毛糸で靴下を編む knit *wool* into socks; knit socks out of *wool*. ▶彼女(手にかけて)差し出している毛糸のかせを彼女は巻き取っていた She was rolling a skein of the *woolen yarn* he was holding out for her.

けいど 経度 longitude. (⇨東経) ●経度を測る calculate [measure] the *longitude*.

けいど 軽度 — 軽度の形 light; (ほんの少しの) slight. (対重度)

*****けいとう** 系統 [組織] a system; [血統] descent. (⇨系, 血統) ●神経[消化]系統 the nervous [digestive] *system*. ●系統立てる systematize. ●そのことを系統立てて話す tell it *systematically* [*in a systematic way*]. ●赤系統の色 a color *belonging to the red group*; *shades* of red. ●事務系統の仕事に向いている be suited for work of the clerical type. (**!** 意味をとって do well in a clerical job などもよい)
— **系統的な** 形 systematic; (秩序だった) methodical.
— **系統的に** 副 ●系統的に本を読む read *systematically*. ●英文法を系統的に勉強する make a *systematic* study of English grammar.
●系統樹 a genealogical tree.

けいとう 継投 — 継投する 動 ▶小林が清水を継投した [野球] Kobayashi *replaced* Shimizu *on the mound*. /(代わって登板した) Kobayashi took the *mound in relief of* Shimizu.
●継投策 a strategy of combining pitchers.

けいとう 傾倒 — (専念する) devote oneself to …; (…の熱心な賞賛者である) be an ardent admirer of ….

けいとう 鶏頭 [植物] a cóckscomb.

けいとう 芸当 (奇術のような早わざ) a trick (**!** 「動物の曲芸」の意もある); (曲芸, 離れ業) a feat, a stunt (**!** stunt の方が高度で人目を引くもの). ●危ない芸当をする (曲芸を) perform [do] a risky *feat* [*stunt*]; 《比喩的》make a risky attempt.

げいどう 芸道 an art. ●芸道に励む devote oneself to the pursuit [洗練] refinement] of one's *art*.

けいどうみゃく 頸動脈 [解剖] the carotid /kərάtɪd/ (artery).

けいとくちん 景徳鎮 [中国の都市] Jingdezhen /dʒɪŋdédʒén/. [参考] 中国一の陶磁器生産地として有名)

げいにく 鯨肉 whale meat.

げいにん 芸人 an entertainer; a performer; (寄席芸人) a vaudevillian /vɔ̀ːdəvíliən/.

げいのう 芸能 public entertainments. ●芸能人 [=芸能界] ●芸能人 an entertainer; (アーティスト) an artist (**!** 以上は a singer, an actor のように具体的にいうことが多い); (テレビタレント) a TV personality [xtalent].

げいのうかい 芸能界 the world of entertainment, show business, 《話》showbiz. ●芸能界の人々 *showbiz* personalities. ●18歳で芸能界で

けいば 競馬 horse racing, the races; (1レース) a hórse ràce. ●競馬に行く go to *the races*. ●競馬に賭(か)ける bet money on a horse; (米) play *the races*. ●競馬で負ける[勝つ] lose [make] money at *the races*. ▶酒は飲まないが競馬はやる I don't drink but I play *the races*.
●競馬馬 a racehorse. ●競馬場 a racetrack; (英) a racecourse.

けいべつ 軽蔑〖身分の低い人〗a person of low rank; (下役) an underling; (未熟者) a greenhorn; (小物)〖話〗small fry (複数扱い).

けいはい(しょう) 珪肺(症)〖医学〗silicosis.

けいはく 軽薄 图 (浅はか) frivolity. ●製品に対する顧客の好みは軽薄短小化の傾向にある People tend to prefer smaller, lighter and thinner products.
── 軽薄な 形 frivolous; (愚かな) silly.

けいはつ 啓発 图
── 啓発する 動 enlighten;〖書〗edify. ●読者を啓発する本 an *enlightening* book. ●氏の講義に大いに啓発される be greatly *enlightened* by his lecture.

*****けいばつ** 刑罰 图 (a) punishment, a penalty. (⇨罰)
●重い刑罰を科す inflict a heavy (⇔a mild) *punishment* [*penalty*] (on him). ●刑罰を受ける receive (a) *punishment*; be punished.

けいばつ 閨閥 a faction whose leading figures are one's wife's relatives.
●閨閥政治 a form of government by the relatives of the ruler's wife; nepotism on one's wife's side.

けいはんざい 軽犯罪 a minor [a petty] offense;〖法律〗a misdemeanor. ●軽犯罪を犯して罰せられる be punished for one's *minor offenses* [*misdemeanors*].
●軽犯罪法 the Minor Offenses Act.

*****けいひ** 経費 (費用) expense(s), cost(s); (維持費) upkeep. (⇨費用) ●必要経費 necessary *expenses* [*expenditure*]. ●車の経費 the *upkeep* of a car. ●経費を抑える keep [hold] down *expenses*. ●経費を30パーセント削減する cut down (on) [reduce] *expenses* by 30 percent. ●接待費を必要経費で落とす deduct entertainment expenses as necessary *expenses*. ▶それには大変経費がかかる It *costs* a great deal./(非常に高い) It's very *expensive*.
●経費削減 cost-cutting; cost [expenses] reduction.

けいび 軽微 ── 軽微な 形 ●軽微な被害をこうむる suffer *slight* [(わずかな) trifling, negligible] damage.

けいび 警備 图〖監視〗guard;〖保安〗security;〖防衛〗defense (⇨防衛). ●会場の警備態勢を強化する strengthen the *security* setup of the meeting place.
── 警備する 動 guard (*against*); stand guard (at the gate); police (the streets); ●厳重に警備されている be heavily *guarded* [*policed*]; be under heavy *guard*.
●警備員 a (security) guard; a security man; (和製語) a guard man. ●警備会社 a security company. ●警備隊 the (coast, border) guard; a garrison. ●警備艇 a guardship.

けいひん 景品 a free gift, a giveaway. ●景品を出す offer *gifts* [*giveaways*].

けいひんかん 迎賓館 a guesthouse (複 -houses /-ziz, (米) -siz/), a guést hòuse. ●赤坂の迎賓館 the Government [State] *Guesthouse* at Akasaka.

けいふ 系譜 (系図) a family tree, a geneálogy.

けいふ 継父 a stepfather.

けいぶ 頸部 图 the neck; (子宮などの)〖解剖〗a cérvix (複 -vices, ~es).
── 頸部の 形 cervical.

けいぶ 警部 (米) a captain, (英) a chief inspector.
●警部補 (米) a lieutenant /luːténənt/, (英) an inspector.

げいふう 芸風 the style [(特徴) characteristic] of one's performances [acting]. ●先代歌右衛門の芸風を受け継ぐ inherit [(守る) follow] the *artistic tradition* of the late Utaemon.

けいふく 敬服 ●敬服する 動 admire, have great admiration 《for》.

けいぶつ 景物 ❶〖季節の風物〗natural features of the seasons. ●竹の雪も冬の景物の一つだ The snow on bamboos is one of the *attractive features of* [*scenes in*] winter. ❷〖景品〗(⇨景品)

けいふん 鶏糞 chicken droppings.

*****けいべつ** 軽蔑 图 contempt /kəntémpt/, (〓無価値だとしてばかにすること); (敵意・怒りに満ちた〓見下すこと)〖書〗disdain. ●彼女のふるまいは級友の軽蔑の的だった Her behavior was an object of *contempt* of her classmates./Her behavior was the *scorn* of her classmates. ▶彼の提案は軽蔑にも値しない His proposal is *beneath* [*below*] *contempt*. (〓「軽蔑に値する」なら …is contemptible.) ●彼女は彼の態度に軽蔑の念を抱いている(=軽蔑している) She has *contempt* [*scorn*] *for* his manner./She is *contemptuous* [*scornful*] *of* his manner./She *holds* his manner *in contempt*.
── 軽蔑的な 形 ●軽蔑的な笑いをする give a *contemptuous* [*scornful*] smile; smile contemptuously [scornfully].
── 軽蔑する 動 despise, 《話》 look down on [upon]… (〓despise は嫌悪感に, look down on は対等に扱っていないことに重点がある); (表情や態度に出して) scorn;〖書〗disdain. ●偽善者をひどく軽蔑する show a great *contempt for* hypocrites. ▶君[君の仕事]を軽蔑するつもりはなかった I didn't mean to *despise* you [your work]. ▶臆病(おくびょう)者だと軽蔑されるのは嫌だ I hate to *be looked down upon as* a coward [*for being* cowardly].

けいべんてつどう 軽便鉄道 a narrow-gauge /-géidʒ/ railway.

けいぼ 敬慕 图 adoration. ●敬慕の念を抱く feel *adoration* 《for》. ●敬慕の念を抱かせる inspire *adoration* (in many people).
── 敬慕する 動 adore.

けいぼ 継母 a stepmother.

けいほう 刑法 criminal law. ── 刑法上の 形 criminal; penal /píːnl/.

けいほう 警報 a warning; (装置) an alarm. ●警報を鳴らす ring [sound] an *alarm*. ●空襲[火災; 暴風雨; 津波]警報を出す give [issue, raise] an air raid [a fire; a storm; a tidal wave] *warning*.

けいぼう 閨房 〖寝室〗a bedroom, (古) a bed chamber;〖婦人の居間〗a woman's private sitting room; (上流婦人の) a boudoir /búːdwaːr/.

けいぼう 警棒 (米) a nightstick, (英) a truncheon; a policeman's club [stick].

けいぼうだん 警防団 volunteer guard; (自警団) a civil defense corps.

けいま 桂馬 (将棋の) a (chess) knight; (囲碁の) a knight jump.

けいみょう 軽妙 ── 軽妙な 形 (軽快な) light; (巧みな)

けいむ 警務 police affairs.

けいむしょ 刑務所 a prison; a jail. (!)(1) いずれも「拘置」の意では ①. (2)《米》では軽犯罪者・未決囚を入れる拘置所や留置場にしか通俗的には jail を用いる方が普通) ●刑務所に入れる put 《him》 in *prison* [*in jail*, *behind bars*]. ●刑務所に入っている *be in prison* [*jail*]; be jailed [imprisoned]. ●刑務所から出る come out of *prison* [*jail*]. ▶彼は殺人の罪で刑務所に入れられた He *was sent to* [*was put in*, (行った) *went to*] *prison* for murder. ▶彼女は彼に面会するため刑務所に行った She went to the *prison* to visit him.

げいめい 芸名 〖舞台俳優の〗 a stage name; 〖映画俳優の〗 a screen name; 〖職業上の〗 a professional name.

けいもう 啓蒙 enlightenment. (⇒啓発)
●啓蒙運動 a campaign for enlightenment; (18世紀のヨーロッパの) the Enlightenment. ●啓蒙時代 an age of enlightenment. ●啓蒙主義 the philosophy of the Enlightenment.

***けいやく** 契約 图 a contract /kántrækt/; an agreement; a bargain, 《話》a deal; a lease.

> **使い分け** **contract** 「契約」の意を表す最も一般的な語. 個人・団体・企業・国家間の売買, 請負, 保険などさまざまな契約に使う.
> **agreement** 幅広く使えるが法的拘束力がないので保険などには使えない.
> **bargain** 取引〖売買〗契約をさす.
> **deal** bargain の口語で軽い意味の契約, 取り決めをさす.
> **lease** 賃貸借契約をさす.

① 【～契約】 ●長期契約 a long-term *contract*. ●仮[本]契約 a temporary [a formal] *contract*. ●雇用[賃貸]契約 an employment [a léase] cóntract. ●専属契約 an exclusive contract. (⇒専属) ●新規契約 a new contract. ●選手を 2 年契約で雇う sign up a player to a two-year *contract*. (⇒④)

②【契約～】 ●契約開始[満了] the commencement [termination] of a *contract*. ●契約のサイン (a) signature. (関連) ファンサービスのサイン (an) autograph)▶彼は契約内容に同意した He agreed to the *contract* terms.

会話 「契約期間はどのくらいですか」「1 年です」 "What's the term of the *contract*?" "It's one year."/"How long does the *contract* run?" "It runs for one year."

③【契約が】 ●契約が成立する reach [come to] a *contract*. ●契約が決まる(=契約することに決める) agree a contract. ●来年契約(期間)が切れる The *contract* expires [runs out] next year. (!) 確実な予定なので will expire [run out] としないのが普通)

④【契約を[で]】 ●契約で by *contract* [*lease*]; on an *agreement*. ●10 年契約で農地を借りている have the farmland *on* a ten-year *lease*. ●契約をする[結ぶ] contract; make [enter into] a *contract*; (署名の上雇う) sign 《him》 up. ●契約を踏みにじる break [violate] a *contract*. ●契約を更新する renew a *contract*. ●契約を履行する carry out [fulfill, perform] a *contract*. ●契約を延長する extend a *contract*. ●契約を取り消す cancel [〖法律〗rescind] a *contract*. ●契約を取る get [win] a *contract*. ▶彼はそのセールスマンと新車を買う契約をした He *contracted* [*made a contract*] *with* the salesman *for* a new car [*to buy a new car*]. ▶球団はそのアメリカ人選手と来シーズンの契約をした The baseball team *signed up* the American player for the next season./The American player *signed on with* the baseball team for the next season.

―― **契約する** 動 contráct, make* a cóntract; sign up. (⇒図③)●契約したとおり as *contracted* [*agreed*]. ▶その歌手はそのレコード会社と契約している The singer *is under contract to* [*with*] the record company./The record company *has* the singer *under contract*.

●契約違反 (a) breach of contract. ●契約解除 cancellation [annulment] of a contract; (賃貸契約の) cancellation of lease; (雇用の) severance. ●契約結婚 contract marriage. ●契約更新 (a) renewal of a contract. ●契約社員 a contract worker;《米話》a just-in-time employee,《英》a temporary (worker) (!)口語では a temp ともいう). ●契約社会 a contractual society. ●契約書 (⇒契約書) ●契約当事者 parties to a contract. ●契約不履行 non-fulfillment [default] of contract.

けいやくしょ 契約書 a contract; (賃貸契約の) a lease (contract). ●売買契約書 a sales *contract*. ●契約書を作成する draw up a *contract*. ●契約書に署名する sign a *contract* [a *lease*].

けいゆ 経由 via /váiə/ …; by way of …; through …. ●ロンドン経由でパリへ飛ぶ fly to Paris *via* [*by way of*] London. (!)後の方が堅い言い方) ▶仏教は朝鮮を経由して日本へ伝わった Buddhism reached Japan *through* Korea.

けいゆ 軽油 light oil.

げいゆ 鯨油 whale oil.

けいよう 形容 ―― **形容する** 動 (描写する) describe; (言い方で) express; (修飾する) modify. ●彼女の美しさは言葉で形容できない She is *inexpressibly* beautiful./Her beauty is *beyond description*.

けいよう 掲揚 ―― **掲揚する** 動 hoist [fly] 《a flag》.

けいようし 形容詞 〖文法〗 an adjective; 〖人につける形容語〗 an epithet. (!)例: John, *the Fool* 馬鹿のジョン) ●限定[叙述]形容詞 an attributive [a predicative] *adjective*.
●形容句 an adjective phrase. ●形容節 an adjective clause.

けいようどうし 形容動詞 〖文法〗 an adjectival verb.

けいら 警邏 patrol. ●警ら中の巡査 a police officer *on patrol*.

けいり 刑吏 (死刑執行人) an executioner; (絞首刑の) a hangman.

けいり 経理 (会計) accounting. ●経理を担当している be in charge of *accounting*.
●経理部 the accóunting division.

けいりし 計理士 〖「公認会計士」の旧称〗 (⇒会計)

***けいりゃく** 計略 〖人を欺く〗 a trick; 〖わな〗 a trap; 〖陰謀〗 a plot; 〖戦略〗 strategy. ●計略を用いる[見破る] use [see through] a *trick*. ●計略を巡らす devise a *plot*. ●敵の計略の裏をかく outwit [outsmart] the enemy. ▶彼は計略にかかった He was caught in a *trap*./(計略に陥った) He fell into a *trap*.

けいりゅう 係留 图 mooring /múəriŋ/.
―― **係留する** 動 moor. ●杭に係留してあるボート a boat *moored* to a post.
●係留所 a mooring.

けいりゅう 渓流 a mountain stream.

けいりょう 計量 图 measurement.

けいりょう

—— 計量する 動 (量を) measure; (重さを) weigh.
・計量カップ a méasuring cùp.

けいりょう 軽量 —— 軽量の 形 lightweight, light.

けいりん 桂林 〖中国の都市〗Guilin /gwíːlín/.

けいりん 競輪 a bicycle [a cycle] race; (日本式の) keirin.
・競輪場 a bicycle racetrack. ・競輪選手 a (professional) cycle racer.

けいるい 係累 ・係累が多い have *a large family* to take care of [to support].

けいれい 敬礼 名 (挙手などして) a salute.
—— 敬礼する 動 salute; give a salute.

*けいれき 経歴 (家族, 学歴, 職業) one's background; (職業的な) one's career /kəríər/; (記録としての) a record; (履歴) one's personal history. ・経歴がすばらしい[芳しくない] have a distinguished [a poor] *record*. ・経歴を調べる look into one's *background*. ・教師としてすばらしい経歴を持っている have a brilliant *career* as a teacher [in teaching]. (⇨キャリア) ・彼の経理の経歴が大変役に立った His accounting *background* came in quite useful.

げいれき 芸歴 a history of one's performances [acting].

けいれつ 系列 a group; (企業体) a *keiretsu* (🌐 ～), a group of affiliated companies. ▶あの会社は松下系列だ That company *is a subsidiary of* [*is affiliated with, has an affiliation with*] the Matsushita group.
・系列会社 an affiliate /əfíliət/; an affiliated company; (子会社) a subsidiary /səbsídièri/ (company). ・系列ノンバンク a non-bank affiliate.

けいれん 痙攣 名 〖医学〗(a) cramp, (a) spasm (⚠ 以上の2語は《英》で Ⓤ); (けいれんによる震え) 〖書〗convulsions; (ぴくぴくするけいれん) a twitch. ・ふくらはぎのけいれん (a) *cramp* in one's calf muscles. ・胃けいれん stomach *cramps*. ・けいれん防止剤 an anti-*convulsant* tablet. ・けいれんを起こす [have] (a) *cramp* (*in* one's leg); have [go into] *convulsions*; go into (a) *spasm*.

—— 痙攣する 動 ▶彼の目はぴくぴくけいれんしていた His eyes *were twitching*.

けいろ 毛色 (人の) hair color; (動物の) fur color.
・毛色の変わった人 a different type of person; (変な) an odd [a *strange*, (風変わりな) a *queer*, (常軌を逸した) an eccentric] person.

けいろ 経路 (道筋) a route, a channel; (方法) means. ・感染経路 a *route* of infection. ・逃走経路 an escape *route*. ・入手経路 *means* [a *channel*] of acquisition.

けいろう 敬老 respect for old people [〖やや書〗the aged].
・敬老会 (give) a party to entertain old people [〖やや書〗the aged]. ・敬老の日 Respect-for-the-Aged Day; (お年寄りの日) Senior Citizens' Day.

ケインズ 〖英国の経済学者〗Keynes (John Maynard ～).
・ケインズ経済学 Keynesian economics.

けう 希有, 稀有 —— 希有 [稀有] な 形 (⇨希(ま)な) ・希有な事例 a *rare* [(珍しい) an *uncommon*, (異常な) an *unusual*] case.

ケー K, k. ・K24 (24 金) 24-karat《米》[24-carat《英》] gold 《略はそれぞれ k., kt.; c., ct.》. ・3K (= kitchen)のアパート (部屋が三つと台所) a 3-room apartment with a kitchen.

ケーオー a knockout; a KO (⚠ KO's). ・ケーオー勝ちする win by a *knockout*; knock ... out.

ケーキ (a) cake. (⚠ 菓子パン・ホットケーキなども含む. a (whole) cake はケーキ丸ごと一つで, 切ったものを a piece [two pieces] of cake などで表す) ・バースデー[クリスマス]ケーキ a birthday [a Christmas] *cake*.
・デコレーションケーキ a fancy [ˣa decoration] *cake*. ・パウンドケーキ《米》pound *cake*, 《英》Madeira /mədíərə/ *cake*. ・ホットケーキ a pancake; a griddlecake; 《米》a flapjack. ・ケーキ屋 a patisserie /pɑtí(ː)səri/; a bakery (⚠ パンも売っている).
・ケーキを焼く [作る] bake [make] a *cake*. ▶ケーキもう一ついかがですか How about another piece of *cake*?
・ケーキ型 a cake mold. ・ケーキカット cake-cutting ceremony.

ケーケー (株式会社の略記号)《米》Inc., 《英》Ltd (⚠《英》の PLC, Plc は Public Limited Company (上場会社)の意). ・社名の後につける ˣK.K. は和製英語》

ゲージ a gauge /géidʒ/.

*ケース 〖入れ物〗a case; 〖場合〗a case. ・ガラスのケース a glass *case*. ・特殊なケース a special *case*.
・ケーススタディー 〖事例研究〗a case study 《of》.
・ケースワーカー a caseworker.

ケースバイケース ・ケースバイケースで (judge) according to the *situation*, as the *case* may be. ▶それはケースバイケースだ (=状況による) That *depends* (*on circumstances*). (⚠ on a case-by-case basis は「個々別々に」の意)

ケーソン 〖潜函(せんかん)〗a caisson /kíːsɑn/.

ゲーテ 〖ドイツの詩人・作家〗Goethe /géitə/ (Johann Wolfgang von ～).

ケーてん K点 〖極限点〗the critical point.

ゲート a gate. ・正面ゲート the front *gate*. ・ゲートインする (競馬で) enter the starting *gate*. ▶JAL の756便は何番ゲートから出発しますか What *gate* is JAL 756 leaving from?
・ゲートウェー 〖コンピュータ〗a gateway.

ゲートボール gateball; (説明的に) a ball game which was invented in Japan on the model of croquet /kroukéi/. ・ゲートボールをする play *gateball*.

ゲートル [<フランス語] 〖脚絆(きゃはん)〗gaiters.

ケーパー (⇨ケッパー)

ケープタウン 〖南アフリカの都市〗Capetown.

ケーブル a cable. ・海底ケーブルを敷設する lay a submarine *cable*.
・ケーブルカー a cable car. ・ケーブルテレビ cable TV.

*ゲーム a game. ・テレビゲーム a video game. ・アウェー(の)ゲーム an away *game*. ・ホームゲーム a home *game*. ・ロードゲーム a road *game*. ・ナイトゲーム a night *game*. ・デーゲーム a day *game*. ・シーソーゲーム a seesaw *game*. ・コールドゲーム a called *game*.
▶ …に 2ゲーム差をつけて [つけられて] いる be two *games* ahead of [behind] …. ▶タイガースに1ゲーム差に迫る move within one *game* of the Tigers. ▶ゲーム差なしで with no game difference. ▶ゲームオーバー[セット] (=試合終了) The *game* is over [ˣset]. / 〖野球〗Game. / 〖テニス〗Game and set. / (和製語) Game over [set].
・ゲームセンター《米》a penny arcade, 《英》an amusement arcade; (テレビゲームの) a video arcade. ・ゲームソフト a video game software.
・ゲームポイント (テニスなどの) a gáme pòint. ・各ゲームの決勝点をあげるチャンス

けおされる 気圧される ・堂々たる門構えにけおされる(=圧倒される) be overcome (威圧される) be overawed) by the imposing gate.

けおとす 蹴落とす ▶彼は同僚を蹴落として (=犠牲にし

けおりもの 毛織物 woolen fabrics [textiles].

***けが** 怪我 名 ❶ [負傷] (事故などで) an ínjury; a hurt (⚠ ínjury より軽い); (武器による) a wound /wúːnd/. ●軽いけが a slight (↔a serious, a severe) *injury* [*wound*]. ●けが人 an *injured* [a *wounded*] person (⚠ 複数形は通例 injured [wounded] people); 《集合的》《やや書》 the *injured*, the *wounded*. ▶彼はたいしたけがじゃないって医者は言ってるよ He's not seriously *hurt* [*injured*], the doctor says.
会話「おけがはありませんか」「大丈夫です」 "*Are* you *hurt?*" "(I'm) all right, thanks." ❷ [過失] ●これといったわけがなくwithout any serious *mistakes*.
── 怪我(を)する 動 (事故などで) get* [be] injured; get [be] hurt, hurt* oneself (⚠ get [be] injured より軽い); (武器などで) get [be] wounded. ▶彼はその自動車事故で大けがをした He *was badly* [*seriously*] *injured* in the car accident. ▶私は転んで右脚にひどいけがをした I *injured* [*hurt*] my right leg badly when I fell down. (⚠ ×I *was injured* [*hurt*] in the right leg. は不可) ▶彼は撃たれて頭に[腕に]けがをした He *was wounded on* the head [*in* the arm] by the shot./The shot *wounded* his head [arm].
会話「この塀から跳び降りるのを見ててね」「やめなさい．けがをするわよ」 "Watch me jump off this wall." "Don't. You'll *hurt yourself*."
── 怪我(を)させる 動 injure; hurt*; wound. ●彼にナイフでけがをさせる *wound* him with a knife; inflict a knife wound on him.
●けがの功名 (偶然の成功) a chance success.

げか 外科 名 surgery; (病院内の) the department of surgery. ●脳[形成]外科 brain [plastic] *surgery*.
── 外科の，外科的な 形 súrgical.
●外科医 a surgeon. (⇨医者) ●外科手術 surgery; a surgical operation.

げかい 下界 (人間の世界) this world; (地上) the earth. ●飛行機から下界を見下ろす look down on *the earth* from the plane.

けかえし 蹴返し [相撲] *kekaeshi*; minor inner footsweep.

けがす 汚す [[名誉などを]] disgrace, dishonor; [[名声などを]] 《書》 sully; [[神聖なものを]] profane. ●家名を汚す *disgrace* [*bring disgrace on*, *dishonor*] one's family; *stain* the family's good name. ●名声を *sully* [*soil*] a reputation. ▶そのスキャンダルは学校の名声を汚すものだった The scandal is a *discredit* to the school's good name.

けがに 毛蟹 [動物] a hairy crab.

けがらわしい 汚らわしい (汚い) dirty; (むかつきそうな) disgusting; (いやな) nasty. ▶それは口にするのも汚らわしいことだった That was a *nasty* thing to say.

けがれ 汚れ [[汚点]] a stain; [[不浄]] uncleanness; [[不純]] impurity. ●家名に汚れを残す leave a *stain* on one's family name; (はずかしめる) disgrace one's family name. ●汚れを知らぬ (=無邪気な)子供 an *innocent* child.

けがれる 汚れる get* dirty; (堕落する) be corrupted. ●汚れたお金 *dirty* money.

けがわ 毛皮 (兎・狐などの柔らかい毛(皮)) fur. (⚠ 毛皮製品の意では (U). ●ミンクの毛皮(製品) a mink *fur*.
●毛皮のコート a *fur* coat; a coat made of *fur*.

*げき 劇 [[芝居]] a play; [[戯曲]] (a) drama (⚠ 「劇文学」の意では (U). play の方が日常的な語) (⇨芝居 ❶); 音楽劇 a musical *play* [*drama*]; 《集合的》(the) musical *drama*. ●劇中劇 a *play* in a *play*. ●新作劇を上演する produce [stage] a new *play* [*drama*]. ●劇を見る see (観賞する) appreciate a *play* [*drama*]. ▶その劇は今国立劇場で上演中だ The *play* is now on [showing] at the National Theatre. ▶彼女はその劇に出ていた She acted [appeared] in the *play*. ▶学園祭で彼らはシェイクスピアの劇を上演した They performed Shakespeare's *play*(s) at their school [campus] festival.

げき 檄 (声明書) a manifesto, a declaration; (訴え) a written appeal; (回状) a circular. ●次の選挙に向けて檄を飛ばす issue a *written appeal* for the next election. (熱弁をふるう) harangue for the next election. [参考] 「檄を飛ばす」を「激励する」の意で用いるのは誤用

げきえいが 劇映画 a film with a story line.

げきか 劇化 名 dramatization.
── 劇化する 動 ●小説を劇化する *dramatize* a novel; *turn* a novel *into a play*; *adapt* a novel *for the play* [*stage*].

げきか 激化 ── 激化する 動 inténsify. ▶最近国際競争が激化した International competition *has intensified* recently. (⚠ 「競争の激化」は growing competition).

げきが 劇画 a story comic.

げきから 激辛 ●激辛カレー fiery (hot) [super hot] curry.

げきげん 激減 ●a marked [a sharp, a sudden, a rapid] décrease. (⇨ 激増)
── 激減する 動 decréase márkedly [sharply, suddenly, rapidly]. (⇨減る，減少)

げきこう 激高，激昂 名 (興奮) excítement; (憤激) (a) fúry, a ráge (⚠ 前の方が強意的).
── 激高[激昂]する 動 get excíted; be enráged; fly into a fúry [a ráge]. ●激高した学生 *enraged* students.

げきさく 劇作 ── 劇作する 動 write a play [drama].
●劇作家 a dramatist; a playwright (⚠ ×a playwriter という).

げきし 劇詩 a dramatic poem; (総称) dramatic poetry [verse].

げきしゅう 激臭，劇臭 a powerful stink; a sickening odor.

げきしょう 劇症 ── 劇症の 形 fúlminant.
●劇症肝炎 [医学] fulminant hepatitis.

げきしょう 激賞 名 (receive) high praise (*for*).
── 激賞する 動 praise (very) highly, 《書》 extól(l).

*げきじょう 劇場 a theater (⚠ (英) a theatre は (米)でも劇場名によく用いられる), a playhouse (⚠ -houses /-ziz, 《米》-siz/).
●劇場街 a theater district [quarter].

げきじょう 激情 [[激しい感情]] a violent [a strong] emotion; [[熱情]] (a) passion. ●激情を抑える hold back one's *violent emotion*. ●激情に駆られて in a fit of *passion*.

げきしょく 激職 (職務) a busy post; (仕事) a busy job. (⇨ 劇 激務)

げきしん 激震 a severe [a violent] shock [earthquake].

げきじん 激甚，劇甚 ── 激甚[劇甚]な 形 ●激甚な競争 keen competition. ●激甚な打撃を敵に与える inflict a *terrible* (《致命的な》a *crushing*) blow on the enemy.
●激甚災害指定地 a terrible disaster area.

げきする 激する ❶ [興奮する] get [be] excited; (激怒する) be enraged; fly into a rage [fury]. ●激しやすい excitable; hot-temperd; (起こりやすい) irritable.
❷ [激しくなる] ▶戦いはますます激してきた The battle *is getting fiercer.*

げきせん 激戦 (戦闘の) hard fighting, a fierce battle; (激しい競争) a close [a hot] contest. ●激戦を交える fight a *fierce battle*《with》.
●激戦地 a hard-fought field; (選挙の) a closely [a hotly] contested constituency.

げきぞう 激増 a marked /mάːrkt/ [a sharp, a sudden, a rapid] increase. (■前の2語は程度が, 後の2語は速度が激しいこと)(⊗ 激減)
── 激増する 動 ▶失業者数が激増した The number of the unemployed *has* [ˣhave] *sharply increased*.(⇨増加)

げきたい 撃退 ── 撃退する 動 敵を撃退する *drive back* [*fight off*, *repel*] an enemy. ●セールスマンを戸口から撃退する(=追い返す) *turn* [*drive*] *away* a salesman from the door.

げきだん 劇団 a theatrical [a dramatic] company; (旅回りの) a theatrical [an acting] troupe /trúːp/. (⇨‐団)
●劇団員 a member of a theatrical company; a trouper.

げきだん 劇壇 the stage; the theatrical world.

げきちゅう 劇中 ▶劇中の人物 the characters *in the play*.
●劇中劇 a play within a play.

げきちん 撃沈 ── 撃沈する 動 (attack and) sink《a ship》.

げきつい 撃墜 图 downing.
── 撃墜する 動 ●敵機を撃墜する *down* [*shoot down*] an enemy plane.

げきつう 激痛 [an acute] pain; (突発的な) a pang. ●激痛が走る[に襲われる] have [be seized by] a *sharp pain*.

げきてき 劇的 ● 劇的な 形 dramatic. ●劇的な事件 a *dramatic* event. ▶彼女の救出は劇的だった Her rescue was *dramatic* [a *dramatic* one].
●劇的に dramatically.

げきど 激怒 图 great anger; (a) fury; (抑えられないほどの)(a) rage. (⇨怒り)
── 激怒する 動 get very angry; fly into a fury [a rage]. ▶彼女は彼に裏切られて激怒していた She was *furious with* [ˣat] him *for* having betrayed her./She was *furious at* [*about*] his betrayal. (⇨怒(る)る) ▶彼は激怒して口もきけなかった He was speechless *with fury* [*rage*].

げきどう 激動 (激変) 图 upheával. ●社会の激動の時代 a time of social *upheaval*.

げきどく 劇毒 a deadly poison. (⇨ 猛毒)

げきとつ 激突 图 (物が) a crash; (意見・利害などが) a clash. (⇨衝突)
── 激突する 動 ▶車は木に激突した The car *crashed* [*smashed*] *into* [*against*] a tree. (■ *into* では食い込む, *against* でははね返される感じ)

げきは 撃破 ── 撃破する 動 defeat《the enemy》, destroy《the enemy battleship》; (敗走させる) rout《the enemy》; (論破する) refute《one's opponent》.

げきはく 激白 ── 激白する 動 speak one's mind frankly; (吐露する) lay bare one's heart.

げきはつ 激発 an outburst. ●感情の激発 an *outburst* of emotion.
── 激発する 動 ▶王に対する反乱が激発した A rebellion *broke* [*burst*] *out* against the king.

げきひょう 劇評 a dramatic criticism.
●劇評家 a drama [a theater] critic. (■後の方はオペラ, ミュージカルも含む)

げきぶつ 劇物 a highly toxic substance.

げきぶん 檄文 (⇨ 檄)

げきへん 激変 图 (突然の) a sudden change; (急激な) a rapid change; (激しい) a violent change; (徹底的な) a drastic change. ●政治の激変 a *violent change* in politics 《■of も可能だが, in が普通》: political *upheaval*.
── 激変する 動 ▶天候が激変した The weather *changed suddenly*./There was a sudden change in the weather. ▶ここ数年で我が国の産業構造は激変した《やや書》 The industrial structure of our country *underwent a drastic change* in the last few years.

げきむ 激務 [仕事] hard work; [職務] a busy post. ●激務についている be engaged in *hard work*; hold a *busy post*.

げきめつ 撃滅 ── 撃滅する 動 destroy ... completely, 《やや書》 annihilate /ənáiəlèit/.

げきやく 激薬 a powerful [a very strong] drug; [毒薬] a (deadly) poison.

げきやす 激安 ▶このシャツを激安で買った I got this shirt *dirtchéap*.
●激安ショップ a dirtcheap store; a store where everything is (as) cheap as dirt.

げきらい 毛嫌い ── 毛嫌いする 動 ●犬を毛嫌いする(=本能的に嫌悪感を持っている) have an *instinctive dislike* of dogs;《やや書》 have an *antipathy* to dogs.

げきりゅう 激流 a violent stream, a torrent. (⇨急流) ●激流にのまれる be caught in the *torrent*.

げきりん 逆鱗 ── 逆鱗に触れる (怒りを買う) incur《his》anger. (⇨怒(いか)り ④)

げきれい 激励 encouragement. ●激励の言葉 words of *encouragement* [*cheer*].
── 激励する 動 ●人を激励していっそう努力を促す *encourage* [*spur*]《him》to make greater efforts. ▶彼をしっかり激励してやらないといけない He needs a lot of *encouragement* [*needs encouraging*]. ▶母親が子供に学校で[何にでも]1番になりなさいと激励する話はよく聞く We often hear (that) mothers *encourage* their children to be [become] No. 1 at school [everything]. (■《話》では that は省略する)

げきれつ 激烈 ── 激烈な 形 fierce, violent; (食うか食われるかの) dog-eat-dog; (情け容赦のない) cutthroat. ●印刷業界の激烈な競争 *fierce* [*dog-eat-dog*] competition in the printing business.

げきろん 激論 (have) a heated argument [discussion, debate]. (⇨議論, 討論)

げくう 外宮 the Outer Shrine of Ise.

げけつ 下血 ── 下血する 動 discharge blood.

けげん 怪訝 ●けげんそうに(=疑わしげに)私を見る give me a *dubious* [変な目つきで] a *strange* look; look at me *dubiously* [*strangely*]. ▶彼はけげんな(=困惑した)顔をしていた He looked *puzzled* [《書》*perplexed*].

げこ 下戸 ▶私はまったくの下戸です(=まったく酒が飲めない) I *can't drink (alcohol)* at all.

げこう 下校 图 ▶下校の際には車に気をつけなさい Watch out for cars *on your* [*the*] *way to and from school*. ▶下校時間です (校内放送で) The school is closing for the day.
── 下校する 動 *go* [*come*] *home from school* (■視点が学校にある場合は go, 家にある場合は come を用いる); leave school (for home).

げこくじょう 下克上 ・下克上の世 'a world where people once deemed low-ranked *take the upper hand of* the high-ranked people'; (社会の激変期) the time of social upheaval.

げこむ 蹴込む ・溝に石を蹴り込む(=けり入れる) *kick* a stone *into* the gutter.

けさ 今朝 this morning. ▶彼は今朝早く出発した He started early (×in) *this morning*.

けさ 袈裟 a surplice; a Buddhist priest's stole.

げざ 下座 ❶ [下位の人が座る席] (⇨下座(ざ)) ❷ [寄席などの] the musicians' seats; (説明的に) the musicians' box on the left side of the stage.

げざい 下剤 (a) laxative /lǽksətɪv/. ・下剤をかける [飲む] use [take] a *laxative*.

けさがけり 袈裟懸り ・袈裟懸けに切る cut (him) *slantwise from the shoulder*. ・輪にしたロープを袈裟懸けにして持ち運ぶ carry a coiled rope worn over one shoulder diagonally to under the other.

げさく 戯作 a light [popular] work of literature; (江戸時代の) a popular novel in the later Edo era. ・戯作者 a writer of popular literature; a writer of a popular novel in the later Edo era.

げざん 下山 ━━ 下山する 動 climb [come] down a mountain; [寺を去る] leave a temple.

けし 芥子 [植物] a poppy; (アヘンを採る) an opium poppy. ・ケシの実 a *poppy* seed.

げし 夏至 the summer solstice /sɑ́lstɪs/.

けしいん 消印 (郵便の) a postmark. ・封筒に押されている消印 the *postmark* on the envelope. ・その手紙は8月20日付けの横浜の消印が押してあった The letter *was postmarked* Yokohama/August 20./The letter bore a Yokohama *postmark*/August 20. ▶はがきは5月31日の消印まで有効です Cards should *be postmarked* not later than May 31.

けしかける [犬などを] set* (a dog) on [upon] (him); [扇動または] incite, egg (him) on (*to do*).

けしからぬ, けしからん (弁解のできない) inexcusable; (許しがたい) unpardonable; (無礼な) rude; (恥ずべき) shameful; (ひどく不愉快な) outrageous; (外聞の悪い) scandalous. ▶あんなふるまいはけしからん Such behavior is *not excusable* [is *inexcusable*, (ひどすぎる) is *too much*].

***けしき 景色** [風景] (全体の) scenery (❗a はつかないことに注意); (個々の光景・場面) a scene (❗人の動きを暗示することが多い); (山・谷・畑など陸地の) a landscape; [眺め] a view. (⇨風景, 眺め) ・田舎の景色 rural *scenery*. ・美しい景色 beautiful *scenery*, a beautiful *scene* [*view*]. ・景色のよい所 a *scenic* place [*spot*]. ・この地方は景色がいい The *scenery* [×scene] is beautiful in this region. (❗この地方の景色 … でも誤りではないが頭でっかち) ・この部屋からの景色はすばらしい The *view* from this room is wonderful./I have a wonderful *view* from this room. ・その看板で景色が見えない The signboard blocks out the *view*.

けしきばむ 気色ばむ (怒りを顔に出す) show (one's) anger (*at*); (むっとなる) become sullen (*at*).

げじげじ a house centipede; (いやなやつ) [話] a skunk, [俗] a creepy-crawly (❗おどけた言い方). ・げじげじ眉 thick, bushy eyebrows.

けしゴム 消しゴム (主に米) an eraser /ɪréɪsər/, (主に英) a [(an India)] rubber. ・消しゴムで消す erase [rub out] (words) *with an eraser*. ▶彼の鉛筆には消しゴムがついている His pencil has an *eraser*.

けしさる 消し去る (消す) [書] erase (文字・記憶な

え) blot (-tt-) out; (取り除く) remove. ・いやな思い出を消し去る *blot out* unpleasant memories.

けしずみ 消し炭 cinders; used charcoal.

けしつぼ 消し壺 a charcoal extinguisher.

けしとぶ 消し飛ぶ ・竜巻で屋根が一瞬にして消し飛ばされた The whirlwind *blew* our roof *off* [*away*] in a flash. ▶ニュースを聞いて不安が消し飛んだ My anxiety *vanished* at the news.

けしとめる 消し止める put*… out, [書] extinguish.

***けじめ** ❶ [区別] (やや書) (a) distinction. ・公私のけじめをつける *draw a line between* public and private matters. ・その男は善 [と] 悪のけじめがつかない He can't *tell* [never *knows*] right *from* wrong. (❗次例より口語的)/He can't *distinguish* [*make a distinction*] *between* right and wrong.

❷ [収拾] (a) settlement; (終結) an end. ・その問題にけじめをつける settle the matter (*finally*); *put an end to* the matter. ・政治家としてけじめをつける (=責任をとる) take *responsibility* as a politician.

げしゃ 下車 ━━ 下車する 動 [バス・列車などから] get* off(…) (↔get on); [車から降りる] get out (of …) (↔get in [into]). (⇨降りる) ・次の駅で下車する *get off* (a train) at the next station. ・熱海で途中下車する *make a stopover* at Atami; (旅行を中断する) break one's journey at Atami.

げしゅく 下宿 名 (下宿屋) a boardinghouse (複-houses /-zɪz, (米) -sɪz/); (食事なしの) a lódging [(米) a róoming, (英) (婉曲的) a guést] hòuse; (通例多数日・週間単位で貸す); (下宿部屋) a room; lodgings, (英語) digs (❗以上の2語は通例家具付きの部屋で, 1 部屋でも複数扱い). ・下宿の主人 a landlord; (女主人は a landlady) ・下宿代はいくらですか How much do you pay for board and lodging [*room and board*]? (❗How much is …?, What are the charges for …? ともいえる)

━━ 下宿する 動 (食事付きで) board; (食事なしで) lodge, (米) room. ▶彼女はおじさんの所に下宿している She *is boarding* [*lodging*, (米) *rooming*] *at* her uncle's (house) [*with* her uncle].

・下宿人 (賄い付きの) a boarder; (食事付きでない) a lodger, (米) a roomer, (英) (婉曲的) a paying guest ともいう. ・下宿人を置く take in boarders [lodgers].

ゲシュタポ [<ドイツ語] [秘密国家警察] the Gestapo /gəstɑ́ːpou/. (❗複数扱い)

ゲシュタルト [<ドイツ語] [形態] (a) gestalt. ・ゲシュタルト心理学 Gestalt psychology.

げしゅにん 下手人 the murderer.

げじゅん 下旬 the end of the month. (⇨上旬)

げじょ 下女 a maidservant; a maid. (⇨下男)

***けしょう 化粧** 名 makeup. ・化粧直しをする touch up [fix] one's *makeup*; (改装する) redecorate (a store). ・化粧気のない顔 a face without *makeup*. ・化粧をする (⇨動) ・化粧を落とす take off [remove] one's *makeup*. ▶彼女は少し化粧をしている She is wearing light *makeup*./She has made up her face a little. ▶彼女は化粧映えのする顔立ちをしている She looks very attractive [beautiful] when she wears makeup./Makeup shows off her face very beautifully.

━━ 化粧する 動 make* (oneself) up; make up [powder, (古) paint] one's face (❗powder は「おしろいをつける」化粧の意. paint は軽蔑的に「はでな色を塗る」の意), put* on one's face, [話] do* one's face, [話] put one's face on; (身じたくをする), (やや古・書) make one's toilet.

・化粧鏡 a toilet [a bathroom] mirror. ・化粧室

けじらみ 毛虱〖昆虫〗a crab louse (圏 〜 lice).

けしん 化身〖権化(ﾞｺﾞﾝ)〗the incarnation 《*of*》;《具体化されたもの》《やや書》the embodiment 《*of*》. ●悪魔の化身 the incarnation [*embodiment*] of evil.

げじん 外陣 an outer sanctum (of a temple [a shrine, a church]); 《砲 内陣》

けす 消す ❶〖火・電灯などを〗put... out,《書》extinguish;《ラジオ・ガスなどスイッチを回して》turn ... off, switch ... off.《英》では put ... off も用いられるが今は《古》 ▶ろうそくを消す *put out* [*blow out*] a candle. ●たばこを消す *put out* a cigarette;《踏み消す》*stamp out* a cigarette; *stub out* a cigarette with one's foot. ▶寝る前にテレビを消しなさい *Turn off* the TV [*Turn* the TV *off*] before you go to bed.(❗)「それを消しなさい」は Turn it *off*. の語順が正しく、ˣ*Turn off* it. は誤り) ▶私は明かりを消して眠った I *switched off* [*turned off*, *put out*] the light and slept./I slept *with* the light *off*.

❷〖文字などを〗(こすり取る) rub (-bb-) ... out [*off*](❗ *out* は消えにくいしみなどをこすって取る.*off*は表面をこすって落とす), (軽ﾞ) erase; (ふき取る) wipe ... off,《書》(線を引いて消す) cross ... out [*off*] ([off ではリストなどから削る, out は誤りや人に知られたくない個所を削除する]; (削除する) delete. ▶その間違いを消せ *rub out* [*erase out*] the error. ●名簿から彼の名前を消す *cross* his name *off* the list; *delete* his name *from* the list. ▶彼はその単語を線で消した He *crossed* the word *out*. ▶黒板(のチョークの跡)を消しなさい *Wipe* the chalk marks *off* the blackboard./(まれ) *Wipe off* the chalk marks *from* the blackboard./《米》*Erase* the blackboard.
[会話]「あの落書き、消しなさいと言ったでしょ」「やったよ、でもどうしても消えないんだ」"Didn't I tell you to *rub out* that graffiti?" "I tried [ˣI did], but it won't *rub out*." (❗I did では消えていることになるので but 以下の内容と矛盾する)

❸〖音声などを〗(弱める) deaden; (弱音器で) damp; (吸収する) absorb; (騒音などが小さな音を消す) drown /dráun/ ... out. ▶音を消してテレビを見る watch (ˣthe) TV *with* the sound *off*. ▶彼らの会話は波の音に消された Their conversation *was drowned out* by the sound of the waves.

❹〖取り除く〗remove; (望ましくないものを) get* rid of .... ▶悪臭を消す *remove* [*get rid of*] a bad smell. ▶痛みを消す *remove* [*kill*] pain. ▶毒を消す(=中和する) *counteract*;《やや書》*neutralize* poison. ▶証拠を消す *destroy*《書》*erase*] evidence. ▶パスコースを消す〖サッカー〗*cut out* the pass. ▶彼は脳裏から記憶を消そうとした He tried to *blot out* [《書》*erase*] the memory from his mind. ▶その事件は彼の名声に消しがたい汚点を残した That incident left an *unremovable* [an *indelible*] stain on [ˣin] his reputation.

❺〖姿を消す〗disappear.(⇨消える❶)

❻〖殺す〗kill; murder,《米話》rub (-bb-) ... out.

げす 下種, 下衆 a low-grade person; (根性のいやしい人) a mean [〖根性の曲がった〗a prejudiced;《心の狭い》a petty(-minded)] fellow.

●げすの後知恵 a fool's hindsight;《ことわざ》Fools are wise after the event.
●げすのかんぐり a prejudiced [a petty-minded] view; a mean people's suspicion.

*げすい 下水《設備》sewerage /súːərɪdʒ/ (❗ 排水システムの全体をさす); drainage 〖排水そのものや方法をさす〗;《排水溝[管]》a drain, a drainpipe;《下水汚水》a sewer /súːər/;《汚水》sewage /súːɪdʒ/, waste water. ▶その地域にくまなく下水道を通す run *waste disposal pipelines* throughout the area. ▶下水が詰まっている The *drain* is clogged [is blocked]. ▶この町には近代的な下水設備がある This town has a modern *sewerage* system.
●下水処理場 a sewage disposal plant.

けすじ 毛筋《1本1本の毛》a hair;《髪をとかした後の筋目》the lines of one's combed hair.

●毛筋ほども ▶この薬品の安全性は毛筋ほども(=少しも)疑いがない There is *no* doubt *at all* about the safety of this medicine.

ゲスト a guest. ●ゲスト出演する appear (on the program) as a *guest*; make a *guest* appearance (*on* the show).

●ゲストハウス a guést hòuse.

けずね 毛臑, 毛脛 hairy legs.

けずりとる 削り取る《はぎ取る》shave ... (off);《こすり取る》scrape ... (off).

けずりぶし 削り節 dried bonito shavings [flakes].

*けずる 削る ❶〖薄くそぎとる〗《板などを》shave; (かんなで) plane; (鉛筆を) sharpen. ●板を数ミリ削る *shave* [*plane*] (a few millimeters *from*) the board. ▶この鉛筆は削るのが難しい. 芯(ｼﾝ)が折れてばかりいるんだ It is hard to *sharpen* this pencil. The point keeps breaking off.

❷〖削除する〗《書》delete, (線を引いて消す) cross ... out; (削減する) cut*; 〖数・量を減らす〗cut ... down, reduce (❗ 前の方が口語的). ●名簿から彼の名前を削る *delete* [ˣomit] his name *from* the list (❗ omit は初めから入れないでおくこと); *cross* his name *off* the list. ▶最後の2語を削る *cross out* the last two words. ▶経費を3割削る *cut down* (*on*) [*reduce*] one's expenses by 30 percent. (❗「10万円削る」ならば ... to 100,000 yen となる) ▶予算は3分の1削られた The budget *was cut* by a third.

げせない 解せない 《理解できない》incomprehensible.

ゲゼルシャフト 〖<ドイツ語〗〖利益社会〗a gesellschaft.

げせわ 下世話 a common saying. ▶下世話にも言うように背に腹は代えられない Necessity knows no law as the *common saying* goes.

げせん 下船 〖 〗(a) disembarkation.
——下船する 〖 〗get off a ship;《やや書》disembark (⇔embark). ▶神戸で下船する *disembark* at Kobe.

げせん 下賤 〖 〗low birth; humble origin.
——下賤の 〖 〗low; humble.

げそ 〖イカの足〗a squid's [a cuttlefish's] arm.

げそく 下足《集合的》footwear, footgear.

けた 桁 ❶〖数字の〗(アラビア数字の0-9 までのうちの一つ) a figure, a digit /dídʒɪt/;《数の位》a place. ●1 [2; 3]けたの数 single [double; three] *figures* [*digits*]. ●6けたの収入 a six-*figure* [a six-*digit*] income; an income of six *figures* [*digits*]. ●計算を1けた間違える miscalculate by one *digit*. ●小数点以下5けたまで計算する calculate (it) to five *places* of decimals [five decimal *places*].

げた / けつあつ

▶伸び率は2けた台にとどまっている The rate of increase remains in double *figures*. ▶小数点以下何けたまで知っていますか How many decimal *places* do you know?
❷〚建物などの〛(建物の主要横材) a beam; (橋・屋根などの) a girder.
●桁が違う ▶中国の領土の広さは日本とは桁が違う In terms of territory, there is no comparison between Japan and China. (⇨桁違い)

げた 下駄 *geta*; (説明的に) a pair of] Japanese (wooden) clogs (❗通例複数形で). ●げたをはいている[はく] wear [put on (↔take off)] *geta*. (❗「げたをはいて歩く」は walk in (one's) *geta*) ●げたばきで来る come in *geta*. ▶勝負はげたをはくまで分からないさ It ain't over till it's over. (❗ain't は《俗》で am not, is not, are not の縮約形)
●げたを預ける ▶最後の決断は彼にげたを預けた(=任せた)かっこうだ It looks as if we *have left* our final decision *to* him.
●げたをはかせる ▶得点にげたをはかせる《話》 *jack up* the marks [scores].
●げた箱 a shoe cupboard /kʌ́bərd/; (棚) shoe shelves. (事情 米英では closet (収納戸棚)を利用するが普通.

けだかい 気高い noble. ●気高い心[行為] a noble mind [〚書〛deed].

けたぐり 蹴手繰り 〚相撲〛*ketaguri*; pulling inside ankle sweep.

けだし 蓋し (おそらく) probably; in all probability; maybe; (結局) after all. ▶けだし(=確かに)名言である It's *definitely* a wise saying [*surely* a good remark]./That's *definitely* [*unquestionably*] well said.

けたたましい 〚やかましい〛noisy; (大きく聞こえる) loud; 〚鋭い〛sharp; (つんざくような) shrill, piercing. ●けたたましい(=つんざくような)叫び声をあげる give a *shrill* [a *piercing*] cry. ▶突然電話がけたたましく鳴り始めた Suddenly the telephone started to ring *noisily* [*loudly*].

けたちがい 桁違い ▶彼の財産はけた違いに(=比較にならないほど)大きい His fortune is *incomparably* large. ▶彼の作品と私のとではけた違いだ(比較にならない) There *is no comparison* between his work and mine./(はるかにすぐれている) His work is *much better than* mine.

げだつ 解脱 ⓝ deliverance of one's soul; salvation from the bondage of this world.
── 解脱する ⓥ be delivered from the bondage of this world; attain salvation.

けたてる 蹴立てる ●砂を蹴立てる *kick up* the sand. ●席を蹴立てて帰る storm out of a room and go home.

けたはずれ 桁外れ ▶彼はけた外れに大きな手をしている He has *extraordinarily* big hands. ▶それをけた外れの安値で買った I bought it at an *incredibly* low price./《話》I bought it *dirt-cheap*. (❗*dirt-cheap* は副詞)

けだま 毛玉 a pill. ●セーターの毛玉をつまみ取る pinch off *pills* on a sweater. ●毛玉ができる pill.

けだもの 〚動物〛〚書〛a beast,〚書〛a brute (⇨動物 [類語];〚残忍な人〛) a beast, a brute. (❗いずれもしばしばおどけて用いられる) ●けだものような男 a *beast* [a *brute*] of a man.

けだるい 気だるい 《やや書》languid; (ものうい)《やや書》languorous /lǽŋɡərəs/; (元気のない) listless.

げだん 下段 (寝台車の) the lower berth. ●刀を下段に構える hold one's sword *low*.

けち ⓝ 〚金などで〛(性質) stinginess; (人) a miser /máizər/; 《主に米話》a cheapskate; 〚心の狭さ〛narrow-mindedness. ▶けち! You *miser* [*cheapskate*]!
── **けちな** ⓐ ❶〚金などで〛(やや話) stingy /stíndʒi/ (↔generous); mean; (話) tight(-fisted); miserly;《米》close (*with*). (⇨けちけち〚文例〛)

> 使い分け **stingy** 最も一般的な語.
> **mean** 金を出ししぶること.
> **tight(-fisted)** 締まり屋で手に入った金を出したがらないこと.
> **miserly** 少し改まった語で, 金をためるのが好きで, 極端に出ししぶること.

▶彼は大変けちな男だ He's a very *stingy* [*tight-fisted*] man./He's very *stingy* [*mean*, *tight*, 〚婉曲的〛*extremely careful*] *with* his money. ▶彼女, ひどくけちなの. ぜったいお金を払わないわよ She's so *cheap*. She never pays for anything. (❗この *cheap* は《米話》で stingy とほぼ同意)
❷〚心の狭い〛narrow-minded, petty, mean. (❗この順で軽蔑の含みは強くなる) ▶あいつはけちなやつだ He is a *narrow-minded* [a *mean*] fellow.
●けちがつく ▶我々のプロジェクトに最初からけちがついた *Something bad* [*unlucky*] *happend to* our project at the (very) beginning.
●けちをつける ▶彼は私の仕事にいつもけちをつけてばかりいる He's always *criticizing* [*finding fault with*] my work. (❗*always* とともに進行形で用いると通例非難の意を表す)

けちけち ▶金にけちけちするな《米》Don't *be so close with* a dollar./(出ししぶるな) Don't *grudge* spending your money.

ケチャップ (tomato) ketchup;《米》catsup.

けちょんけちょん ── **けちょんけちょんに** 副 ▶政府の新政策はけちょんけちょんにやっつけられた The government's new policy was *really* slammed [(酷評される) picked apart].

けちらす 蹴散らす ❶〚足で蹴って散らす〛kick about [around]. ❷〚追い散らす〛▶警官は群集を蹴散らした The police *scattered* the crowd.

けちる (けちけちする) skimp (*on*); (出し惜しみする) be stingy (*with*). ●チップをけちる *skimp on* a tip.

けちんぼう けちん坊 (金や物を出し惜しむ人) a stingy person; (金を遣いたがらない人)《軽蔑的》a miser. (⇨けち)

けつ 欠 ❶〚欠けたところ, 欠乏〛●欠を補う make up for a *lack*. ❷〚欠席〛(⇨欠席)

けつ 尻 buttocks,《米俗》butt,《米話》the ass /ɑːs/,《英卑》the arse. (⇨尻(₁))
●けつの穴が小さい (臆病な) cowardly; (度量の狭い) narrow-minded.
●けつをまくる (けんか腰になる) turn defiant; take a defiant attitude.

けつ 決 ●決を採る ...の決を採る take a *vote on* ...; put ... to the *vote*.

けつあつ 血圧 blood pressure. ●最高[最低]血圧 maximum [minimum] *blood pressure*. ●血圧を測ってもらう have one's *blood pressure* taken [checked, measured]. ▶彼は血圧が高い His *blood pressure* is high (↔low)./He has [suffers from] high *blood pressure* 〚医学〛hypertension (↔hypotension). ▶血圧は上が130で下が90です My *blood pressure* is 130 over 90. (❗130/90 とも言う) ▶この薬を飲めば血圧が下がりますか Will this medicine lower [reduce] my *blood pressure*? ▶血圧が5上がった My *blood pressure* went up [rose] (↔fell, dropped) by 5.
●血圧計 a blood pressure gauge /ɡéidʒ/; 〚医学〛

a (sphygmo)manometer /(sfígmou)mənámitər/. ●血圧降下剤 a hypotensive.

けつい 決意 图 (a) decision; determination; (a) resolution. (⇨決心) ●決意を新たにする make a fresh *resolution* (*to* do).
── **決意する** 動 decide; determine; resolve. ●決意しているbe determined; be resolved. ●たばこをやめる決意をした I (*have*) *decided* [*determined, resolved*] *to* give up smoking.

けついん 欠員 〖空席の職〗a vacant post [position], an opening. ●欠員ができるのを待つ wait for a position to fall [become] *vacant*. ●欠員を補う fill a *vacancy* [*a vacant post*]. ●(その職を欠員にしておく leave the position *vacant*. ▶技師に1人欠員がある We have a *vacancy* [an *opening*] *for* an engineer.

けつえき 血液 blood. (⇨血) ●血液検査を受ける take a *blood* test; have one's *blood* tested. ●血液の循環をよくする improve the circulation of the *blood*; improve [promote] *blood* circulation. ●検査のために血液を取る draw some *blood* for a (*blood*) test.
〈会話〉「血液型は何ですか」「O型です」 "What's your *blood* type [*group*]?" "It's O." 〈事情〉 米英では日本と違って日常会話の話題にはならない)
●血液銀行 a blóod bànk. ●血液製剤 blood products. ●HIVに感染した血液製剤 an HIV-infected blood product. ●血液センター a blood (donor [donation]) center.

けつえん 血縁 〖関係〗a blood relation(ship); 〖人〗a blood relation [relative].

けっか 結果 (a) result; an outcome; a consequence; (an) effect; (a) fruit. (⇨成果)

> 使い分け **result** 最終的結果を表す一般的な語.
> **outcome** 選挙や政策などが注目されている成り行きの結末や, 方法論や研究の最終的な結果を表す.
> **consequence** 事の成り行きとして必然的に起こる結果を表す.
> **effect** ある原因が他に与える影響を表す.
> **fruit** 長期間の努力や政策, 研究の成果を表す.

① 〖~結果〗 ●原因と結果 cause and *effect* [×result]. (❗無冠詞) ●調査[研究]結果 the *findings* of the survey [*research*]. ●...という結果になる[終わる] result in .... ●...の結果として consequently ..., as a result of .... ●必然の結果(=経過)として by a natural *process* (*of*).
② 〖結果~〗 ●結果責任 (⇨結果責任) ▶それは結果論だ(=結果を得た後なら何でも言える) You can say anything after you get the *result*.
③ 〖結果は〖が〗〗 ▶選挙の結果はどうなるでしょうか What will be the election *results* [the *results* of the election, the *outcome* of the election]?/ How will the election *turn out*? ▶結果が出るのを待っているところです We're waiting for the results to come in. ▶ワールドカップは結果が一番大事. 勝ちたかった In the World Cup, the *result* is all that matters. We really wanted [hoped, ×wished] to win. (❗(1) all that matters は「大切なことすべて」の意. (2) wanted to ... は「...することを望んだができなかった」の意. (3) wish は後が不定詞のto win でなく wished that we had won となるのでここでは不適)
④ 〖結果を〗 ▶君の怠惰な生活はいつか悪い結果を招く(=もたらす)だろう Your idle life will bring you bad *results* [*consequences*] someday. ▶彼の決定は重大な結果を招いた His decision had [led to] serious *consequences*.
⑤ 〖...(の)結果~する〗 ▶怠けた結果彼は失敗した As a *result* [*a consequence*] of his laziness he failed. (❗*a* の代わりに the を用いることは不可)/His failure *resulted from* [*was caused by*] his laziness./His laziness *resulted in* failure./His laziness *caused* [*brought about*] his failure./(彼はなまけた. その結果失敗した) He was lazy, *so* (*that*) he failed. ▶検査の結果彼は健康であることが分かった The examination showed that he was in good health.
── **結果的に** 副 ▶彼の言ったことは結果的には正しかった(=最後には正しいと分かった) What he said *turned out* (*to* be) right *in the end*. ▶結果的に(=後に判明したのだが)ミスだった As it turned out [×As a result], it was a mistake. (❗as a result は不適)

げっか 月下 ▶月下に琴を弾く play the *koto in the moonlight* [*under the moon*].
●月下美人 〖植物〗a Queen of the Night. ●月下氷人 (仲人) a go-between; a matchmaker.

けっかい 決壊 ── **決壊する** 動 (ダム・堤防などが) burst. ▶その大雨で川の右岸が決壊した The river *burst* its right bank because of the heavy rain./The rain was so heavy that the right bank of the river *burst* [*broke*].

けっかく 欠格 ●欠格者 (不適格者) an unqualified person.

けっかく 結核 〖医学〗tuberculosis /t(j)u(:)bə:rkjəlóusəs/ 《略 TB》, 〖古〗consumption. ●結核性の 〖にかかった〗 tuberculous, tubercular. ●彼は結核にかかっている He has [is suffering from] *tuberculosis*.
●結核患者 a tuberculous [a TB] patient. ●結核菌 a túbercle bacíllus 《⓿ -li /-lai/》. ●結核療養所 a sanatorium, 《米》a sanitarium.

げっがく 月額 ▶彼の収入は月額20万円以上ある His *monthly* income [His *salary*] is over 200,000 yen. (❗salary は通例「ひと月」の給料をいう (⇨月給))/He has [gets] an income of over 200,000 yen *a month*.

けっかせきにん 結果責任 legal responsibility [liability] for consequences. ●結果責任を負う take the legal responsibility for the consequence 《*of*》. ●結果責任が問われる The liability is asked for [is required for] the consequence ....

けっかん 欠陥 〖欠点〗(重大な) a defect; (軽微な) a fault; (不備) a flaw. ●致命的な欠陥 a fatal *defect*. ●(建造物の)構造上の欠陥 a defect in construction. ●その制度のいくつかの欠陥を是正する correct some *defects* [*flaws, faults*] in the system. (❗in の代わりに ×of は不可) ●彼には肉体的な欠陥もある He has physical *defects*.
●欠陥品 a defective [a faulty] product; 《話》a lemon (❗特に欠陥車 (a defective car) をさす).

けっかん 血管 a blood vessel. ●(興奮したりして)血管を破裂させる burst a *blood vessel*. ●血管(=静脈)の浮き出た手 a veined hand.
●血管圧迫止血 〖医学〗angiopressure /ǽndʒiou-/. ●血管拡張剤 〖薬学〗a vasodilator.

けつがん 頁岩 〖地学〗shale.

げっかん 月刊 ── **月刊の** 形 monthly. ▶この雑誌は月刊です This magazine is issued [appears] *monthly*./This is a *monthly* magazine.
●月刊誌 a monthly (magazine).

げっかん 月間 (月ごとの) monthly. ●月間報告(書) a monthly report. ●月間予定 a monthly schedule.

けっき 血気 (活力) 《やや書》vigor. ●血気さかんな vigorous.
●血気にはやる (性急な) hot-blooded.

けっき 決起 ── **決起する** 動 ●圧制[圧制者]に抗して決起する(=立ち上がる) *rise against* oppression [the oppressor].
●決起大会[集会] (hold [stage]) a rally. (❗特に大規模な政治集会をさす)

けつぎ 決議 图 〖議会などで投票による〗a resolution (❗決議案[文]の意もある); 〖決定〗a decision.
●その案に反対[賛成]の決議を採択する[通す] adopt [pass] a *resolution* against [for, in favor of] the plan.
── **決議する** 動 resolve 《*on* [*upon*]+图; *doing*; *to do*; *that* 節》. ▶委員会はその法案を廃案にすることを決議した The committee *resolved to* abolish the bill [*that* the bill (《主に英》should) be abolished].

けっきゅう 血球 〖生理〗a blood cell [corpuscle /kɔ́ːrpəsl/]. ●赤[白]血球 a red [a white] corpuscle.

けっきゅう 結球 (キャベツ・白菜などの) a head.

*けっきゅう 月給** monthly pay; a (monthly) salary (❗ monthly はつけないのが普通). (⇨給料) ●安月給 a small [a low, a (very) modest] *salary*. ▶彼の月給は25万円だ His *monthly pay* [His *salary*] is 250,000 yen./He gets a *salary* of 250,000 yen./He gets 250,000 yen a month.
●月給泥棒 a worker who isn't well-deserved for his [her] salary. ●月給取り (サラリーマン)

けっきょ 穴居 ── **穴居する** 動 live [《書》dwell] in a cave. ●穴居生活 cave dwelling. ●穴居人 a caveman, a cave dweller.

*けっきょく 結局** after all; (最後には) in the end (❗通例文頭・文尾に置く); eventually, (長い目で見れば) in the long run (❗以上のうち通例 after all のみが否定文でも使える); 〖(一連の事柄の)最後に〗finally, 《やや書》in conclusion; 〖要するに〗in short (❗文頭・文中で); 〖いろいろ考えると〗all in all (❗通例文頭で).

> [解説] after all は通例文尾, 時に文頭で, 「これまでいろいろとやってきた[言ってきた, 起こった]が, それにもかかわらず」の意で, 結果が期待・意図に反することを述べる表現.

▶何度もやってみたが結局だめだった I tried many times, but failed *after all* [but failed *in the end*, only to fail, ×but failed *at last*]. (❗下不定詞の後には予期しない不運な内容がくる. (2) at last は長く待った[努力した]後に望ましい何かがくるという肯定的意味で用いる成句で, この場合は不可 (や×結局) の意は turn out に含まれるので after all は省略可) ▶彼女は結局パーティーに来なかった She didn't come to the party *after all* [×at last]. (❗after all は話し手の待ちかねた気持ちを表す) ▶よいものを買う方が結局安くつく It is cheaper *in the long run* to buy good things./*All in all*, it is cheaper to buy good things. ▶結局私たちは映画を見に行くことにした *Finally*, we have decided to go to the movies. ▶結局君は私の提案に反対なのですね *In short* you're against my proposal, aren't you?
▶まあ, 話せば長くなるが, 結局のところ会社をやめて自分の会社を始めることにしたというわけです Well, it's a long story. But *what it boils down to is that* [*as it turned out*,] I decided to quit the company and start my own. (❗いずれも慣用表現. 後の方は主文の後に置くこともできる. 前の方は But I decided ... own. That's what it boils down to. のようにもいえる)

[翻訳のこころ] 小十郎は半分辞退するけれども, 結局台所のとこへ引っぱられてってまたていねいなあいさつをしている(宮沢賢治『なめとこ山の熊』) Kojuro tries to decline the offer, but in the end he's always taken to the kitchen and there exchanges polite greetings all over again. (❗(1)「半分...する」は try to ... しようとする, 試みる)で表す. (2) decline は「(何らかの申し出を)断る, 辞退する」の意. (3)「結局」は in the end (最終的には)と表す. (4) この文の前後の状況から, 小十郎が訪れるたびにこのような場面が繰り返されているので always を加える)

けっきん 欠勤 图 absence 《*from* work [duty], *from* the [one's] office》. (❗回数や期間を問題にする場合は ⓒ) (⇨欠席) ●無届欠勤 (an) *absence* without notice. ●長期欠勤 a long(-term) *absence*. ▶欠勤が多すぎるのであなたにはやめていただきます I'm firing you because you have missed too much work. (❗fire は「首にする」の意)
── **欠勤する** 動 be absent 《*from*》. (⇨休む ❸) ▶彼は病気のために5日間欠勤した He *was absent* [*stayed away*] *from* work for five days because he was sick. (❗後の方が口語的)/His sickness resulted in a five-day *absence from work*.
●欠勤者 a person who is absent; an àbsentée.
●欠勤届 a report [a notice] of absence. ●欠勤届を出す hand in a *report* [a *notice*] of *absence*; report one's absence 《*to*》.

けづくろい 毛繕い 图 grooming. ── **毛繕いする** 動 groom oneself.

げっけい 月経 〖医学〗menstruation. (⇨生理 ❷)

げっけいかん 月桂冠 laurels; a laurel wreath.

げっけいじゅ 月桂樹 〖植物〗a laurel.

けつご 結語 a conclusion.

*けっこう 結構** ── **結構な** 形 ❶〖好ましい〗good; (すてきな) nice; (とてもすてきな) wonderful; (すばらしい) fine; (並はずれて質の高い) excellent; (とてもおいしい) delicious. (⇨いい ❶) ▶結構なお味です It's *very good*./It's *delicious*. (❗×very delicious とは通例いわない) ▶結構な品物をありがとうございました Thank you very much for the *nice* [*wonderful*] present. ▶お話はまことに結構ですが, 新しい機械を買うには結構お金がかかりますね That's all very *well*, but new machines cost us quite a lot to buy.
[会話]「近ごろどうだい」「うまくいってるよ」「それは結構なことだね」"How are things going?" "Great." "*Good*. *I'm glad to hear it*."
[会話]「先日のお茶会はいかがでしたか」「結構うまくでした」"How was the tea ceremony the other day?" "Everything was absolutely perfect."
❷〖十分〗(間に合う) will do. (⇨いい ❺) ▶運転免許証かパスポートをお持ちでしたらそれでも結構です If you have a driver's license or a passport, that will *be sufficient* [*fine*] as well 〖(どちらでもよろしい) either *will do*〗. ▶ほんの少しで結構ですから時間をいただけませんか Would you please spare me a *little bit* of your time?
[会話]「いくらお入り用ですか」「5,000円で結構です」"How much do you want?" "Five thousand yen *will do* 〖(《やや書》) *answers the purpose*〗." (❗数字は文頭では通例つづり字で表す)
[会話]「おかわりはいかがですか」「いやもう結構です. おなかがいっぱいです」"Would you like another helping?" "*Nó*, ／ *thank you* ＼／ *thanks*. I'm full [I've had enough]." (❗断るときにはこのように理由をそえるのが丁寧)

❸〖許可〗(...してもよい) can*, may* (⇨いい ⓮); (不必要) do* not have to do. (⇨いい ⓫) ▶ドアは開けた

けっこう

ままで結構です You *can* [*may*] leave the door open. (❗ may は目上の人が目下の人に許可を与える場合にのみ用い, 尊大に聞こえるので通例避けられる)/(閉める必要はありません) You *don't have to* [*don't need to*] close the door.

❹ [同意, 満足] ▶現在の仕事で結構です(=満足している) I *am satisfied* [*happy*] *with* my present job.

会話 「9時15分の(飛行機の)便がございます. よろしいでしょうか」「ええ, それでも結構ですが, 10時15分の便があればなお結構なのですが」 "There's a flight at 9:15. Is that all right?" "Well, *it'll be fine* (*with* [*for*] me) [that sounds *good* (*all right*] (*with* [*for*] me)]. If you have one at 10:15, that would *suit* me better." (❗ with [for] me の代わりに by me とするのは《英》)

❺ [拒絶] 会話 「これいりませんか」「結構です」 "Do you want this?" "*I don't think so* [*I think not*]." (❗ 前の方が普通. 積極的に Oh, that *isn't necessary*. という表現もよく用いられる)

── 結構 副 [[かなり]] *rather*, 《話》*pretty* (❗ ともに very より弱いが, quite, fairly より強意的. rather は形容詞・副詞・名詞・動詞を, pretty は形容詞を修飾する);(まあまあ) *fairly* (❗ quite より意味が弱く, 好ましい意味の形容詞・副詞を修飾することが多い);(なかなか)《主に英》*quite* (❗ quite に強勢を置き, 通例形容詞・動詞などを修飾. ❗ かなり [類語]) ▶このワインは結構いける This wine is *rather* [*fairly, pretty, quite*] *good*./(予想よりいい) This wine is better *than* (I) *expected*.

けっこう 欠航 名 the cancellation of a flight [a sailing].

── 欠航する 動 ▶欠航にする *cancel* a flight [a ship]. ▶暴風雨のためその便は欠航になった The flight *was canceled* because of the storm. ▶今夜の佐渡丸は欠航します The Sadomaru for tonight will *not sail*.

けっこう 血行 circulation (of the blood). ●血行が悪い have (a) *poor* (↔ a *good*) *circulation*. ●血行をよくする stimulate *circulation*.

けつごう 決行 ── 決行する 動 (計画などを) carry ... out. ●ストを決行するgo on strike. ▶雨天でも試合は決行する(=予定通り行われる) The game will *be held as scheduled* [*planned*] even if it rains. ▶スト決行中 The strike is on./《掲示》On Strike.

けつごう 結合 名 (a) combination; (a) union.

── 結合する 動 join; combine; unite. (❗ この順に結合の度合いが強くなり, unite は一体化を強調する) ●破片を結合する *join* [*put*] the pieces *together*. ●二つの物を一つに結合する *combine* [*unite*] two things *into* one. ●水素と酸素が結合して水になる Hydrogen and oxygen *unite* to form water.

けつごう 月光 moonlight. ▶月光を浴びて泳ぐ swim *in the moonlight* [*by moonlight*].

＊けっこん 結婚 名 (a) marriage; (式) a wedding.

事情 米英では1年中で最も日が長く, 天気が安定していて美しい6月に結婚する人が多い. 6月 (June) はローマ神話の結婚の女神ジューノー (Juno) にちなんでつけられた月でもあることから, この月結婚した女性は「6月の花嫁 (June bride)」と呼ばれ, 縁起がよく幸福になるといわれる.

① [~結婚] ▶近親結婚 《make》a consanguineous /kὰnsæŋɡwíniəs/ *marriage*;《俗に》intermarriage. ▶国際結婚 an international *marriage*. ▶神前結婚 a *wedding* (ceremony) according to Shinto rites. 事情 米英では church wedding といって教会で行うことが多い ▶政略結婚

(政治的な) a political *marriage*; (打算的な) a *marriage* of convenience. ▶見合い[恋愛]結婚 an arranged [a love] *marriage*. (❗「見合い[恋愛]結婚をする」は get married through arrangement [for love]. (⇨動)) ●できちゃった (結)婚 a shotgun *marriage*. ▶私たちは学生結婚です We got married when we were (college) students.

② [結婚(の)~] ▶結婚適齢期の女性 a *marriageable* woman; a woman of *marriageable* age. ●結婚問題 a *marriage* problem. ▶私は今では定職に就き, 幸せな結婚生活を送っている I have a steady job now, and *are* happily *married*. (⇨動 [第3文例 注]) ▶私と国との関係は結婚のようなものだ My relationship with my country is akin to [like] that in *marriage*. (❗ be akin to は堅い表現)

③ [結婚を[が]] ▶彼は彼女に結婚を申し込んだが断わられた He *proposed to* her [asked her to *marry* him], but she rejected (↔ accepted) him. (❗ (1) 後の方が普通. (2) propose の主語は通例男性) ▶彼は結婚が遅かった[早かった](=遅く[早く; 若くして] 結婚した) He *married* [*got married*] late in life [early in life; young]. (⇨動) ▶恋する若者は結婚を急ぐが, そのような結婚の多くはやがて失敗に終わる Young people in love rush into *marriage*, but many such *marriages* break up soon [(その結婚生活の多くは) their *married* life often ends in failure shortly afterward]. ▶結婚おめでとう Congratulations! 事情 このあいさつは通例新郎に対してのみ用い, 新婦に対しては I wish you every happiness [the best of luck]./My best wishes to you. などというべきであるとされてきたが, 最近では新婦に対しても用いるようになってきた.

④ [結婚に~] ▶父は私たちの[彼女との]結婚に強く反対している My father is strongly against our *marriage* [my *marriage to* her].

── 結婚する 動 marry; get* married《to》.

解説 **marry** は結婚する相手に重点を置くが, **get married** は結婚すること自体に重点を置くより口語的な言い方. 特に自動詞用法の **marry** は通例時・場所・様態などを表す副詞相当語句を伴う.

▶太郎と花子は来春結婚する予定です Taro and Hanako are going to *get married* next spring. ▶彼女はフランス人と結婚した She *married* [*got married to*] a Frenchman. (❗ ×married [got married] *with* a Frenchman は不可) ▶あなた方は結婚して何年になるのですか(=どのくらい長く結婚しているのですか) How long have you *been* [×got(ten)] *married*? (❗ (1) 「結婚している」状態をいうときは be married の形を用いる. (2) How long is it since you got married? は Are you *married*? (結婚しているの)と同様親しい人間の間以外は避ける) ▶彼は生涯結婚しなかった He remained *unmarried* [*single*] throughout his life. ▶彼は娘を自分の部下と結婚させた He *married* his daughter *to* [×with] one of his men. ▶4人の娘を結婚させる(=嫁がせる)のに大変な金がかかった It cost me dearly to *marry off* my four daughters. ▶彼女は結婚するタイプではない She's not the *marrying type*.

● 結婚観 one's view of marriage; an outlook on marriage. ● 結婚記念日 a wedding anniversary. ● 結婚式 (⇨結婚式) ● 結婚行進曲 a wedding march. ● 結婚相談所 a marriage bureau. ● 結婚話 (⇨結婚話) ● 結婚指輪 a márriage [a wédding] ring.

けっこん 血痕 a bloodstain. ▶血痕のついたシャツ a *bloodstained* shirt; a shirt *stained with blood*.

けっこんしき 結婚式 a wedding (ceremony). (❗(1) この意味で marriage を用いるのはまれ. (2) ceremony をつけず単に wedding というときは通例式の後の披露宴を含む.「結婚披露宴」のみは *a wedding* reception [*x*party] または単に a reception という. (3) *a wedding party* は「結婚当事者」) ● ホテルで結婚式を挙げる hold a *wedding* (ceremony) at a hotel. ▶ 彼らは教会で結婚式を挙げた They *were married* [They *got married*, 《ややまれ》They *married*] in a church. (❗この were married は「牧師の主宰による」の意を含む)

けっこんばなし 結婚話 ❶ [結婚相手の提案] a suggestion for a possible marriage partner. ● 親戚が娘への結婚話を持ってきた A relative of mine visited my house with a recommendation of a marriage partner for my daughter. ❷ [結婚の話題] a subject of marriage. ● 昨夜, 息子が私たちに結婚話を切り出した Last night, my son broached the subject of marriage to us.

けっさい 決済 图 《やや書》(a) settlement. ● 現物決済 cash *settlement*. ● 翌日決済 overnight [one-day] *settlement*.
── **決済する** 動 勘定を決済する *settle* an account.
● 決済日 a séttlement dàte [dày].

けっさい 決裁（決定）(a) decision;（承認）approval;《書》sanction. ● 決裁を仰ぐ submit 《it》 for 《his》 *approval*.
── **決裁する** 動 give 《it》 one's approval.

けっさい 潔斎 图 purification. ── **潔斎する** 動 purify oneself.

けっさく 傑作 图 a masterpiece.
── **傑作な** 動 （こっけいな）funny;（ばかげた）absurd;（思いもよらない）incredible. ● この絵は彼の傑作だ This picture is his *masterpiece* [is *one of* his *best works*]. ▶ 彼は傑作な(=こっけいな)男だ He is a *funny* guy.

けっさん 決算 图 settlement (of accounts); closing (the books). ● 決算報告をする make a report on the *closing*;（財務結果を報告する）report the *financial results*. ● 中間決算 interim earnings.
── **決算する** 動 ● 毎年年度末に決算する *settle accounts* [*close the books*] at the end of each fiscal year. ● 粉飾決算する carry out window dressing (*settlement*); window-dress.
● 決算期 a fiscal term. ● 決算日 a clósing [a séttlement] dày [dàte].

げっさん 月産 monthly output [production].

けっし 決死 ● 決死の(=物狂いの)攻撃をする make a *desperate* attack. ● 決死の覚悟で城を守る defend a castle *desperately* [死をものともしないで] *in the face of death*,（命がけで）*at the risk of one's life*].

げつじ 月次（毎月の）monthly.
● 月次報告書 a monthly report.

けっしきそ 血色素 图⇒ ヘモグロビン

けつじつ 結実 图 fruition /fruíʃən/. (❗比喩的に「達成」の意でも用いる)
── **結実する** 動 bear fruit (❗《やや書》では比喩的にも用いる);（現実のものとなる）come [be brought] to fruition.

‡**けっして 決して【決して…ない】** never; not (...) at all /ə túːl/; by no means; a long way from ...,《やや書》far from ...; on no account.

|使い分け| never 最も一般的な語であるが,「いつ何時も...ない(not at any time)」という時間の観念が含まれているので, 必ずしも not の強調語ではない.
not (...) at all, by no means not の否定の意を

さらに強めた言い方. 程度について用い, 時間の観念は含まない.
a long way from, far from「...にはほど遠い」の意で, 名詞, 動名詞, 形容詞を伴って用いる.
on no account「どのような理由があっても...しない」の意.

▶ 彼は決してそんなことはしないだろう He'll *never* do it./He won't do it *on any account*. ▶ あなたは難しいと思っているかもしれないがこの問題は決して難しくはない This problem is *not at all* [*by no means, far from, in no way*] difficult, though you may think so [it is]./This problem is *not* difficult *at all* [*by any means*], though you may think so. (❗この場合 never, on no account を用いることは不可である. なお, by no means は文中に置くが not ... by any means とした場合は文尾)/This problem is *a long way from* [*far from*] (being) difficult, though you may think so. ▶ 彼女は決してうそをつくような人ではない She *never* tells [*never* does tell] a lie. (❗後の方が強意的)/《ややまれ》She is *the last person to* tell [*who* tells] a lie. ▶ 決して暴力をふるってはいけない *Never* [*Don't on any account*] use violence.

|会話|「私がその時計を盗んだと思っているんだろう」「決してそんな(=断じてそんなことはない)」"You think I stole the watch." "*Ábsolutely ˋnot*."

|会話|「こんなレストランに入らなければよかったね」「本当だ. 料理はまずいし値段も高い」「もう決してここには来ないことにしよう」"We shouldn't have come in this restaurant." "You're not kidding. Lousy food and massive prices." "It's *the last time* we'll eat here."

けっしゃ 結社（団体）an association;（組織）an organization;（協会）a society. ● 結社の自由 freedom of *association*. ● 国粋主義者の秘密結社 a secret nationalist *organization* [*society*].

げっしゃ 月謝 a monthly fee [tuition]. ▶ あの学校の月謝は高い The *monthly fee* is high at that school./They charge a high *monthly tuition* at that school. (❗They は漠然と「(学校)当局の人々」をさす)

けっしゅう 結集 ── **結集する** 動（集中させる）concentrate /kɑ́nsəntrèit/;（集める）gather (together), join. ● 我々の総力を結集する *concentrate* all our efforts 《on》.

げっしゅう 月収 a monthly income. (⇒年収)

けっしゅつ 傑出 ── **傑出した** 形（他に抜きん出た）outstanding, distinguished;（優秀な）excellent.
── **傑出する** 動（抜きん出る）stand out 《from, among》;（秀でる）《書》excel 《in, at》. ▶ 彼は画家として傑出している He is *outstanding* [*distinguished*] as a painter./He is an *outstanding* [a *distinguished*] painter.

けつじょ 欠如 图 (a) lack. ● プライバシーの欠如 (a) *lack* of privacy.
── **欠如する** 動 ▶ 彼は創造性が欠如している He *lacks* [*is lacking in*] creativity (❗前の方は皆無を強調).

*****けっしょう 決勝**（決勝戦）the final(s);（引き分け・同点試合の後の）a play-off, a runoff.《決戦》● 決勝戦出場選手 a finalist. ● 決勝まで勝ち進む go on to [《話》make it to,（出場資格を得る）gain] *the finals*. ● 決勝に勝つ(で負ける)] win [lose] *the finals*. ● 決勝に残って競技する [競走する] play [run] *in the finals*. ● ワールドシリーズの決勝戦 the final (and deciding) game of the World Series. ▶ 彼女はテニスの決勝戦に進出した She got

けっしょう

to the tennis *final*(s). ▶ワールドカップの決勝戦でイタリアがフランスを破った Italy beat France in the World Cup *Final*.
- 決勝点《ゴール地点》 the finish (line). ▶決勝点を入れる〖球技〗make the *winning* shot; 〖野球〗score the (game-)*winning* [(game-)*deciding*] run; 〖サッカーなど〗score the *winning* goal.

*けっしょう 結晶 图 （結晶体）a crystal; （結晶作用）crystallization; 〖成果〗fruit. (❗時に複数形で).
- 雪の結晶 a *crystal* of snow; a snow *crystal*.
- 努力［愛］の結晶 the *fruit*(s) of (one's) hard work [the union].
── 結晶する 動 crystallize 《into》.

けっしょう 血漿 〖生理〗(blood) plasma.

けつじょう 欠場 ── 欠場する 動 （出ない）miss a game; do not appear 《in a game》; （プレイしない）do not play 《in a game》. ▶シーズンのうち2か月を欠場する miss two months of the season. ▶10試合に欠場する sit out ten games.

けっしょう 楔状 图 a shape of a wedge.
── 楔状の 形 wedge-shaped.
▶楔状文字 a cuneiform character.

けっしょうばん 血小板 〖生理〗a platelet /pléitlət/.

けっしょく 欠食 動 skip a meal.
- 欠食児童 an undernourished schoolchild.

けっしょく 血色 a complexion (❗顔の色つや, 皮膚のいろいろの状態をさす); （よい顔色, 顔の赤み）(a) color.
- 血色がよい have a good *complexion* [*color*]. (❗血色のよいピンク色の肌の人をさして He [She] has a lot of *color* [a high *color*]. という). ▶血色が悪い have a bad [a poor] *complexion*; have very little [a bad] *color*. ▶血色のよい（＝赤ら顔の）中年の男 a *ruddy*-faced man of middle age; a middle-aged man with a *ruddy* face. ▶彼は血色がよくなった His *color* [*complexion*] has improved./(顔に赤みが戻った) He got his *color* back.

げっしょく 月食 〖天文〗a lunar eclipse; an eclipse of the moon. ▶皆既[部分]月食 a total [a partial] *eclipse of the moon*.

げっしるい 齧歯類 rodents.

‡けっしん 決心 图 (a) decision; 〖決意〗determination; （固い）a resolution.
① 【決心は】● 初志を貫こうとする彼の決心は固い His *determination* [*resolution*] to carry out his original intention is very firm. (❗頭っかちな文なので特別な場合を除き次の例が普通)/He has a firm *determination* to carry out his original intention. ▶彼の決心はぐらついた He wavered in his *determination*. ▶もう決心はついている I *have made up* my *mind*./My mind is made up. (⇨動) ▶彼女の決心は変わらなかった She wouldn't change her mind./Nothing could affect her decision.
② 【決心を】● 決心を固くする[変える] strengthen [change] one's *determination*. ▶彼女のひとことが彼の決心をぐらつかせた Her word weakened [shook] his *determination*.
── 決心する 動 〖心を決める〗decide 《to do; that 節》; make* one's mind 《to do; that 節》; 〖決意する〗〖書〗determine 《to do; that 節》; 《やや書》resolve 《to do; that 節》.

《使い分け》 decide 物事をしようと決心することを表す. 決断が困難な状況や決断の必要性, 決心する人などの過程が問題になることが多い.
make up one's mind decide より口語的で, 決心すること自体に焦点がある.
determine 時間をかけて決意し, それを固く守ろうとすることを表す.
resolve やり遂げようとする意志の固さを表す.

▶私たちはまだ決心していない We *haven't decided* [*made up* our *minds*] yet. ▶彼は子供に立派な教育を受けさせようと決心した He *decided* [*made up his mind, determined, resolved*] to give his children a good education. (❗いずれも節を用いて He *decided* [*made up his mind* …] *that* he would give …. のようにいえるが, to 不定詞が将来の行為に重点があるのに対して, that 節では心理的状態に重点があり, 以前からの決心を暗示する) ▶彼女は二度と彼に会うまいと決心した She *decided* [*made up* her *mind, determined, resolved*] never to see [*that* she would never see] him again. (❗never, not などの否定語は to 不定詞の直前に置く) ▶彼女はピアニストになろうと決心している She *is determined* [《やや書》*is resolved*, ×*is decided*] *to* become a pianist. ▶大学へ行くかどうかまだ決心していない I *haven't decided* [《書》*determined*] *whether* or not I should go [*whether* or not to go] to college. ▶彼の言葉が私に留学を決心させた (＝彼の言葉で私に留学する決心がついた) What he said *has decided* [*determined, resolved*] me to study abroad. (❗(1) この用法では人は主語にこない. (2)《主に米話》では What he said *has convinced* me to study abroad. の方が普通)

けっしん 結審 the conclusion of a trial.
── 結審する 動 ▶その刑事裁判は結審した The criminal trial *was concluded*.

けっする 決する decide. ▶運命を決する *decide* one's fate. ▶雌雄を決する （最後の対決をする）have a showdown 《*with*》.

*けっせい 結成 图 organization; formation. ▶クラブの結成 the *organization* of a club.
── 結成する 動 〖労働組合を結成する〗organize [form, set up] a labor union.

けっせい 血清 〖医学〗(a) serum /síərəm/.
- 血清肝炎 serum hepatitis. ▶血清注射 a serum injection. ▶血清療法 serum therapy.

けつぜい 血税 （納税者の金）taxpayers' money. ▶血税のむだ使い a waste of *taxpayers' money*.

げっせかい 月世界 the lunar world; （月）the moon.

*けっせき 欠席 图 (an) absence. ▶個々の欠席をいうときは ⓒ. ▶電話で欠席を届ける call in sick. ▶無断欠席 (an) *absence* without permission [notice]; （ずる休み）(a case of) truancy. ▶たび重なる授業の欠席 one's frequent *absences from* school. ▶今日の欠席者はだれですか（教室で）Who is *absent* [*missing*] today?/Who is not here today? (❗Is anybody *absent* today? ともいう) ▶会議の欠席者は 3 名だった There were three *absentees* [*people absent*] from the meeting.
── 欠席する 動 《やや書》be ábsent, stay away 《*from*》(❗後の方が口語的. 他に日常会話では do* not go [come], be not here [there] を用いることが多い); 〖書〗absént oneself 《*from*》(❗しばしば意図的に休むことを含意); （授業などを）miss; （ずる休みをする）play truant [《米話》hooky], 〖話〗cut* 《school, a lecture》. (⇨休む, ずる休み) ▶きのうは病気で学校を欠席しました I *was absent* [*stayed away*] *from* school yesterday because I was sick. (❗後の方が堅い言い方) ▶最近就職活動に忙しくてたびたび授業を欠席している Recently I've been so busy hunting for a job and *have missed* a lot of classes. ▶今朝は頭が痛いので先生の授業を欠席させていただきたいのですが As I've got a headache this morning, I'd like to *be excused from* your

class. ▶あすの会合を欠席します(＝出席しません) I won't *attend* the meeting tomorrow./I won't *be* at the meeting tomorrow. (!後の方は口語的)
● **欠席裁判**〖法律〗a trial in absentia. ▶被告人は欠席裁判に付された The accused was *tried in absentia* [*in* 〈his〉 *absence*]. ● **欠席届** (send in) a notice of absence. (!病気の場合 a sick note, a doctor's report などをよく用いる)

けっせき 結石〖医学〗a stone; a calculus /kǽlkjələs/ (㉺ -li /-lai/). ● **腎臓結石** a kidney *stone*; a renal *calculus*. ● **膀胱結石** a *stone* in the bladder; a vesical *calculus*.

けっせん 血栓〖医学〗(a) thrombus. ● **脳血栓症** cerebral thrombosis.

けっせん 血戦 a bloody battle.

けっせん 決戦 图 (戦争の) a decisive battle [action]; (競技の決勝戦) the final, a deciding match [game, race]; (同点終了後の決定戦) a runoff, a play-off. (⇨決勝)
── **決戦(を)する** 動 fight a *decisive battle* 《*with*》.

けつぜん 決然 ── **決然とした** 形〖断固とした〗determined,〖書〗resolute.
── **決然と** 副 determinedly, resolutely.

けっせんしょう 血栓症〖医学〗(a) thrombosis /θrɑmbóusəs/. ● **冠状動脈血栓症** a coronary 《*thrombosis*》.

けっせんとうひょう 決選投票 (最終投票)《take》a final ballot. (!特に同点者間で決定投票を行うことを hold a *runoff* election という)

けっそう 血相 ●**血相を変える** change color. (!恐怖やショックで蒼白になったり(turn pale) 怒りで赤くなったり(turn red [scarlet]) するなどのイメージ) ▶彼は怒りでみるみる血相が変わった He got furious and the expression on his face changed terribly./He changed *color* in a rage.

けっそく 結束 图 〖結合, 合体〗union; 〖統一性〗unity. ●**国民の結束** national *unity*. ●**結束を固める** strengthen one's *union*. ●**結束の固い** close-knit; closely united [linked]. ▶彼らの結束は固い They are very [closely] *united*.
── **結束する** 動 unite 《*to* do》; stand together. ●**結束してその計画に反対する** *unite to* oppose the project; *unite against* the project.

けつぞく 血族 (⇨肉親)
●**血族関係** blood relationship. ●**血族結婚** (近親結婚) marriage between near relations.

げっそり ●**げっそりしたほお** hollow cheeks. ●**げっそりする**(＝失望する) be disappointed 《*at*》. ▶彼は病気の後げっそりやせこけていた He was *very thin and weak* after his illness./He looked *emaciated* after his illness.

けっそん 欠損 (不足) 《やや書》a déficit; (損失) a loss. ●**欠損が出る** show a *deficit*. ●**欠損を埋める** make up [make good] a *deficit*.

けったく 結託 图 (ぐる)〖書〗collusion. ●**結託して** in *collusion* 《*with*》.
── **結託する** 動 collude 《*with*》.

けったん 血痰 bloody phlegm.

*けつだん 決断 图 〖決定〗(a) decision; 〖最終的な決断〗determination; 〖固い決意〗(a) resolution. (!この順に意味が強くなる) ●**決断を下す** (⇨動) ●**決断力のある男** a man of *decision* [*determination, resolution*]; a decisive man. ●**決断力が乏しい** lack *decision*; (優柔不断である) be indecisive [〖話〗 wishy-washy]. ▶それは難しい決断だった It was a difficult *decision* to make. ▶彼は決断が早い [遅い] He is quick [slow] to make *decisions*.
── **決断する** 動 decide, make a decision; determine; resolve. (⇨決心する) ●**その件について早急に決断する** *make* a prompt *decision on* the matter.

けつだん 結団 ── **結団する** 動 form [establish, set up] an organization; organize [set up] a group. (㊦ 解団)
●**結団式** a ceremony celebrating the formation [establishment] of an organization.

げったん 月旦 ●**月旦評** descriptions of people's strengths and weaknesses; comments on [about] people's characters.

*けっちゃく 決着 (解決) (a) settlement; (終わり) an end. ●**決着をつける** (解決する) settle; (終わらせる) put an end 《*to*》; (人と話し合って)〖話〗have it [the matter] out 《*with*》. ▶その紛争はまだ決着をみていない The dispute *is* still not [not yet] *settled*.

けっちょう 結腸〖解剖〗the colon.

けっちん 血沈 「『赤血球沈降速度』の略」〖医学〗erythrocyte sedimentation rate 《略 ESR》. ●**血沈を計る** run the *blood sedimentation* test.

ゲッツー ゲッツーをとる 〖野球〗 make [turn] a double play. (!×get two は和製英語だが, Get two! (ダブルプレーをとろう！)と言うことはある (⇨ダブルプレー))

*けってい 決定 图 (判断の上の) (a) decision; (決意を秘めた) determination; (結論) a conclusion; (解決) (a) settlement.
①【～決定】●**意思決定** decision-making. ●**重大な[急な; 有利な]決定** a crucial [a hasty; a favorable] *decision* 《*about, on*》. ●**自己決定** self-determination. ●**閣議決定** (⇨閣議)
②【決定～】●**決定権がある** have the final say 《*in, about*》. ●**決定力不足に悩む** be hampered with scoring problems; be hampered by a lack of goals. ●**決定(が)次第お知らせします** We'll inform you as soon as the *decision* is made.
③【決定は】 ▶コンテストの参加者の決定は抽選で行われる(＝抽選で決定される) The participants in the contest will *be decided* by lot.
④【決定を】●**決定を下す** (⇨動) ●**その決定をくつがえす** reverse the *decision*. ●**決定をためらう** hesitate to make a final decision [judgment]. ●**決定を迫る** press [しきりに urge] 《*him*》 to decide. ▶彼がそうする[その問題について]最終決定を下した He made the final *decision* to do it [*on* the matter]. ▶私たちはそれについて討議し, 反対する決定をした We talked it over and *decided* against it.
── **決定する** 動 (決める) decide, make* a decision; (決意する) determine (!後の方が意味が強い); (日取り・価格などを) fix, set*, settle (!最初の2語が口語的). ●**計画の実行を決定する** *decide* [*determine*] to carry out the plan. ●**どのような対策を講じるか決定する** *decide* what measures to take. ▶パーティーの日曜日と決定する *fix* [*set, settle*] the date of the party *for* [×*on*] Sunday. ▶遠足で10月に奈良に行くことが決定された It *has been decided* that we (should) go to Nara in October on our school excursion. (! *should* を用いるのは主に《英》) ▶家庭環境が子供の性格を決定する Home environment *determines* children's personalities. ▶その国境線は100年前に条約で決定された The boundary *was settled* in a treaty a hundred years ago.
── **決定的な** 形 decisive; (最終的な) conclusive; (確定的な) definite (⇨確定). ●**決定的な証拠** *decisive* [*conclusive, definitive*] evidence. ●**彼の**

涯の決定的瞬間に at a *decisive* [(重大な) a *crucial*] moment in his career; at the *moment of truth* in his life. ▶後の方は「闘牛士がとどめのひと突きをする瞬間(のような)決定的な」の意) ▶私は決定的瞬間を写真に撮った I took a picture at the *decisive* moment. ▶彼の勝利は決定的となった His victory has become *decisive* [*definite*].
● 決定事項 decisions. ● 決定版戦 (同点の際の) a play-off. ● 決定打〖野球〗a game-winning hit; a key hit. ● 決定版 a definitive edition.
● 決定論〖哲学〗determinism. ● 決定論者 a determinist.

*けってん 欠点 ❶ [不十分な点] (ちょっとした) a fault; (重大な) a defect; (完璧(%)さを損なうちょっとした) a flaw (品物・議論・性格などについて用いる); (不都合な) a drawback, (全体的には好都合な中での) the downside (↔upside); (物事などの) a weak point, shortcomings (!後の方は通例複数形で). (⇨短所)
● 欠点を直す correct one's *shortcomings* [*weak points*]. ▶彼女には欠点がない She is free from *faults*./She has no *faults*./She is faultless. ▶彼の議論には欠点がない There are no *flaws* in his argument./His argument is flawless. ▶駅から遠いのがこの家の欠点だ The (only) *drawback* [*The downside*] of this house is that it is a long way from the station.
❷ [落第点] a failure. (⇨落第)

ゲット — ゲットする 動 ❶[手に入れる] get; (買う) buy, 〖話〗get. ▶ついに重要な情報をゲットした At last, I have got [obtained] the important information. ▶彼は賞金5万円をゲットした He won [got] the reward of fifty thousand yen.
❷ [得点する] score a goal; win a point.

けっとう 血統 blood, stock; (の) a pedigree (!しばしば動物に用いる). (⇨血族, 家系) ● 血統がよい (人が) come from [of] a good family; (人・動物が) come from [of] good stock. ● 血統書 (⇨血統書)

けっとう 血糖 blood sugar, sugar in the blood. ● 血糖値を計る [下げる] test [lower] the *blood sugar* level.

けっとう 決闘 名 a duel. ● 決闘を申し込む [に応じる] challenge 《him》 [accept 《his》 challenge] to a *duel*.
— 決闘する 動 fight a duel 《with》.
● 決闘者 a duelist.

けっとう 結党 — 結党する 動 form [organize, set up] a party. (㊥ 解党)

けっとうしょ 血統書 (動物の) a pedigree /pédigri:/. ● 血統書つきの犬 a *pedigree*(*d*) dog.

ゲットー [<イタリア語] 【特定の社会集団の居住地] a ghetto.

けつにく 血肉 one's flesh and blood. ● 血肉を分けた兄弟 a brother of the same *flesh and blood*; a *blood* brother.

けつにょう 血尿 bloody urine; (症状) 〖医学〗hematuria. ▶血尿が出る pass [have] bloody urine.

ケッパー 〖植物〗a caper. (!通例複数形で)

けっぱい 欠配 ● 給料の欠配 *nonpayment* of wages. ▶米が欠配している We *have no rations of* rice.

けっぱく 潔白 [無罪] innocence; guiltlessness; [無垢] purity. ● 身の潔白を証明する prove one's *innocence*.
— 潔白な 形 (無罪の) innocent; guiltless; (純粋な) pure.

けつばん 欠番 a missing number. ● 永久欠番 (野球で) a retired (uniform) number. ▶16番は欠番になっている No. 16 is *missing*. ▶球団はノーラン・ライアンの34番を永久欠番にした They *retired* Nolan Ryan's #34. (!# is number を表す記号)

けっぱん 血判 a seal of blood.
● 血判状 a petition [a written pledge] sealed with one's blood. (!a written pledge は「誓約書」)

げっぴょう 月評 a monthly report [書評] review].

けっぴん 欠便 the cancellation of a (scheduled) flight [sailing]. (⇨欠航)

げっぷ — げっぷする (ひどい) belch, (軽い) 〖話〗burp; give [let out] a (loud) belch 〖話〗burp. 事情 米英では burp はともかく, 人前での belch はきわめて下品とされる) ● げっぷを抑える suppress [stifle] a *belch* [a *burp*].

げっぷ 月賦 monthly installments [payments] (! an installment は「1回分の分割払い込み金」); (制度) 〖主に米〗(the) installment plan, 〖英〗(monthly) hire purchase. ● 車を月賦で買う buy a car *in* [*by*] *monthly installments* 〖米〗on the *installment plan*, 〖英〗*on hire purchase*. ▶彼はテレビの月賦を毎月5,000円支払う He pays an *installment of* five thousand yen on the TV set every month./He pays for the TV set *in* [*by*] *monthly installments* of 5,000 yen.

けつぶつ 傑物 a giant, a very distinguished person.

げっぺい 月餅 (a) moon cake; (説明的に) a Chinese confection eaten on August 15 of the lunar calendar.

けっぺき 潔癖 — 潔癖な 形 (きれい好きの) tidy, 〖書〗cleanly /klénli/; (不正を嫌う) upright, (やや書) scrupulous. ▶彼は潔癖症だ He is fanatical [very fastidious] about cleanliness.

けつべつ 決別 名 (a) parting.
— 決別する 動 〖主に書〗part from ... 〖別れる〗; (捨てる) break with .... ● 過去と決別する *break with* the past.

けつべん 血便 〖書〗bloody stools. ● 血便が出る have *blood in the stool*; pass blood.

*けつぼう 欠乏 名 (a) deficiency; (欠如) (a) lack. (⇨不足) ▶ビタミンの欠乏 *deficiency in* vitamins; vitamin *deficiency*.
— 欠乏する 動 ▶燃料が欠乏してきた The fuel *is running short* [*running out*].
● 欠乏症 a deficiency disease.

げっぽう 月報 a monthly report [(会の) newsletter, (会社の) bulletin /búlitn/].

けつまく 結膜 〖解剖〗a conjunctiva.
● 結膜炎 〖医学〗conjunctivitis /kəndʒʌŋktəváitis/; (流行性の) pinkeye.

けつまずく stumble 《over a rock》. (⇨つまずく)

けつまつ 結末 [終わり] an end; (映画・物語などの) an ending; [結論] a conclusion. ● 事件の結末 the *end* of an affair. ▶この映画の結末はどうなったか What was the *end* [*ending*] of the movie?/ How did the movie come *to an end*?
● 結末をつける ▶この問題に結末をつけなくてはいけない I have to *bring* this matter *to an end* [*put an end to* this matter]./(解決する) I have to *settle* this matter.

げつまつ 月末 the end of the month. ● 月末までに (近く)に by [near, toward] *the end of the month*. ▶この月末は忙しい I'm busy at *the end of* this *month*.

けつみゃく 血脈 〖血管〗a blood vessel; 〖血筋〗(⇨血筋(%)).

げつめん 月面 the lunar surface, the surface of

けつゆうびょう 血友病 〖医学〗hemophilia /hìːməfíliə/.
• 血友病患者 a hemophiliac;《話》a bleeder.

*げつよう(び) 月曜(日) Monday《略 Mon.》.(⇨日曜(日))
• 月曜病 Monday morning blues [feeling].

けつらく 欠落 图 (欠如) lack; (抜け) a gap. • 記憶の欠落を埋める fill a *gap* in one's memory.
── 欠落する 動 • 道徳心が欠落している be *lacking* in moral sense; *have no* moral sense.

けつりゅう 血流 a blood current (in one's veins).

けつるい 血涙 • 血涙をしぼる shed bitter tears《*over* one's death》.

けつれい 欠礼 ▶喪中につき年賀欠礼いたします Being in mourning, I *shall refrain from offering you* the New Year's *greetings*.

げつれい 月例 ── 月例の 形 (毎月の) monthly.
• 月例会(議) a monthly meeting. • 月例報告 a monthly report.

げつれい 月齢 [月の] the age of the moon; 〖生後1年未満の乳児の〗the number of the month after a baby was born (語源) 米英では1歳以後も乳児の年齢は月数を用いるのが普通).

*けつれつ 決裂 图〖交渉などの〗a breakdown; 〖友好関係などの〗a rupture. • 二国間の友好関係の決裂(=断絶) a *rupture* in [(崩壊) the *breakup of*] the relations between the two countries.
── 決裂する 動 • その交渉は決裂した The negotiations *broke down* [*fell through, came to a rupture*].

けつろ 結露 condensation《on a window》.

⁑けつろん 結論 图 (a) conclusion; 〖決定〗(a) decision.
①【結論に】▶その病気はウイルスが原因であるとの結論に達した We came to [arrived at, reached] the *conclusion* that the disease was caused by a virus./Our [The, ×A] *conclusion* was that the disease was caused by a virus.(! that ... は2例とも同格節) ▶私たちはそのことを徹底的に話し合ったが、結論には至らなかった We discussed (×about) it exhaustively but came to no *conclusions*. ▶いろいろ話し合った末、家を建て替えるという結論に落ち着いた After plenty of discussion, we've finally decided to rebuild our house.

②【結論を】• 結論を先に述べる[書く] state [write] one's *conclusion* first. • 早まった結論を下す jump to *conclusions* [a *conclusion*]; (結論を急ぐ) make a hasty *conclusion*.(⇨動)• 結論を次回に持ち越す[先送りする] put off (making) a *decision* till the next meeting. ▶その統計から三つの結論を導くことができます We can draw three *conclusions* from the statistics.

③【結論として】▶結論として二つのことを提案したいと思います *In conclusion*, I'd like to propose two things.

── 結論を下す[出す] 動 conclude, draw* [form, make*] a conclusion; 〖決定する〗decide. ▶彼らはその計画が実行不可能であるとの結論を下した They *concluded* the plan *to* be impracticable [*that* the plan was impracticable]. ▶足跡からそれはクマの仕業に違いないとの結論を下した From the tracks we saw, we *concluded* [*drew the conclusion*] *that* it must [《話》had to] be the work of a bear. ▶その件に関して早急に結論を出しなさい Decide about [*Make a decision on*] the matter without delay.

ゲティスバーグ 〖米国の都市〗Gettysburg /ɡétizbə̀ːrɡ/. • ゲティスバーグの演説 the *Gettysburg Address*.

げてもの 下手物 odd [weird /wíərd/, bizarre] things [(食べ物) food(s)]. • 下手物趣味がある have odd [weird] tastes in things [food]. ▶彼は下手物食いだ He has *bizarre* tastes in food./He eats *bizarre* foods.

けど【けれども】
会話 「映画に行かない？」「行きたいけど宿題があるんだ」"How about going to see a movie?" "I'd like to, *but* I have some homework [×homeworks]."

げどう 外道 ❶〖仏教以外の教え〗any religion other than Buddhism; (邪教) (a) heresy; (邪教徒) a heretic.
❷〖真理に反した道〗• 外道なことをする人 a brute; (卑劣漢) a wretch, a scoundrel. ▶この外道め You *brute* [*scoundrel*]!

げどく 解毒 图 detoxification.
── 解毒する 動 counteract a poison; detoxify.
• 解毒剤 an antidote.

けとばす 蹴飛ばす kick (hard).(⇨蹴(ʺ)る)

ケトル 〖やかん〗a kettle.

けどる 気取る suspect; (感づく) sense; (かぎつける) (やや話) get wind of .... • うそを気取られないように注意する be careful not to *be suspected of* lying.

けなげ 健気 ── 健気な 形 〖感嘆すべき〗admirable; 〖賞賛に値する〗praiseworthy; 〖雄々しい〗brave.
▶その女の子はけなげにも母が留守の間弟のめんどうをみた The *admirable* girl [*Admirably*, the girl] looked after her little brother while her mother was away.

けなす ▶彼は彼女をけなしてばかりいる He *is* always *criticizing* her./《話》He is busy *running* her *down*.(⇨批判する) ▶「けちん坊」は「倹約家」をけなして言うのに用いられる "A miser" is used *unfavorably* for "a frugal person."(! unfavorably の代わりに in a derogatory way を文尾に用いてもよい)

ケナフ 〖植物〗a kenaf.

けなみ 毛並み ▶この猫は毛並みがよい This cat has a fine (coat of) fur [a beautiful soft coat]. ▶彼は毛並みがよい He comes from [of] a good family.(⇨家柄)

げなん 下男 a manservant.(復 menservants).(対 下女)

ケニア 〖国名〗Kenya /kénjə/; (公式名) the Republic of Kenya.(首都 Nairobi) • ケニア人 a Kenyan.
• ケニア(人)の Kenyan.

けぬき 毛抜き 《a pair of》tweezers.

げねつざい 解熱剤 〖薬学〗an antipyretic.

ケネディ 〖米国の政治家〗Kennedy (John Fitzgerald 〜).
• ケネディ宇宙センター Kennedy Space Center.
• ケネディ国際空港 Kennedy International Airport.

けねん 懸念 图 (a) fear; (an) anxiety; (a) worry.(⇨心配)
── 懸念する 動 fear; be anxious《about》; worry《about》.

ゲノム 〖生物〗genom(e) /dʒíːnoum/. • ヒトゲノム a human *genom(e)*.
• ゲノム計画 the genom(e) project.

けば 毛羽 (布・果実などの) fluff,《話》fuzz; (ラシャ・スエードなどの) nap; (ビロード・じゅうたんなどの) pile. • 布に毛羽を立てる raise the *nap* on cloth.

ゲバ [＜ドイツ語] violence. ▶内ゲバ an internal strife; (説明的に) violence between factions of a student movement.

けはい 気配 [兆候] a sign; (証拠に照らした) (an) indication; [気味] a touch. ▶その家には人のいる気配はなかった There was [I could see] no sign of anyone at the house. ▶景気がよくなる気配がある There are signs [indications] that business is improving. (❗that ... は同格節)/Business is showing signs of improvement. ▶風にはかすかに秋の気配が感じられた There was a faint touch of autumn in the air. ▶彼は自分のそばに人がいるような気配を感じ取った He sensed an unseen presence near him. (❗a presence は「(目に見えない)霊気」の意)

けはえぐすり 毛生え薬 a hair restorer.

けばけばしい (はでで安っぽい) gaudy, tawdry; (これ見よがしの) showy. ▶けばけばしい服 gaudy [showy] clothes. ▶けばけばしい(=どぎつい)色のネクタイ a loud tie. ▶けばけばしい家具 (χa) cheap showy furniture.

けばだつ 毛羽立つ 動 become* fluffy (話) fuzzy.
▶毛羽立たせる fluff (out [up]); fuzz.
— **毛羽立った 形** fluffy; fuzzy.

げばひょう 下馬評 (うわさ) a rumor. ▶下馬評では田中氏が再選されるということだ Rumor has it [There's a rumor (circulating), It's rumored] that Mr. Tanaka will be elected again. / I hear(d) [People say] (that) Mr. Tanaka would be elected again.

ゲバルト [＜ドイツ語] (⇨ゲバ)

けびょう 仮病 a pretended [(書) a feigned] sickness. (⇨病気) ▶彼の病気は仮病にすぎない His sickness is a mere pretense.
▶<u>仮病を使う</u> ▶彼は仮病を使った He pretended [(話) faked, (書) feigned] sickness./He pretended to be [(話) feigned himself (to be)] sick./(やや話) He played sick.

げびる 下卑る 動 ▶下卑ている be vulgar. (⇨下品)

*けひん 下品 —— 下品な 形** vulgar; (粗野の) coarse; (低俗な) low; (みだらな) indecent. ▶下品な冗談 a vulgar [a low, (不快な) a nasty] joke. ▶彼の言葉遣いは粗野で下品だった His language was coarse and vulgar. ▶ぐちゃぐちゃ音を立てて物を食べるのは下品だ It's bad manners to make a loud noise while (you are) eating.

けぶかい 毛深い hairy; [毛むくじゃらの] shaggy. ▶毛深い胸 a hairy chest.

けぶる 煙る (⇨煙(けむ)る)

ケベック [カナダの州・都市] Quebec /kwibék/.

ゲマインシャフト [＜ドイツ語] [共同社会] a gemeinschaft.

けまり 蹴鞠 kemari; (説明的に) a kind of football played by nobles in old Japan.

ケミカル chemical.
▶ケミカルシューズ artificial leather shoes; 《和製語》chemical shoes.

けむ 煙 smoke. (⇨煙(けむり))
▶<u>煙に巻く</u> ▶彼の大げさな言葉に煙に巻かれてしまった I was completely mystified [puzzled] by his big words.

けむい 煙い smoky. ▶この部屋は煙い This room is smoky. ▶たき火が煙いのでせきが出た The smoky fire made me cough.

けむくじゃら 毛むくじゃら ▶毛むくじゃらの大男 a hairy tall man; a tall man who has hair all over his body. ▶毛むくじゃらの犬 a dog with a shaggy coat; a shaggy dog.

けむし 毛虫 a (hairy) caterpillar.

けむたい 煙たい ❶ [煙い] smoky. (⇨煙い)
❷ [敬遠したい] ▶私にとって彼は煙たい存在だ I don't feel at ease with him. ▶その先生は学生に煙たがられている (＝人気がない) The teacher is unpopular with [among] the students.

*けむり 煙** smoke; (刺激性の) fumes. ▶煙の出ている煙突 a smoking chimney. ▶煙に巻かれて死ぬ be choked to death by smoke. ▶煙を家の外へ出し let the smoke out of a house. ▶煙突から煙が出ている Smoke is coming out of the chimney./(煙を吐いている) The chimney is giving off [emitting] smoke. ▶あちこちの家からうっすらと煙が立ち昇っていた Thin columns of smoke rose from houses here and there. ▶彼女は煙にむせた She was choked with [by] smoke. ▶待合室はたばこの煙でいっぱいだった The waiting room was full of cigarette [cigar, tobacco] smoke. ▶火のない所に煙は立たない (ことわざ) There is no smoke without fire.

> **翻訳のこころ** 部屋は煙のように消え，二人は寒さにぶるぶる震えて，草の中に立っていました (宮沢賢治『注文の多い料理店』) The room disappeared as if it had gone up in smoke, and the two found themselves standing in the grass, shaking [shivering] with cold. (❗(1) go up in smoke は「煙になって(のように)消えてしまう」の意の慣用表現．(2)「立っていました」は「立っていたのに(自分たち自身が)気がつきました」と表す．(3) shake は「一般的に震える」，shiver は「寒さや恐怖で瞬間的に震える」の意)

▶<u>煙になる</u> (火葬に付される) be cremated; (焼失する) be burned to ashes [the ground].

けむる 煙る [煙が出る] smoke; (くすぶる) smolder; [かすむ] look dim (-mm-). ▶暖炉が煙っている The fireplace is smoking. ▶家々は雨の中に煙っていた The houses looked dim in the rain.

*けもの 獣** (書) a beast, (書) a brute. (⇨けだもの)
▶獣道 an animal trail.

げや 下野 —— 下野する 動 [官職をやめる] resign (from) one's government post; [野党になる] go out of power.

けやき 欅 [植物] a zelkova /zélkəvə/ (tree).

けやぶる 蹴破る ▶ドアを蹴破る kick the door open; break open the door by kicking it.

けら 螻蛄 [昆虫] a mole cricket.

ゲラ a galley. ▶校正のためゲラを受け取る receive galleys [galley proofs] for correction. ▶ゲラを校正する correct [read] proof(s); proofread (a text).
▶ゲラ刷り a galley (proof); (a) proof (sheet).

けらい 家来 a retainer; (封建時代の) a vassal, a man (複 men).

げらく 下落 图 [価格などの] a fall, a decline, a downturn; (書) (a) depreciation; (一時的な) a dip; (急な) a drop. ▶株式市場はこの数か月下落傾向にある There's been a downturn trend in the stock market for several months.
—— **下落する 動** ▶株価が急に下落した Stock prices fell [dropped] suddenly [大幅に] sharply]./ There was a sudden [a sharp] fall [drop, (やや書) decline] in stock prices. ▶円は暴落に対して10パーセント下落した The yen depreciated ten percent against the dollar.

げらげら ▶げらげら笑う laugh loudly; roar with laughter, have [(古) laugh] a good laugh.
▶彼の冗談にみんながげらげら笑った His joke made everybody roar with laughter.

けり ● けりをつける (終える) finish, get* through (with)...; (解決する) settle; (話し合い・けんかで) have* a showdown 《with》,《話》have it out 《with》. ● その仕事にけりをつける finish [get through (with)] the work. ● ついにその問題にけりがついた The matter *has been settled* at last.

げり 下痢 〖医学〗diarrhea /dàiəríːə/;《話》the runs. ● 下痢をする have *diarrhea* [*loose bowels*]. (〖前の方が普通〗) ● 下痢がひどい I have a bad case [attack] of *diarrhea*. ● 下痢止め a binding medicine.

けりこむ 蹴り込む kick (a ball) in. ● ボールをゴールに蹴り込む kick a ball in [into] the goal.

ゲリマンダー 〖党利党略のための選挙区の不当改変〗a gerrymander /dʒérimændər/.

ゲリラ 〖<スペイン語〗(ゲリラ兵) a gue(r)rilla /gərílə/. ● ゲリラの野営地 the gue(r)rillas' camp. ● ゲリラ戦 gue(r)rilla war(fare) [fighting]. ● ゲリラ部隊 a gue(r)rilla gang [band].

*****ける** 蹴る ❶〖足で〗kick. ● ボールをける *kick* a ball, *kick at* a ball. (❗ kick は実際にけったことを表すが, kick at ... は「...を目がけてける」の意で, 実際にけったか否かは文脈による); give a kick at [×to] a ball. ● ドアを乱暴にける *kick* the door violently; give the door a violent *kick*. (❗〖×give a violent kick to the door は不可〗) ● 彼の横腹[脚]をける *kick* him *in* the side [*on* the leg]. (⇒打つ 〖類語〗) ● 戸をけり開ける *kick* the door open. (❗ open は形容詞で, けった結果の状態を表す) ❷〖要求などを〗reject, refuse, turn ... down. (⇒断わる)

ゲル 〖物理・化学〗gel /dʒél/.

ケルト ● ケルト族 the Celts. ● ケルト族の Celtic.

ゲルニカ 〖スペインの都市〗Guernica /gəːrníːkə/. (参考 ピカソの同名の絵画で有名)

ゲルマニウム 〖化学〗germanium /dʒərméiniəm/《元素記号 Ge》.

ゲルマン ● ゲルマン民族 the Germanic peoples.

ケルン 〖石積みの道程標〗a cairn /kéərn/.

ケルン 〖ドイツの都市〗Cologne /kəlóun/;《ドイツ名》Köln.

げれつ 下劣 ―下劣な 形 (卑しむべき) mean; (見下げた) (やや書) despicable. ● 下劣なことをする act contemptibly. ● 下劣なやつ a contemptible fellow.

*****けれども** (も) (...だけれども) though, although (❗ 後の方が堅い語で, 文頭にくることが多い); (しかし) but; (しかしながら) (やや書) however; (それでもなお) (and) yet. (⇒にもかかわらず, しかし) ● 雪が降っていたけれども, 試合は中止にならなかった It was snowing, *but* they didn't cancel [call off] the game./They didn't cancel the game *though* [*although*] it was snowing./They didn't cancel the game *in spite of* [《書》*despite*] the snow. (❗(1) 第 2, 3 例では though, in spite of 以下を文頭に回すことも可. (2) despite は特に新聞などで好まれる) ● 欠点はあるけれども, 私は彼が好きだ *In spite of* [《書》*Despite*] his faults, I like him. (❗ He has some faults, *but* [Though he has some faults,] I like him. の方が口語的)/*For* [*With*] all his faults, I like him. (❗ With all ... では「欠点があればこそ彼が好きだ」の意にもなるので後半部分を ... I still like him. とする方が明確) ● 彼女は大変もの静かだけれども朗らかだ She's very quiet *and* cheerful. (❗ 対立する関係にない文や語句をつなぐ場合は, 日本語に引かれて but を用いないよう注意) ● (電話で) こちらは池田ですけれども花子さんはいらっしゃいますか This is Ikeda speaking. Can I speak to Masako? (❗ このように単に文を軽くつなぐだけの「けれども」は英訳しない)

-ければ without .... (⇒-なければ)

けんらん 外連 〖人気取りの演技〗playing to the gallery; (見せびらかし) show-off; 〖ごまかすこと〗pretense; (はったり) claptrap. ● けれん味のない 〖ごまかしのない〗unpretentious; unaffected. ● 彼はけれん味がないから好きだ I like him for his *unpretentious nature*./I like him because he *is free from claptrap*.

ゲレンデ 〖<ドイツ語〗a (ski) slope.

げろ (へど) vomit. (⇒へど)

ケロイド 〖医学〗a keloid /kíːlɔid/. ● 腕にケロイドがある have a *keloid* [(傷跡) a (*bad*) *scar*] on one's arm. (❗ scar に修飾語を bad, nasty, ugly などを添えた方が実態に沿う場合が多い)

げろう 下郎 (召し使い) a servant, a valet; (社会的地位の低い人) a person of low social standing.

けろけろ ● カエルがけろけろと鳴いている A frog is *croaking*.

げろげろ ● げろげろ吐く throw up [vomit] all that one has eaten.

ケロシン 〖灯油〗《米, 豪》kérosene;《英》paraffin.

けろり ● けろりとしている (=何とも思わない) feel nothing; (平静でいる) stay [keep] calm. ● ひと晩よく寝ると彼女の風邪はけろりと(=完全に)よくなった She *completely* [*fully*] got over the cold after a good night's sleep. ● 彼の頭痛は海を見るとけろりと治った His headache cleared up *completely* [(たちまち消えた) *suddenly* disappeared] when he saw the sea. ● 彼はひどいけがをしたが, 何もなかったようにけろりとしていた He got seriously injured, but he *behaved as if nothing had happened*.

*****けわしい** 険しい (山・傾斜が) steep; (顔つきが) severe, stern. ● 険しい山 a *steep* mountain. ● 彼は険しい顔つきでいすに座っていた He sat on a chair with a *severe* [a *stern*, a *grim*] look.

けん 券 (切り取り式の) a coupon. (⇒切符) ● 乗車[入場]券 a pássenger [an admíssion, an éntrance] tícket. (❗ いずれも状況によって明らかな場合は単に ticket でよい) ● 会員券 a mémbership cárd.

けん 県 (日本・フランスなどの) a prefecture /príːfektʃər/. (❗「府」にも用いる) ● 青森県 Aomori Prefecture. (❗ the) Aomori prefecture. (事情 米英では prefecture を行政区画に用いないためほど一般的でない. 分かりにくい場合は Aomori Prefecture, which is the northernmost part of Honshu (本州の最北にある青森県)などのように地理的特徴や有名な場所などを添える説明が望ましい) ● 三重県民 a citizen of Mie *Prefecture*. ● (全体) the citizens [people] of Mie *Prefecture*. ● 県営球場 (⇒県営) ● 県知事 a prefectural governor. (❗「愛媛県知事」は the governor of Ehime *Prefecture*.) ● 県会議員 a member of a *prefectural* assembly.

けん 件 ❶〖事柄〗a matter. ● 例の件 the *matter* in question. ● 至急を要する件で on urgent *business*. ● 東京行きの件で何か決まましたか What have you decided *about* going to Tokyo? ❷〖事件〗a case. ● 盗難 2 件 two *cases* of theft [robbery].

けん 妍 beauty; gorgeousness; attractiveness. ● バラ園ではいろいろな品種のバラの花が妍を競うように咲き誇っている All kinds of roses are in full bloom in the rose garden, *vying with* one another *in beauty*. (❗ vying は vie (張り合う) の現在分詞)

けん 兼 ● 居間兼寝室 a bed-*cum*-living room. (❗ cum /kám/ は「...付きの」の意);《英》a bed-sitter (❗《話》a bed-sit,《書》a bed-sitting room ともいう. 通例貸し室) ● 書斎兼応接間 a room used both as a study and for receiving visitors. ● 朝食兼昼食 brunch.

けん 剣 a sword /sɔ́ːrd/ (⇨刀); [短剣] a dagger; [決闘・フェンシング用の] a rapier; [銃剣] a bayonet. ● 諸刃(もろは)の剣 a two-[double-] edged *sword*. (!) 比喩的にも用いられる) ● 剣客 a fencer; a swordsman. ● 剣舞 《do》 a sword dance.

けん 間 [長さの単位] a *ken*. (参考) 約 1.82m) ● この部屋の間数 the length [*breadth*] of this room *in ken*.

けん 腱 [解剖] a tendon.

けん 鍵 (ピアノなどの) 《strike》 a key.

-けん -軒 1 軒家 一戸建ての家) a house, a detached house (働 houses /-ziz, (米) -siz/) (!) 前の方が普通の言い方); (孤立した家) 《主に書》a solitary house. ● 3 軒の家 three houses. ● 1 軒ごとに回って歩く call at *every house*; walk (*from*) *door to door*. ● 角から 2 軒目の家に住む live in *the second house* from the corner. (2 軒先に) live *two doors* (*away*) from the corner. ▶小川さんの家は 1 軒置いて隣です Mr. Ogawa lives *two doors away* from us./[主に英] Mr. Ogawa lives *next door but one* to us. (!) 2 例とも us を our house としない

-けん -圏 (領域) a sphere; (地域) an area; (連合) a bloc. ● 英国の勢力圏 the British *sphere of* influence. ● 首都圏 the metropolitan *area*. ● 共産圏 the Communist *bloc*.

-けん -権 (権利) (a) right. ● スト権 a [the] *right to strike* [*to go on strike*]. (⇨権利)

げん 元 [中国の通貨単位] yuan /júːən/ (働 ~, ~s) (略 Y).

げん 言 a word; a remark; a statement. ● 彼の言のごとく as he *put it*. ● 言を左右にする equivocate; (どっちつかずの返事をする) hedge; (遠回しに言う) beat around the bush. ● 言を待たない ▶21 世紀は高度情報化社会になるということは言を待たない(=言うまでもない) *Needless to say*, [*It goes without saying that*] in the 21st century we will live in a highly information-based society.

げん 弦 (楽器の) a string; (弓の) a bowstring; [数学] a chord. ● ギターの弦 a guitar *string*; a *string on* a guitar. ● ギターに弦を張る *string* a guitar.

げん 現 (現在の) present; (現職の) (書) incumbent. ● 現住所 one's *present* address.

げん 厳 ● 厳たる態度をとる take a *stern* attitude (*toward, to*). ● 警戒を厳にする keep a *strict* [細心の] a *close*] watch (*on*). ● 厳として (⇨厳として)

げん 験 ❶ [縁起] (運) luck; (前兆) an omen. (⇨縁起) ● 験のよい [悪い] こと a good [a bad, an ill] omen; (good) [bad] luck. ● 験をかついでその品を買う [とっておく] buy [keep] the article *for luck*. ● 験直しをする do something to *improve one's luck*.
❷ [効き目] ● 験が現れる take effect. (⇨効き目)

-げん -減 (減少) a decrease in population. ● 水の供給の 10 パーセント減 a 10 percent *cut* [*reduction*] in water supply. ● 鋼鉄の輸出は今年 2 割減となった The export of steel *has decreased* [*reduced, been reduced*] by 20 percent this year.

けんあく 険悪 ——険悪な 形 [表情などが] (険しい) stern; (恐ろしい) fierce; [天気などが] (今にも降り出しそうな) threatening; (荒れ模様の) stormy; [事態などが] (深刻な) serious; (緊迫した) tense. ▶彼は険悪な顔つきで私を見た He gave me a *stern* [(威嚇的な) *menacing*] look. ● 両国間の関係は険悪になった The relations between the two countries have become *serious* [(悪化した) have deteriorated].

げんあつ 減圧 名 reduction of pressure; decompression. —— **減圧する** 動 reduce the pressure (*of*); decompress. ● 減圧室 a decompréssion chàmber.

けんあん 検案 (検死) 《make》 an autopsy; 《carry out》 a postmortem examination. ● 検案書 a certificate of a postmortem examination.

けんあん 懸案 a pending problem [question]. ● 長年の懸案を解決する dispose of a long-*pending* question. ▶その法案は次期国会まで懸案となった The bill *was left undecided* [*pending*] till the next Diet session.

げんあん 原案 [議案] the original bill; [計画] the original plan. ▶法案は原案どおり可決された The bill passed *in its original form* [(草案のまま) *as drafted*, (何の修正もなく) *without any amendment*].

*****けんい 権威** authority 《over, with》; [権力] power (*over*); [権威者] an authority (*on*). ● 権威筋の情報 the information from an authoritative source. ● 権威主義的な authoritarian. ● 経済学 [この道] の最高権威 the greatest *authority* on economics [*in* this field]. ● 権威のある学者 an *authoritative* scholar; a scholar of authority. (!) 後の方が堅く, 時にとりすました感じ) ● 権威をつける give [lend] *authority* 《*to*》. ● 権威に反抗する rebel against *authority*. ▶芥川賞は日本文学中のすぐれた新人に対して年 2 回与えられる権威ある(=高く評価されている)賞である The Akutagawa Prize is a *prestigious* award given semiannually to an outstanding new writer in Japanese literature.
● 権威主義 authoritarianism. ● 権威主義者 an authoritarian.

けんいん 牽引 名 traction.
—— **牽引する** 動 tow (a car); (強制的に移動させる) tow (a car) away. (⇨引っ張る❶) ● 牽引されている(車・船が) be in 《米》[*on* 《英》] *tow*; (人が治療のために) be *in traction*.
● 牽引車 a tractor; (運動・計画などの推進力となる人・国) the motive power 《*of, behind*》. ● 原動力) ● 牽引療法 a traction treatment, [医学] extension.

けんいん 検印 a seal of approval; (著者の) the author's seal [*imprint*]. ● 検印済み approved and sealed [stamped].
—— **検印する** 動 seal, stamp; put [set] one's seal [stamp] of approval 《*to, on*》; affix a seal of approval 《*to*》.

:げんいん 原因 [結果を生み出す] (a) cause; [発端] (an) origin; [根源] the root. ● 原因と結果 *cause* and effect. (!) 無冠詞) ● 原因を突き止める trace the *cause* 《*of* it》; trace (it) to its *origin*. ▶その火事は原因不明だ The *cause* of the fire is unknown [is not known]. (!) 「原因不明の火事」 は a fire of unknown *cause*) ▶その事故の原因は何でしたか What was the *cause of* [*was responsible for*] the accident? (!) 後の言い方は複雑な原因に用いることが多い)/Why [How] did the accident happen [*occur*]? (!) Why は理由を, How はいきさつを表す)/(何が事故を引き起こしたか) What *caused* the accident? ▶彼の病気は粗末な食事が原因だった

けんうん

His sickness *was caused by* [(結果として生じた) *resulted from*] bad food [nutrition]./Bad food [nutrition] was the *cause* of his sickness. (❗「一因」ならば a cause of his sickness) ▶彼の腹痛は食べ過ぎが原因でそうに違いない His stomachache *comes* [*must be*] *from* eating too much. ▶その事故が原因で我々は出発できなかった We couldn't leave *because of* [*owing to*, *on account of*] the accident./(その事故が我々が出発するのを妨げた)《書》The accident *prevented* [*kept*] us *from* leaving.
●原因療法 a causal treatment.

けんうん 巻雲 〖気象〗a cirrus (複 cirri), a cirrus cloud.

けんえい 県営 ── 県営の 形 prefectural; under prefectural management. ●県営陸上競技場[球場] a prefectural athletic field [baseball stadium].

げんえい 幻影 〈幻〉visions;〈幻想〉illusions;〈蜃気楼〉a mirage /mɪrɑ́ːʒ/. ●幻影を見る see *visions*. ●世界平和の幻影を追う pursue the *mirage* of world peace.

けんえき 検疫 名 quarantine /kwɔ́(ː)rəntiːn/.
── 検疫する 動 quarantine.
●検疫官 a quarantine officer. ●検疫所 a quarantine station.

けんえき 権益 〈権利〉rights;〈利益〉interests. ●在外権益を守る protect the *interests* overseas.

*****げんえき** 現役 名 ●現役を退いてコーチ陣に加わる retire from *active play* and join the team coaching staff. ▶彼は現役では最高の投手です He's the best pitcher *playing* [*on the active list*]. ▶彼は現役で大学に入った He got into college *right after graduating from high school*.
── 現役(の) 形 〈活動的な〉active. ●現役選手 an active player. ●現役将校 an officer *on active service* [*on the active list*]. ●現役合格者 a successful candidate who gains *immediate entry*.

げんえき 原液 an undiluted solution.

げんえき 減益 a earnings [a profit] decline; a drop in earnings [profits]. ▶当社は大幅な減益となった Our *earnings* have *collapsed*./We have faced a sharp *drop in earnings*.

けんえつ 検閲 名 〖出版物・映画などの〗censorship;〖検査〗(an) inspection;〈査〉(an) examination. ●新聞[映画]の検閲 press [film] *censorship*. ●検閲を通るに引っ掛かる pass [fail to pass] *censorship*. ●検閲を受けた[受けていない]ニュース censored [uncensored] news. ▶検閲は、これをしてはならない No *censorship* shall be maintained. (参考 日本国憲法第21条2)
── 検閲する 動 censor. ●検閲される[を受ける] be censored.
●検閲官 a censor.

けんえん 犬猿 ・**犬猿の仲** ▶彼らは犬猿の仲だ They lead a *cat and dog* life./They argue [quarrel] violently all the time.

げんえん 減塩 ── 減塩する 動 reduce [cut down on] the amount of salt.
●減塩しょうゆ low salt soy sauce. ●減塩食 a low salt diet.

けんえんけん 嫌煙権 the right to be free from other people's tobacco [cigarette] smoke; non-smokers' rights.

けんお 嫌悪 名 〖好きでないこと〗(a) dislike; 〖憎悪〗(a) hatred; 〖むかむかするほどの嫌気〗disgust; 〖本能的に根深い嫌悪〗〈やや書〉an antipathy /ǽntɪpəθi/ 〈*to*, *toward*, *against*〉. ●自己嫌悪 self-hatred;

げんか

self-hate. ●彼を嫌悪の目で見る look at him *with hatred* [*disgust*]. ▶彼の態度に嫌悪の念を抱いた I *hated* his behavior.
── 嫌悪する 動 ●自由思想をひどく嫌悪する have a deep [strong] *antipathy to* [*toward*] liberal ideas.

けんおん 検温 名 thermometry. ── 検温する 動 take (one's) temperature.
●検温器(体温計) a clinical thermometer.

げんおん 原音 〖再生音に対して元の音〗the original sound; 〖原語での発音〗the original pronunciation.

*****けんか** 喧嘩 名 〖言葉上の〗a quarrel; (論争, ささいな口論) (an) argument; (騒々しい長引かないけんか)《話》a row /ráu/; 〖腕力の〗a fight.

① 【～(の)けんか】●兄弟[夫婦]げんか a *quarrel* between brothers [husband and wife]. (❗後の方は対句のため無冠詞) ●激しいけんか a fierce *quarrel* 〖(なぐり合いの) *fight*〗. ●大げんか a big quarrel [argument]; a fierce fight; a blazing row. ●子供のけんか a children's fight [quarrel]. ●なぐり合いのけんかで鼻血を出す get a bloody nose in the *fight* 〖げんこつによる〗the *fist fight*〗.

② 【けんか～】●けんか腰で belligerently; in a belligerent [(挑戦的な) a defiant] manner. ●けんか別れをする 《話》have a bust-up. ▶彼はけんかっ早い(=けんか好きだ) He's very quarrelsome./《米話》He's scrappy.

③ 【けんかの[を]～】●彼らのけんかの仲裁に入る settle [(やめさせる) stop] their *quarrel*; (割って入る) break up their *fight*. ●けんかを始める start *fighting*; start [get into] a *fight*. ●けんかの原因 the cause of a *quarrel* 〖(争いの種) the seeds of strife〗. ●けんかの仕方 how to *argue* [*quarrel*, *fight*]. ●一対一のけんかをする *fight* one-on-one; have a one-on-one *fight*. ▶主人と私はけんかの後すぐに仲直りした My husband and I soon made up after our *row* [*quarrel*, *argument*].

●けんか両成敗 In a quarrel both parties [sides] are to blame.

●けんかを売る pick a quarrel [a fight] 《*with* him》; provoke 《him》 to a quarrel [a fight]. ▶けんかを売ってきたのはやつの方でおれじゃない It was him, not me, that picked a quarrel. (❗It was he, not I, who... は改まった言い方)

●けんかを買う (挑戦を受ける) accept 《his》 challenge.

── 喧嘩する 動 口論する; quarrel, have* a quarrel 《*with*＋人, *about* [*over*]＋事》; argue, have an argument 《*with*, *about*, *over*》;《話》fall* out 《*with*, *about*, *over*》; 〖なぐり合う〗fight*, have a fight 《*with*, *against*》. ▶子供たちはいちばんいい席を取り合ってけんかした The children quarreled with [argued with, fought 《with》] each other over (who should have) the best seat. (❗初めの二つは口論、最後は取っ組み合い)

けんか 県下 in [throughout] the prefecture.

けんか 献花 名 flower tributes.
── 献花する 動 offer flowers (in tribute) to the dead [deceased].

けんか 鹸化 名 〖化学〗saponification.
── 鹸化する 動 saponify 《*for*》.
●鹸化価 saponification value [number].

けんが 懸河 ・**懸河の弁** an eloquent speech.

げんか 〖幻化〗*Hallucinations*. (参考 梅崎春生の小説)

げんか 言下 ●言下に(=即座に)申し出を断わる refuse [turn down] an offer *promptly* 〖(きっぱりと)

flatly].

げんか 見価 (a) cost. ▶仕入れ原価 purchase [first] *cost*; *cost* of purchase [goods purchased]. ▶製造原価 manufacturing [production, factory] *cost*; *cost* of production [goods manufactured]. ▶原価で[以下で]売る sell at [below] *cost*. ▶原価で買う get [it] for *cost*.
● **原価管理** cost cntrol. ● **原価計算** costing; cost account(ing). ● **原価主義** the cost valuation basis; the cost basis [method, principle]. ● **原価率** (a) cost percentage.

げんか 減価 图 [割引] a reduction in price; a price reduction; [価値の低減] depreciation.
—— **減価する** 動 ▶ロシア貨幣が急激に減価した Russian money *has* sharply *depreciated in value*.
● **減価償却** 減価償却

げんが 原画 the original picture.

げんかい 見解 (意見) (an) opinion; (ものの見方) a view (▪ しばしば複数形で); (▪ 意見) ▶その件についての見解を述べる express one's *opinion* [*views*] on the matter. ▶私はその点では彼と見解が一致する I have the same *opinion* as he does on that point./I *agree with* him *on* that point. ▶私は政治に関しては彼とは見解を異にする I have different *opinions* [*views*] *about* politics from him./He and I have a different political *point of view*. ▶それは見解の相違(=問題)ということですね It's *a matter of opinion*. (▪「あなたの意見に私は不賛成」との含み) ▶その点は見解の相違ということにしておきましょう Let's *agree to differ* [*disagree*] on that point.

けんがい 圏外 out of (↔within) the sphere 《*of*》. ● 優勝圏外にある(= 優勝の見込みがない) have *no chance of* winning the championship.

けんがい 懸崖 an overhanging cliff. ● 懸崖作りの菊 a cascade chrysanthemum.

*　**げんかい** 限界 a limit (▪ しばしば複数形で); [能力などの] limitations (▪ 通例複数形で), (▪ やや書) bounds (▪ 通例複数形で). ▶能力の限界を知る know the *limits* of one's abilities; (自分[自身]の限界を知る) know [recognize] one's own *limitations*. ▶我々たちには限界がある There is a *limit* to [x in] what we can do. ▶それは人知の限界を超えている It exceeds [is beyond] the *limits* [*bounds*] of human knowledge.
● **限界効用** marginal utility. ● **限界収益** marginal profit. ● **限界費用**〖経済〗marginal cost.

けんがい 言外 ▶言外の意味を読み取る(= 行間を読む) read between the lines. ▶そのことを言外にほのめかす hint at it. (⇒ほのめかす) ▶私にとっては「人生」という言葉は闘いと苦痛の意味を言外に含んでいる To me the word "life" connotes [has connotations of] struggle and pain.

げんかいたいせい 厳戒体制 ▶厳戒体制をしく be on *full alert* [*strict guard*] 《*against*》.

けんかく 剣客 a swordsman (おう).

*　**けんがく** 見学 图 a visit《*to*》. ▶工場見学に行く(実地見学の旅行で) *go to* a factory *on a field trip*; (勉強の一環として見学する) *visit* a factory *as part of* [*in connection with*] one's *studies*. ▶博物館の見学は今度が初めてですか Is this your first *visit to* the museum?
—— **見学する** 動 (訪れる) visit; (自由に見て回る) walk around ...; (案内に従って見て回る) make* a tour, tour. ▶学生たちはテレビ局を見学した The students *made* [*did, went on*] *a tour* of the TV station.
● **見学者** a visitor.

げんかく 幻覚 (a) hallùcinátion. ▶彼は時々幻覚を起こす[に襲われる] He sometimes has [suffers from] *hallucinations*./He sometimes gets *the horrors*. (▪ the horrors は「怖いものを見る幻覚」)
● **幻覚剤** (a) hallucinogen /həlúːsənədʒən/.
● **幻覚症状** hallucinosis.

げんかく 厳格 —— **厳格な** 形 (厳正に守る) strict; (妥協を許さない) severe; (情け容赦がない) stern; (窮屈なまでに厳しい) rigid. ▶厳格な規則 *strict* [*severe*, *rigid*] rules. ▶厳格な主人 a *strict* [a *severe*, a *stern*] master. ▶彼は学生に厳格だ He is *strict* [*severe*] *with* his students.
—— **厳格に** 副 strictly; severely; sternly; rigidly.

げんがく 弦楽 string music.
● **弦楽器** (⇒弦楽器) ● **弦楽合奏** the string ensemble /ɑːnsɑ́ːmbl/. ● **弦楽合奏団** a string ensemble [orchestra (band)]. (▪ いずれも単・複数扱い. 前の方は少人数のもの) ● **弦楽四重奏曲** a string quartet. ● **弦楽四重奏団** a string quartet. (▪ 単・複数扱い)

げんがく 衒学 图 pedantry. —— **衒学的(な)** 形 pedantic.
● **衒学者** a pedant.

げんがく 減額 图 (削減) (a) reduction, a cut.
—— **減額する** 動 reduce, cut ... down. (▪ 後の方が口語的)

げんかしょうきゃく 減価償却 图 (a) depreciation.
—— **減価償却する** 動 depreciate.
● **減価償却費** depreciation expense.

けんかしょくぶつ 顕花植物〖植物〗a phanerogam. (▪ 隠花植物)

げんがっき 弦楽器 a stringed instrument; (オーケストラの) the strings (▪ 集合的に用い複数扱い).

けんかみね 剣が峰 〖噴火口の〗a crater's edge; 〖土俵の〗the rim of the ring. ▶剣が峰に立つ(= 絶体絶命の状態になる) be in a desperate situation [state]; have one's back to [against] the wall; 《話》 be in a real bind [pinch]. ▶成否の剣が峰だ(= 予断を許さない) Our success or failure *hangs in the balance*.

けんがん 検眼 an eyesight [an eye] test. ▶検眼してもらった方がいい You should have your *eyesight* [your *eyes*] *tested* [*checked*].

けんがん 献眼 (an) eye donation.

*　**げんかん** 玄関 the (front) door; the (front) entrance; the (front) porch; 〖玄関の間〗the (entrance) hall.

> 使い分け ▶ (**front**) **door** 正面のドアをさす.
> **entrance** exit (出口)に対する語で,「入り口」の意.
> **porch** 主に玄関の外側でひさしや屋根のある部分.

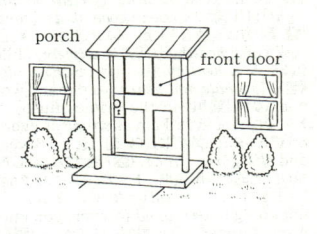

[図: porch / front door のイラスト]

● 玄関から入る enter *at* [*through*, ×*from*] *the front door*. ▶お父さんに会いたいという人が玄関に来ている There's a man *at the door* asking for Daddy. ▶玄関(=応対)に出てもらえませんか Will you answer *the door*? ▶彼を玄関まで見送って別れ

のあいさつをした I saw him to the *door* and said good-by to him. ●成田空港は日本の玄関である Narita Airport is *the gateway to* [×*of*] Japan.
●**玄関払い** ●玄関払いを食わす turn 《him》 away *at the door*.
●**玄関灯** a porch lamp. ●**玄関番** a doorkeeper, a porter, a janitor.

げんかん 厳寒 intense [severe] winter.

げんぎ 嫌疑 《容疑》(a) suspicion;《罪名》a charge.(⇨容疑)

げんき 元気 名 〖健康〗(good) health;〖精力〗energy /énərdʒi/;〖快活〗spirits;〖勇気〗courage, heart;〖体力〗strength.

① 【～元気】 ●空〔付け〕元気 mere *courage*;《酒で》Dutch *courage*. ●食べる元気もない be too tired even to eat anything.

② 【元気～】 ●彼は元気いっぱいだ He's full of *energy* [*vigor, vitality, life*]./He's very much *alive*. ●彼は元気そのものだ He is very *energetic*./He is *energy* itself.

③ 【元気が】 ●元気がある be full of *energy* [*vigor*]; be *energetic* [*vigorous*]. ●元気がない《意気消沈している》be *depressed*; be *in low* [*poor*] *spirits*;《体調が悪い》be out of shape. ●元気が見るからにない He looks *depressed* [《話》*blue*].
▶私はもう一度立ち上がって戦う元気(=勇気)がなかった I didn't have the *courage* [*heart*,《話》*guts*] to get up and fight again. ▶彼は彼女に会って元気が出た He *cheered up* when he saw her./《話》He *got a lift from* seeing her. ▶コーヒーを1杯飲んだら元気が出た I *felt refreshed* with a cup of coffee./A cup of coffee *refreshed* me.
会話「今日はなんだか元気がないね」「風邪を引いているのよ」"You're *not looking well* [《話》*good*] today." "I have a cold."

④ 【元気を】 ●元気を出す gather one's *strength*;《勇気づけられる》take *heart* [*from, at*];《勇気を奮い起こす》pluck up *heart* [one's *courage*]. ●元気を取り戻す《健康を》recover one's *health*;《気力の》recover one's *spirits*; pull *oneself* together.
▶元気を出して *Cheer up*!/《気持ちを取り直せ》Snap out of it./《やや書》Lift up your [Take] *heart*./《気を落とすな》Don't let it get you down./Don't lose *heart*. ●元気をもらう gain strength [energy];《話》get a lift 《*from*》. (⇨③ [第3文例])

── **元気な** 形 《健康な》healthy;《活気のある》lively;《快活な》cheerful;《精力的》enèrgétic, vigorous;《強健な》robúst. ●元気である《健康である》《やや書》be *in good health*;《やや話》be *fine* [*all right*];《体調がよい》be *in good shape* [*condition*](❗後の方は運動選手に用いるのが普通). ●元気な(=健康な)子 a *healthy* [《活発な》*lively*] child. ●元気な老人 a *healthy* [《かくしゃくとした》a *vigorous*,《書・古》a *hale and hearty*] old man [woman].
●元気な[の]盛り in the prime [flush] of life.
●相変わらず元気です I am as *strong* as ever. ▶彼は86歳だがまだ元気だ[にしている] He's 86 years old and still going strong.《「老いてなお盛んである」の意の口語的な慣用表現》●お父さんはいつまでもお元気で(=いらして)いらっしゃるわけじゃないのよ Your *father's not going to be around* forever, you know.《❗not ... forever は「いつまでも...しているとは限らない」の意の部分否定》
会話「ご家族の皆様はお元気ですか」「お陰さまで皆元気です」"How's your family?" "They are all *fine* [*very well*, ×*very fine*, ×*healthy*], thank you."

会話「やあ, 元気?」「うん元気. 君は?」"Hi! How are you?" "(I'm) *fine*, thanks. And you?"(❗いろいろな表現であり, 健康だけについて尋ねているのではない。How are you doing?/How's things?/How's it going? などの方がくだけた問い方。また (I'm) fine. の代わりに Just great./Pretty good./Oh, not (too) bad./All right. などとも答える)

── **元気に, 元気よく** 副 《精力的に》with energy [vigor];《快活に》cheerfully;《上機嫌で》in good [high] spirits. ▶彼は元気よくテニスをしている He's playing tennis *with energy*. ▶元気にしなさい Say "Good morning" *cheerfully*./Give me a *cheerful* "Good morning." ▶早く元気になってください I hope you will get *well* soon./I wish you a (very) speedy *recovery*. ▶花は水につけると元気になる(=生気を取り戻す) Flowers *revive* in water.
会話「もうよろしいんですか」「ええすっかり元気になりました」"Are you all right?" "Yes, I'm quite *all right* [quite *well*], thank you." (⇨形)

げんき 原器 the standard (for weights and measure). ●キログラム原器 a *standard* kilogram *weight*.

げんぎ 原義 the original meaning 《*of* a word》.

けんぎかい 県議会 a prefectural assembly.
●**県議会議員** a member of the prefectural assembly.

けんきせい 嫌気性 ●**嫌気性細菌** anaerobic /ænərόubik/ bacteria.

げんきづける 元気づける《勇気づける》encourage;《活気づける》cheer 《him》 up. ▶私は彼の言葉に元気づけられた I *was encouraged* by his words. ▶彼を少し元気づけてやらないといけない He needs a little *cheering up*.

けんきゃく 剣客 a swordsman; a fencer.
けんきゃく 健脚《足の達者な人》a good [a strong] walker.

けんきゅう 研究 名 (a) study 《*of, on, in*》; research 《*on, in*》 《しばしば複数形で》.

使い分け **study** 知識獲得のための研究・勉強のこと。しばしば one's studies で個人の研究活動などさす。**research** study より学術的で, 新事実などの発見をめざす研究・調査のこと。不可算名詞なので a や数詞などを伴わないが, 複数形で用いることがある。

① 【～研究】 ●文学の研究 the *study of* literature. ●カントの研究(書名で) *Studies on* Kant (❗学問領域には in を用いる: Studies *in* Philosophy); (論文名で) A *Study of* Kant. ●共同研究 (⇨共同[共同研究]) ●物理学の(分野における)最近のすぐれた研究 an excellent piece of recent *research* in (the field of) physics. ●電子工学の基礎研究 basic *research* in electronics.

② 【研究～】 ●研究結果 *research* results [findings]. ●研究目的で for *research*. ▶彼は研究心旺盛(❗)(=研究熱心だ) He is eager in his *studies*./(何でも知りたがる) He is curious about everything.

③ 【研究を】 ●研究を重ねる conduct a series of *studies*. ▶彼はエイズの原因についての研究を始めた He began his *researches into* the causes of AIDS. ▶この結果が正しいことを証明するには, さらに研究を進める必要がある Further *studies* are needed to prove these results right. ▶インフルエンザの流行に備えてワクチンの研究(=探究)を急ぐ必要があります We need to speed up the *search for* a flu vaccine in case the flu epidemic breaks out.

── **研究する** 動 study; make* [do*, conduct] a

げんきゅう study 《*of*》; do [carry out, conduct, ×make] research 《*on, into, in*》; research 《*on, into, in*》. (!)学科については他動詞を用いる。●西田教授のもとで哲学を研究する *study* philosophy under Prof. Nishida. ▶彼は文学を研究している He *is studying* literature. (!)×He is making a study of literature. は不可. a study は「ある一つの study」を示し, literature のような学問全体をさす語とは用いない (⇨図①)) ▶彼らは放射能を研究している They *are doing research* [×a research] *on* [*into*] radioactivity. (!)*into* の方がより精密な研究を示す)/They are engaged in radioactivity *research*.
- **研究員** a reséarch wòrker; a researcher.
- **研究会** a seminar; (小規模な) a workshop.
- **研究開発** research and development (略 R&D). • **研究機関** a research institútion. • **研究室** a study (room); (大学教授個人の) an office; (科学実験の) a laboratory; 《話》 a lab. • **研究者** (文科系の) a scholar; (自然科学系の) a scientist; 《書·古》 a student 《*of*》. • **研究所** (⇨研究所)
- **研究生** a reséarch stùdent. • **研究生活** one's life of research; one's life as a researcher.
- **研究チーム** a reséarch tèam [《グループ》gròup].
- **研究費** reséarch fùnds [expènses]. (!)前の方が「資金」, 後の方が「経費」の意)

げんきゅう 言及 图 (a) reference, (a) mention.
— **言及する** 動 mention; refer (-rr-) to ..., make reference to ...; 《触れる》touch on .... ▶彼は本の中でその理論について言及した He *referred to* the theory in his book.

げんきゅう 原級 《文法》the positive class; 《もとの学年》the same [original] class. ●原級にとどめる keep 《him》in *the same class* [*grade*] for another year; keep 《him》back to repeat *the same grade*.

げんきゅう 減給 a cut in salary, a salary cut. ●1割の減給になる take a ten percent *cut in salary*.

けんきゅうじょ 研究所 (専門的研究を行う) an [a research] institute; (科学実験·調査を行う) a (research) laboratory.

けんぎゅうせい 牽牛星 《天文》Altair /æltéər/.

***けんきょ** 謙虚 图 modesty.
— **謙虚な** 形 (控えめな) modest; (素直な) humble.
● 人の忠告を謙虚に聞く listen *humbly* to 《his》advice; take 《his》advice *humbly*. ▶あの人は自分の行いに非常に謙虚です He is very *modest about* his behavior. ▶あの人は前より謙虚になった He became more *modest* than before. (!)*modester* than は今は《古》)

けんきょ 検挙 图 an arrest. (⇨逮捕) — **検挙する** 動 arrest.

けんぎょう 兼業 ▶ぼくの家は兼業農家です My father is a farmer with a side job. (!)農業が主)/(片手間に農業が主) My father does [is engaged in] farming on the side. (!)農業が従)

げんきょう 元凶 (悪い事の根本的原因) the prime cause of the evils /íːvlz/.

げんきょう 原郷 one's spiritual home; (説明的に) an actual or imaginary home where one can regain one's true self and peace of mind.

げんきょう 現況 the present state [condition].

げんきょく 原曲 the original piece of music; the original melody [song]. ▶この曲の原曲はスコットランドの民謡だ This song *is based on* a Scottish folk song.

けんきん 献金 图 (a) contribution, (a) donation 《*to*》. (!)いずれも「寄付金」の意で [C])●政治献金 a political *contribution* [*donation*].
— **献金する** 動 contribute; donate; make a contribution [a donation] 《*of* 100,000 yen》. (⇨寄付する)
● **献金箱** (キリスト教会の) an óffertory bòx.

***げんきん** 現金 ❶ [お金] cash. ●現金3万ドルを現金で受け取る receive a *cash* downpayment of 30,000 dollars [a downpayment of 30,000 dollars in *cash*]. ▶今手元に現金がない I am out of (↔in) *cash* now./(持ち合わせがない) I have no (ready) *cash* on [with] me. (!)金などの小物はonが普通) ▶この小切手を現金に換えてくれない Can [Could] you *cash* this check for me?/I'd like to have this check *cashed*, please. (!)have + 目的語 + 過去分詞の構文で「換えてもらいたい」の意)/I'd like to change this check, please. ▶株を少し現金化したい I'd like to *redeem* some of my stocks [*turn* some of my stocks *into cash*]. (!)後の方が口語的) ▶そんな多額の現金をそろえるのは無理だ We can't get that much *cash* together. ▶自動車を現金で買った I bought a car *for* [*in*] *cash*./I paid (*in*) *cash* for a car. ▶支払いは現金でも月賦でも結構です You may pay [Payment may be made] either *by cash* or (by) monthly installments. (!)この cash は「即金」の意で, 小切手·手形などを含む) ▶あの店は現金でしか物を売らない That store sells only *for cash*. / (現金取引でのみ商売する) They do business only *on a cash basis* at that store.
会話 「それをいただくわ」「お支払いは現金ですか. それともカードですか」「現金で払います」 "I'll take it." "Would this be *cash* or charge?" "I'll pay (in) *cash*." (!)「ビザカードで」は with Visa, 「小切手で」なら by check という)
❷ [その他の表現] ▶彼は現金(=打算的)なやつだ He is a *calculating* [a *mercenary*] fellow.
● **現金売り** (a) cash sale. ●**現金書留** (by) registered mail. 事情 米英では現金専用の書留はない
- **現金残高** (a) cash balance. ●**現金自動預払い機** an automatic [an automated] teller machine (略 ATM). ●**現金収支** cash flow. ●**現金取引** (a) cash transaction; (a) transaction for cash. ●**現金問屋** a cash-and-carry wholesaler.
- **現金払い** a cash payment. ●**現金販売** a cash sale; a sale for cash. ●**現金割引** a cash discount.

げんきん 厳禁 a strict prohibition. (⇨禁止) ▶ここでは喫煙は厳禁です Smoking *is strictly forbidden* [*prohibited*] here. ▶火気厳禁《掲示》(引火物注意) Flammables.
— **厳禁する** 動 ●生徒の飲酒を厳禁する *strictly forbid* pupils *to* drink; 《書》*strictly prohibit* pupils *from* drinking.

げんくん 元勲 an elder [a veteran] statesman.

げんけい 原形 the original form. ▶山中に墜落した飛行機は原形をとどめていなかった The plane that crashed in the mountains was wrecked beyond recognition.
● **原形質** 《生物》prótoplàsm; plasma.

げんけい 原型 a prótotype 《*of*》; (ひな型) a model 《*of*》.

げんけい 減刑 图 (a) reduction of a sentence; (死刑に対して) 《書》a commutation.
— **減刑する** 動 reduce [commute] a sentence 《*to*》.

げんけい 厳刑 a severe [《重い》a heavy] punishment.

げんけいしつ 原形質 《生理》protoplasm.

けんげき 剣劇 a sword-fighting play.

けんけつ 献血 名 《receive》a blood donation.
―― **献血する** 動 donate [give] blood.
- **献血者** a blood donor. ● **献血車** 《米》a bloodmobile, 《英》a mobile blood donation unit.
- **献血手帳** a blood donor's card.

けんけん ―― **けんけんする** 動 hop [jump] using one leg.

けんげん 権限 [法律などに基づいて命令を強制する] authority 《over＋人, for＋事; to do》; [委任された] (a) power 《of, over; to do》(**!** しばしば複数形で).
- 部下に権限を行使させる exercise one's *authority* [*power*] over one's staff. ● 彼が文書に署名する権限を与える give him the *authority* [*power*] to sign the documents; *authorize* him to sign the documents. ▶彼には最終的な決定を下す権限がある He has the *authority* [*power*] to make the final decision./He *is authorized* to make the final decision. ▶それは営業部長の権限を越える行為です That is an action outside the *authority of* [*as*] a business manager./It is beyond the business manager's *power* to do that.

けんげん 顕現 名 (a) manifestation.
―― **顕現する** 動 manifest itself.

けんけんがくがく 喧々諤々 (⇒侃々(カンカン)諤々)

けんけんごうごう 喧々囂々 名 ▶氏の不注意な発言に喧々囂々たる抗議の声があがった His careless speech sparked *storms* [*howls*] *of* protest.

けんけんふくよう 拳々服膺 ▶その言葉を拳々服膺せよ The words should be engraved in your memory. ▶You must bear the words firmly in mind.

けんご 堅固 ―― **堅固な** 形 (強固な) strong; (しっかりした) firm; (堅くて動かない) solid.
―― **堅固に** 副 strongly; firmly; solidly.
―― **堅固にする** 動 strengthen; make 《it》solid.

げんこ 拳骨 (げんこつ) (a) clenched fist. (⇒拳骨)

***げんご 言語** 名 (a) language; [話し言葉] speech. (⇒言葉❶) ● 二[多]言語使用の bilingual [multilingual]. ―― **言語の** 形 linguistic.
- **言語学** (⇒言語学) ● **言語習得** language acquisition. ● **言語障害** a speech defect [impediment]. ● **言語生活** language life; the linguistic aspects of life. ● **言語政策** language policy; language planning.

げんご 原語 the original language; [原文, 原書] the original (text). ●ゲーテを原語で読む read Goethe /gə́ːrtə/ *in the original*.

けんこう 健康 名 (good) health.
① [健康(の)～] ● 健康診断を受ける have a *check-up*; have a physical (examination) (**!** (1) 《話》 では a physical だけで用いられることが多い. (2) ×a health examination とはいわない); 《やや書》 undergo a medical examination. ● 彼の健康状態を調べる check his physical condition. ● 健康のためにジョギングする jog for one's *health*; jog to improve one's *health*. ● 健康のありがたさは失ってみて初めて分かる You do not appreciate the blessing of *good health* until you lose it. ▶彼は健康上の理由で辞職した He resigned his post [position] for *health* reasons [because of *ill health*]. ▶完全な健康体でなければ宇宙へ行くことは許されません If you are not completely *healthy*, you will not be allowed to go into space. ▶子供たちが暇さえあればゲームセンターに入りびたっているのは健康的ではないと思う I don't think it's *healthy* for kids to spend all their time at the (penny) arcade. ▶彼女は一見健康そうに見えるけれど実際は心臓が悪い She's apparently *healthy* but actually she has heart trouble.

② [健康が[は]] ● 母の健康がすぐれない (一時的に) My mother is not very [quite] *well*. (**!** 修飾語を伴わないで well を単独で用いることはまれ)/My mother's *health* is not very good. (継続的に) 《やや書》 My mother is *in bad* [*poor*] *health*. (**!** My mother is not *healthy*. とはあまりいわない. また ×My mother's body is not *healthy*. は不可) ▶彼の健康は衰えてきた He is failing [declining] in *health*./His *health* is failing [declining]. ▶私は彼の健康が気がかりだ I'm anxious about his *health*. ▶健康は富にまさる 《ことわざ》 *Health is above* [*better than*] *wealth*.

③ [健康を] ● 健康を保つ keep *fit*; 《古》 keep one's *health*; keep [stay, remain] *healthy*. ▶酒を飲みすぎると健康をそこなう(＝危うくする)ことになるよ 《人が主語》 You will risk [(失う) lose] your *health* if you drink too much. (**!** 日常会話では get [get] sick などの方が普通 (⇒病気); 《物が主語》 Too much drinking will damage [ruin, harm] your *health*. ● 健康を害している be out of *health*. ● 健康を取り戻す recover [regain] one's *health*. ● 水泳をして健康を増進する improve [promote] one's *health* by swimming. ▶ご健康を祈りますI wish you *good health*. ▶あなたの健康を祝して乾杯 Your (very) *good health*!/Let's drink to your *health*! ● 彼は今では健康を取り戻して働けるまでになっている Now he is *fit* and able to work.

④ [健康に] ● 健康によい healthy, 《米》 healthful; wholesome. ● 健康によい食事 a *healthy* meal; a meal good for the health. ● 健康に恵まれる be blessed with *good health*. ▶これらの運動は健康によい These exercises are good (↔bad) *for* your *health* [the *health*, 《話》you]. (**!** for の代わりに to は不可) ▶喫煙は健康によくない Smoking is bad for the [your] *health*. (**!** ×for health は不可)/Smoking is injurious to (your) *health*. (**!** ×to the health は不可) ▶Smoking is harmful to (the [your]) *health*. ● 健康にはくれぐれも留意してください Please take good care of your *health* [yourself]. (**!** 聞き手の健康が思わしくないことを暗示することもあるので, 単に Take care. で十分な場合が多い) ▶君がもしたばこをやめればもっと健康になるだろう If you stop smoking, your *health* will improve.

―― **健康な** 形 healthy; well*, 《やや話》fine; fit (-tt-); sound; robust.

> 使い分け **healthy** 身体も心もすこやかで問題がないこと. 人間本来の望ましい健康状態をさす.
> **well** 病気やお産から回復した健康状態をさす.
> **fit** テストや試合, 旅行に堪えるだけの体力があって健康状態が良いことをさす.
> **sound** 心身ともに欠陥のない状態をさす.
> **robust** 頑丈でたくましいことをさす.

● 健康な体[肉体] a *healthy* body. ● 健康な心[精神] a *sound* mind. ● 心身ともに健康な人 a person who is *sound* in mind and body [is *healthy* mentally and physically].
- **健康管理** health care. ● **健康食** a health diet.
- **健康食品** health food(s) (**!** 種類に言及する場合でも単数形の方が普通); (健康によい食べ物) healthy [《米・書》healthful] food(s). ● **健康診断書** a health report. ● **健康法** how to keep fit [healthy]. ● **健康保険** health insurance.

けんこう 兼行 ● 昼夜兼行で働く work *day and night* [24時間休みなく] (a)*round the clock*.

けんこう 軒昂 ● 意気軒昂だ be in high spirits; be elated.

- **げんごう 剣豪** a great swordsman; a master fencer.
- ***げんこう 原稿** (手書き・タイプによる) a manuscript; (草稿, 下書き) a draft; (印刷前の) a copy; (投稿) a contribution. ◆ (400字詰め)原稿用紙 10枚 ten sheets of *manuscript* paper (ruled off into 400 squares). ◆コンピュータで原稿を書く write [prepare] a *manuscript* (on a computer).
  - 原稿料 pay (for the writing).
- **げんこう 言行** one's words and deeds. ▶彼の言行は一致しない His *words* do not agree with his *deeds*./He says one thing and does another.
  - 言行録 one's memoirs; a written record of one's words and deeds.
- **げんこう 現行** ── 現行(の) 形 (現在の) present; (現在通用している) current; (現存の) existing; (今使用されている) now in use; (後位修飾に) (法律などが効力を持つ) in force. ◆現行制度 the *present* [*current, existing*] system. ◆現行の教科書 the textbooks *now in use*. ◆現行法のもとでは under the law *in force*; under the *existing* law.
- **げんごう 元号** (年号) the name of an era; (説明的に) a name given to the period of an emperor's reign.
- **けんこうこつ 肩甲骨** 〖解剖〗a scapula /skǽpjələ/ (⑱ scapulae /-liː/, ~s); (一般的には) a shoulder blade. (🖉 a shoulder bone は《まれ》)
- **げんこうはん 現行犯** ▶彼がさいふを盗んだところを現行犯で捕まえる catch [seize, arrest] him *in the act of* stealing a wallet; catch him *red-handed* stealing a wallet. (🖉 以上いずれも catch では単に目撃する場合も含む)
- **げんごがく 言語学** 图 linguistics. (🖉 単数扱い)
  - ── 言語学(上)の 形 linguistic.
  - 言語学者 a linguist.
- **けんこく 建国** the foundation of a nation.
  - 建国記念の日 National Founding [Foundation] Day.
- **げんこく 原告** a plaintiff (⑱ ~s) (↔a defendant; (告発者) an accuser.
- **げんこつ 拳骨** a fist; (げんこつ打ち)《give him [get]》a punch. (殴る) ◆げんこつで机をどんどんたたく pound a desk with one's *fist*.
- **げんごろう 源五郎** 〖昆虫〗a Japanese water beetle.
- **げんごろうぶな 源五郎鮒** 〖魚介〗a gengoro crucian.
- **けんこん 乾坤** heaven and earth.
  - 乾坤一擲(いってき) risking death [everything]; staking all one's money. ▶その新事業に乾坤一擲の賭けをする stake all one's fortune on the new business. ▶信長は乾坤一擲の(=のるかそるかの)桶狭間の戦いに勝利した Nobunaga won the neck-or-nothing battle of Okehazama.
- **‡けんさ 検査** 图 (綿密に調べること) (an) examination; 〖点検〗a check; (an) inspection; (ある基準に合うか否かを試すこと) a test. ◆ 検査入院をする be hospitalized for *tests*.
  - ①〖~検査〗◆安全検査 a sáfety inspèction; a sáfety chèck. ◆抜き取り検査 a random *inspection*. ◆品物の品質検査 a *check on* the quality of the goods. ◆放射能(を探すための)検査 a radiation *test*; a *test for* radiation.
  - ②〖検査を〗▶私は視力検査を受けた I had an eyesight *test*./(検査してもらった) I had my eyesight *tested* [*checked*]. ▶医者に精密検査をしてもらいなさい See a doctor for a complete *physical* (*examination*). (⇨検診)
- ── 検査する 動 examine, make* an examination (*of*); check, make a check (*of, on*); inspect, make an inspection (*of*); test, give* a test (*of, for*). ◆井戸の水を検査する *examine* [*test*] the water of a well. ◆品物を検査する *inspect* [*make an inspection of*] the goods. ◆大気中の放射能を検査する *test* the air *for* radiation. (⇨図①) ▶私の荷物は税関で入念に検査された My baggage *was* closely *checked* [*inspected*] at the customs.
- **けんざい 建材** 〖「建築資材」の略〗building matèrials. ▶新建材に含まれる化学物質で健康を害している人がいる Some people suffer from chemicals used in the new *building materials*. (🖉 「化学合成物を使った建材」と考え, synthetic building materials と訳すこともある)
- **けんざい 健在** ▶両親はまだ健在です (Both of) my parents are still *in good health* [*alive and well*]. (⇨元気な)
- **けんざい 顕在** ── 顕在(化)する 動 become actual, be actualized; (はっきり分かる) be manifest; (感知できる) be tangible.
  - 顕在失業 actual (↔invisible) unemployment.
- **けんさい 減債** 图 partial payment of a debt.
  - ── 減債する 動 sink 《a debt》.
  - 減債基金 a sinking fund.
- **‡げんざい 現在** 图 the present; (今) now; (こんにち) today. ▶時には現在を将来のために犠牲にしなければならないことがある We must sometimes sacrifice *the present* to the future. ▶現在までのところすべてうまくいっている Up *to the present* [*Up to now, So far*] everything has gone well. (🖉 現在完了形とともに用いる)
  - ── 現在(は) 副 now; today; (今のところは) at present; as of now. (⇨今❶) ▶現在多くの人がこの分野で働いている Many people work in this field *now* [*today*]. ▶現在その件は調査中です The matter is under investigation *at present* [*now*]./The matter is *now* [*currently*] under investigation. ▶当社が発注した商品は今日現在届いておりません《商用文》The merchandise we ordered has not arrived *as of today*.
  - ── 現在の 形 present; (現在ある) existing; (現時点での, 現行の) current. (⇨今❶②) ◆現在の状況では under *present* [*existing*] conditions. ◆現在の市場金利 the *current* rate of interest. ◆2007年4月1日現在の内閣 the Cabinet *as of* April 1, 2007. ▶現在のご住所はどこですか What [×Where] is your *present* address?/Where do you live *now*? ▶現在の生活費では車を買う余裕なんてない With the cost of living *what* [*as*] *it is* (*today*), I can't afford (to get) a car.
  - 現在価値〖経済〗present value [worth]. ◆現在完了〖文法〗the present perfect. ◆現在時制〖文法〗the present tense. ◆現在進行形〖文法〗the present progressive form. ◆現在地 (地図などの掲示) You are here. ◆現在分詞〖文法〗the present participle.
- **げんざい 原罪** original sin.
- **げんざいりょう 原材料** raw [crude] materials. ▶原材料価格の急激な値上がり a sharp rise in the price of *raw materials*.
- **けんさく 研削** 图 grinding. ── 研削する 動 grind 《a stone》.
  - 研削盤 a grinder.
- **けんさく 検索** 图 (参照) reference; (データの呼び出し)〖コンピュータ〗access.
  - ── 検索する 動 refer to 《index cards》;〖コンピュータ〗access; (索引を使う) use an index. ◆コンピュー

けんさく タで情報[ファイル]を検索する *access* information [files] *from* a computer. ●インターネットでデータを検索する *search* the Internet *for* the data. ▶この本には検索しやすいように索引がついている This book has an index for easy *reference*.
●検索エンジン『コンピュータ』a search engine.

けんさく 献策 图 (a) suggestion; advice.
── 献策する 動 ●販売促進について社長に献策する *suggest* sales promotion *to* one's president; *advise* one's president *on* sales promotion.

げんさく 原作 the original (work). ●シェイクスピアを原作で読む read Shakespeare *in the original*.
●原作者（著者）the author;（作家）the writer.

けんさつ 検札 (a) ticket inspection. ▶まだ車掌が検札にやってこない The conductor hasn't come to *inspect* [*check*] our tickets yet.
●検札係 a ticket inspector.

けんさつ 検察 ●検察側 the prosecution. ●検察側の証人 a *prosecution* witness; a witness for *the prosecution*.
●検察官 a (public) prosecutor.（⇒検事）●検察審査会 the Committee for Inquest into the Prosecution. ●検察庁 a public prosecutor's office. ●検察当局 the prosecution.

けんさん 研鑽 hard study. ── 研鑽を積む study hard; devote oneself to one's studies.

けんざん 見参 ── 見参する 動 have the pleasure of seeing [meeting]《him》.

けんざん 検算 ── 検算する 動 check [go over, go through]《the accounts》.

げんさん 原産 图『源』origin.
── 原産の 形 native. ●日本原産の猿 a *native* Japanese monkey. ▶キウイは中国原産だ The kiwi fruit is *native* to China [a *native of* China].
●原産国 the country of origin. ●原産地（⇒原産地）

げんさん 減産 图（自然的）a decrease in production [output];（人為的）a reduction of production [output]. ▶この工場は20パーセントの減産であった The *output* of this factory *has dropped* [*decreased*] (by) 20 percent.
── 減産する 動 ●鋼鉄を15パーセント減産する *cut* [*reduce*,《書》*curtail*] steel production by 15 percent.

げんさんち 原産地 the place of origin; the home《of》. ●コーヒーの原産地 the (*original*) *home* of the coffee plant.
●原産地証明書 a certificate of origin. ●原産地表示 a place-of-origin label.

けんし 犬歯 a dogtooth《(匯) dogteeth》;（特に上の犬歯）an eyetooth《(匯) eyeteeth》;『解剖』a canine (tooth《(匯) teeth》).

けんし 検死, 検視 图 『死因審問』a (coroner's) inquest;[検死解剖] an autopsy /5:tɑpsi/, a postmortem (examination). ▶その子は検死の結果溺死ではなく窒息死したことが明らかになった The *autopsy* *on* the child showed that it had not drowned but had died of suffocation.
── 検死[検視]する 動 hold an inquest《*on* a corpse》; hold [do, carry out] a postmortem《*on*》.
●検死官 a coroner.

けんし 献詞 图（⇒献辞）
けんし 絹糸 silk thread.
けんじ 健児 a vigorous [a stalwart] youth.
けんじ 堅持 图（固守）(an) adherence.
── 堅持する 動《やや書》adhere to ...; stick to ....
●自説を堅持する *adhere* [*stick*] *to* one's opinion.

けんじ 検事 a public prosecutor.
●検事局 the public prosecutor's office. ●検事総長 the Public Prosecutor General;《米》the Attorney General;《英》the Director of Public Prosecutions. ●検事長 a chief public prosecutor;《米》a chief prosecuting attorney. ●検事補 a probational public prosecutor.

けんじ 献辞 图 a dedication.
けんじ 顕示 图 (a) revelation; (a) manifestation.
●自己顕示欲（⇒自己）
── 顕示する 動 show; reveal.

*げんし 原子 图 an atom. ── 原子の 形 atomic;（核の）nuclear.
●原子エネルギー atomic [nuclear] energy. ●原子価『化学』《主に米》a valence,《主に英》a valency. ●原子核 an atomic nucleus《(匯) nuclei /njú:kliəi/》. ●原子記号 an atomic symbol. ●原子雲 an atomic cloud; a mushroom cloud. ●原子構造『物理』atomic structure. ●原子番号『化学』an atomic number. ●原子病『医学』an atomic disease;（放射線病）radiation sickness. ●原子物理学 nuclear physics.《単数扱い》●原子量『化学』atomic weight. ●原子炉 a nuclear reactor.（⇒原子炉）;《和語》an atomic reactor.

げんし 幻視 a visual hallucination.（⇒幻覚）
げんし 原始 ── 原始の, 原始的な 形（文明発達の初期段階の）primitive;（未開で野蛮な）uncivilized. ●原始的な部族 an *uncivilized* tribe.
●原始時代 primitive [primeval /praimí:vl/] ages.（⇒後の方が古い）●原始人 primitive man. ●原始文明 primitive civilization. ●原始林 primeval forests.

げんし 原紙 (謄写版の) a stencil; stencil paper.
げんし 原資 (government) funds for investment and loans. ●ボーナスの原資 *funds* for bonuses.
げんし 減資 a reduction of [a decrease in] capital.
── 減資する 動 reduce capital.

げんじ 源氏 (一族) the Genji clan.（⇒源氏物語）
●源氏名(ˆ) a professional name of a geisha, a bar hostess or the like.

*けんしき 見識 ❶[判断力] judgment;（洞察力）(an) insight;（ものの見方）a view. ●見識のある人 a person of (good) *judgment* [(great) *insight*]. ●高い見識を示す show good [excellent] *judgment*《*in*》. ▶彼は政治に関しては高い見識を持っている He has a great *insight into* politics.
❷[気位] pride;（威厳）dignity. ●見識張る be full of *pride*; stand on one's *dignity*;《やや書》assume an air of importance.

けんじつ 堅実 图（着実）steadiness.
── 堅実な 形（着実な）steady;（信頼できる）reliable, trustworthy;（考えなどが健全な）sound. ●堅実な若者 a *steady* [a *reliable*] young person.
── 堅実に 副（着実に）steadily.

‡**げんじつ** 現実 图 a reality; (an) actuality.（! reality は偽りや作り話でないこと. actuality は想像や夢でなく実際に存在すること）
①【～現実, 現実～】●人生の厳しい現実 the harsh *realities* of life. ●現実離れした（＝空想上の）話 a *fantastic* story. ●超現実的 surreal /sərí:əl/.（⇒シュール）
②【現実は】●現実は違う The reality is different. ●現実は, 日本は今'デフレ状態にある The *reality* is that Japan is now in depression. ▶現実は厳しい *Reality* is cruel.
③【現実に[から]】●現実には in *reality*, in the

real world. ●現実にある (実在する) exist in the *real* world. ●現実に (実際に起こる) happen in *real* life. ●現実にあり得ない be impossible in *real* life [this world, the real world]. ●現実から逃避する escape from *reality*. ●現実に近い作り話 a fiction which is exactly like a true story. ▶私の夢は現実になった (=なった) My dream *has come true*./ My dream *has become* a reality [*has been realized*]. ▶私はその物音で現実に引き戻された (現実の時間に) I was brought back to *the present* by the sound. (現実世界[日常]の世界に) The sound *brought* me *down to earth*. ▶それが現実に起こる (のもそう遠い将来ではないことは歴史を見れば分かる History proves it will *be* (*a*) *reality* in the not-so-distant future.
④【現実を】● 現実を直視[無視]する face [ignore] *reality*. ●現実を否定する deny the real situation [actual conditions]; deny reality. ▶『オリバーツイスト』は人生の悲惨な現実をあますところなく描き出している *Oliver Twist* shows life in all its miserable *reality* [all the miserable *realities* of life]. ▶この問題に現実を踏まえて対処しよう Let's be *realistic* about this problem. ▶現実を現実として認めなければならない We must accept reality as it is [things as they come].
— 現実の 形 real; actual. ▶彼はそこで現実の問題に直面している He is up against a *real* problem there.
— 現実的な 形 realistic. ●現実的な物の見方をする take a *realistic* view 《*of*》. ▶彼は現実的だ He is a *realistic* man [a realist]./He is down to earth [a down-to-earth person].
— 現実に 副 actually; (本当に) really. (⇨実際 ③) ▶現実に事故を目撃した I *actually* saw the accident.
●現実化 realization. ●現実化する (願望・計画などが) be realized. ●現実主義 realism. ●現実主義者 a realist. ●現実性 (⇨現実性) ●現実生活 real [actual] life. ●現実世界 the real [actual] world.

げんじつせい 現実性 〖現実の実態〗reality; practicality; 〖現実に起こりうる可能性〗possibility; reality. ●現実性に富んでいる have a strong [real, distinct] *possibility*. ▶我々は雇用の厳しい現実性を認識した We now realize the harsh *reality* of looking for a job. ▶その話は現実性に乏しい That story is outside the bounds of *possibility*.

げんじてん 現時点 〖今〗at the present time; (今のところ) for the present.

げんしばくだん 原子爆弾 an atòmic bómb; an átom bòmb, 《古》an A-bomb. ▶我が国に2個の原子爆弾が投下された Two *atomic bombs* were dropped on our country.

げんじぼたる 源氏蛍 【昆虫】a *Genji* firefly.

げんじものがたり 『源氏物語』 *The Tale of Genji*. (〖参考〗紫式部の物語)

けんしゃ 検車 an inspection of motor vehicles. ●検車係 an inspector of motor vehicles.

けんじゃ 賢者 a wise man; a sage.

けんじゃのおくりもの 『賢者の贈り物』 *The Gift of the Magi*. (〖参考〗オー・ヘンリーの小説)

けんしゅ 堅守 名 strong [〖頑強な〗stubborn] defense. — 堅守する 動 defend 《a castle》stoutly.

げんしゅ 元首 the head of state; 《書》a sovereign /sávərin/.

げんしゅ 原酒 (日本酒の) unprocessed *sake*; (ウイスキーの) malt whiskey

げんしゅ 原種 (種を取るための) seed stock, seed grain; (改良種などのもとになる) a pure breed [stock]; the wild [original] breed [strain].

げんしゅ 厳守 名 〖厳しく守ること〗strict observance.
— 厳守する 動 ●交通規則を厳守する *observe* traffic rules *strictly*. ●時間を厳守する be punctual. (〖!〗「時間厳守」は punctuality)

けんしゅう 研修 〖研究〗study (〖!〗複数形もほぼ同意で用いる); 〖訓練〗(a) training (〖!〗複数形にしない). ●職場研修 on-the-job *training*. ●サンフランシスコに英語研修に行くよ go to San Francisco to *study* English. ▶我々は3日間の研修を受けた We got [were given] *training* for three days. (〖!〗We received [were provided] *training*.... は《やや書》)
●研修生 a trainee /treiní:/. ●研修旅行 《make, take, go on》a study trip 〖周遊の〗 a study tour》.

けんじゅう 拳銃 a pistol; a gun. (〖!〗ピストル) ●拳銃の名手 a good [〖話〗a dead, crack] shot. ▶表で拳銃の音がした I heard a shot outside.

げんしゅう 減収 a décrease [a drop] in income [(売り上げの) sales, (税収の) tax revenues, (収穫の) the crops]. (⇔ 増収) ▶今月は5万円の減収になった My *income decréased* [*dropped*] by fifty thousand yen this month.

*げんじゅう 厳重 — 厳重な 形 (厳正な) strict; (苛酷(ᵏᵒᵏ)などと厳しい) severe; (綿密な) close; (語調などがきつい) strong. (⇔厳格) ●厳重な点検 a *close* [(徹底的な) a *thorough*] inspection.
— 厳重に 副 strictly; severely; closely; strongly. ▶囚人を厳重に監視している keep a *strict* [a *close*] watch *on* [*over*] a prisoner. ●厳重に罰せられる be *severely* punished. ●厳重な警告を give a *strong* warning 《*to*》. ▶私たちはそのことについて政府に厳重に抗議した We *strongly* protested [made a *strong* protest] against the government about it.

げんじゅうしょ 現住所 the present address.

げんじゅうみん 原住民 an original [a native,《書》an indigenous /indídʒənəs/] inhabitant; 《今はまれ》a native (〖!〗個人をさす場合は, 特に, 貧困・無教養を暗示し蔑視的); an aborigine /æbərídʒəni:/. ●アメリカの原住民 a *Native* American. (〖!〗今は an American Indian に代わってこの言い方が一般) ▶アボリジニはオーストラリアの原住民だ The Aborigines are the *original inhabitants* of Australia.

けんしゅく 厳粛 名 solemnity.
— 厳粛な 形 (荘重な) solemn /sáləm/; (威厳のある) grave; (逃すことを許さない) hard, severe. ●厳粛な光景 〖発表〗a *solemn* sight [announcement]. ●厳粛な儀式 a *solemn* [a *grave*] ceremony. ●厳粛な顔つき a *grave* look. ●厳粛な事実 a *solid* fact. ▶死は人生で最も厳粛な事実である Death is the *hardest* fact in life.
— 厳粛に 副 ▶その決定を厳粛に (=深刻に) 受け止める take the decision *seriously*. ▶彼の葬儀は厳粛に行われた His funeral was *solemnly* performed.

けんしゅつ 検出 名 〖見えないものを探り当てること〗detection.
— 検出する 動 ▶死んだ男の胃の中には毒物は検出されなかった No poison *was detected* [They didn't *find* any poison] in the dead man's stomach. (〖!〗後の方が口語的)
●検出器 a detector.

けんじゅつ 剣術 (⇨剣道)

げんじゅつ 幻術 (⇨⑩ 魔術)

げんしょ 原初 名 the first; (起源) the origin; (根源)

the source. ● 宇宙の原初 the *origin* of universe.
── 原初の 形 *first*; *original*.
げんしょ 原書 the *original* (work [text]). ● ホメロスを原書で読む read Homer *in the original*.
げんしょ 厳暑 severe [intense, extreme] heat.
けんしょう 肩章 a shoulder strap; (将校の) an epaulet(te).
けんしょう 健勝 ● ご健勝にて何よりと存じます I'm glad to hear that you *are in good health*.
けんしょう 検証 图 (検査) (an) inspection; (実証) verification. ● 現場検証 an on-the-spot *inspection*.
── 検証する 動 inspect; 《やや書》verify.
けんしょう 憲章 a charter. ● 国際連合憲章 the *Charter* of the United Nations; the United Nations *Charter*.
けんしょう 顕彰 ── 顕彰する 動 ● 長年の功労を顕彰する *honor* (him) *in public* in recognition of many years of his meritorious services.
● 顕彰碑 a monument in honor of a person who rendered great service [contributed a great deal] 《to the community》.
けんしょう 懸賞 (競争などの) a prize; (謝礼) a reward. ● 懸賞論文 a *prize* essay. (⚠「受賞論文」の意もある) ● 懸賞を取る[に当たる] win a *prize*. ● 懸賞をかける offer a *prize* [a *reward*] 《*for*》; (犯人などに) put [set] a *price* [ˣa *prize*] 《*on* his head》.
● 懸賞コンクールに応募する enter a *prize* contest [competition].
けんじょう 献上 图 presentation.
── 献上する 動 present 《it *to* him; him *with* it》; offer 《it *to* him》.
● 献上品 a gift; a present.
けんじょう 謙譲 (慎み深さ) modesty; (へりくだり) humility. ● 謙譲の美徳 the virtue of *modesty*.
● 謙譲語 (単語) a modest word; (表現) a modest expression.
:げんしょう 現象 a phenomenon (複 phenomena). ● 一時的[まれな、よくある]現象 a passing [rare; common] *phenomenon*. ▶ 虹(にじ)は美しい自然現象である A rainbow is a beautiful natural *phenomenon*. ▶ 大学生の学力低下は世界的な現象らしい The fall of academic performance by college [university] students is apparently a global *phenomenon*.
● 現象論〖哲学〗phenomenalism.
*げんしょう 減少 图 (数量が減ること) (a) décrease; (減らすこと) (a) reduction; (ゆっくりとした下落)《やや書》a decline. ● 客の30パーセントの減少 a 30 percent *decrease* [a *decrease* of 30 percent] *in* the number of customers. ● 人口の減少 a *decrease* [a *decline*] *in* population; a *decreasing* population. ● 貿易黒字の減少 trade surplus *reduction*.
── 減少する 動 décrease; (徐々に) dwindle. (⇨減る) ● 5,000人に減少する *decrease* [*dwindle*] *to* 5,000 people. ▶ その国の人口は減少しつつある The population of the country *is decreasing* [*on the decrease*]. ▶ The country has a shrinking population. ▶ 出生率が徐々に減少してきた There has been a gradual *decrease* [*decline*] *in* the birthrate. / The birthrate has *decreased* [*dwindled*] gradually. / The birthrate has become lower and lower. ▶ 急激な円高により自動車輸出が減少した The sharp appreciation of the yen has caused auto exports to *decline*.
*げんじょう 現状 the present situation [condition, state of things]; the status quo /kwóu/. ● 最後の語は堅い語で主に政治の分野などで用いる) ● 現状では in the *present situation* [*state of things*]; under the *present conditions* [*circumstances*]; as *things are* [*go, stand*]. ● 現状を打破する[に対処する] break [meet] the *present situation*. ● 現状に甘んじる be content with *things as they are*. ▶ 彼の中国に対する認識は現状(=現実の状態)には程遠い His understanding of China is far from *what it* [《やや古》 *she*] *really is*. ▶ 彼らの賃金は現状維持がいいところ(=せいぜい)だろう Their wages will *stay the same* at best. ▶ 現状(=そのまま)でよい It's okay *as it is*.
げんじょう 原状 the original state [condition]. ● 原状に復する return to the *original state*.
けんしょうえん 腱鞘炎 〖医学〗tenosynovitis /tènousainəváitəs/. ● けんしょう炎になる 《患部が主語》develop *tenosynovitis*.
げんじょうしゃ 健常者 a person who is mentally and physically sound.
げんしょく 原色 a primary color. ● 三原色 the three *primary colors*. ● 原色図鑑 a book illustrated in *color*. ● どぎつい原色調のアロハ a *garish*-colored aloha shirt; an aloha shirt in *harsh* colors.
げんしょく 現職 [現在の職] the present post [(官職) office]. ● 現職者 (政治家など公職にある) an incúmbent; (一般に) a person currently in office. ● アメリカの現職大統領 the *incumbent* President of the United States. ● 現職の(=現役の)警官 a police officer *on active service*. ● 現職にとどまる remain [stay] in one's *present post* [*office*].
げんしょく 減食 ── 減食する 動 eat less; reduce one's diet.
げんしりょく 原子力 atomic [nuclear] energy; (動力としての) atomic [nuclear] power. ● 原子力の平和利用 peaceful use of *nuclear energy* [*atomic power*].
● 原子力潜水艦 a nuclear(-powered) [an atomic(-powered)] submarine. ● 原子力発電 nuclear [atomic] power generation. ● 原子力発電所 a nuclear [an atomic] power plant [《主に英》station].
げんじる 減じる 〖数量などを〗reduce, decréase, lessen (⇨減らす); 〖刑を〗《やや書》commute; 〖引く〗subtract (⇨引く ❸). ▶ 彼の刑を死刑から終身刑に減じる *commute* his sentence from death penalty to life imprisonment.
けんしん 健診 a (medical [physical]) checkup (⚠ 通例定期的な健康診断をいう); a medical [a physical] (examination) (⚠ 就職などのための健康診断。また単に an exam(ination)ともいう). ● 胃の集団検診 a group stomach *checkup* [*examination*]. ● 歯の定期検診を受ける have [take] a periodic [regular] dental *checkup*.
けんしん 検針 图 an inspection of a meter; meter-reading.
── 検針する 動 ● ガスのメーターを検針する read a gas meter.
● 検針員 a meter reader [attendant].
けんしん 献身 图 devotion 《*to*》; (自己犠牲) self-sacrifice.
── 献身的の 形 (人・事が) self-sacrificing; (人が) devoted. ▶ その看護師は患者を献身的に看護した The nurse *devoted* herself *to* attending [*devotedly* attended] on her patients./The nurse gave a *self-sacrificing* care to her patients.
── 献身する 動 ▶ 彼は難民救済に献身した He *devoted*

けんじん himself [his energies] *to help*ing refugees.

けんじん 県人 a native of a prefecture. ● 奈良県人会 a society of people from Nara Prefecture.

けんじん 堅陣 a stronghold; a strong position.

けんじん 賢人 a wise person;《書》a sage. ● 賢人会議 a wise men's conference.

げんしん 原審 (原裁判) the original trial; (原判決) the original verdict [decision]; (原判決) the original [judgment] of the lower court. ● 原審を破棄するoverrule [overturn] *the original verdict*; reverse *the decision of the lower court*.

げんじん 原人 a primitive [a primeval] man; (猿人) a pithecanthropus. ● ジャワ原人 Java *man*.

けんしんれい 堅信礼 confirmation.

げんず 原図 the original drawing [plan, map].

けんすい 建水 (水こぼし)《米》a slop jar,《英》a slop basin [bowl].

けんすい 懸垂 图 (1回の)《主に米》a chin-up,《英》a pull-up.
── 懸垂する 動 do chin-ups (**!** 「3回懸垂する」は do three chin-ups); do chinning exercises; chin oneself.

げんすい 元帥 『陸軍』《米》a general of the army,《米話》a five-star general,《英》a field marshal; 『海軍』《米》a fleet admiral,《英》an admiral of the fleet.

げんすいばく 原水爆 atomic and hydrogen bombs, A- and H-bombs (**!** 政治的文脈では the bomb); (核爆弾) nuclear bombs.
● 原水爆禁止運動 a movement against atomic and hydrogen bombs (核兵器) nuclear weapons).

けんすう 件数 (事件の数) the number of cases. ▶交通事故の件数がうなぎ登りだ *The number of* car accidents is [xare] skyrocketing.

げんすんだいの 原寸大の (実物大の) full-scale; (等身大の) life-size(d).

げんせ 現世 this world [life]. ● 現世の楽しみ *worldly [earthly]* pleasures. ● 現世と来世 *this world* and the next.
● 現世利益 divine grace [blessing and favor] in this world.

けんせい 牽制 图 (制止) (a) check; (抑制) (a) restraint. ● 一塁へ牽制球を投げる 『野球』 make a pick-off throw to first; throw over to first. (**!**「牽制球で刺す」は pick ... off) ▶彼は一塁への牽制がうまい He has a good (*pick-off*) move to first.
── 牽制する 動 check; lay a restraint 《on》.
● 牽制プレー a pick-off play.

けんせい 憲政 (立憲政治) constitutional government. ● 憲政を敷く set up [establish] a *constitutional government*. (**!** 政府の意では [C])

けんせい 権勢 (権力) power; (勢力) influence. ● 権勢を振るう wield *power*, 《やや書》exert *influence*.

けんせい 現勢 『現在の情勢』the present [existing] state of things [affairs]; the current [present] situation; 『現在の勢力』the present [existing] strength《of a political party》.

げんせい 厳正 厳正な 形 (厳しく公平な) strict and fair. ● 厳正な審査 *strict and fair* judgment. ● 厳正中立な立場を取る adopt a position of *strict* neutrality; adopt a *strictly* neutral position.

げんぜい 減税 a tax reduction [cut], a reduction [a cut] in tax《on a new car》. (⇔ 増税)
● 所得税減税 an income tax reduction [cut].
● 特別減税 a special tax reduction [cut]. ● 大幅減税を要求する call for big *tax cuts*.
── 減税する 動 ▶5 パーセント減税する *reduce [cut,*

lower] taxes by 5 percent.

げんせいだい 原生代 『地学』 the Proterozoic (era).

げんせいどうぶつ 原生動物 a protozoan.

げんせいりん 原生林 a primeval [a virgin] forest. (**!** 前の方は「太古よりの」、後の方は「人手の入らぬの意」)

けんせき 譴責 图 (職務に関する叱責(しっせき))《やや書》(a) reprimand. ── 譴責する 動 《やや書》reprimánd.

げんせき 原石 raw ore; (鉱石) (an) ore; (宝石の) a gemstone.

げんせき 原籍 (⇔⇨ 本籍)

けんせつ 建設 图 (建築物の) construction; (設立) establishment. ● 道路の建設工事 the *construction* of the road; road *construction*. ● 新空港建設に着手する start [begin] the *construction* of [*constructing*] a new airport. ● ごみ焼却場の建設に反対する oppose [object to] the *construction* of an incineration plant. ▶そのホテルはまだ建設中です The hotel is still *under construction* [*is still being built*]. ▶その橋の建設に 2 年かかった The *construction* of the bridge took two years./It took two years to *construct* [*build*] the bridge. (⇔ 動)
── 建設的な 形 ▶彼は建設的な意見を述べた He expressed a *constructive* opinion.
── 建設する 動 build*, construct (**!** 後の方は堅い語で「大きな物を建造する」の意が強い); establish. (⇔ 建てる) ● ダムを建設する *build* [*construct*] a dam.
● 新しい国家を建設する *build* (*up*) [*establish*] a new state. ▶プールはスーパーマーケットの跡地に建設される予定です A swimming pool is planned [scheduled] to *build* at the site of the supermarket.
● 建設会社 a constrúction [a búilding] còmpany. ● 建設業 the constrúction índustry.
● 建設現場 a constrúction [a búilding] sìte.
● 建設事業 a constrúction pròject. ● 建設省 the Ministry of Construction. (参考 現在は国土交通省に移行) ● 建設費 constrúction còsts [expènses]. ● 建設予定 the constrúction plàn [schèdule].

げんせつ 言説 (意見) an opinion, a remark; (批評) a comment; (述べること) a statement.

けんぜん 健全 ── 健全な 形 sound, healthy. (**!** 前の方が強意的) ● 健全な財政 *sound* finance; (予算が) a *balanced* budget. ● 健全な生活 a *healthy*(↔ an *unhealthy*) life. ● 健全なテレビ番組 *wholesome* TV programs. (参考 道徳的であることを強調) ▶難産でしたが母子ともに健全です It was a difficult delivery, but both mother and child *are doing fine* [*well*].
● 健全なる精神は健全なる身体に宿る 《ことわざ》 A sound mind in a sound body. (参考 教育の理想を述べる言葉)

げんせん 源泉 (出所) a source; (起源) (an) origin. (⇔ 源) ● 活動力の源泉 the *source* of energy.
『翻訳のこころ』 活動のこころ 政治や経済の制度と活動には、学問や芸術の創造活動の源泉としての「古典」にあたるようなものはありません (丸山真男 『「である」ことと「する」こと』) In political and economic institutions and activities, there is nothing that corresponds to the "classics" which serves as the source of creative activities in the arts and scholarship.
● 源泉課税 taxation at source;《英》pay-as-you-earn《略 PAYE, P.A.Y.E.》. ● 源泉徴収 deducting tax at source;《米》withholding.
● 源泉徴収票 a certificate of tax deduction at

げんせん 源泉 ; 《米》a withholding slip.
げんせん 厳選 ── **厳選する** 動 select (carefully), choose (very) carefully; handpick (❗「自ら一つ一つ選ぶ」の意).
げんぜん 厳然 ── **厳然とした** 形 〖厳しい〗 stern; 〖動かしがたい〗 hard; (否定できない) undeniable; (議論の余地のない) indispensable. ● 厳然たる事実 a *hard fact*.
げんぜん 現前 ● 現前の事実に目を向ける turn one's attention to what really is *before one's eyes*.
*****げんそ** 元素 an element.
── **元素記号** the symbol of an element.
けんそう 喧騒 (a) noise; a din. (⇨騒音) ● 通りの喧騒 street *noises*; *noises* from the street. ● 大都会の喧騒を逃れる get away from the *din* [the *hustle and bustle* /bʌ́sl/] of a large city. (❗ hustle and bustle は「せわしくはたらいた活動をすること」をさす)
けんぞう 建造 图 construction. (⇨建設) ● 建造中のタンカー a tanker *under construction*.
── **建造する** 動 ● タンカーを建造する *build* [*construct*] a tanker.
── **建造物** a building.
げんそう 幻想 〖夢のような空想〗 (a) fantasy; 〖錯覚〗 (an) illusion. ● 甘い幻想 a sweet *illusion*. ● 幻想の世界に住む live in a world of *illusion*. ● …という幻想を抱く cherish [be under] the *illusion* that …. ▶ 私は自分の能力に幻想など抱いていない I have no *illusions* about my ability.
げんぞう 幻像 visions; illusions. (⇨ 幻影)
げんぞう 現像 图 development.
会話「このフィルムの現像とプリントをお願いします」「プリントのサイズはいかがいたしましょう」"I'd like my film *processed* [*developed* and printed]." "What size prints do you want?" (❗ process は「(目的物を得るために)必要な工程をへる」の意)
── **現像する** 動 (自分で) develop; (専門家に托して) have 《the film》 developed.
げんそうきょく 幻想曲 〖音楽〗 a fantasia /fæntéiʒə/, a fantasy.
げんそうそっきょうきょく 『幻想即興曲』 *Fantaisie-impromptu*. (〖参考〗ショパンのピアノ曲)
*****げんそく** 原則 〖根本の規則〗 a principle; 〖一般・個人の習慣〗 a rule. ● 平和三原則 the three-point peace *principle*. ● 基本原則を立てる establish a fundamental [an essential] *principle*. ● アメリカの政治の基本原則は憲法に記されている The basic *principles* of American [the U.S.] government are written in the Constitution. ▶ 私は原則的にその計画に賛成だ I agree to the plan *in principle*. ▶ 私は原則として人に金を貸さないことにしている I don't lend money *as a rule*./(金を貸さないのが原則だ) It is my *rule* [It is a rule with me, My *rule is*] not *to* lend money./I *make it a rule* not *to* lend money. ▶ 日本は1967年以来、武器輸出を規制した三原則を持つ Since 1967, Japan has maintained three principles banning arms exports.
げんそく 舷側 the side of a ship.
げんそく 減速 图 a slowdown (⟷(a) speedup), 《やや書》 deceleration (⟷acceleration). ● 経済の減速 a *slowdown* in the economy.
── **減速する** 動 slow down (⟷speed up), 《やや書》 decelerate (⟷accelerate).
げんぞく 還俗 ── **還俗する** 動 return to secular life; renounce the cloth.
けんそん 謙遜 图 〖控えめで慎み深いこと〗 modesty; 〖へりくだり〗 humbleness (❗ しばしば卑屈さを含む). ● 謙遜家 a *modest* person. ● 謙遜な態度 a *modest* [a humble] attitude.
── **謙遜する** 動 ● 謙遜して語る talk *modestly* [with *modesty*]. ▶ 彼は自分の作品について謙遜している He *is modest about* his works.
● **謙遜語** (⇨謙譲〖謙譲語〗)
げんそん 現存 ── **現存する** 動 (生きている) living; (物などが存在する) existing; (文書・絵画などが) 《書》 extant. ● 現存の作家 a *living* writer. ● 現存の生物 *existing* forms of life.
── **現存する** 動 exist.
けんたい 倦怠 fatigue /fətíːɡ/, weariness. (⇨疲れ)
● 倦怠感を覚える feel *tired* [*weary*]. (❗ 後の方は堅い言い方) ▶ 彼らの結婚生活も倦怠期にさしかかった They *have got tired* [*weary*] *of* their married life.
けんたい 検体 (見本) a specimen, a sample.
けんたい 献体 donation of one's body 《*to*》.
── **献体する** 動 donate [leave] one's body 《*to*》.
けんだい 見台 a bookrest, a bookstand.
げんたい 減退 〖衰え〗 a decline 《*in* health》; 〖喪失〗 (a) loss. ● 食欲減退 (a) *loss* of appetite.
── **減退する** 動 ● 食欲が減退する *lose* one's appetite. ● 彼の体力は減退しつつある His strength *is weakening* [*declining*]. (❗ 後の方が堅い語)
*****げんだい** 現代 〖形〗 the present age [day]; (今日) today; (このごろ) these days. ● 現代では電話はなくてはならないものである A telephone is indispensable *in the present age*. ▶ これは現代における最大の問題である This is the biggest problem of *the present day*. ▶ 現代はコンピュータの時代だ *This* [*Today*] *is the age of computers*. ▶ 現代ではだれもそんな考え方はしない Nobody thinks that way *these days* [*now, today*].
── **現代の, 現代的の** 形 〖過去に対して今日の〗 present-day (限定的用法のみ); 〖当世の〗 modern; contemporary; 〖最新の〗 up-to-date (❗ 修飾語のない叙述用法には up to date). ● 現代の若者 *present-day* young people; young people 《of》 *today*. ● 現代アメリカ人作家 *modern* [*contemporary*] American writers. ● 現代の英語 〖科学技術〗 *present-day* English [*technology*]. (❗ Modern English は近代英語 (1475年以降の英語) のこと) ● 現代的な思想 *modern* [*up-to-date*] ideas.
● **現代劇** a modern play. ● **現代社会** modern society. ● **現代人** people of today. ● 現代人は通例考え方などが進んだ人をいう ● **現代っ子** a child 《of》 today (⦅ children ⦆). ● **現代版** (現代の形態で出版されたもの) a modern edition [version] 《*of*》; (過去の人物・物の再現) modern-day [present-day] 《Shylock》.
げんだい 原題 the original title.
げんたいけん 原体験 (説明的に) childhood experiences which are still fresh in one's memory.
ケンタッキー 〖米国の州〗 Kentucky /kəntʌ́ki/ (略 Ky., Ken. 郵便略 KY).
けんだま 剣玉 (遊戯) cup and ball; (説明的に) A popular game using a ball attached by a string to a shallow cup with a handle. The aim is to toss the ball and catch it in the cup. ● 剣玉をする play *cup and ball*.
けんたん 健啖 a healthy [〖大食いの〗 a voracious] appetite; 〖大食い〗 gluttony, voracity. ▶ 彼は健啖家だ He is a *big* [*a heavy, a voracious*] eater./He has *a big* [*a healthy, a voracious*] appetite.
げんたん 減反 ── **減反する** 動 reduce [cut back] rice acreage; cut back the acreage under cultivation.
● **減反政策** a policy of reducing rice acreage.

けんち 見地 a point of view, a viewpoint 《*of*》; a standpoint 《*of*》. ▶この見地からみると、それは重要ではない From this *point of view*, that is not important. (⇨立場❷, 観点)

けんち 検地 a land survey. ── 検地する 動 survey land.

けんち 検知 a detection.
• 検知器 a 《gas》detector.

げんち 言質 《約束》a promise;《誓約》(a) pledge;《身動きをとれなくすること》a commitment. (❗後の二つはやや堅い語) (⇨約束) • 言質を与える give [make] a *pledge* 《*to* do; *that* 節》; commit oneself 《*to* do; *to* doing》. • 言質を取る get [obtain] 《his》*pledge*.

げんち 現地 《特定の地点》the spot;《実地活動の場》the field. • 現地の人たちに現地の言葉で話す speak to the people *there* 《*話*》the *locals* in *their own* language. • 現地に詳しい人 a person who knows the country [the area] well. • 現地の安い労働力を利用する take advantage of the cheap *local* labor. • 言語学者はしばしば現地で仕事をする Linguists often work *in the field*. ▶AZ602便は現地時間14時に到着の予定でございます AZ 602 will arrive at 14:00 *local time*.
• 現地生産 local production. • 現地調査 an on-the-spot investigation; 《ˣa》field work; a field survey. • 現地採用 local procurement. • 現地通貨 local currency. • 現地報告 an on-the-spot [a field] report. • 現地法人 an affiliated company incorporated abroad; an local incorpolated company.

⁑けんちく 建築 名《建築学・様式》architecture;《建造》construction;《建築物》a building, a structure (❗後の方は堅い語). • 現代建築 modern *architecture*. • 木造建築 a wooden *building* [*structure*]. • 和風建築 a Japanese(-style) building; Japanese architecture. • コンクリート建築 a concrete building. • 鉄筋コンクリート建築 (⇨鉄筋)
── 建築(上)の 形 architectural.
── 建築上 副 architecturally.
── 建築する 動 build*, put*...up;《建造する》construct (❗build より堅い語). ▶新しい病院を建築している They're building [constructing] a new hospital./A new hospital *is being built* [*is under construction*].
• 建築科 (大学の) the department of architecture. • 建築家 an architect. • 建築会社 a building [a constrúction] còmpany. • 建築基準法 the Building Standards Law. • 建築業者 a builder. • 建築工事 constrúction wòrk. • 建築士 a registered [a qualified] architect 《*of the firstclass*》. • 建築資材 building matèrials. 《㊙建material》. • 建築事務所 a registered [a qualified] architect's office. • 建築物 a building, a structure;《集合的》the architecture.

げんちゅう 原虫 《原生動物》原生動物.

けんちょ 顕著 ── 顕著な 形 《注目に値する》remarkable;《際立った》marked, noticeable /nóutisəbl/;《前の方が強意的》;《傑出した》outstanding;《印象的な》striking. (⇨著しい) ▶両者の間には顕著な差はない There are no *marked* [*noticeable, striking*] differences between them.

けんちょ 原著 《原作》the original (work).

けんちょう 県庁 《県庁舎》a prefectural government office;《県の行政府》a prefectural government;《県当局》the prefectural authorities.
会話「愛知県の県庁所在地はどこですか」「名古屋です」"What [ˣWhere] is the capital city of Aichi *Prefecture*?" "Nagoya (is)./《古》It is Nagoya." ▶古くは the capital city ... が普通と感じられていたが、今日では What が主語ととられ, それが応答に反映しているのに注意

けんちょう 堅調 (景気・相場などの) strength, goodness. • 堅調な景気指標 strong [good, steady] economic statistics.

げんちょう 幻聴 an auditory hallucination. (⇨幻覚)

けんちんじる 巻繊汁 *kenchinjiru*; (説明的に) vegetable stew in which we cook taroes, carrots, burdocks, tofu and so on with oil.

けんつく 権柄を食わせる (はねつける) give a rebuff 《*to*》; (しかりつける) tell ... off; (どなりつける) yell 《*at*》.

けんてい 検定 名《正式の認可》(official) approval;《検査》a test, (an) examination. ▶この教科書は文部科学省の検定済みだ This textbook *is authorized* [*is approved*] by the Ministry of Education. (⇨文部科学)
── 検定する 動 (認可する) 《書》approve (officially);《書》authorize; (検査する) examine.
• 検定教科書 an authorized textbook. • 検定試験 a certificate [a license] examination. • 英語能力検定試験 an English proficiency test; (日本英語検定協会の) the 《first grade》STEP test in practical English. (❗STEP は The Society for Testing English Proficiency の略.「準一級」は the prefirst grade という)

けんてい 献呈 (進呈) presentation.
── 献呈する 動 present 《it *to* him》.
• 献呈本 a presentation book [copy].

*けんてい 限定** 名《禁止的な》restriction. (⇨制限) ── 限定する 動 limit; restrict. (⇨限る)
• 限定意見《会計》a qualified opinion. • 限定戦争 a limited war. • 限定相続《承認》qualified acceptance of heritage. • 限定版 a limited edition. • 限定販売 a limited sale.

けんでん 喧伝 ▶来年2月に内閣が改造されると喧伝されている It is noised about [abroad] that the Cabinet will be reshuffled in February next year.

げんてん 原典 the original (text). • 原典にあるcheck the original.

げんてん 原点 (出発点) the stárting pòint; (最初) the beginning;《数学》(座標の) the origin. • 原点 (=根本原理) に帰る get [go] back to (the) *basics*.

げんてん 減点 ── 減点する 動 ▶英語のテストで10点減点された I *had* ten points *taken off* [*subtracted*] on the English test. (❗on [ˣat] the test は「試験で」の意)
• 減点法 the demerit system; (レスリングなどで) the bad-mark system. • 減点法で採点する grade the papers on 《ˣwith》the *demerit system*.

けんと 県都 a prefecture's capital; the capital city of a prefecture; (省・県などの中心都市) a provincial capital.

けんと 建都 the foundation of a capital.

*げんど 限度** a limit (❗しばしば複数形で);《能力などの》limitations (❗通例複数形で (⇨限界)). • 最小限度 the minimum. • 最大限度 the maximum. ▶私はたいへん寛大な人間だがそれにも限度があるよ I'm a very generous [forgiving] person, but there is a *limit* (to my generosity). ▶彼の欲望には限度なかった There was no *limit* to his greed./His greed knew no *limit*(*s*) [*bounds*]. ▶日本国憲法は最低限度の生活を保障している The Constitution of Japan guarantees the *minimum* standard

けんとう 見当 ❶〖推測〗a guess; 〖見積もり〗an estimate. ▶私は彼の年齢の見当をつけた I *guessed* (*at*) his age.(I guess は比べて「試み」を強調する)/I *made* [*took*] *a guess at* his age./I *guessed* how old he was. ▶なぜ君がそれを知っているのか見当もつかない I can't *guess* [*imagine*] why you (should) know it. (❗should があると話し手の「驚き」など主観的な感情を表す)/I *have no idea* (*of*) why you know it. (❗of は通例省略る. さらに意味を強めて I don't have the slightest [faintest, (話) foggiest] idea ….ともいえる) ▶私の見当ではこの仕事をやり終えるのに2年かかる I *estimate* that it'll take two years to finish this work. ▶それは見当はずれだ That's *beside the point*. (⇨見当違い)
〖会話〗「まだずっと遠いの?」「だいたいの見当で2マイルだな」"Is it much farther?" "A couple of miles, *at a rough guess*."
❷〖方向〗a direction. ▶青森はだいたいこの見当(＝方向)です Aomori is somewhere *in this direction*./Aomori is about this way.
❸〖ねらい〗aim. (⇨狙(ﾞ)い)
❹〖およそ〗about …. (⇨およそ, 約, くらい)

けんとう 検討 图〖よく調べること〗(an) examination; (細かい調査) a study;〖考慮〗consideration; (討議) discussion. ▶検討中である be under *consideration* [*review*]. (❗主語は事) ▶それはさらに考慮を要する It requires a further *examination* [*discussion*].
── 検討する 動 examine; study (⇨調査する), consider, think about… (⇨考慮する); discuss. ▶弁護士はその事件を(細かく)検討した The lawyer *studied* the case. ▶仕様書の変更が可能か検討してもいいですよ We can *discuss* a possible change in the specifications.

けんとう 拳闘 (ボクシング) boxing. (⇨ボクシング)

けんとう 健闘 图 ▶健闘を祈る Good luck to you!
── 健闘する 動 (善戦する) make [put up] *a good fight*; (懸命の努力をする) make strenuous efforts.

けんどう 剣道 *kendo*; (説明的に) Japanese swordsmanship. ▶剣道の練習をする practice *kendo*. ▶彼は剣道3段です He is a third(-)dan in *kendo*./He is a third(-)dan *kendoist* [*a kendoist* of the third grade].

げんとう 幻灯 a slide.
● 幻灯機 a slide projector.

げんとう 眩灯 a sidelight.

げんとう 厳冬 a severe [a hard] winter. ▶厳冬期に *at the coldest time* [*part*] *of the winter*.

げんどう 言動 (⇨言行) ▶言動を慎みなさい Be careful (about) *what you say and do*./You should try to speak and behave politely./You should make an effort to be polite. (❗polite は「注意して人に失礼でないふるまいをする」の意の形容詞)

げんどうき 原動機 a (prime) motor.

げんとうし 遣唐使 a Japanese envoy to the Tang /táːŋ/ Dynasty [The Tang, China].

けんとうしき 見当識〖心理〗orientation.

けんとうちがい 見当違い ▶それは見当違いだ(＝君の推測ははずれている) You've *guessed wrong*./You're making a *wrong guess*./(的はずれだ) That's *beside the point*. ▶彼は見当違いな(＝的はずれの)答えをした His answer *missed the mark*./He answered *off* [*beside*] *the point*.

げんどうりょく 原動力 motive power; (駆り立てる力) driving force; (動かす力) moving force. ● 平和運動の原動力 the *motive power* of [behind] the peace movement. ▶彼がその計画の原動力でした He was the *driving* [*moving*] *force* behind the program. ▶日本人は恥感を原動力にしている The Japanese are motivated by a sense of shame.

■ **DISCOURSE**
終身雇用は経済成長の原動力のひとつであった. 言い換えれば, 終身雇用なしでは日本は現在の繁栄はなかったであろう The lifetime employment system has been a *driving force* for the economic growth. **In other words**, Japan would not have developed as it has without the system. (❗in other words, 言い換えるとは言い換えに用いるディスコースマーカー. 続けて「原動力」の内容を詳しく言い換えている)

ケントし ケント紙 Kent paper.

げんとして 厳として (いかめしく) sternly; (厳粛に) solemnly; (重々しく) gravely; (断固として) firmly; (動かしがたく) undeniably. ▶彼女は厳として私の申し出を拒絶した She *sternly* [*firmly*] refused (to accept) my proposal.

けんどじゅうらい 捲土重来 ▶捲土重来を期する resolve to make another attempt (for a victory) with redoubled efforts; resolve to try again still harder.

けんない 県内 in [inside, within] a prefecture.

けんない 圏内 ▶イギリスの勢力圏内 *within* the British [✕English] *sphere* of influence. ● 暴風雨圏内 *in* a storm zone. ● 合格圏内にいる have a chance of passing (the exam).

げんなま 現生 cold cash. (⇨動 現金)

げんなり ── げんなりする 動〖疲れきる〗be tired [worn] out; 〖あきてしまう〗be fed up, be bored to death. ▶げんなりして tiredly. ▶彼は夏の暑い日に1日歩き回ってげんなりしている He *is tired* [*worn*] *out* walking all day on a hot summer day. ▶ほとんどの患者は病院の変わり映えしない食事にげんなりしていた Most of the patients *were fed up with* the same hospital meals which were not much different from day to day.

げんに 現に 〖実際に〗actually; (本当に) really;〖自分の目[耳]で〗with one's own eyes [ears];〖今〗now. ▶私は現にそれを見た[聞いた]のだ I have *actually* seen [heard] it./I have seen [heard] it *with* my *own eyes* [*ears*]. ▶現に今戦争で死んでいる人がいる Some people are *actually* [*really*] being killed in battle now. (❗actually は予想や外見と違って「現実に」の意)/(この瞬間にも) Some people are being killed in battle *at this very moment*.

げんに 厳に (厳しく) strictly. ▶厳に言葉を慎め You should be *very careful* when you speak./Watch your words [your language, what you say].

けんにょう 検尿 图 a urine /júərin/ test, examination of one's urine.
── 検尿する 動 (医師が) test [examine] one's urine; (検尿してもらう) get a urine test; have one's urine tested.

けんにん 兼任 ── 兼任する 動 hold the additional post (*of*); concurrently hold the post (*of*).

けんにん 堅忍 ● 堅忍不抜の精神で学問に精進する devote oneself to one's studies *with perseverance* [*patience*].
● 堅忍持久 indomitable [dogged] perseverance.

けんにん 検認 ── 検認する 動〖法律〗(米) probate, (英) prove.

げんにん 現認 ── 現認する 動 witness.
けんのう 献納 名 presentation; (a) contribution; (a) donation.
── 献納する 動 present 《it *to* a shrine》; make contributions [donations] 《*to* a shrine》.
● 献納品 an offering.
げんのしょうこ 現の証拠 〖植物〗a cranesbill.
けんば 犬馬 ● 犬馬の労をとる dedicate oneself [one's life] 《*to* him》; do a great service 《*to* him》.
***げんば 現場** (行為・事故・事件などの) a scene; (地点) a spot 《! 以上2語は通例単数形で》; (建築の) a site (! 事故・事件などにも用いる). ● 事故現場 an accident *scene*; the *scene* of an accident. ● 建築現場 a construction *site*. ● 窃盗の現場を押さえられる *be caught* (*in the act of*) stealing. ● 現場の教師 (=教室で実際に教えている教師) teachers who are actually teaching classes. ● 教育の現場を知らない don't know what is going on at school. ● 現場の意見を聞く listen to [pay attention to] what workers [teachers, etc.] have to say. ▶ そのナイフは犯行現場で発見された The knife was found at the *scene* of the crime.
● 現場監督 a site manager; a field overseer.
● 現場検証 an on-the-spot investigation [inspection]. ● 現場中継 a remote hookup 《with》.
けんぱい 献杯 ── 献杯する 動 offer 《him》 a cup of wine [sake].
げんぱい 減配 名 (配給量の) a reduction of rations; (配当金の) a reduction of dividend payout.
── 減配する 動 ▶ 会社は今期配当を2パーセント減配した The company *reduced its dividend* by two percent this term.
けんばいき 券売機 (切符販売機) a ticket machine.
▶ ぼくは券売機で切符を買った I got a ticket from a *machine*.
けんぱく 建白 名 a petition, a representation;〖法律〗(特に政府などへの) a memorial.
── 建白する 動 ▶ 政府に建白する *petition* [*make a representation to, memorialize*] the government.
● 建白書 an offering.
げんばく 原爆 an atom(ic) bomb, an A-bomb.
● 原爆実験 an atomic test, an A-test. ● 原爆症 illness caused by atomic-bomb radiation.
げんばくししゅう『原爆詩集』 *Anthology of Japanese Atomic Bomb Poems*. 〖参考〗峠三吉の詩集
けんばつ 厳罰 a severe punishment. ● 厳罰に処する (厳しく罰する) punish 《him》 severely.
げんぱつ 原発 〖『原子力発電(所)』の略〗(⇨原子力)
けんばん 鍵盤 a keyboard. (! 個々の鍵は a key)
● ピアノの鍵盤 the *keyboard* of a piano; piano *keys*.
げんばん 原板 a negative.
げんぱん 原版 〖活字組版の〗《米》a form, 《英》a forme; (写真印刷版の) the original plate;〖複製・翻刻の〗the original edition.
げんはんけつ 原判決 ● 原判決を破棄する reverse the *original decision* [*verdict*].
けんび 兼備 ● 才色兼備 (⇨才色兼備) ● 兼備する (⇨㊂兼ね備える)
けんびきょう 顕微鏡 a microscope. ● 電子顕微鏡 an electron *microscope*. ● 100倍の顕微鏡 a *microscope* of 100 magnifications; a 100-power *microscope*. ● 顕微鏡で調べる examine 《it》 under the *microscope*; make a *microscopic* examination 《of》.
● 顕微鏡写真 a microphotograph.
けんぴつ 健筆 ● 健筆をふるう wield a *productive* [(筆達者な) a *facile*] pen.
● 健筆家 a productive [a powerful, (多作の) a prolific] writer.
けんぴん 検品 ── 検品する 動 inspect; make an inspection 《of》; check.
げんぴん 現品 (実際にある品物) the actual article; (手元にある品) the article at hand [(当の) in question]. ● 現品引き替えは cash on delivery. ● 現品限りの last item on stock.
けんぶ 剣舞 (perform) a sword dance.
げんぷ 原父 原風景 a primal scene.
げんぶがん 玄武岩 〖地質〗basalt /bəsɔ́ːlt/; (俗に) whìnstòne.
げんぷく 元服 (説明的に) a ceremony to celebrate one's coming of age in old Japan.
── 元服する 動 celebrate one's coming of age.
***けんぶつ 見物** 名 (名所などの) sightseeing. ● 彼らを見物に連れて行く take them *for sightseeing* [×*to sightseeing*]. ● 京都見物に行く *go sightseeing in* [×*to*] *Kyoto*; go to Kyoto *for sightseeing*; go to Kyoto *to see the sights*. (! *do* the sights は《英俗》)
── 見物する 動 〖場所・建物などを〗visit; (名所などを) see* the sights of …;〖展示品・芝居などを〗see; (試合・行列などを) watch;〖傍観する〗look on 《at》.
● パリを見物する see [《英俗》 *do*] *the sights of Paris*; (見て回る) look around Paris. ▶ 京都ではいろんな所を見物しました I *did* a lot of *sightseeing* in Kyoto./I visited [saw] a lot of places in Kyoto.
● 見物席 (観覧席) (劇場・球場などの) a seat; (競技場などの) (集合的) the stands. ● 見物人 (観光客) a sightseer; a visitor; a tourist; (観客) a spectator; (傍観者) an onlooker; a býstànder.
げんぶつ 原物 the original.
げんぶつ 現物 (the actual) article. ▶ その本には興味がありますが，現物を見ないで買うわけにはいきません I'm interested in the book, but I can't agree to buy it without seeing it [buy it *sight unseen*]. (! *sight unseen* は「(あらかじめ)現物を見ないで」の意の慣用表現) ▶ 米1袋の現物支給だった I got paid *in kind* with a sack of rice.
ケンブリッジ 〖英国・米国の都市〗Cambridge /kéimbridʒ/.
● ケンブリッジ大学 Cambridge University.
けんぶん 見聞 名 〖観察〗(an) observation;〖経験〗(an) experience;〖知識〗(a) knowledge;〖視野〗《やや堅》horizons (! 通例複数形で). ● 見聞を広める see more of the world [of life]; broaden [widen, expand] one's *horizons*. ● 外国のことについて見聞が広い（=よく知っている）know a lot [be well-informed] about foreign countries.
── 見聞する 動 ▶ この本は彼が旅行中じかに見聞したことに基づいている This book is based on his own *experiences* and *observations* [*what he saw and heard* firsthand] while (he was) traveling.
けんぶん 検分 名 (an) inspection; (an) examination.
── 検分する 動 inspect; examine. ● 工場敷地を実地検分する *make* a personal *inspection* of the plant site; *inspect* the plant site in person.
げんぶん 原文 the original (text), the text. ● (原文のママ) (sic). ● (誤記のままの引用に付す．ラテン語で「このように」(= thus) の意) ● 原文に忠実に訳す make a faithful translation of *the original*. ● 原文で読む read (a novel) *in the original*.
げんぶんいっち 言文一致 the unification of the

けんぺい　written and spoken language.
けんぺい　権柄（権威）authority;（権力）power. ● 部下に権柄を振るう exercise one's *authority* over one's subordinates. ▶ その警察官は権柄づくな(=威圧的such)態度で市民に応対した The policeman treated the civilian in an *overbearing*〔いばった〕a *bossy* manner.
けんぺい　憲兵〔陸軍〕a military policeman (複-men), an M.P.;〔海軍〕a shore patrolman (複-men), an S.P.
　● **憲兵隊**〔陸軍〕the military police (**!** 複数扱い);〔海軍〕the shore patrol (**!** 単・複両扱い).
けんぺいりつ　建蔽率'building to land ratio'; the maximum building coverage ratio. ▶ この土地は建蔽率70パーセントです This land has a 70 percent *coverage ratio*.
けんべん　検便　a stool test.（⇨検尿）
けんぽ　健保〔「健康保険」の略〕（⇨健康）
げんぼ　原簿　a ledger;（登記などの）the original register. ● 原簿に記入する make an entry in a *ledger*.
***けんぽう　憲法**　a constitution. ▶ 特定の国の憲法は the C-)（⇨法律）● 憲法を制定[擁護]する establish [defend] the *constitution*. ● 憲法を改正する amend [revise] the *constitution*. **!** amend の方が正式表現）● 憲法を発布する proclaim the *constitution*. ● 憲法で保障された権利 a *constitutional* right. ● それは憲法違反である That is *unconstitutional*./That is *against* [is a *violation of*] the *Constitution*. ▶ これらの権利は憲法で保証されている These rights are guaranteed under the *Constitution*. ▶ 日本国憲法は1947年に施行された The *Constitution* of Japan was enforced [came into force] in 1947. ▶ 憲法は完成したが, 民主主義の出発であって完成ではない Although we have a new *Constitution*, it just signals the start [beginning] of democracy, not its completion [perfection].
　── **憲法（上）の** 形 constitutional.
　● **憲法改正** amendment [revision] of the constitution.（**!** 個々の条の改正は an amendment to the constitution, または a constitutional amendment という）● **憲法記念日** Constitution (Memorial) Day.
けんぽう　剣法　the art of fencing; swordsmanship.
けんぽう　拳法《Shorinji》*kenpo*;（説明的に）a martial art of Chinese origin: it employs fists and legs to knock the opponent down.
げんぽう　減法〔数学〕subtraction.
げんぽう　減俸 名　a pay [a salary] cut; a cut [a reduction] in pay [salary].
　── **減俸する** 動　● 10パーセント減俸された[になる] have one's *pay cut* [*reduced*] by 10 percent.
けんぼうじゅつすう　権謀術数（謀略）〔書〕wiles;（策略）a trick. ● 権謀術数をめぐらす（あらゆるはかりごとを使う）use all kinds of *wiles*.
けんぼうしょう　健忘症（忘れっぽさ）forgetfulness;（記憶喪失）〔医学〕amnesia /æmníːʒə/.（⇨物忘れ）
げんぼく　原木　raw lumber.
けんぽん　献本 名　a complimentary;（特装の）a presentation;（採用検討用の）an inspection [a desk] copy.
　── **献本する** 動　present /prizént/ a copy《to》.
げんぽん　原本　the original (book [文書] document]);（原文）the text. ▶ 契約書の原本と2枚の写しthe *original* contract and two copies.
けんま　研磨 ── **研磨する** 動（研ぐ）grind;（つやを出す）polish.
　● **研磨機** a grinder; a polisher; a polishing machine. ● **研磨剤** an abrasive.
げんまい　玄米　unpolished rice, brown rice.
　● **玄米茶** tea mixed with roasted brown rice.
けんまく　剣幕（ものすごい顔つきやふるまい）a fierce look (and sharp tongue). ● たいへんな剣幕で fiercely; with a *fierce look* (on one's face).
***げんみつ　厳密** 名〔厳密さ〕strictness;〔厳正さ〕rigidity.（**!** 柔軟性のないことを強意）
　── **厳密な** 形　strict; rigid;（綿密な）close. ● その語の厳密な意味では in the *strict* sense of the word. ● 階級間の厳密な区別 a *rigid* distinction between classes.
　── **厳密に** 副　● 厳密に言えば *strictly* speaking; to be exact. ● その問題を厳密に調べる make a *close*〔入念な〕a *careful*,〔徹底的な〕a *thorough*] examination of the matter; examine the matter *closely* [*carefully, thoroughly*].
けんみん　県民（1人）a citizen of a prefecture;（全体）the citizen [people] of a prefecture.
　● **県民性** the character of the people of a prefecture.
けんむ　兼務 名〔兼職〕an additional [《やや書》a concurrent] post.
　── **兼務する** 動　● この学校の校長は教頭を兼務している The principal of this school *holds the concurrent post of* [*concurrently holds the post of*] the vice-principal.
けんめい　件名　a subject line.
けんめい　賢明 名《やや書》wisdom.
　── **賢明な** 形（判断が正しい）wise;（分別のある）sensible;（当を得た）well-advised. ● 賢明な判断 a *wise* decision. ▶ 彼は賢明にもその申し出を断わった He was *wise* (enough) [He had the *wisdom*] to decline the offer./*It was wise* [*sensible*] *of* him *to* decline the offer. ▶ 彼の選択は賢明だった He chose *wisely*.
けんめい　懸命　● 懸命に…しようとする make an all-out [strenuous] effort to do …; go all out to do …. ● 懸命に自分を抑えようとする struggle [try hard] *to* control oneself.
げんめい　言明 名〔宣言〕(a) declaration;〔明確な声明〕a definite statement.
　── **言明する** 動　● そのことについて次のように言明する make a *declaration* [a *definite statement*] about it as follows; *state* it *definitely* as follows. ▶ 彼らは徴兵制度は反対だと言明した They *declared* [*stated clearly*] (*that*) they were against the draft system./《やや書》They *declared* (*themselves*) against the draft system.
げんめい　厳命　a strict order. ● すぐに出発せよとの厳命を受ける be given *strict orders* [be strictly ordered] to start at once.
げんめつ　幻滅　disillusion(ment);〔失望〕disappointment. ▶ 私は彼[彼のとった行動]に非常な幻滅を感じている I *am* very [×much] *disillusioned with* him [*at* his behavior]. (**!** disillusioned は完全に形容詞化しているので強める副詞は very)
げんめん　減免（税金の）reduction of and exemption from taxes;（刑の）mitigation and remission.
げんもう　原毛　raw wool.
けんもほろろ　● けんもほろろに(=にべもなく)私の頼みを突っぱねる refuse my request *flatly*.
けんもん　検問（調べ）(an) inspection. ● 検問でひっかかる（検問所で捕らえられる）be caught at a *checkpoint*.
　● **検問所** a checkpoint.
けんや　原野　the wilds.（⇨荒野）
***けんやく　倹約** 名　economy; thrift; frugality.（**!**

の順で倹約の度合いは強くなる) (⇨節約) ▶母はいろいろ細かい倹約をした My mother practiced many little *economies*. (🅘倹約行為の意では Ⓒ)/My mother was very *careful with* her money.

── **倹約する** 動 [金・時間などを省く] save; [むだ遣いしない] economize ⟨on⟩; (費用などを切り詰める) cut* down ⟨on⟩...; be careful with one's money. ● 経費を倹約する *cut down* ⟨on⟩ expenses. ● 金[食べ物]を倹約する *save* money [food]; *be economical of* one's money [food]; *be frugal of* one's money [food]. ▶燃料を倹約して使いなさい You must *economize on* [*make an economical use of*] fuel./Use fuel *economically*.

● 倹約家 a thrifty [a frugal, a saving, an economical] person. (🅘けなして「けちな人」という意では a stingy person)

げんゆ 原油 crude oil [petroleum].

けんゆう 県有 ── **県有の** 形 prefectural.
● 県有地 prefectural land.

げんゆう 現有 ── **現有の** 形 present; current; existing. ● 現有勢力 current [(実質的)な) effective] strength ⟨of a political party⟩.

けんよう 兼用 名 (⇨兼) ▶この部屋は会議室兼用です This room *is also used* [*also serves*] *as* a meeting place [*for* meetings].

── **兼用する** 動 ▶この車は父と兼用している My father and I *use* this car *together*./Both my father and I *use* this car./I *share* this car *with* my father.

けんらん 絢爛 (きらびやか) gorgeousness. ● 絢爛たる gorgeous. ● 絢爛豪華な衣装 a *gorgeous* dress.

:**けんり 権利** (a) right ⟨*to, of* (do)ing⟩; *to do*⟩; (要求・所有する権利) a) claim ⟨*to, on*⟩. ● 権利と義務 *rights* and duties.
①【〜権利】● 女性の権利 women's *rights*. ● 知る権利 the [a] *right* to know. ● 彼の小説を映画化する権利 the film *rights of* [*to*] his novel. (🅘著作権などには for も可)
②【権利が[は]】▶ 国民は知る権利がある The public has [《英》have] the [a] *right to* know. ▶彼には利益の半分を要求する権利があった He has a *right* [a *claim*] *to* half of the profit. ▶君には私を批判する権利はない You *have* no *right to* criticize me. (🅘否定文では no [not much] right のように Ⓤ扱い)/You *are* not *entitled to* criticize me. (🅘反語的に What *right* do you have to criticize me? (私のことを批判するなんて君にはどんな権利があるのか)のようにもいえる)
③【権利を】● 権利を行使[主張]する exercise [assert] one's *rights*. ● 権利を守る defend [maintain] a *right*. ● 権利を譲る transfer [hand over] (the) *right* ⟨*to*⟩. ● (書類にサインをして)sign away [over]. ● その土地に対する権利を主張する lay *claim* [ˣa claim] *to* the land. ● その会合に出席する権利を獲得[放棄]する acquire [give up] the *right* to attend [*of* attending] the meeting. ● 他人の権利を尊重[侵害]する respect [《書》 infringe ⟨on⟩] other people's *rights*. ▶人間はすべて法の下に平等な権利を有する All human beings [people] have equal *rights* under the law. (⇨人間[類語])
● 権利意識 right consciousness. ● 権利金 (割増金) a premium; (借家の) 《英》 key money. ● 権利書 a title deed; a title document.

*けんり **原理** ❶ [根本原則, 自然や機械などの仕組み] a principle; [実践の基となる理論] a theory. ● アルキメデスの原理 the *principle* of Archimedes /ˌɑːrkɪˈmiːdiːz/. ● 原理原則に従って議論する argue ⟨it⟩ *from* ⟨its⟩ *principles*.
❷ [特定分野の基礎研究] a philosophy; [技術・科学などの] principles. ● 経済学原理 the *philosophy* [*principles*] of economics.
● 原理主義 [宗教] fundamentalism. ● 原理主義者 a fundamentalist.

けんりつ 県立 ● 県立病院 a prefectural hospital. (🅘固有名詞は語頭が大文字: 広島県立 A 高等学校 Hiroshima *Prefectural* A High School) (⇨公立)

げんりゅう 源流 (起源) (an) órigin; (水源) a source, headwaters (🅘複数扱い. 各支流の水源を一括して). ● 文化の源流 the *origin* of culture.

けんりょう 見料 [見物料金] admission, an admission fee; [占い料金] a fortune-teller's fee.

*げんりょう **原料** raw [crude] materials (↔ manufactured goods) (🅘材料)
● 原料油 raw [stock] oil.

げんりょう 減量 名 a loss in weight. ● 減量経営する (＝能率的にする) *streamline* management [a business]; (経営効率をよくする) improve management efficiency, *make* a business *more efficient*. ▶あなたは太り過ぎだから減量が必要です You are overweight and need to *reduce* ⟨your weight⟩.

── **減量する** 動 lose weight; (食事制限などで) reduce ⟨one's⟩ weight, [《主に米話》 reduce; (量を減らす) reduce the quantity ⟨of⟩. ▶間食をやめればあなたは1か月で3キロ減量できる Cut out snacking and you'll *lose* three kilos in a month.

*けんりょく **権力** [支配力] power ⟨*over; to do*⟩; [法律に基づく強制力] authority ⟨*over* ＋人, *for* ＋事⟩; [影響力] (an) influence ⟨*on*⟩. ● 国家権力 state *power*. ● 政治的権力 political *power*. ● 権力を握る seize *power*. ● 権力を振るう[持っている; 失う] exercise [have; lose] one's *power* [*authority*] ⟨*over*⟩. ● 権力の座につく[ついている] come into [be in] *power*. ▶彼は権力をかさに着て私に無理な要求をした He asked too much of me (by) making unfair use of his *authority*. ▶彼は大統領に次いでその国でいちばん権力を持っている After the President, he is the most *powerful* [(影響力のある) *influential*] man in the country.
● 権力者 a person of power [influence]; a person in power. ● 権力闘争 a struggle for power; a power struggle. ● 権力欲 (a) lust for power.

けんろう 堅牢 名 solidity; (長持ち) durability.
── **堅牢な** 形 solid; strong; durable. ● 堅牢な家具 *solid* furniture, *solidly*-constructed furniture.

げんろう 元老 an elder statesman. (複 -men).
● 元老院 (古代ギリシャ・ローマの) the Senate.

げんろくそで 元禄袖 a short kimono sleeve.

*げんろん **言論** [話すこと] speech; [書くこと] writing; [世論] public opinion. ● 言論の自由 freedom of *speech*; (出版関係で) freedom of *the press*. ● 言論を統制する control *speech and writing*.
● 言論界 the press. (🅘一般に新聞・雑誌をさすが, しばしばテレビ・ラジオを含める) ● 言論機関 (マスコミ機関) an organ of (ˣa) public opinion (🅘しばしば organs of ... の形で); the (mass) media (🅘通例複数扱い).

げんろん 原論 a principle. ● 経済学原論 the *principles* of economics.

げんわく 幻惑 dazzlement.
── **幻惑する** 動 dazzle. ● 幻惑される be dazzled ⟨*by*⟩.

こ

こ 子 ❶ [人間の子] a child (閥 children), [話] a kid; (男児) a boy; (女児) a girl; [集合的] a family. ● 里子 a foster child. ● 7歳の男[女]の子 a seven-year-old *boy* [*girl*]. ● かわいい子 [=赤ん坊] a cute *baby*. ● 子のない childfree, childless. ▶前の方が婉曲的で好まれる) ▶あの子は金持ちの子だ She [He] comes from [[書・まれ] of] a wealthy *family*. ▶うちの子はあまり勉強しない My *son* [*daughter*] doesn't study hard. ▶彼は子だくさんだ (⇨子沢山) ● 私はベトナム戦争の子だ I am a *child* of the Vietnam War. (参考) 「ベトナム戦争による思想的影響を受けた世代」の意。アメリカでは, この世代は flower children とも呼ばれる)

❷ [動物の子] a baby (!通例, 後に動物名をつける: a *baby* monkey); [通例集合的] young (!複数扱い); (猫) a kitten; (犬) a puppy, a pup. (!その他の動物については個々の動物を参照) ▶コウモリは通例 1 回に 1 匹しか子を産まない A bat usually has only one *young* at a time. (!2 匹なら two *young*)

● 子はかすがい Children are there to help solidify the bond of their parents.

こ 弧 ● 弧を描く form [[やや書] describe] an *arc*. ● 大きな弧を描いて in a wide *arc*.

こ 個 (個人) an individual.

こ 粉 (⇨粉(z)) ● 身を粉にして働く work oneself [one's fingers] to the bone (*to do*).

コ ● 「コ」の字型の建物 a three-sided building.

―こ ―小 ❶ [ほとんど] almost, nearly. ▶家から事務所まで小1時間かかる It takes (me) *nearly* [*almost*] one hour from my house to the office.

❷ [大したことない] ● 小役人 a minor [a *petty*] official. ● 小利口な (=抜け目のない) 振る舞い smart [*clever*] behavior.

―こ ―故― ● 故田中氏 the *late* Mr. Tanaka.

―こ ―個 ● ケーキ 1 個 (=一切れ) a slice [a *piece*] of cake. ● せっけん 3 個 three *cakes* [*bars*] of soap. ● 桃 3 個 three peaches. (!three pieces of peach は「桃 3 切れ」) ▶このオレンジは 1 個 100 円する These oranges are 100 yen *each* [*a piece*]./These oranges cost 100 yen *a piece*. (!後の方は堅い言い方)

―こ ―戸 (家) a house (閥 houses /háuziz, (米) -siz/). (⇨軒) ● 8 戸の家 eight *houses*.

―こ ―湖 Lake ...; (比較的小さい) ... Pond; (スコットランド・アイルランド) Loch /lák, láx/.... ● 十和田湖 *Lake Towada*; the *Lake* of Towada. (!前の方が一般的。「琵琶湖と十和田湖」なら Lakes Biwa and Towada のように複数形が) ● ウォールデン湖 *Walden Pond*. (参考) 森の哲人 H. D. Thoreau のゆかりの湖) ● ネス湖 *Loch* Ness. ● 火口湖 a crater *lake*.

こ 五 five; [5 番目の] the fifth. (⇨三)

ご 碁 a go game; (説明的に) a Japanese board game in which the players attempt to obtain more area than their opponents. ● 碁を打つ play *go* (*with*).

● 碁石 a *go* stone. ● 碁盤 (⇨碁盤)

ご 語 [単語] a word; [用語] a term; [言語] (a) language. ● 専門語 a technical *term*. ● 800 語で書く write in 800 *words*.

―ご ―後 *after* ...; [今から...後に] in ... (!*after* は ある時間の経過を示し過去に, in がある事が起こるまでの時間の経過を示し未来に用いる); [その後] later; [...以来ずっと] since (!完了形とともに用いる). ● 結婚後 *after* marriage [(he) gets married]. ▶事故の 5 分後に警察が来た The police came (*in*) five minutes *after* the accident. ▶それから 2 時間後に彼は来た He came two hours *later* [*afterward*, *after*]. (!(1) later, afterward の方が普通. (2) ... later than [after] my arrival などが省略された表現. (3)「それから」の意を含まず単に期間をいう場合は He came *after* two hours. (2 時間後に来た) ▶次の電車は (今から) 15 分後に出ます The next train will leave *in* fifteen minutes (from now) [*in fifteen minutes' time*]. ▶その後 (母の死後) 私がずっと社長をしています I have been (the) president of the company *since* then [my mother died].

コア [中核] a core.

● コアコンピタンス [[得意技術[分野]] core competence. ● コアタイム [[拘束時間帯]] core time. ● コアビジネス [[中核事業]] core business.

ごあいさつ ご挨拶 (⇨挨拶) ▶とんだごあいさつだね This is no way to greet someone.

こあきない 小商い small-sized business; a family business; a business based on a small amount of capital.

こあじ 小味 ● 小味の利いた (=ちょっと味のある) 話 a smart [a *witty*, a *spicy*] story.

こあたり 小当たり ― 小当たりする 動 ▶この計画について彼に小当たりしてみよう (=彼の心中を探ってみよう) I'll try to sound [*feel*] him *out* about this plan.

コアラ [動物] a koala /kouáːlə/ (bear).

:こい 濃い 形 ❶ [濃さ・密度が] (スープなどが) thick (↔thin); (茶・酒などが) strong (↔weak); (料理の味つけで) heavily-seasoned (↔lightly-seasoned). (⇨薄い) ● 濃いスープ *thick* soup. ● 濃い霧 a *thick* [a *dense*, a *heavy*, xa *deep*] fog. ● 濃いお茶 [コーヒー] *strong* tea [*coffee*]. ▶このペンキは濃すぎて使えない This paint is too *thick* to use. ▶霧が急に濃くなってきた The fog *was thickening* [*getting thick*] quickly.

会話「韓国料理はいかがでした」「ちょっと味が濃すぎるように思いました」 "How did you find the Korean food?" "Well, it was a bit too *strongly* [*heavily*] seasoned for me, I'm afraid."

❷ [色が] deep; (暗い) dark; [髪などが] thick. ● 濃い青 *dark* [*deep*] blue. ▶彼は髪の毛 [あごひげ] が濃い He has *thick* hair [beard]./(髪 [ひげ] に重点を置いて) His hair [beard] is *thick*. (!beard には heavy も用いられる) ▶彼女の化粧は濃すぎる Her makeup is too *thick* [*heavy*]./She wears *too much* makeup. ▶彼の顔は疲労の色が濃かった His face showed how tired he was.

❸ [可能性が] strong. ▶我がチームは敗北の可能性が濃い There is a *strong* [xa *high*] possibility that our team will lose./(負けそうだ) Our team *is very likely* to lose.

❹ [関係が] (密な) close. ● 濃い親戚 a *close* relative. ▶血は水よりも濃い (ことわざ) Blood is *thicker* than water.

❺ [その他の表現] ▶彼は長いまつげに浅黒い肌, 濃い顔

(=はっきりした目鼻立ちの)印象のせいか女性ファンが多かった His *defined* [*strong*, *sharp*] features [×His dark face] with the long eyelashes and rather dark (skin have attracted many female fans. (🛈(1)「濃い」を dark とすると「色黒」の意。(2)「浅黒い肌」を好ましいとするときは olive (color) ともいう)

── 濃くする 動 thicken; (濃縮する) condense; (味つけを) season strongly [heavily].

*こい 恋 love; (一時的な) a romance. (⇨恋する) ● 夏の日の恋 a summer *romance*. ● 恋する女 a woman *in love*. ● 恋に破れる be disappointed in *love*. ● 恋を打ち明ける confess one's *love* (*to*). ● 恋する,恋に落ちる fall in *love* (*with*). ● 恋がさめる fall out of *love* (*with*). ▶これまでにだれかに恋をしてしまったことがある? それともまだ恋をしたことはないの? Have you ever *fallen in love with* anyone, or are you still fancy-free?
● 恋の鞘当(さや)当て a rivalry between two men for the affections [love] of one woman.
● 恋は思案の外 (恋は理性を失わせるものだ) Love is beyond reason./Love is not a reasonable thing.

こい 鯉 『魚介』a carp (🛈通例単・複同形。種類をいう時は ~s). 事情 carp には無知・貪欲などの好ましくないイメージがあり、日本語のような「威勢のよい魚」のイメージはない)
● 鯉口を切る get ready to fight by loosening one's sword from its scabbard.
● 鯉の滝登り ▶彼は鯉の滝登りのように出世して政界の実力者になった He leaped straight to the great political power.
● 鯉こく *koikoku*, (説明的に) miso soup with carp cut in round slices. ● 鯉幟(のぼり) (⇨鯉幟)

こい 故意 ── 故意の 形 (意図的な) intentional, deliberate. (🛈後の語は熟慮の末であることを暗示し、前の語より口語的)

── 故意に 副 intentionally, deliberately; (わざと) on purpose, (書) purposely. ▶彼は故意にそれをやった。物のはずみではない He did it *deliberately* [*intentionally*, *on purpose*], not by accident.

ごい 語彙 (a) vocabulary. (🛈集合的にある言語・個人などの用いる語をいう。語彙の種類をいうときは [C]) ● 語彙を増やす build [develop, enlarge, expand] one's *vocabulary*. ▶彼は語彙が豊富だ[乏しい] He has a large [a small] *vocabulary*. (🛈... a rich [a poor, a limited] *vocabulary*. ともいえる。×He has many [a few] *vocabularies*. とはいわない)

ごい 語意 the meaning of a word.
こいがたき 恋敵 a rival in love.
こいき 小粋 ── 小粋な 形 (⇨粋) ● 小粋な女 a *smart* [a *stylish*, a *chic*] woman. ● 小粋な身なり a *refined* [a *stylish*] dress.
こいくち 濃口 ● 濃口しょうゆ dark-colored soy sauce.
こいこがれる 恋い焦がれる pine [long, (書) yearn] (*for*). ▶多くの若者は大都市に恋い焦がれて家出する Many young people *are pining* [*longing*] *for* a big city and leave home.
こいごころ 恋心 (愛) love (*for*). 淡い恋心 faint *love*.
ごいさぎ 五位鷺 『鳥』a (black-crowned) night heron.
こいし 小石 a pebble; a small stone.
こいじ 恋路 (恋) love; (情事) a romance; a love affair (*with*). ● 人の恋路を邪魔する interfere with (*their*) *love* (*affair*).
こいしい 恋しい 『親愛な』dear; 『最愛の』beloved.

● 故郷が恋しい (思い焦がれる) *long* [《主に書》*yearn*] *for* one's home; (懐かしがる) *feel homesick for* one's home. ▶あの人がとても恋しい(=いなくて寂しい) I *miss* him very much.

こいしたう 恋い慕う long for 《one's lover》; miss 《him》deeply [desperately, very much];《書》pine for [yearn after] 《one's home》. ▶母の面影を恋い慕う *long for* [《書》*yearn after*] one's mother's image.

こいする 恋する (恋に陥る) fall* in love 《*with*》; (急に) 《話》fall for ...; (好きになる) come* to love. ● 恋する女 a woman *in love*. ● 熱烈に彼女に恋している *love* her passionately; *be madly in love with* her.

こいちゃ 濃茶 (説明的に) (rich-flavored) powdered green tea, whipped into smooth and soft paste.

こいつ **❶**［この者］［この男］《話》this fellow [guy]; (彼) he;［この女］this woman; (彼女) she. ● こいつら (彼ら, 彼女たち) they; these people. (🛈目の前にいる人を he, she, they というのは通例失礼だが、この日本語の感じからは可) ▶こいつめ(おどけて) You rascal!/You villain!/(ののしって) Damn you!
❷［これ］▶こいつはすげえ *This* is great [*fantastic*]!

こいなか 恋仲 ●彼らは恋仲である They *are in love with* each other./They *love* each other.

こいにょうぼう 恋女房 one's beloved /bilʌ́vid/ [dear] wife.

こいぬ 子犬 a puppy, a pup.

こいのぼり 鯉幟 carp-shaped streamers (made of paper or cloth traditionally flown on Children's Day).

こいびと 恋人 ［男性］a boyfriend; a boy; (愛人) a lover;［女性］a girlfriend; a girl; a love (🛈「愛されている人」の意だが、今では呼びかけで Yes, (my) *love*. のように使われる以外はあまり);［男, 女］(やや古) a sweetheart. (🛈以上いずれも通例 one's ~ の形で用いる) ▶彼女はぼくの恋人じゃない,ただの友達だよ She's not my *girlfriend*, she's just a friend of mine. ▶若い恋人たちは手をつないで歩いていた The young *lovers* were walking hand in hand.
● 恋人同士 lovers; a couple.

こいぶみ 恋文 a love letter.

こいめ 濃い目 ●濃い目の化粧 a little heavy [thick] makeup. ▶コーヒーを濃い目に入れてください I'd like my coffee *rather strong* [*a little stronger*], please.

コイル a coil.

こいわずらい 恋煩い, 恋患い lovesickness. ● 恋煩いしている少年 a *lovesick* boy. ▶彼女はボーイフレンドが彼女のもとを去ってからひどい恋煩いをしていて食べることも寝ることもできない She is so *lovesick* since her boyfriend left her that she can't eat or sleep.

コイン a coin.
● コイン入れ a coin purse. ● コイントス coin-toss. ● コイン投げ pitch-and-toss.

ごいん 誤飲 swallowing a foreign object [body].

コインランドリー a coin(-operated) laundry /lɔ́:ndri/, 《話》a coin-op. (🛈(1) laundry は洗濯場の意。(2)《米商標》a Láundromàt,《英》a làund(e)rétte もよく用いる)

コインロッカー a coin-operated [《まれ》a coin] locker,《話》a locker. ● かばんをコインロッカーに預ける leave one's bag in the *locker*.

こう so; like this. ● こういう (⇨こういう) ▶こう言って彼は立ち上がった *So* saying [*With this*], he stood up. ▶こう暑くては何もする気になれない I don't feel

こう **like** doing anything in *this* heat./It's *so* hot *(that)* I don't feel like doing anything. (❗️《話》では that をしばしば省略する) ▶こうしては(=ぐずぐずしてはいられない We have *no time to lose*. ▶こう見えても(=そうは見えないかもしれないが)高校時代は短距離走の選手だったんだから I may not look *it* [×so], but I was a sprinter when I was a high school student.

会話「今年香港へ行こうか,それともお金を貯めて来年ヨーロッパへ行こうか」「じゃこうしたらどう.借金してでもヨーロッパへ行こうよ」「そのほうがよさそうだね」"Shall we go to Hong Kong this year? Or shall we save money and go to Europe next year?" "*Tell you what*. We take out a loan and go to Europe this year." (❗️I'll tell you what. は具体的な提案の前に用いる I'll make you a deal. ともいう.また *Here*'s what you should do. は具体的に指示を与える前に用いる) "That sounds a better way to do it."

こう **公** (公爵) a duke; a prince. ●エジンバラ公 the *Duke* of Edinburgh. ●菅原道真公 *Prince* Sugawara Michizane.

こう **功** (功績) an achivement; (成功) (a) success. ●年の功の知恵 (⇨年の功). ●功なり名遂げる achieve success and win fame.

こう **甲** ❶[甲羅] (亀・カニなどの) a shell. ❷[人間の] (手の) the back (of one's hand); (足・靴・靴下の) the instep. ▶彼は手の甲で口をふいた He wiped his mouth with *the back* of his hand. ❸[順序・等級] (1 番目) the first; (後者に対する前者) the former; (成績の優) grade A, an "A". ●甲と乙 the former and latter. ●甲の薬は乙の毒 (ことわざ) One man's meat is another man's poison.

こう **行** ❶[行くこと] going; (旅) a trip, a journey; (旅立ち) departure. ●逃避行 an escape journey. ❷[行動] an act, action, (書) conduct. ●上司と行を共にする *act* together with one's boss. ❸[銀行] a bank. ●上位行 high-ranking *banks*.

こう **孝** (⇨孝行,親孝行)

こう **坑** [炭坑] a mine; [坑道] a pit; (縦坑) a shaft, (横坑) a level.

こう **劫** [囲碁] *ko*; an alternate-capture situation.

こう **効** (ききめ,効能) (an) effect 《*on*》; (書) efficacy; (書) operation 《*on*》. ▶薬石効なく彼は亡くなった He passed away in spite of all the medical treatment he had received [had been given].
●効を奏する (ききめを現す) be effective 《*against*》; (成功する) be successful 《*in, at*》.

こう **幸** (幸運) luck, good fortune; (幸福) happiness. (❗️「幸不幸」「幸か不幸か」は幸または不幸の一方だけをさすこともある) ▶人の幸不幸はその人の行い次第 Our *happiness* and *únhappiness* depends [×depend] on our deeds. (❗️unhappiness のアクセントは対比のため前に移動) ▶彼は最初の妻に死に別れたが幸か不幸かその妻との間には子供がなかった He lost his first wife, but *fortunately* he had no children by her.

こう **香** incense. ●香をたく burn *incense*.

こう **候** (時候) a season; (気候) weather. ●寒冷の候 《*in*》 the cold *season*.

こう **校** ❶[学校] a school. ●我が校 our *school*. ●名門校 a prestige *school*. ❷[校正] proofreading; (校正刷り) galley proofs, proof sheets. ●初[再;三]校 the first [second; third] *proof*.

こう **高** (高等学校) a high school. ●男子[女子]高 a boys' [a girls'] *high school*.

こう **項** [条 (article) の下位区分] a clause; [本の章 (chapter) の下位区分] a section; (段落) a paragraph; [表などの] an item; [数学] a term. ●日本国憲法第 9 条第 2 項 Article 9, *Clause* 2 of the Constitution of Japan.

こう **稿** (原稿) a manuscript, a copy. ●第 1 稿 the first *manuscript*.
●稿を改める rewrite a manuscript.

こう **請う** [懇願する] beg (-gg-); (必死に) (やや書) implore; [頼む] ask, 《やや書》 request. ●金を請う *beg for* money; *beg* money 《*from* him》. ●許しを請う *implore* [*beg for, ask for*] forgiveness. ●彼に援助を請う *ask* him *for* help. ●許可を請う *request* permission. ▶彼にその会の出席を請うた I *asked* [*begged*] him to attend the meeting. (⇨頼む)

こう- **好**- good; fine; favorable. ●好影響 (a) *good* influence. ●好景気 *good* times. ●好対照 a *good* contrast. ●好天気 *fine* weather.

こう- **高**- (高さ・程度の高い) high; (年上の) older, elder, senior. ●高たんぱく食品 *high*-protein foods. ●高緯度 *high* latitude. ●高学歴の人たち *highly*-educated people. ●高学年 the *upper* grades (米) [forms (英)].

-こう **-港** (⇨神戸港 the port of Kobe; Kobe *Port*. (❗️形の上では上記の二つがあるが,港によっていずれか一方が普通である場合が多い) ●積み出し港 a lóading *port*, a port of loading. (⇨出港,入港)

-こう **-鋼** steel. ●特殊鋼 special *steel*.

ごう **号** [番号] a number; [雑誌などの] an issue, a number; [カンバスの大きさ] a size. ●305 号室 Room (*No.*) 305. (❗️three oh [zero] five と読む. 1625 号室なら one six two five または sixteen twenty-five と読む) ●「キャンキャン」の最新[今月; 4 月; 来月]号 the latest [current; April; next] *issue* of the *CanCam*. (❗️雑誌などの) ●古い号 a back *number* [*issue*]. ●10 号の油絵 a *size* 10 oil painting. ●55 号ホームラン the fifty-fifth home run. ●クイーンエリザベス号 the Queen Elizabeth. (❗️船の名前には the をつける) ▶私のアパートは 520 号室です My apartment is *No.* 520. (❗️five two oh [zero] または five twenty と読む.「520 号室のアパート」は Apartment (*No.*) 520)

ごう **合** ❶[容積の単位] a go. (参考) 約 0.18 リットル) ❷[登山路の 10 分の 1] a stage. ●富士山の 6 合目 the sixth *stage* of Mt. Fuji.

ごう **剛** (強いこと) strength. ●剛の者 a stouthearted [a brave] man.

ごう **郷** ●郷に入っては郷に従え Every country has its fashion, so don't try to contradict it. (❗️「田舎にはその風習があるのだから,あえてそれを否定するようなことはするな」の意); (ことわざ) When in Rome, do [Do in Rome] as the Romans do.

ごう **業** (前世の行いで決定されている将来) [ヒンズー教・仏教の] karma; (宿命) fate; destiny (❗️fate はマイナス方向に向かう運命).●業が深い be very sinful.
●業を煮やす ▶煮え切らない彼女に彼は業を煮やした Her indecision really *annoyed* [*irritated*] him. (❗️後の方が意味が強い)

ごう **壕** (塹壕) a trench; (防空壕) a dugout, an air raid shelter.

こうあつ **降圧** (血圧を下げること) bringing down [lowering] one's blood pressure.
●降圧剤 an antihypertensive drug.

こうあつ **高圧** — **高圧的な** 形 ●高圧的なセールスマン a *high-pressure* salesperson. ●高圧的な(=力ず

こうあん の)手段をとる take *high-handed* [《話》*strongarm*] measures. ●高圧ガス *high-pressure gas*. ●高圧線 a *high-tension wire* [*line*]; a *high-voltage power line*. ●高圧流 a *high-tension current*.

こうあん 公安 *public safety* [*peace*]; (法と秩序) *law and order*. ●鉄道公安官 a *railroad* 《米》[a *railway* 《英》] *police officer*. ●公安を保つ[乱す] *keep* [*disturb*] the *public peace*.
●公安委員 a *public safety commissioner*. ●公安委員会 the *Public Safety Commission*. ●公安条令 the *public safety regulations* [《書》*ordinance*]. ●公安調査庁 the *Public Security Intelligence Agency*.

こうあん 考案 图 《着想》an *idea*; 《工夫》a *device*; 《計画》a *design*.
—**考案する** 動 *devise*; (考え出す) *think... up*; *work... out*; (創作する) *originate*; (発明する) *invent*.
●考案者 a *deviser*; an *originator*; an *inventor*.

‡**こうい 行為** an *act*, (an) *action*, 《主に書》a *deed*; (ふるまい) *behavior*,《書》*conduct*. (⇨行い [類語]) ●残虐行為 a cruel *act* [*action*]; an *act* [*xaction*] of cruelty. ●犯罪行為 a criminal *act*. ●よい行為(=善行)をする do a good *deed*. ▶紳士としてあるまじき行為だ His *conduct* is unworthy of a gentleman.

*こうい **好意** 图 *favor*; *goodwill*, *good will*; [親切な] *kindness*; (愛情) (an) *affection*; (親愛の情) *friendliness*. ●彼の好意に報いる return his *favor* [*kindness*]. ●彼女の好意に甘える[を無にする] *depend on* [*waste*] her *kindness*. ●著者の好意により (転載を許されたよ) *by courtesy of* the author. ▶彼は私たちに好意を示した He showed *favor* [*goodwill*] *toward* [*to*] us. ▶ご好意は決して忘れません I shall [will] never forget (all) your *kindness*. (!*shall* の方が決意の度合いが強い) ▶彼女はあの青年にひそかに好意を寄せている(=愛している) She secretly *loves* the young man.
—**好意的な, 好意ある** 形 *favorable*; (親切な) *kind*; (親しみのある) *friendly*; (気の合った) *sympathetic* (*to*). ●好意的な論評 a *favorable* review. ●好意ある忠告 *kind* [善意の] *well-meant*] *advice*. ●好意的な返事をする give a *favorable* answer. ●彼を好意的に扱う treat him *with favor* [*kindness*]; treat him *favorably* [*kindly*, in a *friendly* way]. ▶彼は我々に好意的だ He is *friendly* [has a *friendly feeling*, has *goodwill*] *toward* us. ▶彼は我々の提案に好意的だ He looks *with favor* on our *proposal*./(賛成している) He is *in favor of* our proposal.

こうい 厚意 (親切) *kindness*; (尽力) *help*. ●あなたのご厚意で *through your kindness*. ●ご厚意深く感謝します I'm very [really, deeply] grateful for your *kindness*./I deeply [really, very much] appreciate your *kindness*. (!後の方は堅い言い方)

こうい 皇位 the (Imperial) *Throne*.
●皇位継承 succession to the Imperial Throne.

こうい 校医 a *school doctor* [*physician*].

こうい 高位 a *high rank*. ●高位高官の *persons of high rank and office*; 《集合的》 *dignities*, *dignitaries*.

ごうい 合意 (mutual) *agreement* [*consent*]. (⇨同意) ●合意に達する come to [reach] (an) *agreement*. ●合意の上で *by mutual agreement* [*consent*]. ●国民の合意 a national *consensus*. ●合意事項を文書化する put *agreement* in writing. ▶この件は細かな点では意見の不一致はあるが大筋では合意に達している We still differ over the details, but we're broadly [(基本的に) basically] *in agreement* on this matter.
—**合意する** 動 ▶彼らはいくつかの点で合意した They *agreed on* several points.

こういう (このような) *... like this*; (この) *this*; (この種の) *this kind of ...*. ●こういう本 a book *like this*; *such a book as this*. ▶いいかい、こういうふうにクラブを握ってごらん Look, try to grip your club *like this* [*in*) *this way*]. ▶こういうことは慎重に扱わなくてはなりません We have to handle *this* matter carefully. ▶こういうわけで酒もたばこもやめました This is why I stopped drinking and smoking.

こういか 甲烏賊 [魚介] a *cuttlefish*.

こういき 広域 a *wide* [a *large*] *area*.
●広域行政 *integrated administration of a large region*. ●広域捜査 *a search conducted over a wide area*. ●広域通信網 [コンピュータ] a *wide-area network* 《略 WAN /wǽn/》.

こういしつ 更衣室 [劇場・テレビスタジオの] a *drèssing ròom*; [体育館・クラブなどの] a *locker room*, 《英》a *chánging* [a *drèssing*] *ròom*.

こういしょう 後遺症 [医学] a *sequela* (櫨 -lae); (なごり) (an) *aftereffect* (*of*). (!2 語ともしばしば複数形で)

こういつ 後逸 —**後逸する** 動 ▶サードがゴロを後逸した The third baseman let the grounder pass by him./The grounder got through the third baseman.

ごういつ 合一 (結合)《書》*union*; (統合)《書》*unification*, *integration*; (統一) *oneness*, 《書》*unity*. ●知行(ちぎょう)合一 *union* [*inseparability*] *of knowledge and practice*.

こういっつい 好一対 ●好一対をなす make a good [a well-matched] *pair* [夫婦が] *couple*].

こういってん 紅一点 (唯一の女性) the only girl [woman] 《*of the members, in the group*》.

こういん 工員 (工場労働者) a (factory) *worker*.

こういん 光陰 ●光陰矢の如し (ことわざ) *Time flies*. (!*like an arrow* をつけるのは和製英語)

こういん 行員 (銀行員) a *bank clerk*. (! a *banker* は「銀行家, 銀行経営者」の意. 「窓口担当者」は a *teller*)

こういん 拘引 图 (逮捕) (an) *arrest*; (拘留) *custody*.
—**拘引する** 動 *arrest*; [法律] *attach*; *take* 《him》into custody.
●拘引状 a *warrant of arrest*.

ごういん 強引 —**強引な** 形 (押しつけがましい) *pushy*; (無理強いの) *forcible*. ●強引なセールスマン a *pushy salesperson*.
—**強引に** 副 ●強引に押し入る *force* one's way 《*into* a building》. ●議案を強引に通過させる *push* [*force*] a bill through the Diet. ▶彼は娘をその男と強引に結婚させた He *made* his daughter marry the man./He *forced* his daughter *to* marry [*into*] marrying the man.

ごうう 豪雨 (a) *heavy* [(a) *torrential*] *rain*. (⇨大雨) ●集中豪雨 a *torrential downpour*; a concentrated *rain*. ▶先週の豪雨のため川は増水した The river has swollen with last week's *heavy rains*.

こううつざい 抗鬱剤 an àntidepréssant (drug [agent]).

こううりょう 降雨量 (a) *rainfall*. ●この地方の平均年間降雨量 the average annual *rainfall* of this region.

こううん 幸運 图 (good*) luck (⇔bad luck), good fortune (⇔misfortune). (⇨運) ●トランプで連続きである have a run [a streak] of (good) luck at cards. ▶幸運を祈る *Good luck* [*Best of luck*] (to you)!/改まって I wish you (good) luck [*the best of luck*]! (❗競技参加者・受験者などに対し「頑張って」という気持ちで言われることがある) ▶四つ葉のクローバーを見つけたら幸運が訪れるよ If you find a four-leaf clover, you'll have *good luck*.
会話「残念ながら負けちゃったよ」「次回に幸運を祈るよ」"I lost, I'm afraid." "*Better luck* next ╱time!"
── **幸運な** 圏 ●幸運な人 a *lucky* person. ▶幸運にも我々はそこで会うことができた *Luckily* [*Fortunately*, (やや書) *Happily*], we met there. (❗It was (×a) *good luck* [*lucky*, *fortunate*, a *happy* thing, ×*happy*] *that* we met there. ともいえる.「会うことができた」を ×*could* meet としないこと)/We *had* a (*good*) *luck* [*good fortune*] *to* meet there./We were *lucky* [*enough*) *to* meet there./We were *lucky that* we met there [(*in*) meet*ing* there].

こううんき 耕耘機 a cultivator.

こうえい 公営 ── ●公営の 圏 (公の) public; (地方自治体の) municipal. ●公営にする place (it) under *public management*.
●**公営ギャンブル** public-managed gambling.
●**公営住宅**(総称) public housing; (1世帯) a unit of public housing;《英》a council-house.

こうえい 光栄 图 〖名誉〗(an) honor; (特別な名誉) a privilege. ●光栄ある地位 an *honorable* position. ▶このようなおめでたいお席にお招きいただきましたこと光栄に存じます It is a great *honor* [*privilege*] (for me) to be invited to this auspicious occasion. (❗I'm very honored [privileged] .... のようにもいえる) ●身に余る光栄です This is an undeserved *honor*./I don't *deserve* this (much) *honor*. ▶彼はこの小説で芥川賞受賞の光栄に浴した He *was honored with* [*had the honor of* receiv*ing*] the Akutagawa Prize for this novel.

こうえい 後裔 a descendant. (⇨子孫)

こうえい 後衛 〖スポーツの〗(テニスなどの) the back player; (フットボール・サッカーなどで) a back; 〖軍隊の〗the rear guard. ●後衛をつとめる (サッカーなどで) play *back*; (軍隊で) bring up the *rear*.

こうえき 公益 the public interest(s) [benefit].
●**公益事業** public utilities. ●**公益質屋** a public pawnshop. ●**公益法人** a public service corporation.

こうえき 交易 trade; commerce. (⇨貿易)

こうえつ 校閲 图 (a) revision. ── **校閲する** 動 revise.
●**校閲者** a reviser.

*こうえん **公園** 图 (通例大きな) a park; (市街地の広場・小さな公園) a square (❗通例四角形). ●**国立[国定]公園** a national [a quasi-national] *park*. ●**円山公園** Maruyama *Park*. (❗固有名詞のときは通例無冠詞) ●公園のベンチに座る sit on [×in] a *park* bench. ▶彼は毎朝公園に散歩に行く He goes for a walk in [×to] the *park* every morning.

*こうえん **講演** 图 〖講義〗a lecture (⇨講義); 〖演説〗a speech (⇨演説); 〖講話〗a talk.
── **講演する** 動 give [deliver, ×make] a lecture (*on*, *about*); give [make, deliver] a speech (*about*, *on*).
●**講演会** a lecture meeting. ●**講演者** a lecturer; a speaker.

こうえん 口演 图 〖書〗an oral narration.
── **口演する** 動 (講談などを)《書》narrate; (浪曲など

を) recite.

こうえん 公演 a (public) performance; a presentation. (⇨上演) ●定期公演 a regular *performance*.
── **公演する** 動 perform.

こうえん 好演 图 (演劇などの) good acting; (演技・演奏などの) an excellent performance (*of* a play). ▶脇役陣の好演が光る The *excellent performance* of the supporting players is outstanding.
── **好演する** 動 put on a good show. ▶彼女は初めてのヒロイン役を好演した She *gave an excellent performance* as the first heroine.

こうえん 後援 图 support; (強力な) backing. ▶その行事は市の後援で行われた The event was held *under the sponsorship* [*auspices*] *of* the city. (❗sponsorship は「金銭的後援」. auspices は「指導的後援」でもったいぶった感じを伴う)
── **後援する** 動 support; back ... (up); 〖金銭的に〗sponsor. ●弁論大会を後援する *sponsor* a speech contest.
●**後援会** a society for the support (*of* Mr. A); a (Mr. A's) supporters' association; (芸能人などの) a fán clùb. ●**後援者** a supporter; (金銭的な) a sponsor; (芸術家などの) a patron.

こうえんきん 好塩菌 〖生物〗halophilic bacteria; halophile.

こうお 好悪 〖好き嫌い〗one's likes and dislikes. (❗対比による強勢の位置に注意)

こうおつ 甲乙 ▶両者に甲乙をつけるのは難しい It is hard to tell which (one of the two) is better./There is little difference between the two. (❗There is no comparison between the two. は「両者の間には差があります甲て比較の対象にならない」の意になる.《ことわざ》Comparisons are odious. にほぼ相当)
●**甲乙丙丁** A, B, C and D.

こうおん 恒温 ●**恒温動物** a homoiotherm; (一般に) a warm-blooded animal.

こうおん 高音 (音声) high (⇔a low) tone; (音調) a high-pitched (⇔a low-pitched) sound.
●**高音部**(最高音部) treble (⇔bass /béis/); (最高音域) sopráno.

こうおん 高温 (a) high temperature. ●高温で at a *high temperature*. ▶この国の高温多湿には耐えられない I can't bear the *high temperature* and high humidity of this country.
●**高温ガス** high temperature gas. ●**高温ガス炉** a high temperature gas-cooled reactor.

ごうおん 号音 (合図の音) a signal sound.

ごうおん 轟音 a roar. ●火山の轟音 the *roar* from the volcano. ●轟音を立てる roar; make a roaring sound. (⇨ごうごう)

*こうか **効果** 图 ❶〖効き目〗(an) effect; (効能) efficacy; (結果) (a) result. ●音響[照明]効果 sound [lightening] *effects*. ●(映画撮影の)特殊効果 special *effects*. ▶彼をしかったがあまり〔あまり〕効果がなかった I told him off, but it didn't have any [much] *effect*. ▶その薬は風邪に効果がない〔大変効果がある〕The medicine has no [a good] *effect on* a cold./The medicine is *ineffective against* [*very effective against*, *very good for*] a cold. (❗good for の方が口語的. ... ineffective [very effective] *in* cur*ing* a cold. ともいえる) ▶その経済政策は効果てきめんだった (= 効果がすぐあらわれた) The economic policy had an immediate *effect* [*worked* immediately].
会話「街灯をつければ犯罪は減るでしょうか」「大いに効果があるでしょう」"Would there be very little

crime, if the streets were lighted?" "It would make a big difference." (❗「大した効果はないでしょう」なら It wouldn't make any difference.)
❷ 〖柔道の判定〗 a *koka*. ●効果をとる score a *koka*.
── 効果的な 形 effective 《*in*》.
── 効果的に 副 effectively. ●効果的に話す speak *effectively* [in an *effective* way].

こうか 工科 〖工学部〗 the school of engineering.
●工科大学 an institute of technology.

こうか 考課 (人の) a performance evaluation; (会社の) a business report. ●人事考課 a performance *evaluation*; an efficiency *rating*.
●考課表 (人事の) a personnel *record*; (会社の) a business record.

こうか 校歌 a school [a college] song.

こうか 降下 图 (a) descént (↔ascent). ●急降下 a sudden *descent*. ▶飛行機はまもなく成田空港に向け最後の降下態勢に入ります We will soon make a final *descent* into Narita Airport.
── 降下する 動 descénd. ●パラシュートで降下する *descend* by parachute; parachute.

こうか 高価 ── 高価な 形 (値段の高い) expensive; (驚くほど高い) (やや略) costly; (貴重で) valuable. ●高価な花びん an *expensive* [a *costly*, a *valuable*] vase. ▶その車は高価な買い物だ The car is an *expensive* purchase. (❗値が高いだけのことをいう.) ▶その若い女性は高価な衣装を身につけていた The young woman was *expensively* dressed.

こうか 高架 ●高架線 (鉄道) 《米》 an elevated railroad, 《米話》 an el /él/; [an L]; 《英》 an elevated [an overhead] railway; (電線) an overhead wire [line]. ●高架道路 《米》 陸橋.

こうか 硬化 ── 硬化する 動 harden; (態度などが[を]) stiffen. ●態度を硬化させる *stiffen* one's attitude. ▶政府の新政策が野党を硬化させた The new government policy *stiffened* the opposition parties.
●硬化症 〖医学〗 sclerosis.

こうか 硬貨 a coin; metallic currency. ●100 円 [10 セント; 1 ペニー] 硬貨 3 枚 three 100-yen *coins* [*dimes*; *pennies*]. ●硬貨で支払う pay in *coin*.

こうか 膠化 图 (ゼリー状に固まること) gelatinization.
── 膠化する 動 gelatinize; jelly.

こうが 高雅 ── 高雅な 形 (優雅な) elegant, refine. ●高雅な雰囲気の貴婦人 a lady with an *elegant* atmosphere.

こうが 黄河 〖〖中国の川〗〗 the Huang He /hwà:ŋ hə́:/, the Yellow River.

*こうが 豪華 ── 豪華な 形 (ぜいたくな) luxurious /lʌɡzúəriəs/, deluxe; (華麗な) splendid, 《話》 gorgeous; (質の高い) of very high quality. ●豪華なホテル a *luxurious* [a *luxury*, a *deluxe*, 《話》 a *posh*] hotel. ●豪華な真珠のネックレス a *gorgeous* pearl necklace. ▶その部屋には豪華な家具が備わっていた The room was *luxuriously* furnished.
●豪華客船 a luxury liner. (❗この場合 luxurious を使うのはまれ) ●豪華版 (本の) a deluxe edition (of a book).

ごうか 業火 (地獄の) 〖〖仏教〗〗 hellfire, the flames of hell; (大火事) a big fire.

*こうかい 公開 ── 公開の 形 (出入り・使用など自由な) open; (公の) public. ●公開の席で話す speak *in public* (↔in private).
── 公開する 動 〖施設などを〗 open; 〖情報などを〗 make (it) public, go public 《*with*》; 〖作品・品物を〗 exhibit; (展示されている) be on display; 〖映画な どを〗 release. ▶その公園は一般に公開されている[た] The park *is open* [*was opened*] to the public. ▶その公式記録は数年間一般公開されなかった The official records *were not made public* for several years. ▶その寺の宝物が一般公開されている The temple's treasures *are on display* [*on show*, *being shown*] now. ▶その映画は去年日本で公開された The film *was released* in Japan last year.
●公開株 an introduced stock. ●公開講座 (大学の) an extension course. ●公開市場 an open market. ●公開状 an open letter. ●公開捜査 (make) an open criminal investigation. ●公開討論(会) an open [a public] debate; a [an open] forum 《*on*》. ●公開入札 a public tender.

*こうかい 後悔 图 (a) regret; 《書》 repentance; 《書》 remorse.
── 後悔する 動 be sorry 《*for, about*; *that* 節》; regret (-tt-) 《*that* 節; *doing*》; 《書》 repent 《*of*》. (❗通例宗教的文脈で). ▶あのように言ったことを後悔している I'm sorry [I *regret*] (*that*) I said that./I'm *sorry for* [I *regret*] saying that. (❗having said も可能だが, 単純形の saying の方が普通)/I'm sorry [I *regret*] *to* have said that. (❗I'm sorry [I regret] *to say*....とは「残念ながら...と言わねばならない」の意) ▶彼は不勉強(= 勉強しなかったこと)をひどく後悔した He was very *sorry* [He much *regretted*] (*that*) he had not studied hard (enough)./He was very *sorry* not to have studied hard (enough)./He much *regretted* not studying [*having* studied] hard (enough). ▶私は自分のしたことを後悔していない I have no *regrets about* what I did. (❗I have no regrets は常に複数で用いることに注意)/I feel no *regret* [I'm not *regretful*, I don't *feel bad* [《話》*badly*]] *for* what I did. ▶後悔することになるよ You'll be sorry for [*about*] this. (❗脅迫としても用いる)
●後悔先に立たず It is too late to grieve [be sorry] when the chance is past./(ことわざ) It's no use crying over spilt milk./(してしまったことは元に戻せない) What is done cannot be undone.

*こうかい 航海 图 a voyage /vɔ́iidʒ/; a cruise /krúːz/; a passage (❗単数形のみ); navigation. (⇨航行)

| 使い分け | voyage 航海を意味する一般的な語で, 長い船旅. |
| cruise 観光のため各地に寄港して楽しみながらする遊覧航海. |
| passage 船または飛行機による長い旅で, その過程を強調する. |
| navigation 「航行」の意でやや堅い語. |

●遠洋航海 an ocean *voyage*. ●航海に出る go on a *voyage* 《*to*》. ▶彼らは間もなく世界一周の航海に出る They will soon go on [take] an around-the-world *voyage* [*cruise*]./They will soon go on [take] a *voyage* [a *cruise*] around the world. ▶その貨物船はインド洋に向けて航海中であった The cargo boat was on its *voyage* toward the Indian Ocean. (❗主語は「人」も可) ▶荒れた航海だった We had a rough [a stormy] *passage*. ▶航海の無事をお祈りします (I wish you) bon voyage /bɑ̀ːn vwɑɪɑ́ːʒ/. (❗フランス語から)/Have a nice trip [voyage]. (❗後の文の方がくだけた表現)
── 航海(を)する 動 make* a *voyage*, 《書》 voyage 《*to*》; sail; navigate. ▶私たちの船はフランスへ処女航海をした Our ship *made* its [her] maiden *voyage to* France. ▶彼は太平洋を航海した He *sailed*

こうかい　(across) the Pacific.
- 航海士 a mate. ● 航海図 a chart.

こうかい 公海　the open sea; the high seas.

こうかい 更改 图　(契約などの更新) renewal; (制度などの変更) (a) change; (改革) (a) reform. ● 契約更改を済ませる finish a contract *renewal*.

── 更改する 動　renew 《a passport》; change [reform] 《a system》.

こうかい 紅海　the Red Sea.

こうかい 降灰　an ash fall [fallout], a fall of ash; (その灰) falling ash.

こうかい 黄海　Huang Hai /hwɑ́ːŋ hái/, the Yellow Sea.

*****こうがい** 公害　(environmental) pollution. (⚠単にpollutionということが多い) 騒音[食品; 産業]公害 noise [food; industrial] *pollution*. ● 公害のない環境 a *pollution*-free environment. ●《人・都市などが》公害で苦しむ suffer from *pollution*. ● 公害防止[規制]の対策を講じる take measures to prevent [control] *pollution*. ▶ 工場が公害をもたらすことはよくある Factories often produce *pollution*. ▶ 自転車は公害を引き起こすことはない Bikes are *pollution*-free.
- 公害対策 anti-pollution measures. ● 公害反対運動 an anti-pollution campaign. ● 公害病 a pollution-related [-caused] disease. ● 公害認定患者 an officially acknowledged victim of a pollution-related disease. ● 公害問題 a pollution [an environmental] problem.

*****こうがい** 郊外　(都市近郊の住宅地帯) the suburbs, 《米話》the burbs; (都市の中心部に対する周辺部) the outskirts. ● 郊外住宅が密集している山裾 a *suburb*-clotted hillside. ▶ 私は京都の郊外に住みたい I'd like to live *in the suburbs* [*in a suburb*, *on the outskirts*] of Kyoto. (⚠ (1) a suburb は the suburbs の中の1地区をさす. (2) 「京都の郊外」は a Kyoto *suburb* ともいえる) ▶ 郊外(= 田舎)を散歩した I took a walk in *the country*.
- 郊外住宅地 a suburban residential district; (特に通勤者の多い) a commuter *suburb*.
- 郊外電車 a suburban train.

こうがい 口外 ── 口外する 動　● このことを口外するな Don't *tell* anybody about this./Keep this *to yourself*./Keep quiet about this.

こうがい 口蓋 〖解剖〗the palate.
- 口蓋音〖音声〗a palatal. ● 口蓋化〖音声〗a palatalization. ● 口蓋垂〖解剖〗the uvula /júːvjələ/ (圈 ~s, -lae /-liː/). ● 口蓋裂〖医学〗cleft palate.

こうがい 光害　light pollution.

こうがい 校外　● 校外の[に, で] outside the school; out of school; off-campus.
- 校外活動 extramural [off-campus] activities.

こうがい 梗概 〖あらすじ〗an outline;〖要約〗a summary;〖論文・小説などの〗《やや書》a synopsis (圈 synopses). ● この戯曲の梗概を述べる *give* an *outline* [a *summary*] of the drama; *outline* [*summarize*] the drama.

こうがい 鉱害　mining [mineral] pollution.

こうがい 構外　● 構外の[に, で] outside [off] the premises [grounds, compound].

ごうかい 豪快 ── 豪快な 形　(大きな) big; (腹の底から) hearty. ● 豪快なホームラン〖野球〗(hit) a long [圈な] *tremendous* home run.

── 豪快に 副　豪快に笑う give a *big* [a *hearty*] laugh; roar with laughter.

ごうがい 号外　an extra [a special] (edition) 《of a newspaper》. ● 毎日新聞の号外 a *Mainichi* extra; an extra to 《×of》the *Mainichi*. ▶ 号外, 号外!《売り声》Extra, extra!

こうかいどう 公会堂　a public hall.

こうかがくスモッグ 光化学スモッグ　photochemical smog.

こうかく 口角　the corner of the mouth.
- 口角泡を飛ばす (さかんに論じる) discuss 《a matter》passionately [heatedly]; argue with 《him》with passion; have a heated discussion 《on, about》.
- 口角炎〖医学〗perlèche, angular cheilitis /kailáitis/.

こうかく 広角　a wide angle. ● 広角に打つ hit to all fields; use the whole field.
- 広角打法〖野球〗spray hitting. ● 広角レンズ a wide-angle lens.

こうかく 降格 图　《やや書》(a) demotion.

── 降格する 動　《やや書》demote 《him *to* +地位, *for* +理由》(↔promote).

こうがく 工学　engineering. ● 機械[土木]工学 mechanical [civil] *engineering*. ● 電子工学 eléctronics. (⚠単数扱い)
- 工学士 a bachelor of engineering. ● 工学修士 a master of engineering. ● 工学博士 a doctor of engineering. ● 工学部 the school [college, 《主に英》faculty] of engineering.

こうがく 光学　optics. (⚠単数扱い)
- 光学器械 an optical instrument. ● 光学顕微鏡 a light [an optical] microscope.

こうがく 後学　● 後学のために (将来の参考のために) (just) for (one's own) future reference.

こうがく 高額　● 高額紙幣 bank notes of [in] large [high] denominations. ● 高額商品 high-priced goods; (高い値札のついた) goods with a high price tag. ● 高額所得者 a person with large [high] income. (⚠「高額所得者層」は (be in) the high income group [bracket])

ごうかく 合格 图　passing 《of》;〖成功〗succéss. ▶ 合格おめでとう Congratulations on (your) *passing* [your *success in*] the exams.

── 合格する 動〖試験などに〗pass (⚠ 《人・物》を合格させる の意にも用いる);〖なんとか合格する〗get* through ...;〖成功する〗succeed 《in》. ▶ 彼は試験に1番で合格した He *passed* first in the exam. ▶ 彼は東大に合格した He *passed* [*succeeded in*] the entrance examination for [of, to] Tokyo University. (⚠ ×passed Tokyo University は不可. 文脈上明らかな場合は目的語の省略が)/(受け入れられた) He *got accepted into* Tokyo University.
- 合格者 a successful candidate. ● 合格証 a certificate of acceptance. ● 合格通知 a letter of acceptance. ● 合格点 a [the] passing grade [mark].

こうがくしん 向学心　a desire to learn [for learning]. ▶ 彼は向学心に燃えている He really *wants* [*is trying hard*] *to learn*. (⚠ He has a strong *desire* [*will*] *to learn*. より口語的)/He is very eager *to learn*.

こうがくねん 高学年　the upper grades《米》[forms《英》]. (⇨学年)

こうかくるい 甲殻類〖動物〗the crustacea. (⚠複数扱い) ● 甲殻類の動物 a crustacean /krʌstéiʃən/.

こうかつ 狡猾 图　cunning. ── 狡猾な 形　cunning; crafty; sly. (⇨ずるい)

こうかん 交換 图　(an) exchange; (古い物・欠陥品などの) replacement; (物々交換) barter; (両替) (a) conversion. ● 2人の間の手紙の交換 an *exchange* of letters between the two. ● 金と物との交換

こうかん *exchange* of money *for* goods. ●等価[不等価]交換 an *exchange* of equivalents (*non-equivalents*). ●電話交換手 a telephone operator; an operator (⚠呼びかけは Operator). ▶(この本との)交換に何をくれる? What will you give me *in exchange* [お返しに] *in return* (*for* this book)? (⇨引き換え) ▶交換です. 内線番号をどうぞ *Switchboard*. Which extension would you like? ▶今の交換レートはいくらですか What [×How much] is the current *exchange rate*?

―― **交換する** 動 ❶ 【取り替える】change; (古い物・破損品などを)replace. (⚠いずれも同種類の物と取り替える) ●おむつを交換する *change* a baby's diaper (●後に *for* another が省略されている); *change* a baby. ●古い電池を(新しいのと)交換する *replace* an old battery (*with* [*by*] a new one). ●シーツを(きれいなのと)交換しない *Change* the sheets (*for* clean ones). (⚠「シーツの交換」は a change of sheets/*Change* a bed. ▶欠陥品は無料で修理または交換いたします A defective product will *be* fixed or *replaced* free.

❷【やり取りする】exchange (⚠「交換し合う」の意では目的語は複数形); (商品などを) trade. ●パーティーで贈り物を交換する *exchange* gifts [×a gift] at the party. ▶私は彼女と席を交換した I *exchanged* [*changed*] seats *with* her. (⚠複数形に注意) ▶彼はバットをミットと交換した He *exchanged* [*made an exchange of, traded*, ×changed] his bat *for* a mitt. (⚠changed が不可の理由は (⇨❶)) ▶この帽子をもっと小さいのと交換していただけますか (店で) Could you *exchange* [*change*] the hat *for* a smaller one?
●交換価値 exchange value; value in exchange. ●交換条件 a bargaining chip [point]; a trade-off. ●交換台 a switchboard; (交換局) a telephone exchange. ●交換手を通しての通話 an operator-assisted call. ●交換部品 a spare part. ●交換留学生 an exchange student. ●交換レンズ an interchangeable lens.

こうかん 公刊 a publication. (⇨出版, 刊行)
―― **公刊する** 動 publish; issue; bring out.
こうかん 公館 an official residence. ●在外公館 diplomatic establishments abroad.
こうかん 交感 『生理』sympathy.
●交感神経 the sympathetic nerve. ●交感神経障害 sympathicopathy.
こうかん 交歓 ―― **交歓する** 動 (溶け込む) mix (*with*).
●交歓会 (懇親会) (やや話) a get-together, 《米》a mixer (*for*).
こうかん 好感 [好ましい印象] a good [favorable] impression; [よい感情] (a) good feeling. ●好感の持てる(=感じのよい)青年 a *pleasant* [A人好きのする] a *likable*] young man. ●その学生は教授に好感を与えた The student *made a favorable impression* on the professor./The student *impressed* the professor *favorably*. ▶私は彼に好感を持っている I *have friendly feelings toward* him./(好きだ) I *like* him.
こうかん 好漢 a good [a nice] fellow; 《米俗》a regular guy.
こうかん 高官 (⇨高級 [高級官僚]) ●政府高官 a high [a high-ranking] government official.
こうかん 巷間 (世間) the world; (町) the town. ▶巷間伝えるところによれば近々空き地に大型店舗が新築されるそうだ People say [《書》*It is rumored that, Rumor has it that*] a new big store will be built in the open.

こうがん 厚顔 (恥を知らないこと) shamelessness; (生意気) impudence. ●厚顔無恥な shameless; impudent; (鉄面皮の) brazen-faced.
こうがん 紅顔 a rosy [a ruddy] face. ●紅顔の美少年 a *handsome* [a *fair*] youth.
こうがん 睾丸 『解剖』the testicles.
こうがん 強姦 名 rape.
―― **強姦する** 動 rape, commit a rape. ●強姦された人 a *rape* victim. ●強姦未遂 an attempted criminal assault.
こうがんざい 抗癌剤 (制癌剤) an anticancer drug [agent].
こうかんど 高感度 ●高感度フィルム high-speed film; fast film.
こうき 工期 a period [a term] of construction.
こうき 公器 (新聞・雑誌・テレビなど) 〖書〗organs of public opinion. ●「世論報道の機関」の意)
こうき 広軌 〖鉄道〗a broad gauge. (⇔ 狭軌)
こうき 光輝 (輝き) brightness, brilliance; (名誉) glory. ●我が母校の光輝ある伝統 a *glorious* [*splendid*] tradition of our old school [Alma Mater].
こうき 好機 a good* opportunity [chance]. (⇨機会) ●好機を逸する miss [let slip] a *good opportunity* [*chance*]; let the *chance* go [slip by]. (⚠ *the* chance は「またとない機会」の意) ▶一生に一度の好機だった It was the *chance* of a lifetime. ▶(いよいよ)好機到来だ Now is the [your] *time*.
こうき 後記 a postscript. (⇨後[書]き)
こうき 後期 (二つに分けた) the second half; the second [latter] period (*of*); (…以降の) post-…; (2学期制の) the second semester. ●江戸時代後期に in the *late* (↔early) Edo *period*. (⇨末期, 後半)
●後期印象派 the Postimpressionism.
こうき 香気 (a) fragrance. (⇨香り)
こうき 校規 school rules [regulations].
こうき 校旗 a school flag.
こうき 高貴 名 nobleness.
―― **高貴な** 形 ●高貴な生まれの人 a person of *noble* birth. ●高貴な顔立ちの紳士 a *noble-looking* gentleman.
こうき 綱紀 (規律) discipline. ●綱紀を正す tighten *discipline*.
●綱紀粛正 the enforcement of discipline.
*こうぎ 抗議 名 (a) protest /próutest/; 〖反対〗an objection. ●不当な措置に対し当局に抗議を申し込む file [lodge] a *protest* with the authorities against the unfair measure.
―― **抗議する** 動 protest /prətést/, make* a protest (*against*). ●性差別に抗議する *protest* (*against*) sex discrimination (⚠against を省略するのは《米》); *make a protest against* sex discrimination. ●監督は走者がアウトになったことについて審判に強く抗議した 〖野球〗The manager *protested* strongly [*made a strong protest*] *to* the umpire *about* the runner being out. ▶国務長官はその戦争に抗議して辞任した The Secretary of State resigned *in protest against* the war.
●抗議試合 a protested game. ●抗議集会 a protest rally. ●抗議声明 (issue) a statement of protest. ●抗議デモ a protest demonstration. ●抗議文 a written protest; a note of protest; a protest note.
こうぎ 広義 a broad [a wide] sense. (⇨意味) ●それを広義に解釈する take it *in a* [*its*] *broad sense*.
こうぎ 交誼 (親交) friendship, friendly relations. ▶学生たちは卒業時に変わらぬ交誼を誓い合った The

students swore eternal *friendship* with each other at graduation.
こうぎ 講義 图 a lecture (*on*, *about*). (❗*on* は専門的内容を暗示) ●歴史の講義 a *lecture in* history (❗*学科*では in を用いる); a history *lecture*. ●講義を聞く listen to [《書》hear] a *lecture*. ●講義ノートを念入りにとる take careful *lecture* notes; take careful notes of [《米》on] the *lecture*. ●講義に出る[出ている] attend [be at] the *lecture*. (⇨出席する)
── 講義(を)する 動 ▶彼は学生に英詩についての講義をした He *lectured* (*to*) [*gave a lecture to*] his students *on* English poetry.
ごうき 剛毅 fortitude. ▶彼女は数々の弾圧にも決して屈することのない剛毅な人であった She was a woman of *fortitude* who never yielded to oppressions.
ごうき 豪気 ── 豪気な 形 brave, bold, 《話》plucky; 《書》stouthearted.
ごうぎ 合議 (協議) talks; (意見の一致) (a) consensus (❗複数形なし). ●合議で物事を決める make decisions *by consensus*.
●合議制 (代表制) the representative system.
こうきあつ 高気圧 [気象] high (atmospheric) pressure; an anticyclone. (⇨気圧) ●移動性高気圧 a migratory *anticyclone*.
*こうきしん 好奇心 curiosity. ●好奇心の強い人 a *curious* person; a person who has (an) intense [(a) keen] *curiosity* 《*about*》. ●好奇心にかられて out of *curiosity*. (⇨駆られる) ●知的好奇心に燃えている be burning with intelléctual *curiosity* 《*to do*》. ●好奇心をそそる arouse [excite] 《one's》*curiosity*. ●好奇心を満たす satisfy one's *curiosity*. ▶その女の子は賢くて何事にも好奇心が強い The girl is very bright and *curious about* everything./The girl is very bright and shows *curiosity about* everything.
こうきせい 好気性 ●好気性細菌 [生物] aerobic bacteria.
*こうきゅう 高級 图 high class [quality].
── 高級な 形 high-class, high-grade; (良質の) quality; (高価なものを売る) expensive 《*stores*》. ▶このカメラは高級だ This camera is (*of*) *high quality*. (❗*of* はしばしば省略される)/This camera is a *high quality* one. (❗one の使い方に注意) ▶この本はぼくには高級すぎる This book is too *serious* [*intellectual*] for me (to understand)./The level of this book is too high for me.
●高級官僚 a high(-ranking) government official. (❗他に top-ranking official, high-level official, top official などともいえる) ●高級紙 [新聞] a quality newspaper. ●高級車 a deluxe [an expensive, 《話》a classy] car. ●高級品 (high) quality goods [articles]; goods [articles] of (high) quality. ●高級ホテル a high-class [《上流の》a fashionable, (品質が5つ星の)a five-star, 《話》a posh] hotel. ●高級レストラン an exclusive [an expensive, 《話》a classy] restaurant. ●高級ワイン quality [choice] wine.
こうきゅう 好球 [野球] a good pitch; an easy ball; a fat pitch. ▶好球必打 Be sure to hit [Don't miss] a *good pitch*.
こうきゅう 後宮 (奥御殿) the Inner Palace.
こうきゅう 恒久 图 《やや書》permanence.
── 恒久の 形 permanent. ●世界に恒久平和を確立する establish *permanent* peace in the world.
こうきゅう 降給 (格下げ) a lowering of position [rank]; 《書》degradation, (a) demotion. (⇔昇

こうきゅう 高給 a high [a large] salary; high pay.
●高給を取る get [draw, earn] *a high salary*; be highly paid. ●高給を取っている編集者 an editor *on high pay*; *a highly-paid* editor.
こうきゅう 硬球 (野球の) a hard ball (⇔ 軟球); (公式のボール) an official baseball.
ごうきゅう 号泣 图 (大声で泣くこと) a bitter cry, 《書》wailing.
── 号泣する 動 cry out in sadness, 《書》wail 《*over*》. ▶彼は母の計報に接し号泣した He *cried bitterly* [《書》*wailed*] *over* his mother's death.
ごうきゅう 剛球 [野球] a blazing fastball; a smoke ball.
●剛球投手 a hard-throwing [a power] pitcher.
こうきゅうび 公休日 a public [《米》a legal, 《英》a bank] holiday; (休暇)《米》a vacation, 《英》a holiday; (定休日) a regular holiday.
こうきょ 皇居 the Imperial Palace. ●皇居前広場 the *Imperial Palace* Plaza.
こうぎょ 香魚 [「アユ」の別称] (⇨鮎)
*こうきょう 公共 图 《公衆》the public.
── 公共の 形 (公衆の) public (⇔private); (社会全体に共通な) common. ●公共の福祉 *public* welfare. ●公共の利益を図る promote the *public* interest; work for the *common* good. (❗the *common* good は「公益」の意) ▶公共の場所での喫煙を禁じる必要がある It is necessary to ban smoking in *public* place. ▶この公園は公共のものでだれでも利用できます This park is *public* property and anyone can use it. ▶彼は公共心に富んでいる He is full of *public spirit*./He is a man with plenty of *public spirit*.
●公共機関 a public institution. ●公共企業体 a public (service) corporation. ●公共建築 a public architecture. ●公共広告 public advertising. ●公共広告機構 the Japan Ad Council (略 AC). ●公共工事 public construction. ●公共サービス a public service. (❗しばしば複数形で) ●公共財産 public property. ●公共事業 a public enterprise; (土木工事の) public works. ●公共施設 public facilities. ●公共職業安定所 public employment security office. ●公共団体 a public organization. ●公共投資 public investment. ●公共放送 public (noncommercial) broadcasting. ●公共料金 public utility charges; (家賃などに対して)《話》utilities.
こうきょう 好況 [繁盛] prosperity; [商況] booming business, a (business) boom; [好況の時勢] good [prosperous] times. ▶産業界は目下好況を呈している The industry shows all the signs of *prosperity* [*is doing very well*] these days.
*こうぎょう 工業 图 (an) industry. (❗集合的に工業全体をいうときは Ⓤ, 具体的に個々の分野をいうときは Ⓒ) ●重[軽]工業 (a) heavy [light] *industry*. ●製造(工)業に従事している人々 people who are [work] in manufacturing *industries*. ▶日本の自動車工業は危機に直面している The Japanese auto(mobile) *industry* is facing [is faced with] a crisis.
── 工業の 形 industrial. ●日本の工業の中心地 an *industrial* center in Japan; one of the centers of Japanese *industry*.
●工業化 industrialization. ▶その国は急速に工業化しつつある The country *is becoming* [*being*] rapidly *industrialized*. ●工業技術 technology. ●工業国 an industrial [an industrialized]

こうぎょう country [nation]. ●工業所有権 an industrial property right. ●工業生産 industrial production. ●工業製品 industrial products. ●工業大学 an institute of technology; a technical college [institute]. ●工業団地 an industrial park. (⚠ park は「広大な敷地」の意) ●工業地帯 an industrial area [region]. ●工業デザイン an industrial design. ●工業都市 an industrial city. ●工業用水 water for industrial use.

こうぎょう 鉱業 the mining industry.

こうぎょう 興行 〖上演〗(1回の) a show, a performance; (連続の) a run; 〖事業〗show business. ●新春歌舞伎大興行 the New Year's special Kabuki program. ●興行成績がよい[悪い] do well [badly] at the box office; be good box office; be a box office success [hit]. (⚠ box office は「劇場の切符売り場; 興行上の集客力」の意) ▶1日2回興行をやる They give two *shows* [*performances*] a day. ▶その芝居は3か月長期興行を続けている The play has had a long *run* of three months.

● 興行権 performance [production] rights. ●興行師 a showman, a show manager (⚠ showman の中立的な言い方); (ボクシングの試合・コンサートなどの) a promoter.

こうぎょう 興業 encouragement and promotion of new industry.

こうきょうがく 交響楽 〖音楽〗a symphony.
●交響楽団 a symphony (orchestra).

こうきょうきょく 交響曲 〖音楽〗a symphony. ●ベートーベンの第九交響曲 Beethoven's Ninth (*Symphony*).

こうきょうし 交響詩 〖音楽〗a symphonic poem.

こうぎょく 紅玉 ❶〖宝石〗a ruby. (⇒ルビー) ❷〖リンゴ〗《米》a Jonathan (apple).

こうきん 公金 public [government] money. (⚠ money の代わりに funds も可)
●公金横領 the embezzlement of public money.

こうきん 抗菌 ── 抗菌性の 形 antibacterial.
●抗菌靴下 antibacterial socks.

こうきん 拘禁 (判決前の留置) 《書》detention; (拘置) 《書》custody; imprisonment; 《書》confinement.

── 拘禁する 動 imprison; confine; 《書》detain. ▶警察はその男を殺人事件で尋問するために拘禁した The police *detained* [*imprisoned*] the man for interrogation in the murder case.

こうぎん 高吟 ── 高吟する 動 recite (a poem) aloud.

ごうきん 合金 (an) alloy. ●銀と銅の合金 an *alloy* of silver and copper. ●銀に銅を混ぜて合金にする *mix* [〖冶金〗*alloy*] silver *with* copper.

こうく 校区 (学区) a school district.

こうぐ 工具 a tool. ●電動工具 a power *tool*. ●工具一式 a set of *tools*.

ごうく 業苦 〖仏教〗(因果応報の苦しみ) karmic sufferings; (罪の報い) the wages of sin.

*****こうくう** 航空 图 aviation. ●国際[国内]航空 international [domestic] *aviation* service. ●日本航空 Japan *Airlines*. ●英国航空 British *Airways*. ●大韓航空 Korean *Air*.

── 航空の 形 aerial /éəriəl/, àeronáutic. ▶ブエノスアイレス-ニューヨーク間に定期航空路を開設した They set up (a) regular *air* service between Buenos Aires and New York. (⚠ They は漠然と関係会社の人々をさす)

●航空医学 aviation medicine. ●航空運賃 an airline [x a plane] fare, an airfare. ●航空会社 an airline. ●航空貨物 air cargo [freight]. ●航空基地 an air (force) base. ●航空協定 a civil air transportation agreement. ●航空券 an airline ticket. ●航空工学 aeronautics. ●航空交通管制 air traffic control 《略 A.T.C.》. ●航空交通管制官 an air traffic controller. ●航空交通管制部[センター] an air traffic control center. ●航空自衛隊 the Air Self-Defense Force. ●航空写真 an aerial photograph. ●航空書簡 an aerogram; an air letter. ●航空神経症 〖医学〗aeroneurosis. ●航空標識 a navigation light. ●航空母艦 an aircraft carrier. ●航空力学 aerodynamics. ●航空料金 an airfare.

こうくう 口腔 (⇔口腔(こう))

こうくう 高空 a high altitude [sky].
●高空飛行 high-altitude flying [flight].

こうぐう 厚遇 〖温かいもてなし〗 a warm reception [welcome]; 〖親切な待遇〗 good treatment 《優遇》. ●厚遇を受ける[される] *get* [*be given*] *a warm reception*; *get* [*receive*] *a warm welcome*; *be warmly received* [*welcomed*].

こうぐう 皇宮 the Imperial Palace. (® 皇居)
●皇宮警察 the Imperial Guards.

こうくうき 航空機 (an) aircraft. (⚠ (1) 空中を飛行する乗り物の総称. (2) 通例無冠詞で集合的. ただし an や数詞を伴うこともある. (3) 単・複同形 〈飛行機〉)
●航空機産業 the aircraft industry. ●航空機事故 an air crash.

こうくうびん 航空便 air(-)mail [xair post]; (封筒の標示)《米》VIA AIR MAIL; 《英》BY AIR MAIL; 《仏》PAR AVION. ●航空便の手紙 an *airmail* [an *air*] letter. ●航空便で送る send ⟨it⟩ *by airmail* 《by はしばしば省略される》; send ⟨it⟩ *by air; airmail* ⟨it⟩.

こうくん 校訓 a school motto, 《書》school precepts.

こうくん 行軍 图 a march; marching.
── 行軍する 動 march. ▶彼らは夜間の中を行軍し続けた They kept *marching* in the rain during the night.

こうけい 口径 a caliber. ●38口径のピストル a 38 *caliber* revolver.

こうけい 光景 〖目に見える眺め〗a sight; 〖事件などの場面, 眺め〗a scene (通例人の動きを暗示); 〖目を見張らせるような〗a spectacle; 〖眺め〗a view. (⇒眺め) ●恐ろしい光景を目にする see a terrible *sight* [*scene*]. ●全体の光景 the whole *scene*. ▶その子供が通行人に物ごいをしている光景は哀れだった The *sight* [*scene*] *of* the child begging from passersby was very pitiful. (⚠ ×The *sight* [*scene*] *that* the child was begging .... は不可)/The child begging from passersby was a very pitiful *sight* [*scene*]./It was very pitiful to see the child begging from passersby. ▶その残酷な光景を今でもはっきり思い出す The cruel *scene* is still vivid in my memory. ▶そのパレードはすばらしい光景だった The parade was a magnificent *spectacle*. ▶それはちょっとした光景だった It was a *sight* to see.

こうげい 工芸 a craft; 〖手工芸〗a handicraft. ●伝統工芸 a traditional *craft*.
●工芸家 (男性) a craftsman, (女性) a craftswoman, (男女共用) craftspeople. ●工芸品 a craft object; (集合的) craftwork. ●工芸品店 a handicraft shop.

*****ごうけい** 合計 图 the sum, the [a] total, the sum total 《*of*》.

使い分け sum 数量を単純に加算した合計の意で、最も一般的な語.
total すべての結果を入れた合計をさし、しばしばそれが大きいことを暗示する.
sum total total とほぼ同じ意味だが、簿記などで用いる名堅い語.

▶7と3の合計は10だ The *sum* of 7 and 3 is 10.
▶被害者の合計は 100 人になった The *total* (number) of the victims came to 100./The victims *totaled* [*amounted to, ran up to*] 100.
▶その惨事で合計 30 人が死亡した A *total* of 30 people died in the disaster./*All told* [*Altogether*], thirty people died in the disaster.
▶彼女は請求書を手にとって合計(額)を見た. 大変な額었った She took the bill and looked at the *total*. It was an enormous amount [*very large*].

会話「おいくらになりますか」「合計 90 ドルになります、お客様」"How much do you make it?" "*All told* that'll make ninety dollars, madam." (*All* that makes ... と現在形でいうよりやわらかい言い方)

会話「合計でいくらになりますか」「2 万円です」"How much is it *in all* [*altogether*]?/What is the *total*?/What does the *total* come to?" "Twenty thousand yen."

── 合計する 動 add [sum (-mm-)] ... up; total ... (up). ● 彼は数字を合計して平均を出した He *added* [*totaled, summed*] *up* the figures and took the average. (**!** figures の代わりに numbers も可)
▶合計しての数字を教えてください *Make up the total* and tell me the figure, will you?

こうけいき 好景気 prosperity; good (↔hard) times; (一時的な) a boom. (⇒景気, 好況) ▶レジャー産業は好景気だ The leisure industry is *booming*./There is a *boom* in the leisure industry.

こうけいしゃ 後継者 a successor. ● (...の)後継者になる succeed 《him》; take over (the business).
● その支配人の後継者に任命される be appointed as a *successor to* [xof] the manager.

こうゲーム 好ゲーム a good game; (接戦) a close [a tight, a seesaw] game.

*こうげき 攻撃 图 ❶【攻めること】(an) attack 《on, against》; (突然の激しい) (an) assault 《on》; (防御に対する)《書》 offense. ● 正面[側面; 背面]攻撃 a frontal [a flank; a rear] *attack*. ● 総[報復; 連続]攻撃 an all-out [a retaliatory; a successive] *attack*. ● 波状攻撃 an attack in waves.
● 背後から敵軍に奇襲攻撃をかける make a surprise *attack on* the enemy from [in] the rear. ● 攻撃を開始する open [launch] an *attack*. ● 攻撃的な(n) an *offensive* 《on, against》. ● 攻撃をしかける begin to attack. ● 猛攻撃を受けている[受ける] be [come] under violent *attack* 《from, of》. ● 攻撃から身を守る defend oneself against an *attack*.
● 攻撃を加える(=攻撃する) (⇒動). ● 攻撃を繰り返す make [execute] repeated attacks; attack repeatedly. ▶ヤンキースが9回の裏の攻撃である The Yankees are batting [at bat] in the bottom of the ninth.
❷【非難】an attack 《on》; (a) criticism, 《書》(a) censure. ● 非難の集中攻撃 a *fire* of reproaches. ● 攻撃(的態度)には取る take the *offensive*. ● 彼は攻撃の的となった He was the object of an *attack* [(激しい非難) severe *criticism*].
── 攻撃的な 形 (防御に対して) offensive; (攻撃態勢の) aggressive (**!**《話》ではほめ言葉として「積極的な」の意でも用いる). ● 攻撃的態度で in an *offensive* [an *aggressive*] manner.

── 攻撃する 動 ❶【攻める】attack; (突然激しく) make* an assault 《on》; (激しく反撃すれば)《書》 assail. ● その町を攻撃する *attack* [*make an attack on*] the town; *make an assault on* the town. (**!** 前の方は町や人が無條のこともあるが、後の方では占拠が含意される) ▶我が軍は夜間に敵を攻撃した Our army *attacked* the enemy during the night.
❷【非難する】attack; criticize; 《書》 denounce; (激しくあるいは道徳的見地から) condemn. (⇒非難する)
● 攻撃は最良の防御である《ことわざ》Attack is the best form of defense.
● 攻撃側【球技】the offense; 【野球】the offensive team; the team [side] at bat. (**!** いずれも集合的に用い、単・複両扱い) ● 攻撃性 the nature of aggression. ● 攻撃目標 an attack objective.
● 攻撃用兵器 offensive [aggressive] weapons [arms]. ● 攻撃力 offensive power [strength].

こうけつ 高潔 图 nobility.
── 高潔な 形 ● 高潔な人格の人 a person of *noble* character; a person of great *nobility*.

こうけつ 豪傑 a hero (~s); (豪放な人) a bold [a daring] person; (規格からはみ出た人) an extraordinary person. ▶彼女は豪傑に見えるがそれでもなかなか繊細なところがある She looks *bold and daring*, but underneath she's very sensitive.

こうけつあつ 高血圧 high (↔low) blood pressure; 【医学】 hypertension (↔hypotension). ▶彼は高血圧だ He has *high blood pressure*./He is suffering from *hypertension*.

*こうけん 貢献 图 (a) contribution 《to》; (助け) a help.
── 貢献する 動 contribute 《to》; help ... out. ▶彼は世界平和に大いに貢献した He *contributed* greatly *to* world peace./He *made a great contribution to* world peace. ▶チームに貢献することが大切だと思っている. 記録は二の次さ I think it's important to *help* the team *out*. I'm not playing for the record.

こうけん 効験 (効き目) (an) effect; (a) virtue, 《書》 efficacy. (⇒効能, 効き目) ● 効験あらたかな薬 an *effective* [《書》an *efficacious*] medicine.

こうけん 後見 ❶【補佐】【法律】 guardianship; wardship;《書》 tutelage, custody. ▶彼は義兄の後見で大学へ入学した He entered college under the *guardianship* [《書》 *custody*] of his brother-in-law.
❷【能・歌舞伎などの】 a prompter.
● 後見人【法律】 a guardian. (**関連** 被後見人 a ward)

*こうげん 高原 a plateau /plætoʊ/ (〜s, plateaux /-z/); (高台) (やや書) a height, a tableland (**!** 2 語ともしばしば複数形で単数扱い); (高地) highlands. ● ゴラン高原 the Golan *Heights*. ● 志賀高原 the Shiga *Highlands*. ● 高原状態に達する reach a *plateau*.

こうげん 公言 ── 公言する 動 (人前をはばからず言う) declare; (感じていることや意見をはっきり言う) profess. ● 信念を公言する *profess* one's beliefs. ▶彼は自分が過激派だと公言してはばからない He openly *declares that* he is a radical./He openly *declares himself* (*to be*) a radical./He *makes no secret of* being a radical.

こうげん 巧言 (お世辞) flattery; fair [honeyed] words. (⇒お世辞)
● 巧言令色(鮮)なし仁(*rén*)(巧みな言葉を使い、いい顔色を作っている者には、人の道を心得た者が少ない)(ことわざ) Fair [Fine, Soft] words butter no pars-

こうげん　nips./Where there is over mickle courtesy, there is little kindness./God in the tongue and the devil in the heart.

こうげん 光源　(映写機などの) a light source; 〖物理〗 an illuminant.

こうげん 抗原　〖医学〗 an antigen.
- 抗原抗体反応 an antigen-antibody reaction.

ごうけん 合憲　合憲である be constitutional.
- 合憲性 constitutionality.

ごうけん 剛健 形　(強健) virility.
- 剛健な 形 virile; (男らしい) manly.

こうげんがく 考現学　modernology; the study of modern phenomena.

こうげんびょう 膠原病　〖医学〗 a collagen disease (略 CD).

こうけんりょく 公権力　public [state, governmental] power; governmental authority.

こうこ 公庫　(住宅金融公庫) the Housing Loan Corporation. ▶ 公庫で 2,000 万円借りる borrow twenty million yen from the *Housing Loan Corporation*.

こうこ 後顧　● 後顧の憂い (後の心配) (将来の) anxiety about one's future; one's future anxieties; (家庭の) anxiety about one's home; one's family cares [worries]. ▶ 君がここに残れば後顧の憂いはない If you stay here we'll have no *anxiety about* our home.

こうこ 香香　pickled vegetables; pickles. (⇨圖 漬物)

*こうご 交互 — 交互に 副 (⇨代わる代わる)

こうご 口語　(話し言葉) spoken language; (くだけたスタイルの言葉) colloquial language. ● 口語体で書く write in a *colloquial* style.
- 口語英語 spoken [colloquial] English. ● 口語文 (a piece of) writing written in a colloquial style. ● 口語訳 (a) colloquial translation; translation into colloquial 《Japanese》.

ごうご 豪語 — 豪語する 動 boast. (⇨自慢する) ▶ 彼は 10 か国語しゃべれると豪語した He *boasted* that he could speak ten languages.

*こうこう 高校　(senior) high school, 《話》 a high. (⇨学校) ● 全日制 [定時制] 高校 a full-time [a part-time] *high school*. (! 「夜間高校」の場合なら a night *high school* という) ● 通信制高校 a correspondence *high school*. ● 実業 [商業; 工業; 農業] 高校 a vocational [a commercial; a technical; an agricultural] *high school*. ▶ 彼は高校では成績がよかった He did well in *high school*. ▶ 私の息子は高校 2 年生です My son is a second-year student in *high school*./《米》 My son is in the 11th grade [an eleventh-grader]. ▶ 太郎は高校時代にはテニス部に所属していた Taro belonged to the tennis club when he was a *high school student* [in *high school*].
- 高校教育 high school education. ● 高校生 a high school student. ● 高校総体 an inter-high school athletic competition [《米》 meet]. ● 高校野球 high school baseball. (! 「全国高校野球大会」は the National Senior High School Baseball Tournament)

こうこう 口腔　the mouth; 〖解剖〗 the oral cavity.
- 口腔衛生 oral [dental] hygiene.

こうこう 孝行　filial piety [duty]. (⇨親孝行)
- 孝行息子 a dutiful [a good] son.

こうこう 後攻　● 後攻する 〖野球〗 take the field first; bat last. ▶ 我がチームの後攻で試合が始まった The game started with our team *taking the field first*.

こうこう 航行　navigation. ▶ 四国沖を航行中の船舶 ships *sailing* off Shikoku.
- 航行区域 a navigation area.

こうこう 皓々　▶ 月が皓々と(=明るく)照っている The moon is shining *bright(ly)*. (! *bright* の方が口語的) (⇨明かり)

こうこう 煌々　▶ 夜空に星が煌々と輝いている The stars are shining *bright(ly)* [*brilliantly*] in the night sky. (! *brilliantly* の方がより明るい)

こうこう 咬合　(歯のかみ合わせ) 〖医学〗 occlusion; bite. ● 不正咬合 malocclusion.

こうごう 皇后　● 皇后陛下 an empress; Her Majesty the Empress; Her (Imperial) Majesty.

ごうごう 囂々　▶ この政策は国民からごうごうたる非難を受けた This policy was *bitterly* [*harshly*] condemned by the public.; The public made a *clamorous* protest against this policy.

ごうごう 轟々　▶ ごうごうと音を立てる roar; (雷のような) thunder; (風が) howl [*through* the trees). ▶ 滝がごうごう音を立てて落ちていた The waterfall came *roaring* down. ▶ 列車がごうごう音を立てて通った The train *thundered* [*roared*] along./The train passed along *with a roar* [*with a thundering noise*].

こうこうがい 硬口蓋　〖解剖〗 the hard palate.

こうこうぎょう 鉱工業　mining and manufacturing.
- 鉱工業生産 industrial production (in manufacturing, mining and utilities). ● 鉱工業生産指数 an industrial production index.

こうごうしい 神々しい　(神のような) divine; (神聖な) heavenly. ▶ 神々しい美しさ *divine* beauty.

こうごうせい 光合成　〖生化学〗 photosynthesis.
- 光合成で by [through] *photosynthesis*. ● 光合成を行う carry on [out] *photosynthesis*; photosynthesize.

こうこうど 高高度　a high altitude.
- 高高度飛行 a high altitude flight; (亜成層圏飛行) substratospheric flying.

こうこうや 好々爺　a good-natured old man (複 men).

こうこがく 考古学 图　arch(a)eology /ɑːrkiɑ́ləʤi/. (! 《米》でも -a- のつづりが多い)
- — 考古学(上)の 形 arch(a)eological.
- 考古学者 an arch(a)eologist.

こうごき 小動き　(株式・為替などの) a minor fluctuation; narrow movements.

*こうこく 広告 图　an advertisement /《米》 ædvərtáizmənt, 《英》 ədvə́ːtɪs-/ 《for》, 《話》 an ad; (広告を出すこと) advertising. (⇨宣伝)

① 〖～広告〗　● 新聞広告 a newspaper *advertisement*. ● 三行広告 a classified *ad* (! 項目別に分類されていることから). ● 《米》 a want *ad* (! 主に求人・求職の広告であることから). ● たばこの広告 cigarette *advertising*. ● 商業広告 commercial *advertising*. ● サブリミナル[閾外(いきがい)]広告 subliminal *advertising*.

▮ **DISCOURSE**
テレビ広告は消費者には一定のメリットがある TV *advertisements* give *certain* benefits to consumers. (! *certain* (特定の) は抽象的内容を述べるディスコースマーカー。続けてメリットの具体的内容を述べる)

② 〖広告(の)～〗　● 広告掲載 advertising. ▶ これは広告の品ですか Is this the thing I saw in *advertisement* [you *advertised*]?

③ 〖広告を [で]〗　● 秘書の求人広告を出す *advertise for* a secretary. ● 英語の家庭教師の求職の広告を出す *advertise for* a job *as* a private English teacher. ●新聞やテレビに新製品の広告を出す *advertise* [*put an advertisement for*] a new product in the newspapers and on television. ●広告で見る see 《it》 in an *advertisement*. ▶新聞広告でこの本はよく売れるようになった After we put an *advertisement* in the newspapers, the book began to sell./(需要が増えた) The *advertisement* in newspapers created a great demand for this book. (*!* 前の方がより口語的)

── **広告する** 動 ádvertise; (人・職などを求めて) advertise for ....
● **広告会社** an advertising [an ad] agency.
● **広告業** advertising (business). ● **広告写真** advertising [ad, commercial] photography.
● **広告収入** an advertising revenue. ● **広告代理店** an advertising agency. ● **広告塔** an advertising tower; (人) a poster child; a person around whom an ad campaign is built; one who acts as a symbol of a group in order to draw others in. ● **広告主** an ádvertiser; (ラジオ・テレビの) a sponsor. ● **広告板** (ポスターなどをはる)《米》a billboard,《英》a hoarding. ● **広告欄** an advertisement column. ● **広告料** an ad rate.

こうこく 公告 图 a public [an official] notice [announcement]. ── **公告する** 動 notify; announce publicly (⇨発表する).

こうこく 公国 (prince) が治める国) a principality, (公爵 (duke) が治める国) a duchy /dʌ́tʃi/. ●モナコ公国 the *Principality* of Monaco. ●ルクセンブルク大公国 the Grand *Duchy* of Luxembourg /lʌ́ksəmbɑ:rg/.

こうこく 抗告 图 『法律』 an appeal.
── **抗告する** 動 ▶最高裁へ即時抗告する *appeal* the decision immediately *to* the Supreme Court.

こうこく 興国 ● 興国の祖 the founder of a country.

こうこつ 恍惚 ●恍惚の人 a *senile* person. ●恍惚として彼女の歌に聞きほれる listen rapturously to her song. (⇨うっとり)

こうこつ 硬骨 (硬い骨) a hard bone; (気丈) backbone; firm character; stubbornness.
● **硬骨漢** (意志強固な人) a man of strong will [firm character]. ● **硬骨魚** a bony fish; a teleost.

こうこつのひと 『恍惚の人』 *The Twilight Years*.(《参考》有吉佐和子の小説)

こうこつもじ 甲骨文字 (説明的に) ancient Chinese pictographs inscribed on beasts' bones and tortoise shells.

こうごに 交互に (順番に) in turn; (次々に) one after the other, alternately. (⇨代わる代わる)

ごうコン 合コン (説明的に) a drinking party, at which there are the same number of men and women who are seeking a chance to find a friend of the opposite sex.

こうさ 交差 ● 立体交差 a two-level *crossing*.
● **平面交差** 《米》a grade *crossing*, 《英》a level *crossing*.
── **交差する** 動 ▶この道はそこで幹線道路と交差している This road *crosses* the main road there./This road and the main road *cross* there.
● **交差点** (⇨交差点)

こうさ 考査 an examination, 《話》an exam, a test. (⇨試験 ❶, テスト ❶)

こうさ 黄砂 yellow sand.

こうざ 口座 an account. ●普通預金口座 a sávings [《英》a depósit] accòunt. ●当座預金口座 a

checking 《米》[a current 《英》] *account*. ●口座を開く[閉じる] open an *account* [close one's *account*] 《*with* [*at*] a bank). ●彼の銀行口座に10万円振り込む put [pay] 100,000 yen into his bank *account*. ●口座から5万円引き出す draw [take] 50,000 yen from [out of] one's *account*. ▶みずほ銀行に口座があります I have an *account* at [with] (the) Mizuho Bank./I keep [hold] an *account* in (the) Mizuho Bank.
● **口座番号** an account number. ● **口座引き落とし** a direct debit. ● **口座振替** an account transfer.

こうざ 高座 (一段高い席) a platform, a dais /déiis/; (寄席などの) the stage. ●高座に上がる go on the *stage*. ●高座をつとめる play [perform] on the *stage*.

こうざ 講座 (連続の講義) a course; (講義) a lecture; (教授職) a chair. ●ラジオ英語講座 a radio English *course*. ●公開講座 an extension *course*.
● **夏期講座** a summer *course*. ●日本史の講座 a *course* in [a *course of lectures on*] Japanese history; a Japanese history *course*. ●大学で英文学の講座を担当する hold the [a] *chair* of English literature at the university. ▶私は金曜日の夜に開かれる講座をとっている I'm taking a *course* that meets on Friday night.

*こうさい 交際 图 『付き合い』《やや書》(an) association; 『面識』《やや書》(an) acquaintance; 『交友関係』(⇨付き合い) a friendship. ●彼女とは以前ちょっとの間交際があった I had a brief *friendship* [*acquaintance, association*] *with* her a while ago. (*!* 恋愛関係をいう場合には) I *was going out with* [*seeing*] her a while ago. (⇨動) ▶彼は交際(=友人の範囲)が狭い He has a small [a narrow] (↔a large, a wide) circle of friends. (*!* narrow はしばしば「閉鎖性」を含意) ▶彼は交際が広いが本当の友人は少ない He has a wide *acquaintance*(*ship*) [(多くの知人がある)] plenty of *acquaintances*] but only a few real friends. ▶彼女に交際(=デート)を申し込んだが断られた I asked her for a *date* [I asked her for out on a *date*], but she refused [turned it down]. ▶うちの学校では男女交際は禁止だ Our school has a rule prohibiting a boy and a girl student from *going out together*. (⇨動) ▶彼女はあまり交際好きではない She does not *socialize* [*mix*] very well./She is not very *sociable* [is rather unsociable]./She doesn't much like being with people. (⇨社交)

── **交際(を)する** 動 『社交として』(交わる) socialize, mix 《*with*》; (好ましくない人と) associate 《*with*》; 『男女間で』go*out 《*with*》, 《複数主語で》go out together (『go steady 《*with*》, go 《*with*》は《古》; (しばしば会って) see*. (*!* 2以上の go はいずれもしばしば進行形で) (⇨图; 付き合う) ▶彼はさまざまな人と広く交際している He *socializes* [*mixes*] *with* a wide variety of people.
● **交際費** social expenses; (接待費) entertáining expènses; (会社払いの) an expense account.

こうさい 公債 (issue, redeem) (国の) government [(地方の) municipal] bonds.
● **公債依存度** a depending rate on government bond issue.

こうさい 光彩《書》luster, brilliance. ●光彩を添える add *luster* 《*to*》.
● **光彩陸離** ^(°) 光彩陸離とした(=光り輝く) 宝石 glittering jewels.
● **光彩を放つ** shine, sparkle.

こうさい 虹彩 『解剖』 the iris /áiəris/.
● **虹彩炎** 『医学』iritis /aiəráitis/.

こうざい 功罪 ●功罪相半(あい)ばする ▶その計画の功罪は相半ばすると思う The *merits* and *demerits* of the plan seem to balance out [even out]. (! 対比によるアクセントの移動に注意)

こうざい 鋼材 steel (materials).

こうざいりょう 好材料 good material; (資料) excellent [sufficient] data; 〖株式〗a positive [a favorable] factor, good news. ●研究推進の好材料 *excellent data for* proceeding with a study.

***こうさく** 工作 图 ❶〖学科〗(手細工) (a) handicraft. ●工作の時間 a *handicraft* class.
❷〖土木・建築工事〗construction (work). ●補強工作 reinforcement *work*.
❸〖策略〗political *maneuvering*; (軽蔑的) politicking. ●裏工作 behind-the-scenes activity.

— 工作する 動 make*; construct; 〖策略する〗maneuver. ●和平工作する *make* a peace move. ●裏面工作 behind the scenes. ●その会議への準備工作をする(=道を開く) *pave the way* for the conference. ▶彼はいとこをいい職につけるため工作をした(=内密に運動した) He *pulled strings* to get his cousin a good job. (! pull strings は〖話〗で,「ひそかに工作する」の意)

● 工作員 a secret agent; an intelligence agency operative. ● 工作機械 a machine tool. ● 工作室 a workshop. ● 工作品 handicrafts. ● 工作物 a construction (work).

***こうさく** 耕作 图 〖田畑を耕して作物を作ること〗cultivation; 〖農作業〗farming.

— 耕作する 動 cultivate; plow /pláu/; till. (➪耕す)

● 耕作機械 a cultivator; a farm(ing) tool. ● 耕作地 cultivated land; plowed land. ● 耕作物 farm [agricultural] products.

こうさく 交錯 图 (混ぜ合わせ) a mixture.

— 交錯する 動 mix together; (やや書) mingle. ●愛憎の交錯する奇妙な感情 a curious *mixture* of love and hatred. ●将来に対する期待と不安が交錯する have excitements for the future *mingled with* fear.

こうさく 鋼索 a wire rope, a cable.
● 鋼索鉄道 [ケーブルカー] a cable car [railway]; a funicular (railway).

こうさつ 考察 图 〖熟慮〗consideration; 〖研究〗a study. ●東洋美術についての考察 a *study of* Oriental art.

— 考察する 動 ●その問題を注意深く考察する *give careful consideration to* the matter; *consider* the matter carefully.

こうさつ 絞殺 图 strangulation.

— 絞殺する 動 strangle (him); choke (him) to death.

こうさてん 交差点 a crossing, an intersection.
● セントラルパークウエストと81番街の交差点にあるヘイドンプラネタリウム館 the Hayden Planetarium, Central Park West at 81st Street. ●道路を交差点で渡る cross the street at the *crossing* [*intersection*].

***こうさん** 公算 〖見込み〗(a) probability; 〖可能性〗a chance. (➪可能, 確率) ●彼がここへ来る公算十分ある There is every *probability of* his coming here [*that* he will come here]. (!It is very [highly] probable that ... ともいえる)/There is a good *chance of* his coming here [*that* he will come here]./He is very *likely* to come here. (!*It is* very *likely that* he will come here. ともいえる)

こうさん 降参 图 (a) surrender (*to*). ●敵は降参に追いやられた The enemy was [were] forced into *surrender*.

— 降参する 動 ❶〖降伏する〗surrender (*to*), give* in (*to*) (後の方が口語的); (投降する) give up (*to*). ▶我々は敵に決して降参しないぞ We shall never *surrender* [*give in*] *to* the enemy. (! shall は will より強い意志を表す) ●敵は戦わずに降参した The enemy *gave in* [*gave up*] without a fight.
❷〖耐えられない〗cannot stand*; 〖あきらめる〗give* up.. ●この暑さには降参だ I *can't stand* [*bear*] this heat. ●この問題には降参だ(=解けない) I *can't solve* this problem./This problem *has got me beaten*. ●もう降参だ(まいった) I give up./(君負けた) You win. ●いずれも現在形に注意 (➪た). 通例 × I lost. とはいわない)

***こうざん** 鉱山 a mine. ●金鉱山 a gold *mine*. ●鉱山で働く work in a *mine*.
● 鉱山労働者 a mineworker; a miner (!〈英〉では通例炭鉱夫をさす).

こうざん 高山 a high mountain.
● 高山気候 an alpine climate. ● 高山植物 an alpine (plant); (集合的) an alpine flora. ● 高山病 mountain [〖医学〗altitude] sickness. ● 高山病にかかる suffer *mountain sickness*.

***こうし** 格子 a lattice. ●鉄格子のついた警察の移送車 a police van with *bars* at the windows. ●防犯 [防護]用の鉄格子 a security *grill*(*e*).
● 格子じま (a) check; (タータンチェック) (a) plaid /plǽd/; a tartan (!× (a) tartan check としない). ● 格子じまのカーテン a *check*(*ed*) curtain. ● 格子造り latticework. ● 格子窓 a lattice window.

こうし 子牛 a calf (覆 calves); 子牛の肉 veal.

こうし 公司 (中国語で「会社」の意) a company.

こうし 公私 〖公的・私的な事柄〗public and private matters [affairs]. ●公私を区別する(=一線を画する) draw the line between *public* (〖公務の〗 *official*) *and private matters*. ●公私を混同する mix up *public and private matters*; (会社の場合) mix *company business with personal affairs*. ▶彼は公私ともに忙しい He is busy both *officially* and *privately*.

こうし 公使 a minister. (➪大使) ●イタリア駐在日本公使 the Japanese *Minister to* Italy.
● 公使館 a legation. ● 公使館員 (個人) a member of the legation staff; (全体) the legation (staff).

こうし 孔子 Confucius /kənfjúːʃəs/. ●孔子の教え *Confucian* teachings; (儒教) Confucianism.

こうし 行使 图 use /júːs/; (権力・権力などの) exercise.

— 行使する 動 ●暴動を鎮圧するために武力を行使する *use* /júːz/ [〖書〗*employ*, (やや書) *resort to*] (armed) force to put down a riot. ●国民としての権利を行使する *exercise* one's rights as a citizen.

こうし 厚志 (親切な気持ちと配慮) kindness and consideration. ▶ご厚志を感謝いたします Thank you for your *kindness*.

こうし 校史 a school history; a history of a school.

こうし 講師 〖講演者〗a speaker, a lecturer; 〖大学の〗(専任の)〈米〉an instructor,〈英〉a lecturer, (日本の) an assistant professor, (非常勤の)〈米〉a lecturer,〈英〉a part-time lecturer (!teacher とすれば中学・高校・大学を問わない), (日本の) a lecturer. ●化学の講師 an *instructor in* [×of] chemistry; a chemistry *instructor*.

‡こうじ 工事 图 construction (work). ●建設工事を始める start *construction work*. ▶「工事中」(掲

こうじ 示)(建設[修理]中)Under *Construction* [*Repair*]./(道路・水道・ガスなどの)Men working [at work]./(道路工事)Róad wòrks. ▶道路は工事中だ The road *is under construction* [*repair*].
── **工事(を)する** 動 ● 電話線に[カーペットの敷き込み]工事をする *install* a phone line [a carpet].
● 工事現場 a site of construction; a constrúction site.

こうじ 麹 *koji*; (説明的に) a kind of yeast prepared from rice or barley.
● 麹菌 ⓢ a *koji* mold spore; an aspergillus /æspədʒɪləs/ (⦅複⦆ -gilli /-dʒɪlaɪ/).

こうじ 小路 an alley; a lane; a narrow street. ● 袋小路 a blind *alley*. (⇨袋小路)

こうじ 公示 a public announcement; 〚公式の通知〛 an official notice.
── **公示する** 動 ● 市長選挙を公示する *make a public announcement* of a mayoral election; *announce* a mayoral election *publicly* [*officially*].
● 公示地価 an assessed value of land.

こうじ 公事 public [official] affairs; official business.

こうじ 好事 a happy event; (よい行い) good conduct.
● 好事魔多し 《ことわざ》(カップを口に持っていく間にもうかつな失敗はたくさん生じる) There's many a slip between the cup and the lip.; (幸運は平手打ちに出くわす) Good luck comes by cuffing.

こうじ 好餌 (うまいえさ) good bait; (誘惑するもの) a temptation, 《書》an allurement; (欲望のえじき) a victim; (a) prey 《*to, for, of*》. ▶彼の小説は批評家の好餌となった His story became an easy *victim* of the critics./His story fell easy *prey to* the critics.

こうじ 後事 (将来のこと) one's future affairs; (死後のこと) one's affairs after one's death. ▶彼は最後の息を引き取るときおじに後事を託した When he breathed his last, he asked his uncle to look after his *affairs*.

ごうし 合祀 ── **合祀する** 動 enshrine together.
▶この神社には戦没者が合祀されている Fallen soldiers *are enshrined together* in this shrine.

ごうし 合資 ● 合資会社 a limited partnership.

ごうし 郷士 a rural [a country] *samurai*; 〚英史〛 a yeoman; a squire.

*こうしき 公式 ❶ 〚数学〛 a formula (⦅複⦆ ~s, formulae). ● 公式で表す express (it) in a *formula*; formulate. ▶その線の長さを計算する公式は難しすぎる The *formula* for calculating the length of the line is too difficult.
❷ 〚おおやけ〛 (公式の) official; (正式の) formal. ● 非公式の記者会見を行う have an *informal* press conference.
● 公式記録 (公認の) an official record. ● 公式戦 a regular game (in a pennant race). ● 公式訪問 an official [a formal] visit.

こうしき 硬式 ● 硬式テニス (hardball) tennis.
● 硬式野球 (hardball) baseball. (⦅補⦆ テニス・野球とも米英では硬式が普通なので、hardball はほぼ不要。逆に軟式の場合には rubberball が必要)

こうしけつしょう 高脂血症 〚医学〛 hyperlipemia /hàɪpərlɪpíːmiə/.

こうじげん 高次元 a high(er) dimension. ● 高次元の話 a high-*dimension* talk.

こうしせい 高姿勢 (高圧的な態度) a high-handed attitude. ● 高姿勢に出る take a *high-handed attitude* 《*toward*》.

こうしつ 皇室 the Imperial Family [Household].

こうしつ 高湿度 high humidity. ● 高温高湿 *high* temperature *and humidity*.

こうしつ 硬質 ⓢ hardness.
── **硬質の** 形 hard. ● 硬質の文体 a *crisp* style.
● 硬質ガラス hard glass. ● 硬質小麦 hard wheat.
● 硬質磁器 hard porcelain; hard earthenware.

こうしつ 膠質 〚化学〛 colloid.

こうじつ 口実 (偽りの理由) a pretext /príːtekst/; (言い訳) an excuse /ɪkskjúːs/. ● もっともらしい口実をつくる make (up) a plausible *excuse*. ● 遅刻の口実 ⦅find⦆ a *pretext* [an *excuse*] *for* being late. ▶彼は病気を口実に学校を早退した He left school early *on* [*under*] *the pretext of* being sick [*that* he was sick]. (⇨理由 ③) ▶そんな口実は通らない That is no *excuse*.

こうじつせい 向日性 〚植物〛 heliotropism /hìːliːátrəpɪzm/. ● 向日性の植物 a hèliotrópic plant.

こうして (in) this way (〚話〛では In を省略することが多い); 《書》thus. ▶こうして彼は彼女の心をとらえた *In this way* [*Thus*], he won her heart./*That's how* he won her heart. ▶こうしてドアに鍵(⦅紛⦆)をかけなさい Lock the door (*in*) *this way* [*like this*]. ▶こうしていただくとありがたいのですが *This is what* we'd like you to do.

こうしゃ 公社 a public corporation.

こうしゃ 公舎 an official house [residence]. ● 知事[警察署長]公舎 an *official residence for* the governor [the head of a police station].

こうしゃ 巧者 (熟練) skill 《*in, on, at*》; proficiency 《*at, in*》; (熟練者) an expert 《*at, in, on, with*》. ● 試合巧者の選手[チーム; 監督] a tactically clever player [team; manager, coach].

こうしゃ 後者 the latter (↔the former); 〚第二のもの〛 the second. (⇨前者)

<blockquote>
■ DISCOURSE
私は後者の見方を選ぶ I would **prefer** the *latter* view to the former. (❗ I would prefer ... (私は ...の方を好む) は二者を表すディスコースマーカー。I prefer よりも丁寧で、論説文に適している)
</blockquote>

こうしゃ 校舎 a school building. ▶ベルが鳴ると子供たちは校舎に入っていった The bell rang and the kids went into the *school*.

こうしゃ 降車 ── **降車する** 動 get off. (⇨降りる ❷)
● 降車口 an exit /éɡzɪt/; 〚揭示〛 Exit; 《英》Way Out. ● 降車ホーム a [an arrival] platform.

ごうしゃ 豪奢 ⓢ 《豪華》luxury; magnificence; extravagance.
── **豪奢な** 形 luxurious; magnificent; extravagant. ● 豪奢な邸宅 a *palatial* [a *magnificent*, a *very luxurious*] residence. ● 豪奢な暮らしをする enjoy a *very luxurious* [《書》an *affluent*] lifestyle.

-ごうしゃ -号車 Car No. ..... ▶食堂車は9号車でございます The dining car is *Car No.* 9.

こうしゃく 公爵 (英国の) a duke; (英国以外の) a prince. (⇨貴族 解説) ● 公爵夫人 (英国の) a duchess; (英国以外の) a princess.

こうしゃく 侯爵 (英国の) a marquess /máːrkwəs/; (英国以外の) a marquis /máːrkwəs/. (⇨公爵) ● 侯爵夫人 a marchioness /máːrʃənɪs/; marquise.

こうしゃく 講釈 ⓢ 〚説明〛 (a) explanation; (講義) a lecture; (くわしい論評) 《書》(an) exposition; 〚講談〛 storytelling. ● 講釈を述べる give ⦅boring⦆ *lectures* ⦅*about* this and that⦆.
── **講釈する** 動 explain; 《書》expound; lecture ⦅*on*⦆.

- **講釈師** a professional storyteller.
- **こうしゃさい 公社債**《公債と社債》public and corporation bonds.
  - 公社債投資信託 a bond investment trust fund.
- **こうしゅ 好守** good fielding; solid [tight] defense. ●好守好走〚野球〛*good fielding* and good running.
- **こうしゅ 攻守** óffense and défense (**!** 対照強勢に注意);〚野球〛batting and fielding.
  - 攻守所を変える《攻める側になる》reverse 《their》positions; turn the tables 《on one's rival》;〚野球〛《the teams》change sides.
- **こうしゅう 口臭** bad [foul] breath;〚医学〛halitosis /hǽlətóusis/. ▶彼は口臭がある He has *bad breath*./His breath smells 《bad》./He suffers from *halitosis*.
- **こうしゅう 公衆** the 《general》public. (**!** 単・複両扱い (⇨大衆)) ●公衆の面前で in public. (⇨人目)
  - 公衆衛生 public health [hygiene]. ●公衆電話《ボックス》a public telephone [a pay phone]《booth》. ▶このあたりに公衆電話はないでしょうか Where can I find a *pay phone* around here?
  - 公衆道徳 public morals [morality]. ●公衆便所 a public lavatory [toilet];《米》a cómfort stàtion [ròom];《英》a 《public》convenience. (**!** 以上はいずれも前の2語の婉曲語) ●公衆浴場 a public bath.
- **こうしゅう 広州**〚中国の都市〛Guangzhou /gwàːŋdʒóu/.
- **こうしゅう 杭州**〚中国の都市〛Hangzhou /hàːŋdʒóu/.
- **こうしゅう 講習**〚課程〛a course;〚授業〛a class;〚講義〛a lecture;〚研修会〛《米》an institute. ●英語の夏期講習を受ける take a summer *course in*〚×of〛English. ●教員の講習会に出席する《米》attend a teachers' *workshop* [*study group*].
- **ごうしゅう 豪州** (⇨オーストラリア)
- **こうしゅうは 高周波** 《a》high (↔《a》low) frequency.
- **こうしゅけい 絞首刑** ●彼を絞首刑にする put him to *death by hanging*; *hang* him. ●殺人罪で絞首刑になる *be hanged* [×*hang*] *for* murder.
  - 絞首刑執行人 a hangman.
- **こうしゅだい 絞首台** a gallows. ●絞首台の露と消える die [be executed] on the *gallows*.
- **こうしゅつ 後出** to be mentioned subsequently. (⇨後述)
- **こうじゅつ 口述** 名 dictation.
  - **—口述の** 形 oral; verbal.
  - **—口述する** 動 ●手紙を秘書に口述する *dictate* a letter *to* one's secretary. ●口述試験 an oral examination. ●口述筆記 dictation.
- **こうじゅつ 公述** ●公述する 動 speak [give one's views, observe one's idea] at a public hearing.
  - 公述人 a speaker at a public hearing.
- **こうじゅつ 後述** 名 ●詳細は後述 Full details will *be mentioned later*.
  - **—後述する** 動 say [mention, write about, describe] 《it》later.
- **こうじゅほうしょう 紅綬褒章** the Medal with a Red Ribbon. (⇨褒章)
- **こうしょ 高所** a high place, a height;《高地》altitudes. ▶だれもあのような高所に長期間滞在することはできない No one can stay for a long time at those *high altitudes*.
  - 高所恐怖症〚医学〛a fear of heights; acrophobia. ●私は高所恐怖症です I'm afraid of [I fear] *heights*.

- **こうじょ 公序** ●公序良俗に反する行為 conduct against public order and morals [public peace and good order].
- **こうじょ 皇女** an Imperial princess.
- **こうじょ 控除** 名〚差し引くこと〛deduction;〚免除〛exemption. ●基礎控除 basic *deduction*. ●税額控除を受ける receive tax credits.
  - **—控除する** 動 deduct; exempt.
  - 控除額 a deduction.
- **こうしょう 交渉** 名 ❶〚話し合い, 協議〛《交渉》negotiation(s) (**!** 通例複数形で);《会談》talks.
  - ①《〜交渉》●和平交渉 peace *negotiations* [*talks*]. ●賃上げ交渉 *negotiations* [*talks*] *for* higher wages. ●団体交渉 collective *bargaining*. ●直接交渉 a direct negotiation.
  - ②《交渉(の)〜》●何週間にもわたる交渉の末 after long weeks of *negotiation*. ●交渉のテーブルにつく sit at the *negotiating* table. ▶その件は交渉中である The matter is *under negotiation*./*Negotiations* are going on [under way] about the matter. ▶価格については交渉の余地がある The price is *negotiable* [open to *negotiation*]./There is room for *negotiation* about the price. ▶それは交渉次第である It is subject to *negotiation*./It is the matter of *negotiation*.
  - ③《交渉が[は]》▶賃金交渉がまとまった The wage *negotiations* [*talks*] have been concluded [completed]. ▶労使間交渉は行き詰まった[決裂した] The *negotiations* between labor and management have been deadlocked [have broken down].
  - ④《交渉を》●交渉を始める open [start, enter into] *negotiations* 《*with*》. ●交渉を再開する reopen [resume] the negotiations [negotiation process]. ●外交交渉を打ち切る break off diplomatic *negotiations*.
  - ❷〚接触, 関係〛《接触》(a) contact;《関係》a relation. ●彼と卒業以来交渉がない I've had no *contact* with him since graduation./I've been out of touch with him since graduation.
  - **—交渉する** 動 negotiate 《*with*》;《値段などについて掛け合う》bargain 《*with*》. ▶政府はその法案について野党と交渉した The government *negotiated with* the opposition party *about* [*over*] the bill. (**!** over は長時間の含意) ▶組合は会社側と交渉して10パーセントの賃上げを取り決めた The labor union successfully *negotiated* a 10 percent wage raise [increase] *with* the employers. ▶彼女は店員と値段を《安くしてくれるよう》交渉した She *bargained with* the clerk *about* the price [*for* a lower price].
  - 交渉相手 a negótiating pàrtner. ●交渉権 a negótiating right. ●交渉団体 a negótiating bòdy [pàrtner]. ●交渉人 a negotiator. ●交渉力 bárgaining pòwer [lèverage].
- **こうしょう 口承** 名《an》oral tradition. (⇨伝承)
  - **—口承する** 動 hand 《a tradition》down [〚書〛transmit 《a tradition》] orally.
  - 口承文学 oral literature.
- **こうしょう 公称** 名《公式の発表》an official [a public] announcement 《about》;《公の名前》an official name.
  - **—公称の** 形《公式の》official;《名目上の》nominal.
  - ●その新聞の公称部数 the *official* circulation of the newspaper.
  - 公称資本〚経済〛nominal capital.
- **こうしょう 公証** ●公証人 a notary 《public》.
  - 公証役場 a notary public's office.

こうしょう 公傷 an injury at work; an industrial injury; an injury suffered while on duty.

こうしょう 考証 图 (時代考証) (a) (historical) background research [study]. ▶時代考証がしっかりしている The *historical background is based on good research*. (❗good に代えて careful, close, full なども文脈により可)
— **考証する** 動 research, study.

こうしょう 哄笑 (大笑い) loud laughter; a roar of laughter. (⇒笑い)
— **哄笑する** 動 laugh loudly; roar with laughter.

こうしょう 校章 a school badge.

こうしょう 高尚 — **高尚な** 形 (知的で洗練された) refined; (高度な) advanced, high(-level); (深遠な) deep. ● 高尚な趣味(＝好み) a *refined* taste.

こうしょう 鉱床 a (mineral) deposit; a mine. ● 金の鉱床 a *deposit* of gold.

:**こうじょう 工場** a factory; a plant; a mill; a works (❗単・複同形).

使い分け **factory** 食料生産や電化製品の製造、機械の組み立てを大量に行う工場。
plant 製紙工場・原子力発電所など工業的な処理や加工を行う工場、または公共施設などをさす。
mill 綿や鉄など原材料を加工する工場。
works 鉄などの加工施設。
shop 建物の中にある店舗と一体化した作業場。
factory 以外の語はしばしば複合語で用いる。

● 工場内 inside a factory. ● 自動車工場 a cár fàctory; an auto(mobile) 《米》 a motorcar 《英》 *factory* [*plant*]. ● セメント[化学]工場 a cement [a chemical] *plant*. ● 製粉[紡績; 材木; 製紙]工場 a flóur [a cótton; a lúmber; a páper] *mill*. ● 修理[塗装; 機械]工場 a repáir [a páint; a machíne] *shòp*. ● 製鋼工場 a steel *mill* [*works*]. ● 再処理工場 a repróceessing plànt. ▶彼はソニーの工場で働いている He works in a Sony *factory*. ▶この工場には工具製造所もある This *plant* includes a tool factory.
● 工場地帯 a factory area. ● 工場長 a factory [a works, a plant] manager. ● 工場主 a factory owner. ● 工場廃水 industrial waste water. ● 工場閉鎖 plant closing [closure]; (工場労働者の締め出し戦術としての) (a) lockout. ● 工場渡し ex works [factory].

こうじょう 口上 (口頭による伝言) an oral [《書》verbal] message; (芝居の) a prologue. ● 口上を述べる deliver a *prologue*.
● 口上書 a verbal note.

こうじょう 交情 (友情) friendship. ▶彼との交情を温めたい I'd like to renew my *friendship* with him.

こうじょう 向上 图 [上昇] (a) rise; [改善] (an) improvement; [進歩] (an) advance, prógress. (⇒進歩) ● 地位の向上 a *rise* in one's position. (❗「昇進」の意では通例 (a) promotion を用いる) ● 生活水準の向上 the *improvement* of living standards. ▶彼には向上心がない He has no desire to *improve* himself./He has no aspiration [ambition].
— **向上する** 動 rise; (改善する) improve; (進歩する) make progress. ● 向上させる (地位などを) raise; (能力などを) improve. ▶女性の社会的地位が向上した Women's social status *has risen* [*has been improved*]./Women *have risen* [*have been improved*] *in* their social status. (❗improve の主語が人の場合、in の後にくるのは技能・知識・健康など)

こうじょう 厚情 kindness; 《書》favor. ▶ご厚情深謝いたします Thank you very much for [I deeply appreciate] many *kindness* you've shown to us.

こうじょう 荒城 a ruined castle.

こうじょう 恒常 ● 恒常性 [生理] homeostasis; [心理] constancy.

ごうしょう 豪商 a rich [a wealthy] merchant.

***ごうじょう 強情** 图 stubbornness; obstinacy. ▶そう強情をはるな Don't be so *stubborn*.
— **強情な** 形 (言いなりにはならない) stubborn; (決めたことは意地でも変えない) obstinate. (⇒頑固) ▶彼女は強情な女だよ She is a *stubborn* [an *obstinate*] woman.

こうじょうけん 好条件 a favorable condition; good [excellent] terms. ▶会社側は従業員に年間9か月のボーナスという好条件を提示した The company offered the employees *favorable conditions* of a nine-month bonus a year. (❗「支払条件」の意では複数形)

こうじょうせん 甲状腺 [解剖] the thyroid /θáiroid/ (gland). ● 甲状腺炎 [医学] thyroiditis. ● 甲状腺機能亢進 hyperthyroidism. ● 甲状腺機能低下 hypothyroidism. ● 甲状腺ホルモン [生化学] thyroid hormone /hɔ́ːrmoun/.

こうじょうのつき『荒城の月』 *The Moon over the Ruined Castle*. (⇒参考) 瀧廉太郎作曲の歌曲

こうしょく 公職 a public office. ● 公職に就く[就いている、とどまる] take [hold; remain in, stay in] *public office*. (⇒公務員) ● 公職を追われる be driven [removed] from *public office*. ● 一切の公職を退く retire from *public life*.
● 公職選挙法 the Public Office Election Law. ● 公職追放 a purge (*of him*) from public office.

こうしょく 好色 图 (セックスの対象としてのみ見ること) léchery; (すぐに性的欲望を起こすこと) 《やや書》lasciviousness.
— **好色な** 形 lécherous, 《やや書》lascívious. ● 好色家 a lecherous person; a lecher.

こうしょくいちだいおとこ『好色一代男』 *The Life of an Amorous Man*. (⇒参考) 井原西鶴の小説

***こうじる 講じる** ❶ [講義をする] 英文学を講じる *lecture* [*give a lecture*] on English literature.
❷ [手段をとる] 手段を講じる *take* measures [steps] 《*to do*》.

DISCOURSE
その発言に賛成する。ただし、以下の対策が講じられる必要がある I agree with the statement; **however**, the following measures must *be put in place*. (❗; however (ただし)は条件付き賛成を表すディスコースマーカー)

こうじる 高じる get* [grow*] worse. ▶胃の病気が高じて何も食えない My stomach condition *has worsened* and I can't eat anything. ▶風邪が高じて肺炎になった The cold *has developed into* pneumonia.

こうしん 口唇 (くちびる) a lip.
● 口唇裂 [医学] a cleft lip.

こうしん 交信 图 [通信] communication; [連絡] (a) contact. ● 交信が途絶える lose (radio) *contact* (*with*).
— **交信する** 動 ● 彼と交信している be *in communication* [*contact*] *with* him. ● 船と無電で交信する *make* radio *contact with* the ship; *communicate with* the ship by radio; *radio to* the ship.

こうしん 行進 图 a march; [祝賀や行事のための] a parade /pəréid/. (⇒パレード) ● 結婚[軍隊]行進曲

こうしん 更新 图 renewal. ●運転免許証の更新 the *renewal* of a driver's license. ●自動更新 automatic *renewal*. ▶来月ご契約の更新です Your contract is up for *renewal* next month.

—— **更新する** 動 (契約などを) renew; (記録などを) break*; (設備などを) replace; (情報などを) update. ●契約を更新する *renew* a contract. ●世界記録を更新する *break* the world record 《*for*》. ▶来月運転免許証を更新しなければならない I have to *renew* my driver's license next month. ▶彼は自分が作ったやり投げの記録を次々と更新した He *broke* all the records he had set in the javelin throw. ▶新しい情報を受け取ったらデータベースを更新しておかなければならない The database must *be updated* whenever new information is received.

●更新手数料 a renewal fee [commission].

こうしん 庚申 ●庚申塚 (説明的に) a roadside standing stone which is engraved with images of a deity and three monkeys.

こうしん 後進 ❶ [若い世代] ●後進を育てる train [coach] *the younger generation*.
❷ [進歩の遅れ] ●アフリカの後進性 *backwardness of Africa*. 《⇒後進国》
❸ [後ろへ進むこと] ●後進させる back (up). 《⇒バック》
●後進に道を譲る [開く] give place to [make room for] *younger people*.

こうじん 公人 (公職にある人) a public official. ●公人の立場で 《やや書》 in an [one's] (public (↔a private, a personal) capacity; (公人として) as a *public official*.

こうじん『行人』 Wayfarer. (参考) 夏目漱石の小説

こうじん 幸甚 appreciation; gratefulness; thankfulness. ▶当方までおいでくだされば幸甚に存じます We would be very *happy* if you would come to us.

こうじん 後塵 ●後塵を拝する (すぐれた人の後についていく) play second field 《*to*》; (人に追い越される) be outstripped 《*by*》.

こうしんこく 後進国 《軽蔑的》 a backward country [nation]; [発展途上国] a developing country [nation].

こうしんじょ 興信所 (人事の) a detective [《英》 an inquiry] agency; (商事の) a credit bureau /bjúərou/ (《複》 ~s, bureaux /-z/).

こうじんぶつ 好人物 a good-natured person.

こうしんりょう 香辛料 (a) spice. ●香辛料を強く [少々] きかせた料理 a very [a mildly] *spicy* dish.

こうしんりょく 向心力 a centripetal force.

こうず 構図 composition. ●絵の構図 the *composition* of a picture. ▶その絵の構図はいい [悪い] The picture *is* well [ill] *composed*.

こうすい 香水 (a) perfume /pɔ́:rfju:m/, 《主に英》 scent; [香水類] 《集合的》 perfumery. ●髪に香水をつける *perfume* /pərfjú:m/ one's hair. ▶彼女は香水石けんのにおいをふんぷんさせている She smells strongly of *perfumed* soap. ▶彼女は濃い [甘い香りの] 香水をつけている She wears a strong [(a) sweet; (a) rose] *perfume*.

こうすい 降水 ●降水確率 probability of precipitation. ●降水量 rainfall; [気象] precipitation. ●年間平均降水量 an average annual *rainfall*.

こうすい 硬水 hard water 《↔soft water》.

*こうずい 洪水 a flood /flʌd/; [大洪水] 《やや書》 a déluge; [洪水の水] floodwaters.
❶ [~の洪水] ●情報の洪水 a *flood* of information. ●質問 [贈り物] の洪水 a *shower* of questions [presents]. ●光の洪水 a flood of light. ▶ノアの洪水 the Flood, the Deluge. ▶道路は車の洪水だ There is a stream of cars on the street./ The streets *are very crowded with* traffic.
❷ [洪水~] ●洪水警報を発令する issue a *flood* warning 《*for* an area》.
❸ [洪水が] ●集中豪雨のためその地方に洪水が起こった A *flood* struck that area as a result of the localized downpour./The localized downpour caused a *flood* in that area.
❹ [洪水に [で]] ●洪水にあった人々 flood victims; (説明的に) people suffering from the *flood*. ●洪水にあった家 *flooded* houses; houses *under water*. ●洪水で崩れる collapse under flood. ▶湾岸の低地は大洪水に見舞われるでしょう There will be serious *floods* on all the low ground around the bay. ▶橋が洪水で流された The bridge was washed [carried] away by the *flood*. ▶度重なる洪水で多くの人が家を失った Frequent *floods* left a lot of people homeless.

こうずか 好事家 (変わった趣味を持っている人) a person of strange tastes; (趣味のいい人, 風流な人) a person of (refined) taste.

こうする 抗する resist. ●抵抗する, 逆らう) ●時流に抗する go [swim] *against* the stream.

ごうする 号する [名づける] name; (呼ぶ) call; [表向きそのように言う] claim. 《⇒称する》●彼は出家して信玄と号された He became a priest and *was called* Shingen.

*こうせい 構成 图 composition; [文などの] a structure; [文法] a construction; [組織化] organization. ●文の構成 the *construction* of a sentence. ▶この小説は構成がなっていない This novel suffers from a lack of *structure*. ▶あなたの家の家族構成を教えてください Please tell [×teach] me how many people you have in your family and who they are.

—— **構成する** 動 make*... up, 《書》compose (!通例受身で); 《書》constitute. ▶私たちのクラスは 40 名で構成されている Our class *is made up of* [*is composed of, consists of*] forty students.
●構成員 a constituent member 《*of* a community》. ●構成要素 a structural element; a constituent (element).

こうせい 公正 图 [公平で正しいこと] fairness; [法的に正しいこと] justice; [依怙贔屓をしないこと] impartiality. 《⇒公平》●公正を期す ensure *fairness*. ▶今こそ, 神の子すべての上に公正を実現すべき時なのです Now is the time to make *justice* a reality for all of God's children.

—— **公正な** 形 fair; just; impartial. ●公正な手段で *fair* 《↔foul》 means. ●公正な判決を下す pass a *just* 《↔unjust》 sentence. ▶彼は常に正しいと信じたことを行った公正な人だった He was a *fair and just* man who always did what he believed was right. ▶あの先生は生徒たちに対して公正でなかった The teacher was not *fair to* [*toward, with*] his students. ●彼の仕事を公正に評価する evaluate his work fairly [*with justice, impartially*]. ●公正に勝負をする [ふるまう] play *fair*. (!play, fight, act の場合は fairly の代わりに fair を用いる)
●公正価格 a fair price. ●公正証書 a notarial deed. ●公正取引委員会 the Fair Trade Commission.

こうせい 攻勢 (攻撃態勢) the offensive. ●平和攻勢 a peace *offensive*. ▶我が軍は攻勢をかけた[に転じた] Our troops took [changed to, turned to] *the offensive*.

こうせい 更生 图 (正常に戻すこと) rehabilitation. ●更生手続きをする *file for Chapter XI*. (⇨更生会社)
— **更生する** 動 be rehabilitated; (改心する) reform oneself.
●**更生会社** a company under Chapter XI [rehabilitation law]. ●米国では『破産法第11章』で会社更生を記載. ●**更生施設** rehabilitation facilities. (参考) 非行・麻薬などの依存症から身体的機能障害などの治療と社会復帰訓練を行うさまざまな施設の総称)

こうせい 厚生 welfare.
●**厚生事業** welfare work. ●**厚生施設** welfare facilities. ●**厚生年金** an employees' pension. ●**厚生年金基金** an employees' pension fund. ●**厚生年金保険** an employees' pension insurance. ●**厚生労働省** the Ministry of Health, Labour and Welfare. ●**厚生労働大臣** the Minister of Health, Labour and Welfare.

こうせい 後世 ●後世の人 *future generations*; posterity (↔ancestry). ●後世に伝統を伝える *hand down the traditions*. ▶彼の名は後世に残るでしょう His name will *live* [*go down*] *in history*./He will be remembered forever.

こうせい 後生 ●後生おそるべし (自分より若い人を軽んじてはいけない. 計り知れない可能性を秘めているのだから) You should not think lightly of your juniors because they have immense potential.

こうせい 恒星 a fixed star; 〖天文〗 a star.
●**恒星日** a sidereal day. (■ sidereal は「星の(運行)による」の意)

こうせい 校正 图 proofreading.
●**校正する** read proof; proofread 《a book》. ●**校正者** a proofreader. ●**校正刷り** a (galley) proof. (■通例複数形で)

ごうせい 合成 图 composition;〖化学〗 synthesis.
— **合成の** 形 (混合の) composite; (複合の) compound;〖化学〗 synthetic.
— **合成する** 動 compose; compound;〖化学〗 synthesize.
●**合成語** a compound (word). ●**合成ゴム** synthetic rubber. ●**合成写真** a composite photograph. ●**合成樹脂** synthetic resin. ●**合成繊維** synthetic fiber [fabrics]. ●**合成皮革** composition [synthetic] leather. ●**合成物** a composition; a compound (substance).

ごうせい 豪勢 图 (ぜいたく) luxury. (⇨豪華)
— **豪勢な** luxurious. ●豪勢に暮らす live *luxuriously* [*in luxury*]; lead a *luxurious* life; lead a life of *luxury*.

こうせいしんやく 向精神薬 a psychotropic (medicine).

こうせいせき 好成績 good results. ●好成績(=よい結果)を上げる get good results 〖学業で〗 good grades; (スポーツで) a good score (点数), a good record (記録).

こうせいねん 好青年 a good [(感じのよい) a pleasant] young man (働 men).

こうせいのう 高性能 high performance. (⇨性能)
●**高性能車** a *high-performance* car.

こうせいぶっしつ 抗生物質 an antibiotic /ǽntibaiátik/.

*****こうせき 功績** services;〖貢献〗(a) contribution;〖業績〗an achievement;〖栄誉〗credit. ▶井上氏は地方文化の発展に著しい功績をあげた Mr. Inoue rendered *remarkable services* to the growth of the local culture.

こうせき 皇籍 an official status as a member of the Imperial Family.

こうせき 鉱石 (an) ore /ɔ́ːr/. ●鉄鉱石 iron *ore*.

こうせきそう 洪積層 〖地学〗 diluvial formations; diluvia /dilúːviə/ (働 a diluvium).

こうせつ 公設 — **公設の** 形 publicly run [established]; (市[町]営の) municipal.
●**公設市場** a municipal [a municipally-run] market.

こうせつ 巧拙 (うまいへた) skill; (できばえ) workmanship. (■中上語は expertness). ▶文章の巧拙は問わない It doesn't matter whether the sentences *are written well or not*.

こうせつ 巷説 (世間のうわさ) hearsay 《about》; (a) rumor 《about, of》. ●出所不明の巷説 a *rumor* from unknown sources.

こうせつ 降雪 snow; a snowfall; (一時的な) snow showers. ●1メートルの降雪 a *snowfall* of one meter (deep). ▶この地方の平均降雪量はどれくらいですか What's the average *snowfall* in this region?

こうせつ 高説 (すぐれた意見) a valuable opinion; (相手の意見) your opinion. ▶将来計画についてご高説を拝聴したい I'd like to hear *your opinion* [*views*] on the future plan.

こうぜつ 口舌 (口先だけの言葉) empty [hollow] words.
●**口舌の徒** 〖口先のうまい人間〗 a smooth talker.

ごうせつ 豪雪 a heavy snowfall. ▶その村は一夜にして3メートルの豪雪に見舞われた The village had a *heavy snowfall* of three meters [ten feet] overnight.
●**豪雪地帯** a heavy snowfall area.

こうせん 口銭 (⇨⑩ 手数料)

こうせん 工船 a factory ship. ●蟹(ᵃ)工船 a crab *factory ship*.

こうせん 公選 图 public election. ●公選による publicly elected.
— **公選する** 動 elect by popular vote. (■ 全党員で党首を選ぶ場合など)

こうせん 交戦 (戦争) (a) war; (戦闘) (a) battle. (⇨戦争) ●交戦状態に入る[ある] enter into [be at] *war* 《with》.
●**交戦国** the belligerent power [nation, country].

こうせん 光線 (ひとすじの光) a ray [a beam] of light; (光) light. (⇨光 [類語]) ●太陽光線 the sun's *rays*; the *rays* of the sun; (書) sunbeams. ●北側からの柔らかい光線 a soft north *light*.

こうせん 抗戦 (抵抗) resistance. ●徹底抗戦 do-or-die *resistance*. ●(徹底)抗戦する resist (to the bitter end). (■口語的慣用表現).

こうせん 高専 〖『工業高等専門学校』の略〗a technical junior college.

こうせん 鉱泉 a mineral spring; 〖鉱水〗 mineral water(s).

こうぜん 公然 — **公然の** 形 (隠しだてしない) open; (広く世間に知られた) public; (公式の) official. ●公然の秘密 an *open* secret.
— **公然と** 副 openly; (人前で) in public. ▶その男性は公然と彼女を批判した The man *openly* [*publicly*] criticized her.
●**公然わいせつ罪** indecent exposure.

こうぜん 昂然 ●昂然と胸を張る throw out one's chest *triumphantly*.

ごうぜん 傲然 ●傲然たる (傲慢な) arrogant, haugh-

ごうぜん 轟然 ● 轟然たる雷鳴 a *roaring* [an *earsplitting*, a *deafening*] thunder.

こうせんてき 好戦的 ── 好戦的な 形 ● 好戦的な国民 a *warlike* nation. ● 好戦的な態度をとる take a *bellicose* [a *belligerent*] attitude.

こうぜんのき 浩然の気 ● 浩然の気を養う (さわやかな気分になる) refresh oneself (*with*); (くつろぐ) feel relaxed.

こうそ 公租 a public tax.
● 公租公課 taxes and other public charges.

こうそ 公訴 『法律』(起訴) prosecution (*against, for*); (主に米) presentment (*to*); (告訴) accusation (*against*). ── 公訴する prosecute.
● 公訴棄却 dismissal of prosecution. ● 公訴権 power [authority] of prosecution; authority to indict. ● 公訴時効 prescription against public action. ● 公訴事実 a charge.

こうそ 控訴 图 (an) appeal. ● 控訴を棄却する[取り下げる] reject [withdraw] an *appeal*. ● 控訴を差しもどす refer the *appealed* case back to the lower court.
── 控訴する 動 appeal, file 《米》 [lodge 《英》] an appeal (*to*). ● 地裁判決を不服として控訴する *appeal* to the higher court *against* the district court ruling.

こうそ 酵素 a ferment; 『生化』an enzyme /énzaim/.
● 酵素洗剤 enzyme detergent.

こうぞ 楮 『植物』a paper mulberry; (説明的に) one kind of mulberry from which Japanese rice paper is made.

*__**こうそう**__ 構想 (計画) a plan; (設計・着想) a design, (a) conception; (着想・思いつき) an idea. ● 具体的な構想を練る work out a detailed *design* (*for*). ▶ その車はまだ構想の段階にある The car is still at the *design* stage.

こうそう 好走 图 a good [a hard] run. (⇒好守)
▶ 彼は3区で区間賞の好走を見せた He ran so well that he won a prize for the third leg.
── 好走する 動 run well; make a good run.

こうそう 抗争 『争い』(a) struggle, strife; (延々と続く) feud /fjúːd/; (*between*). ● 派閥抗争 factional strife. ● 権力抗争(=闘争) a *struggle* 《書》 a *contention*) *for* power; a power *struggle*.

こうそう 高僧 (徳の高い) a priest of (high) virtue; (位の高い) a high priest, 《書》 a dignitary.

こうそう 高層 ● 高層雲 an altostratus (cloud).
● 高層建築物 a high-rise (building); (超高層ビル) a skyscraper. ● 高層マンション 《米》 a high-rise apartment building; 《英》 a block of high-rise flats.

こうそう 高燥 ── 高燥な 形 ● 高燥な土地 high and dry land [ground]. (⇔低湿)

こうそう 鉱層 an ore /ɔːr/ bed.

*__**こうぞう**__ 構造 图 (a) structure. ● 社会[人体]の構造 the *structure* of society [the human body]. ● 経済[文]の構造 economic [sentence] *structure*. ● 人間の遺伝子構造を解読する decode the genetic *makeup* of humans. ▶ スーパーの建物は構造がきわめて単純だ Supermarkets are very simple in *structure*.
── 構造(上)の, 構造的な 形 structural. ● 構造上の欠陥 (a) *structural* defect. ● 構造の問題 a *structural* problem.
● 構造改革 (a) structural reform [change]. ● 構造式 『化学』a structural formula. ● 構造主義 (言語学・哲学の) structuralism. ● 構造不況 structural depression.

ごうそう 豪壮 ── 豪壮な 形 (宮殿のような) (やや書) palatial /pəléiʃl/; (壮大な) grand; (壮麗な) magnificent. ● メイフェアの豪壮なホテル a *grand* hotel in Mayfair.

こうそうるい 紅藻類 red algae /ǽldʒiː/.

こうそく 光速 the speed [velocity] of light. (!×light speed [velocity] としない)

こうそく 拘束 图 (制限) a restriction; 『抑制, 規制』(a) restraint. ● 拘束を解く lift [remove] *restrictions*.
── 拘束する 動 (制限する) restrict; (抑制する) restrain; (束縛する) tie (~d; tying) 《書》 bind* … (down) (⇒束縛する); (身柄を拘留する) take* (him) into custody. ▶ 義務で自分自身を拘束(=束縛)したくない I don't want to *tie* myself *down* with any obligation.
● 拘束時間 total hours spent at work. ● 拘束力 binding force. ▶ この協定は法的には拘束力はない This agreement is not legally *binding*.

こうそく 校則 school rules [regulations]. (⇒規則)

こうそく 高速 (a) high speed; 『高速道路』《米》an expressway; 《英》(a) motorway. ● 高速で運転する drive *at* (×with) (a) *high speed*; drive very fast. ▶ 彼は時速90マイルの高速で車を運転した He drove a car at a speed as high as ninety miles an hour. ▶ 市と市を結ぶ高速バスが運行されている There are *fast* [*highway*] bus services between cities.
● 高速車線 a fast (↔slow) lane. ● 高速度撮影 high-speed photography. ● 高速料金 (collect [charge; pay]) an expressway 《米》 [a motorway 《英》] toll.

こうぞく 後続 (次に来る) following; (次の) next. ● 後続の車に注意 Be careful of the cars *behind* you. ● 後続バッター the following batter; the batter on deck. ● 後続列車 the following train.

こうぞく 皇族 (総称) the Imperial [Royal] Family; (個人) a member of the Imperial Family.

ごうぞく 豪族 a powerful family [clan].

こうそくど 高速度 (⇒高速)

こうそくどうろ 高速道路 《米》 an expressway (!揭示ではしばしば Xpwy と略す), a freeway (!highway は「幹線道路」だが, 高速道路と同じような機能のものも多い); 《英》 a motorway. ● 名神高速道路に乗って(主を使って) on the Meishin *Expressway*. ● 御殿場で高速(道路)に入る[を降りる] enter [leave, turn off] *the expressway* at Gotenba.

こうしょう 江蘇省 『中国の省』Jiangsu /dʒjàːŋsúː/; Province.

こうそつ 高卒 《略》a high school graduate. ● 高卒の資格 (高校の卒業証書) a high school diplóma [《英》certificate].

ごうそっきゅう 豪速球 (『剛球』)

こうた 小唄 a *kouta*; (説明的に) a traditional Japanese song [ballad] sung to the accompaniment of the samisen.

こうだ 好打 图 『野球』good hit.
── 好打する 動 make a key hit; get a clutch [key] hit. ▶ 9回裏彼が左中間に好打し, 我がチームは勝利を収めた He *got a key hit* to left center field in the bottom of the ninth inning and our team won the game.
● 好打者 a good [a clutch] hitter.

ごうだ 豪打 图 a hard [strong] hitting. ● 豪打のレッドソックス the *strong-hitting* Red Sox.
── 豪打する 動 blast [belt, drive, hammer, rip] 《a hit》.

*__**こうたい**__ 交替 图 『変更』a change; 『交互にすること』

こうたい (2者間で) (an) alternation; (3者以上の間で) (a) rotation;〖勤務交替で〗a shift;〖交替人と〗a relief. ● 政権の交替 a *change* of government. ▶ 従業員は3交替制になっていた The workers were organized into three *shifts*.

── **交替で[に]** 副 (3人以上が) by turns (! 繰り返しを暗示する); (交互に) in turn, alternately (⇨やる代わる); 〖輪番制で〗in rotation. ● (8時間ずつ) 3交替で勤務する work in [on] three (rotating) shifts (of eight hours).

── **交替する** 動 〖交替でする〗take* turns, alternate (! 前の方が堅い語 (⇨副)); 〖代理をする〗take 〈his〉place (! 入れ替える, 入れ替わると); change;〖取って代わる〗replace; 〖輪番で〗rotate; 〖交替者と〗relieve. ● 選手を交替する *change* players. ● (複数形に注意) → 選手を交替させる(=退かせる) remove a player. ● 新旧交替する *replace* the old *with* [*by*] the new. ● レフトの選手と交替して守備固めに入る take over defensively for the left fielder. ▶ 警備員は2時間ごとに交替する The guards *rotate* [The guard *is relieved*, They *change* the guards] every two hours.

● **交替勤務** shift work.

こうたい 抗体 〖医学〗an ántibòdy. (! 通例複数形で)

こうたい 後退 图 (退却) (a) retreat; (撤退) (a) withdrawal; (⇨退却, 撤退);〖景気の〗a recession.

── **後退する** 動 draw [move] back; (軍隊などが) retreat 《*from*》, fall back; withdraw 《*from*》; (景気が) go [move] 《*into* recession》. ● 後退させる (車を) back 《a car》up, move 《a car》backward.

こうだい 工大 〖「工業大学」の略〗a university of technology.

こうだい 広大 ── 広大な 形 extensive; (果てしなく広い) vast. ● (広い) 広大な大海原 a *vast* (expanse of) ocean. ● 広大な大学構内 an *extensive* [a *large*] campus.

こうたいごう 皇太后 the Empress Dowager /dáuədʒər/. (! 英国では Queen Mother)

こうたいし 皇太子 〖英国以外〗the Crown Prince (!「皇太子妃」は the Crown Princess);〖英国〗the Prince of Wales. (⇨殿下)

こうたく 光沢 (手を加えた表面的な) (a) gloss; (反射による) (a) luster; (磨いた) (a) polish; 〖布・羽毛・鉱物などの〗a sheen. (⇨艶(2)〖類語〗) ● 絹の光沢 the *gloss* [*sheen*] of silk. ● 美しい光沢の真珠 a pearl with a beautiful *luster*. ● 光沢を出す (磨いて) polish 《it》(up); (光沢剤を塗って) put polish on 《it》.

● **光沢紙** glossy paper.

ごうだつ 強奪 图 (a) robbery; (乗り物・貨物の) hijacking, a hijack. (⇨奪い取る, 強盗)

── **強奪する** 動 ● 彼[銀行]から金を強奪する *rob* him [the bank] *of* money.

こうたん 降誕 (誕生) birth. ● キリストの降誕 the *birth* of Jesus Christ, the Nativity /nətívəti/.

● **降誕祭** Christmas. (⇨クリスマス)

こうだん 公団 a public corporation. ● 日本道路公団 the Japan Highway *Public Corporation*.

● **公団住宅** 〖米〗a government-built apartment complex;〖英〗a council flat [house].

こうだん 降壇 ── 降壇する 動 〖壇上から降りる〗dismount (from) the platform;〖大学教員などが職を辞める〗leave [give up, quit] one's job.

こうだん 高段 (武道・碁・将棋などの) a high rank.

● **高段者** a holder of a high rank.

こうだん 講談 *kodan* (説明的に) the storytelling of war chronicles, heroic episodes or revenge tales.

● **講談師** a kodan narrator.

こうだんし 好男子 a fine gentleman; a nice man; (美男子) a handsome [a good-looking] man; (屈強かつハンサムな男) 〖話〗a hunk.

こうち 巧緻 图 (精巧) elaborateness; exquisiteness; delicacy.

── **巧緻な** 形 elaborate; exquisite; delicate. ● 巧緻な文章 *polished* [*refined*] sentences.

こうち 拘置 图 detention.

── **拘置する** 動 detain 《him》. ● 拘置しておく[されている] hold 《him》 [remain] in *detention*.

● **拘置所** a jail; a prison. (⇨刑務所)

こうち 耕地 〖耕作された土地〗cultivated land, a cultivated field. (! arable land は耕作に適した土地)

● **耕地面積** cultivated acreage.

こうち 高地 highlands; (高台) (やや書) a height (! しばしば複数形で); (丘) a hill; (高原) a plateau /plætóu/ (獲) ~s, plateaux /-z/). (⇨高原)

こうちく 構築 图 building, 《書》construction. ● 平和の構築は戦争するより難しい(=長期間にわたる努力と精力を必要とする) *Building* peace was more arduous than waging war.

── **構築する** 動 build, 《書》construct. ● データベースを構築する *build* [《書》construct] a database.

こうちせい 向地性 〖植物の〗positive geotropism. (⇨ 背地性)

こうちゃ 紅茶 (black) tea. (! 緑茶 (green tea) と区別する場合以外は通例単に tea という. 1杯の紅茶の意では Ⓒ (⇨茶)). ● 紅茶をいれる[出す; 飲む] make [serve; have] *tea*. ● 紅茶を二つ注文する order two *teas*. (⇨コーヒー) ▶ この紅茶は濃[薄]すぎる This *tea* is too strong [weak].

こうちゃく 膠着 agglutination; (交渉などの行き詰まり) (a) deadlock; (停止) a standstill. ● 膠着状態にある be *at a deadlock* [*a standstill*]; be deadlocked. ▶ 和平交渉は膠着状態になった The peace negotiations *reached deadlock* [*came to a standstill*].

● **膠着語** an agglutinative language.

こうちゅう 甲虫 a beetle.

こうちゅう 校注 revision and annotation.

こうちょう 好調 (a) good* condition. (⇨調子❶) ● 絶好調である be in the best *condition* [《運動選手が》in top *form*]. ▶ 好調に事が運んだ Things went *well* [*smoothly*]./Everything was *all right*. ▶ 耐久消費財の売れ行きが好調である Durable goods are selling *well*. ▶ その打者は絶好調である The hitter is red hot.

こうちょう 紅潮 ● (人が)ほおを紅潮させる glow [(さっと) be flushed] 《*with* excitement》.

こうちょう 校長 a principal,〖英〗a headmaster; (一部私学の) a warden, (女性の) a headmistress (! (1)〖米〗では私立学校の校長をさす. (2) 今は a headmaster, a headmistress の代わりに a headteacher を用いる). ● 彼をA高校の校長に任命する appoint him *principal* of A High School. (! 役職が唯一のときは通例無冠詞)

● **校長室** the principal's office.

こうちょう 高潮 〖満潮〗(a) high tide;〖頂点〗the climax. ● 最高潮.

こうちょうかい 公聴会 a public [(公開の) an open] hearing. ● 公聴会を開く hold [open] a *public hearing*.

こうちょく 硬直 图 ● 死後硬直〖医学〗rigor mortis.

── **硬直する** 動 (筋肉・態度などが) stiffen; get [become] stiff. ● 硬直した考え rigid [inflexible]

こうちん 工賃 （請求する側から）charges; （支払う側から）wages, pay.

こうつう 交通 〖車の往来, 交通量〗traffic; 〖輸送〗《主に米》transportation,《主に英》tránsport. (⇨輸送)

①〖交通～〗 ●ひどい交通渋滞にあう get stuck in heavy *traffic*; get stuck in a big *traffic* jam. ●交通規則を守る keep to [×keep] *traffic* rules; obey *traffic* rules. ●交通違反をする break [(やや書) violate] *traffic* rules [regulations]; commit a *traffic* violation [offense]; （歩行者が） jaywalk (!) 違反者はそれぞれ a traffic violator [offender], a jaywalker という. ●交通整理をする direct *traffic*. ▶彼は交通事故で死んだ He was killed in a *traffic* [a *car*, an *auto*] accident.

②〖交通(量)が〗 ●大雪のため1週間にわたって交通が途絶えた［まひした］Because of the heavy snow, *traffic* was held up [(話) crippled] for a week. ▶この通りは交通量が多い There is a lot of [heavy] *traffic* on this street./(The) *traffic* is heavy 《英》busy] (↔light) on this street. ▶この通りは交通量が最も多い時間帯には混雑する This street is congested at peak *traffic* hours.

③〖交通を〗 ●交通を規制する control [regulate] *traffic*. ●交通を遮断する shut off *traffic*.

—— 交通の 形 traffic. ●交通の要衝(ようしょう) an important place along a route. ●交通の発達 the evolution of the traffic system. ●交通の混雑を緩和する ease [relieve, reduce] *traffic* congestion. ●交通の流れはスムーズだった There was a smooth flow of *traffic*./*Traffic* was flowing smoothly. ▶ここは交通の便がよい(= 公共の交通機関を利用するのに便利である) This place is convenient to [《主に英》for] public *transportation*./(便利なところに位置している) This place is conveniently located [situated].

●交通安全運動 a traffic safety campaign.
●交通機関 (a means of) transportation 《米》[transport《英》]. ●交通警官 a traffic policeman. ●交通信号 a traffic light [signal]. (! 通例複数形で. signal は音による信号なども表す) ●交通費 tráveling expènses,《主に米》transportation;（バス・タクシー・電車などの運賃）a carfare. ●交通標識 a traffic sign. ●交通法規《obey》 traffic regulations; ●交通網 (道路網) a network of roads.

ごうつくばり 業突く張り（欲張り）greedy,《書》avarice;（人）a greedy 《書》an avaricious) person, a miser,《話》a scrooge.

こうつごう 好都合 —— 好都合な 形 （時間・場所などが都合のよい）convenient;（状況などが有利な）favorable;（幸運な）fortunate. ●ピクニックに好都合な天気 (x)a *favorable* weather for a picnic. ●好都合なことに conveniently;（運よく）fortunately. (! いずれも文頭で) ▶10時なら好都合だ Ten o'clock is *convenient to* [*for*] me. ▶万事好都合に(=うまく)行った Everything went *favorably* [*well*, *all right*]. ▶何日がいちばん好都合ですか What day would *suit* you best?

*こうてい 肯定 图 (an) affirmation. ●肯定も否定もしない say [answer] neither yes nor no.
—— 肯定的な 形 affirmative; positive.
—— 肯定する 動 （再確認して; 質問に答えて） affirm 《it; that》; （はいと言う［答える］）say [answer] yes; (肯定的に答える)《書》answer in the affirmative (↔negative).
●肯定文〖文法〗an affirmative sentence.

こうてい 工程 （工事などの手順）process of work; （生産・加工の）stage of production. ●生産工程の大半を機械化する automate most steps in the manufacturing *process*.
●工程管理 process control.

こうてい 公定 —— 公定の 形 official. ●公定歩合を0.5ポイント引き上げる［下げる］raise [cut, reduce] the (*official*) discount [*bank*] rate by half a percentage point.
●公定価格 an official price.

こうてい 公邸 an official residence.

こうてい 行程 （旅程）a journey; （旅程表）《やや書》an itinerary /aítinərèri/;（旅行・レースなどの区分）a leg;（距離）(a) distance. ●3日の行程 a three-day *journey*. ●全行程を歩く walk all *the way*. ●会社までは3キロ[たった10分]の行程だ I have a *journey* of 3 kilometers [only 10 minutes] to the office.
●行程表《submit》a road map. (⇨ロードマップ)

こうてい 皇帝 图 an emperor; (帝政ロシアの) a tsar /zá:r, tsá:r/ (! czar ともつづる).
—— 皇帝の 形 imperial.

こうてい『皇帝』*Emperor*. (〔参考〕ベートーベン作曲のピアノ協奏曲)

こうてい 校訂 图 revision.
—— 校訂する 動 revise《a text》.

こうてい 校庭 a playground, a schoolyard.

こうてい 航程 （船の）(a) sail, a leg; （航空機の） a flight, a lap; (話) a leg, a hop. ●ジェット機で8時間の航程 an eight-hour *distance* [*lap*] by jet.

こうてい 高低 〖上がり下がり〗rise and fall; 〖土地の起伏〗rolling, 《書》undulations; 〖音声の〗(a) pitch, modulation; 〖相場の〗fluctuations. ●声の高低 the *rise and fall* of the voice.

こうてい 高弟 （すぐれた弟子）one's best pupil [disciple]; a leading disciple.

こうてい 拘泥 —— 拘泥する 動 （こだわる）stick 《to》,《書》adhere《to》. ●彼はよくつまらないことに拘泥する He often *sticks* [*keeps*,《書》*adheres*] *to* trifles.

ごうてい 豪邸 a luxurious [an expensive] house.

こういえき 口蹄疫 foot-and-mouth disease (略 FMD). (〔参考〕家畜の伝染病)

こうてき 公的 —— 公的な 形 public; (公務上の) official. ●公的な金融支援 an *official* financing package. ●為替市場への公的介入 *official* intervention in the exchange market. ●公的資金を投入する inject *public* [*government*] funds《into》.
●公的介護保険 long-term care insurance. ●公的生活 public life (↔private life). ●公的年金 a public pension plan [scheme]. ●公的扶助 public assistance.

こうてき 好適 —— 好適な 形 （理想的な）ideal; (ぴったりの) right; （必要を満たした）suitable; (よい) good*.

こうてきしゅ 好敵手 a (good*) match《for》; a good rival 《of him, for +主題, in +分野》. (⇨相手 ❸) ●好敵手に出会う meet one's *rival* [×enemy, ×match].

こうてつ 更迭 图 〖人事の入れ替え〗a reshuffle; 〖免職〗(a) dismissal.
—— 更迭する 動 ●3名の閣僚を更迭する *reshuffle* three Cabinet ministers. ▶彼は収賄で更迭[= 免職]された He was *dismissed from* one's post *for* bribery.

こうてつ 鋼鉄 steel.

こうてん 公転 图《make》(a) revolution. (! 1回転の場合は one ~) (⇨回転)
—— 公転する 動 revolve (on its orbit) 《around the

こうてん sun). (⇨回る)
こうてん 交点 an intersection.
こうてん 好天 good* [fine] weather. (⇨晴天)
こうてん 好転 图 ▶天気が好転に向かっている The weather *is changing for the better* [*is improving*].
— **好転する** 動 get [become] better; change [take a turn] for the better. ▶間もなく事態は好転するだろう Things will *be better* [(改善される) *improve*; (上向く) *look up*] soon.
こうてん 後天 — 後天的な 形 acquired (↔innate).
● 後天性免疫 acquired immunity. ● 後天性免疫不全症候群 [医学] acquired immunodeficiency syndrome (略 AIDS).
こうてん 後転 a backward roll.
こうてん 荒天 stormy [rough] weather.
こうでん 香典 *koden*, (説明的に) a monetary offering given to the bereaved family at the funeral. [参考] 米英にはこの慣習はない) ▶勝手ながら今香典,ご供花はご辞退申し上げます Flowers and *monetary offerings* are gratefully declined.
● 香典返し a gift in retun for *koden*.
こうど 光度 lùminósity; (the degree of) brightness.
こうど 高度 ❶ [高さ] (an) altitude; (a) height. (⇨高さ) ● (飛行機の)高度を上げる[下げる] elevate [lower] *its altitude*. ▶この飛行機は高度 3,000 メートルで飛んでいる This plane is flying at an *altitude* [a *height*] of 3,000 meters.
❷ [程度] ● 高度な技術 high [highly-developed] technology. ● 高度な(=進歩した)研究 advanced studies. ▶彼らは高度な文明を誇りに思っている They are proud of their *high* level of civilization.
● 高度記録 an altitude record. ● 高度計 an altimeter /ˈæltɪmətər/. ● 高度経済成長 high growth of the economy; high-growth economy.
こうど 硬度 (鉱物・金属・水などの) hardness.
こうとう 口頭 口頭の 形 oral; (身ぶりなどでなく言葉の) verbal. — 口頭試問を受ける take an *oral* test [examination; (米大学学位審査の) defense]; [話] take an oral; be examined *orally*. ▶口頭での約束(=口約束)では不十分なので文書での約束が必要だ An *oral* [A *verbal*] agreement is not good enough; we must have a written promise [agreement].
— **口頭で** 副 orally; (身ぶりなどでなく言葉で) verbally.
こうとう 公党 a [an officially recognized] political party.
こうとう 好投 图 [野球] nice [good, fine, strong] pitching.
— **好投する** 動 ▶5イニングを好投する *pitch* five *strong* innings. ▶彼はリリーフとしていつも好投する He always *pitches well* in relief.
こうとう 紅灯 ● 紅灯の巷(ちまた) (色町) a red-light district.
こうとう 高等 — 高等な 形 high(er); advanced.
● 高等学校 (⇨高等学校) higher [×high] education. ● 高等技術 advanced technology [technique]. (❶ high technology は「コンピュータ・半導体などを作る先端技術」の意)
● 高等裁判所 a high court. ● 高等数学 higher [advanced] mathematics. ● 高等専門学校 a technical college (❶ 工業系のもの); (英) a tertiary college. ● 高等動物 the higher animals.
● 高等弁務官 a high commissioner.
こうとう 高踏 — 高踏的な 形 (高尚な) high-toned,

(やや書) lofty. (よそよそしい) (話) standóffish.
こうとう 高騰 ● 円の高騰 a *sudden* [a *sharp*] *rise in* the yen; a *jump in* the yen.
— **高騰する** 動 ▶物価が高騰している Prices *are rising rapidly* [*are soaring*]. (⇨暴騰)
こうとう 喉頭 [解剖] the lárynx (複 ~es). ▶喉頭がん(の手術)で声を失う人が多い Many people lose their voices when they are operated on for cancer of the *larynx*.
● 喉頭炎 [医学] laryngitis. ● 喉頭ポリープ a laryngeal polyp.

こうどう 行動 图 [行為] (くり返された) (an) action; (1回の) an act; [ふるまい] *behavior*; [書] *conduct*; [活動] activities (通例複数形で). (⇨行い) [類語]
①【〜(の)行動】● 団体[個人]行動 group [individual] *action*. ● 軍事行動 military *action*. ● 消費行動 (a) consumption *behavior*. ● 問題行動 (a) problem(atic) *behavior*. ▶午後は個人[自由]行動をとってよろしい You may have free *activities* in the afternoon./(好きなことをしてよろしい) You can do whatever you like in the afternoon.
②【行動〜】● 行動力のある[行動的な]人 a man [a woman] of *action* (❶ 強意的に) an *action* man [woman] ともいう; (活発な人) an active person; (積極的な人) an aggressive person. ▶彼は行動半径が広い He has a wide range [(書) sphere] of *action* [*activities*].
③【行動が[は]〜】▶彼らの迅速な行動が彼の命を救った Their prompt [quick, swift] *actions* saved his life. ▶彼の行動は勇敢だった His *act* [*action*, *behavior*] was brave./(勇敢に行動した) He acted [behaved] bravely.
④【行動に[を]〜】● 考えを行動に移す(=実行する) put one's idea into *action*. ● 直ちに行動をとる[起こす] *act* now; act [take *action*] immediately; take immediate *action*. ● 彼の行動(=動静)を見守る watch his *movements*. ● 別行動をとる take a different course [course of *action*] from others. ● 行動を開始する begin [start] an action. ▶自分の行動に責任を持ちなさい You should answer [be accountable] for your *actions* [*what* you *do*]. ▶彼の返事は口先だけで行動に移さなかった His response was merely verbal and he took no *action*. ▶私たちは1日中ずっと行動をともにした(=ともに過ごした) We *spent* the whole day *together*.
— **行動(を)する** 動 [行う] act; [ふるまう] behave. ▶奇妙な行動をする *act* (very) strangely. ▶彼の命令[忠告]に従って行動する *act on* his order [advice]. ● 集団で行動する(=動き回る) go around in groups. ▶今こそ行動すべき時だ Now is the time for *action* [*to act*]./We must *act* now.
▶君は大人なんだからそれ相応に行動すべきだ You're an adult and should *act* [*behave*] accordingly.
● 行動計画 a plan of action. ● 行動主義 behaviorism. ● 行動様式 a behavior pattern; a pattern of behavior.
こうどう 公道 a (public) road, 《書》a public highway. ▶「私道」は a private road (⇨道❶))
こうどう 坑道 (横坑) a tunnel, a gallery, a drift; (縦坑) a shaft, a pit. ● 岩盤に深く坑道を掘る *mine* deep into the rock.
こうどう 黄道 [天文] the ecliptic.
● 黄道光 zodiacal /zoʊdáiəkl/ light. ● 黄道十二宮 the signs of the zodiac.
こうどう 講堂 a lecture hall, 《米》 an auditorium, 《英》 an assembly hall; (ひな段式の) a (lecture) theater. ● 学校の講堂 a school *auditorium*.

ごうとう 強盗 〖人〗a robber; (夜盗) a burglar; (昼間の押し込み強盗) a housebreaker; (路上の) a mugger (⇨泥棒); 〖行為〗(人) a robbery, (人) a burglary. ●銀行強盗 (人) a bank robber; (行為) a bank robbery; (武装強盗による) a bank holdup. ●強盗を働く commit (a) robbery [(a) burglary] 《on+家を, against+人》; rob 《him of it》; (家に押し入る) break in [into (a house)]. ▶彼は強盗容疑で逮捕された He was arrested for robbery [burglary]. ▶昨夜強盗に入られた Our house was robbed [broken into, ×broken in] last night. (⚠(1) break in は自動詞で受身不可. (2) Our house was…. は We were…. ともいえる)
●強盗殺人罪 burglary and murder.

*ごうどう 合同 图 (a) combination; (結合) union; 〖数学〗congruence.
── 合同の 圃 combined; united; (共同の) joint; 〖数学〗congruent 《to》. ●彼と事業を合同でやる(＝協力する) join hands with him in an enterprise. ▶2人の音楽家は合同で演奏会を開いた The two musicians gave a joint concert. ▶この二つの三角形は相似形だが合同ではない These two triangles are similar but not congruent.
── 合同する 動 (結合する) combine; (一体になる) unite.
●合同委員会 a joint committee. ●合同事業 a joint project. ●合同葬 a mass funeral. ●合同労組 a joint labor union.

こうとうがっこう 高等学校 (a senior) high school; an upper secondary school. (⇨高校, 学校)

こうとうぶ 後頭部 the back of the [one's] head.

こうとうむけい 荒唐無稽 ── 荒唐無稽の 圃 (空想的はなはだしい) fantastic; (ばかげた) preposterous, absurd, nonsensical.

こうとく 高徳 high 〖書〗lofty virtue. ●高徳の僧 a priest of high [great] virtue.

こうどく 鉱毒 (鉱害) mining [mineral] pollution; (汚染物質) pollutants produced in mining processes.

こうどく 講読 图 reading. ── 講読する 動 (読む) read.

こうどく 購読 图 (a) subscription 《to》.
── 購読する 動 ●雑誌を(定期・予約)購読する take [〖英〗take in] a magazine (⚠in は〖英〗でも次第に用いられい傾向にある); subscribe to a magazine. (⚠前の方が口語的). 〘事情〙米英では通何郵送による) ●1年間予約購読する take out a year's subscription 《to》. ●本誌の継続購読をご希望の場合は if you wish to receive further copies of this magazine. ▶私はニューヨークタイムズを購読している I take [subscribe to; (読んでいる) read] the New York Times. (⚠この意では進行形不可)
●購読者 a subscriber 《to》; (読者) a reader. ▶その新聞は購読者が多い The newspaper has a large circulation. (⚠circulation は「発行部数」の意)
●購読料 a subscription (fee).

こうとくしん 公徳心 public morality; (公共心) public spirit. ●公徳心に欠ける be lacking in public morality.

こうどくそ 抗毒素 〖薬学〗an antitoxin.

こうとり(い) 公取(委) [「公正取引委員会」の略] (⇨公正)

こうない 坑内 坑内で in the pit [縦坑] shaft]. ●坑内事故 an accident in the pit. ●坑内に閉じこめられる be shut up in the pit.

こうない 校内 ●校内で on the school grounds; (大学の) on (the) campus. ●校内ソフトボール大会 an intramural [(クラス対抗の) an interclass] softball tournament. ▶校内に車を乗り入れてはいけません Don't drive your car onto (the) campus./《掲示》〖学内駐車禁止〗No parking on campus.
●校内暴力 school violence. ●校内放送 the school PA (system). (⚠the PA (system)は the public-address system (拡声装置)の略)

こうない 港内 ●港内で in [within] the harbor; in the port. ▶神戸港は最も近代的な港内設備を備えている Kobe Port is equipped with the most modern harbor facilities.

こうない 構内 ●構内で (駅などの) in a 《railroad》 yard; (教会などの) in the precincts; (工場など壁で囲まれた建物群の) in a compound; (建物とその敷地を含む) on the premises; (大学などの) on (the) campus (⇨校内). ●構内立入禁止 〖掲示〗Keep off the premises.

こうないえん 口内炎 〖医学〗(a) stomatitis /stòuməˈtaɪtɪs/ -titides /-tɪtədiːz/).

こうなん 後難 future troubles; the consequences. ●後難を恐れて口をつぐむ remain silent for [in] fear of the consequences.

こうなん 硬軟 hardness and softness. ▶経営者側は大幅な賃上げ交渉で硬軟両様の措置を取った The management took a hard and soft line in the big raise negotiations.

こうにち 抗日 resistance to Japan.
●抗日感情 anti-Japanese sentiment [feeling].

こうにゅう 購入 图 purchase /pɚːrtʃəs/; buying. ●一括購入 basket [lump-sum] purchase. ●新しい家の購入 the purchase of a new house. ▶大量購入の場合には割引いたします We give a discount on bulk purchases.
── 購入する 動 〖書〗purchase; buy. (⇨買う) ▶パソコンをボーナス一括払いで購入した I purchased a PC with a single payment at bonus season.
●購入価格 a búying [a púrchase] ràte [price].

*こうにん 公認 图 official recognition [approval].
── 公認する 動 (公式に認める) recognize 《it》officially 《as a world record》; (権限を与える) authorize 《it; him to do》; (公式に是認する) approve 《it》officially. (⇨認める)
●公認会計士 《米》a certified public accountant; 《英》a chartered accountant. ●公認記録 an official record. (⚠関連) 未公認記録 an unofficial record) ●公認候補者 a recognized [a nominated] candidate; (党公認の) a party-backed candidate.

こうにん 後任 a successor. ▶彼は A 教授の後任です He is the successor to [×of] Professor A./He is Mr. A's successor 《⇔predecessor》as professor./He has succeeded Mr. A as professor.

こうねつ 高熱 〖体温〗a high fever; 〖温度〗an intense heat. (⚠a high temperature は体温・温度の両方に用いる) ●高熱に苦しんでいる be suffering from a high fever [one's high temperature].

こうねつひ 光熱費 lighting and heating expenses.

こうねん 光年 a light year. ▶その星は地球から4光年の距離にある The star is four light years away from the earth.

こうねん 後年 ▶彼は後年学者として名を成した He has become known as a scholar later in life [in his later years].

こうねん 高年 old age. (⇨高齢)

こうねんき 更年期 (婦人の) the menopause, the change (of life). ▶彼女は更年期に入っている She's going through the change.
●更年期障害 a menopausal disorder [(症状) symptom].

こうのう 効能 (有効性) effectiveness, 《書》 efficacy. ● アスピリンの効能 the *effectiveness* [*efficacy*] of aspirin. ● 効能がある be effective (*against, for*). (⇨効果)
● 効能書き a statement of virtues.

ごうのう 豪農 a rich [a wealthy] farmer.

こうのとり 〘鳥〙 a stork.

こうのもの 香の物 pickles. (⇨⃝漬物)

こうのもの 剛の者 (剛胆(⦅⃝⃝⃝⃝⃝⃝)な人) a stouthearted person; (勇敢な人) a brave person.

こうは 光波 a light wave.

こうは 硬派 ❶ [強硬派] uncompromising politicians; hard-liners. (⇨鷹派) ● 硬派の政治家で鳴らしている be a noted *uncompromising* politician; be famous as a *hard-line* politician.
❷ [男(=腕力)を誇示する若者] a swaggering young man; 《話》 a tough boy.

こうば 工場 a factory. (⇨工場(⦅⃝⃝⃝⃝))

*こうはい 後輩 (学校の)《米》 one's underclass student; (主に組織の) one's junior. (⇨先輩 [解説])
▶ 彼は2年後輩です (年齢が) He is two years *younger than* I am [《話》 *than* me, 《古・まれ》 *than* I]./(学年が) He is two years *behind* me in school.

こうはい 交配 图 (異種交配) crossing, cróssbrèeding.
―― **交配する** 動 cross [cróssbrèd] 《A with [and] B》.
● 交配種 a cross; a crossbreed; a hybrid.

こうはい 好配 〚《話》配偶者〛 one's good wife [husband]; 〚《話》配当〛 a good [a high] dividend. ● その企業は今期好配が見込めそうだ The enterprise seems to hold promise of a *good dividend* this period.

こうはい 光背 (⇨⃝⃝ 後光)

こうはい 荒廃 图 〚破壊〛 ruin; (国土などの) devastation.
―― **荒廃する** 動 come [go] to ruin; fall into ruin. ● 荒廃している be [lie] *in ruins*. ▶ 人心が荒廃した The people's hearts grew hard.
―― **荒廃させる** 動 ruin; devastate. ▶ その内戦で国土は荒廃した The civil war *ruined* [*devastated*] the land.

こうはい 降灰 volcanic ash; a fall of ash; fallen ash.

こうはい 高配 〚気配り〛 consideration, attention, care; 〚高い配当〛 a high [a good] dividend. (⇨好配). ▶ ご高配をありがたく存じます I'm much obliged to you for your *kind consideration*.

*こうばい 勾配 〚傾斜〛 a slant, a slope, an inclination (⇨傾斜); 〚坂〛 a pitch; (鉄道・道路などの) a gradient, 《米》 a grade. ● 屋根の急勾配 a steep *pitch* [*slant, slope, inclination*] of the roof.
● 上り[下り]勾配 an up [a down] *grade*. ▶ この道は勾配がゆるやかだ This road has a gentle *slope* [*slant*]. ▶ この坂は 5 分の 1 [20 度]の勾配がある There is a *grade* [an *inclination*] of 1 in 5 [twenty degrees] in this slope.

こうばい 公売 图 a public auction.
―― **公売する** 動 sell 《goods》 at [《英》 by] auction. ● 公売処分 disposition by public sale; (a) tax sale.

こうばい 紅梅 (説明的に) a Japanese apricot tree with red blossoms.

こうばい 購買 purchase /pə́ːrtʃəs/; buying.
● 消費者の購買意欲をそぐ curb consumers' appetite for *buying*. ▶ コマーシャルが彼のその車に対する購買欲をそそった The commercial induced him to buy the car.
―― **購買する** 動 《書》 purchase; buy. (⇨買う)
● 購買者 a buyer; a purchaser. ● 購買部 (会社の部門) the púrchasing depàrtment; (学校の) a school store. ● 購買力 púrchasing [búying] pòwer.

こうばいすう 公倍数 〘数学〙 a common multiple. (⇨公約数) ● 最小公倍数 the lowest [least] *common multiple* (略 LCM, l.c.m.).

こうはいち 後背地 the hinterland; a region lying inland from the coast.

こうはく 紅白 red and white.
● 紅白戦 (プロ野球などの) an intra-squad game.
● 紅白饅頭(⦅⃝⃝⃝⃝)) a pair of red and white *manju* traditionally given out on an auspicious occasion.

こうばく 広漠 ―― 広漠たる 形 vast; wide; extensive. ● 広漠たる大平原 *vast* [*wide*] plains.

こうばしい 香ばしい sweet-smelling; (香料の) 《書》 aromatic. ● コーヒー豆の香ばしいにおい the *aroma* of coffee beans. (⇨におい, 香り)

こうはつ 後発 ● 後発列車 the train that *started late*. ● 後発メーカー a manufacturer who entered the market late; a late starter. ● 国際市場への後発参入企業 a latecomer to the international market.
● 後発発展途上国 least-developed countries 《略 LDC》.

*こうはん 公判 (a) (public) trial. ● 公判に付する bring 《him》 to [up for] *trial*; put 《him》 on *trial*. (⇨裁判) ▶ 彼は窃盗罪での公判中だ He is (going) *on trial for* theft./His theft case is *under trial*.
▶ その事件の公判はいつ開かれますか When is the *trial* on the case to be held?/When does the case *come to trial*? ▶ 検察は公判を維持できないだろう The prosecutors will not be able to carry the *trial* through.

こうはん 広範 ―― 広範な 形 ● 英文学について広範な (=広い) 知識を持っている have an *extensive* [a *wide*, a *broad*] knowledge of English literature.

こうはん 甲板 (⇨甲板(⦅⃝⃝⃝⃝))

こうはん 後半 the second [latter] half. (❗ はっきり区分できないものには latter (↔former) が好まれる) (⇨前半) ● 1990 年代後半 the *latter* (↔former) *half* [*part*] of the 1990s; the *second* (↔first) *half* [*part*] of the 1990s. ● 8 月後半に休暇を取る take a vacation during the *latter* days [*part*] of August. ▶ その小説の後半は読まなかった I didn't read the *latter part* of the novel. ▶ 彼は 50 代の後半だ He is in his *late* (↔early) fifties.
● 後半戦 (試合の) the second half of a game; (シーズンの) the second half of a season.

*こうばん 交番 a *koban*, a police box [station].
〚事情〛 米英には警察や消防などの緊急連絡用電話ボックスはあるが、日本のような常駐の交番はない)

こうばん 降板 图 (キャスターなどの) a resignation.
● ニュース番組からの降板を発表する announce one's resignation from the news network.
―― **降板する** 動 ● 投手を降板させる (攻撃側が) knock a pitcher out of the box; send a pitcher to the showers; (監督が) remove a pitcher. ▶ (投手が) 降板させられる be removed; get the hook.

ごうはん 合板 plywood /pláiwud/. ● プリント合板 printed [*faced*] *plywood*.

こうはんい 広範囲 a wide range [《研究の》 field].
● 広範囲の知識を持つ have a *wide range* of knowledge. ▶ この雑誌は広範囲の話題を扱っている

This magazine covers a *wide range* of topics. ▶彼の研究は広範囲に及んでいる His research is *wide-ranging* [of *wide range*]./He has a *wide field* of research. ▶台風による災害は広範囲に及んだ There was a *widespread* disaster from the typhoon.

こうはんせい 後半生 the latter half of one's life. (◯ 前半生) ▶彼は後半生を田舎で暮らした He lived in the country during the *latter half of his life*.

こうひ 工費 the cost of construction, constrúction cósts.

こうひ 公費 ●公費で at *public expense*. ●公費(=公金)をむだ遣いする waste *public money*.

こうひ 皇妃 an empress.

こうび 交尾 名《書》mating; copulation.
— 交尾する 動《書》mate 《with》; copulate 《with》.
●交尾期 the máting sèason.

こうび 後尾 (後部) the rear (↔front); the tail (↔head); (船尾) the stern (↔stem). ▶彼女はコンサートのチケットを手に入れるため行列の最後尾に並んだ She stood at the *end* (↔*head*) of the line to get the concert ticket.

ごうひ 合否 (合格か不合格) success or failure; (結果) the result of an examination. ●受験者の合否の判定をする decide whether to *pass or fail* the examinees.

こうヒスタミンざい 抗ヒスタミン剤 〖薬学〗an antihistamine.

こうひつ 硬筆 (ペン) a pen; (鉛筆) a pencil.
●硬筆習字 penmanship.

*こうひょう 公表 名 (an) [(a) public] announcement. (◯発表) ●関係者の氏名の公表を差し控える hold back 〖《書》withhold〗 the names of the people involved.
— 公表する 動 make* (it) public; (公式に) announce; (活字にして) publish; (秘密を) disclose. ●真相を公表する make the facts *public*; *announce* the facts; (握りつぶすわけにはいかない) can't sit on the facts.

こうひょう 好評 〖受けがよいこと〗 a favorable [a good*] reception; 〖人気〗popularity; 〖本・映画などの〗a favorable [a good] review. ●好評を博す meet with [get, have] a *favorable reception*; win *popularity*. (◯評判)

こうひょう 高評 (批評) (a) comment 《on》; (a) criticism 《of, on》. ▶私の論文についてご高評を賜りたい I'd like to have your *comments on* my paper.

こうひょう 講評 名 (a) comment 《on》. (❗直訳的に a critical comment とすると非難の意を強く出るので好ましくない) ▶彼女の作文に対する先生の講評は適切なものだった Her teacher's *comment on* her writing was good and to the point.
— 講評する 動 comment [make a comment] 《on, about; that 節》.

こうひん 公賓 a guest of the government. (◯国賓)

こうひんいテレビ 高品位テレビ a high-definition television (略 HDTV).

こうふ 公布 〖法律の〗《書》promulgation (◯発布); 〖重大な決定の〗proclamation. (◯布告)
— 公布する 動 promulgate, proclaim.

こうふ 交付 — 交付する 動 ●年金を交付する(=与える) give 〖《書》grant〗《him》a pension. ●旅券を交付する(=発行する) issue [give, 《書》grant]《him》a passport.
●交付金 a grant(-in-aid), a subsidy. (❗前方は「上から下に与える金」，後方は「何かを下支えする金」の意で，補助金，助成金のいずれにも当たる) ●教育交付金 a *subsidy* for education.

こうふ 坑夫，鉱夫 a miner.

こうぶ 後部 the back, 《やや書》the rear. (⇨後ろ) ●後部の座席 a *back* seat. ●バスの後部に at the *back* of the bus; in the *back part* of the bus.

こうふう 光風 ●光風霽月(たり) being serene and clear-minded.

こうふう 校風 〖精神〗a school spirit; 〖気風〗the tone of a school; 〖長年の流儀〗(a) school tradition. ▶その学校の校風がきらいだ I don't like the *tone* [〖雰囲気〗*atmosphere*] of the school.

*こうふく 幸福 名 happiness (⇨幸せ); 〖健康で満足な生活〗《やや書》well-being; (特定の人の) welfare. ●真の幸福を得る achieve true *happiness*. ●幸福感を持つ have a feeling of *happiness*; have a sense of *well-being*. ●子供の幸福に責任あるを be responsible for the *welfare* of one's children.
●幸福を求める look for [《書》seek] *happiness*.
●幸福を脅かす threaten one's *happiness* [《やや書》*well-being*]. ▶金で幸福は買えない You can't buy *happiness* with [×by] money./Money cannot buy *happiness*. ▶科学は人類に幸福をもたらすだろうか Does science bring *happiness* [《やや書》*well-being*] to human beings?
— 幸福な 形 happy. ●幸福な家庭 a *happy* home. ▶私は今日ほど幸福だったことはない I'd never felt *happier* than I did today. ▶This was the *happiest* day of my life. ▶私は彼女といる時がいちばん幸福だ I am [feel] *happiest* [×the happiest] when I am with her. (❗他と比較せず叙述的に用いられるときは最上級でも通例 the をつけない)
— 幸福に 副 happily. ●幸福にする make 《him》 *happy* 《×happily》. ▶彼らは幸福に暮らした They lived *happily* [a *happy* life]. (❗前の方が口語的)

こうふく 降伏 (a) surrender 《to》. (⇨降参) ●無条件降伏 unconditional *surrender*. ●敵の降伏の条件を話し合う discuss the terms for the *surrender* of the enemy.
— 降伏する 動 (降参する) surrender 《to》; give* in 《to》. (❗後の方が口語的) ▶敵はそれ以上抵抗せずに降伏した The Enemy *gave in* without further resistance.

*こうぶつ 鉱物 a mineral.
●鉱物学 mineralogy. ●鉱物学者 a mineralogist. ●鉱物資源 mineral resources.

こうぶつ 好物 one's favorite food. ▶私の好物は広島のカキだ Hiroshima oysters are my *favorite food*./My favorite food is Hiroshima oysters./I'm (very) fond of Hiroshima oysters.

*こうふん 興奮 名 excitement; (喜びなどでぞくぞくすること) a thrill; (神経や器官の興奮) stimulation. ●興奮を引き起こす cause [《やや書》arouse] *excitement*.
●興奮を抑える control one's *excitement*; keep one's *excitement* in check.
— 興奮する 動 be [get*] excited 《at, by, about; to do》; be [get] thrilled 《at, with》(いずれも状態または状態の変化を, get は状態の変化を表す); thrill 《at》; (刺激を受ける) be stimulated. ●興奮した群衆 an *excited* [×an exciting] crowd. ●興奮して跳び回る jump about *in excitement* [*excitedly*]. ▶さらに興奮して部屋に入って来る come into a room full of *excitement*. ▶彼女はその知らせを聞いて興奮していた She *was excited at* [*by*] the news./She *was excited to* hear the news. ▶そんなに興奮するな Don't *get* so *excited* [*excite yourself* too much]./(落ち着け) Calm down. ▶その映画に観客は非常に興奮した The audience *was* very

much *thrilled by* [*was very* (much) *excited by*] the film./The film *thrilled* [*excited*] the audience very much.
— **興奮させる** 動 excite; thrill; stimulate. ● 神経を興奮させる excite [*stimulate*] the nerves.
● **興奮剤** a stimulant (drug).

こうふん 口吻 ● 口吻を漏(ﾛ)らす hint at the possibility (*of*).

こうふん 公憤 public indignation 《*at, about, over, on*》; (義憤) righteous indignation. ▶子供の虐待に関する報道は公憤をかきたてた Reports of child abuse aroused *public* [*righteous*] *indignation*.

こうぶん 構文 (文の構造) the construction of a sentence, a sentence structure.

こうぶんし 高分子 a high molecule; (巨大分子)〔化学〕a macromolecule.

こうぶんしょ 公文書 an official document [*paper*]; (保管所収蔵の)《集合的》archives /άːrkaɪvz/. ● 公文書偽造で罰せられる be punished for forgery of an *official document*.

こうべ 首, 頭 (⇨頭)
● こうべを垂れる become modest.
● こうべをめぐらす『振り返る』look around; 『過ぎ去ったことを思い出す』look back 《*on*》.

*こうへい 公平 [『私情・欲望などに左右されないこと』fairness; 『えこひいき・偏見などがないこと』impartiality; 『自己や他の関係者の利害に動かされず正しい規律を守ること』justice.
— **公平な** 形 (公正な) fair; (片寄らない) impartial; (判断などが正しい) just. ● 公平無私な判事 a *fair* [an *impartial*] and disinterested judge. ● 公平な態度で in a *fair* [an *impartial*, a *just*] manner. ● 公平な評価 a fair evaluation. ● 公平な意見を述べる give an *impartial* [《私心のない》*disinterested*] opinion. ● 公平な決定をする make a *fair* [a *just*] decision. ▶議長は各議員に公平でなければならない A chairman [A chairwoman] should be *fair* [*impartial*] *to* each member. ▶彼は態度が公平だ He is *fair* [*just, fair and just*] in his attitude(s).
— **公平に** 副 fairly; impartially; with justice. ● 人を公平に扱う treat people *fairly* [*impartially, with justice*]. ● 彼を公平に評すると to do him *justice*. ● 仕事を公平に割りふる make a *fair* division of the work. ● 公平に分配する distribute (...) fairly 《*among* [*between*]》.

こうへん 後編 『本などの後半』the latter [second] part 《*of*》; 『後の巻』the latter [second] volume 《*of*》. ▶3巻に分かれている場合は the third [last] volume 《*of*》 となる ● その小説の後編 the *latter volume of* the novel; (続編) the *sequel to* the novel.

こうべん 抗弁 图 (抗議) a protest 《*against*》; (被告の)〔法律〕a plea, (a) defense.
— **抗弁する** 動 protest; 〔法律〕plead 《*against*》, defend.

ごうべん 合弁 (共同の) joint. ● 日米合弁事業 a Japan-U.S. *joint* venture. ● A社と合弁会社を設立する form a *joint* venture with A; link up with A in a *joint* business.

*こうほ 候補 (候補者) a candidate; (候補に指名された人・物) a nominee. ● 市長候補 a *candidate for* mayor. ● 公認候補 an official *candidate*. ● タレント候補 an entertainer-turned *candidate*. ● アカデミー賞候補 an Academy Award *nominee*. ● 金メダル候補 (=有望選手) a gold-medal *hopeful*. ▶彼は大統領候補に指名された He *was nominated for* President [*for* the Presidency]. ▶ここが新しい国際空港の候補地です This is the *site proposed for* a new international airport.
● **候補者名簿** a list of candidates; 《米》a slate; (政党の) a ticket. ● **候補生** a (《英》gentleman) cadet.

こうほ 好捕 图〔野球〕a good [a beautiful, a splendid] catch.
— **好捕する** 動 make a good catch of a line drive.

こうぼ 公募 (株式で) a public offering. (⇨募集)
— **公募する** 動 ● 主演男優を公募する (=応募を促す) *invite applications for* the leading actor. ● 債券[株式]を公募する *offer* bonds [stocks, 《英》shares] *for public subscription*.
● **公募価格** a public offering price. ● **公募債** a publicly offered bond.

こうぼ 酵母 yeast.
● **酵母菌** a yeast fungus.

こうほう 工法 a method of construction. ▶この高層ビルは最新の工法で建てられた This skyscraper was built by using the newest *methods of construction*.

こうほう 公報 an official report [bulletin]; (定期的に発行される) a newsletter.

こうほう 広報 (活動) public relations (略 PR, P.R.). (❢ 単数扱い); (広く伝えること) publicity. ▶広報活動は重要な仕事だ *Public relations* is [×are] *important business*.
● **広報課** a public relations office. ● **広報係** a public relations officer. ● **広報誌** a magazine for public relations. ● **広報部** a public relations department.

こうほう 後方 (⇨後ろ) ● 後方にもたれる lean *back* [*backward*]. ● 後方から敵を攻撃する attack the enemy from *behind* [*the rear*]. ▶後方の湖が琵琶湖です The lake *behind* us is Lake Biwa.
● **後方勤務** a rear service. ● **後方部隊** troops in the rear.

こうほう 航法 navigation.

こうほう 高峰 a high peak; (高い山) a high mountain.

こうぼう 工房 (画家などの仕事場) a studio (複 ~s), an atelier; (手工業の作業場) a workshop.

こうぼう 弘法 ● 弘法にも筆の誤り (ことわざ) Even Homer (sometimes) nods.
● **弘法筆を選ばず** (ことわざ) A bad workman blames [quarrels with] his tools.; The cunning mason works with any stone.

こうぼう 攻防 a battle (in alternate óffense and défense). (❢ 対照強勢に注意) ● 激しい攻防(戦)を繰り広げる fight a fierce battle.

こうぼう 興亡 (盛衰) the rise and fall. ● 国の興亡 *the rise and fall* of a country.

ごうほう 合法 — **合法的な** 形 『法律に定められている』legal; 『法に触れない』lawful; 『法律上正当な』legitimate. ● 合法的な行為 a *legal* [a *lawful*] act. ● 合法的手段 a *lawful* means. (❢ 単・複同形) ● 合法的な相続人 a *legitimate* heir.

ごうほう 豪放 — **豪放な** 形 (度量の大きな) large-[broad-, open-] minded; open-hearted. ● 豪放磊落(ﾗｲﾗｸ)な (=度量の大きな)人 an *open-hearted* [an *open-minded*] person.

こうぼく 公僕 a public servant. (⇨公務員)
こうぼく 香木 an aromatic tree.
こうぼく 高木 a (tall) tree.
こうほん 校本 a variorum (edition); an edition containing variant texts of a classic. ● 校本万葉集 a *variorum* (*edition*) *of the Manyoshu*.

こうほん 稿本 (草稿) a manuscript. (⇨草稿)

こうま 子馬 〖小型品種の馬〗a pony; 〖若い馬〗(雄) a colt, (雌) a filly (! 離乳前の子馬は, 特に a foal という).

こうまい 高邁 — **高邁な** 形 lofty (! high の堅い語); noble. ● 高邁な理想を抱く hold a *lofty* ideal.

こうまん 高慢 名 〖自尊心〗pride; 〖尊大・横柄〗arrogance, haughtiness; 〖うぬぼれ〗conceit. ● 高慢の鼻をくじく humble [(傷つける) hurt, (恥をかかせる) humiliate] his *pride*.
● 高慢ちきな overproud.
— **高慢な** 形 proud; arrogant; haughty; conceited (〖話〗では stuck-up とも). ● 高慢な態度 a *proud* [a *haughty*] attitude.

ごうまん 傲慢 名 〖尊大・横柄〗arrogance, haughtiness; 〖傲慢無礼〗insolence.
— **傲慢な** 形 arrogant; haughty; insolent. ● 傲慢な態度で in an *arrogant* manner; arrogantly; haughtily. ▶ 彼は目下の者に傲慢だ He is *arrogant* [*insolent*] to his inferiors.

こうみ 香味 flavor and taste.
● 香味野菜 spicy and flavorous vegetables.
● 香味料 spices; seasoning.

こうみゃく 鉱脈 a vein, a lode. ● 銅のいい鉱脈を発見する discover a rich *vein* [*lode*] (of copper).

こうみょう 巧妙 — **巧妙な** 形 (気の利いた) clever, 《主に米》smart (! いずれも「抜け目のない」という悪い意味を含むことがある); (熟練を示す) skillful; (工夫に富む)《やや書》ingenious. ● 巧妙な手口を使う use a *clever* [a *smart*, an *ingenious*] trick. ● 巧妙に仕組まれたわな a *cleverly* [a *skillfully*] devised trap.

こうみょう 功名 ● けがの功名 (⇨怪我(⁽゚⁾)) [成句]
● 功名心 (野心) (an) ambition. ● 功名心にかられる be driven by *ambition*.

こうみょう 光明 (光) light, a lamp; (希望) hope. ● …の前途に光明を見いだす see a *bright future* ahead of ….

こうみん 公民 (市民) a citizen; (社会科の) civics (! 単数扱い).
● 公民館 a community center. ● 公民権 civil [civic] rights.

こうむ 公務 (an) official duty. ● 公務に就く[就いている] assume [be on] *official duty*. ● 公務で出張する travel on *official business*. ● 公務多忙なために on account of the pressure of *official duties*.
● 公務執行妨害 (an) interference with a government official in the execution [exercise] of his duties.

こうむ 校務 school duties [affairs].

こうむいん 公務員 (職員) a government [a public] employee, a government [a public] worker; (高官) a government [a public] official, (公僕) a civil [a public] servant. ▶ 彼女は国家[地方]公務員です She *works for* the national [(市) city; (県) prefectural] *government*. (! She is a national [a local] *government employee*. より普通. 国家公務員の場合いずれも national は省略可)

こうむてん 工務店 a komuten (; 説明的に) an office or company that does construction and/or engineering works.

こうむる 被る 〖被害・損害などを〗suffer; 〖許しなどを〗receive. ● ごめんをこうむる (⇨御免) ▶ 騒音で迷惑を被るを嫌われる be annoyed by noises. ▶ 彼はその取り引きで多大の損害を被った He *suffered* heavy losses in the transaction.

こうめい 高名 — **高名な** 形 (有名な) (very) famous; (広く知られた) well-known; (傑出した) distin-

guished. ▶ 彼は高名な作家だ He is a very *famous* writer./He is a writer of great [high] *fame*.

ごうめいがいしゃ 合名会社 an unlimited [a general] partnership.

こうめいせいだい 公明正大 — **公明正大な** 形 ● 公明正大な裁判官 a *fair* judge.
— **公明正大に** 副 ● 公明(正大)にする do 《it》 *fairly*; (公正にやる) play *fair* (and *square*). (! 慣用句. square は「真っ正直な, 一点の(不正の)疑いもない」の意) (⇨公正 ③)

こうめいとう 公明党 the New Komeito.

こうもう 孔孟 ● 孔孟の教え the teaching(s) of Confucius and Mencius.

こうもう 紅毛 ● 紅毛碧眼(⁽⁾) a (red-haired and blue eyes) foreigner; a Westerner.

こうもう 膏肓 ● 膏肓(⁽゚⁾)に入る (⇨病) [成句]

こうもく 項目 〖表や目録などの〗an item; 〖題目・新聞の見出しなどの〗a head(ing); (辞書の見出し) an entry (word); 〖要点〗a point. ● 表に載っている 10 の項目 ten *items* on the list. ● 項目ごとに並べる arrange 《them》*item by item*. ● 問題を 4 項目に分けて扱う treat a question under four *heads*. ● 3 項目から成る要求をする make a three-*point* demand [a demand which consists of three *points*]《on him》. ● 勘定を項目別に記す *itemize* a bill. ▶ これはどの項目に出ていますか What *heading* does this come under?

ごうもくてき 合目的 — **合目的的な** 形 purposive.

こうもり 〖動物〗a bat /bæt/.
● こうもり傘 an umbrella.

こうもん 肛門 名 〖解剖〗the anus /éinəs/.
— **肛門の** 形 anal.
● 肛門科 proctólogy.

こうもん 校門 a school gate. (⇨門)

こうもん 拷問 torture /tʃɔːrtʃər/. ● 彼を拷問にかける put him to (the) *torture* [on the rack]; *torture* him. ● 彼を拷問にかけて白状させる make him confess *by torture*; *torture* him to make him confess; *torture* a confession out of him.
● 拷問台 (中世の) the rack.

こうや 荒野 (未開の) the wilds, 《古・詩》the wilderness /wíldərnəs/; (不毛の) a desert /dézərt/,《書》(a) wasteland, the wilderness. ● 荒野を旅する travel across the *wilds* [*wild land*].

こうや 紺屋 (染物屋) a dyer.
● 紺屋の白袴(⁽ᵃᵏ⁾) 'Dyers' pants are never dyed.'/《ことわざ》(靴直しの女房はいちばんひどい靴をはいている) The cobbler's wife goes the worst shod.

こうやく 公約 名 a pledge; (約束) a promise. ● 選挙公約を果たす[破る] fulfill [break] one's campaign *pledges* [*promises*].
— **公約する** 動 ▶ 政府はインフレ抑制を公約した The government *pledged* 《*itself*》 to check inflation.

こうやく 膏薬 〖張り薬〗a plaster; 〖軟膏〗(an) ointment. ● 膏薬を張る[塗る] apply a *plaster* [*ointment*] 《to》.

こうやくすう 公約数 〖数学〗a common divisor. (⇨公倍数) ● 最大公約数 the greatest *common divisor* (略 GCD, g.c.d.).

こうやさい 後夜祭 a closing party 《after》 a festival). (⇨ 前夜祭)

こうやのけっとう 『荒野の決闘』 *My Darling Clementine*. [参考] 米国の映画.

こうやのしちにん 『荒野の七人』 *The Magnificent Seven*. [参考] 米国の映画.

こうやひじり 『高野聖』 *The Priest of Mount Koya*; *The Holy Man of Mount Koya*. (参考] 泉鏡花の小

こうゆ 香油 balm; perfumed hair oil.
こうゆ 鉱油 mineral oil.
こうゆう 公有 ― **公有の** 形 public, publicly-owned.
● **公有地** public land.
こうゆう 交友 〖人〗(友人) a friend; (知人) an acquaintance; 〖関係〗(a) friendship. (付き合い)
▶彼はいろんな人と交友関係がある He has all sorts of *friends*./He has a large circle of *friends*.
こうゆう 交遊 名 《書》(an) association.
― **交遊する** 動 《書》associate [be in association]《*with*》.
こうゆう 校友 (男性) an alumnus /əlÁmnəs/ (複 alumni /-nai/); (女性) an alumna (複 alumnae /-niː/).
● **校友会** a graduates' [an alumni, an alumnae] association.
ごうゆう 豪遊 ― **豪遊する** 動 live it up (extravagantly). ▶ナイトクラブで豪遊する *live it up* in the night club.
こうよう 公用 〖官庁・会社などの職務〗official business; 〖公共の職務〗public [government] business; 〖公務上の使用〗official use. (⇨用 ❶❷)
● **公用語** an official language. ● **公用車** a car for official use. ● **公用文** wording [language] used in official documents.
こうよう 効用 (有用性) use; 《経済》utility; (効き目) (an) effect. (⇨効果) ▶スポーツの効用 the *use* of sports. ●効用がある(役に立つ)be of use; (効き目がある)be effective 《*against*; *in doing*》.
こうよう 紅葉, 黄葉 名 red [yellow] leaves; (紅葉した風景) autumn tints [colors]. ▶谷間は紅葉で燃えるようだ The valley is ablaze [aflame] with *autumn colors*. ▶その時は秋で紅葉がきれいだった It was fall, with lovely *colorings in the leaves*.
― **紅葉[黄葉]する** 動 turn red [yellow; (赤や黄色に) red and yellow].
こうよう 高揚 名 ●愛国心の高揚(=急激な高まり) an *upsurge* of patriotism.
― **高揚する** 動 ●士気を高揚させる(=高める) *lift* the morale. (⇨用 ❶)
こうよう 綱要 (要点) essentials; (基本) elements; the main point; (概要) an introduction 《*to*》.
▶生物学講要の *elements* of biology.
こうようじゅ 広葉樹 a broadleaf [a broad-leaved] tree. (⇨葉樹)
ごうよく 強欲 名 greed; (特に金銭に対して)《書》ávarice. ― **強欲な** 形 greedy; 《やや書》avaricious.
こうら 甲羅 (亀などの) a shell. ●甲羅を干す(=日光浴をする) sunbathe; bask in the sun.
こうらい 高麗 〖朝鮮半島の王朝〗Koryo.
● **高麗人参** (⇨⑨ 朝鮮 [朝鮮人参])
こうらく 行楽 (観光) sightseeing; (旅行) a pleasure trip; (ピクニック) a picnic. ●一日の行楽を楽しむ enjoy one's day *out*. (! out は「外出して」の意の副詞)
● **行楽客** (観光客) a tourist; a sightseer; (保養地で休暇を過ごす人)《米》a vacationer, a vacationist, 《英》a holidaymaker, 《集合的》holiday people. ● **行楽地** a tourist [a holiday] spot; (保養地) a (holiday) resort. ● **行楽日和** ideal [nice] weather for an outing.
こうらん 高覧 ▶私の論文をご高覧に供したく存じます I take pleasure in submitting my paper for your kind *inspection*.
こうり 小売り retail (↔wholesale). ●小売りで買う [売る] buy [sell] 《*it*》*at* [《主に英》*by*] *retail*; buy [sell] 《*it*》*retail*. ●叔父はスポーツ用品の小売りをやっています My uncle is a sporting goods retailer./My uncle *retails* sporting goods. ▶このバットは小売りで 4,000 円です This bat *retails* at [for] 4,000 yen./This bat is 4,000 yen *at* [*by*] *retail*.
● **小売価格** a retail price. ▶「希望小売価格 6 万円」は Recommended *retail* price ¥60,000)
● **小売業** retail business [trade]. ● **小売商人[業者]** a retail dealer; a retailer. ● **小売店** a retail store《米》[shop《英》].
こうり 公理 《書》an áxiom. ●公理の(ような)《書》axiomatic.
こうり 功利 ― **功利的な** 形 《書》utilitárian. ●功利的に考える(実用を重んじる) see from a *utilitarian* viewpoint; (利益を優先する) give priority to *profit*.
● **功利主義** utilitarianism. ● **功利主義者** a utilitarian. ● **功利性** utility.
こうり 行李 a wicker trunk [suitcase].
こうり 高利 (xa) high interest; 〖法外な高利〗usury.
●高利で金を貸す lend money at *high* (↔low) *interest*.
●**高利貸し** (貸し業務) usury; (貸す人) a high-interest money lender, a usurer, 《話》a loan shark.
ごうりか 合理化 名 streamlining, 《主に英》rationalization. ●大規模な[徹底的な; 思い切った]合理化 major [thorough; drastic] *streamlining*.
― **合理化する** 動 streamline 《主に英》rationalize 《an organization, a process》.
ごうりき 強力, 剛力 〖強い力〗great physical strength; 〖登山の荷物運搬人[ガイド]〗a mountain carrier [guide].
●強力犯 a violent crime.
こうりつ 公立 ― **公立の** 形 〖私立に対して〗(公営の) public; 〖地方自治体の〗(区・市・町・村立の) municipal; (道・府・県立の) prefectural; (都立の) metropolitan. (! 以上はいずれも限定用法が普通) ●公立(の)学校《米》a *public* school (! イングランドでは「私立の中高一貫教育校」を意味)、《英》a state school. (⇨学校) ●公立の図書館に勤める work for [at] a *public* library. ▶この学校は公立だ This school is a *public* institution./(市立だ) This school is run by the city [is under municipal management].
こうりつ 効率 名 efficiency. (⇨能率) ●生産効率 production *efficiency* ●機械の効率 the *efficiency* of a machine. ●コスト効率のよい cost-effective.
― **効率的な** 形 efficient (↔inefficient). ●資源の効率的な利用 *efficient* use of resources.
― **効率的に** 副 efficiently.
こうりつ 高率 a high rate. ●高率の課税 a *high* tax *rate*.
ごうりてき 合理的 ― **合理的な** 形 〖理性的な〗rational; 〖理屈に合った〗reasonable; 〖実際的な〗practical. ●聖書の教えを合理的に解釈する interpret the teachings of the Bible *rationally* [*reasonably*]; put a *rational* [a *reasonable*] interpretation on what the Bible says.
こうりゃく 攻略 ― **攻略する** 動 (占領する) capture; (負かす) defeat. ●エースピッチャーを攻略する pound [tag, touch, get to] an ace pitcher.
こうりゃく 後略 名 omission of the rest. ●引用文後略 *omission of the rest* [*latter part*] of the quotation.

── 後略する 動 omit the rest.
こうりゅう 交流 ❶ [交換] (an) exchange; (an) interchange. ●両国間の文化交流を促進する promote cultural *exchanges* between the two countries. ●私たちはパーティーを開いて関係者の交流を図った (= 友情を深める努力をした) We held a party and tried to promote friendship among the attendants. ▶国と国とのつき合いでは人間同士の交流が大事だ (= かぎとなる) People-to-people *exchanges* are the key to promoting good relations between countries.
❷ [電気の] alternating current《略 AC》.
●交流試合 (リーグ間の) [野球] an interleague play [game].

こうりゅう 拘留, 勾留 名 [法律] custody; [判決前の拘留] (主に政治犯の) 《やや書》detention. ●拘留中である be *in custody* [*detention*]. ●拘留を解かれる be discharged [released] from *custody*.
── 拘留 [勾留] する 動 ●殺人容疑で拘留する *take* (him) *into custody* for murder.

こうりゅう 興隆 名 (繁栄) prosperity; (台頭) a rise. ●コンピュータ産業の興隆 the *prosperity* of the computer industry. ●合衆国の興隆 the *rise* of the United States.
── 興隆する 動 prosper; rise.

ごうりゅう 合流 名 ●二つの川の合流点 the *meeting* [*junction*] of the two rivers.
── 合流する 動 ●仲間の一行に合流する (= いっしょになる) *join* the party. ▶小さな流れは山のふもとで大きな流れに合流する The little stream *joins* [*meets*; (流れ込む) *runs into*] a large one at the foot of the hill.

*こうりょ 考慮 名 [よく考えること] (a) consideration; [慎重に熟考すること] (a) deliberation. ●彼の気持ちを考慮に入れない leave his feelings *out of consideration* [*account*]; (無視する) disregard his feelings. ▶我々は現在彼の提案を考慮中だ We *are* now *considering* his suggestions./《事が主語》His suggestions are *under consideration* by us now. ▶彼は慎重な考慮の末、大学に進学することにした After careful *consideration*, he decided to go (on) to college. (❗onをつけると進学の感じが強く出る)
── 考慮する 動 [よく考える] consider, think*...over (口語的に); [考慮に入れる] take...into consideration [account]; [斟酌(しんしゃく)する] allow for.... ●その問題を十分 (= 注意深く) 考慮する *consider* the matter carefully; *give* the matter *careful consideration*; *think* the matter *over*. ●彼の若さを考慮する *consider* his youth [(the fact) that he is young]; *take* his youth *into consideration*; *allow* [*make allowance*(s)] *for* his youth. ▶すべての点を考慮すると、その計画の実現は相当難しい All things *considered*, the plan is rather difficult to realize. ▶費用に関しては、そのことを考慮せざるをえない As for the cost, that will have to *be considered*.

こうりょう 荒涼 ── 荒涼とした 形 bleak /blíːk/; (荒れた) désolate. ●荒涼とした原野 a *bleak and desolate* land; a wilderness.

こうりょう 香料 [香辛料] (a) spice; [香水] (a) perfume; [香典] (⇨香典).

こうりょう 校了 final proofreading. (《参考》校正の符号はO.K.) ●校了にする finish proofreading; OK the proofs.
●校了紙 a press proof.

こうりょう 稿料 (原稿料) a fee for a manuscript [an article]; pay for a piece of writing.

こうりょう 綱領 [基本方針] fundamental principles; (政党などの) plátfòrm. ●...を綱領にかかげて on a *platform of* ....

こうりょく 効力 (薬・法律などの) (an) effect; (法律などの拘束力) force; (法律などの有効性) validity. ●効力を発する (薬・法律などが) take *effect*; (法律などが) come into *effect* [*force*]. ●効力を失う lose *effect* [*force*]. ▶この契約はいまだ効力がある This contract remains *in effect* [*force*]. ▶この条約の効力は1年である This treaty *is valid* [*holds good*] for a year.

こうりん 光輪 (後光) a halo /héilou/; an aureola /ɔːríːələ/; (神の) a glory; (聖人等の) a gloria.

こうりん 光臨 ▶会議へのご光臨を仰ぎたく存じます We request the honor of *your presence* at the meeting.

こうりん 後輪 a rear [a back] wheel.
●後輪駆動車 a car with rear-wheel drive.

こうりん 降臨 (キリストの) Advent; (神仏などが天下ること) descent. ●天孫降臨 the *descent* of the Sun-Goddess's grandson to earth.

こうるい 紅涙 [美人[女性]の涙] a fair's [a woman's] tears.
●紅涙をしぼる ▶その映画は多くの女性の紅涙をしぼった (= 女性を泣かせた) The movie *made* many women *weep* [*moved* many women *to tears*].

こうるさい 小うるさい be fussy [particular] 《about》. ▶彼女は着るものについてはなかなか小うるさい She *is* very *fussy* [*particular*] *about* her clothes.

こうれい 好例 (⇨ 適例)

こうれい 交霊 spiritualism; communication with [sending messages to] the dead [deceased].
●交霊会 a séance. ●交霊現象 a spiritual phenomenon. ●交霊術 spiritualism.

こうれい 恒例 (確立した) an established custom; (年1回の) an annual event.
── 恒例の 形 (習慣的な) customary; (毎年の) annual; (伝統的な) traditional. ●恒例の夏のバーゲン an *annual* [a *traditional*] summer sale. ●恒例により according to (the *established*) *custom*; as usual.

こうれい 高齢 an advanced age. ●90歳の高齢で亡くなる die at the *age* of ninety. ▶日本はいま人口の高齢化が急速に進んでいる Japan is now facing a rapidly *aging* society./Japan is now experiencing a rapid increase of the *aged population*.
●高齢化社会 an aging society. ●高齢者 old people; (集合的) (やや書) the aged (❗婉曲的には the elderly, older [elderly] people, senior citizens などともいう. いずれも複数扱い); (個人) an aged person, a person of advanced age [years]; (⇨ 老人). ●高齢者介護 nursing care for elderly people; elderly care ●高齢出産 late childbearing.

ごうれい 号令 [権威者からの命令] a command; [指令] an order. ●「気をつけ」と先生は号令をかけた "Attention!" the teacher gave [shouted] an *order*.

こうれいち 高冷地 a highland with a low temperature.

こうれつ 後列 the back row.

こうろ 行路 (通り道) a path, a road; (進路) a course; (経歴) a career.
●行路病者 (行き倒れ) a person lying (dead) by the roadside.

こうろ 香炉 an incense burner; (つり香炉) a

こうろ censer.

こうろ 航路 〖船・飛行機の規定航路〗a route, a lane; 〖船の定期航路〗a line; 〖針路〗a course. ●欧州航路船 a steamer on the European *line*; an European *liner*. ▶これがアメリカまでの最短航路です This is the shortest *route* to America. ▶飛行機は正しい航路を[を外れて]飛んだ The plane flew *on* [*off*] *course*.

こうろ 高炉 〖溶鉱炉〗a blast furnace.

こうろう 功労 〖書〗service(s).
● 功労者 a person who has contributed greatly (*to*) [has rendered meritorious *services* (*to*)].

こうろうしょう 厚労省 〖「厚生労働大臣」の略〗(⇨厚生)

こうろく 高禄 ●高禄を食(は)む draw [earn, receive] a *high salary*.

こうろん 口論 图 a quarrel, 〖話〗a row /ráu/; an argument. ▶昨夜父親とお金のことで口論になった I got into a *quarrel* [an *argument*] *with* my father *about* money last night./I quarreled [argued] *with* my father *about* money last night.
── 口論する 動 quarrel [have a quarrel; argue, have an argument; 〖婉曲的〗have words] 〈*with*＋人, *about* [*over*]＋事〉.

こうろんおつばく 甲論乙駁 图 〖賛否の意見〗the pros and cons.
── 甲論乙駁する 動 ▶彼らは新しい家具を買うことで甲論乙駁した They *argued* [*talked over*] *the pros and cons* of buying new furniture./They *discussed for and against* the buying of the new furniture.

こうわ 口話 silent mouthing. (⇨ 手話)

こうわ 講和 peace. ●単独講和条約を結ぶ conclude a separate *peace* treaty.
── 講和する 動 make peace 〈*with*〉.

こうわ 講話 图 a lecture 〈*on*, *about*〉; a talk 〈*on*, *about*〉; 〖書〗a discourse 〈*on*, *upon*〉.
── 講話する 動 lecture 〈*on*, *about*〉; give a talk 〈*on*, *about*〉; give [〖書〗deliver] a discourse 〈*on*, *upon*〉.

こうわん 港湾 a harbor; a port.
●港湾施設 port facilities. ●港湾都市 a port city. ●港湾労働者 a dockworker; 〖主に米〗a longshore worker.

ごうわん 豪腕 a strong [an iron] arm.
●豪腕投手〖野球〗a hard-throwing pitcher; an iron man.

こえ 声

━━━ WORD CHOICE ━━━ 声 ━━━

voice 人の声・声質を表す最も一般的な語. 比喩的に, 物事の立てる音や, 天の声・良心の声などをさす場合もある. ▶彼の声はやがて消えていった His *voice* soon faded.
cry 人の泣き声・叫び声, 鳥の鳴き声のこと. ●苦痛のうめき[助けを求める叫び]声 *cries* of pain [for help].

━━━ 頻度チャート ━━━

voice ▆▆▆▆▆▆▆▆▆▆▆▆▆▆▆▆▆▆

cry ▆▆

　　　20　　40　　60　　80　　100 (%)

❶ 〖人間の〗(a) voice.
①【〜声】 ●小さい[大きな]声 (⇨❺) ●明るい声 a lively [happy, jovial] *voice*. ●美しい[太い; 細い; はっきりした; 甲高い; 穏やかな]声 a beautiful [deep; a thin; a clear; a high-pitched; a soft] *voice*. ●しわがれた声 a hoarse [a husky] *voice*. ●沈んだ声 a subdued [a depressed, a gloomy, a sad] voice. (❗subdue は悲しい, 不幸せなために静かで, 押さえるような声. depressed は失望などのために落ち込んだ様子の声. gloomy は不幸せなために暗い感じを与えるような声. sad は悲しさでよわまれい声) ●ささやき声 a whisper; a whispering *voice*.
②【声の〜】 ▶今日は声の調子がよい[悪い] I am in (good) [in poor] *voice* today. (❗無冠詞に注意)
③【声が】 ●声がよい have a good [a sweet; 〖計量豊かな〗a rich] *voice*. ●風邪で声が出ない lose one's *voice* because of a cold. ●声が出るようになる get one's *voice* back. ●隣の部屋から彼らの声が聞えた I heard their *voices* in [✕from] the next room./I heard them talking in the next room. ▶「こんにちは」という声がした "Hello," said a *voice*. ▶彼は感動のあまり声がつまった His *voice* broke with emotion. ▶その先生は声がよく通る The teacher's *voice* carries (very) well. ▶それを求める声が高まっている The demand for it has increased. ▶彼はぎょっとしてしばらく声が出なかった(＝しゃべれなかった) He was so frightened that he could not speak [he had no *voice*] for a moment. ▶私は大声で叫んで声がかれてしまった I became [〖話〗got] hoarse from shouting./I shouted myself hoarse. ▶反対の声が相次いだ There followed (a succession of) objections. ▶声が遠いんだけど (電話で) I can't hear you.
④【声を】 ●声をそろえて in chorus [unison]. ●声を合わせる say in chorus [unison]. ●声を荒げて(＝怒った声で) in an angry *voice* [*tone*]. ●声を限りに叫ぶ shout at the top of one's *voice* [*lungs*]. ●声を高くする[ひそめる] raise [drop, lower] one's *voice*. (❗raise one's *voice* 〈*to* [*at*] him〉は「(怒って)声を張り上げる」の意味もある) ●声を立てる make a sound; cry. ●声を立てずに泣く cry silently. ●しっ, 声を立てないで Hush! Quiet! ▶学生諸君は自分の習っている英語の文章を声を出して読むのがよい It's good for the students to *read* the English sentences they learn *aloud* [✕loudly].
⑤【声で】 ●小さな[大きな]声で話す talk in [✕with] a low [a loud, a big] *voice*; talk softly [loudly]. ●蚊の泣くような声で答える answer in a feeble voice. ▶もう少し大きな声で言ってください Speak louder, please. (❗Speak more loudly. より普通)/Speak up, please. ▶彼女はできるだけ大きな声で叫んだ She shouted as *loud* as she could.
❷ 〖鳥獣の〗a cry, a call; (小鳥・虫のちいちいと短い) a chirp; (鳥のさえずり) a song, a twitter (❗chirp をくり返す声). ●カモメの鳴く[オオカミのほえる]声 the *cry* of a gull [a wolf]. ●小鳥の鳴き声で目が覚めた I woke to the *call* [*chirp*, *song*, *twitter*] of birds.
❸ 〖意見〗(やや書) a voice; 〖ときの声〗a cry. ●神[良心]の声 the *voice* of God [conscience]. ●国民の声を無視する ignore the *voice* [*opinion*] of the people. ▶税制改革を求める[に反対する]声が高まっている A *cry for* [*against*] tax reform is becoming clamorous./An increasing number of people are for [against] tax reform.
❹ 〖気配〗●春の声を聞く when spring is just around the corner.
●声がかかる be shouted [yelled] at; be asked to do (*it*).
●声無き声 the collective voice of the weak

こえ 肥 (⇨肥料)
- 肥溜め a cesspool.

ごえい 護衛 [名] [警備] (a) guard /gáːrd/; [儀礼上の護衛] (a) protection, (an) escort. ● 大統領の護衛(たち) the President's *guard* [*escort*]. ● 警察に護衛されて *under* police *escort*; *under the escort* [*protection*] *of* the police.
—— **護衛する** 動 ● 王を護衛する *guard* [*protect*, *escort*] the king.
- 護衛艦 an escort ship; 〔集合的〕a convoy (!単・複両扱い). ● 護衛兵 a guard; a (military) escort.

ごえいか 御詠歌 a pilgrim's hymn.

こえがわり 声変わり the change [breaking, cracking] of (one's) voice. ▶彼は声変わりし始めた His *voice* has begun to *change* [*break*, *crack*].

こえだ 小枝 a twig. (⇨枝)

ごえつどうしゅう 呉越同舟 ▶対立する2人が呉越同舟で同じ委員会に入っている Two people hostile to each other *are ironically* on [×in] the same committee.

ごえもんぶろ 五右衛門風呂 a *goemon* bathtub; (説明的に) an iron bathtub heated from beneath with a floating [replaceable] wooden lid.

:こえる 越える, 超える ❶[向こう側へ行く] [越えて行く] go* over …, [限界を越えて] go beyond …; [横切る] cross, go across …. ● 野を越え丘を越えて歩いて行く *walk across* the fields and *over* the hills. ● 国境を越える *cross* the border. ▶ファウルボールはバックネットを越えた〔野球〕The foul ball *went over* the backstop. ▶彼は海を越えてアメリカへ行った He *went across* [*over*] the ocean to America. (!*across* は横切る, *over* は渡って行く感じ). ● 私の故郷は川を越えたところにある My hometown lies *across* [*over*] the river./(越えた向こう側に) My hometown lies *beyond* the river./(反対側に) My hometown lies *at the opposite side of* the river. ● 川の代わりに山なら My hometown lies *over* (うしろに) *beyond*, *at the opposite side of*] the mountain. などという）

❷[上回る] [数量などが超える] be over …; (…より上である) be above …; (…より多い) be more than …; [限度・権限などを超える] exceed. ● 40歳を超えている *be over* [*more than*, *above*] forty. (!*more than* が最も口語的). ● 重量制限を越える *exceed* the weight limit. ● 自己の権限を超えた行いをする *exceed* [*go beyond*] one's authority.

❸[超越する] (…よりまさる) be better than …, [書] surpass, 〔書〕excel (-ll-); (理解などを超えている) be above …, be beyond …. ▶彼は英語の学力で彼女を超えている He *is better at* English *than* she is [〔話〕*than* her]./He *surpasses* [*excels*] her in English. ● その問題は私の理解を超えている The problem *is beyond* [*above*] me. ● 前の方が普通

こえる 肥える ❶[人などが] grow [get*] fat (-tt-); [体重が増える] put* on [gain] weight. ▶彼は肥え気味だ He *is getting* a little too *fat*.
❷[土地が] grow* fertile [rich]. ● 肥えた土地 *fertile* land. ▶この土地は大変肥えている This land is very *fertile*.
❸[目・口などが] ● 目[舌; 耳]の肥えている have a

good eye [palate; ear] 《*for*》. ● 目[舌; 耳]の肥えている人々 *discerning* [*appreciative*] people; people *with discernment*. (!people を palate, ear, drinker, audience などに適宜変えて用いることもできる)

ごー (⇨ごうごう) ▶エンジンがごーっと音を立てて始動した The engine *roared* into life.

こおう 呼応 [名] [文法] cóncord, agreement.
—— **呼応する** 動 agree 《*with*》. ● 互いに呼応して(＝協力して)行動する act *in cooperation with* each other.

ゴーカート a gó-kàrt, a go-cart. (!〔商標〕a Go Kart より)

コーカサス ● コーカサス山脈 the Caucasus (Mountains).

ゴーギャン 〔フランスの画家〕Gauguin /gougǽŋ/ (Paul ~).

コーキング [名] [充填(じゅうてん)材を詰めること] caulking.
—— **コーキングする** 動 caulk.

コーク (商標) Coca-Cola, Coke. (! coke は「コカイン」の意にもなるので注意 (⇨コーラ))

コークス coke.

ゴーグル [オートバイ・スキー・潜水用の保護眼鏡] (a pair of) (motorcycle, ski, diving) goggles.

ゴーゴー gó-gó (dàncing). ● ゴーゴーを踊る dance the *go-go*; enjoy *go-go dancing*.

ゴーサイン ゴーサイン[許可]を出す give the *green light* [*go-ahead*] 《*on* [*to*] the project, *for* [*to* build] the bridge》; 〔米〕green-light 《the project》. ● go sign は和製英語

コージェネレーション (⇨コジェネレーション)

ゴージャス —— **ゴージャスな** 形 ● ゴージャスなドレス a *gorgeous* dress.

:コース ❶[通る道] a route; (山中の) a trail. ● ハイキングコース a híking ròute [tràil, còurse]. ● パレードのコース a paráde ròute. ● コースを外れて飛ぶ (飛行機が) fly *off course*. ▶このコースが観光にはいちばんいい This *route* is the best for sightseeing. ▶彼はヨットがコースからそれないように懸命に操った He worked hard to *keep* his yacht *on course*.

❷[競技の] (ゴルフなどの) a course; (競走・競泳の) a lane. ● 第1コースを走る have [run on] *Lane* No. 1. ● インコース[アウトコース]の球 an inside [an outside] pitch. ● インコース[アウトコース]へ速球を投げる throw a fastball on the inside [outside] (corner). ● マスターズのコースレコード the Masters *course* record. ● コースアウトする go off the *course*.

❸[課程] a course. ● 英語の集中コースをとる take an intensive *course* in English. ● ドクターコースに進む take [enroll in] a Ph.D. [a doctoral, a doctor's] *program* [*course*] 《*in*》.

❹[ディナーの料理の1皿] a course. ● コース料理 〔米〕a special, 〔英〕a set dinner [lunch]. (⇨フルコース)

コースター [コップなどの下に敷く物] a coaster.

ゴースト [幽霊] a ghost.
- ゴーストタウン a ghost town. (!参考 鉱山などの廃止で住む人がいなくなった町) ● ゴーストライター [代作者] a ghost writer.

コーチ [名] coaching; (人) a coach. (!日本語の「コーチ」は an assistant coach [manager] にあたることが多い) ● バスケットボール[テニス]のコーチ a basketball [a tennis] *coach*. ● ピッチングコーチ a pitching *coach*. ● バッティングコーチ a batting [a hitting] *coach*. ● 一塁[三塁]コーチ a first [a third] base *coach*.
—— **コーチ(を)する** 動 coach 《him, a team, him *in*

コーチゾン

tennis). ● 三塁コーチをする *coach* (at) third. ▶うちの兄さんは野球のコーチをしている My brother *coaches* a baseball team.
● コーチボックス 〖野球〗 a coach's box.

コーチゾン 〖薬学〗 cortisone. 〖参考〗 関節炎・リューマチ治療剤〗

コーチャー ● コーチャーズボックス a coach's [a coacher's] box. ● 前の方が普通

コーディネーター a coórdinàtor. ● インテリアコーディネーター an interior *coordinator*.

コーディネート 图 coordinate.
── **コーディネートする** 動 ● 居間の壁紙とカーテンの色調をコーディネートする *coordinate* the colors of wallpaper and curtains in the living room.

コーティング (a) coating. ▶このガラスにはコーティングが施されている This glass has a *coating*.

コーデュロイ corduroy. (⇨コールテン)

*コート 〖衣服〗 a coat. (❗通例上着をいうが、オーバー (overcoat)、レーンコート (raincoat) なども含む) ● コートをお預りいたしましょう Let me take your *coat*.

コート 〖球技の〗 a 《tennis, basketball》 court. ● クレー〖グラス; ハード〗コート a clay [a grass; a hard] *court*. ● センターコート a center *court*. ● コートをかわる change *courts*. ● 選手は (試合をするために)もうコートに出ている The players are already *on court*.

コード ❶〖和音〗 a chord.
❷〖電気の〗 an (electric) cord, 《英》a flex; (延長用の) an extension cord. ● 長いコードのついた電気スタンド a desk lamp with a long *cord*.
❸〖暗号〗 a code. ● 文字コード 〖コンピュータ〗 a character code.
● コードネーム a code name. ● コードブック a code book. ● コードレス cordless. ● コードレスヘッドフォン a pair of cordless headphones.

こおとこ 小男 a little [a small] man (圈 men); a man of small stature.

コートジボワール 〖国名〗Côte d'Ivoire /kòut davwá:/; (公式名) the Republic of Côte d'Ivoire. (首都 Yamoussoukro) ● コートジボワール人 a Ivorian. ● コートジボワール(人)の Ivorian.

こおどり 小踊り ── **小躍りする** 動 ▶私は小躍りして喜んだ I jumped [leaped, danced] for joy.

コードレス (コードのついていない家電製品) cordless electrical appliances.
● コードレスアイロン a cordless iron. ● コードレスホン a cordless phone.

コーナー ❶〖隅、角〗 a corner; 〖競走路の〗 a turn.
● インコーナー 〖野球〗 the inside (*corner*). ● (ストライクゾーンの)コーナーへ投げる make a pitch on the *corner*; hit a *corner*. ● 最終[第 4]コーナーを曲がる round the stretch [fourth] *turn*. ● コーナーに追い詰める back (him) into a *corner*. ● コーナーワークがよく work the *corners*; hit the *corners*.
❷〖特に設けた区分〗 a section. ● 子供服コーナーで in the children's wear *department* [*section*]; (売り台)at the *counter* for children's wear. ● 喫煙コーナー a smóking àrea [zòne].
❸〖「コーナーキック」の略〗● ショートコーナー〖サッカー〗a short corner (kick).
● コーナーキック 〖サッカー〗 a corner kick. ● コーナーフラッグ 〖サッカー〗 a corner flag.

コーナリング cornering.

コーパス 〖言語資料〗a corpus (圈 corpora). (〖参考〗 個別言語・作家のテキストや発話を大規模または網羅的に集めたもの) ● 話し言葉のコーパス a *corpus* of spoken language.

*コーヒー coffee. (❗注文するときなどの)1杯のコーヒー (a cup of coffee)の意では © (⇨③ 〖第 1 文例〗)

①〖~コーヒー、コーヒーの〗● アイスコーヒー iced [ice] *coffee*. ● インスタントコーヒー instant *coffee*. ● 缶コーヒー (a) canned coffee; a can of coffee (❗数える、または容器に重点を置く場合の). ● アメリカンコーヒー 1 杯 a cup of weak *coffee*. (⇨アメリカンコーヒー) ● コーヒー代を払う pay one's *coffee*; pay the coffee bill. ● コーヒー色 〖コーヒー色の〗 *coffee*'s color; (コーヒー色の) coffee-colored.
②〖コーヒーを[の]〗▶コーヒーはいかがですか Would you like [care for] some *coffee*? ▶私はコーヒーは濃いのが好きだ I like my *coffee* strong (↔weak).
〖会話〗「コーヒーのお好みは?」「ブラックお願いします」"How do you like your *coffee*?" "Black, please."
③〖コーヒーに[を]〗● コーヒーを飲む have [drink] *coffee*. ● コーヒーをいれる[出す] have [serve] *coffee*. ▶ブラックコーヒーを二つお願いします Two black *coffees*, please. (❗(1) 日常会話、特に店で注文するときは Two cups of black *coffee*, please. より普通. (2) ミルク入りコーヒーであれば Two coffees *with milk* [*cream*], please. のようにいう。また《主に英》では Two *white* coffees, please. のようにもいう. (3)「ミルクたっぷりのコーヒー」は milky coffee, coffee *with much milk*) ▶私たちはコーヒーを飲みながら 2 時間ほど話をした We talked about two hours over (a cup of) *coffee*. (❗このような場合 ✕ ... over cups of coffee. のようにはいわない)
〖会話〗「コーヒーに砂糖とクリームを入れますか」「クリームだけで結構です」"Do you take sugar and cream in your *coffee*?" "Just cream would be fine."
● コーヒーカップ a cóffee cùp. ● コーヒー牛乳 coffee-flavored milk. (❗✕coffee milk は不可) ● コーヒーシロップ coffee (flavored) syrup. ● コーヒーゼリー 〖商品名〗 coffee(-flavored) jell-O. ● コーヒー専門店 a coffee specialty store. ● コーヒーバッグ a cóffee bàg. 〖関連〗ティーバッグ a tea bag) ● コーヒーブレーク (have [take]) a cóffee brèak. ● コーヒーポット a cóffee pòt. ● コーヒーミル a coffee mill [grinder /gráindər/]. ● コーヒー豆 coffee beans.
● コーヒーメーカー a percolator, a coffee-maker.

コープ 〖生協〗 a co-op /kóuàp/.

ゴーフル(お菓子) waffle.

コーポレート 〖法人〗〖会社〗の] corporate /kɔ́:rpərət/.
● コーポレートアイデンティティー 〖企業イメージ統合戦略〗 (a) corporate identity (略 CI). ● コーポレートイメージ 〖ある企業に対して抱くイメージ〗 a corporate image. ● コーポレートガバナンス 〖企業統治〗 corporate governance. ● コーポレートカラー 〖企業イメージを象徴する色〗 a corporate color.

コーラ cola (❗1 本[1 杯]のコーラは a 〜);《商標》Coca-Cola (❗ Coke, coke ともいう);《商標》Pepsi-Cola (❗ Pepsi, pepsi ともいう).
〖会話〗「お飲み物はいかがですか」「コーラをお願いします」"(Would you like) something to drink?" "I'll have a *Coke* [a *Pepsi*]." (❗注文の際には a Cola では聞き違えることが多いので避ける)

コーラス a chorus. (⇨合唱)
● コーラスガール a chorus girl. ● コーラスグループ a choral group; a chorus.

こおらせる 凍らせる freeze*. ● アイスクリームを凍らせる *freeze* ice cream.

コーラン 〖イスラムの経典〗 the Koran /kərá:n/.

*こおり 氷 ice. (❗「1 片の氷」は a piece of ice)
①〖~氷、氷~〗● かき氷 (普通的に) shaved *ice* with syrup. ● 角氷 (製氷器で作った) an *ice* cube. ● 氷詰めにする pack (it) in *ice*.
②〖氷が〗▶池に氷が張った *Ice* has formed on [(一面に) over] the pond./The pond froze

over. ▶湖の氷が溶け[割れ]始めた The *ice* on [×in] the lake began to melt [break up].
❸《氷の》 ●氷の上 on *ice*. ●氷の張った湖 an *iced* lake; a lake covered *with* [*in*《thick》] *ice*. ●氷のように冷かい風 *icy* winds. ▶彼女の手は氷のように冷たかった Her hands were very cold [*as cold as ice*]．Her hands were *like ice*.
❹《氷に[で]》 ●氷に閉ざされた港 an *icebound* harbor. ●氷に覆われる be covered with ice. ●ワインを氷で冷やしておく keep wine *on ice* [*cooled with ice*].
●氷小豆(ホサミ) shaved ice with boiled adzuki beans. ●氷菓子 an ice. ●氷砂糖 (a piece of) rock《米》[sugar《英》] candy. ●氷豆腐 freeze-dried *tofu*. ●氷ばさみ (a pair of) ice tòngs. ●氷枕 an icy pillow;《氷のう》an ice bag, a cold pack,《英》an ice pàck. ●氷水 iced [ice] water.（❗*icy* water は「氷のように冷たい水」の意）●氷屋 a shop [stall] selling shaved ice with syrup (on it);《製氷業者》an ice dealer.

こおりつく 凍り付く be frozen together;《堅く凍りつく》be frozen hard. ●凍りついた田舎道 a *frozen* [an *icy*] country road. ●凍りつくような寒い朝 a *freezing* [an *icy*] (cold) morning. ▶夜の寒さでワイパーがフロントガラスに凍りついた The wiper *was frozen to* the windshield because of the cold during the night.

***こおる 凍る** freeze*;［凍っている］be frozen. ▶水は摂氏 0 度で凍る Water *freezes* at 0℃.（❗0℃は zero degrees centigrade と読む）▶湖は一面に[すっかり]凍ってしまった The lake *has frozen over* [*up*]. ▶寒さで道がかちかちになった The cold *has frozen* the road hard. ●洗濯物が洗濯ひもに凍りついた The washing *froze* [*was frozen*] *to* the clothesline. ▶外は凍るほど寒かった It *was freezing* cold outside.（❗*freezing* は形容詞の副詞的用法. It *was freezing* outside ともいう）▶恐い映画を見て彼は血が凍る思いをした The horror movie made his blood *freeze* [*froze* his blood, *turned* his blood *to ice*].

コール ❶［通話］a call. ●コレクトコール (料金受信人払い)《米》a collect (phone) *call*.（❗「コレクトコールをかける」は call《him》collect）
❷［短期資金貸借］【金融】call.
❸［判定］a call. ●難しい[遅い]コール a hard [a delayed] call. ●ストライクとコールする call (a pitch) a strike.
●コールガール［電話で呼び出される売春婦］a call girl. ●コールサイン［放送局などの呼び出し符号］a call sign.（参考）NHK の JOAK など）●コール市場 a (money) market. ●コールマネー【金融】call money; money at [on] call. ●コールレート【金融】call rate.

ゴール 图 ［競技の決勝線[点], 球技での得点］a goal.
●（球技で）ゴールを決める get [kick, score, bag] a *goal*. ●サッカーでは kick in home ともいう）●ゴールの枠をとらえる shoot on target. ●ゴールを守る keep goal《for》. ●ゴールインする(レースで) cross [reach] the *goal* (line); cross the finishing line;（テープを胸で切る）breast [break] the tape;（結婚する）get married.（❗goal-in は和製英語）

── **ゴールする** 動 goal, tally.
●ゴールエリア the goal area. ●ゴールキーパー（サッカーなど）a goalkeeper,《米》a goaltender,《話》a keeper, a goalie. ●ゴールキーパーをする be a goal-keeper, play in goal. ●ゴールキック a goal kick. ●ゴールネット a goal net. ●ゴールポスト a goal post. ●ゴールマウス a goal mouth. ●ゴールライン a goal

line.
コールスロー coleslaw.
コールタール coal tar.
コールテン corduroy［kɔ́ːrdərɔi］,《話》cord. ●コールテンのズボン (a pair of) *corduroy* [《口》*cord*] pants; corduroys;《話》cords.
ゴールデンアワー prime (TV) time; peak viewing time;《和製語》golden hour.
ゴールデンウィーク 'Golden Week' holidays（❗golden week, GW などは和製英語なので引用符をつける);（説明的には）a succession [a series] of national holidays from April 29th to May 5th.（事情）Easter holidays [vacation] がこれに当たる）（⇒連休）
ゴールデンタイム（⇒⓵ ゴールデンアワー）
ゴールデンレトリーバー ［動物］(犬) a golden retriever.
ゴールド ［金］gold.
●ゴールドラッシュ a gold rush.
コールドクリーム cóld crèam.
コールドゲーム【野球】a called game. ▶激しい降雨のため試合はコールドゲームとなった The game *was called* because of (the) heavy rain.（❗スポーツ界では its を省略する習慣が普通）
ゴールドコースト ［オーストラリアの都市］the Góld Còast.
コールドパーマ a cold (permanent) wave.（❗a cold wave は「寒波」の意にもなる）
コールドビーフ cold beef.
『**ゴールドラッシュ**』 *Gold Rush*.（参考）柳美里の小説）
こおろぎ 蟋蟀 ［昆虫］a cricket. ▶コオロギが鳴いていた The *crickets* were chirping.（事情）米英人には陽気にひびく）
コーン ［トウモロコシ］(an ear of) corn (❗corn は集合名詞);《英》maize;［アイスクリームの］a cone.
●コーンスターチ《米》cornstarch,《英》cornflour. ●コーンフレーク(ス) cornflakes. ●コーンミール cornmeal; maize flour.
コーンビーフ（⇒コンビーフ）
コカ ［植物］a coca shrub;（葉）coca.

こが 古雅 图 classical grace.
── **古雅な** 形 antique and elegant.
こがい 子飼い bringing up [rearing,《主に米》raising] from infancy. ●子飼いの弟子 a disciple one has trained from an early age.
こがい 戸外 the outdoors《単数扱い》; the open air. ●戸外運動 *óutdoor* exercise. ●戸外に出る go *outdoors*. ▶夏は戸外で遊ぶことが多い We often play *outdoors* [*out of doors*, *in the open air*] in summer.

***ごかい 誤解** 图 ［誤った理解］(a) misunderstanding 《*of*, *about*》（❗具体的には ⓒ);［誤った解釈］(a) misinterpretation. ●誤解を招く説明をする give《him》a *misleading* explanation《*of*》. ▶私たちの間には何か誤解があるようです There seems to be some *misunderstanding* between us. ▶彼に対する妻の誤解は解けなかった His wife's *misunderstanding about* [*of*] him did not go away [was not removed]. ▶そういう言い方は誤解を招きそうだ Putting it that way may cause a *misunderstanding* [*be misleading*].

DISCOURSE
しかし実際は, このような主張は誤解を生む危険がある (But) **in fact**, this kind of argument may be *misleading*.（❗in fact（実際は）は主張を表すディスコースマーカー）

── **誤解する** 動 misunderstand*,《話》get*...

ごかい wrong, 《書》 misapprehend; [誤って解釈する] misinterpret. ▶私の言っていることを誤解してくださ い Don't *misunderstand* me [what I say]./ Don't *take* what I say *the wrong way*./《話》 Don't *get me wrong*.

ごかい 沙蚕 《動物》 a lugworm.

こがいしゃ 子会社 a subsidiary (company) (↔a parent company). ● 完全 [100 パーセント] 子会社 a wholly [a 100 percent] owned *subsidiary*. ● 連結子会社 a consolidated *subsidiary*.

ごかいしょ 碁会所 a go parlor [club]; a go players' club.

コカイン cocain(e) /koukéin/; 《俗》 coke.

ごかく 互角 图 [同等] equality; (対等) evenness.
—— 互角の 形 equal; (対等の) even; (好取り組みの) well-matched, evenly-matched. ● 互角の試合 an *even* [an *equal*, a *well-matched*] game; (接戦) a *close* game. ● 互角に戦う fight *evenly* [*equally*]. ▶太郎は英語の学力では花子と互角だ Taro *is equal to* Hanako in his knowledge of English./Taro and Hanako *are well* [*equally*] *matched* in their knowledge of English. ▶スキーで直樹と互角の勝負をするのは無理だ I *am no match for* Naoki in skiing./I *can't match* Naoki in skiing.

ごがく 語学 (外国語) a foreign language. ▶彼は語学の才能がある He has a talent for *languages*./ He has a *linguistic* talent. ▶彼は語学が強い [弱い] He is strong [weak] in *languages*./He is a good [bad] *linguist*. ▶彼は学生時代には語学がよくできた He did very well in *languages* at school.
● 語学教育 language education. ● 語学教師 a language teacher. ● 語学者 a linguist. ● 語学力 a knowledge of (foreign) languages; linguistic knowledge.

ごかくけい 五角形 a pentagon /péntəgàn/. ● 正五角形 a regular *pentagon*. ● 五角形の建物 a *pentágonal* building.

こかげ 木陰 the shade of a tree. ● 木陰で本を読む read a book in [under] *the shade of a tree*.

コカコーラ 《商標》 Coca-Cola, Coke. (⇨コーラ)

こがす 焦がす burn*; scorch. (⇨焦げる) ● 思いに胸を焦がす *burn* with love (*for*). (⇨焦がれる) ● 肉を焦がさないように気をつけなさい Be careful not to *burn* (the) meat.

こがた 小型 —— 小型の 形 small(-sized); (携帯用の) portable, (ポケット型の) pocket(-sized); (こぢんまりした) compact. ▶デジタルカメラは小型化してきている Digital Cameras are getting *smaller* in size.
● 小型カメラ a pocket [a compact] camera. ● 小型(自動)車 a small car; 《米》 a compact (car) (❗日本車の小型車に相当する a subcompact (car) より一回り大きい).

こがたな 小刀 a (small) knife (復 knives); (折りたたみ式の) a pocketknife, a penknife. (❗ナイフ1枚の単純なもの)

こかつ 枯渇 —— 枯渇する 動 (川などが) go dry (⇨涸(か)る); (資源などが) run out. (⇨尽きる)

*****ごがつ** 五月 May. (⇨一月)
● 五月人形 dolls for the Boy's Festival. ● 五月晴れ (⇨五月(さつき)) ● 五月病 (新入生 [新入社員] の憂うつ神[心気]症) freshman hypochondria /hàipəkάndriə/.

こがね 小金 (わずかなお金) a small sum of money; (かなりまとまったお金) a sizable [《話》 a tidy] sum of money. ▶彼はまさかのときに備えて小金をためこんでいるようだ It seems that he is saving *a sizable sum of money* for a rainy day.

こがね 黄金 (金) gold. ● 黄金色の golden.

こがねむし 黄金虫 《昆虫》 a gold beetle; a goldbug.

こがも 小鴨 《鴨の幼鳥》 a (wild) duckling; [ガンカモ科の水鳥] a teal.

こがら 小柄 —— 小柄な 形 [背が低い] short; [体つきが小さい] small; 《a man》 of small build (structure).

こがら 小雀 《鳥》 a willow tit.

こがらし 木枯らし a cold [(刺すように寒い) a biting] winter wind.

こがれる 焦がれる [切望する] long [《主に書》 yearn] (*for*); [待ち遠しがる] be impatient (*for*; *to* do). ▶彼は彼女の到着を待ち焦がれていた He *was longing* [*impatient*] *for* her arrival./He *was eagerly awaiting* her arrival. ▶彼女は外国に住むボーイフレンドに会いたいと思い焦がれている She *is impatient* [(…したくてたまらない) 《話》 *dying*] *to see* her boyfriend who lives abroad. ▶あの子は音楽の先生に思い焦がれている (= 思いを寄せている) He *has fallen in love with* [《書》 *has lost* his *heart to*] the music teacher.

こかん 股間 (股) a crotch, 《英》 a crutch. ● ボールは投手の股間を抜けた 《野球》 The ball went through [between] the pitcher's *legs*.

ごかん 五官 the five organs of sense; the five sensory organs.

ごかん 五感 the five senses.

ごかん 互換 [互換性] interchangeability; compatibility. ● 互換性がある [ない] be compatible [incompatible] (*with*). ▶テキスト形式上の互換性がないと入力のし直しが必要になる *Incompatibility* between [in] text formats requires rekeying./If text formats *are incompatible* (*with* each other), you have to input data all over again.

ごかん 語感 ● 英語の語感をつかむ get the *feel* for English. ▶彼は語感が鋭い He has a keen *sense of language*. ● [広く言語に対する感覚]

ごがん 護岸 ● 護岸工事 shoreline protection [(補強のための) reinforcement] works. (❗shoreline は寄せる波が作る線)

こかんせつ 股関節 《生理》 a hip joint.
● 股関節炎 《医学》 coxitis.

こき 古希 (数え年70) one's 70th (calendar) year. (⇨還暦)

こき 語気 a tone (of voice); (声) one's voice. ● 語気を荒げる raise one's *voice*. ● 語気を荒げて in a harsh [(怒った) an angry] *tone*. ● 語気を強めて(= 強調して) speak emphatically. ● 語気を和らげる soften one's *voice*.

ごき 誤記 a writing error, an error in writing; (事務上の) a clerical error; (書き損じ) a slip of the pen; (転記の際の誤り) a miscopy; (誤植) a misprint, a typographical error.

ごぎ 語義 the meaning [(定義) definition] of a word.

こきおろす こき下ろす criticize … (strongly), 《話》 run*… down. ▶彼は彼女を無作法だとひどくこきおろした He *criticized* her severely for being rude.

ごきげん 御機嫌 (⇨機嫌) ● ご機嫌伺いに行く go to say hello (*to*). ● ご機嫌いかがですか How are you?/(やや俗) How are you doing? ▶彼は ご機嫌斜めだ He is *in a bad mood*. (⇨不機嫌) ▶今日はご機嫌だね You really *look happy* today, don't you?
● ご機嫌取り (人) a person who flatters [《話》 butters up] someone.

ごきげんよう 御機嫌よう good(-)by, 《話》bye(-bye), so long; 《書》farewell.《⇨さようなら》 ▶(別れる人に) I wish you good luck./Good luck (to you)!(❗「幸運を祈る」の意から単に激励する場合にも用いる)(特に旅立つ人に) I wish you a pleasant journey./Have a nice trip!

こぎざみ 小刻み ── 小刻みに 副 ●小刻みに震える tremble slightly, 《やや書》quiver. ▶小刻みに増加する increase little by little. ▶小刻みに歩く walk with quick and short steps.

こぎたない 小汚い (かなり汚れた) rather dirty,《書》shabby, (行為などが卑劣な) mean, dirty,《話》nasty.《⇨小ぎたない》 ▶小汚い身なり sloppy [rather dirty] clothes. ▶小汚いやり方をするな Don't play mean [dirty, cheap] tricks.

こきつかう こき使う work [drive*] (him) very hard; (次々に指図する) push [order] (him) around. (⇨酷使)

こぎつける 漕ぎ着ける ●合意にこぎ着ける reach [come to] (an) agreement. ▶両国はようやく条約の調印にこぎ着けた The two countries finally managed to agree and sign the treaty.

こぎって 小切手 《米》a check,《英》a cheque.(❗事情)米英では個人も日常生活で気軽に小切手を用いる)▶旅行(者)用の小切手 a traveler's check (略 TC). ●個人用小切手 a personal check. ●不渡り小切手 a dishonored [a bounced,《米話》a rubber] check.(❗「小切手が不渡りになる」は The check is dishonored./The check bounces.) ▶(彼に) 100万円の小切手を切る write (him) a check for one million yen. ▶小切手を現金に換える cash a check. ▶小切手を振り出す issue [write (out), make out] a check (to him); draw a check on a bank. ▶小切手を改ざんする raise a check. ▶小切手で払う pay by check.(❗無冠詞) ▶小切手はどなたあてに切ればよろしいのですか Who do I write [make] out a check to?
●小切手受取人 a check drawee. ●小切手帳 a checkbook. ●小切手振出人 a check writer [drawer].

こぎて 漕ぎ手 an rower; (男の) an oarsman (複 -men),(女の) an oarswoman (複 -women).

ごきぶり 《昆虫》a cockroach,《米話》a roach.

こきみよい 小気味よい ●小気味よい(=気持ちのよい)態度 a pleasant manner. ●小気味よい(=小気味のきいた)答えをする give a smart [a clever] answer; answer smartly [cleverly].

こきゃく 顧客; (常連) a patron. (⇨客)
●顧客管理 customer management. ●顧客サービス customer service. ●顧客志向 customer orientation [focus].(❗参考) 顧客満足を最大限に満足させることを企業目標とする考え方) ●顧客満足 customer satisfaction《略 CS》. ●顧客名簿 a customer list.

コギャル (説明的に) a teenage girl dressed in loud clothing and wearing heavy make-up.

*こきゅう 呼吸 名 ❶【息】breath (❗1 回の呼吸は a breath. 以下の語についても同様);〖呼吸〗breathing; 〖書〗respiration.
①【〜呼吸, 呼吸〜】 ●腹式呼吸 abdominal breathing. ●呼吸困難になる have difficulty (in) breathing.
②【呼吸が】 ●呼吸ができる be able to breathe. ▶呼吸が苦しい I find it painful to breathe. ▶It's hard to breathe. ▶泳ぎ終えたとき彼は呼吸が荒かった He was breathing hard [heavily] when he finished swimming. ▶高度が高い所では呼吸が困難です We have difficulty (in) breathing [It's

difficult to breathe] at high altitudes.(❗《話》では in は通例省略する) ▶彼の呼吸が止まった His breathing stopped./He stopped breathing.
③【呼吸を[に]】 ●呼吸(数)を数える count one's breathing [respiratory] rate. ●呼吸を続ける keep (on) breathing. ●(走った後などに)通常の呼吸に戻る get one's breath back. ●鼻[えら]で呼吸をする breathe through one's nose [its gills]. ●呼吸を整える get one's breath back; (一息つく) catch one's breath. ●呼吸に合わせる adjust to the rhythm of (one's [the]) breathing [breathing rhythm].
❷【こつ】《話》 ●a [the] knack; (上手なやり方) a [the] trick. ●商売の呼吸を覚える learn the knack [tricks] of the trade. ▶彼は数学を教える呼吸を心得ている He has the [a] knack of teaching mathematics.
❸【調子】 ▶彼らは呼吸が合っていた(=仲よくやっていた) They were getting along well [《話》hitting it off] with each other./They were in perfect harmony.
── 呼吸する 動 breathe /brí:ð/.
●呼吸音 a respiratory [breath] sound. ●呼吸停止 a cessation of breathing.

こきゅう 胡弓《楽器》a Chinese violin.

きゅうき 呼吸器 a respiratory organ.
●呼吸器系 the respiratory system. ●呼吸器疾患 a respiratory disease.

‡**こきょう** 故郷 one's hometown [home town] (❗(1) 市町村を問わず用いることができる. (2) 県・島などには用いられない. one's home prefecture [island] という. (3) one's native village [town, place] はあまり用いないが, 固有の地名とともに用いて one's native Nara (故郷の奈良)のようにはいう); one's (old) home;〖出生地〗one's birthplace. ●第二の故郷 one's second home [hometown]. ●故郷に帰る go [go back, return] home.(❗(1) 文脈によって「家に帰る」の意にもなる. (2) この home は副詞) ●故郷を出る leave (one's) home [one's hometown]. ●故郷を恋しがる be [feel] homesick; pine [long] for home (❗通例進行形で). ▶あなたの故郷はどちらですか Where are you [do you come] from? ▶Where have [did] you come from?(❗は出身地に関係なく常に「どこから来たのか」の意)/What's your hometown?(❗×What is your native place? とはいわない)/Where's your home (town)? ▶私の故郷は長野県です Nagano is my home prefecture./My home(town) is in Nagano Prefecture.(❗×My hometown is Nagano Prefecture. とはいわない)/(出身は長野県だ) I'm [I come] from Nagano Prefecture.(❗come を ×came としないこと) ▶故郷に残してきた妻子に会えなくて寂しく思う I miss my family back home.(❗この home は形容詞) ▶私の故郷はペルーですが, 日本は第二の故郷です I'm Peruvian, but I've made Japan my (second) home.

こぎよう 小器用 ── 小器用な 形 a little handy (at, with); a little dexterous 《at》. ▶彼はものを直すのが小器用だ He is a little handy at fixing things.

ごきょう 五経 the Five (Chinese) Classics of Confucianism.

こぎれ 小切れ a small piece of cloth; a strip of cloth. ▶彼女は小切れで座布団カバーを作った She made a cushion cover out of some small pieces of cloth.

こぎれい 小奇麗 ── 小奇麗な 形 (きちんとした) neat; (きちんとして行き届いた) tidy, trim; (しゃれた) smart.《⇨小汚い》 ▶小ぎれいな店 a tidy (little) shop. ●部

こきんわかしゅう『古今和歌集』Kokinshu: A Collection of Poems Ancient and Modern. (参考) 紀貫之ら撰の最初の勅撰和歌集)

こく 石 [単位] a koku (穀 〜). (参考) (1) 容積の単位. 約180ℓ. (2) 和船の積載量の単位. 約0.278m³)

こく 酷 ▶それ以上彼を働かせるのは酷だ It is too much to work him any more. ▶少し酷な言い方をすれば (=かもしれないが)... Although this may sound a little too harsh, ...

こく 濃 [酒・コーヒーなどの] body; [料理の] savor. ▶こくがある become full-bodied. ▶こくのあるワイン full-bodied wine. ▶こくのあるスープ savory soup. ▶こくのある(=深みのある)随筆 a deep [(味わいのある)] a tasteful] essay.

*こぐ 漕ぐ row, [オールで] oar /ˈɔːr/, [かいで] paddle. ▶川を漕ぎ渡る row (a boat) across the river. ▶一生懸命オールを漕ぐ pull hard on the [one's] oars.

ごく 語句 [語] words; [語と句] words and phrases.

ごく 極く [非常に] very; [極度に] extremely; [まったく] quite. (⇨非常に) ▶ごく普通の子 a very ordinary child; just an ordinary child (! a quíte órdinary... は音調上通例不可. この場合は quite an ordinary ... とすればよい.) ▶これは日本ではごくありふれた花です This is a very common flower in Japan. ▶彼が来るのを知ったのはごく最近です I quite [only] recently learned of his coming.

ごくあく 極悪 [名] atrocity; [書] enormity, villainy. (! いずれも行為は[C])

—— **極悪の** [形] most wicked; outrageous; [書] enormous, villainous. ▶極悪非道の振る舞い inhuman [outrageous] behavior.

▶極悪人 an atrocious [an outrageous] fiend; a devil.

こくい 国威 the national prestige [dignity].

ごくい 極意 [真髄] the essence; [深い真理] mysteries; [秘伝] the secret. ▶茶道の極意 the essence [mysteries, secrets, (奥義) heart] of the tea ceremony.

こくいっこく 刻一刻 every moment. (⇨刻々)

こくいん 刻印 [名] a carved seal.

—— **刻印する** [動] put [[書] impress] a seal (on).

ごくいん 極印 a hallmark.

こくう 虚空 [大空の] the sky, the air; [何もない空間] empty space, [書] the void. ▶虚空をつかんで倒れる fall down grasping at the air.

こくうん 国運 ▶国運を賭する stake the destiny [fate] of the nation.

こくえい 国営 [名] state [government] management.

—— **国営の** [形] state-run[-operated] ⟨railways⟩; ⟨railways⟩ run [operated] by the state.

▶国営化 nationalization. ▶炭坑を国営化する nationalize; [⇔denationalize, privatize] coal mining. ▶国営事業 state [government, national] enterprise. ▶国営農場 a state-run farm. ▶国営放送局 a state-run broadcasting station.

こくえき 国益 national interest(s). ▶彼らの国益を計る promote their national interests. ▶国益に反する be against the national interest.

こくえん 黒鉛 [地学] black lead /lɛd/; graphite.

こくおう 国王 a king; [君主] a monarch. (⇨王) ▶スペイン国王 the King of Spain.

こくがい 国外 (⇨海外) ▶国外へ[で] abroad; overseas. ▶国外のニュース foreign news. ▶国外へ追放される be sent into exile; be exiled. (⇨追放) ▶国外に品物を持ち出す(=密輸出する) smuggle goods out of ⟨Japan⟩.

こくがく 国学 the study of Japanese classical literature; the study of ancient Japanese thought and culture.

こくぎ 国技 a [the] national sport ⟨of Japan⟩. (! (1) 特に一つの競技をさす時は the. (2) 球技の場合は sport の代わりに game も可. (3) その国固有のものなら a traditional sport of Japan のようにもいえる)

*こくご 国語 [日本語] Japanese, the Japanese language, (学校として) Japanese language; [英語を母語とする国の] English; [言語] (a) language; [母語] one's native language [mother tongue]. ▶国語の授業 a Japanese class; a class of [in] Japanese. ▶国語辞典 (日本語の) a Japanese dictionary. ▶彼は数[2; 3] か国語が話せる He speaks several [two; three] languages./He is multilingual [bilingual; trilingual].

▶国語学 Japanese linguistics. ▶国語審議会 the Japanese Language Council.

こくこく 刻々 (⇨刻々(こく))

ごくごく ▶ごくごく(のどを鳴らして)飲む gulp ⟨water⟩ down. ▶通例この訳でよいが, gulp ⟨water⟩ loudly [noisily] とか drink ⟨water⟩ with a slurping sound と描写することも可)

*こくさい 国際 —— **国際(的)な** [形] (各国間の) international; (全世界にわたる) cosmopolitan. ▶国際色豊かな町 a town with a rich international flavor. ▶国際感覚を身につける acquire an international way of thinking. ▶国際電話をかける make an international [an overseas] call ⟨to⟩. ▶そのスパイ事件は国際問題に発展した The spy affair developed into an international problem. ▶彼は国際感覚のある人だ He is an internationally-minded man. ▶国際的水準から見れば労働賃金はまだ高いと考えられる By international standards labor costs are still considered high.

—— **国際的に** [副] internationally. ▶彼女は国際的に有名な科学者だ She is an internationally famous scientist.

—— **国際化する** [動] (...を) internationalize; globalize; (...が) go international.

▶国際運転免許証 an international driving permit. ▶国際オリンピック委員会 the International Olympic Committee [略 IOC]. ▶国際化 internationalization. ▶国際会議 (attend) an international conference. ▶国際河川 an international river. ▶国際関係(学) international relations. ▶国際空港 an international airport. ▶国際結婚 (an) international marriage. (関連) 異人種[異宗教]間の結婚 ⇨ mixed marriage) ▶国際語 an international language. ▶国際交流基金 (the) Japan Foundation. ▶国際司法裁判所 the International Court of Justice [略 ICJ]; (通称) the World Court. ▶国際社会 the international community. ▶国際収支 the (international) balance of payments. ▶国際情勢 the international situation. ▶国際人 a cosmopolitan (person). (! 外国での経験が豊富で国家の偏見にとらわれず国際的な視野を持った人のこと. internationalist は「国際協調主義者」) ▶国際政治学 international politics. ▶国際通貨 international [world] currency. ▶国際通貨基金 International Monetary Fund [略 IMF]. ▶国際都市 (多くの国の人々から成る都市) a cosmopolitan city. ▶国際犯罪 an international crime. ▶国際紛争

こくさい an international dispute. ●**国際法** international law; law of nations. ●**国際連合** the United Nations 《略 UN, U.N.》. (⇨国連)
●**国際労働機構** International Labor Organization《略 ILO》.

こくさい 国債 a government bond, public funding [funds],《英》the funds. ▶毎年赤字国債が発行されている Deficit *government bonds* are issued every year.
●**国債依存度** the dependency rate on government bond issue; the ratio of reliance on bond issues to national budget.

ごくさいしき 極彩色 rich [vivid, brilliant] coloring. ●極彩色の絵 a *richly colored* picture.

こくさく 国策 a national policy.

こくさん 国産 ── **国産の** 形 domestic; domestically produced; (日本製の) Japanese (-made). ▶輸入ものより国産のワインの方が好きです I prefer *domestic* wines to imported ones.
●**国産車** a domestic car; (日本車) a Japanese car, a car made [manufactured] in Japan.
国産品 domestic products [goods]; domestically-[(主に英) home-]produced articles.

こくし 国士 (愛国者) a patriot.
●**国士無双** (天下随一の人物) the most distinguished person; (マージャンの) The Thirteen Unique Wonders.

こくし 酷使 图 (xa) rough use. ▶この機械は酷使に耐えた This machine stood *rough use* [*rough handling*].
── **酷使する** 動 ・従業員を酷使する(=こき使う) *work* [*drive*] the employees *too hard*; (次々に指図して)《話》*push* [*order*] the employees *around*.
●**目を酷使して痛める** *strain* one's eyes (*badly*).
▶彼は数週間体を酷使した(=働きすぎた) He *worked too much*《やや書》*overworked* (*himself*)] for several weeks.

こくじ 告示 〘通知〙 (a) notice; 〘正式の〙 (a) notification; 〘公表〙 an announcement. ●**政府告示** a government *notification*.

こくじ 国事 the affairs of state, national [state] affairs. ●**天皇の国事行為** the emperor's constitutional functions.
●**国事犯** (行為) a political crime [offense]; (人) a political offender.

こくじ 国璽 the Great Seal; the Seal of State.
こくじ 酷似 ▶この文章は私が書いたものに酷似している This writing *closely resembles* (×with) [*is very similar to*] mine./There is a *close resemblance* *between* this writing and mine.

ごくし 獄死 图 death in prison. ── **獄死する** 動 die in prison.

こくしびょう 黒死病 the Black Death.《参考》14世紀ヨーロッパで大流行した (⇨ペスト)

こくしょ 国書《参考》〘一国の元首が出す外交文書〙a sovereign diplomatic document [letter]; 〘和書〙 a Japanese book, a book (written) in Japanese.

こくしょ 酷暑 (the) intense [severe] heat. (⇨暑さ)
▶酷暑の折からお体に気をつけてください Please take good care of yourself in this *intense heat* [*heat of midsummer*].

こくじょう 国情 the conditions of [the state of affairs in] a country.

ごくじょう 極上 ── **極上の** 形〘最上の〙 best; 〘精選された〙 choice. ●**極上のワイン** *choice* [*the best*] wine; (最高品質の) wine *of the highest* [*the best*] *quality*.

こくしょく 黒色 black.
●**黒色腫**〘医学〙 a melanoma. ●**黒色人種** the black [Negro, Negroid] race.

こくじょく 国辱 a national disgrace. ▶彼の政治的亡命は国辱に値する His political asylum is worthy of a *national disgrace*.

こくじん 黒人 图 (アメリカの) an African American; 〘古〙 an Afro-American (❗ a black は 1970–80年代には最も普通の語(それ以前は a Negro)だったが、90年代に入って逐次侮蔑(ぶべつ)的な語となり、最近では an Afro-American を経て an African American が代表的な語となった. black も用いられるが, Negro は特別な連語を除いて今は避ける.); 〘集合的に〙 African American people;《英》an African Caribbean.
●**黒人を差別する** discriminate against *African American people*.
── **黒人の** 形 African American. ●**黒人の女性** an *African American* woman.
●**黒人英語** African American [Black] English. ●**黒人居住区** an African American (↔white) neighborhood. ●**黒人霊歌** a Negro spiritual.

こくすいしゅぎ 国粋主義 ùltranátionalism, nátionalism (❗ 後の方は「愛国主義」というよい意味になることもある).
●**国粋主義者** an ultranationalist; a nationalist.

こくせい 国政 (政治) government; (行政) (national) administration. ●**国政を担う** administer a country.
●**国政選挙** a national election.

こくぜい 国税 national taxes.
●**国税庁** (日本の) the National Tax Administration Agency.《参考》米国の the Internal Revenue Service, 英国の の (Board of) Inland Revenue に相当する)

こくぜい 酷税 a heavy tax; heavy taxation. (⇨重税)

こくせいちょうさ 国勢調査 a (national) census.
●**国勢調査をする** take a *census*.

こくせき 国籍 (a) nationality; (市民権) citizenship.
●**国籍不明機** a plane of unknown *nationality*.
●**両親の国籍** the *nationalities* of one's parents.
●**二重国籍** (have) dual *nationality* [*citizenship*]. ▶彼は昨年日本国籍を得た He got [acquired] Japanese *nationality* [*citizenship*] last year.
会話「彼女の国籍はどこですか」「日本です」"What [×Where] is her *nationality*?/What *nationality* is she?" "She is (a) Japanese." (❗(1) 国籍を強調するときは を つける. (2)「彼女は日本国籍だ」は She has [is of] Japanese *nationality*.)

こくせん 国選 selection by the state.
●**国選弁護人** a court-appointed lawyer; an official defense counsel.

こくせんやかっせん『国性爺合戦』 *The Battle of Coxinga*.《参考》近松門左衛門の人形浄瑠璃

こくそ 告訴 图 a charge, (an) accusation; (検察の) (a) prosecution; (民事の) (a) complaint, a (law) suit, an action.
── **告訴する** 動 charge, accuse; prosecute; sue. (⇨訴える ❶ [類語]) ●犯罪のかどで告訴する *charge* 《him》 *with* a crime; *accuse* 《him》 *of* a crime; *prosecute* 《him》 *for* a crime; *bring an accusation* [*a charge*] *of* a crime 《*against* him》. (❗ 被害者となる者の法定代理人が主語. それ以外が主語の場合には「告発する」となる) ●**損害賠償を求めて彼を告訴する** *sue* him *for* damages; *bring a suit* [*an action*] *for* damages *against* him.

こくそう ●告訴状 a (letter of) complaint. ●告訴人 (⇨原告)

こくそう 国葬 a national [a state] funeral. (⇨葬儀)

こくそうちたい 穀倉地帯 a granary /ɡrǽnəri/, a grain-producing area [region], the breadbasket.

こくぞうむし 穀象虫 〖昆虫〗a rice weevil.

こくたい 国体 ❶〖国民体育大会〗the National Athletic Meet〖時に英〗Athletics Meeting〗. ❷〖国家形態〗national polity.

こくたん 黒檀 ébony. ●黒檀の木 an ebony.

こくち 告知 图〖書〗(a) notification. ●がんの告知を受ける be informed of one's cancer.
—**告知する** 動 notify; inform《人の事》. (!前の方が堅い語)

こぐち 小口 (額) a small sum [amount] 《of》; (量) a small amount [quantity] 《of》. ●小口の預金 small deposits. ●小口の注文もお受けいたします We will gladly receive small orders as well as large ones.
●小口現金（会社などで日々の必要のために用意する現金）petty cash.

こぐちぎり 小口切り ●キュウリを小口切りにする cut a cucumber into thin slices.

こくちょう 国鳥 a national bird.

> 関連 各国の国鳥: 米国 bald eagle (ハクトウワシ)/英国 robin (コマドリ)/オーストラリア lyrebird (コトドリ)/日本 pheasant (キジ)

こくちょう 黒鳥 〖鳥〗a black swan.

ごくちょうたんぱ 極超短波 ultra high-frequency 《略 UHF》.

ごくつぶし 穀潰し (ろくでなし) a good-for-nothing, 《話》a good-for-naught; (なまけ者) an idler.

こくてい 国定〖書〗prescription by the state. ●国定教科書 a textbook compiled by the Ministry of Education; a state textbook. ●国定公園 a quasi-national park. ●国定税率 an autonomous [a national, a statutory] tariff.

こくてつ 国鉄〖「国有鉄道」の略〗(⇨国有)

こくてん 黒点 a dark [a black] spot; 〖天文〗(太陽の) a sunspot.

こくど 国土 a country; 〖土地〗land; 〖領土〗(a) territory. ●人口の多い狭い国土 a small, over-populated country.
●国土開発 national land development. ●国土計画 national land planning. ●国土交通省 the Ministry of Land, Infrastructure and Transport. ●国土交通大臣 the Minister of Land, Infrastructure and Transport. ●国土地理院 the Geographical Survey Institute.

こくどう 国道 a national highway [road, route].
●国道171号線 National Highway 171; Route 171. (!171 は one seventy one, 101 なら one oh one と読むのが普通)

ごくどう 極道 图（邪悪な）wickedness;（道楽）〖書〗prodigality;（放蕩(ほうとう)）〖書〗dissipation, profligacy.
—**極道** 形（邪悪な）wicked;（放蕩の）〖書〗dissipated, profligate. ●極道（=やくざ）の世界 the underworld.

こくない 国内 —**国内の** 形 domestic, home. ●国内ニュース domestic news. ●国内消費の落ち込み[急増]a fall [a surge] in domestic consumption.
●国内でも国外でも both at home and abroad.
●国内産業 home [domestic] industries. ●国内市場 the home [domestic] market. ●国内需要 domestic demand. ●国内線（飛行機の）a domestic airline. ●国内総生産 gross domestic product 《略 GDP》.

こくないしょう 黒内障〖医学〗amaurosis.

こくなん 国難 a national crisis. ▶今日(こんにち)日本は国難に直面している Today Japan is faced with a national crisis.

こくはく 告白 图 (a) confession.
—**告白する** 動 ▶彼はその女性に愛の告白をした He confessed [confided] his love to the girl. (⇨白状する)

こくはつ 告発 a charge. (⇨告訴) ●内部告発 whistle-blowing. (⇨内部)
●告発者 an accuser.

こくばん 黒板 a blackboard (!緑色のものにも用いる);（明るい色の）《米》a chalkboard,（緑色の）a greenboard. ❶単に a board ともいう. ●黒板をふく clean [《米》erase] a blackboard. ●チョークで黒板に字を書く chalk a board. (⇨チョーク) ●黒板にあなたの名前を書きなさい Write your name on the blackboard.
●黒板拭き《米》an [a blackboard] eraser,《英》a (board) rubber.

こくひ 国費 (国の費用) national [government] expenditure(s); (国の資金) government funds.
●国費をむだ使いする waste government funds.
●国費の削減 (be hit by) government cuts. ●国費(=国の奨学資金)で留学する study abroad on a government scholarship [(政府の機関による) a scholarship awarded by government institutions].

こくび 小首 ●小首をかしげる have doubts《about》; doubt.

ごくひ 極秘 a top [a strict] secret;《文書の表示》Strictly confidential; 〖極秘の状態〗strict secrecy. ●極秘の情報 top-secret information; strictly [highly] confidential information. 《参考》米国政府・軍隊で機密情報を3段階に分け, 機密性の高い方から, Eyes only, Sensitive, Secret Classified と呼んでいる) ●極秘にする keep《it》strictly [very] secret. ▶会談は極秘のうちに行われた The talks were held in the greatest secrecy.

こくひょう 酷評 图 (a) severe [(a) sharp] criticism. (⇨批判)
—**酷評する** 動 criticize《him》severely [sharply].

こくひん 国賓 a state [a national] guest. ●国賓としてパーティーに招待する invite《him》to the party as a state guest.

こくふく 克服 —**克服する** 動 (打ち勝つ) overcome, (困難・障害などを乗り越える) get over .... ▶彼がこのハンディを克服するのは容易ではなかった It was not easy for him to overcome [get over] this handicap./His victory over this handicap did not come easily.

ごくぶと 極太 —**極太の** 形 very thick. ●極太の糸 (a) very heavy thread [yarn].

こくぶんがく 国文学（日本文学）Japanese literature. (⇨文学)

こくぶんぽう 国文法（日本語の文法）Japanese grammar.

こくべつ 告別 good-by,《書》farewell.
●告別式 (葬儀) a funeral service [ceremony].
●告別式に出る go to [《やや書》attend] a funeral (service).

こくほう 国宝 a national treasure /trézɜr/. ●人間国宝 a living national treasure. ●国宝の指定を受ける be designated as a national treasure.

こくぼう 国防 national defense. ●国防増強５か年計画 a five-year *defense* build-up program. ●**国防(総)省** (米国の) the Department of Defense; 《米話》the Pentagon. ●**国防費** the national defense spending [cost].

ごくぼそ 極細 ●極細のペン a *superfine-pointed* pen. ●極細の毛糸 a *extrafine* woolen yarn. (⇨極太).

こぐまざ 小熊座 〖天文〗the Little Bear; Ursa Minor.

こくみん 国民 〖全体〗a nation (⚠ 通例単数扱い),《書》a people (⚠ 複数扱い);（一般大衆）the public (⚠ 通例単数扱い (⇨大衆));〖個人〗a citizen;《やや書》a national.

> **使い分け** **nation** 主に政治的観点で１国をなす人間集団.
> **people** 主に文化的・地理的観点から１民族をなす集団.
> **citizen** 国籍・市民権を持つ者としての国民 (= 公民).
> **national** 外国在住者の国籍を問題にする場合に用いる.

① 【**～(の)国民**】●日本国民（全体）the *people* of Japan; the Japanese (*people* [*nation*]);（個人）a Japanese. ●ヨーロッパの（諸）国民 the *peoples* of Europe. ●フランス在住の日本国民（＝在留邦人）Japanese *nationals* (living) in France. ●世界のすべての国民 all (the) *nations* [*peoples*] of the world. ▶日本人は勤勉な国民だ Japanese people [The Japanese] are ˟is a hardworking *people*. ▶前の方が普通

② 【**国民(の)～**】●国民の声 the voice of the *nation*; (皆の) public opinion. ●国民の祝日 a *national* holiday. ●国民的英雄 a *national* hero. ▶納税は国民の義務である Paying tax is every *citizen*'s obligation.

③ 【**国民が[は]**】▶次の選挙では全国民が投票するだろう The whole [entire] *nation* will vote in the next election. ▶国民は知る権利がある The *public* has a right to know.

●**国民感情** (a) national sentiment [feeling]. ●**国民休暇村** a national vacation village. ●**国民健康保険** the Nàtional Héalth Insùrance;《英》the Nàtional Héalth (Sèrvice). ●**国民審査** a national review of the Supreme Court Judges. ●**国民所得** national income. ●**国民性** the national character; national characteristics [〖書〗traits]. ●日本人の国民性 the Japanese character. ●**国民生活金融公庫** (the) National Life Finance Corporation. ●**国民総生産** gross national product 《略 GNP》. ●**国民体育大会** (国体) the National Athletic Meet. ●**国民投票** a (national) referendum [a plebiscite] 《on》. ●後の方は「国家的大事に関する投票」の意 ●**国民年金** a national pension. ●**国民年金基金** The National Pension Fund.

こくむ 国務 state affairs. ●国務をつかさどる administer [conduct] *affairs of state*. ●**国務省**《米》the Department of State. ●**国務大臣** a minister of state;（無任所の）a minister without portfolio. ●**国務長官**《米》the Secretary of State.

こくめい 克明 ── **克明な** 〖形〗 (詳細な) detailed. ●克明なメモ a *detailed* note. ●起こった事を克明に記す describe what happened in (great) *detail*.

*****こくもつ 穀物** grain,《英》corn. (⇨穀類) ●穀物畑 a field of *grain* [*corn*].

ごくもん 獄門 〖牢獄の門〗a prison gate; 〖さらし首〗a gibbeted head.

こくゆう 国有 ── **国有の** 〖形〗 national, government-[state-]owned.
── **国有化する** 〖動〗 nationalize.
●**国有化** nationalization 《*of*》. (⇨国立, 国営) ●**国有鉄道** a national railroad 《米》 [railway 《英》]; (英国国鉄) British Rail 《略 BR》; (かつての日本国有鉄道) the Japanese National Railways 《略 JNR》. (⇨ジェーアール) ●**国有林** a national [a government-owned] forest.

こくようせき 黒曜石 〖地学〗obsidian.

ごくらく 極楽 (a) paradise; (天国) heaven. ▶ここはまったく極楽だ This is a real *paradise*. ●**極楽往生** to die peacefully and be reborn in the Pure Land [Paradise]. ●**極楽浄土** the (Buddhist) Pure Land [Paradise]. ●**極楽とんぼ** a happy-go-lucky fellow.

ごくらくちょう 極楽鳥 〖鳥〗a bird of paradise.
ごくらくちょうか 極楽鳥花 〖植物〗a strelitzia /strəlítsiə/.

こくりつ 国立 ●**国立公園** a national park. ●**国立大学** a national university. (⇨公立, 県立)

ごくりと with a gulp.

こくりゅうこうしょう 黒竜江省 〖中国の省〗Heilongjiang /héilɔŋdʒiɑ́ːŋ/ Province.

こくりょく 国力 national power [strength]; (経済力) national wealth. ●国力をつける build up *national power*.

こくるい 穀類 grain,《英》corn. (⚠ corn は《英》では穀物の代表格である「麦類」,《米》では「とうもろこし」の意)

こくれん 国連 the United Nations 《略 UN, U.N.》. (⚠ 単数扱い) ●イギリスの国連大使 Britain's [the British] ambassador 〖*to*〗 *the United Nations*. ●国連の日本代表 the Japanese representative to *the United Nations*. ●国連に加盟する join (↔leave) *the United Nations*. ▶国連は 1945 年 10 月 24 日に創立された *The United Nations* [*UN*] was founded on October 24, 1945.
●**国連安全保障理事会** the United Nations Security Council 《略 UNSC》. ●**国連加盟国** a member (nation) of the United Nations. ●**国連憲章** the Charter of the United Nations. ●**国連事務局** the secretariat of the United Nations. ●**国連事務総長** the Secretary-General of the United Nations. ●**国連総会** the United Nations General Assembly. ●**国連大学** the United Nations University 《略 UNU》. ●**国連本部** the United Nations Headquarters. (⚠《米》複数扱い,《英》単数扱い)

ごくろう ご苦労 ▶ご苦労さま Thank you very much for your trouble [for all you've done]. / You did a good job, thank you.

こくろん 国論 public opinion. (⇨世論) ●国論を統一する unify *public opinion*. ▶その問題で国論は二分されている *Public opinion* is divided in two groups on that problem.

こぐんふんとう 孤軍奮闘 〖名〗▶数々の困難に対して孤軍奮闘の末, 彼女は新商品の開発にこぎつけた After a *long battle against* many difficulties, she managed to develop a new product.
── **孤軍奮闘する** 〖動〗 fight stand alone 《against》.

こけ 苔 〖植物〗moss. ●コケむした庭 [細道] a *mossy* garden [trail]. (⚠ *mossy* は限定用法のみ) ▶岩にコケがはえた Moss has grown on the rocks. / (一面はえている) The rocks are covered (over) with *moss*. ▶転石苔むさず 〖ことわざ〗A rolling stone gathers no *moss*. (⚠《米》ではたえず動き回っている

こけ〔虚仮〕(仏教で)'an untruth'.
こけにする ▶お前, おれをこけにする(=ばかにする)つもりかな Are you trying to *make a fool* [《話》*a monkey*] *(out) of* me? (⇨こけおどし)
こけい〔固形〕a solid.
● 固形食 solid foods; solids. ● 固形スープ a soup cube. ● 固形燃料 a solid fuel. ● 固形物 a solid [substance].
ごけい〔互恵〕— 互恵の 形《書》reciprocal.
● 互恵主義《書》rèciprócity. ● 互恵条約 a reciprocity treaty. ● 互恵通商協定 (make) reciprocal trade agreements.
こけおどし〔底の見えすいた脅し〕an empty threat, (a) bluff;〔派手だが実質のないもの〕a showy but insubstantial thing.
こけくさい〔焦げ臭い〕● 焦げ臭いにおい a burnt smell. ▶何か焦げ臭いぞ I (can) *smell* something *burning*.
こけこっこう〔鳴き声〕(a) cock-a-doodle-doo (圏~s). (❗動詞に用いることもできる)
こけし a *kokeshi* doll.
こげちゃ〔焦げ茶〕dark brown. ● 焦げ茶色の靴 *dark brown* shoes.
こけつ〔虎穴〕● 虎穴に入(い)らずんば虎児を得ず 'Unless you enter a tiger's den, you cannot catch its cub.'/'Only in the den can you get a tiger's cub.'/〈ことわざ〉Nothing venture(d), nothing gain(ed).
こげつく〔焦げ付く〕❶〔焼きつく〕burn*;(表面が) scorch;(真っ黒に) char (-rr-). (⇨焦げる) ● 鍋に焦げ付いた魚をこそげる scrape off the *burnt* fish in the pan. ▶シチューは焦げ付きやすい Stew can *be burned* [《英》*be burnt*] easily.
❷〔貸し金などが回収不能になる〕▶貸した金が焦げ付いた The loan *is irrecoverable* [*is uncollectable*, *is gone forever*].
こけつまろびつ〔転げつ転びつ〕● こけつまろびつ(=あわてふためいて)逃げ帰る run back in a panic.
コケティッシュ ● コケティッシュな顔立ち[目つき] a *coquettish* face [look].
こげめ〔焦げ目〕a burn. ● きつね色に焦げ目のついたトースト *browned* toast. ▶テーブルの上に丸い焦げ目がついている There is a round *burn* on (the surface of) the table.
こけもも〔苔桃〕〖植物〗a cowberry; a bilberry.
こげら〔小啄木〕〖鳥〗a Japanese pygmy woodpecker; a grey-capped woodpecker.
こけらおとし〔柿落とし〕the (formal) opening (of a new theater).
こける(ほおが) become* hollow. ▶ほおのこけた男 a *hollow*-cheeked man.
こける〔転ける〕fall down (⇨転ぶ), (倒産する) go bankrupt; go out of business;(失敗する) fail (*in*, *at*). ▶芝居がこけてしまった(=失敗した) We *failed in* a play.
***こげる**〔焦げる〕burn; (表面が) scorch; (真っ黒に) char (-rr-). ▶肉が焦げた The meat *has burned* [*scorched*]. ▶パンは焦げてかりかりになった The bread *burned* to a crisp. ▶あまりストーブに近づくとスカートが焦げますよ You'll have your skirt *scorched* [Your skirt will *scorch*] if you get too near the heater.
こけん〔沽券〕● 沽券にかかわる be beneath one's dignity.
ごけん〔護憲〕the support of the Constitution.
● 護憲運動 a campaign to protect [defend, support] the Constitution. ● 護憲派 a group supporting the Constitution.
ごげん〔語源〕the origin of a word, an etymology (❗「語源学」の意では ⓤ). ▶この単語の語源はスペイン語だ This word *comes* [《やや書》*derives*, *is derived*] *from* Spanish.

:ここ ❶〔場所〕here (⇔*there*) (❗副詞で「ここに[へ, で]」の意 (⇨①), また, 名詞で「ここ」「この場所」の意 (⇨③) とがある;(この場所) this (place); (❗これ) this.
①〔ここは[が]〕here; this place; this. ▶ここは大阪より暖かい It's warmer *here* [in *this place*] than in Osaka. (⇨こちら❶) ▶ここ(=この土地)はどうも私の性に合いません I don't like it *here*. (❗ この口では「(ここの)雰囲気」といった漠然とした状況をさす) ▶ここが私の家です *This* [《話》*This* here] is my house./(ここが私の住んでいる所です) *This* is (the place) [*Here*'s] where I live. ▶よくここが分かったね I wonder how you found this place.
会話「ここはどこですか(=私(たち)はどこにいますか)」「梅田です」"Where are we [am I] now?" "We're [You're] in Umeda." (❗(1) × Where is *here*? とはいわない. Where is this (place)? は写真などを見ていて尋ねる言い方. (2) 1 人であっても尋ねた相手を含めて we ということも多い)
②〔ここに[へ, で]〕here. (❗他の場所と対比して強意的に to [in] here ということがある) ● ここに泊まる stay here [at this place]. ● ここでの生活 life here. ▶時計はここにあります Your watch is *here*. (❗ *Here* is your watch. は相手の注意を引いて「(ほら)ここに君の時計があるよ」の意) ▶彼女はさっきまで(ちょうど)ここにいた He was (right) *here* a moment ago. ▶なんだここにいたのか. そこら中捜したよ Oh, *here you are*. I've been looking everywhere for you. ▶ここにいる女性が彼の奥さんです The lady *here* is his wife. (❗ このように名詞の後に置いて「ここにいる[ある]…」の意で用いるのは《話》) ▶ここへ来なさい Come (× to) *here*./(遠くの人に向かって) Come *over here*. ▶ここへは 2 時間に 1 本しか電車がない The trains *to here* only run every two hours. ▶ここではたばこはご遠慮ください Please refrain from smoking *in here*. (❗ Thank you for not smoking … のようにいうことも多い) ▶きのうここで彼に会った I saw him *here* [at *this place*] yesterday. ▶(タクシーの運転手に)ここで結構です(=降ろしてください) *This* is fine. ▶ここにも他のサイトへのリンクがある Here too are links to other sites. ▶私は今ここ東京にいます I'm *here* in Tokyo (now). (❗ here でまず大まかな場所を述べ, 次に具体的な場所を述べる)
会話「鉛筆はどこかな」「ここにあるよ」"Where's the pencil?" "﹨*Héré* it ／is." (❗ Right *here*./﹨*Here* you are. も可)
③〔ここから[より]〕from [(内から外へ) out of] here. ● ここから学校まで *from here* to the school. ▶ここから出よう Let's get *out of here* [*this place*]. ④〔ここまで〕up to here. ● ここまで来れば now that one has come this far. ▶ここまで追い込んでしまった have driven [forced] (him) into this situation. ▶さあ, ここまでおいで(赤ちゃんなどに) Now walk *up to me*. ▶京都からここまで歩いてきました I walked *here* from Kyoto.
❷〔この(時)点〕here. (❗通例文頭・文尾で); on this point. ▶ここは君の考えに賛成です I agree with you *here* [*on this point*]. ▶ここで彼は二つのことを強調した *Here* he stressed two things. ▶ここまでは(=今までのところ)万事うまく行った Everything has gone well *so far* [*up to now*]. (❗ so far, up to now は通例現在完了形とともに用いる)
❸〔期間〕▶ここ 3 年間彼らは日本に住んでいる They have lived in Japan *for the past* [*last*] three

years. (📛 ×...*these* three *years*. は今は用いない。ただし...*these past* [*last*] three *years*. は可) ▶2,3日［しばらく］彼は学校を休みます He'll stay away from school *for the next* few days [*for some time to come*].

❹〖その他の表現〗● ここそばかり believing that this is the only chance. ▶ここまで(=これほど)事態が悪化しているとは知らなかった I didn't know that things went *so bad as this*. ▶ここだけの話だけど彼らのおしゃべりにはうんざりした *Confidentially* [《話》(*Just*) *between you and me*, (*Just*) *between ourselves*] I got bored by their chatter. (⇨ここだけ) ▶ここという(=大事な)時にはだれもが浩二を当てにした Everyone looked to Koji at the *critical* moment.

● ここ一番 (at) the most crucial [important] moment.

ここ 呱々 (⇨囲 産声(うぶごえ))
● 呱々の声を上げる ▶赤ん坊が呱々の声を上げた(=生まれた) A baby *was born*.

ここ 個々 — 個々の 形 individual; each. ● すべて個々の判断にまかせる leave everything to *each one's* judgment.
— 個々に 副 individually.

こご 古語 an old word. (📛 廃語 (an obsolete /ɑ́bsəlit/ word) と一般には用いられていないが現在も生きている古風な言葉 (an archaic /ɑːrkéiik/ word, an old-fashioned word) と分かれる)

:こご 午後 afternoon (📛 正午から日没までは終業時までをいう); p.m. [P.M.] (📛 正午から夜の12時までの時刻を示す数字の後につけて用いる (⇨午前)) ▶午後2時 at two (o'clock) *in the afternoon*; at 2 *p.m.* [P.M.] (📛 ×at *p.m.* 2 は不可) ▶彼女は午後買い物に出かけた She went shopping *in the afternoon*. ▶午後遅く雨が降り出した It began to rain late *in the afternoon* [*in the late afternoon*]. ▶私は5日［土曜］の午後は暇です I'll be free *on the afternoon* of the 5th [(*on*) *Saturday afternoon*]. (📛 前の方は on の代わりに in も不可. 時刻を伴う場合はいも可. 後の方は《主に米》では on をしばしば省略する (⇨午前)) ▶今日［明日］の午後テニスをしよう Let's play tennis this [*tomorrow*] *afternoon*.

ココア cocoa /kóukou/; (飲料) (a) cocoa, (a) (hot) chocolate. (📛 1杯のココアの意では ⓒ)

ここう 孤高 孤高の人 a person who has high ideals and is indifferent to worldly affairs.

ごごう 古豪 (かつての一流選手［チーム］をいう) a once top-rated [top-ranking] player [team]; (老練者) a veteran. ▶その新鋭チームは決勝で古豪と対戦した The new team had a game with a *top-ranking one* in the final.

ごこう 後光 a halo /héilou/ (複 ~(e)s); a nimbus (複 ~es, nimbi /nímbai/). ▶仏像の頭に後光が射している The Buddhist image bears a *halo* around its head.

こごえ 小声 (低い声) a low voice. ● 小声で話す speak *in a low voice*; (ささやき声で) speak *in whispers* [*in a whisper*] (📛 whisper (ささやく) 1語でいうのが普通.

こごえじに 凍え死に 名 death from cold. (⇨凍死)
— 凍え死にする 動 freeze [be frozen] to death.

こごえる 凍える freeze*. (⇨凍る) ▶彼は手が凍えないようにすり合わせて暖めた He chafed his hands together to keep them from *freezing*.

ここかしこ (⇨あちこち, ほうぼう)

ここく 故国 one's home (country); one's homeland. (⇨本国)

ごこく 五穀 cereals, grains. ● 五穀豊穣を祈る pray for a rich *harvest* [《話》bumper *crops*].

ごこく 護国 ● 護国神社 a shrine for the war dead.

こごし 小腰 ● 小腰をかがめる (腰をちょっとかがめる) bow slightly; make a slight bow.

ここだけ ここだけ (⇨ここ❹) ▶ここだけの話に願います Please *keep* this *to yourself*./(会議場などで)《話》This will *stay* [×not leave] the room.

ここち 心地 (⇨心地よい) ● はき心地のよい靴 *comfortable* shoes; shoes (which are) *comfortable* to wear. ▶このいすは座り心地がいい This chair is *comfortable* to sit in [on]. ▶夢を見ているような心地がした I *felt as if* I were in a dream. ▶(自分の目を信じられなかった) I couldn't believe my eyes. ▶当地に大きな地震が起きたとき、私は生きた心地がしなかった(=死ぬかと思った) I *felt as if* I were going to die when the strong earthquake hit this area.

ここちよい 心地よい (心身をさわやかにする) refreshing; (気持ちのよい) pleasant; (身体をくつろげる) comfortable. (⇨快適) ● 心地よい(=こじんまりして暖かい)部屋 a *cozy* [《英》a *cosy*] *room*. ▶春の気候はとても心地よい Spring weather is very *pleasant*. ▶そよ風が心地よく吹いていた The breeze was blowing *pleasantly*./A *nice* [A *lovely*, A *pleasant*] cool breeze was blowing. ▶ざらっとした布地が肌に心地よかった The coarseness of the cloth *felt good* on my skin.

こごと 小言 〖年下・目下の者への叱責(しっせき)〗(a) scolding, a telling-off,《話》a talking-to (《~s 言われ); (お説教) a lecture;〖不平〗a complaint. ● 小言を言う(しかる) tell (him) off,《やや古》scold; (がみがみいう) nag (*at*); (不平を言う) complain (*to*). ▶彼女は仕事がまずいとペンキ屋に小言を言った She *complained to* the painter *about* doing such a poor job.

ココナッツ (実) a coconut.
● ココナッツミルク coconut milk, the milk of a coconut.

ここのか 九日 ●九日間 for *nine* days. ▶5月9日に on May 9(*th*). (⇨日付) ●九日目 the ninth. (⇨三つ)

ここのつ 九つ nine. ▶九つ目の子. (⇨三つ)

このところ (⇨このところ)

ココやし ココ椰子 〖植物〗(木) a coconut palm, a coco; (実) a coconut.

こごる 凝る (水などが) freeze, coagulate; (血液などが) jell, congeal.

:こころ 心
WORD CHOICE 心
mind 理性に基づく合理的な精神の働きのこと. 記憶・判断・決心などを含意する. ● 落ち着いた心の状態 a peaceful state of *mind*.
heart 感情・情緒に基づく精神の働きのこと. 愛情・同情・感動・気分などを含意する. ▶君の歌に心を打たれた Your song touched my *heart*.
spirit mind と対立する概念としての魂や精神の働きのこと. soul よりも意味が広く, 思想・理念・民族精神などを含意する. ● 邪悪な心 evil *spirit*.

頻度チャート

	20	40	60	80	100 (%)
mind					
heart					
spirit					

『こころ』 −ごころ

(a) mind; (a) heart; (a) spirit (⇒[類語]); (a) soul (❗時に spirit と交換可能だが、spirit より感情・感性の深さがあり、道徳的性質を帯びる);(感情) feelings;(意志) (a) will.

① 【心が[は]】 ● 心が落ち着く feel [be] calm. ● 心が(=根は)優しい be *basically* kind;《やや書》be kind *at heart*. ● 心が晴れる feel refreshed. ▶私の心は決まった My *heart* is set. ▶君には向上しようとする心がない You have no *mind* [*will*] to improve yourself. ▶期待で心が躍った My *heart* leaped with anticipation. ▶彼の心が見抜けない I can't *understand* [*see through*] him./I can't find out what he is really thinking. ▶そんなことをするとは君には心というもの(=思いやり)がないのか How *heartless* of you to do such a thing!/It's very *heartless* of you to do such a thing. ▶行くかとどまるかで彼の心は揺れた He *wavered* between going and staying. ▶木を見ると心がなごんだ The trees *comforted* [*consoled*] me. (後の方が堅い語) ▶彼らは心が通い合っている(互いに理解し合っている) There's mutual understanding between them./(信頼関係で結ばれている)《主に米》They *are connected with* each other.

② 【心の】 ● 心の優しい人 a kind-*hearted* [a gentle-*hearted*] person. ● 心の広い[狭い]人 a broad-*minded* [a narrow-*minded*] person. ● 心の友《主に書》a *bosom* [bú(:)zəm] *friend*. ● 心の平安 *spiritual* peace; peace of *mind*. ● 心のケア *mental* care. ● 心の糧 food for *thought* [*the mind*]. ● 心の支え an emotional and psychological support. ● 心のどこかに somewhere in one's heart [mind]. ● 心の闇 the darkness in one's mind. ● 心の中で in one's *heart*; inwardly. (⇒内心) ● 心のおもむくままに as one *pleases* [*likes*,《書》*wishes*]. ● 心のこもった贈り物 a *thoughtful* [心の暖まる] a *heart*-warming present. ● 心の準備をする prepare oneself (*for; to* do). ● 心の底から from the bottom of one's *heart*. (⇒⑤) ● 心の暖かい人 He has a warm *heart*./He is a warm-*hearted* man. ● 彼は心のきれいな人だ He is pure *in mind*. ▶彼は心の底では私を嫌っていた He disliked me deep in his heart [《話》deep *down*]./(本当は) He *really* didn't like me. ▶目は心の窓といわれている They say the eyes are the windows of the *soul*.

③ 【心に】 ● 心に残る remain in one's *mind*. ● 心を静める calm oneself (*down*); calm one's mind. ● 都会の生活を心に描く imagine city life;(ありありと) picture city life to oneself. ● 亡き母の思い出を心に抱く《書》cherish the memory of one's dead mother. ● 私の心にかなった部屋 a room *after* my own *heart*. ▶彼の言葉が私の心に重くのしかかった His remarks weighed heavily *on* [*in*] my *mind*. ▶彼女はアニメ作家になろうと固く心に決めている She *is determined* [*is resolved*] to become an animator.

┃ 翻訳のこころ おまえらの望みはかなったぞ。おまえらは、わしの心に勝ったのだ(太宰治『走れメロス』) Your wish has come true. You won over my *mind* [*heart*].

DISCOURSE
音楽は人の心に大きな影響を与える。例えば気分を高めたり、幸せな気分にしたり、心を静めてくれたりする Music has a great impact on our *minds* ― it can excite you, it can make you happy, and it can calm you down. (❗ダッシュ(一)は具体例に用いるディスコースマーカー)

④ 【心を】 ● 心を尽くす do one's best. ● 心を決める make up one's *mind* (*to* do). ● 彼女の心をつかむ(=愛を勝ちとる) win her *heart*. ● 彼に心を打ち明ける open (up) one's *heart* to him. ▶真二は彼女のことで心を悩ましている Shinji worries [is *worried*] *about* her./Shinji is anxious about her. ▶彼の話が彼らの心を打った His story *touched* [*impressed*, *moved*] them. ▶ラフカディオ・ハーンは日本の心を理解した Lafcadio Hearn understood the *spirit* of Japan.

⑤ 【心から】 ● 心から彼を歓迎する give him a *hearty* welcome; welcome him *heartily*. ● 彼女に心からの感謝の手紙を書く write her a *sincere* letter of thanks (a letter of *sincere* thanks). ▶君には心から感謝しています I thank you *from* (the bottom) of my *heart* [*with all* my *heart*]./(たいへん感謝している) I'm most grateful [very much obliged] to you. ▶快適な旅になるよう心からお祈りしています I *dó hope* you have a comfortable journey. (❗do は一般動詞・have 動詞を強調し、強く読む) ▶心から愛してますよ I *dó love* you *dearly* and *truly*.

● 心が痛む ▶彼はその知らせで心が痛んだ His *heart* ached with [at] the news./The news made his *heart* ache.

● 心が動く (…したい気持ちがある) feel like ((*doing*)); be [feel] inclined (*to* do);(感動する) be touched ((*by*)), be moved ((*by*));(後の方が強い);(興味を持つ) be interested ((*in*)).

● 心ここにあらず one's mind is not focusing.
● 心して with great care; with much caution.
● 心して味わう savor ((*it*)) from the bottom of one's heart.
● 心なし ▶心なしか I don't know for sure, (but) ….
● 心にかける ● 心にかけてくださってありがとうございます Thank you for *thinking of* us.
● 心に留める bear [keep] ((*it*)) in mind. (❗通例命令的文脈で)
● 心にも無い ● 心にもないことを言うな Don't say what you don't mean [what is not in your mind].
● 心を合わせる ▶みんなで心(=力)を合わせてその仕事をやり遂げなければならない We must accomplish the task *with* combined efforts.
● 心を痛める ▶その知らせに私は心をひどく痛めた I *was* very *sad* (in mind) to hear the news./It made me very *sad* to hear the news. (❗The news *grieved* me deeply./I *was* deeply *grieved at* [*to* hear] the news. はいずれも《書》)
● 心を入れ替える (行いを悔い改める) reform oneself; mend one's ways;(新しい出発をする) make a fresh start;(改心して生活を一新する) turn over a new leaf.
● 心を奪われる (魅了される) be charmed [fascinated] ((*by, with*));(没頭する) be absorbed ((*in*)).
● 心を鬼にする steel oneself [one's *heart*] ((*against* his plea)).
● 心を砕く think and worry ((for)).
● 心を込める ▶もっと心を込めて仕事をやりなさい You should put more heart into your work.
● 心を許す accept ((*him*)).

『こころ』 Kokoro. (参考 夏目漱石の小説)

−ごころ −心 ● 親心 parental *love*. ● 子供心 a child-ish *mind*. ● 仏心 a merciful *heart*. ● 魚心あれば水心 (ことわざ) Scratch my back and I'll scratch yours. ▶彼には詩心がある He has a poetic mind.

こころあたたまる 心温まる heart-warming; (人の心を喜ばす) cheering.

こころあたり 心当たり [見当] an idea; [手がかり] a clue. ●心当たりの場所を捜す check every likely place [any place (he) can think of]. ▶だれか私に電話をしてきたのか心当たりありませんか Do you have any *idea* (*of*) who telephoned me? (❗［話］では wh- 節の前の of は通例省略される)
会話「(あなたを)手伝ってくれる人はだれかいますか」「3人ほど心当たりがあります(=心に決めている)」"Is there anyone who will help you?" "I *have* three *in mind*."

こころあて 心当て (当て推量) guesswork, a random guess; (心頼み) reliance; (望み) hope. ●心当てにして彼の知らせを待つ wait for his news *with hope*.

こころある 心有る [思いやりのある] thoughtful; considerate; sympathetic (⇨思い遣り); [分別のある] sensible; [趣の分かる] appreciative, discerning.

こころいき 心意気 (気迫) spirit; (決意) detèrmination; (積極性) positiveness. ●心意気に打たれる be impressed [moved] by (his) tremendous *spirit*.

こころいわい 心祝い (心ばかりの祝い) a small congratulatory present [gift].

こころうつり 心移り (⇨心変わり)

こころえ 心得 (知識) knowledge; (規則) rules. ●従業員心得 *rules* for employees. ●休暇中の心得(=過ごし方) *how to* spend the vacation (米) [holidays (英)]. ●心得顔で話す talk *with a knowing look* [*knowingly*]. ●多少医学の心得がある(=訓練を受けた)ボランティア a volunteer with some medical *training*. ●少し柔道の心得(=経験)がある have some *experience* (in) practicing judo. ▶彼は多少ドイツ語の心得がある He has some *knowledge of* [(やや書) some *acquaintance with*] German. (⇨知識) ▶「おれだって多少の心得があるのだ」と彼は言った "I *know* a thing or two myself," he said. ▶そんな行動をするなんて心得違いもはなはだしい You *are* completely *wrong to* do that.

翻訳のこころ 高瀬舟に乗る罪人の過半は、いわゆる心得違いのために、思わぬ料を犯した人であった(森鷗外『高瀬舟』) Half of the criminals on board *Takasebune* (a boat on Takase River) were those who committed crimes unintentionally because of some misunderstandings (on their part). (❗(1)「(船に)乗る」は on board a boat [ship]. (2)「心得」は understanding ((正しい, しかるべきと)承知していること)、「心得違い」は misunderstanding (思い違い)と表す. on their part は「(他人でなく)自分自身がした(思い違い)」. (3)「思わぬ」は unintentionally (意図しないで))

こころえる 心得る [知っている] know*; [承知している] understand*; [気づく] become* aware *of*; *that* 節]; [みなす] regard (*as*), [間違って] take* (*for*). ▶その政治家は聴衆を引きつけるすべを心得ている The politician *knows* how to carry [*has a* [*the*] *knack of*] carrying his listeners [audience] with him. ▶彼は茶の湯についてはかなりいちおう心得ている She *knows* pretty much *about* [has the general knowledge of] tea ceremony. ▶学校を何だと心得ているか What do you take schools *for*? (⇨みなす)

こころおきなく 心置きなく ▶これで心置きなく仕事に専念できる Now I can devote all my energy to my work *without any worry* [*without worrying*].

こころおぼえ 心覚え [記憶] memory, (書) remembrance; [覚え書き] a note, (書) a memorandum (複 ~s, memoranda), (話) a memo (複 ~s).

こころがけ 心掛け [態度] an [a mental] attitude; [注意] attention; care. ▶彼は心がけがいい He is a man of good *intentions* [a right-minded person]. ▶老人に席を譲るとはいい心がけだ It's very kind of you to give your seat to an older [elderly] person. ▶よく遅刻するのは心がけが悪いからだ You are often late because you are not careful enough.
会話「規則正しい生活をするようにしています」「それはいい心がけです」"I'm trying to keep regular hours." "It's a wise policy."

こころがける 心掛ける [努力する] try (*to do*); [留意する] keep* [bear*]... in mind, be careful; [志す] intend (*to do*), aim (*to do*; *at doing*). ▶遅刻しないよう心がけなさい *Try* [*Be careful*] not *to* be late.

こころがまえ 心構え ●心構えをする prepare oneself [get ready] (*for* the worst); to meet the worst] (⇨覚悟); (話) get oneself up (*for* (doing) one's new job). ▶私はそれに対して心構えができていなかった I *wasn't prepared for* it.

こころから 心から (⇨心 ❺)

こころがわり 心変わり 名 a change of mind [heart]; (裏切り) (a) betrayal.
—— 心変わりする 動 (気が変わる) change one's mind; (裏切る) betray. ▶彼女はころころと心変わりする(=移り気だ) She's very *fickle*.

こころくばり 心配り consideration. (⇨心遣い, 配慮)

こころぐみ 心組み (心構え) preparation 《*for*》; an attitude 《*toward*》; intentions. (⇨心構え)

こころぐるしい 心苦しい ▶君にそこまでしてもらっては心苦しい *I'm sorry* to put you to so much trouble. (❗事柄を主語にして, It *pains* [*pricks*] my *conscience* if you do so much as that. というのも(書)) ▶お言葉に甘えるようで心苦しいですが... It *bothers* me to take advantage of you [your kindness], but ....

*こころざし 志 ❶ [意志] (a) will (*to do*); (意向) a wish (*to do*) (❗しばしば複数形で); (意図) (an) intention (*to do*); (決意) (a) resolution; (大望) (an) ambition; (目標) an aim. ●志を遂げる realize one's *ambition* [*aspiration*] 《*to do*》; achieve one's *aim* 《*to do*》. ●政治家になろうと志を立てる *resolve* [*make a resolution*] *to* be a statesman. ▶両親の志を継いで医者になった Following [(やや書) Bowing /báuin/ to] my parents' *will* [*wishes*], I became a doctor.
❷ [好意] (親切・親切な行為) a kindness; (贈り物) a (small) present [gift]. ▶お志ありがとうございます I really appreciate [Thank you very much for] your *kindness*. (❗後の方が口語的) ▶これはほんの志です This is only a *small present* for you./(感謝の印です) This is a *small token* of my *gratitude*.

こころざす 志す [意図する] intend (*to do*); [目ざす] aim 《*at*; *to do*》; [大望を抱く] have* an ambition (*to do*); [決心する] make* up one's mind (*to do*); [したいことを心に決める] set* one's heart 《*on*》. ▶若いころ私は政治家を志した When I was young, I *intended* [*had an ambition*] *to* be a politician.

こころさびしい 心寂しい, 心淋しい lonely, (主に米) lonesome. ●心寂しい日々を送る spend *lonely* [(書) *solitary*] days.

ごろし 子殺し killing one's child [baby]; a child murder.

こころしずかに 心静かに quietly; calmly; peacefully. ●心静かに待つ wait *peacefully*.

こころして 心して 〖注意深く〗carefully; with care. ●心して患者を扱う treat a patient *with* (*great*) *care*.

こころじょうぶ 心丈夫 ●心丈夫である feel safe [secure]. ▶彼女がいっしょにいてくれるなら心丈夫だ I *feel safe* if she is with me.

こころぜわしい 心忙しい restless; uneasy. ▶年末になると何となく心ぜわしい I somewhat *feel restless* at the end of the year.

こころだのみ 心頼み reliance; hope. ●心頼みにする rely [count] 《*on, upon*》. ▶彼女の協力を心頼みにする I *rely* [*count*] *on* his cooperation.

こころづかい 心遣い 〖思いやり〗consideration 《*for*》; thoughtfulness, 〖気遣い, 心配〗concern. ▶お心遣いありがとう Thank you for your (kind) *consideration*./That's very *considerate* of you./I appreciate your *thoughtfulness*.

こころづくし 心尽くし 〖親切〗(心) kindness; (行為) a kindness; 〖思いやり〗consideration. ●心尽くしのもてなし *warm* [*kind*] hospitality. ●客への心尽くしの(=心をこめた)手料理 a dish *carefully* [(とっておきの) *specially*] prepared for the guest. ●彼の心尽くしに感謝する thank him for his *kindness* [*many kindnesses, kind consideration*].

こころづけ 心付け a tip, 《書》a gratuity. (⇨チップ❷). ●心付けをする tip [give a *tip* to] 《him》.

こころづもり 心積もり ━ 心積もりをする 動 (動作) prepare (oneself) 《*for; to do*》; (状態) be prepared [ready] 《*for; to do*》. ▶次の仕事の心積もりをする prepare oneself [get ready] *for* the next job. ▶両親が年をとって足腰が立たなくなったら同居する心積もりでいます I'm *prepared to* live with my parents when they get too old to get about. ▶ひそかに心積もりしていた(=予期していた)とおりに物事が進んでいる Things are turning out just as I *was thinking* [*expecting*].

こころづよい 心強い 〖安心させるような〗reassuring; 〖勇気づける〗encouraging. ●心強い便り *encouraging* [*reassuring*] news. ▶彼の言葉を聞いて心強く思った I *felt reassured* [*was encouraged*] by his words./His words (greatly) *reassured* [*encouraged*] me.

こころない 心ない 〖残酷な〗cruel; (思いやりのない) inconsiderate, 〖思慮のない〗thoughtless. ●心ない言葉 *cruel* [*inconsiderate, thoughtless*] remarks.

こころならずも 心ならずも 〖意志に反して〗against one's will; 〖いやいやながら〗reluctantly; 〖不本意に〗unwillingly; 〖思わず〗in spite of oneself. ▶彼は心ならずもその命令に従った He obeyed the order *against* his *will*./He *reluctantly* [*unwillingly*] obeyed the order. ▶私は心ならずも吹き出してしまった I burst into laughter *in spite of* myself.

こころにくい 心憎い ●心憎い(=目を見張る)演出効果 *dramatic* [(ただただ驚くばかりの) *amazing*, (実に見事な) *marvelous*] stage effects. ▶彼の心憎いばかり(=見事なほど)の配慮 his *admirably* careful [*thoughtful*] consideration. ●心憎いほど(=完璧なまでに)落ち着いている be *perfectly* calm.

こころにもない 心にもない ●心にもないお世辞 flattery. (❗この語の中に「心にもない」の意が同じく含まれている. insincere flattery というと非常にはっきりする) ▶彼女は時々心にもないことを言う She sometimes says what she really does not mean.

こころね 心根 (心情) one's feelings, 《書》one's disposition; (根性) nature, spirit. ●心の優しい

人 a person *of good nature*.

こころのこり 心残り 〖残念〗regret; 〖気が進まないこと〗reluctance. ▶何も心残りはない I have no *regrets*./I have nothing to *regret*. ▶彼女は子供と別れるのが心残りだった She was *reluctant* to part with her child.

こころばかりの 心ばかりの small. (⇨ささやか) ▶ほんの心ばかりの品ですがお納めください I would be very glad if you accept this present *as a small token of* my gratitude. (❗「お世話になっていることへの感謝のしるしとして」の意)
【会話】「これはほんの心ばかりのものです」「まあ、こんなに心遣いはご無用でしたのに. 本当にありがとうございます」"I've brought a *little* something." "Oh, you shouldn't have. Thank you very much."

こころひそかに 心密かに secretly; in one's heart. ▶彼は心ひそかにその女性に思いを寄せている He is *secretly* in love with the woman.

こころぼそい 心細い 〖寂しい〗lonely; (不安な) uneasy (↔secure). ▶ひとり暮らしで心細くないのですか Don't you feel *lonely* [*uneasy*] living alone?

こころまかせ 心任せ ●心任せに歌う sing *as one pleases* [*likes*].

こころまち 心待ち ━ 心待ちにする 動 look forward 《*to doing*》. (⇨楽しみ) ▶彼が帰るのを心待ちにしている be *looking forward to* his return (❗現在形とり進行形の方が話者の強い気持ちが表現される); (待ちかねている) be *impatiently waiting for* him to return; (待ちこがれている) be *eargerly awaiting* his return.

こころみ 試み 〖試みる, 努力〗a try; a trial; an attempt (⇨試みる), 〖試験〗a test; (⇨試験❷); 〖実験〗(an) experiment (⇨実験). ●試みに on *trial*. (⇨試しに) ▶彼は3度目の試みで成功した He succeeded *on* the [his] third *try*.

* **こころみる 試みる** try 《*to do; doing*》; attempt 《*to do; ✗doing*》.

  使い分け try 日常生活の中で目的のために行動すること. 気軽な試みもあれば努力をする場合もある.
  attempt 計略・手間・時間を要する事柄や, 個人レベルでは不可能な行政レベルの事柄を試みること. 努力よりやり遂げる決心に重点があり, しばしば失敗を含意する.

●懸命に試みる *try* hard. ●その方法を3度試みる *try* [*attempt*] the method three times; *have* three *tries* [*make* three *attempts*] *at* the method. ▶彼は減量しようとあらゆる方法を試みた He *tried* everything *to* lose weight. ▶囚人たちは脱走を試みた The prisoners *tried to* escape. (❗実際に脱走するに至ったかどうかは不明)/The prisoners *tried* escaping [an escape]. (❗実際に脱走したかの成否は不明)/The prisoners *attempted to* escape [an escape]. (❗実際に脱走はしたが, 失敗したことを暗示する)

こころもち 心持ち 図 〖気持ち〗a feeling. (⇨気持ち)
━ **心持ち** 副 〖幾分〗rather; (少し) a little, a trifle. (⇨幾らか) ▶心持ちきゅうくつな帽子 a hat *a little too* [*a trifle*] tight. ▶心持ち首を右に向けてください—えぇ, それくらい Turn your head *a little* to the right. —Oh, that's it.

こころもとない 心許ない 〖不安な〗uneasy; 〖頼りない〗unreliable; 〖不安定な〗unstable. ▶将来が心許ないなる be [feel] *uneasy about* the future. ▶その仕事を彼にまかせるのは心許ない He's *unreliable* and we can't leave the work to him.

こころやすい 心安い friendly. (⇨遠慮 ❸, 気心) ●心安い(=親しい)友人 one's *close* /klóus/ friend. ●心安くなる become friends [*friendly*] 《*with* him》.

こころゆくまで ▶彼なら心安く(=遠慮せずに)何でも頼める I can ask him anything *without reserve*.

こころゆくまで 心ゆくまで to one's heart's content; (十分に) fully; to the full. ▶私たちは京都の秋を心ゆくまで楽しんだ We enjoyed an autumn trip in Kyoto *to our heart's content*./We *fully* enjoyed an autumn trip in Kyoto.

*__こころよい 快い__ 形 (人を満足させる) pleasant, (書) pleasing; (さわやかな) refreshing; (甘い) sweet. ●快い涼しいそよ風 a *refreshing* cool breeze. ●快くフルートの調べの *sweet* tones of a flute. ●虫の音が耳に快かった The chirps of insects were *pleasant* [*pleasing*] to the ear.
── **快く** 副 (自ら進んで) readily; (相手の意を汲んで) willingly; (喜んで) gladly. ●快く彼に金を貸す lend him money *willingly*. ●彼はこの案を快く承諾してくれた He *readily* consented to this plan. ●快くご援助いたします I'll *gladly* help you./I'll be *glad* to help you. ▶彼は私のことを快く思っていないらしい He seems to *be displeased* [*doesn't* seem to *be pleased*] *with* me.

こころよし 快し **快しとしない** don't think it is right 《to do》.

ここん 古今 ●古今の文学 ancient and modern literature; literature *of all ages*. ●古今を通じて最大の政治家 the greatest statesman *of all time* [*ages*]. ●古今東西の英雄 heroes *of all ages and countries*. ●これは古今未曽有(ず^ん)の大工事だ This *is the greatest construction in history [that has ever been* undertaken].

ごこん 語根 【言語】 the root (of a word).

ここんちょもんじゅう 『古今著聞集』 *Collection of Tales Heard, Present and Past.* (参考) 鎌倉時代の説話集)

ごさ 誤差 【数学】 an error. ●許容できる誤差の範囲 an allowable margin of [for] *error*; (専門語で, 許容誤差) (a) tolerance. ▶1 パーセント以内の誤差を見込んである[なら許容できる] An *error* of less than one percent will be allowed. ●プラスマイナス 3 パーセントの誤差がある There is a margin of *error* of plus or minus 3 percent.

ござ ●ござを敷く spread a *rush* [a *straw*] mat.

ごさい 後妻 ●後妻をもらう take a woman as one's second wife.

こざいく 小細工 a cheap trick. ●小細工を弄(^^)する play a *cheap trick* 《on》.

ございます 御座います [[「ある」の丁寧語]] (⇨ある) ▶お探しの品はこちらにございます The item you are looking for *is* here. ▶お世話になりましてありがとうございます Thank you very much for your kindness.

コサイン 【数学】 a cosine (略 cos).

こざかしい 小賢しい (抜け目のない) shrewd; (ずるい) cunning; (生意気な) impertinent.

こざかな 小魚 a small fish (魚~).

こさく 小作 tenant farming. ●小作する *tenant* a farm.
●小作制度 the tenant system. ●小作人 a tenant (farmer). ●小作料 (farm) rent.

こさじ 小匙 a teaspoon. (略 大匙) ●小さじ 2 杯分の砂糖 two *teaspoonfuls* of sugar.

こさつ 古刹 (由緒ある古い寺) a historic old temple.

こさつ 故殺 (激情から行う非計画的殺人) 【法律】 manslaughter.

ごさつ 誤殺 图 a wrong murder; killing a person by mistake.
── **誤殺する** 動 kill 《him》 by mistake.

コサック 〖南ロシアの民族〗 a Cossack.
●コサックダンス a Cossack dance.

こざっぱり 〖きちんとした〗 neat, tidy; 〖きれいな〗 clean. ▶彼女はいつもこざっぱりした服装をしている She's always *neatly* (*and plainly*) dressed./She always dresses *neatly*.

こさめ 小雨 (少量の) a light rain; (細かい) a drizzle. (⇨小降り) ▶小雨が降っている It's *raining lightly*./It's *drizzling*.

こさん 古参 (古顔) an old-timer.

ごさん 午餐 (⇨昼食)

ごさん 誤算 图 (a) miscalculation. ▶それは私の大きな誤算でした It was my serious *miscalculation*. ▶彼があんなふうに反応するとは誤算だった I *miscalculated* his reaction.
── **誤算する** 動 (やや書) miscalculate.

ごさんけ 御三家 (ある分野で有力な三つの存在) the big three. ●歌謡界の御三家 the *top three* singers of the song world.

:**こし 腰** 〖胴体のくびれた部分〗 a waist /wéist/; 〖ヒップ, しり〗 a hip (! waist の下で横に張り出た左右の腰骨の部分。通例その両方をさすので複数形で用いられる。日本語の腰は waist と hip を含む); 〖背中の下部〗 the lower back. ▶彼は腰まである流れの中を歩いた He walked through a *waist*-high stream of water.
① 【~型】 ●ほっそりした[太い]腰 a slender [a thick] *waist*. ●くびれた細い腰をしている have a wasp waist.
② 【腰が】 ▶彼は腰が細いのでズボンが落ちそうになる His *hips* are so narrow that his pants tend to fall [slip] down. ▶ベンチに長い間座っていたら腰が痛くなった I got a *backache* from sitting on the bench so long. ▶その老人は年で腰が曲がっている The old man is bent [*stoops*] with age.
③ 【腰の】 ●腰の細い女の子 a slender-[a slim-, a trim-]*waisted* girl. ●腰(=ひざ)の弱い相撲取り a weak-kneed sumo wrestler. (!【話】では比喩的に「弱腰の」の意にも用いられる)
④ 【腰に】 ●腰に巻く wrap 《it》 around the [one's] waist. ●腰に下げる hang 《it》 at the waist. ●彼女の腰に手を回す put one's arm around her *waist*. ▶彼女は両手を腰に当てて立っていた She stood (with her) hands on (her) *hips*./(やや古) She stood, arms *akimbo*. (事情 女性が相手に挑戦するときのジェスチャー) ▶彼女は腰にベルトをしていた She had a belt around her *waist*.
⑤ 【腰を】 ●腰をもむ massage [give massage to] the [one's] lower back. ▶彼は腰を浮かして(=座席から半は立ち上がって)私の方へ(握手のために)手を伸ばした He *half rose* from his *seat* and extended his hand to me. ▶彼は力がよく出るように腰を落としてかまえた He took [assumed] a *low position* [*posture*] so that he was able to [×could] put forth more power. ▶彼はソファの上にどすんと腰を下ろした He *sat down* heavily on the sofa. ▶彼は腰をかがめて来賓の前を通った He passed, *stooping*, before the honored guests. (事情 米英人は通例このような動作はしない) ▶そのおばあさんは腰を曲げて歩く The old woman walks with her *back* bent.
●腰がある ●腰があるうどん firm noodles.
●腰が重い (なかなか行動しない) be slow to act.
●腰が軽い (進んで行動する) be ready [willing] to act; (軽率に行動する) act hastily.
●腰が据(^^)わる become settled; (乳児が) become stabled.
●腰が低い (控えめだ) be modest [humble]; (礼儀正しい) be polite [courteous].
●腰が引ける be reluctant to do; get cold feet.
▶「僕にできるかなぁ…」彼は最初から腰が引けたようなこと

を言った "Well, can I really do it?" he said, looking only half-hearted in his attempt from the beginning.
- 腰を上げる ▶重い腰を上げて(=しぶしぶ)出かける be reluctant to go out; reluctantly go out.
- 腰を入れる (本気になる) become resolute; (腰に力を入れてまっすぐ立つ) straighten up one's back and stand erect.
- 腰を落ち着ける ▶彼はどこに勤めても腰が落ち着かない He never stays long in one place [job].
- 腰を折る 話の腰を折る interrupt (his) conversation [speech]; interrupt (him) in (his) speech.
- 腰を据(ﾌ)える ▶君は腰をすえてその仕事にとりかかりなさい You'd better *settle down to* the work./(打ち込みなさい) You must *concentrate on* [*put your mind to*] the work.
- 腰を抜かす ▶彼は腰を抜かした (立てなくなった) His knees gave under him./(ひどく驚いた) He was scared [frightened] stiff [to death].
- 腰を割る lower the center of gravity of one's body with one's legs apart.

こし 輿 〖昔の一人乗りのかご〗a palanquin (⇒玉の輿); 〖みこし〗a portable shrine.

こし 古紙 old paper; used paper. ● 古紙を再生して新製品を作る recycle *old* [*used*] *paper* and make it into new products.

こし 枯死 〖名〗 (草木が枯れること) death*; wither; blight.
—— 枯死する 〖動〗 die; wither; be blighted.

こじ 固持 —— 固持する 〖動〗 自説を固持する *persist in* one's opinion; *hold steadfastly on to* one's opinion. ● 自己の方針を固持する *stick by* one's principle.

こじ 固辞 —— 固辞する 〖動〗 refuse 《the offer》 firmly.

こじ 居士 〖出家せず仏道の修行をする男性の仏教徒〗a Buddhist layman; 〖男〗a man; 〖成人男性の戒名の下につける称号〗(説明的に) a deceased man's title following his posthumous name. ● 一言(ﾎﾟ)居士 a *man* who has something to say about everything.

こじ 孤児 an orphan (child 《複 children》). 〖!〗 orphan は時に父親または母親と死別した子供をさすことがある。● 戦争孤児 a war *orphan*. ● 孤児になる become [be left] an *orphan*; be orphaned.
- 孤児院 a home for orphans; an orphan home; an orphanage.

こじ 故事 (言い伝え) a legend; (起源) (an) origin.
- 故事来歴 the legend [origin] and history.

こじ 誇示 —— 誇示する 〖動〗 軍事力を誇示する *show off* [*make a show of*] military strength [power].

ごし 五指 the five fingers.
- 五指に入る ▶彼女の歌唱力は芸能界でも五指に入る She is one of *the top five* singers in the entertainment world.

-ごし -越し ❶〖場所〗 ▶肩越しに彼を見る look at him *over* one's shoulder. ▶新聞越しに彼をのぞき見る peep at him *from behind* one's newspaper. ▶垣根越しに隣の庭が見える Over [Through] the hedge I see the neighbor's garden. (〖!〗 over は「上を越えて」, through は「(生け垣のすき間)を通して」の意)
❷〖時〗▶彼とは10年越しの付き合いだ I have been friends [xa friend] with him *for* ten years./We have known each other *for* ten years.

こじ 誤字 〖誤った文字〗a wrong letter (〖!〗 letter はアルファベットの文字. ひらがな[漢字]の場合は wrong *hiragana* [*kanji*]); (英単語の) a misprint. ● 誤字だらけの作文 a composition full of *wrong letters*; a *badly misspelled* composition.

こしあげ 腰上げ (着物の) a tuck at the waist.

こじあける こじ開ける force [break*, wrench] 《a door》 (force は「無理に」, break は「壊して」, wrench は「ねじって」開けるの意); (針金などで錠を) pick 《a lock》. ● ピンで鍵をこじ開ける *pick* a lock with a pin.

こしあん 漉し餡 puréed /pjuréid/ sweet bean paste.

こしいた 腰板 〖障子・壁などの下部に張った板〗〖建築〗a wainscot, 《米》a baseboard, 《英》a skirting board; 〖はかまの〗the back stay.

こしいれる 腰入れる force ... 《into, between》. ▶その力士は腕を相手の腕の下にこじ入れた The *sumo* wrestler *forces* his arm under his opponent's arm.

コジェネレーション 〖熱電併給システム〗cogeneration (system).

こしお 小潮 (干満の差が最小の潮) a neap tide.

こしかけ 腰掛け a stool; (長いす) a bench. (⇒椅子)
- 腰かけ仕事 (仮の) a temporary job; (一時しのぎの) a stop-gap job.

こしかける 腰掛ける sit* down 《on》; take* a seat; seat oneself. (⇒座る)

こしき 古式 ● 古式ゆかしく (古来の慣習にのっとって)《perform》according to the ancient customs; (伝統的かつ優雅なやり方で) in an elegant and traditional way.

こじき 乞食 〖人〗a beggar; 〖行為〗begging. ● 乞食根性 a mean [a mercenary] spirit. ● 乞食をする beg; live by begging; beg for a living [one's meals].

こじき 〖古事記〗*The Record of Ancient Matters*. 〖参考〗太安万侶撰録の日本最古の歴史書

こしぎんちゃく 腰巾着 〖腰に下げる口をひもでくくった財布〗a money pouch [purse] hung at one's side; 〖勢力者のそばにまとわりついて離れない人〗a hanger-on 《複 hangers-on》.

こしくだけ 腰砕け ● 腰砕けになる break down [collapse, fail] (in the middle). ▶資金不足で腰砕けになった計画も数多くある Not a few projects *broke down halfway* [失敗に終わる) *fell through*] because money supply was not enough./Many plans *failed to materialize* for lack of funds. (〖!〗 materialize は「(計画・願望などが)具体化する」の意) ▶税制改革も腰くだけで終わった(=失敗した) The tax reform *has fallen through*.

こしけ 腰気 〚⇒〛下(ｼﾓ)の物.

ごしごし ▶ごしごしこする scrub. ● 石けんをつけて足をごしごし洗う *scrub* one's feet with soap and water. ▶彼女は床のしみをごしごしこすって取った She *scrubbed off* stains on the floor.

こしたんたん 虎視眈々 —— 虎視眈々と 〖形〗 vigilantly. ● 虎視眈々と機会をねらっている be watching *vigilantly* for a chance 《*of*; *to do*》.

ごしちちょう 五七調 alternating lines of five and seven syllables.

ごしちにち 五七日 35th day after 《his》 death.

こしつ 固執 〖名〗 〖しつこさ〗persistence; 〖固守〗adherence; 〖固執〗insistence.
—— 固執する 〖形〗 persist 《*in*》; (固守する) stick 《*to*》, 《書》adhere 《*to*》; (しがみつく) cling 《*to*》; (言い張る) insist 《*on*》. ▶彼は自説に固執する He *persists in*

[insists on, is set in] his opinions./He *never changes* his opinions.
こしつ 個室 one's (own) room; (病院などの) a private room; (寝台車の)《米》a (private) compartment.《❗》トイレつき.
ごじつ 後日 ▶後日(=後で)それをあなたに説明いたしましょう I'll explain it to you *later on* [*afterward*, (将来) *in the future*, (いつか) *someday*].
● 後日談 (続き・結果の話) a sequel《*to* the story [incident]》; (思い出) 《やや書》 recollections.
こしつき 腰付き (身のこなし) (a) bearing, (a) carriage; (足どり) a step, 《書》 a gait; (姿勢) a pose, a position, 《書》 (a) posture. ● 危ない腰つきで with unsteady steps; with an unsteady gait.
ゴシック Gothic.
● ゴシック建築 Gothic architecture. ● ゴシック体 『印刷』(肉太の活字体) boldface; (太字の活字) a bold(-faced) type.
こじつ sophistries, distorted [false] reasoning, stretching the fact.
こじつける use sophistries; (理屈で正当化する) justify … with false [distorted] reasoning; (でっち上げる) make … up.
ゴシップ 《a piece [a bit] of》gossip. (⇨噂(⁰ᵇᵃ)) ゴシップ好きの人, 《話》 a *gossipy* person. ▶彼らはゴシップの種になっている There has been lots of *gossip* about them./People are *gossiping* about them.
● ゴシップ欄 a gossip column.
ごじっぽひゃっぽ 五十歩百歩 ▶五十歩百歩だ They *are much the same*. ▶君の案もよくないが彼のも五十歩百歩だ Your idea is not good and his is *not any better*(, 書).
こしぬけ 腰抜け (臆病者) a coward /káuərd/; (気力のない人) a weak-willed person; (弱虫) a weak-kneed person, 《話》 a chicken; (女々しい男)《話》 a sissy.
こしばり 腰張り papering the lower part of a wall [a door].
こしひも 腰紐 a *koshihimo*; (説明的に) a cord tied around the waist, used under a sash for fixing a kimono.
こしべん 腰弁 『腰に弁当を下げること』hanging a lunch box at one's waist; (その弁当) a lunch box hung from one's waist; 『安月給取り』a low-salaried office worker.
こしぼね 腰骨 『解剖』the hipbone.
こしまわり 腰回り one's waist measurement. ▶彼の腰回りは80センチだ His *waist* is [measures] 80 centimeters *around*.
こしゃく 小癪 ── **こしゃくな** 形 (生意気な)《話》saucy, cheeky. ▶あいつはおれに口答えばっかりしやがるこしゃくながきだ He's a *saucy* brat, always talking back to me.
ごしゃく 語釈 名 an explanation of a word [a phrase].
── 語釈する 動 explain a word [a phrase].
こしゆ 腰湯 《take》 a hip bath.
こしゅ 戸主 the head of a family; a householder.
こしゅ 固守 ── **固守する** 動 (自陣を固守する) *defend* one's position *stubbornly*. ● 古い規則を固守する *stick to* [*keep to*] the old rules.
ごしゅ 語種 a lexical class.
こしゅう 固執 persistence. (⇨固執(ᵏ₃))
***ごじゅう** 五十 fifty; 『50番目の』the fiftieth. (⇨二十) ● 50年前 *fifty* years ago; *half a century* ago.
● 五十肩 (suffer from) a frozen shoulder.《❗》四十肩も同じ英語.
● 五重 ● 五重奏 『音楽』a quintet(te).
● 五重の塔 a five-storied pagoda.
ごじゅうおん 五十音 the Japanese (*kana*) syllabary. 《❗》 syllabary は「音節文字表」のことで, 日本語の場合は「五十音図」だ. ● 用例カードを五十音順に並べる arrange the citation slips in the order of *the Japanese syllabary*.
ごしゅうしょうさま ご愁傷さま (⇨愁傷)
こじゅうと 小舅 one's brother-in-law 《復 brothers-》.
こじゅうと(め) 小姑 one's sister-in-law 《復 sisters-》.
ごじゅうのとう 五重塔 『五重塔』 *The Five-Storied Pagoda*. 《参考》幸田露伴の小説.
ごしゅきょうぎ 五種競技 the pentáthlon. 《❗》その選手はa pentathlete.
こじゅけい 小綬鶏 『鳥』a bamboo partridge.
ごじゅん 語順 word order.
こしょ 古書 (古い本) an old book; (古本) a second-hand [a used] book.
こしょ 古所 the ancient Imperial Palace. (⇨皇居)
● 東宮御所 the Crown Prince's *Palace*.
***こしょう** 故障 名 『機械・からだなどの』trouble; 『機械・車などの突然の』a breakdown; 『機能停止』(a) failure. ● 故障車 a *broken-down* [《やや書》 *disabled*] car. ● 故障者リストに載る[から復帰する]『野球』go on [come off] the *disabled* list. ● エンジンの故障 (have) engine *trouble* [(an) engine *failure*]. ● 故障の原因を突きとめる locate the source of the *trouble*. ● 燃料系統に故障あるThe *trouble* is in the fuel line. ● バスの故障で学校に遅れた I was late for school because of the *breakdown* of the bus [because the bus *broke down*]. ▶その投手は60日故障者リストから戻された The pitcher was activated from the 60-day *disabled* list. ● 故障《掲示》 *Out of order./Out of use*.
── 故障する 動 go* [get*] *out of order* 《❗電話などと公共性の高い機械・機器などについて用いる》; 《車・機械などが》break* down 《❗状態を表すときは be broken down》. ▶エアコンが故障した My air conditioner *has got out of order* [*has gone wrong*]./I've *had* some *trouble with* my air conditioner. ▶彼がどうやってあなたに知らせられたって. あなたの電話は故障してたのよ How could he let you know? Your phone *was out of order* [*wasn't working*]. ▶エレベーターが突然故障して階と階の間で止まってしまった The elevator suddenly *broke down* [*had a* sudden *breakdown*] and stopped between floors. ▶この時計は故障している (=壊れている)This watch *is broken*. 《❗比較的小さいものには be broken down より be broken を用いるのが普通./(動かない) This watch *doesn't work* [*run*, ×*move*]. 《❗「ちゃんと動いていない」なら This watch *isn't working* [*running*] *right*.》/(どこかおかしい) *Something* is [*There is something*] *wrong with* this watch.
こしょう 小姓 a page 《*to* Hideyoshi》.
こしょう 呼称 (呼び名) a name 《*for*》.
── 呼称する 動 call, name; (体操のときの掛け声) call out (the) time.
こしょう 胡椒 (粉末) pepper; (実) a peppercorn.
● スープに胡椒を入れる *pepper* [put *pepper* in] the soup.
● 胡椒入れ《米》 a pépper shàker, 《英》 a pepper pòt. ● 胡椒ひき a pepper grinder [mill].
こじょう 古城 an old [an ancient] castle. ● 古城巡りの旅 a tour around the *old castle*.

こじょう 孤城 〖一つ離れた城〗an isolated [〖書〗a solitary] castle; 〖孤立して援軍のない城〗a helpless [〖書〗a besieged] castle.

ごしょう 後生 ▶後生だからここにいてくれ *For God's* [*Christ's, heaven's, goodness'*] *sake*, stay here (with me!) (⚠ 後の２語の方が響きがやわらかい) ▶彼女は彼からのラブレターを後生大事にしまっている She *treasures* the love letter from him.

こしょうがつ 小正月 the little New Year (January 15 by the lunar calendar).

ごじょかい 互助会 a mutual aid society; (共済組合) 《米》a benevolent [a benefit] society [association]; 《英》a friendly society.

ごしょく 誤植 a misprint, a typographical [a printing] error. ●誤植を直す correct *misprints*. ▶誤植のない本はない There's no book without a *misprint*.

こしょくそうぜん 古色蒼然 ▶古色蒼然とした寺 a very *old-looking* temple.

こしよわ 腰弱 ▶彼は腰弱だ(身体的に) He has *weak knees*. (⚠ 英語では「ひざ」を用いる)/(性格的に) He is *weak-knees*. (⇨弱腰)

*****こしらえる 拵える** ❶〖作る〗make*. (⇨作る) ▶洋服を２着こしらえてもらった I had two suits *made*.
❷〖建てる〗build*, 《やや書》construct. ▶彼らはあの大きな川に鉄橋をこしらえた They *built* [*constructed*] an iron bridge across that large river.
❸〖準備する〗prepare; (整える) arrange. ●朝食をこしらえる *prepare* [《主に米》*fix*] breakfast; *get* breakfast *ready*.
❹〖でっち上げる〗make*... up, invent (⚠ 前の方が口語的); 《やや書》fabricate. ▶彼はもっともらしい口実をこしらえるのがうまい He is good at *making up* [*inventing*] convincing excuses.
❺〖化粧する〗make* (oneself) up. ▶俳優たちは顔をこしらえていた The actors *were making up*.

こじらせる (物事を) complicate; (人間関係・病気を) make* (it) worse. (⇨悪化) ▶彼は風邪をこじらせた He *made* his cold *worse*./His cold *grew* [*got*] *worse*./He is suffering from complications of (the) flu.

ごじる 呉汁 *gojiru*; mashed soybean miso soup.

こじれる (物事が) become* complicated; (人間関係が) become complicated; (話が) go* [turn] sour; (病気が) get* [grow*] worse. ▶それではよけい話がこじれるだろう That will make things *worse*.

こじわ 小皺 fine wrinkles; (目尻のしわ) crow's-feet.
●小じわができ始める begin to get *small wrinkles*.
▶シャツの小じわをアイロンでのばす iron out the *little wrinkles* in a shirt. ▶目尻に小じわが出始めた *Fine wrinkles* started to appear around her eyes.

*****こじん 個人** 图 an individual. ▶社会は個人から成り立っている The community is made up of *individuals*.
── **個人(の)** 形 individual. (⇨個人的) ●個人経営の病院 a *private* hospital. ●英語の個人指導を受ける take *private* lessons [*personal* instruction] in English. ●学生に個人面接をする see [interview] one's students *individually*. ▶個人の権利を侵害してはいけない I don't infringe on [xin] the rights of the *individual* [the *individual's* rights]. ▶個人に関するデータの保護対策が必要である It is necessary to take measures to protect *personal* data.
●個人差 differences among individuals; individual variation(s). ●個人事業 sole proprietorship. ●個人主義 (⇨個人主義) ●個人種目 an individual event. ●個人消費 personal [private, individual] consumption. ●個人タクシー an owner-driven taxi. ●個人年金 a personal pension; an individual annuity. ●個人破産 personal bankruptcy. ●個人プレー an individualistic selfish behavior. ●個人輸入 private import.

こじん 故人 〖書〗【法律】the deceased (⚠ 単・複両扱い), (婉曲的に) the departed (⚠ 単・複両扱い). ●故人となる die; (婉曲的に) pass away. ●故人をしのぶ remember *the departed* [(名前を出して) the late Mr. A].

ごしん 誤診 a wrong diagnosis (翻 -noses /-si:z/).
── **誤診する** 動 ▶その子の病気をはしかと誤診する make [give] *a wrong diagnosis of* the child's sickness *as* measles; *wrongly diagnose* the child's sickness *as* measles.

ごしん 誤審 图 (審判の) (a) misjudgment; (裁判の) miscarriage of justice. 【法律】an error. ▶試合の結果を審判の誤審のせいにしてはならない We should not blame the outcome of the game on an umpire's *misjudgment* [*miscall*].
── **誤審する** 動 misjudge, miscall; make a misjudgment [a miscall]; blow a call.

ごしん 護身 self-defense. ●護身用のピストル a gun for *self-protection* [*self-defense*].
●護身術 an art of self-defense.

こじんしゅぎ 個人主義 图 individualism.
── **個人主義の** 形 individualistic.
●個人主義者 an individualist.

こじんてき 個人的 ── **個人的な** 形 (個人個人の) individual; (個人に関する) personal; (私的な) private. ●個人的な理由でチームをやめる quit one's job for *personal* [*private*] reasons. ▶私の個人的な意見では彼は間違っていないということです My *personal opinion* [*view*] is that he is not wrong./I *personally* think that he is right. ▶それは私の個人的なことです。あなたには関係ありません That's ˇmy *business*. Not ˋyours./That's my *personal* [*private*] affair.
── **個人的に** 副 individually; personally. ▶彼を個人的に知っているわけではない I have no *personal* acquaintance with him./I don't know him *personally*. ▶個人的には君の意見に賛成だ *Personally* [*Individually*], I agree with you.

こじんてきなたいけん『個人的な体験』 *A Personal Matter*. (参考) 大江健三郎の小説

こじんまり cozy. (⇨こぢんまり)

*****こす 越す, 超す** ❶〖越える〗(越えて行く) go* over ...; (横切る) cross, go across ...; (通り越して) pass (越える); 〖困難などを乗り越える〗get* over ..., (切り抜ける) get through .... ●峠を越す *go over* the (mountain) pass; (難関を) *pass* [*get over*] the crisis. (⇨峠) ●競争相手の先を越す(=より前を行く) *go ahead of* one's competitors. ▶暑さも峠を越した The heat *has passed* its peak.
❷〖時を過ごす〗spend*; (退屈しのぎに) pass. ●山小屋で冬を越す *spend* the winter in the mountain cottage.
❸〖超過する〗(数量などが超える) be over ..., (...より多い) be more than ...; (限度・程度を) exceed; 〖まさる〗be better than ..., (危機を) pass; 〖書〗excel (-ll-), surpass. (⇨超える ❷❸) ▶それにこしたことはない Nothing *can be better than* that./There's nothing like that./That *is* certainly *the best*. ▶もちろん安いにこしたことはない(=安ければ安いほどよい) The lower the price is, the better of course. ▶では高価な宝石は身につけない方がいい。用心にこしたこと

はないからね(=絶対安全だということはありえない) You shouldn't wear rich [expensive] jewels here. You can never be safe enough.
❹ [引っ越す] move. (⇨引っ越す)

こす 濾す [濾過,濾紙などを通して] filter; [茶こしなどで] strain. ●飲み水をこす *filter* drinking water.

こすい cunning. (⇨ずるい)

こすい 湖水 (the waters of) a lake.

こすい 午睡 a nap. (⇨⇨ 昼寝)

こすう 戸数 (家の数) the number of houses; [(世帯)] households.

こすう 個数 the number (*of* articles). ●荷物の個数を確かめる make sure of the *number of* bags.

こずえ 梢 the top of a tree, a tree top.

コスタリカ [[国名]] Costa Rica; (公式名) the Republic of Costa Rica. (首都 San José) ●コスタリカ人 a Costa Rican. ●コスタリカ(人)の Costa Rican.

コスチューム [[時代衣装]] a costume. ●ハロウィーンのコスチュームを着てin (a) Halloween *costume*.
●コスチュームプレー cosplay. (❗ *costume play* は「時代衣装を着けて演じる場内演劇」の意)

こすっからい 狡っ辛い (⇨ずるい)

コスト (a) cost. ●生産コスト the *cost* of production; pródúction còst. ●コストを削減する reduce [cut] *costs*. ●その計画はコストがかかりすぎる(=大金がかかる) The plan *costs* a great deal of money.
●コストアップ cost increase; an increase in (the) cost; 《和製語》a cost up. ●コストインフレ cost(-push) inflation. ●コストダウン a cost decrease; a decrease in (the) cost; 《和製語》a cost down. ●コストパフォーマンス cost performance.

ゴスペル [[黒人の宗教音楽]] a gospel (music).
●ゴスペルソング a gospel song.

コスモス [[植物]] a cosmos /kázməs/ (複 ~(es)).

コスモス [<ギリシャ語> [[宇宙]] the cosmos.

コスモポリタン [[世界人, 国際人]] a cosmopolitan /kàzməpálətn/.

*こする 擦る [[摩擦する]] rub (-bb-); [ごしごしみがく] scrub (-bb-); [こすって落とす] scrape. ●手をこすって暖める *rub* one's hands warm [to warm them, to get warmth]. ●泥を靴からこすり落とす *rub* the mud *off* [*from*] one's boots; *scrape* the mud *off* [*from*] one's boots. ●棒をこすり合わせて火をおこす make a fire by *rubbing* two sticks *together*.
●床をごしごしこすってきれいにする *scrub* the floor clean. ●こすった当たりのヒット a scratch hit [single]. ●三遊間へこすった当たりのヒットを打つ scratch out a hit to the hole (on the left side).

ごする 伍する (肩を並べる) rank (*with, among*); (仲間に入る) join; take part (*in*). ●天才に伍する *rank with* a genius. ●世界の列強に伍する *join* the great powers of the world.

ごすんくぎ 五寸釘 a long nail; (説明的に) a nail about six inches long.

*こせい 個性 [[個人の全特徴]] (a) personality; [他と異なる特徴] individuality; [[独創性]] originality.
●個性豊かな人 a person with [who has] a great deal of *personality*; a person of marked *individuality*. ●非常に個性的な作品 a work of great *individuality* [*originality*]; a very *individual* [*original*] work. ●個性が強い have a very strong *personality*. ●個性がある[ない] have [lack] *individuality*. ●個性を発揮できる仕事 a job in which one can show one's *individuality* [*originality*]. ▶生徒1人1人の個性を伸ばす[尊重する]必要がある We should develop [respect] the *individuality* of each student.

ごせい 語勢 [[音声]] emphasis, stress; (口調) a tone (of a voice). (⇨ 語気)

こせいぶつ 古生物 extinct animals and plants.
●古生物学 paleontology. ●古生物学者 a paleontologist.

こせがれ 小倅 (自分の息子の謙称) my son. ▶この小せがれめ！ You young [little] *brat* [《米》*punk*]! (❗ brat は「悪がき」の意で子供に対して, punk は「青二才, ちんぴら」の意で若者に対して用いる)

*こせき 戸籍 a family [a census] register. [[事情]] 米英には日本の戸籍に当たるものはない) ●戸籍を調べる inquire into (his) *family register*. ●戸籍に入れる[から抜く] have (his) name listed in [deleted from] the *family register*. ▶彼は戸籍上は私の息子でないり He is not my son *on the register* [not *lawfully* my son].
●戸籍抄本 an extract copy of 《his》family register. ●戸籍謄本 a full copy of 《his》family register.

こせき 古跡 (旧跡) a historic spot, a place of historical interest; (遺跡) historic remains, ruins.

こせこせ ──こせこせする worry over trifles; be fussy; be petty-minded. ●あの商人は取り引きがこせこせしている The merchant is *narrow and petty* in his dealings.

こぜに 小銭 small money; (small) change; (硬貨) a coin. ●小銭をお持ちですか Do you have some *change* [*coins*]? (「小銭をお願いします」に近い意) ▶小銭がなくなってしまって電話がかけられない I ran out of *coins* and can't make a phone call.
●小銭入れ a cóin [《米》a chánge] pùrse, 《英》a purse.

こぜりあい 小競り合い a (little [short]) skirmish. (❗ 戦闘・口論の両方に使える)

こせん 古銭 an old coin.

ごせん 互選 ●議長を互選で決める (選挙で) elect the chairperson *by vote* [*ballot*]; (話し合いで) choose the chairperson *by discussion*.

*ごぜん 午前 morning; a.m. [A.M.].

解説 **morning** は夜明けから正午まで, または夜12時から正午までの間をいう. **a.m.** [A.M.] は夜12時から正午までの時刻を示す数字のあとにつけて使う. 時刻表や見出し以外は通例小文字かスモールキャピタル (A.M.) が用いられ, 主に書き言葉. 《英》では通例ピリオドは省略される.

●午前3時に at three (o'clock) *in the morning* (❗ 慣用的に the を伴う.「5月1日午前3時に」は at three (o'clock) in [on] the morning of May 1 で, in の場合 morning の後に音の休止がありその時刻であることを, on の場合 on の前に休止があり時刻を強調する. 書き言葉では前の方は On May 1 at three (o'clock) in the morning の方が明確な言い方); at 3 a.m. [A.M.]. (❗ at 3や at 3 o'clock *a.m.* [A.M.] は不可) ●午前7時2分の京都行き電車に乗る take the 7:02 *a.m.* [A.M.] (train) for Kyoto. (❗ 7:02 は seven 6 /óu/ twó と読む. (2) 時刻表は通例24時間制なので, 紛らわしくない場合は take the 7:02 (train) for Kyoto だけでよい) ▶午前中に雨が激しく降った It rained heavily *in the morning*. (❗ It has rained…. と完了形を用いれば午前中に発話されたことになる) ▶私は土曜の午前中に外出しています I'm out (*on*) Saturday *morning*(s). (❗ (1) 特定の曜日の「午前」には前置詞 on をつけるが,《主に米英》は通例省略される. (2) 複数形は「いつも」を強調. 単に「午前中はいつも外出しています」であれば I'm always out *in the morn-*

ごぜん *ing(s)*./《主に米》I'm always out *mornings*. となる. このことは afternoon, evening, night にも当てはまる) ▶彼は今日[昨日]午前中に大阪を発った He left Osaka this [yesterday] *morning*.
- **午前様**〔行為〕coming home in the small hours after having fun;〔人〕a person who comes home in the small hours after having fun.

ごぜん 御前〔天皇・貴人の前〕the presence of the Emperor [a person of high rank].
- **御前会議** an Imperial Council; a conference in the presence of the Emperor. ●**御前試合** a match [a game] in the Imperial presence.

ごぜん 御膳〔『食事, 飯』の丁寧語〕(⇨食事, 飯)●天ぷらご膳 a set meal with a dish of *tempura*, a bowl of rice, a bowl of soup, a simmered dish and a little bowl of delicacies.
●**御膳汁粉** a sweet broth made of smoothly strained adzuki bean paste with a piece of rice cake in it. ●**御膳そば** high-quality white *soba* noodles.

ごせん 五線紙《a sheet of》music paper.
ごせんふ 五線譜 a score.

-こそ ❶【意味を強める】▶これこそ(=これはまさに)私が捜していたペンです This is *the very* pen I have been looking for. ▶自分自身の子供をもってこそはじめて親の愛情が分かる We *cannot* appreciate the love of our parents *until* we have our own children./*It is not until* we have our own children *that* we can appreciate the love of our parents. ▶私こそ一言お礼を申さねばなりません It is I who should express a word of thanks. (❗(1) I を強めた強調構文. (2) 日常的には It's mé that should say thank you. や, 簡単に「こちらこそ」Thank yóu. のようにいう) ▶冬に雪があってこそ北海道だ(=冬に雪のない北海道なんて考えられない) I can't imagine Hokkaido without snow in 《主に米》the) winter. ▶今度こそきっと全力を尽くそう I'm sure I will do my best this time. (❗/ *this* time と強く読む)
会話「座りなさい, 友子. 見えないよ」「あなたこそ立ちなさいよ」"Sit down, Tomoko. I can't see!" "No. You stand up *instead*." (❗ このように強調する場合, 命令文でも よう を使う)
会話「口いっぱいにほおばったままでしゃべらないで」「じゃあ, あんたこそやめてよ」"Don't talk with your mouth full." "Don't you do it, then." (❗ you を強く読む)

DISCOURSE
親こそ子供に食卓での行儀を教えるべきだ *It is* parents *who* **should** teach children table manners. (❗ should (…すべきだ) は主張を表すディスコースマーカー)

❷【一応の肯定を表す】(…だがしかし) but; (…であるけれども) though .... ▶彼は私をほめこそすれ, 決して笑わなかった *Though* he praised me, he never laughed at me.

こぞう 小僧〔少年〕a boy;〔商店の〕a shop boy (❗文脈があれば shop は省略可);〔寺の〕a young Buddhist disciple /dɪsáɪpl/. ▶いたずら小僧 a mischievous *boy*.

ごそう 誤送 wrong shipment.
ごそう 護送〔囚人護送車《米》a police [a patrol,《話》a paddy] wagon;《英》a police van;《英話》a Black Maria /məráɪə/.
── **護送する 動** ●囚人を護送する *send* prisoners *in a patrol wagon* [*under guard*].

ごぞう 五臓 the five viscera. (参考) 肺臓 (lungs)・心臓 (heart)・脾臓 (spleen)・肝臓 (liver)・腎臓 (kidneys)をさす
- **五臓六腑** five viscera and six entrails;〔内臓〕《書》the bowels, the internal organs. ▶暑い日の冷たいビールは五臓六腑にしみわたる A glass of cold beer on a hot day seeps into *every part of my body* [*every pore of my skin*].

こぞうのかみさま 小僧の神様』 *The Shopboy's God*. (参考) 志賀直哉の小説

こそく 姑息 ── 姑息な 形 ●姑息な手段を取る take a *stopgap* [*a makeshift*] measure.
ごそくろう 御足労 ●ご足労いただきありがとうございます Thank you very much for *taking the trouble to come here*./Thanks. I appreciate *your coming* 〈over〉. ▶署までご足労願えませんか Could you come to the police station with me?

こそげる〔削り落とす〕scrape ... out. ●靴底の泥をこそげる *scrape* the mud *off* [《米話》*off of*] the sole of one's shoe.

こそこそ〔ひそかに〕secretly;〔人目を忍んで〕stealthily /stélθɪli/;〔人の陰で〕behind《his》back. ●こそこそささやく whisper. ●こそこそ《部屋から》出て行く *steal* [*sneak*] out (of the room). ▶彼はこそこそ何かやっている He is doing something *secretly* [*behind our back*].

ごそごそ ●ごそごそ動く bustle; rustle /rʌsl/. ●机の中の書類をごそごそかき回す *bustle* papers around in the desk drawer. ▶暗やみで何かごそごそ動いた Something *rustled* in the dark.

こそだて 子育て child raising. (⇨育児) ●子育ての問題をかかえている have a *child raising* problem. ▶子育ての話になると私たちはいつも意見が合わない We always disagree when we talk about *bringing up children* [*child raising*].

こぞって ●その法案にこぞって(=一致して)賛成する agree to the bill *unanimously* [(例外なく) *without exception*]. ●一家こぞって(=家族全員が)そのパーティーに行った The *whole* [*All* the] family went to the party.

こそで 小袖〔昔の袖の短い普段着〕(説明的に) a short-sleeved casual kimono worn in the old days;〔絹の綿入れ〕a padded silk garment.

こそどろ こそ泥 a sneak;〔けちな〕a petty thief (複 thieves); a pilferer;〔壁などを伝って侵入する〕a cat burglar.

こそばゆい ticklish. (⇨くすぐったい)

ごぞんじ 御存知 (⇨知る) ●ご存知のとおり... As you *know*, ... ●ご存知かもしれませんが Perhaps you *know*...; You may *know*.... ▶あとはご存知のとおりです The rest is history. (❗ 身の上話などを締めくくる慣用表現) ▶あれ, ご存知の方だったのですか Well, do you *know* him [her] ?/Well, is he [she] your *acquaintance*?
会話「宮沢さんをご存知ですか(=面識がありますか)」「ピアニストの方ですか. お名前は存じておりますが, お会いしたことはありません」"Do you *know* Ms. Miyazawa ?" "A pianist? I *know* her name [I've *heard of* her], but I've never met her personally." (❗ Do you know... と直接的に聞くより Do you happen to know ... とか Do you know ..., by any chance? (もしやご存知...)とした方が心くばりのある言い方になることがある)

こたい 固体 名 a solid (body). ▶ドライアイスは固体から直接気体になる Dry ice goes directly from a *solid* to a gas.
── **固体の 形** solid.
●**固体燃料** solid fuel.

こたい 個体 an individual.
●**個体差** an individual difference. ●**個体発生**

こだい 〚生物〛 ontogeny, ontogenesis. ● **個体変異** individual variation.

こだい 古代 ancient [old] times. (⚠ 前の方が古い) ● 古代エジプト人 the *ancient* Egyptians. ● **古代史** ancient history. (参考) 西洋史では西ローマ帝国滅亡の476年以前をさす) ● **古代人** ancient people, 《やや書》 the ancients. ● **古代文明** ancient civilization.

こだい 誇大 ― 誇大な 形 ● 誇大な(=誇張された)広告 an *exaggerated* [《おおような》a *sensational*] advertisement. ● 誇大に表現する exaggerate 〈it〉; express 〈it〉 *exaggeratedly*.
● **誇大妄想** 〚医学〛 megalomania /mègəlouméiniə/; delusions of grandeur /grǽnʒəɾ/. ● 誇大妄想の人 a megalomaniac.

ごたい 五体 ● 五体満足な(= 健康で正常な)子 a *healthy and normal* child.

こだいこ 小太鼓 a small drum; 《響線つきの》a snare [a side] drum.

ごだいこ 五大湖 the Great Lakes.

ごだいしゅう 五大州 (⇨五大陸)

ごたいそう ご大層 (⇨大袈裟)

ごたいりく 五大陸 the Five Continents. (参考) アジア(Asia)・ヨーロッパ(Europe)・アフリカ(Africa)・アメリカ(America)・オーストラリア(Australia)をさす. オーストラリアの代わりにアメリカを南北に分けて数えることもある)

***こたえ 答え** 〚解答〛 an answer; 《計算などによる》 a solution; 〚返事〛 an answer, a reply (⚠ 後の方は堅い語); 〚応答〛 a response. ▶私にはその問題の答えが分からない I don't know the (correct) *answer* to the question [解決法] the (correct) *solution* to the problem〉. ▶その生徒の答えは間違っていた The pupil's *answer* was wrong./The pupil gave the [×a] wrong *answer*. (⚠ a を用いると「一つだけ間違っていた」の意となる) ▶ドアをノックしたが、返事はなかった I knocked on [at] the door, but there was no *answer* [*response*]. ▶それでは答えになっていない That's no *answer*./《私の質問に答えていない》 You're not *responding* to my question. (⚠ 後の方が普通) ▶それでお答えになっているでしょうか That *answered* it?

こたえられない ▶暑い日のビールの1杯はこたえられない *There is nothing like* a beer on a hot day. ▶彼の軽井沢の別荘は夏にはちょっとこたえられない魅力がある His villa in Karuizawa is simply *out of this world* in summer.

***こたえる 応える** ❶ 〚痛感される〛 come* [〚やや話〛 be brought] home 〈to〉; 〚つらい〛 be hard 〈on〉; be trying 〈for〉; 〚悪影響する〛 take* one's toll, 《書》 tell* 〈on〉. ▶父の言葉が胸にこたえた(= 痛切に感じられた) My father's words *came home to* me. ▶彼女の死は彼にかなりこたえた Her death *was* pretty *hard on* him./He *took* her death pretty *hard*. ▶働き過ぎると体にこたえますよ Overwork will *take its toll* [*tell*] *on* your health [you]. ▶今日の暑さはこたえる I really *feel the heat* today.
❷ 〚応じる, 報いる〛《反応として》answer, reply 《to》, respond 《to》(⚠ この順に堅い言い方で, respond は内容的主に反応の仕方に重点がある); 《要求などを満たす》meet*. ▶多くの要望にこたえて *in answer* [《やや書》 *reply*, 《書》 *response*] *to* many requests. ● 時代の要請にこたえる satisfy [meet] the demand of the age. ● 期待にこたえる come up to [live up to, meet]〈their〉 expectations. ▶私が手を振ると、彼女はうなずいてこたえた When I waved to her, she *replied* with a nod [*by* nodding]. (⚠ …, she nodded *in reply*. ともいえるが堅い言い方) ▶尚子はスタンドからの大声援にこたえて最後の力をふりしぼってスパートをかけた Naoko *responded to* a great cheer from the stands by putting on a spurt with the last of her strength. ▶助けを求める彼の叫びにこたえる人はいなかった His cry for help went *unanswered*.

*:**こたえる 答える** answer; 《改まって》《やや書》reply 《to》(⚠ 文書で答えることを暗示することがある).

解説 answer が answer A (人)+B (質問など)の文型で用いられるのは, *Answer* me this [that] (question). (この[その]質問に答えてください)のような決まった言い方に限られており, ×Answer this [that] (question) *to* me. の語順は不可.

● はっきりと答える answer definitely; give a definite *answer*. ● 質問に答える answer [reply to] a question. (⚠ ×answer to [reply] a question は不可. answer が名詞のときは to が必要(⇨返答)) ▶彼は私の質問には答えなかった He didn't *answer* [*respond to*] my question./He didn't *answer* me. (⚠ 後の方は質問だけでなく話しかけられて返事をする場合などにも用いる) ▶To my question he didn't *answer*. (⚠ my question を強調する言い方. このような場合以外, 前の他動詞用法が普通) ▶彼はそれには何も答えなかった He gave no *answer* to that./He *made* [*gave*] no *reply* to that. ▶何と答えてよいか分からなかった I did not know what to *reply* [*what* to *say in reply*]./I was at a loss for an *answer*. ▶ 彼はそれを知っていると答えた He answered (me) [*replied* (*to* me)] *that* he knew it./"I know it," he answered [*replied*]. (⚠ 直接話法で用いるのは主に書き言葉. 会話では He said, "I know it." が普通)

こだかい 小高い elevated. ● 小高い丘 a small [low] hill; a (slight) rise.

こだから 子宝 ● 子宝に恵まれる have [《書》 be blessed with] children [a child].

ごたく 御託 (くどくどとした話) a tedious [《書》 a repetitious] talk. ● ごたくを並べる talk *tediously* 《about》; harp on 《about》.

こだくさん 子沢山 ▶彼は子だくさんだ He has *a lot of children*./He has a large family. ▶貧乏人の子だくさん《ことわざ》The poor have *large families*.

ごたごた 名 《もめ事》(a) trouble; (口げんか) a quarrel; (論争) (a) dispute. ● 会社間の賃金をめぐるごたごた a *dispute* 《特に長い》a *wrangle*》 *with* the management over pay. ● ごたごたを起こす cause *trouble*. ▶彼の家にはごたごたが絶えない There is no end to the *trouble* in his family. ▶あの夫婦は何かごたごたがあったそうだ The couple is said to have had a *quarrel* [《話》 a *row* /ráu/]. ▶「何か」にひかれて *some* quarrel [row] としないこと)
── ごたごた 副 ▶彼の部屋にはいろんな物がごたごた置いてあった Various things were lying about *untidily* in his room.
── ごたごたしている 動 ❶ 〚忙しい〛 be too busy, be occupied. ▶私たちは月末はいつもごたごたしている We are always *too busy* toward the end of a month.
❷ 〚乱れている〛 be in disorder, be messy. ▶その部屋はごたごたしていた The room *was* (*in*) *a mess* [*was messy*].

こだし 小出し ● 小出しにする take … out [give …] *little by little* on many occasions. (⚠ take out は「取り出す」の意)

こだち 木立 a grove; a clump of trees.

こたつ 炬燵 a *kotatsu*. ● 電気ごたつ an electric *kotatsu*. ● こたつで丸くなる curl oneself up under

ごたつく a *kotatsu*. ▶日本では冬になると四角いやぐらに布団をかけたこたつと呼ばれる暖房器具を使い、手や足を暖めながらだんらんを楽しむ In Japan in ((主に米)) the) winter, people use a heater called *kotatsu*, which is attached to a square wooden frame and is covered with a thick quilt, and under this they enjoy conversation, warming their hands and feet.

ごたつく (⇨ごたごた) 🈩 🈔 🈕

こだて 戸建 a house. ●一戸建て)

こだね 子種 (子供) a child; 〖法律〗 one's issue; one's offspring. ; (精子) a sperm. ▶彼には子種がない He has no *children* 〖*sterile*〗. (❗*childless* は「欲しいのに子供がない」、sterile は「生殖力がない」の意)
● **子種を宿す** ▶彼女は子種を宿している(=妊娠している) She is *pregnant*.

ごたぶん 御多分 ● **ご多分に漏れず** just like other people [men, women] (例外ではない) not an exception. ▶金持ちは世事に疎いというが、彼らご多分に漏れない I hear that rich people don't know much of the world, and he *is no exception*.

こだま 木霊 🈩 an echo (俚 ~es).
──**こだまする** 🈔 echo. ▶我々の叫び声は山々にこだました Our shouts *echoed* over the hills./The hills *echoed with* [*to*] our shouts./(やや書) The hills *echoed* (*back*) our shouts.

*こだわる ● 服装にこだわる(=うるさい) be particular [(いやになるほどうるさい) fussy] about one's clothes.
● 伝統にこだわる(=固執する) stick to the tradition.
● 結果にこだわる take the result too seriously.

こたん 枯淡 🈩 (さりげない単純さ) casual simplicity.
──**枯淡の** 🈔 simple and refined. ▶彼の絵画は枯淡の境地に達している His painting has attained a state of *subdued refinement*.

こち 鯒 〖魚介〗 a flathead.

こちこち ❶ 〖固くなる〗 stiffen, become* [get*, turn] stiff; (乾燥して固くなる) become dry and hard. ● こちこちに凍る be frozen *hard*. ▶パンは古くなるとこちこちになる Old bread becomes *dry and hard*.
❷ 〖緊張して固くなる〗 become* tense. ▶彼女は大勢の前でこちこちになる She becomes *tense* [*tenses up*] in public.
❸ 〖頑固である〗 be stubborn; (融通がきかない) be inflexible. ▶彼はこちこちの父権主義者だ He is a *stubborn* [〖書〗a *stiffnecked*] patriarchist.
❹ 〖時計がこちこちいう〗 tick. ▶時計がこちこちいうのが聞こえた I could hear the clock *ticking* (*away*). (❗「時計のこちこちいう音」は the *tick*(*ing*) of a *clock*)

ごちそう 御馳走 〖もてなし〗 a treat; 〖豪華な食事〗 a gorgeous dinner, a feast; 〖おいしい食物〗 delicious [excellent] food; 〖すてきな料理〗 a nice dish. ● ごちそうをする prepare *something special* 《*for* dinner》; cook a *special dinner*. ▶わあ、ごちそうだね What a *treat*!/(おいしそうだと) Doesn't this look \ good! ▶どうもごちそうさま I really enjoyed the meal./That was a wonderful dinner [meal]. ●米英では決まった言い方はない。食事に招かれて帰り際には Thank you for the nice dinner. のように食事だけの礼を述べるのは失礼で、It was a wonderful [delightful] evening. とか Thank you for this evening, I've really enjoyed it. などという。▶君に昼食をごちそうする(=おごる)よ I will *treat* you *to* lunch./Let me *buy* you lunch. (❗buy は目上の人には用いない ⇨ 奢(おご)る)

▶彼の家で夕食をごちそうになった(=食事に招かれた) I *was invited* to his house *for dinner*.
〖会話〗「僕は礼子に会うまで、人をこんなに愛せるとは思わなかった」「いやはや、ごちそうさま」 "Before I met Reiko, I didn't believe that I could be so much in love with anyone else." "Well, well, that's very interesting." (❗ (1) I can be in love… は時制の一致で could となる。(2)「ごちそうさま」は…that's very interesting. (興味深い話ですね)といいながらこう言うしかなくて結構です」の意を表し、この後は通例話題を変える)

こちゃく 固着 🈩 sticking, 〖書〗adhesion; 〖心理〗 fixation.
──**固着する** 🈔 stick 〖〖書〗adhere〗《*to*》.
──**固着剤** a binder.

ごちゃごちゃ 🈩 (乱雑な) untidy, messy; (頭が混乱した) confused, 〖話〗mixed-up. ● ごちゃごちゃした部屋 an *untidy* [a *messy*, a *disorderly*] room. ● (小説などの)ごちゃごちゃした筋 a *messy* [a *complicated*] plot. ▶台所はごちゃごちゃしていた The kitchen was (*in*) *a mess* [was *messy*]. ▶私は頭の中がまったくごちゃごちゃだった I *was* utterly *confused*. ▶机の上にはごちゃごちゃいろんな物があった All kinds of things *were jumbled* (*up*) on the desk. (⇨ごちゃ混ぜ)
──**ごちゃごちゃにする** 🈔 mix up, confuse 《*with*》. (⇨混同する)

ごちゃまぜ ごちゃ混ぜ ● ごちゃ混ぜにする (混ぜ合わせる) mix … (up) 《*with*》 (❗up がある方が強意的. up がある場合しばしば受け身で「(他の人・物と)混同する」、「雑然とした状態にする」の意に用いる); (雑然とした状態にする) jumble 《*up*, *together*》 (❗通例受身で). ● 仕事と遊びをごちゃ混ぜにする mix business *with* pleasure; *mix* business *and* pleasure *together*. ▶机の上は本と書類がごちゃ混ぜになっていた Books and papers *were jumbled* [*up together*)] on the desk./Books and papers *were mixed up* on the desk./There was a *jumble* [a *mix*] of books and papers on the desk.

こちょう 誇張 🈩 (an) exaggeration; (言葉の上での) (an) overstatement. ▶彼は天性のスポーツマンだといっても誇張ではない It is no *exaggeration* [It is not too much] to say that he is a born athlete. (⇨過言)
──**誇張する** 🈔 exaggerate; overstate. ● 誇張した exaggerated. ● 誇張して exaggeratingly. ▶それはひどく誇張されている That *is* greatly [grossly] *exaggerated*.

ごちょう 伍長 〖軍隊〗a Corporal.

ごちょう 語調 a tone (of voice); (口調) ● 語調を和らげる [強める] soften [raise] one's *voice*; tone down [up] one's *voice*.

こちょうらん 胡蝶蘭 〖植物〗a phalaenopsis.

*こちら ❶ 〖この場所〗here; 〖この方向〗this way. (⇨こっち) ● 川のこちら側に on *this* side of the river. ● こちらにっては、当地はとても寒い It's very cold *here*./It's very cold *out* [*in*, *over*] *here*. (❗out は屋外にいて、in は屋内にいて、over は遠くにいる人に対していう場合) ● こちらへどうぞ (案内して) (Come) *this way*, please./(離れた所にいる人に向かって) Over *here*, please./(丁寧に) If you (would) come *this way*, sir [madam]. ▶はいこちらです。そちらではありません The station is *this way*, not that way. ▶彼らはそこからこちらへ向けてまだ歩いているのだろう They're probably still walking (to) *here* from there. (❗*to* here は *from* there に対する臨時の名詞用法)
❷ 〖これ、この人〗this. ▶こちらの方がそちらより値段が高い *This* (one) costs more than that (one).

▶(紹介して)こちらは兄の浩です *This is my older brother Hiroshi.* (▶特に必要がなければolder, youngerの区別をして紹介することはない)/(くだけて) *This here's Hiroshi, my brother.*
❸[私], I; (電話で) this; (私たち) we. ▶そちらが悪いのだ. こちらに責任はない *You are to blame. I'm not responsible for that.* ▶こちらは皆元気です *We [My family] are all fine.* (▶*My family is* all fine. ということも多い) ▶(電話で)こちらは山田ですがそちらは田中さんですか *This is Yamada (speaking). Is that* [×*this*] *Mr. Tanaka?* (▶(1) *Yamada here.* ともいえる. ×*I am Yamada.* ×*Are you Mr. Tanaka?* とはいわない. (2) 会社などでは次のような言い方もする: こちらは海星病院です *You've reached the Kaisei Hospital.*)
会話 「5日に帰るから. 会うのを楽しみにしているよ」「こちらもよ. お電話ありがとう」"*I'll be back on the 5th. I'm really looking forward to seeing* [×*to see*] *you.*" "*Same here. Thanks a lot for calling.*"

こぢんまり (暖かくて居心地がよい) cozy, snug (-gg-); (こぎれいで整った) neat. ●こぢんまり(と)した部屋 a *cozy* [a *snug*, a *neat*] *small* room.
翻訳のこころ 目立たないけれどこぢんまりとした, いい美術館だった(江國香織『デューク』) *It was an inconspicuous but cozy art museum.*

こつ (やや話) a [the] knack 《*of, for*》, 《話》the hang 《*of*》; (熟練の要る) (an) art. ●こつは心得ている *have the art of* acting. ●こつを覚える [忘れる] *get* [*lose*] *the knack* [*the hang*] 《*of*》. ▶いったんこつを覚えてしまえば簡単だ *Once you get the knack it's easy.* ▶その戸を開けるにはこつがある *There's a knack to* [*in*] *opening the door.*

こつ 骨 a bone; (遺骨) ashes, remains. ●お骨を拾う [納める] gather [bury] one's *ashes*.
●骨揚げ (説明的に) gathering ashes with chopsticks and putting them in an urn.

ごつい [ごつごつした] rough, craggy; [頑丈な] sturdy, stout; (こわれにくい) rugged /rʌ́gid/. ●ごつい手 a *rough* hand. ●ごつい靴 *sturdy* [*thick*] boots. ●ごつい(=武骨な感じのする)二枚目 a *ruggedly* handsome man. (❗ rugged(ly) は はめ言葉)

*こっか 国家 (民族集団としての) a nation; (政治的な) a state; (主に地理的な) a country (⇨国); [政府] government. ●近代国家 a modern *nation* [*state*]. ●資本主義国家 a capitalist *country*. ●単一[多]民族国家 a one-race [a multiracial] *nation*. ●国家に尽くす serve one's *country*. ●国家的見地から見ると from a *national* point of view. ●国家と個人はどちらが優先するか Which comes first, *nation* or self? (▶対比による無冠詞に注意) ▶その国家の存亡は彼の外交手腕にかかっていた *The fate of the nation rested on his diplomacy.*
●国家管理 state [government] control. ●国家権力 state power; the power of the state. ●国家公務員 a government official. ●国家財政 national [state] finance; (特定の国の) the country's finances. ●国家試験 a national [a state] examination. ●国家主義 nationalism. ●国家主義者 a nationalist. ●国家的行事 a national event.
こっか 国花 a national flower.
こっか 国歌 a national anthem. ●フランス国歌 (sing [play]) *the national anthem of France.*

*こっかい 国会 (日本・デンマークなどの) the Diet; (米国・中南米の共和国の) (the) Congress (❗ 通例無冠詞); (英国・カナダ・英国自治領の) Parliament; (国民の代表の会議) a national assembly (❗ 単・複両扱い); (立法府) a legislature, a legislative body (❗ ともに単・複両扱い); (特に二院制の) the House.

解説 日本以外の国々の国会で, 特に米国や英国などの国会は, 通例日本語では米国議会のように「議会」と呼ばれる.

●通常[特別; 臨時; 延長]国会 an ordinary [a special; an extraordinary; a prolonged] *Diet* session. ●国会を解散[召集]する dissolve [convene, summon] *the Diet*. ●国会は現在閉会[開会]中である *The Diet is now in recess* [《やや書》in session, 《やや書》sitting]. ▶その法案は国会の承認を得た *The bill was approved in the Diet.* ▶日本の国会は英国議会にならって作られた *The Japanese Diet was modeled after the British parliament.* (❗ この場合 parliament の p は小文字)
●国会議員 (日本の) a member of the Diet, a dietman [(女性) a dietwoman]; (米国の) a member of Congress, a Congressman [(女性) a Congresswoman] (❗ (1) いずれも特に下院議員をさす. (2) 女性解放運動家は a Congressperson を好む. (3) 上院議員は a Senator); (英国の) a Member of Parliament (略 an M.P.) (❗ 通例下院議員をさす. 上院議員は a Lord). ●国会議事堂 (日本の) the Diet Building; (米国の) the Capitol (❗ a capitol は米国の州議会議事堂をさす); (英国の) the Houses of Parliament. ●国会審議 consideration in the Diet. ●国会中継 a broadcast from the Diet. ●国会提出 submission to the Diet.
●国会答弁 an answer [a reply] in the Diet.
こっかい 黒海 the Black Sea.
*こづかい 小遣い [定期的に与えられる] 《米》an allowance, 《英》pócket mòney 《書留》米英とも子供の小遣いは通例週1回与えられる); [小遣い銭] 《話》pócket [spénding] mòney. ●小遣いかせぎにアルバイトをする work part-time for [to earn] *pocket money*. ▶彼は月1万円の小遣いをもらっている *He receives* [*is given*] *an allowance of 10,000 yen a month.*

*こっかく 骨格 [体格] (a) build, (a) frame; (特に男の) a physique; [建物などの骨格] a framework. ●骨格のがっちりした男 a man with [(主に英) of] a sturdy *build* [a powerful *physique*]; a sturdily-*built* [《英》a sturdily-*set*] man. ▶彼は骨格がほっそりしている *She has a slender frame.*
こっかん 酷寒 (⇨極寒)
ごっかん 極寒 (the) severe [bitter, intense] cold.
●極寒に耐える bear [stand] *severe cold*.

*こっき 国旗 a national flag; (船舶・軍隊の国旗の colors (⇨旗)) ●国旗を掲揚する hoist [raise] *the national flag*. ●英国国旗を掲げた船 a ship under the Queen's [the King's] *colors*. ▶星条旗はアメリカ合衆国の国旗です *The Stars and Stripes is* [×*are*] *the national flag of the United States.*

関連 各国国旗の呼称: 英国 the Union Jack/米国 The Stars and Stripes/中国 the Five-Star Red Flag/フランス the Tricolor/日本 the Rising-Sun (Flag).

こっきしん 克己心 [自制心] self-control, self-restraint; [禁欲] self-denial. ●克己心のある人 a *self-denying* person.
こづきまわす 小突き回す (つついてゆすり回す) push [shove]... around [about]; (いじめる) ill-treat, tease, bully. ▶彼は胸ぐらをつかまれて乱暴にこづき回された *He was grabbed and roughly shaken by*

the lapels.

こっきょう 国教 a state religion. ● 英国国教会 the Church of England; the Established [Anglican] Church. (!〈英〉で church は国教会の教会のみをさす)

こっきょう 国境 (国境地方) the frontier; (川・山など他国との地理的境界) the border; (国境線) the boundary. ● 国境を侵す violate the border [*frontier*]. ● 国境を越えて逃げる escape across *the border*. ● 中国の国境を越えてモンゴルに入る cross the Chinese *border* into Mongolia. (!「中蒙(ﾓｳ)国境」は *the* Chinese-Mongolian *border*, between China and Mongolia) ▶ フランスは東でドイツと国境を接している France *borders on* [×with] Germany on the east. ▶ 音楽に関する限り国境は急速に消滅してきている The *national border* is rapidly disappearing as far as music is concerned.
● 国境なき医師団 Doctors Without Borders.
● 国境なき記者団 Reporters Without Borders.
● 国境紛争 a border dispute [(武力衝突) clash].

コック 〖水道・ガスなどの栓〗 a tap, a cock; (蛇口) 〈米〉a faucet.

コック 〈オランダ語〉〖料理人〗 a cook /kʊk/.
● コック長 a head [a chief] cook; a chef /ʃef/ (⦿ ~s).

こづく 小突く (指・棒などで) poke; (押す) push; (ひじで) elbow; (注意・合図のため軽くひじで) nudge. (⇨つく)

コックス 〖舵手(ﾀﾞｼｭ)〗a cox, 〈書〉a coxswain /kɑ́ksn, kɑ́kswèin/. ● 早稲田のコックスをつとめる cox [*coxswain*] the Waseda boat [eight]; cox [*coxswain*] for Waseda.

コックピット 〖操縦室(席)〗 a cockpit.

こっくり ● こっくりする nod. (!「居眠りをしていて」,「うなずいて」の両方の意) ▶ 父はテレビを見ながらよくこっくりする Father often *nods* (*off*) while watching television. ▶ 彼女はこっくりとうなずいた(=同意した) She *nodded* her consent.

こづくり 子作り ● 子作りにはげむ try to conceive a child.

こづくり 小作り ── **小作りな** 形 (物が) small (-sized); (人が) small-limbed. ● 小作りのケーキ a *small*(-*sized*) cake. ● 小作りな男 a *little* man. (!「背の低い」だけなら short だが, ここでは不適. a little man には「つまらない男」の意もあるので, a nice little man というこもある)

こっけい 滑稽 ── **こっけいな** 形 〖笑いを誘う〗 funny; comic; (風変わりで) comical (!どっと笑いを誘う); 〖ユーモアのある〗 humorous; (嘲笑を誘う) ridiculous. ● 道化師のこっけいな(=おどけた)しぐさ a clown's *comical* antics. ● こっけいなことを言う say *funny* things; (冗談を言う) tell jokes. ▶ 君はその帽子をかぶるとこっけいに見える You look *funny* [*ridiculous*] in that hat.
● 滑稽本 a witty and humorous type of novel in the late-Edo period Japan, depicting the ordinary people's lives in the city of Edo.

こっけいせつ 国慶節 the Anniversary of the Founding of the People's Republic of China. (参考) 中国の国家記念日. 10月1日)

こっけん 国権 (国家権力) state [national] power; (国家の統治権) sovereign rights. ▶ 日本では国会が国権の最高機関である The Diet is the highest organ of *state power* in Japan.

こっけん 黒鍵 (ピアノなどの) a black key. (⇔白鍵)

こっこ 国庫 (national) treasury.
● 国庫金 treasury funds. ● 国庫支出金 national treasury disbursements. ● 国庫収入 national treasury receipts. ● 国庫負担 state contribution. ● 国庫補助(金) a government [a state] subsidy /sʌ́bsədi/.

ごっこ ● お医者さんごっこをする play doctor [doctors and nurses]. ● 学校[お店屋さん; 泥棒; 戦争]ごっこをする play school [store; cops and robbers; war]. ▶ カウボーイごっこをしようよ Let's *make* [*play*] *believe* (that) we are cowboys. (! make believe は「ふりをする」の意)/Let's *play at* (being) cowboys.

*こっこう 国交 (diplomatic) relations. ● 国交を断絶する[結ぶ; 回復する] break off [establish, restore] *diplomatic relations* [*ties*] 〈*with*〉. ▶ 両国はその事件以来国交がない The two countries have had no *relations* since the incident.

ごつごうしゅぎ ご都合主義 (便宜優先の) opportunism; (日和見的な) timeserving, fence-sitting.
● ご都合主義者 an opportunist; a timeserver, a fence-sitter.

こっこく 刻々 every moment [minute]. ▶ 株価は時々刻々と変化する The stock prices change *every moment* [*minute by minute*].

こつこつ ❶ 〖努力の様子〗(勤勉に) diligently; (着実に) steadily; (一歩一歩) step by step. ▶ 日本ではこつこつ働く人は評価される People who work *diligently* are more valued in Japan. (!「こつこつ働く人」は a diligent [a slow but steady] worker) ▶ 彼は3時間こつこつ登って頂上に達した He reached the summit after climbing [he climbed] *step by step* for three hours. ▶ 彼女は子供の学費にとこつこつお金をためている She is putting away some money *little by little* [*bit by bit*] for her children's school expenses.
❷ 〖軽い連続音〗(軽くたたく音) a rap; (カチッという音) a click. ● ドアをこつこつたたく *rap* [*knock*] on [at] the door. ▶ 彼女がハイヒールをこつこついわせながら歩道を歩いてくるのが聞こえた I heard the *clicks* of her high heels coming up the walk.

ごつごつ ● ごつごつした rugged /rʌ́gid/. (!「でこぼこのある, 岩だらけの」,「(顔つきが)男っぽい」,「無骨な, 粗野な」の意で用いられる); (肌ざわりが) uneven, rough. ● ごつごつした(=岩の多い)山 a *rugged* mountain. ● ごつごつした手 *rough* [節くれだった) *knotted*] hands. ▶ 地面は凍っててごつごつしていた The ground was frozen and *rough*.

こっし 骨子 (要旨) the gist; (重要な内容[観点]) the main point(s) [idea(s)].

こつずい 骨髄 〖解剖〗(bóne) màrrow. ▶ 彼に対して恨み骨髄に徹している I have a *deep-seated grudge against* him./〈話〉 I hate his *guts* 〈*for doing*〉.
● 骨髄移植 a bone marrow transplant. ● 骨髄炎 〖医学〗 osteomyelitis /ɑ̀stioumàiəláitəs/.

こっせつ 骨折 〖医学〗 (a) fracture. ● 単純[複雑]骨折 a simple [a compound] *fracture*. ● 膝骨折の疑いのある suspected *broken knee*. ▶ 彼はころんで左膝を骨折した He fell and broke [〈書〉*fractured*] his left leg. ▶ 医者は彼女の骨折した脚の治療をした The doctor treated her *broken* leg [her for a *broken* leg].

こつぜん 忽然 ── **忽然と** 副 〖突然〗 suddenly, all of a sudden; 〖不意に〗 abruptly; 〖思いがけなく〗 (quite) unexpectedly.

こっそう 骨相 (人相) physiognomy /fiziá(g)nəmi/.
● 骨相学 phrenology. ● 骨相学者 a phrenologist.

こつそしょうしょう 骨粗鬆症 〖医学〗 osteoporosis /ɑ̀stiouparóusəs/.

こっそり（ひそかに）secretly, in secret;（人目を忍んで）stealthily /stélθili/;（自分だけで）in private. ●こっそり部屋に入る steal [sneak, slip] into the room. ▶彼はこっそり外国へ行った He secretly went abroad. ▶会はこっそり開かれた The meeting was held in private. ▶彼女は親にも知らせずにこっそり外国で結婚した She got married abroad in secret, even without letting her parents know.

ごっそり ▶彼は貯めたお金をごっそりだましとられた He was swindled out of all the money he had saved. ●彼の遺産は税金でごっそり持っていかれた Most [A good part] of his estate went for taxes.

ごったがえす ごった返す（ =混雑する）▶その店は買い物客でごった返していた The store was very crowded with shoppers.

ごったに ごった煮 a hotchpotch.

こっち here; this way.（⇨こちら）▶彼がチームにいれば勝利はこっちのものだ With him on our team, we will surely win.

ごっちゃ ●空想を事実とごっちゃにする（ =混同する）confuse [mix up] fancies with facts.

ごっちゃごっちゃ（⇨ごちゃごちゃ）

こっちょう 骨頂（絶頂）the height; the sublimity. ●愚の骨頂（⇨愚 [成句]）

こつつぼ 骨壷 a cinerary [a cremation] urn; an urn.

こつづみ 小鼓〖楽器〗a kotsuzumi; a small hand drum.

***こづつみ 小包**〖主に米〗a package,〖主に英〗a parcel（!いずれも大きさの大小は問わず，持ち歩き・郵送用の包み。package は〖英〗では通例大きなものを指し送には用いない;〖小さな包み〗a packet,〖主に米〗a pack. ●郵便小包 a postal package [packet]. ●速達小包 a special package. ●本を小包郵便で送る〖主に米〗mail a package,〖主に英〗[post 〖主に米〗];小包を郵送する〖主に米〗send a parcel by mail 〖主に英〗[post 〖主に米〗].

こってり〖濃密に〗heavily, thickly;〖厳しく〗severely. ●こってりした化粧 heavy makeup. ●こってり油をつけた頭 a thickly greased head. ●こってりした料理 a rich food [dish]. ●こってり油をしぼられた be severely told off; be given a good telling-off. ▶彼は脂肪の多いこってりした料理を控えるように医者に言われた He was advised by his doctor to refrain from heavily fatty foods.

こっとう 骨董（骨董品）an antique;（珍奇な品）a curio（⊕~s);（時代遅れの人・物）a museum piece（⊕おどけた表現）. ▶英国製家具の骨董品 antique English furniture. ●骨董商 an antique [a curio] dealer. ●骨董店 an antique [a curio] shop.

ゴッドファーザー〖名付け親〗(a) godfather;〖マフィアなどの犯罪組織の首領〗〖米〗Godfather.

コットン〖木綿,（化粧用綿〗cotton.（⇨木綿）●コットン紙 cotton (bond) paper.

こつにく 骨肉（肉親）one's own flesh and blood; a blood relation [relative]. ●骨肉の争い a family quarrel;〖書〗family discord.
●骨肉相食（はむ）（肉親同士が争う）be in ugly conflict with one's blood relations.

こつにくしゅ 骨肉腫〖医学〗an osteosarcoma /ˌàstiousɑːrkóumə/; an osteogenic sarcoma.

こっぱみじん 木端微塵 ▶あらしのため船はこっぱみじんに（ =粉々に）砕かれた The storm smashed the ship into (small) pieces [to bits, to fragments];（マッチの軸木ほどに）to matchwood,〖話〗in(to) smithereens].

こつばん 骨盤〖解剖〗a pelvis（⊕~es, pelves /-viːz/). ●骨盤の狭い女性 a woman with a narrow pelvis.

こっぴどく severely. ●こっぴどくしかられる be severely told off. ●彼をこっぴどくやっつける（ =打ちのめす）beat him up; beat him soundly [〖(やや話)〗to (a) pulp];（批判する）criticize him severely [harshly];（懲らしめる）〖話〗give it to him (straight).

こつぶ 小粒〖小さい種類〗a small kind;〖小さい粒〗a small grain. ●小粒の栗 a small (kind of) chestnut.

***コップ**〖＜オランダ語〗a glass;〖大型で脚も取っ手もない〗a tumbler;〖脚と台つきの〗a goblet;〖取っ手つきの〗a mug;〖大型で取っ手・ふたつきのビール用〗a tankard. ●紙コップ a paper cup. ●使い捨てのコップ a disposable cup. ●コップ1[2]杯の水 a glass [two glasses] of water. ●コップにいっぱいつぐ fill a glass up (to the brim).
●コップの中のあらし a tempest 〖米〗[a storm 〖英〗] in a teacup.
●コップ酒 sake sold by the glass.

こつぶん 骨粉 powdered bones; bone meal [dust].

コッペ(パン) a (bread) roll.（!×a roll bread は不可）

ゴッホ〖オランダの画家〗van Gogh /góu, gɔ́ːx/ (Vincent ~).

こつまく 骨膜〖解剖〗the periosteum /pèriástiəm/.
●骨膜炎〖医学〗periostitis /pèriəstáitis/.

こづめ 小爪 a half-moon;〖医学〗a lunula.

こづらにくい 小面憎い annoyingly cheeky.

こづれ 子連れ ▶彼女は子連れで海外旅行に出かける予定です She is planning to go abroad with her children./She is going to take her children on an overseas trip.

こつん ●ボールにバットをこつんとあてる hit a ball lightly with a bat.

ごつん ●ごつんとぶつける bump (on, against). ▶彼は柱に頭をごつんとぶつけた He bumped his head on the pillar. ▶父親は息子の頭にごつんげんこを食らわせた The father gave his son a rap on the head with his fist./The father thumped his son on the head.

こて 鏝（左官用の）a trowel;（裁縫用の）an iron, a flatiron;（頭髪用の）a curling iron, curling tongs;（はんだ用の）a soldering iron.

こて 小手 ●小手をかざす to shade one's eyes with one's hand to look distantly.

こて 籠手（よろいの）an armed guard;（中世の騎士の）a gauntlet;（剣道の）fencing gloves;（フェンシング・アーチェリーの）a bracer.

ごて 後手 ●後手に回る ▶私は論戦で後手に回った（ =守勢に回った）I stood on the defensive [（機先を制された）〖やや書〗was forestalled] in the debate. ▶政府の打つ手は後手後手に回った Everything the government did was too late [lost good timing].

***こてい 固定 ―― 固定する**〖動〗fix. ●棚を壁にしっかりと固定する fix a shelf to a wall.（⇨取り付ける）
―― **固定した**〖形〗(動かない) fixed;（定まった）regular;（基本的な）basic.
●固定為替相場 the fixed exchange rate.
●固定観念 (have) a fixed idea [a stereotype] (about). ●固定客 a regular customer. ●固定給 a fixed [a regular, a basic] salary. ●固定金利 a fixed rate; a fixed(-rate) interest. ●固定資産 fixed assets. ● 固定資産税 property tax.
●固定費 fixed [constant] cost(s). ●固定票 solid [loyal] votes; solid [loyal] support. ●固定比率 (a) fixed ratio; (a) fixed-assets (to

こてきたい 鼓笛隊 a drum and fife band.

ごてごて thickly, heavily. ●ごてごて(=けばけばしく)飾り立てた部屋 a *gaudily* decorated room. ▶彼女はごてごて(=厚く)化粧をしていた She was *heavily* made up./She wore *heavy* makeup.

こてさき 小手先 ── 小手先の圏 (容易な) easy; (見かけ倒しの) cheap; (間に合わせの) makeshift 《measures》. ●小手先の仕事 an *easy* job. ●小手先の細工をろうする use *cheap* tricks.

こてしらべ 小手調べ (試すこと) a trial. ●小手調べに少し練習問題をやってみる do a few exercises as a *trial*.

コテッジ a cottage.
●コテッジチーズ cottage cheese.

ごてどく ごて得 ⇨ごね得.

ごてまり 小手毬 〖植物〗 a spir(a)ea.

***こてん** 古典 (昔からの一流の作品) a classic; (古典文学) the classics 〖集合的に用い, 単数扱い〗, classical [×classic] literature. 〖参考〗英語では「古典文学」は本来ギリシャ・ローマのものについていうが, 日本などのものにも用いる》 ●古典派の絵画 *classical* 〔↔romantic〕 paintings. ▶私は古典を読むのが好きだ I like reading *the classics*. ▶「源氏物語」は日本の古典です *The Tale of Genji* is one of the Japanese *classics* 〖日本の文学史上の傑作〗 a literary *classic* of Japan〗.
── 古典的な 圏 classic. ●古典的な美しさ *classic* [×classical] beauty. (ᗏclassicalは「ギリシャ・ローマの古典文学[語学]の, 古典派の」の意) ●古典仮名遣い classical *kana* orthography. ●古典主義 classicism (↔romanticism). ●古典籍 Japanese classical literal materials. ●古典落語 classical *rakugo*.

こてん 個展 a private [a one-man] exhibition 〖(話) show〗. ●個展を開く hold [give] a *private show*.

ごてん 御殿 a palace /pǽləs/. ●御殿のような家に住む live in a *palatial* /pəléiʃl/ house.

こてんこてん completely, thoroughly, utterly. ▶我々はこてんこてんにやっつけられた We were *completely* [*utterly*] beaten./We were beaten *to a pulp*./〖英話〗We were *murdered*.

こてんぱん utterly. (⇨こてんこてん)

こと 事 INDEX

名
❶ 事柄　　　　　❷ 出来事
❸ 事情　　　　　❹ やるべき仕事
❺ 経験　　　　　❻ 内容, 意味
❼ 習慣　　　　　❽ 経験
❾ 予定　　　　　❿ 可能性
⓫ 忠告, 伝聞, 決心　⓬ 必要, 価値
⓭ 別名　　　　　⓮ 期間
《終助詞》
❶ 感嘆　　　　　❷ 命令
❷ 質問, 勧誘, 念押しなど

── 事 名 ❶ [事柄] a matter; (事物) a thing; (何かあること) something (ᗏ否定文・疑問文では通例 anything); (…するところのこと) what.
①〖~事〗●残念なこと a *matter* for [of] regret. ●重要なこと an important *matter* [*thing*]; *something* important. (ᗏsomething+形容詞の語順に注意) ●自分のこと one's own thing. ●本当のこと the truth, what is true. ●後のこと what happens after …. ●驚いた[遺憾な]ことに *to* one's surprise [regret]. ●ちょっとしたことで怒る get angry *for nothing*. ●どうすることもできない cannot do anything (about [with] it). ●それは笑いごとではない It's no laughing *matter*. ●そんなことはしたくない I don't want to do such a *thing* [*anything* like that]. ▶後の方が強意的) ●最も重要なことは健康あることです The most important *thing* [*What* is most important] is *that* we are healthy. (ᗏこの that は ❹ の意) ●私にできることが何かありますか Is there *something* [×anything] I can do for you? (ᗏyes の答えを予期・期待する場合は something を用いる) ●あなたのためならとんなことでもしましょう I will do *anything* [*what*(*ever*) I can] for you. (ᗏwhat より whatever の方が強意的)
〖会話〗「あいにく中村が手を引いちまったよ」「まさにあいつがやりそうなことだな」"Nakamura backed out, I'm afraid." "It's just the sort of *thing* he would do."

② 〖~の事〗 (ᗏ前置詞などを用いて) ▶私は試験のことが心配だ I feel uneasy *about* the examination. ▶航空券のことで電話をしました Did you call *about* the airline ticket? ▶金のことと言えば君に 1,000 円の借りがある Talking [Speaking] *of* money, I owe you 1,000 yen. ▶金のことになると彼は意外にけちだ He is unexpectedly stingy *when it comes to* money. ▶太郎のことだから何とかうまくやってのけるだろう Since Taro is Taro, he will manage to carry it off./Taro is the kind of man who will manage to carry it off.

❸ 〖~する事〗 (ᗏ不定詞・動名詞を用いて) ▶時間を厳守するということは大事だ Being [To be] punctual is important./*It* is important to *be* punctual. ▶本を読むことが好きです I like reading./I like *to* read. (ᗏ後者は一般的なこと, 後の方は特定の行為・未来の行為についていう) ▶私にできることはコーヒーをいれることぐらいです All [The only *thing*] I can do is (*to*) make coffee. ▶*to* を省略するのは〖話〗. この thing は ❶ の意) ▶英語を勉強することは私たちにとって大切なことです *It* is important that we [*for us to*] study English.

❹ 〖~だ(という)事〗 (ᗏ that 節を用いて) ▶彼が先生だということを知っています I know *that* he is a teacher. ▶彼が死んだことを知っていますか Do you know *of* [*about*] his death? ᗏof では間接的に知っていること, about では具体的事実を知っていることを含意する. したがって about では that he died を Do you know *that* he died? といってもほぼ同じ意)

❷ [出来事] an occurrence; (重大な) an event; (付随的な) an incident (⇨出来事); (もめ事) (a) trouble. ●事を起こす cause *trouble*. ▶それはよくあることだ That's a common [an everyday] *occurrence*./That happens every day. ▶困ったことに彼は自分のことしか考えない The ˇ*trouble* is that 〖話〗The ˇ*trouble* is,〗 he thinks only of himself. ▶事もなく日が過ぎていった The days have passed *without* (×an) *incident* [uneventfully]. ▶困ったことになった (自分に) I've got into *trouble*./(情勢が) The situation has become *serious*. ▶彼にもしものことがあったらすぐに教えてください Please let me know at once if *anything* happens to him. ▶失敗したら事だろうな It would be *awful* if we failed.

❸ [事情] circumstances; ((漠然と)事態) things, matters, affairs; (事の状態) a situation; (場合) a case. (⇨事情) ●事と次第によっては according to *circumstances*. ●事を甘く見る take *things* [*matters*] easy. ●彼はよくあることだ as is often the *case* with him. ▶どんなことがあっても彼を信じてはいけない Under [In] *no circumstances* must

you trust him. (**!**否定語を含む副詞句が先行する場合の倒置に注意. 文語的な文体)▶事は重大だ The *situation* is serious. ▶それは事によりけりだ It [That] (all) depends (on the *circumstances*). (**!**on the circumstances は通例省略される) ▶事を荒立てるな Don't make *matters* worse. ▶この規則が当てはまらない事もある There are some *cases* where [in which] this rule does not apply.
会話「5万円なら出してあげられるのだが」「でもそれで事は解決するの?」"We could offer him fifty thousand yen." "Will that be the end of *it*, though?"
会話「恵美はどうしたの?」「いつものことだよ, 彼女時間どおりだったことがないもの」"What's happened to Emi?" "It's always *the same*. She's never on time."
❹ [やるべき仕事] work; (かかわり合いのあること) business (**!**否定文で); [個人的な関心事] an affair. ▶それは君の知った事ではない That's none of your *business* [*affair*]./That's no *business* [*affair*] of yours. ▶今日は何もする事がない I have *nothing* to do today.
❺ [話題] a subject. ▶その事は私たちの話には出なかった The *subject* didn't come up in our conversation.
❻ [内容, 意味] ▶私の言うことが分かりませんか Don't you understand *me* [*what* I say]? ▶君は書きたいことを書いていいんだよ You can write *what* you like. ▶それはどういうことですか What do you *mean* by that? ▶臓器移植の問題は事が事だけに(=その特有の性質による)大論争を巻き起こした The problem of organ transplants, *by its own nature*, created a lot of dispute.
会話「私のペン見なかった?」「これのこと?」"Have you seen my pen?" "Is ╱this it?/Do you *mean* this one?"
❼ [習慣] ▶私は毎朝6時に起きることにしている I *get up* at six every morning. (**!**通例単純現在形で)(⇨習慣) ▶彼は1日2キロジョギングすることにしている He *makes a point* [*a practice*] of jogging two kilometers a day./He *makes it a point* [*a practice*] to jog two kilometers a day. (⇨必ず ❷)
❽ [経験] ▶アメリカに行ったことがありますか *Have* you (ever) *been* [*Did* you *ever go*] to America? (**!**現在完了の方が穏やかな質問) ▶以前どこかであったにかかったことがありませんか *Haven't* we met somewhere before? ▶まだ富士山を見たことがない I *have never seen* Mt. Fuji. (⇨経験)
❾ [予定] ▶彼はあすここに来ることになっている He *is to* come [*is coming*] (来ると考えられている) *is supposed to* come] here tomorrow. (**!**supposed to の発音は /səpóustə/ が普通) ▶飛行機は午後5時に着くことになっている The plane *is due* [*is scheduled to* arrive] at 5 p.m. (⇨予定)
❿ [可能性] ▶夏でも寒いことがある It *can* be cold in (the) summer. (⇨ことによると)
⓫ [忠告, 伝聞, 決心] ▶…とのこと be informed [told] that…. ▶胃のレントゲンを撮ってもらうことだね I *suggest* (*that*) you (*should*) have your stomach X-rayed. (**!**should を用いるのは《主に英》) ▶彼はまだ学生だということです People *say* [*They say*, *I hear*] he is still a student. (**!**It is said that…. は堅い言い方) ▶私はたばこをやめることにした I *have made up* my *mind* to give up [quit] smoking.
⓬ [必要, 価値] ▶急ぐことはありません You *don't have to* [*don't need to*] hurry. (⇨必要) ▶その町は訪れてみるだけのことはある The town *is worth* a visit [visiting]. (⇨価値)
⓭ [別名] ●鈴木こと久保 Kubo, *alias* /éiliəs/ Suzuki. (**!**特に犯人について用いる)
⓮ [期間] 会話「でも君は彼が結婚してるって言ったよ」「長いことそうだと思ってたんだよ」"But you said he was married." "*For a long time* I thought he was."

── こと 《終助詞》 ❶ [感動] (⇨なんと) ▶まあご親切なこと *How* kind of you!
会話「で, これが長男の忠之だよ」「まあ, 大きくなったこと!」 "And this is Tadayuki, the oldest." "Hásn't he ╱grown!"
❷ [命令] ▶芝生に入らないこと《掲示など》*Keep off* the grass.
❸ [質問, 勧誘, 念押しなど] (⇨─か)
● 事あれかし ▶事あれかしと願ってもむだである Hoping [Wishing] for a change to happen will get you nowhere.
● 事ここに至る ●事ここに至っては now that [when] things have come this far.
● 事志(こころざし)と違(たが)う ▶事志と違っていたのでこれはほんの短期間しか続きませんでした This only lasted for a short period of time as things didn't turn out as I'd expected.
● 事無きを得る do not become serious.
● 事に当たる undertake the work.
● 事によったら, 事によると quite possibly.
● 事はさように such is the case that, this being the case.
● 事もあろうに of all things.
● 事を構える make trouble (on purpose).
● 事を好む a person with unusual tastes and who likes to stir things up on purpose.
● 事を分ける explain rationally [logically].

こと 琴 a koto (徼 〜(s)); (説明的に) a long Japanese musical instrument having 13 strings resembling a horizontal harp. ●琴を弾く play the *koto*.

こと 古都 an ancient capital.

-ごと (…もいっしょに) (together) with; (…ぐるみ) …and all. ●リンゴを皮ごと食べる eat an apple, peel *and all*. ●車ごとフェリーボートに乗り込む board a ferryboat *together with* cars.

-ごと -毎に (⇨-毎に)

ことあたらしい 事新しい ▶今日の新聞には新しいことは何も載っていない There is nothing *new* in today's newspaper. ▶これは事新しく取り上げる問題ではない This is not a matter to take up *again* [*anew*].

ことう 孤島 a solitary [an isolated] island; (無人島) a desert island. ●陸の孤島 an inaccessible land.

こどう 鼓動 图 ●心臓の鼓動 the *beat* [《主に医学》*pulsation*] of one's heart; (a) heartbeat (**!**a heartbeat は1回の鼓動).
── 鼓動する 動 beat; (激しく) throb. ▶私の心臓は驚きで激しく鼓動していた My heart *was beating wildly* [*was throbbing*] with surprise.

ごとう 語頭 the beginning of a word.
●語頭音『言語』an initial sound.

こどうぐ 小道具 『小さな道具』a small tool; (便利な)(話) a gadget; 《書》props, 《書》properties.
●台所用小道具 kitchen gàdgets.
●小道具方 a prop;《書》a próperty màn [(女性も)hàndler].

ごとうさ 誤動作 (a) mulfunction.

ごとうち 御当地 ●ご当地ソング a popular song whose lyrics include place names and [or]

ことかく 事欠く ▶家は貧乏で三度の飯にも事欠くありさまだった We were so poor that we *couldn't afford* enough food to fill our stomach [we *were always short of* food]. ▶ボランティアには事欠かなかった There was no lack of volunteers.

ことがら 事柄 a matter; an affair. (⇒事) ●政治に関する事柄 political *matters* [*affairs*].

こときれる 事切れる (⇒囲 死ぬ)

こどく 孤独 图 [独りぼっちで寂しいこと] loneliness; [仲間がなく1人でいること] ((書)) solitude (! 寂しさを含まない). ●孤独を楽しむ enjoy *solitude*.

── 孤独な 形 lonely, ((主に米話)) lonesome (! lonely より感傷的); ((やや書)) solitary; [ただ1人の] alone (! 叙述的に). ▶孤独な男 a *lonely* [a *solitary*] man. ▶彼は孤独な生活をしている He leads a *lonely* [a *solitary*] life./He lives *all alone* [*in solitude*]. (! *all alone* で「独りぼっちで寂しい」の意)

ごとく 五徳 (やかんなどを乗せるための三脚) a trivet, a kettle holder.

ごとく 如く (まるで…のようだ) as if [though]…. (⇒まるで❶)

ごどく 誤読 图 ((書)) misreading.

── 誤読する 動 read ((a passage)) wrongly, ((書)) misread.

ことこと ▶次にこれをとろ火で5分から7分ことこと煮立たせます Then we'll let this *simmer* for five to seven minutes on low heat.

ごとごと ●ごとごと音を立てる[がる] rattle, rumble. (! 前の方は「ごとごと」より少し高い音の、後の方は低い音をさす) ▶馬車がごとごと A carriage *rattled* along. ▶貨物列車がごとごと走ってゆく A freight train *rumbles* along./I hear the *rumble* of a freight train. ▶隣の部屋で何かごとごといっている I hear some *rattling* noises in the next room.

ことごとく 悉く (⇒全部) ▶学生はことごとくその計画に反対だった *All* (the) students were [*Every* student was, (each を強調して)*Each and every* student was, *Each and every* one of the students was] against the plan. ▶彼のすることはことごとくうまくいく *Everything* he does goes well.

ことごとしい 事々しい pretentiously exaggerated.

ことこまか 事細か ── 事細かに 副 in (great [full]) detail, (very) minutely /máin(j)ú:tli/.

ことさら (特に) particularly, especially (⇒特に); (わざと) intentionally, on purpose. ▶それはことさら(=特別に)取り上げるまでもない We don't *particularly* need to take it up.

＊ことし 今年 this year. (! 現在(完了)形・過去形・未来形のいずれとも用いる) ●今年の冬に this winter; (過ぎ去った) last winter. (! ×in this [last] winter は不可) ●今年中に (by the end of [within]) *this year*, (今年のいつか) sometime (during) *this year*. ▶今年は2007年です This is the year 2007. ▶今年は学校は4月9日から始まる School begins on [×from] April 9 *this year*.

ごとし 如し (まるで…のようだ) as if [though]…. (⇒まるで❶) ●読んで字のごとし(=文字どおり) literally. ▶過ぎたるはなお及ばざるがごとし Too much of thing is not good.

ことだま 言霊 the miraculous power of language; the spirit of language.

●言霊のさきわう国 the land where the spiritual power of language brings happiness to life.

ことたりる 事足りる (will) do; be enough. ▶これで十分事足りる This *is* quite *enough*./This *will do* well enough.

ことづかる 言付かる (伝言を) be asked to give a message ((to)); (物を) be asked to hand ((it to him)). ▶彼から手紙をことうかってきました I *have been asked to give* a letter from him *to* you.

ことづけ 言付け a message. (⇒私信)

ことづける 言付ける (伝言を) leave* a message ((with him)); (物を) ask ((him)) to hand ((it to her)).

ことづて 言づて a message. (⇒私信)

ことなかれしゅぎ 事なかれ主義 ▶彼はいつも事なかれ主義を通している He always abides by *don't-rock-the-boat principles*.

ことなく 事無く (事故なく) without accident [((話)) a hitch]; (面倒な問題もなく) without troubles. ▶夏休みも事なく終わった The summer vacation ended *without accident* [*troubles*].

＊ことなる 異なる (違っている) be different ((from)), differ ((from)) (⇒違う [類語]); [変化する] vary ((with)). (⇒違う) ▶異なった different. ▶君の方法は私の方法とずいぶん異なる[何ら異なるところはない] Your method *is* very [no] *different from* mine. (! very 以外に completely, entirely, totally なども可) ▶政治制度は国によって異なる Systems of government *are different* [*differ*, *vary*] *from* country to country./*Different* countries have *different* systems of government. ▶彼は今までにアメリカのいろいろ異なる場所に行っている He has been to a lot of *different* places in America.

ことに 殊に [とりわけ、特に] especially, ((格別に)) particularly, in particular (⇒特に); [例外的に] exceptionally; [何よりも] above all, most [best] of all. ▶今年の夏は殊に暑い It is *especially* [*exceptionally*]; (異常に) *unusually*] hot this summer. ▶だれにでもだが、殊に老人に対しては親切にせよ Be kind to everybody, but, *above all* [*most of all*], to older [elderly] people.

-ごとに -毎に (毎…) every; each; (…するごとに) every [each] time… (⇒-置き). ●日曜ごとに *every* Sunday. ●地域ごとの医者の数 the number of doctors *from* region *to* region. ▶バスは15分ごとに出る The buses leave *every* fifteen minutes. ▶彼女は会うたびごとにますますきれいに見える She looks more beautiful *each* [*every*] *time* I see her. ▶1語増すごとに20円払わねばならない We must pay 20 yen for *every* additional word. ▶その雨の後、日ごとに暖かくなった It got warmer *day by day* after that rain. ▶我々は店ごとに(=店から店へと)渡り歩いた We went from shop to shop. (! 無冠詞に注意)

ことにする 異にする differ ((from)). (⇒違う) ▶この点については私は彼と意見を異にする I *differ from* him on this point./I *disagree with* him on this point.

ことによると ((助動詞を用いて)) may, might; ((副詞を用いて)) (ひょっとすると) possibly; (もしかすると) perhaps, maybe. (⇒-かもしれない) ▶ことによると彼はあす来るかもしれない *Perhaps* [*Maybe*] he will come tomorrow./He *may possibly* come tomorrow. (! possibly を may の後で用いるとさらに可能性は弱まる)

ことのほか 殊の外 ▶今日はことのほか(=例外的に)寒い It is *exceptionally* [(異常なほど) *unusually*] cold today. ▶その知らせを聞いて彼はことのほか(=極度に)喜んだ He was *extremely* [*more than*, *only too*, ((書)) *exceedingly*] pleased to hear the news. ▶試験はことのほか(=思っていたよりもずっと)やさしかった The examination was much *easier than I* (had) *expected*.

ことば 言葉

WORD CHOICE 言葉

language 特定の民族・話者が書いたり話したりする言語のこと. body language のように, 言語に相当するものもさす. ▶彼女は世界の言葉に興味を持っている She's interested in world *languages*.

word もともとは個々の語のことだが, しばしば言葉一般を表す. ▶他の言葉で言えば in other *words*.

頻度チャート
language ██████████
word ██████████
20 40 60 80 100 (%)

❶ 【言語】(a) language (!個々の国家・民族の言語をいうときは Ⓒ);〖音声言語〗speech;〖方言〗(a) dialect. ● 話し[書き]言葉 (the) spoken [written] *language*. ● はやり言葉 (流行語) a vogue word, a word in vogue. (⇨流行) ● 言葉の壁[障壁] a language barrier. ● 京言葉 in (a) Kyoto *dialect*. ▶人間には言葉を話す能力がある Human beings have the ability to speak [use *language*]./We have the gift of *speech*. ▶言葉の勉強には根気が必要です The study of *languages* requires patience. ▶音楽は人類共通の言葉である Music is a common *speech* for humanity [human beings]. ▶フランスでは言葉に苦労した In France I had a lot of trouble *making myself understood* [*expressing myself well*] in French. (!前の方は自分の言うことを分かってもらうのに, 後の方はフランス語で自分の気持ちをうまく表現するのに苦労したこと)

❷ 【単語】a word; (句) a phrase. ● 覚えやすい言葉 an easy *word* [*phrase*] to memorize. ● 一言葉で言うと (to put it) in other *words*. ● 考えを言葉で表現する express one's thought in *words*; put one's thought into *words*. ▶うまい言葉が見つからない I can't find the right *word* [the right way to *put* it]. (! put は「表現する」の意) ▶感謝の(気持ちを表す)言葉もありません I have no *words* [I don't know how] to express my gratitude./I can't tell you how grateful I am. (!後の方が口語的に) ▶その苦しみは言葉では言い表せない The pain is *beyond words* [*description*, ×*expression*]. (! description は状況・特徴などを言葉で述べること. expression は言葉だけによる表現とは限らないので不可)/The pain is *unspeakable*. (!不快なものにしか用いない) ▶彼は「報道管制」という言葉の意味を知らなかった He didn't know the meaning of the *word* [×a word, ×the word of] "blackout." (!引用符の内容によって ... the *words* [*phrase*; (表現) ex-*pression*] "freedom of speech" (「表現の自由」という言葉) などとする)

❸ 【実際に話される言葉】(言葉遣い) language; (話しぶり) (通例 one's) speech; (言う[言った]こと) what one has [said]; (発言) a remark; (語) a word.
① 【～の言葉】 ● 日常の言葉で話す speak in everyday [×every day] *language*. ● ひと言歓迎の言葉を述べる say a few *words* of welcome.
② 【言葉～】 ● 言葉たくみに (上手な言い回しで) with a clever *choice of words* [*turn of phrase*]; (甘い言葉で)《謔》with sweet talk [《書》 honeyed *words*]; (お上手を言って) with smooth talk. ● 言葉少なに(=簡潔に)語る tell briefly [in a few *words*]. ▶彼らの言うことを言葉通りにとる take them *at their word* [×words]. ▶彼は言葉遣いが下品[乱暴]だ(=下品[乱暴]な言葉を遣う) He uses vulgar [violent] *language*. ▶人の言葉じりをとらえるのはよせ(=人の言葉のあら捜しをするのはよせ) Stop finding fault with other people's [others'] use of *words*.
③ 【言葉の】 ● 言葉のあや a figure of *speech*. ● 言葉の上の(=口先だけの)約束 a *verbal* promise. ● 言葉の端々で here and there in what one says. ● 言葉のやりとり an exchange of *words*. ● 言葉の使い方 how to use *words*.
④ 【言葉に】 ● 言葉にする put (it) into *words*. ● 言葉に耳を傾ける listen to 《his》 *words*. ● 言葉にしたがう obey one's [the] *words*. ▶言葉につまってしまった(=何と言ってよいか分からなかった) I didn't know what to say./I was at a loss for *words*. (!前の方が普通) ▶言葉(遣い)に気をつけなさい(=言葉の選択を慎重にしなさい) Be careful in your *choice of words*./Weigh your *words* carefully. (!Watch your mouth [language]. は「言葉の口のきき方に気をつけろ」といったりかを売るようなかなり強い語調なので要注意) ▶いまほど言葉に実質がなく, 言葉の枯渇が感じられることはないのではないか I've never felt as strongly as I do now, that *words* have lost their substance or they have simply dried up.
⑤ 【言葉を】 ● 言葉をかける(=話しかける) speak [talk] to 《him》. ● 彼と言葉を交わす(=短い会話をする) have a *word* [a few *words*] with him; talk to [with] him. ● 言葉をはさむ(=人の話をじゃまする) interrupt 《him [a conversation]》. ● 言葉をさえぎる interrupt 《him》 [《his》 *words*]. ● 言葉を繰り返す repeat one's *words*. ● 言葉を失う be at a loss for *words*; (言葉を失う) lose one's *language*. ▶彼が大阪の出身だということは言葉を聞けば分かりますよ You can tell by his *speech* that he comes from Osaka. ▶彼女の言葉を覚えていますか Do you remember *what she said* [*her words*]? (!前の方が普通)

● 言葉に甘える ▶お言葉に甘えてそうさせていただきます I'll accept your *kind* [《寛大な》 *generous*] *offer*.

● 言葉を返す ▶お言葉を返すようですが(=反論するつもりはありませんが)あなたの意見には賛成しかねます I don't mean to contradict [refute] you, but I can't agree with you.

● 言葉を尽くす ▶言葉を尽くして両親を説得したがだめだった I used every *word* to persuade my parents, (but) in vain [but didn't succeed]. (!後の方が普通)

● 言葉を濁す speak ambiguously; (あいまいな返事をする) give a vague answer.

● 言葉遊び a word game [play]. ● 言葉書き (和歌の前書き) a foreword; (絵巻物で) notes; (絵本で) dialogues. ● 言葉数 the number of words used [spoken]. ● 言葉典 a dictionary of words.

『ことばあそびうた』 *A Wordplay — Poetry*. (参考 谷川俊太郎の詩集)

ことばじめ 事始め a beginning; (仕事始め) the beginning of work.

ことぶき 寿 〖祝い事〗a celebration,《書》 festivities; (祝詞) congratulations;〖長寿〗a long life,《書》 longevity.

ことほぐ 寿ぐ, 言祝ぐ (⇨祝う)

こども 子供

WORD CHOICE 子供

child 大人・親の対立概念としての子供をさす最も一般的な語. 14 歳ごろまでを指す場合が多く, 特に幼児をさす場合は young child となる. ● 親子関係 the relationship between a parent and a *child*.

baby 生まれたばかりの赤ん坊のこと. ▶子供を生む have a *baby*.

kid *child* とほぼ同意だが、よりくだけた語で、主に会話に用いられる. the kids の形で子供全般をさす用法が多い. 《米》では大学生あることがある. ▶子供たちは行ってしまった The *kids* were gone.

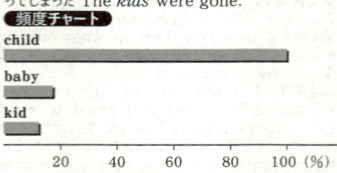

【頻度チャート】
child ██████████
baby   ████
kid   ██

20　40　60　80　100 (%)

a child (複 children), 《話》a kid; (男児) a boy; (女児) a girl; (赤ん坊) a baby; (幼児) an infant (❗ *baby* のやや堅い語で, 《英》では学齢期以前の子供にも用いられ, 《法律》では未成年者をさす); (息子) a son, 《話》a boy; (娘) a daughter; (集合的) offspring (❗単・複両扱い); (一家の子供たち) a family (❗通例複数形にしない). (❗動物の子供は「子」または個々の動物を参照)

①【子供〜】•子供向けの映画 a movie for *children*. •子供好きの男 a man who is fond of children. •子供相手の仕事 a job (dealing) with children. •子供用の (suitable) for children. ▶私は楽しい子供時代を過ごした I had a happy *childhood*. •母は私をいつも子供扱いする My mother always treats me like a *child* [《話》 as if I were [was] a *child*]. ▶子供心にも(=ほんの子供であったが), 両親が兄よりも自分に期待していることが分かった Although I was a mere [only a] *child*, I understood that my parents expected more of me than of my older brother. (❗ an only child は「一人っ子」の意)

②【子供の】•子供のような *childlike*; (子供っぽい) (けなして) *childish*. •子供の教育 the education of *children*; *child* education. •子供のころに when one was a *child*; (書) in one's *childhood*; (書) as a *child*. •子供のころの夢 one's *childhood* ambitions 《to do》. •子供のような大きな目で私を見上げた with one's big, *childlike* eyes. ▶彼は子供のころから機械が好きでした He's loved machines since he was a *boy* [《主に英》 from a *child*]. ▶《書》 since (from) childhood より口語的). ▶子供のようなことをするな Don't be so *childish* [such a *child*]. (❗ *childlike* は「子供らしい純真な」といった意味に使われ、*childish* は大人の考えやふるまいを非難して「子供じみて幼稚な」の意) ▶その坂は子供の足にはきつ過ぎる The slope is too steep for *children* to walk up.

③【子供が[は]】•子供が大きい家庭 a family, the *children* of which have quite grown up. ▶子供は3人です We have three *children* [a *family* of three]. ▶子供(というのは)外へ出て遊ぶのが好きだ The *children* [×*child*] like to go out and play. (❗ 総称的な言い方では *the child* は通例不可) ▶彼女にはまだ子供がない She has no *children* [×*child*] as yet. (❗ 1人もいないということを強調する場合を除き, 複数形を用いる)/《書》She is still *childfree* [*childless*]. ▶前の方が婉曲的 (⇨子). ▶スミス夫妻に子供が生まれた A *baby* was born to Mr. and Mrs. Smith. (⇨生まれる) ▶彼の子供は20歳です His *son* [*daughter*] is twenty years old.

[会話]「子供さんいますか」「ええ, 3人います. 男の子が2人, 女の子が1人です」 "Do you have (any) children [×kids]?" "Yes, three. Two boys and a girl." (⇨[類語])

•**子供ができる** ▶彼女には今月子供ができる She's expecting this month. ▶まもなく私たちに初めての子供ができます My wife and I are going to start a *family* soon. ▶子供ができるとたいへん忙しくなる When a baby comes, we will be very busy.

•**子供の使い** ▶あれではまるで子供の使いだ That was a futile mission. ▶子供の使いじゃあるまいし This mission must not fail.

•**子供会** a children's gathering. •**子供だまし** (⇨子供騙し) •**子供の日** Children's Day. •**子供服** children's wear [clothes]. •**子供部屋** a child's [a children's] room. •**子供料金** children's fare.

こともあろうに 事もあろうに ▶事もあろうに彼が約束を破るなんて I can't imagine how he would [should] break his promise, *of all things*. ▶事もあろうにどうしてあんなやつに頼んだんだ Why did you ask him a favor, *of all people*.

こどもだまし 子供騙し 《米》 kid stuff.
•子供だましの品 (安ぴかの装飾品[宝石]) a gewgaw; a trinket. ▶それは子供だましだ That's (×a) *kids*' stuff.

こともなげ 事もなげ ── 事もなげに 副 •事もなげに(=容易に)問題を解く solve the problem *easily* [(何の困難もなく) *without any difficulty*]. •事もなげにふるまう behave as if *nothing had* [*has*] *happened*.
•事もなげに(=大したことでないように)言う speak *lightly* 《of it》; (無造作に言う) speak *indifferently* [(何気なく) *casually*, (やや書) *nonchalantly*].

ことよせる 事寄せる (口実にする) make an excuse 《for》; (書) make a pretext 《of》. ▶彼は病気に事寄せて会議を欠席した He was absent at the meeting *on the pretext of* ill health.

ことり 小鳥 a (little) bird. •小鳥を飼う have [keep] a (*little*) *bird*. (⇨飼う) •小鳥屋 a *bird* shòp.

***ことわざ** 諺 (言いならわし) a saying; (格言) a proverb; (処世訓) a maxim. •ことわざにもあるように as the *saying* goes; as the *proverb* goes [says, runs]. ▶「光陰矢のごとし」ということわざがある There is a *saying* [a *proverb*], "Time flies."/There is an old *saying* [a *proverb*] *that* time flies.

ことわり 断わり ❶【辞退】declining; (拒絶) (a) refusal. ▶彼は私の招待に断わりの手紙をよこした He sent me a letter *declining* my invitation.
❷【許可】permission, (書) leave (⇨許し); (予告) (a) notice, (警告) (a) warning. •断わりもなく欠勤する stay away from work *without permission* [*leave*, *notice*, (上司に言わずに) *telling*] one's boss]. ▶入場お断わり《掲示》No admittance. ▶はり紙お断わり《掲示》Post *no* bills. ▶犬はお断わり《掲示》No dogs *allowed*. (❗ are allowed の are が省略されている)

ことわり 理 (道理) reason, logic; (理由) (a) reason; (当たり前) a matter of course.

***ことわる** 断わる ❶【拒絶する】refuse; reject; turn ... down; decline.

【使い分け】 **refuse** 要求・申し出・招待などを受け入れる意志がないことを相手にはっきりと示して断ること.
reject 提案・要求などを不要・不適当として断固として拒絶すること. refuse より強意的.
turn down 提案・応募者などを断る口語的な表現.
decline 申し出・提案・招待などを礼儀正しくまた穏やかに断ること.

•わいろを受け取るのを断わる *refuse to* accept a

bribe; *reject* a bribe. ▶彼は彼女にプロポーズしたが,彼女は断わった He proposed to her, but she *refused* (him) [*turned* him *down*]. ▶私たちは太郎を食事に招待したが,彼は断わった We asked Taro to come to dinner, but he *declined* [*refused*, *turned down*, ×*rejected*] the invitation. (**!**「招待」に reject を用いるのは不適切. decline, refuse は the invitation を省略することも可) ▶彼は私たちといっしょに行くのを断わった He *refused* [*declined*, ×*rejected*] *to* go with us. (**!** reject は to 不定詞をとらない) ▶彼は彼の支払いの要求をきっぱりと断わった She flatly *rejected* [flatly *refused*, *gave* a flat *refusal to*] his demand for payment. ▶私たちはコンサートへの入場を断わられた We *were refused* [《や書》*were denied*, 《書》*were not granted*] *admission to* the concert./We *were not admitted to* the concert.

❷ [許可を得る] (許可を求める) ask 《him》 for permission; (予告する) give* 《him》 notice, warn. ● 警察にデモをすると断わる (= 通告する) *warn* the police *of* the demonstration. ▶この部屋を使用するなら,先生に断わった方がいいよ If you want to use this room, you should *ask* your teacher *for permission*. ▶引っ越すときは1か月前にその旨私に断わってください Please *give* me a month's *notice* [《古》*warning*] when you move out.

*こな 粉 [粉末] powder; [穀物の] flour /fláuər/, 粉にする powder; (穀物をひいて) grind [mill] 《wheat》 into *flour*. ● チョークの粉 chalk *dust*.

こなごな 粉々 ▶粉々になる go to pieces; break [smash] into pieces. ▶皿が床に落ちて粉々にこわれた The plate fell to the floor and broke [smashed] *into pieces*./The plate fell *to pieces* on the floor. ▶ボールが当たって窓ガラスが粉々になった The ball *shattered* the window.

こなし ▶身のこなし a movement. (⇨動作, 態度)

こなす [処理する] (終える) finish, complete; (進行させる) get* on with ...; [演じる] perform; [消化する] digest; [自由自在に扱う] 《機械・乗り物などを》manage; (言語を) have* (a) good command 《of》. ● 1週間でその仕事をこなす finish the work in a week. ▶マクベスの役をうまくこなす *play* [*perform*] (the part of) Macbeth very well. ▶一塁と三塁をこなす (can) *play* first and third. ▶仕事はちゃんとこなしていますか How *are* you *getting on with* your work? ▶今では少数の機械で何百人分もの仕事をこなしている A few machines *are* now *doing* the work of hundreds of people. ▶この店では商売を数でこなしている (= 利益を上げる) At this store they *make profits* through quantity sales.

こなせっけん 粉せっけん soap powder.

こなまいき 小生意気 ━ 小生意気な 形 (こしゃくな) cheeky, saucy, 《米》sassy. (⇨生意気) ▶小生意気な小娘 a *cheeky* [a *saucy*] little girl.

こなみじん 粉みじん (⇨粉々 (ぷん))

こなミルク 粉ミルク milk powder; powdered [dried] milk.

こなゆき 粉雪 powdery [fine] snow.

こなれる (消化する) digest. (⇨消化する) ▶彼女はこなれた訳をする She translates *very well* [*in a natural style*, *in a readable style*]. ▶彼は結婚して人間がこなれてきた (= 人間的に成熟した) He *has matured mentally* after he got married.

ごなん 御難 (不運) bad luck; 《書》a misfortune; a disaster. ▶彼女は最近不幸の毒に当たった I'm sorry she has had a series of *misfortunes*.

コナンドイル (⇨ドイル)

こにくらしい 小憎らしい irritating, 《話》aggravating, maddening. (⇨憎らしい) ▶小憎らしい子供 an *aggravating* [a *maddening*] kid.

こにもつ 小荷物 《主に米》a package, 《主に英》a parcel. (⇨小包)

コニャック [フランスのコニャック地方産のブランデー] (a) cognac /kóunjæk/.

ごにん 誤認 ━ 誤認する 動 ● 味方の飛行機を敵機と誤認する *mistake* one's plane *for* [×*as*] an enemy plane.

こにんずう 小人数 (⇨小(氵)人数)

ごにんばやし 五人囃子 *goninbayashi*; (説明的に) the five dolls representing court musicians displayed on the third row from the top tier of the doll stand.

こぬか 小糠 ● 小糠三合持ったら養子に行くな Never marry an heiress, unless you are penniless.

こぬかあめ 小糠雨 a fine [a very light] rain; (霧雨) a drizzle, a drizzling rain. ▶小糠雨が降っている It's *drizzling*./A *very fine rain* is falling.

コネ (縁故) connections; (引き) 《話》pull (**!** 時に a ~). ● コネで就職する get a job through *connections* [*contacts*, *pull*]. ▶「父親のコネ(=影響力)で」なら ... through one's father's *influence*]

こねかえす 捏ね返す ▶何度も繰り返しこねる] knead 《clay [dough]》 repeatedly; [事態をいっそう混乱させる] make the situation more complicate; complicate the situation.

コネクション a good (personal) connection 《with, to》; contacts.

コネクター [接続器具] a connector.

こねこ 子猫 a kitten, a kitty (**!** kitten の愛称).

コネティカット [米国の州] Connecticut /kənétikət/ (略 Conn. 郵便略 CT).

ごねどく ごね得 ▶彼はあれこれ苦情を言ってごね得をした He made a lot of complaints and finally *made them heard*. ▶彼らはどうしてもその金を払おうとしない. このままではごね得になってしまうだろう They won't pay the money. If we give in, they will win *complaining loudly* [(うまく言い逃れをして) *by quibbling*, (不合理な理屈で) *by arguing irrationally*].

こねまわす 捏ね回す (⇨捏ね返す)

こねる [粉などを] knead, work. (⇨練る) ▶理屈をこねる *chop* logic. ▶(投手などが滑りを止めるために新しいボールをこねる rub up a new ball. ▶だだをこねては (= 分からないことを言っては) いけません Don't be (so) unreasonable.

ごねる (文句・不平を言う) complain 《about》; (条件の上で不当にねばる) hold* out for better conditions; (法外な要求を出す) make* an unreasonable demand.

ごねん 御念 (心遣い) care; consideration. ▶ご念の入ったごあいさつ, 痛み入ります I'm much obliged to you for your *considerate* greeting. ▶ご念(=ご心配)には及びません You don't have to *worry* (about that).

ごねんせい 五年生 (小学校の) a fifth-year pupil; 《米》a fifth grader; 《英》a fifth-former. (⇨学年)

この ❶ [指示的に] this (**!** (1) 複数名詞の前では these. (2) 代名詞として「このこと[物, 人]」の意でも用いる). ▶この花とあの花とではどちらが好きですか Which do you like better, *this* flower or that one [《複数》*these* flowers or those]? (**!** 複数名詞を従える場合, 《米》, 《英書》では these, those の後に ones を用いない. ただし these white flowers or those red ones では ones は必要) ▶このことはだれにも言うな Don't tell anyone about *this* (matter). ▶この人は友人の阿部さんです *This* is Mr. Abe, one of my friends./*This* is my friend Abe. ▶彼[漱石]のこの小説が好きだ I like *this* novel of his [Soseki's]. (❗× ...his [Soseki's] *this* novel とはしない) ▶この列車は 50 分で名古屋に到着します *Our* [*This*] train will be arriving at Nagoya in fifty minutes. (❗*our train* は「我々の乗っている列車」, *this train* は他の列車との対比の場合に用いる) ▶いや知ってたよ. このぼくが彼に話したんだもの He did know. I told him *myself*. (❗再帰代名詞の強調用法で I を強めたもの)

[会話]「金をよこしな」「このポケットに入っているから取れよ」"I want your money." "It's *here* in my pocket. Just take it." [事情] 海外で強盗にあったらポケットやバッグに手を入れずに，このように相手に取らせること)

❷ [最近の] (この前の) last; (過去の) past; (次の) next. (⇨ここ ❸) ▶この 1 か月間 (過去) for the *last* [*past*] month; (未来) for the *next* month. ▶この日曜日映画に行きます I'll go to see a movie *next* [(この次に来る) *this* (*coming*)] Sunday. (❗*on* を前に置かない) ▶この 1 週間は忙しかった I've been busy *all through the week*. (❗「その 1 週間」は *all the week*)

このあいだ この間 (先日) the other day (❗1 週間くらい前のことをいう); (数日前に) a few [some, several] days ago; (話) a while back; (最近) recently, lately. ▶この間の晩[夜] the other evening [night]. ▶この間much スピード違反で罰金を取られた He was fined for speeding *the other day* [*several days ago*]. ▶彼はついこの間までこの町に住んでいた He lived in this city *until quite* [*very*] *recently*. ▶彼はこの間からずっと病気で床についている He has been sick in bed *for* (*the last* [*past*]) *several days*. (❗× *since several days ago* は不可) ▶それは今はちゃんと動きますか. この間使おうとしたときには動かなかったんです Does it work now? It didn't (*the*) *last time* we tried it. (❗*the*) *last time* は接続詞的用法)

このうえ この上 (もっと多く) more; (程度・時間などがさらに) further. ▶この上あなたのお世話になるわけにはいきません I won't give you any *more* [*further*] trouble. ▶後の方が堅い言い方) ▶この上, 欲しいものは何もない There is nothing *more* I want./(これに加えて) There is nothing I want *besides* [*on top of*, 《やや書》*in addition to*] *this*./(反語的に) Who could ask for anything *more*? ▶この上は(=今や)逃げる他ない *All* you *can do now* is (to) run away. (❗主に《話》ではしばしば *to* を省略する)/Now you have *no* (*other*) *choice but to* run away. ▶彼はこの上なく幸せだった He was *extremely* happy./He was *as* happy *as* (happy) *can* [×*could*] *be*. (❗(1)《話》では後の happy は通例省略する. (2) *as ... can be* は成句表現で主文の時制の支配を受けない)

このえ 近衛 the Imperial Guards; the bodyguards.
● 近衛兵 (組織) an Imperial Guard; (個人) an Imperial Guard(sman); a soldier in the Imperial Guard.

このかぎり この限り ●この限りではない ▶少なくとも私の場合はこの限りではない At least in my case, it is an exception to this rule.

このかた この方 ● 本校が創立されてからこの方(=以来) *since* the foundation of this school; *since* this school was founded. (❗後の方が口語的) ▶10 年この方 *for the past* [*last*] ten years; 《古》 *these* ten years. ▶生まれてからこの方入院したことがない I have never been in (《主に米》the) hospital *in my*

life.

このくらい〚これほど〛this; 〚そんなに〛so. ▶とても大きなクマを撃った. それはこのくらいの大きさだった I shot a very big bear. It was *about this* big [*about as big as* this, 〚前の方が口語的〛]. ▶その事故までこんなに知らない人がこのくらい多くいる There are *this* many people who know nothing about the accident. ▶子供でもこのくらいは知っている Even a child knows *this much*. ▶今日はこのくらいにしておこう *So much for* today. (❗授業の終わりに先生のいう言葉)/《話》 Let's call it a day. (❗仕事などを終えるときの言葉)

このご この期 ▶この期に及んで私たちに何ができるというのか There's nothing for us to do at *this last moment* [*this final stage*].

このごろ この頃 〚今日では〛these days, nowadays (❗ともに現在時制も用いる. 後の語は主に書き言葉); 〚今〛now; 〚最近〛recently, lately. (⇨最近) ▶このごろの若者 the young people *of today*; young people *today* [*these days*]; *today*'s young people. ▶このごろ物価が高い Prices are high *these days* [*nowadays*].

このさい この際 〚今〛now; 〚この場合に〛on this occasion; 〚こういう事情のもとで〛under the [these] circumstances.

このさき この先 ❶〚前方に〛ahead. ▶駅はこの先 8 キロ行ったところにあります The railroad station is eight kilometers *ahead*. ▶図書館はすぐこの先です The library is *just* [*only a little way*] *ahead*./The library is *only a little way from here*.
❷〚これからずっと〛from now on; (将来) in the future. ▶この先どうするつもりですか What are you going to do *from now on* [*in the future*, (今後) *after this*]? (❗× ...*from now*? は不可)

このしろ 鯑 〚魚介〛a gizzard shad.

このたび この度 ▶この度(=近々)結婚することになりました I am going to get married *soon* [*shortly*]. ▶この度はお世話になりました(=いろいろ助けてくださってありがとうございました) I am grateful (to you) for your kind help [having helped me a lot]./You have been very kind [good] to me. (❗現在完了形で,「いろいろ助けてもらったことが今につながっている」と感謝を新たにする) ▶この度の(=この)選挙に彼は再選をめざして立候補します He will run for a second term in *this* [(予定されている) the *upcoming*] election. ▶この度はご昇進おめでとうございます Congratulations on your promotion. ▶この度はご主人様には, 大変お気の毒に思いますI am terribly sorry about your husband. ▶この度転勤で広島からまいりました大島と申します I have been transferred from Hiroshima. My name is Oshima.

このつぎ この次 〚次の〛next. ▶この次(=次の時)まで待つつもり till *next time*. ▶この次の日曜彼と魚釣りに行きます I'll go fishing with him *next Sunday* [《英古》 *on Sunday next*, ×*on next Sunday*]. ▶この次の駅で降りましょう Let's get off at *the next* station. ▶またこの次(=いつかほかの日に)外で食事をしませんか How about eating out with me *some other time* [*day*]? ▶この次が来るときは私の切手のコレクションを見せであげよう *Next time* you come, I'll show you my stamp collection. (❗(1) Next time は接続詞的用法. (2) When you come next time, ... より普通)

このとおり この通り〚このように〛like this, (in) this way. ▶〚ごらんのように〛*as you see*. ▶すぐこの通りやりなさい Do it *like this* [*(in) this way*, (同じ方法で) *in the same way*] *at once*. ▶列車はこの通り満員で The train is jammed *as you see*. ▶この通り(

このとき **この時** at this [that] time; [この瞬間に] at this [that] moment. (❗それぞれ this は現在の文脈で, that は過去の文脈で用いる) ●この時になってそんなことをしてもだめだ It's no use doing that *at this time [moment]*./(今では遅すぎる) It's too late to do that *now*. ●この時彼はまだ大学生だった He was still in college *at that time [then]*. ●この時はもうコンサートは聴衆の万雷の拍手で始まっていた *By this time*, the concert had begun with thunderous applause of the audience. (❗さらに古い過去(過去完了)と対比しているのでこの場合 this を用いる) ●この時ばかりは彼は真剣な様子だった He looked serious (*just*) *for once*.

このところ **この所** [最近] recently, lately (⇨最近); [このごろ] these days, (主に書) nowadays. (❗最後の二つは現在形と共に用いる) ●彼はこのところあまり酒を飲まない He doesn't drink much *these days [nowadays]*. ●この病院は授業に出ていません He hasn't been to class *recently [lately, (書) of late]*.

このは **木の葉** a leaf (働 leaves). (⇨葉) ●(船が)木の葉のように波にもまれる *be tossed* about by the waves; *toss* about in the waves. (❗「波にもまれている船」は a tossing ship)

このはずく **木の葉木菟** [鳥] a scops owl.

このぶん **この分** [この調子で] at this rate. ●この分でいくと体育館は12月までに完成するでしょう *At this rate*, the gymnasium will be completed by December. ●この分でいくと(=事態がこのように進むと)物価は当分上がり続けるだろう *If things go on like this*, prices will keep rising for some time. ●この分では(=現在の状況から判断すると)両国間に戦争はないだろう *Judging from [by] the present state of affairs*, there will be no war between the two countries. ●この分では(=現状では)株に投資できない *As things are*, I can't invest any money in stocks. ●この分から雪はじきにやむでしょう *By the looks of it*, it will stop snowing soon.

このへん **この辺** [この近くに] near [(米) around] here; [この近所に] in this neighborhood [(書) vicinity]; [近くのどこかに] around. ●この辺にレストランはありますか Is there a restaurant *near [around] here?*/Is there a restaurant *in this neighborhood?* ●この辺の方ですか Do you come from *around here?*

このほか **この他** [これに加えて] besides (this), in addition (to this) (❗通例文頭で); [これを除いて] except for. ●この他に彼女は料理も上手だ *Besides [In addition]*, she is good at cooking.

このまえ **この前** ❶[先日] the other day; (最近) recently, lately. (⇨この間, 先日, 最近) ●この前の嵐の後しばらくして *the recent* storm. ●この前言ったように as I said *before [earlier]*, ... ●この前たまたま彼と出会った I happened to see him *the other day*.
❷[前回] ●この前の日曜日[夏] (に) *last* Sunday [summer]. (❗「この前の夏(に)」は秋にいうような場合は this summer も可)。●この前の市長 the *former* mayor; the *ex-*mayor. ●この前どこで働いていましたか Where did you work *last*? ●この前彼女に会ったときは彼女は幸福そうに見えた She looked happy when I *last* saw her./She looked happy (*the*) *last time* I saw her. ●彼女はこの前は別の男と歩いていた She was walking with a different gentleman *from the last time*. ●この前の授業に出たかい Did you go [come] to *the last class?* (❗you がその授業の教師/出席者なら come, それ以外の者なら go を用いる)

*__このましい__ **好ましい** [すてきな] nice; [感じのよい] pleasant, agreeable; [望ましい] desirable; [好意ある] favorable; [適している] suitable. ●好ましい結果 a *good* result. ●好ましからぬ人物 an *undesirable [a disagreeable]* person. ●好ましい環境 *desirable* surroundings. ●好ましからぬ(=歓迎されない)客 an *unwelcome* guest. ●好ましい印象を与える make a *favorable* [a *good*] impression ((on)).

このまま [あるがままに, そのままに] as it is, as they are. ●この花をこのまま彼の所へ持って行こう I'll take this flower to him *as it is*. ●私の所持品をこのままにしておいてくれ Leave my things *as they are*./Leave [*Let*] my things *alone*. ●今度は彼の失敗をこのままにしておく(=見逃しておく)ことはできない I can't *overlook* his mistake this time. ●このままでいくと(=この調子では)彼は再選されないだろう *At this rate* he won't be reelected. (⇨この分)

このみ **木の実** a nut. (⇨実)

このみ **好み** a liking; (好き嫌い) one's likes and dislikes; [趣味な] (a) taste; [気まぐれな好み] a fancy; [選択] choice, preference. ●服装の好み one's *taste for [in]* dress. ●好みに応じて砂糖を入れる add sugar to *taste*. ●この車は私の好みに合わない This car *isn't to my taste* [(書) *liking*]. ●(後の方は時に気取った表現)/This car *isn't for* me./This car *doesn't suit* my *taste* [*fancy*]./I don't *like* this car. ●人の好みはさまざまだ Everyone has their own *taste* [*likes and dislikes*]. (❗likes との対比のためには強勢移動に注意)/(ことわざ) There is no accounting for *taste* [(今は古) *tastes*]./(ことわざ) One man's meat is another man's poison. (❗meat は「食物」の意) (⇨たで) ●兄と私とでは詩の好みが違う My brother and I have different *taste in* poetry. ●この二つの中ではどちらがお好みですか Which of these two is your *choice* [*preference*]?/Which of these two do you *like better* [*prefer*]? ●私には特別な色の好みはない I have no special *preference for* color. ●好みの色は何ですか What is your *favorite* color?/What color do you *like*? ●彼は服の好みが大変うるさい He is very *particular* [(話) *choosy*, (米話) (けなして) *picky*] *about* what he wears.

会話 「このスカートはどう」「私の好みからすればもうちょっと短くしてほしいな」 "How's this skirt?" "For my *taste*, cut it a bit shorter."

会話 「音楽が大好きです」「好みは?」「クラシックです」 "I like music very much." "What *flavor?*" "Classical [×Classic]."

*__このむ__ **好む** like, be fond of ...; [大好きだ] love (❗ like より意味が強く, 主に女性に好んで用いられる); [...の方を好む] prefer (-rr-). (⇨好き) ●彼はあまりウイスキーを好まない He doesn't *like [care for]* whiskey very much. (❗care for は主に否定文・疑問文・条件文で用いる) ●好むと好まざるにかかわらず, 私は1人でそこへ行かねばならない *Whether* I *like* it or not, I have to go there alone.

このよ **この世** 图 (現世) this world; (人生) this life. ●この世を去る go out of this world; (婉曲的に) pass away. ●彼はもうこの世にはいない He is *no longer alive*./(書) He is *no more*.

── **この世の** 形 (現世の) worldly; (天国に対して地上の) earthly. (❗いずれも限定的に) ●この世の楽しみ *earthly* pleasures.

このような, このように like this. (⇨こんな) ●このよう

このわた にやってください Please do it *like this* [(*in*) *this way*].

このわた 海鼠腸 the salted entrails of sea cucumbers. (参考) 珍味の一つ)

ごば 後場 (証券取引所の) the afternoon session. (⇔ 前場)

こばい 故買 图 (盗品を買う[取引する]こと) buying [traffic in] stolen goods.
— 故買する 動 buy [traffic in] stolen goods.
● 故買品 《米》hot goods.

こばか 小馬鹿 ● 小ばかにする look down on; 《書》 scorn. ▶人を小ばかにしたような態度を取るな Don't take a scornful attitude toward people.

こはく 琥珀 amber. ● 琥珀色の amber(-colored).

ごばく 誤爆 图 (an) accidental [unintentional] bombing. — 誤爆する 動 accidentally bomb 《a hospital》.

ごはさん 御破算 ● 御破算にする 〖元に戻して始める〗 start (all) over again, 《主に米》 start over, 《書》 start afresh; 〖中止する〗 (計画などを) give*... up (⇔止(°)める); (行事・予定などを) call ... off.

こばしり 小走り ▶彼は小走りでやってきた He *trotted* up to me.

こはだ 〖魚介〗a gizzard shad (複 ~, ~s).

こばち 小鉢 a small [little] bowl.

ごはっと 御法度 ● 御法度になっている be forbidden (by law). ▶ここではその話は御法度だよ It's a *taboo* (story) here.

こばな 小鼻 the wings of a nose.
● 小鼻をうごめかす (得意になる) be triumphant; be glowing with pride.
● 小鼻をふくらませる ● 小鼻をふくらませて(=不愉快そうな顔をして)文句を言う complain *looking displeased* [*with unhappy looks*].

こばなし 小話 a funny short story.

こばなれ 子離れ ● 子離れする 動 (子供の自立をうながす) encourage one's child to be independent; (子供と一定の距離を置いて接する) keep one's distance from one's child [children].

こはば 小幅 ● 小幅な値動きを a *small* change in prices. ● 小幅な下方修正 *modest* downward revision.

*こばむ 拒む 〖断わる〗 (きっぱり) refuse; (断固としてきっく) turn ... down (! refuse, reject の婉曲語); (丁寧に) decline; (要求などを) deny. (⇔断わる)
● 彼の要求を拒む *refuse* [*reject, turn down, deny*] his request. ▶彼は命令に従うことを拒んだ He *refused* [×rejected] *to* obey the orders. (! reject は to 不定詞をとらない)

こばら 小腹 ● 小腹がすく ▶小腹がすいた I guess I'm a little hungry./I feel a bit peckish.
● 小腹が立つ ▶彼の見え透いたお世辞に小腹が立つ(=ちょっと腹が立つ) I *get a little angry at* his obvious flattery.

コバルト 〖化学〗 cobalt /kóubɔːlt/ 〖元素記号 Co〗.
● がん細胞にコバルトを照射する a direct *cobalt* radiation to kill cancer cells.
● コバルトブルー cobalt blue.

こはるびより 小春日和 Indian summer. (参考) 米国北部やカナダに 11 月頃訪れる暖かく乾燥した気候)

こはん 湖畔 the lakeside. ● 湖畔で *by* [*beside*] *the lake*. ● 湖畔の宿 a hotel *on the lake*; a *lakeside* hotel. ● 琵琶湖畔で休暇を過ごす spend one's vacation *at* Lake Biwa.

こばん 小判 *koban* (! 単・複同形); (歴史的な) an oval gold [silver] coin formerly used in Japan. (▶猫に小判 (⇒猫 [成句]))
● 小判形 the shape of *koban*.

*ごはん ご飯 rice, (炊いた米) boiled [cooked] rice (⇔飯(°)); (食事) a meal. (解説)いごはん plain rice. (語法) 米英人には物足りなく感じられるので味付けをして食べる傾向がある) (茶碗 1 杯の) 一つあつあつのご飯 a bowl of steaming *rice*. (主に米) fix] a *meal*; make *dinner*. ▶ご飯の時間ですよ (It's) time to eat [have a *meal*]. ▶ご飯ですよ Dinner's ˇready. (! dinner は時間に応じて breakfast, lunch, supper と替えてよい) ▶今日のご飯はとってもふっくら炊けている The *rice* today is cooked nice and /náisənd/ corpulent [fluffy].
● ご飯茶碗 a rice bowl. ● ご飯物 a dish consisting mainly of rice.

ごばん 碁盤 a go-board; (説明的に) a board with 324 squares or 381 intersections on which two players compete to win a larger number of intersections.
● 碁盤の目 碁盤の目(のように) on a grid (pattern [system]).
● 碁盤縞 (a) check ● 碁盤縞に checkerwise; in a checkerboard.

こばんざめ 小判鮫 〖魚介〗 a sharksucker; a remora.

こはんにち 小半日 nearly half a day. ▶彼は日曜日は小半日読書して過ごした He spent *nearly half a day* reading on Sunday.

こび 媚 (a) flattery.
● 媚を売る flatter. (⇔へつらう, おべっか)

ごび 語尾 the end(ing) of a word [(文の) a sentence]. ▶語尾をはっきり発音しない人が多い Many people fail to speak clearly *at the end of a sentence*. ● 語尾変化 〖文法〗 inflection.

ゴビ ゴビ砂漠 the Gobi /góubi/.

*コピー 图 〖複写物〗a copy (! 英語の copy は同時に印刷した本・雑誌などをもいうので two *copies* of the book (その本を 2 冊のようにも用いることができる); 〖複製品〗 a reproduction, 〖広告文〗 (advertising) copy. ● バックアップコピー a backup *copy*. ● 違法コピー an illegal *copy*. ▶この手紙のコピーを 3 部取って くれますか *Make* three *copies of* this letter for me, will you? ▶この書類のコピーを取ってください Take *a second generation copy* of this document.
— コピーする 動 copy, make a copy 《*of*》; (絵画などを) reproduce.
● コピー機 a phótocopy machine; a photocopier. ● コピー食品 (an) imitation food. ● この語は食品見本を指す場合もある) ● コピープロテクト 〖ソフトウェアの違法コピーを防止する機能〗 copy protection.
● コピーライター 〖広告文案作成者〗 a copywriter.
● コピーライト 〖著作権, 版権〗 (a) copyright 《記号 ⓒ》.

こひざ 小膝 ● 小ひざを打つ slap one's knee.

こびじゅつ 古美術 classical art.
● 古美術商 an antique dealer. ● 古美術品(骨董品) an antique /æntiːk/; (古典的形式の作品) a work of a classical art form. ● 古美術品店 an antique shop. (⇒骨董(°))

こひつじ 子羊, 小羊 a lamb /læm/.

こびと 小人 a dwarf (複 ~s, dwarves).

ごびゅう 誤謬 (誤り) an error; a mistake. (⇒誤り)

こひょう 小兵 (体格の小さいこと) a small build [(書) physique]; (体格の小さい人) a short man. ● 小兵の力士 a wrestler of *small build*.

こびりつく ▶泥が私の靴にこびりついた Mud *stuck* [*clung*] *to* my shoes. (⇒くっつく) ▶彼の言葉が私の頭にこびりついて離れない His words *stick* in my

こびる 媚びる flatter. (⇨へつらう)
こぶ 瘤 〖打撲による〗a bump; 〖固いれもの〗a lump; 〖ラクダの〗a hump; 〖木の節の〗a knot. ▶ボールが当たって頭にこぶができた I got a *bump* [a *lump*] on [*x*in] my head when I was hit by a ball.
こぶ 昆布 (⇨昆布(こんぶ))
● 昆布巻き (説明的に) a roll of *kombu* with the core ingredients, cooked with sugar and soy sauce.
こぶ 鼓舞 图 〖激励〗encouragement; inspiration.
── 鼓舞する 動 〖励す〗encourage; 〖奮い立たせる〗inspire. ● 士気を鼓舞する *raise* the morale 《of a team》.
ごふ 護符 a charm; a talisman; (身につける) an amulet. (⇨お守り)
ごぶ 五分 〖利率〗five percent; 〖等しい〗even. (⇨五分五分) ● 年利五分《*at*》an annual interest of 5 *percent*. ● 五分の試合 an *even* game.
こふう 古風 ── 古風な 形 ● 古風(=旧式)な家 an *old-fashioned* house. ● 古風で趣のある》a *quaint* house. ● 古風な考え an *old-fashioned* idea.
ごふく 呉服 (着物の種類) fabrics [cloths] for *kimonos*; (着物) *kimonos*.
● 呉服屋 (店) a *kimono* store [shop]; (人) a *kimono* dealer.
こぶくしゃ 子福者 a (happy) person blessed with many children.
ごぶごぶ 五分五分 ── 五分五分の 形 fifty-fifty; (互角に) even. ▶彼の成功の見込みは五分五分だ His chance of success is *fifty-fifty* [an *even*]./He has a *fifty-fifty* [an *even*] chance of success./It is an *even* chance that he will succeed.
会話 「どっちのチームが勝つと思う」「五分五分かな、どっちにしてもこれといった選手がいないからね」"Which team do you think will win?" "It's a *toss-up*. Neither of them has a star player."
ごぶさた 御無沙汰 ▶すっかりごぶさたして申し訳ありません (手紙で) It's been a long time since our last correspondence./(長いこと手紙を出さないですみません) I'm sorry I have not written (to) you for a long time. 事情 このような形式的なことは通例書かない. ただし, 返事が遅れたときには, First of all, I have to apologize to you for not answering your letter sooner. などと謝る (⇨《巻末 手紙の書き方》))/(親しい間で) (It's) been a long time./Long time. ❗ Long time no see. はこの場合には くだけすぎ
こぶし 拳 a fist. ● こぶしを握り締める clench one's *fist*; clench one's hand into a *fist*. ● こぶしを振る shake [wave] one's *fist*.
こぶし 小節 a tremolo. ▶その歌手は小節をきかせてしみじみと歌った The singer sang very emotionally with a *tremolo*.
こぶし 辛夷 〖植物〗a magnolia kobus.
ごふじょう 御不浄 (go to [use]) a toilet. (⇨便所)
こぶつ 古物 an antique /ænti:k/. (⇨骨董)
こぶつき 瘤付き (a person) with a child. ▶こぶつきの人は再婚しにくい It is difficult for *a person with a child* to marry again.
こぶとり 小太り ── 小太りの 形 (太りぎみの) rather fat; (いくぶんぽっちゃりした) plump; (肉付きがよく胸が豊かな) buxom. (⇨太る)
こぶね 小舟 a small [a light] boat.
コブラ 〖動物〗a cobra. ● ジャイアントコブラ a giant *cobra*.
こぶり 小振り ── 小振りの 形 ● 小振りの(=小形の)茶

こぶり 小降り 〖小雨〗a light rain; 〖霧雨〗a drizzle. ▶雨が小降りになって(=あがって)きた The rain *is letting up*./The rain *has lessened*.
わん a *small-sized* bowl.
コプロセッサー 〖コンピュータ〗a coprocessor.
こふん 古墳 an ancient tomb, a tumulus (復 ～es, tumuli). ● 古墳を発掘する excavate [unearth] an *ancient tomb*.
こぶん 子分 a follower; (集合的) a following; (政界・やくざのボスの) one's henchman (復 -men). ● 子分が多い have a lot of *followers*; have a large *following*.
こぶん 古文 ancient writing; (古典) Japanese classics (❗ 単数扱い) . (the) classics は古代ギリシャ・ローマのものをさす).
ごふん 胡粉 (白色の顔料) chalk; whitewash.
ごへい 御幣 (説明的に) a sacred wand with strips of white paper.
● 御幣をかつぐ be superstitious 《*about*》.
● 御幣かつぎ superstition; (人) a superstitious person.
ごへい 語弊 ● 語弊がある misleading. ▶そういうと語弊があるかもしれないが The expression may be *misleading*, but ….
こべつ 戸別 ── 戸別の 形 door-to-door, house-to-house. ● 戸別訪問する make a *door-to-door* visit [投票・寄付などの依頼で] canvass]; visit [canvass] *from door to door* (❗《話》では from を省略することがある).
── 戸別に 副 from door to door; from house to house.
こべつ 個別 ── 個別の 形 (個人個人の) individual; (各々の) each; (別々の) separate. ● 個別の指導 *individual* guidance. ● 個別の部屋 *separate* rooms.
── 個別に 副 individually; separately. ● 個別に生徒と面談する meet and talk with the students *individually*; have a meeting with *individual* students.
コペルニクス 〖ポーランドの天文学者〗Copernicus /koʊpə́ːrnɪkəs/.
● コペルニクス的大転回 a Copernican revolution.
コペンハーゲン 〖デンマークの首都〗Copenhagen /koʊpənhéɪɡən/.
ごほう 語法 usage. ● 現代米語語法 modern American *usage*; (a) modern *Americanism*.
ごほう 誤報 a false [an incorrect] report.
ごぼう 牛蒡 〖植物〗a burdock. 事情 欧米では食用としない) ● ささがきごぼう shredded *burdock*.
● ごぼう抜き ▶デモ隊をごぼう抜きにする *remove* the demonstrators *bodily one by one*. ▶彼は5人ごぼう抜きで(=一気に追い抜いて)先頭に立った He *overtook* five runners ahead of him *in one spurt* and went into the lead.
ごぼごぼ ▶流しの水がごぼごぼ音を立てて吸い込まれて行った The water in the sink *gurgled* down the drain. ▶小川の底から水がごぼごぼわき出ている Water *is bubbling up* from the bottom of the brook.

__こぼす__ ❶ 〖物をこぼす〗(液体・粉などを誤って) spill; (液体を) slop (-pp-); (涙などを) 〖書〗shed*; (パンくずなどを落とす) drop (-pp-). ● 涙をこぼす *shed* tears. ● パンくずをテーブルにこぼす *drop* crumbs on the table. (❗意図的にそうでない場合がある) ▶床にインクをこぼした I *spilled* some ink *on* [(一面に) *over*] the floor.
❷ 〖不平を言う〗complain 《*about*, *of*》; (ぶつぶつ言う) grumble 《*about*, *of*》. ▶彼は物価が高いといつもこぼしてばかりいる He *is always complaining*

[*grumbling*] about high prices. (▶He always complains .... と人なり, 話し上手のいらだちを含意する)

こぼね 小骨 small [fine] bones. ●喉に小骨が刺さる get a *small* bone stuck in one's throat.
● **小骨を折る** (ちょっと苦労する) take a little pain [trouble].

コボル 〖コンピュータ〗 COBOL 《*common business-oriented language* の略》. (参考) プログラム言語の一種)

こぼれだね こぼれ種 (自然に地面に落ちた植物の種) a self-sown seed; (落胤(いん)) an illegitimate child of a noble.

こぼればなし 零れ話 an episode;《米》tidbits,《英》titbits 《*of*》. ▶彼の少年時代のこぼれ話 a humorous *episode* in his boyhood.

***こぼれる 零れる** (液体が容器などから) spill*, slop (-pp-); (あふれ出る) overflow; (落とす) drop (-pp-). ▶牛乳がグラスからあふれてテーブルにこぼれた The milk *spilled* [*slopped*] over the glass *on* [*一面に*) *over*] the table./The milk *overflowed* the brim of the glass *onto* the table. ▶目から涙がこぼれた (=落ちた) Tears *dropped* [(流れた) *flowed*] *from* my eyes. (⇨落ちる) ▶彼の顔に笑みがこぼれた A smile *broke out* on his face.

こぼれる 毀れる (刃などが欠ける) be chipped [nicked]. ▶刀の刃がこぼれている The edge of the sword *is chipped* [*nicked*].

ごほん(ごほん) ●ごほん(ごほん)と咳(せき)をする cough /kɔ́(ː)f/. ▶ごほんごほんと激しく咳込んでいる be having a bad fit of *coughing*.

こぼんのう 子煩悩 ▶彼は子煩悩だ(=子を溺愛(できあい)する) He *dotes on* [*upon*] his children./He is a *fond* [*a doting*] father.

こま 駒 〖将棋の〗a piece; 〖弦楽器の〗a bridge. ●持ち駒 a captured *piece* for one's own use.
●**駒を進める** 決勝戦に駒を進める(=勝ち進む) *advance to* [*reach*] the finals.

こま 小間 a small gap [room].

こま 独楽 a top. ●こまを回す spin a *top*.

ごま 胡麻 〖植物〗 sesame /sésəmi/; (実) sesame (seeds).
●**ごまをする** grind /gráind/ sesame seeds (▶「ごまを炒(い)る」 は toast *sesame seeds*; 《比喩的に》(へつらう) flatter; (ご機嫌をとる)《話》play up (*to*).
●**ごまあえ** a dish dressed with sesame sauce.
●**ごま油** sesame oil. ●**ごま塩** ⇨胡麻(塩) ●**ごますり** (人) a flatterer.

ごま 護摩 goma; (説明的に) a sacred fire for invocation. ●護摩をたく light a *sacred fire*.

コマーシャル a commercial (message), 《米》a message;《和製語》CM. ●化粧品[その会社]のテレビコマーシャル a TV *commercial* for cosmetics [the company]. ●コマーシャルの時間(=による放送の中断) a *commercial* break. ●ここでちょっとコマーシャルを We'll be right back after this (*commercial*) *message*.
● **コマーシャルソング** a commercial [an advertising] jingle [song]. (▶*song* より *jingle* が普通. また文脈によっては commercial を省略して jingle だけでも可) ●**コマーシャルベース** a commercial basis [footing].

こまいぬ 狛犬 komainu; (説明的に) lion-shaped guardian dogs, sitting facing each other.

:こまかい 細かい ❶ 〖物が小さい〗 small; (微細な) fine (▶通例限定的に). ●細かい砂[ほこり] fine sand [dust]. ●目の細かいレース[絹] fine lace [silk]. ●きめの細かい肌 *fine-textured* skin. ●細かくきざんだキャベツ *finely* chopped [shredded] cabbage. ▶この雑誌は細かい活字で印刷されている This magazine is printed in *small* type. ▶肉を細かく切ってください Cut the meat into (very) *small* pieces./Chop up the meat.

❷〖金額が少ない〗small. ●細かい金で支払う pay in *small* change. ▶この 1,000 円札を細かくしてくださいませんか Can you give me *change for* this 1,000-yen bill?/Can you *change* [*break*] this 1,000-yen bill (for me)?

❸〖綿密な〗(注意深く綿密な) close; (詳細にわたる) detailed; (詳細を極めた) minute /maɪn(j)úːt/. (▶ minute には原則として変化形はないが, 強調のために最上級 minutest が使われることがある). ●細かく closely; minutely; (詳細に) in detail. ●細かい点をいくつか省略する omit some *details*. ●昆虫を細かく観察する observe insects *closely*. ●彼女の話に細かく注意を払った He paid *close* [*careful*] attention to her words. ▶彼は私にその事故を細かく説明した He gave me a *detailed* [*a minute*] explanation of the accident./He explained the accident to me *in detail* [*minutely*]. (▶ ×He explained me the accident ... は不可) ▶細かい点まで触れるな Don't *go into detail*.

❹〖ささいな〗(取るに足らない) small, trivial. ●細かい誤りを指摘する point out 《his》*small* [*trivial*] mistakes. ▶私は今そんな細かい事にかかわっているひまはない I don't have time now for *small* matters like that.

❺〖微妙な〗(感じやすい) sensitive; (繊細な) delicate; (違いなどが微妙な) subtle /sʌ́tl/. ●細かい違い a *subtle* [*a delicate*, (わずかな) *a slight*] difference 《between》. ▶彼女は神経が細かい(=神経過敏だ) She is very *sensitive*.

❻〖金銭〗(慎重な) careful; (けちな)《話》stingy. ▶彼はひどく金に細かい He is very *careful* [*stingy*] with his money. (⇨けち)

ごまかし (あざむく) (a) deception; (だまそうとする策) trickery, a trick; (いんちき) (a) cheating. (▶いずれも具体的行為では ⓒ) (⇨だます) ▶トランプでごまかしをする *cheat* at cards. ▶あの男にはごまかしがきかない You can't play a *trick* on him.

ごまかす ❶〖だます〗deceive,《やや話》take*... in (▶しばしば受身で); (計略を用いて) trick; (だまし取る) cheat; (金銭などをだまし取る) swindle. (⇨だます) ●外見にごまかされる be *deceived* by appearances. ▶彼らは彼女をごまかして金を巻き上げた They *cheated* [*swindled*] her *out of* her money./They got money from her *by a trick*.

❷〖着服する〗(公金を) embezzle; (こっそりと)《やや話》pocket. (⇨着服, 横領.

❸〖数量を細工する〗●年齢をごまかす cheat [(うそをつく) *lie*] *about* one's age. ▶私はそのレストランで釣銭をごまかされた I *was shortchanged* [They *shortchanged* me] at that restaurant. ▶肉屋で目方をごまかされた I *was defrauded* with short weight at the butcher's./(目方をごまかした) The butcher *shortweighted* [*gave short weight*]. ▶私が帳簿をごまかしてるとでも思っているのか Do you think I*'m dishonest about* [《話》*cooking* (*up*)] the accounts?

❹〖場面を取りつくろう〗(過ちなどをうまく弁明する) explain ... away; (質問・税金などをうまくかわす) evade,《話》dodge. ▶彼はえり元の口紅のことを妻になんとかごまかそうとした He tried to *explain away* the lipstick mark on his collar to his wife. ▶彼女は踏み段につまずいたが, すぐそれを笑ってごまかした She stumbled over the step, but at once *laughed* it *off*.

こまぎれ 細切れ 〖細かい切れ端〗a scrap; 〖断片〗a fragment. ●豚肉を細切れにする *chop* [*hash*] the pork. ●細切れの(=断片的な)知識 *incomplete* 〖やや書〗*fragmentary* knowledge.

こまく 鼓膜 an eardrum; 〖解剖〗a tympanum /tímpənəm/ (複 ~s; tympana). ▶彼は鼓膜が破れた He had his *eardrum* split [ruptured]./His *eardrum* split [ruptured].

こまげた 駒下駄 《a pair of》low wooded clogs.

こまごま 細々 細々とした little; 〖詳細な〗detailed, minute /main(j)úːt/. ●細々とした用事 *little* [*small*] things to do; 〖雑用〗chores. ●細々とした指示をする give 《him》*detailed* [*full*] instructions. ●そのことについて細々と述べる explain it *in detail* [*minutely*]; go into detail about it.

ごましお 胡麻塩 a mixture of toasted sesame and salt. ●胡麻塩頭 'a head with mixed white and black hair.' ●胡麻塩頭の男 (白髪まじりの男) a *gray-haired* man; a man with gray hair. (❗ grizzled (hair) は訳語として日本語の口語的な響きと少し合わない) (⇨白髪(しらが))

こましゃくれる 動 talk [act] like a grown-up.
── **こましゃくれた** 形 《生意気な》《話》saucy, 《話》cheeky, 《米話》sassy (⇨生意気); 《ませた》precócious (⇨ませた).

こまた 小股 (また) a crotch, (歩幅が狭いこと) short steps. ▶彼女は小またで歩いた She walked with *short steps*. ●小またの切れ上がった ●小またの切れ上がった(=すらりとした足の長い)女性 a woman *with a good slender figure*; a slender [a stylish] woman. ●小またすくい 〖相撲〗 *komatasukui*; over thigh scooping body drop.

こまち 小町 (美しい娘) a beautiful girl; (美人) a beauty.

こまづかい 小間使い a maid; 《男女共用》a housekeeper.

こまつな 小松菜 *komatsuna*, (説明的に) a kind of colza.

こまどり 駒鳥 〖鳥〗a robin. (参考 英国の国鳥)

こまねく ▶手をこまねいていては(=何もしないでいては)事態はいっそう悪くなる If you go on *doing nothing*, things will get worse.

こまねずみ 独楽鼠 〖動物〗a Japanese dancing mouse. ●こまねずみのように働く work like a beaver [a bee].

こまめ 小まめ ── **小まめに** 副 ●こまめに(=きびきびと)動く move *briskly*. ●こまめに(=最新の状態に)住所録を整理しておく try to keep the address book *up to date*. ▶彼はこまめに働く He is working *briskly*, always doing something different.

ごまめ dried Japanese anchovies. ●ごまめの歯ぎしり to offer vain resistance.

こまもの 小間物 《米》notions, 《英》haberdashery. (❗ いずれも針・糸・ボタン・リボンなどの裁縫用品をいう) ●小間物屋を開く(ヘどを吐く) vomit, 《俗》puke ... up. ●小間物屋 《米》a notion store; 《英》a haberdashery, a haberdasher's shop.

こまやか 細やか ── **細やかな** 形 (温かい) warm; (優しい) tender. ●細やかな愛情 *warm* affection. ●こまやかに看病する look after 《him》*with great care*.

こまらせる 困らせる (迷惑をかける) trouble; (当惑させる) embárrass; (困惑させる) perpléx; (悩ませる) bother; (いらいらさせる) annoy. ●人を困らせる質問をする ask *embarrassing* [*perplexing*; (やっかいな) *disturbing*] questions. ●難しい質問で彼を困らせる *perplex* [*puzzle*] him with difficult questions. ▶つまらないことで私を困らせないでくれ Don't *trouble* [*bother*; (心配させる) *worry*] me with trivial matters. ▶少年は車がほしいと言って両親を困らせ続けた The boy kept (on) *bothering* his parents for a car. (❗ on をつけると継続・反復を強調し, 話し手のいらだちを含意することが多い)

こまりきる 困りきる

〔翻訳のこころ〕私は, 困りきった表情を浮かべたまま, 何と言ってよいのかわからずに呆然としていた (山田詠美『ひよこの眼』) With an utterly troubled look [expression] on my face, I stood there dumbfounded [speechless], not knowing what to say. (❗(1)「困りきった」は be utterly troubled (全く困った)と表す. (2) dumbfounded は驚きで声がでない状態. speechless はしかるべき言葉を思いつかない状態)

こまりはてる 困り果てる be at a total loss.

こまりもの 困り者 (厄介者) a nuisance 《to him》; (んちゃくを起こす人) a troublemaker, 《話》a black sheep; (役立たず) a good-for-nothing.

こまる 困る

▎**WORD CHOICE** 困る
have trouble [difficulty] 何らかの原因で漠然と支障を感じていること. ▶その宿題には困った I *had difficulty* with [(in) doing] the homework.
have a problem ちょっとした問題があって軽く支障を感じていること. ▶その外国人と話すのにだれも困らなかった Nobody *had a problem* talking to that foreigner.

▎**頻度チャート**
have trouble [difficulty]
▬▬▬▬▬▬▬▬▬▬▬▬▬▬▬▬▬▬
have a problem
▬▬▬▬▬▬▬▬▬
    20   40   60   80   100 (%)

❶ 〖困難にあう, 苦労する〗have* trouble [difficulty] 《with+事・人; (in) doing》 (❗ trouble の方が口語的だ); 〖ひどい目にあう〗have a hard time 《with+事; doing》; 〖苦しめられる〗be troubled 《by, with》. ●職探しに(=職が見つからなくて)困る have *trouble* [*difficulty*] (in) finding a job (❗ in は通例省略する); *have a hard time* finding a job. ▶たくさんの宿題で困っています I'm *having trouble* with lots of homework [×homeworks]. ▶彼は借金で困っている He's *troubled* by debt. ▶食料不足で大変困った We *had a hard time* because we didn't have enough food./(苦しんだ) We *suffered* greatly *from* the food shortage./(苦労を引き起こした) The food shortage *caused* us a lot of *trouble*. ▶困ったことに(更に困ったことには)妹はまた病気になった The ˇ*trouble is* (*that*) [To make matters worse,] my sister got sick again. (❗ 前の方は that の直前でやや上昇気味で切る. 次例も同様. 《話》では ˇTrouble is, my .... のようにもいう) ▶何を困っているのですか What's the *trouble* [*problem*]? ▶私は困っている友人を助けるつもりだ I'll help my friends *in trouble*. ▶あの子はよく心配するけるが, いちばん困るのは体が弱いことです She often worries me, but *the worst of it* [*all*] *is that* she has poor health. ▶その時は観光シーズンではなかったので, 手ごろなホテルを見つけるのには困らなかった(=なんなく見つけることができた) It was not the tourist season, so I was able to [×could] find an inexpensive hotel *without difficulty*. (!) could は一回限りの行為の達成には用いられない) My son *gives me a hard time*./(苦労の種だ) My son is a *great trouble* to me [(話) a pain in the neck].

❷ 〖困窮する〗 ・金に困っている be *in* financial *difficulties*; be pressed for money; 《話》 be hard up. ▶彼は生活に困っている (=well off)./(ほとんど生活できない) He can hardly make his [a] living.

❸ 〖迷惑する〗 (しつこくくり返される) be annoyed; (心の平静を乱される) be bothered. (!) 前の方が強意的 (⇒悩ます) ・困らせる (⇒困らせる) ▶彼には困ったもんだ He's *annoying* me./I'm *annoyed* with him./ He *troubles* me. ▶彼には困った癖がいくつかある He has several *annoying* habits. ▶困ったことにとても忙しくしているときにお客さんがあった *To my annoyance*, I had a visitor when I was very busy. ▶彼は時間を守らないので困る It *annoys* me that he is not punctual. ▶何か困ったことでもあるの？ What's *bothering* you?

❹ 〖当惑する〗 (分からなくて) be puzzled, (書) be perplexed; (恥ずかしくて) be embarrassed (⇒当惑する); 〖途方に暮れる〗 be at a loss. ・困らせる (⇒困らせる) ▶困った質問 a *puzzling* [an *embarrassing*] question. (!) ✕a *puzzled* [an *embarrassed*] question は不可) ▶彼女は彼らからほめられて困ってしまった She *was embarrassed* by his praise. ▶言葉に困った He *was at a loss for* words [what to say]. (!) at a loss は wh 節の前ではそれに続く前置詞は省略される) ・(話) He *was stumped for* words./He *was puzzled* [didn't know] what to say. (!) know を用いた最後の言い方が最も普通

翻訳のこころ 父親は、困った、という表情になった、困った、とは言わなかった（竹西寛子『蘭』） My father had a troubled [worried] look, but he did not say that he was troubled [worried]. (!) trouble は比較的長期間にわたって困ること、worry は短期間のささい心配ごと)

❺ 〖都合・具合が悪い〗 be inconvenient. ▶電話がないと困る Not having a telephone is *inconvenient* [an *inconvenience*]./It is [✕We are] *inconvenient* for us not *to* have a telephone./(電話なしではやっていけない) We can't do without a telephone. ▶こういうことが起こるようでは困ります (=起こってほしくない) I *don't want* this sort of thing happen*ing*. (!) ... to be happening の to be の省略された形で、否定文で用いられる傾向がある) ▶ここでは喫煙は困ります (許可されていない) Smoking *is not allowed* 〖やや書〗 *permitted*] here./(禁じられている) Smoking *is forbidden* here. ▶交通事故が毎年増えているのは困った(=残念な)ことだ It is a (great) *pity* 〖やや書〗 *It is regrettable*, ✕It is regretful〗 *that* the number of car accidents is increasing every year. ▶雨が降ると困るから(=場合に備えて)傘を持って行きなさい Take an umbrella (*just*) *in case* it rains [should rain]. (!) 後者を用いる方が可能性が低い)

会話 「彼はすぐ来ると思う？」「来なけりゃ困る(=絶対来なければならない)」"Do you think he'll come at once?" "He'll ábsolutely ˎhave to."

こまわり 小回り ・小回りがきく ▶この車は小回りがきく(=融通のきく)人 a *flexible* person. ▶この車は小回りがきく This car *can easily turn around* [*in a small circle*].

コマンド 〖指令〗〖コンピュータ〗 a command. ・コマンドキー a command key. ・コマンドライン a command line.

ごまんと 五万と ▶そんな例ならごまんとある There are *countless* examples of that kind.

-こみ -込み ・すべての費用込みで at the *all-inclusive* 〖(英)〗 *all-in*〗 expense. ▶この宿泊料金はサービス料込みです(=含んでいる) This hotel rate *includes* [*is inclusive of*, ✕contains] service charges. ▶私の月給は税込みで40万円です My monthly salary is 400,000 yen, tax *included* [*inclusive of* tax, *before* tax].

*ごみ

WORD CHOICE ごみ

trash, rubbish 各種のごみ・くず・ぼろをさす最も一般的な語。ただし、生ごみの意はない。 ・駅にごみを捨てる dump *trash* [*rubbish*] in the station.
garbage 台所・食堂などから出る生ごみを含んだ生ごみ・食べかすのこと。 ・生ごみを種類によって分別する separate *garbage* according to the type.
litter 道などに落ちている紙くずなどのごみのこと。 ・道のごみを掃除する clean the *litter* on the road.

頻度チャート

trash, rubbish ▮▮▮▮▮▮▮▮▮▮
garbage ▮▮▮▮▮▮▮
litter ▮▮

20 40 60 80 100 (%)

〖生ごみ〗 garbage; 〖小型のがらくた〗《米》 trash,《英》 rubbish; (粗大の) refuse /réfjuːs/; 〖くず〗 litter; 〖ちり〗 dust. ・ごみを掃く[払う] sweep [brush off] *dust*. ・道にごみを捨てる drop *litter* on the street. ・ごみだらけの道 a *littered* street. ▶ごみ捨てるべからず (掲示) No *litter*(*ing*)./No *dumping* (here). ▶ごみの収集日は週3日あって燃えるごみは月・金、燃えないごみは水です。だからごみは分けて捨てるようにしてください There are three pick-up [*garbage*] days a week. *Burnables* are picked up on Mondays and Fridays, and *unburnables* on Wednesdays. So please try to keep them separate. ▶目にごみが入った I've got a speck of *dust* in my eye.

会話 「ごみを出してくださる？」「いいとも」"Could you take out the *garbage* [*trash*] for me?" "No problem."

・ごみ収集車《米》 a gárbage trùck,《英》 a dustcart. ・ごみ収集人《米》 a gárbage pèrson [collèctor],《英》 a dustman. (!) 《米》では婉曲的に a sanitation worker ともいう) ・ごみ捨て場 a dúmping gròund; a (refuse) dump. ・ごみ箱《米》 a gárbage [a trásh] càn,《英》 a dustbin. ・ごみ袋 a trásh《米》 [a rúbbish《英》] bàg.

こみあう 込み合う 〖混雑している〗 be crowded; 〖詰め込まれている〗 be packed, be jammed. (⇒込む ❶)
こみあげる 込み上げる 〖出てくる〗 come* to ...; (浮かびくる) rise* to ...; (わき出る) well (up) (*in*). ・熱いものが胸にこみ上げる have a lump in one's throat (!) 原因となるものを主語にすれば bring a lump ... となる) ▶涙が彼の目にこみ上げてきた Tears *came to* [*rose to, welled* (*up*) *in*] his eyes. ▶その光景に怒りがこみ上げてきた Anger *welled up in* me at the sight./I *was filled with* anger at the sight.
こみいる 込み入る 〖複雑である〗 be complicated [intricate, involved]. (⇒複雑) ▶込み入った時計の仕掛け the *intricate* works of a clock. ▶この小説の筋は込み入っている The plot of this novel *is complicated* [*intricate, involved*].

コミカル ― コミカルな 形 〖おどけた〗funny, comical.

ごみごみ ●ごみごみした(=不潔で不快感を起こさせる)スラム a *squalid* slum. ●ごみごみした(=取り散らして汚い)部屋 a *messy* room; (物でごった返した) a *cluttered* room.

こみだし 小見出し a subtitle (↔a main title); a subheading.

こみち 小道 (路地, 田舎道)a lane; (野山の) a path, a footpath, a track; (路地) an alley. (⇨道 ❶)●小道をたどって湖に出る follow the *path [track]* to the lake.

コミック a comic (book). (⇨漫画) ●コミックオペラ a comic opera. ●コミックス(漫画本) a comic book; (4コマ以上の続き漫画, 劇画) the comics. ●コミックソング a comic song.

コミッショナー a commissioner.

コミッション 〖手数料, 歩合〗(a) commission; (リベート) a kickback (*of* 10 percent). (⚠ 英語には日本語のような悪い含みはない ⇨手数料)

コミット ― コミットする 動 〖かかわる, 確約する〗commit.

コミットメント 〖関与, 確約, 公約〗(a) commitment (*to*).

こみみ 小耳 ●小耳にはさむ (ふと耳にする) overhear*; (たまたま聞く) happen to hear; (ちらっと聞く) hear at a glance.

コミューター ●コミューター機 〖短・中距離用の小型旅客機〗a commuter airplane.

コミュニケ 〖<フランス語〗 〖共同声明〗 a communiqué /kəmjúːnɪkéɪ/. ●共同コミュニケを読み上げる[発表する] read [issue, release] a joint *communiqué*.

コミュニケーション communication. ●コミュニケーションがうまくとれている have good *communication* (*with*); communicate well (*with*).
●コミュニケーションギャップ the communications gap (*between, with*). (⚠ 複数形に注意)

コミュニスト 〖共産主義者〗a communist.

コミュニズム 〖共産主義〗communism.

コミュニティー 〖地域社会[共同体]〗a community. ●地域コミュニティー a local *community*.
●コミュニティーセンター 〖交流会館〗a community center. ●コミュニティーバス a community bus.
●コミュニティービジネス community business. ●コミュニティールーム 〖地域交流室〗a community center [room].

こむ 込む, 混む ❶ 〖混雑している〗be crowded; (いっぱい詰め込まれている) be packed, be jammed; 〖車と人で大混雑する〗be congested; (人が群がる) be thronged. (⇨混雑する) ●込んだバス a *crowded* bus. ●込んだ店 a store *full of* shoppers; a *busy* store. ●込み具合 the degree of *crowding*. ▶その店は買い物客でひどく込んでいた The store *was* very *crowded with* shoppers./(すし詰めだった) The store *was* jam-packed [*was* completely *jammed*] *with* shoppers. ▶その高速道路はいつも込んでいる The expressway *is* always *congested* (*with* traffic). (⚠ ×Traffic is always congested. とはいわない)/(交通量が多い) *There is* always *heavy traffic* [*Traffic is* always *heavy*] on the expressway. ▶きょう山口氏は予定が込んでいる(=ぎっしりだ) Mr. Yamaguchi has a *full* [a *heavy*, a *tight*, a *crowded*] schedule today.
❷ 〖精巧である〗(念入りに仕上げた) elaborate; (意匠を凝らした) fancy. ●手の込んだ刺しゅう *elaborate* [*fancy*] embroidery.

***ゴム** 〖<オランダ語〗rubber; gum.

> **使い分け** **rubber** 天然または合成のゴムを表し, India rubber ともいう. 具体的ゴム製品を表すときは ⓒ.
> **gum** 粘着性物質としてのゴムを表す.

●天然[合成; 人造]ゴム natural [synthetic; artificial] *rubber*. ●輪ゴム (⇨輪ゴム)
●ゴム印 a rubber stamp. ●ゴム園 a rubber plantation [estate]. ●ゴム跳び〔遊び〕《米》Chinese jump rope; 《英》French skipping. ●ゴム長《米》(a pair of) rubber boots; 《主に英》(wellington) boots, 《英話》wellies. ●ゴムの木 (観賞用) a rubber plant; (ゴムを産する) a rubber tree, a gum (tree). ●ゴムのり gum; mucilage. ●ゴムひも elastic, an elastic string. ●ゴムボート a rubber boat; an inflatable (boat).

***こむぎ** 小麦 〖植物〗wheat; 《英》corn. ●小麦色の light brown; (肌が) suntanned. ▶小鳥が散らかった小麦をついばんでいる Birds are pecking at scattered grains of *wheat*.
会話 「あの子小い麦色に日焼けしているわ」「あれは日焼けサロンで焼いた色よ」"She has a nice *tan*." "That's a fake bake."
●小麦粉 (wheat) flour /fláʊər/. (関連) 強力粉 hard-[strong-]wheat flour/薄力粉 soft-wheat flour) ●小麦粉をねる knead *flour*. ●小麦畑 a field of wheat; a wheat field.

こむずかしい 小難しい (面倒な) troublesome, bothersome; (回りくどい) tortuous. ●小難しい理屈 a *tortuous* argument.

こむすび 小結 〖相撲〗a *komusubi*; (説明的に) the fourth highest ranking sumo wrestler.

こむすめ 小娘 a young girl.

こむそう 虚無僧 a *komuso*; (説明的に) a Buddhist priest belonging to the Fuke sect of Zen Buddhism, wearing a large braided hat which entirely covers the head.

こむらがえり 腓返り (get [have]) (a) cramp in the calf. (⚠ a cramp とするのは《主に米》)

ごむりごもっとも 御無理御尤も ▶上司にはいつもご無理ごもっともでいくのが彼の主義だ His principle is that his boss is always *right*.

***こめ** 米 rice. ●米をとぐ[たく; 作る] wash [boil; grow] *rice*. ●米を買う buy (some) rice. ▶たいていの日本人は米を主食にしている Most Japanese (people) live on *rice*.

> **DISCOURSE**
> 日本語には米に言及する方法がたくさんある. 例えば, イネ, オコメ, ゴハン, メシなどだ In Japanese, *rice* is referred to in many ways: **for example**, ine (rice plant), o-kome (uncooked rice), gohan (cooked rice), and meshi (a casual name men use for cooked rice). (⚠ : for example (例えば)は具体例に用いるディスコースマーカー)

> **関連** いろいろな米: 精白米 polished [white] rice/玄米 unpolished [brown] rice/胚芽(はいが)米 rice with germs/もち米 glutinous rice.

●米印 (説明的に) the symbol, which is attached to the front of words or expressions in Japanese writing to refer the readers to the notes or comments on them 〖記号 ※〗. ●米俵 a straw rice bag. ●米粒 (もみ (husk) のついた) a grain of rice. ●米どころ a rice-producing district. ●米ぬか rice bran. ●米びつ a rice bin [chest]. ●米屋 (店) a rice shòp; (人) a rice

ごめいさん ご名算 (珠算で) Your calculation is right.

こめかみ 『解剖』 a temple. (❗通例複数形で)

こめつきばった 米搗きばった 『昆虫』(ショウリョウバッタ) a grasshopper; (コメツキムシ) a click beetle; 〖ぺこぺこする人〗 a flatterer; a bootlicker; a yes-man.

コメディアン a comedian.

コメディー 〖喜劇〗(a) comedy.

コメディカル 〖医師以外の医療従事者〗 a co-medical. (参考) 看護師・薬剤師・医療検査技師など)

* **こめる 込める ❶**〖装填(する)〗load, charge. ● 銃に弾丸を5発込める *load* [*charge*] *a gun with 5 bullets*.
❷〖精神を集中する〗● 演技〖演奏〗にもっと心を込める *put more emotion* [*heart, enthusiasm*] *into one's performance*. ● 絵に精魂を込める *put one's heart and soul into a painting*. ● 心を込めて(=誠意をもって)話す〖書く〗 speak [write] *sincerely*. ● ありったけの力を込めて引っ張る *pull as hard as one can*; *pull with all one's strength* [*force, might*].

こめん 湖面 the surface of a lake. ● 湖面に 《a yacht》 *on the surface of*) a lake. ● 湖面を渡る風 the wind blowing *over the lake*.

ごめん 御免 ❶〖許可〗● ごめんをこうむって with your *permission*; 《書》*by* [*with*] *your leave*. ● 天下御免のごめんを許された; licensed.
❷〖免除〗● ごめんをこうむる(=言い訳して断わる) *beg off*. ● お役御免になる(解雇される) *be dismissed* [《話》*fired*]; (責任を解除される) *be relieved of one's duties*. ● 演説はごめんこうむりたい *I would like to be excused from making a speech*.
❸〖拒否〗● 人と競争するのはごめんだね(=するつもりはない) *I'm not going to* compete with people. ▶ そんなことをするのはまっぴらごめんだ *I absolutely refuse to do such a thing*./*I wouldn't do such a thing for (all) the world*. ▶ もう戦争はごめんだ(=たくさんだ) *We have had enough of wars*./*No more wars!*
❹〖謝罪〗● 遅れてごめん *Sorry, I was so late*./*My* [*Many*] *apologies being so late*. ▶ ごめんで済んだ警察はいらないよ *Save that for the jury*. 〖「その発言は陪審員のためにとっておけ」の意〗 ▶ 2年5か月も一緒にいてあげられなくてごめん *We are sorry that we've been with you for only two years and five months*.

── **ごめん** 圕 ● ごめんなさい (⇒御免なさい) ● ごめんください (呼びかけで) Hello!/May I come in? (事情) 米英では他家の訪問の際ベルなどで合図し、外からは呼びかけない/(これで失礼します) See you again. (⇒失礼)

コメンテーター a commentator /kámənteitər/.

コメント 〖論評〗(a) comment 《*on, about*》. ▶ ノーコメント〖話〗 No *comment*! (❗答弁拒否の決まり文句) ▶ 君の意見にはコメントはいたしません *I will not comment on your opinion*. (❗日本語につられて × ... *comment on* your opinion.)

* **ごめんなさい 御免なさい** *I'm sorry*. (❗真に自分の過失を認めて謝る表現. くだけた言い方では I'm をよく省略する. 《米》では, せき払いなどは (米) では Excuse me. の方が普通.) I *bég you* ↘*párdon*. (❗I'm sorry. より丁寧な表現)(⇒すみません) ▶ あんなことをするとは思わなかった I'm *so sorry* I said that. ▶ 時間をそんなに多く取らせてごめんなさい *Excuse me for taking up so much of your time*. ● 間違っていたらごめんなさい(=許してください) *Forgive me if I'm wrong*.

こも 薦, 菰 a straw mat.

ごもくずし 五目鮨 *gomokuzushi*; (説明的に) vinegared rice mixed with several kinds of ingredients.

ごもくならべ 五目並べ *go-moku*; (説明的に) a game in which two players take turns to place a *go* stone in each square. The one who places five stones in a row unblocked by the opponent wins the game.

ごもくめし 五目飯 *gomokumeshi*; (説明的に) lightly-seasoned boiled rice mixed with fish [meat] and vegetables.

こもごも 交々 (⇒代わる代わる, 次々) ● 悲喜こもごも (⇒悲喜) 〖成句〗

こもじ 小文字 a small letter. (⇒大文字)

こもち 子持ち ❶〖親〗● 〖母親〗 a mother. ▶ 彼女は2人の子持ちです *She is the mother of two children*./*She has two children*.
❷〖魚〗● 子持ちのシシャモ a *shishamo* smelt *with eggs* [*roe*].
● 子持ちわかめ (説明的に) *wakame* seaweed covered with herring roe.

こもの 小物 ❶〖こまごました道具〗 small articles; accessories. **❷**〖小人物〗 a petty [an unimportant] person; 《集合的に》 small fry.
● 小物入れ an accessory case; (自動車の) a glove compartment.

こもり 子守 图 〖行為〗 baby-sitting (❗両親が外出中その家へ行って子守をすること. 子供は赤ん坊 (baby) とは限らない); 〖人〗 a baby-sitter (❗通例近くに住む学生に頼む); (本職の) 《米・英古》 a nursemaid.
── **子守(を)する** 囲 baby-sit (❗過去形は baby-sat より did baby-sitting の方が普通); (世話をする) look after [take care of] a baby.
● 子守歌 a lullaby.

* **こもる 籠もる** 〖満ちる〗 be filled 《*with*》; 〖引きこもる〗 (⇒引き籠(ｺ)もる, 閉じ籠(ｺ)もる) ▶ その小さな部屋はたばこの煙がこもっていた The small room was filled *with* [*was full of*] cigarette smoke. ▶ 心のこもった贈り物ありがとう Thank you for your *kind* [*imaginative*] present. (❗*imaginative* は「相手が喜びそうなものをあれこれ想いめぐらした」の意)

こもれび 木漏れ日 dappled /dǽpld/ sunlight; sunlight filtering through the leaves.

コモロ 〖国名〗 Comoros; (公式名) the Union of Comoros. (首都 Moroni). ● コモロ人 a Comoran. ● コモロ(人)の Comoran.

こもん 小紋 a small [a fine] pattern.

こもん 顧問 an adviser 《*to*》 (❗ advisor ともつづる); a counselor 《*to*》, a consultant 《*to*》 (❗ 後の2語は特に専門的な助言を与える意); (会社の) a corporation lawyer; (家庭の) a family lawyer. ● 野球部の顧問 a staff *adviser* to the baseball club. ● 会社の顧問をする act *as adviser to* a company; *be a corporate adviser*. (⇒会社)
● 顧問団 an advisory group. ● 顧問弁護士 a legal adviser

こもんじょ 古文書 (歴史的証拠文書) a historical [(古い) an old; (古代の) an ancient] document; (公的な記録文書)《集合的に》 archives /á:rkaivz/.
● 古文書学 diplomatics. (❗単数扱い)

コモンセンス 〖良識〗 common sense; 〖だれもが知っていること〗 common knowledge.

* **こや 小屋** (掘っ建て小屋) a hut; (丸太小屋) a (log) cabin (❗通例 hut の方が粗末); (物置の) a shed; (家畜のおり) a pen; (納屋) a barn; (定期市などの) a booth. (❗ hut 以外は複合語で) ● 犬小屋 a kennel; 《主に米》 a doghouse. ● うさぎ小屋 a (rabbit) hutch. ● 牛小屋 a cowhouse; a cattle shed. ● 馬小屋 a stable. (❗しばしば複数形で単

ゴヤ　扱い● 鶏小屋 a henhouse; a (hen) coop. ● 豚小屋 《米》a pigpen; 《英》a pigsty /píɡstai/. ● 比喩的に「きたない部屋[家]」の意にも用いる● ストリップ小屋 a strip *joint*. ● 小屋を建てる build [put up] a *hut*.

ゴヤ　〖スペインの画家〗Goya /ɡóiə/ (Francisco José de ~ y Lucientes).

こやぎ　子山羊　a kid; (革) kid.

こやく　子役 (役者) a child actor (男) [actress (女)]; (役) a child's [a boy's, a girl's] part [role].

ごやく　誤訳　图 (a) mistranslation; an incorrect translation; a mistake [an error] in translation. ▶彼は誤訳をたくさんした He *made* a lot of *mistakes* [*errors*] *in translation*. ▶もし誤訳があったら指摘してください Please point out *errors in translation*, if any.
── 誤訳する 動 ●その英文を誤訳する *mistranslate* the English sentence; *translate* the English sentence *incorrectly*.

こやし　肥やし　(a) fertilizer. (⇨肥料)

こやす　肥やす　〖土地を〗fertilize, make* 《the land》 fertile; 〖家畜を〗 fatten 《cattle》 (up); 〖目などを〗 cultivate 《a good eye *for*》.

こやすがい　子安貝　〖魚介〗a cowrie.

こやすじぞう　子安地蔵　a stone statue of a guardian deity of easy childbirth to whom pregnant women pray.

こやま　小山　a hill; a hillock. (❗ hill は「山」の訳が適切であるものまで含むのに対し, hillock は丘より低く塚程度のものまでさす)

こやみ　小止み　▶雨が小やみになった The rain *is letting up*./There is a *lull* in the rain.

こゆう　固有　── 固有の 形　(特有の) peculiar 《*to*》, 《書》proper 《*to*》; (特質などが本来備わっている) inherent 《*in*》; (特徴的な) characteristic 《*of*》; (動植物が土地特有の) native 《*to*》. ▶日本固有の習慣 customs *peculiar* [*proper*] *to* Japan. ▶この本能は人間固有のものだ This instinct is *inherent in* [*characteristic of*] human beings. ▶コアラはオーストラリア固有の動物だ Koalas are *native* [《書》 *indigenous*] *to* Australia.
● 固有名詞〖文法〗a proper noun.

こゆき　小雪　a (very) light snow. ▶小雪が舞っている It's snowing very lightly./A *very light snow* is falling.

こゆび　小指　(手の) the [one's] little finger, 《米話》the [one's] pinkie; (足の) the [one's] little toe. (⇨爪)

こよう　雇用　图 employment. ● 完全[終身]雇用制 a full [a lifetime] *employment* system [plan]. ▶彼の仕事は労働者の雇用と解雇だった His job was *hiring* and firing workers. ▶大型の公共事業は雇用の創出に役立つかもしれない Large-scale public works might help (to) create *employment*. ▶不況の長期化で(=長期化している状況下では)雇用(事情)は厳しい Under the prolonged recession, *employment* is hard to find.
── 雇用する 動　employ, 《米》hire; (一時的に)《英》hire. ●雇う 〖類語〗
● 雇用機会均等法 the Equal Employment Opportunity Law. ● 雇用期間 a period of employment. ● 雇用契約 an employment còntract [agrèement]. ● 雇用者[主] an employer. (関連) 被雇用者 an employee. ● 雇用条件 employment tèrms; terms of employment. ● 雇用対策 (take) employment mèasures. ● 雇用調整 an employment adjústment. ● 雇用保険 unemployment insúrance.

ごよう　御用　❶〖用事〗(⇨用 ❶, ❹) ▶お安いご用です Certainly./Of course./With pleasure./《米話》Surely [Sure]. (❗ いずれも依頼・要求などに対する肯定的な返答として用いる) ▶私にご用ですか Did you *want* me? /Do you want me? より丁寧な言い方 ▶何のご用ですか (受付などで) What can I do for you? (❗ 男性には sir, 女性には ma'am を文尾に置くとより丁寧になる. What do you want (with me)? は「何の用だ」に当たる乱暴な言い方) / (受付・店などで) Can [May] I help you? (❗ may の方が丁寧) ▶ご用は何か承っていますか (店員が客に) Are you *being waited on* [*being attended to*, *being taken care of*, *being helped*, *being served*]? / (すでにだれか用件を聞いているか) Is anyone *taking care of* [*helping*] you? ▶何かご用がございましたらフロントにお電話ください If there's anything you need [If you want anything], you've only to phone the front desk [×the front].
❷〖注文〗(⇨注文) ▶今日は何か御用はございませんか Do you have any *order* today, ma'am [sir]? (❗ ma'am は女性, sir は男性に対して用いる)
❸〖公用〗●宮内庁御用達 a purveyor 《of wine》 to the Imperial Household.
❹〖逮捕〗an arrest. (⇨逮捕)
● 御用納め (日) the last business day of the year (at the government office); (事) the closing of official business for the year. ● 御用聞き an order taker. ▶御用聞きに行く go to take [get] an *order* from [×to] a customer. ● 御用金 〖歴史〗 (説明的に) money temporarily requisitioned from wealthy merchants in Edo and Osaka by the Shogunate or feudal lords in the Edo period in Japan. ● 御用商人 a purveyor to the Goverment [Imperial Household]. ● 御用新聞 a pro(-)government newspaper. ● 御用邸 an Imperial villa. ● 御用始め (日) the first business day of the year (at the government office); (事) the reopening of official business for the year.

ごよう　誤用　图 (a) misuse. (砒 正用) ▶漢字の誤用 the *misuse* [*wrong use*] of Chinese characters. ── 誤用する 動.

ごようてい　御用邸 (皇室の別邸) an Imperial villa.

ごようろん　語用論　pragmatics.

コヨーテ〖動物〗a coyote /kaióuti/.

こよみ　暦　(カレンダー) a calendar; an almanac /ɔ́:lmənæk/ (❗ 日の出, 日没, 潮の干満その他の情報がある書物式暦). ● はぎとり式の暦 a tear-off *calendar*. ● 2007 年の暦 a *calendar* for 2007; a 2007 *calendar*. ● 暦の上ではもう夏だ It is already summer *officially* [according to the *calendar*].

こより　a paper string. ●こよりをよる twist paper into a *string*.

こら　▶こら, そんなことはよせ *Hey, you!* Stop doing that! ▶こら(=おい), 静かにしなさい *Look here!* Be quiet!

コラーゲン〖生化学〗collagen /kάilədʒən/.

コラージュ〖＜フランス語〗〖美術〗(a) collage /kəlά:ʒ/.

こらい　古来　from old [(大昔)] ancient] times. ● 日本古来の風習 an *old* [(昔からの)《書》a *time-honored*; (伝統的な) a *traditional*] Japanese custom.

ごらいこう　御来光　the sunrise (seen from the top of a high mountain).

こらえしょう　堪え性 (忍耐力) patience; (耐え忍ぶこと) endurance; (がんばり通すこと) perseverance. ●こらえ性のない人 a person with no *patience* [*endur-*

こらえる 堪える **❶**【我慢する】bear*, stand* (bear より口語的), put* up with ...; (辛抱強く)(ややあ書) endure. (⇨耐える) ▸こらえきれない悲しみ an unbearable sorrow. ▸痛みをこらえる bear [stand, endure] the pain.
❷【抑制する】(涙・感情などを) hold* [keep*] (one's tears) back; (怒りなどを) control (-ll-), keep (one's anger) in; (笑い・あくびなどを) suppress. ▸笑いをこらえる suppress a smile. ▸あくびをこらえる suppress [stifle] a yawn. ▸私は怒りをこらえることはできなかった I couldn't control my anger [suppress my anger, keep my anger in]. ▸彼女は泣かないでおこうようとした She tried not to cry.

*ごらく 娯楽 (楽しみごと) (an) amusement; (演芸・余興の) (an) entertainment; (休養, 気晴らし) (a) recreation; (暇つぶしの気晴らし) a pastime; (楽しみ) a pleasure. ▸大都市にはたくさんの娯楽がある Big cities have a lot of [many kinds of] amusements. ▸ここでは娯楽にはこと欠きません。演劇, コンサート, 競馬その他いろいろあります There is no lack of amusement here: plays, concerts, races, etc /ètsétərə/. (⇨など) ▸多くの(=たいていの)人にとってテレビを見るのが娯楽だ Watching TV is an entertainment for most people. ▸あなたは娯楽として何をしますか What do you do as a pastime [for amusement, for recreation, for pleasure]?
●娯楽雑誌 an amúsement mägazine. ●娯楽産業 the entertáinment ìndustry [bùsiness]. ●娯楽施設 amusement [recreational] facilities. ●娯楽室 a recreátion [an amúsement] ròom. ●娯楽番組 an entertáinment prògram.

こらしめる 懲らしめる (罰する) punish, discipline; (教訓を与える) teach (him) a lesson. (⇨罰する) ▸その少年はこらしめないといけない You must teach the boy a lesson./The boy needs discipline.

こらす 凝らす ▸彼女は目を凝らしてその写真を見た She looked hard [closely, carefully] at the picture./She strained her eyes to see [fixed her eyes on] the picture. ▸彼らはパーティーのためにいろいろ趣向を凝らした(=念入りに計画を立てた[準備をした]) They made elaborate plans [preparations] for the party.

コラボレーション【共同制作】(a) collàborátion. (!作品をさすときは C)
コラム a column. (! 署名入りの時評・随想など)
コラムニスト【特約寄稿家】a columnist. ▸彼女はタイムズのコラムニストだ She is a columnist for The Times.

ごらん 御覧 **❶**【見る】see*; look (at). (⇨見る) ▸ごらん, 雨が降りそうだ Look [×See]! It's going to rain. ▸あれをごらん Look at that!/Take [Have] a look at that! ▸ごらんのとおりもうすっかり元気です As you (can) see, I'm quite well now.
❷【試みる】▸もう一度やってごらん Try again./Have another try.
 会話 「鉛筆が折れちゃった」「これを使ってごらんよ」"My pencil's broken." "Try this one."
❸【その他の表現】▸それごらん。言わないことじゃないThere (you are)! I told you so! [Didn't I tell you?] (! と省略して Told you so! もよく用いる)
●ご覧に入れる show. (⇨見せる)

こり 凝り stiffness. ▸肩のこり (have) a stiff neck. ▸マッサージをして肩のこりをほぐした I eased stiffness in my shoulders by massaging them.
こり 狐狸 〖キツネとタヌキ〗foxes and badgers; 〖悪事を働く人〗a wrongdoer.

コリアンダー【植物】a coriander.
コリー【動物】a collie (dog).
ごりおし ごり押し ──ごり押しする 動 force [(しゃむに) bulldoze]... through. ▸議案をごり押しする force [bulldoze] the bill through (the Diet).
こりかたまる 凝り固まる 〖熱狂的になっている〗be fanatical 《about, on》; (夢中になっている)《話》be crazy 《about》; (偏執的である) be bigoted. ▸彼は一つの固定観念に凝り固まっている He is fanatical [crazy] about a fixed idea. ▸彼らは盲目的愛国主義に凝り固まっている They are bigoted to [in] chauvinism./They are bigoted [fanatical] chauvinists.

こりこり ▸こりこりした(歯ごたえなどが) crunchy; (手ざわりがかたい) firm; (肩などがこって) stiff. ▸この奈良漬はこりこりしておいしい This narazuke is crunchy and delicious. ▸私の両腕は使い過ぎでこりこりにこってしまった I overworked my arms so that they became stiff.

こりごり (⇨懲りる) ▸あんな連中はこりごりだ(=もうたくさんだ) I've had enough of such people. ▸あそこへ行くのはこりごりだ(=二度と行きたくない) I'll never go there again.

ごりごり ▸ごりごりかく scratch; (へらなどでこそげる) scrape. ▸彼はぼくに刺された腕をごりごりかいた He scratched his arm bitten by a mosquito.

こりしょう 凝り性 ─凝り性の人 (完全主義者) a perfectionist (! 悪い意味でなしで); (熱中する人) an enthusiast. ▸彼は本当に凝り性だ He becomes very enthusiastic about [《話》really gets into] things.

*こりつ 孤立 名 isolation.
●孤立無援・孤立無援で(=1人で)戦う fight alone.
──孤立する[している] 動 be isolated; (友・味方がない)(ややあ書) be friendless. ▸孤立した; (寂しい) solitary. ▸彼女はクラスで孤立している She is isolated [(友達がない) has no friends, is friendless] in her class. ▸私たちの村は大雪のために孤立した Our village was isolated [was cut off] by the heavy snow.
●孤立主義 isolationism. ●孤立政策 an isolationist policy.

ごりやく 御利益 ▸ご利益があった(=私の祈りがかなった) My prayers were heard [were answered]. ▸この神社ではどんなご利益がいただけるのですか What kind of blessings [(キリスト教の) intercessions] can I expect from (the deity of) this shrine?

ごりょう 御料 (皇室の所有物) Imperial property [possessions].
●御料地 an Imperial estate.
ごりょう 御陵 an Imperial mausoleum /mɔːsəliːəm/. ●桃山御陵 the Momoyama Mausoleum.

こりょうりや 小料理屋 a small restaurant serving simple Japanese dishes.
ゴリラ【動物】a gorilla /gərílə/.
こりる 懲りる 〖もうたくさんだ〗have enough 《of》 (⇨こりごり); 〖教訓を学ぶ〗learn a lesson 《from》. ▸これで彼もこりるだろう I hope this will be a good lesson to him.

ごりん 五輪 the Olympic Games, the Olympics. (⇨オリンピック)

*こる 凝る **❶**【熱中する】(⇨熱中) ▸彼らはロックミュージックに凝っている They are crazy about [《話》are into] rock music.
❷【工夫する】▸凝った(=装飾を凝らした)家具 fancy [elaborate] furniture. ▸服装に凝る(=うるさい) be particular about one's clothes.
❸【肩の筋肉が】get* stiff 《from doing》. ▸あまり根をつめて編み物をすると肩が凝りますよ Knitting too

hard will *give* you *a stiff neck*./If you knit too hard, you will *have a stiff neck*. (⇨肩❶②)

コルク cork /kɔ́ːrk/; [栓] a cork (stopper). ● コルクの栓をする cork 《a bottle》. ● ワインのコルクを抜く pull a *cork* from a bottle of wine. (⚠抜くときの音は pop)
● コルク樫 cork; cork oak. ● コルク抜き a corkscrew.

ゴルゴダ [聖書] Golgotha /ɡɑ́lɡəθə/. ([参考] キリストはりつけの地)

コルサコフ ● コルサコフ症候群 [医学] Korsakoff's syndrome. ([参考] 記憶力障害や健忘、作話などの症状がある)

コルセット a corset /kɔ́ːrsɪt/; (一着) a pair of corsets; (首を支えるための) a neck-brace. ● コルセットを着用している女性 a *corseted* woman.

ゴルフ golf. ● ゴルフの試合 a *golf* match. ● ゴルフ練習場 a 《*golf*》 driving range. ● ゴルフ用のジャケット a gólfing jàcket. ● ゴルフに行く go *golfing*. ● ゴルフをする play *golf*; golf. ● ゴルフで 1 ラウンド回る play a round of *golf*.
● ゴルフカート a gólf càrt. ● ゴルフクラブ a gólf clùb. ● ゴルフ場 a gólf còurse. ● ゴルフバッグ a gólf bàg. ● ゴルフボール a gólf bàll.

ゴルファー a 《low handicap》 golfer, a golf player.

***これ** ❶ [この物、この人、この事] this (圈 these).

> [解説] **this** と **that** (1) 場所的・心理的に話し手の近くにある物をさすのが **this**. 遠くの物をさすのが **that**. this は日本語の「これ」に、that は「それ」「あれ」に対応する: これ[あれ]は何 What's *this* [*that*]? (⚠応答は It's a pocket calculator. (電卓だよ)のように it (複数のは they)で受けるのが普通)
> (2) 単独で人にも用いるが通例 this (この人)、that (あの人)が文の主語の場合に限られる: これ[あれ]は私の父です This [That] is my father. きのうあの人に会った I saw *that* man [×that] yesterday.
> (3) 未来のことを述べる場合は this を、過去のことを述べる場合は that を用いる: これはおもしろい *This* will be interesting. あれはおもしろかった *That* was interesting.
> (4) 形容詞として this+图 (この...)、that+图 (その..., あの...)でも用いる: これとあれではどちらがいい Which do you prefer *this* one or *that* one?

▶ これは私が先週とった写真です *This* is a picture (複数) *These* are pictures) I took last week.
▶ これでニュースを終わります And *that*'s the end of the news. (⚠すでに述べたことです. 他の文脈ではthis も用いられる)/(米話) I'm signing off (the news) *now*. ▶ これをもって式を終了いたします *This* is the end of the ceremony. ▶ これゆえ(=この理由で)その問題に興味がなくなった For *this* reason I have lost interest in the matter.

[会話] 「この大きな鍵(鍵)は合わないわ」「じゃあ、これでやってみて」"The big key doesn't fit." "Try *this* one, then."

[会話] 「気に入ったカーペットが見つからないわ」「これならいいかもしれないよ」"I can't find a carpet I like." "*Here*'s one that might do."

❷ [注意を引いて] look (here); listen; 《米話》say, 《古》I say; hey (⚠主に男性語). ● これ…! This is…! ▶ これ、親に向かってその口のきき方は何だ *Look here*, you can't say things like that to your parents! ▶ これ、何がおかしいのか *Say*! What are you laughing at [What's funny]? ▶ これ太郎、ドアをけるのはやめなさい *Hey*, Taro! Stop kicking the door.

[会話] 「これ、何をしようとしていたの?」「何も」"*Now* what have you been up to?" "Nothing." (⚠be up to は「悪事などをたくらんでいる」の意)

ごれいぜん 御霊前 (⇨霊前) ● ご霊前に報告する report (it) to the soul of the deceased [a deceased person].

***これから** (今後はずっと) from now on (⚠現在について用い、過去・未来については from then on を用いる(⇨それから)); (これ以後) after this; (将来) in the future; (今までと違って今後は) 《米》in the future, 《英》in future. ● これからの(=将来の)若者たち the youth of *the future*. ● これからの(=来たるべき)世代 the *coming* [*next*] generation. ▶ これからは仕事に身を入れよう I'll put my back into my work *from now on* [*after this*, *in the future*]. ▶ これからどうなるかだれも分からない Nobody knows what will happen *in the future*. ▶ これから行ってももう間に合うまい It'll be too late to go *now* [×from *now*]. (⚠from now on は単独では用いない (⇨今❶③)) ▶ あなたのこれからの(=将来の)計画を教えてください Tell me about your *future* plans [your plans for the *future*]. ▶ これから出かけるところです I'm (*just*) *going out*. (⇨今❸) ▶ これから勉強しなければならないことがたくさんある I have a lot of work *ahead of* me. ▶ 彼女の弟はこれからというときにがんで死んだ Her brother died of cancer *in the prime of* his *life*. (⚠prime は「盛り」の意)

これきり [この 1 回限りで] once and for all (⚠何かをきっぱりやめるときなどに用いる); [二度と(…しない)] (not [*never*]…) *again*. ▶ 会うのはこれきりにしよう Let's stop seeing each other after this./Let's *not* see each other *again*. ▶ しなくてはならないのはこれきりです This is all you have to do. ▶ 酒はこれきりでやめるよ I shall [will] *never* drink *again*. (⚠shall の方が固い決意を表す)

コレクション a 《stamp》 collection. ● 切手のコレクションをする make a *collection* of stamps; collect stamps.

コレクター a collector. ● コインコレクター a coin *collector*; a *collector* of coins.

コレクトコール [料金受信人払い通話] 《make》 a collect (call) [a reverse(d)-charge 《英》] call. ● コレクトコールをする 《米》call 《him》 collect; 《英》reverse the charges.

[会話] 「木村さんからコレクトコールで電話がかかっております. よろしいでしょうか」「ええ、それで結構です」"I have a *collect call* for you from Mr. Kimura. Will you accept the charges?" "Yes I'll accept it."

コレクトマニア [収集癖] a collectomania.

これくらい ● これくらいの as (+图 圖) as this; 《話》this (+图 圖). ▶ 彼はこれくらいの背の高さをさす He's about *as* tall *as this*./《話》He's *this* tall. ▶ 奈良時代の彫刻はこれくらいにして次に平安時代に入ろう *So much for* the Nara sculpture. Now let's get into [look at] the Heian period.

これこれ ● これこれの場所と時間 *such and such* a time and place. ▶ これこれ静かにしなさい *Come*, *come* [*Come now*; *Now, now*; *Now then*], be quiet.

これしき ● これしきのことでへこたれるな Don't let *this* discourage you from trying again.

コレステロール cholesterol /kəlést∂roʊl/. ● コレステロール値が高い [低い] 《人が主語》have high [low] *cholesterol*. ● 血中のコレステロール値を下げる reduce one's *cholesterol* level in the blood.

これだけ ❶ [上限を示して] ▶ これだけしかくれないの? *Is this all* you give me?/*Is this the most* you can give me?/《驚きあきれて》*How little* you can give

これっぽっち ▶お金はたったこれっぽっちしか残っていない We only have this much money left. (**!** this は(話)の副詞で「こんなに，これほど」の意) ▶この図書館にはどうしてこれっぽっちしか本がないのですか Why are there so [×this] few books in this library?

これで (⇨これ❶)

これでも ▶これでも(=信じられないかもしれないが)昔は町の野球チームのピッチャーでした Believe it or not, I used to be a pitcher on the local team. ▶これでもかというほど殴られた I was all [*relentlessly*] beaten up. (**!** all と up で二重に強調している)

これという (特別な) particular. (⇨これといった)

これといった particular. ●これといった目的もなく without any *particular* purpose. ●これといった理由もなく for no *particular* reason. ▶今日はこれといってすることがない I have nothing *particular* to do today. ▶彼はこれといった(=取り立てて言うほどの)作品を残していない He didn't leave any works *to speak of* [*worth mentioning*].
会話 「ねえ，土曜の夜何か予定ある」「いいえ，これといった予定はないわ」"Say, are you doing anything Saturday evening?" "No, nothing *special*./ No, not *much*."

これは ▶これは Oh dear! ▶これはこれはよく来てくれました Oh, dear. How nice of you to come. ▶これはしたり (My) goodness!

これほど so (＋形) ▶これほど頼んでも(=頼みにもかかわらず) in spite of all one's request. ▶野球がこれほどおもしろいとは思わなかった I didn't realize (that) baseball was *so* [×*such*] exciting [*so much* fun]. ▶これほど笑ったことってちょっと記憶にないや I don't know when I've laughed *so much*. ▶これほど大きなリンゴは見たことがない I've never seen *such a* [×*the*] big apple. (**!** (1) ×a *such* big [a big *such*] apple は不可. (2) *so* big an apple も可だが堅い言い方. (3) a big apple *like this* はくだけた言い方)

コレポン 〖商業通信〗 business [commercial] correspondence.

*__これまで__ ❶ [今までのところでは] so far; [今まで] until [till] now (**!** until の方が堅い語. 文頭では until が普通); up to now (**!** 前の言い方より口語的で強調的. 文頭で用いることが多い); [かつて] ever (**!** 通例疑問文・否定文で); [以前に] before. (**!** 以上の語を用いず単なる現在完了形で表現することも多い) ▶これまでにも増して熱心に働く work harder than *before* [*ever*]. ▶これまでのところ彼は幸せに暮らしてきた *So far* [*Until now*, *Up to now*] he has lived happily. (**!** 「先のことは分からないが」を含意する. 単に He has lived happily. ではその含意はなく「これまでずっと幸せに…」の意. ×He has *ever* lived happily. は不可) ▶これまで最高の点数だ That's my best score *so far*. ▶これまでに彼の本を読んだことがない I've *never* [*haven't* (*ever*)] *read* his books (*before*). (**!** *ever* はない方が普通) ▶これまでにその映画を見たことがありますか Have you (*ever*) *seen* the movie? (**!** *ever* がある方が強意的) ▶これはこれまでに私の見た中で最高の映画だ This is the best movie (that) I *have ever seen* [I *ever saw*]. (**!** この ever は最上級を強める用法. 次例も同様) ▶これまでいちばん低い温度を記録した The temperature reached its lowest *ever*.
❷ [最後] ▶今日はこれまでにしよう That's all [it] for today. ▶授業の終わりの先生の言葉. So much for today. とはいわない)/Let's call it a day. (**!** 仕事などを終わるときの言葉) ▶彼はもうこれまでだ It's all over with him./(回復の見込みがない) There's no hope of his recovery.

これみよがし これ見よがし ── これみよがしの 形 〈やや書〉 òstentátious.
── これみよがしに 副 ●これみよがしに着飾る be ostentatiously dressed; be dressed (up) to attract attention; (その場に合わない華美な服を着ている) be overdressed for the occasion. ▶彼女はこれみよがしにブランドものバッグを持ち歩いている She is carrying a brand-name handbag ostentatiously [just to show it off].

これら these. (**!** this の複数形) (⇨これ) ▶これら[これらの本]は私のです These [*These*] books] are mine.

コレラ 〖医学〗 cholera. ●コレラにかかる catch [contract] *cholera*. ●コレラ患者 a cholera patient; (症例) a case of cholera. ●コレラ菌 a cholera germ.

*__ころ 頃__ 〖特定の時〗 the time; 〖ちょうどよい時〗 (a) time (*for*; *to* do; (*that*) 節). (⇨時) ▶あの[その]ころ in those days; at that time; (back) then. ▶あなたが帰宅するころには私はもう寝ているでしょう I'll be in bed *by the time* (*that*) you get home. (**!** that は通例省略する) ▶私が初めて京都を訪れたころは路面電車が走っていた *The first time* I visited Kyoto [*When* I first visited Kyoto], streetcars were still in service (**!** I could see streetcars running there). (**!** この the first time は接続詞的用法) ▶そろそろバスの来るころだ It's about *time* the bus came [*for* the bus *to* come]. (**!** 前の方は「本来ならもう来ているはずなのに」の含みを持つ言い方で，節内の動詞は直説法過去形が普通. 頻度的には後の不定詞を用いる言い方が多い) ▶子供のころその学校へ通っていた *When* I was a child [〈書〉*As* a child, 〈書〉*In* my childhood] I went to that school.

*__-ころ -頃__ about …, 〈主に米〉 around …. (⇨-頃(ご))
ごろ 語呂 a [the] ring. ●このことわざは語呂がいい This proverb has a nice *ring* to it. ●この二つの言葉は語呂が悪い These two words don't *go* [*sound*] *well together*.
●ごろ合わせ a play on words; a pun.
ゴロ 〖野球〗 a grounder; a ground ball. ●平凡なゴロ a routine *grounder*. ●ぼてぼてのゴロ a slow roller; a trickler. ●三塁にゴロを打つ hit a *grounder* to third. ●ピッチャーゴロに[を]打って一塁で?アウトになる *ground out* to the pitcher. ●ゴロを上手にさばく field a *grounder* successfully. ●ゴロを捕り損ねる fumble [boot] a *grounder*. ●ゴロをすくい上げる pick up [scoop] a *ground ball*.

*__-ごろ -頃__ ❶ [時を漠然と表して] about …, 〈主に米〉 toward …; around …. (⇨今頃)

> **解説** (1) about, around では指定された時の前後を, toward ではその少し手前の時期を示す.
> (2) 日本語では質問の答えに強調で「ごろ」をつける場合があるが，英語には訳さない: いつごろ出発されますか When will you start?

●3時[昼]ごろ (at) *about* [*around*] three o'clock [noon]. (**!** at を用いるのは冗長的ともいわれるが，しば

ころあい 頃合い しば用いられる. ×about [around] at の語順は不可) ▶火曜ごろから彼に会っていない I haven't seen him since *about* Tuesday. ▶パーティーの終わりごろになると疲れてしまった I got tired *toward* the end of the party.
会話「彼女が来たのは何時ごろでしたか」「7 時ごろでした」"What time was it when she came?" "*About* [*Around*] seven."
❷【ちょうどよい時期・状態】▶カキは今が食べごろだ Oysters are now *in season*. (⇨見頃)

ころあい 頃合い 图 ●頃合いを見はからって部屋を出る choose the *right time* [take an *opportunity*] to leave the room.
—— 頃合いの 形 right, good; (条件にかなった) suitable; (扱いやすい) handy. ●頃合いの(時) a *right* [*good*] time. (ℹ️ 時より moment がより適切な場合もある) ●4 人家族に頃合いの家を探す look for a *right house* [a house *big enough*] for a family of four.

ころう 古老, 故老 (老人) an old person. ●昔のしきたりを村の古老にたずねる ask an *old* villager about ancient traditions.

ころがき 転柿, 枯露柿 a dried persimmon.

ころがし 転がし (転売) (a) resale. ●土地転がし land-rolling.

ころがす 転がす ●ボールを床に[彼の方へ]転がす roll *a ball along* the floor [*to* him].

ころがりこむ 転がり込む (大金が転がり込む=思いがけなく手に入る) get a large sum of money unexpectedly. ●友人の家に転がり込む move in on one's friend. ●ボールが草むらに[車の下に]転がり込んだ The ball *rolled* (*off*) *into* the grass [*under* the car].

ころがる 転がる [回転する] roll; [倒れる] fall* (down); (勢いよく) tumble. ▶ボールは溝に[テーブルから]転がり落ちた The ball *rolled* (*down*) *into* the ditch [*off* the table]. ▶彼は階段から転がり落ちた He *fell* [*tumbled*] *down* [×*from*] the stairs. ▶君の探している万年筆は足もとに転がっている(=いる) The (fountain) pen you are looking for *is lying* at your feet. ▶そんな安物の宝石ならどこにでも転がっているよ You can find such a cheap jewel anywhere. ▶水泳客がいなくなった海岸には空びんや空かんがあちこちに転がっていた(= 散らかったままだった) After swimmers were gone, empty bottles and cans *were left scattered* here and there on the beach.

ごろく 語録 analects, a collection of one's sayings. ●『論語』は孔子の語録である "Rongo" is the *analects* of Confucius.

ころげまわる 転げ回る roll about [around]; (のたうち回る) tumble [toss] about, toss and turn.

ころげる 転げる (⇨転がる) ●笑い転げる *roll* (*about*) with laughter.

ころころ ❶【転がるさま】●ころころ転がる roll (*over and over*). (ℹ️ 動詞を重ねて, roll and roll とするのもよい) ▶ボールはころころ転がっていった A ball *rolled down* [*away*].
❷【意見が次々に変わるさま】▶彼の意見はころころ変わる His opinion *often* changes.
❸【女性の笑うさま】●ころころ笑う laugh *happily* [*merrily*].
❹【太っているさま】●ころころした赤ちゃん[子犬] a *chubby* baby [puppy]. ●彼女は小柄でころころしている She is a small and *round* [《話》a *roly-poly*] girl.

ごろごろ ❶【転がるさま】●ごろごろ転がる roll; tumble. ▶大きな石が斜面をごろごろ転がっていった A large stone *rolled* down the hill. ▶目がごろごろします My eyes feel *sandy*.
❷【たくさん転がっているさま】▶彼女程度の歌手ならごろごろいる There are *a lot* [*swarms*] of singers of her talent. (ℹ️ swarms は (ハチやアリなどの)群れ)
❸【鳴る音】▶おなかがごろごろ鳴った My stomach *rumbled*. ▶一晩中雷がごろごろ鳴っていた Thunder *was rumbling* all night. ▶猫はうれしいときごろごろう Cats *purr* when they feel happy.
❹【怠けているさま】▶彼は働きにも行かないで家でごろごろしている He is *lazing* [*hanging*, *loafing*] around at home without going to work.

ころし 殺し (a) murder. (⇨殺人)

ころしもんく 殺し文句 (効果的な表現) a telling phrase [expression] (決め手)《話》 a clincher.

ころしや 殺し屋 (a) (hired) killer; (男性の) a hít mán.

ころす 殺す ❶【生命を奪う】kill; (故意に) murder; (残虐に) slaughter; (大量に) massacre; [暗殺する] assassinate. ●その殺された女性 the *murdered* [×*killed*] woman. (ℹ️ the recently *killed* woman のように副詞を伴う場合は可) ●殺すぞと彼をおどす threaten to *kill* him; threaten him with *death*. ▶その男は彼女を刺し殺した The man *killed* [*murdered*] her *with* a knife./The man *stabbed* her *to death*. ▶彼女はピストルで殺された She *was killed* [×*was murdered*] by a pistol. (ℹ️ 直接原因を表す by の代わりに道具を表す with を用いると「だれかによって」殺されたことが暗示されるので murder も可)/The pistol *killed* [×*murdered*] him. ▶何千ものアザラシがここで毎年殺された Thousands of seals *were slaughtered* [*killed*, *massacred*] here every year. (ℹ️ 目的語が「人」以外では通例用いられない)
❷【抑える】hold*; (こらえる) suppress. ●息を殺す *hold* [×*kill*] one's breath. ●あくびをかみ殺す *suppress* [*stifle*] a yawn. ●投球のスピードを殺す kill a pitch. ●バントの打球を殺す kill [*deaden*] the ball.

ごろつき (悪党) a rogue; (ゆすり) a racketeer; (ちんぴら) a hooligan,《やや古》a hoodlum.

コロッケ [<フランス語] a croquette /króukét/.

コロッセウム [古代ローマの大円形競技場] the Colosseum /kɑ̀ləsí:əm/.

ころっと (⇨ころりと) ●ころっと出てくる pop out; roll out. ●ころっと死ぬ die *suddenly* [*unexpectedly*]. ▶買い物袋からりんごがころっと出てきた An apple *rolled out of* the shopping bag. ▶私は彼と会う約束をころっと忘れていた I *completely* [《話》*clean*] forgot the appointment with him. ▶私はあの男にころっとだまされた I *was nicely* taken in by that fellow. ▶「ものの見事に」の意)

ごろっと (⇨ごろんと)

コロナ【天文】a coróna (~s, -nae /-ni:/).

ごろね ごろ寝 ▶ソファーの上でごろ寝する *fall asleep* [《話》*drop off*, (横になる) *lie down*] on the sofa without changing one's clothes.

ころぶ 転ぶ [倒れる] fall* (down [over]); (勢いよく) tumble. ●石につまずいて転ぶ stumble on [over] a stone and *fall* (*down*); *fall* [*tumble*] *over* a stone. ●階段で転ぶ *fall* [*tumble*] down the stairs. ▶彼は転んでひざをすりむいた He *fell* (*down*) and scraped his knee./He scraped his knee in [*by*, ×*with*] *a fall*. ▶どっちに転んでも(=どちらにしても)損はない I have nothing to lose *either way*.
●転ばぬ先の杖(?)「'Walk with a stick so that you might not fall down.'/《ことわざ》Look before you leap.; Prevention is better than cure.
●転んでもただでは起きない ▶やつはいつも転んでもただでは

ころも

起きない He always gets something even out of his mistakes.

ころも 衣 〖僧の法衣〗a (Buddhist) monk's robe; 〖天ぷらの衣〗(a) coating (❗揚げる前のものは batter); 〖パン粉の〗breading.
• **衣の下のよろい** a hidden animosity; a hidden threat of military force; the potential threat of military force.

ころもがえ 衣替え ── 衣替え(を)する 〖衣服の〗 change into summer [winter] clothes; 〖街路・店舗の〗(模様替え〖改装〗する) redecorate, refurbish; (改造する) remodel. • **店の内外(ﾅｲｶﾞｲ)の衣替えをする** refurbish the store inside and out.

コロラド 〖米国の州〗Colorado /kάlərædou/(略 Colo. 郵便略 CO)).

ころりと ❶〖すっかり〗completely. • **ころりと忘れる** forget completely. (⇨ころっと)▶ 彼は彼女の魅力にころりと参ってしまった He was *completely* captivated by her charm.
❷〖ばたっと〗• **ころりと倒れる** fall flat. ▶ 彼は流れ弾にあたってころりと地面に倒れた He was hit by a stray bullet, and fell *flat* on the ground.
❸〖突然〗suddenly. ▶ 彼は態度がころりと変わった He *suddenly* changed his attitude.

コロン a colon《記号 :》. (⇨巻末〖句読法〗)

ごろんと • **ごろんと横になる** lie down, lie flat on one's side. ▶ 彼は丸太をごろん(=どすん)と置いた He put down the log *with a thud*.

コロンビア 〖国名〗Colombia;《公式名》the Republic of Colombia. (首都 Bogotá) • **コロンビア人** a Colombian. • **コロンビア(人)の** Colombian.

コロンビア 〖米国の都市〗Colúmbia.

コロンブス 〖イタリア生まれの航海者〗Colúmbus (Christopher ~).

コロンボ 〖スリランカの都市〗Colombo /kəlʌ́mbou/.

***こわい 怖い** (⇨恐ろしい)• **こわい(=厳格な)先生** a *strict* teacher. ▶ 彼はこわい(=ものすごい)顔つきをしている He looks *fierce* 〖〈いかめしい〉stern〗./He has a *fierce* [a stern] face. ▶ 彼はこわくて口もきけなかった He was too *afraid* to say anything. ▶ ああ、こわかった Boy, *wás* I *scared*! (❗(1) 感嘆文の一種で常に下降調。(2) 間投詞の boy は男女の別なく用いるが、黒人に対しては侮辱的)▶ きゃー、こわい Ahh! This *is scary* [I'm *scared*]! • **みんなで渡ればこわくない**(=ことわざ) There's safety in numbers.
• **怖いもの知らず** ▶ 彼は怖いもの知らずだ(何も恐れない) He fears nothing./He's not afraid of anything./《主語が》Nothing makes him afraid./《向こう見ずな子》He's a reckless boy.
• **怖いものなし** have nothing to fear [be afraid of].
• **怖いもの見たさ** • **怖いもの見たさだった** My curiosity over came my fear.

こわいろ 声色 vocal mimicry. • **彼の声色を使う** *mimic* [*imitate*, *impersonate*] his *voice*. • **声色を使うのがうまい** be a good *mimic*; be good at *vocal mimicry*. • **声色使い** a mimic.

こわがる 怖がる be afraid (*of*; *that* 節; *to do*), fear 〖前の方にくる情報を強い語に〗;〖突然おびえる〗be frightened, 《やや話》be scared (*at*; *that* 節; *of*; *to do*);〖ひどくおびえる〗be terrified (*at*, *that*; *of*)(⇨恐れる).
• **こわがらせる** make (him) *afraid*; frighten,《やや話》scare; terrify. • **こわがらなくてよい** Don't *be* [*xget*] *afraid*./Dón't be [*get*] ╱ *scared*. (❗下降調は命令口調となるので不適当)▶ 彼はこわい川を泳ぎ渡ることをとてもこわがった He was very (much) *afraid of* swimming [*afraid to* swim] across the river. (❗後の方にはこわくて泳ぎ渡る気にならないことを表

636

こわだんぱん

す(⇨恐ろしい))▶ 彼女は蛇を大変こわがっている She *is* very (much) *afraid* [*frightened*, *scared*] *of* snakes. (❗《話》では very が好まれる. terrified は very (much) *afraid* に相当するので, very で修飾しないで用いる)/She *has a great fear* [*terror*] *of* snakes. ▶ 彼女はその光景を見てこわがった She *was frightened* [*scared*, *terrified*, ×*afraid*] *at* [*by*] the sight. (❗*afraid* は一時的な恐怖には使えない. by は受身的性格が強い場合で, 対応する能動表現を用いて The sight *frightened* [*scared*, *terrified*] her. ともいえる)/She *was frightened* [×*scared*] *to* see the sight. (❗「…was scared to see は「こわくて見られなかった」の意)

こわき 小脇 • **小脇に抱える** • **小脇に本を抱える** carry a book *under* one's *arm*.

こわけ 小分け 图 (a) subdivision.
── **小分けする** 動 subdivide. • **ケーキを5等分に小分けする** *subdivide* a cake *into* five equal parts [portions].

こわごわ (⇨恐(ｵｿ)る恐る)

ごわごわ • **ごわごわしている** coarse; rough /rʌ́f/; stiff. ▶ その布はごわごわしている The cloth feels *coarse*. ▶ そのシャツはのりがききすぎてごわごわしている The shirt is overstarched and *stiff*.

こわざ 小技(相撲・柔道などの)a subtle [a delicate] technique. (⇔ 大技)

ごわさん 御破算 • **御破算(ﾊﾞｼｬﾝ)**

‡**こわす 壊す** ❶〖破壊する〗(物をばらばらにする) break* (❗ 一般的な語); (建物・都市などを完全に破壊する) destroy; (部分的に壊す) damage; (使えなくする) ruin; (めちゃめちゃにする) wreck; (打ち砕く) smash; (大きな建造物を) demolish, pull [tear*]... down (❗ 後の方がくだけた言い方(⇨取り壊す)). • **ドアを壊して家に入る** *break down* the door and [to] enter the house. • **金庫を壊す** *break* [*crack*] a safe. ▶ 誤って模型の帆船を床に落として壊してしまった I dropped the model sailboat on the floor by accident and *broke* [*damaged*] it. ▶ 兵隊たちは玄関のドアをたたき壊して開けた The soldiers *broke* [*smashed*] the front door open. (❗smash の方が破壊の程度がひどい. open は形容詞)▶ 巨大なマンションを建てるために美しい古い家がたくさん壊された They *tore down* lots of beautiful old houses to build a huge condominium. ▶ 自民党をぶっ壊す I will *break up* [*dismantle*, *bust up*] the Liberal Democratic Party. (❗bust up は口語表現)
❷〖だめにする〗(台なしにする) ruin, (価値を) spoil*; (損なう) damage, injure; (体調を狂わす) upset*. • **景観を壊す** *ruin* [*spoil*] the beauty《of》. • **(仕事・たばこなどが)体をこわす** *damage* [*injure*, *ruin*] one's health. • **縁談を壊す** *break* (*off*) a match. • **得点のチャンスを壊す** *kill* a rally. ▶ 子供は食べすぎよくおなかをこわす Children often *have* [*get*] *stomach upsets* by eating too much./Children often *upset* their stomach by overeating. ▶ 先発投手は何とか試合を壊さずにおいた The starting pitcher managed to keep the team in the game.

こわだか 声高 ── **声高に** 副 (大きな声で) in a loud voice, loudly; (強い調子で) forcefully; (強硬に) firmly; (厳しく) severely. • **声高にののしる** curse 《him》*loudly*. • **声高に批判する** criticize 《him》*severely*. • **声高に論じる** argue *forcefully* [*loudly*, *firmly*].

こわだんぱん 強談判 a strong demand. ▶ 強制立ち退きの件で強談判した We made a *strong protest* [*protested strongly*] *against* our forced eviction.

ごわつく (⇨ごわごわ)

ごわっぱ 小童《話》《軽蔑的》a little squirt, a brat.

こわね 声音 a tone of voice. ▶彼女は優しい声音で話す She speaks in a tender *voice* [a soft *tone*].

こわばる 強張る stiffen, become* stiff. ▶彼は表情をこわばらせた His face *was stiffened*./His face *set in stiff* lines.

こわもて 強面 (恐ろしい顔つき) a fierce [a frightening] look; an awful look.
● 強面に出る (強硬な態度に出る) take a strong [an oppressive] attitude 《toward》.

こわれもの 壊れ物 a fragile /frǽdʒəl/ item;《集合的》breakables;《表示》Fragile.
会話「これ壊れ物なんです」「はい、分かりました。ステッカーを貼っておきます」"This is *fragile*." "OK, I'll see to it. I'll put a *fragile* sticker on it."

:こわれる 壊れる 〖破壊される〗(ばらばらになる) break*, be broken; (部分的に壊れる) be damaged; (完全に壊れる) be destroyed; (めちゃくちゃになる) be wrecked (⇨壊す); (機械などの調子が狂う) get* out of order; (故障する) break (down). ▶壊れたおもちゃ a *broken* toy. ▶壊れにくい物《=壊れ物》▶花びんが床に落ちて壊れた The vase fell on the floor and *broke* 《*into* [*to*] *pieces*》.《*into* [*to*] pieces では「粉々に」の意が出る》/The vase fell on the floor and *smashed to pieces*. 《前の言い方より強意的》▶衝突で電車がめちゃめちゃに壊れた In the collision the train *was badly damaged* [*was completely wrecked*]. (!後の方はまったく修理不可能なことを含意) ▶この電話[コンピュータ]は壊れている This telephone [PC] *is out of order* [*is broken, doesn't work*]. ▶この洗濯機はまた壊れた This washing machine *broke down* again. ▶縁談がこわれた The match [Their engagement] *was broken* (*off*).

こん 根 ❶ 〖数学〗a root. ●*x*の*n*乗根 the *n*th *root* of *x*. ▶2 は 4 の平方根であり，8 の立方根である 2 is the square *root* of 4 and the cube *root* of 8. ❷ 〖根気〗 (我慢) patience; (持久力) endurance; (精力) energy. ▶根気，根気，根負け.
● 根を詰める work very hard (*on*); (休憩なしで働く) work without (taking) a break; (全力を傾けて) devote all one's energy [energies] (*to*).

こん 梱 a bale. ▶綿花一梱 a bale of cotton.

こん 紺 〖色〗dark blue. ▶紺色の服を着ている wear a *dark-blue* dress.

こん- 今- ▶今シーズンに during *this* season. ● 今(=今日)4月6日に *today*, on April 6.

こんい 懇意 ── 懇意な 形 friendly; (親密な) close, intimate. (!intimate は性的関係の意を含む場合もあるので注意); 〖親しい〗familiar. ▶彼と懇意になる (友人になる) *make friends with* him《複数形に注意》; (知り合いになる) *get acquainted with* him; (親密になる) *become close to* him. ▶彼と懇意にしている *be* (*good*) *friends with* him; *be on friendly terms with* him.

こんいん 婚姻 a marriage. (⇨結婚)
● 婚姻届 registration of one's marriage.

こんか 今夏 this summer. (⇨今年)

こんか 婚家 one's husband's family.

こんかい 今回 this time. (⇨今度) ● 今回の(=この前の)中国の旅で during the *last* tour of China. ▶今回はあなたとご一緒しましょう I'll go with you *this time*.

こんがい 婚外 ── 婚外の 形 extramarital.
● 婚外子 an extramarital child.

こんがらがる 〖糸などが〗get* tangled [entangled]; 〖事柄などが〗(混乱する) get confused; (複雑になる) get complicated. ▶頭がこんがらがってきた I *am getting confused*.

こんがり ● こんがり焼く (肉を) roast [brown] 《meat》nicely; (パンを) toast (bread). (!toast は「茶色になるまで焼く」の意) ▶彼はこんがり焼いたパンが好きだ He likes *nicely* [*lightly*] *browned* toast./He likes his bread *toasted to a turn*. (!to a turn は「ちょうどよい程度に」の意) ▶彼女は肌をこんがり焼いた She suntanned [✕sunburned] herself *steadily* [(一様に) *uniformly*] *and well*. (!sunburned は炎症を起こした場合に用いて，ここでは不適)

コンカレントエンジニアリング concurrent engineering. (参考) 設計・解析・製造の各工程を同時に平行して進める生産方法)

こんかん 根幹 (基本) a basis; (根本) the root; (本質) essence. ▶民主主義が近代社会の根幹をなしている Democracy forms the *basis* of modern society.

こんがん 懇願 名《書》(an) entreaty;《書》(哀願) a plea (*for*). ▶彼は私の援助の懇願を無視した He ignored my *plea for* help.
── 懇願する 動 beg,《書》entreat; (嘆願・哀願する) plead with ..., implore; (訴える) appeal to .... ● 彼に助けてくれと懇願する *plead with* [*appeal to, entreat*] him *for* help [*to* help me]. ▶彼女は彼に同行してくれるよう懇願した She *begged* (*of*) him to [*begged that he*《(主に英) should》] go with her. (!(1) of がある方が強意的. (2) that 節より to 不定詞の方が一般的)

こんき 今季 this [the present] season.

こんき 今期 this [the present] term. ▶今期最高の視聴率 the highest audience rating in *this term*.

こんき 根気 〖忍耐〗patience, (長期にわたる) endurance; (粘り強さ) perseverance; 〖精力〗energy.
● 根気のある patient (↔impatient); persevering.
● 根気よく働く work *with patience* [*patiently*]. ▶この仕事には大変な根気がいる This work takes a lot of *patience*. ▶彼は根気が続かなくなった He has become less and less *patient*./(以前ほど根気がない) He is not as *patient* as he used to be. ▶根気が尽きた My *patience* has run out./I have run out of my *patience*.

こんき 婚期 〖結婚するのに適した年齢〗(a) marriageable age. ▶婚期に達している 《be of [reach] *marriageable age*. ▶彼女は婚期を逸した She (has) missed a *chance to get married*.

こんぎ 婚儀 (⇨⇨ 結婚式)

『ごんぎつね』 *Gon, The Little Fox*. (参考) 新美南吉の童話)

古今ことばの系譜 『ごんぎつね』

「ごん，お前(ﾏﾞ)だったのか，いつも栗をくれたのは」ごんは，ぐったりと目をつぶったまま，うなずきました．兵十は火縄銃をばたりと，とり落としました．青い煙が，まだ筒口(ﾂﾂｸﾞﾁ)から細く出ていました．

"Gon, was it you? Was it you who gave me those chestnuts?" Gon helplessly nodded, his eyes closed. Heiju dropped his gun. A stream of blue smoke was still issuing from the muzzle of Heiju's gun. (!(1) ごんは，いたずらをした償いに兵十の家の入り口に栗を置こうとし兵十はそれを知らず，またいたずらに来たと思い銃で撃った．(2)「ぐったり」は「もう立ち上がる力もなく」という様子．helplessly (どうしようもなく)と訳した．(3)「ばたりととり落とす」は「(意識して)置いた」(place [lay] down)のではなく「(力が抜けて，思わず)落とした」という意味であるから drop を用いた．(4)「筒口」は「銃口」と言い換える．(⇨晴れる)

こんきゅう 困窮 图 〖貧困〗poverty;〖困苦〗(a) hardship. ●生活困窮者 the poor and needy; needy people.
━━ **困窮する** 動 be poor [in poverty];(貧乏に苦しむ)have a hard up.(⇨困る❷)

*__こんきょ 根拠__ a ground 《for》(❗通例複数形で);(理由) (a) reason 《for; to do; why 節》;(基礎) a basis 《of, for》;(より所) (an) foundation;(典拠) (an) authority. ●その会社の根拠地 the firm's *base*. ●何の根拠もないのに非難される be *baselessly* accused 《of》. ▶そう信じる十分な根拠がある There are sufficient *grounds* [*reasons*] *for* believing it./We have every [good] *reason* to believe it. ▶その話は根拠のないものだ The story is *groundless* [has *no foundation*, is *without foundation*]./(話) There is *nothing* to the story. ▶何を根拠にそんなことを言うのか On what *grounds* [*basis*] do you say that?/What's the *basis for* your saying that?/What *grounds* [*basis*] do you have *for* saying that?/How can you be *certain*?

ごんぎょう 勤行 a religious service.

こんく 困苦 hardship(s); sufferings. ●困苦欠乏に耐える bear hardship [*sufferings*].

ぐんぐ 欣求 ●欣求浄土〖仏教〗a wish to be in Elysian Fields.

ゴング 〖銅鑼〗a góng 《どら》;〖ボクシングの〗a bell;〖古〗a gong.

コンクール [<フランス語] a contest, a competition. ●コンクールに参加する enter [go in for] a *competition*. ●ショパンコンクールで2位に入る[優勝する] get second place in [win] the Chopin *Competition*.

コンクラーベ〖カトリック〗〖教皇選挙会議〗a conclave /kánkleiv/.

こんくらべ 根比べ an endurance contest.

コンクリート concrete. ●コンクリートの建物 a *concrete* building. ●鉄筋コンクリート reinforced *concrete*; ferroconcrete.(⇨鉄筋) ●土手をコンクリートで固める concrete the bank; cover the bank with *concrete*.
●コンクリートジャングル〖[生存競争の厳しい]大都会〗a concrete jungle. ●コンクリートパネル a concrete panel. ●コンクリートブロック a concrete block. ●コンクリートミキサー a concrete mixer.

コングレス 〖公式の会議〗a congress;〖米国連邦会議〗Congress.

コングロマリット 〖複合企業(体)〗a conglomerate (company).

ごんげ 権化 (an) incarnation, the personification. ●美[悪]の権化 the *incarnation* of beauty [evil].

こんけい 根茎 〖植物〗a rhizome /ráizoum/, a rootstock.

こんけつ 混血 ●彼は日本人とアメリカ人の混血だ He is *half* Japanese and *half* American.
●混血児 a child of mixed parentage; a half [mixed] blood.(❗ x a half とはいわない)

*__こんげつ 今月__ this month. ●今月の10日に on the 10th of *this month*. ●今月中に (by the end of [within]) *this month*;(sometime *this month*). ●雑誌の今月号 the *current* issue [number] of a magazine. ▶今月は雨が多かった We have had a lot of rain *this month* [ˣin this month].

こんげん 根源 〖根底〗the root;〖源〗the source. ●諸悪の根源を断つ stamp out the *root* [*source*] of all evil. ●戦争の根源の原因 the *root* cause of the war.

ごんげん 権現 (仏の化身) an incarnation of the Buddha.

*__こんご 今後__ (これ以後) after this;(今までと違ってこれからは) (米) in the future, (英) in future (⇨将来図)(これから) from now on. ●今後5年間で for the *next* five years; for five years *from now*. ▶今後はもっと英語を勉強します I'll study English harder *after this* [*in* (*the*) *future, from now on*]. ▶今後のために言っておくが，ここは禁煙だ *For future reference*, you shouldn't smoke here.

コンゴ〖国名〗(the) Congo /káŋgou/; (公式名)〖コンゴ共和国〗the Republic of Congo (首都 Brazzaville);〖コンゴ民主共和国〗the Democratic Republic of Congo (略 DRC, DR Congo)〖参考〗旧ザイール〗(首都 Kinshasa). ●コンゴ人 a Congolese. ●コンゴ(人)の Congolese.

こんこう 混交 a mixture;(ごちゃ混ぜ) a jumble. ●玉石混交 a *mixture* of wheat and chaff.

こんごう 金剛 ●金剛砂 emery (powder); carborundum. ●金剛石 (a) diamond. ●金剛杖 a pilgrim's staff. ●金剛力 Herculean strength. ●金剛力士 a Deva King.(⇨仁王)

こんごう 混合 图 (a) mixture.
━━ **混合する** 動 mix; mingle; blend.(⇨混じる, 混ざる)
●混合ダブルス mixed doubles. ●混合物 a mixture;(酒・コーヒーなどの) a blend. ●空気は気体の混合物である Air is a *mixture* of gas(s)es.

コンコース 〖駅ビル・空港ビルなどの通路兼ホール〗a cóncourse. ▶北コンコースの本屋のあたりでお待ちしております I'll meet you near the bookstore *on* the north *concourse*.

コンコーダンス 〖用語索引〗a concordance 《to, of》.

ごんごどうだん 言語道断 (ひどい) unspeakable;(許しがたい) unpardonable;(けしからぬ) outrageous.

こんこんと 昏々と ●昏々と眠っている be *deeply* [*heavily*] asleep. ●昏々と眠る sleep *deeply* [*heavily*].

こんこんと 滾々と ●こんこんとわき出る well (out). ▶泉からこんこんと水がわき出ている Water *is bubbling out* of the spring.

こんこんと 懇々と ●こんこんと諭す admonish 《him》 *over and over again*; give 《him》 parental guidance.(❗ admonish は「愛情・親切心があるからこそ言い聞かせる」の意の堅い語)

コンサート a concert. ●コンサートを催す give [hold, (話) do] a *concert*. ▶彼らは8月にロンドンでコンサートを開くそうだ I've heard they are doing a *concert* in London in August.(❗この進行形はすでに決められた未来の予定・計画を表す)
●コンサートホール a concert hall. ●コンサートマスター a concertmaster, (英) a leader.

こんさい 混載 ●混載貨物 a mixed cargo.

こんざい 混在 图 (a) mixture.
━━ **混在する** 動 be intermingled. ▶この小説は事実と虚構が混在している This novel is a *mixture* [a *composite*] of fact and fiction./Fact and fiction *are intermingled* in this novel.

コンサイス 〖簡明な〗concise.

こんさいるい 根菜類 root crops [vegetables].

*__こんざつ 混雑__ 图 〖交通などの〗congestion;〖ぎゅうぎゅう詰め〗a jam;〖人などの殺到〗a rush;〖押し合い〗a [the] crush. ●交通の混雑を緩和する ease [relieve] traffic *congestion*; ease [relieve] a traffic *jam*.(❗後の方が口語的) ●朝夕の混雑(=ラッシュアワー)を避ける avoid morning and evening *rush*(-)*hours*. ▶その店は日曜日の午後混雑のピークに

なる *Congestion* in the store reaches a peak on Sunday afternoons.
── 混雑する 動 〚多くの人で込み合っている〛be crowded; 〚ぎっしり詰まっている〛be jammed; 〚充満している〛be congested. (⇨混む❶) ●混雑した所へ行く go to *crowded* places. ▶バスは子供たちで混雑していた The bus *was crowded* [*jammed, packed*] *with* children. ●休日は道路が混雑する The roads *are congested* (*with* traffic) on holidays./(交通量が多い) Traffic is *heavy* on holidays./Traffic is *heavy* [*a lot of*] *traffic* on holidays. ▶映画館の入り口はたいへん混雑していた There was a big *crush* at the entrance to the movie theater.

コンサルタント a consultant 《*to* a company, *on* economic affairs》. (❗特に専門的知識を持つ医師・弁護士・技師など) ●経営コンサルタント a management *consultant*.

コンサルティング consulting.
●コンサルティング会社 consulting firm. ●コンサルティングサービス consulting service. ●コンサルティング料 a consulting fee.

こんじ 根治 图 (a) complete recovery 《*from*》; (治療) (a) complete cure 《*of*》.
── 根治する 動 recover 《*from*...》 completely; cure 《*of*...》 completely. ●根治できない病気もある。水虫がその一つだ There are some diseases which you are *not cured of completely*. Athlete's foot is one of them.

コンシェルジェ [＜フランス語] 〚ホテルの接客係〛a concierge /kùnsiɛərʒ/.

こんじきやしゃ 金色夜叉 *The Gold Demon*. (参考 尾崎紅葉の小説)

こんじゃくものがたりしゅう 今昔物語集 *Tales of Times Now Past*. (参考 平安時代の説話集)

*こんしゅう 今週 this week. ●今週の火曜日に *this* Tuesday; on Tuesday *this week*; 〚話〛on Tuesday; (過ぎ去った) *last* Tuesday. ●今週中に (by the end of) *this week*; (今週のいつか) sometime *this week*; (今週以内に) within the week. (❗あまり使わない). ●今週数学の試験がある We have a math exam *this week* [×in this week]. ●今週中ずっと暇だった I have been free all [*during*] *this week*. ▶今週は防火週間だ This is fire prevention week.

こんしゅう 今秋 this fall 〚米〛[autumn 《主に英》]. (⇨今年)

コンシューマー 〚消費者〛a consumer.
こんじゅほうしょう 紺綬褒章 a Medal with Dark Blue Ribbon. (⇨褒章)

こんしゅん 今春 this spring. (⇨今年) ●今春は桜の花が咲くのが遅い The cherry trees bloom late *this spring* [×in this spring]./The cherry blossoms come out late *in the spring this year*.

*こんじょう 根性 〚性質〛nature; 〚気力〛spirit; 〚勇気〛courage, 〚話〛guts; 〚闘志〛fight, fighting spirit. ●根性を見せる show *fight* [*spirit*]. ●根性の悪い人 an *ill-natured* person. ▶彼は根性がある He is a man *of spirit*./He is a man *with guts* [*grit*]. ▶彼はそれをする根性がなかった He didn't have the *guts* [*grit*] to do it.

こんじょう 今生 (この世) this world [life]. ●今生の思い出 memories of *this life*. ●今生の別れを告げる bid 《him》 a last farewell.

こんじょう 紺青 Prussian blue; deep blue; ultramarine.

こんしん 混信 图 〚通信〛interférence.
── 混信する 動 interfére. ●この番組に韓国のラジオ放送が混信している A Korean radio program *is interfering with* this one.

こんしん 渾身 ●渾身の力を込めて with all one's strength 〚〚やや書〛might〛. ▶亮子は襲いかかってきた人を渾身の力で投げつけた Ryoko threw the attacker down *with all her strength*.

こんしん 懇親 ●懇親会 a party, 〚話〛a get-together.

こんすい 昏睡 (状態) (a) coma /kóumə/. ●昏睡状態にある[に陥る; から覚める] be in [go into; come out of] a *coma*.

コンスタント ── **コンスタントな** 形 (一定した) constant; (固定した) fixed; (ゆらぎのない) steady.
── **コンスタントに** 副 ●彼女は英語ではコンスタントに80点をとっている She *constantly* gets at least 80 marks in English exams.

こんせい 混成 图 (a) mixture.
── 混成の 形 mixed; (各要素がまじりあった) composite. (❗限定的)
●混成酒 a mixed drink; a cocktail. ●混成チーム a combined team.

こんせい 懇請 图 (an) earnest request; 〚書〛(an) entreaty.
── 懇請する 動 request 《*for; to do; that* 節》; 〚書〛entreat 《*for; to do*》. ●彼女は経営危機乗り切りのためにA氏に社長就任を懇請した The board *earnestly requested* Mr. A *to* become the president and help the company get out of the financial difficulties.

こんせいがっしょう 混声合唱 a mixed chorus /kɔ́ːrəs/. (⇨合唱)
●混声合唱曲 a suite /swiːt/ for a mixed chorus.

こんせいき 今世紀 this century. (⇨世紀)

こんせき 痕跡 〚跡〛(a) trace; 〚(an) evidence; 〚印〛a sign (❗主に否定文で). ●痕跡をとどめる leave a *trace*; show [give, 〚やや書〛bear] *evidence*. ●古代都市の痕跡をたどる *trace* an ancient city. (⇨跡, 形跡)

こんせつ 懇切 ── **懇切(丁寧)な** 形 (細部まで気を配った) kind; careful; attentive. (❗どの語も very で強めることができる)
── **懇切(丁寧)に** 副 kindly; carefully; attentively. ●懇切丁寧に教える teach 《him》 *kindly*; give 《him》 *careful* instructions.

こんぜつ 根絶 ── **根絶する** 動 (⇨撲滅する) ●悪習を根絶する *get rid of* [*root out*] bad practices. ●盗難事件を根絶する *put an end to* the robberies.

コンセプト 〚基本概念〛a concept. ●基本コンセプト a (fundamental) *concept*.
●コンセプトアート 〚概念美術〛a concept [a conceptual] art. ●コンセプトカー 〚試作車〛a concept car. ●コンセプトモデル 〚試作モデル〛a concept model.

こんせん 混戦 ▶パ・リーグのペナントレースは混戦模様である The Pacific League pennant race is *very tight*./The Pacific League pennant is still *bitterly fought for*.

こんせん 混線 ── **混線する** 動 (電話が) get [be] crossed; (話が) get [be] mixed up. ▶この電話は混線している The line *is crossed*.

こんぜん 婚前 ── **婚前の** 形 premarital; antenuptial; prenuptial. ●婚前交渉を持つ have *premarital* sex 《*with*》.

こんぜんいったい 渾然一体 ●渾然一体となっている be in perfect harmony. ▶雲ひとつない青空は紺碧(こんぺき)の海と渾然一体となっている An unclouded blue sky and the deep-blue sea form a *harmonious whole*.

コンセンサス 〚合意〛a [the] consensus. ●コンセンサスを得る achieve [reach, arrive at] a *consensus*.

コンセント
▶この件についてコンセンサスが得られた We reached a *consensus* on this matter./A *consensus* was reached regarding this matter.

コンセント (wall) socket; 《主に米》an (wall) outlet, 《主に米》a power point, a receptacle. (**!** ×consent は「同意(する)」の意) ●ラジオのプラグをコンセントに差し込む plug in (↔unplug) the radio; put the radio plug in(to) a *socket* [an *outlet*]. ●コードをコンセントから抜いてもう一度差し込む unplug and replug the wire.

コンソーシアム 〖共同事業体〗a consortium /kənsɔ́ːrʃiəm/.

コンソール 〖コンピュータなどの制御卓〗a console.

コンソメ [<フランス語] consommé /kɑ̀nsəméi/; clear soup.

こんだく 混濁 ── 混濁した 形 〖水などが〗muddy; 〖意識が〗muddled, confused. ●意識が混濁する[している] fall into [be in] a state of *confused* consciousness.

コンダクター 〖指揮者〗a conductor.

コンタクト ●コンタクトを取る make *contact* [get in *contact*, get in *touch*] 《with him》; contact 《him *by* telephone》. (**!** (1) ×contact *with* him は不可. (2) ×take contact とはいわない) (⇨連絡)

コンタクトレンズ (片方の) a contact lens, 《話》a contact. ●ハード[ソフト; 色付きの; 通気性のある]コンタクトレンズ a hard [a soft; a tinted; a gas-permeable] *contact lens*. ●コンタクトレンズをはめている[はめる; はずす; 消毒する; 洗浄する] wear [put in; take out, remove; disinfect; rinse] *contact lenses* [*contacts*].

こんだて 献立 a menu, a bill of fare (**!** 後の方が堅い表現. 両者とも献立および献立表の両方の意で用いる); 〖食事〗a meal. (⇨メニュー) ●献立をいろいろ考える(=食事の計画を立てる) plan 《his》*meal*(s).

こんたん 魂胆 (隠れた動機) an ulterior /ʌltíəriər/ [a hidden] motive. ●魂胆がある have an *ulterior motive*.

こんだん 懇談 图 a friendly [an informal] talk.
── 懇談する 動 have a friendly [an informal] talk 《with》.
●懇談会 a talk-in; 《話》a get-together.

コンチェルト [<イタリア語] 〖音楽〗〖協奏曲〗a concerto /kəntʃéərtou/. (⇨~曲)

こんちくしょう こん畜生 (人をののしって)〖俗〗Fuck it [you]!; 《話》Damn (you)! (⇨畜生)

コンチネンタル 〖大陸の〗continental.
●コンチネンタルタンゴ a continental tango. ●コンチネンタルブレックファスト continental breakfast. 〖参考〗パンとコーヒーの簡素な朝食

こんちは (⇨こんにちは)

こんちゅう 昆虫 an insect (**!** 害虫・益虫両方に用いられるが, 米英人には悪いイメージでとらえられる場合が多い); 《主に米》a bug. (**!** 害虫のみをさす) ●昆虫採集をする collect *insects*. ●昆虫採集に行く go hunting for *insects*.
●昆虫学 entomology. ●昆虫学者 an entomologist.

コンツェルン [<ドイツ語] 〖企業合同〗a combine; 〖複合企業体〗a conglomerate.

こんてい 根底 (根源) the root; (基礎) a basis; (土台) (a) foundation; (核心) the heart. (⇨根本) ●太陽崇拝の根底にある考え the thought *at the root of* the solar worship. ●の根底を成す form the *basis of* ... ●の理論を根底から覆す overturn the theory from its *foundation*.

コンディション condition, 《話》shape. (⇨体調) ●コンディションがいい be in (↔out of) *condition* [《話》*shape*, *training*] (**!** training はスポーツ・技能試験などに用いる); be in good (↔《やや書》poor) *condition* [〖話〗*shape*]. ●コンディションをくずす[保つ] lose [keep one's] *condition*. ●レースに備えてコンディションを整える condition oneself [(練習に入る) go into training] for the race.

コンテキスト 〖文脈〗a context.

コンテスト a contest; (品評会) a show, an exhibition. ●歌謡コンテストに参加する enter a song *contest*.

コンテナ(ー) a container /kəntéinər/.
●コンテナガーデン a container garden. ●コンテナ貨物列車 a container train. ●コンテナ船 a container ship. ●コンテナターミナル a container terminal. ●コンテナトラック a container truck [《英》lorry].

コンデンサー a capacitor. (**!** condenser は現在は主に自動車に使うもののみをさす)

コンデンスミルク condensed milk.

コンテンツ 〖中身, 情報の内容〗contents.

コント [<フランス語] 〖小喜劇〗(do) a comic skit [sketch]; (perform) a comic short play.

＊**こんど** 今度 图 ❶〖この度〗(今回) this time; (今) now. ▶今度いっしょに行ってあげるからきっとしてね I'll go with you *this time* but never again. ▶今度は(=さあ)彼の打つ番だ *Now* it's his turn to bat./(次は) It's his turn to bat *next*. ▶今度だけは私の好きにさせてちょうだい (*Just*) for once [*Just this once*], let me do as I like. ▶今度は彼女が驚いた *This time* [*Now*] she was surprised. ▶カナダへは今度で 10 回目の出張です *This* is my tenth business trip to Canada.

❷〖最近〗recently, lately (⇨最近); (先日) the other day. ▶彼は今度ロンドンから帰って来た He has *recently* come back from London.

❸〖次回, この次〗next time; (ほかの時) another time, some other time; 〖近いうちに〗shortly, soon; 〖今後〗from now on, in (the) future. ▶今度来るときそれを持ってきなさい Bring it to me *next time* you come. (**!** Bring it to me when you come *next time*. より口語的) ▶それは今度また議論しよう Let's discuss it *another time*. ▶今度はいつ会えるの? *How soon* can I see you again? ▶今度アメリカへ行きます I'm going to America (*shortly*). ▶今度からもっと気をつけます I'll be more careful *from now on* [《米》*in the future*, 《英》*in future*].
〖会話〗「今度はうちへぜひいらしてください」「ええ, そうさせていただきます」"*Next time*, you must come to our place." "Fine, we'd like that."
── 今度の 形 〖新しい〗new; 〖この前の〗last; 〖最近の〗recent; 〖次の〗next, coming. ●今度の金曜日に(×on) *this (coming)* [(次の) *next*] Friday. ●今度の夏休みに in the *next* [*coming*] summer vacation. ▶今度の教授は日本史の権威です The *new* professor is an authority on Japanese history. ▶彼は今度の試験で落第した He failed the *last* [*recent*] exam.

こんとう 今冬 this winter. (⇨今年)

こんとう 昏倒 图 (卒倒) a faint. (⇨卒倒)
── 昏倒する 動 fall down in a faint; (気絶する) faint.

＊**こんどう** 混同 图 confusion 《of, between》. ●"study" と "learn" の混同 the *confusion of* "study" and "learn".
── 混同する 動 confuse [mix up] 《A *with* [*and*] B》; 〖取り違える〗mistake*《A *for* B》. (⇨間違える) ●その双子を混同する confuse [mix up] the twins.

▶個人主義と利己主義を混同するな Don't *confuse* individualism *with* [*and*] egoism.
こんどう 金堂 the main hall of a Buddhist temple.
コンドーム a condom /kándəm/, a (contraceptive) sheath, 《主に米話》 a rubber; 〖医学〗(しばしば婉曲的) a prophylactic. ●コンドームをつける[つけている; はずす] put on [wear; take off] a *condom*.
コンドミニアム 〖分譲マンション〗《米》a condominium.
ゴンドラ (船) a góndola, (作業用の) a cradle, (気球などの) a gondola, a basket; (スキーリフトの) a gondola, a car, a chair; (ロープウェーの) a car.
コントラクトブリッジ 〖トランプ〗contract bridge.
コントラスト 〖対照〗(a) contrast. ▶そのセーターとスカートのコントラストがいい That sweater and skirt are [make] a nice *contrast*.
コントラバス 〖楽器〗a double bass /béis/, 《話》a bass fiddle, (時に) a contrabass. ●コントラバス奏者 a double bassist.
コンドル 〖鳥〗a condor /kándər/.
コントロール 图 control. ●車のハンドルのコントロールを失う lose *control* of the steering wheel. ●(投手の)コントロールミス mislocation. ▶その投手はコントロールがよい[悪い] The pitcher has good [poor] *control*. ●彼はコントロールに難がある[が定まらない] He has some *control* trouble [is *wild* around the plate].
── **コントロールする** 動 control 《one's feelings》. ●カーブをうまくコントロールする control one's curve. ●コントロールキー 〖コンピュータ〗a contról kèy 《略 Ctrl》. ●コントロールタワー 〖管制塔〗a contról tòwer. ●コントロールパネル 〖操作盤〗〖コンピュータ〗a contról pànel. ●コントロールブース a contról bòoth. ●コントロールルーム a contról ròom.
こんとん 混沌 〖混乱〗(a) confusion, (大混乱) chaos. ●混沌としている be in *chaos* [*confusion*]; be *chaotic*. ●混沌とした世界情勢 a *chaotic* world situation. ▶事態はまったく混沌としている Things are in a state of utter [complete] *chaos*.
***こんな** 〖前述の, 後述の〗such (❗冠詞 a, an は such の後に置く); 〖このような〗like this (❗this より口語的); 〖この〗this; 〖この種類の〗this kind [sort] of .... (⇨そんな) ●こんな時に at a time *like this*. ●こんな天気のときには in *this kind of* weather. ▶こんなすばらしい人に会ったことがない I've never met *such* a nice [《書》so nice a] person. ▶こんな時間[夜のこんな時間]でここで何をしているの What are you doing here at *this* hour [*this* time of night]? ▶なんで君がこんなことをするのか僕は理解に苦しむ I can't understand what makes you do *this kind of thing* [*such* a thing (*as this*)]. ▶彼はその箇所はこんなふうに弾いた He played the passage *this way* [*like this*]. /*This is the way* he played the passage. ▶あれ, もうこんな時間ですか. もう帰らなくてはなりません What? Is that *the time*? I must go now. ▶金メダルを獲得できてこんな嬉しいことはありません I couldn't be happier winning the gold medal.
***こんなに** so (＋副, 形) (as this) (❗as this は文脈から明らかな場合は省略される); 《話》this (＋副, 形). ●こんなに夜遅く so late at night (*as this*) ▶こんなに遅いとは/それがこんなに面白いとは思わなかった I didn't realize it could be *this* much fun [*so* much fun *as this*]. ▶こんなに雨が降ってたのではお帰りになれません You can't go home in *all this* rain.
会話 「今出かけた方がいいよ」「今? こんなにすぐ?」"You ought to leave now." "Now? *So* soon?"

‡**こんなん** 困難 图 〖難しさ〗(a) difficulty; 〖苦労〗(a) trouble; 〖苦難〗(a) hardship; 〖苦しみ〗sufferings. ●困難に立ち向かう face [face up to] a *difficulty*. ●(困難が非常に強烈的) ●あらゆる困難に打ち勝つ get over all kinds of *difficulties* [*hardships*]. ●困難に陥る get into *difficulties*. ●財政的困難に陥っている be in financial *difficulties* [*trouble*]. ●困難に耐える bear *hardships* [*sufferings*]. ▶事態がどんなに困難でも彼女は希望を失わなかった No matter how *hard* things were, she never lost hope.
── **困難な** 形 〖難しい〗hard (❗知能・熟練などを要することに用いる); 〖骨の折れる〗hard (❗肉体的・精神的に非常な努力を要することに用いる); 〖面倒な〗troublesome. ●困難な仕事 a *hard* [a *difficult*, a *troublesome*, no easy] task. ●解決困難な問題 a *difficult* [a *hard*] problem *to* solve; a problem *difficult* [*hard*] *to* solve. ▶こんな少ない収入では生活が非常に困難だ I find it very *hard* [*difficult*] (for me) to live on such a small income./I have great *difficulty* [*trouble*] (*in*) living on such a small income. (❗《話》では通例 in を省略する)
***こんにち** 今日 today; 〖このごろ〗(×in) these days, 《主に書》nowadays (❗現在時制とともに用いる). ●今日の日本 Japan *today*; the Japan of *today*; *today*'s Japan. ●今日の世界 the world (*of*) *today*; the *present-day* world. ●今日まで up to *today* [*this day*; (現在) the *present*]. ●今日の問題 a contemporary problem of relevance. ●不安定な社会情勢の今日は in these days [《この時代に》*this age*] of unstable social conditions. (❗these days は修飾語を伴うときは in がつく) ▶彼は懸命に働いて今日の地位を得た He has worked hard to get where he is *today*. ▶今日では教育について親の考えが10年前と変わってきている *Today* [*These days*, *Nowadays*] parents have different ideas about education than [from what] they had ten years ago.
***こんにちは** helló, 《主に米》hi, 《英》hullo, Good morning, Good afternoon.

解説 **hello**, **hi** が親しい間柄で特に名 (first name) とともによく用い, 1日中いつでも使える: *Hi!* Tom [×*Mr. Brown*]. **Good morning** は午後1時ごろまで, **Good afternoon** はそれから日没までに用い, もう少し改まった感じ. Good day は今はまれ. (⇨さよなら)

会話 「こんにちは」「こんにちは, いいお天気ですね」"*Hello*, there!" "Oh, *hi*! (It's a) nice day, isn't it?" (❗一般的なあいさつ. 米国では天気のことはあまりいわない)
会話 「健君, こんにちは」「こんにちは, 田中先生. お元気ですか」"＼*Hello*, ／Ken." "*Good* ／*afternoon*. Mr. Tanáka. How ＼are you?"
こんにゃく 蒟蒻 〖食物〗《a piece of》 *konjak* [*konnyaku*] (jelly); (説明的に) a hard jelly made from the starch of devil's tongue; 〖植物〗devil's tongue.
●こんにゃく玉 a tuber of *konnyaku* root. ●こんにゃく問答 gibberish questions and answers.
こんにゅう 混入 ── **混入する** 動 mix [put] (...) 《*in*》; (液体に少量加える) lace ... 《*with*》. ●コーヒーに毒物を混入する/*put in* poison in one's coffee; *lace* one's coffee *with* poison.
こんねん 今年 (⇨今年(ことし))
こんねんど 今年度 the current [present] year; this year. ●今年度予算 the budget for the *cur-*

コンパ a party, (クラスの) a class party; (集まり)《話》a get-together. ▶新入生歓迎コンパをする have [give] a welcoming *party* for the freshmen.

コンバージョン〖変換〗

コンバーター〖変換装置〗a converter.

コンバート 名〖野球〗conversion.
—— **コンバートする** 動 (選手を別のポジションへ) convert; move. ▶彼は外野手から内野手にコンバートされた He was moved [*converted*] *from* an outfielder *to* an infielder.

コンパイラ〖機械語翻訳プログラム〗〖コンピュータ〗a compiler.
• コンパイラ言語 a compiler language.

コンパクト 名〖携帯用おしろい入れ〗a (powder) compact;〖小さい〗compact. (⇨小型)
—— **コンパクトな** 形〖小さく鋭い〗compact. • コンパクトなスイング a *compact* swing. • コンパクトに振る take a short swing.
• コンパクトカー a compact car. • コンパクトカメラ a compact camera. • コンパクトディスク a compact disc《略 CD》.

コンパス〖<オランダ語〗〖製図用の〗compasses (❗単数扱い), (両脚とも針の) dividers (❗ともに数えるときは a pair [two pairs] of ... を用いる);〖羅針盤〗a (mariner's) compass.
• コンパスが長い ▶彼はコンパス(=脚)が長い[短い] He has long [short] legs.

コンパチブル • コンパチブルである(=互換性がある) be compatible 《*with*》.

コンパニオン a guide, a hostess. (❗この意では ˣa companion は和製英語)

*__こんばん__ 今晩** this evening; (今夜) tonight. (❗ ˣthis night とはいわない) ▶今晩パリに出発します I'm leaving for Paris *this evening* [*tonight*]. (❗ ˣ... in this evening [tonight] とはいわない)

*__こんばんは__** Good ˋevening. (❗日没から寝る時間までは Good evening. Good night は「おやすみ」) (⇨こんにちは)

コンビ〖相棒〗a partner《*to*》;〖2人の組〗a pair, (芸人などの) a duo (複 〜s).〖野球の〗二遊間コンビ a middle-infielder combination; a keystone combination [combo]. • ダブルプレーコンビ a double-play combination. ▶彼らは理想的なコンビだ They are ideal *partners* for each other./They are an ideal *pair*. ▶君とコンビを組みたい I want to *be partners* [*partner up*, *be partnered up*] *with* you.

コンビーフ corned [bully,《米》corn] beef.

コンビナート〖<ロシア語〗a complex, an industrial complex. • 石油コンビナート a petrochemical *complex*.

コンビニ(エンスストア) a convenience store. (❗英国の a corner shop もこの系統の店. 街角にあるとは限らない)
• コンビニ決済 (make) (a) payment at a convenience store.

*__コンピュータ(ー)__** a computer. • パーソナル[家庭用]コンピュータ a personal [a home] *computer*. • オフィス[ホスト]コンピュータ an office [a host] *computer*. • 汎用コンピュータ a general-purpose *computer*. • スーパーコンピュータ a super *computer*. • マイクロコンピュータ a microcomputer. • デスクトップコンピュータ a desktop *computer*. • コンピュータ制御の機械 a *computer*-controlled machine. • コンピュータを立ち上げる boot (up) a *computer*. • コンピュータに入力する put [feed]《data》into a *computer*. • コンピュータで処理する use a *computer* to process (information); process《information》with [in] a *computer*; computerize《information》. ▶我が社は給与部門を完全にコンピュータ化した Our company *has* completely *computerized* its wages department. ▶この辞書は全編コンピュータに入っているので内容の変更は簡単にできる This dictionary is all on a *computer* and can be changed easily.
• コンピュータウイルス computer virus. • コンピュータグラフィックス computer graphics. • コンピュータゲーム (play) a computer game. • コンピュータ言語 (a) computer language. • コンピュータ工学 computer science. • コンピュータ犯罪 a computer crime. • コンピュータマニア (話) a computer fanatic [buff]. (❗前の方は「…狂」と軽蔑的な含みを持つ. 後の方は「…博士, 凝り屋」に近い意) • コンピュータリテラシー[コンピュータを使いこなす能力] computer literacy. • コンピュータワクチン a computer vaccine [vaccination] program.

こんぶ 昆布〖植物〗*kombu*; (説明的に) a kind of kelp (boiled to get Japanese soup stock or cooked to make *tsukudani*).

コンファーム —— **コンファームする** 動〖確認する〗confirm;〖再確認する〗reconfirm.

コンファレンス〖会議〗a conference.

コンプライアンス〖法令遵守〗compliance.

コンフリー〖植物〗a comfrey.

コンプレックス〖心理〗a complex. • コンプレックスを持つようになる get [develop] a *complex*. • 自分の白人コンプレックス(=劣等感)を取り除く rid oneself of [get rid of] one's *inferiority complex toward* the white. (⇨劣等感)

コンプレッサー〖圧縮機〗a compressor. • エアコンプレッサー an air *compressor*.

コンペ a (golf) competition.

こんぺいとう 金平糖〖<ポルトガル語〗confetti.

こんぺき 紺碧 • 紺碧の空 a deep blue sky.

コンベヤー a conveyor. • ベルトコンベヤー a cónveyor bèlt. (❗(1) 単に a conveyor ともいう. (2) a belt conveyor は《まれ》)

コンベンション〖代表者会議〗a convention.
• コンベンションセンター a convéntion cènter. • コンベンションホール a convéntion hàll.

コンポ a stereo component. (❗部品の一つ)

こんぼう 混紡 (紡ぐこと) mixed spinning; (紡いだ糸) a mixture, a mix. • 混紡の mixed. • 綿と麻の混紡糸 a *mixture* of cotton and linen. • ポリエステル50パーセント混紡のズボン (a pair of) pants with an 50 percent polyester *mix*.

こんぼう 棍棒 a club, (短い) a cudgel;〖警棒〗《米》a nightstick,《英》a truncheon. • こん棒を振り回す brandish a *club*.

こんぽう 梱包 名 (包み) a package,《主に英》a parcel; (包むこと) packing. • 梱包を解く open; unpack; unwrap.
—— **梱包する** 動 pack [wrap] ... (up); do one's packing.

コンポスト〖堆肥(たいひ)〗compost /kámpoust/.

*__こんぽん__ 根本** 名〖根底〗the root;〖土台〗(a) foundation;〖基礎〗a basis. (⇨基本, 根底) • 失敗の根本原因 the *root* cause of failure.
—— **根本的な** 形 • 根本的(=基本的)な問題 a *fundamental* [a *basic*] problem. • 根本的な税制改革 a *fundamental* [(抜本的な) *drastic*] tax reform.
—— **根本的に** 副 ▶彼とは根本的に意見が合わない I disagree *fundamentally* [*basically*] with him.

コンマ〖読点〗a comma;〖小数点〗a decimal point. (⇨巻末〖句読法〗) • 2語の間にコンマを入れる put [use, insert] a *comma* between the two

こんまけ 根負け 彼のしつこさに根負けした His tenacity *exhausted* my *patience* [*wore me down*]./I *gave in* to his tenacity.

こんめい 混迷 (a) confusion. ▶政局は混迷の度を加えた The political situation was thrown into greater *confusion* [*was more and more confused*].

コンメンタール [<ドイツ語] 〖注釈書〗a commentary.

こんもう 懇望 图 (ひたすら望むこと)《書》(an) entreaty; an earnest request. (⇨懇願)

── **懇望する** 動《書》entreat 《him (*to do*)》; ask《him》earnestly.

こんもり ▶ブナがこんもり茂っている小さな丘 a small hill *thick* with beech trees. ●こんもりした茂みに隠れる hide in a thicket. ▶丘の上に木がこんもりと茂っている The trees grow *thick* on the hill.

*****こんや 今夜** tonight (**!**×this night とはいわない); (今晩) this evening. ●今夜のテレビニュースで on *tonight*'s TV news. ▶今夜はおじの家に泊る I'll stay at my uncle's *tonight* [*for the night*].

こんや 紺屋 (⇨紺屋(こ󠄀))

*****こんやく 婚約** 图 engagement. ●婚約中の2人 an *engaged* couple. ▶真澄は詩織との婚約を発表した[破棄した] Masumi announced [broke (off)] his [ˣan] *engagement to* [ˣwith] Shiori.

── **婚約する** 動 ▶ジョンはアリスと婚約した[している] John *got* [*is*] *engaged to* Alice./John and Alice *got* [*are*] *engaged*.

●婚約者 (男性) a fiancé; (女性) a fiancée. (**!**いずれも発音は《米》/fiːɑːnséi/《英》/fiɑ́ːnsei/) ●婚約指輪 an engágement ring.

こんよく 混浴 mixed bathing /béiðiŋ/. (⇨風呂) ▶露天風呂は混浴になっています At the open-air hot spring, men and women *use the same bath*.

*****こんらん 混乱** 图 〖入り乱れて個々の区別がつかない状態〗(a) confusion; 〖順序・秩序が乱れている状態〗disorder; 〖手がつけられないほどの無秩序状態〗chaos. ●場内の混乱 the *confusion* [*disorder*] in the hall. ●混乱に陥る be thrown into *confusion* [*disorder*]. ●混乱状態にある be in (a state of) *confusion* [*disorder*, *chaos*]. ●混乱にまぎれて逃げる escape in the *confusion*. ▶その地震で町は大混乱となった The earthquake brought utter *chaos* to the city [*produced utter chaos in the city*].

── **混乱する** 動 (まごつく) be [*get**] *confused*. ●混乱した考え *confused* ideas. ●会議を混乱させる put [*throw*] a meeting into *confusion*. ▶彼は頭が混乱してどうしていいか分からなかった He got so *confused* [*mixed up*] that he didn't know what to do. ▶関係のない事を持ち出して頭を混乱させないでくれ Don't try to *confuse* me *with* irrelevant facts.

こんりゅう 建立 图 building;《書》erection. (⇨建設)

── **建立する** 動 build [set up,《書》erect]《a temple》.

こんりゅう 根粒 a root nodule /nɑ́dʒuːl/.

●根粒菌 root nodule bacteria.

こんりんざい 金輪際 ▶彼とは金輪際口をきかない I shall *never* [I won't *ever*] talk to him *again*.

こんれい 婚礼 a wedding. (⇨結婚)

こんろ a (portable) (cooking) stove,《米》a range,《英》a cooker; (野外用バーベキューコンロ) a barbecue, (小型の) a *hibachi*. (**!**portable をつけると日本の昔のコンロに近づく)

こんわ 懇話 a friendly talk [discussion]. (⇨懇談)

こんわく 困惑 图《書》perplexity; (当惑) (an) embarrassment. ●困惑の表情を浮かべる look *perplexed* [*embarrassed*].

── **困惑する** 動 ●彼の質問に困惑する be perplexed [be embarrassed, be puzzled] *by* his questions.

さ

さ 差 【違い】(a) difference; (大きな隔たり) a gap; (票決などの) a margin. (⇨違い) ●男女間に給与の差をつける make a *difference* in payment *between* men and women. ●差を埋める[縮める] bridge [narrow] the *gap*. ▶彼の考え方と君の考え方とでは大きな違いがある There is a great *difference* [*gap*] *between* his (way of) thinking and yours. ▶彼らの年齢差は10歳です The *difference* in their ages is ten years./There is an age *difference* of ten years between them./There is a ten year *gap* between them. ▶自民党がわずかの差[大差; 200 票差]で敗れた The Liberal Democratic Party was defeated by a narrow [a wide; a 200 vote, ×200 votes] *margin*. ▶彼は2位に200メートルの差をつけて走った He ran ahead of the second runner *by* two hundred meters. (**!** by は「…だけ」という差異を表す)

■ DISCOURSE
依然として, 失業率に関して男女間に差がある There is still a *difference* between men and women **with respect to** the unemployment rate. (**!** with respect to ... (…に関しては)関連を表すディスコースマーカー)

***ざ 座 ❶**【席】a seat. ●座につく take a [one's] *seat*. (⇨席❶)
❷【集まりの席】●座をしらけさせる(=水をさす) cast a chill 《over the gathering》.
❸【地位】a position. ●妻[権力]の座 a *position* of wifehood [power]. ●政権の座につく[ついている] come *into* [be *in*] power. ▶彼は3年間チャンピオンの座を守った He was the champion for three years.

さあ ❶【注意喚起, 催促】●さあ始めるぞ Hére /goes!/*Hére* we ⌄go! (**!** 敢然と立ち上がるときの掛け声) ▶さあ駅に着いたぞ ↘*Hére* we are at the ⌄station. ▶さあバスが来たぞ ↘*Hére* cómes the /bus. (**!** 代名詞なら Hére it ⌄comes. の語順をとる)(⇨ほら) ▶さあどうぞ ↗*Hére* you /are./↘*Hére* it /is. (**!** 人に物を渡しながらいう。前の言い方は相手の「人」に, 後の言い方は渡す「物」に重点がある。 単に Here. ともいう) ▶さあ行こう ↘*Now*, let's ↘go! ▶さあさあ泣かないで (⇨さあさあ) ▶さあ, 落ち着いて Steady, /*now* [*there*]! ▶私はいくつだと思う? さあ当ててみて How old do you think I am? *Go on*, take a guess.
❷【ちゅうちょ, 困惑】 会話 「だれが犯人だと思う?」「さあね」"Who do you think is the culprit?" "*Well*, I can't tell." (**!** この well は通例平担に引きのばす音調)
 会話 「この週末はどうするの」「さあね。たぶん家にいて庭いじりでもするよ」"What are you going to do this weekend?" "*I'm not sure* [*I don't know yet*]. I'll probably stay home and work in the garden."

サーカス a circus. ●サーカスの芸人 a *circus* performer. ▶サーカスを見に行く go to the *circus*.
サーキット 【電気回路】a circuit /sə́ːrkət/; 【自動車レースの走路】a (car racing) circuit.
●サーキットトレーニング【スポーツ】circuit training.
サークル ❶【クラブ】(正式に組織された) a club (**!** 日本語の「サークル」にはこれに当たることが多い (⇨クラブ)); (共通の趣味を持つ人の集まり) a circle, an interest group. ●文芸サークル a literary *club*. ●読書サークル a reading *circle*.
●サークル活動 group activities.
❷【赤ん坊用の】a playpen.

さあさあ (催促) there, there; now, now. (⇨さあ) ▶さあさあ! ↘*Come* /*now*! ▶さあさあ泣かないで *There, there*, [*Come, come; Now, now*] don't cry./↘*Now* [↘*Come on*], stop crying.

ざあざあ ▶雨がざあざあ降った It *poured down* (**!** pour の発音は /pɔ́ːr/.)/It rained *heavily*. (**!** 「ざあざあ降り の雨」は (a) pouring [(a) heavy] rain) ▶上から水がざあざあ流れ落ちてきた Water *flooded down* from above. (**!** 以上2例は適切な副詞がないので, 動詞で工夫する。pour「注ぐように降る」, flood「洪水のように流れる」) ▶川はざあざあ音を立てて流れていた The river *rushed* down. ▶ラジオがざあざあいっている The radio is making loud *crackling* noises./I can hear loud *crackling* noises on the radio.

ザーサイ [<中国語] Szechwan /sètʃwáːn/ pickles.
サーズ 【医学】SARS 《*severe acute respiratory syndrome*(重症急性呼吸器症候群)の略》.
サーチエンジン 【コンピュータ】【検索サイト】search engine.
サーチライト ●サーチライトを当てる shine [play] a *searchlight* 《*at, on*》.
サード 【野球の塁】third (base) (**!** 通例無冠詞); (三塁手) a third base player [(男の) baseman 《-men》] (⇨三塁); 【自動車のギア】(go into) third (gear). ●サードを守る play third.
●サードコーチ【野球】a third base coach; 《和製語》a third coach. ●サードゴロ a grounder to third. ●サードフライ a fly to third. ●サードベース third base. (**!** 通例無冠詞)
サードニックス 【アカシマメノウ】【地学】(a) sardonyx. 〔参考〕8月の誕生石)
サーバー ❶【球技の】a server.
❷【コンピュータの】a server. ●メールサーバー a mail *server*. ●サーバーにアクセスする access (to) a *server*.
❸【料理取り分け用の】a server. ●ケーキサーバー a cake *server*.

‡サービス 図 service /sə́ːrvəs/. (**!** 具体的な行為の場合は ⓒ. 商店での「値引き」などの意はない) ●モーニングサービス(=朝の特別朝食定食) a breakfast special; a bargain breakfast. ●morning service は「朝の礼拝」) ●顧客[カスタマー]サービス customer *service*. ●出血サービス a blowout sale. ●新サービスを提供する offer a new *service*. ▶スミスさんは きのう1日中家庭サービスをした(=家族と過ごした) Mr. Smith spent a whole day with his family yesterday. ▶あの店はサービスがよい You (can) get good *service* at that store./That store gives good *service*./The *service* is good (↔bad) in that store. (**!** The service in that store is good. より普通) ▶あのレストランはサービスが急に悪くなった The *service* worsened [deteriorated] rapidly at that restaurant. ▶この国ではだれでも介護サービスが受けられる Everyone is entitled to get nursing care *services* in this country.
── **サービス(を)する** 動 ▶君に一つサービスをして駅まで車

で送っていくよ I will *do* [*offer*] you a *service* by driving you to the station. ●このコートを3万円にサービスします(=値引きする) We will *reduce* [*cut down*] the price of the coat *to* 30,000 yen. ▶これはサービスです(=無料です) You can get this *gratis* [《話》*for free*]./(おまけとして添えます)《話》I'll *throw* this *in* (!「おまけ」は a thrów-in ともいう).
● サービスエース《テニス》a service ace, an ace. (⇨サーブ) ● サービスエリア a sérvice àrea. ●サービス業 a service industry. ●サービス残業《work》unpaid overtime. ●サービスステーション a fílling státion. (給油のみの) a filling stàtion. ●サービス精神 the spirit of service (×service spirit). ●サービスセンター a service center. ●サービス品 (値引き品) a (special) bargain (《掲示》at Bargain special); (景品) a free gift; 《話》a giveaway. ●サービスマン a repairman. ●サービス料 a service charge.

サーブ 图 a service, a serve. ●サーブが入らない cannot get a *serve* in. ●サーブに失敗する[を落とす] lose [drop] a *serve*. ●サーブを打ち返す[受け損なう] return [miss] a *serve*. ●サーブをキープする hold [stay] one's *service* [*serve*].
会話 「サーブはだれの番だ?」「きみの番だよ」 "Whose *serve* [*service*] is it?" "It's your turn."
── **サーブ(を)する** 動 ●強烈なサーブをする serve a hard slam.

サーファー a surfer.
サーフィン surfing. ●サーフィンに行く go *surfing* (*at* a beach). ●サーフィンをする surf; ride the *surf*. ●ハワイへサーフィンをしに行く go to Hawaii to surf.
サーフボード a surfboard. (!文脈があれば単に a board も可)
サーベイランス 〖調査監視〗 surveillance.
サーベル a saber /séibər/.
サーボ ●サーボ機構 a sérvomèchanism;《話》a servo.
ザーメン [<ドイツ語]〖精液〗〖生理〗semen /síːmən/; sperm.
サーモスタット 〖自動温度調節器〗 a thérmostàt.
サーモン 〖サケ(の身)〗 (a) salmon /sǽmən/. ●スモークサーモン smoked *salmon*.
● サーモンピンク salmon pink.
ザール 〖ドイツの州〗 Saar /sɑːr/. (参考 正式名称は Saarland)
サーロイン 《a piece of》sirloin /sə́ːrlɔin/.
●サーロインステーキ sirloin steak /stéik/.

*さい 際 〖とき〗 when 《+節》(⇨時❷); 〖場合〗 if, in case 《+節》, in case of ... (⇨この際)(!最後はやや堅い言い方で通例文頭にくる (⇨この際)) ●火事の際には *in case of* 《a》fire. ●緊急[非常]の際には *in an emergency*. ▶こちらの方へお越しの際にはぜひお立ち寄りください You've got to drop in 《on us》*when* you happen to come this way [in this neighborhood]. ▶必要の際にはお電話ください Call me up *if* you need me [if necessary].
さい 才 (⇨才能) ●才におぼれる have too much confidence in one's 《own》*ability*.
さい 犀 〖動物〗 a rhinoceros /rainásərəs/;《話》a rhino (複 ~s).
さい 賽 a dice (!単・複同形), 《英古・米》a die. (⇨さいころ)
●さいは投げられた The die is cast.
さい 差異 (a) difference. (!違い)
さい- 再- re-. 〖「再び」の意の接頭辞〗 ●旅券を再発行する *reissue* a passport; issue a passport *again*. ●定年後再就職する(=新たな職につく) get a *new* job after retirement.

さい- 最- (!形容詞の最上級で表す) ●社会の最下層 the lowest class of society. ●最重要課題 the *most* crucial problem. ●最北の地 the northernmost land.

*-さい -歳 ...year(s) old. (!1歳の場合のみ単数形. 乳児の年齢は is twelve *months* old のように月齢でいうのが普通(⇨年〈ど〉, 年齢)) ●5歳の男の子 a five-year-old [×five-years-old] boy; a boy of *five* (years) (!a strong little boy of four では years がなくてもよい); a boy *five* years old (!非標準) ▶あなたのお父さんは何歳ですか *How old* is your father? (!(1) 答えるときは、会話では He is 50 *years old* [《書》 50 *years of age*]. より単に (He is) 50. などという方が普通. ×His age is 50. は不可. (2) *What age* is [×*has*] your father?/*What's* your father's age? という言い方もあるが、これは「お父さんが亡くなった時はあなたは何歳でしたか」 (*What age were you* [*What was your age*]) *when your father died?*) の意味にもとられる (⇨年〈ど〉)) ●私は 30 歳で結婚した I got married when I was *thirty* (years old). (!× ...I was thirty years. は不可/I got married *at* (*the age of*) 30 [*at age* 30]. ▶12歳以上の子供は大人の料金で Children over [above] the *age of* 12 must pay full fare.
-さい -債 (⇨債券) ●外債 a foreign *bond*. ●国債 a government *bond*.
ざい 在 ●東京の在(=少し離れたところ)に住む live on the *outskirts* of Tokyo.
ざい 材 ❶ 〖材木〗(製材)《米》lumber, 《英》timber. ●チーク材 teak *wood*. ●建築用材 building *lùmber*.
❷ 〖材料〗 material.
❸ 〖人材〗 ●有為の材 a person of ability.
ざい 財 a fortune. ●一代で財をなす make a *fortune* in one's lifetime. ●公共財 public *goods*. ●消費財 consumer *goods*.
さいあい 最愛 ●最愛の妻《one's》*beloved* /bilʌ́vid/ wife. ●最愛の人 the person 《one》*loves most*;《one's》*beloved*.
さいあく 最悪 (最悪の事態) the worst (↔the best). ●生涯最悪の日 the *worst* day in one's life. ●最悪の事態に備える prepare for *the worst*. ●最悪の場合には *at* (*the*) *worst*; *if* (*the*) *worst comes to* (*the*) *worst*. ●最悪中の最悪の結果になった It is *the worst possible* thing [《筋書き》scenario] *that could happen*. ▶孤独であることほど人生で最悪のことはない There is *nothing* worse in life than being in solitude.
ざいあく 罪悪 〖宗教・道徳上の〗 a sin; 〖法律上の〗 a crime. (⇨罪) ●罪悪感 (罪の意識) a sense of guilt; a guilty conscience. (⇨罪 ❸)
ざいい 在位 reign /réin/. (!在位期間を表すときは C) ●エリザベス1世の在位中に during the *reign* of Queen Elizabeth Ⅰ. ▶横綱は在位 15 場所を数えた The grand champion has held his *rank* for 15 tournaments.
ザイール Zaire /zɑːíər/. (参考 コンゴ民主共和国の旧称 (⇨コンゴ))
さいうよく 最右翼 ●Aチームが優勝の最右翼にあげられている A is the team *most likely* [(優勝候補の筆頭) A are (the) *favorites*] to win the championship. (!後の方はチームでなく個人を指す場合は単数形を用いる)
さいえい 再映 图 a rerun. ── **再映する** 動 rerun.
さいえん 才媛 a talented [an intelligent] woman (複 women).
さいえん 再演 图 a second performance [presen-

さいえん — **再演する** 動 芝居を再演する perform [give] a play again.

さいえん 再縁 (再婚) (a) remarriage.

さいえん 菜園 a végetable gàrden; (市場向けの)《米》a truck farm, 《英》a market garden; (家庭用の) a kitchen garden.

サイエンス 〖科学〗science.
● サイエンスパーク 〖ハイテク産業地域〗a science park. ● サイエンスフィクション 〖空想科学小説〗science fiction《略 SF》.

さいおう 最奥 —— **最奥の** 形 innermost, inmost.
● 最奥の the *remotest* parts of the earth. ● 心の最奥に in the *innermost* [*deepest*] recesses of one's mind.

さいおうがうま 塞翁が馬 ▶人間万事塞翁が馬 (⇨人間[成句]

さいか 才華 brilliant ability.

さいか 災禍 (天災、災難)

さいか 採火 —— **採火する** 動 (説明的に) kindle a fire from the sun's rays for the sacred torch (as in the Olympic Games).

ざいか 在荷 (a) stock. (⇨在庫) ● 在荷がある[ない] be in [out of] *stock*.

ざいか 財貨 (金銭と品物) money and goods; (財産) property; (富) a fortune. ● 財貨を蓄える accumulate a *fortune*. ● 戦争で財貨をすべて失う lose all one's *property* in the war.

ざいか 罪科 ❶〖罪〗(a) sin. (⇨罪) ❷〖刑罰〗(a) punishment. (⇨刑罰)

ざいか 罪過 (道徳上の) (a) sin; (法律上の) an offense; (過ち) a mistake. ● 罪過を悔い改める repent of one's *sin*.

さいかい 再会 名 (a) reunion.
—— **再会する** 動 meet [see]《him》again; have a reunion《with him》. (⇨会う)

さいかい 再開 —— **再開する** 動 〖中断した後〗resume; 〖閉じた後〗reopen; 〖続ける〗continue. ● 会は午前10時に再開した The meeting *resumed* at 10 a. m./We *resumed* the meeting at 10 a.m. ▶昼食後討論を再開しよう Let's *continue* [《主に米》*carry on*] the discussion after lunch. ● 授業は9月に再開される School *reopens* in September./We go back to school in September. ▶その翌日から工場は生産を再開した The next day, the factory *was back* in production.

さいかい 斎戒 purification. ● 斎戒沐浴する purify oneself.

さいかい 最下位 (順位・競技などで) last place [position], 〖話〗the cellar; (地位) the lowest rank.
● 最下位である be placed last, 《話》be in *the cellar* (❗最下位のチームは a last-place team; a cellar dweller); (最下位に終わる) finish *in last place*. ● 最下位に転落する[を脱する] fall into [escape] *last place*. ● リーグの最下位である be *at the bottom of the league*. ● 最下位は今年も M 高校だった *Last place* went to M High School this year again.

:**さいがい** 災害 (a) disaster, a calamity (❗後の方は被災者の悲しみを強調); 〖大災害〗a catastrophe.
● 自然災害 (=天災) a natural (↔an artificial) *disaster*. ● 洪水による災害 a flood *disaster*. ● 災害をもたらす[防止する] bring [prevent] *disaster*. ● 多くの災害にあう have a lot of *disasters* [*calamities*].
● 災害地 a disaster area; (被災地) a stricken area. ● 災害復興 disáster recòvery.

ざいかい 財界 〖金融界〗the financial world, fi-nancial circles, 〖実業界〗the business world, business circles. ● 財界の大物 a leading financier.
● 財界人 (金融家) a financier; (実業家) a business executive [(男の) a businessman, (女の) a businesswoman].

ざいがい 在外 —— **在外の** 形 overseas.
● 在外研究員 a researcher [a research worker] overseas; (総称) overseas research personnel. ● 在外公館 diplomatic establishments abroad. ● 在外資産 overseas [foreign, external] assets. ● 在外事務所 an overseas agency. ● 在外投資 foreign [overseas] investment. ● 在外邦人 Japanese residents abroad.

さいかいはつ 再開発 名 (a) rèdevélopment. ● 都市再開発 urban *redevelopment* [*renewal*].
—— **再開発する** 動 redevelop.

さいかく 才覚 resource, resourcefulness; (速い頭の働き) ready [quick] wit. ● 才覚に富む男 a man of *resource*; a quick-witted man.

ざいがく 在学 名 (⇨在校, 在籍) ● 彼らは大学在学中に結婚した They (got) married *while* they *were*) in 《米》[*at*《主に英》] college./(大学生のときに) They (got) married *when* they *were* college *students*.
—— **在学する** 動 ▶学校には 2,000 人の学生が在学している There are 2,000 students (enrolled) in the school.
● 在学証明書 a certificate of studentship; a studentship certificate.

さいかくにん 再確認 名 reconfirmation; double-check.
—— **再確認する** 動 reconfirm; double-check. ● ホテルの予約を電話で再確認する *reconfirm* one's hotel reservation by phone. ▶書類に間違いがないか再確認してください Please *double-check* the document for errors.

さいかこう 再加工 名 reprocessing.
—— **再加工する** 動 reprocess.

さいかん 才幹 ability. ● 才幹のある人 an *able* person; a person of *ability*.

さいかん 再刊 a reissue. (⇨復刊)
—— **再刊する** 動 reissue.

さいかん 彩管 a paintbrush.

さいき 才気 ● 才気あふれる会話 conversation full of *wit*.
● 才気煥発(カンパツ) ▶彼は才気煥発だ He is *brilliant* [*quick-witted*].
● 才気走る ▶彼には少しも才気走ったところがない (=才気を外に表わさない) He doesn't appear to be *bright*.

さいき 再起 〖復帰〗a comeback, 〖回復〗recovery. ● 再起不能である be past [beyond] (hope of) one's *recovery*.
—— **再起する** 動 come back; recover. ▶その選手は見事に再起した The player *made* a successful *comeback*.

さいき 債鬼 a merciless bill collector, an importunate creditor. ▶私は債鬼に借金の返済を迫られていた I was pressed for money by an *importunate creditor*.

さいぎ 再議 reconsideration.
—— **再議する** 動 reconsider《a bill》.

さいぎしん 猜疑心 (a) suspicion. ● 猜疑心の強い目で彼を見る look at him suspiciously [with suspicion].

さいきょ 再挙 ● 再挙を図る make another attempt; give《it》another try.

さいきょう 最強 ● 最強のチーム the strongest team.

ざいきょう 在京 ●私が在京中に during my *stay in Tokyo*. ▶彼は在京中だそうだ I hear he *is now (staying) in Tokyo*.

ざいきょう 在郷 ●在郷中 *in* one's *hometown*. ●在郷の友人 a friend in one's *hometown*.

さいきょういく 再教育 图 reeducation; [再訓練] retraining; [現職教育, 社内研修] in-service education [training]; a refresher (course).
── 再教育する 動 reeducate; retrain.

さいきん 最近 副 recently, lately.

> 【解説】通例「現在に近い過去のある 1 点」の意では **recently** を過去形とともに用い,「ある過去の 1 点から現在まで」の意では **recently, lately** を現在完了 (進行)形とともに用いるのだが, いずれの意でも文脈しだいで過去完了形と用いられることもある. 〈英〉では lately は通例疑問文・否定文に, 肯定文では recently を用いる傾向があるが, 〈米〉ではこのような区別はない.

▶最近は就職難だ ✓*Recently* [*Lately*] it's been hard to get a job./*These days* [《主に書》*Nowadays*, ×*Recently*, ×*Lately*] it's hard to get a job. (❗recently を現在形と用いるのはまれ. lately を現在形とともに用いるのは You're not looking well *lately*. のように継続状態や反復的習慣行為を表す場合に限られる (⇒この頃(ᠼ)). ▶最近あまりよく眠れません I haven't been sleeping ✓well /*recently* [*lately*, 《書》*of late*]. ▶彼が病気だと知ったのはごく最近です I only *recently* learned (that) he is sick. (❗lately を過去形と用いるのはまれ)/It's only *recently* that I learned he is sick. ▶つい最近まで そのことを知らなかった I didn't know that until quite [very] *recently*. (❗until の後では lately よ り recently の方が普通). ▶最近 5 年間彼から便りがない I haven't heard from him in [《主に英》for] *the past* [*last*] *five years*. ▶最近彼女が書いた育児書は好評です Her *recent* [《最新の》*latest*, 《一番最近の》*most recent*] book on childcare is very popular. (❗「彼女」が故人の場合は latest は不可)

──最近の 形 recent; 《最新の》the latest. ●最近の出来事 *recent* events; the events of *recent times*. ●最近のニュース the *latest* news; *hot news*. ●最近の若者 the young people *of today*; young people *today* [*these days*]; *today*'s young people.

さいきん 細菌 bacteria /bæktɪəriə/ (❗通例複数形を用いる. 単 bacterium), a germ (❗bacteria の日常語).
●細菌学 bacteriology. ●細菌学者 a bacteriologist. ●細菌性食中毒 bacterial food poisoning. ●細菌戦 bacteriological [germ] warfare; (生物戦争) a biological warfare. ●細菌培養 germ culture. ●細菌兵器 a bacteriological [a germ] weapon. ●細菌療法 bacteriotherapy.

ざいきん 在勤 ── 在勤する 動 ●名古屋支店に在勤する *work* in the Nagoya branch.

さいぎんみ 再吟味 图 (a) reexamination.
── 再吟味する 動 ▶その政策は再吟味する必要がある The policy is in need of *reexamination*./We need to *reexamine* [*review*] the policy.

さいく 細工 图 ❶[職人の技] workmanship, craftsmanship; [製作物]《a piece of》*work*; [手工芸品] a handiwork, a handicraft. ●凝った細工の装飾品 an ornament of elaborate *workmanship* [*craftsmanship*].
❷[ずるい画策] (an) artifice; [ごまかし] a trick.
── 細工する 動 ❶[製作する] *work*.
❷[ずるい手段を用いる] (書類などに不法に手を加える) tamper with …; (帳簿などを)manipulate, 《話》cook … (up). (⇒小細工)
●細工は流々, 仕上げをごろうじろ The end crowns the work.

さいくつ 採掘 ── 採掘する 動 mine. ●石炭を採掘する *mine* coal.

サイクリング cycling,《話》biking. ●サイクリング専用道路 a *cycling* road. ●サイクリングに行く go *cycling* [*biking*]; go on a *cycling* tour [(自転車での遠出) a long *bike* ride].

サイクル [周期, 波長] a cycle. ●4 サイクルエンジン a four-*stroke* engine.

サイクルヒット ●サイクルヒットを打つ [野球] hit for the cycle [the hat trick]. (❗(1) 後の方は主にサッカーなどで 1 試合に 3 ゴール入れることだが, 最近では野球にも転用されている. (2) ×cycle hits は和製英語) ●サイクルヒットのシングルヒットだけ足りない fall a single short of the cycle.

サイクロン [熱帯性低気圧] [気圧] a cyclone.

さいくん 細君 one's wife. (⇒妻)

さいぐんび 再軍備 图 rearmament.
── 再軍備する 動 ●核兵器で再軍備する *rearm with nuclear weapons*.

ざいけ 在家 (在俗の人) a Buddhist layman;《総称》the laity. (⇔ 出家)

さいけいこく 最恵国 a most favored nation《略 MFN》.
●最恵国待遇 《give》most-favored-nation status [treatment].

ざいけいちょちく 財形貯蓄 workers' asset-building savings.

ざいけいほうていしゅぎ 罪刑法定主義 [法律] legalism.

さいけいれい 最敬礼 ── 最敬礼(を)する 動 ●最敬礼をする make a deep [a low, (礼儀正しい) a polite] bow /báu/; bow deeply [low, politely]. (⇒お辞儀)

さいけつ 採決 图 (投票) a vote; (投票権の行使) voting. ●採決で決める decide (a matter) *by vote* [*voting*]. (⇒可決)
── 採決(を)する 動 ▶その動議について採決をしましょう Let's *take a vote on* the motion [*put the motion to the vote, vote on* the motion]. (❗挙手による採決では議長は Can I ask for a show of hands? のようにいう)

さいけつ 採血 ── 採血する 動 take blood《(検査中に) *for* a test; (輸血中に) *for* transfusion》.

さいけつ 裁決 [決定] (a) decision; [判断] (a) judgment. ●その件について裁決を仰ぐ ask for 《his》*decision* about the matter; leave the matter to《his》*judgment*. ●裁決を下す pass *judgment* [*a decision*] 《*on* him》.

さいげつ 歳月 (時) time; (年月) years. (⇒年月(ᡃᠼ))
●歳月がたつにつれて as the *years* pass [go by, roll on]. ▶3 年近くの歳月が流れた Almost [Nearly] three *years* went by.
●歳月人を待たず [ことわざ] Time and tide wait for no man.

サイケデリック [幻覚的な] psychedelic /sàikədélik/.

さいけん 再建 图 reconstruction; (再興) reestablishment.
── 再建する 動 reconstruct, rebuild; reestablish.
●昔の図面を頼りに塔を再建する attempt to *reconstruct* [*rebuild*] the tower from its old plans.

さいけん 再検 图 (a) reexamination.
── 再検する 動 reexamine.

さいけん 債券 a bond; (社債) a debenture. ●貯蓄債券 a savings *bond*. ●債券を発行する issue [float] *a bond*. ●債券を償還する redeem *a bond*.

さいけん ● 債券取引 bond trading.

さいけん 債権 a credit. ● 不良債権を処理する write off a *bad debt* [*loan*]. ● 債権回収 debt collection. ● 債権国 a creditor nation [country]. ● 債権者 a creditor. ● 債権者会議 a creditors' meeting.

さいげん 再現 图 (再生) reproduction.
— **する** 動 ● 忠実に [厳密に] 再現する *reproduce* faithfully [exactly]. ● 祭りの雰囲気を再現する *reproduce* the atmosphere of the festival.

さいげん 際限 — **際限(の)ない** 形 endless, limitless. (⇨果てしない) ● 際限のない競争 an *endless* competition. ● 際限なく続く continue *endlessly* [*without end*]. ● 人間の欲望には際限がない Human desire knows *no bounds*./There is *no end* to human desire.

ざいげん 財源 (国などの) financial resources; (収入源)《やや書》a source of revenue; (資金)《やや話》funds; (金) money. ● 財源が乏しい [豊かだ] be poor [rich] in *financial resources*. ▶国の財源を増やすために新税が導入された New taxes were introduced to increase the nation's *finances*.

さいけんとう 再検討 图 [再検査] (a) reexamination; [再調査] (a) review; [再考] (a) reconsideration. (⇨検討)
— **再検討する** 動 reexamine; study ... again (❗後の方が口語的);review;《やや書》reconsider. ▶その計画は再検討されるだろう The project will *be reexamined* [*be reviewed*]./The project will *come under review*.

さいこ 最古 ● 我が国最古の木造建築物 the oldest wooden building in our country.

サイコ [神経症患者]《話》(a) psycho (徸 ~s). ● サイコセラピー psychotherapy. ● サイコセラピスト a psychotherapist.

***さいご 最後** ❶【一番終わり】the last (↔the first); (結末) an end (↔a beginning).

① 【最後を】 ▶彼は生涯の最後を社長職で飾った He rounded off [made a successful ending to] his career by becoming president (of the company).

② 【最後から】 ● 最後から2番目の席 the second seat from the *last* (one); the second *last* [×last second] seat; the next seat to the *last* (❗the next-to-last seat ともいう);《主に英》the *last* seat but one.

③ 【最後まで】 to the last [end] (⇨終り ⑤);(すっかり) through, out. ● 最後まで戦う fight *to* [*till*] *the last*; fight it *out*. ● 最後まで読む read 《it》 through [*to the end*]. ▶最後の最後まであきらめるな Never give up *till the very end* [*until the last minute*]. ▶最後まで私の言うことを聞いてください Please hear me *out* [*through*]. ▶そのバスケットの試合を最後まで見たい I'd like to see the *end out* [*see out*] the basketball game. ▶やるからには最後までやり通すんだ! If you do this, you do it *all the way*. ▶それがうそだとは最後まで分からなかった *In the end*, we found that it was false.

④ 【最後となる】 ▶先月入院中の彼を見舞ったが、それが最後となった I went to see him in the hospital last month, but that was the *last* time I saw him.

❷ 【いったん…したら】 once (+節). ▶彼はこうと決めたら最後、絶対自分の考えは変えない *Once* he has made up his mind, he never changes it [his mind].

— **最後の** 形 last; final. (❗last は一続きの物事の最後、final は一連の過程の完結を意味する) ● この月の最後の2日間 the *last* two days of this month. (❗×the two *last* days … はほぼ通例使わない) ●この本の最後の章 the *last* [*final*] chapter of this book. ● 最後の列の人 those in the *last* row. (❗「各列の最後(=一端)の人」は a person at the *end* of each line) ● 最後の方(を) the *last* gentleman [lady]. ● 最後の瞬間《at》the *last* moment. ● 最後のチャンス the *last* chance. ● 最後の望みをかける set《the [one's] *last* hope on》. ● 最後の手段として警察に訴える go to the police *in the* [*as a*] *last resort*. ● 最後の一線を越える go 《《古》 go 》 to the *limit*, allow sexual intercourse. ▶熊本にいるのも今日が最後の(日)だ This is my *last* day in Kumamoto. ▶あしたが最後の試験だ It's my *final exam* tomorrow. ▶彼は今試験の最後の追い込みの勉強をしている He's studying for a test in a *last-minute* rush. ● 最後の最後まであきらめるな Don't give up till *the very end*. ▶先月入院中の彼を見舞ったが、それが彼にとった最後(の時)となった I went to see him in the hospital last month. That was the *last* time (that) I had seen [saw] him. (❗(1) 過去のことについていう場合 that 節内は通例過去完了形、時には過去形。現在のことについていう場合は現在完了形、未来のことについては現在形を用いる (⇨初めて). (2) この英語の2文は相互に対立・対照を示す内容なので、日本語の「が」にひかれて but で結びつけることはできない。ただし … month *and* it [《書》, which] was … のように連結性を強化することは可)

— **最後に(は)** 副 last (❗通例文尾で); (文全体を修飾して) lastly, finally (通例文頭で); (とうとう) in the end (❗否定文には用いない). ▶彼女は最後に来た She came *last*./She was the *last* (person) to come. ▶彼女を最後に見たのはいつですか When did you see her *last*? ▶法廷の前列に座っていた彼が最後に法廷を出た He, seated in the front of the court, left *last of all*. ▶最後に皆様のご協力に感謝申し上げます *Lastly* [*Finally, Last of all*], I'd like to thank you all for your help. ▶彼は何度も私を裏切ったが最後には親友になった He betrayed me many times, but *in the end* we became good friends [but we ended up (as) good friends. (❗前の friends は主語が単数の場合でも常に複数形: He became good *friends* with me.) ▶彼はリサイタルの最後にバッハを演奏した He *ended* his recital *with* [*by playing*] Bach. ▶これを最後にきっぱり酒をやめます I'll give up drinking *once and for all*. ▶最後に一言付け加えますと *In conclusion*, let me add a few (more) words. ▶必ず最後にガスの元栓を閉めてから寝ること Be sure to turn off the gas main *last thing at night*. (❗last thing at night は first thing in the morning (朝一番に) と対をなす慣用表現)

さいご 最期 [死] one's [the] death;《婉曲的》one's [the] end; [臨終] one's *last* moment. ● 帝国主義の最期 the *end* [*death*] of imperialism. ● 悲惨な最期を遂げる *die* a miserable [a tragic] *death*; *die* in misery. ● 最期の言葉 one's *last* [*dying*] words. ● 彼の最期を見届ける (= 臨終の床に居合わせる) be there when he dies [is about to die];《やや書》be present at his deathbed.

ざいこ 在庫 (a) stock; (an) inventory. ● 在庫がある [ない] be *in stock* [*out of stock*]. ● 在庫を抱える carry inventory [inventories]. ● 在庫の急激な増加 a drastic rise [increase] in *inventries*. ● 在庫の急激な減少 a sharp decline [depletion] in *inventries*. ● 本の在庫が多い [少ない] have a large [a small] *stock* of books. ▶在庫をすべて処

分した We cleared out entire *inventory*. ▶申し訳ございませんが、その商品は在庫が切れております We are very sorry, but the item is out of *stock*./It is our regret to inform you that we have run out of our *stock* of the item.
● 在庫一掃セール a cléarance sàle. ● 在庫回転率 (improve) an inventory [a stock] turnover. ● 在庫管理 inventory control [management]. ● 在庫整理 inventory shake(-)out. ● 在庫調整 inventory adjustment. ● 在庫品 (a) stock 《of》; goods in stock.

*さいこう 最高 图 〖最大限〗a maximum (⇔a minimum). ▶失業率が過去最高になった Unemployment has now reached its *maximum*. ▶最高100ドルまで使ってよい You may spend a *maximum* of 100 dollars. ▶最高で金，最低でも金 What I want to do is to get a gold at the maximum and a gold at the minimum. I will do it. (❶ will のアクセントに注意)
── 最高(の) 形 〖高さ・程度が最高の〗the highest; 〖一番よい〗the best; 〖程度・質が最高の〗the greatest (❶その他いろいろな形容詞を最上級で用いて「最高の」の意を表せる); 〖頂点の〗top; 〖地位・権力などが最高位の〗《やや書》supreme; 〖最大限の〗《やや書》maximum; 〖記録的な〗record. ▶最高速度で at *top* [*the maximum*] speed. ▶最高タイムでそのレースに優勝する win the race in *record* time. ▶世界で(=現存する)最高のバイオリン the *very best* violin there is. ▶彼は試験で最高点をとった He got *top* [*the highest*] marks in the exam. ▶きのうの気温はこれまでの最高記録を更新した Yesterday's temperature was the *highest* on record./The temperature reached a *new record* [a *new high*] yesterday. ▶そのレストランは最高のイタリア料理を出す They serve the *best* Italian food at that restaurant. ▶彼女は当時最高のオペラ歌手だった She was the *top* [*supreme*] opera singer in those days. ▶公園は最高の人出だった A *record* number of people were out in the park. ▶この夏最高の暑さだ It's the *hottest* this summer. ▶ムーランルージュのショーは最高だった(=見事だった) The show at the Moulin Rouge was *first rate* [*superb*]. (❶superb は主に女性語) ▶湯上がりによく冷えたビールの1杯は最高だ (*There's*) *nothing like* a glass of well-chilled beer after a hot bath. ▶最高！ That couldn't be better. ▶最高の(=この上なく幸せな)気分です I feel *as happy as* (happy) *can be*./I'm *on top of the world*./(これぞ人生だ)《話》This is the life.
● 最高経営責任者 a chief executive officer 《略 CEO》. ● 最高検察庁 the Supreme Public Prosecutor's Office. ● 最高執行責任者 a chief operating officer 《略 COO》. ● 最高指導者 a supreme [a top-ranking] leader. ● 最高殊勲選手 the most valuable player 《略 MVP》.

さいこう 再考 图 reconsideration; (熟考)reflection. ● 再考の結果 on *reflection*; on *second thought* 《米》[*thoughts* 《英》]. ▶再考の余地はない There is no room for *reconsideration*.
── 再考する 動 reconsider; think ... over again; think twice 《about》.

さいこう 再興 图 (a) revival. ● 経済再興 an economic *revival*.
── 再興する 動 ▶日本経済を再興する試み attempt to *revive* the Japanese economy. ● 国を再興する *rebuild* a country.

さいこう 採光 ▶この部屋は採光がいい This room gets much light [sunlight].

さいこう 催行 ● 最少催行人員6名・最大催行人員20名 Participants: Minimum 6/Maximum 20.

ざいこう 在校 ── 在校する 動 (在籍している) be a student [be enrolled] 《at the school; in 1998》 (⇨在学); (学内にいる) be in [《米》at] school 《until noon》. ▶スミス先生は5時まで在校されます Mr. Smith *is at school* until five.
● 在校生 (一同) (all the) students; (卒業生に対して) non-graduates. ● 右，在校生代表 上田幸子 Representing *non-graduates*, Sachiko Ueda.

ざいごう 在郷 ● 在郷軍人 (米) a veteran, an ex-soldier, an ex-serviceman; (予備役の) a reservist. ● 在郷軍人会(米国の) the American Legion.

ざいごう 罪業 a sin.

さいこうがくふ 最高学府 the highest institution [《書》seat] of learning.

さいこうきゅう 最高級 ● 最高級のホテル a hotel of *the highest class* [*grade*]; *the best* hotel; (5つ星印の) a *five-star* hotel (❶ホテル・レストランなどに用いる).

さいこうさい(ばんしょ) 最高裁(判所) the Supreme Court.
● 最高裁長官 the Chief Justice of the Supreme Court.

さいこうちょう 最高潮 a climax; a peak. (⇨絶頂) ▶最高潮に達するreach [come to] a *climax*. ▶会場に着いた時にパーティーは最高潮だった The party was *in full swing* when I got there.

さいこうふ 再交付 a reissue.
── 再交付する 動 reissue 《a licence》.

さいこうほう 最高峰 the highest mountain 《in the world》, the highest peak 《of the Alps》. ● 日本画壇の最高峰 *the greatest* of all painters in Japan. ● 英文学の最高峰(= 最高権威者) *the greatest authority on* [*最高の作品》 the highest pinnacle of*] English literature.

さいこく 催告 《書》(a) notification.
── 催告する 動 notify; (返済を) demand.

さいごつうちょう 最後通牒 an ultimatum /ʌltəméitəm/ (複 ~s, ultimata). ● 最後通牒を出す deliver [issue] an *ultimatum* 《to him to do》; give 《him》 an *ultimatum* 《to do》.

さいごのいっく『最後の一句』 *The Last Phrase*. 〔参考〕森鷗外の小説.

さいごのばんさん『最後の晩餐』 *the Last Supper*. 〔参考〕イエスが十字架につけられる前夜，十二弟子とともにした最後の食事．ダ・ビンチが描いた壁画が有名)

さいこよう 再雇用 图 reemployment.
── 再雇用する 動 reemploy.

さいころ a dice (❶単・複同形.「さいころ遊び[ばくち]」の意では), 《米・英古》a die. ● さいころを振って，出た数だけ進んでいいのです (すごろくゲームなどで) Throw [Roll] (the) *dice*, and the number on the dice will tell you how far you can go.

サイコロジー 〖心理学〗psychology.

さいこん 再婚 图 a second marriage. (⇨結婚)
── 再婚する 動 ▶彼女はすぐに再婚した She *remarried* soon./She *got married again* soon.

さいさい 再々 again and again, over and over again. ▶彼女の名前を再々呼んだが返事はなかった I called her name *again and again*, but there was no response.

さいさき 幸先 ● 幸先(が)いい〖縁起がいい〗be a good (⇔a bad) sign; 〖いいスタートを切る〗make a good (⇔a bad) start, 《やや話》get off to a good [(とてもいい) flying] (⇔a bad) start.

*さいさん 採算 ● (もうけ) (a) profit; gain (❶しばしば複数形で). ● 採算を無視してその製品を売る sell the product without considering one's *profit*. ● 独

立算制 the self-supporting accounting system. ▶そのバス会社は採算割れした This bus company has been *unprofitable*./This bus company *didn't make enough profit*.
● **採算が取れる** ●採算がとれている商売 a *paying* [(もうかっている) a *going*, a *lucrative*] business. ▶この商売は採算がとれる[とれない]だろう This business will *pay* [won't *pay*]./This business will *be profitable* [*unprofitable*].

さいさん 再三 ●再三(再四)警告する warn 《him》 *repeatedly* [*over and over again*]; give 《him》 *repeated* warnings. (⇨何度❷)

＊ざいさん 財産 [土地・建物の] (a) property (❢集合的に Ⓤ,「所有物」の意では Ⓒ); [巨額の金] (a) fortune. (⇨資産)

① **〜財産, 財産〜〉** ●共有財産 common *property*. ●私有[公有; 国有]財産 private [public; national] *property*. ▶健康は私の唯一の財産(=資本)です Good health is my only capital [*asset*]. ▶彼女は財産目当てに彼と結婚した She married him for *money* [for his *fortune*].

② **【財産が[は]】** ●彼には少なくとも 2 億円の財産がある He has a *fortune* of [He is *worth*] at least 200 million yen. ▶その財産はすべて彼の娘のものになるだろう All the *property* will go to his daughter.

③ **【財産の】** ●ばく大な財産の相続人 an heir to [×of] a large *fortune*. ●財産の保全 preservation of *property*. ●財産の整理 liquidation.

④ **【財産を】** ●株で財産を築く make a *fortune* on the stock market. ●多大の財産を受け継ぐ inherit [succeed to, come into] a great *fortune*. ●火事で財産を失う lose one's *money* [*possessions*] in a fire. ●彼の財産を管理する look after his *property* [[法律]*estate*]. ▶彼は全財産をその事業につぎ込んだ He put all his *fortune* in the enterprise. ▶住宅ローンの支払いがなかったので, 銀行は彼の財産を没収した The bank seized [confiscated] his *property* because he could not make the mortgage payments.
● **財産家** a man [a woman] of property; (資産家) a man [a woman] of means. ● **財産刑** (科料) amercement; (科料) a fine; (没収) forfeiture. (❢財産刑には以上の 3 種がある) ● **財産権** a próperty right. ● **財産税** property tàx. ● **財産分与** settlement. ● **財産目録** an inventory.

さいし 才子 a man of talent, a talented [a clever] man. ●主に男性についていう (⇨才女)
● **才子多病** (ことわざ) Too wise to live long.

さいし 妻子 one's wife and children; [家族] one's family. ●妻子のある男 a married man with a *family*; a family man (❢「家庭を大事にしている男」の意の方が普通). ●妻子を捨てる desert [walk out on] one's *wife and children*. ●妻子を養う support one's *family*.

さいし 祭司 a priest.

さいし 祭祀 a rite (❢しばしば複数形で), a ritual.

さいじ 祭事 a festival; a rite (❢しばしば複数形で), a ritual.

さいじ 細字 (こまかい字) a minuscule /mínəskjùːl/ letter (❢米粒に書くような極小文字); (一般に) a small [tiny] letter. ●細字用のペン[ボールペン] a fine pen [ballpoint].

さいじ 細事 a trifling [a trivial] matter; 《書》 a trifle. ●細事にこだわる be particular about *trifles*.

さいしき 彩色 ―― **彩色する** 動 color, paint.

さいじき 歳時記 a *haiku* poet's compendium of seasonal terms.

さいしけん 再試験 a retest, 《米》 a make-up (test [exam]).

さいじつ 祭日 (祝日) a (legal) holiday (⇨祝日); (祭りの日) a festival (day).

ざいしつ 在室 在室中 be in a room.

ざいしつ 材質 the quality of material(s). ●材質のいい[悪い]品物 goods of good [poor] *quality*; good-quality [poor-quality] goods.

さいして 際して [行事などに] on the occasion of ...; [...の時に] on .... (⇨...に当たって) ●結婚式に際して *on the occasion of* the wedding. ●出発に際して *on* 《his》 departure. ●この前の経済危機に際して *in the face of* the last economic crisis.

ざいしゃ 在社 ●在社している be in [at] an office.

さいしゅ 採取 ―― **採取する** 動 [集める] gather; [拾う・摘む] pick ... (up); [指紋を取る] take 《his fingerprints》.

＊**さいしゅう 採集** ⌘ ●昆虫採集に出かける go *hunting for* insects.
―― **採集する** 動 ●貝殻を採集する *collect* shells. (⇨集める❶) ●チョウを採集する *catch* butterflies *for specimens*.
● **採集家** a collector.

さいしゅう 最終 ―― **最終の** 形 (一番最後の) the last; (決定的な) final; (締めくくりの) closing. ●最終電車に間に合う catch the *last* [×*final*] train. ●最終決定をする make the [one's] *final* decision. ●試合の最終日に on the *closing* [*last, final*] day of the game. ●最終講義を聞く hear 《his》 *farewell* [×*final*] lecture.
―― **最終的に** 副 ▶それはまだ最終的に解決されていない It's not *finally* settled.
[会話] 「それは臨時の仕事にすぎないんですよ」「最終的には(=ゆくゆくは)どんな種類の仕事をしたいのですか」 "It's only a temporary job." "*Eventually* what sort of ((話)) a) job would you like [do, have]?"
● **最終局面** the final phase. ● **最終結果** an end result; (決算表の損益を示す最後の数字) the bottom line. ● **最終消費者** (エンドユーザー) an end user [consumer]; the ultimate consumer.
● **最終目標** an end [the final] goal; the ultimate target. ● **最終利回り** (債券の) a yield to maturity.

ざいじゅう 在住 ●在住外国人 a resident alien /éiliən/; a foreign resident. ●パリ在住の日本人 *a Japanese living* [*who lives*] *in* Paris.

さいしゅうしょく 再就職 (⇨就職) ●再就職の斡旋(ｱｯｾﾝ) (an) outplacement.
―― **再就職する** 動 find a new job.

さいしゅうとう 済州島 (⇨済州(ﾁｪｼﾞｭ)島)

さいしゅつ 歳出 (an) expenditure, spending. (⇦歳入)

さいしゅっぱつ 再出発 ―― **再出発する** 動 make a fresh start; start afresh, start over again. ▶彼は再出発する(=心を入れ替えてやり直す)と約束した He promised to *turn over a new leaf*.

＊**さいしょ 最初** [一番初めのもの] the first (↔the last) (❢単・複両形あり, 含意される名詞の数に呼応する); [初め] the beginning (↔the end) the start. (⇨初め)

① **【最初の】** ●最初の方(=人) the *first* person [gentleman, lady]. ●今月の最初の方に at [in] *the beginning of* this month. ●最初の印象 one's first impression of 《him》. ●最初の角を右へ曲がりなさい Turn (to the) right at *the first* corner. ▶それが彼に会った最初(の時)だった It [That] was *the first time* (that) I had met him. (❢ × *...the first time*

to meet him. は不可) (⇨初めて[第2文例]) ▶最初のうちは冗談だと思ったが、後で事実だと分かった At first [In the beginning], I thought it was a joke, but then I realized it was true.
② 【最初に】 ●3章の最初に at the beginning of Chapter 3. ●手紙の最初に(=冒頭に) at the head of the letter. ▶スペイン人が最初にサンフランシスコに定住した Spanish people were the first to settle down [(最初の植民者) the first settlers] in San Francisco./Spanish people settled down in San Francisco first. (■…first in San Francisco. では「他の場所に定住する前にまずサンフランシスコに」の意となる) ▶最初に大津に来たとき琵琶湖の大きさに驚いた The first time I came to Otsu, I was surprised how large Biwa Lake was. (■ When I came to Otsu for the first time, …. より普通) ▶まず最初に彼に電話した I phoned him first (of all)./The first thing I did was phone him.
③ 【最初から】 ▶最初からある計画 the original plan. ●その詩を最初から最後まで暗唱する learn the poem by heart from beginning to end. ▶彼はその考えに最初から反対だった He was against the idea from the start. ▶最初からやり直した方がいいですよ You should start back at the beginning.
④ 【最初は[で]】 ▶最初は彼はよそよそしく見えたが、実にいい人だった He looked unfriendly at first, but he was really a nice man. (■ at first は文頭でも可) ▶ジェットコースターに乗るのはこれが最初で最後だ This is both my first and last roller coaster ride!

さいじょ 才女 a talented woman (複 women).
さいじょ 妻女 (妻と娘) one's wife and daughter; (妻) one's wife.
ざいしょ 在所 ❶【故郷】 one's hometown; (いなか) the country. ❷【人が住んでいるところ】 one's residence.
さいしょう 宰相 the Prime Minister; (ドイツなどの首相) the Chancellor. (参考 ビスマルクのあだ名「鉄血宰相」は the Iron Chancellor). (⇨首相)
さいしょう 最小、最少 ── 最小[最少]の 形 (大きさ・量が) the smallest; (量が) the least; (量・程度などが) minimum (■ 通例限定的に). ●世界最小の腕時計 the smallest watch in the world. ●最少の努力でしかない make only a minimum effort.
●最小公倍数 〖数学〗 the lowest [least] common multiple (略 LCM, l.c.m.).
さいじょう 祭場 (祭りを行う場所) the site of a religious service.
さいじょう 斎場 (葬儀場) a funeral home, (英) a funeral parlor.
さいじょう 最上 ── 最上の 形 the best; [[もっともすばらしい] the finest; [[質などが最も高い] the highest; [[至上の] 《やや書》 supreme. ●最上の品 the best article; an article of the finest [finest, highest] quality. ●最上の幸福 supreme [the greatest] happiness. ●最上階の from the top floor. ▶彼女は私たちの大学の最上級生だ She is in her [the] last year at our university. (〖米〗 She is a senior at our university. (■ senior は大学・高校の最上級生のこと)
●最上級 〖文法〗 the superlative (degree).
ざいじょう 罪状 a crime. (⇨罪)
●罪状認否 〖法律〗 (an) arraignment /ərĕinmənt/. ●強盗殺人の公訴事実について罪状認否を行う arraign [him] on charges of armed robbery and murder.
さいしょうげん 最小限 a [the] minimum (複 ～s, minima). ●損害を最小限に抑える keep the loss

(es) to a minimum; minimize the loss(es).
さいしょく 菜食 名 (野菜[菜食主義者]の食事) a vegetable [a vegetarian] diet.
── 菜食する 動 live on a vegetable diet; (している) be on a vegetable diet.
●菜食主義 vegetarianism. ●菜食主義者 a vegetarian; (厳格な) a vegan /víːɡən/. (⇨肉食 [肉食主義者])
ざいしょく 在職 ── 在職中の[に、で] in office. ●4年間の在職期間中に during a tenure of four years.
●在職している be [stay] in office; hold office. ▶在職中はお世話になりました You were a great help to me while I was in office [during my tenure of office].
さいしょくけんび 才色兼備 ▶彼女は才色兼備だ She has both wit and charm./She is both beautiful and talented.
さいしん 再診 (a) reexamination.
さいしん 再審 (a) retrial /rìːtráɪəl/; (上訴された訴訟に対する) 〖法律〗 (a) review. ●再審請求をする appeal 《to the court》 for a retrial. ●再審を受ける be retried; get a new trial.
●再審裁判所 a court of review.
さいしん 細心 ── 細心の 形 (細かな点まで注意深い) very careful; (細心熟慮の) prudent. ●細心の注意をもって扱う handle 《a vase》 with the greatest care. ▶発言には常に細心の注意を払うべきです You should always be very careful about what you say./You should always pay close attention to your speech. ▶彼はドアの開け閉めに音を立てないよう細心の注意を払って寝室からそっと出た He made sure not to make a noise with the door as he slipped out of the bedroom.
さいしん 最深 ●最深の湖 the deepest lake.
さいしん 最新 ── 最新の 形 the newest; (一番最近の) the latest; (先端的な) up-to-date; (現在広まっている) current. (⇨新しい) ●最新式の設備の工場 a factory with the most up-to-date facilities; an up-to-date factory. ●この雑誌の最新号 the current [latest, newest] issue of this magazine.
●吉本ばななの最新の小説 Yoshimoto Banana's latest [newest] novel; the most recent novel by [of] Yoshimoto Banana. ▶これが今年の春の最新流行のファッションです This is the latest fashion (for) this spring. ▶この雑誌にはここニューヨークの最新情報が満載されている This magazine keeps you up to date with how things are here in New York.
さいじん 才人 a person of talent, a talented [a clever] person.
さいじん 祭神 an enshrined deity.
サイズ (a) size, a measurement. (⇨寸法) ●あらゆるサイズの靴 all sizes of shoes; shoes of all sizes. ●並サイズの練り歯磨き a regular-size tube of toothpaste. ●サイズが合うかどうか上着を着てみる try a jacket on for size. ●サイズを測る take [measure] the size 《of》. ●自分に合うサイズのシャツを捜す look for a shirt one's size. ▶この靴はサイズが合わない。もっと小さいサイズはないかしら These shoes are not my size [(ぴったり合わない) don't fit me]. Do you have them in a smaller size? ▶彼女のスリーサイズは(バスト)90, (ウエスト)60, (ヒップ)90です Her measurements [(英話) vital statistics] are 90-60-90.
会話 「靴のサイズはどのくらいですか」 「7EEだと思います」 "May I have your size, sir?/What size shoes do you wear [《主に英》 take]?/What [×How much] is your shoe size [the size of

your shoes]?/What shoe size are you?" "7EE, I think." (!) ×How large are your shoes? とはいわない。(2) EE は double E と読か。(3)「足」を使って What *size* are your feet?/What *size* feet have you got? などともいう）

ざいす 座椅子 a legless seatback; (説明的に) a legless chair with a backrest (used on *tatami* mats in Japanese-style rooms).

さいする 際する (⇨際して)

さいすん 採寸 ── 採寸する 動 ▶洋服屋は私を採寸した The tailor *took* my *measurements*.

さいせい 再生 图 [新生] (a) rebirth; [失われた器官の] regeneration; [廃物の] recycling, reclamation; [音・場面などの] reproduction; (録音・録画の) a playback, a replay. ●都市の再生 urban *regeneration*. ●再生利用する recycle. ▶そのプレーヤーの再生音はいい The record player *reproduces* well. ▶再生ボタンを押してください Press the *play* button.
── 再生する 動 [蘇生(ポン)する] come* to life again; [廃品を] recycle, reclaim; [失われた器官が[を]] regenerate; [録音・録画を] play ... back, reproduce. ●日本経済を再生する *regenerate* Japan's economy. ●録音[録画した演説]を再生する *play back* the recording [speech]. ▶テープレコーダーは彼の声を生き生きと再生した The tape recorder *reproduced* his voice vividly.
●再生医療 regenerative medicine. ●再生紙 recycled paper. ●再生不良性貧血 [医学] aplastic anemia.

さいせい 再製 图 remanufacturing. ── 再製する 動 remanufacture.
●再製品 a reprocessed article; (廃物の) a recycled article.

ざいせい 在世 ●在世中に during one's lifetime; while one was still alive [living].

ざいせい 財政 图 finance ((!)「財源・財政状態」の意で は複数形で); financial affairs.
① [~財政] ●国家[地方]財政 national [local] *finance*. ●緊縮財政 retrenchment *finance*. ●赤字財政 deficit *financing*; compensatory *finance*.
② [財政~] ●財政赤字を抑制する bring the *budget* deficit under control. ●財政上の理由で for *financial* reasons. ▶その国は財政援助を求めた The country sought *financial* aid. ▶彼は財政面で以前より恵まれている Financially [Financewise], he's much better off than before. ▶その市は財政悪化の一途をたどっている The city *finances* are going on worsening. ▶我が家は財政破たんした Our *finances* have been in a mess.
③ [財政は[が]] ●財政が苦しい be in *financial* difficulties [trouble]; (暮らし向きが楽でない) be badly (↔well) off; (金に困っている) 《話》be hard up (for money). ▶その国の財政は健全です The country's *finances* are sound.
④ [財政を] ●財政を建て直す set its [one's] *finances* in order. ●市の財政(状態)を改善する improve the city's *finances*. ●国家[家庭]の財政を握る hold the nation's [one's family's] *purse strings*.
── 財政の 形 financial.
── 財政的に 副 financially.
●財政家 a financier. ●財政改革 a fiscal reform. ●財政学 the science of finance. ●財政危機 a financial crisis. ●財政構造改革 a fiscal structural reform. ●財政顧問 a financial advisor. ●財政再建 fiscal reconstruction [restructuring]. ●財政政策 a fiscal policy. ●財政投融資 fiscal investment and loan program; 《米》 pump priming.

さいせいき 最盛期 [人生などの] the prime; [黄金時代] the golden age [days]; [出盛り] the season. (⇨出盛り) ▶彼は今が人生の最盛期にある He is now *in the prime of* his life [*in his prime*]. ▶今はカキの最盛期だ Oysters are *in season* now.

さいせいさん 再生産 reproduction. ●拡大[縮小]再生産 expanded [reduced] *reproduction*.

さいせき 砕石 (舗装用の) macadam; (コンクリート用の) (an) aggregate. ●砕石舗装する macadamize a road.

さいせき 採石 ── 採石する 動 quarry /kwɔ́(ː)ri/ (stones).
●採石場 a (stone) quarry.

ざいせき 在席 ●在席している be at one's desk.

ざいせき 在籍 ── 在籍する 動 (している) be registered [be enrolled] (*as a* member [a student]); be enrolled (《米》 [*at* 《主に英》] (a) school); be on the 《school》 register [roll].
●在籍証明書 (学校の) a certificate of registration [studentship]; (団体の) a membership certificate.

さいせん 再戦 图 a return match. ── 再戦する 動 fight again.

さいせん 再選 图 reelection. ●再選をねらう seek *reelection*.
── 再選する 動 ▶彼女は市長に再選された She *was reelected* Mayor./She *was elected* Mayor *again*.

さいせん 賽銭 ●さい銭をあげる make a money offering.
●賽銭箱 an óffertory bòx.

* **さいぜん** 最善 one's [the] best. ●最善を尽くす do [try] one's *best*; do the *best* one can. ●最善の方法を考える think about the *best* way [method]. ▶先生にご恩返しをするため最善を尽くすつもりだ I'll do my *best* to repay the teacher.

さいぜんせん 最前線 ●最前線にいる兵士たち soldiers at [on, in] the *front*. ●平和運動の最前線にいる be in [on, at] the *forefront* of the peace movement.

さいせんたん 最先端 ── 最先端の 形 [最も進んだ] the most advanced; [最新の] the latest [fashion]. (⇨先端) ●最先端の医療 the most advanced medicine; state-of-the-art [cutting-edge] medicine. ▶彼女はコンピュータ技術の最先端で働いている She works at *the latest frontiers* [*the cutting edge*] of computer technology. ((!) いずれもある知識・科学技術の「最先端分野」の意)

さいぜんれつ 最前列 the front row. ▶劇場によっては最前列に座るとかえってステージがよく見えない At some theaters the seats *in the front row* do not give (you) a good view of the stage(, contrary to expectation).

* **さいそく** 催促 ── 催促する 動 (せきたてる) urge; (しつこくせがむ) press. ●彼女に返事を催促する *press* her *for* an answer. ●彼に借金の返済を催促する *urge* him *to* pay back his debt; *press* him *for* payment of his debt.

さいそく 細則 detailed regulations (to execute [carry out] a law).

さいそく 最速 ●最速の乗り物 the fastest vehicle.

さいた 最多 ── 最多の 形 (most の前に「通例 the を省略すると「ほとんどの」の意). ●最多得票を得る get *the most* votes. ●そのレースに最多出場をする make *the most* entries into the race.

サイダー 《米》soda, 《商標》Sprite, 《商標》7-up; 《英》(a) (fizzy) lemonade; 《話》(soda) pop [参考] ふたをとる音から). (!cider は《米》リンゴジュース, 《英》リンゴ酒)

さいたい 妻帯 ― 妻帯する 動（結婚する）get married;（妻がいる）have a wife.
● 妻帯者 a married man.

さいたい 臍帯 〖解剖〗umbilical cord.
● 臍帯血 (umbilical) cord blood.

さいだい 細大 ● 細大漏らさず 細大漏らさず（＝詳細に）報告する report (it) *in full [every] detail*;（ごく細かなことに至るまで）report (it) *to the smallest detail*.

さいだい 最大 ― 最大の 形 the most;（一番大きい）the biggest, the largest, the greatest (⇨大きい[類語]);（最大限の）maximum (!通例限定的に).
● 最大得票数 the most votes. (⇨最多) ● 最大積載量 10 トン a *maximum* load of ten tons. ● 日本最大の発電所 The biggest [*largest, greatest*] power plant in Japan. (!最後は文語的で感情をこめた言い方) ● 20 世紀最大の（＝最も偉大な）作家 the greatest writer of the twentieth century. ● これは過去最大の地震だ This is *the biggest* [*(最悪の) the worst*] earthquake (that) we've ever had.

■ DISCOURSE
原子力は実に 20 世紀最大の発明のひとつである Nuclear power is **indeed** one of *the greatest* inventions of the twentieth century. (! indeed （実に）は主張を表すディスコースマーカー)

● 最大公約数〖数学〗the greatest common divisor《略 GCD, g.c.d.》.

さいだいげん 最大限 a [the] maximum (複 〜s, maxima). ● 最大限の努力をする do one's very best; make *maximum* efforts. ● その機会を最大限に活用する make the most of the opportunity; *make full use of* the opportunity.

さいたく 採択 名 adoption. (⇨採用)
― **採択する 動** ● 決議案を採択する *adopt* (↔reject) a resolution.

ざいたく 在宅 ― 在宅の 形 at home. ● 在宅勤務する work *at home*;（コンピュータの端末機を用いて）telecommute. ● スミスさんはご在宅ですか Is Mr. Smith *in* [*(at) home*]? (! at を省略するのは《英話・米》)
● 在宅医療 home medical care. ● 在宅医療制度 a home-care system. ● 在宅介護 nursing care at home; home care. ● 在宅福祉 home welfare. ● 在宅福祉サービス home welfare services.

さいたる 最たる ● 最たるもの（最適例）a prime [the best] example;（最も目立つもの）the most conspicuous [outstanding] example. ▶ この新市庁舎は税金の無駄づかいの最たるものだ This new city hall is *a prime* [*the worst*] *example* of a waste of tax.

さいたん 最短 ― 最短の 形 the shortest. (対 最長)
● パリへの最短コースを行く take *the shortest* route to Paris. ▶ ここから駅までの最短距離はどのくらいですか What is *the shortest* distance from here to the station?

さいだん 祭壇 an altar. ● 祭壇を設ける prepare [set up] an *altar*.

さいだん 裁断 ❶〖切ること〗cutting.
❷〖判断〗judgment. ● 彼の裁断を仰ぐ（求める）ask for his *judgment*;（委ねる）leave ... to his *judgment*. ● 裁断を下す pass *judgment* (*on*).
― **裁断する 動** cut.
● 裁断機 a cutter.

ざいだん 財団 a foundation. ● ロックフェラー財団 the Rockefeller *Foundation*. ● 日本財団 The Nippon *Foundation*. ([参考] 正式名称は「日本船舶振興会」)
● 財団法人 an incorporated foundation.

さいち 才知（聡明な）intélligence;（頭の回転の速さ）wit, quick-wíttedness. ● 才知にたけた intélligent; brilliant; quíck-witted.

さいち 細緻 ― 細緻な 形 minute;（細かいことに気を配る）meticulous. ● 細緻な描写 a *minute* description.

***さいちゅう 最中 ― 最中に 副** 〖動作の〗in the middle of ...,《やや書》in the midst of ...;（間に）during ...;〖暑さ・人気・戦いなどの〗at the height of .... ▶ 朝食の最中に電話がかかってきた There was a telephone call *in the middle of* breakfast. (! call以下は *while* I was having breakfast の方が普通) ● 彼らはあらしの最中に出航した They set sail *in the middle of* [*at the height of*] the storm. ▶ 稲刈りで忙しい最中に父が病に倒れた My father came down with a disease *when* we were busiest harvesting rice.

ざいちゅう 在中 ▶ 見本在中 Samples (enclosed [only]). (! 封筒などの表書き. only は他に同封物がない場合に用いる)

さいちょう 最長 ― 最長の 形 the longest. (対 最短) ● 日本(の)最長のトンネル the *longest* tunnel in Japan.
● 最長不倒距離〖スキー競技〗the longest jump.

さいづち 才槌 a mallet.
● 才槌頭 a hammer-shaped head.

さいてい 最低 名 〖最低[小]限〗a minimum (↔a maximum) (複 〜s, minima (↔maxima)). ▶ 彼は最低(限)月に 5 本の映画を見る He sees *a minimum of* [*(少なくとも) at least, not* [xno] *less than*] five movies a month. (! 後の二つの方が普通)
― **最低(の) 形** the lowest;（最低[小]限の）《やや書》minimum;（最もひどい）the worst. ● 試験で最低の点をとる get *the lowest* mark(s) in the exam.
● 最低合格点 the *minimum* mark for passing the exam. ● 最低必要条件を満たす meet the *minimum* requirements. ● そんなうそをつくなんて彼は最低だ He is *the lowest of the low* to tell such a lie. ▶ これは今まで読んだ中で最低の本だ This is *the worst* book I've ever read.
会話「休暇はどうでしたか」「最低(＝ひどかった)．どこへ行っても人ばかりでね」"How was your vacation?" "(It was) *terrible*. Crowds everywhere."
● 最低価格 the minimum price; a floor (price).
● 最低生活水準 the minimum standard of living. ● 最低賃金 the lowest wage; a minimum wage.

さいてい 裁定 (a) decision;（仲裁）(an) arbitration;（裁決）a ruling. ● 裁定を下す《him》one's *decision* (*on, about*); decide (*in favor of, against*). ● 彼女は調停者の裁定に従うことに決めた She made up her mind to abide by the mediator's *arbitration*.
― **裁定する 動**（仲裁する）arbitrate (*in* ...);（裁判官・調停者などが）award;（株・商品などを）arbitrage.
● 裁定取引 arbitrage trading.

さいていげん 最低限 (⇨最低)

さいてき 最適 ― 最適の 形 the most suitable;（最善の）the best. ● 子育てに最適の場所 *the most suitable* place to rear children. ▶ これは結婚祝いに最適です This is *most suitable* [*fittest, just the thing*] *for* a wedding gift.

ざいテク 財テク financial engineering;（説明的に）

strategic moneymaking through investment in stocks, bonds, and so on.

さいてん 採点 图 grading;《英》marking;（主に志願者・競技者などの）scoring. ● 採点が甘い［辛い］be generous [severe, strict] in one's *grading* [*marking*].
— **採点する** 動 ● 英語の答案を200点満点で採点する *mark* [*grade*] the exam papers in English on the scale of 200 points.
● 採点者 a grader;《英》a marker; a scorer. ● 採点簿 a márk [《米》a gráde] bòok.

さいてん 祭典 a festival.（⇨祭り）● スポーツの祭典 a sports *festival*.

さいでん 祭殿 a shrine.

サイト （インターネット上の）a site.

さいど 再度 副（再び）again. ;（2回）twice. ● エベレストに再度挑戦するtry to climb Mt. Everest (*once*) *again* [*once more*]; give climbing Mt. Everest *another* try.
— **再度の** 形（もう1回の）another;（2回目の）second.

さいど 彩度 chroma. ● 彩度の高い［低い］色 a high [a low] *chroma* color.

サイド a side.（⇨側）● 逆サイドにボールを送る［展開する］《サッカー》send the ball to the opposite *side*.
● サイドアウト〖テニス，バレー〗(call) a side out. ● サイドカー a sidecar. ● サイドスロー〖野球〗a sidearm pitch;《和製語》a side throw. ● サイドスローで投げる throw *sidearm*.（❗投手・野手の両方に用いる）● サイドテーブル a side table. ● サイドバック〖サッカー〗a side back, a full back. ●《英》では現在サイドバックが普通 a full back が普通 ● サイドビジネス a sideline; a side [a second] job. ● サイドブレーキ《米》an emergency [a parking] brake;《英》a handbrake;《和製語》a side brake. ● サイドボード a sideboard. ● サイドライン〖競技〗a side line. ● サイドリーダー a supplementary reader;《和製語》a side reader. ● サイドワーク (have) a part-time job.

さいどく 再読 — **再読する** 動 read again, reread.

さいとつにゅう 再突入 图 (a) reentry (*into*).
— **再突入する** 動 ● 大気圏に再突入する *reenter* the atmosphere.

サイドミラー《米》a side mirror,《英》a wing mirror. ● サイドミラーを見る look in a *side mirror*.

さいなむ 苛む tórture,《やや書》torment. ● 良心の呵責［自責の念；罪の意識］にさいなまれる be tortured by conscience [remorse; guilt].

*さいなん** 災難〖個人の不幸〗(a) misfortune,（通例軽い）(a) mishap,（不運）bad luck;〖災害〗(a) disaster,（大きな）a calamity（災害）;〖事故〗an accident;〖困った事態〗trouble. ● 災難を招く（軽率なことをして）《やや書》court *disaster*;《話》ask [look] for *trouble*,（引き起こす）cause [bring about] *trouble*.（⇨災い）● 災難にあうを（免れる）meet with [escape] *misfortune* [*disaster*,（事故に）an *accident*]; have [miss (having)] an *accident*. ● 災難だと思ってあきらめる accept (it) as *bad luck*.
〔会話〕「きのう車を盗まれました」「それは災難でしたね」"I had my car stolen yesterday." "What (a stroke of) *bad luck* you have!/(それはお気の毒に) Oh, that was too bad./What a shame [a pity]!"

さいなん 済南〖中国の都市〗Jinan /dʒiːnɑ́ːn/.
さいなん 最南 the southernmost. ● 島の最南端 the southernmost tip of the island.

ざいにち 在日 ● 在日外国人 a foreigner living [resident] in Japan（❗この resident は形容詞）; an alien resident (in Japan). ● 在日米軍 U.S. Forces in Japan [, Japan].（❗後のように in をコンマで代用することが多い）

さいにゅう 歳入 revenue /révən(j)uː/;（❗「歳入の内訳」の意では複数形で）.（⇨ 歳出）

さいにゅうこく 再入国 (a) reentry (*into*).（⇨入国）

さいにん 再任 reappointment. — **再任する** 動 reappoint（him *to* a post）.

ざいにん 在任 图 ● 在任中 while (one is) in office.（⇨在職）
— **在任する** 動 ● 彼は中国に在任した He held a post [特に公務員が] *held office* in China.

ざいにん 罪人〖刑法上の〗(犯人) a criminal, a culprit;（法律違反者）an offender（⇨犯人）;〖宗教上の〗a sinner.

さいにんしき 再認識 — **再認識する** 動 ● 住宅問題を再認識する（再度はっきり理解する）*realize* the housing problem *again*,（新しい見方をする）*see* the housing problem *in a new* [*a fresh*] *light*.

サイネリア〖植物〗a cineraria.（⇨シネラリア）

さいねん 再燃 ● インフレの再燃（＝再発）the return [《やや書》recurrence] of inflation.
— **再燃する** 動《やや書》recur;（活発になる）revive; be revived. ▶その問題が再燃した The problem *has recurred* [*has been revived*]./(再び表面化した)《やや書》The problem *has come to the fore* again.

さいのう 才能 ability; (a) talent; a gift; a genius; (an) aptitude.（⇨能力）

> 〔使い分け〕**ability** 最も一般的な語で，物事を成し遂げるための先天的または後天的な知的・精神的・肉体的能力を表す．諸分野における才能を暗示する場合にはしばしば abilities のように複数形で用いられる．
> **talent** 特定の分野における生まれながらの才能を表す．本人の努力や修練によってさらに高度なものとなることを暗示する．
> **gift** 専門分野から日常的な広い範囲において，類まれな生まれながらの才能を表す．
> **genius** 生まれながらに独創的な才能があり，世界的に有名で歴史に名が残るような天才を表す．相手をほめるときにも用いる．
> **aptitude** ある分野における先天的または後天的な適性能力を表す．しばしば学術・芸術などにおいて習得が早いことを暗示する堅い語．

① **【〜才能】** ● 隠れた才能 a hidden *talent*. ● 生まれながらの才能の持ち主だ He is a man of great *talent* [*ability*]./He has great [a lot of] *talent*.
② **【才能が】** ● 彼は数学の(作曲をする)才能がある He has *ability in* mathematics [the *ability to* compose music].（❗不定詞を伴えば通例定冠詞をつける）● 彼は語学の才能がある He has a *talent* [a *gift*, a *genius*, an *aptitude*] *for* (learning) languages. ● 彼は画家として大変な才能がある He has a great *talent* as a painter./He is a very *talented* painter. ▶彼は特に音楽の才能があるわけではない He's not specially *talented* in music.
③ **【才能を】** ● 才能を伸ばす develop one's *abilities* [*talents*]. ▶彼女は絵の才能を大いに発揮した She showed a great *talent* [*aptitude*] *for* painting.

さいのかわら 賽の河原 'the dry riverbed of the Sanzu River (= the Styx)'.
● 賽の河原の石積み ▶それは賽の河原の石積み(＝むだな努力)だよ That's a futile effort.

さいのめ 賽の目 ● ニンジンをさいの目に切る dice a

carrot; cut a carrot into small cubes.
サイバー 〖電脳の〗cyber.
● サイバーカフェ a cybercafé. ● サイバーカルチャー cyberculture. ● サイバースペース cyberspace. ● サイバー戦争 a cyber war. ● サイバーテロ cyber terrorism.
さいはい 采配 ▶あれは明らかに監督の采配(=指示)ミスだ That is obviously the manager's *mistake* [判断の誤り) *misjudgment*].
── 采配を振る (事業などを指揮する) direct; (組織などを管理する) manage; (責任者として担当する) take charge of ...; (取りしきる)《話》run the show, call the shots [tune]. ● 事業の采配を振る *direct* [*run the show for*] the project.

*さいばい 栽培 图 cultivation, growing; culture (🚩品種改良の意も含む).
── 栽培する 動 cultivate; grow. (🚩後の方が口語的) ▶彼らは温室でイチゴを栽培している They *grow* strawberries in their greenhouse.
● 栽培漁業 fish-farming.

さいばし 菜箸 (説明的に) a pair of long chopsticks used in cooking or serving at the table.
さいばしる 才弾る clever and arrogant.
さいばしる 才走る shrewd; too clever.
さいはつ 再発 図 (回復しかけた病人が病気をぶり返すこと)《やや書》a relapse; 〖病気がぶり返すこと〗a return; 〖問題・病気などが繰り返されること〗《やや書》(a) recurrence. ▶交戦状態の再発は防がなくてはならない We must prevent any *recurrence* of hostility.
── 再発する 動 (人が主語) have a return [a relapse, a recurrence]《of》,《やや書》relapse; (問題・病気などが主語) return, 《やや書》recur. ▶リューマチが再発する *have* [*suffer*] *a return of* rheumatism. ▶彼は退院後まもなく病気が再発した He *got sick again* [*relapsed, had a relapse*] soon after he (had) left the hospital. (🚩 His sickness *got worse again* [*returned, recurred*] soon after .... ともいえる)

ざいばつ 財閥 zaibatsu 〖単・複両扱い〗; 〖企業合同〗a business combine. (🚩米国では財閥とはいわず, the Rockefeller *family* [*clan*] (ロックフェラー一族) のようにいう)

さいはっけん 再発見 图 (a) rediscovery.
── 再発見する 動 rediscover. ● 日本の自然美を再発見する *rediscover* the natural beauty of Japan.
さいはっこう 再発行 图 a reissue. ● パスポートの再発行を申請する apply for the *reissue* of a passport.
── 再発行する 動 issue ... again; reissue.
さいはて 最果て ▶最果ての地 the *farthest* place.
サイバネーション 〖コンピュータによる自動制御〗cybernation.
サイバネティックス 〖人工頭脳学〗cybernetics.
さいはん 再犯 a second offense.
── 再犯者 a second offender.
さいはん 再版 〖第2版〗a second edition; 〖復刻版, 増刷版〗a reprint. ▶再版を出す issue the *second* [(改訂版) *revised*] *edition*; (改訂[復刻, 増版]する) revise [reprint] 《the book》.
さいはん 再販 resale.
● 再販価格 a résale price. ● 再販(価格維持)制度 (keep up) the fair-trade 《米》[resale price maintenance 《英》] system.
*さいばん 裁判 (公判) (a) trial; (通例民事の訴訟) a suit; (訴訟事件) a case; (開廷) court. 【墨事】米英では民事から選ばれた通例12名の陪審員 (jury) が有罪・無罪の評決 (verdict) を行い, それに基づいて裁判官が判決 (sentence) を下す)

① **〜裁判** ▶軍事 [公開] 裁判 a military [an open] *trial*. ▶民事 [刑事] 裁判 a civil [a criminal] *case*. ▶秘密裁判 a secret *trial*. ▶公平な裁判 a fair *trial*.
② **裁判〜** ▶その事件は裁判沙汰(ざた)にならずに解決した The case was settled *out of court*.
③ **裁判は** ▶裁判は原告の勝訴[敗訴]となった The *case* was decided in favor of [went against] the plaintiff./(原告が裁判に勝った[負けた]) The plaintiff won [lost] his *suit*.
④ **裁判に[を]** ▶裁判にかける try 《him for murder》; bring 《him》 to *trial*; take 《him》 to *court* (for trial). ▶事件を裁判に持ち込む bring a case to *trial*; put a case on *trial*. ▶裁判に証人として召喚される be called as a witness at a *trial*. ▶裁判を開く hold a *trial*. ▶裁判に負ける lose a *suit* [a *case*]. ▶彼は窃盗罪で裁判を受けた He *was tried for* [*on the charge of*] theft./He *stood trial for* theft. (🚩 (今) 受けている なら He *is being tried* [*going*] *on trial*] *for* theft.) ▶その証言は彼の裁判に有利である The testimony is in his favor in *court*.
● 裁判員制度 the lay judge system. ● 裁判官 a judge (🚩「川田裁判官」は Mr. Justice Kawada》; (集合的で) the bench (🚩単・複両扱い). ● 裁判記録 court proceedings. ● 裁判所 (⇨裁判所) ● 裁判制度 the jústice sýstem. ● 裁判長 the chief justice; the presiding [chief] judge. (🚩呼びかけは Your Honor). ● 裁判費用 cóurt cósts.

サイパン ● サイパン島 Saipan /sàipǽn/.
さいばんしょ 裁判所 〖法廷〗a court (of justice [law]); (庁舎) a courthouse (⓷ -houses /-ziz, 《米》-siz/). ● 家庭裁判所 (⇨家庭) 地方, 高等裁判所 a family [a summary; a district; a high] *court*.
● 最高裁判所 (⇨最高裁) ● 名古屋地方裁判所 the Nagoya District Court.
さいひ 採否 ● 採否を決める decide to *adopt* [*accept*] 《his idea》*or not*. ▶採否はまだ検討中である be trying to decide to *take* 《him》 *up or not*. ▶採否 (=採用試験の結果) は郵便でお知らせします The *result* will be notified by post.
さいひ 歳費 〖費用〗annual expenditure; 〖国会議員の1年間の給与〗an annual allowance [salary].
さいひつ 才筆 (うまい文章) a clever [a good] style; (文ガ) literary talent.
さいひょうか 再評価 图 (作品などの) reevaluation; (収入・財産などの) revaluation, reassessment.
── 再評価する 動 reevaluate; revaluate, reassess. ▶彼の作品は現在再評価されている His works are being reevaluated [given *more value*] these days.
さいひょうせん 砕氷船 an icebreaker.
*さいふ 財布 〖札と小銭両用の〗《米》a wallet (🚩《米》では札・クレジットカードなどを入れるものを billfold ともいう);《英》a purse; 〖小銭入れ〗《米》a change [coin] purse,《英》a purse. (🚩《米》では, purse は通例女性用ハンドバッグを意味するので注意) ▶軽い[重い]財布 a light [a heavy] *wallet* [*purse*]. (🚩比喩的に〖貧乏[金持]〗の意にもなる) ▶あっ, 財布がないぞ. 盗まれたようだ Oh, no! My *wallet* has gone. I think it was stolen. (⇨盗む)
● 財布の口を締める ▶年末には財布の口を締めるべきだ We should *tighten* the *purse strings* [We should try *not to waste* our *money*] at the end of a year.
● 財布のひもが堅い ▶妻は財布のひもが堅い My wife doesn't *waste* her *money*.
● 財布のひもを締める tighten one's purse strings.

▶財布のひもを締めなくてはいけない(=出費に気をつけなくてはいけない) We have to *be careful with expenses*.
●財布(のひも)をにぎる hold [control] the family purse strings.
●財布のひもを緩める loosen one's purse strings.
●財布(の底)をはたく empty one's purse; spend one's last penny.

さいぶ 細部 a detail. ●その協定の細部 the *details* of the agreement. ●細部(=詳細)にわたる go into *detail* [*particulars*].

さいぶん 細分 图 subdivision.
── 細分化する 動 subdivide (into smaller parts).

ざいべい 在米 in America during one's stay in *America* [*the U.S.*]; while one is staying in *America* [*the U.S.*].
●在米邦人 Japanese people residing [staying] in America; Japanese residents in America.

さいべつ 細別 图 subdivision.
── 細別する 動 subdivide 《into》.

さいへん 再編 (⇨再編成)

さいへん 砕片 a fragment, a broken piece.

さいへん 細片 a small [a slender] piece; (とがった) a splinter.

さいへんせい 再編成 图 reorganization. ●労働組合の再編成 the *reorganization* of a labor union.
── 再編成する 動 ●陸軍を再編成する *reorganize* the army.

*__**さいほう**__ 裁縫 图 sewing /sóuiŋ/; needlework (❗ 刺繍(しゅう)なども含む). ▶彼女は裁縫が上手です She can *sew* very well./She is good at *sewing* [*needlework*].
── 裁縫(を)する 動 sew; do needlework.
●裁縫道具 a séwing sèt; séwing thìngs.
●裁縫箱 a séwing bòx [kìt].

さいほう 再訪 ── 再訪する 動 visit again; (特に長い期間をおいて) revisit. ▶彼はケンブリッジを再訪した He *revisited* Cambridge.

さいほう 西方 ●西方浄土【仏教】the Pure Land of Amida.

さいぼう 細胞 图 a cell. ●がん細胞 a cancer *cell*. ●単細胞 a single *cell*.
── 細胞の 形 cellular.
●細胞遺伝学 cytogenetics. ●細胞学 cytology /saitάlədʒi/. ●細胞診【医学】cytodiagnosis. ●細胞組織 (the) cellular tissue. ●細胞分裂 cell division. ●細胞膜 cell membrane.

ざいほう 財宝【金銀財宝】treasure;【富】wealth,《書》riches.

さいほうそう 再放送 (ラジオ・テレビ番組の) a rebroadcast, a repeat, a rerun. ●音楽番組の再放送 a *rebroadcast* [a *repeat*, a *rerun*] of a musical program.
── 再放送する 動 ●講演を再放送する *rebroadcast* [*rerun*] a lecture.

サイボーグ a cyborg /sáibɔːrg/.

さいほく 最北 the northernmost. ●島の最北端 the *northernmost* tip of the island.

さいほけん 再保険 reinsurance. ●再保険をかける reinsure.

サイホン a siphon /sáifn/.

さいまつ 歳末 the year-end. (⇨暮れ) ●歳末大売り出し a *year-end* grand sale. ●歳末助け合い運動 a *year-end* charity drive.

さいみつ 細密 ── 細密な 形 (細かい) minute; (詳しい) detailed. ●細密な描写 a *minute* [a *minutely detailed*] description.
── 細密に 副 minutely; in (minute) detail; (綿密に) closely.
●細密画 an elaborately painted picture; (しばしば人物画) miniature.

さいみん 催眠 hypnosis /hipnóusis/. ●催眠状態にある be in a *hypnotic* state.
●催眠剤 a hypnótic (drug);《話》knockout drops. ●催眠商法 hypno-selling. ●催眠療法 hypnotherapy.

さいみんじゅつ 催眠術 hýpnotism. ●催眠術をかける hýpnotize. ●催眠術にかかる be 《easily》 hýpnotized. ●催眠術にかかっている be under hypnósis. (❗ hypnosis は「催眠(状態)」の意)
●催眠術師 a hýpnotist.

さいむ 債務【負債】(a) debt /dét/,【金融】liabilities;【法的返済義務】an obligation. ●債務を履行する pay (off)【金融】service) one's debt; meet one's obligation.
●債務国 a debtor country [nation]. ●債務者 a debtor. ●債務不履行 default 《with him》. ●債務保証 (銀行の) a bank guarantee.

ざいむ 財務 (財政上の事務) financial affairs; (財政) finance.
●財務委員会 a finance committee. ●財務官 (やや書) a financier; (財務省の) the Vice Minister of Finance for International Affairs. ●財務局 a local finance bureau. ●財務省 the Ministry of Finance; the Finance Ministry; (米国の) the Division of the Treasury. ●財務諸表 financial statements [tables, sheets]. ●財務大臣 the Minister of Finance; the Finance Minister. ●財務長官 (米国の) the Secretary of the Treasury. ●財務部 a finance division.

さいもく 細目 details; (明細)《書》particulars; (詳しく書かれたもの) specifications. ●報告書の細目 the *details* of a report. (⇨詳細)

*__**ざいもく**__ 材木【用材としての木】wood (❗ 1 本は a piece of *wood*. 材木の種類をいうときは ⓒ); 【製材した木】《主に米》lumber,《英》timber. ●材木を切り出す lumber (*in* the forest). ●材木をひいて板にする saw *wood* into a board. ●材木で家を建てる build a house out of [*of*, ×from] *wood*. (❗ out of の方が口語的) ▶チークやラワンのような材木は家具を作るのに使われます *Woods* such as teak and lauan are used for (making) furniture [×furnitures].
●材木置き場 a lumberyard; a timberyard.

ざいや 在野 ●在野の有力者 an influential figure *out of government offices*. ●在野の政党 an opposition party; a party *out of office*.

さいやく 災厄 (⇨⓷ 災難)

サイヤングしょう サイヤング賞 the Cy Young Award. (参考) 米国メジャーリーグでそのシーズンの最優秀投手に与えられる賞)

さいゆ 採油 ── 採油する 動 (種子などから油を搾り取る) extract oil; (採掘する) drill for oil, drill an oil well; (くみ出す) pump oil.

さいゆうしゅう 最優秀 (⇨最優秀)

さいゆうせん 最優先 (⇨優先)

*__**さいよう**__ 採用 图【意見や方針の】(an) adoption;【従業員の】employment. ●新方式の採用 the *adoption* of a new method. ●採用申し込み an application for *employment*. ●採用の手控え a *hiring freeze*.
── 採用する 動【採り上げる】adopt;【使う】use;【雇う】employ,《米》hire (❗《英》では「ある目的のために一時的に雇う」の意). ●彼の案【計画】を採用する *adopt* his idea [plan]. ●新しい教科書を採用する *use* a new textbook. ▶彼は事務員として採用された He *was employed* [*was hired*] as an office

さいらい 再来 ●モーツァルトの再来 a second Mozart. ●世界大恐慌の再来 *another advent* of the Great Depression.

ざいらい 在来 ── **在来の** 形 (いつもの) usual; (慣例的な) customary; (伝統的な) traditional; (慣習的な) conventional. ●在来種のタンポポ a *native* (*species* of) dandelion. ●在来産業を保護する protect *traditional* [*native*] industries.
●在来線 the old 《Tokaido》 line.

さいりゃく 才略 ● a clever scheme; (才知) resource(s). ▶彼は創意に富み才略に長けた人だ He is inventive and *resourceful*.

さいりゅう 細流 a small stream; (小川) a brook.

ざいりゅう 在留 图 在留期間を延長する extend one's stay 《in Japan》.
── **する** 動 〔住む〕live (⇨在住); 〔滞在する〕stay, remain (⇨滞在する).
●在留外国人 a foreign resident 《in Japan》.

さいりよう 再利用 ── **再利用する** 動 use ... again, reuse. (**!** recycle は「再生利用する」(⇨リサイクル, 再生) ▶ビンを再利用する *reuse* a bottle.

さいりょう 宰領 图 ❶〔荷物・人夫の監督〕(行為) supervision, superintendence; (人) a supervisor, a superintendent.
❷〔団体旅行の世話(人)〕旅行団の宰領 a tour conductor; (主催者) a tour organizer.
── **宰領する** 動 ❶〔荷物・人夫を〕supervise; superintend.
❷〔団体旅行を〕guide 《a tourist party》.

さいりょう 最良 ── **最良の** 形 the best; (最もすばらしい) the finest; (最高の) top. ▶人生最良の日 *the best* [*happiest*] day in one's life.

さいりょう 裁量 〔行動・選択の自由〕(やや書) discretion; 〔判断〕(a) judgment. ▶その件を彼の裁量にゆだねる leave the matter to his *discretion*.

:ざいりょう 材料 (a) material, 〔話〕stuff; 〔資料〕data (**!** datum の複数形であるが単数形が多くなってきている; 〔料理などの〕an ingredient /ɪŋgríːdiənt/. ●建築材料 building 〔construction〕 matèrials. ●実験材料 materials for experiments. ●ケーキの材料 the *ingredients* of the cake. ●本の材料を集める collect material [*data*] for a book. ▶この人形を作るのにどんな材料が必要ですか What *materials* are needed to make this doll?
●材料実験 material testing. ●材料費 the cost of materials; the material cost.

ざいりょく 財力 financial power; 〔資産〕assets; 〔財源〕resources. (⇨資力)

ザイル 〔<ドイツ語〕a climbing rope. ▶我々は安全を考慮してザイルでお互いをより合わせた We *roped ourselves together* for safety.

さいるい 催涙 ●催涙ガス 《fire》tèar gàs. ●催涙弾 a tear gas grenade [shell, bomb].

さいれい 祭礼 a festival.

サイレン a siren /sáɪərən/. ▶外でパトカーか救急車のサイレンの音が聞こえた I heard the *siren* of a police car or an ambulance outside. ▶サイレンが鳴った [鳴りやんだ] The *siren* blew [died]. ▶パトカーがサイレンを鳴らした The police car sounded its *siren*. ▶消防車がサイレンを鳴らしながらやって来た A fire engine came (with its *siren*) wailing.

サイレンサー 〔消音装置〕a silencer.

サイレント 〔無声映画〕a silent film.

サイレントマジョリティ 〔声なき大衆〕the silent majority. (**!** 単・複両扱い)

サイロ a silo 《㲋 ~s》. ●サイロに貯蔵する silo.

さいろく 再録 图 〔再び活字にして載せること〕(a) reprinting; 〔録音〔録画〕し直すこと〕rerecording.
── **再録する** 動 〔再び活字にして載せる〕reprint; 〔録音〔録画〕し直す〕rerecord. ▶その記事は次号に再録される The article will *be reprinted* in the next issue.

さいろく 採録 ── **採録する** 動 (記録する) recórd.
●各地の方言を採録する *record* local dialects.

*さいわい 幸い 图 happiness.
── **幸いな** 形 〔幸運な〕lucky, fortunate; 〔うれしい〕glad (-dd-), happy; 〔満足している〕pleased; (大喜びである) delighted. ▶ここにいたとはあなたは幸いでした You were *lucky* [*fortunate*, ×*happy*] to be here./It was *lucky* [*fortunate*, ×*happy*] (*that*) you were here. (⇨幸せ) ▶お役に立てば幸いです I'll be *glad* [*happy*, *pleased*, *delighted*] if I can be of any help to you. ▶早急にお返事をいただければ幸いです We would *appreciate* it if you could (kindly) respond quickly.
── **幸いにも** 副 luckily, fortunately, 《やや書》happily. ▶今朝地下鉄で事故があったが、幸いにもだれもけがをしなかった There was an accident in the subway this morning, but *luckily* [*fortunately*] no one was injured. (⇨幸運)

さいわん 才腕 (才能) ability 《to do》; (手腕) (a) skill 《in, at》. ▶彼は会社の経営に才腕を振るった He showed [displayed] his *skill in* managing the company. (**!** ... his *ability to* manage ... ともいえる)

:サイン 图 ❶〔署名〕(手紙・正式文書などにする) a signature /sɪɡnətʃər/ (**!** ×sign はこの意で不可); (有名人などの自筆の) an autograph. (⇨署名) ●サイン入りボール an *autographed* ball. ●著者のサイン本 a book *signed by* the author.
❷〔合図〕a sign (⇨合図); (野球などの) a signal, a sign. ●サインを受ける catch [get] a *sign*. ●サインを見落とす miss a *sign*. ▶彼はピッチャーにサインを送った He *gave* a *signal* [*sign*] to [He *signaled*] the pitcher. ▶投手はサイン違いをした The pitcher misread the *sign*.
── **サインする** 動 ●契約書にサインする *sign* (one's *name to*) a contract. ▶ここにサインしてください Please *sign* (your name) here./Please *write* [*put*] *your signature* here. ▶この本にサインしてもらえませんか Could I *have* your *autograph on* this book? (**!** (1) 有名人に「サインしてください」は Could I have your *autograph*, please? または Could I please ...? その人がサインをする場合は通例 sign one's *autograph* という。(2) サインを求める人は an *autograph* hunter/Will you please *autograph* this book?
●サイン会 an autograph session. ●サイン帳 an autograph album [book]; 《和製語》a sign book. ●サインペン a felt pen; a felt tip; 《和製語》a sign pen.

ざいん 座員 a member of a troupe, a trouper.

サウジアラビア 〔国名〕Saudi Arabia /sáʊdi ərébiə/; (公式名) Kingdom of Saudi Arabia. (首都 Riyadh) ●サウジアラビア人 a Saudi (Arabian).
●サウジアラビア(人)の Saudi (Arabian).

サウスカロライナ 〔米国の州〕Sóuth Carolína 《略 S.C. 郵便略 SC》.

サウスダコタ 〔米国の州〕Sóuth Dakóta 《略 S. Dak. 郵便略 SD》.

サウスポー 〖野球〗 a sóuthpàw, a left-hander.
サウナ a sauna /sɔ́ːnə, sáu-/ (bath).
サウンドトラック a sóundtràck.
さえ 冴え ❶ 〖光・色・音などの〗 clearness, clarity. ● 音のさえ clearness [clarity] of sound.
❷ 〖頭脳の働き・技術などの〗知性のさえ sharp intelligence. ● 腕のさえを見せる show great *dexterity* ⟨*in, at*⟩.

:‒**さえ**（副助詞）❶ 〖…ですら〗 even. ▶ これは初めての人 (= 初心 [初学] 者) さえ答えられる簡単な問題です This is an easy question *even* a beginner can answer. (❗ éven a beginner のように修飾される語の方を強く読む) ▶ 彼は日曜でさえ働かねばならなかった He had to work *even* on Sunday. ▶ 彼女は自分の名前を書くことさえできない She can't *even* write her own name.
❷ 〖その上〗 besides, what is more. （⇨その上）▶ 風が激しい上に雨さえ降ってきた It was windy, and *besides* [*what is more*, 〈話〉*on top of that*, 〈さらに悪いことに〉*what is worse*], it began to rain. （❗ 以上いずれも what is… は主文の時制の影響を受けて what was… となることもある）
❸ 〖だけ〗 only, just (❗ 後の方が口語的); （…しさすれば）if only…, 〈やや書〉provided (that)…; 〈…である限りは〉as [so] long as…. ▶ 君さえしっかり勉強さえすればよい *All* you *have to do* is (to) work hard. (❗ 〈口〉ではしばしば to を省略する/You *just have to* study hard. (❗ 命令文で *Just* study hard. ともいえる) ▶ 静かにさえしていればここにいてもよい You can stay here *as* [*so*] *long as* you keep quiet./All you have only to do is to keep quiet to stay here.
会話「今夜芝居に行くっていうのはどう」「もっと早く言ってくれさえしたらなあ！」"How about a play tonight?" "*If only* you had asked me earlier!" (❗ I could go. などの主節を省略した言い方。仮定法が普通だが直説法も可; 雨がやみさえすればすぐ出発します If only it stops raining, I'll leave at once.)

さえかえる 冴え返る 〖鮮やかにさえる〗 be extremely clear; 〖寒さがぶり返す〗 be cold again.
さえき 差益 a margin; a differential profit. ● 円高差益 a yen appreciation [overvaluation] *profit*.
*さえぎる **遮る** 〖中断させる〗 interrupt; 〖妨害する〗 block; 〈物が〉〈やや書〉obstruct; 〈行く手を〉bar (-rr-); 〖中に入れない〗 shut*… out. ● 話を遮る *interrupt* [*break in on, cut in on*]〈his〉talk; 〈話す人を〉*interrupt* ⟨*him*⟩. ● 眺めを遮る *obstruct* [*block, interrupt*] the view. ● 日を遮るためにカーテンを少し引く pull the curtains a little *against* the sun. ● 何一つ視野を遮るもののない荒地 a wild *open* moor. ▶ 彼女は私の行く手を遮った She *barred* [*blocked, stood in*] my way. (❗ この順に口語的) ▶ 厚いカーテンは光を遮る A thick curtain *shuts out* [*blocks, obstructs*] the light.
さえざえ 冴え冴え ● さえざえとした月 a clear [a bright] moon.
さえずり 囀り a song; a chirp; a twitter. （⇨声❷）
さえずる 囀る sing*; chirp; twitter; 〈ヒバリ・カナリアが〉warble. ●〈鳴く〉● さえずっている鳥 a *singing* bird. ● さえずる鳥 (=鳴鳥) a songbird. ▶ 小鳥のさえずる声で目覚めた I was awakened by the *chirping* [*chirp*] of birds.
*さえる **冴える** 〖 動 〗 ▶ 満月が空にさえている (= 明るくかがやいている) A full moon *is shining bright*(*ly*) in the sky. ▶ ベッドに入って本を読むとますます目がさえてきてなかなか眠れなくなります When I read in bed, I become more *wakeful* and can't get to sleep

easily. ▶ さえてるね How *clever* you are! ▶ このときばかりは彼女の第六感が妙にさえていた For once my sixth sense *was on the ball*. (❗ be on the ball は「機敏に働いている」の意)
— **冴えた** 〖 形 〗 ❶ 〖光・色・音などが〗 clear; （明るい）bright. ● さえた考え a *clear* idea. ● トランペットのさえた音 the *clear* tones of a trumpet. ● さえない[さえた] 色 a dull [a bright, a clear] color.
❷ 〖人が〗 （頭がさえた） clear(-)headed; （利口な）clever, bright; （腕のいい）skillful; （手先の器用な）dext(e)rous; （目がさえた）wakeful. ● 腕のさえた外科医 a *skillful* surgeon. ● さえない顔をしている have a *dull* look on one's face. ▶ どうしたの、さえない顔をして What happened? You don't look very happy.
さえわたる 冴え渡る ● さえ渡る音色で in a *very clear* tone. ● さえ渡る青空 a *clear* blue sky.
*さお **竿, 棹** a pole (❗ 特にまっすぐに立てた支柱などに用いる); a rod. ● 竹ざお a bamboo *pole*. ● 旗ざお a flag *pole*. ● 釣りざお a físhing ròd [pòle].
● さおをさす (⇨棹さす)
● さお竹 a (straight) bamboo pole (used to hang washing out to dry).
さおさす 棹さす (説明的に) move a boat along by pushing a long pole against the bottom of the river. ● 時代の流れにさおさす swim with the tide.
さおとめ 早乙女 (田植えをする少女) a rice-planting maiden.
:**さか 坂** ❶ 〖坂道〗 a hill; (斜面) a slope. （⇨下り坂, 上り坂）● 急な坂を上る go up 〖書〗 ascend, （書くように）climb〗 a steep *slope*. ● ゆるやかな坂を下る go down 〖書〗 descend〗 a gentle *slope*. ▶ 寺は坂の上 [下] にある The temple stands at the top [foot] of the *hill*.
❷ 〖年齢や仕事などの〗 ▶ 彼は 60 の坂を越している (= 60 歳になった) He has turned sixty 〖（60 歳を越えている) is over sixty〗. (❗ 「60 代を超している」という解釈もあり, その場合は be no longer in one's sixties, be in one's early seventies などという)
さか 茶菓 refreshments; tea and cakes. ● 客に茶菓を出す serve *refreshments* to a guest.
さが 性 ❶ 〖生まれつきの性質〗 one's nature. ● おのれの愚かな性を恥じる be ashamed of one's foolish *nature*.
❷ 〖ならわし〗 ▶ 浮世の性とはそのようなものだ It's *the way of the world*.
さかあがり 逆上がり （鉄棒で）(do, practice) forward upward circling ⟨*on the bar*⟩.
*さかい **境** 图 〖境界〗 a boundary; 〖国境(地帯)〗 the border. ● 県境 the prefectural *boundary*; the *boundary* between two prefectures. ● 生死の境をさまよう hover between life and death. ▶ 隣の家との境を示すさくがある There is a fence marking the *boundary* [*border*] between our yard and the neighbor's. (❗ この border は自分の家から見た縁 (edge) の意) ● ドイツはフランスと境を接するGermany *borders on* [*xat*] France. ▶ 退職を境にして彼のライフスタイルはがらりと変わった His lifestyle has completely changed *since* he retired from the job. (❗「彼」が故人の場合は過去形で changed completely *after*…. となる)
— **境する** 〖 動 〗 ● 米国は北側でカナダと境する(=隣接している) The US *is bounded* on the north by Canada. ▶ 2 軒の家は低い垣根で境する (=境界を作る) There *is* a low *fence along the boundary* between the two houses.
● 境目 a boundary line; a borderline. ● 当落の境目にいる候補者 a borderline candidate; a can-

さかうらみ 逆恨み ▶私は彼に逆恨みされた My kindness to him met with his resentment to me. ▶彼は彼女の忠告を逆恨みした He *thought badly of* her well-meant advice./He *felt bitterly resentful of* her friendly advice.

＊さかえる 栄える prosper, thrive, flourish.

> **使い分け** **prosper** 最も一般的で、金銭的・物質的に繁栄すること。
> **thrive** ある条件下で成長・発展をとげること。
> **flourish** 発展して全盛期を迎えること。(⇨繁盛, 全盛)

▶その町は昔は栄えていた The town used to *be prosperous* [*prospering*].

さかおとし 逆落とし ❶〖頭から先に落とすこと〗a headlong fall [plunge]. ●逆落としに落ちる fall [plunge] headfirst [headlong]. ❷〖馬などで一気に駆け下りること〗●逆落としに降りる plunge downhill; plunge down a precipice.

さかき 榊 〖植物〗a *sakaki* (tree); (説明的に) a low-spreading, evergreen tree used in a Shinto ritual.

さがく 差額 (a) difference; (残額) the balance. ●後で差額を支払う pay the *difference* later. ●差額ベッド an extra-charge hospital bed.

ざがく 座学 studying at the desk in the classroom only.

さかぐら 酒蔵 a wine cellar [vault].

さかげ 逆毛 ●逆毛を立てる tease 《米》[backcomb 《英》] one's hair.

さかご 逆子 (出産) a breech birth [delivery]. ▶息子は逆子で生まれた My son was born *feet first*.

＊さかさ(ま) 逆さ(ま) 图 (⇨逆)
── 逆さ(ま)の 圏 (上下逆さの) upside-down, 《書》inverted. ●上下逆さまのポスター an *upside-down* [an *inverted*] poster.
── 逆さ(ま)に 副 upside down; (頭から先に) headlong, headfirst (⇨真っ逆様); (後方から) backward. ●アルファベットを逆さまに言う say the alphabet *backward* [in *reverse*(*d*) order]. ▶君は絵を逆さまに見ている You are looking at the picture *upside down*.
── 逆さ(ま)にする 動 〖上下を〗turn ... upside down, 《書》invert; 〖位置・順位を〗reverse. ●びんを逆さまにする turn a bottle *upside down* [〖底を上に〗*bottom up*]; *invert* a bottle. ●逆さまにしたバケツに座る sit on an *upturned* bucket.
●逆言葉 a back slang. ●逆さ富士 an inverted image of Mt. Fuji reflected in the water. ●逆さまつげ ingrown eyelashes; 〖病理〗trichiasis /trikáiəsis/.

さがしあてる 捜し当てる 〖捜して見つける〗find＊; (居場所を突き止める)《書》locate; (気づきにくい物の存在を発見する)《やや書》detect. ●病巣を捜し当てる *detect* the focus.

さかしい 賢しい (⇨賢い)

さがしだす 捜し出す find＊; (時間をかけて組織的に) search ... out; (ようやく) track [hunt] ... down. (⇨捜し当てる) ▶私は職員名簿からあなたの住所を捜し出した(=調べた) I *looked* your address *up* in the personnel file.

さがしまわる 捜し回る look around 〔for〕, 《書》(そこらじゅうを) everywhere 〔for ...〕. ●時計を捜し回る look [search] everywhere *for* one's watch.

さがしもの 捜し物 ▶何か捜し物でもしているのですか Are you looking for something [anything]? (❗後の方は単なる中立的な言い方だが、前の方は「何を捜しているの」に近い言い方)

さかしら 賢しら ●さかしらを言う talk knowing 〔about〕.

ざがしら 座頭 the leader of a troupe.

＊さがす 捜す, 探す

> **WORD CHOICE** 捜す, 探す
> **seek** 利益・幸福・真理・平和など、主に抽象的価値・概念をさがし求めること。●何らかの新しい視点を探し求める *seek* out some new perspective.
> **search** 具体的な人・物を見つけようとして、広い範囲にわたってくまなくさがすこと。また、search for＋名詞の形を取る場合は、seek と同様に抽象的価値・概念を目的語に取ることが多い。●データベースでその単語を捜す *search* the database for the word.
> **look for** 具体的な人・物・場所などをさがすこと。よりくだけた表現。▶息子のためによい学校を探している I'm *looking for* a good school for my son.
> **頻度チャート**
> seek ▬▬▬▬
> search ▬▬▬▬▬▬▬
> look for ▬▬▬▬▬▬▬▬▬▬
>   20 40 60 80 100 (%)

look for ...; 《書》seek＊ (for ...); search (for ...) (⇨〖類語〗); hunt (for ...) (❗獲物のようにとらえにくいものを必死に追い求めること). ●職を探す look [hunt] *for* a job; 《書》seek employment; (見つけようとする) try to find a job. ●犯人を捜す hunt [search *for*, 《書》seek (*for*)] a criminal. (❗search は「捜すべき場所」を目的語に取り,「捜すべきもの」を *for* の後に置くので, search a criminal は「犯人の身体検査をする」の意になる。seek は *for* を伴う方が強意的) ●辞書で単語を探す(=単語の意味を調べる) look up a word *in* a dictionary. ▶これが私がずっと探していた帽子です This is the hat (which) I've *been looking for* [*trying to find*]. (《話》では which は通例省略される) ▶ここを捜してもむだだ. 私が捜したから It's no use *looking for* it here. I've *looked*. (❗日本語につられて ×look for here とはいわない) ▶ポケットに手を入れて小銭を捜した I *searched* [*dug in*] my pocket *for* small change. (❗×I searched small change in my pocket. は不可)/(手探りで) I *felt* [*groped*] around *in* my pocket *for* small change. ▶ノートを見つけようと引き出しをすくなく探した I've *searched* (*through*) [*hunted* (*through*), *looked through*] the drawers *for* my notebook. (❗search, hunt では through を伴う方が強意的. look through は「ひと通りざっと調べる」の意) ▶何かお探しですか (店員が) Can I help you with anything? (❗応答は Yes, please. で医品を求めるか, I'm just looking, thanks. (ちょっと見ているだけです) などという)

会話 「社長が君を捜しているよ(=君に用事がある)」「何のことで私を捜しているのかしら」"You're wanted by the boss." "What *is* he wanting me for, I wonder?"

さかずき 杯 a (*sake*) cup, a drinking cùp; (ワイングラス) a wineglass; (脚つきの) a goblet. ●杯に注ぐ fill a *cup*. ●杯を差す[受ける] offer [accept] a *cup*. ●杯を干す drain [empty] a *cup*. ●杯を交わす exchange *cups*. (❗複数形に注意) ●別れの杯をくむ drink a parting cup [glass].

さかせる

- 杯を返す (返杯する) offer a *sake* cup in return; (縁を切る) break off one's pledge of loyalty.
- 杯事 (杯をとりかわすこと) the exchange of *sake* cups; (酒宴) a drinking bout.

さかせる 咲かせる make* 《a flower》 open. ▶カイラはバラを咲かせる (= 育てる) のがとても上手だ Kayla is very good at *growing* roses.

さかぞり 逆ぞり ── 逆ぞりする 動 shave the wrong way; shave upward.

さかだい 酒代 〖酒の代金〗 money for drinking [a drink]; 〖心づけ〗 a tip, 〖書〗 a gratuity (⇨チップ).

さかだち 逆立ち 图 a handstand; (頭をつけての) a headstand. ── 逆立ちする 動 stand on one's hands [head].

- 逆立ちしても ▶私には逆立ちしても (= どんなにがんばっても) そんなことはできない I *won't in any way* [I'll *in no way*] *be able to* do it. (❗I *won't* be able to do it *in any way*. の語順も可)/There is *no way* I will be able to do it.

さかだつ 逆立つ (動物の毛が) bristle /brísl/; stand* up (stiffly). ▶それを聞くと髪の逆立つ思いがするだろう That'd make your hair *stand on end*.

さかだてる 逆立てる (動物が怒って) 〖毛が主語〗 bristle (up); (鳥が怒ったり寒さを防ぐために) ruffle (up) its feathers [plumage]. ▶犬は怒って毛を逆立てた The dog's hair *bristled* (*up*) with anger.

さかて 逆手 ──鉄棒を逆手で握る grip the horizontal bar *from below* [*with* one's *palms facing upward*].

- 逆手に取る ▶彼は私の論法を逆手に取って攻撃した He attacked me *with* my own logic./He *used* my *own logic against* me.

さかて 酒手 (⇨酒代)

さかな 魚 a fish; (魚肉) fish. (⇨魚屋)

> 解説 fish は一般に「魚」をさすが，広い意味では貝類やクラゲ類を含めることがある．複数形は通例 fish. 個々の魚や種類を強調するときは fishes となることもあるが，最近では kinds of *fish* の方が一般的: いろいろな種類の魚 all kinds of *fish*.

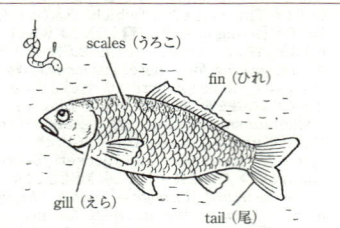

scales (うろこ)
fin (ひれ)
gill (えら)
tail (尾)

- 魚の群れ a shoal of *fish*. ● 魚を5匹つかまえる catch five *fish* [〖まれ〗 *fishes*]. (⇨解説) ▶川に魚釣りに行く go *fishing* in [×to] the river. ● 魚がいっぱいいる池 a pond full of *fish*. ● 魚を焼く broil 《主に米》 [grill 《主に英》] *fish*. ▶その調理器は a broiler, a grill ● 魚を三枚に下ろす fillet a *fish*. ▶晩のおかずに魚を買ってくるわ I'll go and get some *fish* for dinner. ▶この時期この川では魚がよくとれる The river is well *fished* at this time of year. ▶ここの池の魚はあらかたとりつくされた This pond *is* much *fished out*.
- 会話 「魚はお好きですか」「はい，とても好きです」 "Do you like *fish*?" "Yes, I love *them* [*it*]." (❗「生きている魚」なら them, 「魚肉」なら it)

さかな 肴 a side dish for alcoholic drinks. (❗side dish は「添え料理」の意) ▶豆腐はよい酒のさかなになる *Tofu* is a good *side dish for sake*.

さかなで 逆撫で ── 逆撫でする 動 ▶太郎はよく花子の神経を逆撫でする[言う] Taro often *rubs* Hanako (*up*) *the wrong way*. (❗くだけた言い方. 「猫の毛を逆なでして怒らせる」ことから「(思わず)怒らせる」の意. up をとることもある）

さかなみ 逆波 a head sea; a choppy sea.

さかなや 魚屋 (人) a fish dealer, 《主に英》 a fishmonger; (店) a fish store, 《英》 a fishmonger's (shop), 《英》 a fishmonger (❗《英》では a fish shop も可だが，この語は fish and chips の店をさすこともあるので，文脈によっては用いない方が無難）. ▶彼は魚屋です He is a *fish dealer*./He *deals in fish*. (❗の fish は「魚肉」の意)

さかねじ 逆ねじ ●逆ねじをくわせる ▶お金にだらしがないと彼に非難されて，彼女は「あなたほどではないわ」と言って逆ねじをくわせた (= 反撃した) When he criticized her for being careless with the money, she *responded* [*retorted*] by saying she was not as careless as he was.

＊さかのぼる 溯る ❶〖流れを〗 go* up 《a river》; upstream 《along a river》. ● 船で[泳いで]川をさかのぼる sail [swim] *upstream*.
❷〖人・家系などが過去にさかのぼる〗 go* back 《to》; (源泉を) trace ... back 《to》; 〖物・事が年代にさかのぼる〗 date back 《to》; (年代から始まる) date 《from》. ▶その起源を突きとめるには中世にさかのぼらなければならない We must *go back to* the Middle Ages to trace the origin./We must *trace* the origin *back* to the Middle Ages. ▶この寺の創建は17世紀にさかのぼる This temple *dates from* [*dates back to*, *goes back to*] the 17th century. ▶この法律は4月1日にさかのぼって適用される This law *is retroactive* [*is backdated*] *to* April 1st.

さかば 酒場 a bar, 《英》 a pub. (⇨バー)

さかまく 逆巻く ● 逆巻く海 a raging sea.

さかみち 坂道 a slope; a hill. (⇨坂)
- 坂道を転げ落ちるよう ▶内閣の支持率は坂道を転げ落ちるように (= 非常に急激に) 低下している The government's approval rating has been falling *extremely sharply*.

さかむけ 逆剥け a hangnail.

さかむし 酒蒸し ▶マスの酒蒸し *sake*-steamed trout.

さかもり 酒盛り a drinking bout /báut/ [party, (浮かれ騒ぐ) 〖話〗 spree].

さかや 酒屋 〖販売店〗 a líquor stòre [shòp]; (店内では酒を飲ませない) 《米》 a páckage stòre, 《英》 an off-licence; (人) a líquor dèaler, 〖醸造所〗 a brewery; (人) a brewer.

さかやき 月代 ●月代をそる shave the front of one's head.

さかやけ 酒焼け ▶彼の顔は長年の飲酒で酒焼けしていた His face was *red from* long years of *drinking*.

さかゆめ 逆夢 ▶夢は逆夢 In dreams things often go contrary to life./Things will be [turn out] contrary to the dreams you've had.

＊さからう 逆らう 〖願いなどに〗 go* against ...; 〖命令などに従わない〗 disobey; 〖反駁する〗 contradict; 〖抵抗する〗 resist; 〖反対する〗 oppose; 〖公然と反抗する〗 defy. ▶両親〖先生の忠告〗に逆らう *resist* one's parents [one's teacher's advice]. ● 政府の政策に逆らう defy [oppose] the Government's policies. ● 法に逆らって (= 無視して) 行動する act *in defiance of* the law. ● 流れに逆らって泳ぐ swim *against* [(まともに受けて) 〖書〗 *in the teeth of*] the stream. ▶彼の意向に逆らうな Don't *go against* his wishes. ▶彼は彼女に会ってはいけないという私の命令に

逆らった He *disobeyed* [*went against*] my orders not to see her. ▶お言葉に逆らうようですが, ご意見には賛成しかねます I hate to *contradict* you, but I can't agree with you. ▶彼はいちいち私に逆らう He always *takes an opposite view* to mine./He *contradicts* everything I say. ▶彼は逆らわないバッティングをする He hits straightaway./He goes with the pitch.

さかり 盛り ❶ [絶頂] the height. ▶夏の盛りには夕立ほどすがすがしいものはない In the *height of* (the) summer nothing is so *as* [*as*] refreshing as a shower of rain. ▶公園の桜は今が盛りです The cherry blossoms [×flowers] are now *at* their best [*in full bloom*] in the park. ▶花はもう盛りをすぎて(=散って)いる The flowers are already *out of bloom*. (❗「はやもう」の気持ちを強く表す場合はThe flowers alrèady áre.... のようにいう)

❷ [全盛期] the prime, (書) the bloom. ●男[女;娘]盛りである be *in the prime of* manhood [womanhood; youth]. ●人生の盛りに in the *prime of* life; in one's *prime*. ▶彼女は若く見えるが美しさの盛りはすぎている She looks young but she's past her *prime*.

❸ [発情] (雌の) heat; (雄の) rut. ●さかりのついた雌牛 a cow *in* [《英》*on*] *heat*.

さがり 下がり ❶ [下がること] ●南下がりの土地 land which *slants* to the south.

❷ [相撲でまわしの前に下げるもの] *sagari*; (説明的に) the ornamental string apron tucked into the front folds of a *sumo* wrestler's belt.

●下がり目 (物価・相場の) 《show》a downward trend; (たれ目) droopy [(down-)slanted, (down-)slanting] eyes. ▶私は下がり目だ My eyes slant downward.

さかりば 盛り場 [《歓楽街》] an entertáinment àrea; [《繁華街》] busy streets.

さがる 下がる ❶ [位置・価格・数量が] come* [go*] down; (落ちる) fall*; (急に落ちる) drop (-pp-); (滑べり落ちる) slide* down; (地面などが沈下する) sink*; (低下する) lower. ▶オレンジの値段が下がってきた The price of oranges *has come down* [*gone down, fallen*]. (❗消費者の立場からは come down, 生産者にとっては go down となる) ▶その水位が2メートル下がった The water level *dropped* two meters./There was a two meter [×meters] *drop* in water level. ▶温度が急に下がった The temperature *went down* [*fell, dropped*] sharply./There was a sharp *fall* [*drop*] in temperature. ▶熱は下がった The fever *has gone down* [*subsided*]. ▶ドルの価格が108円に下がった The dollar (value) *fell* [*dropped, depreciated*] *to* 108 yen. ▶彼女の彼に対する評価が下がり始めている Her opinion of him *is sinking*. ▶サービスが悪いと店の評判が下がるよ If you don't serve your customers well, your store will *lose* its good *reputation* [will *become unpopular*].

❷ [ぶら下がる] hang*; (ぶらりと垂れる) dangle. ▶屋根からつららが下がっていた There were icicles [Icicles *were*] *hanging* (*down*) from the roof. ▶物干しにたくさん洗濯物が下がっていた There was a lot of washing [A lot of washing *was*] *hung out* on a clothesline. (❗be hung out を「外に出して干される」の意) ▶カーテンのひもが下がっていた The curtain cord *was dangling*.

❸ [退く] (後退する) go* [step (-pp-), move] back; (じゃまにならない所に) stand* back; (引き下がる) retire, withdraw*. ●3歩下がる *go* [*move*] *back* three steps; *take* three steps *back-*

ward(*s*). ●自室へ引き下がる *retire* [*go back*] *to* one's own room. ▶白線の内側に下がってください (駅のアナウンス) Please *step back* and keep behind the line. ▶ロープから[左へ]下がっていなさい *Stand* [*Stay*] *back* from the rope [*to* the left]. ▶下がれ. 爆発するかもしれない *Get back!* It might explode!

❹ [退歩する] (気力・技術などが衰える) fall* off; (練習不足でへたになる) get* out of practice. ▶ゴルフの腕が下がった My skill in golfing *fell off* (↔improved). (⇨腕 ❷ ③) ▶成績が大幅に下がった My grades *fell* greatly./(前よりずっと悪い成績を取った) I *got far worse grades* [《英》marks]. ▶今度の試験で成績が10番下がった I *was* ten places *down on* [*after*] the last exam.

***さかん 盛ん** ── **盛んな** 形 [繁盛している] prósperous, flourishing /fláːrɪʃɪŋ/, thriving (❗prosperous が最も一般的); [成功した] successful; [活発な] (積極的な, 活動的な) active; (精力的な) energetic; (強健で活発な) vigorous; (元気のよい) lively; [熱烈な] enthusiastic; [人気のある] popular. ●盛んな商売 a *prosperous* [*a flourishing*, *a thriving*] business. ▶この国で最も盛んなスポーツ the most *popular* sport in this country. ▶血気盛んな若者 a *hot-blooded* young person. ▶そのランナーは沿道の人々から盛んな声援を受けた The runner received *enthusiastic* [(心から の) *hearty*, (声高な) *loud*] cheers from the people along the route. ▶彼は70歳にしてますます盛んだ He is 70 years old and still very *active* [*energetic*, *vigorous*], (話) He's 70 and still *going strong*. ▶この市では家具の生産が盛んだ The production of furniture *is prospering* [*flourishing*, *a big business*] in this city./(大規模に生産されている) Furniture is produced *on a large scale* in this city. ▶我が国ではウインタースポーツが盛んだ Winter sports are very *popular* in our country./(奨励している) Our country encourages winter sports. ▶その町は以前は田舎町だったが今では商業が盛んだ The town used to be a rustic community, but now it is very commercial.

── **盛んに** 副 (⇨しきりに) ●その計画について盛んに討論する discuss the plan *actively*; have an *active* [a *lively*, (白熱した) a *heated*] discussion about the plan. ●盛んに(=広く)宣伝する advertise (it) *extensively*. ▶犬は盛んに尾を振った The dog wagged its tail *eagerly*. ▶暖炉の中で火が盛んに燃えている A fire is burning *furiously* [*briskly*] in the fireplace. (❗furiously の方が燃え方が激しい)

── **盛んになる**[する] 動 (繁栄する) prosper, flourish; (人気を得る) become* [get*] popular; (促進する) promote; (奨励する) encourage. ▶海外旅行がますます盛んになってきている Traveling abroad *is getting* more and more *popular*. ▶東西文化の交流を盛んにしなければならない We must *promote* [*increase*] cultural exchanges between the East and the West.

さかん 左官 a plasterer.
さがん 左岸 the left bank (of a river).
さがん 砂岩 sandstone.

***さき 先** 名 ❶ [先端] (ペン・針などのとがった先) a point; (指・岬などの突き出た先) a tip; (棒など細長いものの先) an end. ●針の先 the *point* of a needle. ●犬のしっぽの先 a pointed step on the *end* of a dog's tail. ▶この剣は先がとがっている This sword has a sharp (↔a dull) *point* [is pointed]. ▶私は指先をやけどした I burned my fingertip [the *tip* of my finger]. ▶彼は私を頭の先から足の先までじろじろ見た He stared

at me *from head to toe* [*foot*].
❷【未来】the future; (人・国などの前途) a future; (成功の見込み) an outlook 《*for*》,《話》future 《*in*》(⚠ 後の語は通例疑問・否定文で). ▶先のことを考える think of [について] about] *the future*; think [look] *ahead*. ▶先を読む (予測する) predict [forecast] the future (⇨予測する); (推測する) guess (⇨推測する).
①【～先】 ▶これから先(=将来)何が起きるかだれも分からない No one can tell what will happen *in the future*. ▶これから先(=今後は)もっと注意しなさい Be more careful *from now on* [《米》*in the future*, 《英》*in future*]. ▶その問題が解決されるのはそう先のことではない《主に書》It will not be long before the problem is [✗will be] solved./(近い将来解決される) The matter will be settled *in the near future* [(間もなく) *before long*, (やがて) *soon*]. ▶50年先に私たちの木造校舎はどうなっているだろう What will become of our wooden school building fifty years *from now* [*in* fifty years, ✗*after* fifty years]? ▶冬休みはちょうど3週間先だ The winter vacation is just three weeks *away* [*off*, *ahead*].
②【先が[の]】 ▶先が思いやられる I am anxious [feel gloomy] about my *future*. ▶病人はもう先が長くはないだろう I'm afraid the patient doesn't *have long to live*. ▶作家としてやっと先の見通しが立ち始めた(=どうやらうまく行き始めた) Now I'm starting to *get somewhere* as a writer. ▶月旅行できるのもう先の話ではない We will be able to travel to the moon *in the near future*./《主に書》It *won't be long before* we take a trip to the moon. ▶君はまだ若い. 君には先があるよ You're still young. you *have a bright future*. ▶今から先のことを悲観するのはよせ Don't be pessimistic about your *future*.
❸【目的地】one's destination. (⇨行き先) ▶彼の勤め先はどこですか Who does he work for?
会話「ちょっと休みませんか」「いや先を急ごう」"Why don't we take a rest?" "No. Let's *be on our way*."
❹【順序】(まず最初に) first; (…より前に) ahead (of …), before …. ▶先に私が読みますから後について読んでください I'll read *first* and then you follow [read after] me. ▶あすは何よりも先に彼を訪おう I'll visit him *first thing* tomorrow. (⚠ しばしば後に tomorrow, in the morning などを伴う) ▶彼女は私より先に駅に着いた She got to the station *before* me [(より早く) *earlier than* I did,《話》*earlier than* me,《古・まれ》*earlier than* I]. ▶先に行ってくれ. すぐ追いつくから Go *ahead*. I'll catch you in a minute. ▶遊びより仕事が先だ Business *comes before* [(優先する) *takes precedence over*] pleasure. ▶昨夜彼はだれよりも先に帰った He left *earlier than* anybody else last night. ▶大事なことは先にしましょう First things first. ▶宿題を先にすませてから遊びに行きなさい Do your homework *first* and go out to play.
❺【前方】(方方に[へ]) ahead; (離れて) away, off; (向こうに) beyond …. ▶新潟から二つ先の(=向こうの)駅 the second station *beyond* Niigata. ▶目と鼻の先 (⇨目[成句]) ▶その村はここから2キロほど先です The village is about two kilometers (*ahead* [*away*, *off*]) *from* here. ▶彼女は教会の2軒先に住んでいる She lives two doors *away from* [*beyond*] the church. ▶山田さんはここから7, 8軒先で北町 38番に住んでいます Mr. Yamada lives seven or eight doors *along*, 38 Kitamachi. ▶あの床屋の先を右へ曲がりなさい Turn right just *beyond* [(過ぎたところで) *past*] that barbershop. ▶私は大阪から先へ行ったことはない I have never been *beyond* [(より遠くへ) *farther than*] Osaka. ▶彼の事務所ならちょっと先です His office is right *up* [*down*] *there*. (⚠ up [down] there は「あそこ」「そこで」の意で,必ずしも「高い[低い]所」を意味しない) ▶その本はこの先の本屋で買った I bought the book at the bookstore *further* (*up*) *ahead*. (⚠ up がある方が近くを表す) ▶I bought the book at the bookstore *up* [*down*] *the street*. ▶そこから先は道が(=道の残りは)舗装されていない The *rest of the road* is not paved. ▶天気のいい時にはここから 50 キロ先まで見えます On a clear day you can see *for* 50 kilometers from the top floor. ▶その先を話してください(話を続けてください) Go *on* [Go *ahead*] (*with* your story). ▶スティーブンはバイクでランナーの先を走っている Stephen is riding a motorcycle *ahead of* the runners.
❻【以前】 ▶そのことは先に述べたとおりです It is just as I stated *earlier* [*before*, *previously*, *above*]. (⚠ above は横書きの文章で「上に, 前に」の意)
● 先が見える ▶あの事業は先が見えている (将来性がない) There is no *future* in that business./(見通しは暗い) The *outlook* for that business is gloomy. (⇨将来❷)
● 先に立つ ▶行列の先に(=前方に)立って行進する march *ahead of* [(より前に) *before*] the parade; (先頭に) march *at the head of* the parade.
● 先を争う ▶彼らは先を争っての燃えさかるホテルから出ようとした They scrambled [(もがきながら) struggled] *to get out of the blazing hotel*.
● 先を越される ▶タクシーを止めようとしたら, 酔っ払いの男に先を越された I was going to halt a taxi, but some drunken man *beat me to it*. (⚠ beat A to B は《話》で「A (人)よりも先に B (ねらいのもの)を獲得する」の意)

— 先の 形 previous; (前の) former; (この前の) the last. ● 先の経験から from one's *previous* experience(s). ● 先の市長 the [a] *former* mayor; the [an] *ex*-mayor. ● 先の会合 the *last* meeting.

さき 左記 — 左記の 形 (次の) the following. ▶左記のものが必要です—ペンとノート You will need the *following* things—a pen and a notebook. ▶理由は左記のとおり(=次のとおり) The reasons are *as follows*. (⚠ 主語の数・時制とは関係なく例のように用いる。非人称構文 as it follows もされる)

さぎ 鷺 〖鳥〗 a héron. (⚠ サギ類, 特にアオサギ, シラサギは an égret)
● 鷺を烏(カラス)と言いくるめる ▶彼は契約を取るためならさぎをからすと言いくるめることも辞さない He'll be willing to *talk black into white* [*swear black is white*] to get the contract. (⚠「目的のために手段を選ばない」の意の慣用表現で, 未来形・条件節で用いられる)

さぎ 詐欺 〖違法手段で権利などを奪うこと〗 (a) fraud /frɔ́ːd/ 〖具体例は〗Ⓒ; 〖金品などをだまし取ること〗 swindling (⚠ 具体例は a swindle). ● 詐欺を働く commit *fraud*; swindle;《主に法律》defraud (*him of* his money). ● 詐欺で訴えられる be accused of *fraud*. ▶私の父は詐欺にあってなけなしの貯金をだまし取られた My father *was swindled* [*cheated*] *out of* what little savings he had. (⇨だます)
● 詐欺師 a swindler; a fraud; (信用詐欺師) a confidence man [woman];《話》a con man [woman].

-ざき -咲き ▶七分咲きの桜 cherry trees seventy percent *in bloom*. (⇨遅咲き, 早咲き)

さきおくり　先送り —— 先送りする 動 ●決定を先送りする *put off* [*postpone*, *delay*] deciding. (⇨延期, 延ばす❷)

さきおととい　一昨昨日 three days ago.
さきおととし　一昨昨年 three years ago.
さきがい　先買い ●土地の先買いをする buy [*purchase*] land in anticipation of a rise.
さきがけ　先駆け ❶ [先んじること] (先導) the lead; (主導権) the initiative. ●流行の先駆けをする (=先頭に立つ) *lead* the fashion. ▶彼は近代医学の先駆け (=開拓者) となった He was a *pioneer* of modern medicine./He *pioneered* [*led*] modern medicine.

❷ [前触れ] a forerunner, 《書》a herald. ▶クロッカスは春の先駆けである The crocus is a *forerunner* [a *herald*] of spring./《書》The crocus *heralds* the coming of spring.

さきがけて　先駆けて ▶夏に先駆けてツバメがやって来る Swallows come *before* summer./《ツバメは夏の前触れとなる》《書》Swallows *herald* the beginning [coming] of summer. ▶彼らは何年も時代に先駆けて遺伝子操作に取り組んでいた They were years *ahead* of their time in the way they worked on gene manipulation.

さきこぼれる　咲き溢れる ▶庭には花が咲きこぼれていた A lot of flowers were blooming in the garden.
さきごろ　先ごろ not long ago; (先日) the other day; (数日前) a few [some, several] days ago. (⇨先日)
さきざき　先々 ❶ [未来] the (distant) future. ●先々のことを考える think about the *distant future*; (遠い将来に目をそそぐ) look far ahead into the *future*. ●先々のことに備える provide for the *(distant) future*. ▶息子の先々が心配だ I am anxious about my son's *future*.

❷ [行くすべての所] ▶彼女は行く先々で歓待を受けた She was warmly welcomed *everywhere* she went [*at every place* she went to]. (⚠いずれも《書》めいた言い方口語的に)

さきさま　先様 the other party.
さぎそう　鷺草 〔植物〕 a fringed orchid.
サキソホ(ー)ン　〔楽器〕 a sáxophone, 《話》a sax. ●サキソホン奏者 a saxophonist. ●サキソホンを吹く play the *saxophone*.
さきそめる　咲き初める ▶桃が咲き初めた The peach trees *began to blossom*.
さきそろう　咲き揃う (満開になる) be in full bloom [*blossom*]; (⇨満開); [全部咲いている] be all out [*open*].
さきだか　先高 ●先高感 anticipation of a rise.
さきだつ　先立つ ❶ [先行する] go* [*happen*] before ...,《書》precede. (⇨先立って)

❷ [先に死ぬ] ▶妻に先立たれた I lost my wife./My wife *died* (on me). (⚠ (1) on me を添えると「妻に死なれて困る」の意が出る。(2) ×My wife *died before* me. では私も妻といることになるので注意。I *had* my wife *die*. では通例「妻を (人を使って) 殺させた」の意となる).

❸ [優先する] ▶先立つものは金だ Money *comes before* [*precedes*] everything else.

さきだって　先立って [より前に] before ...; earlier than ...; 《書》previous [*prior*] to .... ▶会議に先立って歓迎会が催された A reception was held *before* [*previous to*] the conference./(先行した)《書》A reception *preceded* the conference.

さきづけ　先付け ●先付け小切手 a postdated check.
さきどなり　先隣 ●先隣の女の子 a girl *next door but one*.
さきどり　先取り —— 先取りする 動 take [*receive*] (money) *in advance*. ●時代を先取りする (=見越して対処する) *anticipate* the trend of the times.
さきにおう　咲き匂う ●咲きにおうバラ sweet [*fragrant*] roses *in full bloom*. ●花の咲きにおう季節 a *flowering* season.
さきのばし　先延ばし 名 (a) postponement.
—— 先延ばしする 動 postpone 《the wedding》.
さきのり　先乗り —— 先乗りする 動 go to a place in advance (for preparation).
さきばしる　先走る ▶彼は先走ってその新製品を買った He *jumped the gun* by buying [and bought] the new product.（くだけた言い方。「スタートのピストルが鳴る前に飛び出る」ことから）

さきばらい　先払い 名 payment in advance; prepayment.
—— 先払い(を)する 動 make an advance payment; pay ... in advance. ▶家賃は 1 か月先払いしています I *pay* my rent a month *in advance*.
さきぶと　先太 —— 先太の 形 club-shaped; (動植物について) clavate. ●先太の棒 a *club-shaped* stick.
さきぶれ　先触れ (前兆) a sign. (⇨前触れ)
さきぼう　先棒 (⇨お先棒)
さきほこる　咲き誇る (満開である) be in full bloom [*blossom*], be at its best. ▶公園のバラが今を盛りと咲き誇っている The roses in the park are *at their best* [*in all their glory*].
さきぼそり　先細り ▶あのフィットネスクラブの会員数は先細りの傾向にある Membership in 《米》[*of* 《英》] the fitness club *has tapered off* recently. ▶我が国の輸出は先細りになりつつある (=減少している) Our exports *are* gradually *going downhill* [*declining*].
さきほど　先程 (少し前に) a little [a short] while ago, a short time ago; (しばらく前) some time ago. ▶彼はつい先ほど帰って来ました He came back just *a little while ago* [(たった今) *just now*]. (⇨今❷) ▶あのご婦人が先ほどからお待ちです That woman has been waiting for you *for some time* [*for a while now*, ×since some time ago]. ▶彼なら先ほど (=2-3 分前) までそこにいたのですが He was there until *a few minutes ago*. ▶先ほど言ったように私はパーティーが嫌いなんです As I said, I don't like parties. (⚠単に過去形で「先ほど」の意を表すことも多い)

さきまわり　先回り ▶彼らはそこに先回りして (=先に着いて) 隠れていた They *got* there *before* [*ahead of*] me and were hiding themselves.
さきみだれる　咲き乱れる (一面に) bloom all over; (あふれんばかりに) bloom in profusion. ▶裏庭に色とりどりのバラが咲き乱れていた In the back yard the roses were a *riot* of colors.
さきもの　先物 〔商業〕 futures; forward.
●先物買い forward buying. ●先物価格 a futures [a forward] price. ●先物為替 futures [forward] exchange. ●先物市場 the futures market. ●先物相場 the forward rate [quotation]. ●先物取引 a futures contract; a futures [a forward] transaction.
さきもり　防人 (説明的に) soldiers stationed in the northern parts of Kyushu for its defense in ancient times.
さきやす　先安 (相場で) lower quotations for future months. ●株の先安を見越す anticipate a *decline* in stock prices.

- **先安感** anticipation of a fall.
- **さきゅう 砂丘** (海辺などの低い) a (sand) dune; (砂山) a sandhill. ▶松の木が1本砂丘に生えていた The pine tree was alone on the *sand dunes*.
- **さきゆき 先行き** the future. (⇨将来) ●お金があまりないので先行き不安だ I'm worried [anxious] about *the future* because I don't have much money.
- ‡**さぎょう 作業** 图[仕事] work;[生産工程] an operation. ●時計を組み立てる精巧な作業 a delicate *operation* in watchmaking. ●工場の作業を開始[停止]する begin [suspend] *operations* at the plant. ●作業中立入禁止《掲示》No Admittance During Working Hours.
  - ●作業仮説 a working hypothesis. ●作業療法 occupational therapy《略 OT》. ●作業療法士 an occupational therapist.
  - ── **作業する** 動 work.
  - ●作業員 a worker. ●作業計画 a wórk pròject. ●作業時間 wórking hòurs. ●作業場 a wórkshop. ●作業服 wórk(ing) clòthes. ●作業療法 occupational therapy《略 OT》.
- **ざきょう 座興** (an) èntertáinment (at a party). ●座興に手品をする do a magic trick *to entertain* the company. ●ほんの座興のつもりで just *for fun*.
- **さきわたし 先渡し** (商品の) payment after delivery (❗×delivery before payment は不可);(賃金の) (⇨先払い).
- **さきわれ 先割れ** ●先割れスプーン a spork.《参考》spoon と fork から》
- **さきん 砂金** gold dust. ●砂金を採る pan gold.
- **さきんじる 先んじる** [進度・優劣などで] be ahead of [before]...《❗進歩を暗示する場合は ahead of が普通》;[率先してやる] take* the initiative (*in* doing);[競争・勉強などの開始時に]《やや話》get* [have*] a head start (*on* [*over*]+人)《❗ have は状態を表す》. ●時代に[他の人より]ずいぶん先んじている be well *ahead of* the times [others]. ▶この分野では日本が他の国に先んじた Japan *got ahead* (*of* other countries) in this field.
  - ●先んずれば人を制す《ことわざ》First come, first served.《❗「早い者勝ち」の意》
- ***さく 策** (計画) a plan; (対策) measures; (方策) a policy; (策略) a trick. ●策を練る work out a *plan*. ●策を講じる take some *measures*.
  - ●策を弄(ろう)する use a dirty [a mean, a nasty] trick.
- ***さく 咲く** (一般に花が) flower; (特に観賞用の花が) bloom; (特に果樹の花が) blossom;[開く] come* out, open;[咲いている] be in flower [blossom, (満開) (full) bloom]. ▶たいていの植物は春に花が咲く Most plants *flower* [*bloom*] in (the) spring. ▶桜の花は間もなく咲くだろう The cherry trees will *flower* [*blossom*] soon./The cherry blossoms will *come* [*be*] *out* soon. ▶庭のバラが咲いている[咲き出した] The roses *are in flower* [*have come into bloom*] in the garden.
- ***さく 割く** [分け与える] (時間などを) spare;(紙面などを) give*...(*to*), devote...(*to*). ▶読書に割く時間がない I have no time to *spare* [I cannot make time] for reading. ▶2-3分時間を割いていただけませんか Could you *spare* me a few minutes [a few minutes *for* me]? ●彼はその論文で数ページを割いてその問題を論じている He *has given* [*devoted*] several pages *to* the discussion of the subject in his paper.
- ***さく 裂く** [二つ以上に分離する] (ナイフなどで) cut*... up, (縦に) split*; (紙などを手で) tear*... (up), (手荒に) rip (-pp-) ... (up);(人と人との仲を) separate, 《書》sever. ●紙をずたずたに裂く[切り裂く] *tear* (*up*) [*cut up*] (a sheet of) paper into pieces. ▶彼は私たちの仲を裂こうとしている He is trying to *separate* [*come between*] us. ▶大きな氷山がその船の船体を裂いた A big iceberg *split* [*broke*] the body of the ship.
- **さく 作** ❶[作品] a work. ●会心の作 one of one's best *works*. (⇨品, 駄作)
  ❷[作柄] a crop. ●平年作 an average [a normal] *crop*. ●今年は米の作がいい We have a good *crop* of rice this year.
- **さく 柵** a fence; (横木を組んだ) a railing (❗ しばしば複数形で); (先のとがったくいを並べた) a stockade. ●畑に柵をめぐらす *fence* (*in* [*around*]) the field; *rail* (*in*) the field. ▶彼は柵を跳び越えた He jumped over the *fence*.
- **さく- 昨-** ●昨春(に) *last* spring; in ((主に米)) the) spring *last year*. ●昨シーズン(に) *last* season.
- **さくい 作為** [不自然なこと] artificiality; [意図的なこと] deliberateness. ●作為的にふるまう behave in an *artificial* way.
  - ●作為犯《法律》a crime of commission.
- **さくい 作意** [故意] intention; [製作意図] (意匠) a design; (構想) a conception; (主題) a motif /mouti:f/ (⑱ ~s). ▶私は作意があってしたわけではない I didn't do it *intentionally* [*deliberately*, *on purpose*]. (⇨故意)
- **さくいん 索引** an index. ●索引を引く consult [look (it) up in] the *index* (*of* a textbook). ▶この本は索引が不備である This book *is poorly indexed*./The *index* of this book is not well compiled.
- **さくおとこ 作男** a farmhand.
- **さくが 作画** ── **作画する** 動 (絵を) draw [paint] a picture; (写真を) take a photograph.
- **さくがら 作柄** ●米の作柄がよい[悪い] have a good [a bad] rice *crop*; have a rich [a poor] *harvest* of rice. (⇨豊作, 不作)
- **さくがん 削岩** ── **削岩する** 動 drill a rock; drill holes in a rock.
  - ●削岩機 a róck drìll.
- **ざくぎり ざく切り** ●キャベツをざく切りにする cut cabbage *roughly*.
- **さくげつ 昨月** last month. (⇨先月)
- **さくげん 削減** 图 a cut (*in*), a cutback (*in*); (縮小) (a) reduction. ●人員削減 a staff [a personnel] *cut* [*cutback*, *reduction*]; a *cut* [a *cutback*, a *reduction*] in staff [personnel]. ●思い切った経費削減 drastic cost *cuts* [*reductions*].
  - ── **削減する** 動 cut, curtail, cut back (*on*...); (縮小する) reduce. ●出費を10パーセント削減する make a ten percent *reduction* [*cut*] in spending; *reduce* [*cut* (*down*), *cut back* (*on*)] the expenses by ten percent. (❗ 後の二つの方が口語的 (⇨減らす))
- **さくご 錯誤** (誤り) a mistake, a fallacy. ●錯誤に陥る make a *mistake*. ●時代錯誤 an anachronism. ▶これはよく見られる錯誤だ This is a common *fallacy*.
- **さくさく** ●さくさく噛む crunch. ●リンゴのさくさくした歯ざわり the *crisp* bite of an apple. ▶私は霜の上をさくさく歩いた I walked *crunching* the frost under my feet./As I was walking, the frost *crunched* under my feet. (❗ 2例とも under my feet の使い方に注意)
- **ざくざく** (⇨さくさく) ●白菜をざくざく(=荒く)切る cut Chinese cabbage into big pieces. ▶箱の中には金貨銀貨がざくざく(=たくさんあった) There were *plenty of* [*a lot of*] gold and silver coins in the

さくさん 酢酸 〖化学〗acétic ácid.
さくし 作詞 ● 作詞作曲する write the music and (the) words for [of] a song. (!(1) 両方の the を省略することも. (2) music と words の入れ替えも可)
● 作詞家〔歌謡曲の〕a songwriter.
さくし 作詩 ― 作詩する 動 write [compose] a poem;〔韻文を〕write verse.
さくし 策士〔駆け引きのうまい人〕a tactician;〔策略家・軽蔑的〕a schemer /skíːmər/.
● 策士策に溺れる Craft brings nothing home.
さくじつ 昨日 yesterday. (⇨昨日(きのう))
***さくしゃ** 作者〔著者〕an author;〔執筆者〕a writer. (!ともに女性にも用いる (⇨作家)) ● 作者不明の詩 an *anonymous* poem. ● この小説の作者はだれですか Who is the *author* of [Who wrote] this novel?
さくしゅ 搾取 名 exploitation. ● 中間搾取 intermediary *exploitation*.
― 搾取する 動 ● 小作人を搾取する *exploit* [*squeeze*] the peasants. (後の方が口語的)
● 搾取階級 the exploíting cláss. (関連 被搾取階級 the exploited class)
さくしゅう 昨秋 last autumn [〔米〕fall].
さくしゅん 昨春 last spring.
さくじょ 削除 名〔線を引いて文字を消すこと〕deletion;〔不要なものを取り除くこと〕(an) elimination.
― 削除する 動 ● delete;〔線を引いて消す〕cross... out; eliminate. ● 最後の語を本文から削除する *delete* [*eliminate*, *cross out*] the last word *from* the text. ● 彼の名を名簿から削除する *cross* [*strike*] his name *off* the list.
● 削除箇所 a deletion.
さくず 作図 ― 作図する 動〔図を書く〕draw a figure [a diagram];〖幾何〗construct (!名詞は a construction).
さくする 策する devise, work ... out. (⇨図る)
さくせい 作成 ― 作成する 動〔文書などを〕make; draw ... up;〔書類・請求書などを正式に〕make ... out;〔草稿などを〕prepare. (⇨作る) ● 遺言書を作成する *make* [*draw up*] a will. ● リストを作成する *make* (*out*) [*draw up*] a list. ● 請求書を作成する *make out* a bill.
さくせい 作製 ⇨作製
サクセスストーリー a success story.
さくせん 作戦 〖軍隊の行動〗(military) operations,〔英話〕ops; (大演習) maneuvers /mənúːvər/; 〖戦略〗(全体的な) a strategy; (個々の戦闘で) tactics (!単・複両扱い). ● 共同作戦 concerted *operations*. ● 作戦上重要な地点 a place of *strategic* importance. ● 作戦を考える map out a plan (of *operations*); plan one's *strategy*. ▶作戦は予定どおり進んだ The *operations* went ahead as scheduled.
● 作戦会議 a strategy meeting.
さくそう 錯綜 ● 錯綜した (複雑に入り組む) be complicated [(解きほぐしがたく) entangled, (細分までからみ合って)〔やや書〕intricate]. ● 状況はひどく錯綜している The situation is extremely *complicated*.
さくちゅう 作中 ● 作中の人物 a character in a novel [a play, a movie].
さくちょう 昨朝 yesterday morning.
さくづけ 作付け planting. ● 米の作付け面積 an acreage for rice *planting*.
さくてい 策定 ― 策定する 動 ● 都市計画を策定する *draw up* [*work out*] a city plan.
さくとう 昨冬 last winter.
さくどう 策動 名〔巧妙な策略〕(a) maneuver;〔陰謀〕a plot, a scheme. (⇨画策)
― 策動する 動 plot [scheme] (*to do*).
● 策動家 a maneuverer; a plotter; a schemer.
さくにゅう 搾乳 名 milking.
― 搾乳する 動 ● 日に2度搾乳する *milk* a cow twice a day.
● 搾乳器 a milking machine.
さくねん 昨年 last year. (⇨去年)
さくばく 索漠 ― 索漠とした 形 bleak;〔わびしい〕dreary. ● コンクリートのアパートが立ち並ぶ索漠とした町 a *bleak* city of concrete apartment blocks.
さくばん 昨晩 last night [evening], yesterday evening. (⇨昨夜)
***さくひん** 作品 〖文学・芸術などの〗a work;〔小品〕a piece;〖音楽の作品番号〗an opus /óupəs/〔略 op.〕(複 opera, ―es)〔通俗単数形で〕. ● 芸術作品 *works* of art. ● 文学作品 literary *works*. ● 宮澤賢治作品集 Miyazawa Kenji's collected *works*; the collected *works* [*writings*] of Miyazawa Kenji. ● ハイドンの作品76番を演奏する play Haydn's *Opus* 76. ▶『武器よさらば』はヘミングウェイの作品だ *A Farewell to Arms* is Hemingway's *work* [is (a *novel*) by Hemingway]. ▶この人物画はだれの作品ですか Who painted this portrait? (!By whom was this portrait painted? より普通) ▶何てすばらしい作品を作ったんでしょう! What a fine *piece of work* you've produced!
さくふう 作風 characteristics of one's work; (文体・作り方) a style. ● 独自の作風がある have a *style* of one's own.
***さくぶん** 作文 a composition (!「作文を書くこと」の意では Ⓤ), essay writing;〔書かれたもの〕an essay,〔米やや古〕a theme 〔学校の課題作文 (a school composition) のこと〕. ● 英作文の練習をする do exercises in English *composition*. ▶私の家族について作文を書いた I wrote a *composition* [an *essay*] *about* my family.
さくぼう 策謀 名〔陰謀〕an intrigue.
― 策謀する 動 ● クーデターを策謀する *plot* a coup d'état.
***さくもつ** 作物 a crop (!しばしば複数形で);〔農産物〕farm products. ● 換金作物 a cash *crop*. ● 作物を栽培する grow [raise] *crops*. ● 作物を取り入れる gather [harvest] a *crop*. ▶8月に収穫される作物は多い Many *crops* are harvested in August.
さくや 昨夜 last night, yesterday evening. ▶昨夜ふしぎな夢を見た I had a curious dream *last night*. (×yesterday night は不可. ただし tomorrow night (明晩)は可) ▶昨夜の宴会は楽しかったかい Did you have a good time at the party *yesterday* [×last] *evening*?
さくゆう 昨夕 yesterday evening; last night.
***さくら** 桜 〖植物〗(木)(花) cherry tree; cherry blossoms [flowers];〔露天商などの〕(話) a come-on, a decoy;〔劇場などの〕a claqueur /klækɚ/;〔集合的〕a claque. ▶上野公園へ桜見物に出かけないか. あそこの桜は今が見ごろらしい Why don't we go to see *cherry blossoms* in [×to] Ueno Park? I've heard they are now at their best [in full bloom]. ▶一面桜吹雪だった The petals of *cherry blossoms* were fluttering down all over the ground.
● 桜色 (pale) pink. (!cherry red は「(さくらんぼの)あざやかな赤 (bright red)」の意. 実際の桜の色は (pale) pink, (bright) red, dark [blackish] red とさまざま) ● 桜狩り an excursion for viewing cherry blossoms. ● 桜前線 a cherry-blossom front. ● 桜肉 (馬肉) horseflesh; horsemeat.

さくらえび
● 桜吹雪 a shower of cherry blossoms. ● 桜餅 *sakuramochi*, (説明的に) a pink-tinted rice cake filled with sweetened bean paste, wrapped in a salt-preserved cherry leaf. ● 桜湯 *sakurayu*, (説明的に) an infusion of salted cherry blossoms (drunk on happy occasion).

さくらえび 桜海老 [動物] a pinkish shrimp.
さくらがい 桜貝 [魚介] a tellin, a cherry shell.
さくらじま 『桜島』 *Sakurajima*. [参考] 梅崎春生の小説]
さくらそう 桜草 [植物] a primrose.
さくらん 錯乱　a mental disorder, (mental) derangement. ● 精神錯乱に陥る《やや書》become (mentally) deranged.
さくらんぼ 桜ん坊 [植物] a cherry. ● 色については (⇨桜[桜色])] ● さくらんぼのように赤い唇 *cherry*-red lips.
さぐり 探り ● 探りを入れる　[[人の意向を打診する]] sound 〈him〉 out 〈*about*, *on*〉; [間接的に] feel 〈him〉 out 〈*on*〉; [不正行為などを調査する] probe (a scandal), investigate [make an investigation into] 《the matter》(without attracting attention).
さぐりあてる 探り当てる ● 手探りで電灯のスイッチを探り当てる feel around [grope about] for the light switch and find it. (⇨捜し当てる)
さぐりだす 探り出す　find*...* out; (秘密を) search [spy, (徹底的に捜して)《やや話》ferret] *...* out. ● 彼の意向を探り出す *sound out* his intentions. ● 秘密を探り出す *search* [*spy*] *out* a secret.
さくりゃく 策略 (⇨計略)

*****さぐる** 探る　● 鍵(ぎ)がないかポケットを探る(＝捜す) *search* [*feel in*] one's pockets *for* the key. ● 火事の原因を探る(＝調査する) *investigate* the cause of the fire. ● 人の腹を探る *sound out* 〈his〉 mind; sound 〈him〉 out. (⇨探り) ● 人の行動をこっそり探る *spy on* 〈him〉 (❗ 受身可); *spy into* 〈his〉 actions. ▶彼女は探るような目付きで彼を見た She looked at him *searchingly*. ▶単刀直入に話し合いましょう. 腹の探り合いは時間のむだですから We'll get right to the point. I think it's a waste of time to *beat around the bush*. (❗ 成句表現)

さくれい 作例 [作り方の手本] a model; [説明などのために作った用例] an example.
さくれつ 炸裂 —— 炸裂する 動 explode. (⇨爆発)
ざくろ 石榴 [植物] (実, 木) a pomegranate /pάmə-grænət/.
● 石榴石 (a) garnet.

*****さけ** 酒　[[アルコール飲料類]] alcohólic drinks [beverages], álcohol, [英] liquor /líkər/; [強い] spirits, [米] liquor]; [日本酒] *sake*; [ワイン] wine; [ビール] beer; [果実酒] fruit wine.

┌──────────────────────┐
│ **使い分け** alcoholic drinks, alcohol 「アルコール飲料」の意の一般的な言い方.
│ **liquor** 《英》では広く酒を意味する堅い語だが,《米》では spirits と同様, ウイスキーやブランデーなど特に強い酒を意味する.
│ **spirits** ウイスキーやブランデーなど特に強い酒をさす.
└──────────────────────┘

①【～酒】● 1 杯の酒 a cup of *sake*; a glass of *wine*. ● 一合の酒 a [one] *go* of *sake*; 180 milliliters of *sake*. ● 強い[弱い]酒 a strong [a weak] *wine*; a hard [a light] *liquor*. ● 甘口[辛口]の酒 sweet [dry] *sake* [*wine*, ×*sake*]. ● 苦い酒 bitter *sake* [*wine*]. ● うまい(＝味のよい)酒 good [風味のある], delicate, (まろやかな) mellow] *sake* [*wine*].
②【酒～】● 酒癖がよい[悪い] be a good [a bad]

さけびごえ
drinker. ● 酒びたりになる get alcoholic. ● 酒太りする become fatter from drinking.
[会話] 「あの方は何で亡くなったのですか」「ウォッカです. 酒びたりになって死んだのですよ」"What did he die of?" "Vodka, sir. He *drank* himself to death."
③【酒[は]】● 酒が弱い be a light [×a weak] drinker; (すぐ酔う) get drunk [×drunken] easily. ● 酒が強い (たくさん飲める) can drink quite a lot; (大酒飲みである) be a heavy drinker; be a boozer. ▶酒が飲みたい I'd like [I want] to *drink*. ▶酒が回ってきた The *sake* has started to take effect./(酒に酔ってきた) I'm getting drunk. ▶酒はつきあい程度です I only drink socially./I'm only a social drinker. ▶浩は酒が好きだ Hiroshi likes to *drink*./Hiroshi is fond of *drinking*.
④【酒の】● 酒の席 a drinking bout. ● 酒の上でのけんか a drunken brawl. ● 酒の相手 a drinking partner [companion, pal, buddy]. ▶それは酒の上でしたことだ I did it under the influence of *liquor*.
⑤【酒で】● 酒に酔う get [be] drunk;《書》get [be] intoxicated. (❗ be では「酔っている」という状態を表す) ▶彼は酒におぼれている He's given himself up to *drink*. ▶この drink は「飲酒」の意)/《話》He's *on the bottle*. ● 「酒におぼれるようになる」は take to *drink* [《話》*the bottle*])
⑥【酒を】● 酒を飲む drink alcohol (❗ (1) 酒の種類によって, *sake*, wine, whiskey などを用いる. (2) 単に drink ですますことも多い) ● 酒をやめる give up [quit] drinking. ● 酒をつぐ pour out *sake*. ● 酒を酌(く)み交わす help one another to *sake*. ● 酒をしきりに勧める press *sake* on 〈him〉. ▶彼はイスラム教徒で酒を 1 滴も飲まない He is a Muslim and never *drinks* [《やや書》touches a drink]. ▶1 杯は人酒を飲み, 2 杯は酒酒を飲み, 3 杯は酒人を飲む With the first cup, the man drinks *sake*. With the second cup, *sake* drinks *sake*. But with the third cup, *sake* drinks the man.

● **酒に飲まれる** ▶私はときに酒に飲まれる I'm sometimes *completely drunk*. ▶太郎は酒に飲まれない Taro can hold his *liquor*./Taro is *temperate in drinking*. ▶酒に飲まれるな Drink moderately.

● **酒は百薬の長** (ことわざ) Good wine makes good blood.

● 酒かす *sake* lees. ● 酒飲み a drinker; (大酒飲み) a heavy drinker; (飲んだくれ)《軽蔑的》a drunkard.

さけ 鮭 [魚介] a salmon /sǽmən/. 《複》～(s). 「サケ肉」の意では ⓤ] ● 塩ザケ salted *salmon*.
● 鮭缶 canned 《米》[tinned《英》] salmon.
さげ 下げ ❶ [下げること] ▶彼は速度の下げを感じた He felt the *lowering* of velocity. ❷ [相場の] (⇨下落) ❸ [落語などの落ち] (⇨落ち)
さけい 左傾 [名] ▶船は激しく右傾左傾を繰り返した Our boat continued to list strongly to port and then to starboard. (❗ は船にのみ用いる)
—— **左傾する** 動 lean to the left; (思想的に) turn leftist. 《反》右傾)
さけしお 下げ潮　an ebb tide. (⇨引き潮)
さけすむ 蔑む　despise;《話》look down (up)on 〈him〉. (⇨軽蔑) ▶憎しみ合ったり蔑み合ったりしたくありません We don't want to hate or *despise* one another.
さげどまる 下げ止まる ▶株価が下げ止まった Stock prices have *stopped falling*.
さけびごえ 叫び声　a cry; [大声] a shout; a yell (❗ shout より鋭い); [金切り声, 悲鳴] a scream, a shriek (❗ scream より甲高い); (甲高すぎて不快な)

screech. (⇨ふぶ) ● 苦痛の叫び声をあげる give [let out] *a cry* of pain. ▶通りから助けを求める叫び声が聞こえた A *cry* [A *shout*, A *scream*] *for* help came [was heard] from the street.

さけぶ 叫ぶ ❶ 〖叫び声をあげる〗 cry ... (out); shout ... (out); yell ... (out); scream, shriek, 《書》exclaim.

【使い分け】
cry (out) 感極まって泣き叫ぶこと.
shout (out) 人が一瞬驚くほど大声で叫ぶこと.
yell (out) 怒りや恐怖, 痛みのあまり鋭い声で叫ぶこと. shout より口語的.
scream 驚き・恐怖・感動で女性や赤ん坊などが甲高い声を出すこと.
shriek scream よりも耳をつんざくような金切り声で女や子供などが泣き叫ぶこと.
exclaim 感情が高ぶって突然に声を出すこと. 必ずしも大声とは限らない.

● 痛くて叫ぶ *cry* [*shout*, *scream*] with pain; *give a cry* [*a shout*, *a scream*] *of* pain. ▶「勝った」と彼は叫んだ "I won!" he *cried* [*shouted*, *exclaimed*]. (❗he の代わりに名詞の主語を用いる場合は "I won!" *cried* my brother [Taro]. のように「動詞＋主語」の語順も可) ▶彼女は助けを求めて大声で叫んだが, 彼には聞こえなかった She *cried out* [*shouted out*, *yelled out*, *screamed*] *for* help, but he couldn't hear her. ▶彼は私たちに止まれと叫んだ He *shouted* [*cried* (out)] *for* us *to* stop./He *yelled at* us *to* stop. ▶クモを見て京子はきゃっと叫んだ Kyoko *screamed* [*shrieked*] when she saw a spider.
❷ 〖強く要求する〗 clamor. ● 改革[増税反対]を叫ぶ *clamor for* reform [*against* higher taxes].

さけめ 裂け目 〖地面や壁などの〗 a crack, 〖岩・地面などの〗 (やや書) a cleft 《*in*》 (⇨われ目, 亀裂(ぷっ)); 〖服などの〗 a tear /téər/, a rip (⇨ほころび).

さける 避ける 〖意識的に好ましくない人・物・事に近づかない〗 avoid (❗最も一般的な語), 〖嫌がって〗 《やや書》 shy of ...; 〖《やや書》 shun (-nn-); 〖近寄らないでおく〗 keep* away from ...; 〖義務・質問などから要領よく逃げる〗 《やや書》 evade; 〖未然に防ぐ〗 《やや書》 avert. ● 夏の暑さを避けて木陰で休む take a rest *from* the summer heat in the shade of a tree. ▶彼は私を避けているみたいだ I think he's *avoiding* [*keeping away from*] me. ▶車はなんとか電柱にぶつかるのを避けた The car narrowly *avoided* (*running* into) the utility pole. (❗この場合 ✗evade は不可) ▶達也は私の質問に答えるのを避けた(関わり合いたくないので) Tatsuya *avoided* [〖答えるべきだが〗 *evaded*] (answering) my questions. ▶両国間の戦争は外交交渉で避けられるかもしれない The war between the two countries may *be avoided* [*be averted*] through diplomatic negotiations. ▶雪による列車の遅れは避けられない The delay in [xof] the trains *can't be avoided* [*is unavoidable*] due to snowfalls. ▶それは避けて通れないよ We must not *avoid* it./There's no *getting around* it. (❗後の方は口語的慣用表現) ▶死は避けられない(=必ずやって来る) Death *is inevitable* /inévətəbl/./ It *is inevitable* that we will die.

DISCOURSE
多文化主義は避けられないとする筆者の見方に賛成する I share the author's view which states that multiculturalism *is inevitable*. (❗I share one's view which states that ... (...とする...の見方を共有する)は賛成を表すディスコースマーカー)

さける 裂ける 〖紙・布が〗 tear* /téər/, 〖ぐいっと強く〗 rip (-pp-); 〖板などが縦に〗 split*. (⇨裂く) ▶シャツは裂けひ ざはすりむけていた The shirt *was torn* and the knee was barked.

さげる 下げる ❶ 〖低くする〗 (位置・程度などを) lower; (減ずる) reduce. ● 頭を下げる (物に当たらないように) *lower* one's head; (敬意をかくてあいさつする) bow 《*to*》; (謝る) apologize 《*to him for* one's failure》; (頼む) ask 《*him for* money》. ● その机を 1 万円に [5,000 円] 下げる *lower* [*reduce, bring down*] the price of the desk *to* 10,000 yen [*by* 5,000 yen]. ▶ボリューム[ラジオのボリューム]をちょっと下げてくださいな *Turn* the volume [the radio] *down* a bit, would you?
❷ 〖つるす〗 hang*; (身につけている) wear*. ● 天井からランプを下げる *hang* a lamp *from* the ceiling. ● ペンダントを下げている *wear* a pendant.

翻訳のこころ 近所のスーパーの袋を両手にさげて, 母が帰ってきた (吉本ばなな 『みどりのゆび』) My mother got [came] home, holding shopping bags from the neighborhood super market in both hands. (❗(1)「…を両手に提げる」は hold ... in both hands と表す. (2)「帰ってくる」は came [got] (back) home. (3) 文の中心は「母が帰ってきた」ことなので語順を日本語とは逆にする)

❸ 〖後方へ動かす〗 ● いすを下げる move 〖引いて〗 pull, 〖押して〗 push] back a chair.
❹ 〖片づける〗 ● お膳(菓)(の皿や湯飲みを)下げる *clear* the plates and cups *from*) the table.

さげわたす 下げ渡す grant.
さげん 左舷 〖海事〗 port; 〖左舷(の側)〗 the port side. ● 舵輪を左舷に取る put the wheel *to port*.
ざこ 雑魚 〖集合的〗 small fish [fry] 《❗複数扱》. small fry は 《話》で「取るに足らない連中, 小物」の意でも用いる)
● 雑魚の魚(ё)交じり The stupid simpleton sits among the doctors.
ざこう 座高 one's sitting height. ● 座高が低い(=胴が短い) be short-trunked.
さこうべん 左顧右眄 (⇨右顧左眄)
さこく 鎖国 图 seclusion; 〖孤立〗 isolation. ● 鎖国政策をとる adopt a policy of *seclusion*; carry out a *closed-door policy*. ▶彼らは鎖国か開国かでもめた They argued for a long time, whether they should continue their *closed-door policy* or open their doors to foreign countries.
── **鎖国(を)する 動** ▶過去において日本は鎖国をした In the past, Japan *closed* its *doors to* foreign countries.
さこつ 鎖骨 a collarbone, 〖解剖〗 a clavicle /klǽvikl/.
ざこつ 坐骨 the hipbone.
● 坐骨神経痛 〖医学〗 《suffer from》 sciatica /saiǽtikə/.
ざこね 雑魚寝 ── **雑魚寝する 動** sleep crowded together (in the same room).
ささ 笹 bámboo grȧss; (葉) a bámboo lèaf [blàde]. (❗(1) 単独の bamboo がアクセント移動することに注意. (2) leaf の複数形は leaves)
● 笹舟 a bàmboo-leaf bóat. ● 笹藪 a bamboo thicket; a thicket of bamboos.
ささい 些細 ── **些細な 形** (取るに足らない) trivial, 《書》 trifling (ちょっとした) slight. ● ささいな誤り a *trivial* [*a trifling, a slight, a small*] error. ● さいなことで口論する argue about *trivial* [*trifling*] matters. ▶子供たちはほんのささいな失敗でもしかられ罰せられた The children were scolded and punished even for the *slightest* fault. ▶この頃はささいなこと(=重大とは思えないこと)が重大事件になるこ

ささえ 支え (a) support; (つっかい棒) a prop. (⇨支柱)
● 橋の支え(=支柱) the *supports* of a bridge. ▶子供が私の支えだろう My children will *support* me [will give me *support*]. (❗精神的激励の意での支援を moral support, 人の情緒を安定させる支援を emotional support と明示的にいうこともある)

さざえ 栄螺 〖魚介〗a turban [a top] shell.

ささえる 支える support; (下から) hold*... up,《書》sustain; (人が…っかい棒などで) prop (-pp-) ... (up).
● バルコニーを支えている柱 pillars *supporting* [*holding up*] the balcony. ● 一家(の暮らし)を支える *support* [*keep*, *sustain*] one's family. ● 財政的に支える provide financial *support* (*for* the team). ▶彼は塀をつっかい棒で支えた He *supported* the wall with a prop./He *propped up* the wall. ▶困ったときでも希望が[彼が]私を支えてくれた Hope [He] *supported* me in time of trouble. ▶お父さんが精神的に支えてくれた My father gave me moral *support*. ▶氷は私たちを支えるほど厚くない The ice is not thick enough to *hold* our weight.

ささがき 笹搔き 〖料理〗shavings. ● ゴボウをささがきにする shave a burdock root into slivers; cut a burdock root as if you were sharpening a pencil with a knife.

ささくれ (木材・竹材などの) a fine split; (甘皮の) a hangnail. ▶親指にささくれができる[できている] get [have] some *hangnails* on one's thumb.

ささくれる 〚木・竹などが〛get* splintery, splinter; (指が…) 〚気持ちが〛become* irritable; get upset. ▶気持ちがささくれている be irritable; be upset.

ささげ 大角豆 〖植物〗a cowpea, a black-eyed pea.

ささげもつ 捧げ持つ hold《a thing》up before one's eye.

ささげもの 捧げ物 an offering.

ささげる 捧げる ❶〚生命・努力・時間などを〛(犠牲にする) sacrifice; (専念する) devote. ● 国のために命を捧げる *sacrifice* one's life for one's country. ● 歴史の研究に一生を捧げる *devote* [*give*,《やや書》 *dedicate*] one's life *to* the study of history.
❷〚神などに〛● 神に祈り[感謝]を捧げる *offer* prayers [*render* thanks] *to* God. ▶彼は著書を友(の国)に捧げた(=献呈した) He *dedicated* his book *to* (the memory of) his friend.
❸〚高く上げる〛● 両手を捧げる *hold up* [*lift up*] both hands. ●(物を)捧げ持つ *hold* 《it》up respectfully.

ささつ 査察 图 (an) inspection. ● 空中査察 an aerial *inspection*. ● 国連の査察を無条件で受け入れる submit unconditionally to the UN *inspection*.
—— 査察する 動 inspect.
● 査察官 an inspector.

さざなみ a ripple. ▶そよ風が湖面にさざなみを立てた A breeze rippled [made *ripples* on] the surface of the lake./The lake rippled in the breeze.

ささまくら 『笹まくら』 *Grass for My Pillow*. (参考) 丸谷才一の小説

ささみ 笹身 white [breast] meat (of a chicken).

さざめき 笑いのさざめき a *ripple* of laughter.

さざめく 笑いさざめく laugh and talk merrily.

ささめゆき 細雪 (⇨粉雪)

ささめゆき 『細雪』 *The Makioka Sisters*. (参考) 谷崎潤一郎の小説

ささやか 細やか —— 細やかな 形 (小さい, 小額の) small; (わずかな) modest. ● ささやかな家 a *small* [(ごく小さい) a *tiny*] house. ● ささやかな夕食会を催す have a *small* dinner party. ● ささやかに暮らす live in a *small* way; (ささやかな収入で) live on a *small* [a *modest*] income.

ささやき 囁き a whisper; 〖小川などのさらさらという音〗 a murmur. ● ささやき声で話す speak *in whispers* [a *whisper*]. ● 小川のささやき the *murmur* of a stream. ● 風のささやき《書》the *whisper* of a breeze.

> **翻訳のこころ** 先刻の，あの悪魔のささやきは，あれは夢だ．悪い夢だ．忘れてしまえ (太宰治『走れメロス』) A whisper of a devil [A devil's whisper] that you heard a minute ago was a dream, a bad one. Forget all about it. (❗(1)「悪魔がささやく」という概念は英語ではあまり一般的ではないので, that you heard を入れてささやいたのが悪魔であることを明らかにする. (2) 「先刻の」は a minute ago (わずか前のと表す)

ささやく 囁く 〚小声で言う〛whisper; 〚低い声でほそぼそ言う〛 murmur. ● 愛の言葉を彼女の耳元にささやく *whisper* [*murmur*] words of love in her ear. ▶「愛してるわ」と彼女はささやいた She *whispered* [*murmured*], "I love you." (❗ "I love you," she *whispered* [*murmured*]. の語順も可) ▶彼らは離婚するといううわさがささやかれている(=うわさされている) *It is rumored* [*is whispered*] *that* they will be divorced. (❗It is said [They say] that ... でも言うことは通じる)

ささら a bamboo whisk.

ささる 刺さる stick*; (矢などが) pierce. (⇨突き刺さる) ▶魚の骨が彼女ののどに刺さった A fish bone *stuck* in her throat.

さざれいし さざれ石 a pebble.

さざんか 山茶花 〖植物〗a sasanqua /səsǽnkwə/ (camellia).

サザンクロス 〖南十字星〗〖天文〗the Southern Cross.

さし 差し ● 差しで話し合う talk *face-to-face*《with》.

-さし -止し ● 読みさし(=読んでいる途中)の本 a *half-*read book.

さじ 匙 a spoon; 〖小さじ, 茶さじ〗a teaspoon; 〖中さじ〗《主に英》a dessertspoon; 〖大さじ〗a tablespoon. ● 砂糖1[2]さじ a *spoonful* [two *spoonfuls*, two *spoonsful*] of sugar. ● 砂糖大さじ山盛り[すり切り]2杯 two heaping [level] *tablespoonfuls* of sugar. ● さじですくう *spoon* (the ice-cream) up [out]. ● さじ加減 (⇨さじ加減)
● さじを投げる ▶その事件についてはさじを投げた(あきらめた) I *have given up on* the case./(力が及ばない) The case *is beyond* my *power*.

さじ 些事, 瑣事 a trifle, a trivial matter [thing]. ● 些事にこだわる worry about *little thing*.

ざし 座視 —— 座視する 動 (傍観する) look on, sit* and watch; (構わずに放っておく) leave*《him》alone. ▶彼の窮状を座視するにしのびなかった I *couldn't just look on* him in his plight./He was in a difficult situation and I *couldn't leave* him *alone*.

さしあげる 差し上げる ❶〚持ち上げる〛lift [*hold*] ... up; (重量挙げ) jerk《a barbell》. ● 優勝カップを高々と差し上げる *lift* [*hold*] *up* the championship cup high above one's head.
❷〚人に上げる〛give*. (⇨与える) ▶よろしかったらこれはあなたに差し上げます You can *keep* it if you want. /I'll give this to you. (というより丁寧, さらに Can I offer you this one? など疑問文の形でもいくる)
会話「何か差し上げましょうか」「ジンでももらおうか

"(Can I) get you something?" "I'll have a gin."
さしあし 差し足 ❶〖抜き足〗(⇨抜き足) ❷〖競馬で〗
● 差し足が鋭い spurt when overtaking other horses.
さしあたって 差し当たって (⇨差し当たり)
さしあたり 差し当たり (当分の間) for the time being, for the moment, for the present; (今現在) now, at present, at the moment; (まず) for a start, first (of all). (⇨まず ❶) ▶適当なアパートが見つかるまでさしあたり私のところにいなさい You can stay with me *for the time being* [*for the moment*] until you can find a good apartment. ▶さしあたり必要なものを言ってください Tell me what you need (*just*) *now* [*at the moment*]. ▶さしあたりこの詩文集で19世紀の英詩を読むことにしましょう Let's read 19th century English poetry using this anthology *for a start*.
さしあみ 刺し網 a gill net.
さしいれ 差し入れ (慰労のための) présents 《*for* one's friends》; (刑務所への) necessary articles presented [sent in] to a prisoner. ▶彼は従業員たちの労をねぎらってビールの差し入れをした He *gave* beer *to* his employees as a recognition of their services.
さしいれる 差し入れる présent 《them *with* beer》; (中間にはさむ) insert.
さしえ 挿し絵 an illustration; 〖カット〗a cut; 〖図〗a figure. (⇨絵) ● カラー挿し絵 a colored *illustration*. ● 挿し絵をかく draw an *illustration*; (本に) illustrate a book. ● 挿し絵入りの本 an *illustrated* book. ▶この本には挿し絵がたくさんある This book has a lot of *illustrations*./This book *is* fully *illustrated*.
● 挿し絵画家 an illustrator.
サジェスチョン 〖示唆, 提案〗(a) suggestion; 〖勧め〗(a) recommendation.
さしおく 差し置く (意図的に無視する) ignore, 《やや書》disregard. ▶親を差し置いてそんな大事なことを決めてはいけない You shouldn't make such an important decision *ignoring* your parents' opinion [(親と相談しないで) without talking to your parents]. ▶彼は部長を差し置いて(=飛び越えて)社長のところへ文句を言いに行った He *went over the head of* the general manager to complain [and complained] to the president. ▶今日は何ををさし置いても(=何よりもまず)しなければならないことがある There is something I have to do *before anything else* [*first of all*] today.
さしおさえ 差し押さえ seizure /síːʒɚr/; 〖法律〗attachment; (動産の)〖法律〗distraint. (⇨差し押さえる) ▶差し押さえ令状 a writ of *attachment* [*seizure*]; a warrant for *attachment* [*seizure*].
さしおさえる 差し押さえる seize /síːz/; 〖法律〗attach; (財産などの)〖法律〗distrain. (⇨差し押さえる) ▶彼は財産を差し押さえられた His property *was seized*./He *had* his property *attached* [*distrained*].
さしかえる 差し替える replace 《A *with* B》; (取りかえ) change. (⇨入れ替える) ▶この写真をあれと差し替えてください Please *replace* this photo *with* that one./Please *change* this photo *for* that one./Please *use* that photo *instead of* this one.
さしかかる 差し掛かる (来る) come*《*to*》; 〖近づく〗approach, come near 《*to*》. (⇨近付く) ▶坂道にさしかかる come to a slope [a hill]. ▶新しい段階にさしかかる(=入る) enter (*on*) a new phase. (❗on を伴う言い方は《書》)
さしかけ 指し掛け (将棋で) an unfinished game.

さしかける 差し掛ける ● 彼に傘を差し掛ける *hold* the umbrella *over* him.
さじかげん さじ加減 ● さじ加減する(=配慮する) take (it) into consideration; (手心を加える) make allowance(s) for (it, him). ▶成否は彼のさじ加減ひとつで決まる The success (all) depends on how he considers handling [×to handle] it. ▶それは君のさじ加減ひとつだ(=君の裁量に任されている) It is left to your *discretion*.
さしかざす 差しかざす ▶私たちに見えるようにそれを差しかざしてください *Hold* it *up* so that we can see it.
さしがね 差し金 (教唆(ᵏˠᵒᵘˢᵃ))instigation. ▶だれの差し金であの男は金貸しを殺したのか Who *led* him to kill the moneylender? (❗lead (*him*) to do は「彼を導いて…する気にさせる」の意)
さしき 挿し木 (切った枝) a cutting. ● 挿し木をする plant a cutting.
さじき 桟敷 〖劇場の〗(上階の) a balcony; 〖相撲の〗a box seat. ● 天井桟敷 a gallery.
***ざしき** 座敷 a *zashiki*, (説明的に) a Japanese-style guest room with *tatami* mats on the floor (❗単なる guest room は「来客用寝室」の意); 〖客間〗a drawing room (❗普通の家庭では a living room を接客用に使うので, a drawing room は改まった古めかしい感じの語になっている); 〖居間〗a living ròom, 《主に英》a sítting ròom. ● 座敷に通す show (*him*) into the *living room*.
● 座敷牢 a confining room, a room for confinement.
さしきず 刺し傷 (剣などの) a stab (wound); (虫などの) a bite; (とげなどの) a puncture (wound); (針の) a prick. ● 体の左側の深い刺し傷 a deep *stab* in the left side. ● 指の刺し傷 a *prick* in the finger.
さしこ 刺し子 quilted clothes; (説明的に) a garment made of one or more layers of cotton fabrics and quilted in various patterns; (縫うこと) quilting.
さしこみ 差し込み ❶〖挿入〗(an) insertion. ● 差し込み原稿 an insert.
❷〖腹部の急激な痛み〗(have) a sudden sharp pain in the stomach.
❸〖電気の〗(プラグ) a plug; (コンセント)《米》an outlet, 《英》a socket; (端子) a jack.
さしこむ 差し込む ❶〖挿入する〗● 鍵(ᵏᵃᵍᵘⁱ)穴に鍵を差し込む put [*insert*, *fit*] a key *into* a lock. ● アイロンのプラグを(コンセントに)差し込む *plug* the iron *in* (*at* the outlet).
❷〖光が〗▶日が窓から(部屋に)差し込んでいた The sun *was coming* [(いっぱい) *streaming*, *pouring*] in [*into* the room] *through* the windows.
さしころす 刺し殺す stab (-bb-) (*him*) to death.
さしさわり 差し障り 〖気を悪くすること〗offense; 〖差し支え〗an obstacle. ▶差し障りがあるといけないから for fear of giving *offense* 《*to*》. ● 差し障りのある[ない]ことを言う make *offensive* [*inoffensive*, (当り障りの) *noncommittal*] remarks.
さししめす 指し示す point 《*at*, *to*》 (⇨指す ❶)
***さしず** 指図 〖省〗 directions; (指示) instructions; 〖指揮〗direction; 〖命令〗an order (❗しばしば複数形で); (権威者による) a command. (⇨命令) ● 彼の指図どおりに行動する act according to his *directions* [*instructions*]; follow his *directions* [*instructions*]. ● 彼の指図の下に働く work under his *direction*. ▶君から指図は受けない I won't take *orders* from you./I don't want you to give me any *directions*.
—— 指図(を)する 動 〖命令する〗 order; (公式に) command, 《書》direct; 〖指示する〗instruct. (⇨命令

さしずめ 差し詰め ❶ [結局, つまるところ] after all; [要するに] in fact; [言ってみれば] as it were. ▶その役にはさしずめ彼がぴったりだ *After all* [[いろいろ考慮してみると] *All things considered*], he is the right actor for that role.
❷ [差し当たり] (⇨差し当たり)

さしせまる 差し迫る (⇨迫る❶) ▶差し迫った(=緊急の)問題 an *urgent* [a *pressing*] problem. ●差し迫った(=今にも起こりそうな)危険 (an) *imminent* [(an) *impending*] danger. ▶後の方は文語的で, 心配・不安をかき立てる時間的余裕がある) 我々はそれが差し迫って(=すぐに)必要というわけではない We are in no *immediate* need of it.

さしだしにん 差出人 a sender 《*of* the letter》. ●差出人の住所 a *sender*'s [(返送先の)a *return*] address.

さしだす 差し出す [手などを] hold*... out; [伸ばす] reach ... out; [提出する] hand ... in; [上位の者に] submit (-tt-). ●本を受け取ろうと手を差し出す *reach* [*stretch*] *out* one's hand *for* the book. ▶彼は私に手を差し出した(=握手を求めた) He *held out* his hand *to* me./He *offered* me his hand. ▶報告書を彼に差し出した I *handed in* [*submitted*] a report *to* him.

さしたる 然したる (⇨大した) ▶その二つの事実にさしたる違いは見られなかった We did *not see much* [(特別な)any *particular*] difference between the two facts.

さしちがえる 刺し違える stab each other.
さしちがえる 指し違える [将棋] make a wrong move.
さしちがえる 差し違える (相撲で行司が) misjudge; make a mistake in deciding the winner.

さしつかえ 差し支え [異議] an objection; [支障] a hindrance.

さしつかえない 差し支えない ●差し支えなければ(=かまわなければ) if it's all right with you; if you don't mind (▮前の方がくだけた言い方); [都合がよければ] if it's convenient (for [to] you). ▶差し支えなければ教えてほしいのですが, お仕事は何をなさっているのですか *If you don't mind* my asking, what do you do? (▮必要があって女性に年齢を尋ねるときにも使える. その他 Would you mind if I asked your age?/Forgive me for asking, but could you tell me your age? など) ▶彼の意見はもう決まっていると言って差し支えない *It's safe to say* 《*that*》 his opinion is already set.
会話 「窓を開けても差し支えありませんか(=よろしいですか)」「いいですよ」"*Can* [*Could*, *May*] I open the window?" "Sure. (▮この順に丁寧な言い方)/"*Do you mind* [*Would you mind*, 《話》*Mind*] *if* I open the window?" "Of course not." (▮ほかに No, I don't mind. など. 《話》では Sure., Certainly. などと答えることもある)
会話 「散歩に行こうと思っていたんだ」「差し支えなければ私も行くわ」"I thought of going for a walk." "I'll come too, *if I* ᵛ *may* [*if you don't* ᵛ *mind*]."
会話 「何時にうかがいしましょうか」「いつでも差し支えありません」"What time shall I come?" "*Any time will do*."

*****さしつかえる 差し支える** [じゃまする] interfere 《*with*》; [悪影響を及ぼす] affect; [苦労する] have* difficulty [trouble] 《(*in*) *doing*》. (▮in は省略されるのが普通) ▶仕事に差し支えるようなら, そんなことはやめなさい You should give it up if it's going to *interfere with* [*affect*] your work.

さして (⇨大して, そんなに)
さして 指し手 ❶ [将棋の駒の動き] a move. ●次の指し手 one's next *move*.
❷ [(上手に)将棋を指す人] ▶彼はなかなかの指し手です He is a very good *shogi* player.
さして 差し手 ●差し手争い [相撲] a struggle to force one's hand or hands under one's opponent's arms.

さしでがましい 差し出がましい [行動などがずうずうしい] presumptuous /prizʌ́mptjuəs/; [でしゃばりな]《話》pushy; intrusive; [厚かましい]《話》forward; [おせっかいな]《話》nosy; [厚かましくて無礼な] impertinent. ●差し出がましい行為 *presumptuous* conduct; an intrusion. ●差し出がましい質問 a *nosy* question. ●差し出がましいことを言う make *impertinent* remarks. ●差し出がましいことをする push [put] oneself forward. ▶差し出がましいようですが(=干渉したくないのですが), あんな人たちとかかわらないほうがいいと思います *I don't like to interfere* [(私のことではないのですが) *It's really not my business*, (よけいなこととは思いますが) *I know it's an intrusion*], but I think you'd be wiser not to mix up with such people.

さしでぐち 差し出口 ▶いらぬ差し出口をきくな Mind your own business. ▶彼女はいつでも私たちの話に差し出口をはさむ She is always *butting in* on our conversation.

さしでる 差し出る (⇨でしゃばる) ▶差し出たことをしてすみません Excuse me for being *too forward* 《*with*》.

さしとおす 刺し通す pierce; run 《a sword》through 《him》. ●針を衣服に刺し通す *run* a needle *through* clothes.

さしとめる 差し止める (禁止する) forbid*; (法的に) ban (-nn-); (一時的に) suspend. ●彼が私の家へ出入りするのを差し止める *forbid* him to come [*tell* him *not to* come] to my house. ●記事を差し止める《やや書》*suppress* an article. ▶その出版社は最新号の発売を差し止められた The publisher *was banned from* putting the latest issue on sale.

さしぬい 差し縫い quilting.
さしね 差し値 [証券] (指定した値段) a limit (price); (買い手の) a bid (price). ●指し値で買う[売る] buy [sell] *at limits*. ●指し値以内[以下]で within [below] *the limits*.
●指し値注文 a limit order.

さしのべる 差し伸べる ●援助の手を差し伸べる give [lend] a helping hand 《*to*》; give help [(公的な) aid] 《*to*》.

さしば 差し歯 (義歯) a false tooth.
さしはさむ 差し挟む (⇨はさむ❹)
さしひかえる 差し控える [衝動を抑える]《書》refrain 《*from*》; [ちゅうちょしてやめる] hold* back 《*from*》. ▶この件に関しての段階でコメントすることは差し控えたい At this moment [point], I'd like to *refrain* from commenting on this matter. (▮日本語の「段階」に対応する stage は英文では一般的でない)

さしひき 差し引き [差し引くこと] deduction; [差額] the balance. ●差し引き 500 円の損 a loss of 500 yen *on balance*. ●貸借を差し引きする strike a *balance*.

さしひく 差し引く take*... 《*off*》, deduct ... 《*from*》. (▮前の方が口語的) ●給料からその費用を差し引く *take* the cost *off* one's pay; *deduct* the cost *from* one's pay. ●値段の10パーセントを差し引く

さしまねく　差し招く beckon. ▶彼はジェーンに近くへ来るようにと差し招いた He beckoned (to) Jane to come up.

さしまわす　差し回す ●車を差し回す send a car around [round]. ●スパイをフランスに差し回す send agents into France.

さしみ　刺身 /sǽsimi/; sliced raw fish. ●マグロの刺身 (a dish of) sliced raw tuna. ●刺身のつまa garnish served with sashimi. ▶私は刺身のつまみたいなものです《比喩的》I play second fiddle. ●刺身包丁 sashimi knife; a kitchen knife for sashimi.

さしみず　差し水 ── 差し水(を)する動 ▶沸騰しているお湯に差し水をした I poured some water into the boiling water.

さしむかい　差し向かい ▶恋人たちは差し向かいに座って食事をした The couple had dinner across from each other. 《電話や手紙のやりとりによってではなく「じかに会って」の意》

さしむける　差し向ける send* (him) around [along].

さしもどす　差し戻す 〚事件を下級裁判所に〛send*... back, 《やや書》remand, 〚法案などを〛《やや書》refer (-rr-) 《to》. ●その事件を第一審に差し戻す send back [remand] the case to the court of first instance. ●法案を委員会に差し戻す refer a bill back to a committee.

さしゅう　査収 ── 査収する動 check and receive.

さじゅつ　詐術 詐術にたけた男 a man who is good at swindling.

さしょう　些少 《⇨僅か》 些少な金額 a small amount of money. ▶些少ながら感謝の気持ちとしてお収めください Please accept this small token of my appreciation.

さしょう　査証 a visa /víːzə/. 《⇨ビザ》

さしょう　詐称 図 (a) misrepresentation. ●身分詐称 misrepresentation of one's identity [position]. ●学歴詐称 a false statement about [of] one's academic background [career].
── 詐称する動 (偽の身分を名乗る) misrepresent 《as》, (偽名を使う) use a false name. ▶彼は大学生だと詐称した He misrepresented himself as a college student.

さじょう　砂上 ─ 砂上の楼閣 〚もろい物〛 a house built on the sand; 〚実現不可能なこと〛castles in the air.

ざしょう　座礁 ── 座礁する動 (浅瀬に) go [run] aground; (岩礁に) go [run] on the rocks; (岸に) be stranded. ●座礁した船 a stranded ship.

ざしょう　挫傷 〚医学〛 a contusion. ●脳挫傷 cerebral contusion; contusion of the brain.

さしわたし　差し渡し a diámeter. 《⇨直径》

さじん　砂塵 (a cloud of) dust. 《⇨砂埃(ぼこり)》 ●砂塵をまき散らす scatter dust.

***さす　指す** ❶ 〚指示〛point 《at, to》《❕ at は対象そのものを、to では対象の位置の方を表す》, 《書》 indicate; 〚指名する〛call (on ...). ●地図上の場所を指で指す point at [indicate] a place on a map. ●授業中にさされる get called (on) in class. ●人を指すのは失礼だ It's rude to point at people. ●その矢印は彼の家の方をさしていた The arrow points (to) the east [to his house]. 《❕ to より漠然とした方向は toward; in the direction of で示す》●気圧計は 1,000 をさしている The barometer reads [The hand of the barometer points to] 1,000.
❷ 〚意味する〛 mean*; (言及する) refer (-rr-) 《to》. ▶「彼」とはだれをさしているのですか Who do you mean by "he"?

***さす　差す** ❶ 〚光が〛(輝く) shine*; (入る) come* [get*] into (a room) (⇨差し込む❷); (雲間から) break* through the clouds.
❷ 〚帯びる〛(身につける) put*... on; (薄く着色される) be tinged 《with》. ●刀を腰にさしている wear a sword at one's side. ▶彼女の頬に赤味がさした She blushed a little.
❸ 〚注ぐ〛 put*... 《into, on》. ●機械[ドアのちょうつがい]に油をさす oil a machine [the hinges of a door]; put some oil into a machine [on the hinges of a door].
❹ 〚傘を〛 put*... up; (開く) open. ●傘をさして歩く walk under an umbrella [with an umbrella up]. (「傘をささずに」なら with no umbrella)
❺ 〚その他の表現〛

> **翻訳のこころ** 私の心に何か小さな影がさすと、本人よりも早く気づいて私の好物のさつまいもの天ぷらを作ってくれた祖母 (吉本ばなな『みどりのゆび』) Whenever some little worry got into [cast a shadow in] my mind, my grandmother would sense it before me and cook [make] my favorite deep-fried yam potatoes. ❕ (1)「影がさす」は...worry got into mind (心配事が心に浮かぶ), ...cast a shadow (気がかりなことがちらっと心に浮かぶ、心をよぎる)と表す。(2)「本人(より早く)」は文脈から「私」なので、before me と表す

***さす　刺す** ❶ 〚突き刺す〛(刃物などで) stab (-bb-); (ぐさりと) thrust; (特に先のとがった先端で) pierce 《❕ pierce は突き通ることを含意》; (ちくりと) prick; (虫がかむ) bite*; (虫・植物が刺す) sting*. ●刺すような痛み a stabbing [a stinging] pain 《in》. ●刺すような視線 a piercing look. ●とげで指を刺す prick one's finger on a thorn. ●柄の長いフォークにウインナを刺す put a wiener onto one's toasting fork. 《バーベキューのときなど》▶彼はその男の背中を刺した He stabbed the man's back [the man in the back]. 《❕前の方は体中、後の方は人に重点を置いた言い方》▶私は体中ハチに刺された I was stung all over (my body) by bees. 《❕「蚊に刺された」は I was bitten... by a mosquito.》
❷ 〚アウトにする〛〚野球〛(送球で) throw*... out; nail; (けん制球で) pick ... off.

***さす　挿す** ❶ 〚ものの間に入れる〛insert, put... 《in》. ●花びんに花をさす put 〚生ける〛arrange flowers in a vase. ▶ガードマンはドアの前で止まり鍵をさした The guard stopped before a door and inserted the key.
❷ 〚挿し木をする〛plant. 《⇨挿し木》

さす　砂洲 (波でできた) a sándbàr; (河口にある) a sándbànk.

ざす　座す (座る) sit. ●座して待つ sit without doing anything.

***さすが** ① 〚さすがは(...だけある)〛(...に値する) worthy of ...; (...に似つかわしい) (just) like ...; (期待どおりに) as might be expected 《of ...》. ▶彼はさすがは父の子です He is a son worthy of his father. ▶そうするとはさすが(だ)A さんだ It is just like Mr. A to do so. ▶さすがは勇士だけあって彼は危険に臨んでも冷静だった He remained calm in the face of danger, as might be expected of a hero.

会話 「母さん、試験でぼくがトップだったんだよ」「へえっ、すごいじゃない。さすがだわ(=あなたならきっとそうなると思っていた)」"Mom! I got the top score on the test."

"Oh, that's wonderful. *I knew* you *would.*"
②【さすが…も】 even; (…だけれども) though…. ▶その光景を見てさすがの彼も顔色を失った Even ˇhe turned pale at that sight. (❗必ずhe に強勢を置く) ▶さすがの勇敢な彼もおじけづいた *Though* [*Although*] he was a brave man [《書》Brave man *as* he was], he got frightened. (❗as の前の名詞は無冠詞)
③【さすがに】 (本当に) indeed; truly. ▶彼はさすがに偉大な政治家である He is *indeed* [*truly*] a great statesman. ▶さすがにびっくりした *Naturally*, I was surprised. ▶さすがに言えなかった I could not find it in myself [my heart] to say so.

さずかりもの 授かり物 a blessing. ●天からの授かり物 a *blessing* [a *gift*] from Heaven.

さずかる 授かる (神などから与えられる) be blessed (*with*); (手ほどきを受ける) be initiated (*into*). ●子を授かる be given [《書》be blessed with] a child. ●茶道の奥伝を授かる(=伝授される) be *initiated into* the innermost secrets of tea ceremony. ●豊かな知性を授かっている(=生まれながらに持っている)《書》be well endowed with intelligence.

***さずける 授ける** 【授与する】(金銭・権利などを)《書》grant; (学位・称号などを)《書》confer 〈-rr-〉…(*on*) (⇨与える); 【伝授する】(やや書) initiate, (教える) teach*. ●日本料理の技術を授ける initiate ⟨his⟩ pupils *into* Japanese cookery [cooking]. ●知恵を授ける teach ⟨him⟩ wisdom; teach wisdom (*to* him).

サスペンス suspense. ●サスペンスもの a thriller; a mystery story. ▶この映画はスリルとサスペンスに満ちている This film is full of thrills and *suspense*.

サスペンダー 【ズボンつり】《米》suspenders, 《英》braces.

サスペンデッドゲーム 【野球】a suspended game.

さすらい wanderings. ●さすらいの旅人 a *wandering* traveler. ●さすらいの旅に出る go on a *wandering* journey.

さすらう wander (around [about]); (自由に楽しく) roam (around [about]); (あてもなく) drift. (⇨放浪)

さする【こする】gently rub [stroke]. ▶母親は痛がる子供のお腹をしばらくさすってやった The mother *gently* [*tenderly*] *rubbed* her boy's aching stomach for a while.

***ざせき 座席** a seat. (⇨席) ●バスの座席を予約する reserve a *seat* on the bus. ●窓側[通路側]の座席を確保する secure a window [an aisle /áil/] *seat*. ▶この車の後部座席には3人が十分座れる The back *seat* of the car is wide enough for three people. ●座席におつきください。まもなく公演が始まります Please take your *seats*, the play begins soon. ▶私の座席は5Fです。どこにありますか I'm in *Seat* 5F. Where's that? ▶込んだ電車で幸い座席につけた I was lucky [had the good fortune] to get [find] a *seat* on [×in] the crowded train. ●座席指定券 a reserved-seat ticket. ●座席番号 the seat number. ●座席表 a seating chart.

させつ 左折 图 a left turn.
── **左折する** 動 turn (to the) left; make a left (turn). (⇨右折)

ざせつ 挫折 图【失敗】(a) failure; (希望の挫折, 計画の失敗) (a) frustration; 【行き詰まり】a setback. ●挫折感を味わう feel frustration [a sense of *failure*]; feel [be] frustrated. ●挫折を乗り越える get over [overcome] one's *frustration* [*failure*]. ▶その失敗は我々にとって大きな挫折であった The failure was quite a *setback* to us.
── **挫折する** 動 ▶彼の計画は挫折した His plan(s) *fell through* [*failed*, *met with a setback*]./He *failed in* his plan(s).

:**させる** ❶【AがBに…させる】(無理やり) A (人・事など) make* B (人など) do, A force B to do (❗ make より強意的); (やわらかく命令して) A (人) have* B (人) do (❗主に《米》で, make より使役的意味は弱い); (説得して) A (人) get* B (人など) to do; (望みどおり) A (人) let* B (人など) do, A allow B to do. (❗ let, allow も「望みどおりに」の含意があるので against one's will などとともに用いることはできない) ▶私は彼らにその部屋の掃除をさせた I *made* [*had*] them *clean* the room. (❗ make, have は B が目上の人の場合には用いない)/I *got* them *to clean* the room. ▶いやがるのを何とか説得してさせたことを含意)/I *had* [*got*, ×*made*] the room *cleaned* by them. (❗ get の方が口語的。「…してもらう」の意にもなる。by 以下を示さない場合が多い) ▶私は辞職させられた I *was made* [*was forced*, ×*was had*, ×*was gotten*] *to* resign. (❗受身では to 不定詞を伴うことに注意. have, get はこのような受身はとらない) ▶何が彼をそうさせたのか What *made* [×*had*] him do so?/(何が原因で彼はそんなことをしたのか) What *caused* [×*got*] him *to* do that? (❗ have, get は物主語にもとらない。cause より make の方が口語的) ▶吹雪で車をこれ以上は走行させることはきない I can't *get* the car *to* go on [*going on*] any farther because of the snowstorm. (❗前の方は努力してやることを含意する) ▶彼が行きたがらないのなら無理に行かせるわけにはゆかないが, 行きたがっているのだから行かせてやりなさい If he does not want to go, you can't *make* him. Since he does want to, you should *let* him. (❗いずれもով が省略されているが, 文脈上明らかな場合は原形不定詞は省略可) ▶自己紹介をさせてください *Let* me [*Allow me to*, ×*Let's*] introduce myself. (❗(1) let me には /lémi/ と読む。(2) 後の方は堅い言い方) ▶子供たちはその川で泳がせてもらえなかった The children *were* not *allowed* [*permitted*, ×*let*] *to* swim in the river. (❗ let は通例受身では用いない) ▶彼を満足させるのは難しい It's hard to *please* him./He's hard to *please*. (❗ please のように他動詞に「させる」の意が含まれている場合がある)

❷【その他の表現】▶それはとてもおいしかった。君にも食べさせたかったよね It was delicious. I wish you could have had some, too. ▶私がいっしょにいる限り, 君に不自由はさせない As long as I am with you, you will have all you need [《書》you shall want for nothing]. ▶決して損はさせません You can't lose, I promise. ▶その仕事させていただきます I think I'll accept the job.
会話 「機長に会わ(さ)せろ(=会うことを要求する)」「まあまあ落ち着いてください。パーサーが承ります」"I demand to see the captain." "Just take it easy, sir! Our purser will attend to you."

させん 左遷 ▶彼は地方の支店に左遷された He *was sent* [格下げされた] *was demoted*, *was degraded*] *to* a post in a provincial branch.

ざぜん 座禅 *zazen*; (説明的に) *Zen* meditation conducted in the lotus position. ●座禅を組む practice *zazen* [*Zen* meditation].

さぞ(…に違いない) must 〈*do*〉. (❗ do は通例状態を表す動詞) (⇨きっと) ▶さぞお疲れでしょう You *must* be tired. (❗ I'm afraid を前につけると同情の気持ちが加わる) ▶彼の成功の知らせを聞いて彼女はさぞうれしく思ったことでしょう How glad she *must* have been to hear the news of his success! ▶彼らは彼の演技にさぞ(=きっと)満足していることでしょう I'm sure they

さそい 誘い (招き) (an) invitation; (誘惑) temptation. ▶ (異性に対する誘い)文句 (話) a *pick-up* line. ● パーティーへの誘いを受ける receive an *invitation* to the party; be invited to the party. ● **誘い球** 〖野球〗 a bait pitch.

さそいかける 誘いかける (求める) ask, invite. ▶ 大統領は彼に政権への参加を誘いかけた The President *asked* him *to* join the administration.

さそいこむ 誘い込む (人・動物を) lure ... 《in, into doing, ×to do》; (人を) tempt ... 《into doing; to do》. ● 彼を悪の道に誘い込む *tempt* him *to* evil. ▶ネズミたちを青かびチーズで取りに誘い込もう Let's *lure* mice *into* the trap with blue cheese.

さそいだす 誘い出す lure 《him》 out; ask [invite] 《him》 out. ▶ 彼女を映画に誘い出すつもりだ I'm going to *lure* [*ask*] her *out* to the movie.

さそいみず 誘い水 ● ポンプに誘い水を差す prime a pump. ▶彼の発言が議論の火種となった(=議論を引き起こした) What he said *sparked* some discussion.

* **さそう 誘う** ❶ 〖招く〗 invite; ask. (⇨招待する) ● お誘い合わせの上 ... Will you please *get* your friends *together* and .... ● 彼を飲みに誘う *invite* him [*ask* him *out*] *for* a drink; *invite* [*ask*] him *to* go out for a drink. ▶ きのう彼に誘われたんだけど断われなくて He *asked* me yesterday, and I couldn't say no.
会話「ダンスパーティーにだれを誘うつもりなの」「まだ決めてないんだ」 "Who are you going to *ask to* the dance?" "I haven't made up my mind yet."
❷ 〖誘いに立ち寄る〗 call for .... ▶7時に誘いに行きます I'll *call for* you at seven./(車で) Let me *pick* you *up* at seven.
❸ 〖誘発する〗 induce. ▶ 彼の退屈な講義は眠気を誘う His dull lecture *induces* sleep./His dull lecture *makes* us *sleepy* [*drowsy*]. ▶彼の話は私たちの涙を誘った(=感動させて涙を流させた) His story *moved* us *to* tears.
❹ 〖誘惑する〗 tempt; lure; entice; (特に若い女性を) seduce; (異性を引っ掛ける) (話) pick 《her》 up. (⇨誘惑する) ● 彼を悪の道に誘う *tempt* [*lure*] him *to* evil. ● 打者を誘ってボール球を振らせる *entice* [*tease*] a batter into swinging at a bad pitch. ▶ すばらしい陽気に誘われてハイキングに出かけた The fine weather *tempted* me *to* go on a hike.

ざぞう 座像, 坐像 a seated [a sedentary] figure [image, statue].

さぞかし (⇨さぞ)

さそくつうこう 左側通行 《掲示》 Keep (to the) left. (⇨左側)

さそり 蠍 〖動物〗 a scorpion.

さそりざ 蠍座 〖占星・天文〗 Scorpio (!) the はつかい); (天蠍(てんかつ)宮) 〖占星〗 the Scorpion. (⇨乙女座)
● 蠍座(生まれ)の人 a Scorpio (働 〜s), a Scorpian. (● 後の方は形容詞にも用いる)

さそん 差損 a loss (on a balance sheet).

さた 沙汰 ● 狂気のさた an *act* of madness. ● 裁判ざたになる be brought to court. ● 警察ざたになる be reported to the police; become a police case.
● **沙汰の限り** ▶そのように考えるなど沙汰の限り(=もってのほか)だ The idea is a most *preposterous* one.

さだか 定か 〖はっきり〗 clearly; 〖確かに〗 (話) for sure. ▶ 彼が生きているかどうかは定かではない It is not *certain* whether he is alive.

ざたく 座卓 a Japanese-style low table (used especially on tatami mats).

さだまる 定まる (決まる) be decided; (固定する) be fixed; (落ち着く) settle. ▶ このごろは天候が定まらない The weather *hasn't* (*been*) *settled* recently./(変わりやすい) The weather *is changeable* these days.

翻訳のこころ 言うまでもなく, 水にはそれ自体として定まった形はない (山崎正和『水の東西』) Naturally, water does not have any definite [fixed] shape of its own. (!) (1) 「言うまでもなく」は naturally (当然のこととして) と表す. (2) 「定まる」 は 「一定の, 固定された」 の意なので, definite, fixed と表す. (3) 「それ自体として」 は of its own (それ自身の)と表す)

さだめ 定め ❶ 〖法律〗 a law; 〖規則〗 a rule; (公の) a regulation.
❷ 〖運命, 天命〗 fate; destiny. (!) destiny には天が人になさしめる使命を含む. fate は通例悪い方向に向かう) ▶ この世の定め the *fate* of this world.

さだめし 定めし (⇨きっと)

* **さだめる 定める** ❶ 〖制定する〗 (規則などを) lay* ... down; (規定する) stipulate, (書) provide 《that 節》; 〖基準・罪などを〗(書) prescribe. ● クラブの規則を定める *lay down* [*make*] rules in the club. ● 議決は過半数の賛成で成立すると定められている It *is stipulated* [*is provided*] *that* a decision 《(主に英) should》 be made by a majority. ● 法律は脱税には重い刑罰を定めている The law *prescribes* heavy penalties for tax evasion.
❷ 〖決定する〗 decide; (目標を) set*. ▶ 行く先を定める *decide* where to go. ▶ 会う時間を定めよう Let's *set* the time (when) we'll meet.
❸ 〖落ち着ける〗 settle. ▶ 身を定める settle (down) 《in Kyoto》; settle oneself 《in》.

さたやみ 沙汰止み ▶彼らはその計画をさたやみにすることに決めた They decided to *abandon* [*give up*] the project.

サタン 〖キリスト教での悪魔〗 Satan /séitn/.

ざだんかい 座談会 a round-table talk [discussion]; a discussion meeting; (公開の) a symposium.

さち 幸 ❶ 〖幸福〗 happiness; (幸運) good* luck. ▶ 幸多かれと祈ります I wish you *good luck.*/I wish you *well*.
❷ 〖産物〗 ● 山[海]の幸 *products* from the land [sea]. ● 海の幸, 山の幸に恵まれている be rich in *products* from land and sea. (!) land と sea を並列する場合には the がつかないことに注意).

さちゅうかん 左中間 〖野球〗 left center. ● 左中間へ大きなフライを打つ hit a long fly ball to *left center*.

ざちょう 座長 〖劇団の〗 the leader of a theatrical troupe; 〖懇談会などの〗 (男性) a chairman, (女性) a chairwoman, (男女共用) a chairperson. ● 座長を務める act as *chairman* 《*of* the meeting》; chair (the meeting); be *in the chair*.

* **さつ 札** paper money; (米) a bill, (英) a note. (⇨紙幣, 札), 札入れ, 札束, 札びら)

さつ 察 (警察) (話) a cop.

* **-さつ -冊** 〖同一書物の1冊〗 a copy; 〖本〗 a book; (書) a volume (!) a book の堅い言い方. 書籍・書巻など). ● この本を2冊買う buy two *copies* of the book. ▶学校の図書館には5万冊以上の蔵書がある Our school library has over 50,000 *volumes* [*books*].

ざつ 雑 — 雑な 服 (不注意な) careless; (いい加減な) slipshod; (話) sloppy; 〖大まかな〗 rough. (⇨大雑把, 粗雑) ● 雑な仕事 a *slipshod* [*sloppy, careless*] piece of work. (!) 「雑な仕事をする人」 は a slipshod [a sloppy] worker) ● 体育館のような雑

な(=大まかな構造の)建物 a building of simple structure like a gymnasium. (!)「安い材料で手間ひまかけずに粗雑に造った家」は a jerry-built house)
── 雑に 副 ▶このシャツは縫い方が雑だ This shirt is poorly sewn.
さつい 殺意 殺意を持って〖法律〗with intent to kill; with murderous intent. ● 殺意のある目つきで彼を見る look at him with murder in one's eyes.
さついれ 札入れ a wallet.《米》a billfold.
さつえい 撮影 图 〖写真の〗photography /fətágrəfi/; 〖映画の〗filming, shooting. ● 高速度撮影 high-speed photography. ▶〖揭示〗No photography [cameras]./Photography forbidden.
── 撮影する 動 〖写真を〗photograph, take a photograph /fóutəgræf/ 〖写真〗a picture,《話》a photo /fóutou/《of》;〖映画を〗film, shoot. 《を撮る》● 彼女が泳いでいるところを撮影する《写真に》photograph [take a photo(graph) of] her swimming;《映画に》film [shoot] her swimming. ▶その映画は一部パリで撮影された Part of the film was shot 〖×was filmed〗in Paris.
● 撮影所 a móvie [a film] stùdio.
ざつえき 雑役 《雑多な仕事》《やや書》miscellaneous work;《こまごました仕事》small jobs. (⇨雑用)
● 雑役夫〖婦〗an odd-jobber;《公共施設の》《主に米》a janitor,《英》a caretaker.
ざつえき 雑益 miscellaneous income.(⇔雑損)
ざつおん 雑音 (a) noise (⇨音⦅き⦆);〖電波障害〗static. ● ラジオの雑音 radio noise; static on the radio. ▶このレコードは雑音がひどい This record makes very harsh noises.
*さっか 作家 a writer;〖筆者〗an author;〖小説家〗a novelist. ● 女流作家 a woman writer [author]. (!)(1)特に女性であることを強調する言い方で、通例は単に writer と表す.(2)複数形は women writers と woman も複数化する. ● 推理〖短編小説〗作家 a mystery [a short story] writer. ● 陶芸作家 a ceramic artist. ▶作家として身を立てるのは容易なことではない It is no easy matter for you to establish yourself as a writer [in writing].
さっか 作歌 writing poems [poetry].
さっか 昨夏 last summer.
ざっか 雑貨 sundry goods (supplies),《米》notions,《書》sundries;〖食料品雑貨〗groceries.
● 雑貨屋 (人) a grocer; (店) (⇨雑貨店).
サッカー soccer,《英》(association) football. ● サッカーの試合 a soccer 〖《英》football〗match. ● サッカーをする play 〖×a〗soccer. ● 日本サッカー協会 Japan Football Association 〖略 JFA〗. ● 国際サッカー連盟 Fédération Internationale de Football Association 〖略 FIFA〗. ▶サッカーの真実とはフィールドの中で起きること、それがすべてだ With soccer games, it's all about what happens on the field. (!)be all about は about で以下のことが「すべて、最も重要である」の意) ▶英国では、サッカーは元々労働者階級のスポーツとされてきた In Britain, soccer has traditionally been viewed [regarded, considered] as a working-class sport [a sport for blue-collar people].
● サッカーくじ《英》the (football) pools;《日本の》toto.
さつがい 殺害 图 killing;《故意の》(a) murder.
── 殺害する 動 kill; murder. ● 米民間人ファルージャで殺害される (新聞の見出し) American Civilians Slain in Fallujah. (!)見出しには kill より強烈な響きを持つ slay が好まれ、受動態 (were slain) の be 動詞は省略される)

● 殺害者 a killer; a murderer.
さっかく 錯覚 (an) illusion; a trick of the eye. ● ...という錯覚をいだいている have the illusion that...; be under the [an] illusion that.... ▶赤い色を見ると暖かいように錯覚する Red gives [creates] an illusion of heat. ▶ニューヨークにいるような錯覚を起こした(=まるでニューヨークにいるみたいだった)I felt as if I were 〖《話》was〗in New York. ▶目の錯覚だよ、だれもいないじゃないか You're seeing things. There's nobody. (!)通例進行形で用いる)
ざつがく 雑学 knowledge of various [《やや書》miscellaneous] things. ▶うちの息子は雑学の大家だ My son has some knowledge about everything.
さっかしょう 擦過傷 a graze, an abrasion. ● 擦過傷を負う suffer abrasions.
ざっかてん 雑貨店 (通例田舎の) a general store; (安価な商品を扱う)《米》a variety [a dime] store (通例食料品は売っていない); (食料品雑貨店)《米》a grocery (store),《英》a grocer's (shop); (薬・日用雑貨なども売る)《主に米》a drugstore.
サッカリン 〖化学〗saccharin. (参考) 人工甘味料)
ざっかん 雑感 miscellaneous thoughts [impressions].
さつき 五月 〖暦の〗May;〖花の〗an azalea /əzéiljə/.
● 五月雨 (an) early summer rain. ● 五月晴れ beautiful [glorious, lovely] weather in May; (梅雨の晴れ間) sunny [clear] weather during the rainy season. ● 五月闇 gloomy [dismal] weather during the rainiy season.
さっき (少し前に) a little [a short] while ago; (しばらく前) some time ago. (⇨先程) ● さっきから for some time; (今まで) all this while. ▶何、さっきの話と違うじゃないか What? That's a different story from what you told me only a short time ago. ▶さっきからどこへ行ってたの Where have you been all this while?
さっき 殺気 殺気立った (興奮した) excited; (騒然とした)〖書〗seething; (血に飢えた) bloodthirsty. ● 殺気立った群衆 an excited crowd.
ざつき 座付き ● 座付き作家 a playwright working for a theater.
ざっき 雑記 miscellaneous notes [writings]. ● 身辺雑記 a miscellany /mísəlèini/ from one's daily life.
● 雑記帳 a notebook;《米》a scratch pad.
さつきしょう 皐月賞 the Satsuki-sho Derby.
さっきゅうに 早急に (⇨早急⦅きゅう⦆に)
ざっきょ 雑居 ● 雑居ビル a building tenanted by various kinds of stores, offices or restaurants.
さっきょう 作況 ● 米の作況指数 the rice-crop index.
さっきょく 作曲 图 (交響曲などの) composition.
── 作曲する 動 (交響曲などを) compose (a piece of music); write* music. (!)write* a song は「作詞・作曲する」の意. 単に「歌詞に曲をつける」は put* [set*] the words to music) ▶ベートベンは偉大な交響曲を作曲した Beethoven composed great symphonies.
● 作曲家 a composer; (歌謡曲などの) a songwriter. (!)後の方は「作詞家」の意もある)
さっきん 殺菌 sterilization (⇨消毒);〖牛乳などの低温による〗pasteurization. ▶日光は殺菌作用がある Sunshine kills germs.
── 殺菌する 動 ● 殺菌した牛乳 sterilized milk. (!)低音殺菌処理したものを pasteurized milk, 超高温

殺菌したものを UHT (=ultraheat-treated) milk という. ●器具を煮沸して殺菌する *sterilize* the instrument by boiling.
● 殺菌力 stérilizing pòwer.
ざっきん 雑菌 various kinds of harmful germs [bacteria].
サックコート a sack coat.
サックス (話) a sax. (⇨サキソホ(-)ン)
ざっくばらん ── **ざっくばらんな** 形 (率直な) frank; (形式ばらない) informal. ● ざっくばらんな人 a *frank* [(隠しだてしない) *a straightforward*] person.
── **ざっくばらんに** 副 frankly; informally. ▶みんなの意見をざっくばらんに言ってもらおう (話) I need to get everyone's input *up front*.
ざっくり ● ざっくり割れたスイカ watermelon *broken into several pieces*. ● ちょうど耳の下でざっくり切りそろえた髪 hair *cut straight just under the earline*. ● ざっくりした生地 a *coarse* fabric; a *loosely-woven* fabric. ● ざっくりと(=くだけてゆったりと)着る wear *casually* [*off-handedly*].
ざっけん 雑件 miscellaneous matters.
ざっこく 雑穀 (miscellaneous) cerials; (米) grain, (英) corn (❢ (米)では「トウモロコシ」の意).
さっこん 昨今 (最近) recently, lately (⇨最近); (このごろ) these days, nowadays. (⇨この頃(ご))
さっさと (すばやく) quickly; (迅速に) promptly; (間を置かずに) immediately, without delay. ● さっさと返事を書く reply *promptly* to the letter. ● さっさと(=急いで)逃げ出す run away *in a hurry*. ● さっさと仕事をしなさい Do your work *quickly*. ▶彼女は仕事が終わるとさっさと帰る She goes home *right after* work./She *hurries* home after work. ▶彼はさっさと(=時を移さず)次の仕事に取りかかった He *lost no time* in starting the next work.
さっし 察し (推察) a guess; (理解) understanding. (⇨察する) ● 察しのよい人 a person with fine *understanding*; (頭の回転の速い人) a *quick-witted* (⇔a slow-witted) person. ▶彼は察しが早い He is quick to *understand*. ▶お察しのとおりです You've *guessed* it (right)!
さっし 冊子 (本) a book; (小冊子) a booklet. (⇨小冊子)
サッシ a (window) sash [frame]. ▶アルミサッシ an aluminum (window) *sash*.
*ざっし 雑誌 (一般に) a magazine; (専門雑誌) a journal; (定期刊行物) a periodical. (❢ 日本語と異なり、英語の magazine は book (本・単行本) に含まれないことに注意) ● 月刊[週刊]雑誌 a monthly [a weekly] (*magazine*). ● 総合[婦人]雑誌 a general [a women's] *magazine*. ● 旅行[ファッション]雑誌 a travel [a fashion] *magazine*. ▶彼はその雑誌の5月[今月]号を買った He bought the May [the current] issue of the *magazine*. ▶私は毎月5種類の雑誌をとっている(=定期購読している) I take [*subscribe to*] five kinds of *magazines* every month. (❢ 後の方が堅い言い方) ▶タイムはありますか Do you have a *Time magazine*? (❢ 日本語では「…誌」と言わないことも多いが、英語では上のようにするのが普通)
● 雑誌記事 a magazine article. ● 雑誌記者 a magazine writer [reporter]; a journalist. ● 雑誌社 a magazine publisher.
ざつじ 雑事 ●身辺の雑事を整理する settle one's *personal* [*private*] *affairs*. (⇨雑用)
サッシュ a sash.
ざっしゅ 雑種 a cross, a crossbreed, a hybrid (❢ いずれも動物・植物の異種交配の意); (犬の) (軽蔑的な) a mongrel. ▶レオポンはヒョウとライオンの雑種 A leopon is a *cross between* [a *hybrid of*] a leopard and a lion.
ざっしゅうにゅう 雑収入 miscellaneous income [(公共団体の) revenue], income [revenue] from miscellaneous sources.
ざっしょ 雑書 miscellaneous books.
さっしょう 殺傷 ── **殺傷する** 動 kill or wound (three people).
● 殺傷事件 a case of bloodshed.
ざっしょく 雑食 ── **雑食性の** 形 omnivorous. ●ヒグマは雑食です Brown bears are *omnivorous*.
さっしん 刷新 (改革) (a) reform; (革新) (an) innovation. ●政界の刷新 political *reform*. ●人事の刷新 (=大異動) a personnel *shake-up*.
── **刷新する** 動 reform; innovate 《in》.
さつじん 殺人 (故意の) murder; (過失の) (法律) manslaughter; (故意・過失の) (法律) (a) homicide. ●殺人を犯す[2件犯す] commit *murder* [two *murders*]. ▶警察からは事故で処理したが、私はあれは殺人だったと思う The police decided it was an accident, but I thought it was *murder*. ▶彼は殺人の容疑[罪]で逮捕された He was arrested on suspicion of [on a charge of, for] *murder*.
── **殺人的な** 形 ●殺人的な暑さ deadly heat. ●殺人的なスケジュール a hectic schedule. ▶そのプラットホームの混雑ぶりは殺人的だった The platform was *horribly* crowded.
●殺人罪 a charge of murder; a murder charge. ●殺人事件 a murder case. ●殺人犯 a murderer. ●殺人未遂 an attempted murder.
さっすう 冊数 ●多くの冊数を売る sell a great many *copies*.
*さっする 察する [推測する] guess; suppose; gather (⇨推測する); [感じとる] sense; [想像する] imagine. ●危険を察する *sense* [*be aware of*] danger. ▶彼の口ぶりから察して from what he says; I *gather* from what he says (*that* 節). ▶察するところ彼は彼女のことが好きらしい I *guess* [*suppose*, *think*] (*that*) he likes her. (❢ この順に根拠は強くなる. He likes her, I／*guess*[…]. のように一人称の主語では文尾にも置ける (⇨思う)) ▶彼の心労は察するにあまりある I can just *imagine how* worried he is. (❢ この just は強意語) ▶胸中お察しします I can *imagine* how you feel./(心から同情します) I truly feel for you./I do sympathize with you. (❢ do は強意の助動詞で強く読む)
ざつぜん 雑然 ● a mess. ●雑然とした部屋 a *messy* [an *untidy*] room. ▶台所は雑然としていた The kitchen was (*in*) *a mess* [*in* (*a state of*) *disorder*]. ▶本が雑然と積んであった Books were left in an *disorderly* pile [heap].
さっそう 颯爽 ● さっそうとした姿の青年 a *dashing* [a *smartly-dressed*] young man. ● さっそうと(=堂々と)歩く walk *jauntily* [(堂々と) in a *dignified* way].
ざっそう 雑草 weeds. (⇨草) ●雑草のようにたくましい be (as) tough as nails [old boots]. (❢ like weeds は「(人が)多数で」の意)
*さっそく 早速 [すぐに] at once, 《話》 right away [off], immediately. (⇨すぐ❶) ▶早速彼に返事を書いた I answered his letter *at once* [*immediately*, *right away*]. ▶彼は帰宅すると早速宿題を始めた *As soon as* [*Soon after*] he got home, he sat down to his homework. ▶では早速最初のゲストの方をご紹介いたしましょう So, *without more* [*much*, *further*] *ado* /əˈduː/, let's bring on our first guest.

ざっそく 雑則 miscellaneous rules.
ざっそん 雑損 miscellaneous losses. (⇨ 雑益)
• 雑損控除 casualty loss deduction.
ざった 雑多 ── **雑多な** 形 (寄せ集めの) miscellaneous; (種々の) various. ● 種々雑多な職業の人々 people of *various* occupations. ● 雑多な用事を片づける get *miscellaneous* duties straight.

さつたば 札束 a wad [(巻いて折ったりした), (積み重ねた)] a stack] of bills; 《米》bank notes 《英》.
• 札束が舞う ▶ 今回の選挙戦では大量の札束が舞った This election campaign *was awash with a big sum of money*.

ざつだん 雑談 名〔つまらない話〕idle [small] talk; 〔気楽なおしゃべり〕a chat.
── **雑談する** 動 chat [have a chat] 《about + 事, with + 人》.

さっち 察知 ── **察知する** 動 (推測する) gather, infer; (感づく) sense; (かぎつける)《話》get wind of .... (⇨察する)

サッチャー 〔英国の政治家〕Thatcher (Margaret ～).

さっちゅうざい 殺虫剤 (an) insecticide; (粉の) (sprinkle) (an) insect powder. ● 野菜に殺虫剤をかける spray vegetables with *insecticide*(s); spray *insecticide*(s) over vegetables.

さっと ❶〔突然に〕suddenly, all of a sudden. ▶さっと風が舞い上がった All of a sudden [Suddenly] there rose a puff of wind.
❷〔すばやく〕quickly; (敏しょうに) nimbly; (急いで) in a hurry. ● さっと身をかわす dodge *quickly* [*nimbly*]. ● 辞書をさっとめくって単語を調べる *flip* [*have a quick flip*] through one's dictionary to look up a word. ▶ 彼はドアをさっと開けた He *threw open* the door [the door open]. ▶ 彼はTシャツをさっと脱いで洗濯機に放り込んだ He *slipped off* [*out of*] his T-shirt and threw it into the washing machine. ● 「さっと着る」は slip ... on, slip into ...)
❸〔すぐさま〕(迅速に) promptly; (直ちに) immediately. ▶ その質問はとても難しかったのですぐに答えられなかった The question was so difficult that I couldn't answer *promptly* [《話》*right away*].
❹〔その他の表現〕● ホウレンソウをさっと(=軽く)ゆでる boil spinach /spɪnɪtʃ/ *lightly*. ▶ 彼はその知らせに顔色がさっと青くなった He *turned* pale at the news. ▶ 彼女は彼の言葉にさっと赤くなった She *flushed* [×*blushed*] at his words. (❗ blush はただ「顔を赤らめる」だけで「さっと...」の意はない)

*__ざっと__ ❶〔丁寧でなく〕(大まかに) cursorily; (すばやく) quickly; (手短に) briefly. (❗ 副詞でなく,「大まかに...する」に類する動詞を用いてもよい: glance (ざっと見る), skim (ざっと触れる[通る, 読む, 見る]), skip through (ざっと飛ばし読みする)) ▶ 私はざっと家の掃除をした I cleaned the house *quickly*. ▶ 彼はざっと本に目を通した He went through the book *quickly* [*cursorily*]./He had a *quick* [a *cursory*] look through the book. ▶ 彼女は自分の考えをざっと述べた She *briefly* told us what she thought. ▶ 彼は報告書にざっと目を通した He *skimmed through* [*over*] the report.
❷〔数量などがおおよそで〕(大ざっぱに) roughly; (約) approximately. ● さっと見積もった損害額の *rough* estimate of the damage. ▶ ざっと 100 万円かかった It cost *roughly* [*approximately*, (約) *about*] one million yen.

さっとう 殺到 ── **殺到する** 動 〔駆けつける〕rush 《to, into》; 〔どっと押し寄せる〕pour 《洪水のように》flood 《into》. ● 大勢の野球ファンが球場に殺到した A crowd of baseball fans *rushed* [*poured*, *flooded*] *into* the stadium. ▶ 全国から苦情の手紙が殺到した Letters of complaint *poured* [*flooded*] *in* from all over the country. ▶ 毛皮コートの注文が殺到している There is a *flood* [a *rush*] of orders for fur coats.

ざっとう 雑踏 〔押し合いへし合い〕a [the] crush; 〔群衆〕a crowd, a throng. ● 雑踏に巻き込まれる be caught in the *crush*. ● 大都会の雑踏(=にぎわい) the *hustle and bustle* of a big city. (❗ (1) /hʌ́sl/ /bʌ́sl/ の /-sl/ の部分は発音しないことによって人のにぎわいの感じがよく出る. (2) 上の語順で用いる. またいずれか一方を用いて the hustle [bustle] of... ともいえる)

ざつどく 雑読 reading at random.
ざつねん 雑念 ● 雑念が次々に浮かんで読書に集中できなかった All kinds of *thoughts* crossed my mind and I wasn't able to concentrate on reading.

ざつのう 雑嚢 a duffel [a duffle] bag; 《米》a gunnysack.

ざっぱく 雑駁 ── **雑駁な** 形 (非体系的な) unsystematic; (筋の通らない) incoherent; (一貫しない) inconsistent. ● ざっぱくな(=非体系的な)知識 *unsystematic* knowledge.

さつばつ 殺伐 ── **殺伐とした** 形 〔人・事が〕(冷酷非情な) cruel; (血なまぐさい) bloody; 〔場所が〕(寒々とした) bleak; (住む人のない) desolate /désəlɑt/.

*__さっぱり__ 副 ❶〔まったく(...ない)〕(not) at all. ▶ 私はドイツ語がさっぱり分からない I *don't* understand German *at all*. ▶ あの男がなんであんなに怒ったのか, おれにはさっぱり分からない Why the guy was so angry, I'll *never* know. ▶ レストランの客の入りはさっぱりだ There are *very few* customers at the restaurant.
[会話] 「景気はどう」「さっぱりだよ」"How's business?" "*Not good at all./Very bad*."
── **さっぱりした** 形 ❶〔味などが〕refreshing; (あっさりした) plain; (軽い) light. ● さっぱりした味 a *refreshing* taste.
❷〔人柄などが〕(率直な) frank. ▶ 彼はさっぱりした人です He is *frank* [*straightforward*].
❸〔服装などが〕clean and neat [tidy]. (❗ 2 語重ねる方が日本語に近くなる) ▶ 彼女の子供たちは着ているものがさっぱりしている Her children are *clean and neat* [*tidy*] in what they wear.
❹〔気分などが〕(すがすがしい) refreshed; (ほっとした) relieved. ● ふろに入ってさっぱりしなさい Have a bath and feel *refreshed*. ▶ 私は借金をみな返してさっぱりした I felt *relieved* to have paid off all my debts.

ざっぴ 雑費 miscellaneous expenses; (臨時費)incidental expenses.

さっぴく 差っ引く (⇨差し引く)

さつびら 札びら 《米》a bill, 《英》a bank note.
• 札びらを切る (気前よくお金を使う) pay very generously (showing off a wad of bills); spend money freely.

ざっぴん 雑品 miscellaneous articles [objects].
さっぷうけい 殺風景 ── **殺風景な** 形 (荒涼とした) desolate /désəlɑt/, bleak; (単調でおもしろみのない) dull, drab 《-bb-》. ● 殺風景な眺め a *bleak* [a *dull*] sight. ▶ テーブルといすが一つずつあるだけで殺風景な(=がらんとした)部屋だ Only with a table and a chair, the room looks *bare*.

ざつぶつ 雑物 miscellaneous articles [objects].
ざつぶん 雑文 miscellaneous writings [(随筆) essays].

ざっぽう 雑報 general [miscellaneous] news; miscellaneous information.
• 雑報欄 the general [miscellaneous] news

ざっぽん column.
ざっぽん 雑本 miscellaneous books.
さつまあげ 薩摩揚げ a *satsuma-age*; (説明的に) a deep-fried patty of fish paste containing minced vegetables or seaweed.
さつまいも 薩摩芋 〖植物〗a sweet potato (働 ～es).
さつまじる 薩摩汁 (説明的に) thick *miso* soup made with chicken, pork and vegetables.
ざつむ 雑務 (⇨雑用)
ざつよう 雑用 (ちょっとした仕事) small jobs; (はんぱ仕事) odd jobs; (家の) chores. ● 雑用に追われる busy oneself with *small jobs*. ● 雑用をする do *odd jobs*; do the *chores*.
さつりく 殺戮 〖名〗(大虐殺) slaughter; mássacre; a holocaust (!⃝ (1) 人間を殺すときのみに用いられる. (2)「ナチによるユダヤ人の大虐殺」は the H-).
── 殺戮する 〖動〗 slaughter; massacre.
ざつろく 雑録 miscellaneous records.
ざつわ 雑話 a random talk.
＊さて now;《話》well. (⇨ところで, では) ▶ さて休憩にしよう *Now* [*Well*], let's have a break. ▶ その問題は片づいた. さて次に移ろう The problem is settled. *Now* for the next one.
〖会話〗「何か飲みますか」「さてな. 紅茶かな」 "Would you like something to drink?" "*I don't know*. Perhaps some tea."
さてい 査定 〖名〗 assessment. ● 課税額〖損害額〗の査定 the *assessment* of taxes [damages].
── 査定する 〖動〗 assess. ▶ 損害額は 3,500 ドルと査定された The damage *was assessed* at 3,500 dollars.
● 査定額 an assessment; an assessed value.
サディスティック ── サディスティックな 〖形〗 sadistic /sədístik/.
サディスト a sadist /séidist/.
サディズム 〖〖加虐趣味〗〗 sadism /séidizm, sæ-/.
さておき ▶ 冗談はさておき joking *aside* [*apart*]. ▶ 費用はさておき, とても時間がかかるでしょう *Apart* [《米》 *Aside*] *from* the cost, it will take a lot of time. ▶ 何はさておき(=まず第一に), ごみの山を片づけなければならない *First of all* [*Before anything else*], we must clear a pile of rubbish away.
さておく (⇨さておき)
さてさて ▶ さてさて, 微妙な質問だね *Well, well*, it's a delicate question to answer. ▶ さてさてやっかいなやつだ What a nuisance he is!
さてつ 砂鉄 iron sand.
さてつ 蹉跌 (失敗) a failure; (後退) a setback, 《書》 a reverse. ● 蹉跌をきたす suffer a *setback*.
さてね well. (⇨さて)
さては 〖その上〗 besides (!⃝ 接続詞的に); 〖それでは〗 then; 〖きっと〗 surely, certainly. ▶ さてはお前がやったんだね You must have done it. / *Then*, it was you who did it. / *So* that was your job. (!⃝ 悪事についていう)
サテライト 〖衛星〗 a satellite.
● サテライトオフィス a satellite office. ● サテライト局 a satellite station. ● サテライトスタジオ a satellite studio.
さてん 茶店 (⇨喫茶店)
さと 里 〖小集落〗 a (small) village; 〖実家〗 one's parents' home. (⇨さと, 里帰り)
サド 〖サディズム〗 sadism; 〖サディスト〗 a sadist.
さとい 聡い ❶〖賢い〗 clever.
❷〖感覚が鋭い〗● 利にさとい have a *quick* eye for a profit [for gain]. ▶ 私は耳がさとい I have a *sharp* ear. (!⃝ ×sharp ears とはいわない)
さといも 里芋 〖植物〗 a taro /táːrou/ (働 ～s).

＊さとう 砂糖 sugar. (!⃝ 角砂糖やスプーン 1 杯分をいうときはしばしば 〖C〗) ● 角砂糖 a lump [cube] of *sugar*; (角砂糖 1 個) a (lump [cube]) of *sugar*; a *sugar* cube. ● 白[黒, 赤]砂糖 refined [raw; brown] *sugar*. ● 氷砂糖 rock 《米》 candy. ▶ 私はコーヒーに砂糖は入れません I don't take [have] *sugar* in my coffee. / I drink coffee without *sugar*. / (ブラックで飲む) I drink my coffee black.
〖会話〗「紅茶にいくつ砂糖を入れますか」「二つ入れてください」 "How many *sugars* (do you want) in your tea?" "I want two (*sugars*)." (!⃝ 状況によって two spoonfuls [lumps, (小袋) packets] of *sugar* で表すこともできる)
● 砂糖入れ a súgar bòwl.
さとう 左党 ❶〖左翼政党〗 a leftist party.
❷〖酒の好きな人〗 a drinker.
さどう 作動 ── 作動する 〖動〗 work, run, operate. ● 機械を作動させる set the machine going [in *motion*]; start the machine.
さどう 茶道 tea ceremony (first practiced by *Zen* priests to achieve a contemplative calm); the Way of Tea.
ざとう 座頭 (盲人) a blind man; (あんま) a blind masseur.
さとうきび 砂糖黍 〖植物〗 sugar cane.
さとうだいこん 砂糖大根 〖植物〗 a sugar beet.
さとおや 里親 a foster parent. (働 里子)
● 里親制度 a foster-parent system.
さとがえり 里帰り ▶ 彼女は来月里帰りするつもりだ (結婚後初めて) She is going to *go home to see* her *parents* [*visit* her *parents* at her *old home*] *for the first time after* (her) *marriage*. (!⃝ 精 米英ではこのような決まった言い方はない) ▶ 5 年ぶりに里帰りします I'm visiting my parent's home for the first time in five years.
さとかた 里方 (妻の実家) one's wife's parents' home; (妻の家族) one's wife's family.
さとご 里子 a foster child. (働 里親) ● 里子に出す give (away) one's baby [child] to its [her, his] foster parents.
さとごころ 里心 ● 里心がつく get homesick; 《書》 yearn to return home (to one's parents).
＊さとす 諭す (穏やかに注意する) admonish; (じっくり説いて) persuade; (理を説いて) reason. ● 不作法をいけないと諭す *admonish* him for his misbehavior. ● 少女に彼の申し出を受けるよう諭す *persuade* the girl to accept his offer. ▶「申し出を受けた」結果まで含意する. 単に「諭す」だけなら try to persuade (の説得)
さとやま 里山 a country hill.
さとゆき 里雪 snow on the plains.
さとり 悟り 〖理解〗 understanding, 〖心が目覚めること〗 spiritual awakening [enlightenment]. ● 悟りがよい[悪い] be quick [slow] of *understanding*; be quick-witted [slow-witted]; be quick [slow] *on the uptake*. ▶ 彼は 40 歳になって悟りを開いた He *was spiritually awakened* [He attained *enlightenment*] at forty. ▶ 彼は悟り澄ましたような顔つきだ He looks as if [《話》 like] he *knows everything*.
＊さとる 悟る 〖認識する〗 realize (!⃝ 進行形・受身不可), become＊ aware [conscious] (*of*); 〖気づく〗 notice; (感ずく) sense, 《書》 perceive; 〖悟りを開く〗 achieve [attain] enlightenment. ▶ 彼は自分のあやまちを悟った He *realized* his mistake. / He *realized* [*found, saw*] (*that*) he had made mistakes. ▶ 待ち伏せしていることを敵に悟られないようにせよ

サドル (馬などの) (raise [lower]) a saddle.
● サドルバッグ a saddlebag.

サドンデス 〖競技〗sudden death. (参考 延長戦で先に得点した方を勝ちとする方式)

さなえ 早苗 rice sprouts, sprouts of rice.

さなか 最中 (...の) in the middle of .... (⇨最中). ● 夏の最中に in the height of the summer. (⇨真夏) ● 冬の最中に in the depths of the winter. (⇨真冬)

さながら as if [though]...; just like .... (⇨まるで❶)

さなぎ 蛹 (昆虫の) a pupa /pjúːpə/ (複 pupae /pjúːpiː/); (チョウなどの) a chrysalis.

さなだひも 真田紐 a braid; a narrow braided rope.

さなだむし 真田虫 〖動物〗a tapeworm.

サナトリウム 〖療養所〗a sanatorium /sænətɔ́ːriəm/ (複 ~s, sanatoria).

さにあらず 然に非ず ▶ 実はさにあらず It is *not the case* in reality.

サニーサイドアップ 会話 「卵はいかがなさいますか」「サニーサイドアップにしてください」"How would you like your eggs?" "*Sunny-side up*, please."

サニーレタス 〖植物〗(a) red leaf lettuce.

さね 実, 核 (果実の) a seed, a stone, a pit.

さのう 左脳 the left hemisphere, the left side of the brain.

さのう 砂嚢 ❶〖砂袋〗a sandbag. ❷〖鳥類の胃の一部〗a gizzard.

さは 左派 (人) a leftist;《集合的》the left (wing) (❗単・複両扱い), (政党内部の) the left faction. (⇨右派) ● 左派の leftist; left-wing.

さば 鯖 〖魚介〗a mackerel (複 ~(s)). (❗その肉は Ⓤ) ● さばを読む cheat in counting. ▶ 彼女は 2 歳さばを読んだ She lied about her *age taking off [adding on]* two years. (❗前の方は少なめに, 後の方は多めにいう場合) ● さば雲 (いわし雲) the mackerel sky. (⇨鰯(°))

サパー 〖夕食〗supper. ● サパークラブ 〖高級ナイトクラブ〗a supper club.

さはい 差配 ── 差配する 動 act as (an) agent. ● 差配人 (土地の周旋業者) a land [家屋の) a house] agent; (不動産の) a real estate agent, a realtor.

サバイバル 〖生き残り〗survival. ● サバイバルキット a survival kit. ● サバイバルグッズ survival goods. ● サバイバルナイフ a survival knife.

さばき 裁き (a) judgment. ● 公平な裁き a fair *judgment*. ● (...の罪で)裁きを受ける be tried 《*for*》.

*__さばく__ 砂漠 图 a desert /dézərt/. ● サハラ砂漠 the Sahara /səháːrə/; the Sahàra Désert. (❗二つ以上の砂漠名を併記したり, 固有名詞の一部として意識されない場合は D を小文字で表す: サハラ砂漠とゴビ砂漠 the Sahara and Gobi deserts. /アリゾナの砂漠 the Arizona desert) ● 砂漠の植物 *desert* plants. ▶ ボツワナは巨大な国だが大部分が砂漠である Botswana is huge but mostly *desert*. (❗この desert は形容詞. 類例: Most of the land is *hill*. (陸地の大部分は山だ))

── 砂漠化する 動 desertificate.
● 砂漠化 desertification.

*__さばく__ 捌く ● その難問をうまくさばく(=解決する) *settle* [処理する) *deal with*] the difficult problem successfully. (⇨処理する) ● 在庫品をさばく(=売る) *sell* [*dispose of*] the goods in stock. ● ゴロをさばく *field* a grounder. ● ワンバウンドの送球をさばく handle a one-hop throw. ● 魚をさばく(下ごしらえをする) *dress* [内臓を取り除く) *clean*, (3枚に下ろす) *fillet*] a fish.

*__さばく__ 裁く (裁判にかける) try; (判決を下す) judge, pass judgment 《*on*》. (⇨裁判) ● その事件を裁く *try* the case. ▶ 彼は盗みの容疑で裁かれた He *was tried* [He *stood trial*, He *went on trial*] *for* stealing [theft].

さばく 佐幕 the policy of supporting the Tokugawa Shogunate. ● 佐幕派の人 a supporter of the Tokugawa Shogunate.

さばけた 捌けた (ざっくばらんな) frank; (もの分かりのよい) understanding; (心の広い) liberal, open-minded; (気取らない) down-to-earth.

さばける 捌ける be sold. (⇨売れる, 捌く)

さばさば ▶ そのことを言ったのでさばさばした I got it off my chest and *felt fine* [*better*]. (❗*get ... off one's chest* は「心につかえていることを人に言う」の意) ● 彼女は会社を辞めて実にさばさばした(=すごい解放感を覚えた) He *felt a* terrific *sense of freedom* when he left the company. ● さばさばした人だ He is a man who *never niggles*. (❗*niggle* は「つまらないことにこだわる」の意)

サバティカル 〖大学教員などの長期有給研究休暇〗sabbatical (year [leave]). ● サバティカルをとっている be on sabbatical. ● サバティカルをとる take a sabbatical.

さはんじ 茶飯事 an everyday incident [occurrence]; a daily routine. (⇨日常)

サバンナ 〖<スペイン語〗(a) savanna(h) /səvǽnə/.

*__さび__ 錆 rust. (⇨錆びる) ● ナイフのさびを落とす clean the *rust* of a knife; (こすって(みがいて)) rub [scour] the *rust* off a knife. ● さびを止める prevent [protect against] *rust*. ▶ 鉄はさびがつきやすい Iron gathers *rust* [*gets rusty*] easily. ● ステンレス鋼はさびがつかない Stainless steel resists *rust* [does not rust]. /Stainless steel is *rust*-proof. ● さび止め (塗料) antirust paint; (さび止め剤) an anticorrosive; a rust inhibitor.

さび 寂 〖古びたものの落ち着いた趣〗a special kind of beauty that results from aging; antique look; 〖閑寂(た)〗〖枯淡(た)の趣〗quiet simplicity. ● 寂のある茶碗 a *beautiful old-looking* cup. ● 寂のある(=深く渋みのある)声 a *deep, sonorous* voice.

:**さびしい** 寂しい, 淋しい 〖人, (比喩的に)物・場所が〗lonely,《米》lonesome;《書》solitary;《書》forlorn; 〖人がいない〗deserted. (⇨ひとりぼっち)

使い分け **lonely** ひとりぼっちで寂しいことを強調する一般的な語.
lonesome lonely より感情で, 特に親しい人と別れて寂しい場合に用いる.

● 寂しい晩[場所] a *lonely* evening [place]. ● 寂しい曲 a *sad* [ⓧa lonely] tune. ● 寂しい思いをする feel *lonely*; (人がいなくて) miss 《him, it》. ● 寂しく暮らす lead a *lonely* [〖書〗a *solitary*] life; live *in loneliness* [*solitude*]. ▶ あなたがいなくてとても寂しかった I was very *lonely* [I missed you so much] with you away. (❗with you away a while [because] you were away ともいう)
会話「とても寂しくなるよ」「私もよ」"I'm going to miss you very much." "I (miss you) too./〖話〗Me too."

さびしがりや 寂しがり屋, 淋しがり屋 〖孤独感を感じやすい人〗a person who feels lonely [《米》lonesome] easily; (1人でいるのを嫌がる人) a person who does not like to be alone.

さびしがる 寂しがる, 淋しがる feel* lonely [《米》lonesome]; miss 〈him〉. (⇨寂しい)

さびしさ 寂しさ, 淋しさ loneliness;《書》solitude. (⇨孤独)

さびつく 錆び付く (さびる) rust; (徐々に) rust away. (⇨錆びる) ▶ちょうつがいはすっかりさびついている The hinges *are* badly *rusted* [*are rusted up*]. ▶私の英語は少しさびついている My English *is* a little *rusty*./I am a little *rusty* on [×in] English.

ざひょう 座標 〘数学〙a coordinate. ● X 座標 an x *coordinate*. ● 座標を求める find [locate] the *coordinates*.
● 座標系 〘数学〙coordinate system. ● 座標軸 a coordinate axis.

***さびる 錆びる** rust, get* [become*] rusty; gather rust. (⇨錆び付く) ●さびたナイフ a rusty knife; a knife covered with *rust*. ●鉄の門はさびてしまった The iron gate *rusted* (*away*) [*got rusty*]. (❗*away* を伴うと「腐食する」の意) ▶ナイフは真っ赤にさびていた The knife was red with *rust*.

***さびれる 寂れる** (衰える) decline. ●さびれてゆく[さびれた]村 a *declining* [(住む人のいない) a *desolate* /désəlat/, a *deserted*] village. ▶あの酒場もさびれ(=以前ほど繁盛しなくなって)きた That bar *has become less prosperous*. (❗「さびれた酒場」は a run-dòwn bár)

サブ 〘控え〙a substitute.

サファイア a sapphire.

サファリ (a) safari /səfɑ́ːri/.
● サファリジャケット a safari jacket. ● サファリスーツ a safari suit. ● サファリパーク《米》an animal park, 《主に英》a safari park.

ざぶざぶ (水しぶきを飛ばして) with a splash, with splashes. (⇨じゃぶじゃぶ)

サブタイトル 〘副題〙a subtitle.

ざぶとん 座布団 a *zabuton*, a (seat) cushion; (説明的に) a Japanese square cushion used when sitting on the *tatami* mat. (⇨布団) ▶客に座布団を勧めるask one's guest to sit on a *cushion*; push a *cushion* toward one's guest. (❗push は相手に対して強く押しつける感じを表す)

サブマリン・サブマリン〘投法〙a submarine delivery.

サプライサイド 〘供給側〙supply-side.

サプライヤー 〘供給者〙a supplier.

サフラワー 〘ベニバナ〙〘植物〙a safflower.

サフラン 〘植物〙a saffron. (香辛料・染料など) saffron.

ざぶり (⇨ざぶん)

サブリミナル (潜在意識に働きかける映像表現方法について) subliminal.
● サブリミナルアド[広告] 〘閾外(いきがい)広告〙subliminal advertizing.

サプリメント 〘栄養補助食品〙a supplement.

サブルーチン 〘コンピュータ〙a subroutine.

ざぶん (水を飛ばして) with a splash. ▶その男は橋の上から川へざぶんと飛び込んだ The man jumped off the bridge into the water *with a* (big [loud]) *splash*. (❗big splash はしぶき, loud splash は音を表す)/The man *splashed* the river from the bridge. ▶ぼくらは波が岸にざぶんざぶんと打ち寄せるのをみつめていた We watched the waves *break* (*ing*) on the shore for a while. (❗進行形の方が繰り返す動作をよりはっきり示す)

***さべつ 差別** 图 discrimination 《*against*》. ● 男女差別 sex(ual) *discrimination*; sexism. ● 高齢者差別 [老人]差別 age *discrimination*; agism. ● 逆差別 reverse *discrimination*. ● 男女の差別なく(=に関係なく)regardless [irrespective] *of* sex. ● 彼らを差別なく(=えこひいきせずに)扱う treat them *without partiality* [(平等に) *equally*]. ● 差別待遇を受ける receive [be given] *discriminatory* treatment. ● 大人も子供も無差別に撃つ shoot grown-ups and children *indiscriminately*. ▶国家があるから，人間の差別がある Because there is the nation state, there is [exists] *discrimination* against some people. ▶自分が社長になれないのは人種差別によるものだ Racism is what's blocking me [holding me back] from making it to president. (❗make it to …は「…を成就する」の意)
—— 差別的な 形 discriminatory.
—— 差別する 動 discriminate 《*against*》. ▶人種差別を *discriminate against* race. ▶その会社は採用に当たって女性を差別した The company *discriminated against* women in its hiring. ▶教師はできる生徒とできない生徒を差別してはいけない Teachers should not *discriminate between* bright *and* dull pupils [*treat bright and dull pupils differently*].
● 差別用語 discriminatory language [words].

さへん 左辺 〘(不)等式〙the left side. ▶左辺の項を the *left side* of a mathematical equation.

さほう 作法 manners; etiquette. (⇨行儀, 礼儀) ▶日本は作法を重んじる国だ Japan is a country where *manners* are important [prized].

さぼう 砂防 erosion control.
● 砂防ダム an erosion control dam. ● 砂防調査 erosion control research. ● 砂防林 an erosion control forest.

さぼう 茶房 (⇨喫茶店)

サポーター ❶ 〘支持者〙a supporter. ▶イアン・シャープは幼い頃からのスパーズサポーターだといわれる Ian Sharp is said to have been a Spurs *supporter* [*fan*] since his early days.
❷ 〘運動用の〙a supporter; (男性の股間を保護する)《話》a jockstrap. ●サポーターをしている[つける] wear [put on (↔take off)] a *supporter*.

サポート 图 support. (⇨支持) —— サポートする 動 support.

サボタージュ 〘フランス語〙《米》a slowdown,《英》a go-slow. (❗sabotage はひそかに機械類を破壊したりして, 生産活動を低下させる妨害行為) ▶サボタージュをする《米》stage a *slowdown*;《英》go slow, go on a *go-slow*.

サボテン 〘スペイン語〙〘植物〙a cactus (複 ～es, cacti /kǽktai/). (参考)和名は弁慶柱.

さほど〘それほど〙(=さほど)…でない not so《big》(as …). (⇨それほど)

サボる 〘仕事を〙be lazy 《*at*》, (のらりくらりと) loaf (*around*); 〘学校・授業を〙(ずる休みする) play truant [《米話》hook(e)y] (*from* school) (⇨ずるける);(欠席する)《話》cut* 《a class》. ● 授業を二つサボる *cut* [《主に米》*skip*] two classes. ▶あいついつも仕事をサボっている He *is* always *loafing* on the job. ▶あと 1 回授業をサボったら退学してもらうよ If you *cut* [*skip*] one more class, you'll be kicked out of school.

ザボン 〘ポルトガル語〙〘植物〙a shaddock, a pomelo (複 ～s).

さま 様 ● さまになる look good [right]. ▶彼は何をやってもさまになる He does everything smartly and elegantly. ▶彼のスーツ姿は全然さまにならない He looks terrible [(不かっこうな) very awkward] in suits./He doesn't have what it takes to wear suits.

-さま -様 〘男〙Mr.; 〘女〙(未婚) Miss; (既婚) Mrs.; (区別なく) Ms.; (手紙などで) 《主に英書》Esq. (❗(1)

Esquire の略で Mr. より改まった敬称. John Brown, *Esq.* のように用いる. (2)《米》では弁護士・国会議員に限って男女にかかわらず用いられることがある).

解説 (1) 親しい人にあてる手紙の冒頭に Dear Mr. [Mrs., Miss] Brown などと敬称をつけて書くと妙に改まった感じになる. 封筒の表書きではこの限りでないが, 敬称をつけないで姓名だけの場合もある.
(2) 公的な手紙では相手が既婚か未婚かに関係なく女性には Ms. ..., と敬称をつけるのが好まれる.
(3) 性別不詳の相手には敬称をつけない. (⇒さん)

ざま ざまをみろ(=当然の報いだ) It serves [Serves] you right! (**!** you はさし示す相手によって him, her, them なども可) ▶何てざまだ What a *sight* you are!/(恥を知れ) Shame on you!
サマーウール a light(weight) wool fabric.
サマースクール (a) summer school.
サマータイム [夏時間]《米》daylight(-saving) time (略 DST), 《英》summer time;[夏季] summertime. ▶東部夏時間午前 8 時に at eight a.m. Eastern *Daylight* Time.
さまがわり 様変わり 名 a complete change.
—— **様変わりする** 動 change completely. ▶この一帯もすっかり様変わりした This area *has completely changed*./This area *looks entirely different from* what it was.
さまざま 様々 ▶...様々である(おおいに感謝している) All one's thanks go to ...; cannot thank ... enough;(賞賛する) give 〈him〉a lot of credit 〈*for*〉; take one's hat off 〈*to*〉.
さまざまな 様々な ―― **様々な** 形 various;[違った] different. (⇒色々) ▶さまざまな意見 *various* opinions. ● さまざまな種類の動物 *various* kinds of animals; *many different* kinds of animals. ● さまざまな年齢の男女のグループ a group of men and women of *varying* ages. ● 客に対する応対の仕方は国によってさまざまである The proper behavior for guests *varies* from country to country. ▶日々さまざまな事件が起こる *A variety of* things happen [keep happening] every day. (**!** keep happening は「次から次へと生じる」様子を表す)

DISCOURSE
動物園には有益な目的がないと言う人もいるかもしれないが, 一般市民にとって動物園はさまざまな点で有益だ Some people may say the zoo has no useful purpose, *but* for ordinary citizens it is useful *in many ways*. (**!** but (しかし)は逆接を表すディスコースマーカー)

***さます** 冷ます [冷やす] cool;(冷めさせる) let*... cool 〈⇒冷やす〉;[興味・熱意などをなくす] spoil. ▶お茶を冷ましてから飲みなさい Let your tea *cool* before you drink it.
***さます** 覚ます ❶[目を覚まさせる] wake*... (up), 《書》waken, 《書》awake*. (⇒覚める ❶) ▶彼を眠りから覚ます wake him (*up*) from sleep. ● 変な音で目を覚ました(=目が覚める) be woken [《書》be wakened] by queer sounds. ▶すっかり目を覚ましている be wide 〈×very〉awake. ▶彼は今朝早く目を覚ました He woke (*up*) early this morning.
❷[迷いを] bring*〈him〉to his senses. (⇒覚める❷)
❸[酔いを] sober〈him〉up. (⇒覚める❸) ▶酔いを覚ますためにコーヒーを 1 杯飲んだ I drank a cup of coffee to *sober* (*myself*) *up*.
さまたげ 妨げ [人, 物] an obstacle 〈*to*〉, a hindrance 〈*to*〉;[行為] obstruction 〈*of*〉, 《書》hindrance 〈*of*〉. (⇒邪魔, 妨害) ▶その事件が彼の出世の妨げになっている The affair is *in the way of* [*is an obstacle to*] his success in life. ▶彼らがその気になってるんだから妨げになるものは何もない Since they're willing, what's to *stop* them?

さまたげる 妨げる [遅らせる] hinder; [障害になる] get*... in the way 〈*of*〉;[不可能にさせる] prevent [keep*, stop (-pp-)]...〈*from doing*〉(**!** 後の 2 語の方が口語的);[邪魔する] interfere 〈*with*〉. (⇒邪魔(を)する) ▶粗末な食事がその子供の成長を妨げている Poor food *hinders* the growth of the child./Poor food *hinders* [*keeps*] the child *from growing*. ▶彼らは私が会に出席するのを妨げた They *prevented* me 〈*from*〉attending the meeting. (**!** (1) from を省略するのは《主に英》で,《米》ではれ. (2) from を省略すると彼らが私が出席している最中に妨害したことになる (⇒[次例]). (3) 受身形では《米》《英》を問わず from は省略されない) ▶そのことが状況の正しい理解を妨げている That *prevents* our correct understanding of the situation./That *prevents* us *from* [《書》our] understanding the situation correctly. ▶安眠を妨げるな(=妨害するな) Don't *disturb* my sleep [me while I am sleeping].
さまつ 瑣末 ―― **瑣末な** 形 trivial, trifling. ● さまつな事柄 a *trivial* matter.
さまよう 彷徨う wander, roam (around [《主に英》about]). (**!** wander はあてもなくぶらぶら歩き回る. roam は通例広い範囲を自由負気ままに歩き回ること) ▶町をさまよう *wander around* (*in*) the town. (**!** in は放浪の範囲を示すので, 町自体に関心がある場合は省略される) ▶丘をさまよう *wander* (*over*) the hills. ▶世界中をさまよう *roam around* the world. ▶生死の境をさまよう *hover* between life and death. ▶彼は森をさまよっているところを発見された He was found *wandering* (*around*) in the forest.
さまよえるオランダじん 『さまよえるオランダ人』 *The Flying Dutchman*. (参考) ワグナー作曲のオペラ)
サマリー [要約] a summary. ▶議長サマリー [議長総括] a chairperson's *summary*.
さみしい 寂しい, 淋しい lonely. (⇒寂(さび)しい)
さみせん 三味線 (⇒三味線(しゃみせん))
さみだれ 五月雨 (an) early summer rain. ▶五月雨式のスト sporadical strikes. ▶抗議行動は五月雨式に 1 か月間続いた Protests continued *sporadically* [*intermittently*] for a month.
サミット [首脳会談] 《hold》a summit (meeting). ▶東京サミット〈*at*〉the Tokyo *Summit*. ▶サミットを成功させよう Make the *Summit* a success!/Let us make a success of the *summit*. (**!** スローガンのときは前の方のような命令形にすると強まる)

‡さむい 寒い ❶ [気温が低い] cold; chilly. (⇒暑い)

使い分け cold 「寒い」の一般的な語.
chilly cold より意味が弱く, 何となく肌寒いぞくぞくする感じの不快な寒さ.

▶今朝は寒いですね (It's) a *cold* [a *chilly*] morning, isn't it? ▶そんな薄着で寒くないですか In such thin clothes, aren't you *cold* [don't you feel *cold*]? ▶明け方はやっと寒かった It was *chilly* [There was a chill in the air] toward dawn. ▶外はいてつくように寒い It's freezing (*cold*) outside. ▶日が落ちると一段と寒くなった When it got dark, it turned much *colder*. (**!** 比較級の強めには very は用いない) ▶こう寒くてはたまらない I can't stand this *cold*./This *cold* is unbearable to me. (**!** この cold はいずれも名詞)
❷ [その他の表現] ▶お寒い(=貧弱な)福祉予算 a *poor* welfare budget.

さむがり　寒がり ▶彼はとても寒がりだ He is very *sensitive to the cold*.

さむがる　寒がる（寒いと訴える）complain of the cold; （寒さがこたえる様子である）seem to feel the cold.

さむけ　寒気（身震い）a chill,《話》the shivers.
● 寒気がする feel [have] a chill; feel [be] chilly; (寒い) feel cold. ▶何だか寒気がする I feel kind of *chilly*. ▶その写真を見ただけで寒気がした Just looking at the snapshot gave me *the shivers* [《話》 *the creeps*].

***さむさ　寒さ**（the）cold; cold weather;（ぞくっとする不快な）a chill（通例単数形で；⇨寒い）● 冬の厳しい寒さ the bitter [intense, severe] *cold* of winter. ● 寒さをしのぐ keep out the *cold*. ▶寒さが身にこたえる I feel *the cold*. ▶彼は寒さに震えていた He was shivering with *cold*. ▶一日一日と寒さがつのった The weather got *colder* day by day.

さむざむ　寒々 ● 寒々とした風景 a wintry scene.
● 寒々とした（＝もの寂しい）部屋 a *dreary* room; (冷え冷えとした) a *chilly* room.

さむぞら　寒空 a wintry sky;（冬の寒い天候）cold [wintry] weather. ▶寒空の中，彼らは三々五々やって来た They came in twos and threes in *cold weather*.

サムターン〖内鍵(ﾅｲｶﾞｷﾞ)つまみ〗a thumbturn.

さむらい　侍 a samurai（**!**単・複同形），a (*samurai*) warrior. ● 七人の侍〖映画名〗 *The Seven Samurai*.

さめ　鮫〖魚介〗a shark.
● さめ肌 dry and scaly skin.

さめざめと ● さめざめと泣く continue to cry quietly [softly].

さめやらぬ　覚めやらぬ be not completely [fully] awake. ▶彼らは勝利の興奮覚めやらぬ状態だ Their excitement about the victory lingers on [hasn't worn off (yet)].

***さめる　冷める** ❶〖熱い物が〗cool (down);（冷たくなる）get* cold. ● 熱湯を冷めないようにしておく keep boiling water hot. ▶早く来ないとスープが冷めてしまうわ Come to the table quick [quickly]. Your soup *is getting* [*going*] *cold*. (**!**(1) 命令文では quickly より quick が普通。(2) go は「好ましくない状態への変化」を示す。(3) …quick, or your soup will get cold. では「冷めますよ」といった冷静な言い方）▶おふろの湯が冷めないうちに（＝十分温かい間に）入りなさい Take a bath while it's warm enough. (**!** 日本語につられて x … before the hot water doesn't get cold. とはしない）

❷〖情熱などが〗cool off;〖興味が〗be spoiled; be chilled. ▶仕事に対する熱が冷めた My love for work *has cooled off*./（興味を失った）I have lost interest in work.

***さめる　覚める** ❶〖眠りから〗wake* (up),《書》waken (up),《書》awake*. ● 眠りから覚める wake (*up*) from [out of] (one's) sleep. ● 目の覚めるような青 *bright* [*vivid*] blue. ● 真夜中に目が覚めた I *woke* (*up*) in the middle of the night. ▶目が覚めると寝汗をかいていた I woke *up* (to find myself) sweating. ▶彼は火事で目が覚めた He was *woken* (*up*) by a fire./He *woke* (*up*) to a fire. (**!** せき・悪夢など内的刺激が原因で目が覚める場合は　wake・(up) with a cough [one's nightmare] のように用いる）▶《事が主語》A fire *woke* him *up*.

❷〖迷いから〗come* to one's senses. ▶あの人にうんとられて目が覚めた He gave me a good telling-off, and I *came* [*was brought* (*back*)] *to* my *senses*./《書》His severe scolding *brought* me *to* my *senses*.

❸〖酔いから〗get* [become*] sober; sober up.
▶コーヒーを1杯飲めば酔いがさめるよ A cup of coffee will *sober* you *up*.

❹〖興奮・友情などが〗cool down. ● さめている（＝冷静である）be calm and collected; keep one's head; be sober. ▶事態をさめた目で（＝現実的に）見る look at the situation *realistically*. ▶近頃の若い者はさめている Young people today *are cool* [*have a cool attitude*] *to* [*toward*] things.

さめる　褪める lose color, discolor; fade (away). (⇨褪(ｱ)せる) ● さめやすい色 a color which *fades* easily. ▶このシャツは洗っても色がさめない This shirt washes well./The color of this shirt will not wash out.

さも (just) like ….（⇨いかにも）
● さもあらばあれ さもあらばあれ（＝何があろうとも），私にはそれをする覚悟ができている Come what may, I am prepared to do it.
● さもありなん （彼は勝たなかったが，さもありなんと思った（＝予想したとおりだった）He didn't win, which was *what I had expected*.

サモア〖南太平洋の群島〗Samoa /səmóuə/;（公式名）the Independent State of Samoa. (首都 Apia)
● サモア人 a Samoan. ● サモア語 Samoan. ● サモア（人）語の Samoan.

さもしい (人が卑劣な) mean;（偏狭な） narrow-minded. ● さもしい了見 a *narrow-minded* idea.

ざもち　座持ち ● 座持ちのよい（＝楽しませるのがうまい）人 a deipnosophist /daipnásəfist/.

ざもと　座元〖興行の主催者が〗the manager, the producer;〖興行場の持ち主〗the proprietor of a theater.

さもないと，さもなければ otherwise; or (else) (**!** else がある方が強意的。以上二つはしばしば肯定命令文の後で);〖もし…でないなら〗if not. (**!** 否定命令文の後なら or, if so: 動くな，さもないと（＝動くなら）撃つぞ Don't move, *or* [*if so*,] I'll shoot you.) ▶急ぎなさい，さもないと遅れるよ Hurry up, *or* (*else*) [*if not*,] you'll be late. ▶スピードを落とさないと。さもないとはその角を曲がれないよ Slow down, *otherwise* your car can't turn the corner. (**!** *otherwise* は文尾に用いて Slow down. Your car … otherwise. のようにもいえる)/If you *don't* slow down, your car can't turn the corner.

サモワール /＜ロシア語/ a samovar /sǽməvɑːr/. (参考)ロシアの伝統的なお茶用湯沸かし器)

さもん　査問 图 (an) inquiry. ● 公式の査問 《hold》an official *inquiry*. ● その件を査問に付す lay the matter before the commission of *inquiry*.
── **査問する** 動 inquire (*into*); investigate.
● 査問委員会 the commission of inquiry.

さや　莢〖豆などの〗a pod; a hull;（固くなった）a shell. ● エンドウのさやをむく shell [*pod*, *hull*] peas.

さや　鞘（刀剣・刃物などの）a sheath /fiːθ/;（刀剣の）a scabbard. ● 剣をさやに納める put one's sword back into the *sheath*; sheathe /fiːð/ one's sword.
● **さやを払う** ● 剣のさやを払う（＝さやから抜く） draw [unsheathe] one's sword.

さやあて　鞘当て ● 恋のさや当て rivalry in love (*between* A and B).

さやいんげん　莢隠元 a string bean,《英》a French bean. (**!** 通例複数形で)

さやえんどう　莢豌豆 a field pea. (**!** 通例複数形で)

さやか 清か ── 清らかな ● さやかな月の光 *bright*, *clear* moonlight. ● さやかな声 a *clear* voice.

ざやく　座薬 a suppósitòry.

さやさや ● そよ風にさやさやと揺れる sway *gently* in the

さゆ 白湯 (plain) hot water.

さゆう 左右 名 ▶左右をよく見て通りを渡りなさい Look *right and left* [(両側を) *both ways, either way*] carefully before you cross the street. (❗Look *to the right and the left*.... も❗)/(あたりを見回す) Look *around* carefully before crossing the street.

── **左右に** 副 (左と右に) right and left (❗時に left and right ともいう); (左右横に) from side to side. ▶船はあらしで左右に揺れた The ship rolled *from side to side* in the storm. ▶通りの左右(=両側)にしだれ柳がある There are weeping willows *on both sides* [*on either side*] *of* the street. ▶その振り子は左右に動いていた The pendulum is swinging *back and forth* [*from side to side*]. (❗前の方の日英表現の違いに注意)

── **左右する** 動 [影響する] (間接に) influence; (直接に) affect; [意見などを動かす] sway. ●感情に左右されるbe carried away by one's emotion. ●米の収穫は天候に大いに左右される The rice crop *is* greatly *influenced by* the weather./The weather greatly *influences* the rice crop. ●人の人生観はその時々の健康状態に左右されることが多い Our philosophy often *depends on* our condition [the condition of our health] at the time. ▶その事件がその政治家の運命を左右した The scandal *affected* [(決定した) *decided*] the fate of the politician.

●左右対称 symmetry.

ざゆうのめい 座右の銘 ▶「誠実」を座右の銘とする have "sincerity" as *one's motto*; "Sincerity" is one's *motto*.

‡**さよう** 作用 名 ❶[働き] (法則に従った) operation (❗作用の仕方に重点がある); (結果の面から見た) action (❗物理的・化学的作用にも用いる); (原因から見た) agency; [影響] (an) effect. ●呼吸作用 the *operation* of breathing. ●作用と反作用 *action* and *réaction*. (❗対比による reaction の強勢の移動に注意) ●岩に対する波の作用 the *action* of water *on* rocks. ●熱の作用で by [through] the *agency* of heat. ●アルコールと薬の相互作用で by the *interaction* between alcohol and medicine.

── **作用する** 動 [働く, 効果がある] operate 《*on*》, act 《*on*》, work 《*on*》; (不利に) affect. ▶その毒は神経系に作用し, 10分ぐらいで死にます The poison *operates on* [*acts on, works on, affects*] the nervous system, bringing death in about ten minutes.

●作用点 an application point.

さよう 左様 so. (➾そう, そのように)

さようなら good-by(e). (➾さよなら)

> **翻訳のこころ** あの小父さんは, 自分はさきにさようならしたからいいようなものの, この女のひとはこれからどうやって生きていくのだろう (竹西寛子『蘭』) That man [×uncle] doesn't have anything more to worry about, because he's already said 'Good-by [Farewell]' to life. But I just wonder how this woman is going to live from tomorrow [now on]. (❗(1) 英語の「おじさん」にあたる uncle は血縁関係だけに用いる. (2)「さようならをした」は比喩的に用いられており, Farewell が文の雰囲気には合っている. (3)「いいようなものの」は have anything worry about (心を煩わすことがない) を表す)

さよきょく 小夜曲 [音楽] a serenade /sèrənéid/.

さよく 左翼 ❶[政治上の] (派) the left (wing) (❗集合的. 単・複両扱い); (人) a leftist (❗以上は, しばしば L-(W-); L- と書く) ●左翼的な思想 left-wing [*leftist*] ideas.

❷[野球の] left field. (➾レフト)
❸[飛行機・隊列などの] the left wing.
●左翼手 [野球] a left fielder. (➾レフト) ●左翼団体 a left-wing [a leftist] organization. ●左翼分子 left-wing elements.

***さよなら** 間 good-bye (❗goodbye, good-by, goodby ともつづる); [話] bye (now), bye-bye, so long; [書] farewell (❗長く別れるときに 《注意》); (また会いましょう) (I'll) see you later [soon] (❗See you again. は長い間または永久に会えない人に用いる); (じゃまた) Be seeing you. (❗次にいつ会うか分かっているときは See you then [on Monday; tomorrow]. (そのとき) 月曜日; あした] またね) のように); (夜に) Good / night.

── **さよなら** 名 ▶お父さんにさよならを言いなさい Say *good-bye* to your father. ▶子供たちは手を振って [キスをして] 私にさよならをした The kids waved [kissed] me *good-bye*.

●さよならパーティー a farewell [a good-bye] party. ●さよならヒット [野球] a game-ending hit.
●さよならホーマー [野球] a game-ending homer; a walk-off homer.

さより [魚介] a halfbeak (複 ~(s)).

***さら** 皿 ▶[料理を盛りつける深い大皿] a dish (❗the dishes はナイフ・フォークを含めた食器類一般をいう); (米) a platter; [dish に入れられた料理を盛り分ける浅い皿] a plate; [茶わんの受け皿] a saucer; [1皿の料理] a dish, a plate; [コース料理の中の一品] a course. ●スープ皿 a soup *plate*. ●牛肉と野菜の料理1皿 a *dish* [a *plate*] of beef and vegetables. ●料理を皿に入れて出す serve the food in a *dish* [*on a plate*]. ●食卓の皿類を片づける clear away *the dishes* on the table; clear *the dishes* from the table. ●6皿の料理を注文する order a six-*course* dinner [a dinner of six *courses*]. ●目を皿のようにする (➾目 [成句]) ▶彼に豆を3皿平らげたHe ate three *dishes* [(3人分) three *helpings*] of beans.

●皿洗い (➾皿洗い) ●皿時計 a plate clock.

ざら (➾さらに)

さらあらい 皿洗い (行為) dishwashing, (英) washing-up; (人) a dishwasher, (英) a washer-up (複 washers-). ●皿洗いをする do [wash (up)] the dishes; (英) wash up, (英話) do the *washing-up*.

●皿洗い機 a dishwasher.

さらいげつ 再来月 the month after next.

さらいしゅう 再来週 the week after next. ●再来週の今日に two weeks from today.

「会話」「来週の土曜日は難しいなあ」「再来週の方が都合がいい？」 "Next Saturday's difficult." "Will the Saturday *after* suit you better?"

「会話」「ピカソの展覧会はいつ終わるかご存じですか」「再来週の土曜日です」 "Do you know when the Picasso exhibition ends?" "*A week next* Saturday."

さらいねん 再来年 the year after next.

さらう review. (➾おさらい)

さらう 浚う ❶[奪い去る] carry ... off; (波などが) sweep* [wash] ... away; (演説などが人の心を奪う) sweep ... along. ●1等賞をさらう *carry off* (the) first prize. ●(主役をさらう)人気[評判]をさらう steal the show. ▶彼の演説は聴衆の人気をさらった His speech *swept* the audience *along* with him.

❷〖川底などを〗(網などで) drag (-gg-); (浚渫する)船〖機〗などで) dredge;〖溝などを〗clean ... out. ●池をさらってナイフを捜す *drag the pond for the knife.*

サラエボ 〖ボスニア・ヘルツェゴビナの首都〗Sarajevo /sǽrəjéivou/.

ざらがみ ざら紙 pulp [rough] paper.

サラきん サラ金 〖消費者金融業〗consumer loan business; 〖高利貸し〗(行為) loan sharking; (人)〖話〗a loan shark. ●サラ金〖業者〗から金を借りる borrow money from a *loan shark* (at *a consumer loan company* 〈at an exorbitant rate of interest〉).

さらけだす さらけ出す (はっきり示す) reveal; (暴露する) expose (⇨暴露する); (感情などを) show* 〈one's feelings〉openly. ●そのことについて自分の無知をさらけ出す *reveal* one's *ignorance of the matter.* ●手の内をさらけ出す put [lay] one's card on the table. ●すべてをさらけ出す (=白状する) *confess* everything 〈*to him*〉. ●危機に直面すると人は弱点をさらけ出す People *show* their *weakness unintentionally* when they face a crisis.

さらさら ❶〖音が〗(木の葉・紙など) rustle; (流れなど) murmur; (風など) whisper. ●木の葉が風にさらさら鳴る音が聞こえる I can hear the leaves of trees *rustling in the wind.* ●小川がさらさらと音を立てて流れているのが聞こえる The running water in the stream is heard *murmuring.* (●「小川のさらさらという流れの音」は *the murmur of a stream* という)
❷〖感触などが〗●さらさらと契約書にサインする sign the contract *smoothly* [*quickly*]. ●砂は握るとさらさらで指の間からさらさらとこぼれ落ちた The sand felt *dry and smooth* in my hand and *trickled* through the fingers. (● trickle は「(液体のように) 少しずつ流れる」様子を表す)

さらさら 更ара ●さらさら(=少しも)...ない (⇨少しも)

ざらざら ●さらざらした rough, coarse; (砂で) sandy; (ほこりで) dusty. ●壁面はざらざらしている The wall surface is *rough*. ●この砂糖はざらざらしている The sugar is *coarse*. ●床は砂でざらざらしていた The floor was *sandy* [*gritty*]. ●母の手は長年の水仕事でざらざらしていた My mother's hands felt *rough* [*coarse*, (ひび割れで) *chapped*] from years of kitchen work.

さらし 晒し (さらすこと) bleaching; (さらして白くした布) bleached cloth.
●さらし飴(あめ) glutinous rice jelly. ●さらし餡(あん) powdered bean-paste. ●さらし木綿 bleached cotton cloth.

さらしくび 晒し首 a gibbeted head. ●さらし首にされる[なる] have one's head exposed [gibbeted] to public scorn.

さらしこ 晒し粉 bléaching pòwder.

さらしにっき 更級日記 *As I Crossed a Bridge of Dreams.* (〖参考〗菅原孝標女の日記)

さらしもの 晒し者 ●彼はさらし者にされた He was deeply disgraced in public.

***さらす 晒す** 〖日光などにあてる〗expose; 〖漂白する〗bleach. ●雨[日光]にさらす *expose* 〈it〉 *to the rain* [*the sun*]; (放置する) leave 〈it〉 *in the rain* [*sun*]. ●危険に身をさらす *expose* oneself *to danger*. ●恥をさらす *be put to shame*. ●みじん切りの玉ねぎを水にさらす *soak* minced onion *in water*. ●日にさらしておくとにおいが抜けます The smell will go if you *leave* it *out in the sun*.

さらそうじゅ 沙羅双樹 〖植物〗a sal (tree).

サラダ (a) salad. ●ハムサラダを作る make [prepare, ×cook] a ham *salad*. ●ぱりっとした野菜サラダを食べる have some (crisp) vegetable *salad*. (●レタスなど青野菜のサラダを green salad という)●サラダはよく混ぜ合わせてから召し上がれ Toss the salad well before you eat.
●サラダオイル salad oil. ●サラダ菜 lettuce; salad. ●サラダバー a salad bar.

サラダきねんび『サラダ記念日』 *Salad Anniversary.* (〖参考〗俵万智の歌集)

さらち 更地 vacant land (to build a house on); (主に米) a vacant lot; (建物用) (主に米) a building lot. (⇨空き地) ●地震によって倒壊した家屋は全部撤去されて更地となっていた After the earthquake, all of the collapsed houses had been carried away leaving *vacant lots* behind.

ざらつく be [feel*] rough /rʌ́f/ [(砂で) sandy]. (⇨ざらざら)

さらっと (⇨さらりと)

さらなる 更なる ●さらなる飛躍を期待しております I hope you will make more progress *than* this.

***さらに 更に ❶**(なおいっそう) (比較級を強めて) much, far, still, even, 〈話〉a lot, lots; (ますます) more and more (● more に限るその他の形容詞・副詞の比較級も用いる); (程度・距離などが) further (● 距離の意では〈主に英〉で, 〈米〉では farther が普通). ●彼らはさらに多くのお金を要求した They asked for *much* [*far, a lot*] *more* money. ●台風が近づくにつれて雨はさらに激しくなった As the typhoon approached, it rained *harder and harder*. ●本校の学生はすべてが20歳前後というわけではない. 30歳代の人も, さらにはもっと年上の人もいる Not all our students are about twenty years old. Some are in their thirties. Some are *even* older. ●彼はその問題をさらに調査した He looked into [investigated] the matter *further*./He made a *further* investigation into the matter. ●我々はさらに 8 キロ進んだ[さらに南下した] We went ahead eight *more* kilometers [went *farther south*]. (● eight more kilometers の代わりに eight kilometers more を用いるのは文語的, ×more eight kilometers は不可)
❷〖その上〗besides, what is more (●後の方が強意的で, 〈話〉ではしばしば what's more と略す), 〈やや書〉moreover; 〈書〉further(more) (● besides や moreover などをすでに用いた後で用いることが多い); (それに加えて)〈やや話〉on top of that (● 不快なことに用いることが多い), in addition (to that). (⇨その上) ●その家は駅からも遠いし, さらに値段が高すぎた The house was a long way from the station, and *on top of that* [(さらに悪いことには) *what's worse, worse still*], it was too expensive.
❸〖再び〗(over) again; (新たに)〈書〉afresh,〈書〉anew. ●彼はさらに試みた He tried *again*. ●三度目をいうときは yet again)/He had *another* try.
❹〖もう一つ〗another. ●さらに 2 週間待つ wait *another* [an *extra*] two weeks.

ざらに ●ざらにある (ありふれた) common. ●ざらにはない (まれな) rare. ●ざらにある出来事 an *everyday* occurrence; a commonplace. ●そのような間違いはざらにある Such mistakes are very *common* [(どこにでも見つかる) are found everywhere].

さらば ●さらば友 *Farewell*, my friends.

サラブレッド a thoroughbred (horse). (● 馬の場合通例 T- で表す)

サラミ salami /səlɑ́:mi/.

ざらめ 粗目 a rough surface.
●粗目糖 granulated sugar; raw sugar. ●粗目雪 corn snow.

さらゆ 新湯 さら湯を使う take a bath first in one's family.

サラリー 〖給料, 月給〗(a) salary; (×a) pay.

サラリーマン a salaried worker [employee] (❗以下の言い方の方が普通); (会社員) an office worker, a company employee; (ホワイトカラー) a white-collar worker; (一般的に) a working adult. (❗(1) 以上のような漠然とした言い方より He works for Sony. や He is an engineer at Sony. などのように具体的会社名や職名をいう方が普通。(2) 日本に住んでいるか生活したことのある米英人はしばしば a salary man というが、これは一種の和製英語)
- サラリーマン金融 (⇨サラ金)

さらりと ❶ [しつこくなく] lightly, plainly, simply. ▶彼女はサラダをいつもさらりとした味付けします She always dresses her salad *simply*.
❷ [思い切って] resolutely; (ためらいもなく) without hesitation. ▶彼は仕事をさらりと辞めてしまった He quit his job *without hesitation*.
❸ [その他の表現] ・さらりとした粉末 *dry* powder. ●手触りがさらりとしている(=なめらかだ) be *smooth* to the touch. ▶彼女はさらりと[=巧みに]その質問をかわした He parried the question *skillfully*. ▶彼女は人柄がさらりとした(=率直な人である) She is a *frank* [an *open-hearted*, (人柄がよい) a *good-natured*] woman.

サランラップ (商標) (米) Sarán Wràp. (⇨ラップ)
サリー a sari, a saree. (❗発音はともに /sάːri/)
ざりがに (動物) a crayfish, (主に米) a crawfish (⛁ ~(s)).
さりげなく さり気ない (⇨何気ない) ・さり気なく(=気取らずに)話す talk *unaffectedly* [(自然に) *naturally*]. ・さり気なく(=むとんちゃくに)言う say *carelessly*.
さりとて 然りとて (しかし) and yet; (それにもかかわらず) nevertheless. ▶私は勝った。さりとてそれが何の役に立ったのか I won, *yet* what good has it done?
サリドマイド (薬学) thalidomide.
・サリドマイド児 a thalidomide baby.
サリン sarin /sάːrin/ (gas). ・猛毒サリンガス the lethal [deadly] gas *sarin*.
さる 去る ❶ [場所・人のもとを離れる] leave*, go* away (*from*); (地位・団体などをやめる) resign (*from*...), (話) quit*; (退職する) (通例定年で) retire (*from*); (辞める) ・東京を去る *leave [go away from]* Tokyo. ・職を去る (職場を) *leave* one's office; (要職を) *resign* one's office; (話) *quit* one's job. ・委員会を去る *leave [resign from]* the committee. (❗resignの方が堅い語。通例団体・機関には from がつく) ・政界を去る *retire from* the political world. ・この世を去る(=死ぬ) die; (婉曲的) pass away. ▶彼は妻のもとを去った He *left* his wife. ▶(彼は妻を残して死んだ,の意になる) ・欲張りすぎると運も去ってしまう(=逃げてしまう) If you try to get too much, the luck might *go away*.
❷ [過ぎ去る] ▶冬が去り今は春だ Winter *has gone* and spring is here (with us). ▶音楽会は去る 10日に行われた The concert *was* held on the tenth of this month. (❗過去形で「去る」の意が表されることがある) ▶彼は去る 5 月に死んだ He died *last* May. (❗ただし、去年の 5 月と誤解されることがあるので、come this May ということもある)
・去る者は追わず Not to pursue a person who wants to leave. ((ことわざ)) Who can hold that will away?
・去る者は日々に疎し ((ことわざ)) Out of sight, out of mind./Seldom seen, soon forgotten.
さる 申 the Monkey.
・申年 (十二支) the year of the Monkey. (⇨干支 関連)

さる 猿 (動物) a monkey /mʌ́ŋki/; (大形で尾のない) an ape.
・猿も木から落ちる 'Even monkeys sometimes fall down from the trees'./((ことわざ)) Even Homer sometimes nods.
●猿ぐつわ a gag. ●猿芝居 a monkey show; (たくらみ) a stupid [a cheap] trick. ●猿知恵 shallow cunning. ●猿回し a monkey entertainer [showman]. ・猿回しの猿 a performing monkey.

ざる 笊 (竹製かご) a bamboo basket [(盆) tray]; (料理用水切り) a colander.
・ざる法 (抜け穴だらけの法律) a loophole-ridden regulation [law].
さるがしま 猿が島 *The Island of Monkeys*. (参考)
さるかにがっせん 猿蟹合戦 *The Quarrel of the Monkey and the Crab*. (参考 日本の昔話)
ざるご 笊碁 unskillful go playing. ・ざる碁を打つ人 a poor go player.
さること 然る事 ・自己犠牲もさることながら、... Self-sacrifice is all very well, but .... ▶それもさることながら、それは疑いもなく最古のスペイン語の詩である *Be that as it may*, it is unquestionably the oldest poem in the Spanish language.
さるすべり 百日紅 (植物) a crape myrtle.
ざるそば 笊蕎麦 *zarusoba*; (説明的に) chilled *soba* served on a basketwork plate with a cup of cold dipping sauce.
ザルツブルグ (オーストリアの都市) Salzburg /sɔ́ːlzbəːrg/.
サルトル (フランスの哲学者・小説家) Sartre /sάːrtrə/ (Jean-Paul /ʒɑːnpɔ́ːl/ ~).
さるのこしかけ 猿の腰掛け (植物) a pore fungus [mushroom]; a shelf fungus.
サルビア (植物) (a) sálvia; (薬用) sage.
サルファざい サルファ剤 (薬学) (米) a sulfa drug, (英) a sulpha drug.
サルベージ salvage /sǽlvidʒ/.
・サルベージ船 a salvage boat.
さるまた 猿股 shorts (米) [underpants (英)] for men.
さるまね 猿真似 ・猿まねをする人 an ape, (話) a copycat. ・猿まねをする ape.
サルモネラ (菌) (a) salmonella.
・サルモネラ食中毒 salmonella food poisoning.
さるもの 去る者 ・さる者 a smart person; (手ごわい相手) a tough negotiator [(俗) customer]; (並でない人) no ordinary person. ▶敵もさる者、そう簡単にはうんと言うもんか He is a real *tough customer*. He won't say yes so readily.
-ざるをえない -ざるを得ない ▶私は計画をあきらめざるを得なかった(=仕方なくあきらめた) I *was compelled* [*was forced*] *to* give up my plan. (❗force を用いる方が強意的)/I *had to* [*had no* (*other*) *choice but to*] give up my plan. ▶彼の冗談に笑わざるを得なかった I *couldn't help* laughing [((主に米式)) *couldn't help but* laugh, (書) *could not but* laugh] at his joke.
ざれうた 戯れ歌 a comic song.
されき 砂礫 gravel.
されこうべ a weatherbeaten skull.
ざれごと 戯れ言 a joke. (⇨冗談) ・され言はさておき *joking* aside.
されど 然れど (⇨しかし)
-される (⇨れる)
サロン a salon; (応接間) a reception hall.
●サロンエプロン a sarong apron.

さわ 沢 [[沼地]] (a) swamp, (a) marsh (⇨沼); [[谷川]] a mountain stream.

サワー [[カクテル]] (a) sour.

サワークリーム sour cream.

さわかい 茶話会 a tea party.

***さわがしい 騒がしい* ❶**[やかましい] noisy. (⇨やかましい) ▶騒がしい教室 a *noisy* classroom. ▶騒がしく noisily. ●騒がしさ noisiness; (騒音) (a) noise. (⇨騒ぎ, 騒音) ▶子供たちは1日中騒がしかった The children *were noisy* all day.

❷[物騒な] troubled. ▶騒がしい世の中 the *troubled* world.

さわがせる 騒がせる [平静・治安などを乱す] disturb. ▶心を騒がせるニュース *disturbing* [(扇情的な) *sensational*] news. ▶お騒がせしてすみません I'm sorry *to have disturbed* you. ▶(大変面倒をかけてすみません) I'm sorry *to have given* you *so much trouble* [*have troubled* you so much]. ▶彼女の死は大いに世間を騒がせた(=センセーションを巻き起こした) Her death *produced* [*caused*] *a great sensation*./Her death was very *sensational*.

さわがに 沢蟹 [[動物]] a small river crab.

さわぎ 騒ぎ ❶[騒がしさ] (a) noise; 《話》a racket (!単数形で). (⇨騒ぐ ❶, どんちゃん騒ぎ) ▶この騒ぎは何事 What's all this *noise* [*racket*] about?/Why are they making so much *noise* [such a *racket*]?

❷[騒動, 混乱] (政治的・社会的暴動) (a) disturbance, 《婉曲的》trouble(s) (!不定冠詞はつけない); (混乱) (a) confusion; (大混乱) (a) panic; (大騒ぎ) (an) uproar (⇨大騒ぎ). ▶学校でちょっとした騒ぎがあった We had a small *disturbance* [some *trouble*(s)] at school. ▶騒ぎが起こった[静まった, 鎮圧された] A *disturbance* arose [settled down; was put down]. ▶情報不足が騒ぎを大きくした Lack of information made the *confusion* [*commotion*] greater. ▶彼らはまた騒ぎを起こした[私を騒ぎに巻き込んだ] They *got* [got me] *into trouble* again. (!警察・教師などの権威者にとがめられるようなことをいう) ▶近所で火事騒ぎがあった There was a fire *panic* in the neighborhood. ▶近所に火事があってパーティーどころの騒ぎではなくなった(=大きくて不可能だった) A fire broke out in my neighborhood and the party was *out of the question*.

さわぎだてる 騒ぎ立てる make* a big [so much] fuss 《over, about》; 《話》make [raise] a big stink 《over, about》.

***さわぐ 騒ぐ ❶**[騒がしくする] make* (a lot of) noise; 《話》carry on, 《話》make [kick up] a racket. ●飲んで歌って騒ぐ enjoy oneself together [《話》make merry] by drinking and singing. (⇨どんちゃん騒ぎ) ▶ひどく騒いでしかられた We were told off for *making* so much *noise*. (!×so many noises は不可) ▶そんなに騒ぐな Don't make so much *noise*. (!Don't make such a noise. は「そんな音を立てるな」の意)

❷[要求・不満を訴えて] clamor 《for, against; to do》. ●金を返せと騒ぐ *clamor for* the money back; *clamor to* pay back the money.

❸[空騒ぎをする] make* [《話》kick up] a fuss 《about, over》. ▶ささいなことでがたがた騒ぐな Don't *make* a big [so much] *fuss about* little things./Don't *fuss about* nothing.

❹[その他の表現] ●胸が騒ぐ (⇨胸騒ぎ) ▶彼は若いころまだいぶん女の子に[マスコミに]騒がれたもので He used to *be* really *popular with* girls [*get* a lot of *attention from* the media] when he was young.

さわさわ ▶さわさわと葉のそよぐ音がする I hear a *soft rustle* of leaves [the sound of leaves *rustling softly*].

ざわざわ 副 ▶ざわざわ音がする (物がこすれ合って) rustle (⇨ざわざわ); (小声で話す) murmur. ▶どこまでも続くトウモロコシ畑を風がざわざわ音をたてて渡る The wind *rustled* the endless field of corn. ▶この部屋はざわざわしている(=うるさい) This room is *noisy*.

> **翻訳のこころ** 風がどうと吹いてきて、草はざわざわ、木の葉はかさかさ、木はごとんごとんと鳴りました (宮沢賢治『注文の多い料理店』) When the wind blew, the grass made rustling sounds; the tree leaves, dry sounds; and the trees, heavy knocking sounds. (!英語には「ざわざわ」「かさかさ」「ごとんごとん」にあたる擬音語はないので, sound をそれぞれの音を表す形容詞で修飾する)

— ざわざわする 動 ▶聴衆は講演者が現れるとざわざわするのをやめた The audience stopped *murmuring* [*talking*] when the speaker showed up.

ざわつく [[やかましくなる]] get* noisy; [[がやがや言う]] buzz. ▶その知らせで教室がざわついた The classroom *got noisy* [*buzzed*] with the news./The news *caused a stir* in the classroom.

ざわめく ●ざわめく声 a buzz [a hum] of conversation; (ざわついた声) a stir (!「ざわめき立つ声」は a great stir; (さわぎ立てる声) (an) uproar. ▶町中がそのニュースでざわめいていた(=大騒ぎをしていた) The whole town *was astir with* the news./(興奮してさわいでいた) The whole town *was buzzing with excitement* because of the news. (!「ニュース」を主語にして The news caused a *stir* in the town. などのようにもいえる)

***さわやか 爽やか —爽やかな* 形 ❶**[すがすがしい] fresh, refreshing. ▶さわやかな朝の空気 *fresh* [*refreshing*] morning air. ●さわやかな秋の朝 a *nice* (and) *cool* [(ひんやりと身のひきしまるような) a *cool and crisp*] autumn morning. ▶ひと眠りしたので気分がさわやかになった I felt *refreshed* [*fresh and fit*] after a nap. ▶冷たい水を飲むとさわやかな気分になった A glass of cold water *refreshed* me.

❷[弁舌が] (言いたいことをはっきりと力強く伝えられる) eloquent; (言葉などを上手に話せる) fluent. ●弁舌さわやかな人 a *fluent* speaker. (⇨弁舌)

さわら 椹 [[植物]] a *sawara* cypress.

さわら 鰆 [[魚介]] a Spanish mackerel (複 ~(s)). (!その肉は [U])

さわり 触り [[the best]] [最も印象的な] most impressive] part, the climax.

さわり 障り [[障害]] an obstacle, a hindrance (⇨障害); [[悪い影響]] a bad effect, harm. ▶このパーティーに私が参加してもさわりはないでしょうか Will I [it] cause any inconvenience [trouble], if I come to the party? / Can [May] I come to the party? (!後の方が会話としては自然)

***さわる 触る* [[接触する]] touch; (さわって知る) feel*. (⇨触れる) ▶体を前に折って爪先に指が触れますか Can you bend down to *touch* your toes with your fingers? ▶足に何かさわった I felt something *touch* [×touched] my foot./I felt *a touch* on my foot. ▶それはさわると冷たい It *feels cold*./It is cold *to the touch*. ▶彼女はしこりが出来ていないか乳房をさわってみた She *felt* her breasts to see if there were any lumps. ▶さわるべからず 《掲示》Hands off./Don't *touch*.

●触らぬ神にたたりなし 《ことわざ》Let sleeping dogs lie.

***さわる 障る ❶**[健康を害する] be bad 《for》, be harmful 《to》; (悪い影響を与える) affect. ▶夜ふかし

をすると体にさわります Staying up late (at night) will *be bad for* your health [《話》*for* you]./ Staying up late (at night) will *affect* your health.
❷ [感情を害する] hurt* one's feelings; (いらだたせる) irritate; (不愉快にさせる) annoy; (怒らせる) offend. ▶騒音が神経にさわった The noise *got on my nerves*.

さわんとうしゅ 左腕投手 〖野球〗a left-hander, a left-handed pitcher, a southpaw.

*さん 三 three;〖3番目の〗the third. ▶京都の三大祭り the *three* biggest festivals of Kyoto.

さん 桟 〖横木〗a crosspiece;〖障子・戸の骨〗(障子の) a frame, (戸の) a bolt. ▶戸の桟を下ろす *bolt* the door.

さん 算 〖算木〗(⇨算木);〖計算〗calculation, reckoning.
● 算を乱す (列がばらばらになる) be in total [utter] confusion.

さん 酸 〖化学〗(an) acid; (酸類) acids.

さん 賛, 讃 〖人・事物をほめる文〗〖書〗a panegyric, (a) eulogy. ▶ビートルズ賛 a *tribute* to the Beatles.
❷ [絵に書き入れた文章] ●絵に賛を入れる add an *inscription* to a picture.

*-さん 〖男〗Mr. (徽 Messrs.);〖女〗(未婚) Miss; (既婚) Mrs. (徽 Mmes.); Ms. /míz/ (徽 Mses., Ms's) (未婚・既婚の区別が不明または不要な場合にも用いる). ⚠
(1) Miss にはピリオドをつけない. (2)《英》では Mr., Mrs., Ms. およびその複数形のピリオドを省略することが多い. (3) 職業によっては Mr. Driver (運転手さん) などとして用いる ●鈴木(薫)さん Mr. [*Miss, Mrs., Ms.*] (Kaoru) Suzuki. (⚠ 日本語では名だけの場合にはつけない: 薫さん ×Mr.) Kaoru. (2) 複数形は the *Miss* Suzukis, the two *Miss* Suzuki(s) (2人のお姉さん)のようにいう。the *Misses* Suzuki は《古》) ●鈴木さんと田中さん (男性2人) *Mr.* Suzuki and *Mr.* Tanaka; *Messrs*. Suzuki and Tanaka. ●田中さんご夫妻 *Mr.* and *Mrs.* Tanaka [xTanakas].
▶小田さんこんにちは Good afternoon, *Mr.* Oda. (語法) (1) 米英では親しい間柄の呼びかけに敬称をつけず名を用いる: Hello, Kenji. (2) 姓名で呼びかけるのは不自然: ×Hello, Kenji Oda.) ▶留守中に伊藤さんという方がお見えになりましたよ *A Mr.* Ito came to see you while you were out. (⚠ 自分の知らない人をいうときは a をつける) ▶お父さんによろしく Please say hello to your father.

-さん -山 Mt. ~, Mount ~. ●富士山 (×the) *Mt*. [*Mount*, ×Mountain] Fuji. (⚠ (1)《英》では *Mt* Fuji のようにピリオドを省略するのが普通。(2) 二つ以上の山をいう場合は Mounts Fuji and Asama)

-さん -産 ●北海道産のジャガイモ potatoes *from* Hokkaido. ●県産のたばこ (県)の tobacco *produced* in the prefecture. ●外国 [内地] 産のオレンジ *foreign-grown* [*home-grown*] oranges.

さんい 賛意 ●賛意を示す express (うなずいて) nod (-dd-)] one's approval (*to*). (⇨賛成 ❷)

さんいつ 散逸 — 散逸する 動 be scattered and lost; 〖書〗be scattered to the (four) winds.

さんいん 参院 [『参議院』の略] (⇨参議院)

さんいん 産院 a maternity home [hospital].

ざんえい 残映 ●〖夕映え, 夕焼け〗 the evening glow.
❷ [名残] a vestige. ▶その場所はジョージ王朝の華やかさの残映をまだ十分に保っていた The place still retained sufficient *afterglow* from its Georgian gaiety.

サンオイル 〖日焼け止めオイル〗suntan oil [lotion].

(⚠ sun lotion [oil] ということもある)

:**さんか** 参加 图 participátion (*in*).
— 参加する 動 take* part (*in*), 《やや書》participate (*in*) (⚠ 日常会話では come*, go* が用いられることも多い); (行われているスポーツ・会議などに) join (*in*); (競技会などに) go in (*for*); (競技などに参加を申し込む) enter (for...). (⇨加わる) ●討論会に参加する take part [*participate*, *join*] in a discussion. ●クラブ活動に積極的に参加する *take an active part* [be actively *involved*] in club activities. ●テニス部の夏の合宿に参加する (=行く) *go to* the summer training camp of one's tennis club. ●ゴルフに参加する *take part in* [×join] the golf. (⚠ ゴルフは途中から参加はできないので join は不適切) ▶私どもの京都へのバス旅行に参加なさいますか Are you *coming* on [×for] our bus trip to Kyoto?
● 参加国 a participating nation. ● 参加者 《やや書》a partícipant (*in*); (競技の参加申し込み者) an entrant (*for*); an entry (*for*). ▶レースの参加者は何人ですか How many *entrants* [*entries*] are there for the race?/How many competitors *have entered* (*for*) [*gone in for*] the race?

さんか 山高 roving mountain tribes, mountain nomads.

さんか 惨禍 a (terrible) disaster. ▶terrible は冗言的として避ける人もいる ●戦争の惨禍 the *ravages* /rǽvidʒiz/ of a war.

さんか 産科 〖医学〗obstetrics /əbstétriks/. (⚠ 単数扱い) (⇨病院)
● 産科医 an òbstetrícian. ● 産科病院 a maternity hospital. ● 産科病棟 a maternity ward.

さんか 傘下 — 傘下の 形 〖子会社の〗subsidiary; 〖系列下の〗affiliated. ●東芝傘下の会社 the *subsidiary* [*affiliated*] companies of Toshiba.
●共産党の傘下に入る come *under the umbrella* [(影響) *the influence*, (支配) *the control*] of the Communist Party.

さんか 酸化 图 〖化学〗oxidation /ɑksidéiʃən/; oxidization /ɑksədaizéiʃən/.
— 酸化する 動 oxidize /ɑksədàiz/.
● 酸化鉄 iron oxide. ● 酸化物 an oxide /ɑksaid/.

さんか 賛歌 a song of praise. ●愛の賛歌 (=愛をたたえる歌) a *song in praise of* love.

さんが 山河 mountains and rivers.

さんが 参賀 a New Year's visit to the Imperial Palace. ●参賀に行く visit the Imperial Palace (and see the Emperor) to celebrate the New Year.

さんかい 山海 ●山海の珍味 all kinds of delicacies.

さんかい 山塊 〖地学〗a massif. ●モンブラン山塊 the Mont Blanc *Massif*.

さんかい 散会 — 散会する 動 (解散する) break up; (閉会する) close; (一定期間の延期・休会する) adjourn.

さんがい 三界 (この世) this whole world.
● 三界に家なし ●女三界に家なし Women are not allowed to lead an easy life in this whole world./Women have no place to settle in.
● 三界の首枷 ●子は三界の首枷 One's children will be a burden as long as one lives.

さんがい 三階 《米》the third floor; 《英》the second floor. (⇨階)

さんがい 惨害 (⇨惨禍)

ざんがい 残骸 remains; (乗り物・建物の) a wreck, (集合的) wreckage; (廃墟(きょ)) ruins. ▶飛行機の残骸 the *remains* of a wrecked plane; the

さんかいき 三回忌 《*on*》 the second anniversary of 《his》 death.
さんかいしゃ 参会者 an attendant (at a meeting).
***さんかく** 三角 図 a triangle. ● 三角形の頂点[底辺; 高さ] the vertex [base; altitude] of a *triangle*. ● 目を三角にする(=怒ってにらみつける) look angrily at 《him》. 《話》 look daggers at 《him》. ▶正三角形の三辺は等しい All sides of an equilateral *triangle* are the same length [equal in length]. (!) 底辺以外の辺は a leg)
── 三角(形)の 形 triangular. ● 三角形の布[鏡] a *triangle* of cloth [mirror, ×a mirror]. ● 逆三角形の(=ハート型の)顔 a *heart-shaped* face. ▶パイは三角形の小片に切り分けられた The pie was divided into *triangular* pieces.
● 三角関係 a love [the eternal] triangle. ● 三角関数 〘数学〙 a trigonométric(al) function. ● 三角巾 a sling, a triangular bandage. ▶ 彼は左腕を三角巾でつっていた His left arm was in a *sling*. ● 三角筋 〘解剖〙 a deltoid muscle. ● 三角コーナー (流しの) a sink strainer. ● 三角州 a delta. ● 三角錐 〘数学〙 a triangular pyramid. ● 三角測量 triangulation. ● 三角測量する triangulate. ● 三角点 〘測量〙 a triangulation point. ● 三角柱 〘数学〙 a triangular prism. ● 三角定規 《米》 a triangle; 《英》 a set square. ● 三角波 a choppy wave.
さんかく 参画 ── 参画する 動 take part [《やや書》 participate] 《*in*》. (⇨参加する)
さんがく 山岳 mountains.
● 山岳地帯 a mountainous /máuntənəs/ district [region]. ● 山岳部 a mòuntainéering [a mountain climbers', an alpine] club.
さんがく 産学 ● 産学協同 industry-university cooperation; academic-industrial collaboration. ● 産学共同研究 a joint industry-university research project.
ざんがく 残額 (差引残高) the balance; (残った金額) the remainder, the remains; 〘借金の未払い分〙 arrears.
さんかしゅう 『山家集』 *The Mountain Hermitage.* (参考) 西行の歌集
***さんがつ** 三月 March (略 Mar.). (⇨一月) ● 3月に in *March*. ● 3月3日に on *March* 3. (!) on March (the) third と読む)
さんがにち 三箇日 the first three days of the new year.
さんかん 山間 ● 山間のへき地 a secluded place *in* [*among*] *the mountains*. ● 山間の村 a *mountain* village.
● 山間部 a mountainous /máuntənəs/ area.
さんかん 参観 ● 参観する 動 visit; (観察する) observe. ▶私は息子の授業を参観した I *visited* [*observed*] my son's class.
● 参観者 a visitor. ● 参観日 (授業参観日) a parents' observation day; an open house 《米》 [day 《英》].
さんかんおう 三冠王 ● 三冠王になる 〘野球〙 get [win, take] the *triple crown*.
さんかんしおん 三寒四温 (説明的に) a cycle of three cold days and four warm days (in wintertime).
さんかんば 三冠馬 a Triple Crown horse.
さんき 山気 bracing mountain air; crisp, fresh mountain air.
さんぎ 算木 (占いに使う) divining sticks [blocks].
ざんき 慚愧 ● 慚愧の涙 〘shed〙 tears of *remorse*

[*shame*]. ● 慚愧(の念)に堪えない be filled [be overcome] with *remorse* 《*for*》; be deeply ashamed of oneself.
さんぎいん 参議院 the House of Councilors; the Upper House.
● 参議院議員 a member of the House of Councilors; a Councilor. ● 参議院議長 the President of the House of Councilors; the Upper House President.
ざんぎく 残菊 the last chrysanthemums of the season.
さんきゃく 三脚 a tripod /tráipad/. ● 三脚を立てる set up a *tripod*.
ざんぎゃく 残虐 図 atrocity; (残忍) brutality (!) いずれも「残虐な行為」の意では通例複数形で); 〘残酷〙 (a) cruelty (⇨残酷). ● 戦争中行われた数多くの残虐行為 many *atrocities* [acts of *atrocity*] which were committed during the war. ● 警察の黒人に対する残虐行為 police *brutalities* against black people.
── 残虐な 形 ● 残虐な犯罪 an *atrocious* crime.
さんきゅう 産休 maternity leave, leave for childbirth. ● 産休を取っている be on *maternity leave*. ● 産休に入る go on *maternity leave*. ▶ケイトは3か月間の産休を取った Kate took three months' *maternity leave*.
サンキュー Thanks (a lot) (!) (1) 軽い調子の言い方。a lot は口ぐせでいう人が多い。(2) Thank you. は日本語でいうほど軽い表現ではない) (⇨ありがとう)
さんきょう 山峡 a gorge, a ravine.
***さんぎょう** 産業 図 (an) industry. (!) 「産業部門」の意では [C]. ● 第一[二; 三]次産業 the primary [secondary; tertiary] *industry*. ● 基幹産業 a key *industry*. ● 次世代産業 the next-generation industry. ▶観光がその町の主要な産業だ Tourism is the chief [major, main] *industry* of the town.

┌─────────────────────────────────────┐
│ 〘関連〙 主な産業: アパレル産業 the clothing in- │
│ dustry/観光産業 the travel [tourist, lei- │
│ sure] industry/軍需産業 the munitions in- │
│ dustry/鋼鉄産業 the steel industry/コンピュー │
│ タ産業 the computer industry/自動車産業   │
│ the auto(mobile) industry/情報産業 the in- │
│ formation industry/繊維産業 the textile in- │
│ dustry/バイオ産業 the bioindustry; the bio- │
│ tech industry/ハイテク産業 the high-tech in- │
│ dustry/リース産業 the leasing industry.   │
└─────────────────────────────────────┘

── 産業の 形 indústrial. (!) industrious は「勤勉な」) ● 産業の合理化 the rationalization of *industry*. ● 産業の育成 industrial development. ▶産業の発展が途上国には欠かせない The development of *industry* [The *industrial development*] is essential to developing countries.
● 産業界 the industrial world; (産業人) industry (!) 集合的に用い単数扱い). ● 産業革命 the Industrial Revolution. ● 産業活動 industrial activity [activities]. ● 産業基盤 (an) industrial infrastructure. ● 産業別組合 an industrial [a vertical] union. ● 産業構造 an industrial structure. ● 産業資本 industrial capital. ● 産業スパイ (人) an industrial spy; (行為) industrial espionage. ● 産業廃棄物 industrial waste. ● 産業排水 industrial wastewater. ● 産業用ロボット an industrial robot; a steel collar (worker).
さんぎょう 蚕業 sericulture, the sericultural industry. (⇨養蚕)
ざんきょう 残響 (a) reverberation. (!) 通例複数形

ざんぎょう 　て）．●**残響時間** reverberation time. ●**残響室** a reverberation room.

ざんぎょう 残業 图 overtime work. ●サービス残業 unpaid overtime work.

── **残業する** 動 work [do] overtime; (会社で遅くまで働く) work late at the office. ●2時間残業して work two hours *overtime*; do two hours' *overtime*. ▶彼は毎月相当量の残業をする He does a lot of *overtime* every month. ●**残業時間** overtime. ●**残業手当** overtime pay [payment].

さんきょく 三曲 (説明的に) an ensemble of three musical instruments: *koto, shamisen* and *shakuhachi*.

ざんきん 残金 〚残った金〛 the money left over (❗×the left-over money とはいわない); 〚差引残高〛 the balance. ●残金を支払う pay *the balance* [〚残り〛*the remainder*].

さんきんこうたい 参勤交代 〚歴史〛(説明的に) a system of alternate attendance under which feudal lords were forced to go up to Edo and reside there to serve the *shogun* in alternate year.

サンクスギビングデー Thanksgiving Day.

サンクチュアリー 〚聖域〛 a sanctuary.

サングラス 《a pair of》 sunglasses, dark glasses. (⇨眼鏡) ●サングラスをかけている wear *sunglasses*. ●サングラスの男 a *dark-glassed* man; a man with *dark glasses* on.

さんぐん 三軍 〚全軍〛 the armed forces; 〚陸軍・海軍・空軍の総称〛 the army, the navy and air force.

さんけ 産気 ●産気づく start [go into] labor; begin having a baby. ●産気づいている be in labor.

ざんげ 懺悔 图 〚悔い〛(書) repentance, penitence; 〚告白〛 confession.

── **懺悔する** 動 go to confession; confess (one's sins) *to* a priest); repent (*of*).

さんけい 山系 a mountain range. ●大雪山系 the Daisetsu *Mountain Range*.

さんけい 参詣 ●参詣する visit (*to*). (⇨参拝)

さんげき 惨劇 〚惨事〛 a tragedy; (大きな) a disaster, a calamity; 〚流血事件〛(やや書) bloodshed.

さんけつ 酸欠 a lack [a shortage] of oxygen; an oxygen shortage. ●酸欠になる be starved [deprived] of *oxygen*. ●酸欠で死ぬ die from *lack of oxygen*.

ざんげつ 残月 a morning moon, the moon at dawn.

さんげつき 『山月記』 *Tiger Poet*. (参考 中島敦の小説)

さんけん 散見 ▶あちこちにその動物の足跡が散見された Here and there I found traces of the animal.

さんげん 三弦 〚『三味線』の別称〛(⇨三味線)

ざんげん 讒言 图 (a) slander; a false charge.

── **讒言する** 動 slander; make a false charge (*against*).

さんげんしょく 三原色 the three primary colors.

さんけんぶんりつ 三権分立 the separation of the three powers (of the executive, the legislature and the judiciary).

さんこ 三顧 ●**三顧の礼** ●三顧の礼をもって with *great courtesy*.

さんご 珊瑚 〚動物〛 coral. ●サンゴを採集する fish for *coral*.

●**サンゴ珠** a coral bead. ●**サンゴ礁** a coral reef; 〚環礁〛 an átoll. ●**サンゴ虫** a coral.

さんご 産後 ●産後1週間で退院する leave (the) hospital (×in) a week *after delivery* [(やや書) *childbirth*]. ▶彼女は産後の肥立ちがとても悪い She has hardly recovered *from the birth of* her *last baby*. ▶母子とも産後の経過は順調である Mother and child are both doing well *after delivery* [×childbirth].

＊**さんこう** 参考 reference; 〚情報〛 information.

①〚参考のため〛●後々の参考のためそれをファイルしておく file it *for future reference*. ▶ご参考のため新製品の見本をお送りします *For your information*, we take pleasure in sending you a sample of the new product.

②〚参考にする〛●その課題に関して数冊の本を参考にする (=参照する) *refer to* [*make reference to, consult*] several books on the subject. (❗いずれも堅い言い方で, 日常会話では use [see] several books ... が普通) ●彼の意見を参考にする (=考慮する) *take* his suggestions *into account* [*consideration*]; (活用する) *make use of* his suggestions. ●参考になる (=役に立つ)情報 *useful* [*helpful*] information. ▶なるほど,参考になりますね Well, that's something./Well, that sounds *useful* [*helpful*]. ▶それはあなたが彼らの考え方を理解する上で参考になる (=助けになる)でしょう It will *help* you (to) understand their ways of thinking. (❗(話)では to は省略されることが多い) ▶これはあの小説を書いたときに参考に見た地図です These are the maps I *referred to* when I wrote that novel.

会話 「どんな車でしたか」「トヨタです」「色は」「シルバーグレー,それぐらいしか覚えていません」「奥さん,ありがとうございます. 大変参考になります」"What kind of car was it?" "A Toyota." "What color?" "Silver gray. And that's really all I remember, officer." "Thank you, ma'am. You've been a big *help*."

●**参考意見** a reliable opinion. ●**参考書** (参考図書) a reference book; (学習参考書) a study aid. ●**参考書目** a bibliography. ●**参考資料** reference material (*for*). ●**参考人** (証人) a witness (*for*). (❗(国会の)「参考人」は an unsworn witness, 「証人」は a sworn witness という)

●**参考文献** a reference.

さんこう 山行 〚山の中を歩いていくこと〛 a walk in the mountains; mountain climbing. ; 〚山の中に遊びに行くこと〛 a hike, hiking.

ざんこう 残光 an afterglow.

ざんごう 塹壕 ●塹壕を掘る dig a *trench*.

さんごく 三国 (三つの国) three countries [powers]; (世界) the (whole) world. ●彼女は三国一の幸せ者だ She's the happiest [luckiest] person in the whole world. ●**三国協定** a tripartite agreement. ●**三国間貿易**(取引) tripartite [trilateral] trade. ●**三国同盟** a triple alliance; (第二次世界大戦時の日独伊の) the Tripartite Pact.

＊**ざんこく** 残酷 图 cruelty; 〚けだもののような残忍さ〛 brutality; 〚残虐〛 atrocity. (❗いずれも「残酷な行為」の意では通例複数形で使う〚虐待, 残虐〛)

●**残酷** 形 cruel; brutal; atrocious; (無慈悲な) merciless. ●残酷な独裁者 a *cruel* [a *brutal*, a *merciless*] tyrant. ●動物を残酷に扱うな Don't treat animals *cruelly*./Don't be *cruel* to animals. ●その犬をけるなんて君は残酷だよ It is *cruel* of [×for] you [You are *cruel*] to kick the dog.

さんこつ 散骨 the dispersal of one's ashes.

サンサーンス 〚フランスの作曲家〛 Saint-Saëns /sænsá:ns/ (Camille ～).

さんさい 山菜 edible wild plants [grass].

さんさい 山塞, 山砦 a mountain stronghold [fort].

さんざい 散在 ── **散在する** 動 be scattered (❗物が主語);〔点在する〕be dotted 《with》(❗場所が主語)(⇨点在).・散在する家々 *scattered* houses.・日光浴をしている人が散在している海岸 the beach *dotted with* sunbathers. ▶ 公園にはごみが散在していた Trash *was scattered around* in the park./ The park *was littered with* trash.

さんざい 散財 ── **散財する** 動 spend a lot of money 《on》;〔浪費する〕waste [squander] money 《on》.・ずいぶん散財させて申し訳ありません I'm sorry to have *put* you *to so much expense*. ▶ 大変な散財だったでしょう It must have *cost a fortune*. (❗ a fortune は《話》「多額の金」の意)

ざんざい 斬罪 beheading, decapitation.・斬罪に処する behead, decapitate.

さんさく 散策 图 a walk;(ゆっくりとくつろいだ) a stroll;(目的もなく広範囲の) a ramble. (⇨散歩)
── **散策する** 動 ▶ しばらく公園を散策した I *took a walk* [*a stroll*] in the park for a while.

さんざし 山査子〖植物〗(木) a hawthorn (tree); (花) hawthorn.

さんさしんけい 三叉神経〖解剖〗the trigeminal nerve.
・三叉神経痛〖医学〗trigeminal neuralgia.

ざんさつ 惨殺 图 a brutal [a cruel] murder.
── **惨殺する** 動 murder 《him》brutally [cruelly]. ▶ 彼は昨夜惨殺された He *was brutally murdered* last night.

さんざっぱら 散々っ腹〖「さんざん」の強意語〗(⇨散々)

さんざめく make merry.・子供たちのさんざめく声 the *merry* [*cheerful*] voices of children.

さんさろ 三叉路 a three-way junction [intersection].

さんさん 燦々 ・日差しがさんさんと差し込む居間 a *sunwashed* living room.・太陽がさんさんと(=明るく) 輝く The sun shines *bright(ly)* [〔まぶしく〕*brilliantly*].

さんざん 散々 〔徹底的に〕completely, thoroughly; 〔ひどく〕badly, terribly; 〔激しく〕severely; 〔まったく〕quite; 〔容赦なく〕mercilessly.・にわか雨でさんざんな(=ひどい)目にあう have a *hard* time (of it) in a shower.・さんざん(=ありとあらゆる)不平を並べる make *all sorts of* complaints. ▶ 私たちのチームはさんざん打ち負かされた Our team was *completely* [*thoroughly*] beaten. ▶ 私はそのことでさんざんしかられた I was *severely* told off for it./《話》I got a *good* telling-off for it. ▶ さんざん待たされた I was kept waiting 《for》 such [*quite*] *a long time*. ▶ 彼は私にさんざん(=多大の)迷惑をかけた He gave me *a great deal of* [*a lot of*] trouble.
会話「どうだった？」「さんざんだったよ」"How did you get on?" "*Terribly*."

さんさんくど 三三九度; *sansan-kudo*;（説明的に）a ceremony in which the bride and bridegroom sip *sake* three times from each of the three cups and make their pledge of matrimony.・新郎新婦は三三九度の杯を交わした The bride and bridegroom exchanged *sake* cups to seal their vow.

さんさんごご 三々五々・三々五々に by [in] twos and threes.・客は1人で来る人も、三々五々連れ立って来る人たちもいた Guests arrived in ones, *twos and threes*.

さんじ 三時 3時(=おやつ)にしよう Let's have (*afternoon*) *tea*.

さんじ 参事 a (chief) advisor (to the director);（参事官）a councilor.

さんじ 惨事〖突発的な大災害〗a disaster;〖悲劇的事件〗a tragedy.・交通の大惨事 a traffic *disaster*; a terrible traffic accident.

さんじ 賛辞 (a) tribute (of praise); praise.・賛辞を呈する speak *words of praise* 《to》; pay a *compliment* 《to him, on his courage》; pay *tribute* 《to him for his courage》.

ざんし 残滓 (残りかす) leavings;（コーヒーなどの）dregs.・奴隷制度の残滓(=名残) the *vestiges* of slavery.

ざんし 惨死 图 (a) violent death.
── **惨死する** 動 meet a violent death.

ざんじ 暫時 (⇨しばらく)

さんしきすみれ 三色菫〖植物〗a pansy.

さんじげん 三次元 three dimensions.
── **三次元の** 形 three-dimensional 《space》(略 three-D, 3-D).

さんしすいめい 山紫水明 scenic beauty.・山紫水明の地 a *scenic* spot.

さんじせいげん 産児制限 (practice of) birth control.

さんしつ 産室 a maternity room; (分娩室) a delivery room.

さんしゃ 三者 three people [persons].・三者間伝達のシステム a system of *three-way* communication.・三者凡退に打ち取る〖野球〗retire the side in order [in one, two, three].・三者三様の結論に達した Each of the three reached his own conclusion.
・三者会談 a tripartite meeting.

さんじゃく 三尺・三尺下がって師の影を踏まず Always have respect for your teacher(s).
・三尺の秋水(さんすい) a sharp long sword.

さんじゅ 傘寿 one's 80th year [birthday]. (⇨還暦)

ざんしゅ 斬首 图 beheading; (切られた首) a decapitated head.
── **斬首する** 動 behead, decapitate.

さんしゅう 参集 (⇨集まる, 集合)

*__さんじゅう 三十__ thirty;〖30番目の〗the thirtieth. (⇨二十, 五十)

さんじゅう 三重 ── **三重の** 形 triple. (⇨二重)・三重の塔 a *three-storied* pagoda.・三重にする triple.
・三重苦 a triple handicap.・三重奏〖音楽〗a trio /tríou/ (複 ～s).

さんしゅうき 三周忌 (⇨三回忌)

さんじゅうさんかいき 三十三回忌・父の三十三回忌 the 32nd anniversary of my father's death.

さんじゅうさんしょ 三十三所 the 33 temples sacred to the Kannon, Buddhist saint.

さんじゅうしょう 三重唱 a trio.

さんじゅうろっかせん 三十六歌仙 the 36 great poets (of the Heian period).

さんじゅうろっけい 三十六計・三十六計逃げるにしかず The best way to do is to run away.

さんしゅつ 産出 图 production; (産出量[高]) (an) output.・石炭の年間産出量 the annual *output* of coal.・石油産出国 an oil producer; an oil-*producing* country.
── **産出する** 動 produce; yield. ▶ この鉱山はダイヤモンドを産出する This mine *produces* diamond.

さんしゅつ 算出 图 calculation, computation.
── **算出する** 動 calculate, compute; work [figure] ... out 《the cost》. ▶ 私たちは1週間の出費を算出した We *calculated* our weekly expenditure.

さんじゅつ 算術 arithmetic. (⇨算数)
・算術平均〖数学〗an arithmetic(al) mean.

さんしゅのじんぎ 三種の神器 (天皇家の) the three sacred imperial treasures, the mirror, the sword and the jewel). ▶ デジカメ・薄型テレビ・DVD

レコーダーが現代の三種の神器と呼ばれている A digital camera, a Flat Screen TV, and a DVD recorder are the three most wanted items of people today.

さんじょ 賛助 ● 賛助出演する appear as a guest performer.
● **賛助会員** a suppórting mèmber. ● **賛助会費** a supporting membership fee.

ざんしょ 残暑 the heat of late summer. ▶日中は残暑まだ厳しく、秋とは名ばかりである The *heat of* day is still severe though it's already autumn in calendar.

***さんしょう 参照** 图 reference ⟨*to*⟩. ● 相互参照 (a) cross-reference. ▶詳細は第9節参照 For details, *see* §9. (❗ §は section と読む) ▶次例参照 Compare [*Cf.*; *Cp.*] the following examples. (❗ cf. はラテン語 *confer* の略で *compare* と読む。cp. は *compare* の略)
── **参照する** 動 [調べる] refer (-rr-) to ..., consult; [見る] see*; (特定のページ・書籍などを) turn to ...; [比較する] compare. ▶単語の意味を調べるために辞書を参照する *refer to* [*consult*] a dictionary *for* the meaning of a word (❗ 堅い言い方で, 日常会話では use [see] a dictionary and find out the meaning ... などの方が普通); (辞書で単語を調べる) *look up* a word *in* a dictionary. ▶30 ページの16行目を参照せよ *Refer* [*Make reference*] *to* page 30, line 16.

さんしょう 三唱 ● 万歳三唱 three cheers. (⇨万歳)
▶彼らは彼の健康のために乾杯し、万歳を三唱した They drank to his health, and they gave him three cheers.

さんしょう 山椒 [植物] (木) a Japanese pepper tree; (香辛料) Japanese pepper. [参考] サンショウ属には a prickly ash (アメリカサンショウ) という木があるが、この木は皮を歯の鎮痛剤に使う。日本とは用途が違う)
● **山椒は小粒でもぴりりと辛い** (ことわざ) (よいものは小さい個に入ってくる) Good things come in small packages.

さんじょう 三乗 图 [数学] cube. ● 3 乗根 the *cube root* (*of*). ● 3 の 3 乗は 27 The *cube* of 3 is 27./3 *cubed* is 27.
── **三乗する** 動 cube.

さんじょう 参上 ── **参上する** 動 visit. ▶明日参上いたします We will *visit* you tomorrow.

さんじょう 惨状 [ひどい光景] a terrible sight [spectacle]; [ひどい状態] a miserable condition [state]. ● 惨状を呈する present a *terrible* [a *horrible*] *sight*.

ざんしょう 残照 an afterglow. ▶残照の上に小さく輝く月が見えた I saw a very brilliant little moon shining above the *afterglow*.

さんしょううお 山椒魚 [動物] a (giant) salamander.

さんしょううお 『山椒魚』 *Salamander*. [参考] 井伏鱒二の小説)

さんしょうだゆう 『山椒大夫』 *Sansho the Steward*. [参考] 森鷗外の小説)

さんじょうのすいくん 山上の垂訓 【聖書】 the Sermon on the Mount.

さんしょく 三色 ── **三色の** 形 three-color; tricolor(ed).
● **三色旗** a tricolor; (フランス国旗) the Tricolor.

さんしょく 蚕食 图 encroachment; inroads.
── **蚕食する** 動 encroach ⟨*on*⟩; make inroads ⟨*into*, *on*⟩.

さんじょく 産褥 [書] confinement. ● 産褥に就くbe confined to bed.

● **産褥期** a lying-in period, 【医学】 puerperium.
● **産褥熱** 【医学】 puerperal [childbed] fever.

さんしょくすみれ 三色菫 (⇨三色(さんしき)菫)

さんじる 参じる [参上する] (⇨参上); [参加する] participate ⟨*in*⟩.

さんじる 散じる [散り散りになる] disperse, scatter; [なくす, 散らす] (金を) squander; (痛みを) kill.

さんしろう 『三四郎』 *Sanshiro*. [参考] 夏目漱石の小説)

┌─ **古今ことばの系譜** **『三四郎』** ─┐
すると男が、こう言った。(略)「日本より頭の中のほうが広いでしょう」と言った。「とらわれちゃだめだ。いくら日本のためを思ったって贔屓の引き倒しになるばかりだ」 But then the man said ... Don't ever surrender yourself — not to Japan, not to anything. You may think that what you're doing is for the sake of the nation, but let something take possession of you like that, and all you do is bring it down. (Jay Rubin) ❗
(1) 日露戦争の勝利のあと強まり出した自国を尊大視する傾向に警告を発した言葉。 (2)「囚われる」は「敵に囚伏して囚われる」の意ではなく「小さいことに執着し広く物事を見ることをしない」という意味と思われる。そうすると Don't stick to something particular — neither to Japan, nor to anything. などと訳せる。
└──────────────────┘

さんしん 三振 图 【野球】 a strikeout. ● 奪三振王 a *strikeout* king. ● 200 奪三振 200 *strikeouts*.
● 15 三振を奪う *strike out* 15 (batters); get 15 *strikeouts*. ● 速球で三振に打ち取る *strike* ⟨*him*⟩ *out* with a fastball.
── **三振(を)する** 動 strike out; be [get] struck out; fan. ● 空振りの三振をする be struck out *swinging*. ● 3球三振をくらう *be struck out on* three *pitches*. ▶彼は見逃し(=見送り)の三振をした He was called out on strikes./He struck out looking. (❗「見逃しの三振」は a called strikeout; strike three called)

さんしん 三線 a *sanshin*, an Okinawa's snakeskin *samisen*.

ざんしん 斬新 ── **斬新な** 形 (新しい) new; (独創的な) original; (新鮮な) fresh; (新奇な) novel. (⇨新しい)
● **斬新な発想** an *original* [a *novel*, a *fresh*] idea.

さんしんとう 三親等 the third degree of kinship. (⇨親等)

さんすい 山水 ● 山水画 a landscape painting (in Eastern Asia). ● 山水画家 a landscape painter.

さんすい 散水 ── **散水する** 動 sprinkle water ⟨*on*, *over*⟩.
● **散水装置** a sprinkler.

さんすう 算数 arithmetic; (数学) mathematics,《米話》math,《英話》maths; (単純な計算) 《do》 sums. ● 算数の練習問題をする do exercises in *arithmetic*.

さんすくみ 三すくみ ● 三すくみになっている[なる] be in (touch, to reach) a three-cornered deadlock.

サンスクリット Sanskrit /sǽnskrɪt/.

さんずのかわ 三途の川 the Styx /stɪks/. ● 三途の川を渡る cross the Styx. (❗ die の婉曲表現)

さんする 産する produce, yield. (⇨産出する)

:**さんせい 賛成** 图 [同意] agreement; [是認] approval; [好意, 支持] favor; [支持] support. ▶賛成 *Yes!* (↔*No!*)/(米国議会) *Yea* /jéɪ/! /(英国議会) *Aye* /áɪ/! /(↔*Nay*!)
[会話]「海岸へしようよ」「賛成」 "Let's go to the beach, shall we?" "*Yes, let's.* /(それいいね) *I'm up for that.*"
① 【賛成(の)~】 ● その法案に賛成投票をする vote

for the bill; vote *in favor* [*support*] *of* the bill.
● この計画に賛成の意を表す show [express] one's *approval to* the plan; (理由・根拠を挙げて) argue the case *for* (↔*against*) the plan. ▶賛成多数により引取 The *ayes* have it. ▶賛成の方はご起立願います Those (who are) *in favor* [*who approve*], please stand up. ▶賛成票は反対票を上回った There were more *yeses* [*yeas, ayes*] than noes [*nays*]. ▶彼に賛成の票は 50 票で反対は 3 票だった Fifty votes were *in favor of* him and three were against. ▶委員会は賛成多数で決議案を通した The committee passed a resolution by *a majority vote*.
②《賛成を》● 彼らの賛成を求める ask (for) their *approval*. ● その決定は委員会の過半数の賛成を得た The decision won [met with] the *approval of* the majority of the committee.

── 賛成する 動 〘同意する〙 agree 《*with*＋人・意見, 〘承諾する〙 *to*＋事》;〘よいと認める〙 approve 《*of*》; 〘支持する〙 support, be in favor 《*of*》, be for ... (↔against); 〘動議・提案などを採択する〙 second.
● 賛成してうなずく nod *in agreement* [*approval*]. ● 私も(それについては)まったく賛成です I quite *agree* [I do *agree*, I couldn't *agree* more] (*about* that). ● 私は彼の提案にすぐ賛成した I *agreed with* [*agreed to, accepted*] his proposal at once. ● その件に関してあなたの意見に全面的に賛成しかねます I can't entirely *agree with* you [*your opinion*] on the matter. (⚠ agree が認可でなく, 単に意見の一致を表すので with の代わりに xto を用いるのは不可) ▶太郎の両親は彼が花子と結婚することに賛成した Taro's parents *have agreed to* his marrying Hanako [*to* let him marry Hanako, *that* he will marry Hanako]. (⚠ 前の二つは認可を表すが, 最後は単なる意見の一致を表す) /Taro's parents *have approved* (*of*) his marrying [marriage to] Hanako. ▶私は日本人は働きすぎだという考えに賛成できない I can't *approve* [*support, accept*] the idea that Japanese people work too much. (⚠ I don't like the idea.... のようにいう方が口語的だ) ▶「議長, 私はその動議に賛成です」"Mr. Chairman [〘女性〙 Ms. [Madam] Chairperson], I second the motion." ▶彼は男女同権に賛成している He *favors* [*is in favor of*] equal rights for men and women.
会話 「あなたは彼の言うことに賛成ですか反対ですか」「大賛成です」"*Are* you *for* him or against him?" "I'm all *for* him [his idea]."

■ **DISCOURSE**
費用がかかりすぎない限りはその計画に賛成だ I *agree with* the plan, **as long as** it doesn't cost too much. (⚠ as long as ... (...の限りにおいて) は条件付き賛成を表すディスコースマーカー)

● 賛成者 a supporter. ● 賛成論 a supporting view; a positive view.
さんせい 三世 〘日系米人〙 a Sansei 《〜(s)》, a second-generation Japanese American (⚠「二世」の意でも用いられる (⇨一世, 二世)).
さんせい 三省 ── 三省する 動 reflect on what one has done many times a day.
さんせい 酸性 图 ── 酸性の 形 ácid; acidic. ● 酸性にする[なる] acídify; make (it) [become] *acid*.
● 酸性雨 acid rain. ● 酸性岩 acid rock. ● 酸性紙 acid paper. ● 酸性食品 acid food. ● 酸性土壌 acid soil.
さんせいけん 参政権 suffrage, the vote. ● 婦人参政権 woman [women's] *suffrage*. ● 参政権がある have *suffrage*. ● 参政権を与える[獲得する] grant [get] *suffrage*.
さんせき 山積 ── 山積する 動 pile up, be piled. (⇨山積み) ▶問題が山積している We *have piles* [*heaps*] *of* problems (to solve).
ざんせつ 残雪 remaining [lingering] snow.
さんせん 参戦 图 entry into [participation in] a war.
── 参戦する 動 《やや書》participate in [《書》enter into] a war; (戦争を始める) go to war 《*against*》; (宣戦布告する) declare 《xa》war 《*on, against*》.
▶第一次世界大戦では日本はイギリス側に参戦した In the First World War Japan *entered into the war* on the English side.
さんぜん 参禅 ● 本山に参禅する practice Zen (meditation) at a head temple.
さんぜん 産前 before childbirth.
さんぜん 燦然 ── 燦然たる 副 brilliantly. ● さん然と輝く宝石 *brilliant* jewels. ▶星がさん然と輝く The stars shine *brilliantly*.
さんそ 酸素 〘化学〙 oxygen (元素記号 O). (⇨酸欠)
● 酸素化合物 an oxygen compound, an oxide.
● 酸素呼吸 aerobic respiration; oxygen respiration. ● 酸素吸入 oxygen inhalation. ● 酸素吸入をする inhale oxygen. ● 酸素吸入器 an oxygen inhaler. ● 酸素テント (be in) an oxygen tent. ● 酸素マスク (wear) an oxygen mask.
ざんそ 讒訴 ── 讒訴する 動 make a false charge 《*against*》.
さんそう 山荘 a mountain cottage [〘立派な別荘〙 villa].
ざんぞう 残像 〘心理〙 an áftimage.
さんぞく 山賊 a bandit (榎 〜s, 〘まれ〙 〜ti /-ditti/).
さんそん 山村 a mountain village.
ざんぞん 残存 ● 残存部数 the number of *remaining* copies.
── 残存する 動 remain; (生き残る) survive.
さんだい 三代 (三つの世代) three generations. ● 三代にわたって収集してきた美術品 the art collection (made) by the three generations of one's family.
さんだい 参内 ── 参内する 動 visit the Imperial Palace.
ざんだか 残高 〘収支の差額〙 a balance 《*of* 100,000 yen》. ● 銀行預金残高 the bank *balance*. ● 繰越残高 the *balance* carried forward.
● 残高照会 an inquiry for the balance. ● 残高表 (貸借対照表) a balance sheet.
サンタクロース Santa Claus /sǽnta klɔ́ːz/, 《主に英》Father Christmas. ▶サンタクロースを見た人が誰もいない(＝誰も見ていない)からといって, サンタクロースがいないという証拠にはなりません Nobody sees *Santa Claus*, but that is no proof [doesn't mean] that there is no *Santa Claus*.
サンダル 《a pair of》sandals.
さんたん 惨憺 ● 惨たんたる(＝ぞっとする)光景 a *frightful* [a *dreadful*, a *horrible*] sight. ● 惨たんたる(＝ひどい)失敗 a *terrible* [a *miserable*] mistake.
● 惨たんたる(＝壊滅的な)敗北を喫す suffer a *crushing* defeat; be *soundly* defeated. ● 惨たんたる結果に終わる end *in disaster*. ● 苦心惨たんする take great 《xmany》pains 《*to* do》.
さんたん 賛嘆 图 admiration; praise.
── 賛嘆する 動 admire; praise.
さんだん 三段 ● 三段構えの手段 《take》three-way means [measures].
● 三段跳び the triple jump; the hop, step and

さんだん jump. ● 三段跳びの選手 a triple jumper. ● 三段腹 a spare tire. ● 三段目『相撲』*sandanme*;(説明的に) the third division from the bottom on the official listing of rank. ● 三段論法『論理』a syllogism /síləʤizm/. ● 三段論法を使う use syllogism; talk in a syllogístic way.

さんだん 散弾 《集合的》shot; a pellet.
● 散弾銃 a shotgun.

さんだん 算段 ── 算段(を)する『準備する』get ... ready, prepare; 『計画を練る』work ... out; 『考える』think of ...; 『何とか処理する』manage; 『工夫する』《やや書》contrive. ● 金の算段をする get money ready; (調達する) raise money. ● 逃げる算段をする work out [think of] a way to escape.

さんたんげん 三単現『文法』『「三人称単数現在形」の略』a third person singular present form.

*****さんち** 産地 a prodúcing dístrict [cènter]. ● 産地(=農園)直送の桃 peaches direct from (the) farm; farm-fresh peaches. ● 宇治はお茶の産地として名高い Uji is famous as a tea-*producing district* 〔お茶の(生産)で〕for its (*production* of) tea).

さんち 山地 a mountainous /máuntənəs/ [a mountain] district [region]; (高地) highlands.

さんちゅう 山中 ● 山中に in the mountains. ▶山中深く入ったところでライオンがほえるのが聞こえた Far up *in the mountains* I heard a lion roar.
● 山中暦日なし Those who live a leisurely life in the mountains tend to forget the time.

さんちょう 山頂 the top [summit] of a mountain, a mountaintop; (とがった山頂に) a peak. (⇨頂上)

さんちょく 三直 ▶警備員は三直で働いている The guards work *on* [*in*] *three 8-hour shifts*.

さんちょく 産直 ● 産直のリンゴ apples *fresh* [*sent direct*] *from* the orchard [*producers*]; *farm-fresh apples*.

さんてい 算定 ── 算定する 動 (計算する) cálculate; (見積る) éstimàte. ● 費用を算定する *calculate* what the expense is; *estimate* the expense (*at*).

ざんてい 暫定 ── 暫定的な 形 provisional; (一時的に) témporàry.
── 暫定的に 副 provisionally; temporarily; for the time being.
● 暫定協定 a provisional [(仮の)《やや書》a tentative] agreement. ● 暫定政府 a provisional [《やや書》an interim /íntərim/] government. ● 暫定措置 temporary measures. ● 暫定予算 a provisional [《やや書》an interim] budget.

サンティアゴ『チリの首都』Santiago /sæntiːáːgou/.
サンディエゴ『米国の都市』San Diego /sæn diéigou/.
サンデー [氷菓] a (chocolate) sundae /sándei/.
サンデー [日曜日] Sunday. (⇨日曜)
ざんてき 残敵 the remnants of the enemy army.

*****さんど** 三度 three times, 《古》thrice. ● 月に3度 *three times* a month. ● 3度に1度は (at least) once *in three times*. ● 1日に3度の食事をする have [eat] *three meals a day*.
【三度目[で]】 ● 彼の3度目の転居 his *third* move. ▶彼は3度目の優勝を果たした He won the championship *for the third time*. ▶彼は3度目で最後のチャンスをもらえた He was given *a third* and last chance. (❗*a* third is one, another に続いて「さらにもう1度の」の意)
● 三度の飯より ▶ゴルフが三度の飯より好きだ I'd rather play golf than eat.
● 三度目の正直 (That is a case of) third time lucky./The third time plays for all.

ざんにん

● 三度笠 (さんどがさ) a sedge hat.
ざんど 残土 surplus construction soil.
サンドイッチ a sandwich /sǽndwitʃ/. (❗パン3枚のものは a double-decker (sandwich), 1枚のものは an open sandwich という) ● ハム[ツナ]サンド(イッチ)を hàm [a tùna] sándwich. ● パンにハムをはさんでサンドイッチを作る put slices of ham between slices of bread and make some *sandwiches*. ● 昼食にサンドイッチが食べたい I want to eat *sandwiches* for lunch.
● サンドイッチマン a sándwich màn; 《男女共用》a sándwich bòard ádvertiser.

さんとう 三等 (第3位) third place; (第3等級) the third class [rate]; (3等賞) (the) third prize. (⇨一等)
● 三等親 a relative in the third degree. (⇨親等)

さんどう 山道 a mountain path.
さんどう 参道 the approach to [×of] a shrine.
さんどう 桟道 a plank bridge.
さんどう 産道 the birth canal.
さんどう 賛同 (⇨賛成, 同意) ● 多くの人の賛同を得る win [receive] *approval* of many people.
── 賛同する 動 approve 《of》, agree 《with》.

ざんとう 残党 the remnants [survivors, remaining members] 《of the Heike clan》.
サンドウェッジ『ゴルフ』a sand wedge.
さんとうきん 三頭筋『解剖』the triceps.
さんとうしょう 山東省 『中国の省』Shandong /ʃàːndóːŋ/ Province.
サンドトラップ『ゴルフ』《米》a sand trap,《英》a bunker.
サンドバギー [浜[砂丘]用自動車] a beach buggy; a dune buggy.
サンドバッグ『ボクシング』a púnching bàg. (❗sandbag は護岸用などの砂袋)
サンドペーパー sandpaper.
サントメ・プリンシペ『国名』São Tomé and Príncipe; (公式名) the Democratic Republic of São Tomé and Príncipe. (首都 São Tomé)
サントラ『「サウンドトラック」の略』a soundtrack.
さんにゅう 参入 動 (a) entry 《into》. (❗「参入する権利[機会]」の意では Ⓤ) ● 新規参入 new *entry*. ● 新製品のヨーロッパ市場への参入 the new model's *entry* into the European market.
── 参入する 動 enter. ● 出版業へ参入する *get into* publishing [the publishing business].
さんにゅう 算入 名 inclusion.
── 算入する 動 include. ▶すべての経費をそこに算入してください Please *include* all the expenses in it.
ざんにょう 残尿 residual urine. ● 残尿感 sense of residual urine.
さんにん 三人 three people [persons].
● 三人寄れば文殊の知恵 (ことわざ) Two heads are better than one./Two eyes can see more than one.
● 三人官女 the three court ladies in waiting (displayed on the Doll Festival). ● 三人称『文法』the third person. ● 三人称単数現在形 (⇨三単現)

ざんにん 残忍 名 brutality;[残酷] cruelty. ● 残忍性を示す show one's *brutality* [one's *brutal nature*].
── 残忍な 形 brutal; (人が) cruel; (冷酷な) cold-blooded. ● 残忍な[残忍きわまる]行為 an act of *cruelty* [*dreadful cruelty*]. ● 残忍な殺人 *brutal* [*cold-blooded*] murder. ● 残忍な暴君 a *brutal* [a *cruel*] tyrant.

ざんねん 残念 ── 残念な [形] sorry; regrettable, regretful; 〖失望させる〗disappointing; 〖悔しがらせる〗(やや書) mortifying.

> [使い分け] **sorry** 「残念な」の意を表す最も一般的な語。「残念な」の意では必ず人が主語になり、叙述的に用いる: 私は試験に落ちて残念だ I am *sorry (that)* I failed the test. (⚠️ ×It is *sorry* I failed the test. は誤り)
> **regrettable, regretful** regrettable は「人を残念がらせる、後悔すべき」の意で通例物・事に関してのみ用いるが、regretful は人にも物にも用い「人が残念がっている」または「(表情などが) 残念な気持ちを表す」の意: 彼の残念そうな顔 his *regretful* [×regrettable] face./残念な知らせ *regretful* [×regretful] news./彼はそのことを残念がっている He is *regretful* [×regrettable] about that.

▶昨今の若者があまり本を読まないのは大変残念なことである《書》 It is very *regrettable* [It is much *to be regretted*, It is *a matter of* great regret, ×It is a great regret] *that* young people today do not read many books. (⚠️ *Regrettably*, young people …. ともいえる) ▶あの本をなくしたのは残念だ I'm *sorry (that)* [It's *a pity (that)*, 《やや書》 I *regret that*] I (have) lost that book. (⚠️ that 節中を … I *should have lost* …. とするのは驚き・意外さを表す堅い言い方)/《やや書》I *regret* losing [having lost] that book. (⚠️ I *regret doing* [*having done*] は過去のことについて用いる) ▶まことに残念ですがご招待には応じられません I very much *regret to say that* [*Much to my regret, To my deep regret*], I can't accept your invitation. (⚠️(1) いずれも堅い言い方で、くだけた言い方では、I'm very *sorry to say (that)* [(I'm) *sorry*, but I'm *afraid*] I can't accept your invitation. などという。(2) ×I *regret saying* …. とはしない)

[会話]「残念ながらうまくいかなかったよ」「それは残念」"I didn't make it, I'm *afraid*." "(I'm) *sorry to hear that*./What *a pity* [《話》 *a shame*]!/(がっかりだね) What *a disappointment* for you!/(不運だ) That's too bad./Bad [Hard] luck."
[会話]「同窓会に来なかったね」「忙しかったんだ」「みんな残念がっていたよ」"I didn't see you at the reunion." "I was busy." "You *were missed*."

● **残念賞** a consolation prize. (⚠️ consolation は「慰め」の意)

さんねんせい 三年生 ❶ 〖生徒〗 (⇨一年生, 学年) ❷ 〖植物〗 a triennial (plant).
● **さんば 産婆** a midwife. (⇨助産師)
サンバ 〖音楽〗 the samba; (曲) a samba. ● サンバを踊る dance the *samba*.
*さんばい 三倍 three times. (⇨倍) ● 5 の 3 倍 *three times* five.
さんぱい 参拝 ── **参拝する** [動] 伊勢神宮に参拝する visit [go worshipping at] Ise Shrine. ▶小泉首相は 2006 年 8 月 15 日に靖国神社に参拝した Prime Minister Koizumi visited Yasukuni Shrine on August 15, 2006.
● **参拝者** a visitor (*to, at*); a worshipper (*at*).
さんぱい 酸敗 [名] acidification.
── **酸敗する** [動] acidify.
ざんぱい 惨敗 [名] a crushing [a complete] defeat. (⚠️ 前方が主観的で意味が強い)
── **惨敗する** [動] suffer [go down to] a crushing defeat.
さんぱいきゅうはい 三拝九拝 ── **三拝九拝する** [動] bow many times. ● 三拝九拝して彼に許しを請う

ask his pardon *on* one's *knees*; *go down on* one's *knees* and ask his pardon.
サンバイザー a sun visor.
さんばいず 三杯酢 three-flavor vinegar; (説明的に) a mixture of soy sauce, vinegar, and sugar or sweet sake.
サンパウロ 〖ブラジルの都市〗 São Paulo /saum páulou/.
さんばがらす 三羽烏 a distinguished trio /trí:ou/. (⚠️ 集合的, 単・複両扱い) ● 政界の三羽がらす the *three most able persons* in the political world.
さんばし 桟橋 a pier; (小さい) a jetty; (浮き桟橋) a landing stage. ● 船は桟橋に着いた The ship docked at the *pier*.
さんぱつ 散発 [名] ● (投手が) 散発 3 安打に抑える scatter three hits.
── **散発的な** [形] sporadic. ▶ 散発的な銃声がまだ聞えていた The sound of *sporadic* shooting could still be heard.
── **散発的に** [副] sporadically. ▶ 雷鳴が散発的に続いた The distant thunder continued *sporadically*.
さんぱつ 散髪 [名] a haircut, hair cutting.
── **散髪する** [動] get [have] a haircut; have one's hair cut (⚠️ cut one's hair は自分で切ること).
ざんぱつがみ 散ばら髪 disheveled hair.
ざんぱん 残飯 the remains of a meal; (捨てるつもりの食べ物) food scraps. (⚠️ leftovers は「残りもの」で必ずしも「残飯」ではない) ● 夕食の残飯を犬にやる feed the *leftovers* [the *remains*, the *remnants*] of dinner to a dog.
さんはんきかん 三半規管 〖解剖〗 three semicircular canals.
さんぴ 酸鼻 ● 酸鼻を極めた appalling, disastrous, horrible.
さんび 賛美 ── **賛美する** [動] praise. (⇨賞賛)
さんぴ 賛否 〖賛成か反対〗 yes or no; 〖承認か否認〗 approval or disapproval; 〖賛否両論〗 the pros and cons. ● その提案の賛否を論じる argue *the pros and cons* of the proposal; argue the proposal *pro and con*; argue *for and against* the proposal. ● その議題の賛否を問う (= 票決に付す) *put* the subject *to the vote*. ● 賛否同数の場合私に決定権があることを念のため申し上げます In the event of a *tie*, I would like to remind you that I have the casting vote.
ザンビア 〖国名〗 Zambia /zǽmbiə/; (公式名) the Republic of Zambia. (首都 Lusaka) ● ザンビア人 a Zambian. ● ザンビア(人)の Zambian.
さんびか 賛美歌 a hymn /hím/.
● **賛美歌集** a hýmn bòok; a book of hymns; (教会用語) a hymnal.
さんぴょう 散票 ▶ 彼らには少し散票が入った There were a few *scattered votes* for them.
さんびょうし 三拍子 ● 三拍子の曲 a tune *in triple time*.
● **三拍子そろう** ● 三拍子そろった (= 万能の) 運動選手 an *all-around* [《理想的な》an *ideal*] athlete. ● 三拍子そろった野球選手 a five-tool player. (⚠️ 英語では攻と守をそれぞれ二つに分けて 5 拍子とする)
さんぴん 産品 (主に工業製品) a product; (主に農産品) farm products.
ざんぴん 残品 the remaining [(売れ残り) unsold] goods. ● 残品を半額で整理する sell off *the remaining goods* at half price.
さんぶ 三部 three parts.
● **三部合唱** a chorus in three parts; 《play》 a trio. ● **三部作** 〖劇〗 a trilogy.
さんぷ 産婦 (出産直前の) a woman who is about to

give birth to a child; (直後の) a woman who has just given birth to a child.
さんぷ 散布 — **散布する** 動 (まき散らす) scatter; (液体・粉などを振りかける) sprinkle; (粉を) dust; (液などを吹きかける) spray. ▶芝生に除草剤を散布する *scatter [sprinkle, spray] weedkiller on the lawn*; *scatter [sprinkle, spray] the lawn with weedkiller*. ▶農薬[肥料]を空中散布する 《米》 *crop-dust*; 《英》*crop-spray*. (!空中散布用ヘリコプター[軽飛行機]は *crop-duster* [*sprayer*])
ざんぶ 残部 ❶ (残りの部分) the rest, the remainder, the remnant; (書籍などの売れ残りの部数) copies in stock. ▶その仕事の残部 the *rest* [*remainder*] of the work. ▶残部僅少 We have a small *stock* of the book./We have few *copies* of the book *in stock*.
さんぷく 山腹 ▶山腹の家 a house *on the mountainside* [*hillside*]; a house *halfway up the mountain* [*hill*]. (⇨中腹)
さんふじんか 産婦人科 obstétrics and gỳnecólogy, ob-gyn /óubi:dʒi:wàien/.
▶産婦人科医 an obstetrícian (and gỳnecólogist); an ob-gyn.
***さんぶつ** 産物 『工業製品に対する農[天]産物を集合的に』*próduce* (⇨製品 [類語]); 『成果』 a *fruit*, a *result*. ▶主要産物 the main *products* [*prodúce*]. ▶農[海]産物 agricultural [marine] *products*. ▶努力の産物 the *fruit*(*s*) [*product*] of one's efforts. ▶ジャガイモがその国の主要産物の一つだ Potatoes are one of the *main crops* [the *staples*] of the country.
サンフランシスコ 『米国の都市』Sàn Francísco. (!略称 Frisco だが市民は San Fran または S.F. の方を好む. ×Cisco は不可)
サンプリング 『見本抽出』sampling. ▶無作為抽出のサンプリングを行う *survey* a *random* sample.
▶サンプリング調査 sampling.
サンプル 『見本』a sample, a specimen. ▶商品サンプル a product *sample*. ▶血液サンプル a blood *sample* [*specimen*]. ▶ただいま無料サンプルを差し上げております Free *samples* are available now.
さんぶん 散文 prose. ▶散文で書く write in *prose* (↔verse). ▶散文的な prosaic /prouzéiik/.
▶散文詩 (1 編の) a prose poem; 《集合的》prose poetry.
ざんぺん 残片 a remaining piece.
***さんぽ** 散歩 图 a walk; (ゆっくりとくつろいだ) a stroll; (目的もなく広範囲の) a ramble. ▶公園に散歩に行こう Let's go (out) for a walk in the park. /(散歩する) Let's walk [take a walk, have a walk] in the park. (!walk [take a walk] to the park だと「公園まで散歩する」の意. この場合は ×have a walk to the park とはいわない) ▶彼は朝食前に海岸へ散歩に出かけた He went (out) for a stroll along [on] the beach before breakfast. ▶彼は朝の散歩に出かけている He is out for [on] his morning walk. (!for は目的を表す. on は「最中で」の意) ▶テーブルの上のグラスには父があげその朝散歩のときに摘んだ草花がさしてあった The flowers she picked on her walk that morning were put in a glass on the table. ▶家でダックスフントを 2 匹飼っていたのでその河川敷によく犬を散歩に連れていったものだった We had a pair of duchshunds and often used to walk them [take them for walks] on that riverbed terrace. (!人の場合は普通 take (a child) for a walk のようにいう)
会話 「とても楽しい散歩だったわ」「どのあたりまで行ったの」"We had a very pleasant walk." "How far did you go?"
— **散歩する** 動 ▶湖の周りを散歩する take a walk [walk] around the lake.
▶散歩道 a walk; (遊歩道) a promenade.
さんぼう 三方 ❶ 『供物台』a small wooden offering stand. ❷ 『三方向』 ▶私の田舎は三方を山に囲まれている My hometown is surrounded by [with] hills *on three sides*.
さんぼう 参謀 ▶『軍の』(個人) a staff officer; 《総称》the staff (!単・複両扱い); 『会社などの』(ブレーン) an adviser (!しばしば advisor ともつづる), 《話》a brain.
▶参謀長 the chief of staff. ▶参謀本部 the General Staff Office.
さんぽうかん 三宝柑 『植物』a *sampokan*, a navel-like orange.
さんま 秋刀魚 『魚介』a (Pacific) saury /sɔ́:ri/ (働 sauries), a saury pike (働 ~(s)).
さんまい 三枚 ▶魚を三枚に下ろす fillet a fish; cut a fish into two boneless fillets and the third piece with the skeleton. ▶三枚に下ろしたヒラメ fillet of sole; sole fillet. (!その 1 切れは a fillet of sole, a piece of sole fillet などという)
▶三枚肉 (ばら肉) ribs; spareribs.
さんまい 三昧 (⇨—三昧 (ざんまい))
—ざんまい —三昧 ▶彼は読書三昧の日々を送っている (没頭して) He spends his days *absorbed in* books. ▶あのぜいたく三昧の生活はそうもつまい I don't think their *life of luxury* [*high life*, 《話》*life in clover*] will last (for) a long time.
さんまいめ 三枚目 (おどけて面白い奴) 《話》a scream (!複数形なし); 《米》a cutup; (道化役者) a comedian.
サンマリノ 『国名』 San Marino; (公式名) the Republic of San Marino. (首都 San Marino) ▶サンマリノ人 a San Marinese. ▶サンマリノ(人)の San Marinese.
さんまん 散漫 ▶散漫な人 (思考が) a loose thinker; (注意力が) 《話》a scatterbrain. ▶散漫な話 [手紙] a rambling speech [letter]. ▶騒音で注意が散漫になった I [My attention] *was distracted by* the noise./The noise *distracted* my attention.
さんみ 酸味 acidity, sourness. ▶酸味のある sour, acid. ▶酸味がする taste 《quite》sour [acid]; have a sour [an acid] taste.
さんみいったい 三位一体 the Trinity. ▶親と学校と地域が三位一体となって子供を守る The parents, the school and the community, all together, protect [watch over] children.
▶三位一体論者 a Trinitarian.
さんみゃく 山脈 mountains, a mountain range [chain], a range (a chain) of mountains. ▶中国山脈 the Chugoku *Mountains*. ▶アルプス山脈 the Alps. (!複数扱い)
ざんむ 残務 remaining work [business]. ▶残務整理をする clean [clear up, (終える) finish] one's *remaining work*.
さんめんきじ 三面記事 《米》city news; 《英》home news.
さんめんきょう 三面鏡 a three-way [a triple] mirror.
さんめんろっぴ 三面六臂 ▶三面六臂の仏像 a Buddhist image with three faces and six arms.
▶三面六臂の大活躍をする (⇨八面六臂)
さんもん 三文 ▶三文の値打ちもない be dirt cheap; be worthless.
▶三文小説 a cheap [《米》a dime] novel.

- 三文判 (安物の判) a cheap seal; (実印でない判) one's unregistered seal. ● 三文文士 a hack writer.
さんもん 山門 a gate of a temple, a temple gate.
さんや 山野 fields and mountains.
● 山野草 wild grass.
さんやく 三役 ❶ 〖三つの要職〗 the three highest posts [positions]; (人) the three most important executives; (政党の幹部)《集合的》the caucus (⚠単・複両扱い).
❷〖相撲の上位〗 the three top [highest] ranks in *sumo*; (力士) the *sumo* wrestlers of the three top [highest] ranks 〖いずれも横綱を含む場合は最後に counting *yokozuna* and *ozeki* as one, 含まない場合は except [excluding] *yokozuna* をつける〗.
さんやく 散薬 a powder; powdered medicine.
さんゆうかん 三遊間 〖野球〗 the hole (between third and short [on the left side]). ▶ ゴロは三遊間を抜けた The grounder went through the hole between third and short.
さんゆこく 産油国 an oil-producing country [nation].
さんよ 参与 图 (政府など公共機関の) a councilor; (学校・病院や民間の会社などの相談役) a counselor.
── 参与する 動 ● その計画に参与する participate [take part] in the plan.
ざんよ 残余 (⇨残り)
さんよう 山容 ● 崇高な山容 the sublime *shape of a mountain*.
さんようすうじ 算用数字 Arabic numerals [figures].
さんようちゅう 三葉虫 〖古生物〗 a trilobite.
さんらん 産卵 图 ▶ サケは産卵のため川を逆上る Salmon swim upstream to *spawn*.
── 産卵する 動 (鳥などの) lay [(魚・カエルなどが大量に) spawn] (eggs); (ハエなどが…に卵を産みつける) blow.
● 産卵期 (魚・貝・カエルなどの) the spáwning sèason; (鳥・魚 などの繁殖期) the brèeding sèason.
さんらん 散乱 ── 散乱する 動 be scattered; (ごみなどが) be littered 《with》(⚠主語は場所 (⇨散らかる)). ▶ おもちゃが床に散乱している Toys *are scattered* on the floor./The floor *is littered with* toys.
▶ トラックがひっくり返って積んでいたオレンジがあちこちに散乱した A truck was overturned and the oranges it had been loaded with *were thrown far and wide*.
さんらん 燦爛 ── 燦爛たる 形 glittering, brilliant.
● 太陽の燦爛たる光輪 a *glittering* halo around the sun.
さんりゅう 三流 ── 三流の 形 third-rate, third-class. (⇨二流)
ざんりゅう 残留 ── 残留する 動 stay behind; remain (behind). ● 中国残留孤児 Japanese children *left behind* in China after World War II.
● 残留農薬 residual agricultural chemicals.
さんりん 山林 〖山と森〗 mountains and forests; 〖森林〗 a forest; 〖山林地帯〗 woodland. ● 山林を伐採する deforest [disafforest] a mountain.
さんりんしゃ 三輪車 a tricycle /tráisikl/, 《英話》 a trike.
さんるい 三塁 〖野球〗 third (base). (⇨二塁) ● 三塁線にファウルを打つ hit a foul down the *third base* line. ● 三塁側スタンド the stands on the third-base side [behind third base].
● 三塁コーチ a third base coach. ● 三塁手 a third base player; (男の) a third baseman. ● 三塁打 a three-base hit; 《口》 a triple.
ざんるい 残塁 ── 残塁となる be left on base; be stranded. ● 残塁 12 になる leave 12 runners *on base* [×bases]; *strand* 12 runners. ▶ 彼は三塁に残塁となった He *was left at* third [*on third base*]. ▶ その投手は(相手チームに) 10 残塁させた The pitcher left ten runners *stranded* [*on base*].
サンルーフ a sunroof (車 〜s), a sunshine roof.
サンルーム a súnroom, a sún párlor. ● サンルームを付け足す build a *sunroom* onto the house.
さんれつ 参列 图 (an) attendance; presence. (⇨出席)
── 参列する 動 attend; be present 《at》. ▶ 彼の葬儀に多数の人が参列した A large number of people *attended* [*were present at*] his funeral./There was a large *attendance* at his funeral.
● 参列者 those (who are) present; (参列者数) an attendance. (⚠単数扱い)
さんろく 山麓 (at) the foot [base] of a mountain.
● アルプスの山麓 (をなす連なった丘) the *foothills* of the Alps; the Alpine *foothills*.
さんわり 三割 thirty percent. ● 三割を打つ bat [hit] (at) .300. (⚠ .300 は three hundred と読む)
● 三割打者 a three-hundred [a .300] hitter.

し

し 死 (a) death; 【法律】 decease. (⇨死ぬ)
① 【～死】 ● 溺死[(で)]焼死] death by [×from] drowning [fire]. ● 安楽死 euthanasia. ● 過労死 karoshi, death from overwork. (⇨過労死) ● 尊厳死 death [dying] with dignity. (⇨尊厳死) ● 脳死 brain death. ● 安らかな死 a peaceful death. ● 胃がんによる死 a death from [caused by, (まれ) of] stomach cancer. ● 事故[自然]死する die an accidental [a natural] death; die in an accident [of natural causes, naturally].
② 【死が】 ● 死が迫っている Death is near at hand [approaching]./(人が主語) He is going to die very soon.
③ 【死の】 ● 死の恐怖 the fear of death. ● 死の灰 (=放射性降下物) (radioactive) fallout; radioactive dust.
④ 【死に】 ● 死に直面する face death. ● 死に至る諸病状 medical conditions leading to death. ▶彼は死に臨んで(=死ぬ間際に)妻に何か言おうとしていた He was trying to say something to his wife just before he died [on the point of dying, at the point of death, (死の床で)(やや書) on his deathbed].
⑤ 【死を[と]】 ● 死を選ぶ choose death. ● 彼の娘の死をいたむ mourn his daughter's death [the death of his daughter]; mourn (for) his daughter. ● 長い間死と戦う run a long race with death. ▶その出来事が彼の死を早めた[招いた] The event quickened [caused] his death. ▶人は死を逃れることはできない People [We] cannot escape [×escape from] death./(死ぬ運命にある) Man is mortal. ▶彼なら死を覚悟していた He was ready to die then. ▶動物は死を予感するではないようだ Animals do not seem to anticipate death.
⑥ 【死で】 ● 彼の突然の死で家族は路頭に迷った His sudden [unexpected] death left his family without support.
● 死を賭す sacrifice one's life.

*し **氏** 【人の姓・姓名につける敬称】 Mr. /místər/ (⇨さん); 【彼】 he. ● 鈴木氏 Mr. Suzuki. ● 蘇我氏(=一族) the Sogas.

*し **四** four; 【4番目の】 the fourth. (⇨三) ● 四半分に折りたたむ fold (it) into quarters. ● 第3四半期の授業料 the third quarterly tuition. ● 四半世紀 a quarter (of a) century. (⇨分(*))

*し **市** a city. ● 福岡市 the City of Fukuoka. (❶(1) 堅い表現で日常的には単に Fukuoka が普通. (2) Fukuoka City のような言い方は New York City のように一部の市に限られ一般的でない. (3) 手紙の住所などでは Fukuoka-shi とも書く)
● 市議会議員 (⇨市議会) ● 市町村 cities, towns and villages; (地方自治体) municipalities.
● 市当局 the municipal authorities.

*し **詩** (1編) a poem; 【集合的】 poetry; (散文に対する韻文) verse. ● 散文詩 a prose poem. ● 抒情詩 a lyric poem. ● 英詩を数編朗読する recite several English poems [several pieces of English poetry]. ● シェリーの詩から1行[1節]引用する quote a line [a stanza] from Shelley. ● 愛の詩を書く write a love poem [a poem about love].

―― **詩の, 詩的な** 形 poetic /pouétik/, poetical. ● 詩の才能 《have》 a poetic talent. ● 詩的描写をする give a poetic description 《of》; write poetically.

し **士** 【侍】 a samurai (複 ～); 【男の人】 a man, (紳士) a gentleman. ● 同好の士 a person who shares the same interest.

し **子** a child. ● 第一子 one's first child.

し **指** a finger; (親指) a thumb. ● 第一指 a thumb.

し **師** a teacher, (英語) a master. (⇨先生)

し **資** 【資金】 capital; (財源) funds; 【資材, 材料】 material; 【資質】 nature, a gift. ● 労資 capital and labor.

―し 《接続助詞》 ❶ 【事柄を並べあげて示す】 besides, what's more, 《やや書》 moreover. (⇨その上) ▶彼は健康だし頭もいい He is in good health, and besides [what's more], he is bright./Besides being healthy, he is bright.
❷ 【一つの条件だけをあげて, あとをほのめかす】 ▶もう子供でもあるまいし(=じゃないのだから), 1人でやりなさい Do it yourself—you are no longer a child.

―し ―史 a [the] history of .... ● 現代史 modern history. ● アメリカ史 (×the) American history; the history of America.

―し ―視 【...を特別視[重要視; 異端視]する】 regard ... as (being) special [important; 《やや書》heretical]. (❶(1)「特別視」は「例外的」と考えれば special に代えて exceptional. (2) regard に代えて consider, look on も可. また「...視する」を「...として扱う」と考えれば treat も可)

*じ **地** 【地面】 the ground; 【織物などの】 (素地) a background; 【肌】 texture; 【素肌】 one's skin; 【本性】 one's real character. ● 地ならしをする level the ground. ● 地の人間 people of the place; the locals. ● 白地に赤い水玉模様 a pattern of red dots on a white background. ● 地が黒い be dark-skinned. ● 地を出す reveal one's real [true] character; give oneself away. ● (会話文に対して)地の文 a narrative part. ▶彼女の一生は恋愛小説を地で行ったようなものだった Her life was just like a real-life love story.

*じ **字** 【漢字などの】 a character; 【アルファベットの】 a letter; 【筆跡】 handwriting, a hand (❶ 単数形のみ; 《字の書き方》 penmanship; 【活字】 type, print.
① 【～の字】 ● あの生徒は英語のエの字も知らない That pupil does not know (even) a word [the ABC] of English.
② 【字が[は]】 ● 彼は字が上手である He has good handwriting./He writes (in) a good hand. (❶前の方が普通) ● あなたの字は読みにくい Your handwriting is hard [not easy] to read. ▶その子は字が書ける[読める] The child can write [read]. (❶ letters などは不要) ● 私は字が下手で自分の書いたものが読めないことがある My penmanship is so bad [I write so badly] (that) I sometimes can't read it myself.
③ 【字を】 ● 字を削る[加える] erase [add] a character. ● 誤字を直す correct a wrong character (a misspelling). (❶前の方は日本語, 後の方は英語の字の場合) ● 字を練習する practice penmanship. ● 字を教える teach letters [characters]. ▶彼はきれいな

筆跡ですらすらと字を書いた He *wrote* rapidly with a fine clear hand.
④【字に[で]】● 太[細]字で書く write *in* [×with] heavy [slender] *characters*. ● 大きい字[ローマン体]で印刷された本 a book printed *in* large [roman] *type*. ● 細かい字でぎっしりと thickly in small *letters* [*characters*]. ● 大の字になる lie on one's back with one's arms and legs spread out.

じ 痔 piles, 〖医学〗hemorrhoids /hémərɔ̀idz/. (**!** いずれも複数扱い) ● 痔が悪い have [suffer from] *piles*.

じ 辞 an address; a speech (**!** address より口語的). ● 開会[閉会]の辞を述べる give an opening [a closing] *address*.
● 辞を低くする maintain [keep] a low profile.

じ- 次- the next.

*-じ -時 o'clock. (**!** (1) of the clock の省略形. (2) 分までいう場合は a.m. (午前), p.m. (午後) とともには用いない: ×6 o'clock p.m. (3) o'clock の前では数字より six などと書く方が普通) (⇨分, 何時) ● 2 時ちょうどに at two (*o'clock*); at just two (*o'clock*). ● 午後 6 時ごろに (at) around [about] 6 p.m.; (晩の 6 時ころに) (at) around [about] six (*o'clock*) in the evening. ● 18 時のようにいうときは 1800 hours と書き eighteen hundred [(やや話) nothing] hours と読む ● 9 時 [9 時 1 分] の列車に乗る take the nine *o'clock* [9:01] train. (**!** 前の方は 9:00 [(英) 9.00] とも書き nine o'clock と読む. 後の方は nine-o /ou/ -one と読む. 文脈から明らかな場合, train は省略可) ● 私たちは午前 10 時に駅で会うことになっている We are to meet at the station at ten (*o'clock*) in the morning.

-じ -寺 (⇨寺) ● 法隆寺 (the) Horyuji *Temple*.

-じ -児 ● 2 歳児 a two-year-old *child*. ● 革命児 a revolutionary; a revolutionist.

-じ -路 ● 伊勢路 the Ise Road.

*しあい 試合 〖団体球技の〗a game; (公式の) a match (**!** (米) では通例 ball のつく球技には game を用いる) (⇨①); 〖個人またはペア対抗の〗a match; (格闘技の一勝負) a bout /báut/; 〖競技会〗a competition; (勝ち抜き戦) a tournament; (総当たり戦) (米) a round robin; (選手権試合) a championship (**!** しばしば複数形で), a title match. (⇨勝負, ゲーム)
①【～の試合, 試合～】● 野球の試合 a baseball [a ball] *game*. ● サッカーの試合 (米) a soccer *game*; (英) a football *game* [*match*]. ● ボクシング[レスリング]の試合 a boxing [a wrestling] *match*. ● 練習[対校]試合 a practice [an interscholastic] *match*. ● 国際試合 an international *match* [*game*]. ● 試合中 *game* underway. ● 試合中に during a *game*. ● 試合消化が一つ少ない with a *game* in hand. ● 昨シーズンの同じ対戦試合 [サッカー] the same fixture of last season. ● 阪神と広島の試合は 3 対 0 で阪神の勝ちだった The *game* between Hanshin and Hiroshima ended with the score of three to nothing, in Hanshin's favor. ▶ テニス[ゴルフ]の試合の結果はどうでしたか What was the outcome of the tennis [golf] *match*? ▶ 両チームともうまい試合運びだった Both teams *were playing* well.
②【試合に】● 試合に勝つ[負ける] win [lose] a *game*. ● 試合に出る play [(参加する) take part, appear] in a *game*. ● 試合に欠場する miss a *game*. ● 試合に臨む enter a *game*. ● 一方的な試合になる end in a one-sided [×a one-side] *game*. (**!** ×a *oneside* game とはいわない) ▶ 彼ったら, 腕を折ってしまったんだよ. だから試合には出られないんだって He

broke his arm. So he couldn't *play*.
③【試合を】● 試合をする play a play; play [have] a game 《*with*, *against*》. ● ホームランで試合を終える end a game with a homer. ▶ 私ともう 1 試合をしませんか Won't you *play* another *game* with me [*play* me another *game*]? ▶ 我々はきのう中国チームとバレーボールの試合をした We *played* the Chinese team *at* volleyball yesterday./We *played* volleyball *against* the Chinese team yesterday.
▶ どことどこが試合をしているの Who's *playing* who?
▶ 彼のホームランが試合を決めた He hit a home run that won the *game*./(米話) His homer put the *game* on ice. (**!** on ice は「勝利が確かな状態に」の意)

じあい 自愛 ● ご自愛ください Please *take* (*good*) *care of yourself*.

じあい 慈愛 〖愛情〗affection, love. (**!** 前の方は love より温和で永続的な愛情) ● 親の慈愛 parents' *affection* [*love*] 《*for*》. ● 慈愛深い母 one's *affectionate* [*loving*] mother. ● 慈愛に満ちたほほえみ an *affectionate* smile.

しあがり 仕上がり 〖出来栄え〗workmanship; 〖終了〗(a) finish; (終えること) finishing; (完成) 《やや書》completion, accomplishment. ▶ この作品は見事な仕上がりを見せている This work shows exquisite *workmanship*.
会話 「作品の仕上がりはどう?」「なかなかいいよ」 "How has the work *come out*?" "Very well [Not too bad]." (**!** come out は「(結果が)…になる」の意)

しあがる 仕上がる be finished; 〖完成される〗be completed. (⇨完成する, 出来上がる) ▶ 写真がきれいに仕上がった The picture *has come out* (very) well.

しあげ 仕上げ ● finish; (仕上げること) finishing. ● つや出し仕上げ a shiny *finish*. ● その絵に仕上げの筆を入れる put *the finishing* touches to the painting. ▶ この木製机は仕上げが美しい This wooden desk has a beautiful *finish* [is beautifully finished].

じあげ 地上げ ── 地上げする 動 buy plots of land up by force (to sell at a much higher price).
● 地上げ屋 〖話〗a land shark.

*しあげる 仕上げる 〖終える〗finish ... (off) (**!** off がつくと「完全に終える」と強意的になる); (完成させる) complete (**!** finish より堅い語); (やっと終える) get* through 《*with*》... (**!** 困難さを暗示する). ▶ 宿題は仕上げましたか Have you *finished* (doing, ×to do) your homework? ▶ その仕事は今日中に仕上げなければいけない I have to *finish* (*off*) [*complete*] the work today [×within today]. ▶ 早く仕上げてしまおうよ Let's *get finished* quickly. ▶ 私は 10 日でなんとかその仕事を仕上げた I managed to *get through* (*with*) the work in ten days.

しあさって 明明後日 two days after tomorrow, three days later (from today [from now]). (**!** 具体的に日や曜日でいうことが多い)

ジアスターゼ 〖生化学〗diastase /dáiəstèis/.

シアター 〖劇場〗a theater. ● レストランシアター《米》a dinner *theater* 《**!** ディナーショーをするレストラン》;《和製語》a restaurant theater.

しあつ 指圧 (療法) acupressure, *shiatsu* /ʃiːɑ́ːtsuː/.
● 指圧療法師 an acupressurist.

シアトル 〖米国の都市〗Seattle /si(ː)ǽtl/.

じあまり 字余り ● 字余りの俳句[短歌] a *haiku* [a *tanka*] with an extra syllable [extra syllables].

*しあわせ 幸せ 名 happiness (⇨幸福, 幸い); 〖喜び〗 pleasure.

—— 幸せな 形 happy. ▶美しい音楽を聞くことほど幸せなことはない Nothing makes me *happier* [私を楽しませてくれる] *gives me greater pleasure*] than to listen to beautiful music. (❗*happier* の意味上の主語は me であるが, ×Nothing is happier to me than .... のように物事を主語にとらない(⇒③)) ● 幸せな結末 a happy ending. ▶こんな幸せなことは今まで一度もなかった I've never felt *happier* in my life. ▶私は[あなたに]いい妻を持っていて幸せだ I'm [You must be] *happy* to have a good wife. (❗(1) ×You're *happy* .... のようにつけて他人の感情を断定することになり, この場合不自然. (2) ×It is happy that you have a good wife. は不可) ▶うわー, 最高に幸せだわ Wow, I'm the *luckiest* woman *on earth*. (❗うれしい気持ちを強調する言い方)

—— 幸せに happily. ●幸せに暮らす live *happily*; lead [live] a *happy* life. ▶人はみな幸せになりたいと思う Everybody wants to be [become, get] *happy*./(書) Everybody desires *happiness*. ▶お幸せに I wish you every *happiness*./I hope you'll be very *happy*. (❗前の文よりくだけた言い方)/Be *happy*, dear. (❗親しい人に用いる)
会話「その男といっしょになっても幸せにはなれないよ」「彼に会ってもいないのによくもそんなことが言えるわね」"You'll never be *happy* with him." "You've never even met him! How can you say such a thing?"

しあん 私案 one's (own) plan [proposal].
しあん 思案 名 [[思考]] thought; [[熟慮]] consideration. ●思案に=考え込んだ]顔で with a *thoughtful* [(心配げな) a *worried*] look. ▶どうしたのかと思案に暮れる do not know [(話) be at one's wits' end to know, (書) be at a loss] what to do. ▶ここが思案のしどころだ This is where we need to *think hard* [*consider carefully*].
●思案投げ首 deep in thought what to do.
—— 思案する 動 think (*about*); consider; (あれこれ考える) ponder. ▶彼は行くべきかどうか思案していた He *was considering* [*pondering*] whether to go.
しあん 試案 (やや書) a tentative plan.
シアン [[化学]] cyanogen.
●シアン化物 [[化学]] cyanide /sáiənáid/.
しい 椎 [[植物]] a chinquapin.
●椎の実 a chinquapin.
しい 思惟 thinking; a profound thought.
しい 恣意 —— **恣意的な** 形 árbitràry. (⇒任意)
しい 示威 ●示威運動 a demonstration. (⇒デモ)
しい 自慰 masturbation. —— **自慰(を)する** 動 masturbate.
じい 侍医 a court physician [doctor].
じい 辞意 one's intention [decision] to resign. ●辞意をひるがえす abandon one's *intention to resign*; (思いとどまる) stop short of *resigning*; (考え直す) rethink [(やや書) reconsider] one's *resignation*. ▶彼は辞意を明らかにした He announced his *intention to resign*./He announced that he *would resign*. ▶彼は辞意が固い He is firmly determined to *resign* [*give up* his *post*].
シーアイ a CI 《*corporate identity system*》 の略.
シーアイエス CIS 《*Commonwealth of Independent States* の略》. (参考 旧ソ連内の12か国で構成)
シーアイエフ 《運賃保険料込み値段》[[条件]] CIF, c.i.f. 《*cost, insurance and freight* の略》.
シーア派 シーア派 (イスラム教の) the Shiah sect. (関連 スンニ派 the Sunni sect)
ジーエイト G8 《*the Group of Eight* (先進8か国首脳会議)の略》.
シーエス a CS 《*customer satisfaction*》の略.

ジーエヌピー [[国民総生産]][[経済]] GNP 《*Gross National Product* の略》.
シーエム a commercial. (❗ a commercial message といったり, それを CM と略すのは一般的ではない)
しいか 詩歌 [[集合的]] poetry; (1編の) a poem.
しいく 飼育 名 ●動物園の飼育係 a zoo keeper. ● 羊の飼育場 a sheep farm.
—— 飼育する 動 (育てる) raise; rear; (繁殖のために) breed; (飼う) keep. (⇒飼う) ▶羊を飼育する *raise* sheep.
しいく『飼育』 *Prize Stock*. (参考 大江健三郎の小説)
シークきょう シーク教 Sikhism.
●シーク教徒 a Sikh.
シークタイム [[コンピュータ]] seek time.
シークレット a secret. ●オープンシークレット [[公然の秘密]] an open *secret*. ●トップシークレット a top *secret*.
シークレットサービス 《米》 Secret Service; (その一員) a Secret Service person. (❗大統領など要人の特別警護をする)
じいさん (⇒おじいさん)
シージー [[コンピュータ]] CG 《*computer graphics* の略》.
じいしき 自意識 self-consciousness. ●自意識過剰の self-conscious.
シーズ [[種(☆)]] seeds. ●技術シーズ 《*sow*》 the *seeds* of technology, technological *seeds*.
シースルー ●シースルーのブラウス a *see-through* blouse.
シーズン a season. (⇒季節, 旬(☆)) ▶受験シーズンを迎えて with the coming of the entrance examination *season*. ●フットボールのシーズン the football *season*. ●レギュラーシーズン a regular *season*. ●(今)シーズン最多の連勝 a *season*-high winning streak. ●ホームランのシーズン記録を持っている hold the *season* record for home runs. ●野球は今シーズンオフだ This is the *óff-sèason for* baseball. (❗ ×*season off* は和製英語) ▶ホテルはシーズン中は込んでいます Hotels are crowded *in season*. (❗「シーズンオフでがらがらだ」は ... are almost empty *in the off-season*)
ジーセブン G7 《*the Group of Seven* (先進7か国蔵相会議)の略》.
ジーせんじょうのアリア『G線上のアリア』 *Air for the G string*. (参考 バイオリン独奏曲)
シーソー (a) seesaw, 《米》 a teeter(-totter). (❗遊具は C, 遊びは U) ●シーソー遊びをする play (at) *seesaw*; play on a *seesaw*.
●シーソーゲーム (接戦) a close game [match].
しいたけ 椎茸 [[植物]] a *shiitake* mushroom; (説明的に) a flat Japanese mushroom cultivated on Japanese oak logs.
しいたげる 虐げる [[圧迫する]]《やや書》oppress; [[迫害する]] persecute; [[虐待する]] treat cruelly; [[暴政を行う]]《やや書》tyrannize ... (over). ●虐げられた人々 *oppressed* people; 《やや書》the *oppressed*. ▶独裁者は人々を虐げた The dictator *oppressed* [*tyrannized* (*over*)] the people. ▶貧しい人々を虐げてはいけない Don't *treat* poor people [《やや書》the *poor*] *cruelly*.
シーチキン tuna /t(j)ú:nə/; 《米商標》 Chicken of the Sea. (❗ ×*sea chicken* は日本の商標)
シーツ a sheet. ●ベッドのシーツを変える change the *sheets* on the bed.
しーっ [[静かにさせるとき]] hush!; sh!; 《やや話》 shush!; [[動物などを追い払うとき]] shoo! ▶しーっ! だれかがやって来る *Hush* [*Sh*]! Someone is coming here. ▶彼女は強くしーっと言って子供を黙らせた She hushed

her child firmly. ▶彼は猫をしーっ(しーっ)と追い払った *"Shoo!"* he shouted, chasing the cat away./ He shooed the cat away.

しいて 強いて 〖力ずくで〗by force; 〖意に反して〗against one's will. ●強いて彼に小切手をきかせる *make* him sign [*force* him *to* sign] the check; make him sign the check *against his will*. ▶強いてとおっしゃるならすっかりお話ししましょう I'll tell you the whole story, if you *insist*. ▶どちらもお似合いですが、強いて言えば、こちらの方がいいかもしれません Both of them look good on you, but if I *have to* make a choice, this one is a little better.

シーティー 〖断層撮影〗CT 《*computed* [*computerized*] *tomography*の略》.

シーディー 〖コンパクトディスク〗(a) CD 《**®** ～s》《*compact disc*の略》. ●CDをかける put on [play] a *CD*. ●暇なときにCDを聴く listen to *CDs* in one's free time. ▶その曲はCDに入っている The music is available on *CD*. ●CDプレーヤー a CD player.

ジーディーピー 〖国内総生産〗〖経済〗GDP 《*Gross Domestic Product*の略》. 会話「日本のGDPは世界で何番目ですか」「2番目です」"Where does Japan's *GDP* rank in the world?" "(It ranks) second."

シーディーロム (a) CD-ROM 《**®** ～s》《*compact disc with read-only memory*の略》.

シート ❶〖座席〗a seat. (⇨シートベルト)
❷〖覆い〗a cover; 〖防水シート〗a waterproof canvas; 〖タールなどを塗った〗(a) tarpáulin.
❸〖1枚の紙〗a sheet. ●切手シート a *sheet* of stamps.

シード ●第1シードの選手 a top-*seeded* player; a top *seed*. ●第5シードの選手 a No. 5 *seed* player; a 5th-*seeded* player. ▶彼は昨年の柔道大会では第4シードだった He *was seeded* fourth [No. 4] in the grand *judo* tournament last year.

シートノック 〖野球〗pre-game fielding practice; 《和製語》seat knock.

シートベルト a seat [a safety] belt. ●肩掛けシートベルト a harness. ●シートベルトをお締めください Fasten your *seat* [*safety*] *belts*, please. ●みんなシートベルトをつけていますか Is everyone strapped in?

シートン 〖米国の作家・博物学者〗Seton (Ernest Thompson ～).

ジーパン jeans; 《和製語》G-pants. (⇨ジーンズ)

ジーピーエス GPS 《the *global positioning system*の略》.

シーピーユー 〖コンピュータ〗a CPU 《*central processing unit*の略》.

ジープ 〖商標〗a jeep.

シーフード (a) seafood. ●シーフードを食べる eat *seafood*. ●シーフードレストラン a seafood restaurant.

シームレス ── シームレスの 〖形〗〖縫い目のない〗seamless. ●シームレスストッキング 《a pair of》seamless stockings.

シーラカンス 〖古生物〗a coelacanth /síːləkænθ/.

シーリング 〖賃金・予算などの最高限度額〗a ceiling. ●予算シーリング a budget *ceiling*.

*******しいる 強いる** 〖強制する〗〖無理に〗force; 〖仕方なくやらせる〗〖書〗compel (-ll-) (⇨強制する); 〖意見・義務などを押しつける〗impose. ●彼に自白を強いる *force* [*compel*] him *to* confess; *force* a confession out of him. ●自分の意見を他人に強いる *impose* [*force*] one's opinions (*up*)*on* other people [others].

シール a seal /síːl/, a sticker. (**!** 後の方が一般的) ●封筒にクリスマス用シールを張る put a Christmas *sticker* [*seal*] on the envelope.

シールドこうほう シールド工法 a shield method. (参考 トンネル掘進技術の一つ)

しいれ 仕入れ (a) purchase; buying.
●仕入れ価格[値段] a púrchase [a búying] price. ●仕入れ係 a púrchase clèrk. ●仕入れ先 a supplier; a vendor. ●仕入れ品 stock (on hand); goods on hand.

シーレーン 〖海上交通路〗a sea lane.

*******しいれる 仕入れる** 〖買い入れる〗buy*; 〖大量に〗stock up (*on* goods); 〖手に入れる〗get*. ▶食料品をたくさん仕入れた We *have bought* a lot of foodstuffs [*stocked up on* foodstuffs]./〖在庫に対して〗We *have* a large *stock of* foodstuffs. ▶どこでそんな情報を仕入れたのか Where *have* you *got* such (×an) information?

じいろ 地色 the ground color.

しいん 子音 〖音声〗a consonant (⇔a vowel). ●有[無]声子音 a voiced [a voiceless] *consonant*.

しいん 死因 the cause of death. 会話「死因は?」「心臓まひだ」"What did he *die of*?" "Heart failure." (**!** 詳しくは He *died of* heart failure. 堅い言い方では Heart failure was the *cause of* his *death*. も可)

しいん 試飲 ── 試飲する 〖動〗sample, try; taste. ●ワインの試飲会 a wine-*tasting* party.

シーン 〖場面〗a scene. ●ラブシーン a love *scene*.

じいん 寺院 a temple; 〖イスラム教の〗a mosque.

ジーン 〖遺伝子〗a gene. ●ジーンセラピー〖遺伝子治療〗gene therapy. ●ジーンバンク〖遺伝子銀行〗a gene bank.

ジーンズ 《a pair of》《米》blue》jeans, 《商標》Levi's /líːvaiz/; 〖(米) denims; 《和製語》G-pants. ●ジーパンをはく put on 《a pair of》*jeans*. ●ひざで切ったジーパンをはいた少年 a boy in cutoff *jeans*; a boy wearing cutoffs.

しいんと ●しいんとなる fall silent. (⇨静まり返る) ▶先生から級友の死を知らされた教室はショックでしいんとなった There reigned a *shocked* silence in the classroom [〖沈黙して〗(The whole) class listened *in shocked silence*] when the homeroom teacher broke the news of their friend's death. (**!** reignは「支配する」の意で、代わりに was も可) ▶森は風もなくしいんと静まり返っていた The forest was *perfectly still* [There was a *perfect stillness* in the forest] when the wind was dead.

じいんと ●じいんとさせる〖感動させる〗move, touch. (**!** 前の方が意味が強い) ●じいんとくる場面 a *touching* scene. ▶その悲しい出来事に私は目頭がじいんとなった/I *was moved to tears* at the sad incident./I felt tears coming to my eyes at the incident. ▶彼女の言葉がじいんときた(=心にしみた) Her words *came home to me*. ▶水に手をひたすと、冷たくてじいんとしてきた(=無感覚になった) When I dipped my hand in the water, I felt it *going numb* from cold. ▶エレベーターで降りる途中耳がじいんとなった On my way down by elevator a drum seemed to be beating in my ear.

じう 慈雨 〖ありがたい雨〗a welcome rain. ●干天の慈雨 (⇨干天 [成句])

じうた 地唄 (説明的に) a folk song accompanied on the *samisen*.

しうち 仕打ち 〖扱い〗treatment. ●彼からひどい仕打ちを受ける be treated very badly by him; get a raw *deal* from him. ▶彼の仕打ちは決して忘れないI shall [will] never forget *what he did to me*. (**!** shall は自分の決意の度合いが強い)

しうん 紫雲 a purple cloud.

しうんてん 試運転 〖名〗〖列車・車などの試運行〗a trial [a test] run; 〖車などの〗a test drive.

シェア
—— **試運転する** 動 ●機械を試運転してみる put a machine to trial; give a machine a trial run. ▶車を試運転した I made a trial [a test] run of a car./ I test-drove a car.

シェア 名 〖市場占有率〗(a) (market) share. (❢単数形で) ●シェアを伸ばす increase one's *share of the market*. ▶この会社はパソコン業界では30パーセントのシェアを占めている This company has an 30 percent *market share* in personal computers.
—— **シェアする** 動 〖分かち合う, 共有する〗share.

しえい 市営 名 〖市で経営されている〗city-run. ●市営の 形 municipal; (市で経営されている) city-run. ●市営アパート a *municipal* apartment house. ●市営バス a *municipal* [a city] bus. ▶このプールは市営です This swimming pool *is run* [*is operated*] *by the city*.
●じえい業者を営む be a *self-employed* builder.
—— **自営する** 動 run one's own 《store》; run 《a store》 of one's own; be self-employed.
●自営業者 a self-employed person, 〖集合的〗(やや書) the self-employed (❢複数扱い) 〖独立した実業家〗an independent businessman [businesswoman] (履 -men) (❢会社・商店などの所有者をいう); (小売業者) a retailer.

じえい 自衛 名 self-defense. ●自衛上 in *self-defense*. ●自衛手段を講じる 〖国家が〗take *self-defense* measures; 〖個人が〗take measures to *protect* oneself.
—— **自衛する** 動 defend [protect] oneself. (⇨守る)
●自衛官 a (Japan) Self-Defense Force official.
●自衛艦 a Japan Maritime Self-Defense Force ship; a JMSDF ship. ●自衛権 〖exercise〗the right of self-defense. ●自衛隊 the (Japanese) Self-Defense Forces 〖略 JSDF, SDF〗. ●自衛隊員 a Self-Defense official.

シェイクスピア 〖英国の劇作家・詩人〗Shákespeare (William ～).

シェイプアップ getting (oneself) into shape; (美容体操) beauty excercises, 《書》calisthenics /kæləsθénɪks/. ●シェイプアップする get (oneself) into shape (❢ shape up は「体調をよくする」の意で, 日本語のように「体形をよくする」の意には用いない); do beauty excercises.

ジェーアール 《愛称》JR (*Japan Railways* の略).
●JR 西[東]日本 West [East] Japan Railway Company.

ジェーオーシー 〖日本オリンピック委員会〗JOC (*Japan Olympic Committee* の略).

シェーカー (カクテルを作る) a shaker.

シェークハンド shaking hands; 〖テニス・卓球などのラケットの握り方〗the handshake grip for the racket.

シェーバー 〖電気かみそり〗a [an electric] shaver.

シェービングクリーム (put on) sháving crèam.

ジェービイ 〖共同企業体〗a JV; a joint venture.

ジェーリーグ J. League. (❢正式名称は Japan Professional Football League)

しえき 私益 private [personal] interest. (⇨私利)

しえき 使役 名 ●使役する 動 make 〈him〉 work [do 〈it〉]; set 〈him〉 to work.
●使役動詞〖文法〗a causative verb.

ジェスチャー (身ぶり) a gesture. (⇨身振り) ▶彼は本当はそんなつもりじゃないんだ. ただのジェスチャー(= 見せかけ)だよ He doesn't really mean it; it's just a *show* [《話》an *act*].
●ジェスチャーゲーム 〖play〗 a game of charades /ʃəréɪdz/.

ジェット 〖噴出(物)〗a jet.

●ジェットエンジン a jet engine. ●ジェット気流 a jet stream. ●ジェットコースター a roller coaster, 《米》a coaster, 《英》a big dipper, 〖和製語〗a jet coaster. ●ジェットスキー a jet ski. ●ジェットスキーに乗る ride a jet ski; go jet skiing. ●ジェットバス a jet bath. ●ジェットフォイル 〖噴射推進式水中翼船〗a jetfoil.

ジェットき ジェット機 a jet (plane [airplane]); 〖定期ジェット旅客機〗a jetliner, a jet airliner. ●ジェット機でアメリカへ行く fly *by jet* to America.

ジェトロ 〖日本貿易振興会〗JETRO (*Japan External Trade Organization* の略).

ジェネリック ●ジェネリック医薬品〖後発医薬品〗a generic drug.

ジェネレーション 〖世代〗a generation.
●ジェネレーションギャップ a generation gap.

ジェノサイド 〖集団殺害〗genocide.

ジェノバ 〖イタリアの都市〗Genoa /dʒénoʊə, dʒenóʊə/. 〖参考〗イタリア名 Genova)

シェパード 〖動物〗《米》a German shepherd (dog); 《英》an Alsatian.

シェフ 〖コック長〗a chef (履 ～s) (❢フランス語「長(head)」の意), a head cook. ●シェフのおすすめ料理 (掲示などで) chef's special(ty) [suggestion].

ジェラシー 〖しっと〗jealousy 〖dʒéləsɪ/. ▶彼女には彼が勝ったときジェラシーを感じた She felt *jealous* when he won.

シエラレオネ 〖国名〗Sierra Leone; (公式名) the Republic of Sierra Leone. (首都 Freetown) ●シエラレオネ人 a Sierra Leonean. ●シエラレオネ(人)の Sierra Leonean.

シェリー (酒) (a) sherry.

シェルター a shelter. ●核シェルター a nuclear (fallout) *shelter*.

シェルパ 〖チベット系の高地民族・山岳ガイド〗a Sherpa.

しえん 支援 名 support; backing. (⇨援助)
—— **支援する** 動 support; back ... up. ●平和運動を支援する *support* the cause of peace.
●支援者 a supporter.

しえん 私怨 a grudge (*against*); (a) personal enmity (*toward*). ▶ジョンはアンが昇進してからずっと私怨を抱いている John has had a *grudge against* Ann ever since she was promoted.

しえん 紫煙 (blue) tobacco smoke. ●紫煙をくゆらす puff (away); smoke.

しえん 試演 a trial performance, a preview.

じえん 自演 ●自作自演する (⇨自作)

ジェンダー 〖文化的・社会的役割としての性〗(a) gender. ●ジェンダーフリー gender-free.

しお 塩 salt. (❢ (1) 海水からとった塩 (sea salt) および岩塩 (rock salt) からとった普通の塩をさす. (2) common salt ともいう; (食卓塩) table salt. ●塩1つまみ [1さじ] a pinch [a spoonful] of *salt*. ●塩を振りかける salt; sprinkle *salt* on 〈it〉; sprinkle 〈it〉 with *salt*. ▶このスープは塩がききすぎている[足りない] This soup is too salty [needs more *salt*].
▶塩を取ってもらえますか(食卓で) Will [Could] you pass (me) the *salt*? (❢事情 米英では, 食卓で腰を上げて人の前に手を伸ばすて取るのはマナーに反する) ●娘をなめても(= 塩だけを食べて生きようとも)娘は高校を出す My daughter shall receive [get] a high school education, even if I must live on *salt* alone.

●塩をまく ●塩をまいて清める scatter some *salt* for luck.

●塩入れ (振り出し式) a salt shaker; (つぼ式) a salt cellar.

しお 潮 a tide; 〖潮流〗a current; 〖海水〗séa [sált].

しおあん 塩餡 salty bean jam.

しおかげん 塩加減 ●塩加減をほどよくする be properly *salted*; be well-*seasoned*. ▶真紀はスープの塩加減を見た Maki tasted the soup to see if she put enough *salt* in it.

しおかぜ 潮風 a salty ocean [sea] breeze; a sea [a salt] breeze.

しおから 塩辛 ●(説明的に) finely-cut fish meat salt-pickled with its entrails and fermented. ●イカの塩辛 cuttlefish *shiokara* preserve.

しおからい 塩辛い salty. ●塩辛い水[食べ物] *salty* water [food].

しおからとんぼ 塩辛蜻蛉 [昆虫] a *Shiokara* dragonfly.

しおき 仕置き (⇨お仕置き)

しおくり 仕送り 图 (郵送された金)(やや書) a remittance; (保護者が与える金) an allowance. ▶母からの月々の仕送りで暮らしています I live on the *money* my mother sends me every month./I live on a monthly *remittance* from my mother.
── 仕送りする 動 ▶東京の息子に月10万円仕送りする *send* 100,000 yen each month to one's son in Tokyo.

しおけ 塩気 图 (塩分) salt /sɔ́ːlt/; (塩味) a salty taste. ●塩気がある taste [be] salty. ●塩気を抜く remove the salt (*from* seaweed).

しおこしょう 塩胡椒 ●肉に塩こしょうをする season meat with *salt and pepper*.

しおさい 潮騒 the sound of the sea [waves].

しおさい『潮騒』*The Sound of Waves*. (参考) 三島由紀夫の小説)

しおざけ 塩鮭 a salt(ed) salmon.

しおさめ 仕納め ▶これが今年のスキーの仕納めだ This is my *last* skiing *for* [*of*] this year.

しおじ 潮路 [潮の流れる道] a tideway; [航路] a sea lane [route].

しおし(と) dejectedly; with a heavy heart. ●しおしとしている be in *low* [*poor*] spirits.

しおせんべい 塩煎餅 a *shiosembei*; (説明的に) a rice cracker seasoned with soy sauce.

しおだし 塩出し ── 塩出しする 動 ▶数の子を塩出しする *remove the salt* from salted herring roe *by soaking it in water*.

しおだち 塩断ち 图 abstinence from salt food.
── 塩断ちする 動 abstain from (eating) salt food.

しおたれる 潮垂れる 〖しょぼくれる〗look miserable; 〖泣く〗weep; (涙を流す) shed tears.

しおづけ 塩漬け ●キュウリの塩漬け *pickled* cucumber. ●野菜を塩漬けにする keep [pickle] vegetables in *salt*.

しおどき 潮時 high time; (適した時)(a) time. ▶引きあげる潮時だ《話》It's *high time* (that) we left. ▶that は通例省略し, 従節の動詞は直説法過去形が普通)/It's *high time* for us to leave. ●潮時(=好機) を見計らって引退した I *seized an opportunity* to resign. ▶何事にも *潮時*(= 時機)というものがある There is a *time for* everything.

しおひがり 潮干狩り ●潮干狩りに行く go *shellfish gathering* 《on the beach》; go 《to the beach》to *gather shellfish*.

しおみず 塩水 salt [salty] water.

しおもみ 塩揉み ●キュウリの塩もみ paper-thin slices of cucumbers sprinkles with salt and squeezed.

しおやき 塩焼き (魚の) broiled 《米》[grilled 《英》] fish with salt.

しおやけ 潮焼け ── 潮焼けする 動 ●潮焼けしている be tanned by the sun and salty ocean breezes.

しおらしい 〖控えめな〗modest; 〖おとなしい〗gentle, meek; 〖かわいらしい〗sweet; 〖いじらしい〗touching. ●しおらしい娘 a *sweet* girl. ●彼は今日はいやにしおらしい He is unusually *modest* today.

しおり 枝折り, 栞 (本にはさむ) a bookmark; (案内書, 手引き) a guide, a guidebook. ●しおりをはさむ put [slip] a *bookmark* between the pages.

しおりど 枝折り戸 (説明的に) a (garden) gate (made) of twigs and branches, or of bamboos.

しおれる 〖しぼむ〗wither; 〖色・生気を失う〗fade; 〖たれる〗droop. ▶花が寒さでしおれた The flowers *withered* in the cold./The cold *withered* the flowers.

しおん 紫苑 〖植物〗an aster; an Michaelmas daisy.

じおん 字音 the pronunciation [sound] of a Chinese character.
●字音仮名遣い *kana* orthography for pronunciation of Chinese characters.

しか 〖動物〗a deer (⇨ーだけ); (雄) a stag, a buck; (雌) a hind, a doe; (子鹿) a fawn. ●シカの皮 deerskin, buckskin. ●シカの角 an antler; (1対) a pair of antlers. ●シカの肉 venison. ▶奈良にはシカがたくさんいる There are a lot of *deer* 《*deers*》 in Nara.
▶鹿を追う者は山を見ず Those who are absorbed in one thing lose sight of other things.

しか 市価 a market price [value]. ●市価の変動 *market* fluctuations.

しか 歯科 dentistry, dental surgery.
●歯科医 a dentist; a dental surgeon. ●歯科医院 a dentist's (office); a dental office [clinic].
●歯科技工士 a dental technician. ●歯科大学 a dental college.

***-しか** (副助詞) only. (❗ 日本語では「しか」は必ず否定語とともに用いられ, 「…しか…ない」となるが, 英語では通例肯定で表す) (⇨ーだけ) ▶昨夜は5時間しか寝ていない I slept *only* (for) five hours last night. ▶《話》言葉ではI ónly slept (for) ˇfive hours. .... の位置が普通) ▶母しか私を本当に理解してくれる人はいません *Only* my mother really understands me./My mother is the *only* person who really understands me. ▶待つしかない I'll *just* have to wait. ▶彼女は泣くしかなかった The *only* thing [*All*] she could do was (to) cry. (❗ to を省略するのは主に《話》)/She had *no choice but to* cry. (❗

ここは「泣くしか選択肢がない」ことで, She did nothing but cry. では「ただもう泣くばかり」の意で状況描写しているだけなので不適切(⇨唯(ゆい)❷)) ▶ 彼に頼むしか方法がない There's *no* way *but to* ask him./We have *no* (other) choice *but to* ask him. (⚠会話体では2文にする You should ask him. It's the *only* way to go. のようにいうことが多い) ▶ 箱の中には古新聞しか(=古新聞以外何も)なかった We found *nothing but* old newspapers in the box.
会話「どうしよう」「もう一度やってみなさい. それしかないでしょう」"What shall I do?" "Try again. That's *all* you can do."

しが 歯牙 ● 歯牙にもかけない take no notice (*of*); not care at all (a straw).

じか 自家 ● 自家薬籠(やくろう)中の物 自家やくろう中の物とする acquire a perfect command of; gain full control of.
● 自家営業 (a) family business. ● 自家受精〘生物〙self-fertilization. ● 自家受粉〘植物〙self-pollination. ● 自家中毒〘医学〙autointoxication. ● 自家撞着(どうちゃく) self-contradiction. ● 自家発電装置 one's own power plant.

じか 時下 recently; lately. (⇨最近) ▶ 時下ますますご健勝のこととお慶び申しあげます(手紙で) I hope that you are healthy and happy.

じか 時価 the current price. ● 絵を時価で売る sell a picture *at the current price.* ▶ このダイヤは時価(=現在の金で)1,000万円です This diamond *is worth* ten million yen *in today's money.*/(今日1,000万円と評価されている) This diamond *is valued* [*is quoted*] *at* ten million yen *today.*
● 時価総額 the aggregate market value; market capitalization. ● 時価発行 an issue at the market price.

じか 磁化 图〘物理〙magnetization. ── 磁化する 動 magnetize.

じが 自我 〘自己〙the (one's) self; 〘哲学〙(the) ego. ● 自我の形成 the formation of one's *self* [*ego*]. ● 自我に目覚める become conscious of *oneself.* ▶ 彼は自我が強い(=自己中心的だ) He is *self-centered* [*egotistic,* (利己的な) *egoistic*].

しかい 司会 ● T氏の司会で under the *chairmanship* of Mr. T. ▶ 彼がその会議の司会をした He *presided at* [*chaired*] the meeting.

── 司会する 動 take* [be in] the chair (*at* a meeting), preside (*at* a meeting); act as host (master of ceremonies) (*at* a show), 《米話》emcee 〖(英) compere〗(a show).
● 司会者 〖会議の〗a chairman (匾-men) (⇨議長); 〖討論会などの〗a moderator; 〖番組・パーティーなどの〗a host, a master of ceremonies (略 MC), 《米話》an emcee /émsiː/, 《英》a compere /kámpeər/ (⚠以上は女性にも用いる); 〖ニュース放送の総合司会者〗(主に米) an anchorperson, an anchor; (男性) an anchorman (匾-men), (女性) an anchorwoman (匾-women).

しかい 四海 〖四つの海〗the four seas; 〖世の中全体〗the whole world.

しかい 市会 〖「市議会」の略〗(⇨市議会)

しかい 死海 the Dead Sea.

しかい 視界 (見通しのきく距離) visibility; (視野) view, sight; (視域) a field of vision. (⇨見通し) ▶ 視界500メートル a *visibility* of 500 meters (⚠具体的には冠詞がつく). ● 視界がきかないために for lack of *visibility.* ● 視界に入ってくる[から消える] come into [disappear from, go out of] *view.* ● 視界を妨げる block [obstruct] one's *view.* ▶ 視界が悪い(ゼロの)ため空港は閉鎖された The airport was closed because of poor [zero] *visibility.*/It was difficult to *see* and (so) the airport was closed.

しかい 斯界 ● 斯界の権威 an authority in the *field* [on the *subject*].

しがい 市外 ● 市外に住む live in [×on] the suburbs [a suburb] (*of*). (⇨郊外)
● 市外局番 (米) an area code, (英) an STD code (subscriber trunk dialling code (電話加入者市外通話コード)の略). (参考) 東京の03, 神戸の078などに当たる. ● 市外通話 (米) a long-distance call; (英) a trunk call.

しがい 市街 (通り) a street; (町) a town, a city. ● 旧市街 the old (section of the) *town.* ▶ 市街地へのバスは1時間にせいぜい1本程度しかない The bus to the city center [downtown] is limited to one [a single] service per hour at most. (⚠downtown は郊外に対して, 街中で商店や公共の建物などが多くある地域をさす)
● 市街戦 street fighting. ● 市街地図 a city map. ● 市街電車 (米) a streetcar; 《英》a tram(car).

しがい 死骸 (人・動物の) a (dead) body; (人の) a corpse; (動物の) a carcass. (⇨死体)

じかい 次回 next; next time. (⇨次) ▶ 次回の会議はいつ開かれますか When will the *next* meeting be (held)? ▶ 次回完結 To be concluded.

じかい 耳介 〘解剖〙an auricle.

じかい 自戒 ● 自戒の念 a self-reproach.
── 自戒する 動 admonish oneself.

じかい 自壊 图 disintegration. ── 自壊する 動 disintegrate.

じがい 自害 ── 自害する 動 kill oneself.

しがいせん 紫外線 ultraviolet /ʌltrəváiələt/ rays; 〘光学〙ultraviolet light.
● 紫外線療法 ultraviolet treatment [therapy].

しかえし 仕返し 图 revenge.
── 仕返し(を)する 動 〘話〙get back (*at*+人, *for*+事); get even (*with*+人, *for*+事); pay (him) back (*for*); (復讐(ふくしゅう)する) take revenge (*on*+人, *for*+事). ● 彼におまけをつけて仕返しをする *pay him back* with interest. ▶ 彼に侮辱されたので仕返ししてやった I *got back at* him *for* insulting me./(同一行為で) I was insulted, so I insulted him *in return.*/I *returned* his insult.

しかがり 鹿狩り *Deer Hunting*. (参考) 国木田独歩の小説)

古今ことばの系譜『鹿狩り』

「鹿狩りに連れて行こうか」と中根の叔父がだしぬけに言ったので僕はまごついた.
「だって僕には鉄砲がないもの」
「あハハハハばかを言ってる, お前に鉄砲が撃てるものか, ただ見物に行くのだ」
僕はこの時やっと十二だった. 鹿狩りのおもしろい事は幾度も聞いているから, 僕はお伴をることにした.
Uncle Nakane asked me, "Would you like to go deer hunting with us?" His question was so sudden that I did not know what to answer.
"But I have no gun," I said.
My uncle chuckled and said, "Of course, you are too young to use a gun. You just watch."
I was only twelve. But I had heard that deer hunting was interesting, so I decided to go. ⇒(1)「まごつく」は「どう答えたらよいか, すぐには分からなかった」と解釈した. (2) 笑い声を hahaha などとそのまま擬音語にせず, chuckled など動詞の選択で表現する方がよい. 機嫌のいい笑い)

しかく 資格 (地位・職業などの) (a) qualification; (必要以上) a requirement (❗しばしば複数形で); (免許) a license.

① 【〜資格, 資格〜】 ● 有資格者 an eligible (person). ▶彼は受験資格がない He has no *qualification(s)* [is not qualified] to take the examination. ▶彼は大学の入学資格(=要件)を満たしている He meets the *requirements* for entering college. ▶彼は英語の資格試験を受けた He took a *qualifying* examination in English.

② 【資格が[は]】 ● 資格がいる need a certificate. ▶彼には音楽を教える資格がある He *is qualified for* teaching [*to* teach] music. /(音楽の教師の資格がある) He *is qualified as* [*to* be] a teacher of music. ▶彼は年金をもらう資格がある He is *eligible* (↔ineligible) *to* receive a pension [*for* a pension]. (❗eligible は「法的に資格がある」の意) ▶君にはそんなことを言う資格(=権利)はない You don't have the *right* [You have no *right*] to say that. ▶私にはそのような賞をもらう資格(=価値)はない I *am unworthy of* [*don't deserve* (*to* receive), 《書》 *am not deserving of*] such a prize.

③ 【資格を】 ● 資格を持つ have *qualification* (*for*). ● 資格をとる obtain [get] a *qualification* (*for*). ▶彼は去年医師の資格を得た He got a doctor's *license* [a medical *qualification*] last year. (❗いろ例より口語的)/He *qualified* [gained a *qualification*] *as* a doctor last year. (❗He qualified himself as a doctor last year. は今はまれ) ▶彼女はオリンピックの出場資格を得た[失った] She *qualified for* [*was disqualified from*] the Olympic Games. ▶協会は彼に指導員[その仕事]の資格を与えた The association *qualified* him *as* an instructor [*for* the job]. /The association gave him a *qualification as* an instructor [*for* the job].

④ 【資格で】 ▶彼は法律顧問の資格でその会議に出席した He joined the meeting *in the capacity of* (*in his capacity*) *as* a legal adviser.

***しかく 四角** 图 〖正方形〗 a square; 〖四辺形〗 a quadrilateral. ● 四角に切る cut (*it*) *square*.
● **四角四面** 〖四角形〗の square. ● 四角四面な人 a square; a quadrate; a prim 《話》stuffy person.
— **四角い** 形 square. ● 四角いテーブル a *square* table. ● 大きな四角い紙 a large *square* piece of paper.

しかく 死角 (見えない方向) a blind side; (運転手にとっての) a blind spot (❗比喩的に「盲点」の意にも用いる (➪盲点).

しかく 刺客 an assassin.

しかく 視角 〖物理〗 the optic angle, the angle of vision; 〖見地, 観点〗 a viewpoint, a point of view.

しかく 視覚 (the sense of) sight; 〖視力〗 eyesight, vision. ● 視覚を失う lose one's *eyesight* [*sight*].
● 視覚に訴える appeal to *the eye*. ▶彼は視覚を失って聴覚が発達した Having lost *the sense of sight*, his hearing improved.
● **視覚器官** the visual organ. ● **視覚教具** visual aids.

しかく 史学 history; study of history.
● **史学科** the History Course.

しかく 私学 a private school; (大学) a private college [university].

しかく 歯学 《やや書》 dentistry.
● **歯学部** the Department [School] of Dentistry. (➪学部)

しかく 詩学 (詩論) poetics; (韻律論) prosody.

***じかく 自覚** 图 consciousness; awareness. ▶公害をなくすには市民の自覚が必要だ Citizens have to *be aware* (*of*) what they should do to control pollution. (❗wh- 語の前では of は省略されることが多い)
— **自覚する** 動 become* [be] aware (conscious) [of] 〖悟る〗 know*, realize. ▶自分の欠点は自覚している I *am aware of* [*know*] my own faults. ▶彼は指導者であることを十分自覚している He fully *realizes* [*knows*] (*that*) he is the leader.
● **自覚症状** subjective symptoms.

じかく 字画 the (number of) strokes of [in] a Chinese character.

じかく 痔核 piles; 〖医学〗《米》hemorrhoids, 《英》haemorrhoids.

じがくじしゅう 自学自習 self-instruction; learning by oneself.

しかくばる 四角ばる be too formal; 《やや話》stand* on ceremony. ● 四角ばった文字 an *angular* character. ▶結婚式は四角ばらずにやります We're going to have an *informal* wedding.

しかけ 仕掛け 〖装置〗 a device; 〖機械装置〗《書》 a mechanism; 〖ごまかしの〗 a trick. ● 機械仕掛けの mechanical *device*. ● ネズミをとる簡単な仕掛け a simple *device* 〖話〗 a *gadget*) *for* catching rats. ▶この時計はぜんまい仕掛けで動きます This clock works by a spring [on a spring *mechanism*]. ▶それには種も仕掛けもない There is no *trick* in it.
● **仕掛け人** a mastermind (*behind* a crime).

しかける 仕掛ける ❶ 〖着手する〗 begin*, start. ● 仕掛けた仕事 the job (which) we *have just begun* [*strated*] *to* do; 《やや書》 the job *in hand*. ▶彼にけんかを仕掛ける (=売る) *pick* (*up*) a quarrel *with* him. ● 戦争を仕掛ける *make* [*wage*] war 《*on*, *against*》.
❷ 〖装置する〗 set*; (爆弾など) plant. ● キツネにわなを仕掛ける *set* [*lay*] a trap for a fox. ● 大使館に爆弾を仕掛ける *set* [*plant*] a bomb at the Embassy. ▶その爆弾は触ると爆発するように仕掛けられていた The bombs *were set* to *go off* on contact.

シカゴ 〖米国の都市〗Chicago /ʃikáːgou/.

しかざん 死火山 an extinct volcano (働 〜e)s).

***しかし but** (❗反対・対立を示す最も一般的な語); (しかしながら) 《やや書》however (❗but とほとんど同じ意味だが, 文頭・文中・文尾いずれにも置かれる. 通常コンマで区切る); (それでもなお) (and) yet, 《やや書》(but [and]) still (❗以上の二つは but, however より強い反対・対立を表す); (それにもかかわらず) (話) all the same (❗文頭・文尾に置かれる), 《書》nevertheless (❗文頭・文中・文尾いずれにも置かれる); (けれども) (話) though (❗通例コンマを添えて文尾に置く. although にはこの用法はない). ▶彼は一生懸命働いた. しかしうまく行かなかった He worked hard, *but* [*(and) yet*] he didn't succeed. /He worked hard; *however*, he didn't succeed. /(期待に反して失敗に終わった) He worked hard *only to* fail. ▶雨が激しく降っている. しかし私たちは出発しなければならない It's raining hard. *However* [*All the same*, *Nevertheless*, (たとえそうでも) *Even so*], we must start now. ▶なかわらず ❶ ▶列車に乗り遅れた. しかし田中君が車に乗せてくれた I missed the train; Tanaka gave me a ride, *though* [*although*].

じがじさん 自画自賛 图 self-praise.
— **自画自賛する** 動 praise oneself; 《主に英話》blow one's own trumpet; 《話》pat oneself on the back.

しかず 如何ず ▶逃げるにしかず(=逃げるのが一番だ) It is *best* for you to run away./It is *best* that you (should) run away. ●百聞は一見にしかず (⇨百聞〖成句〗)

じかせい 自家製 ●自家製(の)ジャム *homemade* jam. ●自家製のビール *home-brewed* beer; (a) *home brew* 〖他のアルコール飲料をさすこともある〗.

じかせん 耳下腺 〖解剖〗the parotid (gland). ●耳下腺炎〖医学〗parotitis; (おたふくかぜ) (the) mumps 〖単数扱い〗.

じがぞう 自画像 a self-portrait. ●自画像を描く paint 〖線画で draw〗 one's *own portrait*.

しかた 仕方 a way; (系統だった) a method; (...のやり方) how to (do); (うまく対処するこつ) 《話》the ropes. (⇨方法) ▶彼のあいさつの仕方が気にくわない I don't like the *way* he greets me./I don't like his *way* of greeting. ▶彼の実験の仕方は間違っていた The *method* of his experiment was wrong. ▶この留学生にここでの生活の仕方をよく教えてあげてね。頼みますよ I'm counting on you to teach these foreign students the *ropes* around here.
〖会話〗「その料理の仕方をごぞんじですか」「ええ, 数年前に習いました」"Do you know *how to* cook it?" "Yes, I learned *how* some years ago."
●仕方咄(ばなし) *rakugo* performed with gestural movements.

じかた 地肩 ▶トムは地肩が強い Tom has a powerful *throwing arm*.

*****しかた(が)ない 仕方(が)無い** ❶〖どうすることもできない〗can't help (it); 〖甘受せざるをえない〗have[＊ not to] accept (it); 〖避けられない〗cannot be avoided, be inevitable, be unavoidable; 〖選択の余地がない〗have no choice. ▶彼の悪声は仕方がない He *can't help* his coarse voice. ▶列車が遅れたって〖遅れるのは〗仕方がないよ I *can't help* it if (that) the train is late. ▶多少の批判は仕方がない Some criticisms *are inevitable*./You *have to* accept some criticisms. ▶彼女に真相を言うより仕方がない(=真相を言うよりほかにどうしようもない) You *have no (other) choice* [*There is nothing for it*] *but* to tell her the truth. ▶済んだ事は仕方がない What is done is done [cannot be undone].
〖会話〗「金曜日までは出発できないんだ」「じゃあ仕方がないな」"We can't leave till Saturday [×Friday]." "Well it *can't be helped*."
〖会話〗「いったいどうして彼にお金を払ったりしたのよ」「仕方がなかったのよ」"Whatever made you pay him?" "It *couldn't be avoided*."
❷〖当然だ〗it is natural (that).... (⇨当然) ▶彼女が彼を恨むのも仕方がないよ It's only *natural (that)* she should have [she has, ×she have] a grudge against him. ▶不注意だと言われても仕方がない I'm ×careless, if you ×like.
〖会話〗「家賃が払えなくなってアパートを追い出されたんだ」「そりゃ仕方がないな(=世の中そういうものだ)」 "I was kicked out of my apartment because I couldn't pay the rent." "That's *the way it goes* [*is*]."
❸〖むだだ〗it is [there is] no use (*doing*) (⇨無駄); 〖役に立たない〗won't do. ▶砂漠を横断するのにこんな車じゃ仕方がない This car *won't do* for driving across the desert.
❹〖...ずにいられない〗can't help (*doing*); 〖どうしても...したい〗be eager [anxious] (*to do*), 《話》be dying (*to do*; *for*). ▶心細くて仕方がなかった I *couldn't help* feeling lonely. ▶彼女に会いたくて仕方がない I'd very much like [I badly want] to see her. (❗前の方が控えめな言い方)/I just *can't wait*

[《話》I'm *dying*] to see her. (❗最後の言い方は女性が好んで用いる傾向がある) ▶彼は娘がかわいくてしかたがない He really dotes on his daughter. (❗ dote on ... で「...を溺愛する」の意)

しかたなしに 仕方無しに 〖選択なく...する〗be compelled (*to do*); (法律などによって) be obliged (*to do*); 〖渋々〗unwillingly; 〖しぶしぶ〗reluctantly; 〖意志に反して〗against one's will. ▶彼は仕方なしに職務を辞めた He *was compelled to* resign his office./He *had to* leave his office. (❗後の方が口語的) ▶私たちは彼の提案を仕方なしに受け入れた We *unwillingly* [*reluctantly*] accepted his proposal. ▶彼女は脅されて仕方なしに秘密をばらした She was threatened and revealed the secret *against* her will. ▶彼は差し出されたグラスに手を伸ばし, 仕方なしに少しずつ飲んだ He reached for the offered glass, taking the *obligatory* sip.

じかたび 地下足袋 rubber-soled *tabi* [socks, footwear].

じがため 地固め —— 地固め(を)する 動 harden [(ならす) level] the ground; (下地を作る) lay the groundwork (*for*) (❗比喩的にも用いる); (下準備をする) 《やや書》make preparatory [preliminary] arrangements (*for*).

じかだんぱん 直談判 direct negotiations. ●直談判に及ぶ negotiate (*with* him) directly [in person, personally].

-しがち apt, liable, prone. (⇨-がち) ●間違いをしがちだ be apt [liable, prone] *to* make mistakes.

しかつ 死活 life and [or] death. (❗語順に注意) ▶それは我が社にとって死活問題である For our company it's a matter of *life and death* [a *life-and-death* matter].

*****しがつ 四月** April (略 Apr.). (⇨一月)
●四月ばか April Fools' [Fool's] Day. (⇨エープリルフール)

じかつ 自活 图 self-support. ●自活の道 a means of *supporting oneself*.
—— 自活する 動 ●自活している学生 a *self-supporting* student. ●タクシーの運転手をして自活する *support oneself* [*earn one's own living*] (by) driving a taxi [as a taxi driver].

しかつめらしい 鹿爪らしい 〖顔つきが〗(いかめしい) stern; (もったいぶった) solemn; (深刻な) grave; 〖態度が〗(堅苦しい) stiff; 〖形式ばった〗formal.

しかと 確と 〖確かに〗certainly; 〖正確に〗exactly; 〖明白に〗clearly, distinctly; 〖しっかりと〗tightly, firmly. ●しかと考える think (it) over; consider (it) carefully. ▶しかとは見えなかった I couldn't see it *clearly* [*distinctly*].

じかとりひき 直取引 direct transaction.

しがない (つまらない) humble; (惨めな) 《やや書》wretched /rétʃɪd/. ●しがない暮らしをする lead [live] a *wretched* [a *miserable*] life. ▶田舎の小さな学校でしがない教師をしています I'm just a *humble* [a *lowly*] teacher at a small school in the country.

*****じかに 直に** directly; (伝聞でなく) at first hand. (⇨直接(に)) ●その事を彼からじかに聞く hear about it *directly* [*at first hand*] from him. ●肌にじかに着る put (it) on *next to* one's skin. ●ウイスキーをボトルからじかに飲む drink whiskey *straight* from the bottle.

じがね 地金 〖めっきの素地〗base metal; 〖未加工の金属〗raw metal. ●地金を出す(=本性を現す) betray oneself.

-しかねない (⇨-かねない)

じかばき 直履き ▶大輔はスニーカーをじかばきするのが好き

だ Daisuke likes *wearing* her sneaker *with no socks*.

しかばね 屍 a corpse; a dead body.
- 屍に鞭(むち)打つ blame a dead person for what he [she] did or said.

しかばん 私家版 a private edition.

じか び 直火 direct heat. ▶魚を直火で焼く roast [《米》broil, 《英》grill] fish over open fire.

しがみつく しがみ付く cling* to ...; (しっかりとつかまる) hang* onto ...; (しっかり握っている) hold* onto ....
- 母親にしがみついて離れない cling to one's mother.
- その大枝にしがみつく hang onto the bough; hold onto the bough; hold the bough tightly.

しかめっつら しかめっ面 a frown(ing face); a grimace /grímæs/. ▶しかめっ面をする (⇨しかめる)

しかめる ● 顔をしかめる (まゆをひそめる) frown /fráun/ 《at》; (痛みや不快で) grimace /grímǝs/ 《at》; (いやな顔をする) make [pull] a face 《at》. ⓘ a face is faces とも する ▶彼に向かって[彼の行儀の悪さに]顔をしかめる *frown at* him [his bad behavior]. ● 顔をしかめてそれを見る look at it with a *frown*. ● 痛くて顔をしかめる *grimace* with pain; make [give] a *grimace* of pain.

*しかも ❶ 《その上》(⇨その上) ▶彼女は気だてがよく, しかも器量よしだ She is good-natured, *and besides* [*what is more*, 《書》*moreover*], she is pretty. ▶彼は自信が持てる, しかも絶対的にね He is sure of it, *yes*, (*and*) positive. ⓘ 前言よりさらに強い言い方を導く ▶私はそこへ行かなければならない, しかも(=それも)すぐに I must go there, *and* that *at once*. ⓘ *and* that の後は通例副詞 ▶私は傘をなくした, しかも(=それも)買ったばかりのを I've lost an umbrella, (*and*) a brand-new one *at that*. ⓘ *at that* の前は通例名詞, 時に副詞

会話「これが長男の太郎か」「まあ大きくなったこと！しかもお父さんにそっくりじゃないの」 "This is Taro, the oldest." "Hasn't he grown! *And* /ǽnd/ isn't he (just) like his father!"

❷ 《それにもかかわらず》(⇨かかわらず) ▶この魚は安くてしかも栄養がある This fish is inexpensive, (*and* [*but*]) *yet* (it is) nourishing [*but* (it is) *nevertheless* nourishing]./This fish is inexpensive *but* [*and* /ǽnd/] *nourishing*.

じかよう 自家用 (家庭用) family use; (個人用) private use.
- 自家用車 a private car, a family('s) car; (マイカー) one's (own) car, a private car [《英》public transportation (公の車)に対して]. (⇨マイカー)

しからしめる otherwise; or; or else. ▶それは時勢のしからしめるところだ That is *due to* the tendency of the times./That is *caused by* the trend of the age.

しからずんば ▶我に自由を与えよ, しからずんば死を Give me liberty, *or* give me death!

しからば 〖それならば〗if so; in that case; 〖そうすれば〗then.

しがらみ 柵 ▶恋のしがらみ *bonds* of love. ▶家のしがらみ family *ties*.

しかり 叱り ▶叱り a telling-off, a scolding. ▶読者からお叱りを受けた I was *criticized* [(反語的に) got *compliments*] from readers.

しかり 然り ▶その男は「しかり」と答えた The man said [answered] *yes*. ▶逆もまた然り The same with the converse.

しかりつける 叱り付ける (ひどくしかる) tell* 《him》off severely, give* 《him》 a good telling-off (⇨叱る); (声を荒げて) 《米話》bawl 《him》 out.

しかる 叱る 〖こうるさく〗scold (ⓘ《米》では先生・親が子供をしかる場合に用いる.《英》では今は古風な語), give 《him》 a scolding; (先生・親・上司などが) tell* 《him》 off, give 《him》 a telling-off; (上司などが) (やや強) reprimand (⇨叱責(しっせき)); 〖罰する〗punish; 〖とがめる〗reproach (⇨とがめる). ▶先生は彼が授業中に話をしていたと言ってひどくしかった The teacher *told* him *off* severely [*scolded* him severely, (怒った)*got* very *angry with* him] *for* talking in class [*because* he talked in class].

▶言うことを聞かないといけない He needs *a good scolding* [*telling-off*, 《話》*talking-to*]. ▶スピード違反をしたドライバーは巡査に厳しくしかられたThe speeding driver *was* severely *reprimanded by* [*received* a severe *reprimand from*] the policeman. (ⓘ この文脈で scold を用いるのは不自然)

しかるに 然るに 〖しかし〗however; 〖それにもかかわらず〗《書》 nevertheless; 〖ところが一方〗while; 〖他方では〗on the other hand. (⇨しかし, 他方)

しかるべき 然るべき 形 (本来そうあるべき) proper; (必要・条件を満たした) suitable; (最適の) right; (社会的にちゃんとした) respectable; (相応の) due. ▶しかるべき方法でその仕事をする do the work in a *proper* way. ▶しかるべき理由もなしに彼を逮捕する arrest him without *proper* [*due*] cause. ▶彼はあんなことをしたのだから非難されてしかるべきだ(=非難に値する) He *deserves* criticism [*to be criticized*] for having done it.

—— **然るべく** 副 (適切な方法で) appropriately; (きちんと) properly; (一番いいと思う方法で) as one thinks best [fit, right]. ● しかるべく処置する take *appropriate* [*proper*] measures; cope with 《the situation》*appropriately* [*properly*]. ▶彼が会議に参加できるようしかるべく取り計らいます I'll *see to* (*it*) *that* he can attend the meeting. (ⓘ 節中は通例現在形)

シガレット 〖紙巻きたばこ〗a cigarette.
- シガレットケース a cígarette càse.

しかん 士官 an officer, a commissioned officer.
- 士官候補生 a cadet.

しかん 子癇 〖医学〗eclampsia.

しかん 支管 (ガス・水道の引込管) a service pipe.

しかん 仕官 —— **仕官する** 動 be in the government's employ.

しかん 史観 one's [a] view of history.

しかん 弛緩 图 relaxation. —— **弛緩する** 動 relax.
- 筋弛緩剤 《a》 muscle /mʌ́sl/ relaxant.

しかん 私感 one's personal impression.

しかん 歯冠 a crown (of a tooth).

しがん 志願 图 〖申し込み〗(an) application; 〖自発的奉仕〗volunteering.
—— **志願する** 動 〖申し込む〗apply 《for＋仕事など, to＋人・団体》; 〖自発的に申し出る〗volunteer 《for, to do》. ▶看護師を志願する *volunteer* (*to* work) *as* a nurse. ▶兵役を志願する *volunteer for* military service. ▶彼は A 大学に入学を志願した He *applied* (*for* entrance [admission]) *to* A University.
▶その仕事を志願する者はだれもいなかった There was no *volunteer for* (*doing*) the job./No one *volunteered for* [*to do*] the job.
- 志願者 (応募者) an applicant; (立候補者) a candidate; (自発的に申し出る) a volunteer. ● 大学入学志願者 an *applicant for* entrance [admission] to a university. ● 志願兵 a volunteer.

じかん 時間 ❶〖時間の単位〗(1 時間) an hour. ● 長時間の重労働 long *hours* of hard work. ● 時間給で働く work for hourly pay; be paid *by the* [*an*] *hour*; be paid on an hourly basis. (⇨

給)●何時間も働く work *for hours*. ▶1日は24時間ある There are 24 *hours* in a day./A day has twenty-four *hours*. ▶3時間が経過した Three *hours* have elapsed [passed]. ▶このガソリンスタンドは24時間営業です This gas station is open (for) 24 *hours* (昼夜ぶっ通しで)《やや話》around the clock. ▶会議は午後1時から3時まで2時間続いた The meeting continued for two *hours* between 1 and 3 p.m. [×p.m. 1 and 3] ▶1時間もすれば彼は到着するでしょう He will arrive in an *hour* [(in) an *hour* from now]. (🅘 within an *hour* は「1時間以内に」の意) ▶1時間も(=まる1時間)お待たせしてすみません I am sorry (that) I have kept you waiting for a whole *hour*. ▶成田は私の家から3時間ほどかかる Narita is about three *hours* from my house. ▶日曜は2時間に1本しか電車がない There's only one train every two *hours* on Sunday(s). ▶船は1時間ごとに[1時間に1回]出ます Boats leave *every hour* [*hourly*]. (🅘 (every hour) on the hour は「正時ごとに」) ▶2時間ほど歩いたら湖に出た After about two *hours'* walk, we got to the lake./About two *hours'* walk took [brought] us to the lake. (🅘 brought は聞き手が話し手と同時に湖にいる場合) ▶礼拝は4時間に及んだ The service lasted as long as four *hours*.

会話「ここから東京まで何時間かかりますか」「歩いて[車で]2時間半です」"How many *hours* [How long] does it take to go from here to Tokyo?" "It takes two *hours* and a half to walk [drive] there./It is two and a half *hours'* walk [drive] there." (🅘 there is to Tokyo の代用副詞)

❷【時】time.

①【時間〜】 ●時間と空間 *time* and space. ●時間切れ (⇨時間切れ)

②【時間が[は]】 ▶残り時間がほとんどない There's very little [hardly any, almost no] *time* left. ▶私はその小説を読む時間がない I have no *time* to read [*for reading*] the novel. ▶時間がなくなってきたので急がなければならない *Time* is running out [We are running out of *time*, We don't have much *time* left], so we must hurry. ▶時間が十分あるので急ぐ必要はない There's no need to hurry, we've got plenty of *time*. ▶時間が許せばあなたのパーティーに出ます I'll come [×go] to your party if *time* permits [×allows]. (🅘 相手のいる(または行く)所へ「行く」はcome) ▶この試合が始まってからほんの少ししか時間がたっていない It's only been a short *time* since this game began. ▶答えを書きなさい。(制限)時間は1分です Write down the answers. You have one minute. ▶今お時間はありますか(=お手すきですか) Are you *free* now?/Do you *have time* now? (⇨④) ▶時間は足りますか(=充分ですか) Is the time enough? ▶彼を納得させるには少々時間がかかるだろう It'll take a bit of *time* to convince him. ▶いったい何でまた船で行くのさ? えらく時間がかかるぞ Why ever go by boat? It'll take a lot of *time*. (🅘 ever は why を強調する) ▶時間はとらせません I won't keep you long. ▶もっと時間が欲しい I want more *time*. ▶時間はあと8分です The time left is eight minutes.

③【時間の】 ●時間のむだ a waste of *time*. ●時間のかかる仕事 a *time*-consuming job. ▶彼女は夢中でテレビを見ていて時間のたつのを忘れた She was so absorbed in watching TV that she lost track of *time*. ▶川はぐんぐん増水していて、警察水位に達するのは時間の問題だ The river is swelling rapidly. It's a matter [a question, ×a case] of *time* before the water rises up to the danger level.

④【時間に】 ▶毎日時間に追われるのはいやだ I don't like being pressed for *time* every day. ▶年齢とともに時間は速度を増し、やがて時間に追いすがるように生きるようになる Time moves faster as people grow older, eventually forcing them to live as if hanging on to time [following closely at its heels]. (🅘 follow closely at its heels は「すぐ後を追いすがるようについて行く」と言う意の慣用表現)

⑤【時間を】 ●時間をつぶす kill *time*. (⇨暇つぶし) ●時間を惜しむ be economical with [of] one's time. ●時間を忘れる forget about time. ●時間を浪費するな Don't waste your *time*. (🅘「時間の浪費」は a waste of *time*) ▶お時間をさいてくださってありがとうございます Thank you very much for your *time*. ▶彼はいろいろ口実をつけて時間をかせごうとした He tried to buy [play for, 《話》stall for] *time* by giving a lot of excuses. ▶ゴングが鳴ってから彼は自分のコーナーでぐずぐずして時間をかせいだ After the bell rang, he lingered on his corner, *running down the clock*. (🅘 サッカーなどで時間切れをねらう時間かせぎは run out the clock) ▶彼は研究に多くの時間をかけた He spent a lot of *time* on his studies. ▶それには好きなだけ時間をかけなさい Take as much *time* [as *long*] as you like over it. ▶データのバックアップを取るのに5時間を要した It took five *hours* to back up the data. ▶少なくとも6時間おきなさい Leave an *interval* of at least 6 hours 《*between*》.

会話「少しお時間を拝借できますか」「いいですよ」"Can you *spare* me a few minutes [a minute]?" "Yes, sure."

⑤【時間と】 ▶当分の間は時間と競走しなくてはならない We have to race against *time* [*the clock*] for the time being.

❸【時刻】 (the) time; (時計に示される時刻) an hour. ●標準[現地]時間 standard [local] *time*. ●夏時間 《米》daylight(-saving) time 《略 DST》, 《英》summer time. ●時間帯 (同一標準時の) a *time* zone; (テレビなどの) a (*time*) slot. ▶もう寝る時間ですよ It's *time* you went to bed. ▶節内の動詞は今は直説法過去形が普通)/It's *time* (for you) *to* go to bed./It's bedtime [*time* for bed]. ▶彼は時間どおり[時間どおり8時]にそこに着いた He got there right *on time* [*punctually* at eight o'clock]. ▶列車は時間どおりに着いた The train arrived *on time* (予定どおりに) on schedule, (遅れずに) without delay. ▶彼は約束の時間に来なかった He didn't turn up at the appointed *time* [*hour*].

①【時間が[は]】 ▶もう時間がきました *Time* is up. ▶私の時計は時間が正確だ My watch keeps good [correct, perfect] *time*. ▶運命を決する時間が刻々と迫っている The fatal *hour* is approaching every moment. ▶その事故の起こった時間は午後6時半だった The *time* of the accident was 6:30 p.m./It was at 6:30 p.m. that the accident occurred. ▶うちの夕食の時間は7時です Our dinner *time* [*hour*] is 7:00.

②【時間に】 ▶彼はときどき時間に遅れる He *is* sometimes *late* [*behind time*]. ▶彼は約束の時間に大変正確だ He *is* very *punctual for* an appointment [*in* keeping an appointment]. ▶いつもの時間に遊びに来てください Please come to see me at the usual *hour* [*time*]. ▶こんな時間に彼が家にいるはずがない He can't be at home at a *time* like this.

じかん

③【時間を】▶彼に時間を尋ねてごらん Ask him the *time* [*hour*]. ▶彼の到着時間を教えてください Please let me know the *time* of his arrival [*what time* he is arriving]. ▶彼女は時間を間違えて音楽会に出かけた She went out to the concert at the wrong *time*. ▶私は腕時計の時間をテレビの時報に合わせた I set my *watch* by the time-signal on TV.

❹ [授業・勤務・営業などの時間] an hour (**!** しばしば複数形で); (学校の時限) a period; (教室の授業時間) a class. ● 授業時間 school *hours*; a class. ● 自習時間 a free study *period*; (自習室での) (米) study hall. ● 営業時間 business [office] *hours*. ● 勤務時間中に during working *hours*. ▶今日の2時間目に英語のテストがある We have an English test in the second *period* today. ▶水曜日は6時間授業がある We have six *classes* [*lessons*] on Wednesday. ▶開店時間は9時30分です Opening time is 9:30./We open at 9:30. ▶彼女は英語の時間に居眠りをした She dozed off during the English *lesson* [*class*]. ▶休み時間にキャッチボールをしましょう Let's play catch [×catch ball] *at recess* (米) [*break*〔英〕].

- 時間講師 a part-time (↔a full-time) lecturer.
- 時間差攻撃 an attack preceded by a feint.
- 時間表 (授業の) a (class) schedule.

じかん 次官 a vice-minister; 《米》an assistant secretary;《英》an undersecretary. ● 外務事務次官 the Administrative *Vice-Minister* of [for] Foreign Affairs.

じかんがい 時間外 ── 時間外の 形 overtime.
- 時間外勤務 overtime work. (⇨残業) ● 時間外勤務をする work *overtime*. ● 時間外手当 overtime pay.

じかんぎれ 時間切れ ● 時間切れとなる (人が) pass the time limit; (時間が) Time runs out. ▶すでに時間切れだ(=すでに遅い) It's too late now.

じかんわり 時間割り 《主に米》a (class) schedule;《英》a timetable;〔カリキュラム〕a curriculum (圈 curricula, ~s).

***しき** 式 **❶ [儀式]** 〔式典〕a ceremony; (特に宗教上の) a rite (**!** しばしば複数形で). ● 結婚式 a wedding (*ceremony*); marriage *rites*. ● 式を挙げる[に参列する] hold [attend] a *ceremony*. ● 式の司会をする preside at a *ceremony*. ▶式の日取りを決めましたか Have you fixed the date for the *ceremony*? ▶開式式ははなばなしく行われた The opening *ceremonies* were spectacular.

❷ [数式] an expression;〔方程式〕an equation;〔公式〕a formula (圈 formulae, ~s);〔不等式〕an inequality. ▶水の分子式 a molecular *formula* for water. ● 式を立てる set up an *equation*.
- 式次第 the program [order] of a ceremony.
- 式服 a ceremonial dress [robe], (正式な) a formal dress. (⇨礼服)

***しき** 指揮 图 command (**!** 国王や軍隊の長や船長などによる指揮); direction (**!** 実務的な事の指揮・管理). ● 会社の総指揮をとる take the general *direction* of the company. ● 指揮系統において規律を守る keep discipline in a chain of *command*. ● 指揮(=命令)を仰ぐ ask《him》for *orders*. ▶彼の指揮に100人の部下がいる He has one hundred men under his *command* [*direction*]. (**!** 単に ... under him. ともいえる) ▶小沢氏の指揮でその交響曲が演奏された The symphony *was conducted* by Mr. Ozawa./The symphony was performed *under the baton* of Mr. Ozawa.

── 指揮する 働 command; direct; (楽団を) conduct. ● 交響楽団を指揮する *conduct* a symphony orchestra. ▶国王は軍隊を指揮した The King *commanded* [*took command of*] the army. (軍隊は国王の指揮下にあった) The army *was under* the King's *command*.

- 指揮官 a commander;〔陸軍〕a commanding officer. ● 指揮者 (指導者) a leader; (音楽の) a conductor. ● 指揮台 a rostrum. ● 指揮棒 a baton.

しき 士気 /mǽrəl/;〔闘志〕fighting spirit. ● 選手の士気を高める boost [lift, raise] the *morale* of the players. ▶チームの士気は上がった[下がった, くじかれた] The *morale* of the team rose [sagged; was destroyed]. ▶彼らの士気は盛んである Their *morale* is high (↔low).

しき 四季 the (four) seasons. (⇨季節) ● 四季の美しさ the beauty of the *four seasons*. ● 四季を通じて at all *seasons* of the year; (1年中) all the year around. ▶四季おりおりの眺めがある Scenery changes from *season* to *season*.

しき『四季』〔曲名〕*The Four Seasons*(〔参考〕ビバルディ作); *The Seasons*(〔参考〕チャイコフスキー作).

しき 死期 (the time of) death, (婉曲的) one's end. ● 死期を早める quicken one's *death*. ▶彼の死期が近づいている He is dying [is near *death*, is nearing his *end*].

しき 紙器 (紙製の容器) a paper container.

-しき 一式〔やり方, しきたり〕a way;〔流儀〕a fashion (**!** way より堅い語);〔建築などの様式・やり方〕(a) style;〔体系的方法〕a system. ● アメリカ式の生活 the American *way* [*style*] of living. ● ルネッサンス式建築 the Renaissance *style* of architecture; architecture *in* the Renaissance *style*. ● インド式に生活する live *in* Indian *style*. ● アメリカ式に歓迎する welcome《him》in the American *way* [*fashion*]. ● ヘボン式 the Hepburn *system*. (〔参考〕ローマ字つづりの一方式)

しぎ 鴫〔鳥〕a snipe (圈 ~, ~s).
しぎ 仕儀〔なりゆき〕the course of events;〔事情〕circumstances.
しぎ 市議〔「市議会議員」の略〕(⇨市会議)
しぎ 試技 3度目の試技で at one's third *attempt*.

***じき** 時期 〔(その)時〕time;〔季節〕a season;〔期間〕a period. ● 毎年この時期には at this *time* of (the) year. ● 種まきの時期に in the sowing *season*; in the *season* for sowing. ● 歴史におけるある時期に at certain *periods* in history. ▶そろそろ決意すべき時期に来ている It is almost *time* when we must decide./It is almost *time* (for us) *to* decide./It's about *time* (*that*) we made up our minds. (**!** that は通例省略される. 節内は直説法過去形であることに注意) ▶十代は多くの点でいちばん大変な時期だ The teens are the hardest *period* in many ways. ▶その計画を持ち出すにはまだ時期尚早(ショゥ)だ It is still too early [*premature*] to bring up the plan.

じき 次期 〔次の〕next. ● 次期会長 the *next* president.
じき 時季 a season. (⇨季節)
じき 時機 (a) time; (機会) an occasion;〔好機〕a chance, (an) opportunity. (⇨機会, 潮時) ● 時機を見計らって(...する) take *occasion* (*to do*). ● 時機を待つ wait for an *opportunity*. ● 時機を逸する miss [〔話〕pass up] a [one's] *chance*; let an *opportunity* slip by. ▶今は真実を告げるべき時機ではない Now is not the *time* [The *opportunity* has not come] (for us) *to* tell the truth. ▶あなたの発言はいろいろな意味で時機を得ている Your remark is

じき *timely* in more ways than one.
じき 磁気 magnetism. ● 磁気の[を帯びた] magnetic. ● 磁気を与える magnetize.
● 磁気あらし a magnetic storm. ● 磁気カード a magnetic card. ● 磁気テープ magnetic tape. (❗ カセット化したものを ⟨C⟩)
じき 磁器 porcelain /pɔ́ːrsəlin/, china(ware).
じき 直 ━ 直に ⦅副⦆ ❶ [一瞬にして] in a moment [a minute]; [間もなく] soon, shortly (⇨すぐ ❶❷, 間もなく); [ほとんど] almost, nearly (⇨殆(ほと)ど). ▶じきに戻ってきます I'll be back *in a moment* [*a minute*]. ▶じき夏が来る Summer will *soon* be here. (❗ 強めて Summer will be here *very soon*. ともいえる) ▶彼はもうじき40歳だ He is *almost* [*nearly*] forty. (❗ almost の方が40歳に近い) ▶じきにお昼ごはんよ. みんな手を洗って入ってらっしゃい (外にいる子供たちに) Kids! Lunch is *about* ready! You all wash your hands and come on up.
❷ [容易に] easily. (⇨さ ❸)
じぎ 字義 the meaning of a word. ● 字義どおりに解釈する interpret ⟨a word⟩ *literally*.
じぎ 児戯 ● 児戯に類する, 児戯に等しい be childish; be child's play [kid stuff, kids' stuff].
じぎ 時宜 (⇨時機)
しきい 敷居 [入り口の] the threshold /θréʃhould/; [戸の] a doorsill. ● 敷居をまたぐ cross the *threshold*. ● 敷居の中から中をのぞく look over the *threshold* and look inside. ▶この家の敷居を2度とまたぐな Never darken my door again. (❗ 日本語と同じくらい古くさい表現)
● 敷居が高い ▶彼の家は敷居が高い(=訪問するのは気が進まない) I don't feel like visiting him.
しきいし 敷石 a flagstone, a flag; [舗装用の] a paving stone [⦅英⦆ slab]. ● 庭の小道に敷石を敷く lay *flagstones* on the garden path.
しきうつし 敷き写し (a) tracing. ▶あの教授の論文は弟子の論文の敷き写しだった The professor's paper was a *mere copy* of his [her] student's paper.
━ 敷き写しする ⦅動⦆ ● 地図を敷き写しする *trace* [*make a tracing* of] the map; copy the map using tracing paper.
しぎかい 市議会 a municipal [a city] assembly, a municipal [a city] council.
● 市議会議員 a member of the municipal assembly. ● 市議会議員である be a member of the *municipal assembly*; be on the city council.
しきかく 色覚 color sense.
● 色覚障害 color (vision) deficiency [impairment]. ● 赤緑色覚障害 a red/green color deficiency.
しきかん 色感 [色覚] a color sense; [色から受ける感じ] the impression of a color.
しきぎょう 私企業 a private company [enterprise].
しききん 敷金 a (security) deposit. ▶3か月分の敷金を入れる pay [make, leave] a *deposit* of three months' rent. ▶敷金は出になるときに全額または一部が返ってきます You'll get back all or part of your *security deposit* when you move out.
しきけん 識見 judgment. (⇨⦅和⦆ 見識)
*****しきさい 色彩** [色] (a) color; [彩色] coloring; [色合い] a tint, a tinge. [色] ● 色彩感覚は優れた sense of *color*. ● 色彩豊かな場面 a scene *full of color(s)*; a *colorful* scene. ● 色彩に乏しい文体 a *colorless* [a *dull*] style. ● 政治的色彩のあるクラブ a club with political *coloring*; a politically-*colored* [a politically-*tinged*] club. ● 色彩を添える give *coloring* ⟨*to*⟩. ● そのトーテムポールは鮮やかな色彩で塗られていて, 見栄えがした The totem pole was painted in bright *colors* and lovely to look at.
しざきざき 四季咲き ● 四季咲きのバラ a *perpetual* rose. (❗ perpetual は「絶え間なく繰り返す」の意)
じきさん 直参 a direct [an immediate] vassal [retainer] of a *shogun*.
しきし 色紙 a square piece of thick paper(, often used to write a poem or to paint a picture on). ● 色紙切りにした (料理) cut ... into thin squares.
しきじ 式辞 ● 式辞を述べる give [deliver] an *address* (at a ceremony). (❗ 後の方が堅い語)
しきじ 識字 (develop, promote) literacy.
● 識字率 the literacy rate.
じきじき 直々 ● 直々に ⦅副⦆ (本人が直接に) personally, in person.
しきしま 敷島 ● 敷島の道 (和歌の道) the art of *tanka* poetry.
しきしゃ 識者 an intellectual; ⦅集合的⦆ the intellect(s) (⇨インテリ); [専門家] an expert.
しきじゃく 色弱 partial color blindness. ● 色弱である be partially color-blind.
しきじょう 式場 a ceremonial hall. (❗ 時に「告別式場」(a funeral home ⦅米⦆ [parlour ⦅英⦆)をさすことがある) ● 結婚式場 a wedding (reception) hall.
しきじょう 色情 (a) lust; sexual desire.
● 色情狂 【医学】 (病気) erotomania; (人) an erotomaniac, a sex maniac.
しきしん 色神 color sense [vision]. (⦅和⦆色覚)
● 色神検査 a color vision test; a test for color blindness.
しきそ 色素 【生物】 (a) pigment. ● メラニン色素 melanin.
じきそ 直訴 ━ 直訴する ⦅動⦆ make a direct appeal [petition] ⟨*to*⟩.
しきそくぜくう 色即是空 All is vanity.
しきたり (a) custom. (⇨慣習, 慣例) ● 古いしきたりを守る observe an old *custom*.
ジギタリス 【植物】 a digitalis; a (purple) foxglove. (⦅参考⦆ この乾燥葉は強心薬として用いられる)
しきち 敷地 [用地] a site ⟨*for*⟩; [区画地] ⦅米⦆ a lot; (小区画地) a plot ⟨*用地*⟩; [構内] (建物の周囲の) grounds; (建物を含めた) premises (⇨構内). ▶敷地は一律横15メートル, 縦20メートルに区画されている The *plots* each measure 15 meters by 20 meters.
しきちょう 色調 a tone; [色合い] ⦅書⦆ a tint; (濃淡の) a shade (of color). ● 暗い色調の絵 a dark-toned [-tinted, -shaded] picture. ● 色調(=色の調和)がいい have good *color coordination*.
しきつめる 敷きつめる lay* [spread*] ⟨a carpet⟩ all over ⟨the floor⟩. ● じゅうたんを敷きつめた応接室 a *fully* carpeted reception room; a reception room with *wall-to-wall* carpeting. ● 道に砂利を敷きつめる cover the road with *gravel*.
じきでし 直弟子 one's pupil [disciple]. (⇨弟子)
しきてん 式典 a ceremony. ● 式典を執り行う perform [carry out] a *ceremony*. ● 式典に参列する attend a *ceremony*.
じきでん 直伝 ● 師匠直伝の奥義 a secret art *handed down directly from* one's teacher [master].
じきとりひき 直取引 (⇨直(じき)取引)
じきに 直に (⇨直(じき))
じきひつ 直筆 『その人自身の筆跡』 one's own hand [handwriting]. ● 女王直筆の書簡 the letter written *in the Queen's own hand* [*handwriting*]; the letter written by the Queen *herself*.

しきふ 敷布 a sheet. ●週1回敷布を替える change *sheets* every week.

しきぶとん 敷き布団 a mattress. (⇨布団)

しきべつ 識別 图 (a) distinction, discrimination. (⇨区別) ●色の識別 the *distinction* of color. ●正邪の識別 *discrimination* between right and wrong [*of* right *from* wrong].
── **識別する** 動 distinguish, discriminate 《A *from* B, *between* A and B》. (⇨区別する, 見分ける, 分かる) ●識別できる be distinguishable (↔indistinguishable) 《*from*》.

しきま 色魔 a sex maniac.

しきみ 樒〚植物〛 a star anise.

しきもう 色盲 color blindness.
── **色盲の** 形 color-blind. ●緑色盲の green-blind.

しきもの 敷物 (じゅうたん) a rug; (じゅうたん) a carpet; (マット・畳・ござ類) a mat, (集合的) matting. ●敷物をしいてない床 a bare floor.

しきゃく 刺客 (⇨刺客(し))

じぎゃく 自虐 图 self-torment; masochism /mǽsəkìzm/.
── **自虐的な** 形 self-tormenting; masochistic.

*****しきゅう 支給** 图〚供給〛supply; provision; 〚支払い〛payment. ●現物支給 *payment* in kind.
── **支給する** 動〚供給する〛(不足の物を) supply; (必要な物を) provide; 〚与える〛give*; 〚支払う〛pay*. ▶政府は被災者に毛布を支給した The government *supplied* [*provided*] the sufferers *with* blankets. (❗《米》では with の省略も可)/The government *supplied* blankets *to* [*for*] the sufferers./The government *provided* [*distributed*] blankets *for* [《米》*to*] the sufferers. ▶年2回ボーナスが支給される We *are given* a bonus twice a year.

しきゅう 子宮 the womb /wúːm/; 〚解剖〛the uterus /júːtərəs/ (複 uteri /júːtəràɪ/, ~es). ●子宮萎縮〚医学〛uterine atrophy; metratrophy. ●子宮外妊娠 ectopic [extrauterine] pregnancy. (❗ectopic は「異常な場所に生じる」の意) ●子宮がん uterine cancer; cancer of the womb. ●子宮筋腫 fibroid; hysteromyoma /hìstəroumaiómə/. ●子宮後屈 retrodisplacement [retroversion] of the uterus. ●子宮出血 uterine bleeding. ●子宮摘出 hysterectomy. ●子宮内膜炎 endometritis.

しきゅう 四球〚野球〛a base on balls, a walk, a (free) pass. (⇨フォアボール) ●敬遠の四球 an intentional *walk*. ●四球を得る [draw, take] a *base on balls*. ●四球を与える give up [issue] a *walk*; walk a batter.

しきゅう 死球 ●死球を受けて hit by (a) pitch (略 HBP). ●死球を受けた打者 a hit batter [batsman]. ●死球を与える hit a batter with a pitch; hit a batsman. ▶打者は死球を受けた The batter was *hit by a pitch*. (⇨デッドボール)

しきゅう 至急 副〚今すぐに〛at once, right away, immediately (❗right away が最も口語的. immediately はやや堅い語だがしばしば日常会話でも強意的に用いる); 〚大至急〛as soon as possible (略 ASAP) (❗as soon as *one can* は「できるだけ早く」で穏やかな言い方); 〚迅速に〛promptly (❗自発的態度を暗示); 〚緊急に〛urgently. ▶至急お願いします Please get back *at once* [*right away*, *right off*]. ▶至急ご返事ください Please reply to this letter *promptly* [*immediately*, *as soon as possible*]. ▶身を守るヘルメットが至急欲しい We must have [*urgently*] need helmets to protect ourselves.
── **至急(の)** 形〚緊急の〛urgent; 〚即座の〛immediate; 〚迅速な〛prompt; 〚差し迫った〛pressing. ●至急の用件 *urgent* business. ●至急便(=速達)で送る send (it) (by) *express*. ▶至急の場合には電話をください Please call me in an *urgent* case [《緊急の場合》in an *emergency*].

じきゅう 自給 ●米を自給する be *self-sufficient in* rice.
●自給自足 self-sufficiency, self-support. ●自給自足の生活(様式) a *self-sufficient* [a *self-supporting*] life (style).

じきゅう 時給 an hourly wage; (時間単位の支払い) payment by the hour. ▶時給はいくらですか How much can I *get an hour* [*by the hour*]? ●時給制 the hourly-wage system.

しきゅうしき 始球式〚野球〛a first-ball ceremony. 〖参考〗米国では大統領・市長などがスタンドから投げ込むのが一般的であったが, 引退した選手などが打者を立たせずにマウンドから投げることもよくある) ●始球式のボールを投げる throw out the *first ball*.

じきゅうせん 持久戦 (消耗戦) 《wage》a war of attrition; (待機戦術) 《play》a waiting game. ▶彼らは持久戦の構えだ They are prepared to *hold out* until their enemy gives in.

じきゅうそう 持久走 an endurance run.

じきゅうりょく 持久力 ●持久力がない have no *staying power* [(スタミナ) *stamina* /stǽmənə/].

しきょ 死去 图 (a) death. (⇨死)
── **死去する** 動 die; (婉曲的に) pass away.

じきょ 辞去 ── **辞去する** 動 take one's leave 《of him》; say goodbye 《to him》.

しきょう 司教 a bishop.
●司教(管)区 a bishopric; a diocese.

しきょう 市況 a market; market conditions [activity]. ●株式市況 the stock *market*. ●活発な市況 an active [an animated] *market*. ●閑散とした市況 an inactive [a narrow, a thin] *market*.

しきょう 詩興 ▶天の川を見ていたら詩興がわいた I *was inspired to compose poems* by the Milky Way./The Milky Way *inspired* me *to compose poems*.

しぎょう 始業 ▶学校は8時半始業です School *begins* [*starts*] at [×from] eight-thirty. ●始業式 the opening ceremony [《米》exercises].

じきょう 自供 图〚白状〛(a) confession. (⇨白状)
── **自供する** 動 ▶彼は犯行を自供した He *made a confession of* his crime./He *confessed* (*to*) his crime./He *confessed* (*that*) he had committed the crime.

:**じぎょう 事業**〚仕事〛(商売上の) (a) business; (一般に) 〚大きな計画〛(公的利益をめざす) an enterprise; (個人的な) an undertaking; (大規模な) a project; (冒険的な) a venture.
① 〖~事業〗 ●主要〖中核〗事業 major [core] *business*. ●社会〖慈善; 福祉〗事業 social [charitable; welfare] *work*. ●非営利事業 non-profit [noncommercial] *undertaking*. ●政府〖市〗の事業 a government's [a municipal] *enterprise*. ●公共事業 a public(-)works *project*. ●住宅〖鉄道建設〗事業 a housing [a railroad construction] *project*. ●共同事業 a joint *venture*《between》. ●記念事業 a commemorative *project*. ●インターネット関連事業 an internet-related *business*. ▶ホテルを経営するのはなかなかの大事業だ Managing a hotel is rather a large *undertaking*.
② 〖事業が〗 ●事業が軌道に乗った(=うまくいき始めた) Our *business* has taken off [has gotten into gear]. ▶その地域で昨年開発事業が行われた

The development *projects* were undertaken in the region last year.
③〖事業に〖を〗〗● 事業に参入する enter into a *business*. ● 事業を展開する develop a *business*. ● 事業を拡張する extend [expand] one's *business*. ● 事業に失敗する fail in one's *business*. ● 事業を起こす launch a *business*. ● 新しい事業を始める start a new *business* [*enterprise*]. ● 共同で[手広く]事業をする do *business* together [on a large scale]. ● 難事業に着手する launch [embark on] a difficult *enterprise*.
● 事業家 a businessman. ● 事業計画 a business plan. ● 事業債 industrial bonds. ● 事業資金 a business fund. ● 事業者 people responsible for an enterprise. ● 事業所 an office. ● 事業所税 office [business facility] tax. ● 事業所得 income from business activities. ● 事業税 business [enterprise] tax. ● 事業戦略 a business strategy. ● 事業年度 a business year. ● 事業費 working expenses. ● 事業部 a division [department]; a [an internal] group company. ● 事業部制 a divisional system.

しきょうひん 試供品 a (free) sample.
しきよく 色欲 (a) lust; sexual desire. (⇨色情)
しきょく 支局 a branch (office). (⇨支店) ▶ ニューヨーク支局 a [the] New York *branch*. ● FBI 支局 an FBI *field office* (*in* Texas). (❗支局員 is a field agent)
じきょく 時局 a situation. (⇨情勢)
じきょく 磁極 〖物理〗 a magnetic pole.
しきり 仕切り 〖部屋などの〗 a partition; 〖列車・箱などの〗 a compartment; 〖小さな仕切られた個室〗 a cubicle; 〖境界〗 a boundary; 〖相撲の〗 toeing the mark. (⇨仕切る) ● ガラスの仕切り a glass *partition*. ● 仕切り壁 a partition (wall). ● 仕切りが三つある箱 a box with four [×three] *compartments*. ● 仕切りを入れる put up a *partition*.
***しきりに** ❶〖頻繁に〗 often, frequently (❗後の方が堅い語); (繰り返し) repeatedly. (⇨度々, 絶えず) ▶ 彼女はこのごろしきりに君の話をする She *often* [*frequently*] talks about you these days. ▶ 彼はしきりに(=何度も)うなずいた He nodded *many times*.
❷〖程度を強めて〗 ▶ 朝からしきりに(=激しく)雨が降っている It has been raining *hard* [*heavily*, (絶え間なく)《文章》 *incessantly*] since (this) morning. ▶ 彼はそのことをしきりに(=非常に)気にしていた He was *very* anxious about that.
❸〖熱心に〗 ● しきりにしっぽを振る wag one's tail *eagerly*. ● しきりに彼女の気を引こうとする try *hard* to attract her attention. ▶ 彼がしきりに君に会いたがっている He *is anxious* [*eager*,《話》*dying*] *to* meet you. (❗最後の語が一番強意的) ▶ 彼はしきりに私に入会を勧めた He *urged* me *to* be [become] a member.
しきる 仕切る ❶〖分割する〗 divide; (仕切り壁などで) partition, (カーテンで) curtain ... off, (ついたてで) screen ... off. ● カーテンで部屋を二つに仕切る *divide* [*partition*] the room *into* two parts *with* a curtain.
❷〖管理する〗 manage. (⇨取り仕切る)
ジキルはかせとハイドし『ジキル博士とハイド氏』 *The Strange Case of Dr. Jekyll and Mr. Hyde*. 〖参考〗スティーブンソンの小説
−しきれない ▶ 今は多忙で彼の世話をしきれない(=よく世話ができない) I'm so busy that I *can't* take (×a) good care of him. ▶ 彼はお金を使いきれないほどもうけた He earned *more than* he *could* possibly spend.

しきわら 敷き藁 (動物の) litter.
***しきん** 資金 〖特別な資金〗 a fund (❗「手持ち金, 財源」の意では通例複数形で); 〖資本金〗 capital. (⇨資本) ● 育英資金 a scholarship *fund*. ● 運転資金 working [a circulating] *capital*. ● 回転資金 a revolving *fund*. ● 政治[選挙]資金 political [electoral] *funds*. ● 結婚資金 a marriage *fund*; *money* to marry on. ● 公的資金を注入する inject public *money* (*into*). ● 資金繰りが難しい have difficulty (in) raising *funds*. ● 資金集めの夕食会を催す give a *fund* raising [(慈善目的の) benefit] dinner. ● その計画に資金援助をする *fund* [〖話〗 bánkròll] the project. ● 資金を引き上げる pull the *funding*. ▶ 資金不足である We are short of *funds*. ▶ 資金不足のためにその事業は中止になった Lack of *funds* halted the project. ▶ 彼らは難民救済のために資金を募った They raised a *fund* for the relief of [a relief *fund for*] refugees.
● 資金運用 application [use] of funds; fund management [operation]. ● 資金管理 fund administration [management]. ● 資金源 a source of money; a money source. ● 資金調達 funding; financing; fund [capital, money] raising. ● 資金難 (財政難) financial difficulties; (資金不足) lack of funds.

しぎん 市銀 〖「市中銀行」の略〗(⇨市中)
しぎん 詩吟 recitation [chanting] of a Chinese poem.
しきんきょり 至近距離 ● 至近距離から撃つ shoot (him) *at point-blank range* [×*distance*]; shoot him *point-blank* (*in* the chest).
しきんせき 試金石 a touchstone; 〖試すもの〗 a test. ● 試金石になる become the *touchstone* (*of*).
:しく 敷く 〖敷物・鉄道などを〗 lay*; 〖広げる〗 spread*; 〖覆う〗 cover; 〖舗装する〗 pave. ● 床にじゅうたんを敷く *lay* [*spread*] a carpet *on* the floor; (床一面に) *cover* [*lay*, *spread*] the floor *with* a carpet. ● 鉄道を敷く *lay* [*build*] a railroad. ● 街路にアスファルトを敷く *pave* a street *with* asphalt. ● 鳥かごの底にきれいな新聞紙を敷く *put* clean newspaper *on* the bottom of a bird cage. ● 自分でふとんを敷く *make* one's own bed. ● 座ぶとんを敷く *sit on* a cushion.
しく 市区 (市外の区画) a block; (市と区) a city and a ward.
しく 詩句 (詩の1行) a line; (詩の1節) a stanza, a verse.
しく 如く ▶ 用心するに如くはなし(=用心するのが一番よい) You'd better make assurance absolutely sure.
***じく** 軸 〖心棒〗 an axis (❸ axes /ǽksìːz/); (車輪の) an axle; 〖機械の〗 a shaft, a pivot; 〖茎〗 a stem, a stalk; 〖掛け物〗 a scroll, a roll; 〖数学〗 axis. ● 軸のついたリンゴ an apple with the *stem*. ● 軸を床の間にかける hang a *scroll* in the alcove. ▶ 地球は地軸を中心に回る The earth turns *on* its *axis*. ▶ 小説全体がこの事件を軸に展開するThe entire novel turns *around* this incident.
じく 字句 (用いた言葉の意味・その表現の仕方) wording. ● 字句を修正する change the *wording*; make some changes in the *wording*. (❗修正の度合いによって, some は considerable, a lot of など言を換える) ● 字句にこだわる be particular [fussy] about the *wording* [*use of words*]. ● 字句どおりに受け取る take [interpret] (it) *literally*.
じくあし 軸足 a pivot foot; (重点) (an) emphasis. ● 軸足に力を入れる put one's weight on one's *pivot foot*.

じくう 時空 time and space.
じくうけ 軸受け a bearing.
しぐさ 仕種, 仕草 〘身振り〙(a) gesture; 〘演技〙 acting; 〘ふるまい〙 behavior. ● 大げさなしぐさで話す speak *with exaggerated gestures*. ● 子猫のしぐさがとてもかわいい(することすべてが) *Everything (that) our kitten does is adorable*./(動作が) *Our kitten's movements are adorable*.

ジグザグ ● ジグザグの道 a *zigzag* road. ● 坂道をジグザグに上る *zigzag* [*go zigzag*] up a slope; go up a slope in a *zigzag*.

じくじ 忸怩 ● 忸怩たる思いである(恥ずかしい) be [feel] *deeply ashamed*.

しくしく ● しくしく泣く cry softly [quietly]; (涙を見せて) weep. (**!** sob は「むせび泣く」(cry noisily) でここでは不適) ▶ 少女は母親の顔を見るとしくしくと泣くのをやめた The little girl stopped *weeping* [*crying softly*] when she saw her mother.

じくじく ● じくじくしている(水などがにじむ) soggy, (湿気のある) damp; (ぬれている) wet; (水を吸った) sodden. ● じくじく(しみ)出る ooze. ▶ 雨のあと地面はじくじくしている The ground is *soggy* after the rain. ▶ 切り口から血がじくじく出ていた Blood *was oozing* out of the cut.

しくじり (a) failure. (⇨失敗)
しくじる fail, (試験に)〘米話〙flunk. (⇨失敗する)
ジグソーパズル 《do》a jigsaw puzzle, a jigsaw. (**!** 〘米〙では単に a puzzle ともいう)

しぐち 地口 a pun; a wordplay.
しくつ 試掘 ― 試掘する 動 prospect 《for gold》; drill 《for oil》.
シグナル 〘信号〙a signal.
しくはっく 四苦八苦 ― 四苦八苦する 動 〘苦労する〙have trouble (difficulty) 《in doing》; 〘つらい目にあう〙have a hard time 《doing》; 〘奮闘する〙struggle hard 《to do》; 〘話〙sweat blood 《over》. (⇨苦労する)

じくばり 字配り spacing of letters [characters]; letterspacing.

*****しくみ** 仕組み 〘構造〙(a) structure; 〘機構〙(a) mechanism. ● 現代社会の複雑な仕組み the complicated *structure* of today's society. ● 脳の仕組み the *mechanism* of the brain.

*****しくむ** 仕組む (たくらむ) plot (-tt-); (練って作る) work ... out. ● 巧妙に仕組まれたわな a cunningly *worked-out* trap. ● 彼をつかまえるためのわなを仕組む *set* a trap to catch him. ▶ それは偶然ではなく仕組まれたことのように見えたが It didn't look accidental but *contrived*. (**!** contrived は「わざとらしい」の意)

シクラメン 〘植物〙a cyclamen /sáikləmən, sík-/.
しぐれ 時雨 a shower in late fall [early winter]; a drizzling [a drizzly] rain.
● 時雨煮 (説明的に) various kinds of seafood such as clams, bonito and tuna boiled down in soy sauce with sweet *sake* and ginger.

しぐれる 時雨れる ▶ 1 日中しぐれていた It *was raining off and on* [*on and off*] all day.

しけ 時化 〘あらし〙a storm, stormy weather; 〘不漁〙a poor catch (of fish). (⇨時化る) ● しけにあう be hit by a *storm*.

じげ 地毛 one's own hair.
しけい 死刑 the death penalty; (極刑) capital punishment. ● 死刑を執行する carry out [hold] the *execution*. ● 死刑を廃止する abolish the *death penalty*. ● 彼は死刑の宣告を受けていた [The man] He was under (×the) sentence of *death* [was sentenced to *death*, received a *death* sentence].

● 死刑囚 a condemned criminal.
しけい 私刑 a lynching. (⇨リンチ)
しけい 紙型 〘印刷〙a matrix (複 ~es, matrices); a mat.
しけい 詩形 verse; a verse form.
しげい 至芸 excellent [outstanding] arts and crafts.
じけい 字形 the form of a character [a letter]; (印刷の) type.
じけい 次兄 one's second oldest [eldest] brother.
じけいだん 自警団 a vigilance committee; a vigilante group.
● 自警団員 a vigilante; a member of a vigilance committee [a vigilante group].
じけいれつ 時系列 a time series.
:**しげき** 刺激 名 stimulation; (a) stimulus (複 stimuli /stímjəlài/); 〘興奮〙(an) excitement; 〘励み〙(an) encouragement, 《やや書》(an) incentive; 〘動機うけ〙(a) motivation.

┌─────────────────────────────────────
│ 使い分け **stimulation** 精神・器官・物事の進展に
│ 刺激を与えること. 通例よい意味で用いる.
│ **stimulus** 精神・器官・物事の進展に刺激を与えるもの.
│ **excitement** 興奮した状態や興奮させるようなもの.
└─────────────────────────────────────

● 刺激のない(＝単調な)生活を送る lead a *monotonous* (退屈な) *a dull, a boring*] life. ▶ 彼には何か刺激が必要だ He needs some *stimulation* [*encouragement*]. ▶ その出来事は私にとって大きな刺激となった That event was a great *encouragement* [*stimulus*, (動機うけ) *motivation*] to me. (**!** was の代わりに gave, acted as も可/I *was* greatly *encouraged* [*motivated*] *by* that event. ▶ その少年はスピードに刺激を求めた The boy looked for *excitement* [(スリル) *thrills*] in speed. ▶ 田舎の生活は刺激がない Country life lacks *excitement*.

— 刺激する 動 〘書〙stimulate; (興奮させる) excite; (怒らせる) provoke; 〘けりさせる〙irritate; 〘励ます〙encourage; (鼓舞・扇動する) 〘やや書〙incite; (動機うけ) motivate. (⇨名)

①〘事・物を刺激する〙● 国内生産を刺激する *stimulate* domestic production. ▶ スープは食欲を刺激する Soup *stimulates* the appetite. ▶ その本は学生たちの好奇心を刺激した The book *excited* [呼び起こす] 〘書〙*aroused*] curiosity in the students. ▶ 濃い黒い煙が目を刺激した The dense black smoke *irritated* my eyes.

②〘(人)を刺激して〜させる〙stimulate [excite, incite] 《him》to do [to+名]; provoke 《him》into do*ing* [to+名, 《まれ》to do] (いずれも名詞は感情・行為などを表す); (勇気づけ) encourage [motivate] 《him》to do. ● 彼を刺激して怒らせる *excite* [*incite*] him *to* get angry [*to* anger]. ● *provoke* him *into* getting angry [*to* anger]. ▶ その成功に刺激されて彼はさらに努力した The success *encouraged* [*motivated*] him to make greater efforts./The success *stimulated* [*incited*] him *to* (make) greater efforts.

— 刺激的な, 刺激の強い 形 stimulative; (興奮を呼びおこす) exciting; (扇情的な) sensational; (挑発的な) provocative /prəvǽkətiv/, (刺すような) 《やや書》pungent. ● 刺激(的な)策をとる take *stimulative* measures. ● 煙の刺激の強いにおい a *pungent* smell of smoke. ● 刺激の強い小説 a *sensational* novel. ● 刺激的なことを言う make *provocative* [*pungent*] remarks. ▶ なんて刺激的な経験だろう What a *stimulating* experience!

しげき 「ニューヨークは好き?」「ええ, とっても. 刺激的な街だから」"Do you like New York?" "I like it a lot. It's an *exciting* place to live [city to live in]." (❗ place では in は省略可だが city では必要)
● 刺激剤 【医学】a stimulant. ● 刺激物 a stimulant. ● コーヒー・酒など

しげき 史劇 a historical play.

しげき 詩劇 a verse drama, a drama (written) in verse.

しげしげ (何度となく) (very) often, frequently (❗ 後の方が堅い語); (いつも) all the time. ● しげしげと = じっと見る look *hard [fixedly] ⟪at⟫*; gaze [stare] *fixedly ⟪at⟫*; watch (closely [carefully]). (⇔見詰める, 見る)

しけつ 止血 图 【医学】a hemostasis (複 hemostases).
── 止血する 動 stop (the) bleeding.
● 止血剤 【医学】a hemostat /híːməstæt/; (収斂(½ぇ)剤) a styptic /stíptik/. ● 止血帯 a tourniquet.

じけつ 自決 [自己決定] sélf-determinátion; [自殺] suicide /súːəsàid/. (⇔自殺) ● 民族自決 racial self-*determination*.

しげみ 茂み (下生え) a bush; (下生えと低木) a thicket; (草の) a tuft [a clump] of grass, (やや書) a tussock. (⇔藪(な)) ● かん木の茂み a *clump* of bushes. ● 雑草の茂み a *growth* of weeds. ▶ 茂みに潜んでいるのはだれ Who is lurking [hiding] in the *bushes* [*thicket*]?

しける 時化る be stormy; (海などが) become* rough. ● 海がしけている The sea is *rough*.

しける 湿気る become* [get*] damp; dampen.

＊しげる 茂る (植物が主語) grow* thick(ly) (❗ これの方は結果の状態に重点がある); (場所が主語) be covered [(手入れされないために) be overgrown] ⟪with⟫. ● 草の生い茂った庭 a garden *overgrown with* weeds. ▶ 山腹には木がうっそうと茂っていた Trees *grew* [×were growing] *thick* over the hillside./The hillside *was thick* [*was thickly covered*] *with* trees.

＊しけん 試験 图 ❶ 【学校などの試験】an exam /igzǽm/, (正式) an examination; a test; 《主に米》a quiz (複 ~zes).

> **使い分け** **examination** 学生・志願者の知識・資格などを調べる特に重要な各種の試験. 主に書き言葉で, 一般に今は exam が普通.
> **test** 単に学習の定着度を調べる小試験, または客観テスト.
> **quiz** 授業中に行う簡単な小テスト.

① 【～試験】● 算数の試験 an arithmetic *exam* [*test*] (❗ 次の言い方より口語的); an *exam* [a *test*] in [×of] arithmetic. ● 学科名には in を用いる: 3課[不規則動詞]の試験 an *exam* [a *test*] *on* Lesson three [irregular verbs]. ● 筆記試験 a written *exam* [*test*]. ● 口述[頭]試験 an oral *exam* [*test*]. ● 面接試験 (就職の) an employment [job] *interview*. ● 二次試験 a secondary *exam(ination)*; the second(-)stage *exam*. ● 最終試験 the final(-)stage *exam*. ● 前期試験 a first term *exam*; an *exam* at the end of the first semester. ● 模擬試験 a trial [mock] *exam*. ● 追試験 a make up exam. ● 係長の昇進試験 the promotion *exam for* sub-section chief. ②【試験(の)～】● 試験中 an *exam* is in progress. ● 試験中に during an *exam*. ● 試験勉強をする a study [(準備をする) prepare, (詰め込み勉強をする) cram, do a cram] for an *exam*. ▶ 試験のときはよく勉強しました I worked hard at (the) *exam* time. ▶ 試験の結果はいつ分かりますか When will we know [get] the *exam* results?/(出ますか) When do our *exam* results come out?

③ 【試験が[は]】▶ 試験が近づいてきた The exam is approaching. ▶ いったん試験が始まると... Once an exam starts ....

> **会話** 「今日試験が終わったんだ」「いいなあ, ぼくはあともう二つあるんだ」"I've finished my *exams* today." "Great. I have two more (*exams*) to go." (❗ to go は名詞の後に用いて「残っている」の意)

> **会話** 「数学の試験はどうだった?」「簡単だったよ[ひどかったよ]」"Whát was the ＼math *exam* [*paper*] like?" "＾Simple [＾Horrible]." (❗ paper は《書》an examination paper の略で「試験問題」の意)

④【試験に】● 試験に備える prepare for an exam. ▶ 彼は試験に落ちた [合格した] He failed [passed, succeeded in] an *exam*. ▶ その問題は試験に出た The question was given [asked] in the *exam*.

⑤【試験を】● 試験を受ける(=受験する) take [(話) do, (英) sit (for)] an *exam*. ● 試験(を)する give an *exam* (to); hold [conduct] an *examination*. (❗ 後の方が堅い言い方) ● 試験を放棄する abandon an *exam*. ▶ 先生は私たちが宿題をやってきたかどうか確かめるために試験をした The teacher gave us a *test* [tested us] to see if we had done our homework.

⑥【試験で】▶ 彼は物理の試験でよい成績をとった He got a good grade 《米》[good marks 《英》] *on* the physics *exam* [*in* physics]./He did well (↔poorly) *on* the physics *exam*. (⇔点 ❷)

❷ 【試すこと】 a test; a trial; an experiment.

> **使い分け** **test** 試した結果, ある基準に達しているか確かめること.
> **trial** 試す過程を強調する.
> **experiment** trial より系統的に新発見などを目指す試み.

● 走行試験 a road *test*. ▶ この製品は十分試験済みです This product *is* well *tested* [*tried*].

── 試験的な 形 test; trial; 《正式》 expèriméntal; (仮の) tentative. ● 試験(的)飛行 a *test* [a *trial*] flight. ● 試験(的)段階にある be in an *experimental* [a *test*] stage.

── 試験的に 副 (試しに) on trial; (仮に) experimentally; (仮に) tentatively. ● 試験的に1か月間雇ってみる employ 《him》 for a month *on trial*; give 《him》 a month's *trial*.

── 試験する 動 test (for...); experiment ⟪on, with⟫. (⇔実験(をする)) ● 機械を試験運転する (⇔試運転) ● (ロープの)強度を試験する test (a rope) *for* strength.

● 試験科目 exam(ination) subjects; subjects for an exam. ● 試験官 an examiner, 《米》a proctor, 《英》an invigilator. ● 試験管 (⇔試験管) ● 試験場 an examinátion ròom [hàll]. ● 試験制度 an examination system. ● 試験範囲 the area covered in an exam. ▶ 試験範囲はどこ[何課]ですか What [How many lessons] is the *examination* going to cover?/What [How many lessons] will we *be tested on*? ● 試験問題 exam(ination) questions; questions for an exam. ● 試験用紙 an exám pàper [shèet]. (❗ この場合の paper は 🄲)

しけん 私見 (個人的見解) one's personal opinion

[view]. ●私見では in *my opinion* [*view*]. (🔲 〜の代わりに according to be を用いるのは避ける)

*しげん 資源 resources. ●天然[海底;人的]資源 natural [submarine; human] *resources*. ●観光資源 *resourses* of tourism. ●鉱物資源を開発する develop [exploit] mineral *resources*. ▶その国は天然資源にも人的資源にも恵まれていた The nation was rich (↔poor) in natural *resources* and manpower.
●資源エネルギー庁 the Agency for Natural Resources and Energy. ●資源開発 resource development. ●資源ごみ recyclable waste.

しげん 至言 〖時宜にかなった言葉〗an apt [an appropriate] remark; (名言) a (wise) saying. ▶「時は金なり」とは至言である It *is well* [*truly*] *said that* 'time is money.'

‡じけん 事件 〖法律上の〗a case; 〖出来事〗an event; (付随的な) an incident; (世間に知られた) an affair; 〖醜聞〗a scandal. ●出来事

①〖〜事件〗●殺人事件 a *case* of murder; a murder *case*. ●刑事事件 a criminal *case*. ●贈[収]賄事件 a bribery *scandal*. ●歴史上の一大事件 a great historical *event*. (🔲「小事件」は a minor *incident*) ●ダイヤモンド窃盗事件 an *affair* of the stolen diamonds. ●心中未遂事件 a *case* of an attempted double suicide that failed.

②〖事件が〗▶今日その店で珍奇な事件が起こった There was a strange *incident* [A strange *incident* occurred] in the store today. ▶この事件が戦争を引き起こした This *incident* caused a war. ▶間もなくその事件は解決される The *case* will be solved soon. ▶事件が続いている There has been a series of *incidents*.

③〖事件の〗●事件の発生 the occurrence of an *incident* [*affair*]. ●事件の衝撃 the shock of an *affair*. ●事件の経過 how the *affair* progressed. ●事件の現場 the scene of an *affair*. ●事件の鍵を握る hold the key to the *case*. ●事件の全容を明らかにする reveal the *case* entirely; bring the whole *case* to light.

④〖事件を〗●その事件を解明する[調べる;担当する] clear up [investigate; work on] the *case*. ●その事件をもみ消す cover up the *incident* [*affair*]. ●事件を目撃する witness an *affair*. ▶彼はその事件を劇の題材にした He used the *incident* as a theme for the play.
●事件記者 a news reporter on the police beat. (🔲 beat は「パトロール地域」の意)

じげん 字源 the origine of a (Chinese) character.

じげん 次元 〖数学・物理〗a dimension. ●第三次元 the third *dimension*. ●二次元の 2 two *dimensions*; two-*dimensional*. ●次元(=水準)が違う be on a different *level* [(領域) *sphere*]; belong to a different *level* [(部類) *category*]. ●次元の低い(=低俗な)考え a *vulgar* (↔an elevated) notion.

じげん 時限 a time limit; 〖授業時間〗a period. ●第 2 時限は英語です The second *period* is English./ We have English (in the) second *period*. (🔲 in the は省略することが多い; 2 時限目は歴史, 3 時限目は化学です We have history class *second period* and chemistry *third*.)
●時限ストの労働者 a limited-hour strike. ●時限ストを行う have a *limited-hour* strike; go on (a) strike for a *limited number of hours*. ●時限装置 a time [a timing] device. ●時限爆弾《plant》a time bomb. ●時限立法 legislation of specified duration.

しけんかん 試験管 a test tube.

●試験管ベビー a test-tube baby; an in vitro baby.

しこ 四股 ●四股を踏む 〖相撲〗stamp one's feet.

しこ 指呼 ●指呼の間に《stay》within hail [hailing distance] (of).

しご 死後 ●死後の世界 the world *after death*. ●死後に出版された彼の作品 his work published *after his death*; his posthumous /pástʃəməs/ work. ▶その人は死後数時間たっていた The man *has been dead* for several hours.
●死後硬直 〖医学〗rigor mortis.

しご 死語 〖すたれた言葉〗an obsolete /ɑ̀bsəliːt/ word; 〖使われなくなった言語〗a dead language.

しご 私語 (ひそひそ話) a whisper. ▶授業中私語はしないように You shouldn't *talk* during the class.

しご 詩語 (詩的語法) poetic diction; (詩的文体) poetic language; (詩的単語) a poetic word.

‡じこ 事故 ❶〖出来事〗an accident; (ちょっとした不運な) a mishap; (激突事故) a crash.

①〖〜事故, 事故〜〗●衝突事故 a collision; a car crash. ●列車事故 a train [a railroad (米), a railway (英)] *accident*. ●飛行機事故 an air (plane) *accident*; (墜落事故) a (plane) *crash*. ●ひどい事故 a bad [a serious] *accident*. ●事故発生 the occurrence of an *accident*. ●事故原因 the cause of an *accident*. ●交通事故で死ぬ be killed [die] in [×by] a traffic *accident*.

②〖事故が[は]〗●自動車事故が起きた A car [An automobile] *accident* occurred [happened]. ▶事故は多くの場合不注意から起こる Many *accidents* occur through carelessness [are caused by carelessness]. ▶この事故は起こるべくして起こった This was an *accident* waiting to happen.

③〖事故に〗●事故に繋がる lead to an *accident*. ●事故に巻き込む involve (him) in an *accident*. ●事故に巻き込まれる be involved in an *accident*. ▶彼は途中で事故にあった He had [met with] an *accident* on the way.

④〖事故を〗●事故を起こす cause an *accident*. ●事故を防ぐ prevent an *accident*. ▶あなたは自転車で(=自転車に乗っていて)事故を起こしたことがありますか Have you ever had an *accident* on your bicycle?

⑤〖事故で〗in an accident (⇨①); (故意でなく) by accident, accidentally. ▶タンカーで事故で数百万リットルの油が流出した The tanker *accidentally* spilt millions of liters of oil into the sea.

⑥〖事故も〗▶両親は事故もなく(=無事に)到着した My parents have arrived *without accident* [*mishap*].

❷〖事情〗circumstances. ●事故のため欠席する be absent (from school) because of unavoidable *circumstances*.
●事故現場 the scene of an accident; (特定の) the accident. ▶彼が最初に事故現場に駆けつけた He was the first person to rush to *the accident*. ●事故死 an accidental death; death by accident. ●事故防止 accident prevention.

‡じこ 自己 (one's) self (🔲通例 self の形で合成語を作り, 単独で用いることはまれ); 〖自分自身〗oneself. (自分) ●9.9 秒の自己ベストで 100 メートル競走を制する win the 100-meter dash in a *personal* best of 9.9 seconds. ●自己を見つめる reflect on one's *own* [(内なる) *inner*] *self*. ▶彼は自己主張が強い[非常に自己中心的だ] He is very *self-assertive* [*self-centered*]. ▶彼は自己顕示欲が強い He always wants to make *himself* conspicuous [stand out].

じこ ── **自己暗示**〔心理〕autosuggesstion, self-suggestion. ● 自己暗示にかかる suffer from *autosuggesstion*. ● **自己嫌悪** self-hatred. ● 自己嫌悪に陥る hate oneself. ● **自己資本**〔経済〕equity capital; net worth; (株主資本) stockholder's [shareholder's] capital. ● **自己資本比率**〔経済〕the equity [capital] ratio. ● **自己紹介** self-introduction. ● 自己紹介をする introduce oneself 《to》. ● **自己申告** a self-return. ● **自己申告制度** a self-return system; (納税の) a self-assessment system. ● **自己疎外** self-estrangement. ● **自己破産** (⇨自己破産) ● **自己批判** self-criticism. ● 自己批判する criticize oneself. ● **自己満足** self-satisfaction. ● 自己満足をさせる satisfy oneself 《with》. ● **自己矛盾** self-contradiction. ● 自己矛盾に陥る contradict oneself.

じご **事後** ── **一事後の** 形 ex post facto /éks pòust fæktou/. ● 彼らの決定に事後承認を与える give one's *ex post facto* approval to their decision.
● 事後報告 an ex post facto report.

じご 持碁 a draw in *go*.

しこう 至高 supremacy.

しこう 伺候 ── **伺候する** 動〔仕える〕wait on;〔ご機嫌伺いする〕pay one's respects 《to》.

しこう 志向 ● 政治志向の若者 a politically *oriented* young person. ● ブランド志向である *have a weakness* for brand names.

── **志向する** 動 (目指す) aim 《at》; (究極の目標を設定する) set the ultimate goal 《to》.

しこう 思考 名〔考えること, 思考力〕thought;〔考えること〕thinking. (⇨考え) ● ここのところ思考力の衰えを感じる I feel I'm losing my *faculty for thought*. ▶彼には思考力がない He has no *thinking* ability [no ability to *think*].

── **思考する** 動 think. (⇨考える)

しこう 指向 ── **指向性の** 形 directional; directive.
── **指向する** 動 point 《to》.
● 指向性 directivity. ● 指向性アンテナ a directional antenna. ● 指向性マイク a directional microphone.

しこう 施行 名〔法律などの〕〔執行〕enforcement; (実施) operation; (効力) effect, force.

── **施行する** 動 ● 法律を施行する put a law into *effect* [*force, operation*]; enforce a law. ▶その法律は来週から施行される The law will take *effect* [*become effective*] next week./The law will *come into effect* [*force, operation*] next week.

しこう 歯垢〔医学〕(dental) plaque /plǽk/; (歯石) tartar /tάːrtər/. ● 歯垢がたまる *Plaque* builds up [accumulates]. ● 歯垢を取る remove *plaque*.

しこう 嗜好〔好み, 趣味〕(a) taste; 〔好き〕(a) liking. ▶このワインは私の嗜好に合わない This wine is not to my *taste* 〔書〕*liking*〕. (⚠後の方は時に気取った表現)/This wine does not suit my *taste*./I don't like this wine.
● 嗜好品 (好きな食物) one's favorite food; (ぜいたく品) luxury goods, a luxury.

じこう 事項〔事柄〕matters;〔項目〕an item;〔題目〕a subject. ● 調査事項 *matters* for investigation. ● 関連事項 relevant [related] *matters*; a relevant *item* [*subject*].

じこう 時効〔法律〕(権利・義務などの) prescription; (公訴時効) the statute of limitations. ▶その事件はあす時効になる The *statute of limitations* on the case *runs out* tomorrow./Time runs out on the *statute of limitations* for the case tomorrow.
● 時効期間 the period of prescription.

じこう 時候〔季節〕the season;〔天候〕(the) weather. (⇨季節, 時季) ● 時候のあいさつを交わす〔する〕exchange a few words about the *weather*. ▶私は時候の変わり目にはぜんそくが出る I suffer from asthma at the change of *seasons*.

じごう 次号 the next number [issue]. ▶次号に続く To be continued. ▶次号完結 To be concluded.

しこうさくご 試行錯誤 ● 試行錯誤で〔試行錯誤の結果〕by trial and error.

じごうじとく 自業自得 ● 自業自得とあきらめる take *the natural consequences of* one's *own misdeed*. ▶彼はよく勉強せずに悪い成績をとった。自業自得さ(=自分で求めたのだ) He didn't study hard and got bad grades—he *asked for it* 〔当然の報いだ〕 he *had it coming* 《to him》].

会話「安部先生にレポートで不可をもらっちゃった。インターネットから写し取ったのがばれて」「それは自業自得だね」"Mr. Abe gave me an F for my paper. He found out that I downloaded it from the internet." "(It) *serves* you *right*./(自分のせいだ) You *have only* yourself *to thank* 《for it》."

じごえ 地声 one's natural voice. ▶彼は地声が大きい He has (got) a loud voice. (⚠ by nature (生まれつき)はつけなくてよい)

しごき 扱き a grueling drill (imposed by senior members).

しこく 四国 (地方) the Shikoku district; (島) Shikoku Island, the island of Shikoku.

しごく 至極 ● 至極ごもっともです(=まったくおっしゃるとおりです) You are *quite* right. ▶獲物を逃がして至極(=この上なく)残念だ It is *extremely* regrettable that I missed the game.

しごく ❶〔なでる〕● ひげをしごく stroke (down) one's beard.

❷〔訓練する〕(徹底的に) put*... through the mill; (技能などを反復して) drill ... hard 《in》, train and drill 《to do》. ▶英語の広木先生にはしごかれた I *was drilled hard* by my English teacher, Mr. Hiroki.

‡じこく 時刻 (時間) time; (24 時間制の) an hour. (⇨時間❸) ● 到着〔出発〕時刻 the arrival [departure] *time*. ● バス〔列車, 飛行機〕の時刻表 a bus [a train; an airplane] *schedule*《主に米》[*timetable*《主に英》]. ● 早い〔遅い〕時刻に来る come at [in] an early [a late] *hour*. ▶時刻は 10 時 5 分です It [The *time*, The *hour*] is 10:05. (⚠交通機関や軍隊など 24 時間制では ten-(hundred-)o/óu/- five, 一般には five (minutes) past [《米》after] ten,〔話〕ten five と読む) ▶列車は時刻どおりにそこへ着いた The train got there *on time* [*on schedule*]. ▶夜のこの時刻に何をしているのか What are you doing at this time of night?

じこく 自国 one's (own) country; 〔本国〕⇨本国. ● 自国語 one's native language. ● 自国語しか話さない韓国の映画スターに通訳を介してインタビューする interview the *monolingual* Korean film star through an interpreter.

じごく 地獄, Hell (↔Heaven); (地獄のようなひどい場所・状態) (a) hell. ● 受験地獄 an 'examination *hell*'. (⇨受験) ● この世の地獄 a *hell* on earth. (⇨生き地獄) ▶地獄へ落ちろ(=くたばっちまえ) Go to *hell*!
● 地獄で仏(に会ったよう) It's like meeting a good samaritan (in my hour of need).
● 地獄のさたも金次第 Everything [Anything] can be settled by money even in hell.;《ことわざ》Money makes the mare to go. (⚠雌馬

(mare) はしぶとく御しがたいことから. to は調子を整えるために入れたもの)
- **地獄絵** a hell picture. - **地獄耳** 《have》 big ears.

じごくへん『**地獄変**』*The Hell Screen*. [参考] 芥川龍之介の小説)

しこしこ ❶ [歯ざわり] - しこしこした chewy; (堅ゆでで歯ざわりよい) al dente /æl déntei/. (!) rubbery は堅い肉をかむときの感触を表し, ここでは不適切)
❷ [粘り強さ] - しこしこと (忍耐強く) patiently, with a lot of patience; (1歩1歩) step by step; (地道に) steadily. - しこしこと原稿を書く write one's manuscripts *steadily*.

しごせん **子午線** [地学] a meridian /mərídiən/.

しこたま a lot of.... - しこたまもうける《話》make pots [a pot] of money; (話) rake it in, (話) rake in *a lot of* money (!) 後の二つはしばしば進行形で).

しごと **仕事** [働くこと] work; a job; labor; business; a task; [職業] an occupation, a job (=職業); [任務] a duty (!) 通例複数形で); (割り当てられた仕事) an assignment (⇨務め).

[使い分け] **work** 「仕事」の意を表す最も一般的な語. 職業や勤務だけでなく労働・作業・任務など幅広い意味を持つ.
job 給与のある仕事, またはすべき義務.
labor 肉体労働, またはそのような仕事に従事すること.
business 商業や経済, 生産と関わる仕事. 複合語で使用されることが多い.
task 他から課せられた任務や具体的な仕事・課題.

①【~の(仕事)】- やさしい仕事 an easy [a light] task. (! ×easy [light] labor は不可) - 骨の折れる [困難な] 仕事 hard [heavy] work; a hard job. - パートタイムの仕事 a part-time (→a full-time) job. (⇨パート❸) - 引き合う [引き合わない] 仕事 (×a) paying [(×an) unprofitable] business. - 安定した仕事 a secure job. - やりかけの仕事 work in progress. - はんぱ仕事 an odd job [×labor]. - 新しい仕事 a new job. - 毎日の決まりきった仕事 one's routine (work). - 一生の仕事 one's lifework [life's work]; one's career /kəríər/. - 辞書編集の仕事 the work [job] of compiling a dictionary. - 手仕事 handiwork. (⇨手仕事) - 畑仕事 farming. - 家の仕事 a household job; housework. ▶彼を説得するのはひと仕事だ It's quite *a job* to persuade him. ▶そこへ行くのは一日仕事だ It will take you a whole day to get there.

②【仕事(の)~】- 仕事ぶり one's performance at *work*. - 仕事の虫 (軽蔑的) a workaholic; (仕事の鬼) a demon for *work*; (仕事大好き人間) a *work*-addict. - 仕事熱心な人 a hardworking person. - 仕事上の約束がある have a *business* appointment. - 仕事の都合で because of one's working; for the convenience of the work. - 仕事の件でon the matter of work. - 仕事の手を休める take a break from one's work. ▶お仕事中失礼します I am sorry to interrupt you while you *are working* [*at work*, *on the job*]. (! on the job は通例工具に用いる) ▶彼に英語教師の仕事の口を見つけてやった I found him *work* [a *job*, 《書》a *position*] as an English teacher. ▶2006年の仕事納めの日 the last *business* day of the year in 2006.

③【仕事が[は]】- 仕事がない (することがない) have nothing to do; (失業中) be out of *work* [a *job*]. - 仕事がたくさんある have a lot of *work* [jobs,

works] to do [×to be done]. - 仕事が忙しい busy with [at, over] (one's) *work*. - 仕事が雑 [丁寧] である be sloppy [precise] in one's *work*. ▶私の仕事はあなたの質問に答えることです My *job* [*task*] is to answer your questions. - 仕事ができよくできる He does well on the *job*./He is good at his *job*./He is an able worker. - 彼は仕事が早い [遅い] He works quickly [(too) slowly]./He is a quick [a slow] worker. - 私は仕事が手につかない I can't settle down to *work*./I am in no mood for *work* [to *work*]. - 前の方は「仕事に落ち着いて始められない」の意, 後の方は「仕事をする気になれない」の意) ▶私はまだ仕事が終わっていない I haven't finished [I haven't done with, 《話》I'm not through with] my *work* yet. ▶彼女の仕事は(=商売)はうまく行って[軌道に乗って]いた Her *business* was doing well. - 自分の人生のために仕事はある There's a *job* for your life.

[会話] 「お父さんのお仕事は何ですか」「銀行員です」"What [kind of] *work* [*job*] does your father do (for a living)?/What (line of) *business* is your father in?/What's your father's *work* [*occupation*, ×*job*]?" "He is a bank clerk [works for a bank]." (!(1) 最初が最も普通の尋ね方. (2) job は目上の人には避けた方がよい (⇨❺[会話]))

[会話] 「仕事はうまく行ってますか」「ええ, なんとか」"How is your *work* going?/How are you getting on with your *work*?" "Fine."

④【仕事に】- 仕事に(とり)かかる start *work* [to *work*, working]; get (down) [set] to *work*; be [set] about one's *work*. - 仕事に追われる be pressed with *work* [*business*]. - 仕事に精を出す attend to one's *business*; apply oneself to one's *business*. (! 日常会話では work hard が普通) - 仕事に没頭する plunge (oneself) into the *work*. - 仕事に向く be cut out for a *job*. - 仕事につながる lead to a *job*. - 英語を使う仕事につく get a *job* using English. ▶朝何時に仕事に出かけますか(=会社に行く) What time [When] do you go to *work* [the office] in the morning? ▶私は教育を生涯の仕事に選んだ I chose education for [as] my *career*. - 彼はいろいろな仕事に手を出したが, 何一つ成功したものがない He tried his hand at all kinds of *business*, but he hasn't succeeded in any of them. - 趣味であったことが仕事になった What was once a hobby has become my job.

⑤【仕事を】- 仕事をする(=働く) *work*. - 通訳の仕事をする *work as* an interpreter. - コンピュータ(関連)の仕事をしている *work* [*be*] *in* computers. - いい[まずい] 仕事をする do a good [a bad] *job*. - 仕事を覚える learn how to do the *job*. - 仕事を続ける continue [go on with] one's *job* [*work*]. - 仕事を与える give (him) a *job* [*work*]. - 仕事を頼む ask (him) to do the *work*. - 仕事を怠る neglect one's *task* [*duties*]. - 仕事を始める(=仕事にとりかかる)(⇨④) - 仕事を休む be absent [stay away] from *work*. (! 後の方が口語的) - 仕事をやめる (中断する) stop [(話)quit] *working*; (終了する) get (話) leave] off *work*; (辞職する) leave [(話)quit] one's *job*, resign from one's *job*, (通例定年で) retire from one's *job*. - 仕事を探す look [《やや話》hunt] for a *job*; 《書》seek *employment*. - 仕事を片づける finish one's *work*. - 仕事を失う(=失業する) lose one's *job* [*employment*]. - 仕事を家に持ち帰る take *work* home. - 仕事を持つ母親 a *working* mother. - 仕事を離れると(就業時間以外に) when not at *work*; outside the office. ▶彼女はK&Kという会社で仕事を見つけた(=就職した) She found [got] *a job with a firm called K&K*. ▶どうしてその仕事をされるようになったのですか How did you get into that line of *work*? ▶私は田中芳行と申します. 会計の仕事をしております. 今は請求書のチェックが仕事です I'm Yoshiyuki Tanaka. *I'm in* accounts. *I'm responsible for* checking invoices. ▶仕事を二つ持っているのでとても忙しい I'm really busy because I have two *jobs* [×*works*]. ▶彼はよく仕事を変える He often changes his *job* [*occupation*]. ▶今日はここで仕事を打ち切ろう Let's stop *working* for today./(話) Let's call it a day. ▶金を使って仕事をするなら営業マンはいらない If you can generate *business* by (simply) spending money, you don't need salespersons.

会話 「で，どんなお仕事をなさってるんですか」「仕事ですか，脳外科をやってます」 "So what's your line of *business*?" "Line of *business*? I'm a brain surgeon." (⇨③ 会話)

❻【仕事で[から]】 ●仕事から帰る get [come, go] home from *work*. (⇨帰る) ▶彼は仕事でパリへ行った He went to Paris *on business*./He went *on a business trip* to Paris. (!仕事を主眼にして《やや書》 Business took him to Paris. ともいえる (⇨出張))

• 仕事着 wórk(ing) clòthes, overalls; (勤務先などでの) a wórking ùniform. • 仕事師 (土木工事の労働者) a construction worker; a steeplejack; (事業を計画・経営する人) a shrewd entrepreneur. • 仕事場 a workshop; one's place of work, (家の) one's home office. • 仕事部屋 a workroom. • 仕事量 workload.

しこな 四股名 【相撲】 a (sumo wrestler's) ring name.

じこはさん 自己破産 a personal [voluntary] bankruptcy. • 自己破産の申請 one's *personal* [*voluntary*] *bankruptcy* petition.

しこみ 仕込み ●英国仕込みの紳士 a gentleman *trained* [(教育を受けた) *educated*] in England; an English-*trained* gentleman.
• 仕込み杖 a sword cane [stick].

しこむ 仕込む ❶【訓練する】train; (教える) teach*. ▶馬を競馬用に仕込む *train* horses *for* a race. ▶猫に芸を仕込もうとしてもむだだ It's useless [a waste of time] to try to *teach* a cat to do tricks.
❷【仕入れる】stock up 《*on*》. ●パーティー用に食料をたくさん仕込む *stock up on* food for the party; (買う) *buy* a lot of food for the party.

しこり 痼り 【はれもの】a lump; (腫瘍[はが]) a tumor (!しばしば「がん」を暗示); (感情の) bad [ill] feelings. • 胸にしこりができる develop a *lump* in one's breast. • 後にしこりを残す leave *bad* [*ill*] *feelings*.

じこりゅう 自己流 one's own style [way, fashion]. • 自己流のやり方 one's *own style*. • 自己流に after [in] one's *own style* [*fashion*]; in one's *own way*. ▶私の絵は自己流です I am a *self-taught* painter.

しこん 紫紺 purplish dark blue.

しこん 歯根 the root of a tooth.

しさ 示唆 图 (a) suggestion; [ヒント] a hint. (⇨暗示, ヒント) ● 示唆に富む論文 a *suggestive* [*stimulating*, *thought-provoking*] essay; an essay full of *suggestions* [*ideas*]. • 有益な示唆をいただく have a helpful *suggestion* 《from my teacher》.
—— 示唆する 動 suggest 《*that* 節; *doing*》; hint 《*that* 節; *at*》.

しざ 視座 a point of view; a viewpoint. (⇨視点)

じさ 時差 time difference. ▶まだ時差ぼけが治っていないみたいだ I guess I still have [get, suffer from] (xa) jet lag. (! 米国帰りの人なら I guess my body's still on U.S. time. (体はまだ米国時間みたいだ)ともいえる)

会話 「東京とパリとの時差はどのくらいありますか」「8時間です. 東京の方が8時間早いんです」 "What is [Can you tell me] the *time difference* between Tokyo and Paris?" "Eight hours. Tokyo is eight hours ahead." (!an eight-hour time difference between A and Bのように数値を伴う言い方では不定冠詞を伴う)

• 時差出勤 staggered working hours. (! flextime は勤務時間帯の自由選択制度)

しさい 子細 图 【事情】circumstances; 【詳細】details.
—— 子細に 副 in detail; minutely.

しさい 司祭 a priest.

しさい 詩才 poetic genius [talent].

しざい 死罪 capital punishment. (⇨死刑)

しざい 私財 one's (private) property, one's (own) money. ▶彼は私財を投じて医学校を創った He used his *own money* to found a medical school.

しざい 資材 materials. • 建築資材 búilding matérials. • 資材置き場 a place [a storehouse] for *materials*.

じざい 自在 —— 自在の 形 • 伸縮自在のセーター an *elastic* sweater.
—— 自在に (自由に) freely; (意のままに) at will; (簡単に) easily.
• 自在鉤 a pothook.

しさく 思索 [思考] thought; [考えること] thinking; [深く考えること] contemplation, meditation (! 後の方がさらに深く真剣な思索を暗示). • 思索にふける be lost in *thought* [*contemplation*, *meditation*].
—— 思索的な 形 contemplative /kəntémplətɪv/, meditative /médətèɪtɪv/.
—— 思索する 動 think reflectively; cóntemplàte; meditate 《*on*》.
• 思索家 a thinker.

しさく 施策 (政策) a measure; (方針) a policy. • 施策を講じる take *measure* 《*to* do》. • 施策を行う carry a *policy* out.

しさく 詩作 —— 詩作する 動 write [compose] a poem.

しさく 試作 图 【試験的に製造すること】trial manufacture [production]; 【画家などの】a study.
—— 試作する 動 雪上車を試作する *make* [*produce*] a snowmobile *experimentally*.
• 試作車 an experimental car. • 試作品 a trial product.

じさく 次作 (芸術作品) one's next work of art; (文芸作品) one's next literary work.

じさく 自作 • 自作の (自分で作った[書いた]) of one's own making [writing, composing]; (something) which one made [wrote, composed] (for) oneself. (! 一般には関係代名詞を用いた言い方の方が普通) • 自作自演する(=自作の劇の中で演じる) act in a play of one's *own writing* [in one's *own play*].
• 自作農 a landed farmer.

じざけ 地酒 (*sake* of) local brew /brúː/; locally brewed *sake*; a local brand of *sake*.

しさつ 刺殺 —— 刺殺する 動 stab (-bb-) 《him》 to death; 【野球】make a putout; put out 《a runner》.

しさつ 視察 图 (an) inspection.
— **視察する** 動 inspect, make an inspection《of》; (視察に訪れる) visit. ● 水害地を現場視察する make an on-the-spot inspection [an inspection tour] of a flood-stricken district.
● **視察団** an inspéction tèam [pàrty]. ● **視察旅行** an inspéction tòur, a tour of inspection.

* **じさつ 自殺** 图 (a) suicide. ● 焼身[ガス]自殺をする burn [gas] oneself to death. ● ピストル自殺をする shoot oneself to death; take one's own life with a gun. ● 屋上から飛び降り自殺をする jump to (one's) death from the rooftop. ● 列車に飛び込み自殺をする kill oneself by jumping in front of a train. ▶彼は服毒[首つり]自殺をした He killed himself by taking poison [hanging]./He poisoned himself to death [hanged himself]. ▶彼は昨夜自殺をはかった He attempted suicide [tried to kill himself] last night. ▶そんなむちゃな運転は自殺行為だ Driving so recklessly is suicidal.
— **自殺の** 形 suicidal.
— **自殺する** 動 kill oneself; commit (-tt-) suicide (⚠ 後の方は堅い言い方);〚自分の命を断つ〛take* one's own life. ▶時々自殺したくなる I sometimes feel like killing myself [committing suicide]./ I sometimes feel suicidal.
● **自殺者** a suicide. ● **自殺点** (score) an own goal. ● **自殺幇助(ほうじょ)罪** the crime of aiding and abetting suicide. ● **自殺未遂** an attempted suicide. ● **自殺率** a suicide rate.

しさん 四散 — **四散する** 動 scatter away;〚書〛be scattered to the (four) winds.

しさん 試算 图 an estimate, a rough [(仮の) a provisional] calculation.
— **試算する** 動 ● 旅行費用を試算する estimate the cost of the trip.

しさん 資産 〚財産〛(a) property;〚巨額の金〛(a) fortune;〚資力〛means;〚個人・会社の〛an ásset (⚠ 通例複数形で).(⇨財産)● **総[純]資産** total [net] assets. ● **固定[流動]資産** fixed [current] assets. ● **海外[国内]資産** foreign [domestic] assets. ● 資産を公開する make one's property public; disclose all one's financial interests. ● 資産を売却する sell [liquidate] the assets; (処分する) sell off [down] the assets. ● 資産を相続する come into a fortune. ▶地価の上昇によって含み資産が倍増した As a result of the increase in the price of land, the value of hidden assets has doubled.
● **資産運用** assets management. ● **資産家** a rich [a wealthy] person; a man of means (⚠ 男性についていう). ● **資産株** income stock. ● **資産勘定** an asset account. ● **資産管理** asset-management. ● **資産凍結** assets freeze. ● **資産評価** assets valuation.

しざん 死産 图 (a) stillbirth.
— **死産する** 動 ▶彼女は赤ん坊を死産した She had a stillbirth [a stillborn baby]./Her baby was stillborn [was born dead].

じさん 持参 — **持参する** 動 (持って来る) bring*; (持って行く) take*. ● 印鑑をご持参ください Please bring your seal with you.
● **持参金** a dowry /dáuəri/. (⚠ この語には不動産も含まれる). ● **持参人** (小切手などの) a bearer.

しし 四肢 the limbs.
● **四肢まひ**〚医学〛quadriplegia. (参考) 両上肢・両下肢の運動・知覚のまひ

しし 死屍 a (dead) body; a corpse. (⇨死体, 死骸) ▶戦場は死屍累々としていた There were heaps of corpses on the battlefield.
● **死屍に鞭打つ** ▶死屍にむち打つようなことはよせ Don't speak ill of [criticize] the dead.

しし 志士 a patriot.

しし 嗣子 (男) an heir; (女) an heiress. (⇨相続人)

しし 獅子 a lion; (雌) a lioness.
● **獅子身中(しんちゅう)の虫** an ungrateful and treacherous friend.
● **獅子頭** a lion mask (for shishimai). ● **獅子鼻** a snub [a pug] nose.

* **しじ 支持** 图 support;〚後援〛backing. ● 現内閣の支持率 the approval rate of the present cabinet. ● その計画に対する彼の厚い支持 his warm support for the plan. ● 彼の支持を得る[得ている] get [have] support from him; get [have] his support. ● 国民の支持を失う lose the support of the (general) public. ● その計画は世論の全面的な支持を得た The project won the full support [backing] of public opinion.
— **支持する** 動 support;(主に議論などで) back ... (up). ● 彼の計画を支持する support his plan; (支持している) be in favor [favor] of his plan. ▶選挙ではどの候補者を支持しますか Which candidate will you support [back] in the election? ▶人々はその新党を支持しなかった People didn't support [gave no support to, didn't favor] the new political party. ▶彼はその議論で私を支持してくれた He backed me up [stood up for me] in the argument.
● **支持者** a supporter; (後援者) a backer.

* **しじ 指示** 图〚指図〛directions;〚明細な〛instructions (⚠ 特に書面のものをさすことが多い);〚助言〛advice;〚さし示すこと〛(an) indication. ● 上司の指示を受ける receive instructions from the boss. ● 医者の指示をあおぐ ask a doctor for advice; ask for a doctor's advice. ▶私は彼の指示に従った I followed his directions [instructions, advice].
— **指示する** 動 direct; (やや書) instruct; indicate. ● 彼に退出するよう指示する direct [instruct, 命ずる] order] him to leave the room; direct [instruct him, order] that he (《主に英》should) leave the room.
● **指示語**〚文法〛a demonstrative word. ● **指示代名詞**〚文法〛a demonstrative pronoun.

しじ 死児 (死んだ子) a dead child; (死産児) a stillborn child.
● **死児の齢(よわい)を数える** wish things had not been like this; (言っても甲斐のないことの愚痴(ぐち)をこぼす) complain about one's fate; (ことわざ) cry over spilit milk.

しじ 私事 a private [a personal] matter; private [personal] affairs. ▶私事にわたって恐縮ですが Excuse me for being personal, but ....

しじ 師事 — **師事する** 動 (学問上で) study under 《Professor K》; (芸術分野などで) take lessons from 《K》; (弟子入りする) become 《K's》pupil [disciple].

しじ 侍史 (手紙の脇付け) respectfully.

じじ 時事 current events; the events of the day.
● **時事英語** current English. ● **時事解説** comments on current topics. ● **時事解説者** (放送の) a (news) commentator. ● **時事評論** a review of current events. ● **時事問題** current topics [affairs]; a current issue. ● **時事問題を論じる** discuss current events [the events of the day].

じじ(い) 爺 an old man; (祖父) a grandpa.

ししおどし 鹿威し a *shishiodoshi*; (説明的に) a device for making high-pitched sounds in a traditional Japanese garden.

シシカバブ 【料理】shish kebab.

ししき 司式 ── **司式する** 動 officiate 《*at*》. ▶あの牧師が結婚式を司式した That priest *officiated* at the wedding.

ししきゅう 四死球 【野球】a base on balls [a walk] and a hit batsman. (⇨四球, 死球)

じじこっこく 時々刻々 momentarily; every moment; from moment to moment. (🚩 hourly, hour も上と同じ形式で用いることができる) ▶五色沼は時々刻々その色を変える Goshiki Pond changes color *from hour to hour*. ▶私は一度死んで生き返った. 今は私を一生懸命に生きる I once died and came back. I live *every moment* with all my energy.

ししざ 獅子座 【占星・天文】Leo /líːoʊ/ (🚩 the はつけない); 《獅子宮》【占星】the Lion. (⇨乙女座) ▶獅子座(生まれ)の人 a Leo (複 ~s).

ししそんそん 子々孫々 ●子々孫々に至るまで down to the remotest descendants. ●子々孫々に伝える hand (it) down *from generation to generation*.

ししつ 私室 a private room.

ししつ 紙質 the quality of paper. ▶紙質がよい [大変よい] The paper is of good [high] *quality*.

ししつ 脂質 【生化学】lipid.

ししつ 資質 【素質】the makings; 【才能】(生まれつきの) (a) talent, a gift; (潜在的な) (a) capacity; (努力でさらに伸ばした) (an) ability; 【由来の性質】nature. ●資質に恵まれた若者たち *talented* [*gifted*] young people.

しじつ 史実 historical [×historic] evidence; 【歴史的事実】a historical fact. ▶この物語は史実に基づいている This story is based on *historical evidence* [*facts*]. ▶彼の著書は細部に至るまで史実に忠実なことでよく知られている His books are well known for their accurate *historical* detail.

じしつ 自室 one's (own) room. ●自室に引きこもる stay in one's *room*.

じしつ 痔疾 ●痔疾にかかる have [suffer from] hemorrhoids [piles].

じじつ 事実 a fact; 【真実】truth; 【現実】(a) reality; 【実情】the case.
① 【~事実】●明らかな事実 an obvious [a clear] *fact*. ●既成事実 an established *fact*. ●意外な事実 a startling [an unthinkable] *fact*. ●決定的な事実 a decisive *fact*. ●よく知られた [紛れもない] 事実 a well-known [an unquestionable] *fact*. ●観察によって知り得た事実 the *truth* (which) we learned from observation. ●衝撃の事実 a shocking *fact*. ▶彼が無実だという事実が分かった We have discovered (the *fact*) that he is innocent. (🚩 that 節を従える動詞の後では the fact は省略する方が簡潔でよい)/The *fact* that he is innocent [of his innocence] has been discovered.
② 【事実(の)~】●事実問題 a question of *fact*. ●事実関係を明らかにする reveal the details of a *fact*. ▶それは事実上の(=実質的な)敗北だった It was a practical [a virtual] defeat. ▶実際 [実際は] ▶事実上一銭も残っていなかった I had *practically* [*virtually*] no money left.
③ 【事実に】●これらの事実に照らしてみて in view of these *facts*. ●事実に矛盾する [反する] be contrary to the *fact*. ▶君の報告は事実に基づいていない Your report is not based [founded] on *fact*.
④ 【事実を】●事実を認める [曲げる; おおい隠す; 明らかにする] admit [distort; cover up; reveal] a *fact*. ●事実をありのままに語る tell the (whole) *truth*; give 《him》the bare *facts*. ●事実を直視する face (the) *facts*. ●事実を誇張する exaggerate a *fact*. ▶意見ではなく事実を述べなさい Give us the *facts*, not (your) opinions.
⑤ 【…は事実だ】▶彼が我々を裏切ったのは事実だ It is *true* [a *fact*] that he betrayed us./(実を言えば) The *fact* [The *truth*] is (that) he betrayed us. (⇨実は) ▶彼は病気だと言ったが, それは事実ではなかった He said he was sick, but it was not *true* [the *case*].

■ DISCOURSE
テレビに多くの利点があることは事実だ. しかし私は, テレビは自分で考える力を弱めたと思う It is *true* that TV has many benefits. **Nevertheless**, I would say it has weakened the people's ability to think for themselves. (🚩 nevertheless (しかし) は逆接を表すディスコースマーカー.「…は事実だ」などの譲歩表現と組み合わせて用いると効果的)

●事実は小説より奇なり (ことわざ) Truth [Fact] is stranger than fiction.
●事実無根 ●事実無根のうわさ a *groundless* [an *unfounded*] rumor.
── **事実** 【本当に】really; (意外かもしれないが) actually; (さらにはっきり言えば) in fact, as a matter of fact. ▶実は 【類語】▶彼は事実そう言ったのだ He *really* [*actually*] said so. ▶彼は健康ではなかった. 事実しょっちゅう入院していた He was in poor health. *In fact*, he was very often sent to (《主に米》the) hospital.

じじつ 時日 ❶ 【日にち】a date. ▶次の会合の時日を決めよう Let's fix the *date* of the next meeting.
❷ 【時間】 time. ●時日がかかる take (some [much]) *time*.

ししとう 獅子唐 【植物】a small green pepper.

ししふんじん 獅子奮迅 ●獅子奮迅の勢いで 《run [walk]》 like fury; with great energy.

しじま silence. (⇨静寂) ▶夜のしじまに in the *still* of the night.

ししまい 獅子舞 *shishimai*; (説明的に) a dance performed in a lion's mask (developed from an act of exorcism on New Year's Day) (🚩 exorcism は「悪魔払い」の意).

しじみ 蜆 【魚介】a *shijimi* mussel; (説明的に) a kind of very small mussel used as a popular ingredient for *miso* soup.

ししゃ 支社 a branch (office). (⇨支店)

ししゃ 死者 (1人の) a dead person; (複数の) the dead (🚩 1人の人にも用いるのは《古》); 【事故・災害などの】(死亡者) fatalities 【統計などで用いる】, (死者総数) the death toll. (⇨死傷者) ▶その事故による死者の数は100人に達した The *death toll* from [The number of (×the) *fatalities* in] the accident reached one hundred./(100人の死者が出た) One hundred people were killed [(100人の命が失われた) One hundred lives were lost] in the accident.

ししゃ 使者 a messenger; (使節) an envoy. (⇨使い) ●使者を送る [立てる] send a *messenger* 《*to*》. ▶コマドリは春の使者です Robbins are the *messengers* of spring.

ししゃ 試写 a preview; (映画関係者だけの) a trade première /prɪmiər/ [show]. ●映画の試写会を行う give [hold] a *preview* of a film; preview a film.

ししゃ 試射 ── **試射する** 動 test-fire 《a gun》. ●試射場 a firing range.

じしゃ 自社 one's company [corporation, firm].
ししゃく 子爵 a viscount /váikàunt/. (⚠ 称号：(英国で) Lord ...; (英国以外で) Viscount ... (⇨貴族 解説))
● 子爵夫人 a viscountess.
じしゃく 磁石 图 a magnet;【方位計】a compass.
● 棒[馬蹄(てい)形]磁石 a bar [a horseshoe] *magnet*. ▶ この金属には磁石はつかない *Magnets* don't attract this metal.
── 磁石の 形 magnetic.
じしゃく 自若 self-possession. ● 泰然自若としている (⇨泰然)
ししゃごにゅう 四捨五入 ── **四捨五入する** 動
● 3.7532 の小数点以下第 4 位を四捨五入する *round* 3.7532 *off to* three decimal places [*to* the third decimal place].
ししゃのおごり『死者の奢り』 *Lavish Are The Dead*. (参考) 大江健三郎の小説
ししゃも 柳葉魚【魚介】a *shishamo* smelt (複 ~(s)).
ししゅ 死守 ── **死守する** 動 defend desperately [最後の最後まで] to the bitter end].
ししゅ 詩趣 poetic(al) feelings. ● 詩趣に富む be *poetic(al)*; be full of [rich in] *poetry* [*poetic feelings*].
じしゅ 自主 图 independence; (自主性) autonomy.
● 自主独立の self-independent.
── **自主的な** 形 independent; (自発的な) voluntary. ● 自主的な活動 (a) voluntary activity.
── **自主的に** 副 independently; voluntarily; of one's own (free) will. ● 自主的に判断する judge independently.
● 自主管理 self-management. ● 自主規制 self-restraint; voluntary restriction [restraint]. ● 輸出品に対する自主規制 self-restraint on exports. ● 自主財源 independent revenue sources. ● 自主トレ(ーニング) voluntary (spring) training.
じしゅ 自首 ── **自首する** 動 surrender (oneself) to the police;《話》turn oneself in [give oneself up] (to the police).
ししゅう 死臭 the putrid smell of a dead body;《書》the stench of death [decaying flesh].
ししゅう 刺繍 图 embroidery. (⚠ 作品は an ~)
── **刺繍する** 動 ▶ 金糸でイニシャルをハンカチに刺繍する *embroider* one's initials *on* a handkerchief [a handkerchief *with* one's initials] *in* gold thread.
● 刺繍糸 embroidery thread.
ししゅう 詩集 a collection of poems; (名詩選集) an anthology. ● エミリー・ディキンスン全詩集 The *Poems* of Emily Dickinson. (⚠ 書名としては、Collected Poems of ..., Poetical Works of ... などがある)
***じしゅう 始終** [始めから終わりまで] from beginning to end (⇨一部始終); [いつも] always, all the time (⇨いつも 解説); [絶えず] (繰り返し) continually; (変わりなく) constantly; [しばしば] often, frequently (⇨度々). ▶ 彼は始終テレビを見ている He is *always* watching TV. (⚠ always を伴って進行形で用いると通例話し手のいらだちを表す) ▶ 彼は始終図書館に通っている He *very often* [*frequently*] goes to the library.
しじゅう 四十 forty. (⇨四十(しじゅう))
● 四十にして惑わず You are advised not to suffer from perplexities any more when you become forty.
しじゅう 次週 (来週) next week; (その翌週) the next week (⚠ 過去・未来を基準にして).
じしゅう 自修 self-study. ▶ 剛は自修で(=独学で)韓国語を話せるようになった Tsuyoshi learned to speak Korean by *self-study*.
じしゅう 自習 ── **自習する** 動 study by oneself.
● 自習時間 a free study period [hour]; 《米》a study(-hall) hour; 《米》study hall. ● 自習室 《米》a study hall.
じじゅう 自重 dead weight.
じじゅう 侍従 a chamberlain /tʃéimbərlin/.
● 侍従長 the Grand Chamberlain to the Emperor.
ししゅうえん 歯周炎【医学】periodontitis /pèriːədəntáitis/.
しじゅうかた 四十肩 《suffer from》a frozen shoulder. (⚠ 日本語と同じ英語)
しじゅうから 四十雀【鳥】a great tit; a titmouse (複 -mice).
しじゅうしょう 四重唱【音楽】(a) four-part chorus.
しじゅうそう 四重奏【音楽】a quartet(te). ● 弦楽四重奏 a string *quartet*.
ししゅうびょう 歯周病【医学】periodontitis /pèriədəntáitis/.
ししゅく 私淑 ── **私淑する** 動 ▶ 彼女は K 先生に私淑している She admires Mr. K and is very much influenced by his books [and has learned a lot of things from his books].
しじゅく 私塾 a private school.
じしゅく 自粛 图 [自制, 克己] self-control; [自己訓練] self-discipline.
── **自粛する** 動 ● 選挙運動を自粛する *use* [*exercise*] *self-control over* one's election campaign. ● 喫煙を自粛する(=控える) *refrain from* smoking.
ししゅつ 支出 图 (an) expenditure (↔revenue) (⚠ expense より堅い語); spending; an outgo (複 ~es) (↔an income); (出費) (an) expense (↔earnings) (⚠「必要[所要]経費」の意では複数形).
● 個人支出 personal *spending*. ● 民間[公共; 政府]支出 private [public; government] *spending* [*expenditure*]. ● 本代に 10 ドルの支出 the [an] *expenditure* of 10 dollars *on* books. (⚠ the では「支出すること」, an では「支出額」の意) ● 支出を切り詰める cut down (on) [reduce] one's *expenses* [*expenditure(s)*]. ● 収入と支出のバランスを保つ keep income and *outgo* [revenue and *expenditure*] in balance.
── **支出する** 動 [支払う] pay*; [金を費やす] spend*.
● 研究に多くの金を支出する *spend* a lot of money *on* the research. ● 先月は衣服代に多額の支出をした I had to *pay* great *expenses for* clothing [*to* buy clothes] last month. (⚠ 単に I had to *pay* a lot (of money) *for* [*to* buy] clothes last month. ともいえる)
● 支出額 an expenditure.
しじゅほうしょう 紫綬褒章 the Medal with Purple Ribbon. (⇨褒章 関連)
しじゅんかせき 示準化石【地質】an index fossile.
ししゅんき 思春期 adolescence /ædəlésns/; puberty /púːbəti/. (⚠ 前の方は「期間」, 後の方は「開始時期」をさす) ● 思春期の子供 an *adolescent* (person). ● 思春期特有の感情 the feelings characteristic of *adolescence* [ˣ*puberty*]. ● 思春期になる arrive at *puberty* [ˣ*adolescence*].
ししょ 支所 a branch (office).
ししょ 支署 a branch office.
ししょ 司書 a librarian /laibréəriən/.
ししょ 史書 a history book.

ししょ 死所, 死処 (死ぬべき場所) a place to die; (死んだ場所) a deathplace.

ししょ 子女 a child (⑳ children) (⇨子供); (女の子) a girl, (娘) a daughter. ●帰国子女 a returnee (student [child]).

***じしょ** 辞書 a dictionary. (⇨辞典) ●辞書を編さんする compile a *dictionary*. ●単語を辞書で調べる look up a word in a *dictionary*. ●その単語の意味を調べるため辞書を引く use [see] a *dictionary* to find the meaning of the word; 《やや書》 consult [refer to] a *dictionary* for the meaning of the word. (❶軽く単に check [look in] the dictionary… ということも多い) ▶その単語は私の辞書には載っていない The word is not (given [found]) in my *dictionary*./I can't find the word in my *dictionary*.

じしょ 地所 (土地) land; (広大な家屋敷) an estáte. (⇨土地)

じしょ 自署 a signature; an autograph. (⇨サイン❶)

じじょ 次女 the [one's] second daughter.

じじょ 自助 self-help.
●自助具 a self-help tool (for the disabled).

じじょ 侍女 a waiting maid [woman]; (女王・王女の) a lady-in-waiting.

***ししょう** 支障 【行く手に立ちふさがるじゃま物】an obstacle; (行動の障害) (a) hindrance; (一時的な) a hitch. ▶その事件は我々の計画の支障となるだろう The matter will be an *obstacle* [a *hindrance*] to our project. ▶計画に支障が生じた The program had developed a *hitch*. ▶式は支障 (=滞り) なく行われた The ceremony went off *without a hitch* [*without hindrance*, (円滑に) *smoothly*].

ししょう 師匠 a teacher (↔a pupil); (特に芸の) a master. ●お花の師匠 a *teacher* of flower arrangement.

***しじょう** 市場 a market.
① 【~市場】 ●国内[海外]市場 the home [foreign, overseas] market. ●外国為替市場 the foreign-exchange *market*. ●買い手[売り手]市場 a buyer's [a seller's] *market*. ●金融市場 the financial [money] *market*. ●自由市場 an open *market*. ●先物市場 forward *market*; (商品・債券の) future *market*. ●その製品をアメリカ市場で販売する sell the products on [xin] the U.S. *market*. ▶株式市場は今日は活況[不振]だった The stock *market* was active [dull, slack] today.
② 【市場(の)~】 ●市場の動き the activity of the *market*. ●市場のニーズ (meet) the needs of the *market*. ●市場の規模 the scale of the *market*. ●金の市場価格 the *market* value [price] of gold. ●市場占有率を高める build up a *market* share; increase one's share of the *market*. ▶アメリカは日本にコンピュータ市場の開放を求めてきた The U.S. has asked Japan to open (up) its *market* for computers. ▶EUは日本の自動車市場の拡張[開拓]をねらっている The EU is aiming at expanding [developing] a *market* for automobiles in Japan.
③ 【市場に[から]~】 ●市場に参入する enter [penetrate, move into] the *market*. ●市場から撤退する get out of [pull out of, exit] the *market*. ▶4月には新型車が市場に出回るだろう In April new model cars will be (put) on [xin] the *market*.
④ 【市場を~】 ●市場を開拓する explore [develop, pioneer] the *market*. ●市場を独占する monopolize the *market*.
●市場介入 market intervention. ●市場開放 market opening [liberalization]. ●市場価値 market value. ●市場経済 the market(-oriented) economy. ●市場原理 a market mechanism. ●市場参入 market entry. ●市場操作 market operation (不正に) manipulation). ●市場調査 market research. ●市場分析 market analysis. ●市場崩壊 a market crash. ●市場予測 a prediction of the market.

しじょう 史上 (歴史上) in history; (記録的な) record; (空前の) all-time. ●史上最大のショー the greatest show *in history*; the best show *ever*. ●史上空前の収穫 a *record* [an *unprecedented*] crop. ▶「タイタニック」は映画史上最高の興行成績をあげた 'Titanic' was the biggest moneymaker *in* movie *history*./'Titanic' was an *all-time* box-office hit.

しじょう 至上 ── 至上の 形 supreme. ●至上の幸福 *supreme* blessedness. ●芸術至上主義 art for art's sake.
●至上命令 a supreme command [order].

しじょう 至情 sincere [genuine] feelings; sincerity. ●至情を吐露する show one's *sincerity*; express [show] one's *genuine feelings*.

しじょう 私情 one's personal feelings. ●私情を交える bring one's *personal feelings* (*into*). ●私情に左右される be influenced by one's *personal feelings*.

しじょう 紙上 ●紙上の (新聞で) in [xon] the newspaper; (紙の上だけの) on paper. ●紙上の計画 a plan *on* [xin] *paper*; a *paper* plan.

しじょう 詩情 poetic sentiment. ●詩情豊かな人 a person full of *poetic sentiment*.

しじょう 試乗 名 a test drive [ride].
── 試乗する 動 (車に) test-drive; (自転車に) test-ride.
●試乗車 a demonstration car [bicycle].

しじょう 誌上 ●誌上の (雑誌で) in [xon] the magazine. ●タイムの今週号の誌上で in the current number of *Time*.

じしょう 自称 (自分で勝手に名乗る) self-styled; (見せかけの) would-be. ▶彼は自称音楽家だ《軽蔑的》 He is a *self-styled* [a *self-proclaimed*] musician./(自称している) He *calls* himself a musician./(通例偽って)《書》 He *represents* himself *as* [*to be*] a musician.

じしょう 自傷 [医学] self-mutilat; self-injury; self-laceration.

じしょう 事象 [現象] a phenomenon (⑳ phenomena); [出来事] an event.

:**じじょう** 事情 ❶ (周囲の境遇) circumstances; (事の状態) a situation, conditions (❶ situation より身近なものについて用いる); (漠然とした事態) affairs, matters, things; (場合) a case.
① 【~事情】 ●国内[国際; 海外]事情 domestic [international; foreign] *affairs*. ●食料[住宅]事情 the food [housing] *situation*. ●詳しい事情 details. ▶交通事情はよくなりつつある Traffic *conditions* are getting better [improving].
② 【事情~】 ●政界の事情通 a person well-informed on [about, xof] political *affairs*. ●事情聴取を受ける be summoned for *voluntary questioning*. ▶彼はその事件に関して警察に事情聴取された He was questioned by the police about the incident.
③ 【事情が】 ●事情が許す限り as far as the *circumstances* permit. ●いかなる事情があっても under [in] any *circumstances*. ▶そのことがあってから事情が変わった Since that happened, *things*

じじょう
have changed. ▶事情があって彼はやむなく退職した He was forced by *circumstances* to quit his job.
④【事情の】●事情の許す限り as far as *circumstances* permit. ●その事情のもとではできるだけのことはした He did everything he could do under the *circumstances*.
⑤【事情に】●世事にうとい do not know much about the world. ●彼は中国の事情に明るい He is well-informed (↔uninformed) on [about] Chinese *affairs*.
⑥【事情を】▶私に事情を皆話してくれ Tell me all the *circumstances*.
⑦【事情で】●やむを得ない事情で because of unavoidable *circumstances*. ▶こういう事情でごいっしょできません Such being the *case* [Under these *circumstances*], I can't come with you.
❷【理由】a reason. ●家庭の[言われぬ]事情で for family [some secret] *reasons*.

じじょう 自乗 图【平方, 2乗】【数学】a square. ▶3の自乗は9です The *square* of three is nine./Three *squared* is [makes] nine. ●4乗以上は the 《fourth》 power of ...; ... to the 《fourth》 (power) のようにいう (⇒三乗)
── 自乗する 動 ●5を自乗する *square* five; *multiply* five *by* itself.
● 自乗根 a square root.

じじょう 自浄 self-purification [cleansing /klénziŋ/]. ●海の驚異的な自浄作用 the wonderful *self-cleansing* action of the sea. ▶時に政界は自浄能力を失っていると言われる People sometimes say [It is sometimes mentioned] that the political world has lost its power to *cleanse itself* [正常に戻る] put itself to rights].

じしょうこつ 耳小骨【解剖】the auditory ossicles.

じじょうじばく 自縄自縛 ▶彼は自縄自縛に陥った He was caught in his own trap.

ししょうしゃ 死傷者 casualties /kǽʒuəltiz/. (⚠通例複数形で《死者》) ▶その事故で10人の死傷者が出た There were ten *casualties* in the accident. ▶死傷者は非常に多かった The *casualties* were very high.

ししょうせつ 私小説 a private life novel; a novel based on a writer's personal experiences; an "I" novel; (自伝風小説) an autobiographical novel. (事情) 米英では「私小説」はない

ししょく 試食 图 ▶スーパーではソーセージの試食品がつまようじに刺して配られていた There were *samples* of the sausage given out on toothpicks at the supermarket.
── 試食する 動 sample.
● 試食会 a sámpling pàrty.

ししょく 辞職 图 (a) resignation /rèzignéiʃən/. ●辞職願いを出す hand [send] in one's *resignation*.
── 辞職する 動 resign /rizáin/, (話) quit*. ▶彼は辞職した He *resigned* (from his post [position])./《話》 He *quit* (his job). ●内閣は総辞職した All the members of the Cabinet *resigned*./《書》 The Cabinet *resigned* en bloc /ɑ:ŋ blɑ́k/. (⚠内閣総辞職》 the general *resignation* (of the Cabinet) ▶彼は議長を辞職した He *resigned as* chairman. ▶スキャンダルを起こしたあと彼は辞職することになった After the scandal he *was eased out of* his job. (⚠ease out は「巧妙な手口でやめさせる」の意)

じじょでん 自叙伝 an àutobióğraphy. ●バートランド・ラッセル自叙伝【書名】*The Autobiography of Bertrand Russell*.

ししょばこ 私書箱 a Post-Office Box 《略 P.O. Box, POB》. ●...を中央郵便局私書箱150号に送る send ... to Chuo *P.O. Box* 150.

ししん 私心【利己心】selfishness; 【利己的動機】a selfish motive. ●私心のない人 an *unselfish* [a *disinterested*] person.

ししん 私信 one's private [personal] letter.

ししん 指針 ❶【指標】a guide; (指導原理) a guiding principle. ▶宗教は時には人生の指針となる Religion is sometimes a *guide to* [a *guiding principle in*] our life.
❷【計器の針】●速度計の指針 an *indicator* [a *pointer*, a *needle*] of a speedometer /spidámitər/. ●磁石の指針 a compass *needle*.

ししん 視診【医学】the inspection.

ししん 詩心 (have) a poetic turn of mind; (good) taste in poetry.

ししん 詩神【ギリシャ神話】a Muse.

しじん 私人 a private (↔a public) person. ●私人として in a *private* capacity.

しじん 詩人 a poet. ●女流詩人 a woman *poet*. (⚠特に女性を強調する場合以外は poet だけで表す. poetess は避ける) ●ロマン派の詩人 a Romantic *poet*. ●詩人肌である have a poetic turn of mind, be something of a *poet*.

***じしん** 自信 (self-)confidence.
❶【自信～】●自信不足 (a) lack of *confidence*. ●自信過剰である be overconfident; be too confident. ●自信満々[たっぷり]である have so much [a lot of] *confidence*; be full of *confidence*; be very [really, 《話》real] *confident*. ▶彼は大変な自信家である He's quite a *confident* person./《軽蔑的の》He's very *sure* of him*self*.
❷【自信が】●自信がなくなる lose one's confidence. ▶(答えに)自信がありますか (=確かですか) Are you *sure* (of the answer)? ▶彼は試験に受かる自信がある He is *sure* [*confident*] of passing the test./He is *sure* [*confident*] (that) he will pass the test. (⚠He is *sure* to pass the test. とすると話し手から見て「彼はきっと受かる」の意になる) ▶この計算の正確さには自信がない I have no *confidence* in the accuracy of this account. (⚠日本語では「の正確さ」を省いても文は成り立つが、英語では the accuracy of を省くことはできない. 同様に「よい英語を書く自信がある」は I have confidence *in* my *ability* to write good English. となる) ▶私は足[テニスの腕]には自信がある I am a good walker [tennis player].
❸【自信の[に]】●自信のある顔つきで with a *confident* look. ●自信に満ちた be filled with *confidence*. ▶私はこんなに自信のない人を見るのは初めてだ I've never seen a person so *unsure of* him*self* [her*self*]. ▶彼に自信のほどを尋ねる ask how confident he is about it.
❹【自信を】●自信を持つ[失う, つける] gain [lose; develop] *confidence* (*in*, *over*). ●自信を持って with *confidence*; confidently. ●自信を回復する resotre [recover] (one's) *confidence*. ●自信を深める come to have more *confidence*; deepen one's *confidence*. ●自信を持ちなさい You should have more *confidence* in yourself. ▶今や彼は書くことに自信をつけてきた He has been gaining *confidence over* [*in*] his writing now.

***じしん** 地震 an earthquake, 《話》a quake; 《米》a temblor; (小さい) a tremor. (⇒震災)
❶【〜(の)地震, 地震〜】●大地震 a major [a strong, a severe] *earthquake*. (⚠(1) この場合 big, huge は主に《話》.《書》では「大」の字から予想されるほどには用いられない. (2) 阪神大震災の際にある

紙の見出しに *Killer Earthquake* Slams Kansai. とあったが、これは「超大型地震関西を直撃」とでも訳されようか） ▶マグニチュード7の地震 an *earthquake* measuring 7.0 on the Richter scale; an *earthquake* of magnitude 7.0 on the Richter scale. ●海底地震 a submarine [an undersea] *earthquake*. ●群発地震 *earthquake* swarms ●新潟地震 the Niigata *Earthquake* [*earthquake*]. ●地震対策をとる take anti-*earthquake* procedures [measures]. ▶日本は地震国だ Japan is a land of [has a lot of] *earthquakes*.
②【地震が[は]】 ▶東京は地震が多い（しばしば起こる）*Earthquakes* often occur [There are frequent *earthquakes*] in Tokyo./(しばしば襲う) *Earthquakes* often hit [strike, shake] Tokyo. ▶今朝、弱い[強い]地震があった We had [We felt, There was] a slight [a strong] *earthquake* this morning./A slight [A strong] *earthquake* occurred [happened, ×broke out] this morning. ▶地震は火山のある地域でよく発生する Earthquakes often occur in the same areas as volcanoes. ▶地震は国籍や民族の違いなどに関係なく、大地の上のすべての人々に襲いかかる *Earthquakes* affect all people living on the earth [globe], regardless of nationality or race.
③【地震で】 ▶大部分の家は地震で壊れた Most of the houses were destroyed by [in] the *earthquake*. ▶地震で家が揺れるのを感じた I felt the house shake from [in] the *earthquake*.

> 関連 地震に関することば: 震度 seismic intensity [scale]/耐震の earthquake-resistant/免震の earthquake-proof/免震工法 seismic isolation/有感[無感]地震 a felt [an unfelt] earthquake/震源 the hypocenter, the seismic center [focus]/震央 the epicenter/マグニチュード magnitude/リヒタースケール the Richter /ríktər/ scale (参考) 地震の規模を示す尺度)/本[前;余]震 main [fore; after] shocks.

●地震雷火事おやじ ▶昔はよく「地震雷火事おやじ」と言ったものだ We used to say there were four frightening things on earth—*earthquakes*, thunder, fires, and fathers.
●地震学 seismology /saizmɑ́lədʒi/. ●地震学者 a seismologist. ●地震活動 (a) seismic activity. ●地震観測 seismómetry. ●地震計 a séismogràph; a seismómeter. ●地震研究所 an earthquake research institute. ●地震帯 an earthquake [a seismic] zone [belt]. ●地震探査 seismic prospecting [exploration, survey]. ●地震断層 an earthquake fault. ●地震波 an earthquake wave; a seismic wave. ●地震予知 an earthquake prediciton; a prediction of earthquakes.

じしん 自身 oneself (⇨自分); [自己] (one's) self (⇨自己). ●自分自身の齒 one's *own* teeth. ▶彼自身がそこへ行った He *himself* went there. (!he を強調する。次の訳のように文尾に置くことも可)/He went there *himself* [*in* *person*]. ▶あなた自身のことも伺わせていただけませんか Would you tell me something about *you*?

じしん 時針 the hour hand.
じしん 自刃 ── 自刃する 動 commit suicide [kill oneself] with a sword.
じじん 自陣 one's army camp [battle positions]. ●自陣深くからの攻撃（サッカーなどに) an attack from the defensive end.
ししんけい 視神経 [解剖] the optic nerve.
しす 資す (⇨資する)
しす 辞す (⇨辞する)
ジス JIS ((Japanese Industrial Standard(日本工業規格)の略)．
●ジスマーク the JIS mark.
しずい 歯髄 [解剖] (dental) pulp.
●歯髄炎 [医学] pulpitis.
じすい 自炊 ── 自炊する 動 cook for oneself; cook [fix] one's own meals.
しすう 指数 an index (number). ●物価[消費者物価]指数 [経済] a price [a consumer price] *index*. ●株価指数 a stock (market) *index*. ●不快指数 a discomfort *index* (略 DI).
しすう 紙数 ●紙数が尽きてきたので[の都合で] owing to lack of (the alloted) space. ●紙数が不足する run short of space.
じすう 字数 the number of letters [characters].
しずか 静か ── 静かな 形 quiet, still, silent; calm (⇨穏やか); peaceful (⇨平和 ③); soft, gentle (⇨柔らかい).

> 使い分け quiet 人が寡黙で話をしない状態や、静かな場所、穏やかな生活や時間を表す．
> still 風・水などが一時的に動きがなく静かな状態や、人が動かずにじっとして静かな状態を表す．
> silent 音や声が聞こえない完全に静かな状態や、人が無言で沈黙している状態を表す．

●静かな通り a *quiet* street. ●静かな夜 a *quiet* [a *silent*, a *still*] night. ●静かな海 a *calm* [a *quiet*, a *still*] sea. ●静かな声 in a *quiet* [a *soft*, a *gentle*] voice. ▶その部屋は水を打ったように(=針1本落ちても聞こえるくらい)静かだった It was so *quiet* [*still*] in the room that you could have heard a pin drop. (!it を主語にして副詞(句)で場所を表す言い方。従節の仮定法に注意。The room was so *quiet* that .... も可) ▶そのエンジンはとても静かだ The engine is very *quiet*.

── 静かに 副 quietly, silently; calmly; peacefully; softly, gently. (⇨形) ●静かに歩く[話す] walk [talk] *quietly*. ●静かに座る[座っている] sit *quietly* [*quiet*]. (!動作を表す動詞は副詞で修飾するが、状態を表す動詞の後には形容詞を用いる。以下同様) ●子供たちを静かにさせる make the children *quiet*; *quiet* the children (*down*). (!*down* を伴う方が強意的) ●静かにドアをたたく knock *gently* [*softly*] on the door. ▶彼はもの静かにしゃべった He spoke *quietly*. ▶静かにせよ Be [Keep] *quiet*. (!(1) 単に *Quiet*. ともいう。Be silent. はまれであるが、名詞形で Silence! (静粛に)は掲示や議長発言などによく用いられる。(2) Be [Keep] *still*. は「動かずにじっとしていよ」、Be *calm*. は「(興奮している人に)落ち着け」の意)/(しっ! 黙って) Hush!/(吠えてくる犬に) Easy! ▶夜がふけるにつれてあたりはいっそう静かになった All became *more quiet* as the night went on. (!*quieter* より普通)

── 静かさ 名 quiet(ness). (⇨静か, 静寂)

しずく 滴 a drop; (ぽたぽた落ちるもの) a drip. ●雨のしずく *drops* of rain; raindrops. ●ひとしずくの涙 a tear (drop). ●蛇口からぽたぽたと落ち続ける水のしずく the steady *drips* of water from the tap. (!単数形 drip は「1 滴」と音をさす) ●しずくとなって落ちる fall *in drops*; drip. ▶ひとしずくの涙が彼女のほおを伝った A tear rolled down her cheek. (⇨しずける)
しずけさ 静けさ [静寂] stillness; [音を立てないこと] silence; [騒音・動きがないこと] quiet, quietness (!状態を静かに強くいうときは前の方が普通). [平穏] calm. ●夜の静けさを破る break the *stillness* [*silence*, *quiet*] of the night. ●あらしの前の静けさ the *calm* [*quiet*] before the storm. ▶その教室は

しずしずと 水を打ったような静けさになった A dead *silence* [A *hush*] fell over the classroom. (⚠*silence* を強調する形容詞にはほかに complete, perfect, deep なども用いられる)

しずしずと 静々と 《音を立てないように》quietly; softly; 《優雅に》gracefully. ◆しずしずと歩く walk *quietly* and *slowly*.

システマチック systematic.

システム a system. (⇨組織, 体制, 方式) ◆ソーラーシステム a solar *system*. ◆物流システム a logistics [a physical distribution] *system*.
◆システムアドミニストレーター[管理者] a system administrator;《略》sysadmin. ◆システムインテグレーション system integration. [参考] 企業内情報システムの立案から設計・開発・保守までを一貫して請け負うサービス) ◆システムインテグレーター a system integrator. ◆システムエラー a system error. ◆システムエンジニア a system engineer《略 SE》. ◆システムオペレーター a system operator;《略》a sysop. ◆システム環境 systems requirements. ◆システム管理 system administration. ◆システムキッチン a fully-fitted kitchen;《和製語》a system kitchen. ◆システムクロック『コンピュータ』a system clock. ◆システム工学 systems engineering. ◆システム障害 (a) system disturbance. ◆システム設計 a systems design. ◆システムソフト『コンピュータ』a system(s) software. ◆システムダウン『コンピュータ』a system failure. (⚠crash ともいう) ◆システムディスク『コンピュータ』a systems disk. ◆システム手帳 a personal organizer. ◆システムファイル『コンピュータ』a system file. ◆システムプログラム『コンピュータ』a system(s) program. ◆システム分析 system(s) analysis. ◆システムボード『コンピュータ』a system board. (⚠mother board が普通)

ジステンパー 『犬などの伝染病』distemper.

ジストマ 『動物』《寄生虫》a distome.
◆ジストマ症『医学』distomiasis.

ジストロフィー 『医学』dystrophy. ◆筋ジストロフィー muscular *dystrophy*.

じすべり 地滑り 《大規模の》a landslide; 《小規模の》《英》a landslip; 『地質』(a) dislocation. ◆総選挙で地すべり的勝利をおさめる win [get] a *landslide* victory in the general election; win [get] the general election in a *landslide*.

しずまりかえる 静まり返る become completely quiet; 《急に話をやめる》fall silent. ◆小泉氏が演説を始めると聴衆はしいんと静まり返った Just as Mr. Koizumi began to speak, the audience *fell silent*. (⇨静けさ)

しずまる 静まる, 鎮まる become* quiet [calm, still], quiet 《主に米》[quieten 《主に英》] down (⇨静か); 『音・あらしなどが』calm [die [=d; dying), go*] down, 《書》abate; 『興奮・あらしなどが』《やや書》subside; 『反乱などが』be put down, be suppressed; 『痛みが』be relieved. ◆風がやっと静まった The wind *has calmed* [《徐々に》*died*] *down* at last.

しずみこむ 沈み込む become* [get*] depressed. (⇨沈む ❸, 塞(ふさ)ぎ込む)

‡しずむ 沈む ❶『水中で』sink*, 《船・人などが》go* down [under]. ◆沈みかけている[沈んだ]船 a *sinking* [a *sunken*] ship. ◆水の底深くに沈む *sink* deep into the water. ◆水は木に沈まない Wood does not *sink* in water. ◆2 隻の船が銚子沖で沈んだ Two boats *sank* [*went down*, *went under*] off Choshi.
❷『太陽・月が』set*《↔rise》, go* down; sink*. ◆太陽が西に沈みかけていた The sun *was setting* [*going down*, *sinking*] in the west. (⚠「海[巨大なピラミッド]の向こうに...」なら ...setting over the sea [a great pyramid]. という) ◆太陽は山の陰[水平線下]に沈んだ The sun *sank* behind a mountain [below the horizon].
❸『気分が』《意気消沈する》feel* [get*] depressed; 《憂うつである》feel gloomy [《話》blue]. ◆《塞(ふさ)ぎ込む》彼女は今日は沈んだ顔をしている She looks *depressed* [*gloomy*, 《話》*blue*] today. ◆彼は悲しみに沈んでいる He *is deep* [*is buried*] *in* grief. ◆彼女に会って私の心は沈んだ(=悲しくなった) I *felt* [*was*] *sad* when I saw her.

しずめる 沈める 『船などを沈没させる』sink*; 『水中に入れる』submerge. ◆敵艦を沈める *sink* an enemy ship; *send an enemy* ship *to the bottom*. ◆いすに身を沈める *sink into* a chair. ◆俊介は湯舟に体を沈めた Shunsuke *let* himself *down into* the bathtub.

しずめる 静める, 鎮める calm ... (down); 《主に米》quiet [《主に英》quieten] ... (down); 『なだめる, 和らげる』soothe /súːð/; 『騒ぎなどを』suppress, put*... down (⚠後の方が口語的). ◆彼の怒りを静める *soothe* [《やや書》*appease*] his anger. ◆痛みを鎮める *soothe* [《除く》*relieve*] the pain. ◆神経を鎮める *calm* [*settle*] one's nerves. ◆反乱を鎮める *put down* [*suppress*] the rebellion. ◆気を静めよ *Calm down./Calm yourself* (*down*)./《自制心を取り戻せ》*Pull yourself together*. ◆母親は泣いている子を静めようとしていた The mother tried to *calm* (*down*) [*soothe* (*down*), 《黙らせる》*hush*] the crying baby.

しする 資する ◆人類の福祉に大いに資する *contribute greatly to* the welfare of mankind. ◆世界平和促進に資する *make for* world pease; *be helpful to promote* world peace.

じする 辞する 『去る』leave*; 『断る』《やや書》decline; 『辞任する』resign (*from*). ◆職を辞する *leave* [《話》*quit*] one's job; *resign* (*from*) one's post [position]. ◆大学を辞する *resign from* the university. ◆彼は議会も辞さない決意である(=会から身を引く覚悟はできている) He is ready to *withdraw from* the society.

‡しせい 姿勢 ❶『身体の構え』(a) posture; 《一時的な》a position; 《意識的な》a pose. (⇨ポーズ) ◆姿勢がよい[悪い] have good [bad, poor] *posture*. ◆立った[座った]姿勢で in a standing [a sitting] *posture*. ◆正しい姿勢で(=背筋を伸ばして)読書する read with one's back straight; read straightening oneself. ◆私たちは先生の前で気をつけの姿勢で立っていた We stood in an upright *posture* [at attention] in front of our teacher. ◆彼は楽な姿勢で横になっていた He lay in a comfortable *position* [*posture*]. ◆そのモデルはいろいろな姿勢をとった The model adopted various *poses* [took various *postures*].
❷『態度』an attitude. ◆低姿勢で with a humble [a modest] *attitude*. ◆彼はその問題に強い[前向きの]姿勢をとった He took a strong [a positive, a forward-looking] *attitude toward* the problem.

しせい 四声 the four tones of Chinese characters.

しせい 市井 ◆市井のうわさ (a) rumor, gossip.
◆市井の人 《庶民》the common people; 《書》the populace. (⚠単・複両扱い)

しせい 市制 a municipal system. ◆市制を敷く incorporate 《a town》 as a city; organize as a municipality. ◆この町は来年市制が敷かれます This

しせい town will *get city status* [*be municipalized*] next year.

しせい 市政 *municipal government* [*administration*], (🔼の方は「政治」、後の方が「行政」) ● 市政に参加する *participate in municipal government.*

しせい 市勢 *the state* (*of the economy*) *of a city.*
● 市勢調査をする take a *census of a city.*

しせい 死生 *life and* [*or*] *death.*
● 死生命(めい)にあり *death is out of control.*

しせい 至誠 *absolute sincerity.* (⇨🔼 真心)

しせい 私製 ── 私製の形 *private.*
● 私製はがき a *postcard.* **関連** 英国には「官製はがき」がない。米国では a postcard は官製[私製]はがき、a postal card は官製はがきをさす)

しせい 施政 (行政) *administration;* (政治) *government.*
● 施政方針演説 a *policy speech*; an *administrative policy speech*; a *speech on one's administrative policies.*

しせい 詩聖 *a great poet.*

じせい 自生 ── 自生する動 *grow wild.*
● 自生植物 a *wild plant*; a *volunteer* (*plant*).
● 自生地 a *habitat.*

じせい 自制 名 *self-control; self-restraint.* ● 自制心を失う *lose one's self-control*; *lose control* (*of oneself*); (パニックに陥る)《話》*freak out.* ● 自制心を取り戻す *get oneself together.* ▶ 彼には自制心が欠けている He *lacks* [*is lacking in*] *self-control.*/He has no *control over himself.* ▶ 私はかっとなってまったく自制心を失った I just *lost control of* myself in a fit of anger.
── 自制する動 *control* [*restrain*] *oneself*; *exercise self-restraint.*

じせい 自省 *reflection; introspection.*

じせい 自製 ── 自製の形 (自作の) *of one's own making*; (手製の) *handmade, homemade.*

じせい 時世, 時勢 (*the*) *time*(*s*). (⇨時代❷)

じせい 時制 〖文法〗 a *tense.* ● 現在[過去]時制 the *present* [*past*] *tense.* ● 時制の一致 *sequence of tenses.*

じせい 辞世 ● 辞世の句 (この世を去るに臨み詠んだ詩歌) a *tanka* [*a haiku*] *poem composed just before one's death.* ● 辞世の言葉 *one's last words.*

じせい 磁性 *magnetism.* ● 磁性を帯びた *magnetic* 《needles》.

しせいかつ 私生活 (*one's*) *private* (↔*public*) *life.*
▶ 大統領にも私生活はある Even Presidents have [are entitled to] *private lives.*

しせいじ 私生児 (婉曲的) a *love child*; (非嫡出(ちゃくしゅつ)子)《書》an *illegitimate* /ɪlɪdʒɪtəmət/ *child* 《of children》; (やや古)《軽蔑的》a *bastard.* ● 私生児である be *illegitimate.*

しせき 史跡 a *historic* [*historical*] *spot* [*place*], a *spot* [*place*] *of historical* [×*historic*] *interest.* ● 史跡を訪ねる *visit a historic spot.*

しせき 歯石 ● 歯石をとる *remove* [(こそげる)*scale*] *tartar* /táːrtər/ (*from the teeth*). (⇨歯垢(こう))
● 歯石除去 *scaling.*

しせき 次席 ── 次席の形 *second; second best;* (副…) *assistant.* ● 次席検事 the *assistant public prosecutor.*

じせき 自責 *self-reproach.* ● うそをついて自責の念に駆られている(＝罪悪感に苦しんでいる) *suffer from a guilty conscience about* having told a lie. (⇨良心❷)

● 自責点〖野球〗an *earned run* (略 ER). ● 3 自責点を許す *allow* [*yield*] *three earned runs.*

じせだい 次世代 *the next generation.* ● 次世代携帯電話 an *advanced* cell(ular) *phone.*

:しせつ 施設 〖学校・児童福祉などの公共の社会施設〗an *institution;* 〖公共または私設の設立物〗an *establishment;* 〖図書館・病院など便宜を与える設備〗*facilities.* ● 教育施設 an educational *institution* [*establishment*]; educational *facilities; facilities for* education. ● 老人施設 an *institution* [*a home*] *for* the aged; an old people's *home.*
● 教護施設 a correctional *institution.* ● 軍事施設 military *facilities* [*installations*]. ● 公共[娯楽, 文化; 医療]施設 public [recreational; cultural; medical] *facilities.* ● 施設の子供たち *children* in *institutions.* ● その孤児は施設に入れられた The orphan was put in an *institution* [*a home*].

しせつ 私設 ── 私設の形 *private.*
● 私設秘書 a *private* [a *personal*] *secretary.*

しせつ 使節 (外交上の) an *envoy,* an *ambassador;* (会議などに派遣される) a *delegate.* ▶ 彼は親善使節として日本へやって来た He came to Japan as a goodwill *envoy* [親善の使命を帯びて] on a goodwill *mission.*
● 使節団 a *delegation;* (特別任務を帯びた) a *mission.* (🔼 いずれも集合的に) ● 文化使節団を派遣する *send a cultural mission* (*to*).

じせつ 自説 *one's opinion* [*views*]. (⇨説)

じせつ 時節 〖時期〗*time;* 〖機会〗 an *opportunity,* a *chance;* 〖天候〗*weather.* ● 時節の到来を待つ *wait for an opportunity* [*the time*]. ▶ 時節が来れば彼は行動を開始するだろう When the *time* [*opportunity, chance*] *comes,* he'll *take action.* ▶ 時節はまだ到来していない The *time* [*opportunity*] has not yet *come.* ▶ 時節柄くれぐれもお体を大切に Be sure to take good care of yourself in this hot [cold] *weather.*

しせん 支線 *a branch line.*

しせん 死線 ● 死線をさまよう *hover between life and death.* ● 死線を越える *narrowly escape death.*

しせん 視線 an *eye* (通例複数形で); (目つき) a *look;* (注視) a *gaze;* (一瞥(べつ)) a *glance.* ● 視線をそらす *look away* (*from*). ● …に視線を向ける *turn one's eyes upon* [*on, toward*]…; *look at*….
● 視線を落とす *drop one's eyes.* ● 視線を交わす *make an eye contact* (*with*). ● 迷惑そうな視線を投げる *shoot a nasty look* (*at*). ▶ 2 人の視線が合った Their *eyes met.* ▶ 彼女と視線を合わせるのが恥ずかしくて、ついⅠ目をそらせてしまった I felt too embarrassed to meet her *gaze* and [so] I looked away. ▶ 私は彼女の視線を背に感じながら歩み去った As I walked away, I felt she must *be looking at* my back. /(熱い視線を) I walked away, feeling her *eyes burning into my back.*

しせん 詩仙 *a great poet.*

:しぜん 自然 〖天然〗 *nature* (↔*art*). (🔼 通例 the を伴わない。代名詞でさすときはしばしば *she, her* を用いる) ● 美しい自然 the beautiful *natural environment; natural beauty;* the *beauties* [*beauty*] *of nature.* ● 美しい自然とはいわない

❶〖自然(の)〜〗● 自然のままの *natural* (🔼 通例限定的に)、(人の手が加えられていない) *wild.* ● 自然の恵み[驚異] the *blessings* [*wonders*] *of nature.*
▶ その行為は自然の理に反している The deed goes against *nature.* ▶ 自然体で(＝いつもの自分で)いきなさい Just *be yourself.*

❷〖自然が[は]〗● 自然が豊かだ be *rich in nature.* ▶ 大都市周辺では自然が日に日に失われている *Nature is being destroyed day by day* on the outskirts of big cities.

じせん

DISCOURSE
自然は極小の微生物から植物や動物,そして地球全体といったさまざまな要素から構成される *Nature* consists of many elements, from the smallest microorganisms(,) to plants and animals, and to the whole planet. (📒 A consists of ... (A は…から構成される)は定義に用いる表現)

③ 【自然に[と]】 ●(文明世界を去って)自然に帰る go back to *nature*. ●自然に反す against *nature*. ▶夏は自然に親しむよい季節さ Summer is the best season to be in close contact with *nature*. ▶彼は田舎の自然にあこがれている He longs for rural surroundings [a *natural* environment]. (📒 通例 × ... rural *nature* [*nature* in the country]. とはいわない/(田園の暮らしにあこがれている) He longs to *live in* [longs for] *the country*. ▶彼らは自然とともに生きるよう努めている They try to live with *nature*.

── 自然(な[の]) 形 (当然な) natural (⇨当然); (人の手を加えない) natural (📒 通例の限定的のみ); (自然発生的な) spontaneous. ▶母親が子供を愛するのは自然だ It is *natural* that a mother should love [loves, ×love] her child./It is *natural* for a mother to love her child. ▶その地は自然のままの状態で残されていた The land was left as it was [(手つかずで) untouched].

── 自然に 副 (普段どおりに, 天然に) naturally; (自然発生的に) spontaneously; (ひとりでに) (all) by oneself; (自動的に) automatically. ▶彼はまったく自然にふるまった He behaved quite *naturally*. ▶彼はその技術を自然に身につけた He acquired the skill *naturally*. ▶自然に拍手がわき起こった There was a *spontaneous* outburst of applause. ▶火は自然に消えた The fire went out *by itself*. ▶その傷は自然に治るだろう The wound will *heal itself*.

● 自然塩 natural salt. ● 自然界 the natural world. ● 自然科学 natural science. (📒 学科を示すときは ⓒ) ● 自然河川 wild rivers. (参考 護岸工事などしていない自然のままの川) ● 自然環境 a natural environment. ● 自然減 (人口の) a natural decrease (in population); (労働力の) natural wastage. ● 自然現象 a natural phenomenon. ● 自然災害 (天災) a natural disaster. ● 自然死 《die》 a natural death. ● 自然児 a child of nature. ● 自然主義 (⇨自然主義) ● 自然食品 natural food(s) [(有機栽培の) organic] food(s). (📒 nature food(s) ともいう) ● 自然数 『数学』a natural number. ● 自然石 natural stone; field stone. ● 自然葬 a natural burial. ● 自然治癒 spontaneous healing; autotherapy. ● 自然淘汰 natural selection. ● 自然農法 organic [chemical-free] farming. ● 自然破壊 the destruction of nature. ● 自然発火 spontaneous combustion. ● 自然発生 spontaneous generation. ● 自然法 the natural law. ● 自然保護 (the) conservation of nature. ● 自然療法 a nature cure; naturopathy.

じせん 自選 one's personal [own] selection 《*from* among one's works》. ● 自選短編集 a *collection* of short stories *selected by the author*.

じせん 自薦 one's own recommendation. ▶自薦他薦を問いません a recommendation required (whether by yourself or another).

じぜん 次善 ● 次善の策 the next [*second*] best measure.

じぜん 事前 ● 選挙の事前運動 *preelection* campaigning. ▶事前に(= 前もって)知らせてください Please let me know *beforehand* [*in advance*]. ● 事前協議 prior consultation. ● 事前準備 advance preparations.

じぜん 慈善 图 charity. ▶彼は定期的に慈善のために [慈善事業に]寄付をしている He gives money regularly to *charities* [*charity*].

── 慈善の 形 charitable.

● 慈善家 a charitable person. ● 慈善興業 a charity show. ● 慈善事業 (仕事) charitable work; (施設, 団体) charities. ● 慈善事業を(経営)する run a *charity*. ● 慈善団体[施設] a charitable organization [institution], a charity.

しぜんしゅぎ 自然主義 naturalism.
● 自然主義者 a naturalist.

しせんしょう 四川省 [[中国の省]] Szechwan /sètʃ-wáːn/ [Sichuan /siːtʃwáːn/] Province.

しせんりょうり 四川料理 Szechwan [Sichuan] cooking.

しそ 始祖 (元祖) a founder, an originator

しそ 紫蘇 『植物』 a beefsteak plant.

*しそう 思想 [考えること] thought, thinking; [考え] (a) thought, an idea (⇨考え [類語]); [思想形態] an ideology (⇨イデオロギー).

① 【〜思想, 思想の〜】 ●近代思想 (×a) modern *thought*. ●科学的思想 scientific *thought* [*thinking*]. ●社会主義思想 socialist *thought* [*ideas*]. ●東洋思想 Eastern *thought* [*ideas*]. ●危険思想の持ち主 a person with dangerous *ideas*. ●思想の自由 freedom of *thought*.

② 【思想は[が]】 ●思想がある[ない] have an ideology [no ideology]. ▶彼の思想は進歩的だ His *thought* is progressive./He has progressive *ideas*. ▶多くの場合思想は言葉によって表現される Most *thoughts* are expressed by (means of) words. ▶この本には作者の思想(= 意見)がよく表れている This book reveals the author's *thoughts* [*ideas*].

● 思想家 a thinker. ● 思想史 a history of ideas [thoughts]. ● 思想統制 control of thought; (検閲) censorship of ideas. ● 思想犯 an ideological offender.

しそう 死相 a shadow of death. ▶彼の顔に死相が現れている The *shadow of death* is on his face./His face shows that he is nearing his end [he is dying].

しそう 志操 principle. ● 志操堅固な人 a person of (high) *principle*.

しそう 詩想 a poetic(al) imagination; poetic(al) sentiment.

しそう 試走 a pre-contest run; (車などの) a test drive (⇨試乗).

しぞう 死蔵 ── 死蔵する 動 store [keep] 《it》 lying idle [without any intention of using it].

じぞう 地蔵 a *Jizo*; (説明的に) a guardian deity who protects the souls of children from falling into hell, whose stone statue in the form of a Buddhist monk is often found by the roadside.

しそうのうろう 歯槽膿漏 『医学』pyorrhea /pàiərí:ə/; (歯周病) Riggs' disease (▶歯槽膿漏にまで至る).

シソーラス [[分類語彙(ぃ)集]] a thesaurus /θisɔ́ːrəs/.

しそく 子息 one's son (used when referring to another's son).

しそく 四則 the four operations of arithmetic: addition, subtraction, multiplication and division.

しぞく 士族 a family of the *samurai* class. ● 士族の出 a descendant of *samurai*.

しぞく ・士族の商法 amateurish business methods.
しぞく 氏族 a family, a clan.
・氏族制度 the clan [family] system.
じそく 自足する 動 (自ら満足する) be satisfied 《with》.
じそく 時速 (⇨速度) ・時速50キロで車を走らせる drive a car *at (a speed of)* 50 kilometers /kilámətər/ *an* [*per*] *hour*. (!50 kph と略す) ・時速150キロの速球を投げる throw a fastball 150 kilometers an hour. ・彼の速球は時速100マイルを記録した His fastball clocked (at) 100 miles per hour.

じぞく 持続 图 duration. (⇨長続き)

DISCOURSE
「持続可能性」とは，物質的発展と環境保護の間のバランスのとれた方法を意味する *"Sustainability"* **refers to** a balanced approach between material progress and the preservation of the environment. (!A refers to ... (A は...を意味する)は定義に用いる表現)

—— 持続する 動 (続く) last, continue; (維持する) keep 《it》 up, maintain.
しそこなう (⇨—損なう)
しそちょう 始祖鳥 an archaeopteryx /ɑ̀ːrkiɑ́ptəriks/.
*しそん 子孫 a descendant; (集合的)《書》posterity; (子供たち) offspring (!単・複同扱い). ・彼は西郷隆盛の子孫だ He *is descended from* [is *a descendant* of, 《話》 *comes from*] Saigo Takamori. (!He *descends* from .... は今は稀) ・これは子孫に残さ[伝え]ねばならない This must be kept for *posterity*./This must be handed down [on] from generation to generation.

しそんじる 仕損じる [失敗する]fail 《*to* do》; (...する時に間違う) make* a mistake 《*in* do*ing*》; [しのがす] miss 《do*ing*》. (⇨急〈せ〉く)
じそんしん 自尊心 pride; self-respect. (!pride は悪い意味でも用いる) ・自尊心の強い proud; self-respecting. ・自尊心を傷つける hurt [wound] 《his》 *pride*. ・そんなことをするのは自尊心が許さなかった His *pride* didn't allow him to do that./(あまりに自尊心が強すぎた) He had too much *pride* [was too *proud*] to do that. (!×He had too high pride... とはいわない)

:**した** 下 ❶ [下部] the lower part, 《話》(the) underneath; [下の階] the downstairs (!単数扱い).
① 【下(の)〜】[下部の] lower (↔upper) (!二つに分けたうちの「下の方の」の意); [階下の] downstairs (↔upstairs); [下方への] dównward (↔upward). ・下半分 *below* half (area). ・下くちびる the *lower* lip, the underlip. ・下の方 the area *below*. ・下の部屋 a room *downstáirs*. (!a dównstairs room より普通)
②【...の下の[に，を，へ，で]】[場所，位置] (...より低い位置に) below ... (↔above); (...の真下に，におおわれて) under ..., underneath ...,《書》beneath ... (↔over); [移動] (...の下を通って) under ... (↔over); [方向] (...の下方へ) down ... (↔up ...).

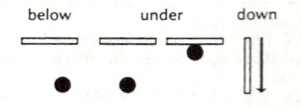

below　　under　　down

解説 (1) **below** と **under**: 「...から離れて下に」の意で交換して用いられることが多い。ただし below が単に上下関係を示すのに対し，under は真下(directly below)にあること，または上からおおう物との接触を示し，その下を何かが移動することを暗示することもある。
(2) **beneath** と **underneath**: beneath は under の代わりに用いられ，間にある程度の距離があることを暗示する。また特に上からおおわれて隠れている状態やおおう物との接触を強調する場合には underneath が用いられることがある。

・窓の下 *below* [*under*] the window. ・上着の下にセーターを着ている wear a sweater *under* [*underneath*] the jacket. (!wear a jacket with a sweater *underneath* [×under] は上着に焦点を当てた言い方) ・彼女は線の下に自分の名前を書いた She wrote her name *below* [*under*] the line. ・太陽は地平線の下に沈んだ The sun sank *below* [×under] the horizon. ・橋の下に船がある There is a boat *under* the bridge. (!*below* the bridge は「橋の下流に」の意)

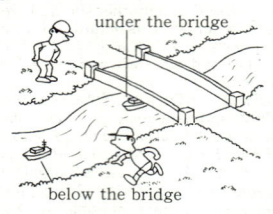

under the bridge

below the bridge

・この通りの下を地下鉄が走っている The subway runs *under* this street. ・彼の家は坂の下にある His house is *under* [*at the foot of*, (下りていった所に) *down*] the slope. (⇨❷) ・猫がテーブルの下から出て来た A cat came out [There appeared a cat] from *under* the table. (!under the table 全体を from で受けている)

③【下に[を，へ，で]】below; [階下に] dównstairs, below; [下(方)に向かって] down, dównward. ・下に置く put *under* [*beneath*] 《it》. ・下を見る[向く] look *down*; lower one's eyes. ・下へ降りる go [come] *down*; go [come] *downstairs*. ・下へ落ちる fall *down*; (地面へ) fall to the ground. ・下を通る pass *under* [*beneath*, *below*] 《it》. ・下を歩く walk *under* [*beneath*, *below*] 《it》. ・下は下宿している He is *downstairs*. ・ずっと下に海が見えた We saw the sea far *below*. (!below us なら ② の用法) ・彼は下を向いたまま立っていた He stood with his eyes cast *down*. (!*cast* は過去分詞) ・下で待っていて，すぐ行くわ Wait for me *downstairs*; I won't be long.

❷ [最下部] the bottom (↔top); [足部] the foot (↔top); [土台] the base. ・階段の下に at the *bottom* [*foot*] of the stairs. ・下から3行目に on the third line from the *bottom*. ・写真のいちばん下の段の右端の男の人はだれですか Who is the man at the *bottom* right-hand corner of the picture?

❸ [年下] (...より若い) younger (↔older, elder) 《*than*》; junior (↔senior) 《*to*》; (年齢が...未満の) under ..., below ..., less than ... (⇨以下). ・下の息子 a *younger* son. ・彼のいちばん下の息子[弟] his *youngest* son [brother].

❹ [下位] (地位・価値・数量的に下の) below ...

under …; lower 《than》; (より劣った) inferior 《to》(!主に物事が主語. 地位・階級などについて用いるのは堅い言い方(⇨劣る)). ● 点数が下 marks are *lower*. ▶彼は私より3学年下だ He's three years *under* [*behind*, ×*under*] me in school. ▶我々は彼の下で働いている We work *under* him. (!彼の直属の部下であることを含意する. below を用いると単に地位の上下関係をさす)

❺【下記, 後述】▶下を見よ See *below*.
● 下にも置かない 下にも置かないもてなしをする give 《him》 a very warm reception.

した 舌 a tongue. (⇨舌足らず)
①【舌が[は]】 ▶舌が荒れている My *tongue* is rough [(炎症をおこしている) sore]. ● 舌がもつれる one's tongue twists. ▶舌はいちばん重要な発音器官である The *tongue* is the most important organ of speech.

②【舌を[で]】● 舌を鳴らす click one's *tongue*. (不満・いらだちのしぐさ) ● 舌をかむ bite one's *tongue*. ▶舌をかみそうな名前 a *tongue* twister of a name. ● (あいって)舌をだらりと出す hang [loll] out one's *tongue*. ● (舌の先)で虫歯の穴を触る feel a cavity in one's tooth with (the tip of) one's *tongue*. ▶彼女は彼に向かって舌を出し「べー」と言った She put [stuck] her *tongue* out at him and said "Bleah!" 事柄 軽蔑のしるし
● 舌が回る ▶彼はよく舌が回る(=おしゃべりだ) He is very *talkative*./(けなして) He has a glib *tongue*. (⇨口❹①)
● 舌の根の乾かぬうちに while the words are fresh out of [from] one's mouth.
● 舌を巻く (驚嘆する) be amazed [astonished] 《at, by》; (感嘆する) be filled with admiration 《for》.

-した 羊歯 『植物』a fern. (!集合的には Ⓤ)
じた 自他 ● 自他ともに許す ▶彼は自他ともに許す(=だれもが認める)当代随一のピアニストだ He is *universally* recognized as the greatest pianist of the day. (!It is *universally* recognized that he is …. ともいえる)
じだ 耳朶 (耳たぶ) a lobe, an earlobe; (耳) an ear.
したあご 下顎 the lower jaw. (⇨顎)
したあじ 下味 ▶おろしニンニクとしょうゆで豚肉の切り身に下味をつけなさい Season the slices of pork with grated garlic and soy sauce (before cooking them).
したあらい 下洗い preliminary wash(ing).
したい 死体 『人間・動物の』a (dead) body (!「死んだ」の意を強調する以外は通例 dead は用いない; (特に人間の) a corpse (!死体を客観的に見た冷たい感じの語); (動物の) a carcass, a carcase. ● 身元不明の死体 an unidentified *body* [*corpse*]. ▶母親は息子の死体を確認した The mother identified the *body* of her son. ▶彼は死体遺棄の容疑で逮捕された He was arrested for abandonment of a *corpse*. ▶彼は死体で発見された He was found *dead*.
したい 肢体 (手足)『書』limbs /lɪmz/; (身体) a body. ● 肢体不自由児 a crippled [《婉曲的》 a (physically) handicapped] child. (!通例後の方を用いる)
したい 姿態 『姿』a figure; 『ポーズ』a pose. ▶彼女は美しい[ほっそりした]姿態をしている She's got a lovely [a slim] *figure*.
-したい (⇨-たい)
しだい 次第图 ❶【順序】● 式・祝典の次第 the order [(予定) *program*] of the ceremony.
❷【事情】▶こういう[そうい う]次第です This is

[That's] how it is. ▶そういう次第で申し訳ありませんが何もできません And so [『書』 *Such being the case*], I'm sorry I can't do anything. ▶それは事と次第による That (all) [It all] *depends*. (!on the circumstances が省略されている (⇨[次例]))
▶事と次第によっては彼自ら行くかもしれない *According to circumstances*, he may go himself.
❸【次第だ】● …にかかっている) depend on [upon] … (!進行形は不可); (…に任されている) be up to ….
▶行くか残るかはあなた次第です It's *up to* you whether you go or stay./Whether you go or stay *is up to* you. ▶君の人生は君次第なのだ(=君が作るのだ) Your life is what you make of it.
|会話| 「その事業はどのくらい期間がかかる?」「分からないね, まあ金次第かな」"How long do you think the project will take?" "There's no telling. It *depends on* the funding."

── 次第 腰 (…したとすぐに) as soon as …, immediately (after) … (!after を用いないのは《英》, (話) right after …. (⇨すぐ) ▶家に着き次第電話します I'll call you up *as soon as* [*immediately after*, 《話》 *right after*] I get [×*will get*] home./『書』 *On getting* home, I'll call you up. ▶ご都合がつき次第手紙の返事をください Please answer my letter *at your earliest convenience* [*as soon as it is convenient for* you, (できるだけ早く) *as soon as possible*]. (!最初の表現は堅い言い方で主に商業文で用いられる)

── 次第に 副 (徐々に) gradually, by degrees; (少しずつ) little by little, (!話) bit by bit; (ますます) more and more. (⇨段々副, 徐々に) ▶彼は次第に健康を回復した He *gradually* recovered his health.
しだい 私大 a private university [college].
じたい 事態 a situation, a state of affairs [things]; (漠然とした事柄) things, matters. ● 困った事態 an awkward *situation* [*state of affairs*]. ● 非常事態 a *state* of emergency. ● 事態に対処する meet the *situation*. ● 困難な事態に直面しうる事態 be faced [be confronted] with a difficult *situation*. ● 事態を緩和する ease the *situation*. ● 事態を悪化させる make *things* worse. ● 事態を収拾する settle the *situation*. ▶事態はまだ楽観を許さない(=まだ重大だ) The *situation* is still serious [*grave*]. (!grave の方が深刻さの程度は強い)
▶事態はどうなっているのか知らせてください Let me know how the *situation* stands [*things* stand]. ▶事態は悪く[よく]なってきた *Things* are going worse [getting better]. ▶嘆いたところで事態はよくなりはしない Mourning won't improve *things* [help *matters*].
じたい 辞退 ── 辞退する 動 [穏やかに] decline; [きっぱりと] refuse; [断固としてきつく] reject. (⇨断わる ❶) ● 招待を辞退する *decline* [*refuse*, 《話》 *turn down*, ×*reject*] an invitation. ● 彼の申し出を辞退する *decline* [*refuse*] (to accept) his offer; *reject* [*turn down*] his offer.
じたい 字体 the form of a character; (活字の) type. ● 斜字体 italic *type*.
じたい 自体 itself (屢 themselves). ▶その計画自体は悪くない The plan *itself* is not bad. (!*itself* は plan を強調する. 文尾に置くことも可)/(それ自体では) The plan is all right *in itself*.

じだい 時代
> **WORD CHOICE** 時代
> age 一定の長さを持った歴史上の特定の時期のこと. しばしば, 時々の支配者や大きな事件などによって特徴づけられる. ● 輝かしい大英帝国時代に in the golden *age* of the British Empire.

period さまざまな長さを持った歴史上の特定の時期のこと. ▶植民地時代に during the colonial *period* [*era*].

era 他と区別されるような特色・特徴をもち, 始まりが明確に languages 歴史上の特定の時期のこと. ▶IT革命という新しい時代に入った We've entered a new *era* of IT revolution.

▼頻度チャート

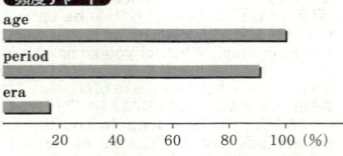

age ████████████████████
period ████████████
era ███

0 20 40 60 80 100 (%)

❶ 『歴史上の期間』 a period, an age, an era, an epoch (! era は初期の, 画期的な出発点となる時代). ▶不況の時代 a *period* of depression; a depression *era*. ▶原子力[宇宙]時代 the atomic [space] *age*. ▶シェイクスピアの時代 the *age* of Shakespeare. ▶原始時代 the primitive *ages*. (! 複数形にするのは、一時代一時代と意識しないから). ▶革命の時代 a *period* [an *age*, an *epoch*] of revolution. ▶封建[江戸]時代の終わりに at the end of the feudal [the Edo] *period*. ▶明治時代に in the Meiji *era*. ▶車の発明は新時代を画するものだった The invention of cars marked a new *epoch* [was *epoch-making*]. ▶ベートーベンはゲーテと同時代の人だった Beethoven was *contemporary with* [a *contemporary of*] Goethe.

❷ 『時勢, 世の中』 (the) time(s), day(s). (! いずれも複数形で用いることが多い)

①【~(の)時代】 ▶古きよき時代 the good old *times* [*days*]. (! good old の語順に注意) ▶今日のような高度技術の時代に in these *days* [this *day*] of high technology. ▶ケネディの時代に in Kennedy's *time*(s) [*day*(s)]; in the *time*(s) [*day*(s)] of Kennedy. ▶いつの時代にも at any *era*. ▶これからの時代の future *age*. ▶当時は金持ちだけが飛行機で旅行できる時代だった Those were the *days* [×*day*] *when* only rich people were able to travel by plane. ▶現代は原子力の時代だ This is [We live in] the *age* of atomic energy. (⇒❶) ▶このEメールの時代, 人々は以前ほど手紙を書かなくなった In this *age* of e-mail, people don't write letters as much as they used to.

②【時代~】 ▶時代遅れの武器 an óld-fàshioned [an óut-of-dàte, an òutdàted] wéapon. ▶彼の考えは時代遅れだ His ideas are *behind the times* [*out of date*]./He's not up-to-date in his ideas any more. ▶時代がかって聞こえるかもしれないが Though it might sound old-fashoned.

③【時代は[が]】 ▶時代は変わった (The) *times* have changed. ▶君たちの時代がやって来る Your *time* will come. ▶やがてだれもが宇宙旅行のできる時代が来るであろう The *time* will soon come *when* everybody can enjoy space travel. ▶ The time when everybody ... will soon come. の語順より普通 (⇒❷②)) ▶昔とは時代が違う We are in a different *age* than we used to be.

④【時代の】 ▶時代の要請に応える meet the demands of the *times*. ▶時代の先端を行く産業 a *frontier* industry. ▶時代の流れに反して against the current of the *time*.

⑤【時代に[を]】 ▶時代に遅れないようについてゆく (try to) keep up [keep in step] with the *times*.

▶時代を反映する reflect the *times*. ▶時代を築く build [construct, create] a new *age* [*era*]. ▶時代を超える transcend the age-gap. ▶この計画は時代を何年も先取りしている This plan is years ahead of (↔behind) the *times*.

❸ 『古いこと』 antiquity. ▶非常に時代物のつぼ a pot of great *antiquity*; a very *old* pot. (! 「時代物(=古物)」は an antique), ▶時代物(=年代物)のスポーツカー an *antique* sports car.

❹ 『人の一生のうちの期間』 days. ▶青春[子供; 高校]時代 in one's *youth* [*childhood*, high school *days*]. (! when one was young [a child; a high-school student] とする方が口語的也) ▶彼にも全盛時代があった(が今は落ちぶれている) He has seen better *days*./He has had his *day* [×*days*]. (! one's day は「全盛期」) ▶彼は独身時代によく一人旅をした He would often travel alone *before he was married*. (! in his bachelorhood [pre-marriage days] より普通)

▶時代感覚 the sense of the times. ▶時代区分 a periodization (of history). ▶時代劇 a historical [a period] play; (日本の) a *samurai* drama. ▶時代考証 the background research (for a historical novel [drama]). ▶時代錯誤 an anachronism. ▶時代小説 a *samurai* novel; a *samurai* story. ▶時代精神 the spirit of the times.

じだい 地代 (a) land [(a) ground] rent. ▶年50万円の地代で土地を借りる rent the land *for* 500,000 yen a year. (! 賃貸しする場合は for の代わりに at も可)

じだい 次代 [次の時代] the next era [age]; [次の時代の人々] the next [coming] generation (! 単・複数扱い) ▶次代をになう若者 the younger [×next] generation who will build up the *next era*.

じだいしゅぎ 事大主義 toadyism, sycophantism; (日和見主義) timeserving.
▶事大主義者 a toady, a sycophant; a timeserver.

*****したう 慕う** [愛する] love; [思い焦がれる] long 《*for*》, 《主に書》 yearn 《*for*》; [敬慕する] adore; [いなくて寂しく思う] miss. ▶遠くに住む母を慕う *long for* one's mother who lives far away. ▶その教授を慕う *adore* [《敬慕する》 *admire*] the professor. ▶彼女は彼を心から慕っていた She *loved* him dearly./(彼に愛着を抱いていた) She *was* deeply [very] *attached to* him.

したうけ 下請け 图 ▶その会社は仕事を下請けに出した The company *farmed* [*contracted*] *out* the work to its subcontractor.
― 下請けする 動 subcontract, get a subcontract 《*from*》.
▶下請け業者(会社, 企業) a subcontractor. (!「先請け」は a primary contractor,「孫請け」は a sub-subcontractor) ▶下請け工場 a subcontract factory. ▶下請け仕事 subcontracted work.

したうち 舌打ち ― **舌打ちする** 動 (不満を表して) click one's tongue; (いらだち・困惑・不賛成などを表して) tut(-tut); [舌打ちの音は tut, tut!]. ▶いらいらして舌打ちする a *tut(-tut)* with impatience. ▶舌打ちして不満を表す give a *tut(-tut)* of disapproval.

したうちあわせ 下打ち合わせ (make) preliminary arrangements 《*for* a thing *with* him》.

したえ 下絵 (make) a rough sketch 《*of* a face》; (図案) a design 《*for* a dress》.

したおび 下帯 a loincloth; a waistcloth.

:したがう 従う ❶ 『随行する』 (後について行く[来る]) follow; (いっしょに行く) go* with..., 《やや書》 ac-

したがえる 従える ——[伴う]be attended by ...; (同行される)be accompanied by .... ▶彼は2人の秘書を従えて入って来た He came in, attended [followed] by his two secretaries. ▶大統領は私服警察を従えていた The president had some plain clothes police officers with him./The president was accompanied by some plain clothes police officers. (!前の方が口語的)
❷[征服する]conquer; (打ち破る)defeat. ● 敵を従える conquer an enemy.

したがき 下書き [草稿] a draft. ● 講演の下書きを書く draft [make a draft of] a speech. ● 下書きなしで演説する speak without a draft; (即席で) make an offhand speech [a speech offhand].

***したがって 従って** ❶[だから](それ故)(やや書)therefore; (当然の結果として)consequently; (このようにして)(書)thus; (その状態に合わせて)(書)accordingly. (⇒だから) ▶彼は55歳だ. 従って年金をもらう資格はない He is 55 and therefore not eligible to receive a pension.
❷[...どおりに, 応じて]according to ...; in accordance with .... (!後の方が堅い表現) ● 交通規則に従って車を運転する drive a car according to [in accordance with] traffic regulations. ● 会社への貢献度に従って給料が支払われる You will be paid according to [(比例して) in proportion to] the contribution you make to the company.
❸[...につれて]as .... ▶彼は年をとるに従って温和になった As he grew older, he got gentler [has mellowed]./The older he grew, the gentler he became.

したがり 下刈り —— **下刈りする** 動 clear underbrush. 《米》[undergrowth 《英》]; remove weeds.

-したがる [欲する]want [(書)desire] (to do); [思い焦れられる]long to do; [熱心にしたがる]be eager (to do); be anxious (to do). (⇒-たがる)

***したぎ 下着** an undergarment; 《集合的》underwear, underclothes, underclothing; (女性の)lingerie /lɑ̀ːnʒəréi/. ● 玄関のブザーが鳴ったとき私は下着だけだった I had nothing but my underwear on when the doorbell rang. ● 私は下着を替え, バッグには何枚か着替えの下着を入れた I changed my underwear and packed some extra (underwear [ones]). (!「着替えの下着」(a change [a set] of underwear) は, この文では同じ言葉が重なるので不

じだきゅう 自打球 one's own foul tip. ● 自打球をすねに当てる take a foul tip off one's shin. ▶彼は自打球をした He hit his own foul tip.

したきりすずめ『舌切り雀』 The Tongue Cut Sparrow. (参考 日本の昔話)

***したく 支度** [準備] preparation(s); arrangements (⇒準備, 用意); [身支度] dressing.
—— **支度(を)する** 動 ● 冬支度をする prepare [make preparations] for the (coming of) winter. ● 夕食の支度をする prepare [(主に米) fix] dinner; get dinner ready. ● 旅支度をする get dressed for [dress (oneself) for] a journey. (!後の方が堅い言い方. oneself は省略されることが多い; (準備をする) prepare [get ready] for a trip.

したく 私宅 one's (private) house [home, residence].

***じたく 自宅** one's home [house]. (!(1) house は通例一戸建ての家屋をいう. (2) house の複数形は (houses /-zɪz, 《米》-sɪz/)). ● 自宅の住所 one's home address. ● 自宅にいる be (at) home (! at を from を省略するのは《英語・米》); be in. ● 自宅監禁されている be under house arrest. ▶彼は自宅待機中だ He is waiting at home.
● **自宅療養** home treatment; home remedy.

したくさ 下草 《米》underbrush, 《英》undergrowth.

したげいこ 下稽古 図 a rehéarsal.
—— **下稽古する** 動 rehéarse (a show); give [have] a rehearsal.

したげんこう 下原稿 a (rough) draft; a manuscript.

したけんぶん 下検分 a preliminary inspection. (⇒ 回 下見)

したごころ 下心 [自分を利するための隠れた動機] a hidden agenda, 《書》an ulterior motive. ▶彼に下心がある He has an ulterior motive [(秘密の意図) a secret intention, a secret design]. ▶彼の提案には何か下心があるに違いない There must be some hidden agenda [behind] his proposal.

したごしらえ 下ごしらえ 図 (準備) preparations.
—— **下ごしらえ(を)する** 動 ● 料理できるように魚の下ごしらえをする prepare [dress] fish for cooking.

-したことがある (⇒こと ❸)

したさき 舌先 the tip of the tongue.
● **舌先三寸** 舌先三寸でごまかす equivocate; explain it away.

したざわり 舌触り ● 舌触りがよい[悪い]be pleasant [unpleasant] to the palate.

したじ 下地 [基礎]groundwork, a foundation; [基礎知識]a grounding. ● 民主主義の下地を作る lay the groundwork [foundation] for democracy. ▶彼は英文法の下地がしっかりしている He has a good grounding in English grammar.

したし 仕出し catering /kéɪtərɪŋ/ (for). ● 仕出しをする cater (for a party); deliver dishes to order. (! to order は「注文に従って」の意) ● 仕出し弁当 a box lunch for delivery. ● 仕出し屋 a caterer.

***したしい 親しい** [仲のよい] friendly; [なじみ深い] familiar; [親密な] close, intimate.

使い分け **friendly** 友人のように仲がよく, 気軽な関係を表す.
familiar 家族間に見られるような打ち解けた親しさを表す.
close friendly より親密な, 身近な関係を表す.

> **intimate** close よりさらに親密で何でも話せる間柄を表す. しばしば異性間では性的な関係を暗示する.

● 彼と親しくなる (友人になる) make [become] friends [ˣa friend] with him; (知り合いになる) get acquainted with him. ▶あの人はだれとも大変親しくする He is very *friendly* to [*toward*] everybody. ▶父は彼と親しい My father is *friendly* [*familiar*] *with* him./My father is good *friends with* him./(親しい間柄である) My father is *on friendly* [*familiar, good*] *terms with* him. ▶彼は親しげに話しかけてきた He talked to me *in a friendly manner* [*way*]. (❗friendlily という副詞は口調がよくないので避けられる)

● 親しき中にも礼儀あり (ことわざ) A hedge between keeps friendship green. (❗「間に垣根があることが友情を新鮮に保つ」の意)

したじき 下敷き 〖机の上に置く〗a desk pad; 〖筆記用具の〗a plastic sheet. 〖参考〗米英にはない ● 車の下敷きになる be buried [crushed, caught] under a car. ● A を下敷きにして (=手本にして) after [on] the model of A. ▶その登山者は大きな岩の下敷きになって死んだ The climber was crushed to death *under* a massive rock.

したしさ 親しさ (⇨親しみ)

したしみ 親しみ 〖友好〗friendship; 〖友好的気持ち〗(a) friendly feeling; 〖心の安らぎ〗familiarity. ● 親しみのある微笑 a *friendly* smile. ● 親しみのある雰囲気 a *friendly* [a *familiar*, (親密な) an *intimate*] atmosphere. ● 親しみやすい (=社交的な) 人 a *sociable* person. (⇨親しむ) ▶彼に親しみを感じる have *friendly* feelings *toward* him; feel *friendship for* him.

*****したしむ** 親しむ ● 読書に親しむ *enjoy* reading; *spend a lot of time* reading. ● 自然に親しむ *live with* (親しく交わる) *be in close contact with*, 〖書〗*commune with*] nature. ● 英語に親しむ (=精通する) *get familiar with* English. ● 子供に親しまれている (=人気のある) 遊び a game *popular among* children. ▶彼は親しみやすい人だ He's a *friendly* person./(一緒にいると楽しい人だ) He's *easy to be with*.

したじゅんび 下準備 preliminary arrangements; (骨の折れる) spadework; (基礎を作る) groundwork; (予習的な) homework. ● 会合の下準備をする *prepare* [*get ready*] *for* the meeting; *arrange* a meeting. ● 下準備をする *make* preparations [*arrangements*] *for* ... も可) ▶交渉担当者が下準備をしてこなかったのは明らかだった The negotiator clearly didn't do his *homework*.

じだしゃ 次打者 〖野球〗the batter on deck; the on-deck batter.

したしらべ 下調べ ── 下調べ(を)する ⦅動⦆ make a preliminary inquiry (*into*). ● 授業の下調べをする (=予習をする) *prepare* (*for*) one's lessons. (❗*for*は「…に備えて」の意)

したそうだん 下相談 ⦅have⦆ preliminary talks ⦅*with*⦆.

したたか ⦅形⦆ ● したたか者 (不屈な) a *tough* /tʌ́f/ person; (扱うのが難しい者) a person (who is) *very hard to deal with*. ● したたかな交渉相手 a *tough* negotiator.
── したたか ⦅副⦆ 〖強く〗hard; 〖激しく〗severely; 〖たくさん〗a great deal. ● したたか飲む drink *a great deal* [⦅話⦆*a lot, heavily*]. ● 頭を木にしたたかぶつける strike one's head *hard* against the tree. ▶私はしたたか殴られた I was beaten up *severely*./I got a *good* [a *sound*] beating.

したためる 認める 〖書く〗write ⦅a letter⦆; 〖食べる〗have ⦅eat⦆ ⦅lunch⦆.

したたらず 舌足らず ── 舌足らずな ⦅形⦆ ● 舌足らずな (=不十分な) 説明 an *inadequate* explanation. ● 舌足らずなしゃべり方をする speak with a *lisp*. ⦅話⦆ talk *baby talk*.

したたる 滴る (ぽたぽたと) drip (-pp-), drop (-pp-) (この意では drip の方がよく使われる); (細い線となって) trickle (ぽたぽた落ちる意もある). ● 緑したたる青葉 *fresh* green leaves. ● 彼の手から血がしたたり落ちていた Blood *was dripping from* his hand./His hand *was dripping* (*with*) blood. ▶彼女の目から涙がしたたり落ちた Tears *dropped* [*dripped*] *from* her eyes./(ほおを伝って) Tears *trickled down* her cheeks.

したつづみ 舌鼓 ● 舌鼓を打つ smack one's lips ⦅*over*⦆.

したっぱ 下っ端 〖軽蔑的〗an underling. ● 下っ端役人 a *minor* [a *petty*] official.

したづみ 下積み 〖社会の底辺〗the bottom; 〖無名〗obscurity. ● 下積みから身を起こす rise from the *bottom* (*rung of the ladder*); rise from *obscurity*. ▶彼は下積みが長かった He experienced long years of *obscurity*.

したて 仕立て 〖仕立て方〗tailoring; 〖裁縫〗sewing; 〖裁断の仕方〗a cut. ● 仕立て下ろしの (真新しい) brand-new] clothes. ● 仕立て上がりの服 newly made clothes. ● 仕立てのうまい人 a good *tailor* [*dressmaker*]. ● 仕立物をする do the sewing (of the clothing). ● 仕立てのよいオーバー a well-*tailored* overcoat. ▶彼のスーツは仕立てがよい His suit *is* well (↔*badly*) *tailored* [*made*]. ▶その服を仕立て直してください Please *alter* [ˣ*reform*] the dress. ▶その一行は特別仕立ての (=特別の) 列車でそこへ行った The party went there on a *special* train.

● 仕立て代 tailoring charges; the charges for the tailoring. ● 仕立て屋 (紳士服の) a tailor; (婦人服の) a dressmaker.

したて 下手 ● 下手に出る (へりくだった態度を取る) take a humble [a modest] attitude ⦅*toward*⦆; behave humbly [modestly] ⦅*toward*⦆; 〖書〗humble oneself. (❗humble, humbly はしばしば卑屈さを含意する)

したてなげ 下手投げ 〖相撲〗an underarm throw; 〖野球〗an underhand throw [delivery, pitch]. ● 下手投げの投手 an *underhand* pitcher; a submariner. ● 下手投げで投げる throw *underhand*. (❗投球にも送球にも用いる. pitch underhand とすると投球のみをさす)

したてる 仕立てる ❶ 〖服を〗make*, (主に男物を) tailor. ● 娘に洋服を仕立てる make a dress *for* one's daughter. ▶その背広はどこで仕立てた (=仕立ててもらった) のですか Where did you *have* the suit *tailored* [*made*]?
❷ 〖人を〗train. (⇨仕込む) ● 彼を法律家に仕立てる *train* him *to be* a lawyer.
❸ 〖乗り物などを〗(用意する) prepare ⦅a bus⦆; (差し向ける) send*, dispatch ⦅a bus⦆.

したどり 下取り a trade-in. ● カメラの下取り価格 a camera's *trade-in* value. ● 2,000 ドルで下取りしてもらう get 2,000 dollars on a *trade-in*. ▶下取りしてくれませんか Will you give me a *trade-in*? ● 今乗っている本を下取りに出して新しい車を買った I *traded in* my present car *for* a new model.

したなめずり 舌なめずり ── 舌なめずりする ⦅動⦆ ⦅話⦆ lick [smack] one's lips [chops]. (❗比喩的に「期待して待つ」の意でも用いられる)

しためり 下塗り an undercoat. ▶まず下塗りをしなさい Apply the *undercoat* first.

したね 下値 a lower price.

したばえ 下生え 《米》underbrush, 《英》undergrowth.

したばき 下穿き (男性用の) underpants, 《話》pants; (女性用の) panties, 《英》knickers; (男性・女性用の) briefs.

したばき 下履き outdoor shoes.

じたばた — **じたばたする** 動 struggle; (虫などが) wriggle; (抵抗する) resist. ▶じたばたするな Don't *struggle*. / Don't *resist*. / (うろたえるな) Don't *panic*. / (しっかり腰をすえろ) Just sit tight. ▶落ちたセミが地面でじたばたしていた A fallen locust 《米》[cicada 《英》] *was wriggling* on the ground. ▶じたばたしてもしようがない It's no use *resisting*.

したばたらき 下働き (助手的仕事) a job of an assistant; (人) an assistant. ▶私は彼のところで下働きを何年かした I *worked under* him (as an assistant) for some years.

したはら 下腹 the lower abdomen [belly]; (動物の) an underbelly. ▶下腹がしくしく痛む There is a dull pain in the *lower part of* my *abdomen*.

したばり 下張り — **下張り(を)する** 動 cover 《a wall》 with paper before a facing.

したび 下火 動 《火の勢い・人気などが》die down (〜d; dying); 〖需要・インフレなどが〗tail off; drop* (-pp-); 〖流行などがすたれる〗go* out of fashion. ▶火事は間もなく下火になるでしょう The fire will *die down* [抑制される] *be under control* soon. ▶彼の人気は下火になってきた His popularity *is dying down* [(衰えて)《やや書》*declining*, 《やや書》*waning*]. ▶新車の需要が下火になり始めた The demand for new cars began to *decline* [*tail off*].

したびらめ 舌平目 〖魚介〗a sole. (❗ 通例単・複同形)

-したほうがいい —した方がいい (⇨い ⓯)

じたまご 地卵 a locally-produced egg.

したまち 下町 the traditional shopping and entertainment districts (of Tokyo). ▶浅草・神田・深川・日本橋などいう。 ❷ 英語の downtown はビジネス街やショッピング街のある今の中心地区をさすので、the old downtown district のようにもいえる）
● **下町言葉** the language spoken particularly in the old downtown district of Tokyo.
● **下町風** the carefree, humane life style in old downtown district of Tokyo.

したまわる 下回る 〖数量などが〗…より以下である〗be below …; […より少ない(低い)] lower than …. ▶平均を下回る be *below* (↔*above*) average. ▶この工場の生産高は昨年の水準を大幅に下回っている［下回った］ The output of this factory *is* [*has fallen*] far *below* last year's level. ▶私たちの賃金はあなたがたより下回っています Our wages *are less* [*lower*] *than* yours. ▶その選挙の結果は私たちの予想を下回った(=期待はずれだった) The results of the election *came* [*fell*] *short of* our expectations. / The results of the election *were not as good as* we had hoped for.

したみ 下見 图 a preliminary inspection.
— **下見(を)する** 動 (前もって調査する) 《やや書》make a preliminary inspection 《of》; (強盗目的で)《話》case 《the place》. ▶試験場は下見をすることにしている have a look at the examination hall *in advance*.

したむき 下向き ❶ (下向きになる) (衰える) 《やや書》decline; (相場などが下がる) go down. ❷ 顔を下向きに *a lower* one's face. ● コップを下向きに置く(底を上にして) put a glass *with the bottom up*; (上下逆さまにして) put a glass *upside down*. ▶相場は下向きだ The market *is going down* [*falling*, *declining*].

したむづかい 下目遣い ● 下目遣いに…を見る look at … *with a downward eyes*; cast a *downward glance* at ….

したやく 下役 a subordinate.

したやく 下訳 subcontract translation; 'ghost-translation'.

したよみ 下読み 图 preparatory reading.
— **下読みする** 動 read 《a book》 beforehand.

-したら (⇨-たら ❶)

じだらく 自堕落 ● 自堕落な(=だらしない)生活を送る lead a *slovenly* [(いくじなしの) 《ふしだらな》*loose*] life.

したりがお したり顔 (得意な) a proud [(勝ち誇った) a triumphant, (してやったりの) smug] look. ● したり顔をして proudly; triumphantly; smugly; with a *proud* [*triumphant*, *smug*] *look* on one's face.

しだれざくら 枝垂桜 〖植物〗a weeping cherry (tree).

しだれやなぎ 枝垂柳 〖植物〗a weeping willow.

しだれる 枝垂れる droop; hang down.

したわしい 慕わしい dear; beloved.

したん 紫檀 〖植物〗(木) a rosewood; (材) rosewood.

しだん 指弾 — **指弾する** 動 (排斥する) reject, shun; (非難する) criticize.

しだん 師団 〖軍隊〗a division.
● **師団長** the divisional commander; (自衛隊の) the Commanding General of the Division.

しだん 詩壇 the world of poetry; poetic(al) circles.

じたん 時短 the reduction of working hours. ● 時短への動き a trend toward *shorter working hours*.

じだん 示談 〖法廷外の決着〗an out-of-court settlement, a settlement out of court; 〖個人的決着〗a private settlement. ● 示談に応じる agree to an *out-of-court settlement* 《of one million yen》. ▶会社はその件を100万円の示談(金)で解決した The company *settled* the case *out of court* [*without going to law*] for one million yen.
● **示談屋** a person who deals in out of court settlements 《of car accident cases》.

じだんだ 地団太 ● **地団太を踏む** ● 地団太を踏んで悔しがる stamp one's feet in frustration.

*****しち 七** seven; [7 番目の] the seventh. (⇨三)

しち 質 pawn, 《話》hock; (担保) pledge. (⇨質入れ)
● 指輪を質に入れる put a ring *in pawn* [*in hock*]; pawn 《話》hock one's ring. ● 質に入れてある be *in pawn* [*in hock*].
● **質流れ** (⇨質流れ) ● **質札** a pawn ticket. ● **質屋** (店) a pawnshop; (人) a pawnbroker.

しち 死地 ● 死地に赴く go into *the jaws of death*. ● 死地に陥る be in [fall into] *the jaws of death*.

じち 自治 图 self-government; 《やや書》autonomy. ● 自治を認める recognize the *self-government* 《of

しちかいき 七回忌 (⇨七回忌)
***しちがつ** 七月 July 《略 Jul.》. (⇨一月)
しちかっけい 七角形 a héptagòn.
しちごさん 七五三 shichigosan; (説明的に) the festival held on November 15 to celebrate the healthy growth of one's children aged seven, five and three (especially, boys of three or five, girls three or seven).
しちごちょう 七五調 ▶七五調の詩 a poem in the *seven-and-five syllable* meter.
しちさん 七三 ▶髪を七三に分ける part one's hair *at the side*.
***しちじゅう** 七十 seventy. (⇨七十)
しちしょう 七生 (仏教で) seven rebirths; (七代) seven generations.
じちたい 自治体 a self-governing [《やや書》 an autonomous] body. ▶地方自治体 a local government; a municipality.
しちてんばっとう 七転八倒 ── 七転八倒する 動 toss and turn [toss about, 《やや書》 writhe /ráid/ (about)] in great pain.
しちながれ 質流れ (a) foreclosure. ▶質流れになる become unredeemed; be gone.
▶質流れ品 an unredeemed article [item].
しちなん 七難 (いろいろな災難) various misfortunes.
▶七難八苦 a great many misfortunes
しちふくじん 七福神 the Seven Gods of Good Fortune.
しちぶそで 七部袖 three quarter [³/₄, bracelet] sleeves.
しちみ(とうがらし) 七味(唐辛子) shichimi*-togarashi*; (説明的に) a mixture of seven dried and ground flavors: red peppers, *sansho* pepper pods, mandarin orange peel, black hemp seeds, white poppy seeds, dark green seaweed bits and white sesame seeds.
しちめんちょう 七面鳥 [鳥] a turkey (獲 ~s, ~). (🛈 肉は Ⓤ)
しちめんどう 七面倒 great [much] trouble. (⇨面)
▶七面倒臭い extremely troublesome.
しちゃく 試着 ── 試着する 動 try 《a suit》 on. ▶サイズが合うか、どうぞご試着ください Please *try* this coat *on* for size.
● 試着室 a fitting ròom.
しちゅう 支柱 a prop; a post; (中心的存在) the mainstay; (一家のかせぎ手) a breadwinner. ▶日本経済の支柱 the *mainstay* of Japanese economy.
しちゅう 市中 ● 市中銀行 (民間銀行) a commercial bank; (都市銀行) a city bank. ● 市中金利 the money [market] rate; the open market rate.
しちゅう 死中 ▶死中に活を求める seek (to find) a way out of a desperate [a fatal] situation.
シチュー (a) stew /st(j)úː/. ● ビーフ[タン]シチュー beef [tongue] *stew*. ● シチューにする stew 《meat》.
しちゅうすいめい 四柱推命 (説明的に) a kind of fortune telling: telling a person's fortune with four periods of one's birth time, day, month and year.
シチュエーション 〖状況〗 a situation. ▶彼は今難しいシチュエーションにいる He is in a difficult *situation*.
● シチュエーションコメディー (テレビやラジオの連続ホームコメディー) a situation comedy; 《話》 a sitcom.
しちよう 七曜 ● 七曜星 the Big Dipper. ● 七曜表 a calendar.
しちょう 支庁 a branch office.
しちょう 市庁 a city hall. (⇨市役所)
しちょう 市長 a mayor. ▶神戸市長 the *Mayor* of Kobe. ● ~市長 Mayor Suzuki (🛈 人名が続く場合は無冠詞) ● 一日市長をする act as *mayor* for a day. ● 市長の職[任期] mayoralty. ▶彼女は 5 年間この市の市長をしています She has been *mayor* of this city for five years. (🛈 mayor は今では女性にも用い、女性形 mayoress は通例「市長夫人」の意)
● 市長選挙 a mayoral election.
しちょう 思潮 the trend [current] of thought. ▶アメリカ文芸思潮 the main *current* of American literature.
しちょう 試聴 ── 試聴する 動 listen 《to a CD》 before buying 《it》.
● 試聴室 a lístening bòoth.
しちょう 次長 an assistant manager.
しちょう 自重 ── 自重する 動 〖慎重に行動する〗《話》 watch oneself [one's step]; 〖用心深くなる〗 be prudent. ▶自重しろよ *Watch* yourself. ▶もっと自重してほしい I want you to be more *prudent*.
しちょう 自嘲 [名] self-mockery. ▶自嘲的な笑いを浮べる wear a *self-mocking* smile; smile *self-mockingly*.
── 自嘲する 動. mock [laugh at] oneself.
しちょうかく 視聴覚 ● 視聴覚教育 audio(-)visual education [instruction]. ● 視聴覚教室 an audio(-)visual classroom. ● 視聴覚機器[教員] audio(-)visual aids; audio(-)visuals.
しちょうしゃ 市庁舎 a city hall.
しちょうしゃ 視聴者 (特にテレビの) a viewer; 《集合的》 an audience, 《書》 the viewing public (🛈 ともに単・複両扱い 《⇨聴衆》). ● 視聴者参加番組 an *audience* participation program; (電話での) 《米》 a call-in, 《英》 a phone-in.
しちょうそん 市町村 cities, towns and villages; (自治体) municipalities.
しちょうりつ 視聴率 a [an audience] rating, 《主に英》 a viewing figure. (🛈 ともに通例複数形で) ▶視聴率の高い[よい]テレビ番組 a TV program with a high [a good] *rating*. ▶彼の番組は視聴率がいちばん高い His program is (the) highest in the *ratings* [is at the top of the *ratings*, (最も人気がある) is (the) most *popular*]. ▶彼がその番組に出るようになって視聴率が 10 パーセント上がった After he (had) joined the program, the *ratings* (for it) went up [improved, 《やや書》 rose] (by) ten percent.
しちょく 司直 (裁判官) a judge. ● 司直の手にかける bring 《him》 to *justice*.
シチリア 〖イタリアの島〗 Sicily /sísəli/. ● シチリア(人)の Sicilian.
しちりん 七輪 a portable clay cooking stove.
じちん 自沈 ── 自沈する 動 scuttle [sink] 《one's own ship》. (🛈 scuttle は「船に穴を開けて沈める」の意)
じちんさい 地鎮祭 a ground breaking ceremony.
しつ 質 quality. ▶質の高い製品 goods of high *quality*; (high) *quality* goods. ● 質をよくする[落とす] improve [lower] the *quality* 《of》. ● 量より質を重んじる put *quality* before quantity. ▶そのワインは質がよい The wine is of good (⇔poor) *quality*./The wine is good (⇔poor) *in quality*./(上等のワインだ) It is *quality* wine. (🛈 最後の quality は

容詞的用法)
- **しつ** 室 a room. (⇨部屋) ●実験室 a laboratory. ●406 号室 Room number 406.
- **しっ** hush /hʌʃ/; sh(h), ssh /ʃ:/; silence; 〖鳥や猫を追い払う声〗shoo, scat /skæt/. (❗命令形で) ●子供に強くしっと言って黙らせる *hush* the child firmly. ●しっと言って鳥を追い払う *shoo* a bird away [off]. ▶しっ, 赤ん坊が起きますよ *Hush* [*Sh*]! You'll wake the baby!
- ***じつ** 実 〖真実〗truth; 〖現実性〗reality; 〖誠実〗sincerity; 〖成果〗(good) results. (⇨実に, 実の, 実は) ●実を言うと (⇨実は) ●実をあげる (成果をあげる) achieve (good) results.
- **しつい** 失意 〖失望〗disappointment; 〖絶望〗despair. ●失意のどん底にある be in the depths of *despair*. ●失意(=不遇)の時代 one's period of *adversity*.
- **じついん** 実印 one's (officially) registered seal. (⇨印鑑)
- **しつう** 歯痛 (have [get]) toothache. ▶昨夜は一晩中ひどい歯痛に悩まされた I had terrible *toothache* all last night.
- **しつうはったつ** 四通八達 ●鉄道が四通八達している(=複雑な鉄道網を持っている) have a complicated railroad [(米) rail(way) (英)] network.
- **じつえき** 実益 《書》profit; 〖実利〗practical use. ▶この仕事は趣味と実益を兼ねている(=おもしろいだけでなく実益がある) This work is *profitable* [*useful*] as well as interesting./This work gives me *profit* and pleasure at the same time.
- **じつえん** 実演 图 〖実地教授〗a demonstration,《話》a demo; 〖上演〗a performance. ●ダンスの実演 a dancing *demonstration*.
- — **実演する** 動 demonstrate; perform. ●その機械の使い方を実演する *demonstrate* [《話》*give* 《him》a *demo of*] how to use the machine.
- **しつおん** 室温 (a) room temperature. ▶赤ワインは普通室温で(=冷やさずに)供される Red wine is usually served at *room temperature*.
- **しっか** 失火 图 an accidental fire. ▶火事は失火であった The fire broke out *through* [*was caused by*] *carelessness*.
- — **失火する** 動 start a fire through carelessness.
- **じっか** 実科 a practical course.
- **じっか** 実家 one's parents' home [house]. (❗文脈により単に one's home [house] でも表せる); (両親の家族) one's parents' family. ●実家に帰る go [come] back to one's *parents' home* [*house*]; visit one's parents. ▶私の実家は青森です My (*parents'*) *home* is in Aomori.
- **しつがい** 室外 ●室外に[で] outside the room; outdoors; out of doors. ●室外機 (エアコンの) an outdoor unit.
- **じっかい** 十戒 〖聖書〗the Ten Commandments.
- **じつがい** 実害 actual harm (物への害) damage]. (⇨害) ▶実害はほとんどなかった There was hardly any *damage*./There was (very) little *harm* [*damage*] done. (❗harm は人に用いる)
- **しつがいこつ** 膝蓋骨 〖解剖〗the kneecap; the patella《書》~s, patellae).
- ***しっかく** 失格 图 disqualification.
- — **失格する** 動 ●ルール違反で失格した(=資格を奪われた) He *was disqualified* [(競技から外された) *was put out of a competition*] for breaking rules. (⇨落第 ❷)
- **じつがく** 実学 practical learning.
- **しっかと** tightly; securely. (⇨しっかり 副 ❷)
- ***しっかり** ❶〖丈夫に〗strongly. ▶その海辺の家はしっかり建てられていた The beachfront house was *strongly* [*solidly*] built.
- ❷〖きつく〗tight(ly); (堅く) firmly; (安全に) securely. ●母親は赤ん坊をしっかり抱いた The mother held her baby *tight(ly)*. ▶私は彼女の手をしっかり握った I held her hand *firmly*. ▶彼は彼女をしっかりしばった He fastened it *tight(ly)* [*firmly, securely*].
- ❸〖きちんと〗properly; (十分に) well. ●しっかり睡眠をとる sleep *well*; have a *good* sleep. ▶朝食はしっかり取らなければいけない You must eat your breakfast *properly*.
- ❹〖抜け目なく〗shrewdly, wisely. ▶彼は自分の払った金の分だけはパーティーでしっかり食べたり飲んだりした He ate and drank enough to *shrewdly* recover what he had paid for the party.
- ❺〖力いっぱい〗hard. ●しっかり勉強する study *hard*. ▶しっかり努力すれば報われるよ If you try *hard*, you will be rewarded.
- — **しっかりした** 形 ❶〖ゆるぎない〗firm; (ぐらつかない) steady; 〖丈夫な〗strong; (がっしりした) sturdy. ●しっかりした基礎 *firm* foundations. ●しっかりした箱 a *strong* box. ●しっかりしたいす a *sturdy* chair. ●しっかりした足どりで歩く walk with *steady* steps; walk *steadily*. ▶トキのひなは日に日に体がしっかりしてきた The baby ibis has grown *stronger* day by day.
- ❷〖頼りになる〗reliable, dependable. ▶彼はとてもしっかりした人です He is a very *reliable* man.
- ❸〖抜け目ない〗shrewd, clever. ▶由美子は実にしっかりしてるよ Yumiko is a *shrewd* woman indeed.
- ❹〖その他の表現〗▶彼は死ぬ直前まで意識がしっかりしていた He had been *fully* conscious just before he passed away. ▶しっかりしろ! (あきらめるな) Don't give up!/(戦い抜け) Fight it out!/(元気を出せ) Cheer up. ▶しっかりしろ(=気を失うな) 傷は浅い. Don't pass out. You are not seriously wounded.
- 会話 「しっかりやれよ, 太郎」「君もだよ, 健次」"*Good luck*, Taro." "Same to you, Kenji."
- **シッカロール** baby powder; 《商》Siccarol.
- **しっかん** 質感 the texture (《of》wool [stone]).
- **しっかん** 疾患 (a) disease /dɪziːz/. (⇨病気) ●心臓疾患 a heart *disease*. ●内臓疾患 a *disease* of internal organs.
- **じっかん** 十干 the ten calendar signs in China and Japan.
- **じっかん** 実感 图 〖認識〗(a) realization; 〖信念〗(a) belief (《~s》). ●実感をこめて話す speak with *feeling*. ▶彼は父が死んだという実感がわかなかった He didn't *realize* (信じられなかった) couldn't *believe*] that his father was dead./He couldn't *make himself believe that* his father was dead. ▶この絵は実感がよく出ている(=真に迫っている) This picture is *true to life* [*nature*].
- — **実感する** 動 (fully) realize; make oneself believe. ●都市生活の欠陥をつくづく実感する *fully realize* the shortcomings of city life.
- **しっかんせつ** 膝関節 〖解剖〗a knee joint.
- **しっき** 漆器 〖集合的〗lacquer ware; japan (ware); lacquered [japanned] ware. (❗数える時は a piece of ...)
- **しつぎ** 質疑 a question.
- ●**質疑応答** questions and answers. ●(講演の後の)質疑応答の時間 a *question*-and-answer session.
- **じつぎ** 実技 (理論に対して) practice; (実践技術)

しっきゃく 失脚 图 (地位の喪失) loss of position; (破滅) one's [the] downfall.
— **失脚する** 動 彼は不正事件で失脚した He lost his post [position] because of the scandal./The scandal led to his *downfall*.

しつぎょう 失業 图 unemployment. ▶不況で若者の失業(率)が増大しつつある Youth *unemployment* is rising because of the recession. ▶その国は失業者数が多い There is a lot of *unemployment* in the country./(失業率が高い) In the country un*employment* is high. (❗「高い失業率」は high (↔ low) *unemployment*) ▶私は今失業手当をもらっていますが, 大した額ではありません I'm on *unemployment* (compensation 《米》[benefit 《英》]), but I don't get much. (❗ on は「依存して」の意)
— **失業する** 動 lose* one's job; become* unemployed. ▶彼は今失業している He *is unemployed* [*jobless*] now./He *is out of a job* [*out of work, out of employment*] now.
• **失業者** an unemployed person; (無職の人) a jobless person; (集合的で) the unemployed [jobless] (❗複数扱い). • **失業対策** a relief measure for the unemployed; an unemployment policy. • **失業保険** unemployment [jobless] insurance. • **失業問題** an unemployment problem. • **失業率** an unemployment [a jobless] rate; (the level of) unemployment.

じっきょう 実況 (状況) the actual condition; (ありさま) the actual scene. ▶ライブコンサートの(テレビ)実況 a live concert telecast.
• **実況放送** (⇨実況放送)

じつぎょう 実業 图 business. • 実業に従事している be (engaged) in *business*. • **実業界に入る** go into [enter] the *business* world; (実業につく) go into [enter] *business*.
• **実業家** (男) a búsinessman, (女) a businesswoman (❗(1) 特に経営者・役員などをさすことが多い. (2) 男女平等の視点から a business person (⇨people) も用いる); (大実業家) an industrialist. (⇨ビジネス [ビジネスマン]) • **実業学校** a vocational school. • **実業教育** vocational education.

じっきょうほうそう 実況放送 图 《ラジオの》an on-the-spot broadcast; 《テレビの》an on-the-spot telecast; 《テレビ・ラジオの》a (running) commentary; (スポーツの) a play-by-play commentary.
— **実況放送(を)する** 動 ▶野球の実況放送をする do a running [a play-by-play] *commentary* of a baseball game; *broadcast* a baseball game *on the spot*.

しっきん 失禁 图 《医学》incontinence.
— **失禁する** 動 have a toilet accident; (常習的に) be incontinent. (❗尿・排便の両方の場合, 特に be doubly incontinent ということがある)
• **失禁パッド** an incontinent pad.

しっく 疾駆 — **疾駆する** 動 run at full [high] speed. (⇨疾走する)

シック ▶シックなドレス a *chic* [(いきな) *stylish*] dress. (⇨粋(*い*))

しっくい 漆喰 (壁・天井などへの) plaster; (仕上げ用の) stucco. • しっくいを塗る plaster; put *plaster* (*on*).

シックハウスしょうこうぐん シックハウス症候群 《医学》sick building syndrome (略 SBS). (❗ sick house syndrome とはいわない)

しっくり — **しっくりする** 動 ❶ 《仲よい》get* along well 《*with*》; be on good terms 《*with*》. ▶彼らはしっくりいっていない They *are* not *getting along* [*on*] very *well*./They *are* not *on good terms* (*with* each other).
❷ 《うまく合う》suit; fit (-tt-); go* [match] (well, perfectly) with .... ▶このカーテンはこの部屋にしっくりしない This curtain *doesn't suit* [*go well with*] the room.

じっくり (注意して) carefully; (細部を大事にして) meticulously; (申し分なく) perfectly. • その絵をじっくり見る study the picture *carefully*. • じっくり考える think *well*; think (*it*) over; ponder. • じっくり(=時間をかけて)やる do (*it*) *taking* one's *time*. • じっくり話し合う have a *good* talk. ▶それをじっくり考えなさい You'd better *think* it *over* [急がずに *stop to* [*and*] *think about* it].

しつけ 躾 《訓練》(知性・体力の) training; (知性・徳性の) discipline; [行儀] manners. (⇨躾ける) • 家庭のしつけ home *discipline* [*training*]. • しつけのよい [よくない]子供 a well-*trained* [an undisciplined] child. • (幼児の)用便のしつけ toilet *training*.

しつけ 仕付け (仮縫い) a tack; basting. • 仕付けをする tack; baste.
• **仕付け糸** bastings.

しつけ 湿気 《空気・気候の湿度》humidity; 《じめじめして不快》damp(ness); 《少量の湿り気》moisture. • 適度な湿気 a fair degree of *moisture*. ▶台所が床下からの湿気でやられている The kitchen has got [suffers from] rising *damp*. ▶湿気の多い気候は健康によくない A *damp* [A *humid*] climate is not good for our [the] health.

しつげい 漆芸 Japanese lacquer art.

しつけい 失敬 — **失敬な** 形 rude; impolite. (⇨失礼)
— **失敬する** 動 (無断で持って行く) take ... without 《his》permission; (盗む) steal, 《話》lift.

じっけい 実兄 one's own [real] older [elder] brother.

じっけい 実刑 (刑務所に入れること) imprisonment, prison. (❗後の方は「刑務所に入れられること」の意にもなる) (⇨刑) ▶彼は懲役3年の実刑判決を受けた He was sentenced to three years in *prison* [to *prison* for three years, to three years' *imprisonment*]. ▶彼女は実刑は免れないであろう She will have to go [to *be sent*] to *prison*.

じつげつ 日月 《月日》time; years (⇨月日); 《太陽と月》the sun and the moon.

しつける 躾ける 《訓練する》train; discipline; [行儀を教える] teach* (him) manners [how to behave]. • 自分のことは自分でするように彼をしつける *train* him to look after himself. • 子供を厳しく[きちんと]しつける *discipline* one's child strictly [properly].

しっけん 失権 图 forfeiture (of one's right); the loss of one's right.
— **失権する** 動 (権力を失う) forfeit the right 《*to* do》.

しっけん 執権 (a) regency; (人) a regent.

しつげん 失言 图 《不適切な意見》an improper remark; (言い間違い) a slip of the tongue. • 失言を取り消す take back one's *improper* [(無思慮な) *indiscreet*] *remark*.
— **失言する** 動 make an improper remark [a slip of the tongue].

しつげん 湿原 (a) marsh, (a) marshland, a marshy plain. • 釧路湿原 Kushiro *Marsh*.

じっけん 実験 图 (an) experiment; a test. (❗前の方は新発見や理論の実証, 後の方は基準に合うか否か

じっけん の検査が目的) ●化学(分野における)実験 a chemical *experiment*; an *experiment in* chemistry. ●動物実験 an *experiment on* [*with*, *using*] animals (⚠ *on* は動物を直接の実験対象とする場合, *with* は動物を用いての実験を行う場合に用いる); an animal *experiment*. ●核実験 a nuclear *test*.

── **実験の, 実験的な** 形 experimental. ●実験(的な)段階にある be in the *experimental* [*test*] stage. ●実験的な試み an *experimental* trial.

── **実験的に** 副 experimentally; by way of [as an] experiment.

── **実験(を)する** 動 experiment 《*on*, *with*》; do [conduct, perform, carry out] an experiment. ●化学の実験をする *experiment in* chemistry; *do* a chemistry *experiment*. ●人体実験をする *experiment on* human beings; *do experiments on* human beings. ▶研究チームは最も安全な治療法を見つけるためにさまざまな薬の実験をした The research team *experimented* with various medicines to find the safest cure. (⚠ experiment は自動詞なので with が必要)/The *experiments* with various medicines *were conducted* by the research team for the purpose of finding the safest cure.

●実験科学 an experimental science. ●実験結果 an experimental result; the result of an experiment. ●実験材料 (a) material for experiment; (an) experimental material. ●実験式 an empirical formula. ●実験所[室] a laboratory, 《話》a lab. ●実験小説 an experimental novel. ●実験台 (モルモット) (be used as) a guinea pig. ●実験動物 an experimental animal.

*****じっけん 実権** (実際の権力) real power; (支配力) (full) control. ●実権のない(=名ばかりの)経営者 a manager *in* name *only*. ●政治の実権を握る[握っている] take [have] (*full*) *control of* [*over*] the government; take [hold] *actual* political *power*. ▶彼は名目上は党首だが実権はほとんどない While he is nominally the head of the party, he has hardly any [almost no] *real power*.

じっけん 実見 ── **実見する** 動 witness; observe ... in person; see ... with one's own eyes.

*****じつげん 実現** 名 realization, fulfillment. ●夢[希望]の実現 the *realization* of one's dreams [hopes]. ●実現可能な計画 a *feasible* plan. ●彼の計画は実現の運びとなった The plan has reached the stage of *realization*.

── **実現する** 動 realize, fulfill; [夢・予言などが] come* true. ●計画を実現する *realize* [*fulfill*] one's plan; bring one's plan *to realization*. ●懸命に努力して夢を実現する(=達成する) *achieve* one's dream [ambition] through hard work. ▶彼の希望は実現した His hopes *came true* [*became a reality*, 《やや書》*were realized*].

●実現性 feasibility; the possibility (of becoming reality).

*****しつこい** 形 ❶ [執拗(しつよう)な] persistent; insistent (⚠ persistent は執拗さを, insistent は主張の強さを強調); [うるさくせがむ] 《書》importunate; [頑固な] stubborn, obstinate; [詮索好きの] inquisitive /inkwízətiv/. ●しつこい人 a *persistent* person. ●しつこい風邪 a *persistent* [*a stubborn*] cold. ●しつこい子供たち *importunate* children.

❷ [食べ物が] (腹にもたれる) heavy; (脂っこい) greasy; [色あいが] loud, showy. ●しつこい食物 *heavy* [*rich*] food. ●しつこい色 a *loud* [a *showy*] color.

── **しつこく** 副 persistently. ▶彼は私にしつこく質問した He *persistently* [*insistently*] asked me questions./He asked me *persistent* questions./He *pestered* me *with* questions. ▶他人の事をそんなにしつこく聞くな(=せんさくするな) Don't be so *inquisitive about* other people's affairs. ▶彼はその車を買えと私にしつこく勧めた He (*repeatedly*) *urged* me *to* buy the car. (⚠ repeatedly (再々)を用いると意味が強まる) ▶母は夜ふかしをしないようにしつこく言った(=言い続けた) My mother *kept* (*on*) *telling* me [✗*persistently told* me] not to stay up late. (⚠ on のある方がしつこさを強調する) ▶彼は彼女にしつこく答えを迫ったが, 彼女は彼の要求をそらした He *pressed her for* an answer, but she put him off. ▶梅雨前線が西日本にしつこく居座っている The seasonal rain front has refused to go away from the western part of Japan.

しっこう 失効 名 (法律・保険などの) lapse.

── **失効する** 動 lose effect; lapse; become null and void.

しっこう 執行 名 [命令・法律・死刑などの] (an) execution. ●命令[判決]の執行 《書》the *execution* of one's order [the sentence]. ●強制執行 《書》forcible *execution*. ▶昨年は3件の死刑執行がなされた Three *executions* were carried out last year.

── **執行する** 動 《書》execute; [実行する] carry ... out. ●職務を執行する *execute* [果たす] *perform*, *carry out*, *do*] one's duties. ▶後の方は口語的》 ▶大統領は議会が制定した法律を執行する The President *executes* what the Congress legislates. ▶殺人犯の死刑が執行されるだろう The murderer will *be executed*./(殺人罪で処刑されるだろう) He will *be executed for* murder.

●執行委員 a member of the executive committee. ●執行委員会 an executive committee. ●執行官 an enforcer. ●執行権 (exercise) (an) executive power. ●執行停止 a stay [suspension] of execution. ●執行人 (遺言の) 《法律》an executor; (死刑の) an executioner. ●執行部 (組合・政党の) the executive. ●執行猶予 a suspended sentence. (⇨猶予)

*****じっこう 実行** 名 [理論に対する] practice; [行動] (an) action; [命令・計画などの] execution.

① 【実行〜】 ●実行可能な計画 a *practicable* [a *workable*] plan. ●彼には実行力(=行動力)がある He is a man of *action* [an *action* man]. (⚠ 後の方がきびきびした言い方で広告などでよく用いられる) ▶その計画は実行不可能だ The plan is impossible (for us) to *carry out*. (⇨動)/That is an impracticable plan.

② 【実行が】 ●彼は口先ばかりで実行が伴わない He is all talk and no *action* [*deed*]./He seldom *does* what he says. (⇨言行)

③ 【実行に】 ●彼の考えは直ちに実行に移された His idea *was* at once *put into practice*. (⇨動)

── **実行する** 動 carry ... out; (する) do*; [実行に移す] put*... into practice; [命令・計画などを]《書》execute. ●計画を実行する carry out 《書》*execute*] a plan; *put* a plan *into practice*. ▶約束をしたら実行しなければならない If you make a promise, you should *carry it out* [履行する] *fulfill* it, (守る) *keep* it.

●実行委員会 an executive committee. ●実行犯 a perpetrator.

じっこう 実効 an actual effect. ●実効性のある[ない]法律 an *effective* [an *ineffective*] law.

しっこく 桎梏 fetters; the yoke. ●桎梏を脱する break the *fetters* 《of conventions》.

しっこく 漆黒 ▶森の中は漆黒の闇だった It was *pitch-dark* [*(as) dark as pitch*] in the woods.

しつごしょう 失語症【医学】aphasia /əféiʒə/.
● 失語症患者 an aphasic (patient).

じっこん 昵懇, 入魂 ― 昵懇[入魂]の 圏 intimate; close; friendly. ▶彼女とはじっこんの間柄だ I am *on friendly terms with* her./She and I *are close friends*.

:**じっさい 実際** 图〖事実〗a fact;〖真実〗truth;〖現実〗(a) reality;〖実地〗practice;〖実情〗the actual conditions. (⇨実地) ▶想像と実際 imagination and *reality*. ● 理論と実際 theory and *practice*.
● 自動車産業の実際 the *actual conditions* of the automobile industry. ▶この写真ではあなたはありもよく写っている In this photo you look better than you *actually* [*really*] are./This photo flatters you.

【実際は】in fact, as a matter of fact; (実を言えば) to tell the truth; (現実は) actually (⇨実は); (本当のところは) really, in reality; (実質上は) virtually. ▶彼は医者と言ったが実際はそうでなかった He said he was a doctor, but *in fact* [*actually*] he was not. ▶実際は彼がその会社の社長だ He is *virtually* [*practically*] the president of the company./He is the *virtual* [*practical*] president of the company.

― **実際(の), 実際の** 圏 real; actual; (実地の) practical. ● 実際の価値 *real* [*actual*] value. ● 実際の費用 *actual* cost. ● 実際問題 a *practical* problem. ▶実際の見地から from the *practical* point of view. ● 実際のところ (⇨图 [実際は]) ▶この計画は実際問題としてうまくいかないだろう This plan won't work *in practice*./*Practically*, this plan won't work.

― **実際(に)** 圏 (現に) actually; (本当に) really; (真に) truly; (実際に) practically, in practice; (強意的に)〖indeed (⇨実に). ▶彼が実際に言ったこと what he *actually* [*really*] said. ▶私はこの目で実際に見た I *actually* saw it with my own eyes. ▶その事件は実際にあった The accident *really* [*actually*] happened. ▶彼はテニスがうまいそうだが, 実際にやっているところは見たことがない I hear he is a very good tennis player, but I've never seen him play (tennis). ▶君は実際軽率だった You were *really* [*truly*] thoughtless./That was very thoughtless of you, *indeed*. (❗ 前には通例 very ... と呼応してよく用いる) ▶実際彼は来たのだ He *did* come. (❗ この did は動詞 come を強調する助動詞) ▶アトランティス大陸は実際に存在した 'The Atlantis' *really* existed.
● 実際家 a practical person.

じつざい 実在 图 existence. ● 神の実在を信じる believe in (the existence of) God; believe that God really *exists*.

― **実在の** 圏 (本当に存在する) real (↔imaginary); (実際の, 現存の) actual; (人・物などが存在する) existent. ● 実在の人物 a *real* [an *actual*] person.

― **実在する** 動 exist. ● 実在しない non-existent; (現実のものでない) unreal; (想像上の) imaginary. ● 実在論 realism.

しっさく 失策 a mistake, an error. (⇨失敗, エラー)

*じっし **実施** 图 〖実行〗practice;〖法律などの〗enforcement;〖効力〗effect.

― **実施する** 動 ● 計画を実施する *carry out* a plan. (⇨実行する) ● 法律を実施する(=施行する) *put* a law *into effect* [*force*, *operation*]; *enforce* a law. ▶その調査は来月実施される(=行われる) The investigation will *be carried out* [*be conducted*] next month.

じっし 十指 ― **十指に余る** ▶彼は十指に余る特許を取った He got *more than ten* patents.
● 十指のさすところ ▶彼が偉大な政治家であることは十指のさすところだ *Everyone agrees* that he is one of the greatest statesmen.

じっし 実子 one's own child; a child of one's own.

じっし 実姉 one's own older [elder] sister.

しっしき 湿式 ― **湿式の** 圏 wet. (㊉ 乾式)

じっしつ 実質 图 substance. ▶私は外見よりも実質を選びたい I prefer *substance* to appearance.

― **実質的な** 圏 substantial. ● 実質的な援助 *substantial* help.

― **実質的に** 圏 substantially; in substance. ▶実質的には減税にならない There is [We have] no *substantial* tax reduction. ▶彼らの考えは実質的には同じだ Their opinions are *substantially* the same [the same *in substance*]. ▶それは(名目上はそうではないが)実質的には敗北だ It's a *virtual* defeat./It's *virtually* a defeat.
● 実質金利 a real interest rate. ● 実質所得 real (aftertax) income. ● 実質成長率 a real growth rate. ● 実質賃金 real wages.

しつじつごうけん 質実剛健 ▶我が校の校訓は質実剛健である Our school motto is *simplicity and sturdiness* [*fortitude*].

― **質実剛健な** 圏 simple and sturdy.

じっしゃ 実射 ― **実射する** 動 fire (live) shells.
● 実射訓練 rifle (shooting) [gun] practice with full charge.

じっしゃかい 実社会 the (real) world. ● 実社会に出る go [get] out into the *world*; get a start in *life*, start in *life*.

じっしゅう 実収 (⇨手取り)

じっしゅう 実習 图〖訓練〗(a) training;〖練習〗(a) practice;〖科目の〗a laboratory 《on》. ● 料理の実習を受ける have (practical) *training in* 《×of》 cooking. ● 教育実習をする practice teaching; do one's teaching *practice*; teach as a student teacher.

じっしゅきょうぎ 十種競技 the decathlon /dikǽθlən/.

しつじゅん 湿潤 ― **湿潤な** 圏 moist; humid; damp.
● 湿潤材 【化学】a wetting agent.

しっしょう 失笑 ● 失笑を禁じ得ない cannot help *laughing* 《at》.
● 失笑を買う be laughed at; meet with a contemptuous laugh.

じっしょう 実証 〖確証〗positive proof; proof positive. (⇨証拠, 証明) ▶...であることは実証済だ It *has been proved* that .... (⇨証明する)

― **実証的の** 圏 positive.

― **実証的に** 圏 positively.

― **実証主義**【哲学】positivism.

*じつじょう **実情** the actual situation [circumstances, conditions]; the real state of things [affairs]. (⇨現状) ▶実情をふまえる take the *actual situation* [*circumstances*] into account. ▶彼は事態は好転すると言っていたが, 実情では(=実のところ)むしろ悪化している He said things would go better, but *actually* [*as it is*] they are getting worse. (❗ actually は「意外だと思うだろうが実際は」の意)

しつしょく 失職 unemployment. (⇨失業)

しっしん 失神 a faint.

― **失神する** 動 faint; (意識を失う) lose conscious-

しっしん ness [one's senses], 《やや話》pass out. ● 失神している[倒れる] be [fall down] in a *faint*. ● ニュースを聞いて失神する *faint* at the news. ▶ 彼は彼女を殴って失神させた He knocked her *senseless* [《話》*cold*]./He *stunned* her with a blow.

しっしん 湿疹 a rash (❗種類をいう場合以外は単数形のみ); 〖医学〗eczema /éksəmə, égzə-/. ● 湿疹ができる〈人・体の部分が主語〉come [break] out in a *rash*; 〈人が主語〉have *eczema* [a *rash*] (*on the back*). ▶ 子供のころひどい湿疹ができたことがある I suffered from a bad case of *eczema* when I was a child.

じっしんほう 十進法 〖数学〗the decimal system. ● (図書の)十進分類法 the (Dewey) decimal classification. (❗《話》では the Dewey system とも) ● 十進法に切り変える go *decimal*. ● 十進法で on the *decimal system*.

じっすう 実数 〖数学〗a real (↔an imaginary) number.

しっする 失する ● 礼を失する be rude (*to him*); behave rudely (*toward him*). ● 遅きに失する (遅すぎる) be too late; (機会を逸する) miss the [one's] chance (*to do*).

しっせい 叱正 ▶ ご叱正を請う Will you please *correct* any errors *without reserve*?

しっせい 失政 misgovernment, misrule. ▶ 10年にわたる失政で国民が飢餓状態に追い込まれた A decade of *misgovernment* drove the people to starvation.

しっせい 執政 government; administration. ● 執政官 an administrator.

じっせいかつ 実生活 〖現実の生活〗real [actual] life, practical life. ● 実生活では in *real* [*practical*] *life*. ▶ 私が大学で学んだことは実生活ではほとんど役立っていない What I learned at the university has been of little *practical* use to me.

しっせいしょくぶつ 湿生植物 a hydrophyte.

しっせき 叱責 图 (a) scolding; a reprimand.
— 叱責する 動 reprimand, give (him) a reprimand; 〖書〗rebuke. ▶ 彼は上司から誤認逮捕したことを厳しく叱責された He *was* severely *reprimanded by* [*received a* severe *reprimand from*] his boss *for* arresting the wrong person.

しっせき 失跡 disappearance. (⇨失踪)

じっせき 実績 〖実際の成果〗an actual record; (a) performance; 〖業績〗an achievement; (これまでのすべてを網羅した) a track record. ● 過去の実績 past *performance*. ● 彼女の女優としての実績 her *achievements* as an actress. ▶ 仕事の実績が上がらなかった The work didn't give *actual results*./We didn't see any *concrete results* from the work. ▶ その予備校は大学入試合格率で高い実績がある The cram school has a strong *track record* in getting its students through college entrance exams.

しつぜつ 湿舌 〖気象〗moist tongue.

じっせん 実戦 actual fighting [battle]. ● 実戦の経験がある have experience in *actual fighting*. ▶ 演習は実戦を想定したものだった The exercise simulated *actual battle* condition.

じっせん 実践 图 practice. (⇨実行)
— 実践する 動 practice, put ... into practice. (❗後の方が口語的) ● 聖書の教えを実践する *practice* the teachings of the Bible.
● 実践躬行 Actions speak louder than words.

じっせん 実線 a solid line.

*しっそ 質素 图 simplicity, plainness.

— 質素な 形 (簡素な) simple; (飾り気のない) plain; (倹約する) frugal. ● 質素な服 a *plain* dress. ● パンとチーズの質素な食事 a *simple* [a *frugal*] meal of bread and cheese. ▶ 彼は質素な生活をしている He leads a *simple* [a *plain*, a *frugal*] *life*./He lives *simply* [*plainly*, *frugally*].

しっそう 失踪 图 disappearance.
— 失踪する 動 disappear (*from one's home*); (逃げる) run away; (行方不明になる) go missing. ▶ 彼が失踪して3日になる He's *been missing* for three days.
● 失踪者 a missing person; a runaway. ● 失踪宣告 a declaration of a missing person's death. ● 失踪届 a report of (*his*) *disappearance*.

しっそう 疾走 — 疾走する 動 run at high speed; speed. ▶ 高速道路を車が疾走していくのが見えた I saw cars *speeding* along the expressway 《米》[motorway 《英》].

じっそう 実相 the actual [true] state 《*of society*》. (⇨実情)

じつぞう 実像 〖光学〗a real image (❗「虚像」は a virtual image); 〖実態〗the actual conditions [circumstances]. (⇨実態)

しっそく 失速 图 a stall; (勢いを失う) lose momentum. ● 失速状態に陥る go into a *stall*; (勢いを失う) lose momentum.
— 失速する 動 stall.

じっそく 実測 图 a survey, measurement.
— 実測する 動 survey; measure.
● 実測図 a survey. ● 実測値 a measurement. (❗通例複数形で)

じつぞんしゅぎ 実存主義 图 〖哲学〗existentialism.
— 実存主義の 形 〖哲学〗èxisténtial; èxistentialist.
● 実存主義者 an existentialist.

しった 叱咤 — 叱咤する 動 〖しかる〗《やや書》rèprimánd; 〖激励する〗encourage. (⇨励ます, 激励) ● 叱咤激励する greatly [strongly] encourage (*him to do*); spur.

しったい 失対 〖「失業対策」の略〗(⇨失業)

しったい 失態 a blunder. ● 大失態を演じる make [commit] a terrible *blunder*.

*じったい 実態 the actual conditions [circumstances]; 〖現実の状態〗the real state of affairs [things]. ● 少年犯罪の実態を調べる investigate the *actual conditions* of juvenile delinquency. ● 実態は (= 現状は) as *things* are [*stand*]. (❗挿入句として) ▶ その宗教団体の実態は明らかでない Not much is known with any certainty about the religious body.
● 実態調査 actual condition survey; survey on actual situation; field study.

じったい 実体 〖哲学〗sùbstance; 〖内容〗content; 〖事実〗a fact. ● 実体のある (実在する) substántial (↔unsubstantial); 〖中身のある〗solid (↔hollow). ▶ 夢の実体についてはまだ多くのことが分かっていないままだ Many things are still unknown about dreams.

しったかぶり 知ったかぶり ● 知ったかぶりをする人 《話》《軽蔑的》a know(-it)-all. ● 知ったかぶりに話す talk *knowingly* [*in a knowing way*]. ▶ 彼は何でも[それについて]知ったかぶりをする He *pretends to know* all the answers [all about it].

じつだん 実弾 ❶〖弾丸〗live /láiv/ ammunition; (小銃・ピストルの) a bullet; (大砲の) a live [a loaded] shell. ● 実弾入りのピストル a *loaded* revolver.
❷〖金銭〗(現金) cash. ▶ この前の選挙戦では相当の

しっち 実弾が使われたそうだ It is said that there was a lot of *cash flow* in the last election.
● **実弾射撃** (小銃・ピストルの) live shooting; (大砲の) target practice with live shells. ● **実弾包** a ball (⇔blank) cartridge.

しっち 失地 ● 失地を回復する recover the *lost territory*.

しっち 湿地 damp ground; (低湿地) (a) swamp, (a) marsh. 🚨 marsh は swamp, bog (沼地)を含む広い湿地帯）
● **湿地帯** wetlands.

じっち 実地 practice. ● 実地に即した practical. ● 実地の経験 an *actual* [a *practical*] experience.
● **実地運転試験** (新車の) a road test; (運転免許取得のための) a driving skill test. ● **実地検証[調査]**をする make an *on-the-spot* investigation [survey]; (⇔現地) ● その理論を実地に応用する *put* the theory *into practice*.

しっちゃかめっちゃか a complete mess.

じっちゅうはっく 十中八九 ●十中八九これは本当だ This is *almost certainly* true./Very likely [Probably, 《話》Ten to one] this is true. 🚨 (1) most likely, quite likely も可だが、×Likely this is true. のように単独では文頭では用いない。(2) nine times out of ten は almost always (ほとんどいつでもの意で用いる)

しつちょう 室長 (事務所の) the head of an office; (実験室の) the head of a laboratory.

じっちょく 実直 ― 実直な 形 (良心的な) conscientious /kànʃiénʃəs/; (誠実な) sincere; (正直な) honest.

しっつい 失墜 名 loss.
― **失墜する** 動 lose. (⇔失う) ● 権威を失墜する lose one's dignity. ▶例のスキャンダルで彼の名誉は完全に失墜した His honor *was* completely *lost* by that scandal./(例のスキャンダルが彼の名誉を台無しにした) That scandal ruined his reputation.

じつづき 地続き ●うちの庭と公園とは地続きになっている Our garden *adjoins* /ədʒɔ́isnt/ *to*] the park. (⇔隣接) ●この辺の島はみな大陸と地続き(=大陸の一部)だったそうだ They say all these islands were *part of* the continent.

じって 十手 (説明的に) a short metal policeman's nightstick in the Edo period.

じってい 実弟 one's own [real] younger brother.

しつてき 質的 ― 質的な 形 qualitative. ▶この2台のコンピュータは質的にはほとんど差がない There is little *qualitative* difference [difference in *quality*] between these two computers.

しつてん 失点 ❶ [失した点数] a point lost in a game [a match]; [野球] a run allowed. ● 無失点に抑える (完封する) shut ... out; 《話》blank; whitewash. ● 無失点イニングを30に延ばす stretch one's scoreless streak to thirty innings.
❷ [失策] a mistake, (大きな) a blunder. ● 失点を重ねる make repeated *mistakes*.

*しっと 嫉妬 名 (a) jealousy /dʒéləsi/; envy. 🚨 envy は人の幸運・能力などを見て自分も持ちたいとうらやむ気持ち。jealousy はそれらが自分にないのは不当だとして相手を憎悪する気持ち） ● 嫉妬深い夫 a *jealous* husband. ● 彼の名声に対する激しい嫉妬 fierce *jealousy for* his fame. ● 嫉妬心から彼は *out of jealousy* [*envy*]. ● 嫉妬のあまり in a fit of *jealousy* [*envy*]. ● 嫉妬に燃える be consumed by *jealousy*. ● 嫉妬を覚える feel *jealousy* [*envy*].
― **嫉妬する** 動 ▶同僚たちは彼の異例の昇進に嫉妬していた His coworkers *were jealous of* his exceptional promotion./His coworkers *envied*

(him) his exceptional promotion.

*しつど 湿度 humidity. (⇔湿度) ● 湿度の高い気候 a *humid* [a *damp*] climate. 🚨 後の方はしばしば不快を暗示。a wet climate は「雨の多い気候」) ●日本の夏は暑くて湿度が高い Japan is very hot and *humid* in summer.
【会話】「湿度はいくらですか」「50パーセントです」"How high is the *humidity*?" "It's 50 percent."
● **湿度計** a hygrometer /haigrάmətɚ/.

*じっと ❶ [動かずに] still. ●彼はじっと座っていた He sat *still*. ●じっとしろ! Stand *still*!/(動くな) Don't move!/Freeze! ●最後の言い方は俗語で強盗などが言う言葉) ●バスを降りたら私が迎えに行くまでそこでじっと待っていてください When you get off the bus, please *stay put* till I come to pick you up. ● stay put は《話》「動かずに同じところにとどまっている」の意)

❷ [視点を定めて] ●じっと見る look *fixedly* [(注意を集中して) *intently*] (*at*); (感情をこめて、興味を持って) gaze (*at*); (好奇心で目を大きくして) stare (*at*); (動きに注意して) watch. ▶彼はその美しい人をじっと見た He *gazed at* the beautiful lady./(見とれて) He *drank in* the beautiful lady *with his eyes*. ▶人をじっと(=じろじろ)見るのは失礼だ It is rude to *stare at* someone. ▶あの男をじっと見張ってろ *Watch* that man.

❸ [辛抱して] patiently; (文句一つ言わずに) uncomplainingly. ▶彼はじっと順番を待っていた He was waiting *patiently* for his turn. ▶彼はその会社で30年間じっと働いてきた He has worked for the company *uncomplainingly* for thirty years.

❹ [その他の表現] ▶じっとしていたのでは問題は解決しない You can't solve the problem *by sitting and waiting* [(何もしないのでは) *by doing nothing*]. ▶じっと(=のらくら)してないで何かしなさい Don't *be idle* [*lazy*]. Do something useful. 🚨 idle は「することがなくて」、lazy は「やる気がなくて」ぶらぶらしている意)

しっとう 失投 名 [野球] a mistake.
― **失投する** 動 pitch an easy ball by mistake; make a mistake.

しっとう 執刀 ― 執刀する 動 óperàte 《*on*＋人, *for*＋病気》. ▶谷口先生が父の(胃がん)手術の執刀医(=執刀する医師)と決まった It was decided that Dr. Taniguchi would *operate* [*perform an operation*] *on* my father (*for* his stomach cancer).

じつどう 実働 ●実働8時間 《*work*》eight hours a day.
● **実働時間** actual working hours.

しつどくしょう 失読症 [医学] dyslexia.

しっとり ― **しっとりした** 形 ❶ [湿った] moist. ▶この花壇はしっとりしている This flower bed is *moist*. ▶このクリームをお使いいただくとお肌がしっとりしてきます If you continue to use this cream, you'll get beautiful, *moist* skin [your skin will *moisten*].

❷ [落ち着いた] calm, peaceful. ▶この町はどこかしっとりしている There is something *peaceful* about this town.

じっとり ― **じっとりした** 形 (湿っぽい) damp; (暑くてべとつく) sticky; (ぬれた) wet. ▶今日は暑し暑いぞ It's hot and *damp* [*sticky*, ×*wet*] today. 🚨 wet では雨天になる) ▶汗で手がじっとりしていた I felt my hands *damp* [*sticky*, *wet*] with sweat.

しつない 室内 the inside [interior] of a room. ●室内にいる stay *in a room* [屋内に] *indoors*].
● **室内楽** chamber music. ● **室内楽団** a chamber orchestra. ● **室内装飾** interior design [decora-

tion]. ● **室内装飾家** an interior designer [decorator]. ● **室内遊戯** an índoor game.

じつに 実に (本当に) really; (真に) truly; (非常に) very, very much; (まったく) quite; (極度に) extremely, (⇔非常に, 本当) ▶彼女は実にいい子だ She is a *really* nice girl. (❗ She is a *really* nice girl. さらに She *really* is a nice girl. のように really を前に移動させるほど意味が強くなる)/She is *very* nice (*indeed*). (❗ indeed はしばしば very＋形・副 の後で強調のためにつけ加えられる) ▶実に愉快だった I *really* enjoyed myself./I enjoyed myself *very much*. (❗ I *very much* enjoyed myself. ともいえる)/I had a *very* good [enjoyable] time. ▶それは実に不可解だ That's *quite* a [a *real*] mystery./It's *all very* puzzling. ▶実に困った I am *quite* at a loss. ▶実にくだらない What rubbish indeed! ▶この問題は実に難しい This problem is *extremely* [《すごく》 *terribly*, 《話》 *awfully*] hard./This problem is *much* [*far*, ×*too*] too difficult. ▶実におもしろい小説 How interesting this novel is!/This is *súch* an interesting novel. (❗ 後の方は女性に好まれる) ▶ローラースケートは実に楽しい It's *great* [a *lot of*, *such*] fun skating on the road. (❗ It is skating 以下を受ける形式主語)/What *fun* (it is) to skate on the road! ▶ロンドンで実に多くの日本人と出くわした I've seen a *great* [a *good*] many Japanese in London. (❗ great を用いる方が強意的. 不可算名詞が続く場合は a great [a good] deal of … となる)

【会話】「分からないよ」「そう？ 実に簡単なのよ」"I can't understand it." "Can't you? It's simple, *really*."

じつねん 失念 ― **失念する 動** (completely) forget. (⇔忘れる)

じつねん 実年 ― **実年の 形** mature; middle-aged. (⇔中高年)

じつの 実の (真の) true; (本当の) real; (現実の) actual. (⇔本当) ▶実の母親 (継母に対して) one's *true* [*real*] mother; (義母に対して) one's *own* mother. ▶実の子 one's *own* [*real*, *biological*] child. ▶口先ばかりで実のない(＝不誠実な)人 a plausible and insincere person. ▶実のところ to tell (you) the truth; in fact, as a matter of fact.

***じつは 実は** in fact, as a matter of fact; to tell (you) the truth; actually.

【使い分け】 **in fact, as a matter of fact** 前述の内容をさらに詳しく補って「もっとはっきり[具体的に]言えば」の意を表す場合や，聞き手の期待や予想に反することを自信を持って切り出す場合に用いる.

to tell (you) the truth 今まで黙っていたことや言いにくいことを伝えるときに「本当のことを言えば」の意で用いる.

actually as a matter of fact などと同様に期待や予想に反することを伝える際に用いるが，「意外だと思うかもしれないが」という気持ちのこもった丁寧な表現.

▶彼はネクタイをしていなかった. 実はネクタイを持っていないのだ He wasn't wearing a tie. *In fact* [*As a matter of fact*, 《そのわけは》《話》*The thing is*], he doesn't have a tie. ▶彼は宿題を自分でやったと言ったが, 実は彼のお姉さんがやったのだ He said he did his homework by himself, but *in fact* [*actually*, 《主に米》*really*], his sister did it (for him). ▶実は(＝実を言うと)私はあなたが怪しいと思っていたのです *To tell the truth* [《白状するけど》I must confess], I suspected you. (❗ ×If I tell the truth とはいわない)/*The truth* [*fact*] (*of the matter*) *is* (*that*) I suspected you. (❗ 《話》ではしばしば that を省略する. また, *The truth* [*The fact*, *Fact*] *is*, I …. ともいう) ▶実はね You know what [something]? (❗ 興味深い話などの前置き)/Let me explain.

【会話】「コーヒーでもどうですか」「実は今飲んだばかりなんです」"How about a cup of coffee?" "Well, *actually* [×*really*], I've just had a cup [×it]." (❗ Well, ＼really, は「あれまあ」など戸惑いや失望を表し, ここでは不適当)

【会話】「ツインの部屋を頼んでおられたことになっておりますが」「実はそうではなくてダブルの部屋を頼んだのです」"I see here you asked for twin beds." "(No), *actually* not. I asked for a double bed." (❗ この文脈では Not ＼really. (まさか)ともいえる)

ジッパー 《主に米》a zípper, 《主に英》a zip (fastener). (⇔チャック)

***しっぱい 失敗** ❶【目的が達成されないこと】(一般に) (a) failure 状態は ⓤ, 個々の事例は ⓒ; (ねらったものを取り逃がす[撃ちそこなう]こと) a miss. ▶彼は成功するまでに何度も失敗を重ねた He (had) had [met with, ×met] many *failures* before he succeeded. (❗ meet は人・物に用い, 事には用いない) ▶その作品は完全な失敗作だ The work is a complete *failure* [《話》*flop*]. ▶たとえ失敗でも全然やらないよりはまし Even *failure* is better than doing nothing at all. ▶そんな失敗くじけないでもう一度挑戦しなさい Don't let that *failure* discourage you from trying again. ▶(射撃で)最初の1発は失敗だった The first shot was a *miss*. ▶彼の研究生活は失敗の連続だった A succession of *failures* marked his life as a reseacher. (❗ of の後には複数名詞)

❷【誤り】a mistake, an error (⇒間違い); (愚かさ・不注意による大失敗) a blunder. ▶ひどい失敗をやらかす make a terrible *blunder*; blunder badly.

● **失敗は成功のもと** 《ことわざ》Failure is the highroad to success./Failure teaches success.

― **失敗する 動** fail, 〘物事がうまくいかない〙 go* wrong. ● バントを失敗する *fail* to bunt. ● 盗塁を失敗する be caught stealing. ● セーブを失敗する blow a save. ▶彼は試験に失敗した He *failed* the test./He *failed* to pass the test. (❗ (1) He didn't pass the test. の方が口語的. (2) failed *in passing* the test は避けた方がよい) ▶計画は失敗した The plan *failed* [*was a failure*]./(失敗に終わった) The plan ended in *failure*./The plan *fell through*.

じっぱひとからげ 十把一絡げ ● それらを十把一からげに(＝無差別に)扱う treat them *indiscriminately* [(価値のないものとして) as worthless]; (いっしょくたにする)《話》lump them together. ▶私たちをあんなテロ集団と十把一からげにするなんて, 冗談じゃないわ Do you *lump* us *with* that terrorist group? Don't be ridiculous.

しっぴ 失費 (needless) expenses; expenditure.

じっぴ 実否 ▶そのニュースの実否を確かめよう Let's find out the *truth* of the news [whether the information is *true or not*].

じっぴ 実費 〘実際にかかる費用〙actual expenses. ▶実費は負担しないといけない You must pay the *actual expenses*.

しっぴつ 執筆 名 writing.

― **執筆する 動** write 《an article *for* a magazine》.

● **執筆者** a writer; (寄稿者) a contributor.

しっぷ 湿布 ▶看護師は私の足に冷湿布をしてくれた The nurse *put* a cold *compress on* [*applied* a cold *compress to*] my leg.

● **湿布薬** a poultice.

じっぷ 実父 one's own [real] father.

しっぷう 疾風 a gale, a strong [a violent] wind; 〚気象〛a fresh breeze. (❗気象学ではこれよりはるかに強い風を「疾風」(a fresh gale) という) ●疾風迅雷のごとく like lightning [a whirlwind]; (as) quick as lightning [a flash]. ●疾風怒濤(ど)の時代 a *stormy* age; the age of 'Sturm und Drang /stùrm unt drɑ́ŋ/ (= storm and stress)'. (参考 ドイツのゲーテ・シラーなどを輩出した時代)

***じつぶつ** 実物 〚実際の物[人]〛the real thing [person]; 〚本物〛the genuine object; 〚美術の〛life. ●実物の花 a *real* flower. ●実物大の写真 a *life-size*(d) photograph; a photograph *as large as life*. ●この銅像は実物そっくりだ This bronze statue is quite *lifelike* [is true to *life*, looks just *like a real person*]. ●実物を見ないと何とも言えない I can't tell unless I see the *thing itself*.
●実物教育 an object lesson. ●実物取引 a cash [a spot] transaction.

しっぺい 疾病 a disease /dizíːz/. (⇨病気)

しっぺがえし しっぺ返し 〚仕返し〛〘話〙tit for tat; 《やや書》retaliation; 〚口答え〛a retort. ●彼にしっぺ返しをする give him *tit for tat*; *get even with* him; 《やや書》*retaliate against* him.

***しっぽ** 尻尾 a tail (⇨尾); 〚端〛the end. ●しっぽを振る wag a *tail*. ●その犬のしっぽは垂れ下がって[ふさふさして]いた The dog had a drooping [a furry] *tail*.
●しっぽを出す(本性を出す) show one's true colors.
●しっぽをつかまえる(過失を見つける) find 〈his〉fault; (うそ・不正などを見破る) catch 〈him〉out.
●しっぽを振る ●彼は上司にしっぽを振っている(こびへつらう) He *is fawning on* [〚おべっかを使う〛*flattering*] his boss.
●しっぽを巻く ●おびえた犬はしっぽを巻いて逃げた The frightened dog ran with its *tail* between its legs. (⇨人にも用いる)

じつぼ 実母 one's own [real] mother.

***しつぼう** 失望 图 〚期待はずれ〛disappointment; 〚落胆〛discouragement; 〚絶望〛despair, loss of hope; 〚失望させるもの・こと〛a disappointment, 《話》a letdown. ▶私は失望のどん底にあった[落ちた] I was [fell into] the depths of *despair*.
— **失望する** 動 〚希望や期待を裏切られる〛be disappointed 《with [at, about] +事, with [in] +人, about [at] doing》, feel* let down; 〚やる気や自信をなくす〛be discouraged 《at, by》; 〚希望を失う〛lose* (one's) hope(s).

解説 **(1)** disappointed と disappointing の違いに注意。「彼は失望した」は He *was disappointed*. と必ず受身にする。He *was disappointing*. とすると「彼は人を失望させるような人だった」という他動詞的な意味になる。discouraged と discouraging についても同様。**(2)** disappointed は discouraged より形容詞的性格が強く，(very) much のほかに very 単独でも修飾できる。

▶その結果[彼，レース敗退]には失望した I *was disappointed at* the result [*in* him; *about* losing the race]. ▶彼が試験に落ちたことを聞いて私は大変失望した I *was* very (much) [terribly, bitterly, deeply] *disappointed* (*to* hear) *that* he failed the test. ▶それは省略可. ややオーバーに I *could have wept* to hear…. (泣きたいくらいだ)ということも多い/His failure in the test very much *disappointed* me. ▶前の方より堅い言い方. 名詞形が用いて…was a great disappointment to me. のようにもいえる)/(私が大いに失望したことに) To my great *disappointment*, he failed the test. ▶彼は選ばれ

なくて失望した He *was disappointed* not *to* be chosen [*about* not being chosen]. ▶失望するな Don't *lose heart*./Don't *be disappointed* [*discouraged*]. ▶私を失望させないでくれ Don't *disappoint* me./Don't *let me down*. ▶そこにいい所ではありません. 行かれても失望されるだけでしょう It's not a good place. You'll go there only to *find disappointment*.

しっぽうやき 七宝焼 cloisonné /klɔ̀izənéi/.

しつぼく 質朴 ―質朴な 形 simple and gentle [mild].

じつまい 実妹 one's own [real] (younger) sister.

しつむ 執務 ●執務中である be at work; be at one's desk.
●執務時間 búsiness [óffice, wórking] hòurs.
●執務室 an office; (米国大統領の) the Oval Office.

じつむ 実務 business. ●実務経験が十分ある have enough *business* experience.
●実務家 a (good) businessman [businesswoman]. (❗通例修飾語を伴う)

じづめ 字詰め the number of characters on a page [in a line]. ●400字詰めの原稿用紙 manuscript paper for four hundred *characters*.

しつめい 失明 ―失明する 動 (視力を失う) lose one's sight [eyesight]; (盲目になる) go blind.
●左目を完全に失明している be completely [totally] *blind* in one's left eye. ●(…で)失明寸前である be very blind (with …).

じつめい 実名 one's real name.

***しつもん** 質問 图 a question /kwéstʃən/, (問い合わせ) 《やや書》(an) inquiry.
① 【質問～】 ▶大統領は記者の質問攻めにあった The President met with a rush [〘話〙a lot, lots] [〘書〙faced a barrage] of *questions* from reporters. (⇨【質問を浴びせる】)
② 【質問が】 ▶フロアから質問が出た A *question* was asked from the floor. ▶このクラスでは質問が多い Students ask many questions in this class. ▶何か(他に)質問がありますか (Do you have [Are there]) any (other) *questions*? (❗any の代わりに some を用いると，質問があることを期待する言い方)

会話 「ちょっと質問があるんですが」「はい，どうぞ」 "I have some *questions* (to ask you.)/Can I ask you something?" "Sure, go ahead." (❗この something は一種の丁寧語. 先生に生徒が質問するような場合はもっと率直に Can I ask you questions? といえばよい)

③ 【質問に】 ▶次の質問に答えなさい Answer the following *questions*.
④ 【質問を】 ●彼に質問をする ask him a *question*; put a *question* to him (❗改まった場面で用いる); 《まれ》ask a *question* of him. ●質問を提起する raise a *question*. ●質問を投げかける throw a *question* (at him). ●質問を浴びせる[ぶつける] shower [bombard, flood] ⟨him⟩ with *questions*. ●質問を受け流す[そらす] turn a *question* aside; evade [〘書〙parry] a *question*. ●質問を受ける be asked; be questioned. ●質問を続ける keep asking *questions*. ●質問を変える change *questions*.

— **質問する** 動 ask ⟨him⟩ a question; question (❗連続的に一連の質問をする); ask, 《やや書》inquire. (⇨尋ねる) ●矢つぎ早に質問する shoot [fire] *questions* (at him). ▶両親は私にいろいろ質問した My parents *asked* [×made] me a lot of *questions*./My parents *asked* [*questioned*] me [×to

しつよう

me) *about* a lot of things. ▶その中の1人が手をあげて堤防は決壊するでしょうかと質問した One of them put his hand up and *asked* if the banks of the river would ever break.
● **質問者** a questioner. ● **質問書** a written inquiry; (アンケート) a questionnaire /kwèstʃənéər/.

しつよう 執拗 ── **執拗な** 形 (しつこい) persistent.
● しつように説明を求める demand an explanation *persistently*.

*__**じつよう 実用**__ 名 practical use.
── **実用的な** 形 ▶これは実用的だ This is *useful* [*of practical use*]./(実用向きに作られている) This is designed for *practical use* [*purposes*]. ▶この本は理論的というよりむしろ実用的だ This book is *practical* rather than theoretical.
── **実用化する** 動 put (it) to practical use; put (it) into practice.
● **実用英語** (実際の役に立つ英語) practical English. ● **実用主義** pragmatism. ● **実用書** a how-to book. ● **実用新案** a utility model. ● **実用品** a useful article; (日用品) daily necessities.

じづら 字面 the appearance of written words.
● 字面を追う follow words. ▶字面がよい[悪い] The appearance of the written words is good [bad].

しつらえる 設える [[準備する]] prepare; [[設備する]] equip.

じつり 実利 (実際の利益) an actual profit. ● 実利を重んじる(=利益を優先する) give priority to *profits*.

しつりょう 室料 the room rent; the rent for a room.

しつりょう 質量 [[物理]] mass. ● その物体の質量 the *mass* of the body.
● **質量数** mass number. ● **質量保存の法則** the law of conservation of mass.

*__**じつりょく 実力**__ ❶ [[能力]] one's ability [power]; [[功績]] merit(s).
①【実力が[の]】● 実力のある able; capable; competent. ● 英語の実力がある[ない] have a good [a poor] command of English; be proficient [poor] in English. ▶彼はいちばん実力のある生徒だ He is the most *able* of our students.
②【実力に】● あの会社は実力に応じた給料を出している Every employee in that firm gets his salary according to his *ability* [*on* his (*own*) *merits*].
③【実力を】● 実力を発揮する show [display] one's *ability*. ● 実力を示す prove oneself to be really capable. ● 実力を認める recognize (his) ability. ● 英語の実力を養う develop one's *ability in* English. ▶肩書きよりも実力を重んじる value *ability* above [beyond] titles.
④【実力で】▶彼は実力でその大学に入った He got into the university through *ability*.
❷ [[武力]] arms; [[暴力]] force. ● 実力を行使する use *force*; (武力に訴える) appeal to *arms*; (ストライキをする) go on *strike*.
● **実力行使** use of force; (ストライキ) a strike. ● **実力者** (政界などの) an influential [a powerful] person; (陰の実力者) a power behind the throne. ● **実力主義** (任用・昇進制度の) the merit system; (成績第一主義) (a) meritocracy /mèritákrəsi/. ● **実力テスト** an academic ability test.

*__**しつれい 失礼**__ 名 ❶ [[無礼]] rudeness; impoliteness. (⇨形)
❷ [[謝罪, 断り]] ▶失礼ですが[します, しました] Excúse me./(I bég your) párdon./Párdon me./(I'm)

しつれん

sórry. (❗( )内を省略するのはくだけた言い方) (⇨すみません)

解説 Excúse me は(ⅰ)知らない人に話しかけたり頼んだりする, (ⅱ) 人の体に触れたり足を踏んで謝る, (ⅲ)人の前や間を通る, (ⅳ)せき払いやくしゃみをして謝る, (ⅴ)座を外す, (ⅵ)異議を唱えたり発言を訂正する場合などに用いる軽い断りやわびの表現. (I beg your) pardon, Pardon me. はより丁寧な堅い言い方で, 主に(ⅱ)(ⅳ)(ⅵ)の場合に用いるのは《米》. 上昇調で言うと「失礼ですがもう一度言ってください」の意だが,《米》では Excúse me? (↗),《主に英》では Sórry? (↗) なども用いられる. (I'm) sorry. は以上の表現より謝罪の意が強く, 自分の非をはっきりと認める言い方. 人の体に触れたときなど《英》では (I'm) sorry. と言う方が普通.

▶ちょっと失礼します(=中座させてください) Excuse me (for) a moment. (❗目上の人には Would you excuse ...? や May I be excused...? のように言う方が丁寧で適切) ● お話し中失礼します Excuse [Pardon, Forgive] me *for* interrupting you. (❗(1)《話》では Excuse me の後の for は省略されることもある. (2) Excuse my interrupting you. は《まれ》) ▶こんな時間にお電話をして失礼ではなかったでしょうか I hope I'm *not* calling you up at a bad time. ▶これで失礼します I think I must be going now. (❗職場などで先に帰る場合も, 単に I'm going. で十分で, 日本語的に Sorry to leave ahead of you. (お先に失礼します) のようには普通いわない) ▶失礼ですがどちら様ですか May I have your name, please?/(電話で) May I ask who's calling?/(電話で) Who is this [《英》that], please? (❗最後はややくだけた言い方)

会話「大変長くお待たせして失礼しました」「いいえ, そんなに待っていません」"*I'm sorry* I have [*I'm sorry to* have] kept you waiting so long." "No, it's not too long."

── **失礼な** 形 rude (❗人の気持ちを無視し粗野で厚かましい); impolite (❗礼儀や丁寧さに欠ける); impertinent (❗目上や尊敬すべき人に対して無作法な). (⇨無礼) ● 失礼な男 a *rude* [an *impolite*] man. ● 失礼なことを言う say *rude* things; make a *rude* [an *impolite*, an *impertinent*] remark. ▶先生に対してそんな失礼なことを言うな[するな] Don't be so *rude to* your teacher. ▶人を指さすなんてあなた失礼ですよ It's *rude* [*impolite*] *of* you *to* point at people./You're (being) *rude* [*impolite*] *to* point at people. (❗being は一時的状態を表す) ▶失礼な! ✓Sorry!/Excuse ↗me! (❗名 ❷ の謝罪の場合と音調の違いに注意)

会話「それはお送りいたします」「もし失礼でなければ, それはいつごろになりますか」"I'll send it to you." "Just when, if that isn't a *rude* [an *impertinent*] question?" (❗..., if I may ask?/if you don't mind me asking? の方が普通)

じつれい 実例 [[代表的な]] an example; [[個別的な]] an instance; [[説明のための]] an illustration. (⇨例) ● 実例をいくつかあげる give some *examples* [some *instances*].

しつれん 失恋 名 disappointed [lost] love; [[失意]] a broken heart.
── **失恋する** 動 ● 失恋した男 a *broken-hearted* man. ▶彼女は失恋した She *failed* [*was disappointed*] *in love*. (❗was disappointed は「(恋に)失望した」の意) ▶まったく人を愛したことがないよりは愛して失恋したことがある方がよい It's better to *have loved and lost* rather than never to have loved at all.

じつろく 実録 a true [a documentary, a factual] record.
- **実録物** an entertaining fictional novel based on historical facts (written mainly in the Edo period).

じつわ 実話 a true story. ▶実話をもとにした映画 a film (that [which] is) based on a *true story*.

して 仕手 (能の) the protagonist, the leading part [role];【株式】a speculator, an operator.
- **仕手株**【株式】a speculative stock. ● **仕手相場** a speculative market.

して 四手〖植物〗a hornbeam.

してい 指定 图 appointment;《書》specification;《書》designation. ● 学校指定の本屋 a bookstore *designated* by the school. ● そこへ指定の時間に行く go there at the *appointed* time.
── **指定する** 動〚日時・場所を〛《書》appoint;〚特定する〛specify;〚明確に示す〛《書》designate. (⇨指名する) ▶面接の日時と場所を指定する *appoint* [*specify*, *designate*] the time and place for an interview. ▶その地域は国立公園に指定された That area *was designated* (*as*) a national park.
- **指定席** a reserved seat 《*in a train*》. ● **指定都市** a designated city. ● **指定銘柄**【株式】specified stocks.

してい 子弟 children. ▶良家の子弟 *children* of a good family.

してい 私邸 one's (private) house [《書》residence].

してい 師弟 ▶彼らは師弟の関係です They are *teacher and student* [《主に英》*master and pupil*].(❗いずれも冠詞はつけない)

じてい 自邸 one's (private) residence.

シティー〖(都)市〗a city.
- **シティーホテル**〖都心のホテル〗a hotel in the center of the city.(❗a city hotel とはいわない)

-(し)ていた (⇨-(し)ている)

INDEX
❶ 過去に進行中の行為・できごと
❷ 過去の状態
❸ 過去の習慣・行為の繰り返し
❹ 現在まで継続されていた行為・できごと・状態
❺ 過去のある時点以前の行為・できごと・状態
❻ 未来のある時点での完了
❼ 現在の事実に反する仮定
❽ 過去の事実に反する仮定
❾ 丁寧な依頼   ❿ 名詞を修飾

❶ **[過去に進行中の行為・できごと]**〚過去進行形で〛was [were]《*doing*》.

解説 Ⅰ 過去のある時点を基準として、その時点より前に始まり、その時点以後も続いたと思われる行為やできごとを表すときには、英語では過去進行形を用いる.行為やできごとの始点と終点には関心を払わない言い方.

▶1時ころにはまだ昼食を食べていた About one o'clock I *was* still *having* lunch.(❗(1) 行為・状況の期間がないことを強調するときは still を添える.(⇨まだ [類語])(2) 単純過去形を用いて About one o'clock I had lunch. では「1時ころに昼食を食べ始めた」ことを表す) ▶秀雄は一晩中[その時]本を読んでいた Hideo *was reading* all night [then, at that time].(❗しばしば all night, all day (long), all yesterday, all the afternoon など all … で始まる語句を伴って継続を強調する) ▶妻は部屋で仕事をしていて、私は台所で夕食をつくっていた My wife *was working* in her room while I *was cooking* dinner in the kitchen.(❗while 節と進行形で同時進行を強調)

解説 Ⅱ 「...ていた」は英語では過去進行形?
「...ていた」は必ずしも過去進行形を用いるとは限らず、表現したい内容やいっしょに使う副詞句等を考慮する必要がある.「さっきまで雨が降っていた」は It *was raining* a little while ago [×until a little while ago].(少し前の時点では雨が降っていた)で表せるが、これだけの文では雨が降っているかどうかは不明.現在やんでいることをはっきりさせたい場合は、… but it has stopped now. を添えるか、代わりに It rained until a little while ago.(少し前までは雨が降っていた)/It has just stopped raining.(ちょうど今雨がやんだところだ)/It stopped raining a little while ago./《米》It just stopped raining (a little while ago).(少し前に雨がやんだ)などといえばよい.

❷ **[過去の状態]**〚過去時制の状態動詞を用いて〛《*did*》.

解説 過去の状態を表すには、過去時制の「be＋形」、「be＋過去分詞」をはじめ、一般に状態動詞と呼ばれる動詞を使うことで表すことができる.状態動詞は通例進行形では用いられない.

▶健太郎は一晩中起きていた Kentaro *was* [*stayed*] awake all night. ▶彼はずっと黙っていた He *kept* [*remained*, *stayed*] silent.(❗keep は「変化しないで黙っている状態を保ち続ける」ことをいうが、remain は「故意にずっと黙っている」か「相変わらず黙っている」のあいまい.stay は「ある理由のために故意に黙っている」こと) ▶見ると彼はぐっすり眠っていた(＝彼がぐっすり眠っているのを発見した) I *found* him fast asleep. ▶彼らはドアを開けっ放しにしていた They *kept* [*left*] the door open.(❗(1) keep [leave]＋目的語＋補語の構文.open は形容詞. (2) keep は「意図的に...しておく」, leave は「...の状態に放置しておく」に意味の重点がある) ▶ロンドンで暮らしていたころ長男が生まれた We *lived* in London when our first son was born.(❗… were living と進行形にすると「たまたま [一時的に]暮らしていた」の意となる (⇨-(し)ている ❷ **(b)**))

会話「佐藤さんが会社を辞めたことを知っていましたか」「もちろん、知っていましたよ」"*Did* you *know* that Mr. Sato quit the company?" "Of course, I *knew* that."(❗このような場合 Did you know …? は実質的に Do you know …? に近くなるので、"… I know that." のように単純現在形で答えることもある)

❸ **[過去の習慣・行為の繰り返し]** (a) **[過去時制で]**《*did*》.

解説 過去にある一定期間続いた状態・習慣や繰り返された行為を表すには単純過去時制を用いる.

▶私は毎朝5時に起きていた I *got* up at 5 o'clock every morning.(❗副詞句 every morning によって過去の習慣を表すことが明確になる.単なる過去の事実を表す I got up at 5 o'clock this morning.(私は今朝5時に起きた)と比較)

(b) **[過去進行形で]** was [were]《*doing*》.(❗驚くほどの頻度で起きていることを強調する (⇨-(し)ている ❹ **(b)** 解説)) ▶彼女は人の悪口ばかり言っていた She *was* always *saying* bad things about other people.

❹ **[現在まで継続されていた行為・できごと・状態]**〚現在完了(進行)形で〛have* (*been doing*); have 《*done*》. (⇨-(し)ている ❶ **(b)**)) ▶午前中ずっと眠っていました I've *been sleeping* [I've *slept*] all morning. ▶これまでずっと英語は難しいものと考えていました I've

−(し)ている

always *thought* that English is difficult.
❺【過去のある時点以前の行為・できごと・状態】〖過去完了(進行)形で〗had (done). (❹過去におこる二つの行為・できごと・状態のうち，古い方を過去完了形で表すことによって両者の前後関係をはっきりさせる (⇨−た))
▶私が真夜中に電話したときには，彼女はすでに家を出ていた Mami *had* already *left* her home when I called her. (❹ I called Mami after she (*had*) *left* her home./Mami (*had*) *left* her home before I called her. などでもほぼ同じ内容を表すことができるが，接続詞の after や before によって二つの出来事の前後関係が明らかなので過去完了形の代わりに過去形ですますことが多い)
▶私は疲れていた．ずっと部屋で勉強をしていたからだ I was tired. I *had been studying* [*had studied*] in my room. (⇨−(し)ている ❶ (b))
▶太郎はその年弁護士になった．東京へ出てきて10年がたっていた Taro *became* a lawyer in that year. He *had been* in Tokyo for 10 years.
❻【未来のある時点での完了】〖未来完了(進行)形で〗will have (done); will have been (doing).
▶今度の10月で6年間ここで働いていたことになる By next October I'*ll have worked* [*been working*] here for six years. (⇨−(し)ている ❶ (b))
❼【現在の事実に反する仮定】〖仮定法過去で〗(did). (⇨−しる ❷)
▶その本を持っていたら君に貸してあげるのだが If I *had* that book, I *would* lend it to you.
❽【過去の事実に反する仮定】〖仮定法過去完了形で〗had (done). (⇨しる ❸)
▶あと10分早く来ていたら間に合ったのに If you *had come* ten minutes earlier, you *would have been* in time.
▶もしあの飛行機に乗っていたら，今はみんな死んでいたね If we *had taken* that plane, all of us *would be* dead now. (❹前半は過去のことに触れているので仮定法過去完了形，後半は現在のことに触れているので would have done ではなく would do の形が使われていることに注意)
❾【丁寧な依頼】〖過去進行形で〗was [were] (doing).

解説 (1) 英語は過去形でも現在の文脈で，主に wonder, hope, think などの動詞とともに用いる．(2) この用法では，進行形が不完結を暗示して主語である話し手の「まだはっきりそう思っているわけではない」といったためらいの気持ちを表し，さらに過去形にすることによって現在との関係を断ち切って，「以前はそう思っていた(が今は違う)」というふうに最終的決定は聞き手の自由に任せる態度を示して丁寧な表現となっている．

▶あなたにお手伝いいただければと思っていたのですが I *was wondering* if you could help me. (❹(1) 最も丁寧な言い方．ほかに，丁寧な順に I'*m wondering* if you could help me./I *wondered* if you could help me. ともいう．(2) I *wonder* if you could help me. では聞き手が断わる余地がない)
❿【名詞を修飾】(a)【現在分詞で】(doing). (⇨−(し)ている ❸ (a))
▶私の前に座っていた人はずっとたばこを吸っていた The man (who was) *sitting* in front of me was smoking all the time.
(b)【その他の修飾節】▶その物音にぎょっとして，捕えていた鶏を放してしまった〖前置詞, 関係詞節〗I was startled by the sound and let go off the chicken *in* my hands (*that*) I had caught, (米)(*that*) I caught, × (that) I was catching. (❹(1) 目的格の関係代名詞は通例省略される．(2) catch は瞬間的動作を表す動詞なので，進行形は「(まさに)捕まえようとしていた」の意となる．ただし目的語が複数の文脈では反復を表す: I was catching chickens and putting them back in the henhouse. (次々に鶏を捕まえて鶏小屋に入れていった))

---

*−(し)ている
INDEX

❶ 進行中の行為・出来事
❷ 状態
❸ 名詞を修飾
❹ 習慣的行為
❺ 完了・結果
❻ 観察・意見
❼ 伝聞
❽ 丁寧な依頼
❾ 現在の事実に反する仮定
❿ 過去の事実に反する仮定
⓫ 経験
⓬ 過去の事実

❶【進行中の行為・出来事】(a)【現在進行形で】is [am, are]《doing》.

解説 Ⅰ 話し手が話しているときに進行途中の行為やできごとを表すときには，英語では現在進行形を用いる．話し手は問題となっている行為・できごとについて，「まだ終わっていない」とか「途中でありまだ続く」といったとらえ方をしている．

▶勉強しているときは話しかけないでください Don't talk to me when I'*m studying*. (❹ このように進行中の行為 (I'm studying) は話している時点に限定されないこともある)
▶秀雄がベッドの上で飛び跳ねている Hideo *is jumping* on the bed. (❹ hit, jump, kick, nod などの瞬間的動作を表す動詞を現在進行形で用いると，同じ動作が繰り返されていることを表す)
会話「何をしているの」「宿題をしているところなんだ」"What *are* you *doing*?" "I'*m* (just) *doing* my homework." (❹ (1) 現在進行形は文字どおりそのその行為をしている最中でなくて，ちょっと休憩しているときにも用いる．(2)「いま，まさに，ちょうど[…の最中[しているところ]である]」の意を強調したいときは，just, now, at the moment などを添える (⇨今 ❶))
会話「雨はまだ降っていますか」「いいえ，もう降っていません」"*Is* it still *raining*?" "No, it's not *raining* now." (❹ (1) 行為・状況の期間が長いことを強調するときは still を添える (⇨まだ[類語])．(2) 答え の部分は No, it (has) stopped raining now. (もう降りやんだ)ともいえる)

解説 Ⅱ 「…している」は英語では現在進行形？
「…している」という現在進行形をすぐ思い浮かべるかもしれないが，現在進行形は本来「…する途中である」「…しかかっている」の意を表す「現在途中形」とでもいうべきもの．特に状態の変化を表す arrive, become, die, fall, get, go, leave, stop などの動詞では，He'*s arriving* [*coming*; *going*; *leaving*] soon. (彼はもうすぐ到着します[来ます; 出かけます])/The bird *is dying*. (その鳥は死にそうだ)/It'*s getting* [*becoming*] *warmer*. (だんだん暖かくなってきた)などのように，必ずしも日本語の「…している」とは一致しないことに注意．(⇨❷ (a) [第2文例])

(b)【現在完了(進行)形で】have* been《doing》; have《done》.

解説 Ⅲ 過去のある時点に始まった状態・行為が現在まで続いていることを表すには英語では現在完了(進行)形を使う．通例，状態動詞及び継続的行為を表す動詞 (expect, hope, keep, learn, lie, live, play, rain, sit, sleep, snow, stand, stay, study, teach, wait, want, work など)とともに用いられる．現在完了進行形ではしばしば，現在完了形では通例，for 句や since 句[節]など，期間を表す副詞相当語句を伴う．

▶2月からここに来ています I'*ve been* (*staying*) here since February.
▶私は彼女を子供のころから知っている I *have known* [×have been knowing] her since she was a child. (❹ know は状態動詞なので

―(し)ている

進行形不可）▶私は3年間英語を勉強しています I've been studying English for three years. (❢話している時点でまだ勉強の途中でこれからも勉強し続けることを暗示する場合にも, 勉強が少し前に完結しその余韻がまだ現在残っている場合にも用いる)/I've studied English for three years. (❢まだ勉強を続けているかはともかくこれまで3年間勉強してきたことを表す)

解説 IV (1) **現在完了進行形と現在完了形の違い**: 継続的行為を表す動詞の場合, 現在完了進行形と現在完了形ははぼ同じ意味で用いられ交換可能なことが多いが, 現在完了進行形の方がより継続性を強調する. 現に日常会話では lie, sit, stay, wait など通例あまり長くない継続動作を表す動詞の場合, 現在完了進行形の方が好まれる.
(2) **単純過去時制との違い**: 単純過去時制を用いた I studied English for three years. は不特定な過去の3年間, 勉強をしたことを伝える言い方で, その終了時点と話している時点との時間的隔たりが感じられる場合に用いる.

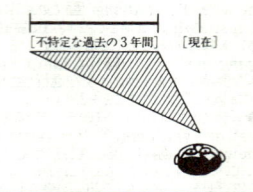

[不特定な過去の3年間] [現在]

(c) **[未来進行形で]** will be 《doing》. ▶明日の今ごろは我々は何をしているかな I wonder what we'll be doing about this time tomorrow.
(d) **[過去進行形で]** was [were] 《doing》. ▶太郎は私が電話をかけているときに新聞を読んでいた Taro was reading a newspaper while I was talking on the phone. (❢英語では時制の一致で過去進行形となる. while は同時進行を強調)
❷ **[状態]** (a) **[現在時制の状態動詞を用いて]** 《do》.

解説 I 現在の状態を表すには, 現在時制の「be＋形」,「be＋過去分詞」をはじめ, 一般に状態動詞と呼ばれる動詞を使うことで表すことができる. 状態動詞は通例進行形では用いられない.

▶戸が開いて[閉まって]いる The door is open [is closed, is shut]. (❢ The door is opening [is closing,《まれ》is shutting]. は「開いて[閉まって]いる状態」ではなく「開き[閉まり]つつある」の意)/救急車が学校の前に止まっている An ambulance is [is parked] in front of the school. (❢《米》is standing 〈一時停車している〉ともいえるが, is stopping は「〈速度を落として〉止まりかけている」の意となるので不可 (⇨❶ **解説** I))/あの建物は角に立っている The building stands [×is standing] at the corner. (❢主語が移動可能なものでは, 進行形も可. その場合, 一時的動作を表す (⇨[第2文例])) ▶彼女は和服がとても似合っている She looks very nice in the kimono. (❢和服一般をさす「彼女は和服がとても似合う」(She looks very nice in kimonos.) と異なり, 特定の和服をさすので, 日本語に着物を特定する語がなくても, 英語では the のような限定詞が必要)/The kimono looks very nice on her.
(b) **[現在進行形の状態動詞を用いて]** be 《doing》.

解説 II いつもとは違った一時的な行為や状況, 一時的な傾向に表すには現在進行形を用いる. 一般に状態動詞は進行形にはできないが, この用法では使用可.

▶まゆ子, なぜめがねをかけていないの Why aren't you wearing glasses, Mayuko? (❢現在形を使った Mayuko wears glasses. (まゆ子は《習慣的に》めがねをかけている)と比較) ▶今日は君は頭がさえているね You are being very clever today. (❢ You are very clever. は主語の永久的性質を表すが, 進行形を用いると「さえたことをする[言う]」の意で一時的性質を表す. 同様の進行形が可能な形容詞: careful, foolish, formal, funny, generous, mean, polite, stupid, wise など)
(c) **[知覚動詞]** ▶サイレンの音が聞こえていますか Do you hear [×Are you hearing] the sound of the sirens? ▶私は真由美が家を出て行くのに気がついていた I noticed [×was noticing] Mayumi leave the house.

解説 see, hear, smell, observe, feel, taste, notice などの知覚動詞は通例進行形にしない.

❸ **[名詞を修飾]** (a) **[現在分詞で]** 《doing》.

解説 (1)「眠っている赤ん坊」のように「…している」が名詞を修飾する場合, 動詞の現在分詞形を用いる: a sleeping baby. (❢ sleeping car (寝台車)のように「…のための」の意で用いられる動名詞と比較)「私の隣に眠っている赤ん坊」のように現在分詞の部分がさらに修飾語を伴う場合は現在分詞を名詞の後に置く: a baby sleeping next to me.
(2) この用法の現在分詞は通例進行形では用いられない consist, expect, hope, want, wish などの動詞でも使用可 (❢ like を除く): 我々は10人のメンバーからなっている委員会を作った We set up a committee consisting of ten members.

(b) **[その他の修飾語句]** ▶大金の入っている財布をなくした **[前置詞]** I've lost my wallet with a lot of money in it. ▶あのひょろっとしている若者はだれですか **[形容詞]** Who's that thin young man? ▶彼が書類を入れている金庫は2階にある **[関係詞節]** The safe (that) he keeps his papers in is upstairs. (❢目的格の関係代名詞は通例省略する. that のけわりに which も可能だが堅い言い方)/《書》The safe in which he keeps his papers is upstairs. (❢ which は省略不可)

❹ **[習慣的行為]** (a) **[現在時制で]** 《do》.

解説 I 現在を含み, ある一定期間続くと思われる習慣・繰り返される行為や事柄を表すには単純現在時制を用いる. しばしば every day, always, often, usually などの頻度を表す副詞(句)を伴う.

▶おじは農業をやっている My uncle runs [keeps] a farm. (❢ My uncle is running [keeping] a farm. は一時的に農業をやっていることを表す (⇨❷(b)))/My uncle is a farmer. ▶彼は毎日バスで大学に通っている He goes to college by bus every day. (❢ He is going to college by bus now. (今はバスで大学に通っている)は, 限られた期間で反復される活動を表す (⇨❷(b))) ▶淀川は琵琶湖に端を発し, 大阪湾に流れ込んでいる The Yodo River rises in Lake Biwa and flows into Osaka Bay.
(b) **[現在進行形で]** be 《doing》.

解説 II 継続的に繰り返される行為を表すのに, 単純現在時制 (⇨(a)) と比べて驚くほどの頻度で起きていることや偶然繰り返されていることを強調する場合, 英語では現在進行形を使う. hear, think などの一部の状態動詞も進行形で用いられる. 通例 always, constantly, continually, forever, perpetually, repeatedly などの副詞を伴い, しつこさに対するいらだちや非難の気持ちを表す表現となることが多い.

▶君は勉強もしないでいつもテレビばかり見ているね You *are* always *watching* TV without studying.

❺【完了・結果】

解説 行為や出来事が, 現在(⇨(a))や将来(⇨(b))や過去(⇨(c))のある時点で完了していることや, さらにその時点とそれ以前においても何らかの結果を残していることを表すには英語では完了形を使う. 通例動作動詞とともに用いる. また, 行為やできごとが完了したことを明確にするために, just (⇨今 ❷), already (⇨もう 解説), still, yet [類語] などの語句をしばしば伴う.

(a)【現在完了形で】have 《done》. ▶彼ならもう帰ってきている He *has* already *come* back. (❗状態を表す be 動詞を使って He *is* back already. ともいえる (⇨❷ (a))) ▶彼女は宿題をまだすませていない She hasn't *finished* her homework yet./She still hasn't [*has* still not] *finished* her homework. (❗still は常に否定語より前に置く)/《書》She *has* not yet *finished* her homework.
(b)【未来完了形で】will have 《done》. ▶8時までにはそこへ着いているよ I'*ll have gotten* there by eight o'clock./I'll be there by eight o'clock.
(c)【過去完了形で】had 《done》. ▶彼女はそのことならずに美和に話しているよと言った She said that she *had* already *told* it to Miwa.

❻【観察・意見】【現在時制で】《do》. (❗話者の観察や意見を表す think, hope, suppose, understand, see, hear, smell, love, hate などの状態動詞とともに) ▶彼は無罪だと思っています I *think* [*dó think*] (that) he is innocent. (❗後の方が強意的. I'm thinking ... では「...と思うようになってきた」の意. ただし「...しようかと思っている」の意では I'm thinking of doing .... のように進行形となる (⇨思う ❸, つもり ❶ ③))

❼【伝聞】【現在時制で】《do》. (❗最近聞いた内容を伝える hear, learn, say, tell などの動詞とともに) ▶天気予報は明日は曇りだと言っている The weather forecast *says* it will be cloudy tomorrow.

❽【丁寧な依頼】【現在進行形で】be 《do*ing*》. (❗主に「...と思っているのですが」の意で wonder, hope, think などの動詞とともに用いる (⇨(し)ていた ❾ 解説) ▶明日ここへ来ていただければと思っているのですが I'*m hoping* you will come over here tomorrow.

❾【現在の事実に反する仮定】【仮定法過去形で】《did》. (⇨もし ❷) ▶彼の住所を知っているのなら教えてあげるのですが If I *knew* his address, I would tell (it to) you. ▶君が富山に住んでいればなあ I wish you *lived* in Toyama.

❿【過去の事実に反する仮定】【仮定法過去完了形で】had 《done》. (⇨もし ❸) ▶あのときその本を買っていればなあ I wish I *had bought* the book at that time. ▶I am sorry I didn't buy the book at that time. や, より強意的には If only I *had bought* [If I *had* only *bought*] the book at that time! (♥) でも表現可

⓫【経験】【現在完了形で】have* 《done》. (⇨こと ❽) ▶彼はこれまでに何度か私に会いにここへ来ている He *has been* [×*has* seen] here to see me several times. (❗ever は通例肯定文では用いない (⇨これで ❶)

⓬【過去の事実】【過去時制で】《did》. ▶その殺人犯は午後10時ごろ実家に立ち寄っている That murderer *dropped* in at his parents' house about 10:00 p.m.

しでかす 仕出かす (go and) do. (⇨やらかす) ▶とんだことをしでかしてくれたものだ You'*ve gone and done* it now. (❗ have gone and done は《話》で「そんなばかなことをしたのか」という話者の驚きを表す) ▶あの(男の)子は何をしでかすか分からない We never know what the boy will (*go and*) *do* next.

* **してき** 指摘 ── 指摘する 動 point ... out; show; 《書》indicate. ● 彼の誤りを指摘する *point out* his mistakes; *point out that* he made mistakes [he is wrong].

してき 史的 ── 史的な 形 histórical. (⇨歴史的な)
● 史的唯物論 *historical* [×*historic*] materialism.

してき 私的 ── 私的な 形 (公に対して) private; (個人に関する) personal. (⇨個人的) ● 私的なこと *private affairs*; *personal* matters.

してき 詩的 ── 詩的な 形 poetic /pouétik/, poétical. ● 詩的な描写 a *poetic* description.
── 詩的に 副 poetically.

-してしまう (⇨-しまう)

* **してつ** 私鉄《米》a private railroad;《英》a private railway.

しでのたび 死出の旅 ● 死出の旅に出る go to the next world; depart this world.

しでのやま 死出の山 the mountain in Hades [the underworld, the world of the death].

-しては (⇨-にしては)

-してみる (⇨やってみる)

してみると then. (⇨そうすると)

-しても ▶【たとえ...でも】even if [though] (❗even though の方が堅い表現);【仮に認めても】granted 《that 節》;【どんなに...でも】however, no matter how (+副); ❗whenever, whoever, however などの wh-ever 語または「no matter＋wh-語」で譲歩の意を表す. 後の方が口語的). ▶今すぐ出たとしてもその列車に間に合わない *Even if* I (×*will*) *leave* right away, I won't catch the train. (❗*even if* [*though*] 節は未来のことであっても will, shall を用いない) ▶本[金]は持っているとしてもごくわずかです I have very few books [little money], *if* any. (❗可算名詞では few, 不可算名詞では little を用いる (⇨少し) ▶たとえ何も言わなくても彼の気持ちは分かる I know how he `feels *if* he says `nothing at /all. (❗*even if* と同義の *if* 節は条件節により, 主節の後に付加的に置かれることが多く, 下降上昇調で発音する) ▶彼が好投手だとしてもそのチームには勝てないかもしれない *Granted that* [*Even if* it is true (that), (...であるが) *Although*] he is a good pitcher, he may not beat [×*win*] the team. ▶どんなによく勉強しても1年では英語を習得できない *No matter how* [*However*] hard you study, you can't master English in a year. (❗*However* hard you *may* study, ... は文語的) ▶だれが電話をしてきてもいないと言ってください *No matter who* [*Whoever*] phones, please say I'm not in.

-してもらう (⇨もらう ❸)

してやられる ▶彼にまんまとしてやられた I *was* nicely *tricked* [*taken in*] by him.

してん 支店 a branch (office). ● 京都支店 the Kyoto *Branch*《*of* a company》. ● 支店を作る[出す] establish [set up, open] a *branch*. ● 支店を閉じる close (down) a *branch*. ● 我が社は日本各地に支店を持っている Our company has *branches* in every part [all parts] of Japan.
● 支店長 the manager of a branch (office); a branch manager. (❗後の方が口語的) (⇨会社)

してん 支点《物理》a fúlcrum (複 ~s, fulcra).

してん 始点 a stárting pòint.

してん 視点【見地】a point of view, a viewpoint.
● いくつかの視点から話す speak from several *points*

しでん 史伝 a biography based on historical evidence.

しでん 市電 《米》a streetcar, 《米》a trolley (car); 《英》a tramcar. (⇨電車)

***じてん** 辞典 a dictionary. (⇨辞書, 事典) ●英和[和英]辞典 an English-Japanese [a Japanese-English] *dictionary*. ●学習辞典 a learner's *dictionary*. ●同義語[シノニム]辞典 a *dictionary* of synonyms.

じてん a dictionary of Chinese characters.

じてん 次点 ●次点の者[候補者] the [a] runner-up (復 runners-, 〜s). ●次点になる be (a) *runner-up* (*for*) (! be 動詞の後ではしばしば無冠詞); finish *second* [*in second place*].

じてん 自転 图 『天体の』(a) rotation. (! 1 回転の場合は《make》a 〜) (⇨回転) ●地球の自転 the *rotation* of the earth.

── **自転する** 動 ▶地球は24時間で1回自転する The earth *turns* [*rotates*] *on its axis* once every twenty-four hours.

じてん 事典 (百科[専門]事典) an encyclop(a)edia /ensàikləpí:diə/; (通俗的に、または特定分野の) a dictionary. (⇨辞書, 辞典) ●音楽事典 an encyclop(a)edia [a *dictionary*] of music.

じてん 時点 (⇨時②) ●現時点では at this *time* [*moment*]. ●彼が結婚した時点では at the *time* [*moment*] of his marriage; when he got married.

じでん 自伝 an autobiography /ɔ̀:toubaiɑ́grəfi/.

***じてんしゃ** 自転車

WORD CHOICE 自転車

bicycle 自転車をさす最も一般的な語. ●自転車で移動する travel on a *bicycle*.
bike bicycle の省略形. 自転車のほか, 時に小型のオートバイのこともさす. ●マウンテンバイク a mountain *bike*.

頻度チャート

bicycle ▬▬▬▬▬▬▬▬▬▬▬▬▬
bike ▬▬▬
 20 40 60 80 100 (%)

a bicycle, a cycle; 《話》a bike. ●子供[婦人]用自転車 a child's [a lady's, a woman's] *bike*. ●室内トレーニング用自転車 an exercise *bike*. ●競技用自転車 a racing *bike* [*cycle*]; a racer. ●電動アシスト自転車 an electronically assisted *bicycle*. ●自転車をこいで[押して]坂を上る pedal [push, wheel] a *bicycle* up a slope. ●自転車から降りる[に乗る] get off [onto, on] a *bicycle*. ●自転車で学校へ行く go to school *by* [*on* a] *bicycle* (⇨バス⑤); cycle [ride a *bicycle*] to school. ●自転車をとばす drive one's *bicycle* fast. ●自転車で通る travel along *by bicycle*. ▶私はよく父の自転車の(後ろ)に乗せてもらった I often ride on my father's *bicycle*. ▶あの会社は自転車操業のようだ It seems like the company is barely getting by.

会話 「自転車に乗れますか」「乗れるようにはなりましたが, まだあまりうまくないんです」"Can you ride a *bicycle*?" "I've just learned how to ride, but I'm not a good *cyclist* yet."

●自転車置き場 a bicycle park; a bicycle parking place. ●自転車競技 a bicycle race. ●自転車乗り a bicyclist; a cyclist. ●自転車屋 a bicycle store. ●自転車旅行 《take》a bicycle trip [a cycling tour].

してんのう 四天王 ❶『仏教』the Four Devas. ❷『最も優れた4人』the best four (wrestlers).

しと 使徒 an apostle /ǝpásl/, a disciple /disáipl/. ●使徒行伝『聖書』the Acts of the Apostles.

しと 使途 ●金の使途を明らかにする explain *how* the money *was spent*. ●使途不明金 unaccounted-for money.

しど 示度 a reading. ▶示度は2度である The *reading* on the thermometer is 2 ℃.

しとう 死闘 a fierce battle [struggle] 《*against, with*》. ●死闘を繰り広げる fight a *fierce battle*; make a *fierce struggle*.

しとう 至当 ── 至当な 形 just; reasonable; fair and right. ●至当な報酬[罰] a *just reward* [*punishment*].

しとう 私闘 fighting based on [stemming from] one's (own) personal grudge.

***しどう** 指導 图 guidance; (指揮, 統率力) leadership; (競技などの) coaching; (指図) direction; (教授) instruction.

①【指導(の)〜】 ●学習指導要領 a course of study. ●彼の指導の下で[に] under his *guidance* [*direction, leadership, lead*]. ●指導的役割を果たす play a *leading* part [role] 《*in*》; take the *lead* 《*in*》. ●指導の任にあたる take [assume] the *leadership* 《*of*》; (競技などの) undertake the task of *coaching*. ●指導を受ける receive [《受け入れる》accept] an *instruction*. ▶彼は指導力のある人だ(指導者の素質がある)He is a natural *leader*. (! He has leadership. は「先頭に立って(何かをする)」の意) ▶彼は指導のしようがない, やる気がないんだから He can't *be coached*. He doesn't want to learn. ▶ご指導のほどよろしくお願い申し上げます I would be most grateful for any *guidance* [*advice*] you may be able to give me.

②【指導を】 ●指導を仰ぐ look to 《him》for *guidance*. ●指導を誤る misguide; misdirect.

── **指導(を)する** 動 guide; lead*; coach; instruct; direct. ●勉学の指導をする *guide* 《him》 *in* 《his》 studies. ●合唱隊[消費者運動]の指導をする *lead* a chorus [a consumer movement]. ●彼に受験[数学の]指導をする *coach* him *for* his exam [*in* math]. ●スキーの指導をする *instruct* 《him》 *in* [《about, of》] skiing. ▶君は彼が指導するとおりにしさえすればよい You have only to do as he *directs*. ●指導案 a guidance plan; (授業の) a teaching plan. ●指導員[者] a leader; a coach; a director; an instructor; a guide. ●フットボールの指導員(=コーチ) a football *coach*. ●スキーの指導員 a ski *instructor*. ●指導教員 a guidance teacher; (米) a counselor; (大学の) an (academic) adviser, a mentor. ●指導原理 guiding principles; guidelines. ●指導主事 a teacher's consultant; a supervisor (of school education). ●指導書 a guide 《to》; an instruction book; (教科書の) a teacher's manual. ●指導法 a method of guidance; (授業の) a teaching method.

しどう 市道 a municipal [a city] road.

しどう 私道 a private road [path]. (! path は「人が歩いてできた小道」)

しどう 始動 ── 始動する 動 start. ●モーターを始動する *start* the motor.

しどう 斯道 ●斯道の大家 an authority *in the field* [*on the subject*].

じとう 地頭 an official in charge of a manor; a lord of a manor. ▶泣く子と地頭には勝てぬ (⇨泣く[成句])

じどう 自動 — 自動の, 自動的な 〖形〗 automatic.
- 自動巻きの時計 an *automatic* [a *self-winding*] watch.

— **自動的に** 〖副〗 automatically; 〖機械的に〗 mechanically. ▶ドアは自動的に開いた The door opened *automatically*.
- **自動化** automation. ● **自動化する** automatize. ● **自動改札機** an automatic ticket gate. ● **自動拳銃**(けんじゅう) an automatic (pistol). ● **自動修正** an automatic correction. ● **自動小銃** an automatic (rifle). ● **自動食器洗い機** an automatic dishwasher. ● **自動制御** automatic control. ● **自動装置** an automation (**●** ~s, automata). ● **自動扉** an automatic door. ● **自動販売機** a vending machine [《英》a slot machine] (*for* coffee). ● **自動引き落とし** automatic deduction. ● **自動翻訳** automatic translation. ● **自動翻訳機** an automatic translation machine. ● **自動列車制御装置** an automatic train control system.

じどう 児童 〖子供〗a child (**●** children); 〖総称〗children, boys and girls; 〖学童〗a schoolchild (**●** -children). ▶児童向けの本を多数購入した We bought a great number of books for (*young*) *children*.
- **児童館** a children's [a juvenile] library. ● **児童虐待** child abuse. ● **児童教育** children's education; the education of children. ● **児童憲章** the Children's Charter. ● **児童自立支援施設** a children's self-reliance support facility. ● **児童心理(学)** child psychology. ● **児童相談所** a child consultation center; a children's welfare center. ● **児童手当** child benefit. ● **児童福祉** child welfare. ● **児童福祉法** Child Welfare Law. ● **児童文学** juvenile /dʒúːvənàil/ literature. ● **児童ポルノ** child pornography.

じどうし 自動詞 〖文法〗an intransitive verb.

***じどうしゃ 自動車** 〖乗用車〗a car;《米書》an automobile,《米話》an auto (**●** ~s);《主に英書・やや古》a motorcar;〖タクシー〗a taxi (⇨タクシー);〖トラック〗a truck;《英》a lorry (⇨トラック);〖バス〗a bus (**●** ~es) (⇨バス);〖各種自動車の総称〗a motor vehicle. (⇨車). ● 営業用車[自家用]自動車 a trade [a private] *car*. (**!** 後の方は one's own car ともいえる (⇨マイカー). ● 大型[小型]自動車 a long-sized [a compact, a small] *car*. ● 電気自動車 an electric *car*. ● 自動車に乗る[から降りる] get in [out of] a *car*. ● 自動車を運転する drive (a *car*). ● 自動車にひかれる be run over by a car. ● 彼女をそこまで車で送る drive her there by car. ▶自動車で行く？ それとも電車にする？ Shall we *drive* or take the train?
- **自動車会社**[メーカー] an automobile [a car] manufacturer; a car [an auto] maker. ● **自動車学校** a drívíng [ˣa car] schòol. ● **自動車競走** a car [an auto] race. ● **自動車産業** the auto (mobile) [《米》motor 《英》] industry. ● **自動車事故** (be killed in) a car [《米》an automobile, 《英》a motor] accident. ● **自動車修理工** a car [an automobile, a garage] mechanic. ● **自動車ショー** a motor show. ● **自動車電話** a car(-)phone. (**!** a carphone ともつうる) ● **自動車道** 《米》an expressway;《英》a motorway. ● **自動車販売店** a car dealer.

しだらない slovenly. (⇨ふだらしない).

しとげる 仕遂げる 〖し終える〗finish 《doing》;〖完成する〗complete;〖成しとげる〗accomplish. (⇨完成する, 終える).

しどころ ▶ここが我慢のしどころだ Now is *the time for*

you to be patient [to show patience].

しとしと ● しとしと雨が降る rain softly [gently];（こぬか雨が降る）drizzle. ▶1日中雨がしとしと降った A *soft rain* was falling all day (long)./It *was drizzling* all day.

じとじと （湿っぽい）damp;（ぬれた）wet (-tt-);（暑くてじめじめした）sticky. ● じとじとした天気 *damp* [*sticky*] weather. (**!** wet weather は「雨天」) ▶床がじとじとだ The floor is *damp* [*wet*]. ▶干してある洗濯物が雨でじとじとになった The washing [《米》wash] on the line got *wet* in the rain.

じとっ (⇨じとじと) ▶このタオルはじとっとしている This towel is *damp*.

しとど しとどにぬれる get thoroughly wet; get soaked to the skin. (⇨びしょ濡れ)

シドニー 〖オーストラリアの都市〗Sydney.

しとめる 仕留める （殺す）kill;（銃で鳥を）shoot* [bring*]... down;（銃でけものなどを）shoot... dead.

しとやか 淑やか — **淑やかな** 〖形〗〖優美な〗graceful;〖慎み深い〗modest;〖穏やかな〗gentle. ▶彼女はすらっとしていてしとやかな人だ She is slim and *graceful*.

じどり 地取り 〖地面の区画〗a layout;〖囲碁で地を取ること〗taking territory in *go*.

しどろもどろ ● しどろもどろの返答をする（筋道の立たない）give an incoherent [（うろたえてめちゃくちゃの）a confused] answer. ● しどろもどろになる be thrown into (utter) confusion; be (utterly) confused.

***しな 品** ❶ 〖品物〗（個々の）an article;（商品）goods (⇨品物, 品⑵ ❷);（在庫品）(a) stock (**!** しばしば複数形で). ● お祝いの品 a gift, a present. ● 品数が多い have a wide range [selection] 《of shoes》. ▶所変われば品変わる (⇨所 〖成句〗)
❷ 〖品質〗quality. ● 品がよい[悪い] be of good [poor] *quality*. ● 品が違う be different 《*from* it》in *quality*;（品が優れている）be superior 《*to* it》in *quality*. ● 品を落とす lower the *quality*.

しな 科 ● **科をつくる** be coquettish [flirtatious]; flirt.

しない 市内 ● 市内見物をする[に出かける] see the sights of [go sightseeing *in*] *the city*. ● 市内を行進する march *through the city*. ● 市内配達無料 free delivery *within the city* (limits). ▶私は福岡市内に住んでいます I live *in the city* of Fukuoka. ▶市内をご案内しましょう I'll show you around [over] *the city*.
- **市内通話** a city [a local] call.

しない 竹刀 a bamboo sword.

シナイ ● **シナイ半島** the Sinai /sáinài/ (Peninsula).

-しない (⇨-ない)

しなう 撓う 〖曲がる〗bend*;〖曲げやすい〗be flexible;〖ばねのように弾力のある〗be springy. ● よくしなう竹 (a) *flexible* bamboo. (**!** 「竹材」を表すときは ⓤ) ▶私の重みで枝がしなった The branch *bent* [*gave*] under my weight.

しなうす 品薄 ● **品薄である** be in short supply;《人が主語》be low 《*on* gasoline》. (⇨品 ❶) ▶現在この製品は品薄だ This product is *in short supply* [（不足している）is *running short*] at present.

しなおす do over again. (⇨遣り直す)

しながき 品書き a list;（目録）a catalog(ue);（献立表）a menu.

しなぎれ 品切れ ● **品切れである** be out of stock. ▶その店ではろうそくが品切れだ[になった] The store *is* [*has run*] *out of* candles./Candles *are* [*have run*] *out of* stock at the store.

しなさだめ 品定め — **品定めする** 〖動〗（価値を見定

しなす 死なす ●愛児を死なす(=失う) lose one's dear child. ●石を投げて犬を死なせる stone a dog *to death*. ▶死なせてください Please *let me die*.

しだれかかる (⇨しだれる)

しだれる 〖甘えて擦り寄る〗nestle [snuggle] up 《*to*》;〖誘うようにもたれかかる〗lean* invitingly 《*against*》.

しちく 支配竹 (⇨メンマ)

しなびる 〖水分がなくなってしわがよる〗shrivel;〖しおれる〗wither. ●しなびた手[リンゴ] a *shriveled* hand [apple]. ▶しなびた野菜 *withered* vegetables.

シナプス 〖神経細胞の接合部〗〖解剖〗a synapse.

しなぶそく 品不足 (⇨品薄)

***しなもの 品物** 〖個々の〗an article;〖商品〗goods (⚠ (1) 複数扱い. 数詞はつけないが many, some, any など漠然と数を表すものはつける. (⇨品物 (2)) 以上2語は,〖話〗では thing(s) で代用されることも多い;〖在庫品〗(a) stock (⚠ しばしば複数形で). ●品物で返す pay 《him》back *in kind*. ▶ in kind は「金銭ではなく品物で」の意) ▶彼女のハンドバッグにはたくさんの品物が入っていた There were many *articles* in her purse. ▶あの店はあらゆる種類の品物を置いている That store carries *things* [*articles*, *goods*] of all kinds.

シナモン cinnamon /sínəmən/.
●シナモントースト cinnamon toast.

しなやか 〖物が〗(曲げやすい) flexible, pliable;〖曲げてももどる〗elastic;〖やわらかい〗soft;〖人・体が〗supple,〖書〗limber (↔stiff). ●しなやかな針金 a *flexible* wire. ▶彼女は考え方がしなやかだ She is *flexible* in thinking.

> **翻訳のこころ** 少年はきびきびと準備体操を済ませて, しなやかに水に飛び込んだ(江國香織『デューク』) The boy did warm-up exercises briskly [energetically] and jumped into the water gracefully [with agility]. (⚠ (1) briskly は無駄なく自信に満ちた動作, energetically は「精力的に動く」の意. (2) gracefully は見た目のしなやかさ[美しさ], with agility は動きのしなやかさ[機敏さ]を表す)

じならし 地ならし ── **地ならし(を)する 動** level the ground.

じなり 地鳴り the rumble of the earth. ▶地鳴りがした The earth rumbled.

シナリオ 〖脚本〗a scenario /sənǽriòu/ (複 ~s), a script.
●シナリオライター a scenario [a script] writer.

しなる 撓る (⇨撓う)

しなん 至難 ── **至難の 形** most difficult, hardest.
●至難のわざ a *most difficult* task;〖書〗a *herculean* /hə̀ːrkjəliːən/ task (⚠ しばしば Herculean.) ▶市民を巻き添えにしない攻撃は至難である Mounting attacks without involving civilians is *next to impossible* [*extremely difficult*].

しなん 指南 图 instruction; teaching.
── **指南する 動** instruct; coach; teach.
●指南役 a master; a coach; instructor.

じなん 次男 the [one's] second son.

シニア 〖老齢者〗a senior citizen,〖米〗a senior;〖上級者, 年長者, 上級生〗one's senior;〖老齢の, 上級の, 年長の〗senior.
●シニアセンター a center for senior citizens [〖米〗seniors]. ●シニアプレーヤー a senior player, (スポーツ) a senior.

しにいそぐ 死に急ぐ court death.

しにおくれる 死に後れる outlive [survive] 《him》.

しにがお 死に顔 a face of a dead person. ▶父の死に顔は穏やかだった Father looked peaceful when he died.

しにがね 死に金 〖むだ金〗idle capital;〖ためておくだけの金〗dead capital.

しにがみ 死に神 Death (■語 米英では手に鎌を持ち黒い服を着た骸骨の姿で表される);〖主に書〗the (Grim) Reaper (■語 手に大鎌を持った収穫者の姿で表される). ●死に神にとりつかれている be obssessed with [by] *Death*.

しにぎわ 死に際 ●死に際に when one is just about to die;〖やや書〗on one's deathbed. (⇨死 ④)

しにく 死肉 dead flesh;〖腐肉〗carrion.

しにく 歯肉 〖解剖〗a gum (■通例複数形で); a gingiva (複 gingivae).
●歯肉炎〖医学〗gingivitis.

ジニけいすう ジニ係数 〖所得格差指標〗Gini('s) co-efficient.

しにげしょう 死に化粧 ●死に化粧をする make the face of a dead person up; make a dead person up.

しにざま 死に様 the way 《he》dies [died].

しにせ 老舗 an old(-established) store [〖会社〗firm]; a store [a firm] with a long history.

しにそこなう 死に損なう 〖死のうとして失敗する〗fail to kill oneself;〖死にそうになる〗be almost killed 《*in* an accident》.

しにたい 死に体 ●死に体である〖相撲〗be in a hopeless position; have little or no chance of winning.

しにたえる 死に絶える die (~d; dying) out; become* extinct.

しにどき 死に時 a time to die.

しにどころ 死に所 a place to die.

しにばしょ 死に場所 (⇨死に所)

しにばな 死に花 ●死に花を咲かせる die a glorious [an honorable] death.

しにみず 死に水 ●死に水を取る attend 《him》on 《his》deathbed.

しにめ 死に目 ▶彼女は父親の死に目に会えなかった She couldn't see her father *on* his *deathbed*. /Her father had already died [was already dead] when she came to him.

しにものぐるい 死に物狂い ── **死に物狂いの 形** 〖必死の〗desperate;〖狂気のような〗frantic. (⇨必死)
●死に物狂いの競争 a *desperate* competition.
── **死に物狂いで 副** desperately;〖話〗like hell;(命がけで) for dear [one's] life. ●死に物狂いで働く work *desperately* [*frantically*].

しにょう 屎尿 (human) wastes; excrement.

しにわかれる 死に別れる lose*,〖やや書〗be bereaved of .... ▶彼は去年奥さんに死に別れた He *lost* [*was bereaved of*] his wife last year.

しにん 死人 a dead person,〖集合的〗〖やや書〗the dead. (⇨死者) ●死人のような顔つき a *deathly* look.
●死人に口なし Dead people cannot talk any more.

しにん 視認 a visual confirmation.

じにん 自認 ── **自認する 動** ▶彼はテニスの第一人者をもって自任している He *thinks of himself as* the best tennis player./He *flatters himself that* he is the best player in tennis. (⚠ 後の方は「勝手にそう思い込んでいる」という含みがある)

じにん 辞任 图 (a) resignation. (⇨辞職)
── **辞任する 動** resign (one's job [post]); step down. ●大使を辞任する *resign as* ambassador.

しぬ 死ぬ 動

WORD CHOICE　死ぬ

die 人・動物が自然に死ぬこと。また、植物などが枯れること。●がん[心臓発作;戦争]で死ぬ *die from cancer* [*of a heart attack; in a war*].

be killed 戦争や不慮の事故などで、本人の意に反して死ぬこと。deに比べ被害性が強く含意される。▶銃火を浴びて[事故で]死んだ He *was killed* by gunfire [*in an accident*].

頻度チャート
die
be killed
20　40　60　80　100 (%)

❶ [命がなくなる] (一般的に) die (〜d; dying); 《婉曲的》 pass away, pass on; (事故・戦争などで) be killed; [自殺する] kill oneself (⇨自殺). ▶祖母はもう death しました My grandmother *is* [xwas] already *dead*. (**!** is dead は現在死んでいる状態を表す)/My grandmother *has* already *died*. (**!** 前の訳は死後かなりの時間が経っていることを暗示するのに対して、最近死んだことを含意する)/《婉曲的》My grandmother *is no longer living*.

①【死因で死ぬ】●老衰で死ぬ *die of* old age. ▶彼は何で死んだのですか What did he *die of*?/(死因は何ですか) What is the cause of his death? ▶彼はがんで死んだ[死にかけている] He *died* [*is dying*] *of* [*from*] cancer. (**!** of は病気など直接的・内的な原因に用い、from は負傷など間接的・外的な原因に用いるとされるが、この区別はなくなりつつある。次例参照)/(死因が主語) Cancer *killed* [*is killing*] him. ▶彼は銃傷がもとで死んだ He *died from* [*of*] a gunshot wound. ▶彼は交通事故で[落雷で; 落馬して]死んだ He *was killed in* a traffic accident [*by* a thunderbolt; *by* falling *off* a horse]. ▶不慮の死の場合は direct より普通 ▶多くの子供たちが食糧不足から次々に死んでいった A lot of children *were dying off* through [*from*, xof] lack of food. (**!** 主語は複数に限る)

②【(ある状態で)死ぬ】●苦しんで死ぬ die in anguish [agonizingly]. ●123 歳で死ぬ die at the age of 123. ●あっけなく死ぬ die too suddenly [all-too-soon]. ▶彼は畳の上で安らかに死んだ He *died* peacefully in [xon] his bed. ▶彼は若くして死んだ He *died* young. (**!** die の補語としては他に happy, rich, poor, a rich man, a beggar などが主なもので、old は不可 (⇨①))/He was (still) young when he *died*.

③【死ぬまで】●死ぬまで君を愛する I shall love you till my *death* [till my *dying day*, (生涯) all my life, (今後死ぬまで) for the rest of my life, (生きている限り) as long as I live].

④【死ぬほど】●死ぬほど笑う laugh oneself silly [sick], 《話》 die laughing (**!**「笑い死にする」の意もある) ▶死ぬほど空腹だ I'm *dying* [*almost die*] *of* hunger. (**!** 前の方が普通。進行形でないときは almost, nearly などを伴う) ▶死ぬほどコーヒーを飲みたい 《話》 I'm *dying for* [*to drink*] some coffee. ▶彼女が死ぬほど好きだ 《話》 I'm *madly* in love with her. ▶靴がきつくて死ぬほど痛い My shoes are so tight that they *are killing* me. ▶私は蛇が死ぬほど怖い I'm scared *to death* of snakes. (scared の他に worried (心配して), bored (退屈して) などの意の語に用いる)

⑤【死んで】▶父が死んで 10 年になる It's [It's been] ten years since my father *died*./My father *died* ten years ago./My father has *been dead* [xhas died] for ten years. (**!** die は継続を表す完了形では用いない) ▶部屋の中で男の人が死んでいる There's a *dead* [xa dying, xa died] man in the room. (**!** a dying man は「死にかけている男」の意)

⑥【死なれる】▶夫には4年前に死なれた I *lost* my husband four years ago./My husband *died* [*passed away*] (on me) four years ago. (**!** (1) on は「...を犠牲にして」の意。(2) I *had* my husband *die* (*on me*)…. は日本的発想と一致するが(まれ)。xI was died by my husband …. は不可) (⇨死に別れる)

❷ [その他の表現] ●生きるか死ぬかの問題 a life-and-death matter. ▶人間は死ぬものだ Human beings are *mortal*. ▶死ぬことは恐れていません I am not afraid to *die*. ▶私は死ぬ覚悟で(=命をかけて)戦います I shall [will] fight *at the risk of my life*. (**!** shall の方が決意の度合いが強い) ▶その額縁では絵が死んでしまう That frame may *kill* a good picture. ▶彼とペアを組むなんて死んでも願い下げだ(=ならピストル自殺する方がましだ) I'd rather *shoot myself* than being partner with him. ▶彼は死んでも死にきれないだろう He might carry his regrets beyond the grave. ▶お前の命を奪うまで死ぬに死ねない I won't *die* till I kill you. ▶君のためなら死んでもいい I could *die* for you.

●死んで花実が咲くものか Nothing is achieved by dying.

―― 死んだ 形 dead; 《法律》 deceased. ●死んだ人 a *dead* person (⇨⑤); (集合的) the dead. ▶彼女は子供を死んだものとあきらめた She gave her child up for *dead* [*lost*]. ▶彼は死んだふりをした He pretended to be *dead*. ▶彼は死んだも同然だ He is as good as *dead*. ▶彼は死んだように(=ぐっすりと)眠っていた He slept *like a log*. He was *dead* asleep. ▶君とこの家に一緒に住むくらいなら死んだほうがまし I'd rather die than live in this house with you.

●死んだ子の年を数える (⇨死児 [成句])

じぬし 地主 a landowner, a landlord.
●地主階級 the landed class.

じねずみ 地鼠 [動物] a shrewmouse, a shrew.

じねつ 地熱 (⇨地熱(ちねつ))

シネマ [映画] (米) the movie, 《英》 the cinema.
●シネマコンプレックス [複合型映画館] a cinema complex. ●シネマスコープ [[ワイドスクリーン映画の一種]] 《商標》 CinemaScope.

シネラマ [[ワイドスクリーン映画の一種]] 《商標》 Cinerama.

シネラリア [植物] a cineraria. (参考)「死」を連想させることから日本ではサイネリアと呼ばれている)

じねんじょ 自然薯 [植物] a Japanese yam.

しの 篠 (⇨篠竹)

しのうこうしょう 士農工商 (説明的に) the four classes of warriors, farmers, craftsmen and tradesmen in the Edo period in Japan.

しのぎ 鎬 ●しのぎを削る compete keenly [fiercely] 《with him; for the title》; be in keen [fierce] competition. (⇨競争)

-しのぎ ●一時しのぎの makeshift. ●その場しのぎの temporary. ▶退屈しのぎに本を読む read a book to *kill time*. ●寒さしのぎに to *keep out* the cold.

しのぐ 凌ぐ ❶【勝る】 be superior 《to》; 《書》 surpass; 《書》 exceed 《in》. (⇨勝る) ▶すべての学科で人をしのぐことはできない。自分の好きなのを選びなさい You can't *be superior to* others in every subject; choose your favorites.

❷【耐える】stand*; bear*.（❗いずれも通例 can を伴って否定文・疑問文で用いる）▶しのぎにくい夏 an *unbearably* hot summer. ▶しのぎやすい（= 穏やかな）冬 a *mild* winter. ▶この暑さはとてもしのげない I can't *stand* [*bear*] this heat.
❸【防ぐ】keep*... out. ▶雨をしのぐ *keep out* the rain;（雨宿りをする）*take shelter from* the rain.
❹【切り抜ける】▶危機をしのぐ *get through* [《やや話》*tide over*] a crisis. ▶草の根をかじって飢えをしのぐ（= いやす）satisfy one's appetite *on* grass roots. ▶この金で1週間はしのげる This money will *last* me (for) a week./《やや話》This money will (be able to) *tide* me *over* for a week.

しのこす 仕残す leave* (it) unfinished [half-done].

しのごの 四の五の ●**四の五の言わずに** without grumbling [complaining]. ▶四の五の言わずに働け *Stop grumbling* and get down to work.

しのだけ 篠竹【植物】*shinodake*; a small kind of bamboo.

しのつく 篠突く ▶しのつく雨 a (torrential) downpour; a heavy [a driving, a torrential] rain.

しのとげ『死の棘』*Sting of Death.*（参考 島尾敏雄の小説）

シノニム【同義語】a synonym.

しのはい 死の灰（radioactive）fallout; radioactive dust.

しのばせる 忍ばせる【隠す】hide*,《やや書》conceal.
●机の下に参考資料を忍ばせる *hide* reference data under the desk. ●足音を忍ばせて（= 忍び足で）(⇨忍び足) ●声を忍ばせて（= ひそひそ声で）talk *in whispers* [*a whisper*]. ▶彼はポケットにピストルを忍ばせていた He *hid* [*concealed*] a pistol in his pocket./（ひそかに携帯していた）He *carried* a pistol *secretly* in his pocket.

しのび 忍び【忍者, 忍術】(⇨忍者, 忍術)；【ひそかにすること】(⇨お忍び)
●忍び会 a secret meeting. (⇨密会) ●忍び歩き walking stealthily;（高貴な人が）traveling incognito. ●忍び声 a whisper; a suppressed voice.

しのびあし 忍び足 ▶忍び足で歩く walk softly [stealthily /stélθiliː/];（つま先立ちで）tiptoe（quietly）, walk on tiptoe(s). (⇨抜き足)

しのびこむ 忍び込む steal* [sneak] in. ▶泥棒はこの窓から部屋に忍び込んだに違いない The thief must *have stolen* [*sneaked, crept*] *into* the room through this window.

しのびない 忍びない (⇨忍び❷) ▶彼がそんなふうに扱われるのは見るに忍びなかった I *couldn't bear seeing* [*to see*] him treated like that./I *hated* to see him treated that way.

しのびなき 忍び泣き ━ **忍び泣きする** 動 weep silently.

しのびよる 忍び寄る creep* [《書》steal*] up. ▶背後から彼に忍び寄る *creep* [*steal*] *up on* him from behind. ▶老いがいつしか彼に忍び寄っていた Old age *had crept up on* him unawares [《米》*unaware*].

しのびわらい 忍び笑い 名 a titter, a snicker, a snigger. ━ **忍び笑いする** 動 titter, snicker, snigger 《at》.

***しのぶ 忍ぶ** ❶【隠れる】hide* (oneself). ▶人目を忍んで in secret. ▶彼らがみな通り過ぎるまで彼は木陰に忍んでいた He (had) hid (himself) behind the bush until they all passed away.

❷【我慢する】bear*;（長い間耐え強く）《やや書》endure;《話》（不便などを）put* up with .... (⇨忍ない)

***しのぶ 偲ぶ** ●亡き母を偲ぶ（= 思い出す）remember [recall, think of] my dead mother. ▶その文豪を偲んで（= 記念して）銅像を建てる erect a bronze statue *in memory of* the great writer. ●...を偲ぶ会 a gathering in memory of Mr. [Mrs., Ms.].....

しのぶぐさ 忍ぶ草【植物】a hare's foot fern.

シノプシス【映画などのあらすじ】a synopsis (複 -ses /-siːz/).

しば 芝【植物】（芝草）the grass;（芝生）a lawn;（移植用芝土（の一片））(a) turf (複 〜s);【サッカー】a pitch. ▶よく手入れされた芝 a carefully groomed *lawn*. ●芝を植える turf 《a garden》; lay *turf*《in a garden》to make [create] a *lawn*. ●芝を刈る mow the *lawn*.
●芝刈り lawn mowing. ●芝刈り機 a lawn mower.

しば 柴（小枝, そだ）brushwood;（たきぎ）firewood.
●柴を刈る gather *firewood*. ●柴垣 a brushwood fence. ●柴刈り firewood gathering. ▶おじいさんは山へ柴刈りに行きました The old man went into the woods to gather *firewood*.

じば 地場 (⇨❻ 地元)
●地場産業 (traditional) local industry.

じば 磁場 a magnetic field.

ジハード【イスラム擁護の聖戦】a jihad.

しはい 支配 名（絶対的権力による）rule;（優勢な力による威圧的な）domination;（統制による）control. ▶イギリスの植民地支配 the British colonial *rule*. ▶軍の支配下にある be under military *rule*. ▶...を支配下に置く take [seize, gain] *control of* ....▶ボール支配（率）ball possession. ▶第二次大戦後日本はアメリカの支配下にあった Japan was *under the control* [*domination*] of the U.S. after World War Ⅱ.
━ **支配的な** 形 ▶支配的な考え dominant [（数の上で）predominant] ideas.
━ **支配する** 動 rule;（政治的に）govern;（権力で）dominate;（統制する）control (-ll-).（⇨治める）
●感情に支配される be controlled [ruled] by one's emotions. ●自然の法則に支配される be subject to the laws of nature. ▶1人の独裁者がその国を支配していた A dictator *ruled* (over) [*governed, dominated, controlled*] the country. ▶私はだれのことも支配したり征服したりしたくありません I don't want to *rule* or conquer anyone.
●支配階級 the ruling [governing] class(es).
●支配者 a ruler. ●支配人 (⇨支配人) ●支配力 one's control (*over*).

しはい 紙背 ▶眼光（がんこう）紙背に徹する (⇨眼光［成句］)

しはい 賜杯 the Emperor's Trophy [Cup].

***しばい 芝居** ❶【劇】a play;（戯曲）(a) drama,《集合的》the theater. (⇨劇) ▶芝居をやる play, act a *play*;（劇を上演する）give [present,《話》do] a *play*, put a *play* on a stage. ▶芝居を見る see [×watch] a *play*. ▶芝居がはねる（= 終わる）a *play* ends. ▶今度の新しい芝居は大当たり［大入り］だった The new *play* was a big hit [had a large audience]. ▶今夜芝居のけいこをします I will rehearse a *play* this evening. ▶彼はよく芝居を見に行く He often goes to see a *play*./He often goes to the *theater*. (❗この *theater* は「劇場」の意で,「映画を見に行く」の意にもなる. ×... goes to *a* theater. とはいわない)／（芝居の常連だ）He is a *playgoer* [a *theatergoer*]. ▶彼女は音楽と芝居が大好きです She loves music and *the theater*.

❷ 〖作り事〗 ● 芝居気のある having a *theatrical* /θiǽtrɪkl/ character [quality]. ▶彼は芝居がうまい He is a good *actor*./(人をだますのがうまい) He is good at *deceiving people*. ▶彼は本当は怒っていなかった。単なる芝居だった He was not really angry. He *was* only *pretending* [*acting*, *faking*]. (**!**後の文は He was just putting it on. ともいう) ▶彼のふるまいは芝居がかっていた His behavior was *theatrical*.
● 芝居を打つ put on a play.
● 芝居小屋 a playhouse; (劇場) a theater.
● 芝居茶屋 a teahouse in a theater.

しばい 試売 (a) trial sale.
● 試売品 goods on trial sale.

じばいせき 自賠責 〖「自動車損害賠償責任保険」の略〗 compulsory automobile liability insurance.

しばいにん 支配人 a mánager. (**!**(1) 呼びかけには用いない。(2) 男性・女性の区別なくこの語を用いる。a manageress (女支配人) は差別語とされ, 今ではまれ)
● 総[副]支配人 a general [an assistant] *manager*.

しばいぬ 柴犬 〖動物〗a *Shiba* (dog); (説明的に) a Japanese breed of small dog with erected ears and a curled tail.

しばえび 芝海老 〖動物〗a (white) prawn /prɔ́ːn/.

じはく 自白 图 (a) confession. (⇨白状) ● 容疑者から自白を引き出す beat a *confession* out of a suspect.
—— 自白する 動 ● 犯行を自白する *confess* (to) one's crime.

じばく 自爆 图 suicide bombing.
—— 自爆する 動 ● kill oneself by suicide bombing; commit(ted) suicide bombing (**!**自爆をしようとしたが自分は死ななかった可能性もある).
● 自爆テロ a suicide bombing (attack). ● 自爆犯 a suicide bomber.

しばくり 柴栗 〖植物〗a small chestnut.

しばざくら 芝桜 〖植物〗a moss phlox; a moss pink.

しばしば 屡 often. (⇨たびたび)

じはだ 地肌 〖皮膚〗(a) skin; 〖土地の表面〗the ground.

しばたたく 瞬く blink one's eyes.

じばち 地蜂 〖昆虫〗a wasp.

しはつ 始発 (始発便) the first run; (始発列車・電車) the first train.
● 始発駅 the starting station.

しばづけ 柴漬け *shibazuke*; (説明的に) vegetables (such as eggplants, cucumbers, red *shiso* leaves, small green peppers) chopped and pickled together.

じはつてき 自発的 —— 自発的な 形 voluntary /váləntèri/.
—— 自発的に 副 voluntarily; of one's own accord.
● 自発的に援助を申し出る make a *voluntary* offer of help; offer one's help *voluntarily*.

しばふ 芝生 a lawn; 〖芝草〗grass; (土〜) turf. ▶手入れの行き届いた芝生 a manicured [a carefully tended] *lawn*. ▶芝生を刈る[に水をまく] mow [sprinkle] the *lawn*. ▶芝生に入るべからず《掲示》Keep off the *grass*.

しばぶえ 柴笛 a (young-)leaf flute [pipe].

じばら 自腹 ● 自腹を切る pay 《one's travel expenses》out of one's own pocket [with one's own money].

＊しはらい 支払い (a) payment. (**!**1 回の支払い・支払金の場合は 〖C〗) ● 支払いを延期する put off [postpone] *payment*. ● 支払いを停止する stop [(一時的

に) suspend] *payment*. ● 請求書の支払いとして小切手を同封する enclose a check *in payment for* the bill. ▶この支払いは済んでいる This *has been paid for*./(支払い済) (表示) Paid. ▶お支払いはどのようになさいますか。カードですか How *are you paying*? Credit card? ▶借金は支払い済みだ My debts *are all paid up*. (**!**pay up は借金などを「(しぶしぶ) 支払う」こと) ▶彼は車の支払いを滞(とどこお)らせた He fell behind in his car *payments*. ▶テレビに月 5,000 円の支払いをしなければならない I must *pay* 5,000 yen *for* the TV a [every] *month*./I must *make monthly payments of* 5,000 yen for the TV. (⇨月賦) ▶今のところ 1 日 1 万円の支払いを受けている I'*m being paid* ten thousand yen a day.
● 支払い回数 the number [frequency] of payments. ● 支払い期日 the due [maturity] date. ● 支払い先 a payee. ● 支払い条件 the terms of payment. ● 支払い請求 a claim. ● 支払い高 the amount of payment. ● 支払い停止 suspension [stopping] of payment. ● 支払い手形 a bill payable. (**!**payable は「支払い可能な」の意で, 名詞の前には置かない) ● 支払い人 a payer. ● 支払い能力 the ability [capability] to pay; solvency. ● 支払い日 the date of payment; (給料の) (a) payday. ● 支払い不能 the failure to pay; insolvency. ● 支払い不能者 an insolvent. ● 支払い方法 the means [method] of payment. ● 支払い猶予 a moratorium.

＊しはらう 支払う pay*. ● 現金[小切手]で支払う *pay in cash* [*by check*]. ▶前の方は *pay* cash ともいう) ● 借金を支払う *pay* [*clear*] (*off*) one's debts. (**!**pay [clear]... off は「皆済する」の意) ● 雑誌代を支払う *pay for* [×pay] the magazine. ▶彼に家賃を支払う *pay* him *for* the rent. ▶このラジオに 100 ドル支払った I *paid* one hundred dollars *for* this radio./(100 ドルで買った) I *bought* this radio *for* 100 dollars.

＊しばらく 暫く ❶ 〖短い間〗(少しの間) for a (little) while; (ほんの少しの間) for a moment [a minute]. (⇨ちょっと) ▶彼はしばらく眠った He slept *for a while*. ▶しばらくお待ちください Wait *a moment* [*a minute*], please./Just *a moment* [*a minute*], please./One moment [One minute], please. (**!**いずれも minute を用いる方が口語的) ▶しばらくして中村君がやって来た Nakamura came [appeared, turned up] *after a while* [*some time later*]. (**!**過去の文脈では after や later を用いる)/(書) It *was not long* [*It was some time*] *before* Nakamura came. (⇨経つ) ▶しばらくすれば宿題は終わります I'll finish my homework *in a while*. (**!**未来の文脈では in を用いる)
(会話)「行きましょうか」「しばらく待つ方がいいと思わない？」"Should we go?" "Don't you think it would be wiser to wait (*for*) *a while*?" (**!**(話) では継続を表す動詞の後では for は省略されることが多い)
❷ 〖当分〗for the time being. ▶しばらくはこれで間に合う This will do *for the time being* [(今のところ) *for the present*, 《やや話》*for now*; (ある期間) *for some time*]. (**!**some に強勢が置かれると「かなり長い間」の意)
(会話)「あとでまた来るよ」「じゃあしばらくしてから。またね」"I'll be back later." "Good-by *for now*. See you then."
❸ 〖長い間〗for a long time. ▶しばらく彼とは話していない I haven't talked to him *for a long time*. ▶私はしばらくぶりに彼を訪ねた I visited him *for the first time in a long time* [(話) *in ages*]. (**!**in の代わりに for を用いるのは《英》(⇨久しぶり)) ▶ずいぶん

しばりあげる しばらくぶりですね(=この前会って以来長い時間がたっている) It's [It's been] *a long time* [《話》*ages*,《話》*years*] *since I last saw you*./*I haven't seen you for such a long time* [《話》*for ages*,《話》*for years*]./《話》Long time, no see.

しばりあげる 縛り上げる tie [bind]... (up) securely [firmly]; truss... (up). ▶泥棒は守衛をロープで縛り上げた The thieves *tied* [*bound*] the guard (*up*) *firmly with* ropes./The thieves *trussed* the guard *up with* rope.

しばりくび 縛り首 (a) hanging.

しばりつける 縛り付ける tie [bind]... (up). (⇨縛る)

しばる 縛る ❶ [くくる] tie (~d; tying); bind*... (up); fasten.

> 使い分け tie ひも・ロープなどでくくること, またはある物にくくりつけること.
> bind tie よりしっかり縛る[縛りつける]ことで tie より堅い語. また「巻きつけて縛る」の意でも用いる.
> fasten 固定すること.

● 縄で彼の手足を縛る tie [bind] his arms and legs *with* (a) rope. ● 旗をさおにきつく縛りつける *fasten* the flag tight *to* [*on*] the pole. ▶その囚人は柱に縛られていた The prisoner *was tied* [*bound*] *to* the post. ▶彼らは彼の手を縛り目隠しをした They *tied* his hands *together* and blindfolded him. ▶彼女は髪がじゃまにならないように縛った(=くくった) She *bound up* her hair so it wouldn't get in the way.

❷ [束縛する] (仕事・場所などに拘束する) tie (~d; tying); (義務などで拘束する) bind*. ● 規則に縛られている *be bound* [*be tied down*] *by* rules. ● 時間に縛られている *be bound* [*be restricted*] *by* time; (時間がなくて困っている) *be pressed for* time. ● 私は仕事に縛られている I *am tied* [*am chained*] (*down*) *to* my work./My work *ties* me (*down*).

しばれる 凍れる (凍る) freeze; (厳しく冷え込む) be terribly cold. ▶今夜はしばれるなあ It's *freezing* (*cold*) tonight./It's *terribly* [*awfully*] *cold* tonight.

しはん 市販 ── 市販する 動 (市場に出す) put... on the market. ▶この薬は市販されていない This medicine *isn't* (*put*) *on the market*./This medicine *hasn't come onto the market*./You can't *get* this medicine *over the counter*. ⚠ *over the counter* は「(処方箋なしで)店頭で」の意で, そのような薬を *over-the-counter drugs* という)

● 市販品 goods *on the market*; (店で販売されている品物) goods on sale [sold] *at a store*.

しはん 死斑 a death spot.

しはん 師範 (先生) a teacher, an instructor.

● 師範学校 a téachers còllege. ● 師範代 (補助の) an assistant instructor; (代理[臨時]の) an acting instructor.

しはん 紫斑 a purple spot.

● 紫斑病 [医学] purpura.

じはん 事犯 a criminal offense; a crime.

じばん 地盤 ❶ [土地] ground. ▶地盤が沈下している The *ground* is sinking [subsiding]. (⚠「地盤沈下」は the subsidence of the *ground*) ▶この辺の地盤はやわらかい The *ground* is not hard around here./The *ground* around here is soft [not firm].

❷ [足場] a foothold; a footing; (基礎) the foundations. ● 市場の地盤を固める establish a *foothold* in the market. ● 地盤を築く lay the *foundations* (*of* one's success)).

❸ [選挙区] one's constituency. ● 地盤を固める strengthen one's *constituency*; 《米》(議員が) mend [look after] one's *fences*.

しはんき 四半期 a quarter of the (fiscal) year. (⚠ 通例会計年度の区分なので fiscal をつけるのが普通)

● 2008 年度第 1 四半期 The *first quarter* [*first three months*] of fiscal 2008. ▶景気は 3 四半期連続で落ち込みを見せた The economy actually contracted for three consecutive *quarters*.

じはんき 自販機 『「自動販売機」の略』 a vénding machìne 《米》.

しひ 市費 ● 市費で at the *city expense*; at *the expense of the city*.

しひ 私費 (⇨自費)

● 私費留学生 (海外からの) an overseas student (who is) studying at his [her] own expense; (海外への) a student (who is) studying overseas at his [her] own expense.

しひ 詩碑 a stone [a marble] monument inscribed with a poem.

じひ 自費 one's own expense(s). ● 自費留学[出版]する study abroad [publish a book] *at* one's *own expense*. ● 費用は自費で払う pay expenses *out of* one's *own pocket*.

じひ 慈悲 mercy; [情け深さ] charity; [哀れみ] pity. (⇨情け) ● 慈悲を請う beg (him) for *mercy*. ● お慈悲に[で] for *mercy*'s [*pity*'s] sake. ● 慈悲深い判事 a *merciful* [*寛大な*a *lenient*] judge. (*情け深い*) ● 彼はいつも慈悲的の心で人を見る He always judges other people *out of charity* [*mercy*].

> 翻訳のこころ お上のお慈悲で, 命を助けて島へやってくださいます (森鷗外『高瀬舟』) The official had shown mercy to spare [×save] my life and send me to the island. (⚠ (1)「お上」は an official (役人)と表す. (2)「お慈悲で」は show mercy (慈悲を示す, 与える)と表す. (3) spare は「危害(=死刑になること)が及ばないように特別に配慮する」の意. save は「身の安全を守る」の意なのでここでは不適切)

シビア ── シビアな 形 severe. ● シビアな批評 *severe* criticism.

じびいんこうか 耳鼻咽喉科 otolaryngology /òutoulæ̀riŋgάlədʒi/. ● 耳鼻咽喉科の医院 an ear, nose, and throat hospital.

● 耳鼻(咽喉)科医 an ear, nose, and throat doctor [specialist] (略 an ENT specialist); an otolaryngologist.

じびき 字引 a dictionary. (⇨辞書)

じびきあみ 地引き網, 地曳き網 a seine /séin/ (net), a dragnet. ● 地引き網をする draw the *seine* ashore.

じひつ 自筆 ● 漱石の自筆の原稿 manuscripts *in* Soseki's *own handwriting*.

じひびき 地響き [重々しい音] a thud; [轟音] a roaring sound; [地鳴り] the rumble of the earth. ● 地響きを立てて倒れる fall with a (heavy) *thud*. ▶ダンプカーが地響きを立てて我が家の前を通り過ぎた A dump truck *rumbled* past my house.

しひょう 死票 a wasted vote.

しひょう 指標 [書] an index (複 ~es, indices); (経済の) an indicator; (政策などの) guidelines. ● 経済指標 economic *indicators*. ● その数字は今後の土地の相場の指標となるだろう The figures will act as a *barometer* for the market price of land.

しびょう 死病 a fatal [an incurable] disease.

じひょう 時評 a comment [a review] on current affairs. ● 文芸時評 a literary *comment* [*review*].

● 時評欄 an editorial page.

じひょう 辞表 a resignation. ● 辞表を提出[撤回]する hand in [withdraw] one's *resignation*. ● 辞表を受理[却下]する accept [refuse] 《his》 *resignation*.

じびょう 持病 《慢性病》a chronic disease. ▶ぜんそくの持病に悩んでいる I am suffering from my *chronic [old] asthma*.

シビリアン 〖一般市民, 文民〗a civilian.
● シビリアンコントロール〖文民統制〗civilian control.

しびれ 痺れ 〖感覚をなくすこと〗numbness; 〖血行がはたげらわれて起きる手足のしびれ〗《話》pins and needles. (⇨痺れる)
● **しびれを切らす** ▶私は長い間彼女を待ったがしびれを切らして(=我慢ができず)帰ってきた I waited for her for a long time, but I *got impatient* and came home.

*****しびれる 痺れる** 〖無感覚になる〗go* numb, 《やや話》go to sleep; 〖ひびする〗get* paralyzed. (⇨麻痺(¾))
▶ぼくはあのロックにしびれた I *was carried away [was enthralled]* by the rock. ▶足がしびれた My legs *have gone numb [gone to sleep]*./I *got pins and needles* in my legs. ▶腕がしびれている My arm *is numb [asleep]*.

しびん 溲瓶, 尿瓶 a chamber pot; a urinal.

しふ 師父《師と父》one's teacher and father; 《敬愛している師》a fatherly teacher.

しぶ 渋 astringent juice; (柿の) persimmon tannin.
● 渋を抜く remove the *astringency* 《of persimmons》.

しぶ 支部〖本店・本部に対して〗a branch 《office》; 〖クラブ・協会などの〗a chapter; 〖労働組合などの〗《米話》a local.
● 支部長 the manager of a branch office.

じふ 自負 图 〖誇り〗pride; 〖自信〗(self-) confidence; 〖うぬぼれ〗(self-) conceit. ● 彼は自負心が強い He is very *confident*./He has great *confidence* in his abilities./He *thinks* very *highly of himself*.
── 自負する 動 be self-confident 《of; *that* 節》; take pride in 《do*ing*》; flatter oneself 《*that* 節》.

じふ 慈父〖愛情深い父〗a loving [an affectionate] father.

*****しぶい 渋い** ❶〖味が〗(柿などが) astringent; (酒などが舌ざわりが悪い) harsh. ● 渋い(=苦い)お茶 *bitter* [《濃い》*strong*] tea.
❷〖趣味・色などが〗(簡素な) austere; (洗練された) elegant, refined; (地味な) subdued, quiet, 《米》sober, 《英》sombre; (控えめな) low-key. (〖日本語の「渋い」に当たる英語はないので、訳語を工夫する必要がある〗) ● 渋い色 an *austerely elegant* [a *subdued*] color. ● 彼は渋いネクタイをしている He is wearing a *quietly refined* tie.
❸〖表情が〗 渋い顔をする make a sour /sáuər/ face 《不機嫌で気難しい顔をする》; frown 《*at*》《不機嫌・不賛成を表してまゆをひそめる》.
❹〖けちな〗stingy; 《話》tight-fisted.

シフォン chiffon /ʃifán/. ● シフォンベルベットのイブニングドレス chiffon velvet evening dress.
● シフォンケーキ a chiffon cake.

しぶおんぷ 四分音符 〖音楽〗《米》a quarter note, 《英》a crotchet.

しぶがき 渋柿 an (immature) astringent persimmon.

しぶがっそう 四部合奏 〖音楽〗a quartet(te) /kwɔːrtét/.

しぶがみ 渋紙 paper plastered with persimmon tannin.

しぶかわ 渋皮 the astringent inner skin 《of a chestnut》.
● 渋皮のむけた 渋皮のむけた(=あかぬけした)女性 an urbane [a *refined*, a *sophisticated*] woman.

しぶき 飛沫《水煙》a cloud 《of》spray; 〖はねかかる水〗a splash. ● しぶきがかかる get covered with *spray*; get splashed with water. ● 水しぶきをあげてプールに飛び込む dive into the pool with a *splash*; splash into the pool.

しふく 至福《この上もない幸福》《やや書》《feel, be filled with》《pure [*sheer*]》bliss.

しふく 私服《制服に対して》plain clothes. (〖❗〗(1) plain clothes は警官の私服. (2) 米国の私立校などでは制服 (uniform) を着ないで登校してよい日を設けている学校がある. これを a free dress day という)
● 私服警官 a plain-clothes police officer; an officer in plain clothes.

しふく 私腹 ● 私腹を肥やす line one's (own) pockets; feather one's nest.

しふく 紙幅 the number of pages available. ● 紙幅に制限があるので because of *limited space*.

しふく 雌伏 ── 雌伏する 動 bide /báid/ one's time.
● 雌伏3年 *waiting for a good opportunity* for three years.

ジプシー a gypsy. (〖❗〗しばしば G-. 軽蔑的な響きがあるため,《英》では「旅の人」(a traveler, a traveling person) と呼ぶこともある. ジプシー自身は Romany と自称する)

しぶしぶ 渋々〖気の進まぬまま〗reluctantly, grudgingly; 〖不本意に〗unwillingly. (⇨渋る) ● 《金などを》しぶしぶ出す grudge 〖《話》cough up〗《money》.
● 彼は依頼をしぶしぶ承諾した He *reluctantly* [*unwillingly*] consented to the request./He gave *reluctant* [*unwilling*] consent to the request.

ジブチ〖国名〗Djibouti /dʒibúːti/; 《公式名》the Republic of Djibouti. 《首都 Djibouti》 ● ジブチ人 a Djiboutian. ● ジブチ(人)の Djiboutian.

しぶちゃ 渋茶 《苦い》bitter tea; 《濃い》strong tea.

しぶつ 私物 《自分の持ち物》one's personal belongings. (〖❗〗複数扱い. 数える時は a piece of ..., two pieces of ...) ● 公用車を私物化する use an official car *as if it were* 〖《話》*was, is*〗one's *own car*; 《書》*appropriate* an official car *to* one's *own use*.

*****じぶつ 事物** things. ● 日本の事物(=風物) *things Japanese*. (〖❗〗(1) この意では通例形容詞を後に置く. (2) Japanese things は物質的な物のみをさす)

じぶつどう 持仏堂 a private Buddhist shrine.

ジフテリア 〖医学〗diphtheria /difθíəriə/.
● ジフテリア血清 〖薬学〗antidiphtheria serum /síərəm/.

シフト〖移行〗a shift. ● シフト勤務(=交代勤務)をする work on rotating *shift*. (〖❗〗「シフト勤務」は shift work) ● 王シフト(野球の守備の) Oh *shift*. ● シフトを破る beat the *shift*. ● 引っ張り専門の打者に対して極端なシフトをとる make a *radical shift* against the dead-pull hitter. ▶シフトが敷かれている The *shift* is on.
── シフトする 動 shift. ▶多くの企業が生産拠点を海外にシフトした Many companies *shifted* manufacturing overseas.
● シフトキー a shift key. ● シフトジスコード shift JIS code.

しぶとい 〖粘り強い〗persistent; 〖生まれつき強情で頑固な〗stubborn; 《考え方などが》obstinate; 〖屈しない〗unyielding. ● しぶとい奴 an *impudent* [a *stubborn*, an *obstinate*] fellow. ● しぶとい相手 an *unyielding* opponent.

シフトダウン 图 〖低速ギアへ切り換えること〗a downshift. (⚠ ×shiftdown とはいわない)
── シフトダウンする 動 《米》downshift, shift down;《英》change down.

じふぶき 地吹雪 a blizzard; a severe snowstorm.

しぶみ 渋味 (⇨渋い) ● 渋味のある柿 an *astringent* persimmon. ● 渋味のある(=抑制のきいた)演技 a *low-keyed* performance.

ジブラルタル ● ジブラルタル海峡 (the Strait of) Gibraltar /dʒɪbrɔ́ːltər/.

しぶりばら 渋り腹 〖医学〗tenesmus.

しぶる 渋る 〖気が進まない〗be unwilling 《to do》;〖いやがってなかなかしない〗be reluctant 《to do》;〖ちゅうちょする〗hesitate 《to do》;〖与えるのをいやがる〗grudge;〖遅らせる〗delay 《doing》. ● 寄付を出すのを渋っている *be unwilling* to make a contribution. ▶彼は1日休暇をくれるのを渋った He *grudged* [*was reluctant to* give] us a one-day leave. (⚠ unwilling と異なり、結局は休暇をくれたことを含意)

しぶろく 四分六 ● 四分六に分ける divide 《the profits》*at the ratio* /réɪʃoʊ/ [*in the ratio*, *by a ratio*] *of 6 to 4*.

しぶん 私憤 a personal grudge.

しぶん 脂粉 〖化粧〗makeup;〖化粧品〗cosmetics.
● 脂粉の香(か)に迷う 〈女に迷う〉be captivated by a woman.

しぶん 四分 ● 4分の1 a [one] fourth; a quarter. ● 4分の3 three *fourths*, three *quarters*. (⚠「4分の1マイル」は a *quarter* mile が普通)

しぶん 死文 ● 死文化する become a *dead letter*; be inoperative.

:**じぶん 自分** ❶〖自身〗oneself. (⚠ (1) 主語に応じて myself, himself, ourselves などと変化する. (2) 動詞・前置詞の目的語になる用法(通例無強勢)と、単に意味を強める用法(強勢を置く)とがある. (3) 主語には用いない) ● 自分としては満足している As for myself [As for me, ✓Personally], I am satisfied.

①〖自分~〗● 自分中心の考え方 a *self-centered* way of thinking. ● 自分探し trying to find out what career planning is all about. ● 自分持ちto pay for the expenditure used for one's company's sake. ▶彼はまったく自分勝手な男だ。自分のことしか考えないんだ He's a very *selfish* man [He's very *self-centered*]. He only thinks of [about] *himself*. ▶自分らしく(=あなたらしく)振舞いなさい Act like yourself.

②〖自分〗〖が[は]〗● 自分はどうなっても whatever happens to one. ▶彼は自分(自身)が間違っていることを知らない He doesn't know he (*himself*) is wrong. (⚠ himself は強意用法にで省略可)

③〖自分(自身)の〗one's own…; …of one's own. (⚠ (1) own は代名詞の所有格の後に用いられて意味を強める. (2) 冠詞 a, no, any, this, that などとともに用いるときは後の方を使う) ● 自分の家を持つ have *one's own* house [a house *of one's own*, ✓a one's own house]. (⚠ さらに意味を強める場合は very を用いる: have one's *very* own house [a house of one's *very* own]) ● 自分のものにする make 《it》*one's own*; 〖習得する〗learn, master. (⚠ 後の方が完全に習熟する意が強い) ● 〈何でも自分の思うようにする have 〈everything〉 *one's own* way. ● 鏡の中の自分の姿を見る look at *oneself* [*one's reflection*] in the mirror. ▶彼らはその子を自分たちの子供のように愛している They love the child as if he were *their own* [✓their *own* one]. ▶彼はそれを自分の前に置いた He put it in front of *him* [×himself]. (⚠ 通例場所を表す前置詞の後では oneself でなく人称代名詞を用いる) ▶異質

の文化を自分のものにする(=吸収同化する)のは容易なことではない It's no easy matter to *assimilate* a different culture.

④〖自分に〗● 自分に言い聞かせる tell [convince] *oneself*. (⚠ 後の方は「納得させる」の意) ● 自分に厳しい be strict with *oneself*. ● 自分に合う職を見つける find a job that suits me.

⑤〖自分(自身)を〗● 自分を知る[犠牲にする; 抑える] know [sacrifice; control] *oneself*. ● 自分を殺す〈自殺をする〉kill *oneself*; 〈自我を抑える〉suppress *oneself*. ● 自分を励ます encourage *oneself*. ● 自分を見失う lose sight of *oneself*. ▶自分(の体)を大切にせよ Take care of *yourself*.

⑥〖自分で〗〈人の助けを借りずに〉by oneself, on one's own; 〈他人がするのではなく〉for oneself (⚠「自分の利益になるように」を含意). ● 自分で言うのも何だが… If I do say so *myself*, …. ▶それは自分でできるI can do it (by) *myself* [on my own]. ▶自分のことは自分でしなくてはならない You have to do things *for yourself* [look after *yourself*]. (⚠ 後の言い方は経済的に扱いていくこと) ▶これは私が自分で作った〈デザインした〉ブラウスです This is a blouse I made [designed] (by) *myself*. (⚠ 次例より口語的)〖今はまれ〗This is a blouse *of my own making* [*design*].

会話「料理はすべて自分で作っています」「本当ですか。ご自分で料理を？」"I do all my *own* cooking." "Really? You cook *for yourself*?"

会話「もし君がぼくだとしたらどっちを選ぶ」「自分で決めろよ」"Which would you choose, if you were me?" "Make up your *own* mind."

❷〖私〗I. (⇨私(わたし))
● 自分史 a memoir of one's life.

じぶん 時分 ❶〖時〗time. (⇨頃(ころ)) ● クリスマスの時分に at Christmastime; at Christmas *season*. (⚠ on Christmas はクリスマス当日のみをいう) ● 1日[夜、1年]の今時分に at this *time* of day [night, (the) year]. (⇨今頃) ● 昼の時分時(どき)に at [×in] lunchtime.

❷〖当時に〗(⇨頃, 当time)

しぶんおんぷ 四分音符 (⇨四分(しぶ))音符.

しぶんごれつ 四分五裂 ● 子供たちは四分五裂して(=四方八方に)逃げた The kids ran away *in all directions*.

しぶんしょ 私文書 a private document.
● 私文書偽造(罪)〖法律〗the forgery of a private document.

*****しへい 紙幣** paper money [currency]; 《米》a bill; 《英》a (bank) note. (⇨札(さつ)) ● 高額[低額]紙幣 a large [a small] *bill*. ● 5ポンド紙幣 a five-pound [×-pounds] *note*. ▶本の代金を10ドル紙幣で支払った I paid with a ten-dollar *bill* for the book.

会話(銀行で)「紙幣の種類はどういたしましょうか」「10ドル紙幣9枚と残りは5ドル紙幣でお願いします」"How do you want it?" "Let me have nine tens and the rest in fives."

じへいしょう 自閉症〖医学〗autism /ɔ́ːtɪzm/. ● 自閉症の子供 an *autistic* child.

しべつ 死別 ● 死別する 動 lose. (⇨死に別れる)

シベリア Siberia /saɪbíəriə/.
● シベリア鉄道 the Siberian Railroad.

しへん 紙片 a piece [a slip, a strip] of paper. (⚠ strip は「細長い片」)

しへん 詩編〖聖書〗the Book of Psalms /sάːmz/.

しべん 至便 ● 至便な 形 very convenient. (⇨便利)

しべん 思弁 图 speculation. ── 思弁的な 形 speculative.

じへん
- 思弁哲学〖哲学〗speculative philosophy.

じへん 事変 an incident (*!* riot, war などの婉曲語);〖紛争〗(a) trouble〖disturbance の婉曲語〗. ●満洲事変 the Manchurian *Incident*.

じべん 自弁 at one's own expense. ●自弁する pay one's own expense.

しへんけい 四辺形 a quadrilateral /kwɑ̀drəlǽtərəl/, a quadrangle /kwɑ́dræŋgl/. ●四辺形の建物 a *quadrangular* building.

しぼ 私募〖金融〗private placement.

しぼ 思慕 图 (あこがれ) longing;(思い焦がれること)《書》yearning. ●思慕の情に堪えかねる have a desperate *yearning* (*for*).
— **思慕する** 動 feel [form] a strong [a deep] attachment (*to*); be very attached (*to*). ●亡き母を思慕する miss one's dead mother (a lot).

じぼ 字母 the letters of the alphabet;(活字の母型) a matrix (複 ～es, matrices); a type.

じぼ 慈母〖愛情深い母〗a loving [an affectionate] mother.

*__しほう__ 四方 〖周囲(全体)に〗(all) around;〖あらゆる方面に〗on all sides [every side];〖あらゆる方向に〗in all directions [every direction]. ●四方八方から人が集まる gather from *all directions*. ●ここから 50 マイル四方にある(=半径 50 マイル以内の)すべての湖 every lake *within a radius of* 50 miles from here. ●四方(八方)に逃げる run away in *all directions*. ●四方八方(=至る所)を探す look *everywhere* for .... ▶彼の家は四方を柵(?)で囲ってある His house is fenced *all around* [*on all sides*]. ●日本は四方を海で囲まれている Japan is surrounded by the sea. (⇨囲む) ●この花壇は 5 メートル四方(=平方)ある This flower bed is 5 meters *square*./(5 メートル四方の花壇) This is a flower bed 5 meters *square*.

しほう 司法 图 the administration of justice.
— **司法の** 形 judicial /dʒuːdíʃəl/. ▶外交官に対して司法権は及ばない We have no *judicial* power [*jurisdiction*] over diplomats.
- 司法解剖 a legally-ordered autopsy. ●司法官 a judicial officer. ●司法研修所 the Legal Training and Research Institute. ●司法試験 a bar [a judicial] examination. ●司法修習生 a legal trainee. ●司法書士 a judicial scrivener. 〖語彙〗米国には日本の書士に相当する職業はない)
- 司法制度 the judicial system.

しほう 至宝 the greatest treasure. ▶彼女は我が校の至宝だ She is a *great asset* to our school.

しほう 私法 private law.

*__しぼう__ 死亡 图 (a) death; (法律) decease /disíːs/. (⇨死) ●死亡した dead; (法律) deceased. ▶彼の死亡の原因は何ですか What is the cause of his *death*? ▶がんは死亡率の高い病気である Cancer is a disease with a high *death* [*mortality*] rate. ▶彼の死亡が確認された His *death* was confirmed.
— **死亡する** 動 die 〜d; dying); (婉曲的に) pass away;(事故などで) be killed. (⇨死ぬ) ●彼は 10 月 1 日午前 3 時に死亡した He *died* [*passed away*] at three o'clock in the morning on October 1st. ●毎年交通事故で多くの人が死亡する Every year a lot of people *are killed* in [×by] traffic accidents.
- 死亡記事 an obituary (notice). ●死亡時間 the time of death. ●死亡者(死者) the dead. ●死亡証明書 a death certificate. ●死亡通知 a notice of death.

*__しぼう__ 志望 图 〖望み〗(a) wish;(強い) (a) desire;(大望) (an) ambition;〖選択〗a choice. ●第一志望の大学 one's *first-choice* university. ▶私は作家志望だ I *want* [*wish*] *to* be a writer. (*!* wish の方が実現の可能性が低く、丁寧または控えめな表現)/I have a *desire* [an *ambition*] *to* be a writer. (*!* 後の文は堅い言い方) ▶君の志望校はどこですか Which college [school] do you *want to* enter?/Where do you *want to* go to college [school]?/Which college [school] *have* you *applied* [*are* you *applying*] *to*?/Which is the school of your (first) choice?
— **志望する** 動 want; wish;《書》desire;〖申し込む〗apply (*to*+人・団体, *for*+仕事など). (⇨希望する)
- 志望者 an applicant (*for*); a candidate (*for*).

*__しぼう__ 脂肪 (動植物の) fat (!種類をいうときは C); (溶けて柔らかい獣脂) grease; (豚の) lard; (クジラなどの) blubber. ●植物脂肪〖動物脂肪〗vegetable [animal] *fat*. ●中性脂肪 (neutral) fat; 〖医学〗triglyceride. ●皮下脂肪 subcutaneous fat. ●内臓脂肪 visceral fat. ●低脂肪の牛乳 low-*fat* milk. ●脂肪の多い[少ない]肉 *fatty* [*lean*] meat. ●おなかの周りに脂肪がつく put on *fat* around the waist. ●(肉から)脂肪を取り除く remove *fat*; cut *fat* off. ●(食事の脂肪を減らす[取らない]) cut down on [cut out] *fat*.
- 脂肪肝〖医学〗a fatty liver. ●脂肪吸引 liposuction. ●脂肪血症〖医学〗lipemia. ●脂肪酸〖化学〗fatty acid. ●脂肪代謝〖生理〗fat metabolism. ●脂肪太り being fat from eating too much fatty food.

しぼう 子房〖植物〗an ovary.

じほう 時報 a time signal. ●時計を 9 時の時報に合わせる set one's watch by the 9 o'clock *time signal*.

じぼうじき 自暴自棄 desperation. (⇨自棄(ʲ₎))

しほうじん 私法人 a private corporation.

しぼう 死没 (a) death; decease. (⇨死亡)

しぼむ 〖しおれる〗wither;〖空気が抜ける〗deflate. ▶切り花はすぐしぼむ Cut flowers soon *wither*. ▶風船がしぼんだ The balloon *deflated*.

しぼり 絞り ❶〖レンズの〗〖光学〗diaphragm /dáɪəfræm/; (F ナンバー表示による) an f-stop. ●絞り 3.2 で写す take a picture at *f*.3.2. (*!* three point two と読む)
❷〖絞り染め〗(染め方) tie-dyeing; (染め物) a tie-dye. ●絞りの羽織り tie-dye. ●絞り(染め)の羽織り a *tie-dye*(*d*) half-length *kimono* coat.

しぼりあげる 絞り上げる 〖強くしかる〗give 《him》a good telling-off [scolding] (*for*);〖金を搾り取る〗squeeze (⇨絞り取る). ▶父から絞り上げられた I *was severely told off* [*scolded*] by Father.

しぼりこむ 絞り込む ▶私たちは候補者を 10 人から 2 人に絞り込んだ We *narrowed* the list of candidates *down* from ten to two.

しぼりとる 絞り取る 〖絞って取る〗squeeze 《*from, out of*》(⇨絞る ❶);〖搾取する〗squeeze 《*from, out of*》; (金などを) extort 《*from*》. ●彼から金を搾り取る extort [*squeeze, wring*] money *from* him.

__しぼる__ 絞る, 搾る ❶〖水分などを取り去る〗(押して) squeeze; (ねじって) wring; (軽くねじって) twist; (圧縮加工して) press. ●チューブから歯みがき剤を絞り出す *squeeze* toothpaste *out of* [*from*] the tube. ●タオルを水気がなくなるまで絞る *wring* [*squeeze*] *out* a towel. ●ぬれた服を絞る *twist* the wet clothes. ▶レモンの汁を絞ってくださらない？ Could you *squeeze* (juice *out of*) a lemon?
❷〖無理に出させる〗(不法に) extort 《*from*》; (無理に同意させて) squeeze [wring*] 《*from, out of*》. (⇨絞り取る) ●無い知恵を絞る *rack* one's brains;

❸ 【厳しく尋問する】〖話〗grill 《him for it》; 〖厳しく訓練する〗drill 《in》; 〖ひどくしかる〗〖話〗tell* 《him》 off. ▶スピード違反で警察にこってり絞られた I *was grilled by the police for speeding*. ▶英文法では高校時代に絞られた I *had* English grammar *drilled into* me [I *was drilled in* English grammar] when I was a high school student. ▶宿題を忘れて先生にこってり絞られた I *was severely told off by the teacher for forgetting my homework*. ▶私は先生にこっぴどく絞られた The teacher *gave* me a severe *telling-off*. ▶今日はクラブで絞られた(=鍛えられた) I *was put through the mill during club training today*. (❗ be put through the mill は「苦しい経験をさせられる」の意.「苦しい経験をする」は go through the mill)

❹ 【範囲をせばめる】narrow ... down, limit 《to》. ●論点を絞る *narrow down* the subjects for discussion. ●候補者を3人に絞る *narrow* the candidates *down* to three.

❺ 【小さくする】▶ラジオの音量を絞る *turn down* (the volume of) the radio.

しほん 資本 capital. (❗修飾語がつくときはしばしば a ~)

① 【～(の)資本】●個人[外部]資本 private [borrowed] *capital*. ●総資本 total *capital*. ●外国資本 foreign *capital*. ●自己資本 net worth. ●固定[流動]資本 fixed [circulating] *capital*. ●人的[独占]資本 human [monopolistic] *capital*. ▶彼はその金を商売の資本に遣った He used the money as *capital* for his business. ●体が資本です Health is the most precious resource.

② 【資本が】●新しい事業を始めるには多くの資本が必要です We need a lot of *capital* to start a new business.

③ 【資本の】●資本の論理 *capital* logic. ●資本の自由化 liberalization of the *capital* market. ▶商売がうまく行く(成功する)かどうかは資本の運用方法次第だ Success in business depends on how to use *capital*.

④ 【資本を】●資本を調達する raise *capital*. ▶彼らはその映画製作に多額の資本を投じた They invested a great deal of *capital* in the film production.

⑤ 【資本で】▶彼はわずかな資本で手広く商売をしている He's doing (an) extensive business with (a) small *capital*.

●資本家 a capitalist; (経営陣) the management (❗このままで複数扱いもある). ●資本回転率 a turnover (ratio) of capital. ●資本家階級 the capitalist class. (❗単・複両扱い) ●資本勘定 a capital account. ●資本金 capital. ▶その会社の資本金は8億円です The company has a *capital* of 800 million yen [800 million yen *capital*]. ●資本財 capital goods. ●資本市場 capital market. ●資本主義 (⇨資本主義) ●資本準備金 a capital reserve. ●資本提携 capital tie-up. ●資本投下 capital investment. ●資本取引 a capital transaction. ●資本流出 capital outflow. ●資本流入 capital inflow.

しほんしゅぎ 資本主義 图 capitalism.
── 資本主義の 形 capitalist; capitalistic.
●資本主義経済 a capitalist economy. ●資本主義国家 a capitalist country. ●資本主義社会 a capitalist society. ●資本主義者 a capitalist.

しほんろん 『資本論』 *The Capital*. [参考] マルクスの経済学書]

しま 島 an island /áilənd/; (詩) an isle (❗散文では通例固有名詞の一部としてのみ用いられる (⇨諸島)). ●淡路島 the *Island* of Awaji; Awaji *Island*. ●カリブ海の島々 the *islands* of the Caribbean. ●小さな島に住む live *on* a small *island*. ●島めぐりの観光船 a (tourist) ship making a tour of the *islands*. ▶その島には1軒しか店がない There's only one store *on* the *island*.

しま 縞 a stripe; (細い) a pinstripe. ●縞柄(模様) a striped pattern. ●白い縦[横]縞のあるカーテン a curtain with white vertical [horizontal] *stripes*. ●黄と緑の縞模様の服 a yellow and green *striped* dress. ●格子縞のシャツ a plaid /plǽd/ shirt. ●細い縞の黒っぽいスーツ姿の男性 a man in a dark *pinstripe* suit. ▶会社の役員や弁護士などの定番の服装) ▶アメリカの国旗には13本の縞がある The American flag has thirteen *stripes*.

しまい 姉妹 ❶ 〖姉と妹〗sisters. (⇨兄弟) ●3人姉妹 three *sisters*.

❷ 〖関係の深いもの〗▶京都はパリと姉妹都市です Kyoto is a *sister* city 〖(英)〗 a twin town] 〖*of*〗 Paris. (❗通例 of を用いる)/Kyoto and Paris are *sister* cities 〖(英)〗 twin towns]. (❗それぞれ /s/ /s/, /t/ /t/の頭韻に注意)
●姉妹校 a sister school. ●姉妹編 a companion volume [piece] 《to》.

しまい 仕舞い 〖終わり〗an end; 〖閉じること〗a close. (⇨御仕舞い) ●店じまいする *close down* a store; (廃業する) go out of business. ●しまい湯に入る take *the last* bath. ▶彼はしまいには勝つだろう He will win *in the end*. ▶討論はしまいにはどなり合いになった The discussion ended *in* (an) uproar. ▶もう1杯やってしまいにしよう(=切り上げよう) Let's have one more glass *to end* [*finish*] *up with*. (❗ with を落とさないこと) ▶もっと体に気をつけないとしまいに入院するはめになるよ If you don't take better care of yourself, you'll *end up* in the hosptal. ▶私はその映画をしまいまで見た I saw the movie *to the end* [*last*]./I sat *through* the movie. (❗後の方は「興味がないのに最後まで座って見ていた」という含みがある)

しまい 仕舞 *shimai*; (説明的に) a Noh dance in plain clothes.

-じまい ▶あの映画は見ずじまいになってしまった I wanted to see the movie, but I *lost the chance* to see it. (❗「見る機会を失った」の意. 単に I had no time to see it./I didn't see it. などともいえる) ▶だれかに聞こうと思っていたが, あのことは分からずじまいになっている I should have asked someone about it. It remains *an unsolved question*. [I *still don't know* about it.]

しまいこむ 仕舞い込む (押し込んで) tuck ... away [*in*], tuck 《*into*, *under*, *among*》; (見えない所に) put* ... away. (⇨仕舞う ❷)

しまう 仕舞う ❶ 〖終了する〗 (仕事などを) stop (-pp-) (*working*); (店などを) close, shut*. ▶店をしまう時間だ It's time to *close* [*shut*] the store.
❷ 〖片づける〗 (見えない所に) put* ... away; (元の場所に戻す) put ... back; (保存する) keep*; (必要なときに備えて) store; (大切に) treasure. ●服をたんすにしまう(=しまっておく) *put* the clothes *away* [*keep* the clothes] in the chest. (❗ *store* the clothes *away* とすれば「しまう」の意でも「しまっておく」の意)
▶本をかばんにしまう *pack up* one's books. ▶私は初恋の思い出を心にしまっている I *treasure* the memory of my first love. ▶彼がその話を胸にしまっておいたのは賢明だった He was wise to *keep* the news to *himself*.

会話「この金どうしよう」「金庫にしまっておきなさい」 "What about this money?" "*Lock it up* in the

—**しまう** 〖完了, 結果〗 ▶本を読んでしまいましたか Have you *finished* reading the book? ▶彼の名前を忘れてしまった I *forget* [I've *forgotten*, ×*forgot*] his name. (**!** forgot だと「忘れていた」の意) ▶最終電車に乗り遅れてしまった I *missed* the last train. ▶彼の言動にはあきれてしまった I *was* very much *disgusted* with [by] his behavior. (**!** 以上 2 例のように, 日本語の「…してしまった」はあまり好ましくない結果を強調することがあり, 英語では必ずしも完了形で表現するとは限らない)

しまうま 縞馬 〘動物〙 a zebra /zíːbrə/.

じまえ 自前 ▶自前で at one's own expense(s). (⇨自賞)

しまかげ 島影 the (dim) outline of an island. ▶遠くに島影を認めた An *island* could be seen dimly in the distance.

じまく 字幕 (せりふの) subtitles. ●字幕スーパーつきの映画 a film with 《Japanese》 *subtitles*.

しまぐに 島国 an island country [nation]. ●島国根性 insularity /ìnsəlǽrəti/.

—**しませんか** (⇨ーか④)

しまだ 島田 the *shimada* hairstyle; (説明的に) a Japanese hairstyle for a (young) lady.

*****しまつ** 始末 图 ❶〖結末〗▶事の始末(＝事態がどうなったか)を聞きたい Let me hear *how things turned out.*
❷〖解決, 処理〗●紛争の始末 the *settlement* of a dispute. ●けんかの始末をつける *settle* [〚やや話〛 *patch up*] the quarrel.
●始末が悪い difficult to deal with.
●始末に負えない ●始末に負えない(＝扱いにくい)子供 an unmanageable [(言うことをきかない) an *unruly*] child.

── 始末(を)する 動 〖処理する〗 deal* with …; (うまく) manage; 〖解決する〗settle; 〖処分する〗 dispose of …; (片づける) put* … away. ●廃物を始末する *dispose of* rubbish. ●床に散らかったおもちゃを始末する *put away* the toys scattered around on the floor. ▶この問題はどう始末したらいいでしょうか How shall we *deal with* this problem?

会話 「和夫が窓を割っちゃったよ」「彼はそれをどう始末したの」 "Kazuo's broken a window." "How did he *deal with* that?"

●始末書 a written apology; a written explanation. ●始末屋 (倹約家) a frugal person.

しまった ▶しまったと思う feel [be] sorry. ▶しまった, また間違った Oh, *no* [*Oh, dear*] I've made a mistake again. (**!** 後の方は主に女性に好まれる言い方) ▶しまった, 鍵(鷙)をなくした *Oops* [*Damn it, Darn it*]! I've lost my key. (**!** damn [darn] は下品な言い方で, 「ちぇっ」に近い感じ (⇨畜生)

会話 「しまった！」「どうしたの？」「出発する前に車を満タンにするのを忘れたんだ」「まあ, つまりガス欠になったってことなの？」 "*I could kick myself!*" (**!**「ばかなことをしてしまった」とự惜の念をこめた成句表現)"Why?" "**!** I forgot to fill up the tank before we left." "Oh! Do you mean to say we're out of gas?"

しまながし 島流し ●島流しにする exile 〚〚やや書〛 banish〛 《him》 to an island.

しまふくろう 島梟 〘鳥〙 a Blakiston's fish owl.

しまへび 縞蛇 〘動物〙 a Japanese fore-striped rat snake.

しまらない 締まらない ▶刑事がすりにあったんだって. 締まらない話だね I hear a detective had his pocket picked. *How foolish!* [*What a fool* 《he is*》!/(かっこうがつかない》 It'll be the *loss of* his *face*.]

しまり 締まり ▶締まりのない顔 a *stupid-looking* face; (うつろな表情) a *vacant* look. ●お金の面で締まりのない(＝ルーズな)人 a person who is *careless with* 《his》 money. ▶あの男は口元に締まりがない His *lips are* always *hanging loose.*

しまりす 縞栗鼠 〘動物〙 a chipmunk.

しまりや 締まり屋 (倹約家) a thrifty person. (**!** 逆に金遣いの荒い人は a big spender あるいは a spendthrift という)

*****しまる** 閉まる, 締まる ❶〖閉まる〗 (ゆっくり) close /klóuz/; (急に) shut* (**!** この 2 語は通例交換して用いられるが, closed は閉じた状態, shut は閉じる動作に重点がある); (ばたんと閉まる) slam (-mm-). ●閉まっているドア a *closed* [×a *shut*] door. ▶この戸は閉まっている This door *is closed* [*is shut*, (鍵(鷙)がかかっている) *is locked*]. ▶窓が風ではたんと閉まった The window *slammed* (*shut*) [*shut with a slam*] in the wind.

会話 「このふたはぴっちり閉まらないよ」「逆方向に回してみてごらん」 "This lid doesn't *close* properly [*doesn't fit*]." "Try turning it the other way around."

会話 「店は何時に閉まりますか」「6 時に閉まります」 "What time does the store *close*?" "It *closes* at six."/"When do they *close* the store?" "They *close* it at six."

❷〖締まる〗(ひもなどが締められる) be tied; (筋肉などが締まっている) be solid. (⇨ふ締まらない) ▶彼は筋肉が締まっている He has *solid* (⇨flabby) muscles.

*****じまん** 自慢 图 〖誇り〗pride; 〖自賛〗self-praise; 〖ほら話〛(a) brag. ●自慢げに proudly; boastfully. ▶美人の妻が彼の自慢(の種)だ His beautiful wife is his *pride* (*and joy*)./His *pride* is the beauty of his wife. ▶そんなことは自慢にならない That's nothing to *be proud of* [*brag about*]. ▶お前の自慢(話)は聞きあきた I'm sick (and tired) of your *bragging*.

翻訳のこころ 自慢ではないけれど, わたしは泳げない (江國香織『デューク』) It's nothing to be proud of [×boast about], but I can't swim [don't know how to swim]. (**!** boast about は「(…ができることを)自慢する」の意なのでここでは不適切)

── 自慢する 動 be proud 《*of; that* 節》, take* pride 《*in*》, pride oneself 《*on*》; boast 《*of, about; that* 節》; brag 《-gg-》《*of, about; that* 節》.

使い分け be proud 最も一般的な表現でよい意味にも悪い意味にも使う.
boast 悪い意味で, 自慢げに述べることを表す.
brag 悪い意味で, 大げさに自慢してほら話をすることを表す.

▶彼は美人の娘[娘が美人であること]を自慢している He *is proud of* his beautiful daughter [*of his* daughter being beautiful, *that* his daughter is beautiful]. ▶彼女はみんなにその映画スターに会えたことを自慢している She *boasts to* everyone *of* having met [*that* she met] the movie star. ▶自慢するつもりはないけれども, ぼくはクラスで 1 番だった I don't mean to *brag*, but I was at the top of the class. ▶彼は 50 匹も魚を釣ったと自慢した He *bragged that* he had caught fifty fish. ▶彼女はいつも自分のことを我々に自慢している She *is* always *bragging to* us *about* herself.

しみ 染み a stain; (まだらな) a spot; (にじんだ) a blot; 〖汚れ〗(こすってできた) a smudge; (油性の) a smear; 〖顔の〗a blotch. ●血のしみ a blood *stain*; a *stain* (a *speck*) of blood. ●インクのしみ an ink *blot* [*stain*, *spot*]; a *smudge* of ink. ●ペンキのしみ a *smear* of paint. ●消えないしみ an indelible

しみ

stain 《on》. ● しみを抜く remove [get out] stains [spots, stain] 《from》. ● しみだらけの顔 《have》 a blotchy face. ▶ 果物のしみは落ちにくい Fruit stains are difficult to get out. ▶ ネクタイにしみがついているよ You have a spot on your tie. ▶ こぼしたソースでカーペットにしみができた The sauce I spilt has made a stain [a spot] on the carpet./The sauce I spilt has stained [spotted] the carpet. (⚠ 後の文ではしみは一つとは限らない) ▶ しみは洗濯しても落ちなかった The stain did not come out after the washing. (⚠ out では染み込んだしみ, off では表面についているしみを暗示する) ▶ そのドレスを染み抜きに出した I sent the dress to the cleaner's to have the stain removed. ▶ 心配するな. ただの水だからしみにはならない Don't worry, it's just water, it won't stain.

しみ 衣魚 〖昆虫〗 a silverfish; (本につく) a bookworm, (衣類につく) a (clothes) moth.

＊じみ 地味 ― 地味な 形 〖服装などが〗(目立たない) quiet; (飾りのない) plain, simple; (控えめな) (やや古) modest (⚠ 特に女性に関して用いる); (モダンでない) conservative; 〖色調が〗 quiet; (落ち着いた) subdued; (くすんだ) dull; (黒っぽい) dark. ● 地味な女性 a quiet [a modest] woman. ● 地味な生活 a simple [a modest] life. ● 地味な服装をする dress plainly. ▶ このネクタイは彼には地味だ This tie is too plain [quiet, conservative] for him. ▶ 彼は地味に物事をする He does things in a small way.

じみ 滋味 〖味わい〗 (a) taste; (a) flavor. (⇨味❷) ● 滋味豊かな作品 a work with a lot of flavor in it.

しみいる 染み入る soak. (⇨染み込む)

しみこむ 染み込む (液体が) soak 《into, through》 (⚠ into は「染み透る」, through は「染み渡る」の意); (液体・においなどが)《書》permeate 《into》. ● 染み込ませる(=吸い取る) soak … up. ▶ インクがこぼれてカーペットに染み込んだ The spilt ink has soaked into the carpet.

＊しみじみ 〖心から〗heartily; 〖感慨深く〗deeply, with deep emotion; 〖もの静かに〗quietly, softly. (⇨じっくり) ▶ 彼としみじみと話す talk quietly with him; (腹を割って) have a heart-to-heart talk with him. ▶ 過ぎし日をしみじみ振り返る look back on one's days with deep emotion [よかったことを] with great nostalgia. ▶ 戦争の悲惨さがしみじみ分かった I fully realized the misery of war.

しみず 清水 (澄んだ水) clean [(crystal-)clear, fresh] water; (湧き出る) spring water.

じみち 地道 ― 地道な 形 (着実な) steady; (まじめな) serious.

― 地道に 副 steadily. ● 地道に努力する make steady [serious] efforts. ● 地道にこつこつと(生活費を)かせぐ grind out one's living.

しみつく 染み付く cling* 《to》; (くせが) get* the habit 《of doing》. ▶ たばこのにおいが服に染みついている The smell of tobacco has clung to my clothes./My clothes smells badly of tobacco.

しみったれ stinginess; (人) a stingy person, 《米》a tightwad 〖くだけた言い方〗. ▶ 彼は思っていた以上にしみったれだ He is far stingier 《with his money》 than I expected.

しみでる 染み出る (液体・気体・においなどが) seep 《into, out》. ▶ その花びんの割れ目から水が染み出ていた Water was seeping out through cracks in the vase.

しみとおる 染み透る soak [pénétràte, 《書》pérmeàte] 《into, through》. (⇨染み込む, 浸透)

しみゃく 支脈 (水脈の) a branch; (山脈の) an offset; (葉脈・血管の) a veinlet.

シミュレーション 〖模擬実験〗 (a) simulation. (参考 近年サッカーでは「審判のファール宣告を促すための演技的行為, 特に倒れ込む行為」を「シミュレーション」, もしくは口語で「ダイビング」と称している) ● シミュレーションを使ってテストする a test through simulation.

シミュレーター a simulator. ● フライトシミュレーター 〖模擬飛行装置〗 a flight simulator.

＊しみる 染みる ❶ 〖にじみ込む〗 soak 《into, through》. (⇨染み込む)

❷ 〖痛む〗(うずくように痛む) smart; (刺すように痛む) sting*. ▶ 煙が目に染みた The smoke made my eyes smart [sting]./My eyes smarted [stung, were sore] from the smoke. ▶ 少し染みるかもしれませんがこれで傷がきれいになります This may sting [bite] a little, but it'll cleanse the wound.

❸ 〖強く感じる〗 ▶ 寒さが骨身に染みた The cold pierced me to the bone./I was chilled to the bone [marrow (of the bones)]. ▶ 彼の親切が身に染みた His kindness touched [moved] me greatly./I was greatly touched [moved] by his kindness.

-じみる ▶ 子供じみたしゃべり方をする talk like a child; (軽蔑的) talk in a childish way.

＊しみん 市民 a citizen. (⚠ 投票権のある者の意. 並記する地名により国民, 県民, 町民ともなる) ● 大阪市民 (個人) a citizen of Osaka; an Osakan /óusəkən/ (⚠ 「大阪人」「浪速っ子」といった感じの語で主に新聞用語. cf. Tokyoite /tóukiouàit/ (東京人, 江戸っ子)); (総称) the citizens [people] of Osaka. (関連 大阪府民 a citizen of Osaka Prefecture/ニューヨーク人[っ子] a New Yorker/ロンドン人[っ子] a Londoner) ● 一般市民 a civilian; the ordinary citizens. ● 世界市民 a world citizen; a citizen of the world; a cosmopolitan. ● 市民の関心[反応] concern [a reaction] from citizens. ● 納税はすべての市民の義務である Paying taxes is every citizen's obligation.

● 市民運動 a citizens [a grass-roots, a civic] movement. ● 市民オンブズマン a citizen('s) ombudsman [〖男女共用〗 ombudsperson]. ● 市民階級 bourgeoisie /bùərʒwɑ:zí:/. ● 市民革命 a civil revolution. ● 市民権 (⇨市民権) ● 市民社会 a civil society. ● 市民税 a municipal tax. ● 市民体育館 a municipal gymnasium; a city gymnasium. ● 市民大学 a citizens' college. ● 市民団体 a citizens' group.

しみん 四民 (⇨士農工商)

しみん 嗜眠 〖医学〗 lethargy. ● 嗜眠性脳炎 〖医学〗 sleeping sickness; lethargic encephalitis.

しみんけん 市民権 (国民の資格) citizenship. ● 米国の市民権を得る gain [〖書〗 be granted] U.S. citizenship; become a U.S. citizen. (⇨国籍)

しみんとう 自民党 the Liberal Democratic Party (略 LDP). ● 自民党員 a Liberal Democrat; a member of the Liberal Democratic Party (⚠ しばしば a LDP member とも書かれる).

＊じむ 事務 名 〖机に向かう仕事〗 office [clerical] work, deskwork; 〖実務・職務上の仕事〗 business. (⇨仕事) ● 事務用機器[コンピュータ] a business machine [computer]. ● 事務多忙のため by the pressure of business. ● 事務に就く get an office [a clerical, a desk] job. ● 事務能力がある have business ability. ● 事務処理をする transact [conduct] one's business [affairs]. ● 事務レベルの working-level. ● 事務の引き継ぎ to inform one's successor of the details of one's work. ▶ 彼はその会社で事務を執っている He does office

ジム ━━*clerical*] *work* at the company.
━━**事務的な** businesslike. ●事務的な応対 a *businesslike* [*a matter-of-fact*] *way* of receiving people. (❗前の方は手際のよさ，後の方は味気なさを含意) ●事務的な口調 a *businesslike* tone. ●その件を事務的に扱う handle the matter in a *businesslike way*.
●**事務員，事務官，事務局員** a clerk, an office worker. (❗後の方が普通) ●**事務官** a government official. ●**事務規定** office regulations. ●**事務局** a secretariat. ●**事務局長[総長]** a secretary-general. ●**事務室** an office. (⇨事務所) ●**事務用品** stationery; office supplies.

ジム (体育館) a gym; (ボクシングの) a boxing gym. (❗gym は gymnasium の略)

しむけ 仕向け (商品などを送ること) shipping.
●**仕向先[地]** the (place of) destination.

しむける 仕向ける ●彼が辞職するように仕向ける(＝働きかける) approach [*speak to*] him about his resignation. ●彼女に友人を裏切るよう仕向ける(＝そのかす) *entice* her *to* betray [*into* betraying] her friends. ●我々は彼に決断するよう仕向けた(＝せき立てた) We *pushed* him to make [*into* making] a decision.

じむし 地虫 〖昆虫〗a grub.

じむしょ 事務所 an office. ●きゅうくつな事務所 a cramped *office*. ●法律事務所に勤める work in [at] a lawyer's *office*.

しめ 〖鳥〗a hawfinch.

しめ 締め 〖束〗a bundle 《*of*》; 〖合計〗the total, the sum (total). ●締めにケーキを食べる eat cake at the end of a meal.

しめあげる 締め上げる 〖きつく締める〗tighten ... up; (ひも・錠などで) fasten ... up [*tightly*]; (ボルトで) bolt ... up; (ねじで) screw ... up; 〖厳しく追求する〗question [*interrogate*] (*a suspect*) severely.

***しめい 氏名** (名と姓) one's given name and family name (❗語順に注意); a full name (❗略さない姓名全部のこと); (名前) one's name (⇨名前). ●あなたの氏名と住所をブロック体で書いてください Please write down your (*full*) *name* and address in block letters.

***しめい 使命** (a) mission. ●使命を果たす carry out one's *mission*.
●**使命感** a sense of mission; (天職意識) (《strong》 sense of) vocation 《*for* teaching》.

しめい 死命 life and death.
●**死命を制する** (運命を決する) decide [*seal*] one's fate.

しめい 指名 名 nomination; 〖書〗designation; appointment. ●(選挙などで)指名を獲得する win the *nomination*. ●殺人容疑で警察に指名手配される *be wanted for* murder by the police. (❗「指名手配中の男」は *a wanted man*)
━━**指名する** 動 〖名指す〗name; (公式に)〖書〗designate /dézignèit/; 〖任命する〗appoint; 〖候補に〗nominate; 〖指名하는〗call on 《him *to* do》. ●彼を議長に指名する *name* [*designate*, *appoint*] him (*as* [*to be*]) chairman. (❗(*as* [*to be*]) の後の名詞は通例無冠詞) ●大統領候補に指名される be *nominated for* President [the (office of) presidency].
●**指名競争入札** designed (competitive) bidding. ●**指名打者** 〖野球〗a designated hitter 《略 DH》. ●**指名投票** a nomination vote.

じめい 自明 ●**自明の理** a self-evident [*an obvious*] truth; 《書》an axiom /ǽksiəm/. ●それは自明の理だと思います It is *self-evident*./It speaks for itself. ●そ

れは自明の理だと思います I accept it as an *axiom*.

しめきり 注連縄 (⇨注連縄)

しめきり 締め切り ●a deadline 《*for*》. (❗closing time は通例「営業終了時間」の意) ●締め切り日 (応募などの) the *closing* date (*for* applications); (支払いなどの) the due date. ●明日の締め切りまでに by tomorrow's *deadline*. (❗次例の the に注意) ●4月1日[午後5時]の締め切りまでに by the April 1 [5 p.m.] *deadline*. ●締め切り時間に間に合わせる [遅れる] meet [*miss*] the *deadline*. ●締め切り日を延期する push back the *deadline* 《*until*》. ●レポート提出の締め切りはいつですか When is the *deadline for* (handing in) the paper?

しめきる 閉め切る，締め切る ❶〖戸・家などを〗shut* [*close*] ... (up). ●窓を閉め切っておく *keep* the windows *closed* [*shut*].
❷〖申し込みなどを〗close. ●申し込みを締め切る *close* applications 《*for* the job》.

しめくくり 締めくくり 〖結論〗a conclusion; 〖要約〗a summary; 〖終わり〗an end. ●しめくくりとして in *conclusion* [*summary*]. ●仕事のしめくくりをつける *finish* the work; *get through* (《主に米》*with*) the work; 《やや書》*put an end to* the work.

しめくくる 締めくくる ●みんなに感謝してスピーチを締めくくる(＝終える) *finish* [*close*, 《やや書》*conclude*, (首尾よく) *round off*] one's speech *by* thanking everybody. (⇨結ぶ❹) ●試合を締めくくる close out a game.

しめこみ 締め込み (まわし) a sumo wrestler's cloth belt.

しめころす 締め殺す strangle, suffocate [*choke*] 《him》to death; (蛇が) squeeze ... to death.

しめさば 締め鯖 *shimesaba*; (説明的に) raw mackerel sprinkled with salt and pickled in vinegar.

しめし 示し ●**示しがつかない** ●彼のだらしない生活ぶりでは子供たちに示しがつかない His loose way of living *is* [*sets*] *a bad example for* his children.

しめじ 〖植物〗a *shimeji* mushroom.

しめしあわせる 示し合わせる ●示し合わせた合図 a *prearranged* signal. ●彼らは示し合わせて(＝あらかじめ取り決めて)逃亡した They escaped as they *had arranged beforehand* [*previously*, *in advance*].

しめしめ 《話》I've got it!; 《話》I made it! (⇨しめた)

じめじめ ━━**している** ❶〖水分が多い〗damp; (ぬれた) wet (-tt-). ●梅雨で部屋がじめじめしている The room is *damp* because of the rainy season. ●雨の後で地面がじめじめしている The ground is *wet* after the rain.
❷〖性格などが暗い〗gloomy, somber, dismal. ●彼はじめじめしている He is *gloomy*.

しめす 示す ❶〖見せる〗show*; 《書》display; (表現する) express; (例などを) give*; (それとなく示す) indicate; (例証する) illustrate. ●身分証明書を示す *show* an ID card. ●英語に興味を示す *show* [*display*] interest in English. ●例を示す *give* an example. ●子供によい手本を示す *set* an example for one's child. ●その数字は生活費の著しい増加をはっきり示している The figures clearly *show* a marked increase in living costs. ●彼はうなずいて賛成の意を示した He *showed* [*expressed*, *indicated*] his approval with a nod. ●その行為は彼が勇敢であることを示している The deed *shows* [*illustrates*, (証拠である) *is evidence of*] his bravery. The deed *shows* [*indicates*, (立証する) *proves*] that he is brave.
❷〖指し示す〗point ... (out); (記号などが) mark, 《書》designate /dézignèit/; 〖表示する〗(印などで)

《書》indicate; (計器などが) read*. ▶駅へ行く道をさし示す point [indicate, (地図を書いて) show] the way to the station. ▶地図の赤丸は学校を示す Red circles on the map mark [designate] schools. ▶アクセント記号は一つの語における強勢を示す An accent mark indicates stress in a word. ▶温度計が零度を示している The thermómeter reads [shows, indicates, stands at] zero degrees. (⚠ ✗zero degree とはいわない) ▶その記号は何を示している(=表す)のですか What does the symbol stand for?

しめた 《話》I've got it!; 『いいぞ』Good!; 『ありがたい』Thank God [goodness]! (⇨しめしめ)

しめだし 閉め出し (労働者の工場からの) a lockout.

しめだす 閉め出す shut* [(錠をかけて) lock] ... out.
• 彼を部屋から閉め出す shut [lock] him out of the room. ▶労働者は争議中に工場から閉め出された The workers were locked out during the dispute.

しめつ 死滅 图 《絶滅》extinction.
—— **死滅する** 動 become extinct; (死に絶える) die out.

じめつ 自滅 —— **自滅する** 動 destroy [ruin] oneself; bring about one's ruin; (自分で自分の首を絞める) cut one's own throat. ▶大事な試合で(緊張のあまり)自滅する 《米話》choke in a big game. ▶彼らはエラーを連発して自滅した They lost the game by making a succession of errors.

じめつく (⇨じめじめ)

しめつけ 締め付け ❶ 『強く締めること』▶ねじの締めつけが甘い The screw is not tightened enough./The screw is loose.
❷ 『強い取り締まり』▶上からの締めつけがきびしい 『強い』be under tight control.

しめつける 締め付ける ❶ 『強く締める』tighten. • ねじを締めつける tighten a screw; fasten a screw tight(ly).
❷ 『圧迫する』(押しつける) squeeze, 《やや書》compress; (心をひどく悲しませる) distress, 《やや書》wring*. ▶相手をヘッドロックで締めつける(=締めあげる)(レスリングで) squeeze the opponent in a headlock. ▶日本を経済的に締めつける(=経済上の制裁を加える) impose economic sanctions on Japan. ▶胸が締めつけられるような(悲しい)事件 a heart-wrenching [a heart-wringing] incident. ▶何かに胸を締めつけられるような気がした I had a tight feeling in my chest. (⇨圧迫) ▶彼の話を聞いて私の胸は締めつけられる思いだった I was distressed to hear his story.
❸ 『取り締まる』▶生徒は校則で締めつけられている The students are tightly [strictly] controlled by the school rules.

しめっぽい 湿っぽい ❶ 『空気などが』(じめじめした) damp, ▶不快な感じを伴う), (湿度の高い) humid, (湿気を適度に含んだ) moist; (ぬれた) wet (-tt-). • 冷たくて[暑くて]湿っぽい空気 (a) cold and damp [hot and humid] air; (特定の場所の) a cold and damp [a hot and humid] atmosphere. ▶雨の日は湿っぽい It is damp in rainy weather.
❷ 『沈みがちの』(陰気な) gloomy.

しめて 締めて ▶その数を締めて100になる The figures add [sum] up to 100. ▶締めていくらになりますか How much does it come to [make] altogether?/What is the total?

しめなわ 注連縄 a shimenawa rope; (説明的に) in Shinto religion, a thick, twisted straw rope with stripes of white paper hung around a place [a thing] to ward off evil spirits.

しめやか —— **しめやかに** 图 (悲しみの中に) sorrowfully; (厳粛に) solemnly; (静かに) quietly. ▶彼の葬儀はしめやかに執り行われた His funeral was solemn [was conducted solemnly].

しめらせる 湿らせる make*... slightly [a little bit] wet; dampen; moisten. (⇨湿る) ▶彼は舌で唇を湿らせた He moistened his lips with his tongue./He made his lips wet with his tongue.

しめり 湿り wet; dampness; moisture; humidity. ▶いいお湿りですね It's a welcome rain, isn't it?

しめりけ 湿り気 moisture; dampness. (⇨湿気) ▶湿り気がある moist. (⇨湿る)

*:**しめる 閉める，締める，絞める** ❶ 『閉じる』(ゆっくり) close; (急に) shut* (⇨閉まる); (くぎ・錠などで) fasten, 《やや書》secure. ▶門を閉める close [shut, fasten] the gate. ▶引き出しを閉める close a drawer. • カーテンを閉める close [draw, pull] the curtains. • 窓を閉めておく keep the window closed [shut]. • 戸をばたんと閉める bang [slam] the door shut; shut the door with a bang [a slam]. • 窓を閉めてください。風が強すぎるよ Close [Shut] the windows, please. The wind is too strong. ▶店は午後7時に閉めます Our store is closed at seven p.m. (⚠「(すでに)閉まっている」の意にもなる)/We close (the store) at seven p.m.
❷ 『締め付ける』(しっかり留める) fasten; (身につけている) wear*; (結ぶ) tie (～d; tying). ▶頭に鉢巻きを締める tie a towel around one's head. • シートベルトを締める [締めている] fasten [wear] one's seat belt. • ネクタイを締める [締めている] tie [wear] a tie. ▶彼はトランクに皮ひもをかけて締めた He fastened a strap around the trunk.
❸ 『引き締める』(きつく) tighten; (ねじって) screw ... (up). • ねじ [ベルト] を締める tighten a screw [one's belt]. • バイオリンの弦を締める tighten [screw up] the strings of a violin.
❹ 『節約する』• 燃料費を締める economize (on) [save] fuel. • 経費を締める(=切り詰める) cut down (on) [(減らす) reduce, (削減する) slash, 《やや書》curtail] one's spending.
❺ 『きびしくする』▶学生を締める be strict [firm] with the students; 《やや話》keep a tight rein on the students.
❻ 『合計する』(⇨締めて)

*:**しめる 占める** ❶ 『空間・地位などをふさぐ』occupy, take*... up; (ある割合を) account for ...; 『座席などにつく』take; 『手に入れる』get*; 『持っている』have*; 『確保している』hold*. • 彼の心を占める [占めている] occupy his mind. ▶過半数を占める get a majority. ▶その地域はほとんど工場が占めていた Most of the areas were occupied [were taken up] by factories. ▶女性の参加者は全体の6割を占めた Women participants occupied [accounted for, (達した) amounted to, (構成した) made up] 60 percent of all. ▶彼がその地位を6年間占めていた He held [occupied] the position for six years. ▶53パーセントの米国人が「人生で宗教がたいへん重要な役割を占めている」と考える Fifty three percent of Americans think religion plays a very important role in their lives.
❷ 『その他の表現』▶(成功の)味を占める get a taste of success; be encouraged [elated] by one's success.

*:**しめる 湿る** become* [get*] damp [moist] (⚠ moist は適度の, damp は不快な湿気を意味する); (ぬれる) get [become] wet. • 湿った空気 moist [(高温多湿の) humid] air. ▶洗濯物はまだ湿っている The washing is still damp [wet]. ▶湿った木はなかなか燃えなかった The damp [wet] wood didn't burn

しめん 四面 four sides. (⇨四方) ▪(正)四面体 〖幾何〗 a (regular) tetrahedron /tètrəhíːdrən/.
▪ **四面楚歌** ▸四面楚歌である be surrounded [be besieged] by enemies.

しめん 紙面 ❶〖紙の表面〗the surface of the paper.
❷〖記事を載せるページ〗space. ▸紙面を割く give *space* (*to*); allow *space* (*for*). ▸紙面の都合で(=に限りがあるので) on account of limited [for lack of] *space*. ▸紙面が許せば if *space* permits; if there is enough *space*. ▸紙面の許す限りを to the limit of *space*. ▸そのスキャンダルが新聞の紙面をにぎわせた The scandal was splashed across the *page* of the newspaper.

しめん 誌面 ▸誌面で on the *page* of a magazine. ▸就職申し込みについての詳細は誌面 15 ページをご覧ください For further details on how to apply a job, see *page* 11.

***じめん** 地面 the ground; 〖(空に対する)地〗the earth.
▪地面に倒れる[横たわる] fall to [lie on] the *ground*. ▪地面に円を描く draw a circle *in the ground*. ▸20 秒間にわたり地面が揺れた For twenty seconds the *earth* shook. ▸雨がやんと地面はさわやかな土のにおいがした The *earth* smelled fresh after the rain.

***しも** 霜 frost. (**!** 霜の種類や霜がおりることをいうときは Ⓒ) ▪一面に霜がおりている校庭 the *frost*-covered school ground. ▸昨夜は霜がおりた We had [There was] a *frost* last night. ▸今朝野原に霜がおりていた The fields were frosty [were covered with *frost*] this morning. ▸ひどい霜で植物がやられた The plants were damaged [were killed] by the heavy *frost*./The heavy *frost* damaged [killed, did damage to] the plants.

しも 下 ❶〖下流〗the lower reaches (of a river).
▪下の方へ流されるで carried away *downstream*. ❷〖後半〗the latter part. ▪下の句 the *latter part* of a *tanka* poem. ▪数字の下 2 桁 the *last two digits* of a figure.
❸〖下座〗(⇨下座)
❹〖大小便〗▸老人の下の世話をする take care of the old man's [woman's] *toilet function*; help the old man [woman] to relieve himself [herself].

しもがかる 下掛かる ▸彼はよく下がかった話をする His jokes are often a bit blue.

しもがれ 霜枯れ ▪霜枯れの *frost*-bitten; frosted.
▪霜枯れした植物 frost-bitten plants. ▪霜枯れ時 dreary winter; when trees are frosted; 〖景気の悪い時期〗time especially at the end of the year when the business is weak.

しもがれる 霜枯れる be nipped [killed] by frost.

しもき 下期 (⇨下半期)

しもく 耳目 ▸耳目を引く attract *public attention*.
▪耳目を驚かす startle the *world*; cause [create] a *sensation*.

しもごえ 下肥 night soil; human excrement.

しもざ 下座 ▪下座に座る(食卓で) sit at the bottom of a table; 〖部屋で〗take *the lower* [*the last*] *lowest*] seat; 〖横 1 列に並ぶ場合〗sit far removed from one's superior.

しもじも 下々 the common people; the masses; 〖下層階級〗the lower class.

しもたや 仕舞屋 a dwelling house in the shopping district.

しもつき 霜月 〖11 月〗November; 〖陰暦の〗the eleventh month of the lunar calendar.

しもて 下手 〖舞台の〗the right (of the stage), the right(-hand) side of the stage (**!** 舞台側から見て); 〖川の〗下下流, 下 ❶. ▸舞台の下手から登場[へ退場]する enter [exit] *stage right*. ▪*stage right* (↔*stage left*) は副詞句

じもと 地元 ▪地元の 〖(地域の)〗local; 〖(本拠地の)〗home. ▪地元チーム a *home* [a *local*] team. ▪地元の人 a *local* (area) person (↔a stranger to the area (よその人)) ▪地元民 *local* people [inhabitants]; people of the *district*, 〖話〗locals; (一時的な訪問者に対して) natives.

しもどけ 霜解け a thaw, thawing. (⇨雪解け)

しもネタ 下ネタ a dirty joke.

しもばしら 霜柱 frost like ice needles. (**!** 英語には対応する訳語はない) ▸霜柱が立った *Frost* has formed into ice needles on the ground.

しもはんき 下半期 the latter [second] half of the (fiscal) year. (**!** 通例会計年度の区分なので fiscal をつける方が普通)

しもぶくれ 下ぶくれ ▪下ぶくれである be full-cheeked; have chubby cheeks [full jawline]. (**!** chubby は「感じよく肉つきのよい」の意)

しもふり 霜降り 图 〖牛肉〗well-marbled sirloin beef. ── 霜降りの 厖 〖肉の〗marbled 《meat》.

しもやけ 霜焼け chilblains; 〖凍傷〗frostbite. ▪霜焼けができるを get [suffer] *frostbite*. ▪霜焼けのできた耳 *chilblained* [*frostbitten*] ears. ▸足に霜焼けができている I have *chilblains* on my toes./My toes are *frostbitten*.

しもよけ 霜除け ▪霜よけをする shelter 《plants》 from frost; protect 《plants》 from [against] frost.

しもん 指紋 a fingerprint, 〖話〗a print. (**!** 通例複数形で) ▪指紋を取る take [get] 《his》 *fingerprints*.
▪指紋を残す leave one's *fingerprints* 《on》. ▪ナイフから指紋を採取する lift 《his》 *fingerprints* from a knife. (**!**「指紋採取」は fingerprinting) ▪指紋を照合する match the *fingerprints* 《with》.

しもん 試問 ▪口頭試問 an oral exam.

しもん 諮問 ── 諮問する 動 consult … (for advice). ▸審議会に諮問する *consult* the council (*for* technical advice).
▪諮問機関 an advisory panel [organization].
▪首相の私的諮問機関 a private *advisory* panel to the prime minister.

じもん 地紋 a pattern.

じもん 自問 ── 自問する 動 ask oneself.

じもんじとう 自問自答 ── 自問自答する 動 answer one's own question; 〖思索する〗wonder to [think to, argue with] oneself 《*about*; *wh*- 節》.

***しや** 視野 ❶〖視界〗view, sight; 〖視域〗a field of vision. ▸視野を遮る shut out one's *view*. ▸湖が視野に入ってきた The lake came into *view* [*sight*].
❷〖思考などの範囲〗horizons. ▪視野を広める broaden one's *horizons*. ▸彼女の視野は狭い[広い] Her *horizons* are narrow [broad]./(彼女は視野の狭い[広い]人だ) She is a woman of narrow [broad] *horizons*. ▸(…a woman with a narrow [a broad] *outlook*. ともいえる)

しゃ 社 〖会社〗a company; 〖神社〗a shrine.

しゃ 紗 (silk) gauze.

しゃ 斜 ▪斜に構える stand ready 《*to do*》.

じゃ 蛇 a serpent; a snake.
▪蛇の道はへび Set a thief to catch a thief./An old poacher makes the best keeper.

じゃ(あ) 〖ところで〗well; 〖さて〗now; 〖そうすると〗then.

(⇒では, それでは) ▶じゃ, さようなら ▽Bye (now)!/(じゃ, また) See you./Good by(,) then. ▶じゃ, それまで Right, that's all [it].
会話 「もう行かなくっちゃ」「そうかい, じゃあな」"I gotta go now." "OK. Take it easy." (! gotta /gátə/ は have got to の短縮形 (主に米語))

ジャー [魔法びん] a vacuum bottle [《英》flask], a thermos (bottle). (! 英語の jar は「(陶器・ガラスなどでできた広口の)びん」の意)

ジャーキー 《a stick of》jerky.

じゃあく 邪悪 ● 邪悪な 形 evil /íːvl/, wicked /wíkid/ (! 後の方が強意的) (⇒悪い); (悪徳に満ちた) vicious. ▶邪悪な力がひつぎを背負ってやって来ようとしている Evil forces are coming with coffins on their backs.

ジャーク (重量挙げの) clean and jerk.

シャーシー a chassis /ʃǽsi/, 徴 chassis /ʃǽsiz/.

ジャージー [服地] jersey /dʒə́ːrzi/ (cloth); [セーター] a sweater; (運動選手の着るシャツ) a jersey; (競技の前後に着る上下そろいの) a tracksuit; 《米》a sweat suit.

しゃあしゃあ ● しゃあしゃあしている (非難などを感じない) be thick-skinned; (鈍感な) be insensitive (to); (恥じない) be shameless. ▶彼女は他人に何を言われてもしゃあしゃあしている She is insensitive to whatever other people may say. ▶彼女は浮気がばれてもしゃあしゃあしている When she was found having an affair, she didn't bat an eye [an eyelid]. (! この成句は「顔に感情の変化を少しも出さない」の意)

じゃあじゃあ [水をかけるさま] ● 水をじゃあじゃあかける splash water 《on》.

ジャーナリスト a journalist. (⇒記者)

ジャーナリズム journalism. ▶ジャーナリズムの仕事につく go into journalism.

ジャーナル a journal.

シャープ ❶[音楽] a sharp (↔a flat).
❷[鋭い] ● 頭がすごくシャープだ be 《as》sharp as a razor; be razor-sharp; have a razor-sharp mind.

シャープペンシル a mechanical《米》[a propelling《英》] pencil. (! 単に a pencil ともいう. a sharp pencil は「先のとがった鉛筆」)

シャーベット 《米》(a) sherbet,《英》(a) sorbet.

シャーマン a shaman /ʃɑ́ːmən/ (徴 ~s).

シャーレ [<ドイツ語] a lab(oratory) dish.

シャーロックホームズ [コナン・ドイルの推理小説の主人公] Sherlock Holmes.

しゃい 謝意 gratitude, appreciation. ▶彼の援助に対して謝意を示す express one's gratitude [appreciation] (to him) for his assistance.

シャイ — シャイな 形 [内気な, はにかみ屋の] shy. (⇒恥ずかしい) ▶彼はシャイなのでダンスに誘えない He is too shy to ask a girl to dance with him.

ジャイアント ● ジャイアントスラローム [スキー] giant slalom.

ジャイカ [国際協力事業団] JICA (Japan International Cooperation Agency の略).

ジャイロコンパス a gyro compass.

ジャイロスコープ [回転儀] a gyroscope.

しゃいん 社印 the official seal of a company.

しゃいん 社員 [従業員] an employee (of a company) (⇒会社員); [職員] a staff member (of a company) (⇒職員). ● 平[正]社員 an ordinary [a regular] employee. ● 契約社員 a contract worker. ● 派遣社員 a temp. ● 新入社員 a new employee; a (new) recruit. ▶彼はこの出版社の社員です He is an employee of this publishing company. / He works for this publishing company. (! 後の方が口語的)
● 社員研修 (企業内教育訓練) personnel training within industry; staff training. ● 社員証 an employee ID card. ● 社員割引 an employee discount.

しゃうん 社運 ● 社運をかけた新事業 a new project which will determine the future of a company.

しゃおく 社屋 an office building, the building of a company.

しゃおんかい 謝恩会 a thank-you party given by the graduates [the graduating class] in honor of their teachers.

しゃか 釈迦 (the) Buddha, (釈迦牟尼) S(h)akyamuni. ▶花祭りは釈迦の誕生を祝う祭りです Hanamatsuri is the festival to celebrate the birth of Buddha.
● 釈迦に説法 There is no need to teach a fish how to swim.

しゃが 射干, 著莪 [植物] a fringed iris.

ジャガー [動物] a jaguar.

シャガール [ロシア生まれのフランスの画家] Chagall (Marc ~).

しゃかい 社会 图 ❶[生活共同体] society (! 通例無冠詞だが同じ習慣・法律・組織などを持つ特定の集団をいうときは (a) society); (世間) the world (! 日本語の「社会」はこの意のことも多い); (共同体) a community. (⇒世間, 世の中)
①(~社会) ● 産業社会 industrial societies. ● 上流[中流, 下層]社会 the upper [middle; lower] class(es). ● 西欧社会 Western society. ● 文明[豊かな]社会 a civilized [an affluent] society. ● 人間社会 human society. ● 多民族社会 a multi-racial society. ● 地域社会 a local community. ● ニューヨークのプエルトリコ人社会 the Puerto Rican community in New York.
②【社会は[が]】 ▶現代の社会は実践的な政治家を必要としている Modern society needs practical politicians.
③【社会の】 ● 社会のおきて the laws of society. ▶家族は社会の最小単位である The family is the smallest unit of 《×the》society. ▶新聞はいわば社会の鏡である The newspaper is, so to speak, the mirror of 《×the》society.
④【社会に】 ● 社会に出る go [get] out into the world 《×the society》. (! ここでは「世間」の意) ● 社会に溶け込む be assimilated into society. ▶青年は社会に何らかの貢献をしようと努力すべきだ Young people should try to do something good to (benefit) society [for the benefit of society]. ▶日本の社会には階級差や身分差が比較的少ない There are relatively few class and status distinctions in 《×the》Japanese society.
⑤【社会を】 ● 社会を担い前進させる shoulder and advance society. ● 持続可能な社会を目指す aim at a sustainable society. ▶日本は民主主義に基づいた社会を築き上げた Japan has built her society on a democratic basis.
❷[教科目] social studies. (! 単数扱い)

関連 高校の社会科の科目名: 世界史 World History/日本史 Japanese History/地理 Geography (! 以上三つをまとめて「地理・歴史」 Geography & History と呼ぶ)/現代社会 Contemporary Society/倫理 Ethics/政治・経済 Politics & Economy (! 以上三つをまとめて「公民」 Civics と呼ぶ).

— 社会の, 社会的(な) 形 social. ●社会的地位 one's *social* position [status]. ▶日本では医師の社会的地位は高い Doctors enjoy their high (*social*) *status* in Japan.
- ●社会の窓があいている 社会の窓(=ズボンのファスナー)が開いているよ Your fly is undone [open].; (書) Your stable door is open. (!いずれも慣用表現)
- ●社会悪 a social evil; a social wrong. ●社会意識 social consciousness. ●社会運動 a social movement. ●社会科学 social science. ●社会現象 a social phenomenon. ●社会工学 social engineering. ●社会事業 social work. ●社会情勢 social conditions [circumstances, situation]. ●社会人 a member of society. ●社会性 sociality. ●社会生活 social life. ●社会正義 social justice; social righteousness. ●社会政策 public policy; social policy. ●社会秩序 a (*disturb*) social order. ●社会鍋 (hold) a charity pot. ●社会不安 (*cause*) social unrest. ●社会復帰 a return to society. ●社会保障 social security. ●社会保障制度 a social security system. ●社会民主主義 social democracy. ●社会面 the third human-interest page. ●社会問題 a (*serious*) social problem.

しゃがい 社外 ▶社外持ち出し厳禁 This is for internal company use only. (参考 資料などの表紙にある表示)
- ●社外取締役 an outside director.

しゃかいがく 社会学 图 sociology /sòusiàládʒi/.
— 社会学(上)の, 社会学的な 形 sociological.
- ●社会学者 a sociologist.

しゃかいしゅぎ 社会主義 sócialism.
- ●社会主義経済 a socialist economy. ●社会主義国 a socialist nation [country]. ●社会主義者 a socialist.

しゃかいふくし 社会福祉 social welfare.
- ●社会福祉士 a social worker. ●社会福祉事業 social welfare work. ●社会福祉法人 a social welfare juridical person.

しゃかいほけん 社会保険 social insurance. ▶社会保険料は毎月給料から天引きされている The *social insurance* contribution is deducted from one's salary every month.
- ●社会保険制度 a social insurance program. ●社会保険労務士 a certificated social insurance and labor consultant.

じゃがいも じゃが芋 (a) potato (徴 ~es). (!米 ではサツマイモ (sweet potato) と区別して Irish [white] potato ということがある) (参考「ジャガタラ(ジャワのジャカルタ芋)」から)

じゃかじゃか じゃかじゃか金をもうける make money *hand over fist*. ●じゃかじゃかドラムを叩く beat the drums *incessantly*.

しゃかっこう 斜滑降 traversing. ●斜滑降で下りる *traverse* the slope.

しゃがみこむ しゃがみ込む squat (down). ▶長時間しゃがみこんでいたので足が痛み出した My legs began to ache from *squatting* (*down*) for so long.

しゃがむ (つま先でバランスをとって) squat /skwát/ (-tt-) (down); (曲げた脚を体に寄せて) crouch (down); (かがみこむ) stoop [bend*] low.

しゃかりき ●しゃかりきに働く work *like anything* [*crazy*, *mad*]; work *frantically*.

ジャカルタ [[インドネシアの首都]] Jakarta /dʒəká:rtə/. (!Djakarta は古いつづり字)

しゃがれる 嗄れる (⇨嗄(しゃが)れる)

しゃかん 舎監 a dormitory superintendent [(女性) matron]; (主に英) a housemaster, (女性) a housemistress.

しゃかんきょり 車間距離 the distance between two cars. ▶事故を起こしたときは十分車間距離をとっていなかった When I had an accident, I wasn't *keeping a good distance from [was too close to*) *the car* in front (of me). (!車間距離を極端に詰めて走ることをタッチゲートという: トラックが車の直後について いる A truck *is tailgating* a car.)

じゃき 邪気 ●邪気のある malicious. ●邪気のない innocent. ●邪気を払う purge human bodies of noxious vapors.

しゃきしゃき ●しゃきしゃきとした [[動作が]] (手際のいい) efficient; (きびきびした) brisk; (生き生きした) lively; [[歯ざわりが]] crisp. (⇨しゃきっと) ●しゃきしゃき仕事をする work *efficiently* [*briskly*].

しゃきっと ●新鮮でしゃきっとした野菜サラダ fresh and *crunchy* vegetable salad. ▶彼はシャワーを浴びて気分がしゃきっとした He *felt refreshed* after (taking) a shower. ▶ほらみんなしゃきっとしろ Look *alive*, guys!

しゃきょう 写経 handwriting of a sutra, copying of a sutra by hand; (写した経文) a handwritten sutra.

じゃきょう 邪教 (a) heresy /hérəsi/, a heretical religion.

しやく 試薬 [化学] a reagent.

しゃく 勺 [[容積・面積の単位]] a *shaku*. (参考 容積では 0.018 リットル, 面積では 0.033m³)

しゃく 尺 [[長さの単位]] a *shaku*. (参考 30.3cm)
- ●尺を取る (寸法を計る) measure ... (up); take measurements of ....

しゃく 杓 a ladle; a dipper. (⇨柄杓(ひしゃく))

しゃく 酌 ●酌をする fill [pour] 《a glass of wine》(for him). ▶お酌をしましょうか Let me *fill* your glass [*cup*]./Shall I *pour* some *sake*?

しゃく 笏 (王笏) a scepter; (職杖) a mace.

しゃく 癪 ❶ [[かんしゃく]] (いらだち) (an) annoyance; (腹立ち) anger, (話) (an) aggravation. ●しゃくの種は [a *cause of*] *annoyance*; an *irritation*.
▶しゃくだな How *annoying* [*aggravating*]!
会話「何をそんなにかりかりしてるんだい」「私はね、うそをつかれることほどしゃくなことはないのよ」「うそをついたことはないよ」"What are you on edge about?" "It's being lied to that really *aggravates* me." "I never lied."
❷ [[さしこみ]] a sudden sharp stomachache; 《get [have]》 a cramp.
- ●しゃくにさわる しゃくにさわる態度 an *annoying* [*an irritating*] attitude. ▶彼の言うことはいちいちしゃくにさわった I *got annoyed* [*irritated*, (腹が立った) *offended*] *at* his every word./His every word [Every word of his] *made me angry* [*irritated me*, (話) *got on my nerves*] (!最後は「神経にさわる」の意).

じやく 持薬 the medicine one regularly takes; one's regular medicine.

-じゃく -弱 [[...よりすこし少ない]] a little less than ....
▶5キロ弱 *a little less than* [*a little under*] five kilograms. ▶この学校には 100 人弱の生徒しかいない This school has *not more than* 100 students.
▶その会社は 30 万ドル弱(=30 万ドル近く)の純益をあげた The company earned *almost* [*nearly*] $300,000 net.

しゃくい 爵位 (a) peerage; a title (of the nobility).

じゃくおんき 弱音器 a mute; a damper.

じゃくし 弱視 图 (have) weak eyesight [sight].
— 弱視の 形 weak-sighted.

ジャグジー (商標) a Jacuzzi /dʒəkú:zi/.

しゃくしじょうぎ 杓子定規 —— 杓子定規な 形 ●杓子定規な考え inflexible thinking. ●杓子定規な人 a stickler for (the) rules. ●杓子定規にやる stick to rules; go [do everything] by the book.

じゃくしゃ 弱者 weak people, 《集合的》《やや書》the weak. (!複数扱い)

しゃくしょ 市役所 a town [《米》a city] hall, a city [《米》a municipal] office.

しゃくじょう 錫杖 (高僧の) a staff; (主教などの) a crosier, a crozier.

じゃくしょう 弱小 —— 弱小の 形 (small and) weak.
●弱小国家 a small, powerless country; (マイナーな扱いを受ける) a minor country.

じゃくしん 弱震 a weak earthquake. (!字義どおりの訳.日本の震度分数による「弱震」は震度3に相当するので a rather strong earthquake くらいがよい)

しゃくぜん 釈然 ●彼の説明はどうも釈然としない(＝満足していない) I *am not* quite *satisfied* [*happy*] *with* his explanation.

じゃくたい 弱体 —— 弱体の 形 weak. (⇨弱い)
—— 弱体化する 動 weaken.

しゃくち 借地 名 leased land.
—— 借地する 動 (土地を借りる) lease a land.
●借地権 a lease. ●借地人 a tenant;《書》a leaseholder. ●借地料 (a) ground [land] rent.

じゃぐち 蛇口 《米》a faucet, 《英》a tap. (⇨栓) ●蛇口をひねる(＝水を出す) turn on (↔off) a *faucet*.

じゃくてん 弱点 a weak point, a weakness;〖欠点〗a shortcoming. (!通例複数形で) (⇨短所) ●人の弱点をつく hit other people's *weak points* [(痛い) *sore spots*]; hit other people *where it hurts*. ▶彼は弱点の克服に努力した He tried to overcome his *weaknesses* [*shortcomings*].

じゃくでん 弱電 a weak electric current.
●弱電機器 a light electrical appliance.

*しゃくど 尺度 〖度量の単位, 評価などの基準〗a measure;〖変化・世論などの指標〗《やや書》a barometer /bərámətər/;〖判断の基準〗《やや書》a criterion /kraitíəriən/. ▶メートルは長さの尺度である A meter is a *measure* of length. ▶富だけが成功の尺度ではない Wealth is not the only *criterion* [*measure, barometer*] of success in life. ▶株価は商活動の尺度である The stock prices are a *barometer* of business activity.

しゃくどういろ 赤銅色 名 brown.
—— 赤銅色の 形 brown. ●赤銅色に日焼けしている漁師 a tanned fisher [男の fisherman].

しゃくとりむし 尺取り虫 〖昆虫〗a looper; an inchworm; a measuring worm.

しゃくなげ 石楠花 〖植物〗a rhododendron /ròudədéndrən/.

じゃくにくきょうしょく 弱肉強食 (ジャングルの掟(おきて)に) (follow) the law of the jungle. ●弱肉強食の世界 a world where the stronger prey *on* [*upon*] the weaker.

しゃくにゅう 借入 borrowing.

しゃくねつ 灼熱 ●灼熱の(＝激しい)恋 a *burning* [*passionate*] love. ●灼熱の(＝焼きつくように熱い)太陽 a *scorching* sun.

じゃくねん 若年 (a) young age.
●若年性糖尿病 〖医学〗juvenile diabetes. ●若年層 the young-age group [bracket]; the young people.

じゃくはい 若輩, 弱輩 (未熟者) an inexperienced [〖話〗a green] person;〖話〗a greenhorn. ▶若輩者ではありますが Though I'm young and inexperienced, ...

しゃくはち 尺八 〖楽器〗a shakuhachi; (説明的に) a Japanese bamboo flute with five holes.

しゃくほう 釈放 名 (a) release, (a) discharge 《from》.
—— 釈放する 動 release [discharge] 《him》from prison; set 《him》free (!くだけた表現. 目的語が長いときは *set free* all those prisoners who ... のような語順も可).

しゃくま 借間 a rented room.

しゃくめい 釈明 〖説明〗(an) explanation;〖言い訳〗(an) excuse /ikskjúːs/. ●釈明を求める (説明を要求する) demand an *explanation*《*about*＋事, *from*＋人》; (説明の機会を求める) ask for an opportunity to explain《*about*》.

しゃくや 借家 a rented house (働 houses /-ziz, 《米》-siz/) ●借家住まいをする live in a *rented house*. ●借家を探す look for a *house for rent*《米》[*to let*《英》, *to rent*]. ●借家人 a tenant.

しゃくやく 芍薬 〖植物〗a peony /píːəni/.

しゃくよう 借用 borrowing, loan. ▶金3万円借用, 井上太郎 IOU ¥30,000, Taro Inoue. (!借用証に書く書式)
—— 借用する 動 (無料で) borrow; (有料で) rent. (⇨借りる)
●借用語 a borrowed word; a loanword. ●借用証書 a bond of debt [loan]. (!メモ程度の借用証は an IOU (＝*I owe you*), または a loan note という)

ジャグラー 〖投げ物曲芸師〗a juggler.

しゃくりあげる sob (-bb-) convulsively; (突然激しく) dissolve into (big) gasping sobs.

しゃくりょう 酌量 —— 酌量する 動 make allowance(s) for ...; take ... into consideration [account]; consider. (⇨斟酌(しんしゃく), 情状酌量)

しゃくる 杓る 〖すくう〗bail ... (out), ladle ... out, scoop (⇨掬(すく)う);〖あごを〗scoop one's head arrogantly.

しゃくれる 杓れる ●しゃくれたあご a *turned-up* chin.

しゃくん 社訓 the motto of a company.

しゃけい 斜頸 〖医学〗torticollis; wryneck.

しゃげき 射撃 名 shooting; (1回の) a shot;〖鉄砲, 砲火〗fire. ●ライフル[クレー]射撃 rifle [clay] *shooting*. ●一斉射撃 a volley. ●射撃を始める[やめる] open [cease] *fire*. ▶彼は射撃がうまい[へただ] He is a good [a bad] *shot*./He is good [bad] at *shooting*.
—— 射撃する 動 shoot; fire. (⇨撃つ)
●射撃場 a shóoting ränge (屋内の) gàllery.

ジャケット 〖上着〗a jacket;〖カバー〗(本の) a (book [dust]) jacket, a dust cover, a wrapper; (レコードの) a (record) jacket (《米》a sleeve《英》).

しゃけん 車券 a betting ticket on a bicycle race.

しゃけん 車検 a vehicle inspection;《英》an MOT test. ●車検に出す have one's car *inspected*, put a car in for its *inspection*,《英話》*MOT* a car.

じゃけん 邪険 —— 邪険な 形 (無情な) harsh; (無慈悲な) merciless; (冷酷な) cruel. ●邪険な人 a *cruel* [a *merciless*] person.
—— 邪険に 副 ▶邪険にする treat《him》*cruelly* [*mercilessly*].

しゃこ 車庫 〖自動車の〗a garage /gərάːdʒ/; (屋根と支柱だけの) a carport;〖電車などの〗a train shed. ●車が2台入る車庫つきの家 a house with a two-car [a *double*] *garage*. ●車庫に車を入れる put [park]《his》car in the *garage*.

しゃこ 蝦蛄 〖動物〗a squilla /skwílə/.

しゃこう 社交 〖交際〗《書》society.
—— 社交的な 形 ▶彼女はとても社交的だ She is very

しゃこう *sociable* (↔*unsociable*, *antisocial*). (▮×She is *social*. とか ×She has *sociability*. とはいわない) ▶She is a very *sociable* woman. (▮「外向的で社交的」であれば, ... an *outgoing*, *sociable* woman. といえる) ▶彼女はそう言ったのは社交辞令(=外交辞令)に She said so but she *was* just being *diplomatic*./She said so just to be *polite* [just out of *politeness*].
- 社交家 a *sociable* person;《話》a good *mixer*.
- 社交界 fashionable society [*circles*]. • 社交クラブ a social club. • 社交性 *sociability*. • 社交ダンス *ballroom dancing*.

しゃこう 斜光 *slanting rays* [*light*].
しゃこう 斜坑 *an inclined mine shaft*.
しゃこう 遮光 图 *shading*. —— 遮光する 動 *shade*, *shield*.
- 遮光板 a *gobo*. • 遮光幕 a *shade*.

じゃこう 麝香 *musk*.
じゃこうじか 麝香鹿〖動物〗a *musk deer*.
じゃこうねこ 麝香猫〖動物〗a *rasse*.
じゃこうねずみ 麝香鼠〖動物〗a *muskrat*.

しゃさい 社債 a *corporate bond*, a *debenture* (*bond*) (▮《米》では通例無担保のものをさす). • 転換社債 a convertible *bond* [*debenture*]. • 額面50ドルの社債を発行する issue [sell] *bonds* in the face amount of 50 dollars.

しゃざい 謝罪 图 (an) *apology*. • 謝罪を求める demand an *apology* 《*from* him》.
—— 謝罪する 動 *apologize*, make an *apology* 《*to* him *for* one's behavior》. (⇨詫(わ)びる, 謝る) ▶彼は迷惑をかけたことを私たちに公式に謝罪した He *apologized to* us publicly *for* causing trouble.

しゃさつ 射殺 —— 射殺する 動 *shoot* 《him》 dead [*to death*].
しゃし 社史 a history of a company, a company history.
しゃし 斜視 图 a *squint* (▮外斜視をさす場合が多い); (内斜視) *cross-eye*; (斜視の目) *cross* [*squint*] eyes. ▶ひどい斜視である have a bad *squint*.
—— 斜視の 形 *cross-eyed*, *squint-eyed*.
しゃし 奢侈 *luxury*. (⇨贅沢(ざい)) • 奢侈に流れる live in *luxury*; lead [live] a life of *luxury*.
しゃじ 謝辞 words of gratitude [*appreciation*, *thanks*]; (わび) (an) *apology*.
しゃじく 車軸 an *axle*.
- 車軸を流す ▶車軸を流すように(=激しく)雨が降った The rain fell [came down] *in buckets* [*torrents*].

しゃじつ 写実 图 *realism*.
—— 写実的な 形 *realistic*. • 写実的な犬の絵 a *realistic* painting [*drawing*] of a dog.
- 写実主義 *realism*. • 写実主義者 a *realist*. • 写実小説 a *realistic novel*.

じゃじゃうま じゃじゃ馬 an unruly horse;《比喩的》《書》a *shrew*. (▮御しがたい[気性の激しい]若い女性 (an *unmanageable* [a *fiery-tempered*] girl) の意)

しゃしゃりでる しゃしゃり出る ▶しゃしゃり出るんじゃない Don't *butt in*./Don't be *too forward* [*pushy*].
しゃしゅ 社主 the proprietor of a company.
しゃしゅ 車種 the type of car. • 最新の車種 the latest *model*.
しゃしゅ 射手 (弓の) an *archer*; (銃の) a *shot*, a *shooter*.
じゃしゅう 邪宗 (a) *heresy* /hérəsi/, a heretical religion.
しゃしゅつ 射出 —— 射出する 動〖発射する〗*shoot*, *fire*;〖噴出する〗*spout*, *eject*;〖放射状に出る〗[出す]〗*radiate*.
- 射出座席 an *ejection* [an *ejector*] seat.

しゃしょう 社章 a *badge* [a *button*] of a company.
しゃしょう 車掌 〖路面電車・バスの〗 a *conductor*;〖列車の〗《米》a *conductor*,《英》a *guard*. • バスの車掌 a bus *conductor*. (▮(1) 性別に関係なく a bus conductor ということが多い. a bus conductress は性差別的で〖廃〗. (2) 英語では a bus girl は「ウェーターの助手の女性」の意)

しゃしょう 捨象 图 *abstraction*. —— 捨象する 動 *abstract*.
しゃじょう 車上 ▶車上の人となる(車に乗る) get into a car.
しゃじょう 射場 (弓の) an *archery range*; (射撃の) a *shóoting ránge* [*屋内の*].
しゃしょく 写植〖印刷〗*photocomposition*, *photo-typesetting*; *filmsetting*.

しゃしん 写真

WORD CHOICE 写真

photograph, **photo** 「写真」の意の最も一般的な語. photo は省略形で, くだけた文脈で広く用いる. • 写真に写っているかわいい男の子 a pretty boy in the *photograph*.
picture 写真・絵画のこと. photograph よりいくぶんくだけた文脈で用いる. • その俳優の写真を撮る take [snap] a *picture* of the actor.

a phótograph, a picture (▮*photograph* より口語的の,《くだけて》 *photograph* より多く用いる);《話》a *photo* 《*米》~s》;〖スナップ〗a *snapshot*,《話》a *snap*;〖写真術〗*photography*. • 記事と写真 words and *pictures*.
① 〖~(の)写真〗• 家族[卒業]写真 a family [a graduation] *photograph*. • カラー[白黒]写真 a color [a black and white] *photograph*. (▮×a white and black photograph とはいわない) • 肖像写真 (1枚) a portrait *photograph*;《集合的》portrait *photography*. • 色あせた写真 a faded *picture*. • 航空写真 an aerial *photograph*. • スチール写真 a still (*photograph*). • 全身[上半身]の写真 a full-length [a half-length] *photograph*. • 私の父の写真 (父が写っている) a *picture* of my father; my father's *picture*; (父が写した[所有する]) my father's *picture*, a *picture* of my father's (父が写したことをはっきりさせる場合は a *picture* of my father's own taking). ▶このお孫さんの写真はとてもかわいいですね This photograph of your grandson [granddaughter] is very cute. (▮主語が長いので次例の方が普通) / This is a very cute *photograph* of your grandson [granddaughter].
② 〖写真~〗• 写真判定で競走に勝つ win a race in a *photo* finish. ▶彼女は写真うつりがよい She (always) comes out well (↔badly) in *photographs*./She *photographs* [《話》*photos*] well./She is *photogénic*.
③ 〖写真は[が]〗▶写真は全部よく撮れていた All the *pictures* came out well. (▮写っている(=he)を主語にして He looked really [very] good in all the *pictures*. ともいえる) ▶この写真はピンボケだ This *picture* is out of [not in] focus. (ぼやけている) This *picture* is blurred. • 私の友だちが撮ってくれたこの写真はどうですか How do you like the photo my friend took of me? (▮*of* に注意) ▶もしいい写真が撮れないとしたら, 近寄り方が足りないからだ If your *picture* hasn't turn out right, you did not get close enough to the object. (▮英語と日本語の

じゃしん

制の違いに注意)
④[写真に[で]] ▶写真に犬が写っている There is a dog *in* [✗*on*] the *picture*. ▶彼らに写真で何度か見たことがある I've seen him *in pictures* several times.
⑤[写真を] ●写真を現像する[焼きつける; 引き伸ばす] develop [print; enlarge] a *photograph*. (❗ D. P. E. is developing, printing, enlarging からの和製英語) ●写真を見せる show 《him》 a *photograph* [*picture*]. ●ネガからの写真を2枚焼増しする make two prints of this *picture* from the negative. ▶私は彼が公園を散歩している写真を撮った I took a *picture* [a *photograph*, a *photo*, a *snapshot*] of him walking in the park./I *photographed* him walking in the park. ▶私は彼に写真を撮ってもらった I had [got] my *picture* taken by him. ▶私の趣味は写真(を撮ること)です My hobby is *photography* [taking *pictures*, ✗*pictures*, ✗*photographs*].
[会話]「すみませんが、写真を撮っていただけますか」「いいですよ。 城をバックに撮りましょうか」 "Excuse me. Would you please take a *photograph* for me?" "No problem. Would you like me to take a *picture* of you in front of the castle?"
●写真家 a (professional) *photographer*. (❗(1)男女の別なく用いる。 (2) cameraman, camera-woman はテレビ・映画の撮影技師) ●写真機 a camera. ●写真コンテスト a *photográphic* contest. ●写真撮影 *photography*. ●写真雑誌 a photo magazine. ●写真集 a *photográphic* album 《of》. ●写真植字 *photocomposition*; photo typesetting; photo typography. ●写真製版 *photomechánical processes*. ●写真立て a *photo*(*graph*) *stand*; (額状の) a photo frame. ●写真帳 (アルバム) a *photograph* [[話] a *photo*] *album*. ●写真屋 (写真館) a *photográphic studio*; (現像などの店) a camera store. (❗[米] a drugstore,《英》a chemist's (shop) でフィルム・現像などを取り扱っており、ここを利用する人が多い)

じゃしん 邪心 an evil intent [spirit, heart]; a malicious intent.

じゃしん 邪神 an evil [a wicked] god [deity].

しゃす 謝す (⇨謝する)

ジャス [[日本農林規格]] JAS 《*J*apanese *A*grícultural *S*tandard の略》.

ジャズ [[音楽]] jazz /dʒæz/ (music). ●モダンジャズ modern *jazz*. ●ジャズバンド a *jazz* band. ●ジャズ演奏家 (男の)(男女の別なく) a *jazzman*; a *jazz* musician [*player*]. ●ジャズを演奏する play *jazz* (*music*).

-しやすい (傾向がある) be apt [liable] to 《do》; tend to 《do》; be inclined to 《do》 (⇨傾向①); (容易である) be easy to 《do》. ▶彼は風邪を引きやすい He *is apt* [*liable*] *to* catch 《a cold》./He *is subject* [*susceptible, sensitive*] *to* colds. ▶この本は読みやすい This book *is easy to* read./This book *is easy* (for you) *to* read this book./You can read this book *easily* [*with ease*].

じゃすい 邪推 [[理由なく疑うこと]] a groundless suspicion; [[単なる想像]] just one's imagination.
—— **邪推する** suspect 《him》 without reason.

ジャスティフィケーション [[行末そろえ]][[印刷]] justification.

ジャスト ▶5時ジャストに *exactly* [*just*] at five o'clock; at five o'clock *sharp* [✗*just*]. ▶1,000円ジャストで at *exactly* [✗*just*] 1,000 yen. ●ジャストミートする just meet the ball; hit the ball *squarely* [on the nose].

● ジャストインタイム方式 a just-in-time (production) system. (⇨ジャストインタイム方式)

ジャスミン [[植物]] (a) jasmine; (香水) jasmine.
● ジャスミンティー jasmine tea.

しゃする 謝する ❶[礼を言う] express one's gratitude 《*to*》; thank 《*him* for a thing》. (⇨礼❶)
❷[謝る] apologize. (⇨謝る) ❸[断わる] refuse. (⇨断わる)

しゃぜ 社是 a company's policy.

しゃせい 写生 [名] sketching. ▶田舎へ写生に出かける go into the country to *sketch*; go *sketching* in [✗*to*] the country.
—— **写生する** [動] sketch, make* a sketch 《*of*》. ▶彼女の姿を写生する *sketch* her figure. ▶海岸の景色を絵の具を使ってざっと写生する *make* a rough *sketch of* coast scenery in color. ●写生画 a *sketch*; a picture drawn from life. ●写生帳 a sketchbook; a sketchpad. ●写生文 a (literary) sketch.

しゃせい 射精 [名] (an) ejaculátion. —— **射精する** [動] ejaculàte.

しゃせつ 社説 an editorial; 《英》a leader, a leading article. ▶首相支持の社説を載せる carry [run] an *editorial* in support of the prime minister. ●社説で政府を攻撃する hit the government *in* an *editorial*. ●社説欄 the editorial column.

しゃぜつ 謝絶 [名] refusal. ▶面会謝絶《掲示》No Visitors. ▶その患者は面会謝絶です The patient *is not allowed to* see any visitors.
—— **謝絶する** [動] (断固として) refuse; (丁寧に) decline.

じゃせつ 邪説 an evil creed [theory, doctrine] (❗creed は「宗教上の信条」、theory は「学説」、doctrine は「教義」の意); (異教, 異説) (a) heresy.

しゃせん 車線 a (traffic) lane. ●対向車線 the opposite *lane*. ▶4車線の道路 a four-lane road [highway]. ●車線を変更する change *lanes*. (❗複数形に注意)

しゃせん 斜線 a sloping [a slanting,《やや書》an oblique] line; (区切り記号「/」) a slash (mark), an oblique (stroke). ▶地図の斜線の部分が大学です The *shaded* part on the map is the university.

しゃそう 社葬 《conduct [hold]》a company funeral.

しゃそう 車窓 a car [a train] window. ●車窓の景色 the scenery seen from a *train window*. ▶荒野が車窓に広がった The wild land opened out *beside the train*.

しゃそく 社則 company regulations [rules].

しゃたい 車体 the body (of a car).

しゃだい 車台 a chassis /ʃǽsi/ (複 ~ /ʃǽsiz/).

しゃたく 社宅 a company house (複 houses /-ziz, (米) -siz/); (集合的) company housing.

しゃだつ 洒脱 —— **洒脱な** [形] (さっぱりした) frank; (あか抜けした) refined, polished.

しゃだん 遮断 —— **遮断する** [動] shut* ... off; (光・熱などを) shut ... out; (退路・電気などを) cut* ... off; (交通を) block ... off. ●騒音を遮断する shut out noises. ●彼らの逃走経路を遮断する *cut off* their escape routes. ▶その盆地は高い山で外界から遮断されている The valley *is shut off* by the high mountains from the rest of the world. ▶地すべりで交通が遮断された Traffic *was blocked* (*off*) by a landslide. (❗block off の方が長期間の遮断を意味する)
● 遮断機 a (crossing) gate [barrier].

しゃだんほうじん 社団法人 a corporation aggre-

しゃち gate;〔法律〕a corporate juridical person.

しゃち 鯱 〔動〕a killer whale, an orca.

しゃちほこ 鯱 a *shachihoko*;(説明的に) an imaginary sea animal with a tiger-like head and a fish-like body.

しゃちほこだち 鯱立ち a handstand; a headstand. (⇨逆立ち)

しゃちほこばる 鯱張る become* stiff, stiffen (up).
・しゃちほこばった態度 a *stiff* attitude. ▶そんなにしゃちほこばらないで Don't be so *stiff* (〔堅苦しい〕*formal*).

しゃちゅう 社中〔社内〕(⇨社内);〔芸人などの一座〕a troupe.

しゃちゅう 車中 ・車中で on [in] a train. ▶車中泊はありません(バス旅行パンフレットで) There is no overnight stay *on the bus*.

しゃちょう 社長〔主に米〕the president〔《英》(男の) chairman,（女の）chairwoman〕《*of* a firm [a company]》(▲特に大会社の社長・会長を the chief executive officer(最高業務執行者)《略 CEO》と呼ぶ),《話》the boss(▲Boss と無冠詞・大文字で呼びかけにも用いられる)・副社長 a vice-*president*. ▶彼はホンダの社長だ He is (the) *president* of Honda Motor. (■補語の位置では the は《話》でしばしば省略される) ▶社長は夏休みはとらないのですか Aren't you taking a summer vacation, Boss? (■英語では、話している相手は王[皇]室の人などに対する以外は 'you' で表す。「社長、先生」などの敬称は、文頭や文末で呼びかけの形にして表す)

・社長室 the president's office.

***シャツ** 〔〔肌着〕《米》an undershirt,《英》a vest(■通例ではない);〔ワイシャツ〕a shirt /ʃɚːrt/. ・ランニングシャツ an undershirt;《英》a vest. ▶彼はピンクのシャツ[スポーツシャツ]を着ている He's wearing a pink [a sport(s)] *shirt*.
・シャツブラウス a shirt blouse.

じゃっか 弱化 ――弱化する 動 (弱くする) weaken; (弱くなる) become weak.

ジャッカル 〔動物〕a jackal.

しゃっかん 借款 a loan. ・借款を申し込む ask [apply] for a *loan*. ・借款を供与する give [provide, (やや書) grant] a *loan*. ・多額の円借款を得る get [obtain] a massive *loan* from Japan.

じゃっかん 若干 圖 (多少) somewhat. ▶シーズン中はホテルの料金が若干高くなる Hotel rates are *somewhat* higher in season.

――**若干の** 形 some;〔少数の〕a few;〔少量の〕a little. ・若干の間違いをする make some [a few] mistakes. ▶今若干の金を持ち合わせている I have some [a little, ×a few] money on me. (■on の代わりに with も可能だが、小さな物については on が普通)

じゃっかん 弱冠 ▶彼は弱冠 18 歳でショパン・コンクールを制した He was the winner at the Chopin Competition when he was *only* eighteen years old. (■簡単には He won the Chopin at eighteen. で、特に「弱冠」を表す必要はない)

しゃっかんほう 尺貫法 the *shakkan* system of weights and measures.

じゃっき 惹起 ――惹起する 動 cause; bring about. (⇨引き起こす)

ジャッキ a jack. ・ジャッキで上げる *jack* (the car) *up*.

しゃっきり (⇨しゃきっと) ・動作がしゃっきりしている move about *briskly*.

***しゃっきん** 借金〔個人間での〕a debt /det/《「借金状態」の意では 〕;〔銀行などの貸付金〕a loan.

①〔**借金が**〕 ・私は彼に 5 万円の借金がある I *owe* him 50,000 yen./I owe 50,000 yen to him. (■前の方は金額に、後の方は人に重点を置いた言い方)/I'm *in debt to* him *for* 50,000 yen. ▶借金がますますかさんできた I'm getting deeper and deeper into *debt*./I'm running up more and more *debts*./(どんどん) My *debts* are piling up on me and on. ・現在は借金がありません I am *out of debt* now. ▶ジャイアンツは借金(が)3 である The Giants are three games below [under] .500. (■.500 is five hundred と読む)

②〔**借金を**〕 ・借金を負う be saddled with *debt [loan]*. ・彼からいくらか借金をする *borrow* some *money from* him. ・銀行から借金をする *borrow*《50,000 dollars, money》*from* a bank; take out a *loan from* a bank. ・借金をするために家を抵当に入れる mortgage /mɔ́ːrɡɪdʒ/ one's house in order to get a *loan*. ・借金を催促する press (him) to pay a *debt*. ・銀行に 500 万円の借金を申し込む ask the bank for a *loan* of five million yen. ・借金を全部返済する pay [clear] off all one's *debts*. ・借金を帳消しにする(=免除する) forgive a *debt*. ▶彼は私に借金を返さなかった He didn't pay his *debt* back to me./He didn't pay me back his *debt*. ▶彼はギャンブルで多額の借金を抱えている He is heavily *in debt* from gambling. ▶彼はとうとう借金を踏み倒した He dodged payment of his *debts* after all.

③〔**借金で[の]**〕 ・借金で家を建てる build a house with *borrowed money* [(住宅ローンで) *on* a home *loan*]. ・借金で首が回らない be deeply [up to the ears] *in debt*. ・借金の利子を払う pay the interest on a *debt*,《英》service one's *debt*. ・借金のかたとして取る hold (it) as (a) security for a *debt*.

・借金の取り立て the collection of a *debt*.
・借金取り a debt collector.

じゃっく 惹句 a catch phrase.

ジャック 〔トランプの 11〕a jack, a knave.

ジャックナイフ a jackknife (複 -knives).

しゃっくり 图 a hiccup, a hiccough /híkʌp/. ・しゃっくりが止まらない cannot stop *hiccuping*.

――**しゃっくりする** 動 hiccup, have [get] the hiccups. (■(1)《英》では the をつけない。(2) 人前では Hic. Hic―cuse me (=Excuse me). などという)

ジャッグル ――ジャッグルする 動〔野球〕juggle [bobble]《a ball》.

しゃっけい 借景 (説明的に) making use of a beautiful surrounding landscape of mountains in the distance or of the neighborhood trees in the layout or design of a garden.

しゃっこう 『赤光』Red Light. (参考 斉藤茂吉の歌集)

じゃっこく 弱国 a weak country [nation].

ジャッジ 图 (審判員) a judge;(審判) (a) judgment.

――**ジャッジする** 動 judge; pass judgment《on》.
・ミスジャッジする misjudge; judge wrongly.

シャッター ❶〔カメラの〕a shutter /ʃʌ́tər/. ・1,000 分の 1 秒のシャッタースピード a *shutter* speed of one thousandth of a second. ・(カメラの)シャッターを切る press [release,《話》click,《話》fire, ×push] the *shutter* (of a camera). (■click は「かしゃっと音を立てる」の意)

❷〔よろい戸〕(one of) the shutters. ・シャッターを下ろす close [pull down] (↔open) the *shutters*. ・すべての窓はシャッターが下りていた All the windows *were shuttered*.

・シャッターチャンス a chance for a good shot [picture];《和製語》shutter chance. ▶シャッターチャンスを逃してしまった I missed the right moment for taking a good picture.

しゃっちょこだち (⇨鯱(しゃち)立ち)

しゃっちょこばる (⇨鯱(しゃち)張る)
シャットアウト 图 〖野球〗〖米〗a shutout; (完封負け) a whitewash.
── **シャットアウトする** 動 〖野球〗shut 《them》 out; win a shutout victory 《over》 the Giants. whitewash 《them》. ● ジャイアンツをシャットアウトする *shut out [whitewash; blank]* the Giants. ● 3 安打シャットアウトを果たす pitch a three-hit shutout. ● 日本製品をシャットアウトする(=通商を停止する) *embargo* Japanese goods. ● 通りの騒音をシャットアウトする(=さえぎる) *shut [screen] out* street noises.
シャッポ ● シャッポを脱ぐ admit one's defeat.
しゃてい 舎弟 〖弟〗one's younger brother; 〖弟分〗a sworn brother.
しゃてい 射程 〖距離〗(a) range. ● 射程内[外]にある be within [out of] the *range*. ● この銃の射程距離は 200 メートルである This gun has a *range* of 200 meters.
しゃてき 的的 shooting. ● 射的場 a shóoting rànge [(屋内の) gàllery].
しゃでん 社殿 the main building of a (Shinto) shrine.
しゃど 斜度 a slant.
しゃとう 斜塔 a leaning tower. ● ピサの斜塔 the *Leaning Tower* of Pisa /píːzə/.
しゃどう 車道 a roadway. ● 車道を歩く walk *on the roadway*.
じゃどう 邪道 (ふさわしくないやり方) an improper way 《*to* do; *of* doing》; (よこしまなやり方) an evil way. ▶そうするのは邪道だ That's *the wrong way [off the rails]*./That's *not the right way* to do it.
シャトー 〖大邸宅〗a chateau, a mansion.
シャドー 〖影〗shadow. ● シャドーキャビネット 〖影の内閣〗a shadow cabinet. ● シャドーボクシング shadow boxing.
シャトル ❶〖バトミントンの〗a shuttlecock. ❷〖織機の〗a shuttle. ❸〖折り返し運転〗a shuttle (service). ● シャトルバス a shuttle bus.
しゃない 社内 ● 社内で in one's company. ● 社内の ín-hòuse. ● あの出版社には社内にデザイナーをかかえている That publishing company has *in-hòuse* artists [artists *in-hóuse*]. (❗後の in-house は副詞) ▶我々は社内の情報ネットワークを強化した We strengthened our *inter-company [in-house]* communication network. ▶彼は社内結婚をした He married a woman working *in* the same *company [office]*.
● 社内教育 in-house training ● 社内報 an in-house newsletter.; (実地訓練) òn-the-jòb [ín-sèrvice] tráining. ● 社内放送 an in-house PA system. (❗PA system は pùblic-addréss sýstem (拡声装置)の略)
しゃない 車内 ● 車内で in the 《米》 on) a train. (⇨車内[車中で]) ▶最近では車内で化粧する女性は珍しくない It's not rare these days to see women putting on make-up *on the train*./Women putting on make-up *on the train* are not a rare sight these days.
● 車内改札 an inspection of passengers' tickets. ● 車内販売 sales on the train.
しゃなりしゃなり ● しゃなりしゃなりと歩く (上品ぶって) walk *with affected grace*; (気取って体を左右に振りながら) walk *affectedly* swaying one's body from side to side; sashay 《*along*》.
しゃにくさい 謝肉祭 the carnival. (〖参考〗カトリック教国で四旬節 (Lent) 前の 3 日間行われる祭典)
しゃにむに 〖無謀に〗recklessly; 〖無理に〗by force;

〖猛烈に〗furiously; 〖荒々しく〗fiercely. ● しゃにむに敵陣に突っ込む dash *recklessly* [make a *furious* dash] into the enemy.
じゃねん 邪念 ● 邪念(=悪い考え)を払う free oneself of [a *wicked* [evil] *thought*.
じゃのめ 蛇の目 〖太い輪の形〗a bull's-eye; 〖傘〗an umbrella with a bull's-eye design.
しゃば 娑婆 〖世の中 [earth]; 〖拘束などされている人にとっての〗the outside world.
しゃばく 射爆 firing and bombing. ● 射爆場 a firing and bombing range.
しゃばけ 娑婆気 (worldly) ambitions. ● 娑婆気がある be (very) ambitious.
じゃばら 蛇腹 (建物の軒の) a cornice; (カメラなどの) a bellows (複 ～).
ジャパン 〖日本〗Japan. ● ジャパンバッシング Japan bashing. ● ジャパンマネー Japan money.
しゃひ 社費 the company expense; the expense of the company. ● 社費で留学する study abroad at *the expense of the company*.
しゃびせん 蛇皮線 〖楽器〗a snake-skin *samisen*.
しゃふ 車夫 a rickshaw man.
ジャブ a jab. ● ジャブを出す jab 《*at*》; throw a jab 《*to*》.
しゃふう 社風 the company's style [tradition]. (❗style は「やり方」, tradition は「伝統」) ● この方式は社風に合わない This method doesn't fit in with [is contradictory to] our *company's style*.
しゃぶしゃぶ *shabushabu*; (説明的に) a one-pot dish whose ingredients (such as thin-sliced meat and vegetables) are swished in boiling broth and eaten with a soy-based sause.
じゃぶじゃぶ (水をはねさせて) with a splash, with splashes of water. (❗splash は複数形もとるが水しぶきのときは with a splash が普通なので, それも起こるときは(じゃぶじゃぶ)は with splashes *of water* で工夫する) ● じゃぶじゃぶ洗濯をする wash *with splashes* of water; wash *vigorously*. ● じゃぶじゃぶ水をかける *splash* water 《*on, over*》. ● 彼は小川をじゃぶじゃぶ歩いて渡った He walked across the stream, *splashing* water about./He *splashed* (his way) across the stream.
しゃふつ 煮沸 ── 煮沸する 動 boil. ● 煮沸消毒する sterilize 《the towel》 by *boiling* [with *boiling water*].
シャフト 〖心棒, 柄〗a shaft.
しゃぶる suck. ● あめをしゃぶる suck 《*at* [*on*]》a piece of candy. ▶親指をしゃぶってはいけません Don't *suck* 《(や)なさい》 Stop *sucking*] your thumb.
しゃへい 遮蔽 ── 遮蔽する 動 screen; cover (up). ● 遮蔽物 a screen.
*****しゃべる** 喋る talk (❗speak とは異なり, 打ち解けた会話をしたり, とりとめのない話をしたりするときに用いられることが多い); 〖気楽に談笑する〗chat (-tt-) (❗talk よりくだけた語); 〖くだらないことをぺちゃくちゃ喋る〗chatter; 〖秘密などを漏らす〗let*... out. ● しゃべりまくる *talk* away; *talk* and *talk*; *talk* on and on. (❗on は継続の意を表す副詞) ▶しゃべるのをやめろ Stop *talking*./(そんなにしゃべるな) Don't *talk* so much./(口を閉じなさい) Close your mouth./(黙れ) Shut your mouth./(〖話〗Shut up! ● 彼はよくしゃべる人だ He *talks* a lot./He is very *talkative*. (⇨おしゃべり) ▶彼にしゃべらせるのは大変だった It's been very difficult [〖話〗quite a job] *to get him to speak*. ▶コーヒーを飲みながら彼と長い間しゃべった I *chatted with* him for a long time [I *had a long chat with* him] over a cup of coffee. ▶子供と

シャベル 子供が部屋を出るとぺちゃくちゃしゃべり出した The children began to *chatter* when the teacher left the room. ▶この秘密を人にしゃべるな Don't *let out* [*disclose*] this secret./Don't *tell* this secret *to anyone*./(人に秘めておく) *Keep* this secret *to yourself*. ▶彼は自分の過去については何もしゃべらない He never *says* anything about his past.

シャベル a shovel /ʃʌvl/. ●シャベル1杯の土 a *shovel* [a shovelful] of earth. ●シャベルですくう shovel (up)《coal》.

ジャポニカまい ジャポニカ米 Japonica rice.

しゃほん 写本 【本】a manuscript (!専門用語); a handwritten [a manuscript] copy;〔書き写すこと〕transcription [copying] 《*of a book*》. ●現存する古代の写本 surviving ancient *manuscripts*.

シャボンだま シャボン玉 a (soap) bubble. ●シャボン玉を吹く blow (*soap*) *bubbles*.

***じゃま** 邪魔 图 ❶【妨害, 障害】an obstacle; (a) hindrance; (an) interruption; (a) disturbance; (an) interference. (⇨動❶) ▶私の仕事には多くの邪魔が入るだろう I'll get a lot of *interruptions* in my work./I expect a lot of *troubles* in my work. (!expect は「悪いことを覚悟している」の意) ▶お邪魔でしょうか Am I *disturbing* [*bothering*, *interrupting*] you? ▶これは役に立たないどころか邪魔だ This thing is worse than useless. It's *in the way*. ▶邪魔だ, どけ Get out of my [the] way!/ Get out of here!
会話「お邪魔じゃないかしら」「どうぞそのまま, 場所は十分ありますから」"I'm afraid I'm *in your way*." "Don't move. There's plenty of room."
❷【邪魔な人・物】a hindrance; (人に迷惑な人・物) a nuisance (⇨邪魔者) ▶君は助けになるより邪魔だよ You are more of a *hindrance* than a help.
── 邪魔(を)する 動 ❶【妨害する】(人が) disturb; interrupt;(物・事が) interfere 《*with*》;(人・物が) hinder,《やや書》obstruct, be [get*] in the way 《*of*》. (⇨妨害する, 妨げる)

> 使い分け **disturb** 個人の時間・空間・言動が邪魔され, 正常・平穏な状態や雰囲気が壊されることを表す。
> **interrupt** 進行中の作業や話が中断されることを表す。
> **interfere** 他から活動・過程・状況が邪魔されて, 干渉されることを表す。
> **hinder** 進行中の事柄が途中で中断されることを表す。
> **obstruct** 進行中の活動・動作や眺めなどに対する障害があって邪魔されることを表す。
> **be [get] in the way** 行く手をふさいでいる[ふさぐ]ことを表す。比喩的に活動の邪魔になっている[なる]ことも表す。

▶お邪魔して申し訳ありませんが, 2-3分お時間をいただけませんか I'm sorry to *disturb* you, but would you spare me a few minutes? ▶彼は彼女の演説の邪魔をした He *interrupted* her speech./He *interrupted* her while she was speaking. ▶君は私の仕事の邪魔をしている You *are disturbing* (me *in*) my work. ▶この部屋なら邪魔されずに勉強できる I can study *undisturbed* in this room. ▶通りの騒音が勉強の邪魔になる Street noises *interfere with* my studying./Street noises *hinder* (me *in*) [*are a hindrance to*] my studying. ▶倒れた木が通行の邪魔になっている The fallen tree *obstructs* [*blocks*] the traffic. ▶彼女は長い髪が(仕事の)邪魔にならないように縛った She tied back her long hair so (that) it wouldn't *get in the way* (*of* work). (!that を省略するのは《話》) ▶女性の帽子が邪魔になって舞台がよく見えなかった The woman's hat *obstructed* [*interrupted*, (台無しにした) *spoiled*] my view of the stage. ▶重い箱が邪魔になって戸が開かない I can't open the door, because there is a heavy box *in the way*.
❷【訪問する】▶あすお邪魔してもよろしいですか May I *come to see* [*come and see*,《話》*come see*] you tomorrow? ▶大変長い間お邪魔いたしました I'm sorry I've taken (up) so much of your time. (!感謝の気持ちを表して Thank you for taking a long time. のようにいうことも多い) ▶(そろそろおいとましましょう) I think I must be going. (!帰り際の「お邪魔しました」は Thanks for your time. や単に Thank you. とか Good-by. ですますことも多い)

ジャマイカ 【国名】Jamaica /dʒəméikə/ (!公式名も同じ). (首都 Kingston) ●ジャマイカ人 a Jamaican. ●ジャマイカ(人)の Jamaican.

じゃまもの 邪魔者 (⇨邪魔❷) ▶彼を邪魔者扱いにする treat him as a *nuisance*.

しゃみせん 三味線【楽器】a samisen (!shamisen ともつづる);(説明的に) a three-stringed Japanese banjo-like musical instrument played by plucking with a large plectrum. ●三味線を弾く play the *samisen*. (!楽器には通例 the を付ける)

ジャム (a) jam; (a) jelly (!通例つぶ状の果肉の入っていないものをいう). ●リンゴジャム apple *jam* [*jelly*]. ●パンにイチゴジャムをつける spread strawberry *jam* on a slice of bread.

しゃむしょ 社務所 a shrine office.

シャムねこ シャム猫 【動物】a Siamese /sàiəmí:z/ (cat).

しゃめい 社名 the name of a company, a company name. ●社名入りの封筒 an envelope with the *company name* printed on it. (!「社名入りの便箋」は letterhead)

しゃめい 社命 ●社命により by *order of* [on the *orders of*] *a company*.

しゃめん 斜面 a slope. ●急な[ゆるやかな]斜面 a steep [a gentle] *slope*. ●山[丘]の斜面 a hillside.

しゃめん 赦免 图《やや書》(a) pardon; (神による)《書》(a) remission. ●罪の赦免を求めて祈る pray for the *remission* of sins.
── 赦免する 動《書》pardon; (神が)《書》remit. ●赦免される be pardoned; be granted a 《presidential》*pardon*.

しゃも 軍鶏 a gamecock. (!「闘鶏」は cockfighting)

しゃもじ a rice paddle [scoop]. ●しゃもじで茶碗にご飯をよそう put rice into a bowl with a *paddle*.

しゃゆう 社友 (その会社に関係のある人) a friend of a company;(会社の仲間) a colleague.

しゃゆう 社有 ●社有の company-owned《land》.

しゃよう 社用 company business. ▶彼は社用で東京に行った He went to Tokyo *on* (*company*) *business*.
●社用車 a company car. ●社用族 (説明的に) company employees who are allowed to put their eating and drinking on the expense account when they entertain clients in connection with their business.

しゃよう 斜陽 ●斜陽産業 a declining [a has-been, a sunset] industry. ●斜陽族 the new poor; 'the declining upper class'.

しゃよう『斜陽』*The Setting Sun*. (〖参考〗太宰治の小説)

じゃよく 邪欲 (不正な欲望) an improper desire; (私欲) a selfish desire; (みだらな情欲) a lewd [a lustful] desire.

しゃら 沙羅〚植物〛a sal (tree). (⇨沙羅(ﾗ)双樹)

しゃらくさい 洒落臭い impudent; cheeky; saucy. ▶しゃらくさいまねはよせ That's enough of your *cheek*!/I've had enough of your *impudence* [*cheek*]!

じゃらじゃら ●じゃらじゃら音を立てる jingle; rattle. ▶鍵(ｶｷﾞ)の束が彼のベルトでじゃらじゃら鳴った A bunch of keys *jingled* on his belt. ▶硬貨がブリキの箱の中でじゃらじゃらいっている Coins *rattled* in the tin box. (❢ポケットにある硬貨が触れ合って音を出すような場合は jingle が適している)

じゃらす 猫をじゃらす *play* with a cat.

しゃり 舎利 ❶〚仏陀・聖者の遺骨〛the ashes of the Buddha [a saint]. ❷〚火葬した後の骨〛one's ashes. ❸〚米〛(grains of) rice. ●銀しゃり polished *rice*.

じゃり 砂利 (道路補修用の) gravel /grǽvl/; (海・川などの自然にできた) pebbles. ●道路に砂利を敷く *gravel* [spread *gravel* on] a road.
●砂利置き場 a gravel yard. ●砂利採取場 a gravel pit. ●砂利道 a gravel road [path].

じゃりじゃり ●じゃりじゃりしている(＝砂がまじっている) gritty. ●じゃりじゃりした道(＝砂利道) a *gravel* road. ▶この貝はじゃりじゃりする The shellfish are *gritty*. ▶口の中が砂でじゃりじゃりする My mouth feels *gritty* with sand.

しゃりっと ●しゃりっとしたレタス a *crisp* lettuce. ●しゃりっとした肌ざわりの生地 *cool* and *elastic* material.

しゃりょう 車両〚乗り物〛a vehicle;〚鉄道の〛《米》a car,《英》a carriage. ●車両故障 a breakdown.
●車両乗り入れ禁止地域 a car-free [an auto-free] zone. ▶この道は車両通行禁止です This road is closed to *vehicles* [*traffic*].

****しゃりん** 車輪 a wheel. ▶車輪が脱落した The *wheel* fell off. ●「外れる,取れる」なら come off)

しゃれ 洒落 ❶〚冗談〛(やや古) a jest;〚ごろ合わせ〛a pun. (⇨冗談) ●うまい[気のきいた; おもしろい; 古い]しゃれ a good [a clever; a funny; an old] *joke*. ●言葉のしゃれ a *play* on words. ●へたなしゃれを言う tell [make,《話》crack, ×say] a bad *joke*; make a bad *pun*. ●しゃれが分かる see [get, understand] (his) *joke*. ●しゃれで言う say (it) for [as] a *joke*. ▶まともに取らないで, ほんのしゃれですから Don't take it seriously. I'm only *joking* [That's only a *joke*]. ▶彼はしゃれの通じない人です He can't take a *joke*. ▶こんなことがしゃれや冗談で言えるか I can't say such a thing [a thing of that kind] as a *joke*./(本気だ) I'm serious [in earnest].
❷〚おしゃれ〛(⇨おしゃれ) ●しゃれ男 a fop. (❢けなしていう)
❸〚その他の表現〛▶休暇にはハワイ旅行としゃれ込んだ We treated ourselves to a trip to Hawaii for a vacation.

しゃれい 謝礼 (報酬) a reward;(専門職業者に払う) a fee. ▶ダイヤのブローチを見つけてくれた人には 10万円の謝礼をさしあげます A *reward* of 100,000 yen will be offered to the person who finds the diamond brooch. ▶彼らは行方不明の飼い犬を見つけてくれた謝礼として彼に 500 ドル払った They gave him 500 dollars as a *reward* for finding their lost dog. ▶その弁護士への謝礼はいくらどしょうか What [How much] is the lawyer's *fee*? ▶彼は相談料として法外な謝礼を要求した He demanded an unreasonable *fee* for his consultation.

しゃれき 社歴 ▶彼の社歴は 20 年だ He's worked for [been with] the company for 20 years. (❢ He's worked for ... はすでに会社を退職している場合,

He's been with ... はまだ勤務している場合) ▶あなたの社歴は何年ですか How many years have you worked for [been with] the company?

しゃれこうべ 洒落頭 a weatherbeaten skull.

しゃれた 洒落た ❶〚気・言葉が機知のある〛witty;〚服装などがいきな〛stylish, smart (❢前の方は smart より行の先端たる含みがある);〚趣のある〛tasteful. ●しゃれたことを言う make *witty* remarks. ●しゃれた帽子 a *stylish* [a *smart*] hat. ●しゃれた飾り *tasteful* [(手のこんだ) *fancy*] decorations.

しゃれっけ 洒落っ気 ●しゃれっ気がない (ユーモア感覚がない) have no *sense of humor*;(服装に無頓着(ﾄﾝﾁｬｸ)である) be indifferent to one's clothes.

しゃれる 洒落る ❶〚おしゃれをする〛dress oneself up; dress [be dressed] stylishly [smartly].
❷〚冗談を言う〛joke, crack [make] a joke. (⇨洒落た)

じゃれる play 《with》. ▶子猫がまりにじゃれていた The kitten *was playing with* a ball.

じゃれん 邪恋 an illicit love affair.

ジャワ ●ジャワ島 Java /dʒá:və/. ●ジャワ原人 the Java-man. (❢ Java man ともつづる)

シャワー a shower (bath). ●シャワーつきの部屋(ホテルの) a hotel room with (a) *shower*. ●シャワーを浴びる have [take] a *shower*. ●シャワーを出す[止める] turn on [off] the *shower*. ▶シャワーを浴びて着替えをしたい I want a *shower* and a change [to *shower* and get changed].
●シャワー室 a shówer stàll [ròom].

しゃん (⇨しゃんと)

ジャンクション〚合流点〛《主に米》an intersection,《主に英》a junction.

ジャンクフード junk food.

ジャンクボンド a junk bond [issue]. (❢参考 格付けが投資適格である「BBB 以上」に満たない社債)

ジャンクメール (郵便物の) junk mail;(E メールの) spam (mail).

ジャングル (a) jungle. (❢通例 the ～) ●ジャングルの動物 jungle animals. ●アフリカのジャングルで in the *jungles* of Africa. ●ジャングルの掟(ｵｷﾃ) (follow) the law of the *jungle*.

ジャングルジム《米》a jungle gym (❢もと商標),《米》monkey bars,《英》a climbing-frame.

じゃんけん janken,〚the (game of) rock-paper-scissors. ●2 人はじゃんけんをした. 彼女がぐーを出して彼のちょきに勝った They played *janken* [*rock-paper-scissors*]. The rock she showed beat his scissors. ●じゃんけんで決めよう Let's decide by *janken*. (❢事情 米英ではコインを投げて決めるので Let's toss up!/Let's decide by a toss-up. などという)

しゃんしゃん ●しゃんしゃんと手拍子を打つ *clap* one's hands. ▶父は 90 歳だがしゃんしゃんしている(＝丈夫だ) Father is 90 years old, but he *is still going strong*. (❢〈話〉で進行形で用いる)

じゃんじゃん (絶えることなく) continuously, incéssantly;(たっぷり) plentifully;(むだにするよう) wastefully;(次々と) one after another;(たくさん) in plenty, a lot. ▶彼らは警鐘をじゃんじゃん鳴らした They rang the alarm *continuously*. ▶彼女はいつもふろ場で水をじゃんじゃん使う She always uses water *wastefully* in the bathroom. ▶彼らは私に料理をじゃんじゃん持って来た They brought me dishes *one after another*. ▶すき焼き好きよね, じゃんじゃん(＝好きなだけたくさん)食べて You like /sukiyaki, \do you? Eat *as much as you like*. (❢下降調に読んで念を押す) ▶新製品の宣伝を始めてまもなく注文がじゃんじゃん入ってきた Soon after we started advertizing our new product, the orders came

rolling in.
シャンゼリゼ 〖パリの大通り〗 the Champs Élysées /ʃɑːnzeilizéi/.
シャンソン ＜フランス語＞ a chanson /ʃɑːnsɔ́ːn/.
シャンツェ ＜ドイツ語＞ 〖スキーのジャンプ台〗 a ski jump.
シャンデリア ＜フランス語＞ a chandelier /ʃændəlíər/.
しゃんと ● しゃんとした[して] upright (❗「姿勢などがまっすぐな[に]；人格がきちんとした，正直な」などの意);（まっすぐな[に]) straight. ●しゃんと座る sit *upright*; sit up *straight*. ▶母は90歳だがまだしゃんとしている My mother is ninety but still very *healthy and active* (❗まだ元気はつらつとしている) still looks *alive*. ▶あなたもう大人でしょ. 少しはしゃんとしなさいよ (＝責任ある行動をとりなさい) You're an adult now. Be *more responsible*.
ジャンヌダルク 〖フランスの国民的英雄〗 Jeanne d'Arc /ʒɑ̀ːn dɑ́ːrk/. (❗英語では Joan of Arc /dʒóun əv ɑ́ːrk/ ともいう)
ジャンパー ❶ 〖上着〗 a jacket;（特にスポーツ用の防寒ジャケット）《米》a windbreaker (❗本来は商標). (❗英語の jumper は《英》では「セーター」のこと) ❷ 〖陸上・スキーのジャンプ選手〗 a jumper.
● ジャンパースカート《米》a jumper;《英》a pinafore (dress).
シャンハイ 上海 〖中国の都市〗Shanghai /ʃæŋhái/.
シャンパン (⇒シャンペン).
シャンピニオン ＜フランス語＞ a champignon.
ジャンピング ●ジャンピングキャッチ (make) a leaping [×jumping] catch.
ジャンプ 图 a jump. ── ジャンプする 動 jump. (⇒跳ぶ)
● ジャンプ競技 〖スキー〗the ski jump. ●ジャンプシュート 〖バスケット〗a jump shot [×shoot]. ●ジャンプスーツ 〖上下ひと続きのスーツ〗a jumpsuit. ●ジャンプ台 〖スキー〗a ski jump. ●ジャンプボール 〖バスケット〗a jump ball.
シャンプー 图 (洗髪) a shampoo /ʃæmpúː/ (複 ～s);（洗髪剤) a shampoo.
── シャンプーする 動 shampoo one's hair; have a shampoo.
シャンペン ＜フランス語＞ (a) champagne /ʃæmpéin/.
ジャンボ ●ジャンボサイズの（話）jumbo(-sized).
● ジャンボ(ジェット)機 a jumbo jet; a jumbo.
ジャンル ＜フランス語＞ a genre /ʒɑ́ːnrə/, a type.
しゅ 主 〖神〗the Lord. (❗キリスト教の神，呼びかけのときは Our Lord を用いる)
しゅ 朱 vermilion /vərmíljən/. ●朱塗りの箱 a *vermilion*-laquered box.
● 朱に交われば赤くなる 《ことわざ》(悪友と交われば悪くなる) He who touches pitch will be defiled. (❗「ピッチにさわると手が汚れる」から今は touch pitch は「悪友と交わる」の意)
● 朱を入れる ●答案に朱を入れる *correct* exam papers.
● 朱を注ぐ（顔を真っ赤にする）one's whole face turns red.
しゅ 種 〖生物分類上の〗a species (複 ～);〖種類〗a kind, a sort. ●サルにはいくつかの種がある There are several *species* of monkey. ●その種の事件が増えている Incidents of that *kind* are on the increase. ●日本には約200種のトンボがいる About 200 *varieties* of the dragonfly live in Japan./We have about 200 *varieties* of dragonflies in Japan.
しゅい 主位 (主要な) a central position.
しゅい 主意 (主眼) the main idea.
しゅい 首位 (the) first [the top] place;〖指導的地位〗the leading position;〖競争過程で〗the lead.
● クラスで首位に立つ be [×become] (at) the *top* of the class; be the *best* in the class. ●コンテストで首位になる get (*the*) *first place* in the contest. ●セントラルリーグで首位を奪い返す regain [lose] their *first place* in the Central League. ●首位に5ゲーム差をつけられる fall into five games out of first place [off the pace].
● 首位打者 a batting champion [king]. (❗a leading hitter はシーズン途中での，またはチーム内の首位打者)
しゅい 趣意 (⇒趣旨) ●趣意書 a prospectus.
じゅい 樹医 a tree specialist; a tree surgeon.
しゅいん 手淫 masturbation.
しゅいん 主因 (主な原因) the main [major, primary] cause (*of*);（主な要因) the major [chief, leading] factor (*in*).
じゅいん 樹陰 the shade of a tree.
しゅいんせん 朱印船 〖歴史〗a shogunate-licensed trading ship [vessel].
しゆう 市有 ── 市有の 形 municipal; city-owned.
● 市有の建物 *municipal* buildings.
● 市有地 city lands.
しゆう 私有 ── 私有の 形 private, privately owned.
● 私有権 private ownership. ●私有財産 private property. ●私有地 private land;（建物も含めて） private property.
しゆう 雌雄 male and female. ●雌雄を鑑別する distinguish the *male* from the *female*.
● 雌雄を決する fight ... out; fight (on) to the finish.
● 雌雄異株 〖植物〗dioecism. ●雌雄異体 〖動物〗dioecism. ●雌雄同株 〖植物〗monoecism.
● 雌雄同体 〖動物〗hermaphrodite.
しゅう 週 a week. (❗日曜から土曜までの7日間も，不特定の7日間もさす) (⇒週間，今週，先週，来週，毎週) ●週単位で by the [×a] *week*. ●週の初め[終わり]に at the beginning [end] of the *week*. (⇒週末) ●週5日制（学校の）a five-day school *week*;（職場の）(⇒週休). ●週に40時間働く work a 40-hour *week*. ▶彼は1週間に何度東京へ来ますか How many times does he come up to Tokyo a *week* [in a *week*, every *week*]?/How many times a *week* does he come up to Tokyo? ▶2週間の休暇を取る予定だ I'm going to take a vacation for two *weeks*./I'm going to take two *weeks*' [a two-*week*] vacation. (⇒週間) ●委員会は週に1回開かれます The committee meets *weekly* [once a *week*, every *week*]. (❗「週に2回 [2-3回]」は twice [two or three times] a week/The committee has a *weekly* meeting.
しゅう 州（行政区画）《米・豪》a state,《英》a county,《カナダ》a province. ●カリフォルニア州 the *State* of) California. (❗×California *State* とはいわない) ●サンフランシスコ州立大学 San Francisco *State* University. ●合衆国には50の州がある There are fifty *states* in the United States. ▶アトランタはジョージア州の州都です Atlanta is the (*state*) capital of Georgia. (❗この文では state はなくてもよい)
● 州議会 a state assembly [législature]. ●州知事 a governor.
しゅう 衆 ●若い衆 the young people. ●烏合(うごう)の衆 (⇒烏合の衆). ●衆を頼む rely on [upon] one's *numerical superiority*. ▶みなの衆，さあやろうじゃな

か *Everyone*, let's get going!

-しゅう -周 (⇨一周)
会話「(トラックをあと何周(=何回)走るの)」「あと3周だ」"How many more times should we run around the track?" "Three more times."

-しゅう -宗 a sect. (⇨派) ●日蓮宗 the Nichiren Sect.

-しゅう -臭 ●刺激臭 a pungent *smell* [*odor*].

-しゅう -集 a collection. ●漱石作品集 the collected works of *Soseki*.

じゆう 自由 图 (a) freedom; 《主に書》liberty;《書》license.

> 使い分け **freedom** 拘束・障害などがないことを表す幅の広い語。
> **liberty** freedom と同義だが、束縛・強制からの解放や行動に際しての選択の自由を暗示する。
> **license** 行動・言論・思想などの自由を表すが、しばしば軽蔑的に勝手気ままに自由が乱用された状態をいう。

① 【～(の)自由】 ●言論[選択;出版]の自由 *freedom* of speech [choice; the press]. (❗この場合は liberty とは普通いわない) ●宗教的自由 *freedom* of religion; religious *freedom* [*liberty*]. ●個人の自由 indivisual [personal] *freedom* [*liberty*]. ●学問の自由 academic *freedom*. ●精神の自由 *freedom* of spirit. ▶行こうと行くまいと君の自由だ You *are free* to go or not. (⇨⑤)/(君次第だ) *It's up to* you *whether* you go or not.

② 【自由～】 ▶彼は自らの自由意志でそこへ行った He went there of his own *free will*. ▶京都では自由行動はありません You *aren't free* to go around in Kyoto. (⇨⑤) ▶スペイン語かフランス語のいずれかを自由選択できる You *have the option of* (taking) Spanish or French. ●「自由選択」は *free choice*)

③ 【自由が】 ▶彼にはそれをする自由がある He has the *freedom* [*liberty*] *to do* it. ▶今の女性は昔よりずっと自由がある Women have a lot more *liberty* [*freedom*] (*to do*); (*to do*). ▶彼は自動車事故で右足の自由がきかなくなった He *lost the use of* his right leg in the car [《米話》auto] accident.

④ 【自由の】 ●自由のために戦う fight for *freedom*. ●自由の身となる be set free [at liberty] (*from* jail); be liberated.

── **自由な** 形 free. ▶忙しくて自由な時間があまりない I'm so busy (that) I don't have much *free* [《余分の》*spare*] time. (❗ that は《話》ではしばしば省略する)

── **自由に** 副 ❶【制限なく】freely; (好きなように) as one likes [pleases, 《書》wishes]; (意のままに)《書》at will; (自由に...できる・してよい) be free [《書》at liberty] (*to do*); (遠慮なく...する) feel free (*to do*) (❗通例命令文で). ●自由になる (解放される) become *free*. ●自由にやる do *freely*. ●自由に出入りする come in and out freely. ▶私たちは図書館を自由に使ってよいことになっている We can use the library *freely*./We *are free* [*at liberty*, ×*at freedom*] *to use* the library./We have the *freedom* [《ややまれ》*liberty*] *of using* the library. (❗ freedom は「出入り・使用の自由」の意) ▶私の車をご自由にお使いください Please *feel free* [*You are free*] *to use* my car. (❗ May I use your car? などに対して応答する場合には Feel free! (どうぞどうぞ), Help yourself! のように to 以下を省略する)/You can use my car *freely* [*at will*, (いつでも好きなときに) *any time you like*]./My car is *at your disposal*. ▶服装自由 You may dress *as you like*

[*please*]. ▶彼は数か国語を自由に操る He speaks several languages *very well* [(流暢に) *fluently*]./He has a *perfect command* of several languages. ▶彼は自由自在にその機械を操った He operated the machine *at will* [(簡単に) *easily*, (上手に) *skillfully*].

❷【その他の表現】 ▶ご自由にお取りください (掲示) Please take one. (❗ビラ・パンフの類だけに限らない) ▶試食品はご自由にお召し上がりください Please *help yourself to* the samples. ▶彼は自分の自由裁量でその仕事ができる He has a *free hand* to do [*in doing*] the job.

── **自由にする** (解放する) free, set*... free (❗後の方が口語的の), release, 《書》liberate. ▶その囚人はいつ自由にしてもらえますか When will the prisoner *be freed* [*be set free*, *be released*]? ▶その政治家は人々を奴隷の身から自由にしてやった The statesman *set the people free* [*released the people*] *from* slavery.

●**自由演技** an optional routine; 『フィギュアスケート』(シングル) a free program; (ペア・アイスダンス) free-skating. ●**自由化** (⇨自由化). ●**自由形** (自由形). ●**自由業** (a) free-lance profession. (⇨フリー) ●**自由競争** free [open] competition. ●**自由経済** a free economy. ●**自由契約選手** a free agent. ●**自由研究** (an) independent research. ●**自由作文** a free composition (*on*); an essay. ●**自由思想** liberal ideas. (❗「自由思想家」は *liberal* thinker; a freethinker) ●**自由主義** liberalism. ●**自由主義国** a free nation. ●**自由主義者** a liberalist, a liberal. ●**自由人** 『奴隷でない』 a freeman; 『慣習にとらわれない人』 a liberal. ●**自由世界** (共産圏に対し) the free world. ●**自由席** a nonreserved [an unreserved] seat. ▶(観劇などで) 自由席を2枚ください Could I have two seats in the *unreserved* [×*free*] section? (❗ free は「無料」の意となり不適切) ●**自由の女神像** the Statue of Liberty. ●**自由貿易** free trade. ●**自由貿易地域** a free trade area. ●**自由放任主義** the laissez faire (principle); permissiveness principle. ●**自由民主党** (日本の) the Liberal Democratic Party (略 LDP); (英国の) the Liberal Democrat Party, the Liberal Democrats (略 Lib Dems). ●**自由律** free-style *haiku*.

じゆう 事由 a reason. (⇨理由)

じゅう 十 ten; 『10番目の』 the tenth. (⇨三) ▶何十人もの人々 *dozens* [×*tens*] of people. ▶何十回も (=何度も何度も) *scores* of times. (❗ a score は「20」の意)

じゅう 銃 a gun (❗以下の銃を含む最も意味の広い語); (拳銃(ぢゅう)) a pistol; (ライフル銃) a rifle; (猟銃, 散弾銃) a shotgun; (連発銃) a machinegun. ●**空気銃** an air *gun*. ●**銃を携帯**[装填; 発砲]する carry [charge; fire] a *gun*. ●彼に銃を向ける aim one's *gun* at him. ▶銃を捨てて出て来い Throw down your *gun* and come out! ▶彼は銃でライオンを撃った He shot [shot at] a lion with a *gun*. (❗ shot は実際に命中したことを意味するが、shot at は単にねらい撃っただけで命中したとは限らない. 後の意では He shot [fired] a *gun* at a lion. ともいえる)

じゅう ▶熱いフライパンに水をかけたらじゅうっと音がした The hot frying-pan *hissed* as I dashed water over it. (⇨じゅうたん)

じゅう 柔 ●柔よく剛を制す 'Softness overcomes Hardness.'

じゅう 従 ── **従の** 形 subórdinate; (二次的な) sécondary. (⇨従属)

:-じゅう -中 ❶【期間】(ずっと) all through...,

しゅうあく throughout ...; over ...;（期間内に）within ...（⇨ －中(*3)）;〚範囲〛（最上級とともに）(...の中で) (up + all + 複数名詞), in（＋単数名詞）;〚場所〛(あちこち回って) around ...;（すみずみまで）all over (...), throughout (...). ▶ 1日中 all day (long);（1日の大半）for most of the day. ▶ 1年中 all the year around; *throughout* the year; every day of the year. ▶ 一晩中起きている sit up all night (long) [*all through* the night]. ▶ 世界中を旅行する travel *around* [*all over*, *throughout*] the world; travel the world *over*. (❗ *over* は副詞) ▶ 彼は夏の間中そこに滞在した He stayed there *over* [*through(out)*, *during*] the summer. (❗ *during* は文脈によって「夏の間の特定期間」の意にもなる (⇨ 間(*3))) /I spent the *whole* summer there. ▶ 今週[今日]中に彼に電話を入れねばならない I have to call him (*sometime*) *this week* [*today*]./I have to call him *by the end of this week* [*by tonight*, *by the end of the day*]. (❗「今週中に」は *within the week* も可能だが上例の方が普通, *within this week* は避ける. 「今日中に」は ×*within today* [*this day*] は不可) ▶ 彼はクラス中でいちばん背が高い He is the tallest *in* the class [*of* all his classmates]. ▶ 私は部屋中時計を捜した I looked *for* the watch *all over* the room. ▶ 彼は体中がぬれていた He was wet *all over* [*through*]./(徹底的に) He was *thoroughly* wet. ❷〚すべての〛all; whole (❗ the 〜). ▶ うち中みんな元気です The *whole* family is [×*are*] in good health./The family is [are《英》] *all* in good health. (⇨家族)

しゅうあく 醜悪 ── 醜悪な 形 ugly /ʌgli/; (ぞっとするほど醜い) hideous /hídiəs/, disgusting.

しゅうあけ 週明け ▶ 週明けに at *the beginning of next week*; early next week.

じゅうあつ 重圧 ▶ 重圧に耐える bear great pressure.

***しゅうい** 周囲 图〚円周〛(a) circúmference;〚周りの状況〛surróundings;〚環境〛(an) envíronment. (⇨環境).

① 〚周囲は〛▶ その町の周囲は景色が美しい The town has beautiful *surroundings*. ▶ 周囲は大変静かだった It was very quiet *all around* (us).
会話「その木の周囲はどれくらいありますか」「5メートルです」"How big [×*long*] is the tree *around*?" "It is five meters *around* [*in circumference*, 《やや書》*in girth*]."/"What is the *circumference* of the tree?" "It is five meters."

② 〚周囲に(は)〛around. (⇨周り ③) ▶ 周囲に集まる gather *around* (*her*). ▶ 周囲にはだれもいなかった There was nobody *around*.

③ 〚周囲を〛▶ 周囲をうかがう have a look *around* to see what the situation is. ▶ 彼は周囲を見回した He looked *around* [《主に英》 *round*, 《書》 *about*] (him). ▶ その公園は高いビルに囲まれている The park *is surrounded by* tall buildings.

── 周囲の 形 surrounding. (❗限定用法のみ) ▶ 周囲の景観[国々] the *surrounding* scenery [nations]. ▶ 周囲の雰囲気 the atmosphere *around* here. ▶ 周囲の変化 change of the *surroundings*. ▶ 周囲の状況[事情]から判断して judge from the *surroundings* [*circumstances*]. ▶ 彼女は周囲の人みんなに愛されていた She was loved by all *around* [親しい) *close to*] her. ▶ 周囲の目を(＝周囲の人々がどう思おうと)気にする Don't care what other people [others] think.

じゅうい 獣医 (話) a vet, 《米》 a veterinarian /vètərənéəriən/, 《英書》 a veterinary /vétərənèri/, surgeon.

● 獣医学 veterinary science [medicine]. ● 獣医学部 a veterinary school. ● 獣医大学 a veterinary college.

じゅういち 十一 eleven. ▶ 11 番目(の) the eleventh.

***じゅういちがつ** 十一月 November (《略 Nov.》). (⇨一月) ▶ 11月に in *November*.

しゅういつ 秀逸 图 excellence; (最も優れた作品) a masterpiece, a masterwork.
── 秀逸な 形 excellent; splendid; superb.

しゅういん 衆院 〚「衆議院」の略〛(⇨衆議院)

しゅうう 秋雨 (an) autumn rain.

しゅうう 驟雨 a shower. (⇨夕立)

しゅうえき 収益 (利益) (a) profit; (販売・取引などの) proceeds; (企業などの) earnings; (販売・投資などの) (a) return. ▶ 大きな収益をあげる make a large [a big, (巨大な) a huge] *profit*.

● 収益性 profitability. ● 収益率 the rate of profitability [return]; an earning rate. ● 収益力 earning power [capacity].

しゅうえき 就役 ▶ その軍艦はなお就役中である The warship is still *in commission*.

しゅうえん 終焉 (終わり) the end; (死) death. ▶ 芭蕉終焉の地は大阪の御堂筋の喧騒(*3)の中にある Basho's *deathplace* (⇔*birthplace*) [The place where Basho *died*] is now in the din of Midosuji Avenue in Osaka.

しゅうえん 終演 ▶ 終演は午後9時である The *performance ends* at 9 p.m./The *curtain falls* at 9 p.m.

じゅうおう 縦横 ● 縦横に〚縦と横に〛crosswise and lengthwise (❗地図で見るような場合は vertically and horizontally); (四方八方に) in all directions;〚自由に〛freely;（意のままに）《書》 at will. ● 縦横の活躍をする play a very active part 《*in*》. ● 縦横無尽たらしめる act to one's heart's content without any constraints from any parties. ▶ 国中を鉄道が縦横に走っている A network of railroads covers the whole country.

じゅうおく 十億 a [one] billion (❗数字の後では bn と略すことがある: 250億ドル ＄25*bn*). ▶ 何十億ドル *billions* of dollars.

しゅうおん 集音 ● 集音マイク a highly directional microphone.

しゅうか 秀歌 an excellent *tanka* [*waka*].

しゅうか 臭化 ● 臭化物 〚化学〛bromide.

しゅうか 衆寡 ▶ 衆寡敵せず 彼らは敗れた They were (heavily) *outnumbered* and defeated.

しゅうか 集荷 图 collection of baggage [(産物) products]. ── 集荷する 動 collect; pick ... up.

しゅうか 集貨 collection of freight [goods].

じゆうか 自由化 liberalization; ▶ 貿易の自由化 trade *liberalization*; *liberalization* of trade. ▶ 金融自由化に対する外圧がますます強まってきた External pressure for financial *liberalization* has been increasingly built up.

── 自由化する 動 liberalize. ▶ 技術導入を自由化する *liberalize* technology imports.

じゅうか 銃火 fire;（小銃による）rifle fire;（銃器による）gunfire. ● 銃火を浴びて under *fire*. ● 敵と銃火を交える exchange *fire with* the enemy.

しゅうかい 周回 图 ● 周回遅れの最終走者 an anchor who is one *lap* behind. ● 周回(＝周囲) 10キロの池 a pond ten kilometers *around* [*in circumference*].

── 周回する 動 ▶ 地球を周回する *go around* [*round*] the earth.

しゅうかい 集会 (an) assembly; 《やや書》 a gathering; a meeting (❗ 以上3語は前の語とは特定の目的を意識した言い方); (政治・宗教的な大集会) a rally; (宗教的な集会) a congregation. ● 大集会 a mass meeting. (共通の関心事を討論する大衆集会[国民大会]) ● 集会の自由 freedom of assembly [association]. ▶全校集会は(いつも)8時半からだ School assembly begins [is] at 8:30. ▶これは日本の学校の朝礼に当たる. ×...from 8:30. (は不可)
● 集会場 (定期的集会場所) a méeting plàce; an assembly hall [room].

しゅうかい 醜怪 ── 醜怪な 形 hideous; extremely ugly.

しゅうかいどう 秋海棠 〔植物〕 a begónia.

:**しゅうかく 収穫** 名 ❶ 【作物などの】 a crop (❗ しばしば複数形で); (主に穀物の) (a) harvest. ● 小麦の収穫時期 during the wheat harvest. ▶今年は小麦の収穫がよい We have a good (↔a poor) crop [harvest] of wheat this year. (⇨豊作) ▶今年の米の収穫(高)は今までで最高だった We've had the biggest (bumper) rice crop [harvest] ever this year./ We've brought in a record rice crop [harvest] this year. ▶この農場の小麦の収穫はヘクタール当たりどのくらいですか What is the yield of wheat per hectare on this farm?/How much wheat does this farm yield per hectare?
❷ 【獲物, 成果】 ▶今日の釣りは大した収穫がなかった I didn't get much fish today.
会話 「今日は何か収穫があった？」「いや大したことはないよ」"Did you get anything today?" "Not really."
── 収穫する 動 (取り入れる) harvest, bring *... in (❗ 後の方は口語的な言い方); (刈り取る) reap. ● 小麦を収穫する harvest [bring in, reap] wheat.
● 収穫高 (1農場または1種類の作物の) a crop; (1地方・1季節の全農作物の) the crops; a harvest.

しゅうかく 臭覚 (a sense of) smell. (⇨嗅覚)

しゅうがく 就学 名 ● 就学[就学前]児童 a school-age [a preschool] child. ● 就学年齢に達する reach school age.
── 就学する 動 enter [be enrolled in] school.

しゅうがくしょう 終楽章 ── 〔音楽〕 the last [final] movement; a finale /fɪnάːli/.

しゅうがくりょこう 修学旅行 a (three-day) school trip (《やや書》 excursion). ▶私たちは京都に修学旅行に行った We went on a school trip to Kyoto./ We went to Kyoto on [for] a school trip.

じゅうかさんぜい 重加算税 a heavy additional tax.

じゆうがた 自由形 (水泳・レスリングの) freestyle.
● 100メートル自由形種目 a 100 meters freestyle swimming event.

***じゅうがつ 十月** October (略 Oct.). (⇨一月) ● 10月に in October.

:**しゅうかん 習慣** 名 (習性) (a) habit (❗ 個人の癖や習慣); (慣習) (a) custom (❗ 主に社会的な習慣. 個人の習慣についても用いられることもある. ❗ habit の方が一般的); (社会のしきたり) (a) convention; (慣行, 慣例) (a) practice (❗ custom の意でしばしば軽蔑的に用いるが, 商業・法律上の慣行についても指す).
① 【～習慣】 ● よい食習慣 a good diet habit. ● 生活習慣病 a life-style disease.
② 【習慣が】 ● 悪い習慣がつく(=に陥る) fall into (↔out of) a bad habit. (⇨癖(ᆨ)) ▶朝早く起きる習慣が身についた I got into [形成された] formed] the habit of getting up early in the morning. ▶欧米ではクリスマスに贈り物をする習慣がある Westerners have the custom of giving [×to give] presents at Christmas./In Europe and America it is customary [a custom] to give presents at Christmas. (❗ It is the Western custom to....ともいえる) ▶私にはそのようなことをする習慣がない I don't have a habit of doing this sort of thing.
③ 【習慣に】 ● 昔からの習慣に従って according to an old custom. ▶彼は日曜日にはその博物館に行くのが習慣になっていた He used to go to the museum on Sundays. (❗ 過去のその人の長期間にわたるその人の特徴的な習慣を表す) ▶私は寝る前に散歩するのが習慣になっている I am in the [have the, have a] habit of going [×to go] for a walk before I go to bed./ It is my habit [practice] to go for a walk before going to bed./I always [usually] go for a walk before going to bed. ● 最後が一番口語的な言い方. I make it a rule to go for a walk .... (散歩することである)ともいえるが, 実際にはあまり用いられない) ▶たばこは習慣になる Tobacco is addictive [habit-forming]. (❗ addictive は「(麻薬・酒などが)習慣的になる」の意で通例悪いことに用いる)
④ 【習慣を】 ● 読書の習慣を身につける form [acquire] a habit of reading. ▶彼女はつめをかむ習慣をやめることができなかった She couldn't get out of [break] the habit of biting her nails.
⑤ 【習慣から】 ● つい習慣からたばこを吸ってしまった I just smoked out of [from] habit.
⑥ 【習慣で】 ● クリスマスカードを出すのは古くからある習慣だ Sending Christmas cards is an old custom.
── 習慣的な 形 habitual; customary.
── 習慣的に 副 habitually; customarily.

しゅうかん 収監 名 imprisonment, confinement.
── 収監する 動 put 《him》 in prison; imprison; confine.
● 収監状 〔法律〕 a mittimus.

しゅうかん 終刊 ● 終刊号 the final number (of a magazine).

しゅうかん 週刊 ── 週刊の 形 weekly. (⇨月刊)
● 週刊誌 a weekly (magazine).

しゅうかん 週間 a week. (旬, 一週間) ● 愛鳥[読書; 交通安全]週間 Bird [Book; Traffic Safety] Week. (❗ 大文字で) ● 2[1]週間おきに every two weeks [other week]. ● 何週間もの間 for weeks. ● 数週間で完成する complete 《it》 in several weeks. ▶冬に2週間の休暇がある We have two weeks' [a two-week, 《主に英》 a fortnight's] vacation in winter. (⇨週)

じゅうかん 重患 ● 重症 [重症患者].

じゅうかん 縦貫 ● 九州縦貫道路 a north-south highway through Kyushu.

じゅうかん 銃眼 a loophole; a porthole.

***しゅうき 周期** 名 a period, a cycle. (❗ 前の方は線状の, 後の方は循環的な反復) ● 3年周期で in a three-year cycle [period].
── 周期的な 形 periodic(al), cyclic.
── 周期的に 副 periodically, cyclically. ● 周期的に出る熱 periodic [×cyclic] attacks of fever.
● 周期律 the periodic law.

しゅうき 秋季, 秋期 autumn, 《米》 fall. (⇨秋) ● 秋季運動会 the autumn athletic meet [meeting 《英》]. (語法 米英には日本のような習慣はない)

しゅうき 臭気 a bad [an unpleasant, a nasty] smell; (かすかな) a stink. (⇨悪臭) ● 臭気を放つ give off [《書》 emit] a bad smell.

しゅうき 終期 the close; the end.

-しゅうき -周忌 the (first, second) anniversary of 《his》 death. (❗ 三周忌は死後満2年のときの法要なので second であって third ではない)

しゅうぎ 祝儀 ❶ 【祝い事】 a happy occasion; (婚礼)

しゅうし　終始 [ずっと] all the time; throughout; [始めから終わりまで] from beginning to end. ▶彼は終始冷静でした He kept his calmness *all the time [throughout]*. ▶会議は活発な討論に終始した They had a heated discussion *throughout [all through]* the meeting. ▶彼は終始一貫軍国主義に反対した He was *consistently* against militarism.

しゅうじ　習字 [書道] calligraphy /kəlígrəfi/; [書法] penmanship. ●習字の練習をする practice *calligraphy [penmanship]*. ●習字を習う take lessons in *calligraphy*.

***じゅうし　重視** ── 重視する 動 [強調する] put [lay, place] emphasis [stress] on …; [重要だと考える] regard … as important, attach (great) importance to …; [真剣に受けとめる] take … seriously. ●その問題についての彼の意見を重視する *attach importance to* his opinion on the matter; *take* his opinion on the matter *seriously*. (⇨重要)

じゅうし　十四 fourteen.

じゅうじ　十字 a cross. ●十字を切る cross oneself. ●十字懸垂 [体操] the crucifix. ●十字砲火 [軍事] crossfire.

じゅうじ　従事 ── 従事する 動 [仕事・研究などに] be engaged, engage (*in*); [職業に] (従う) follow 《the law》; (追求する) pursue 《*one's* business [studies]》. ▶彼は20年間農業に従事してきた He *has been engaged in* agriculture for the last twenty years. ▶彼は医業に従事した He *followed* the medical profession./He *pursued* medicine as a profession.

ジューシー juicy.

じゅうじか　十字架 a cross; (キリストがはりつけにされた) the Cross. ●十字架(上のキリスト)像 a crucifix. ●十字架にかける crucify 《him》; put 《him》 on the *cross*. ▶キリストは十字架ではりつけにされた Christ was crucified on a *cross*. ●十字架を背負う ▶我々は一生十字架(=苦難)を背負っている[背負わなければならない] We *have a cross to bear* [*must bear our cross*] as long as we live.

しゅうじがく　修辞学 (やや書) rhetoric /rétərik/.

じゅうじぐん　十字軍 ●十字軍の遠征 the Crusades /kru:séidz/. ([!] 通例複数形で、1回の遠征に言及する場合は、例えば the First [Second, etc.] Crusade のようにいう)

じゅうしち　十七 seventeen. ●17番目(の) the seventeenth.

じゅうしちかいき　十七回忌 the sixteenth anniversary of one's death.

しゅうじつ　終日 all day (long). ([!] long をつけると意味が強まる) ▶きのうは終日雨降りだった It rained *all day* (*long*) yesterday [*all yesterday*]. ▶彼は終日畑仕事をした He worked in the fields *all day* (*long*) [(朝から晩まで) *from morning till night*].

しゅうじつ　週日 a weekday. (⇨ウイークデー)

***じゅうじつ　充実** ●充実感 a sense of *fulfillment*. ●国防の充実 *completion* of national defense.

── 充実した 形 [十分な] full; [完全な] complete; [内容のある] substantial; [実り多い] fruitful. ●充実した生活を送る lead [live] a *full* life. ▶彼は気力が充実している He is *full of* energy.

しゅうしふ　終止符 (主に米) a period; (主に英) a full stop. ▶文尾に終止符を打つ put a *period* at the end of a sentence. ●論争に終止符を打つ(=終わらせる) put an *end* [a *period*, a *stop*] to the dispute; bring the dispute to an *end* [*stop*].

▶人類は戦争に終止符を打たなければならない. そうでなければ戦争が人類に終止符を打つことになる Mankind must *put an end* to war, or war will *put an end* to mankind.

じゅうしまつ　十姉妹 [鳥] a *jushimatsu*; a kind of common finch.

じゅうしゃ　従者 an attendant; a follower.

***しゅうしゅう　収集** 名 (a) collection. ●収集物は C
▶私の趣味は切手収集です My hobby is *collecting* stamps [stamp *collecting*]. ▶ごみの収集日は毎週金曜日だ Trash *collection* is [Trash is picked up] every Friday.

── 収集する 動 [趣味・研究などのため目的をもって集める] collect; [散らばっているものを一つに集める] gather. ●外国の硬貨を収集する *collect* foreign coins; *make a collection of* foreign coins. ●その惑星に関するデータを収集する *gather* [*collect*, (集積する) *accumulate*] data on the planet. ▶彼は古刀をたくさん収集している He *has a large collection of* old swords /sɔ́:rdz/.

●収集家 a collector.

しゅうしゅう 会話 「あのおしゅうしゅういっているのは何の音だろう」「やかんの湯がわいているのよ」 "What is that *hissing* sound?" "Oh, the kettle's boiling."

しゅうしゅう　収拾 [名] ●事態の収拾がつかなくなった Things [The situation] *got out of control [hand]*.

── 収拾する 動 [扱う] handle; [統制する] control (-ll-); [解決する] settle; [危機を脱する] save. ●その場をうまく収拾する *handle* [*save*, *control*] the situation; *get* [*bring*] the situation *under control*; (問題を解決する) *settle* the matter.

しゅうしゅう　修習 to study and learn [master] (English).

じゅうじゅう ▶肉がフライパンでじゅうじゅう焼けている The meat *is sizzling* in the frying pan.

じゅうじゅう　重々 (大変) very well [much] (⇨大変); (十分に) fully. ▶不利は重々承知の上だ I know *very well* that I am in a bad position.

しゅうしゅく　収縮 名 [金属・筋肉などの] (a) contraction; [素材・布などの] shrinkage.

── 収縮する 動 contract; shrink. (⇨縮む)

じゅうじゅく　習熟 名 proficiency /prəfíʃənsi/ (*in*). (⇨熟達, 熟練)

── 習熟する 動 ●コンピュータの操作に習熟する acquire *proficiency* [*become proficient*] *in* computing.

じゅうしゅつ　重出 ── 重出する 動 ▶その本には例の聖書からの1節が重出している That passage from the Bible *appears several times* in the book.

じゅうじゅん　従順 名 obedience /oubí:diəns/.

── 従順な 形 obedient; (優しやすい) docile /dásl/; (文句や反論を言わない) meek /mí:k/. ●しつけがよくて従順な子供 a well-trained and *obedient* child.

***じゅうしょ　住所** one's address /ədrés, ǽdres/. ●家の住所 one's home *address*. ●住所不定の男 a man of no fixed *address* [書] *abode*]; (浮浪者) a *homeless* man; [法律] a vagrant /véigrənt/. ●現住所を書く write down one's present *address*.
▶彼女の住所[会社の住所]はどこですか What [×Where] is her *address* [her office *address*]?
▶住所が変わったら知らせてください Let me know if you change your *address*./Please notify me of any change of *address*. (●後の方は堅い表現)
▶ご住所とお名前をおっしゃってください (Give [Tell] me) your name and *address*, please. (●語順に注意) ●住所不明(表示) *Address* unknown.

会話 「ご住所はどちらですか」「神戸市東灘区森北町1-1-3です」 "May I have [Would you give me]

your *address*?" "My *address* is 9-1-3, Morikita-cho, Higashinada-ku, Kobe."
● 住所変更通知 a change-of-address note.
● 住所録 an address book.

しゅうしょう 周章 ● 周章狼狽(ろうばい) 周章ろうばいする be disconcerted; be thrown into confusion; fall [get] into a panic.

しゅうしょう 愁傷 (⇨お悔やみ) このたびはまことに御愁傷様です Please accept my *sincere condolences*./You have my *sincere sympathy*. (!たとえば君の母親がなくなった場合、少しくだけた言い方としてI'm sorry to hear about your mother./I'm sorry your mother has passed away [is gone]. などがある)

*じゅうしょう 重傷 a serious injury [wound]. (!injury は事故などによるもの。wound は銃・凶器などで意図的に負わされた傷をいう) ● 事故で重傷を負う be *seriously injured* [*hurt*] *in* the accident. ● 頭に重傷を負う get a *serious injury* [*wound in*] the head; *be seriously wounded in* the head. ▶ 犯人はその女性に重傷を負わせた The criminal *wounded* her *seriously*. /The criminal inflicted a *serious wound* on the woman.
● 重傷者 a seriously injured [wounded, 《まれ》hurt] person (⑳ people), 《やや書》《集合的》 the seriously injured [wounded].

じゅうしょう 重症 (重い病気) a major [a severe] sickness, a serious [a critical] illness. ● 重症患者 a serious [a critical] case. (!「重患名簿」を(on) the danger list という; 「彼は重症だ」は He is *on the danger list*. ということもある)

じゅうしょう 重唱 ● 二重[三重；四重]唱 《音楽》(play [sing]) a duet [a trio; a quartet].

じゅうしょう 重障 『「重度身体障害」の略』a serious handicap.
● 重障児[者] a seriously handicapped child [person]; 《集合的》 the seriously handicapped.

じゅうしょうしゅぎ 重商主義 《経済》mercantilism.
―― 重商主義の 形 mercantile.
● 重商主義者 a mercantilist.

*しゅうしょく 就職 one's place for employment. ● 就職の面倒を見る help 《him》 get a *job*. ▶ 彼はすでに就職活動を開始している (= 就職口を探している) He has already started looking [hunting] for a *job*. ▶ 就職活動はうまくいっているかい How's your *job-hunting* going? ▶ 今年は就職難だ (= 就職口が不足している) It is hard to get [find] a *job* this year./We have trouble finding *jobs* this year. (⇨動)/(就職口が不足している) There is a shortage of *jobs* [We have a *job* shortage] this year. ▶ その大学には学生のための就職(あっせん)課がある The college has a (job) *placement* bureau [office] for students. 《事情》 米国では a career center, 英国では a job centre などで就職をあっせんする (⇨職業 [職業紹介所])
―― 就職する 動 (職を見つける) get* [find*] a job [work, employment, 《書》a position] (雇われる) get employed. ▶ 彼女は銀行に就職している She *has a job with* [*in, at*] a bank. (! with は会社の一員であること, in は就職している場所を強調する. at も場所を表すが活動・従事を暗示する)/She *is employed in* a bank./(銀行に勤めている) She *works for* a bank. (⇨勤める)
● 就職あっせん a (job) placement. ● 就職試験 (take) an employment exam [an exam for employment]; (面接の) (have) a job interview [an interview for a job]. ● 就職情報誌 a job

placement magazine. ● 就職説明会 a briefing for job applicants. ● 就職戦線 the employment front. ● 就職率 an employment rate; a rate of employment.

しゅうしょく 秋色 (秋の景色) autumn scenery; (秋の気配) signs of autumn.

しゅうしょく 修飾 名 『文法』modification.
―― 修飾する 動 modify.
● 修飾語 a modifier.

じゅうしょく 住職 the chief priest 《of a Buddhist temple》.

じゅうしょく 重職 a responsible post. (⇨⑳ 要職)

じゅうじろ 十字路 a crossroads. (! 単数扱い) (⇨交差点, 四つ角)

しゅうしん 修身 moral training; morals; (科目) ethics.

しゅうしん 執心 ―― 執心する 動 (愛着を感じる) feel [be] attached 《to》; (欲しいと思う) set one's heart 《on》; (熱心する) be devoted 《to》. ▶ 君は知子にご執心のようだね 《話》 You're crazy *about* Tomoko, aren't you?/(特別な感情を持っている) 《話》 You have a thing *for* [*about*] Tomoko, don't you?

しゅうしん 終身 名 a lifetime.
―― 終身の 形 lifetime. ● 終身刑の宣告を受ける be sentenced to *life* imprisonment [imprisonment *for life*].

DISCOURSE
確かに終身雇用制度は戦後日本の経済発展に効果的であった。しかし昨今は時代にそぐわないようだ The *lifetime employment system* was, **indeed**, effective for Japan's economic development in the postwar period; lately, however, it seems to have become outdated. (!indeed (たしかに)は譲歩を表すディスコースマーカー)

● 終身会員 a life member. ● 終身官 an irremovable officer; an official appointed for life. ● 終身雇用制度 the lifetime employment system. ● 終身年金 a life pension; 《やや書》annuity. ● 終身保険 whole life insurance.

しゅうしん 就寝 ▶ 就寝中 while one *is asleep* [*is sleeping*]. ▶ 就寝の時間ですよ It's time for bed.
―― 就寝する 動 go to bed.
● 就寝時間 bedtime.

しゅうじん 囚人 a prisoner, a prison inmate.

しゅうじん 集塵 ● 集塵機 a dust chamber [collector].

じゅうしん 重心 『重力の中心点』the center of gravity; 『釣り合い』(a) balance. ● 重心を保つ keep (↔lose) one's *balance*. ● 片足で体の重心をとる *balance* 《oneself》 on one foot.

じゅうしん 重臣 a senior subject [vassal]; a chief vassal [retainer].

じゅうしん 銃身 a barrel 《of a gun》.

しゅうじんかんし 衆人環視 衆人環視の的 the focus of public attention. ▶ 衆人環視の中で処刑が行われた時代もあった There was a time when the execution was held [carried out] *in* (*the full view of the*) *public*.

*ジュース 『飲料』juice (! 種類をいうときは ⓒ. 果実・野菜などからしぼった汁で, 果汁は 100 パーセントのものに限る); (炭酸水入りの) a soft drink; (果汁 100% でない) a fruit [juice] drink. ● オレンジジュース orange *juice*; (果汁 100 パーセントでない) an orange *drink*.
● ミックスジュース a mixture of fruit *juices*; mixed (fruit) *juice*.

ジュース 『競技の』deuce. ● ジュースになる [に持ち込む

go [get] to deuce.

じゅうすい 重水〖化学〗heavy water.
● **重水素** heavy hydrogen; 〖化学〗deuterium /d(j)u:tˈi(ə)riəm/〖元記号 D〗. ● **重水炉** a heavy water reactor.

しゅうせい 修正 图 〖計画・意見などの部分的変更〗(a) modification; 〖文書などの〗(a) revision; 〖法律などの語句の〗〖誤りの〗(an) amendment; 〖誤りの〗(a) correction; 〖数字などの調整〗(an) adjustment. ● 上方[下方]修正 upward [downward] revision [adjustment(s)]. ● 論文に数か所修正を加える make some modifications to one's thesis. ● 議案の修正(案)を提出する propose an amendment to a bill. ▶この計画[考え]は少し修正の必要がある This plan [idea] needs some modification.
— **修正する** 動 modify; revise; amend; 〖誤りを〗correct; 〖調整する〗adjust. ● 原稿を修正する revise [make revisions to] a manuscript. ● そのデータを修正する adjust the data. ▶設計図が一部修正された The design was modified.
● **修正液**《主に米》whiteout,《商標》White Out;《主に英》correction fluid,《商標》Tipp-Ex. ● **修正主義** revisionism. ● **修正予算** a revised budget.

しゅうせい 修整 — **修整する** 動 (写真を) retouch /riːtˈʌtʃ/; touch (it) up.

しゅうせい 終生 ● 終生変わらない友情 a lifelong friendship. (!) lifelong は叙述的には用いない) (⇨生涯, 一生)

しゅうせい 習性 (a) habit. (⇨癖, 習性) ● サルの習性 the habits [behavior] of apes. ● 夜ふかしの習性がある have a habit of staying up (till) late.

しゅうせい 集成 — **集成する** 動 collect;《やや書》compile. (⇨集大成)
● **集成材**〖建築〗laminated wood [lumber].

しゅうぜい 収税 tax collection.
● **収税官吏** a tax collector.

じゅうせい 銃声 a shot, a gunshot;《書》a report (!「伝わってくる音＝爆発音」の意). ● 銃声が聞こえる hear a shot [a gunshot]; hear a report of a gun.〖発砲〗a shot.

じゅうせい 獣性 the beast; 〖残忍〗brutality. ● 彼の中に潜んでいた獣性をむき出しにする reveal the beast in him.

じゅうぜい 重税 ● **重い税金** a heavy tax; 〖輸出入品などにかかる税〗a heavy duty (!) しばしば duties); 〖重い課税〗heavy taxation. ● 宝石に重税をかける impose [lay] a heavy tax [duty] on jewels. ● **重税に苦しむ** suffer from the heavy taxes [taxation]. ▶ 我々は重税を課せられている We are heavily taxed./We are subject to heavy taxation.

じゅうせき 重責 ● 重責を担う take (on) [accept, bear, shoulder] a heavy responsibility.

じゅうせきかいろ 集積回路 an integrated /ˌɪntəˈɡreɪtɪd/ circuit (略 IC).

しゅうせん 周旋 〖世話〗《書》〖his〗good offices; 〖仲介〗agency. ● …の周旋で through the good offices of ...; by [through] the agency of ....
● **周旋業** brokerage; an agency. ● **周旋業者** a broker; an agent. ● **周旋料** brokerage; (a) commission.

しゅうせん 終戦 ● 終戦後の日本 postwar Japan. ● 終戦後20年間 for twenty years after the war.
● **終戦記念日** the anniversary of the end of the war.

しゅうぜん 修繕 图 repair(s) (!)「修繕作業」の意では通例 ~ s); fixing; 〖主に衣類の〗mending. ● 家の修繕 house repairs. ● 修繕がきかない beyond repair.
— **修繕する** 動 repair, fix; mend (⇨修理する); 〖分解点検修理する〗overhaul. ● 壊れたドアを修繕する repair [fix, mend] a broken door. ● エンジンを修繕する repair [overhaul] an engine.
● **修繕費** the cost of repairs; repáir còsts.
● **修繕屋** a repairman. ● **修繕用具** repáir tòols.

じゅうぜん 十全 — **十全な** 形 perfect, complete. (⇨完全, 万全)

じゅうぜん 従前 (⇨従来)

しゅうそ 宗祖 the founder of a religious sect.

しゅうそ 臭素 〖化学〗bromine /brˈoʊmiːn/〖元記号 Br〗.

しゅうそう 秋霜 ● **秋霜烈日(の)** ● 秋霜烈日のごとき(＝非常に厳しい)権力 relentless authority.

しゅうぞう 収蔵 — **収蔵する** 動 (作物を蓄える) store ... (away [up]); (手元にしまっておく) keep.

じゅうそう 重曹 〖化学〗bicarbonate /baɪkˈɑːrbənɪt/ (of soda), sodium bicarbonate, baking soda,《話》bicarb.

じゅうそう 銃創 a bullet wound.

じゅうそう 縦走 — **縦走する** 動 ● 日本アルプスを縦走する traverse /trəvˈɜːrs/ the Japan Alps.

しゅうそく 収束 图 ❶〖収拾〗● 事態の収束を図る try to settle the situation. ❷〖数学〗convergence.
— **収束する** 動 〖数学〗converge.

しゅうそく 終息 图 ● 終息に向かう draw to an end; be ending. — **終息する** 動 come to an end; end. (⇨終わる)

しゅうぞく 習俗 (世の中のならわし) manners, customs; 〖民俗学〗folkways (!)複数扱い).

じゅうそく 充足 — **充足する** 動 ● 欲望を充足する satisfy a desire. ● 充足した生活を送る lead [live] a full life.
● **充足感** a sense [a feeling] of fulfillment.

じゅうぞく 従属 图 〖被支配〗subordination; 〖依存〗dependence.
— **従属的な** 形 subordinate; dependent.
— **従属する** 動 be subordinate (to); be dependent (on).
● **従属国** a dependency. ● **従属節**〖文法〗a subordinate clause. ● **従属接続詞**〖文法〗a subordinate conjunction.

しゅうたい 醜態 disgraceful behavior. ● 醜態を演じる disgrace oneself (by doing); make a sight of oneself.

じゅうたい 重体 ● 父は重体だった My father was in (a) serious [(a) critical] condition./My father was critical [critically ill, seriously ill]. (!) critical は「危篤(きとく)の」の意. ill に代えて sick も可) (⇨危篤)

じゅうたい 渋滞 图 (交通の) a tráffic jàm,《やや書》tráffic congestion /kəndʒˈɛstʃən/. ▶ 渋滞にひっかかった We were caught in a traffic jam./We got caught [stuck] in traffic.
— **渋滞する** 動 ● ひどく渋滞している道路 a heavily congested road. ▶ その通りは交通渋滞していた The street was crowded [jammed] with cars./There was a traffic jam [a traffic hold-up] in the street./(車はじゅずつなぎであった) The traffic was bumper-to-bumper on the street. ▶ 数台のオートバイが渋滞(＝立ち往生)している車の間を縫うように走って行った Several mortorcycles wound /wˈaʊnd/ in and out through the stalled traffic.

じゅうたい 縦隊 (a) line; (軍隊の) a file (↔a rank), a column. ● (何列もの)縦隊で行進する march in columns [files]. (!)「4列縦隊で」は in a column [a file] of four, in four columns [files]) ● 1[2]列

縦隊で歩く walk in a straight *line* [in two straight *lines*]; walk (in) single *file* [(in) double *file*].

*じゅうだい 重大 图 〖重要さ〗importance; 〖深刻さ〗seriousness; 〖ゆゆしさ〗《書》gravity. ▶ 重大視する take 《the matter》(very) seriously. ▶ 首相は事態の重大性を認識した The Prime Minister realized the *importance* [*seriousness*, *gravity*] of the situation.

— **重大な** 形 〖重要な〗important (▪ 最も一般的な語); 〖深刻な〗serious; 〖重要な意味を持つ〗significant; 〖ゆゆしい〗grave. ● きわめて重大な問題 a very *important* matter [a matter *of* great *importance*]; a *serious* matter. ● 重大な過失を犯す make a *serious* [a *grave*, a *big*] mistake. ● 重大な事実 a *significant* fact. ● 重大な結果 a *grave* consequence. ▶ 事態はますます重大になってきている The situation is getting *more and more serious*./(悪くなってきている) Things are getting *worse and worse*.

- 重大視 regard ⟪it⟫ as problematic.

じゅうだい 十代 one's teens. (⇒ティーンエージャー)
● 十代の少年[少女] a teen-ager; a teenage boy [girl], a boy [a girl] *in* his [her] *teens*. (▪ いずれも語尾に -teen のつく 13–19 才の年齢) ● 十代 in one's *teens*. ● 十代前半[後半]である be *in* one's early [late] *teens*.

しゅうたいせい 集大成 图 〖いろいろの資料を集めて編集すること〗compilation. (▪ 編集した物は ⓒ) ▶ これは政党政治に関する彼の研究の集大成である This is a *compilation* of his studies on party politics.

— **集大成する** 動 ● 日本の詩歌を集大成する(=編集して1冊にまとめる)《や書》*compile* Japanese poetry *into* one book.

*じゅうたく 住宅 a house (⚐ houses /-ziz, 《米》-siz/); a home; (高級住宅)《書》a residence; 〖集合的〗housing /háuziŋ/. ● 公営住宅 public *housing*; (新しい)《米》a (*housing*) project. ● 住宅問題 a *housing* problem. ● 住宅難に苦しむ suffer from a *housing* shortage. ● 住宅事情を改善する improve *housing* [the *housing* situation]. ● 新興住宅地 a newly-developed *residential* area; a new *housing* area. ● 二世帯住宅 a *house* with living facilities for two related families. ▶ その都市では住宅[2万戸の住宅]が不足している There is a shortage of *housing* [20,000 *houses*] in the city. ● 彼らは住宅街に住んでいる They live in a *residential* area [quarter, district].

- 住宅金融公庫 The Housing Loan Corporation.
- 住宅手当 a housing allowance.
- 住宅ローン a home [a housing] loan.

しゅうだつ 収奪 — **収奪する** 動 〖奪い取る〗《や書》deprive ⟪人...of+物⟫; 〖取り去る〗take ... away ⟪from⟫;《書》wrest ⟪from⟫.

*しゅうだん 集団 a group; a band; a mass.

> 使い分け **group** 何らかのつながりを持った人々の小さな集団.
> **band** リーダーのもとに集まった集団.
> **mass** 多くの人や物の集まり.
> group や band は原則として全体をひとまとまりとして見るときは単数扱いだが, 個々のメンバーに重点を置くときは《英》では複数扱い, 《米》では単数動詞, 複数代名詞で呼応させるのが普通.

① 〖～の(集)団, 集団～〗● 少年たちの集団 a *group* of boys. ● テロリスト集団 a terrorist *group*. ● 年齢集団 an age *group*. ● 小数民族集団 a minority *group*. ● 先頭集団 the leading *group* ⟪of runners⟫. ● 集団志向の社会 a *group*-oriented society.

② 〖集団を[に, で]〗● 集団を作る form a *group*; (集団になる) *group* together. ● 小さな集団に分かれて行動する act *in* small *groups*. ● 大集団で行進する march *in* a huge *mass*. ● 集団を率いる lead a *group*; head up a *group*. ● 集団で作る make ⟪it⟫ in a large *group*.

- 集団安全保障 collective security. ● 集団移住 migration as a group. ● 集団演技 a mass game. ● 集団下校 leaving school in groups. ● 集団検診 a group medical examination. ● 集団行動 a group activity. ● 集団自衛権 the right of collective defense. ● 集団自殺 ⟪commit⟫ a mass [group] suicide. ● 集団就職 employment as a group. ● 集団食中毒 mass [group] food poisoning. ● 集団登校 going to school in groups. ● 集団治療 group therapy. ● 集団発生 an outbreak.

じゅうたん 絨緞, 絨毯 (床・階段に敷きつめる) (a) carpet; (床の一部に敷く) a rug. ● 床にじゅうたんを敷く lay a *carpet* on the floor; carpet the floor; cover the floor with a *carpet*. ▶ 床にはじゅうたんが敷きつめてあった The floor had a wall-to-wall *carpet*.

- 絨緞爆撃 a carpet bombing.

じゅうだん 銃弾 a bullet /búlət/. ● 銃弾の跡 a *bullet* hole. ● 銃弾に倒れる be shot to death.

じゅうだん 縦断 — **縦断する** 動 (縦に切る) cut ⟪it⟫ vertically; (大陸などを) go [travel] through .... ▶ アンデス山脈は南米大陸を縦断している The Andes /ǽndiːz/ run through South America.
- 縦断面 a vertical [a longitudinal] section.

しゅうち 周知 ● 周知の事実 a well-known fact; (a matter of) common knowledge (▪ やや堅い言い方). ● 周知のように as everybody knows; as is generally [well] known.

しゅうち 衆知 ▶ 青少年犯罪防止のために衆知を集めなければならない (多くの人の助言[意見]を聞かなければならない) We must *ask a lot of people for advice* [*opinion*] to prevent juvenile delinquency./(多くの人の英知を結集する)《書》We must *gather the wisdom of many people* to nip juvenile delinquency in the bud.

しゅうちしん 羞恥心 〖良心に訴える恥ずかしさ〗shame; 〖自信を欠いたはにかみ〗shyness. (⇒恥ずかしい) ● 羞恥心で顔を赤らめる blush *for* [*with*] *shame*; blush *shyly*. ● 羞恥心のない人 a *shameless* person.

*しゅうちゃく 執着 图 (⇒固執(ĩ₀)) ● 執着心が強い be very *persistent* [《やや書》*insistent*, *tenacious*].

— **執着する** 動 〖意見などに〗insist ⟪on⟫; 〖かたくなに〗cling [《書》adhere] ⟪to⟫; (理不尽に) persist ⟪on⟫; (あくまで)《やや書》be tenacious /tənéiʃəs/ ⟪of⟫; 〖愛情をもって〗be attached ⟪to⟫. (⇒執心する) ● 古いしきたりに執着する persist in [cling to] old customs.

しゅうちゃく 終着 ● 終着の列車 the *last* (↔first) train.
- 終着駅 a terminal station; a terminus (⚐ ~es, termini); a railroad terminal (▪ 建物を含めて).

*しゅうちゅう 集中 图 〖注意・努力などの集中〗(a) concentration; 〖人口・権力などの集中〗centralization. ● 集中力を養う develop the ability to *concentrate*. ● 集中力を必要とする仕事 work that requires *concentration*. ● 人口の都市集中化 *concentration* of population in cities; urban cen-

tralization. ▶人間が集中できるのは(=人間の集中力は)1時間か1時間半である Human power of *concentration* lasts only an hour or an hour and a half.
── **集中する** 動 (1点に集める) concentrate /kánsəntrèit/ 《*on*》; (注意などを) focus, center 《*on*》; (機能などを) centralize 《*on*》. ▶彼の言うことに注意を集中する *concentrate* (one's attention) [*focus* one's attention] *on* what he says. ▶彼はそれにあまり気持ちを集中できなかった He couldn't *concentrate on* it very well. ▶質問はその点に集中した Questions *centered on* that point. ▶ほとんどの工場がこの地域に集中している Most of the factories *are concentrated* in this area. ▶権力がすべてこれら数人に集中している All of the power *is centralized* among these few people.
● **集中豪雨** (get) a very heavy outbreak of rain; a concentrated heavy rain; (局地的な豪雨) a localized torrential rain. ● **集中講義** an intensive course 《*in*》. ● **集中攻撃** (野球の) a rally. ● **集中治療室** an intensive care unit 《略 ICU》.
じゅうちゅうはっく 十中八九 (⇨十中(ǰǔ)八九)
しゅうちょう 酋長 a chief 《他 〜s》.
じゅうちん 重鎮 an important [指導的な] leading, (影響力の強い) an influential figure 《*in* the political world》.
しゅうてい 舟艇 a boat; a small craft. ● **上陸用舟艇** a lánding cráft.
じゅうていおん 重低音 a heavy bass sound.
しゅうてん 終点 [鉄道・バスなどの] the terminal; the terminus; [路線の終わり] the end of (the) line. ▶列車は終点に到着した The train arrived at [pulled into] the *terminal* (station). ▶上越新幹線の終点は新潟です The *terminal* [The *end of the line*] *for* the Joetsu Shinkansen is Niigata. ▶彼は終点の一つ手前で降りた He got off at the stop before the *end* of (the) line.
しゅうでん 終電 the last train. ● **終電に乗り遅れる** miss *the last train*.
***じゅうてん** 重点 名 [重要な点] an important point; [強調] (an) emphasis; [優先] priority. ▶日本では重点がとかく東京に傾きがちだ In Japan, both politics and economy tend to *be focused on* Tokyo.
● **重点を置く** あの大学は運動に重点を置いている The college *puts emphasis* [*stress*] *on* athletics./The college *emphasizes* [*stresses*] athletics.
── **重点的に** 副 ● **重点的に**(=集中的に)歴史を研究する study history *intensively* ● [選択的に] *selectively*》.
● **重点主義** the priority system.
じゅうてん 充填 a filling.
── **充填する** 動 fill. ▶奥歯に金を充填してもらった I had one of my back teeth *filled with* gold.
● **充填材** filler; (虫歯用の) filling.
じゅうでん 充電 charge. ● **充電式の** rechargeable 《shavers》.
── **充電する** 動 charge [再充電する] recharge] a 《car》 battery; (元気を取り戻す) recharge one's batteries; relax and get back one's energy. ▶最大限に充電してある *be on* full *charge*.
● **充電器** a (battery) charger.
じゅうでんき 重電機 heavy electric equipment.
しゅうでんしゃ 終電車 (⇨終電)
しゅうと 姑 (夫[妻]の母) a mother-in-law 《他 mothers-,《英話》〜s). (⇨義母)
しゅうと 舅 (夫[妻]の父) a father-in-law 《他

fathers-,《英話》〜s). (⇨義父)
しゅうと 州都 a state capital.
しゅうと 宗徒 a believer; a devotee.
シュート 名 (野球の) a screwball (「シュート」に正しく対応する英語はない。実際は a tailing fastball という); (ゴールへの) a shot. ● **ミドルシュート** a middle (range) shot. ● **ゴールの枠に飛んだ[枠を外れた]シュート** a shot on [off] target. ▶彼はロングシュートをねらったがそれた He tried a long *shot* but missed the target.
── **シュートする** 動 shoot (《主に命令文で》); have [try] a shot (at [on] goal) (《入ったかどうかは不》)
ジュート [黄麻(ǔ)の繊維] jute.
じゅうど 重度 ── **重度の** 形 severe. (⇨軽度)
● **重度障害者** a severely handicapped person; 《集合的》the severely handicapped.
しゅうとう 周到 ── **周到な** 形 (最善の準備をした) best-laid; (注意深い) careful; (完璧な) thorough /θə́:rou/; (綿密な) scrupulous. ● **周到な準備をする** make *careful* preparations; prepare *carefully*.
じゅうとう 充当 名 (an) appropriation /əpròupriéiʃən/.
── **充当する** 動 make an appropriation; 《やや書》appropriate. ● **100万円を借金の支払いに充当する** *appropriate* [*make an appropriation of*, 《違う》 *use*] one million yen for payment of debts.
じゅうどう 柔道 judo. ● **放課後柔道をする** practice [do, ×play] *judo* after school. (!格闘技には play は使わない) ▶彼は柔道5段だ He is a 5th dan [grade] *judoka*./He is a *judoka* of the fifth (dan [grade]).
● **柔道着** a *judoka*; a judoist. ● **柔道着** a suit for *judo* practice. ● **柔道選手** a *judo* fighter.
しゅうどういん 修道院 a religious house (他 houses /-ziz, 《米》-siz/); (男子の) a mónastery; (女子の) a cónvent. (!) (1) 個々の「修道士」は a monk /mʌ́ŋk/;「修道女」は a nun, a sister. 男女の区別をしない a religious という語もある. (2) sister は修道女の呼びかけに用いることが多い: *Sister* Yamada (シスター山田)) ● **修道院生活** the monastic [the *convent*] (way of) life.
じゅうとうほう 銃刀法 [「銃砲刀剣類所持等取締法」の略] [法律] the Firearms and Swords Control Law.
***しゅうとく** 修得 ── **修得する** 動 (単位を取る) earn [take, acquire] a credit 《*in* math》(!4 単位なら four credits となる); (課程を終える) finish a course 《*in* math》.
● **修得単位** earned credits.
***しゅうとく** 習得 名 acquisition /ǽkwiziʃən/; (熟達) mastery. ● **言語の習得** the *acquisition* of language [language *acquisition*]; *mastery* of language. (!前の二つは母語の習得に使われる傾向がある) ▶彼は物事の習得が早い He is quick *at learning* [*to learn*]./He is a quick learner.
── **習得する** 動 ● **英語を習得する** (=習って身につける) learn [努力の末] *acquire*, (達人になる) *master*] English. (⇨learn)
しゅうとく 拾得 ── **拾得する** 動 (見つける) find.
● **拾得物** a thing found. (!xa found thing とは言わない)
しゅうとめ 姑 a mother-in-law 《他 mothers-,《英話》〜s). (⇨義母)
じゅうなん 柔軟 ── **柔軟な** 形 (体・筋肉がしなやかな) supple; (曲げ[ねじり]やすい) pliable; (融通のきく) flexible; (適応性のある) adaptable. ● **柔軟な精神** [態度] a *flexible* mind [attitude].

- 柔軟性 flexibility. ● 柔軟体操 calisthenics.
じゅうに 十二. ● 12番目(の) the twelfth.
● 12時に at *twelve* (o'clock); (正午に) at *noon*; (夜の12時に) at *midnight*.
じゅうにおんかい 十二音階 a twelve-tone scale.
*****じゅうにがつ** 十二月 December《略 Dec.》. (⇨一月)
● 12月に in *December*.
じゅうにきゅう 十二宮 the twelve signs of the zodiac.

> **関連** 十二宮: 白羊宮 Aries /éəri:z/, (牡羊座) the Ram/金牛宮 Taurus /tɔ́:rəs/, (牡牛座) the Bull/双子宮 Gemini, (双子座) the Twins/巨蟹(きょ)宮 Cancer, (蟹(かに)座) the Crab/獅子(し)宮 Leo /li:ou/, (獅子座) the Lion/処女宮 Virgo, (乙女座) the Virgin/天秤(びん)宮 Libra, (天秤座) the Balance [Scales]/天蠍(かつ)宮 Scorpio, (蠍(さそり)座) the Scorpion/人馬宮 Sagittarius /sædʒitéəriəs/, (射手座) the Archer/磨羯(きつ)宮 Capricorn, (山羊(やぎ)座) the Goat/宝瓶(ほう)宮 Aquarius, (水瓶座) the Water Bearer [Carrier]/双魚宮 Pisces /páisi:z/, (魚座) the Fishes.

じゅうにく 獣肉 meat.
じゅうにし 十二支 (⇨干支(し))
じゅうにしちょう 十二指腸 〖解剖〗a duodenum /d(j)u:ədí:nəm/ (複 duodena).
● 十二指腸潰瘍〖医学〗a duodenal ulcer.
じゅうにしんほう 十二進法 〖数学〗duodecimal.
じゅうにひとえ 十二単 (説明的に) a ceremonial dress [attire] of a Japanese court lady.
じゅうにぶん 十二分 ▶君は十二分にやった You have done *more than enough* [(期待された上に) *more than you were expected to*]. ▶食糧は十二分にありますか Do you have *more than enough* food? ▶十二分にいただきました I've had *enough*. (❗単に enough だけで「十二分に」の意は表せる)
*****しゅうにゅう** 収入 〖定期的な所得〗(an) income; 〖稼ぎ高〗earnings; 〖売上高〗a sale (❗ しばしば複数で); (演奏会などの収益) proceeds (❗ 〖税金などによる歳入〗revenue /révənjù:/ (❗ 総収入の意では複数形).
①**【〜を得る】** ●総収入 gross *income* [*earnings*].
● 実[年間，平均]収入 net [annual; average] *income* [*earnings*]. ● 税収入 tax *revenues*; *revenue* from taxes. ● 興行収入 box office. ● 現金収入 a cash *income*. ● 低収入で暮らしている人々 people *on* low [↔high] *incomes*. ● 無収入の人 a person with no *income*. ● 少ない収入で家族を養う support one's family *on* a small [a low] *income*.
②**【収入〜】** ▶ 収入以上の生活をする live beyond one's *income* [〖やや書〗*means*]. ▶ 物価がこう上がったのでは収入の範囲内で生活するのは難しい With prices going up the way they are, it is hard to live within my *income* [(収支を合わせる) to make ends meet].
③**【収入は［が］】** ▶ 彼は収入が多い His *income* is large./He has [earns, enjoys] a large *income*. ▶ 彼の収入はどのくらいですか What [×How much] is his *income*? ▶ 彼女は月に50万円の収入がある She *has* an *income* of five hundred thousand yen a month./Her monthly *income* is [Her monthly *earnings* are] five hundred thousand yen. (⇨年収) ▶私の収入は5年前の2倍になった My *income* is twice as large as it was five years ago./(2倍かせぐ) I *earn* double what I did five years ago. ▶ 先月より収入が増えた[減った] My *income* has increased [decreased] over last month./I

have earned a larger [a smaller] *income* than last month.
④**【収入を】** ● バザーの収入を慈善事業に寄付する give the *proceeds from* [*of*] a bazaar to charity.
● 収入印紙 a revenue stamp. ● 収入源 a source of revenue [income]; a revenue producer.
● 収入役 a revenue officer; a treasurer.
しゅうにん 就任 图 (任につくこと) (an) assumption (*of*); (式を行う正式な) installation, (an) inauguration (❗米国大統領には後の方を用いる).
── 就任する 動 ▶ 部長に就任する assume [take] the post of general manager (❗ take の方が口語的); be installed (❗ (公職につく)〖やや書〗*take office*] as manager. ▶ 彼は1月20日に米国大統領に就任する He is to *be inaugurated* [*take office*] *as* (the) President of the United States on January 20. (❗この日を the Inauguration Day と呼ぶ)
● 就任演説 (give, make) an inaugural speech.
● 就任式 an inauguration.
じゅうにん 住人 an inhabitant, a resident. (⇨住民)
▶ そのアパートには50人の住人(=間借り人)がいた There were fifty *tenants* in the apartment house.
じゅうにん 重任 ❶**【重大な任務】** an important duty; a responsible task. ● 重任を引き受ける assume [take on] an *important task*.
❷**【再任】**(⇨再任)
じゅうにんといろ 十人十色 《ことわざ》So many men, so many minds. ▶ この世は十人十色だな(=いろいろの人たちが世の中を作っている) It takes all sorts to make a world./The world is made up of all sorts of people.
じゅうにんなみ 十人並み ── 十人並みの 形 (平均的な) average; (普通の) ordinary; (容貌(ぼう)が) average-looking. (⇨人並) ● 十人並みの能力の人たち people of *average* ability.
しゅうねん 執念 〖固執〗persistence;《やや書》tenacity. (⇨執心(しん)) ▶ 彼は焼き物づくりに executive kept している(=専念している) He *is* very *devoted to* making [×make] pottery./He makes pottery *with such ardor*.
-しゅうねん -周年 ● 学校創立100周年を祝う celebrate the 100th [centénnial] *anniversary* of the foundation of the school. (⇨記念 [記念日])
じゅうねん 十年 ten years; a decade. ● ここ数十年間に in the recent several *decades*.
● 十年一日のごとく (毎年毎年) year and year; (飽きずに) tirelessly. ▶ 十年一日のごとく平凡な生活が続く Year and year I lead an ordinary life.
● 十年一昔 A lot changes in ten years.
しゅうねんぶかい 執念深い 〖しつこい〗persistent; 〖復讐(しゅう)心の強い〗(性質として) vindictive; (ある行為に対して) revengeful. ▶ 警察は執念深く犯人を追った The police chased the criminal *persistently*./ The police kept (on) chasing the criminal. (❗後の方が普通。on は行為の継続・反復を強調する副詞)
しゅうのう 収納 图 storage /stɔ́:ridʒ/. ● 収納スペースが足りない do not have enough *storage* [《主に米》*closet*] space.
── 収納する 動 (貯蔵する) store; (しまう) put... away (*in* a chest).
しゅうは 宗派 〖分派〗(時に軽蔑的に) a sect; 〖教派〗a denomination (❗しばしば sect より大きく，正統性，独立性が強い).
● 宗派争い sectarian differences; sectarian strifies. ● プロテスタントの諸宗派 the Prótestant *denominations*.

しゅうは 秋波 ●**秋波を送る**(色目を使う) make eyes at ...; give 《him》 the eye; make sheep's eyes at ....

しゅうはい 集配 图 collection and delivery.
── **集配する** 動 collect and deliver.
●**集配人** (郵便の)《主に米》a mail [a letter] carrier, (男の) a mailman;《英》a postal carrier, (男の) a postman.

しゅうはいいん 集配員 (⇨集配[集配人])

じゅうばこ 重箱 a *jubako* (饅 ~s); (説明的に) a tier of lacquered boxes with a lid on top used mainly for transporting cooked food for a short distance.
●**重箱の隅をほじくる** ▶重箱の隅をほじくるような話はやめよう Let's stop splitting hairs.

しゅうバス 終バス the last bus.

しゅうはすう 周波数 〖物理〗(a) frequency. ●837キロヘルツの周波数で放送する broadcast *on* [*at*] *a frequency of* 837 kilohertz.

じゅうはち 十八 eighteen. ●18番目(の) the eighteenth.
●**18金** 18-karat gold. ●**十八番** (⇨十八番(^は))

じゅうばつ 重罰 a severe punishment.

しゅうばん 終盤 the last [final] stage (*of*). ●試合は終盤にさしかかった The game reached the *last stage.*/We've entered the *last stage* of the game.

しゅうばん 週番 weekly duty; (週番の生徒) a student on weekly duty. ▶今週はぼくが週番です I'm *on duty this week.*

じゅうはん 重版 (版) a second edition; (刷) a second [another] impression [printing].

じゅうはんしゃ 従犯者 〖法律〗an accéssory 《*in a crime*》; (共犯者) an accomplice.

しゅうび 愁眉 ●**愁眉を開く** feel [be] relieved 《*to do; that* 節》.

じゅうひ 獣皮 an animal skin; a hide.

しゅうひょう 集票 ── **集票する** 動 gather votes.

じゅうびょう 重病 ●重病である have a *serious* [a *critical*, ×a *heavy*] *illness*; be *seriously* [*critically*] *ill* [*sick*]. (❗*critical*(*ly*) は「危篤の[で]」の意)
●**重病人** a serious [a critical] case.

しゅうふく 修復 图 (a) restoration, (a) renovation. (❗修復作業を表すときはしばしば複数形で) ●その絵は現在修復中です That painting *is now under restoration* [*renovation*]./That painting *is being restored* [*is being renovated*] now.
── **修復する** 動 restore, renovate (❗ともにやや堅い語); improve relations 《*between*》, mend (one's) fences 《*with*》. ●我々は彼との関係を修復した We *patched up* relations with him./We *made up* with him.

しゅうぶん 秋分 the autumn(al) equinox /í:kwənɑ̀ks/.
●**秋分点** the autumnal equinox point. ●**秋分の日** Autumnal Equinox Day.

しゅうぶん 醜聞 (a) scandal. (⇨噂(^{うわさ}), スキャンダル)

じゅうぶん 十分 ── **十分な** 形 〖数・量的に〗(必要に足りるだけの) enough /ɪnʌ́f/ (❗複数可算名詞または不可算名詞と用いる); 《やや書》 sufficient (↔insufficient); (あり余るほどの) ample; (質・量的に) ádequate (❗量的には) good (❗a ~ で); (欠けるところのない完全に) full. ●十分な食事をとる have [eat] a *good* meal; make a *full* meal. ●今十分な食料があるWe have *enough* [*sufficient, adequate*] food now. (❗前の二つは純粋に量を問題にするが, adequate では「質的に満足のできる」の意にも解される)/(ま れ) We have food *enough* [×sufficient, ×adequate] now. (❗enough は名詞の前に置く方が普通) ▶1 か月 20 万円では家族を養うには十分でない Two hundred thousand yen a month is not *enough* [*adequate*] to support my family. (❗主語には数量を含意する語句がくる) ▶そのバスには我々全員が座れるだけの十分な座席はない The bus doesn't have *enough* [*sufficient, adequate*] seats *for* us all. (❗adequate は複数名詞とは用いない) ▶この家はあなたの家族には十分な大きさです This house is large *enough* [×*enough* large] *for* your family *to* live in (it). (❗(1) 副詞の enough は形容詞・副詞の後に置く. (2) for your family がない場合, it は通例省略される) ▶十分な時間の余裕を見て音楽会に出かけた We went to the concert in *plenty of* [*ample*] time. ▶私はできることは精一杯やっています. たとえそれが十分ではないにしても I'm doing the best I can, if that's not *good enough*.
[会話]「いかにも見てくれだけじゃないの, そのスーツ」「ぼくには十分さ(=間に合う)」"That suit is so shoddy." "It'*ll do* for me."
── **十分に** 副 sufficiently; (豊富に) amply; 〖完全に〗fully; (徹底的に) thoroughly /θˈɜːrouli/; (最大限に)《書》to the full (⇨存分). ●資金が十分に供給されている be *sufficiently* provided with funds. ●その事件を十分調査する investigate the incident *thoroughly* [《入念に》*carefully*]. ▶それに十分満足しています I'm *fully* [*completely, entirely, totally*] satisfied with it. ▶十分に報いられた I was *fully* [*amply*] rewarded. ▶駅まで3 マイルは十分ある It's *fully* [*a good, a full,*《古》*full*] three miles to the station. (❗It's three full miles .... ともいえるが, ×... a three *full miles* は不可) ▶あなたの言いたいことは十分わかっています I know well *enough* [×*know enough*] what you want to say. (❗副詞の enough は単独では用いない) ▶その展覧会は十分訪れる価値がある The show is *well* [*quite*] worth visiting. ▶彼は地図を十分に利用できなかった He couldn't make *good* use of the map.
[会話]「もう少しどう?」「もう十分いただきました」"Would you like some more?" "No, thank ╱you, I've had *enough* [*plenty*]. (❗いずれも名詞)(/《満腹です》I'*m full*, thank ╱you." (❗日本語になくても英語では通例添える方がよい)

じゅうぶん 重文 〖文法〗a compound sentence.

じゅうぶん 重文 〖「重要文化財」の略〗(⇨重要)

シューベルト 〖オーストリアの作曲家〗Schubert (Franz Peter ~).

***しゅうへん 周辺** 〖郊外〗the outskirts (❗都市から遠い周辺部), the suburbs (❗郊外の住宅地域);〖周りの〗surroundings (⇨周囲);〖近所の〗a neighborhood (⇨近所, 付近). ●パリの周辺部に on the outskirts [*in the suburbs*] of Paris. ●その湖の周辺の地域 the area *around* the lake. ●東京とその周辺に in and *around* Tokyo; in Tokyo and its *surrounding* areas.
●**周辺機器** peripheral (equipment).

しゅうほう 週報 (報告) a weekly report; (会報, 公報) a weekly bulletin; (新聞[雑誌]) a weekly (paper [magazine]).

しゅうぼう 衆望 〖人気〗popularity; (支持) popular support; (期待) popular expectation; (信頼) popular confidence [trust].

じゅうほう 重砲 a heavy gun;《集合的》heavy artillery.
●**重砲隊** the heavy artillery.

じゅうほう 銃砲 guns; (主に小さい)《やや書》fire-

じゅうぼく 従僕 a manservant; a valet.
じゅうほんぽう 自由奔放 ● 自由奔放な生活を送る lead an *independent*, *freewheeling* life; (好きなように生きる) live as one likes.
シューマイ 焼売 a shaomai /ʃáumai/; (説明的に) a small Chinese steamed dumpling filled with minced pork and vegetable mixture.
しゅうまく 終幕 〖劇などの最後の場面〗 the last scene; (最後の1幕) the final act;〖行事などの終わり〗the end (*of* an event). ● 終幕となる end; come to an end [a close].
しゅうまつ 終末 an end. ● 事件の終末 the *end* of an event [an affair]. ● 終末を迎える come to an *end*.
● 終末医療 〖医学〗 terminal care; terminal treatment.
しゅうまつ 週末 a weekend. (🛈 土曜の午後から、週休二日制では金曜の夜から日曜の晩まで) ● 週末に 《米》 [at 《英》] the *weekend*. (🛈 (1) this, that, next, last がつくときは前置詞は不要. (2)「毎週末に」の意のときは every weekend または on 《米》 [at 《英》] weekends, 《米話》 weekends) ● 週末旅行 a *weekend* trip. ● 週末亭主 a *weekend* husband. ● 週末を田舎で楽しく過ごす spend a lovely *weekend* in the country. ▶よい週末をお過ごしください Have a nice *weekend*! ▶次の週末は特別に予定はありません I have no special plan for the *weekend*.

会話「そこには長いこと滞在しておられますか」「少なくとも週末いっぱいはいます」"Will you be staying there long?" "Until *the end of the week* [Over *the weekend*] at least." (🛈 前の言い方は「日曜の朝まで」ともとれる)

シューマン 〖ドイツの作曲家〗 Schumann (Robert 〜; Clara 〜).
じゅうまん 十万 a [one] hundred thousand [×thousands]. ● 数十万人の労働者 hundreds of thousands of workers.
じゅうまん 充満 ── 充満する 動 be full (*of*); be filled 《with》. ▶煙が部屋に充満した Smoke *filled* the room./The room (was) *filled with* smoke./The room *was full of* smoke.
しゅうみつ 周密 ── 周密な 形 exhaustive; very careful and thorough. (⇨周到)
しゅうみん 就眠 ── 就眠する 動 go to bed [sleep].
● 就眠時間 one's bedtime.
:じゅうみん 住民 an inhabitant, a resident. (🛈 前の方はその地に長く住む集団に属する者. 後の方は特定の地域の居住者で、一時的居住者も含む) ● この村の住民 the *inhabitants* of this village. ● 彼は東京の住民だ He lives in Tokyo./〖書〗 He is a *resident of* [is *resident in*] Tokyo.
● 住民運動 a resident's movement. ● 草の根住民運動 a grassroots movement of local residents. ● 住民基本台帳ネットワーク Basic Residential Registers Network System. ● 住民税 a resident tax. ● 住民団体 the residents' association. ● 住民投票 a (local) referendum; the inhabitants' poll [《米》 voting]. ● 住民登録 resident registration. ● 住民票 a resident card.
しゅうめい 襲名 ● succession to the name of ....
── 襲名する 動 succeed to the name of .... (⇨継ぐ)
じゅうめん 渋面 a grimace; a frown. (⇨しかめっ面, しかめる)
じゅうもう 絨毛 〖解剖〗 a villus (複 villi).
しゅうもく 衆目 ● ...は衆目の一致するところである It is

universally acknowledged that ....
じゅうもく 十目 ● 十目の見る所 It is universally [unanimously] recognized that ....
しゅうもん 宗門 (分派) a (religious) sect; (宗派) a denomination.
じゅうもんじ 十文字 a cross. ● 十文字(の)形の cross-shaped. ● 十文字に cross-wise.
しゅうや 終夜 ● 終夜運転する run *all through the night* [*throughout the night*]. ▶その店は終夜営業している The shop is open *all night* (*long*).
しゅうやく 集約 ── 集約する 動 〖まとめる〗 gather; collect; put ... together (⇨まとめる);〖整理する〗 arrange.
● 集約農業 intensive agriculture [farming].
じゅうやく 重役 an executive (officer). (⇨役員)
● 重役会 the board of directors; the executive committee. ● 重役会議 a meeting of (the board of) directors; a board of directors' meeting. ● 重役室 a boardroom; an executive suite /swiːt/.
じゅうやく 重訳 a secondhand translation.
じゅうゆ 重油 heavy oil.
しゅうゆう 周遊 (旅行) a (circular) tour; 《英》 a round trip (🛈 《米》 では「往復旅行」の意). ● 九州周遊の旅に出かける go on a *tour of* [《英》 go on a *round trip to*] Kyushu.
● 周遊券 an excursion [a tourist] ticket; 《英》 a round-trip ticket.
***しゅうよう** 収容 名 ▶このホテルは500人の客を収容できる This hotel *has accommodations for* [*can accommodate*] 500 guests. ▶この劇場の収容人員(=座席数)はいくらですか How many *seats* does this theater have? ▶この劇場は300人収容できる This theater *has a* (*seating*) *capacity of* [*has seats for*, *seats*, *holds*, *admits*] 300 people.
── 収容する 動 ❶ 〖収容力がある〗(ホテルなどが宿泊設備を持つ) accommodate; (座席がある) seat; (余裕がある) admit (-tt-).
❷ 〖運び入れる〗 ▶彼らはけが人を病院に収容した They took [(担架などで) *carried*] the injured (people) *to* (《主に米》 the) hospital. (🛈 people のある方が口語的)
● 収容所 (捕虜などの) a concentration camp; (難民の) a réfugee cámp. ● 収容力 (ホテルなどの宿泊設備) accommodation(s) 《*for*》 (🛈 通例 《米》 では複数形で, 《英》 では単数形で); (劇場などの座席数) a seating capacity 《*of*》.
しゅうよう 収用 名 〖書〗 (an) expropriation /ekspròupriéiʃən/. ● 土地の強制収用 the compulsory land purchase. ● 土地収用法 the Land Expropriation Act.
── 収用する 動 〖書〗 expropriate. ● 農民の土地を収用する *expropriate* land *from* farmers; *expropriate* farmers *of* their land.
● 収用権 the right of expropriation; 〖法律〗 (the) right of eminent domain ▶公の目的のために個人の財産を強制的に取得する権利).
しゅうよう 修養 ● 修養を積む discipline [train] oneself (訓練); cultivate one's mind. (⇨教養)
● 修養を積んだ人 a *well-cultured* [a *well-disciplined*] person. ▶彼は修養が足りない He lacks *self-discipline* [*self-control*].
:じゅうよう 重要 名 (重要さ) importance; (意義) (やや書) significance. (⇨形 〖類語〗) ▶彼は水の重要さ [重要性] が分かっていない He doesn't know the *importance* of water [how *important* water is].
── 重要な 形 important; (やや書) significant; 《書》 crucial; essential; key; major; vital.

じゅうよう

> **使い分け** **important** 価値・効果・影響力があり重要なこと.
> **significant** 特に意義深い, または優れているなどの理由で人目を引き, 将来に影響を及ぼす可能性があること.
> **crucial** 将来や生死を決するほど重要で欠くことができないこと.
> **essential** あるものにとって根本的で欠くことができず絶対必要であること.
> **key** 他に依存されるほど重要で要となっていること.
> **major** 他と比較して重要性・重大さなどにおいてまさっていること.
> **vital** 全体が機能していく上で基本的で欠くことができないこと.

● 重要な産物 major [key, (主な) main] products.
● 重要視する regard [look upon, look on]... as *important*; think highly [much] of... (❗ much は通例否定文で用いる); have a high opinion of...; attach great *importance* to... (❗ 意味によって great の代わりに no, (too) much, some, little なども可 (⇨ 第2文例)). ▶ 読書は学生にとって重要だ Reading is *important* [*crucial*, *essential*] to [for] students. (❗ to は対象を, for は目的・利益を意識した言い方) ▶ 彼が金持ちかどうかは(私にとって)重要ではない It's not *important* [It doesn't matter] to [for] me whether [if] he is rich or not. (❗ matter は通例 it を主語にして否定文・疑問文で用いる)/(重要な問題ではない) It's not an *important* matter [《書》 It is a matter of no *importance*] (to me) whether [if] he is rich or not. ▶ 彼がそこにいることは重要だ It is *important* that he is [(should) be] there. (❗ that 節内に (should) を用いると命令的な響きを伴う. この場合, should を用いるのは《主に英》)/It is *important* for [×of] him to be there. (❗ (1) 「for＋人」は文脈によって to不定詞の意味上の主語ではなく「彼にとって」の意にもなるが, その場合「to＋人」も可. また, for [to] 句は文脈から明らかな場合省略可. (2) ×He is important to be there. は不可. また ×It is important his being there. のように動名詞を続ける構文も不可) ▶ 今日は人類の歴史上重要な日である Today is a *significant* day in the history of human beings. ▶ この計画を成功させるためにはみんなの協力がきわめて重要だ Everybody's cooperation is *vital* to [for] the success of this plan. ▶ 最も重要なのは質である Quality is what *counts* most.

■ DISCOURSE
スポーツで重要なのは勝つことだけという意見に賛成[反対]だ I am for [against] the opinion that winning is all that *matters* in sports. (❗ I am for [against]... (私は...に賛成[反対]だ)は賛成・不賛成を表すディスコースマーカー)

● 重要参考人 〖法律〗 a material witness.
● 重要書類 an important document; important papers. ● 重要人物 an important person; 《話》 a VIP (❗ a *very important person* の略).
● 重要(無形)文化財 〖集合的〗 important (intangible) cultural property [assets].

じゅうよう 重用 ― **重用する** 動 give 《him》 a responsible [a high, a leading] position [post]; appoint 《him》 to a position of trust.
じゅうよく 獣欲 animal [carnal] desires; (a) lust.
しゅうらい 襲来 〖攻撃〗 (an) attack 《on》 (⇨攻撃); (突然の) a raid 《on》; 〖侵入〗 (an) invasion.
― **襲来する** 動 (あらしなどが) hit, 《書》 visit; (敵が) attack; raid 《on》, invade. (⇨襲う)

じゅうりょう

じゅうらい 従来 副 (今まで) until [up to] now; (今までのところ) so far. (⇨仕 ❶ ⑤) ● 従来どおり as *usual*; as *before*; as *in the past*. ▶ 従来は(＝以前は)こんな犯罪は日本になかった Such a crime has never been committed *before* in Japan.
― **従来の** 形 (いつもの) usual; (伝統的な) traditional; (昔からの) old. ● 従来の物の考え方 the *traditional* [*conventional*] way of thinking.
● 従来の体育館 the *old* [(前の) *former*] gymnasium. ▶ この爆弾は従来型のものよりはるかに破壊力がある This bomb has more destructive power than any *conventional* bomb.
しゅうらく 集落 a village; (小さな) a hamlet.
しゅうらん 収攬 ● 人心を収攬する *win* the hearts of the people; *win* people's hearts.
じゅうらん 縦覧 图 (⇨閲覧) ● 名簿の縦覧を許可される be permitted to *look through* the list.
― **縦覧する** 動 look 《at》; (調べる) inspect.
しゅうり 修理 图 repair(s); 〖修理作業〗の意では通例 ～ s); fixing; (主に衣類の) mending. ▶ トラックの修理サービス truck *repair* service. ● 車を修理に出す send one's car *for repair*(s); take one's car to the garage *for repair*(s); (修理点検してもらう) have one's car *serviced*. ▶ この車は修理がきかない This car can't *be repaired*./This car is beyond *repair*.
会話 「田中ですが, 車の修理はもうできていますか」「まだです. 今修理中です」"This is Mr. Tanaka. Has my car *been repaired* yet?" "Not yet. It's *being repaired* [It's under *repair*] right now."/《人が主語》"This is Mr. Tanaka. Have you finished working on my car?" "Not yet. We're still working on it." (❗ 後の方が普通)
― **修理する** 動 repair, make* repairs 《on》; mend; fix. (❗ repair は車・機械類などの比較的複雑で熟練を要する修理. mend は小さな穴・破れなどの簡単な修理.《米》では主に布製品の修理に用いられる. fix はいずれにも用いる) ▶ パンクしたタイヤを修理する *repair* [継ぎをする *patch*] a flat tire. ● 道路を修理する *repair* [《英》*mend*] roads. ▶ この電気かみそりは修理しないといけない This electric razor needs *to be repaired* [needs *repairing*, needs some *repairs*, is in need of *repair*]. (❗ 以上の例より I have to *repair* this electric razor. の方が口語的) ▶ 私は時計を修理してもらった I *had* my watch *repaired* [*fixed*]. (❗ この場合は mended も用いられる)
● 修理工 a mechanic; a repairer. ● 修理工場 a repáir shòp; (車の) a garage.

しゅうりょう 終了 图 an end; (閉じること) a close.
― **終了する** 動 end; 〖会などが[を]〗 close; 〖仕事などが[を]〗 finish. (⇨終わる, 終える) ▶ 試合は終了しました The game *is* [×was] *over*. ▶ 本日の作業は終了しました Today's work *has finished*.
しゅうりょう 収量 (a) yield; (1年間[シーズン]の) a crop, a harvest. ▶ 当地では1エーカーあたりの米の収量はどのくらいですか What is the rice *yield* per acre here?
しゅうりょう 修了 图 completion.
― **修了する** 動 ● 全課程を修了する *finish* [*complete*] the whole course of study.
● 修了証書 a certificate 《in nursing》; a diploma 《in》.
じゅうりょう 十両 〖相撲〗 (地位) the jyuryo; (説明的に) the second highest division on the official listing of rank; (十両の力士) a jyuryo wrestler.
じゅうりょう 重量 weight. ● 重量制限を設ける set [place] a *weight* limit. ▶ 重量が10キロ不足[超過]している be *underweight* [*overweight*] by ten

じゅうりょう kilos. ● 小包の重量を計る weigh the package; take [×measure] the weight of the package. ▶この石の重量は1トン以上ある This stone weighs more than 1 ton [×is heavier than 1 ton]. 会話「積み荷の総重量はどれくらいですか」「5トンです」 "What is the total weight of the freight?" "It is 5 tons."
● 重量あげ weight lifting. (❗「重量あげをする」は lift weights, その選手は a (weight) lifter) ● 重量トン a deadweight ton.

じゅうりょう 従量 ● 従量税 specific duties.

じゅうりょく 重力 〖物理〗(地球引力) gravity; (一般の引力) gravitation. ● 重力の法則 the law of gravitation. ● 無重力 zero gravity. (⇨無重力)

じゅうりん 蹂躙 ── 蹂躙する 動 ❶ [踏みにじる] ● 先住民の権利を蹂躙する trample on the rights of the native people.
❷ [侵害する] ● 他人の権利を蹂躙する infringe upon the rights of other people.

シュール [<フランス語「シュールレアリスム」の略] 名 surrealism /səríːəlìzm/.
── シュールな 形 ● シュールな(=超現実的な)顔 a surrealistic face.

しゅうれい 秀麗 ● 秀麗な 形 graceful. ● 眉目(びもく)秀麗 (⇨眉目 [成句])

しゅうれい 秋冷 cool autumn weather. ▶秋冷の候となりました The cool autumn has just come./We are now in the cool autumn.

じゅうれつ 縦列 a column (↔row); a file (↔rank).
● 縦列で進む march by files.
● 縦列駐車 parallel parking.

しゅうれっしゃ 終列車 《catch, miss》 the last train.

しゅうれん 収斂 名 astringency; contraction; 〖数学〗convergence.
── 収斂性の 形 astringent; contracting.
── 収斂する 動 contract; 〖数学〗converge.
● 収斂剤 〖薬学〗an astringent. ● 収斂レンズ 〖光学〗a converging [a positive] lens.

しゅうれん 修練 training; practice. (⇨訓練, 練習)
● 修練を積んだ trained 《drivers》.
── 修練する 動 train; practice.

しゅうろう 就労 ── 就労する 動 (仕事を始める) start working [to work].
● 就労許可書 a work permit. ● 就労時間 wórking hòurs. ● 就労者 a worker. ● 就労日数 workdays; wórking dàys.

じゅうろうどう 重労働 hard work; (刑罰としての) hard labor.

しゅうろく 収録 名 〖録音, 録画〗recording, taping.
● ラジオ番組の収録 the recording of a radio program. ▶この64メガビットの集積回路には新聞256ページ分の活字が収録できる This 64 megabit IC chip is capable of holding 256 pages of newspaper print.
── 収録する 動 ● オペラをライブで収録する record an opera on tape [tape an opera] before a live audience. ▶この本には英文学に関する彼の講義が収録されている (記載されている) This book contains his lectures on English literature./(印刷されている) His lectures on English literature are printed in this book.

しゅうろく 集録 名 (a) compilation. ● 現代詩集録 a compilation of modern poetry.
── 集録する 動 compile.

じゅうろく 十六 sixteen. ● 16番目(の) the sixteenth. (⇨三)

じゅうろくしんほう 十六進法 〖数学〗hexadecimal (notation).

じゅうろくぶおんぷ 十六分音符 〖音楽〗《米》a sixteenth note; 《英》a semiquaver.

じゅうろくミリ 十六ミリ 〖フィルム〗16-mm [millimeter] film; 〖映画〗a 16-mm [millimeter] film [movie].

しゅうろん 修論 〖「修士論文」の略〗(⇨修士)

しゅうわい 収賄 bribery /bráibəri/, 《主に米》graft; 〖わいろを受け取ること〗acceptance of a bribe.
── 収賄する 動 accept [take] a bribe; take graft; 《話》get money under the table. ● 1,000万円収賄したため逮捕される be arrested for accepting a bribe of ten million yen.
● 収賄罪 bribery. ● 収賄事件 a bribery [a payoff, 《米》a graft] case [scandal]. (❗ case は「犯罪がらみの事件」の意) ● 収賄者 a bribetaker.

ジューンブライド 〖6月の花嫁〗a June bride. 〖参考〗June はローマ神話の Jupiter の妻で結婚の女神 Juno の月であることから、この月に結婚した花嫁は幸せになれると信じられている.

しゅえい 守衛 a guard; (学校などの)《米》a janitor, 《英》a caretaker; (特に, 門衛) a doorkeeper, a gatekeeper.

じゅえき 樹液 sap. ● 樹液を採る sap; collect sap 《of》.

じゅえきしゃ 受益者 (遺産などの受取人) 〖法律〗a bèneficiary; (利益を得る人) a person who benefits. ● 受益者負担の原則 the benefit principle that the beneficiaries share the cost.
● 受益者課税 taxation of [tax on] beneficiaries.

ジュエリー jewelry /dʒúːəlri/, jewels. ● ジュエリーをつけている wear jewelry [jewels].

しゅえん 主演 名 ▶マイケル・フォックス主演の映画 a film starring [featuring] Michael Fox.
── 主演する 動 ▶その映画は彼女が主演した She (was) starred [played the lead, played the leading role] in the movie./The movie starred [featured] her.
● 主演男優[女優] a leading actor [actress]; a leading man [woman, lady].

しゅえん 酒宴 a carousal; (飲み会) a drinking party; (饗宴(きょうえん)) a feast. ● 酒宴を開く give [throw] a carousal [a drinking party]. (❗ throw は受身不可)

しゅおん 主音 the keytone; the tonic.

しゅか 主家 one's master's [employer's] house.

しゅか 樹下 ▶樹下に under a tree. (砂 樹上)

シュガー 〖砂糖〗sugar.
● シュガーカット a low-calorie sweetener. ● シュガーポット 〖卓上砂糖入れ〗a sugar bowl. ● シュガーレス a sugarless sweetener.

しゅがい 酒害 the harmful [ill, injurious] effects of drinking.

じゅかい 樹海 a sea of trees; wide [broad, vast] expanses of woodland.

しゅかく 主格 〖文法〗the nominative [subjective] case.
● 主格補語 〖文法〗a subjective complement.

じゅがく 儒学 Confucianism; the teachings of Confucius.
● 儒学者 a Confucianist, a Confucian (scholar).

しゅかくてんとう 主客転倒 (砂本末転倒)

*しゅかん 主観 名 (主観性) subjectivity (↔objectivity).
── 主観的(な) 形 《しばしばけなして》subjective. ▶それは大変主観的な見方だ That's a very subjective point of view.

しゅかん ― 主観的に 副 subjectively. ●主観的[客観的]に物事を見る see things *subjectively* [*objectively*].

しゅかん 主幹 a chief (覆 〜s); a head; (編集の) the chief editor, the editor in chief (覆 editors 〜). (!いずれも執筆者一覧の欄では the はつけない)

しゅかん 主管 图 superintendence, supervision; (人) a superintendent, a supervisor.
― 主管する 動 supervise; have charge of ....

しゅがん(てん) 主眼(点) (主たるねらい) the chief aim; (主目的) the main purpose; (要点) the main point. ▶この事業は国際交流に主眼を置いている The *main purpose* of this program is to promote international exchange./This program *aims chiefly at* [*is intended chiefly for*] international exchange.

しゅき 手記 〖メモ〗notes; 〖体験記, 回想録〗memoirs /ménwa:rz/. ●手記する take [make] *notes* 《*of, on*》. ●手記を書く (自分の体験をもとに) draw on one's personal [first-hand] experience 《*of*》; (回想録を書く) write one's *memoirs*.

しゅき 酒気 the smell of alcohol. ●酒気を帯びている smell of alcohol; have alcohol on one's breath; be drunk.
●酒気帯び運転 《be arrested for》drunk(en) driving [〖話〗driving drunk]. ●酒気検査 a breath [a breathanalyzer] test.

しゅきゃく 主客 a drínking vèssel.

***しゅぎ** 主義 (生活・行動などの方針) a principle (!しばしば複数形で); (個人の習慣) a rule; (宗教上の) a doctrine (!政策について用いるのは《主に米》). ●保護貿易主義 protection*ism*. (!- ism は「...主義」を表す接尾辞) ●主義を守る be true [faithful] to one's *principles*; (がんとして) stick [hold fast] to one's *principles*. ●主義を捨てる abandon [desert] one's *principles*. (!abandon は「やむなく」, desert は「故意に」を含意する) ▶うそをつくことは私の主義に反する Lying is against my *principle*(s) [*rule*]./It is against my *principle*(s) [*rule*] to tell lies. ▶金を貸さないのが彼の主義だ He makes it a *rule* never to lend money./It is his *rule* [a *rule with* him] never to lend money. ▶あの学校はもうけ主義だ(=金のために経営されている) That school is run for money [profit].

しゅきゅう 守旧 conservatism. (覆 保守)
●守旧派 the conservatives, the old guard; (改革の抵抗勢力) the resistance force, the die-hard opponents to reforms. (⇨抵抗[抵抗勢力])

じゅきゅう 受給 ― 受給する 動 receive 《a pension》.
●受給者 a recipient. ●年金受給者 a *recipient* of a pension; a pensioner.

じゅきゅう 需給 supplý and demánd. (!語順は日本語と逆) ●需給のバランス supply-demand balance. ●需給ギャップ a gap between supply and demand.

しゅきょう 主教 a bishop. ●総主教 Ecumenical /èkjəménikl/ *Patriarch*. (参考) ギリシャ正教の最高位聖職者)

しゅきょう 酒興 (an) entertainment at a (drinking) party.

***しゅぎょう** 修行 (宗教的苦行) religious austerities. ●寺で修行を積む practice *religious austerities* at a temple; try to cultivate truly Buddhist conduct in a temple.

しゅぎょう 修業 图 (見習い) apprenticeship; (訓練) (a) training
― 修業(を)する 動 ●彼の下でコックの修業をする train oneself for a professional cook under him. ●花嫁修業をする *learn* social skills and the art of home-making.

じゅきょう 儒教 图 Confucianism. ― 儒教の 形 Confucian.

翻訳のこころ 例えば儒教の有名な五倫という人間の基本的関係を見ますと, 君臣, 父子, 夫婦, 兄弟, 朋友ということ (丸山真男『「である」ことと「する」こと』) Consider the renowned Confucian five ethical relationships which applies to basic human relationships; they are the relationships between lord and subject, father and son, husband and wife, older and younger brothers, and friend and friend.

***じゅぎょう** 授業 a (school) lesson; (a) class; school.

使い分け **lesson** 個人授業またはクラスの集団的授業.
class 集団的授業をさす. 《米》では lesson より普通.
ともに個々の授業を表すときは可算名詞として用いる(⇨③). また, 両語とも授業時間の意でも用いる: フランス語の授業時間中に during the French *class* [*lesson*].
school 授業が行われる場所としての学校を機能的な意味で用いた語で, 無冠詞で用いる.

① 【〜授業】 補習授業 a supplementary *lesson*. ●課外授業 an extracurricular *lesson*. ●歴史の授業 a history *lesson* [*class*]; a *lesson* [a *class*] *in* history (!特定の分野には on を用いる. of は不可 (⇨⑤)).
② 【授業〜】 ●授業内容 the contents of a *class* [*lesson*]. ●45分の授業時間 a *teaching* period [a *school hour*] of 45 minutes. (!文章でいうときは Each class lasts 45 minutes. など) ●授業開始のベル a (school) bell summoning children [students] to *class*. ▶山田先生は今授業中です Mr. Yamada is teaching (his *class*) now. (!生徒から見た場合は He is now *in* [in a history] *class*. のようにいう) ▶彼は授業中居眠りをした He dozed off *in* [*during*, ×at] *class*.
③ 【授業が[は]】 ●授業終わってから after *class* [*school*] (is over). (!後の言い方は「放課後に」の意. 特定の授業の場合は after *the* class (is over) という) ●授業が分かる can understand the contents of the *class* [*lesson*]. ▶加藤先生の授業は厳しい Mr. Kato is demanding [relentless] in *class*. ●英語の授業は1週間に何時間ありますか How many English *classes* [*lessons*] do you have a week? ▶あすは午前中授業がありません We have no *school* [*classes*, *lessons*] tomorrow morning./We have no morning *classes* [*lessons*] tomorrow. ▶3時から英語の授業がある I have an English *class* [*lesson*] at [from] 3 o'clock. ▶授業は8時半に始る *School* begins [*Classes* begin] at [×from] 8:30. ▶授業が終わると彼は家に走って帰った When *classes* were finished, he ran [raced] home. ▶2時間目の授業は何ですか What *class* [*lesson*] do you have (at the) second period? ▶その授業は進むのが早い[遅い] The *class* is fast [slow]. ▶今日の授業はこれで終わり That's all [it] for today./I think that will be all for today. (!先生の言葉で, 後の方が丁寧. ×So much for today ['s lesson']. は「もううんざりだ」の含みあるので不適当)

会話「今晩は授業は何時からだった」「7時です」 "What time is *class* tonight?" "It's at 7:00."

④【授業に】● A 先生の授業に出る attend Mr. A's *class* (⚠️堅い言い方。日常会話では go [come] to Mr. A's *class* の方が普通); take *lessons* from Mr. A.
⑤【授業を】● 英語の授業を受ける take an English *lesson* [*lessons* in English]. ●授業を(担当)する give [hold, teach] a *class*; give a *lesson*.
●授業を休む(=出席し損なう) miss a *class* [a *lesson*]. (⇨休む) ●授業をさぼる cut *school* [a *class*, a *lesson*]. (⇨サボる) ▶先生の授業を受けたいのですが I'd like to join your *class*./May I be in your *class*?
●授業参観 a (class) visitation. ●授業時数 school hours. ●授業料 school fees; (大学の) tuition (fees).

しゅぎょく 珠玉 a (beautiful) jewel [gem]; [小逸品] (やや話) a (literary) gem. ●珠玉の随筆 a *gem* of an essay.

じゅく 塾 a *juku* (school), a private-tutoring school; (補助的な) a supplementary private school (⚠️a cram school は「一時的な詰め込み」で不適)。●週に 2 回塾に通う go to a *juku* (school) twice a week.

しゅくい 祝意 (事に対して) (a) celebration; (人に対して) congratulations. ●祝意を表す offer ones *congratulations* (*on* him); congratulate (him *on* it). ●彼の成功に祝意を表して in celebration of his success.

しゅくえい 宿営 ⓒ quartering.
— 宿営する 動 quarter; (野営する) camp.
●宿営地 a billet.

しゅくえん 祝宴 ●祝宴をはる give a *feast* [a *banquet*]. (⇨宴)

しゅくえん 宿縁 fate; destiny; (仏教・ヒンズー教の) karma.

しゅくが 祝賀 — 祝賀する 動 (行動で) celebrate; (言葉で) congratulate.
●祝賀会 (have [hold]) a celebration. ●祝賀パレード a celebration parade.

しゅくがん 宿願 (書) one's long-cherished wish; (夢みてきたこと) one's dream. ●宿願を果たす realize one's *long-cherished wish*; realize [achieve] one's *dream*. ▶ピアニストになるのが私の宿願だった I have always dreamed of being a pianist. (⚠️この場合はその希望が実現したかしなかったかは不明。しかし, I have dreamed of being [wanted to be] a pianist for a long time. というと夢は実現していないことを暗示する)

じゅくぎ 熟議 ⓒ (much) deliberation; careful discussion.
— 熟議する 動 deliberate (*about, on, over*).

しゅくげん 縮減 ⓒ (a) curtailment (*of*); a cutback (*in*); reduction.
— 縮減する 動 curtail; cut back [down] (on).

じゅくご 熟語 [慣用句] an idiom (⚠️慣用語法も含み, 次の語よりも意味が広い); a set [an idiomatic] phrase; [日本語の] a set of *kanji*.

しゅくさいじつ 祝祭日 a (legal) holiday. (⇨祭日)

しゅくさつ 縮刷 — 縮刷する 動 print (a book) in (photographically) reduced size.
●縮刷版 a reduced-size edition.

しゅくじ 祝辞 [祝いの演説] a congratulatory /kɒŋɡrǽdʒələtɔːri/ address; [祝いの言葉] congratulations. ●祝辞を述べる make a *speech of congratulation* [(書) deliver a *congratulatory address*] (*at* a ceremony); offer one's *congratulations* (*to*).

じゅくし 熟柿 a ripe persimmon.
●熟柿臭い ▶彼の息は熟柿臭かった(=酒臭かった) His breath reeked of alcohol.

じゅくし 熟視 — 熟視する 動 (じっと見つめる) gaze (*at*), look intently (*at*); (驚き・好奇心などのために) stare (*at*).

しゅくじつ 祝日 a (legal) holiday; (国民の) a national [a public] holiday (⚠️public holiday は《米》では用いない;《英》a bank holiday.

関連 主な祝日

〖日本〗元日 New Year's Day (1 月 1 日)/成人の日 Coming-of-Age Day (1 月第 2 月曜日)/建国記念の日 National Foundation Day (2 月 11 日)/春分の日 Vernal Equinox Day (3 月 20 日ごろ)/昭和の日 Showa Day (4 月 29 日)/憲法記念日 Constitution Day (5 月 3 日)/みどりの日 Greenery Day (5 月 4 日)/こどもの日 Children's Day (5 月 5 日)/海の日 Marine Day (7 月第 3 月曜日)/敬老の日 Respect-for-the-Aged Day (9 月第 3 月曜日)/秋分の日 Autumnal Equinox Day (9 月 23 日ごろ)/体育の日 Health and Sports Day (10 月第 2 月曜日)/文化の日 Culture Day (11 月 3 日)/勤労感謝の日 Labor Thanksgiving Day (11 月 23 日)/天皇誕生日 The Emperor's Birthday (12 月 23 日)

〖米国〗 New Year's Day (1 月 1 日)/Martin Luther King Jr.'s Day (1 月第 3 月曜日(州により異なる))/Lincoln's Birthday (2 月 12 日(州により 2 月第 1 月曜日))/Washington's Birthday (2 月 22 日(大部分の州で 2 月第 3 月曜日。この日に Lincoln's Birthday を統合して President's Day とし 1 日にする州もある)/Memorial [Decoration] Day (5 月最後の月曜日)/Independence Day (7 月 4 日)/Labor Day (9 月第 1 月曜日)/Columbus Day (10 月第 2 月曜日。最近はこの日を祝日としない州もある)/Veterans Day (11 月 11 日)/Thanksgiving Day (11 月第 4 木曜日)/Christmas Day (12 月 25 日)

〖英国(イングランドとウェールズ)〗 New Year's Day (1 月 1 日)/Good Friday (復活祭前の金曜日)/Easter Monday (復活祭の翌日の月曜日)/May Day (5 月第 1 月曜日)/Spring Bank Holiday (5 月最後の月曜日)/Late Summer Bank Holiday (8 月最後の月曜日)/Christmas Day (12 月 25 日)/Boxing Day (12 月 26 日)

〖カナダ〗 New Year's Day (1 月 1 日)/Good Friday (復活祭前の金曜日)/Easter Monday (復活祭の翌日の月曜日)/Victoria Day (5 月 25 日の直前の月曜日)/Canada Day (7 月 1 日)/Labour Day (9 月第 1 月曜日)/Thanksgiving Day (10 月第 2 月曜日)/Remembrance Day (11 月 11 日)/Christmas Day (12 月 25 日)/Boxing Day (12 月 26 日)

〖オーストラリア〗 New Year's Day (1 月 1 日)/Australia Day (1 月 26 日)/Good Friday (復活祭前の金曜日)/Easter Monday (復活祭の翌日の月曜日)/Anzac Day (4 月 25 日)/Queen's Official Birthday (6 月第 1 月曜日)/Christmas Day (12 月 25 日)/Boxing Day (12 月 26 日)

〖ニュージーランド〗 New Year's Day (1 月 1 日)/Day after New Year's Day (1 月 2 日)/Waitangi Day (2 月 6 日)/Good Friday (復活祭前の金曜日)/Easter Monday (復活祭の翌日の月曜日)/Anzac Day (4 月 25 日)/Queen's Official Birthday (6 月第 1 月曜日)/Labour Day (10 月第 4 月曜日)/Christmas Day (12 月 25 日)/Boxing Day (12 月 26 日)

しゅくしゃ 宿舎 (宿泊所) a lodging; (ホテル・旅館) a hotel. ●公務員宿舎 *housing* for government employees. ●国民宿舎 a people's *hostel*.

しゅくしゃ 縮写 a reduction.
— **縮写する** 動 make a reduced copy 《*of*》; copy 《...》 on a smaller scale. ●75パーセントに縮写するcopy on a scale of 75 to 100.

しゅくしゃく 縮尺 a (reduced) scale. ●大[小]縮尺地図 a large-*scale* [a small-*scale*] map. ●縮尺5万分の1の地図 a map *on* [drawn to, drawn with] a *scale* of 1:50,000 (1 を *one* to fifty thousand と読む); a one-to-fifty-thousand *scale* map. ●その地図の縮尺はどのくらいですか What is the *scale* of that map?
— **縮尺する** 動 scale ... (down).

しゅくしゅ 宿主 (寄生虫などの) a host.

しゅくしゅく 粛々 ― 粛々と 副 solemnly and silently.

じゅくじゅく ●じゅくじゅくした soggy. ●雨後のじゅくじゅくした芝生を歩く walk on the *soggy* lawn.

しゅくしょ 宿所 (宿泊所) one's lodging. (⇨宿泊)

しゅくじょ 淑女 a lady.

じゅくじょ 熟女 an attractive mature woman.

***しゅくしょう 縮小** 名 (a) reduction; [削減] (a) curtailment; [書] (a) cutback. ●軍備縮小 disarmament; the *reduction* of armaments. (⇨軍備) ●特権の縮小 the curtailment [制限] of《his》privileges. ●生産の縮小 the *reduction* of [*cutbacks* in] production.
— **縮小する** 動 [大きさ・数量などを減らす] reduce; [費用などを切り詰める] cut*... down,《書》curtail; [生産・営業などを小さくする] cut ... back. ●サイズを半分に縮小する *reduce* the size to half. ●経費を20パーセント縮小する *reduce* [*cut down*《on》] expenses by 20 percent. ●国内での事業を縮小する *cut back* domestic operations. ●平時には軍備は縮小されるべきだ In time of peace, the army should *be reduced* in size.

■ DISCOURSE
実際, ここ数十年間, 国内の産業は縮小し続けている **In reality**, the domestic industry has been *shrinking* during the last few decades. (**!** *in reality* (実際は) は主張を表すディスコースマーカー)

●縮小コピー a reduced-size copy.

しゅくしょう 祝勝 ●祝勝会を催す hold a *victory celebration*; (宴会) hold [give] a *banquet in celebration of* [*to celebrate*] *a victory*

しゅくず 縮図 a reduced drawing; [小形] a miniature 《copy》. ●アメリカの縮図 America *in miniature*. ●機械の10分の1の縮図をかく *draw* a machine *to a scale of* 1:10. (⇨縮尺) ●彼の苦難の物語は現代生活の縮図(=典型)である The story of his hardships is the typical example [書] the (very) *epitome* [*ipitəmi*] of modern life.

しゅくず『縮図』 *Miniature*. (参考) 徳田秋声の小説)

***じゅくす 熟す** ripen, get* [become*] ripe. (**!** *get* の方が口語的) ●トマトは赤く熟すまで採ってはいけません Don't pick the tomatoes until they *are red and ripe*. ●反乱の機は熟している The time is *ripe* [It is *high time*] for revolt.

じゅくすい 熟睡 名 a sound [a deep, a dead] sleep.
— **熟睡する** 動 have a sound [a deep] sleep; sleep soundly [deeply]; (話) sleep like a log. ●熟睡している be fast [sound, ×very] asleep.

しゅくする 祝する celebrate. ●...を祝して in celebration [honor] of ....

しゅくせい 粛正 (腐敗・汚職などの浄化) a cleanup.
— **粛正する** 動 clean ... up.

しゅくせい 粛清 a purge.
— **粛清する** 動 (やや書) purge.

じゅくせい 熟成 aging.
— **熟成する** 動 (ワイン・ウイスキー・チーズが[を]) age; mature. ●ワインによってはほんの数か月で熟成するものもある Sóme wines *are aged* in only a few months.
— **熟成した** 形 aged; matured; (熟成の終わった) finished. ●熟成したワイン *finished* wine.

しゅくぜん 粛然 ― 粛然と 副 silently; solemnly. ●粛然と襟を正す be struck with awe.

***しゅくだい 宿題** ❶ [家庭学習] homework (**!** 数えるときは a piece [two pieces] of *homework* のようにいう); (米) an assignment. ●数学の宿題 math *homework*. ●その1節を暗記する宿題 an *assignment* of memorizing the passage. ●宿題をする do one's *homework*. ●今日の宿題はその練習問題をすることです Today's *assignment* is to do the exercise. ●今日の宿題忘れた人はいますか 手をあげて Did anyone forget the *homework* for today? Raise your hand. ●先生は夏休みの宿題をたくさん出した The teacher gave us a lot of *homework* [*assignments*] for the summer vacation. (**!** ×a lot of homeworks は不可)
❷ [懸案] a pending question. ●その問題は2年越しの宿題だ The question *has been pending* for two years. ●その問題は月曜まで宿題となった The question *is left open* till Monday.

じゅくたつ 熟達 名 (a) mastery; [技能] proficiency. (⇨熟練)
— **熟達する** 動 ●英語に熟達する get *mastery* [(a) *good command*] of English; *master* [become *proficient in*] English. ●心臓手術に熟達した外科医 a surgeon *skilled* in heart surgery.

じゅくち 熟知 ― 熟知する 動 [よく知っている] know ... very well [thoroughly]; [精通している] be familiar 《*with*》; [状況などに通じている] (やや書) be well-informed 《*about, on*》. ●彼はこの機械を熟知している He *knows* this machine *thoroughly* [*very well*]./He has a thorough [a *full*] knowledge of this machine./He *is familiar with* this machine. ●彼は国際情勢を熟知している He *is well-informed* [*knows a lot*] *about* the international situation.

しゅくちょく 宿直 night duty. (⇨夜勤)
●宿直員 a person on night duty. ●宿直室 a night duty room. ●宿直手当 a night duty allowance.

しゅくてき 宿敵 ●宿敵である be an old enemy [rival]; (対抗関係がある) there is a long-standing rivalry 《*with, between*》.

しゅくてん 祝典 a celebration; [祭り] a festival (⇨祭り); [記念祭] a jubilee (dʒúːbəliː/. ●祝典を催す hold [have] a *celebration*.

しゅくでん 祝電 (send) a telegram of congratulations, a congratulatory telegram.

じゅくどく 熟読 careful reading. ●熟読する read 《a book》carefully [through and through]; pore over 《a book》.

しゅくとして 粛として ●満場粛として声なし All are in *dead* [*absolute*] *silence*.

じゅくねん 熟年 mature age. ●熟年の紳士 a gentleman *of mature age*.

しゅくば 宿場 a stage. ●宿場町 a post town.

しゅくはい 祝杯 a toast. ●山本先生のために祝杯をあげ

しゅくはく 宿泊 图 (a) lodging, (滞在) a stay. (⇨泊まり) ── **宿泊する** 動 (⇨泊まる)
- 宿泊客 a guest [a visitor] at a hotel; a house guest. 宿泊施設 accommodation(s). (❗s をつけるのは《米》) 宿泊所 (one's) lodgings. (❗1 部屋でも複数形で用いる複数扱い) (⇨下宿) 宿泊人 a lodger; (下宿人) a boarder. 宿泊料 hotel charges [expenses]. 宿泊料を払う pay a hotel bill.

しゅくふく 祝福 图 (a) blessing.
── **祝福する** 動 〖神・聖職者が〗bless*; (幸運を祈る) wish 《him》good luck. ▶彼に神の祝福がありますように May God *bless* him. ▶彼らは新婚夫婦の前途を祝福した They *wished* the newly married couple a happy future.

しゅくべん 宿便 the retention of feces (in the intestines).

しゅくほう 祝砲 (fire) a salute /səlúːt/. ● 21 発の祝砲を放つ give a 21-gun *salute*.

しゅくぼう 宿坊 (a) lodging for pilgrims in a temple.

しゅくぼう 宿望 one's cherished hopes. (⇨宿願)

しゅくめい 宿命 (a) fate; (a) destiny. ● 運命》▶海外駐在は商社マンなら宿命のようなものだ(=不可避だ) Overseas postings *can't be avoided* if you work for a trading company. ▶戦争は人類の宿命ではない Humans are not destined [fated] to fight in war.
── **宿命的な** 形 ● 宿命的な出会い a *fateful* meeting. (❗fateful は「将来を決定する重要な」の意だが, しばしば悪い結果を暗示する fatal, ill-fated と似た意でも用いられる)
- 宿命論 fatalism. 宿命論者 a fatalist.

しゅくやく 縮約 ── **縮約する** 動 (簡約する) abridge 《a book》.
- 縮約版 an abridged edition.

しゅくりつ 縮率 a (reduced) scale. (⇨图 縮尺)

しゅくりょ 熟慮 ● 熟慮の末 after *careful consideration* [*much deliberation*]. (⇨熟考) 熟慮断行する take decisive action after (careful) deliberation.

じゅくれん 熟練 图 〖磨いた技能〗skill; 〖技能をきわめること〗mastery. ● 射撃に非常な熟練ぶりを発揮する show great *skill in* [*at*] shooting. 熟練の要る仕事 a *skilled* job; (説明的に) a job which requires a lot of *skill*.
── **熟練した** 形 〖腕の立つ〗skillful, (訓練を積んで) skilled 《*at, in, with*》; 〖専門家的な〗éxpert 《*at, in, on; at* [*in*] *doing*》; 〖経験を積んだ〗experienced 《*in*》. ● 教育に熟練している be *experienced in* teaching; be éxpert [an expert] *at* teaching (❗at の代わりに in も可. 形容詞の expert も名詞と同様, 位置強勢が普通) ▶その理容師はハサミさばきが非常に熟練していた The barber was very *skillful* [very *skilled*] *at* using scissors.
- 熟練工 a skilled worker.

しゅくん 主君 one's lord, the lord one serves.

しゅくん 殊勲 〖きわだてて尽力すること〗distinguished services. ● 最高殊勲選手 the most valuable player (略 MVP). 最高殊勲選手賞 the most valuable player award. 殊勲を立てる 〖書〗render *distinguished services*; 《やや書》distinguish oneself. 殊勲打を打つ 〖野球〗get a (game-)winning hit [a key hit].
- 殊勲賞 〖相撲〗the outstanding performance award.

じゅくんしゃ 受勲者 a recipient of a decoration [an order].

しゅけい 主計 an accountant; (軍隊の) a paymaster.
- 主計局 (財務省の) the Budget Bureau.

しゅげい 手芸 handicraft(s). (❗通例複数形で. Ⓒ「手芸品」の意にもなる)
- 手芸教室 a handicraft class. 手芸展 an exhibition of handicrafts.

じゅけい 受刑 ── **受刑する** 動 serve time 《*for* murder》; serve a sentence 《*for* fraud》.
- 受刑者 a cónvict. 〖prisoner の報道用語〗

しゅけん 主権 〖最高の権力〗sovereignty /sɑ́vrən/ power; 〖他国から独立した統治権〗sovereignty. ● 隣国の主権を侵す violate the *sovereignty* of the neighboring country. ▶主権在民 *Sovereign power* lies [rests, resides] with the people.
- 主権国家 a sovereign state. 主権者 a sovereign (ruler).

じゅけん 受験 图 ▶昨年 T 大学の受験に合格した I passed the entrance *examination for* [*of, to*] T University. (⇨入学試験) ▶彼は受験勉強をしている He is studying [準備をしている] preparing, (詰め込んでいる) cramming] for the *examination*. ▶彼は受験資格がない He is not qualified [has no qualification] to take the *examination*. ▶何人の受験生が合格しましたか How many of the *examinees* [(志願者) *applicants*] passed?
── **受験する** 動 take* [《英》sit* for] an examination 《*for, of, to*》 (❗米英とも take が普通); (出願する) apply to ... 《身分可》. ▶来年は T 大学を受験するつもりです I am going to *take the entrance examination for* [*apply* (*for admission*) *to*] T University next year.
- 受験科目 a subject for [of] an examination. 受験産業 the examination industry. 受験地獄 the 'examination hell'. (❗日本語をなぞった直訳なので通例引用符をつける) 受験番号 an examinee's (seat) number. 受験票 an applicant's identification card; (許可証) an examination admission card. 受験料 an examination fèe.

しゅげんじゃ 修験者 a mountain ascetic.

しゅげんどう 修験道 *shugendo*; a sect of Esoteric Buddhism.

しゅご 主語 〖文法〗a subject.

しゅご 守護 protection; guard. ● 神の守護 divine protection.
── **守護する** 動 protect; guard.
- 守護神 〈⇨守護神〉 a patron [a tutelary] saint. 守護天使 a guardian angel.

しゅこう 手稿 a manuscript.

しゅこう 首肯 ── **首肯する** 動 (うなずく) nod; (賛成する) agree; (同意する) consent.

しゅこう 酒肴 food and drink.
- 酒肴料 charges for food and drink.

しゅこう 趣向 〖考え〗an idea; 〖計画〗a plan. ● 新しい趣向を思いつく think of a new *idea*. ● パーティーの趣向を凝らす make *plans* for the party. ● 趣向を変えて(=気分転換に)庭で食事をしよう Let's have dinner in the garden *for a change*.

しゅごう 酒豪 a heavy [a hard] drinker.

じゅこう 受講 ── **受講する** 動 ● 西教授の講義を受講する take [《出席する》attend] Professor Nishi's *lecture* [*class*]. 英語の夏期講習を受講する take [〖参加する〗*take part in*, 《やや書》*participate in*] a summer course in English.
- 受講者 (授業・講義などの) a student attending a

しゅこうぎょう class [a lecture]; (実技・講習などの) a participant. ● 受講ার a tuition fèe; tuition.

しゅこうぎょう 手工業 〖手を使う〗(a) manual industry; 〖手先の器用を要する〗(a) handicraft (industry).
● 手工業者 a handicraftsperson; (男の) a handicraftsman.

しゅこうげい 手工芸 handicrafts; manual arts and crafts.
● 手工芸品 a handicraft. (!通例複数形で)

しゅごじん 守護神 a guardian god [deity /díːəti/]; 〖野球〗(抑えの切り札) a closer; a bullpen ace.

しゅさ 査査 (論文審査などの) a chief examiner; (調査などの) a chief investigator.

しゅざ 首座 the top; the head. (⇨首席)

しゅさい 主宰 superintendence; supervision. ▶ ...の主宰のもとに under the superintendence [supervision] of ....
── **主宰する** superintend; supervise; preside at [over] 《the meeting》.
● 主宰者 the president; the chairman.

しゅさい 主催 图 ▶その展覧会はある出版社の主催で開かれた The exhibition was held under the auspices /ˈɔːspɪsɪz/ [sponsorship] of a publishing company.
── **主催する** (組織・企画する) organize; (興行などを行う) promote; (金を出して後援する) sponsor; (主人役を務める) host. ● パーティーを主催する organize [host] a party. ● ゴルフの試合を主催する promote a golf match.
● 主催国 the host country 《for the World Cup》. ● 主催者 an organizer; a promoter; a sponsor.

しゅざい 取材 ── **取材する** 動 (記事を取る) cover; (取材訪問する) interview 《him》; (資料を集める) collect [gather] material 《for》. ● 事故を現地取材する cover an accident on the spot.
● 取材記者 a reporter.

しゅざん 珠算 (an) abacus calculation. ● 珠算をする calculate [do sums] on an abacus.

じゅさん 授産 ── **授産する** 動 give employment [work] 《to》; provide employment [work] 《for》.
● 授産施設 a vocational aid center. ● 授産所 a work center.

*__しゅし 趣旨__ 〖目的〗an aim; 〖意味〗a meaning; 〖旨〗《書》 the effect. (⇨旨(ど)) ● その計画の趣旨に反することを be against the aim of the plan. ● ...という趣旨の手紙を彼らからもらう receive a letter from him saying [《書》to the effect] that .... ▶私の話の趣旨(=言わんとすること)は分かるか《話》Do you follow my drift?

しゅし 主旨 ▶彼の講演の主旨(=要点)が分かる get the main point [《要》the gist] of his lecture.

しゅし 種子 a weed. (⇨種(衫))
● 種子植物 a seed plant

しゅじ 主事 (人) a superintendent; (地位) 《やや書》 superintendency. ● 指導主事 a teacher's consultant; a supervisor (of school education).

じゅし 樹脂 (液体) resin /rézin/; (固形状のもの) a resin. ● 合成樹脂 synthetic resin. ● 樹脂加工する plasticize.

しゅじい 主治医 (担当の) a [the] doctor in charge; (かかりつけの) a family doctor.

しゅじく 主軸 the principal axis 《※ axes》. ● チームの主軸を打つ bat cleanup in a lineup.

じゅしゃ 儒者 a Confucianist, a Confucian (scholar).

しゅしゃせんたく 取捨選択 图 choice; selection. (⇨選択)
── **取捨選択する** 動 choose; select.

しゅじゅ 種々 ── **種々の** 形 (いろいろな) various; (多くの) many. ● 種々の果物 various [many] kinds of fruit; fruit of various [many] kinds. ● 種々の理由で for various reasons.

じゅじゅ 授受 ── **授受する** 動 deliver [give] and receive.

しゅじゅう 主従 master and servant; lord and vassal. ▶彼らは主従の関係にある They are master and servant.
● 主従関係 master-and-servant relationship; the relation between master and servant.

*__しゅじゅつ 手術__ an operation; surgery (!特に外科的な手術の技術). ● 手術室 [台; 着] an óperating ròom [tàble; ùniform]. ● 外科手術 a surgical operation. ● 心臓切開手術 an open-heart operation; open-heart surgery. ● 移植手術 transplant surgery. ● 大〖難しい; 簡単な〗手術 a major [a difficult; a simple] operation. ● 緊急手術 an emergency operation. ● 鼻〖胃かいよう〗の手術を受けるhave [undergo] an operation on one's nose [for a stomach ulcer]. ▶彼の(受けた)手術はうまく行った The operation he had [×His operation] was successful./He was successfully operated on.
── **手術する** 動 operate 《on+人＋for+病名》, perform [do*, carry out] an operation. ● 彼の肺がんを手術する operate [perform an operation] on him for lung cancer. (!...on his lung for cancer. も可)

じゅじゅつ 呪術 mágic; (まじない) a spell.
● 呪術師 a magician; (シャーマン) a shaman /ʃάːmən/.

しゅしょ 朱書 ── **朱書する** 動 write in red ink.

*__しゅしょう 首相__ (日本・英国の) the Prime Minister 《略 PM》(!新聞・放送では the Premier も用いる); (フランス・イタリア・中国などの) the Premier; (ドイツ・オーストリアなどの) the Chancellor. ● 吉田首相 Prime Minister Yoshida. (! ×the Prime Minister Yoshida とはいわない. ただし「吉田元[前]首相」は the former Prime Minister Yoshida という) ● 首相官邸 the Prime Minister's official residence.
● 首相代理 an acting prime minister. ▶彼は次期首相になるだろう He will be the next prime minister.

しゅしょう 主将 a captain. ▶彼はチームの主将に任命された He was appointed captain of the team.

しゅしょう 主唱 ▶...の主唱で at the proposal [《書》instance] of ....
── **主唱する** 動 《書》advocate; take the lead 《in doing》.
● 主唱者 (考えなどの) an advocate 《of》; (事業などの) a promoter.

しゅしょう 首唱 ── **首唱する** 動 advance 《a new theory》.
● 首唱者 the first (person) to advance 《a plan》.

しゅしょう 殊勝 ── **殊勝な** 形 praiseworthy; admirable. ▶なかなか殊勝な心がけだ(=君の決意に感心している) I really admire your determination.

しゅじょう 衆生 (一切の生物) all living things [creatures]; (一切の人類) all mankind [humankind, human beings]. ● 衆生を済度する save all mankind.

じゅしょう 受章 ── **受章する** 動 be awarded with a medal.

じゅしょう 受賞 图 ▶受賞の連絡を受けたときには何のことか分からなかった When I was told I had won the

award, I did not understand what it was all about.
── **受賞する** 動 receive [be awarded, honored with] a prize. (⇨賞) ▶彼が監督賞を受賞した He is the *winner* of the best director prize./The best director *award* went to him.
● 受賞作品 a prize(-winning) [an award-winning] work. ● 受賞作家 a prize(-winning) [an award-winning] writer. ● 受賞者 a prize [an award] winner; a recipient of a prize [an award]. ● ノーベル化学賞受賞者 a Nobel (prize) *winner* in chemistry.

じゅしょう 授賞 ── **授賞する** 動 award [give] a prize.
● 授賞式 an award ceremony.

じゅじょう 樹上 ●サルは樹上で生活する Monkeys live *in trees*. (⇨ 樹下)

*しゅしょく 主食 a staple food [diet]. (⇨常食) ▶彼らの主食は米だ Their *staple* [*principal*] *food* is rice.

しゅしょく 酒色 ●酒色にふける lead a dissipated [a dissolute] life.

しゅしょく 酒食 ●酒食のもてなしをする wine and dine 《him》; entertain 《him》 with *food and drink*.

しゅしん 主神 the chief god [deity].

しゅしん 主審 the chief umpire [referee]; 【野球】 the umpire-in-chief.

*しゅじん 主人 ❶ [夫] one's husband; 【家長】 the head of the family. ▶主人は今留守です My *husband* is not at home now. (❗ 改まった言い方では Mr. 《Tanaka》. くだけた言い方では Taro のように本人の名を用いることもある) ▶ご主人はご在宅ですか (田中太郎宅で) Is Mr. Tanaka [《話》 Taro, ×your husband] at home?/Is Mr. Tanaka [《話》 Taro] in? ▶私と主人はパーティーに出席しますが、あなたとご主人はどうなさいますか My *husband* and I will go to the party, but how about you and your *husband*? (❗ 語順に注意. ×I and my husband ... とはいわない)
❷ [雇い主] an employer, 《今はまれ》 a master; [飼い主] a master. ▶犬は主人のもとへ走った The dog ran to its *master*.
❸ [店主] 《米》 a storekeeper, 《英》 a shopkeeper; (オーナー) an owner, a proprietor; [旅館・下宿などの] (男) a landlord; (女) a landlady (❗ 呼びかけも可). ▶肉屋の主人(=所有者) a méatstore òwner [経営者] mánager]. (❗ a butcher は必ずしも主人とは限らない) ▶宿屋の主人 the *landlord* [*landlady*] of an inn; 《今はまれ》 an innkeeper.
❹ [接待者] ●主人役 a host; (女) a hostess. (❗ 女性にも host を用いる傾向にある) ▶パーティーの主人役を務める act as *host(ess)* at the party; *host* a party. (⇨務める) ▶主人役の人が我々を紹介してくれた Our *host* introduced us. (❗ one's がつくことに注意)

じゅしん 受信 图 (状態) reception (↔transmission). ▶当地では受信状態が悪い *Reception* is poor here. ▶この機械は受信専用です This machine is for *receiving* only.
── **受信する** 動 ●船からの遭難信号を受信する receive an SOS (message) from the ship.
● 受信機 a receiver; a receiving set. ● 受信局 a receiving station. ● 受信人 (名あて人) an addressee. ● 受信料 a license fee.

じゅしん 受診 ── **受診する** 動 consult [see] a doctor. (⇨診察 ②)
● 受診料 a medical fee.

しゅじんこう 主人公 a hero (複 〜es) (❗ 男女いずれにも用いる); (女性の) a héroine.

しゅす 繻子 satin. ●しゅすの服を着ている wear a *satin* dress.

じゅず 数珠 a *juzu* prayer /préər/ beads (used by Buddhists); (説明的に) a rosary-like string of beads used for Buddhist prayer. ● 数珠玉カーテン a *beaded* curtain.
● 数珠つなぎ ▶ 1 キロにわたって車が数珠つなぎになっている There is a one kilometer *string of* crawling cars./The cars are crawling along *bumper to bumper* for as long as one kilometer.
● 数珠球 a bead; 【植物】Job's tears.

しゅすい 取水 图 ●ダムからの取水制限をする control *the amount of water taken* from a dam.
── **取水する** 動 take water 《from》.
● 取水口 a head gate.

じゅすい 入水 ●入水自殺をする commit suicide by throwing oneself into the water (❗ water の部分に特定の単語 Lake Biwa, the Tone (River), the sea を入れることもできる); drown /dráun/ oneself.

しゅせい 守勢 the defensive. ●守勢に回る[回っている] go [be] *on the defensive*.

しゅぜい 酒税 a liquor tax.

じゅせい 授精 图【生物】fertilization.
── **受精する** 動 be fertilized.
● 受精卵 a fertilized egg.

じゅせい 授精 人工授精 artificial insemination.
● 人工授精する inseminate 《a cow》 (artificially).

しゅせき 手跡 handwriting. (⇨㊙筆跡)

しゅせき 主席 ●国家主席 (中国の) the Chairman.

しゅせき 首席 (最上位) the top; (先頭) the head. ●クラスの首席である (at) the top [head] of the class. ▶勇介は首席で卒業した Yusuke graduated *at the top of* the school (大学を) with top *honors*].
● 首席検事 the chief public prosecutor. ● 首席判事 the chief judge.

しゅせき 酒石 tartar.
● 酒石酸 【化学】 tartaric acid.

しゅせん 主戦 ●主戦投手 【野球】 an ace (pitcher). ● 主戦論 jingoism. ● 主戦論者 a jingoist; an advocate of war.

しゅせん 酒仙 a son of Bacchus; a heavy drinker.

じゅせん 受洗 ── **受洗する** 動 be baptized [christened].

しゅせんど 守銭奴 (けちな) a miser, 《話》 a skínflint; (貪欲な) a moneygrubber.

じゅそ 呪詛 a curse. (⇨呪(ﾉﾛ)い)

しゅぞう 酒造 (醸造酒の) brewing; (蒸留酒の) distilling.
● 酒造会社 a brewing company, a brewer; a distilling company, a distiller. ● 酒造業 the brewing industry; the distilling industry. ● 酒造場 a brewery; a distillery.

じゅぞう 受像 图 (状態) reception; (映像) a picture.
── **受像する** 動 (映像を受信する) receive a picture.
● 受像機 (テレビ) a television (set).

しゅぞく 種族 [部族] a tribe (❗ 文明が遅れているという含みを持つ); [人種] a race; [動物の] a family, a species /spíːʃiːz/ (❗ 単・複同形). ● 種族保存の本能 the instinct of preservation of the *species*.

*しゅたい 主体 图 【哲学】the subject. ●主体と客体 *subject* and object. ● 主体性 (⇨主体性) ▶このグループは学生が主体です(=学生で構成されている) This group is made up mainly of [*mainly consists of*] students.
── **主体的に** 副 ●主体的に行動する act *independ-*

しゅだい 主題 a subject; a theme /θiːm/ (**!** 後の方は特に議論・文芸作品・音楽などの一貫した基本テーマのこと);〖劇・音楽などの繰り返される〗(やや書) a motif 〜s).
• 主題歌 a theme song [tune].

じゅたい 受胎 图 conception. ── 受胎する 動 〖医学・聖書〗conceive.
• 受胎告知 (聖母マリアへの) the Annunciation.
• 受胎調節 a birth control.

じゅだい 入内 the Empress(-to-be)'s official entry into the Imperial Palace.

しゅたいせい 主体性 (自主性) independence; (個性) individuality. • 主体性のある人 an *independent* person; a person of *individuality*. ▶主体性のない学問が大成するはずない (Scholary) learning without *self-direction* cannot possibly be of a great success.

じゅたく 受託 ── 受託する 動 be entrusted 《with》; take charge of ….
• 受託収賄 (公務員の) accepting a bribe in connection with one's own work. • 受託人[者] a trustee; (商品の) a consignee. • 受託販売 (a) sale on consignment.

じゅだく 受諾 图 (an) acceptance;〖承諾〗(やや書) consent.
── 受諾する 動 ▶彼の提案を受諾する give (one's) *consent* to his proposal; *accept*〖やや書〗*consent to*, (同意する) *agree to* his proposal.

しゅたる 主たる main, chief; (第1の, 最重要の) primary, principal. (⇒主(ｼｭ)な)

:**しゅだん** 手段 (一般的に) a means (֎ 〜);(方策) a measure (**!** しばしば複数形で); (段階的処置) a step; (頼るもの) a resort.
①【〜手段】 • 生計[交通, 通信]の手段 a *means* of livelihood [transportation, communication]. • 表現手段 a *means* of expression.
②【手段を】 ▶彼は入国ビザを取るのに不法な手段を使った He used illegal *means* to get an entry visa. ▶目的は手段を正当化しないが恋と戦争は手段を選ばない The end doesn't justify the *means*, but all is fair in love and war. ▶目的を果たすために彼はあらゆる手段を尽くした He tried [took] every possible *means* to achieve his purpose. ▶損失を最小限にするための有効な手段を取らなないといけない We must take effective *measures* [*steps*] to minimize the losses.
③【手段で[だ]】 ▶彼女は不正な手段で欲しいものを手に入れた She got what she wanted by unfair [foul] *means*. ▶教育は目的を達成するための単なる手段だ Education is only a *means to an end*. (**!** 慣用的な表現)
④【手段として】 • …のための手段として as a means of 《doing》. ▶彼は最後の手段として車を売った He sold the car as a [in the] *last resort*.

しゅちしゅぎ 主知主義〖哲学〗intellectualism.
• 主知主義者 an intellectualist.

しゅちにくりん 酒池肉林 a sumptuous feast [banquet].

しゅちゅう 手中 ▶彼の手中にある(所有[支配]されている) be in his hands; (所有されている) be in his possession; (意のままになっている) be at his mercy.
• 手中に収める ▶彼はばく大な富を手中に収めた He *came into* (*possession of*) a large fortune./He *got* (*possession of*) a large fortune./A large fortune *came* [*fell*] *into* his *possession*.

しゅちゅう 主柱 a principal pillar; (中心となる人[もの]) the mainstay 《of》.

じゅちゅう 受注 图 orders received. • 国内の[海外からの]受注 domestic [overseas] *orders*. ▶新規の受注は著しく減っている New *orders* are falling off sharply.
── 受注する 動 receive [get] an order 《from》.
• 受注残高 a back order; a backlog. • 受注生産 production-to-order.

しゅちょ 主著 one's chief [major] book [work].

:**しゅちょう** 主張〖言い張ること〗(an) insistence;〖権利などの主張〗(a) claim;〖自説・要求などの主張〗(an) assertion;〖意見〗one's opinion;〖論点〗one's argument, one's point;〖唱道〗advocacy.
• 最後まで主張を曲げない stick to one's *opinion* to the last. ▶彼の無罪の主張は却下された His *claim* of (×to) innocence [to be innocent] was rejected.
── 主張する 動〖強く言い張る〗insist 《on》;〖事実であると〗claim;〖断言する〗assert;〖自己の立場を守ろうと〗maintain;〖強く力説する〗urge;〖理論的に〗argue;〖唱道する〗advocate;〖強調する〗emphasize. • 自己の権利を主張する assert [claim, insist on] one's rights. • その土地の所有権を主張する *claim* ownership of the land; lay claim to the land. • 改革を主張する *advocate* reform. ▶彼は無実を主張した He *insisted* on [*asserted*, *maintained*] his innocence./He *insisted* [*asserted*, *maintained*] that he was innocent. (**!** (1) 節内は直説法過去で, 事実の主張を表す. (2) He *insisted that* he (*should*) be innocent. では「無実であるべきだ」と要求・願望を述べている)/(被告人が法廷で) He *pleaded* not guilty. ▶彼はその仕事をすべて1人でやったと主張した He *claimed* to have [*that* he had] done all the work by himself. ▶コロンブスは西へ行けばインドに着くと主張した Columbus *argued that* he could reach India by going west.

しゅちょう 主潮 the main current 《of Japanese literature》.

しゅちょう 主調〖音楽〗the keytone; the tonic.
• 主調音 the tonic.

しゅちょう 首長 the head (of a local government); (イスラム教国で) an emir /əmíər/. • アラブ首長国連邦 the United Arab *Emirates* /émərəts/ (略 UAE).

しゅつ 術 (技術) the art 《of》; (秘訣(ﾋｹﾂ)) the secret 《of》. • 出世術 the *art of* getting on in the world.

* **しゅつえん** 出演 图 • リズ・テーラー出演の映画 a movie with Liz Taylor; a Liz Taylor movie. ▶その芝居の出演者はおよそ20人です The *cast* of the play includes about 20 characters.
── 出演する 動 (テレビ・舞台などに) appear, make* one's appearance; (役を演じる) perform, play, present. (⇒演じる). • テレビ[舞台; 劇; コンサートホール]に出演する *appear* on television [on the stage; in the play; in the concert hall]. • ロメオ役で出演する *perform* in the role of Romeo; *play* [*perform*, *present*] Romeo. ▶劇団は彼を犯人役で出演させた The theater company *presented* him as a criminal. ▶彼が出演していたころはそのテレビ番組が大好きだった I really liked the TV show when he *was on* (it) [*was appearing* in it].

しゅっか 出火 图 an outbreak of fire; (火事) a fire.
• 出火の原因 the cause of the *fire*.
── 出火する 動 ▶奇妙なことに空き家から出火した Strange to say, the *fire started* [*broke out*] in an unoccupied house.

しゅっか 出荷 (出荷した荷物) a shipment; (発送) shipping. • 国内[海外への]出荷 a domestic [an overseas] *shipment*.

じゅっかい 十戒 (⇨十戒)

じゅっかい 述懐 图 (回想) rèminíscence; (思い出) recollections.
— **述懐する** 動 ●過去の思い出を述懐する《書》relate one's past *recollections*. ●幼い頃を述懐する(=思い出話をする)《書》*reminisce about* one's childhood.

しゅっかん 出棺 ●出棺は(=霊柩車が出るのは)午後3時の予定です The hearse is to leave the house at three in the afternoon. (**!**be+to 不定詞は予定を表す堅い表現)

しゅつがん 出願 图 (an) application. (⇨申し込み)
— **出願する** 動 ●大学に出願する apply [make an application] (for admission) to a college. ●**出願期限** the deadline for application. ●**出願者** an applicant (for). ●**出願手続き** application procedure.

しゅっきん 出金 图 (支払い) payment; (投資) an investment; (寄付) a contribution; (経費) expenses. ●**入金**
— **出金する** 動 pay; invest money (in); contribute money (to); (投資する) sink money (into, to).

しゅっきん 出勤 ●時差出勤 staggered working hours.
— **出勤する** 動 (職場へ向かう) go to work [the office]; (職場に着く) get to the office; (職場に出る) report for work [duty]. ●出勤している be *at the office*. ●バスで出勤する go to work by bus; take the bus to work. (**!**work はとも に名詞) ▶彼は午前9時に出勤する(=職場に着く) He *gets to the office* at 9:00 a.m.
●**出勤時間** (家を出る時間) the time to go to the office; the office-going hour; (始業時間) the time for reporting; the start of office hours. ●**出勤日数** the number of days attended. ●**出勤日** a workday; a working day. ●**出勤簿** an attendance book.

しゅっけ 出家 图 (仏教の僧) a bonze (⇨坊主); a (Buddhist) priest [monk].
— **出家する** 動 leave (one's) home to become a priest.

しゅつげき 出撃 《書》a sally; 《書》a sortie. (**!**両方とも自陣地に戻ることを前提としている)
— **出撃する** 動 sally; make a sally [a sortie] (into an enemy camp).

しゅっけつ 出欠 attendance. (⇨出席) ●出欠の記録 one's *attendance* record.

しゅっけつ 出血 bleeding, loss of blood; [内部の] hemorrhage /hémərɪdʒ/. ●内出血 internal *bleeding*; [医学] internal hemorrhage /héməridʒ/. ●脳出血 cerebral *hemorrhage*. ●傷口の出血 the *loss of blood* from a wound. ●**出血サービスをする**(=大割引で売る) sell goods at great bargains. ●傷口を包帯でしばって出血を止めた I bandaged the cut to stop the *bleeding*. ▶彼は出血がひどい He's *losing a lot of blood* [*losing blood fast*]. ▶その患者は出血多量で死んだ The patient died from *loss of blood*./The patient bled to death [×to die].
— **出血する** 動 bleed*, lose* blood; have* a hemorrhage. ▶傷口からひどく出血している He *is bleeding* badly [a lot] *from the cut*./His cut *is bleeding* badly. ●**出血性貧血** [医学] hemorrhagic anemia.

しゅっけとそのでし 出家とその弟子 *The Priest and his Disciples*. (参考) 倉田百三の戯曲

***しゅつげん** 出現 an appearance,《やや書》emergence;(重要な事物・人の)《やや書》the ádvent. ●新興国の出現 the *appearance* of new nations. ▶通信衛星の出現でテレビ放送は地球上のどこででも生中継が可能になった With the *advent* of communications satellites, TV broadcasts could be transmitted live to any point on the globe.
— **出現する** 動 appear; emerge (from). (⇨現れる)

しゅっこ 出庫 — **出庫する** 動 (蔵出しする) take goods out of a warehouse; (車などを車庫から出す) get a car out of a garage. ▶始発のバスは5時に出庫する The first bus *leaves* the carbarn at 5 a.m.

じゅっご 述語 [文法] a predicate /prédɪkət/.

じゅつご 術語 a technical term,《書》(a) tèrminólogy. ●法律上の術語 a legal *term*; (集合的) legal terminology [terms].

しゅっこう 出向 — **出向する** 動 ▶彼は関連会社に出向している(=転出させられている) He *is lent out* [*is on loan*] *to* a related company.
●**出向社員** a loaned worker.

しゅっこう 出校 — **出校する** 動 attend [go to] school.

しゅっこう 出航 — **出航する** 動 sail, set sail (from). ▶その船は神戸から横浜に向けて出航した The ship *sailed from* [(出発した) *left*] Kobe *for* Yokohama.
●**出航時間** sailing time.

しゅっこう 出港 图 departure (from (a) port). ●出港を延期する put off [postpone] one's *departure from* (a) port; put off [postpone] *leaving port*.
— **出港する** 動 [出発する]] leave* (↔enter) (port),《書》depart (from (a) port); [出航する] sail, set* sail. ▶あらしのため船は出港できなかった The storm prevented our ship from *leaving* [*sailing*]./(港にとどまった) The storm kept our ship in port.

しゅっこう 出稿 ●広告出稿 an advertisement placement.

しゅっこう 出講 — **出講する** 動 give [deliver] a lecture (at); teach (at).

じゅっこう 熟考 图 [熟慮] (careful) consideration; [慎重な考慮] deliberation. ●熟考の上 after *careful* [*due*] *consideration* (**!**due は「十分な」の意); after (long) *deliberation*; after *thinking* (it) *over*. ▶その提案はなお熟考中だ The proposals *are still under* (*careful*) *consideration*./We *are still considering* the proposals carefully.
— **熟考する** 動 consider... (carefully), think*... over (**!**後の方が口語的); (あれこれ考える) ponder (on, over...); 《書》 deliberate (on, over...).

しゅっこく 出国 图 departure from a country. (⇔入国) ●不法出国 illegal *departure*.
— **出国する** 動 leave [《書》depart from] a country.
●**出国手続き** departure formalities. ●**出国ビザ** (obtain) an exit visa.

しゅつごく 出獄 — **出獄する** 動 (出所する) be released from prison; get out of prison.

しゅっこんそう 宿根草 [植物] a perennial (plant).

じゅっさく 術策 (策略) a trick; (わな) a trap; (陰謀) (an) intrigue /ɪntríːɡ, íntriːɡ/; (巧妙な手段)《書》(an) ártifice; (計略, 作戦)《書》a strátagem. ●術策をろうして by a *trick*. ●術策をろうする try a *trick* [a *stratagem*] (on him). ●敵の術策にはまる fall

しゅっさつ 出札 (切符を売ること) the sale of tickets.
- 出札係 《米》a ticket agent; 《英》a booking clerk. ・出札口 a ticket [《英》a booking] window; a wicket.

しゅっさん 出産 图 (a) birth, childbirth; (過程) a delivery. ・出産に立ち合う be present at the *delivery*. ・出産のとき死ぬ die *in childbirth*.
会話「いつご出産の予定ですか」「6月です」"When is your baby due?/When are you going to [×will you] *have a baby*?" (! 確定的な予測では will は用いない)/When *are* you *expecting* (a *baby*)?" "In June."
── 出産する 動 ▶ 彼女は女の双子を出産した She *gave birth to* [《書》*was delivered of*, ×bore] twin girls. (! *female twin* とはあまりいわない)/She *had* two baby girls at one *birth*. (! ×two girl babies は通例いわない)
・出産休暇 a maternity leave. ・出産予定日 one's [the] due date (of one's baby).

しゅっし 出資 (投資 (an) investment; (寄付金) a contribution. ・共同出資 a pool; (a) joint *investment*. ・弟の会社に多額の出資をする *invest* a large sum of money *in* one's brother's company; *make* a heavy *investment in* one's brother's company. ▶ 彼らは共同出資をして新しいプロジェクトに着手した They *pooled* resources and entered on a new project.
── 出資する 動 invest; contribute. ▶ 合弁事業に出資する *invest* [*make an investment*] *in* a joint venture.
・出資金 an investment. ・出資者 an investor; (資金調達者) a financier.

しゅつじ 出自 the source; the origin.

しゅっしゃ 出社 ── 出社する 動 go [come] to the office. (! go と come の使い分けは (⇨行(い)く❶))
▶ 9時までに出社したことはないんですよ。9時 30分 (の約束)ではどうでしょうよ I never *get in* before 9:00. Could we say 9:30? ▶ 申し訳ございませんが寺田は休暇をいただいております。来週の月曜には出社いたします I'm sorry, but Mr. Terada is on vacation. He will be back next Monday.

しゅっしゃ 出車 driving out of a parking lot [garage].

じゅっしゅきょうぎ 十種競技 (⇨十種(じっ)競技)

しゅっしゅっ ▶ しゅっしゅっと音を立てる hiss; make a hiss. ▶ (蒸気機関車が)しゅっしゅっぽっぽと走る chug along. (! その音は choo-choo /tʃúːtʃúː/, púff-púff で幼児語の「汽車ぽっぽ」の意でも用いる) ▶ 蒸気が破れたパイプからしゅっしゅっと出ていた Steam *was hissing* through the leaks in the pipe. ▶ 彼女は部屋のにおいを消すために香水をしゅっしゅっとまいた She *sprayed* perfume *lightly* in order to get rid of the unpleasant smell in the room.

しゅっしょ 出処 ・出処進退 whether to stay in a position or not.

しゅっしょ 出所 ❶ [出所] (情報などの) a source. ▶ そのうわさの出所を突き止める trace the *source* of the rumor. ▶ そのニュースの出所は信頼できる The news comes from a reliable *source*.
❷ [刑務所から出ること] ・出所する be released from prison; get out of prison.

しゅっしょう 出生 (⇨しゅっせい)

しゅっしょう 出場 图 [参加] participation 《in》; [加入] (an) entry. ・選手を3日間出場停止処分にする suspend a player for three days; *give a three-day suspension to* a player. ▶ ベラミーは以後2試合出場停止処分になる見込みだ Bellamy will be suspended for the next two games. ▶ 彼はそのコンテストへの出場を取り消した He canceled his *participation in* [withdrew from] the contest.
▶ 彼女はそのレースの出場資格を失った She was disqualified from (*taking part in*) the race.
── 出場する 動 [参加する] take* part 《in》, participate 《in》 (やや堅い語); [競う] compete 《in》; [参加を申し込む] enter 《for》. ・初出場する make one's first *appearance*. ・100試合以上に出場する play over 100 games. ・ピンチランナーとして出場する be inserted in a game as a pinch runner. ・チームの全試合に先発出場する start every one of one's team's games. ・代打出場でホームランを打つ hit a home run in one's pinch-hit appearance. ▶ 彼は円盤投げに出場して優勝した He *entered* [*competed in*] the discus throw and won.
・出場者 a participant 《in》; (競技などの) an entry 《for》; (コンテストの) a contestant; (クイズ・番組などの) a panelist. ▶ レースの出場者は何人もいなかった There were only few *entries* in the race.

しゅっしょく 出色 ── 出色の 形 (目立ってすぐれている) outstanding; excellent; exceptionally good.

***しゅっしん** 出身 ❶ [出身地] one's hometown (! 子供時代を過ごした所やずっと住んでいる所をさすこともある); (通例有名人の) one's birthplace. ▶ 彼はベルギー人のブリュッセルの出身です He is (a) Belgian, *from* Brussels. (! 国籍を強調するときは冠詞をつける)
会話「あなたの出身(地)はどちらですか」「神戸です」"Where *are* you *from*?" "(I'm from) Kobe. *From* Kobe."/"Where do you *come from*?" "(I *come from*) Kobe." "Where *did* [*have*] you *come from*? は出身地に関係なく「どこから来たのか」の意)/"What is your *hometown*?" "(It's) Kobe./Kobe is." "*Where* is your *hometown*? に対する答えは It's in Hyogo Prefecture. など)

❷ [卒業した学校] (母校) 《書》one's alma mater /ǽlmə mάːtər/. (! 通例単数形で)
会話「出身大学はどちらですか」「M大学です」"What college *did* you *graduate from*?" "(I *graduated from*) M University."/"I'm a graduate *of* M University./M University is my *alma mater*. などの及び方)

❸ [以前の職業] ▶ 作家出身の政治家 a writer-*turned*-politician. (! *turned* は「変更した」の意)
▶ 彼は官僚出身の (= 元官僚だ) He was *originally* a government official [《軽蔑的》a bureaucrat /bjúərəkræt/].

しゅつじん 出陣 ── 出陣する 動 go to war; go to the front.

じゅっしんほう 十進法 (⇨十進(じっ)法)

しゅっすい 出水 a flood. (⇨洪水)
── 出水する 動 flood. ▶ 川が氾濫して町全体に出水した The whole town *flooded* when the river burst its banks.

しゅっせ 出世 图 (人生における成功) success in life; (会社などの昇進) promotion. ▶ 彼は出世コースに乗っている He *is on* his *way to the top*./He *is running up* [*climbing*] *the ladder of success*.
▶ 彼はいちばん下積みから出発して出世街道を登りつめた He started at the bottom and *has worked* his *way up to the top*. ▶ 彼は同級生の出世頭だ He is *the most successful* man of our classmates.
▶ これは彼の出世作だ This work established him as a writer.
── 出世する 動 succeed [win 《great》 success] in life; rise [get ahead] in the world; (昇進する)

しゅっせい 出生 (a) birth. ●出生率の増加[低下] a rise [a fall] in a birthrate.
●**出生地** the place of one's birth. (!the place where one was born の方が口語的に); (特に有名人の) one's birthplace. ●**出生届** the registration of one's birth.

しゅっせい 出征 图 ●出征中 in the field; 《soldiers》 at the front.
── **出征する** 動 go to war; go to the front.

‡**しゅっせき** 出席 图 presence 《at》; (an) attendance 《at》 (! 出席回数のときⒸ). (参考) 出欠の返信用葉書の書き方の1例: 御出席 *WILL ATTEND* 御欠席 *WILL NOT ATTEND* ●出席調べ a roll call.
●出席をとる (名前を呼んで) call the roll; take [do] the roll call; check *attendance*. (《英》では call [mark] the register が普通) ●出席不良であの先生に落とされるかもしれないと心配だ I'm worried that the professor may fail me for poor [不十分な] *insufficient*] *attendance*. ▶万障お繰り合わせの上ご出席ください Your *attendance* is requested.
〖会話〗「出席をとります. 阿部君」「はい」 "Let me call the roll. Abe." "Here!"
── **出席する** 動 《やや書》 attend (! 日常会話ではgo*, come* で表すことが多い); (会合などに顔を出す) turn out 《for》; (出席している) 《やや書》 be present 《at》 (! 日常会話では be here [there, at ...] で表すことが多い). ●彼女の送別会に出席する go [come] to her farewell party; *attend* [《まれ》*attend at, ×attend to*] her farewell party. ▶会合には70人出席していた There were 70 people *present* at the meeting. ▶披露宴に出席できるかどうかお知らせください Please let me know if you can *attend* the wedding reception or not.
〖会話〗「昨夜会合があったんだよ」「ぼくは出席すべきだったの?」 "We had a meeting last night." "Should I *have been* there?"
●**出席者** (⇨出席者) ●**出席簿** a roll (book); 《英》 a register.

しゅっせきしゃ 出席者 (全体) those (who are) present; (出席者数) an attendance 《of 100》 (!単数扱い). ●講演には多数の出席者があった A lot of people *came to* (hear) the lecture. ●最も口語的(⇨出席する))/The lecture *was* well (↔poorly) *attended*./There were a large (↔a small) number of people *present* at the lecture. (!There was a large *attendance* at the lecture. より普通) ●私が部屋に入ったとき会議の出席者の半分が起立した Half *the meeting* stood up when I went in. (!the meeting は集合的に「参加者一同」の意)

しゅつだい 出題 ── **出題する** 動 (作る) make an examination [a test] question; make [draw] up an examination; (出す) set a question [a problem]. ▶今度の試験は教科書からは出題しません In the next exam I'm not going to *make questions* from your textbooks.
●**出題傾向** the tendency of examination questions. ●**出題者** a person who makes (examination) questions. ●**出題範囲** the range of examination questions.

しゅったん 出炭 ── **出炭する** 動 produce [mine] coal. ●**出炭量** coal output.

じゅっちゅう 術中 ●敵の術中に陥る play into the enemy's hands; fall into the enemy's trap; be entrapped.

じゅっちゅうはっく 十中八九 (⇨十中(じっちゅう)八九)

しゅっちょう 出張 图 (会社員の) a business trip; (公務員の) an official trip; [修理のためなどの] a service call. ●短期[長期]出張 a brief [an extended] (business) trip. ●日帰り出張 a day's [one day] (business) trip. ●海外出張 an overseas (business) trip. ●仙台に出張を命じられる be sent to Sendai *on business*; be ordered to go to Sendai *on business*. ▶申し訳ございませんが, 寺田は出張中でございます I'm sorry, but Mr. Terada is now out of town [*on a business trip*, *away from the office*, *away on business*] now.
── **出張する** 動 make* [go* on] a business [an official] trip 《to Osaka》; go 《to Osaka》 on business; travel on business 《to Osaka》.
●**出張所** a branch office. ●**出張手当** a travel(ing) allowance. ●**出張費** travel(ing) expenses.

しゅってい 出廷 ── **出廷する** 動 appear in court.

しゅってん 出典 the source; 〖信頼するに足る典拠〗 an authority. ●この引用文の出典を調べる[明らかにする] check [name] the *source* of this quotation. ▶この1節の出典は聖書です(=引用されている) This passage *is quoted* from the Bible. ▶典拠を示すべきだ You should quote your *authorities*. (!説・事実・数字などについての出典を求める言い方)

しゅってん 出店 图 the opening of a new store.
── **出店する** 動 open [build] a new store; (出店などを) set up a booth. ●同社はついにニューヨークに出店した At last the company *opened* their *new store* in New York.

しゅってん 出展 ── **出展する** 動 ●絵画展に絵を出展 (=出品)する *exhibit* one's painting at the picture show. (⇨出品)

しゅつど 出土 ── **出土する** 動 be dug up, 《やや書》 be unearthed. ▶このつぼはその丘から出土した This vase *was dug up* [*was unearthed*, *was excavated*] on that hill.
●**出土品** an unearthed article [(原始的な工芸品)] artifact.

しゅっとう 出頭 图 (出廷) 〖法律〗 an appearance. ●出頭命令を受ける 〖法律〗 receive a summons; 〖書〗 be summoned.
── **出頭する** 動 report 《to the police》; 〖法律〗 appear 《in court》 present oneself] 《in court》.

しゅつどう 出動 ── **出動する** 動 〖派遣される〗 be dispatched; 〖動員される〗 be mobilized. ▶反乱を鎮圧するために機動隊が出動した Mobile units *were dispatched* to suppress the revolt.

しゅつにゅうこく 出入国 ●**出入国管理** immigration control. ●**出入国管理官** an immigration officer. ●**出入国管理法** Immigration Control Law. ●**出入国記録カード** an embarkation and disembarkation card; an E/D card).

しゅつば 出馬 ── **出馬する** 動 〖立候補する〗 run (主に米) [stand (主に英)] 《for+職》; [自ら赴く] (行く) go [(来る) come] in person (⇨行(い)く). ●市長選には5人の候補者が出馬した[している] Five candidates *have run* [*are running*] *for* mayor [in the mayoral election].

‡**しゅっぱつ** 出発 图 a start; 〖交通機関などの〗 (a) departure. ▶出発地点に引き返そう Let's turn back to *where we started*. ▶私は出発を2時間延ばした I

put off [postponed] my *departure* for two hours.
— 出発する 動 (場所を離れる) leave* 《*for*》,《書》depart 《*for, from*》; (動き出す) start 《*from, for*》; (旅などに出る) start [set] out [off]; (飛行機が離陸する) take* off; (船が出航する) sail, set sail.

> 使い分け　leave ある場所を離れることに重点がある。start 移動を開始することに重点がある。

●旅行に出発する start (out [off]) on a [one's] trip; set out [off] on a journey. (⇨旅行) ▶私たちはあす朝早く出発しなければならない We must *start* [*leave*] early tomorrow morning./We must make an early *start* tomorrow morning. ▶一行はパリに向けて出発した The party *left* [*started*, 《書》 *departed*] for Paris. ▶私たちは東京からハワイへ向かって出発した We *left* [xleft from] Tokyo *for* [xto] Hawaii. (❗The train *left from* Tokyo Station (Track 5). のように乗り物が「駅」や「(駅の何)番線」などから出発するというときは from は可)/We *started* (飛行機で) *took off*, (船で) *sailed*] *from* Tokyo *for* [xto] Hawaii. ▶あなたの乗る飛行機は何時に出発しますか When [What time] does your plane *take off* [*leave*]?/What is the *departure* time of your flight? ▶その船は1時間したら出発します The ship *sails* [*leaves*] in an hour. (❗start を示す sail, leave, start などの動詞は、現在時制で確実な未来の出来事を表す) ▶ようやく私たちの乗ったバスは出発した(=動き出した) At last our bus *started*. ▶この文脈では left を使うと不自然になる) ▶さあ出発しよう Come on. Let's *be off* [*get going*]. ▶彼は弁護士として出発したが後に政界入りした He *started out* as a lawyer, but he got into politics later.
●出発時刻 the time of departure; the departure [starting] time. ●出発点 (⇨出発点)

しゅっぱつてん 出発点 (旅行・議論などの) the starting point; (競技などの) the starting mark [line]; (飛躍・発展などの) the takeoff 《*for*》. ▶ガイドつきの町めぐりの出発点はマーケット広場です The *starting* point for the guided tour of the town is in the market square. ▶このことが実質的な交渉の出発点となった This became the *takeoff for* substantive negotiations.

じゅっぱひとからげ 十把一絡げ (⇨十把(ジャ)一絡げ)

* **しゅっぱん 出版** 名 publication. ●限定出版 limited *publication*. ●出版društvoの仕事をする have a job in *publishing*. ●その小説の出版を禁止[停止]する suppress [suspend] the *publication* of the novel.
— 出版する 動 [本・定期刊行物を] publish (❗売ることに重点がある); 〖新聞・雑誌・公的文書を〗 issue, put*... out (〖発行することに重点がある〗) (⇨発行); 〖出版物を出す〗 bring*... out (くだけた言い方); 〖活字にして出す〗 print. ▶新しい本を出版する *publish* [*bring out, print*] a new book. ●小説を自費(限定)出版する *publish* a novel at one's own expense [in a limited edition]. ●来月出版される予定の新刊書 new books which *are coming out* [*are to appear*, *are scheduled for publication*] next month. (❗書物や論文などで「5月出版予定」というとき、題目の後に 'To appear in May.' と書く) ▶この辞書は三省堂から出版された This dictionary *has been published* [*issued*] *by* [xfrom] Sanseido. ▶その本はまだ出版されていない The book *is not in print* [*has not been published*, *has not come out*, *has not appeared (in print)*] yet.
●出版業 (engage in) publishing business. ●出版業界 the publishing world; publishing circles; 《集合的》 the press. ●出版権 a publishing right. ●出版社 a publishing company [house] (❗後の方は小規模な); a publisher (❗しばしば複数形で). ●出版物 a 《monthly》 publication ●コンピュータに関する出版物 a publication about computers. ●出版部数 the number of copies published.

しゅっぱん 出帆 — 出帆する 動 sail, set sail. (⇨出航)

しゅっぴ 出費 (種々の支払い) expenses. ●出費を切り詰める[抑える] cut down (on) [reduce] *expenses*. ▶その指輪は彼女には大変な出費だった The ring *cost* her a lot of money./(人が主語) She bought the ring at a vast *expense*. ▶今月は出費が多かった I've had a lot of *expenses* this month./(多くの金を遣った) I *'ve spent* a lot of *money* this month.

しゅっぴん 出品 — 出品する 動 (展覧会などに展示する) exhibit /ɪɡzíbɪt/; (品物を陳列する) display. (⇨展示) ●絵画展に絵を出品する *exhibit* one's painting at the picture show. ●品評会には新製品が出品されている New products *are displayed* [*on display*] at the fair.

しゅっぺい 出兵 — 出兵する 動 send 《書》dispatch] troops 《*to*》.

しゅつぼつ 出没 — 出没する 動 (よく現れる) appear (frequently). ▶かつてこの海域には海賊がよく出没していた Pirates once *appeared frequently* in this area of the sea.

しゅっぽん 出奔 — 出奔する 動 (逃げる) run away [off]; (行方をくらます) abscond 《*from*》; (駆け落ちする) elope 《*with*》.

しゅつもん 出問 — 出問する 動 set a question.

しゅつらん 出藍 ●出藍のほまれ *be superior to* [(やや書) *excel*, 《書》*surpass*] one's teacher (*in* achievement).

しゅつりょう 出漁 ▶貧しい漁師はしけの日も出漁しなくてはならなかった The poor fisher [fisherman] had to *go fishing* on a stormy day.
●出漁区域 a fishing area.

しゅつりょく 出力 〖電気装置・コンピュータの〗 output; 〖発電力〗 generating power. ▶この発電所は出力100万キロワットです The *output* of this power plant is one million kilowatts./This power plant *generates* one million kilowatts.
●出力装置 an output device [unit].

しゅつるい 出塁 — 出塁する 動 〖野球〗 get to [(して いる) be on] first base. ●エラーで出塁する get on board on an error.
●出塁率 on-base average [percentage].

じゅでん 受電 — 受電する 動 receive a telegram [wire, (海外電報) a cable].

* **しゅと 首都** the capital (city),《書》the metrópolis (❗a metropolis は 「主要都市」の意). ●日本の首都 the *capital* of Japan; Japan's *capital* (city).
会話 「日本の首都はどこですか」「東京です」 "What [xWhere] *is the capital of* Japan?" "Tokyo (is)./〈古〉It's Tokyo." (❗今日では the capital ではなく what が主語ととらえられる)
●首都圏 the Metropolitan area. ●首都高速道路 the Metropólitan Expressway.

しゅとう 種痘 〖医学〗 (a) vaccination (against [for] smallpox. ●赤ん坊に種痘をする *vaccinate* a baby *against* [*for*] smallpox.

しゅどう 手動 — 手動の 形 manual; (手で操作する) hand-operated, operated [worked] manually [by hand].
●手動制御装置 a manual control (↔an automatic control. ●手動ブレーキ a hand brake.

しゅどう 主導 图 ●政治主導の politically oriented 《projects》; 《projects》 under the political leadership.
── **主導する** 動 take the lead.
● **主導権**〔⇨主導権〕● **主導者** a prime mover; a leader.

じゅどう 受動 ── **受動的な** 形 passive (↔active).
● 受動的な態度をとる take a *passive* attitude 《toward》.
● 受動喫煙 passive [secondhand] smoking.
● 受動態〔文法〕(the) passive voice.

しゅどうけん 主導権 ● 主導権争い the struggle for *the leadership*. ● 主導権を握る[失う] take [lose] *the initiative* 《in》.

しゅとく 取得 图 《やや書》 acquisition. ●不動産取得税 a real estate *acquisition* tax.
── **取得する** 動 acquire; 《やや書》 obtain 《a driver's license》. ● 同社の株式の7パーセントを取得する *acquire* 7 percent of the company's stocks. ● 免許証を取得する get [gain, obtain] a license. ● その土地を1億円で取得する *purchase* the land for a hundred million yen.
● 取得物 an acquisition.

しゅとして 主として mainly, chiefly. (⇨主に)

シュトラウス 〔オーストリアの作曲家〕 Strauss (Johann ～); 〔ドイツの作曲家〕 Strauss (Richard ～).

じゅなん 受難 sufferings; 〔試練〕 ordeals. ●キリストの受難 the *sufferings* of Jesus Christ; the Passion; the Crucifixion. (❗The Passion は最後の晩餐(ばん)から十字架上での死まで, the Crucifixion は十字架上での死にいたる受難をさす)

ジュニア (年少者, 下級生) one's junior; (年少の, 下級の) junior. ●フィリップ・モリス・ジュニア(＝二世) Philip Morris, *Jr*. ●ジュニア(＝十代の人)向きのファッション (a) fashion for *teenagers*.

しゅにく 朱肉 cinnabar seal ink; a vermilion inkpad.

じゅにゅう 授乳 ── **授乳する** 動 feed [suckle,《やや古》nurse] 《a baby》. (❗詳しくは母乳の場合はbreast-feed, ミルクの場合は bottle-feed という)
● 授乳期 the period of lactation.

しゅにん 主任 (権限を持った) a chief (複 ～s); (長) a head; (管理者) a manager; (上司) 《話》 a boss. ●経理部主任 the accounting *manager*; the *chief* of the accounting division. ●調理主任 the *chief* cook. ●1年生の主任である be *in* (full) *charge* of the first-year classes.
●主任研究員 a primary investigator (略 PI).
●主任制 (学校の) a chief teacher system.
●主任弁護士 a lead counsel.

しゅぬり 朱塗り ── **朱塗りの** 形 vermilion.

ジュネーブ 〔スイスの都市〕 Geneva /dʒəníːvə/.

しゅのう 首脳 (長) a head; (指導者) a leader; (最高位の人) a top. ●各国首脳 *heads* of states.
●首脳会談 a summit (meeting [conference]); summit talks 《between》. ●出席者 a summiteer) ●首脳部 (政府の) the heads of the government; (会社の) the (top) management of a company (❗単・複両扱い)

じゅのう 受納 图 receipt. ── **受納する** 動 receive.

シュノーケル 〔水中呼吸器具〕 a snorkel.

しゅのきげん 『種の起源』(*On*) *the Origin of Species* (*by Means of Natural Selection*). (参考 ダーウィンの生物学書)

しゅはい 酒杯 a (sake) cup. (⇨ 杯(さかずき))

シュバイツァー 〔フランスの医師・神学者・音楽家〕 Schweitzer (Albert ～).

じゅばく 呪縛 ● 呪縛をかける spellbind; cast [put] a

spell 《on him》. ● 呪縛を解く break the *spell*.

しゅはん 主犯 the principal offender, the initiator.

しゅはん 首班 the head (of a cabinet). ● 内閣の首班に指名する designate 《him》 as [to be] (the) *prime minister*.

しゅひ 守秘 secrecy.
● 守秘義務 the duty of confidentiality. ● 守秘義務違反 an abuse of confidentiality.

*しゅび **守備** defense; 〔野球〕fielding. ● 守備側 the defense; 〔野球〕the *fielding* team; the team in the *field*, the *field*. (❗いずれも集合的に用い, 単・複両扱い) ● 守備につく play *defense*; take the *field*. ● 定位置の守備をとる play straightaway. ● 前進守備の内野を抜くヒットを打つ hit a single past the drawn-in infield. ● 彼は守備がうまい He is a good *fielder*. ●a fielder は「守手」の意)/He fields (a ball) very well./He has a good glove. (❗「うまい守備だ！」は Oh, well fielded! となる) ● そのショートは守備範囲が広い The shortstop has good range. ● 内野陣は前進[中間; 普通]守備をとった The infielders played in [halfway; back].
● 君はどの守備位置を守っていますか What position do you play? / What's your position? ● 私たちのチームは守備が弱い. 守備の堅いチームになるにはうんと守備練習をしなければならない Our team is weak in *defense* [in *fielding*]. It takes a lot of *fielding* practice to be a team with tight [solid] *defense*.
● 守備妨害 interference. ● 守備要員 a defensive replacement.

しゅび 首尾 ❶[不変] ● 首尾一貫して consistently. ● 彼の態度は首尾一貫している He is *consistent in* his attitudes.
❷[結果] ● 首尾よく (うまく) well; successfully; (都合よく) fortunately. ● 首尾よく試験に合格する *succeed in* passing an examination. ● 万事首尾よくいった Everything went [came off] (quite) *well*.

じゅひ 樹皮 bark. ● 樹皮をはぐ *bark* a tree.

ジュピター Jupiter.

しゅひつ 主筆 (編集長) the (chief) editor; the editor(-)in(-)chief (複 editors(-)). (⇨主幹) ● 副主筆 an assistant editor; a subeditor.

しゅひつ 朱筆 ● 朱筆を入れる red-pencil 《written material》; correct errors.

しゅびょう 種苗 seeds and saplings.
● 種苗会社 a nursery company. ● 種苗業者 a nurseryman, (女性) a nurserywoman; 《男女共用》 nursery manager [owner, operator].

じゅひょう 樹氷 hoarfrost [ice] on a tree.

しゅひん 主賓 the guest of honor, the chief [principal] guest. ● 彼[田中氏]を主賓としてパーティーを開いた We had a party *in* his *honor* [*in honor of* Mr. Tanaka].

*しゅふ **主婦** a housewife (複 -wives), 《米》 a homemaker. (❗主夫 (house husband) も含む言い方で, 最近では前の語より一般的) ● 彼女は主婦であり3児の母でもある She is a *housewife* and mother of three children.
● 主婦連(合会) the Housewives' Federation.

しゅふ 主夫 a househusband.

しゅふ 首府 the capital (city). (⇨首都)

シュプール 〔＜ドイツ語〕 ski tracks [the tracks of skis] (on [in] the snow). ● 彼らは美しいシュプールを描いて斜面を滑り降りた They skied down the slope leaving beautiful *tracks* in the snow.

じゅぶつ 呪物 a fetish. ● 呪物崇拝 fetishism.

シュプレヒコール 〔＜ドイツ語〕 a chorus of shouts

しゅぶん 799 **しゅよう**

[yells], a chant. ▶デモ隊は「消費税粉砕」とシュプレヒコールをした The demonstrators *yelled in chorus* [*chanted*], "Down with the consumption tax."

しゅぶん 主文 (判決文の) the text (of a judicial decision).

じゅふん 受粉 图〖生物〗pollination. (**!**「授粉」の意もある) ● 自家受粉 self-pollination. ● 他家受粉 cross-pollination.

── **受粉する** 動 (やや書) be pollinated.

じゅふん 授粉 图〖生物〗pollination. (**!**「受粉」の意もある)

── **授粉する** 動 (やや書) pollinate.

しゅほ 酒保 a canteen;《米》a post exchange《略 PX》.

しゅほう 手法 (操作・美術的技巧) a technique /teknítk/; (技術上の腕まえ) téchnical skíll.

しゅほう 主峰 the highest peak [mountain].

しゅほう 主砲 the main gun [cannon];〖野球〗(強打者) a slugger;(4 番打者) a cleanup [hitter].

しゅぼうしゃ 首謀者 〖悪者や暴動などの〗a ringleader; 〖黒幕〗a mastermind.

しゅみ 趣味 a hobby;〖関心〗(an) interest;〖好み〗(a) taste;〖余技〗a pastime.

> **解説** 一般に日本人は hobby を使いすぎる傾向がある. hobby は主に積極的, 創造的に行う趣味のことで, その道は人にひけをとらないほどの本格的なものをいうことが多い. したがって My *hobby* is playing cards [eating]. とは普通いわない. また「趣味は読書[音楽鑑賞]です」は My *hobby* is reading [music]. とするより I *like* reading [listening to music]. や I *enjoy* reading [music]. の方が普通.

① 【〜趣味】 ▶ 上品な趣味 (a) refined *taste*.
② 【趣味は[が]】 ▶ 趣味は合う one's *taste* agrees with 《his》; have [share] common *interests*. ● 趣味が広い have a wide range of *hobbies*. ▶ 趣味は何ですか What *are* you *interested in*?/What are your main *interests* [your favorite *pastimes*]?/What is your *hobby*? (**!** (1) 最後の文は hobby のあることを前提としているので親しい人でない限り失礼にあたるから注意. 初対面の人には③の第 1 例などが適切. (2) 日常的には What [What do you do in] your free time? (暇なときはどのようにお過ごしですか)などのようにいえば相手の趣味が聞き出せる) ▶私の趣味は絵を描くこととピアノを弾くことです I'*m interested in* painting (pictures) and playing the piano./My *hobbies are* ×My hobby is] painting (pictures) and playing the piano. (**!** My hobbies are *to paint* .... のように不定詞はあまり用いない) ▶彼は音楽に趣味がある He has a *taste for* music. (**!** His *taste is for* music. ともいえる. 日常会話では He likes music. という方が普通) ▶彼女は服の趣味がいい[悪い] She has good [poor] *taste* in clothes./Her clothes are in good [poor] *taste*. ▶特に趣味はありません I have no *hobbies* worth mentioning. ▶趣味が高じて仕事になった Their *hobby* developed with a business.

③ 【趣味を[で, に, と]】 ▶ あなたは趣味をお持ちですか Do you have any *hobbies*? ▶ 趣味で切手収集を始めた I have taken up stamp collecting [collecting stamps] *as a pastime* [*as a hobby*, *for pleasure*]. (**!** 「趣味と実益を兼ねて」なら for business [profit] and *pleasure* となる) ▶彼は探偵小説が趣味になった He has developed a *taste for* detective stories. ▶これは私の趣味に合わない This isn't *to my taste*. ▶趣味と実益を兼ねるのは難しい It is difficult to combine one's *hobby* with benefits.

シュミーズ [<フランス語] a slip.

しゅみせん 須弥山 *Shumisen*, (説明的に) a high mountain believed to be in the center of the world (by Buddhists).

しゅみゃく 主脈 (山脈の) the main range;〖植物〗a costa (複 costae); a midrib; the main vein.

***じゅみょう 寿命** 〖命の長さ〗the span of life, a lifespan;〖生命〗(a) life (複 lives);〖一生〗a lifetime;〖耐久時間〗a life.

① 【〜寿命】 ▶彼の選手寿命も終わりに近い His playing *life* [His *life* as a player] is nearly over. ▶日本人の平均寿命が延びた The average *lifespan* of the Japanese has been extended [prolonged].

② 【寿命は[が]】 ▶彼女の寿命は長[短]かった She was *long-lived* [*short-lived*]./She had a *long* [a *short*] *life*. ▶彼女は大きな蛇を見て(= 見た瞬間)寿命が縮めと思いました She *was frightened* [*was scared*] *to death* at the sight of [when she saw] the big snake. ▶この電池は寿命がとうとうきた This battery *has run down* at last. (**!** 電球なら The bulb *has burned out*....)

■ **DISCOURSE** ■
医学の進歩により, 人の寿命は延びた People now *live* longer *due to* advances in medicine. (**!** due to ... (... が原因で)は理由に用いるディスコースマーカー)

③ 【寿命を】 ▶彼は寿命を全うした He lived out his (*natural*) *life*./(自然死した) He died a natural death.
● 寿命が縮む ▶彼は十分な休息を取らず寿命を縮めた He shortened his *life* because he did not get enough rest. ▶あのことが心配で彼女は寿命を縮めている That anxiety *is killing* her.

しゅむ 主務 ● 主務官庁 the competent authorities. ● 主務大臣 the competent minister.

しゅもく 種目 (競技の) an event. ● 陸上競技種目 track and field *events*.

しゅもく 撞木 a wooden bell hammer; (木うち) a mallet.

じゅもく 樹木 trees. ● 樹木葬 a burial in a forest.

しゅもくざめ 撞木鮫 〖魚介〗a hammerhead shark.

じゅもん 呪文 〖魔法の力を持っている〗a spell 〖 = 魔法〗;〖魔よけの〗a charm. ▶ 呪文をかける cast a *spell* 《*on* [*over*] her》. ● 呪文を解く break the *spell*. ● 呪文に縛られる under a *spell*; spellbound. ● 悪霊よけの呪文を唱える recite a charm *against* evil spirits.

***しゅやく 主役** (役) the leading part [role]; (俳優) a leading actor [(女の) actress]. (**!** 今は女優自身も actor ということが多い). ● 主役を務める play the *leading* [*main*] *part*; act the *leading character*; star 《*in* a play》. ▶ 彼は会議で主役を演じた He played a *major role* at the meeting.

じゅよ 授与 图 (学位などの)《書》conferment. ● 名誉学位の授与 the *conferment* of an honorary degree.

── **授与する** 動 (学位・称号などを)《書》confer ...《*on*》; (賞などを) award ...《*to*》. ▶田中耕一氏にノーベル化学賞を授与された Mr. Koichi Tanaka *was awarded* the Nobel Prize in chemistry.

***しゅよう 主要** ── **主要な** 形 chief; main; major; principal; leading; important. (⇨主な) ▶ その戦争の主要な原因は the *chief* [*main*, *major*, *principal*] cause of the war. ▶ その国の主要な産物は何ですか

しゅよう What are the *chief* [*main, major, principal*] products in the country? ▶アメリカの主要な都市をあげよ Name the *chief* [*major*] cities of the U.S. ▶彼はその紛争の解決に主要な役割を果たした He played a *leading* part [role] in settling the dispute.

しゅよう 腫瘍 〖医学〗a tumor /t(j)úːmər/. ●悪性[良性]腫瘍 a malignant [a benign /bənáin/] *tumor*.
●脳腫瘍 a brain *tumor*.

*__じゅよう 需要__ demand (⇔supply). ●需要と供給 supply and *demand*. (❗*demand* and *supply* より普通) ●買い換え需要 replacement *demand* (*for* home-electronics products). ●需要を満たす meet [supply] the *demand*. ▶石油はこのごろ需要が多い There is a great *demand* [a good *market*] for oil these days. (❗逆に「需要が少ない」の意では no [very little, a poor] の形容詞をつける)/Oil is in a great *demand* these days. ▶8月は電力の需要が急激に伸びる There is a sharp rise in *demand* for electric power in August. ▶価格は需要によって変化する The price varies with *demand*.
●需要インフレ(-ション)〖経済〗demand(-pull) inflation. ●需要供給の法則 the law of supply and demand.

じゅよう 受容 图 (an) adoption. ── **受容する** 動 adopt (a foreign culture). ── **受容力** receptivity.

じゅよう 需用 (消費すること) the use [comsumption] (*of* electricity).

しゅよく 主翼 the wings (of an aircraft).

しゅら 修羅 (⇒阿修羅) ●修羅の巷 (⇒修羅場)

しゅらば 修羅場 〖芝居の戦闘場面〗a battle scene; 〖激しい戦闘〗a fierce battle; (血みどろの) a bloody battle; 〖悲惨な光景〗a terrible sight; (流血の現場) a scene of bloodshed. ●修羅場と化す turn into a *scene of bloodshed*. ▶彼は何度も修羅場をくぐってきた He has had a lot of *terrible experiences*.

ジュラルミン duralumin /d(j)uərǽləmən/.

しゅらん 酒乱 〖酒癖が悪いこと〗a drink(ing) problem; 〖人〗a problem drinker. ●酒乱になる get violent [cause trouble] when drunk.

じゅり 受理 图 acceptance.
── **受理する** 動 (受け取る) receive; (承諾する) accept. ●彼の辞表を受理する *accept* his resignation.

しゅりけん 手裏剣 a throwing knife.

じゅりつ 樹立 图 establishment. ●新党の樹立 the *establishment* of a new political party.
── **樹立する** 動 ●外交[友好]関係を樹立する *establish* diplomatic [friendly] relations. ●世界記録を樹立する *make* [*establish, set up*] a world record (*for*).

しゅりゅう 主流 the mainstream, the main current. ●米文学の主流 the *main currents* of American literature.
●主流派 the leading [mainstream] (⇔antimainstream) faction; the faction in power.

しゅりゅうだん 手榴弾 a (hand) grenade /grənéid/.

しゅりょう 狩猟 a hunt; hunting; (銃猟) shooting. (❗hunt, hunting は,《米》では銃猟を含めて広く狩猟をすのに対し,《英》では通例銃を用いないで猟犬によるキツネ狩り・ウサギ狩りなどに用いる) ●彼は山に狩猟(=狩り)に出かけた He went *hunting* [went on a *hunt*] in the mountains. (❗in の代わりに to は不可)
●狩猟家 a hunter; (特にキツネ狩りの)《英》a huntsman. ●狩猟期 the hunting season. ●狩猟場 a

hunting ground. ●狩猟民族 a hunting people.

しゅりょう 首領 (かしら) a head; (権限のある) a chief (働 ~s); (指導者) a leader. (⇒長)

しゅりょう 酒量 one's drinking capacity. ●酒量が多い drink heavily; be a heavy drinker. ●酒量が増える[減る] drink more [less] (than before [one used to]). ▶酒量が多いよ, 少し減らしたら You drink too much. You should cut down (on your drinking).

じゅりょう 受領 图 receipt /risíːt/. (⇒受け取り) ●小包受領の判を押す *sign for* the parcel. (事情 米英ではこのような場合の判はない)
── **受領する** 動 receive. ●受領している be in *receipt* (*of*). ▶2月20日付貴信, 確かに受領いたしました This is to acknowledge our *receipt* of your letter of February 20th. (❗商業文で, 感情を交えない書き方)
●受領者 a receiver. ●受領証 a receipt.

しゅりょく 主力 the main force [strength]. ●主力を注ぐ concentrate one's *efforts* [*energy*] 《*on*》. ▶ビールは当社の主力商品です Beer is one of our *main* sales items.
●主力艦隊 the main fleet. ●主力メンバー leading [xmain] members. (❗main は人には用いない)

しゅりょく 呪力 incantatory power; magical power of incantation.

:**しゅるい 種類** a kind, a sort (❗sort の方が主観的でくだけた語); 〖同類のなかで異なった〗a variety; 〖型〗a type; 〖部類〗a class.
① 〖種類が〗 ▶このトンボとあのトンボでは種類が違う This dragonfly is different *in kind* [the different *kind*] from that one. ▶この2匹の犬は種類が同じです These two dogs are *of the same kind*. (❗ 種類をいうときは性質を表す of は省略不可)/These dogs are two *of a kind*. (❗of a kind は「同種類の」)
② 〖種類の〗 ●あらゆる種類のバラ all *kinds* [*sorts, varieties*] of rose(s) (❗roses と複数にする方が口語的); roses of all *kinds* [*sorts, varieties*] (❗この語順は種類を強調した言い方. 以下同様). ▶こういう種類のホンは値段が高い This *kind* [*sórt*] of book(s) is expensive. (❗kind [sort] を主語とするやや堅い言い方. of の後は通例無冠詞)/Books of this *kínd* [*sórt*] are expensive. (❗A book of this *kínd* is .... はまれ)/《話》Thése *kínd* [*sòrt*] of books are expensive. (❗kind [sort] of は /káind/, /sò:rtə/ となり, ひとまとまりの形容詞として主語の books を修飾する. Thèse *kínds* [*sórts*] of books ... は通例2種類以上の本をさす) ▶あの店ではたくさんの種類のアイスクリームを売っています They sell a lot of *flavors* of ice cream [ice creams in a lot of flavors] at that shop. (❗flavor は「風味」)/Many *sorts* of ice cream are [A (great [wide]) *variety* of ice cream is] sold at that shop. ▶新しい種類の車が発売された A new *týpe* of car [xa car] was put on sale./Cars of a new *týpe* were put on sale. ▶お宅の農園では何種類[どんな種類]のリンゴの木を植えていますか How many *kinds* of apples [What *kind* of apple, What *kinds* of apples] do you have on your farm? (❗what kind of の後に *an* apple や apples を用いるのは《話》)
③ 〖種類に〗 ▶それらは3種類に分類される They fall [are divided] into three *classes* [〖範ちゅう〗 *categories*].

しゅるい 酒類 alcoholic drinks [〖書〗beverages]; liquor.

じゅれい 樹齢 the age of a tree.

会話「この木の樹齢はどのくらいですか」「たぶん500年くらいでしょう」"How old is this tree?" "What's the *age of this tree?*" "Probably about five hundred years old."

シュレッダー 〖不要文書細断機〗 a shredder.

しゅれん 手練 ── 手練の 形 skillful; dexterous.
- 手練の早業で with the swiftness of a *practiced skill*.

しゅろ 棕櫚 〖植物〗 a hemp palm /pá:m/. ▶シュロの木[葉] a palm tree [leaf].

じゅろうじん 寿老人 the God of Longevity.

しゅわ 手話 sign language,《主に米》sign. ●手話で話す use [talk in] *sign language*. ●手話通訳する interpret (what (he) says) (for her) *in sign language*. (!「手話通訳者」は a *sign language interpreter*)

じゅわき 受話器 a (telephone) receiver. ●受話器を取る[持ち上げる] [pick up, take up] the *receiver*. ●受話器を置く replace [put back, put down] the *receiver*; hang up (the *receiver*) (! hang up on him とすると,「一方的におしゃべりな彼との電話を切る」の意). ●受話器を耳に当てる put the *receiver* to one's ear. ●受話器をはずしたままにする leave the *receiver* off the rest (cradle, (かぎ状の) hook]. ●受話器を手で押さえる put one's hand over the phone.

しゅわん 手腕 ability. (⇨能力) ▶政治的手腕を発揮する[振るう] show [exercise] one's political *ability* [*skill*].
- 手腕家 an able person; a person of ability (!後の方は堅い表現).

しゅん (⇨しゅんと)

しゅん 旬 the (apple) season. ▶リンゴは今が旬だ Apples are now *in* (⇔*out of*) *season*. (!「これからが旬だ」は ... are just coming into season)

*****じゅん** 順 〖順序〗order; 〖順番〗one's turn. (⇨順番)
- 順不同に in random *order*. ▶順を追って説明する explain (it) in *order*.

── 順に 副 〖順序よく〗in order;《2人が交替で》in turn, alternately; 《3人以上が順に》in turn, by turns. ▶〖年の言い方は繰り返しを暗示〗年齢[身長;大きさ;成績]順に in *order* of age [height; size; merit]. ▶彼女は物事を順に取り上げた She took things *in order*. ▶彼らは順に(=順繰りに)その質問に答えた They answered those questions *in turn*. ▶彼は名前を五十音[ABC]順に並べた He listed the names *in the order* of the Japanese syllabary [*in* alphabetical *order*, alphabetically].

じゅん 純 ── 純な 形 〖純粋な〗pure;〖純真な〗simple;〖本物の〗genuine. ▶純日本式家屋 a house in *pure* [*all*] Japanese style. ●純で誠実な人 a *simple* sincere person.
- 純文学 *pure* [*polite*] literature.

じゅん- 準- 〖半...〗semi-; 〖擬似の〗quasi- /kwéizai-/.
- 準礼装 *semi*formal dress. ●準公式報告書 a *quasi*-official report. ●〖公式文書で修正もありうる文書〗準会員 an *associate* member. ●〖英検の〗準一級 the *pre*-first grade.

じゅんあい 純愛 platonic [innocent, pure] love.

じゅんい 順位 〖序列〗ranking;〖順序〗order. ●順位(=優位)を争う contend for the *lead*. ▶彼女はクラスの成績順位がトップだ She *ranks* highest in her class./She is (at) the top (⇔bottom) of her class.
- 順位決定戦 《同点の場合の決勝戦》 a play-off.
- 順位表 the standings.

しゅんえい 俊英 〖すぐれていること〗genius;〖人〗a genius. ▶数学の俊英 a math [a mathematical] *genius*.

じゅんえき 純益 (a) net profit. ●その取り引きで100万円の純益を上げる *net* [*make a net profit of*] one million yen on the deal.

じゅんえん 巡演 ▶その楽団はヨーロッパを巡演中だ The band *has been on the road* [*on tour*] in Europe.

じゅんえん 順延 (a) postponement. ●〖雨天順延〗運動会は雨天順延です In case of rain, the athletic meet 《米》 [meeting 《英》] *will be put off* [*will be postponed*] *till the next fine day*.

じゅんおくり 順送り ── 順送りする 動 〖順に次へ回す〗 pass (it) on (to); 〖ぐるりと回す〗 pass (it) round [around]. ●その話を順送りする *pass* the story *on* (to the next person); *pass* the story *around*.

しゅんが 春画 pornography,《話》porno; an obscene 《a dirty》 picture.

じゅんか 純化 名 purification. ── 純化する 動 purify.

じゅんか 順化 名 acclimatization,《米》acclimation.
── 順化する 動 acclimatize,《米》acclimate.

*****じゅんかい** 巡回 名 〖巡視〗a round (! しばしば複数形で), 《警備員・警官の》patrol; 〖歴訪〗a tour. ●巡回中の警官 a police officer *on patrol* [his [her] *round*(s), his [her] *beat*, the *beat*].

── 巡回する 動 go* on [make*] one's rounds (*of*); 〖巡視する〗patrol (-ll-). ▶数人の警官が通りを巡回していた I saw several police officers *patrolling* the streets.
- 巡回区域 one's round [beat]. ●巡回講演 (make) a lecture tour (*of* a district).
- 巡回図書館《米》a bookmobile,《英》a mobile [《主に英》a traveling] library. ●巡回保健師《米》a visiting nurse.

しゅんかしゅうとう 春夏秋冬 〖四季〗the four seasons; 〖1年中〗all (the) year round [around].

じゅんかつゆ 潤滑油 lubricating oil, (a) lubricant. (! 「円滑にするもの」の意で比喩的にも用いる)

しゅんかん 瞬間 名 a moment; an instant (! 後の方が緊急・移ろいやすさ・瞬間性を強調する);《話》a minute. (⇨一瞬) ●人生の劇的瞬間 a dramatic [決定的な] a critical] *moment* in life. ●ほんの一瞬間 for an *instant*. ●次の瞬間[その瞬間]彼は地面にばったり倒れた The next *moment* [At that *moment*] he fell flat to the ground. ▶そのニュースを聞いた瞬間彼は真っ青になった He turned white *the moment* [*instant*, *minute*] (*that*) he heard the news. (! as soon as he heard the news. よりぐだけた言い方で強意的. that は通例省略する) ▶彼はかっとなった瞬間妹をなぐってしまった He hit《ややぞ》[struck] his sister in a *moment* of anger. ●あの瞬間は忘れることができないと思う I don't think I'll ever forget that *moment*./I'll never be able to forget that *moment*.

── 瞬間的な 形 momentary; instantaneous.
- 瞬間最大風速 the maximum instantaneous wind velocity. ●瞬間湯沸器《英》a geyser /gí:zər/.

*****じゅんかん** 循環 名 〖流れ〗circulation; 〖周期〗a cycle. ●血液の循環 the *circulation* of blood; (blood) *circulation*. (! 血の循環(=血行)が悪い」は have poor *circulation*) ●景気の循環 the business《英》trade》 *cycle*.

── 循環する 動 circulate; run* in cycles. ▶血液は体内を循環する Blood *circulates* through [around] the body.
- 循環型社会 a recycling-oriented society.

じゅんかんき 循環器 a circulatory organ. ●**循環系**【解剖】(心臓・血液などの) the circulatory system. ●**循環小数**【数学】repeating decimals.

じゅんかん 旬刊 ●旬刊〔=10日ごとに発行される〕誌 a magazine *published* [*issued*] *every ten days*.

じゅんかん 旬間 a period of ten days. ●交通安全旬間 a *ten-day* traffic safety campaign.

じゅんかんごし 準看護師 《米》a practical nurse; 《英》a state enrolled nurse.

しゅんき 春季 春期 spring, springtime. (⇨春) ●春季演奏会 the *spring* concert.

しゅんぎく 春菊【植物】a crown daisy.

しゅんきはつどうき 春機発動期 the age when they begin to have vague notion of love and sex.

じゅんきゅう 準急 《米》a local express (train).

じゅんきょ 準拠 ●この CD は教科書準拠だ These CDs *are based on* [《やや書》*are edited in accordance with*] the textbook.

じゅんきょう 殉教 图 martyrdom /mɑ́ːrtərdəm/.
―― **殉教する** 動 become a martyr; die for a religious cause.
●**殉教者** a martyr /mɑ́ːrtər/.

じゅんきょう 順境 (*in*) favorable circumstances. (⇔ 逆境)

じゅんぎょう 巡業 a (provincial [whistle-stop]) tour. ●劇団を巡業に連れて出る take the theater company *on tour*. (❗on tour は成句で無冠詞。ただし「ヨーロッパ[地方]巡業に」なら冠詞をつけて on *a tour* of Europe [*a provincial tour*] という)

じゅんきょうじゅ 準教授 an associate professor. (⇨教授 関連)

じゅんきん 純金 pure [solid] gold. ●純金の指輪 a *solid gold* ring.

じゅんぎん 純銀 pure [solid] silver. ●純銀のスプーン a *solid silver* spoon.

しゅんきんしょう 『春琴抄』 *Portrait of Shunkin*. (参考) 谷崎潤一郎の小説

じゅんぐり 順繰り in turn; by turns.

じゅんけつ 純血 ―― **純血の** 形 pure-blooded.

じゅんけつ 純潔 图 purity, chastity.
―― **純潔な** 形 (道徳的・性的に汚れのない) pure; (若い女性が性的に汚れのない) chaste; (処女・童貞の) virgin. ●心の純潔な人 a *pure-*hearted person.

じゅんけっしゅ 純血種 ―― **純血種の** 形 (馬) a thoroughbred. ―― **純血種の** 形 pure-bred.

じゅんけっしょう 準決勝 (全体) the semifinals; (1試合) a semifinal (game [match]). ●決勝に進む go on [《話》make it, 《やや書》advance] to a *semifinal*. (❗go on は get through とすると, 途中の困難を強調する)

しゅんけん 峻険 ―― **峻険な** 形 (険しい) steep 《mountains》.

しゅんげん 峻厳 ―― **峻厳な** 形 (厳しい) strict; severe.

しゅんこう 竣工 图 (完成) completion.
―― **竣工する** 動 ●新校舎が竣工した The new school building *was completed*. (❗「…は3月竣工の予定である」は … is due for *completion* in March.)
●**竣工式** a ceremony to celebrate the completion 《*of*》.

じゅんこう 巡航 a cruise /krúːz/ 《on Nippon-maru》. ●巡航中の旅客機 a liner *on a cruise*.
―― **巡航する** 動 ●当機は高度1万メートルで巡航しております The plane *is cruising* [We *are cruising*] at an altitude of 10,000 meters.
●**巡航速度** a cruising speed. ●**巡航ミサイル** a cruise missile.

じゅんこく 殉国 ●殉国の士 an ardent patriot.

じゅんさ 巡査 a police officer; (男の) a policeman 《愛 -men》, 《話》a cop; (平の) 《英》a police constable. (⇨警官) ●山本巡査 《米》*Officer* Yamamoto, 《英》*Constable* Yamamoto.
●**巡査長** a senior policeman. ●**巡査部長** a (police) sergeant.

しゅんさい 俊才 genius; (人) a genius, a talented person.

じゅんさい 蓴菜【植物】a water shield [target].

じゅんざや 順鞘【商業】a positive spread 《↔a back [a negative] spread》.

しゅんじ 瞬時 ●瞬時にして (瞬間的に) in an instant; instantly. ●コンピュータは瞬時にすべての計算をやってのけた The computer did all the calculations *instantly*. ▶グローバル化の時代にあって, 情報は瞬時に世界を駆けめぐる In this age of globalization, information gets around the world *in a flash*.

じゅんし 巡視 图 patrol /pətróul/.
―― **巡視する** 動 ●校内を巡視する *patrol* the school grounds.
●**巡視艇** [船] a patrol boat.

じゅんし 殉死 ―― **殉死する** 動 kill oneself on the death of one's lord [master].

じゅんじ 順次 in order. (⇨順に)

じゅんじつ 旬日 (a period of) ten days. ●旬日もせずして in less than *ten days*.

じゅんしゅ 遵守 图 【法律・慣例などの】observance. ●交通規則の遵守を励行する enforce the *observance* of traffic rules.
―― **遵守する** 動 ●法を遵守する observe [*obey*, *abide by*] the law.

しゅんじゅう 春秋 【春と秋】spring and autumn; 〖1年〗a year; 〖年齢〗age.
●**春秋に富む** be still young. ●春秋に富む若者 a youth with a promising future.
●**春秋の筆法** to write an opinion with one's own value judgment.

しゅんじゅん 逡巡 图 (ためらい) hesitation.
―― **逡巡する** 動 be undecided 《about …》; hesitate 《*about doing*》. (⇨ためらう)

*****じゅんじゅんに** 順々に ●順々に 副 (順を追って) in order; (順番に) in turn, by turns; (1人[一つ]ずつ) one by one; (次々と) one after another. (⇨順番)

じゅんじゅん 諄々 ●諄々と説く explain *patiently and minutely* [*in minute detail*].

じゅんじゅんけっしょう 準々決勝 the quarterfinals.

:**じゅんじょ** 順序 ❶【決まった並び方】order; (連続して起こる順序) sequence. ●順序立てて(=秩序立てて)説明する explain (it) *systematically* [*in a systematic way*]. ●事件の起こった順序をたどる follow the *order* [*sequence*] of the event. ▶この名簿は順序が逆だ[狂っている] This list is in reverse *order* [*out of order*, in wrong *order*]. ▶彼の本はいつも順序正しく並んでいる His books are always arranged *in* (the right) *order* [*in an orderly way*].
❷【手順】●順序を誤る follow the wrong *order*. ●順序を踏む go through due *formalities* [the proper *procedure*]. ▶式は順序どおりに進んだ The ceremony went *as was arranged* [*as was planned*, (順調に) *smoothly*].
●**順序不同** No set [fixed] *order* is observed. (事情) 米英ではこの種の断わり書きをつける習慣はない)

しゅんしょう 春宵 a spring evening.
●**春宵一刻値(あたい)千金** One hour of a spring evening is worth billions of yen.

じゅんしょう 準将 【米陸軍・空軍・海兵隊】a brigadier

じゅんじょう 〘米海軍・海兵隊〙 a commodore; 〘英陸軍・英海兵隊〙 a brigadier; 〘英空軍〙 an air commodore.

じゅんじょう 純情 〘清純な心〙 a pure heart; 〘純真〙 naivety /nɑːiːvəti/. ●彼は純情だ He has a *pure heart*./He is *pure in heart*.

しゅんしょく 春色 spring scenery [landscape].

じゅんしょく 殉職 — 殉職する 動 die while on duty; die in the line of duty; (自分の持ち場で) die at one's post. (⇨死ぬ)

じゅんしょく 潤色 图 embellishment.
—— **潤色する** 動 embellish; add [give] color 《to》. ●私は事故のことを潤色して話していた気持ちを抑えきれなかった I couldn't resist *embellishing* the story of the accident.

じゅんじる 殉じる (殉死する) follow the death of 《him》 by killing oneself; (信仰のために) die 〜d; dying) a martyr /máːrtər/ to 《one's faith》.

じゅんじる 準じる ●収入に準じて(=比例して)種々の税金を払う pay taxes *in proportion to* [(応じて) *in accordance with*] one's income. ●正会員に準じる扱いを受ける be treated *in the same way as* regular members. ▶以下これに準じる(=これはまた次のものにも適用される) This also *applies to the following cases*.

***じゅんしん** 純真 图 (無邪気) innocence; (うぶ) naivety /nɑːiːvəti/.
—— **純真な** 形 innocent; naive (❗前の方は「悪を知らない」、後の方は「未熟・未経験でまだ世間を知らない」ことを強調); (子供のように) childlike. ●彼はまだ若くて純真だ He is still young and *innocent*.

じゅんすい 純粋 —— **純粋な** 形 pure; (本物の) genuine. ●純粋な心 a *pure* heart. ●純粋な愛 *genuine* love. ●純粋の(=生っ粋の)フランス人 a Frenchman *born and bred* in France; a *trueborn* Frenchman. ●純粋な野生のサルは人間を襲わない Monkeys that are *truely* wild do not attack [(傷つける) harm] humans.

じゅんせい 純正 ●純正な 形 pure; genuine.
●純正科学 pure science. ●純正中立 strict neutrality. ●純正品 genuine products.

じゅんせい 準星 〘天文〙 a quasar.

しゅんせつ 浚渫 —— **浚渫する** 動 dredge.
●浚渫機 a dredging machine; a dredge.
●浚渫船 a dredger; a dredge.

じゅんぜん 純然 ●純然たる(=まったくの)失敗 an *absolute* [*downright*] failure. ●純然たる(=正真正銘の)芸術家 a *genuine* artist. ▶これは純然たる詐欺だ This is a *downright* [an *utter*] fraud /frɔːd/./This is *nothing but* a fraud.

じゅんぞう 純増 a net increase (*in* coal consumption).

しゅんそく 駿足 (足の速い人) a fast runner; a speedster. ▶彼は駿足を飛ばしてヒットを二塁打にした With his *great speed*, he stretched the single into a double. ●彼は俊足を飛ばして一塁から生還した He sped home from first.

じゅんそく 準則 〘規則に従うこと〙 the observance of a rule; 〘守るべき規則〙 a rule, a regulation.

じゅんたく 潤沢 ●潤沢な 形 abundant. ●潤沢な資金 *abundant* [*ample*] funds.

しゅんだん 春暖 warm spring weather. ●春暖の候となりました The *warm spring* has just come./We are now in the *warm spring*.

***じゅんちょう** 順調 —— **順調な** 形 (好都合の) favorable; (申し分のない) satisfactory; (円滑な) smooth.
●順調にいかない go wrong. ▶すべて順調にいけば、その橋は年内に完成する If everything goes well

[smoothly, (支障なく) *without a hitch*], the bridge will be completed by the end of this year. ▶順調にいっている(=順調にある)ときは自分ではそれに気づかない人もいる Some people don't know when they're *well off*.

会話「すべて順調かい」「今までのところはね」 "Is everything *all right*?" "So far."/"How's everything coming?" "So far *so good*."

じゅんて 順手 ●鉄棒を順手に握る grip a horizontal bar *overhand*.

しゅんと ●しゅんとなる(=しょげて静かになる) become depressed and fall silent.

じゅんど 純度 purity, (やや書) (a) degree of purity. ●純度の高い金 gold of high (↔low) *purity*.

しゅんとう 春闘 a spring labor offensive.

***じゅんとう** 順当 —— **順当な** 形 (本来そうあるべき) proper; (当然の) natural; (道理にかなった) reasonable. (⇨当然)
—— **順当に** 副 (都合よく) well. ●順当にゆけば if everything goes well; if nothing [no accident] happens; in the ordinary [normal] course of events [things]. ▶我がチームは順当に(=予想どおり)勝ち進んだ Our team went on winning *as we had expected*.

***じゅんのう** 順応 图 adaptation /ædæptéiʃən/《to》.
●環境への順応 adaptation *to* the environment.
—— **順応する** 動 (環境などに) adapt (oneself)《to》; (規則・習慣などに) conform《to》. ▶彼女は簡単に外国生活に順応した She easily *adapted* [*adjusted*] (*herself*) *to* life in a foreign country. (❗再帰代名詞を入れると努力の気持ちを含意する) ▶彼は校風に順応できなかった He could not *conform to* the atmosphere of the school.
●順応性 (適応性) adaptability. ●順応性のある flexible; adaptable. (❗後の方は通例叙述的にのみ用いる)

じゅんぱく 純白 pure white. ●純白のウエディングドレス a *snow-white* [a *pure white*] wedding dress.

しゅんぱつりょく 瞬発力 instantaneous muscular strength [muscle power].

***じゅんばん** 順番 (番) one's turn; (順序) order. (⇨番、順序、順に) ●歯医者の順番を待つ wait (one's *turn*) to see the dentist. ▶やっと順番がきた My *turn* has come (around) at last. (❗around は定期的順番を暗示) ▶太郎押さないで、順番を待ちなさい Don't push, Taro. Wait (❗まれ) *for*) your *turn*. ●少しの間列の順番を取っておいてくれませんか Will you save my *place* in line for a few minutes?

***じゅんび** 準備 图 〘用意〙 preparation(s); (手はず) arrangements. (⇨用意) ●準備運動をする warm up, have [go through] a warm-up. ▶テストの準備はできています We *are ready* for the test. ▶準備万端整ったよ、火曜日の9時に出発だ (It's [We're]) all *set* [Everything's *ready*. We have everything *ready*]. We leave on Tuesday at nine. (❗set はここでは ready と同意の形容詞) ▶だれもが楽しくなるように準備が整えられた The *arrangements* were made so as to make everyone happy.
—— **準備(を)する** 動 prepare (for...); get*(...)* ready (*for*) (❗prepare より口語的で、直前の最終的準備を暗示する); (手配する) arrange. (❗make preparations [arrangements]《for》は prepare や arrange より長期的及び準備過程を強調するに行く) ●最悪の場合に備えて[彼の言葉を聞く前に]心の準備をする *prepare* (*oneself*) *for* the worst [*to hear what he says*]. (❗「準備ができている」という状態は be prepared《*for*; *to do*》で表す) ▶彼女は(我々の

めに)夕食の準備をしてくれた(=作ってくれた) She *prepared* [《主に米》*fixed*] dinner (*for* us). (**!**) (1) 日常会話では fix の方が普通. (2) prepare dinner は料理など直接手を加える準備をさすのに対して, prepare for dinner は食器・手洗いなど間接的準備をさす. (3) 「for＋人」のときは次の語順も可: She prepared [fixed] us dinner./She got dinner *ready* (for us). ▶ 彼は試験準備をするのに忙しい He is busy *preparing for* [*getting ready for*, *preparing to* take, *with preparations for*] the exam. (**!**) 教師が試験を準備する場合は *prepare* the exam) ▶ 6 時までに(出発する)準備ができますか Will you *be ready* (*to* start) by six? ▶ 旅行会社が私たちの旅の準備をしてくれた The travel agency *arranged for* our journey [*for us to travel*]./The travel agency *made arrangements for* our journey [*for us to travel*]. (**!**)(1) arrangements を主語にして受身可 (⇨図). (2) ×did arrangements とはいわない
• 準備委員会 an arrangement committee.
• 準備金 a reserve. • 準備預金制度 the reserve deposit requirement system.
しゅんびん 俊敏 ― 俊敏な 形 agile; bright and quick; quick-witted.
しゅんぷう 春風 a spring breeze.
• 春風駘蕩(たいとう) 春風駘蕩たる穏やかな日和 a peaceful [a calm] spring day.
じゅんぷう 順風 a fair [a favorable] wind. • 順風(=その時の風)に乗って進む sail *with* [*before*] *the wind*.
• 順風に帆を上げる ▶ すべて順風に帆を上げるがごとくだった Everything proceeded smoothly just like a boat before the wind.
• 順風満帆(まんぱん) ▶ 彼は父親が生きている間は順風満帆であった Everything *was smooth sailing* for [*went smoothly with*] him until his father died.
じゅんぷうびぞく 醇風美俗 a humane atmosphere.
じゅんふどう 順不同 ▶ 順不同に in random order.
しゅんぶん 春分 the vernal [spring] equinox /íːkwənəks/.
• 春分の日 Vernal Equinox Day.
しゅんべつ 峻別 ― 峻別する 動 sharply distinguish 《A *from* B, *between* A *and* B》; make [draw] a sharp distinction 《*between* A *and* B》.
じゅんぽう 旬報 a ten-day report; a bulletin issued every ten days.
じゅんぽう 遵奉, 順奉 observance.
じゅんぽう 遵法, 順法 ― 遵法 [順法] の 形 law-abiding; obedient to the law.
• 遵法精神 the law-abiding spirit. • 遵法闘争 《米》 a slowdown, 《英》a work-to-rule. (**!**)いずれも婉曲語法) • 遵法闘争をする 《米》slow down, 《英》work to rule.
じゅんぼく 純朴 ― 純朴な 形 • 純朴な(=純真な)人 a *naive* [a *simple*, (悪ずれしていない) an *unsophisticated*] person.
しゅんみん 春眠 • 春眠暁を覚えず In spring we are liable to oversleep [to sleep very late] without noticing dawn breaking.
しゅんめ 駿馬 a swift horse.
じゅんめん 純綿 pure cotton; 100-percent pure cotton.
じゅんもう 純毛 pure wool.
• 純毛製品 all-wool [pure-wool] goods.
じゅんゆうしょう 準優勝 図 (人, チーム) a runner-up (複 runners-up).
― 準優勝する 動 be a runner-up; finish a runner-up; come [finish] second. ▶ 彼女はマラソンで準優勝した She *was* [*came*, *finished*] *second* to the champion in the marathon.
じゅんよう 準用 ― 準用する 動 apply 《a rule》 correspondingly 《*to*》. ▶ 彼らはその規則を新会員に準用した They *applied* the rule *correspondingly* to new members.
じゅんようかん 巡洋艦 a cruiser.
しゅんらい 春雷 spring thunder.
じゅんり 純利 (a) net profit.
じゅんり 純理 pure logic [reason].
じゅんりょう 純良 ― 純良な 形 pure 《water》.
じゅんりょう 順良 ― 順良な 形 gentle and good.
じゅんれい 巡礼 (a) pilgrimage /pílɡrəmɪdʒ/. • 四国へ巡礼の旅に出かける go on [make] *a pilgrimage* to Shikoku; *go in pilgrimage* to Shikoku.
• 巡礼者 a pilgrim. • 巡礼地 a place of pilgrimage.
じゅんれき 巡歴 ― 巡歴する 動 make a tour 《*of* Europe》; tour (in).
じゅんれつ 峻烈 ― 峻烈な 形 scathing; severe; sharp. • 峻烈な批評 *scathing* [*severe*, *sharp*] criticism.
じゅんれつ 順列 〖数学〗a permutation.
• 順列組み合わせ permutations and combinations.
じゅんろ 順路 • 順路(=一定の道筋)で by the *fixed* [*regular*] *route*.
しょ 書 〖書道〗calligraphy, penmanship; 〖手紙〗a letter; 〖書物〗a book; 〖書いたもの〗writing; 〖書類〗a document.
しょ 署 • 消防署 a fire *station*. • 警察署 a police *station*. • 税務署 a tax [a taxation] *office*.
しょ 緒 (⇨緒(ちょ))
しょー 諸ー (いろいろな) various; (いくつかの) several.
• 諸外国語 *several* foreign languages.
しょ 序 (始め) a beginning; (序文) a preface /préfəs/; (序論) an introduction.
しょあく 諸悪 ▶ 拝金主義が諸悪の根源 The love of money is the root [source] of *all evil*.
じょい 女医 a wóman [a fèmale] dóctor (⍟ women doctors). (**!**)(1) 特に女性を区別する場合に限る. 一般的には a doctor を用いる. (2) a lady doctor は丁寧すぎてかえって見下げた感じになるので避ける. (3) a wóman dòctor は「婦人科医」
じょい 叙位 図 the conferment of a rank.
― 叙位する 動 confer 《a rank [a title] *on* him》.
しょいこむ 背負い込む • 背負い込む(=重荷・責任などを負っている) be saddled [burdened] 《*with*》. • 彼に借金を背負い込ませる *saddle* [*burden*] him *with* debts. • やっかいな子を背負い込む(=面倒を見る) have a troublesome child *on* one's *hands*.
ジョイスティック 〖テレビゲームなどの操作レバー〗a joystick.
しょいちねん 初一念 • 初一念を貫く carry out one's *original intention*. (⇨ 初志)
しょいん 所員 a staff member, a staffer; (総称) the staff, the personnel.
しょいん 書院 a *shoin*; (説明的に) a traditional Japanese formal reception room.
• 書院造り 〖建築〗(説明的に) a traditional style of Japanese residential architecture established in the Momoyama period and still lives in present-day Japanese style houses.
しょいん 署員 • 警察署員 a police officer. • 消防署員 a fireman, 《男女共用》firefighter • 税務署員 a tax officer.
ジョイント 〖接合部〗a joint. • ジョイントコンサート a joint concert. • ジョイントベン

チャー 〖合弁事業〗 a joint venture.

しよう 使用 图 use /júːs/. (**!**「用途」の意味ではしばしば 〖C〗) (⇨利用)

① 【使用〜】 ●使用済み[未使用]の切手 a *used* /júːzd/ [an *unused*] stamp. ●機械の正しい使用法を知る learn the proper *use* of the machine; learn how to *use* the machine properly. ●使用上の注意を守る observe the *instructions*. (**!**複数形で用いる) ●使用不能の掲示 an out of *use* sign. ●使用許可を得る obtain permission to *use* 《it》. ●核兵器の使用禁止 prohibition of the *use* of nuclear weapons. ▶この会議室は現在使用中です The meeting room is *in use* now. ▶使用中 Occupied. 〖参考〗部屋・トイレなどの掲示

② 【使用に[を]】 ●辞書の使用を許す[禁じる] allow [forbid] the *use* of a dictionary; allow [forbid] 《him》 to *use* a dictionary. ●使用を認める admit the *use* of 《it》. ●使用を防ぐ prevent the *use* of 《it》. ▶この電球は5,000時間の使用に耐える This bulb *lasts* [*can be used*] for 5,000 hours.

— **使用する** 動 use /júːz/; make* use /júːs/ of .... (⇨使う, 利用) ▶彼は仕事に車を使用する He *uses* his car for work.

●**使用価値** (物の有用性・効用) 〖経済〗 value in use; use value. ●**使用者** (雇い主) an emplóyer; (利用者) a úser /júːzər/. ●**使用人** (雇用者者) an emplóyee; (召し使い) a servant. ●**使用料** (料金) a fee. (a) charge (**!**しばしば複数形で); (賃貸[賃借]料) (a) rent, rental. ●車の使用料は the *rent* for the car. ●**使用量** the amount used; the quantity consumed.

しよう 子葉 〖植物〗 a seed leaf [lobe]; a cotyledon /kɑ̀tɪlíːdn/.

しよう 止揚 图 〖哲学〗 sublation.
— **止揚する** 動 sublate.

しよう 仕様 ❶ 〖方法〗 a way. ▶他にしようがない There is no other *way*. (⇨仕方が無い) ▶あなた私がいなければどうしようもない He is *helpless* without me./He can't do anything without me. ▶すみません, どうしようもなかったのです I'm sorry, I *couldn't help it*. ▶しようがない人ねえ！ Yóu *\helpless* man! ▶どうしようもなくなったらあなたのお世話になります I'll come to you when I'm desperate. ▶それ以外にどうしようもないもの What more [*else*] could I do?
❷ 〖設計〗 a design.
●**仕様書** specifications.

しよう 私用 ●私用に使う *use* 《it》 for private purposes; (公金を) turn 《public money》 to *private use*. ●彼は私用で不在です He is away on *private* [*personal*] *business*. (**!** private は「公用」と対照して用いることが多い (⇨公用)) ▶会社の電話は私用に使わないでください Don't use office telephones for *personal* calls.

しよう 枝葉 — **枝葉末節** の 形 (重要でない) unimportant.
●**枝葉末節** ●枝葉末節にこだわる be too particular [fussy] about *trifles*.

しよう 試用 图 (a) trial.
— **試用する** 動 give ... a trial; (テストする) have [make] a trial 《of》; try ... out. ●新薬を試用する *make a trial of* [(十分にテストする) *try out*] a new medicine 《on some patients》.
●**試用期間** a trial [a probationary] period.

-しよう-使用 (⇨使う ① ②)

*しよう 賞 (特別な功績に対する) a prize; (一定の条件を満たした) an award. ●最優秀男優賞 the Best Actor *Award*; an Oscar for the Best Actor. 〖参考〗これを含むアカデミー賞(全体)は the Academy *Awards*, the Oscars という) ●コンテストで全部の賞をさらう carry off [away] all the *prizes* in a contest. ●彼に賞を与える award [give] him a *prize*. ●芥川賞を取る win (受賞する) be awarded] the Akutagawa *Prize* 《for the novel》. ▶残念賞としてこれを差し上げます I'd like you to have this as a consolation *prize*.

しよう 抄 (抜粋) an extract.

しよう 性 (生来の性質) (a) nature. (⇨性格) ●性に合った仕事 a congenial /kəndʒíːnɪəl/ job. ▶その仕事は彼女の性に合わない He is not *suited for* [*to*] the task./The task does not *suit* him./〖話〗He is not *cut out for* [*to do*] the task. (**!**最後の文は通例否定文で) ▶私はどうも彼と性が合わない Somehow I don't *agree with* him. (**!**肯定文では通例用いない) /〖仲よくやってゆけない〗 Somehow I don't *get along* [*on*] well *with* him.

しよう 省 〖官庁の〗 a ministry; (米国の) a department (**!**〖英〗でも新設のものには用いる); (英国の) an office. ●財務省 the *Ministry* of Finance. ●〖中国の行政区間〗 a province. ●山東省 Shandong *Province*.

しよう 将 a commander.
●将を射(‵)んと欲すればまず馬を射よ He that would the daughter win must with the mother first begin.

しよう 商 (商業) commerce; (商売) business, trade; (商人) a trader; 〖数学〗 the quotient.

しよう 章 〖書物の〗 a chapter (略 chap., ch.). ●第2章 the second *chapter*; *chapter* two [Ⅱ].

しよう 笙 〖楽器〗 a sho; (説明的に) a traditional Japanese wind musical instrument.

しよう 証 (証拠) evidence, proof; (証明書) a certificate; (身分証明書) an ID card.

しよう 衝 ●衝に当たる be in charge 《of》; bear the responsibility 《for》; be responsible 《for》.

しよう 礁 a reef. ●サンゴ礁 a coral *reef*.

しよう 背負う (⇨背負(しょ)う, 背負い込む)

しょう- 小-, 少- ●小アジア Asia *Minor*. ●少人数の晩餐(ばん)会 a *small* dinner party. ▶高山は小京都といわれる Takayama is called a *little* [(小型の) a *miniature*] Kyoto.

しょう- 正- ●正2時に just [exactly, promptly] at two; at two sharp [on the dot].

-しょう -勝 a win (↔a loss). ▶彼らとの対戦成績は4勝3敗だ We've had four *wins* and three losses [four *victories* and three defeats] *against* them.

じょう 滋養 (栄養物) nourishment. ●滋養物 nourishing [(栄養のある)〖書〗 nutritious] food.

じょう 上 ❶ 〖標準よりすぐれたこと〗 ●上の上 the very best. ❷ 〖上巻〗 the first volume.

じょう 情 〖愛情〗 (a) love; (温和で長く続く) (an) affection; (愛着) (an) attachment; 〖心情〗 a heart; 〖感情〗 feeling(s); (涙もろさ) (a) sentiment. ●親子の情 the *love* [*affection*] between parent and child; parental *love* [*affection*]. ●愛と哀れみの情を同時に覚える have mixed *feelings* of love and pity. ●情の薄い[ない]人 a *cold-hearted* [a *hard-hearted*] person. ●情のこもった手紙 an *affectionate* [a *very kind*] letter. ●情に縛られる get *emotionally* caught up. ▶彼は自分の子供に何の情も示さなかった He didn't show his children any *affection*. ▶彼は情のある人だ He's *warm and loving*./He is a *kind-hearted* [a *warm-hearted*] person.
●**情が移る** ●彼に情が移る become *attached to* him.

- **情にもろい** ▶彼は情にもろい He is a *sentimental* man./(すぐ感動して涙を流す) He *is easily moved to tears*.
- **情を通じる** have an intercourse with 《him》.

じょう 嬢 [未婚の女性の姓または姓名につける敬称] Miss; [娘] a daughter; [女の子] a girl. (⇨お嬢さん) ▶二村(知子)嬢 *Miss* (Tomoko) Futamura. (! ×Miss Tomoko とはいわない) ●案内嬢 (劇場などの) an usherétte. ▶こんにちは、お嬢ちゃん。お名前は何 ていうの Hello, *darling* [*little girl*]. What's your name? ▶男女を問わず幼い子の呼びかけには darling が普通

じょう 錠 ❶[錠前] a lock; (南京錠) a padlock. (⇨鍵(ぎ))
❷[錠剤] a tablet; [丸薬] a pill. ●ビタミン錠 a vitamin *tablet*. ●毎食後に2錠の薬を飲む take [×drink] two *tablets* after each meal.

-じょう -上 ●教育上 from an educational point of view. ●政治上の理由で for a political reason.

-じょう -条 ●一条の光 a *ray* [a *stream*] of light. ●一条の稲妻 a *streak* of lightning. ●憲法第9条 the ninth *article* [*Article* 9] of the (Japanese) Constitution.

-じょう -帖 ●紙1帖 a quire of paper.

-じょう -乗 ●5の2乗 the second *power* of five. ▶5の2[3]乗は25[125]です 5 squared [cubed] is 25 [125]./The square [cube] of 5 is 25 [125]./The second [third] power of five is 25 [125].

-じょう -城 ●姫路城 Himeji *Castle*. (⇨城)

-じょう -畳 ●8畳間 an eight-*mat* room.

じょうあい 情愛 (an) affection. ●情愛深い人 a person of deep *affection*; an *affectionate* person.

しょうあく 掌握 图 (支配) control.
── **掌握する** 動 (人などを) get control 《over》; (政権などを) come into power. ●掌握している (人などを) have control 《over》; (政権などを) be in power.

しょうい 小異 a minor conflict.
●小異を捨てて大同につく make common cause by putting aside [sinking] *minor differences*.

しょうい 少尉 [陸軍・米空軍・英海軍] a second lieutenant; [米海軍] an ensign; [英空軍] a pilot officer.

じょうい 上位 ●上位にある be in a high(er) rank [position], be high(er) in rank; be above [superior to]... in rank. (⇨位 ❹, 優位) ●クラスで上位を占める *rank high* in one's class; (平均より上である) be *above average* in one's class; (トップグループにいる) be among the best students in one's class. ●上位10位以内に入賞する win a prize for the *top* 10 *rankings*.

じょうい 攘夷 the exclusion of foreigners from Japan.
●攘夷論 exclusionism. ●攘夷論者 an exclusionist; an exclusivist.

じょうい 譲位 ── **譲位する** 動 abdicate (from) the throne.

じょういうち 上意討ち a seizure of *samurai* rebels by the command of their master.

じょういかだつ 上意下達 ── **上意下達の** 形 top-down 《plans》.

しょういぐんじん 傷痍軍人 《米》a disabled veteran, 《英》a disabled ex-serviceman.

しょういだん 焼夷弾 an incendiary bomb.

しょういん 勝因 the cause of victory.

しょういん 証印 a seal. ●証印を押す put [set] the *seal* 《on a document》.

じょういん 上院 the Upper House; 《米国の》the Senate; 《英国の》the (House of) Lords. (! 後の二つは単・複両扱い)
●上院議員 a member of the Upper House; 《米国の》a Senator; 《英国の》a Lord.

じょういん 冗員 a supernumerary; a supernumerary [an extra] person [employee, official]. ●冗員を整理する weed *supernumeraries* out.

じょういん 乗員 a crew member, (男の) a crewman (慶 -men); (集合的) a crew (! 単・複両扱い).

じょうえん 常打ち a regular performance (at a regular place).

しょううちゅう 小宇宙 a microcosm /máikrəkὰzm/.

しょううん 勝運 ▶勝運に恵まれた[恵まれなかった] Luck was with [against] us.

じょうえい 上映する show, run; (やや書) present; (上映されている) be on. ▶あの映画館ではどんな映画を上映していますか What movie *is showing* [*playing*, *on*] at that movie theater?/What movies *are* they *showing* [*presenting*] at that movie theater? ▶その映画はまだ上映されている The movie *is* still *running* [*on*]. ▶「ダイハード」近日上映 "Die Hard," *coming soon* 《to your town》./"Die Hard" *is coming*.
会話「上映は何時からなの」「7時のと9時10分のとがあるよ」"What time *is* it *showing*?" "There're *shows* at 7 and 9:10."

しょうエネ 省エネ energy(-)saving; energy(-)efficiency. ●省エネ型冷蔵庫 an *energy-saving* (type of) refrigerator. ●省エネ技術 *energy-saving* technology. ●省エネ対策を講じる take measures for *energy-saving*. ●省エネ投球 economical pitching. ●省エネ投手 an economical pitcher.

しょうえん 小宴 (give [hold]) a small [a private, an informal] party.

しょうえん 荘園 a manor (in medieval Japan).
●荘園制 the manorial system. ●荘園領主 the lord of a manor.

しょうえん 消炎 ── **消炎する** 動 reduce inflammation.
●消炎剤 [薬学] an anti-phlogistic (agent); an anti-inflammatory.

しょうえん 硝煙 ●硝煙反応 (gun) powder smoke.

しょうえん 上演 图 a performance; a presentation. ●「オセロ」の上演 the *performance* [*presentation*] of Othello. ●ショーの上演時間 the *running* time for the show. ▶その上演はすばらしかった The *performance* was wonderful./(それは立派に上演された) It *was* well *acted* [*performed*]. ▶上演中入場お断わり (掲示) No admittance *during* (the) *performance*.
── **上演する** 動 (演じる) perform, give* a performance 《of》; (公開する) put*... on, 《やや書》present; [劇を演じる] play; (舞台で演じる) stage, bring* (it) to the stage. ▶その劇団は「ハムレット」を上演した The theater company performed [played, staged, put on] Hamlet. ▶あの歌劇場では何が上演されていますか What's *on* at that opera house? ▶このミュージカルは2か月にわたって上演されている This musical *has been running* [*playing*] (for) two months.

しょうおう 照応 图 correspondence 《between, with》. ── **照応する** 動 correspond 《with, to》.

じょうおう 女王 a queen (⇨女王(ぎ))

しょうおん 消音 ●消音装置[器] (エンジンの) a muffler; (銃の) a silencer. ●消音ピアノ a silencer-equipped piano.

じょうおん 常温 normal temperature; (ワインなどの)

しょうか 【室温】 ▶常温で保存する keep (wine) at *room temperature*.

しょうか 消化 图 (a) digestion /daidʒéstʃən/. ●消化のよい[悪い]食物 *digestible* [*indigestible*] food; food that *is easy* [*difficult*] *to digest*. ●消化を助ける help [promote] one's *digestion*. ●消化を妨げる disturb [upset] one's *digestion*. ●消化不良を起こす get [suffer from] *indigestion*. (●状態をいうときは have indigestion [digestive trouble]) ▶これらの野菜は消化がよい These vegetables are easy to *digest* [good for *digestion*, *digest* well].

── **消化する 動 ❶**[食物・知識などを]digest. ▶食物は胃の中で消化される Food *is digested* in the stomach. ▶この学説は難しくて私は消化できない This theory is too difficult for me to *digest*.

❷[計画・注文などを]meet*; [製品などを](消費する)consume; (売り切る)sell*... out; [仕事などを]finish. ●勉強のスケジュールを消化する *meet* [遅れずについていく *keep up with*] one's study schedule.

●消化液 digestive juices. ●消化器官 a digestive organ. ●消化器系統 『解剖』the digestive system. ●消化酵素 a digestive enzyme. ●消化剤 a digestive. ●消化力 digestive power.

しょうか 昇華 图 『化学』sublimation.
── **昇華する 動** sublimate.

しょうか 消火 图 fire fighting [extinguishing].
── **消火する 動** put out [〘書〙extinguish] a fire. ●消火器 a fire extinguisher. ●消火栓 a (fire) hydrant; a fireplug.

しょうか 消夏 ●消夏法 a way of summering, a way to cope with the summer heat.

しょうか 商科 (●商学部)
●商科大学 a commercial college.

しょうか 商家 『人』a merchant; (その家族) a merchant('s) family; 『店』a house (●houses /-zɪz, (米)-sɪz/; (米)a store, 〈主に英〉a shop. ▶春子は商家の出である Haruko comes from a *merchant family*.

しょうか 唱歌 (歌うこと) singing; (歌) a song.
●唱歌集 a collection of songs; a songbook.

しょうか 頌歌 an anthem; a hymn of praise.

しょうが 生姜 『植物』ginger /dʒíndʒər/. ●紅ショウガ red-dyed *ginger*. ●ヒョウガの根. ●豚肉のショウガ焼き *ginger*-flavored pork sauté.

じょうか 城下 ●城下の盟(ちかい) a promise to surrender made by a *daimyo* when his territory is invaded by an enemy force.
●城下町 a castle town.

じょうか 浄化 图 purification; (腐敗などの) a cleanup. ●町の浄化 a *cleanup* of the city.
── **浄化する 動** purify〈water〉; (腐敗などを町などから) clean (the city) up. ●浄化槽(汚水の) a septic tank. ●浄化装置 a purifier.

‡**しょうかい 紹介** 图 introduction. ●自己紹介 self-*introduction*. ●日本への新製品の紹介 the *introduction of* a new product *into* Japan.

── **紹介する 動 ❶**『人を』introduce. ●(目上の人・聴衆に)〘書〙present /prizént/.

> [事情] 人を紹介するときには，異性の場合は年齢に関係なく男性を女性に，同性の場合は年少者を年長者に，また，女性の場合は未婚者を既婚者に先に紹介するのが一般的な順序である．

▶彼は友達を父親に紹介した He *introduced* his friend *to* his father. ▶自己紹介します．ぼくは奥田祐樹です Let me *introduce* myself. My name's [I'm] Yuki Okuda. (●(1) May I introduce myself? の方が丁寧．(2) Yuki を省略するのはぞんざいな言い方) ▶私たちはお互いに紹介し合った We *introduced* [×presented] ourselves *to* each other. ▶私のことを彼女に紹介してもらいたいのですが I'd like *to be introduced to* her. ▶あの有名な歌手ブレント・ウォッツを紹介いたします(劇場で) Let me *present* [It is my great pleasure to introduce] that great singer, Brent Watts. (●以上の社交上の「紹介」のほかに，[医者/弁護士を]紹介するは *refer* ⟨*him*⟩ *to* a doctor [a lawyer] と *refer* を用いる) ▶お母さん，紹介したい(＝会ってもらいたい)人がいるんだけど Mom, I'd like you to *meet* someone. ▶安藤敏子さんを紹介ください．彼女は私の学校の先生です I'd like to *introduce* Miss Toshiko Ando to you. Miss Ando [×She] is a teacher at our school. (●目の前にいる人や目上の人の場合，代名詞で受けることは通例避ける)

会話「みなさん，新入生を紹介します．ケイティ・ケネディーさんです」「こんにちは，ケイティ」「こんにちは，よろしく」"Everybody, I'd like you to say hello to your new arrival. Miss Katy Kennedy." "Hello, Katy." "Hi! Nice to meet you."

❷[物事・言葉を]introduce. ▶彼女は彼のニューアルバムを視聴者に紹介した She *introduced* his new album *to* the audience. ▶シェイクスピアを初めて日本に紹介したのはだれですか Who first *introduced* Shakespeare *to* Japan? ▶私はホームステイ先の家庭に日本の文化について少し紹介した I *told* my host family some things about Japanese culture. (●このような文脈では introduce は不適当) ▶そう口を尖らせないでくれよ．ぼくは彼女に言われたことを紹介しているに過ぎないのだから Don't pout, I'm just *telling* you what I've been told by her. (●pout は不服や怒りの気持ちを表すときに口を尖らす表情．pout one's lips は「キスを求めるように」の意になるので注意)

▰▰ **DISCOURSE** ▰▰
ストレスを緩和するための三つの方法を紹介しよう．　第一に，健康な生活様式を保つことだ I would like to *introduce* **three** ways of reducing stress: first, try to maintain a healthy lifestyle. (●**one** [two; three; several (1つ[2つ; 3つ; いくつもの)]は列挙される数を示すディスコースマーカー．続けて具体的内容を列挙する)

❸[世話・斡旋(あっせん)をする](⇒世話する **❷**)
●紹介状 a letter of introduction.

しょうかい 哨戒 a patrol /pətróul/.
●哨戒機 a patrol plane.

しょうかい 商会 a firm; a company (略 Co.). ●スミス商会 the *Firm* of Smith; Smith *and* [&] *Co*. (●(1) ×Smith Co. とはしない．Smith Trading Co. に可．(2) Co. は /kʌ́mpəni/, 〖話〗/kóu/ と読む)

しょうかい 照会 图 (an) inquiry /ínkwəri/. (人物・身元などの) (a) reference. ●照会の上 on *inquiry*. ●照会中 under *inquiry*. ●あなたの(身元の)照会先はどちらですか Who are your *references*?

── **照会する 動** ▶私の経歴については山本教授に照会してください Please *refer* [*make reference*] to Professor Yamamoto *for* my career.
●照会状 a letter of inquiry; a reference.

しょうかい 詳解 ⟨*give*⟩ a full [a detailed] explanation ⟨*of*⟩.

‡**しょうがい 障害** ❶[妨げとなるもの](進行を止めるもの)an obstacle; (進行を遅らせるもの) a hindrance; (大きな壁を) a barrier; (困難な状況・問題) a difficulty. (⇒邪魔) ●3,000メートル障害 the 3,000-meter stéeplechàse. ▶その迷信はその種族の進歩を遅らせる

しょうがい 障害となっている The superstition is an *obstacle* [a *hindrance*] to the tribe's advancement. ▶輸入規制は貿易の障害になっている Import restrictions are *barriers to* trade. (**!**「貿易障害」は trade *barriers* という) ▶私は多くの障害に出合ったが,何とかそれも乗り越えた I ran into [met with] a lot of *difficulties*, but managed to get over them. ❷ [身体の](病気) trouble; (機能の欠陥) a defect; (不調) (a) disorder. ●心臓障害 heart *trouble*.
●腎臓の機能障害 an *impaired* kidney function. ●言語障害者 a person with a speech *defect* [*impediment*]. (**!**後の方は専門用語で,軽度のものをさす) ●脳[神経; 感情; 血行]障害 a brain [a neurological; a mood; a circulatory] *disorder*. ●身体障害者 (⇨障害者) ▶(身体)障害者は人の助けがなければ生きていけない Disabled people [The disabled] cannot live without the help of [from] others.
●障害児教育 education of the disabled [x handicapped] children. ●障害年金 a pension for the disabled. ●障害物競走 (陸上競技から) a hurdle race, the hurdles (**!**単数扱い);(運動会の) an obstacle race.

しょうがい 生涯 [人生] one's [a] life (**複** lives); [職業的経歴] one's career /kəríər/; [存命期間] one's [a] lifetime. (⇨一生) ●生涯を終える end one's life [days]. ●生涯の伴侶(はんりょ) a partner *for* [*in*] life, a life partner. ●政治家としての彼の生涯 his *career* as a statesman; his political *career*. ●生涯に五つの小説を書く write five novels *in* one's *lifetime*. ●生涯独身で通す remain single *all* [*throughout*] one's *life*. ▶彼は生涯の大半をウィーンで過ごした He lived most of his *life* in Vienna /viénə/. ▶生涯ご恩は忘れません I'll [shall] never forget your kindness *as long as* I *live* [*all* my *life*]. (**!** shall の方が決意の度合いが強い)▶生涯に負債をあなたに He *was* forever in-debted to you *for life*. ▶彼らの友情は生涯続いた Their friendship lasted *all* their *lives*. (**!**「生涯の友情」は a *lifelong* friendship) (⇨終生)
●生涯教育 lifelong [生涯続ける) on-going, 《米》continuing) education.

しょうがい 渉外 (連絡, つながり) liaison /liːazɑːn/; (打ち合わせ, 交渉) arrangements, (a) negotiation.

しょうがい 傷害 (an) injury. ▶彼は傷害罪で逮捕された He was arrested on the [a] charge of (inflicting) *bodily injury*.
●傷害事件 a case of bodily injury. ●傷害致死 [法律] a bodily injury resulting in death.
●傷害保険 accident insurance.

じょうがい 場外 a place outside 《the place》.
●場外ホームランを打つ hit an out-of-the-park homer; hit a homer out of the park [over the roof]. (**!** over the roof 以外の表現は,スタンドに入るホームランを表すのが普通)
●場外馬券売り場 an off-track betting place.

しょうがいは 小会派 a minority party.

しょうかく 昇格 图 (a) promotion. (⇨昇進)
━━**昇格する** 動 promote. ●メジャーリーグへ昇格する go [come] up to the major leagues; break into the majors. ●彼は部長に昇格した He *was promoted* to manager.

しょうがく 小額, 少額 a small amount [sum] 《*of* money》.
●小額紙幣 a small bill 《米》 [note 《英》].

じょうかく 城郭 [城] a castle /kǽsl/; [城の囲い] castle walls.

じょうがく 上顎 the upper jaw; [解剖] a maxilla (**複** maxillae). (⇨下顎(したあご))

しょうがくきん 奨学金 a scholarship /skálərʃip/. ●大学へ奨学金を申し込む[もらう] apply for [win, gain, get] a *scholarship* to the university. ●奨学金をもらって留学する study abroad *on a scholarship*.

しょうがくせい 小学生 a schoolchild (**複** -children), (男子生徒)《主に英》a schoolboy, (女子生徒)《主に英》a schoolgirl; (総称) schoolchildren. ●中学生・高校生などと区別して《米》で an elementary [a grade] school student, 《英》a primary school pupil のようにもいう) (⇨生徒)

しょうがくせい 奨学生 a scholarship student, a student on a scholarship.

しょうがくぶ 商学部 the department [college] of commercial science.

しょうがつ 正月 [新年の数日間] the New Year (⇨新年); [元日] New Year's Day (⇨元日); [1月] January. ●正月に (年始に) at the *New Year*; (元旦に) on *New Year's Day*. (**!**前置詞に注意) ▶まだ生徒たちは正月気分が抜けないようだ The students seem to feel as if they were still in the *New Year*.
●正月休み the New Year holidays.

しょうがっこう 小学校 《米》 an elementary [a primary] school, a grade school 《州によって学制が異なり修業年数に違いがある》, 《英》 a primary school 《5歳から11歳まで》. (**!**英国では私立の小学校でa preparatory school 《8歳から13歳まで》というのが別にある) (⇨学校)

しょうがない 仕様がない (⇨仕様, 仕方(が)無い)

じょうかまち 城下町 a castle town.

しょうかん 小寒 shokan; (説明的に) the first half of the coldest season (January 6-19).

しょうかん 召喚 [法律] a summons (**複** ~es); (証人に対しての) a subp(o)ena.
━━**召喚する** 動 summon. ▶彼は裁判所に召喚された He *was summoned* to appear in court.
●召喚状 [法律] a summons; a subp(o)ena.

しょうかん 召還 ━━**召還する** 動 recall; call back. ●駐インド大使を本国に召還する order [summon] the ambassador to India (to come) home; recall the ambassador *from* India.

しょうかん 将官 (陸軍の) a general; (海軍の) an admiral.

しょうかん 商館 (説明的に) an office of a foreign merchant in the Edo period.

しょうかん 償還 图 (返済) (a) repayment; (a) refund; (債券などの)《書》redemption.
━━**償還する** 動 ●負債を償還する *repay* a loan. ●公債を償還する 《書》 *redeem* a bond.
●償還期限 (final) maturity; a maturity [a due] date. ●償還基金 redemption fund.

じょうかん 上官 a superior] officer.

じょうかん 乗艦 ━━**乗艦する** 動 go on board a warship; board a warship.

じょうかん 情感 feeling. ●情感を込めて歌う sing with great *feeling*. ▶その女優は50にしてなおみずみずしい情感(=感じ)を漂わせている At fifty, the actress gives us an *impression* that she is still young.

しょうかんしゅう 商慣習 a business [a commercial] practice.

しょうき 正気 图 (one's) senses; (one's right) mind; (意識) consciousness; (狂気でないこと) sanity; (酔っていないこと) soberness. ●正気に返る (意識が戻る) recover *consciousness* [one's *senses*]; come to (one's *senses* [*oneself*]) (**!**come to 単独で用いる場合は /kʌ́mtúː/ と読む);

しょうき　　なる) become *sane*. ●正気を失う lose one's *senses*; (意識を失う) lose *consciousness*; (発狂する) go mad.
── 正気の形 *conscious*; *sane*; *sober*. ▶彼はその時はまだ正気だった(=しらふだった) He was still *sober* at that time. ▶彼は正気でない He is *out of his senses* [*mind*]./He is not *in his right mind*./(気が狂っている) He is *insane* [*mad*]./《話》では否定文で I don't think he's *all there*. のようにもいう.

しょうき　商機 a business opportunity [chance].

しょうき　勝機 ●勝機をつかむ[逸する] seize [let slip] the *chance of victory*.

しょうき　鍾馗 *Shoki*; (説明的に) the God believed to drive (the god of) plagues.

しょうぎ　床几 a stool; a folding stool.

しょうぎ　省議 (内閣各省の会議) a departmental meeting [conference].

しょうぎ　将棋 *shogi*; (説明的に) a Japanese chess-like board game for two players. ●将棋をさす play *shogi*.
●将棋倒し ●将棋倒しになる fall (down) like (a lot of) dominoes [《主に英》ninepins].

しょうぎ　商議 (評議) (a) conference; (相談) (a) consultation.

じょうき　上気 ── 上気する動 (顔が赤らむ) be flushed; (興奮する) be excited. ●上気した顔 a *flushed* face. ▶彼女は湯上がりでほんのり上気していた She looked slightly *flushed* after her bath.

じょうき　上記 ●上記の(=上に述べ)理由で for reasons *mentioned above*. ▶上記電話にご連絡ください Please call me up on the *above* phone number.

じょうき　常軌 ●常軌を逸した(=風変わりな)行動 *eccentric* [《異常な》*abnormal*] conduct. (⇨逸する)

じょうき　蒸気 (熱を加えて出る) steam; (空中に見える) 《米》(a) vapor. ▶蒸気が地面から立った *Steam* [*Vapors*] rose from the ground. ▶その船は蒸気で動く The ship is driven by *steam* [is *steam-driven*].
●蒸気機関 a steam engine. ●蒸気機関車 a steam locomotive. ●蒸気船 (小型の) a *steam*-*boat*; (汽船) a steamer; a steamship.

＊じょうぎ　定規 a ruler, a rule; [直角・T 形・L 形の] a square; [三角の]《米》a triangle,《英》a set square. ●T 定規 a T-*square*.

じょうきげん　上機嫌 good humor. ●上機嫌である be in a *good* (↔a bad) *humor*; (意気込んで) be in *good spirits*.
── 上機嫌な形 ●上機嫌な男たち good-humored (↔ill-humored) men.

しょうきち　小吉 good luck.

しょうきぼ　小規模 ── 小規模の形 small-scale.
●小規模の農業経営 *small-scale* farming. ▶彼は小規模ながら駅前でレストランをやっている He runs a restaurant in front of the station, though it is *on a small scale*.

しょうきゃく　正客 (主賓) the guest of honor; (茶道の) the main guest (at a tea ceremony).

しょうきゃく　消却 名 ［消去］(a) deletion; ［消費］consumption; ［返済］(a) repayment.
── 消却する動 ●名前をリストから消却する delete a name *from* the list. ●財産を消却する run one's fortune *through*.

しょうきゃく　焼却 名 incineration /ɪnsɪnəréɪʃən/.
── 焼却する動 burn ... up;《やや書》incinerate.
●焼却場 (ごみの) an incineration plant; garbage incineration facilities. ●焼却炉 (ごみの) an in-cinerator.

しょうきゃく　償却 名 (a) repayment; (公債などの) 《書》redemption, an amortization (⇨償還); (貸し倒れ償却, 全額減価償却) a write-off. ●減価償却 《やや書》depreciation. ●不良債権の償却 a *write-off* of bad debts.
── 償却する動 (債権・公社債などを) amortize; (不良債権などを) write [charge] ... off; (減価償却する) depreciate.

じょうきゃく　上客 (正客) a guest of honor; (大事な顧客) a good [a valued] customer.

じょうきゃく　乗客 a passenger; (乗客から見た他の客) a fellow passenger. ▶その飛行機の乗客の中に日本人はいなかった There were no Japanese among the *passengers* on the plane [the plane *pas-sengers*].
●乗客係 a passenger agent [clerk]. ●乗客席 a passenger seat. ●乗客名簿 a passenger list.

じょうきゃく　常客 a regular customer.

しょうきゅう　昇級 (a) promotion. (⇨昇進)

しょうきゅう　昇給 名 a pay [a wage] raise [《英》rise] (単に a raise, a rise ともいう); a raise [《英》a rise] in (one's) pay [salary]. (⇨給料) ●定期昇給 a periodic [a regular, 《年に 1 度の》a set annual] *pay raise*. ▶組合は月額 1 万円の昇給を要求している The union has asked for a *wage raise* [*increase*] of 10,000 yen a month.
── 昇給する動 ▶今年 4 パーセント昇給した This year I *got* a four percent *raise in* (my) *pay*./This year I had my four percent *raised*.
●昇給率 the rate of pay raise.

じょうきゅう　上級 名 a high(er) rank [level], an upper grade.
── 上級の形 higher; ［水準が］advanced; ［階級が］superior. ▶彼は私より 2 年上級です He is two years *senior to* me [*ahead of* me] at school.
●上級課程 an advanced course. ●上級公務員 (高官) a high-ranking [a high] official. ●上級将校 a high-ranking officer. ●上級生《米》an upperclassman,《英》a senior (pupil, student) (《米》では大学・高校の最上級生をさす).

しょうきょ　消去 名 ［書いたもの・録音したものを消すこと］《やや書》(a) deletion,《書》erasure; ［除去］(an) elimination. ●消去法 by elimination.
── 消去する動《やや書》delete,《書》erase; (やや書) elíminàte.

しょうきょう　商況 business (conditions). (⇨景気) ●商況は活発［不振］だ Business [The *market*] is brisk [dull].

＊しょうぎょう　商業 ［工業に対する］(商品・サービスの売買) commerce (銀行・保険業など関連するすべての商活動も含む); (主に商品売買) trade; ［一般に営利を目的とした特定の商活動］business. ●商業道徳の低下 a decline in business morality. ●商業に従事している［する］be engaged [engage] in *commerce* [*trade*, *business*]. ▶スポーツはあまりにも商業化されてしまった Sport *has become* too *commercialized*. ▶携帯電話は 1980 年代後半に日本で初めて商業化された The cell phone was commercialized in Japan in the late 80's. (仏「初めて」(for the first time) は文脈からあるので, 英文ではで示さなくてもよい)
●商業英語 business English. ●商業界 the business [commercial] world; the world of business [commerce]. ●商業高校 a commercial high school; a commerce high school. ●商業主義 commercialism. ●商業地区 a commercial district. ●商業通信(文) 《総称》business corre-spondence; (手紙) a business letter. ●商業手形

(a) commercial paper [bill]; (a) mercantile paper [bill]. ●**商業デザイン** a commercial design. ●**商業都市** a commercial city. ●**商業放送** (民間放送) commercial broadcasting.

じょうきょう 状況 (物事の状態) a state (常に単数形で); (一時的な) (a) condition; (置かれた立場) a situation; (周囲の状況) circumstances. (⇨状態)
● このような状況にあっては in a *state of affairs* like this; in [under] these *circumstances*. ● 危機的状況にある be in a critical *condition*; be at a crisis. ● 日本の現在の財政状況 the present financial situation of Japan. ● いかなる状況でも in [under] any *circumstances*. ▶彼は状況を把握してすばやく行動した He sized up the *situation* and took (×a) quick action. ▶状況が好転［悪化］した The *situation* improved [got worse, 《やや書》deteriorated]. ▶その時の状況が一番最善そうった Under the *circumstances*, it was the best thing to do.
● **状況証拠** 〖法律〗circumstantial evidence.
● **状況判断** circumstantial judgment.

じょうきょう 上京 ─ **上京する 動** go [come] (《英》up) to Tokyo. (**!** up to Tokyo は《米》では東京へ向けて北上することをさす(⇨行く)) ▶上京している be in Tokyo.

*****しょうきょく 消極** ─ **消極的な 形** 〖否定的な, 積極性を欠いた〗negative (↔positive); 〖受け身の, 活発でない〗passive (↔active). ▶その計画に消極的である(= 不賛成である) be *negative* about the plan. ●消極的な(=言うだけの)忠告 *negative* advice. ▶彼女は何事にも消極的な態度だった She took a *passive* attitude about everything. ▶彼は消極的な気質だ He has [is of] a *passive* disposition./He has a *negative* personality [is a *negative* person]./ (内向的な人だ) He is an introvert (↔an extrovert).

しょうきょく 小曲 a short piece of music.

しょうきん 賞金 prize money, a prize. ●**賞金を出す［かける］** offer a *prize* (*for*). ▶だれがゴルフで1,000万の賞金を獲得するのだろうか Who will win a *prize* of ten million yen for golf?
● **賞金王** a top [leading] prizewinner. ●**賞金獲得者** a prizewinner.

じょうきん 常勤 ─ **常勤の 形** full-time. (↔part-time) ●**常勤の仕事** a full-time job. ●**常勤で働く** work *full-time*.

じょうく 冗句 (むだな句) a redundant phrase; (冗談) a joke.

じょうくう 上空 〖空〗the sky, the skies. (⇨空) ▶はるか上空に far [way] up in *the sky*. ▶水戸上空を飛ぶ fly *over* Mito. ●3,000 メートルの上空(=高度)で at an *altitude* [a *height*] of 3,000 meters. ▶その UFO は千葉市の上空で観測された The UFO was sighted *over* Chiba City.

しょうぐん 将軍 a general; 〖幕府の〗a shogun. ●**乃木将軍** *General* Nogi. ●**冬将軍** 'General Winter'; Jack Frost.

じょうげ 上下 图 (物・数値などの移動) the rise and fall (*of*, *in*). ●**金価格の上下**(=変動) *fluctuations* in the prices of gold. ●**背広上下** a (two-piece) suit. ●**上下2巻の辞書** a dictionary in [×of] two volumes. ▶彼は絵を上下逆さまに持っている He holds a picture *upside down*. ▶そこには上下(=身分)の別なく多くの人が集まった A lot of people came there, regardless of *rank*. ▶軍隊には階級的な上下関係が守られている The army observes a hierarchy of *superior-inferior* relationships.
─ **上下の 形** up and down (**!** 方向以外に, 交通機関の上り下りに用いるのは《英》); (垂直方向の) vertical.
─ **上下に 副** up and down; vertically. ▶地震で家が上下に揺れたのを感じた I felt the house shake [jolt] *up and down* in the earthquake. ▶船[飛行機]が上下に揺れた Our ship [plane] *pitched*. (**!**「左右に揺れる」は roll)
─ **上下する 動** rise* and fall*, go* up and down. (**!** 後の方が口語的) ▶彼女の熱は38度を上下していた Her temperature *rose and fell* [*went up and down*] around 38 degrees centigrade.
> 翻訳のこころ 高瀬舟は京都の高瀬川を上下する小舟である (森鴎外『高瀬舟』) *Takasebune* is a small boat which goes up and down River *Takasegawa* in Kyoto. (**!**「(船が)上下する」は go [×do] up and down)
● **上下動** the heave.

しょうけい 小計 图 a subtotal. ─ **小計する 動** subtotal.

しょうけい 承継 succession. (⇨継承)

*****しょうけい 情景** 〖光景, 場面〗a scene; 〖眺め〗a sight. ▶のどかな情景 an idyllic *scene*.

しょうけい 上掲 ●**上掲の写真[表]** the *above* photograph [chart].

しょうけいもじ 象形文字 (古代エジプトの) a hieroglyph /háiəraglif/; a hieroglyphic (character); (中国・日本の) a pictograph.

しょうげき 衝撃 〖物理的, 精神的〗(a) shock; 〖物体間の衝突, 強い効果〗(an) impact. ●**衝撃を与える** shock, give 《him》a *shock*; have [make] an *impact* (*on*). ●**爆発の衝撃で** by the *shock* [under the *impact*] of the explosion. ▶そのニュースを聞いて我々は大きな衝撃を受けた We were greatly *shocked* to hear [*at*] the news./The news gave us a great *shock* [×a great shock to us]./The news came as a great *shock* to us.
─ **衝撃的な 形** shocking. ●**衝撃的な出来事** a *shocking* accident.
● **衝撃波** a shock wave.

しょうげき 笑劇 a farce.

しょうけつ 猖獗 ▶校内で流感が猖獗をきわめていた A flu epidemic *was raging* through the school.

しょうけん 正絹 pure silk.

しょうけん 商圏 a trading area.

しょうけん 商権 commercial rights.

しょうけん 証券 〖有価証券〗securities; 〖証書, 手形〗a bill; 〖債券, 社債〗a bond. ●**有価証券** (negotiable) *securities*.
● **証券会社** a securities company. ●**証券業務** securities business [activities]. ●**証券市場** a securities market. ●**証券取引** securities trading. ●**証券取引委員会**《米》the Securities and Exchanges Commission《略 SEC》. ●**証券取引所** a stock exchange.

しょうげん 証言 图 (a) testimony. ●**法廷で彼に不利な証言をする** *testify* [*witness*] against (↔for, on behalf of) him in court.
─ **証言する 動** testify 《*to*; *that* 節》, give* testimony 《*that* 節》; witness 《書》bear* witness 《*to*》. ▶彼女は容疑者が家に入るのを見たと証言した She *testified that* she had seen the suspect enter the house./She *witnessed* to having seen the suspect enter the house.

しょうげん 象限 〖数学〗a quadrant.

*****じょうけん 条件** a condition; 〖支払い・契約などの〗terms; 〖資格などの必要条件〗a requirement 《*for*》(**!** しばしば複数形で); 〖前提条件〗a precondition 《*of*》《書》a prerequisite 《*of*, *for*》.

じょうげん

①【～条件】
- 絶対条件 an absolute *condition*.
- 支払い条件 the *condition* [*terms*] of payment.
- 世界平和の第一条件 the first *condition* for world peace.
- 必要十分条件 a necessary and sufficient *condition* 《*for*》.
- 成功の前提条件は a *prerequisite* for [*of*] success.
- 人質解放の交換条件 the *terms* for release of the hostages.
- 金は必ずしも幸福になるための条件ではない Money is not necessarily a *condition* of happiness.

②【条件(の)～】
- (労働)条件のいい仕事 a job with good working *conditions*.
- 彼はそれを条件付きで承認した He approved of it *on* certain *conditions* [*conditionally*]. (！後の方が堅い言い方)/《やや堅》He gave a *conditional* approval of it.

③【条件を[に]】
- 条件を提示する offer the *terms and condtions*.
- 条件に恵まれる be blessed with good *conditions*.
- この条件に合う[を満たす]人ならだれでも採用しよう We'll employ anyone who meets these *conditions* [*requirements*].
- 樹木は気候条件によっていろいろな高さになる The trees may reach various heights depending upon climatic *conditions*.
- 彼は我々が彼の事業に 25 パーセント出資するという条件をつけた[出した; 受け入れた] He made it [proposed; accepted] a *condition that* we make 25 percent invest in his business enterprise.

④【条件で】
- よい条件で雇われる be employed on favorable *conditions* [*terms*].
- 彼は給料の前払いという条件でその仕事を引き受けた He took the job *on condition* (*that*) [*provided* (*that*)] he got paid in advance. (！いずれも (only) if より堅い言い方)

- 条件検索 a conditional search. ● 条件節【文法】a conditional clause. ● 条件闘争 a compromise in a labor dispute to settle it. ● 条件反射【心理】a conditioned reflex [*response*] 《*to*》.

じょうげん 上弦
- 上弦の月 a waxing (↔waning) moon; the moon at the first quarter.

じょうげん 上限 the upper limit; (最大限) maximum; (法令による賃金・料金・物価などの) a ceiling.
- 原油生産量の上限を決める put [set] a *ceiling* on oil production.

しょうこ 証拠 (Xan) evidence 《*of, for; to do; that* 節》; proof 《*of; that* 節》.

> **使い分け** evidence 何かを信じるだけの理由になり得るもの.
> proof 何かが正しいことをはっきり証明するもの. 具体的な証拠の品・事実をいうときは a piece [a bit, a scrap] of *evidence*, a proof (働 ~s).

①【～証拠, 証拠～】
- 状況[物的]証拠 circumstantial [physical, tangible] *evidence*. (！material evidence は「(判決を左右するような)重要な証拠」) ● 有力な[確かな]証拠 strong [reliable, convincing] *evidence*. ● 直接[伝聞]証拠 direct [hearsay] *evidence*. ● 証拠立てる verify.
- 彼は証拠不十分で釈放された He was released on insufficient *evidence* [for lack of *evidence*].

②【証拠が[は]】
- 証拠が見つかった (a piece of) *evidence* was found.
- 彼が無実だという証拠がありますか Is there any *evidence* [*proof*] *that* he is innocent?/Do you have any *evidence* [*proof*] *of* his innocence?/(証明できますか) Can you *prove that* he is innocent [*prove him* (*to be*) innocent]? (！that 節か of 句が)
- 彼の陳述を信じるに足る十分な証拠がありますか Do you have enough *evidence to* believe his statement?
- 証拠がないのだから彼をどうすることもできない In the absence of *evidence* [*proof*], you can't do anything to him. (！Without any *evidence* [*proof*], ... ともいえる)
- その証拠は彼に有利[不利]だ The *evidence* is in his favor [is against him].

③【証拠に】
- 証拠に基づいて訴訟を裁く judge a case on the *evidence*.
- その証拠に彼は来なかった As *proof of* it, he didn't come. (！×As its proof, ...とはしない)

④【証拠を】
- 証拠を固める(＝集める) gather [collect] *evidence*.
- 証拠を隠滅する destroy the *evidence* 《*of*》.
- 証拠を残す leave *evidence* behind.
- 決定的な証拠を提出する give [produce] conclusive *evidence*.
- 私は動かぬ証拠をつかんだ I obtained hard [(反証の余地のない) indisputable] *evidence*.
- 少しでも証拠を見せてくれれば君の言うことを信じよう Show me *a scrap of evidence* [*proof*] and I'll believe you.

⑤【証拠だ】
- 彼の顔がこわばっているのは緊張している証拠だ His stiff look *is the proof* [(示している) *shows*] *that* he is tense.

● 証拠隠滅 destruction of evidence. ● 証拠金 margin requirement. ● 証拠写真 a picture for evidence. ● 証拠書類 documentary evidence. ● 証拠調べ the taking of evidence. ● 証拠能力 admissibility of evidence. ● 証拠品 an article [item] of evidence.

しょうこ 礁湖 a lagoon.

しょうこ 正午 noon; (12 時(ごろ)) midday.
- 彼は正午に家を出た He left home at noon [*midday*].

じょうこ 上古 ancient times.
- 上古史 an ancient history.

じょうご 上戸 a (heavy) drinker. ● 笑い[泣き]上戸 a merry [a maudlin] drinker.

じょうご 漏斗 a funnel.

しょうこう 小康 a lull /lʌl/.
会話「先生, 彼の病状はいかがでしょうか」「今のところ小康を保っています(＝悪くなっていない)」"How is he, doctor?" "He's *holding* his *own* now." (！決まり文句)

しょうこう 昇降 图 ascent and descent; rise and fall.
— 昇降する 動 go up and down; ascend and descend; rise and fall.
● 昇降機 an elevator. (⇨エレベーター) ● 昇降口 an entrance; [船の] a hatch(way). ● 昇降舵(だ) (飛行機の) an elevator.

しょうこう 将校 an officer, (正式には) a commissioned officer. ● 陸軍[海軍]将校 a military [a naval] *officer*. ⇨軍人.

しょうこう 症候 a symptom. (⇨兆候) ● 症候群 a syndrome. (⇨症候群)

しょうこう 商港 a commercial [a mercantile] port.

しょうこう 焼香 — 焼香する 動 (香をささげる) offer [(焼く) burn] incense /ínsens/.

しょうごう 称号 (肩書き) a title; (学位) a degree.
- 女王は彼に貴族の称号を与えた The queen conferred a noble *title* on [×to] him.

しょうごう 商号 a trade name. ● 商号を登記する register one's *trade name*.

しょうごう 照合 图 a check.
— 照合する 動 写しを原本と綿密に照合する *check* a copy carefully [thoroughly] *against* the original.

じょうこう 上皇 a retired emperor; an ex-emperor.

じょうこう 条項 (条約・法律・契約などの) a clause; a provision; a stipulation. ● 契約条項 a contract

じょうこう *clause.* ● 罰則条項 a penalty *clause.* ● この契約書の中の二つの条項を削除する eliminate [remove, get rid of] two *clauses* in this contract.

じょうこう 情交 (sexual) intercourse. ● 情交を結ぶ have (sexual) intercourse 《*with*》.

しょうこうかいぎしょ 商工会議所 the 《Japan》 Chamber of Commerce and Industry (⚠ その会頭は chairman); (米国の) the Chamber of Commerce of the United States.

じょうこうきゃく 乗降客 passengers getting on and off (the train).

しょうこうぎょう 商工業 ● 日本の商工業 the Japanese *commerce and industry*; the *commerce and (the) industry* of Japan. (⚠ 複数扱い) ● 商工業の中心地 a *commercial and industrial* center.

しょうこうぐん 症候群 a syndrome. (⚠ 病名には Ⓤ)

しょうこうし 小公子 a little prince.

しょうこうねつ 猩紅熱 〖医学〗 scarlet fever; scarlatina.

しょうこく 小国 (小さい国) a small country; (弱小国) a minor country. (⇔ 大国)

しょうこく 生国 one's native country; the land of one's birth.

じょうこく 上告 图 〖法律〗 (an) appeal (to a higher court).
— 上告する 動 ● 最高裁に上告する *appeal to* the Supreme Court.
● 上告審 〖法律〗 an appellate trial.

しょうこと ● しょうことなしに (仕方なく) as there is no other (good) way 《*to do*; *of doing*》.

しょうこり 性懲り ● 性懲りもなく (過去の重なる失敗から何も学ばずに) without learning anything from one's failures; incorrigibly. (⇔懲りる)

しょうこん 商魂 (商売のセンス) business sense; (営利主義) commercialism. ▶ 商魂たくましい男だ He has a good [a shrewd] *business sense*./(もうけ一辺倒だ) He is bent on gain [is very commercial].

しょうさ 小差 a narrow margin. (⇔僅差)

しょうさ 少佐 〖海軍〗 a liutenant commander; 〖陸軍・米空軍〗 a major; 〖英空軍〗 a squadron leader.

しょうさ 証左 evidence; proof. (⇔即 証拠)

しょうさい 商才 ● あの男はなかなか商才がある The man has a good *head for business*./The man has considerable *business* [*commercial*] *acumen* /əkjúːmən/.

しょうさい 詳細 图 details /díːteilz, ditéilz/; particulars. ▶ 彼はその事故の詳細を話した He gave (all) the *details* [*particulars*] of the accident./He went into *detail(s)* about the accident. ▶ 詳細は追ってお知らせします I will let you know further [×farther] information later.
— 詳細な 形 detailed; (一部始終の) full; (過度に綿密な) minute /main(j)úːt/. ● 詳細な説明 a *detailed* [a *full*] account 《*of*》. ● 詳細な記述 a *minute* description.
— 詳細に 副 in detail; minutely; (長々と) at (full) length. ● もっと詳細に *in more detail*. ▶ 彼はその計画を詳細に説明した He explained the plan *in detail* [gave a *detailed* explanation of the plan].

じょうさい 城砦 a fort, a fortress.

じょうざい 浄財 (寄付金) a donation.

じょうざい 錠剤 a tablet; 〖丸薬〗 a pill. ● 錠剤を飲む take [×drink] *tablets* [*pills*].

じょうさく 上策 the best plan [idea, policy, way].

じょうさし 状差し a letter rack.

しょうさつ 笑殺 — 笑殺する 動 (一笑に付す) laugh ... off. ▶ ジョンに飲みすぎだよと言ったが、彼は笑殺した I told John he was drinking too much, but he just *laughed* it *off*.

しょうさっし 小冊子 〖パンフレット〗 a brochure /brouʃúər/, a pamphlet; 〖通例紙表紙の〗 a booklet.

しょうさん 消散 — 消散する 動 (消えてなくなる) vanish; (蒸発する) evaporate; (雲・霧が) lift.

しょうさん 勝算 〖勝利・成功の見込み〗 a chance of winning. ▶ この試合には勝算が十分ある We have a good [a fair] *chance of* winning this game. ▶ 我々に勝算がある[ない] The chances [*odds*] are in our favor [against us].

しょうさん 硝酸 〖化学〗 nitric /náitrik/ acid.
● 硝酸アンモニウム ammonium nitrate. ● 硝酸塩 nitrate. ● 硝酸カリウム potassium nitrate. ● 硝酸銀 silver nitrate.

しょうさん 賞賛 图 (ほめること) praise; 〖感嘆〗 admiration; 〖拍手かっさい〗 applause. ● 賞賛の目で見る give 《him》 an *admiring* look [×give an admiring look to 《him》]. ▶ 彼の行為は大いに賞賛に値する His conduct deserves [is worthy of] *great praise*. ▶ 彼は級友の賞賛の的である He is the *admiration* of his classmates. ▶ 彼の小説は賞賛を博した His novel won [received] *high praise*./He won [received] *high praise for* his novel./He was highly praised for his novel.
— 賞賛する 動 praise; admire; speak* highly of .... (⇒褒める) ● 彼の作品を賞賛する *praise* his work. ● 賞賛すべき praiseworthy; admirable. ● 彼の故郷を賞賛する(=たたえる)詩 a poem *in praise of* his hometown. ▶ だれもが彼の勇気を賞賛した Everyone *praised* [*admired*] his courage [him *for* his courage]. (⚠ × ... praised [admired] *that* he was courageous. は不可)
● 賞賛者 an admirer 《*of*》.

しょうし 小史 a short history.

しょうし 小誌 one's (little) magazine [journal].

しょうし 少子
🟥 **DISCOURSE** 🟥
少子化の一因として、グローバル競争で何とかやっていくために必要な教育を子供に与えるには多額のお金が必要だとの思いがある Many couples today tend to raise fewer children **because** they understand that it costs a lot of money to give the proper education for them to survive in the competitive global society. (⚠ because (of)... (なぜなら..., ...のため)は理由に用いるディスコースマーカー)

● 少子化・男女共同参画担当大臣 the Minister of State for Gender Equality and Social Affair.
● 少子高齢化社会 an aging society with a low birthrate. ● 少子社会 a society where fewer babies are born; (低出生率社会) a low-birthrate society; (少子化社会) a declining birth society.

しょうし 焼止 ● 笑止千万 extremely ridiculous [absurd]; ludicrous.

しょうし 焼死 death by fire.
— 焼死する 動 (焼け死ぬ) be burned to death; (火事で命を落とす) lose one's life [be killed, die] in a fire.
● 焼死体 (黒焦げになった) a charred body.

しょうし 証紙 a certificate stamp.

しょうじ 障子 a *shoji*; (一般的に) a set of light-weight sliding doors made of wooden framework covered with thin paper that allows light to pass through. (cf. 襖) ● 障子を開ける

しょうじ
slide the *shoji* open.
- 障子に目(あり) We may be overseen without our knowing it.
- 障子紙 (a sheet of) *shoji* paper.

しょうじ 小事 a trifle; a trivial matter. ・小事にこだわらない do not worry about *trifles*.
- 小事は大事 Take care of the pence, and the pounds will take care of themselves.

しょうじ 正時 ▶バスは毎正時に発車している Buses leave every hour *on the hour*.

じょうし 上司 (直属の) one's boss (!最も一般的な語. 男女の区別なく用いることができる), one's senior, 《書》one's superior; (大組織での)《書》one's supervisor; (⇨部下) ▶彼[彼女]は私より若いが私の上司 He [She] is my *boss* [is *senior to* me, is my *senior*], though he [she] is younger.

じょうし 上肢 the arms; the upper limbs; (動物の前足) the foreleg; the front legs.

じょうし 上梓 — 上梓する publish (a book).

じょうし 城址, 城趾 (廃墟) the ruins [(城のあった場所) site] of a castle.

じょうし 情死 a lover's suicide.

じょうじ 常時 always. (⇨いつも) ・インターネットの常時接続 (a) 24(-)hour internet connection.

じょうじ 情事 (have) a love affair (*with*).

じょうじいれる 招じ入れる invite (him) in.

しょうしか 少子化 (⇨少子)

しょうじがいしゃ 商事会社 a commercial [a business] company. (⇨商社)

＊しょうじき 正直 图 honesty /ánisti/; truthfulness; frankness. ▶三度目の正直 (ことわざ) Third time lucky.
- 正直の頭に神宿る God protects honest people.
—— 正直な 形 (偽りのない) honest /ánist/ (↔dishonest); (うそをいわない) truthful (!前の方は率直・誠実でうそや偽りのないことを強調するのに対し、後の方はうそを言わない点を強調する); (隠し立てせずに) straight. ・正直な人 an *honest* [a *truthful*] person. ▶私の作品について正直な意見を言ってほしい I want your *honest* opinion of my work.
会話 「だけど彼はそれが必要なんだって言ってるよ」「そうね、でも honestlyところ彼にそれが必要なの?」"Well, he says he needs it." "Yes, but ˋdoes he, *in all honesty*?"
—— 正直に 副 honestly; truthfully; straight. ▶「それは知りません」と彼女は正直に答えた "I don't know about it," she answered *honestly*. ▶正直に言って彼は信頼できない *Honestly* (*speaking*) [*To be honest* (with you)], I can't trust him. (!相手に不都合・不愉快なことをいうときの前置き表現) ▶正直に本当の事を言いなさい Be *honest* and tell me the truth. (!Tell me the truth honestly. より普通) ▶よく正直にそう言ってくれました It was *honest* of [×for] you to say so./You were *honest* to say so.
会話 「私も、他の人が好きになってしまったの. 彼にどう言えばいいのか分からなくて」「(隠さず)正直に言う方がいいと思うわ」"I've fallen in love with somebody else and I don't know how to tell my boyfriend." "I think you should tell him *straight* [(話) *level with* him]."

＊じょうしき 常識 图 (生活体験から得た思慮分別) common sense, (良識) sense; (だれもが知っていること) common knowledge; (世間一般の知識) general knowledge. ・常識を働かせる use [(書) exercise] (one's) *common sense*. ・常識を身につける acquire *common sense*; increase one's *general knowledge*. ▶彼は常識がある He has (×a) *common* *sense*./He is a man of *common sense* [(分別がある) a *sensible* man]. (⇨非常識) ▶彼は常識をまったく欠いている He has no [doesn't have any] *common sense*. ▶そんなふるまいは常識外れである It is *senseless* to behave like that.
会話 「私たち夜明け前に出発するわよ」「少しは常識をわきまえなさいよ」"We'll leave before dawn." "Have a bit of *sense*./Where's your *common sense*?"
会話 「電話料金は深夜は安いのね」「知らなかったの? そんなの常識よ」"The telephone rates are lower at late night." "Didn't you know? That's *common knowledge* [×common sense]./(だれもが知っていることだ) That's what everyone knows."
—— 常識的な 形 ・常識的な解釈 a *commonsense* [(普通の) an *ordinary*] interpretation. ・常識的な(=平凡な)言葉 a *commonplace* remark.
- 常識テスト a general knowledge test.

じょうしき 定式 a formula.
- 定式幕 tableau curtains used in a *Kabuki* stage.

しょうしげん 省資源 resources saving.

しょうしつ 消失 —— 消失する 動 disappear; vanish.

しょうしつ 焼失 图 ・焼失を免れる escape [×escape from] the *fire*.
—— 焼失する 動 burn down, be burned [(英) be burnt] down; be destroyed by (a) fire. ・焼失した工場 a *burnt-out* factory. (!形容詞的限定用法では (米)(英) とも burnt が普通) ▶その大火で多くの家が焼失した A lot of houses *burned down* [*were burned down*] in the big fire.

じょうしつ 上質 fine [good, high] quality.
- 上質紙 paper of fine quality.

じょうじつ 情実 (個人的な配慮) private [personal] considerations; (えこひいき)《やや書》favoritism.
- 情実にとらわれる be influenced [swayed] by *personal considerations*. ・情実で昇進する be promoted through *favoritism*.

しょうしみん 小市民 a petit bourgeois (復 petits ～); (階級) the petite bourgeoisie; the lower middle class.

しょうしゃ 小社 one's small company [office].

しょうしゃ 商社 a commercial [a business, (貿易の) a trading] company. ・総合商社 a *sogoshosha*; a general *trading company*.

しょうしゃ 勝者 〖試合の〗a winner; 〖戦争の〗a conqueror, 《書》a victor.

しょうしゃ 照射 (放射線の) irradiation.
—— 照射する 動 irradiate. ・X 線を照射する apply X-rays (*to*).

しょうしゃ 瀟洒 —— 瀟洒な 形 elegant; (さっぱりした) neat. ・瀟洒な家 an *elegant* house.

＊じょうしゃ 乗車 图 ・乗車を拒否される[する] refuse [be refused] a *ride*. ・(発車のときに)みなさん(急いで)ご乗車ください All aboard!
—— 乗車する 動 get* on [(乗って行く) take*] (a train [a bus]); get in (a car). (⇨乗る ❶) ・タクシーに乗車する *get in* [*into*, ×on] a taxi. (!into では乗り込む動作が強調される)
- 乗車券 a (train [railroad]) ticket. ・乗車券売場 a ticket window;《英》a booking office.
- 乗車賃 (バス・電車などの) a fare. ・乗車ホーム a boarding platform.

じょうしゃひっすい 盛者必衰 What gets up must come down.

しょうじゃひつめつ 生者必滅 All living things must die.

じょうしゅ 城主 the lord of a castle; a castellan.

じょうしゅ 情趣 ●情趣に富んだ(=趣のある)庭 a tasteful garden. (⇨処世, 風情(ふぜい).)

じょうじゅ 成就 〘達成〙achievement; 〘完成〙accomplishment; 〘実現〙realization.

—— **成就する 動** achieve; accomplish; realize. (⇨成し遂げる) ▶ついに大願が成就した (⇨大願)

しょうしゅう 召集 图 〘集合命令〙a call 《to》; 〘議会などの〙a summons (複 ~es); 〘軍隊などの〙mobilization.

—— **召集する 動** (国会を) call [summon, convene] (the Diet); (軍隊などを) mobilize (the army).
●**召集令状** (米) a draft card; (英) one's call-up papers.

しょうしゅう 招集 —— **招集する 動** (会を) call 《a meeting》; (会議・人を) 〘書〙summon, convene.
▶市議会はその問題の協議のために招集された The city council was called to discuss the matter.

しょうしゅう 消臭 —— **消臭する 動** get rid of [(抑える) reduce, (隠す) hide] a bad smell.
●**消臭剤** a (room) deodorizer.

しょうじゅう 小銃 a rifle; 〘小銃類〙small arms, firearms. (!いずれも複数扱い) ●自動小銃 an automatic rifle.
●**小銃弾** a bullet.

じょうしゅう 常習 habitualness.

—— **常習的な 形** (癖による) habitual; (凝り固まった) confirmed. ●麻薬常習者 a habitual drug-user; a drug addict. ●賭博(とばく)の常習者 a chronic gambler.
●**常習犯** a habitual [a confirmed] criminal.
▶彼は会に遅刻してくる常習犯だ(=常習的に遅刻する) He is habitually [(いつも) always] late for our meetings. (!後の方が普通)

じょうじゅう 常住 ●**常住坐臥**(ざが) (いつも) always, all the time.

しょうしゅうかん 商習慣 a business practice.

しょうじゅつ 詳述 —— **詳述する 動** ●その事件の様子を詳述する explain the event in detail [fully]; give a detailed [a full] explanation of the event.

じょうじゅつ 上述 ●上述の問題 the problem above mentioned; 〘書〙the above-mentioned problem; 〘書〙the said problem. ●上述のごとく as stated [mentioned] above.

じょうしゅび 上首尾 图 a great [a huge, a big] success. ▶彼の映画は上首尾だった His film was a great success. —— **上首尾の 形** successful.

しょうじゅん 照準 (銃などの) a sight (!前後にある照準器を表してしばしば複数形で); (ねらい) aim. ●…に照準を合わせる set one's sights on …, have … in one's sight; (ねらう) take aim at …, aim at …

じょうじゅん 上旬 the beginning of the month; (説明的に) the first ten days of the month. (!英語では上旬・中旬・下旬の区分をせず、前のように漠然と表す) ●来月 [1 月] 上旬に at the beginning of next month [January]; early next month [in January]. (!early in next month, ×early the next month としない)

しょうしょ 証書 〘債券の〙a bond; 〘署名なつ印した権利証書〙〘法律〙a deed; 〘文書〙a document; 〘学位を伴わない〙修業証明書〙a certificate. ●卒業証書 a diplóma. (⇨卒業) ●信託証書 a trust deed. ●証書を作成する draw up [write out] a deed.

しょうしょ 詔書 an Imperial edit [rescript].

***しょうじょ 少女** a girl. (!通例 7-12 歳くらいまでの女の子をさすが,〘話〙では日本語と異なり一般に女性の意で用いる) ●少女らしい girlish. ▶彼女は少女時代にとてもかわいかった She was very pretty [cute] when she was a (little) girl [in her girlhood]. (!

when 節で表した前の方が口語的)
●**少女趣味** girlish tastes. ●**少女小説** a story for young girls. ●**少女マンガ** a comic for young girls.

じょうしょ 浄書 a clean copy. (⇨⓵ 清書)

しょうしょう 少々 a little; a few. (⇨少し)

しょうしょう 少将 〘陸軍・米空軍〙a major general; 〘海軍〙a rear admiral; 〘英空軍〙an air vice-marshal.

しょうじょう 症状 〘徴候〙a symptom; 〘病状〙the condition of a patient [a disease]. ●自覚症状 a subjective symptom. ●はしかの症状を呈する[ある] show [have] symptoms of measles. ▶糖尿病の予備軍のときには自覚症状がない In the early stages of diabetes, the patients don't notice any symptoms themselves. ▶風邪の症状あり。頭痛, 体の痛み, 熱はなし Has cold symptoms—headache, sore throat—but not fever. (!医師の診断書に書く文句)

しょうじょう 猩猩 (オランウータン) 〘動物〙an orangutan.

しょうじょう 賞状 a certificate of merit. ▶彼女は勇気をたたえられて賞状をもらった She was given [awarded] a certificate of merit for (her) bravery.

***じょうしょう 上昇 图** 〘物価などの〙a rise (↔a fall); 〘昇ること〙〘書〙an ascent (↔a descent). ●温度の上昇 a rise in temperature. ●3 パーセントの物価上昇 a three percent price rise. ●気球の上昇 the ascent of a balloon. ●物価の上昇傾向 the upward trend in [of] prices; the upward price trend. ●急上昇 a rapid [a sharp, a steep, a drastic, a strong] rise; a surge.

—— **上昇する 動** rise*, go* up (後の方が口語的); 〘書〙ascend; (急に上がる) shoot* up. (⇨上がる) ●人気が上昇中 a rise in popularity. ▶物価は上昇している Prices are rising [are on the rise, are going up]. ▶飛行機は上昇して雲の中に入った The plane ascended into the clouds.
●**上昇気流** an ascending air current; 〘気象〙a thermal.

じょうしょう 常勝 ●常勝チーム an invincible [an unbeaten] team. ●常勝のチャンピオン an unbeaten [an undefeated] champion.

じょうじょう 上々 excellent; (最高の) the (very) best; 〘商業〙〘極上の〙superfine. ▶結果は上々(=大成功)だった The result was a great success.
●**上々吉** the very best fortune; the very best luck.

じょうじょう 上場 图 listing. ●東証上場 the listing on the Tokyo Stock Exchange. ▶これらの会社は上場を廃止しようとしている These companies are in the process of delisting.

—— **上場する 動** list (stocks); (会社が) go public. ▶その株式は上場されている The (company) stock is listed.
●**上場会社** a listed company; a public company [《米》corporation]. ●**上場株** listed stocks. ●**上場基準** (initial) listing requirements; the listing standard. ●**上場廃止** delisting.

じょうじょうしゃくりょう 情状酌量 ●彼の罪には情状酌量の余地はない There's no circumstances to be considered [〘書〙no extenuating circumstances] in his offense.

—— **情状酌量する 動** (考慮に入れる) make allowance(s) for circumstances; (罪を軽くする) extenuate.

しょうじょうばえ 猩々蝿 〖昆虫〗a fruit fly; a vinegar fly.

しょうじょうぶっきょう 小乗仏教 the Hinayana /hiːnəjáːnə/ (↔the Mahayana), Hinayána Búddhism. (参考) サンスクリット語で「小さい乗り物」の意.

しょうしょく 小食 ●彼女は小食である(=あまり食べない) She *doesn't eat much*./She *eats a little*./She is a *light eater*./She eats like a bird.

じょうしょく 常食 〖重要な食べ物〗a staple food [diet]; 〖日常の食物〗a daily food. ▶日本人は米を常食にしている Japanese people *live on* (a *diet* of) rice./Rice is the *staple food* [*diet*] of Japanese people.

＊しょうじる 生じる 〖起こる〗(偶然に) happen, occur (-rr-); (起こるべくして) take* place (⇨起こる); 〖問題などが発生する〗arise* (*from*); 〖…の結果として生じる〗result (*from*); 〖引き起こす〗cause; 〖生み出す〗create. ▶事故は彼の不注意から生じた The accident happened [occurred, ×took place] through [×from] his carelessness./The accident *was caused by* [*resulted from, arose from*] his carelessness. ▶戦後日本には大きな変化が生じた Big changes *have taken place* in Japan after the war. ▶彼の話は疑惑[誤解]を生じた His story *created* suspicions [misunderstanding]. ▶どうして貿易不均衡が生じたのですか What *caused* [*brought about*] the trade imbalance?/(原因は何ですか) What is the *cause of* the trade imbalance?

じょうじる 乗じる ❶〖つけ込む〗take* advantage of ...; (...から利益を得る, 利用する) profit from [by] ...; (話) cash in on ...; (機会などを捕える) seize. ▶彼女の無知に［この機に］乗じる *take advantage of* her ignorance [this opportunity]. ●他人の弱味に乗じる *take advantage of* [*profit from*] the weakness of other people.
❷〖掛け算をする〗▶3 に 4 を乗じると 12(=3×4＝12) Three *multiplied by* four is twelve. (⇨掛ける)

しょうしん 小心 图 timidity; (臆病(おくびょう)) cowardice. ●小心翼々(よくよく) ●小心翼々としている very timid; meticulous.
── 小心な 圏 timid; cowardly.
●小心者 a timid [(狭量な) petty-minded] person; a coward.

しょうしん 昇進 图 (a) promotion 《*to*》, 《書》advancement; (地位が上がること) a rise in rank. ▶年功序列による昇進 *promotion* by seniority /síːnjərəti/. ▶課長への昇進 one's *promotion to* section chief. ▶この会社には昇進の見込みがない There are no chances of *promotion* in this firm. ▶彼は昇進が早かった He got [was given] a rapid *promotion*./His promotion was rapid.
── 昇進する 動 be [get*] promoted, get [gain, win*] (a [one's]) promotion, 《やや書》advance; rise* in rank. ▶業績と能力で昇進する *be promoted* [*win a promotion, rise in rank*] by merit and abilities. ▶彼は校長に昇進した He *was promoted to* (the position of) principal. (❗役職名は通例無冠詞)
会話「田中は今部長だよ」「彼ここ 2, 3 年でずいぶん昇進したね」"Tanaka's general manager now." "*Hasn't* he *got on* in the last few years!" (❗応答文は感嘆文の一種で, 下降調で発音)

しょうしん 焼身 ●焼身自殺をする burn oneself to death; suicide by fire.

しょうしん 傷心 〖悲しみ〗《やや書》sorrow; (深い悲しみ) grief; (悲痛な思い) a broken heart. ▶傷心のあまり in *grief* [*deep sorrow*]; heart-brokenly (broken-heartedly ともいう).

しょうじん 小人 a person of little importance [worth]; a nobody; a lightweight.
●小人閑居して不善をなす An idle brain is the devil's workshop. ; The devil finds work for idle hand to do.

しょうじん 精進 图 (献身)《やや書》devotion.
── 精進する 動 devote [apply] oneself (*to*); (肉食をしない) live on a vegetarian diet; 《書》abstain from fish and meat. ●研究に精進する *devote oneself to* one's study.
●精進揚げ deep-fried vegetables. ●精進落ち〔明け〕the end of the period of abstinence. ●精進日 a day of abstinence (from fish and meat). ●精進料理〔菜食〕 a vegetarian diet; vegetarian cooking; (説明的に) vegetarian dishes in which no meat or fish is used: they are prepared mainly for religious reasons.

じょうしん 上申 ── 上申する 動 report 《*to* one's superior official》; submit a report 《*to*》.
●上申書 a (written) report.

じょうしん 上伸 an upturn; an upward turn; a jump; a rise.

じょうじん 常人 an ordinary [a common] person.

しょうしんしょうめい 正真正銘 ●正真正銘の(=本当の)詩人 a *true* [a *real*] poet. ●正真正銘の(=本物の)ピカソの絵 a *genuine* [an *authentic*] Picasso.

‡じょうず 上手 图 〖お世辞〗(a) flattery. (⇨お世辞)
●お上手を言う flatter 《him》; say nice things 《*to* him》.
●上手の手から水がも(れ)る Even Homer sometimes nods.
── 上手な 圏 (巧みな) good* 《*at, in, with*》; (熟練した) skillful 《*at, in, with*》; (専門的知識・技能のある) expert /ékspəːrt/ 《*at, in, on*》(❗叙述用法でも使われ, ×/ikspə́ːrt/ の発音は用いられない); (器用な) clever 《*at, with*》. (⇨うまい❶〖類語〗) ▶彼女はピアノが上手だ She is a *good* pianist./She is *good* [*skillful, skilled,* (an) *expert*] *at* playing the piano./(上手に弾く) She plays the piano (*very*) *well*. (❗最初の例文が最も普通の言い方) ▶あなたは本当に話し[聞き]上手だね You're a *good* talker [listener], indeed. ▶彼女が字が上手だ She has *good* handwriting./She writes *well* (《書》a *good* hand). ▶彼は商売上手だ［言葉の使い方が上手だ］ He is *clever at* business [*with* words].
会話「で, これが明の絵よ」「6 歳の子にしてはけっこう上手だね」"And this is Akira's drawing." "You know it's rather *good,* for a six-year-old."
── 上手に 副 well*; (巧みに) skillfully. ●上手にタイプする type *well*. ●はしを上手に使う use chopsticks *skillfully*. ▶彼は英語を上手に話す He is a *good* speaker of English./He speaks English (*very*) *well*. ▶英語が上手になりたい(=上達したい) I want to *improve* my English. ▶彼は時間を上手に(=有効に)使った He made *good* [(最も有効に) the *best*] *use of* his time.

しょうすい 小水 (小便) urine.

しょうすい 憔悴 ── 憔悴した 圏 (病的にやつれた) haggard; (やせてごつごつした) gaunt. ●憔悴した顔 a *haggard* face [(表情) look]. ▶彼は憔悴した様子だった He looked *haggard*.

じょうすい 浄水 clean water.
●浄水器 a water purifier; (大型の) a water purification system. ●浄水工場 a water filtration [purification] plant.

じょうすいどう 上水道 (給水設備) water-works. (❗

単·複両扱い)

しょうすう 小数 〖数学〗a decimal. ▶小数第3位まで計算せよ Calculate down to the third *decimal* (place) [three *decimal* places]. ▶小数点以下は切り捨てること Discard *decimals* [the numbers below the decimal point]. (❗前の方が普通)
会話「君, 円周率の値(ネェ)を知ってる?」「あの 3.14 なんとかいうやつかい」「小数点何位まで知っている?」 "You know the value of *pi*?" "You mean that 3.14 and what's it [(何やかや) whatnot]?" "How many *decimal places* do you know?"
● 小数位 a decimal place. ● 小数点 a decimal point.

しょうすう 少数 a minority (↔a majority). ▶少数の(少ない数がある) a few; (少ない数の) a small number [small numbers] of .... ▶その場所は少数の地元の人しか知らなかった The place was known only to *a few* local people. ▶彼は少数派だ He is *in the minority* [*in a minority group*]. ▶会の出席者は少数であった A *small number of* people (たった数人しか) Only *a few* (people) were present at the meeting./There was a *small* number of people present at the meeting./There was a *small* attendance at the meeting. / The number of (×the) people present at the meeting was *small*.
● 少数精鋭 the able minority; elitism (❗後の方はしばしば軽蔑的). ● 少数民族 a minority race; an ethnic minority.

しょうすう 乗数 〖数学〗a multiplier.

しょうする 称する ❶〖名乗る〗▶山田と称する男があなたに会いに来ていました A man *called* [*by the name of*] Yamada came to see you./A Mr. Yamada came to see you. (❗後の方が普通)
❷〖言う〗▶彼は自分のことを辞書の専門家と称していた He *represented himself as* an expert on dictionaries. (❗実際はそうでないという含みがある (⇨自称)) ▶彼は病気と称して(=を口実に)学校を休んだ He stayed away from school on [under] the *pretext of* sickness [*that* he was sick].

しょうする 証する (証明する) prove.

しょうせい 小生〖男性が自分をへりくだっていう語〗I.

しょうせい 招請 图 (an) invitation.
── 招請する 動 invite 〈him *to* a conference〉.
● 招請状 a letter of invitation.

しょうせい 勝勢 ▶彼には勝勢があった The odds were in his favor./He gained [got, had] the upper hand./He stood a good [a fair] chance of winning the game.

*じょうせい 情勢 a situation; circumstances (❗ circumstances は人や物事に影響を及ぼす周囲の状況. それの集まったものが situation); 〖事態〗the state of things [affairs]. (⇨状況)〖国際[経済, 政治] 情勢 the international [economic; political] *situation*. ▶現在の情勢では under the present *situation* [*circumstances*, *state of affairs*]. ▶やっかいな〖緊迫した; 微妙な〗情勢にある be in an awkward [a tense; a delicate] *situation*. ▶情勢が(どのように進展するか)を見る see how the *situation* develops. ▶情勢を見て取る〖に対処する〗 take in [meet] the *situation*. ▶情勢に明るい〖暗い〗《話》 be in [out of] the swim. ▶情勢が好転した The *situation* has [*Things* have] improved (↔worsened). ▶それで情勢が一変した That changed the whole *situation*.

じょうせい 上製 ── 上製の 形 superior.
● 上製本 a hardcover; a deluxe edition.

じょうせい 醸成 ── 醸成する 動〖酒などを〗brew (beer); 〖引き起こす〗cause; bring ... about.

しょうせき 硝石 saltpeter /sɔːltpiːtər/.

じょうせき 上席 (⇨〖敬〗上座)

じょうせき 定石 ❶〖囲碁で, 決まった打ち方〗standard moves. ❷〖決まった仕方〗▶定石どおりにする〈話〉do 〈it〉 by the book; (試験済みで信頼できる戦術を使う) use tried and true 《米》[tested 《英》] tactics.

じょうせき 定席 (決まった席) one's regular seat [place].

じょうせき 定跡 〖将棋で, 決まった打ち方〗 standard moves.

*しょうせつ 小説 (長編の) a novel; (物語) a story; (超現実的空想小説) a romance; (架空の話) fiction (❗集合的. 作品一つは a work [a piece] of fiction). ● 空想科学小説 science *fiction* (略 SF). ● 大衆[歴史]小説 a popular [a historical] *novel*. ● 恋愛小説 a romantic *novel*. ● 探偵小説 a detective *story* [*novel*]. ● 短編小説 a short *story*. (❗novel と対比するときは short はしばしば省略する) ● 連載小説 a serial (*story* [*novel*]) 《*in a magazine*》. ● 私小説〖⇨私小説〗● 実際の出来事を小説にする make a *novel* out of a real event. ● 小説を読む read a *novel* [a *story*]. ▶これは三浦綾子の小説です This is a *novel* by [×of] Ayako Miura./This *novel* was written by Ayako Miura. ▶事実は小説より奇なり (⇨事実 [成句])
● 小説家 (小説を書く人) a novelist; (作家, 著述家) a writer.

しょうせつ 小節〖音楽〗a bar, 《やや古》a measure.

しょうせつ 詳説 图 a detailed [a full] explanation 〈*of*〉. ── 詳説する 動 explain in great detail; elaborate 〈*on*〉.

じょうせつ 常設 ── 常設の 形〖永久的な〗permanent; 〖常置の〗standing. ● 映画の常設館 a movie theater.
── 常設する 動 (永久的に設置する) establish ... permanently.
● 常設委員会 a standing committee. (⇨委員会)

じょうぜつ 冗舌 ● 冗舌をろうする talk a lot; (相手がうんざりするまでしゃべる) talk 〈his〉 head 〖《話》 ear〗 off.
── 冗舌な 形 (話好きな) talkative; (多弁な)《書》(軽蔑的に) garrulous /ɡǽrjələs/.

しょうせっかい 消石灰 slaked lime.

しょうせつしんずい『小説神髄』*The Essence of the Novel*. (参考) 坪内逍遙の評論

しょうせん 商船 a merchant ship.
● 商船大学 a mercantile marine college.

しょうせん 商戦 (go into) a sales battle (competition). ▶年末商戦 a year-end *sales battle*. ▶クリスマスシーズンにはデパートが激しい商戦を展開する Department stores *compete* fiercely during the Christmas season.

しょうぜん 悄然 ▶悄然としている (しょんぼりしている) be depressed.

じょうせん 乗船 图 (an) embarkation; boarding.
── 乗船する 動 go* [get*] aboard, go [get] on board; 《やや書》embark (↔disembark). (⇨乗る ❶). ▶フェリーに乗船する go aboard [on board] a ferry; board a ferry; embark in [on] a ferry.
● 乗船券 a boarding card [pass]. ● 乗船港 a port of embarkation.

じょうせん 情宣 information and propaganda.

しょうせんきょく 小選挙区 (1区1人の選挙区) a single-seat constituency [electoral district]; (小さな選挙区) a small constituency [electoral district].

●小選挙区制 the single-seat constituency system.

しょうそ 勝訴 a winning (↔a losing) suit. ▶その裁判は被告の勝訴になった The defendant *won* (↔ lost) *the suit* [*case*]./The case *resulted* [*was decided*] *in favor of* the defendant.

じょうそ 上訴 图 〖法律〗(lodge) an appeal 《to a higher court》.
── **上訴する** 動 appeal 《to》.

しょうそう 少壮 ── 少壮の 形 young. ●少壮気鋭の学者 a spirited *young* scholar.

しょうそう 尚早 ── 尚早の 形 too early; (まだ熟していない) premature /priːmət(j)úər/; unripe. ▶まだ了測するのは時期尚早だ It is still *too early* to do that [tell]. (**!** *too early to tell* は選挙結果などの予測によく使われる)

しょうそう 焦燥 impatience. ●焦燥に駆られる get *impatient* [(落ち着かない) *restless*].
●焦燥感 a feeling of impatience.

しょうぞう 肖像 a portrait /pɔ́ːrtət, -treit/. ▶これは母の[を描いた]肖像です This is a *portrait* [a *picture*] of my mother. (**!** *my mother's portrait* [*picture*] ではこの意のほかに「母が描いた」「母の所有する」の意もある)
●肖像画 a portrait (painting). ●肖像画を描いてもらう have one's *portrait* painted; (ポーズをとる) sit for one's *portrait*. ●肖像画家 a portrait painter. ●肖像権 one's portrait rights.

じょうそう 上層 〖地層などの〗an upper layer; 〖空の〗the upper air; 〖建物の〗the upper stories; 〖階級の〗the upper classes. ●会社の上層部 (集合的) the top leadership of a company.
●上層雲 a high cloud. ●上層気流 〖気象〗an upper-air current.

じょうそう 情操 (a) séntiment; (よい趣味) good taste.
●情操教育 the cultivation of aesthetic, moral, and religious sentiments.

じょうぞう 醸造 ── 醸造する 動 (酒・ビールなどを) brew 《beer》.
●醸造家 a brewer. ●醸造酒 a brew. ●醸造所 (ビールの) a brewery; (ワインの) a winery.

しょうそく 消息 〖知らせ〗news 《*of*, *about*; *that* 節》 (**!** 単数扱い); 〖情報〗information. ▶難破した船の消息が分かる learn the *news about* the wrecked ship. ●亡命者らの消息を伝える bring the *news of* the refugees. ●消息筋によれば according to (well-)informed sources. ●消息通 a well-informed person. ▶彼は家を出たきり消息が不明で He left home and *was* not *heard of* any more. (**!** *hear of* は間接的にうわさを聞くこと. 受身でもよく用いられる)/(居所が知れない) His *whereabouts* has [have] been unknown since he left home. ▶昨年以来彼らの消息を聞いていない I haven't *heard anything* [*have heard nothing*] of them since last year.
会話「木村の消息を何か知ってるかい」「もう何年も彼からは音沙汰(さた)がないんだ」 "Do you have any *news of* Kimura?" "We haven't *heard from* him for ages." (**!** *hear from* は本人から直接手紙や電話をもらうこと. *hear of* については (⇒〖第 1 文例〗))

しょうぞく 装束 costume; dress; 〖書〗attire; (式服) a robe. ●白黒]装束をつける be dressed in white [black].

*__しょうたい 招待__ 图 (an) invitation. ●招待に応じる[を受ける, を断わる] accept [receive, get; decline] an *invitation* 《*to* a party》. ▶ご招待いただきありがとうございます Thank you for *inviting* me. (**!** *invit-*ing の代わりに *having* を用いると子供っぽくひびく)/Thank you for your *invitation*. ▶彼は去年英国政府の招待でロンドンに行った He went to London *at the invitation of* the British government.
── **招待する** 動 invite [ask] 《him》《*to*＋場所・催し, *for*＋催し》(**!** *ask* の方が口語的); (家に) have* 《him》over (通例近くから招待することをいう). ▶彼は我々を自宅[夕食; 結婚式]に招待した He *invited* us *to* his house [dinner; his wedding].
会話「いつ彼を招待するつもりなの」「日曜日に招待するよ」 "When will you *ask* him?" "I'll *invite* him on Sunday."
●招待客 a guest, an invited guest. ●招待券 (一般に) an invitation ticket; (無料券) a free [a complimentary] ticket. ●招待状 an invitation (card); a letter of invitation. (**!** 後の方が堅い表現) ●結婚式の招待状を出す send out *invitations* to one's wedding.

しょうたい 小隊 a platoon.
●小隊長 a platoon leader.

しょうたい 正体 ❶〖本当の姿〗(本性) one's true [real] character; (身元) identity. ●殺人犯の正体 the murderer's *identity*. ●彼女の正体をあばくunmask her. ▶彼は正体を現した He showed his *true character* [*colors*].
❷〖正気〗●正体なく眠る《話》be *dead* asleep (**!** *dead* は「すっかり (completely)」の意);《話》sleep *like a log* (**!** 慣用句で「ぐっすり眠る」の意).

‡じょうたい 状態 a state (**!** 常に単数形で); (a) condition,《話》shape; a situation; circumstances.

> 使い分け **state** 特定の時の人・事柄の状態を表す一般的な語.
> **condition** 特定の原因・環境のもとでの一時的な状態を表す.
> **circumstances** 人・事柄に影響を及ぼす周囲の状況を表す.
> **situation** 特定の時・場所における個別の状況や立場・境遇を表す.

●天候状態 the weather *conditions*; the *state* of the weather. ●目下の経済状態 the present economic *situation*. (**!** ... *conditions* なら家計など日常生活の経済状態をいう) ●健康状態がよい be in a good (↔a poor) *state* of health; be in good physical *condition*; be in good *health* [《話》*shape*]. ▶両国は戦争状態にある The two countries are in a *state* of war [at war]. ▶彼は危篤状態だ He is in a critical *condition*. ▶そんな状態では退院できない You can't leave the hospital in that *condition*./(まだ退院できる状態ではない) You are in *no condition to* leave the hospital. ▶その絵は理想的な状態で保存されてきた The painting has been preserved under ideal *conditions* [×an ideal condition]. ▶その銀行の経営状態はかなり悪い[申し分ない]らしいよ The bank is in pretty bad [tip-top] *shape*, I hear.

じょうたい 上体 the upper part of the body; the upper body. ●上体を前に倒す bend down (↔bend backwards).

じょうたい 常態 a normal state. ●常態に復する be restored to *normal* [*normálity*,《主に米》 *nórmalcy*].

じょうだい 上代 ancient times.
●上代文学 ancient literature.

じょうだい 城代 ●城代家老 (説明的に) a daimyo's senior [chief] retainer in charge of the castle during his master's absence.

しょうたく 小宅 (小さな家) a small house; (我が家)

しょうたく one's (own) house.
しょうたく 妾宅 a mistress's house.
しょうたく 沼沢 (a) marsh; (a) swamp; (a) bog.
● 沼沢植物 a helophyte; marsh plants. ● 沼沢地 marshy ground [fields]; swampy ground.

***しょうだく** 承諾 图 [申し出や要求に応じること] (やや書) consent; [熟慮の上での同意] (書) assent; [話し合いなどによる同意] agreement; [受諾] acceptance; [許可] permission; [是認] approval. ● 事後承諾 (⇨事後) ● 彼の承諾を得て [得ないで] with [without] his *consent*. ● 双方の承諾の上でそれをする do it by mutual *consent* [*agreement*]. ▶私は車の使用の承諾を彼らから得て I got his *consent* [(許可) *permission*] to use his car.

── 承諾する 動 (やや書) consént; (書) assent, agree 《*to*; *to do*》 (⇨同意する); [受け入れる] accept. ● その提案を承諾する *consent* [*agree*] *to* the proposal; give (one's) *consent to* the proposal; *accept* the proposal. ▶彼らは資金援助を承諾した They *consented* [*agreed*] *to* give financial aid.

***じょうたつ** 上達 图 [進歩] progress; [向上] improvement.

> **DISCOURSE**
> 海外で英語を学ぶしか, 英語上達の道はないのだろうか. 私はそうは思わない Is studying English abroad the only way to *become fluent* in the language? I do not think so. (❗「疑問文→答え」のパターン. 序論でよく用いられる)

── 上達する 動 ▶彼の英語はめきめき上達した His English *has improved* remarkably./He *has made* remarkable [rapid] *progress* in English.

じょうだま 上玉 [『美人』の俗語] (⇨美人)
しょうだん 昇段 图 (a) promotion. (⇨昇進)
── 昇段する 動 be promoted 《*to*》; advance in rank.
しょうだん 商談 business talks; a (business) negotiation; a business deal. ● 商談を進める go ahead with *business talks*. ▶商談がまとまった The *business talks* have been settled./We've got the deal. (❗ deal は「取引契約」の意. It's a deal. ともいう)

***じょうだん** 冗談 a joke (❗もともと joke には「ばかげた事」という含みはなく, むしろ日本語の「ユーモア」に近い);《話》(気のきいた) a crack.

① 【冗談～】 ● 冗談まじりで half *jokingly*. ● 冗談抜きで without *joking*. ● 冗談半分に (=半ばまじめな口調で) say in a half-serious tone. ▶あの川を泳ぎ渡るなんて冗談事ではない (=大変な事だ) It's not a *joking* matter [(話) It's no *joke*] swimming across that river. (❗ It is swimming ... を受ける形式主語. swimming ... は to swim ... でも可)

② 【冗談が [は]】 ▶彼は冗談が分からない [通じない] 男だ He doesn't get [see] the [×a] *joke*. (❗この joke は「こっけいな事」という抽象的な意)/He has no sense of humor. ▶冗談が過ぎるぞ (=冗談にもほどがある) You are carrying a *joke* too far./It is [has gone] beyond a *joke*. ▶冗談はさて置き本題に戻ろう *Joking apart* [*aside*], let's return to the main subject. ● 冗談はよしてください None of your *jokes* on me.

③ 【冗談を】 ● 冗談を言う tell《him》[make,《話》crack, say] a *joke*, joke《with + 人, about + 事》;《話》make a *crack*《*about*...》;《話》kid. ● 冗談を真に受ける take a *joke* seriously. ▶彼は私に頭以外とも悪いところはないという冗談を言った He joked with [×to] me *that* there was nothing wrong with him, except (for) his brains. ▶前の週末にいつものように彼と冗談を交わしていた Last weekend I *was joking* with him. (❗この進行形は日常茶飯事のように繰り返し行われることをさす)

④ 【冗談で [として]】 ▶冗談で (=面白半分の気持ちで) 言ったまでだ I only said it *in joke* [(自分では冗談のつもりで) *for a joke*, (冗談と受け取ってもらうつもりで) *as a joke*]./I just said it *for* [*in*] *fun*. ▶僕にご冗談としては受け取れない I can't [I'm not able to] take a *joke*.

⑤ 【冗談だ】 ▶気にするな. ほんの冗談だよ Don't be upset. I *was* only *joking* [It was only a *joke*.]./(話) I *was* just *kidding*. ▶彼が怠け者だって？ 冗談じゃない (=ばかを言うな) Are you saying he's lazy? Don't be ridiculous.

会話「(まさか冗談でしょう)」「いいえ, 本気よ」"You múst [háve to] *be joking* [(話) *kidding*]!/You're *joking* [(話) *kidding*]!/You're nót ˇserious." "I mean it."

じょうだん 上段 ❶ [上の段] an upper row [tier]; (寝台車の) an upper berth; (船の) an upper bunk; (上座) an upper seat. ● レストランド上段へ打ち込をhit a pitch high into the left field stands [deep into the left field seats].
❷ [剣道などの構え] ● 刀を上段に構える hold the sword over one's head.

***しょうち** 承知 ▶ご承知のとおり彼は一流のピアニストです *As you know*, he is one of the best pianists. ▶彼は承知の上でしたのです He *knew* really well what he was doing.

── 承知する 動 ❶ [知っている] know*, be aware 《*of*》. ▶そんなことは十分 [百も] 承知している I *know* that very [full] well./I'm well [fully] *aware of* that.

❷ [承諾する] consent《*to*》; (同意する) agree《*to*》; (是認する) approve《*of*...》(「(権威のある人・当局が)正式に承認する」の意では of は用いない); [許す] (権威をもって) permit (-tt-,), (好きにせよと) allow. ▶両親は私のアメリカ留学を承知してくれました My parents *permitted* [*allowed*] me *to* study in the United States./My parents *approved of* [*consented to*, *agreed to*] my *studying* in the United States. ▶彼の車を本人が承知しているのなら使ってもいいよ You can use his car if he *is agreeable*. ▶だましたら承知 (=容赦) しないぞ If you deceive me, I *won't forgive* you for it.

会話「手伝っていただけませんか」「承知しました」 "Could [Would] you help me?" "Surely《主に米》[*Certainly* 《主に英》]./*All right*, sir [ma'am]." (❗くだけた言い方は Sure. OK. などともいうが, 改まった言い方での「承知する」とは多少ずれる)

しょうち 招致 图 ● 2016 年のオリンピックの招致合戦を繰り広げる compete to *bring* the 2016 Olympic Games 《*to* one's *capital*》.
── 招致する 動 invite.
じょうち 常置 ── 常置の 形 permanent; standing. (⇨常設)
じょうち 情痴 (an) infatuation《*with*, *for*》; blind love; a foolish passion.
しょうちくばい 松竹梅 a pine, a bamboo, and an apricot tree.
しょうちゅう 掌中 ▶ぼくの命は彼の掌中にある My life is *in* his *hands*./My life is [lies] *at* his *mercy*. ● 掌中の玉 one's treasure [jewely]; one's treasured child.
しょうちゅう 焼酎 *shochu*; (説明的に) Japanese liquors distilled from sweet potatoes, wheat, etc.

じょうちゅう 条虫 〖昆虫〗a tapeworm.

じょうちゅう 常駐 ●軍を常駐させる《やや書》station troops.
● 常駐 (駐留軍) stationed troops. ● 常駐プログラム a resident program; TSR (program) 《*Terminate-and-Stay-Resident* の略》.

じょうちょ 情緒 (an) emotion;〖雰囲気〗an atmosphere. ●情緒不安定だ be *emotionally* unstable. ▶この市は江戸情緒がある This city has [retains] an Edo *atmosphere*.
●情緒障害〖心理〗an emotional disorder.

*****しょうちょう 象徴** 图 a symbol;〖絵や図案などによる〗an emblem. ▶ハトは平和の象徴である The dove is the *symbol* [*emblem*] of peace./The dove is *symbolic* [*emblematic*] of peace./The dove *symbolizes* peace.
—— 象徴的な 形 symbolic;《書》emblematic.
—— 象徴する 動 symbolize.
●象徴詩 symbolic poetry. ●象徴主義 symbolism.

しょうちょう 小腸 〖解剖〗the small intestine.

しょうちょう 省庁 (中央官庁) ministries and other government agencies. (⇨官庁)

しょうちょう 消長 rise and fall; ups and downs; the ebb and flow 《*of*》.

じょうちょう 冗長 —— 冗長な 形 (長たらしい) lengthy;(くどい) wordy;《書》verbose /vəːrbóus/. (⇨冗漫な)
●冗長な報告書 a *lengthy* [a *wordy*] report.

しょうちょく 詔勅 an Imperial edict [proclamation].

しょうちん 消沈 ●意気消沈する become depressed. (⇨意気消沈)

しょうつき 祥月 the month of a person's death.
●祥月命日 the anniversary of a person's death.

じょうてい 上程 —— 上程する 動 introduce.; present ▶その議案は本会議に上程された The bill *was introduced* [*was presented*] to the plenary session.

しょうてき 小敵 a weak enemy [opponent].

じょうでき 上出来 —— 上出来な 形 very good;〖すぐれた〗excellent;〖見事になされた〗well-done. (⇨出来) ▶彼の作品は上出来だ His work is *excellent* [*very good*, *well-written*, *well-made*]. ▶彼の試験は上出来だった He *did very well* [*better than expected*] on [《主に英》in] the exam.

*****しょうてん 商店** 《主に米》a store;《主に英》a shop. (⇨店 [解説])
●商店街《go shopping at [×to]》the shopping street [(区域) district [×region]; (ショッピングセンター) center, 《米》mall]. 〖*mall* は屋内施設〗
●商店主 《米》a storekeeper;《主に英》a shopkeeper.

*****しょうてん 焦点** 〖レンズなどの〗a focus (複 ~es, foci /fóusai/). ▶この写真は焦点が合っている This picture is *in* [*out of*] *focus*. ▶彼は女優にカメラの焦点を合わせた He *focused* his camera *on* the actress./He brought the actress *into focus*.
●焦点距離 the focal distance [length].

しょうてん 昇天《書》ascension; (キリストの) the Ascension.
—— 昇天する 動 (死ぬ) die;《婉曲的》pass away, go to heaven.

しょうでん 小伝 a short biography.

しょうでん 昇殿 (説明的に) stepping into the holy of holies [sanctum sanctorum] of a Shinto shrine.

じょうてん 上天気 beautiful [fair, fine, good] weather. ▶明日は上天気だろう The weather will be *fine* tomorrow.

しょうと 商都 a commercial [a business] city.

しょうど 焦土 ●焦土と化す be burned (《英》burnt) to the ground; be reduced to ashes (❗地域全体を表す語を主語とする).
●焦土戦術 (敵軍の攻勢を妨害する) a scorched-earth strategy [policy].

しょうど 照度 〖光学〗illuminance; (intensity of) illumination. ●照度計 an illuminometer.

じょうと 譲渡 图 (権利・財産などの) a tránsfer. ●権利の譲渡 the *transfer* of rights.
—— 譲渡する 動 hand ... over;〖法律〗transfér; (手形などを)〖金融〗negotiate. ▶彼は子供たちに財産の大半を譲渡した He *transferred* a large part of his property to his children.
●譲渡証書 a transfer deed. ●譲渡所得 capital gains; the income from transfer assets.
●譲渡性預金 certificate of deposit (略 CD).
●譲渡人 a transferor.

じょうど 浄土 ●浄土 the Pure Land. ●極楽浄土 the (Buddhist) Paradise.

しょうとう 小刀 a short sword; a dagger.

しょうとう 小党 a small [a minor] (political) party.

しょうとう 消灯 —— 消灯する 動 turn [switch] off the light; put out the light. ▶消灯! (指示) Lights out!
●消灯時間 lights-out (time).

しょうどう 商道 business ethics; commercial morality.

しょうどう 唱道 图 advocacy. —— 唱道する 動 advocate.
●唱道者 an advocate《*of*》.

しょうどう 唱導 —— 唱導する 動 (導く) lead; (仏道に導く) convert ... to Buddhism; (唱道する) (⇨唱道). ●平和運動を唱導する *lead* a peace movement.

しょうどう 衝動 图 (an) impulse; an urge (❗*impulse* より強意的). ▶彼を殴りたいという衝動を抑える resist the *impulse* to hit him. ▶その鳥を盗みたい衝動に駆られた I had [felt,《書》was seized with] an *impulse* [an *urge*] *to* steal the bird.
—— 衝動的な 形 impulsive. ●衝動的な男 an *impulsive* man; a man of *impulse*.
—— 衝動的に 副 impulsively. ●衝動的に行動する act *impulsively*; act *on* (an) *impulse*.
●衝動買い impulse buying [purchase]. (❗品物[人]は an *impulse* buy [buyer]. 「衝動買いする」 は (it) *on impulse*. 最近では impulse-buy (it) の動詞用法も生まれてきた)

*****じょうとう 上等** —— 上等の 形 good*;〖優秀な〗excellent;〖質のよい〗of good quality;〖より優れた〗superior 《*to*》. ●上等の品 an *excellent* article. (⇨高級 [高級品]) ●いちばん上等のワイン the *best* wine; wine of the *highest* quality. ▶これはあれより上等だ This is *better* than that./This is *superior to* [×than] that.
●上等兵 (旧日本陸軍) a private first class. (❗自衛隊で a private first class は「二等陸士」の意)

じょうとう 上棟 ●上棟式 (棟上げ式) the ceremony of the completion of the framework of a house.

じょうとう 常套 ●常套的な 〖陳腐な〗stock; (文句などが) hackneyed; (いつもの) the same old. ▶それは彼の常套手段だ (=いつものやり方だ) That's how [the way] he usually does it. / That's his old

trick./That's *the same old trick* of his.
● 套句 a stock [a hackneyed] phrase; a cliché. ▶「善処します」は政治家の使う常套句だ "We'll take proper measures" is one of the *stock* [*hackneyed*] *phrases* politicians usually use.

じょうどう 常道 a proper [a right] way; a regular [a usual] manner; a regular method.

しょうとく 生得 ── 生得の 形 innate; by nature. (⇨生まれつき)

しょうとく 頌徳 ● 頌徳碑 (説明的に) a monument in commemoration of a person's greatest service.

*****しょうどく** 消毒 图 disinfection. ● 消毒済みのコップ a *sterilized* glass.

── 消毒する 動 disinfect; (殺菌する) sterilize /stérəlaɪz/. ● ふとんを日光消毒する *disinfect* the *futon* in the sun [*by* solar heat]. ● 水を塩素で消毒する *disinfect* the water *with* chlorine. ● 傷口を消毒薬で(=をつけて)消毒する *sterilize* [*disinfect*] the wound by applying some antiseptic (to it).
● 消毒薬[剤] (器具などの) (a) disinfectant; (人の皮膚の) (an) antiseptic.

じょうとくい 上得意 a good [a regular] customer.

*****しょうとつ** 衝突 图 ❶ [車などの] (動いているもの同士の) (a) collision; (激突) a crash, a smash. ● 正面衝突 a head-on *collision*. ● バスと電車の衝突(事故)は a *collision between* a bus and a train. ▶ 十字路で三重衝突があった There was a three-way *collision* [a three-car *crash*] at the crossroads.
❷ [意見・利害などの] a clash; (a) conflict (❶ 前の方は「ぶつかり合い」、後の方は「闘争」の意味合いがある); (口げんか) a quarrel. ● 両者の利害の衝突 a *clash* [a *conflict*, 《比喩的に》 a *collision*] of interests between the two. ● 武力の衝突 (an) armed *conflict*.

── 衝突する 動 ❶ [物・人などがぶつかり合う] collide 《with》, come* into collision 《with》; [激突する] crash [❶ crush は「押しつぶす」), smash 《into》. (❶ crash は激突する音で, smash はその際の損傷に重点がある); [当てる] hit*. (⇨ぶつかる) ▶ あぶない！衝突するよ Look out! We're going to *crash*. (❶ ×We'll *crash*. とはいわない) ▶ 彼の車は街灯柱に激しく衝突した His car *collided with* a lamppost./His car *crashed* [*smashed*] *into* [×at, ×against] a lamppost./His car *ran* [*bumped*] *into* a lamppost. ▶ バスがトラックと正面衝突した A bus *collided* head-on *with* a truck./A bus and a truck *collided* head-on (*with* each other). (❶ There was a head-on *collision between* a bus and a truck. ともいえる)/A bus *crashed* [*smashed*] *into* a truck head-on. (❶ *hit* into の前でも可) ▶ 停めておいた車がトラックに衝突された The parked car *was hit* by a truck.
❷ [立場の相反する人・集団が争う] clash 《with》; conflict 《with》; (口論する) argue, quarrel 《with》. ▶ 学生は警官隊と衝突した(=ぶつかって格闘した) The students *clashed with* the police./*There was a clash* [*A clash took place*] between the students and the police. ▶ その件では彼の意見と私の意見はよく衝突する His opinions often *clash* [*conflict*, 《比喩的に》 *collide*] *with* mine over the matter./(意見が合わない) He often *disagrees with* me over the matter. (❶ *collision* を比喩的に用いて次のようにもいえる: 政府は労働組合と衝突した The government *came into collision with* the trade unions.) ▶ あの 2 人はいつも衝突している The two *are* always *arguing* [*quarreling*] with each other.

しょうとりひき 商取引 a business deal; a commercial [a business] transaction.

じょうない 場内 ● 場内で (会場内で) in the hall; (敷地内) on the grounds [premises]. ● 場内放送される be announced on [over] the PA (system). (❶ PA system は「場内用拡声装置 (*p*ublic *a*ddress system)」の意) ● 場内整理をする control the crowd *in the hall* [*on the grounds*].

しょうに 小児 an infant; a little [a small] child (⑧ children); [よちよち歩きの] a toddler.
● 小児科 pediatrics /piːdiǽtrɪks/. ● 小児科医 a children's doctor; a pediatrician. ● 小児虐待 child abuse. ● 小児ぜんそく 【医学】 infantile asthma. ● 小児まひ 【医学】 infantile paralysis; poliomyelitis /pòʊliəʊmaɪəlάɪtɪs/; 《話》 polio.

しょうにゅうせき 鍾乳石 a stalactite.

しょうにゅうどう 鍾乳洞 a limestone cave [《大洞窟》 cavern].

*****しょうにん** 承認 图 [是認] approval; [同意] (やや書) consent; [許可] permission; [正式な認可] recognition. (⇨認める, 承諾) ● 承認を得る get [obtain]《his》 *approval* [《話》 *O.K.*]. ● 委員会の承認を求める ask for the *approval* of the committee. ▶ それは彼女の承認を得てやるべきだ You should do it *with* her *approval* [《同意》 *consent*, 《許可》 *permission*]. ▶ 彼は社長からその契約をしてもよいという承認を得た He received the president's *approval* to sign the contract.

── 承認する 動 [是認する] approve; [同意する]《やや書》 consent; [許可する] permit; [正式に認可する] recognize. ▶ 委員会はその計画を承認した The committee *approved* [×*approved of*, 《やや書》 *consented to*] the plan. ▶ ほとんどの国がその島国を(国家として)承認している Most countries *recognize* the island state (*as* [*to be*] a nation). (❶ 通例進行形不可)

*****しょうにん** 商人 (一般に) a merchant (❶《英》では卸売商、特に貿易商をいう); (貿易業者) a trader; (個別の商品を扱い専門的知識を持った) a dealer; [店主] 《米》 a storekeeper, 《英》 a shopkeeper; (小売商人) a tradesperson; (集合的に) tradespeople. ● 毛皮商人 a fur *trader*; a *trader* in furs. ● 中古車商(人) a used-car *dealer*; a *dealer* in used cars. ● 死の商人(=戦争屋) a *merchant* of death. ▶ あの人は木材商人だ He is a timber *merchant*.
● 商人根性 (営利主義) commercialism; the mercenary spirit.

*****しょうにん** 証人 a witness (❶ しばしば無冠詞で); (目撃者) an eyewitness. ● 検事[被告]側の証人 a prosecution [a defense] *witness*; a *witness for* the prosecution [defense]. ● 生き証人 a living *witness*. ● 証人台に立つ《米》 take the *(witness) stand*;《英》 go into the *witness box*. ● 証人を審問する hear [examine] a *witness*. ● 証人に立てる call [take] ⟪him⟫ *to witness*. ▶ 弁護士は証人に反対尋問をした The lawyer cross-questioned the *witness*. ▶ 彼がうそをついていないことは私が証人になります I will *testify* [《書》 *bear witness*] *to* his honesty./I will *testify that* he is honest. ▶ 彼は証人として喚問された He was called as a *witness* in court [at the trial].

しょうにん 上人 a holy priest; a saint. ● 日蓮上人 Saint Nichiren.

しょうにん 小人 a child. (⇨子供)

しょうにん 昇任 (a) promotion. (⇨昇進)

じょうにん 常任 ── 常任の 形 (常置の) standing;

しょうにんずう 小人数 a small number of people.
● 小人数(制)のクラス a *small* class. ● 授業を小人数制で行う teach a *small* class; give lessons to *a small number of* students.

しょうね 性根 ●性根が腐っている (まったく堕落している) be utterly corrupt; (芯まで) be corrupt to the core.
●性根がすわる ▶あの男は性根がすわっている He is strong-willed.
●性根を入れ替える (改心して新しい生活を始める) turn over a new leaf; start a new life.

***じょうねつ 情熱** 图 [理性を圧倒するほど激しい] (a) passion; (燃える) (an) ardor; (変わらぬ) fervor (⇨熱情); [熱狂的な] enthúsiàsm. ●政治に情熱を持っている have a *passion* for politics; be *enthusiastic* [an *enthusiast*] about politics. ●教育に情熱を燃やす burn with *enthusiasm for* education. ▶今でもその仕事に情熱をかけられるかどうか自問してみるべきかもしれないね Maybe you should ask yourself if your *heart's* still in the job.
── **情熱的な** 形 passionate; ardent; enthùsiástic.
●情熱的な人 a *passionate* [an *ardent*] person; a person *of passion*.
── **情熱的に** 副 passionately; ardently; enthusiastically. ●情熱的に語る speak *passionately*.

しょうねつじごく 焦熱地獄 the blazing inferno; scorching [burning] hell.

***しょうねん 少年** a boy; [青少年] a juvenile /dʒúːvənàil/.

> **使い分け** **boy** 比較的若い十代までの男子を表す。また, 年齢に関係なく親しみをこめて呼びかけや息子さす場合に用いる。
> **juvenile** 少女も含めた青少年。報道でよく用いられる正式な表現。

● 少年の頃の思い出 one's *boyhood* memories. ●少年のような笑み a *boyish* /bɔ́iiʃ/ smile. ●非行少年 a *juvenile* delinquent. ▶私は少年時代田舎で楽しく過ごした I spent happy days in the country when I was a *boy* [in my *boyhood*]. (**!** when 節を用いた言い方の方が口語的)/I had a happy *boyhood* in the country.
●少年老い易く学成り難し (学ぶべきことは多くて, 学び取られることのなんと少ないことか) How much to learn and how little learned.
●少年院 《米・英古》a reformatory, 《英》an approved school. ●少年鑑別所 a juvenile classification home. ●少年非行[犯罪] juvenile delinquency. ●少年野球 boys [boy's, boys'] baseball.

じょうねん 情念 (an) emotion; (a) passion 《for》.

しょうねんエッチ『少年H』 *A Boy Called H*. [参考] 妹尾河童の小説

しょうねんば 正念場 (重大な局面) the crucial moment [point]; (決断の時) the time for decision; (大詰めの対決) (話) a (final) showdown.
▶元気を出せ, 正念場はこれからだ Cheer up! The *showdown* [(最悪の事態) The *worst*] is yet to come.

しょうのう 小脳 [解剖] the cerebellum /sèrəbéləm/ (國 ~s, -bella /-lə/).

しょうのう 小農 a small farmer; a peasant; (集合的) the peasantry.

しょうのう 笑納 ▶どうぞ笑納ください Would you please accept this little gift?/I'd be very happy if you accepted this little gift.

しょうのう 樟脳 camphor /kǽmfər/; (虫よけ玉) a camphor ball, a mothball.

じょうのう 上納 (a) payment.
●上納金 the money paid to the government [authorities]. ●上納米 rice delivered to the government [authorities] as a tax.

しょうのつき 小の月 a month of 30 days or less.

しょうは 小破 slight damage.

じょうば 乗馬 图 horseback 《米》 [horse 《英》] riding. ▶乗馬が好きだ I like *riding a horse*.
── **乗馬する** 動 ride (on) a horse; get on [《やや書》mount] a horse; (乗馬をしに行く) go horse-riding.
●乗馬靴 riding boots. ●乗馬クラブ a horse riding club.

しょうはい 勝敗 victory or defeat. (⇨勝ち負け) ▶そのホームランが勝敗を決した The home run decided the game. ▶勝敗はともかく最善を尽くしなさい *Win or lose*, you should do your best. ▶その投手は勝敗にかかわらず降板した The pitcher left the game without a decision.

しょうはい 賞杯 《win》a cup; a trophy.

しょうはい 賞牌 a medal. ●賞牌を得る[授与する] earn [give, award] a *medal* 《for》.

***しょうばい 商売** ❶ [商い, 商活動] business, trade.
●もうかる商売 profitable *business*, (a) profitable *trade*. ●商売に向いている be suited to a *business* career [a career in *business*]. ●商売を始める[やめる; している] go into [go out of; be in] *business*. ●商売が上手である have a good head for *business*. ▶当社は外国の数社と商売をしている We do *business* with several foreign companies. ▶このところ商売が振るわない[好調である] *Business* is slack [brisk] these days.
会話 「商売はどうですか」「ぼちぼち[さっぱり]です」"How's *business*?" "So-so [Very poor]." (**!**特定の商売・事業・店をさすと How's the [your] *business*?)

❷ [職業] a job, an occupation (**!**後の方が堅い語); (ある特定の) 《話》line; (商活動に関する職業) a business, (a) trade. (**!**後の方は手先の技術を要する職業の意でも使い, 時に軽蔑的響きがある) ●家の商売(=家業)を継ぐ take over [carry on, 《やや書》succeed to] the family *business*. ●商売柄いつもネクタイを締めていなければならない I always have to wear a tie because of my *job*./《米》My *job* requires me to wear a tie at all times. ▶生徒を教えるのが先生の商売(=職務)でしょう Isn't it a teacher's *job* [*duty*] to teach his students?
会話 「何の商売をなさっているのですか」「食品雑貨の商売をしています」"What is your *line* (of *business*)?/What (line) of *business* are you in?" "I run a grocery store./I'm in the grocery *business* [*line*, *trade*]./(卸業として) I deal in groceries." (**!**What's your *business*? はあいまいなことば。この形では What's your *trade*? の方がよい)
●商売気質(かたぎ) the merchants's way of thinking. ●商売敵(がたき) a business [a trade] rival. ●商売気(ぎ) a commercial motive [spirit]. ●商売人 (⇨商人)

じょうはく 上膊 (⇨❶ 上腕)

しょうばつ 賞罰 (ほうびと罰) reward and punishment. ▶賞罰なし No reward and no punishment. (事情) 米英の履歴書にはこの項はないので,

じょうはつ 蒸発 图 evaporation.
— 蒸発する 動 evaporate /ivǽpərèit/; (人が) disappear. ▶太陽は水を蒸発させる The sun *evaporates* water. ▶彼の父親は彼が小さい頃に彼と母親を残して蒸発したきりだった His father *ran away*, leaving him and his mother when he was a young child.

しょうはブロック 消波ブロック a dissipating block.

しょうはん 相伴 — 相伴する 動 (接待を受ける) partake of 《a meal *with* him》 at his request; (利益を受ける) have [get] a share in the profits. ▶そのグループに加わって中華料理のお相伴にあずかる I joined the group to share a meal at a Chinese restaurant.

じょうはんしん 上半身 the upper half of the body.
- 上半身裸になる strip (oneself) *to the waist*; (裸になっている) be naked *from the waist up*. (⇒下半身)
- 上半身写真 a head-and-shoulders photo; (説明的に) a picture of the upper part of the body [(ウエストから上の) from the waist up]; a half-length photograph. (⇒顔写真)

しょうひ 消費 图〖物資など使い尽くすこと〗consumption; 〖金・時間などの支出〗expenditure. ●国内[家庭]消費 home [household] *consumption*. ●個人消費 personal *consumption*. ●時間の消費 *expenditure* [浪費] (a) *waste*] of time. ●エネルギー[燃料]の消費 the *consumption* of energy [fuel]; energy [fuel] *consumption*. ●待機消費電力 standby electricity *consumption*. ●ガソリンの消費量 the *consumption* of gasoline. ●消費の伸び[回復／減少] a growth [a pickup; a decline] in *consumption*. ●消費を抑える hold down [cut down on] *consumption*. ●消費を刺激する encourage *consumption*.
— 消費する 動 (燃料・労力・時間などを)《書》consume; (使う) use, (使い果たす) use ... up (! consume より日常的な語); (費やす) spend*. ●時間の大半をその仕事に消費する spend [*consume*] most of one's time on the task. ▶あなたの家では毎月どれくらい電気を消費しますか How much electricity does your family *consume* [*use*] every month?
- 消費行動 a consumption behavior. ●消費財 (⇒消費財) ●消費支出 consumer [consumption] spending [expenditure]. ●消費者 (⇒消費者) ●消費社会 a consumption society. ●消費税 a consumption [《米》sales] tax; (付加価値税)《英》a value-added tax (VAT). ●消費生活 consumer life. ●消費生活アドバイザー an advisory specialist for consumers' affairs. ●消費生活協同組合 a consumers' [a consumer's] cooperative (society). ●消費生活センター the Consumer Affairs Center. ●消費性向 a propensity to consume. ●消費文化 consumer culture (! 主に消費者が持っている、または消費者を取りまく文化); Culture of consumerism (! 消費主義に影響を受けた文化).

しょうび 焦眉 ●焦眉の急 an urgent need; a matter of the great(est) urgency.

しょうび 賞美 — 賞美する 動 praise; admire. (⇒褒める)

じょうひ 冗費 wasteful [unnecessary] expenses [expenditure]. ●冗費を省く cut down (on) *wasteful expenses*.

じょうび 常備 — 常備の 形 standing.
— 常備する 動 have [keep]《a thing》ready.
- 常備軍 a standing army. ●常備薬 (家庭の薬) household medicine; (救急箱) a first-aid kit.

しょうひざい 消費財 consumer(s') [consumption] goods. ●耐久消費財 durable *consumer goods*; *consumer* durables.

しょうひしゃ 消費者 a consumer. ▶消費者の動向に敏感な企業が現在の経済危機を乗り切ることができるだろう *Consumer*-sensitive companies could survive the present economic crisis. ▶不況克服のかぎは消費者が握るといわれる *Consumers* are said to be holding the key to overcoming the recession.
- 消費者運動 consumerism; a consumer movement [campaign]. ●消費者価格 a consumer [a consumers'] price. ●消費者金融 consumer credit. ●消費者心理[マインド] consumer sentiment [confidence]. (参考) 消費者の景気感とそれに基づく消費態度) ●消費者センター a consumer information center. ●消費者団体 a consumer organization. ●消費者物価指数 the consumer price index《略 CPI》. ●消費者米価 the consumer rice price. ●消費者保護 consumer protection.

じょうびたき 尉鶲 〖鳥〗a redstart.

しょうひょう 商標 a trademark (略 TM) (! a trade mark ともつづる); 〖銘柄〗a brand. ●登録商標 a registered *trademark* (記号 ®). ●商標を登録する register a *trademark*. ●商標を侵害する infringe 《his》*trademark*.
- 商標権 trademark rights. ●商標名 a trade [a brand] name.

しょうひょう 証票 a certificate.

しょうびょう 傷病 ●傷病手当金 the sick benefit.
- 傷病兵 sick and wounded soldiers.

しょうひん 商品 goods; merchandise; (農業・鉱業における産物) a commodity; (在庫品) (a) stock; (製品) a product.

> **使い分け** **goods** 移動可能な商品を総称的に表す最も一般的な語。複数扱いで数詞はつけないが many, some, any などはつける。
> **merchandise** 商品を総称的に表すが、取り引きを意識した堅い語。数えるときは a piece of merchandise のようにいう。
> **commodity** 農産物・鉱物などを商品として大量に扱うときに用いる堅い語。

- 主要商品 staple *commodities*. (! 1国の経済の中心となる特に農業、鉱業における重要産物をさす) ●ヒット商品 a hit *product*. ●売れ筋商品 a strong seller. ●目玉商品 a loss leader; 《米話》a special. ●商品を仕入れる lay in *goods* [*a stock*]; stock *goods*. ▶あの店はとびきり上等な商品を扱っている That store carries really excellent *goods*./They sell really excellent *goods* at that store. (! good *goods* は口調が悪く避けられる) ▶我が社の商品は常に保証つきです Our *merchandise* is always guaranteed.
- 商品化 commercialization. ●商品化する commercialize. ●商品回転率 the merchandise turnover (rate). ●商品券 a gift certificate《米》[token《英》]. ●商品先物 commodity futures. ●商品取引所 the commodity exchange. ●商品見本 a trade sample. ●商品名 a brand [a trade] name. ●商品目録 a catalog(ue).

しょうひん 賞品 a prize. (⇒賞)

しょうひん 小品 (短い作品) a short piece [work]; (絵画) a small painting.

じょうひん 上品 图〖洗練〗refinement; 〖優美〗(優な

しょうふ 的な) elegance; (生まれつきの) grace.
— **上品な** 形 〖知的で洗練された〗 refined; 〖優美な〗elegant; graceful (!後の方は自然に備わっている気品を含意する). ● 非常に上品な婦人 a very *refined* [*elegant*, *graceful*] lady;《やや書》a lady of great *refinement* [much *elegance*, much *grace*]. ● 上品な話し方 a *refined* way of speaking. ▶この部屋は上品にまとめられている This room is *elegantly* furnished [furnished in *excellent* taste].

しょうふ 娼婦 a próstitùte.

***しょうぶ** 勝負 图 〖試合〗a game;《主に英》a match; 〖勝ち負け〗victory or defeat.
① 〖～勝負, 勝負(の)～〗 ● 互角の[負け] 勝負 an even [a losing] *game*. ● 名勝負 one of the best *games* [*matches*] ever. ● 勝負強い succeed when it is needed most. ● 真剣勝負をする *play* [*fight*] for real. ● 出たとこ勝負をする(=下準備なしでする) *play* it by ear. ● 勝負の世界(=力の支配する世界) the world where power rules. ● 長いラリーの続くいい勝負 a good close *game* [*match*] with many long rallies. ▶チェスを一勝負どうですか How about (having) a *game* of chess?
② 〖勝負が[は]〗 ▶やっと勝負がついた The *game* is over at last. / At last, the *game* has ended [come to an end]. ▶勝負はこっちのものだ The *game* is mine [ours].
③ 〖勝負に〗 ● 勝負に勝つ[負ける] win [lose] a *game*. ● 勝負にこだわる stick to winning. ● 勝負に出る make a decisive move. ● 勝負に徹する think about winning from the beginning to the end. ▶チェスでは彼はない I'm *no match for* him in chess.
④ 〖勝負を〗 ● 勝負をする(⇒動) ● 勝負をつける(=最後まで戦う) fight it out; (同点試合の決勝戦をする) play off. ● 勝負をおりる give up the idea of participating in a game because there is little hope of winning.
— **勝負(を)する** 動 have a game [a match]《with》; (競技をする) play《with》; (戦う) fight《with》. ● 逃げずに四番打者と勝負する challenge the cleanup. ● 正々堂々勝負をしよう Let's play fair [a fair game].
● **勝負は時の運** 勝負は時の運 *Victory or defeat* [*Whether you win or not*] is just luck. ● **勝負事** a game, a match; 博(*)け事 gambling. ● **勝負師** a gambler. ● **勝負下着** attractive underwear for special occasions. ● **勝負球** 〖野球〗a finishing pitch; a money pitch. ● **勝負服** attractive clothes for special occasions.

しょうぶ 菖蒲 〖植物〗a sweet flag. (!an iris /áiəris/ (⊕ ~es, irides /íradi:z/) はアヤメ属の植物を幅広くさう. アヤメ・イチハツ・ショウブなど)
● **菖蒲湯** (説明的に) a bath with a bunch of iris leaves (and mugworts) on May 5.

じょうふ 情夫 a lover.

じょうふ 情婦 a mistress.

‡**じょうぶ** 丈夫 图 good health.
— **丈夫な** 形 ❶ 〖健康な〗healthy; (強い) strong; (強健な) robust /roubʌ́st/. ● 丈夫な子供 a *healthy* [a *strong*] child. ● 丈夫である be *healthy*; be in [have, enjoy] *good health*. ● 彼女はそう丈夫ではない. よく病気をする She isn't very *strong*. She's frequently sick. ▶体を丈夫にすることが大切です It is important to *improve* your health.
❷ 〖物が頑丈な〗(強い) strong, (しっかりした) sturdy /stə́ːrdi/; (堅い) firm; (もちがよい) durable; (こわれにくい) tough. ● 丈夫な作りのいす a *strongly*-built [a *strong*, a *sturdy*] chair. ▶このコートは丈夫な生地でできている This coat is (made) of *durable* material.

じょうぶ 上部 the upper part. ● 建物の上部 *the upper part* of the building. ● ページの上部に at the *head* [*top*] of the page.
● **上部構造**〖組織〗a superstructure.

しょうふく 承服 图 consént; 〖受諾〗acceptance.
— **承服する** 動 consént 《*to*; *to do*》; accept. (⇒同意)

しょうふだ 正札 a price tag [label], a (price) ticket. ● 車を正札の値段で売る sell a car at *sticker price*. ● 5,000円の正札がついている be marked [be labeled]"¥5,000". ● 正札をつける(=値段をつける) mark [set, put] a price 《on a hat》.

じょうぶつ 成仏 — **成仏する** 動 rest in peace; (死ぬ) die, (婉曲的に) pass away. ● 彼の霊よ成仏してください(=安らかれ) May he rest in peace. ▶あんなふうに死んだ人たちはまだ成仏できていないと思うよ People that died that way are still hanging around, I'm afraid.

しょうぶん 性分 〖先天的な性質〗(a) nature; 〖気質〗a disposition, (やや書) (a) temperament. (⇒性質) ● (生まれつき)臆病(*)な性分である be cowardly (by nature); have a cowardly *nature*. ● おとなしい性分である have [be of] a placid *disposition*. ▶うそを言うのは私の性分に合わない It isn't *in my nature* [It goes *against the grain* for me] to tell lies. (!It goes *against my grain*.... ともいえる)

じょうぶん 条文 〖序文・付録に対して本文〗a text; 〖条項〗(!article は箇条) ● 憲法の全条文 a full *text* of the Constitution. ● 昨年定められた法律の条文によれば according to the *provisions* of the law made last year.

しょうへい 招聘 an [a cordial] invitation. (!cordial は「正式で礼儀を尽くした」の意) ● 招聘を受ける[断る] accept [decline] an *invitation*.
— **招聘する** 動 invite 《him *to do*》.

しょうへい 将兵 officers and men.

しょうへき 障壁 (乗り越えうる障害) a bárrier; (大きな障害) an óbstacle. ● 関税など通商の障壁となるもの trade *barriers* such as import taxes. ● 最初, 探検隊と現地人との間に言葉の障壁があった At first, there was a language *barrier* between the local inhabitants and the explorers. ▶アルプスは旅人たちの眼前に越えがたい障壁となって立ちはだかっていた (やや書) The Alps rose over the travelers as an insurmountable *obstacle*.
● **障壁画** paintings on walls; sliding doors, freestanding screens and folding screens.

じょうへき 城壁 a castle wall; a rampart. ● 城壁を巡らす surround 《a castle》 with *walls* [a *rampart*].

しょうへん 小片 a small piece; a bit; (破片) a fragment.

しょうへん 小編 (短い文学作品) a short story.

しょうへん 掌編 (非常に短い文学作品) a short short story.

しょうべん 小便 图 urine /júərin/; 〖話〗a pee (!小児語); (小便をすること) urination. (⇒おしっこ, 立ち小便) ● 小便が近い have to *urinate* frequently. ● 小便をこらえる hold one's *water*. ● 小便をもらす wet one's pants. ● 小便臭い childish; (俗) pissy.
— **小便する** 動 urinate, pass [discharge] (one's) urine; pee, have a pee, 《書》make [pass] water.
● **小便所** a urinal. (!「小便器」「しびん」の意もある)

***じょうほ** 譲歩 图 (a) concession 《*to*》; 〖妥協〗(a)

しょうほう compromise.
—**譲歩する** 動 (しぶしぶ認める) concede 《to》; (屈する) give way 《to》, 《書》 yield 《to》. (⇨譲る) ● 譲歩して彼の要求をいれる concede [make concessions, give way] to his demands.

しょうほう 商法 the commercial law.

しょうほう 唱法 the singing technique; the way of singing (songs).

しょうほう 勝報 the news of a victory.

しょうほう 詳報 a detailed [a full] report 《on [of] the accident》.

しょうぼう 消防 (活動) fire fighting.
● 消防士 a firefighter; (男の) a fireman.
● 消防自動車 a fire engine. ● 消防署 (建物) a fire station. ● 消防団 a fire department [《英》brigade] (🔍 the をつけると組織としての消防署をさす: 消防署に電話する call the fire department) ● 消防艇 a fireboat.

じょうほう 情報 information 《about, on; as to wh-節, that 節》(🔍 数えるときは a piece [a bit] of ... を用いる); (秘密の) intelligence 《of》; (目新しい) news.

① 【～情報】 ● 内部 [秘密; 機密] 情報 inside [secret; classified] information. ● 役に立つ情報 a useful piece of information; a piece of useful information. (🔍 後の言い方は useful を強調する) ● 最新の情報 the latest information [news]. ● 個人情報 personal data. ● イベント情報 a listing of events. ● (クレジット) カード情報 credit-card data [information]. ● 顧客情報 customer information. ● さらなる情報 further [additional] information. ● 確かな情報源 a reliable source of information. ● (米国の) 中央情報局 the Central Intelligence Agency 《略 CIA》.

② 【情報を】 ● 彼に情報を伝える relay [convey, transmit] information to him. ● 情報を公開する make information [《記録》records] available to the public; release records to the public. ● 情報を扱う deal with information. ● 情報を交換し合う share information 《with》. ● 情報をもとに act on a piece of information. ● 彼が日本に来るという情報を流す release information that he will come to Japan. ● その問題に関する情報を集める collect [gather] information about [on] the subject. (🔍 about では一般的な, on では専門的な情報を示す) ● 情報を盗む steal information. ● 情報を共有する share information 《with》. ● 情報をもらす leak information 《to》. ● 情報を操作する manipulate information. ▶ その本からたくさんの貴重な情報を得ることができる We can get [obtain] a lot of valuable information [×informations] from the book./The book gives us [provides us with] a lot of valuable information. ● さらに詳しい情報については、お近くの代理店にお問い合わせください For further information, please contact our agent nearest you.

● 情報科学 information science. ● 情報格差 an information gap. ● IT時代の情報格差を是正する bridge the digital divide. ● 情報革命 an information revolution. ● 情報 (化) 社会 an information(-oriented) society. ● 情報家電 an information appliance. ● 情報管理 management of information; information management. ● 情報機関 an intelligence [《英》a secret] service. ● 情報機器 information equipment [products]. ● 情報技術 information technology 《略 IT》. ● 情報源 a source of information. ● 情報検索 information retrieval 《略 IR》.

● 情報公開 [開示] disclosure of official information. (🔍 米国の「情報公開法」は Freedom of Information Act) ● 情報工学 information engineering. ● 情報産業 the information industry. ● 情報紙 a listing paper. ● 情報誌 a listing magazine. ● 情報時代 the information age. ● 情報収集 information gathering. ● 情報処理 information processing. ● 情報スーパーハイウェイ an information superhighway. (参考) 米国内におけるデジタル情報通信基盤整備構想) ● 情報戦争 an information war(fare). ● 情報操作 information manipulation. ● 情報通信技術 information and communication(s) technology 《略 ICT》. ● 情報通信ネットワーク an information and communication network. ● 情報提供者 (調査・研究のための) an informant; (警察などへの) an [a police] informer. ● 情報部 [局] an intelligence bureau [department, office, 《米》agency]. ● 情報部員 an intelligence officer [agent]. ● 情報網 an information network. ● 情報流出 (a case of) information leakage; a leakage of information.

じょうほう 上方 図 the upper part.
—**上方の** 形 upper.
—**上方に** above; upward. ▶ 12月の消費者物価指数が大幅に上方修正された The consumer price index for December was revised *upward* substantially.

じょうほう 定法 the usual way [method].

じょうほう 乗法 《数学》multiplication.

しょうほん 正本 (原本) the original; (芝居の台本・脚本) the script of a play.

しょうほん 抄本 (抜粋したもの) an extract 《from》.
● 戸籍抄本 an *extract from* [an *extract copy of*] one's family register.

じょうまえ 錠前 a lock. ● 戸に錠前をかける lock (↔unlock) a door.
● 錠前屋 a locksmith.

じょうまん 冗漫 —**冗漫な** 形 [必要以上に言葉数の多い] 《軽蔑的》wordy, 《書》verbose; [散漫な] 《書》diffuse. ● 冗漫な文体で in a *wordy* [*verbose*, a *diffuse*] style. ▶ 彼の作文は冗漫だ His composition is *wordy*.

しょうみ 正味 ● 正味の目方 *net* weight. ● 正味3時間働く work for three *full* [a *full* three] hours. (⇨丸一) ● 正味20ドルをかせぐ have *net* earnings of 20 dollars; earn a *clear* 20 dollars.

しょうみ 賞味 —**賞味する** 動 relish [enjoy] 《a meal [a drink]》.
● 賞味期限 the best before date; (店頭販売期限) 《米》púll dàte, 《英》séll-by dàte. ● 賞味期限 2010.4.5 (表示) Best before April 5 2010.

じょうみ 情味 ● 情味のある話 a story full of *human feelings*. ▶ あの女性は情味がある She is *warm-hearted*.

じょうみゃく 静脈 《解剖》a vein. (🔍「動脈」は an artery) ● 大動脈 the main *vein*.
● 静脈血 venous blood. ● 静脈注射 an intravenous injection. ● 静脈瘤 《医学》a varix /vǽriks/ (《複》varices /vǽrɪsiːz/); (症状) varicósis.

じょうむ 常務 a senior [a managing] director. (⇨会社)
● 常務取締役 a managing director.

じょうむいん 乗務員 a crew member; (男の) a crewman (《複》-men); (集合的) the crew. ● ジェット旅客機の乗務員 the *crew* on [of] a jetliner.
● 乗務員室 a crew's cabin.

しょうむしょう 商務省 the Department of Com-

しょうめい 証明 图 (a) proof (⟨複⟩ 〜s), (a) testimony (⟨!⟩ proof より堅い語); (a) demonstration. ●(出生)証明書 a (birth) certificate. ●身分証明書 an *identification* [an *identity*] card; an *ID* (card). (学生証) a student's *ID* (card).

—— **証明する** 動 (証拠・論法によって真実であることを示す) prove*; (明らかにする) show*; (口頭で証言する) testify (*to*); (学説・事実などを立証する) establish; (例示・論理的説明などで) démonstràte; (文書で) certify. (⇨証拠, 証言) ●身分を証明する *prove* [*establish*] one's identity; identify oneself. ●定理を証明する *prove* [*demonstrate*] a theorem. ▶私は(彼らに)彼が有罪であることを証明した I *proved* his guilt (*to* them)./I *proved* (*to* them) *that* he was guilty. (⟨!⟩(1) wh-節が続く場合は them は通例文尾; あなたはどこにいたか彼らに証明できますか Can you *prove* where you were *to* them? (2)「…に」を表す句を伴わない場合は I *proved* him (*to be*) guilty. ともいえるが that 節の方が口語的)/I *showed* (them) (*that*) he was guilty. (⟨!⟩「…に」を伴わない場合 I *showed* him *to be* guilty. ともいえるが that 節の方が一般的) ▶この事実は彼女の誠実さを証明している This fact *proves* [*shows*,《書》*testifies* (*to*)] her integrity./This fact *proves* [*shows*,《書》*testifies*] *that* she is honest. (⟨!⟩通例進行形不可)/This fact *is proof of* her honesty [*that* she is honest]. ▶…に相違ないことをここに証明します《証明書の文句》I hereby [This is to] *certify that* ….

しょうめい 照明 lighting; illumination. (⟨!⟩後の方が堅い語) ●クリスマスツリーの照明 the *lighting* [*illumination*] of the Christmas tree. ●直接照明 direct (↔indirect) *lighting* [*illumination*]. ●舞台照明 stage *lighting*. ●やわらかい照明の寝室 a softly *lit* [*illuminated*] bedroom. ●照明を当てる light … (up); illuminate 《the street》. ▶その部屋は照明がよい[悪い] The room is well [poorly] *lit*.

●照明係 a lighting technician. ●照明効果 lighting effects.

しょうめつ 消滅 图 ⟦消失⟧ disappearance; ⟦絶滅⟧ extinction.

—— **消滅する** 動 (消失する) disappear; (死滅する) become extinct; (権利などが) expire; (時効を怠ったために)《法律》lapse. ●自然消滅する *die out* in the course of time. ▶その協定は 5 月 1 日に消滅した The agreement *expired* [*ceased to exist*] on May 1.

しょうめん 正面 ❶⟦前部⟧ the front; (建物の装飾的な) the facade /fəsɑ́ːd/. ●正面玄関 the *front* entrance. ●建物の正面で待つ wait *at the front of* the building. ●正面の方を見る look *to* [*one's right/front*. ●もう帰るの. 正面出口で待っているわね I'm ready to go. I'll meet you out *front*. ▶その宮殿の正面は非常に装飾的だ The *front* [*facade*] of the palace is very décorative. ●その家の正面には大きな庭がある There is a big garden *in front of* [xbefore] the house. (⟨!⟩before は漠然と「…の前・前方で」だが, このように静止した物に通例用いない)
❷⟦相対すること⟧ ●彼女の顔を正面から見る look ⟨xat⟩ her *straight* [*right*] in the face. (⟨!⟩look (at) her face straight [from the front] などは通例いわない) ●三塁正面のゴロ[センター正面のライナー]を打つた hit a grounder at the third baseman [a liner straight away to center field]. ▶銀行は私たちの家の正面(=真向かい)にある The bank is *just opposite* (*to*) [《主に米話》*across from*, xin front of] our house. (⟨!⟩to は省略する方が普通)
❸⟦その他の表現⟧ ●その案に正面切って(=真っ向から)反対する *directly* oppose the plan; set [put] one's face against the plan. ●正面からの疑問に取り組む squarely tackle the problem.

しょうめんしょうとつ 正面衝突 a head-on collision ⟨*between* two cars⟩; a head-on ⟨*car*⟩ crash. (⇨衝突する ❶ [第 3 文例])

しょうもう 消耗 图 ⟦ひどく疲れること⟧ exhaustion; ⟦消費⟧ consumption; ⟦磨耗⟧ wéar and téar.

—— **消耗する** 動 (物・精力などを) consume; (体力を) exhaust. ▶私は激しい労働で体力を完全に消耗した I *was* completely [absolutely, xvery] *exhausted from* [*by*] hard work.

●消耗品 consumables.

じょうもの 上物 excellent [choice] goods; high(-) quality goods; goods of the highest quality.

しょうもん 小問 a subquestion.

しょうもん 証文 a bond. ▶彼の口約束は証文と同じ(=絶対確かだ) His word is (as good as) his bond. (⟨!⟩（ ）内は通例省略される)

じょうもん 定紋 a family crest.

じょうもん 城門 a castle gate.

じょうもん 縄文 ●縄文時代 the *Jomon* period; (説明的に) an archaeological period in Japan down to the third century B.C. when *Jomon* pottery was used [in use]. ●縄文土器 *Jomon* pottery; (説明的に) cord-marked pottery made during the *Jomon* period.

しょうや 庄屋 a village headman in the *Edo* period.

しょうやく 生薬 a [《米》an] herbal medicine; a crude drug.

しょうやく 抄訳 图 (部分訳) translation of selected chapters [passages]; (全体を縮めた訳) an abridged translation.

—— **抄訳する** 動 translate selected chapters [passages] ⟨*from*⟩; make an abridged translation ⟨*of*⟩.

じょうやく 条約 a treaty. ●日米安全保障条約 the U.S.-Japan Security *Treaty*. ●条約加盟国 a *treaty* power. (⟨!⟩通例複数形で) ●通商条約を結ぶ conclude [enter into, make] a commercial *treaty* ⟨*with*⟩. (⟨!⟩「条約を結んでいる」という状態をいうときは have a *treaty*) ●平和条約に調印する sign a peace *treaty* ⟨*with*⟩. ●3 国間の条約を改正[批准; 破棄]する revise [ratify; abolish] a *treaty between* the three countries. (⟨!⟩between は通例 2 者間に用いるが, 個別性を強調するときは 3 者以上でも among ではなく between を用いる)

じょうやど 定宿 one's usual inn [hotel].

じょうやとい 常雇い regular [full-time] employment; (人) a ful-time employee [worker].

じょうやとう 常夜灯 a nightlight; an all-night light.

しょうゆ 醤油 soy(/) sauce, soy. ▶しょうゆ顔(=柔らかい目鼻立ち)の男 a guy with *soft*, *gentle* features. ●顔の目鼻立ちについていう場合は face でなく features を用いる)

しょうよ 賞与 a bonus /bóunəs/. ●年末賞与 a year-end *bonus*.

じょうよ 剰余 ⟦余分の額⟧ (a) surplus; ⟦残額⟧ (a) bálance.

●剰余価値 surplus value. ●剰余金 a surplus (fund).

しょうよう 小用 urine. (⇨小便)
しょうよう 従容 ●従容として composedly; calmly.
しょうよう 称揚 praise. (⇨賞賛)

しょうよう 商用 business. (⇨仕事) ● 商用でニューヨークに行く go to New York *on business*.

しょうよう 逍遙 ── **逍遙する** 動 go for [on] a ramble; go for [have] a stroll. ● 森を逍遙する *go for [on] a ramble* in the woods; *ramble* [through] the woods.

しょうよう 慫慂 ── **慫慂する** 動 advise; suggest; (強く勧める) urge.

しょうよう 常用 名 habitual [regular] use. ● 麻薬常用者 a drug addict.

── **常用する** 動 use ... habitually [regularly]. (!薬の場合は take を用いる)

じょうようしゃ 乗用車 a (passenger) car. (⇨車)

しょうようじゅりん 照葉樹林 a broadleaf evergreen forest.

じょうよく 情欲 ● lust; sexual desire [drive].

:**しょうらい 将来** 名 ❶ [未来] the future; (人・国などの前途) a future.

①【将来は】● ▶彼女の歌手としての将来は明るい She has a bright [a great] *future* (ahead of her) as a singer./(有望な歌手だ) She is a (very) promising singer.

②【将来に】● ▶遠い将来に目を向ける look far ahead into *the future*. ● 将来に向けて資格をとる gain qualification for one's *future*.

③【将来を】● ▶人類の将来を予想する foretell *the future* of human beings. ● 息子の将来を心配[悲観]する be anxious [feel gloomy] about one's son's *future*. ● 将来を考える think about the [one's] *future*. ▶その決定は慎重かつ将来をよく見通したものでした The decision was discreet and *far-sighted*.

❷ [見込み] (物・事の) an outlook, prospects (*for*) (!前の方が客観性が高い); 《話》 future (*in*) (!通例疑問文・否定文で); (有望) promise. ● 将来性のある会社 a *promising* firm; a firm with great *promise* [good *prospects*]. ▶この事業には将来性がない There is no *future in* this business./This business has no *future* [*prospects*]./(この事業の将来性は暗い) The *outlook for* this business is [The *prospects for* this business are] gloomy. ▶彼は将来が大変楽しみな人です He is a person of great [extraordinary] *promise*.

── **将来の** 形 future; (予想される) prospective. ● 将来の妻 one's *future* [*prospective*] wife. ● 将来の夢 one's *future* dream. ● 将来のある国 a country with a *future*. ● 将来のため for the sake of one's *future*. ● 将来の計画を立てる make one's plan for *the future*; plan one's *future*. ▶君は自分の将来のことをもっと真剣に考えるべきだ You should think about your *future* more seriously.

── **将来(に)** 副 (遠い将来) in the future; (今後は) in (the) future (!な をつけるのは 《米》); (いつか) someday, one day. ● 近い将来 *in the near future; in the* not too distant *future*. ▶私は将来 [xwinning rate]に I want to be a teacher *in the future* [(大人になったら) when I grow up]. ▶日本は将来どうなるのであろうか What will become of Japan *in (the) future*?/What will be *the future* of Japan? ▶私もいつか将来アメリカに行くことがあるかもしれない I may go to America *someday* [*one day*, sometime *in the future*, (遠い将来) *in the distant future*].

しょうらい 招来 ── **招来する** 動 (招く) invite; (引き起こす) cause.

じょうらく 上洛 ── **上洛する** 動 go [come] (up) to Kyoto.

しょうらん 笑覧 ▶近著をお送りいたします. ご笑覧ください Let me send you a copy of my recent book. I'd be very happy if you would *read* it.

しょうらん 照覧 ▶神もご照覧あれ Heaven be my witness!

***しょうり 勝利** 【【戦争・競技などでの】】 (a) victory (⇔(a) defeat) (!最も一般的な語); 【競技での】 a win (⇔(a) loss) (!*victory* より口語的); 【大勝利】 (a) triumph (*over*) (!勝利の喜びを含意する). ● 敵に対する正義の勝利 the *triumph* of right *over* might. ● 勝利の女神 the goddess of *victory* (!ギリシャ神話では Nike). ● 勝利の歓声 shouts of *triumph*. ● 軍[チーム]を勝利に導く lead the troops [team] to *victory*. ● 選挙で圧倒的勝利をおさめる win a sweeping *victory* in the election. ▶その戦いで我が軍は大勝利をおさめた Our troops won [had, gained] a great *victory* at the battle./The battle ended in a great *victory* for our troops. ▶試合は 7 対 5 でタイガースの勝利となった The game ended with the Tigers *winning* (by a score of) 7 to 5. ▶我々はかなり勝利に近づきつつあった We were well on the way to *winning*.

● 勝利者 (ゲームなどの) a winner; (主に書) a victor.
● 勝利投手 [野球] a winning pitcher; a winner.
● 最多勝利投手 [野球] the winningest pitcher.

じょうり 条理 ● reason; logic. ● 条理に反する生き方 one's *immoral* (way of) living.

> 翻訳の観点から 喜助の話はよく条理が立っている. ほとんど条理が立ちすぎているといってもいいくらいである (森鷗外『高瀬舟』) Kisuke's story [talk] is very [quite] logical. In fact, it can even be said [You might as well say] that it is too logical. (!(1) story, talk は「(だれかが)語ること」の意. (2)「条理にかなっている」は logical (論理的な, 筋が通った)と表す. (3)「…といってもいいくらいである」は "You might as well say ... と表す話者の意図が強調され, 一般的な言い方の it can even be said ... より口語的)

じょうり 情理 ▶彼に情理を尽くして私の提案を受け入れさせた I persuaded him *warmheartedly and logically* to accept my offer.

じょうりく 上陸 名 (a) landing.

── **上陸する** 動 (海・空から陸の目的地に着く) land; (浜・陸に上がる) go [come] ashore (!船員が一時的に上陸する場合に用いられる); (下船する) get off a ship, 《書》 disembark; (台風などが襲う) hit, strike. ● 島に上陸する *land on* the island. ▶乗客は神戸に上陸した The passengers *went ashore* [*landed*, *disembarked*] at Kobe. ▶台風が昨夜九州に上陸した The typhoon *hit* [*struck*, x*landed on*] Kyushu last night.

● 上陸作戦 《the Normandy》 landing operations. ● 上陸用舟艇 a landing craft.

しょうりつ 勝率 the rate of winning; (投手の) winning percentage. ▶チームの勝率 won-lost percentage. ▶勝率は 5 割だ *The rate of winning* [xwinning rate] is 0.5.

***しょうりゃく 省略** 名 【省くこと】 (an) omission; 【語句などを文字を略して短くすること】 (an) abbreviation (*of*, *for*). ● 前置詞の省略 the *omission* of the preposition. ● Sept. は September の省略形である 'Sept.' is an *abbreviation of* [*for*] 'September.'/'Sept.' is *short for* [(表す) *stands for*] 'September.' ● 以下省略 The rest *is omitted*.

── **省略する** 動 omit (-tt-), leave*... out (!後の方が口語的); (縮約による) abbreviate; (短くする) shorten. ● その章を省略する *omit* [*leave out*] the chapter. ▶「真理子」という名前はしばしば「真理」と省略される The name 'Mariko' *is* often *abbreviated* [*is*

shortened] to 'Mari.'/(略して呼ばれる) Mariko *is often called Mari for short*.
- 省略符号 an apostrophe (′). ● 省略法 『文法』(an) ellipsis.

じょうりゅう 上流 ❶『川の』the upper stream; (地域) the upper reaches (of a river). ● 長良川上流の温泉郷 a hot spring village on the *upper reaches of the Nagara River*. ● 上流へ向かって泳ぐ swim *up the river*; swim *upstream*. ● 上流でアユ釣りをする enjoy *ayu* fishing [angling] in the *upper reaches (of the river)*. ● 橋はここから1キロ上流にある The bridge is one kilometer *up the river* [*upstream*] from here./The bridge is one kilometer *above* this place.
❷『社会の』▶ 彼女は上流(=上流家庭)の生まれである She was born in [(出である) comes of] an *upper-class family*.
- 上流階級 the upper class(es). ● 上流社会 high [fashionable, polite] society.

じょうりゅう 蒸留 distillation.
—— **蒸留する 動** distill. ▶ ウイスキーは大麦を蒸留して作られる Whiskey *is distilled from* barley.
- 蒸留酒 spirits; (米) liquor. ● 蒸留酒製造所 a distillery. ● 蒸留水 distilled water.

しょうりょ 焦慮 ● 焦慮の色が濃い look worried [impatient].
—— **焦慮する 動** (気をもむ) be worried (*about, over*); (いらだつ) be impatient (*with, at*).

しょうりょう 少量 ● 少量のバター *a little* butter; *a small amount* [*quantity*] *of* butter. ● ごく少量の塩 only *a little* [(ひとつまみの) *a pinch of*] salt; (話) just *a little bit of* salt.

しょうりょう 渉猟 —— **渉猟する 動** (広く読む) read 《books》 extensively; (山野などを渡り歩く) wander around mountains and fields.

しょうりょう 精霊 the spirit of a dead person.
- 精霊流し lantern floating, lantern-offering on the water.

しょうりょうばった 精霊ばった 『昆虫』 an oriental longheaded locust.

しょうりょく 省力 (労働を減らすこと) (a) reduction of labor; (経費の節約) saving of labor. ● 省力化を図る try to *save* [*reduce*] *labor*.
- 省力装置 a labor-saving device.

じょうりょくじゅ 常緑樹 an evergreen (tree).

しょうるい 生類 living things; creatures. (⇨生き物)

じょうるり 浄瑠璃 *joruri*; (説明的に) a narrative chanted to the accompaniment of the *samisen*.

***しょうれい 奨励 名** encouragement; (刺激) stimulation; (促進) promotion. ● 社会奉仕の奨励 the *encouragement* of social service.
—— **奨励する 動** encourage 《him *to do*》. (⇨勧める, 薦める) ▶ 父は私に貯蓄を奨励した My father *encouraged* me *to* save.
- 奨励金 a bounty 《*on*》.

しょうれい 省令 a ministerial ordinance.

しょうれい 症例 a case 《*of*》.

じょうれい 条例 a regulation. (⇨法律, 規則) ● 市条例 the municipal *regulations*.

じょうれん 常連 『店の』a regular customer 《*at*》, (話) a regular 《*at*》; a patron /péitrən/ 《*of*》; 『興業の』a 《concert》 goer. ▶ goer の前に行く先の名前がくる ▶ あの人はうちの常連客の1人だ He's one of our *regular customers*.

しょうろ 松露 『植物』a truffle.

じょうろ 如雨露 a watering can.

しょうろう 鐘楼 a bell tower; (教会堂に付属する) a belfry.

しょうろく 抄録 an extract; an excerpt.

しょうろん 小論 a short article [essay]; (自分の) one's article [essay].

しょうろん 詳論 名 a full [a detailed] discussion; a thorough debate.
—— **詳論する 動** discuss ... fully [in (great) detail].

しょうろんぶん 小論文 an essay; a short essay; 『試験』an essay exam [test].

しょうわ 昭和 Showa. (⇨平成)

しょうわ 笑話 (こっけいな話) a funny story; (ユーモアのある話) a humorous story.

しょうわ 唱和 ▶ A君のために万歳三唱しますのでご唱和願います Let's all give three cheers [*Banzai*] for Mr. A.

じょうわ 情話 a love story; a romance.

しょうわくせい 小惑星 『天文』an asteroid /ǽstərɔ̀id/. (■通例複数形で)

しょうわるい 性悪 —— 性悪な 形 ill-natured; wicked and malevolent.

じょうわん 上腕 『解剖』the upper arm; the brachium.

しょえん 初演 the first performance 《*of*》; the premiere 《*of*》. ▶ 新ドイツオペラを東京で初演された The first performance [The premiere] of a new German opera *was given* in Tokyo./A new German opera *was first performed* [*was first staged*, *was premiered*] in Tokyo.

じょえん 助演 —— 助演する 動 support; act 《*with*》; play a supporting role [part].
- 助演女優 a supporting actress. ● 助演男優 a supporting actor.

ショー a show. ● バラエティショー a variety *show*. ● モーターショーを開催する hold an auto [a car, (英) a motor] *show*. ● きのうはショーを見に行った I went to the *show* yesterday.
- ショービジネス show business [(話) biz].

じょおう 女王 a queen. ● エリザベス2世女王 *Queen* Elizabeth Ⅱ. (■ Ⅱ は the second と読む) ● 英国女王 the *Queen* of England. (■ ただし単に統治者として「女王」というときは Queen (無冠詞)) ● 桜祭りの女王 the *queen* of the cherry blossom festival.
- 女王のようにふるまう queen it 《*over her friends*》. ● 女王アリ 『昆虫』a queen ant. ● 女王バチ 『昆虫』a queen bee.

ショーウインドー a (show) window. ● ショーウインドーをのぞき込む look at the displays in the *window*.

ジョーカー 『トランプ』a joker.

ジョーク a joke. (⇨冗談)

ショーケース 『陳列用ガラスケース』a showcase.

ジョージア 『米国の州』Georgia (略 Ga. 郵便略 GA).

ショーツ 『運動用短パン』shorts 《米》では「(男性用)パンツ」の意にもなる); 『女性用パンツ』panties, 《英》pants.

ショート 名 『短絡』『電気』a short circuit, (話) a short; 『遊撃手』『野球』a shortstop (■守備位置の意では short ともいえ, 無冠詞). ● ショートを守る play *shortstop*.
—— **ショートする 動** (電気が) short-circuit; short out. ▶ 停電して停電した The electric current was cut off owing to a *short circuit*.
- ショートアイアン 『ゴルフ』a short iron. ● ショートカット a short haircut [cut]. ● ショートケーキ (主に米) 《a slice of》 《strawberry》 shortcake (■日本語のものとは少し異なる。この short は「ショートニング (shortening) が多くてさくさくする」の意); cake with

cream and fruit on top. ●ショートショート a short-short story. ●ショートステイ a short stay in a residential care or nursing home. ●ショートストップ a shortstop. ●ショートトラック〖競技〗short track speed skating; (競走路) a short track. ●ショートドリンク a short drink. ●ショートバウンド a short hop. ●ショートバウンドでボールを捕る field a ball on the short hop. ●ショートパンツ (短ズボン) short pants (主に米) [trousers (主に英)]; shorts (‼(米)では「(男性用)パンツ」の意もある). ●ショートプログラム (フィギュアスケートの) the short program. ●ショートヘア (have) short hair. ●ショートホール〖ゴルフ〗a par-three hole. (‼ a short hole は通例「短い穴」の意)

ショートニング shortening. (参考) 菓子をさくさくさせるためのバターなど)

ショーボート〖演芸船〗a showboat.

ショーマンシップ showmanship.

ショール〖肩掛け〗a shawl.

ショールーム a showroom. ●電気製品[ガス器具]のショールーム an electricity [a gas] *showroom*. ●電気製品のショールームで炊飯器を買う buy a rice cooker from an electricity *showroom*.

しょか 初夏 ●初夏に in early summer, early in summer.

しょか 書架 a bookshelf (複 -shelves); (図書館の) a stack. (‼ しばしば複数形で)

しょか 書家 a calligrapher.

しょかい 初回 the first time; 〖野球〗the first inning.

*じょがい 除外 名 〖締め出すこと〗exclusion (↔inclusion); 〖例外にすること〗(an) exception.
── 除外する 動 〖締め出す, 仲間に入れない〗exclude; 〖例外として省く〗〖書〗except; 〖名簿・グループから省く〛omit, leave*... out; 〖数に入れない〗count ... out (⇔除く); 〖可能性を考えない〗rule ... out. ●その可能性を除外して考える *rule out* the possibility.

しょがかり 諸掛かり sundry costs [expenses].

しょがくしゃ 初学者 a beginner. ●初心(者)・初学者向けの本 a book (intended) for *beginners*.

じょがくせい 女学生 a schoolgirl; (米) a girl [a female] student.

しょがこっとう 書画骨董 (説明的に) objects of art—calligraphic works and paintings drawn with Chinese ink—and curiosities.

しょかつ 所轄 (管轄) (やや書) jurisdiction. (⇒管轄) ●所轄の税務所 the district tax office; the tax office in charge of one's district. ●所轄官庁 (関係当局) the authorities concerned.

じょがっこう 女学校 a girls' (high) school.

しょかん 初刊 the first publication.

しょかん 所感 ●それについて所感(=思い)を述べる make *remarks* [(論評) *comments*] on it.

しょかん 所管 jurisdiction. (⇒所轄, 管轄)

しょかん 書簡 (手紙) a letter; (集合的) (やや書) correspondence. ●書簡文例集 a letter-writer. (‼「手紙を書く人」の意もある) ●往復書簡 (集合的) correspondence.
●書簡体小説 an epistolary novel.

じょかん 女官 a court lady; a lady-in-waiting.

しょき 初期 名 the beginning; the early part (*of*); the early years [days]; (病気などの) an early stage. ▶その実験はまだ初期段階だ The experiment is still at an *early* stage [in its *early stages*].
── 初期の 形 early (↔late). ●彼の初期の作品 his *early* work.

── 初期に 副 early (↔late). ●1980年代の初期に in the *early* 1980's [1980s]. (‼ 1980(')s は nineteen eighties と読む) ●17世紀初期に in the *early part* of the 17th century. ▶禅は鎌倉時代初期に中国から伝わった Zen was introduced from China at the *beginning* of [in the *early, early* in the] Kamakura period.
●初期微動〖地質〗preliminary tremor.

しょき 所期 ── 所期の 形 expected. (⇒期待) ●所期の成果をあげる achieve the *expected* results.

しょき 書記 a clerk, a secretary. ●大使館・領事館官 the First *Secretary* at [of] the Embassy.
●書記局 a secretariat. ●書記長 a chief clerk [secretary]; (政党の) a secretary-general.

しょき 暑気 〖暑さ〗heat; 〖暑い気候〗hot weather. ●暑気あたりする (=暑さにやられる) be affected by the *heat* [*hot weather*]. ●暑気払いに to forget [beat] the summer *heat*.

しょきか 初期化 ── 初期化する 動 〖コンピュータ〗initialize; format.

しょきゅう 初級 ── 初級の 形 elementary. ●初級英語 elementary English; English for *beginners*.
●初級課程 an *elementary* [a *beginners'*] course.
●初級者用テキスト a textbook for *beginners*.

しょきゅう 初球 〖野球〗(打者に対する) the first ball [pitch]; (試合・各イニングの) the first pitch. ●初球打ちの打者 a *first-ball* hitter. ●打者に対して初球を速球から入る throw a fastball on the *first pitch* to a batter; start a batter off with a fastball.

じょきょ 除去 ── (a) removal.
── 除去する 動 remove; get rid of .... (⇒除く) ●腎臓の結石を除去する *remove* the kidney stones.
●害悪を除去する remove [*get rid of*] evils.

しょきょう 所行, 所業 behavior; conduct. (⇒行い)

じょきょうじゅ 助教授 (米) an associate [an assistant] professor, (英) a reader. (⇒教授 関連) ●T大学物理学助教授、田中健 Ken Tanaka, *Associate Professor of* [*Reader in*] Physics at T College.

しょぎょうむじょう 諸行無常 Everything is evanescent [Nothing is permanent] in this world.

じょきょく 序曲 〖音楽〗an óverture (*to*). (‼ 比喩的にも用いる)

ジョギング 名 jogging; (1回の) a jog. ●公園にジョギングに行く go *jogging* [go for a *jog*] in the park; go to the park for a *jog*. ●公園のジョギングコース a *jogging* track in the park.
── ジョギングする 動 jog.
●ジョギングシューズ (a pair of) jogging shoes.

しよく 私欲 (私利) (やや書) (*from, out of*) self-interest; (利己的な欲望) selfish desires. (⇒私利) ●私欲に目がくらむ be blinded by *selfish desires*.

> 翻訳のこころ　人間は、もともと私欲のかたまりさ。信じては、ならぬ (太宰治『走れメロス』) Human beings are by nature [in nature] full of egotistic desire. You should not believe them. (‼ (1)「...のかたまり(である)」は be full of ... (...で満ちている, 一杯である) と表す. (2)「もともと」は by nature (生来), in nature (=本質において) と表す. in nature の場合は、前後にコンマを入れる. (3)「私欲」は egotistic desire (利己的[自己中心的]な欲望) と表す)

*しょく 職 ❶〖仕事〗(具体的な) a job; (働くこと) work; 〖雇われること〗employment; 〖職業〗(an) occupation; 〖地位〗(責任のある) a post; (相対的・社会的な) (書) a position. (⇒職業, 地位)
①〈～職〉●事務職 clerical [desk] *work*. ●専門職 a professional *occupation*. ●管理

managerial [an administrative] *position* [*post*].
❷【職を】● 職を得る get a *job*; get *employment*. (⇨就職する) ● 職を失う lose one's *job*; lose *employment*; (解雇される) be dismissed [《口》fired]. ● 職を変える change one's *job* [*occupation*]. ● 職を退く resign one's *post* [*position*]; (公職を) leave [resign] *office*; (嫌になって仕事を放り出す) walk out of one's *job*. (⇨職探し) ● 職を探す look [hunt] for a *job*; seek *employment*. ▶この年になって秘書の職を探すのも容易ではありません It isn't easy to try to get a *job as* a secretary at my age. ▶ 職を求む (掲示) *Position* [*Situation*] wanted.
❸【職が】▶ 彼らには職がない(=失業している) They are *out of work* [*a job*, *employment*]./They are *jobless* [*unemployed*].
❹【職に】● 職につく(⇨❷【職を得る】) ▶ 今の守衛の職につく前は彼は警官でした He was a policeman before taking this *job* as a guard. ▶ 彼は政府内で重要な職にある He holds an important *post* [*position*] in the Government.
❷【技術】skill; (熟練を要する) (a) trade. ● 手に職をつける acquire some kind of *skill*; learn a *trade*.
❸【任務】duties (!通例複数形で). (⇨職務, 任務) ● 職を果たす fulfill [perform, carry out] one's *duties*.

しょく 食 ❶【食物】food. (!通例複合語を形成するのでその第1要素の見出し、または複合語見出しを参照のこと) ● 食と健康の関係 a relationship between *food* [*diet*] and health. (! diet は「人が定期的に摂取する食物」の意。また、栄養価の高も含む場合もある)
❷【食事】a meal. (⇨食事) ● 1泊2食つきで9,500円 9,500 yen per [a] night including two *meals*. ▶ 彼女は1日2食しか食べない She has only two *meals* a day.
❸【食べること】(食欲) (an) appetite /ǽpətàit/. ● 食が進む ● 食が進む[進まない] have a good [a poor] *appetite*; eat much [cannot eat much]. ● 食が細い ▶ その子は食が細い The child is a small [a light] *eater*. (⇨小食)
● 食生活 (⇨食生活)

しょく 食, 蝕 《天文》 an eclipse. ● 日[月]食 a solar [a lunar] *eclipse*.

-しょく -色 ● 保護色 protective *coloration*. ● 地方色 local *color*.

しょくあたり 食あたり ● ひどい食あたり a bad case of *food poisoning* /pɔ́izəniŋ/. ● 食あたりする get [come down with, ×suffer from] *food poisoning*. (! suffer は「今食あたりにかかっている」状態をさすからここでは不適切)

しょくいき 職域 (職場) one's place of work; one's workplace; (職務の範囲) the area of work.

しょくいん 職員 [ある部門や組織の一員] a staff member, 《集合的》 the staff 《米》 では通例単数扱いだが、《英》では職員全体を一つの単位と考えるときは単数扱い、1人1人を問題にするときは複数扱い); (特に公的な仕事に用いる複数扱い); [働く人] a worker; (従業員) an employee.
● ホテルの職員になる join the hotel *staff*; become a hotel *clerk*. ● 図書館の職員 library *staff*. ● 市役所職員 a city *worker* [*employee*]; (庁舎内勤務者) a city office *worker*; (市の役人) a city official. ▶ 彼は経理部の職員だ He is a *staff member* [*on the staff*] of the general accounting division. (! ×He is a *staff* of .... としない) ▶ この図書館には20人の職員がいる There are 20 *staff members* [is

a *staff* of 20, 《英》are 20 *staff*] in this library. ▶ その部には職員が多い The department has a large (↔a small) *staff* [×many *staffs*]. ▶ この病院には十分な職員がいる(=十分配置されている) This hospital *is* well *staffed*.
● 職員会議 a staff meeting; (先生の) a teachers' meeting (!大学の、また《米》の高校の職員会議は a faculty meeting). ● 職員室 a teachers' room. ● 職員録 a directory of government officials.

しょくぐう 処遇 图【待遇】(a) treatment. ● 親切な処遇を受けた I received kind *treatment*./I was kindly *treated*.
—**処遇する** 動 ● 彼を冷たく処遇する give him cold *treatment*; 《話》 give him the cold shoulder, cold-shoulder him.

しょくえん 食塩 (一般に) salt; (食卓用の) table salt. ● 食塩入れ (振り出し式)《米》a saltshaker; 《英》a saltcellar. ● 食塩水 a salt [a saline /séilin/] solution. (! salt water は「塩水で主に海水をさす)

:しょくぎょう 職業 an occupation; a profession; a trade; a vocation; a career /kəríər/; a job; work; business.

> **使い分け** occupation 職業をさす最も一般的な語で、正式な文書などにも使うやや堅い語.
> **profession** 医師・弁護士・教師など知的な専門知識や訓練を必要とする職業.
> **trade** 技術や熟練を要求する職業.
> **vocation** 利害を離れ社会に貢献する職業.
> **career** 一生にたずさわる、また経歴になるほど長くたずさわる職業.
> **job** 賃金をもらってする仕事・勤め口.
> **work** 職業や勤務だけでなく、労働・作業・任務など幅広い意味を持つ一般的な語.
> **business** 商業や経済、生産と関わる仕事. 複合語で用いられることが多い.

❶【職業～】● 職業的自立 professional independence. ● 職業上の occupational; vocational. ● 職業別の according to *occupation*. ● 職業柄室内にいることが多い the nature of my *job* keeps me indoors often.
❷【職業は】▶ 彼の職業は何ですか What is his *occupation* [*job*]?/What kind of *work* [*job*] does he do?/What's his *line*?/(何をしている) What does he do? (!(1) job を用いる言い方は目上の人には避ける. (2) What is he? も職業を問うが、相手に向かって What are you? と尋ねるのは失礼なので避ける. Who is he? は通例名前を聞く表現だが、職業に用いることもある. (3) What is he doing? は一時的な職業であることを暗示する. (4) 答え方はいずれも He is a teacher./He teaches at a high school. などでよい) ▶ 彼女の職業はプログラマーです She is a (computer) programmer *by occupation*. (!無冠詞に注意. 職種に応じて by profession, by trade も用いる: He is a doctor *by profession*.)
❸【職業に】● 教師を職業に choose teaching as one's *occupation* [*profession*, *vocation*]; choose teaching for one's *career*. ● 著述業を職業にする make writing one's *profession* [*career*]. ● 医学関係の職業に就く enter a medical *profession*. ▶ 彼はどんな職業に向いていますか What (kind of *occupation* [*work*]) is he fit [suited] for?
❹【職業を】● 職業を変える change one's *occupation* [*job*]; (次々と) change *jobs*. ● 職業を探す look for *work* [*a job*]; 《書》seek *employment*.
● 職業安定所 a job placement [security] office. ● 職業意識 job consciousness. ● 職業教育 voca-

しょくげん

tional education. ● 職業訓練 vocational training. ● 職業(訓練)学校 a vocational (training) school. ● 職業指導 vocational guidance. ● 職業紹介所《米》a recruitment [an employment] agency, a career center;《英》an employment office, a job centre. (⇒就職〔第4文例〕) ● 職業適性検査 a vocational aptitude test. ● 職業病 an occupational [a vocational, a job-related] disease. ● 職業婦人 a career woman [girl] (❗a career man は通例「官公庁に勤める男性」の意); a professional woman. ● 職業別労働組合 a trade-specific [a craft] union. ● 職業倫理 professional ethics.

しょくげん 食言 —— 食言する 動 (約束をたがえる) break one's promise (❗eat one's words は「前言の誤りを認めて〔撤回する〕」の意); (food) eat.

しょくご 食後 食後に after a meal. ● 食後の休憩時間 a recess *after a meal*. ● 食後の果物[菓子] (a) dessert.

しょくざい 贖罪 图 redemption. —— **贖罪する** 動 redeem 《him》from sin.

しょくさがし 職探し job hunting. ● 職探しをする look [hunt] for a job;《書》seek a position.

しょくさん 殖産 the promotion of industry.

しょくし 食指 (人さし指) one's index [first] finger; one's forefinger.
 ● 食指が動く be interested 《in it》; want 《to get it》. ▶ そのワイングラスを見てちょっと食指が動いた I *felt like buying* the wine glass when I saw it.

:しょくじ 食事 a meal, a diet; dinner.

〈使い分け〉
meal 1回分の食事のことで, 朝食(breakfast), 昼食(lunch), 夕食(supper)を総称する語. 個々の食事名が明らかなとき meal は用いない: 今朝は遅い食事をした We had a late *break-fast* [×meal] this morning. また meal は冠詞がつくのに反し breakfast, lunch, supper は通例無冠詞. ただし形容詞が形容詞を伴う場合は a をつけ, 特定の食事を強調するときは the をつける: その翌朝の食事は質素なものだった *The breakfast* we were served the next morning was a simple [a frugal] one.
dinner 1日のうちで最も主要な食事. (⇒夕食)
diet 病気治療や体重調整のための規定食.

① **【～食事】** ● 毎日3度の食事 daily *meals*. ● おいしい[まずい]食事 a good [a poor] *meal*. ● フルコースの食事 a full-course *dinner*. ● バランスのとれた食事 a balanced *diet*. ● 軽い食事をする have a light *meal*; 《話》have a bite (to eat).
② **【食事(の)～】** ● 食事の作法 *table* manners. ● 食事制限をする[している] go [be] on a *diet*. ● 食事の後片づけをする clear the table (and do the dishes). ● ( )内は皿洗いまで含めた表現. ● 食事代を払う pay a *meal*. ● 食事つきの学生寮 a campus dormitory with meals. ● 彼の食事の世話をする make *meals* for him. ● 食事の席につく sit at a dining table. ▶ 食事中にそんなことを話すのはよくない It's not good to talk about that while (we are) *eating* [during the meal,《米》*at the table*,《英書》*at table*]. ▶ 食事の時間です It's time to *eat*.
③ **【食事に】** ● 彼女を食事に誘う ask her out for a *meal* [*dinner*, ×*supper*]. ● 彼らを食事に invite 《them》to dinner [a *dinner*]. (❗後の方は正式の晩さん会などの場合) ● 食事に招かれる be invited to dinner [a *dinner*]. ● 食事にワインを飲む drink wine with [at] one's *meal*. ▶ 彼は朋子と食事に出かけた He went (out) for a *meal* with Tomoko.
④ **【食事を】** ● 急いで食事をする(=とる) have [eat]

しょくたく

a quick *meal*. ● 外で食事をする eat [《書》*dine*] out; (レストランで) *eat* (dinner) at a restaurant. ● 食事を用意する (料理) prepare [cook, make,《米話》fix] a *meal*; (お膳立て) set the table. ● 食事をぬく skip one's *meal*. (❗miss one's meal は食べそこなうの含みがある) ● 食事を出す serve《him》*a meal*. ● 食事を注文する order a *meal*. ● 食事を済ます finish *eating*. ● 食事をおごる treat him to a *meal*. ▶ 私たちは道路沿いのレストランで食事をした We *ate* at a roadside restaurant. ▶ 1日3度の食事をする We have [eat] three *meals* a day./We *eat* three times a day.

〈会話〉「いっしょに食事をしていかれませんか」「ありがとう. 喜んで」"Would you like to *eat* [*have dinner*] with me?" "Thank you. I'd love to."
 ● 食事時間 a mealtime. ● 食事時間に at *meals*.

しょくしゅ 触手 (昆虫の) a feeler;(植物・タコなどの) a tentacle.
 ● 触手を伸ばす (人が) try to get《it》by illegal means.

しょくしゅ 職種 the kind [type] of job. ▶ どんな職種につきたいですか What *kind* [*type*] *of job* would you like to engage in?

しょくじゅ 植樹 —— 植樹する 動 ● …を記念して植樹する *plant a tree* in commemoration of …. ● 植樹祭 a tree-planting ceremony. 〈事情〉Arbor Day (植樹の日)は米国・カナダの春の年中行事の一つ)

しょくしょう 食傷 ▶ 彼の話には食傷した(=うんざりした) I was sick and tired of [was fed up with] his talk./(もうたくさんだ) I had (more than) enough of his talk.

しょくしょう 職掌 ● 職掌柄, 匿名を希望する Due to the nature of my position, I herein request anonymity.

しょくじょ(せい) 織女(星)【天文】Vega /víːɡə/.

しょくじりょうほう 食餌療法 a diet therapy; a dietary cure. ● 低塩[カロリー]食餌療法 a low-salt [-calorie] *diet*.

しょくしん 触診 图【医学】palpation.
—— **触診する 動** palpate; examine by touch.

しょくじんしゅ 食人種 (人食い人種) a cannibal tribe. (⇒人食い)

しょくせい 食性 dietary habit.

しょくせい 植生 vegetation.

しょくせい 職制 [職場の人員組織]the staff organization of an office; [管理職]the management (❗単・複両扱い). ● 職制を改める reorganize an office.

しょくせいかつ 食生活 ● 食生活(=食習慣)を改善する improve one's *eating habits*; (より栄養価の高い食物を食べる) eat more nourishing food [better food]. ● 食生活が貧しい eat poor food. ▶ 日本人の食生活は最近よくなった The *diet* of Japanese people [《やや書》the Japanese] has improved recently.

しょくせき 職責 (義務) one's duty. ● 職責を果たす fulfill [《書》discharge] one's *duty*; do one's *duty*. ● 職責を果たせない fail to do [fail in] one's *duty*.

しょくぜん 食前 ● 食前に before a meal. ● 食前の祈りを唱える say grace before the meal.
 ● 食前酒 an aperitif /ǽpəriːtíːf/.

しょくぜん 食膳 (⇒→ 食卓)
 ● 食膳に供する ● 客の食膳に供する serve《fish》to the guests.

しょくだい 燭台 a candlestick, a candlestand.

しょくたく 食卓 a (dining) table. (⇒テーブル) ● 食

しょくたく 〔につく〕 sit down to [at] (the) *table*. (❗the を省略するのは《英》) ●食卓の用意をする lay [set, spread] the *table*. ●食卓(の上)を片づける clear the *table*. ●食卓を離れる leave the *table*; (中座する) be excused from the *table*. ●彼らは食卓を囲んで座っていた They were sitting around the *table*. ▶食卓で(=食事中に)鼻をかんではいけません You shouldn't blow your nose *at the table* 《米》[*at table* 《英書》]. (❗やや堅く大げさな言い方. ... while you are eating. の方が普通)
〔会話〕「食卓の用意ができましたのでどうぞ」「ありがとう」 "Please come to the *table*." "Thank you." (❗ホストと客の対話)
●食卓塩 table salt.

しょくたく 嘱託 (正規でない従業員) a nonregular employee.
●嘱託殺人 murder by contract.

しょくちゅうしょくぶつ 食虫植物 〖植物〗 an insectivorous /inséktivərəs/ plant.

しょくちゅうどく 食中毒 food poisoning. (⇨食あたり)

しょくちょう 食長 a foreman (複 foremen); an overseer.

しょくつう 食通 〖美食〗 a gourmet /gυərméi/, an épicure, 〖食道楽〗 epicuréanism.

*****しょくどう 食堂** (家・ホテルなどの) a dining room; (レストラン) a restaurant; (24時間営業の安食堂) 《米》 a diner; 〖軽食屋〗 a café /kæféi/ (❗《英》では酒類を出さない), a lunchroom (❗学校などの昼食室にも用いる); (セルフサービスの) a cafeteria /kæfətíəriə/; (カウンター式の) a snack bar (❗酒類は出さない); (列車内・駅などの) a buffet /bəféi/. ●彼はいつも学校の[社員]食堂で昼食を食べる He always eats lunch in the school [company] *cafeteria*.
●食堂車 a dining [《英》a restaurant] car; 《米》a diner. 〖参考〗食堂車への案内放送の1例: Passengers are invited to proceed to the restaurant. (❗proceed は「(ある方向に)進む, 向かう」の意の堅い語)

しょくどう 食道 a gullet; 〖解剖〗 an esophagus /isǽfəgəs/.
●食道がん 〖医学〗cancer of the esophagus.

しょくどうらく 食道楽 (美食) epicureanism /èpikjυəríːənizm/; (美食家) 《やや書》 an épicure; (食通) 《やや書》a gourmet /gυərméi/.

しょくにく 食肉 meat. (⇨肉❷)
●食肉動物 (肉食動物) a carnivorous [a flesh-eating] animal; a cárnivòre.

*****しょくにん 職人** (男の) a craftsman (複 -men), (女の) a craftswoman (複 -women); 〖書〗an artisan /ɑ́ːrtəzən/. ●腕のいい[わるい]職人たち good [bad, poor] *craftspeople*.
●職人気質 the artisan [craftsman] spirit. ●職人芸 craftsmanship.

しょくのう 職能 (能力) ability for some work; (はたらき) function.
●職能給 the wages on job evaluation. ●職能代表制 the functional representation. ●職能別労働組合 a trade-specific [a craft] union.

*****しょくば 職場** one's place of work, one's workplace; work (❗《英》では, 職場の種類を具体的に表現するのが普通》; (作業場) a workshop. ●彼は2年後職場に復帰した Two years later he returned to *work*. (❗work は名詞) ▶職場のセクハラに対する問題意識が次第に高まってきた The awareness of sexual harassment in the *workplace* has gradually increased. ▶職場に電話してこないで Try not to call me up *at work*.

●職場環境 the office [working] environment; office conditions. ●職場結婚 a marriage between coworkers. ▶彼は職場結婚をした He married a woman working in the same company [office]. ●職場保育所 a workplace nursery. ●職場放棄 a strike; a walkout. (⇨ストライキ)

しょくばい 触媒 〖化学〗 a catalyst.

しょくはつ 触発 ━ 触発する 動 ▶彼のほかな発言がけんかを触発した His stupid remark *touched off* [引き金となった] *triggered* a fight.

しょくパン 食パン bread; (薄く切った) sliced bread. (⇨パン) ●食パン1枚 a slice of *bread*. ●食パン2山 two loaves of *bread*.

しょくひ 食費 (家計の中の) food expenses; (下宿などでの食事代) the charge for board. ▶月にどのくらい食費がかかりますか How much do you pay for *food* a month?

しょくひ 植皮 图 〖医学〗skin grafting; dermatoplasty. ━ 植皮する 動 graft.
●植皮術 a skin graft.

*****しょくひん 食品** a food (個々の食品をいう); (食品1点) an article [a piece] of food; (総称) foodstuffs. (⇨食べ物) ●健康[冷凍]食品 health [frozen] *food*(s).
●食品衛生 food hygiene /háidʒiːn/. ●食品添加物 an [a food] additive. ●食品業界 the food industry.

‡**しょくぶつ 植物** a plant; 《集合的》vegetation; (一地方・時代の) the flora (複 〜s, florae). ●熱帯[高山]植物 tropical [alpine] *plants*. ●野生[栽培]植物 wild [garden] *plants*. ●西インド諸島の植物 the *flora* of the West Indies. ●植物を栽培する grow *plants*. ▶植物に水をやるのを忘れた I forgot to water the *plants*. ▶すべての植物が霜でだめになった All the *plants* were destroyed by the frost. ▶植物を愛することは, 私にとって一つの宗教である For me it's a religion to love *plants*.
●植物園 a botanical garden. (❗しばしば複数形で) ●植物界 the plant [vegetable] kingdom. ●植物学 botany. ●植物学者 a botanist. ●植物採集 plant(-)collecting. ●植物状態人間 (a human) vegetable [《英》 cabbage]. ●植物性 vegetable; botanical. ●植物(性)油 vegetable oil. ●植物性脂肪 vegetable fat. ●植物標本 a botanical specimen. ●植物分布 the distribution of plants. ●植物ホルモン a plant hormone; a phytohormone.

しょくぶん 職分 one's duty. (⇨勤め, 職務)

しょくべに 食紅 red food coloring.

しょくぼう 嘱望 ▶将来を嘱望される(=前途有望な)青年 a promising youth; a young person of promise. ▶彼は我が校で将来を嘱望されている学生の1人だ(=我が校のホープだ) Our school *has* [*puts its*] *hopes* on him and several other students.

しょくみんち 植民地 图 a colony. ●英国の植民地 a British *colony*. ●「入植者」は a colonist) ●植民地にする colonize 《a foreign country》.
━ 植民地の 形 colonial. (❗通例限定的に)
●植民地化 colonization. ●植民地支配 colonial rule. ●植民地主義 colonialism. ●植民地政策 a colonial policy.

しょくむ 職務 〖義務, 任務〗(a) duty (⇨任務); 〖仕事〗 work. ●職務上の調査 an official inquiry. ●職務を遂行する perform [carry out] one's *duty* [*duties*]. ●職務を怠る neglect one's *duty* [*work*]. ●職務に専念する attend to one's *work* [*duties*]. ●職務に忠実だ be faithful to one's duties. ●職務についている be *on duty*. ▶彼は職務怠

慢で解雇された He was dismissed for neglect of duty 〔neglecting his *duties*〕.
● 職務規定 office regulations. ● 職務給 job(-)based pay. ● 職務質問 police questioning.

しょくめい 職名 (職務の名前) (the name of) one's title 〔position〕; (職業の名前) (the name of) one's occupation.

しょくもう 植毛 图 a hair transplant 〔implant〕.
—— 植毛する 動 transplant 〔implant〕 hair.

しょくもく 嘱目 —— 嘱目する 動 pay attention to …; watch; expect much 〔*of*, *from*〕.

しょくもたれ 食もたれ (脂身の多い食べ物は食もたれする Fatty food *lie heavy on* stomach.

*****しょくもつ 食物** food. (!集合的に用い種類のときは [C]) (⇒食べ物) ● 栄養のある食物 (a) nourishing /nɔ́ːriʃiŋ/ 〔[書] nutritious〕 *food*. ● 質素な食物 simple 〔plain〕 *food*. ● 消化のよい〔悪い〕食物 digestible 〔indigestible〕 *food*. ▶レバーは栄養のある食物である Liver is (a) nourishing *food*.
● 食物アレルギー food allergy 〔intolerance〕. ● 食物繊維 dietary fiber. ● 食物連鎖 a food chain.

しょくやすみ 食休み 《have 〔take〕》a short 〔a little〕 rest after a meal.

しょくよう 食用 ▶このキノコは食用にはならないがおいしい This mushroom *is good to eat*〔《やや書》 *edible*, *fit to be eaten*〕 but does not taste (very) good.
● 食用油 (料理用油) cooking oil. ● 食用花 an edible flower. ● 食用リンゴ an éating 〔料理用〕 a cooking〕 àpple.

しょくよく 食欲 (an) appetite /ǽpətàit/. ▶今日は食欲がない〔旺盛(おぅ)だ〕 I have no 〔a good, a healthy〕 *appetite* today. ▶最近は食欲不振だ I'm suffering 〔a lack of *appetite* these days. (! suffer は状態動詞が進行形で用いることが多い) ▶お菓子を食べすぎると食欲がなくなる Eating too much candy will spoil 〔take away, make you lose〕 your *appetite*./If you eat too much candy, you will spoil 〔lose〕 your *appetite*. ▶軽い運動は食欲を増進させる A little exercise will give you a good *appetite* 〔improve your *appetite*〕.

*****しょくりょう 食料** food (!種類のときは 《食料雑貨類》 groceries, 《食料品類》 foodstuffs. ▶戦時中は多くの食料品は配給制だった Many *foodstuffs* were rationed during the war.
● 食料貯蔵室 a pantry. ● 《英》台所・食堂に隣接する》● 食料品店 a grocery; 《米》a grocery store, 《英》a grocer's (shop).

*****しょくりょう 食糧** food; 〔蓄えられた〕 provisions; 〔軍隊・探検隊などの〕 rations /rǽʃənz/. ▶兵士たちの 3 か月分の食糧 the soldiers' *rations* for three months. ▶数日のうちに冬の食糧なくなるだろう The *provisions* for winter will run out in a few days.
● 食糧事情 the food situation. ● 食糧生産 food production. ● 食糧不足 a food shortage. ● 食糧問題 the food problem.

しょくりん 植林 图 afforestation. —— 植林する 動 plant trees; afforest 〔hills〕.

しょくれき 職歴 〔職業上の経歴〕 a 〔one's〕 professional career, an 〔one's〕 occupational career, one's employment history; 〔仕事上の経験〕 work experience. ● 法律家としての長い職歴 a long *professional career* in law. ● 職歴 30 年の (= その仕事に 30 年たずさっている)英語教師 an English teacher with thirty years *on the job*.
会話 「ご職歴をうかがわせていただけませんか」「ここに来る前は IBM にいました」"Could you tell me what kind of *work experience* you've had?" "My last position was with IBM." (!事語 職歴は最も最近のものから順次さかのぼって答える)

しょくん 諸君 〔呼びかけ〕(男性のみに) Gentlemen; (男女全員に) Ladies and gentlemen; (教師が生徒などに) Everybody; (同志に) My friends. (⇒皆さん)

じょくん 叙勲 〔書〕 (a) conferment of a decoration. ● 春の叙勲者名簿 the spring honors list. ▶彼は医学に対する偉大な貢献により叙勲の栄に浴した He *was awarded* Japanese Legion of Honor *for* his great contribution to medical science.

しょけい 処刑 图 〔死刑執行〕 execution.
—— 処刑する 動 execute 《him *for* murdering his parents》; carry out an execution.
● 処刑台 a scaffold.

しょけい 書痙 〔医学〕 writer's cramp.

しょけい 諸芸 various accomplishments.

じょけい 女系 the female line. (⇔ 男系)

じょけい 叙景 a description of scenery.
● 叙景文 descriptive sentences 〔paragraphs〕 about scenery.

じょけつ 女傑 (勇敢な女) a brave 〔a heroic〕 woman 《women》; an amazon.

しょげる 〔気落ちしている〕 be depressed 〔dejected〕 (! 後の方が堅い語); 〔落胆している〕 be discouraged; (元気がない) be in low spirits. ▶彼女はしょげた様子をしていた She looked *depressed* 〔*dejected*, (失望した) *disappointed*〕./She had a *dejected* look. ▶さあ太郎、そんなことでしょげるな ヽCome on, ／Taro. Don't *let it get* you *down*. (! get … down は〔人を落ちこませる〕の意).

しょけん 初見 〔音楽〕 sight-reading. ▶ショパンの小品を初見で弾く play Chopin's short piece by sight(-reading).

しょけん 所見 〔意見〕 an opinion; (見解) a view; (簡潔で形式ばらない意見) a remark; (観察に基づく意見)〔書〕 an observation. (⇒意見) ● 所見を述べる give 〔express〕 one's *opinion(s)* 〔*view(s)*〕. ● カルテに患者の所見を書き留める write down one's *observations* of a patient in the medical record.

じょけん 女権 women's rights.
● 女権拡張運動 the women's right 〔feminist〕 movement. ● 女権拡張論 feminism. ● 女権拡張論者 a feminist.

じょげん 助言 图 advice /ədváis/; 〔書〕 (熟慮ののち与えられる専門的な) counsel /káunsl/; (提言) a suggestion. ● 一つの助言 a piece 〔a bit, a word〕 of *advice*. (! ×an advice とはいわない) ● 助言に従う follow 〔act on, (聞き入れる) take〕《his》 *advice*.
● 助言を求める ask 《his》 *advice*; ask 《him》 for *advice*; (専門家に) consult 《him》. ▶彼はカウンセラーのところへ助言を求めに行った He went to the counselor for *advice*. ▶医者の助言に従って彼はたばこをやめた On his doctor's *advice* he gave up smoking.
—— 助言する 動 advise 〔counsel〕《him》《*to do*》 (! advise の発音は /ədváiz/); give* 《him》 advice 〔counsel〕. ● その件に関して彼に助言する *advise* him *about* 〔*on*〕 the matter. (! about は一般的な事柄, on は専門的な事柄について) ▶彼はそこへ行かないよう助言してくれた He *advised* me not *to* go there./He *advised* me *against* going there. (! 前の方が普通).
● 助言者 an adviser, a counselor.

しょこ 書庫 (個人住宅の) a library; (図書館の) the stacks.

しょこう 曙光 dawn; the first light of the day. ● 希望の曙光 the *rays* of hope; a *gleam* of hope.

しょこう 曙光 the *dawn* of civilization.

しょごう 初号 the first number (*of* a magazine).

じょこう 徐行 ── 徐行する 動 slow down; go slow(ly). ▶徐行(標示) Go slow. ▶列車は終着駅に近づき徐行した(=向けて)徐行した The train *slowed down* for the terminal station.

しょこく 諸国 various countries. ●近隣諸国 neighboring countries.

しょこん 初婚 one's first marriage.

しょさ 所作 しとやかな所作(=身のこなし) a graceful *carriage*.

しょさい 所載 名 ●本紙所載の漫画 the cartoon series *carried* in this newspaper.
── 所載する 動 (載せる) carry.

しょさい 書斎 a study, (家の仕事場) a home office; (書庫) a library. ●書斎に閉じこもっている shut oneself up in one's *study*.

しょざい 所在 〖建物などの占める位置〗 a location; 〖人の居所〗one's whereabouts 〖単・複両扱い〗; 〖活動の中心地〗〖書〗 a seat. ●所在ない have nothing to do; don't know what to do. ●隠れ家の所在を見つけ出す find out the *location* of the hide-out; *locate* the hide-out. ●県庁の所在地 the *seat* of the prefectural government. ▶彼の所在が分からない I don't know his *whereabouts* (彼がどこにいるか) *where* he is)./His *whereabouts* are [is] unknown. ▶彼らは責任の所在(=だれに責任があるか)を突きとめた They found out *who was responsible for* it [*who was to blame for* it, *whose fault* it was]./They found out *where the responsibility lay*.

じょさい 助祭 〖カトリック〗 a deacon.

じょさいない 如才ない tactful, (気のきいた) clever (and skilled); (巧妙な) (やや書) adroit. ●如才ない答え (give) a *tactful* [an *adroit*] answer. ▶彼女は如才がない She is a *tactful* woman./(如才なくふるまう) She acts *tactfully* [*adroitly*].

しょさん 所産 ●長年の研究の所産 the *fruit*(s) [*product*] of years of research. ▶この小説はアイルランド人特有の想像力の所産だ This novel is the *product* of Irish imagination.

しょざん 初産 one's first childbirth.
●初産婦〖医学〗a primipara; a woman bearing [expecting] her first child

じょさんし 助産師 a birthing assistant [nurse], a midwife (⑱ -wives).

しょし 初志 (最初の目的) one's original intention.
●初志を貫徹する[翻す] carry out [give up] one's *original intention*.

しょし 庶子 an illegitimate /ɪlɪdʒɪtəmət/ child (⑱ children), a child born out of wedlock.

しょし 諸氏 ladies and gentlemen.

しょじ 所持 名 ●所持金を全部なくす lose all the money (*he*) *has* (*on* him). ●麻薬の不法所持で逮捕される be arrested for *possessing* [*being in possession of*] illegal drugs.
── 所持する 動 have, (書) possess; (持ち歩く) carry.
●所持品 (⇨所持品)

しょじ 諸事 everything; all; all affairs.

じょし 女子 〖女〗a woman (⑱ women), a lady, a female; (少女) a girl.
●女子学生 a girl [a woman, a female] student; 《米》(共学の)a co-ed. ●女子教育 the education of women [girls]. ●女子(高)校 a girls' (high) school. ●女子大学 (⇨女子大)

じょし 助詞 〖文法〗 a particle.

じょし 序詞 ❶〖序文, 序言〗(著者が書いた) a preface; (著者以外の人が書いた) a foreword; (プロローグ) a prologue. ❷〖和歌, 詩の〗a modifier.

-じょし -女史 〖女性の姓・姓名の前につけて〗(未婚) Miss; (既婚) Mrs.; (未婚・既婚) Ms. (!今はこの形が最も一般的) (⇨-さん). (彼女) she.

じょじ 女児 a girl. (⇨女子)

しょしがく 書誌学 bibliography.
●書誌学者 a bibliographer.

しょしかた 処し方 ●身の処し方(=いかにやっていくか)を心得ている know *how to get on in the world* [(いかにふるまうか)〖書〗*how to conduct oneself*].

しょしき 書式 a form. ●書式に記入する fill out [in] a *form*. ●書式どおりに(=指示された書式に従って)書く write according to the *form* prescribed.

じょじし 叙事詩 an epic (poem); 《集合的》 epic poetry.

じょしだい 女子大 a women's college [university].
●女子大生 a women's college [university] student; 《米・やや古》(男女共学の)a coed.

じょしつ 除湿 dehumidification.
── 除湿する 動 dèhumídify (the air).
●除湿器 a dehumídifier.

しょしひん 所持品 one's belongings, one's personal effects. (⇨持ち物)

しょしゃ 書写 名 copying; transcription.
── 書写する 動 copy; transcribe.

じょしゅ 助手 an assistant. ●運転助手 an *assistant* driver. ●A 氏の助手を務める work as Mr. A's *assistant* [*assistant to* Mr. A].
●助手席 the seat next to the driver('s seat); the passenger seat.

しょしゅう 初秋 ●初秋に in early fall 《米》[autumn 《英》]; early in fall [autumn].

しょしゅう 所収 ●第1巻所収のエッセイ an essay *included* in volume 1.

じょしゅう 女囚 a female prisoner [convict]. (⇨囚人)

しょしゅつ 初出 the first appearance.

じょじゅつ 叙述 名 an account; (物語ること) narration. ── 叙述する 動 give an account 《*of*》;〖書〗 narrate.
●叙述形容詞〖文法〗a predicative adjective.

しょしゅん 初春 ●初春に in early spring; early in spring; at the beginning of spring.

しょじゅん 初旬 the beginning of the month. (⇨上旬)

しょじょ 処女 〖人〗a virgin (!「童貞」の意にもなる); 〖書〗 a maiden; 〖処女性〗 virginity. (⇨童貞) ●処女を失う lose one's *virginity*.
●処女作 one's maiden [first] work. (! 性差別を意識する人は first または premier を好む) ●処女地 virgin soil. ●処女飛行 one's maiden [first] flight. (! 性差別を意識する人は first または premier を好む) ●処女峰 a virgin peak. ●処女膜〖解剖〗a hymen /háɪmən/.

しょしょう 所掌 ●契約を所掌する役人 the officer *in charge of* contracting.

しょじょう 書状 a letter.

しょしょう 序章 an introduction.

じょじょうし 叙情詩 a lyric (poem); 《集合的》lyric poetry.
●叙情詩人 a lyric poet.

じょじょうしょうきょくしゅう 抒情小曲集『抒情小曲集』 *Short Lyrics*. 〖参考〗室生犀星の詩集)

じょじょうふ 女丈夫 a brave woman. (⇨⑱ 女傑)

じょしょく 女色 ●女色に迷う be captivated [infatuated, smitten] by a woman's charms

じょじょに 徐々に (段階を追って) gradually, 《やや書》by degrees; (ゆっくりと) slowly; (少しずつ) little by little; (着実に) steadily, step by step. ▶ぼくの健康は徐々に回復している My health is *gradually* improving./I'm getting better *by degrees*. ▶私は徐々に彼女の言ったことが分かってきた I *slowly* began to realize [understand] what she meant.

しょしん 初心 the initial enthusiasm. ●初心に帰る go back to the *initial enthusiasm*. ▶初心忘るべからず Don't forget the *enthusiasm* you *had at the beginning*./Remember your *initial* [*first*] *enthusiasm*.

しょしん 初診 the first medical examination. ●初診の患者 a new patient.
●初診料 the first visit charge; the fee charged for a patient's first visit.

しょしん 所信 [意見]one's opinion [view]; [信念]one's belief (霸 ~s), one's conviction. ●首相の所信表明演説 Prime Minister's general policy speech. ▶…について所信を述べる express [give] one's *opinion* [*view*] *on* [*about*]…

しょしんしゃ 初心者 a beginner. ●テニスの初心者 a *beginner* in tennis. ●初心者コース a *beginners'* [初歩の] an *elementary* course; a course for *beginners*.

じょすう 序数 〖数学〗 an ordinal (↔ a cardinal) number.

じょすう 除数 〖数学〗 a divisor.

じょすうし 助数詞 〖文法〗 a classifier.

しょずり 初刷り a first impression [printing].

しょする 処する ❶[対処する] ●難局に処する cope [deal] with difficulties.
❷[処理する] ●事を処する deal with; [(うまく)(can) manage, (最終的に) dispose of] the matter.
❸[処罰する] ●彼を厳罰に処す punish him severely. ▶彼は5年の禁固刑に処せられた He was sentenced to five years' imprisonment.

じょする 叙する ❶[述べる] describe.
❷[爵位などを授ける] confer …(*on*).

しょせい 処世 ▶彼は処世術をよく心得ている He knows well *how to get along* [*on*] *in* life. (⇨世渡り)
●処世訓 a maxim.

しょせい 書生 (学生) a student; (玄関番) a houseboy, a houseman (霸 -men).
●書生論 an argument that is too theoretical and impracticable.

*****じょせい 女性** 图 a woman (霸 women); a lady; (若い) a girl. (⇨女) ●女性のタクシー運転手 a *woman* taxi driver. ▶彼女はとても美しい女性だ She is a very beautiful *woman* [*lady*]. ▶その広告は女性客に受けた The advertisement appealed to *female* buyers.
—— **女性的な** 形 feminine, 《やや書》 womanly (!前の方は女性・物について, 後の方は女性の行為・性格・外見などについていう (⇨女らしい); (男性について) (軽蔑的) womanish. ▶彼は女性的な歩き方をする He walks in a *womanish* [柔弱な] an *effeminate*] way. (!ともに軽蔑的)
●女性解放運動 women's lib [〖書〗 liberation]. (!今は女性の movement を用いる方が普通) ●女性解放運動家 a women's liberationist [libber]. ●女性学 women's studies. ●女性語 women's language. ●女性雑誌 a women's magazine. ●女性上位 female dominance. ●女性美 feminine beauty.

じょせい 女声 a female voice.
●女声合唱 a female chorus.

じょせい 女婿 one's son-in-law (霸 sons-, 《英話》-laws).

じょせい 助成 —— **助成する** 動 (政府が企業・事業などを) subsidize /sʌ́bsədàiz/; (財政的に援助する) support; (後援する) sponsor; (補助的に助ける) 《書》 assist.
●助成金 (⇨助成金) ●助成産業 subsidized industries.

じょせい 助勢 help; assistance. (⇨助力, 助け)

じょせいきん 助成金 (政府が企業などに交付する) a subsidy; (政府が公共事業・教育機関に交付する) a grant, a grant-in-aid. ●食糧[住宅]助成金 food [housing] *subsidies*. ●大学への政府助成金 a Government *grant* to university. ▶政府はこれ以上その計画に助成金を出すのを拒否した The government refused to *subsidize* the program any further. ▶彼は留学の研究助成金を得た He obtained a research *grant* to study abroad.

じょせいと 女生徒 a schoolgirl, 《米》 a girl student. (⇨生徒)

しょせき 書籍 a book. (⇨本)
●書籍目録 (図書目録) a catalog of books. (⇨図書) ●書籍売り場 (デパートなどの) a book department; (掲示) Books.

じょせき 除籍 —— **除籍する** 動 (戸籍から) remove one's name from the register [(学籍から) school register]; (学校・組織から) expel (him) from …. ▶その生徒は除籍された(=退学処分になった) The boy *was expelled* from school.

しょせつ 所説 one's opinion [view].

しょせつ 諸説 various opinions.
●諸説紛々 ▶この部分の解釈は諸説紛々としている(=諸説が入り乱れている) *Opinion is* [*Opinions are*] *divided on* the interpretation of this passage.

じょせつ 序説 an introduction.

じょせつ 除雪 —— **除雪する** 動 (道路の雪を除く) remove snow from the road; clear snow away from the road; clear the road of snow; (ショベルで) shovel snow off [away from] the road.
●除雪車[車] a snow-plow.

しょせん 初戦 the first match [game]. ●初戦敗退 the defeat in the first round (of a tournament).

しょせん 所詮 (とうてい…できない) can't possibly (!possibly は can't を強調する); (最終的には) in the end; (結局) after all; (どうせ) anyway, anyhow. ▶その患者はしょせん助からないだろう The patient *can't possibly* recover. ▶彼が昇進できるか否かはしょせん部長の考え次第だ His promotion depends, *after all*, on how the general manager thinks about him. ▶彼の計画はしょせんうまくいかないだろう His plan will fail *anyway*.

しょせん 緒戦 the beginning [early stages] of a war [a match, a game].

しょそう 諸相 various aspects 《*of* Japanese culture》.

しょぞう 所蔵 ▶この絵は石田氏の所蔵である This painting *is owned by* [(…に属する) *belongs to*] Mr. Ishida. /(…の所有[コレクション]である) This painting is *in* Mr. Ishida's *possession* [*collection*].

じょそう 女装 —— **女装する** 動 disguise oneself as a woman [in a woman's clothes].
●女装趣味 transvestism.

じょそう 助走 an approach run, 《主に英》 a run-up.
●助走路 (走り幅跳びなどの) a runway; (スキージャンプの) an approach.

じょそう 序奏 〖音楽〗 an introduction.

じょそう 除草 图 weeding.
— **除草する** 動 weed 《a garden》; (雑草を抜く) pull up [remove] weeds.
● 除草剤 (a) weedkiller; (a) herbicide.

じょそう 除霜 — **除霜する** 動 defrost, 《英》 demist.
● 除霜装置 a defroster, 《英》 a demister.

しょぞく 所属 图 ●共産党所属の国会議員 a Diet member of [belonging to] the Communist Party.
— **所属する** 動 ▶私は野球部に所属している I belong [×am belonging] to the baseball team. ▶彼は営業部に所属している He works [is] in the sales department./He belongs to the sales department. (❗この文脈では前の方が普通。「A 会社に所属して(=勤めている)」は work for [in, with] A Company といい, 通例 ×belong to A Company とはいわない) ▶彼はその部隊に所属している He is attached [is assigned] to the unit. (⇨配属)

しょぞん 所存 (an) intention. (⇨考え, つもり) ▶全力を尽くす所存でおります I am planning to do my best.

じょそんだんぴ 女尊男卑 predominance of women over men. (⇔男尊女卑)

*****しょたい** 所帯 a household; 〔家庭〕a family; 〔家政〕housekeeping. ● 1 人所帯 a one-person household. ● 男所帯 (男やもめの) a widower's 〔未婚者の〕 a bachelor's household. ● 所帯染みる be domesticated. ● 所帯持ちがよい be a good (↔a bad) householder; be good (↔bad) at housekeeping; run one's household effectively. ● 所帯やつれする be worn (out) with domestic cares. ▶所帯を持って(=結婚して) 10年になります It is [has been] ten years since I got married. (↔一家を構えて) I set up house]. ▶私のところは大所帯です I have a large family./My family is large [a large one]. (⇨家族)
● 所帯道具 household goods. ● 所帯主 the head of the household; a householder.

しょたい 書体 (活字文字の) a typeface; (手書き文字の) a style of handwriting.

しょだい 初代 ●初代首相 the first prime minister. ● 初代春団治 Harudanji I [the first].

じょたい 女体 (⇨女体(にょたい))

じょたい 除隊 (a) discharge from the army. ●傷病のため除隊になる be discharged from the army due to medical problems.
● 除隊兵 a discharged soldier.

しょたいけん 初体験 the first experience. (⇨初(はつ)体験)

しょたいめん 初対面 ●初対面の人 a person whom one met for the first time. ▶彼女とはその時が初対面でした That [It] was the first time I met her./ (その時初めて彼女に会った) Then I met her for the first time. ▶彼らは初対面のあいさつをした(=お互いに「はじめまして」と言った) They said to each other, "How do you do?"/(お互いに自己紹介した) They introduced themselves to each other.

しょだな 書棚 a bookshelf (④-shelves).

しょだん 初段 shodan, the first dan.

*****しょち** 処置 a measure (to do; against); 〔方策〕(通例複数形で); (一つの手段) a step (to do); 〔処分〕 disposal; 〔治療〕(a) treatment. ●台所のごみの処置 the disposal of garbage. ● 応急処置 emergency [first-aid] treatment. ▶政府はテロ行為に対して強硬な処置を取った The government took strong measures [steps] against the terrorism. ● 処置なしだ(=どうしてよいかわからない) I

don't know what to do with it./(何もすることができない) Nothing can be done.
— **処置する** 動 dispose of...; (対処する) deal* with ...; (解決する) settle; 〔治療する〕 treat. ● 問題を処置する dispose of [deal with, settle] the matter. ● 傷を処置する treat the wound.

しょち 書痴 a bibliomania.

じょちゅう 女中 a (house)maid. (⇨お手伝い)

じょちゅうぎく 除虫菊 〔植物〕a pyrethrum /paɪríːθrəm/.

じょちゅうざい 除虫剤 (an) insecticide.

しょちゅうみまい 暑中見舞 ●暑中見舞を出す send 〈him〉 a summer greeting card; write (to) 〈him〉 asking after 〈his〉 health in the hot season.

しょちょう 初潮 〔医学〕menarche /mənáːrkiː/; one's first (menstrual) period. ●初潮は何歳のときでしたか At what age did your periods start?

しょちょう 所長 a head, a chief (④ ~s); (組織・活動の責任者) a director.

しょちょう 署長 (警察) ●警察署長 the chief of a police station. (⇨chief の ④ は ~ s)

じょちょう 助長 图 〔促進〕promotion; 〔激励〕encouragement; 〔強化〕strength.
— **助長する** 動 promote; encourage; strengthen. ●世界平和を助長する promote [(さらに進める) further] world peace. ●それでは彼の怠惰を助長するだけで That will simply [just] make him lazier.

しょっかい 職階 a job classification.
● 職階制 (a) job classification system.

しょっかく 触角 a feeler; (特に昆虫の) an antenna /ænténə/ (④ antennae /-niː/). ●触角を伸ばす put out its feelers [antennae].

しょっかく 触覚 (the sense of) touch. ●敏感な触覚 a delicate sense of touch. ●触覚に頼って歩く walk by touch.

しょっかん 食間 ●食間に between meals. ▶食間に服用のこと To be taken between meals.

しょっかん 食感 ▶そのアイスクリームは普通のアイスクリームとは食感が異なる The ice cream has a different feel in the mouth from regular ice cream.

*****しょっき** 食器 〔食器類〕tableware (❗集合的. 総称的に皿・コップ・フォーク・スプーンなどをいう); (正餐(せいさん)用の) a dinner service [set]; (1 回の食事に使用する食器類) the dishes. ●(食後)食器を下げる[洗う] put away [wash, do] the dishes.
● 食器洗い機 a dishwasher. ● 食器棚 a cupboard /kʌ́bərd/. (❗発音に注意)

しょっき 織機 a loom. ●織機できれいな布を織る make a pretty fabric on one's loom.

ジョッキ 〔ビールの〕a beer mug. ●ジョッキ 1 杯のビール a mug of beer.

ジョッキー a jockey.

ショッキング ●ショッキングな事故 a shocking [an appalling] accident.

*****ショック** (a) shock. (❗具体的には C. 日本語の「ショック」よりはるかに強烈な精神的ア道徳的な非難の気持ちを含意する) ●ショックを与える give 〈him〉 a shock (❗×give a shock 《to him》とはいわない); shock 〈him〉. ●ショックを受ける get [receive] a shock (from); be shocked (at, by). ●注射でショック死する die of shock from injection. ▶彼女はそのショックから立ち直りつつある She is getting over the shock. ▶彼の死はには非常にショックだった His death was a great shock to me./His death was very shocking to me. (❗shocking は形容詞) / His death shocked me greatly. (❗受身表現は I

しょっけん 食券 a meal ticket (bought at the entrance of some Japanese restaurants). (!(1)《米》の a meal ticket は店が出す食事割引券または (2)《英》では昼食券として従業員に配られるものを a luncheon voucher /váutʃər/ という)

しょっけん 職権 (公の権能) one's (official) authority; (権力) power. ●…に対して職権を乱用[行使]する abuse [use,《書》exercise] one's *authority over*…. ●彼に…する職権を与える give him an *authority to do* [*for doing*]…; (やや書) authorize him *to do*…. ●職権で *on* one's own *authority*. ●職権乱用 an abuse of authority [power], an authority [a power] abuse.

しょっこう 燭光 candlepower (略 cp).

しょっちゅう all the time; (いつも) always; (たいてい) most of the time; (しばしば) often. (⇨よく❷) ▶彼はしょっちゅう宿題を忘れる He *often* forgets to do his homework./He is *always* forgetting to do his homework. (!後のように進行形で用いると非難の意を含む) ▶彼はしょっちゅう来るわけではない He doesn't come *very often*. ▶彼はしょっちゅう留守だ He is out *most of the time*.

しょってたつ 背負って立つ ●会社をしょって立つ become an indispensable person for the prosperity of a company.

しょってる (うぬぼれている) be puffed up, be stuck up, be full of oneself, (話) be big-headed; (大口をたたく) 《俗》be full of hot air.
会話「クラスの女の子はみんなおれにほれてるんだ」「ずいぶんしょってるわね」"All the girls in my class have a crush on me." "You *are full of hot air*."

ショット ❶【球技の】a shot. ●ナイスショット (=いい当たり) a good *shot*. ❷【撮影の】a shot. ●ツーショットの写真 a two-*shot*.

ショットガン 【散弾銃】a shotgun.

ショットバー a shot bar.

しょっぱい (塩辛い) salty /s(ː)lti/.

しょっぱな 初っ端 ●しょっぱなから from the very beginning; right from the start.

しょっぴく pull (him) in; arrest.
会話「どうもべンが容疑者くさいぞ」「よし,おれがしょっぴいてやる」"Ben looks like a suspect." "I'd *pull him in*."

ショッピング shopping. (⇨買い物) ●カタログ[テレホン; テレビ; インターネット]ショッピング catalog [telephone; television; internet] *shopping*. ●ショッピングに行く go *shopping* (*at* a department store).
●ショッピングカート a shopping cart [《英》 trolley]; (スーパーなどの) a pushcart. ●ショッピングセンター a shopping center [《米》 mall]. ●ショッピングバッグ a shopping bag. ●ショッピングモール a shopping mall.

ショップ 【店】a shop, a store. ●ペットショップ a pet *shop*. ●100円ショップ a 100-yen *shop*. ▶おじは横浜でハンバーガーショップを開いています My uncle has [runs] a hamburger *shop* [*restaurant*] in Yokohama.

しょて 初手 【将棋】the [one's] first move. ●初手 (=最初) から from the (very) beginning; (right) from the start.

しょてい 所定 ━ 所定の 形 (約束の) appointed; (確定した) fixed; (規定された) prescribed. ●所定の場所で at an *appointed* [a *fixed*] place. ●所定の用紙 a *prescribed* form. ●所定の位置につく take *one's* place; take up *one's* position. ●所定の時間内に within a *given* period of time. ●本を所定の場所に戻す put books back in their *correct* place [*to* where they *should* belong].

じょてい 女帝 an empress; (女王) a queen.

しょてん 書店 《主に米》a bookstore, 《主に英》a bookshop. (!書店名は英語では Cody's Books (コーディー書店), B-Doulton (ダルトン書店)など similar の名前を用いることが多い)

じょてんいん 女店員 a salesperson; (女の) a saleswoman. (!婉曲的に a sales clerk ともいう. a salesgirl (若い女店員)は避ける方がよい)

しょとう 初冬 ●初冬に in early winter, early in winter.

しょとう 初等 ━ 初等の 形 elementary. (⇨初歩)
●初等科 an elementary course. ●初等教育 elementary education. ●初等数学 elementary mathematics.

しょとう 初頭 the beginning. ●16世紀初頭に *at the beginning of* the 16th century.

しょとう 諸島 (a group of) islands /áiləndz/; an archipelago /ɑːrkəpéləɡoʊ/ (@ ～(e)s). ●ハワイ諸島 the Hawaiian *Islands*. ●マレー諸島 the Malay *Archipelago*. ●イギリス諸島 the British *Isles*. ●尖閣諸島 the Senkaku [Diaoyutai] *Islands*. (!後の方は中国・台湾での言い方)

しょどう 書道 (Japanese) calligraphy /kəlígrəfi/.
●書道をする[習う] practice *calligraphy*.
●書道家 a calligrapher.

じょどうし 助動詞 【文法】an auxiliary (verb) (略 aux., auxil.).

しょどうそうさ 初動捜査 an initial (criminal) investigation.

*****しょとく** 所得 (an) income. (⇨収入)
①【～所得】●多い所得 (a) large *income*. ●総[純]所得 (a) gross [net] *income*. ●勤労[不労]所得 (a) earned [unearned] *income*. ●国民所得 national *income*. ●給与所得 employment *income*. ●個人所得 an individual's *income*.
●平均所得 an average *income*. ●課税所得 (a) taxable *income*. ●可処分所得 a disposable *income*. ●高[低]所得家庭[層] a high- [a low-] *income* family [bracket, group].
②【所得を[が]】●高い所得を得る earn a high *income*. ▶彼には年間 1,000万円以上の所得がある He has an annual [a yearly] *income* of ten million yen or over./His annual [yearly] *income* is over ten million yen./He earns ten million yen or more a year.
③【所得で】●彼の少ない所得で家族を養う support his family on his small *income*.
●所得額 (the amount of) one's income. ●所得隠し income concealing; concealment of income. ●所得格差 an income gap [differential]. ●所得控除 tax deductions and allowances. ●所得水準 the level of income. ●所得税 (⇨所得税) ●所得政策 an incomes policy. (!複数形に注意)

しょとくぜい 所得税 income tàx. ●所得税増税[減税] an *income tax* hike [cut, reduction]. ▶所得税は3月半ばまでに納めなければなりません Your *income tax*es are due by the middle of March.
●所得税率 an income tax rate.

しょなのか 初七日 ●初七日の法要を行う hold a Bud-

じょなん dhist memorial service *on the seventh day after* ⟨his⟩ *death*.

じょなん 女難 ▶女難の相が出ていますな You'll get into *trouble with women*. I can see it on your face.

しょにだん 序二段 〖相撲〗*jonidan*; (説明的に) the second division from the bottom on the official listing of rank.

しょにち 初日 〖開幕の日〗the opening [(最初の) first] day; 〖映画・オペラ・演劇などの〗the opening [first] night; 〖映画・オペラ・演劇などの〗the premiere /primíər/. ●その劇の初日の切符 a ticket for the *opening night* [to the *premiere*] of the play. ●(芝居・オペラなどを)初日必ず見に行く人 a first-nighter.
●初日を出す〖相撲〗get the first win in a *sumo* tournament.

しょにんきゅう 初任給 a [one's] starting salary [pay]. (⇨給料) ●大卒の初任給は20万円だった The *starting salary* [*pay*] for college graduates was 200,000 yen./College graduates *started with* [*on, at*] *a salary of* 200,000 yen.

しょねつ 暑熱 the summer heat.

しょねん 初年 (初めの年) the first year; (初期の) early years. ●初年兵 new [raw] recruits.

しょねんど 初年度 the first year. ●会計初年度 the *first* fiscal [*the*] *year*.

じょのくち 序の口 ❶〖始まり〗a beginning ▶これはほんの序の口だ This is just the *beginning*.
❷〖相撲〗*jonokuchi*; (説明的に) the lowest division on the official listing of rank.

しょは 諸派 (党派) various parties; (分派, 派閥) various factions.

じょはきゅう 序破急〖舞楽・能楽〗introduction, development and finale.

しょばつ 処罰 图 a punishment. (⇨罰)
—**処罰する** 動 ▶彼はお金を盗んで厳しく処罰された He *was* severely *punished for* stealing money. (⇨罰する)

しょはん 初犯 the first offense; (人) a first offender.

しょはん 初版 the first edition. ●希少価値のある初版本の収集家 a collector of rare *first editions*.

しょはん 諸般 —**諸般の** 形 various; several. ●諸般の事情から for *various* reasons.

ショパン 〖ポーランドの作曲家・ピアニスト〗Chopin /ʃóupæn/ (Frédéric François ～).

じょばん 序盤 ●序盤戦 be in the early part [stage(s)] of the game [(選挙の) of the election campaign]. (▶選挙の場合 stages が好まれる)

しょひょう 書評 a book review. ●書評をする *review* a book.
●書評欄 a book-review column.

しょふう 書風 a style of handwriting [calligraphy].

*****しょぶん** 処分 图 〖処理, 始末〗〖書〗disposal; 〖罰則〗(a) punishment (⇨罰). ●売却処分 *disposal* by sale. ●ごみの処分 garbage *disposal*; the *disposal* of garbage. ●退学処分 (⇨退学) ●在庫処分 stock clearance [*removal*]. ●(在庫の)処分品 clearance goods.
—**処分する** 動 〖始末する〗dispose of ...; (売り払う) sell *... (off);* (取り除く) get* rid of ...; (捨てる) throw*... away; 〖処罰する〗punish ...● ▶この家を処分するかが問題だ (＝問題はこの家をどう処分するかだ) The question is how to *dispose of* [*what to do with*] this house. ▶彼は土地を処分した He *disposed of* [*sold*] the land. ▶彼は古いおもちゃを処分した He *got rid of* [*threw away*] the old toys. ▶これらの品は特別価格で処分してかまいません You can *dispose of* [*sell off*] these items at special prices.

じょぶん 序文 a preface /préfis/; a foreword (▶後の方はしばしば著者以外の人の手による). ●その本の序文で in the *preface* to [×of] the book.

ショベルカー a power shovel, a mechanical excavator;《和製語》a shovel car.

ショベルローダー a shovel loader.

しょほ 初歩 图 〖知識〗the rudiments ⟨*of*⟩; the elements ⟨*of*⟩; the ABC's《米》[ABC《英》]《*of*》; 〖段階〗the first step ⟨*of*⟩. ●英語の初歩 the *rudiments* [*elements*, *ABC*('*s*)] of English. ●英語を初歩から学ぶ learn English from the *beginning*.
—**初歩の, 初歩的な** 形 elementary, (軽蔑的に) rudimentary; 〖基本の〗basic. ●日本語の初歩の知識 an *elementary* knowledge of Japanese. ●初歩的な間違いをする make a *basic* [a *simple*] mistake.

しょほう 処方 图 (a) prescription. ●医師の処方で薬を受け取る obtain a drug on a doctor's *prescription*. —**処方する** 動 prescribe.
●処方箋 (⇨処方箋)

しょほう 書法 one's style of writing; calligraphy, penmanship.

じょほう 除法〖数学〗division.

しょほうせん 処方箋 a prescription. ●処方箋を書く make out [write (out)] a *prescription* ⟨*for*⟩; prescribe ⟨*for*⟩. ●その処方箋に従って調剤してもらう get the *prescription* filled [made up]. ●処方箋なしで買える薬 an over-the-counter drug [medicine]. ▶多くの薬は処方箋がないと買えない Many drugs are only available *on prescription*.

しょぼくれる (しょげる) be depressed; (みじめな様子になる) look miserable.

しょぼしょぼ ▶彼は寝不足で目をしょぼしょぼさせている He is bleary-eyed for lack of sleep./His eyes are *bleary* because he didn't have enough sleep.
▶雨がしょぼしょぼ(＝小雨が)降っている It *is drizzling*.

しょぼんと lonely; depressed. (⇨しょんぼり)

じょまく 序幕 〖第一幕〗the first [opening] act; 〖物事の始まり〗a prelude ⟨*to* civil war⟩.

じょまく 除幕 图 (an) unveiling.
●除幕式 an unveiling (ceremony). ●故山本元帥の記念碑の除幕式を行った They *unveiled* the monument of the late Dr. Yamamoto.

しょみん 庶民 图 〖貴族に対する平民〗(全体) the (common [ordinary]) people; (1人) a commoner; 〖公衆〗the (general) public; ordinary citizens. (⇨大衆) ●庶民の声に耳を傾ける listen to the voice of *the people*.
—**庶民的な** 形 ●庶民的な(＝取り澄ましたのところのない)レストラン an *unpretentious* restaurant. ▶大阪は庶民的な町だ Osaka is a town for *ordinary citizens*.

しょむ 庶務 ●庶務課 the general affairs section, the section of general affairs.

しょめい 書名 the title of a book, a book title.

しょめい 署名 图 (手紙・正式文書などにする) a signature /sígnətʃər/; (有名人などの自筆の) an autograph /ɔ́:təɡræf/. ●署名運動をする carry on [《やや書》conduct] a *signature*-collecting campaign. ●署名入りの本 an *autographed* book; a book with an *autograph*. ●署名者 a signer. ▶我々はこの嘆願書に1万人の署名を集めた We have collected 10,000 *signatures* for [on] this petition.

― 署名する 動 sign; autograph. ● 著書に署名する *autograph* a copy of one's book 《*for* him》. ▶ With Mr. Tanaka's compliments/With the compliments of Mr. Tanaka (謹呈田中より)／(下に署名してください Can we *have* your *signature* [*Sign* (your name)] at the bottom, please. ▶ 彼はその書類に署名した He *signed* (his name *on*) the document./He put [wrote, ×sign] his *signature* on the document. 🚨 契約書は署名捺印(なついん)されていた The contract *was signed* and sealed. 書類 米英では日常は署名だけで済ませることが多い)

じょめい 助命 图 ▶ 彼の妻は王に夫の助命を請うた His wife *begged* [《書》*entreated*] the King *for* her husband's *life*.
― 助命する 動 spare a person's life.

じょめい 除名 图 《追放》(an) expulsion.
― 除名する 動 (学校・クラブ・組織などから) expel; (リストから) strike* 《his》name off a list. ▶ 彼は労働組合から除名(=追放)された He *was expelled from* [《話》*was kicked out of*] the labor union.

しょめん 書面 (文書) writing; (手紙) a letter. ● 書面で申し込む apply *in writing* [*by letter*]; (申し込み書を送る) send (in) an application form [a written application]. ● 取り決めを書面にする put an agreement *in writing*; make a written agreement. ▶ 私はそのことを書面で確認してほしいと彼に頼んだ I asked him to confirm it *in writing*.

しょもう 所望 图 a wish; a desire. ▶ ご所望の本をお送りいたします We will send the desired book.
― 所望する 動 wish for ...; desire; ask for ....

しょもく 書目 (書物の名前) a title of a book; (書物の目録) a catalog of books.

***しょもつ 書物** a book. (⇨本)

しょや 初夜 one's wedding night. (🚨 ×one's bridal night とはいわない)

じょやく 助役 (副市長) a deputy mayor; (駅長補佐) an assistant station official [*manager*].

じょやのかね 除夜の鐘 the tolling of temple bells at midnight on New Year's Eve. (⇨大晦日(おおみそか))

***しょゆう 所有** 图 possession; 《所有権》ownership. ● 個人[共同]所有 individual [collective] *ownership* [*property*]. ▶ その土地はその会社の所有だった [になった] The land *was in* [*came into*] *the possession of* the company./The company *was in* [*came into*] *possession of* the land. ▶ 彼女はとても所有欲が強い She is very *possessive*.

― 所有する 動 own; 《書》possess; (持っている) have*. (🚨 いずれも進行形なし) ● ヘロインを所有する *possess* heroin /hérouɪn/. ▶ この車はあなたの所有していますか Who *owns* [*has*, ×possesses] this car? (🚨 (1) possess は通例不特定の目的語をとる。(2) have は手元でいつでも使える状態で所有していることを含意)/Who is the *owner* of this car? ▶ その家は彼が所有している The house *is owned* [×is possessed] by him. (🚨 ×possess は受身不可)/(彼に属する) The house *belongs to* him.

● 所有格『文法』the possessive case. ● 所有権 ownership. ● 所有者 an owner. ● 所有地 one's (own) land. ● 所有物 one's possessions; (所持品) one's belongings; (財産) one's property.

じょゆう 女優 an actress. (⇨俳優, 役者)

しょよ 所与 ▶ 所与の条件のもとで under these *given* conditions.

しょよう 所用 business. (⇨用❶) ● 所用で on *business*.

しょよう 所要 ▶ 東京駅までの所要時間は約 1 時間です It will take about an hour to get to Tokyo Station.

:**しょり 処理** 图 《取り扱い》management; 《処分》disposal; 《コンピュータ》processing. ● 下水処理 sewage /súːɪdʒ/ *disposal*. ▶ 御社のご注文につきましては, 必ず迅速な処理を行うようにいたします Your orders will certainly receive very prompt attention.
― 処理する 動 《事を》handle, (問題などを) deal* with ...; (うまく) (can) manage; (解決する) settle; 《物を》(処分する) dispose of ...; (薬品で処置する) treat; 《コンピュータ》process. ● 産業廃棄物を処理する *dispose of* industrial waste. ● ある物質を酸で処理する *treat* a substance with acid. ● データをコンピュータで処理する *process* the data in a computer. ● ゴロを処理する field [take care of] a grounder. ▶ その問題は簡単には処理できない We can't *manage* [*handle*, *deal with*, *settle*, *dispose of*] the problem easily.

じょりゅう 女流 ― 女流の 形 woman, 《古》《今は軽蔑的》lady. ● 女流作家 a woman [a *female*] writer.

しょりょう 所領 (feudal) domains; a manor; a territory.

しょりょく 助力 help, assistance; aid. (⇨助け) ▶ 彼の助力で with [×by] his *help* [*assistance*]. ▶ 彼の助力をあおぐ ask for his *help*.

***しょるい 書類** (筆記・印刷による文書一般) a paper (🚨 通例複数形で公の文書や身分証明などの文書を表す); (資料・証拠としての) a document; (記入用紙) a form.

① 《～書類》 ▶ 正式書類 an official *document*. ● 重要書類 important *papers* [*documents*]. ● 機密書類 secret [*classified*] *documents*. ● 必要書類を提出する hand in the necessary *papers* [*forms*].

② 《書類(の)～》 ▶ 書類送検する send 《his》 *papers* to the prosecutor's office. ● 書類選考する select 《the candidates》 by examining their career *papers*. ▶ この書類のコピーを 3 部とってください Please make three copies of this *document*.

③ 《書類を》 ▶ 書類を整理する (分類する) sort (out) [classify] *papers*; (整理保存する) file (away) *papers*. ▶ 彼は顧問弁護士に書類を作成してくれるよう頼んだ He asked his lawyer to draw up the *document* for him.

④ 《書類に[が]》 ▶ これらの書類に(必要事項を)記入してください Fill out [in] these *forms*, please [if you could]./《話》If you'll fill in these *forms*. ▶ この書類にざっと目を通していただけますか Would you please take a look at the *papers*?/Could you please glance down [over, through] the *documents*? ▶ 書類があちらじゅう散らばっていた The *papers* were scattered all around [over the place].

● 書類かばん a briefcase.

ショルダー 《肩》 a shoulder.
● ショルダーバッグ a shoulder bag.

じょれつ 序列 (順位) order; (地位) rank; (格付け) ranking. ● 序列に従って名前を呼ぶ call names in proper *order* according to *rank*. ▶ 彼は会社では序列が私より上だ He *ranks above* me in the office./He is in a higher position than I in the company.

じょろ 如露 a watering can. (⇨如雨露(じょうろ))

じょろう 初老 ― 初老の 形 elderly; in one's early sixties. (⇨年配)

じょろう 女郎 a prostitute. ● 女郎屋 a brothel.

じょろうぐも 女郎蜘蛛 〖動物〗a silk spider.
しょろん 所論 (意見) one's opinion; one's view.
じょろん 序論 an introduction 《to》.
しょんぼり (寂しい) lonely, 《主に米話》lonesome; (気がくじけて) depressed, (人の方が堅い話) しょんぼりと(=ひとり寂しく)《主に米話》lonesomely. ▶彼女はしょんぼりして帰ってきた She came back looking *depressed* [(みじめな) *miserable*, (ひどくがっかりして) *dejected*].

しら 白 ▶しらを切る (⇨しらばくれる)
しらあえ 白和え *shiraae*; (説明的に) vegetables (and fish meat) dressed with a mixture of pureed *tofu*, ground white sesame and white *miso*.
じらい 地雷 a (land) mine. ●地雷を埋める[に触れる; を除去する] lay [strike; remove] a mine.
しらうお 白魚 〖魚〗an ice fish. ●白魚のような(=白くて細い)指 delicate white fingers.
しらが 白髪 (xa) white [(白髪まじりの) gray, (銀髪) silver] hair. (⇨髪 解説) ●白髪頭の男 a *gray-haired* [a *gray-headed*] man; a *white-haired* man. ●白髪まじりの髪 gray [*grizzled*] hair; hair streaked [*sprinkled*, *shot*] with gray. ▶彼は心配事のために急に白髪が増えてきた His *hair* is rapidly going [*turning*] *gray* [×white] with worry. (**!** 主語は He も可)
●白髪染め a hair dye.
しらかば 白樺 〖植物〗a silver [a white] birch.
しらかわよふね 白河夜船 ●白河夜船である(=ぐっすり眠っている) be sound [fast] asleep.
しらき 白木 plain (unvarnished, unpainted) wood. ●白木造りの神殿 a (Shinto) shrine built of plain wood.
しらぎく 白菊 〖植物〗a white chrysanthemum.
しらくも 白癬 〖医学〗ringworm; tinea.
しらける 白ける 〖興ざめる〗《主に書》become* chilled; 〖台なしになる〗be spoiled; 〖無感動である〗(やや書) be apathetic /æpəθétik/. ●〈宴会などで〉座をしらけさせる人 a killjoy; 《話》a wet blanket. ●しらけた態度 an *apathetic* attitude. ●しらけた顔をする look *apathetic* [(退屈した) *bored*]. ▶彼の発言でパーティーはしらけた His remarks *spoiled* [*chilled*, (やや書) *cast a chill over*] the party./The party *was spoiled* [*was chilled*] by his remarks. ▶あの男は政治に対してしらけている(=熱意がない) That guy doesn't *show any enthusiasm for* politics./(無関心である) That guy *is apathetic about* [*toward*] politics.
しらこ 白子 ❶〖魚の〗soft roe; milt.
❷〖色素の少ない人〗an albino /ælbáinou/ (優 ～s).
しらさぎ 白鷺 〖鳥〗an egret /í:grət/, a white heron.
しらじらしい 白々しい ●白々しい(=明白な)うそ an *obvious* [(見え透いた) a *transparent*] lie. ●白々しい(=うわべだけの)お世辞 *hollow* compliments. ●白々しく (知らないふりをして) with an air of innocence; with feigned ignorance; (ずうずうしく) shamelessly.
しらす 白子 〖魚介〗a whitebait; the young of sardines. ●しらす干し boiled and dried young sardines.
しらす 白州 a white sand bar.
しらす 白砂 the deposits of volcanic ash and sand.
●シラス台地 a volcanic ash plateau.
-しらず -知らず ▶そこは暑さ知らずの所だ The place is *free from* the summer heat. ▶彼は怖いもの知らず (どんな危険にも立ち向かう) He will *face up to* any danger./(好んで危険なことをする人だ) He is a daredevil.
じらす 焦らす 〖待てない気持ちにさせる〗irritate, (特に性的に) tease; 〖宙ぶらりんの状態にしておく〗keep* 《him》hanging [in suspense]. ▶彼女はいつも彼をじらしてばかりいる She always *irritates* him./She always *keeps* him *hanging* [*in suspense*].
しらずしらず 知らず知らず ▶私たちは知らず知らず(=無意識に)誤りを犯すことがある We sometimes make *unconscious* mistakes./We sometimes make mistakes *unconsciously* [〖書〗*unawares*, (そうとは知らずに) *without knowing it*]. ▶私は知らず知らずのうちに大声を上げて助けを求めていた I was crying out for help *before I knew it*.

*****しらせ 知らせ** news, word 《of; that 節》. (**!** word は無冠詞に注意) (⇨ニュース) ▶彼からうれしい[重大な; すばらしい]知らせがあった I've received 《xa》good [big; great] *news* from him. ▶彼の死亡の知らせがあった I received the *news of* his death [*that* he had died]./《書》Word [×The word] came *of* his death [*that* he had died].

*****しらせる 知らせる** let* 《him》know 《about; that [wh-]節》, 《書》inform 《him》《of [about]; that [wh-]節》; 〖告げる〗tell* 《him》《about [of]; that [wh-]節》(**!** about は詳しく, of は簡単に知らせる場合); (公式に文書で)《やや書》notify (**!** inform と同様の構文で用いる). (⇨通知する) ●知らせずにおく(=秘密にしておく) keep 《it》secret from 《him》; keep 《it》to oneself. ●殺人事件を警察に知らせる(=通報する) *notify* the police *of* a murder; *report* a murder *to* the police. ▶出かける用意ができたら知らせてください Please *let me* know when you are [×will be] ready to go. ▶そのことについては手紙でお知らせいたします We'll *let* you *know about* it [〖書〗*make* it *known to* you] by letter./I'll write 《to》 you about it. (**!**《英》では to がつくのが普通) ▶彼女は母親の死を知らされた She *was informed of* her mother's death./She *was informed that* her mother had died. ▶お知らせしたいことがあります I have something to *tell* you./There is something I have to *tell* you. (**!** くだけた言い方では Guess what!/(Do) you know what? などということもある) ▶試験に合格したと彼が知らせてくれた He *told* me *that* I had passed the examination. ▶だれかが彼女に母親の死を知らせなくてはならないだろう Someone'll have to *break* the news of her mother's death *to* her. (**!** break は通例悪い知らせを打ち明けるときに用いる) ▶お知らせいたします《アナウンス》May I have your attention, please! ▶ご利用の階をお知らせ願います〈エレベーターで〉Please *call* your floors. ▶英国航空より BA547 便の到着をお知らせいたします British Airways *announces* the arrival of Flight BA547.
しらたき 白滝 whitish stringy *konnyaku*.
しらたま 白玉 rice flour dumplings.
●白玉粉 rice flour.
しらちゃける 白茶ける 〖動〗fade; discolor.
―― 白茶けた 〖形〗faded; discolored.
しらっと ●しらっとした(=しらけた)有権者 an *apathetic* electorate.
しらつゆ 白露 dew; dewdrops.
しらとり 白鳥 (白い鳥) a white bird; (ハクチョウ) a swan.
しらなみ 白波 white-topped waves;《米》white-caps,《英》white horses.
しらぬ 知らぬ (⇨知る)
●知らぬが仏 〖知らなければ傷つくことはない〗(決まり文句で) What he doesn't know won't hurt him.;《ことわざ》Ignorance is bliss. ▶彼は知らぬが仏でカメラ

しらぬい 不知火 (説明的に) mysterious lights on the Yatsushiro Sea in Kyushu in the summer night.

しらは 白刃 a naked sword.

しらは 白羽 ●**白羽の矢が立つ** ▶次期社長として彼に白羽の矢が立てられた He *was singled out* as the next president.

しらばくれる [知らないふりをする] pretend not to know, pretend to be ignorant; [書] feign ignorance; [無実のようにふるまう] play innocent. ▶少年はその事故についてしらばくれたがだめだった The boy tried to *pretend not to know* [*feign ignorance of*] the accident, but failed [(やや書) *but in vain*]. ▶しらばくれても分かりますよ Even if you *play innocent*, I can tell.
会話 「太郎、ぼく何かしたかい、どうしたのさ」「しらばくれてからに(＝まるで知らないかのように)」 "Taro, what did I do wrong? What's the matter?" "*As if you didn't* [《話》*don't*] *know*."

シラバス [講義要項] a syllabus (⑱ ～es, syllabi /síləbai/).

しらはりちょうちん 白張り提灯 a white paper lantern.

しらふ 素面 ⃞ sobriety /soubráiəti/.
—**素面の** ⃝ sober. ▶彼は車の事故を起こしたときしらふだった He was *sober* [*was not drunk*] when he caused the car accident.

シラブル [音節] [言語] a syllable.

しらべ 調べ ●[調査] (an) investigation; (an) examination, (an) inquiry (⇒調査); [尋問] questioning; examination (⇒尋問); [調子] (音色) a note; (曲) a tune; (旋律) (a) melody. ▶美しい調べ a beautiful *melody* [*tune*].

しらべもの 調べ物 something to look into [check up on]. ▶例の件で調べ物があるので図書館に行かなくてはならない I'll have to go to the library to *do* [×*make*] *some research on* it.

*****しらべる** 調べる
◆**WORD CHOICE** 調べる◆
check 物事が適正であるかどうかを一通り確認するため、すばやく簡単に調べること。より丁寧に調べる場合にはcheck on。▶書類を(じっくり)調べる *check* (*on*) the documents.
examine 主に医師・研究者などの専門家が、職務として具体的・個別的な対象物を綿密に観察・調査すること。▶警察が遺体を調べた The police *examined* the body.
investigate 専門家が、事実を明らかにするため事件・状況などを組織的・専門的に調査すること。▶探偵はその殺人事件を調べている The detective is *investigating* the murder case.

◆**頻度チャート**◆
check ▬▬▬▬▬▬▬▬▬▬
examine ▬▬▬▬▬
investigate ▬▬▬
     20   40   60   80   100 (%)

❶ [調査する] examine; investigate; check (⇒[類語]); [念入りに点検する] inspect; [さわって知る] feel*; [見て確認する] see*; [じっくり見る] study. ●その問題を調べる examine [investigate, go into] the problem. ●脈を調べる feel one's pulse. ●地図を調べる study a map. ●書類を調べる(＝目を通す) look over [through] papers. ●答案を調べる(＝採点する) grade 《米》 [mark 《英》] examination papers; (点検する) check one's paper. ●人数を調べる(＝数える) count the number of people. ▶彼はその石を顕微鏡で調べた He *examined* the rock with a microscope. ▶警察はその事件を調べている The police *are investigating* [*looking into*] the incident. ▶国境でパスポートを調べられた The passports *were inspected* [*were checked*] at the border. ▶別の方法をやってみて効果があるかどうか調べてごらん Try another approach and *see* if it works. ▶警官は私がポケットに何か持っているか体に触って調べた The policeman *felt whether* I had anything in my pocket.
会話 「かけてもいない通話料金が請求されたのですが」「調べてみます。お名前と電話番号をお願いします」 "You overcharged me for calls I didn't make." "Let me *check*. What's your name and phone number, please?"

❷ [参考書などで捜す] look ... up; [参考書などを引く] see*, 《書》 consult. ●電話帳で番号を調べる look up [find out] the number in a telephone book. ▶その単語の意味を辞書で調べなさい *Look up* the word *in* the dictionary./*See* [《書》 *Consult*] your dictionary *for* the meaning of the word.

❸ [捜す] search. (⇒捜す)

❹ [尋問する] question; examine. ▶彼らは警察に調べられた They *were questioned* by the police.

しらほ 白帆 a white sail.

しらみ 虱 [昆虫] a louse (⑱ lice). ●シラミがわく be infested with *lice*. ●シラミを駆除する get rid of *lice*.

しらみつぶしに しらみ潰しに (徹底的に) thoroughly /θʌ́rouli/. ●手掛かりがないかしらみつぶしに建物を捜索する search the building *thoroughly* for clues; comb /kóum/ the building for clues. ▶警察は行方不明の子供をしらみつぶしに(＝あらゆる手段に訴えて)捜索している The police *are turning every stone* in their search for the missing child.

しらむ 白む ▶東の空が白んできた The eastern sky *is getting light*. (⇒明ける❶)

しらゆき 白雪 white snow.

しらゆきひめ 白雪姫 Snow White.
●『白雪姫と七人の小人』 *Snow White and the Seven Dwarfs*. (参考) グリム童話

しらゆり 白百合 [植物] a white lily; a Easter lily.

しらん 紫蘭 [植物] a *shiran* orchid; a bletilla.

しらんかお 知らん顔 ▶彼女が困っているのに知らん顔(＝無関心)だ He is *indifferent to* her trouble. ▶手を上げたのに先生は知らん顔(＝無視［気づかないふり］)をした The teacher *ignored* me [*pretended not to notice* me, *looked the other way*] when I raised my hand.

しらんぷり 知らん振り ▶街でジョンに会ったが、彼は知らんぷりをした I saw John in town, but he *pretended not to recognize me* [*ignore me deliberately*; just *cut me dead*].

*****しり** 尻 ❶ [人・動物の] 《書》 buttocks /bʌ́təks/ (❗ 腰掛けるといすに触れる部分をいう); 《話》 a bottom, 《話》 a behind, 《話》 a rear (❗ 3語は婉曲語に); (ヒップ) hips (❗ 腰骨の周囲の盛り上がった部分。片方だけをさす場合は単数形で); (けつ) 《卑》 an ass, backsides; [牛などの] a rump.

しり【~尻】 ● 大きな尻 large [big] *buttocks*; broad [heavy] *hips*. ● まるまると太った尻 plump *hips*.

❷【尻が[の]】 ● 尻のあたり around one's *buttocks*. ● 彼女は尻が大きい She has broad [big, plump] *hips*./She is broad-[large-, plump-]*hipped*./She has a rather big *bottom* [is rather big-*bottomed*].

❸【尻を】 ● (罰に)彼の尻をぶつ smack his *buttocks* [*bottom*, *behind*, *rear*]; give him a smack on the *buttocks* [*bottom*, *behind*, *rear*]. ▶尻をはしょる the tail end of one's *kimono* into its *obi* loop; omit the tail end of (a story). ▶尻をふく clean up (after a BM). ▶尻をつくことなく跳び箱をとんだ I jumped over a vaulting horse without my *bottom* touching the seat. ▶彼女はお尻を左右に振りながら歩く She sways her *hips* from side to side as she walks. ▶お客さんに尻(=背)を向けてはいけない Don't turn your *back* to your guest(s). (⇨背)

❷【なべ・ズボンなどの】 ● なべの尻(=下面) the *undersurface* [*bottom*] of a saucepan. ▶ズボンの尻が薄くなっている The *seat* of the pants is thin. ▶彼は尻のポケットに財布を入れていた He carried his wallet in his *hip* pocket.

❸【後方, 席次】 ● 彼らの尻(=後方)からついて行く follow them in the *rear*. ● 列の尻(=終わり)に座る sit at the *tail end* of the line. ▶彼はクラスの尻にいた He was at the *bottom* of his class.

● 尻が重い (なかなか行動しない) be slow to act.
● 尻が軽い (進んで行動する) be ready [willing] to act; (軽率に行動する) act hastily.
● 尻が長い ▶彼は尻が長い He tends to outstay [overstay] his welcome.
● 尻に敷く ▶女房の尻に敷かれた男 a henpecked husband. ▶彼女は亭主を尻に敷いている(=思いのままに操る)《話》She can *twist* her husband *around* her *little finger*./Her husband is *under* her *thumb*./She wears the *pants*《米》[*trousers*《英》]. (!ズボンは男がはくものであることから (⇨かかあ天下))
● 尻に火がつく be pressed by urgency.
● 尻に帆をかける turn tail and run away; show a clean pair of heels.
● 尻の毛を抜く deprive 《him》 of 《his》 property.
● 尻を追い回す ▶女の尻を追い回す chase after women [girls].
● 尻を拭(ぬぐ)う bear the consequences of 《his》 mistake; clear up 《his》 mess.

しり 私利 one's own interests, 《やや書》self-interest. ● あの男はつねに私利私欲で行動する That guy always acts *in* his *own interests* [out of *self-interest*, (利己的な動機で) *from selfish motives /móutɪvz/*].

じり 事理 reason. ● 事理をわきまえる be reasonable; be sensible.

シリア 〖国名〗Syria; (公式名) the Syrian Arab Republic. (首都 Damascus) ● シリア人 a Syrian. ● シリアの Syrian.

*しりあい 知り合い 〖人〗(知っている人) an acquaintance, a person (who(m)) one knows (!後の方が口語的な言い方で, 通例懇意な間柄を含意); 〖関係〗acquaintance(ship). (⇨友達 解説)) ● 知り合いの 知り合い one's *acquaintance's acquaintance*. ● 知り合いがいない have no *acquaintances*. ● 彼とはちょっとした(=会釈する程度の)知り合い I have a nodding *acquaintance* with him./(単なる知り合いだ) He is just [only] an *acquaintance*./He is a slight *acquaintance* (of mine). ● 彼とは昔からの知り合いだ I have known [×have been knowing, ×know] him for years./(友達同士だ) I have been *friends* [×a *friend*] with him for years.

❶【知り合いが】 ● 知り合いが多い have many *acquaintances*; have a wide [a large] circle of *acquaintances*.

❷【知り合いの】 ● 私の知り合いの医者 a doctor (who(m) I *know*; a doctor of my *acquaintance*. ▶横浜に住みたいと思いますが, どなたか知り合いの方はいらっしゃいますか I'm interested in living [×to live] in Yokohama. Do you know anybody (who could help me? (!内は知らぬ土地なので何かと世話になることを考えて英語ではつけ加える方がよい)

❸【知り合いに】 ▶駅で知り合いに出会った I met a person I *know* [an *acquaintance* (of mine)] at the station. (!my *acquaintance* は不自然 (⇨友達 解説)(2))) ● お知り合いになれてうれしく存じます (通例初対面で紹介されて) I'm glad [(It's) nice] to *meet* [*get to know*] you./(改まって) I'm pleased to *make* your *acquaintance*. (⇨知り合う) ▶きっと彼と知り合いになってよかったと思うでしょう I know you'll enjoy knowing him.

しりあう 知り合う (つき合うようになる) get [come] to know 《him》(!come は改まった言い方); (紹介などされて) meet 《him》; (浅く知り合う) get [become] acquainted with 《him》; (書) make 《his》 acquaintance [the acquaintance of 《him》]. ▶お 2 人はどのように知り合われたのですか How did you *come to know* (each other)? ▶君たち知り合ってからどれくらいになるの How long *have* you *known* each other? ▶今の若者はしばしば出会い系サイトで知り合う These days young people often *get to know* each other through encounter sites on the cell phone.
会話 「君たちは最初どこで知り合ったの?」「飛行機でよ」"Where did you first *meet*?" "On a plane." (!on を省くのはぶっきらぼうな言い方)

しりあがり 尻上がり ● 尻上がりの口調で(=上がり調子で)話す speak with a *rising intonation* [*tone*]. ▶彼女の演奏は尻上がりによくなって, 後半は本当に魅力的だった Her performance *got better and better* and the latter half of it was really beautiful. (⇔ 尻下がり)

シリアル 〖コーンフレークなど〗a cereal /síəriəl/.
シリアル 〖連続, 直列〗serial.
● シリアルナンバー a serial number. ● シリアルポート〖コンピュータ〗a serial port. ● シリアルマウス〖コンピュータ〗a serial mouse.

シリーズ a series /síəri(:)z/ (働 ~). ● シリーズものの a serial; (⇨連続) a serial. ● 日本文学シリーズ the Japanese Literature *Series*. ● 日本シリーズ〖野球〗the Japan *Series*. ● 地下鉄シリーズ〖野球〗a subway *series*. ● 3連戦シリーズ a three-game series. ● ワールドシリーズに進出する make it to the World *Series*.

しりうま 尻馬 ● 尻馬に乗る(盲目的に従う) follow [(まねる) imitate] 《him》 blindly.
しりおし 尻押し (⇨後押し)
シリカゲル 〖化学〗silica gel /sílɪkə dʒèl/. (参考) 乾燥剤)
しりがる 尻軽 ── 尻軽な 厖 fickle; unfaithful. (⇨浮気な)
じりき 地力 (もともと持っている能力) ability. (⇨実力)
● 地力のある able. ● 地力を発揮する display [show] one's *ability*.

じりき 自力 ●自力で生活する live *by oneself* [*on one's own*]. (⇨独力) ●自力でたたき上げた男 a *self-made* man. ●自力更生 regeneration by one's own efforts; self-help.

しりきれとんぼ 尻切れとんぼ ●何事も尻切れとんぼ(=途中までで完結しない状態)にするな Don't leave anything *half-done* [*unfinished*].

しりごみ 尻込み 名 (ためらい) hesitation.
— **尻込みする** 動 (ためらう) hesitate (*to do*); (ひるむ) shrink (*from*); (逃げ腰になる) back away (*from*). ●怖くて尻込みする *back away* [*shrink back*] in fear.

シリコン 【化学】 silicon 《元素記号 Si》; (シリコン樹脂) silicone /sílikoun/.
●シリコンチップ a silicon chip. (!単に a chip ともいう) ●シリコン注入物 (整形美容用の) (a) silicone implant. ●シリコンバレー 《米国の半導体関連企業が集中する〜》Silicon Valley.

しりさがり 尻下がり ●尻下がりの音調 (a) falling intonation. ●尻下がりの傾向 a downward trend; a falling [a downward] tendency. (⇔ 尻上がり)

じりじり ❶【ゆっくりと】slowly; (徐々に) gradually; (着実に) steadily. ▶敵はじりじりと迫ってきていた The enemy was closing in (on us). (!close in は「周囲からじりじりと迫る」の意)/The enemy was *slowly* [*gradually*] surrounding us. ▶物価がじりじりと上がり始めた Prices have begun to *edge up*.
❷【焼きつくように】scorchingly. ▶夏の日はじりじりと暑かった The summer day was *scorchingly* [《話》*scorching*] hot./It was a *scorching* summer day. ▶太陽がじりじりと照りつけていた The sun was burning (down) *fiercely*.
❸【いらだって】●じりじりさせる(=人をいらいらさせる) irritate. ▶試験の結果をじりじり待つ wait *impatiently* [《熱心に》*eagerly*] for the result of the exam. ▶私は受付のいいかげんな応対にじりじりした I *was irritated by* the receptionist's sloppy response.

しりすぼみ 尻すぼみ ●尻すぼみになる weaken toward the end; gradually lose interest [energy]; fizzle. ▶騒動は尻すぼみになった The disturbance *has gradually lost its energy* [*drive*]. ▶宇宙飛行士になるという彼女の夢は尻すぼみに終わった Her ambition to become an astronaut *fizzled out*.

しりぞく 退く ❶【後ろへ下がる】draw* back; move back; (1歩) take* a step backward; (兵が) withdraw*, (不利になって) retreat. ●彼女は蛇を見て退いた She *drew* [*stepped*] *back* when she saw a snake. ●軍隊は前線から退いた(=撤退した) The army *withdrew* from the front.
❷【職などを】(通例定年で) retire 《*from*》; (辞職する) resign, leave* 《one's post》 (!後の方が口語的). ●公の生活から退く *retire from* public life. ●教授の職を退く *retire* as professor. ●代打を送られて退く *leave* a game [*retire*] for a pinch hitter.

しりぞける 退ける ❶【却下する】reject, turn down (!後の方が口語的). ▶委員会は彼の提案を退けた The committee *rejected* [*turned down*] his proposal.
❷【撃退する】beat* (an attack) off; beat (an enemy) back. ●最初の7人の打者を退ける retire [set down] the first seven batters. ●四番打者を二塁のポップフライに退ける get the cleanup to pop up to second.
❸【遠ざける】(近寄らせない) keep* (him) away; (退席させる) ask (him) to leave.

じりだかい じり高 【経済】a gradual rise (in the market price). (⇔ じり安) ▶相場はじり高である The market *is gradually rising*.

しりつ 市立 ── 市立の 形 municipal. ●市立病院 a *municipal* [*a city*] hospital. (⇨公立, 県立)

しりつ 私立 ── 私立の 形 private. ●私立大学 a *private* college [university].

じりつ 自立 名 self-support; independence (*from*).
— **自立する** 動 (自活する) support oneself; (独立する) become [be] independent (*of*), 《やや話》stand on one's own feet. ●自立した女性 an *independent* woman. ●経済的に親から自立する become [be] financially *independent of* [ˣ*from*] one's parents. ▶息子はもう(経済的に)自立している My son is *on his own* now./My son *is* financially *independent* now.
●自立語 【文法】an independent word.

じりつしんけい 自律神経 【解剖】an autonomic nerve.
●自律神経 the autonomic nervous system.
●自律神経失調(症) 【医学】autonomic imbalance [atáxia].

しりとり 尻取り *shiritori*; (説明的に) a Japanese word-chain game. ●尻取りをする play *shiritori*.

しりぬぐい 尻拭い ●尻ぬぐいをする(=他人のごたごたを清算する) straighten out 《his》 mess. ●彼の借金の尻ぬぐいをする *straighten out* his financial mess. ●彼の失敗の尻ぬぐいをする clean up after his mistake.

しりぬけ 尻抜け (すぐ忘れてしまうこと) forgetfulness; (抜け道があること) a loophole (*in* the rule).

しりはしょり 尻はしょり ── 尻はしょりする 動 tuck up one's kimono [skirts].

じりひん じり貧 《やや書》a gradual decline. ●じり貧になる(=下り坂になる) go downhill; get worse. ▶今のままでは会社はじり貧だ If we don't do anything, our company will *get worse* (*and worse*).

しりめ 尻目 ●不景気を尻目に(=不景気でも[不景気などまるでよそごとみたいに])かせぎまくっている連中もいる Some people are making a lot of money even in hard times [as if the depression were someone else's problem].
●尻目にかける (軽視する) ignore; 《俗》give 《him》 the go-by.

しめつれつ 支離滅裂 (つじつまの合わない) incoherent /ìnkouhíərənt/. ▶彼の説明は支離滅裂だ(=一貫性を欠いている) His explanations *are lacking in coherence*.

しりもち 尻もち ●尻もちをつく fall on one's buttocks [《話》bottom, 《話》behind, rear (end)]. (!end を省略する方が口語的の) (⇨尻)

じりやす じり安 【経済】a gradual fall [drop] (in the market price). (⇔ じり高) ▶株価はじり安だ Stock prices *are gradually falling*.

しりゅう 支流 (本流から分岐した) a branch; (本流に注ぐ) a tributary (stream). ●アマゾン川の支流 a *tributary* of the Amazon River.

じりゅう 時流 the current of the times. ●時流に乗る(=迎合する) swim with [against] *the current of the times*; (流れに身を任せる[任せない]) go [move] with [against] *the flow*. ●時流に乗っている keep up with *the times*; 《話》be in (↔out of) *the swim*; 《積極的に》《話》jump on the *wagon* [*bandwagon*].

しりょ 思慮 【考え】(a) thought; 【用心深さ】prudence; 【思慮分別】discretion. ●思慮深く thoughtfully; with *prudence* [*discretion*]. ●思慮深い人 a *thoughtful* [a *prudent*, a *discreet*]

しりょう person. ▶そんなことをするとはあなたは思慮が足りない *It is thoughtless [imprudent, indiscreet] of* [×*for*] *you to do such a thing.*

しりょう 資料 (素材) material; (データ) data. (⇨データ) ●研究資料 research *data*. ●参考資料 reference *materials* [*data*]. ●一次資料 primary *sources*. ▶本を書くための資料を集める collect *material* [*data*] *for a book.* ▶御社の採用に関する資料をお送りください Please send me *information concerning employment opportunities with your company.*

しりょう 史料 a historical document.
●史料編纂(ﾍﾝｻﾝ) historiography.

しりょう 飼料 feed. (⇨餌(ｴｻ))

しりょう 死霊 the spirit of a dead person; a ghost; (怨霊(ｵﾝﾘｮｳ)) a vengeful ghost.

しりょく 死力 ●死力を尽くす (死に物狂いの努力をする) make desperate efforts; make an all-out effort.

しりょく 視力 eyesight, sight; 《やや書》vision. ●視力検査を受ける have an *eye* [《やや書》an *eyesight*] test; (測ってもらう) have one's *eyesight* tested. ●視力検査表 an eyechart. ●動体視力 dynamic visual acuity. ▶彼は視力がいい[弱い] He has good [poor] *eyesight*./His *eyesight* is good [poor]./He has good [poor] *vision*. ▶彼の視力は衰え始めている His *eyesight* [*sight*] is failing. ▶左眼の視力は1.0[0.5]だ I have twenty-twenty [twenty-forty] *vision* in my left eye. (❗(1) 20/20[20/40]とも言う. (2) 20フィート(約6m)の位置から視標番号20[40] (1/3 [2/3] インチの大きさの文字)を確認できる視力) ▶彼は右目の視力を失った He lost his *eyesight* in [×of] the right eye.

しりょく 資力 (財力) means; (資産) resources; (富) wealth; (資金) funds; (金) money. ▶彼にはかなり資力がある He is a man of considerable *means* [*resources, wealth*]. / He is a very *rich* [*wealthy*] man. ▶新しい家を買うだけの資力がない I don't have enough *funds* [*money*] to buy a new house./I can't *afford* (to get) a new house.

じりょく 磁力 〖物理〗 magnetic force.
●磁力線 a line of magnetic force.

シリンダー a cylinder /sílindər/.
●シリンダー錠 a cylinder lock.

しる 知る

INDEX

❶ 情報を得る ❷ 面識がある
❸ 知識がある ❹ 認識する
❺ 発見する   ❻ 経験する
❼ 関係する

WORD CHOICE 知る

know すでにある内容・情報を「知っている」状態にあること. ▶あなたも知っているように as you *know*. ▶君のことは知っているよ I *know* (of [about]) you.

learn 知らない内容・情報を新たに「知る」こと. 直接的に知るのではなく, 見聞によって間接的に知る場合は, learn of. ▶その事故のことはニュースで知ったんだ I *learned of* the accident from the news.

頻度チャート

know ████████████████████
learn ████

20 40 60 80 100 (%)

❶ **[情報を得る]** (すでに知っている) know* 《*of*+人[物, 事, *about*+事; (*that*) 節, *wh-*節》 (❗*about* は具体的に知っている場合, *of* は直接知らない場合に用いる); (人から聞いて知る) 《書》learn* 《*of, about*; (*that*) 節, *wh-*節》 ▶どうして彼を知るようになったの How did you get to *know* him? ▶私の知るかぎりでは, 彼はレースに勝ったことは一度もありません As [So] *far as I know*, he has never won a race./To (the best of) *my knowledge*, he has never won a race. (❗ともに文尾に置くことも可) ▶彼が試験に合格したかどうか知りたき[知りたい] I don't *know* [I'd like to *know*] *whether* he passed the examination. ▶あの山は知っていますが, まだ登ったことはありません I *know of* the mountain, but I've never climbed it. ▶いつそこへ行ったらよいか知っていますか Do you *know when* we should go there [*when* to go there]? ▶彼は私の過去を知りたがった He *was curious about* my past. ▶そんなこと知っているわけないだろう Don't ask me. (❗質問を突っぱねるときの慣用表現)

会話 「彼は失業中だ」「知っているよ」"He is out of work." "I *know* (it, that, ×so)." (❗先行する平叙文を受ける代用形 it, that は通例省略する. ×I'm *know*ing. は不可)

会話 「彼は何歳ですか」「さあ知りません」"How old is he?" "(I'm) sorry but I don't *know*./(見当がつかない) I've no idea." (❗(1) 先行する疑問文を受ける場合, *know* の後に it は不要. 節末を省略して単に "I don't know." とするのはぶっきらぼうな言い方. (2) I've no idea. は「そんなこと知らないよ」といらだちを含んだ言い方にもなる. また強調形として I don't have *the slightest* [*faintest*] idea. (さっぱり知りません) (⇨分かる ❷)/How should I know? (知ってるはずがないでしょ/知るもんか)などという)

① **【…に知られる】** ▶その病気は医学の専門家の知るところであったが一般には知られていなかった The disease *was known by* specialists in medicine but not *to* the public. (❗受身では *to* の方が普通. ただし *by* は動作主が知ろうとした結果としての状態を, *to* はいつの間にか知るようになることを含意する) ▶彼女はその町ではみんなに知られるようになった She has become *known to* [×*by*] everybody in the town. (❗*become* の後では *known* は完全に形容詞化していて *by* はとらない)

② **【…から[で]知る】** ▶お父さんがお亡くなりになったことを息子から聞いて今知ったばかりです I *have just learned of* your father's death *from* my son./I *have just learned from* my son (*that*) your father passed away. (❗*that* を省略する方が口語的. pass away は die の婉曲的な言い方) ▶私はその事故を新聞[ラジオ]で知った I *learned of* the accident *from* the newspaper [*on* the radio]. (❗I *saw* the accident *in* the newspaper./I *heard* the news of the accident *on* the radio. という方が普通)

❷ **[面識がある]** know*, 《書》 be acquainted 《*with*》 (❗後の方は単に「顔見知りである」の意であるが, *know* は通例「熟知している」ことを含意する) ▶顔[名前]だけは知っています I *know* him only by sight [*name*]. (❗前の方は ×... *by face* としない) ▶あの人のことはうわさには聞いて知っているが, 個人的には知りません I *know of* him, but I don't *know* him personally. (❗*know* him は実際に知っている, *know of* him は間接的に知っていること (⇨❶))

会話 「岡田さんを知っていますか」「よく知っています」"Do you *know* Mr. Okada?" "Yes, I *know* him well." (❗個人的つき合いを問題にしないときは例えば *Do you know who* Michael Jackson *is*?/Have

you ever heard of Michael Jackson? などという)
❸ 〖知識がある〗 know*, have* knowledge 《of》, be familiar 《with, to》; 〖知識を得る〗learn*. ▶駅へ行く道を知っていますか Do you *know* the way to the train station? ▶博多はよく知っています I *know* Hakata well./I *know* a lot about Hakata./I have (a) good *knowledge* of Hakata. (❗(形+) knowledge of の型にはしばしば不定冠詞を伴う)/I am *familiar* with Hakata. (❗Hakata is *familiar* to me. は「博多は見慣れている」程度の意) ▶どうして音楽のことをそんなによく知っているの How do you *know* so much about music? ▶あなたは自分の国のことをもっと知るべきだ You should *learn* [*get to know*, ×know] more *about* your own country. (❗know はすでに知っている状態をさすので不可) ▶目が覚めたとき, 私は知らない部屋にいた When I woke up, I was in a *strange* room. ▶この辺のことはよく知りません I'm a *stranger* in this neighborhood. (❗「まったく知りません」は I'm a complete [a total] *stranger*...) ▶私はフランス語はほとんど知らない I *know* French very little./I *know* very little about French./I *have* very little *knowledge* of French. ▶彼はその金庫の開け方を知っていた He *knew* how to open the safe.

会話「英語をどれくらい知っていますか」「あまりよく知りません」"How well do you *know* English?" "I don't *know* it very well [much]. (❗このように「実際的な知識を身につけている」の意(以下 2 例も同様)では well や much を単独で文尾に用いない: ×I don't know that *well* [*much*].)/I never well [much] *know* that./I don't *know* much about it. (❗この much は代名詞)/I don't *have* much *knowledge* of it."

❹ 〖認識する〗(事実として認めている) know*; (悟る) realize; (気づく) notice; (気づいている) be aware 《of》; (真価を的確に判断する) appreciate. ▶彼が有名な作家であった[である]ことは知っています I *know (that)* he was [is] a well-known writer. (❗that は省略可)/(《書》) I *know* him to have been [*to* be] a well-known writer. (❗世間一般の評判を伝える場合には受身にして He *is known* to have been [*to* be, *as*] a well-known writer. のようにいう方が It *is known that*.... より普通) ▶その映画を見て平和の大切さを知った When I saw the movie, I *realized* [×knew] the importance of peace. ▶彼はそれがどんなに危険かということをよく知っていた He *was* fully *aware* 《*of*》 [*knew* very well] how dangerous it was. (❗ wh- 節の前の of は通例省略される) ▶彼女は途中その駅を通り過ぎたことを知らなかった She didn't *notice* (*that*) she passed the station on the way. ▶それは私の知らないうちに起こった It came about [happened] without my *knowledge* [without my *knowing* about it, before I *knew* it]. (❗最後の言い方は「あっという間に」のように速さを強調する (⇒いつの間にか)) ▶昨夜の地震は知りませんでした(=感じなかった) I didn't *feel* the earthquake last night. ▶恥を知れ Be ashamed (of yourself)./Shame on you! ▶知らぬが仏 (⇒知らぬ)

❺ 〖発見する〗 find* (*it*) (*out*) (❗find out は「調査・観察の結果知る」ことで, find とは異なり偶然性を含まない); (思いがける) discover. ▶彼はとても正直であることを知った I *found* [*discovered*, ×knew, ×found out] (*that*) he was very honest./I *found* [《まれ》 *discovered*] him *to* be very honest. ▶先生はその学生がカンニングしていたことを知った The teacher *found out that* the student had been cheating on [in] the exam./(しているところを見つけた[つかまえた]) The teacher *caught* the student cheating on [in] the exam. ▶勤めて初めて教育が大事であることを知った I didn't *discover* [*realize*, ×find] how important education was until I went to work./It wasn't until I went to work that I *discovered* [*realized*] how important education was.

❻ 〖経験する〗 experience; (経験して知る) know*. ▶我々は戦争を知りません We *have* never *experienced* war. ▶商売のことはあまり知りません(=経験がない) I'm not very [little] *experienced* in business work. (❗(1) little は単独では堅い言い方. (2) experienced は形容詞) ▶貧乏がどんなものか知っています I *have known* poverty./I *know* what it is like to be poor. ▶彼は世間をよく知っている[知らない] He *knows* a lot *about* [is ignorant of] the world.

❼ 〖関係する〗 have* something to do with...; 〖気にする〗 care (通例否定文・疑問文で用いる). ▶(忠告を聞かない人に)もうどうなっても知りませんよ Well, no matter what happens, don't say I didn't warn you.

・知ったことじゃない ▶それはぼくの知ったことじゃない(=何の関係もない) I *have nothing to do with* it./It *has nothing to do with* me./It's not my concern [business]. (❗It's no concern [business] of mine./It's none of my business. は感情的・強調的な言い方) ▶彼がどうなろうとぼくの知ったことじゃない I *don't care* [《話》 *couldn't care less*] what will become of him.

● 知る人ぞ知る only a connoisseur would know.

*しる 汁 〖液体, 水分〗 liquid; 〖果実・野菜・肉などの〗 juice; 〖樹液〗 sap; 〖肉汁〗 gravy; 〖汁物〗 soup; broth; 〖煮出し汁〗 stock (⇒だし). ▶汁の多いナシ (水々しい) a *juicy* (a *succulent*) pear /péər/; (水っぽい) a watery pear. ▶この取り引きでうまい[甘い]汁を吸っているやつがいる There is somebody who gets [makes] unfair profits out of this business.

● 汁椀 a soup bowl.

シルエット a silhouette /sìluét/. (参考) フランスの政治家の名から) ● カーテンに映った男のシルエット the *silhouette* of a man on the curtain.

シルク 〖絹〗 silk. (⇒絹)
● シルクスクリーン silk screen. ● シルクハット a top hat, 《話》 a topper. (❗a silk hat は主に絹製の top hat をさす)

シルクロード the Silk Road [Route].

しるけ 汁気 juice. ●汁気のある juicy.

しるこ 汁粉 *shiruko*; (説明的に) sweetened *azuki* soup with rice cakes or rice-flour dumplings in it.

:しるし 印 〖○や×などの〗 a mark; 〖ある意味を表す記号など〗 a sign; 〖ある感情を思い起こさせるもの〗 a token; 〖照合・点検my〗 a √印; 〖英〗 a check, 《英》 a tick (❗日本語のような否定的なイメージはない). ▶○[×]印のついた単語 words *marked* (with) circles [crosses]. ▶その印はどういう意味ですか What does the *mark* [*sign*] mean? ▶顔色がよいのは健康なしるしだ A ruddy face is a *sign* of good health./A ruddy face *indicates that* you are in good health. ▶ご親切に対するお礼が(=感謝)の印としてこの本をお送りします I'll send you this book as a *token* [*in token*] of my gratitude for your kindness. ▶印ばかりの品ですがお礼です This is just a small *token* of gratitude for you. ▶心なしか肩を落としたように見えた. 元気印の(=非常に元気なことで知られている)姉さんらしくもなかった Her shoulders seemed to have somewhat drooped. That

was not at all like her because she was known for all her vitality [as a symbol of vitality]. (🛈 droop は元気がないために体の一部が下がっている状態を表す)
- 印をつける mark, put* a mark (*on*); check (米) [tick (英)]... (off). ● かばんに(目)印をつける mark [*put a mark on*] a bag. ● 地図に出ている彼の家に赤鉛筆で[赤で]印をつける mark his house on the map *with a red pencil* [*in red*]. ● 基本単語に星印(*)をつける mark basic words *with* asterisks [stars]; *put* asterisks *against* basic words. ▶ 読みたい本に√印をつけなさい Check (*off*) [*Put checks beside*] the titles of the books you want to read.
- 印半纏(はんてん) (説明的に) a Japanese version of a livery coat, which is worn by traditional workers and has the name of a shop on it.

しるし 徴 a sign; an indication. (⇨兆し, 兆候)

*しるす 印す (印を)つける) mark. (⇨印) ▶ 彼は成功の第一歩を印した He *has taken* the first step toward success.

しるす 記す (書き留める) write [put*]... down; (記録として本や碑などに) (書) inscribe. ● 忘れないうちに自分の考えを書き記す write [*put*] *down* one's idea before one forgets it. ● 彼の言葉を心に記す *inscribe* his words *on* one's heart; *keep* [*bear*] his words *in* mind. ▶ トロフィーに第 1 回の優勝者の名前が記された The trophy *was inscribed with* the name of the first winner.

ジルバ a jitterbug. (参考 日本語の「ジルバ」は jitterbug の崩れた音から) ▶ ジルバを踊る dance the jitterbug; jitterbug.

シルバー ● シルバーグレーの髪 silver gray hair.
- シルバーエージ 'silver age'; (実年, 熟年) vintage years. ● シルバーシート (⇨優先席) ● シルバーパス a free transportation pass for elderly.

しれい 司令 a command. ● 部下に攻撃の司令を出す give a *command for* [*command, order*] one's men to attack. (🛈 command は通例軍隊で用いる)
- 司令官 a commander; a commandant.
- 司令長官 a Commander-in-Chief. ● 司令塔 〖サッカー〗 a playmaker, a schemer; the manager on the pitch; the director on the pitch.
- 司令部 the headquarters. (🛈 単・複両扱い)

しれい 『死霊』 Spirits of the Dead. (参考 埴谷雄高の小説)

しれい 指令 an order; (軍隊などの) a command. (⇨命令)

じれい 事例 an example, an instance; a case; (先例) a precedent.
- 事例研究 a case study.

じれい 辞令 ❶ 〖任命書〗 a written appointment.
- 販売部長の辞令を手渡される receive an *appointment* as sales manager.
❷ 〖言葉〗 ● 外交辞令 diplomatic *language*. ● 社交辞令でそう言うだけ say so just to be polite.

しれつ 熾烈 ― 熾烈な 〖形〗 (戦いなどが) fierce, raging; (競争が) keen, fierce, cutthroat. ● 大学入学の熾烈な競争 keen [*fierce, stiff*] competition for getting admission [admitted] to college [(the) university]. ▶ 自由を求める闘争は熾烈の度を加えた The struggle for freedom became *fiercer*.

しれつきょうせい 歯列矯正 〖医学〗 orthodontics /ɔːrθəˈdɒntɪks/; straightening of irregular teeth.
- 歯列矯正をする have one's teeth straightened.
- 歯列矯正の金具をはめている wear braces 《米》 [a brace 《英》] on one's teeth.

じれったい 焦れったい 〖人がいらいらする〗 be irritated 《*at, by*》; 〖人がもどかしがる〗 be impatient 《*at, about*》; 〖物事がいらいらさせる〗 be irritating. ● じれったげに彼の到着を待つ wait *impatiently* for his arrival. ▶ 彼の話し方はいささかじれったい I *am a little irritated* [*impatient*] *at* the way he speaks./The way he speaks *is a little irritating* to me.
▶ じれったいなあ 早く本当のことを言ってくれ 〖話〗 Don't keep me *dangling*! Tell me the truth right away.

しれっと ▶ 次郎はどんなに大酒を飲んでもしれっと(=平然)としている No matter how much Jiro drinks, he *looks calm and sober*.

しれる 知れる ❶ 〖知られるようになる〗 become* known (*to*). ▶ 彼の名は世界に知れ渡っている[渡った] His name *is* [*has become*] well *known to* the world. (🛈 well-known ともつづる) ▶ 彼が仮病を使ったことが先生に知れた(=耳に入った) It came to his teacher's *knowledge* that he had faked sickness.

❷ 〖ばれる〗 (見破られる) be found out 《調査の結果わかることで, 後の二つのように偶然性はない》; (明るみに出る) be out, come* to light. ● お里が知れる (⇨お里 〖成句〗) ▶ 彼がわいろを受け取ったことが警察に知れた The police *found out* (*that*) he had taken a bribe./The police *found out* about him taking a bribe. ▶ 最近になってそのスキャンダルが世間に知れた The scandal *has* recently *come to light*.

じれる 焦れる 〖いらいらする〗 be irritated 《*at, by*》; 〖もどかしがる〗 be impatient; 〖やきもきする〗 fret (-tt-). (⇨焦れったい)

しれん 試練 〖災い, 困難〗 a trial; 〖試験〗 a test. ● 私にとって厳しい試練 a severe *trial for* [*to*] me. ● 大きな試練を受ける[に直面する] undergo [face] a great *trial*. ● 時の試練に耐える stand the *test of time*.

ジレンマ a dilemma /dɪˈlemə/. (🛈 どちらを選んでもよくないことを意味する) ▶ 八方ふさがりのジレンマ an impossible *dilemma*. ● ジレンマに陥っている be (caught) in a *dilemma* 《*whether* 節》. ● ジレンマに追い込む put [place] 〈him〉 in a *dilemma*.

‡**しろ** 白 〖白色〗 white; 〖潔白〗 innocence. ▶ 彼は白(=無罪)だ He *is innocent* [*not guilty*].

*しろ 城 a castle /ˈkæsl/. (🛈 固有名詞では Himeji Castle のように) ● 城跡(=廃城(は い じょ う)) the ruins [(あった場所)] site) of a *castle*. ● 城を築く build a *castle*. ● 城を攻める attack [(包囲して) lay siege to] a *castle*. ● 城を攻め落とす take [capture] a *castle*. ● 敵に城を明け渡す surrender a *castle* to the enemy. ● 海辺で砂の城をつくる build a sand *castle* at [on] the beach.

しろあり 白蟻 〖昆虫〗 a termite, a white ant.

しろあん 白餡 white bean paste.

*しろい 白い ❶ 〖色が〗 white. ● 他の色と並べている場合には white は後に置く: 白とピンクの服 a pink and *white* dress); 色肌が色白の fair (⇨色 ❷). ● 白い服を着た少女 a girl wearing [in] a *white* dress; a girl (dressed) in *white*. (🛈 この white は「白い服」の色の名前) ● 壁を白く塗る paint a wall *white*. ● 髪に白いもの(=白髪)が混じる have some *white* hair in one's head. ▶ 彼の髪は白くなった His hair has turned *white* [*gray*]./His hair has whitened [is quite *gray* now].

❷ 〖その他の表現〗 ▶ 君の吐く息が白い(=霧状になる) Your breath *turns to mist* in front of you. ▶ 自分の吐く息が冷たい空気に触れて白くなった I saw my breath form a tiny cloud in the cold air.
- 白い歯を見せる show one's (*white*) teeth.

● 白い目で見る ▶彼は私を白い目で(=冷たく)見た He looked coldly on [at] me.
しろう 屍蝋 adipocere; grave wax.
じろう 痔瘻 〖医学〗(an) anal fistula /éinl fístʃələ/. (⇨痔)
***しろうと** 素人 〖プロに対して〗an amateur /ǽmətʃùər/ (!「未熟者」の意もある); 〖専門家に対して〗a lay person, (男の) a layman (圈 -men); (女の) laywoman (圈 -women) (!特に法律・医学などの). ● 素人画家 an amateur painter; an amateur in [of] painting. ● 素人向きの医学書 a medical book for laymen. ● 素人目には to one's amateurish eyes. ▶彼は素人にしてはゴルフがうまい He can get to golf for an amateur. ▶出版業ではずぶの素人です I'm just an amateur [(話)quite green] in the publishing business. ▶それは素人考えだ That's a non-professional idea [way of thinking]. ▶彼らは素人離れしていた They were as good as professionals.
じろうものがたり 『次郎物語』 The Tale of Jiro. (参考) 下村湖人の小説)
しろうり 白瓜 〖植物〗an oriental pickling melon.
しろかき 代掻き ● 代掻きをする plow a rice field before rice plants transplanting.
しろがね 白金 (銀) silver; (銀貨) a silver coin.
しろかび 白黴 mildew.
しろくじちゅう 四六時中 〖1日中〗all day; 〖いつも〗always, all the time. ● 四六時中机に向かっている spend all day (working) at the desk. ▶君は四六時中不平ばかり言っている You are always complaining. /You are complaining all the time. ▶言うのは簡単だが,四六時中彼女を見張っているなんてことは無理だ It's easy enough to say, but I just can't watch her every minute (of the day).
しろくばん 四六版 duodecimo; twelvemo.
しろくま 白熊 〖動物〗a polar (=white) bear.
しろくろ 白黒 ●白黒の写真[映画] a black-and-white [×white-and-black] photo [film]; a photo [a film] (which is) in black and white. ●驚いて目を白黒させる roll [blink] one's eyes in surprise. (!roll ぐるぐる, blink ぱちぱちさせること)
● 白黒をつける ●どちらが正しいか白黒をつける(=きっぱりと決着をつける) get it settled once and for all which one is right.
しろざけ 白酒 (sweet) white sake.
しろざとう 白砂糖 white [refined] sugar.
しろじ 白地 (白い布地) white cloth; (白い地色を) a white background.
しろしょうぞく 白装束 white clothing. ● 白装束をしている be dressed in white.
じろじろ ●じろじろ見る stare《at》. ▶人をじろじろ見るのは失礼です It is rude to stare at people.
しろたえ 白妙 (白い布) white cloth; (白色) white.
しろタク 白タク an unlicensed taxi.
じろっと ●じろっと見る stare hard [sharply]《at》(怒りなどで) glare《at》; (視線をすばやく投げかける) shoot a glance [a sharp look]《at》. ▶彼は向きを変えながら私をじろっと見た He shot a glance at me as he turned. ▶彼は知らない人をじろっと見ることがよくある He often stares hard at strangers.
シロップ syrup, (米) sirup. ● メープルシロップ maple syrup.
しろっぽい 白っぽい whitish; whity.
しろつめくさ 白詰め草 〖植物〗(a) white clover.
しろながすくじら 白長須鯨 〖動物〗a blue whale; a sulphur-bottom whale.
しろなまず 白癜 〖医学〗leucoderma; vitiligo.

しろぬき 白抜き white on black.
しろネズミ 白鼠 〖動物〗a white mouse; (忠実な雇い人) a faithful employee [servant].
しろバイ 白バイ a police motorcycle (painted white). ● 白バイ警官 a motorcycle police officer; 《話》a speed cop. (⇨警官)
『**しろばんば**』 Shirobamba: A Childhood in Old Japan. (⇨伊) 井上靖の小説)
しろぼし 白星 (勝利) a win; a victory.
シロホン 〖木琴〗a xylophone /záiləfòun/.
しろみ 白身 ●卵の白身 (of an egg), (an) egg white [「黄身」は yolk]; (魚の) white flesh. ● 白身の魚 a fish with white flesh; (英) a whitefish. (⇨身 ④) ▶卵の白身と黄身を分けなさい Separate the egg white from the yolk. (!複数個の卵の場合は whites, yolks となる)
しろみそ 白味噌 light brown miso.
しろむく 白無垢 a white kimono [dress]. ● 白無垢姿で be dressed in white.
しろめ 白目 the white of the [one's] eye. (!通例複数形で)
しろもの 代物 stuff. (!この語は,はっきりする必要のない「物」などに用いる) ▶彼にとんでもない代物をつかまされた He passed off this (terrible) stuff on me.
じろりと (⇨じろっと)
しろん 史論 a historical review; an essay on history.
しろん 試論 an essay《on》《of》.
じろん 持論 (お得意の理論) one's (pet) theory. ● 持論を曲げない stick to [hold fast to, persist in] one's opinion. (!いずれも one's opinion を主語に受身可. persist in は堅い表現) ▶…というのが彼の持論だ His theory is that …. /He has a theory that ….
***しわ** 皺 〖皮膚・衣服などの〗a wrinkle; 〖皮膚の〗a line; (深い)〖やや書〗a furrow〖特に額の〗; 〖布・紙などより〗a crease. (⇨しわくちゃ,小皺) ● しわだらけのコート[顔] a wrinkled coat [face].
①【しわが[は]】 ▶彼女は顔にしわが多い(=しわだらけだ) Her face is all wrinkled./Her face is full of wrinkles./Her face is covered with lines. ▶彼女は怒るとみけんにしわが寄る She gets wrinkles in her brows when she gets angry.

> 翻訳のこころ その王の顔は蒼白で,みけんのしわは,刻みこまれたように深かった (太宰治『走れメロス』) The king looked very pale [The king's face was very pale]. The lines [wrinkles] on his forehead [furrows on his brow] were so deep that they looked as if they had been etched there. (!(1) a line, a wrinkle は「(額の)しわ」の一般的な語. furrow は書き言葉として用いられることが多い. (2) there は on the forehead [brow] をさす)

②【しわを】 ●包装紙のしわをのばす smooth (down [out]) the creases in the wrapping paper. ●ブレスしてズボンのしわをのばす press [iron] out the wrinkles in the pants; press [iron] the wrinkles out of the pants. ▶彼女は額にしわを寄せて考え込んでいた She wrinkled (up) her brow [forehead] in thought.
③【しわに】 ●しわになる wrinkle; crease. ▶麻はしわになりやすい Linen wrinkles [gets wrinkled] easily. ▶上着はかけておかないとしわになるよ Your jacket will crease [You will get creases in your jacket] unless you hang it up.
しわがれる 嗄れる (声が) become* hoarse [husky]《from shouting, a cold》. (!前方は耳ざわりな声, 後の方はのどがかれたような声) ● しわがれた声で話す

しわくちゃ speak in a *hoarse* [a *husky*] voice; speak *hoarsely* [*huskily*]. ▶大声を出して声がしわがれる shout oneself *hoarse*; shout until one *is hoarse*.

しわくちゃ 〚皮膚・衣服などが〛wrinkled; 〚皮膚が〛lined; 〚紙・布などが〛creased. ●しわくちゃにする wrinkle; crease; make 《it》wrinkled [creased]. ●しわくちゃになる wrinkle; crease; become wrinkled [creased]. ●しわくちゃの紙 a *creased* sheet of paper. ●年をとってしわくちゃの老女 an old woman *wrinkled* [*lined*] with age. ▶彼女のスカートはしわくちゃだ Her skirt is all *creased* [*wrinkled*]. / Her skirt is full of *creases*.

しわけ 仕分け 图《分類》classification.
— **仕分けする** classify;《えり分ける》sort ...《out》.
●書類を仕分けする *classify* papers; *sort* 《out》papers.

しわけ 仕訳 图〖簿記〗journalizing. — **仕訳する** 動 journalize.
●仕訳帳 a journal.

しわざ 仕業 the work. ▶砂浜にできたこの見事な模様は風の仕業です This fantastic pattern on the sands is the *work* of the wind. ▶これはいったいだれの仕業だ Who on earth 《the hell》did this? (! on earth, the hell は疑問詞を強める)

じわじわ 《ゆっくりと》slowly;《徐々に》gradually;《着実に》steadily. (! 最後の2例のように動詞で表した方が適切な場合がある) ▶その痛みは普通じわじわくる The pain usually comes *slowly*. ▶その製品の売上げはじわじわ低下してきた The sales of the product have *steadily* declined. ▶血が包帯からじわじわ出した Blood *oozed* through the bandage. ▶雨水がじじわじわ地面に吸い込まれていった The rainwater *seeped into* the ground.

しわす 師走 December.

じわっと (⇔じわじわ)

しわよせ 鎮寄せ《悪い影響》a bad influence. ●労使紛争のしわ寄せを受ける be subject to the *bad influence* of labor disputes.

じわり 地割り 图 allotment of land.
— **地割りする** 動 allot land; mark《a car park》out.

じわれ 地割れ a crack [《やや書》a fissure] in the ground. ▶きのうの地震で滑走路に何か所か地割れができた Yesterday's earthquake caused some *cracks* in the runway.

*しん 心 〚心〛a heart;〚意識〛(a) sense;〚精神〛(a) spirit;〚意志〛(a) will. ▶彼の愛国心 his patriotic *spirit*; his patriotism. ▶あの男はがさつだが心は(=本当は)なかなかいいやつだ He is vulgar, but he is *really* a nice fellow [心に he is good *at heart*]. ▶辞書の校正は心が(=頭が)疲れる Proofreading a dictionary is *mentally* exhausting. ▶彼女は心が強い(=奥の方に強い性格[意志]がある) She *has a strong character* [*will*] *underneath*. (⇔芯①)

*しん 芯 〚鉛筆の〛lead /léd/ (! 種類をいうときは C);〚ろうそく・ランプなどの〛a wick;〚果物などの〛a core, a heart. ●柔らかい[硬い]芯の鉛筆 a soft [a hard] *lead* pencil; a pencil with a soft [a hard] *lead*.
●リンゴの芯 an apple *core*; the *core* of an apple. (! 「リンゴの芯を取る」は *core* an apple) ●芯のある(=生炊きの)ご飯 half-cooked rice. ●速球を(バットの)芯でとらえる connect solidly with a fastball; meet a fastball on the nose. ▶このナシは芯まで[まで]腐っている This pear is rotten *at* [*to*] *the core*. ▶寒くて体の芯まで冷え込んだ It was so cold that I was chilled *to the bone* [*marrow*].

しん 臣《家来》a retainer; a vassal;《臣下》a subject.

しん 信《信用》trust.
●信を置く believe; trust.
●信を問う《国民の信を問う》make an appeal for the confidence of the whole nation.

しん 神 ●神に入る be divinely skilled.

しん 真 truth; reality. ●真善美 *truth*, good and beauty.
— **真の** 形《偽りのない》true;《本当の》real;《実際の》actual;《正真正銘の》genuine. ●真の友 a *true* [*real*] friend. ●真の友情 *true* friendship. ●真の意味 a *true* meaning. ●真のダイヤ a *genuine* diamond. ▶まさかの友は真の友 (⇔まさか [成句])
— **真に** 副 truly; really. (⇔本当に①)
●真に迫る 真に迫った(=生き生きとした)戦争描写 the *vivid* description of the battle. ▶彼の話は真に迫っている His story is (very) *true to life*.

しん 秦 the Qin dynasty.

しん 清 the Qing dynasty.

しん- 新- new; neo-/ní:ə-/ (↔old). 《新しい》●新印象派の画家 a *Neo*- [a *neo*-] Impressionist. ●新人類と旧人類 the *new* youth and the old-fashioned adults. ●新雪 *newly* fallen snow.

しん- 親- pro- (↔anti-). ●親米政権 a *pro*-American government. ▶彼は大変な親英家です He is very *pro*-British./《英国崇拝者だ》He is an Anglophile (↔an Anglophobe).

じん 仁《儒教の》perfect virtue.

じん 陣 ●〚陣営〛《陣地》a position. ●山頂近くに陣を張る *camp* [*set up a camp*] near the mountaintop. ●強襲によって敵陣を奪取する carry an enemy *position* by assault.
❷〚主義・信条などを同じくする集団〛a group. (! 単・複両扱い) (⇔-団) ●がん研究陣 a research *group* ●〚スタッフ〛*staff*》of cancer. ●報道陣 a *group* of newspaper reporters; the press. ●教授陣 the faculty. (⇔教授)

ジン gin. ●ジントニック a gin and tonic. ●ジンフィズ (a) gin fizz.

-じん -人 ●都会[地方]人 city [country] *people*. ●西洋人 a Westerner. ●芸能人 an entertainer.

しんあい 親愛〚愛〛《優しく温かい愛》(an) affection. ●彼女に親愛の情を持つ[示す] have [show] (a) deep *affection for* her. ●親愛なるジョージ *Dear* George, (! (1) 親しい友人間などで手紙の初めに用いる。(2) 名前の後にコンマを添える)

じんあい 仁愛 benevolence; humanity.

じんあい 塵埃 dust.

しんあん 新案 a new idea《design, device》.
●新案特許 a patent on a new design [device].
●新案特許を申請[取得]する apply for [take out, obtain] a *patent on a new design* [*device*].

しんい 神意 devine [God's] will.

しんい 真意《本心》one's real [true] intention. (⇔本心);《本当の意味》the true meaning. ▶私の真意が彼らに伝わっていないようだ They don't seem to understand *what I want to say* [*what I mean*].

しんいき 神域 the precincts of a shrine.

じんいてき 人為的 — **人為的な** 形《人が造った》artificial; man-made (⇔人工);《人が引き起こした》man-made. ●人為的災害 a *man-made* disaster; a disaster *caused by human error*.

しんいり 新入り a newcomer,《話》a rookie. ●新入りの選手 a rookie. ●新入りの警官 a *rookie* cop.

しんいん 心因 — **心因性の** 形 psychogenic.
●心因性疾患 a psychogenic disorder. ●心因性症状 a psychogenic symptom.

しんいん 真因 the true cause.

じんいん 人員 〖人数〗the number of people 〘書〙persons; 〖人数全体〗the staff, 〘書〙the personnel /pə̀ːrsənél/. (⇨職員) ● 人員整理(=削減) a *personnel* cut [reduction]; a cut [a reduction] in *personnel*; (婉曲的) (縮小化) downsizing; (適正サイズ化) rightsizing. (❗後の方がより婉曲的) (⇨リストラ) ● 人員を増やす[減らす] increase [reduce] *the staff* [*personnel*]. ● 人員を配置する arrange *the personnel*. ● 人員が過剰である[不足している] be overstaffed [understaffed, not well-staffed].

じんう 腎盂 〖医学〗the renal pelvis.
● 腎盂炎 〖医学〗pyelitis /pàiəláitis/.

しんうち 真打ち a first-class *rakugo* storyteller; a *rakugo* headliner. ▶ よっ, 真打ち登場! Here he comes, the best [star] performer!

しんえい 新鋭 ● 最新鋭の(=最新の技術を採用した)戦車 a *state-of-the-art* tank. ● ゴルフ界の新鋭 an *up-and-coming* golfer.

じんえい 陣営 a camp. ● 反対陣営 the opposing *camp*. ● 保守[革新]陣営を擁護する defend a conservative [a reformist] *camp*.

しんえいたい 親衛隊 one's bodyguard (❗集合的, 単・複両扱い. 隊員1人にも用いる); (熱狂的ファン) an ardent fan, 〘話〙a groupie.

しんえん 深淵 (奈落) 〖文〗an abyss /əbís/; (深い所) the depths. ● 人の心の深淵に触れる look into *the depths* of human heart.

しんえん 深遠 深遠な思想 a deep [〘やや書〙a profound] thought.

じんえん 腎炎 〖医学〗nephritis /nəfráitis/.

しんおう 心奥 ● 心奥から from the (bottom of one's) *heart*.

しんおう 深奥 the depths.

しんおう 震央 the epicenter. (⇨震源地)

しんおん 心音 (a) heartbeat.

しんおん 唇音 〖音声〗a labial (sound [consonant]).

しんか 臣下 a subject; a vassal; a retainer.

しんか 真価 true [real] worth; true [real] value. (⇨値打ち) ● 彼の本の真価は認められなかった The *true worth* [*value*] of his book went unrecognized. ▶ 彼は真価を発揮した He showed [displayed] his *real worth*.

しんか 深化 图 deepening. ● 不安の深化 a *deepening* sense of fear.
―**深化する** 動 deepen. ● 世界情勢の理解を深化する(=深める) *deepen* one's understanding of world affairs.

しんか 進化 图 evolution.
―**進化する** 動 ▶ ヒトはサルから進化した Human beings *evolved* from the apes.
● 進化論 the theory [doctrine] of evolution; (ダーウィン説) Darwinism.

じんか 人家 a (dwelling) house (徴 houses /-ziz, 《米》-siz/). ● その地域は人家が多い[少ない] The area is densely [sparsely] populated.

シンカー 〖野球〗a sinker; a sinkerball. ● シンカー投手 a sinkerballer.

シンガーソングライター a singer-songwriter.

しんかい 深海 the deep sea; (大洋の) the ocean depths.
● 深海魚 deep-sea fish.

しんがい 心外 ―心外な 形 (意外な) unexpected; (残念な) regrettable. ▶ そんなことを言われるとは心外だ I'm very *sorry* [I *didn't expect*] to hear such a remark. ▶ 彼の告訴は心外だ Nothing is more *regrettable* than his complaint. ▶ それは心外な(=不当な)批判だ That's an *unjust* [an *unfair*] criticism.

しんがい 侵害 图 (侵入) (an) invasion 《of》; (違反) (a) violation 《of》; (抵触) (an) infringement 《of》; (私事への立ち入り) (an) intrusion 《on, into》; (権利などへの徐々の侵入) 〘書〙(an) encroachment 《on》. ● プライバシーの侵害 an *invasion of* [an *infringement of*, an *intrusion on*] privacy.
―**侵害する** 動 ● 人権を侵害する violate [invade, 〘書〙infringe (on), 〘書〙encroach on] human rights.

じんかい 塵芥 (⇨ごみ)

じんかいせんじゅつ 人海戦術 ● 人海戦術で employing human-wave tactics; (人手だけに頼って) by human labor alone, by the labor of innumerable workers.

しんかいち 新開地 (開発した土地) (a) newly-opened land; new land.

しんがお 新顔 〖新しく来た人〗a newcomer; (新人) a new face (↔an old-timer); 〖見知らぬ人〗a stranger.

しんがく 神学 theology /θi(ː)ɑ́lədʒi/. ● 神学上の論争 a *theological* debate.
● 神学校 a theological seminary 《米》[college 《英》]. ● 神学者 a theologian. ● 神学生 a theological student.

しんがく 進学 图 ● 大学進学希望者 a *college-bound* student. ● 大学進学塾 a preparatory school for university entrance exams. (⇨予備校)
―**進学する** 動 go (on) to high school [(大学) university, college]. (❗on は「続けて」の意の副詞) ▶ 彼は大学に進学することを希望している He wishes to *go* (*on*) *to* college.

*じんかく 人格 (性格, 人柄) (a) personality; (徳性) character. (❗前の方は対人関係における個人の内面的な特徴のすべてをいうのに対し, 後の方は道徳的な面における個人の性質をいう) ● 二重人格者 a person with a double [a dual, (分裂した) a split] *personality*. ▶ 子供の人格を無視してはいけない We shouldn't disregard a child's *personality* [the *personality* of a child]. ▶ 彼の人格は環境によって形成されたものである His *character* was formed by his environment. ▶ 健太はなかなかの人格者だ Kenta is a man of very good *character* [×*personality*].
● 人格権 〖法律〗a personal right.

じんかくか 神格化 图 deification /dìːəfikéiʃən/.
―**神格化する** 動 deify /díːəfài/.

じんがさ 陣笠 ● 陣笠連 the rank and file; 《英》the backbenchers.

しんがた 新型 a new type; (車・機械などの) a new model. ● 新型のインフルエンザ a *new type* of influenza. ● 新型の車 a *new* [(最新の) the *latest*] *model* car.

しんがっき 新学期 a new (school) term. ● 新学期用に用意しておくお金 one's *back-to-school* budget.

しんかなづかい 新仮名遣い the new [modern] *kana* orthography.

しんかぶ 新株 〖経済〗new stocks, 《英》new shares.

シンガポール 〖国名〗Singapore /síŋ(g)əpɔ̀ːr/; (公式名) the Republic of Singapore. (首都 Singapore) ● シンガポールの Singapórean. ● シンガポール人 a Singapórean.

しんから 心から from the (bottom of one's) heart; sincerely.

しんがら 新柄 a new pattern [design].

しんがり [後部] the rear; (行列などの) the tail; [はずれ] the end. ● 行列のしんがりに at the *rear* [*tail*, *end*] of a parade. ● しんがりを務める《やや書》bring up the *rear*.

しんかん 心肝 ● 心肝を寒からしめる make one's blood freeze [curdle, run cold].

しんかん 信管 a fuse /fjúːz/. ● 爆弾から信管を外す remove the *fuse* from a bomb; defuse a bomb.

しんかん 神官 a Shinto priest.

しんかん 新刊 ● この本は新刊です This book *was just* [*has just been*] *published*. ● 新刊予定 Near Publication. (❗目録などに書く)
● 新刊書 a newly published book; a new book [publication]. ● 新刊書評 book reviews.

しんかん 新患 a new patient.

しんかん 新館 a new building; (別館) an ánnex.

しんかん 震撼 ── 震撼させる 動 (揺さぶる) shake; (衝撃を与える) shock. ● 世界を震撼させるような声明 a world-*shaking* announcement.

しんがん 心眼 one's mind's eye.

しんがん 真贋 ● 真贋の区別がつきにくい絵もある Some paintings are difficult to tell whether they are *authentic* [*genuine*] or not [*false*].

しんかんせん 新幹線 the *Shinkansen*; (…新幹線) the New ... Line; (弾丸列車) a bullet train. ● 東海道新幹線 the *New Tokaido Line*. (❗the Tokaido *Shinkansen* Line と書くこともある) ● 新幹線で宇都宮に行く go to Utsunomiya by [on the] *Shinkansen*; take the *Shinkansen* to Utsunomiya.

しんき 心悸 ● 心悸亢進[亢進] [医学] palpitation; tachycardia.

しんき 新奇 图 novelty. ── 新奇な 形 novel; (独創的な) original.

しんき 新規 ● その商社と新規に(=新しい)取り引きを始める start a *new* business with the firm.
● 新規まき直し ● 新規まき直しをする(=再出発する) make a *fresh* start; 《書》start afresh; (もう一度初めからする) start all over again.

しんぎ 心技 ● 心技ともに万全である be in perfect condition both *mentally* and *technically*.

しんぎ 信義 [誓いを守ること] faith; [忠誠] loyalty. ● 信義を重んずる男 a man of *good faith* [(名誉) *honor*]; a *faithful* [a *loyal*] man. ● 彼はだれに対しても信義を守る[破る] He *keeps* [*breaks*] *faith* with everyone./He *is faithful* [*unfaithful*, *disloyal*] to everyone.

しんぎ 真偽 truth (or falsehood). ● 彼の陳述の真偽を確かめる confirm [《書》ascertain] the *truth* of his statement. ● 真偽はともかく、それは子供にとってためになる話だ *True* or not, that is a story instructive [good] for [×to] children.

しんぎ 審議 图 [話し合い] (a) discussion; [熟考] consideration, (議会などによる正式な) [《書》deliberation (❗しばしば複数形で). ● 審議中である (議会などが) be discussing [deliberating (on)] (a question); (議案などが) be under *discussion* [*deliberation*]; be being discussed [deliberated]. (❗×be discussed [deliberated] とはいわない). ● 審議を打ち切る close the *discussion*. ● 審議を重ねたあと after much *discussion* [*deliberation*]. ● 法案を審議未了で(=棚上げして) shelve a bill; 《米》table a bill [《英》では「審議に付す」の意]. ● その問題は委員会の審議に付された(=委員会に提出された) The matter was submitted to the committee.
── 審議する 動 discuss; consider; 《書》deliberate.
● 審議会 a council.

じんぎ 仁義 humanity and justice; (やくざの) *yakuza*'s moral code. ● 仁義に外れる be against the *moral code*.
● 仁義を切る exchage formal greetings.

じんぎ 神器 a sacred treasure. ● 三種の神器 (⇨三種の神器)

しんきいってん 心機一転 ── 心機一転する 動 change one's mind; (改心する) turn over a new leaf.

しんきくさい 辛気臭い ● 辛気臭い人 a privatistic and asocial person.

しんきじく 新機軸 (革新) (an) innovation; (発展) a departure. ● 学習辞典編集に新機軸を打ち出す introduce *innovations* [make a *new departure*] in editing learner's dictionaries.

しんきしょう 心気症 hypochondria.

ジンギスカン [モンゴル帝国の創設者] Genghis Khan /dʒéŋgis káːn/.
● ジンギスカン料理 Mongolian mutton barbecue. (事情 この料理は米英にはない)

しんぎたい 心技体 spirit, technique and physical strength.

しんきゅう 進級 ── 進級する 動 move up to [be promoted to] the next grade 《米》[form 《英》]. ▶彼は3年生に進級した (小学校で) He *moved up to* the third grade [*form*]./(高等学校で) He *became* a senior.

しんきゅう 新旧 ── 新旧の 形 old and new. ● ×new and old (としない) ● 今や新旧交代の時期だ It's time to replace *the old* with *the new*. ▶新旧社長の記者会見が開かれた The *incoming* and *outgoing* presidents gave [held] a press interview.

しんきゅう 鍼灸 ácupùncture and moxibustion.
● 鍼灸師 a practitioner of acupuncture and moxibustion.

しんきょ 新居 one's new house [《米》home]. ● 新居を構える make a *new home*.

*****しんきょう** 心境 (精神状態) a state of mind; (気分) a mood. ● これが私の現在の心境(話) This is how I feel. ● その本を読んで心境の変化をきたした The book brought about a change *in my mind*./After I read the book, I began to *think differently*.

しんきょう 信教 religious belief. ● 信教の自由を圧迫する suppress freedom of *religion* [*religious freedom*].

しんきょう 進境 ● 進境著しい make remarkable progress (*in*). (⇨進歩)

しんきょう 新教 Protestantism.
● 新教徒 a Protestant.

しんきょく 新曲 (メロディー) a new tune; (歌) a new song; (新発売曲) a new release.

しんきろう 蜃気楼 《やや書》a mirage /mərá:ʒ/. ● 暑いときにはよく蜃気楼が立つ *Mirages* often appear [(見える) We often see *mirages*] in hot weather.

しんきろく 新記録 a new record; [最高記録] an all-time high (record). ● 100メートル競走で世界新記録を作る make [(樹立する) set, establish] a *new* world *record* in the 100-meter dash.

しんきん 真菌 fungus; eumycete.
● 真菌症 [医学] mycosis.

しんぎん 呻吟 ── 呻吟する 動 moan; groan. (⇨うめく)

しんきんかん 親近感 a sense of closeness [《やや

書) affinity]. ●新しい先生に親近感を覚える *feel close [attached] to* one's new teacher; *have an affinity for [toward]* one's new teacher.

しんきんこうそく 心筋梗塞 【医学】 myocardial /màiəkɑ́ːrdiəl/ infarction.

しんく 辛苦 [苦難] (a) hardship. (⇨辛酸) ●辛苦をなめる suffer *hardships*.

しんく 深紅 ─深紅の 形 crimson; (緋色の) scarlet.

シンク [台所の流し] a sink.

しんぐ 寝具 bedding (!寝具全体をさす); bedclothes (!シーツや毛布など).

じんく 甚句 *jinku*; (説明的に) a kind of Japanese folk song.

しんくう 真空 a vacuum /vǽkjuəm/ (働 ~s, vacua).
●真空包装の魚 a *vacuum*-packed fish. ●フラスコを真空にする *evacuate* a flask. ●音は真空中には伝わらない Sound doesn't travel in a *vacuum*.
●真空管 a vacuum tube. ●真空放電 vacuum discharge.

じんぐう 神宮 a (Shinto) shrine. ●明治神宮 the Meiji *Shrine*.

しんくうちたい『真空地帯』 *Zone of Emptiness*. (参考) 野間宏の小説)

ジンクス [一般の人に信じられている考え) a popular belief; (悪い縁起) [やぎ話] a jinx (on). (!日本語のジンクスと異なり jinx は悪い意味でのみ用いる)・ジンクスを破る break [smash] the *jinx*. ●ジンクスをかつぐ believe in the *popular belief*. ▶読売ジャイアンツは10点以上得点された次の試合に負けるというジンクスがあった There was a *popular belief* [It *is* popularly *believed*] that the Yomiuri Giants will lose the next game when they get more than ten scores in a game.

シンクタンク [政策研究機関] a think tank. (!単・複両扱い。その一員は a think tanker)

シングル [シングルヒット] [野球] a single, a one-base hit, a base hit; [和製語] a single hit; [ホテルの] a single (room); [服の] a single-breasted coat [jacket]. ●シングルキャッチで捕る make a one-hand(ed) catch (of a liner). (! ×a single catch は和製英語) ●シングルヒットを打つ single (to center); make a *one-base hit*; get a *base hit*. ●シングルヒットで 1 点取る *single* in a run; score a run on a *single*. ●シングルカットする cut [release] (a song) as a *single*. ●シングル幅の布地 8 ヤード eight yards of *single width* cloth.
●シングル盤 a single. ●シングルプレーヤー [ゴルフ] a low handicapper. (!具体的に数字を示して a 5-handicapper (ハンデ 5 の人) のように用いることが多い) ●シングルベッド a single bed. ●シングルマザー a single [an unmarried] mother. ●シングルライフ (lead) a single life.

シングルエー (マイナーリーグの) Single A; Class A.

シングルス (play) singles (↔doubles). (!単数扱い)
●テニスの男子シングルスで彼を破る beat him in the men's tennis *singles*.

シンクロナイズ synchronize. ●唇の動きに声をシンクロナイズさせる synchronize the sound of a person's voice with the movement of their lips.

シンクロナイズドスイミング synchronized swimming. ●シンクロナイズドスイミングの選手 a synchronized swimmer.

しんぐん 進軍 图 a march.
── 進軍する 動 ─とりでに向かって進軍する march on a fortress.

‡**しんけい** 神経 【解剖】 a nerve; [神経過敏] (話) nerves.

①【~神経】 ●自律神経 autonomic *nerves*. ●視[歯]神経 the optic [dental] *nerve*. ●無神経に insensible; indelicate. ●運動神経がない not athletic enough (to be ...). ▶彼は運動神経が抜群だ He has excellent motor *nerves* [*coordination*, (反射神経) *reflexes*]./(すぐれた運動選手だ) He's an excellent athlete.

②【神経~】 ●神経性の nervous; due to nervousness. ▶彼は神経過敏だ He's *very sensitive*./ He's *hypersensitive*. ●彼女は神経衰弱にかかっていた She had [suffered from] a *nervous* breakdown.

③【神経が】 ●神経が疲れる run on *nervous* energy. ●神経がおかしくなる suffer from *nervous disorder*. ●彼は神経が細かい He is *sensitive* (↔*insensitive*)./(話) He has a thin skin. ●彼は神経が太い He has a lot of *nerve*./(動じない) He has no *nerves*./(話) He has a thick skin. ▶そのニュースを聞いて彼は神経が高ぶった(= 強い神経の緊張を与えた) The news *gave him strong nervous tension*. ●彼はそのニュースを聞いてカッとなった He *got excited* [(話) *edgy*] over the news. ▶神経がまいった My nerves are wrecked./(話) I'm a *nervous* wreck.

④【神経に】 ▶その耳ざわりな音が神経にさわった The harsh noise *got on my nerves*./(私をいらだたせた) The harsh noise irritated me.

⑤【神経を】 ●神経を病む suffer from *neurosis*. ●神経を麻痺させる paralyze the *nerve*. ●背中の神経を痛める damage a *nerve* in one's back. ●神経を静める soothe [(主に米) quiet, (落ち着かせる) steady] one's *nerves*. ●神経を使いすぎる overstrain one's *nerves*. ●神経を逆なでする rub (him) (up) the wrong way. ▶彼は暗がりでものを見ようと神経を集中させた He strained every *nerve* to see in the darkness. ▶彼はくだらぬことに神経を悩ましている He is *nervous* [(心配している) *is worried*] about trifles. ▶彼は神経をとがらせている His nerves are all on edge.

── 神経の 形 nervous. ●神経の病気 a *nervous* disease [disorder].
●神経科 the department of neurology. ●神経科医 a neurologist. ●神経学 neurology. ●神経ガス nerve gas. ●神経細胞 【解剖】 a nerve cell. ●神経症 (ノイローゼ) 【医学】 (a) neurosis /n(j)uəróusis/. (cf. 心身症) ●神経症患者 a neurotic. ●神経性胃炎 【医学】 nervous gastritis /gæstráitis/. ●神経戦 (心理戦) psychological warfare. ●神経組織 【解剖】 the nervous system. ●神経中枢 the nerve center. ●神経痛 【医学】 (have) neuralgia /n(j)uərǽldʒə/. ●神経ブロック a nerve block.

じんけい 陣形 (a) (battle) formation. ●陣形を整えて行進する march in *formation*.

しんけいしつ 神経質 图 nervousness.
── 神経質な 形 nervous. ●神経質な人 a *nervous* person; a person with a *nervous* temperament. ▶彼は神経質なたちだ He has [is of] a *nervous* temperament./He is *nervous* by temperament.

── 神経質に 形 nervously. ▶たいていの選手は大きなレースの直前にはひどく神経質になります Most runners will be very *nervous* [(話) all *nerves*] just before a big race. ▶彼の手は神経質そうに震えていた His hand was shaking *nervously*.

しんげき 進撃 图 [前進] an advance; [攻撃] an attack (on). ●敵の進撃 the enemy's *advance* (on the city).
── 進撃する 動 ●敵に向かって進撃する make an

attack on the enemy; *attack* the enemy.

しんげき 新劇 the new [modern] drama.
● 新劇運動 the new-drama movement.

しんけつ 心血 (⇨口)
● 心血を注ぐ ▶ 彼はそれに心血を注いだ He put his *heart and soul* into it.

しんげつ 新月 a new moon.

*****しんけん** 真剣 ［名］ seriousness; ［まじめ］ earnestness; ［誠実］ sincerity. ● 彼の表情の真剣さ the *seriousness* of his expression. ● 真剣味に乏しい lack *sincerity*.
—**真剣な** ［形］ serious; ［まじめ］ earnest. ● 真剣な顔をしている look *serious*. ● 冗談ではありません. 私は真剣です I'm not joking ［(話) kidding］. I am *serious*.
—**真剣に** ［副］ seriously; (本気に) earnestly, in earnest. ● 真剣に試みる make an *earnest* attempt. ● 真剣に(=一生懸命)勉強する study *hard* ［(書) *diligently*］. ▶ そのことについて真剣に考えてもらいたいのです I want you to think *seriously* [*hard*] about it. / I want you to give it some *serious* thought. ▶ 彼は真剣に話し始めた He began to speak *in earnest*.

しんけん 神権 (神の権威) the authority of God; the devine authority.
● 神権政治 theocracy.

しんけん 新券 《米》a new bill, 《英》a new (bank) note.

しんけん 親権 parental rights; (離婚後などに生じる養育権) (child) custody. ● 親権を行使する exercise *parental rights*. ● 親権をめぐってもめる fight a *custody* battle; fight a battle for [to get] *custody* of the child.
● 親権者 a person with parental rights.

しんげん 進言 ［名］［助言］ (a piece of) advice; ［提案］ a suggestion, a proposal. ● 前の方が控えめな提案を示す
—**進言する** ［動］ ▶ 彼にその問題について一言進言する give him a piece of (good) *advice on* the matter. ● 改革案を委員会に進言する *suggest* a reform plan *to* the committee. ▶ 私たちは市長に新計画を直ちに実行するように進言した We *advised* [*suggested*, *proposed*] *that* the mayor (《主に英》 should) carry out the new plan immediately. (⇨提案)

しんげん 震源 a hypocenter. ● 震源の深さ the focal depth.

しんげん 箴言 a maxim; a proverb; an aphorism. (旧約聖書中の1書) Proverbs.

じんけん 人権 human rights. ● 基本的人権 fundamental *human rights*. ● 世界人権宣言 the Universal Declaration of *Human Rights*. ● 人権を尊重［侵害; 擁護］する respect [violate; uphold] *human rights*. ▶ 彼のしたことは人権蹂躙(じゅうりん)だ What he did is an outrage against *human rights*. ▶ 人権と平和の関係はとっても大事. 平和の基礎は人権を大切にすることです *Human rights* have a critical relevance to [a vital bearing on] peace, which is based on [stems from] valuing *human rights*. ▶ 人権とは, すべての人の尊厳, 平等, 安全を確保すること *Human rights* is about securing dignity, equality and safety for everyone.
● 人権侵害 a violation [an infringement] of *human rights*; *human rights* violations.
● 人権擁護局 the Civil Liberties Bureau.

しんけんざい 新建材 new building materials.

しんげんち 震源地 the hypocenter /háipəsèntər/, the seismic center ［focus］; (震央) the épicènter (❗震源の真上にあたる地点または海面上の地点).

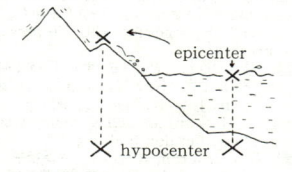

epicenter

hypocenter

じんけんひ 人件費 personnel expenses [expenditures]; personnel [staff] cost(s). ● 人件費が高い high *personnel expenses* [*expenditures*]. ● 人件費を削減する cut (down on) [bring down] *personnel expenses*. ▶ こう人件費が高騰しては会社をやっていくのも大変だ It's difficult to get the company going with *personnel expenses* running [going up] as high as this.

しんげんぶくろ 信玄袋 shingenbukuro; a square bottom draw-string pouch.

しんこ しん粉 rice flour.
● しん粉餅 rice-flour dough.

しんこ 新香 (⇨口 ❚ 漬物)

しんご 新語 a new word; (新造語) a newly invented [newly-coined] word; 《やや書》a coinage.

じんご 人後 ● 人後に落ちない be as+形容詞(句)+as the next man [woman, fellow]. ▶ 人を思いやる点では人後に落ちないつもりでいる I think I'm *as thoughtful of others as the next fellow*. ▶ うちの母は料理では人後に落ちない My mother is *the most wonderful cook I know*.

じんご 人語 ● 人語を解する馬 a horse which can communicate with us.

*****しんこう** 信仰 ［名］ (a) faith; (a) (religious) belief (複～s). ● 信仰の自由 freedom of *faith* ［(宗教) *religion*］. ● 信仰心の厚い人 a *religious* [a *pious*] (↔an irreligious) person. ▶ 彼は信仰心が少しもない He has no *faith* [no *belief in religion*]. / (書) He is completely *irreligious*. ▶ 信仰によって彼女は幾多の辛苦にも耐えることができた (=信仰が耐える力を与えた) Her *faith* gave her the strength to endure many hardships.
—**信仰する** ［動］ ▶ 彼はキリスト教を信仰している He *believes in* [*has faith in*] Christianity. (❗前の方が普通. ×He believes in Christianity. は不可) / He is a Christian.

*****しんこう** 進行 ［名］ prógress. ● 議事の進行 the *progress* of proceedings. ● がんの進行を阻止する arrest the *growth* [*progress*] of cancer.
—**進行する** ［動］ ❶［乗り物が］move; run*. ▶ 列車はゆっくり進行している The train *is moving* [*going*, *traveling*, *running*] slowly (on).
❷［事が］make* prógress, progréss; ［さらに高いレベルへ］《やや書》advánce; ［続行される］ go* on, 《やや書》proceed; ［はかどる］get* along [on] (⇨はかどる). ▶ 工事はゆっくり［早く］進行している The construction work *is making* (˟a) slow ［(˟a) rapid］ *progress*. / The construction work *is progressing* slowly [rapidly]. / They *are making* slow [rapid] *progress with* the construction work. ▶ 損害賠償の訴訟は予定どおり進行している The damage suit *is proceeding* [*going on*] as arranged. (❗「進行中の訴訟」は an on-

しんこう

going suit) ▶その仕事は現在進行しています(=進行中です) The work is now *in progress* [*under way*]. ▶彼のがんは進行している He is at an *advanced* stage of cancer. (! *advanced*は形容詞) ▶彼が議事を進行させた(=司会した) He *led* [*was in charge of*] the meeting./《書》He *presided at* the meeting.
会話「仕事の進行具合はどうですか」「うまく進行して(=はかどって)います」"How *is* your work *getting along* [*going*]?" "It's *getting along* [*going*] nicely."/"How are you *getting along with* your work?"《話》I'm doing all right.
• 進行係 a program director. • 進行形〖文法〗the progressive form. • 進行性ジストロフィー〖医学〗progressive muscular dystrophy.

しんこう 侵攻 图 an invasion. ▶ドイツ軍のフランスへの侵攻 the German *invasion* of France; the *invasion* of France by the German army.
— **侵攻する** 動 ▶フランスへ侵攻する *invade* France.

しんこう 振興 图 promotion;〖奨励〗encouragement. ▶学問の振興 the *promotion* [*encouragement*] of learning.
— **振興する** 動 ▶産業を振興する *promote* the development of industries; *encourage* industries.

しんこう 進攻 图 an advance; an attack.
— **進攻する** 動 advance; attack.

しんこう 新興 图 — 新興の 形〖新しい〗new;〖成長中の〗rising;〖急成長の〗boom, mushroom(ing);〖開発途上の〗developing.
• 新興国 a *rising* [a developing] nation. • 新興宗教 a new religion. • 新興住宅地 a newly-developed residential area. • 新興都市 a *boom* [a *mushroom*] town.

しんこう 親交 图 (a) [a close] friendship, friendly relations. (⇨付き合い) ▶我々の親交は年とともに深まった Our *friendship* grew [deepened] through the years. ▶彼とは親交がある He is a good friend of mine./I am good friends with him. (! (1) 複数形に注意. (2) I'm on friendly terms with him. は必ずしも friend であることを含意しない)

*****しんごう 信号** ❶〖交通信号灯〗a (traffic) light [signal]. (! (1) 《米》では単数形、《英》では複数形で用いる傾向がある. (2) 通例 a red light (赤信号), a yellow〖《英・カナダ》an amber〗light (黄信号), a green light (青信号) の 3 種.《米》では歩行者用は Don't Walk (止まれ) と Walk (進め) の 2 種);〖信号機〗a signal. • 信号のある横断歩道 a light controlled crossing. • 信号を守る obey *traffic lights* [*signals*]. • 青信号で道を渡る cross the street *on* the *green light* [when the *light* is *green*, when the *lights* are green, when the *green light* is on]. (! green の代わりに日本語的に blue は用いない) • 赤信号で止まる stop at [for] a red *light*. • 信号を無視する ignore [go through] a (red) *light*;〖無視して横断する〗cross against a (red) *light*, jaywalk;〖(車が)〗run a red *light*. ▶信号が変わるのを待った We waited for the *light*(s) to change./(青信号を待った) We waited for the green light. ▶次の信号を左に曲がってください Turn (to the) left at the next *light*(s). ▶赤信号みんなで渡れば恐くない《ことわざ》There is safety in numbers.
❷〖合図〗a signal. • 遭難信号 a distress *signal*; (船などの) an SOS; (船舶・航空機の) Mayday. • 遭難信号を送る send an SOS [a Mayday]. • 明かりを点滅させて危険信号を送る send a danger *signal* by blinking a light.
• 信号灯 a signal light [lamp].

じんこう

*****じんこう 人口** (a) population (! 具体的に 1 地域の人口では a ~);〖住民〗inhabitants.
①**〖~人口、人口~〗** • 昼間[夜間]人口 the day [night] *population*. • 全人口 the total *population*. • サッカーの競技人口 a soccer *population*. • 従業者数の人口比 the employment to population ratio.
②**〖人口が[は]〗** • 人口が 300 万の大都市 a large city of three million *inhabitants* [*people*]. (! この場合は population を使うのはまれ); a large city with a [×the] *population* of three million. ▶その町は人口が多い[少ない] The city has a large [a small] *population*. (! ×many [×a few] *population* とはいわない) ▶日本の人口はどれくらいですか What [How large, ×How many] is the *population* of Japan? (! 「日本の人口」は他に the Japanese population, Japan's population も可) / How many people are there in Japan? ▶この町の人口は 5 万人です This city has a *population* of 50,000. / The *population* of this city is 50,000. / This city's *population* is 50,000. / This city has 50,000 inhabitants. ▶農業人口は毎年減っている The farm(ing) *population* is decreasing (↔increasing, growing) each year. ▶人口が着実に増えている The *population* has been increasing steadily.
③**〖人口の〗** • 人口の増加[減少] an increase [a decrease] in *population*. ▶世界の人口の半分以上が北半球に住んでいる More than half of the world's *population* live(s) in the Northern hemisphere. (! このように「一定地域の全住民」の意では単・複両扱い)
• 人口に膾炙(かいしゃ)する ▶そのことわざは人口に膾炙している The phrase is very well known.
• 人口過剰 overpopulation. • 人口過疎地域 an underpopulated area. • 人口過密地域 an overpopulated area. • 人口規模 a population scale. • 人口構造 a population structure. • 人口集中 condensation of population. • 人口調査 (国勢調査)《take》a census (of the population). • 人口爆発 a population explosion. • 人口密度 population density. • 人口密度の高い都市 a densely [a thickly] *populated* city (↔a thinly [a sparsely] *populated* city); (人口の多い都市)《書》a *populous* city. • 人口問題 a population problem.

*****じんこう 人工** 图 art.
— **人工の** 形 (人為的な) artificial; (人の造った) man-made. • 自然と人工の調和 the harmony between [×of] nature and *art*. • 彼に人工呼吸を施す practice *artificial* [〖口移し式の〗mouth-to-mouth] respiration on him. ▶彼らは人工衛星を軌道に乗せることに成功した They succeeded in putting an *artificial* [a *man-made*] satellite in orbit. ▶彼は人工呼吸装置につながれていた He was on a respirator.
— **人工(的)に** 副 artificially. ▶ほとんどの工業用ダイヤモンドは人工的に作られている Most industrial diamonds are *artificially* made. ▶その湖は自然のものではなく人工的に造られたものである The lake is made not by nature but by *art*./The lake is not natural but *man-made* [*artificial*].
• 人工栄養児 a bottle-fed baby. • 人工関節 an artificial joint. • 人工甘味料 an artificial sweetener. • 人工肛門 an artificial anus. • 人工芝 artificial turf [grass]. • 人工授精〖医学〗artificial insemination. • 人工授粉 artificial pollination. • 人工心臓 a mechanical

heart. ● 人工心肺 a heart-lung machine. ● 人工頭脳 a mechanical brain. ● 人工臓器 an artificial (internal) organ. ● 人工知能 artificial intelligence. ● 人工着色料 artificial food coloring. ● 人工着色料を含まない free of *artificial food coloring*. ● 人工中絶 (an) abortion. (⇨中絶) ● 人工透析 artificial dialysis.

じんこう 沈香 〖植物〗 an agalloch.

しんこきゅう 深呼吸 ── 深呼吸(を)する 動 take a deep breath; breathe in [out] deeply.

しんこきんわかしゅう 『新古今和歌集』 *Shinkokin Wakashu*. (参考) 鎌倉時代の勅撰和歌集

***しんこく** 申告 图 (税関の) (税務署の) a return; (履修の) a registration. ● 青色〖確定〗申告 a blue [the final] *return*. ● 所得税の申告をする make a *declaration* of one's income tax; make [file] one's income tax *return*.

── する 動 declare; (予約を) register. ● 1 年次に専攻科目を申告する *declare* a major in one's freshman year. ● 前[後]期の履修を申告する *register* for the first [second] semester. 会話「申告するものが何かありますか」「何もありません」(税関で) "Do you have anything to *declare*?" "(No, I have) nothing to *declare*."
● **申告書** (税関の) a declaration form; (税務署の) a return form; (履修の) a registration form.

***しんこく** 深刻 形 serious; (重大な) grave. ● 深刻な経済危機 a *grave* economic crisis. ● 深刻な顔をしている look *serious*; have a *serious* look on one's face. ● あまり深刻に考えるな 遊びなんだから Don't be so *serious*. [Don't take it so *seriously*./(やや話) Don't let it get to you.] It's only a game. ▶ 不況はますます深刻化している The depression *is deepening* [*is getting worse and worse*]. ▶ 米国人の肥満はかなり深刻な事態に(=危機的な程度にまで)立ち至っている The obesity problem among Americans has reached crisis proportions.

しんこく 親告 〖法律〗 (bring [file]) (a) (formal) complaint from a victim.
● **親告罪** 〖法律〗 an offense subject to prosecution only on complaint.

じんこつ 人骨 a human bone.

しんこっちょう 真骨頂 : 真価値(=本当の価値)を示す [発揮する] show one's *true worth* [(実力) *real ability*].

しんこん 心魂 one's heart [soul].
● **心魂を傾ける** ▶ 彼はその仕事に心魂を傾けた He devoted himself *heart and soul* to the work./He put his *heart and soul* into the work.

しんこん 新婚 (夫婦) a newly married [a newly-wed] couple; newlyweds (!通例複数形で). ● 新婚生活を送る lead a *newly married* life. ▶ 新婚旅行でハワイに行った We went to Hawaii *for our honeymoon*./We went on *our honeymoon* to Hawaii. ▶ 彼らは新婚はやほやだ They('ve) just got married./They('ve) got married quite recently.

***しんさ** 審査 图 〖検査〗 (an) examination; (an) inspection; 〖判定〗 (a) judgment; 〖選抜〗 (a) screening.

── **する** 動 (優劣を) judge; (検査する) examine; inspect; (志願者などを) screen. ▶ 応募者は慎重に審査選別される Applicants *are* carefully *examined* and *screened*.
● **審査委員会** a judging [a screening] committee. ● **審査員** (競技会などの) a judge; a juror (!「審査員団」は a panel of judges [a jury という).

(検査官) an examiner; an inspector. ▶ 彼は弁論大会で審査員を務めた He *judged* [*acted as judge at*] the speech contest./He was on the panel of judges at the speech contest.

しんさい 震災 an earthquake (disaster). (⇨地震)
● 1995 年の阪神・淡路大震災 the Great Hanshin-Awaji *Earthquake* of 1995. (!単に the Hanshin Earthquake とも the Kobe Earthquake ともいう) ● 震災にあう (人が) suffer (from) an *earthquake* (!from がつくと「地震で被害をこうむる」の意); (場所が) be hit [struck] by an *earthquake*.
● **震災地** an area damaged [destroyed] by an earthquake; an earthquake-stricken area.

じんさい 人災 a man-made disaster, a disaster caused by human carelessness [negligence].

じんざい 人材 (有能な人) a capable person; (才能のある人) a talented person, (英) a (musical) talent (!通例修飾語を伴う), (集合的) talent (!複数扱い). ● 人材を集める gather *capable* [*talented*] *people*. ● 広く人材を求める look for *talent*. ● 人材を育成する nurture *human resources*. ▶ あの会社には優秀な人材がある That company has an *excellent staff*. ▶ 管理職として適格な人材の育成が急務である It is a matter of great urgency to train qualified management *personnel*.
● **人材銀行** a job placement agency. ● **人材派遣会社** a temporary employment agency. ● **人材派遣業** worker dispatching undertaking; temporary help service. ● **人材募集** (新聞の求人欄などに) help wanted.

しんさく 真作 a genuine [an authentic] work.

しんさく 新作 (作品) a new work; (新しい曲) a new composition. ● 新作を発表する publish a *new work*; (音楽など) perform a *new work*.

***しんさつ** 診察 图 a medical examination [consultation], a checkup. ● 診察中を under *medical examination*. ● 診察を受ける (=診察してもらう) see [consult] a doctor. (!see の方が口語的だ) ● 大学病院で診察(=健康診断)を受ける have a *medical examination* [a *checkup*] in the university hospital. (!後の方が口語的だ)

── **する** 動 examine; (人を) see*. ● 患者を診察する examine [see] a patient. (!後の方が口語的だ) ▶ 私は山田先生に胃を診察してもらった I had my stomach *examined* [×*seen*] by Dr. Yamada. (!see は人を診察する場合にのみ用いる)
● **診察結果** the result of an examination.
● **診察券** a consultation ticket. ● **診察時間** consultation [doctor's office] hours. ● **診察室** a consultation [an examination] room; (主に米) a doctor's office. ● **診察台** an examination bed. ● **診察日** (病院の) a consultation day; (患者の) one's consultation day; one's medical examination day. ● **診察料** a doctor's fee.

しんさつ 新札 (米) a (brand-)new bill, (英) a (brand-)new (bank) note.

しんさん 辛酸 (a) hardship.
● **辛酸をなめる** 幾多の辛酸をなめる suffer [go through] many *hardships*; have a bitter, hard life.

しんざん(もの) 新参(者) a newcomer, a novice.

しんざんゆうこく 深山幽谷 the depths of the mountain and a deep secluded valley.

しんし 紳士 a gentleman (複 -men /-mən/). ● 本当の紳士 a true [a real] *gentleman*. ● 紳士的な態度 *gentlemanly* behavior. ● 紳士服売り場 the

しんし men's suit department. ●紳士協定を結ぶ make a *gentleman's* [a *gentlemen's*] agreement. (⚠性差別を意識する人は an informal agreement または an oral contract を好む)
●紳士録《米話》a blue book; 〖各界の〗who's who [Who's Who].

しんし 真摯 ― 真摯な 形 ●真摯な態度 a *sincere* [真剣な] an *earnest* attitude 《*to, toward*》; one's sincerity.

しんじ 神事 神事を行う perform *Shinto rites*.

じんじ 人事 personnél affairs [matters]. ▶人事担当者はだれですか Who is in charge of *personnel* (*affairs*)?
●人事不省(ﾌｾｲ) (⇨人事不省)
●人事を尽くして天命を待つ《ことわざ》Do your best and leave the rest to Providence.
●人事異動 personnel transfers [changes]; a personnel [a staff] reshuffle. ●人事院 the National Personnel Authority. ●人事課 a personnel section [department]. ●人事管理 personnel management [administration]. ●人事考課 a merit [a man, a performance] rating.
●人事考課表 a performance assessment sheet.
●人事部 a personnel department [division]. (⚠単に personnel ともいう) ●人事部長 a personnel manager.

しんしき 神式 Shinto rites. ●神式で式を挙げる hold [conduct, perform] a 《wedding》ceremony according to *Shinto rites*.

しんしき 新式 新式(=新型)の車 a *new type* of car; a *new-type* car. ●新式(=新方式)の教授法 a *new method* of teaching.

シンジケート a 《drug(s) [banking]》syndicate.
●シンジケートローン a syndicated loan [credit].

しんじこむ 信じ込む 〖固く信じる〗believe firmly; 〖決めてかかる〗assume 《*that* 節》; 〖一瞬たりとも疑わない〗never for a moment doubt 《*that* 節》▶ぼくは太郎は彼女の実の弟だと信じ込んでいた I *firmly believed* [I assumed, I've never doubted for a moment] *that* Taro was her real brother.

しんしつ 心室 〖解剖〗a ventricle. ●右[左]心室 the right [left] ventricle.

しんしつ 寝室 a bedroom. ●夫婦の寝室(=主寝室) the master *bedroom*. ●来客用の寝室 a guest room.

*****しんじつ 真実** 名 truth; 〖現実性〗reality. ●真実を語る[= 話] (speak, ×say) the *truth*. ●真実を曲げる distort the *truth*. ●真実を突き止める find out the *truth*. ●真実を打ち明ける confess the *truth*. ●真実味のある言葉 *sincere* words. ●報告(書)の真実性を疑う doubt the *truth* [*reality*] of the report. ▶彼の話は真実味に欠けている His story lacks *reality*. ●彼の話には真実味があった(=真実のように聞こえた) His story rang *true* (↔false)./There was a ring of *truth* in what he said.
― 真実の 形 true; (本当の) real. ●真実の話 a *true* story. ▶大統領が暗殺されたのは真実だ It is *true* that the president was assassinated.

しんじついちろ 『真実一路』 *The One Road of Truth*. (〖参考〗山本有三の小説)

じんじふせい 人事不省 ●人事不省に陥る become *unconscious*; fall into *unconsciousness* (↔regain consciousness); (気絶する) faint, pass out (↔come to).

しんしゃ 深謝 ❶〖感謝〗grateful [heartful, sincere] thanks. ▶ご厚情深謝いたします I *deeply appreciate* your kindness./I am *deeply grateful* to you *for* your kindness./I'd like to express my *deepest gratitude* to you *for* your kindness.
❷〖おわび〗sincere [heartfelt] apologies. ▶深謝いたします I'd like to offer [make] my *sincere apologies*.

しんしゃ 新車 a new car.

しんじゃ 信者 a believer 《*in*》. ●マルクスの信者(=信奉者) a *follower* of Marx. ▶彼女はキリスト教信者だ She is a *Christian*./She *believes in* [×believes] *Christianity*.

*****じんじゃ 神社** a (Shinto) shrine. ●成田神社 (the) Narita *Shrine*. ●元旦に家の近くの神社にお参りした I visited the *shrine* near my house on New Year's Day.

ジンジャー 〖しょうが〗〖植物〗ginger.
●ジンジャーエール ginger ale.

しんしゃく 斟酌 ― 斟酌する 動 (特別の事情を考慮して対処する) make allowance(s) for ..., allow for ...; take ... into consideration [account], consider. ▶90歳という高齢を斟酌して, 彼は厳罰には処せられなかった In consideration of [*for*] his age of ninety, he was not punished severely.

しんしゅ 進取 ●進取の気性に富む青年 an *enterprising* young man; a young man with *enterprise*. ▶彼は進取の気性に欠ける He lacks *initiative*.

しんしゅ 新酒 young [fresh] sake.

しんしゅ 新種 a new kind. ●新種のダリア a *new kind* [*variety*] of dahlia. (⇨種類)

しんじゅ 真珠 a pearl. ●真珠のネックレス a *pearl* necklace; a necklace of *pearls*. ●模造真珠 an imitation [(人工の) an artificial] *pearl*. ●養殖真珠 a cultured *pearl*. ●真珠のような白い歯 *pearly* white teeth. ●真珠を採る fish [dive] for *pearls*.
●豚に真珠をやる (⇨豚) 〖成句〗
●真珠貝 a pearl oyster [shell]. ●真珠養殖 pearl cultivation [culture]. ●真珠養殖場 a pearl farm [bed].

*****じんしゅ 人種** 名 a race. ▶アメリカは人種のるつぼである America is a melting pot [《米》a salad bowl, a kaleidoscope] of *races*. (⇨るつぼ)
― 人種の 形 racial.
●人種差別 race [racial] discrimination; (黒人に対する) segregation; (南アフリカの) apartheid /əpάːrthèit/. ●人種差別を受ける be racially discriminated against; suffer (from) *racial discrimination*. (⚠「人種差別を受けた[ている]人」は a victim of *race discrimination*) ●人種差別主義 racism; 《英やや古》racialism. ●人種差別主義者 a racist. ●人種差別廃止 integration. ●人種問題 a race [a racial] problem [issue].

しんじゅう 心中 (a) double suicide; (恋人同士の) (a) love suicide. ●一家心中 (a) family *suicide*. ●無理心中 (a) murder [forced *double*] *suicide*. ●病気の妻と無理心中をはかる attempt to kill one's sick wife and oneself.
― 心中する 動 commit double [love] suicide.
●心中立て proof of one's fidelity.

しんしゅく 伸縮 名 〖広がり縮むこと〗expansion and contraction; 〖伸縮性〗elasticity. ●伸縮自在のゴム *elastic* rubber. ●伸縮性のあるズボン *stretch* pants. (⚠stretch は「伸縮加工した」の意の形容詞)
― 伸縮する 動 expand and contract; be elastic.

*****しんしゅつ 進出** 名 an advance. ▶その会社は海外進出をねらっている(=海外へ事業を広げようとしている) The company is trying to *expand* [*extend*] (its) *business* overseas.
― 進出する 動 ●決勝に進出する *advance to* [*reach*] the finals. ●海外市場に進出する make one's way

しんしゅつ into foreign markets. ●政界へ進出する(=入る) go into [enter] politics. ●その会社は電子産業に進出した(=手を広げた) The company *has branched out into* the electronic industry.

しんしゅつ 新出 ●新出語 a new word.

しんしゅつ 滲出 图 ooze; exudation.
── 滲出する 動 ooze (out); exude.
●滲出性体質『医学』exudative diathesis.

じんじゅつ 仁術 benevolence. ▶医は仁術 (⇨医[成句])

しんしゅつきぼつ 神出鬼没 ●神出鬼没である appear as if from nowhere and vanish without trace.

しんじゅわん 真珠湾 Pearl Harbor. ▶真珠湾奇襲攻撃 a surprise attack on *Pearl Harbor*.

しんじゅん 浸潤 图 saturation.
── 浸潤する 動 saturate; (感情・思想などが) permeate. ▶その制度に対する不満が国中に浸潤していた Dissatisfaction with the system *has permeated* (throughout) the country.

しんしょ 信書 a personal letter; 《総称》personal correspondence.

しんしょ 新書 (新刊書) a new book [publication]; (新書判) a small-sized paperback.

しんしょ 親書 ❶[元首・首相などの公式書簡] President's [Prime Minister's] official letter.
❷[自筆の手紙] a handwritten [(自分で署名した) an autograph] letter.

しんしょう 心証 ●心証がよい[悪い] give 《him》 a good [a bad, an unfavorable] *impression*. ▶彼女はとても心証を害していた She was very *wounded*./…には裁判官の心証を害する結果になった…would have caused the judge to form an unfavorable opinion of 《him》 or: would have disposed the judge against 《him》 ●心証を得る(=確信を持つ) feel convinced 《that…》; be certain 《of…》. ▶裁判官は被告の供述に心証を得た The judge was convinced by the defendant's testimony./His Honor felt the defendant's statement had *merit*.

しんしょう 心象 an image.
●心象風景 (心理的情景) a mindscape; (心に残る場面) scenes that remain (imprinted) in one's mind; (印象的な風景) an impressive landscape.

しんしょう 身上 ❶[財産] a property.
❷[所帯の切り回し] ▶彼女は身上持ちがよい[悪い] She is a good [a bad] housekeeper.

しんしょう 辛勝 a narrow victory.
── 辛勝する 動 win a narrow victory; (わずかの差で勝つ) win by a narrow margin (🔺主に選挙などで用いる).

しんじょう 心情 (考え) one's thought (based on feelings); (感情) one's feelings. ●彼の心情は理解できる can understand *what he thinks* [*how he feels*]. ●被害者の家族の心情を察する(=同情する) *sympathize with* [*feel sorry for*, 《やや書》*feel for*] the victim's family. ●心情的には理解できますが… *Emotionally* I can understand 《him》, but…

しんじょう 身上 (長所) one's merit, one's good point; (宝) one's asset. ▶時間厳守が彼の身上だ Punctuality is his *merit*.
●身上書 a résumé /rèz(j)uméi/.

しんじょう 信条 〖生活・行動などの〗one's principle (🔺通例複数形で) (⇨主義); 〖信念〗a belief (🔺~s); 〖教義〗a creed. ●生活の信条 one's *principles* of life. ●私の宗教的な信条 my religious *beliefs* [(article of) *faith*]. ●あらゆるチャンスを逃すな—それが私の信条です Take every opportunity — that's my *philosophy*.

しんじょう 真情 true [genuine] feelings; sincere sentiments. ●真情を吐露する express [show] one's *true feelings*.

しんじょう 進上 presentation.

じんじょう 尋常 ●尋常な(=普通の)手段では by *ordinary* [*usual*] means. ▶彼は尋常一様(=普通の)の学者ではない He is no mean scholar.

しんしょうしゃ 身障者 a disabled [a (physically) handicapped, 《米婉曲》a physically challenged] person, a person with a disability ; 《米》ではさらに婉曲的にa differently abled person; a person with different abilities といぅ呼び方が好まれる; 《集合的》《やや書》the (physically) handicapped, the disabled.

しんしょうひつばつ 信賞必罰 ●信賞必罰を行う give fitting rewards and punishment.

しんしょうぼうだい 針小棒大 ▶彼はいつも針小棒大に言う He always *makes* a *mountain out of* a *molehill*./(誇張する) He always *exaggerates*.

しんしょく 神職 (神主) a Shinto priest.

しんしょく 浸食 erosion. ●海岸の浸食 coastal *erosion*; the *erosion* of the coast.
── 浸食する 動 erode. ▶海岸が徐々に浸食されている The coast *is* [*has been*] gradually *eroded* [*eaten away*]./The coast suffers (from) gradual *erosion*.

しんしょく 寝食 ●彼と寝食を共にする *live with* him *under the same roof*; live together. ▶数日の間彼女は寝食を忘れて働いた For several days She worked, almost *without food or sleep*. ▶彼は寝食を忘れてアフリカの病人の治療に当たった(=生涯[身]をささげた) He *devoted* his *life* [*himself*] *to* curing sick people in Africa.

しんじる 信じる ❶[本当と思う] believe. (🔺通例進行形不可. 単に「思う」の意にもなる (⇨思う ❶ (a))) ●信じるに足る[信じがたい]話 a *believable* [an *unbelievable*] story; a *credible* [an *incredible*] story. ▶信じられないかもしれないが,あの紳士は実はスパイだった *Believe it or not*, that gentleman turned out to be a spy. ▶彼女は信じられないほど美しかった She was *unbelievably* beautiful./She was beautiful *beyond (all) belief*.
①［…を信じる］自分を信じる *believe* in oneself.
●運命を信じる *believe* in one's destiny. ▶私の言うことを信じてよ *Take* my *word for* it. (🔺通例命令文で用い Believe me. より軽く, 口語的) ●私は君の言うことを信じます I *believe* you [*what you say*]. (🔺 *believe* in you は「君の人柄を信用している」の意 (⇨ ❷)) ●初めのうち自分の耳[目]を信じることができなかった(=が信じられなかった) At first I couldn't *believe* my ears [eyes]. (🔺この言い方は否定文で用いる) ●あの子は幽霊(の存在)を信じている That child *believes in* ghosts [*believes that* ghosts exist]. ●月面に着陸するという考えは最初は信じられなかった The idea of landing on the moon *was incredible* at first.
会話「また同じ間違いをしたのね」「おればかじゃないかな! 信じられないよね」 "You've made the same mistake again." "Ain't I a fool? Would you *believe* (it)?" (🔺(1)いずれも感嘆文の一部で, 疑問文は頭り文末を大きく下降調で言い切る. (2) Ain't は Aren't や Am I not より会話では一般的)
②［…であると信じる］ believe (*that* 節); (A が B であると信じる)《書》believe A to be B. (🔺(1) B は名詞・形容詞. (2) この型は A を主語にした受身でよく用いられる). ▶私はこの話は本当だと信じています I *believe* (*that*) the story is true. (🔺口語では次例より普通)/I *believe* the story *to be* true. (🔺単に I *believe* the story. ともいえる)/It is my *belief* [My *belief* is] that the story is true. ●彼のチームが優勝したなんて信じられない I don't *believe* [I find it hard to *believe*, It's *unbelievable*, It's *incredible*] *that* his team won the championship. ●彼は無実だと信じられている He *is believed to be* innocent. (🔺 *It is believed that* he is innocent.

より好まれる)/They *believe that* he is innocent. (⚠ 信じる in 口語的)
❷【信用する】(直感的に) trust; (根拠もなく心情的に) have* faith in .... (⇨信用する) ▶夫を信じています I *trust* [*have faith in, believe in*] my husband. (⇨❶①) ▶彼はすぐ人を信じる性格です He has a very *trusting* nature.
❸【信仰する】believe [have faith] in .... (⇨信仰) ●キリスト教を信じなくなる lose faith in Christianity.
❹【確信する】be sure [certain] 《*of*; *that* 節》. (⇨確信する) ▶私は昇進するものと信じていた I *was sure* [*certain*] *of* being promoted./I *was sure* [*certain*] (*that*) I would be promoted.
会話「彼は月曜までにそれを渡してくれるでしょう」「あんまり信じなさんな. あまり当てにならない人だから」"He'll let me have it by Monday." "Don't be too *sure*. He's not very reliable."

しんしん 心身 mind and body. ●心身共に健全である be sound in *mind and body*; be *mentally and physically* sound. ●心身を打ち込む(=専心する) devote oneself 《*to*》. ▶彼は心身の疲労で倒れた He collapsed from *mental and physical* exhaustion.
●心身症 a psychosomatic disease. (cf. 神経症)

しんしん 心神 spirit; mind.
●心神耗弱(ニュウ)【法律】feeble-mindedness. ●心神喪失【法律】non compos mentis.

しんしん 津々 ●興味津々 be *deeply* interested 《*in*》.

しんしん 新進 ── 新進の 形 (地位や名誉を得つつある) rising; (将来が有望な) promising. ●新進の作家 a *rising* [*a promising*] writer. ●新進気鋭の学者 a *young and energetic* [an *up-and-coming*] scholar.

しんしん 深々 ▶雪がしんしんと降っている The snow is falling *silently*. ▶夜がしんしんと更けていく The night advances *silently and* [*but*] *steadily*. ▶しんしんと冷え込む夜になった It has turned into a *penetratingly* cold night.

しんじん 信心 (信心深さ) piety /páiəti/; (信仰) (a) faith; (a) religious belief (⊛ ~s). (⇨信仰) ●信心深い婦人 a *religious* [a *devout*] woman. (⚠ pious は「いかにも信心深そうだが実はそうではない」の意にも解されるので避ける) ▶彼は信心深い.日曜日はいつも教会へ行く He is very *religious*. He goes to church every Sunday.

しんじん 深甚 ●深甚なる謝意を表する express one's *deep* [*profound, sincere*] gratitude 《*to* him *for* his kindness》.

しんじん 新人 (芸能界の) a new star 《xface》; (スポーツ界などの) 《話》 a rookie; (職場の) a recruit. ●映画界の新人 a *new* movie 《film (主に英)》 *star*. ●党の期待の新人 the *new hope* of a party. ▶今日では日本の多くの会社が新人を採用する手段としてインターネットを利用している Many Japanese companies now use the Internet as a *recruiting* tool.
●新人王 the rookie king. (⚠「今年の新人王」は the *Rookie* of the Year, その賞[タイトル]は the *Rookie-of-the-Year award* [*title*])

じんしん 人心 the hearts of the people. ●人心を得る[失う] get [lose] the *support of the people*.

じんしん 人身 ●人身攻撃 (make) a personal attack [*personal remarks*] 《*on* him》. ●人身事故 (cause) an accident resulting in injury or death. ●人身売買 human traffic [trafficking]. (⚠ その売買人は human trafficker)

しんじんるい 新人類 a new breed of people.

しんすい 心酔 ── 心酔する 動 ▶彼は教授に心酔している(=敬い慕っている) He *adores* [崇拝する) *worships*] the professor.

しんすい 浸水 ── 浸水する 動 ▶豪雨で500軒以上の家が床上[床下]まで浸水した(=水浸しになった) Over five hundred houses *were flooded* above [below] the floor level by the heavy rain. ▶船が浸水して(=に水が入って)沈んだ The boat *leaked* and sank.

しんすい 進水 ── 進水する 動 ▶船を進水させる *launch* a ship.
●進水式 a launching /lɔ́:ntʃɪŋ/ ceremony. ●進水台 a launching platform.

しんずい 神髄, 真髄 (本質) the essence, 《書》 the quintessence; (精神) the spirit, the soul. ●東洋美術の神髄 *the essence* of Oriental art. ●簡潔は機知の神髄 Brevity is *the soul* of wit.

しんせい 申請 (申し込み) application 《*for*》.
── 申請する 動 ●役所にビザを申請する *apply to* the public office *for* a visa.
●申請書 (fill out [【法律】file]) an application form. ●申請料 a filing charge.

しんせい 神聖 sanctity; holiness; sacredness. ●神聖を汚す violate the *sanctity* 《*of*》.
── 神聖な 形 holy; sacred. (⚠ 前の方が意味が強く,絶対的・本質的な神聖さを表す. 後の方は宗教的崇拝を受けるに足るものに用い, 表面的な神聖さを表す) ●神聖な書物 a *holy* [a *sacred*] book. (⚠ 聖書やコーランなどの聖典) ●その建物[動物]を神聖なものとみなす regard the building [animal] as *sacred*. ●神聖にして侵すべからざる権利 a *sacred and inviolable right*.
●神聖家族 the Holy Family.

しんせい 神性 divinity.

しんせい 真正 authenticity; genuineness.
── 真正の 形 authentic; genuine; true.

しんせい 真性 ── 真性の 形 genuine /dʒénjuin/. ●真性のコレラ (a case of) *genuine* cholera. (⚠ case は「症状」,「患者」の意)

しんせい 新生 a new birth; (新生活) a new life. ●新生児 (⇨新生児) ●新生タイガース the newborn Tigers.

しんせい 『新生』 *Vita Nuova*. (参考 ダンテの詩集)

しんせい 新制 a new system. ●新制大学 a university under the *new system* of education.

しんせい 新星 [星]【天文】a nova /nóuvə/ (⊛ ~s, -vae /vi:/); [新しいスター] a new star.

しんせい 親政 the direct government by *Mikado*.

*****しんせい** 人生 (a) life (⊛ lives). (⚠ 個人の一生・暮らし方の意では [C])
① 【人生(の)〜】●人生の目的[岐路] one's aim [a break] in *life*. ●人生の門出にある若者 a young man on the threshold of *life*. ▶彼は人生経験が豊富である He has seen much of the world [much of *life*]. ▶彼は人生設計を語った He talked about what he was going to do with his *life*.
② 【人生(は)〜】●人生およそ80年 People live for about eighty years [are to be about eighty]./人の寿命は約80年 Man's *life* span is about eighty years. ▶人生は楽しいことばかりではない *Life isn't all fun* [*roses*]./(ことわざ) *Life* is not all beer and skittles. (⚠ skittles はボウリングに似た遊び) ▶人生とはそういうものだ(=仕方がない) *That's life*./That's the way things happen. (⚠ 不快・不幸を経験したときにいう. 逆に幸せな気分のときには This is the life. (これぞ人生だ)を用いる) ▶人生は一度きりだ You only *live* once./You only have

one *life* to live. ▶人生は人が作るもの *Life is what you make of it.*
③〖人生を〗・人生を大いに楽しむ enjoy (one's) *life* to the full. ・充実した人生を送る lead [live] a full *life*. ・人生を楽観[悲観]的に見る look on the bright [dark] side of *life*. ▶どんな人生を送るかは, 人それぞれに異なる *What kind of life to lead differs according to the individual* [*is different from person to person*]./*People choose what kind of life to lead.* (⚠️米ではうしろの方が一般的な言い方)
・人生意気に感ず be moved impetuously; moved by (his) earnest request.
・人生観 an [one's] outlook on life; a [one's] view of life. ・人生行路 one's long difficult passage through life.

しんせいじ 新生児 a newborn baby.
しんせいめん 新生面 (局面) a new phase; (領域) a new field. ・新生面をひらく open up a new field (*in*).
しんせかい 新世界 a new world; 〖米大陸〗the New World (▶これに対しヨーロッパなど旧世界は the Old World).
しんせかいより 『新世界より』*From the New World*. 〖参考〗ドボルザーク作曲の交響曲
しんせき 親戚 a relative. (⚠️この英語は「(夫や妻の)父, 母」なども含む意味の幅の広い語であることに留意) (⇒親類)
じんせき 人跡 ・人跡未踏の untrodden. (⇒未踏)
シンセサイザー a synthesizer /sínθəsàizər/.

*しんせつ 親切 图 (a) kindness (▶行為をいうときは ⓒ); 〖好意〗goodwill, (やや書) a favor; 〖親切にもてなすこと〗hospitality. ・親切心から out of *kindness* [*goodwill*]. ・ちょっとした親切 small acts of *kindness*. ▶ご親切ありがとう *Thank you for* [*I appreciate*] *your kindness.* (⚠️後の方が丁寧ややや堅い言い方)
── 親切な 圈 kind, kindly, nice, good*; (心のやさしい) kindhearted; (人のもてなしが親切な) hospitable.

〖使い分け〗 **kind**, **kindly** しばしば同義的に用いられるが, **kind** は人を助けるなどの具体的行為において「親切な」こと. **kindly** は外見・性質・態度などから見て「親切な」ことで, 通例弱者に対する態度をいう. 限定的にのみ用いられる.
nice **kind** よりくだけた語で細かいところまで心を配って「親切な」の意.
good 道徳的によいという意から「親切な」の意.

・親切な人 a *kind* [a *kindly*, a *kindhearted*] person. ・他人に親切にしなさい *Be kind* [*good*, *nice*, ×*kindly*] *to other people.* ▶彼は今は親切にしてくれている *He is being kind.* (⚠️このように進行形で用いると, 生来の性質を表す *He is kind.* と異なり, 一時的な性質を表し, 「親切にふるまっている, 親切なふりをしている」の意) ▶ご親切に助けてくださってありがとうございました *It was kind* [*nice*, *good*] *of you to help me.* (⚠️*It was kind of you that you helped me.* も可. *It was nice* [*good*] *that…*. は「…はすばらしかった[好都合だった]」の意) ▶*You were kind* [*nice*, *good*] *to help me.* (⚠️*It was ….* の構文の方が間接的で穏やかな言い方) ▶彼は親切にも私にお金を貸してくれた *He was kind enough* [*was so kind as*, (書) *had the kindness*] *to lend me some money.* / *He kindly lent me some money.* (⚠️日常会話では単に *He lent me some money.* ということも多い)
▶彼は私にいろいろ親切にしてくれた *He has done* [*shown*] *me many kindnesses.* (⚠️a *kindness*, many *kindnesses* とはいうが, 数詞をつけて ×*one*

kindness, ×*two kindnesses* のようにはいわない)
▶村人は訪問客に親切だった *The villagers were kind* [*friendly*, *hospitable*] *to their visitors.* / *The villagers treated their visitors with hospitality.* (▶(友好的に) *in a friendly manner*).
会話 「それいつでも貸してあげるよ」「それはご親切にありがとう」"*You can borrow it any time.*" "*That's very kind of you./How nice* [*sweet*] *of you!*" (⚠️後の方が親しみのある言い方. *sweet* は女性の好む言い方)
・親切気 one's willingness to be kind. ・親切ごかし a pretense of kindness.

しんせつ 深雪 deep snow.
しんせつ 新設 ── 新設の 圈 ・新設の会社 a *new* [a *newly-established*, a *newly-organized*] company.
── 新設する 動 〖設立する〗set up, establish; (創設する) found; 〖組織・編成する〗organize. ・大学を新設する *found* [*establish*, *set up*] a university. (⚠️*set up* が最も口語的)
・新設校 a new [a newly-founded] school.

しんせつ 新雪 fresh [new-fallen] snow; (人が踏んだことのない) virgin snow. ▶当地に新雪が降った *There was a fresh fall of snow here.*
しんせつ 新説 (新しい学説) a new theory; (新しい見解) a new idea [view].

*しんせん 新鮮 图 freshness. ・新鮮味に欠ける lack *freshness*.
── 新鮮な 圈 (新しく生き生きしている) fresh; (新しい) new. ・新鮮な野菜[果物; ミルク] *fresh* vegetables [fruit; milk]. (▶「生(㌔)の, 未加工の」の意にもなる)
・新鮮な空気を吸う breathe some *fresh* air. ・新鮮なアイディアをある have a *fresh* [a *new*] idea. ▶朝は空気が新鮮だ *The air is fresh in the morning.* ▶その野菜は畑から取り立てで新鮮です *The vegetables are fresh from the field.*

しんせん 新線 a new line.
しんせん 新選 ── 新選の 圈 (新たに選んだ) newly-selected; (新たに編集した) newly-compiled, newly-edited.
しんぜん 神前 ・神前に供える offer 《a thing》 to the gods; make an offering 《of a thing》 to the gods.
・神前結婚 《perform》 a Shinto wedding [a wedding according to Shinto rites].
しんぜん 親善 〖好意〗góodwill; 〖友好〗(a) friendship, friendly relations. (⇒友好) ・国際親善 international *goodwill* [*friendship*]. ・親善使節として中国へ行く go to China as a *goodwill* envoy [親善使命を帯びて] on a *goodwill* mission].
・親善試合 a friendly match [game]. ・親善訪問 a goodwill visit. ・親善旅行 a goodwill tour.
じんせん 人選 ・人選に漏れる be left out in the *selection of the right person(s)* 《*for*》; be not shortlisted; be not *on the short list* (▶*on the short list* は人選の最終名簿に(のって)の意). ・人選を誤る select a wrong person.
しんぜんび 真善美 truth, good and beauty.
しんそ 親疎 ▶彼女は親疎の別なく人を招待する *She invites anyone whether she knows them well or not.*

*しんそう 真相 the truth; the real [true] facts; the true [real] state of things; 〖事実〗a fact. (⇒真実) ・真相を追求する search for the *truth*. ・事件の真相を知っている[明らかにする; 隠す] *know* [*reveal*, *conceal*] *the* (*real*) *facts of the case.* ▶事の真相は何ですか *What is the truth of the matter?* ▶実

しんそう 相がついに明らかになった The *truth* has come out at last. ▶その委員会が事の真相究明にあたった(=詳しく調査した) The committee investigated [(事情聴取をして) inquired into] the matter.

しんそう 深窓 ●深窓の令嬢 a girl of gentle birth [high society].
● 深窓に育つ be brought up with tender loving care in a good family.

しんそう 深層 ●深層構造〖言語〗deep structure. ●深層心理学 depth psychology. ●深層水 deep ocean water.

しんそう 新装 图 〖内装または外装の改変〗(a) refurbishment; (内装の改変) redecoration; 〖改造〗remodeling. ▶7月20日新装オープン(広告で) Completely *redecorated* [*remodeled*]. Reopening July 20.
—— 新装する 動 refurbish [redecorate] 《a theater》.

*__**しんぞう** 心臓__ ❶〖人体の〗a heart.
① 【心臓が】▶彼は心臓が悪い He has (×a) *heart* trouble [a *heart* complaint, a bad *heart*]. ●心臓がどきどきしていた I felt my *heart* beat rapidly.
② 【心臓の】●心臓の鼓動 the beat(ing) [throb(bing)] of the *heart*; (1回の鼓動) a heartbeat. ●心臓の働き the function of the *heart*. ▶彼が時々めまいを起こすのは最近発見された彼の心臓の異常と関連があるのかもしれない His dizzy spell may have been related to a recent *heart condition*. (!この condition は「異常な状態・病気」の意)
❷〖中心部〗the heart. ●東京の心臓部 the *heart* [*center*] of Tokyo.
❸〖図太さ〗(a) nerve; cheek. ▶彼はなんて心臓だ(=ずうずうしい) How *brazen-faced* [〖大胆な〗*bold*] he is!/What a *nerve* he's got! ▶彼は心臓が弱い(=臆病(おくびょう)だ) He is *timid* [(内気の) *shy*, (勇気がない) *lacking in courage*, 〖書〗*faint-hearted*].
● 心臓が強い have a lot of nerve [guts].
● 心臓に毛が生えている be thick-skinned. ▶別れた女房にお金をせびるなんて心臓に毛が生えたような(=厚かましい)人だね He's got *a lot of nerve* asking his ex(-wife) for money.
● 心臓移植 a heart transplant. (!「心臓を移植する」は transplant a heart) ● 心臓外科 heart [cardiac] surgery. ● 心臓外科医 a heart specialist. ● 心臓死 cardiac death; heart death. ● 心臓肥大 cardiac hypertrophy. ● 心臓病 heart [cardiac] disease; heart trouble. ● 心臓弁膜症 valvular disease of the heart. ● 心臓発作 (have [suffer]) a heart attack. ● 心臓麻痺(まひ) heart [cardiac] failure.

じんぞう 人造 —— 人造の 形 (人工の) man-made, artificial; (模造の) imitation; (合成の) synthetic.
● 人造絹糸(けんし) artificial silk; rayon. ● 人造湖 a man-made [an artificial] lake. ● 人造人間 an android. ● 人造皮革 an imitation [a fake] leather.

じんぞう 腎臓〖解剖〗a kidney. ▶腎臓が悪い(=腎臓病だ) I have (×a) *kidney* trouble [a *kidney* complaint].
● 腎臓結石〖医学〗a kidney stone.

しんぞく 親族 a relative, a relation. (!前の方が普通) (⇨親類)
● 親族会議 a family [×a relative] meeting.

じんそく 迅速 —— 迅速な 形 (すばやい) quick, speedy; (即座の) prompt; (速い) swift. ● 迅速な行動をとる act *quickly* [*speedily*, *promptly*]; take *quick* [*prompt*] action.
—— 迅速に 副 quickly; promptly; speedily. ● 迅速に事を運ぶ do [carry out] the work *quickly* [*speedily*, *promptly*].

しんそこ 真底, 心底 ▶彼女は真底から(=心から)私を助けたいと望んでいた She *sincerely* hoped that she could help me./She was completely *sincere* about helping me./She wanted to help me *from the bottom of* her *heart*.

しんそつ 新卒 a new graduate. ● 新卒の英語の先生 an English teacher *fresh from college*. ▶今年その企業は大学の新卒を採用したがっている The company is seeking *new* college *graduates* this year.

*__**しんたい** 身体__ a body. (⇨体❶) ● 身体各部 the parts of the *body*.
● 身体検査 (健康診断) a physical [a medical] examination (⇨健康); (空港などでの危険物などを見つけるための) a body search, a security check (! ×a body check とはいわない), (話) a frisk (!衣服の上から触って行う). ● 麻薬を隠し持っていないか彼を身体検査をする *search* 〖話〗*frisk*〗him *for* hidden drugs. ● 身体障害者 (⇨身障者) ● 身体髪膚(はっぷ) every part of a human body.

しんたい 進退 ❶〖運動〗●進退きわまる cannot either *go forward or backward*; cannot advance nor [or] retreat; (板ばさみになる) be *in a dilemma*. (⇨板挟み)
❷〖進路〗one's course of action; 〖態度〗one's attitude; 〖行為〗one's conduct. ●進退を明らかにする decide on one's *course of action*. ●進退伺いを出す(=辞表を出す) send [hand] in one's *resignation*.

しんだい 身代 property; (a) fortune. ●身代を作る make a *fortune*. ●身代を潰す dissipate [run through, squander] a *fortune*.
● 身代限り (破産) bankruptcy.

しんだい 寝台 a bed (⇨ベッド); 〖船・列車の〗a berth, a bunk. ●折りたたみ式の寝台 a folding bed. ●上の[下の]段の寝台 an upper [a lower] *berth*.
● 寝台券 a (sleeping-)berth ticket. ● 寝台車 a sleeping car; a sleeper. ● 寝台料金 a berth charge.

じんたい 人体 a human body.
● 人体解剖図 an anatomical chart. ● 人体実験 an experiment on human beings. (⇨実験)

じんたい 靱帯〖解剖〗a ligament. ● 足首の靱帯を損傷する(人が主語) tear a *ligament* in one's ankle.

じんだい 甚大 —— 甚大な 形 ▶地震で建物が甚大な(=重大な)被害を受けた The earthquake did *serious* [*great*] damage to the building./The building was *badly* [*seriously*] damaged by the earthquake.

しんたいししょう 『新体詩抄』 *A Selection of New Style Verse*. (参考) 外山正一らの詩集)

しんたいそう 新体操 rhythmic /ríðmik/ gymnastics. (!複数扱い) (⇨体操)

しんたいりく 新大陸 the New Continent; (新世界) a new world.

しんたく 信託 a trust. ●貸付[投資]信託 a loan [an investment] *trust*.
● 信託会社 a trust company. ● 信託業(務) trust business. ● 信託銀行 a trust bank. ● 信託契約 a trust agreement. ● 信託財産 trust estate [property]; fiduciary estate [property]. ● 信託者 a truster. ● 信託統治 trusteeship. ● 信託統治地域 (国連の) a trust territory. ● 信託預金 a trust deposit.

しんたく 神託 (お告げ) an oracle, a divine message.

シンタックス 〖統語論〗〖文法〗syntax.

- シンタックスエラー [コンピュータ] a syntax error.
- **しんたん** 心胆 • 心胆を寒からしめる make one's blood freeze [curdle, run cold]; freeze [curdle] one's blood. • 心胆を寒からしめる光景 a blood-curdling sight.
- **しんだん** 診断 图 (a) diagnosis /dàiəgnóusis/, (徸 diagnoses /-si:z/). • 診断を誤る make a wrong *diagnosis*. • 健康診断を受ける (⇨健康)
  — **診断する** 動 diagnose /dáiəgnòus/, (!通例受身で), make a diagnosis 《*of*》. ▶医者は誤って彼の病気をはしかと診断した The doctor incorrectly *diagnosed* his illness as measles [*diagnosed* him *as* having measles]. ▶彼女はインフルエンザと診断された Her flu *was diagnosed*.
  • 診断書 a medical certificate; a diagnosis. ▶診断書を1通書いていただきたいのですが I'd like to have a copy of my *medical certificate*. • 診断テスト a diagnostic test.
- **じんち** 人知 human intelligence [intellect]. • 人知の及ばない beyond *human knowledge* [*understanding*]. • 人知の限りを尽くす try every possible means 《*to do*》.
- **じんち** 陣地 a position. (⇨陣 ❶) • 陣地を敷く take up a *position*; set up a *camp*. • 砲兵陣地を爆破する《守る》blast [hold] an artillery *position*.
- **しんちく** 新築 图 (新しい家) a new [a newly-built] house. (徸 houses /-ziz/, 《米》-siz/).
  — **新築する** 動 ▶家を新築した We had a (new) house built.
  • 新築祝い (パーティー) a housewarming (party) (!文脈によりほかに party ともいう); (贈り物) a housewarming present.
- **じんちく** 人畜 men and beasts. • 人畜無害 No harm is done to *humans or animals*.
- **しんちゃ** 新茶 the first tea of the season.
- **しんちゃく** 新着 • 新着の図書 newly-arrived books; (掲示・広告などで) new arrivals. (! arrival は「到着したもの」という広い意の語)
- **しんちゅう** 心中 • 心中では in one's heart [mind]; at heart. • 心中おだやかではない be far from calm; be upset 《*about, with*》; (気分を害する) feel hurt. • 心中を打ち明ける take 《*him*》into one's confidence; confide in 《him》. ▶ご心中をお察しいたします I deeply *sympathize with* you./I know how you feel.
- **しんちゅう** 真鍮 (製品, 色) brass. • 真ちゅうのボタン a *brass* button.
- **しんちゅう** 進駐 图 occupation. — **進駐する** 動 occupy.
  • 進駐軍 the occupation army [force].
- **じんちゅう** 陣中 • 陣中で(陣地の中で) in camp; (戦場で) at the front, in the field. • 陣中見舞いをする visit and encourage 《workers, athletes》with a present of food and drinks [《金一封で》with a donation].
- ***しんちょう** 身長 height /háit/, 《書》stature. • 身長を測る measure one's *height*. • 身長順に line up in order of *height*. • 身長が5センチ伸びる grow [become] five centimeters *taller*. (! 乳児には taller の代わりに longer を用いる) (事情 米英では身長の単位としてはフィートとインチを用いることが多く,特に米では普通) ▶身長はいくらありますか How *tall* [×How] are you?/What is your *height*? (! 前の言い方の方が普通) ▶彼は身長170センチです He is 170 centimeters *tall* [*in height, in stature*]. (!《話》では《 》内はしばしば省略する)/His *height* is 5.5 feet. (! 5.5 は five point five と読む (⇨フィート))

- ***しんちょう** 慎重 图 (注意) carefulness; (用心) caution; (思慮分別) discretion; (熟慮) deliberation.
  — **慎重な** 形 careful; cautious; discreet (! つつしみ注意し); deliberate. ▶彼はその質問に慎重な答え方をした He gave a *careful* [*a cautious, a deliberate*] answer to the question. ▶彼は *careful about* [*cautious about, discreet in, deliberate in*] answering the question. ▶彼は慎重な人で,秘密をもらすようなことはなかった He was *discreet* enough not to give away any secrets.
  — **慎重に** 副 carefully; cautiously; discreetly; deliberately. ▶その問題を慎重に考慮する consider the matter *carefully*; give *careful* consideration to the matter. ▶もっと慎重に運転しなさい Drive more *carefully*. (!「慎重に運転する人」を *careful* driver という) ▶その件はもっと慎重に扱ってはしい I'd like you to handle the matter more *carefully*./I'd like you to be more *careful* with the matter. ▶ほとんどの化学薬品は慎重に扱わなければ危険である Most chemicals are dangerous if people aren't *careful with* them. ▶彼は非常に慎重にものを言う He is very *deliberate* when he speaks./(慎重に言葉を選ぶ) He weighs his words *carefully* when he speaks.
- **しんちょう** 伸張 • 貿易の伸張(=拡張) the *expansion* [*extension*] of a trade. • 中国の勢力が東南アジアで大いに伸張している Chinese influence *has* greatly *extended to* [*expanded in*] South-east Asia.
- **しんちょう** 深長 • 深長な 形 meaningful; significant. • 意味深長 (⇨意味深長)
- **しんちょう** 新調 — **新調の** 形 (新品の) new; (真新しい) brand-new; (新作の) newly-made. • 新調のドレス a *newly-made* [*a brand-new*] dress.
  会話「これが新調した背広です」「よくお似合いですよ」"This is my *new* suit." "It looks good on you."
- **じんちょうげ** 沈丁花 《植物》a daphne /dǽfni/.
- **しんちょく** 進捗 • 大いに[目覚ましく]進捗する make great [remarkable] *progress*.
- **しんちんたいしゃ** 新陳代謝 《生物の》(a) metabolism; 《新旧交代》renewal. • 新陳代謝が激しい have a high (↔a low) *metabolism*. ▶流行語は新陳代謝が激しい Vogue-words *are* constantly *replaced by* [*with*] others.
- **しんつう** 心痛 [心配] (a) worry; [不安] anxiety. (⇨心配) • 心痛の種 a source of *worry* 《*to* him》. • 心痛のあまり病気になる become sick with *worry* [*anxiety*].
- **じんつう** 陣痛 (have) labor pains. • 陣痛が始まる 《人が主語》start [go into] *labor*. • 陣痛を起こしている女性 a woman in *labor*.
- **じんつうりき** 神通力 (have) supernatural [(魔力の)] magical] powers.
- **しんてい** 心底 • 心底から from the (bottom of one's) *heart*; sincerely.
- **しんてい** 進呈 图 presentation. ▶見本無料進呈《広告文》Samples *sent* free [*are available*] on request. (! be available は「手にすることができる」, on request は「請求あり次第」の意)
  — **進呈する** 動 (与える) give; (贈る) present 《him *with* a book, a book *to* him》. ▶あなたにこれを進呈します This is for you. (! 相手を目の前にして I'll *give* it *to* you. などのようにいうのは恩着せがましく失礼なことがある)
- **しんてい** 新訂 a revision.
  • 新訂版 a newly-revised edition 《*of*》.
- **じんてい** 人定 • 人定尋問[質問]をする establish a person's identity.
- **じんてき** 人的 human. ▶我々は国際機関に対する人的

しんてきがいしょう

貢献度を高めるべきである We should increase *human* participation in international organizations.
- 人的資源 human resources. ● 人的資本 human capital.

しんてきがいしょう 心的外傷 〖医学〗trauma /tráumə/.
- 心的外傷後ストレス障害〖医学〗post-traumatic stress disorder 《略 PTSD》.

シンデレラ 〖童話の主人公〗Cinderella /sìndərélə/.
- シンデレラコンプレックス a Cinderella complex.
- シンデレラボーイ[ガール] a Cinderella boy [girl].

しんてん 進展 图 (展開) development; (進行) prógress. ●事件の進展を見守る see the *development* of the event [how the event *develops*].
—— 進展する 動 develop; make progress.

しんてん 親展 (手紙の上書き)(秘密の) Confidential; (個人的な) Personal. ●親展の手紙 a *confidential* [a *personal*] letter.

しんでん 神殿 a shrine; (教会・神殿などの神聖な場所) a sanctuary.

しんでんず 心電図 〖医学〗an electrocardiogram 《略》《米》EKG, 《主に英》ECG; a cardiogram. (⚠ EKG は元のドイツ語つづりの略). ●心電図を撮ってもらう have one's *EKG* taken.

しんでんづくり 寝殿造り the *shinden* style; (説明的に) an style of palace architecture in the Heian period

しんと ●しんとする be utterly [deadly] quiet; (急に話をやめる) fall silent. ●人のいない街はしんとしていた The deserted street was *utterly* [*deadly*] *quiet*. ●ホールはしんとしていた There was *complete* [*absolute*] *silence* in the hall. ●彼の言葉にみんなしんとなった All the people fell *silent* at his words.

しんと 信徒 a believer. ●キリスト教の信徒 a *believer in* Christianity; a Christian.

しんど 深度 ●湖の深度を測る measure [sound] the *depth* of the lake. (⚠ 単に sound the lake ともいう)

しんど 進度 progress. ●英語の進度はクラスによって違っている *Progress* in English is different from class to class.

しんど 震度 seismic /sáizmik/ intensity; 〖マグニチュード〗magnitude. (⇒マグニチュード, 地震) ●その地震は大阪で震度3でした(=を記録した) The quake registered [(測定された) measured] (an *intensity* of) 3 on the Japanese scale in Osaka. ●震度を尋ねるときは How strong did the quake register in Osaka? となる)

じんと (⇒じいんと) ●じんと来る [[感動して]] be deeply touched [moved] 《by》, (悲しみなどで) have [feel] a lump in the throat; [しびれて] feel (one's arm) grow numb; [痛む] (患部が主語) ache, sting (⇒染みる).

しんどい 〖疲れた〗tired; 〖きつい〗hard; (精神的に) tough. ●しんどい仕事 a *hard* job. ●しんどそうな顔をしている look (very) *tired*; wear a *tired* expression. ●今日はしんどかった I had a *tiring* [*hard*] day today. ●きみは落第だと告げるのはしんどい仕事だ It's *tough* to tell that he [she] has to repeat the grade.

しんとう 心頭 the heart; the mind. ●怒り心頭に発するfly into a passion [a rage, a temper, a fury]; be in a towering rage.
- 心頭滅却すれば火もまた涼し The resolved mind has no cares.

しんとう 神道 Shinto(ism); (説明的に) the native religion of Japan, chiefly a system of worship of natural forces and ancestors.

しんとう 浸透 图 〖思想などの〗penetration; infiltration (⚠ 後の方が積極的な浸透); 〖液体などの〗《書》permeation /pəːrmiéiʃən/; 〖化学・物理〗osmosis /azmóusis/. ●新興宗教の労働者への浸透 the *infiltration* of a new religion *into* laborers.
—— 浸透する 動 penetrate; infiltrate (into …); 《書》permeate. ●新しい思想を人民に浸透させる *penetrate* [*infiltrate*] a new idea *into* people. ▶水が土壌に浸透した Water *permeated* (through [into]) the soil.
- 浸透圧 (an) osmótic préssure. ●浸透作用 (an) osmotic action.

-しんとう -親等 ●1[2, 3, 4]親等親族 a relative /rélətiv/ [a relation /riléiʃən/] in the first [second, third, fourth] degree. (⚠ 《米》では relative が好まれ, 《英》では relation が好まれ, relative は …)

***しんどう** 振動 图 (a) vibration; (振り子のような) 《書》oscillation.
—— 振動する 動 vibrate; 《書》oscillate. ▶爆音で窓ガラスが振動した The explosion *vibrated* the windowpanes.
- 振動計 〖物理〗a vibrograph.

***しんどう** 震動 图 a shake; (激しい) a shock; (速い小刻みな) (a) vibration; (地面の大きな) a quake; (微動) a tremor. ●爆発の震動 the *shock* of an explosion.
—— 震動する 動 shake*; vibrate; tremble; 〖車など〗(がたがたと) jolt. (⇒揺れる) ▶足もとで大地が震動した The earth *shook* [《やや書》*quaked*] under us. (⚠ quake は地震などで) ▶交通量が多いので橋が震動した The bridge *shook* [*trembled*] under the heavy traffic. ▶でこぼこ道ではこの車は震動がひどい This car *jolts* terribly [badly] on a rough road.

しんどう 神童 a child prodigy; (⑱) child prodigies; an infant genius.

じんとう 陣頭 ●陣頭に立つ be at the head 《of》; 《や古》lead the van. ●捜索隊の陣頭指揮をとる lead the search party.

じんどう 人道 图 (人間愛) humanity /hjuːmǽnəti/. ▶彼らの捕虜の取り扱い方は人道に反する Their treatment of prisoners is against *humanity*.
—— 人道的な 形 (人道主義的な) humanitarian /hjuːmæ̀nitéəriən/; (人道にかなった, 思いやりのある) humane /hjuːméin/; (⇔inhumane). ●人道的な立場[見地]から from a *humanitarian* point of view. ●最も人道的なやり方で問題を解決する solve the problem in the most *humane* way. ▶それは人道的理由で許しがたい That is unforgivable for *humanitarian* reasons.
- 人道主義 humanitarianism. (⚠ この意味で humanism を使うのはまれ) ● 人道主義者 a humanitarian.

じんとうぜい 人頭税 a poll tax; a capitation.

じんとく 人徳 one's virtue. ●人徳のある人 a man of (great) *virtue*. ●あの難しい局面を切り抜けられたのは彼の人徳のおかげです We got over the difficult situation smoothly because he had such a *charming character*.

じんとり 陣取り *jintori*; (説明的に) a children's outdoor game in which two teams try to take the opponent's land.

じんどる 陣取る occupy. ▶多くの記者たちが門の前に陣取った(=位置を占めた) Many reporters *took* of their *position* in front of the gate. ▶宮殿が市の

中心の広い場所を陣取っている The palace *occupies* a large area in the center of the city.

シンドローム 〖症候群〗〖医学〗a syndrome /síndrəum/

シンナー (paint) thinner. ● シンナーを吸う sniff *glue* [*solvent*]. ● 塗料をシンナーで薄める thin (down) [dilute] paint with some *thinner*.
● シンナー遊び glue-sniffing (**!** glue は「接着剤」の意); (書) solvent sniffing (**!** solvent は「溶剤」の意), (**!** いずれも sniffing を abuse に代えると「習慣的な乱用」の意となる)

しんなり soft. (⇨しなやか)

しんに 真に truly; really. (⇨実(じ), 真, 本当)

じんにく 人肉 human flesh.

しんにち 親日 ── 親日の 形 pro-Japanese.
● 親日家 a pro-Japanese person; a Japanophile. ▶彼は大の親日家だ He really *loves* [*likes*] *Japan*. ややくだけた話し言葉では He's really *pro Japan*.

しんにゅう 之繞 ── 之繞をかける exaggerate.

しんにゅう 侵入 名 (an) invasion; (an) intrusion.
● イラクのクウェートへの侵入 the Iraqi *invasion of* [×to, ×into] Kuwait.
── 侵入する 動 〖領土などに〗invade; 〖家に〗break* (*into*); 〖土地などへの不法侵入する〗trespass (*on*); (コンピュータへ) hack. ● その地区に侵入する *invade* the area. ▶強盗が裏口から彼の家に侵入した A burglar *broke into* his house by the back door. (**!** by は「…を通って」の意)
● 侵入軍 the invading army. ● 侵入者 (領土などへの) an invader; (他人の土地などへの不法の) an intruder, a trespasser; (コンピュータへの) a hacker.

しんにゅう 進入 名 (滑走路などへの) approach. ● 名神高速道路への進入路 an *approach* to the Meishin Expressway. ▶進入禁止 (掲示) Do not *enter*.
── 進入する 動 (中に入る) get into …

しんにゅうしゃいん 新入社員 a recruit; a new employee.

しんにゅうせい 新入生 a new student; 〖高校・大学の1年生〗a freshman (複 -men); (⇨一年生). ● 新入生らしい態度 a *freshman* attitude.

しんにん 信任 (信頼) confidence (↔ nonconfidence). (⇨不信任) ● 信任を得る win [gain] 《*his*》 *confidence*. ▶彼は社長の信任が厚い(=得ている) He has the *confidence* of the president.
● 信任状 (大使などに授ける) credentials. ● 信任投票 a vote of confidence.

しんにん 新任 ── 新任の 形 (今度来た) new; (新たに任命された) newly-appointed. ● 新任の音楽教師 a *new* music teacher; (大学出たての) a music teacher *fresh from* university. ● 新任の(=得たての)あいさつ (大統領・首相などの)(make) an *inaugural* speech; (一般の)(make) the *first* speech in a new position.

しんにん 親任 ── 親任する 動 ▶首相に親任される be *appointed* as Prime Minister by the Emperor.
● 親任式 a ceremony of Imperial investiture.

しんねりむっつり sullen; morose.

***しんねん** 新年 〖元日, 元日からの数日間〗the Nèw Yéar (1) New の前に形容詞がつくときは冠詞は a. (2)「元日」の意を明確にする場合は Nèw Year's Dáy; 〖新しい年〗a new year (特定の年をさすときは the). ● 新年の決意 one's *New Year's* resolutions. ● 新年を祝う celebrate the *New Year*. ● 新年を迎える see the *New Year* in. ▶新年になったら in [at] the *new year*. (**!** in は「新しい年に」,は「年始に」の意) ● 新年早々 at the very beginning of the *year*; as soon as the *new year* begins [comes]. ▶新年おめでとう A Happy *New Year*. (**!** (1)(話)では通例 a を省略する. (2) 前に I wish you をつけるとより堅い表現になる. (3) 答えは Thank you very much. (The) same to you./I wish you the same. (親しい人に) Thanks. You, too. などという. (4) この英語は 1 月 2 日以後は用いない. (5) 年の瀬の 1 週間ほどの間で用いると,「どうぞよいお年を」の本来の意にもなる)

■ DISCOURSE
私たちは新年を年越しそば, 言い換えると「新しい年へと運んでくれる麺」で祝う We celebrate the New Year's Eve by eating *toshikoshi-soba*, or "noodle soup which is believed to carry you safely into the New Year." **!** or (言い換えれば) は言い換えに用いるディスコースマーカー)

● 新年会 a New Year's party.

しんねん 信念 (a) belief 《*in*》(複 ~s); 〖理屈抜きの確信〗(a) faith 《*in*》; 〖根拠のある確信〗(a) conviction; 〖自信〗confidence; 〖行動の指針〗(a) principle. ● 私の堅い信念 my firm *belief*. ● …という確固たる信念に基づいて行動する act in the firm *belief* [*conviction*] *that*…. ● 信念を貫く stick to one's *faith* [*principles*]; carry through one's *conviction*. ▶彼は信念を持っている He is a man of *principle*.

しんのう 心嚢 〖解剖〗a pericardium (複 pericardia).
● 心嚢炎 〖医学〗pericarditis.

しんのう 親王 an Imperial prince. (複 内親王)

しんぱ 新派 a new school; 〖新派劇〗*Shimpa* drama; (説明的に) a form of Japanese drama, developed in the middle of the *Meiji* period.

シンパ a (communist) sympathizer.

じんば 人馬 ● 人馬一体 a man and horse. ● 人馬一体となって in a good collaboration.

‡**しんぱい** 心配 名 (a) worry 《*about*, *over*》; (an) anxiety /æŋzáɪəti/《*about*, *for*, *over*》; (a) care (**!** 以上はいずれも「心配事, 心配の種」の意では〖C〗); concern 《*about*, *for*, *over*》; uneasiness; (a) fear 《*of*》(**!** 時に複数形で). (⇨不安)

| 使い分け | worry いろいろ悩み思うこと. しばしば取り越し苦労を意味する. |

anxiety 将来起こりそうな事に, または何が起こるか分からないので漠然と不安を感じること.
care 強い関心や責任感から気がかりになること. 前の 2 語より意味が弱い.
concern 人や物の安否などを気にかけることや危険や危機に対する懸念.
uneasiness 不安で気持ちが落ち着かないこと.
fear 悪い事が起こるのではないかと恐れること.

① 〖心配〜〗 ● 心配性の人 a worrier; (主に米話) a worrywart. (⇨心配性) ● 心配事があります I have something to *worry about*./I have something *on* [×in] my *mind*. ▶彼には心配事がない He has no worries [nothing to *worry about*]./He is free from [×of] *worry* [*anxiety, care*]. (**!** He is *carefree*. ともいえる)
② 〖心配が[は]〗 ● 彼女の最大の心配は子供の教育だ Her greatest *worry* is her child's education. ● 金の心配はいらない There's no need to [You don't have to] *worry about* money. ▶雨の心配(=恐れ)はない There's no *fear* of rain [raining].
③ 〖心配で〗 ● 心配のあまり病気になる be sick from too much *anxiety*. ▶病弱な息子は私の心配の種です My sickly son is a *worry* [an *anxiety*, a source of *worry*, a *cause* of *anxiety*] *to* me.

④【心配に】▶彼女が約束の時間に来ないので私は心配(=不安)になった When she didn't come at the appointed time, I grew *uneasy* [*anxious*].
⑤【心配を】▶帰りが遅くなって母にすごく心配をかけた I was late coming home and *got* my mother *worried* to death./My late hours *worried* my mother very much. (⚠前の方が口語的) ▶ご心配(=迷惑)をかけてすみません I'm sorry to *have troubled* you.
⑥【心配で】▶彼女は子供の体のことが心配で眠れなかった She was so *worried* [*anxious*] *about* her child's health that she couldn't sleep./She couldn't sleep *with anxiety* [*worry*] *about* her child's health./(事が主語) Her *anxiety* [*worry*] *about* her child's health kept her awake. ▶私は中の様子が心配でドアの外に立っていた I *was worried* (*about*) what was going on inside, and stood behind the door. (⚠ wh- 節の前では about が省略可)
⑦【心配そうな】(気にかかって) anxious; (思い悩んで) worried; (不安で落ち着かない) uneasy. ● 心配そうな母親 an *anxious* [a *worried*] mother. ● この anxious は堅い言い方で, 日常会話では a mother who looks worried の方が普通 ● 心配そうに言う say *anxiously* [*worriedly*]. ● 彼女うなまなざしを向ける turn *anxious* eyes (*to*). ▶彼は心配そうな顔つきで私を見た He gave me a *worried* [an *anxious*, *an uneasy*] look. /(心配そうに) He looked *worriedly* [*anxiously*, *uneasily*] at me. ▶彼女は心配そうな様子だった She looked *worried* [*anxious*, *uneasy*, *troubled*].
── 心配する 動 worry (*about*); (心配している) be worried [anxious, concerned] (*about*); 〖恐れる〗fear (*that* 節); 〖不安で落ち着かない〗feel* uneasy (*about*). ● そのことはあまり心配しないでください Don't *worry* too much *about* it./It's nothing to *worry about*. ▶彼は息子のことでとても心配している He *is* very *worried* [very *anxious*, (病気になるよと) *worried sick*] *about* his son. (⚠この worried は形容詞化しているので very とともに使えるが受身形では不可: He *is* greatly [(very) much, ×very] *worried by* his son.) ▶彼女は夫の安否あんぴを心配していた She *was anxious about* [*for*] her husband's safety./She *was concerned about* [*for*] her husband's safety. ▶彼がまだ姿を見せないので心配している I *am worrying* [I *am worried*, It *worries* me] that he has not shown up yet. (⚠ It is that 節の内容を示す) ▶何を心配しているのだ What's *worrying* [*bothering*] you? ▶母親は息子が入試に失敗するのではないかと心配だった The mother *feared* [*was afraid*] (*that*) her son might fail the entrance exam. (⚠両方とも悪い事を予想しての心配すること. be afraid の方が口語的) ▶彼女の両親は彼女が１人で そこへ行くのをとても心配した Her parents *were* [*felt*] very *uneasy about* her going there alone.
〖会話〗「もう大丈夫だ」「ああよかった. ちょっと心配したわ」"I'm feeling all right now." "Oh, that's fine. You *had us worried* for a moment." (⚠取り越し苦労だと分かったときに用いられる表現)

しんぱい 心肺 ● 人工心肺 a heart-lung machine.
● 心肺機能 〖医学〗cardiopulmonary function. ● 心肺機能蘇生法 cardiopulmonary resuscitation 《略 CPR》.
じんぱい 塵肺 〖医学〗pneumoconiosis.
しんぱいしょう 心配性 ▶母はとても心配性です (心配し過ぎる) My mother *worries too much*./(心配性の人だ) My mother is a worrier [〖米話〗a worrywart].
しんぱく 心拍 (心臓の鼓動) (a) heartbeat; (脈拍) a pulse. ▶運動すると心拍が速くなる Your *heartbeat* [*pulse*] quickens after exercise.
● 心拍数 one's pulse rate. ● 心拍数を数える (脈を取る) feel [take] a person's *pulse*. ● 心拍停止 〖医学〗a cardiac arrest [failure].
しんぱつ 神罰 divine punishment. ● 神罰を受ける be punished by god; incur *divine punishment*.
しんぱつじしん 深発地震 a deep(-)focus earthquake.
ジンバブエ 〖国名〗Zimbabwe /zimbá:bwei/; (公式名) the Republic of Zimbabwe. (首都 Harare) ● ジンバブエ人 a zimbabwean. ● ジンバブエ(人)の Zimbabwean.
しんばりぼう 心張り棒 a bar.
シンバル 〖楽器〗cymbals /símblz/. ● シンバルの(じゃんという)音 a [the] clash of (the) *cymbals*. ● シンバルを鳴らす 叩 [clash] the *cymbals* (together).
しんぱん 審判 ❶〖事件などの〗judgment; (⇨裁決, 判決) ● 最後の審判 The Last Judgment. ● 審判を下す pass *judgment* (*on* him). ❷〖審判員〗(競技などの) a judge (⇨審査 [審査員]); (野球・テニスなどの) an umpire; (ボクシング・フットボールなどの) a referee; 〖判定〗a decision.

〖関連〗いろいろな審判: 〖野球〗主審 an umpire-in-chief/球審 a plate umpire/塁審 a base umpire.
〖サッカー〗主審 a chief referee/副審 an assistant referee/第四の審判 a fourth official/審判団 match official(s).

● 審判をする [務める] judge; umpire; referee. ▶だれが(野球の)審判を務めますか Who are going to *umpire* (the baseball game) [*call the ball game*]?
しんぱん 信販 〖「信用販売」の略〗a credit sale.
しんぱん 侵犯 图 (a) violation.
── 侵犯する 動 ▶日本の領空を侵犯する *violate* Japanese airspace.
しんぱん 新版 (新刊) a new publication; (改版) a new edition.
しんぴ 神秘 图 a mystery. ● 神秘(のベール)に包まれている be wrapped [lost] in *mystery*. ● 神秘のベールをはぐ remove the *mystery* (*from*). ● 宇宙の神秘を探る explore the *mysteries* of the universe.
── 神秘的な 形 mysterious /mistíəriəs/; (宗教的に) mystic(al) (〖限定的に〗). ● 神秘的な笑み a *mysterious* smile. ● 神秘的な儀式 *mystic* rites.
● 神秘主義 mysticism.
しんぴ 真否 ● 真否を確かめる ascertain [find out] whether it is true or not.
じんぴ 靭皮 〖植物〗bast.
しんびがん 審美眼 (美的感覚) an aesthetic /esθétik/ sense; a sense of beauty. ● 審美眼がある have a sense of beauty; have an eye for the beautiful.
シンビジウム 〖植物〗a cymbidium.
しんぴつ 真筆 one's own handwriting.
しんぴつ 親筆 handwriting by a person of high rank.
しんぴょうせい 信憑性 reliability. ● 信憑性のある[ない] reliable [unreliable].
しんぴん 新品 a new article. ● 新品のドレス a *new* [a *brand-new*] dress. ● 私の時計は新品同様だ This watch is (as) good as [is practically] *new*. (⚠《表示》では 'As new')
じんぴん 人品 ● 人品卑しからぬ refined; 《a woman》

しんぶ 深部 the depth(s) 《of》.

しんぷ 神父 a priest;《尊称, 呼びかけ》Father. ● ブラウン神父 *Father* Brown.

しんぷ 新婦 a bride.《⇨新郎》

しんぷ 新譜 (CD など) a new release;(曲譜) a new score.

しんぷう 新風 ● 政界に新風を吹き込む breathe *new life* into the political world.

シンフォニー [[交響楽[曲]]][[音楽]] a symphony.

しんぷく 心服 —— 心服する動[[書]] revere; respect and admire《him》very much; hold《him》in high [great] esteem.

しんぷく 振幅 [[電気]] amplitude (of vibration).

しんふぜん 心不全 heart failure; [[医学]] cardiac insufficiency.

じんふぜん 腎不全 [[医学]] renal /riːnl/ failure.

しんぶつ 神仏 gods and Buddha. ● 神仏の加護を祈る pray for *divine* protection.

じんぶつ 人物 ❶[[人]] a person, (男性) a man (複 men), (女性) a woman (複 women);《⇨人, 男》;(有名・重要) a figure (⇦ 前に形容詞を伴う); (劇・小説などの登場人物) a character; (変わっている, おもしろい, 個性的な)《話》a character. ● 実在の人物 a real *person*. ● 重要人物 an important *person [figure]*; a *man [figure]* of importance;《話》a VIP /víːàipíː/ (*a very important person* の略). ● 偉大な人物 a great *man [woman, figure, character]*. ● 歴史上の人物 a historical *figure [character]*. ▶彼は大した人物だ He is quite a *man*./He is (a) *somebody*.《⇔*nobody*》. ▶彼は要注意人物だ He is a *man* you should keep your eye on.
❷[人柄, 性格] (人から見た印象を総合した) personality;(道徳的に言う)character. ((人格, 性格, 人間)) ▶彼の人物は保証します I (can) assure you he's a good [nice] *man*. ▶彼の言うことを聞くと彼がどんな人物かが分かる His remarks show the *kind of man he is*.
❸ 上半身の絵をさす

シンプル —— シンプルな 形 simple.《⇨簡素》

＊しんぶん 新聞 a newspaper,《やや話》a paper;(集合的)the press 単・複両扱い》.
① [~新聞, 新聞~] ● 日刊新聞 a daily (*newspaper [paper]*). ● 英字新聞 an English *newspaper*. ● 朝日新聞 *the Asahi*. ● 地方新聞 a local *newspaper*. ● 大新聞 a major [leading] *newspaper*. ● 水曜日の新聞発表 a newspaper [a news] report published on Wednesday. ▶新聞報道は否定的だった The *press* report was negative.
②[新聞が[は]] ▶すべての新聞がその事故を簡単に報道した All *newspapers* covered the accident briefly./All *newspapers* gave brief coverage to the accident. ▶すべての新聞はその記事を1面に載せた All *newspapers* put the story on their front page./All *newspapers* frontpaged the story. ▶新聞は世界の出来事を教えてくれます The *newspapers* tell us what is happening [(話) going on] in the world. ▶新しい新聞が出た A new *newspaper* was launched.
③[新聞の] ● 新聞の切り抜き《米》a *newspaper* [a *press*] clipping;《英》a *newspaper* [a *press*] cutting. ● 新聞の見出し a *newspaper* headline.(❗単にa headlineのことが多い) ● 新聞の三面記事 a human interest page; the third human interest page. ▶ヨーロッパの新聞の論調 the tone of the *press* in Europe. ▶彼は地元の新聞のスポーツ記者です He is a sportswriter for [on] the local *newspaper*.
④[新聞に] ● 新聞に広告を出す put [place] an advertisement in the *newspaper*. ● 新聞に眼を通す browse a *newspaper*. ▶それは新聞に載るだろう It will appear [be reported] in *papers*. ▶今日の新聞にはいい記事は一つもない Today's *newspaper* carries no fine articles.
⑤[新聞を] ● 新聞を広げる open a *newspaper*. ● 新聞を家々に配達する deliver newspapers to houses [(from) door to door]. ▶あなたは何新聞をとっていますか What *paper* do you get [take, read]?/What *paper* do you buy [receive] regularly?《⇨購読》▶彼の汚職事件は新聞をにぎわした His corruption scandal made him big *news*.(❗この news は「新聞種」の意)《⇨マスコミ》
⑥[新聞によると] ▶それは新聞で読み [知り] ました I read [saw] it in the *newspaper*. ▶今日の新聞によるとチリで大地震があったそうです Today's *paper* says (that) there was a great earthquake in Chile./《やや書》According to today's *newspaper*, there was a great earthquake in Chile./《書》It says [It is reported, ×It is said] in today's *newspaper* that there was a great earthquake in Chile.
● 新聞売り場 (駅などの) a newsstand. ● 新聞記事 a newspaper article《on, about》; a story. ● 新聞記者 a newspaper reporter [editor]; a newsperson [(男の) a newspaperman]. ● 新聞雑誌 newspapers and magazines. ● 新聞紙 (a piece of) newspaper. ● 新聞社 a newspaper company. ● 新聞社に勤める work for a *newspaper*. ● 新聞小説 a serial [serialized] novel in a newspaper. ● 新聞少年 a newsboy; a paperboy.(❗a newspaper boy ともいう) ● 新聞種 a news matter [item]. ▶あの歌手はまた新聞種になっている That singer is in the *news* [has made *news*] again. ● 新聞配達 newspaper delivery;(仕事としての) (do) a paper route《米》[round《英》]. ● 新聞販売人《米》a newsdealer;《英》a newsagent. ▶店は a newsagent's (shop). ● 新聞屋 a newspaper man. ● 新聞連載 a newspaper serial.

じんぷん 人糞 feces; excrement; (下肥) human manure,《婉曲的》night soil.

じんぶんかがく 人文科学 the humanities;(学科)humane studies.(❗cultural studiesは「教養学科」の意)

じんぶんしゅぎ 人文主義 humanism.

しんぺい 新兵 a recruit /rikrúːt/.

じんべい 甚平 *jinbei*;(説明的に) indoor summer clothes [clothing, wear] for men.

しんぺいけものがたり『新平家物語』*The Heike Story*.《参考》吉川英治の小説

しんぺん 身辺 ● 身辺を警護する (人を守る) guard《him》. ● 身辺(の事柄)の整理をする put one's *affairs* in order. ● 身辺の世話をする《⇨身の回り》

しんぺん 新編 a new edition.

＊しんぽ 進歩 名 [[目標に向かっての着実なまた著しい前進]] prógress; [[前進していくレベルに達すること]] (an) advánce; [[改良, 向上]] (an) improvement. ● 急速な科学技術の進歩 rapid technological *progress [advance]*. ▶科学の進歩によって世界はだんだん狭くなる The world is growing smaller with the *progress [advance(s)]* of science. ▶彼は学業にあまり進歩(の跡)が見られない He doesn't show much *progress* in his studies. ▶彼の最近作は前作に比べ進歩がある His latest work is an *advance* [an *improvement*] on his previous one.(❗いずれも

しんぼう

「進歩したもの」の意で ⓒ ▶このチームは進歩が早い This team is *improving* quickly. ▶小さなころから今日までもっとも進歩しなかったし，ものの考え方も変わらない I've made no *progress* since my childhood, and my way of looking at things has not changed, (either).

■**DISCOURSE**
ここの「進歩」という言葉で私は，すべての人が健康で快適な生活を送ることができることを意味している By "*progress*" here(,) I mean that every person can live a healthy and comfortable life. (By ... here I mean that〜. (...によってここでは〜を意味する)は定義に用いる表現)

── **進歩的な** 形 (革新的な) progréssive; (進んだ) advanced. ●進歩的な思想 a *progressive* [an *advanced*] idea. ●進歩的な人物 a *progressive* (person); an avant-garde person.

── **進歩する** 動 make* prógress [an advance] 《in》, (やや書) prógress 《in》; (やや書) advance 《in》; improve 《in》. ▶彼は英語が著しく進歩した He has made (ˣa) remarkable *progress* in English./He has *improved* [*progressed*, *advanced*] remarkably in English./His English (ability) has remarkably *improved*. ▶医学はここ10年間に大いに進歩した Medicine has made great *advances* [*progress*] during the last ten years./There have been great *advances* in medicine during the past ten years.

●進歩主義 progressivism.

***しんぼう 辛抱** 名 patience; (長期の忍耐) endurance (⇨我慢); [積極的な努力] perseverance. (⇨根気)
●辛抱強い patient. ●辛抱強く patiently, with patience; (頑張って) with perseverance. ▶近頃の若い者は辛抱が足らぬ Young people these days lack *patience* [*perseverance*]. ▶私は辛抱強く彼が戻るのを待った I waited *patiently* for him to return.

── **辛抱する** 動 (話) put* up with ... (❗耐えることよりあきらめを含意する); (苦痛・悲しみなど重みに) bear*; (忍耐強く耐え忍ぶ) (やや書) endure (⇨我慢する); [頑張り続ける] persevére 《in, with》. ▶彼のいやがらせを辛抱する *put up with* his dirty [nasty] trick.
●辛抱して成し遂げる persevére in carrying it out. ●苦労を辛抱する覚悟がなくてはならない You must be ready to *bear* [*endure*] hardships.

しんぼう 心房 [解剖] an atrium (電 atria, 〜s). ●右[左]心房 the right [left] atrium.

しんぼう 心棒 (車軸) an axle; (機械類の) a shaft; [活動の中心人物] a key figure.

しんぼう 信望 [信用] cónfidence, [人気] populárity. ●上司の信望を得る[失う] win [lose] the *confidence* of his boss. ▶彼は上司の信望が厚い He is trusted by [has the *confidence* of] his boss.

しんぼう 深謀 a well-thought-out plan [strategy]; a prudent scheme.
●深謀遠慮 the sagacity of the far-sighted and considerate.

しんぽう 信奉 名 フロイトの信奉者 a believer in [(追随者) a follower of, (熱烈な支持者) an adhérent of] Freud /frɔ́ɪd/.

── **信奉する** 動 フロイトを信奉する believe in [(信じきる) have faith in] Freud.

しんぽう 新法 (法令) a new law; (方法) a new method.

じんぼう 人望 populárity. ●人望を集める[失う] win [lose] *populárity*; become popular [unpopular]. ●人望がある be popular 《with, among》; enjoy *populárity* 《with, among》.

しんぼく 神木 a sacred tree.

しんぼく 親睦 (友愛) friendship. ●親睦を深める promote *friendship* 《between》; cement one's *friendship* 《with》; (理解を深める) know each other better.
●親睦会 a party; (話) a get-together; a social gathering. ●親睦試合 (play) a friendly game.

シンポジウム a sympósium (電 〜s, sympósia). ●国際エイズシンポジウム an international AIDS *symposium*; an international *symposium* on AIDS. ●大気汚染についてのシンポジウムを行う[組む] hold [organize] a *symposium* on air pollution.

シンホニー [交響楽[曲]]. (⇨シンフォニー)

シンボリック symbolic.

シンボル [象徴] a symbol.
●シンボルマーク a symbol; (学校・市・国などの) an emblem; (会社の) a logo /lóʊɡoʊ/; (和製語) a symbol mark.

しんぽん 新本 a (brand-)new book; (新刊) a newly published book.

しんまい 新米 ❶ [経験の浅い人] a novice, 《やや書》a fresh hand; [初心者] a beginner. ●新米写真家 a *novice* photographer; a *novice at* photographing [in photography]. ❷ [米] new rice.

じんましん 蕁麻疹 [医学] hives (❗単・複両扱い); 《英》(a) nettle rash. ●ビールを飲むとひどいじんましんが出る get [develop] severe *hives* from drinking beer. ▶じんましんが出た I broke out with *hives*.

しんみ 新味 ●新味を出す add something new; show originality 《in》. ●新味のない commonplace; (使い古された) trite. ●新味のある計画 a *novel* plan.

しんみ 親身 ●親身の(=親切な)指導 kind [(心遣いのある) careful, (その人には特別な) special] instruction. ●その子を親身になって世話する look after that child *kindly* [(愛情を持って) affectionately, (やさしい心遣いで) with tender [loving] care]. ●親身になって聞く give a sympathetic ear 《to her problem》; be an empathetic listener.

しんみつ 親密 ── **親密な** 形 good, close, great; (慣れ親しい) familiar; (仲のよい) friendly. (⇨親しい)
▶彼とは親密だ I am *friendly* [*good*] *friends* with him./(親しい気遣いで) He is my *close* friend./(親しい間柄だ) I am on *close* [*friendly*] terms with him. ▶彼らはすぐに親密になった(=友達になった) They made [became] friends [ˣa friend] with each other at once.

じんみゃく 人脈 personal connections [relationship]; a network. ●しっかりした人脈を持つ [have] a strong *network* of friends [business people, etc.] ▶その会合は人脈を作る[広げる]いい機会だった The meeting was a good opportunity to do some *networking*.

しんみょう 神妙 ── **神妙な** 形 [おとないし] gentle; meek; [従順な] docile /dάsɪl/; [忠実な] faithful. (⇨おとなしい) ●神妙な態度 a *docile* attitude. ●神妙な(=まじめな)顔つき a serious look.

しんみり ●しんみりと(=静かに)話す speak *quietly*. ●しんみりする(=悲しくなる) become *sad*. ●しんみりとした話 a *sad* [(心を動かす) *touching*, a *moving*] story.

しんみん 臣民 a subject.

じんみん 人民 the people. (❗複数扱い) (⇨国民)
●中国人民 the *people* of China; the Chinese (*people*). ●人民の権利を尊重する respect civil [*people's*] rights. ●人民の人民による人民のための政

治 government óf the *people*, bý the *people*, fór the *people*. (参考 Lincolnの民主主義の理念を述べた言葉)
- 人民公社 a people's cómmune. ● 人民裁判 a people's court; 《婉曲的》 popular justice.
- 人民戦線 a popular front.

しんめ 新芽 (茎・枝になるべき) a sprout; (若芽) a shoot; (葉芽、花芽) a bud. (⇨芽)

しんめい 身命 one's life. ● 身命を捧げる sacrifice one's life 《for》.
- 身命を賭(と)して ▶身命を賭して(=命を危険にさらして)戦う fight at the risk of one's life.

じんめい 人名 a person's name.
- 人名漢字 a limited number of Chinese characters whose use for personal names is authorized. ● 人名辞典 a biographical dictionary.

じんめい 人命 (a) life (複 lives). (!個人の人命では ⓒ) ▶その災害で多くの人命が失われた A lot of *lives* were lost in the disaster. ▶彼は人命救助で表彰された He was honored for saving a *life* [for the rescue work].
- 人命救助法 lifesaving.

じんめん 人面 a face (of human being).
- 人面獣心(じゅうしん) ● 人面獣心の輩 a heartless fellow; a fellow as heartless as a brute.
- 人面魚 'a human face-fish'; a fish that seems to have a human-like face.

しんめんもく 真面目 one's true worth [ability, self]. ● 真面目を発揮する prove one's worth [ability]; show [display] one's ability.

しんもつ 進物 (贈答品) a gift; (贈り物) a present. ▶これを進物用に包んでいただきたいのですが I'd like this *gift-wrapped* [*wrapped as a gift*]./Could you *gift-wrap* this for me?

しんもん 審問 图 《法律》 (an) examination; (聴聞) a hearing; (調査) an inquiry.
── **審問する** 動 examine; hear.

じんもん 尋問 图 questioning; (法廷での) (an) examination; (警察での) (an) interrogation. ● 反対尋問 《法律》 (a) cross-*examination*. ● 誘導尋問 a leading *question*. ▶誘導尋問をする lead a witness. ▶容疑者は警察のきびしい尋問を受けた The suspect *was* severely *questioned* [(きびしく尋問された)(話) *was grilled*] by the police.
── **尋問する** 動 question; examine; interrogate.

しんや 深夜 midnight. (⇨真夜中) ● 深夜営業をしている be open till late at night. ▶試験に備えて深夜まで勉強した I studied until *midnight* [*late at night*] preparing for the exam. ▶彼らは深夜まで話し合った They talked *far into the night*.
- 深夜映画 a midnight movie. ● 深夜バス a late-night bus (service). ● 深夜番組 a midnight [a late-night] program. ● 深夜料金 a late-night charge [rate].

しんやく 新薬 a new medicine [drug].

しんやくせいしょ 新約聖書 the New Testament (略 N.T., NT).

しんゆう 親友 a close [a good, a great, 《書》 a bosom /búzəm/] friend, one's best friend. (! intimate, familiarは異性間では性的な関係を暗示するため使われない方がよい) ▶ぼくたちは大の親友になった We became *the best of friends*. ▶彼女は親友といえる友達はあまりいない She doesn't have many *good friends*.

‡しんよう 信用 图 《信頼》(主観に基づく本能的な) trust; (頼りにして信頼すること) reliance; (証拠に基づく確信のある) confidence; (信念に基づいた一方的で強い) faith (⇨信頼); (取り引き上の) credit; 《評判》 reputation.
① 【信用が】 ● 信用がおける reliable; dependable; trustworthy. ▶彼は彼女に大変信用がある He enjoys her great *confidence* [*trust*]./(信用されている) He *is* much *trusted* by her. ▶その店の信用が落ちた The store's *credit* [*reputation*] has suffered (=has increased). ▶その店は信用がある That store has [enjoys] a *good reputation*./That is a *reputable* store. ▶私はこの銀行に信用がない I'm not *trusted* by the bank.
② 【信用を】 ● 信用を勝ち得る win 《his》 *confidence*. ▶彼は彼女の信用を失った[得た] He has lost [won, gained] her *confidence*. ▶その不祥事が店の信用を傷つけた The scandal has injured our store's *credit* [*reputation*].
③ 【信用で】 ▶彼は信用(=つけ)でそれを買った He bought it *on credit*.
── **信用できる** 形 trustworthy; reliable; (評判のよい) réputable (⇨图①). ● 信用できる店 a *reputable* store. ● 信用できる友人 a *trustworthy* [a *reliable*] friend; a friend *to be trusted* [*to be relied upon*]. ▶じゃあ君は彼が信用できない(=不正直だ)と言うんだね So you're saying he's *dishonest*. ▶彼が強盗にあったという話はどの程度信用できる? How *believable* is his story that he was robbed?
── **信用する** 動 trust; put* trust 《confidence, faith》《*in*》(! 「信用している」の意には have*を用いる); (信じる) believe. ● 彼を信用して金を預ける *entrust* [*trust*] him *with* the money; *entrust* [*trust*] the money *to* him. ▶おれのことを信用してくれ、すべてちゃんとやるから Please *trust* me [*put your trust in* me] and I will take good care of everything. ▶私は彼の言うことを信用していない I *have* no *trust* [*confidence*, *faith*] *in* what he says./I *distrust* [(やや書) *mistrust*, (疑う) *doubt*] what he says. (!distrustの方が mistrustより不信の念が強い)/I don't believe him [what he says]. (! I don't *believe in* him. は「彼の(人格)を信用していない」の意) ▶彼は絶対に飛行機で旅行しない。飛行機を信用していないから He never travels by air because he doesn't *trust* airplanes.
- 信用買い margin buying [purchase]. ● 信用貸し付け a loan on credit. ● 信用金庫 a credit bank. ● 信用組合 a credit union. ● 信用状 a letter of credit 《略 L/C》. ● 信用性 credibility; reliability; believability. ● 耐震信用性 seismic credibility. ● 信用調査 a credit check. ● 信用取引 a credit transaction. (!しばしば複数形で) ● 信用販売 a credit sale.

じんよう 陣容 ❶【陣立て】(a) battle formation. ▶陣容を整えた軍勢 troops in *battle formation*.
❷【顔ぶれ】a lineup; (構成員) staff (! 単・複両扱い). ▶次の試合のために陣容を変える change one's *lineup* for the next match. ▶この大学の教授の陣容は立派だ This university has a fine teaching *staff* [《米》 a fine *faculty*].

しんようじゅ 針葉樹 a coniferous tree, a conifer. (⇔ 広葉樹)

‡しんらい 信頼 图 《主観に基づく本能的な》 trust; (頼りにして信頼すること) reliance; 《証拠に基づいた理性的な》 confidence; 《信念に基づいた一方的で強い》 faith. (⇨信用) ● 教師を生徒との信頼関係を築く establish a relationship of mutual *trust* between teachers and students. ● 人々の警察に対する信頼 people's *confidence* in the police. ▶皆さんの信頼に応えるようがんばります I will work hard to live up to the *trust* you *have* placed in me. ▶彼は私の信

頼を裏切った[得た；失った] He betrayed [won; lost] my *trust* [*confidence*] *in* him. ▶彼の判断は信頼がおける His judgment is *reliable*./His judgment is something you can *have faith in*. ▶そのデータの信頼性は高い The *reliability* of the data is high.
── 信頼できる 形 trustworthy; reliable; (頼りになる) dependable. ●信頼できる筋によれば according to *reliable* [*authoritative*] sources; I have it on *good authority* 《*that* 節》. ▶彼は信頼できる人ですか Is he *trustworthy* [*reliable, dependable*]? (⇨信用できる)
── 信頼する 動 trust; put* trust 《confidence, faith》《in》. ●彼は両親を全面的に信頼している He *has* complete *trust* [*perfect confidence*] *in* his parents./He *trusts* his parents completely. ▶彼の教師としての能力をもっと信頼すべきです You should *put* more *confidence in* his teaching ability. ▶彼は上司から信頼されている He has [enjoys] his superiors' *confidence* [*trust*]./He *is trusted* by his superiors. ▶彼女なら信頼して赤ん坊の世話を任せられる You can *trust* [*put your trust in*] her *to* look after your baby.

しんらい 新来 ── 新来の 形 new; newly-arrived. ●新来の客[患者] a *new* guest [patient].

しんらつ 辛辣 ── 辛辣な 形 (人・規則などがきびしい) severe; (言葉・気性などが激しい) sharp; (痛烈な) biting. ●しんらつな批評をする make a *severe* [a *sharp*] criticism 《against him》; criticize 《him》 severely [*sharply*]. ●しんらつな発言をする make a *cutting* remark. ●しんらつな皮肉で非難する condemn 《him》 in *biting* [*bitter*] irony. ▶しんらつな男だ(=毒舌の持ち主だ) He has a *sharp* [a *biting*] tongue.

しんらばんしょう 森羅万象 everything in the universe [under the sun].

*しんり 心理 名 a state [a frame] of mind; psychology /saikáləd ʒi/; mentality.

> 使い分け **a state of mind** 一時的な精神状態や気分を表す.
> **psychology** 心理学的に見た心的状態・気持ちを表す.
> **mentality** 考え方やものの見方, 態度を表す.

●戦争心理 a war *mentality*. ●群集心理 mass [mob] *psychology*. ▶彼女は夫の心理がよく分からない She doesn't understand her husband's *psychology* [*state of mind*]./(何を考えているのか分からない) She doesn't understand *what* her husband *is thinking about*.
── 心理の, 心理的な 形 psychological; mental. ●その女性の心理描写をする give a *psychological* description of the woman. ▶彼女の犬嫌いは心理的なものだ Her fear of dogs is a *psychological* one.
●心理作用 a mental process. ●心理小説 a psychological novel. ●心理療法 psychotherapy.

*しんり 真理 (a) truth. ●科学的真理 scientific *truths*; the *truths* of science. ●永遠の真理 an eternal *truth*. ●真理の探求 the pursuit of (the) *truth*. ●真理を探求する pursue [seek] (the) *truth*. ▶君の言うことには一応の真理がある There is some *truth* in what you say.

しんり 審理 名 (裁判) trial. ●審理中 be on *trial*.
── 審理する 動 try, judge.

しんりがく 心理学 psychology /saikáləd ʒi/. ●児童[教育; 異常; 犯罪]心理学 child's [educational; abnormal; criminal] *psychology*.

●心理学者 a psychologist. ●心理言語学 psycholinguistics.

じんりきしゃ 人力車 a rickshaw. ●人力車に乗る ride in a *rickshaw*. ●人力車を引く pull a *rickshaw*.

*しんりゃく 侵略 名 〔不当に戦争をしかけること〕aggression; 〔侵入〕 (an) invasion. ●日本軍による中国侵略 the *invasion of* 《✕into, ✕to》 China by the Japanese army; the *invasion of* the Japanese army *into* China. (❗前の方の of は目的格, 後の方の of は主格)
──侵略する 動 (侵入する) invade. ▶その国はヒットラーに侵略された The country *was invaded* by Hitler.
●侵略行為 an act of aggression. ●侵略国 an aggressor (nation). ●侵略者 an aggressor; (侵入者) an invader. ●侵略戦争 an aggressive war; a war of aggression.

しんりょう 診療 〔治療〕medical treatment [care] (⇨治療); 〔診察〕a medical examination, consultation (⇨診察).
●診療時間 consultation hours. ●診療室 an examination room. ●診療所 a clinic; (工場などに附属している) an infirmary.

しんりょうないか 心療内科 psychosomatic medicine; (病院内の) the department of psychosomatic medicine.

しんりょく 深緑 dark [deep] green.

しんりょく 新緑 ●春の木々の新緑 the *new* [*fresh*] *green leaves* of the trees in spring; 《書・詩》 the *fresh verdure* of spring. ●新緑の季節 the season of *fresh green* 《書・詩》 *fresh verdure*).

じんりょく 人力 human power [strength]. ▶それは人力ではどうすることもできない It is beyond *human power* [*control*]./It is humanly impossible.

じんりょく 尽力 名 〔骨折り〕good offices (複数形で); 〔努力〕《やや書》 (an) exertion; 〔助力〕help, support. ●彼の尽力で through [owing to] his *good offices*. ●その方々から尽力を賜る receive a great deal of *support* from them.
──尽力する 動 (精一杯の努力をする) make every (possible) effort 《*to* do》; (最善を尽くす) do one's best 《*to* do》.

*しんりん 森林 (a) forest; a wood. (⇨森) ●深い森林 (a) dense [(a) thick] *forest*. ▶南米の森林には多くの野生動物が生息している Many wild animals live in the *forests* of South America. ●森林浴をする do *forest* [*sylvan*] *breathing*; (説明的に) breathe healthy air [take a therápeutic walk] in the *woods* [*mountains*].
●森林火災 forest fires. ●森林資源 forest resources. ●森林巡視員 a (forest) ranger. ●森林地方[地帯] a forest area; a wooded region; woodland(s). ●森林鉄道 a forest railway. ●森林破壊 the destruction of forests; (大規模の乱伐[伐採]) deforestation. ●森林保護 forest conservation. ●森林浴 forest therapy.

じんりん 人倫 (道義) morality; (人情) humanity. ●人倫にもとる be immoral [inhuman, against *humanity*].

*しんるい 親類 〔人〕 a relative /rélətiv/, a relation /riléiʃən/. (❗《米》では relative が好まれる. 《英》では relation が好まれ, relative は《書》. (2) ともに親子兄弟を含み広く身内・親族を表す. (3) 米英では血のつながる親類を a blood relation, 結婚による親類を a relation by marriage という) ●私の父方の親類 a *relative* on my father's side; 《書》 a paternal *relative* of mine. ●親類づきあいをしない do not associate as *relatives*. ▶彼はぼくの遠い[近い]親類だ He is a distant [a close] *relative* of mine. (❗通例 × ...*my* relative とはいわない)/He is distantly [closely] *related* to me. ▶彼らはよく似ているが親類ですか They rather look alike. Are they *related to* each other?

●**親類縁者** one's relatives by blood and marriage [《書》in blood and law]. ●**親類書き** written information on one's relatives. ●**親類関係** relationship 《*to*》.

しんるい 進塁 ── **進塁する 動**〖野球〗advance [move]《*to* second》. ●バントで走者を進塁させる move a runner along [over] on a bunt. ▶そのパスボールで 2 走者が進塁した The two runners *advanced* on the passed ball.

*じ**んるい 人類**《集合的》mànkind. (❗無冠詞. 通例単・複両扱い. 代名詞は it, they); the human race,《書》humanity;〖動物に対して〗human beings (❗無冠詞. 複数扱い); man (❗無冠詞).

┌─使い分け─ **mankind** 過去・現在・未来にわたるすべての人類を集合的に表す語.
the human race, humanity mankind と同様に人類を集合的にいうが, humanity はもっぱら好ましい性格をいうときに用いられる.
human beings 動物に対して「人」を表す語.
man mankind の意で用いられる堅い語で人間の普遍的性質を強調する. 男性中心を避けて the human race, humanity, human beings, humans, people などを用いることが多くなってきた. ┘

●**人類の歴史** human history; the history of *mankind*. ▶核兵器は人類の最大の敵だ Nuclear weapons are *man*'s greatest enemy [the greatest enemy of *mankind*]. ▶人類は自ら絶滅を招くかもしれない The human race may cause its own extinction.

●**人類学** anthropology. ●**人類学者** an anthropologist.
しんれい 心霊 psychic /sáikik/. ●**心霊作用を受けやすい** psychic.
●**心霊現象** a psychic phenomenon (㉘ phenomena). ●**心霊能力** psychic powers.
しんろ 針路 a course. ●**針路を東にとる** set *course* for east; head east (❗この east は副詞 (⇨向かう)). ●**針路からそれる** go off [《やや書》deviate from] the *course*.
しんろ 進路 a course; (将来の) one's future course [career]. ●**進路を変更する** change one's *course*. ●**進路指導をする** counsel《a student》on his *future course*. ●**台風の進路(=通り道)に当たる** be in the *path* of a typhoon. ▶卒業後の進路は決まりましたか Have you decided what to do [on your *future course*] after graduation? (❗後の方は堅い言い方)
しんろう 心労〖気苦労〗care;〖心配〗worry, anxiety (❗3 語とも具体的なものをいうときは複数形になる);〖精神的緊張〗(a) strain. ▶心労が重なって彼女は病気になった Cares [*Anxieties, Worries*] made her sick. ▶彼は心労で倒れた He collapsed *under the strain*.
しんろう 新郎 a (bride)groom. (❗今は a groom が普通) ●**新郎新婦** the bride and (×the) *groom* (❗語順にも注意); the bridal couple.
じんろく 甚六 ●**総領の甚六** (⇨総領 [成句])
しんわ 神話 a myth /miθ/;《集合的》mythology. ●**ギリシャ神話** the Greek *myths*; Greek *mythology*. (❗ローマ神話と合わせて classical mythology ということもある) ●**神話上の英雄** a *mythical* hero.
●**神話学** mythology.
しんわ 親和 (親睦) friendship.
●**親和力**〖化学〗affinity.

す

す 巣 ❶ 〖鳥・虫・小動物・爬虫(はちゅう)類・魚など〗a nest (❗ミツバチ以外のハチも含む); (ミツバチの) (a) honeycomb, (人工の) a beehive; (クモの) a (spider's) web, a cobweb, 《米》a spider web; (野獣の) a lair; a den. ● 鳥の巣 a bird's [a birds', a bird] nest (鳥の巣は birds' nests). ● アリの巣 an ants' nest. ● 悪の巣 a *den* of iniquity; (売春婦の) a *den* of vice. ● 盗賊の巣 a *den* of thieves. ● 愛の巣 one's warm *nest*. ● 巣ごもり nesting. ● 巣ごもり(鳥などが)作る (鳥などが) build [make] a *nest*. ● (クモが)巣をかける spin [weave] a *web*. ● 巣につく sit on [in] a *nest*; nest.
❷ 〖遊び場, たまり場〗a haunt /hɔ́ːnt/. (❗悪人の「巣」にも用いる)

す 州 a sandbar, a sandbank, a shoal. (❗いずれも満潮時に水没する)

す 酢 vinegar /vínigər/. ● 野菜を酢につける pickle vegetables in *vinegar*. (⇨酢漬け)
● 酢の物 (⇨酢の物) ● 酢水 lightly-vinegared water.

す 鬆 〖大根などの〗a pore; 〖鋳物の〗(空洞部分) a cavity.; (気泡) a blowhole. ▶ この大根にはすが入っている This white radish is *pithy*.

***ず** 図 〖説明のための〗(簡単な) a diagram; (番号を打った) a figure (❗後の語は通例 Fig. 1, Fig. 2 (第1図, 第2図)のように用いる); 〖絵〗a picture; (鉛筆・ペンなどでかいた) a drawing; (大ざっぱな) a sketch; (さし絵, 説明図) an illustration; 〖気象・統計などの〗a chart; 〖平面図〗a plan; 〖グラフ〗a graph. ● 排水システムの図 a [the] *diagram* of the drainage system. ● 気象〖統計〗図 a weather [statistical] *chart*. ● コンサートホールの座席図 a seating *plan* of a concert hall. ● 家の見取り図をかく make a *sketch* [draw a *plan*] of a house. (❗後の方は本格的な図面をかくことをいう) ● 9ページ第5図に示されている図を be shown in *Fig*. [*Figure*] 5 on page 9. ● 図で説明する illustrate 〖it〗 by a *diagram*.
● 図に当たる ▶ 新企画は図に当たった(=うまく行った) The new plan worked (out) well [成功した] went (on) successfully, proved a (great) success].
● 図に乗る ▶ 彼は試験に満点をとって図に乗っている(=思い上がっている) He *is conceited* because he got full marks in the exam.

ず 頭 ● 頭が高い be arrogant, be stuck up; (人を人とも思わない) not be respectful.

すあし 素足 a bare foot (複 feet). (⇨裸足(はだし))

すあな 巣穴 a nest (hole), a burrow.

ずあん 図案 a design; (繰り返し模様) a pattern. (⇨デザイン)
● 図案家 a designer.

すい 粋 图 〖精髄〗(やや書) éssence, 《書》the quintéssence; 〖最良の部分〗the best (part); the cream. ● 最先端技術の粋を集めたロケット a rocket built with the very *essence* of the most advanced technology.
—— 粋な 形 ● 粋な人 (=人情の機微に通じた人) a man [a woman] of the world.

すい 酸い sour /sáuər/. (⇨酸っぱい)
● 酸いも甘いもかみ分けた ▶ 酸いも甘いもかみ分けた(=世事に明るい)人 a man [a woman] of the world. ▶ 彼女は酸いも甘いもかみ分けた人だ She is well experienced in the way of the world./She knows [has tasted] the sweets and bitters of life. (❗最も日本語に近いが, 文学的な表現)

ずい 隋 〖中国の王朝〗the Sui (dynasty).

ずい 髄 (動物の) marrow; (植物の) pith.

すいあげる 吸い上げる suck [(ポンプで) pump] ... up 《from》. ● 水を吸い上げる suck [absorb] water 《from the soil》. ● 意見を吸い上げる take up the opinion; get [draw] the ideas 《from the consumers》. ● 人の利益を吸い上げる exploit.

すいあつ 水圧 water pressure. ▶ 水圧が高い〖上がる〗The *water pressure* is high 〖↔low〗 [rises 〖↔drops〗].

すいい 水位 water level. ▶ 水位が高い〖上がった〗The *water level* is high [went up, rose].

すいい 推移 图 〖変化〗a change; 〖進展〗development; 〖移行〗(a) transition. ● 時代の推移とともに with the *change* of the times. ● 事態の推移(=進展)を見守る watch the *development* of the situation; watch how things will turn out.
—— 推移する 動 ● 徐々に推移する change [develop] gradually; undergo a gradual change [transition]. ● ほぼ現状のまま推移する remain [stay] almost as it is; *change* (very) little.

ずいい 随意 — 随意(の) 形 〖自由選択できる〗optional; (自由の) free; (自発的な) voluntary /válantèri/. ▶ 服装随意 (パーティーなどの招待状で) Dress *optional*. ● 私の机をご随意にお使いください Please feel [You *are*] *free* to use my desk. (⇨自由に)/You can use my desk *freely* [(好きな時はいつでも) *whenever* you *like*]. ▶ 寄付は随意です Contributions are *optional* [*voluntary*]./You have the *option* of contributing or not.
● 随意筋 〖解剖〗a voluntary muscle.

すいいき 水域 an area 〖地帯〗a zone] (of the sea). ● 200 海里漁業専管水域 a 200-mile exclusive fishery *area* [*zone*]. ● テムズ川上流の水域 the upper *reaches* of the Thames.

ずいいち 随一 ● 当代随一の作家 the greatest writer of our age [today]. ● セントラルリーグ随一の打者 the *best* hitter in the Central League. ● 日本随一の名勝地 *the most* picturesque place in Japan.

スイート (⇨スイートルーム)

スイートコーン sweet corn.

スイートスポット 〖スポーツ〗a sweet spot. (〖参考〗ボールが当たると最もよく飛ぶ部分) ● バットのスイートスポットでボールを打つ hit a ball with the *sweet spot* of a bat.

スイートハート 〖恋人, 愛人〗a sweetheart.

スイートピー 〖植物〗a sweet pea.

スイートホーム 〖楽しい家庭〗a happy [a loving] home. (❗この意では a sweet home とはいわない)

スイートポテト (サツマイモ) a sweet potato; (焼菓子) a sweet potato cake.

スイートルーム a (hotel) suite /swiːt/; 〖和製語〗a suite room.

スイーパー 〖サッカー〗a sweeper. (⇨リベロ)

ずいいん 随員 (身辺の世話をする人) an attendant (❗通例複数形で); (随行団) a retinue (❗集合的に用い

複数扱いが普通). ▶大統領の随員たちはみな武装していた The President's *retinue* were all armed.

すいうん 水運 water transportation [《主に英》transport].

すいうん 衰運 declining fortunes. ● 衰運をたどる be *on the decline* [*wane*] (衰え始める) begin to *decline* [*wane*].

すいうん 瑞雲 auspicious clouds.

*__**すいえい**__ 水泳 图 swimming, (ひと泳ぎ) a swim; 〖水浴〗bathing /béiðiŋ/, a bathe /beið/. ● 水泳が上手[へた]である be a good [a poor] *swimmer*; be good [poor] at *swimming* (**!**前の方が普通の言い方). ● 水泳を習う learn how to *swim*; take *swimming* lessons. ▶水泳は健康によい *Swimming* is good for the [your] health. ▶湖へ水泳に行きましょう Let's go *swimming* [go for a *swim*] in [×to] the lake.

―― 水泳する 動 swim*; (ひと泳ぎする) have* a swim.

● 水泳着 《主に米》a báthing sùit, 《英》a swímming còstume. (⇨水着) ● 水泳選手 a swimmer.
● 水泳帽 《米》a báthing càp, 《英》a swímming càp.

すいえき 膵液 〖医学〗pancreatic /pæŋkriætik/ juice.

すいえん 垂涎 (⇨垂涎(ぜん))

すいえん 膵炎 〖医学〗pancreatitis /pæŋkriətáitis/.

すいおん 水温 water temperature.

すいか 水火 fire and water.
● 水火の苦しみ severe hardship and agony.
● 水火も辞さない 水火も辞さない覚悟だ I am prepared to *go through fire and water*.

すいか 西瓜 〖植物〗a watermelon.

すいか 誰何 ― 誰何する 動 (呼びとがめる) challenge. ▶見張りが兵士に誰何するのが聞こえた We heard a guard *challenge* a soldier.

すいがい 水害 〖洪水〗a flood /flʌd/ (**!**1 回の水害でもしばしば複数形で); 〖氾濫(はんらん)〗flooding; 〖被害〗flood damage. ● 水害にあう (人・場所・家などが) suffer *floods*; (場所・家などが) be damaged [be destroyed] by *floods*; be badly flooded. ● 大水害を引き起こす cause heavy *floods*.
● 水害地 a flooded [a flood-stricken] area.
● 水害被災者 a flood victim. ● 水害防止対策 (take) flood-control measures.

すいかずら 忍冬 〖植物〗(a) Japanese honeysuckle.

すいがら 吸い殻 a cigarette butt [end]; (葉巻の) a cigar stub. ● 吸い殻でいっぱいになった灰皿 an ashtray full of *cigarette butts*; a full ashtray.
● 吸い殻入れ (灰皿) an ashtray.

すいかん 酔漢 a drunkard; a drunk.

すいがん 酔眼 ● 酔眼もうろうとして with bleary eye.

ずいかん 随感 occasional thoughts [impressions]. (⇨随想)

ずいき 芋茎 a taro stalk [stem], the stalk [stem] of a taro.

ずいき 随喜 ● 随喜の涙を流す (うれし泣きする) weep for [with] joy; shed tears of joy.

すいきゃく 酔客 (⇨酔っ払い)

すいきゅう 水球 《play》water polo.

すいぎゅう 水牛 〖動物〗a water buffalo (復 ~(e)s).

すいきょ 推挙 图 a recommendation, (a) nomination. (⇨推薦(せん))
―― 推挙する 動 rècomménd [nóminàte] 《him *for* [*as*] deputy governor》.

すいぎょ 水魚 ● 水魚の交わり a very close friendship; (不変の) a fast friendship. ▶彼らは水魚の交わりを結んでいる They are very close friends.

すいきょう 酔狂 ● 酔狂な (=風変わりな) *eccentric* [(気まぐれな) *whimsical*] behavior. ● 酔狂で (=おもしろ半分で) そうするdo it just *for fun*. ▶あんなおんぼろ車を買うなんて君も酔狂(=物好き)だね You're *crazy* to buy such an old wreck.

すいぎん 水銀 〖化学〗mercury /mə́ːrkjəri/《元素記号 Hg》.
● 水銀汚染 mercury contamination. ● 水銀温度計 a mercury thermometer. ● 水銀気圧計 a mercury barometer. ● 水銀柱 (気圧計・温度計の) the mercury. ● 水銀中毒 mercury poisoning.
● 水銀灯 a mercury(-vapor) lamp.

すいくち 吸い口 (キセルの) a mouthpiece; (紙巻きたばこの) a cigarette filter [tip].

すいくん 垂訓 (教えること) teaching; instruction.
● 山上の垂訓 〖聖書〗the *Sermon* on the Mount.

すいけい 水系 a river [a water] system.

すいけい 推計 calculation; (見積もり) an estimate /éstimit/.
―― 推計する 動 calculate; estimate /éstimèit/.

すいげん 水源 (川の) the source (of a river); (給水の) the source of water supply.
● 水源地 the source; (貯水地) a reservoir /rézərvwɑ̀ːr/.

すいこう 水耕 hydroponics; tank farming; aquiculture. (⇨⦿水栽培)

すいこう 推考 图 (推察) inference. ―― 推考する 動 infer (-rr-).

すいこう 推敲 ▶原稿はまだ推敲が必要だ The manuscript still needs *polishing* [needs to be *polished*]. (**!**need doing は受身的意味になる)
―― 推敲する 動 ● (みがきをかける) polish; (修正する) revise; (改良する) improve.

すいこう 遂行 图 〖成就〗accomplishment; 〖実行〗(仕事・任務などの) performance; (計画・命令などの) execution.
―― 遂行する 動 ● 仕事を遂行する *accomplish* [*perform*] a task. ● 職務を遂行する *perform* [*carry out*] one's duties.

すいごう 水郷 a beautiful countryside along the river (canal /kənǽl/, lake); (水郷地帯) a scenic riverside [lakeside] district.

ずいこう 随行 ―― 随行する 動 ● X 氏に随行して(=同行して)アメリカに行く *accompany* Mr. X to America; (随行員として) go to [visit] America *as a member of* Mr. X's party.
● 随行員 an attendant; a member of the retinue. ● 随行団 a retinue.

すいこみ 吸い込み ❶〖吸い込むこと〗▶この煙突は吸い込みが良い This chimney *draws* very well. ❷〖下水槽〗a cesspool, a cesspit.

すいこむ 吸い込む ● 新鮮な空気を胸いっぱい吸い込む *take* [*draw*] *a deep breath of* fresh air; *breathe (in)* [*inhale*] fresh air deeply. ● 渦巻きに吸い込まれる *be swallowed up* by a whirlpool; *be sucked (down) into* a whirlpool. (**!**suck の方がずっと強力な動き) ● (掃除機が)よくごみを吸い込む *suck (up)* dirt very well; (吸引力が強い) have great suction. ▶彼の姿は人込みに吸い込まれた His figure *was swallowed up* among the crowd.

すいさい 水彩 ● 水彩絵の具 watercolors. ● 水彩画 a watercolor, a water-color painting. ● 水彩画家 a water-color painter.

すいさし 吸いさし a half-smoked cigarette; (短くなったたばこ) a cigarette butt [stub].

すいさつ 推察 〖推測〗a guess; 〖想像〗(an) imagination. (⇨推測)

すいさん　水産 ●**水産業** the marine products industry; (漁業) fishery. ●**水産国** a fishing country. ●**水産大学** a fisheries college. ●**水産庁** the Fisheries Agency. ●**水産物** marine products; (食品) sea food.

すいさんか　水酸化 ●**水酸化カルシウム** calcium hydroxide. ●**水酸化ナトリウム** sodium hydroxide. ●**水酸化物** (a) hydroxide.

すいさんき　水酸基 〖化学〗 a hydroxyl /háidrɔ́ksl/.

すいし　水死 图 (death by) drowning.
── **水死する** 動 ▶子供が川で水死した A child drowned [was drowned] in the river. (⇨溺(おぼ)れる)
●**水死体** a drowned body.

すいじ　炊事 图 cooking, kitchen work.
── **炊事する** 動 ▶炊事をする cook, do the cooking. (⇨料理)
●**炊事係** a cook. ●**炊事道具** kítchen [cóoking] utènsils; kitchenware (❢ 数える時は a piece [two pieces] of kitchenware). ●**炊事場** a kitchen.

ずいじ　随時 (いつでも) at any time; (必要に応じて)《やや書》 as occasion arises; (要求ありしだい) on demand [request]. ▶欠員は随時(=そのつど)補充している We fill (up) the vacancy every [each] time it occurs (happens, opens (up)].

すいしつ　水質 water quality. ●**水質を検査する** examine [analize] the water (quality).
●**水質汚染** water pollution. ●**水質検査** water analysis.

すいしゃ　水車 a waterwheel.
●**水車小屋** (水車による製粉所) a water mill.

すいじゃく　衰弱 ── **衰弱する** 動 become* [grow*] weak, weaken, waste away. (⇨弱る❶) ▶病気で彼は衰弱していった He has grown weak [wasted away] from illness./Illness has weakened him. ▶母は急速に衰弱している. あと1週間はもたないだろう Mother is weakening [sinking] fast. She won't last a week.

すいしゅ　水腫 〖医学〗dropsy; edema /edí:mə/.

*__すいじゅん　水準__ a level; (標準) a standard. ●**文化水準** the cultural level. ●**高い知的水準** a high level of intelligence [intellectual level]. ●**高い[低い]生活水準** a high [a low] standard of living. ●**生活水準を引き上げる** improve the standard of living. ●**水準以上[以下]である** be above [below] standard. ●**水準に達する** reach the level; come up to the standard. ●**世界的水準を維持する** maintain the world level [standards]. ▶日本の学問の水準は高い The level of learning [The academic level] is high in Japan. ▶その文明は最高水準に達した The civilization reached the highest level [the peak]. ▶彼の作品は芸術家のものと同じ水準だ His work is on a level with the artists'. (❢ は「同じ」の意) His work is on the level of artists.
●**水準器** 〖測量〗a (spirit) level. ●**水準点** 〖測量〗a benchmark.

ずいしょ　随所 〖至る所〗everywhere, all over the place; 〖あちこち〗here and there. ▶彼のレポートには誤植が随所にある There are a lot of misprints in his report./His report is full of misprints.

すいしょう　水晶 (a) crystal. ●**水晶製品の意では** Ⓒ ●**紫水晶** amethyst /ǽmiθist/. ●**水晶の首飾り** a necklace of crystals; a crystal necklace. ●**水晶のように透明な**〘書〙crystalline; (as) clear as crystal.
●**水晶婚式** a crystal wedding (anniversary). (〘参考〙結婚15周年記念) ●**水晶体** 〖解剖〗a (crystalline) lens. ●**水晶時計** a quartz(-crystal) clock [watch].

すいしょう　推賞, 推奨 〖賞賛〗praise; 〖推奨〗recommendation (⇨推薦(せん)). ▶彼の行為は推賞に値する What he did is worthy of praise.

すいじょう　水上 ●**水上で** on [ˣat] the water. ●**水上で生活する** live on the water.
●**水上競技** water [(水上で行う) aquatic] sports. ●**水上スキー** waterskiing. ●**水上タクシー** a hydrotaxi. ●**水上飛行機** a seaplane. ●**水上レストラン** a floating [(boat)] restaurant.

ずいじょう　瑞祥 a good omen; an auspicious sign.

すいじょうき　水蒸気 (熱を加えたときに出る) steam; (主に自然に発生する) vapor.

*__すいしん　推進__ 图 (前進させること) propulsion; (促進) promotion.
── **推進する** 動 (船などを前進させる) propel (-ll-); (促進する) promote; (計画などを押し進める) push on [ahead, forward] (with one's plans). ▶小泉氏はその改革を推進するのに重大な役割を演じた Mr. Koizumi played a vital role in pushing through the reform. (❢ push through ... は「...をやり遂げる」の意)
●**推進器** (飛行機などの) a propeller; (船の) a screw. ●**推進力** propelling power; (促進力) driving force. (⇨推力)

すいしん　水深 the depth of water. (⇨深さ) ▶この湖の水深は最大で3.8メートルだ The lake is 3.8 meters at its deepest.

すいじん　水神 the god of water.

すいじん　粋人 ❶〖風流を好む人〗a person with [of] refined tastes; (洗練された人) a sophisticated person. ❷〖物分かりのよい人〗a sensible [an understanding] person.

スイス 〖<フランス語〗〖国名〗Switzerland; (公式名) the Swiss Confederation. (首都 Bern) ●**スイス人** a Swiss (圈 ~); (総称) the Swiss. ●**スイス(人)の** Swiss.

すいすい (素早く) quickly, swiftly, speedily; (すべるように) glidingly; (なめらかに) smoothly; (容易に) easily. ●**すいすい事が運ぶ** Things go smoothly. ▶小さな魚がすいすい泳いでいる Small fish are swimming swiftly this way and that. ▶ヨットがすいすい走っていた A yacht sailed glidingly. ▶数学の問題がすいすい解けた I solved the math problems easily [speedily].

すいせい　水生 ── **水生の** 形 〖生物〗aquatic.
●**水生植物** an aquatic plant. ●**水生動物** an aquatic animal.

すいせい　水性 ── **水性の** 形 water.
●**水性ペイント** water paint.

すいせい　水星 〖天文〗Mercury.

すいせい　水勢 the force of water; (強い流れ) a strong current.

すいせい　彗星 a comet. ●**ハレー彗星** Halley's comet [Comet]. ●**百武彗星** Comet Hyakutake. (❢ 専門的には (C/1996 B2) を添えて用いるのが普通) ▶彼は彗星のごとく(=突然)文学界に現れた He emerged into the literary world all of a sudden.

すいせいがん　水成岩 aqueous rock.

*__すいせん　推薦__ 图 (a) recommendation. ●**強い[消極的な]推薦** a strong [a negative] recommendation. ●**彼女の推薦状を書く** write a (letter of) recommendation for her. ▶彼女はその大学に推薦入学した She was admitted to the college on [through] the recommendation of her high school.
── **推薦する** 動 recommend 《物+to+人; as, for》.

すいせん 〘候補者に指名する〙 nominate. ●彼女を通訳に〘その職に〙推薦する *recommend* her as an interpreter [*for* the job]. ●彼を議長候補に推薦する *nominate* him *for* chairman [the chairmanship]. ▶先生は彼をわが会社に強く推薦した His teacher strongly *recommended* him *to* the firm. ▶気軽に読める本を推薦してくださいませんか Could you *recommend* a book for light reading *to* me? (⚠*recommend* me a book …? の文型は今は不可)
●推薦者 a recommender; (指名者) a nominator. ●推薦図書 recommended [×recommending] books.

すいせん 水仙 〘植物〙〘総称〙 a narcissus /nɑːrsísəs/ (働 ~es, narcissi); (らっぱ水仙) a daffodil; (黄水仙) a jonquil.

すいせん 垂線 〘数学〙 a perpendicular (line). ●垂線を引く draw a *perpendicular*.

すいぜん 垂涎 ●垂涎の的 みんなの垂涎の的 the *envy* of everyone.

すいせんべんじょ 水洗便所 a flush toilet. ●水洗便所を流す flush the *toilet*. ▶水洗便所が流れない The *toilet* doesn't flush./I can't get the *toilet* to flush.

すいそ 水素 〘化学〙 hydrogen /háidrədʒən/ 〘元素記号 H〙.
●水素イオン a hydrogen ion /áiən/. ●水素爆弾 a hydrogen bomb; an H-bomb.

すいそう 水葬 water burial /bériəl/, (a) burial at sea. ▶彼らの遺体は水葬にふされた Their bodies *were buried at sea*.

すいそう 水槽 a water tank.

すいぞう 膵臓 〘解剖〙 a pancreas /pǽŋkriəs/.
●膵臓炎 〘医学〙 pancreatitis. ●膵臓がん 〘医学〙 pancreátic cáncer

すいそう 随想 (折にふれて浮かぶ考え) occasional [random] thoughts.
●随想録 essays. ●モンテーニュ随想録 〘書名〙 *The Essays of Montaigne* /mɑntéin/.

すいそうがく 吹奏楽 wind(-instrument) music.
●吹奏楽団 (主に金管からなる) a brass band; (軍楽隊) a military band. ●吹奏楽器 a wind instrument.

*****すいそく** 推測 图 a guess; 〘書〙 (a) speculation; 〘書〙 (a) supposition; (an) inference; 〘書〙 surmise. ●推測で(=当て推量して) by guess [*guesswork*], at a *guess*; (十分な根拠に基づいて) by *inference*. ▶推測が当たった[はずれた] My *guess* was right [wrong]./I *guessed* right [wrong]. ▶それは推測の域を出ない(=にすぎない) That is a mere [only a] *guess*.

── 推測する 動 〘根拠もなしに〙 guess (at …); (あれこれと)〘書〙 speculate (*on, about*); 〘不十分な根拠から〙 suppose,〘書〙 surmise; 〘十分な根拠から〙 infer (-rr-); (印象・観察などから)〘書〙 gather. ●だいたいの数を推測する *guess* (*at*) [*make a guess at*] the number. ▶彼は推測しているだけ(=推測で言っているだけ) He *is* only *guessing* [*speculating*]. ▶あの塔の高さはどのくらいか推測できますか Can you *guess* the height of that tower [how high that tower is]? (⚠ how 節の方が口語的) ▶彼女は50歳だと我々は推測した We *guessed* [×supposed] her age at 50./We *guessed* [*supposed*] her to be 50 (*that* she was 50). (⚠ *that* 節の方が口語的) ▶彼の言葉から推測すると仕事に不満があるようだ I *infer* [*gather*] from his remark *that* he is not satisfied [happy] with the job. (判断すると) (Judging) from what he says, he does not seem satisfied with the job.

すいぞくかん 水族館 an aquarium /əkwéəriəm/ (働 ~s, aquaria).

すいたい 衰退 图 (a) decline. (⚠ 単数形のみ) ●勢力の衰退 a *decline* in power. ▶その帝国は衰退に向かっていた The empire *was declining* [*on the decline*].

── 衰退する 動 decline. ▶今後50年で環境問題を解決できなければ文明は衰退します Failure to resolve environmental issues in the next 50 years will cause human civilization to *decline*.

すいたい 推戴 ── 推戴する 動 ▶我々は彼を名誉総裁として推戴した We had him as honorary president.

すいたい 酔態 drunkenness;〘書〙 intoxication.

すいだし 吸い出し ●吸い出し膏薬 a blister plaster; a plaster for a boil.

*****すいちゅう** 水中 〘陸に対して水〙 the water. ●水中(に) underwater; (水中に)in [under] *the water*. ●水中に飛び込む jump [dive] into *the water*; dive *underwater*. ●水中から彼を助ける help him out of *the water*. ●水中で目を開けて泳ぐ swim with one's eyes open *in the water*; swim *underwater* with one's eyes open. ▶魚は水中に住む Fish live in (the) *water*. ▶その船は水中に没していた The ship was *under water* [*underwater*]. (⚠「水中に没する[沈む]」は sink *into* the water)
●水中花 an artificial flower that opens when immersed in water. ●水中カメラ an underwater camera. ●水中銃 an underwater gun.
●水中眼鏡 (箱眼鏡) a water glass; (水泳用) swimming gòggles. ●水中翼船 a hydrofoil.

*****すいちょく** 垂直 ── 垂直の 形 (水平面に) vertical (↔ horizontal) (⚠正確に 90°でなくても用いる); (表面や線に 90°の) 〘数学〙 perpendicular (*to*) (⇨直角).
●垂直方向に 上または下に動く move in a *vertical* direction. ▶そのがけは地面に対してほとんど垂直です The cliffs are nearly *vertical* to the ground.

── 垂直に 副 ▶この柱は垂直に立っている This pole stands *vertically* [*upright*].
●垂直感染 〘医学〙 vertical transmission [infection]. ●垂直思考 vertical thinking. (働 水平思考) ●垂直線 a vertical [a perpendicular] (line). ●垂直跳び a vertical jump. ●垂直分布 〘生物〙 vertical distribution. (働 水平分布) ●垂直離着陸機 a vertical takeoff and landing aircraft (⚠単・複同形); a VTOL /víːtɔ(ː)l/.

すいつく 吸い付く stick* (*to*); (磁力で引き寄せられる) be attracted (*to*). ▶ヒルが私の足に吸いついた A leech *stuck to* my leg.

すいつける 吸い付ける ▶磁石は鉄を吸いつける(=引き寄せる) A magnet *attracts* iron. ▶あいつはたばこを吸いつけていない(=吸い慣れていない) He *is not used to* smoking [×to smoke].

*****スイッチ** a switch. ●タイム[電源; 電灯の]スイッチ a time [a power; a light] *switch*. ●ツリーの点灯のスイッチを入れる flick a *switch* to illuminate the tree's light. ●スイッチオン[オフ]にする turn on [off] the *switch*. ●ラジオのスイッチを入れる[切る] *switch on* [*off*] the radio; *turn on* [*off*] the radio. ▶そのエアコンは指定した時間にひとりでにスイッチが入る[切れる] The air conditioner *switches* itself on [*off*] at the set time.
●スイッチバック 〘鉄道〙 a switchback. ●スイッチヒッター 〘野球〙 a switch hitter.

*****すいてい** 推定 图 〘見積もり〙 an estimate /éstəmət/; (見積もること) (an) estimation (⚠複数形なし); 〘仮定〙 (a) presumption; (根拠の薄弱な) (a) supposition. ●推定で by *estimate*.

すいてい 推定する 動 ▶費用は100万ドルと推定されている The cost *is estimated it* [*to* be] a million dollars. ▶その樹木の年齢を推定することは容易ではない It is not easy to *estimate* how old the tree is. ▶彼らは彼を無罪だと推定している We *presume* [×*suppose*] his innocence./We *presume* [*suppose*] him *to* be innocent [*that* he is innocent]. (! *that* 節の方が口語的)

すいてい 水底 the bottom of the water. (⇨海底)

すいてき 水滴 a drop of water; (窓ガラスなどの) condensation.

すいでん 水田 a paddy (field); a rice field. (⇨田んぼ)

ずいと ▶彼がずいと寄ってきた He *abruptly* advanced toward me.

すいとう 水痘 〔医学〕chicken pox.

すいとう 水筒 (米) a canteen, (英) a wáter bòttle. ●水筒に水をいっぱい入れる fill (up) the *canteen*.

すいとう 水稲 paddy [wet-field] rice.

すいとう 出納 (お金の出し入れ) payment and receipt /rìsí:t/ of money. ●出納簿をつける (継続的に) keep a cashbook [(会計簿) an account book]. ▶前の方は個人・組織のいずれの場合にも用いる。後の方は慣用的に keep accounts という。特定の1回の記入をいうときは write in a cashbook [an account book].)
●出納係 (店・ホテルなどの) a cashier /kǽʃiər/; (銀行の)(米) a teller, (英) a cashier.

*****すいどう 水道** ❶ [給水設備] waterworks (!(1) 単・複両扱い。(2) 貯水池・送水管・水圧ポンプ・浄化装置などの給水設備全体をさす); (送水システム) water supply [service]; (水道の水) tap [running] water. ●水道を出す [止める] turn on [off] a faucet. ●水道を引く lay a *water* pipe. ●水道を出しっ放しにしている They leave a tap running./(出しっ放しになっている) The *water* is left running. ▶水道が止まった The *water supply* failed. ▶この村には水道がない We have [There is] no *water supply* [*service*] in this village. ▶今日はとても寒くて水道の水が出なかった It was really cold today, and I couldn't get the *water* to come out.
❷ [海峡] a channel. ●紀伊水道 the Kii Chánnel.
●水道管 (本管) a (water) main; (引き込み管) a water pipe [line]. ●水道局 a water board; the bureau of waterworks. ●水道栓 (米) a faucet, (英) a tap. (⇨蛇口) ●水道料金 wáter chàrges; a wáter ràte. ●水道屋 (配管工) a plumber.

すいどう 隧道 a tunnel. (⇨トンネル)

すいとうしょう 水頭症 〔医学〕hydrocephalus.

すいとりがみ 吸い取り紙 blótting pàper; (机上に置く) a blotter.

すいとる 吸い取る suck ... up; (しみ込ませて取る) soak ... up. ▶こぼれた牛乳をスポンジで吸い取った I *soaked up* the spilled milk with a sponge.

すいなん 水難 (水害) a flood disaster; (溺死) drowning; (難破) a shipwreck. ●水難にあう drown; be drowned; be shipwrecked.
●水難救助作業 a rescue operation at sea.

すいのみ 吸い飲み (病人の) a féeding cùp.

すいばく 水爆 a hydrogen bomb, an H-bomb.
●水爆実験 a thermonuclear [an H-bomb] test.

すいはん 垂範 ── **垂範する** 動 (お供をする) set* an example 《*for* [*to*] children》.

すいばん 水盤 a basin; (生け花用の) a shallow flower container.

ずいはん 随伴 ── **随伴する** 動 (お供をする) accompany; 〔書〕 attend.

●随伴現象 an accompanying phenomenon.

すいはんき 炊飯器 a rice cooker.

すいび 衰微 图 (a) decline (! 単数形のみ); decay.
── **衰微する** 動 decline; decay; fall* into decline [decay]. ●衰微していっている be *in decline*; be decaying [*in decay*]. ▶その国は衰微して二流国に転落している The country *has declined* to a second-class power.

ずいひつ 随筆 an essay. ●随筆を書く write an *essay* 《*about*, *on*》.
●随筆家 an essayist. ●随筆集 a collection of 《his》essays.

すいふ 水夫 a sailor. (⇨船乗り)

すいぶん 水分 (水) water; (湿り気) moisture; (汁) juice. ●水分の多いナシ a *juicy* pear.

*****ずいぶん 随分** [非常に] very; much (!動詞・比較級を修飾。肯定文平叙文を修飾する場合、very などの修飾語を伴わないまたは堅い言い方); [ものすごく] extremely, terribly, (話) awfully; [大いに] a great deal, (話) a lot, (やや書) greatly. (⇨大分 解説) ●ずいぶん長い間 for a *very* long time. ▶彼女は彼がいなくなってずいぶん寂しがっている She misses him *very much*. ▶今年はずいぶん暑い夏でした It has been *very* [*extremely*, *terribly*, (話) *awfully*] hot this summer. ▶こちらは日本よりずいぶん物価が安い Prices are much [(話) *a lot*, (かなり) *considerably*] lower here than in Japan. (! いずれも比較級を強める) ▶このことについては今まで日本でずいぶんといろいろなことが言われている So much has been said about this. ▶彼はずいぶん変わった He has changed *greatly* [*so much*, (話) *a lot*]. ▶彼女は衣服にずいぶんお金を遣う She spends *a great deal of* [*an awful lot of*] money on her dresses. ▶ずいぶん久しぶりですね It's [It has been] *quite a long time* [(話) *ages*] since I last saw you. (⇨久しぶり) ▶わが町はしばしば「ベッドタウン」と呼ばれる。ベッドの街、眠るための街とは、ずいぶんな (=失礼な) 呼び方ではないか People often call the town we live in a "bed town." A town of beds or a town where people go to sleep, isn't it indeed a *very degrading* name?

すいへい 水平 图 a level.
── **水平な** 形 ●水平線 [面] a horizontal /hɔ̀(ː)rəzɔ́ntl/ line [plane]. ▶このあたりは地面がほぼ水平である The ground is almost *level* [*horizontal*] around here.
●水平思考 lateral thinking. (翻 垂直思考) ●水平動 a horizontal movement [motion, (震動) vibration]. ●水平分布 〔生物〕 horizontal distribution. (翻 垂直分布)

すいへい 水兵 a sailor, (男の) a seaman (複 -men).
●水兵服 a sailor's uniform. (! sailor suit は男児のセーラー服) ●水兵帽 (子供の) a sailor cap.

すいへいせん 水平線 the horizon /həráizn/. (!「地平線」の意にもなる) ●水平線上に on the *horizon*. ▶太陽が水平線の上に昇った [下に沈んだ] The sun rose *above* [sank *below*] *the horizon*.

すいほう 水泡 foam.
●水泡に帰す ▶彼のすべての計画は水泡に帰した All his plans *have gone down the drain* [*gone up in smoke*, *come to nothing*].

すいほう 水疱 (水ぶくれ) a blister; (小水疱) 〔医学〕 a vesicle.

すいぼう 水防 (水害を防ぐこと) prevention of floods; (水害防御) flood control. ●水防対策をする take measures to *prevent floods*.
●水防訓練 a flood drill. ●水防工事 flood-control works.

すいぼう 衰亡 图 (衰退) a decline; (滅亡) a fall; (汚

すいぼくが 水墨画 a black-and-white [a monochrome] painting (in Chinese ink).

すいぼつ 水没 图 《やや書》submergence.
― **水没する** 動 ▶多くの村がアスワンハイダムの建設で水没した A large number of villages went under water [《やや書》were submerged] after (the) completion of the Aswan High Dam.

すいま 水魔 a disastrous flood. ▶村全体が水魔に襲われた A disastrous flood engulfed the whole village.

すいま 睡魔 drowsiness, sleepiness. ●睡魔に襲われる get very sleepy [drowsy]. ●睡魔と闘う(=振り払おうとする) try to fight off one's drowsiness [the urge to sleep]. ●睡魔に負ける be overcome by drowsiness.

ずいまくえん 髄膜炎 〖医学〗meningitis /mènindʒáitəs/.

すいません Excuse me. (⇨すみません)

すいみつとう 水蜜桃 a (white) peach.

すいみゃく 水脈 a water vein, a vein of water. ●水脈を掘りあてる hit [《やや書》strike] a (rich) vein of water.

*__すいみん__ 睡眠 (a) sleep (❗「睡眠時間」の意にもなる); (快い)《書》(a) slumber (❗ しばしば複数形で).
① 〖睡眠～〗 ▶睡眠時間を 5 時間に減らす cut one's sleep down to five hours. ●睡眠中に in one's sleep; while one is sleeping. ●睡眠不足で体がだるい feel languid from (a) lack of sleep. ▶このところ睡眠不足です I am short of sleep these days./I haven't been getting much [enough] sleep recently. ▶毎晩どれくらい睡眠時間が必要ですか How many hours' sleep [How much sleep] do you need every night? ▶睡眠中〖掲示〗Do not disturb. (❗ ホテルのドアなどにかけておくもの)
② 〖睡眠を〗 ▶昨夜は十分〖9時間〗睡眠を取った I had a good sleep [nine hours' sleep, nine hours of sleep] last night. ❗ 通例 a sleep of nine hours とはしない/I slept well [(for) nine hours] last night. ▶「十分睡眠を取らなかった」は I didn't get much sleep.
● 睡眠時無呼吸症候群〖医学〗sleep-apnea /slíːpæpniːə/ syndrome (略 SAS). ●睡眠障害(⅗) a sleep disorder. ●睡眠薬(錠剤などの) a sleeping pill [tàblet]. ●睡眠療法 sleep therapy [cure].

スイミング 〖水泳〗swimming.
●スイミングスクール a swímming schòol; (水泳教室) a swímming clàss.

すいめつ 衰滅 (⇨〘同〙衰亡)

すいめん 水面 the surface of the water. ▶潜水艦が水面に浮上した A submarine came up to the surface./《やや書》A submarine surfaced. ▶油が水面に浮かんでいる There's some oil floating on the water.
● 水面下 ●水面下の(=見えないところでの)折衝 ((conduct)) negotiations in secret [behind the scenes]; secret [behind-the-scenes] negotiations.

すいもの 吸い物 Japanese clear soup. ●吸い物を吸う have some clear soup.

すいもん 水門 a water gate; 〖ダム・貯水池などの〗a sluice (gate); 〖運河・水路の〗a floodgate; 〖運河の〗a lock.

すいよう 水溶 ― **水溶性の** 形 water-soluble.
● 水溶液 (a) solution.

*__すいよう(び)__ 水曜(日) Wednesday 《略 Wed.》. (⇨

日曜(日))

すいよく 水浴 bathing /béiðiŋ/. (⇨水浴び)

すいらい 水雷 (魚雷) a torpedo; (機雷) a mine.
●水雷艇 a torpedo boat.

すいり 水利 〖〖給水設備〗〗water supply; 〖〖灌漑(かんがい)〗〗irrigation. ▶ここの土地は乾燥していて水利もよく，住居を構えるのに適している The land here is dry and well watered and is fit to build a house on.
●水利権 water [irrigation] rights.

すいり 推理 图 〖〖論理的な〗〗reasoning; 〖〖事実などに基づいた〗〗(an) inference; 〖〖演繹(えんえき)的な〗〗(a) deduction. ●彼の推理によると according to his reasoning.
― **推理する** 動 reason; infer; 《書》deduce. ●資料から推理する infer [deduce] from the data.
●推理作家 a mystery [a detective story] writer. ●推理小説 a mystery (story); a detective story.

すいりく 水陸 land and water. (❗ 語順に注意) ●水陸両用の戦車 《やや書》an amphibious /æmfíbiəs/ tank.

すいりゅう 水流 a current.
●水流ポンプ a water-jet pump.

すいりょう 水量 the volume of water.
●水量計 a water gauge /géidʒ/ [meter /míːtər/].

すいりょう 推量 图 (当て推量) a guess; (不十分な根拠による) (a) supposition; (十分な根拠による) (an) inference.
― **推量する** 動 guess; suppose; infer (-rr-). (⇨推測)

すいりょく 水力 water power.
●水力発電 hydroelectric power generation, waterpower generation. ●水力発電所 a hydroelectric power station [plant].

すいりょく 推力 (エンジンの) thrust.

すいれい 水冷 water cooling.
●水冷式エンジン a water cooled engine.

すいれん 睡蓮 〖植物〗a water [a pond] lily (❗「睡蓮の葉」は a lily pàd).

すいれん『睡蓮』Water Lilies. (〖参考〗モネの絵画)

すいろ 水路 a waterway; (人工の) a canal /kənǽl/; (灌漑(かんがい)用の) a watercourse. ●水路で行く go by sea; go by ship.

すいろん 推論 图 reasoning; (an) inference; (a) deduction. (⇨推理)
― **推論する** 動 reason; infer; 《書》deduce. ▶私はそういうのが実情かもしれないと推論した I reasoned that such was the case.

スイング 〖競技〗a swing; 〖音楽〗swing (music).
●強烈なスイング (take) a powerful swing. ●フルスイング a clean [a full] swing. ●ハーフスイング a half swing. ●アッパースイング an uppercut (swing). ●大きな[小さな]スイング a long [a short] swing. ●止めたスイング a check(ed) swing. ●自分の(ゴルフの)スイングを鏡に映して直す look at one's swing in a mirror to correct it.
●スイングアウト〖野球〗a swinging strikeout. ●スイングアウトになる strike out [go down] swinging. ●スイングジャズ swing (jazz). ●スイングドア〖自在ドア〗a swinging door; 《主に英》a swing door.

*__すう__ 吸う ❶ 〖口で吸い込む〗(液体を) suck ... (in); (気体を) breathe /bríːð/ ... (in), inhale (⟷exhale) (❗後の方が堅い語 (⇨吸い込む)). ●ストローでソーダ水を吸う suck soda through a straw. ●毒へびの傷から毒を吸い出す suck out poison from a snakebite. ●たばこを吸う smoke (a cigarette); have a smoke. ▶赤ん坊は哺乳(ほにゅう)びんのミルクをちゅうちゅう

吸った The baby intently *sucked* (the milk *from*) the bottle.

翻訳のこころ なめとこ山は，一年のうちでたいていの日は冷たい霧か雲かを吸ったり吐いたりしている（宮沢賢治『なめとこ山の熊』）*Nametokoyama* (mountain) *is breathing in and out a cold fog or cloud almost every day through* [*in*] *the year*. (!) (1)「なめとこ山」は固有名詞で，日本語なので斜字体で表す．さらに mountain をつけて山であることを示す．(2)「(気体を)吸う」は breathe in. (3) through は「一年中を通して」と強調の意を表す)

❷ [吸い上げる] suck ... up; (吸い取る) soak ... up, absorb. ▶ 植物は根から水分を吸う Plants *suck* (*up*) moisture from the soil through their roots.

❸ [しゃぶる] ● 親指を吸う *suck* one's thumb.

すう 数 (a) number. (⇨数(ᡃ))

すう- 数- a few; several; a number of ...; some. (⇨いくつか [類語]) ● 数日すればin a *few* days. ● 数回 *several* [*a number of*] times. ● 数冊の本 *some* [*several*] books.

スウェーデン [国名] Sweden /swíːdn/; (公式名) the Kingdom of Sweden. (首都 Stockholm) ● スウェーデン人 a Swede; 《総称》the Swedish [Swedes]. ● スウェーデン語 Swedish. ● スウェーデン(人[語])の Swedish.
● スウェーデン体操 Swedish gymnastics.
● スウェーデンリレー [陸上] the Swedish relay.

*__**すうがく 数学**__ 图 mathemátics, 《米話》math, 《英話》maths. ● 数学の問題 a math [a *mathematical*] problem. ▶ 数学は私のいちばん苦手な科目です *Mathematics* is [X*are*] my weakest (↔ strongest) subject.
── 数学的な 形 mathematical.
── 数学的に 副 mathematically.
● 数学者 a mathematician.

解説 学科目や学問の分野を表す名詞の中には -ics という語尾で終わるものがあるが，これはギリシャ語やラテン語から外来語として入ってきたときの影響によるもの．通例単数扱いするが，学科目や学問の分野以外の意味で用いられるときは通例複数扱いとなる： economics (単数: 経済学; 複数: 経済状態[問題])/ethics (単数: 倫理学; 複数: 倫理観)/gymnastics (単数: 体育; 複数: 体操)/linguistics (単数: 言語学)/mathematics (単数: 数学)/physics (単数: 物理学)/politics (単数: 政治(学); 複数: 政治観[活動]).

すうき 数奇 ── 数奇な 形 [波乱の多い] checkered, full of ups and downs; [幸運から見離された]《書》hapless;《限定的》without luck, unlucky. ▶ 彼女は数奇な生涯を送った She led a *hapless* life./All through her life, she followed a *checkered* career.

すうききょう 枢機卿 a cardinal. (参考) ローマ教皇に次ぐ高位の司教)

すうけい 崇敬 图 reverence (*for*); veneration. ● 祖先に崇敬の念を表す *hold* one's ancestors *in reverence*; *revere* [*venerate*] one's ancestors.
── 崇敬する 動《書》revere;《書》venerate.

すうこう 崇高 图 sublimity; (気高さ) nobility.
── 崇高な 形 sublime; (気高い) noble. ▶ 彼は崇高な心の人である He is a man of *noble* mind./He has a *noble* mind.

スーザ [米国の作曲家] Sousa (John Philip ~).
すうし 数詞 [文法] a numeral.
*__**すうじ 数字**__ a figure; a number; [数の書記体系] a numeral.

使い分け figure 0 から9 までの数字で，それを並べて書き表した数は figures.
number 数学的概念としての数で，数体系中のある数をさす．文脈では数字の方がよい．

● アラビア(=算用)数字 Arabic *numerals* [*figures*]. ● ローマ数字 Roman *numerals* [*figures*]. ● 漢数字 Chinese *numerals* [*figures*]. ● 大きな[小さな]数字 a high [a low] *number*. ● 数字の3 a *figure* three (!) a figure of three は「3 の字形」の意). ● 正確な数字 exact [*precise*] *figures*. ● 天文学的な数字 astronomical *figures*. ● 数字で示す put a *figure* on (*it*); state [express] (*it*) in *figures*; give [cite] *figures* to state (*it*). ● 数字を挙げる give [cite] *figures*. ● 数字で答える reply in terms of *figures*. ● 数字(=計算)に弱い be no good at *figures* [*numbers, calculation*]. (!) figures, numbers は複数形で用いると「計算，算数」の意にもなる) ▶ 七は縁起のよい数字だと言われる They say [It is said] that seven is a lucky *number*.

すうじ 数次 several times. ● 会議は数次に及ぶ hold conferences *several times*.
● 数次旅券 a multiple passport.

すうしき 数式 a numerical formula.

すうじく 枢軸 (中枢) a central part; the center.
● 悪の枢軸 an axis of evil(s).
● 枢軸国 the Axis powers. (関連) 連合国 the Allies)

すうすう ❶ [空気の出入り] (寝息が) quiet; (すきま風が) drafty. ▶ 子供がすうすう寝息を立てている The child is asleep, *breathing quietly*. (!) この場合音調上 breathing との関係で sleeping は避ける) ▶ 窓をもっときちんと閉めてよ，すうすうして寒いから Please close the window tightly. I *feel* cold *currents of air* [It's *drafty* here and I feel cold].

❷ [順調な動き] (⇨すいすい)

❸ [その他の表現] ▶ メンソレータムを塗ったらすうすうした When I applied Mentholatum, I *felt refreshing coolness*.

ずうずうしい 図々しい 形 (厚かましい) impudent, (特に子供に) cheeky; (恥知らずな) shameless; (無礼な) impolite. ▶ あいつはなんて図々しいやつだ What an *impudent* [a *shameless*] fellow he is! ▶ この仕事は図々しくないとやっていけない We have to be *thick-skinned* in this business.

会話「彼は支払いを拒否しているよ」「なんて図々しい！」"He refuses to pay." "What a *nerve*!/The *cheek* of it!" (!)《米》では前の方が好まれる)

── 図々しく 副 (図々しく...する) have* the impudence [《話》nerve] (*to do*); (厚かましく) impudently; (恥知らずにも) shamelessly. ▶ いくら図々しくても借金は君に頼めない I *haven't* got *the nerve* to ask you for a loan. ▶ 彼は図々しくも口答えした He was *impudent* enough to talk back./He *impudently* talked back.

会話「あの本あと2週間手元に置いておこうよ」「図々しいわね，そんなに長いこと置いておくなんて」"Let's keep the book for another two weeks." "Do we *dare* (*to*) keep it as long as that?" (!) to はしばしば省略される)

ずうずうしさ 図々しさ impudence,《話》cheek;《話》nerve (!) 通例 a, the をつける). ▶ あの子の図々しさには驚いた I was surprised by the *nerve* of that boy.

ずうずうべん ずうずう弁 ▶ 彼はずうずう弁だ He speaks *with a strong* [(丸出しの) *a broad*] *Tohoku accent*.

すうせい 趨勢 ● 近ごろの美術や音楽の趨勢(=動向) is

ずうたい 図体 〖体〗a body; 〖骨格〗a frame; 〖巨体〗a bulk. ● 図体の大きい男 a man with a large *body* [*frame*]; a bulky fellow.

すうだん 数段 ▶この考えの方が数段(=はるかに)上だ This idea is *much* better. (⇒通(১)か)

スーダン 〖国名〗(the) Sudan (sú(:)dən/); (公式名) the Republic of the Sudan. (首都 Khartoum) ● スーダン人 a Sudanese (圈 ~). ● スーダン(人)の Sudanese.

すうち 数値 〖数学〗numerical value.
● 数値目標 a numerical target.

スーツ a suit (of clothes). (❗(1) 男性用は上着とズボン, 時にチョッキも加える。女性用は上着とスカート. (2) ×suits とはいわない) ● 既製のスーツ a ready-made *suit*. ▶彼はグレーのスーツを1着あつらえた He had a gray *suit* made to order.

スーツケース a suitcase. ● スーツケースを運ぶ carry a *suitcase*.

すうっと ❶ 〖軽快に, 静かに〗softly; quietly. ● すうっと部屋から出て行く *slip* (*quietly*) out of the room. (❗slip だけでもこの意は表せる) ▶ 1台の車が私のそばにすうっと止まった A car came and stopped *noiselessly* beside me.
❷ 〖まっすぐに伸びてゆくさま〗● けやきのすうっと伸びた枝 a branch of a *Keyaki* tree *spreading* [*shooting up*] *to the sky*. ● すうっと彼女のほおを伝わる涙 a drop of tear running [×*streaming*] down her cheek. (❗streaming では大量に流れること)
❸ 〖さっぱりするさま〗▶思い切って言ったら胸がすうっとしたI built [screwed] up my courage and said it. It was *a load off* my *chest*.

すうとう 数等 ▶こちらの方が数等上だ This is *much* [*far*, 《話》*a great deal*] better. (⇒っと)

すうどん 素うどん (説明的に) *udon* noodles served in hot broth.

スーパー 〖スーパーマーケット〗a supermarket (⇒スーパーマーケット); 〖字幕スーパー〗subtitles.
● スーパーインポーズ superimposition. (参考) 映画などの画面に字幕などを重ねること) ● スーパーコンピュータ a supercomputer. ● スーパー301条 Super 301 (Clause of the Omnibus Trade and Competitiveness Act of 1988). (参考) 米国の包括通商法の条項の1つ) ● スーパースター a superstar. ● スーパーバイザー 〖監督者〗a supervisor. ● スーパーマン a superman. (❗漫画の主人公は S-)

スーパーマーケット a supermarket. ▶駅前のスーパーマーケットで買い物した I did some shopping at the *supermarket* near the station.

すうはい 崇拝 图 worship; (敬愛) adoration; (賞賛) admiration. ● 英雄崇拝 hero *worship*.
── 崇拝する 動 worship; adore; admire. ▶歴史上の人物で最も崇拝する人物はだれですか What historical character do you *admire* most?
● 崇拝者 a worshiper; (賞賛者) an admirer.

すうひょう 数表 mathematical tables; (対数表) 〖数学〗a table of logarithms.

スープ (a) soup. (❗種類のいうときは C). ● 濃いスープ thick (↔thin) *soup*; 《corn》potage /poʊˈtɑːʒ/; cream (*of corn*). ● スープのもと (ベースとなる肉などの煮出し汁) stock; (固形) a stock cube; (粉末) a soup packet. ● スープを飲む (スプーンで) eat [have] *soup*; (容器口をつけて) drink *soup*. ● スープを作る make [×*cook*] *soup*. ● 鳥のがらでスープのベースをとる make stock of *soup* from chicken bones. ● スープの冷めない距離(=ごく近く)に住む live very near [just around the corner]. (❗後の方はよく使う慣用表現) ▶冷めないうちにスープを召し上がれ Eat your *soup*, or it'll get cold. (⇒冷める)
会話 「これは何のスープですか」「チキンスープです」"What kind of *soup* is this?" "It's chicken *soup*." (❗料理名としては chicken broth [consommé] ともいう)
● スープ皿 a sóup plàte [bòwl].

スーベニア 〖土産, 記念品〗a souvenir /sùːvənɪər/.
● スーベニアショップ a souvenir shòp.

ズーム ● ズームアウト (画像が遠ざかること) zooming out.
● ズームイン (画像が近づくこと) zooming in. ▶カメラはスタンドの市長にズームインした The camera *zoomed in* on the Mayor in the stands. ● ズームレンズ a zoom lens.

すうよう 枢要 ── 枢要な 形 (大切な, かなめの) (very) important; (主要な) principal. ● 国際社会で枢要な地位を占める hold a *very important* position among the countries of the world.

すうり 数理 图 〖数学的理論〗a mathematical principle; 〖計算〗(数字計算) figure; (計算能力) arithmetic. ● 数理に弱い be poor at [have a poor head for] figures [arithmetic].
── 数理的な 形 mathematical.
● 数理経済学 mathematical economics. ● 数理言語学 mathematical linguistics. ● 数理哲学 mathematical philosophy. ● 数理統計学 mathematical statistics.

すうりょう 数量 图 (a) quantity; (an) amount. (⇒量) ● 販売数量 sales *quantity*.
── 数量的に quantitatively /kwάntəteìtivli/.
● 数量詞 〖文法〗a quantifier.

すうれつ 数列 〖数学〗(a) progression. ● 等差[等比]数列 an arithmetic(al) [a geometric(al)] *progression*.

***すえ** 末 ❶ 〖終わり〗an end. ● 末の息子 one's youngest son. (⇒末っ子) ▶今月の末 [来ごろ] 日本をたってアメリカに行きます I will leave Japan for America at [toward] the *end* of this month.
❷ 〖後〗after ... ● (人を挙げ句) よく考えた末それをしたI did it. *after* careful consideration [a lot of thought]. / I thought it out [hard] *and* put it into action.
❸ 〖将来〗(a) future. ● 末頼もしい(=前途有望な)学生 a *promising* [a *hopeful*] student. ● 末永く (⇒末永く) ● 行く末 (⇒行く末) ▶彼らは末は結婚するだろう They will get married *in* (《米》the) *future*.

ずえ 図会 ● 日本名所図会 a *collection of pictures* [*paintings*] showing the Japanese sights.

スエーデン Sweden /swíːdn/. (⇒スウェーデン)

スエード suede /swéid/. ● スエードの靴 (a pair of) *suede* shoes.

すえおき 据え置き 〖支払いの〗deférment. ▶定価据え置き We keep the price tag *intact*. / (揭示) No Price Increase.
● 据え置き期間 a period of deferment. ● 据え置き年金 a deferred annuity.

すえおく 据え置く 〖支払いを延ばす〗defer (-rr-); 〖賃金などを凍結する〗freeze*, peg (-gg-); 〖貸し付けなどを償還しないでおく〗leave*... unredeemed. ▶賃金の支払いは翌月まで据え置かれた The payment of wages *was deferred* [*was put off*] until the next month. ▶郵便料金は6か月据え置かれた The postal charges *were frozen* [*were pegged*] for six months. ▶バス料金はここ数年据え置かれている (=同じである) Bus fares *have stayed the same* for several years now.

すえおそろしい 末恐ろしい ▶この子は末恐ろしい(=将来何か非常に悪いこと[偉大なこと]をするだろう) This child will *do something terrible* [*great*] *in the future*.

スエズ ●スエズ運河 the Suez Canal /súːez kənǽl/.

すえぜん 据え膳 a table set before 《him》 for a meal. ●上げ膳据え膳の男

すえたのもしい 末頼もしい promising.

すえつける 据え付ける ●部屋にストーブを据え付ける(=取り付ける) *install* 《固定する》*fix* a stove in the room. ●屋上に望遠鏡を据える(=立てる) *set up* a telescope *on* the roof.

すえっこ 末っ子 the [one's] youngest child [son, daughter]. ●6人子供がいるうちの末っ子 the *youngest* of a family of six (**!** この場合の family は「(...家の)子供」の意).

スエット ●スエットシャツ(トレーナーの上着) sweatshirt. ●スエットスーツ a sweat suit; 《米話》sweats. ●スエットパンツ sweatpants.

すえながく 末永く ▶末永く仲よくしてね Be my friend *forever*.

すえひろがり 末広がり ▶家運が末広がりにひらけた Our family prospered *more and more*.

***すえる 据える** ❶[置く] put*, place, set* (⇒置く[類語]); 《固定する》fix. ●机を窓ぎわに据える *place* [*set*] a desk by the window. ●上座に据える *give* 《him》the seat of honor.
❷[任命する] ●彼をその学校の校長に据える *appoint* him [*place him as*] principal of the school.
❸[目を](視線を固定させる) fix one's eyes 《on him》; (じっと見つめる) stare 《at him》.
❹[腰を] settle down 《to one's work》.

すえる 饐える(腐ってすっぱいにおいがする)(飲み物が) turn [go*] sour /sáuər/; sour (**!** 他動詞にも用いる); (食べ物が) go bad [off]. ▶牛乳がすえる Milk *turns sour*. ▶暑かったのでごはんがすえた Rice *went* bad [*off*] in hot weather.

すおどり 素踊り dancing without (a) costume; uncostumed dancing. ●素踊りをする dance without (a) costume.

***ずが 図画**(絵の具による) painting; (鉛筆・ペンなどによる) drawing; 〚作品〛a painting; a drawing; 《集合的》art. ●子供の図画展 an exhibition of children's *art*.
●図画工作 arts and crafts.

***スカート** a skirt. ●ひざまでのスカート a knee-length *skirt*. ●スカートのひだ a pleat [a gather] on a *skirt*. ●スカートの丈を短く[長く]する raise [lower] the hemline; make the *skirt* shorter [longer]. ●スカートをはく[脱ぐ;整える] put on [take off, step out of; straighten] one's *skirt*. ▶座ったときスカートが持ち上がって太ももが出た Her *skirt* rode up her thighs when she sat down. ▶今ロング[ミニ]スカートが流行している Long *skirts* [*Miniskirts*] are now in fashion.

> **関連** いろいろなスカート：ギャザースカート a gathered *skirt*／キュロットスカート culóttes／ジャンパースカート《米》a jumper,《英》a pinafore (dress)／タイトスカート a sheath *skirt*／プリーツスカート a pleated *skirt*／フレアースカート a flared *skirt*.

スカーフ a scarf (**@** ~s, scarves). ●首にスカーフを巻く wrap one's *scarf* around one's neck.

ずかい 図解 〖説明に伴う絵図〗an illustration; 〖構造・系統図〗a diagram. ●図解入りの手引書 an *illustrated* manual.
── **図解する 動** illustrate; (表で示す) show* 《it》by a diagram.

ずがいこつ 頭蓋骨 a skull /skʌl/; 〖解剖〗a cranium (**@** ~s, crania). ●頭蓋骨を骨折する fracture [(ひびが入る) crack] one's *skull*.
●**頭蓋骨骨折** a skull fracture; a fracture of [to] the skull.

スカイジャック(行為) skyjacking, hijacking (**!** 前の方がより口語的); (1回の事件を) a hijack.

スカイダイバー a skydiver.

スカイダイビング skydiving. ●スカイダイビングする skydive; (楽しむ) enjoy *skydiving*.

スカイブルー 图〖空色〗sky blue.
── **スカイブルーの 形** sky-blue.

スカイライン(山・建物などが空に描く輪郭) a skyline; (山の観光自動車道) a mountain drive.

スカウト 图〖スポーツ・芸能の〗(人) a (talent) scout; (行動) scouting; 〖企業の〗(人) a headhunter; (行動) headhunting. ●スカウトの目に留まる be spotted by a *scout*.
── **スカウトする 動** ●有能な新人を求め(国中を)スカウトして回る *scout* (around the country) *for* (×a) new talent.

すがお 素顔 ●彼女の素顔(=化粧していない顔) her *face without makeup*; her *unpainted face*. ●政治家の素顔(=本当の顔) the *real* [*true*] *face* [*nature*] of a politician. ●パリの素顔 the *real* Paris; (あるがまま) Paris *as it is*.

すかさず[すぐに] at once, immediately (⇒すぐ❶); 〖即座に〗instantly; 〖すばやく〗quickly, promptly; 〖ちゅうちょせずに〗without hesitation.

すかし 透かし(紙の) a watermark. ●透かしが入っていない have no *watermark*; be not watermarked.
●**透かし彫り**〖細工〗openwork.

スカジー〚コンピュータ〛SCSI /skú:zi/《small computer system interface の略》.

すかしっぺ 透かしっ屁 silent fart.

***すかす 透かす** ❶[...を通して見る] look at [see*] 《it》through ... (⇒見る); (光にかざして見る) hold* up 《it》to the light. ●闇を透かして(=目を凝らして)見る peer (out) into the darkness.
❷[...の間をあける] leave* some space between .... ●枝を透かす thin the branches. ●着物のえりを透かす wear the collar of one's kimono *as low as the nape of* one's *neck shows*. (**!**「うなじが見える程度に下げて」の意)

すかす 空かす(腹を) get* hungry. (**!**「腹をすかしている」は be hungry)

すかす 賺す(機嫌を取って...させる) flatter 《him into doing》; (うまく口説いて...させる) coax 《him into doing》[to do]》. (⇒なだめる) ▶脅したりすかしたりして彼をうんと言わせた *flatter* and terrify him *into* saying yes.

すかすか ▶このオレンジはすかすかだ(=水気がなくなっている) This orange is *dry*./This orange isn't *juicy at all*.

会話「この箱はりんご10個ではすかすか(=空きがありすぎる)だね」「15個にすればちょうどよくなるだろう」"Ten apples *leave too much space* in this box." "Fifteen apples will do."

ずかずか ●ずかずか入り込む barge in. ▶彼は私の部屋にノックもせずにずかずか入ってきた He *barged into* my room without knocking.

すがすがしい 清々しい refreshing; (clean and) fresh. (⇒さわやか) ●すがすがしい朝の空気 *refreshing* morning air. ▶今朝は気分がすがすがしい I feel *refreshed* this morning.

‡**すがた 姿** ❶[外見](体つき) a figure; (外形) a shape, (a) form (⇒形); (見かけ) (an) appear-

すがたに

ance; (映像, 面影) an image. ▶彼女は均斉のとれた姿をしている She has a well-proportioned *figure* [*form*]./She is well-proportioned. ▶天使の姿をした像がホールに飾られていた The statue in the *shape* [*form*] of an angel was displayed in the hall. ▶吸血鬼は夜間はコウモリの姿になって現れた The vampire showed the *form* of a bat during the night. ▶人を姿形(= 外見)で判断してはいけない Don't judge people by their *appearances*. ▶彼女は自分の姿を鏡に写してみるのが好きだ She likes to look at her *image* [look at her *reflection*, look at *herself*] in the mirror. ▶彼女は彼の姿(=面影)を忘れないだろう She will not forget his *image*. ▶この辺りではまだ野鳥の姿を見ることができる We can still see *wild birds* around here. (❗このように「…の姿」は英語では訳出しないことも多い) ▶太陽は地平線上に姿を現した The sun *appeared* above the horizon. ▶彼女はパーティーに姿を見せなかった She didn't *show* [*turn*] *up* at the party. (❗以上の3例のように, 日本文中の「姿」が「消える」「現れる」などの出現・消失に関する動詞の目的語となる場合, 英語では自動詞1語で表現されるのが普通) ▶街角の公衆電話が姿を消している Pay (×public) phones on [×in] street corners are disappearing.

❷ [様子, 状態] a state; (描かれた) a picture. ▶我々はその国の実際の姿を知らなかった We didn't know the actual *state* of the country. ▶その映画は自然のありのままの姿を描いている The movie gives us a true *picture* of nature./The movie shows nature as it is.

● 姿を消す ▶彼が姿を消してから3年になる It has been three years since he *disappeared* [(私の前から姿を消した)he *walked out of my life*]. (❗後の方は「彼」が生活を共にする人の場合).

すがたに 姿煮 ▶魚の姿煮 a fish boiled whole.
すがたみ 姿見 a full-length mirror. (⇨鏡)
すがたやき 姿焼き ▶タイの姿焼き a sea bream broiled whole on skewers.
スカッシュ ❶ [飲み物] a fizzy drink. ●レモンスカッシュ (a glass of) fizzy lemon; 《米》 lemon soda; 《英》 lemonade /lèmənéid/. (❗ 《英》 lemon squash は通例無炭酸で「レモネード」に相当する)

❷ [球技] squash rackets (❗単数扱い); squash tennis. (❗いずれも単に squash ともいう)
スカッと (さっぱりした) refreshing; (竹を割ったように) frank and sincere; (すっきりした) clean, clear (-cut); (服装などが) smart, neat, clean and simple. ●スカッとする飲み物 a *refreshing* drink. ●スカッとした服装をしている be *smartly* dressed. ▶1時間昼寝するとすっかりスカッとするよ You'll feel [be] *refreshed* after an hour's nap. ▶言いたいだけ言ったら胸がスカッとした After I said all I wanted to say, I felt *free and relaxed*.
スカッド a Scud. ([参考]湾岸戦争でイラクが使用したミサイル)
すがめ 眇 (斜視) a squint (eye).
すがめる 眇める squint. ●右目をすがめて針に糸を通した I *narrowed* my right eye and passed a thread through a needle.
-すがら ●道すがら on one's [the] way. ●夜もすがら all night (long).
ずがら 図柄 (図のパターン) a pattern; (デザイン) a design.
スカラシップ [奨学金] a scholarship. ▶彼は留学のためにスカラシップを得た He won a *scholarship* to study abroad.
すがりつく (⇨すがる) ▶彼は母にすがりついた [すがりついていた] He *clung to* [*held onto*] his mother.

すがる ❶ [しがみつく] (抱きつくように) cling* (*to*); (しっかりつかまっている) hold* (*onto*); (つえなどにもたれる) lean* (*on*). ●つえにすがって歩く walk *leaning on* a stick.

❷ [頼る] (依存する) depend [rely] (*on*); (人に頼る) look [turn] (*to* him). ●彼の援助にすがる *depend on* his help; *look* [*turn*] *to* him *for* help.

すかれる 好かれる ●人に好かれる人 a likable [(感じのいい) a *pleasant*] person. ●人に好かれない(=不愉快な)奴 an *unpleasant* [a *disgusting*] fellow. (❗後の方は「むかつくような」の意で強意的) ▶彼は親切なので人に好かれている People *like* him because he is kind. (❗*He is liked by* people …. より普通) ▶あの先生は生徒に好かれている(= 人気がある) The teacher *is popular with* [*among*] his students.

ずかん 図鑑 [図版・さし絵入りの] an illustrated book; [絵の] a picture [a pictorial] book. ●日本植物図鑑 An *Illustrated* [*A Pictorial*] *Book* of Japanese Flora.
スカンク [動物] a skunk.
スカンジナビア ●スカンジナビア半島 the Scandinavian /skæ̀ndənéiviən/ Peninsula.
ずかんそくねつ 頭寒足熱 (説明的に) keeping one's head cool and one's feet warm.
すかんぴん 素寒貧 (人) a penniless person. ▶すかんぴんだ I *have no money at all*./I am *completely* [*flat, stony*] *broke*.
すかんぽ [植物] a (wood) sorrel.
すき 好き ― 好きである 動 like; be fond of …; love; care for …; prefer (-rr-).

使い分け like 「好き」の意を表す最も一般的な語.
be fond of like より口語的で強意的.
love 「愛している」の意. また「大好き」の意で主に女性に用いられる.
care for いちばん軽い言い方で疑問文・否定文で用いることが多い.
prefer 「…より…の方が好き」と比較の気持ちがある場合に用いる.
以上いずれも通例進行形では用いない.

---

① [好きです] ▶映画は好きですか Do you *like* [*care for*] movies? ▶私は猫が大好きです I *like* cats very much./I'm very *fond of* cats./I *love* cats. (❗いずれも ×a cat は不可)/I am a cat person. (⇨大好き) ▶私はここが好きです I *like* this place./I *like* it here. (❗後の方はここが場所限定好きといった感じ. it は漠然とした状況をさす) ▶私は豚肉よりも牛肉の方が好きです I *like* beef better than pork./I *prefer* beef to pork. (❗(1) 前の方が口語的. (2) like を修飾する副詞 much は通例 much-better-best と比較変化する. love の場合は much-more-most の方が普通) ▶彼は一人旅が好きです He *likes* [*loves*] *to* travel alone./He *likes* [*loves*] traveling alone. (❗like [love] to do と like [love] doing はほぼ同意だが, 特定の行為・臨時的な行為には to do が, 一般的な行為・常時の行為には doing が好まれる) He *is fond of* traveling [×to travel] alone./(一人旅では) He *prefers* to travel [traveling] alone. ▶コーヒーは甘いのが好きですが太るのでね I *like* my coffee sweet, but it's fattening. ▶私はあなたが歌うのがとても好きです I *love* you to sing./I *love* it when you sing. (❗どちらも「どうか歌ってください」という意の間接的な言い方にもなる. the の後の it は when 以下の内容をさし, その雰囲気が好きだといった感じを表す) ▶彼女が好きで好きでたまらない I'm madly in love with her./《話》 I'm crazy about her.

すき

DISCOURSE
個人的には在宅労働より会社で働くのが好きです Personally, I *prefer* working in the office to working at [from] home. (🔍 *personally* (個人的には)は主張を表すディスコースマーカー. 個人的な好みなどを述べるときに用いる)

②【好きになる】▶彼はひと目で彼女が好きになった He came to like [got fond of, took to, (恋に陥った) fell in love with] her at first sight. (🔍 ×became to like は不可)

③【好き(なよう)に】▶君が決めることだ. お好きなように It's your decision. Do *as you please* [*like*]. (🔍「好きにしろ」と怒りや皮肉を含む言い方は Please [Suit] yourself. また許可はしないが黙認するという含みで Have it your (own) way. という)▶私の好きなにやらせてください Let me do it (*in*) *my own way*.
④【好きなだけ】 as much (+不可算名詞) as [as many (+可算名詞複数形) as] one likes. ▶好きなだけ食べてよろしい You can eat *as much as you like* [*want*]. ▶パンフレットは無料です. 好きなだけ持ち帰りください The pamphlets are free and you can take *as many* (copies) *as you like*.
⑤【好きで】▶彼は金のためではなく好きでそれをした He did it *for love*, not for money. (⇒大好き(だ)いで)
●好きこそものの上手なれ You will do well what you like.

── 好きな 形 favorite. (🔍限定的) ▶いちばん好きな小説[作家] one's (×most) *favorite* novel [writer]. (🔍 *favorite* 自体に「最も[いちばん]」の意を含んでいるので most はつけない) ▶青は彼の好きな色です Blue is his *favorite* color. ▶紅茶かコーヒーか好きな方を選べます You *have* a choice of either tea or coffee./You can *choose between* tea and coffee. ▶どちらでも好きな方を取りなさい Take whichever you *like*. ▶正直に答えてほしいのだが, ほかに好きな人でもいるのか Tell me, honestly, *are you in love with* someone else? (⇒②)

会話「君のいちばん好きな作曲家はだれ？」「モーツァルトがいちばん好きです」"Who's your *favorite* composer?" "Mozart. I like his music best (of all)."

*すき 隙 **❶【油断】** (無防備な時間) an unguarded moment; (不注意) carelessness. (⇒油断, 不注意) ▶隙に乗じる take advantage of an *unguarded moment*. ▶隙を見せない(=警戒している) stay *alert*. ▶ちょっとした心の隙が事故を生む A little *carelessness* causes an accident. ▶隙のつけ入る隙がない He is always *on his guard*./He doesn't leave any *openings*. ▶隙を突かれて一撃を食らった I *was caught off guard* [《米》*flatfooted*] and was given a blow.
❷【機会】 a chance. ●逃げる隙をうかがう wait [watch] for a *chance* to escape. ▶隙あれば人をだまそうとする連中 people who *are ready to* cheat us. ▶彼は見張りが寝ている隙に(=間に)逃げた He ran away *while* the guard was asleep.
❸【欠陥】 a fault, 《話》 a hole. ●隙だらけの理論はない A theory with a lot of *holes* in it. ▶彼の仕事には隙がない(=完璧だ) His work is *perfect* [(欠陥がない) *faultless, flawless*].
❹【余地】 room. (🔍無冠詞) ▶割り込む隙はなかった I had no *room* to step in.
すき 鋤 (牛馬・トラクターなどに引かせる) a plow /pláu/; (シャベル状のもの) a spade.
すき 数寄 (風流であること) (a) refined taste; (風流の道) elegant pursuits.
●数寄を凝らす ●数寄をこらした茶室 an *artistically* [*tastefully*] *designed* teahouse.

すぎ 杉 『植物』 a Japanese cedar /síːdər/. (🔍「杉材」の意では U)
*-**すぎ -過ぎ ❶【時】** after.... (🔍 「…以後」の意にもなるので, 直後の意味を明確に表すには just [soon] after... とする); (時刻) past ...; 『年齢』over ..., past .... (⇒過ぎる❹) ▶彼は5時半過ぎに帰宅した He came home *after* [*past*] five-thirty. ▶「5時10分過ぎに...」なら *...at ten past* (《米》*after*) *five*) ▶来月の20日過ぎにまた会おう Let's meet again (soon) *after* [×past] the 20th of next month. ▶彼は60を過ぎ(=越し)ている He is *over* [*past*] sixty.
❷【過度】▶働き過ぎは病気のもとだ Working *too hard* [《やや書》 *Overworking*] is the cause of illness./*Excessive* working causes sickness. (⇒過ぎる❺)▶それは言い過ぎだよ You've said *more than* enough./You've gone *too far*.
-ずき -好き (⇒愛好家, 愛好者) ▶彼はとてもきれい好きだ He's very (neat and) tidy.

*スキー 〖行為, 競技〗 skiing; 〖スキー板〗 (a pair of) skis. ●スキーをする ski. ●スキーがうまい be a good skier; be good at *skiing*. ●斜面をスキーですべる *ski* (*down*) *a slope*; glide down a slope *on skis*. ●スキーをはいている少年 a boy *on skis*. ▶近ごろスキーは人気のあるスポーツだ Skiing [×Ski] is a popular sport these days. ▶私は毎年北海道にスキーに行きます I *go skiing* in [×to] Hokkaido every year. (🔍 ×go to [for] *skiing*, ×go for a *ski* は不可)/I go to Hokkaido to *ski* [×for skiing] every year. ▶私はスキーが大好きだ I like *skiing* [×ski] very much.
●スキー学校 a skí schòol. ●スキー競技会 a ski competition. ●スキー靴 skí bòots. ●スキー指導員 a ski instructor. ●スキー場 (ゲレンデ) a skí rùn [slòpe], a skíing gròund; (ホテルなどを含めたスキー場全体) a skiresort. ●スキーストック 《米》 skí pòles; 《英》 skí stìcks. ●スキーズボン ski pants. ●スキー大会 a ski meet. ●スキー服 a ski sùit. ●スキー用品 〖集合的〗 skíing equipment.
スキーム 〖体系立った公的な計画〗 a scheme /skíːm/.
スキーヤー a skier.
すきかって 好き勝手 ▶好き勝手なことをする get [have] one's own way; do what one wants; (好きなように行動する) act as one likes [pleases]. (⇒好き③)

すききらい 好き嫌い likes and dislikes /láiks ən disláiks/. (🔍 *dislíke* が普通のアクセントだが対照を示すために *dís* に強勢を置く) ▶彼は食べ物の好き嫌いが激しい[多い] She has strong [many] *likes and dislikes* in [about] food. (🔍 前置詞の選択を避けて when it comes to food ともいえる)/She is *choosy* about food.

すきこのんで 好き好んで▶だれも好き好んでそんな重労働はしない Nobody *wants* to do that hard work./Nobody will do such hard work *by choice*.
すぎさる 過ぎ去る pass. (⇒経つ, 過ぎる❸)
すぎし 過ぎし ●過ぎし日の思い出 memories of *bygone days* [*days long past*].
すきずき 好き好き▶それは好き好きで(=趣味の問題だ) It's a *matter of taste*.
ずきずき ── ずきずきする 動 throb (-bb-). ●ずきずきする痛み a *throbbing* pain. ▶傷が痛くてずきずきする The wound *throbbed* with pain. ▶頭が(頭痛で)ずきずきする My head *throbs* [*aches*]. (🔍 (1) throb は通例ひどい頭痛をさすので特に with pain でなくてもよい (2) ache は throb ほどひどくはない)
スキット 〖寸劇〗 a skit.
すきっぱら 空きっ腹 an empty stomach. ●空きっ腹で酒を飲む drink *sake* on an *empty stomach*.

スキップ 图 (軽く跳んで移動すること) a skip (-pp-).
— **スキップする** 動 skip.
すきとおる 透き通る ● 透き通った (透明な) transparent /trænspǽrənt/; (澄んだ) clear.
すぎな 杉菜〚植物〛a field horsetail.
-すぎない -過ぎない only. (⇨-に過ぎない)
すきま 隙間 〚あいた空間〛an opening; 〚細長く開いた〛a gap (⇨穴); 〚ひび割れ, 裂け目〛a crack; 〚空気・水・光が通る〛a chink. (❗crack より小さい) ▶彼はフェンスのすきまを見つけて中庭に入った He found an *opening* in the fence and got into the court [*courtyard*]. ▶この家はすきま風が入る This house is *drafty* 《米》[*draughty*《英》]./There's a *draft*《米》[a *draught* /drǽft/《英》] in this house.
● **隙間風が吹く** ▶その事件以来両国の間にはすきま風が吹いている (=関係が冷え込んでいる) Since the incident the two countries have been cold toward each other./Since the incident the relations between the two countries have been cooling off.
● **隙間産業** niche industry.
スキミング skimming.
すきもの 好き物 〚好色家〛a lecherous person, a lecher; 〚好事(ゔ)家〛a dilettante.
すきや 数寄屋 (茶室) a teahouse.
● **数寄屋造り** (説明的に) a house built in the style of a teahouse.
すきやき すき焼き 〚料理〛*sukiyaki*; (説明的に) a dish of thin slices of beef, bean curd, and vegetables put in a shallow pan and cooked at the table usually by the diners themselves.
スキャナー a scanner.
スキャン a scan.
● **スキャンデータサービス** scan(ner) data service.
スキャンダラス — **スキャンダラスな** 形 scandalous.
● **スキャンダラスな事件** a *scandalous* event.
スキャンダル (a) scandal. ▶スキャンダルをもみ消す [暴露する] cover up [expose, uncover] a *scandal*. ▶映画スターのスキャンダルを話題にする [すっぱ抜く] talk *scandal about* a movie star. (❗talk の後にくる scandal は無冠詞) ▶スキャンダルに巻き込まれる get involved in a *scandal*.
スキャンティ《a pair of》scanties.
スキューバダイビング scuba diving. ▶スキューバダイビングをする scuba-dive; scuba.
すぎゆく 過ぎ行く pass. (⇨経つ)
スキル 〚技能〛(a) skill. ▶スキルアップを図る aim to improve one's skills.
:**すぎる 過ぎる** ❶ 〚通過する〛(通り過ぎる) pass. (⇨通り過ぎる). ▶あらしが過ぎるのを待つ wait for the storm to *pass*. ▶京都はもう過ぎましたか Have we *passed* Kyoto yet? ▶彼は尋ねた相手なども含めた言い方. 乗り物などに乗っている場合に多く用いる)
❷ 〚時が経つ〛pass (by [away]); go* (by); (飛ぶように) fly*. (⇨経つ) ▶日曜はすぐに過ぎる Sunday *goes* quickly.
❸ 〚終わる〛(特定の期間・催しなどが) be over; 〚過去のものとなる〛be past; 〚期限が切れる〛(契約・許可などが) (やや書) expire; (契約・時間などが) run* out. ▶厳しかった冬も過ぎ春が来た The severe winter *is over* [*past*] and spring has come [is now with us]. ▶君の免許証は期限が過ぎたよ Your driver's license *has expired*. ▶過ぎたこと (=過去) は忘れろ Forget (about) *the past*. ▶過ぎたことは仕方がない [してしまったことは元に戻せない]《ことわざ》*What's done* cannot be *undone*./《ことわざ》It is no use crying over spilt milk.
❹ 〚越える〛(年齢・数量などが) be over; (時刻などが) be past; (期限などが) be overdue. ▶彼女は 20 歳を過ぎている She *is over* [*past*] twenty. ▶彼が来たときには約束の時間はとうに過ぎていた When he came, it *was* well *past* the appointed time. ▶あなたのレポートは提出期限を 3 日過ぎています Your report *is* three days *overdue*./You've three days *too late* handing in your report.
❺ 〚度を越す〛《形容詞・副詞・数量詞を伴う名詞を修飾して》too ...; 《動詞・形容詞の接頭辞として》over-.

> 解説 over- について: 比較的自由に動詞や形容詞の前に置かれ複合語を作るが, 総じて堅い語: 食べ[働き, 重] 過ぎる *overeat* [*overwork*; *be overweight*]. (❗それぞれ eat *too much*; work *too hard* [*much*]; be *too heavy* [*fat*] の方がくだけた言い方)

▶彼女はリンゴ [砂糖] を買い過ぎた She bought *tóo mànȳ ápples* [*mùch súgar*]. ▶この肉は固過ぎる This meat is *too* tough. (❗×This is *too* tough meat. は不可) ▶あの絵はあまりにも高過ぎる That picture is much [a lot, far] *too* expensive. (❗too を強めるのは very を用いるのは不可. 逆に too を弱めて「ちょっと...すぎる」なら a little [a bit] *too* ... などとする) ▶彼は来るのが遅過ぎた He came *too* late. ▶(いすが) 一つ多過ぎる There is one (chair) *too* many. ▶この紙は大き過ぎてその封筒に入らない The paper is *too* big for the envelope. ▶この本は難し過ぎて読めない This book is *too* difficult *to* read (×it) [*for me to* read (it)]. (❗(1) for 句がない場合は it は省略されるのが普通. (2) 単に This book is *too* difficult *for* me. ともいえる)/This book is *so* difficult (*that*) I can't read it. (⇨非常に) ▶彼女は君には過ぎた (=とてもよい) 女房だ She is *only too* good *to* be your wife [*only too* good a wife for you, ×a *too* good wife for you]. (❗She is *much too* good to be your wife. では「女房になるにはよすぎる」で 以下は否定の意味になり結局「女房にはならない」となって不可. only too では very の強意表現で, to 以下は否定の意にならない) ▶その仕事をするときはいくら注意しても過ぎることはない You *cannot* be careful *enough* [*too* careful] when you do the job. ▶冗談が少し過ぎるよ You are carrying your joke a bit [a little] *too far*.
● **過ぎるは及ばざるがごとし**《ことわざ》Too much is as bad as too little.
スキン 〚皮膚〛(a) skin; 〚コンドーム〛a rubber (⇨コンドーム).
● **スキンクリーム** a skin cream; skin food. ● **スキンケア** 〚肌の手入れ〛skin care.
ずきん 頭巾 a hood /húd/. (⇨フード) ● **赤ずきんちゃん** 〚童話名〛*Little Red Riding-Hood*.
スキンシップ body [physical] contact; 《和製語》skinship. ▶スキンシップが足りている赤ん坊は心身ともに健全であると言われている It is said that babies who receive enough *physical contact* are healthy in mind and body.
ずきんずきん (⇨ずきずき)
スキンダイビング skin diving. ▶スキンダイビングをする skin-dive.
スキンヘッド 〚丸刈り頭の若者〛a skinhead. (〘参考〙しばしば暴力的な人種差別主義集団の一員ともみなされる)
*****すく 空く** ▶腹がすく feel [be] *hungry*. ▶今夜手がすいていますか Are you *free* tonight? ▶電車はすいていた (混雑していなかった) The train was *not crowded*. ▶(ほとんど乗客はいなかった) There were *few* [*hardly any*] *passengers* in [on] the train. ▶道路がすいていたので思ったより早く来られました I got here earlier than I (had) expected because the

すく road *was clear* [(the) traffic *was light* on the road].
会話「お腹がすいたでしょう．何か用意しましょうか」「コーヒーだけお願い．実はまだおなかがすいていないのよ」"You must be *hungry*. Shall I get you something to eat?" "Just a cup of coffee, please. Actually, I'*m* still *stuffed*."

すく 好く [[好む]]like, be fond of ...; [[大好きだ]]love. (⇨好む, 好かれる, 虫❷)

すく 透く thin (-nn-). (⇨透ける) ▶少し毛をすいてください Could you *thin* my hair a little?

すく 梳く （髪を）comb /kóum/. (⇨透く)

すく 漉く ●紙をすく *make* paper.

すく 鋤く plow /pláu/ (a field).

すぐ ❶ [[ただちに]] at once, right away [off], right now, now; immediately, directly; right; instantly.

> **使い分け** at once 「(ぐずぐずしないで)ただちに」の意の最も一般的な語．
> right away [off] at once とほぼ同義でくだけた言い方．《米》では at once より好まれる．
> right now「今すぐ」という感じ．
> immediately 時間的な間隔を置かずすぐにという意のやや堅い語．《話》ではしばしば強意的に用いる．
> directly immediately と同義だが，《話》では「ほどなく (very soon)」の意で用いられる．
> right immediately とほぼ同意だが，ややくだけた語で通例副詞・前置詞の前で用いる．
> instantly「即座に」の意でさらに強意的．

▶すぐ参ります I'll come [×go] *at once* [*right away*, *in no time*]./I'*m coming*. （進行形により動作がすでに始まっていることを表す）/I'll *be right there* [*with you*]. ▶ちょっと失礼します．すぐ戻ってきますので Would you excuse me? I'll *be right back*./I'll be back *right away* [*in a moment, in a minute*]./I won't *be long*. （❗「長くはかかりません」の意で I'll be back *soon*. とほぼ同意 (⇨❷)) ▶すぐに返事をください Please send an *immediate* reply./Please write (me) back [respond (to me)] *soon*. （❗ write back は「返事を書く」の意） ▶科学部は放課後すぐに(会を始めます The science club will meet *right* after school. （❗ right は after を強める）
会話「コーヒーをもう少し持ってきてくれませんか」「はい，すぐお持ちします」"Could you bring us some more coffee, please?" "Yes, *right away*."
会話「これまでは時間がなかったんだよ」「じゃあ今すぐ始めなさい」"So far I haven't had time." "Start (*right*) *now* [Get *right* on with it]," then."

【...するとすぐ(に)】 as soon as .... ▶家に着くとすぐ彼女に電話した As soon as [*The moment*, *The instant*, *The minute*, 《英》 *Immediately*, 《英話》 *Directly*] I got home, I called her./When I got home, I called her *at once* [*immediately*]. / *Right* [*Immediately*] after I got home, I called her./《書》*On getting* home, I called her.

> **解説** the moment, the instant, the minute は as soon as とほぼ同意だが，やや強意的で「...すると同時に」の意に近い．《英》では immediately, directly も接続詞的に as soon as と同じ意味で用いられる．no sooner ... than と hardly [scarcely] ... when は通例過去の文脈で用いられ，前の方は as soon as の強意的表現で，後の方は「...した途端に（何か他の事が起こった）」の意を表す：家に着くとすぐ雨が降り出した I *had no sooner* gotten home *than* [I *had hardly* gotten home *when*] it

began to rain./*No sooner had* I gotten home *than* [*Hardly had* I gotten home *when*] it began to rain. （❗いずれも主節の動詞は be 動詞以外は通例過去完了形．no sooner, hardly を文頭に出した後の方が強意的で堅い表現．倒置が起こることに注意）

会話「いつ出発しましょうか」「君の準備ができたらすぐに出発しなさい」"When shall I leave?" "Leave *as soon as* [*whenever*] you're ready." （❗未来のことを述べる場合でも副詞節なので ×... you'*ll* be ready. のようには未来形は用いない）

❷ [[間もなく]] soon, presently (❗後の方が堅い語); (ほどなく) before long (❗ soon とほぼ同意だが，やや文語的); (じきに) shortly (❗以上の語より短い時間で very soon とほぼ同意); (ほとんど) almost, nearly. ▶彼はすぐにここに到着するでしょう He will *soon* arrive [《まれ》 soon will arrive] here./He will arrive here *soon* [*before long, shortly*]./《主に書》*It will not be long before* he arrives [×will arrive] here. ▶事故の後すぐ警察がやって来た *Shortly* [*Soon*] after the accident, the police came. (⇨間もなく) ▶彼は試合が終わるとすぐにフィールドから走り去った As soon as the game was over, he ran out of the field. ▶正月はもうすぐそこだ The New Year *is coming soon* [*is drawing near*]./The New Year *is just around the corner*. ▶もうすぐ３時だ It is *almost* [*nearly*] three.

❸ [[容易に]] easily, with ease, 《やや書》 readily. ▶紙袋はぬれるとすぐに破れる Paper bags break *easily* when they are wet. ▶彼はすぐ(＝快く)その計画に同意した He *readily* agreed to the plan.

❹ [[距離的に]] (ごく近くに) close /klóus/ (⇨近い ❶); (まさに) right; (ちょうど) just. ▶彼は学校のすぐ近くに住んでいる He lives *near* [*close to*] the school. （❗後の方が接近の度合が強い）▶彼女は私のすぐそばに座った She sat *just* beside me./（隣に座った）She sat *next to* me. ▶エチオピアの選手が彼女のすぐ後ろについて走っている An Ethiopian runner is (running) *close* behind her. ▶その事故はすぐ目の前で起こった The accident occurred *right* in front of me [*right* before my eyes].

会話「バス停はここからすぐですか」「ええ，すぐそこです」"Is the bus stop very *near* here [×near from here]?" "Yes, (it's) *just a little way from* here [*just around the corner*]."

会話「その店はどこですか」「駅のすぐ隣です」"Where is the store?" "It's *right* next door to the station."

-ずく [[...によって]] by ...; [[...のために]] for ...; for the sake of ... (❗ for より強意的). ● 腕[力]ずくで彼から金を奪う take money from him *by* force; use force to take money from him. ● 相談ずくで(＝よく相談した上で)決めたこと a decision *reached by* mutual consent; a decision *as the outcome of* one's discussion. ● 損得ずくで (金のために) *for* (*the sake of*) money; (名声のために) *for* one's name's *sake*. ● 計算ずくで *with* calculation.

すくい 救い [[助力]]help; [[救助]]rescue; [[救援]]relief; [[神の]]salvation; [[取り柄]]a saving grace, a redeeming feature. ● 救いようのないばか a *hopeless* [an *incurable*] idiot. (⇨救いがたい) ● 救いを求める ask for *help*. (⇨助け) ▶その患者は救いようがない The patient is *beyond help* [*hope*]. （❗前の方は「手の施しようがない」，後の方は「回復の見込みがない」の意) ▶親切なのが彼の救い (＝欠点を補うとりえ)だ He has the *saving grace* [*redeeming feature*] of kindness./His one *redeeming feature* is his

すくいあげる

kindness.

すくいあげる 掬い上げる ● シャベルで雪をすくい上げる *shovel up* snow. ● ゴロをすくい上げる *scoop [pick] up* a grounder. ● 内角球をすくい上げてレフトへホームランを打つ *golf* an inside pitch over the left-field fence.

スクイーザー 〖レモンなどの圧搾器〗a squeezer.

すくいがたい 救いがたい ● 救いがたい(=矯正できない)悪党 an *incorrigible* rogue. ● 救いがたい奴(=ろくでなし) a good-for-nothing.

スクイズ 〖野球〗a squeeze /skwíːz/ (play). (❗普通の「スクイズ」は a suicide [running] squeeze, 「セーフティースクイズ」は a safety squeeze) ● スクイズをする run [try] a *squeeze*. ● スクイズバントをする make a bunt on a *squeeze play*. ● スクイズで1点取る *squeeze* in a run.

すくいぬし 救い主 ● 救い主の出現を予言する foretell the advent of *the Saviour [the Messiah]*. (⇨救世主)

*__すくう__ 救う 〖救助する〗save; rescue; help (⇨助ける❷); 〖救援・救済する〗relieve; 〖罪から〗save, 《医》redeem 《us *from* our sins》. ● 彼の命を救う *save* [×rescue, ×help] his life. ● おぼれている子を救う *save* [*rescue, help*] a drowning child; *save* [*rescue*] a child *from* drowning. ● 苦境[危険]から彼女を救い出す *help* her *out of* difficulties [danger]. ● その食料で多くの人が飢餓から救われた The food *saved* many people *from* starvation. ▶彼が私を支持してくれるのを知って救われた(=ほっとした) I *felt relieved* to learn that he supported me.

すくう 巣くう 〖鳥が〗nest, build* a nest; 〖悪い者たちが〗be based 〖have* a base〗《in》; infest. ● ソーホーに巣くっている暴力団の一味 a Soho-*based* gang.

〖翻訳のこころ〗もう、どうでもいいという、勇者にも似合いなふてくされた根性が、心の隅に巣くった(太宰治『走れメロス』) I thought, "I don't care anymore (what happens next)." Such a sulky [sullen] thought as is unbecoming to a brave man became lodged in a corner of my mind. (❗(1) spirit や gut は一般的によい意味での「根性」. したがって、ここでは sullen [sulky] thought (ふてくされた考え方)とする. (2)「(根性が)巣くった」は become lodged (しっかりと食い込んだ)と表す)

すくう 掬う ❶〖液体などを手・スプーンなどで〗scoop. ● アイスクリームを容器からすくう *scoop* ice cream *out of* the container; *scoop out* ice cream *from* the container. ● しゃくしでスープをすくって皿によそう *ladle (out)* soup *into* the plates.

❷〖足を〗《物・人が》trip (-pp-)《him》up; 《波などが》sweep*《him》off《his》feet. ▶マットに足もとをすくわれて(=つまずいて)倒れた I *tripped on* the mat and fell down./The mat *tripped* me *up* and I fell.

スクーター a (motor) scooter. (⇨自転車)

スクープ 图〖新聞などの特ダネ〗a scoop. ▶その記事は大スクープだった The news story was a big [a great, a major] *scoop*.

── **スクープする** 動 ▶朝日新聞はその収賄(しゅうわい)事件をスクープした The Asahi *got a scoop on* [*scooped*] the other newspapers with the story of the bribery case.

スクーリング 〖学校授業〗schooling. ● ホームスクーリング 〖在宅授業〗home *schooling*.

スクール 〖学校〗a school. ● スクールカラー (学校を象徴する) school colors; (校風) school tradition. ● スクールゾーン a school

---

すくない

zone. ● スクールバス a school bus.

スクエアダンス a square dance. ● スクエアダンスをする square-dance.

スクエアパス 〖サッカー〗a square pass. (参考) フィールドを横切るパス)

すぐさま (⇨すぐ)

すくすく ▶両親は子供がすくすく育っていくのを見てうれしかった The parents were happy to see their child grow *healthily*. ▶稲がすくすく育っている The rice is growing *very well*.

*__すくない__ 少ない

● WORD CHOICE ● 少ない

little 量や程度が少なくて、ほとんどないこと. a ～ の場合は「少しはある」という肯定的意味に変化する. ▶水はほとんどなかった[ごく少なかった] There were *little* water.

few 人や物の数が少なくて、ほとんどないこと. a ～ の場合は「少しはある」という肯定的意味に変化する. ▶勉強が好きな生徒なんてほとんどいない[ごく少ない] Very *few* students like studying.

a small number [amount] of 数 (number) や 量 (amount) が少ないながらあること. 通例, 否定的含意は伴わない. ● 教室には, 生徒が少し残っていた There remained *a small number of* students in the classroom.

◆頻度チャート◆

little ████████████████████

few ████████████

a small number [amount] of ████

20　40　60　80　100 (%)

〖数が〗few (❗複数可算名詞の前で); 〖量が〗little* (❗不可算名詞の前で); 〖数・量・額が〗small (↔ large), low; 〖量・重さ・額が不足して〗short.

〖解説〗few, little は少数・少量を「ほとんどない」と否定的にとらえる言い方. 話し言葉では、「少しはある」と肯定的にとらえる a few, a little と区別がつきにくいため、通例, very, so, too などに修飾されたり、not ... many [much], only a few [a little], hardly any が代わりに用いられる.

▶100歳まで生きる人は少ない Very *few* [(多くない) *Not many*, (少しの人数しか) *Only a small number of*] people live to be one hundred years old. ▶彼は口数が少ない He doesn't talk *much*./He talks *very little*./He is a man of *few words*. ▶私は彼より間違いが少なかった I made *fewer* [(話) *less*] mistakes than he did. (❗ I didn't make *as many* mistakes *as* he did. の方が口語的) ▶彼の成功の見込みは少ない There is *very little* [*not much*] hope of his success. ▶私は妹よりも収入が少ない I earn *less* money than my sister. の方が口語的)/My income is *smaller* (×less) than my sister's. (❗「人口 (population)」「家族 (family)」「群衆 (crowd)」などにも用いる) ▶燃料が残り少なくなってきた We are getting *low on* [*running short of*] fuel./The fuel is getting *low* [*running short*]. ▶彼は家にいることが少ない(=めったにない) He *hardly ever* [*almost never*] stays (at) home. (❗前の方が口語的)/He *rarely* [〖書〗*seldom*] stays (at) home. ▶おいしいコーヒーを飲ませる店は少なくなった The number of shops which serve good coffee *has* [×have] *decreased* [(少なかったのさら

すくなからず

に) has become less and less]. (**!** The shops which ... とはいわない) (⇒減る) ▶本学の本年度入学学生数は今までで最も少ない Enrollment in our college reached a new low this spring. (**!** new low は「新たな最低値」の意)

すくなからず 少なからず 副 《書》not a little (**!** 遠回しな言い方で実際には「大いに」); (大いに) greatly (**!** 主に過去分詞・動詞を修飾); (大変) very much; (たくさん) a great [a good] deal. ▶その光景を見て少なからず驚いた I was not a little [was greatly] surprised at the sight. (**!** ×I wasn't a little ... としない) ▶彼に少なからず世話になっています I owe a great deal [**話** a lot] to him.

──少なからぬ 形 no small, 《書》not a few [a little] (**!** few は複数可算名詞の前で, little は不可算名詞の前で); (相当の) considerable. ▶少なからぬ金額 no small amount of money; a considerable [a good, 《まれ》not a little] sum of money. ▶少なからぬ本が紛失していた Not a few (かなり多くの) [Quite a few, 《話》A good few] books were missing.

***すくなくとも 少なくとも** at least (↔at (the) most) (**!** 修飾しようとする語句の直前・直後以外では at the least が好まれる); not fewer than..., not less than... (**!** 前の方は数のみ, 後の方は原則として量に用いるが, 《話》では数に用いることも多い). ●少なくとも1日に4時間勉強する study at least four hours a day; study four hours a day at the least. ▶少なくとも30人の労働者が負傷した At least [Not less than, Not fewer than] thirty workers were injured.

すくなめ 少な目 ●塩を少なめに入れる do not put in much salt; put in a moderate amount of salt.

すくに (⇒すぐ)

すくむ 竦む ●血を見てすくむ(=ひるむ) shrink (ちぢこまる), cower, (後ずさりする) draw back, (動けなくなる) freeze] at the sight of blood. ●足がすくむ(恐怖などで) be paralyzed [be petrified, freeze] (with fear). ▶緊張のあまり足がすくんで(=ひざがだめになって)歩けなかった I was so nervous (that) my knees gave way and I couldn't walk.

-ずくめ [すべて(の)] all; [...でいっぱいの] full of .... ●黒ずくめの服装をしている be (dressed) all in black. ●つらい事ずくめの一生 a life full of anguish. ●規則ずくめでうんざりだ I am sick and tired of rules and regulations. ●人生いいことずくめにいかないものだ Life isn't all beer and skittles [all cakes and ale]. (**!** (1) 前の方は《英》に多い. skittles は「九柱戯」と訳すボウリングに似た遊び. (2) 後の方はシェイクスピアの方が多い)

すくめる 竦める ●肩をすくめる shrug one's shoulders. 《事情》肩を上げ両手を上に向けて, あきらめ, 困惑, うんざりした気持ちなどを表す動作) ●肩をすくめて with a shrug of the [one's] shoulders. ●首をすくめる duck one's head [×neck]. (**!**「頭上の障害物を避けるために頭を下げる」の意)

スクラッチ scratch (**参考** レコードの回転を手でわざと変えて作り出す音[技法]); (行為) scratching.
●スクラッチカード a scratch card. (**参考** 表面をこすり取ると「当たり」「はずれ」などが出てくる) ●スクラッチプレーヤー[ゴルフ] a scratch player. (**参考** ハンデ 0 のプレーヤー) ●スクラッチノイズ a scratch; (a) scrachy noise. (**参考** レコードなどが傷や溝のために出す不快な音) ●スクラッチヒット[野球] a scratch hit [single].

スクラップ (廃物) scrap (**!** scraps とすれば残飯の意); (新聞などの切り抜き) 《米》a clipping, 《英》a cutting. ●金属のスクラップ metal scrap; scrap metal.

スケート

●鉄をスクラップにする scrap iron. ▶その車はスクラップとして売られた The car was sold as [for] scrap.
●スクラップアンドビルド scrap and build. (**参考** 効率の悪い部門を整理し, 新しい部門を設けること) ●スクラップブック a scrapbook.

スクラム [ラグビー] a scrum, 《書》a scrummage /skrʌ́mɪdʒ/. ●スクラムを組む scrummage, form [line up for] a scrummage; (比喩的に) join forces [hands] 《to do》.
●スクラムハーフ a scrum half.

スクランブル [緊急発進] a scramble. ●スクランブルをかける scramble.
●スクランブルエッグ[炒(い)り卵] scrambled egg(s). (**!** 複数形でも単数扱い) ●スクランブル交差点 (説明的に) a crossing where vehicles from all directions are stopped at a time for pedestrians.

すぐり [植物] a gooseberry.

スクリーニング [ふるい分け] screening.

スクリーン [映写幕] a screen; [映画(界)] the screen.
●スクリーンセーバー a screen saver. ●スクリーンテスト (映画の出演者を選考するための) a screen test. ●スクリーンプレー[映画のシナリオ] a screenplay. ●スクリーンプロセス[映画] a screen process.

スクリプト a (TV [movie]) script. ●テレビドラマのスクリプトを書く write a script for a TV play.

スクリュー a screw; (船の) a screw (propeller).
●スクリュードライバー a screw driver. ●スクリューボール[野球] a screwball. (**参考** 回転も曲がる方向もカーブと逆)

すぐれもの 優れ物 an object of great utility.

***すぐれる 優れる, 勝れる** ● be excellent, excel (-ll-) /ɪksél/ 《in, at》; [勝る] be better 《than》, 《書》surpass /səːrpǽs/. ●人よりすぐれる excel [be superior to] others. ▶彼は英語[スポーツ]にすぐれている He is excellent in English [at sports]. (**!** in は学科・能力, at は運動・技術などに用いられることが多い)/(得意である) He is very good at English [sports]. (**!** good in とすれば「学科」がすぐれていることをいう) ▶この辞書はあれよりすぐれている This dictionary is better than [superior to, ×superior than] that.

── すぐれない 動 [気分・体の調子が] don't feel* [be not] well*; [健康が] be in poor [bad*] health, 《話》be out of sorts; [顔色が] look pale [unwell, 《主に米》sick, 《主に英》ill]. ▶今日は気分がすぐれない I don't feel well today. (**!** I am not feeling well. のように進行形で用いると特に一時的状態を強調) ▶どうしたんだい. 今日は顔色がすぐれないね What's the matter? You don't look well [look pale] today.

── すぐれた 形 very good; excellent; (傑出した) òutstánding; prominent. ●すぐれた作品 a great [an excellent] work; a masterpiece. ●すぐれた点 a good point; (利点) a merit. ●非常にすぐれた仕事をする do quite éxcellent [òutstánding] wórk. (**!** (1) quite は次の形容詞より弱く発音することに注意. (2) quite の代わりに very は用いない) ▶物理ですぐれた成績をとる get a very good [an excellent, a high] grade in physics. ▶これは今まで見た中で最もすぐれた映画だ This is the best [the most excellent] movie (that) I have ever seen.

スクロール ── **スクロールする** 動 [コンピュータ] (上に) scroll (up [down]).

すげ 菅 [植物] a sedge. ●菅笠 a sedge hat.

ずけい 図形 a figure. ●平面図形 a plane figure.

***スケート** [競技, 行為] skating; [靴] (a pair of) skates. ●スケートをする skate. ●スケートが上手だ [へ

ただ] be a good [a poor] skater; be good [poor] at *skating*. ●スケートをはく put on *skates*. ●スピード[フィギュア]スケート speed [figure] *skating*. ▶我々は湖へスケートに行った We *went skating* on [×to] the lake./We went to the lake to *skate* [×for skating].
●スケート場[リンク] a skáting [an íce, ×a skate] rìnk.

スケートボード (板) a skateboard; (遊び) ⟪enjoy⟫ skateboarding.

スケープゴート 〖身代わり〗a scapegoat. ●…のスケープゴートにされる be made [be used as] a *scapegoat* for ….

スケール 〖規模〗(a) scale; 〖人物の度量〗(a) caliber. ●スケールの大きい計画 a *large-scale* plan. ●世界的なスケールで on a world [a global] *scale*. ●スケールの大きい人 a person *of high caliber*.

スケールメリット 〖規模(拡大)効果〗the merit of scale; (和製語) scale merit.

すげかえる すげ替える change; (AをBと) replace ⟪A *with* B⟫. ▶監督の首をすげ替えてもあのチームは強くならないだろう I don't think the team would be stronger even if the manager *is replaced* [*is changed*].

スケジュール a schedule. (!通例単数形で) ●非常にきついスケジュールで on a very tight *schedule*. ●スケジュールの遅れを取り戻す(＝に戻る) get back on *schedule*. ●スケジュールを調整する arrange one's *calendar*. ▶彼のスケジュールはきつい His *schedule* is tight [hectic, crowded, ×hard]./He has a tight [a crowded, a demanding] *schedule*. ▶あなたは冬休みのスケジュールをもう立てましたか Have you made up [laid out] a *schedule for* the Christmas holidays yet? ▶今週のあなたのスケジュールはどうなっていますか What does your *schedule* look like this week? ▶計画は今のところスケジュールどおりに進行している The project is right *on schedule*./The project is going *as scheduled* [*according to* (*the*) *schedule*].

すけすけ 透け透け　― 透け透けの 形 see-through; (極薄の) sheer. (⇨透ける)

ずけずけ ●ずけずけ言う speak bluntly [brusquely, (率直に) frankly]; be outspoken in one's remarks. ●経営陣をずけずけ(＝遠慮なく)批判する人 an *outspoken* critic of the management. ▶ずけずけ言わせてもらいますが，きみの仕事は雑ですね To be blunt, your work is sloppy.

すけそうだら 助宗鱈 (⇨介党(すけとう)鱈)

すけだち 助太刀 〖助力〗help, ⟪やや書⟫ assistance; 〖助力者〗a helper; (加勢要員) a backup. ●けんかの助太刀をする *help* [⟪書⟫ *assist*] him *in* a fight.

スケッチ 名 〖写生画〗a sketch; 〖写生〗sketching.
― スケッチする 動 ●木をスケッチする *sketch* trees; make [draw] a *sketch* of trees.
●スケッチブック a sketchbook.

すけっと 助っ人 a helper. ●メジャーからの助っ人 an *outside help* from the majors.

すけとうだら 介党鱈 〔魚介〕an Alaska pollack.

すげない ●すげない(＝そっけない)返事をする give a *curt* answer; answer curtly. ●彼にすげなくする(＝を冷淡に扱う) treat him *coldly*; give him the cold shoulder. ●すげなく(＝きっぱりと)断る *flatly* refuse; refuse *point-blank*; give ⟪him⟫ a flat [a point-blank] refusal.

すけばん 助番 (女の番長) the girl leader of a group of juvenile delinquents.

すけべい 助平 名 a lecher; ⟪話⟫ a lech. (!主に男性に用いる)
― 助平な 形 (性的にうずうずしている) lecherous; (みだらな) dirty, ⟪やや書⟫ lewd. ▶彼は助平根性から株に手を出した He tried to push his luck by speculating in stocks.

すける 透ける 〖透明である〗be transparent; 〖透けて見える〗be seen through. ●肌が透けて見えるブラウス a *transparent* [a *see-through*] blouse. (!sheer は極薄の生地をさすが，透けて見えるとは限らない) ▶彼女のブラウスは透けて見える Her blouse *is transparent* [*see-through*].

スケルツォ [<イタリア語]〖三拍子の急速で快活な音楽〗〔音楽〕scherzo /skéərtsou/ (複 ～s, scherzi /-tsiː/).

スコア a score. (⇨得点) ●スコアをつける keep (the) *score*.
●スコアカード a scorecard. ●スコアシート a scoresheet. ●スコアブック a scorebook. (参考 スコアカードを1冊にとじたもの) ●スコアブックをつける fill out a scorecard. ●スコアボード a scoreboard.

スコアラー 〔野球〕a scout. (!a scorer は安打か失策かなど，試合中のプレーを判定する記録員) ●先乗りスコアラー an advance *scout*.

スコアリングポジション 〔野球〕scoring position. ●スコアリングポジションに走者を進める move a runner into *scoring position*.

***すごい 凄い** 形 〖恐ろしい〗terrible; horrible; 〖すばらしい〗wonderful, ⟪話⟫ great, ⟪話⟫ fantastic (!この順で強意的); 〖はなはだしい〗(程度・数量など) great, ⟪話⟫ awful (!限定的に); (程度・量・強さなど) terrific; (まったくの) real. (⇨大変)
① 【すごい～】 ●すごい光景 a *terrible* [a *horrible*] sight. ●すごい読書家 a *great* [(熱烈な) an *avid*] reader. ●すごい風 a *violent* wind. ●すごい雨 a *heavy* rain. ●すごい音 an *awful* [(耳をつんざくような) a *deafening*] sound. ●すごい人気 *great* [*huge*, ⟪話⟫ *immense*, *fantastic*] popularity. ●すごい速度で at a *terrific* speed. ▶それをするのにはすごい技術がいる It takes *great* [⟪話⟫ *a lot of*] skill to do it. ▶彼の姉さんはすごい美人だ His sister is a *real* beauty. (!驚き・意外性を暗示)/His sister is *very* [*really*, ⟪主に米話⟫ *real*, ⟪話⟫ *awfully*] beautiful.
② 【…が[は]すごい】 ●英語力がすごい have a *wonderful* command of English.
会話 「15歳の少年がプロサッカーの試合で決勝点を決めたんだよ」「そいつはすごい」 "A 15-year-old boy scored the winning goal in the pro soccer game." "↘That's ↗*great* [*fantastic*, *amazing*]! (!くだけた言い方では That's はしばしば省略される)/(大したものじゃないか) Ísn't that ↘*something*! (!感嘆文の一種)" (!他に What an achievement! (すごいお手柄だ)/That's like a fairy tale. (うそみたいな話だ)/⟪米話⟫ He's awesome. (すごい子だね) などのようにもいえる)
― すごく 副 〖非常に〗very much, very, so (!so は主に女性に好まれる); ⟪話⟫ terribly, ⟪話⟫ awfully (!いずれもよい意味にも悪い意味にも用いる. awfully は主に女性語); (実に) really. ●すごく急いで in a *terrible* [⟪話⟫ an *awful*] hurry; in *such* a hurry. ●すごくたくさんの人 a *great* [a *good*] many people; an *awful* lot of people. (⇨たくさん) ▶電車はすごく混雑していた The train was *very* [*terribly*] crowded. ▶ジャズがすごく好きだ I like jazz *very much* [⟪話⟫ *a lot*, ×much]. (!Much I like jazz. のような倒置文の場合を除き，肯定文では much は単独では用いない)/I *really* like jazz./I'm *very* [*awfully*] fond of jazz. ▶すごくいい味だわ It ↘*does* taste [*really* tastes] ↗nice! (!does は助動詞で taste を強める)/It tastes ↘*so* ↗nice!

ずこう 図工 (学科の図画・工作) drawing and manual arts. ●図工の時間 the *art* class [lesson]. ●図工の先生 an *art* teacher.

すごうで 凄腕 ●すご腕の人 (抜け目のない人) a shrewd person; (敏腕家) a go-getter, (米話) a hustler. ●すご腕の実業家 a *shrewd* [《米俗》(飛ぶ切りすばらしい) a *crackerjack*] businessman [businesswoman].

スコール a heavy shower (in the tropic). (!squall は「雨[雪]まじりの突風」)

すごさ 凄さ (⇒凄味(ホシ))

すこし 少し ❶ 〖数，量〗 (少数の) a few; 《やや書》a small number [small numbers] of ... (!以上は複数可算名詞の前で); (少量の) a little; 《やや書》a small quantity [small quantities] of ... (!以上は不可算名詞の前で); (数・量が少ない) some /sʌm/ (!複数可算名詞・不可算名詞の前で); (数・量・額が小さい) small (!主に数量を表す名詞・集合名詞の前で).

> **解説** a few, a little は少数・少量を「少しはある」と肯定的にとらえる言い方。「ほとんどない」のように否定的にとらえる場合は few, little を無冠詞で用いるが、話し言葉では a few, a little と区別がつきにくいため、通例、very, so, too などに修飾されたり、not ... many [much], only a few [a little], hardly any が代わりに用いられる。some (疑問文・否定文・条件文では any) が不特定の数量を漠然と表し、数を表す場合は通例三つ以上に用いる。日本語に「少し」という言葉が特にない場合でも、数量を明確に表す必要がない場合は、不定冠詞の複数形の働きをするものとして用いられる。ただし、以上はいずれも相対的な表現で、話し手の感じ方や文脈によって同じ数量に用いられる可能性がある。

●少し買い物[散歩]をする do *some* shopping [walking]. ●(選挙などで)少しの差で敗れる be defeated by a *small* [a *narrow*] margin. ▶少し (⇒もう ❸ ③) ▶私はパリに友達が少しいる I have *a few* [*some*] friends in Paris. ▶彼女に少し迷惑をかけた I gave her *a little* [*some*] trouble. (!some を /sʌm/ と発音すると「かなりの」の意) ▶それにはんの少し塩を加えなさい Add just *a touch of* [《くだけて》*a pinch of*] salt to it. ▶本が少し図書館から盗まれた *A few* [*Some*, *A small number of*] books were stolen from the library. ▶少しでも疑問があったら、私に聞いてください Please ask me if you have *any* questions at all. ▶彼だって少しは息抜きが必要だ Even he needs *a bit of* relaxation.

【少ししか...ない】▶テストでは少ししか間違えなかった I made *very few* [*only a few*, *hardly any*, 《書》*few*] mistakes on the test. ▶時間は少ししか残っていない There is *very little* [*only a little*, *hardly any*, 《書》*little*] time left.

❷ 〖程度〗 (少し) a little, (話) a bit, a little bit; (いくぶん) rather, 《やや書》somewhat (!rather は本来は控えめな表現だが、しばしば「かなり、ずいぶん」の意を暗示する); (わずかばかり) slightly; (ちょっと...するところ) almost, nearly. ▶右に少し動いてください Move *a little* to the right. ▶彼は少し英語が話せる He can speak English *a little* [*a little* English]. ▶少し疲れた I am *a little* [*a* (*little*) *bit*] tired. ▶そのニュースを聞いて少し驚いている I am *rather* [*somewhat*] surprised at the news. ▶*rather* の方が主観的な語) ▶この靴は少し大きすぎる These shoes are *a little* [*a bit*, *rather*] too big for me. ▶彼は転んで少しけがをした He was *slightly* hurt when he fell down. ▶少し頭痛がする I have a *slight* headache. ▶彼は少しずつ回復した He got better *little by little* [《徐々に》*gradually*, 《やや書》*by degrees*]. ▶今日は少し気分がいい I feel *a little* [*slightly*, *rather*, 《話》*somewhat*] better today. ▶もう少しで車にひかれるところだった I was *almost* [*nearly*] run over by a car. (⇒もう ❸ ③)

会話「このナイフはだめだ」「ぼくのは少しはましかな」"This knife's hopeless." "Well, would mine cut *any* better?" (!any は副詞として否定文・疑問文で比較級を強め「少しは, 少しも」の意)

❸ 〖時間〗 (少しの間) a little [a short] while; some time; (瞬間) a moment, a minute, a second. ▶彼は少したら戻ってきます He'll be back in *a little while*./(まもなく) He'll be back *soon*. ▶彼女は少し前に帰ってきた She came back *a little* [*a short*] *while* ago. ▶私たちは 5 時少し前に到着した We arrived *shortly* [*some time*] before five. (!shortly は「寸前」に近い) ▶図書館の完成までにまだひと月かかる It will be *some time* before the library is [×will be] completed. ▶少しお待ちください Please wait (*for*) *a moment* [*a minute*]. /*One moment*, please. ▶少しあとで(=もう少ししてから)また いらっしゃい Come again *a little later*. ▶この薬を飲んで少し眠った方がいい You should take this medicine and get *a little* sleep [sleep *for a little while*].

❹ 〖距離〗 (短い距離) a short distance; (少しの道のり) a little way [《主に米話》ways]. ●少しずつ進む advance *inch by inch*. ▶駅までほんの少しです It is *only a short distance* [*a little way*] to the station. ▶この道を少し行くと市役所がある If you go *a little way* along [down] this road, you will find the town [city] hall. ▶村はまだ少し先だ The village is still *some distance* [*way*] *off*.

すこしも 少しも 【少しも...でない】not(...) *at all* (!最も一般的な言い方); not(...) *in the least* [*slightest*] (!強調的な言い方); (話) not *a bit*, not *one* (little) *bit*; 《やや書》no+名+*whatever* (!no+名 の代わりに not(...) *any*+名, *nothing*, *none* なども可). ▶コンパは少しも楽しくなかった I *didn't* enjoy the party *at all* [*in the least*]. /The party *wasn't at all* [*in the least*, *a bit*] enjoyable. (!The party *wasn't* enjoyable *at all* [*in the least*, *a bit*]. のように at all などを後に置くことも可。しかし前に置く方が語調が強い)/The party was *far from* enjoyable. ▶彼が何を言おうとしているのか少しも分からない I *don't* understand *at all* [*in the least*] what he is trying to say. (!このように目的語として従節が来る場合 at all, in the least は文末には置かない)/I *don't have the slightest* idea [I *don't have any* idea *at all*, I *don't have any* idea *whatever*] (*about*) what he is trying to say. (!(1) I have *no* idea (about).... ともいえる. (2) 最上級を用いた最初の言い方については (⇒分かる ❶)) ▶世間がなんと言おうと少しも気にならない I *don't* care *a bit* [《話》give *a damn*] what other people say. (!後の方は無作法) ▶そのことについて少しも疑わしい点はない There is *no* doubt *at all* [*whatever*] about it. ▶今日は少しも風がない There *isn't the least* [*slightest*] wind today.

すごす 過ごす ●〖時を〗 (ある目的を持って) spend* (⇒費やす); (退屈しないように) pass (!pass の方が堅い語). ▶我々はそこで 1 か月過ごした We *spent* [*passed*] a month there./(滞在した) We *stayed* (for) a month there. (!継続・状態を表す動詞の後では for はしばしば省略される) ▶彼は夜はテレビを見て過ごした He *spent* [*passed*] the evening watching TV. (!この構文では spend を用いるのが普通) ▶このごろいかがお過ごしですか How are you *getting along* [*on*] these days? (⇒暮らす, 生活する) ▶いかがお

ごしでしたか(=お元気でしたか) How have you been? ▶彼は2,3日怠けて［遊んで］過ごした He *idled* a few days *away*. ▶我々はトランプをして楽しく過ごした We *had a good time* [*had fun*] playing cards. ▶私はつまらない本を読んで時間をむだに過ごした I *wasted* my time read*ing* a worthless book./I *wasted* my time *on* a worthless book.
会話 「楽しい休暇を過ごしてね」「あなたもね！」"*Háve a good* ╱*hóliday*." "Ánd ╱*you* [You, *too*]!"
❷ [限度を] (⇨過ぎる❺)

すごすご(と) (気をくじかれて) dejectedly; (情けなく) miserably; (面目をつぶして) dishonorably; (傷心で) with a broken heart. ●敗軍はすごすごと町に戻ってきた The defeated army returned *dejectedly* to the town.

スコッチ [ウイスキー] Scotch (whisky); [服地] (Scotch) tweed. ▶スコッチの水割りを(1杯)ください A *Scotch* and [with] water, please. (⚠ 注文するときは可算名詞扱いにしてaをつける) (⇨オンザロック)
●スコッチエッグ [料理] a Scotch egg. ●スコッチテリア [動物] a Scotch terrier.

スコットランド Scotland. ●スコットランド(人)の Scottish; 《やや古》 Scotch; Scots. (⚠ (1) 形容詞では Scottish がよく用いられる: the *Scottish* education system (スコットランドの教育制度)/a *Scottish* soldier (スコットランド兵). (2) スコットランド人は Scotch を嫌うので, an Scotch egg, Scotch whisky などを除いて今は用いない方がよい) ●スコットランド語 Scotch, Scots. ●スコットランド人 a Scot, (男性) a Scotsman, (女性) a Scotswoman; 《総称》 the Scottish (⚠ the Scots は《やや古》で軽蔑的と受け取られることが多い).

スコットランドヤード [ロンドン警視庁] Scotland Yard. (参考 現在の公式名は New Scotland Yard)

スコップ [<オランダ語] [移植ごて] a trowel; (砂糖・小麦粉なとをすくう小シャベル) a scoop; (シャベル) a shovel.

すこぶる very; highly; extremely. (⇨非常に)

すごみ 凄味 すごみのある (=威嚇的な)声で a *threatening* (恐ろしい) a *frightening*, a *horrible* voice.
●すごみを利(か)かせる ▶刑事は体罰を加えるぞとすごみをきかせた The detective *threatened* me *with* physical punishment.

すごむ 凄む 暴力に訴えるぞとすごむ(=おどす) threaten 《him》 with violence; *threaten* to use violence.

すごもり 巣籠もり (鳥の) nesting; (卵・ひなを抱くための) brooding, (動物の冬眠) hibernation.

すごもる 巣籠もる (鳥が) nest; (卵を抱く) sit* (on eggs), brood.

すこやか 健やか ― 健やかな 形 healthy; (心身ともに) sound.
― **健やかに** 副 ●健やかに育つ grow *healthily*.

スコラてつがく スコラ哲学 Scholasticism.
●スコラ哲学者 a Scholastic.

すごろく 双六 *sugoroku*, a backgammon-like board game played with dice by several players. ●すごろくをする play *sugoroku*.

すさび 遊び (気晴らし) a pastime; (a) diversion; (娯楽) (an) amusement. ●筆のすさび writing *for amusement's sake*.

*__すさまじい 凄まじい__ (恐ろしい) terrible, horrible; (ものすごい)《話》 terrific, tremendous; (激しい) violent.
●すさまじい形相 a *terrible* [(怒り狂った) a *furious*] look. ●すさまじい光景 a *terrible* [a *horrible*] sight. ▶車はすさまじい勢いで走っている The car is running at a *terrific* [a *tremendous*] speed.

▶彼は試合に勝つためすさまじい努力をした He made a *violent* [(必死の) a *desperate*] effort to win the match.
会話 「小説にかぎらず, 活字となると見たくもないの」「じゃあ, 新聞もか」「ええ」「すさまじいな(=本当にきらいなのだな)」 "I just don't want to see printed words, let alone reading novels." "Then, not a newspaper, either?" "No." "You really do hate reading."

すさむ 荒む [心が荒れる] grow* [get*] wild; [堕落してゆく]《やや書》 become* degenerate. ▶すさんだ(=自暴自棄の)生活をする lead a *desperate* life. ▶長引く不況で人の心はしだいにすさんでいった The people *have become morally decayed* in the prolonged economic depression.

ずさん 杜撰 ― 杜撰な 形 [ぞんざいな]《やや書》 slipshod; [だらしない]《やや話》 sloppy; (注意の行き届かない) careless; [欠点のある] faulty. ●ずさんな管理のため become of *slipshod* [*faulty*] management. ▶彼の仕事はずさんだ His work is *slipshod* [*sloppy*]./He does *sloppy* [*careless*] work./He works *sloppily* [*carelessly*].

すし 寿司 *sushi*, (説明的に) vinegared rice topped with raw fish or shellfish. ●箱[巻き; 散らし]寿司 boxed [rolled; garnished] *sushi*.
●寿司種 a *sushi* topping. ●寿司屋 a *sushi* bar [shop]. ●寿司 bar カウンター式の店

*__すじ 筋__ ❶ [道理] reason; [論理] logic; [一貫性] coherence /kouhíərəns/. ●筋の通った[通らない]要求 a *reasonable* [an *unreasonable*] demand. ●筋の通った[通らない]議論 a *logical* [an *illogical*] argument. ●筋の通った[通らない]説明 a *coherent* [an *incoherent*] explanation. ●筋違い (⇨筋違い) ▶君の主張は筋が通っていない Your argument isn't *logical* [(一貫していない) isn't *consistent*]. ▶彼女は筋を通した She *acted according to* her (*moral*) *principles*. (⚠ moral を入れると「義理を通す」に近くなる) ▶この問題では筋を通した方がよい You'd better *be reasonable* (*and just*) on this problem. ▶確かに筋論ではこの問題についての彼の意見は正しいが賛成はしかねる I know his opinion about the matter is logically right, but I can't agree with him.

❷ [情報源] a source (⚠ しばしば複数形で); [...界] circles; [経路, 道筋] a channel; [専門分野] (研究の) a field, (特に商売の) a line. ●消息筋 (well-)informed *sources* [*circles*, 《やや書》 *quarters*]. ●確かな筋からの情報 information from a reliable *source* [a good *quarter*]. ●外交筋を通して through diplomatic *channels* [*circles*]. ●その筋 (⇨その筋)

❸ [線] a line (⇨線); [しま] (模様をなす) a stripe; (光・液体などの流れるような) a streak (⇨縞(じ)); [道筋] an avenue (⇨通り). ●板に筋を引く draw a *line* on a board. ●白い筋の入ったカーテン a curtain with white *stripes*; a white-*striped* curtain. ●水平線上の一筋の光 a *streak* [a *beam*] of light on the horizon. ●ズボンの筋(=折り目) the *crease* in one's pants. ●道筋 Midosuji *Avenue*. ●涙がいく筋も彼女のほおを伝って落ちた *Streams* of tears trickled down her cheeks.

❹ [腱(けん)]《やや書》 a sinew /sínju:/, 《書》 a téndon; [動植物の繊維] a fiber, (豆などの) a string. ●筋の多い肉 *sinewy* meat. ●神経の筋 a nerve *fiber*. ●豆から筋を除く *string* [remove the *strings* from] the beans. ●筋をちがえる (手・足の) sprain 《one's wrist》; (首・背中の) crick [get a crick in] 《one's neck》. ●青筋 blue veins. (⇨青

ずし 筋) ▶彼は足の筋を痛めた He has damaged a *tendon* in his leg.
❺〖小説などの大筋〗a plot; 〖具体的な話の展開〗(a) story line. ●単純な[こみ入った]筋 a simple [a complicated] *plot*. ●芝居の筋 the *plot* of the play. ●歴史上の出来事から話の筋を取る take the *plot* from a historical event. ▶その小説には面白い筋がない The novel has a very thin *story line*. ▶彼は話の筋が分からなくなった He lost the *thread* of the story.
❻〖素質〗▶君はチェスの筋がいい(=生まれつきの適性がある) You *have a natural bent* [*aptitude*] *for* chess.

ずし 図示 图 illustration. (⇨図)
── 図示する 動 ●家の位置を図示する *illustrate* the location of a house. ●車のエンジンの部分を図示する show the parts of a car engine in [by] a *diagram*; draw a *diagram* showing the parts of a car engine.

ずし 厨子 (仏具) a miniature shrine.

すじあい 筋合い 〖理由〗(a) reason; 〖権利〗(a) right. ▶君にあんなひどいことを言われる筋合いはない He has no *right* to say awful things like that to me.

すじかい 筋交い (斜めに入れる材) a diagonal brace. ●窓に筋交いを支(ざさ)う (筋交いで補強する) reinforce the windows with *braces*.

すじがき 筋書き 〖小説などの〗a plot (⇨筋 ❺); 〖概略〗an outline; 〖企て〗a design; 〖計画〗a plan. ▶何もかも筋書きどおりにいった Everything went *according to the plan* [*as planned*, *as arranged*].

すじがね 筋金 ●筋金入りの (信念の強い) stalwart; (芯からの) dyed-in-the-wool; (頑迷一徹な) hardcore; (圧力などに屈しない) unyielding. ●筋金入りの保守党員 a *stalwart* Conservative; a Conservative *stalwart*. ▶彼の頭は筋金入り(の стал) は名訳(=誰もそうは訳していないが)

ずき 図式 ●図式で示す (幾何学的な図で) show (it) in [by] a *diagram*; (地図や絵などで) show (it) on a *chart*; (グラフで) make a graph of (it). (⇨図示)

すじこ 筋子 salted salmon roe.

すじすじ 〖重々しく〗heavily. ●すじすじ揺れる shudder; tremble. ●すじしじ(=重い足取りで)歩く walk *with heavy steps*.

すじだて 筋立て a plot. (⇨筋, 粗筋)

すじちがい 筋違い ▶彼に腹を立てるのは筋違いだ(=根拠がない)*There's no reason* to get angry with him./Don't get angry with him. You're *barking at the wrong tree*. (⇨お門違い)

しずめ 鮨詰め ▶その列車はすし詰めだった The train *was overcrowded* [〖話〗*jam-packed, packed to capacity*]./The passengers *were packed* (*in*) *like sardines* in the train. (❗like sardines は〖話〗で、「缶詰のイワシのように」の意)

すじばった 筋ばった (やせ書) sinewy /sínju(ː)i/.

***すじみち** 筋道 〖道理〗reason; 〖論理〗logic; 〖話〗the thread. (⇨筋(❺)) ●筋道の立った(道理にかなった) reasonable; (論理的な) logical; (首尾一貫した) coherent. ●筋道の立たない unreasonable; illogical; incoherent. ●筋道を立てて語る give a *coherent* account (*of*).

すじむかい 筋向かい ●筋向かいの(=ななめ向こうの)家 the house *diagonally opposite* (*to*) mine. (⇨向かい)

しずめ 節目 〖折り目〗a fold, a crease (⇨折り目); 〖血統〗(a) lineage, (a) pedigree; 〖筋道〗(⇨筋道). ●節目の正しい家 a family of good *lineage*.

すじょう 素性 one's background (❗家族関係・学歴・経験・社会的身分などをいう); (祖先, 経歴) 〖書〗antecédents; (生まれ) birth, origin(s). ●素性のいかがわしい[分からない] 男 a man of shady [unknown] *antecedents*. ▶私は彼の素性を知らない I don't know his *background* [what he is].

ずじょう 頭上 ●頭上の[に] over [above] one's head; overhead. ●(本などが)頭上に落ちる fall *on* one's *head*. ▶飛行機が頭上を飛んだ A plane flew *above us* [*our head*]./A plane flew *overhead*. ▶頭上注意《掲示》Watch [〖主に英〗Mind] *your head*.

ずしり heavily. (⇨ずっしり)

ずしんと with a thud. (⇨ずんと)

すす 煤 soot /sút/; (すすで固まったほこり) grime. ●すすだらけの sooty; grimy. ●壁のすすを払う sweep [clean] the *soot* off the wall. ●すす払い (⇨煤払)

すず 鈴 a bell. ●鈴の音 the jingle [tinkle] of a *bell*. ●鈴を鳴らす ring [jingle, tinkle] a *bell*. ●鈴を張ったような ▶彼女は鈴を張ったような(=大きく魅力的な)目をしている She has big, bright, charming eyes.

すず 錫 tin. ●すず製の tin 《cups》.
●錫婚式 (結婚 10 周年の) a [one's] tin wedding (anniversary). ●錫製品 tinwork; 《集合的》tinware. ●錫箔(ばく) tinfoil.

すずかけ(のき) 篠懸(けの木) 〖植物〗a plane (tree), a platan; (⇨) a sycamore.

すずかぜ 涼風 a cool breeze.

すずがも 鈴鴨 〖鳥〗a scaup (duck); a greater scaup.

すすき 薄 〖植物〗Japanese pampas grass.

すずき 鱸 〖魚介〗a sea bass. (❗通例単・複同形. 肉は ⓤ)

すすぐ 濯ぐ, 漱ぐ ❶〖洗い落とす〗rinse ... (out). ●きれいな水でシャツをすすぐ *rinse* (*out*) one's shirt in clean water. ●口を水ですすぐ *rinse* [*wash*] (*out*) one's mouth with water. (❗rinse の方が普通) ●タオルをすすいで石けんを流す *rinse* the soap *out of a* towel. ●それをよく〖3回〗すすぎなさい *Rinse* it well [*three times*]./Give it a good *rinse* [*three rinses*].
❷〖不名誉などを除き去る〗●汚名をすすぐ *wipe out* a disgrace.

すすける 煤ける become* sooty. ▶その釜はすすけていた The iron pot *was sooty* [*stained with soot*].

‡**すずしい** 涼しい ❶〖気温が〗cool (↔warm); (さわやかですがすがしい) refreshing. ●涼しい風 a *cool* [*a refreshing*] breeze. ●涼しそうなドレス a *cool*(*-looking*) dress. ▶涼しい場所でひと休みしよう Let's have a rest in a *cool* place. ▶高い山は夏でも涼しい It is *cool* on high mountains even in 〖主に米〗(the) summer. ▶夕方には涼しくなった It became *cool* in the evening. (❗「夕方が近づくにつれて...」なら As the evening was drawing near, it became *cooler*.)

❷〖目・音などが〗(澄んで美しい) bright; clear. ●涼しい風鈴の音 the *clear* tinkling of a wind-bell. ●涼しい目をした少女 a *clear-eyed* girl.

> 翻訳のこころ あのびいどろほど幽(かすか)な涼しい味があるものか (梶井基次郎『檸檬』) Nothing's more delicate and refreshing than the taste I get from those flat glass marbles (when I put them in my mouth). ❗(1)「涼しい(味)」は refreshing とある。(2)「びいどろ」は marble (子どもが遊ぶ通例球形のガラス玉). ここでは前後の文から「おはじき」のように平たいものをさしているので, flat を入れる。(3)「...があるものか」は nothing is more ...(...より以上のものはない)と表す)

- **涼しい顔** ▶彼はそのことについては涼しい顔(=無関心な様子)をしていた He *looked unconcerned about* [*indifferent to*] the matter.
すずしろ [[『大根』の古称]] (⇨大根)
すずな 菘 [[『かぶ』の古称]] (⇨かぶ)
すずなり 鈴なり ●鈴なりになる grow *in clusters* [*a cluster*]. ▶小さなリンゴが鈴なりになっている There are a lot of small apples on [xin] the tree./The tree is *heavy* [*loaded*] *with* small apples. ▶人が窓から鈴なりになってパレードを見下ろしていた The windows of the buildings *were full of* [*were crammed with*] people looking down on the parade.

すすはらい 煤払い housecleaning. ●すす払いをする(大掃除をする) do the (general) *housecleaning*; clean the house; (すすを払い取る) sweep soot off.

すすみ 進み progress; advance. ▶勉強の進みが速い[遅い] make (x a) rapid [slow] *progress* in one's studies. ●文化の進みを促進する promote the *advance* [*progress*] of culture. ▶あなたの研究の進み具合はどうですか How *are* your studies *getting along* [*on*]?/How *are* you *getting along* [*on*] *with* your studies?

すずみ 涼み ●夕涼みする *cool oneself* in the evening; *enjoy the cool* of the evening.
- **涼み客** people cooling themselves [enjoying the cool]. ●**涼み台** an outdoor bench for enjoying the cool (of the evening). ●**涼み舟** a summer pleasure boat.

:すすむ 進む

> **WORD CHOICE** 進む
>
> **advance** 強い目的・意志のもと、目標に向かって障害を乗り越えて力強く進むこと。軍隊が進軍すること、チームが勝ち進むこと、技術が進歩することなどを含意する。●急速に進む今日の科学技術 today's rapidly *advancing* technology.
>
> **move [go] forward** ある地点を離れ、別の地点に自然に移動すること。go よりも move のほうがより多く用いられる。go は意志に基づく人の前進をも含意し、move はそれに加え、科学や技術の前進・進歩をも含意する。●そのプロジェクトを前に進めないといけない We have to *move forward* on that project.
>
> **make one's own way** しばしば苦労して道を切り開きながら前に進むこと。●ビジネスの世界で苦労しながら前に進んできた We've *made our own way* in the business world.

❶ [[前進する]] advance 《toward, on》; 《やや書》 proceed 《to》; move; move forward; go*, 《やや書》 make* one's way; (…に向かう) head 《for, toward》; (歩いて) walk; (歩み出る) step (-pp-) forward; (ある距離を) cover, make; (行進して) march; (音・光などが) run*, (車・列車などが) run*, go. ▶彼らは1日に50キロ進んだ They *advanced* [*covered, made*] fifty kilometers a day. ▶3番ゲートに進んでください(空港で) Please *go* [*proceed*] *to* Gate 3. ▶進め Go (ahead)!/(軍隊の号令) Forward!/March! ▶「ずっと中ほどへお進みください」(バスの運転手などが) "*Move along*, please!" (❗go along は「止まらずに先へ」の意)/"Please *move* [*step*] to the rear." (❗rear は「うしろ」の意) ▶彼は「早く」の方へ進んだ He *made for* the door. (❗通例「素早く」の意を含む) ▶彼は人込みをかき分けて進んだ He *made* his *way* through the crowd. ▶その電車は時速100キロで進む(=走る) That train *runs* [*goes, travels*] (at) 100 kilometers an hour.

❷ [[進歩[進展]する]] (着実に) make* prógress; (前進する) advance; (進行する) go*; (仕事などがはかどる) get* along [on]. ●文明が進むにつれて as civilization *advances*; with the advance of civilization. ●進んだ考え方(=進歩的思想)の持ち主 a person with *progressive* ideas. ▶計画は遅々として進まなかった We made little *progress* [didn't *make* much *progress*] on the project. ▶交渉はゆっくりと進んでいる(=進展している) The negotiations *are going* slowly. ▶その仕事は予定より早く進んでいる The work *is going* ahead of schedule. ▶さて(授業は)この前までこの進みましたね Let's *see* where we were. ▶教育制度の点では西洋の国々は日本よりはるかに進んでいた In an educational system Western countries were far *in advance of* [were far *ahead of*] Japan. ▶(引き続き)次の話題に進みましょう Let's *go on to* the next subject. ▶酒が進む(=酒を飲み続ける)につれ、職場の話に戻ってくる When [x As] we *keep on* drinking, we always get around to talking about matters [gossiping] at our workplace.

❸ [[進級する]] (地位・レベルが上がる) advance, move up 《to》; (昇進する) be promoted 《to》; (進学する) go* on 《to college》; (入学する) get* into ...; (肩書) enter; (職業などにつく) go into .... ▶トーナメントの決勝に進む *advance to* [*reach*] the finals of a tournament. ●上級のクラスに進む *move up to* a more advanced class. ●大学に進む *go on to* college [(the) university]. (❗on には「(高校から)さらに」という含みがある) ●A大学の英文科に進む *get into* the English department of A University. ●芸能界に進む *go into* [*enter*] show business. ▶あなたはどの道に進む(=進路を取る)つもりですか What *course* are you going to *take*?

❹ [[時計が]] gain (↔lose*). ▶私の時計は1か月に10秒進む My watch *gains* 10 seconds a month. ▶この時計は5分進んでいる This watch is five minutes *fast* (↔slow).

❺ [[気持ちが]] (…したい気がする) feel* like 《doing》; (喜んで…する) be ready to 《do》, be willing to 《do》 (⇨進展). ▶今日はあまり食が進まない I don't *feel like* eating much today./I have a *poor* (↔a good) appetite today. ▶彼に来るようにと勧めたのですが気が進まないようでした I urged him to come but he seemed *reluctant*. ▶気が進まなかったが(=意に反して)、その仕事を引き受けた I took the job *against* my *will*.

❻ [[病気が]] (悪くなる) get* worse. ▶彼は病気が進んでいる He *is getting worse* [*worsening*]. ▶彼の胃がんはだいぶ進んでいた His stomach cancer was already *advanced* [*in an advanced stage*].

すずむ 涼む ●木陰で涼む *enjoy the cool air* in the shade of a tree; rest in the cool *shade* of a tree. ●庭に出て涼む go out into the garden to *cool off*.

すずむし 鈴虫 [[『昆虫』]] a "bell-ringing" cricket. ▶聞こえるのは鈴虫の声だけだった The only sound was a "bell-ringing" cricket chirping. (❗事情) 一般に米英人はこの鳴き声を好まない)

すすめ 勧め [[『助言』]] advice; [[『提案』]] (a) suggestion; [[『推薦』]] (a) recommendation. ●彼の勧めで買う buy 《it》 *at* [*on*] his *suggestion*; buy 《it》 *on* his *recommendation*. ▶医師の勧めで1日中寝ていた On my doctor's *advice*, I stayed in bed all day long. (❗日常的には I *took* my doctor's *advice* and stayed .... のように言う方が普通) ▶何かお勧めの料理はありませんか I'm afraid you'll have to *recommend* something. (❗(1)「何を食べくらいのかよく分からないので伺うのですが」の含みでいう。単に What's good here? (このお店では何がおいしいのか)と尋ねてもよい)

すずめ 雀 〚鳥〛 a sparrow.
- すずめの涙 ● すずめの涙ほどの(=ほんの少しの)お金 a meager sum of money; 《話》chicken feed; 〚話〛peanuts.
- すずめ百まで踊り忘れず 〚ことわざ〛What is learned in the cradle is carried to the tomb. (!日本語の方は「幼い頃についた(悪い)癖は一生直らない」といった悪い意味だが、英語の方は幼児期のしつけの大切さを強調することわざ)

すずめばち 雀蜂 〚昆虫〛a hornet, a wasp.

*すすめる 進める ❶ 〚前進させる〛(兵などを) advance, move 〔troops〕 forward; (馬などを) urge 〔a horse〕 on; (将棋のこまなどを) move 〔a piece〕. ▶ 彼は門の方へ歩を進めた He made (a move) for the gate.
❷ 〚進展させる〛(促進する) advance; (事業などを推進する) further; (進行をはかどらせる) speed*... up; (さらに続ける) go* on 《with》; (先へ進める) go ahead 《with》. ●近代化を進める advance modernization. ●その計画を進める further [go ahead with] the plan, 《ややかた書》make one's way through] the plan. ●工事を進める speed up the construction. ●仕事を進める go [carry] on with the work. ●調査を進める carry the investigation forward [further]. ▶ 会議はいつもどおりに進められた The meeting was conducted in an ordinary way.
会話「君の兄貴の意見はどうだい」「兄は話を進めるべきだという考えだ」"What's your brother's opinion?" "He thinks we ought to go ahead."
❸ 〚時計を〛●時計を5分進める set the watch forward (by) five minutes. ●時計の針を進める advance the hands on the clock.

*すすめる 勧める ❶ 〚勧告する〛(忠告する) advise; (一番いいと勧める) recommend; (控えめに提案する) suggest; (催促する) urge; (しきりにせがむ) press. ▶ 上司は私に休暇を取るよう勧めた My boss advised (me) [recommended (to me), suggested (to me)] that I (《主に英》should) take a vacation./My boss advised [recommended, suggested] my taking a vacation. (!advise, recommend は my を省略しても意味は変わらないが、suggest は my を省略すると「休暇を取ろうよと言った」の意味になる)/My boss advised [《英》recommended, ×suggested] me to take a vacation. (!suggest は to 不定詞をとらない)/My boss advised [recommended, ×suggested] me a vacation. ▶ タクシーの運転手はそのホテルを私に勧めた The taxi driver recommended [suggested, ×advised] the hotel to me. (!advise の目的語には「物」は不可) ▶ 彼にもう1日泊まっていくようにしきりに勧めた I urged [pressed] him to stay another day. (!(1) 結果は不明。したがって but he wouldn't. (しかし彼は泊まろうとしなかった)を続けることができる. (2) to stay は into staying ... とすると「その結果彼は泊まった」の意となる)
❷ 〚提供する〛offer. ▶ 彼にたばこを勧める offer him a cigarette. ●酒を勧めて(=注いで)回る drift around serving drinks. ●勧められもしないのにいすに腰をおろす sit down without being asked.
❸ 〚奨励する〛encourage. ●学問を勧める encourage (増進する) promote] learning. ●彼にその大学を受けるよう勧める encourage him to apply to the university.

すすめる 薦める recommend. (⇒推薦する)

すずやか 涼やか ●涼やかな目元の少女 a girl with clear [bright] eyes. (⇒涼しい ❷)

すずらん 鈴蘭 〚植物〛a lily of the valley.

すずり 硯 an inkstone.
- 硯箱 an inkstone case.

すすりなき すすり泣き 〔声〕a soft weep; 〔声・事〕soft weeping.

すすりなく すすり泣く weep* softly.

すする 啜る (音を立てずに) sip (-pp-); (音を立てて) 〚話〛slurp; 〚鼻を〛sniff. ●泣きながら鼻をする cry and sniff. ▶ 彼は熱いみそ汁をゆっくりとすした He sipped [took a sip of, slurped] the hot miso soup slowly. ▶ スープをずるずるすするな Don't slurp your soup!

*すすんで 進んで 〚快く〛willingly; 〚自発的に〛voluntarily. (!進んでそれをする do it willingly [voluntarily] (!前の方は頼まれたり必要からするのをいわない、後の方は頼まれなくとも自分から進んですること); be ready [willing] to do it (進んで は willing または willing より積極的な気持ちで、いつでも喜んでするという含みあり); voluntéer to do it. ●情報を進んで提供する volunteer (to give) some information. ●進んでその運動に参加する volunteer for the campaign. ▶ 彼には進んで学ぼうという気持ちがうかがえる He shows great willingness [readiness] to learn.

ずせつ 図説 (⇒図解) ●世界経済図説 explanatory illustrations of the world economy.

すそ 裾 ❶ 〚衣服の〛a hem (!縁の部分); a skirt (!特に女性のドレスの腰から下の部分); a train (!婦人礼服の後方に長くひきずるすそ); a bottom (!主にズボンのすそで,「折り返しのあるすそ」に a cuff). ●スカートのすそ上げをする take the hem of a skirt up. ●すそを引きずって歩く trail one's skirt. ●すそをたくし上げて歩く walk with one's skirt tucked up. ●ワイシャツのすそをズボンの中に押し込む tuck one's shirttails into one's pants; tuck one's shirt in. ●ズボンのすそをまくる roll up one's trousers. ▶ この服はすそ上げをしないといけない This dress needs taking up at the hem.
❷ 〚山の〛the foot. ●山すその家 a house at the foot of the mountain.
●すそさばき the way one carries oneself while wearing kimono. ●すそ回し the lining at the bottom of a kimono. ●すそ模様 a design on the skirt of a lady's dress.

ずぞう 図像 an icon.

すその 裾野 the foot.

スター a star. ●大スター a big star. ●映画スター a movie [a film] star. ●スター選手 a star player. ●スター総出演の出し物 an all-star performance; a performance with an all-star cast. ●スターの座にのし上がる achieve [rise to] stardom ▶ あの少女にはスター性がある The girl has the makings of a star.

スターウォーズ 《米話》Star Wars. (参考「戦略防衛構想」(strategic defense initiative) の別称)

スターズアンドストライプス 〚米国国旗, 星条旗〛the Stars and Stripes.

スターター 〚始動係〛a starter; 〚始動装置〛(自動車の) a starter; (オートバイの) a kick-start(er); 〚先発投手〛〚野球〛a starter.

スターダスト 〚星くず〛stardust.

スターダム 〚スターの地位[身分]〛stardom. ▶ その映画で彼は一躍スターダムに躍り出た He shot to [burst into] stardom in the movie.

スターチス 〚植物〛a statice; a sea lavender.

スターティングメンバー 〚先発メンバー〛a starting lineup. (⇒先発, スタメン) ●スターティングメンバーに入っている[から外れている] be in [out of] the starting lineup.

*スタート 图 〚出発〛a start. ●スタートをする[切る]

スターリン

make a *start*; start;《野球で走者が》break [take off]《*for* second》. ●下手な[いい]スタートをきる make a poor [a good] *start*. ●スタートの合図をする give a *starting* signal. ▶彼は新聞記者として人生のスタートを切った He *began* his career as a newsman.
──スタートする 🈩 start. ▶ピストルが鳴って，彼らは一斉にスタートした The pistol sounded and they *started* [*went off*] at the same time [all at once]. (..they made a clean start. ともいえる)
●スタート係 ●スタート台《競泳用の》a stárting blòck. ●スタートダッシュ〖陸上〗an initial spurt. ●いい[悪い]スタートダッシュを切る 《一般に》make a good [bad] *start*. ●スタートライン《*on*》the stárting lìne;《和製語》start line. ●スタートラインに並ぶ line up at the *start*，《スタートラインにつま先をつける》toe the *line*〖《米》*mark*〗.

スターリン 〖旧ソ連の政治家〗Stalin (Joseph V. ～).
スタイリスト 〖服飾家〗a stylist, a fashion coordinator (🈩 整髪・インテリアの専門家にも stylist を用いる);〖めかし屋〗a smart dresser;〖名文家〗a stylist.

*__スタイル__ 〖型，様式，文体〗(a) style;〖容姿〗a figure;（体格）a physique /fízik/. ●最新の(服装などの)スタイル the latest *styles* (in clothes). ●独特のスタイルで書く write in his own *style*. ●髪をショートスタイルにする have one's hair in a short *style*. ▶彼女はスタイルがいい She has a nice [a good, a lovely] *figure*〖×*style*〗. (🈩 「スタイルが悪い」は She has a poor figure. より She is fat and short. のように具体的に表現する方が普通)
●スタイルブック a stylebook. ▶彼女はスタイルブックから抜け出たような服装をしている She looks as if she stepped out of a bandbox. (● bandbox は「円形の帽子の箱」)

スタウト 〖黒ビール〗stout. (⇨ビール 解説)
スタグフレーション 〖経済〗stagflation. (参考 不景気 (stagnation)とインフレ (inflation) の併存)

すたこら ▶すたこら逃げ出す scurry [scuttle] away.
スタジアム a stadium /stéidiəm/. (複 ～s, stadia).
●スタジアムジャンパー a warm-up jacket.
スタジオ a studio /st(j)úːdiòu/ (複 ～s). ●テレビスタジオ a TV [a television] *studio*. ●レコーディングスタジオ a recording *studio*.

すたすた ▶すたすた歩く（元気よく）walk *briskly*, take a brisk walk;（大また）walk with long steps, stride;（早足で，急いで）walk quickly [at a quick pace], walk in a hurry. ▶若いビジネスマンが通りをすたすた駅の方へ歩いていくのが見えた I saw a young businessman *walking briskly* [*striding*] down the street toward the station.

ずたずた ▶ずたずたに破る tear /téər/《a letter》to pieces; shred. ▶彼は彼女の拒絶の手紙をずたずたに破った He *tore* her letter of refusal *to* [*into*]《*small*》*pieces*. ▶彼らは不要の書類をずたずたに裂いた They *shredded* useless papers. ▶私の心は悲しみでずたずただ My heart *is broken* with sorrow. ▶スキャンダルで彼女の名誉はずたずたになった The scandal *has torn* her honor *to* shreds.

すだち 巣立ち leaving the nest. (⇨巣立つ)
すだち 酢橘 〖植物〗a *sudachi*; (説明的に) a small green citrus fruit used as a garnish.
すだつ 巣立つ 〖鳥が〗leave* [fly*] the nest;〖卒業して社会へ出る〗finish school [graduate 《*from* college》] and go* out into the world.
スタッカート 〖音楽〗staccato /stəkáːtou/. ●スタッカートで弾く play《it》*staccato*.
スタッドレスタイヤ a studless (snow [winter]) tire, a winter tire.

スタッフ 〖集合的〗a staff (🈩 単・複両扱い); (1 人) a staff member. (⇨職員) ▶彼女は編集スタッフの 1 人です She is on [a member of] the editorial *staff*./She is a *staff* member [×a staff] of the editorial department. ▶私たちのスタッフは親切で有能です Our *staff* is《米》[are《英》] friendly and efficient.

スタビライザー 〖飛行機・船などの水平安定装置〗a stabilizer.
ずだぶくろ 頭陀袋（大型手さげかばん）《米》a carryall,《英》a holdall.
スタミナ stamina /stǽmənə/. ●スタミナをつける build up [increase] *stamina*. ▶彼にはマラソンを走りきるスタミナがない He doesn't have the *stamina* to complete a marathon.
スタメン 〖「スターティングメンバー」の略〗a starting lineup. ●スタメンに入っている be (included) in the *starting lineup* for (for the next game).
すたり 廃り ▶名前はちょうど服同様にはやりすたりがある Names, just like clothes, go in and out of fashion.
すたる 廃る (⇨廃れる) ▶そんなことをすれば男が廃る That would *stain* your *honor*〖（評判を傷つける）*hurt* your *reputation*〗./（こけんにかかわる）It would be *beneath* your *dignity*〖（面子を失わせる）*lose* your *face*〗to do that.
すだれ 簾 （竹製の）a bamboo /bæmbúː/ blind〖《米》(window) shade〗. (🈩 籐(ᴛᴏ)製のものは rattan を，葦(ᴀsʜɪ)製のものは reed を bamboo の代わりに用いる)
●すだれを上げる lift [raise (↔let down, lower)] a *bamboo blind*. ●「巻いて上げる」ことを明示する場合は roll up...》●南の窓に[軒下に]すだれをかける hang a *bamboo blind* over the south window [from the eaves].

__すたれる__ 廃れる 〖使われなくなる〗go out of use;（消滅する）die (～d; dying) out;〖流行遅れになる〗go out of fashion;〖時代遅れになる〗get* [go] out of date. ▶この言い回しは廃れつつある This expression *is going out of use* [*becoming obsolete*]. ▶このスタイルはもう廃れた This style *is no longer the fashion* [*is now out of fashion, has gone out*]. ▶無声映画は廃れて久しい Silent movies *have been out of date* for many years./Silent movies *died out* years ago.

スタンガン a stun gun. (参考 護身用)
スタンス 〖足の構え，態度，立場〗a stance;〖野球〗a batting stance. ●オープン[クローズ，スクウェア]スタンス an open [a closed, a square] *stance*.
スタンダード 🈔 スタンダードな standard.
●スタンダードナンバー（音楽の）a standard.
スタンダール 〖フランスの小説家・批評家〗Stendhal /stendáːl/.
スタンディングオベーション ●スタンディングオベーションを送る[受ける] give [receive, win] a standing ovation.
スタンディングスタート 〖陸上〗a standing start. (関連 クラウチングスタート a crouch start)
スタンド 〖屋台店〗a (coffee) stand,《主に英》a stall;〖観客席〗the stands (🈩 座席のある部分をさす. 立ち見席＝terrace);（屋根あり安い）《米》the bleachers;〖電灯〗《机上のの》a désk làmp;《床上の》《米》a flóor làmp〖×stand〗,《英》a stándard làmp;〖ガソリンスタンド〗《米》a gás (a fílling) stàtion;《英》a pétrol stàtion;《和製語》a gasoline stand. ●ライト[レフト]スタンド the right [left] field *stands*. ●スタンドにファウルを打ち込む hit a foul into the *stands*.

スタンドイン 〖映画での代役〗a stand-in. ▶スタンドインする(打球がホームランになる)〖野球〗clear the fence; carry into the stands.

スタンドオフ 〖ラグビー〗a standoff half.

スタンドカラー 〖立ち襟(½)〗a stand-up collar.

スタンドプレー 《米》(a piece of) grandstanding, 《米話》a grandstand play;《和製語》stand play. ● スタンドプレーをする play to the grandstand (gallery);《米話》make a *grandstand play*;《米話》grandstand.

スタンドプレーヤー 《米話》a grandstander.

スタントマン a stunt man [woman] (❗複数形はともに - men); a stunt person (❓ ~ people).

スタンバイ standby /stǽndbài/. ▶緊急事態に備えて救助隊がスタンバイしている A rescue party is *on standby* in case of emergency.

スタンプ a stamp; 〖郵便の消印〗a postmark, a date stamp. ● 記念スタンプ a commemorative *stamp*. ● スタンプを押す put a *stamp* (*on*); stamp. ● スタンプ台 an inkpad; a stamp pad. ● スタンプラリー (説明的に) a race in which participants have their cards stamped at some check points along a prescribed course.

スチーム 〖蒸気〗steam; 〖暖房装置〗a steam heater, a radiator /réidièitər/. ▶この部屋にはスチームが入っている This room is *steam*-heated [heated by *steam*]. ● スチームアイロン a steam iron. ● スチームバス a steam bath.

スチール 〖盗塁〗〖野球〗a steal. ▶ダブルスチール a double *steal*. ▶ディレードスチール a delayed *steal*. ● ホームスチール a *steal* of home.

スチール 〖鋼鉄〗steel. ● スチールギター a steel guitar.

スチール 〖映画の〗a still (photograph).

スチュワーデス an airhostess. (❗(1) stewardess と steward を一括した flight attendant がよく用いられる. (2) stewardess を用いるのは避けた方がよい)

*ずつ 〖それぞれ〗each; 〖ごとに〗every; 〖…につき〗a; 〖反復〗by …. ● 少しずつ (⇨少し❷) ● 彼らに2個ずつリンゴをやる give them two apples *each*. ● 2人に1本ずつペンを渡す give a pen to *every* two people. ● 3か月に1回ずつ once *every* three months. ● 1日に3回ずつ three times *a* day. ● 2人ずつ部屋から出てくる come out of the room two *by* two [*in* twos, (1度に2人ずつ) two at a time]. ▶(ある程度ずつ上の人数の場合でも, たとえば *in groups of* ten (10人ずつ)のようにいう) ▶彼らは500円ずつ持っている They *each* have 500 yen./*Each* of them has [have] 500 yen. (❗(1) 後の方が. (2) They have 500 yen *each*. も可)

*ずつう 頭痛 a headache /hédeik/. ▶激しい頭痛がする have a racking [(頭が割れるような) a splitting, (ずきんずきんする) a throbbing] *headache*. (❗時に a head で表すこともある: ものすごい頭痛なのが, 寝たら治ると思うわ I have an awful *head*. [My *head* hurts [is hurting] awfully.] I'm going to sleep off.) ● 頭痛を訴える complain of a *headache*. ▶今日は軽い[ひどい]頭痛がする I have a slight [a bad] *headache* today. ▶彼女は頭痛持ちだ She suffers from [is troubled with] chronic *headaches*. (❗慢性的な痛みには通例複数形で) ● 頭痛の種 ▶資金不足がそのキャンペーンの[彼の]頭痛の種である《話》Lack of money is a big *headache for* the campaign [*to* him]. ● 頭痛薬 héadache mèdicine.

スツール 《sit [perch] *on*》a stool.

すっからかん ▶財布がすっからかんになった《話》I'm (*flat* [*stony*]) *broke*. I'm penniless.

*すっかり ❶〖なくなってしまうまで〗▶彼はお金をすっかり(=すべて)遣ってしまった He *has used up* [*spent*] *all* his money. ❷〖とても〗very much, 《話》a lot, quite; (完全に) thoroughly, completely; (本当に) really. ▶彼女はすっかり変わった She has changed *very much* [《話》*a lot*]./She has [is] *really* changed. (❗後の方が変わっている状態に重点を置いた言い方)/She is *quite* another woman now. ▶彼の髪はすっかり白くなった His hair is *quite* gray now. ▶(この意では quite より gray を強く読む) ▶彼女は部屋をすっかりきれいにした She cleaned the room *thoroughly*./She gave the room a *thorough* cleaning. ▶それをすっかり忘れていました I completely [《話》*clean*] forgot it. ▶すっかり晴れ上がった The weather [It] *has cleared up*.

ずつき 頭突き ▶頭突きを食らわせる butt 《him》; hit 《him》hard with one's head.

ズッキーニ 〖植物〗《米》a zucchini (❓ ~(s));《英》a courgette /kuərʒét/.

すっきり 副 (簡素に) simply; (はっきりと) clearly; (きれいに) neatly. ● すっきり引かれた眉(½) *clearly*-drawn eyebrows. ● すっきりと均斉のとれた姿 a *beautifully* balanced figure. ● すっきりとした(=簡素な)生き方をする live *simply*; live a *simple* life. ● すっきり組み立てられた文[段落] a *neatly* composed passage.

—**すっきりした** 形 ● すっきりした[すっきりしない]天候 *clear* [*cloudy*] weather. ● すっきりした飲み物 a *refreshing* beverage [drink].

—**すっきりする** 動 ● 心がすっきりする *feel at ease*; *be relieved*. ▶私は長い間胸にたまっていたそのことを言ったのですっきりした I had a thing that had worried me for a long time. I got it off my chest and *felt relieved* [(*much*) *better*]. ▶熱い緑茶を1杯飲んで頭がすっきりした I *refreshed* myself with a cup of hot green tea./I *was* [*felt*] *refreshed* after drinking a cup of hot green tea./A cup of hot green tea *refreshed* me.

ズック 〖<オランダ語〗〖布地〗duck (❗テント・帆布・ズック靴などに用いる); 〖ズック靴〗(a pair of) canvas shoes; 《米》(a pair of) sneakers.

すっくと ▶すっくと立ち上がる stand up *straight* [*upright*, *erect*]; rise *abruptly* to one's feet; *spring* to one's feet.

すづけ 酢漬け pickles. ● 酢漬けのニシン *pickled* herring. ● キャベツを酢漬けにする *pickle* cabbage in vinegar.

ずっこける ❶〖ずり落ちる〗▶いすからずっこける *slide* off one's chair. ❷〖ばかなことをする〗make ⁓a fool of oneself; (自分をばかげた人のように見せる) make one look ridiculous.

ずっしり (重々しく) heavily; (質量感にあふれて) massively. ▶その心配事が心にずっしりとのしかかった The worries weighed *heavily* on [*in*] my mind. ▶その食事が胃にずっしりきた The meal lay *heavy* on my stomach. ▶庭には巨大な一対の岩がずっしり立っていた A pair of huge rocks stood *massively* in the garden.

すったもんだ ▶すったもんだの挙げ句(=大いに口論し大騒ぎしてから) after an awful fuss; after making a lot of fuss.

すってんころり(ん) ▶バナナの皮を踏んですってんころりんと転んだ I *slipped* (*and fell*) on a banana peel.

すってんてん ▶賭け事ですってんてんになる(=有り金をすべて失う) *lose all* one's *money* in gambling. ▶商売に失敗して彼はすってんてんになった(=破産した) He

すっと ❶ [すっきりとするさま] [《ふきっきり、さっぱり》]
❷ [急に軽く動くさま] すっと(=突然)立って戸口へ行く stand up *abruptly* and go to the door. ▶幽霊はすっと(=音もなく)消えた The ghost vanished *silently*.

ずっと ❶ [程度がはるかに] much; far; 《口》 a lot; a great deal. (!以上ずれも形容詞・副詞の比較級を修飾する. much が最も一般的な語 (⇨大分(ﾀﾞｲﾌﾞ))
[解説]) ▶彼はずっとよくなっている He is getting *much* [*far*, *a great deal*, 《口》*a lot*] better. ▶この小説はあの小説より読み終えるのにずっと日数[時間]がかかった This novel took (me) *many more days* [*much more time*] to finish than that one. (!)(1) 可算名詞の days では many, 不可算名詞のtime では much を用いることに注意. (2) far a lot は可算名詞・不可算名詞のいずれにも用いる. それぞれ a great many more days, a great deal more time とするとさらに強まる)
[会話]「バスで行く方が安いの?」「ずっとね」 "Is it cheaper by bus?" "*Much*."
❷ [時間・距離が離れて] (ずっと前に) a long time ago, long ago;(遠く) a long way (!通例平叙文で), far (!通例疑問文・否定文で); (話) way;(はるか遠くに) far away. ▶ずっと前に彼に会ったことがある I remember meeting him *a long time ago*. ▶5時よりずっと前に目が覚めていた I was awake *well* [*long*] before five o'clock. (!ともに before にかかる) ▶ずっと下の方に湖が見えた We saw the lake *far* [*way*] below. ▶その島はずっと北にある The island is *far* [*way*] to the north. ▶ずっと向こうに何が見えますか What do you see *far away* [《遠くに》*in the distance*]? ▶私は駅からずっと離れたところに住んでいる I live *a long way* (*off*) [×*far*] from the station. (! far は肯定文では避ける) ▶給料日はずっと先だ Payday's *a long way off*.
❸ [続けて] (長い間) for a long time; (始めから終わりまで) all [right] through(...), throughout(...); (道のりなどずっと) all the way; (その間ずっと) all the time. ▶1日中[午後]ずっと *all day* [*afternoon*]. ▶一晩中ずっと *throughout* [*all through*] the night; the whole night *through*. ▶ずっと留守にするの? Will you be away *long*? (!long は通例否定文・疑問文でのみ可) ▶彼は3週間前からずっと病気で寝ている He *has been* sick in bed for three weeks [×since three weeks ago]. (!現在完了形で「ずっと」の意が出る) ▶今までずっとどこにいたの? Where have you been *all the time* [*all this while*]? ▶今週はずっと残業ばかりでもうへとへとだ I've had to work overtime this whole week [*all this week*]. I'm dead tired. ▶電車が混んでいたので上野までずっと立ち通しだった(=立っていなければならなかった) The train was so crowded that I had to stand *all the way* to Ueno. (!kept standing は不可 (⇨続ける)) ▶彼は望遠鏡でずっと空を眺めていた He *kept* on *watching* at the sky through the telescope. (!on をつける方が継続の意が強い) ▶不景気がずっと(=永久に)続くなんてことはあり得ない Depression can't last *forever*.
[会話]「パパ、私ずっとママのお手伝いしてたのよ」「えらい子だね」 "*I've been* helping Mommy, Daddy." "That's a good girl."
[会話]「ずっとこちらにお住まいなのですか」「いいえ、5年前からです」 "Have you *always* lived here?" "No. I've lived here for the past five years." (! この always は完了形とともに用い「かねてよりずっと」の意)
❹ [真っすぐ] straight, 《やや話》 right. ▶この道をずっと行きなさい Go *straight* (*on*) along this road. ▶ずっと奥の方へお詰め願います (バスなどで) Move *right* back, please.

すっとばす すっ飛ばす drive* like hell.

すっとぶ すっ飛ぶ hurtle (+圃). ▶すっ飛んで来る come running [《車で》come driving]. ▶石をけろうとしたら、靴がすっ飛んでしまった When I tried to kick a stone, my shoe *hurtled away* instead.

すっとぼける 素っとぼける (⇨とぼける) ▶こんな時にすっとぼけるんじゃないよ Don't *act* [*play*] *dumb* at a (hard) time like this.

すっとんきょう 素っ頓狂 ▶すっとんきょうな男 a *stupid* [《口》*a dumb*] man;《口》a dope. ▶すっとんきょうな声を出す give [let out] a shrill cry. (! 後の方が口語的)

すっぱい 酸っぱい (未熟でまずい) sour /sáuər/; (本来酸味の強い) acid. ▶酸っぱいリンゴ a *sour* apple; an apple with an *acid* flavor. ▶レモンは酸っぱい Lemons are *acid*. ▶その果物は酸っぱい味がした The fruit tasted *sour* [had a *sour* taste]. ▶牛乳が暑さで酸っぱくなった The milk has gone *sour* [has *soured*] in the heat. ▶口が酸っぱくなるほど(=何回も何回も)しっかり勉強するように言ったのに、彼はしなかった I told him to study hard *again and again* [*over and over* (*again*)], but he didn't.

すっぱだか 素っ裸 — 素っ裸の[形]《話》 stárk-náked /-néikid/. (⇨丸裸) ▶素っ裸の赤ちゃんが a *stark-naked* baby. ▶浜辺で素っ裸で遊ぶ play on the beach *stark naked*.

すっぱぬく 素っ破抜く break* the news;《話》 debunk.

すっぱり (⇨きっぱり)

スッペ [《オーストリアの作曲家》] Suppé /súːpei/ (Franz von 〜).

すっぽかす [人と会う約束を破る] break* an appointment (*with*); (デートの相手などを) stand* ... up. ▶授業をすっぽかす(=ずる休みをする) play truant [《米話》*hooky*] *from* school. ▶仕事をすっぽかす(=怠る) *neglect* one's task. ▶彼女はデートをすっぽかした She *stood* me *up*. ▶デートをすっぽかしやがったな I think *I've been stood up*.

すっぽぬける すっぽ抜ける slip (-pp-) out (*of* one's hand). ▶ボールがすっぽ抜けて暴投になった The ball *slipped out of my hand* and went wide. ▶そんなに引っ張らないで。腕がすっぽ抜ける(=関節からはずれる) Don't pull so hard. My arm will *go out of joint*.

すっぽり [完全に] completely, entirely. (⇨完全に) ▶赤ちゃんをすっぽり毛布にくるむ wrap a baby *up* in a blanket; wrap a blanket *all* around a baby. ▶庭はすっぽりと雪で覆われていた The garden was *completely* covered [was covered *all over*] with snow. / The garden *was* blanketed *with* snow. ▶大きなかぶは力いっぱい引っ張るとすっぽり抜けた The large turnip came *clean* out when I pulled on it with all my strength.

すっぽん [動物] a soft-shelled turtle. ●月とすっぽん (⇨月 [成句])
●スッポン料理 turtle dishes.

すっぽんぽん (⇨圃 丸裸, 素っ裸)

すで 素手 ❶ [手そのもの] a hand; (むき出しの手) a bare hand. ▶素手で魚をつかむ catch a fish with one's *hand*(*s*). ▶素手で熱いなべをつかもうとする try to carry a hot pan with one's *bare hands*. ▶素手で小フライをつかむ make a *bare-handed* catch of a short fly ball.
❷ [何も持たないこと] ▶武装した強盗に素手で(=武器

を使わずに)立ち向かう fight *unarmed* with an armed robber. ● 素手で(＝お金をほとんど持たずに)商売を始める open a business *on a shoestring*.

ステイ 〖滞在〗a stay. ● ホームステイ a homestay. (⇨ホームステイ)

すていし 捨て石 〖囲碁の〗a sacrifice, a sacrificed stone; 〖護岸工事などで水中に投入する石〗a riprap; 〖庭に据えておく石〗a garden rock.
● **捨て石になる** ▶彼はその主義のために捨て石となった(＝自分［命］を犠牲にした) He *sacrificed himself* [*his life*] for the cause.

すていん 捨て印 an extra seal impression. ● 捨て印を押す put [affix] one's seal in an extra place 《*on* a document》.

すてうり 捨て売り〖投げ売り〗a sacrifice (sale). (⇨投げ売り)

ステーキ (a) steak /stéik/. ● サーロインステーキ a sirloin *steak*. ● フィレステーキ a fillet *steak*. ● サーモンステーキ a salmon /sǽmən/ *steak*. ● 骨つきステーキ a T-bone *steak*. ● 肉汁のしたたるステーキ a *juicy steak*. ● ステーキを焼く broil [grill] a *steak*. ▶ステーキはレアにして［中ぐらいに焼いて；よく焼いて］ください I'd like my *steak* rare [medium; well-done], please.

ステージ 〖舞台〗a stage.
● ステージママ a stage mother.

ステーション 〖駅, 拠点〗a station.
● ステーションワゴン《米》a station wagon;《英》an estate car.

ステータス 〖地位〗status /stéitəs/.
● ステータスシンボル a status symbol.

ステート 〖国家, 米国などの州〗a state.
● ステートアマ a state-aided amateur (athlete).

ステートメント 〖声明〗a statement.

すておく 捨て置く leave*; (そのままにしておく) let* [leave]《him》alone; leave《it》as it is.

すてがね 捨て金 (むだな金) wasted money.

すてき 素敵 ── 素敵な 形 〖すばらしい〗wonderful,《話》great; 〖驚くべき〗marvelous; 〖美しく心ひかれる〗lovely (⇨素晴らしい); 〖感じのよい〗nice; 〖(かっこいい) cool;〖魅力的な〗attractive; (うっとりするほどの) charming;〖美しい〗(女が) beautiful; (男が) handsome; (男女ともに) good-looking. ● すてきな服 *wonderful* [*lovely*, *nice-looking*] clothes.
▶すてきな女の子 a *beautiful* [*a good-looking*, *an attractive*, *a charming*] girl. ▶すてきな新車 a *nice* new car. ▶彼ってすてきね He's *nice* [《話》*terrific*], ＼isn't he?
会話 「あした映画見に行かない」「すてきだわ」"How about going to the movies tomorrow?" "That's *great*／*Great*."
会話 「これ, あなたにあげる」「まあ, すてき」"This is for you." "How ＼*lovely*! [Isn't it ＼*lovely*!]" (!いずれもैを用いた表現)
会話 「すてきな車をお持ちですね」「どうも！ 乗り心地はなかなかいいんですよ」"You have a *charming* car." "Thank you. It rides very well."
会話 (洋服売り場で試着してみて)「どうかしら」「うわっ, すごくすてきですわ」「でしょ, 私もいい感じだと思うの」 "How do you like it?" "Wow, you look really *cool*." "Yeah, it looks *cool* on me, too."

すてご 捨て子 a deserted [an abandoned] child (⤴ children).

すてさる 捨て去る ● 過去を捨て去る(＝忘れる) put one's past *out of* one's *mind*. (⇨捨てる)

すてしあい 捨て試合 a giveaway game.

すてぜりふ 捨て台詞 ▶彼は「おぼえろ」と捨てぜりふを残していった "I'll remember this." was his *part-ing shot* [(脅迫の言葉) *threat*].

ステッカー a sticker. ● ステッカーを張る put a *sticker* 《*on*》.

ステッキ a (walking) stick; a cane. (⇨杖(ｦ))

ステッチ a stitch.

ステップ 〖踏み台〗(乗り物の) a step; (成功への) a stepping-stone. ; 〖ダンスの〗a step ▶ワルツのステップを踏む go through the waltz *steps*; dance a waltz.

ステップ 〖大草原〗a steppe (!シベリア・アジアのステップをさすのは the Steppe)

ステップバイステップ 〖段階的な〗step-by-step. ● その計画をステップバイステップで実行に移す put the plan into practice *step by step*.

すててこ (a pair of) knee-length underpants.

すてどころ 捨て所 (⇨捨て場) ▶ここが命の捨て所(＝命をかけるところ)だ This is where we *risk our neck* [人生を終える] *end our life*.

* **すでに 既に** already (!肯定文で); yet (!疑問文・否定文で)(⇨もう); (以前) before, previously; (本などで上記に) above. ● すでに(＝上に述べたように) as mentioned *above* 〖前に〗*before*. ▶駅に着いたときには列車はすでに出ていた When I got to the station, the train had *already* left.

すてね 捨て値 ● 家を捨て値で(＝ただみたいな値で)売る《話》sell one's house *dirt cheap* [*for a song*].

すてば 捨て場 a place for dumping waste material. ● ごみ捨て場 a dúmping gròund; a (refuse) dump.

すてばち 捨て鉢 ● 捨て鉢になる(＝やけになる) become desperate; give oneself up to desperation. ● 捨て鉢になって in desperation.

すてみ 捨て身 ● 捨て身で(＝命をかけて)敵と戦う fight the enemy *at the risk of* one's *life*.

: **すてる 捨てる** ❶ 〖不要物を処分する〗throw*... away (!「投げ捨てる」という動作をいうこともある); get* rid of...; discard (!前の二つの表現より堅い語); (ごみなどをどっさと投げ捨てる) dump. ● 古いコートを捨てる *throw away* an old coat; *get rid of* [*discard*] an old coat. ● 書類をくずかごに捨てる *throw* papers *in* [*into*] a waste basket. ▶空き缶を車の窓から捨てるな Don't *throw* an empty can *out of* 《《主に米》*out*》the car window. ▶たばこの吸いがらを路上に捨てるな Don't *throw* cigarette butts *out* on the street./(路上を散らかすな) Don't *litter* 《*up*》the street with cigarette butts. ▶銃を捨てて出て来い *Throw down* [*Drop*] your gun and come out! ▶廃棄物は海中に捨てられた The wastes *were dumped into* the sea. ▶彼は旧式の蓄音機を捨てた(＝手放した)がらない He doesn't want to *part with* his old-fashioned record player. ▶ごみ箱があふれる前にごみを捨てましょう(＝空にしましょう) Let's *empty* the trash can before it gets too full.
❷ 〖見捨てる, 放棄する〗(職・信仰・望みなどを持つことをあきらめる) give*... up (!最も一般的な語); (決定的に見捨てた他人に任せる) abandon; (義務・信用などを破って) desert,《話》walk out on...; (...のものを去る) leave*; (自ら職などをやめる) resign. ● 地位を捨てる *give up* [*abandon*, *desert*, *leave*, *resign*] one's position. (!*desert* は自分の持ち場を放棄すること)
● 故郷を捨てる *abandon* [*leave*] one's hometown. (!前の方は永久に, 後の方は一時的な意味も加わる) ● 恋人を捨てる *walk out on* [*leave*,《話》*drop*] one's boyfriend [girlfriend]. ● 友人のため命を捨てる *give up* [(犠牲にする) *sacrifice*, *lay down*] one's life for one's friend. ● 偏見を捨てる(＝取り除く) *get rid of* one's prejudice. ● 試合を捨てる *give away* a game. ▶彼女は息子が帰るという希望をどうしても捨てきれなかった She couldn't *give*

ステレオ 《ステレオ装置》a stereo /stériòu/ (複 ~s), a stereo set; 《立体音響方式》stereo. ●ステレオ音響で録音する record 《a song》 *in stereo*. ●その曲をステレオで聞く [にかける] listen to [play] the music *on* [*in*, *by*] *the stereo*.
● ステレオ放送 a stereophonic broadcast.

ステレオタイプ 〖紋切り型〗a stereotype /stériou-tàip/. ●ステレオタイプな考え a *stereotyped* idea.

ステロイド 〖生化学〗steroid. ●ステロイドホルモン steroid hormones.

ステンシル 〖型板〗a stencil.

ステンドグラス stained /stéind/ glass. ●ステンドグラスをはめた窓 a *stained-glass* window. (事情▶ 西欧ではもっぱら教会で使う)

ステンレス stainless /stéinləs/ steel. ●ステンレスの流し台 a *stainless steel* sink.

スト a strike; a walkout.
①【〜スト】●交通ストa traffic *strike*. ●ゼネ[ハン]ストa general [a hunger] *strike*. ●全面[部分]ストan all-out [a partial] *strike*. ●時限[24時間]スト a limited-time [a 24-hour, a one-day] *strike*.
②【スト〜】●スト破りをする break up a *strike*. ▶スト決行中である The *strike* is on./They are (out) on *strike*.
③【ストに[を]】●ストを指令[宣言; 中止; 解決]する call [declare; call off; settle] a *strike*. ●労働者は賃上げを要求してストに入った The workers *went* (out) *on strike* for higher wages. (❗「賃金カットに反対して」なら for 句の代わりに *against* a cut in wages. となる)
●ストを打つ (行う) stage a strike.
●スト権 the right to strike. ●スト破り (行為) strike-breaking; (人) a strike-breaker; a scab; 〈米俗〉a fink; 〖英話〗a blackleg.

ストア 〈主に米〉a store, 〈主に英〉a shop. (⇨店) ●コンビニエンスストア a convenience *store*. ●チェーンストア a chain [〈主に英〉a multiple] *store*. ●ドラッグストア 〈主に米〉a drug*store*.

ストイック — **ストイックな** 形 〖禁欲的な〗stoic.

ストーカー a stalker. ●ストーカー行為をする stalk (her). ●ストーカー行為を罰する法律 a law against *stalking*.

すどおし 素通し ●素通しの(=度のない)眼鏡 a pair of glasses *with plain-glass lenses*; (a pair of) *plain* glasses. ●素通しの(=透明な)ガラス *transparent* glass.

***ストーブ** a heater, a stove (❗(1) 石油・石炭・まきを使うものを除いて heater の方が普通. (2) stove は通例複合語で用い、単独では主に料理用意味がさす). ●ガス[電気; 石油]ストーブ a gas [an electric; 〈米〉a kerosene, 〈英〉a paraffin] *heater*. ●オイルヒーター a oil heater (オイルヒーターのこと). ●石炭[まき]ストーブ a coal [a wood] *stove*. ●ストーブの煙突 a stovepipe. ●ストーブをたく light a *heater*; make a fire in a *heater*. ●ストーブをつける[消す] turn on [off] a *heater*. ▶ストーブが消えている The *heater* is out. ●このストーブは全開にしていてもあまり暖かくない This *heater* isn't very warm even though it's full on.
●ストーブリーグ a (hot) stove league.

すどおり 素通り — **素通りする** 動 (通り過ぎる) pass (by...). ●彼の家の前を素通りする *pass* (*by*) his house.

ストーリー 〖物語〗a story; 〖筋書き〗a plot.
●ストーリーテラー a storyteller.

ストール a stole. ●ストールをまとう put on a *stole*.

ストーンウォッシュ ●ストーンウォッシュする stonewash. (参考▶ ジーンズなどを砕石とともにもみ洗いして、古着の味わいをもたせること) ●ストーンウォッシュのジーンズ stonewashed jeans.

ストーンサークル 〖環状列石〗〖考古〗a stone circle.

ストッキング 《a pair of》stockings; 〖野球〗stirrup /stǽrəp/ socks (❗この下にはく白いソックスは sanitary socks). ●パンティーストッキング 〈主に米〉pantyhòse (❗複数扱い), 〈英〉tights, 〈和製語〉panty stockings. ●ストッキングをはく pull *stockings* on. ●ストッキングを脱ぐ pull [peel] *stockings* off. (❗peel は pull より描写的) ●彼女はストッキングをはいていなかった She had no *stockings* on. ●私のストッキング(の片方)が伝線した My *stocking* had a run 〈主に米〉[a ladder 〈英〉]./I got a run [a ladder] in my *stocking*.

ストック 〖在庫品〗(a) stock (⇨在庫); 〖株〗(a) stock. ●その布のストックはたくさんあります We have a large *stock* of the cloth. ●その商品は現在ストックがありません The goods are *out of stock* (↔*in stock*) now.
●ストックオプション 〖自社株購入権〗a stock option. ●ストックヤード 〖一時保管用〗a stockyard.

ストック 〖植物〗a stock.

ストック [<ドイツ語] 〖スキーの〗a (ski) pole, 〈英〉a (ski) stick.

ストックホルム 〖スウェーデンの首都〗 Stockholm /stάkhoʊ(l)m/.

ストッパー 〖留め具, 止める人・物〗a stopper; 〖抑え(の切り札)〗a closer; 〖サッカー〗a stopper (参考▶ ディフェンダー以外でゴールキーパーのこともさす).
●連敗ストッパー a *stopper*.

ストップ 名 stop (-pp-). ●ストップをかける order 《him》 to *stop*.
— **ストップする** 動 stop. ▶地下鉄はストライキ中ストップ(=運行停止)した The subways were *out of operation* during the strike.
●ストップウォッチ a stopwatch. ●ストップ高 a limit high of a stock price. ●ストップモーション 〖映画〗freeze-frame. (❗画像・装置の意では [C]) ●ストップ安 a limit low of a stock price. ●ストップライト a stoplight.

すどまり 素泊まり ●素泊まりで1泊する (日本の旅館で) stay overnight *without meals*.

ストライカー 〖サッカー〗a striker.

ストライキ a strike. (⇨スト)

ストライク 〖野球・ボウリング〗a strike. ●ツーストライクツーボール two balls and two *strikes* (❗日本語とは順序が逆). ●ストライクをとる have a *strike* (*on* a batter). ●ストライクを投げる throw *strikes*. ●ストライクを見逃す take a *strike*. ●キャッチャーへストライク送球する throw a *strike* to the catcher. ▶バッターはツーストライクをとられた The batter had two *strikes* against the pitcher./The batter was down two *strikes*.
●ストライクゾーン the strike zone.

ストライド 〖歩幅〗a stride. ●大きなストライドで走る run with long strides.
●ストライド走法 stride running.

ストライプ 〖縞(じま)〗a stripe. ●幅広のストライプ wide [broad] *stripes*. ●細いストライプ narrow [thin, fine] *stripes*. (❗特に、織り物の極細のストライプ

ストラップ a strap. ●調節[取り外し]のきくストラップ《a bag with》an adjustable [a detachable] *strap*.

ストラテジー 〖戦略〗 strategy.

ストラビンスキー 〖ロシア生まれの米国の作曲家〗 Stravinsky (Igor ～).

ストリーキング streaking. (参考 全裸で公共の場所を走り回ること)

ストリート a street. ●メインストリート a main *street*. ●ストリートチルドレン street children. ●ストリートマーケット a street market.

ストリキニーネ 〖薬剤〗 strychnine /stríkni:n/. (参考 神経興奮剤)

ストリッパー a stripper, a stripteaser.

ストリップ(ショー) (a) striptease; a strip(-tease) show. ●ストリップを見る see a *striptease*. ●ストリップをする strip; do a *striptease*.

ストリングス 〖オーケストラの弦楽器部〗 the strings.

ストレート ❶〖続けざま〗●ストレートで勝つ win a *straight* victory 《over》. ●ストレートで負ける suffer a *straight* defeat 《from》. ●ストレートのフォアボール a walk on four (*straight*) pitches.
❷〖酒類を水で薄めないこと〗●ウイスキーをストレートで飲む drink (one's) whiskey *straight* [*neat*].
❸〖回り道をしないこと〗●ストレートな言い方 a *straightforward* use of the word. ●彼はストレートで京都大学に合格した He got *straight* into Kyoto University.
❹〖直球〗a fastball. (⚠ a straight ball とはいわない)
❺〖ポーカーの役〗〖トランプ〗straight.
●ストレートフラッシュ〖トランプ〗straight flush.

ストレス (a) stress. ●ストレスの多い仕事[時代] a *stressful* job [time]. ●ストレスの多いサラリーマン *stressed-out* working adults. ●ストレスを解消する get rid of [remove], (緩和する) relieve, reduce] *stress*. ●最近かなりストレスがたまっている I've been under a lot of [great] *stress* recently./(たまってきている) I feel *stress* increasing [building up] these days. ▶彼女は職場でのストレスでまいってしまった She broke under *stress* at work.

ストレッチ ❶〖競争路の最後の直線コース〗the homestretch. ❷〖運動〗●ストレッチ体操をする do *stretching* exercises.

ストレッチャー 〖担架〗a stretcher.

ストレプトマイシン 〖薬学〗strèptomýcin. (参考 抗生物質の一種)

ストロー a (drinking) straw. ●ストローで飲む drink 《juice》 with a *straw*; suck [(少しずつ) sip] 《juice》 through a *straw*.
●ストロー級〖ボクシング〗strawweight.

ストローク 〖手足〗〖オール〗の一かき、ゴルフの1打〗a stroke. ●その子供はクロールで20ストロークほど泳いだ The boy did about twenty *strokes* of crawl.
●ストロークプレー〖ゴルフ〗a stroke [a medal] play.

ストロベリー a strawberry.

ストロボ 〖写真〗a strobe /stróub/ (light); an electronic flash.

すとん(と) ●すとんと(=すとんと)倒れる fall *flat*; take a fall. ●すとんとマンホールに落ちる fall *right* into a manhole.

ずどん(と) ●ずどんという銃声 the *bang* of a gun. ●ずどんと鳴る bang; make a bang. ●ずどんと落ちる take a *thumping* fall 《on the ground》.

***すな** 砂 sand. ●砂の(多い) sandy. ●細かい砂 fine *sand*. ●一粒の砂 a grain of *sand*. ●道に砂をまく sand a road; sprinkle a road with *sand*. ▶目[靴]に砂が入った I've got some *sand* in my eye [shoes]. ▶私の靴は砂だらけだ My shoes are all *sandy*.
●砂をかむような 砂をかむような(=無味乾燥な)講義 a dry-as-dust lecture.
●砂嵐 a dust storm; (砂漠の) a sandstorm. ●砂地 sandy soil. ●砂時計 a sandglass; (1時間用の) an hourglass. ●その他 a half-hour glass; an egg glass (ゆで卵用)などもある. ●砂場 (遊び場の)《米》a sandbox; 《主に英》a sandpit. ●砂袋 a sandbag. ●砂風呂《take [have]》a sand bath.

すなあそび 砂遊び ●砂遊びをする play with sand [in the sand].

***すなお** 素直 名 (従順) obedience; (穏やかさ) gentleness, mildness.
—— 形 (従順な) obedient /oubí:diənt/, docile /dásl/; (穏やかな) gentle, mild; (おとなしい) meek (⚠ 通例悪い意味で). ●素直な気持ち (おとなしい) *gentle* feeling; (偏見のない) an open mind. ▶あなたと一緒にいると素直な(=自分に正直な)気持ちになれる I can be *honest with myself* when I'm with you. ▶彼女は大変素直な子供だ She is a very *obedient* [*docile*] child. (⚠ いずれも「未成熟」という負の価値を含む語なので、日本語のよい意味での「素直な」の訳語として大人に用いるのは不適切)
—— 素直に 副 obediently. ▶素直に医師の忠告に従った I followed the doctor's advice *obediently*. /I obeyed the doctor's advice. ▶彼の親切な申し出を素直に(=快く)受けた方がいい You should *be willing to* accept his kind offer.

すなぎも 砂肝 a gizzard.

すなけむり 砂煙 ●砂煙を立てる raise [throw up, kick up] a (cloud of) dust. ●砂煙を立てて走り去る (自動車が) drive off *in a cloud of dust*.

スナック 〖食べ物〗(つまみの類) a snack food (ピーナッツの類); (軽食) a small meal; 〖店〗(軽食堂) a snack bar (⚠ 通例酒類を置いていない; (酒場) a bar.

スナッチ 〖重量挙げ〗a snatch.

スナップ ❶〖留め金具〗a press [(主に米) a snap] fastener,《米》a snap,《主に英》a (press) stud.
●スナップを留める[はずす] do up [undo] one's press fastener.
❷〖写真〗a snapshot, (やや書) a snap. ●スナップ写真をとる take a *snap(shot)* 《of》,《話》*snap* (a photograph of) 《him》.
❸〖手首の動き〗●スナップをきかせる *snap* one's wrist. ●スナップスローで一塁へ送球する make a *snap* throw to first.

スナップショット a snapshot. (⇒スナップ ❷)

すなのうえのしょくぶつぐん 『砂の上の植物群』 *Flora on Sand*. (参考 吉行淳之介の小説)

すなのおんな 『砂の女』 *The Woman in the Dunes*. (参考 安部公房の小説)

すなはま 砂浜 sand(s) (⚠ 通例複数形で); a sandy beach. (⇒浜辺) ●はだしで砂浜を走る run barefoot on the *sand(s)*.

すなぼこり 砂埃 dust; (舞い上がる) a (cloud of) dust. (⇒砂煙) ▶南風が吹くと黄色い砂ぼこりでそこらじゅうがざらざらなる When the wind blows from the south, everything gets gritty with yellow *dust*.

***すなわち** 即ち 〖つまり〗that is (to say); namely; 〖言い換えると〗in other words. (⇒つまり) ●2人の近代日本の有名な作家、すなわち漱石と鷗外 the two modern Japanese famous writers, *namely* Soseki and Ogai.

スニーカー 《主に米》sneakers,《英》plimsolls,《英》

ずぬける 図抜ける (⇨⇨ ずば抜ける)
すね 脛 〖向こうずね〗 a shin; 〖脚部〗 a leg. ●いすねをぶつける bang one's *shin* on a chair. ●すねをけとばす kick [him] in [on] the *shin*.
● すねに傷を持つ have a guilty conscience; have something to hide.
● すねをかじる ~親のすねをかじる *be dependent on* one's parents; 《通例けなして》*live off* [《話》*sponge off*] *one's parents*.
● すね当て shin guards [pads].
すねかじり 脛かじり 《話》《けなして》a sponger /spǽndʒər/. (⇨脛②)
すねる 拗ねる （不機嫌で口をきかなくなる）become* [get*] sulky, sulk; （ふくれつらをする）pout (sulkily). ▶その子はすねている The child *is sulking* [*is in a sulky mood, is in the sulks, has got the sulks*].

> **翻訳のこころ** すぐにすねるたちで、すねた横顔はジェームス・ディーンに似ていた（江國香織『デューク』）He got sulky easily. When he was sullen, his profile looked [was] like that of James Dean. (❗「横顔」は profile.「ジェームス・ディーンの横顔に似ている」ので that (=the profile) of James Dean とすることに注意）

*ずのう 頭脳 〖知力〗(a) brain 《通例複数形で》; a mind; 〖頭の働き〗a head. (⇨頭❸) ●知力のたくましい〖弱い〗頭脳 a powerful [a weak] *brain*. ▶彼は頭脳明晰〖めいせき〗だ He has a clear *head* [*brain*]./頭の切れる）He has a sharp *mind*.
●頭脳集団 a think tank. ●頭脳プレー a clever play. ●頭脳流出 brain drain. ●頭脳流入 brain gain. ●頭脳労働 brainwork, mental work. ●頭脳労働者 a brainworker.
スノー 〖雪〗snow.
●スノータイヤ a snow tire. ●スノーボート a snow boat. ●スノーボード（板）a snowboard;（競技）snowboarding. ●スノーマシン 〖人工降雪機〗a snowmaker, a snowmaking machine; 《和製語》a snow machine. ●スノーモービル〖雪上車〗a snowmobile.
すのこ 簀の子 （台所の）《米》a drainboard, 《英》a draining board; （風呂場の）duckboards.
すのもの 酢の物 〖料理〗a vinegared dish. ●キュウリとカニの酢の物 vinegared cucumbers with crab meat.
スパークリングワイン sparkling wine. (〖参考〗シャンパンがその代表格)
スパート ●スパートをかける put on *a spurt*. (⇨ラスト)
スパーリング 〖ボクシング〗sparring. ●スパーリングをする spar.
スパイ 图 〖人〗a spy, a secret 《an intelligence》agent (❗ spy は非難の意を含み、最近では secret agent の方が好まれる); 〖行為〗espionage /éspianɑːdʒ/. ●産業スパイ（人）an industrial *spy*; （行為）industrial *espionage*. ●二重スパイ a double *agent*. ●敵国のスパイ a *secret agent for* the enemy country.
―― スパイする 動 ●敵の動静をスパイする *spy on* the enemy's movements.
●スパイ映画 a spy [an espionage] movie. ●スパイ衛星 a spy [an intelligence] satellite.
スパイク 图 ❶ 〖靴底などの〗a spike;〖靴〗spikes, 《スパイク付き靴》spiked shoes, spikes, 〖サッカー〗boots, 《和製語》spike shoes.
❷〖バレーボールの〗a spike.
―― スパイクする 動 ❶〖野球などで〗spike 《him》.

❷〖バレーボールで〗give* 《a ball》a spike, spike 《a ball》.
●スパイクタイヤ a spiked tire; 《和製語》a spike tire.
スパイス (a) spice. (❗集合的には〖U〗) ●スパイスのきいたソース a *spicy* [a *highly spiced*] sauce.
スパイラル 〖らせん形(の)〗spiral.
スパゲッティ spaghetti /spəɡéti/. ●スパゲッティを作る（料理として）cook *spaghetti*.
●スパゲッティナポリタン spaghetti Napolitana; spaghetti with tomato sauce. ●スパゲッティミートソース spaghetti with meat sauce; (ボロネーゼ) spaghetti Bolognese.
すばこ 巣箱 （野鳥の）a birdhouse (覆 -houses /-ziz, 《米》-siz/; （ミツバチの）a beehive. ●巣箱を木に付ける fasten [put up] a *birdhouse* in a tree.
スパコン 〖「スーパーコンピュータ」の略〗(⇨スーパー)
すばし(っ)こい 〖機敏な〗quick;〖軽快な〗nimble, agile. (⇨敏捷②)
すぱすぱ ●たばこをすぱすぱ吸う *puff (away) at* [*on*] a cigarette; *puff (away) at* one's pipe.
ずばずば (⇨ずけずけ)
すはだ 素肌 bare [naked] skin. ●素肌にワイシャツを着る wear a shirt next to the *skin*. ▶彼女は素肌がきれいだ She has beautiful (, clear) *skin*./She has a beautiful *complexion*. (❗顔の肌についていう)
スパッツ 《a pair of》leggings. (〖参考〗婦人・子供用の脚にぴたりとつく伸縮性のあるズボン)
すぱっと ❶〖切る様子〗●青竹をすぱっと切る *slash off* a bamboo.
❷〖すばやい処理〗（きっぱり）once and for all (❗and を省略することもある《古》); （すっかり）completely. ▶彼女はたばこをすぱっとやめられたらと思っている She wishes to give up [stop] smoking *once and for all* [*決意してその場で*] *then and there*]. ▶アメリカとの関係をすぱっと切る(=きれいさっぱり)断つのは政治的冒険である It's a political adventure [risk] to break off relations with the USA *completely*.
ずばっと ❶〖刺したり切ったりするさま〗▶矢は金的にずばっと刺さった The arrow *hit the bull's-eye* [《ど真ん中》*the dead center*] 《xstraight》. (❗(1) hit … で「ずばっと」を含意し、これに straight をつけるのは冗言的。(2) hit … は慣用句で比喩的に「核心を突く」意に用いられる（⇨ずばり①）
❷〖ためらわずに言い切るさま〗▶お前はケチだとずばっと言ってやった I told him *straight out* that he was a miser. (⇨ずばり❶)
スパナ《米》a wrench, 《英》a spanner. ●スパナでナットを締める fasten (↔unfasten)〖堅く〗tighten (↔loosen)] a nut with a *wrench*.
すばなれ 巣離れ （巣立ち）leaving the nest.
ずぬける ずば抜ける (⇨優れる) ●ずば抜けた演技 an *outstanding* performance. ●ずば抜けて(=例外的に)背の高い子供 an *exceptionally* tall child. ▶彼はずば抜けてよくできる He is *by far* [*much*] the best student in the class. (❗(1) by far, much は最上級を強める。(2) by far は He is the best student *by far*…. のように後ろから修飾することも可) ●英語〖テニス〗がずば抜けている He far excels in English [at tennis]. ▶彼らはみな頭がよいが、その中では彼女がずば抜けて〖=突出している〗They are all bright, but she *stands out* among them.
スパムメール 〖迷惑メール〗〖インターネット〗spam (mail).
すばやい 素早い quick, swift. ●素早く動く *move quickly* [《話》*quick, swiftly*]. ●危険を素早く察知する be *quick to* sense the danger.

すばらしい 素晴らしい

WORD CHOICE すばらしい, すごい

great 人・本・機会・日々・作品などが特に価値が高く, すばらしいこと. ●オーストラリアではすばらしい時間を過ごせるだろう You'll have a *great* time in Australia.

wonderful 人・物事・時間・作品・旅行・季節などがすばらしく魅力にあふれていること. ●なんてすばらしい世界なんだろう What a *wonderful* world!

fantastic 夢・土地・景色・アイデアなどがこの世の物とも思えぬぐらいすばらしいこと. ●すばらしいプランを思いついたよ I've just come up with a *fantastic* plan.

頻度チャート

great	██████████				
wonderful	███				
fantastic	█				
20	40	60	80	100 (%)	

wonderful, 《話》great (!他に fantastic, fábulous, magnificent, splendid なども用いる); 〖快い〗nice; 〖見事な〗fine; 〖すぐれた〗excellent; 〖驚くべき〗marvelous; 〖素敵な〗lovely. ▶すばらしい考え a splendid [a marvelous, a great,《話》a terrific] idea. ▶彼は実にすばらしい芸術家だ He's really a *wonderful* artist. (!*absolutely* wonderful とは言うが, *very* wonderful とは通例いわない)/He's *quite* an artist [a good artist]. (!「quite+a+単数名詞」は《主に米》) ▶すばらしいね (That's) *wonderful* [*great, fantastic, fine*]! (!fine は肉声にも用いる) ▶すばらしい天気だった The weather was *nice* [*wonderful, marvelous*]. (!順に意味が強くなる)/We had (×a) *nice* [*wonderful, marvelous*] weather. ▶とてもすばらしいプレゼントだわ It's a *lovely* [a *magnificent*] present. ▶ハイキングとはすばらしい It's *wonderful* to go hiking. (!この意では ×It's *wonderful that* we go hiking. は不可)

[会話]「あの芝居はどうだった」「すばらしかったよ」"What was the play like?" "*Excellent* [*Splendid, First-rate*]."

ずばり ❶〖言いにくい事をずばり言う〗say bluntly. ▶ずばり言って彼にはその能力はない To put it *bluntly*, he has no ability to do that. ▶彼はずばりと(＝無遠慮に)ものを言う人です. He is *outspoken* [〖正直に〗*straightforward*].

❷〖ずばり当てる〗hit* the nail on the head;《話》hit the bull's eye (!的の中心を射る の意. 比喩的にも用いる). ▶彼の一言がずばり核心をついた His words *hit the nail on the head* [*hit the bull's eye*]./His words *came straight to the point*.

すばる 昴 〖天文〗the Pleiades /plí:ədìz/. (!その一つは Pleiad)

スパルタ 〖古代ギリシャの都市国家〗Sparta /spá:rtə/. ●スパルタ人 a Spartan. ●スパルタ式教育(＝厳しいしつけ)をする impose rigid [severe] discipline 《on one's child》. (!Spartan education [discipline] とはあまりいわない)

スパン 〖期間, 間隔〗a span. ●10 メートルのスパン a *span* of ten meters. ▶辞書編集はスパンの長い仕事である It takes a long *span* of time to make a dictionary.

ずはん 図版 〖さし絵〗an illustration; 〖別丁扱いの〗a plate; 〖図・図解〗(簡単な) a diagram.

スパンコール a spangle, a sequin /sí:kwin/. (!いずれも通例複数形で)

スピーカー a (loud)speaker; 〖拡声装置〗the public-address [PA] (system). ●スピーカーで呼び出す call 《him》 *over a loudspeaker* [*the PA (system)*].

スピーチ a speech; (特に公式の) an address; (くだけた, 軽い) a talk. (⇨演説, テーブルスピーチ) ▶結婚披露宴でスピーチをする give a (small) *talk* at a wedding reception. (!make a speech も可能だが, かしこまって大げさな話をすることになる)
●スピーチセラピスト 〖言語治療士〗a speech therapist. ●スピーチライター a speechwriter 《for the president》.

スピーディ ─ スピーディな 形 speedy, quick.

***スピード** (a) speed. (⇨速度)
①【～(の)スピード】●フルスピードで *at full speed*. (⇨全速力) ●ものすごいスピードで *at* (a) *terrific* [(a) *furious*] *speed*.
②【スピード(の)～】●スピードの出る車 a *fast* car. ●スピード違反で捕まる be caught *speeding* [〖ネズミ取りに〗in a *speed trap*]. ●意思決定のスピード化 a *speedup in* decision-making. ●スピードダウンする slow [×speed] *down*. ●スピードアップせよ (車を) Step on it [the gas]. (!(1) 通例命令形で. (2) 比喩的に, たとえば「仕事を急げ」(*Speed up your work*.) の意にも用いる)
③【スピードを】●投球のスピードを殺す kill a pitch. ●スピードを殺した投球 an off-speed pitch. ▶我々の車はスピードを出して高速道路を走った Our car *sped* [ran *at speed*] along the expressway. (!(1) Our car の代わりに We とすることも可. (2) この「疾走した」の意では speeded も用いるが sped の方が普通だ) ▶我々は直線道路に出たので車のスピードを上げた We were on a straightway, so I picked up [built up] *speed*. ▶突然列車はスピードを落とした Suddenly the train *slowed down*. (!×speeded down とはいわない) ▶彼は仕事のスピードを上げた He *hurried up* his work./He *speeded up* (the rate of) his work./He *quickened* the pace of his work. (!後の方ほど堅い言い方) ▶そんなにスピードを出すな Don't drive so fast.
●スピード感 a feeling of speediness. ●スピードガン a radar gun; a speed gun. ●スピード狂 a speed maniac /méiniæk/; a speeder. ●スピード時代 the age of speed. ●スピード写真 a fast [an instant] photo. ●スピードスケート speed skating. ●スピードボール a fastball; a speedball.

スピッツ ［＜ドイツ語］〖動物〗a spitz.

スピットボール 〖野球〗a spitball. (参考) 唾液など異物を塗りつけた反則球) ●スピットボール(を投げる)投手 a spitballer.

ずひょう 図表 〖地図・図解・グラフ・表など〗a chart; 〖図解〗(簡単な) a diagram, (番号を打った) a figure. ●文法［歴史］図表 a grammar [a historical] chart. ●図表 1 figure 1; fig. 1. ●図表を作る draw a *chart* [a *diagram*]. ●気温を図表で示す show temperature on a *chart*; *chart* temperature.

スピロヘータ ［＜ドイツ語］a spiroch(a)ete /spáiərəkì:t/. (参考) 梅毒の病原菌)

スピン 〖回転〗a spin. ●ボールにスピンをかける put a *spin* on the ball; give the ball a *spin*; *spin* the ball.

スピンアウト (a) spin-out. (⇨回 スピンオフ)

スピンオフ (a) spin-off. (参考) ある組織から分離・独立をして別会社を作ること)

スフィンクス a sphinx. (!the Sphinx とすればエジプトの Giza 付近の大スフィンクス像)

スプーン 〖匙(さじ)〗a spoon. ●スープ(用)スプーン a soup *spoon*. ●デザート(用)スプーン《主に英》a dessert-

spoon. ● 計量スプーン a méasuring *spòon*. ● スプーン2杯の砂糖 two spoons [*spóonfuls*] of sugar. ▶彼女はスプーンで子供に食事を食べさせた She fed her child with a teaspoon.
● スプーンレース a spoon race. (!an egg-and-spoon race からできたという説や和製英語という説もある)

すぶた 酢豚 sweet-and-sour pork.

ずぶっと ●注射針をずぶっと腕に刺す jab [*plunge*] a hypodermic needle *into* one's arm. ▶一歩ごとに長靴がずぶっと雪の中に沈んだ My booted feet sank *into* the snow at every step.

ずぶとい 図太い (厚かましい) impudent; (特に女性が) bold. ▶彼は図太いやつだ He is an *impudent* fellow./What a *nerve* he has! (⇨図々しい)

ずぶぬれ ずぶ濡れ (⇨びしょ濡れ)

ずぶの ● ずぶの素人(ੱ) a *rank* amateur. (!rank は「(好ましくないこと)が極めつき」の意)

スプラッタームービー 〚血みどろ映画〛 a splatter movie.

すぶり 素振り 图 a practice swing.
── **素振りする** 動 take practice swings; take shadow swings. ▶バット[ラケット]を素振りする *practice swinging* a bat [a racket].

スプリット 〚ボウリング〛 a split.
● スプリットタイム 〚区間タイム〛〚マラソンなど〛 a split (time). ● スプリットフィンガー(ドファストボール) 〚野球〛 a split-finger; a split-fingered fastball; a splitter.

スプリング 〚ばね〛 a spring; 〚春〛 spring.
● スプリングキャンプ spring training. ● スプリングコート a topcoat, a topper; 〚和製語〛 a spring coat. ● スプリングボード 〚踏み切り板〛 a springboard.

スプリンクラー 〚消火システム〛 a sprinkler system.

スプリンター 〚短距離選手〛 a sprinter.

スフレ [<フランス語] 〚料理〛 (a) soufflé /suːˈfleɪ/.

スプレー 〚液〛 spray; 〚器具〛 a spray(er). ● ヘアスプレー hair spray. ● スプレー式殺虫剤 insect *spray*; a *spray* insecticide; 〚話〛 a bug bomb.

スプレッド 〚値幅, 利ざや, 金利差〛〚経済〛 a spread.
● スプレッド貸し a spread loan; spread lending. ● スプレッド取引 a spread transaction.

スプレッドシート 〚表計算ソフト〛〚コンピュータ〛 a spreadsheet.

すべ 術 (方法) a way. ●なすすべを知らない(=どうしていいか分からない) don't know [have no idea] what to do. (⇨途方 [第 1 文例]) ▶そのような不慮の災難から身を守るすべはありません (There's) no *way* we can guard against those kind of unexpected disasters. ▶彼は足を折ってなすすべもなく(=何もできずに)地面に横たわっていた He broke his leg and lay *helpless* on the ground.

スペア 〚予備部品〛 a spare; 〚詰め替え用品〛 a refill. (⇨予備) ▶その機械の部品のスペア *spare* parts for the machine.
● スペアインク a refill for a pen. ● スペアキー a duplicate /djúːplɪkət/ key. ● スペアタイヤ a spare (tire).

スペアミント 〚植物〛 spearmint.

スペアリブ spareribs.

スペイン 〚国名〛 Spain (!公式名も同じ). (首都 Madrid) ● スペイン人 a Spaniard; the Spanish. ● スペイン語 Spanish. ● スペイン(人[語])の Spanish.

スペース a space; (余地) room. (⇨余裕) ● スペースがないので for lack of *space*. ● スペースをあける make *room* 《*for* another desk》. ● スペースを作る 〚サッカー〛 create a *space*. ▶スペース(=紙面)をさく (⇨紙面 ❷) ▶ピアノを入れるのにどのくらいスペースが必要ですか How much *room* [*space*] do you need for a piano? ▶そのテーブルはスペースを取りすぎている The table takes up too much *space*.
● スペースキー a space key [bar].

スペースオペラ 〚宇宙冒険もの〛 a space opera.

スペースシャトル a space shuttle. ● スペースシャトルエンデバー Space Shuttle Endeavour. (!英国つづりに注意)

スペード a spade. ● スペードの 5 the five of *spades*.

すべからく (=是非(ಒ)とも)

スペキュレーション 〚投機〛 (a) speculation.

スペキュレーター 〚投機家〛 a speculator.

スペクタクル 〚大仕掛けな見せ場〛 a spectacle.

スペクトル [<フランス語] 〚光学〛 a spectrum (複 -tra).
● スペクトル分析 spectrum analysis.

スペシャリスト 〚専門家〛 a specialist. ▶彼女は教育のスペシャリストです She is a *specialist* in education.

スペシャル special. ● (…についての)スペシャル番組 a *special* [a *feature*] 《*on*》. ● スペシャルコース a *special* course.

すべすべ ● すべすべした smooth /smúːð/; (絹のように) silky. ▶彼女の肌はすべすべしている Her skin is *very smooth*./She has a very *smooth* skin. ▶彼女はいつも床をすべすべにきれいにする She always *makes* the floor *shining clean*. (!shining は「輝くばかり」の意の副詞用法)

スペック 〚仕様〛 a specification, a spec. ● 基本スペック a basic *specification*.

:すべて 图 〚ひっくるめてすべて〛 all; 〚一つ一つすべて〛 everything. (⇨全部) ▶私たちのすべてがそのことを知っている *All of* us [×All us] know it./We *all* know it. ▶金がすべてではない Money isn't *everything*. ▶一つのことにすべてをかけるな 《ことわざ》 Don't put all your eggs in one basket.
── **すべての** 形 all; every; 〚全体の〛 whole, entire. (!entire の方が強意的) ●世界中のすべての人 *all* the people of the world; *all* the world; the *whole* world. (!最後の二つは単数扱い) ▶すべての子供が愛情を必要としている *All* children need [*Every* child needs] love. ▶すべての学生がその提案に同意した *All* students [*All* (*of*) the students] agreed to the proposal. (!限定的な語がくる場合は of を伴う. この of は省略可) ▶すべての学生が試験に合格したわけではない Not *all* the students [Not *every* student] passed the exam. (!部分否定を表す. All the students did not pass.... は全否定なのか部分否定なのかあいまいなので書く場合は避ける方がよい (⇨全部 图①)) ▶すべての真相を話そう I'll tell you the *whole* [*entire*] truth. (!× ... all the truth. は不可)
── **すべて** 副 (まったく) entirely, completely, all. ▶彼の生活はすべて音楽に向けられている His life is *entirely* given up to music./His *whole* life [*All* his life] is given up to music. ▶それはすべて君の落ち度だ It's *all* your fault. ▶彼は持っていた物をすべてなくした He lost *everything* [〚書〛 *all*] he had.

すべらす 滑らす slip (-pp-). (⇨滑る)

すべり 滑り a slip; (滑るように進むこと) a slide. ▶このふすまは滑りがよい This *fusuma slides* well.

すべりおちる 滑り落ちる ▶ウナギが彼女の手から滑り落ちた The eel *slipped out of* her hands. ▶子供が木から滑り落ちた The child *slipped off* [*from*] the tree. ▶彼は一本目(の滑走)が終わった時点では 5 位であったが, 最終的には 9 位に滑り落ちた He was fifth after the first leg but *slid to* ninth in the end. (!スキーなどの滑走競技で用いられる表現)

すべりこみ 滑り込み ●ホームに滑り込みセーフ safely slide home. ●遅れて先生にレポートを提出する submit the paper to one's teacher *just in time*.

すべりこむ 滑り込む ●二塁に滑り込む[滑り込んでセーフになる] slide [slide safely] into second (base); (頭から)dive in for second and make it. ●後の方が口語的) ●学校に滑り込む(=ぎりぎりに来る) come to school *just in time* [《米話》*in the nick of time*].

すべりだい 滑り台 a slide. ●滑り台で遊ぶ play on the slide; (滑る) go down the slide.

すべりだし 滑り出し (初め) a beginning, a start. ▶滑り出しは上々だ We've made a good *start*.

すべりだす 滑り出す ❶【滑り始める】begin* to slide [glide, slip]. ❷【物事が進行し始める】▶新事業が順調に滑り出した The new business *got off to a good start*.

すべりどめ 滑り止め a skid (🅘坂道などで車輪につける止め木); (タイヤの) a nonskid tread /tréd/; (階段・浴室の) a nonskid strip. ●T大学の滑り止めにF大学を受ける take the entrance exam for F University as an *insurance against failure at* [as a *safe second choice to*, 《米話》as a *safety to*] T University.

スペリング 〘つづり〙 a spelling. ●「菊」という単語のスペリングを知っていますか Do you know the *spelling* of [how to spell] the word "chrysanthemum"? ▶君の作文にはスペリングのミスが多い There are a lot of *misspellings* [You've made a lot of *spelling mistakes*] in your composition.

*****すべる 滑る** ❶【滑走する】(表面に接触して) slide*; (静かにすいすいと) glide; (水面などをかすめて) skim (-mm-); (スケートで) skate; (スキーで) ski. ●スキーで斜面を滑り降りる ski down the slope; go [slide] down a slope on [×with] skis. ●氷の上で滑ろう Let's *slide* [*take a slide*] on the ice. ▶ドアがすべるように(=するすると)開いた The door *slid* open. (🅘引き戸の場合の表現) ▶車はすべるように動いて立ち去った The car moved *smoothly* away. ▶ボートは湖面を滑るように進んだ The boat *skimmed over* [×on] the lake.

> 翻訳のこころ 月の光が青白く山の斜面を滑っていた(宮沢賢治『なめとこ山の熊』) The pale moonlight slid down over the mountain slope. (🅘「青白い」は pale. (2)「(斜面を)滑る」は slid down over として、斜面を覆うように照らしている様子を表す)

❷【誤って滑る】slip (-pp-); (乗り物などが) skid (-dd-) (⇨スリップ). ●口が滑る (⇨口[成句]) ▶コップが手からすべってがちゃんと落ちた The glass *slipped out of* [*from*] my hand and fell with a crash. ●階段で[バナナの皮を踏んで]滑って転んだ拍子に腕を折った I *slipped on* the stairs [*on* a banana peel] and broke my arm. (🅘このように slip は「転ぶ」を含むこともある)

会話「足もとに気をつけて」「どうして？」「道が凍って滑りやすいのよ」「そう、教えてありがとう」"Watch your step!" "Why?" "The road is icy and *slippery*." "Thanks for warning me."

❸【試験などに滑る】fail, 《主に米話》flunk. ▶彼は英語の試験に滑った He *failed* [*flunked*] the English exam.

スペル 〘つづり〙 a spelling. (🅘spell は動詞では「(単語を)つづる」、名詞では「まじない」などの意). (⇨スペリング)
●スペルを間違える spell 《a word》wrongly; misspell.
●スペルチェッカー〖コンピュータ〗a spell(ing) checker.

スポイト [<オランダ語] a dropper.

スポークスマン (男) a spokesman; (女) a spokeswoman (🅘複数形はともに -men); (男・女) a spokesperson (🅰 -people). ●大統領[政府]のスポークスマン a presidential [a government] *spokesman*.

*****スポーツ** (a) sport. (🅘(1) 集合的に用いる場合、《米》では通例 sports, 《英》では sport. 個々の競技には a sport を用いる傾向がある。(2) 魚釣り・狩りなども含む。 ●プロスポーツ a professional *sport*. ●テレビでスポーツを見る watch *sports* 《米》[*sport* 《英》] on TV. ●ラジオのスポーツニュースを聞く listen to the *sports* report on [×of] the radio. ●あなたはどんなスポーツをやりますか What *sport(s)* do you enjoy [take part in, go in for]? (🅘play [do] *sport*(s) は《英》では普通にある表現だが、《米》では不可とする意見もあり、避けた方がよい。play は個々のスポーツについて play football [basketball, tennis] のように用いる) ●卓球はだれでも手軽に楽しめる室内スポーツです Ping-pong is an indoor *sport* anyone can enjoy very easily. ●スポーツを通じてフェアプレーの精神を養うべきだ We should cultivate the spirit of fair play through *sports*.
●スポーツカー a sports car. ●スポーツ記者 a sports reporter. ●スポーツ行事 a sporting event. ●スポーツシャツ a sport(s) shirt. ●スポーツ新聞 a sports newspaper. ●スポーツセンター a sports center [complex]; a fitness center. ●スポーツドリンク an athletic [a sports] drink. ●スポーツバッグ a sports bag. ●スポーツ用品店 a sporting goods store; a sports shop. ●スポーツ欄 a sports page.

スポーツマン 〘運動の得意な人〙an athlete /æθlíːt/; 〘スポーツ好きな人〙 a sports lover, a sports person. (🅘sportsman は狩り・釣り・競馬などを含むスポーツ好きの男のこと) ●スポーツマン精神 (⇨スポーツマンシップ) ●スポーツマンらしい態度 *sportsmanlike* behavior. ●彼女はなかなかのスポーツマンだ She is quite an *athlete* [*very athletic*]./(スポーツが得意だ) She is *very good at* sports 《米》[*sport* 《英》]. (🅘後の言い方の方が口語的)

スポーツマンシップ spórtsmanship. ●スポーツマンシップにのっとり正々堂々と戦う play in a sportsmanlike way. (🅘sportsmanlike を好まない人は play fair and square という)

スポーティー ●スポーティーな(=派手でカジュアルな)ジャケット a *sporty* jacket.

ずぼし 図星 ●図星を指す (正しく推量する) guess 《it》right; (正確に言い当てる) 《話》hit the nail on the head.

スポッと ●穴にすぽっと(=ともに)落ちる fall *right into* the hole. ●栓がすぽっと(=ぽんと)抜けた The cork *popped*.

スポット ❶【短い出演】(やや話) a spot. ●テレビのスポット広告 a television *spot*. ❷【スポットライト】a spotlight. (⇨スポットライト)

スポットライト a spotlight, 《話》a spot. ●スポットライトを浴びる [浴びている] come into [be in] the *spotlight*.

ずぼむ (⇨すぼむ)

すぼむ 窄む (狭くなる) become* narrow, narrow.

すぼめる 窄める (狭くする) make* (it) narrow, narrow. ●唇をすぼめる pucker up one's lips [the mouth]. ●肩を丸くすぼめる hunch one's shoulders. ●傘をすぼめる(閉じる) shut [close] an umbrella; (折りたたむ) fold an umbrella; (巻く) roll an umbrella; (さしていた傘を)ささなくする let [take] down an umbrella.

ずぼら ── ずぼらな 形 ●ずぼらな(=だらしのない)人 a

slovenly [(怠慢な) a *negligent*; (不注意な) a *sloppy*] person; 《話》 a *slob*.

ズボン 《米》pants, 《英》trousers /tráuzərz/. (**!**《米》では trousers は堅い語); (替えズボン) 《やや古》slacks. (**!** 以上いずれの語も複数扱い. 数えるときは a pair of 〜 を用いる)

① 【〜ズボン】● 細い [太い] ズボン narrow [full, baggy] *pants*. ● 半ズボン *shorts*; *breeches*. ● 作業ズボン work *pants* [*trousers*]. ● すそが折り返しになったズボン *pants* with cuffs 《米》[turn-ups 《英》].

会話「このズボンどうだい」「いいんじゃない」 "Do you think these *pants* look all right?" "Yes, they look fine."

② 【ズボンの〜】● ズボンのポケット a *pant* [a *trouser*] pocket. (**!** a *pants* [a *trousers*] pocket は《まれ》) ▶ ズボンのファスナーがあいているよ(=社会の窓があいている) (⇨社会) [成句]

③ 【ズボンを〜】● ズボンをはく [脱ぐ; 引き上げる] put on [take off; pull up, hitch up] one's *pants*. ● ズボンを詰める shorten [alter] one's *pants*. ● 新しいズボンを1着買うよ buy a new pair of *pants*. (**!** new の位置に注意. ただし「茶色のズボン」などの場合は buy a pair of brown *pants* とするのが普通)
● ズボン下 underpants, 《米》suspenders, 《英》braces. (いずれも複数形で) ● ズボンプレッサー a trouser [a pant] press.

スポンサー 【番組提供者】a sponsor. ● 番組のスポンサーになる *sponsor* a program. ▶ ここでスポンサーからのお知らせです And now, a word from our *sponsor*.

スポンジ (a) sponge /spʌ́ndʒ/. ● スポンジで体を洗う wash oneself with a *sponge*; sponge (down) [one's] body.
● スポンジケーキ (a) sponge cake.

***スマート** — **スマートな** 形 ❶【体つきが】(ほっそりした) slim (-mm-), slender. (**!** この意では ×smart は不可) ▶ スマートになりたい I wish I could be *slimmer* [could *slim* (down)]. ▶ スマートに見えるように彼は腹を引っこめた He kept his stomach in, trying to look better.

❷【服装が】(しゃれた) smart; stylish. ● 彼女はスマートな服装をする She is a *smart* dresser. / She dresses *smartly*.

❸【世渡りが】sophisticated.

翻訳のこころ ケイシーはおしつけがましいところのない、スマートな人物で、教養もあった (村上春樹『レキシントンの幽霊』) Casey was not at all pushy. He was a man of refined manners and well educated [a man of refined tastes and sophisticated], too. (**!** a man of refined manners and well educated は「振る舞いがスマートで教養[教育]もあった」. ... of refined tastes and sophisticated は「好み・趣味などがスマートで、知的にも優れていた」の意)

● スマート爆弾 (テレビ映像やレーザー光線で誘導する) a smart bomb. ● スマートボール a Japanese pinball game. ● スマートメディア 【コンピュータ】《商標》SmartMedia. 参考 切手氏のメモリーカード

すまい 住まい 【家】a house (優 houses /-ziz/, 《米》-siz/); a home; 《やや話》a place; 《書》a residence; 《書》a dwelling; 《住所》one's address. ▶ 彼は東京の郊外に住まいを定めた He had [made] his *home* in the suburbs of Tokyo. ▶ お住まいはどちらですか Where do you live (now)?/What [×Where] is your address (, please?) (**!** 後の方は住所を尋ねる言い方) ▶ いいお住まいですね You have a nice *home* [*place*].

スマイリー 【コンピュータ】a smiley ((:-)).
スマイル 【ほほえみ】a smile. 《:微笑み》

すましじる 澄まし汁 (おすまし) clear soup; consommé; broth. ● エビの澄まし汁 clear soup with shrimp.

すましや 澄まし屋 a smug [(気取った) an affected] person; a prig (**!** 軽蔑的に男女いずれにも用いる).

***すます** 済ます ❶【終える】finish; get* through .... (⇨終える ❶) ● 仕事を済ます *finish* [*get through* (*with*)] the work. (**!** with をそえるのは《主に米》) ▶ 食事を済ませてしまおう Let's *finish* in a hurry. ▶ その新聞お済みですか(= もう読んでしまいましたか) Have you *finished* reading [×to read] the newspaper? (**!** 単に Have you *finished* [*read*] the newspaper? ともいえる)/Are you *through* with the newspaper? ▶ 朝食を済ませてから(= 朝食後)出かけよう Let's go out *after* breakfast.

❷【間に合わす】(不十分な物で) make* do 《with》; ((...) なしでやっていく) do* [go*] without (...) (⇨無しで). ● 昼食はカレーで済ませた I *made do* with curry and rice for lunch.

会話「彼らにはあまり会いたくないのよ」「会わずに済ませられる(= 会うのを避けられる)かなあ」 "I don't really want to meet them." "Will you be able to *get out of* it?"

❸【支払う】pay*. ● 勘定を済ませる *pay* [*settle*] a bill.

❹【処理する】deal* with ...; 【解決する】settle. ● 電話で用事を済ませた I *dealt with* the business on the phone.

すます 澄ます ❶【耳などを】● 人の気配がしないかと耳を澄ます *listen for* a sound of life. ▶ 耳を澄ましたが、何も聞こえなかった I *listened* [×*heard*] *carefully*, but heard nothing. ▶ 私は彼の話に耳を澄ました(= 話を注意深く聞いた) I *listened to* his story very carefully [*attentively*].

❷【態度などを】● 彼女はいつも(つんと)澄ましている She is always prim and proper. (**!** prim and proper で一つの成句) ▶ 彼は試験に落ちても澄ました(= 平気な)顔をしていた Even when he failed the test, he *looked unconcerned* [*composed*].

❸【液体を】make* 《water》 clear.

スマッシュ 图 (テニスなどで) a smash. ● 強烈なスマッシュで点をかせぐ gain points with one's powerful *smashes*.
— スマッシュする 動 smash.

スマトラ ● スマトラ島 Sumatra /sumɑ́:trə/. ● スマトラ(島)の Sumatran.

すまない 済まない (謝って) I'm sorry 《for》; (感謝して) Thank you 《for》. (⇨すみません)

***すみ** 隅 a corner. ● 隅のテーブルに座る sit at a *corner* table. ● 部屋の隅に座る sit *in* [×at] *the corner* of a room.

● 隅から隅まで ▶ その部屋の隅から隅まで(= 隅々まで)捜す (⇨隅々) ● 隅から隅まで(= 十分に)知っている know *every detail of* it. ● 隅から隅まで読む read 《a book, a newspaper》 *from cover to cover*.

● 隅に置けない ▶ お前は世間知らずのような顔をしているけれど隅に置けないな(= 見あなどりを抜け目がないな) Although you look as if you haven't seen much of life, you are smarter than you look [(見た目以上のものがある) there's more to you than meets the eye].

すみ 炭 charcoal. ● 炭を焼く burn *charcoal*. ● (⇨炭火, 消炭)

すみ 墨 (汁) India [China] ink; (固形の) an India ink stick; (イカ・タコの) ink. ● (すずりで)墨をする rub an *India ink stick* on [×with] an inkstone.

- 墨絵 a monochrome [a black-and-white] painting.

-ずみ -済み ●領収済み Paid. ●売約済み Sold. ●それはすでに決定済みだ It *has* already *been decided*.

すみか 住み家 a house (⑱ ~s /-ziz, 《米》-siz/); 《書》a dwelling; a residence. (⇨家)

すみきる 澄み切る (晴れ上がる) clear up; be (perfectly) clear. ●澄み切った秋空 a *clear* [(澄み渡った) a *serene*] autumn sky. ●澄み切った心で with a *serene* [(平静な) a tranquil] mind.

すみごこち 住み心地 ●この家は住み心地がよい This house is *comfortable to live in*. (⇨住む [第3文例])

すみこみ 住み込み ●住み込みで働く live [sleep] in. ●住み込みのお手伝い a *live-in* [a *sleep-in*] maid.

すみこむ 住み込む live in .... ●雇い主の家に住み込む *live in* one's employer's house.

スミス 〘スコットランドの経済学者〙 Smith /smiθ/ (Adam ~).

すみずみ 隅々 〘いたる所で〙 all over(...), throughout ...; 〘隅々に〙 in every corner. ●その部屋の隅々まで捜す search *all over* [《話》*every nook and cranny of*] the room; (徹底的に) search the room *from top to bottom*. ●彼らは世界の隅々からやって来た They came from *all over* [*throughout, all the corners of*] the world. ●法の力は社会の隅々にまで及ぶ The arm of the law reaches *throughout* [*into every corner of*] society.

すみそ 酢味噌 vinegared *miso*. ●イカの酢味噌あえ cuttlefish dressed with *vinegared miso*.

スミソニアン ●スミソニアン協会 the Smithsonian Institution. ●スミソニアン合意 the Smithsonian Agreements.

すみぞめ 墨染め (墨染めの衣) a black robe.

すみつく 住み着く settle (down). (⇨居着く) ●彼は結婚して京都に住み着いた He married, and *settled* [(住居を構えた) *took up residence*] *in* Kyoto.

すみっこ 隅っこ a corner. (⇨隅)

すみなれる 住み慣れる get* used to living (*in*). ●住み慣れた家 one's *dear old house* [*home*].

すみび 炭火 (a) charcoal fire.
●炭火焼き charcoal-grilled [《米》charbroiled] meat.

***すみません** ❶ 〘謝罪〙 (主に米) Excuse me./(主に英) (I'm) sorry./Pardon me./I beg your pardon./ (過失を犯したことに対して) I'm sorry.

> **解説** (1) 人にぶつかった場合など軽く謝るとき，《米》では `ˇExcuse me.` が普通．《英》では **(I'm) `ˋsorry.`**，**`ˋPardon me.`** はそれより丁寧だが，これは大げさな感じを与えることもある．くだけた言い方ではしばしば I'm を省略する．以上より丁寧な表現は **I bég your `ˋpardon.`** これらに対する応答は That's [It's] all right., 《話》OK., No problem. (どういたしまして)/Don't worry (about it)., Never mind. (気にしないで)/It doesn't matter. (大したことではありません)/Excuse [Pardon] mé. (！ me を強く) (こちらこそ)/You're right. (あなたが悪いんじゃありません)/Forget (about) it. (忘れてください)など．語尾をやや上昇調にするとよりやわらかい応答になる．
> (2) 自分の過失に対して非を認めきちんと謝るときは **I'm `ˋsorry.`** が普通．この発言に対しては場合によっては責任や補償を伴うので注意．強調する時は I'm réally [só, áwfully, térribly] `ˋsorry.` (！ 後の3語は主に女性に好まれる)/《書》I dó beg your `ˋpardon.` さらに重大な非を認めるときは，I apologize., Forgive me. などを用いる．

▶すみません. 大丈夫ですか (人の足などを踏んだ時に) *I'm sorry. Are you all right?* ▶騒がしくてすみません *Excuse* me *for* being [ˣto be] so noisy./*I'm sorry for* [*about*] this noise. ▶長くお待たせしてすみません *I'm sorry* I have kept [*I'm sorry* to have kept] you waiting for a long time./(長くお待たせしたのでなければいいのですが) I hope I haven't kept you waiting long./(長い間お待ちいただいてありがとうございます) Thank you very much for waiting so long. (！ 後の方ほど米英人らしい発想の表現 (⇨❸)) ▶今朝ほどはすみませんでした *I'm sorry about* this morning. (！ 日本語と同様にこのように事実をぼかしていうこともある．今謝っているので過去形にしないことに注意) ▶ご面倒かけすみませんが，この荷物を運ぶのを手伝っていただけませんか *I'm sorry* [*Sorry*] *to* trouble you, but could you give me a hand with this package? (！ 何かをしてもらった後では *I'm sorry* [*Sorry*] *to have troubled* you, ... のようにいう) ▶車をこわして (本当に)すみません I must *apologize to* you [ˣ*apologize*] *for* damaging your car./Please *forgive me for* damaging your car.

> 会話 「旅行に出かけるので，すみませんが室内の鉢植えの水やりをお願いできるでしょうか」「いいですとも．何ならお庭の方もしておきますよ」「ご親切にありがとうございます」 "*Do you think you could* (*possibly*) water my houseplants for me? We're going away on vacation." (！ このように人に頼み事をする場合は，押しつけがましくならないように控えた表現を用いて「すみません」の気持ちを伝える (⇨いただく ❸)) "I'd be glad to. I'll water your garden plants if you like." "That'll be great."

❷ 〘呼びかけ〙 Excuse me. (！ 見知らぬ人への問いかけなどは上昇調で (⇨❸ 会話)，道をあけてもらうときなどは下降調で発音する) ▶ちょっとすみませんが (話に割りこむ際に) (*Excuse me,*) could I say some words?

> 会話 「すみません．ちょっと通してください」「どうぞ」 "`ˋExcuse me` [*us*] (, `ˊplease`). *May I* get through, please?" "Certainly." (！ (1) us は 2 人以上のとき． (2) 応答には certainly 以外に《米》surely,《米話》sure, all right, right,《話》OK なども用いられるが，何もいわないことも多い)

❸ 〘感謝〙 Thank you. (⇨ありがとう) ▶手伝ってもらってすみません *Thank you for* your help [*for helping me*]./*I appreciate* your help. ▶お忙しい中，時間を割いていただいてすみません *Thank you for* taking time out of your tight schedule. (！ 日本式の *I'm sorry to* interrupt your tight schedule. の言い方より普通)

> 会話 「すみませんが，最寄りの銀行はどこでしょうか」「すみません，分からないんですよ」「すみませんでした」 "`ˇExcuse me`. Where's the nearest bank, please?" "I'm sorry. I don't know." "*Thank you anyway.*" (！ このように相手が質問に答えられなかったときだけでなく，相手から注意を受けたときでも Thank you for warning. などというのが普通)

❹ 〘異議〙 `ˇExcuse me.`/(I'm) `ˇsorry.`/(書) I beg your `ˇpardon.` ▶すみませんがそれは違います *Excuse me* [*I'm sorry, Sorry, I beg your pardon*], but you are wrong.

❺ 〘聞き返し: 何と言いましたか〙 (I bég your) `ˊpardon?`/`ˊExcuse` [Pardon] mé?/ `ˊSorry?`/《話》What did you `ˊsay?`/`ˊWhat?` (！ 最後はぞんざいな言い方なので親しい人以外は避ける方がよい) ▶お名前がよく聞き取れなかったのですが *Pardon?* I didn't quite catch your name.

❻ 〘訂正〙 sorry; (アナウンサーが) (or) rather. ▶彼は東京で，すみません，京都で生まれ... He was born in

すみやか 速やか ━━ **速やかな** 形 (すばやい) quick, speedy; (迅速な, 即座の) prompt; (即刻の) immediate. (⇨速い❷) ▶彼らにその地域からの速やかな軍隊の撤退を求める demand of them a *quick* withdrawal of the troops from the area; demand that they (should) *quickly* withdraw the troops from the area.
━━ **速やかに** 副 quickly; promptly; immediately.

すみやき 炭焼き (炭を作ること) the charcoal making [burning]; (人) a charcoal maker [burner]. ●炭焼きがま a charcoal kiln.

すみれ 菫 『植物』a violet. ●三色スミレ a pansy. ●すみれ色の violet.

すみわけ 棲み分け (生物の生息地の) habitat segregation.

すみわたる 澄み渡る (空が) become* cloudless [spotlessly clear]; be clear (and shiny [sunny]). ▶あらしが過ぎると空は澄み渡った After the storm the sky *became* spotlessly *clear*.

:**すむ** 住む

WORD CHOICE 住む

live 特定の場所に居住し，生活を営むことをさす最も一般的な語． ▶両親と京都に住んでいる I'm *living* in Kyoto with my family.
reside 一定期間にわたって特定の場所に継続的に居住すること．とくに外交官などが任地に駐在することを含意する． ▶その外交官はパリに住んでいる The diplomat *resides* in Paris.

頻度チャート

live ████████████████████
reside ▌

20 40 60 80 100 (%)

live; (やや書) reside /rizáid/; 《書》dwell*; 《書》inhabit.

解説「住む」を意味する動詞は「(広がりを持つ場所の)中に」の意識を伴うために *in* が多く用いられるが，番地を示す場合には *at* (live *at* 100 Park Avenue)，街路・階・農場・島に住む場合には *on* (live *on* a street [the third floor, a farm, an island]) を用いる．

▶私は京都に住んでいます I live [I'm living] in Kyoto. (♪前の方が定住き，後の方は一時的在住を表す) ▶彼女はおばの家に住んでいる She lives with her aunt [*at* her aunt's]. (♪前の言い方の方が普通) ▶水戸はとても住みよい所です Mito is a very comfortable [such a nice] place to *live* (*in*). (♪後の方は女性に好まれる言い方．place では in は省略することが多いのに対して，より具体的な town, country, などの名詞を用いる場合は，通例 in は省略しない) ▶その島にはどんな動物が住んでいるのかだれも知らなかった No one knew what animals *inhabited* the island. ▶その小屋には人が住んでいるようだった The cottage looked (as if it were [《話》was]) *lived in* [*inhabited*]. (♪このように live in が受身で用いられるのは主語が特定の建物の場合に限る．したがって ×*A cottage* [*Some cottages*] looked lived in. は不可) ▶その島には人が住んでいない The island *is* not *inhabited* [*is deserted*]. (♪後の方は「昔は住んでいたが今は無人でさびれている」ことを表す)

●**住めば都** Once you live in a place, you'll come to like it.

*:**すむ** 済む ❶ [終わる] finish, be finished; (出来事・期間などが) be over (♪「終わっている」状態を表す). (⇨済ます, 終わる) ▶授業が済んだらすぐ集まろう Let's get together right after the class *finishes* [*is over*]. ▶やっと済んだぞ Now I'm *finished* [*done*]. (♪Now I've *finished doing* it. より口語的) ▶It's over and done with. (♪It's は It is で, It was ではない) ▶もうお済みでしょうか(=まだ食べていますか)(レストランで皿を下げるときに) Are you still working?
[会話]「もう 1 回やってみてもいい？」「彼女の番が済んだらね」"Can I have another go?" "When she *has had* a turn, you can." (♪このように完了形によって「済む」の意を表すこともある)

❷ [用が足りる] do*. ▶ここでは車がなくても済む We can do [*manage*] without a car here. ▶1 週間の旅行には下着の着替えは 3 組あれば済む Three changes of underwear will *do* for a week's trip. ▶彼が電話してきたので手紙を書かずに済んだ(=書く必要がなかった) I didn't have to [need to] write to him because he called me./(書く手間が省けた) His phone call *saved me the trouble to* write to him. ▶(費用は)100 円で済んだ It cost *only* 100 yen. ▶このままじゃ済むまい(=罰せられずに済む)まい We can't *get away with it*.
[会話]「ママ，ごめんなさい，本当に」「ごめんなさいだけでは済まないわよ(=十分ではない)」"I'm sorry, Mom. I really am." "Well, sorry isn't *good enough*."

すむ 澄む [液体・気体が] become* clear [(透明に) transparent]; [色・音が] become clear; [心が] become serene. ●澄んだ目 *clear* [*liquid*] eyes.
▶ここは空気が澄んでいる The air is *clear* here.

スムーズ ━━ **スムーズな** 形 smooth. (⇨円滑, 順調)
━━ **スムーズに** 副 smoothly /smúːðli/. ▶モーターはスムーズに動いている The motor is running *smoothly*. ●会議はスムーズに運んだ The meeting went on *smoothly*. ▶仕事はスムーズにいっている My work *is going well*.

スメタナ 『チェコの作曲家』 Smetana /smétənə/ (Bedřich /bédərʒɪk/ ～).

ずめん 図面 (設計図) a plan; (設計図の青写真) a blue print; (絵図面) a drawing. ●家の図面を引く draw a *plan for* a house.

すもう 相撲 *sumo* (wrestling); (説明的に) Japanese style wrestling. ●大相撲 professional *sumo*; a grand *sumo* tournament. ●相撲の取り組み(=試合) a *sumo* match [bout]. ●相撲をする do [×play] *sumo wrestling* (*with* him). (♪状況がはっきりしていれば単に wrestle with でもよい)

関連 力士の位: 横綱 a grand champion/大関 a champion/関脇 a champion second-class/小結 a champion third-class/幕内 the senior grade division/幕下 the junior grade division/十両 a *juryo* wrestler.

●**相撲に勝って勝負に負ける** ▶彼は相撲に勝って勝負に負けた(=有利に進めながら結果的に負けた) He was gaining a (big) advantage over his opponent, but he lost the bout at the last moment.
●**相撲にならない** (勝負にならない) be no match for 《the opponent》. (⇨勝負)
●**相撲界** the *sumo* world. ●**相撲取り** a *sumo* wrestler. ●**相撲部屋** 《話》a *sumo* stable. (♪井筒部屋は Izutsu Stable. その親方は a stable master)

スモーク ●スモークサーモン smoked salmon. ●スモークハム smoked ham.

スモール 『小さい』small.
●スモールベースボール 『守備と小技を重視する野球』《play》small [little] ball.

スモッグ smog. ●ひどいスモッグ heavy *smog*. ●スモッグのかかった smoggy. ●光化学スモッグ photochemical *smog*. ●スモッグ警報 a *smog* warning. ●スモッグの町 a *smoggy* town. ▶ここはスモッグがよく出ます It often gets *smoggy* here.

すもも 李 〖植物〗(木) a plum (tree); (実) a plum.

スモンびょう スモン病 〖医学〗 SMON 《subacute myelo-optico-neuropathy (亜急性脊髄視神経症)の頭文字》.

すやき 素焼き 图 (上薬をかけずに焼いた陶器) unglazed pottery; biscuit.
—— **素焼きの** 形 unglazed 《pot》.

すやすや ●すやすやと(=静かに) calmly; peacefully. ●すやすや眠る sleep soundly; be sound asleep (**!** この場合の sound は副詞).

すよみ 素読み ●映画の台本を素読みする(=意味を考えずに音読する) read a scenario *without comprehending its meaning*. ●初校を素読みする(=原稿と照合せずに校正する) *read* the first proof *without checking it with the manuscript*.

-ずら even. (⇨さえ)

スラー 〖音楽〗a slur.

スライス 图 ❶〖薄い1切れ〗a slice. ❷〖ボールの〗a slice.
—— **スライスする** 動 ❶〖薄く切る〗slice 《bread [onions]》. ❷〖ボールを〗slice.
●スライスハム sliced ham.

スライダー 〖野球〗《throw》a slider.

スライディング a slide. (**!** sliding は動詞 slide の -ing 形) ●ヘッドスライディング a headfirst *slide*. ●スライディングなしの二塁打 a stand-up double. ●彼は三塁にスライディングを試みた He tried *sliding* into third (base).
●スライディングキャッチ a sliding catch. ●スライディングタックル a sliding tackle.

スライド (顕微鏡・幻灯用の) a slide; (オーバーヘッドプロジェクター用の) a transparency. ●スライドを映す project a *slide* on a screen. ▶賃金は物価スライド制です Wages are to *slide* with prices./You are paid on a *sliding scale*.
●スライド映写機 a slide projector. ●スライドガラス a slide.

ずらかる (姿をくらます) 〔話〕skip (-pp-). ●町からずらかる *skip* town. ▶ずらかろうぜ Let's get out of here./〔米俗〕Let's *skip* [*beat*] it.

ずらす 〖移す〗move, 〖やや話〗shift; 〖勤務・食事などを〗stagger. ●家具を少し左にずらす *move* [*shift*] the furniture a little *to* the left. ●会社の出勤時間をずらす *stagger* office hours. ▶会議を3日先へずらそう(=延期しよう) Let's *put off* [*postpone*] the meeting for three days.

すらすら (円滑に) smoothly; (容易に) easily, without any difficulty; (すごさ) readily; (滑るように) glidingly. ▶彼らは商談をすらすら進めることができた They managed *smoothly* to [×could smoothly] carry on their business talk. ▶彼女はギリシャ語がすらすら読める〔話せる〕She can read Greek *easily* [speak Greek *fluently*]. ▶彼は自分の過去をすらすら告白した He *readily* confessed his past. ▶彼は記憶ですべての人の名前をすらすら言った He *reeled off* the names of all the people from memory.

ずらっ —— **ずらっと** 副 (すんなりと) smoothly, easily.
—— **ずらっとした** 形 slim (-mm-), slender. (⇨すらり)

スラッガー 〖野球〗〖強打者〗a slugger.

スラックス 〈a pair of〉slacks. (⇨ズボン)

スラッシュ 〖斜線〗a slash (/).

スラブ ●スラブ人 a Slav. ●スラブ民族 the Slavs. ●スラブ語 Slavic. ●スラブ人〔民族, 語〕の Slavic.

スラム (スラム街) a slum. (**!** しばしば複数形で) ●東京のスラム街 the *slums* of Tokyo. ●スラム化する turn into a *slum*.

すらり ●すらりと (人・物が細身で) slenderly, slimly; (スムーズに) smoothly.
—— **すらりとした** 形 slim (-mm-), slender. ●背の高いすらりとした男性 a tall, *slender* [*slim*] man. ●彼女はすらりとしている She is *slim* [*slender*]./She has a *slim* [a *slender*] figure.

ずらり (適切な副詞がないので文で工夫する) ●ずらりと(=列をなして) in a row /róu/ [rows] (**!** 横並びに); in a line [lines] (**!** 縦または横並びに). ▶丘には新しい家がずらりと建っている There are *rows of* houses [Houses stand *in rows*] on the hillside. ▶人々が劇場の前にずらりと並んでいた People *lined up* [*queued up*] in front of the theater. ▶店には春向きの品物がずらりと並べてあった(=いろいろ取りそろえてあった) They [The store] had a *large* assortment [*choice*] of spring goods.

すられる 掏られる (⇨掏る)

スラローム 〖<ノルウェー語〗the slalom /slá:ləm/.

スラング slang; (個々の語) a slang word.

スランプ (一時的な心の調子の衰え) a slump; 《婉曲的》mental fatigue. ●打撃のスランプ a hitting *slump*. ●スランプに陥っているを is in a *slump*. ●スランプに陥る get [sink, fall] into a *slump*. ●スランプから抜け出す get through [〔話〕snap [break] out of] a *slump*.

すり 刷り printing; (増刷) an impression. ●刷りが鮮明である be clearly *printed*. ●2色刷りの辞書 a dictionary 《*printed*》in two colors. ▶哲学書でも数回刷りを重ねるものもある Some of the philosophical books go into several *impressions*.

すり 掏摸 〖人〗a pickpocket; 〖行為〗pickpocketing. ●すりを働く pick 《his》pocket. ▶すりにご用心 《掲示》Beware of *pickpockets*. ▶人込みですりにやられた I had my pocket *picked* in the crowd.

すりあがる 刷り上がる be off the press. ●きれいに刷り上がる be printed beautifully [(鮮明に) clearly].

ずりあがる ずり上がる move up [upward]; (スカートなどが) ride* up.

すりあし 摺り足 ●すり足で歩く (ちゃんと足を上げずに) shuffle, walk with a shuffle; (すべるように静かに) glide one's steps. ▶老人が病院の廊下をすり足でゆっくり歩いている An old man *is* [There's an old man] *shuffling* slowly *along* the hospital corridor.

すりあわせる 摺り合わせる (羽などを) rub (-bb-) together; (意見などを) adjust the differences of opinions. ●手をすり合わせて大喜びする rub one's hands in glee. (**!** 喜び・満足の動作)

スリーエー (マイナーリーグの) Triple A; Class AAA.

スリーカード 〖トランプ〗three of a kind. (**!** ×three card とはいわない)

スリークォーター 〖ラグビー〗a three-quarter (back); 〖野球〗a three-quarter(s) delivery. ●スリークォーターで投げる pitch three-quarter(s) overhand.

スリーサイズ one's (bust, waist and hip) measurements; 〖英話〗one's vital statistics; 〖和製語〗three size.

スリーディー 〖三次元〗3-D.
●3D 映画 a 3-D movie.

スリーバント 〖野球〗a two-strike bunt; 〖和製語〗three bunt. ●スリーバントをする do [try] a two-strike bunt; bunt on third strike [with two strikes].

スリーピース 〚三つ揃いの服〛 a three-piece (suit).
スリーピングバッグ 〚寝袋〛 a sléeping bàg.
スリーフィートライン 〚野球〛 a three-foot line.
スリーラン 〚野球〛 a three-run home run.
すりえ 摺り餌 ground food (for bird).
ずりおちる ずり落ちる slip off [down] (-pp-). ▶毛布がベッドからずり落ちた The blanket *slipped off* the bed. ▶このズボンはずり落ちる These pants *slip down*.
すりかえる 擦り替える ●かばんをすりかえる secretly change bags. ●話題をすりかえる *switch* the subject *skillfully* 《*to*》.
すりガラス 擦りガラス frosted [ground] glass.
すりきず 擦り傷 a scrape; 〚かすり傷〛a scratch; 〚すりむき〛a graze. (⇨傷)
すりきり 摺り切り ▶塩小さじすりきり2杯を入れてください Add two *level* teaspoons of salt.
すりきれる 擦り切れる (布が) wear* out, become* worn-out [threadbare]; (表面のけばなどが) wear off. ▶すり切れた上着 a *worn-out* [a *threadbare*] jacket. ▶この上着のひじがもうすり切れちゃった The elbows of this jacket *have worn out* already. ▶私のジーンズはすり切れて薄くなった[ぼろぼろになった，穴があいた] My jeans *have worn thin* [*to rags*; *into holes*]. ▶このじゅうたんはだいぶすり切れてきた (The pile of) this carpet *is wearing off*.
すりこぎ 擂り粉木 a wooden pestle. (関連) すり鉢 an earthenware mortar. ▶すりこぎでゴマをする grind sesame seeds with a *wooden pestle*.
すりこみ 刷り込み 〚生物・心理〛imprinting.
すりこむ 擦り込む rub ... in. ●顔にクリームをすりこむ *rub* cream *into* one's face. ●よくすりこみなさい *Rub* it *in* well.
すりつける 擦り付ける rub (-bb-) 《A against B》. ▶猫は私に体を擦りつけてのどを鳴らした The cat purred, *rubbing* itself *against* me.
スリット a slit. ●スリットの入ったスカート a skirt with a *slit*.
スリッパ (a pair of) mules, 《米》scuffs. (！slippers は低いかかとのついた軽い室内用の靴 (⇨靴)). 〚事情〛日本のように玄関に置いて客に勧めるような使い方はしない ●スリッパをはく[脱ぐ] put on [take off] one's *mules*.
スリップ 图 ❶〚滑ること〛a slip; a skid (！車の横滑りには skid の方が普通。
❷〚婦人用下着〛a slip. ▶スリップが出ているよ Your *slip*'s showing.
━━ **スリップする** 動 ▶その車はスリップし，衝突した The car *skidded* [*went into a skid*] and crashed. (！×The car slipped... とはいわない)
●スリップダウン〚ボクシング〛a slip.
すりつぶす すり潰す (やわらかいものを押し潰す) mash; (固いものを細かく砕く) grind*. ●ジャガイモをすり潰す *mash* potatoes. ●ゴマをすり潰す *grind* sesame /sésami/.
スリナム 〚国名〛Suriname; (公式名) the Republic of Suriname. (首都 Paramaribo) ●スリナム人 a Surinamese. ●スリナム(人)の Surinamese
すりぬける 擦り抜ける ●人込みをすり抜ける(=通り抜ける) *pass* [(すばやく) *slip*, (ウナギのように) *eel one's way*] through the crowd.
すりばち すり鉢 an earthenware mortar. (関連) すりこぎ a wooden pestle.
すりへらす 磨り減らす (人・物・事を) wear*... down [away, out, off], (磨り減る) wear away. ▶神経をすり減らす *wear out* one's nerves. ▶でこぼこ道は車のタイヤをはやくすり減らす Rough roads *wear* my tires *out* quickly.
すりへる 磨り減る wear* down; (すり減って駄目になる) wear out; (これて消え去る) wear away. ▶ぼくの靴のかかとはいつも片方に傾いてすり減る The heels of my shoes *are* always *worn down* on one side. ▶タイヤ(の模様)がすり減っている The tire treads *are worn*.
すりみ 擦り身 ground fish; fish paste. ●エビのすり身 ground shrimps; shrimp paste.
スリム ━━ スリムな 形 slim (-mm-). ●スリムな体型[女性] a *slim* figure [woman]. ●運動をしてスリムな体型を維持する keep *slim* by getting some exercise. ▶テニスのおかげで彼女の腰はスリムになった Playing tennis *slimmed* her waist./Tennis *made* her waist *slim*.
すりむく 擦りむく 〚ひざ・手など〛skin (-nn-); 〚こすって傷つける〛scrape. ●転んでひざをすりむく fall down and *skin* [*scrape*] one's knee. ●ひざの皮がすりむけている have a *skinned* [a *grazed*] knee.
すりもの 刷り物 (印刷物) printed matter [papers]; (講演会などの配布資料) a handout.
すりよる 擦り寄る draw* closer 《*to*》; (にじり寄る) sidle [edge] up 《*to*》; (寄り添う) nestle up 《*to*》. ●(赤ん坊が)母親に顔をすりよせる *rub* [*press*] its face *against* [×*to*] its mother.
スリラー (小説，映画) a thriller.
スリランカ 〚国名〛Srì Lánka; (公式名) the Democratic Socialist Republic of Sri Lanka. (首都 Sri Jayawardanapura Kotte) ●スリランカ人 a Sri Lankan. ●スリランカ(人)の Sri Lankan.
スリリング ━━ スリリングな 形 thrilling. ▶なんてスリリングなゲームなんだろう What a *thrilling* game!
スリル a thrill. (！英語の thrill は喜び・恐怖・興奮などでぞくぞく，わくわくすること[させるもの]) ●スリルを味わう enjoy [experience, get] a *thrill* 《*from*, *out of*》. ●スリル満点である《事が主語》 be full of *thrills*. ▶彼らが万引きするのはスリルを味わいたいからだ They steal from stores just for the *thrill* [〚話〛*kick*] of it.
‡**する** 為る do*.
① 【图＋する】〚行う〛do*. ●さっさとしろ *Do* it quick [quickly]! (！急げ) Hurry up! ●好きなようにしなさい *Do* as you like. (⇨好き) ●どうぞ楽にしてください *Make* yourself at home [comfortable](, please). ●午前中はどうしてた(=どのように過ごしたの)? How did you *spend* the morning?
②【...を(を)する】 (a) 〚行為・動作を行う〛 do*; have*; make*; take*.

〚解説〛Ⅰ (1) 日本語ではしばしば「图＋(を)する」の型が用いられるが，英語では次のような型を用いて1語の自動詞と同じ意味を表すことができる。これらは一般に口語的な表現で，不定冠詞を伴う場合は1回限りの行為・動作を強調する。
(i) do＋a [an])＋名詞 (！与えられたやるべきことについてのことが多い): 買い物(を)する *do* some shopping; shop.
(ⅱ) do＋the＋動名詞 (！日常の決まりきった仕事についてのことが多い): 掃除(を)する *do* the cleaning; clean./料理(を)する *do* the cooking; cook.
(ⅲ) have＋(a [an])＋名詞 (！1語の動詞と異なり主語がその行為を楽しんでいることを暗示): 話をする *have* a talk; talk./ひと泳ぎ(を)する *have* a swim; swim.
(ⅳ) make＋(a [an])＋名詞 (！何らかの変化を与える行為について用いることが多い): 準備(を)する *make* (a) preparation [preparations]; prepare./演説(を)する *make* a speech; speak.
(ⅴ) take＋(a [an])＋名詞 (！1語の動詞と異なり主語がその行為を楽しんでいることを暗示): 散歩(を)する

する *take* a walk; walk./旅行(を)する *take* a trip; travel.
(ⅰ)〜(ⅴ) の用法に関して詳しくは日本語の名詞の部分の見出し語を参照。ここでは「する」がさまざまな動詞の代用として用いられる場合を扱う。
(2) 1語の動詞で表す方が普通の場合もある: 勉強(を)する study; *do* the studying.
(3) 1語の動詞で表せない場合もある: 皿洗いをする(=皿を洗う) *wash* [*do*] the dishes.

▶もう宿題をしましたか(= 終えましたか) Have you *done* [*finished*] your homework yet?
会話「彼女は私がしなさいと言ったことをどうしてもしようとしない」「じゃあ私がします」"She won't *do* what I told her to (*do*)." "Then, I'll [×I'm going to] *do* it." (❗I を強く読む。発話の瞬間に決めた意図なのでwill を用いる (⇨**⑨** **(a)**))
会話「彼女は仕事をやめたよ」「どうしてそんなことをしたんだろう」"She's quit her job." "I wonder why she *did* it [that, so]." (❗it に比べ there は強意的でくだけた言い方, so はやや堅い言い方 (⇨そう))
(b) 【…として働く】 work 《*as*》; 【役を務める】 act [*serve*] 《*as*》; 【従事する】 be engaged 《*in*》.

解説 Ⅱ 現在就いている職業について述べる場合、習慣的行為を表すので、日本語が「…している」となっていても通例単純現在形で表す.

▶彼はレストランをしている(= 経営している) His uncle *runs* [*is in charge of*] *owns*] a restaurant.
会話「(お仕事は)何をしていらっしゃいますか」「会社員をしています」"What do you *do* (for a living)?" "I'm an office worker. (❗×I'm doing an office worker. とはいわない)/(会社で働いています) I work [×am working] at an office [×at office]." (❗進行形は一時的な状態を表すのでここでは不適当。"What are you doing now?" に対する答えとしては可。職業を尋ねられた場合は、米英では I'm [I work as] an engineer. のように具体的な職種で答えるのが普通)
(c) 【競技などをする】 play. (❗主に球技・遊技に用いる)
●トランプ[テニス]をする *play* cards [tennis]. ●スキーをする ski; enjoy [×play, ×do] skiing. ●エアロビックスをする *learn* [*practice*, *do*, ×play] aerobics.
(d) 【食べる】 eat*. ● 1 日に 3 回食事をする *have* [*eat*, *take*] three meals a day.
(e) 【経験する】 have*; experience; 【傷などを受ける】 get*. ●苦い経験をする *have* a bitter experience [(つらい目にあう) a hard time]. ●指にけがをする *get* injured [an injury] in one's finger.
(f) 【開催する】 hold*; give* (❗後の方が口語的); 【持つ】 have*. ●会議をする *hold* [*have*] a conference. ●パーティーをする *give* [*hold*, *have*, 《話》*throw*] a party.
(g) 【処理する】▶あの花束を(=…)どうしましたか What have you *done* with that bunch of flowers? (❗ do with は疑問詞 what とともに用い, 通例進行形不可)

③【(…に)…をする】

解説 Ⅲ ② と同様に 1 語の動詞で同じ意味を表すことができるが、行為・動作を行う対象を明示するものもある: 彼女にキス(を)する *give* her a kiss; kiss her./手に包帯をする *put* a bandage on a hand; bandage a hand.

●彼に質問(を)する(= 尋ねる) *ask* him a question; 《まれ》*ask* a question of him. ●肉に塩コショウをする(= 味つける) *season* the meat *with* salt and pepper.

④【A(人・物)をB(状態)にする】 (無理に) make* A

B (❗B は形容詞・過去分詞・名詞); 【A(人・物・事)をB(物・事)に変える】 change [turn] A into B. ●彼を議長にする *make* [(任命する) *appoint*, (選ぶ) *choose*] him chairman. (❗B が 1 人しかいない役職名の場合は通例無冠詞) ●ポンドをドルにする *change* pounds *into* dollars. ▶彼は彼女を幸せ[妻]にした He *made* her happy [his wife]. ▶彼は息子を医者にした He *helped* his son (to) become a doctor./He *encouraged* his son to be a doctor./(素材を生かして) He *made* a doctor of his son./(やる気を起こさせて) He *made* his son become a doctor. (❗このような文脈では通例 ×He made his son a doctor. とはいわない)

⑤【…にする】 【決定する】 decide; (選ぶ) choose*, (選び取る) take*. ▶私は行くことに[行かないことに]した I *decided to* [not to] go. ❗I *decided on going* [not going]. も可能だが、to で不定詞の方が普通) ▶私たちの結婚式の日取りは 5 月の第 2 日曜にしました We *decided on* [*chose*] the second Sunday of May for our wedding. ▶これは聞かなかったことにします。いいですか You didn't hear it from me. Do you understand me? (❗(1)「…しなかったことにする」という場合の表現で、しばしば念押しの表現が直後に付加される。(2)「これはなかったことにします」なら This never happened. さらに強調的に None of it ever happened, ⤴OK? などとなる)
会話「どっちのラケットにしますか」「こっちにしよう」"Which racket will you *take*?" "I'll *take* this one."
会話「何になさいますか」「ステーキにします」 (レストランで) "What would you like, sir?" "I'd like (to have) some steak, please."

⑥【…がする】 【音がする】 sound; 【においがする】 smell*; 【味がする】 taste; 【感じがする】 feel*. ▶ベルの音がした(ベルが鳴った) The bell *rang* [*sounded*]./(ベルが鳴るのが聞こえた) I heard the bell ring. ▶それはいいにおい[味]がする It *smells* [*tastes*] good. (❗進行形不可) ▶何か変なにおいがする I *smell* something strange. ▶食後によく吐き気がした I often *felt* sick after meals. ▶頭痛が[のどがひりひり]する I *have* a headache [a sore throat]. (⇨② **(e)**)

⑦【…(の値が)する】 cost*. ● 5 万ポンドもする真珠のネックレス a string of pearls *worth* as much as fifty thousand pounds. ▶その花びんはいくらしましたか How much was the vase [did the vase *cost*]?/How much did you pay for the vase?

⑧【…しようと[するように]する】 **(a)** 【努める】 try 《*to* do》. (⇨試みる) ▶彼は笑おうとしたがだめだった He *tried to* smile, but he couldn't. ▶彼は健康を維持しようと毎朝ストレッチ体操をしている He does some stretching exercises every morning *in an effort to* keep in (good) shape. (⇨よう **④**)
会話「6 時までにそこへ行くようにするよ」「遅れないようにしてね」"I'll *try to* [《話》*try and*] be there by six." "*Try* not *to* be late." (❗and は tries, trying, tried の後には用いず, 原形 try の後に限る)
(b) 【…しそうである】 be going to 《do》 (❗現在の状況から予想される未来を表す); be about to 《do》 (❗前の方より堅い言い方で, 近い未来を強調し, 通例未来を表す副詞とともに用いられる) ▶あなたが電話してきたとき, 私はちょうど出かけようとしていました I *was just going to* [*was about to*] leave when you telephoned.

⑨【…することにしている】 **(a)** 【…する予定だ】 be going to 《do》; (公式に)予定する;《書》be to 《do》. (⇨予定) ▶私たちは今日は午後テニスをすることにしている We're *going to* play [We're *playing*] tennis this afternoon. (❗現在進行形は通例時の

副詞を伴って近い未来の取り決められた予定を表す) ▶(**b**) 『...する習慣だ』(=習慣) ▶彼女は毎日散歩に行くことにしている She goes for a walk every day. (!現在形を用いて習慣的行為を表すのが最も口語的で、通例習慣を示す副詞などを伴う)(行く習慣がある) She has a habit [*is in the habit*] *of going* for a walk every day./She *makes it a practice* [《まれ》*a rule*] *to go* for a walk every day.

⑩ 『...すれば』 (**a**) 『時間が経てば』 in .... ▶彼女は2, 3日すれば戻るでしょう She will be back *in a few days* [*after a few days*; ×*a few days later*]. (!(1) in は未来の時に, after, later は過去の時に用いる: She came back *after a few days* [*a few days later*]. (2,3日すると彼女は戻ってきた). (2) in a few days' time のように time を添えていうことも多い)

(**b**) 『(仮定)すれば』 if; suppose. (⇨もし)

⑪ 『...しないで...する』 (一方をやめて他方を選択して) instead of ...; (するべきことを怠って) without .... ▶私はみんなと出かけないでホテルに残っていた I stayed behind at the hotel *instead of going* out together with the other people./I *didn't* go out together with the other people *but* (I) stayed behind at the hotel. ▶彼はノックもしないでいきなり中へ入ってきた He burst in *without* even knock*ing*./He *didn't* even knock *as* he burst in.

⑫ 『...しよう』 会話 「そのことは彼には内緒にしておきましょう」「そうしましょう[それはよしましょう]」 "*Let's* keep it secret from him (, shall we?)." "Yes, *let's* [*No, let's* not; 《米》No, let's don't; 《英》No, don't let's]." (⇨る❹)

会話 「まあ広いお庭ですね」「さあご案内しましょう」 "What a large garden!" "Well, *let me* show you around." (!意思未来を表す I'*ll* show you around. より普通)

会話 「お皿洗いましょうか?」「いいのよ, 気にしないで. 皿洗いくらい何でもないわ」「まあそう言わずに, たまには私にさせてよ」 "*Do you want me to* [*Would you like me to, Shall I*] do the dishes?" (!最初は親しい間柄のくだけた言い方。次はその丁寧な言い方, 最後は提案・申し出を表す一般的な言い方) "No (, thanks). Don't worry about it. I don't mind doing the dishes." "(Oh,) come on! Let me, for a change."

する 刷る print. (⇨印刷する)

する 掏る pick. ▶私は込んだバスの中で財布をすられた I *had* my wallet *stolen* [《話》*lifted*] in the crowded bus. (!×I *was stolen* [*was lifted*] my wallet .... とはいわない)/I *had* my pocket *picked* in the crowded bus./Somebody *picked* my wallet (out of my pocket) [*pick-pocketed* my wallet] in the crowded bus.

する 擦る 『こする』 rub (-bb-); (やすりで) file; (マッチを) strike*; 『金を失う』 lose*; (遣い果たす) run* out of 《money》. ▶マッチをすって火をつける *strike* [*light*] a match to make a fire. ●ごまをする (⇨胡麻(ごま)) ●競馬で大金をする *lose* a lot of money in the horse race.

ずる ずるをする cheat 《at cards》. (⇨ずるい❷)

*ずるい ❶ 『狡猾』(ずるがしこい)(だまずのがうまい) cunning /kʌ́nɪŋ/ (!日本語の「カンニング」とは意味が異なることに注意 (⇨カンニング));(策を弄(ろう)する) crafty; (ずる賢い) sly (!比較級・最上級は slyer [×slier], slyest [×sliest]). ▶彼女のずるいやり方にだまされるな Don't be fooled by any of her *cunning* [*crafty*, *sly*] tricks. ▶彼はずるそうな顔をしている He has a *cun*-*ning* look about him.

❷ 『不公正な』 unfair; (不正直な) dishonest. ▶それはずるいぞ That's *unfair* [*not fair*]! ▶彼はずるい方法で金をもうけた He got money by *dishonest* means. ▶彼はいつもずるいことをして公正な勝負をしない He *is* always *cheating* and doesn't play fair.

スルーパス 【サッカー】 a through-pass.

ずるがしこい ずる賢い cunning, crafty; (悪賢い) sly; (油断のならない) tricky. (⇨ずるい)

ずるける be lazy; (怠る) neglect one's work. ●ずるけて学校へ行かない do not go to school *out of laziness*; play truant [《米話》*hooky*] (from school) (!家は休けが学校へは行かないことをいう).

するする ●するする滑る slip; (滑るように動く) glide. ●うどんをするする食う suck noodles in *quickly*. ●シャッターをするすると巻上げる roll up the shutter *smoothly*. ▶少年は木にするすると登っていった The boy *nimbly* climbed the tree. ▶うなぎが手からするすると滑り落ちた The eel *slipped* smoothly from my hands.

ずるずる ●ずるずると(=徐々に)悪習に陥る be *gradually* getting into bad habits; (いつの間にか) slide into bad habits. ●ずるずる音を立ててストローでジュースを飲む *noisily* suck up juice through a straw. ▶その登山者は斜面をずるずる滑って降りた The climber *slid* down the slope. ▶少年は上着をずるずる引きずって歩いていた A little boy walked *dragging* [*trailing*] his coat. ▶会議はずるずると10時間も続いた The meeting *dragged on* [*went on and on*] for ten hours. (! on は副詞で継続の意を表す)

ずるずるべったり ●ずるずるべったりに(=わけも分からないままに) for vague [no definite] reasons. ▶そのことがあってからずるずるべったりに一緒になり, 今では2人の子の親となった After that we *just* began to live together and now we are parents of two children.

するっと ●するっと滑る slip 《*on the floor*》. ▶少年は柵の間からするっと抜け出た The boy *slipped through* the fence.

すると 『それから, そうすると』 then; 『そして』 and. (⇨それでは) ▶彼はその錠剤を飲んだ. すると眠くなってきた He took the pills [tablets], *and* [(*and*) *then*] he felt sleepy. ▶すると(=それじゃ)君は彼には会ったことはないのね Well, you haven't met him, have you?/(ということは) *You mean* you haven't met him?

*するどい 鋭い ❶ 『刃物などが』 sharp; keen. ●鋭いナイフ a *sharp*(-edged) knife; a knife with a *keen* edge. ▶この鉛筆は先が鋭くとがっている This pencil has a *sharp* point./This pencil is *sharply* pointed. ▶彼は鋭い(=鋭リリの)目つきをしている He has a *sharp* look in his eyes.

❷ 『痛み・叫びが』 (突然の) sharp; (強烈な) acute. ▶彼は背中に鋭い痛みを覚えた[があった] He felt a *sharp* pain [was in *acute* pain] in the back.

❸ 『頭脳・感覚が』 (迅速で抜け目のない) sharp; (識別力・洞察力のすぐれた) keen; (微妙な差異・刺激にも鋭敏な) acute. ●鋭い質問 a *sharp* [a *keen*, a *point*-*ed*] question. ▶犬は鋭い嗅覚(きゅうかく)を持っている Dogs have a *keen* [a *sharp*, an *acute*] sense of smell./Dogs have good noses. ▶彼は観察が鋭い He is a *keen* [an *acute*] observer.

-するほうがいい -する方がいい should 《do》. (⇨いい ⑮)

するめ a dried squid [cuttlefish]. (!通例単・複同形)

ずるやすみ ずる休み 图 truancy, truanting.
── **する休みする** (許可なく休む) stay away from 《school, work》 without permission; (さぼる) 《話》skip (-pp-) 《a class, a meeting》; (学校をさぼる) play truant [《米話》hook(e)y] (from school).

ずれ　[[時間の遅れ]] a lag; [[意見などの相違]] (a) difference; [[隔たり, 不一致]] a gap. ● 時間のずれ a time lag. ●2人の意見のずれをうまく調節する iron out differences of opinion between the two. ● 世代のずれ(=断絶) a gap between generations; the generation gap.

▶彼は風邪だと言って会社をずる休みした(=風邪で休むと言ったがそれはうそだった) He said he would *stay away from* work because he had a cold, but it was a lie.

ずれあう 擦れ合う rub (-bb-) against each other. ▶木の葉と葉がれあう The leaves of the tree *rubbed against* one another.

スレート a slate. ● スレートで屋根をふく cover the roof [roof a house] with *slates*.

ずれこむ ずれ込む [[延期される]] be put off; [[遅れる]] be delayed. ●来年の初めまでずれ込みそうである will be put off [delayed] until the beginning of next year.

すれちがう ❶ [[物と物が触れそうになって]] ▶その車は壁すれすれで通っていった The car passed *almost touching* the wall. ▶道は狭いので2人がすれすれでしか通れなかった The road was so narrow that two people were able to pass each other *only with difficulty*. ▶彼はふちすれすれまでグラスを満たした He filled the glass *to the brim*. ▶鳥が湖面すれすれに飛んでいるのを見た I saw birds *skimming over* the lake.
❷ [[限度にやっと近く]] (かろうじて) barely; [[危ないところで]] narrowly. ▶彼はすれすれでその試験に合格した He *barely* [*narrowly*] passed the examination. ▶彼はまさか時間に間に合った He was *just* in time. ▶あの政治家はいつも犯罪すれすれのことをやって金を集めている The politician collects money by always doing things that are *very close to* a crime.

すれちがう 擦れ違う ▶涼子とすれ違う(そばを通り過ぎる) *pass* (*by*) Ryoko. (!) by を省略した「追い越す」の意にもなる) (互いに会えずに終わる) *miss* Ryoko. ▶2台のバスが狭い道ですれ違った Two buses *passed each other* on the narrow street.

すれっからし ▶あの女はすれっからしだ(世間ずれしている) She's *too worldly-wise*./(恥知らずの女だ) She is a *shameless woman*./(慎みがなくなった) She *no longer has modesty*.

すれる ❶ [[磨減する]] wear* out; [[無邪気さを失う]] lose* one's innocence. ▶うちのじゅうたんは(どれも)すれて薄くなっている Our carpets *are worn out*.

ずれる [[ずれ落ちる]] slip (-pp-) off ...; [[傾く]] slant; [[行動などが正しい基準から外れる]] turn aside, 《やや書》 deviate. ● 左に少しずれる *slant* a little *to* the left. ▶スカーフが彼女の肩からずれ落ちた The scarf *slipped off* her shoulders. ▶彼女の行動は常道からずれている Her behavior *turns aside* [*deviates*] *from* the normal course of action./Her behavior *has gone off* the normal course of action. ▶彼の議論はずれている(=要点からそれている) His argument *is off* [《やや書》*beside*] *the point*.

スローイン [[サッカー・バスケット]] a throw-in.
スローガン a slogan ● [[主に政治的・商業的な標語]]; a motto 《複》 ~(e)s. ● ...をスローガンに掲げる have [use] ... as one's *slogan* [*motto*].
スローダウン 名 [[減速]] a slowdown; [[怠業戦術]] 《米》 a slowdown, 《英》 a go-slow.
―― スローダウンする 動 slow down.
スロープ a slope. ● ゆるやかな[急な]スロープ a gentle [a sharp] *slope*.
スローフード slow (↔fast) food.
スローモーション slow motion. ● スローモーションの

slow-motion. ● スローモーションで見る watch 《it》 in *slow motion*.
ズロック 図錄 a record in pictures; a pictorial record.
スロット [[コンピュータ]] a slot. ● 拡張スロット an expansion *slot*. (!) 単に slot ともいう)
スロットマシン a slot machine.
スロバキア [[国名]] Slovakia /slouváːkiə/; (公式名) the Slovak /slóuvæk/ Republic. (首都 Bratislava) ● スロバキア人 a Slovakian. ● スロバキア語 Slovak. ● スロバキア(人)の Slovak.
スロベニア [[国名]] Slovenia /slouvíːniə/; (公式名) the Republic of Slovenia. (首都 Ljubljana) ● スロベニア人 a Slovenian; a Slovene. ● スロベニア語 Slovene. ● スロベニア(人)の Slovenian; Slovene.
すわ (おや, まあ, とんでもない) Good Heavens!; (これは驚いた, 困った) Good [My, Oh] God! ● すわという時に in case of [in an] *emergency*; in the hour [moment] of danger [peril]. ▶すわ一大事 That's serious.
ずわいがに ずわい蟹 [[動物]] a snow [a queen] crab.
スワジランド [[国名]] Swaziland /swáːzilænd/; (公式名) the Kingdom of Swaziland. (首都 Mbabane) ● スワジランド人 a Swazi. ● スワジランド(人)の Swazi.
スワッピング 名 [[夫婦交換]] a swap.
―― スワッピングする 動 swap.
スワップ a swap. ● スワップ協定 [[経済]] a swap agreements. ● スワップ取引 [[経済]] a swap transaction [deal].
すわり 座り ● 座りがいい(=安定感がある) be stable; (バランスがよい) be well-balanced. ● 座りのいい鼻は政治家の顔にとって重要である A *dignified* nose is important in a politician's physiognomy. (!) 鼻翼のはった鼻は a wide nose ともいう)
すわりごこち 座り心地 ▶このいすは座り心地がいい This chair *is comfortable* (*to sit on* [*in*]).
すわりこみ 座り込み (デモやストでの) a sit-in, a sit-down (strike). ● 工場で座り込みをする stage a *sit-in* at a factory; *sit in* at a factory. ● 座り込みストライキをする go on [stage] a *sit-down* strike.
すわりこむ 座り込む ❶ [[中に入って座る]] ▶彼は部屋に入って座り込んだ He came [got] into the room and *sat down*.
❷ [[座ったまま動かない]] (急にしゃがみ込む) crouch /kráʊtʃ/ down, drop (-pp-) *into a crouch*; (抗議のため) sit* in (⇒座り込み). ▶気分が悪くて座り込んでしまった I felt sick and *crouched down*.
すわりだこ 座り胼胝 ● 座りだこができている have calluses on one's knees and ankles because of the habit of sitting.
:すわる 座る [[動作]] sit* down, take* [have*] a seat; [[状態]] sit; be seated. (!) 後の方は改まった言い方) ● 丸いす[安楽いす]に座る *sit on* a stool [*in* an easy chair]. (!) on はちょこんと, in は深く座る感じ. したがってこの例では on と in は入れ替えられない) ● 深々と[くつろいで]いすに座る *sit back* [*at one's ease*] *in* a chair. ● いすにきちんと[=背すじを伸ばして]座る *sit up* straight *on* a chair. ● 机に向かって座る *sit at* a desk. ● いすにどかっと座る *sink* [*drop*] *into* a chair; *flop oneself down in* a chair. ● 子供をひざに座らせる *sit* [*set*] a child *on* [*in*] one's lap. ● 座った姿勢のままいびきをかいて眠る snore, sleeping in a *sitting* position. ▶どうぞお座りください *Sit down*, ╱*Take* [*Have*] *a seat*, please./*Please be seated*. (!) 後の方はより丁寧な言い方)/(通例女主人が客に)《主に米》 Would you like *to sit* here? ▶こっちへ来て私のそばに座りなさい Come and *sit by* me.

▶彼は本を読んで[黙って]何時間も座っていた He *sat reading* [*silent*, ×*silently*] *for hours*. ▶看護師は彼を座らせて傷の包帯を替えた The nurse *sat him down* and changed the bandages on the wound.
会話「この席に座ってもよろしいですか」「もちろんです」"May I *take this seat* [*chair*]?" "Certainly."
会話「(バスに)いつも座れることもありますか」"Do you usually *get a seat* (on the bus)?" "Sometimes, but not often."

すわる 据わる ❶[動かない状態になる] ●目を据わらせて with one's eyes *set* [*fixed*]. ▶もう3か月もすれば赤ちゃんの首は据わるでしょう In three months, the baby's neck will be strong enough to hold its head up.
❷[動じない] ●度胸が据わっている have lots of guts; have steady nerve.

すん 寸 ❶[長さの単位] a *sun*. (参考 約 3.03cm)
❷[長さ] ▶その服は寸が足りない The dress *is a little too short*.

すんか 寸暇 [[暇な時]] a spare moment. ▶あの学生は寸暇を惜しんで勉強している That student gives [devotes] every *spare moment* to his study./That student spends all his *spare time* studying.

ずんぐり ●ずんぐりした short and fat [thick]; squat /skwάt/, dumpy. ▶彼は40代はじめの小柄でずんぐりした体つきの男だった He was a little *squat* man in his early forties.

すんげき 寸劇 a (comic) sketch (*!* 時に劇の一部として); a skit (*!* 短い風刺劇. 例: a *skit* on politicians (風刺的に政治家を扱った短い笑劇)).

すんげん 寸言 (短くて意味の深いことば) a short clever remark; 《話》a wise-crack.

すんごう 寸毫 ▶私はそれを寸毫も(=少しも)疑わない I haven't *the least* [*slightest*] doubt about it./I *don't* doubt it *at all*.

すんこく 寸刻 (⇨寸秒)

すんし 寸志 (感謝のしるし) a small [(粗末な)] humble] token of gratitude; (ささやかな贈り物) a small gift.

すんしゃく 寸借 ── 寸借する 動 borrow some money (for a short time).
●寸借詐欺 swindling a small loan 《out of him》; (人) a swindler.

ずんずん ❶[早く] (素早く) quickly; (速く) rapidly.
●ずんずん上達する make *rapid* progress 《*in*》. ▶あの子はずんずん背が伸びた The boy has grown tall *quickly*.
❷[活発に] briskly, actively, energetically. ▶彼はずんずん仕事を進めていった He *briskly* carried on his work.
❸[先へ進むさま] ▶彼は振り向かずにずんずん先へ行った He went *straight on* without looking back.

すんぜん 寸前 ▶彼は始業寸前に教室に入った He got into the classroom *just before* (the) class started./The class *was just going to* start *when* he got into the classroom. ▶ゴール寸前に彼に抜かれた I was outstripped by him *just before* the finish line. ▶その会社は倒産寸前だ The firm *is on the verge of* bankruptcy./The firm will go bankrupt *very soon*. ▶アメリカバイソンは乱獲の結果一時絶滅寸前になったこともある American bisons were once heavily hunted *to the brink* of extinction.

すんたらず 寸足らず ❶[寸法が足りない] (⇨寸 ❷)
❷[普通より少し劣る] ●寸足らずの解説 an *insufficient* explanation.

すんだん 寸断 ── 寸断する 動 cut*... to pieces. ▶地震で東京の交通網は寸断された(=地震により大混乱に陥れた) The earthquake *disrupted* Tokyo's transportation system.

すんづまり 寸詰まり ▶彼は寸詰まりの浴衣を着ている He wears a *yukata too short* for him. ▶この新しいジーンズは洗濯すると寸詰まりになるだろう These new jeans will *shrink* after being washed.

すんてつ 寸鉄 ●身に寸鉄(=武器)を帯びず carry no weapon(s); be unarmed [(素手で)barehanded].
●寸鉄人を刺す A *biting* [*cutting*] *remark pierces us to the heart*.

すんでのところで ▶すんでのところで車にひかれるところだった I was *very nearly* [I came *very close to being*] knocked down by a car./(かろうじてひかれるのをまぬがれた) I *narrowly escaped* [*had a narrow escape from*] *being run over by a car*. ▶霧が深くて私はすんでのところで道に迷いそうになった The mist was so thick that I *almost got lost*.

ずんどう 寸胴 ▶彼女はずん胴だ She has *no waist*.
●寸胴鍋 a cylindrical pan; (深鍋) a saucepan.

すんどめ 寸止め ●パンチを顔の前で止めきれる narrowly escape getting a blow in [on] the face.

すんなり ❶[支障なく] smoothly; (容易に) easily, without any difficulty. ▶私はそれはすんなりいかないと思っていた I don't expect it to go *smoothly* [*easily*]. ▶彼らはすんなり(=文句を言わないで)私の提案を受け入れた They accepted my proposal *without any complaints*.
❷[すらりと] ▶すんなりした slender, slim (-mm-). ▶彼女はすんなりした体つきをしている She has a *slender* [a *slim*] figure./She is a *slender* [a *slim*] girl.

スンニ派 (イスラムの) the Sunni sect. (関連 シーア派 the Shiah sect)

すんびょう 寸秒 ▶寸秒を争う We have [There is] *no time to lose*.

すんびょう 寸描 a brief [a concise] sketch 《*of*》.

すんぴょう 寸評 a brief comment 《*on*》.

すんぶん 寸分 ●寸分たがわない be exactly alike; be the same in every detail; be identical /aidéntikl/. ●寸分も...ない(少しも...ない) not a bit.
●寸分のすきもない服装をしている be *perfect* [《やや書》*immaculate*] in one's clothing; be *impeccably* dressed.

すんぽう 寸法 ❶[尺度] (a) measure, (測った詳しい寸法) measurements; (衣類・商品などの大きさ) (a) size (⇨サイズ). ●寸法の合っていない[ぴったり合った]服を着た男 a man in ill-[well-]fitting clothes. ●寸法を測り違える take a wrong *measurement*. ●彼のウエストの寸法を測る take the *size* of his waist. ▶この机の寸法は縦1メートル横2メートル This desk *measures* [*is*] one meter by two meters. ▶洋服屋は私の新しい服の寸法を測った The tailor took my *measure* [*measurements*] *for* a new suit./The tailor *measured* me *for* a new suit. ▶ズボンの寸法直しをしてもらいたいのですが、やってもらえますか I'd like to *have* my pants *altered*. Do you handle *alterations*?
❷[計画] a plan. ▶丘で昼食という寸法だ The *plan is to* [(打ち合わせてある) We have arranged to] have lunch on the hill.

せ

せ 背 ❶ [背中, 後方] one's back. ●壁を背にして立つ stand with one's *back* to [(もたれて) *against*] the wall. ●背を伸ばす straighten (up) one's *back*; hold one's *back* erect. ●窓に背を向ける turn one's *back* to the window. (**!** 「窓に背を向けて立っている」は stand *with* one's *back* to the window.) ●青空を背にくっきりと山が見えた We could see the mountain clearly *against* the blue sky. (**!** against は「…を背景にして」の意) ●浜辺は白亜の断崖(だんがい)を背にしている The beach *is backed* by the chalk cliffs.

❷ [背状のもの] the back. ●いすの背 the *back* (*support*) of a chair. ●本の背表紙 the *spine* of a book.

❸ [背丈] height, 《書》 stature. (⇒身長) ●背の高い[低い]男性 a *tall* [a *short*] man. (**!** (1) 米英では背が高いことは日本のようには偏重されない. 相手に You're incredibly tall. (すごく背が高いのね)などというのは避けた方がよい. (2)「背の低い」は婉曲的に differentially sized (高さが違うのように)という) ●その少女は背が高くほっそりしていた The girl was *tall* and slender. ●その川は深くて背が立たない(＝底に足がつかない) The river is so deep that we *can't touch* (*the*) *bottom* [we *are out of* our *depth*].

❹ [尾根] a ridge. ●山の背 a mountain *ridge*; the *ridge* of a mountain.

●背に腹はかえられぬ (必要なことに法律はない) 《ことわざ》 Necessity knows [has] no law./(他に選択の余地はない) There is no other choice [no alternative].

●背を向ける ●物質文明に背を向ける(＝を捨てる) turn one's *back on* material civilization. ●敵に背を向ける(＝敗走する) turn tail (and run). ●この機会に背を向けたら二度とめぐり会えないよ If you *walk away from* this opportunity, you'll never see another one like it again. (**!** walk away from は「拒んで逃げる」の意)

せ 瀬 (早瀬) rapids; (浅瀬) shallows; (川の浅瀬) a ford. ●それでは私の立つ瀬がない (⇒立つ瀬)

ぜ 是 ●是とする(＝よいと思う) apprpve (*of* it). ●是が非でも (⇒是が非でも) ●いずれが是か非かは決定できない We cannot decide which is *right* or wrong.

*せい 性 ❶ [性別] sex. (⇒性別)

❷ [性的な事柄] sex. (**!** 文脈によって「性描写」などの意になる) ●性の sexual. (⇒性的な) ●性交渉を持つ have *sex* (*sexual*) *intercourse*] (*with*); make love (*to*, *with*); go to bed (*with*). ●後の二つは婉曲的な言い方 ●性描写の多い本 a book with a lot of *sex* in it. ●性に目覚めるようになる become *sexually* aware. ●彼は息子に性に関する話をしてやる勇気がなかった He didn't have the heart to explain *sexual* matters [《婉曲的》 the facts of life] to his son.

❸ [本性] nature. ●悪にそまりやすいのが人の性です Human *nature* is prone to evil.

❹ [文法上の] (a) gender. (⇒男性, 女性, 中性)

●性科学 sexology. ●性差別 sex [sexual] discrimination; sexism. (**!** いずれも特に女性差別をさす) ●性染色体 《生物》 a sex chromosome. ●性体験 (have) (a) sexual experience. ●性倒錯 sexual perversion. ●性倒錯者 a sexual pervert. ●性犯罪 a sex offense. ●性犯罪者 a sex offender. ●(⇒性教育, 性交, 性転換, 性欲)

*せい 所為 ❶ [責任] (責め) blame; (過失) a fault. ●彼はいつも自分の失敗を人のせいにする He always *blames* [*puts the blame for*] his failure on others./He always *blames* [*puts the blame on*] others *for* his failure./(失敗を他人に帰する) He always *puts* his failure *down to* other people. ●遅れたのは私のせいではない It's not my *fault* (that) I'm late./(責任がない) I'm not *responsible* [I'm in no way *to blame*] for being late. (**!** in no way は not の強意語で《話》) ●それはだれのせいだったんだい Whose *fault* was it?/Who *was to blame for* it? (**!** これに対する答えは前の方は Tom's., 後の方は Tom. のようになる)

❷ [原因] because of. ●年のせいで物忘れがひどくなった I have become very forgetful *because of* (old) age. (⇒ため ❷) ●コーチは試合に負けたのはチームワーク不足のせいだと言った The coach *attributed* [*ascribed*] the loss *to* lack of teamwork. ●あいつのせいで(＝おかげで)ひどい目にあった *Thanks to* him, I had a terrible experience./I have him to *thank for* my terrible experience. (**!** 皮肉を込めた言い方)

せい 正 ❶ [正しいこと] right; (正義) justice; (正確) correctness. ●正誤 (⇒正誤)

❷ [正規] ●正選手 a regular (player). ●正捕手 a regular [an everyday] catcher. ●正会員 a *regular* [a *full*] member.

❸ [原本] ●契約書を正副 2 通作成する prepare the contract *in duplicate*.

❹ [正数] ●正の数 a plus [a *positive*] number.

せい 生 (a) life (複 lives). (⇒命, 生命) ●生あるもの (all) *living* things; 《集合的》 《やや書》 the *living* 《複数扱い》.

●生を享(う)ける ●この世に生をうける(＝生まれる) be born into this world.

せい 姓 one's family name, one's surname. (⇒名字) ●彼は母方の姓を継いでいる He takes his mother's *family name* before marriage.

せい 背 height; 《書》 stature. (⇒背(*), 身長)

せい 聖 St. /séint/ 《Saint の略》. (**!** 人名の前につける) ●聖パウロ教会 *St.* Paul's Church. ●聖なる holy; sacred. (⇒神聖な)

せい 精 ❶ [霊魂] a spirit; (山・森などの精) a nymph /nimf/. ●花の精 the *spirit* of a flower. ●水の精 a water *nymph*; an undine. ●森の精 a forest *nymph*; a dryad.

❷ [精力] energy; (活力) vigor; (体力) strength. ●精をつける gain *strength*. ●精のつく(＝栄養のある)食物 a *nourishing* [a *nutritious*] food.

●精が出る ●精が出ますね How *hard* you *work*!/You really *work hard*, don't you?

●精も根も尽き果てる be completely [absolutely] exhausted.

●精を出す ●仕事に精を出す work *hard*; (打ち込む) apply all one's *energies* [*oneself*] *to* one's work.

せい 静 (じっと動かないこと) stillness; (静かなこと) quiet, quietness. ●静中, 動あり There is movement amid *stillness*.

- **-せい -世** ● ヘンリー 5 世 Henry V [the Fifth]. ● 長嶋 2 世 Nagashima, Jr. [Junior]. (⚠ Jr. は 2 人兄弟の弟, 同名父子の息子, 同名男性 2 人の年少者に用いる)
- **-せい -制** a system. (⇨制度) ● 定年制 an age-limit system; a mandatory retirement system. ● 六三制 the six-three school system. ● 旧制大学 a university under the old (educational) system.
- **-せい -製** (材料を示して) made of ...; (生産地を示して) -made. ● 外国製の家具 foreign-made furniture. ▶ 彼の車はどこ製ですか What make is his car? ▶ この机はスチール製です This desk is made of steel./This is a steel desk. ● このカメラはドイツ製です This camera is of German make [was made in Germany, is German].
- **ぜい 税** (a) tax; (物品などの) (a) duty (⚠ しばしば複数形で単数扱い). (⇨税金). ● 直接[間接]税 direct [indirect] taxes. ● 税制度 (⇨税制) ● 税負担 tax burden. ● 税別[税込み]で 1 泊 100 ドル one hundred dollars a night without [plus] tax. ● 税引き後の利息 an interest after tax. ● 税込み[引き]で年収 500 万です My yearly income is five million yen before [after] tax. (⇨税込み, 税引き)

  関連 いろいろな税: 国税 a national tax/固定資産税 a real estate [property] tax/自動車税 a car [an automobile] tax/消費税 a consumption tax/所得税 an income tax/住民税 a resident tax/相続税 an inheritance tax/地方税 a local tax/付加価値税 a value-added tax 《略 VAT》/物品税 a commodity tax/法人税 a corporation tax/輸入税 import duties.

- **ぜい 贅** (⇨贅沢) ● 贅を尽くしたプレゼント[パーティー] an extravagant present [party].
- **せいあい 性愛** sexual love.
- **せいあくせつ 性悪説** the view that humans are born evil. (⇨ 性善説)
- **せいあつ 制圧** control.
  — **制圧する** 動 control. ● 敵を制圧する control the enemy; bring the enemy under control. ● 首都を制圧する(= 支配権を握る) take [《やや書》gain] control of the capital.
- **せいあん 成案** a definite plan; (具体的な計画) a concrete plan.
- **せいあん 西安** [中国の都市] Xi'an /fiːɑ́ːn/.
- ***せいい 誠意** 名 [誠実] good faith; [言行に表裏のないこと] sincerity /sínsərəti/. ● 誠意を示す show one's good faith [sincerity] 《to, toward》. ● 誠意をもって謝罪する make a sincere apology. ● 誠意をもって行動する act in good faith [with sincerity]. ▶ 彼は何事も誠意をもって当たる He's sincere in everything he does.
  — **誠意(の)ある** 形 sincere /sínsɪər/ (↔insincere); (信義に厚い) faithful (↔faithless); (正直な) honest (↔dishonest). ● 誠意のある人 a sincere [a faithful, an honest] person; a person of sincerity [good faith].
- **せいい 勢い** (⇨勢力) ● 勢いを振るう exercise influence [wield power] 《in》.
- **せいいき 西域** (古代中国の) the Western Regions [Marches].
- **せいいき 声域** a (vocal) range. (⇨音域)
- **せいいき 聖域** (侵すことのできない場所) a sánctuary; a sacred /séikrid/ place; (神聖な地) holy ground. ● 聖域なき構造改革 structural reform without sacred cows. (⚠ sacred cow は「神聖視され, 批判や攻撃の許されぬもの[人]」の意)
- ▶ 予算の 5 パーセント削減に聖域はない(= どんな例外もない) 5 percent badget cut will be done in all sectors, without any exceptions.
- **せいいく 生育, 成育** growth. ▶ さつまいもの生育には砂地が一番だ Sweet potatoes grow [do] best in sandy soil.
- **せいいっぱい 精一杯** ▶ 彼は精一杯(= 全力をあげて)働いた He worked with all his might./He worked as hard as possible [he could]. (⚠ 後の言い方の方が口語的な) ▶ 精一杯やったが彼を救えなかった I did the most I could [I tried my best], but I couldn't save him. ▶ 家族を養うのが精一杯です It is all [as much as] I can do to support my family./The best I can do is (to) support my family. ▶ 阿部先生の授業についていくのが精一杯です I'm struggling to keep up with Mr. Abe's class. (⚠ struggle to do は「四苦八苦してどうにか...する」の意)
- **せいいん 成因** (原因) a cause; (根源) an origin.
- **せいいん 成員** (構成員) a member 《of》. ● 家族の成員 a member of a family.
- **せいう 晴雨** ● 晴雨にかかわらず whether it rains or not; rain or shine; in all weathers. (⇨天気 ⑤) ● 晴雨計 a barometer.
- **せいうち 海象** [動物] a walrus (複 ～, ～es).
- **せいうん 青雲** ● 青雲の志 ● 青雲の志を抱く have great [高邁な] lofty] ambitions.
- **せいうん 星雲** 名 [天文] a nebula (複 nebulae, ～s); [銀河系外の] a galaxy.
  — **星雲(状)の** 形 nebular.
- **せいうん 盛運** ▶ 盛運におもむく(= 運が向いてくる) Luck is running 《his》 way.
- **せいえい 清栄** ▶ 秋冷の候, ますますご清栄のこととおよろこび申し上げます I am very glad (that) you are healthy and doing very well at the cool season of autumn.
- **せいえい 精鋭** (最もよいもの) the best; (えり抜き) 《やや書》the pick. ● 陸軍の精鋭 the pick [best] of the army. ● 少数精鋭の科学者集団 a small elite group of scientists.
- **せいえき 精液** [生理] semen /síːmən/; (精子の集合) sperm.
- **せいえん 声援** cheering, a cheer; [激励] encouragement. ● 声援を送る (競技で) cheer (the team) (on) (⇨応援する); (励ます) encourage 《him》. ● 沿道からランナーに声援を送る cheer the passing runners from the sides of the road.
- **せいえん 凄艶** — **凄艶な** 形 (とても魅惑的な) extremely enchanting; (うっとりするほど美しい) bewitchingly [(気味の悪いほど) uncannily] beautiful.
- **せいえん 製塩** salt manufacture.
  ● 製塩業 the salt industry. ● 製塩業者 a salter. ● 製塩所 a saltern; a saltworks.
- **せいおう 西欧** [西洋] the West (⚠ 主に欧米をさす); [ヨーロッパ] Europe (⇨西洋); [ヨーロッパ] West [Western] Europe (⚠ West Europe は政治的に区分された地域をいう).
- **せいおん 清音** [音声] (無声音) a voiceless sound.
- **せいおん 静穏** 名 (落ち着き) calmness; (安らかさ) quiet(ness); (平静) tranquility; serenity. (⇨平穏)
  — **静穏な** 形 calm; quiet; tranquil; serene.
- ***せいか 成果** [結果] (a) result; (期待される) outcome; (努力の末の) (a) fruit (⚠ しばしば複数形で). (⇨結果) [類語] ● 30 年にわたる研究の成果 the result [outcome, fruit(s)] of 30 years of study. ● 成果の多い会合 a fruitful meeting. ● 成果が

る produce *results*. ● その分野ですぐれた成果を収める achieve [produce] good [splendid] *results* in the field. ▶ その治療法はかなりの成果をあげた The remedy had a very successful *result* [*turned out* (*to be*) very *successful*, *bore fruit*]. ▶ この調査で何の成果も得られそうにない We're getting *nowhere with* this investigation. (**!** get *nowhere* は「何も成し遂げない」の意) ▶ あなたの音はぐんぐんよくなってきた．練習の成果が出てきたね The sound you make is getting better and better. Your practicing is *paying off*.
会話 「成果はあったか」「これというものはない」 "Have you seen any *results*?" "Nothing in particular [(重要な) significant]."

せいか 正価 a net price. ● 正価 500 円 a *net price* of 500 yen. ● 正価販売する sell at a *net price*.

せいか 正貨 specie.
● 正貨準備(高) specie [gold] reserve.

せいか (必修科目) a compulsory [《米》a required] subject.

せいか 生花 〖自然の花〗a fresh flower; 〖生け花〗(⇨生け花).

せいか 生家 ▶ その作家の生家を訪ねてみたい I want to visit the *house where* [*in which*] the writer *was born*. (**!** one's *birthplace* (誕生の地[場所])で生家を示すこともある)

せいか 青果 〖農産物〗fruit(s) and vegetables (**!** v- and f- の語順も可); 《英》greengrocery.
● 青果市場 a fruit and vegetable market. ● 青果商 (⇨八百屋)

せいか 盛夏 ● 盛夏に in the height of summer. (⇨真夏)

せいか 聖火 the sacred fire [flame]; 〖リレーで運ぶ〗a sacred torch. ● オリンピックの聖火 the Olympic (*Sacred*) *Flame*; (リレーで運ぶ) the Olympic *Torch*.
● 聖火台 the flame holder; (オリンピックの) the Olympic Flame Holder (**!** 《書》では the Olympic Caldron [《英》Cauldron], 「聖火点火者」は the Olympic Caldron Lighter という). ● 聖火ランナー a flame [torch] bearer. ● 聖火リレー an Olympic-torch [an Olympic-fire] relay.

せいか 聖歌 a sacred song; (賛美歌) a hymn /hím/; (クリスマスの) a (*Christmas*) carol.
● 聖歌隊 a choir /kwáiər/. ● (1) 単・複両扱い．(2) 隊員は a chorister) ● 聖歌隊で歌う sing in a *choir*.

せいか 精華 (精髄) 〖書〗the quintessence; (本質) the essence. ● 武士道の精華 the *essence* [*quintessence*] of chivalry.

せいか 製菓 confectionery.
● 製菓会社 a confectionery company. ● 製菓業 the confectionery industry. ● 製菓業者 a confectioner.

せいか 製靴 shoemaking.
● 製靴業 the shóemaking ìndustry. ● 製靴業者 a shoemaker. ● 製靴工場 a shóemaking fàctory.

せいが 聖画 a sacred picture [painting].

せいかい 正解 〖名〗a correct [a right] answer [solution]. (⇨答)
— 正解する 〖動〗 answer (a question) [solve a problem] correctly.

せいかい 政界 〖名〗 (政治の世界) the political world, political circles; (政治生活) (a) political life; (政治活動) politics (**!** 単・複両扱い). ● 政界に入る enter [go into] *politics* [*the political world*]. ● 政界を退く retire from *political life* [*politics*].

— 政界の 〖形〗 political. ● 政界のドン a *political* boss.

せいかい 盛会 a successful [a good] meeting.
▶ その会は盛会であった The meeting was a *great success* [*very successful*]./(出席者が多かった) The meeting *was well attended*.

せいかいけん 制海権 ● 制海権を握る take (↔lose) command of the sea [naval supremacy]; command the sea.

せいかがく 生化学 〖名〗 biochemistry.
— 生化学の 〖形〗 biochemical.
● 生化学者 a biochemist.

:せいかく 正確 〖名〗 correctness; accuracy; precision; exactness.
— 正確な 〖形〗 correct; áccurate; precise; exact; 〖完璧(次発)な〗 perfect; 〖時間に正確な〗 punctual.

使い分け **correct** 計算や分析，解釈などに誤りがなくて正しく，標準や規則に合っていること．
accurate 事実に一致するように積極的に努力して，誤りなく的確であること．
precise 細心綿密な正確さを強調する．
exact 寸分の違いもなく厳密で正確なこと．

● 正確な答え a *correct* answer. ● 正確な円 a *perfect* circle. ▶ 私の時計は正確だ My watch keeps *correct* [*accurate*, *good*] time./My watch is *correct* [*accurate*, *right*]. ▶ ニュースの報道は正確でなければならない They should try to be *accurate* [×correct] *in* news reporting. ▶ 私は正確な数字は思い出せない I can't remember the *exact* figures. ▶ 彼女のその夜の記憶は非常に正確だ Her memory of the night is very *exact* [*precise*]. ▶ 彼は約束の時間に正確だ He is (very) *punctual for* appointments.

DISCOURSE
二酸化炭素がどれだけ排出されているかに関して，我々はより正確な統計を得る必要がある We should obtain more *precise* statistics **as to** how much carbon dioxide is being emitted. (**!** as to ...（…に関して)は関連を表すディスコースマーカー)

— 正確に 〖副〗 correctly; accurately; exactly; precisely. ● 正確に言い当てる guess *right*; guess *with accuracy* [*precision*]. ▶ その語を正確に発音できない I cannot pronounce the word *correctly* [*accurately*, *properly*]. ▶ だれも地震を正確に予知できない No one can predict an earthquake *accurately* [*with accuracy*]. ▶ 正確に言うと列車は 7 分遅れました *To be exact* [*precise*], the train was seven minutes late.
会話 「それから大学に進学されたのですか」「正確にはそうじゃないんです」 "And then you went to college?" "No, not *exactly*."
会話 「火曜日の午前中に着いたんだ」「正確には何時に？」 "I arrived on Tuesday morning." "At *exactly* what time?"

:せいかく 性格 〖人の〗(固有の性格) (a) character; (全特徴) (a) personality; 〖他と区別する性質〗(the) nature. (⇨性質)
① 【～性格】 ● 人あたりのよい [強引な] 性格の人 a person *with* [×of] a pleasing [forceful] *personality*; a (person of) pleasing [forceful] *character*. ● 軟弱な性格 a weak *character*. ● 派手な性格 a striking *personality*. ● その任務の性格 the *nature* of the task. ● 彼はどんな性格の人ですか What is his *character* like?/What is he like? ▶ 彼はよい性格をしている He has a good *character* [*personality*]./He is a man *of* [×with] good

せいかく *character*. (❗(1) 後の方は堅い言い方. (2) 後の方は人格者の意にもなる) ▶彼は頼まれたら断れない性格だ His *character* is such that he cannot refuse when (he is) asked. (❗(1) such that は「…のような種類のもの」の意. 堅い書き言葉だが, 最近一般化してきた. (2) ×He has the *character* that …. は不可)

② 【性格(の)～】 ●(小説・脚本での)性格描写がうまい be good at *characterization*. ●性格的に欠陥がある have a defect [(小さな) a flaw] in one's *character*; have *character* flaws. ●彼らは性格の不一致が理由で離婚した They divorced on (the) grounds of *incompatibility* [because they were *incompatible with* each other].

③ 【性格が[は]】 ▶その姉妹は性格が違う The sisters have different *characters* [*personalities*]./The sisters are different in *character*. ▶私の性格は母親ゆずりです I've got my mother's *personality*. ▶イタリアの生活に慣れてくるにつれて私の性格が変わり始めた As I was getting used to the Italian lifestyle, my *personality* began to change. ▶しゃべり方からある程度性格がうかがえる A person's *character* can be inferred from the way he or she speaks. ▶この二つの仕事は性格が異なる These two jobs are different in *nature*.

●性格異常 *character disorder*. ●性格劇 a *character drama*. ●性格検査 a *personality test*. ●性格俳優 a *character actor* [(女優) *actress*].

せいかく 精確 名 *precision*; *exactness*.
―**精確な** 形 *precise*; *exact*. (⇨正確な) ▶科学的な研究には精確な観察を必要とする Scientific study requires *exact observation*.
―**精確に** 副 *precisely*; *exactly*.

せいがく 声楽 *vocal music*. ▶佐藤教授について声楽を習う take *voice* [*singing*] *lessons* from Professor Sato; study *singing* [*voice*] under Professor Sato.
●声楽科 a *vocal music course*. ●声楽家 a *singer*; (バンドに属している) a *vocalist*.

ぜいがく 税額 *the amount of tax*; (査定額) *taxation*.

せいかぞく 『聖家族』 *the Holy Family*. (参考) 幼児キリスト・聖母マリア・聖ヨセフを描いた絵画)

:**せいかつ** 生活 [[暮らし]] (a) *life* (圏 *lives* /láivz/); *living*; [[生計]] a *living*, a *livelihood* /láivlihùd/. (❗ともに通例単数形で).

> 解説 (1) life は生活の「状態」をさすときは抽象名詞であるが, 通例修飾語を伴って生活の「仕方」をいうときは普通名詞として a をとり, 複数形にもなる (⇨ ①).
> (2) 生活を一般的・集合的に見た場合には単数形, 特定的・個別的に見た場合は複数形を用いる: 彼らの生活はきびしいものであった Their *life* was a hard one./彼らはそれぞれ自分の生活を楽しんだ They enjoyed their own *lives* respectively.
> (3) living, livelihood はともに生きてゆくための手段や暮らしの立て方をいうが, living の方が口語的で, 生きて[生活して]ゆく上, 特定の生活様式などを表すときにも用いる意味の広い語.

① 【～生活】 (❗この場合はしばしば a を伴う (⇨ 解説)). ●家庭生活 one's *family* [*home*] *life*. ●私生活 (one's) *private* (↔*public*) *life*. ●学生[大学生活] *student* [*college*] *life*. ●社会生活 one's *social life*. ●集団生活 *group life*. ●忙しい[充実した]生活 a *busy* [a *full*] *life*. ●生きがいのある生活 a *life worth living*; a *life* with *purpose*. ●怠惰な生活 an *idle life*; a *life* of *idleness*. (❗後の方が強意的) ●寮生活を送る live in a *dorm*.

▶都会の生活はどうですか How do you like [find] your *life* in the city [city *life*]? ▶二人の結婚生活は破綻した Their married *life* has broken up. ▶車は日常生活には必要ないと言う人もいる Some people say a car isn't needed for everyday [our daily] *life*.

② 【生活の～】 ●生活の手段 a means of (making a) *living*; a *livelihood*. ●生活の質 the quality of *life* 《略 QOL》. (❗特に精神面についていう) ●生活のために働く work for a *living* [one's *bread*].

③ 【生活が[は]】 ▶以前より生活が楽だ[苦しい] I'm *better* [*worse*] *off* than before. (❗原級は be well [badly] off) ▶年金で何とか生活ができる I can make ends meet on my *pension*./I managed to live on my *pension*. ▶今日ではテレビのない生活は想像できない Today it's hard to imagine *living* [*life*, ×a *life*] *without TV*. (❗*living* は live の動名詞. また特定の個人の「生活」ではないので無冠詞) ▶ここ数年私の生活は少しもよくなっていない My *living* [*livelihood*] hasn't improved at all for the past few years. ▶観光事業に島の人々の生活がかかっている(=は島の主要産業である) 《話》Tourism is the island's *bread and butter*. ▶人にはそれぞれの生活がある We each have our own *lifestyle*.

④ 【生活に】 ●生活に困る find it difficult [be hardly able] to make a *living*. ●毎日の忙しい生活に疲れる get tired of the busy daily *life*. ▶妻は生活に追われていた My wife was trying very hard to make ends meet.

⑤ 【生活を】 ●幸福な生活をする *lead* [*live*] a *happy life*; *live happily*. (❗前の方は形容詞に強勢を置いて発音され, 後の方より強意的に好まれる. ただし, この型は life が修飾語句を伴わない場合は不可. たとえば lead [live] a life of poverty (貧困生活を送る)とはいうが, 単に ×lead [live] a life とはいわない) ●かなりよい[かつかつの]生活をする *make* a *fairly good* [a *bare*] *living*. (❗後の方は *scrape* [*scratch*] a *living* ともいえる) ●苦労の多い生活を送る(=多くの苦難を経験する) *go through* a lot of *hardships*; *lead a dog's life*. (❗後の方は慣用表現だが, 最近はペットブームで「何一つ心配のないぜいたくな生活をする」意でおどけて用いられることもある) ●生活を共にする(=いっしょに暮らす) *live together*; *live under* [*share*] *the same roof*. ▶彼女は一家の生活を支えている She *supports her family*.

―**生活する** 動 *live* (⇨⑤); 暮らす); [[生計を立てる]] *make*` a *[one's] living*. ▶物を書いて生活する *live by writing* [*by one's pen*]; *make* [*earn*, 《やや書》*gain*] *one's* [a] *living by writing* (❗… *as* a *writer* ともいえる). ●月給[年金]で生活する *live on one's salary* [a *pension*]. ●ひと月 10 万円で生活する *live on 100,000 yen a month*.

会話 「失業している間ずっとどうして生活していたの」「建築現場でバイトをしてなんとか生活していたんだ」"How did you *support yourself* all the time you were out of work?" "I managed to *make a living from* [*by*] *working part-time at a construction site*." (❗*support oneself* は「自活する」の意)

●生活環境 *living environment*. ●生活給 a *living wage*. ●生活協同組合 (⇨生協) ●生活苦 the *hardships of life*. ●生活指導 *educational guidance*; *student guidance*; *counseling*. ●生活習慣病 a *lifestyle-related disease*. ●生活状態 *living conditions*. ●生活水準 *living standards*; *the standard of living*. ●生活設計 *life planning*; a *plan for one's life*. ●生活反応 a *vital reaction*. ●生活必需品 the *necessities* [*necessaries*] *of life*. (❗前の方は衣食や水のように

せいかつ なければ生きていけないもの, 後の方より強意的) ● 生活様式 a [one's] way of life; a [one's] life style (⚠ lifestyle ともつうる); a [one's] style of living. ● (後の二つは個人・集団の個性的生き方をいう) an urban [a rural] lifestyle (都会[田舎]の生活様式) ● 生活力 (経済力) one's earning power; (活力) vitality. ● 生活力欠如【医学】abiosis.

せいかつひ 生活費 the cost of living, living còsts [expènses]. ● 教師をして生活費をかせぐ(=生計を立てる) make [earn, gain] one's [a] living by teaching [as a teacher]. (⚠ earn a livelihood ... ともいえる) ▶ 1 か月の生活費はいくらかかりますか What is the monthly cost of living?/How much does it cost to live here [there] a month? ▶ 生活費は親に出してもらっています I depend on my parents for living costs. ● 神戸は生活費の安いところだ Kobe is a cheap [an inexpensive] city to live in. (⚠ 生活事情などのことを話している文脈があれば単に Kobe is cheap. ともいえる)/The cost of living is low in Kobe./(安上がりの生活かできる) We can live cheap in Kobe.

せいかつほご 生活保護 livelihood protection, welfare aid. ● 生活保護を受ける[受けている] go [be, stay] on welfare (⚠) [social security (英)]. (⚠ social security は (米) では「老人福祉」のこと) ● 生活保護家庭 a welfare family; a family on welfare.

せいかん 生還 ━ 生還する 動 ❶ [生きて帰る] come back [return] alive; (無事に帰る) return safe [safely]. ▶ その兵士たちは激戦地から生還した The soldiers came back alive [returned home safely] from the hard-fought field.
❷ [野球で] get [reach; come] home, cross the plate; (得点する) score (a run). ● 三塁から走者を生還させる score [bring in] a runner from third; bring [send] a runner home from third. ▶ 走者は清原の二塁打で生還した The runner got home [scored] on Kiyohara's two-base hit.
● 生還者 a survivor.

せいかん 性感 sexual feeling.
● 性感帯 an erogenous zone.

せいかん 清閑 quiet(ness); (平穏) tranquility; (安らぎ) peace. ● この街の清閑な(=穏やかな)たたずまい a peaceful [(静穏な) a calm] atmosphere of this town.

せいかん 盛観 a grand [(荘厳な) a magnificent] spectacle; a splendid [(荘重な) a stately] sight.

せいかん 精悍 ● 精悍な顔つきの男 a masculine-looking man.

せいかん 精管 【解剖】(輸精管) a spermaduct.

せいかん 静観 名 ● ...に対して静観的態度を取る take [《やや書》 assume] a wait-and-see attitude toward ....
━ 静観する 動 (成り行きを待つ) wait and see; (落ち着いて見守る) watch [observe]... calmly. (⚠ observe の方が客観的に冷静に見守る意が強い) ▶ 私たちは事態を静観すべきだ We should watch the development of the situation calmly./We should wait and see what will happen./(事態が進むにかかせるべきだ) We should let things take their own course.

せいがん 正眼 ● 剣を正眼に構える hold one's sword with its point aimed at one's opponent's eyes.

せいがん 西岸 the west coast.

せいがん 制癌 ● 初期癌に対し制癌作用がある be effective against primary cancer.
● 制癌剤 an anti-cancer drug; a drug inhibiting cancer.

せいがん 誓願 名 a vow.
━ 誓願する 動 make a vow; vow. (⇔誓う)

せいがん 請願 名 a petition 《for; against》. ● 空港建設反対の請願書に署名する sign a petition against the construction of an airport. ● 新空港建設反対の請願する a petition against the construction of a new airport.
━ 請願する 動 petition. ● 政府に減税を請願する petition the government to reduce taxes.

ぜいかん 税関 (the) customs (⚠ しばしば the Customs で単数扱い. 施設にも機関の総称としても用いる); (主に港の) a customs house (⚠ houses /-ziz, (米) -siz/), (米) a customhouse. ● 神戸税関 the Kobe Customhouse. ● 税関を通る get [go] through (the) customs. ● 税関で調べられる get (it) inspected at (the) customs. ● 税関で申告すべき宝石類を持っていますか Do you have any jewelry to declare at customs?
● 税関員 a customs officer. ● 税関検査 customs inspection. ● 税関申告 customs declaration. ● 税関手続き customs formalities.

せいかんせんしょう 性感染症 【医学】 (a) sexually transmitted disease (略 STD). (⚠参考) エイズ・梅毒・癲病・クラミジア感染症など)

*せいき 世紀 a century. ● 21世紀 the 21st [twenty-first] century. (⚠ 省略形は通例大文字の 21st C) ● 今世紀末 the end of this century. ● 紀元前 4 世紀初め[終わり; 半ば]に in the early [late; mid-] 4th century B.C. ● 17-8 世紀に in the 17th and 18th centuries. ● 今世紀最大の作曲家 the greatest composer of this [the present] century. ● 世紀の偉業[大発明品] the greatest achievement [invention] in history. ▶ 彼は 1 世紀近く生きた He had lived nearly a century.

せいき 正規 ━ 正規の 形 regular; [正式の] formal; [正当な] proper. ● 正規の会員 a regular member. ● 正規の手続きを踏む go through the regular procedure; go through proper [due] formalities.

せいき 生気 ● 生気のある full of life; active.

せいき 生起 名 occurrence.
━ 生起する 動 occur; happen. (⇔起こる)

せいき 性器 the sex organs; (外性器)【医学】 the genitals /dʒenɪtəlz/, the genitalia /dʒenɪtéɪlɪə/. (⚠ いずれも複数扱い)

せいき 精気 (元気, 活力) energy; vigor. ● 精気を取り戻す regain one's (former) energy [vigor]. ● 精気に満ちている be full of energy [vigor].

*せいぎ 正義 justice; (正しさ) right. ● 正義の味方 a friend of justice [right]. ● 正義のために戦う fight for [in the cause of] justice. ▶ 彼は正義感が強い He has a strong [no] sense of justice. ▶ 最後は正義が勝つものなのだ Justice will prevail [×win] in the end. ▶ あらゆる戦争は正義の名の下で行われる All wars are fought in the name of justice.

*せいきゅう 請求 名 a request; a demand; a claim. (⇔要求) ● 請求書 (請求書) ● 請求権がある have a claim 《to》. ● 請求に応じて身分証明書を見せる show one's ID card on demand. ▶ 申込書はご請求があり次第お送りいたします Application forms will be sent on request [at your request].
━ 請求する 動 ask, (正式に) request (⚠ よりかたい語); [権限をもって] demand; [当然の権利として] claim; [代金などを] charge. ● カタログを請求する ask for a catalog. ● 彼に勘定を払うよう請求する demand payment of a bill from [of] him;

せいきゅう *request* [xdemand] him *to* pay a bill; *request* (of him) [(主に英)should] pay a bill. ●空港で手荷物を請求する *claim* one's baggage at an airport. ●彼に損害賠償を請求する *claim* [*make a claim for*] damages *against* him. ▶本の代金として1,000円請求された They asked [told] me [made (me) to pay), *charged* (me)] 1,000 yen *for* the book. (❗×They charged me *to* pay .... は不可)

せいきゅう 制球 [野球] *control*; *location*. (⇒コントロール) ●あの投手は制球がよい[悪い] The pitcher has good [bad] *control*. (❗「制球力がない」は ... has no *control*.)

せいきゅう 性急 ── 性急な 形 [あわてた] *hasty*; [軽率な] *rash*. ●性急な決定をする make a *hasty* [a *rash*, (衝動的な)an *impetuous*] decision; decide *hastily* [*rashly*, *impetuously*].

せいきゅうしょ 請求書 a bill (*for*); (飲食店の)(米)a check, (英)a bill. ●高額の請求書 a large *bill*. ●請求書を送る send out a *bill*. ●ガス[電話, 電気]代の請求書を受け取る receive a gas [a phone; an electricity] *bill*. ●請求書をください Check [Bill], please./Can [Could] I have the check [bill], please? (❗後の方が丁寧な言い方)

せいきょ 逝去 图 *passing*. ── 逝去する 動 *pass away*.

せいぎょ 生魚 (生きている魚)a live fish; (新鮮な魚)a fresh fish.

せいぎょ 成魚 an adult fish; (十分に成長した魚)a full-grown [a fully-grown] fish.

せいぎょ 制御 □ *control*. ▶その機械は制御がきかなくなった The machine got [went] out of *control*./We lost *control* of the machine.
── 制御する 動 *control*; (巧みに扱う)*manage*. ●馬を制御する *manage* [*hold*] a horse. ●制御装置 a control device [system]; a controller. ●制御棒(原子炉の) a control rod.

せいきょう 生協 [『生活協同組合』の略] a cooperative society, 《話》a co-op /kóuàp/; (売店)a co-op store.

せいきょう 盛況 ●盛況である(会などが)be well attended; (店などが)be flourishing (⇒流行)❷. ▶慈善コンサートは大盛況だった(=多くの人が行った) *A lot of people went to* the charity concert./(大成功だった) The charity concert was a *great success*.

せいきょう 精強 形 very strong. ●精強な(=とても強い)軍隊 a *very strong* [(強力な)a *powerful*] army.

せいぎょう 生業 (職業)an occupation; (書)a calling. ▶彼は文筆を生業としている He writes *for a living*.

せいぎょう 成業 ── 成業する 動 complete one's study [work; (事業) undertaking].

せいぎょう 盛業 ●盛業中の店 a store which *is prosperous* [*is doing very well*].

せいきょういく 性教育 sex education. ▶その学校では性教育をしている They teach *sex education* in the school. (❗この場合誤解を避けるため teach sex などとしない)

せいきょうかい 正教会 the Orthodox Church. ●ギリシャ正教会 the Greek *Orthodox Church*.

せいきょうと 清教徒 a Puritan /pjúərətən/. ●清教徒革命 the Puritan Revolution.

せいきょうぶんり 政教分離 the separation of religion and state [politics].

せいぎょき 盛漁期 the fishing season.

せいきょく 政局 the political situation. ●政局の危機 a *political* crisis. ●政局を打開する break the *political* deadlock. ●政局は安定している The *political situation* is stable.

せいきん 精勤 hard work; (勤勉)diligence; (きちんと出勤すること) regular attendance.
── 精勤する 動 work hard; be diligent; attend regularly.
●精勤者 a worker [(従業員)an employee; (学生)a student] with a regular attendance record; (会などの)a regular attender. ●精勤賞 a prize for regular attendance.

ぜいきん 税金 (a) tax (*on*). (❗文脈により public [government] money (公金), taxpayer's money (血税)などという: 税金の無駄遣い a waste of *taxpayer's money*) ●(高い)税金を払う pay a (high) *tax*. ●税金を上げる(=増税する)increase [raise] *taxes*. ●税金に1万円払う pay ten thousand yen in *taxes*. ●税金を徴収する collect *taxes* (*from*). ●税金の払い戻しを受ける receive a *tax refund*. ●5パーセントの税金をかける *tax* (an item) at five percent. ●酒には重い税金が課されている A heavy *tax* is imposed on alcohol./There is a heavy *tax on* [×of] alcohol./Alcohol is heavily taxed. ●これらの物には税金がかからない These things are *tax-free* [*free of tax*] (↔taxable). ▶税金で収入の半分がなくなる I lose half my income *in tax*./Half my income goes *in tax*. ▶その税金(=課税)は私には大きな負担でした The *tax levy* was a great burden for me. ▶私の月給は税金を差し引いて(=税引きで)30万円です My salary is 300,000 yen *after tax*.
●税金泥棒 a tax parasite; a parasite on taxes.

せいく 成句 [慣用句] an idiom, a set phrase. (⇒熟語)

せいくうけん 制空権 ●制空権を握る take (↔lose) command of the air [air supremacy]; command the air.

せいくらべ 背比べ ●背比べをする measure [compare] one's height (*with* him).

せいけい 生計 a living, a livelihood /láivlihùd/. (❗ともに通例単数形で用いる (⇒生活)) ●教師として生計を立てる earn [make, gain] one's [a] *living by teaching* [*as a teacher*]. ●地道にかせいで[そこそこに]生計を立てる make an honest [a *moderate*] *living*. ●彼らは生計の道を断たれた(=奪われた) They were deprived of their *living* [*livelihood*]. (❗複数形にしない)
[会話]「彼は何をして生計を立てているの」「銀行員だったんだけど, 今は独立して商売をしてるよ」"What does he do *for a living*?" "He was a bank clerk. But now he's in business on his own."
●生計費 the cost of living; líving expènses.

せいけい 成形 图 (形を作ること) molding, 《英》moulding.
── 成形する 動 mold, 《英》mould.

せいけい 成型 图 casting.
── 成型する 動 cast. ●青銅を成型して像を作る *cast* bronze *into* a statue; *cast* a statue in bronze.

せいけい 西経 west longitude. ●西経30度 Long. 30° W. (❗longitude thirty degrees west と読む)

せいけい 政経 politics [(政治学)political science] and economics.
●政経学部 the college [faculty] of political science and economics.

せいけい 整形 ●整形手術を受ける have *plastic* [(美容の)*cosmetic*] surgery 《on one's nose》; have an *orthopedic* operation. ▶しわとり美顔整形手術

はずいぶん高くついた The face-lifting cost me a fortune.
●整形外科 plastic surgery;〖医学〗orthopedics /ɔːrθəpíːdiks/.●整形外科医 a plastic surgeon; an orthopedic specialist; an orthopedist.

***せいけつ** 清潔 图 cleanness; cleanliness /klénlinis/. (❶しばしば比喩的に用いる)
—— 清潔な 形 〖きれいな〗clean;〖きちんとしている〗neat;〖きれい好きな〗cleanly /klénli/. (⇨奇麗) ●清潔な政治 *clean* politics〖clothes〗.
—— 清潔にする 動 clean, make*... clean;（化学処理をして）cleanse /klenz/. ▶ 彼女はいつも手を清潔にしている She always *keeps* her hands *clean*.

せいけん 生検 (生体組織検査)〖医学〗a biopsy.
せいけん 政見 one's political views [opinions].
●政見を発表する state one's *political views*.●政見放送 a broadcast of political views; a political opinion broadcast.
せいけん 政権〖政治的権力〗(xa) political power;〖政府〗a government;（特にアメリカの）an administration;〖体制〗a regime.●小泉政権 the Koizumi *Government*.●ブッシュ政権 the Bush *Administration*.●連立政権 a coalition *government*.●かいらい政権 a puppet *regime*.●政権争い a struggle [a scramble] for *political power*;a *power* struggle.●政権の交替 a change of *government* [*power*, *regime*].●政権を握る〖にぎる〗come to [be in] *power*.●政権を失う fall from [go out of] *power*.●政権につかせる put (him) into *power*.●新政権を樹立する establish a new *government* [*regime*].

***せいげん** 制限 图〖ある範囲内に制限すること〗(a) restriction (*on*);〖限界,限度〗a limit (*to*);（制限するもの）(a) limitation (*on*).

① 【～制限】●生産(の)制限 *restriction* of production.●輸出制限 export *restrictions*; *restrictions* [*limitations*] *on* exports.●軍備制限(=軍縮) armament *limitations*; disarmament.●産児制限 birth *control*.●無制限に without *restriction* [*limit, limitation*]. ▶ 私は食事制限をしている I am on a *restricted* diet.

② 【制限が[は]】▶ 入場券は数に制限がある There's a *limit* to [xin] the number of (xthe) admission tickets./The admission tickets *are limited* in number. ▶ その競技の参加者に男女の制限はない The race *is open* to participants of either sex.

③ 【制限を】●輸入制限を撤廃する lift [remove] import *restrictions*.●外国貿易に制限を加える put [place, impose] *restrictions* on foreign trade; set *limits* [a *limit*] on foreign trade. ▶ 彼は年齢制限を越えていたので軍隊に入れなかった He couldn't join the army because he was over the age *limit*.

—— 制限する 動〖範囲内に制限する〗restrict;〖限界を定める〗limit.●出版の自由を制限する *restrict* [〖はまれ〗*limit*] freedom of the press.●酒の量を制限する（限られた量の酒を飲む）take a *limited* amount of alcohol;（減らす）*cut down* on drinking. ▶ 我々の活動は狭い範囲に制限されている Our activities *are restricted* within narrow limits. ▶ 彼はたばこを1日1箱[10本]に制限した He *restricted* [*limited*] himself *to* (smoking) a pack [ten cigarettes] a day.（『たばこの量は箱数で数えることが多い』）
●制限時間 time *limit* (*for*). ▶ 制限時間いっぱいだ(=時間切れだ) Time's *up*.●制限選挙 a restricted [limited] suffrage. (⇨普通選挙)●制限速度 the speed limit [restriction]. ▶ この道路の制限速度は

80 キロです The speed *limit* [*restriction*] on this road is 80 kilometers per hour./Speed *is limited* [*is restricted*] *to* 80 kilometers an hour on this road.
せいげん 税源 a source of tax revenue.
せいげん 誓言 (言葉数の多いこと)《書》verbosity. ▶ 教育の重要性については誓言を要しない We *need not dwell on* the value of education.
せいご〖魚介〗a young sea bass. (《参考》スズキの幼魚)
せいご 正誤●正誤表《書》a list of errata /iráːtə/;〖erratum の複数形で〗(表題として)《書》errata;（本などに挿入される紙片)《書》an erratum slip.●正誤問題 true-and-false questions.
せいご 生後 ▶ 生後1年2か月の赤ん坊 a fourteen-month [x- months]-old baby; a baby fourteen months old. (❶年齢は月齢でいうのが普通) ▶ その男の子は生後1週間で死んだ The baby boy died (xin) a week *after he was born* [*after his birth*].

***せいこう** 成功 图（一般に）(a) success. (❶状態は 〖U〗, 個々の事例は〖C〗);〖興行などの〗a hit.●大成功を収める He achieved *success* through hard work. (❶私は成功をお祈りします I wish you (xa) *success*./I hope you (will) *succeed*./（受験者などに）Good luck (to you)! ▶ その映画は大成功だった The film was a *big hit* [a great *success*, very *successful*]. (⇨型) ▶ 成功は99パーセントの失敗に支えられた1パーセントである Failure makes up 99 percent of every *success*.
会話「パーティーはどうだった」「おかげさまで大成功だったよ」"How did your party go off?" "*Very well*, I'm glad to say."(❶I'm glad to say the party went off *very well*.❶very well が文頭に置かれたもの)

—— 成功する 動〖人・事が〗succeed, be successful (*in*). (❶後の方が堅い言い方);〖人が〗have* success,〖話〗make* it;〖出世する〗succeed in life. (⇨出世) ▶ 彼は事業で成功する *succeed* [*make it*] in business. ▶ 彼はその実験に成功した He *succeeded* [*was successful*] *in* the experiment. ▶ 彼は新しいワクチンの発見に成功した He *succeeded in* discovering [xto discover] a new vaccine. (❶succeed は「目的を達成する」の意なので, xcan [be able to] succeed, xsucceed well などの連語では通例用いない) ▶ 彼女は女優として成功した She *succeeded* [*was a success, was successful*] as an actress./She *made* it as an actress./She was [became] a *successful* actress. ▶ 彼は一生懸命やったが成功しなかった He tried hard, but *without success* [*failed*]. ▶ 彼は今までに4回成功している He *has succeeded* four times [*has had* four *successes*] so far. (⇨图)
●成功者 a success, a successful person. (❶ xa *succeeded* person は不可)●成功談 a success story.
せいこう 生硬 (a) crudity.●生硬な訳 a *crude* translation.
せいこう 性交 (sexual) intercourse,〖医学〗coitus;《婉曲的に》love-making,《やや話》sex. (⇨セックス, 性❷)
●性交恐怖症〖医学〗coitophobia.●性交不能（男性の）impotence.
せいこう 性向 one's inclination; one's disposition.
せいこう 性行 one's disposition [character] and conduct.
せいこう 政綱 a political perform; a political pro-

せいこう 精巧 図 eláborateness. ●精巧を極めた彫刻 an *elaborate* [an *exquisite*] carving; a carving of *exquisite* workmanship.
— **精巧な** 形 (緻密(ちみつ)で美しい) exquíste; (高度で精密な) sophísticated. ●精巧な機械 an *elaborate* [a *sophisticated*] machine.
せいこう 製鋼 steel manufacture.
●製鋼所 a steel mill; a steelworks.
せいごう 整合 consistency. (⇨整合性)
せいこううどく 晴耕雨読 ●晴耕雨読の生活を送る lead a life, *working in the fields on fine days and reading* (books) *on rainy days.*
せいこうかい 聖公会 (米) the Protestant Episcopal Church, (英) the Anglican Church. (⚠ 会員は(米) an Episcopalian, (英) an Anglican) ●日本聖公会 the *Episcopal Church* of Japan.
せいごうせい 整合性 consistency. ●整合性がある be consistent ((*with*)); ●整合性に欠ける lack *consistency*; be inconsistent ((*with*)).
せいこうとうてい 西高東低 ●西高東低の気圧配置 a distribution of atmospheric pressure, in which *the high pressure area lies to the west and the low pressure area lies to the east.*
せいこうほう 正攻法 (正統的方法) an orthodox method. ●正攻法でいく use [(書) employ] an *orthodox method*; (公正に戦う) (やや話) play fair (and square) (⇨公正 图 ③). ●正攻法で(=公正に)問題を処理する deal with the problem *squarely* [*fairly*].
せいこく 正鵠 (要点) the point; (急所) a vital point.
●正鵠を射る ●正鵠を射た質問 a question that is *very much to the point.*
●正鵠を失する miss the point; be very wide of the mark.
せいこつ 整骨 — 整骨する 動 reset (his arm).
●整骨医 an osteopath /ástiəpæθ/. ●整骨療法『医学』 osteopathy /ὰstiápəθi/.
せいごびょう 正誤表 (⇨正誤)
ぜいこみ 税込み ●税込みの[で] before tax. ●税込みの値段 the price *before tax*; the price *with taxes included.* (⇨税)
せいこん 成婚 (a) marriage. (⇨結婚)
●成婚式 an Imperial marriage [wedding] ceremony.
せいこん 精根, 精魂 (精力) (an) energy /énərdʒi/; (精魂) heart and soul. ●…に精根[精魂]を傾ける devote *oneself* [all one's *energies*] to ((*it*; do*ing it*)). ▶精根が尽き果てた I am completely [absolutely] exhausted.
せいさ 性差 a sex difference; sexual distinction; a gender gap.
せいさ 精査 图 (細心の調査) a minute [a thorough, a careful] investigation; (細心の検査) a minute [a thorough, a careful] examinaiton; (精密な調査[吟味]) scrutiny.
— **精査する** 動 ●事故の原因を精査する make a minute [thorough] investigation of the cause of the accident; *investigate* the cause of the accident *minutely* [*thoroughly*].
せいざ 星座 a constellation; 『占星』the sign of the zodiac (⇨十二宮). ▶私の星座はやぎ座で血液型はB型です My *sign* is Cápricòrn [*Cápricòrnus*] and my blood type is B.
[会話]「星座は何座ですか」「しし座です」 "What is your *sign of the Zodiac*?" "Mine is Leo./I am a Leo."
●星座表 a star map [chart].

せいざ 正座 — 正座する 動 sit on the floor (in) Japanese style; (説明的に) sit up straight with one's legs folded underneath.
せいさい 正妻 one's legal [lawful] wife.
せいさい 生彩 life. ●生彩を欠く lack *life*; be lifeless; be dull. ●生彩を放つ be lively; be full of *life*.
せいさい 制裁 『国際間の』『書』a sanction (⚠ しばしば複数形で); 『処罰』(a) punishment. ●その国に経済制裁を加える impose economic *sanctions* against the country. ●制裁を解除する lift *sanctions*. ●社会的制裁を十分に受ける suffer severe social *punishment*.
せいさい 精彩 ●精彩を放つ(=目立ってすぐれている) be remarkable; be outstanding. ▶松井のバットは精彩を欠いていた Matsui's batting was regrettably poor [struggling at the plate].
せいさい 精細 图 minuteness.
— **精細な** 形 ●精細な調査 a *minute* [(徹底的な) *thorough*; (入念な) *careful*] investigation.
— **精細に** 副 ●…を精細に調べる investigate … *minutely* [*thoroughly*].
せいざい 製材 图 sawing.
— **製材する** 動 ●丸太を製材する saw [cut] up a log into lumber.
●製材業 the sáwing índustry; (米) lumbering.
●製材所 a sawmill; (米) a lumbermill.
せいざい 製剤 ●血液製剤 blood products.
●製剤会社 a pharmaceutical company.
***せいさく** 政策 (a) policy ((*toward, on*; *to do*)).
① (〜政策) ●日本の対中国[その問題に関する]政策 Japan's *policy toward* China [*on* that matter]. ●経済[金融; 外交]政策 an economic [a financial; a foreign] *policy*. ●長期[短期]的政策 a long-[a short-]term *policy*.
② (政策を[に]) ●保護貿易政策を採る[実行する] adopt [carry out] a protective trade *policy*. ●新しい産業政策を立てる shape [formulate] a new industrial *policy*. ●政策を引き継ぐ take over [succeed] the *policy*. ▶産業を国有化するという政府の政策には同意できない[従わなければならない] We don't agree with [must follow] the government('s) *policy to* nationalize industries.
●政策協定 a policy agreement. ●政策決定 a policy decision. ●政策綱領 a (policy) platform. ●政策立案 policymaking. ●政策論争 a policy argument.
せいさく 制作 图 production. ●映画[ビデオ]制作 film [video] *production*.
— **制作する** 動 ●芸術作品[テレビ番組]を制作する produce a work of art [a TV program].
●制作者 a producer. ●その映画の制作者 the producer of the film. ●制作費 (high) production costs.
せいさく 製作 图 『生産』production; 『大規模な』manufacture. (⇨製造)
— **製作する** 動 (作る) make (⚠ 一般的な語); (製造する) manufacture. ●家具を製作する *make* [(工場で大規模に) *manufacture*] furniture.
せいさつよだつ 生殺与奪 ●生殺与奪の権を握る have absolute control [power] ((*over* him)); have (his) life in one's hands.
:**せいさん** 生産 图 production.
① (〜生産) ●大量生産 mass *production*. ●食料生産 food *production*. ●受注生産 *production* by order. ●海外[現地]生産 overseas [local] *production*. ●再生産 reproduction. ●国内総生産 the gross domestic *product* ((略 GDP)).

せいさん

②【生産〜】 ●生産性を向上させる increase productivity. ▶中国は世界一の小麦生産国である China is the largest wheat-*producing* country [wheat *producer*] in the world./China *produces* the largest amount of wheat in the world.

③【生産を】 ▶ 生産を高める［ふやす］increase [boost, 《やや書》step up] *production*. ●生産を削減する cut back (on) *production*.

④【生産が［は］】 ▶鉄鋼生産が10パーセント落ちた［伸びた］ Steel *production* has fallen [increased] by 10 percent. ▶その新しい機械の生産は来月から始まる *Production* of the new machine will start next month./The new machine will *go into production* (↔ go out of production) next month. ▶生産が需要に追いつかない *Production* has not kept with demand.

—— 生産的な 形 productive (↔ unproductive).
—— 生産する 動 produce; (手作りの так) (大量に機械で) manufacture. ▶この工場では小型車を生産している This factory *produces* [*manufactures*] compact cars.

●生産過剰 overproduction. ●生産管理 production control. ●生産効率 production efficiency. ●生産コスト production [manufacturing] costs. ●生産施設 production facilities. ●生産者 (⇨生産者) ●生産手段 a means of production. ●生産高 (総生産量) production; (単位・期間あたりの) (an) output (❗通例単数形で); (農作物の) a yield (❗通例単数形で). ●生産地 a producing district. ●生産調整 production adjustment. ●生産物 (主に工業製品の) products; (農作物の)《集合的》produce. ●生産ライン a production line. ●生産力 production [producing] capacity.

せいさん 正餐 (a) dinner. (⇨夕食)
せいさん 成算 （成功する見通し）hope of success. ▶成算はまったくない There is no *hope of success*. ▶成算があるのか Are you *sure of success* [*sure* (*that*) you can *make it*]? (❗ make it は「成功する」の意)

せいさん 凄惨 —— 凄惨な 形 （身の毛のよだつ）gruesome, spine-chilling; (ぞっとする) frightful; (恐ろしい) dreadful.

せいさん 清算 图 （破産者の）liquidation; (小切手・手形などの) clearing.
—— 清算する 動 （会社を）liquidate /líkwidèit/《the company》; （完済する）pay off [liquidate] 《a debt》. ▶その会社を清算する *liquidate* the company; *put* the company *into liquidation*. ●過去を清算する bury [liquidate] one's past. ●彼女との関係を清算する end [break off] one's relationship with her.
●清算会社 a company in liquidation. ●清算人 a liquidator.

せいさん 精算 图 adjustment. ●運賃精算所 a fare *adjustment* office. (❗窓口での掲示は FARE ADJUSTMENT)
—— 精算する 動 （差額を）adjust; （勘定・借金などを）settle ... (up). ▶改札口で精算する pay the *adjusted* fare at the ticket barrier. ▶勘定を精算する *settle* one's account. ▶今は私が払っておく。後で精算しよう I'll pay it now and you can *settle with me* [*pay me back*] later.

せいさんかっけい 正三角形 an equilateral triangle. (⇨三角)
せいさんカリ 青酸カリ 【化学】(シアン化カリウム) potassium cyanide /sáiənàid/; (シアン化物) cyanide.

せいさんしき 聖餐式 (Holy) Communion.
せいさんしゃ 生産者 a producer (↔ a consumer); (作る人, 製造会社) a maker; (大規模な製造業者・会社) a manufacturer.
●生産者価格［物価］a producer(s') price. ●生産者物価指数 a producer price index (略 PPI). ●生産者米価 a producer(s') rice price; a producer(s') price of rice.

せいし 正史 （政府で編集した史書）an official [(公認された) an authorized] history.
せいし 正使 （中心となる使者）a chief envoy. (㊑ 副使)
せいし 正視 —— 正視する 動 look (straight) 《at him》. ▶私は母の顔が正視できなかった I could not *look* my mother *in* [xat] the face (❗ the に注意。「目をまともに見る」は look ... in the eye(s)). ▶その現場は正視するに堪えなかった We could not bear to look at that scene.

せいし 生死 【生と死】life and [or] death. ●生死にかかわる問題 a matter of *life* and [*or*] *death*. ●生死 (=生き残り) がかかっている状態 a *survival* situation. ●生死の境をさまよう hover between *life and death*. ▶彼は生死不明だ It is unknown whether he's *alive or dead* [*or not*].

せいし 制止 —— 制止する 動 【止める】stop 《him, a quarrel》; 【前進させない】keep [hold] 《the crowd》back. (⇨止(ど)める ❹)
せいし 姓氏 one's family name. (⇨名字)
せいし 精子 【生理】a sperm (複 ~s). (❗集合体は Ⓤ)
●精子銀行 a sperm bank.
せいし 製糸 【紡績】spinning; (生糸の巻き取り) silk reeling.
●製糸業 the spinning industry; the silk industry. ●製糸業者 a silk manufacturer.
せいし 製紙 paper manufacturing, papermaking.
●製紙会社 a paper manufacturing [a papermaking] company. ●製紙業 the paper industry. ●製紙工場 a paper mill.
せいし 誓詞 an oath; (誓約) a pledge.
せいし 静止 —— 静止する 動 come to rest [a standstill]. ●静止している (じっと立っている) stand *still*; (動かないでいる) 《やや書》remain *stationary*, (休止している) be *at rest*.
●静止衛星 a stationary satellite. ●静止画像 a still frame. ●静止軌道 a stationary orbit.

‡**せいじ** 政治 图 politics (❗単・複両扱い); (統治, 行政) government. ●官僚［議会；民主］政治 bureaucratic [parliamentary; democratic] *government*. ●政党［地方］政治 party [local] *politics*. ●国際政治 international *politics*. ●独裁政治 dictatorship; dictatorial *government*; despotism. ●政治に無関心である be indifferent to [not interested in] *politics*; be apolitical [nonpolitical]. ●政治 (=国事) をつかさどる administer the affairs of state. ●政治を論じる talk [discuss] *politics*. ▶政治には国民の意見が大切だ Public opinion is important in *politics*. ▶政治の貧困は大きな社会問題である Lack of *political* ingenuity is a big social problem.

—— 政治(の) 形 political. ●政治的手腕 *political* ability; statesmanship; (外交の) diplomacy. ●政治的解決 a *political* solution. ▶彼は何の政治的意見も持たない He has no *politics* [*political opinions*]. (❗ politics はこの意では常に複数形扱い)
—— 政治的に 副 politically. ▶両国間の問題は政治的に決着を見た The problems between the two countries were solved [were settled, were resolved] *politically*.

- 政治意識 political awareness. (❗「政治意識が発達している」は be politically aware [minded])
- 政治運動 a political movement [campaign].
- 政治家 (⇨政治家) ● 政治改革 a political reform [reformation]. ● 政治学 politics (❗単数扱い); political science. ● 政治活動 political activities. ● 政治機構 (a) political structure. ● 政治経済 politics and economics. ● 政治経済学 political economy. ● 政治経済学部 the college [faculty] of political science and economics. ● 政治結社 a political organization [group]. ● 政治献金 a political donation [contribution]. ● 政治資金 a political fund. ● 政治資金規制法 the Political Fund Control Law.
- 政治情勢 the political situation. ● 政治生命 one's political career [life]. ● 政治責任 one's political responsibility. ● 政治団体 a political organization [group]. ● 政治犯 a political offender [prisoner]. ● 政治不信 a distrust of politics. ● 政治面 (新聞の) the political page(s) (of a newspaper). ● 政治問題 (解決が必要な) a political problem; (争点としての) a political issue. ● 政治屋 a politician. (⇨政治家) ● 政治力 political influence 《on, over》. ● 政治倫理 political ethics.

せいじ 青磁 celadon (porcelain).

セイシェル [[国名]] Seychelles /seiʃélz/; (公式名) the Republic of Seychelles. (首都 Victoria) ● セイシェル人 a Seychellois. ● セイシェル(人)の Seychellois.

せいじか 政治家 a politician; a statesman (複 -men), (女性) a stateswoman (複 -women).

> 解説 politician は《米》では「政治屋」という悪い意味で用いることが多い. statesman は《米》《英》とも「立派な政治家」という意味で用い,《英》では特に下院議員のことを politician, 閣僚などの重要ポストにいる政治家を statesman と呼ぶことがあるが, 性差別的な - man を避けて a political leader の方を好む人が多い.

- 政治家になる go into [enter] politics; become a politician. ▶ 彼はまともな政治家で, 自分の政治力をもって私腹を肥やすような政治屋ではない He is a respectable statesman, not the kind of politician to take advantage of his political influence and line his own pocket.

*__せいしき__ 正式 — 正式の, 正式な 形 (形式にかなった) formal; (正規の) regular; (公式の) official; (合法的な) legal; (適切な) proper. ● 正式の決定 a formal decision. ● 正式の手続きを踏む go through the regular procedure. ● ナイフとフォークの正式な使い方 the proper way to use knife and fork.

—— 正式に 副 formally; regularly; officially; legally; properly. ● 新政府を正式に承認する formally [officially] recognize the new government. ● 正式に結婚している be legally [officially] married. ● 正式に訪問する pay an official [a formal] visit 《to》. ▶ 彼は正式に大統領選出馬を表明した He formally [officially] announced his candidacy for the presidential election. ▶ 彼は入国を正式に認められた He was officially admitted into the country.

*__せいしつ__ 性質 ❶【人の】(生まれつきの) (a) nature; (行動・感情の一般的傾向の) (a) disposition; (感情の面から見た) (a) temper; (行動・考え方を方向づけるもの)《やや書》(a) temperament; (性格) (a) personality, (a) character (⇨性格). ▶ 彼の性質はやさしい He has a gentle nature./He is a man of 《×with》 gentle nature. (❗後の方が堅い言い方)/He is gentle 《by nature》. ▶ 彼は陽気な[すぐかっとなる; 神経質な]性質だ He has a cheerful disposition [a quick temper; a nervous temperament]. ▶ 彼女は他人の悪口の言えない性質だ It's not in [It's against] her nature to say bad things about other people. (⇨性分)

❷【物の】(本来の) (a) nature; (固有の) a property. ● 原子の性質 the nature of the atom. ● さびない性質の金属 a metal with rustproof properties. ▶ 私は仕事の性質上よく海外へ行く The nature [character] of my job requires me to go abroad quite often. ▶ 砂糖には水に溶ける性質がある Sugar has the property of dissolving 《×melting》 in water. (❗つづり字に注意. ×disolving としない)

せいしつ 正室 one's legal [lawful] wife.
せいしつ 声質 ● 澄んだ声質をしている have a clear voice.

*__せいじつ__ 誠実 图 (うそ・偽り・ごまかしのないこと) honesty; (裏表がないこと) sincerity /sinsérəti/; (信念をつらぬくこと) integrity. ● 芸術家としての誠実さ artistic honesty [integrity]. ▶ 彼女は誠実さに欠ける She lacks sincerity.

—— 誠実な 形 sincere /sinsíər/; honest; (忠実な) true (↔false). ▶ 誠実な人 a sincere [an honest] person; a person of integrity. ▶ 彼は恋人に対して誠実ではなかった He was not true [was untrue] to his girlfriend.

—— 誠実に 副 誠実に生きる lead an honest life; live honestly. ● 誠実に義務[職務]を果たす do one's duties faithfully [in good faith]. ▶ 彼は生徒に対して誠実に対処する He is honest with his students.

せいじほう 正字法《書》orthography.
せいじゃ 正邪 right and wrong. (⇨善し悪し)
せいじゃ 聖者 a saint /séint/.
せいじゃく 静寂 quiet(ness); stillness; silence; (騒がしさのあとの) (a) hush. (⇨静けさ)
ぜいじゃく 脆弱 —— 脆弱な 形 (体質的に) weak, frail, fragile /frǽdʒəl/; (精神的に)《やや書》vulnerable.
- 脆弱性 vùlnerabílity.
せいしゅ 清酒 refined sake.
せいじゅう 成獣 an adult animal; a fully-grown animal.
ぜいしゅう 税収 (tax) revenue. ● 税収不足 a shortfall [shortage] in 《tax》 revenue. (❗新聞などでは前の方が多く用いられる)
せいしゅく 静粛 图 quiet.

—— 静粛な 形 quiet; (声を出さない) silent; (動かない) still. (⇨静か) ● 静粛にする keep 《be》 quiet. ▶ 演奏中の部屋は静粛そのものだった The room was perfectly quiet during the performance. ▶ 静粛に願います (Be) quiet, please. /(裁判長などの注意) Order! ▶ 議長は「静粛に」と言った The chairperson called the committee to order. (❗call ... to order は議長が開会を宣言して「静粛を命じる」こと)/"Silence!" thundered the chairperson. (❗thunder は「大声で言う」の意)

せいじゅく 成熟 图 maturity /mətúərəti/; ripeness. (❗前の方が成熟する過程に重点がある)

—— 成熟した 形 (動植物・果物などが) mature; (果物などが) ripe; (人が) adult. ● 成熟したリンゴ ripe apples.

—— 成熟する 動 mature, become mature; ripen, become ripe.

せいしゅん 青春 (青年期)(one's) youth; (子供と大人の中間期) adoléscence (🚹 17-8 歳ぐらいの青春時代への入口にある若者を含む). ●青春(時代)の young; adolescent. ▶私の青春も過ぎ去ってしまった I am past my *youth*. ▶彼女は青春のまっただ中にいる She is in the middle of her *youth*. ▶彼は青春時代に多くの経験をした He had a lot of experiences *when he was young./In* (his) *youth*, he had a lot of experiences. (🚹 後の方は堅い言い方)

せいじゅん 清純 (清らかさ) purity.
── **清純な** 形 pure. ●清純(無垢)な乙女 a *pure* (and innocent) young girl.

*__せいしょ__ the (Holy) Bible (🚹 (1) 日常的には単に the Bible. (2)「1 冊の聖書」の意では a Bible とする: 彼は聖書を1冊持っている He has *a* Bible.); Scripture (🚹 新約と旧約の両方または一方をさす. the (Holy) Scriptures ともいう). ●新約[旧約]聖書 the New [Old] Testament. 欽定(訳)訳聖書 the Authorized Version《略 AV》. ●聖書の文句 a *biblical* expression. ●聖書には…と書いてある The *Bible* says [tells] that ….

せいしょ 清書 ── **清書する** 動 make a clean copy 《*of*》.

せいじょ 聖女 a saint; a saintly [(聖人らしい)a saintlike, (高徳な) a holy] woman.

せいじょ 整除 【数学】(割り切れること) divisibility. ▶ 21 は 7 で整除できる 21 *is divisible* by 7. / 21 *can be divided* by 7.

せいしょう 正賞 the main prize. (⇔副賞)

せいしょう 斉唱 ●斉唱する sing in unison.

せいしょう 政商 a businessman with political contacts.

せいしょう 清祥 ▶ますますご清祥の段お喜び申し上げます I'm glad to hear (that) *you are better and are living a happier life*.

せいじょう 正常 图 normality, 《米》normalcy; [正気] sanity.
── **正常な** 形 normal (↔abnormal). ●正常な行動 *normal* behavior. ●正常に作動する work *normally*. ▶列車の運行は正常に戻った Train services are now back to *normal* [*normal* conditions]. (🚹 前の normal は名詞) ▶思春期の若者が親の権威にいどむのは正常である It is *normal* for the adolescent to challenge parental authority. ▶彼女が正常であることは疑いない His *sanity* is beyond doubt. ●正常運転 normal operation. ●正常化 normalization. ●外交関係を正常化する *normalize* diplomatic relations 《*between, with*》.

せいじょう 性状 ❶ 【ものの性質と状態】(特性) a property. (🚹 通例複数形で) ●金属の性状 the *properties* of metal. ❷ 【人の性質と行状】●変わった性状の持ち主 a person of a peculiar *character*.

せいじょう 性状 (生まれつきの性質) (a) nature; (その人の行動を決定する生来的な性質) (a) disposition; (性格) (a) character.

せいじょう 政情 ●アメリカの政情に通じている be familiar [《書》well-acquainted] with the *political situation* in America. ●不安定な政情 unstable [uncertain] *political situation*. ●政情不安 *political* unrest. ●日本の政情を安定させる make stable the *political situation* [*状態*) *conditions*] in Japan.

せいじょう 清浄 cleanness. ●清浄な空気 *clean* air. ●空気清浄器 an air *purifier*.
● **清浄野菜** clean vegetables.

せいじょうき 星条旗 the Stars and Stripes (🚹 単数扱い), the Star-Spangled Banner (🚹 大げさな言い方),《愛称》the Old Glory.

せいじょうきよえいえんなれ『星条旗よ永遠なれ』 *The Stars and Stripes Forever*. [参考] スーザ作曲の行進曲

せいしょうねん 青少年 young people.(⇨青年)
●青少年犯罪 juvenile delinquency.

せいしょく 生色 (いきいきとした顔色) a fresh [(健康そうな) a healthy] complexion; (元気のよい様子) a lively look. ●生色がない look pale. ●生色を失う turn [go] pale.

せいしょく 生殖 [繁殖] reproduction; [発生] generation; [出産] [書] procreation.
── **生殖する** 動 reproduce; generate.
● **生殖期** a period of reproduction. ● **生殖器** the reproductive [generative, sex] organs; the genitals (🚹 特に外部に見える部分をさす). ● **生殖細胞** [生物] a reproductive [a generative] cell.

せいしょく 聖職 (神聖な職業) a sacred profession; (天職) a vocation. ●聖職につく (牧師になる) take holy orders. ●聖職に叙せられる (神父になる) be ordained. ▶教職は聖職であると主張する人もいる Some people maintain that teaching profession is *sacred*.
●聖職者 a priest; a clergyman (⇨牧師).

せいしょほう 正書法 [書] orthography.

*__せいしん__ 精神 图 (心) (a) spirit (🚹 肉体 (flesh) に対する語で知力を強調しない); (知力) (a) mind (🚹 物質 (matter) に対する語で、知的・理性的な心); (魂) (a) soul (🚹 肉体 (body) に対する語); (意志) (a) will; (注意力) attention; (精神状態) mentality. (⇨心)
❶【~(の)精神】●時代精神 the *spirit* of the age. ●憲法の精神を尊重する respect the *spirit* of the Constitution. ●独立の精神に富んでいる be rich in the *spirit* of independence.
❷【精神〜】●5歳の精神年齢をしている have a *mental* age of five. ●精神異常をきたしている be out of one's *mind*; be *mentally* ill [disturbed]; be insane. ●精神修養 [鍛練] をする cultivate [train] one's *mind*. ▶その学生はその科目を修了するだけの精神力がなかった The student lacked the *mental* vigor [*spiritual* strength] to complete the course. ▶彼女は精神面で成長した She has grown up [has matured] *emotionally*. ▶それは精神衛生上悪い That has a bad effect on your *mental* health.
❸【精神は】●健全なる精神は健全なる身体に宿る (⇨健全 [成句])
❹【精神を】●彼はその仕事に全精神を打ち込んだ He put his *heart and soul* into the work./(全身全霊を) He devoted himself *heart and soul* to the work./He did the work *heart and soul*. (🚹 後の二つの例の heart and soul (全身全霊を込めて) は副詞句) ▶もっと勉強に精神を集中しなさい Concentrate [Focus] more *attention* on your studies. ▶彼は精神を入れ替えた (= 改心して生活を一新した) He turned over a new leaf./(新しい出発をした) He made a fresh start.
●精神一到何事か成らざらん《ことわざ》《話》Where's a will there's a way. (🚹 英語と日本語の文体の違いに注意)
── **精神的(な)** 形 spiritual (↔material); mental (↔physical); (道徳的な) moral; (感情的な) emotional. ●精神的な指導者 a *spiritual* leader. ●精神的成長 *mental* development. ●患者の精神的な状態 the *emotional* state of a patient. ●精神的な生活を送る lead a *spiritual* life. ●精神的疲労で苦しむ suffer from *mental* fatigue. ●精神的ショックを受ける experience an *emotional* shock. ●精神的動揺を静める suppress an *emotional* disturbance

[upset]. ●精神的勝利を得る win a *moral* victory.（❗実際は敗北したが自分の正しさは認められたという意味の勝利）

——**精神的に** 副 spiritually; mentally; morally; emotionally. ●精神的に支援する give ⦅*him*⦆ *moral* support; support ⦅*him*⦆ *morally*. ▶彼女は肉体的にも精神的にも疲れきっている She is physically and *mentally* tired [worn] out.

●精神安定剤 (a) tranquilizer. ●精神医学 psychiatry. ●精神科 psychiatry. ●精神科医 a psychiatrist /sáikiətrist/; a mental specialist;⦅話⦆a shrink. ●精神鑑定 a psychiatric /sàikiætrik/ test. ●精神構造 one's psychological [mental] makeup. ●精神主義⦅論⦆ mentalism; spiritualism. ●精神障害 a mental disorder. ●精神薄弱 mental deficiency;（人）a mental defective. ●精神薄弱児 a mentally retarded [handicapped] child. ●精神病 a mental illness [disease]. ●精神病院 a mental hospital [home, institution]. ●精神病患者 a mental patient. ●精神病質 psychopathy. ●精神分析 psychoanalysis /sàikouənǽləsis/. ●精神分析医 a psychoanalyst. ●精神分裂症⦅医学⦆ schizophrenia. ⦅参考⦆現在は「統合失調症」という. ●精神療法 psychotherapy.

せいしん 西進 —— **西進する** 動 move west(ward).
せいしん 清新 —— **清新な** 形 new, fresh.（⇨新しい, 新鮮な）
せいじん 成人 图 an adult,⦅話⦆a grown-up;（男性）a man ⦅複 men⦆,（女性）a woman ⦅women⦆.（⇨大人）

> 使い分け adult 法律上成年に達した者. 通例⦅英⦆では18歳以上,⦅米⦆でも18歳以上だが一部の州では21歳以上.
> grown-up 子供に対して成人の意で adult のくだけた語として用いられる.

▶彼はもう立派な成人だ He's a *fully-grown man*.
——**成人する** 動 come of age（❗法律上の成人年齢に達すること）; reach [grow to] manhood [womanhood];（大人になる）grow up. ▶彼は成人して偉大な学者になった He *grew up into* [to be] a great scholar. ▶彼には成人した娘が2人ある He has two *grown-up* daughters.
●成人映画 an adult movie [⦅英⦆film]; an X (-rated) film. ●成人教育 adult education,⦅米⦆continuing education,⦅英⦆further education. ●成人式 a coming-of-age ceremony. ●成人の日 Coming-of-Age [×Adults'] Day. ●成人病 an adult disease.

せいじん 聖人 a saint. ●聖人にふさわしい生涯 a *saintly* life. ●聖人ぶる play the *saint*.
せいしんせいい 誠心誠意（= 真心を込めて）その件に当たる deal with the matter *wholeheartedly*;（解決に最善を尽くす）do one's very best to solve the matter.
せいず 星図⦅天文⦆ a star chart.
せいず 製図 图⦅設計図などの下書き⦆drafting;⦅図を引くこと⦆drawing; cartography.
——**製図する** 動 draft⦅a plan⦆; draw⦅a plan⦆.
●製図家 a draftsman（❗性別をなくして a draftsperson などともいう）;（地図の）a cartographer. ●製図機 a dráfting machìne. ●製図器械 a dráfting [a dráwing] instrument. ●製図板 a dráfting [a dráwing] bòard.（❗これなどれは a ~ easel)
せいすい 盛衰 the rise and fall,（人生の）(one's) ups and downs. ●ローマ帝国の盛衰 *the rise and fall*

of the Roman Empire.
せいずい 精髄 ●文学の精髄（=真髄）the *essence* [⦅書⦆*quintessence*] of literature.（⇨本質）
せいすう 整数⦅数学⦆an integral number; an integer.
せいする 制する（抑える）suppress, put*... down（❗後の方が口語的）;（支配する）control (-ll-). ●暴動を制する *suppress* [*put down*] a riot. ●過半数を制する *get* a majority.
せいせい 生成 图（創造）creation;（形成）formation. ●宇宙の生成 the *creation* of the universe.
——**生成する** 動 create; form.
●生成文法⦅言語⦆ generative grammar.
せいせい 製鋼 refining. ●石油精製所 an oil refinery.
——**精製する** 動 refine. ●原油[砂糖]を精製する *refine* crude oil [sugar].
せいせい 清々 —— **清々する** 動（うれしい）be glad;（ほっとする）feel relieved. ▶彼がやっといなくなってせいせいした I *am glad* (that) he's gone at last./⦅話⦆He's gone at last, and *good riddance* (*to* him)!（❗*riddance* は「厄介払い」の意）▶試験が終わってせいせいした I *feel relieved* now (that) the exams are over.（❗この場合の that は⦅英⦆では通例省略される）/The exams are over. What a *relief*!
せいぜい 精々 ❶⦅できるだけ⦆●せいぜいがんばる work *as hard as possible* [*as hard as one can*];（せいぜい努力する）make *every* (*possible*) *effort*⦅*to do*⦆;（最善を尽くす）do one's *best*⦅*to do*⦆. ▶家族旅行なんて何年ぶりかな. せいせい楽しまなくっちゃ How many years ago was it that we took a family trip, I wonder? Let's *make the most of it*.（❗「最大限に利用する」の意）❷⦅たかだか⦆（よくみても）at best;（多くて）at (the) most, not more than ...;（長くても）at (the) longest. ●せいぜい10日 ten days *at* (*the*) *longest*. ▶せいぜい去年の半分しかできないだろう *At best* we will be able to do only half as much as last year. ▶彼女はせいぜい15歳くらいだ She's about fifteen *at* (*the*) *most*./She's *not more than* [*barely*] fifteen or so. I *barely* は「かろうじて」の意）▶彼の知恵もせいぜいそのくらいだろう That's the *extent* of his wisdom. ▶君の力になりたいが, 今すぐにということなら私に出せるのはせいぜい100万円だ I want to help you, but if it must be right now, then one million yen is *the best* I can do.

ぜいせい 税制 a taxátion [a táx] sýstem; a system of taxation. ●税制面で有利[不利]な点 a *tax* advantage [disadvantage].
●税制改革 a tax reform. ●税制年度 tax year. ⦅参考⦆米国では1月1日, 英国では4月6日に新年度が始まる)
ぜいぜい ●ぜいぜいいう wheeze. ▶彼は冬になるとぜいぜいい始める He begins to *wheeze* in winter.
せいせいどうどう 正々堂々（公明正大に）fair (and square);（反則をしない）clean. ▶正々堂々戦うことを誓います We swear to play *fair* (*and square*).
せいせいるてん 生々流転（すべてのものはたえず変化する）All things are in a state of flux.
*__**せいせき** 成績⦅試験などの結果⦆a result（❗通例複数形で）;⦅評価⦆⦅主に米⦆a grade;⦅主に英⦆a mark（❗A（優）・B（良上）・C（良）・D（可）・F（不可）の5段階, または点数で示す）.⦅成績記録⦆a school record.
①¦**成績は**[が]¦ ▶私の理科の成績は不可だった My *grade* in [for] science was an F./I got an F [an F *grade*, a *grade* F] in [for] science. ▶今学期私の成績が上がった[下がった] My *grades* have

improved [fallen, dropped] this term. ▶彼女は学校の成績がいい She *is doing well* (↔*poorly, badly*) *in school./*She has a good school *record.*/(優秀な生徒である) She's an excellent student. ▶会社の成績(=業績)は良好だ The firm *is doing well* [*doing good business*]. (⚠ ×make good business とはいわない) ▶当社の販売成績は落ちてきた Our sales *record* is falling [*suffering*].
会話 「きのうの試験の成績が発表されたんだ」「どうだった？」 "The exam *results* were announced yesterday.*/*(もらった) I got my exam *results* yesterday." "How did you do?"

②《成績を[で]》●生徒の成績をつける *grade* students. ▶我々は期待したような成績をあげられなかった We couldn't achieve [《やや書》obtain] the expected *results*. ▶私は試験でいい成績をとった I got [×took] high *grades* [*marks*] on the exam. (⚠ good grades [marks] ともいう。「悪い成績」は bad [poor, low] grades [marks]。「いい成績で試験に受かった」は I passed the exam with very good *grades* [*marks*].) ▶彼は英語で90点の成績をとった He got [×took] a *grade* of 90 《米》[90 *marks* 《英》] in English. (⇒点 ❷) ▶私たちは高校時代成績を競った We competed with each other for good *grades* while in high school. ▶彼はテニスの試合で3対2の成績で勝った He gained a 3-2 [three to two] *record* in the tennis match. ▶静香はフィギュアスケートで好成績を残した Shizuka made an excellent *record* in figure skating.

●成績証明書 a transcript (of academic record). ●成績表《米》a report (card);《英》a (school) report. (類語 米英では通例郵送される)

せいせき 聖跡 a sacred [a holy] place of historic interest.

せいぜつ 凄絶 ●凄絶な戦い an *extremely fierce* battle.

せいせっかい 生石灰〔化学〕calcium oxide; burnt [caustic] lime.

せいせん 聖戦 a holy war; (宗教上の) a crusade; (イスラム教の) a jihad.

せいせん 精選〖慎重に選ぶこと〗careful selection. ●果物の精選品(=極上の果物)《書》*choice* fruits; fruits of the finest quality.

── **精選する 動** ●材料を精選する *select* [*pick out*] materials *carefully*. ●精選した収集美術品 a *carefully selected* collection of art objects.

せいぜん 生前 ●生前の[に] in one's lifetime; while (one was) alive; before one's death. ●生前の意志により in accordance with《his》wishes. ▶彼は生前すでに伝説的人物になっていた He was a legend *in his lifetime*.

●生前贈与〔法律〕a gift inter vivos /ɪntərviː-voʊs/.

せいぜん 整然 ── **整然とした 形**〖秩序ある〗orderly, well-ordered;〖きちんとした〗neat. ●整然と1列に並んで立ち上がる line up in *an orderly manner*《*way*》. ●整然とした街並みの住宅地区 a residential district with *straight* streets. ▶書類は机の上に整然とあった The papers were *neat* and *orderly* on the desk. ▶芝生は整然と(=均一にきちんと)刈りそろえられていた The lawn was *uniformly* trimmed.

せいせんしょくひん 生鮮食品 〖新鮮な食品〗fresh food [×foods];〖傷みやすい食品〗perishable food, perishables.

せいぜんせつ 性善説 the view that humans are born good. (対 性悪説)

せいそ 清楚 ── **清楚な 形** 〖きちんとして清潔な〗 neat and clean. ●清楚な身なりをしている be *neatly*

dressed.

せいそう 正装 名 full [formal] dress. ●正装して in *full* [*formal*] *dress* 〖書〗*attire*. ●正装用のくつ *dress* shoes. ▶正装無用《招待状の文句》Don't *dress up*.

── **正装する 動** dress (oneself) up; (状態) be dressed up;《書》be formally attired《in black》.

せいそう 政争 a political issue;《やや書》political strife. ●税制改革を政争の具にする make a *political issue* of a tax reform.

せいそう 星霜 ●幾星霜を経て after a lapse of *many years*. ▶幾星霜を重ねる(=何年もたつ) *Many years* have passed.

せいそう 凄愴 ●凄愴たる光景 a *desolate* scene.

せいそう 清掃 名 cleaning. (⇒掃除)

── **清掃する 動** clean (up). ●道路を清掃する *clean* a street; (ほうきなどで掃いて) *sweep* a street *clean*. ●清掃工場 a garbage incineration plant. (⚠ incineration は「焼却」の意) ●清掃作業員《米》a garbage person [collector],《英》a dustman. (⚠《米》では婉曲的に a sanitation worker ともいう) ●清掃車《米》a gárbage trùck,《英》a dustcart.

せいそう 盛装 ●盛装している be in one's best clothes; be dressed up to the nines (*in* a Chanel suit). (⇒着飾る)

せいそう 精巣〔解剖〕(睾丸) a testis /téstɪs/ (複 testes /-tiːz/).

***せいぞう 製造 名** 〖大規模な〗manufacture;〖生産〗production. (⇒生産) ●自動車[武器]の製造 the *production* of automobiles [arms]. ▶彼は靴の製造に従事している He is engaged in the *manufacture* of shoes./(靴の製造業者だ) He is a shoe [×shoes] manufacturer. (⚠ shoemaker (靴屋)とは違い，大規模に製造する工場経営者のこと)

── **製造する 動** (原materials から大規模に) manufacture (⚠ make より堅い語); (商品を大量に) produce; (作る) make*. ▶多くの会社が海外で商品を製造し始めた A good number of companies have begun to *manufacture* goods abroad. ▶あの工場は月1万台のテレビを製造している That factory *produces* 10,000 television sets a month.

●製造業 a manufacturing industry. ●製造業者 a manufacturer; a producer; a maker. ●製造コスト[原価] manufacturing [production] cost(s). ●製造番号 a serial number. ●製造品 manufactured goods. ●製造物責任 product(s) liability (略 PL). ●製造物責任法 Product Liability Law. (⚠ ×PL Law は不可)

せいぞう 聖像 a sacred image [portrait]; (ギリシャ正教の) an icon.

せいそうけん 成層圏〔気象〕the strátosphere. ●(ロケットが)成層圏を突破する fly through *the stratosphere*.

●成層圏飛行 stratosphere [(成層圏の) stratospheric] flying.

せいそく 正則 a regular system [method].

●正則関数〔数学〕a regular function.

せいそく 生息 ●トラの生息地 the tiger's (natural) hábitat; the *habitat* of tigers.

── **生息する 動** ▶トラがこの森に生息している Tigers *live* in [《書》*inhabit*] this forest.

●生息動物 an inhabitant.

せいぞろい 勢揃い ── **勢揃いする 動** (整列する) line up; (多くの人が集まる) get [meet] together.

***せいぞん 生存 名** existence;〖生命〗life;〖生き残ること〗survival. ●適者生存 the *survival* of the fittest. ●動物世界での生存競争 the struggle for

せいたい *existence* in the animal world. ▶あの状況下では彼の生存は疑問だった His *survival* was doubtful under the circumstances. ▶その事故の生存者は1人だけだった There was only one *survivor* of [from] the accident./Only one *survived* [×survived in] the accident.
— **生存する** 動 *exist*; 〚生きる〛*live*; 〚なんとかして生き続ける〛*subsist*; 〚生き残る〛*survive*. ▶人間は空気がないと生存できない We cannot *exist* [*live*] without air.
- **生存権** the right to live. • **生存能力** viability.

せいたい 正対 — 死と正対する(=に直面する) *face up to death*.

せいたい 生体 a living body.
- **生体解剖** 〚解剖〛vivisection. • カエルを生体解剖する vivisect a frog. • **生体学** somatology.
- **生体肝移植** a liver transplant from a living donor. • **生体腎移植** a renal transplant from a living donor. 〖！donorは臓器提供者〗. • **生体工学** bionics; bioengineering. • **生体実験** an experiment on a living creature. • **生体組織検査**〚医学〛(生検)〚do〛a biopsy. • **生体反応** (a) vital reaction. • **生体力学** biodynamics.

せいたい 生態 〚生物と環境との関係〛ecology; 〚生活様式〛 a mode of life. • ライオンの生態 *ecology* [the *life and habits*] of lions. • その地域の植物の生態(系)を乱す damage the plant *ecology* of the area. • 今日の十代の若者の生態 the *way* teen-agers *live* today; the *life* of today's teen-agers.
- **生態学** ecology. • **生態学者** an ecologist.
- **生態系** an ecological system; an ecosystem.

せいたい 成体 an adult; (成虫体)〚昆虫〛an imago /iméigou/.

せいたい 声帯 〚解剖〛the vocal cords [chords]. 〖！複数扱い〗 ▶彼は声帯を痛めた He damaged his *vocal cords*.
- **声帯模写** vocal mimicry; imitation of 《his》 voice 《his》way of speaking》. • **声帯模写をする** mimic [imitate] 《his》 voice.

せいたい 政体 (a form of) government; 〚政権〛《書》 a regime /rədʒíːm/. • 立憲政体(=立憲制) constitutional *government*. • 新しい政体のもとで under the new *regime*.

せいたい 聖体 • **聖体拝受** Holy Communion.

せいたい 整体 〚医学〛(脊椎矯正) chiropractic; (整骨療法) osteopathy.

せいたい 臍帯 (⇨臍帯(さい))

せいだい 盛大 — **盛大な** 形 〚堂々とした〛grand; 〚繁栄した〛prosperous; 〚大成功の〛very successful. ▶彼に盛大な拍手を送る give him a *big* [a *great*] hand. ▶盛大な送別会が昨夜行われた They gave a *grand* farewell party [gave a farewell party on a *grand scale*] last night.

せいたかあわだちそう 背高泡立草 〚植物〛a tall goldenrod.

せいたかしぎ 背高鷸 〚鳥〛a black-winged stilt.

せいたく 請託 名 (a) solicitation.
— **請託する** 動 ▶彼に便宜を図ってくれるよう請託する *solicit* special favors *from* him; *beg* him *to exercise* his *influence in favor of....*

せいたく 清濁 • **清濁併せ呑む** (だれでも受け入れる) be open-minded; (寛大である) be generous; (寛容である) too. ▶

*ぜいたく** 贅沢 名 luxury /lʌ́gʒəri/; (過度の) extráv-agance. ▶ペルシャじゅうたんはぜいたく品だ Persian carpets are *luxuries* [*luxury* goods]. 〖！×luxury thingsとはいわない〗 ▶うちの車はぜいたく品ではなく必需品です Our car is a necessity, not an *extravagance*. ▶彼は食べ物にはぜいたくしている(=食べ物に金を気前よく遣う) He *lavishes money on* food./He *spends generously* [*is generous in spending* 《money》] *on* food. ▶君はぜいたくを言いすぎる(=求め[期待し]すぎる) You are asking [ex-pecting] too much.
— **ぜいたくな** 形 (物が豪華な, 人がぜいたく好みの) luxuri-ous /lʌgʒúəriəs/; (人・物が金遣いの荒い) extráv-agant; (人が気前のよい) lavish; (値が高価な) expen-sive. • ぜいたくな毛皮のコート a *luxurious* fur coat. • ぜいたくなパーティー an *extravagant* party. • ぜいたくな暮らしをする lead a *luxurious* life; live in *luxury*. ▶一等で旅行してとてもぜいたくな気分だった I felt very *luxurious* traveling (by) first class.
— **ぜいたくに** 副 • ぜいたくに暮らす lead [live] a *luxuri-ous* life; lead [live] a life of *luxury*; live *in* (the *lap of*) *luxury*. • ダイヤをぜいたくにあしらった(=ふんだんに使った)ブローチ a brooch with *a lot of* dia-monds.

せいだす 精出す work hard; (…に努力する)《やや書》 exert oneself 《*to* do》; (…に専心従事する) apply oneself 《*to*》. • 精出して (勤勉に) diligently; assiduously. • 仕事に精出す work *very hard*. • 庭仕事に精出す *work hard at* gardening.

せいたん 生誕 birth. • 鷗外生誕百年祭 the centénnial 《米》[centénary 《英》] of Mori Ogai's *birth*; the 100th anniversary of Mori Ogai's *birth*.

せいたん 西端 the western tip. • 最西端の町 the *westernmost* town (*of the country*).

せいだん 政談 ❶ 〚政治・政局についての議論〛political talk. ❷ 〚政治〖裁判〗の講談〛a historical narra-tive about politics [law case].

せいだん 星団 〚天文〛a cluster of stars, a star cluster. • 球状星団 a globular *cluster*.

せいたんさい 聖誕祭 (⇨⑧ クリスマス)

せいち 生地 one's birthplace.

せいち 聖地 a sacred place, holy ground; (パレスチナの別称) the Holy Land. • 聖地に巡礼する make [go on] a pilgrimage to *sacred places* [*the Holy Land*].

せいち 精緻 名 (微細) minuteness; (細かさ) fine-ness; (繊細) delicacy; (念入りに仕上げること) elab-oration.
— **精緻な** 形 • 精緻な筆使い *minute* [*fine*] brush-work. • 精緻なデザイン an *elaborate* design.

せいち 整地 — **整地する** 動 (土地を) level [整える] prepare] the land [ground] 《*for*; *to* do》; (土壌を) prepare the soil. • 建築のために整地する *level the ground for* construction.

ぜいちく 筮竹 a set of divining sticks.

せいちゃ 製茶 tea processing.
• **製茶業** the tea-processing industry. • **製茶業者** a tea processor. • **製茶工場** a tea factory.

せいちゅう 成虫 〚昆虫〛an imago /iméigou, imáː-/ (複 ~(e)s, imagines /iméidʒəniːz/).

*せいちょう** 成長, 生長 名 growth.
❶ 〚~成長〛▶産業の成長 the *growth* of in-dustries. • 経済[高度]成長 economic [high] *growth*. • ゼロ成長 zero *growth*.
❷ 〚成長~〛• 成長過程 the process of *growth*. • 我が子の成長記録 a record of one's child's *growth*.
❸ 〚成長が〛▶子供は成長がとても早い Children *grow* very fast. • 成長がピークに達した[減速した] The *growth* has peaked [slowed down].
❹ 〚成長を〛• 成長をはばむ check [hinder, stop]

せいちょう

growth. ▶そのアメリカスギは成長を続けた The redwood continued *growing*. ▶彼女は子供の成長を楽しみにしている She delights in watching her child *grow up*. ▶この薬はがん細胞の成長を止める[促進する] This medicine halts [accelerates] the *growth* of cancer cells. ▶この会社はここ10年間で急成長をとげた This company has seen (ⓧa) very rapid *growth* [*has grown* rapidly] in the last ten years.

── **成長[生長]する** 動 〖育つ〗grow*; (大人になる) grow up; 〖発展する〗develop. ▶彼は成長する(＝年をとる)につれ親に反抗するようになった As he *grew older*, he rebelled against his parents. ▶彼は成長して立派な若者になった He *grew up* to be [into] a fine young man. (❗ to be の場合，up は省略不可)/▶その国は急成長(＝発展)している The country *is developing* rapidly.

● **成長株** (株) a growth stock; (人) a promising [an up-and-coming] person, a person with potential. ● **成長期** a growth stage. ● **成長企業** a growth company. ● **成長産業** a growth industry. ● **成長点**〖植物〗a growing point. ● **成長ホルモン**〖生化〗growth hormone. ● **成長率** a growth rate.

せいちょう 正調〖音楽〗the orthodox tune [melody].

せいちょう 成鳥 an adult bird.

せいちょう 声調 ❶〖声の調子〗a tone (of voice). ❷〖中国語などのアクセント〗a tone.

せいちょう 性徴 a sexual characteristic. ● **第一次[第二次]性徴** a primary [a secondary] *sexual characteristic*.

せいちょう 政庁 a government office.

せいちょう 清澄 名 clearness.

── **清澄な** 形 clear. ● 清澄な空気 *clear* air.

せいちょう 清聴 ▶ご清聴ありがとうございました Thank you very much for *your* (*kind*) *attention*. ● **静聴** ▶ご静聴願います *Attention*, please.

せいちょう 整腸 ● 整腸作用がある have a good effect on [be effective against] *intestinal disorders*. ● **整腸剤** (a) medicine for intestinal disorders.

せいちょう 整調 (ボートの) a stroke.

***せいつう 精通** ── **精通する** 動 (親しくよく知っている) be familiar (*with*); (扱い慣れている) be at home (*in*); (熟練・熟達した) 〖書〗be well versed (*in*); (熟知している)〖書〗be well-acquainted (*with*).

▶彼は法律に精通している He *is familiar with* [*at home in*] law. (❗ Law *is familiar to him*. は「法律にかかわったことがある」という意味)/He is *very knowledgeable about* law./(専門家である) He *is an expert in* law (a legal *expert*).

せいてい 制定 名〖法律などの〗〖法律〗enactment; 〖制度・法などの〗establishment.

── **制定する** 動 ▶新しい税法を制定する *establish* 〖法律〗*enact* a new tax law.

せいてき 性的 ── **性的な** (性に関する) sexual; (性の) sex. (❗「性別[差]による」「セックスに関する」の両方の意で) ▶彼女には性的魅力がある She has (a lot of) *sex* appeal./She is *sexually* attractive./〖話〗She's (very) *sexy*.

● **性的いやがらせ** sexual harassment. ● **性的興奮** sexual excitement. ● **性的差別** sexual [sex, gender] discrimination. ● **性的倒錯** sexual perversion.

せいてき 政敵 a political opponent [rival, 《やや書》antagonist].

せいてき 静的 ── **静的な** 形 static.

せいてつ 製鉄 iron [steel] manufacturing. (❗

せいど

steel は厳密には「鋼」) ● **新日本製鉄** Nippon *Steel* Corporation.

● **製鉄会社** an iron [a steel] (manufacturing) company. ● **製鉄業** the iron [steel] industry. ● **製鉄所** an ironworks; a steelworks. (❗ ともに単・複同形)

せいてん 青天 a blue sky.

● **青天の霹靂** (㊟) ▶彼の辞職は青天の霹靂だった His resignation was (like) *a bolt from* [*out of*] *the blue*.

● **青天白日** ▶彼は青天白日の身となった(無罪が証明された) He had his innocence proved./(容疑が晴れた) He was cleared of the charge(s).

せいてん 晴天 clear [fair] weather (❗ 気象では clear (快晴), fair (晴れ)と区別するが，天気予報では fair の中に clear を含めている) (⇨晴明); 〖晴れた空〗a clear [a fair] sky. ▶晴天のもとで under the *clear* [*sunny*] *skies* [*sky*]. (❗ skies は広がりを強調する) ● 晴天が続き(have) a long spell of *fair weather*. (❗ spell は「ひと続き」の意. 「先週は晴天続きだった」は We had fair weather all last week. といえる)

せいてん 聖典〖神聖な本〗a sacred book;〖経典〗scriptures;〖聖書〗the (Holy) Scriptures; the Bible;〖イスラム教の教典〗the Koran.

せいでん 正殿〖神社の本殿〗the main shrine [temple]; 〖表御殿〗the State Chamber.

せいてんかん 性転換 sex change.

● **性転換者** a transsexual. ● **性転換手術** sex-change [a transsexual] operation.

せいでんき 静電気 static electricity, static. ▶ナイロンの下着はよく静電気を起こす Nylon underwear often causes [generates] *static electricity*. ▶このシャンプーを使うと静電気が起こらなくなり髪がとかしやすくなります This shampoo leaves your hair *static*-*free* and easy to comb.

***せいと 生徒** a pupil, (米) a student; (学童) a schoolchild (複 -children), 〖話〗a schoolkid, (男性) a schoolboy, (女性) a schoolgirl.

> 使い分け **pupil** 《米》では小学生，《英》では小・中学生をさす。米・英に関係なくピアノなどの個人レッスンを受けている人にも用いる。
>
> **student** 《米》では原則として小・中・高・大学生，時に小学生にも用いる。《英》では大学生のみに用いたが，最近は中・高生も school *student* と呼ぶようになってきた。(⇨学生, 児童)

● このクラスの男子[女子]生徒 the boy [girl] *students* in this class; the boys [girls] in this class. ● **全校生徒** the whole school. (❗ 集合的に用い単数扱い) ▶その学校の生徒数は1,000人です The school has 1,000 *pupils* [*students*]/There are 1,000 *pupils* [*students*] in the school.

● **生徒会** a student council. ● **生徒指導** pupil [student] guidance 〖しつけ〗discipline. ● **生徒総会** a students' [a student] meeting.

せいと 成都〖中国の都市〗Chengdu /tʃǎːndúː/.

せいと 聖徒 a saint. (⇨聖者)

***せいど 制度** (組織的な) a system; (慣習的な) an institution. ● 教育制度 an education(al) *system*; a *system* of education. ● 結婚制度 the *institution* of marriage. ● 制度を設ける[採用する; 廃止する] establish [adopt, abolish] a *system*. ● 現行の制度では under the present [current] *system*. ▶養子縁組みは重要な社会制度になりつつある Child adoption is becoming an important social *institution*.

── **制度化する** 動 institutionalize.

せいど 精度 (精密) precision; (正確) accuracy. ●

せいとう 正当 名 [正当性] justice, rightness; (議論などの) validity /vælidəti/. ● 正当防衛でその男を射殺する shoot the man dead in *self-defense*. ▶彼が言ったことの正当性は明らかだった The *justice* [*validity*] of his remarks was clear.

── **正当な** 形 just (!以下のすべての意味を含むやや堅い語); [道徳・規範上]正しい] right; [理にかなった] reasonable; [適切な] proper; [公平な] fair; [合法な] legal, lawful. ● 正当な要求 a *just* [a *reasonable*] claim. ● 正当な手段で by *fair* means. ● 正当な権利 one's *legal* right. ● 正当な(=十分な)理由なしに without *good* [*sufficient*] reasons.

── **正当に** 副 justly; rightly; reasonably; fairly, properly; legally. ▶彼らは私を[その問題を]正当に取り扱った(=評価した) They *did* me [the subject] *justice*./They *did justice* to me [the subject].

── **正当化する** 動 justify. ● 自ら(=自分の行為)を正当化する *justify* oneself; *justify* one's actions. ▶いかなる理由でも、核兵器の使用は正当化すべきではない No matter what the reason is, the use of nuclear weapons should not [never] be *justified*. ● 目的は手段を正当化する (ことわざ) The end *justifies* the means.

せいとう 正答 a correct [a right] answer. (⇨正解)

せいとう 正統 名 [世間に正しいと認められているもの] (やや書) orthodoxy; [正当な血筋] legitimacy.

── **正統(派)の** 形 (やや書) orthodox; legitimate. ● 正統派の人 an *orthodox*. ● 正統派の経済理論 *orthodox* economic theories. ● 正統な王位継承者 the *legitimate* heir to the throne.
● 正統学派 the orthodox school.

せいとう 政党 a political party. (⇨党) ▶アメリカには二大政党がある There are two major *political parties* in the U.S.
● 政党助成金 government subsidy to a political party. ● 政党政治 government by political parties; party politics. ● 政党内閣 a party cabinet.

せいとう 精糖 (精製した白砂糖) refined sugar; (砂糖の精製) sugar refining.
● 精糖所 a sugar refinery.

せいとう 製陶 (陶器[磁器]製造) pottery [porcelain] manufacture.
● 製陶業 the pottery [porcelain] industry. ● 製陶所 a pottery.

せいとう 製糖 ● 製糖業 the sugar industry.
● 製糖会社 a sugar manufacturing company.

せいとう 正道 the right path; the path of righteousness. ● 正道を踏む[歩む] tread [walk] *the path of righteousness*. ● 正道から外れる stray [deviate] from *the right path*.

せいどう 制動 ── **制動する** 動 brake; (スキーで制動回転する) stem.
● 制動回転 [スキー] a stem turn. ● 制動滑降 [スキー] a stem, stemming; [登山] a glissade. ● 制動機 a brake. ● 制動灯 (米) a stoplight, (英) a brake light.

せいどう 青銅 bronze. ● 青銅の像 a *bronze* statue; a statue in *bronze*.
● 青銅器(器具) a bronze implement. ● 青銅時代 [考古] the Bronze Age.

せいどう 聖堂 ❶ [キリスト教の] a church. ● 大聖堂 a cathedral /kəˈθiːdrəl/. ● サンピエトロ大聖堂 St. Peter's (Basilica). ❷ [孔子の] a shrine of Confucius.

せいとく 生得 ── 生得の 形 inborn, (やや書) innate (↔acquired). (⇨先天的)

せいどく 精読 名 intensive reading.
── **精読する** 動 read (it) closely [intensively].

せいとん 整頓 ── 整頓する 動 [きれいに片付ける] clear ... up; [きちんとする] tidy [straighten] ... (up), put* [things] in order. ● 整頓された部屋 a *tidy* room. ● 整頓されていない部屋 an *untidy* [(話) a *messy*] room; a room *in disorder*. ▶彼女は母親が来る前に部屋を整頓した She *cleared up* [*tidied (up)*] the room before her mother came. ▶彼は自分の机をきちんと整頓している He *keeps* his desk *nice and clean* [*neat and tidy*].

せいなる 聖なる holy; sacred. (⇨⇨ 神聖な)

せいなん 西南 the southwest (略 SW). (!語順に注意)(⇨東, 北西)

せいなんせい 西南西 the west-southwest (略 WSW).

せいにく 精肉 (良質の肉) (quality) meat.
● 精肉業 the meat industry. ● 精肉商 a butcher. ● 精肉店 a butcher('s) shop.

ぜいにく 贅肉 flab; (余分な肉[脂肪]) unwanted flesh [fat], (《話) a messy. ● ぜい肉がつく get *flabby*. ● ぜい肉を落とす get rid of *flab*; fight the *flab*.

せいねん 青年 [男性] a young man (複 men), a youth (!後の方はしばしば軽蔑的); [女性] a young woman (複 women); [総称] young people, the youth (!単・複両扱い). (⇨若者) ● 前途有望な青年 a promising *young person*. ● 青年男女 *young men* and *women*. ● 今日の青年 *young people* [*the youth*] (of) today; today's *youth*. ▶彼は青年時代をアメリカで過ごした He spent his *youth* [his *young days*] in America.
● 青年実業家 a young businessman [businesswoman]. ● 青年団 a youth association.

せいねん 成年 [大人になる年] full age; (法律上の) one's majority (!(英) では 18 歳, (米) では 18 歳だが, 一部の州では 21 歳); [大人] an adult, (米) a grown-up. ▶彼は成年に達している[いない] He is *over* [*under*] *age*. ▶彼は成年に達した He *has come of age* [(大人になった) *grown up* now]./He *has reached* his *full age* [his *majority*]. (!He's an *adult* now. でもこの意は伝えられない)(⇨未成年)

せいねんがっぴ 生年月日 (one's) date of birth. 会話 「生年月日は?」「平成 2 年 11 月 7 日です」 "What [×When] is your *date of birth*?" "(It's) November 7, 1990." /(話) "When were you born?" "I was born on November 7, 1990." (!(1) 7 は (the) seventh と読む。(2) 年号は特別の目的がなければ西暦を用いる)

せいのう 性能 [作業能力] performance; [能力] power; [効率] efficiency. ● 高性能の high-*performance* [(力の強い) high-*power*(*ed*)] (cars, machines); highly *efficient* (machines); (強力な) *powerful* (engines); (質のよい) (cameras) of high quality. ● コンピュータの性能を高める promote [develop] the *efficiency* of the computer.

せいは 制覇 名 [征服] (a) conquest; [支配] domination. ▶彼女はテニスで世界制覇を果たした(=世界選手権を獲得した) She *won* the world tennis *championship*.
── **制覇する** 動 ● 世界を制覇する *conquer* [*dominate*] the world.

せいばい 成敗 [刑罰] (a) punishment; [裁き] (a) judgment. ● けんか両成敗 [喧嘩] [成句]

せいはく 精白 ― **精白する** 動 (米などを) polish; (砂糖などを) refine.
● 精白糖 refined suger. ● 精白米 polished rice.
せいばつ 征伐 名 (征服) cónquest.
― **征伐する** 動 ● 敵を征伐する cónquer [make a conquest of] an enemy.
せいはつりょう 整髪料 hairdressing. (🖉 hair cream [gel, liquid, mousse, oil, spray] など)
せいはん 正犯 图 the principal offense 《米》[offence 《英》].
● 正犯者 the principal offender.
せいはん 製版 图 plate-making. ― **製版する** 動 make plates.
● 製版機 a platemaker. ● 製版所 a platemaker's shop.
せいはんたい 正反対 图 the (exact) opposite [reverse] 《of》. (⇨反対)
― **正反対の** 形 (位置・行動・意味などが) opposite; contrary (🖉 opposite は対立の意味が強く加わった語); (面・順序・方向などが) reverse. ● 正反対の方向に行く go in the opposite [reverse] direction. ▶彼らの性格はまったく正反対だ Their characters are completely opposite.
せいひ 正否 (正と不正) right or wrong. ● 事の正否を見極める make sure whether it is right or wrong.
せいひ 成否 success (or failure); 〖結果〗 (a) result. ▶成否にかかわらず regardless of the result. ▶成否は努力次第だ Success [Whether we succeed or not] depends on our efforts.
▶成否は五分五分です The chances of success or failure are even./We have an even chance of success.
***せいび 整備** 图 〖道路などの保全・維持〗 maintenance /méɪntənəns/; 〖改善, 改良〗 improvement. ● 道路の整備 the maintenance of roads. ● 車の整備 the maintenance of a car; car maintenance. ● 環境整備 (the) improvement of the environment; environmental improvement.
― **整備する** 動 maintain /meɪntéɪn/; improve; (販売後, 車・電気製品などを修理点検する) service; (エンジンなどを調整する) tune ... (up). ● 自動車を整備する service a car. ● 野球場を整備する put a baseball ground in good condition; (手入れをする) take care of a baseball field. ● よく整備された設備 well- (↔poorly-) maintained equipment. ▶エンジンはよく整備されていた The engine was finely tuned.
● 整備員 a maintenance man [engineer]; (球場などの) a ground keeper; (自動車の) a car mechanic. ● 整備工場 (自動車などの) a service station.
ぜいびき 税引き ● 税引きの[で] after tax. ● 税引き収入 the income after tax; the income net of tax. (⇨税)
せいひつ 静謐 peace and calm [tranquility].
― **静謐な** 形 peaceful, (穏やかな) calm; tranquil.
せいひょう 青票 (反対投票に使う青い票) a blue ballot. (⇨白票) ● 青票を投じる cast a blue ballot.
せいひょう 製氷 (大規模に) ice manufacture; (小規模に) ice making.
● 製氷会社 an íce còmpany. ● 製氷工場 an íce plànt. ● 製氷皿 (冷蔵庫の) an ice (cube) tray. (🖉 ice cube は「四角い角氷」.)
せいびょう 性病 a venereal /vənɪəriəl/ disease (略 V.D.); (婉曲的に) a social disease. (⇨性感染症)
せいひれい 正比例 图 direct proportion. (🔄 反比例) (⇨比例)

― **正比例する** 動 ▶AはBに正比例する A is in direct proportion [directly proportional] to B.
***せいひん 製品** 图 a product; manufactured goods, manufactures; 〖商品〗 goods.

> **使い分け** **product** 工業製品・農産物を含めて広い意味での生産物をいう。
> **manufactured goods, manufactures** 主に織物など機械で大量に生産されたものをいう。

● 工業製品 industrial products. ● 日本製品 Japanese(-made) goods. ● 外国製品 foreign products; (輸入品) imported goods. ● 新製品 a new product; (新型商品) a new line (of products). ● 電器製品 electrical appliances [goods, products]. ● 製品ラインの多角化を図る try to diversify product line. ▶この会社の製品は売れ行きがよい The products of this company sell well.
● 製品開発 product development. ● 製品計画 product planning; a product design. ● 製品コンセプト a product concept. ● 製品ライフサイクル a product life cycle.
せいひん 正賓 a guest of honor. (⇨⑲ 主賓)
せいひん 清貧 ● 清貧に甘んじる be contented to live in honest poverty; live uprightly by rejecting the chances of lining one's (own) pockets.
***せいふ 政府** a government (🖉 しばしば G-. 集合的に政治機関を表す. 《米》では単数扱い,《英》では単・複両扱い); (米国の政権) the Administration; (内閣) a cabinet. (⇨内閣)
① 【~政府】 ● 現政府 the present government. ● 中央政府 the central government; 《米》the Federal Government. ● 州政府 a State government. ● 日本[米国]政府 the Japanese [the US] Government; the government of Japan [the United States]. ● 本国政府 the home government.
② 【政府~】 ● 政府内の intragovernmental. ● 政府内統一見解 a government consensus. ● 政府間協定 an intergovernmental agreement.
③ 【政府を[は]】 ● 新政府を作る form a new government. ● 政府を倒す overthrow a government. ▶政府は増税を検討している The Government has [have] been considering tax increases.
● 政府開発援助 official development assistance (略 ODA). ● 政府機関 a government agency. ● 政府軍 government forces. ● 政府高官 a high (-ranking) government official. ● 政府筋 government sources [circles]. ● (政府)税制調査会 the Tax Commission. ● 政府当局 the government authorities.
せいぶ 西部 the west; (西の地方) the western part; (米国の) the West. (⇨南部) ▶その島は日本の西部にある The island is in the western part of Japan [is in Western Japan, 《米》is in the west of Japan]. ▶アメリカでは開拓地は東部から西部へと広がって行った The frontier moved from the East to the West in the United States.
● 西部劇 a Western (movie); a cowboy movie [film].
せいぶ 声部 〖音楽〗 a voice part.
せいふう 西風 (⇨西風(にし))
せいふう 清風 (さわやかな[すがすがしい]風) a fresh [a refreshing] breeze. ▶政界に清風を吹き込む send a breath of fresh air through the political world.
***せいふく 制服** 〖軍隊・警察などの〗 a uniform; 〖学校の〗 (a) school uniform. (🔄 日米英の学校では特別の学校を除き, 通例制服は着用しない) ▶警官は制服を着用する

せいふく ている Police officers wear *uniforms*. (❗「制服を着た警官」は police officers in (⇔out of) *uniform*; *uniformed* police officer) ▶私立の学校では制服で通学させるところが多い In many private schools they make their students come to school *in uniform*.

せいふく 征服 图 (a) conquest. ▶1066年にノルマン人によるイングランド征服があった The Norman *Conquest* of England [The *conquest* of England by the Normans] took place in 1066./(ノルマン人がイングランドを征服した) The Normans *conquered* England in 1066.

— **征服する** 動 conquer. ▶彼は冬のエベレストを征服した He *conquered* the summit of Mount Everest in winter./(登頂に成功した) He *succeeded in reaching* the summit of Mount Everest in winter.

● **征服者** a conqueror. (関連) 被征服者《集合的》the conquered)

*__**せいぶつ 生物**__ 『生き物』a living thing; (人間, 動物を除く) creature (❗植物は含まない);《集合的》life;〚科目〛biology. ▶火星に生物はまだ見つかっていない No *life* has been found on Mars.

● **生物化学兵器** a biochemical weapon. ● **生物学**(⇔生物学) ● **生物工学** biotechnology. ● **生物室** a biology room. ● **生物時計** (体内時計) a biological clock; a body clock. ● **生物物理学** biophysics. (❗単数扱い) ● **生物兵器** a biological weapon.

せいぶつ 静物 still life.
● **静物画** (paint) a still life (霾 -lifes [《非標準》-lives]); a still life painting [picture].

せいぶつ『静物』 *Still Life*. (参考) 庄野潤三の小説)

せいぶつがく 生物学 图 biology.
— **生物学(上)の, 生物学的な** 形 biological.
— **生物学的に** 副 biologically.
● **生物学者** a biologist.

せいふん 製粉 图 flour /fláuər/ milling.
— **製粉する** 動 mill flour. ▶トウモロコシを製粉して(=ひいて)あら粉にする grind corn into meal; grind meal from corn.
● **製粉機** a flour mill.

せいぶん 正文 the official text. ● 条文の正文 the *text* of a treaty.

せいぶん 成分 图〚混合物の材料〛an ingredient;〚複合物の(不可欠な)構成要素〛〚書〛a constituent. ▶アイスクリームの成分 the *ingredients* of ice cream. ▶水素と酸素は水の成分だ Hydrogen and Oxygen are the *constituents* [*elements*] of water. ▶この石の成分は何か(=何でできているか) What *is* this rock *composed of*?

せいぶんか 成文化 图 codification.
— **成文化する** 動 ▶その法律は成文化された The law *was codified*.

せいぶんほう 成文法 written [statutory] law.

せいへい 精兵 (えり抜きの兵士) elite soldiers.

せいへき 性癖 〚癖〛a habit 《*of* doing》;〚性向〛a tendency 《*to* do》.

せいべつ 生別 lifelong separation [parting]. (⇔(四)生き別れ)

せいべつ 性別 sex;〚性の区別〛the distinction of sex. ● 年齢や性別に関係なく regardless of age or *sex*; without regard to age or *sex*. ● 申込用紙に性別を示す indicate one's *sex* on the application form.

せいへん 正編 the principal [main] part《*of* a book》. (霾 続編)

せいへん 政変 a political change; (クーデター) a coup (d'état) /kú:(deitá:)/; (革命) a revolution; (内閣の更迭) a change of government. ▶政変が起こるかもしれない A *political change* [A *revolution*] may take place.

せいほ 生保 〚『生命保険』の略〛(⇔生命)

せいぼ 生母 one's real mother.

せいぼ 歳暮 a year-end gift [present]; (説明的に) It is customary for most Japanese to exchange or send gifts as a token of gratitude in December. (事情) 歳暮を贈る習慣は西洋にはないが, クリスマスプレゼントを贈る. この習慣はビジネスの場でも見られる》(⇔お中元) ● お歳暮にウイスキーを贈る give 《him》 a bottle of whiskey as a *year-end gift*.

せいぼ 聖母 the Holy [Blessed] Mother. ● 聖母マリア the Virgin Mary; Saint Mary.

せいほう 西方 the west. (⇔東方) ● 西方からの風(=西風) a 《*warm*》 *west* wind. ● この市の西方は *west* of this city. ● 西方へ急ぐ hurry *west* [*westward*].

せいほう 製法 a method; (過程) a process; of manufacturing; (作り方) how to make.

せいぼう 声望 ▶声望が高い have a good *reputation*.
● **声望を得る** win [gain] *fame*.

せいぼう 制帽 (学校の) a school cap; (一般の) a regulation cap. ● 制帽姿の警官 a policeman [a policewoman] *in uniform*.

ぜいほう 税法 the tax law(s).

せいほうけい 正方形 a (regular) square. (⇔四角)

せいほく 西北 the northwest (略 NW). (❗語順に注意)(⇔東)

せいほくせい 西北西 the west-northwest (略 WNW).

セイボリー savory. (参考) 香辛料の一種)

せいほん 正本 (謄本) an officially certified copy; (原本) the original copy.

せいほん 製本 图 (book)binding. (⇔装丁(きき)) ▶その本は今製本中です The book *is binding* [*being bound*] now.
— **製本する** 動 bind a book. ● 3巻を1巻に製本する *bind* (*up*) three volumes *into* one.
● **製本所[工場]** a (book)bindery. ● **製本屋** a (book)binder.

せいまい 精米 图 rice polishing; (精白米) polished rice.
— **精米する** 動 polish rice.
● **精米機** a rice-polishing machine. ● **精米所** a rice mill.

*__**せいみつ 精密**__ 图 precision; minuteness.
— **精密な** 形〚『正確な』〛precise;〚『寸法たがわぬ』〛exact;〚徹底的な〛thorough /θá:rou, θárə/;〚細部に留意した〛minute /main(j)ú:t/;〚詳細な〛détailed.
● **精密な測定** a *precise* [an *exact*] measurement.
● **精密な調査をする** make a *thorough* [a *minute*, a *detailed*] examination 《*of*》; examine 《*it*》 *thoroughly* [*minutely*]. ▶その患者は精密検査を受けた The patient had a *complete* [《深い所まで徹底的な》 an *in-depth*] physical examination 《話》a *close* checkup. (❗ a *minute* [a *precise*] examination とはあまりいわない)
● **精密機械** a precision [(精巧で最新の) a sophisticated] machine.

せいみょう 精妙 — **精妙な** 形 elaborate. ● 精妙な仕掛け an *elaborate* device.

せいむ 政務 (国事) state affairs; (公務) official business. ● 政務を執る administer [《書》attend to] the *affairs of state*.
● **政務官** a parliamentary secretary 《*for*》. ● **政務次官** a parliamentary vice-minister.

(参考) 現在は「副大臣」と称される) ●政務調査会 the Policy Affairs Research Council.

ぜいむ 税務 tax matters; taxatioin business.
●税務官 a revenue officer; (税務署員) a tax collector. ●税務署 (⇨税務署) ●税務相談所 a tax information office.

ぜいむしょ 税務署 a tax office.
●税務署員 (収税吏) a tax collector; (事務員) a tax(-office) clerk. ●税務署長 the tax-office superintendent [supervisor].

＊せいめい 生命 ❶ 【人命】(a) life (注 人の一命は Ⓒ) (⇨命)
① 【生命が[は]】 ▶地球以外に生命が存在するとは思わない I don't believe *life* exists outside of Earth. ▶その事故で10人の生命が失われた Ten *lives* were lost [Ten people lost their *lives*] in the accident./Ten people *were killed* in the accident. ▶人の生命は全地球より重い A person's *life* is heavier than the whole world.
② 【生命の[と]】 ●生命の起源 the origin(s) of *life*. ●生命と財産 *life* and property. ●生命の危険を冒す risk one's *life*. ▶そのとき私は生命の危険を感じた I felt my *life* was in danger at that moment.
③ 【生命に】 ●生命にかかわる(=致命的な)傷 a *fatal* [a *mortal*] wound.
④ 【生命を】 ●生命を奪う take 《his》 *life*; (殺す) kill. ▶妊娠期間中の喫煙は胎児の生命をおびやかす Smoking during pregnancy endangers your baby's *life*. ▶彼はその贈収賄事件で政治生命を失った The bribery case put an end to his political *life* [*career*].
❷ 【物事の精髄】the life; (核心) the soul. ▶時計の生命は正確さにある Precision is the *life* of a clock. ▶民主主義の生命は個人の自由にある Individual freedom is the *soul* of [is what gives *life* to] democracy.
●生命を賭(と)す ▶彼は黄熱病の研究に生命を賭した He *devoted* his *whole life* to the study of yellow fever.
●生命維持装置 life-support system. ●生命科学 a life science (注 通例複数形で); bioscience. ●生命現象 a life phenomenon. ●生命線 (生死にかかわる大切なもの) one's lifeline; (手相の) the lifeline, the line of life. ●生命体 an organism; a living organism. ●生命保険 life insurance [《英》 assurance]. (⇨保険) ●生命力 one's life force; (活力) vitality. ●生命倫理 bioéthics. (注 単数扱い)

せいめい 声明 图 a statement 《on, about》. ●共同[公式]声明 a joint [an official] *statement*. ●声明を発表する issue [make] a *statement* 《on the matter》.
── 声明する 動 declare; (発表する) announce. (⇨発表する, 表明する) ▶我々はその法案に賛成[反対]を声明した We *declared* ourselves for [against] the bill./We *declared* that we were for [against] the bill.

せいめい 姓名 (⇨氏名)
●姓名判断 (説明的に) telling one's fortune by the number of strokes [lines] used in the *kanji* characters of one's given and family name.

せいめん 製麺 noodle making.
●製麺機 a noodle-making machine.

せいもん 正門 the main [front] gate; (入口) the main [《正面》 front] entrance. (⇨門)

せいもん 声門 【解剖】 the glottis.
●声門閉鎖音 【音声】 a glottal stop.

せいもん 声紋 a voiceprint, a vocal print.

せいもん 誓文 a written oath.

せいや 聖夜 a holy [a sacred] night.

せいやく 成約 ──成約する 動 reach a contract [《協定》 an agreement] 《for》; (署名する) sign a contract [an agreement] 《for》.

せいやく 制約 图 【人・行為などを制限すること】(a) restriction 《on》; 【行為などの限定・制限】《やや書》 (a) limitation 《on》; 【束縛, 拘束】(a) restraint; 【条件】a condition. ●厳しい制約を受ける[受けている] come [be] under strict *restrictions*. ▶この国には輸入に関する多くの制約がある There are a lot of *limitations* on imports in this country. ▶この契約には何の制約もつけません I will make no *conditions* on this contract.
── 制約する 動 restrict; limit. ●政治活動を制約する *restrict* [*impose restrictions on*] political activities. (注 *impose* の他に place も可) ▶私は時間に制約されてそれをしなければならない I must do it *in a limited length of* time.

せいやく 製薬 medicine [drug] manufacturing [making]; 【製薬術】 pharmacy.
●製薬会社 a pharmaceutical company. ●製薬業 the pharmaceutical industry. ●製薬業者 a drug maker.

せいやく 誓約 (神にかけての) an oath, a vow /váu/; (固い約束) 《やや書》 a pledge. ●誓約を守る[破る] keep [break] an *oath*.
── 誓約する 動 swear an oath; make a vow 《to do》.
●誓約書 a written oath.

せいゆ 精油 oil refining.
●精油業者 an oil refiner. ●精油所 an oil refinery.

せいゆ 製油 oil manufacturing.
●製油業 the oil industry. ●製油工場 an oil refinery [factory].

せいゆう 声優 a voice actor (男) [actress (女)]; (説明的に) an actor who does voices for animation or cartoons; (ラジオの) a radio actor (男) [actress (女)]; (吹き替えの) a dubber; (ナレーションだけの) an unseen narrator.

＊せいよう 西洋 图 the West; 《書》 the Occident; (西洋諸国) the Western countries. ▶彼は西洋かぶれしている He admires [《米話》 He's big on] the *Western* way of life.
── 西洋の 形 Western, western; 《書》 Occidental.
── 西洋化する 動 ▶日本は明治維新後急速に西洋化した Japan *became westernized* very fast after the Meiji Restoration.
●西洋医学 western medicine. ●西洋化 westernization. ●西洋思想 Western ideas [thoughts]. ●西洋人 a Westerner. ●西洋風 a Western style. ●西洋風の家 a *Western-style* house. ●西洋文明 Western civilization. ●西洋料理 Western food [dishes]; (料理法) Western cooking [cuisine].

せいよう 正用 correct [proper] use [usage]. (⇨誤用)

せいよう 静養 图 (休息) (a) rest; (骨休め) relaxation; (病後の) 《書》 recuperation (⇨保養). ●静養のために to get some *rest*; for one's *rest* [*relaxation, recuperation*]; (健康のために) for one's *health*
── 静養する 動 rest; take [have] a rest; relax; 《書》 recuperate. ●静養して体力を回復する *rest*

and regain one's strength.

せいよく 性欲 (a) sexual desire; (激しい欲情)《軽蔑的》lust. ●性欲が強い have strong *sexual desire(s)*. ●性欲を起こさせる[抑える] arouse [control] one's *sexual desire(s)*.

せいらい 生来 ▶彼は生来(=生まれながら)の臆病(おくびょう)者だ He is a *born* coward./He is cowardly *by nature.* ▶おれは生来金とは縁のない男だ I was *born* poor and I'm a stranger to money. ▶彼は生来の外国人ぎらいである He has a *built-in* hatred of foreigners.

*__せいり__ 整理 图 ●交通整理をする direct [control, regulate] traffic. ●整理整頓(してあくこと) keeping everything *in order.* ■putting ... は「...すること」

――**整理する** 動 ●[きちんとする] (場所を) tidy [straighten]... (up); (物を) put* [set*]... in order; [きれいに片付ける] clear ... up; [整とんしておく] keep*... tidy [neat] (■neat では清潔さも含意する); [きちんと並べる] arrange; [分類する] classify; (仕分けする) sort ... (out). ●部屋を整理する clear up a room; tidy [straighten] (up) a room. ●本棚に本をきちんと整理する *arrange* the books neatly on the shelves (■ *arrange* 《his》 room のように場所を目的語にすると、中にある物の配置替えをすること); put [set] the books on the shelves *in order.* ●書類を整理する sort (out) [整理保存する] file (away) papers. ●帳簿を整理する [しておく] adjust (the) accounts [keep (the) accounts straight]. ●負債を整理する(=完済する) pay off [clear (off)] one's debts. ●考えを整理する(=まとめる) organize one's thoughts [ideas]; get one's head straight. ▶彼の部屋はいつもきれいに整理されて(=整然としている) His room is always (kept) *tidy* [*neat (and tidy), in (good) order*].

❷【不必要なものを除く】●古着を整理する get rid of [throw away] one's old clothes. ●人員を整理する(=減らす) reduce [《やや話》cut down] the staff [the number of employees]; reduce the work force.

●整理券 a numbered ticket. ●整理箱 a chest (of drawers). ●整理だんす a chest (of drawers). ●整理箱 (書類などの) a file. (■整理用キャビネット (a filing cabinet) の意でも用いる)
●整理番号 a reference number.

せいり 生理 图 ❶【生物の体の働き】physiology /fìziálədʒi/.

❷【月経】a period,《書》a menstrual period; 【医学】(a) menstruation, the menses (■単·複両扱い). ▶生理がきちんとありますか Do you have regular *periods*? ▶彼女は今生理だ She is having her *period* [*hormones*]./She's having the *menses*. (■前の方が婉曲的で普通)

――**生理的(な)** 形 physiological. ●生理的変化[現象] *physiological* changes [phenomena]. ●生理的(=体の)要求を満たす satisfy the needs of the body.

●生理学 physiology. ●生理学者 a physiologist. ●生理休暇 a period [a menstrual] leave. (■事情《米》ない) ●生理食塩水 a physiological salt [saline /séili:n/] solution. ●生理痛 period pains; menstrual cramps. ●生理用品 a sanitary napkin [《米》towel《英》].

ぜいり 税吏 a taxation official; (収税吏) a tax collector.

ぜいりし 税理士 a licensed tax accountant.

*__せいりつ__ 成立 图 【発生】birth; 【形成】formation; 【条約などの締結】conclusion; 【実現】realization. ●古代文明の成立 the *birth* of an ancient civili-

zation. ●条約の成立 *conclusion* of a treaty.

――**成立する** 動 ❶【出来る】(生まれる) come* into being [existence]; (形成される) be formed; (組織される) be organized; (設立される) be established, be set up. (■後の方が口語的) ●委員会が成立した A committee *was formed* [*was established, was set up, was organized*]. ▶国際連合は1945年に成立した The United Nations *was established* [*was set up*] in 1945.

❷【まとまる】(取り決められる) be arranged; (条約などが結ばれる) be concluded; (実現する) be realized. ●協定が成立する reach [come to] an agreement. ▶A 氏と B 嬢の縁談が成立した A marriage *has been arranged* between Mr. A and Miss B. ▶両国間の和平条約が成立した A peace treaty *was concluded* between the two nations. ▶予算案が国会で成立した(=国会を通過した) The budget bill *passed* [承認された] *was approved* by the Diet. ▶商談が成立した[しなかった] Their business talk *came off successfully* [*fell through*].

❸【存立する】(⇒成り立つ❷) ▶そんな言い訳は成立しないよ Such an excuse *is not valid* [*will not do*]. (■後の方が口語的)

❹【構成されている】consist of..., be made up of..., be composed of.... (⇒成り立つ❶)

ぜいりつ 税率 tax rate; the rate of tax. ▶税率が改正された[引き上げられた] The *tax rate* was revised [raised].

せいりゃく 政略 (政治上の戦術)《use》political tactics (戦略) strategy; (工作) a political maneuver /mənúːvər/.

●政略結婚 a political marriage; (金や力が目当ての結婚) a marriage of convenience.

せいりゅう 清流 a clear stream.

せいりゅう 整流 【電気】rectification; commutation.

●整流管 a réctifying tùbe. ●整流器 a rectifier. ●整流子 a commutator. ●整流子電動機 a commutator motor.

せいりゅうとう 青竜刀 a Chinese broadsword.

せいりょう 声量 ●声量がある have a powerful [a rich, a full] *voice*. ●声量がない have a weak [thin] *voice*.

せいりょういんりょう 清涼飲料 (アルコールを含まない飲み物) a soft drink; (気分がすっきりする飲み物) a refreshing drink.

せいりょうざい 清涼剤 ●一服の清涼剤となる《事が主語》give a breath of fresh air; be refreshing; (気持ちを高揚させる) be uplifting.

*__せいりょく__ 勢力 power; force; 【力】strength; 【影響力】influence.

①【〜の勢力, 勢力〜】●世界の二大勢力(=大国) the two *powers* [*forces*] of the world. ●新興勢力 a growing [an emergent] *power*. ●武装勢力 an armed group; military *forces*. ●抵抗勢力 resistance *forces*. ●勢力下に under《his》*power* [*influence*]. ▶台風の勢力が増した[衰えた] The typhoon has increased [diminished] in *strength* [×*force*]./The *strength* of the typhoon has increased [diminished].

②【勢力がある】●勢力がある have great *power* [*influence*]《over [with]+人, in+場所》. ●勢力のある powerful; influéntial. ●勢力のない powerless. ▶宮廷での彼の勢力はだれにも負けなかった His *influence* at court was second to none. ▶世界平和に勢力が均衡することが必要だ The balance of *power* is necessary for world peace.

せいりょく ③【勢力を】●勢力を振るう[広げる] wield [extend] one's *power*. ●勢力が強くなる become stronger. ●勢力を失う lose one's *power* [influence].
●勢力争い a power struggle. ●勢力争いをする struggle for *power*. ●勢力図 a map showing one's scope of influence. ●勢力範囲[圏] one's sphere of influence.

せいりょく 精力 图 energy /énərdʒi/ (❗しばしば複数形で); vitality. ●精力のつく食物 food that gives us *energy*. ●精力が尽きる exhaust one's *energy*. ●精力を発散させる let off steam [work off one's *energies*] (at tennis, by playing tennis). ●精力絶倫である have boundless *energy*. ▶彼は宗教改革に全精力を注いだ He applied [devoted] all his *energy* [*energies*] to religious reform. ▶彼は精力旺盛(おうせい)なので3人分の仕事をこなせる He is so *energetic* [has so much *energy*] that he can work as hard as three men.
── **精力的な** 形 energétic; vigorous.
── **精力的に** 副 energetically; vigorously. ▶彼はこの問題では精力的に私たちを支持していた He has supported us *energetically* [*vigorously*] on this issue.
●精力家 an energetic person; a person of great energy [vitality].

せいりょう 声涙 ●声涙ともに下る（涙ながらに語る）speak with tears in one's eyes.

せいれい 政令 （政府の命令）《書》a government ordinance; (内閣の命令) a cabinet order.
●政令指定都市 《書》an ordinance-designated city.

せいれい 聖霊 【キリスト教】the Holy Spirit [Ghost].
●聖霊降臨節 Pentecost. (参考 復活祭から7週目の日曜日)

せいれい 精励 hard work; (勤勉) diligence; industry. ●刻苦精励する work very hard [diligently]; (専心する) apply [(専念する) devote] oneself 《to》.

せいれき 西暦 （キリスト紀元）the Christian era [Era]; (キリスト紀元後) A.D. (❗紀元前を表す B.C. と区別して紀元後を明示するときに用いる) (⇨ZC) ▶彼は西暦5世紀前半 [420年] に死んだ He died in the early fifth century A.D. [in 420 A.D.]

せいれつ 清冽 ── **清冽な** 形 ●清冽な谷川の水 the cool, clear water of a mountain stream.

せいれつ 整列 ── **整列する** 動 (縦または横1列に) line up (❗2列以上のこともある), stand in (a) line; form a line; fall in (❗fall in は軍隊調。しばしば命令文で); (横1列に) stand in a row. ●整列させる get them to *line up*; *line* them *up*. ▶全生徒が校舎の前に整列した All the students *lined up* [*stood in lines*, *formed lines*] in front of the school building. (❗lined up が最も普通)

せいれん 精練 ── **精練する** 動 ●羊毛を精練する scour wool. ●生糸を精練する *degum* raw silk.

せいれん 精錬 图 (金属の) refining; (鉱石の) smelting.
── **精錬する** 動 refine; smelt.
●精錬所 a refinery; a smelter. ●精錬工場 a refíning plànt.

せいれんけっぱく 清廉潔白 ●清廉潔白な(=非の打ち所なく誠実な人)《やや書》a person of great [complete, absolute] integrity.

せいろ 蒸籠 (⇨蒸籠(せいろう))

せいろう 晴朗 ── **晴朗な** 形 clear; fine; serene. ▶天気晴朗なり The weather is *clear* [*fine*].

せいろう 蒸籠 a steaming basket; a basket for steaming food.

せいろん 正論 a (logical and) sound argument. ●正論を述べる put a *sound argument*.

せいろん 政論 (a) political argument [discussion]. ●政論を戦わせる discuss *politics* [*political matters*].

セイロン Ceylon /sɪlán/. (参考 スリランカの旧称)
●セイロン紅茶 Ceylon tea.

ゼウス Zeus /z(j)úːs/. (参考 ギリシャ神話のオリンポス山の最高の主神)

セージ 【植物】a sage.

セーシェル (⇨セイシェル)

セーター a sweater /swétər/. ●手編みのセーター a handknit(ted) [a knitted] *sweater*. ●セーターを編む knit a *sweater*. ●厚ぼったい[厚い; ぶかぶかの]セーター a chunky [a thick (↔thin); a baggy] *sweater*. ●とっくり襟の[タートルネックの]セーター a roll-neck [a turtle-neck] *sweater*. ●セーターを着る[着ている; 脱ぐ] put on [wear; take off] one's *sweater*.

セーヌ ●セーヌ川 the Seine /séin/.

セーフ safe; safely. ●二塁へ滑り込みセーフ slide into second *safely*. ▶一塁はセーフだった The runner was *safe* on first base [reached first base *safely*].

セーブ 图 (投手が) 10 セーブをあげる get [gain, earn, pick up] ten *saves*. ●セーブに失敗する blow a *save*. ●15 セーブ機会に登板して 10 セーブをあげる convert 10 of one's 15 *save* opportunities.
── **セーブする** 動 ●金をセーブして(=倹約して)使う use one's money *sparingly*. ●これからの仕事のために力をセーブする(=蓄えておく) *save* one's strength for later work.
●セーブポイント【野球】a save; 《和製語》a save point.

セーフガード 【緊急輸入制限措置】a safeguard. (❗しばしば複数形で) ●輸入抑制のためにセーフガードを発動する invoke *safeguards* to put the brakes on some imports 《from China》.

セーフティー 【安全】safety.
●セーフティースクイズ a safety squeeze. ●セーフティーゾーン【安全地帯】《米》a safety zone [island]; 《英》an island, a traffic island, a refuge. ●セーフティーネット【安全網[保障制度]】a safety net. ●セーフティーバント【野球】an individual offensive bunt; 《和製語》a safety bunt. ●セーフティーボックス a safe(ty)-deposit box; 《和製語》a safety box.

セーラーふく セーラー服 【子供用の上下そろいの】a sailor suit; 【女子用の】(上着) a middy blouse; (上下) a middy blouse and skirt; (ワンピース型の) a sailor's dress.

セール 【安売り】a sale; (大安売り) a bargain [a discount] sale. ▶セール中《表示》Now on *sale*. ▶これはセール品ですか Is this item for *sale*? ▶このコートはセール除外品です This coat is not in the *sale*.

セールス (販売の) sales /seilz/; selling. ▶セールスの経験はありますか Do you have any actual *sales* experience?
●セールスエンジニア a sales engineer. ●セールストーク a sales talk. ●セールスプロモーション【販売促進】sales promotion. ●セールスポイント a selling point 《*of* a product》. ●セールスマン (⇨セールスマン)

セールスマン a (traveling) salesperson (褒 -people) [(男の) a salesman (褒 -men)] (❗「(店頭の)販売員」とまぎらわしい時には traveling をつける); 《主に英》a (sales) representative 《(英話) rep》. ●保険の

せおいなげ

セールスマン an insurance *salesperson*; a *salesperson* for an insurance company.

せおいなげ 背負い投げ a shoulder throw. ▶相手に背負い投げをかける *throw* one's opponent *over* one's *shoulder*.

せおう 背負う ❶〖背中でかつぐ〗put*〖運ぶ〗carry ... on one's back. ▶彼女は赤ちゃんを背負っていた She *was carrying* her baby *on her back*.
❷〖借金などを〗▶重荷を背負う bear [*shoulder*] a (heavy) burden. ▶彼はかなりの借金を背負っている He *is deeply in debt*. ▶いまの学校は、何もかも背負い込みすぎているんやないか Schools seem to be trying to *take on* too many tasks these days.
❸〖支える〗▶彼は一家を背負っていた He *supported* his family./(一家の大黒柱だった) He was the breadwinner in his family.

せおよぎ 背泳ぎ (swim) the backstroke. (⇨背泳)

セオリー a theory. ▶セオリーどおりならば〖的には〗in *theory*.

せかい 世界 图 the world; (地球) the globe.
①〖～(の)世界〗▶子供[大人]の世界 the *world* of children [adults]. ▶新世界 a new *world*; (南北米大陸) the New *World*. ▶政治[学問]の世界 the political [academic] *world*. ▶第三世界 the Third *World*. ▶今全世界(=世界の人々)がその首脳会談に注目している The whole *world* is [All the *world* is, People all over the *world* are] watching the summit talks now. (❗(1) 最初の二つは単数扱いに注意. (2) The entire *world* ... ともいえる)
②〖世界(の)～〗▶世界の果てまで to the end of the *world*. ▶世界平和を願う pray for *world* peace [the peace of the *world*]. ▶世界(新)記録を破る[作る] break [set, establish] a *world* (new) record. ▶世界1周旅行をする make a round-the-*world* trip [tour]; make a trip around the *world*. ▶世界各地から来た人々 people from all over the *world*; people from every part [corner] of the *world*. ▶その陸上競技大会には世界各国(=各地)から選手が参加した Athletes from all over [every part of] the *world* took part in the track and field meet.
③〖世界が[は]〗▶世界は日ごとに狭くなりつつある The *world* is becoming smaller day by day. ▶前途に新しい世界が開けた A new *world* opened up before me.
④〖世界に〗▶政治[教育]の世界に入る enter the political [educational] *world*. ▶これは日本が世界に誇るものの一つだ This is one of the things we can boast of to the *world*. (❗外国人が発言する場合は we の代わりに the Japanese を用いる) ▶この作品で彼は作家として世界に通用するようになった This work has given him *worldwide* recognition as a novelist. ▶その国は世界に先駆けて無農薬野菜を栽培した The country was the first in the *world* to grow organic vegetables. ▶彼は自分の世界に引きこもりがちだ He tends to shut himself in his own *world* [*a world* of his own]. ▶どこの世界に(=いったいぜんたい)我が子がかわいくない者があろうか Who *in the world* [*on earth*] doesn't love his own child? (❗いずれも疑問詞を強調する)
⑤〖世界を〗▶世界を相手に in opposition to the *world*. ▶彼は世界を股(また)に掛けて精力的に演奏活動をしている He is energetically engaged in giving his recitals *all over* [*throughout*] *the world*.
⑥〖世界(中)で〗▶世界で最も強い国 the most powerful country *in the world*. ▶英語は世界中で話されている English is spoken *all over the world* [*the world over*, *worldwide*, *throughout the world*, *in every part of the world*]. (⇨副)

── 世界的な 形 (世界中に及ぶ) worldwide; (世界中で有名な) world-famous; (世界で一流の) world-class. ●世界的な不景気 a *worldwide* [a *global*] depression. ●世界的な名声を得る gain a *worldwide* reputation. ●世界的規模 (*on*) a *world* scale.

── 世界的に 副 ▶カラヤンは世界的に有名な指揮者だった Karajan was a *world-famous* conductor.
●世界遺産 the world heritage. ●世界遺産条約 the World Heritage Convention. (❗正式には the Convention Concerning the Protection of the World Cultural and Natural Heritage (世界の文化遺産および自然遺産の保護に関する条約))
●世界観 a view of the world; an outlook on the world; a world outlook [view]. ●世界銀行 the World Bank; (公式名) (国際復興開発銀行 the International Bank for Reconstruction and Development (略 IBRD). ●世界史 world history. ●世界情勢 the world situation. ●世界選手権大会 a world championship (meet). ●世界大戦 a world war. (⇨大戦) ●世界保健機関 the World Health Organization (略 WHO).

せかいのおわりとハードボイルド・ワンダーランド 『世界の終りとハードボイルド・ワンダーランド』 *Hardboiled-Wonderland and the End of the World*. (参考 村上春樹の小説)

せがき 施餓鬼 ●施餓鬼の法要をする hold a Buddhist service for the repose of the soul of the dead.

せかす 急かす 〖急がせる〗hurry ... (up); (しきりに勧める) 《やや書》press; 〖強引に押し進める〗push. ●彼女をせかせて結婚させる *hurry* her *into getting* married [*into* marriage]; *press* her to get married. ▶せかさないで、よけい混乱してくるわ Don't *hurry* [(せきたてる) *rush*] me. I'm getting all the more confused. (❗「急がせる」という肯定の意では *hurry* me *up* と通例 up をつける)

せかせか ●せかせかした (落ち着きのない) restless; (忙しい) busy. ●せかせかする(=忙しくする) busy oneself 《*with*》. ●せかせかした人 a *restless* person. ●せかせかした生活をする lead a *busy* life. ▶彼はいつもせかせかと(=急いで)部屋に入ってくる He always walks *hurriedly* into a room./He always *hurries* into a room. ▶お客を迎えるときは母はよく台所でせかせか立ち働く My mother often *bustles around* [*busies herself with* this and that] in the kitchen when we are expecting guests.

せかっこう 背格好 ▶彼は背格好(=外見)が父親とそっくりだ He is very much like his father in *appearance*./(体格がよく似ている) He is built very much like his father.

ぜがひでも 是が非でも 〖どんな犠牲を払っても〗at all costs; 〖何事が起ころうとも〗no matter what happens, whatever happens. (⇨是非) ▶この仕事は是が非でも仕上げなといけないわ I must finish this work *at all costs* [*whatever the cost*, ×*by all means*]. (❗ by all means は許可・同意を強調する慣用句なのでここでは不可)

せがむ (うるさく) pester; (へりくだって) beg (-gg-). (⇨ねだる) ▶「お話ししてよ」とその子はせがんだ "Tell me tales," *begged* the child.

せがれ 息子 one's son. (⇨息子)

セカンド ❶〖二塁〗〖野球〗second (base); 〖二塁手〗 a second base player 〖男の〗baseman 《複 -men》. (⇨塁) ●セカンドランナー the runner on [at] *second*. ●セカンドゴロ[フライ]を打つ hit a grounder [a fly] to *second*.

せき ❷〖自動車のギア〗second (gear). ▸セカンドにいれる go [shift] into *second gear*.
- セカンドオピニオン〖第2診断〗a *second opinion*.
- セカンドハウス〖別荘〗a cottage; (広壮な) a villa. (⚠a second home は「第2の家」の意. a second house とも通例いわない) ●セカンドバッグ〖かかえ式の小型ハンドバッグ〗a clutch; 《和製語》a second bag.
- セカンドハンド〖中古の〗secondhand. ●セカンドベスト〖次善〗the second best. ●セカンドボール〖サッカー〗the second ball. ●セカンドライフ〖定年後の生活〗a life after retirement; 《和製語》a second life.

せき 席 ❶〖座る場所〗a seat; (場所) a place.
① 【~の席】 ●窓側の席 (乗物の) a window *seat*. 関連 通路側の席 an aisle /áil/ *seat*; (レストランの) a *table* near the window.
会話「そこ私の席なんですけど, いいでしょうか」「もちろん」「どうも」 "You're sitting in my *seat* [*place*], I'm afraid./You happen to be in my *seat*. Can I have it?" (⚠相手のばつの悪さをやわらげるために I'm afraid や happen to (意図的でなくたまたま) が用いられる) "Yes, of course." "Thank you."
② 【席が [は]】 ●コンサート [飛行機] の席がとれる get a *seat for* the concert [*on* the plane]. ▸そのコンサートでは席が全部埋まった The *seats* were all filled at the concert. ▸いい席はすぐ埋まる The good *seats* soon fill up.
会話「この席はあいて (=ふさがって) いますか」「ええ, あいていますよ. どうぞ」 "Is this *seat* [*place*] taken [*vacant*]?" "No. It's free [*unoccupied*]. Go ahead." (⚠(1) vacant は通例地位・職などについて用いる. (2) あいていない場合には Ah, I'm saving [*taking*] it for my friend. (えーと, 友達に取っているのですが)/Well, I'm expecting my friend soon. (あの, 友達がまもなく来るのですが) などという)
③ 【席に】 ●席につく take a [one's] *seat*; (座る) sit down (⚠(1) 単に sit だと通例席についている状態を表す. (2)「夕食の席につく」は sit down to dinner). ▸席に戻りなさい Go back to your *seat*. ▸彼女はトムを席に案内した She ushered Tom to his *seat*. ▸彼は私の隣の席に座った He *sat* down next to me [*my* seat]. ▸前の席に1人, 後ろの席に3人乗せてタクシーは走りだした With two passengers in the front *seat* and three in the back, the taxi began to move.
④ 【席を】 ●席を離れる [立つ] leave [stand up from, 《書》 rise from] one's *seat*. ●席をとっておく save [keep] (*him*) a *seat*; save [keep] a *seat* (*for* him). ●バスの中でおばあさんに席を譲る give one's *seat* [*place*] to an old woman on the bus. (⚠「…に席をあける」は make room for…) ▸彼女に私の席をすすめた I offered her my *seat*. ●席を替わっていただけませんか Would you mind changing *seats* [*places*] with me? (⚠複数形に注意) ▸試験の時間が終わるまで席を離れてはいけません Please keep [remain on] your *seats* until the exam period ends. ▸もう少し席を詰めてください Please *sit* a little closer./Please *squeeze up* a little. ▸彼は今席を外しています He isn't here right now./He *isn't at his desk* right now. ▸席を外してくれませんか Will you *leave* us alone now? ▸ちょっと席を外してよろしいですか May I *be excused* for a while? (⚠トイレに行くときなど. Excuse me a minute. ということも多い)
❷〖地位〗a position; (責任のある) a post. ●課長の席 the *position* of the section chief. ▸会長の席は今空いている The *post* of (board) chairman is vacant now.

❸〖場〗(⇨席上) ●宴会の席で醜態を演じる behave disgracefully *at* a feast. ●公の席でその事について話すな Don't talk about it *in public* [*where other people are there*]. (⚠後の方が口語的) ▸平松さんのために席を設けよう Let's give [hold] a (little) party for Mr. Hiramatsu.
- 席の暖まる暇がない (たえず活動している) be on the move; be always busy.
- 席を蹴る ▸彼は席をけって立った (=怒って出て行った) He stormed off [out of the room].

せき 咳 图 a cough. ●しつこい咳 a persistent *cough*. ▸まだ微熱があるがせきは出なくなった I'm still running a slight fever, but my *cough* is gone. ▸彼はせきがひどい. たばこをやめるべきだ He *coughs* a lot [has a bad *cough*]. He should stop smoking.
― 咳をする 動 cough. ●空せきをする have a dry *cough*. ●せきをして魚の骨を吐き出す *cough up* [*out*] a fishbone. ●せきをして血を吐く *cough up* blood. ▸彼は一晩中ひどいせきをしていた He *was coughing* badly [violently] all night long.
- せき止め (薬) (take) (a) cough medicine; (ドロップ) a cough drop; (水薬) cough syrup. ●せき払い (⇨咳払い)

せき 堰 (ダム) a dam; (小さなせき) a weir /wíər/ (⚠川に魚獲りなどのために作る). ●可動堰 a movable *dam*. ●川にせきを作る build [construct] a *dam across* a river; dam a river (up).
- せきを切ったように ▸彼女はせきを切ったようにしゃべりだした She burst into a talk./He began to talk as if a *dam* inside him had broken.

せき 関 a barrier. (⇨圈 関所)
せき 積 图 the product.
せき 籍 (戸籍) a family register; (一員) a member.
●籍に入れる [を抜く] have one's name put on [removed from] the *family register*. ●K大学に籍をおいている be enrolled at K University. ●野球部に籍をおく be a *member* of the baseball club.

-せき -石❶〖時計の〗●21の石の時計 a watch of 21 *jewels*; a 21-*jewel* watch. ❷〖ラジオの〗●6石ラジオ a 6-*transistor* radio.

-せき -隻 ●数隻の船 a few ships. ●びょうぶ一隻 one folding screen.

せきあく 積悪 a series of evil deeds. (翻 積善)
せきうん 積雲 〖気象〗(a) cumulus; (@ cumuli).
せきえい 石英 〖鉱物〗quartz /kwɔ́ːrts/.
- 石英ガラス quartz [silica] glass.

せきがいせん 赤外線 infrared /ìnfrəréd/ (rays).
●赤外線カメラ an infrared camera. ●赤外線写真 an infrared photograph. ●赤外線療法 〖医学〗infrared (ray) therapy.

せきがく 碩学 a person of great learning [《書》 erudition]; a great [《書》 an erudite] scholar.
せきかっしょく 赤褐色 reddish-brown; auburn.
●赤褐色の髪 *reddish-brown* [*auburn*] hair.

せきがん 隻眼 图 one eye.
― 隻眼の 形 one-eyed.

せきぐん 赤軍 〖旧ソ連の正規軍〗the Red Army.
せきこむ 急き込む ●急き込んで (=せかせかと) 話す talk impatiently [very fast, (先を急いで) hurriedly] 《about》; (あえぎながら言う) gasp.

せきこむ 咳込む have* a fit of coughing /kɔ́(ː)fiŋ/.
●たばこを吸っては咳き込む *cough* (*badly*) *over* one's cigarette.

せきさい 積載 ― 積載する 動 (積む) load; (乗せて運ぶ) carry.
- 積載トン数 capacity [freight] tonnage. ●積載排水量 load displacement [draft]. (⚠draft は

せきざい 石材 (building) stone.
● 石材商 a stone dealer.

せきさん 積算 ⓖ〚累計〛adding up;〚見積もり〛(an) estimation.
— **積算する** 動 add up; estimate. ● 各支店の売上高を積算する *add up* 〚(合計する) *total*〛 the sales amount of each branch (store).
● 積算電力計 a watt-hour meter.

せきじ 席次 (成績順位) (academic) standing; ranking. ▶ぼくは席次が7番上がった I went up (↔came down) seven places in my class. ▶先学期クラスの席次は3番だった I ranked [came, was] third in my class last term.

せきじつ 昔日 old days; former times. (⇨⑯ 昔)
▶彼には昔日の面影がない He is not *what* he *used to be*.

せきじゅうじ 赤十字 ●赤十字社 the Red Cross; (公式名) the International Red Cross Society. (❗通例集合体と考えて単数扱いだが, 構成要素を考える場合は複数扱い) ● 日本赤十字社 the Japanese *Red Cross*. ● 赤十字病院 a Red Cross hospital.

せきしゅつ 析出 ⓖ〚化学〛separation;〚沈殿物・堆積物〛deposition.
— **析出する** 動 separate; deposit.

せきしゅん 惜春 (a) lamentation for the passage of spring [one's youth].

せきじゅん 席順 the order of seats, the seating places. ● 生徒の席順を決める decide *the seating places* of one's students.

せきしょ 関所 a barrier;(検問所) a checkpoint.
● 関所を越える〚破る〛pass through [break through] a *barrier*.

せきじょう 席上 ● 国際会議の席上で(=場で) *at* [(時に) *on the occasion of*] the international conference.

せきしょく 赤色 ❶〚赤い色〛a red color.
❷〚共産主義〛communism.

せきずい 脊髄〚解剖〛a spinal /spáinl/ cord.
● 脊髄炎 myelitis /màiəláitəs/. ● 脊髄神経 the spinal nerve. ● 脊髄注射 a spinal injection.
● 脊髄麻酔 spinal anesthesia.

せきせいいんこ 背黄青鸚哥〚鳥〛a budgerigar; a shell [a grass] parakeet.

せきせつ 積雪 (fallen) snow;〚積雪量〛a snowfall.
▶積雪は3メートルぐらいです The *snow* is [lies] about three meters deep. ▶高速道路は積雪(=大雪)のため通行止めになった The expressway was closed because of the *heavy snow*.

せきぜん 積善 a series of good deeds. (㊙ 積悪)

せきそう 積層 ● 積層乾電池 a layered dry cell [battery].

せきぞう 石造 ● 石造の家 a house *built of stone*; a *stone* [a *stone-built*] house.

せきぞう 石像 a stone statue.

せきたてる せき立てる〚せかせる〛(急かせる) hurry [him] (up) (⇨急ぐ); make* [him] hurry;〚駆り立てる〛urge [him] (on [forward]);(精神的に)押迫して) press [him]. ● 決心するようせき立てる *urge* [*press*] [him] *to* make a decision. (❗press の方が強意的で堅い語)

せきたん 石炭 (物質としての) coal (❗数えるときは a piece [a stone, a lump] of coal のにように); (1個の) a coal (❗特に燃えている石炭の塊のこと.「砕いた」燃料用石炭」の意では(英)では coals, (米)では ⓤ). ● 燃えている石炭 a live /láiv/ [a burning] *coal*. ● 石炭をたく burn *coal*. ▶ストーブに石炭をくべる put *coal* [(英) *coals*] in the stove. ● 石炭を掘

せきちく 石竹〚植物〛a (Chinese) pink.

せきちゅう 石柱 a stone pillar.

せきちゅう 脊柱 the spine /spáin/,〚解剖〛the spinal column.
● 脊柱後湾症 kyphosis /kaifóusis/. ● 脊柱側湾症 scoliosis /skòulióusis/. ● 脊柱湾曲 spinal curvature.

せきちん 赤沈 〚「赤血球沈降速度」の略〛(⇨赤血球)

せきつい 脊椎〚背骨〛the backbone;〚脊柱〛〚解剖〛the spinal /spáinl/ column; the vertebrae /və́ːrtəbriː/. (❗複数形で. 脊椎骨の一つは a vertebra).
● 脊椎カリエス spinal caries /kéəriz/. ● 現在は「結核性脊椎炎」tuberculous spondylitis /-láitəs/ という) ● 脊椎動物 a vertebrate (↔invertebrate) (animal).

せきてい 石庭 a rock garden;(説明的に) a Japanese-style garden with rocks and sand deliberately arranged to represent something philosophical.

せきとう 石塔 a tombstone, a gravestone.

せきどう 赤道 the equator /ikwéitər/ (❗しばしば the E-); the line. ● 赤道を横切る cross *the equator* [*line*]. ▶赤道付近は大変暑い It is very hot at around *the equator*. ▶船は赤道直下に来ている The ship is right *on* [ˣunder] *the equator*.
● 赤道祭 Neptune's revel;(説明的に) the ceremony of crossing the equator.

せきどうギニア 赤道ギニア〚国名〛Equatorial Guinea;(公式名) the Republic of Equatorial Guinea. (首都 Malabo) ● 赤道ギニア人 an Equatorial Guinean. ● 赤道ギニア(人)の Equatorial Guinean.

せきとめる 堰き止める, 塞き止める (ダムを作って) dam (-mm-);(a river)(up);(抑制する) keep* [hold*] ... back. ● 水の流れをせき止める *stop* the water *from* flowing. ● さくで人の流れをせき止める *keep back* the flow of people with a barrier.

せきとり 関取 a *sekitori*;(説明的に) professional sumo wrestlers in the top two ranks, *makuuchi* and *juryo*.

*****せきにん 責任** (a) responsibility 《for》 (↔irresponsibility); charge; the blame 《for》; one's [the] fault; duty; liability; accountability.

使い分け
responsibility 自分の仕事や義務を遂行する責任.
charge 人や組織に対して管理や世話をする責任.
blame 失敗など悪いことに対して負う責め.
fault 望ましくない状態を引き起こした責任や過失の原因.
duty 社会的・職業上の責任や道徳上の義務, 法律上の(債務)義務.
liability 特に借金の支払い・損害賠償などの法律上生じる義務.
accountability その立場のある人が他の人に説明する責務.

①〚~責任〛● 共同責任 (a) joint [(a) shared] *responsibility*. ● 経営責任 management *responsibilities*; *responsibilities* for the management. ● 刑事責任 criminal *liability*. ● 説明責任 accountability.

②〚責任~〛● 責任者 (⇨責任者) ● 責任問題 a question of where the *responsibility* lies; a question of who is to blame [is *responsible*].
● 責任逃れをする pass the buck 《to him》. (❗⑥ 第5文例]) ▶私は責任逃れはしない I won't evade

my *resposibility* for it./The buck stops here. ▶彼は責任感が強い[ない] He has a strong [no] sense of *responsibility*. ▶責任重大だ That is a great [a grave, a heavy] *responsibility*.

③《責任が[は]》 ▶責任はすべて私にある All the *responsibility* [The full *responsibility*] is mine./ I am fully *responsible for* it. ▶それに対しての最終的な[道義的]責任は彼にある The ultimate [moral] *responsibility* for it lies [rests] with [on] him./He has the ultimate [moral] *responsibility for* it./He is ultimately *responsible for* it. ▶それに対しては会社側に責任がない There is no *responsibility* on the company's part *for* it. ▶彼はこの借金を支払う責任がある He has the *responsibility to* pay this debt./He is *liable for* this debt. ▶当該大臣の責任が問われるべきだ The minister concerned should be brought [called] to account for it.

④《責任の》 ▶この責任には私にもある I am partly *responsible* [*to blame*] *for* this./This is partly my (own) *fault*. ▶彼は大変責任のある地位についている He holds a position of great *responsibility* [a very *responsible* position]. (❗「責任のある地位の人」は *a person* in *a position* of *responsibility*, 複数形は *people* in positions of ...) ▶責任の所在(＝だれに責任があるか)が明らかでない It is not clear who is *responsible* [*to blame*]./(どこに責任があるか) It is not clear where the *responsibility* lies.

⑤《責任に》 ▶彼はそれを自己の責任において(＝で)やった He did it *on* his own *responsibility*. (❗「独断で」という悪い意味を含むことがある) ▶ここは自分の責任において横断しなさい (当カ汀書は責任を負いません)〈揭示〉 Cross here *at your own risk*. (❗日本の「横断禁止」に相当する)

⑥《責任を》 ▶責任を感じる feel *responsible* (*for*). ▶責任を問う bring [call] 〈him〉 to account. ▶子供に対する親の責任を果たす[回避する] meet [avoid, evade] parents' *responsibilities to* their children. ▶彼はその火事の全責任を負った[取った] He took all the *blame* for the fire./He took [accepted, assumed] full *responsibility for* the fire. ▶勘定は私が責任を持って払います I'll take the [×my] *responsibility for* [*of*] paying the bill. ▶...*to* pay the bill は不可/(面倒をみる) I'll *look after* the bill. ▶自分の言ったことに責任を持つべきだ You should *be responsible for* what you said./(言ったことはすべきだ) You should do what you said. ▶彼は立派に自分の責任を果たした He carried out his *responsibility* splendidly./ He did his *duty* well. ▶責任を人に転嫁してはいけない You should not shift your *responsibility* [《話》 pass the *buck*] *to* other people. (❗《米話》で「責任転嫁」は buck-passing, 「責任転嫁をする人」を *a buck passer* という)/(人に責任を押しつけるな) You should not thrust your *responsibility* on other people. ▶我々はその事故に対する彼の責任を追求した We accused him of *responsibility* for the accident./(事故を彼のせいだとした) We blamed him *for* the accident [《話》the accident *on* him]./We put the *blame for* the accident *on* him. ▶何が起きても私はあなたに一切責任を負いません I will not be *responsible* [I will not *answer*] *to* you *for* anything that happens.

⑦《責任が》 ▶子供に行儀を教えるのは親の責任だ It is parents' *responsibility* [《義務》 *duty*] to teach their children manners. ▶遅れたのは私の責任ではない It's not my *fault* [×my *blame*] (that) I am late. (⇨所為(ぜい))

せきにんしゃ 責任者 a person in charge. ●最高責任者 the chief executive. ●最高経営責任者 a chief executive *officer* (略 CEO). ●最高業務執行責任者 a chief operating *officer* (略 COO). ▶ここの[この店の]責任者はだれですか Who is *in charge* here [*of* this store]?

せきねん 積年 ●積年の努力のおかげで thanks to (*many*) *years* of efforts [hard work]. ●積年の確執 a *long-standing* feud.

せきのやま 関の山 ●あの試験は 50 点が関の山だ (期待できる最高の点だ) In the exam 50 percent is about *the highest* I *can expect*./(...を得るのが精一杯だ) It is *all* I *can do* to get 50 percent in the exam. ▶私の頭ではその大学が関の山だ With a brain like mine that college is *the best* [×*highest*] I *can expect*. (❗ best の部分は文脈によって most (最多), biggest (最大)などとなる)

せきはい 惜敗 ――惜敗する 動 (選挙などでわずかの差で負ける) lose [be defeated] by a narrow margin; (試合で接戦の末負ける) lose a close game.

せきばく 寂寞 desolation; (孤独) loneliness. ●寂寞とした光景 a *desolate* sight.

せきばらい 咳払い ―― 咳払いをする 動 (注意・警告のため) give a (*warning*) *cough* /k5(:)f/; (のどのつかえを取るため) clear one's throat (❗くしゃみなどの時と同様に Excuse me! (失礼)を添える). ▶彼はえへんと咳払いをしてから話し始めた He cleared his *throat* a bit [話] *coughed* a *frog* out of his *throat*] and began to speak. (❗frog は「声のかすれ」)

せきはん 赤飯 red rice, happy rice; (説明的に) glutinous rice steamed with adzuki beans or *sasage* beans (often served on happy occasions).

せきばん 石版 ●石版印刷 lithógraphy. ●石版画 a lithográph.

せきひ 石碑 ●A氏を記念して石碑(＝記念碑)を建てる build a *stone monument* to the memory of Mr. A. (⇨石塔)

せきひん 赤貧 ●赤貧洗うがごとし ▶彼の暮らしは赤貧洗うがごとしである(＝非常に貧しい) He lives *in extreme* [*grinding*, 《書》*abject*] *poverty*. (❗be as poor as a church mouse は今では古い句)

せきふ 石斧 a stone ax.

せきぶつ 石仏 a stone Buddhist image.

せきぶん 積分 图《数学》 integration; (積分学) integral calculus.
―― 積分する 動 íntegrate.

せきへい 積弊 ●積弊を除く get rid of *long-standing* [(深く根ざした) *deep-rooted*] *evils*.

せきべつ 惜別 reluctance to part (*from* him). ●惜別の情を述べる express one's *sorrow of parting*.

せきむ 責務 [務め] duty; (責任を強く感じる務め) (an) obligation. ●責務を果たす do one's *duty*.

せきめん 石綿 asbestos.

せきめん 赤面 图 a blush; (さっと赤くなること) a flush.
―― 赤面する 動 ●恥ずかしくて赤面する blush [(さっと) *flush*] *for* [*with*] shame. ●冗談に赤面する *blush at* a joke. ●赤面させる make 〈him〉 *blush*.

*****せきゆ** 石油 oil, petroleum /pətróuliəm/ (❗後の方が正式); 〔灯油〕《米》 kerosene /kérəsìːn/, 《英》 paraffin (oil). ●石油を掘り当てる strike [hit] *oil*. ●石油を精製する refine *oil*. ●石油を産出する produce *oil*. ●石油資源を開発する develop *oil* [*petroleum*] resources. ●石油採掘のボーリングをする drill *for oil*. ▶莫大な量の埋蔵石油が海底に眠っている Vast *oil* deposits repose beneath the ocean floor.

- **石油会社** an oil company. • **石油化学** petrochemistry. • **石油化学コンビナート** a petrochemical complex. • **石油危機** an oil crisis. (⇨オイル[オイルショック]) • **石油産業** an oil industry. • **石油ストーブ** an oil [a kerosene (米), a paraffin (英)] heater. • **石油製品** oil-based products. • **石油タンク** an oil tank. • **石油輸出国機構** the Organization of Petroleum Exporting Countries (略 OPEC).

セキュリティー 〖安全, 防犯〗security. • **サイバーセキュリティー** (インターネット社会の安全性) cyber security. • **ホームセキュリティー** (家庭向け防犯) home security. • **ナショナルセキュリティー** (国家安全保障) national security.

せきらら 赤裸々 ── 赤裸々な 形 • 赤裸々な(=ありのままの)告白 a naked [(率直な) a frank] confession. • 赤裸々な(=むきだしの)真相 a bare [a naked, (包み隠しのない) a plain] truth.
── 赤裸々に 副 • 自分の過去を赤裸々に話す speak one's past frankly [candidly, plainly].

せきらんうん 積乱雲 〖気象〗(a) cumulonimbus /kjùːmjəlouníməbəs/ (複 -bi /-bai/). (⇨入道雲)

せきり 赤痢 〖医学〗dysentery /dísəntèri/.
• **赤痢菌** a dysentery germ.

せきりょう 席代 (室代) a charge for the room; (レストランなどの) a cover charge. (✕ a table charge は和製英語)

せきりょくしきもう 赤緑色盲 〖医学〗red-green blindness.

せきれい 〖鳥〗a water wagtail. (❗ 英国では a pied wagtail (セグロセキレイ)をさす)

せきわけ 関脇 〖相撲〗sekiwake; (説明的に) the third highest position on the official listing of sumo rank.

せく 咳く (咳をする) cough. (⇨咳をする)

せく 急く 〖急ぐ〗hurry; 〖軽率に急いでやる〗rush. • 結論をせく rush [jump] to conclusions. ▶そんなにせいてはいけない Don't be in such a hurry./(焦っていらするな) Don't be so impatient./(そうむきになるな) Take it easy.
• **急いては事を仕損じる** 〘ことわざ〙Haste makes waste.

せく 塞く, 堰く • 川の水をせく stop the water in a river from flowing; (ダムを造って) dam up a river.

セクシー ── セクシーな 形 《話》sexy. • セクシーな女の子[ドレス] a sexy girl [dress].

セクシャルハラスメント (⇨セクハラ)

セクション a section.

セクター 〖部門, 区域〗a sector; 〖ディスクの記録単位〗〖コンピュータ〗a sector. • **第三セクター** (半民半官) a joint venture of a local government and private businesses; 《和製語》a third sector.

セクト a sect. • 党内のセクト間(=派閥間)の抗争 factional disputes in the party.
• **セクト主義** sectionalism.

セクハラ 〖性的嫌がらせ〗sexual harassment. (❗ harass は「繰り返し嫌がらせをする」の意) • 言葉によるセクハラ verbal sexual harassment. ▶この会社には上司による女性の部下へのセクハラが何件かあった In this office there were some cases of sexual harassment of [against] women by their supervisors. ▶彼女たちはセクハラを受けたとして上司を訴えた They sued their supervisor, claiming they had been sexually harassed.

セグメント 〖部分, 区分〗a segment.
• **セグメント情報** (financial) information by segment; segment [segmental] information. (〖参考〗部門別・地域別の売り上げ損益を示す会計報告)

セクレタリー 〖秘書〗a secretary.

せぐろいわし 背黒鰯 〖魚介〗an anchovy.

せぐろかもめ 背黒鴎 〖鳥〗a herring gull.

***せけん** 世間 〖世の中〗 the world; (現実社会) the real world; (世の習い) the ways of the world; (人生) life; 〖一般の人々〗the public; (人々) people.

① 【世間~】• 世間一般の風潮[考え] a prevailing trend [view]. •(⇨世間体, 世間話)

② 【世間は[が]】▶世間は(広いようで)狭いものですね It's (such) a small world, isn't it? [, indeed.] ▶世間が何を言っても気にしない I don't care what people say. ▶世間はとかくうるさいものだ People will talk. (❗ この will は習性を表す)

③ 【世間の】• 世間の常識 conventional wisdom. • 世間の注意をよく引きつける attract public attention. ▶彼は世間のことをよく知っている He has seen much of life [the world]./He is a man of the world. (⇨世間ının) ▶その番組は世間の批判で放送中止にせざるを得なかった Public criticism forced the program off the air. ▶世間の評判をとても気にする人がいる Some people care too much about what people say about them. ▶彼は世間の眼を気にかけない He doesn't care (a bit) about his public reputation./He is indifferent to what others think about him. ▶そのことで彼は世間の物笑いの種になった That made him a laughingstock (of the world).

④ 【世間に】• 世間に出る go [get] out into the world. ▶彼の名は世間にほとんど知られていない His name is little known to the world [the public]. ▶世間にはいろいろな人がいるものだ 〘ことわざ〙It takes all sorts (to make a world). ▶恥ずかしくて世間に顔向けできない I'm ashamed to show myself in public. • 渡る世間に鬼はない (⇨渡る 〖成句〗)

⑤ 【世間を】• 世間を避ける [渡る] live out of [go through] the world. • 世間を騒がす cause a (great) sensation; (恐怖に陥れる) cause panic. ▶あの人は頑固なので自分で世間を狭くしている(=交際範囲が狭い) He is stubborn, so he has a small circle of acquaintances.
• **世間が狭い** • 私は世間(=交際範囲)が狭い I have a narrow [a small] circle of acquaintances.
• **世間知らず** • 彼女は世間知らずだ She knows nothing of the world./She doesn't understand the ways of the world./She hasn't seen life./(経験不足だ) She's so naive [inexperienced]./《話》She hasn't been around much.
• **世間擦れ** • 世間擦れしている have too much worldly experience; be too wise to the ways of the world; be too sophisticated.
• **世間並みの[に]** (普通の) ordinary; (平均の) average. • 世間並みの暮らしをする lead [live] an ordinary life. ▶彼は世間並みに言って物分かりのいい人だ He is a sensible man as the world goes.

せけんてい 世間体 • 世間体がよい[悪い] look [do not look] respectable. • 世間体をつくろう keep up [save] appearances.

せけんばなし 世間話 • 世間話をする make small talk; (おしゃべりをする) have a chat, 《話》chitchat.

せけんむねさんよう『世間胸算用』Worldly Mental Calculations. (〖参考〗井原西鶴の浮世草子)

せこ 世故 • 世故にたけている know a lot about the world; be worldly-wise; be a man [a woman] of the world.

せこ 勢子 (狩猟の獲物を駆り立てる人) a beater.

せこい 〖ずるい〗(策をろうする) crafty; (こすい) sly; (こそこそした) 《話》sneaky; 〖けちな〗stingy; 《話》tight-fisted; 《米話》cheap; (みみっちい)《話》measly; (了見の狭い) petty(-minded).

せこう 施工 图 〖建設〗construction; building.
—— **施工する** 動 construct; build.

せこう 施行 〖法律〗enforcement. (⇨施行(しこう))

セコハン •セコハンで[の] secondhand. (⇨中古)

セコンド 〖ボクシングの介添人〗a second, a handler.

-せざるをえない -せざるを得ない (⇨-ざるをえない)

セザンヌ 〖フランスの画家〗Cézanne /seizá:n/ (Paul ~).

セし セ氏 centigrade. (⇨摂氏(せっし))

せじ 世事 worldly affairs. •世事にうとい know little of the world [worldly affairs]. (⇨世故)

せじ 世辞 (⇨お世辞)

せしめる •彼の金をせしめる(=だまして取る) cheat [swindle] him out of his money; (ゆすって取る) extort money from him; (甘言で取る)《やや書》wheedle money from [out of] him.

せしゅ 施主 〖寄進者〗a donor; 〖葬式の喪主〗the chief mourner; 〖建築・設計などの注文主〗the client of the builder.

せしゅう 世襲 —— **世襲の** 形 hereditary /hərédəteri/. ▶天皇の地位は世襲制である The position of the emperor is hereditary.
•世襲財産 hereditary property [estate].

せじょう 世上 (世の中)the world.

せじょう 世情 •世情(=世間の複雑な事情)に通じている [うとい] know a lot [be ignorant] of (the ways of) the world.

せじょう 施錠 图 locking.
—— **施錠する** 動 •ドアに施錠する lock a door.

せじん 世人 people; (一般の人) people in general, the (general) public.

せすじ 背筋 〖背骨〗the spine /spáin/. •背筋を伸ばして straighten one's spine [(背中)back]. •背筋を伸ばして座る sit up straight. •背筋が痛む I have a pain in my back. ▶彼は背が高く, 背筋もぴんとしていた He was tall and straight-backed./He was straight and tall.
•背筋が寒くなる ▶背筋が寒くなった(=ぞっとした) Cold shivers ran up my spine./I felt a chill [chills] go down my spine./It sent shivers along [down] my spine. (**!** it の代わりに the ghost story, the sound in the kitchen などが主語になる)

ゼスチャー a gesture. (⇨ジェスチャー)

-せずに without 《doing》; (...する代わりに)instead of 《doing》.

ぜせい 是正 —— **是正する** 動 •誤りを是正する(=改める) correct [〖書〗rectify] a mistake [an error].
•貿易のひどい不均衡を是正する correct [put right] the serious trade imbalance.

せせこましい •物の見方がせせこましい be rather narrow in outlook; take narrow(-minded) views. •せせこましい(=狭苦しい[息苦しい]大都会を離れて暮らす live far away from the closeness [stuffiness] of a big city.

ぜぜひひ 是是非非 •是是非非主義 the principle of being fair and just. •是是非非主義(=公平無私)である be impartial; be fair and just.

せせらぎ (小さな流れ) a small [a little] stream; (小川)《やや書》a brook. •せせらぎの音 the murmur of a small stream; the babbling of a brook.

せせらわらい せせら笑い a sneer.

せせらわらう せせら笑う sneer [laugh sneeringly] 《at》.

せそう 世相 〖社会情勢〗social conditions; 〖世間の様相〗a phase [an aspect] of life. ▶犯罪は現代のさまざまな世相を反映する Crimes reflect various aspects of the present society [life].

ぜぞく 世俗 图 •世俗(=世間)にとらわれない keep [stand] aloof from the world [(世間的なこと)《やや書》worldly things]. •世俗(=大衆)にこびる curry favor with the masses.
—— **世俗の, 世俗的な** 形 worldly. •世俗的な人たち《やや書》worldly people.

せたい 世帯 (同居人を含めた家族) a household; (家族) a family. •2 人世帯 a two-person household. •2 世帯用住宅 a two-family [《米》a duplex] house.
•世帯数 the number of households. •世帯主 the head of the household.

*せだい 世代 a generation. (**!**(1) 約 30 年間をさす. (2) 集合的に 1 世代の人々をさす. その場合単・複両用い) •2 世代前 two generations ago. •世代間の隔絶 a generation gap. •母の世代の人々 the people of my mother's generation. ▶その料理法は母から娘へ何世代にもわたって受け継がれてきた The recipe has been handed down from mother to daughter for long generations. (**!**「母から娘へ」をとると次のようになる: The recipe has been handed down from generation to generation.) ▶私たちはテレビ世代である We belong to the television generation. ▶若い世代の人々は適応能力がある The younger [rising] generation (↔the older generation) is [are] adaptable. ▶相撲界では世代交代が行われている A change of generations is taking place in the sumo world.

せたけ 背丈 height /háit/. (⇨身長)

セダン 《米》a sedan, 《英》a saloon (car).

せちがらい 世知辛い (無情な) cold; (暮らしにくい) hard. ▶世知辛い世の中だ It's a cold [a hard] world (to live in).

せつ 節 ❶ 〖時〗when 《+節》; at the time of .... (⇨時(とき), 際) ▶その節はどうもありがとう Thank you very much for your kindness at that time. (**参考** 米英ではそのときに礼をいうだけで後々繰り返して礼を言う習慣はない)
❷ 〖文章などの〗(まとまりのある一部分) a passage; (章の下位区分) a section; (段落) a paragraph; 〖文法〗a clause. •聖書の 1 節 a passage from the Bible; a Bible passage. •聖書の第 3 章 12 節という場合は chapter three, (**!**verse twelve) •難しい節〖最後の 2 小節〗をテンポをあえて弾く play difficult passages [the last two bars] in slower tempo. •名詞〖形容詞; 副詞〗節 a noun [an adjective; an adverb] clause. ▶金融情報は報告書の第 7 節に載っている Financial information is contained in section seven of the report. ▶6 ページの第 2 節を読みなさい Read the second paragraph of page six.
❸ 〖節操〗one's principles. (⇨信念)

せつ 説 〖意見〗(考え) an opinion; (見解) a view (**!** しばしば複数形で); 〖学説〗a theory; 〖風評〗(a) rumor. •説(=自説)を曲げる[曲げない] change [stick to] one's (own) opinion [views]. •説を同じく[異に]する agree [disagree] with 《him》 (in opinion). (**!**通例進行形で, 受身不可) •新しい説(=学説)を唱える put forward [establish, 《やや書》advance] a new theory. (**!** put forward が最も口語的) ▶彼の説では..., 私の opinion, ... ×according to his opinion とはいわない); he says (that).... ▶(その点では)お説のとおりです I quite agree with [×to] you (on that point). ▶それに関しては いろいろな説がある There are a lot of different opinions about it. ▶その盗難は内部の犯行との説がある People say [It is said, There is a rumor, 《やや書》

せつえい 設営 construction.
— **設営する 動** ●中継局を設営する *construct* [*build*] a relay station. ●テントを設営する *pitch* [*put up, set up*] a tent.

ぜつえん 絶縁 图 ❶ [電気・熱などからの] insulation. ❷ [縁を切ること] breaking off relations 《*with*》.
— **絶縁する 動** ❶ [電気・熱などから] insulate. ❷ [縁を切る] ●彼女と絶縁する *break* (*up*) *with* her; *break off relations with* her. ●絶縁線 (an) insulated wire. ●絶縁体 an insulator. ●絶縁テープ fríction [insulating] tàpe.

せっか 石化 petrifaction. — **石化する 動** petrify.

せっか 赤化 — **赤化する 動** (共産主義化する) go [turn] communist; (共産主義者になる) become a communist.

せっか 雪加, 雪下 [鳥] a fan-tailed warbler.

せっか 舌禍 ●舌禍事件 a trouble one has caused by one's slip of the tongue [one's careless remarks].

ぜっか 絶佳 ●風景絶佳 a superb view 《*of*》.

せっかい 切開 图 [医学] (an) incision. ●切開[心臓切開]手術 a surgical [an open-heart] operation.
— **切開する 動** incise; make an incision 《*in*》 (切り開く) cut ... open [*out*]; (手術する) operate 《*on* him》. ●患部を切開する *cut* the affected part(s) *open* [*out*].

せっかい 石灰 图 lime /láim/. ●生(₅)石灰 quicklime. ●消石灰 slaked *lime*. ●石灰質の calcareous; calcic.
— **石灰化する 動** calcify. ●石灰石[岩] limestone. ●石灰洞 a limestone cavern [cave]. ●石灰乳 [化学] milk of lime.

せっかい 節介 (⇨お節介)

せつがい 雪害 snow damage; damage from snow. ▶この地方の樹木は雪害をひどく受ける The trees in this region *are badly damaged by the snow*.

*せっかく **折角** ❶ [骨を折って] ▶我々のせっかくの(=すべての)苦労が水の泡になった *All* our efforts came to nothing. ▶彼はせっかく(=こつこつ)ためた金を全部なくした He lost all the money he saved (up) *steadily*. ▶せっかく(=はるばる)東京まで行ったのに会議は中止になった I went *all the way to* Tokyo, but the meeting was canceled.
❷ [親切な] ●彼のせっかくの忠告をむだにする throw away his *kind* advice.
会話 「あした来れるかい」「せっかく(のお誘い)だけれどだめなんだ」 "Can you come tomorrow?" "*Thanks for asking*, but I'm afraid not [I can't]." (❗ I'm afraid は「申し訳ない」の気持ちを伝えるが, I'm sorry ほどその気持ちは強くない)
❸ [たまにしかない] [貴重な] precious, valuable; (まれな) rare; (待ち望んだ) long-awaited; (特別の) special. ●せっかくの時間をむだにする waste (one's) *precious* time. ●せっかくのチャンスを逃がす miss [lose] such a *rare* chance. ▶悪天候でせっかくの日曜日がだめになった The bad weather spoiled the Sunday we had been so much looking forward to./Because of the bad weather, the *long-awaited* Sunday was ruined. (❗前の方が口語

的)

ぜっかせん 舌下腺 [医学] the sublingual gland.

せっかち — せっかちな 形 hasty; (軽率な) rash; (辛抱できない) impatient; (そわそわしている) restless. ▶彼は生まれつきせっかちだ He is *hasty* by nature. ▶私はとてもせっかちなので船旅は好きになれない I'm too *impatient* to enjoy a sea trip.

せっかっしょく 赤褐色 《⇨赤(₅)褐色》

せっかん 石棺 a stone coffin; (彫刻などを施した古代の) a sarcophagus (榎 sarcophagi).

せっかん 折檻 — **折檻する 動** punish (a child) by beating (severely), 《書》chastise /tʃæstáiz/. ●言うことを聞かないといって子供をきびしく折檻する *chastise* a child severely *for* disobedience.

せつがん 切願 图 《書》an entreaty.
— **切願する 動** entreat (him *to do*).

せつがん 接岸 — **接岸する 動** come alongside a pier [a quay /ki:/]. (❗ pier は「桟橋」, quay は「埠頭(⅝ڑ)」の意)

ぜつがん 舌癌 cancer of the tongue.

せっき 石器 a stone implement [tool]. ●新[旧]石器時代 the New [Old] Stone Age; the Neolithic [Paleolithic] Age. ●石器時代の道具 a *Stone Age* tool.

せっきゃく 接客 ●接客態度が悪い be impolite to a customer.
— **接客する 動** attend to [serve, wait upon] a customer [a guest]. (❗ customer は商店などの客, guest はホテルなどの客)
●接客業 a hospitality business; a service trade.

せっきょう 説教 图 [宗教の] a sermon; [お説教の] a lecture. (⇨小言) ●説教壇に立つ stand in a pulpit. ▶説教はもうたくさんだ, 放っておいてくれ [話] I'm fed up with your *preaching at* me—just leave me alone!
— **説教(を)する 動** (宗教の) preach (a sermon) 《*to*》, preach 《him》 a sermon; (訓戒する) lecture, give 《him》 a lecture; (くどくどとさとす) 《けなして》 preach (*at*); (こらしめる) teach 《him》 a lesson. ●聴衆に聖書について見事な説教をする *preach a beautiful sermon* to the audience *on* [*about*] the Bible. ▶彼は遅刻したことについてさんざん説教された He was severely *lectured about* being late [(したために) *for* being late]. (❗「しないように」の意で ... lectured *not to* be late ということもある)

ぜっきょう 絶叫 图 a scream, a shriek. (⇨叫び声)
— **絶叫する 動** give a terrible cry; (声を限りに叫ぶ) cry out [shout, scream] at the top of one's voice. (⇨叫ぶ)

せっきょくせい 積極性 agressiveness. ▶彼女は積極性に富む She is *agressive*.

*せっきょくてき **積極的 —積極的な 形** (肯定的な, 建設的な) positive (↔negative) 《*in*+事, *with*+人》; (活動的な, 精力的な) active (↔passive) 《*in*》; (攻撃的な) aggressive (❗特にセールスなど積極性が必要な場合に用いられる); (熱心な) enthusiastic; (いつでも喜んでする) be willing [ready] (*to do*). ●積極的な態度をとる take a *positive* attitude 《*toward*》. ●積極的な(=押しの強い)セールスマン an *aggressive* salesman. ▶彼は地域社会の仕事に積極的でした He *was active in* community affairs. ▶彼は人助けに積極的だ He's *willing* [*ready*] to help people. (❗ willing には頼まれたり必要からするという含みがあり, ready の方が積極的な態度を示す)/He *willingly* [《やや書》*readily*] helps people.
— **積極的に 副** positively; actively; (快く) willingly. ●積極的に考える think *positively*. ●(運動competitions)

が積極的にプレーする play *aggressively*. ●積極的に進む go ahead [on] with (the plan); push on with (the work). ●その計画に積極的に参加する take an *active* part [participate *actively*, (参加している) be an *active* participant] in the project. ▶彼女は積極的にその問題に取り組んだ She attacked the problem *actively*. ▶もっと積極的に話すようにしなさい Try to be more assertive./Learn to assert yourself.

せっきん 接近 图 approach; access /ǽkses/. (! 前の方は単に場所的・時間的に近づくこと。後の方は物理的に接近し目ざす物に触れたり、入り込むこと) ●台風の接近 the *approach* of a typhoon.

—— **接近する** 動 approach, come* near (...). (⇨近付く) ▶台風が九州に接近している A typhoon *is approaching* [×approaching to] Kyushu. ▶彼らは実力が接近している(=ほとんど等しい) They are *almost equal* in (their) ability. ▶彼らは年齢が接近している They *are almost the same* age./Their ages *are* [Their age is] *very close*.

せっく 節句 a seasonal festival. ●端午の節句 the Boys' *Festival*. ●桃の節句 the Doll's *Festival*. ▶怠け者の節句働き Idle folks [people] have the most labor.

ぜっく 絶句 —— **絶句する** 動 〖言葉が見つからない〗 cannot find words (to say); (驚いて) be struck speechless; be dumbfounded /dʌ́mfáundid/; 〖泣きくずれる〗 break down (and cry). ▶事故の知らせを聞いたときしばし絶句した(=しゃべれなかった) I *was unable to speak* [*was left speechless*] (for) a while when I heard the news of the accident.

セックス 图 (性交) 〖書〗(sexual) intercourse; sex (! 本来は男女の性別、雌雄の区別の意). (⇨性) ●セックスアピールがある have (a lot of) *sex* appeal; be sexy. (! 後の方が少し意味が強い) ●セックスに関心を持つようになる become *sexually* aware.

—— **セックスする** 動 have sex [(sexual) intercourse] 《with》; make love 《to, with》; sleep 《with》. (!最後の二つは婉曲的な言い方)
●セックスシンボル a sex symbol. ●セックスセラピー sex therapy. ●セックスチェック (運動選手の) the gender examination; the sex check. ●セックスフレンド a bedmate.

セックスレス —— **セックスレスの** 形 sexless. ●セックスレスの夫婦 sexless couple.

せっくつ 石窟 a stone cave; (地下の洞窟) a cavern. ●石窟寺 a cave temple.

せっけい 設計 图 a plan; (形や構造などの外観の) a design. ●生活[人生]設計 life planning.

—— **設計する** 動 plan (-nn-); design; (配置を考慮して) lay*... out; (設計図をかく) draw* a plan 《for》. ▶庭を設計する *plan* [*design*, *lay out*] a garden. ▶彼は自分の人生を設計したが、そのとおりにはいかなかった He *planned* his (own) life, but it didn't work out that way.

●設計技師 a designer. ●設計図 a plan (for a building); (下書きの) a draft; (青写真) a blueprint; (仕様書) specifications.

せっけい 雪渓 a ravine (谷間) [a slope (斜面)] with perpetual snow.

ぜっけい 絶景 〖雄大な眺め〗 a grand [(壮大な) a magnificent, (壮麗な) a superb] view; 〖すばらしい眺め〗 a wonderful sight; 〖絵のように美しい風景〗 picturésque [grand] scenery. ▶絶景だなあ! What *a grand view* [*sight*]!

せっけいもじ 楔形文字 cuneiform characters.

せっけっきゅう 赤血球 【生理】a red corpuscle /kɔ́ːrpəsl/; a red (blood) cell.

●赤血球沈降速度 (measure) the erythrocyte sedimentation rate (略 ESR).

*****せっけん** 石鹸 soap.

> 解説 「1個の石けん」は a cake [a bar, a cube, a tablet, 〖話〗a piece] of *soap*. cake は「一定の形をしたかたまり」, bar は「棒状」, cube は「立方体」, tablet は「板状小片」。

●化粧[洗濯]石けん tóilet [láundry, wáshing] sóap. ●薬用[香水入りの]石けん medical [perfumed] *soap*. ●粉石けん *soap* powder. ●石けんの泡 *soap* bubbles; (石けん水を振ってできた) lather. ●ひげをそる前に顔に石けんを塗る lather one's face before shaving. (! lather は「石けんの泡を塗る」の意) ●石けんで顔を洗う *soap* one's face and then wash the soap off; wash one's face with *soap* and water. ▶この石けんは泡立ちがよい This *soap* lathers (up) well. ▶目に石けんが入った I got *soap* in my eyes.

●石けん入れ a sóap cáse. ●石けん水 soapy water; (泡立った) (soap) suds (! 複数形で, 複数扱い). (!「石けん水で洗う」は wash (clothes) with *soap and water* という)

せっけん 席巻 —— **席巻する** 動 sweep 《over》; (征服する) conquer.

せっけん 接見 图 (謁見) an audience 《with》.
—— **接見する** 動 grant (him) an audience; grant an audience 《to him》.
●接見室 an audience room; a formal interview room.

せっけん 切言 图 (心からの説得) earnest persuasion.
—— **切言する** 動 ●あらためて出直すよう彼に切言する *strongly persuade* him *to* make a fresh start.

せっけん 雪原 a snowfield, a snowy field.

せつげん 節減 图 (減らすこと) (a) reduction; (切り詰めること) 〖書〗(a) curtailment.
—— **節減する** 動 ●そのプロジェクトの経費を節減する *reduce* [*cut*, *cut down* (on), 〖書〗*curtail*] the expenses for the project.

ゼッケン [<ドイツ語] (番号) a player's [an athlete's] number; (番号を書いた布) a number cloth. ●ゼッケン8番の選手 a player (wearing) number 8.

せっこう 斥候 ●斥候を出す send out a *scout*.

せっこう 石工 a mason /méisn/, a stonemason.

せっこう 石膏 (鉱物) gypsum; (粉末の) plaster (of Paris). ▶警察は石膏でその足跡の鋳型を作った The police made *plaster* casts of the footprints.
●石膏細工 plaster work. ●石膏像 a plaster figure [statue]; (胸像) a plaster bust. ●石膏板 《a sheet of》 sheetrock. (! 壁板に使う建材)

せっこう 拙攻 poor offense.

せっこう 拙稿 my manuscript. (⇨拙宅)

せつごう 接合 图 〖つなぎ合わせること〗joining; (接続) a connection; 〖細胞・固体の〗【生物】zygosis; conjugation.
—— **接合する** 動 join 《A to B; A and B (together)》.
●2枚の金属板をはんだで接合する *join* two sheets of metal (*together*) with solder.
●接合剤 a bonding agent; cement.

ぜっこう 絶交 —— **絶交する** 動 break* off [〖書〗sever] relations 《with》; 〖話〗break off [up] 《with》 (! 恋人・夫婦などが別れるときによく用いる). ▶彼女と絶交した I *have broken off* [*up*] *with* her. ▶彼とは totally 二度と会いたくない I'm *through with* him. I never want to see him again.

ぜっこう 絶好 —— **絶好の** 形 (最もよい) best; (まさしく最適の) perfect; (理想的な) ideal. ▶スキーには絶好の

ぜっこうきゅう

日和だ It's a *perfect* [an *ideal*] day *for* skiing. ▶留学するには絶好の機会だ This is the *best chance to study abroad*.

ぜっこうきゅう 絶好球 an easy ball; a fat pitch.
ぜっこうちょう 絶好調 絶好調である be in the *best condition* [(運動選手が) in *top form*]. (⇨好調)
せっこつ 接骨 图 bonesetting.
—**接骨する** 動 (骨折を) set a broken bone; (脱臼(だっきゅう)を) set a dislocated bone.
●接骨医 an osteopath /ástiəpəθ/; (無資格の) a bonesetter.
せっさく 拙策 (まずい策略) a poor [an inadequate, an unsatisfactory] policy [plan]. ▶そんなことをすると拙策だ It *would be unwise* [*unadvisable*] to do so.
せっさたくま 切磋琢磨 ●切磋琢磨して(=お互いに競争して)学問に励む study [work] hard by *competing with* [*against*] *each other*.
ぜっさん 絶賛 图 ●絶賛を博す win [receive] *the highest praise* 《*from* ＋人, *for* ＋事》. ●批評家の絶賛を浴びる win *critical acclaim*; win *acclaim* from the critics. (❗acclaim は「大声でほめること」)
—**絶賛する** 動 praise 《it》 very highly; praise 《it》 to the skies. (⇨ほめる)
せっし 摂氏 céntigrade 《略 C., cent.》; Célsius 《略 C., Cels.》. 事情 米英では日常生活に摂氏でなく華氏を用いるのが普通. (⇨温度) ▶気温は摂氏12度だ The thermometer stands at 12 ℃. (❗twelve degrees centigrade [Celsius] と読む)
せつじ 接辞 〖文法〗an affix.
せつじつ 切実 ●切実な 形 〖緊急的〗urgent, pressing (⇨緊急); 〖切なる〗earnest; 〖深刻な〗serious. ●切実な問題 〖要求〗an *urgent* problem [request]. ●切実な願い an *earnest* desire [wish]. ▶英語を身につけなければと切実に思う I *keenly* feel the need of learning English.
せっしゃ 接写 图 close-up; (接写写真) a close-up, close-up photography.
—**接写する** 動 ●昆虫を接写する take a close-up [a *close-up picture*] *of* an insect.
せっしゃくわん 切歯扼腕 ●切歯扼腕した(=ひどく悔しがった) ▶彼は選挙に負けて切歯扼腕した He *was deeply chagrined at his defeat at the election*. / *To his great chagrin*, he was defeated at the election.
せっしゅ 拙守 a poor defense; 〖野球〗poor [bad] fielding [defense].
せっしゅ 窃取 图 a theft. —**窃取する** 動 steal.
せっしゅ 接種 (⇨予防接種)
せっしゅ 摂取 图 〖栄養などの〗(an) íntake; 〖文化・知識などの同化〗assimilation; 〖方針などの採用〗(an) adoption. ●1日の食物摂取量 the daily *intake* of food. ●アルコール摂取量を抑える check one's *alcohol intake*; (制限された量を飲む) take a limited amount of alcohol.
—**摂取する** 動 ●西洋文化を摂取する *assimilate* [*adopt*] the Western civilization.
せっしゅ 節酒 〖書〗temperance.
—**節酒する** 動 cut down on one's drinking; 《書》be temperate in drinking [in the consumption of alcohol].
せつじゅ 接受 (受け取ること) reception; (受け入れること) (an) acceptance.
—**接受する** 動 ●公文書を接受する *receive* an official document.
●接受国 a recipient country.
せっしゅう 接収 图 〖軍事目的のために取り上げること〗(a) requisition.

—**接収する** 動 requisition.
せつじょ 切除 图 〖書〗excision; (外科的除去) surgical removal.
—**切除する** 動 ●おできを切除する *cut off* [〖書〗*excise*] a boil; *remove* a boil *surgically* [*by surgery*].
せっしょう 折衝 图 〖交渉〗(a) negotiation. (❗しばしば複数形で) ●折衝のうまい人 a clever [(したたかな) a tough] negotiator. ●敵と休戦の折衝を開始する begin [enter into, open] *negotiations with* the enemy *for* an armistice. ●経営者側と折衝中で be *under negotiation with* the management. (❗主語は「労働時間」などの事柄) ▶労働時間について折衝が行われている *Negotiations* are underway [going on] about working hours.
—**折衝する** 動 《やや書》negotiate 《with》. ▶私たちはその件について市長と折衝した We *negotiated with* the mayor *on* that matter./We *discussed* the matter *with* the mayor.
せっしょう 殺生 ▶むやみに生き物を殺生してはならない Don't *kill* animals just for the sake of it. ▶そんな殺生な(=薄情な) It's *heartless* of you.
せっしょう 摂政 regency; (人) a regent.
せっしょう 絶唱 (すぐれた歌[詩]) a superb song [poem]; an excellent piece of poetry.
—**絶唱する** 動 sing with great feeling [emotion].
せっしょう 絶勝 ●絶勝の地 a place of *superb scenic beauty*; a place with a *superb view*.
せつじょうしゃ 雪上車 a snowmobile.
*せっしょく 接触 图 ●物体の双方の表面が接触すること. また「電気の接触」「人との交際・連絡」などの意にも用いる)); (a) touch 《特に人がある物体や人と一時的に触れ合うこと》. ●個人的接触 personal *contact*. ●両国間の接触 *contact* between the two countries. ●彼と接触を保つ keep [stay, be] *in contact with* him. ●私は彼と個人的接触がある[ない] I am *in* [*out of*] personal *contact with* him.
—**接触する** 動 contact, get in contact 《with》; (触れる) touch (⇨触れる❶); (接触させる) put 《him》 contact [in touch] 《with》. ●パリにいる彼と接触する(=連絡する) *contact* [*get in contact* [*touch*] *with*, *make contact with*] him in Paris. (❗最後は接触の2本の電線が接触すると機械が動き出す When these two wires *touch* [*come into contact*], the machine starts. ▶ぼくの車が彼女の車と接触して(=こすって)傷をつけてしまった My car *scraped* hers.
●接触感染 (病気の) contagion. ●接触事故 a near collision.
せっしょく 摂食 ●摂食障害 (suffer from) an eating disorders.
せっしょく 節食 ●節食する 動 eat less 《*of*》 sweets》(❗less を代名詞として用いれば of が必要); be moderate in eating; (ダイエットする) diet, go on a diet.
せつじょく 雪辱 ●雪辱を果たす (試合で) wipe out the disgrace of a former defeat; get one's *revenge*. ●雪辱戦 a return game [match].
ぜっしょく 絶食 (絶食すること) fasting; (絶食期間) a fast. (⇨断食) ●2日間の絶食 a two-day *fast*.
—**絶食する** 動 fast; go without food.
セッション 〖会合, 会議〗a session.
せつすい 節水 图 water saving [〖やや書〗conservation].
—**節水する** 動 ▶長い干ばつのため節水しなければならなかった We had to *save water* owing to a long spell

of dry weather.

せっする 接する ❶ [隣接する] (国境・境を接する) border (on [upon]...); (隣り合う) adjoin. ● 道路に接する(=沿いの)家 a house *on* the road. (⚠家が何軒もある場合は houses *along* the road) ▶彼の土地は私の土地に接している His land *borders* (*on*) [*adjoins, is adjacent to*] mine.
❷ [接触する] (手で触れる, 接触する) ▶この市は北側が海と接している This city *touches* the sea on the north.
❸ [応接する] (来客を迎える) have*, receive; (会う) see*; (接触する) have contact 《*with*》; (世話する) take* care of..., (病人・客などを) attend (to)...; (店の客に応対する) serve. ▶彼は毎日たくさんの来客に接する He *has* [*receives, sees*] a lot of visitors every day. ▶その村では外国人と接する機会がほとんどなかったので, 外国人に接したらよいのか(=どんな態度をとるべきか)とまどう人も多い The villagers have had very few opportunities to *have contact with* foreigners; many people [there are many who] do not know how to *behave toward* them. ▶彼女は愛情をもって生徒たちに接する She *takes* loving *care of* her pupils.
❹ [知らせなどに] (聞く) hear*; (受け取る) get*, receive. ▶彼の訃報(*)に接する *get* [*receive*] the news of his death. ▶彼は朗報に接して喜んだ He was delighted *at* [*to hear*] the good [happy] news. ▶彼は毎日英語に接するようにしている He tries *to expose himself to* English every day.

ぜっする 絶する ▶私の味わった苦悩は言語に絶した The agonies I underwent *were far beyond description.*/I went through *unspeakable* [*indescribable*] agonies. ▶その地震は想像を絶する被害をもたらした The earthquake caused *unimaginable* damage./The damage caused by the earthquake *was beyond* (*all*) *imagination*.

せっせい 摂生 — **摂生する** 動 be careful about [take care of] one's health.

せっせい 節制 图 moderation, (特にアルコールの)《書》temperance; (書) abstinence 《*from*》.
— **節制する** 動 ● 酒を節制する be *moderate* [《書》*temperate*] in drinking; (酒の量を減らす) cut down on drinking; (たくさん飲まない) do not drink too much. (⇒控える)

せつぜい 節税 lawful tax avoidance.
— **節税する** 動 legally avoid tax(es).

ぜっせい 絶世 ● 絶世の(=またとない)美女 a *rare* [(ほれぼれする)《話》*raving*,《話》*real*] beauty; (並外れた) a woman of *extraordinary* [(比類のない) *matchless*] beauty; (この世のものとも思えない) an *ethereal* beauty.

せつせつ 切々 — **切々たる** 形 (熱烈な) ardent, passionate; (真剣な) earnest. ● 切々たる願い an *ardent* [an *earnest*] wish.

せっせと ❶ [一生懸命に] (very) hard, diligently. (⚠後の方には慎重または徹底の意が含まれる) ▶彼女はいつもせっせと働く She always works (*very*) *hard*. ▶鳥がせっせと何かを巣に運ぶのが見えた Birds were seen carrying something *diligently* to their nest.
❷ [忙しく] busily; [休みなく] incessantly. ▶彼女は山積みの皿をせっせと洗っていた She was *busy* doing a pile of dishes.

せっせん 接戦 [[せり合い] a close /klóus/ game [match, race, contest]; [抜きつ抜かれつの] a seesaw game. ▶接戦の末についに勝った We [*Our* team] finally won a *close game*. ▶この選挙は最後まで接戦になる(=勝敗が予測できない)だろう This election is going to be a real *cliffhanger*.

せっせん 接線 [数学] a tangential line; a tangent.

ぜっせん 舌戦 verbal warfare; (激論) a heated discussion. ● 舌戦を繰り広げる be engaged in a *heated discussion*; discuss 《*it*》 hotly 《*with*》.

せつそう 節操 (信条) principles; (高潔さ) integrity; (志操堅固) constancy, (忠実) fidelity; (貞節) chastity. ● 節操のある人 a person of *principle* [*integrity*]. ● 節操のない男 a man who has no [without] *principles*; an *unprincipled* man. (⚠後の方が堅い言い方)

せつそう 雪像 a statue [an image] in snow; a snow statue [image].

せっそく 拙速 ● 拙速主義 a rough and ready [a quick but slipshod] method. ▶辞書の編集では拙速主義は避けなければならない When you make a dictionary, you must not rush through the job. (⚠rush (it) through は「よく考えないでさっさとやってしまう」の意)

せつぞく 接続 (a) connection.
— **接続する** 動 connect; join; link. (⇒つなぐ, 連絡する)

せつぞくし 接続詞 [文法] a conjunction.

せつぞくどうぶつ 節足動物 an arthropod.

せった 雪駄 *setta*; (説明的に) Japanese leather-soled sandals.

セッター ❶ [犬] a setter. ❷ [バレーボールの] a setter.

せったい 接待 图 [もてなし] entertainment; [応接] reception. ● お茶の接待をする *serve* tea. ▶私は接待の係です I am in charge of *reception* [*receiving visitors*].
— **接待する** 動 (もてなす) entertain; (応対する) receive. ▶彼女はお客を *entertain* one's guest(s). ● 接待係 a receptionist. ● 接待費 (費用) entertáinment expènses; (手当) an entertáinment allòwance.

ぜったい 絶対 — **絶対の, 絶対的な** 形 ábsolute. ● 絶対的な権力 *absolute* power [authority] 《*over*》. ● 絶対の真理 the *absolute* truth. ● 絶対視する regard 《*it* [*him*]》 as absolute. ▶彼は絶対安静が必要だ He needs (an) *absolute* [(完全な) (a) *complete*] rest.
— **絶対に** 副 ábsolutely, 《話》 positively, 《話》 dead; (確かに) certainly, surely, positively. ▶それは絶対に不可能だ It is *ábsolùtely* impóssible. (⚠アクセント移動に注意)/《話》*I bet* (*you*) it's impossible. ▶そのことについては絶対に知らない I know *absolutely* nothing about it. (⚠absolutely は否定を強める) ▶私はその計画に絶対(に)反対だ I am *positively* [*dead* (*set*)] against the plan. ▶あなたが車を買うのは絶対に認めませんよ I *won't ever* [《話》I'll *never ever*] hear of your buying a car. (⚠いずれも甘 never... より強意的であるが, 後の方がさらに否定を強める言い方)

会話 「君にはそれはできないよ」「絶対にできるさ」 "You can't do that." "*Certainly* [*Surely*] I cán./I'm (*quite*) *sure* [*positive*] I cán."

会話 「そこからの夕日は格別だって書いてあるわ」「じゃ絶対行きましょうよ」 "It says the sunset is superb up there." "Well, let's *be sure to* go there."

会話 「彼女はこれまで一度も会ったことはないんだね」「ええ, 絶対にありません」 "You never saw her before at any time?" "No, *never*."

会話 「彼はそのことを知っているのかなあ」「絶対にそんなことはないよ」 "I wonder if he knows it." "*Definitely nót*."

会話 「いっしょに連れて行ってよ」「絶対だめだよ」 "Will

you take me with you?" *"No way."* (⚠ 依頼に対する返事に用いる no のくだけた強意表現)
- 絶対音感 perfect pitch. ● 絶対者〖哲学〗the Absolute. ● 絶対主義 absolutism. ● 絶対多数 (gain [win]) an absolute majority. ● 絶対値〖数学〗absolute value. ● 絶対評価〖教育〗absolute evaluation. (関連) 相対評価 relative evaluation) ● 絶対服従 absolute [unconditional] obedience. ● 絶対量 an absolute quantity. ● 絶対零度〖物理〗absolute zero. 〖参考〗−273.15℃)

ぜつだい 絶大 ── **絶大な** 形 ● 絶大な(=非常に大きい)影響を与える have an *enormous* influence 《*on*》. ● 絶大な権力を手中にする gain *enormous* [絶対的な *absolute*] power. ● 絶大な(=惜しみない)支援をする give 《*him*》 *generous* [*full*] support. ● みなさん, 彼に絶大な拍手を Give him a *big* hand, ladies and gentlemen.

ぜつたいぜつめい 絶体絶命 ● 絶体絶命である (まさに危機である) be in a real pinch; (追い詰められる) be driven into a corner; (後がない)《話》have one's back to the wall.

せったく 拙宅 my house [home,《書》abode]. (⚠ 米英ではへりくだった言い方はしない ×my *humble home* などとはいわない)

せつだん 切断 名《書》severance (⚠ 比喩的にも用いる); (手足の) (an) amputation; (a) disconnection.
── **切断する** 動 cut ... off,《書》sever; (手術で) amputate; (電源を) disconnect. (⇒切る) ● 彼は第一関節から指を切断した He *cut off* his finger at the first joint. ▶あらしで電話線が切断された(=切れた) The telephone line *was broken* because of the storm.

ぜつたん 舌端 (舌の端) the tip of the tongue.
- 舌端火を吐く make a fiery speech; make [give, deliver] a harangue.

せっち 接地 ── **接地する** 動 (地面に接する) touch [reach] the ground; (飛行機などが着陸する) land.

せっち 設置 名 (機関の) (設立) establishment; (創立) foundation; (結成) formation;〖機械の〗installation.
── **設置する** 動 (学校・事務所などを) set ... up; establish, (機械を) install. ● 委員会を設置する *establish* [*form*, *set up*] a committee.

せっちゃく 接着 ● **接着剤** (⇒接着剤) ● **接着テープ** adhesive tape. ● 接着テープでとめる tape, put ... on with *tape*.

せっちゃくざい 接着剤 glue; (ゴム・にかわなどの) (an) adhesive. (⚠ 種類をいうときは C) ● 木工用接着剤 *glue* for wood. ● かけらを接着剤でくっつける *glue* the pieces *back together*. ▶ガラスと鉄をくっつけるには特別な接着剤が必要だ It takes a special *adhesive* to glue glass and iron together.

せっちゅう 折衷 (妥協) (a) compromise. ● 和洋折衷 (和洋)
── **折衷案** a compromise (proposal).

せっちゅう 雪中 ● 雪中行軍 a march in [through] the snow.

せっちょ 拙著 my book [(作品) work]. (⇒拙宅)

ぜっちょう 絶頂 ❶〖最高〗(幸福などの) the height; the peak; the zenith /zíːniθ/; (興味などの) a climax;〖最盛期〗one's [the] heyday. ● 人気の絶頂にある be at the *height* [*zenith*, *peak*] of one's popularity; be in the heyday of one's popularity.
❷〖頂上〗the top; the summit.

せっちん 雪隠 (便所) a toilet,《米》a bathroom. (⇒便所)
- 雪隠詰めにする (窮地に追い込める) corner 《*him*》; drive 《*him*》 into a tight corner [spot].

せっつく ● 私に計画の変更をせっつく(=しきりに促す) *urge* [強く促す]《やや書》*press*] me *to* change my plans. (⇒せき立てる)

せってい 設定 ── **設定する** 動 (基準・機関などを) establish, set ... up; (特定の状況などを) assume, suppose. (⇒仮定).

セッティング (設置) a setting; (用意) an arrangement. ● 国際会議をセッティングする make *arrangements* for an international conference.

せってん 接点 〖数学〗a point of contact. ● 討論に接点 (=一致点) を見いだす find a *point of agreement* [(共通点) find *common ground*] in one's discussion.

せつでん 節電 名 (electric) power saving.
── **節電する** 動 《switch off the light to》 save electricity.

***セット** ❶〖ひとそろい〗(道具・茶器などの) a set; (家具の一式) a suite /swiːt/. ● コーヒー [ティー] セット a cóffee [a téa] sèt. ● ゴルフクラブ1セット a *set* of golf clubs. (⚠「完全なセット」は a full set,「不完全なセット」は a broken set) ● 3点セット a three-piece *suite* [×set]. ● 通例ソファー (settee) とひじかけいす (chair) 二つ) ● 食堂セット a dining room *suite*. ▶この机はいすがセットになります This desk makes a *set* with the chair./This desk and the chair make a *set*. ▶寝室用の家具はセットで売ることが多い Bedroom furniture is often sold *in sets*.
❷〖テニスなどの〗a set. ● 3セットの試合 a three-*set* match. ● 第1セットを取る [落とす] win [lose] the first *set*. ▶試合は3セットまで行った The match went to three *sets*.
❸〖髪の〗a set.
❹〖映画の〗a set. ● 最初の映画をセットで撮影する shoot one's first film *on a set*. ▶あの俳優はセットに入っている The actor is *on* (↔off) (*the*) *set*. (⚠ the のつく方が多い)
❺〖調整〗a setting.
❻〖メニューで〗● ケーキセット cake with tea or coffee. (⚠ ×a cake set とはいわない) ● ランチセット《米》a lunch special;《英》set lunch [dinner]. (⚠ ×a lunch set とはいわない)
── **セットする** 動 ❶〖髪を〗● 美容院で髪をセットしてもらう have one's hair *set* at a beauty salon. ● 私は月に2回髪をセットします I *set* my hair twice a month.
❷〖調整する〗set. ● 目覚まし時計を6時にセットする *set* the alarm clock for six. ● ビデオカメラを台にセットする *set up* a video camera on a stand.
- セットオール〖競技〗a tied set count. ● きょう, セットオールだ The set count is tied. ● セットショット〖バスケット〗a set shot. ● セットプレー〖サッカー〗a set piece. ● セルティックはセットプレーからの得点が多い Celtic score a lot from *set pieces*. ● セットポイント a set point. ● セットポジション〖野球〗a set position. ● セットポジションに入る take one's *set position*; move into a *set position*. ● セットローション sétting lòtion.

せつど 節度 moderation; (節制) temperance. ● 節度のある moderate /mάdərət/; temperate /témpərət/. ● 節度を守る be moderate 《*in*》. ● 何事にも節度が大切だと思う I believe in the value of *moderation* [*temperance*] *in* all things.

セットアッパー 〖中継ぎ投手〗〖野球〗a setup man;《和製語》a setupper.

セットアップ 名 〖コンピュータ〗a setup.
── **セットアップする** set up.
せっとう 窃盗 (a) theft. ● 窃盗を働く commit a theft. ● 窃盗罪で刑務所に入れられる be jailed for stealing [theft].
● 窃盗犯 a thief.
ぜっとう 舌頭 (舌の端) the tip of the tongue.
せっとうご 接頭語 (⇨接頭辞)
せっとうじ 接頭辞 〖文法〗a prefix /priːfiks/.
ゼットき ゼット旗 ● ゼット旗を掲げる (非常事態を乗り切るためにみんなの努力を求める) demand everyone to work hard to get through a crisis.

*****せっとく** 説得 名 persuasion. ● 説得力のある話者 a persuasive [a convincing] speaker. (❗前の方は感情に訴えて行動をとらせるような, 後の方は理性に訴えて納得させるような説得方法を含意) ● 説得に失敗する fail to persuade (her). ▶彼は我々の説得に折れた He gave in to our persuasion. ▶彼は説得に応じなかった He refused to be persuaded [be reasoned with]. (❗「簡単に説得に応じた」は He was easily persuaded.)

── **説得する** 動 persuade; 〈主に米〉(道理で) convince; (論じて) argue; reason 《with》; (しきりに) urge; (なだめすかして) coax; (繰り返し理由を添えて) talk 《him》 around [round 〈英〉] 《to; to doing》; talk.

① **…を説得する** ▶どうやっても彼女を説得するのは無理だろう Nothing would persuade her. ▶今(なお説得中です 《やや話》 I'm (still) working on [at] it. (❗慣用表現. 通例進行形で)
会話 「そんなお金のむだ遣いだって言われるに決まってるわ」「彼を説得できると思う？」"I bet he'll say it's a waste of money." "Do you think you can get him around [説得して支持を得る] win him over, (うんと言わせる) get him to agree]?"

② **〔説得して…させる〕** ▶私は彼を説得してそこへ行かせた I persuaded him to go there. (❗単純過去時制で用いるとその説得が成功したことを含意するので, 説得はしたが成功しなかった場合は tried to persuade him to go, urged [coaxed] him to go を用いる)/ I coaxed [talked] him into going there. ▶彼らは彼を説得してその計画を断念させた They persuaded him not to carry out the plan./They persuaded him out of (carrying out) the plan.《書》They dissuaded him from carrying out [×to carry out] the plan./They argued [talked, coaxed] him out of carrying out the plan. (❗以上いずれも説得が成功したことを含意する) ▶両親は彼女を説得してとうとう家業を継がせた Her parents talked her around finally to succeeding to their business.

セットバック 〖壁面後退〗〖建築〗a setback.
せつな 刹那 (瞬間) an instant; (一瞬) a moment.
● 刹那的快楽にふける indulge in the pleasures of the moment [momentary pleasures, 《つかの間の》transient pleasures]. (❗instant には長さがないのでここでは不可)
● 刹那主義 the principle of living only for the pleasure of the moment.
せつない 切ない ● 切ない(=つらい)思い painful feelings. ● 切ない思いをする feel painful [sad, 《非常に》heartbroken].
せつなる 切なる ● 切なる(=熱心な)願い an ardent [an eager, 〈心からの〉an earnest] wish. (⇨願い)
せつに 切に 〖心から〗sincerely; 〖心の底から〗from the bottom of one's heart; 〖熱烈に〗ardently; 〖切望して〗eagerly; 〖熱心に〗earnestly. ▶彼の援助を切に願う sincerely [ardently] hope for his help.

▶私たちは平和を切に願っている We eagerly wish for peace. ▶我々は平和を切に願う We are eager [anxious] for peace.
せっぱく 切迫 ● 切迫した(=急を要する)事態 an urgent [a pressing] situation. ● 切迫した(=張りつめた)空気 a tense [緊張した a strained] atmosphere.
▶論文提出の期限が切迫している The deadline for submitting the essay [thesis] is near at hand.
● 切迫流産 (a) threatened miscarriage.
せっぱつまる 切羽詰まる ▶〖窮地に追い込まれている〗be driven into a corner 〖to the wall〗; 〖窮地に立っている〗be in a (tight) corner,《話》be in a fix; 〖途方に暮れている〗《話》be at one's wit's end. ▶せっぱつまって(=最後の手段として)人のものに手をかける steal 《it》 as a last resort 〖《必要に迫られて》out of necessity〗. ▶彼はせっぱつまって心にもないことを言った He was driven to the wall and said what he didn't mean.
せっぱん 折半 ── **折半する** 動 go fifty-fifty [halves] 《with 人, on + 事》. ● 利益を折半する go fifty-fifty on the profit(s); split the profit(s) evenly; (半分にする) halve the profits. ▶彼とその費用を折半した I split the cost with him.
ぜっぱん 絶版 ● 絶版になる go out of print. ▶その本はすでに絶版になっている The book is out of print now.

*****せつび** 設備 名 〖集合的に装備・備品〗equipment (❗数えるときは a piece of …); 〖学校・病院など便宜を与える施設〗facilities; 〖宿泊・収容設備〗accommodation(s) (❗単数形は〈米〉); 〖衣食住に便利な設備〗conveniences. ● 研究設備 facilities for study. ● 近代的設備のある工場 a factory with modern equipment. ● 設備の整った well-equipped [well-furnished]《office》. ▶この船は設備がよい This ship is well equipped./This is a well-equipped ship./This ship has fine equipment [×equipments]. ▶このホテルは 1,000 人の客を収容する設備がある This hotel has accommodations for 〖(収容できる) can accommodate〗 1,000 guests. ▶そのモデルハウスにはあらゆる近代的設備が整っている The model house has all modern conveniences.

── **設備する** 動 equip (-pp-) 《the school with computers》; 〖あらかじめ備える〗provide. ▶このマンションには非常階段が設備してある This apartment house is equipped [is provided] with emergency stairs.
● 設備資金 equipment funds. ● 設備投資 investment in plant and equipment; (広い意味で) capital investment. ● 設備費 the cost of equipment.
せつぴ 雪庇 〖登山〗a cornice.
せつびご 接尾語 (⇨接尾辞)
せつびじ 接尾辞 〖文法〗a suffix.
ぜっぴつ 絶筆 ● この小説が彼の絶筆(= 最後の作品)となった This novel was his last work./This novel was the last piece he wrote before he died.
ぜっぴん 絶品 〖すぐれた作品〗a superb [an exquisite] piece of work; 〖珍品〗a rare object; a rarity. ▶そのガーリックパン食べてみた？ 絶品だわ Did you try that garlic bread yet? It's something special.
せっぷく 切腹 名 seppuku; harakiri; (説明的に) suicide by ritual disembowelment practiced by the Japanese samurai to avoid a disgraceful execution.

── **切腹する** 動 commit harakiri.
せつぶん 節分 ▶日本では 2 月 3 日の節分の日には「鬼は外, 福は内」と叫びながら家の内外に豆をまきます On

せっぷん 接吻

せっぷん 接吻 图 a kiss.
── 接吻する 動 kiss 《her on the cheek》; give 《her》a kiss 《on the cheek》. (⚠ ×give a kiss to her とは通例いわない)

ぜっぺき 絶壁 (⇨崖)

せっぺん 切片 a slice; (生物の器官や組織などの) a section; [数学] an intercept.

せっぺん 雪片 a snowflake.

せつぼう 切望 an earnest desire. (⇨熱望)

せっぽう 説法 (意見すること) (an) admonition. ● 釈迦に説法 (⇨釈迦) [成句]

***ぜつぼう 絶望** 图 despair /dispéər/, loss of (all) hope. ● 深い絶望感 a sense of deep *despair*. ▶ 彼は絶望のあまり自殺した He killed himself in [*out of*] *despair*. ▶ 患者[事態]は絶望的だ The patient [situation] is *hopeless* [*beyond hope*].
── 絶望する 動 despair 《*of*》, give* [give up] hope 《*of*》. ▶ 彼女は愛のない結婚生活に絶望した She *despaired of* her loveless marriage./(彼女を絶望させた) The loveless marriage *drove* her *to despair*. ▶ 絶望するな Don't *despair* [*give up your hope*].

ぜっぽう 舌鋒 ● 彼の政策を舌鋒鋭く攻撃する attack his policy *sharply* [非常に痛烈な言葉で] *in most cutting terms*.

ぜつみょう 絶妙 ● 絶妙な手際 *exquisite* [驚くべき *marvelous*] workmanship. ● 絶妙の(=神技のよう)コントロール *miraculously good* control.

ぜつむ 絶無 ● 彼の合格の見込みは絶無である He has *no* chance *at all* [*whatever*] of passing the examination. (⇨皆無)

***せつめい 説明** 图 (an) explanation (⚠ 行為は Ⓤ, 説明となる事実・理由は Ⓒ); [物事の理由・内容などの筋道立った説明] (an) illustration; [例示解説] (an) illustration; [外見・状況描写] (a) description; [写真・絵に添える] a caption. ● (物事が)説明のつかない[できない] inexplicable. ● (物事が)説明を必要としない need no *explanation*.
── 説明(を)する 動 explain; (理由を) account for ...; (実例などをあげて) illustrate; (状況・特徴などを) describe; (告げる) tell*. ● 分かりやすい[十分な; 満足のいく; 納得のいく]説明をする give 《him》an intelligible [a full; a satisfactory; a convincing] *explanation*. ▶ 私はその意味を彼女に説明した I *explained* the meaning *to her*. (1) ×explain *her* the meaning は不可. (2) 直接目的語が比較的長い場合やそれを強調する場合には to her なら前置も可: 私はその文章の意味を彼女に説明した I *explained to* her the meaning of the sentence./I *explained to* her *what* the sentence meant. (⚠ wh-節[句]や that 節が続くときは to her はその前に置く)/I *gave* her *an explanation of* the meaning. ▶ この現象をどう説明しますか How do you *explain* [What is your *explanation of*] this phenomenon? ▶ 君は欠席の理由を説明しないといけない You have to *account* [*give an explanation*] *for* your absence. ▶ 彼はそれを図で[図をかいて]説明した He *illustrated* it *with* [*by* drawing] diagrams. ▶ 私はその男の特徴を警官に説明した I *described* the man *to* the policeman. ▶ それについては彼は何も説明してくれなかった He *told* me nothing about it. ▶ いったいこれはどういうことか手短に説明してくれませんか Can you *tell* me in brief what this is all about?

DISCOURSE
本稿では，災害に対し諸団体がどのような対応を見せたかを説明する **In this paper, I will** *explain* how various organizations responded to the disaster. (⚠ In this paper, I will explain [demonstrate, analyze, show, suggest]... (この論文では, ...を説明する[明らかにする, 分析する, 示す, 提案する]は論文の目的を紹介する表現. 序論でよく用いられる)

● 説明会 an explanatory meeting. ● 説明書 an explanatory note; (薬などの) directions; (機械操作の) instructions, (小冊子) an operating manual. ● その薬を説明書どおりに服用する apply the medicine *as directed* [*according to* (*the*) *direction*]. ● 説明図 an illustration. (⇨図解)

ぜつめい 絶命 ── 絶命する 動 die; (息を引き取る)[書] breathe one's last, expire.

***ぜつめつ 絶滅** 图 [生物などが死滅すること] extinction; [有害生物などを全滅させること] (an) extermination. ▶ その鳥は絶滅寸前だ[絶滅の危機にひんしている] The bird is on the verge of [in danger of] *extinction*./(絶滅寸前の種になった) The bird has become an *endangered* species.
── 絶滅する 動 become extinct; die out; [絶滅させる] exterminate (⇨撲滅); (完全に滅ぼす) destroy ... completely (⇨全滅). ● 絶滅した動物[民族] an *extinct* animal [*race*]. ▶ マンモスが絶滅してから久しい The mammoth *has been extinct* [*has been gone*] for a long time.

せつもん 設問 a question. (⇨質問)

***せつやく 節約** 图 [むだ遣いしないこと] ecónomy, (a) saving; [倹約] thrift, frugality. (⇨倹約) ● 節約に努める practice *economy*. ▶ 彼は節約家だ He *is economical* [*thrifty, frugal*]. (⚠ (1) ×He is *economic*. は不可. (2) He is stingy. は「彼はけちだ」の意)/He *is a man of economy*. ● いいかばんを買うと節約になりますよ It's *economical* [*an economy*] to buy good bags.
── 節約する 動 [むだ遣いしない] ecónomize 《*on*》; (金・時間などを) save; (燃料・食物などを) save (on)...; (費用などを削減する) cut* down (on).... ● 光熱費を節約する *economize on* [*save* (*on*)] light and fuel. ▶ バーゲンで買って金を節約する *save* (money) by buying at a sale. ▶ 水を節約して使いなさい You must *economize on* [*save* (*on*)] water. ▶ 車で行けば時間を節約することになるよ If you go by car, you [it] will *save* time. ▶ 食器洗い機のおかげで時間も労力もたくさん節約できる The dishwasher *saves* (you) a lot of time and labor. ▶ 天井のファンによってどれだけ燃費が節約できるか知りになればびっくりなさいますよ You'll be surprised to see how much a ceiling fan can *cut down* (*on*) your energy costs.

せつゆ 説諭 图 (訓戒) (an) admonition; (叱責) (a) reproof, (やや堅い語) (a) reprimand.
── 説諭する 動 admonish; (説教する) preach; reprove; (小言を言う) give 《him》a lecture.

せつり 摂理 (divine) providence. (⚠ しばしば P-) ● 神の摂理で by Providence.

せつりつ 設立 图 [資金を整えての創設] foundation; [永続性を伴う創設] establishment (⚠ やや堅い語); [組織・導入すること] institution (⚠ 永続性は暗示せず堅い語); [組織すること] organization.
── 設立する 動 [学校・会社などを] set*... up, establish (⚠ 後の方が堅い語); (創設する) found; [会などを][書] institute, organize. ● 新しい学校を設立する *set up* [*establish*] a new school. ▶ 彼は商事会

社を設立した He *established* [*started*] a business firm. ● 設立者 a *founder*; an *institutor*; an *organizer*.

ぜつりん 絶倫 ── **絶倫の** 形 (無類の) *matchless*, *unequaled*. ▶彼は精力絶倫だ He has *unequaled* [*boundless*] energy.

せつれつ 拙劣 ── **拙劣な** 形 ・拙劣な演技 a *poor* [*bad*, (ぎこちない) a *clumsy*] performance.

せつわ 説話 (架空の物語) a *tale*; (事実に基づく,または架空の物語) a *story*; (事実に基づく物語) a *narrative*. ● 説話体の小説 a novel in *narrative* form. ● 説話文学 narrative literature.

せと 瀬戸 (狭い海峡) a *strait*; a *channel* (❗ strait より大きくて広い).

せとぎわ 瀬戸際 ●瀬戸際になって at the *crucial* [(*very*) *last*] *moment*. ▶ここが生きるか死ぬかの瀬戸際だ We are *on the point* [*brink*, *verge*] of *death*.

せとないかい 瀬戸内海 the *Seto* Inland Sea.

せともの 瀬戸物 (陶磁器) *ceramics*; *china*, *chinaware* (❗後の二つは日常語); (陶器) *pottery*. (❗以上はいずれも集合的で, 1個は a *piece of* ～ のようにいう) (⇨陶器) ● 瀬戸物の皿 a *china* [a *pottery*] *dish*.
● 瀬戸物屋 a china shop.

*せなか **背中** a *back*. (⇨背 ❶) ● 背中合わせに座る *sit back to back with* each other. ● 彼に背中を向ける *turn one's back on* [*to*] *him*. (❗ on は怒ってなど拒絶・嫌悪の意を含み, to は体に方向を示す) ● 背中を丸くする *hunch up* (one's *back*). ● 背中のボタンをはずす *undo* the buttons in the *back*. ▶その人は背中が曲がっていた The man's *back* was bent. ▶彼は私の背中をぽんとたたいた He *patted me on the* [×*my*] *back*. (事情 激励・賞賛のしぐさ) ▶猫は背中を丸めてうなった The cat *arched its back* and *growled*.

ぜに 銭 *money*. (⇨金(⅃)) ● 銭のかせげる選手 a *player who draws in a lot of spectators*.
ぜにあおい 銭葵 〔植物〕 a *mallow*.
ぜにかね 銭金 *money*. (⇨金)
ぜにがめ 銭亀 〔動物〕 (イシガメの子) a baby Japanese pond turtle.
ぜにごけ 銭苔 〔植物〕 a *liverwort*.
ぜにん 是認 图 *approval*. ── **是認する** 動 *approve* (of...). (⇨認める)
せぬき 背抜き ●背抜きの(= 裏のついていない)上着 an *unlined jacket*; a *jacket with an unlined back*.
セネガル 〔国名〕 *Senegal* /sènəɡɔ́:l/; (公式名) the *Republic of Senegal*. (首都 Dakar) ● セネガル人 a *Sènègalèse*. ● セネガル(人)の *Senegalese*.
ゼネコン a major construction company.
ゼネスト a *general strike*. (⇨スト, ストライキ)
ゼネラルマネージャー a *general manager*.
せのび 背伸び ── **背伸びする** 動 ❶〔体を伸ばす〕●背伸びして垣根の向こうを見る *stretch oneself* [(つま先で立って) *stand on tiptoe*] and look beyond the fence.
❷〔能力以上のことをしようとする〕▶背伸びしてはいけないよ Don't *try to do anything beyond your ability* [*power*]. /(手に余るような仕事をやろうとするな) Don't *bite off more than you can chew*. /(あまり高望みをするな) Don't *aim too high*.
せばまる 狭まる *narrow*, *become* narrow*.
会話「その交渉は何か進展がありましたか」「双方の意見のへだたりはせまってきました」「それはよい兆しだ」 "Has there been any progress in the negotiation?" "Well, the gap between their opinions *is*

narrowing [*closing*]." "That's a good sign."
せばめる 狭める ●人生に対する見方を狭める *narrow one's views on life*. ●活動範囲を狭める *narrow down the range of one's activities*; (限定する) *limit one's activities*. ●歩幅を狭める *shorten one's stride*.
セパレーツ 〔上下に分かれた婦人服〕 *separates* /sépərəts/.
セパレート ●セパレートコース 〔陸上・水泳〕 a lane.
せばんごう 背番号 a *uniform number*. ● 背番号1の選手 a player (wearing) *uniform number* 1. ● 背番号を永久欠番にする (⇨永久)
せひ 施肥 图 *fertilization*. ── **施肥する** 動 *fertilize*; *manure*.
*ぜひ **是非** 图〔よしあし〕 *right and* [*or*] *wrong*. ▶我々はその方法の是非を論じた We discussed whether the method was *right or wrong*. /We discussed the *right and wrong* of the method. ▶是非もない (= やむを得ないことだ It can't be helped. /There is no help for it. ▶早期英語教育の是非については判断しかねる I'm ambivalent about whether English education in the early childhood is going to be *a good or bad*.
● 是非に及ばず (仕方がない) It cannot be helped.
── **是非** 副〔必ず〕(何としても) *at all costs*, 《否定文で》 *at any cost*; (必ず…する) *be sure* 《*to do*》; (ぜひどうぞ) (やや書) *by all means* (許可・承諾を表す); 〔本当に〕 *really*, *indeed*; 〔間違いなく〕 *without fail*. ▶まもがいに日本に来たいと思います I hope *very much* to come back to Japan. ▶我々はぜひそういった事態は避けなければならない We must avoid such a situation *at all costs* [(書) *whatever the cost*]. ▶ぜひパーティーにいらしてね I'd *really* like you to [*Be sure to*, *Do*, ×*By all means*] come to the party. (❗ do は come より強く発音され命令文を強める. by all means は要請は強い言い方) /Come to the party *without fail*. ▶ぜひとも助けていただきたい I'm *begging* you to help me. (❗ must ask より堅い言い方で, 進行形は控えめな言い方)/(どうしてもあなたの助けが必要です) I *badly* [*desperately*] need your help.
会話「とても楽しかったですよ」「よかったわ. そのうちまたぜひお出かけください」 "We enjoyed ourselves a lot." "I'm glad. You *must* [*You've got to*] come again soon." (❗相手に強く勧めており, 義務の意味はない)
会話「うまくいくかどうか分からないけど, 彼女に会ってみたらどうだろう」「ぜひ会いたいわ, あなたさえよければ」 "I don't know if it works out, I think you should meet her." "I *would love to*, if you don't mind." (❗ I would like to の女性的な感じの言い方)
会話「今晩おうかがいしてもいいですか」「ぜひどうぞ」 "Can I come over tonight?" "(Yes), sure [*of course*, *certainly*]. /*Of course* you can. /*By all means* (do)." (❗ ×*Please*. は不可 (⇨どうぞ))

セピア *sepia* /sí:piə/ ●古ぼけたセピア色の写真 an old *sepia* photograph.
ぜひとも 是非とも at all costs. (⇨是非 副)
せひょう 世評 (評判) (a) *reputation*; (うわさ) *rumor*. (⇨評判) ●世評がよい *have a good* (↔*bad*) *reputation*. ●世評(= 人が言うこと)を気にしない *do not care* [(恐れる) *not be afraid of*] *what people say*.
せびらき 背開き ●背開きの魚の干物 a dried fish *with its back slit open*.
セビリア 〔スペインの都市〕 *Seville* /səvíl/.
せびる 親に小遣いをせびる (=うるさくせがむ) *pester* (話) [*press* (やや書)] one's parents *for* pocket money.

せびれ 背びれ a dorsal fin.

せびろ 背広 [上下] a suit; (通勤用に) a business suit, 《英・やや古》 a lounge suit; [上着] a (suit) jacket. ▶シングル[ダブル]の背広 a single-breasted [a double-breasted] suit. ▶背広姿の男性 a man wearing a *suit* and tie.

せぶみ 瀬踏み ── 瀬踏みする 動 ❶ [瀬の深さを測る] ●湖の瀬踏みをする sound [調べる] check] the depth of a lake; sound a lake.
❷ [様子を探る] ▶この問題について彼の出方を瀬踏みしてみよう Let's sound him out (探りを入れる) put out a feeler about him] on this matter.

ゼブラゾーン [《横断歩道》]《米》a crosswalk;《英》a zebra crossing.

ゼブラフィッシュ [魚介] a zebra fish.

せぼね 背骨 (やや話) [解剖] a backbone, [解剖] a spinal column; (背筋) a spine. ▶背骨が曲がっている have a curved *spine*.

:せまい 狭い ❶ [幅・面積が] (幅が) narrow (↔wide); (面積が小さい) small (↔large). ●狭い部屋 a *small* [✕a narrow] room. ●この道は狭すぎてバスは通れない This road is too *narrow* for buses to pass. ●ベニスの街は狭い Venice is a *small* place. ●この地点で海は狭くなって海峡となっている At this point the sea *narrows* into a strait. ●世界はだんだん狭くなってきた The world is getting *smaller* (and *smaller*). ▶固定観念にとらわれてしまうと、将棋盤が狭いものになってしまう(=自由に将棋がさせなくなる) If you have a certain mindset, you won't be able to play Shogi freely.
会話 「会議は小会議室で行われます」「あそこじゃちょっと狭いんじゃない」 "The meeting's in the small hall." "That won't be big enough, will it?"
❷ [範囲が] narrow, (限られた) limited, restricted. ●狭い交際範囲 a *narrow* circle of friends. ▶彼女は視野が狭い She has *limited* [*narrow*] views./(広くない) Her view of things is *not broad*. ●この問題についての私の知識はかなり狭い My knowledge of this subject is rather *limited*.
❸ [その他の表現] ●心の狭い人 a *narrow-minded* [a *small-minded*] person. ▶世の中って狭いものですね It's (such) a *small* world, isn't it? [indeed].

せきもん 狭き門 [《狭い門》] a narrow gate; [《聖書》] the strait gate; [入試などの難関] (a) difficulty (⇨難関). ●入試の狭き門を突破する get over the difficulty [pass the *narrow* gate] of the entrance exam. ●東京大学は狭き門だ(=入学するのが大変難しい) Tokyo University is very hard to enter [get into]./It is very hard to get into Tokyo University.

せまくるしい 狭苦しい ●狭苦しい台所 a *cramped* kitchen. ●この部屋は小さくて狭苦しい This room is small and *cramped*.

＊せまる 迫る ❶ [近づく] approach; (時が近づく) draw* near; (間近である) be near [close] at hand (⇨近付く); (事が差し迫っている) press; (…の瀬戸際である) be on the verge of.... ●眼前に迫った危険 a *pressing* [an *imminent*] danger. ●台風が四国に迫っている The typhoon *is approaching* Shikoku. (❗✕approaching to ... とはしない) ●試験が間近に迫っている The examination *is near at hand* [*is just around the corner*]. ●開会(式)まであと1週間に迫っている The opening is only a week *away* [*off*]. ●時間が刻々と迫っている Time *is pressing* every moment. ●彼は死が迫っている He *is dying*./He *is on the verge* [*brink, point*] *of* death. ●津波はものすごい速さで私たちの背後に迫ってきた The tsunami *bore down on* us from behind very quickly. (❗ bear down on は脅威を感じさせる大きなものに用いる)
❷ [強いる] (人がせがむ) press 《him》《*to do*; *for*＋事》; (人・事がしきりに勧める) urge 《him》《*to do*》; (人・事が強制する) force [compel (-ll-)] 《him》《*to do*》. ●必要に迫られ urged [compelled] by necessity; (必要から) from [out of] necessity. ●私は小切手に署名するように迫られた I *was pressed* [*was forced*] *to* sign the check. ●政府は彼に研究をやめるように迫った The government *forced* [*compelled*] him *to* give up his studies. (❗やめたことを含意。彼がやめなかった場合は The government *tried to* force [compel] .... とする)/(圧力をかけた) The government *put pressure on* him *to* give up his studies. ●私たちは難しい選択を迫られている We *have to* make a hard choice./We *have* a hard choice to make. (❗ We're forced to make .... では他社の圧力を受けていることを示すのに対して、状況的にそうせざるを得ない場合の言い方)
❸ [近接する] ●家の裏手に崖が迫っている There is a cliff *just behind* my house. (❗ behind の代わりに at the back of を用いると、位置関係の接近は表すが、迫ってくる威圧感は伝わらない) ●その描写は真に迫っている The description *is quite realistic*.

セマンティックス [意味論] semantics.

せみ 蝉 [昆虫] a cicada /sikéidə/,《米》a locust. ▶セミが鳴いている Cicadas are chirping [singing]. 事情 米英人は日本人のように風物詩的親近感は持たない.
●蝉時雨 (じゆ) a continuous chorus of cicadas.

ゼミ [[「ゼミナール」の略]] (⇨ゼミナール, セミナー)

せみくじら 背美鯨 [動物] a right whale.

セミコロン a semicolon 《;》. (⇨巻末 [句読法])

セミナー a seminar 《*on*》. ●英国史のセミナーを開く give a *seminar on* English history.

ゼミナール a seminar /séma:nɑ:r/ 《*on*》. (⇨セミナー)

セミプロ [半職業的な人・選手] a semiprofessional, 《話》a semipro (略 ～s). ●セミプロの運動選手 a *semiprofessional* [a *semipro*] athlete.

せめ 攻め [攻撃] ●攻めに転じる take *the offensive*. ●攻めの態勢にある be *on the offensive*.

せめ 責め [とがめ] blame; [責任] responsibility. (⇨責任) ●損失に対し責めを負う take the *blame* [*responsibility*] for a loss.

せめあぐむ 攻め倦む 〈有効な攻め方が分からないで困っている〉be at a loss how to attack effectively; cannot find an effective way of attack. ▶反乱軍はその城を攻めあぐんだ The rebel army *found it very hard to capture* [*carry*] the castle./The rebels *had a hard time capturing* [*carrying*] the castle.

せめいる 攻め入る ●大挙して隣国に攻め入る(=侵入する) *invade* a neighboring country in (great) force. ●敵の領土に攻め入る(=入り込む) *penetrate* [(侵略する) *make inroads into*] enemy territory.

せめおとす 攻め落とす ●要塞を攻め落とす (強襲して占領する) *take* a fortress *by storm*; (攻取る) *capture* [*carry*] a fortress.

せめぎあい 鬩ぎ合い ▶戦争終結間際に両軍の激しいせめぎあいが繰り広げられた A *fierce battle was fought* between two armies toward the end of the war.

せめぎあう 鬩ぎ合う ●最後の5メートルで2人の泳者がせめぎあった In the last 5 meters, the two swimmers *competed fiercely* for the lead.

せめく 責め苦 (ひどい苦痛) (a) torture. ●地獄の責め

苦 the torture [[苦痛の種] the torments] of hell.
● 責め苦にあうを be tortured; be put to *torture*.

せこむ 攻め込む 〘侵入する〙 make inroads upon [into]…; 〘侵略する〙 invade; 〘入り込む〙 penetrate (into)…. (⇨攻め入る)

せさいなむ 責め苛む treat 《him》 cruelly; ill-treat; torture, torment.

セメスター [[2学期制の学期] a semester /səméstər/.
● セメスター制である be on the *semester* system; operate on *semesters*.

セメダイン 〘接着剤〙 glue. 〘参考〙「セメダイン」は商標名

せたてる 攻め立てる 〘猛烈に[容赦なく]攻める〙 attack fiercely [scathingly]; make* a fierce [a scathing] attack 《on, against》.

せたてる 責め立てる [[厳しく責める] torture 《him》 severely [(しきりに) repeatedly]; [厳しく詰問する] cross-question 《him》 closely, 〘話〙 grill; [しつこく催促する] press [urge] 《him to do》. ● 彼を責めて自白させる *torture* him *severely into* confession; (無理に自白させる) *extort* (a) confession *from* him. ● いくら責めたてられたって、ないそでは振れないわ No matter how hard they *press* me to pay a debt, they can't possibly get a stocking off a bare foot.

せめて [[少なくとも] at least; [[…だけ] just; [多くて…] not more than …. ● 彼はせめて電話くらいよこしてもよさそうなものだ He might *at least* (tele)phone me. ● 彼が苦しまずに死んだのがせめてもの慰めだった It was *at least* a consolation that he died without suffering. ● せめてそのくらいしたっていいじゃないか It's *the least* you can do. ● せめてもう10分待ってくれませんか Can't you wait *just* ten more minutes [[まれ] ten minutes more]? ● それが私のせめてもの (= 唯一の) 慰めです That is my *only* comfort [*sole* consolation].

せのぼる 攻め上る (都へ攻めて行く) march towards the capital.

せよせる 攻め寄せる ● 敵が攻め寄せてきた (= 包囲の輪を縮めてきた) The enemy *closed in on* [*upon*] us.

せめる 攻める attack. (⇨攻撃する, 襲う) ● 敵を一気に [じわじわと] 攻める *attack* the enemy *at a stretch* [*gradually*]. ● 四番打者を慎重に攻める work carefully on the cleanup. ● 打者の外角低目を攻める pitch a batter low and away.

せめる 責める [非難する] blame 《him》 《for+事》; accuse 《him》 《of+事》. ● 彼は私の不注意を責めた He *blamed* [*reproached*] me *for* my carelessness. 〘!〙 (1) blame は「責任があると言って」、reproach は「失望や悲しみの気持ちで」責めること. (2) xHe blamed [reproached] my carelessness. は不可) ● 彼がそれをしなかったからといってあまり責めてはいけません You should nót bláme him too ↘much *because* [xfor] he dídn't ↗do it. 〘!〙 because の前にコンマを置き ╱much, …╲do の音調で読むと「…しなかったのだから」の意となる) ● 彼はお金を盗んだといって責められた He *was accused of* stealing [*having* stolen] the money. 〘!〙「訴えられた」の意にもなる) ● 世の中がうまくいかなくなると人々は大統領を責めるる When things don't go well, people like to [will] blame the presidents.

セメント /səmént/. ● セメントを塗る cement 《the floor》; cover 《the floor》 with cement. ● このセメントは固まるのが早い This *cement* hardens [sets] soon.
● セメント工場 a cemént plànt [fàctory].

セメントだるのなかのてがみ『セメント樽の中の手紙』 *Letters Found in a Cement Barrel*. 〘参考〙 葉山嘉樹の小説)

せもじ 背文字 the book's title on the spine.

せもたれ 背もたれ a back (support). ● 背もたれのある [ない] 椅子 a chair with [without] a *back*. ▶ 背もたれを少し倒してごらん。楽ですよ Recline your seat a little. It will make you more comfortable.

セラー [[地下貯蔵室] a cellar.

ゼラチン gelatin(e) /dʒélətɪn/. ● ゼラチン状の gelátinous.

ゼラニウム [[植物] a geranium /dʒəréiniəm/.

セラピー [[治療] (a) therapy. ● アロマセラピー aromatherapy.

セラピスト [[治療士] a therapist.

セラミック [[陶磁器] ●の形 ceramic. ● セラミックのタイル a *ceramic* tile.

セラミックス ceramics /sərǽmɪks/. 〘!〙 単数扱い)

せり 競り (an) auction. (⇨競売) ● 牛の競り市〘俗〙 a cattle *auction* market. ● 競りで花びんを買う buy a vase *at* [[英] by] *auction*. ● その絵を競りに出す put the painting up *for auction*.

せり 芹 [[植物] a water dropwort.

せりあう 競り合う ● 両候補は知事の座を競り合った (= 競争した) The two candidates *raced for* the office of governor. ▶ 少年たちはその賞を目当てに競り合った The boys *competed with* each other *for* the prize. (⇨競争する)

せりあげる 競り上げる bid … up. ● その絵を50万円まで競り上げる *bid up* (the price of) the picture to 500,000 yen.

ゼリー 〘米〙〘商標〙 jello, Jell-O 〘!〙 フルーツ味のものをいう); 〘主に英〙 (a) jelly 〘!〙 jelly は 〘米〙 では果汁を煮つめて作るジャムのこと).

セリーグ [[野球] the Central League.

せりうり 競り売り (an) auction. (⇨競売)

せりおとす 競り落とす ▶ その絵は2,000ドルで彼に競り落とされた (= 競売で買われた) The picture *was bought at auction* by him (安値で) *was knocked down* to him] for two thousand dollars.

せりかつ 競り勝つ win in close [[激しい] keen] competition. (⑳ 競り負ける) ● 彼は米国大統領選に競り勝った He *won* the race for the White House *in close* [[激しい] *fierce*] *competition*.

せりだす 迫り出す ❶ [押し出す] push … out.
❷ [突き出る] stick* out. ▶ 腹がせり出してきた He is beginning to *spread in the middle*./His stomach has begun to *stick out*. ▶ その建物は上階が一階よりせり出している The building has the *overhanging* upper stories. (〘!〙 overhanging は「突き出ている」の意の形容詞)

せりふ 台詞 [[芝居などの] one's lines; [[語] a word.
● せりふがなかなか憶えられない take a long time to learn one's *lines*. ● せりふをとちる fluff [mess up] one's *lines*. ▶ あいつのせりふ (= 言うこと) が気に入らない I don't like *what he says*.
● せりふ回し elocution.

せりまける 競り負ける lose in close competition. (⑳ 競り勝つ)

せりょう 施療 ⦿ free medical treatment. ● 施療を受ける receive *free medical treatment*; be treated free of charge.

—— **施療する** ⦿ give 《him》 free medical treatment; treat 《him》 free of charge.
● 施療患者 a free [a charity] patient. ● 施療病院 a charity hospital.

せる 競る ❶ [しのぎを削って競う] have a fierce [a keen] competition 《with》. (⇨競争する)
❷ [競売で相手より高い値をつける] bid [make a bid] 《for》. ▶ 業者たちはその貴重な絵画を競っていた The dealers *were bidding higher prices for* the

valuable paintings.

セルビア 〖国名〗 Serbia /sə́ːrbiə/; 《公式名》the Republic of Serbia. (首都 Belgrade) ●セルビア人 a Serb; a Serbian. ●セルビア語 Serb; Serbian. ●セルビア(人)語)の Serb; Serbian.

セルフケア self-care.

セルフコントロール 〖自制〗self-control; 〖自動制御〗automation.

セルフサービス self-service. ●セルフサービスの食堂 a self-service restaurant; a cafeteria.

セルフタイマー a self-timer.

セルモーター 〖エンジンの自動始動機〗a (self-)starter; 《和製語》a cell motor.

セルロイド 〖商標〗celluloid /séljəlɔ̀id/, Celluloid.

セルロース 〖繊維素〗〖化学〗cellulose.

セレナーデ [＜ドイツ語] a serenade /sèrənéid/. ●彼女のためにセレナーデを歌う〖演奏する〗serenade her.

セレブ 〖有名人〗a celébrity, 《話》a celéb.

セレモニー a 《closing》ceremony.
●セレモニーホール a funeral hall.

*ゼロ 〖数〗 a zero /zíərou/, 《英》 ~(e)s); 《英》 (a) nought /nɔːt/ 《主に小数の読み方に用いる》(⇒零)); nothing; nil. (⚠ 電話番号・部屋番号などでは例えば 1003 は one-o /ou/ - o-three, one-double-o-three と読む)
●4 対ゼロで勝つ win (by a score of) four to *nothing* [*zero*]; (ラグビーなどで) win four-*zip* 《米》[four-*nil* 《英》]. ●視界ゼロで前進する go on in *zero* visibility. ●ゼロ(=何もないところ)から始める start (it) from *zero* [*nothing*, *nil*]. ●ごみゼロ作戦 *no* litter campaign. ●赤ちゃんはまだゼロ歳だ The baby is *0* [*zero*] years. (⚠ 複数形に注意) ▶はかりの針はゼロをさしていた The indicator on the scale pointed to *zero*. ▶私の物理の知識はゼロに等しい I know practically *nothing* about physics.
●ゼロエミッション 〖廃棄物〗排出ゼロ zero-emission.
●ゼロ金利政策 the zero interest policy. ●ゼロクーポン債 a zero-coupon bond. 〖参考〗表面利率がゼロのかわりに、額面を大幅に下回る価格で販売される割引債）●ゼロサムゲーム a zero-sum game. ●ゼロシーリング a budget with no increase over the previous year; 《和製語》a zero ceiling. ●ゼロ成長 zero growth. ●ゼロベース予算 a zero-base(d) budget (略 ZBB). 〖参考〗前年実績に関係なく優先順位の高いものから予算をつける方法）

ゼロックス 〖商標〗Xerox /zíərɑks/. (⚠ 一般の用法では Xe-, xe-. ゼロックスしたものは ©(⇒コピー)) ●ゼロックスコピー a *xerox(ed)* copy; 《機械》a *xerox* copier [machine]. ●その手紙をゼロックスする take [make] a *xerox* of the letter; *xerox* the letter.

セロテープ 〖商標〗cellophane tape, 《米》〖商標〗Scotch tape, 《英》〖商標〗Sellotape. ●セロテープで留め合わせる scotch tape [sellotape] 《two pieces of paper》.

セロハン [＜フランス語]〖商標〗cellophane /séləfèin/.
●セロハン包装 *cellophane* wrapping. ●花束をセロハンで包む wrap a bouquet of flowers in *cellophane*.
●セロハンテープ (⇒セロテープ)

セロリ(ー) 〖植物〗celery /séləri/. ●セロリ 1 本 a stick of *celery*. (⚠ 1 株を a head of celery ということもある)

せろん 世論 public opinion. ●国際世論 international *opinion*. ●世論の動向 the trend of *public opinion*. ●世論を無視する [反映する; 操る] defy [reflect; manipulate] *public opinion*. ●世論を喚起する arouse [stir up] *public opinion*. (⚠ stir up の方が口語的で意味が強い) ●世論に訴える [耳を傾ける] appeal [pay careful attention] to public opinion. ●世論調査を行う 《take [conduct]》 a public opinion [an opinion] poll; a poll. ▶世論は学生たちに味方していた *Public opinion* was in favor [on the side] of the students. ▶世論はガソリン税に反対している *Public opinion* is opposed to [is against] the gasoline tax. ▶それに関して世論は二つに分かれている *Public opinion* is divided on it. [(真っ二つに割れている) There is a polarity of *public opinion* on it. ▶世論に従って政治をすると間違う場合もある You may make mistakes, if you (try to) run the country based on *public opinions*.

*せわ 世話 图 ❶ [面倒をみること] care; 〖管理責任〗charge. (⇒動 ❶) ●彼のためにいろいろ [パーティーの] 世話をする *see to* things for him [the arrangement for the party]. ▶赤ん坊の世話はベビーシッターがしている The baby is *in the charge* [《米》*in charge*] *of* the babysitter./The baby is *in the care of* the babysitter./The babysitter is *in charge* [✗*care*] *of* the baby. (⚠ (1) charge を用いる際、原則的には、受身的に世話される者が主語に来る場合は in the charge of を、能動的に世話をする者が主語に来る場合は in charge of を用いるが、《米》では後の方を受身的にも用いる。(2) 特に世話をする人が代名詞のときは in 《his》 charge, in [under] 《his》 care の形をとることが多い: 赤ん坊の世話を彼に任せる leave one's baby *in his charge* [*care*]) ▶リンゴの木は比較的世話が簡単である Apple trees are relatively simple to *take care of*. ▶彼は犬の世話をよくする He *takes good care of* his dog [*looks after* his dog very well].

❷ [斡旋(あっせん)] ●宣教師 [彼] の世話で留学する 《書》 study abroad through the *good offices of* a missionary [his *good offices*]. (⇒斡旋) ▶私は彼女の結婚の世話をした I *acted as* (a) *go-between* in her marriage (*to* Mr. A). (⇒仲人)

❸ [助力] help, 《やや書》assistance. ●世話になる receive *assistance* (*from* him). ▶大変お世話になりました Thank you very much for your *kind help* [*assistance*]. (⇒ありがとう)/You were a great *help* [very *helpful*] to me. (⚠〖事情〗日本語のように単なるあいさつには使わず、実際に世話になったときにいう)/I owe a great deal *to* you. ▶私は何かとおばの世話になっている I am *dependent on* my aunt *for* everything. ▶《商取引先などに対して》いつもお世話になっております We enjoy doing business with you. ▶私は夏の間お世話になった(=役に立った)網戸を外し水洗いした I took off the screen doors I had made a *good use* of during the summer and washed them in water.

❹ [やっかい] trouble. ●あの子は世話がほとんどいらない He *gives* almost no *trouble*./He is *easy* [*no trouble*] *to look after*. ▶お世話をかけてすみません. タクシーを呼んでいただけますか I'm sorry to *trouble* you, but will you call me a taxi? (⇒面倒)

❺ [おせっかい] ▶よけいなお世話だ(=君の知ったことではない) It's none of your business [no business of yours]./Mind your own business.

●世話が焼ける ●世話が焼ける(=やっかいな)子 a *troublesome* child.

●世話を焼く ●何から何まで身の回りの世話を焼く(=面倒をみる)《軽蔑的》*wait on* 《him》 hand and foot. ▶この子は世話を焼かせてばかりいる This child always gives me a lot of *trouble*./This child is a source of constant *trouble*. ▶要らぬ世話を焼かないでくれ Don't *interfere* [*meddle*] *in* my affairs./《話》Don't *poke* your *nose into* my affairs.

—世話する ❶ 【面倒をみる】 take* care of ...; care for ...; look after ...; see* to ... (❗意味が広くやや婉曲的). ▶彼女は長年病気の父親を世話してきた She has taken care of [cared for] her sick father for (many) years. ▶私の留守中赤ん坊を世話してくれませんか Could you look after [take care of, mind] the baby while I am out? (❗ mind は「臨時に世話をする」の意)

❷ 【斡旋(あっせん)する】 (見つけてやる) find*; (得させる) get*; (手配をする) see* about .... (⇨斡旋する) ▶彼が就職を世話してくれた He found me a job [a job for me]./He helped me (to) find a job. ▶娘に家庭教師を世話していただけませんか Would you get my daughter a tutor [a tutor for my daughter]? ▶私がコンサートの切符をお世話しましょう I'll see about your ticket for the concert.

•世話女房 a good housewife; a devoted wife.
•世話人 (会などの世話役) a manager; (発起人) an organizer; (仲立ちをする人) a go-between, an agent. •世話焼き a busybody.

せわしい せわしい人 a busy [落ち着かない) a restless] person. ▶せわしい息 (= 早い) 息遣い fast breathing.

せわしさ (多忙) busyness /bíznəs/. (❗ business /bíznəs/ との違いに注意)

せわしない 忙しない busy; (落ち着きのない) restless, 《話》 fidgety; (大急ぎの) hurried. ▶せわしなく出発する leave in a hurry [hurriedly]; 《書》 make a hurried departure. ▶彼は動作がせわしない He is restless in his movement. ▶彼は夕食の支度でせわしなく動き回っている He is bustling around cooking supper in the kitchen.

せわた 背腸 (エビの) the sand vein. ▶エビの背わたを抜く devein a prawn.

せわり 背割り ❶ 【裂け目】 (衣服の) a slit in the back 《of a coat》; (建材の) a split in the back 《of a pillar》. ❷ 【魚の】 (⇨背開き)

:せん 千 ❶ 【直線などの】 a [one] thousand (⇨百); 【千番目の】 the thousandth. ▶1,000 ドル a thousand dollars. ▶5,050 冊の本 five thousand [xthousands] (and) fifty books. (❗(1) 百の位にある場合に限り千の位の後に and を用いるが, (2) 《米》 ではしばしば省略される. (2) 日常的には fifty hundred (and) fifty と読むこともある) ▶1,001番目の one [the] thousand and first. (❗1,001st とも書く) ▶何[数]千人もの学生 thousands [xthousand] of students.

***せん** 線 ❶ 【直線などの】 a line. •平行線 parallel lines. •太い[細い] 赤の二重線を引く draw a double bold [fine] red line. •線の入った紙 lined [ruled] paper. •38度線 the 38th parallel. ▶白線から前へ出ないでください Please stay behind the white line.

❷ 【電話・鉄道などの】 (電線) a wire, a line; (鉄道・バスなどの路線) a line; (鉄道線路) a track; (道路の車線) a lane; 〖航送〗 a route. •電話線 a telephone line [wire]. •国際線のパイロット a pilot on an international route. •4 車線の幹線道路 a four-lane highway. ▶東京から中央線で西へ行く travel west from Tokyo on the Chuo Line. ▶その列車は 5 番線より発車します The train leaves from track 《米》 [platform 《英》] (No.) 5.

❸ 【行動などの方針】 a line; (基本方針) a principle. •安全第一の線に沿って行動する act on the principle that safety comes first. ▶この線で(=この方針に従って)計画を進めよう Let's go on with our plan on these lines.

❹ 【その他の表現】 ▶彼の学校の成績はかなりいい線をいっている He's doing pretty well in school. ▶交渉はいい線をいっている The negotiations are getting somewhere [《米話》 someplace]. ▶あの人は線の細い(=神経質な)感じの人 He looks sensitive [かぼい) fragile].

〖会話〗 「どうだ, 当たったろう」「いや, でもいい線いってるよ」 "So have I hit it?" "No, but you're (getting) warm."

せん 栓 〖びんなどの〗 a stopper; 〖コルク栓〗 a cork (stopper); 〖たるの〗 a tap, a bung; 〖穴をふさぐ〗 a plug; 〖水道・ガスなどの〗 《米》 a faucet, 《英》 a tap. •コルクでびんに栓をする cork a bottle; put a cork (stopper) in a bottle. •びんのコルク栓を抜く uncork [pull a cork (stopper)] out of a bottle. •綿を丸めて試験管に栓をする stop a test tube with a wad of cotton; use a wad of cotton as a stopper to a test tube. •水道の栓を開ける[閉める] turn on [off] the (water) faucet (❗ 普通は文脈があるので water は省略される).

せん 腺 图 〖解剖〗 a gland. **—腺(状)の** 圏 glandular.

せん 選 (選択) (a) selection; (a) choice; (編集) (a) compilation; (選挙) (an) election. •名曲百選 a selection of one hundred musical masterpieces. ▶その作品は選に漏れた That work was not selected [chosen; (採用されなかった) accepted]./That work was left out of selection.

—せん -戦 ▶彼は 21 戦 20 勝だ He won 20 of 21 races [matches].

ぜん 前 〖かつての〗 ex-; 〖時間・順序などのその前の〗 previous; 〖すぐ前の, 前述の〗 《書》 preceding. •この市の前市長 the ex-mayor [the former mayor] of this city. (❗ 後の方が口語的) •前近代的な考え a premodern [《旧式の》 an old-fashioned] idea. •前ページに on the previous [preceding] page.

ぜん 善 (よいこと) good; (正しいこと) right. •善をなす do good.
•善は急げ Do good things as soon as you can.; (チャンスのがすな) Make hay while the sun shines.

ぜん 禅 Zen. •禅を実践する practice Zen. ▶禅は座禅を組んで静かに瞑想(めいそう)することによって悟りの境地に達することを目ざしています Zen aims to attain spiritual enlightenment by means of sitting cross-legged in silent meditation.
•禅宗 Zen (Buddhism). •禅僧 a Buddhist priest of the Zen sect; a Zen Buddhist priest. •禅問答 a dialogue between Zen priests; (意味の分からない問答) an incomprehensible exchange.

ぜん 膳 (食卓) a table; (食事) a meal; (米飯など1杯分) a helping. •膳につく sit down to the table [a meal]. •10人前の膳をすえる set [lay] the table for ten persons. •三の膳 the third course.

***ぜん—** 全— 〖すべての〗 all; 〖全体の〗 whole (❗ 通例 the [one's] —の形で); 〖欠けることなく全体の〗 entire (❗ whole より強意的); 〖総計の〗 total; 〖全部そろっている〗 complete; 〖十分な〗 full. (⇨全部) •全国民の entire [whole] nation. (❗単数扱い) •全世界 (の世界 ①) •全人格 one's total character. •全4巻の英語辞典 an English dictionary complete in four volumes [with a total of 4 volumes]. •全責任をとる accept full responsibility.

—ぜん -然 ▶学者然としてふるまう behave quite like a scholar. ▶彼は芸術家然としたところがある He has an artistic air about him./There is something artistic about him.

—ぜん -膳 ▶ご飯 1 膳 a bowl(ful) of rice. •はし 1

ぜんあく 善悪 right and wrong. (⇨善し悪し)

せんい 繊維 [動植物の]《集合的》fiber (❗ 繊維の1本をいうときは [C]); [織物の] (a) fiber. ● 食物繊維 dietary fiber. ● 筋肉繊維 muscle fibers. ● 化学(合成)繊維 (a) chemical [a synthetic] fiber. ● ガラス繊維(=グラスファイバー) glass fiber, fiber glass. ● 繊維質のものを食べる eat fiber [fibrous food]. ● 繊維産業 the textile industry. ● 繊維素 (動物細胞の) fibrin; (植物細胞の) cellulose. ● 繊維製品 textile products [(商品) goods].

せんい 船医 a ship's doctor.

せんい 戦意 fighting spirit, the will to fight. ● 戦意を失う lose one's fighting spirit.

ぜんい 善意 (誠意) good faith; (よい意図) good intentions; (好意) goodwill; (親切心) kindness. ● 善意の贈り物 a present of [given out of] goodwill. ● 彼のことを善意に解釈する give him the benefit of the doubt. ▶ [慣用的な言い方] 彼は善意で(=だますつもりなどなく)そうした He did it in good faith [(親切心から) out of kindness]. ▶ 彼をとがめないで. 善意で言ったのだから Don't blame him. He meant well.

せんいき 戦域 a war area; a theater of war. ● 太平洋戦域を拡大する expand the Pacific war area [theater of war].

ぜんいき 全域 the whole area. ● 関西全域にわたり all over the Kansai district; over the whole Kansai district. ▶ ダーウィンの「種の起源」は当時の学問の全域に強い影響を与えた Darwin's The Origin of Species had a strong influence on every field of study at his time.

せんいつ 専一 学問を専一にする devote oneself exclusively [(まったく) completely] to one's studies; study earnestly [in earnest]. ▶ ご自愛専一になさってください Please take good care of yourself.

せんいん 船員 [乗組員] a crew member, a member of the crew, (男の) a crewman (@-men);《集合的》crew (❗(1) 通例高級船員以外. (2) 単・複両扱い《⇨乗組員》); [船乗り] a mariner, a sailor, (男の) a seaman (@-men).

ぜんいん 全員 ▶ 委員会員がそれに反対した All the members of the committee were against it. / The whole committee was [×were] against it. (❗ ここでは全委員を一まとまりとしてとらえているため複数扱いにしない) ● 家族は全員元気です My family is [(英) are] all well. / All my family is [(英) are] well. ● その法案は全員一致の承認により採択された The bill was accepted with unanimous approval [was unanimously approved]. / They approved the bill unanimously. / They were unanimous in approving the bill.

せんうん 戦雲 a war cloud. ● 戦雲が極東に垂れ込めている War clouds hang over the Far East.

せんえい 先鋭 ── 先鋭(的)な 形 radical. ● 先鋭的思想 radical ideas.
── **先鋭化する** 動 turn [become] radical.
● 先鋭分子 (過激主義者たち) radicals; radical elements.

せんえい 船影 ▶ 船影は認められない There is [We see] no sign [trace] of a ship.

ぜんえい 前衛 ❶ [軍隊の] a vanguard (❗ 集合的に用い, 単・複両扱い), an advance guard.
❷ [球技の] a forward. ● 前衛を守る play forward.
❸ [芸術の] the avànt-gárde.
● 前衛芸術 avant-garde /ɑːvɑ̀ːngɑ́ːrd/ árt. ● 前衛派 the avànt-gárde. (❗ 単・複両扱い)

せんえつ 僭越 [[出過ぎること]]《書》presumption;[[ずうずうしさ]]《書》audacity. ● 僭越な行為《やや書》presumptuous [audacious] conduct. ▶ 彼が私に干渉したのは僭越なことだ It was presumptuous of him [He had the presumption] to interfere with us. ▶ 僭越ながらこの案を委員会に進言させていただきます Allow me to suggest this plan to the committee. (❗ Let me suggest ... の改まった丁寧な言い方)

せんおう 専横 名 (独断) arbitrariness; (専制) despotism.
── **専横な** 形 arbitrary; high-handed. ● 専横にふるまう behave very high-handedly [arbitrarily]; have one's own way.

ぜんおん 全音 《音楽》a whole tone [《米》step].

ぜんおんかい 全音階 《音楽》the diatonic scale.

ぜんおんぷ 全音符 《音楽》《米》a whole note, 《英》a semibreve /sémaibriːv/.

せんか 専科 a special course. ● デザイン専科 a design course.
● 専科生 a special course student.

せんか 戦火 war. (⇨戦争)

せんか 戦果 military results [(獲得したもの) achievements]. ● はなばなしい戦果をあげる achieve brilliant military results [(利益) gains]; have [produce] brilliant military achievements.

せんか 戦禍 war damage. ● ひどい戦禍を被る be greatly damaged [ravaged] by war; suffer great damage [《書》 the ravages] of war.

せんか 選果 ── 選果する 動 sort (out) fruit (by (its) size and whether it has any bruises or not).

せんか 選科 an elective [(特別の) an special] course; (正課ではない過程) a non-regular course.
● 選科生 a non-regular [special] student.

せんか 選歌 the selection of poems; (選ばれた歌) a selected [a chosen] poem.

せんが 線画 (ペンまたは鉛筆の) (a) line drawing. (❗「線画法」の意のときは [U])

ぜんか 全科 (過程) the whole [complete] course; (科目) all the subjects.

ぜんか 前科 [犯罪の前歴] a criminal [a jail] record. ▶ 彼は前科がない He has no criminal record. ▶ 彼は前科3犯だ He has been convicted three times. / He has three previous convictions.
● 前科者 an ex-convict, 《話》an ex-con.

せんかい 仙界 (仙人の住居) an abode of hermits [(不死の人) immortals]; (俗界を離れた清浄な所) a secluded and clean place far from worldly cares.

せんかい 先回 (⇨前 前回) ● 先回(=この前)の会議 the last meeting.

せんかい 浅海 a shallow sea.
● 浅海魚 a shallow-water fish.

せんかい 旋回 ── 旋回する 動 (円を描いて) circle; (方向を変えて) turn. ▶ 飛行機は船上を旋回した The plane circled (over) the ship. ▶ ヘリコプターは北に旋回した The helicopter turned [took a turn] to the north.

せんがい 船外 ● 船外に落ちる [投げ出される] fall [be thrown] overboard.
● 船外(発動)機 an outboard motor.

せんがい 選外 ● 選外佳作になった作品 a work that won an honorable mention.

ぜんかい 全快 名 a complete [a full] recovery.
── **全快する** 動 ▶ 彼は全快した He completely [fully] recovered (from (his) sickness [illness]). / He made a complete [a full] recovery

(*from* (*his*) *sickness* [*illness*])./He *got quite well*.

ぜんかい 全開 ● エンジンを全開にする run the engine in *full force* [*at full blast*]; (スロットルバルブを大きく開ける) throw the throttle wide open.

ぜんかい 全壊 ── 全壊する 動 be completely destroyed 《*by* the earthquake》.
● 全壊家屋 a completely destroyed house.

ぜんかい 前回 ● 前回の講義 the *last* [*previous*] lecture. ● 前々回の会合 (⇨前々回) ● (連載物の)前回までの物語のあらすじ an outline of the story up to the *last installment*. ▶ 前回(=この前)はどこへ行きましたか Where did you go (*the*) *last time*?

ぜんかいいっち 全会一致 ● 全会一致でその報告を承認する approve of the report *unanimously* [(満場一致の票決で) *by a unanimous vote*].

せんがく 先学 past [earlier] scholars; scholars in the past.

せんがく 浅学 shallow knowledge. ● 浅学非才を顧みず in spite of my *lack of knowledge and ability*; though I have only *limited learning and ability*.

ぜんがく 全学 the whole university [college]. ▶ 本日全学休校 *The whole university* is closed today.
● 全学集会 an all-campus meeting.

ぜんがく 全額 [[総額]] the total [full] amount. ● 月末までに全額を支払う make *full* payment by the end of the month. ● 借金を全額返済する *pay off* one's debt [*off* は debt から「離れて」の意); pay one's debt *in full*. ● 旅費の全額(=全体)を払い戻す pay 《him》 back *all* (*of*) the traveling expenses; (やや書) refund 《him》 *the whole* traveling expenses.

ぜんがく 前額 (人間の) the forehead; (動物の) a frontlet.

せんかくしゃ 先覚者 [[創始者]] a pioneer /pàiəniər/; [[学問・徳のある人]] a luminary.

せんかくしょとう 尖閣諸島 the Senkaku [Diaoyu (-tai)] Islands. (❗後の方は中国・台湾での言い方)

ぜんがくれん 全学連 [[「全日本学生自治会総連合」の略]] the National Federation of Students' Self-Government Associations.

せんかたない 詮方無い (⇨(似)仕方(が)無い) ▶ せんかたなく(=しぶしぶ)赤ん坊の世話をする take care of the baby *with reluctance*.

せんかん 戦艦 a battleship.

せんかん 潜函 〘工学〙 a caisson.
● 潜函工法 the caisson method. ● 潜函病 〘医学〙 caisson disease; (話) the bends.

せんかん 選管 [[「選挙管理委員会」の略]](⇨選挙)

せんがん 専願 ▶ あの大学の入試は専願制だ The decision of acceptance by that college is *binding* (on the accepted applicants). (❗binding は「拘束力がある」の意)

せんがん 洗眼 [名] eyewashing.
── 洗眼する 動 wash one's eyes.
● 洗眼剤 eyewash; (an) eye lotion; 〘医学〙 a collyrium.

せんがん 洗顔 ── 洗顔する 動 wash one's face.
● 洗顔クリーム facial cleansing cream.

せんがん 腺癌 〘医学〙 adenocarcinoma, glandular cancer.

ぜんかん 全巻 (書物1冊全体) the whole volume; (すべての巻) the complete set. ● シェイクスピア全集全巻 a set of the complete works of Shakespeare.

ぜんかん 全館 ▶ この建物は全館冷暖房になっている This building has central heating and air conditioning [is centrally heated and air conditioned].

ぜんがん 前癌 ● 前がん症状 〘医学〙a precancerous condition.

せんき 戦記 (記録) a record of war; (実録) commentaries of war; (年代順の記録) a war chronicle [memoirs /mémwɑːrz/]; ánnals of war. ● シーザーのガリア戦記 Caesar's *Gallic Wars*.

せんき 戦機 the time for fighting. ▶ 戦機が熟した *The time* has come to *fight a battle* [*to open hostilities*]./*The time* is ripe *for a battle*.

せんぎ 先議 [名] (先に審議すること) prior deliberation(s).
── 先議する 動 deliberate [debate] 《a matter》 first.
● 先議権 the right to debate [deliberate on] 《a budget》 first.

せんぎ 詮議 ── 詮議する 動 (調べる) examine.

ぜんき 前記 ── 前記の 形 above; above-mentioned; 《書》the said (❗法律用語). ● 前記の質問 the *above*(-*mentioned*) question; the question (*mentioned*) *above*. ● 前記のとおり as (*is*) *mentioned* [*stated*] *above*.

ぜんき 前期 〘1年の前半〙the first half (year); 〘2学期制の前半〙the first term [(米) semester]; 〘時代の初期〙an early period. ●(大学の)2学年の前期に in *the first semester* of the second year. (⇨半, 初期)

せんきゃく 先客 a visitor before 《me》. ▶ 先客があったので出直すことにした When I visited [《主に英》called on] him [her], there was *another visitor before me*, so I left a message I would come again and went home.

せんきゃく 船客 a passenger on board (the ship). (❗passenger だけでも文脈によって「船客」の意になる) ● 1等船客 a first-class *passenger*. ● まりも丸の船客 the *passengers* on (*board*) the *Marimo*.

せんきゃくばんらい 千客万来 ▶ 我が家は今朝から千客万来だ We *have had a lot of* [*so many*] *visitors* since this morning.

せんきゅう 選球 ── 選球する 動 wait for a good pitch to hit.
● 選球眼 〘野球〙 a batting eye; an eye. ● その一番バッターは選球眼がいい The leadoff man has a good (*batting*) *eye*.

ぜんきゅう 全休 ● かぜのため全休する (丸1日休む) *be away from school* [(仕事から) *be off work*] *the whole day* [(その期間全部) *throughout the whole of the term*] because of a cold.

:せんきょ 選挙 [名] (an) election.
①〖〜選挙〗● 大統領[知事; 市長]選挙 a presidential [a gubernatorial; a mayoral] *election*. ●(大統領)予備選挙 a primary *election*. ● 衆議院[参議院]選挙 the House of Councillors [the House of Representatives] *election*. ● 統一地方選挙 a nationwide local *election*. ● 国政選挙 a national *election*. ● 総選挙 a general *election*. ● 補欠選挙 a special *election*; 《英》a by-*election*. ● 普通[直接; 間接]選挙 a popular [a direct; an indirect] *election*. ● 公職選挙法 the Public Office *Election* Law.
②〖選挙が〗▶ 4年ごとに市長選挙が行われる A mayoral *election* is held [takes place] every four years./(選挙をする)We *elect* [have an *election for*] mayor every four years.
③〖選挙の〗▶ 選挙のときには投票所に投票に行かねばならない We have to go to the polling place to

せんきょ

vote *at elections*. ▶選挙の結果は今夜放送されるでしょう The *election* results [(投票区)The result of the *poll*] will be broadcast tonight.

④【選挙に】● 選挙に行く go to vote. ▶彼は次の選挙に出る[勝つ;負ける]だろう He will run for [win; lose] the next *election*. (❗run for は《米》で、《英》では stand for を用いる. また《米》では run in も用いられる)

⑤【選挙を】● 選挙をする[行う] (⇨②) ● 選挙を管理する委員会が設置された The commission was set up to oversee the *election*.

⑥【選挙で】▶あす次期会長を選挙で選びます We will *elect* a new chairperson tomorrow./We will *choose* a new chairperson tomorrow. ▶この前の選挙で彼は国会議員に選ばれた He was elected a member of parliament *in* the last *election*.

── 選挙する 動 elect; choose*... by election [(投票で) by vote]. (⇨②, ⑥)

● 選挙違反 (a) violation of the election law; (an) election law violation. ● 選挙運動 an election campaign,《米》a campaign. ● 選挙運動員 a campaigner. ● 選挙演説《make》a campaign speech. ● 選挙カー a campaign van. ● 選挙管理委員会 the Election Administration Committee. (❗《米》では the board of elections, the election board) ● 選挙区 a constituency; an electoral [an electoral] district. ● 選挙区民 a constituent. ● 選挙権 the vote; the right to vote,《書》suffrage. ● 選挙公報 an election bulletin. ● 選挙公約 a campaign promise [pledge]. ● 選挙資金《raise》campaign funds. (❗「選挙資金集め」は fund-raising for a campaign) ● 選挙事務所 an election campaign office [headquarters]. ● 選挙制度 the election system. ● 選挙戦 an election [an electoral] campaign. ● 選挙対策委員会 an election polling committee. ● 選挙人 a voter. ● 選挙人名簿 the electoral roll [register]; the list of voters [electors]. (❗《米》では elector は下院議員および大統領選挙の特別選挙人のこと) ● 選挙日 an election day;《米》Election Day (偶数年の11月の第1月曜日の次の火曜日で多くの州では法定休日). ● 選挙法 the election [electoral] laws. ● 選挙妨害 (election) campaign obstruction. ● 選挙民 the electorate.

せんきょ 占拠 图 occupation.
── 占拠する 動 occupy; take ... over;《話》grab. (⇨占領) ● 建物を不法占拠する take illegal [unlawful] *possession* of the building.

せんぎょ 鮮魚 《集合的》fresh fish.

せんきょう 宣教 (布教) propagation; (特にキリスト教の) missionary work.
● 宣教師 a missionary.

せんきょう 船橋 a bridge; (浮き橋) a pontoon bridge.

せんきょう 戦況 (戦争の状況) the military [war] situation. ● 戦況を見守る watch [observe] the progress of the war. ▶戦況は我が方に有利だ The *war* is going in our favor.

せんぎょう 専業 a full-time job.
● 専業主婦 a (full-time) housewife,《主に米》a (full-time) homemaker. ● 専業農家 a full-time farmer.

せんきょく 戦局 (戦争の形勢)the tide [state] of the war. ● 戦局に重大な変化が見られる witness a significant change in *the progress of the war*. ▶戦局は我が軍に不利に展開している *The tide of the war*

せんけつ

is turning against our army.

せんきょく 選曲 图 selection of music.
── 選曲する 動 ▶クラシックから1曲選曲する *select* a piece of *music* from among classical music.

せんきょく 選局 图 tuning.
── 選局する 動 tune in《to》. ▶NHKを選局してニュースを聞いた I *tuned in to* the NHK to hear the news.

ぜんきょく 全曲 全曲演奏 a *full-length* play.

せんぎり 千切り 千切りにする shred. ● キャベツの千切り *shredded* cabbage.

せんきん 千金 ● 千金の値打ちがある be priceless. ● 一獲千金 (⇨一獲千金) ● 一刻千金(の値) (⇨一刻 [成句])

せんきん 千鈞 ● 千鈞の重み ▶彼の言葉は千鈞の重みがある His words *have* [*carry*] *great weight* with us.

ぜんきんだい 前近代 ── 前近代的な 形 (近代以前の) pre-modern; (古風な) old-fashioned; (封建的な) feudalistic.

せんく 線区 a railroad [《英》a railway] section.

ぜんく 前駆 前駆症状《医学》a premonitory [a prodromal] symptom; a prodrome.

せんぐう 遷宮 ── 遷宮する 動 (神霊を新しい神殿に移す) install (the sacred symbol of) a deity in a new shrine.
● 遷宮式 the dedication of a new shrine.

せんくしゃ 先駆者 a pioneer /pàiəníər/; (学問・流派などの創始者)《書》a progenitor. ● この道の先駆者 a *pioneer* in [×of] this field. ● 心臓移植の先駆者 a heart transplant *pioneer*; a *pioneer* of heart transplant. (⇨草分け)

せんくち 先口 (先約) a previous engagement; (先の申し込み) a previous application.

ぜんくつ 前屈 ● 前屈をする bend forward.

ぜんぐん 全軍 the whole army [(部隊) force]; (スポーツの) the whole team.

せんぐんばんば 千軍万馬 (たくさんの兵と軍馬) a large number of soldiers and war horses. ● 千軍万馬の(=戦闘の経験が豊かな)古つわもの a veteran of many battles.

せんけい 線形 線形動物 nemathelminthes.

ぜんけい 全景 (全体の眺め) a complete view; (パノラマ)《やや書》a pànoráma. ● その市の全景 《enjoy (高い場所から) command》a *panoramic view* of the city; a *view* of the *whole* city. ▶まもなく湖の全景が見えてくるだろう We'll soon be in *full view* of the lake.

ぜんけい 前掲 ● 前掲の図 the diagram *mentioned above*; the *above-mentioned* diagram.

ぜんけい 前景 (景色・絵画などの) the foreground (↔ the background).

ぜんけい 前傾 前傾姿勢で in a *forward-bent* posture.

せんけつ 先決 ▶その紛争の解決が先決だ(=まず最初に紛争を解決しなければならない)*First* (*of all*) [*Before anything else*], we must settle the dispute.
● 先決問題 (ある問題に先立って解決しなければならない第一の問題) the first question to be settled beforehand; (優先的な問題) a priority (matter); (第一に考慮すべき事柄) the first consideration.

せんけつ 専決 ▶市長が市議会の委任によって専決した(独断で決めた) The mayor *decided on* his *own* by commision from the city assembly.

せんけつ 潜血《医学》occult blood.
● 潜血反応検査 an occult blood test.

せんけつ 鮮血 fresh blood. ▶傷口から鮮血がほとばしった *Blood* gushed out from the wound.

せんげつ 先月 last month. ●先月の5日に on the fifth of *last month*. ●先月の最後の月曜日に on the last Monday (*of*) *last month*. ●先月号は *last month*'s issue. ▶彼は先月亡くなった He died *last month*.

せんけん 先見 ━ **先見の明()** ▶彼は先見の明がある He is farsighted [foresighted, *a man of foresight*]./He has *foresight*. ▶父は先見の明がない My father is shortsighted [lacking in *foresight*]. (「先見の明がないこと」は a lack of *foresight*)

せんけん 専権 exclusive rights; arbitrary power.

せんげん 宣言 图 (a) declaration /dèkləréiʃən/; (a) proclamation /pràkləméiʃən/. ●独立宣言 the *declaration* of independence. (合衆国の「独立宣言」の場合は the *Declaration* of Independence) ●平和宣言 *proclamation* of peace. ●奴隷解放宣言 the Emancipation *Proclamation*. ●共産党宣言 the Communist *Manifesto*. ●独立宣言をする *declare* (one's) independence. ●爆弾宣言をする《話》drop [explode] a bombshell.
━ **宣言する** 動 [はっきりと] declare; [国家的関心事を高らかに]《書》proclaim. ▶彼はオリンピックの開会を宣言した He *declared* the Olympic Games (to be) open./He *declared* the opening of the Olympic Games. ▶ついに終戦が宣言された At last the end of war *was proclaimed*.

ぜんけん 全権 (一切の権限) full [《書》plenary] powers, full authority; (絶対的権力) absolute power. ●全権を委任する entrust (him) with [give (him)] *full powers* (*to do*). ▶彼は会社の全権を握っている He has *absolute power* in the company.
●**全権委員** a plenipotentiary. ●**全権大使** an ambassador plenipotentiary /plènipəténʃəri/.

ぜんげん 前言 前言を取り消す take back [withdraw] one's *previous remarks*.

ぜんげん 漸減 图 a gradual decrease. ●漸減傾向にあるをon the decrease. (特に形容詞を添えなくても on で減少が基調になっていることが示されている)
━ **漸減する** 動 decrease [diminish] gradually.

せんけんたい 先遣隊 an advance party [team, (部隊) troop].

せんげんばんご 千言万語 ●千言万語(＝非常に多くの言葉)を費やす use *a great many words*.

せんこ 千古 [遠い昔] great [remote] antiquity; [永遠] eternity. ●千古不滅の eternal; everlasting.

せんご 戦後 [戦後の時期・時代] the postwar period [days]; [戦後数年たって[数年間]] several years [for several years] *after the war*. ●戦後の日本 *postwar* Japan; Japan *after the war*. ▶戦後60年たった It's [It has been] 60 years since the war (was over). (Sixty years has passed since .... ともいうがやや堅い言い方) ▶もはや戦後ではない The nation is no longer [We no longer live] in an immediate *postwar period*.
●**戦後派** the postwar generation.

ぜんこ 全戸 [一家全体] the whole family [house]; [全部の家] all houses. ▶村の全戸が停電した There was a blackout *in all the houses* in the village.

*****ぜんご 前後** ❶ [場所] (前と後ろに) before and behind, before and after; (後の方は時間を「前後に」の意にも用いるが); (前面と背面に) in front and in (the) rear, 《話》 front and rear; (前後に動いて) back and forth. ▶彼女をよく見ないな Look carefully *before and behind* [*to the front and the rear*]. ▶車をバックで車庫に入れるときには前後左右をよく見なさい Look *around* [*about*] (you) carefully when you back your car into the garage. ▶彼らは城を前後から攻撃した They attacked the castle *in front and in the rear* [*front and rear*]. ▶彼らは音楽に合わせて体を前後に揺り動かした They were swaying *back and forth* [《やや書》*to and fro*] to the music.
❷ [時間] (前後ともに) before and after .... ▶教師は試験の前後が特に忙しい Teachers are busy especially *before and after* the exams. ▶2人は前後して部屋に入って来た The two of them came into the room *one after the other*. (3人以上は one after another)
❸ [およそ] about ..., (主に米) around ..., (口) around .... ●30分前後の女性 a woman *about* [*around*] thirty (years old). ▶彼は10時前後にここに来ます He comes here *about* [*around*] ten (o'clock). ▶(10時かそこらに) He comes here at ten or so [*or thereabouts*].
❹ [順序] order; [文脈] a context. ▶前後が逆転している The *order* is reversed. ▶前後関係から語の意味を推測できる We can guess the meaning of a word *from* its *context*. ▶彼の言葉は前後関係なく引用され, 誤解された His words were quoted *out of context* and were misunderstood. ▶彼はよく話が前後する(＝混乱する) He often *gets confused* in his speech./He often *gets mixed up* while (he is) speaking.
●**前後の見境もなく** ▶前後の見境もなく(＝衝動的に)彼は社長をけった He kicked his president *on the spur of the moment*.
●**前後不覚** ●前後不覚に陥る lose consciousness.
●**前後不覚に眠る**《話》sleep *like a log* [*a top*]. ▶前後不覚になるまで飲んだ I drank till I *fell unconscious* [《話》*passed out* (*cold*)].
●**前後を忘れる** ●怒りで前後を忘れる(＝逆上している) be beside oneself with rage.

せんこう 先行 ━ **先行する** 動 〈先に行く〉go ahead 《*of* others》; (順序などが)《書》precede. ▶彼の考えは時代に先行している His ideas *are ahead of* his time./He *is ahead of* the times in his ideas. ▶英語では動詞が目的語に先行する In English the verb *precedes* [*comes before*] the object. ▶地元チームが6対4で先行している(＝リードしている) The home team *is leading* [*is ahead*] six to four. (six to four は副詞句)
●**先行指標**《経済》a leading indicator [signal]; a leader. ●**先行投資** a prior investment.

せんこう 先攻 ━ **先攻する** 動 attack first; 《野球》bat first [in the top].

せんこう 専攻 [専門] one's specialty /spéʃlti/ [field]; one's special study. ▶専攻は文学です(専門家として) My *specialty* [*field*] is literature./I'm studying [*specializing in*] literature. (《主に米》では大学での専攻には My *major* is [I'm *majoring in*] literature. や I'm a literature *major*. を, 大学院での専攻には I'm *studying* literature. を区別して用いる. また, 《英やや書》では大学での専攻に I *am reading* literature. も用いる)
●**専攻科目** one's specialty [special subject]; 《主に米》 (大学の学部学生の) one's major. (関連) 副専攻科目 a minor)

せんこう 穿孔 图 perforation; (パンチによる) punching; (ドリルなどによる) boring, drilling.
━ **穿孔する** 動 perforate; punch; bore, drill.
●**穿孔器** a perforator; a puncher. ●**穿孔機** a bóring machine; a drill.

せんこう 閃光 a flash. ▶雷の閃光がフォーク状に夜空を横切り, 雷鳴がとどろいた Forked lightning *flashed*

せんこう 戦功 distinguished war services. ●戦功を立てる distinguish oneself in battle.

せんこう 潜行 图 ●(地下)潜行運動 underground activities.
— **潜行する** (地下に潜る) go underground; (隠れる) go into hiding. ▶脱走犯が市内に潜行している The escaped prisoner *is* [*stays*] *in hiding* in the city.

せんこう 潜航 图 submarine [(水面下の) underwater] navigation.
— **潜航する** 動 navigate [cruise] underwater.
●潜航艇 a submarine (boat); an underwater boat.

せんこう 線香 an incense stick (made from fragrant woods or grasses). ●仏壇に線香をあげる offer *incense sticks* to the (family) Buddhist altar. (**!**) burn incense sticks at … ともいえる)
●線香代 (香典) a monetary offering. (⇨香典)
●線香花火 a sparkler.

せんこう 選考 [[選抜]] selection; [[審査選別]] screening. ●選考にもれる be not [fail to be] selected.
— **選考する** 動 select; screen. ●書類選考する *screen* [*examine*] 〈his〉 papers. ▶就職希望者たちは慎重に選考された Applicants for the position *were carefully considered* [*screened*]. (**!** ×selected とすれば applicants を選んだことになるので不可)
●選考委員会 a selection [a screening] committee. ●選考基準 the criteria for selection [screening].

ぜんこう 全校 (全校生徒(および先生)) the (whole) school. (**!** 集合的に用い, 通常単・複両用扱い)
●全校生徒 all the students in [of] the school.

ぜんこう 前項 [前にあげた条項] the preceding clause; [前の段落・節] the previous paragraph; [[数学]] the antecedent.

ぜんこう 善行 [よい行い] a good deed; [よい行状] good conduct [behavior]. ●善行で表彰される be commended for one's *good deed*. ●善行を施す do 〈him〉 *a good turn*.

ぜんごう 前号 (ある号の一つ前) the preceding [(現在の号の一つ前) the last] issue [number]. ▶前号から続く Continued from *the last issue*.

＊せんこく 宣告 图〔書〕a pronouncement; [[刑の]] (a) sentence. ●死刑の宣告 the death *sentence*.
— **宣告する** 動 pronounce /prənáuns/; (刑を) sentence. ●彼に死刑を宣告する (刑を) *pronounce* [*pass*] the death sentence *on* him; *sentence* [*condemn*] him *to* death (**!** sentence の方が普通). ▶彼は殺人で有罪を宣告された (= 有罪判決を受けた) He *was convicted of* murder. ▶医師は父の死亡を宣告した The doctor *pronounced that* my father was dead./The doctor *pronounced* my father (*to be*) dead.

せんこく 先刻 (ちょっと前に) a short while [time] ago; (既に) already. ●先刻ご承知のとおり as you *already* know.

ぜんこく 全国 图 the whole country; [[全国各地]] all [a lot of different] parts of the country. ▶インフルエンザが全国に広がっている Influenza has spread *all over the country* [*throughout the country*, (日本中に) *throughout Japan*]. ▶全国からやって来た People came from *all parts of* [*from all over*] *the country*.
— **全国的な** 形 (地方に対し) national; (全国規模の) nationwide. ●全国的な運動を起こす start a *nationwide* campaign [movement]. ●全国的な規模で on a *nationwide* scale. ▶天気は全国的によいでしょう The weather will be nice *all across the country*. ▶その試合は全国ネットで放映された The game was televised *nationwide*.
●全国区 the national constituency. ●全国紙 a national newspaper.

せんごくじだい 戦国時代 the age [period] of civil war(s).

ぜんごさく 善後策 ●善後策(= 改善する手段)を講じる 《やや書》take *remedial measures* 《*against, for*; *to do*》; (後始末の策) take measures to settle the matter satisfactorily.

せんこつ 仙骨 [[解剖]] the sacrum (複 sacra).

ぜんざ 前座 (寄席などの最初の演技) an opening performance [act]; (開幕劇) a curtain raiser; (人) a minor performer. ●前座を務める act as a *curtain raiser*; work an *opening act*.
●前座試合 an curtain-raiser match [game].

センサー a sensor.

せんさい 先妻 one's former wife, one's ex-wife.
●先妻の子 a child by one's *former wife*.

せんさい 戦災 [[被害]] war damage; [[荒廃]] war devastation. ●ひどい戦災を被る; [[免れる]] suffer [escape] great *damage in a war*.
●戦災者 a war victim; (空襲による) an air-raid victim. ●戦災孤児 a war orphan.

せんさい 繊細 图 [繊細さ] (感覚・趣味などの) delicacy; (感覚・観察眼などの) fineness. ●彼の文学趣味の繊細さ the *delicacy* of his taste in literature.
— **繊細な** 形 delicate /délikət/; fine; (感覚などが鋭敏な) exquisite /ekskwízit/. ●繊細な感受性を持つ音楽家 a musician of *delicate* [*fine*] sensibilities. ▶彼女には繊細な美的感覚がある She has an *exquisite* [a *delicate*, a *fine*] sense of beauty.

せんざい 洗剤 (a) detergent /dɪtə́ːrdʒənt/; (a) cleaner /klíːnər/; [みがき粉] (a) cleanser /klénzər/. ●合成[中性]洗剤 a synthetic [a neutral] *detergent*.

せんざい 潜在 — **潜在的(な)** 形 (表に出ていない) latent /léɪtənt/; (可能性のある) potential.
— **潜在する** 動 ▶両国間には戦争の危機が潜在していた The war crisis *remained latent* [*lay hidden*] between the two countries.
●潜在意識 the [one's] subconscious; subconsciousness. ●潜在失業(者数[率]) latent unemployment. ▶潜在失業者数が増加傾向にある *Latent unemployment* is on the increase. ●潜在出血 [[医学]] occult bleeding. ●潜在需要 potential demand. ●潜在成長力 the potential growth rate. ●潜在病原菌 [[医学]] latent disease germs; a masked virus. ●潜在能力 (have [show]) potential; latent ability. ▶子供の潜在能力を見つけることが必要だ It is necessary to find out the child's *potential*.

ぜんさい 前菜 (オードブル) an hors d'oeuvre /ɔːrdə́ːrv/ (複 hors d'oeuvres).

ぜんざい 善哉 (⇨汁粉)

せんざいいちぐう 千載一遇 ●千載一遇のチャンスを逃す lose a *one-in-a-million* chance [*one chance in a million*; (一生に一度の機会) the chance *of a lifetime*, a *once-in-a-lifetime* chance].

せんさく 詮索, 穿鑿 图 ●せんさく好きな inquisitive /ɪnkwízətɪv/; curious (▶よい意味で「好奇心が強い」の意もある); 〔軽蔑的〕〈話〉nosy.
— **詮索する** 動 ●他人のことをせんさくする pry [〈話〉poke one's *nose*] *into* other people's affairs. ▶私の仕事のことをそんなにせんさくするな Don't be so

inquisitive about my job.
ぜんさく 前作 (この前の作品) the last [(先行する) preceding] work.
せんさばんべつ 千差万別 ●千差万別の意見 *various* [*divergent*] views. ●人の趣味は千差万別である Tastes *vary* [*differ*] *from person to person.*
せんし 穿刺 〖医学〗centesis; puncture.
せんし 戦士 a soldier, 《書》a warrior.
せんし 戦史 (a) war history, the history of a war.
せんし 戦死 图 death in (the) war [battle].
── **戦死する** 動 ●夫は第二次世界大戦で戦死しました My husband *was killed* in World War Ⅱ. (🔲 My husband *died*... とも いう)
●**戦死者** a person killed in (the) war [battle]; 《集合的》the war dead (🔲 複数扱い)
せんじ 戦時 图 wartime. ●戦時中に in wartime. ●平時にも戦時にも be in *war* and *peace*. (🔲 語順に注意)
── **戦時の** 形 wartime.
●**戦時経済** wartime economy. ●**戦時産業** wartime industry. ●**戦時体制** a war(time) regime. ●**戦時統制** wartime regulation. ●**戦時内閣** a war cabinet.
ぜんし 全史 the whole history. ●自然科学全史 *the whole history* of natural science.
ぜんし 全紙 (全紙面) the whole [entire] space; (新聞全体) the whole newspaper; (すべての新聞) all newspapers. ●全紙が内閣総辞職を報じた *All the newspapers* reported the general resignation of the Cabinet.
ぜんし 前肢 a foreleg; a front leg.
ぜんじ 漸次 ●漸次(=しだいに)東へ移動する move (to the) east *gradually* [《書》*by degrees*].
せんじぐすり 煎じ薬 a medical decoction.
せんしじだい 先史時代 the prehistoric ages; prehistoric times. ●先史時代の動物 a *prehistoric* animal.
ぜんじだい 前時代 图 the preceding [previous] period [era].
── **前時代的な** 形 old-fashioned; outdated. ●前時代的な考え方 an *old-fashioned* way of thinking.
せんしつ 船室 a cabin. ●1等船室 a first-class *cabin*.
*****せんじつ** 先日 the other day; (数日前に) a few [some, several] days ago; (最近) recently (⇨最近). ●先日東京で強い地震があった *The other day* there was a strong earthquake in Tokyo. ●彼は先日来ずっと欠勤している He has been away from work *for several days* [ˣsince the other day]. (⇨この間)
ぜんしつ 全室 all rooms. ●全室冷暖房完備 *All (the) rooms* are air-conditioned.
ぜんじつ 全日 (1日中) all day (long). (⇨働 終日)
ぜんじつ 前日 ●前日に the day before; (on) the previous [《書》preceding] day. ●彼の父は彼が到着する前日に死んだ His father died *the day before* he arrived [his arrival].
せんじつめる 煎じ詰める ●彼の長い説教は煎じ詰めると「正直に働け」ということだ His long sermon *comes* [《話》*boils*] *down to* "work honestly".
せんじゃくがん 千姿万態 ●千姿万態の火山岩 《書》*multifarious* volcanic rocks; *a large variety of* volcanic rocks.
せんしゃ 洗車 ── **洗車する** 動 wash a car.
●**洗車場** a car wash.
せんしゃ 戦車 a tank. ●重[軽]戦車 a heavy [a light] *tank*. ●対戦車砲 an antitank gun.

●**戦車隊** a tank corps [unit]. ●**戦車兵** a tankman.
せんしゃ 選者 a selector; (審査員) a judge; (科学論文などの) a referee /ˈrɛfəri/.
ぜんしゃ 全社 (全部の会社) all companies; (会社全体) the whole company. ●全社をあげて彼を心から迎えた *The whole company* welcomed him with all their hearts. ●そのニュースはあっという間に全社に広まった The news spread [got around] *through* [*throughout*] *the company*.
●**全社的品質管理** total quality control 《略 TQC》.
ぜんしゃ 前車 (前の車) a car in front [(going) ahead].
●**前車の覆(続)るは後車の戒め** We should learn from 〈his [her, their]〉failure.
●**前車の轍(⑤)を踏む** (前の人の失敗を後の人が繰り返す) repeat one's predecessor's failure.
ぜんしゃ 前者 the former (↔the latter). (🔲(1) 複数名詞を受けるときは複数扱い。(2) 代名詞としても (⇨[第 1-2 文例]) 形容詞としても (⇨[第 3 文例]) 用いる); 〖最初のもの〗(一方は) the one (↔the other) (⇨[第 4 文例]); 〖第一のもの〗the first (↔the second). ●前者の方が後者よりよい *The former* is better than the latter. ●我が家には自転車 2 台と自動車 1 台がある。前者は父と私が、後者は母が使っている We have two bicycles and a car. *The former* are for my father and me. The latter is for my mother. (🔲(1) the former が two bicycles をさすので, are, the latter は a car をさすので is. (2) ただしこのような日常的な文脈ではあまり用いない方がよい) ●前者の案が実行に移された *The former* plan was put into practice. ●ここに小説と漫画の 2 冊の本がある。前者(=一方)は後者(=もう一方)よりすっと厚い Here are two books, a novel and a comic book. *The one* is much thicker than the other. (🔲 この例は特定の場合だが, Here are two books. *One* is a novel and the other is a comic book. では不特定となり the one とはならない)
せんじゃふだ 千社札 a *senjafuda*; (説明的に) a slip of paper printed with the name of a pilgrim on it, who pastes it on the pillar of the shrine or temple.
せんじゃまいり 千社参り a pilgrimage to one thousand shrines and temples.
*****せんしゅ** 選手 〖運動選手〗an athlete /ˈæθliːt/; 〖球技の〗a player; 〖走者〗a runner. ●その他、水泳は a swimmer, スキーは a skier, 走り高跳びは a high-jumper など競技によって異なる) ●プロ選手 a professional *athlete*. ●フィールド選手 a field *athlete*. ●万能選手 an all-round *athlete*. ●野球選手 a (base)ball *player*. ●正[補欠]選手 a regular [a substitute] *player*. ●マラソン[長距離]選手 a marathon [a long-distance] *runner*. ●短距離選手 a sprinter. ●一流選手 a first-class [a first-rate] *player*; a top-ranking [a top-notch] *player*. ●主力選手 a key [a leading] *player*. ●彼女はオリンピックの代表選手に選ばれた She was selected for the Olympic team. ●彼はどのチームの選手ですか What team *is* he [does he *play*] on? ●あの監督は選手交代が早い That manager removes [pulls] *players* so quickly. ●彼は選手起用がうまい He is good at picking *players*. ●ボクサーの選手生命(=ボクサーとしての生涯)は短い Boxers' *careers* do not last long.
●**選手会** a players association. ●**選手権** (⇨選手権). ●**選手村** (オリンピックの) the Olympic Village.
せんしゅ 先取 图 ●先取点を上げる score first.

―― 先取する 動 ●3点を先取する score the first three points [野球] runs].

せんしゅ 船主 a shipowner.

せんしゅ 船首 the bow(s) /báu(z)/. (**!** しばしば複数形で) ●船首から沈む sink from the bow [head].

せんしゅう 千秋 (千年) a thousand years; (長年月) many years. ●一日千秋 (⇨一日千秋)

せんしゅう 先週 last week. ●先週の今日 (⇨今日(*ᵏʸᵒᵘ*) 解説) ●先週の火曜日に (×on) last Tuesday (**!** 同じ週の木-土曜日くらいにいえば「今週の火曜日」の意にもなり紛らわしい); on Tuesday last week. ●彼は先週帰国した He returned home last week.

せんしゅう 選集 (代表作品集) a selection, the select(ed) works (*of* Shakespeare); (名詩名文集) an anthology.

ぜんしゅう 全集 ●漱石全集 Soseki's complete [collected] works; the complete works [writings] of Soseki.

せんしゅうがっこう 専修学校 a special training [vocational] school.

せんじゅうしゃ 専従者 (労働組合の) a full-time union official.

せんじゅうみん 先住民 (原住民全体) aborigines /ǽbərídʒəniːz/; (個人) an aborigine, an aboriginal. (⇨原住民)

せんしゅうらく 千秋楽 the final [closing] day 《of》. ●春場所の千秋楽 the final day of the Spring Sumo Tournament.

せんじゅかんのん 千手観音 the thousand-armed Kannon.

せんしゅけん 選手権 a championship. ●世界選手権を獲得する[失う] win [lose] the world championship [title]. ●選手権大会 a championship tournament. ●選手権保持者 a champion; a title holder.

せんしゅつ 選出 图 (an) election. ●東京選出の代議士 a Diet member for [from] Tokyo; a Diet member who represents Tokyo.
―― 選出する 動 elect. (⇨選出) ●彼は議長に選出された He was elected (as) chairman.

せんじゅつ 仙術 ●仙術を使う practice the supernatural [miraculous] arts.

せんじゅつ 戦術 〔〔個々の戦闘に対する〕〕 tactics (**!** 単・複両扱い. 「駆け引き」の意のときは複数扱い); 〔〔全体の作戦計画〕〕 strategy (⇨戦略). ●戦術上の要点 a tactical [a strategic] point. ●巧みな戦術で敵を破る defeat the enemy by clever tactics. ●その状況を戦術的に利用する take tactical advantage of the situation. ●野党側の引き延ばし戦術で国会は混乱した The opposition's delaying tactics put the Diet into confusion.
●戦術家 a tactician; a strategist.

ぜんじゅつ 前述 ●前述の文 the above(-mentioned) sentence; the sentence (mentioned) above. ●前述のとおり as (is) mentioned [stated] above.

せんしゅぼうえい 専守防衛 an exclusively defensive national security policy.

せんしょ 選書 selected works; (叢書) a library; (選集) an anthology.

ぜんしょ 全書 a complete book; (百科全書) an encyclopedia; (大要) a compendium (複 ~s, -dia). ●英文学全書 a compendium of English literature.

ぜんしょ 善処 **―― 善処する** 動 ●その件を善処する(=適当な措置をとる) take proper measures about the matter. ●問題を善処する(=適当にうまく処理する) deal with the problem right and properly.

せんしょう 先勝 **―― 先勝する** 動 win the first game [match].

せんしょう 戦勝 (a) victory.
●戦勝記念日 an anniversary of a victory.
●戦勝国 a victorious nation [country].

せんしょう 戦傷 a war wound.
●戦傷死者 war casualties. ●戦傷者 a person wounded in a war; a wounded soldier [(軍人)] serviceman; (集合的) the war wounded.

せんしょう 選奨 图 (a) recommendation.
―― 選奨する 動 ●良書を生徒に選奨する recommend a good book to the students.

せんじょう 洗浄 ―― 洗浄する 動 (洗う) wash ... (out); (きれいにする) clean; (すすぐ) rinse (out); (傷口などを) 〔医学〕 irrigàte. ●胃を洗浄する wash out a patient's stomach.

せんじょう 船上 ●船上で[に] on a ship; on board ship.

せんじょう 戦場 a battlefield, a battleground. ●その市は戦場と化した The city turned into a battlefield [a scene of battle]. ●彼は戦場に散った He fell [died, was killed] on the battlefield./(戦死した) He fell [was killed, died] in battle. (**!** いずれも fall を用いるのは《主に書》)

せんじょう 線上 (線の上) on a line. ●彼は当落線上にある There is a fifty-fifty chance of his being elected.

ぜんしょう 全勝 a complete victory; a sweep.
●全勝優勝をする win the championship with a complete victory. ●全勝街道をばく進している keep the slate clean. (**!** 普通は「(試合の)予定表」の意) ●3連戦の全勝 a three-game sweep. ●パイレーツに (4戦)全勝でワールドシリーズに優勝する sweep the Pirates in the World Series. ●琴欧州は全勝(=無敗)で朝青龍と共に首位を守っている Kotooshu stays unbeaten to keep [share] the lead with Asashoryu.
―― 全勝する 動 win all one's games.

ぜんしょう 全焼 ―― 全焼する 動 burn [be burned] down, be burned to the ground [ashes]; be completely destroyed by fire. ●校舎はその火事で全焼した The school building (was) burned down in the fire [was completely destroyed by the fire].

ぜんじょう 前条 (前の箇条) the preceding [foregoing] clause [provision]; (前項) the preceding [foregoing] item [article].

ぜんじょう 禅譲 图 (退位) abdication.
―― 禅譲する 動 abdicate. ●女王は息子に王位を禅譲した The Queen abdicated in favor of her son.

せんしょうこく 戦勝国 a victorious nation [country].

ぜんしょうせん 前哨戦 《やや書》a preliminary skirmish. ●(選挙などが)前哨戦に入る(=予備段階に入る) 《やや書》enter its preliminary stages (↔its final stages).

せんじょうち 扇状地 〔地学〕an alluvial fan; a fan.

せんじょうてき 扇情的 ―― 扇情的な 形 (興奮・興味をあおるような) sensational; (性的に挑発的な) suggestive. ●扇情的新聞 a sensational newspaper. ●扇情的な写真 a suggestive picture.

ぜんしょうとう 前照灯 a headlight. (⇨ヘッドライト)

せんしょく 染色 dyeing.

せんしょく 前職 the past [(前の) former] post [office].

せんしょくたい 染色体 〔生物〕 a chromosome /króuməsòum/. ●X[Y]染色体 an X [a Y] chromosome.
●染色体異常 (a) chromosome aberration.

- 染色体地図 a chromosome map.

せんじる 煎じる a decoct [(煮詰める) boil down] herbs; (書) make a decoction of herbs.

せんしん 先進 ── 先進の 形 advanced; developed. ● 先進の科学技術 advanced [high] technology.
- 先進工業国 an advanced industrial [industrialized] nation. ● 先進国 (⇨先進国). ● 先進8か国首脳会議 the Group of Eight 《略 G8》.

せんしん 専心 名 一意専心の wholehearted.
── 専心する 動 〖努力を集中する〗 concentrate (on); 〖献身する〗《やや書》 devote oneself (to). (⇨ 専念)

せんしん 線審 a linesman. ● ライト[レフト]の線審〖野球〗 a right [a left] field umpire.

せんじん 千尋 ● 千尋の谷 a bottomless ravine; an abyss.

せんじん 先人 (前人) one's predecessor(s); (祖先) one's ancestors. ● 先人の跡をたどる follow in the footsteps of one's predecessors.

せんじん 先陣 the vanguard, 《古風》 the van. ● 先陣を切る(戦いで) go into battle first. ● 先陣に立つ be in the vanguard (of). ● 先陣争いをする(競争で) compete for first place.

せんじょう 戦場 (戦場) a battlefield, a battleground; (陣形) battle formation.

せんじん 戦塵 (戦場の砂塊) the dust of battle. ● 戦塵(=戦場の騒ぎ)を逃れる escape from the tumult of war.

ぜんしん 全身 〖体全体〗 the whole body; (体のいたる所) every part of the body; 〖写真などの〗 the full length. ● 全身運動をする get [take] exercise for every part of the body. ● 全身がだるい feel sluggish all over. ▶ 彼は全身にやけどをした He suffered burns over his whole body [all over (his body)]. ▶ 彼女は全身(=頭のてっぺんからつま先まで)黒ずくめの服装をしていた She wore black clothes from top to toe [from head to foot]. (❗ clothes はここでは帽子・靴を含む)
- 全身全霊 (⇨全身全霊) ● 全身像 a full-length portrait. ● 全身麻酔 general anesthesia.
- 全身麻痺 total paralysis.

ぜんしん 前身 ● 彼の前身(=過去)を洗う look into [《やや書》inquire into] his past. ▶ この女子大の前身は洋裁学校であった This women's college [university] started as [was originally] a dressmaking school.

ぜんしん 前進 名 an advance. ● 敵の前進をくい止める check the advance of the enemy [the enemy's advance]. ● 交渉には大きな前進があった We made a great advance in the negotiations. /(進展した) The negotiations made (ˣa) great progress.
── 前進する 動 〖目標に向かって〗 advance (toward, on); (敵を後退させて) gain ground; 〖先へ進む〗 go ahead, move forward; 〖前進させる〗 advance (troops), move (troops) forward. (⇨進む) ▶ 軍隊は町に向かって前進した The troops advanced toward [on] the town. (❗ on では特に攻撃を暗示) ▶ 雪で私たちは前進できなかった We could not go ahead [forward] because of the snow. ▶ センターは前進してフライを捕った The center fielder came on [drifted in] to catch the fly. ▶ 三塁手はバント処理のために猛然と前進した The third baseman charged in the bunt [to field the bunt]. ▶ 内野は前進シフトを敷いた The infield played in.

ぜんしん 前震 a foreshock.

ぜんしん 漸進 名 gradual progress; steady advance.

── 漸進的な 形 gradual.
── 漸進的に gradually; step by step.
── 漸進する 動 make gradual progress; progress gradually.
- 漸進主義 gradualism.

ぜんじんきょういく 全人教育 an all-(a)round education.

ぜんしんこく 先進国 an advanced [a developed] country.
- 先進国首脳会議 a summit (meeting) of industrialized nations. (❗「パリ先進国首脳会議」は簡略化の Paris summit)

ぜんしんぜんれい 全身全霊 ● 彼女はその仕事に全身全霊を打ち込んだ She threw herself heart and soul into the work. (❗ heart and soul は副詞句)/(一身をささげた) She devoted herself entirely to the work.

ぜんじんみとう 前人未到 ── 前人未到の 形 (研究・調査されていない) unexplored; (足を踏み入れていない) untrodden (⇨未到); (先例のない) unprecedented. ● 前人未到の記録 an unprecedented record.

せんす 扇子 a (folding) fan. ● 扇子を使う[であおぐ] use a fan; fan oneself.

センス (感覚) (a) sense; (直感力) (a) flair; (審美眼) taste. ● センスのある男性 a man of taste [ˣsense]; a tasteful man. ● ユーモアのセンスがある have a sense of humor. ▶ 彼女は色のセンスがよい She has good (↔bad) taste in color. ▶ 彼のマーケティングのセンスのよさは抜群だ He has a real flair for marketing. ▶ あら、そのネクタイとてもセンスがいいわ Say, your tie looks very classy. (❗ classy は「おしゃれで上品な」の意のくだけた語。人・場所にも用いられる)

ぜんず 全図 ● 日本全図 a complete map of Japan.

せんすい 泉水 a fountain; (庭の池) a garden pond.

せんすい 潜水 ── 潜水する 動 (人・動物が) dive; (潜水艦などが) submerge /səbmə́ːrdʒ/.
- 潜水艦 a submarine. ● 潜水病 caisson disease; the bends. ● 潜水夫 a diver. ● 潜水服 a diving sùit [drèss].

せんする 宣する (宣言する) declare; proclaim; (表明する) announce. ● 開会[閉会]を宣する declare the meeting open [closed].

ぜんせ 前世 the previous existence. ● 前世での姿 a previous incarnation. ▶ 彼は前世では猫だったと信じている He believes that he was a cat in the previous incarnation [former life].

せんせい 先生 〖教員〗a teacher; (小学・中学・高校の) a schoolteacher, 《主に英》(パブリックスクールの) (男性) a schoolmaster, (女性) a schoolmistress; (大学の) a professor, 〖指導員〗 an instructor (in); 〖医師に〗 a doctor, 〖話〗 doc.

> **使い分け** teacher 教職についている人すべてにあてはまる最も一般的な語。 小・中学校の先生をさす場合は女性教師が多いので She で受けるのが普通。
> **instructor** スキー・水泳・自動車教習所の先生など特殊な技術を教える人をさす。

> **解説** 先生に呼びかける場合
>
> | | 「先生」 | 「阿倍先生」 |
> | --- | --- | --- |
> | 医者に | doctor, (話) doc | Dr. [Doctor] Abe |
> | 男性教師に | sir | Mr. Abe |
> | 既婚の女教師に | ma'am | Mrs. Abe |
> | 未婚の女教師に | | Miss Abe |

せんせい 先制 ● 先制のホームランを打つ hit a homer to score the game's first run(s). ● 先制点をあげる score the *first* run. ● 先制攻撃 (⇨先制攻撃)

せんせい 宣誓 图 an oath /óυθ/. ● 宣誓をする an *oath* taker. ● オリンピックの宣誓 the Olympic *oath*. ● 選手宣誓 a *declaration* by (a representative of) the athletes (球技の場合) (*players*). (⚠進行係は "Athletes' *oath*!" のようにいう)

── **宣誓(を)する** 動 ● 彼に宣誓させる〖書〗 administer an *oath* to him; put him on [under] *oath*. ● 大統領は就任の宣誓をした The President took the *oath* of office [was sworn into office; was sworn in]. (⚠「宣誓式」は a swearing-in ceremony) ▶ 法廷で彼は右手を上げて真実を述べると宣誓した In court he raised his right hand and *swore* [*took*, *made*] an *oath* to tell the truth. (⇨誓う)

● 宣誓証人 a person who testifies on [under] *oath*; a sworn witness.

せんせい 専制 图 (専制政治) tyranny /tírəni/, 《軽蔑的》despotism; (絶対主義) absolutism.

── **専制の** 形 tyrannical /tirǽnɪkl/, despotic; absolute.

● 専制君主 an absolute monarch; (暴君) a tyrant /táɪərənt/, a despot. ● 専制君主国 an absolute monarchy.

ぜんせい 全盛 the height [zenith /zí:nɪθ/] of prosperity. ● 全盛期[時代] the [one's] heyday; the [one's] *prime*; one's best; (かつての) palmy days; (国・芸術などの黄金期) the golden age. ▶ 英国はビクトリア時代に全盛をきわめた Great Britain reached *the height of* its *prosperity* [was *in all* its *glory*] in the Victorian Age. ● 彼の全盛時代は過ぎた He has seen *better days*./He had his *days*.

ぜんせい 善政 (よい政治) good government. ● 善政をしく govern well; (立派に人民を統治する) rule the people well.

ぜんせいき 前世紀 (今世紀の前) the last century; (その前の世紀) the preceding century. ● 前世紀(=古い昔)の遺物 a relic of the *ancient* [*old*] *times*; (時代遅れの人・物) a museum piece.

せんせいこうげき 先制攻撃 (軍事的) a preemptive /priémptiv/ attack [strike]; (ボクシングの) a leadoff attack. ● 敵に先制攻撃を加える make a *preemptive attack* against the enemy; carry out a *preemptive* [*first*] *strike* against the enemy; *attack* [*strike*] the enemy *first*.

せんせいじゅつ 占星術 astrology /əstrάlədʒi/. ● 占星術師 an astrólogẹr.

せんせいりょく 潜勢力 latent [potential] power [force].

センセーショナル ● センセーショナルな殺人事件 a *sensational* murder.

センセーション ● センセーションを巻き起こす cause [create] a 《great》 *sensation*.

せんせき 船籍 the nationality of a ship. ● リベリア船籍の船 a ship of Liberian *registry*. ● 船籍港 a port of registry.

せんせき 戦跡 an old battlefield; the site [(現場) scene] of a former battle.

せんせき 戦績 (戦争の) a war record; (競技の) a record; a score. ● 30勝わずか1敗という素晴らしい戦績のチーム a team with [having] a brilliant *record* of 30 wins and only 1 loss.

せんせん 宣戦 the declaration of war. (⇨布告)

せんせん 戦線 (戦地) the front. ● 戦線へ行く[送られる] go [be sent] to *the front*. ● 敵に対して共同戦線を張る form a *united front* against the enemy. ▶ 就職戦線は冷え込んでいる The job *market* is dull.

せんぜん 戦前 〖戦前の時期・時代〗 the prewar period [days]. (⇨戦後) ● 戦前に(は) before the war; in (*the*) *prewar days* [*times*]. ● 戦前のヨーロッパの状況 the conditions in *prewar* Europe. ● 戦前から from *before the war* generation. ● 戦前派 the prewar generation.

ぜんせん 全線 ● 台風のため総武線は全線にわたって不通になっている The train service has been stopped *all along* the Sobu Line by the typhoon./(全線が) *All* train services have been suspended *on* the Sobu Line by the typhoon.

ぜんせん 前線 ❶〖戦場の最前線〗the front (line); the battle front. ● 前線にいる息子 a son at *the front*. ● 前線へ出る go to *the front*. ▶ 前線で激しい戦闘が行われた A fierce battle was fought at *the front*.

❷〖気象の〗a front. ● 寒冷前線 a cold *front*. ● 梅雨前線 a seasonal rain *front*. ● 温暖前線が北上した[南下した] A warm *front* advanced north [south].

ぜんせん 善戦 ── **善戦する** 動 (戦い・選挙などで) fight well [hard], put up a good fight; (競技などで) play well; (全力を尽くす) do one's best. ▶ ヤンキースは善戦したが3対2で敗れた The Yankees *played well*, but lost the game by a score of three to two.

*****ぜんぜん 全然** 〖少しも…でない〗 not (…) at all (⇨少しも); (一度も…しない) never; 〖まったく〗 quite, completely. ▶ 私は彼を全然知らない I d*on't* know him *at all* [*in the least*]./He is a *complete* [a *total*, a *perfect*] stranger to me. ▶ それ以来彼に全然会っていない I have *never* met him since then. ▶ それは全然違う It is *quite* [*entirely*, *totally*] different./(とんでもない) Far from it! (⚠通例先行の否定を強める)/(その逆だ) It's the other way around [about].

会話 「うるさいでしょうか」「いいえ, 全然」 "Does the noise bother you?" "*Not at all!/Not in the least!*"

会話 「歌舞伎に行かれることがありますか」「いいえ全然。歌舞伎は好きではないものですから」 "Do you ever go to *kabuki*?" "*No, never* [*I don't ever*]. I don't really like [care for] it."

会話 「もう一つキャンデー欲しいな」「全然(=少しも)ないわ。あなたがみんな食べちゃったのよ」 "I'd like another piece of candy." "There *aren't any*. You've eaten them all."

ぜんぜんかい

[会話]「彼はなぜ会社をやめたんだろう」「全然見当がつかないわ」"Why did he quit his job?" "I don't have *the slightest* idea." (❢ I have *no* idea. ともいえる)
[会話]「そんなこと全然言ってないよ」「じゃあ、何て言ったのさ」"I said *nothing whatever* of the kind [*no* such thing *whatever*]." "What did you say, then?" (❢ whatever は no を伴う名詞の直後に置いて否定を強調する)

ぜんぜんかい 前々回 ●前々回の会合 the meeting before last;《主に英》the last meeting *but one*. (❢ この but は except の意。the last …, the next … とともに用いる)

せんせんきょうきょう 戦々恐々 ●彼は新しい証拠をねるみに出せぬかと戦々恐々として(=ひどく恐れて)いた He *was* very afraid that they might discover (xa) new evidence. (❢ His great fear was that …. ともいえる) ●彼らは戦々恐々として(=大変恐れて)そこに立っていた They stood there *in great fear [filled with fear]*.

せんせんげつ 先々月 the month before last.

ぜんぜんじつ 前々日 two days ago; (おととい) the day before yesterday (⇨おととい); (ある過去の日を基準にして) two days before.

せんせんしゅう 先々週 the week before last.
▶先々週事故でけがをした I was injured in an accident *the week before last* [*two weeks ago*].

*****せんぞ** 先祖 an ancestor /ǽnsestər/. (❢ 女性形 ancestress は《古》); 《集合的》ancestry; forefathers.

> [使い分け] ancestor 通例祖父母より以前の祖先。
> forefather 遠い祖先で、主に男性。また民族・国家の先祖を表す。
> どちらも通例複数形で用いる: その村の先祖 the *forefathers* of the village.

①【先祖の〜】●先祖代々の家屋敷 one's *ancestral* /ænséstrəl/ estate. ●先祖の墓 a *family* tomb. ●先祖伝来の宝物 a *family* heirloom /éərlù:m/. ●先祖返り(したもの) a thrówback 《*to*》. ●先祖の教えを忘れるな Remember what our *forefathers* said. ▶彼らは先祖代々(=何世代も)この家に住んでいる They have lived in this house *for generations*.

②【先祖は】●ぼくの先祖は武士だ My *ancestors* were samurais. (❢ 過去形に注意)

③【先祖を】●先祖を敬う honor one's *ancestors*. ●先祖をまつる (霊を慰める) worship one's *ancestors*; (儀式を行う) hold services for one's *ancestors*. ●300年前 [6代前]まで先祖をたどる trace one's *ancestors* [*ancestry*] back to 300 years ago [*through six generations*].

*****せんそう** 戦争 (a) war; (a) battle. (⇨戦闘)

> [使い分け] war 最も一般的な語で国家間における大規模な戦争をいう。戦争状態の意では Ⓤ。
> battle 通例 war を構成する局地的な戦闘。

①【〜戦争】●冷たい[本格的な]戦争 a cold [a hot] *war*. ●長期にわたる戦争 a long [a drawn-out] *war*. ●全面[局地]戦争 an all-out [a local] *war*. ●核戦争 (a) nuclear *war*. ●侵略[防衛]戦争 an aggressive [a defensive] *war*. ●解放戦争 a *war* of liberation, a liberation *war*. ●市民戦争 a civil *war*. ●宗教戦争 a religious *war*. ●貿易戦争 a trade *war*. ●受験戦争 an entrance examination *war*; a fiercely competitive entrance examinations. ●日清戦争 the Sino-Japanese *war*. (❢ 戦争名には the をつける)

②【戦争〜】●戦争責任がある be responsible for (starting) the *war*. ▶両国は戦争中だった The two countries *were fighting against* each other [*were at war* (*with* each other)]./There was a *war* going on [a state of *war*] between the two countries. ▶戦争反対！No war!

③【戦争が[は]】●その2国間で戦争が起こった A *war* broke out [started, ×happened] between the two nations. ●戦争が激化した The *war* escalated [raged]. ●その戦争は拡大[長期化; 泥沼化]している The *war* is spreading [is drawn out; is stalemated]. ●その戦争は終わった The *war* came to an end./The *war* ended. ▶よい戦争はありはしない There can be no such thing as a good *war*.

④【戦争に[で]】●戦争に勝つ[負ける] win [lose] a *war*. ●戦争に行く go to *war* ([「開戦する」の意もある); (前線に出る) go to the front. ▶両国は戦争に突入した The two countries plunged into the *war*. ▶その政治問題が戦争に発展した The political problem developed into [led to] *war*. ▶その戦争で多くの人が命を落とした Many people were killed in [by] the *war*. (❢ (1) by では「戦争で殺された」という被害者意識が強調される。(2)「(一般に)戦争で」は in war [battle] となって無冠詞)/戦争が多くの命を奪った The *war* claimed so many lives. ▶私たちは戦争に反対だ We are against [are opposed to] any *war*.

⑤【戦争を】●戦争を続ける[防止する; 引き起こす; 始める] carry on [prevent; provoke; start] *war*. ●戦争を終わらせる bring the *war* to an end; put an end to the *war*. ●戦争を放棄する renounce *war*. ▶連合国はその国と戦争をした The Allies made [《やや書》waged] war on [*against*, *with*] the country. (❢ on, against では「戦争をしかける」、with では単に「戦争をする」の意味合いがある)/(始めた) The Allies *went to war against* the country./(宣戦布告をした) The Allies *declared war on* [*against*] the country.
●戦争映画 a war movie [film]. ●戦争犠牲者 war victims, victims of war. ●戦争行為 an act of war. ●戦争孤児 a war orphan. ●戦争犯罪 war crimes. ●戦争犯罪人 a war criminal. ●戦争文学 war literature. ●戦争放棄 a [the] renunciation of war. ●戦争未亡人 a war widow.

せんそう 船倉 a hold. ●船倉に荷物を積み込む stow the *hold*.

せんそう 船窓 a porthole.

ぜんそう 禅僧 (禅宗の僧) a Zen priest.

ぜんぞう 漸増 图 a gradual increase.
——漸増する 動 increase gradually [by degrees; (少しずつ) little by little]. ▶我が国の輸出は漸増している Our exports *are gradually increasing*.

ぜんそうきょく 前奏曲 a prelude 《*to*》.

せんそうとへいわ 『戦争と平和』 *War and Peace*. (参考) トルストイの小説)

せんぞく 専属 ●我が社専属の女優 an actress *under* (*exclusive*) *contract* to our company. ▶彼はその楽団の専属です He *belongs exclusively to* the band.

ぜんそく 喘息 [医学] asthma /ǽzmə/. ●気管支ぜんそく bronchial *asthma*. ●ぜんそくで悩んでいる人 an asthmatic; an *asthma* sufferer. ●ぜんそく発作 〈have〉an *asthma* attack. ▶あの子は小児ぜんそくです The child is *asthmatic*./The child is suffering from *asthma*.

ぜんそくりょく 全速力 full [top] speed. ●全速力を出す develop *full speed*. ▶彼は全速力で走った He

ぜんそん 全損 (a) total loss.
- 全損担保 free from all average 《略 FAA》; security for total loss only 《略 TLO》.

センター ❶『野球』《中堅》 center field; 《中堅手》 a center fielder. ● センターフライを打ち上げる[打ち上げてアウトになる] fly [fly out] to *center*. ● センターを守る play *center field*. ● センターオーバーの二塁打を打つ hit a double over the *center fielder*. ● センター返しの打球を打ち返す hit back to the middle. ● センターラインの守備陣 the up-the-middle defense.
❷『活動の中心地』● 医療[ショッピング]センター a medical [a shopping] *center*.
- センターサークル 『サッカー』 the center circle.
- センター試験 (日本の) National Center Test for University Admissions; (米国の) Scholastic Aptitude Test 《略 SAT》, American College Test 《略 ACT》. ● センターバック『競技』 a center back, a center half. (!)《英》では近代サッカーの常識的フォーメーションが固まる以前から用いられている center half が現在では一般的で, center back を用いるのはまれ). ● センターフォワード『競技』 a center forward. ● センターパンツ『服飾』 a (rear) center vent. ● センターポール (競技場の) a central flagpole; 《和製語》 a center pole. ● センターライン a centerline. ● センターラインを越える cross the *centerline*.

せんたい 船体 〖船・飛行船の〗(a) hull; 〖船の〗the body of a ship. ● 白く塗られた船体 the *hull* (of the ship) painted white.

せんたい 船隊 a fleet (of ships).

せんたい 戦隊 a squadron.

せんたい 選対 〖『選挙対策委員会』の略〗(⇒選挙)

せんたい 蘚苔 〖植物〗 moss. (⇒⇒ 苔(こけ))
- 蘚苔類 bryophyta.

せんだい 先代 〖家系の1代前の人〗《やや書》 one's predecessor /prédəsèsər/ (in the family line); 〖亡父〗 one's (late) father. ● 先代染五郎 the late Somegoro. (!)「今はその芸名を使っていない」の意にも「先ごろ亡くなった」の意にもとれる. 前の方の意味をはっきりさせたい場合は last Somegoro の方).

せんだい 船台 (造船台) stocks; (水中に傾斜した造船台) slips; (修理用の) a slipway.

*****せんたい** 全体 图 ❶〖すべて〗all. (⇒全部)
- 社会全体 the *whole* society. ● ヨーロッパ全体 the *whole* of Europe; 《やや書》 *all* Europe. (!) *whole* は地名に直接つけて ×the whole Europe とするのは不可). ● 国際社会全体 the international community *as a whole*. ● システム全体 the *whole* system. ▶ クラス全体がその案に賛成であった The *whole* class was in favor of the plan./*All* the class was [《英》were] in favor of the plan. (!) *all* the classes は「すべてのクラス」の意). ● 町全体が静まり返っていた The *whole* [*entire*] town was hushed and still. ● 港全体に(=至る所に)霧がかかっていた Fog hung *all over* the harbor [over the *whole* harbor]. ▶ ニュースは町全体にひろがった The news spread *all through* the town.

── 全体の 形 whole (!) 通例 the [one's] ~ の形で); (欠けたものがない) entire; all (⇒①); (全般的な) general; (全体にわたる) overall. ● 全体の[全体的な]傾向 a *general* tendency [trend]. ● クラス全体の問題 a problem for the *whole* class. ● 全体像をつかむ get the (general [big]) picture. ● 全体敷物の鮮やかなオレンジ色は部屋の全体の色調と合わない The rug's bright orange does not go with the *overall* color scheme of the room. ▶ 私は両腕を広げて全体のバランスをとった I spread out my arms to keep my balance.

── 全体として 副 as a whole; (あらゆる点から見て) on the whole; (一般に) generally. ▶ 全体として私たちの旅行は成功だった Our trip was successful *as a whole*./On the whole, our trip was successful. ▶ 全体として見れば日本の大学生はあまり勉強しない *Generally* (speaking) [*In general*], Japanese university students don't study so hard.
- 全体会議 a general meeting. ● 全体主義 totalitarianism. ● 全体主義者 a totalitarian.

ぜんだいみもん 前代未聞 〖聞いたこともない〗 unheard-of; 〖前例のない〗 unprecedented /ʌnprésədntid/. ▶ それは前代未聞のスキャンダルだ That's an *unheard-of* scandal./I've never heard anything like that scandal. ▶ それは前代未聞の出来事だった It was an *unprecedented* event *in history*.

*****せんたく** 洗濯 图 a wash (!) 複数形では用いない); (洗うこと) washing. ● シャツを洗濯に出す send a shirt to the wash [洗濯屋へ] the *laundry*. ● 洗濯に出してある〈物が主語〉 be at the wash [the *laundry*]. ● 洗濯機で洗濯ができる machine-washable. ● これは洗濯がきく This is *washable*./This will *wash*.

── 洗濯(を)する 動 ❶〖衣服などを洗う〗 wash, do the wash [washing, laundry]; 〖洗濯してアイロンをかける〗《書・古》 launder. ● 洗濯すると縮む shrink in *washing* [the wash]. ● 汚れた衣服を手で洗濯する *wash* the dirty clothes by hand. ▶ 彼は週に2度洗濯をする He *does the washing* twice a week. (!) He *washes* twice a week. は「体を洗うこと」ともなりかねない. He does *washing*. は「彼は(職業が)洗濯屋だ」の意) ▶ そのシャツは洗濯しているところです The shirt is being washed [is in the wash]. (!)後の方は「(洗うべき)洗濯物の中にある」の意にもなる)
❷〖その他の表現〗● 命の洗濯をする 《話》 recharge one's batteries.
- 洗濯板 a washboard. ● 洗濯機 (wash clothes in) a wáshing machìne [《米》 a washer]. ● 洗濯石けん (粉末) wáshing pòwder; (固型) a láundry [a wáshing] sòap; (合成洗剤) detergent. ● 洗濯代 laundry charges. ● 洗濯ばさみ 《米》 a clothespin, 《英》 a clothes(-)peg. ● 洗濯物 (集合的) washing [《米》 wash], laundry. (!) 数えるときは a piece of washing のように言う). ● 洗濯物を外に干す hang out the washing [《米》 wash, laundry]. (!)「シャツを外に干す」は hang a shirt outside to dry). ● 洗濯屋 (店) a laundry /lɔ́:ndri/; (ドライ専門の) a dry cleaner's, the cleaner's, the cleaners (⇒クリーニング); (人) a laundry keeper [worker], (男の) a laundryman, (女の) a laundrywoman.

*****せんたく** 選択 图 〖二つ以上から選ぶこと〗 (a) choice; 〖三つ以上から最適なものの選抜〗 (a) selection. ● 良書の選択 the *choice* of good books. ● 選択の自由 freedom of *choice*. ● スーツに合うネクタイの選択 the *selection* of a tie to go with a suit. ● 職業の選択を誤る make a mistake in the *choice* of one's career; make a wrong [a bad] *choice* of one's career; miss one's calling. ▶ メニューの選択の幅はごく狭い There isn't [We don't have] much *choice* in the menu. ▶ この件では私にまったく選択権はない I have no *choice* at all in this matter. ▶ どちら[何]にするか選択に迷います I don't know which to *choose* [what to *choose*, what *choice* to *make*].

── 選択する 動 choose*; (三つ以上から最適なものを) select; (行動を) opt (*for; to do*). (⇒選ぶ) ● これがあれかどちらかを選択する *choose* [×select] between

せんだつ this and that. ●慎重に選択する *choose* [*select*] (it) deliberately; *make a deliberate choice* [*selection*] (*of* it). ●5 科目選択する(=取る) *take* [《米》*elect*] five courses. ▶この材料の中から自由に選択できます You can *choose freely from* [*among, from among, out of*] these materials. (⚠ You *have a free choice from*.... ともいえる) ▶危機に直面したとき、人は最悪の行動[進路]を選択しがちだ In time of danger, people would *choose* [*opt for*] the worst action.
● 選択科目 《米》an elective (subject); 《英》an optional subject. ● 選択肢 the choices.

せんだつ 先達 (開拓者) a pioneer; (先輩) a senior; (先駆者)《書》a precursor; (指導者) a leader; (案内人) a guide. ●日本教育界の先達 a *pioneer* [*a precursor*]; (先覚者) a *forerunner*] in Japanese education.

せんだって 先だって (先日) the other day; (何日か前) some days ago; (少し前) some time ago.

ぜんだま 善玉 (映画・物語などの) a good guy, 《話》the goodie. (⚠通例複数形で)

センタリング 图 a center, 《まれ》a centering. (⇨クロス) ── **センタリングする** 動 center.

せんたん 先端 (剣の先端(=鋭い先)) the *point of* a sword /sɔ́ːrd/. ●指の先端 the *tip* of one's finger. ●先端に網をつけた棒 a stick with a net *on the end*. ●流行の先端を行く *set* [*lead*] the fashion; (消費者が) follow the latest fashion. ●時代の先端を行く *set the trend* [*go ahead*, 《書》*lead the van*] of the times. (⚠「先端を行っている」の意では be ahead, be in the van)
● 先端技術 (a) high technology. ● 先端技術社会 a high-technology [a high-tech] society.

せんたん 戦端 (戦闘状態)《書》hostilities.
● 戦端を開く open (↔cease) hostilities 《with》; (武器を取る) take up arms 《against》.

せんだん 専断 图 (an) arbitrary decision.
── **専断する** 動 make an arbitrary decision.

せんだん 栴檀 【植物】a chinaberry.
● 栴檀は双葉より芳(かんば)し Great talent shows [displays] itself early in childhood.

せんだん 船団 (商船などの) a fleet; (護衛されている) a convoy. ●捕鯨船団 a whaling *fleet*. ●護衛艦付きの輸送船団 a *convoy* of transport ships.

ぜんだん 全段 (新聞の) a whole [an entire] page.
● 全段抜き大見出し a banner (headline); 《米》a streamer (headline).

ぜんだん 前段 (前半) the first half; (前の部分) the former [first] part; (前の段落) the preceding paragraph.

せんち 戦地 the front. ●戦地の兵隊 soldiers at *the front*. ●戦地へ行く[送られる] go [be sent] *to the front*.
● 戦地勤務 field service.

センチ (⇨センチメートル)

ぜんち 全治 complete healing, a complete recovery. ▶全治 1 か月のけがをした I got [suffered] an injury that would take a month to *heal* (*up*) [*recover*] *completely*.

ぜんちし 前置詞 【文法】a preposition.

ぜんちぜんのう 全知全能 ● 全知全能の神 Almighty God; the Almighty; 《書》the omniscient and omnipotent God.

センチメートル a centimeter (略 cm).

センチメンタル (感傷的な) sentimental; (お涙ちょうだいの)《話》tear-jerking. ●センチメンタルな詩 a *sentimental* poem. ●センチメンタルになる become [get] *sentimental*.

せんちゃ 煎茶 green tea (of medium grade).

せんちゃく 先着 图 ●先着順に(到着順に) in order of arrival; (早い者勝ちで) on a first-come-first-served [a first come, first served] basis. ▶座席は先着順に割り振ります Seating is *first come, first served.*/Seats will be allocated *in order of arrival*. ▶先着 500 名様に限り粗品を進呈いたします Gifts will be given to 500 people *on a first come, first served basis* [*to the first 500 people*].
── **先着する** 動 arrive [come] first; arrive [come] earlier than 《me》.

せんちゅう 船中 ●船中で on a ship; on board (a ship). ●船中で一夜を明かす pass a night *on a ship*.

せんちゅう 戦中 ●戦中戦後の困窮の時代には in times of austerity *during* and after *the war*. (⚠単に「戦中の耐乏生活」は *wartime* austerity という) ▶彼は戦中派だ He belongs to *the war generation*.

せんちゅう 線虫 【動物】(回虫) a nematode, a roundworm; (ぎょう虫) a threadworm.

せんちょう 船長 (艦長も;《漁船などの》) a skipper; ●鈴木船長 *Captain* Suzuki.
● 船長室 the captain's cabin.

ぜんちょう 前兆 an omen /óumən/; (⚠宗教的・迷信的な響きがある); 【しるし】a sign; (病気や悪いことの) a symptom. ●それをよい[悪い]前兆ととると take it as a good [a bad, an ill, an evil] *omen*. ●地震の前兆 *signs* [*symptoms*] of an earthquake. ▶あの黒雲はあらしの前兆だ Those dark clouds are a *sign* of a storm. ▶高熱は肺炎の前兆のこともある High fever can be a *symptom* [a *sign*] of pneumonia /n(j)uːmóuniə/.

ぜんちょう 全長 the full [total] length. ▶この鉄橋の全長は約 1,000 メートルです The *full* [*total*] *length* of this railroad bridge is about one thousand meters./(1,000 メートルの長さがある) This railroad bridge *is* about one thousand meters *long*.

せんつう 疝痛 【医学】colic; (腹痛)《話》the gripes.

ぜんつう 全通 ▶その鉄道は全通している The *whole* railroad *has been opened to traffic*.

せんて 先手 ❶【囲碁・チェスなどの】the first move. ●先手を打つ人 the first mover. ●先手でチェスを打つ make *the first move* in a chess game. ▶碁で相手に先手を譲った I let my opponent have *the first move* in the go game.
❷【機先を制すること】● 先手を打つ (機先を制する) forestall, 《話》get the jump on ...; (主導権を取る) take the initiative 《*in doing*》. ▶我々は先手を打って敵を攻撃した We *forestalled* [先制攻撃をした] *made a preemptive attack against*] the enemy. ▶彼は先手を打ってその計画を実行した He *took the initiative in* carrying out the plan.

せんてい 剪定 ── **剪定する** 動 (形を整える) trim 《the hedge》; (余分な枝を切除する) prune 《the roses》.
● 剪定ばさみ 《米》(a pair of) pruning shears, 《英》(a pair of) secateurs. (⚠複数扱い (⇨はさみ))

せんてい 船底 the bottom of a ship.

せんてい 選定 (a) choice, (a) selection. (⇨選択)

ぜんてい 前提 (an) assumption, 《書》a premise.
● 大[小]前提【論理】the major [minor] *premise*. ▶最悪の事態が起こるかもしれないことを前提に立って行動しなくてはいけない We must act *on the assumption* [*premise*] *that* the worst can happen. ▶我々は結婚を前提に(=結婚するつもりで) 付き合っている We're going together *with the intention of* getting married. (⚠ go together は「特定の異性と付き合う」の意の口語表現)

- 前提条件 a precondition.
ぜんてい 前庭 a front yard [garden]; (耳・鼻などの)〖解剖〗a vestibule.
―― 前庭の 形 〖解剖〗vestibular.
- 前庭器官 a vestibular organ.
ぜんてき 全摘 total excision [removal] 《of》. ● 胃の一部摘手術を行う remove the whole stomach.
せんてつ 先哲 (賢人) a sage [(すぐれた学者) a great scholar] of ancient times.
せんてつ 銑鉄 pig iron.
ぜんてつ 前轍 (説明的に) ruts [wheel tracks] left by the vihicles that have passed before.
- 前轍を踏む repeat one's predecessors' errors [(失敗) failures].
ぜんでら 禅寺 a Zen temple.
***せんでん** 宣伝 图 (商品の)an advertisement,《話》an ad《for》(❗ 特にラジオ・テレビによる宣伝は a commercial という (⇨コマーシャル)); (広く知らせるための) publicity; (政府などによる)〖通例,悪い意味を伴う〗propaganda (❗通例,悪い意味を伴う). (⇨広告) ● 宣伝活動をする carry on a publicity [a propaganda] campaign《for》.
- 宣伝用スローガン a slogan for an advertisement. ▶宣伝は大変な効果があった The advertisement had a great effect. ▶宣伝がまずかったので劇場入りが少なかった Because of (×a) poor [bad] publicity, there was a small [a poor] attendance at the theater. ▶たばこの危険性についてはずいぶん宣伝がなされてきた There has been a great deal of publicity about the dangers of smoking.
―― 宣伝する advertise; publicize; propagandize. ● 自己宣伝する advertise oneself. ● 新聞で新製品を宣伝する advertise new products in the newspapers; put [place] an advertisement for new products in the newspapers. ● 息子のことを宣伝して回る(=みんなに言う)tell everybody about one's son.
- 宣伝カー a sound truck. ● 宣伝係 a publicity man [woman, person]; a publicity agent (略 PA). ● 宣伝活動 public relations《略 PR》.(❗単数扱い) ● 宣伝効果 advertising effectiveness. ● 宣伝者 an advertiser; (俳優・芸品などの)a publicity agent, a publicist; (特に政治の宣伝を行う)a propagandist. ● 宣伝費 advertising expenses. ● 宣伝ビラ a handbill; a leaflet. ● 宣伝部 the public relations department. ● 宣伝文 an advertising copy; (本の表紙の)a blurb. 宣伝文句 (キャッチフレーズ) a catchphrase.
ぜんてん 全店 (全部の店) all stores [shops]; (その店全体) the whole store [shop]. ● 全店大売出し (have) a storewide sale.
ぜんてん 全点 (すべての品物) all goods [articles]. ● 全点半額で売る sell all goods at a 50 percent reduction [discount].
ぜんてんこう 全天候 ―― 全天候型の 形 ● 全天候型のテニスコート an all-weather tennis court. ● 全天候機 an all-weather airplane.
せんてんてき 先天的 ―― 先天的な 形 〖性質・能力などが〗(生まれながら備わった) innate /inéit/(↔acquired), inborn, natural; (病気などが) congenital /kəndʒénitl/. ● 先天的な音楽の才能 a natural ability in music; an innate [an inborn] talent for music. ● 先天的な障害 a congenital disorder. ● 先天的に心臓に欠陥のある子供 a child with congenital heart defects.
せんと 遷都 图 the tránsfer of the capital.
―― 遷都する 動 ● 京都から東京に遷都する《やや書》transfér the capital from Kyoto to Tokyo.
セント a cent (略 C, 記号 ¢).(❗参考 米国・カナダなどの貨幣単位で1ドルの100分の1) ● 10 セント 10¢; ten cents. ● 4 ドル 70 セント $4.70; four seventy (❗ (1) ¢ は $ と異なり数字の後につける。(2) 正式には four dollars and seventy cents という).
せんど 先途 ● ここを先途と(=必死に)戦う fight desperately.
せんど 鮮度 ● 鮮度が落ちる[落ちている] lose its freshness [be no longer fresh].
ぜんと 前途 (人・国などの) a future (❗一般的な「将来」は通例 the 〜); (見込み) an outlook, prospects《for》;(有望) promise. (⇨将来 ❷)
① 【前途〜】▶彼は前途有望な学者だ He is a very promising scholar [a scholar of great promise]./He shows a lot of promise in the academic world. ▶彼は前途洋々だ His future is bright. ▶我々は前途多難だ(=多くの困難が我々の行く手にある) A lot of difficulties lie ahead of us [in our way].
② 【前途を[を]〜】● 前途を悲観している be pessimistic about one's [the] future. ▶君たちの前途を祝し乾杯！Let's drink to wish you happy [rosy] futures. (❗「君たち」が新婚夫婦など共通の未来を持つ者の場合には a ... future と単数形を用いる) ▶君たちの前途は明るい You have a bright future ahead of you. ▶外国貿易の前途は暗い The outlook for foreign trade is [The prospects for foreign trade are] gloomy.
ぜんど 全土 ● 日本全土 the whole of Japan (❗ whole は地名に直接つけて ×the whole Japan とするのは不可); (官・書) all Japan. ● 全土にわたって all over [throughout] the country. (⇨全国)
せんとう 先頭 (先端) the head; (最前の位置) the front; (先導, 率先) the lead. ● パレードの先頭集団 [先頭の車] the head group [the front car] of a parade. ● マラソンの先頭集団についていく stay with the leaders [the leading (group of) runners] in the marathon. ▶我々は列の先頭で待った We waited at the head [front] of the line. ▶彼は折り返し地点で先頭に立っていた He had [was in] the lead at the halfway point. (❗「先頭に立った」は went into the lead, 「先頭に飛び出した」は shot ahead) ▶ブラスバンドがパレードの先頭に立った The brass band led (the way for) the parade. ▶彼は先頭に立って教育改革を進めた He took the lead [(先立して) the initiative] in carrying out the educational reform.
- 先頭打者 〖野球〗 a lead-off man [hitter, batter]. ● 先頭打者ホームランを打つ hit a leadoff homer.
せんとう 尖塔 〖とがり屋根〗a spire; a steeple (❗ この先端が spire); 〖小尖塔〗a pinnacle. ● 教会の高い尖塔 the tall spire of the church.
せんとう 戦闘 a combat; (戦争を構成する局地的な戦闘) a battle (❗戦闘状態を表すときは Ｕ); (戦い) a fight; (戦闘行為) action. (戦い) ● 戦闘的な部族 a militant tribe. ● 戦闘態勢をとっている be in combat conditions. ● 戦闘を開始する go into battle [action]. ● 戦闘を中止する break off a battle [an action]. ● 戦闘に参加する take part in a battle; (実戦を経験する) see action [combat]. ● 戦闘中に殺される be killed in action [battle]. (❗無冠詞に注意)
- 戦闘員 a combatant. ● 戦闘機 a fighter. ● 戦闘部隊 fighting forces. ● 戦闘力 fighting power.
せんとう 銭湯 a public bath. 事情 米英で似たものに a bathhouse がある）
せんどう 先導 ―― 先導する 動 (案内する) lead,

せんどう guide; (…に先立つ)《書》precede /prisí:d/. ▶ブラスバンドに先導されてパレードは大通りをゆっくり進んだ *Led by a brass band, the parade marched slowly along the main street.*
● 先導車 a leading car.

せんどう 扇動 图 (an) agitation 《for》; instigation; incitement. ● 指導者の扇動でストをする go on strike *at* [*by*] *the instigation of* the leader.

—— **扇動する** 動 〖世論を喚起する〗agitate 《for, against》; 〖そそのかして...させる〗(を) instigate; 〖鼓舞して...させる〗incite. ● ストライキを扇動する *agitate for* [*instigate, incite*] a strike. ▶彼は群衆を扇動して政府に対し反乱を起こさせた He incited [instigated] the crowd *to* rise against their government.

—— **扇動者** an agitator; an instigator.

せんどう 船頭 a boatman; 〖渡し船の〗a ferryman. (⚠) はいずれも (-men))
● 船頭多くして船山に登る《ことわざ》Too many cooks spoil the broth./A pot that belongs to many is ill stirred and worse boiled.

ぜんとう 全島 (すべての島) all islands; (その島全体) the whole island.

ぜんどう 善導 图 proper guidance.

—— **善導する** 動 guide (him) properly.

ぜんどう 禅堂 a temple for Zen study.

ぜんどう 蠕動 〖身をよじること〗writhing; (体をくねらせること) wriggling; (胃腸の動き)『生理』peristalsis.

—— **蠕動する** 動 writhe; wriggle.
● 蠕動運動 a peristaltic motion.

ぜんとうこつ 前頭骨 〖解剖〗the frontal bone.

ぜんとうぶ 前頭部 the front (of a head); (額) a forehead.

ぜんとうよう 前頭葉 〖解剖〗the frontal lobe.

セントクリストファー・ネーヴィス 〖国名〗St. Kitts and Nevis; (公式名) Saint Christopher and Nevis. (首都) Basseterre)

せんとちひろのかみかくし 『千と千尋の神隠し』 *Spirited Away*. (〖参考〗宮崎駿の映画)

セントバーナード 〖動物〗a Saint Bernard.

セントビンセントおよびグレナディーンしょとう セントビンセントおよびグレナディーン諸島 〖国名〗Saint Vincent and the Grenadines. (首都 Kingstown)

セントポーリア 〖植物〗a saintpaulia.

セントラルパーク (米国ニューヨーク市の公園) (×the) Central Park.

セントラルヒーティング (集中暖房装置) central heating; a central heating system. ▶ この建物はセントラルヒーティングを備えている This building has *central heating* [*is centrally heated*].

セントラルリーグ (野球) the Central League.

セントルイス (米国の都市) St. Louis /séint lú:is(s)/.

セントルシア 〖国名〗Saint Lucia (⚠ 公式名も同じ). (首都 Castries) ● セントルシア人 a Saint Lucian.
● セントルシア(人)の Saint Lucian.

せんない 船内 ● 船内で[に] on [in] a ship; on board ship.

せんない 詮無い (⇨仕方(が)無い)

せんなり 千生り ● 千生り瓢箪(ひょうたん)『植物』a bottle gourd; 〖指物〗an ensign bearing a cluster of gourds.

ぜんなんぜんにょ 善男善女 pious people [folk; men and women].

せんにちこう 千日紅 〖植物〗a globe amaranth.

ぜんにちせい 全日制 the full-time schooling system.
● 全日制高校 a full-time (senior) high school.

(関連) 定時制高校 a night [a part-time] high school)

せんにちて 千日手 〖将棋〗an endless repetition of moves leading to a draw.

ぜんにほん 全日本 ● 全日本選手権 the all-Japan championship. ● 全日本チーム the all-Japan team.

せんにゅう 潜入 —— 潜入する 動 〖部屋などに〗sneak [steal]《into》; 〖敵地・組織などに〗infiltrate; 〖密航する〗smuggle oneself 《into》.

ぜんにゅう 全入 (『全員入学』の略) granting all applicants admission to a school [a college].

せんにゅうかん 先入観 (やや書) a preconception, a preconceived idea [notion]; (偏見) (a) prejudice, (a) bias (⚠ bias はよい意味にも用いられる). (⇨偏見) ● 先入観を持っている have a *preconception* 《about》; have a *prejudice* [*be prejudiced*] 《against》; (初めから決めてかかっている) have a fixed opinion to begin with.

せんにょ 仙女 a fairy; a nymph.

せんにん 仙人 〖山に住む隠者〗a mountain hermit; 〖俗念のない人〗an unworldly person.

せんにん 先任 ● 先任の(= 先輩の)将校 a senior officer.
● 先任者(先輩) a senior; (前任者) a predecessor.

せんにん 専任 —— 専任の 形 (常勤の) full-time (↔ part-time). ● 英語の専任講師 a *full-time* teacher [〖大学の〗(米) instructor, (英) lecturer] of English.

せんにん 選任 图 (選出) (an) election; (任用) (an) appointment, (a) nomination.

—— **選任する** 動 (選ぶ) elect; (任用する) appoint; nominate. ● 副知事に選任される *be nominated* deputy governor 《of Osaka prefecture》.

ぜんにん 善人 a good person; (お人よし) a good-natured person.

ぜんにんしゃ 前任者 (やや書) one's predecessor /prédəsèsər/ (in a job).

せんにんばり 千人針 a *senninbari*; (説明的に) a good-luck-charm cotton belt for soldiers with 1,000 red stitches made by 1,000 women.

せんにんりき 千人力 the strength of a thousand men. ▶ あなたがいれば千人力だ(= 心強い) As long as you are here with us, we *feel reassured very much*./Your presence inspires us with *complete confidence*.

せんぬき 栓抜き (コルク栓の) a corkscrew; (びんの) a cap [a bottle] opener.

せんねつ 潜熱 〖物理〗latent heat.

せんねん 先年 a few [some] years ago.

せんねん 専念 —— 専念する 動 〖努力・注意を集中する〗concentrate 《on》; 〖ささげる〗devote oneself [one's energy] 《to》; 〖一心に従事する〗occupy oneself, be occupied 《in, with》; 〖熱中する〗be absorbed 《in》. ● 庭造りに専念する(=精を出す) *work hard at* gardening. ● 休日は読書に専念する *devote* the holiday *to* reading. ▶ 彼は1日中その仕事に専念した He concentrated on [devoted all his *energies to, occupied himself with, applied himself to*] the work all day long. ▶ 彼女は子育てに専念するために仕事をやめた She quit the job to *devote herself to* motherhood. ▶ 彼女はその小説の執筆に専念している She *is fully occupied in* writ*ing* the novel. (⚠ ...occupied *with* the novel. ともいえる)

ぜんねん 前年 ● 前年に〖その前の年に〗(in) the year before; (in) the previous [《書》preceding] year; 〖昨年に〗last year. (⇨前日) ● 前年同期

せんのう 洗脳 brainwashing.
— **洗脳する** 動 brainwash《him *into* believing the idea》.

ぜんのう 全能 ● 全能の神 Almighty God;《書》the Omnipotent God.
● **全能者(神)** the Almighty.

ぜんのう 前納 名 (前払い) payment in advance.
— **前納する** 動 ● 100万円を前納する *pay* one million yen *in advance*; pay an *advance* of one million yen.

ぜんば 前場 (証券取引所などの) the morning session. (⇔後場)

せんばい 専売 名 〖専売権, 専売品〗a monopoly /mənápəli/. ● その国では塩が政府の専売になっている In that country the government has a *monopoly in [of,《米》on]* salt./In that country salt is a government *monopoly*./In that country salt *is monopolized* by the government.
— **専売する** 動 make a monopoly《*of*》; monopolize.
● **専売特許** a patent. (⇒特許)

***せんぱい 先輩** one's senior,《米》(学校の) one's upperclass student,《書》one's elders.

> 解説 米英, 特に米では日本のように先輩・後輩の関係をあまり重視しないため, 説明的な訳が必要. one's **senior** は年長者を表すが, 年齢より今はむしろ組織などにおける年功序列や学校などの上級生を表すことが多い. one's **elders** は自分より年上の人を集合的に表す語.

▶彼は2年先輩です(年齢が)He is two years *older than* I me,《話》*than* me,《書·まれ》*than* I]./He is two years my *senior*./He is *senior to* me by two years. (⚠最初が最も普通の言い方)/He is two years *ahead of* me at [《米》in] school. (⚠高校·大学の場合,《主に米》では He is in the class two years *ahead of* me. も可)/《主に英》He is two years my *senior* at school. (⚠《米》では senior は高校·大学の最終学年を表すので避けた方がよい) ●彼は仕事ではずっと先輩です(=経験豊富だ) He *has* much more *experience* on the job than I do.

ぜんぱい 全敗 — **全敗する** 動 ▶我がチームは全敗した Our team lost all its games [matches].

ぜんぱい 全廃 名 〖完全な廃止〗total abolition. ● 奴隷制度の全廃 the (*total*) *abolition* of slavery.
— **全廃する** 動 ▶政府は食品への課税を全廃するべきだ The government should *abolish* the tax on food (*altogether*).

せんぱく 浅薄 — **浅薄な** 形 (浅はかな) shallow; (薄っぺらな) superficial. ● 浅薄な知識 a *shallow* [a *superficial*] knowledge《*of*》.

せんぱく 船舶 a ship,《書》a vessel;《集合的》shipping. (⇒舟)
● **船舶会社** a shipping company. ● **船舶業** the shipping industry. ● **船舶保険** hull insurance.

せんばつ 選抜 名 selection. (⇒選ぶ, 選考) ● **全国選抜高校野球大会** the National Invitational High School Baseball Tournament.
— **選抜する** 動 select. ▶多くの応募者の中から選抜される be selected [be picked out] from (among) many applicants. (⚠後の方が口語的)
● **選抜試験** a selective examination.

せんぱつ 先発 — **先発する** 動 (先に出発する) start in advance. ●新人投手を先発させる start a rookie pitcher.
● **先発隊** an advance party. ● **先発投手** a starting pitcher; a starter. ●スワローズの先発投手として登録される *start for* the Swallows. (⇒投手) ● **先発メンバー** (全員) a starting lineup; (一員) a starter. (⇒スタメン) ● **先発ローテーション** the starting rotation.

せんぱつ 染髪 ● 褐色に染髪する *dye* one's *hair* brown.

せんぱつ 洗髪 名 hair-washing; (シャンプーによる1回の洗髪) a shampoo /ʃæmpúː/ (⑲ ~s).
— **洗髪する** 動 wash [shampoo] one's hair; give one's hair a shampoo.

せんぱつじしん 浅発地震 a shallow-focus earthquake. (⇔深発地震)

せんばづる 千羽鶴 one thousand paper cranes (which are often used in praying for recovery from illness).

せんばん 千万 ▶千万手を尽くす try *every* means in one's power. ▶失礼千万だ It's *very* rude of you. ▶千万かたじけない *Many* thanks for your kindness./I am *very much* obliged.

せんばん 旋盤 a lathe /léið/.
● **旋盤工** a turner.

せんぱん 先般 (先日) the other day. (⇒この間)

せんぱん 戦犯 (人) a war criminal; (罪) war crimes.
● **戦犯法廷** a war crimes court.

ぜんはん 前半 the first [former] half. (⇔後半)
● **前半戦** (試合の) the first half of a game; (シーズンの) the first half of a season.

ぜんぱん 全般 名 〖全体〗the whole. (⇔全体) ●組織全般 the *whole* organization. ●学生全般 students *in general*. ●情勢全般を見渡す take an *overall* view of the situation.
— **全般的な** 形 general; (全体にわたる) overall.
— **全般的に** 副 in general; generally; on the whole. ●全般的に言うと generally (speaking).

ぜんはんせい 前半生 the first half of one's life. (⇔後半生)

せんび 船尾 the stern (↔the bow /báu/). ●船尾から沈没する sink *from the stern*.

せんび 戦備 war preparations, preparations for war. ●戦備を整える prepare for war.

せんぴ 戦費 war expenditure.

ぜんび 善美 ●善美を尽くした建物 (華美な) gorgeous [(きわめて美しい) exquisite; (壮麗な) splendid] architecture.

ぜんぴ 前非 ●前非を悔やむ repent of one's *past misdeeds* [(悪行) *follies*; (罪) *sins*].

せんびき 線引き ● 線引きする draw a line. ●両地帯の線引きをする *draw lines of demarcation between two zones*. ●仕事とレジャーの間をはっきりと線引きする *draw clear lines of demarcation between work and leasure*.

せんびょう 線描 a line drawing.

せんぴょう 戦評 (a) comment《*on* a game [*go*]》.

せんぴょう 選評 — **選評する** 動 (俳句を選評する=選んで批評する) select and comment on haiku poems.

せんびょうし 戦病死 — **戦病死する** 動 die of a disease contracted at the front.
● **戦病死者** those who died of diseases they contracted at the front.

せんびょうしつ 腺病質 名 delicate health.
— **腺病質の** 形 delicate; (病弱な) sickly. (⇒虚弱)

ぜんびん 前便 (前便(=前回の手紙)で) in one's *last letter*. ●前便でロンドンに出発する (前の航空便で)

ぜんぴん 全品 all goods. ●全品半額セール a half-price sale of *all goods*.

せんぷ 先負 (説明的に) an unlucky day for urgent business, a lawsuit, etc. on the oldstyle calendar.

せんぷ 先夫 one's former husband; one's ex-husband (⇨先妻).

せんぷ 宣布 名 a proclamation.
—— **宣布する** 動 proclaim; make a proclamation.

ぜんぶ 全部 名 〘すべてひっくるめて〙 all (! 複数名詞を修飾したり複数概念を表すときは複数扱い.単数名詞を修飾したり単数概念を表すときは単数扱い); 〘一つ一つすべて〙 every ... (! 単数可算名詞を修飾し,通例単数扱い), everything (! 単数扱い); 〘まとまった全体〙 the whole (! 単数扱い.名詞として用いるのは《やや書》); 〘総計〙 a total.

① 〘全部(の,を)〙 ● 有り金全部を違う spend *all* (*of*) one's [×one's whole] money. (! one's [the] whole は物質名詞的には用いない) ▶全生徒は自分のラップトップコンピュータを持っている *All* (*of*) *the* [×The whole] students have their own lap(-)top computers. (! (1) the whole は通例複数名詞を修飾しない. (2) 「(一般に)学生は全部」の意では All students .... となり of は用いない. (3) 数詞を伴う場合は the の有無にかかわらず常に特定の学生をさす: all (the) fifty students)/The students *all* have their own lap(-)top computers. (! 主語と同格の all は一般動詞の前または be 動詞・助動詞の後に置く)/*Every* student has their [his] own lap(-)top computer. (! (1) 今では them で受けるのが普通. (2) 特定の学生であることを明示する場合は *Èvery óne of the* students has their [his] own lap-top computer. とする) ▶それらを全部買った I bought *all of* them. (! 人称代名詞を従えるときの of は省略不可)/I bought them *all*. (! 人称代名詞が動詞の目的語の場合 all はその直後の位置を占め,その方が強意的) ▶全部の学生がそこへ行ったわけではない *Nót ↘all* the students [*Nót ↘every* student] went ↗there. / *Àll* the students [*Èvery* student] didn't go ∨there. ともいえるが,下がり調子でいうと,「学生はだれもそこへ行かなかった(*None of the* students [*No* students] went there. / *The whole of the* students didn't go there.)」の意の全部否定を表し,書き言葉ではあいまいなので避ける) ▶一晩でその本を全部読んだ I read *the whole* book [*the whole of the* book] in one evening. (! (1) 後の方は「部分的にではなく」を含意する言い方で,不定のものには用いない: 「ある本1冊を全部」は *a* whole book で, ×the whole of *a* book ではない. (2) I didn't read *the whole* book [*the whole of the* book] in one evening. は「一晩で全部を読んだ」の意で部分否定)/(終わりまで読んだ) I read *through* the book [read the book *from cover to cover*] in one evening. ▶君に話したことは全部本当だ *Everything* [《やや書》*All*] I've told you is [×are] true. (! of の句やこの場合のように関係詞節などの修飾句を従えない場合, all を代名詞として用いるのは特定の慣用的な言い方を除いてまれ. 通例代わりに everything, everyone, everybody などを用いる)/*The whole* thing I've told you is true. ▶あの人の言いたいことは全部分かる I understand *everything* he means. ▶谷崎の作品は全部そろっている I have a *complete* set of Tanizaki's works. ▶彼の本は全部全部退屈というわけではない *Not all* of his books are boring. ▶バターは加減して使いなさい.それだけ(で)全部だから Go easy on the butter; that's *all* there is.

会話 「ピーナツはどこ?」「全部食べちゃったよ」 "Where are the peanuts?" "I've eaten them *all*."

② 〘全部で〙 altogether, in all; (合計で) in total. ▶全部で500人が出席した There were 500 people present *altogether* [*in all, all told*]. / A *total* of 500 people were present. (⇨合計)

会話 「全部で7,000円です」「6,000円になりません か」 "Seven thousand *yen in all* [《英話》*the lot*]." "Could you come down to six thousand?"

—— **全部** 副 〘まったく〙 entirely; completely; all. (⇨すべて 副) ▶急いで全部すませてしまおう Let's finish it *up* [*off*] in a hurry. (! up, off は特定の動詞と結びついて「完結」の意を表す)

ぜんぶ 前部 the front (part). (⇨前 ❶) ●船の前部 *the front* [*fore*] (part) of a ship. ▶エレベーターは建物の前部にあった The elevator 《米》[*lift* 《英》] was *at the front* [*in the front part*] of the building.

ぜんぶ 膳部 (料理) (a) dinner. ●膳部を整える set [lay] *dinner*; lay [set] the table.

ぜんぷ 前夫 (⇨先夫).

せんぷう 旋風 〘つむじ風〙 a whirlwind; 〘大反響〙 a sensation. ▶かつてビートルズは若者の間に大旋風を巻き起こした The Beatles created a great *sensation* among young people.

せんぷうき 扇風機 an electric fan, a fan; (天井につるした) a ceiling [an overhead] fan. ●扇風機をかける[止める] turn on [off] a *fan*.

せんぷく 船幅 the beam.

せんぷく 船腹 〘船の胴体にあたる部分〙 the side(s) of a ship; 〘積載トン数〙 tonnage.

せんぷく 潜伏 —— **潜伏する** 動 hide* out; hide [conceal] oneself. ▶犯人はこの町に潜伏している The criminal *is hiding out* [*concealing himself*] in this city.

●潜伏期間 (病気の) a latency [an incubation] period. (! latency は潜んでいることに, incubation は内部で発達していることに重点がある) ▶その病気の潜伏期間は2週間だ This illness has an *incubation* period of two weeks.

ぜんぷく 全幅 ● 彼に全幅の(=十分な)信頼を置く put *full* [(完全な) *complete*; (絶対的な) *absolute*] confidence [*trust*] *in* him; trust him *fully* [*completely, absolutely*]. (! put を have に換えると「信頼を置いている」の意)

せんぶり 千振り 〘植物〙 a Japanese green gentian.

ぜんぶん 全文 (書物・文書の本文全体) the full [whole] text; (段落全体) the whole passage; (1文全体) the whole sentence. ●声明の全文 *the full text* of a statement.

ぜんぶん 前文 (法律・条約などの) 《書》a preamble /príːæmbl/ 《to》; (上記の文) the above (sentence [(1節) passage]).

せんぶんりつ 千分率 permillage; (a) rate per thousand.

せんべい 煎餅 a *sembei*; (説明的に) Japanese rice crackers (seasoned with salt, soy sauce, sugar, etc.).

●せんべい布団 a *futon* mattress as thin and hard as a rice cracker; a very thin and hard *futon* mattress.

せんべい 先兵, 尖兵 an advance guard; (部隊) an advance detachment.

ぜんべい 全米 ●全米ゴルフ選手権を獲得する win the *American* golf championship. ▶フットボールの全

せんべつ 選別 ── 選別する 動 (えり分ける) sort (out [through]); (精選する) select. (⇨分ける❹) ● よいリンゴと悪いリンゴを選別する *sort out* the good apples *from* the bad.

せんべつ 餞別 ● 餞別をもらう[あげる] be given [give 《him》] a *farewell* [a *going-away*, a *parting*] *present*.

せんべん 先鞭 ● 先鞭をつける (開拓する) pioneer; (率先してする) take the initiative 《in doing》. ▶ 彼は新科学技術導入の先鞭をつけた He *took the initiative in* introducing the new technology.

ぜんぺん 全編 the whole book [(物語) story]. ▶ 全編に平和を愛する心がみなぎっている The story is full of peace-loving ideas./(書) The love of peace pervades the *whole story*. (❗ pervade は「…全体に満ちている」の意)

ぜんぺん 前編 〖本などの前半〗 the first part 《of》; 〖先の巻〗 the first volume 《of》. ● その小説の前編 the *first volume* of the novel.

せんぺんいちりつ 千篇一律 ● 千篇一律の文章 (単調な) a *monotonous* (退屈な) a *dull* composition. ● 千篇一律の(=型にはまった)意見 a *stereotyped* opinion.

せんぺんばんか 千変万化 ── 千変万化の 形 (常に変わっていく) ever-changing; (めまぐるしく変化する) kaleidoscopic /kəlàidəskápík/.
── 千変万化する 動 change kaleidoscopically.

せんぼう 羨望 envy. ● 羨望のまなざしで彼を見る look at him *with envy*; look *enviously* at him; cast *envious* glances at him. ▶ 彼女の美しさは級友たちの羨望の的であった Her beauty was the *envy* of her classmates./(羨望していた) Her classmates *envied* [*were envious of*] her beauty.

せんぽう 先方 (法律文で) the other party (❗ 1 人の人・一つのグループをさす); (普通の文で) he, she, they. ● 先方の言い分 the *other party's* version; *his* [*her*, *their*] version; what *he* has [*she* has, *they* have] to say.

せんぽう 先鋒 〖先駆〗 the vánguàrd. (❗「先駆者(たち)」の意では単・複両扱い) ● 社会改革の先鋒に立って *in the vanguard* [*in the》 van*] of social reform. ● 改革運動の急先鋒に立つ(=指導者である) be a *foremost leader in* the reform movement.

せんぽう 戦法 〖戦術〗 táctics (❗ 単・複両扱い); 〖戦略〗 strategy /strǽtədʒi/. ● 奇襲戦法で勝つ win by surprise *tactics*.

ぜんぼう 全貌 the whole picture. ● 汚職事件の全貌を明らかにする give the *whole picture* of the corruption case; make the corruption case *fully* clear.

ぜんぽう 前方 ● 前方へ進む move *forward* [*ahead*]. ● 前方の建物 the building *ahead* 《of us》 [*in front of* us],《書》*before* us]. ● 後の二つでは進行中であることを含意する) ▶ 300 メートル前方に給油所がある There's a gas station 300 meters 《up》 *ahead* [*forward*]. (❗ up is up (the road)のことで「道をさらに行ったところに」)

ぜんほうい 全方位 ● 全方位外交をすすめる carry on *omnidirectional* diplomacy.

せんぼうきょう 潜望鏡 a périscòpe.

ぜんぽうこうえんふん 前方後円墳 〖歴史〗 (説明的に) a keyhole-shaped ancient Japanese burial mound.

せんぼつしゃ 戦没者 《やや書》those who fell in the war;《やや書》the war dead (❗ 複数扱い).
● 戦没者慰霊碑 a war memorial.

せんまい 洗米 consecrated rice [(洗米) cleansed rice] offered to God.

ぜんまい a spring. ● ぜんまい仕掛けのおもちゃ a windup /wáindʌp/ [《英》a clockwork] toy. ● 時計のぜんまいを巻く wind 《up》a clock [a watch]; wind a clock *spring*. ▶ ぜんまいが緩んでいる[切れている] The *spring* has unwound /ʌnwáund/ [broken]. ● この時計はぜんまいで動く This watch works by a *spring* [by clockwork]. (❗ このような時計は a *spring* [a *clockwork*] watch という)

ぜんまい 薇 〖植物〗 (a) royal [(a) flowering] fern. (❗ 集合的には Ⓤ)

せんまいだ 千枚田 terraced paddies; terraced rice (paddy) fields.

せんまいづけ 千枚漬 (説明的に) pickled vegetables by seasoning thin-sliced turnips by adding sea tangles to them alternately with *koji*, *mirin*, and so on.

せんまいどおし 千枚通し an eyeleteer; a bodkin.

せんまいばり 千枚張り ── 千枚張りの 形 (多層の) multilayer(ed). ● 面の皮が千枚張りだ (無礼で生意気だ) be very impudent; have plenty of cheek [《話》gall]; (鉄面皮だ) be brazen-faced.

せんまん 千万 ten million. (❗ million の用法は (⇨百万)) ● 何千万人という人 *tens of millions of* people.

ぜんみ 禅味 an unworldly flavor [savor] (of Zen Buddhism).

せんみん 選民 ● 神の選民 the Chosen People. (参考 イスラエル民族)
● 選民思想 the elitism.

せんむ 専務 (専務取締役) an executive (managing) director; a senior managing director. (⇨会社)

せんめい 鮮明 ● 鮮明な 形 (色・記憶などが) vivid; (輪郭の明瞭(ᵐⱽ᷒)な) distinct; (形・輪郭のはっきりした) clear. ● 鮮明な色 *vivid* [*bright*] colors. ● 鮮明な画像 a *clear* [a *distinct*] picture. ● 彼女の顔を鮮明に覚えている I remember her face *vividly*.

ぜんめつ 全滅 名 total [complete] destruction; annihilation /ənàiəléiʃən/.
── 全滅させる 動〖町・敵などを完全に滅ぼす〗destroy ... completely,《書》annihilate /ənáiəlèit/, wipe ... out 《口語的》; 〖有害生物などを完全に死滅させる〗exterminate. (⇨撲滅) ● 敵を全滅させる *destroy* the enemy *completely*; (粉砕する) crush the enemy. ▶ その市は地震で全滅した The city *was completely destroyed* by the earthquake. ▶ その疫病で村民が全滅した The plague *wiped out* all the villagers./The plague *annihilated* the whole (population of the) village./(村民はだれも生き残らなかった) *None of* the villagers *survived* the plague. ▶ 霜でとうもろこしが全滅した The frost *spoiled* the corn crop *completely*. ▶ その森のシカは乱伐で全滅しかけている The deer in the forest *are being wiped out* by deforestation.

せんめん 洗面 ● 洗面器《米》a washbowl,《英》a washbasin. ● 洗面所 a bathroom. (⇨便所) ● 洗面道具 toilet articles.

ぜんめん 全面 名 ● 湖の全面(=全表面) the *whole* [*entire*] *surface* of the lake.
── 全面的な 形 (完全な) complete; (すべての部分がそろっている) entire; (全力をあげての) all-out; (一切を含む) overall; (全般的な) general; (心からの) wholehearted. ● 全面的な支持 one's *entire* support. ● 全面ストライキ an *all-out* [a *general*] strike. ▶ 彼は我々の計画に全面的支持を約束した He prom-

ised to support our plan *wholeheartedly* [*heartily*]./He promised a *wholehearted* [a *hearty*] support to our plan.

— 全面的に 副 completely; entirely; generally; wholeheartedly; (まったく) quite. ▶ぼくは彼の意見に全面的に賛成だ I *completely* [*entirely, quite*] agree with you. (⇨全く❶) ▶委員会はその規約を全面的に改正した The committee made an *overall* [(完全な) a *complete*, (大規模な) a *wholesale*] revision of the rules./The committee revised the rules *overall* [*completely*]. ▶君は何も言うな，それは全面的にぼくに任せてくれ Don't say anything at all. Leave it *entirely* to me. ▶全面的に(＝すべて)彼に責任があるわけではない He is not *entirely* to blame.
● 全面広告 a full-page advertisement 《*in the Asahi*》. ● 全面戦争 (総力戦) an all-out [a total] war; a full-scale war.

ぜんめん 前面 the front, the face; (建物の装飾的な) the facade /fəsɑ́ːd/. ● 建物の前面 the *front* of a building.

せんもう 繊毛 (細い毛) thin hair; (細胞の表面の) 《生物》cilia.
● 繊毛運動 《生物》ciliary movement. ● 繊毛虫類《動物》ciliates.

ぜんもう 全盲 ▶この娘は全盲だ This girl is *totally blind*.

:**せんもん** 専門 图 specialty /spéʃlti/; (得手，職業)《話》one's line; (研究・活動の分野) one's field; (学部学生の専攻科目) a major.
①【専門～】 ▶専門性の高い仕事 a highly *specialized* job. ▶それは私の専門外だ It's out of my *line* [*field*].
②【専門は】 ▶あなたの専門は何ですか What is your *specialty* [《米》*major*]?/What do you *specialize* [《米》*are you majoring*] *in*?
③【専門に】 ▶彼は日本史を専門にしている He *specializes* [《米》*is majoring*] *in* Japanese history./Japanese history is his *specialty* [《米》*major*]. (❗いずれの major も大学院生には用いない)/(専門に研究している) He is making a *special study of* Japanese history. ▶彼女は源氏物語を専門にしている She *specializes on* [×*in*] *The Tales of Genji*. (❗日本文学の研究では in だが，その中の特定の分野では on)
④【専門だ】 ▶このレストランはフランス料理専門だ This restaurant *specializes in* [The specialty of this restaurant is] French cuisine /kwiːzíːn/. ▶彼は食い気専門だ(＝彼の唯一の関心事は食べることだ) His *only interest* is (in) eating.

— 専門的な 形 (専門化した) specialized; (技術上の) technical; (特殊な) special; (職業の) professional. ▶それは専門的な立場からいうと間違っている It is wrong from a *technical* point of view. ▶弁護士は専門的な仕事をする人だ A lawyer is a *professional* (person). ▶その仕事はかなり専門的だ The work *is* highly *specialized*./That is a highly-*specialized* job. ▶彼の講義は専門的すぎて私たちには理解できない His lecture is so *technical* that we can't understand it.
● 専門医 a specialist 《*in* plastic surgery》. ● 専門家 (⇨専門家) ● 専門学校 (各種学校) a college; (職業学校) a professional school. ● 専門課程 a special(ized) course. ● 専門技術 expertise; technical [specialist] skill. ● 専門教育 technical [professional] education. (❗ special education は「特殊教育」の意で，必ずしも専門的知識を教えるものではない) ● 専門雑誌 a technical jour-

nal. ● 専門士 a professional [a vocational] school graduate; a technical college graduate. ● 専門書 a technical book. ● 専門職 a profession. ● 専門知識 specialized [special, technical] knowledge; expertise /èkspɜːrtíːz/. ● 専門店 (⇨専門店) ● 専門病院 a special (⇔general) hospital. ● 専門用語 a technical term;《集合的》terminology.

ぜんもん 全問 all questions. ● 全問正解する answer *all the questions* correctly.

ぜんもん 前門 a front gate.
● 前門の虎，後門の狼 between the devil and the deep blue sea.

せんもんか 専門家 (熟練者) an éxpert《*in, at*》; (現職) a specialist《*in* plastic surgery, *on* Dante》; (玄人) a professional. ● 経済学［ケーキ作り］の専門家 an *expert in* economics [*at* baking cakes]. ● 専門家としての意見 a *professional* opinion.

せんもんてん 専門店 a specialty store. ● 舶来品専門店 a store that *specializes in* [*sells only*] imported items.

せんや 先夜 the other night [evening].

ぜんや 前夜 ● 前夜に the night before; the previous [《書》preceding] night. (⇨前日) ● 彼の出発の前夜に the night *before* he leaves [his departure]. ● 競技会の前夜に *on the eve of* the athletic meet. (「前日」の意にもなる)
● 前夜祭 an eve. (⊕ 後夜祭)

せんやいちやものがたり 『千夜一夜物語』*The Thousand and One Nights*. (《参考》アラビア語の説話集)

せんやく 仙薬 an elixir.

せんやく 先約 a previous [a prior] engagement; (人と会う) a prior [a previous] appointment. (⇨約束) ▶先約があるので彼はその会に行けません He can't go to the meeting because he has [because of] a *previous engagement*.
[会話]「ねえジョージ，明日ブランチに来ない？日本料理を作るんだけど」「行きたいけど，あいにく先約があって出かけることになっているんだ。あー，残念」"Hi, George! Can you come round for brunch tomorrow? I'm cooking Japanese food." "Oh, I'd love to, but I'm afraid I'm *already* going out. Oh, what a shame!"

せんやく 煎薬 a decoction; (液体の) an infusion.

ぜんやく 全訳 图 a complete translation《*of* Shakespeare》.

— 全訳する 動 ● 日本語に全訳する *translate*《*a book*》*completely into* Japanese.

せんゆう 占有 图 occupation; (所有)《書》possession.

— 占有する 動 occupy; possess, take possession of ....
● 占有権 the right of possession. ● 占有率 the (market) share《*of* our cars [40 percent]》.

せんゆう 専有 图 exclusive possession. ▶このタウンハウスの占有面積は130平方メートルです This town house has an *area* of 130 square meters for *exclusive use*.

— 専有する 動 (独占する) monópolize《the market》; make a monopoly of ...; (自分だけのものにする) take solo possession of ....
● 専有権 (a) monopoly《*of*》; an exclusive right《*to*》.

せんゆう 戦友 a comrade at arms [in battle], a fellow soldier. (❗comrade はやや堅い語) ▶彼らは戦友だった They had been *comrades at arms*. (❗×fighting friends とはいわない)

ぜんゆう 全優 ● 全優をもらう get *straight A's*. ● 全

せんよう の学生 a *straight-A* [an *all-A*] student. ● 全優で卒業する graduate with *straight A's*.

せんよう 占用 图 (独占的使用) exclusive use; (個人的使用) private use. ―― **占用する** 動 make [(している)] have *exclusive use* 《*of*》.

せんよう 宣揚 图 (高揚) (an) enhancement. ―― **宣揚する** 動 ● 国威を宣揚する *enhance* national prestige.

せんよう 専用 one's exclusive [private, personal] use. (❗最後の語は使用する人が1人のときに使う) ● 我々専用の車 our *private* car. ● 自転車専用道路《米》 a bikeway; a bike lane; a bicycle path. (❗歩行者も含むときは a greenway) ● この車は市長専用です This car is *for* the mayor's *exclusive* [*personal*] *use*./This car is *for the use of* the mayor *only*. ● 職員[会員]専用《掲示》 Staff [Members] *only*. ● この船は貨物専用で乗客を乗せません This ship carries *only* freight; no passengers.

ぜんよう 全容 the whole picture. (⇨全貌(ぜんぼう))

ぜんよう 善用 good use. ―― **善用する** 動 ● 金を善用する *put* one's money *to good use*; *use* one's money *for a good purpose*.

ぜんら 全裸 ● 全裸の女性 a woman *in the nude*;《話》 a *stark-naked* /-néikid/ woman. ● 全裸の写真 a *nude* photograph. ● 全裸で寝る《話》 sleep *stark naked*; (何もつけず) sleep *with nothing on*.

せんらん 戦乱 [戦争] (a) war; [戦闘] a battle. ● 戦乱の南アフリカ *war-torn* South Africa. ▶ その村は戦乱のちまたと化した The village was turned into a scene of *a battle* [戦場] *a battlefield*.

せんり 千里 a thousand *ri*. ● 千里眼 (⇨千里眼) ● 千里の道も一歩から A journey of a thousand miles must start with the first step.

せんりがん 千里眼 (能力) second sight, clairvoyance; (人) a clairvoyant. ● 千里眼の clairvoyant. ▶ 彼は千里眼だ He has *second sight*./He is (a) *clairvoyant*.

せんりつ 旋律 [音楽] a melody, a tune. ● 旋律の美しい melodious. ● 美しい[悲しい]旋律 a sweet [a melancholy] *melody*. ● 主旋律を歌う sing the lead.

せんりつ 戦慄 ● 戦慄を感じる feel a shudder of fear [horror]. ● 身震い.
翻訳のこころ 戦慄が私の背を走る (太宰治『猿が島』) A sense [A feeling] of horror [fear] runs down my back. (❗)(1)「戦慄」は a feeling of fear [a sense of horror] と表す. (2)「(恐怖・戦慄が)背を走る」は英語にも run down one's back という慣用表現がある.

ぜんりつせん 前立腺 [解剖] the prostate (gland). ● 前立腺炎 prostatitis /pràstətáitis/. ● 前立腺癌 prostate cancer. ● 前立腺肥大 enlargement of the prostate.

せんりひん 戦利品 (戦勝記念品) a trophy /tróufi/; (略奪品) loot,《主に書》booty.

せんりゃく 戦略 图 (a) strategy /strǽtədʒi/. (❗具体的には C) ● メディア[イメージ;販売]戦略 a media [an image; a marketing] *strategy*. ● 戦略を立てる work [map] out a *strategy*.
―― **戦略(上)の** 形 strategic(al).
―― **戦略的に** 副 ● ここは戦術的だけでなく戦略的にも重要な場所だ This is an important place not merely tactically, but *strategically* as well. ● 戦略家 a strategist. ● 戦略核兵器 strategic nuclear weapons [arms]. ● 戦略爆撃機 a strategic bomber. ● 戦略兵器削減条約 the Strategic Arms Reduction Treaty《略 START》.

ぜんりゃく 前略 (❗英文手紙ではすぐ用件に入るのが普通なので,「前略」に相当する英語はない)

せんりゅう 川柳 a *senryu* poem, a 17-syllable satirical poem; (説明的に) a witty, joking or satirical poem in seventeen syllables.

せんりょ 千慮 ● **千慮の一失** ● だれしも千慮の一失(=思いがけない失敗)がある Even a very attentive person sometimes *make an unexpected mistake* [*error*, *slip*]./《ことわざ》Even Homer sometimes nods.

せんりょ 浅慮 (無分別) imprudence; (思慮のなさ) thoughtlessness. ● 先生に口答えするとは君は浅慮だった It *was imprudent* [*thoughtless*] of you to answer your teacher back.

せんりょう 千両 [植物] a *senryo*, (学術名) *Chloranthus* [*Sarvandra*] *glabra*. ● 千両箱 a chest for gold coins. ● 千両役者 a great actor.

せんりょう 占領 图 occupation; [占有]《書》possession. ● 米国の占領地 an American *possession*. ● 占領下の日本 Japan under the *occupation* 《*of*》; occupied Japan.
―― **占領する** 動 occupy (❗状態にも用いる); [所有する] possess; [攻略する] capture, seize; [専有する] have* (it) to oneself. ● 敵地を占領する *occupy* the enemy's territory. ▶ 劇場内の前5列までの座席は子供たちが占領していた The seats of the first five rows in the theater *were* all *occupied* [*taken*] by children. ● 占領軍 an occupation army, the occupation forces. ● 占領政策 an occupation policy.

せんりょう 染料 dye; dyestuff (❗しばしば複数形で).

せんりょう 選良 (国民の代表) a representative of the people; (代議士) a Diet member, a member of the Diet.

ぜんりょう 善良 图 goodness.
―― **善良な** 形 good (⇨いい); (人のよい) good-natured (⇔ill-natured). ● 善良な市民 a *good* citizen. ▶ 昔は人々は善良で親切だった People *were good* and kind to each other before.

ぜんりょうせい 全寮制 ● 全寮制の学校に行く go to *boarding* school. (❗無冠詞に注意) ▶ うちの学校は全寮制です This [Our school] is a *boarding school*./At our school all the students are supposed to live in the dormitories [《話》 dorms].

せんりょく 戦力 (兵士) military strength; (潜在的戦事力) war potential; (戦闘力) fighting power. ● 戦力を増強する build up *military strength* [*war potential*]. ▶ その選手はチームにとって戦力(=貴重な人材)となるだろう The player will be a *powerful* [a *valuable*] *asset* to the team.

せんりょく 鮮緑 (鮮やかな緑) bright green; (新緑) fresh green;《詩》 verdure.

****ぜんりょく** 全力 ① 【全力を】● 全力を尽くして (全力で) with *all* one's *strength* [*might*]; at *full strength*;《話》 for all one's worth; (能力の及ぶ限り) to the best of one's *ability*. ● 全力を尽くす do one's best [*utmost*] (*to do*); do everything in [《書》 within] one's *power*;《話》 go all out 《*for*; *to do*》. ● その仕事に全力を傾ける give the task *all* you've got (❗最も日常的な言い方); devote *all* one's *energies to* [(全力をそそぐ) put all one's *energies into*] (doing) the task; (自分の全存在をかける) do the task *with all the power of* one's *being*. ▶ 山田さんは英語教育に全力を注いだ Mr. Yamada devoted *all* his *energies* to English teaching./Mr. Yamada put *all* his *energies*

into English teaching. ▶彼らは彼女の説得に全力をあげた They *did* their *best* [*did all* they *could*] *to* persuade her. ▶成功したいなら全力を出すことだ You have to exert yourself in order to be successful. ▶そのランナーは勝つために全力をふりしぼった The runner did his *utmost* to win the race./The runner pushed himself to the *utmost*.
② 【全力で】●全力で走る run at *full speed* [*strength*]; run *as* fast *as* one *can*. ●全力でロープを引く pull a rope with *all* one's *strength* [*might*]; use *all* one's *strength* to pull a rope; (全力をふりしぼって) gather *all* one's *strength* to pull a rope. ●(打撃後)一塁まで全力疾走する hustle down the line. ▶彼女は全力で(=真正面から)難問に取り組んだ She tackled a difficult problem *head-on*. ▶最初は抑えぎみでいき, ここぞというときを待ってあとはゴールまで全力疾走しなさい Hold back at first, wait for an opportunity, and then *sprint* to the finish.

ぜんりょくとうきゅう 全力投球 ── 全力投球する 動 〖精一杯する〗do one's (very) best. (⇒全力①)
▶会社のために全力投球してきた I *have done* my *best* [*all I could*] for the company. ▶あのピッチャーは全力投球しなかった(=力を尽くして投げなかった) The pitcher didn't bear down to [on] the batter.

ぜんりん 前輪 a front wheel.
●前輪駆動 front-wheel drive 《略 FWD》.

ぜんりん 善隣 ●善隣のよしみで for the sake of *good neighborly relations*. ●善隣外交政策をとる adopt a *good-neighbor* policy.

せんれい 先例 (a) precedent /présədənt/; [前の例] the previous instance. (❗前の方が堅い言い方)
●先例のない事態 a matter *without precedent*; an *unprecedented* matter. ●その先例に従う follow the *precedent* [*previous instance*]. ●先例を作る [になる] set [serve as] a *precedent* 《*for*》. ▶それには先例がない There is no *precedent* for it./It has no *precedent*./It is *unprecedented*.

せんれい 洗礼 (a) baptism; (洗礼・命名式) (a) christening /krísnɪŋ/. ●洗礼者ヨハネ John the Baptist. ▶私は5歳のときキリスト教の洗礼を受けた I received Christian *baptism* [*was baptized* a Christian] when I was five years old. ▶まだ文明の洗礼を受けない種族がいる There are still tribes who *know nothing of* civilization.
●洗礼名 one's Christian [baptismal] name. (❗通例 first [given] name という)

せんれい 鮮麗 ●鮮麗な色彩 a *bright* [《鮮やかな》a *vivid*] color.

ぜんれい 全霊 ●入試の準備に全霊を傾ける *devote oneself heart and soul to* preparing for the entrance exam.

ぜんれい 前例 a precedent. (⇒先例)

ぜんれき 前歴 war experience; war service.

ぜんれき 前歴 〖過去の経歴・履歴〗one's past record [history]; 〖一身上の経歴・履歴〗one's personal record [history]; 〖人の過去〗one's past (❗a past は「いかがわしい過去」をさす). ●いかがわしい前歴の女 a woman with *a past*. ●彼の前歴を調べる check [《たどって調べる》trace] his *past record*. ▶彼の前歴を何かご存じですか Do you know anything of his *past* [his *personal record*]?

せんれつ 戦列 a battle line, a line of battle. ●戦列に加わる[を離れる] join [leave] the *line* 《*of battle*》. ●戦列を維持する hold *the line*. ▶エースが戦列を離脱した[に復帰した] The ace left the team [returned to the lineup].

せんれつ 鮮烈 ●鮮烈な印象を与える make a *vivid* [《際立った》a *striking*] impression 《*on* him》.

せんれつ 前列 the front row [rank]. (❗後の方は主に兵隊・タクシーの列についていう) ●前列に座る[席をとる] sit [take a seat] in the *front row*. ●前列の左から3番目の学生 the third student from the left in the *front row*.

せんれん 洗練 ●洗練された話し方 a *refined* [a *sophisticated*, 《優雅な》an *elegant*] way of speaking. ●非常に洗練された(=磨きのかかった)演奏[演技]をする give a very *polished* performance. ●服装が洗練されている be *refined in* dress; 《着こなしも含めて》be *elegantly* dressed.

***せんろ** 線路 a (railroad 《米》[railway 《主に英》]) track [line] (❗枕木・バラスなども含む); rails (❗通例レールそのものをさす). ▶線路を横断するな Don't cross a (*railroad*) *track*. ▶彼女の家は線路ぎわにある Her house is right by the *railroad track*.
●線路工事 《線路敷設》tracklaying; 《補修など》track maintenance [repairing]. ●線路作業員 《米》a trackman; 《英》a platelayer. (❗敷設と補修を行う)

ぜんろう 全聾 ▶彼は全聾だ He is *totally deaf*.

せんろっぽん 千六本 ●大根を千六本に切る cut a radish into *long thin strips*.

ぜんわん 前腕 the forearm.
●前腕骨 〖解剖〗the antebrachial bone.

そ

そ 祖 〖祖先〗an ancestor; (父ён)《書》forefather; 〖始めた人〗(先駆者) an originator, a father; (創設者) a founder. ● 英詩の祖チョーサー Chaucer, the *father* of English poetry.

そ 粗 (粗い) rough, coarse; (未精製の) unrefined.

-ぞ さあ行くぞ Now, let's ╱go.(❗上昇調で読むことで強調を表す)｜しっかり見張りをしてるんだぞ *Be sure* to keep watch!

そあく 粗悪 ── 粗悪な 〖 poor, bad* (❗後の方が口語的); (より劣った) inferior.
● 粗悪品 goods of poor [bad, inferior] quality; poor [bad] quality goods.

そあん 素案 a rough plan [draft]. ● 素案を示す give a *rough* [a *working*] *draft*; give a *plan in draft*.

-ぞい -沿い 〖…沿いの[を]〗along…. ● 道沿いの家 houses *along* the street; a house *on* the street. (❗*on* は「…に面した」の意) ● 海沿いの暖かい場所で a warm place *by* the sea. ● 川沿いの(道)を歩く walk *along* (the road *next to*) the river.

そいそしょく 粗衣粗食 (質素な生活) a simple [a plain] life. ● 粗衣粗食に甘んじている be content [contented] with one's *simple life*; be under poor living conditions.

そいつ 〖人〗that fellow [man], 《米話》that guy, 《英話》that chap; 〖物・事〗that, (❗*that* の方が指示性が強い). ● そいつを捕まえてくれ Catch [Stop] *that fellow!* ｜ そいつはすばらしい That's great [wonderful]!

そいとげる 添い遂げる ❶〖一生夫婦でいる〗live all one's lives as man and wife; live together till death them [us] do part (❗till 以下は結婚式での誓いの言葉から). ❷〖困難を乗り越えて夫婦になる〗● 彼らは双方の両親の猛反対を押し切って添い遂げた They *got married* though their parents strongly opposed their marriage.

そいね 添い寝 ── 添い寝する 動 lie* by the side of (one's baby); sleep* with (one's baby).

そいん 素因 〖おおもとの原因〗the primary cause [factor, reason]; 〖病気にかかりやすい素質〗〖医学〗a predisposition *(to)*. ● この子にはぜんそくの素因がある This child *is predisposed* to asthma.

そいん 訴因 〖法律〗a charge; (訴因項目) a count. ● 訴因の認否を問う arraign 《him》on the *charge* 《*of* murder》.

そいんすう 素因数 〖数学〗a prime factor.
● 素因数分解 factorization in prime numbers.

:そう ❶〖前述の内容をさして〗(a)〖語・句・節の代用として〗so; it; that.

> **解説** (1) so は「そのように」の意で, it, that などが漠然としており, 話し手の消極的な態度を暗示する語. 次のような用法がある: (ⅰ) 思考を表す think, hope, believe, suppose, imagine,《主に米語》guess, expect, fear, presume, reckon, be afraid など, 発話を表す say, tell 《him》などの後で, that の代わりに目的語として用い, (ⅱ) so の形で先行する動詞句の代わりにも用いる. 主に堅い言い方で用いられ, 副詞相当語句を従えることが多い. 通例主語の意志による行動について用い, like, remember, think, fall, lose などの代用としては用いない.
>
> (ⅲ) seem, appear, remain, find, be, become などの補語〖目的格〗補語として先行する形容詞・名詞の代わりに用いる. (ⅳ) believe, gather, hear, notice, see, understand; say, tell 《him》; it seems [appears] so などの場合, so を主節の前に置いて自分の意見の根拠が別にあることを示すことがある.
> (2) **it** は先行する名詞・代名詞・文の内容などをはっきりと指し示し, so より話し手の積極的な態度を暗示する. **that** は it とほぼ同様に用いられ, it より強意的.

▶ 彼は1人でそこへ行くと言った. しかも自信を持ってそう言った He said he would go there alone, and he said *so* [(そのことを) *it*, (そのことは) *that*] confidently. (❗(1) *so* を用いると話し手の不満を暗示することがある. (2) *that* は他にいろいろ言ったことの対照を強調する) ▶ そう言ったじゃないか(=それごらん) I ＼told you *só*. [×told *so*]. (⇨それ 圏) ▶ たぶんそうだろう Perhaps [Probably] *so* (↔not). (❗(1) 後の方が確率が高い. 単に Perhaps./Probably. ですますことも多い. (2) Ábsolutely [Súrely] ＼*not* (×so). のように高い確信を示す場合は, もなじくぜ [(話) I bét] it ＼is./It ＼must be. などを用いる)/ *That* ＼may be (❗, but …). ▶ 彼女はとても怒っていた. 顔にそう書いてあった She was very angry. She looked *it* (×so). ▶ 彼女は私に二度とそうしないと約束した She promised me not to do *so* [*that*, *it*] again. ▶ カンニングをしたって？もしそうなら彼を合格させるわけにはいかない He cheated? If *so* (↔not) [(それが事実なら) If such is the case, If that is true], I can't pass him. ▶ そうとは知らなかった I didn't know *that* [*it*, ×so]. ▶ そう言って彼は部屋を出て行った With ＼*that*, he left the room.

会話「なに, この札は偽物だって？」「残念ながらそうみたいです」"What? Is this bill a counterfeit?" "I'm afraid *so*./I regret *so*." (❗regret は後に続く部分が事実であることを前提とする場合は I regret *it*. で「それは残念ですね」の意になる)

会話「彼はあす来ると思いますか」「そう思います」"Do you think he will come tomorrow?" "I ˇthink *so* [×it, ×that]." (❗否定的に「そうは思いません」とる答える場合は I don't think *so*., I think ＼not. の両方が可能だが, 前の方が穏やかで普通の言い方)

会話「あすは降らない[降る]と思うわ」「そうだといいね」"I don't think [I think] it will rain tomorrow." "I ˇhope *nót* [*so*]." (❗I hope not. の代わりに ×I don't hope so. とはいわない. 同様のことが be afraid, fear, guess, gather などについてもいえる)

会話「車で行くのはどうと思うね」「私もそう思うわ(=同感だわ)」"I don't think it's a good idea to go by car." "I *agree* (*with* you)." (❗日本語にひかれて ×I think *so*, too. とはいわない)

会話「彼は準備ができていますか」「そうみたいですね」"Is he ready?" "It appears [seems] *so*./*So* it appears [seems]." (❗「そうとは思われませんね」なら It doesn't appear [seem] *so*./It appears [seems] not./×So it doesn't appear [seem].)

会話「あの人は70を越えているのよ」「そうは見えないや」"He is over seventy." "He doesn't look *it* [×so, ×like it, ×one]."

会話「彼らはあす出発します」「そうらしいですね」

"They're leaving tomorrow." "*So* I've heard [I hear]." (❗この用法は think, hope, suppose などには不可. 否定の形も不可: ×*So* I've not heard.)
会話 「君はすごくついてるね」「みんなにそう言われるよ」 "Aren't you ＼*lucky*!" "*That's* what everybody says." (❗Everybody says *so*. より強調的)
会話 「ぼくのグローブどこか知らない?」「これがそう?」 "Can you see my glove anywhere?" "Is this *the one* (you're looking for)?" (❗これに対する答えは ＼That's *it*. (そうなの?) などという)
(b)【同様】(同じこと) the same; (...も同様である) So ＋励＋主語 (❗先行文が肯定文の場合); Nor＋励＋主語 (❗先行文が否定の場合). (⇨立 ❶ 解説) ▶日本でもそうだといいねI wish I could say the *same* for Japan.
会話 「野球は大好きだ」「私もそうよ」 "I'm ＼crazy about baseball." "Í am, ＼*too*./Só am ＼I./《話》Me *too*."/"I really love baseball." "Í do, ＼*too*./Só do ＼I./《話》Me, *too*." (❗《話》では Same here! とも)
会話 「泳げないんだ」「私もそうなの」 "I can't swim." "I cán't, ＼*either*./*Néither* can ＼I./*Nór* can ＼I./《話》Me *neither*./《話》Nor me."
(c)【接続詞的に】● そうすると (⇨そうすると) ● そうしたら (⇨そしたら) ● それが難しいことは分かっているが、そうは言っても(＝しかしまた一方ではやらざるをえないことも確かだ I know it's difficult *but then* [だがたとえそうでも] *but even so*] I also know I must try.
❷【返答、あいづち】(肯定) yes; (否定の疑問に対して) no. (⇨いいえ, はい)
会話 「あれはあなたのノートですか」「そうです」 "Is that your notebook?" "*Yes*, it [×that] *is*." (❗単に Yes. あるいは It is. というう)
会話 「あまり混んでいないね」「そう」 "It isn't so ＼crowded, ＼is it?" "*No*." (❗Yes といわないことに注意)
会話 「田中君じゃないかい」「ええ、そう(＝そのとおり)です」 "Aren't you Tanaka?" "Yes, *that's* ＼*right*."
会話 「彼は英語を話すのが実にうまいね」「本当にそうですね」 "He speaks very good English." "*Só* he ＼*does*./He *dóes*, ＼*indeed*!/＼*Indeed*, he *dóes*!"/"Isn't he so good at English?" "*Yes*, ＼*isn't he*!" (❗感嘆の気持ちを表す応答 (⇨なんと))
会話 「あの人いい人みたいね」「ええ、そうよ」 "He seems nice." "Yes, I ＼*know*." (❗「そうかなあ」なら Oh, I don't know.)
会話 「彼は来ないと思うわ」「そうですか」 "I'm afraid he won't come [I don't think he will come]." "＼*Won't he*?" (❗(1) ×Are you?, ×Do [Don't] you? とはしないことに注意. (2) 音調 ＼は冷静な反応でこれを低い調子で言うと「そうかしら」といった不賛成や疑いの気持ちを含む. 一方、小幅の下降調 ＼は「あっそう」といった無関心を、大幅の ＼、および語末を変えて Óh he ＼won't. やさらに短く ／No? は興味深さ・驚き、意外さを伝える. (3) 他に、「本当ですか」という驚きや疑いには Is that so [right]?/Really?, 「そうですか(なるほど)そうですか」と納得するときは I see も用いる)
❸【程度】so,《話》that. (⇨そんなに, それほど)
会話 「疲れた?」「そうでもないや」 "Are you tired?" "Not ＼*really* [＼*very*]."
❹【思案、ためらい】▶そうですね(＝おおよそのところを言えば)、50 人ほど出席していました There were, (*let's*) *say*, fifty people present. (❗数詞の前に挿入する. ほかに「具体的に言えば」の意で具体例の直前にも用いる (⇨会話 [第 2 例]))
会話 「どの燃料がいいと思いますか」「そうですね、石油がいちばん安上がりですか」 "Which fuel would you advise?" "＼*Well* [*Let me* ＼*see, Well, let's* ＼*see*], oil's the cheapest." (❗いずれもやや下降調で)
会話 「木曜日はだめなんだ」「じゃほかにというと、そうだなあ、土曜日は都合つくかな」"Thursday is impossible." "Well then, can you make it another time, *say*, Saturday?"
❺【その他の表現】 ▶(ああ)そうそう思い出した (⇨ああ 圖 ❷ 〔第 2 文例〕) ▶そうかそれで分かった *Now* I *understand* [×*understood*]. ▶そうだ, いい考えが浮かんだ I've just had a good idea!(⇨こうしよう) Tell you what. (❗この後に具体的な提案が続く)
● そうは問屋がおろさない You're [That's] expecting too much./You'll never get away with it.

そう 壮 ▶壮とする admire [respect]《one's dignified attitude》; approve of《one's highly-motivated ambition》.

そう 相 〚内容を表す姿〛(ある一面から見た姿) an aspect;《人相》looks,《書》physiognomy (⇨人相); 〚現れては消える姿〛a phase. ● 言語の諸相 *aspects* of language. ● 世相の一つ an *aspect* [a *phase*] of everyday life. ▶氷は水の一つの相である Ice is a *phase* of water.

そう 僧 a (Buddhist) priest; 〚修道僧〛a monk; 〚尼僧〛a nun.

そう 層 a layer; 〚地層・社会の〛a stratum (腹 strata, 〜s); 〚所得層などの〛a bracket. ● 粘土の層 a *layer* of clay. ● 年齢層 an age group [《まれ》 *bracket*]. ● 低[高額, 中]所得者層 the low-[high-; middle-] income *bracket*. ● 層状に in *layers*. ● 投手層を厚くする increase pitching depth. ▶このケーキは 4 層だ This cake has four *layers*. ▶この本は若い読者層が対象だ This book is intended for young readers. ▶我がチームは選手の層が厚い Our team has depth [in deep].

そう 躁 (⇨躁病) ▶躁状態にある be in a *manic* state.

そう 沿う, 添う ❶〚…に沿って〛along .... (⇨沿い) ▶道路は線路に沿って走っている The road runs *along* [(平行して) *parallel to*, (脇を) *by the side of*] the railroad track. ● 既定方針に沿って(＝従って)行動せよ Act *according to* [*in accordance with*] the prearranged plan.
❷【期待などに添う】come* up to ..., live up to ...; (必要・要求などに応じる) meet*. (⇨期待) ▶彼女は彼らの期待に添うよう努力した She tried to *come up to* [*live up to*] their expectations. ▶ご希望に沿うよう努力はいたしますがお約束はできません I'll try to *meet* your wishes, but I can't promise anything.

そう 総ー 〚総体の, 総計の〛total, gross; 〚一般の, 全体的な〛general. ● 総人口 the *total* population《*of*》. ● 総所得 a *gross* income. ● 総選挙 a *general* election. ● 総支配人 a *general* manager.

-そう -双 ● 六曲のびょうぶ一双 a pair of six-panel *byoubu*.

-そう -走 ● 50 メートル走 the 50 meter *sprint* [《主に米》*dash, race*].

-そう -葬 ● 社葬を執り行う hold [conduct] a company funeral 《for Mr. A》.

-そう -艘 ● 1 艘の船 a ship, a boat. ● 2 艘の船 two ships [boats]. (❗艘に当たる英語はないので数詞で表す)

ぞう 象 〚動物〛an elephant (腹 〜s,《集合的》〜). ● 雄[雌]の象 a bull [a cow] *elephant*. ● 子象 a calf *elephant*. ● 象の群れ a herd of *elephants*. ▶象は鼻が長い The *elephant* has a long trunk [×nose].

ぞう 像 (姿) an image /imidʒ/; (彫像) a statue; (画像) a picture; (肖像) a portrait. ● 石[木]像 a

stone [a wooden] *statue*. ●鏡に映る像 a mirror *image*; an *image [reflection]* in the mirror. ●未来像 a vision. ●彼の描いた現代の若者像 his *portrayal* of present-day young people. (⇒描写) ●像を建てる put up [《書》erect] a *statue*. ●像を刻む carve an *image (in* stone). ●像を結ぶ focus into an *image*. ●像を投影する throw a *picture* [an *image*] 《on a screen》.

ぞう 増 (⇒増加) ●32ページ増 an *increase* of 32 pages. ●売り上げ15パーセント増 a 15 percent *increase [rise]* in sales.

-ぞう -蔵 徳川家蔵の古文書 old documents in the *possession of* [which belong to, which are the property of] the Tokugawa family.

そうあい 相愛 mutual love. ●相思相愛 (⇒相思相愛)

そうあたり 総当たり a round-robin (tournament [competition]). (関連 勝ち抜き戦 a knockout (tournament))

そうあん 草案 a draft. ●演説の草案を書く make out a *draft* of a speech; draft a speech.

そうあん 草庵 a thatched house.

そうあん 創案 图 an original idea; (an) invention.
── **創案する** 動 think* up a new idea [way]; invent.

そうい 相違 图 〖差異〗(a) difference; (対比的に) a contrast; 〖区別, 差別〗(a) distinction; 〖意見・考えなどの不一致〗(a) disagreement. (❗いずれの語も具体的には C)(⇒違い)
① 【〜の相違】 ●外観[質]の相違 a *difference in* appearance [quality]. ●詩と散文との相違 the *distinction between* poetry and prose. ▶両親と私の間には価値観の相違があります My parents and I have *different* values./I have a *different* set of values from my parents.
② 【相違が[は]】 ▶その2か国語の間にはあまり相違(点)がない There are not many *differences* [There is not much *difference] between* the two languages. (❗「相違がない」なら, There is no *difference* between ...) ▶この点で我々は[3人の間では大きな意見の相違がある There are great [big] *differences of* opinion between us [among the three of us] on this point.
③ 【相違点】 ●相違を生む make a *difference*.
④ 【相違ない】 ▶上記のとおり相違ありません I *affirm* the above to be *correct* and *correct* in every particular. (❗書類など) ▶あの男がそれを盗んだに相違ない That man *must* have stolen it. (⇒違いない)
── **相違する** 動 differ, be different《from》. (⇒違う①)

そうい 創痍 a wound; a scar. ●満身創痍 (⇒満身[成句])

そうい 創意 (新しい考え) a new [(発明的な) an inventive, (独創的な) a creative, an original] idea. ●創意に富んだ inventive; original; creative. ●創意工夫を生かす use an *inventive* idea.

そうい 僧衣 a Buddhist monk's [priest's] robe.

そうい 総意 国民の総意(=意志) the will [《意見の一致》consensus] of the people [the nation]; the national will [consensus].

そういう 〖そのような〗such, ... like that; 〖その〗that; 〖その種の〗that kind of .... (⇒そんな) ▶そういうことだ (話の最後で) That's it. ▶それはそういう問題じゃないのだ (=それとは関係ない) That has nothing to do with it./(それは肝心のことなどではない) That's not the point.

そういえば ▶そういえば(=それで思い出したが)彼の息子も教師だった *That reminds* [×reminded] *me*. His son was a teacher, too. (⇒それで) ▶そういえば思い当たることがあるよ *That reminds me* of something. ▶それでは少し顔色が悪いね(=顔色が悪いのはそういう理由によると分かった) *I see, that's why* you look a little pale.
会話 「お腹がすいているだろうと思ってサンドイッチを持ってきたわ」「そういえばほんとぺこぺこだ」"Perhaps you're hungry. I've brought some sandwiches." "*Come [Now (that) I come]* to think of it, yes, I'm starving."

そういん 僧院 (主に男子の修道院) a mónastery; (尼僧院) a cónvent. ●僧院の生活を送る lead a *religious* life [a life of a *religious*]. (❗ a religious は「修道士[女]」の意)

そういん 総員 a total membership; the entire strength; (乗船全員) all hands. (⇒全員) ●総員1万人の組織 an organization with a *total membership* of ten thousand.

ぞういん 増員 图 an increase of the staff; a staff expansion.
── **増員する** 動 ●スタッフを10人に[3人]増員する *increase* [*enlarge*] *the staff to* ten [*by* three].

そううつびょう 躁鬱病 〖医学〗 a manic-depressive illness; manic depression.
●躁鬱病患者 a manic-depressive.

そううん 層雲 〖気象〗 a stratus /strétrəs/ (複 strati /-tai/).

ぞうえい 造営 图 construction; building. ●造営中の新宮殿 the new palace *under construction*.
── **造営する** 動 construct; build*.

ぞうえいざい 造影剤 〖医学〗 a contrast medium.

ぞうえき 増益 profit increase; an advance [an increase] in profits [earnings]. ●増収増益 increase both in sales and profit. ▶その会社は今年大幅な増益となるだろう The company will *earn* significant *profits* this year.
●増益率 the rate of profit increase.

そうえん 桑園 a mulberry orchard [farm, plantation].

ぞうえん 造園 图 landscape gardening.
── **造園する** 動 (庭を設計する) lay* out a garden.
●造園家 a landscape gardener; a garden designer.

ぞうえん 増援 ── **増援する** 動 reinforce /rìːnfɔ́ːrs/.
●増援 reinforcements. (❗複数扱い)

ぞうお 憎悪 图 (a) hatred; detestation; loathing. (❗順に意味が強くなる)
── **憎悪する** 動 hate, have* a hatred 《for》; detest; loathe. ●憎悪すべき犯罪 a *hateful* [a *detestable*, 《書》 a *loathsome*] crime.

そうおう 相応 ── **相応の** 形 〖ふさわしい〗(事情などに) suitable 《for》; (目的などにぴったり) fit 《for》; 〖似つかわしい〗becoming 《to》; 〖妥当な〗adequate 《to》. ●年相応にふるまう act one's age. ▶彼女はその場に相応した服装をしていた She was wearing clothes *suitable for* the occasion. ▶彼の態度は紳士に不相応だ His attitude is not *becoming to* a gentleman. ▶彼は仕事相応の賃金をもらっている He gets (×an) *adequate* pay for his work. ▶彼らは身分相応の(=収入の範囲内の)家を見つけた They found a house *within* (↔beyond) *their income*. (《やや書》 *means*).
会話 「これはもうひとつだね」「まあ, 値段相応ってとこかな」"This isn't really very good." "Well, you get what you pay for."

そうおん 騒音 (a) noise; (打ち続く大きくて不快で) a din. (⇒音(⁂)) ●町[隣]の騒音に悩まされる be annoyed by street *noises* [the *noise(s)* next door]. ●都会の騒音(=喧噪(⁂)) the din (and

そうか bustle) of the city. ▶彼女は通りを走る車の騒音がいやだった She didn't like the *noise* from the cars in the road. ▶このあたりは騒音がひどい There is a lot of *noise* [a terrible *din*] around here. ▶あまり騒音を立てないように気をつけなさい Take care not to make so much *noise*. ▶騒音で彼の言うことが聞きとれなかった I couldn't hear him through all the *noises* [over the *din*].
●騒音公害 noise pollution.

そうか 喪家 a family in mourning.

そうが 爪牙 claws and fangs.
▶爪牙にかかる(えじきになる) fall (a) victim [a sacrifice] 《*to*》; fall into the clutches 《*of*》.

そうが 挿画 an illustration. (⇨挿し絵)

***ぞうか** 増加 图 〖数量の〗 (an) increase; 〖伸び〗 (a) growth; 〖上昇〗 (a) rise; 〖重量・能力などの〗 a gain. ●人口の急激な増加 a sudden *increase* [*growth, rise*] *in* 〖×of〗 population. (❗「人口の爆発的増加」は a population explosion) ▶体重の増加 a *gain in* weight. ▶生産高は先月に比べ10パーセントの増加(量)を示している The production shows a 10 percent *increase* [an *increase* of 10 percent] over last month. (❗「先月に比べて」は as compared with *that* of last month ともいえるが, over *that of* last month も可) ▶犯罪が増加の一途をたどっている(=着実な増加がある) There is a steady *increase in* crime./Crime *is increasing* steadily.

── 増加する 動 incréase. (⇨増える) ▶その町の人口は増加している The population of the town *is increasing* [*on the increase*]. (❗ on the increase は every year などの時の副詞とともには用いない)/The town *is increasing* in population. ▶日常会話では The town's population is becoming larger and larger. などということも多い ▶会員数は500人[5割]増加した The membership *has increased by* 500 [(*by*) 50 percent]. (❗(1)「5割」は by half も可. (2)「500人に」なら …*to* 500)

DISCOURSE
しかし実際, CO_2 レベルはこの数年で急激に増加したした (But) **as a matter of fact**, CO_2 levels have **risen** sharply in the past few years. (❗ as a matter of fact (実際)は主張を表すディスコースマーカー. 統計など, 事実に基づく主張に用いる)

●増加率 the rate of increase.

ぞうか 造化 God's creation; nature. ●造化の妙 the wonders of nature. ●造化の神(=造物主) the Creator.

ぞうか 造花 an artificial [an imitation,《古》a made] flower.

そうかい 壮快 ── 壮快な 形 (気力の充実した) full of vigor; energetic; 《気色の高揚した》stirred.

そうかい 掃海 ●掃海艇 a minesweeper.

そうかい 爽快 refreshment. ●爽快な朝の空気 *refreshing* [*bracing*] morning air. ▶気分爽快だ I feel *refreshed* [*fresh and fit*]. (❗後の方が口語的. ×refreshing は不可)

そうかい 総会 a general meeting [assembly] (❗後の方は正式);〖書〗a plenary /plíːnəri/ session (❗有権者全員出席の). ●株主総会 a *general meeting* of stockholders. ●国連総会 the United Nations *General Assembly*.
●総会屋 a sokaiya; a (corporate) racketeer.

そうがい 窓外 ▶窓外の景色をぼんやり眺めている *gaze out the window* blankly.

そうがい 霜害 frost damage. ●ひどい霜害をこうむる suffer badly from frost; be badly damaged by frost.

そうがかり 総掛かり ▶子供たちは総掛かりで(=皆いっしょになって)お相撲さんに飛びかかった The children ran at the sumo wrestler *all together* [(一団となって) *in a body, in one body*]. ▶総掛かりでピアノを動かした Working *together*, we were able to move the piano./We *combined* our *efforts* to move the piano.

そうかく 総画 ●総画索引 an index by stroke counts. ●総画数 a total stroke count 《*of* Kanji》.

そうがく 奏楽 (演奏)a musical performance;(音楽)music.

そうがく 総額 〖合計, 計〗the total, the sum (total);〖全体の額〗the total amount [sum]. ●売り上げ〖受注〗総額 *total* sales [orders]. ●損害総額 the *total* loss. ●総額1,000万円の小切手 checks for a *total* of ten million yen. ▶総額いくらになりますか What is *the total*?/What does *the total* come to?/(全部でいくらか) How much is it *altogether* [*in all*]? ●総額100万円になった The *total* (*amount*) came to one million yen./It *totaled* (*up to*) one million yen.

ぞうがく 増額 图 (増加) (an) increase 《*in*》. ●賃金の増額を要求する demand a wage *increase* [an *increase* in wages]; demand a (pay) raise 《米》[rise 《英》].

── 増額する 動 (増す)increase;(上げる)raise.

そうかつ 総括 图 〖まとめ〗a summary; 〖反省〗a review.

── 総括的な 形 overall.

── 総括する 動 ▶その討論を総括する make a *summary* [a *review*] of the discussion; *sum up* the discussion.

●総括質問 (国会の) an overall interpellation /ɪntərpeléɪʃən/.

ぞうがめ 象亀 〖動物〗an elephant [an elephantine] tortoise.

そうかん 壮観 〖壮大な眺め〗a grand sight [view]; (雄大さ)《やや書》grandeur /ɡrǽndʒɚ/; 《目をみはらせる光景》a spectacle. ●ロッキー山脈の壮観 the *grandeur* of the Rockies. ●ハリウッドスターたちがあれだけ揃うのは壮観だ The galaxy of Hollywood stars *is absolutely wonderful*.

そうかん 相姦 (an) adultery. ●近親相姦《commit》incest 《*with*》.

そうかん 相関 ── 相関的な 形 correlative.
●相関関係 (a) correlation 《*with, between*》. ●相関関係がある have a《high》*correlation*《*with*》;《highly》correlate《*with, to*》.

そうかん 送還 ── 送還する 動 (送り返す) send* … back; (捕虜などを本国へ) repatriate /riːpéɪtrieɪt/. ▶…を本国へ(強制)送還する (forcibly) *send …home* [*back*]; *repatriate …* (forcibly).

そうかん 創刊 ── 創刊する 動《a new magazine》. ▶この雑誌は1930年に創刊された This magazine *was first published* [*issued*] in 1930.
●創刊号 the first issue [number].

そうかん 総監 a superintendent-general (⟨複⟩ superintendents-). ●警視総監 the *Superintendent General* (of the Metropolitan Police).

ぞうかん 増刊 图 ●『ヴォーグ』の夏季増刊号 a *special* summer *issue* [*number, edition*] of "Vogue" (magazine).

── 増刊する 動 issue an extra number.

ぞうがん 象眼 图 (an) inlay.

── 象眼する 動 inláy*. ▶金で象眼した箱 a box *inlaid with* gold; a box *with* gold *inlay*.

そうがんきょう ●象眼細工 inlay; inlaid work.
そうがんきょう 双眼鏡 binoculars /báinəkjələrz/; (携帯用小型の) field glasses; (劇場用の) opera glasses. (❗数えるときは a pair [two pairs] of ~ を用いる) ●双眼鏡で鳥を見る watch birds through *binoculars* [*field glasses*].

そうき 早期 图 an early stage.
— **早期の** 形 early. ●早期診断, 早期発見 *early* diagnosis and detection 《*of*》. ●問題の早期解決を目指す try to solve the problem *as soon as possible*. ▶早期のがんは治る Cancer can be cured *in its early stages* [*at an early stage*, 早く見つかれば] if it is found soon enough.

そうき 想起 —— **想起する** 動 recall, 《書》bring* [call]... to mind. (⇨囲 思い起こす)

そうき 総記 (図書分類法の) general works.

***そうぎ 葬儀** a funeral (service); funeral rites. ●仏式の葬儀 a *funeral* in Buddhist rites. ●火災の犠牲者の合同葬儀 a mass *funeral for* the fire victims. ●葬儀の参列者[しきたり] *funeral* attendants [customs]. ●葬儀の列 a *funeral* procession. ●葬儀に出る attend a *funeral* 《*service*》. ▶彼の葬儀は厳粛に執り行われた His *funeral* was solemnly held [performed, conducted].
●葬儀場 a funeral home, 《英》a funeral parlor.
●葬儀屋(人) an úndertaker (❗以下の二つはその婉曲語); 《やや書》a funeral director, 《米》a mortician; (店) an úndertaker's (office), a funeral parlor [《米》home], 《米》a (mortuary) chapel. (❗後はむ婉曲的. 遺体を安置し, そこで葬儀を行うこともある)

そうぎ 争議 [『労働争議』] a labor dispute; [『ストライキ』] a strike, a walkout. ●争議権を求めて交渉する negotiate for the right to *strike*. ●争議を起こす[解決する] start [settle] a *dispute*. ▶賃上げを要求して争議が起こった A *dispute* arose for higher wages.

ぞうき 臓器 internal organs. ●人工臓器 artificial (internal) organs.
●臓器移植 an (internal) organ transplant.
●臓器提供者 a donor.

ぞうきばやし 雑木林 a copse, 《主に英》a coppice; [『低木の茂み』] a thicket.

そうきゅう 早急 —— **早急な** 形 (即座の) immediate; (敏速な) prompt; (行動が素早い) quick; (差し迫った) urgent. ●早急な処置 *immediate* [*prompt*] treatment.
— **早急に** 副 (直ちに) immediately; (間をおかずに) without delay; (緊急に) urgently; (素早く) quickly. ▶この問題に早急に取り組まなければならない We must deal with this problem *immediately*. / This problem demands our *immediate* attention. ▶早急に金が要る I need some money *urgently*.

そうきゅう 送球 图 『野球』a throw. ●送球エラー a *throwing* error.
— **送球(を)する** 動 ●一塁へ悪送球をする make a bad [a wild] *throw* to first (base). ●二塁へ送球するランナーを刺す *throw* out a runner at second base. ●捕手へワンバウンドのストライク送球をする *throw* a one-hop stirke to the catcher.

そうきゅうきん 双球菌 a diplococcus (圏 -cocci).

そうきょ 壮挙 (偉大な仕事) great work; a great undertaking; (勇気ある企て) a heroic [a daring] attempt. ●サハラ砂漠徒歩横断の壮挙を成し遂げて succeed in a *great undertaking* to walk across the Sahara.

そうぎょ 草魚 『魚介』a grass carp (圏 ~, ~s).

そうぎょう 早暁 (a) dawn. (⇨囲 明け方, 夜明け)

そうぎょう 創業 图 [『創立』] foundation; [『設立』] establishment. ●1881年創業 *Established* 1881; *Since* 1881. ▶来年我が社は創業10周年を祝う Next year our company will celebrate the tenth anniversary of its *foundation* [*establishment*].
— **創業する** 動 found; establish; (事業を始める) start business.
●創業者 a founder.

そうぎょう 僧形 the appearance of a Buddhist monk [priest].

そうぎょう 操業 图 operation(s). (❗しばしば複数形で) ●工場の操業を開始する[停止する] begin [suspend] *operations* at the plant. ●沖合で操業中の漁船 a fishing boat *working* [*operating*] off the coast. ●工場は完全操業中です The factory is *in full operation*.
— **操業する** 動 operate; (工場などを動かす) run*. ▶彼らは24時間操業をしている They *operate* on a twenty-four hour basis.
●操業時間 operating hours. ●操業短縮 the reduction [curtailment] of operations; (生産減) a cutback in production. ●操業率 the rate of operation.

ぞうきょう 増強 图 [『補強』] reinforcement; [『強化』] strengthening; (力の) a build-up; [『増大』] (an) increase.
— **増強する** 動 ●兵力を増強する *reinforce* troops; *build up* military strength. ●体力を増強する *strengthen* oneself; *build up* one's strength.
●生産を増強する *increase* [*boost (up)*] production.

そうきょういく 早教育 (就学前教育)《give one's child》a preschool education.

そうきょく 筝曲 *koto* music; (1曲) a *koto* piece.

そうきょく 総局 a head office.

そうきょくせん 双曲線 『数学』a hypérbola (圏 ~s, hyperbolae); a hyperbolic curve.

そうぎり 総桐 ●総桐のたんす a chest of drawers [《米》bureau] made of paulownia wood.

そうきん 送金 图 remittance; (送金額)《書》a remittance.
— **送金する** 動 《書》remit, send* [make*] (a) remittance; send money. ●支払いを小切手で送金する *remit* payment by check. ▶私は時々息子にわずかの送金をしてやります I sometimes *send* my son a small *remittance* [a small amount of *money*].
●送金為替 a remittance bill; bank remittance.
●送金小切手 a remittance check. ●送金手数料 a remittance charge. ●送金人 a remitter.

ぞうきん 雑巾 (ほこり用の) a duster, a dustcloth; (床用の) a floorcloth; (柄つきの) a mop. ●雑巾がけをする wipe [clean] 《it》with a *duster* [a *mop*]; mop.

そうく 痩躯 a thin [a lean] figure [body]. (⇨痩身)
●長身痩躯の老人 a *lean* and tall older man.

そうぐ 葬具 a funeral outfit.

そうぐ 装具 equipment; (用具一式) an outfit. ●登山装具を点検する check if one is properly equipped [*fitted out*] for mountain climbing.

そうぐう 遭遇 —— **遭遇する** 動 (事故・困難・敵などに) meet* with ...,《書》encounter. ▶彼はスペインを旅行中に事故に遭遇した He *met with* [*had*] an accident while traveling in Spain. ▶彼は多くの困難に遭遇しながらも所期の目的を達成した He achieved his aim *though there were a number of*

そうくずれ 総崩れ 〖壊滅的敗走〗(a) rout /ráut/; 〖崩壊〗(a) collapse. ● 総崩れになる 《やや書》be routed; (敗走する) take (to) flight; (崩壊する) collapse completely.

そうくつ 巣窟 a den. ● 悪の巣窟 a den of iniquity. ● 盗賊の巣窟 a den of thieves.

そうぐるみ 総ぐるみ ▶ 私たちは家族総ぐるみで由美を歓待した All our family [All the members of our family] welcomed Yumi.

そうけ 宗家 〖本家〗the head family; 〖家元〗the head of a school.

そうげ 象牙 ivory. ● 象牙色の皮膚 an ivory skin.
● 象牙の塔 ・象牙の塔に閉じこもる be shut up in an ivory tower; (学究生活を送る) lead an academic life.
● 象牙細工 ivory work.

*****そうけい** 総計 the total, the sum, the sum total (⇨合計); 〖総額・量〗the total amount [sum]. ▶ 経費は総計3万円になる The total of our expenses is [comes to] 30,000 yen./Our expenses total 30,000 yen [are 30,000 yen in all].

そうけい 早計 ● 早計な(=性急な)決定 a hasty [a rash] decision.

そうげい 送迎 ▶ コンコースは送迎客でごった返していた The concourse was jammed with people who came to meet [welcome] or see [send] off passengers. ▶ うちの事務所ではお客の送迎用に車を買った Our office bought a car to pick up our customers and drive them home [to trasport our customers].
● 送迎デッキ (空港の) a send-off [an observation] deck. ● 送迎バス a pick-up bus; (学校の) a school bus; (ホテルなどの) a courtesy bus. (❗送迎バス運行) をさすときは ... bus service とする)

ぞうけい 造形 molding /móuldɪŋ/.
● 造形美術 the formative arts. (❗絵画と彫刻をさし、建築や工芸は含まない)

ぞうけい 造詣 ▶ 彼は英文学に造詣が深い He has a deep [a profound] knowledge of [(精通している) 《書》is well versed in] English literature.

ぞうげかいがん 象牙海岸 Ivory Coast. (⇨コートジボワール)

そうけだつ 総毛立つ ● 総毛立つような (身の毛のよだつ) hair-raising; (血も凍るような) blood-curdling; spine-chilling.

ぞうけつ 造血 blood producing [formation]; 〖医学〗hemopoiesis. ● 造血機能に障害がある have trouble with blood-producing functions.
● 造血器官 blood-producing [hemopoietic] organs. ● 造血剤 a blood-forming medicine; 〖医学〗a hematínic.

ぞうけつ 増血 an increase of blood.
● 増血剤 a blood-forming medicine; 〖医学〗a hematínic.

ぞうけつ 増結 ─ 増結する 動 add (to). ▶ この列車は高崎で3両増結します We will add three cars to this train at Takasaki./Three cars will be added to this train at Takasaki.

そうけっさん 総決算 (最後のしめくくり) (a) conclusion; (成果) the fruit(s). ▶ この本は彼の40年にわたる研究の総決算である This book concludes [is the fruits of, represents the culmination of] his forty-years' research.

そうけん 双肩 ● 双肩に掛ける (すべて…次第である) rest [fall] on one's shoulders.

● 双肩に担う (責任などを負う) carry [bear, have] (responsibilities) on one's shoulder.

そうけん 壮健 ─ 壮健な 形 (高齢者が健康で活動的な) hale and hearty 〖❗決まり文句〗, (very) healthy. ▶ ご壮健で何よりです I'm very glad (that) you're healthy [in good health].

そうけん 送検 ─ 送検する 動 ● 容疑者を送検する (= 裁判するために送る) commit a suspect for trial [(検察官へ) to the (public) prosecutor]. ● 書類送検する send case file to the prosecutor; file charges.

そうけん 創見 (新しい考え) a new idea; (独創的な考え) an original [a creative] idea.

そうけん 創建 ▶ 本寺は鎌倉時代初期の創建と伝えられている According to tradition, this temple was (first) built early in the Kamakura period. (❗first を入れると現在の寺は再建されたものということになる)

そうけん 総見 ▶ 歌舞伎座は初日の総見でにぎわった Members of fan clubs for their favorite actors rushed to the Kabuki-za Theatre on the opening day.

そうげん 草原 grassland, a grassy plain (❗(1) 2 語とも複数形で大草原の意. (2) 特定地域の草原に特定の語がある: the prairie(s) (北米), the pampas (南米), a steppe (シベリア), a savanna(h) (熱帯アフリカ), a veld (南アフリカ).

ぞうげん 増減 名 increase or [and] décrease. ▶ 私の収入はここ数年増減がない My income hasn't varied [has neither increased nor decreased] for the past few years. (❗後の方の対照強調によるアクセント移動に注意)
─ 増減する 動 incréase or [and] decréase; (変わる) vary; (変動する) fluctuate.

そうこ 倉庫 a warehouse (複 -houses /-zɪz, 《米》-sɪz/); a storehouse (❗《英》では主に「食糧倉庫」の意で用いるが 《やや古》) 〖書〗a depósitory. ● 貯蔵 [流通] 倉庫 a storage [a distribution] warehouse. ● 倉庫に預ける [保管する] put [store] (goods) in a warehouse. ▶ ハロッズの商品倉庫 Harrod's Depository. ▶ 売り上げが低迷し、売れ残った品が倉庫に山積みとなった Sluggish sales caused unsold goods to pile up at warehouses.
● 倉庫会社 a warehouse company. ● 倉庫係 a storekeeper; 《米》a stockman; a warehouseman. ● 倉庫業 warehousing. ● 倉庫業者 a warehouser.

*****そうご** 相互 ─ 相互の 形 mutual, 《書》reciprocal.
● 相互不可侵条約に調印する sign a mutual non-aggression pact. ● 国際交流は国家間の相互理解に役立つ International exchange promotes mutual understanding between [among] nations. (❗between は国と国との個別関係を, among では集合体としてとらえている)
─ 相互に 副 mutually, 《書》reciprocally. ▶ 彼らは相互に助け合った They gave mutual help to each other./They helped each other [one another]. (⇨互い) 解説
● 相互関係 a mutual [a reciprocal] relationship. ● 相互主義 mutualism; 《書》reciprocity.
● 相互通商協定 a reciprocal trade agreement.
● 相互乗り入れ two or more railway companies sharing tracks. ● 相互扶助 mutual [reciprocal] help. ● 相互貿易 a reciprocal [a two-way] trade. ● 相互保険 mutual insurance. ● 相互保険会社 a mutual insurance company.

ぞうご 造語 名 〖新語を作ること〗coinage; 〖造られた語句〗a coined word [phrase], 《書》a coin-

そうこう age.
── **造語する** 動 coin a word [a phrase].
● **造語成分** the smallest meaningful component [constituent] of a word.

そうこう ● そうこうするうちに in the meantime; meanwhile. ● 風が起こった。そうこうするうちに(=さほど間を置かずに)雨も降りだした The wind rose, and *it was not long* before the rain began to fall.

そうこう 走行 图 ● 走行中の moving. ▶危険ですから走行中は席を立たないでください Please don't leave your seats while we *are moving* [*running*]. It's dangerous.
── **走行距離** mileage /máilidʒ/. (**!** 走行距離の多い，少ないは high, low で表す) ▶この車の走行距離はどれくらいですか What's the *mileage* on this car?/ What *mileage* has this car done? ● **走行距離計** 《米》an odometer /oudámətər/; 《英》a mil(e)ometer. ● **走行車線** a cruising [a slow] lane.

そうこう 奏効 ▶その薬は彼女の頭痛には何の奏効もなかった The medicine *had* no *effect* on her headache.

そうこう 送稿 ── **送稿する** 動 send* one's manuscript 《*to*》.

そうこう 草稿 (下書き) a (rough) draft (**!** 《英》も同じつづり); (手書き・タイプなどの原稿) a manuscript. (⇨原稿) ● **草稿を書く** make a *draft* 《*of*》.

そうこう 糟糠 ● **糟糠の妻** one's wife who has shared joys and sorrows with him all through his life; one's life partner.

:そうごう 総合 图 (a) synthesis /sínθəsis/. (**!** 総合体[物]の意では [C] 《複 syntheses》) ● **総合優勝する** win the all-around competition.
── **総合的な** 形 synthetic; (全般的な) general; (全体的な) total; (包括的な，広範囲の) comprehensive. ● **総合的品質管理** total quality management 《略 TQC》.
── **総合する** 動 synthesize; (総合して考える) put*... together. ▶これらの要因を総合する *put* these factors *together*. ●(考慮する) take these factors *into consideration*. ▶彼の論文は総合するとよくできている(全体として見ると) His thesis is satisfactory [well written] *as a whole*. / (概して) *On the whole*, his thesis is satisfactory.
● **総合医療**[診療] comprehensive medical care. ● **総合開発** comprehensive development. ● **総合科学** a synthetic science. ● **総合科学技術会議** the Council for Science and Technology Policy. ● **総合学習** integrated studies. ● **総合課税** a general tax; comprehensive [consolidated] income taxation. ● **総合芸術** an integrated art project. ● **総合口座** a general cash account. ● **総合小売業** a general merchandise store 《略 GMS》. ● **総合雑誌** a general interest magazine. ● **総合収支** the total [overall] balance. ● **総合商社** a general trading company; a *sogo shosha*; (説明的に) a major Japanese company that trades internationally in a comprehensive range of goods. ● **総合職** the managerial [career, integrated] track; a career-track position. (関連) 一般職 the general track) ● **総合大学** a university. ● **総合調査** a comprehensive survey. ● **総合病院** a general hospital.

そうこう 相好 ● **相好を崩す** break into a smile 《*at* the offer》; grin; beam.

そうこうかい 壮行会 ● **壮行会を開く** have a send-off party [送別会]《書》a farewell party] 《*for* him》.

そうこうげき 総攻撃 ● **総攻撃をかける** make [launch] an *all-out attack* 《*against* the enemy》.

そうこうしゃ 装甲車 an armored car [《米》truck].

そうこうしゅ 走攻守 ● 走攻守三拍子揃った選手 a player good at the plate, on th bases and in the field; a five-tool player (**!** 英語では攻を打率と長打力，守を捕球と送球に分けて五拍子とする).

そうこうせい 走光性 [生物] phototaxis.

そうこく 相克 图 ● 理性と感情の相克(=争い)《やや書》 (a) *conflict* between reason and sentiment.
── **相克する** 動 conflict 《*with*》.

そうこん 早婚 (an) early marriage. ▶彼は早婚だ He married young [early]. (⇨結婚する)

そうこん 草根 the roots of grass.
● **草根木皮** grass roots and tree bark; (漢方薬) Chinese herbal medicine.

そうごん 荘厳 图 solémnity, magníficence.
── **荘厳な** 形 solemn /sáləm/; (⇨厳粛); (崇高な)《書》sublime; (壮大な) magnificent. ● 荘厳なミサ曲 a *solemn* mass. ● 荘厳な美[景観] *sublime* beauty [scenery]. ● 荘厳な宮殿 a *magnificent* palace.

ぞうごん 雑言 ● 悪口[罵詈(ばり)]雑言を浴びせる call 《him》(all sorts of) names (**!** call names 《*at* him》ともいう); taunt and jeer 《*at*》.

***そうさ 操作** 图 [[機械などの]] operation, handling (**!** 後の方は比喩的にも用いる); [[市場・人・機械などの巧みな]] manipulation. ● 遠隔操作 remote *control*. ● その装置の操作 (the) *operation* of the device. ● 操作の簡単な機械 a machine of simple *operation*. ● 株価の人為的操作 artificial *manipulation* of stocks. ● ハンドル操作を誤る lose control of a car. ● **!** car の代わりに the steering wheel (ハンドル) としない.
── **操作する** 動 operate. ● 機械を操作する *operate* [work, run] a machine. ● 世論を操作する *manipulate* public opinion.

そうさ 捜査 图 [[犯罪などの]] (an) investigation (⇨調査); [[捜索]] (a) search (⇨捜索). ● 殺人事件の捜査を行う carry out [conduct] a murder *investigation*. ● (組織的な)犯人捜査をする carry out [conduct] a manhunt. ● 捜査網をくぐり抜ける[敷く] slip through [spread, mount] a dragnet. ▶警察はまだその事件を捜査中である The police *are* still *investigating* the case./The case is still *under investigation*.
── **捜査する** 動 investigate 《a crime》; search 《*for* a criminal》.
● **捜査員** an investigator; (家宅捜査員) a searcher; (刑事) a (police) detective. ● **捜査本部** the investigation headquarters. ● **捜査令状** a search warrant.

ぞうさ 造作 (⇨面倒) ▶それをするのは何の造作(=手数)もない *I have* no *trouble* [(困難) *difficulty*] doing it./I can do it *without any difficulty*.

そうさい 相殺 ── **相殺する** 動 offset*. ● 金融規制緩和の影響を相殺する *offset* the consequences of financial deregulation. ▶賃金の増加分は物価の上昇で相殺されるだろう The wage increases will be *offset* by higher prices.
● **相殺関税** countervailing duties.

そうさい 葬祭 funerals and memorial services.
● **冠婚葬祭** (⇨冠婚葬祭)
● **葬祭料** fúneral expénses.

そうさい 総裁 a president; (官庁・銀行などの) a governor. ● 自民党総裁 the *President* of the LDP. ● 日銀総裁 the *Governor* of the Bank of Japan.

そうざい 惣菜，総菜 (説明的に) dishes served with

そうさく 創作 图 [新しくつくること](x a) creation; (執筆すること) writing; [作品] a creation; (独創的作品) an original work; (小説) a novel; [つくりごと] (a) fiction; (an) invention. ▶それは彼女の創作(= 作り話)だろう I think she *made up* [*invented*] that story.
── 創作する 動 create; (執筆する) write*; (でっちあげる) make* ... up, invent.
● **創作意欲** zeal for creation [writing]. ● **創作活動** (創作的な) creative activity; (小説の) story [novel] writing. ● **創作ダンス** creative [(現代的な) modern] dance. ● **創作力** creativity, (x a) creative power; (独創力) originality.

そうさく 捜索 图 (a) search /sɔ́:rtʃ/ (*for, of*).
①【～(の)捜索】 ● 行方不明の子供の捜索 a *search for* a missing child. ● 湖の捜索が行なわれた call off the *search of* a lake. ▶彼らはそのビルの捜索に出かけた They went to *search* [*in search of*] the building. (⚠ search は人や物を求めてビルの中を見る意, go in search of は捜し求めるものを目的語にとるので, ビルがどこにあるかを捜しに行く意となる) ▶彼は警察の家宅捜索を受けた He had his house *searched* by the police.
②【捜索～】 ● 捜索隊を編成する organize a *sêarch pàrty* [(救助隊) a *réscue pàrty*]. ▶彼女は警察に(行方不明の)夫の捜索願いを出した She asked the police to *search for* her missing husband. (⚠ missing は, 日本語で省略されていても常に必要)
── 捜索する 動 search; hunt. (⇨捜す) ▶警察は逃亡囚を追って町中を捜索している(= 捜索中である) The police *are searching* [*making a search of, hunting*] the town *for* the escaped prisoner.

ぞうさく 造作 图 (作り付けの設備) a fixture; (備品) fittings. ● 顔の造作が整っている[悪い] have regular [poor] *features*; have a good [a bad] *profile*. ● 家の造作をする make *alternations* to a house.

そうさくいん 総索引 the general index.
そうさせん 走査線 (テレビの) scanning lines.
そうさつ 相殺 (⇨相殺(蔡))
そうさつ 増刷 图 (an) additional printing.
── 増刷する 動 ● 1,000 部増刷する *print another* [*an additional*] one thousand *copies*. ▶彼の小説は数回増刷された(= 数回刷られた) His novel went through several *printings*.

ぞうさない 造作ない ▶そんなことは造作ない(= まったく簡単だ) That's quite easy [(少しも面倒でない) no trouble at all]. **── 造作に**(⇨造作(蔡))

そうざらい 総浚い ── 総浚いする 動 (もれなく取り上げる) take* up everything concerned; (習ったこと全部をさらう) review all over; do* an overall review (*for* an exam); (舞台げいこで) have* a final rehearsal.

そうざん 早産 a premature birth. ● 早産で産まれる be born *prematurely*.
● **早産児** a premature baby.

ぞうさん 増産 图 an íncrease in production, a production íncrease.
── 増産する 動 ● 自動車[米]を増産する *increase the production of* automobiles [the *yield of* rice].

ぞうざんうんどう 造山運動 【地学】 orogeny; orogenic movement.

そうし 壮士 a vigorous, sanguine man (in his prime); (自由民権運動の闘士) a freedom fighter; (正義をたてにする脅迫屋) a political blackmailer [extortioner].

そうし 創始 ── 創始する 動 found 《a school》; originate 《an idea》.
● **創始者** a founder; an originator.

そうじ 掃除 图 cleaning. ● 大掃除 (⇨大掃除) ● 掃除の行き届いた部屋 a *clean* [a *tidy*] room. ● 母は午前中は料理と掃除で忙しくしている My mother is busy cooking and *cleaning* in the morning. (⚠ be busy doing の型で, 「...するのに忙しい」の意)
── 掃除(を)する 動 clean (⚠ 完全にきれいにすること. 日本語より徹底さを含意するので注意); [掃いて] sweep*; [ふいて] wipe, (モップで) mop (-pp-); [こすって] scrub (-bb-); [ほこりを取る] dust. (⇨掃く, 拭(⛶)く) ● 部屋を掃除する *clean* a room; (掃いて) *sweep* a room. ● 部屋をきれいに掃除する *clean* a room *up* [*out*] (⚠ up は「徹底的に」, out は「不用なものなどを取り除いて」の意); (掃いて) *sweep* a room clean; *give* a room a good *cleaning* [*sweeping*]. ● 棚を(ほこりを払って)掃除する *dust* a shelf. ▶彼女は1日がかりで家を掃除をした She spent the whole day *cleaning* [✕sweeping] the house. ▶寝室は掃除しないといけない The bedroom needs *cleaning* [*to be cleaned*].
● **掃除機** a vacuum cleaner; 《話》 a vacuum. ● **掃除機をかける** run a vacuum cleaner [《話》 a vacuum] 《over a carpet》; 《話》 vacuum 《a carpet》. ● **掃除道具** cléaning tòols. ● **掃除人** a cleaner. ● **掃除婦** a housekeeping cleaner, a cléaning wòman.

そうじ 相似 similarity. ▶この二つの三角形は相似であって合同ではない These two triangles are *similar* and not congruent.
● **相似形** a similar figure 《to》.

そうじ 送辞 ● 送辞を述べる make a *farewell speech*. (⇨答辞)

ぞうし 増資 图 a capital increase; (新株発行) a new issue. ● 第三者割り当て増資 an *capital increase* through third-party allocation.
── 増資する 動 (会社が) increase 《its [their]》 (capital) stock 《米》 [*shares* 《英》].

そうしき 葬式 a funeral. ● 葬儀

そうじしょく 総辞職 general resignation, resignation in a body [《やや書》 en masse /ɑːŋ mǽs/]. ▶内閣は総辞職した The cabinet *resigned in a body* [*en masse*].

そうしそうあい 相思相愛 ▶2人は相思相愛の仲である They are deeply in love with each other./He loves her as much as she loves him.

そうした such. (⇨そんな)

そうしたら and (then) (⚠ (1) 命令文・命令の内容を含む文の後で. (2) 後にはしばしば will を含む文が続く); then. ▶タクシーに乗りなさい. そうしたら時間内にそこに着きます Take a taxi *and* (*then*) you'll get there in time./(もしタクシーに乗れば) If you take a taxi, (*then*) you'll get there in time. (⚠ if 節がこのように短い場合は then はない方が普通)

そうしつ 喪失 图 (a) loss. ● 一時的に記憶喪失に陥る suffer a temporary *loss* of memory [*memory loss*].
── 喪失する 動 ● 記憶を喪失する *lose* one's memory.

そうして ▶彼は演奏し, 彼女は歌を歌い, そうして(= そして)私は切符を売った He played, she sang, *and* I sold the tickets. (⇨そして (a)) ▶彼は仕事をすませ, そうして(= それから)外出した He finished his work, (*and*) *then* went out. (⇨それから ①) ▶そうして(= その方法で)やってみなさい Try (*in*) *that* way. (⚠《話》では in は通例省略される) ▶そうして(= そのままにして)おきなさい Let it remain *as it is*. (⚠ it is は they were など

そうじて 総じて [一般に] generally, in general; [一般に言って] generally speaking. (⇨一般(的)に)

そうじまい 総仕舞い (年末の) the close of business [work] at the year end; (売り切ること) a sell-out.

そうしゃ 壮者 a man in his prime; a youth. ● 壮者をしのぐ元気な老人 an older man more energetic than many *younger men*.

そうしゃ 走者 a runner; (野球の) a runner, a baserunner. ●(リレーの) 最終走者 the anchor (man [person]); the last *runner*. 【関連】第一走者 the lead-off person, the first runner) ● 打者走者を batter-*runner*. ● 走者を二塁に置いて with a *runner* on second. ● 走者なしで with nobody on. ● 走者を一掃する clean [clear] the bases. ● 走者一掃の二塁打を打つ hit a bases-clearing double.

そうしゃ 奏者 a player. (！大多数の楽器は - ist でその奏者を表します。「楽器名+player」も可。例：a guitarist, a guitar *player*）● フルート奏者 a flute player; (米) a flutist; (英) a flautist /flɔ́ːtɪst/. ● ビオラ奏者 a viola *player*; a violist (！バイオリンの前身 viol の奏者の意もある).

そうしゃ 掃射 ● 機銃掃射を浴びせる machine-gun; (戦闘機から) strafe.

そうしゃ 操車 marshaling. ● 操車場 (米) a switchyard, (主に英) a márshaling yàrd.

そうしゅ 宗主 a suzerain /súːzərən, -rèɪn/.
● 宗主権 suzerainty《over》。● 宗主国 a suzerain (state).

そうしゅ 送受 ● 送受(話)器 a handset. (！送話部分は a mouthpiece, 受話部分は an earpiece)

そうじゅう 操縦 图 operation, handling; (かじをとること) steering. ● トラクターの操縦 the *operation* [*handling*] of a tractor. ● 操縦ミス (飛行機の) cockpit *mishandling*. ● 船は操縦がきかなくなって暗礁にぶつかった The boat *went out of control* and struck the rocks.

—— 操縦する 動 (機械などを) (人・動力が) operate; (人が) handle; [船・車などのかじをとる] steer; [飛行機・船を] pilot, fly*; [人・物を] (うまく) manage; (思いのままに) manipulate; [物を巧みに動かす] maneuver /mənúːvər/. ● 機械をうまく操縦する operate [*work*] a machine skillfully; (レバーを巧みに操り) *manipulate* the levers of a machine. ● 飛行機を操縦する pilot [*fly*] an airplane. ● 船を操縦する steer a ship. ● 彼は車をうまく操縦して車庫に入れた He *maneuvered* his car *into* (↔out of) the garage. ● 美里は夫をうまく操縦している Misato *manages* her husband well.

● 操縦桿(ﾝ) a contról stìck. ● 操縦士 (飛行機の) pilot. (！「副操縦士」は a co-pilot) ● 操縦席 (飛行機・レーシングカーなどの) a cockpit.

ぞうしゅう 増収 an increase in income [(売り上げの) sales, (税収の) tax revenues, (収穫の) the crops], (⑲ 減収) ● 増収増益 increase both in sales and profit. ● 今月は5万円の増収になった My income *increased* by fifty thousand yen this month./I had a fifty thousand yen *increase* [an *increase* of fifty thousand yen] in my income this month. ● 今年度の下半期は増収が見込まれる Revenue is expected to grow in the second half of this year.

そうしゅうへん 総集編 a summarized version of a long serial play [program].

ぞうしゅうわい 贈収賄 bribery, (米話) graft. ● 贈収賄汚職(事件) a bribery [話] a payoff] scandal. ● 大規模の贈収賄事件に発展する develop into a large-scale *bribery* case. ● 彼は贈収賄で有罪判決を受けた He was convicted of *bribery*.

そうじゅく 早熟 —— 早熟な 形 precocious /prɪkóuʃəs/, forward; (作物が) early (⇨早生(生)). ● 早熟な子供 a *precocious* [a *forward*] child. ● その少年は早熟だった(=年の割に大人びていた) The boy was very *mature for his age*.

そうじゅつ 創出 图 creation.
—— 創出する 動 ● その工場のリバプール進出で500人の雇用が創出されるだろう Five hundred jobs will be *created* when the plant is built in Liverpool.

そうじゅつ 槍術 the art [skill] of using a spear.

そうしゅん 早春 早春に in early spring; early in spring.

そうしょ 双書, 叢書 (一連の本) a series; (同じ体裁でそろえた文庫) a library. ● 双書として出版する publish in a *series*. ● ペンギンシェイクスピア双書 Penguin Shakespeare *Library*. ● ペンギン双書 Penguin *Books*.

そうしょ 草書 the cursive style (of Chinese character writing).

ぞうしょ 蔵書 (所蔵の総体) a library; a collection of books. ● 彼は3万冊の[たくさんの]蔵書を持っている He has a *library* of 30,000 volumes [a large *library*].
● 蔵書印 an ownership stamp. ● 蔵書目録 a library catalog.

そうしょう 宗匠 a master; a teacher.

そうしょう 相承 ● 父子相承の技 the art *handed down* from father to son.

そうしょう 創傷 a wound. (⇨傷)

そうしょう 総称 a generic name [term]; a general term.

そうじょう 奏上 —— 奏上する 動 report 《it》 to the Emperor.

そうじょう 相乗 ● 相乗効果[作用] (a) synergy; synergism; (a) synergistic effect. ● 合併による相乗効果 the *synergies* gained by the merger.
● 相乗平均 [数学] geometric average [means].

そうじょう 僧正 a bishop ● 大僧正 (an archbishop) の次の位でキリスト教での階級); a high(-ranking) priest.

そうじょう 層状 stratification.
● 層状岩 [地学] stratified rock.

ぞうじょう 増床 ● 国立病院の増床が早急に求められている It is demanded to *increase the number of beds* immediately in state hospitals.

ぞうしょう 蔵相 [「大蔵大臣」の略] the Finance Minister.

そうじょうかじょ 総状花序 [植物] a raceme /reɪsíːm/.

そうしようしょくぶつ 双子葉植物 a dicotyledon /dàɪkətɪlíːdn/.

そうしょく 草食 ● 草食(性)の動物 a *herbivorous* [a *plant-eating*, a *grazing*] animal; a herbivore.

そうしょく 装飾 图 (飾ること) decoration; (飾り立てること) ornament. ● 装飾としてダイヤをちりばめる stud 《it》 with diamonds *for ornament*. ● 装飾用の花びん an *ornamental* [a *decorative*] vase. ● 室内装飾 interior design (decoration).

—— 装飾する 動 decorate; ornament. (⇨飾る)
● 装飾音 [音楽] an ornament; a grace (note). ● 装飾品 an ornament. (⇨飾り)

そうしょく 僧職 (やや書) the (Buddhist) priesthood. ● 僧職につく enter the (*Buddhist*) *priesthood*; (僧になる) be [become] a (*Buddhist*) priest.

ぞうしょく 増殖 图 (増加) (an) increase 《in》; (動

そうしるい 物）multiplication. ●異常増殖 an abnormal *increase*《*in*》. ●高速増殖炉 a fast breeder reactor.
── 増殖する ■ incréase; multiply /mʌ́ltəplài/.
そうしれいぶ 双翅類《昆虫》two-wing flies.（参考 ハエ・カなど）
そうしれいぶ 総司令部 the General Headquarters（略 GHQ）.（❗️単・複両扱い）
そうしん 送信 图 transmission（↔reception）.
── 送信する ■ transmit (a message)《*to*》.
●送信器 a transmitter.
そうしん 喪心, 喪神 (a) stupor. ●喪心状態にある be in a *stupor*.
そうしん 痩身 a lean [a thin] figure [body].（❗️ lean は健康的な, thin は病的な身について用いる）
●痩身術 how to reduce weight; how to slim down.
ぞうしん 増進 ［増加］(an) íncrease;［促進］promotion;［改善］(an) improvement. ●健康増進 the *promotion* of [an *improvement in*] health.
── 増進する ■ ●学力を増進する improve [develop] one's academic ability.
そうしんぐ 装身具［特に婦人用の］an accessory（❗️しばしば複数形で（⇨アクセサリー））; (装飾品)《米》(男性用) furnishings, (女性用) women's clothes and accessories;《宝石入りの》jewelry.
そうず 挿図 an illustration; a figure.（⇨挿し絵）
そうすい 送水 图 water supply. ── 送水する ■ supply water.
●送水管 a wáter pipe.
そうすい 総帥 the chief commander; a leader.
ぞうすい 増水 图 the rise《*of* a river》.
── 増水する ■ ●増水した川 a swollen [a swelled] river.（❗️状態的意味が強いときは swollen の方を用いる）▶その川は大雨で増水した The river *rose* [*swelled*, *was swollen*] *with* the heavy rains.
ぞうすい 雑炊 ［料理］*zosui*;（説明的に）seasoned rice-porridge with vegetables, fish, shellfish, and other ingredients.（⇨かゆ）
そうすいせい 走水性《生物》hydrotaxis.
そうすう 総数 the total number. ▶出席者の総数は 500 人だった The total number of those who were present was [達した reached] 500./The people who were present totaled [numbered] 500.
そうすかん 総すかん ▶部長の案は総すかんを食った *Everyone refused* to accept the manager's proposal. / The manager's proposal *got the thumbs down from everyone*.
そうする 奏する ●効を奏する（⇨効［成句］）
そうする 草する write* 《an article》; （下書きを作る）draft; write a preliminary version《*of*》.
そうすると［それでは］then（❗️通例文頭・文尾で）; so（❗️文頭で, 相手の意向を確かめて）;［もしそうならば］if so. ▶そうするとすぐにそこへ行った方がいいな *Then* we'd better go there right away./We'd better go there right away, *then*. ▶そうするとおいでにはならないのですね *So* you're not coming. ▶彼は忙しくなるというのか. そうすると別の人を探さなきゃ Are you saying he is too busy? *If so* [（その場合は *In that case*], we have to find another man. ▶そうするとこの問題は結局未解決のままだったということになりますね（=そのことは…ということを意味する）*That means* (*that*) this matter remained unsettled after all.
そうすれば（⇨そうしたら）
そうせい 早世 图 an early [a premature] death.

── 早世する ■ die young.
そうせい 創成 图 creation; formation; foundation.
そうせい 創成 ■ create; form; found.
●創成期 the early period.
そうせい 総勢（全部で）in all; strong（❗️数詞の後に用いる）. ●総勢 20 名のコーラス（グループ）a twenty *strong* chorus;（歌）a chorus sung by a team twenty *strong*.（❗️×a team of twenty strong とはしない）▶私たちは総勢 20 人で洞穴の中の探検に出かけた We, *twenty in all*, went exploring in the cave.
ぞうせい 造成 图（開発）devélopment. ●宅地造成 *development* of building lots.
── 造成する ■ devélop.
●造成地 land developed for building lots.
ぞうぜい 増税 图 a táx increase. ▶増税により個人消費支出が落ち込んでいる The tax increases [*hikes*] have depressed consumer spending.
── 増税する ■ increase [raise] taxes.
●増税法案 a tax increase bill.
そうせいき 創世記（旧約聖書の）Genesis.
そうせいじ 双生児 twins.（❗️1 人は a twin）●一卵性［二卵性］双生児 identical [fraternal] *twins*.
そうせいじ 早生児 a premature baby.
そうせき 僧籍 ●僧籍に入る enter the Buddhist priesthood; become a Buddhist priest.
そうせつ 創設 foundation.（⇨創立）
そうせつ 総説 general remarks; an outline;（序論）an introduction.
そうぜつ ── 壮絶な 形 ［勇壮な］héroic /həróuik/;［激烈な］violent, fierce;（死力を尽くしての）all-out. ●壮絶な最期を遂げる die *heroically*; die a *heroic* death. ●壮絶な戦いを繰り広げる fight an *all-out* battle 《*with*, *against*》.
ぞうせつ 増設 ── 増設する ■（施設などを）establish more;（電話を）install more. ●支店を 2 か所増設する set up [establish] two *more* branch offices.
そうせん 操船 图 steering. ── 操船する ■ steer.
そうぜん 蒼然 ●古色蒼然（⇨古色蒼然）
そうぜん 騒然［混乱］(a) confusion;［大騒ぎ］(an) uproar,［騒動］(a) commotion. ●騒然とした confused;（騒々しい）noisy. ●場内は騒然となった The hall got *confused*./The hall was thrown into a *confusion* [an *uproar*, a *commotion*].
ぞうせん 造船 shipbuilding.
●造船会社 a shipbuilding company. ●造船業 the shipbuilding industry. ●造船所 a dockyard; a shipyard.
そうせんきょ 総選挙 a general election.（⇨選挙）
そうそう 圓 ●そうそう［=(いつも いつも) 彼女に従ってばかりはいられない］I can't obey her *all the time* [*always*].（❗️前の方が口語的）▶いくら好きだってそうそう（=そんなにいつも）にいつも）は食べられません He likes it, but he won't be able to eat it *so often*［そんなにたくさん］*so much*. ▶いくらずうずうしくてもそうそう（=そんなにいつまでも）彼のところに居候はしていられないよ I don't have the nerve to live on [off] him *so long* [*forever*].
そうそう 圓 Oh, yes;（思い出して）Now I remember;（同意を表して）I agree. ; ˇThat's it. ;（激励として）(That's the) way (to go). ▶そうそう, 矢野に電話しなくちゃ *Oh, yes*, I have to call up Yano. ▶そうそう, あいつっても最後へ来てそうだよな *I agree*. He backs out at the last moment, always. ▶いいぞ, そいつでそう（=あきらめないで）Great! *Keep it up!* 会話「今年は受験に失敗したけれど, 来年再挑戦するよ」「そうそう, その意気だ」"I've failed the exam this year. I'll give it another try next year." "Way to go!"

そうそう 早々 ❶ [[急いで]] in a hurry; quickly. ● 早々に立ち去る leave *in a hurry*; hurry away [off].
❷ [[…してすぐ]] immediately [right] after …; (早く) early. ●来月早々 *early* next month. ●2人は新年早々結婚します They are going to get married *at the beginning of* the new year. ▶帰宅早々彼は勉強を始めた He began to study *immediately* [*right*, *soon*] *after* he got home./*As soon as* he got home, he began to study. (⇨すぐ ❶)

そうそう 草々 Sincerely. (❗ Yours sincerely, Sincerely yours と異なり, 堅苦しさがない。これにコンマを添え, 行を改めて署名する)

そうそう 草創 ● 草創期の日本の鉄道事業 the Japanese railroad enterprise in its *early days* [its *infancy*].

そうそう 葬送 ●葬送行進曲 a funeral march. (参考 ショパン作の曲名は *Funeral March Sonata*)

*そうぞう 想像 图 (an) imagination; (気まぐれ) (a) fancy (⇨空想); [[当て推量]] a guess (⇨推測).
① [[想像(の)～]] ●想像上の怪物 an *imaginary* monster. ●想像力 (⇨想像力) ●想像の産物 a product of *fancy*. ●想像以上である be beyond one's *imagination* [what one imagined possible]; be better than one can imagine. ▶ハワイの海の美しさは想像どおりだった The sea of Hawaii was beautiful as I (had) imagined. ▶それは彼にとって想像外の出来事だった The event was (entirely) unexpected to him./The event was beyond his *imagination*.
② [[想像が]] ▶彼の年齢はどのくらいか想像(＝見当)がつかない I *have no idea* (*of*) how old he is. (❗《話》では wh- 語の前では of を通例省略する)
③ [[想像に]] ▶あとはご想像にお任せします I leave the rest to your *imagination*./You can *imagine* [*guess*] the rest.
④ [[想像を]] ●想像をたくましくする stretch [give a free rein to] one's *imagination*. ●想像を超える be beyond one's imagination; be more than one can imagine. ●想像を裏切る be contrary to one's imagination; be not what one imagined. ▶それは想像を絶する光景だった The sight was beyond all *imagination*./(信じられない) That was an incredible sight. ▶どんなに想像をたくましくしても犯行の動機は不明だった We could not find the motive for the crime by any stretch of the [our] *imagination*.

── **想像する 動** imagine /imǽdʒin/ (❗ 原義の「心に描く」から「推測[量]する, 仮定する, 思う, 考える」の意で用いられる。通例進行形を取らない; (気まぐれに) fancy; [[推測する]] guess; [[仮定する]] suppose. ▶彼の驚きを[彼がどんなに驚いたか]まあ想像してごらん Just *imagine* his surprise [how surprised he was]! ▶(仮に)彼女がここにいると想像してみてください Suppose [*Supposing*] (*that*) she were here. (❗ この場合 that 節内は仮定法または直説法) ▶彼が歌手だなんて想像できない I can't *imagine* that he is a singer./《書》I can't *imagine* him (*to be*) a singer [*as* a singer]. ●電気なしの生活を想像するのは難しい It's hard to *imagine living* [×*to live*] without electricity. ▶彼は想像していたよりずっと親切だった He was much more kind than I *had imagined* [*had supposed*, *had thought*] (he would be).
会話 「君がオートバイに乗っている光景など想像できますか」「できません」"Can you *imagine* me rid*ing* [×*to ride*] a motorcycle?" "No, I can't *imagine* it [*that*, ×*so*]." (❗ to 不定詞には通例状態動詞がつく)

●想像図 an imaginary drawing [picture].
●想像妊娠 an imaginary [a pseudo] pregnancy.

**そうぞう 創造 图 creation. ●(神の)天地創造 the Creation. ●創造性, 創造力 (⇨創造性, 創造力).
── **創造的な 形** creative.
── **創造する 動** ●新しいものを創造する *create* [*make*] something new. (❗ 後の方は口語的)
●創造主 (万物の) the Creator; (キリスト教で) God.

*そうぞうしい 騒々しい ●[[雑音を出す]] noisy; (音の大きい) loud. (⇨やかましい) ●騒々しい子供たち *noisy* children. ▶我々の住んでいるあたりは大変騒々しい We live in a very *noisy* neighborhood. ▶なんて騒々しい音楽だ What *loud* music!
── **騒々しく 副** noisily.

そうぞうしさ 騒々しさ noisiness.

そうぞうせい 創造性 creativity, creativeness; (独創性) originality. ●創造性を養う[生かす; 抑圧する] cultivate [use; repress] one's *creativity* [*creativeness*, *originality*]. ▶彼は創造性に富んでいる He's very *creative*.

そうそうたる 錚々たる (傑出した) distinguished; (高名な) eminent; (よく知られた) well-known. ●そうそうたる財界の人の集まり a gathering of *distinguished* financiers [businessmen]. ●そうそうたる学者 *eminent* scholars.

そうぞうりょく 創造力 creativity; creative power.
●創造力豊かな音楽家[作品] a *creative* [an *original*] musician [work]. (❗ 音楽家の場合, a musician with *creative power* [*creativity*] ともいえる) ▶あの作家の創造力は破綻をきたしている The writer is creatively bankrupt.

そうぞうりょく 想像力 (an) imagination. ●想像力を働かせる use one's *imagination*. ●想像力をかき立てる stir 〈his〉 *imagination*. ●想像力を欠く lack *imagination*; be unimaginative. ●想像力が豊かである be very imaginative; have a rich *imagination*. ▶作曲には大変な想像力がいる It takes great *imagination* to write music.

そうそく 総則 general rules.

そうぞく 相続 图 [[遺産の]] inheritance; [[継承]] succession.
── **相続する 動** ▶彼は父の財産を相続した He *inherited* [*succeeded to*, (手に入れた) *came into*] his father's property./He *inherited* the property *from* his father.
●相続権 the right of inheritance. ●相続財産 an inheritance; inherited property. ●相続税《米》(an) inheritance [(a) death] tax;《英》death duty. ●相続人 (⇨相続人)

そうぞくにん 相続人 (男性) an heir /éər/ (*to*); (女性) an heiress /éəris/. ●法定(推定)相続人 an *heir* apparent. ▶彼は莫大な財産の相続人である[になった] He is (an) *heir* [fell *heir*] *to* a large fortune. (❗ an がある場合は何人かの相続人のうちの1人であることが含まれる。fall *heir* ── の時は無冠詞)

そうそふ 曾祖父 one's [a] great-grandfather.
そうそぼ 曾祖母 one's [a] great-grandmother.
そうそん 曾孫 one's [a] great-grandchild (複 -children).

そうだ 操舵 图 steering; steerage. ── **操舵する 動** steer (a ship).
●操舵室 a pilothouse; (小型船の) a wheelhouse.
●操舵手 a steersman; (小型船の) a wheelsman.

*─**そうだ** ❶ [[…という話である]] I hear*; People [They] say*,《主に書》It is said that …. ▶彼らはこの春結婚するそうだ I hear [People say] (that) they will get married this spring. (❗ I hear は「人から伝え

そうたい 聞いている」の意で, I heard のように過去形で用いられることもある. また They will get married this spring, *I hear*. のように文末に置くこともも可) ▶日本の輸出額は今年はかなり減ったそうだ *It is said that* the amount of Japanese exports has considerably decreased this year./The amount of Japanese exports *is said to* have considerably decreased this year.

❷ [思える] seem, appear; (見たところ) look; (聞いた[読んだ]ところ) sound. (⇨よう❷) ▶彼女は健康そうだ She *looks* [ˣis looking] very well./She *seems* [*appears*] (*to be*) very well. ▶その計画はおもしろそうだ That plan *sounds* interesting. ▶彼は楽しそうに笑った He had a merry laugh./He laughed merrily. ▶彼は忙しそうにしているだけだ(=忙しいふりをしている) He's just *pretending to* be busy./His busyness *is* just *pretended*.

❸ [可能性として...しそうだ] (たぶん...だろう) be likely to ⟨do⟩; (...する寸前である) be about to ⟨do⟩. ▶物価が上がりそうだ[そうにない] Prices *are likely* [*are not likely, are unlikely*] to go up./*It is likely* [*unlikely*] that prices will go up. ▶彼女が沈みそうになったちょうどそのときに救助員が彼女をつかまえた A lifeguard reached her just as she *was about to* [*was just going to*] go under. ▶寝不足で死にそうだ I'm *almost* [*nearly*] dead from lack of sleep.

そうたい 早退 ― 早退する 動 ▶彼は学校[会社]を早退した(=早く下校[退社]した) He *left* school [work, the office] *early* (いつもより早く) *earlier than usual*].

そうたい 相対 ― 相対的な 形 relative.
• 相対価格 a relative price. • 相対主義 [哲学] relativism. • 相対性理論 the theory of relativity. • 相対評価 [教育] relative evaluation. (関連) 絶対評価 absolute evaluation)

そうたい 総体 ― 総体的に 副 (全体的に見て) on the whole; (一般に) generally. (⇨全体❺)

そうだい 壮大 图 grandeur /ɡrǽndʒər/; magnificence. (❶前の語は規模の大きさを, 後の語は外観の華麗さを強調する)

― 壮大な 形 grand; magnificent. • 山の頂上からの壮大な眺め a *grand* [a *magnificent*] view from the top of the mountain.

そうだい 総代 图 [代表者] a rèprèsentátive; (会議などに派遣される) a delegate; [卒業生総代] ⟨米⟩ a valedictorian /vælədɪktɔ́:riən/. ▶彼女は卒業生総代として別れのあいさつをした She made a valedictory speech as a *representative of* [(代わって)(やや書) *on behalf of*] the graduating students [class].

そうだい 増大 图 (an) íncrease ⟨in⟩. • 大幅な[相当な; 着実な] 需要の増大 a large [a considerable, a steady] *increase in* [ˣof] demand.

― 増大する 動 (増加する) incréase; (大きくなる) grow*. • 勢力が増大する *increase* in power. • 増大する危機 (やや書) a *mounting* crisis. ▶ガリレオ以来我々の宇宙に関する知識は増大してきた Our knowledge of space *has grown* since Galileo.
• 増大号 (雑誌の) an enlarged number.

そうだがつお 惣太鰹, 宗太鰹 [魚介] a frigate mackerel.

そうだち 総立ち ― 聴衆総立ちの拍手 a *standing* ovation. ▶観衆は総立ちになって大喚声(誇)をあげた All the spectators *got* [*rose*] *to* their *feet* with loud cheers./All the spectators *on* their *feet* cheered loudly.

そうたつ 送達 图 (送り届けること) delivery.
― 送達する 動 deliver; (送る) send*; (裁判所などが) serve. • 召喚状を送達する *serve* a summons ⟨on him⟩; *serve* ⟨him⟩ with a summons.

そうだつ 争奪 ― 争奪する 動 scramble ⟨*for*⟩; struggle ⟨*for*⟩; compete ⟨*for*⟩.
• 争奪戦 (奪い合い) a scramble ⟨*for*⟩, a struggle ⟨*for*⟩, (a) competition ⟨*for*⟩.

そうたん 操短 [「操業短縮」の略] a cutback in operations.

*ˣ**そうだん** 相談 图 ❶ [話し合い] (a) talk; (専門家との) (a) consultation; (重要問題に関する) (a) conference; [助言] (a piece of) advice; [申し出] an offer; [提案] a proposal; [取り決め] (an) arrangement; (合意) (an) agreement. (⇨話❹)

①【~相談】• 身の上相談 *advice* on personal problems. • 身の上相談欄 a personal-*advice* column. • 進路相談 a guidance about one's course after graduation.

②【相談〜】▶相談相手がだれもいない I have no one to *talk to* [頼る) *turn to* ⟨*for advice*⟩]. ▶これはもう相談済みです We have finished discussions about this.

③【相談が】• 相談がまとまる (=合意に達する) come to [reach] (an) *agreement*. ▶正午に出発することで相談がまとまった We agreed to [agreed that we (《主に》 should)] start at noon./We *agreed on* starting at noon. ▶ちょっとご相談があるのですが I'd like to have a *talk* with you. ▶全国から彼のもとに多くの相談が寄せられた A lot of requests for *advice* were sent to him from all over the country.

④【相談の】• 相談の上で after talking [consulting] ⟨*with*⟩; (合意の上で) by *agreement*.

⑤【相談に】• 相談に行く go ⟨*to* him⟩ for *advice*.
• 相談に乗る (⇨[成句])

⑥【相談を】• 相談をまとめる arrange ⟨*with* him, about it⟩. ▶私はその問題について相談を受けた(=助言を求められた) I was asked for *advice* about the matter.

❷ [その他の表現] ▶それはできない相談だ(=無理な要求だ) That's an impossible request./(法外な注文だ) (話) That's a tall order. (❶「それ」の内容を具体的に示す場合は It's not possible for ... to do. の形を用いることができる) ▶彼女は私には何の相談もなく結婚を決めてしまった She decided to get married without any *consultation* with me [asking for my *advice*]. ▶ものは相談だが, このテーブルを運ぶのを手伝ってくれないか May I ask you a favor? Please help me carry this table.

• 相談に乗る (忠告を与える) give ⟨him⟩ advice; (申し出に応じる) accept ⟨his⟩ offer [proposal]. ▶相談に乗ってほしいのですが (買い物客が店員に) Maybe you could *advise* [*help*] me.

― 相談する 動 [話し合う] talk ⟨*to* [⟨主に米⟩ *with*⟩ him, *about* it⟩; consult ⟨*with* him, *about* it⟩. (❶堅い語で日常会話では talk の方が普通. consult は医師・弁護士などに専門的意見を聞く場合, consult with は対等に意見を交換する場合に用いる. ⟨米⟩ では consult with と consult の意で用いることもある); (徹底的に話し合う) talk ⟨it⟩ over ⟨*with* him⟩, discuss ⟨it *with* him⟩ (❶前より堅い語 (=話し合う)); [助言を求める] ask ⟨his⟩ advice ⟨*on, about*⟩. ▶それについては父と相談しなければなりません I must *talk to* [*with*] my father about it. (⇨話す❻) [注]) ▶彼は契約書に署名する前に弁護士と相談した He *asked* his lawyer *for* his *advice* [*consulted ⟨with*⟩ his lawyer] before signing the contract. ▶君に相談したいことがある I have something to *talk about* [*talk over, discuss*] with you. ▶その問題は両親と相談してから決めます I will

そうち decide the matter after *consultation with* my parents. ▶自分の体と相談しながら走っていくと思います I think I will listen [be listening] to my body when I run.
●**相談員** an adviser [an advisor], a counselor; (専門的な) a consultant. ●**相談室** (学校などの) a consultátion ròom. ●児童相談所 a child guidance clinic. ●**相談役** (会社の) a senior (corporate) adviser (❗old な adviser は「顧問」).

そうち 送致 ── **送致する** 動 ●容疑者を所轄警察署へ送致する send the suspect *to* the district police station.

そうち 装置 〖仕掛け〗a device (❗機械などの一部・部品); 〖考案品〗a contrivance /kəntráivəns/; 〖ある目的に用いる器具一式〗(an) apparatus /ǽpərétəs/; 〖舞台装置〗a setting 〖設備〗equipment. ●安全装置 a safety *device*. ●防火装置 fire prevention *equipment [devices]*. ●家に新しい照明装置をつける install a new lighting *system* in a house. ▶リモコン装置のついたミサイル a missile *equipped for* remote control. ▶その装置のことは分からないが動かすことはできる I don't understand the *apparatus*, but I can make it work. ▶彼らは船に新しいエンジンを装置した They *equipped* [取りつけた) *fitted*] the ship *with* new engines.

ぞうちく 増築 图 (拡張) (an) extension (❗「増築部分」を表すときは [C]); (拡大) (an) enlargement. ●家の増築 the *extension* of one's house.
── **増築する** 動 (拡張する) extend 〖(やや書) en-large〗 a house; (建て増しする) build* an addition [an extension, an annex] 〖*to* a house〗; add 〖a room〗 *to* a house; build 〖a room〗 *on* to a house.

そうちゃく 装着 ── **装着する** 動 ●put* ... on; fit. ●車に新しいタイヤを装着する *fit* a new tire *to* one's new car; *fit* one's car *with* a new tire. ▶シートベルトを装着するのをお忘れなく Don't forget to *fasten* your seat belt.

そうちょう 早朝 early morning. ●早朝の散歩 an *early morning* walk. ▶早朝に早くに起きる in the morning; in the *early morning*; (早い時刻に) at an early hour. ●土曜早朝にロンドンをたつ leave London *early on* Saturday *morning*. (⇨朝)

そうちょう 荘重 图 solemnity /səlémnəti/.
── **荘重な** 形 solemn. (⇨厳粛, 荘厳) ▶荘重な口調で in a *solemn* [a *grave*] tone. (❗後の方は「重々しい」の意が強い)

そうちょう 曹長 a sergeant major.

そうちょう 総長 (大学の) a president, a chancellor. (⇨学長) ●国連事務総長 the *Secretary General* of the United Nations.

ぞうちょう 増長 ── **増長する** 動 (思い上がる) be puffed up 〖*with*〗; (話) have* [get*] a swelled 〖米〗[a swollen 〖英〗] head. (❗付け上がる)

そうっと (⇨そっと)

そうで 総出 ▶この時期になると彼の家では一家総出でじゃがいもを収穫する At this time of the year *all* his family go out to harvest potatoes. (❗... *his whole family* [*the whole of his family*] goes out .....のようにもいえる) ▶新村役場の完成祝賀会は村民総出で行われた *All* the villagers [*Everyone* in the village] attended a party to celebrate the completion of the new village office. (❗後の方は単数扱い)

そうてい 送呈 ▶彼女から初めての著書の送呈を受けた She *sent* me a complimentary copy of her first book.

そうてい 装丁 〖製本〗binding /báindiŋ/; 〖表紙のデザイン〗a design. ●革装丁の本 a book in leather *binding*; a leather-*bound* book. ▶この本は装丁がよい This book *is well* (↔*poorly*) *bound* [*designed*].

そうてい 想定 图 (a) supposition; (仮定) (an) assumption. (⇨仮定)
── **想定する** 動 ▶そのホテルで5階客室から火災が発生したことを想定して非難訓練が行われた A fire drill was conducted at the hotel *on the assumption* [*supposition*] *that* a fire broke out at a guest room on the fifth floor. ▶自然はしばしば人間の想定を裏切る Nature often betrays human expectations.

ぞうてい 贈呈 图 prèsentátion. ●賞の贈呈 the *presentation* of the prizes.
── **贈呈する** 動 presént. (⇨贈る) ▶協会は彼女にメダルを贈呈した The association *presented* her *with* a medal [a medal *to* her].
●**贈呈式** a presentation ceremony. ●**贈呈本** a presentation [a complimentary] copy.

そうてん 争点 (要点) the point (at issue); (問題点) an issue. ●今度の選挙の争点 the *issue* of this coming election. ▶彼の発言は争点をはずれている His remarks are *off* (↔*to*) *the point*.

そうてん 装填 ── **装填する** 動 load [charge] 〖a gun〗. ●カメラにフィルムを装填する *load* a film *into* a camera.

そうてん 総点 a total score. ●総点で820点取る get a *total score* of 820 (*in* the exam).

そうでん 相伝 inheritance. ●父子相伝の所領 (先祖伝来の) one's ancestral fief; (父から子へ) the fief inherited [handed down] from father to son.

そうでん 送電 图 (電気 [電力] 供給) electricity [power] supply.
── **送電する** 動 send* electricity; supply electricity [power].
●**送電線** a pówer lìne.

そうと 壮図 a large-scale [a grand] project.

そうと 壮途 ●壮途につく start out on an adventurous trip.

*****そうとう** 相当 ── **相当な** 形 ❶〖かなりの〗considerable; (十分な) good; (並でない) quite a; (なかなか立派な) decent. ●相当な距離 a *considerable* [a *good*] distance. ●相当な数の人 a *considerable* number of people. ●相当な名医 *quite a* [〖米話〗] *some*] doctor. ●相当な生活をする make a *decent* living. ▶彼は株で相当の金をもうけた He made a *considerable* sum of money on the stock market. ▶火事で相当な損害をこうむった We suffered *considerable* losses from the fire. ▶そ れをするのには相当な勇気がいった It took *a lot of* courage to do that.
❷〖適合・相応した〗(ふさわしい) fit (-tt-), suitable (⇨適当な); (妥当な) appropriate; (価値がある) worth.
●相当な処置をとる take *appropriate* measures. ●1万円相当の贈り物 a present [a gift] *worth* ten thousand yen.
── **相当(に)** 副 〖ずいぶん〗considerably (❗通例動詞・比較級を修飾); 〖かなり〗(普通以上に) rather, (話) pretty; (過度にならぬ程度に) fairly; (思ったより) quite. (⇨かなり) ●相当険しい坂 *rather* [*quite*] a steep slope; a *rather* [a *pretty*] steep slope. (❗定冠詞をつける場合は後の語順なのも可) ▶彼は昨年より相当やせている He is *considerably* thinner than (he was) last year. (❗much の控えめな表現) ▶今日は相当に暑いIt is *pretty* [*rather*, *fairly*, (非常に) *extremely*] hot today. (❗rather では不快さで、

そうとう fairly では適度な暑さを含意)
—— **相当する** 動 (…に当たる) correspond to …; (…に等しい) be equivalent [equal] to …; (受けるに値する) deserve. ●彼に相当した仕事 a job *fit* [*suitable*] for him. (⇨ふさわしい) ●アメリカの議会には国会に相当する The Congress in the United States *corresponds to* the Diet in Japan. ▶1ドルは日本の円でいくらに相当しますか What *is* a dollar *equivalent* to in Japanese yen? ▶彼は厳罰を受けるに相当する He *deserves* a severe punishment./ He *deserves* to be severely punished.

そうとう 双頭 ●双頭の鷲 a *double-headed* eagle.
●双頭政治 (a) dyarchy, (a) diarchy.

そうとう 掃討 —— **掃討する** 動 clean … up; mop … up; stamp … out; sweep* … (away).
●掃討作戦 a mop-up [a clean-up] operation.

そうとく 総statekode a generalissimo (複 〜s); (台湾の) the President; (ナチスドイツの) the Führer.

そうどう 僧堂 a Zen-priests' meditation hall.

そうどう 騒動 [騒ぎ] (社会的・政治的な) (a) disturbance; (空騒ぎ) (a) fuss; [混乱] (a) confusion; [もめごと] trouble(s); [紛争] a dispute; [暴動] a riot. (⇨騒ぎ, 騒乱) ●お家騒動 family *troubles* [*strifes*]. ●学園騒動 a campus *dispute*; campus *troubles*. ●つまらないことで大騒動をする make a *fuss about* trifles. ▶学生たちはキャンパスで騒動を起こした The students caused [created] a *disturbance* on the campus. ▶機動隊がその騒動を鎮圧した The riot police suppressed [put down] the *riot*.

ぞうとう 贈答 an exchange of gifts. ●贈答品売り場 a gift counter.

そうどういん 総動員 general mobilization. ▶家族を総動員して隣の家の引っ越しを手伝った I *mobilized all the members* of my family to help the next-door people move out.

そうどうせん 双胴船 a catamaran.

そうとく 総督 a governor general (複 governors general).

-そうな (⇨そうだ ❷ ❸)

そうなめ 総なめ ●出場チームを総なめにする(=全部を負かす) *defeat* [《話》*lick*] *all* the teams. ▶火事は町を総なめにした(=次から次へと町のすべてを焼き尽くした) The fire *spread rapidly and destroyed the whole* town.

***そうなん** 遭難 图 [惨事] (a) disaster /dizǽstər/; [事故] an accident; [船の難破] (a) (ship)wreck (in a mountain accident); [航空機の墜落] a (plane) crash (⇨墜落).
—— **遭難する** 動 [事故にあう] meet* with an accident [a disaster]; [船などで死ぬ] be killed (in a mountain accident); [行方不明になる] get* lost, go* missing; [船・船員などが] (船が) be wrecked; (人が) be shipwrecked. ▶昨夜スキーヤー一行がで遭難した A group of skiers *met with an accident* [*got lost*] in the mountains last night. ▶漁船[漁師]が室戸沖で遭難した A fishing boat *was wrecked* [Fishermen *were shipwrecked*] off Muroto.
●遭難救助隊 a réscue pàrty. ●遭難現場 the scene of a disaster [an accident]. ●遭難者 (犠牲者) a victim (*of* a mountain [a marine] accident). ●遭難信号 (send) a distress signal [an SOS].

-そうに (⇨そうだ ❷ ❸)

ぞうに 雑煮 *zoni*; (説明的に) a Japanese *miso* or *sumashi* (=clear) soup with rice cakes, vegetables, and other ingredients (mainly served at the New Year dinner).

そうにゅう 挿入 图 (an) insertion 《*into*》.
—— **挿入する** 動 ●演説の中に戦時中のエピソードを挿入する *insert* [*put*] a war-time episode *in(to)* one's speech.
●挿入語句 a parenthesis (複 parentheses).

そうねん 壮年 ●壮年期 one's prime, the prime of life. ●壮年期にある[達する] be in [come into] *the prime of life*.

そうねん 想念 (思い) a thought; (明確な形をとっていない考え) a notion.

そうは 走破 —— **走破する** 動 run* the whole distance.

そうは 搔爬 图 [医学] curettage /kjùərətáːʒ/
—— **搔爬する** 動 curette.

そうば 相場 ❶ [市価] (商品などの) a market price [value]; (単に a market ともいう); (外国為替などの) a rate; (実勢の) the going rate; (株式などの相場表) a quotation 《*on*》; (投機) speculation.
① 《~相場》 ●為替相場 the *rate* of exchange; the exchange *rate*. ●株式相場 the stock *market*. ●強気相場 a bull [a bullish] *market*. ●弱気相場 a bear [a bearish] *market*.
② 《相場は(が)》 ▶相場は安定[沈滞]している The *market* is steady [dull]. ▶ダイヤモンドの相場が上がった[下がった] The *market* price of diamond has risen [fallen]. ▶相場は活況を呈している The *market* is getting active [picking up]. ▶ベビーシッターの相場(=現在の慣行料金)はいくらですか What [How much] is the *going rate for* baby-sitting?
③ 《相場で[に]》 ●相場で大もうけする make a large profit on the *market*. ▶それらの好材料はすべて相場に織り込み済みである All the good news is in the *market*./All the good news is built into the *market*.
❷ [一般評価] ▶親は子供に甘いものと相場が決まっている(=一般的に考えられている) Parents *are generally considered* to be indulgent toward their children./(一般的に言って) *Generally speaking*, parents are indulgent toward their children.
●相場師 a speculator. ●相場操縦 manipulation.

ぞうは 増派 ●特派員をさらに3名増派する send three *more* special correspondents.

ぞうはい 増配 a dividend increase; an increase in dividends.

そうはく 蒼白 (⇨真っ青)

ぞうはつ 増発 —— **増発する** 動 ▶JR東海は東京-名古屋間の列車を増発した(=列車の数を増した) The JR Tokai *has increased the number of* trains between Tokyo and Nagoya. ▶冬は蔵王まで臨時バスが増発される(=臨時バスを走らせる) They *operate* [*run*, 《英》*put on*] *extra* buses to Zao in winter. ▶政府は国債を増発しようとしている(=追加発行する) The government are planning to *issue additional* national bonds.

そうはつき 双発機 a twin-engine(d) plane.

そうはつせい 早発性 —— **早発性の** 形 〖医学〗proleptic.
●早発性脱毛症 premature alopecia. ●早発性痴呆 dementia praecox.

そうばな 総花 —— **総花的な** 形 (一律の) across-the-board. ●総花的な予算編成 the *across-the-board* compilation of the budget.

そうばん 早晩 sooner or later. (⇨遅かれ早かれ)

ぞうはん 造反 图 (反逆) (a) rebéllion; (裏切り) (a) betrayal.
—— **造反する** 動 rebél 《*against*》; betray.

- 造反者 a rebel; a betrayer.
そうび 装備 ●兵士の装備(一式) a soldier's *equipment* [*outfit*]. ●船以航海のための装備をする *equip* a ship for a voyage. ●その登山家は完全装備をしていた The climber *was fully outfitted* [*equipped*].
そうひょう 総評 〖概評〗a general comment 《on》.
ぞうびょう 躁病 〖医学〗mania. (⇨鬱(ゥ)病)
- 躁病患者 a manic.
ぞうひょう 雑兵 a soldier of the lowest rank; (兵卒) a private soldier.
ぞうびん 増便 图 ●夏の間1日5本の増便を行う run five *extra trains* a day during the summer.
— 増便する 動 incréase the number 《of flights [buses, trains]》; (飛行機を) fly extra planes; (バス・電車を) run* extra buses [trains].
そうふ 送付 — 送付する 動 send*.
- 送付先 the receiver's address. ●送付状(送り状) a letter of transmittal; a transmittal letter.
そうふ 総譜 〖音楽〗a (full) score.
ぞうふ 臓腑 entrails; entrails. (⇨内臓)
そうふう 送風 图 ventilation. — 送風する 動 ventilate.
そうふく 僧服 a priests' [a monk's] robe.
ぞうふく 増幅 图 〖電気〗amplification.
— 増幅する 動 amplify.
- 増幅器 an amplifier.
ぞうぶつしゅ 造物主 the Creator; the Maker; God.
そうへい 僧兵 an armed Buddhist priest [monk], a Buddhist priest [monk] warrior.
ぞうへい 増兵 图 reinforcement. — 増兵する 動 reinforce (the troops).
ぞうへいきょく 造幣局 a mint /mínt/.
そうへき 双璧 ●双璧をなす the two greatest 《philosophers》; the best two 《war novels》.
そうべつ 送別 〖書〗(a) farewell, 〖話〗a send-off.
- 送別の辞を述べる make a *farewell* speech. ●彼の送別会を開く give a *send-off* [a *farewell*] party for him. (!気軽な「お別れ会」は a good-by (e) [a going-away] party ともいう)
そうほ 相補 — 相補的な 形 complementary.
— 相補する 動 complement each other; (相補関係にある) be complementary to each other.
ぞうほ 増補 (an) enlargement. ●改訂増補版 a revised and *enlarged* edition.
ぞうぼ 増募 (金額の) the increased amount (of money) to be raised; (定員の) the increased number (of new members) to be admitted.
そうほう 双方 both. (⇨両方, 両者) ●当事者双方 the two parties [sides]. ●双方の言い分を聞こう Let's hear *both* sides.
そうほう 走法 a way [a style] of running. ●マラソンの走法 how to run a marathon.
そうほう 奏法 the way [技法] art] of 《piano》 playing; how to play 《the piano》.
そうぼう 双眸 〖a pair of〗eyes. ●双眸を輝かせて with bright [sparkling] *eyes*.
そうぼう 相貌 〖顔つき〗looks; (表情) an expression, 〖書〗a countenance; 〖ありさま〗(状態) (a) condition; (光景) a sight.
そうぼう 僧房, 僧坊 the residential quarters in a (Buddhist) temple.
そうぼう 蒼茫 ●蒼茫たる(=青々とどこまでも広がっている)大海原 the blue, green ocean spreading [stretching] far and wide.
そうほうこう 双方向 — 双方向の 形 two-way; interactive.
- 双方向通信 interactive communications.
- 双方向テレビ interactive TV.
そうぼうべん 僧帽弁 〖解剖〗(心臓の) the mitral valve.
そうほん 草本 〖植物〗a herb; (総称) herbage. ●1年生[多年生]草本 an annual [a perennial] plant.
ぞうほん 造本 bookmaking (!本を作るすべての要素を含む); (製本) bookbinding. ●辞書の造本は堅牢(鷺)でなくてはならない Dictionaries must be made durable [be bound strongly].
そうほんざん 総本山 the head temple 《of Soto sect》; 《比喩的》 the headquarters (!単・複両扱い)
そうまくり 総捲り ●利殖術総まくり all about moneymaking; a comprehensive guide to moneymaking. ●政界総まくり the political world laid bare.
そうまとう 走馬灯 a revolving lantern. ●中学の頃の思い出が走馬灯のように(=次から次へと)浮かんでは消えた Memories of my junior high school days came back to me *one after another* [*in quick succession*].
そうみ 総身(全身) the whole body. ●大男総身に知恵が回りかね 'A giant does not have enough wits about him.'/(のっぽの利口者やちびの謙遜家はめったにいない) 《ことわざ》 Seldom is a long man wise or low man lowly.
そうむ 双務 — 双務的な 形 〖主に法律〗bilateral.
- 双務協定 a bilateral agreement. ●双務契約(conclude) a bilateral contract.
そうむ 総務(仕事) general affairs; (人) a director in charge of general affairs.
- 総務課 the general affairs section. ●総務省 the Ministry of Internal Affairs and Communications. ●総務大臣 the Minister of Internal Affairs and Communications. ●総務部 the general affairs department.
ぞうむし 象虫 〖昆虫〗a weevil; (コクゾウムシ) a rice [granary] weevil.
そうめい 聡明 — 聡明な 形 (賢い) wise; (分別のある) sensible; (知能の高い) intelligent. (⇨賢い [類語])
そうめいきょく 奏鳴曲 〖音楽〗a sonata.
そうめん 素麺 *somen*; (vermicelli-like) thin noodles.
そうもく 草木 plants; 《書》 vegetation.
そうもくろく 総目録 a (general) catalog.
ぞうもつ 臓物 (鶏・家禽(Ꭹⳤ)の食用のもつ) giblets /dʒíblɪts/ 《複数扱い》; (特に牛などのはらわた) 《話》guts.
そうもん 僧門 ●僧門に入る become a Buddhist priest.
そうもん 総門 (正門) the front gate(s); the main entrance.
そうもんか 相聞歌 *somonka*; a love song [poem].
そうゆ 送油 ●送油管 an oil pipeline.
ぞうよ 贈与 — 贈与する 動 ●彼は妻に全財産を贈与した(=与えた) He *gave* his wife all his property [all his property *to* his wife]./(譲渡した) He *made* all his property *over* [〖法律〗*transferred* all his property] *to* his wife.
- 贈与税 a gift tax.
そうらん 争乱 (a) conflict; 《書》 strife; (a) war. ●その2国の間で争乱が絶えない There is never-ending *strife* between the two countries.
そうらん 総覧 ●英文法総覧 A *Comprehensive Guide* to English Grammar. ●園芸総覧 The Gardener's *Compendium*.
そうらん 騒乱 a riot; 〖騒動〗a disturbance. (!後の

方は騒動の程度に幅がある. 暴動もこの中に含まれる) (⇨騒動, 暴動) ● 騒乱罪を適用する apply the anti-*riot* law 《*against*》. ● 騒乱罪で逮捕される be arrested for [on a charge of] raising a *riot*. ● 騒乱を起こす cause a *disturbance*.

そうり 総理 〘総理大臣〙 the Prime Minister. (⇨首相, 総理大臣) ● 副総理 the Deputy *Prime Minister*.
● 総理府 the Prime Minister's Office. (〘参考〙現在は内閣府に移行)

ぞうり 草履 *a zori*; (説明的に)《a pair of》Japanese sandals (with V-shaped thongs, originally made of rice straw); (ビーチ用のゴムぞうり)《a pair of》flip-flops.
● 草履取り (説明的に) a retainer who accompaniese his lord and takes care of the lord's *zori*.

そうりだいじん 総理大臣 the Prime Minister; the Premier. (〘!〙後の方は主に新聞用語 (⇨首相))

そうりつ 創立 图 foundation; establishment; organization. ● 新しい会社の創立 the *foundation* [*establishment*] of a new company. ● 会社の創立 10 周年(記念日)を祝う celebrate the tenth anniversary of the *foundation* [*founding*] of the company. ▶ この学校は創立以来 10 年になります It's [It's been] ten years since the *foundation* of this school [since this school *was founded*]./This school is ten years old.

—— 創立する 動 found; establish; organize.

〘使い分け〙 **found** 資金を整えて設立すること. **establish** found するだけでなく, 永続できるように確立すること. **organize** 創立のみでなくひとつの組織機関を設置して機能を遂行するような措置をとること.

● 大学を創立する *found* [*establish*, *set up*] a college. (〘!〙set up は口語的)
● 創立者 a founder.

ぞうりむし 草履虫 〘動物〙 a paramecium (圈 -cia).

そうりょ 僧侶 a (Buddhist) priest. (⇨僧)

そうりょう 送料 (郵送料) postage; (貨物などの運送料) freight (rates), carriage; (配達料) a delivery [handling] charge. ● 送料込み[別]で 1,500 円 1,500 yen *postage* included [with *postage* extra]. ▶ この手紙をアメリカへ出したいのですが送料はいくらですか What is the *postage* for [on, ×of] this letter to America? ▶ この本の送料は 500 円です The *charge* for the *delivery* of this book is 500 yen.

そうりょう 総量 (重量) gross weight; (体積) gross volume.

そうりょう 総領 the oldest son [daughter]; an heir /éər/.
● 総領の甚六 'The oldest son has proverbially less wits than his brothers.'/(〘ことわざ〙) The younger brother has the more wit.

ぞうりょう 増量 图 ▶ 10 パーセント増量, 定価据え置き (広告で) *Increase* of 10%, Price Held.

—— 増量する 動 increase. ● (話) step ... up. ▶ 薬があまり効かないから少し増量してみましょう The medicine has little effect, so we'll *step up* the quantity.

そうりょうじ 総領事 a consul general.
● 総領事館 a consulate general.

そうりょく 総力 all one's strength. ● 総力をあげて with *all* one's *strength* [*might*].
● 総力戦 an all-out war.

そうりん 叢林 a thick [a dense] wood.

ぞうりん 造林 〘植物〙 afforestation.

● 造林事業 afforestation projects.

ソウル 〘音楽〙 soul (music). ● ソウルの歌手 a *soul* singer.

ソウル 〘韓国の首都〙 Seoul /sóul/.

そうるい 走塁 〘野球〙 baserunning. ● 走塁をする run the bases. ● 走塁ミスを犯す make a *baserunning* mistake. ▶ イチローは走塁がうまい Ichiro is good at *baserunning*.
● 走塁妨害 obstruction.

そうるい 藻類 〘植物〙 algae /ǽldʒi:/. (〘!〙複数扱い)
● 藻類学 algology. ● 藻類学者 an algologist.

ソウルミュージック (⇨ソウル)

そうれい 壮麗 图 —— magnificence, grandeur /ɡrǽndʒər/ (〘⇨壮大〙); (華麗) splendor(s) (〘!〙種々の特徴をいうときは複数形で).

—— 壮麗な 形 ● 壮麗な宮殿 a *magnificent* [a *grand*, a *splendid*] palace.

そうれい 葬礼 (⇨葬儀)

そうれつ 壮烈 —— 壮烈な 形 ● 壮烈な最期を遂げる(= 英雄らしく死ぬ) die a *heroic* death.

そうれつ 葬列 a funeral procession.

そうろ 走路 ❶〘陸上競技場などの〙a track; (一般の) a course. ❷〘野球〙a basepath. (〘参考〙6 フィート幅の塁間走路. タッチを逃れる目的でこの外側に出るとアウト)

そうろう 早老 premature ag(e)ing.

そうろう 早漏 premature ejaculation.

そうろうぶん 候文 an old style of writing letters [letter writing].

そうろん 総論 the general [basic] principle. ● 総論から各論へ進む go from *the general* to *the particular*.

そうわ 送話 (伝送) transmission. ● 送話器 a transmitter; (電話の送話口) a mouthpiece.

そうわ 挿話 an episode /épəsòud/.

そうわ 総和 the sum [grand] total.

ぞうわい 贈賄 图 (わいろ) a bribe; (贈収賄行為) bribery /bráibəri/. ● 贈賄罪で逮捕される be arrested on a charge of *bribery*. ▶ 彼は贈賄で告発された He was charged with *offering bribes*.

—— 贈賄する 動 bribe; commit bribery. (〘!〙後の方には「収賄する」の意もある)
● 贈賄事件 a bribery [〘話〙a payoff] scandal.

ぞうわく 増枠 (an) increase. ● 予算の増枠を求める demand an *increase* in the budget; demand a *larger chunk* of the budget.

そえがき 添え書き (短い手紙) a note; (追伸) a postscript; (推薦状) a recommendation; (写真・挿し絵などの説明文) a caption.

そえぎ 添え木 〘草木の支柱〙a support(er); 〘骨折部分に当てる板〙a splint. ● 折れた腕に添え木をしてもらう have one's broken arm *splinted*.

そえじょう 添え状 a covering letter; a (short) letter [a note] sent with a parcel.

そえぢ 添え乳 ● 添え乳をする suckle [nurse] one's baby in his [her] bed.

そえもの 添え物 (付け加えたもの) an addition; (景品) 《米》a premium; a giveaway.

〘翻訳のこころ〙 樹木も草花もここでは添え物にすぎず, 壮大な水の造形がとどろきながら林立しているのにわたしは息をのんだ (山崎正和 『水の東西』) Trees and flowers were secondary [had only a secondary role] here. It took my breath away to see the pillars [structures] of water standing side by side, making roaring [rumbling] sounds. (〘!〙(1)「添え物」は secondary (脇役的存在) と表す. (2)「...で息をのむ」は ... takes one's breath away と表す)

そえる　添える　[添付する] attach 《to》; [付け加える] add 《to》; [取り合わせる] garnish 《with》.
- 書類に署名を添える attach [affix] one's signature to a document. (❗後の方は特に公的な場合に用いる)・ステーキにパセリを添える garnish a steak with parsley /pάːrsli/.・写真を添えて願書を出す send an application (form) (together) with one's photo.・彼らは飲み物にチーズやクラッカーを添えて出した They served cheese and crackers with the drinks.・彼は世界新記録の上に優勝に花を添えた He established a new world record, and this added glory to his victory.

そえん　疎遠　(an) estrangement; [ご無沙汰(ᘔ)] (one's) long silence.・疎遠にする estrange.・疎遠になる become estranged 《from》. (⇨仲)

ソークワクチン　[医学] the Salk vaccine.

ソーシャル　social.
- ソーシャルエンジニアリング [社会工学] social engineering.・ソーシャルコスト [社会的費用] social cost.・ソーシャルダンス [社交ダンス] social dancing.・ソーシャルワーカー [社会福祉士] a social worker.・ソーシャルワーク [(社会(福祉)事業] social work.

ソース　[調味料] sauce.・料理・菓子などにかける種々の液体調味料のことで、日本で普通ソースといわれるのは Worcester(shire) /wústə(ʃər)/ sauce. しょうゆも soy sauce という.・小エビのチリソースあえ shrimps in chili sauce.・ソースをかける put [pour] sauce 《on》.

ソース　[出所] a source.・ニュースソースを明らかにする name a (news) source.

ソースパン　a saucepan.

ソーセージ　(a) sausage /sɔ́(ː)sidʒ/.・ウインナーソーセージ (a) Vienna sáusage, 《米》(a) wiener /wíːnər/, 《米話》(a) wienie, 《和製語》wiener sausage.

ソーダ　soda.・クリームソーダ an ice-cream soda. (❗単に a soda ともいう)
- ソーダガラス soda-lime glass.・ソーダ水 (味のない炭酸飲料水) soda water; (味付きの炭酸清涼飲料水) 《話》pop, 《米話》soda (pop).

ソート　名 [コンピュータ] sorting.　——**ソートする**　動 sort.
- ソートキー a sort key.

ゾーニング　[都市計画などの地域区分] zoning.

ソープ　[石けん] (a) soap.
- ソープオペラ [連続メロドラマ] a soap opera.・ソープランド a massage parlor; 《和製語》a soap land.

ソーホー　SOHO (small office/home office の略).

DISCOURSE
SOHO は「スモールオフィス・ホームオフィス」の略称で、個人が家庭内にいながら企業のために働いたり、または自身で小さな会社を経営することである SOHO stands for "small office/home office", **in which** individuals work out of their home for a company, or run a small company in their home. (❗, in which ... (そこでは...)は定義に用いるディスコースマーカー)

ソーラー　(太陽光線[熱]を利用した) solar /sóulər/.
- ソーラーカー a solar car.・ソーラーシステム a solar heating [energy] system. (❗the solar system は「太陽系」の意)・ソーラー電卓 a solar-powered calculator.・ソーラーハウス a solar house.

ゾーン　a zone.

そかい　租界　a concession.

そかい　疎開　名 強制疎開 forced [compulsory] evacuation.
　——**疎開する**　動　▶我々は戦時中大都市から田舎に疎開させられた We were evacuated from a large city to the country during the war.
- 疎開者 an evacuee /ivækjuːíː/.

そがい　阻害　名 [障害] (a) hindrance.
　——**阻害する**　動 [妨げる] hinder; [成長を遅らせる] 《文書》retard; [まともな成長を妨げる] stunt.・作物の成長を阻害する retard [stunt] the growth of the crops.

そがい　疎外　alienation /èiliənéiʃən/.・クラスで疎外感を抱く feel alienated [a sense of alienation, left out] in the class.
　——**疎外する**　動 [無視する] leave*... out; [人・事が人を遠ざける] alienate 《out of, from》.

そかく　組閣　the formation of a (new) government [cabinet]. (❗cabinet より government の方が普通)
　——**組閣する**　動 form [organize] a (new) government.

そがものがたり　『曾我物語』　The Tale of the Soga Brothers. (参考) 室町時代の軍記物語)

そぎおとす　削ぎ落とす　shave [slice]... off.・リンゴの腐った部分をそぎ落とす slice a rotten part off the apple.

そぎぎり　削ぎ切り　▶牛肉をそぎ切りにする slice beef very thin (against the grain).

そぎとる　削ぎ取る　shave [scrape]... off.

そきゅう　訴求　(an) appeal 《to》.　▶このコマーシャルは 20 代の女性に訴求力がある This commercial appeals to [has appeal for] women in their twenties.

そきゅう　遡及　——**遡及する**　動 be retroactive; act retroactively 《to》.　▶この法律は 5 月 10 日に遡及して施行される This act will be retroactive to May 10.

そく　即　❶ [すぐに] at once, immediately; (...するとすぐに) as soon as ....・用意ができたら即出発だ We'll get started as soon as everything is ready.
❷ [そのまま] directly.　▶練習不足は即敗退につながる Lack of proper practice directly leads you to the loss of a game.
❸ [すなわち] A ＝ B. ▶(二者が結局同一であることを表して)色即是空 All is [that exists is] vanity.

-そく　-足　・新しい靴 1 足 a new pair of shoes; a pair of new shoes. (❗前の方が普通)・ストッキング 5 足 five pairs of stockings.

そぐ　削ぐ　[けずり取る] shave ... off; [くじく] dampen, damp down ....　▶彼は私のやる気[気力]をそいだ He dampened my enthusiasm [my spirit(s)].

ぞく　俗　(⇨俗っぽい, 俗に).

ぞく　族　[家族] a family; [種族] a tribe (❗固有の種族名をいう場合は、その名詞を複数形にして the をつける: ピグミー族 the Pygmies).・阿部一族 the Abe family; the Abes.・印欧語族 the Indo-European family (of languages).

ぞく　属　[生物] a genus /dʒíːnəs/ (複 genera /dʒénərə/, ~es).

ぞく　続　(続き) a sequel /síːkwəl/ 《to》.

ぞく　賊　[泥棒] (こそ泥) a thief 《of thieves》; [強盗] a robber; (夜盗) a burglar (⇨泥棒); [反乱などの] a rebel /rébl/, a traitor.・国賊 a traitor to one's country.

ぞくあく　俗悪　名 (a) vulgarity.
　——**俗悪な**　形　vulgar.・俗悪な番組 a vulgar program.

そくい　即位　名 (an) enthronement.
　——**即位する**　動 (やや書) be enthroned.
- 即位式 an enthronement [(戴冠式) a corona-

ぞくうけ 俗受け ── 俗受けする 動 appeal to popular taste.

ぞくえい 続映 ▶あの映画は5週間続映(すること)になった That film [movie] will *be shown* five more weeks.

ぞくえん 続演 ▶その芝居の続演が決まった They decided to *continue to put on* [*stage*] *the play*.

そくおう 即応 ── 即応する 動 (対処する) cope with …. ▶時代の流れに即応する *cope with* the trend of the times; go with the current.

そくおん 促音 【音声】a double consonant (in Japanese).

そくおんき 足温器 a foot warmer.

ぞくがら 続柄 (family) relationship.

ぞくぎいん 族議員 (説明的に) a Diet member who represents a special interest group.

そくぎん 即吟 图 (an) improvisation.

── 即吟する 動 improvise.

ぞくぐん 賊軍 a rebel army; rebels.

ぞくけ 俗気 (世俗) worldliness; (野心) worldly ambition; (俗悪) vulgarity. ▶あの男はいい年をしてまだ俗気が抜けない He is still interested in *worldly success* at his age.

ぞくご 俗語 (総称) slang; (個々の) a slang(y) word. ● 俗語をつかう *slang* [*×*a slang]. 「豚箱」は「留置所」の俗語である "Lockup" is *slang* [(俗語表現) a *slang* expression] *for* "detention cell."

そくざ 即座 ── 即座に 副 (ただちに) (⇨すぐ❶); (その場で) then and there (!❷there and then ともいう), on the spot. ● 即座に返答する answer *at once* [*immediately*, *right away*]; give an *immediate* [(迅速な) a *prompt*] answer. ▶頼んだら即座に1万円貸してくれた When I asked him for a loan, he lent me ten thousand yen *on the spot*. ▶ショーウインドーの中のきれいな服を見て，彼女は即座にそれを買う決心をした She saw a beautiful dress in the shop window, and decided to buy it *there and then*.

そくさい 息災 ●無病息災である (⇨無病)

そくさん 速算 图 a rapid calculation.

── 速算する 動 make* [do*] a rapid calculation 《*of*》. ● 速算術 the art of rapid calculation.

そくし 即死 图 instant death, 《やや話》 death on the spot.

── 即死する 動 be killed instantly [《やや話》 on the spot].

そくじ 即時 (すぐに) immediately, at once (⇨すぐ❶); (その場で) on the spot. ● 即時に行動を起こす take *immediate* action; act *immediately* [(迅速に) *promptly*]. ▶ボストンは即時電話できますか Can I call Boston by *direct* dialing?/Can I call Boston *direct*? ● 即時抗告 【法律】an immediate appeal [complaint]. ● 即時通告 an immediate notice. ● 即時払い spot [*immediate*] payment; cash on the spot.

ぞくじ 俗字 a simplified Chinese character for common use.

ぞくじ 俗耳 ●俗耳に入りやすい (一般の人に容易に理解される) be easily understood by ordinary people.

ぞくじ 俗事 worldly affairs; (雑事) miscellaneous affairs. ● 俗事に追われる be busy with *worldly affairs* [*trifles*].

そくじつ 即日 (on) the same day. ● 即日開票 ballot counting done on the day of voting. ● 即日仕上げ same-day service.

そくしゃ 速射 [shooting].

── 速射する 動 fire shots rapidly [quickly]. ● 速射砲 a rapid-fire gun.

そくしゅう 速修 ●イタリア語速修コースをとる take a *crash* [an *intensive*] course in Italian.

── 速修する 動 learn … intensively in a short period.

ぞくしゅう 俗臭 ●俗臭ふんぷんたる学者 a *worldly-minded* [a *very vulgar*] scholar.

ぞくしゅつ 続出 ── 続出する 動 (問題・困難などが) arise* in succession, 《話》 crop up one after another; (事件などが) (⇨続発する). ● 質問が続出する *have a crop of* questions.

ぞくじょ 俗女 your [his, her, their] daughter.

ぞくしょう 俗称 a common [a popular] name 《*for*》. (!*for* … を伴うと冠詞 a は the となる)

*****そくしん 促進** 图 [増進] (a) promotion; [進歩させること] advancement; [奨励] encouragement. ● 公共の福祉の促進のために for the *promotion* of public welfare.

── 促進する 動 promote; advance; encourage; [早める] hasten, quicken. ● 世界平和を促進する *promote* [(さらに推し進める) *further*] world peace. ▶化学肥料は植物の成長を促進する Chemical fertilizer *encourages* [*quickens*] the growth of plants.

ぞくしん 俗信 (一般に信じられていること) popular belief; (民間の迷信) popular superstitions.

ぞくしん 続伸 图 continued strength 《*in* stock prices》.

── 続伸する 動 continue to rise [strengthen]. ▶相場は2日続伸した The market *continued to rise* [*rally*] for two consecutive [straight] days.

ぞくじん 俗人 a worldly person (複 ~ people) (⇨俗物); (聖職者に対して) a layman (複 -men); (凡人) an ordinary person.

ぞくじん 俗塵 ●俗塵を避ける be secluded from *the bustle of the world*.

そくしんじょうぶつ 即身成仏 the attainment of the mental state of Buddha while one is still in life.

そくする 即する (適合する) conform to …; (基づく) base oneself on [upon] …. ● …に即して in conformity with …; on the basis of …. ▶彼らの決定は信頼できる情報に即して行われた Their decision was made *on the basis of* reliable information.

そくする 則する ● 法に則して判断する judge 《the case》 *according to* [《書》 *in accordance with*] the law.

*****ぞくする 属する** 【所属する】(教会・クラブなどに) belong 《*to*》 (⇨所属); (学校・会社には用いない); (項目などに) come* [be, fall*] 《*under*》. ▶彼はそのテニスクラブに属している He *belongs to* [*is a member of*] the tennis club. (!×He *is belonging to* …. としない) ▶その本は文芸批評の部類に属する The book *comes under* the heading of literary criticism.

そくせい 即製 ● 即製の (間に合わせの) いすを作る make a *makeshift* chair.

そくせい 促成 ● 促成栽培 forcing culture. ● 促成栽培のトマト a *forced* tomato.

そくせい 速成 ● 速成科 an intensive [a crash] course (in English). ● 速成法 a quick method.

ぞくせい 属性 (本来備わっている性質) an áttribute 《*of*, ×*to*》.

そくせき 即席 ● 即席のスピーチをする make an *impromptu* [an *off-the-cuff*] speech; speak im-

そくせき 即席 *promptu [off the cuff]*.
● 即席ラーメン instant Chinese noodles. ● 即席料理 instant meals [food]; a quickly prepared dish; (有り合わせの材料で作る) potluck (⚠ただし、《米》では「料理持ち寄りのパーティー」の意でも用いるので注意).

そくせき 足跡 [足あと] a footstep; a footprint (⚠いずれも複数形で. footprint には「業績」などの意の比喩的用法はない (⇒足跡(ぁと))); 〖業績〗 an achievement; (貢献) a contribution 《to》. ● 彼の足跡を振り返る look back on his *achievements*. ▶ダーウィンは生物学史上偉大な足跡を残した Darwin *made a great contribution to* [*made his lasting mark on*] the history of biology. ▶彼は植村直己の最後の足跡をたどるためにマッキンリーに向けて出発した He set out for Mount Mckinley to retrace Naomi Uemura's last *footsteps*.
● 足跡をしるす ▶芭蕉は東北各地に足跡をしるした(=訪れた) Basho visited various districts of the northern part of Japan (and left his *footprints* there).

ぞくせけん 俗世間 the world; (宗教的世界に対し) secular society. ● 俗世間から離れて暮らす live apart from *the world*; live in seclusion.

ぞくせつ 俗説 popular belief. ● 俗説によれば according to *popular belief*.

ぞくせんりょく 即戦力 ▶即戦力になる宣伝マン[ピッチャー]を捜しているところです We are looking for a man who *can readily work* as an adman [as a pitcher in a game].

ぞくぞく ── ぞくぞくする 動 ❶ [寒さで震える] shiver 《with cold》. (⇒ぞっと) ▶少し熱っぽくて背中がぞくぞくします I'm a bit feverish and *feel a shiver* [*feel shivers*], (寒気を感じる) *feel a chill*》 running down my back. (⚠ a shiver, shivers は恐怖・嫌悪の気持ちを表す場合が多い.
❷ [喜びなどでわくわくする] be thrilled 《at》, be excited 《at》 (⇒わくわく); (喜びで震える) burst with joy. ▶私は彼を負かしてぞくぞくするほどうれしかった I *was thrilled* to have defeated him.

ぞくぞく(と) 続々(と) (次々と) one after another. ▶そこでは子供たちが栄養失調で続々と死んでいきます The children there are dying of malnutrition *one after another*. ▶最近外国の歌手が続々と(=おびただしい数の外国の歌手が)来日している Recently a great [a large] number of foreign singers have come to Japan. ▶礼状が続々と来た(=殺到した) Letters of thanks *poured* [*flooded*] *in*. ▶劇場から続々と人が出て来た A stream [Streams] *of* people came out of the theater.

そくだい 即題 a subject for impromptu verse [haiku].

*****そくたつ** 速達 《米》 special delivery; 《英》 express (delivery). ● 速達で手紙を出す send a letter *by special delivery* [*express*]; send a *special delivery* [*an express*] letter.
● 速達郵便 《米》 special delivery mail; 《英》 express post; (手紙) 《米》 a special delivery letter; 《英》 an express letter. ● 速達料金 a special [an express] delivery charge.

そくだん 即断 an immediate decision.
── 即断する 動 decide immediately [there and then, on the spot].

そくだん 速断 ── 速断する 動 (早まった決定をする) decide hastily; make* a hasty decision.

ぞくちょう 族長 《書》 (男の) a patriarch /péitriɑːrk/, (女の) a matriarch; (家長) the head of a family.

ぞくっと (⇒ぞくぞく)

ぞくっぽい 俗っぽい (下品な) vulgar; (世俗的な) worldly. ▶あの男は何とも俗っぽい奴だ He is a very *worldly-minded* fellow.

そくてい 測定 图 measurement. ● 時間の測定 the *measurement* of time.
── 測定する 動 measure. (⇒測る)

*****そくど** 速度 (a) speed; 〖物理〗 (a) velocity.
①【~の速度】● 最高速度《at》maximum [top] *speed*. (⚠後の方は「全速力」の意 (⇒全速力)) ● 平均速度 the average *speed* [*velocity*]. ● 普通の速度《at》(an) ordinary *speed*. ● 高速道路での最低速度 the minimum *speed* on an expressway. ● 光の速度 the *speed* [*velocity*] of light. ● 制限速度を超える exceed [break] the *speed* limit. ▶その車は時速 50 キロの速度で走っている The car is traveling at a *speed* of 50 kilometers /kəlɑ́mətərz/ an [per] hour. (⚠ (1) 50 kilometers per hour は 50 k(m)ph とも略せる. (2) くだけた言い方では The car is going 《at》 50 kilometers an hour. ともいえる. (3) 話し手が乗っている場合は We are driving at .... と人主語が普通.
②【速度~】● 速度計はちょうど 31 マイルをさしている The speedometer /spidɑ́mətər/ is right *at* 31./ The speed indicator reads exactly 31 miles. (⚠前の方が口語的. 31 マイルは約 50 キロに当たる)
③【速度が[は]】● 速度が速い run [travel] fast [at high *speed*(s)]; (変化が) change rapidly [at a rapid rate]. ● 速度が遅い run [travel] slowly [at slow *speed*(s)]; (変化が) change slowly [at a slow rate]. ● 列車[生産]の速度が上がった The train [The production] *speeded* up. ▶その船の速度は 15 ノットです The ship's *speed* is fifteen knots./The ship is making [doing] fifteen knots./The ship is going at the rate of fifteen knots.
会話 「新幹線の速度はどれくらいですか」「平均 200 キロです」"How fast does the *Shinkansen* run?" "About 200 kilometers (per hour) on average."/"What is the average *speed* of the *Shinkansen*?" "(It's) about 200 kilometers an hour."
④【速度~】● 速度を計る measure the *speed* [*velocity*] 《of》. ▶その車は時速 50 キロに速度を上げた[下げた] The car *speeded up* [*slowed down*, *reduced speed*, *speeded down*] to 50 kph. ▶町を出ると列車は速度を上げ始めた The train began to pick up [gather] *speed* after leaving the city. ▶スクールゾーンでは速度を落とせ Drive slow(ly) in [×at] school zones. (⚠ slow の方が slowly より口語的) ▶車は速度を落として止まった[角を曲がった] The car *slowed* to a stop [to turn the corner].
● 速度制限 the speed limit [restriction].

そくとう 即答 图 an immediate [a ready] answer.
── 即答する 動 give* [×make] an immediate [a ready] answer 《to him》; answer 《him》 immediately [迅速に] promptly.

ぞくとう 属島 an island belonging to a continent [本島に the main island].

ぞくとう 続投 ▶岡田監督の続投が決まった It was decided that Mr. Okada would *continue to manage* the team next season.
── 続投する 動 continue to pitch; (職務を続ける) continue 《to do》. ▶監督は松坂を続投させた The manager *left* Matsuzaka *in*./The manager *stayed with* Matsuzaka.

ぞくとう 続騰 (⇒続伸)

そくどく 速読 图 rapid [speed] reading.

── 速読する 動 read* 《a book》 rapidly.

ぞくに 俗に (一般に) commonly. ●俗に言われているように as is *commonly* said [called]; (ことわざにあるとおり) as the saying goes [is]. ▶あいつは俗に言うマザコンだ He is *what is called* [*what you call*] a mama's boy.

ぞくねん 俗念 a worldly desire. ●俗念を捨てる free oneself from *worldly desires*.

そくのう 即納 immediate delivery.

── 即納する 動 (金を払う) pay* 《money》 down [immediately] 《for》; (品物を渡す) deliver 《a computer》 immediately 《to him》; (品物を供給する) immediately supply 《him *with* a computer》. (**!** immediately の代わりに promptly, quickly, speedily, without delay も可)

そくばい 即売 图 (その場の現金取り引き) a spot sale. ●展示即売会 an exhibition and sale 《of dolls》.

── 即売する 動 sell* on the spot.

*****そくばく** 束縛 图 [抑制, 拘束] (a) restráint; [制限] (a) restriction; [拘束物] a tie; [足かせ] 《やや書》 fetters. ●病気[貧困]による束縛を脱する break loose from the *restraints* of illness [poverty]. ●結婚[因襲]の束縛から逃れる break (away) from the *fetters* of marriage [conventions]. ▶自由とは束縛がないことである Liberty is the absence of *restraint*.

── 束縛する 動 (抑制する) restráin; (制限する) restrict; [縛りつける] tie [(法的に)[書] bind*]... (down); (通例受身で); [足かせをする] 《やや書》 fetter. ●人を束縛する restrain a person. ●言論の自由を束縛する *restrict* freedom of speech. ▶私は1日中仕事に束縛されている I *am chained* [*am tied* (*down*)] *to* my work all day. ▶私は束縛されるのはいやだ I don't want any *ties*./I don't want to *get tied down*. ▶この国の国民である限りは国の法律に束縛される In so far as you are a citizen of this country, you *are bound by* its law.

ぞくはつ 続発 图 a succession [a rash] 《*of* + 複数名詞》.

── 続発する 動 ▶事件が続発した We had a *succession of* incidents [*one* incident *after another*]./Incidents happened [*followed*] *one after another*.
●続発症 [医学] deuteropathy. ●続発性貧血 [医学] secondary anemia.

ぞくひつ 速筆 ▶彼は速筆だ He is a quick writer. (⇔ 遅筆)

ぞくぶつ 俗物 a snob. (**!** 地位や富を異常に尊重し、自分より地位の低い者を見下す人)
●俗物根性 snobbery.

そくぶつてき 即物的 practical (and realistic); (情に左右されない) unsentimental; (現実的な) down-to-earth. ▶今の若者たちは即物的だと言う人がいる Some people say that young people today tend to be *practical and unidealistic*.

そくぶん 側聞 ●側聞するところによれば… I hear [understand]…; I am told …; (たまたま聞いた) I happened to hear …; (直接聞いたのではないが) I heard it indirectly ….

ぞくへき 側壁 a side wall.

ぞくへん 続編 /síːkwəl/ 《*to*》; a continuation 《*of*》. ●…の続編を書く write a *sequel to* ….

そくほ 速歩 a fast walk; (馬の) a trot.

そくほう 速報 图 a prompt report. ●ニュース速報 (テレビ・ラジオなどの) a néwsflàsh (**!** 単に flash ともいう); 《米》 a (news) bulletin.

── 速報する 動 ●開票の結果を速報する *report* the election results *up to the minute*.

ぞくほう 続報 图 a follow-up; a subsequent [a follow-up] report 《*on, of*》. ▶列車事故現場からの続報が入りました Further news from the spot of the train accident has just come in.

ぞくみょう 俗名 (生前の姓名) one's secular name; (出家以前の姓名) one's name as a layman.

ぞくむ 俗務 (⇔ ⑯ 俗事)

ぞくめい 属名 (生物分類上の) a generic name.

そくめん 側面 图 (一面) an aspect; (建物・山・部隊などの) a flank. ●技術的側面 the technical *side*. ●道の側面に(=わきに)立つ stand *by the side of* the road. ●敵を側面から攻撃する attack the enemy *on the* left *flank*; attack the left *flank* of the enemy. ●彼を側面から(=間接的に)援助する aid him *indirectly*; give him *indirect* aid. ▶彼は酔っ払ったらいつもとは違った性格の側面を見せる When (he is) drunk, he shows a different *side* [*aspect*] of his character. ▶その車は赤信号を無視して私の車に側面からぶつかった The car jumped the red light and hit my car side-on. (**!** 「側面衝突」は side-on collision)

ぞくよう 俗謡 a popular song; (民謡) a folk song.

ぞくらく 続落 continued weakness.

── 続落する 動 continue to fall [retreat].

ソクラテス [古代ギリシャの哲学者] Socrates /sɑ́krətiːz/.

ぞくりゅうけっかく 粟粒結核 [医学] miliary tuberculosis.

そくりょう 測量 图 (一般の) measurement; (土地の) (a) survey.

── 測量する 動 méasure; survéy; (水深を) sound. ●海の深さを測量する *measure* [*sound*] the depth of the sea. ●建設用地を測量する *survey* [*make a survey of*] the construction site.
●測量器 a survéying instrument. ●測量技師 a surveyor; a survéying engineer. ●測量図 a survey (map).

ぞくりょう 属領 a dependency; (領地) a possession.

そくりょく 速力 (a) speed. (⇔速度, 全速力)

ぞくろん 俗論 (通俗的な意見) a popular, unscientific opinion [view]; (月並みな議論) a conventional view [opinion].

そぐわない ▶彼らの計画は現状にそぐわない(=釣り合わない) Their plans don't *match* the present state of things. ▶そのドレスはパーティーにそぐわない(=ふさわしくない) The dress is *unsuitable* [*isn't fit*, 場違いな *is out of place*] for the party.

そけいぶ 鼠蹊 鼠蹊部 [解剖] the groin. ●鼠蹊ヘルニア [医学] inguinal hernia.

そげおちる 削げ落ちる (⇒削げる)

そげき 狙撃 ─**狙撃する** 動 ●3階の窓から彼を狙撃する *snipe 《at》* [*shoot 《at》*] him from a third floor window. (**!** at ではねらいを定めただけで必ずしも命中するとは限らない)
●狙撃兵 a sniper.

ソケット (電球の) a (lightbulb) socket; (壁に設けられた電気プラグの) a wall socket, 《主に米》 an outlet, 《英》 a power point. ●充電器をソケットに差し込む plug a battery charger into a *socket*.

そげる 削げる be shaven [sliced] off. ●ほおがげっそりそげた顔 a face with *hollow* [*deeply sunken*] cheeks.

そこ ❶ [場所] (そこに[へ, で]) there (↔here); (その向こうに[へ, で]) over there (**!** 通例 there より遠くをさす); [その場所] that place. ▶彼の家はすぐそこだ His house is just *over there* [《話》 around the

corner]．
会話「ここかい」「そう．そこそこ，そこがかゆいのよ」"Just here?" "Right, ✓that's it. *That's* where it itches."

① 【そこに［へ，で］】 there; over there. ▶そこに署名してください Sign your name *there*. ▶10時にそこへ行くよ I'll go *there* [×go to there] at ten. ▶ボールはそこのいすの下にある The ball is *there* under the chair. (**!** there で大まかな場所を述べ，次に具体的な場所を述べる) ▶そこにいる人が君を捜しています The [That] man *there* is looking for you. (**!** このように名詞の後に置いて「そこにいる［ある］…」の意で用いるのは《話》. 強勢は the mán there, thát màn there となる) ▶そこには10軒の家があった There were ten houses *there*. (**!** 最初の there は存在を表す there)
会話「私の本はどこ」「そこにあるよ」"Where are my books?" "They are *there*./*Thére* they ✓are." (**!** 後の方は相手に注意を促す言い方)
会話「そこにいるのはだれだ」「私です．花子です」"Who's (*in*) *there*?" "It's me. Hanako." (**!** in は内部や奥まった所を暗示する．状況によって out（外），under（下），up（上方），down（下方）なども用いられる）
② 【そこから［まで］】 ●そこから駅まで from *there* [*that place*] to the station. ▶彼は車で名古屋駅に行き，そこから新幹線で新大阪に向かった He drove to Nagoya Station, *where* he took the Shinkansen for Shin-Osaka. (**!**, where is and there (そしてそこで) と交換に) ▶ちょっとそこまで送りましょう. I'll send you *a bit of the way*./Let me go *part of the way* with you.
❷【その点】 that; 【そこまで】 that much; 【その時】 then. ▶そこが彼の長所です *That*'s his strong point. ▶そこまではまったく正しい *That much* is quite correct. ▶そこまで覚えていない I don't remember *that much* [(それも) *that*]. ▶そこへ彼が戻って来た He came back just *then* [*at that time*]. ▶そこで言葉を切って彼はコーヒーをひと口飲んだ *There* he paused to take a sip of the coffee. (**!** He paused *there* and took …. の位置も可) ▶じゃ，そこまで (それで万事 OK) Right, *that's it*.

*そこ 底 (最低部) a bottom; (川・海・湖などの) a bed; (靴の) a sole; (物の基底部) a base; (景気の) a trough; (価格の) a floor.
① 【〜底】 ●谷底 the bottom of a valley [ravine, gorge]. ●川の底 the *bottom* [*bed*] of a river, the river-*bottom*; (川床) the riverbed. ●ゴム底の靴 rubber-*soled* shoes. ▶この箱は上げ［二重］底だ There's a raised [a double] *bottom* to this box.
② 【厚の〜】 ●底の厚いなべ a thick-*bottom* pan. ●底の底 the very *bottom*; (状況が) the worst situation; (レベルが) the lowest level.
③ 【底に［は］】 ▶そのバケツは底が抜けている The bucket is broken at the *bottom*./The *bottom* has fallen out of the bucket. (**!** The *bottom* of the bucket has fallen out. は自然な語順. 現在完了は「抜けてしまった」結果としての底抜けの状態を含意) ▶この靴のスプリングのきいた底が気に入っています I like springy *soles* on my shoes. ▶景気後退の底は近いだろう The *bottom* of recession is probably near. ▶翌朝は底が抜けたような晴天(=限りないほどの高い青空)だった The next morning we found a brilliant day with a limitless blue sky.
④ 【底に】 ▶底に落ちる fall to the *bottom*. ●底にたまる (水やほこりが) gather [collect] on the *bottom*; (徐々に) accumulate on the bottom. ▶茶わんの底にお茶の葉が少し残っている There are some tea leaves at [on, in] the *bottom* of the cup. (**!** at が葉の残っている底の部分を示しているのに対し，on は葉が底にあるといった感じを与える．in は少し残っているお茶の中に葉があるといった感じ) ▶船は海の底に沈んだ The ship sank [went, was sent] to the *bottom* (of the ocean). ▶靴の底に穴があいている There is a hole in the *sole* of my shoe.

●底が浅い ● 底の浅い(＝浅薄な)知識 *superficial* knowledge.
●底が割れる (見破られる) be revealed [disclosed].
●底を入れる (底値になる) bottom out; touch [hit] the bottom (price).
●底を打つ (景気・相場が) bottom out; touch [hit, reach] (a [the]) *bottom*. ▶景気は底を打った Recession *has bottomed out*.
●底をつく ▶食料が底をついた(=なくなった) Our food *has run out*./We *have run out of* the food.

そご 齟齬 (食い違い) a contradiction; 《書》 (a) discrepancy; (不一致) (a) disagreement. ▶両者の報道は齟齬をきたしている There are *contradictions* between their reports.

そこあげ 底上げ ▶賃金の底上げをする(＝最低額を引き上げる) raise the wage floor.

そこい 底意 real intention; (底にある動機) a ulterior [an underlying] motive; (底にある意味) a core meaning. ▶彼女は彼の底意をはかりかねていた She couldn't see *what he really meant*.

そこいじ 底意地 ●底意地が悪い be spiteful, 《やや書》 be malicious. (⇨意地悪) ▶彼女は底意地が悪い She's *really spiteful*./She's *spiteful at heart*. (**!** このように何らか副詞を伴った方がはっきりする)

そこいら (⇨そこら) ▶2時間かそこいらで戻ってくるよ I'll be back in two hours *or so*.

そこいれ 底入れ 图 (景気・相場の底打ち) bottoming out; hitting [touching] (a [the]) bottom.
—— 底入れする 動 bottom out; hit* [touch, reach] (a [the]) bottom. ▶ブラジルのインフレは底入れした Inflation *has bottomed out* in Brazil.

そこう 素行 behavior, conduct. (⇨品行)
そこう 粗鋼 crude steel.
そこう 遡行 —— 遡行する 動 go* [walk, (船で) sail] up the river; go [walk, sail] upstream.

そこうお 底魚 bottom fish, a groundfish.
そこうち 底打ち (⇨同 底入れ)
そこかしこ here and there. (⇨あちこち)
そこがたい 底堅い ▶市場は底堅い状況が続いている The market has been firm in its undertone./The undertone of the market has been steady./The tone underlying the market has been firm.

そこがため 底固め (相場の) slight fluctuations along a bottom.

そこきみわるい 底気味悪い weird /wíərd/; eerie. (⇨気味（成句）)

そこく 祖国 one's own [home] country, 《書》 one's homeland; (移住民にとっての) 《やや書》 one's mother country [motherland]. (⇨本国)
●祖国愛 love for one's own country.

そこここ (あちこち) here and there. ▶庭のそこここに水たまりができている There are tiny pools (of rain water) *about* the garden. (**!** about は限られた比較的狭い範囲をおす)

そこしれない 底知れない 《やや書》 bottomless, 《主に書》 fathomless.

そこそこ ① 【だいたいそのくらい】 (…くらい) or so; (やっと) just …; 【せいぜい】 at (the) most, not more than …; 【以下】 less than …. ▶費用は2万円そこそこでしょう It *won't cost more than* twenty thousand yen./The cost will be twenty thousand yen *or so.* ▶彼は50そこそこなのに頭はまっ白だ Though he's *just* turned fifty, his hair is all white. ▶学校まで歩いて10分そこそこです It is *less than* a ten-minute walk to the school./(以内で行ける) You can get to the school *within* [*in less than*] ten minutes. ▶彼は食事もそこそこにして出かけた He left home soon after he had a *quick* [*a hasty*] meal.

そこぢから 底力 (真の力) 《have》real power. ● 底力を発揮する show *real power*.

そこつ 粗忽 ── 粗忽な 形 (不注意な) careless; (軽率な) rash.
● 粗忽者 a blunderer; a careless fellow.

そこで 〘だから〙so, therefore (❗ so より堅い語); 〘それから〙then; 〘そして〙and. (⇨だから) ▶この仕事は1人ではできない. そこで君に手伝ってもらいたい I can't do this work by myself, (*and*) *so* I want you to help me. (❗ and は省略する方が普通) ▶太郎がまずぼくをなぐった. そこではくなぐり返した Taro hit me first, *and* (*then*) I hit him back.

*そこなう **損なう** 〘いい状態を失わせる〙spoil*, mar (-rr-); (❗ 後の方は少し堅い語); 〘すっかりだめにする〙ruin; 〘傷つける〙hurt*, injure. ▶たくさんの目ざわりな建物で通りの美観が損なわれた A lot of eyesore buildings *spoiled* [*marred*] the beauty of the streets. ▶彼女の機嫌[感情]を損なったようだ I'm afraid I *have hurt* [*injured*] her feelings.

-そこなう ─損なう 〘失敗する〙fail (*to* do); 〘機会を失う〙miss. ● 最終電車に乗り損なう *fail to* catch the last train; *miss* the last train. ● ハンドルを切り損なう *lose control of* one's car. ● 弁当を食べ損なった I *missed* (my) lunch.

そこなし 底無し ── 底無しの 形 (底の無い)《やや書》bottomless; (限りのない) unlimited; (極度の) extreme; (どうしようもない) hopeless. ● 底なしの不況 a *bottomless* depression. ● 底なしの飲んべえ a *hopeless* tippler.
● 底なし沼 a bottomless lake.

そこぬけ 底抜け ▶彼は底抜けのお人好しだ He is *extremely* good-natured./He is *such a* good-natured fellow. (❗ such に強勢を置く)

そこね 底値 a bottom [a floor] price; a rock-bottom price; a low. ● 底値を更新る hit [reach] a new low.

そこねる 損ねる 〘健康などを〙ruin; 〘感情などを〙hurt*, injure. (⇨損なう) ▶彼が健康を損ねたのは長年きつい仕事をしたからだ He *ruined* his health because he had worked very hard for many years.

そこのけ ▶彼女はバイオリンで先生そこのけの上達ぶりらしい I hear she is making such progress that she'll soon be a *better* violinist *than* her teacher.

そこはかとなく (何となく) somehow; (うっすらと) faintly. ▶そこはかとなく梅の香がただよっていた The air was faintly scented with *ume* blossoms.

そこばく (いくらか) some. (⇨幾らか)

そこひ 底翳 〘医学〙(黒内障) amaurosis; (白内障) a cataract; (緑内障) glaucoma.

そこびえ 底冷え ▶今夜は底冷えがする Tonight the cold *chills* me *to the bone* [*the marrow*].

そこびかり 底光り 《give》a soft [a quiet] luster [shine].

そこびきあみ 底引き網 a trawl (net); a dragnet.
● 底引き網漁船 a trawler; a dragnet fishing boat. ● 底引き網漁法 fishing with a trawl.

そこふかい 底深い deep-rooted; deep-seated. (⇨根深い)

そこほん 底本 (⇨底本(てい))

そこまめ 底豆 〘医学〙a bunion /bʌ́njən/; a blister on the sole.

そこら ▶1年やそこらで中国語は習得できない We can't learn Chinese in a year *or* /ə/ *so*. ▶どこかそこらで一服しよう Let's take a rest somewhere *around* [*about*] *there*. ▶そこらじゅうに(=至る所に)ごみが散らかっていた There were heaps of rubbish *everywhere* [*all over* (*the place*), *all around*]. ▶そこらの(=あんな普通の人間といっしょにしないでほしいな I don't like to be lumped with *those ordinary* people. (❗ この those は軽蔑の意を含む)

そさい 蔬菜 vegetables.

そざい 素材 〘材料〙(a) material; 〘小説などの〙a subject matter. 〘材料〙・執筆素材 writing *material*. (❗ writing materials はペン・鉛筆などの筆記用具の意)

そざつ 粗雑 〘注意の行き届かない〙careless; (いいかげんな) sloppy (⇨雑); 〘大ざっぱな〙rough, crude.

そさん 粗餐 dinner. ▶英語では日本語のようにへりくだって a plain meal (粗末な食事)などとはいわない ▶会の後で粗餐を差し上げたく存じますのでよろしくお願い申し上げます We would really like you to stay for *dinner* after the meeting, if you could make it. (❗ make it は「都合をつける」の意)

*そし **阻止 ── 阻止する** 動 〘中止させる〙stop; 〘計画などを妨害する〙block; 〘抑える〙check; 〘起こらないようにする〙prevent [stop] ... 《*from* doing》 (❗ stop の方が口語的). 〘進行などを遅らせ妨げる〙hinder. ● 計画を阻止する *block* [〘やや書〙*obstruct*] a plan. ● ダブルプレーを阻止する break up a double play. ● 盗塁を阻止する throw out a potential base stealer. ▶警察は街頭デモを阻止しようとした The police tried to *stop* [*put a stop to*, *check*] the street demonstration. ▶それは科学の進歩を阻止するだろう It will *stop* [*prevent*, *hinder*, (行く手に立ちふさがる) *stand in the way of*] the progress of science. ▶捕手は走者の本塁突入を阻止した The catcher *blocked* the runner off the plate.

そし 祖師 the founder (*of* the Zen sect).

そし 素子 〘電子工学〙an element; a device.

そじ 素地 〘素質〙the makings 《*of*》; 〘基礎〙the groundwork 《*for*》; (基礎知識) a grounding 《*in*》. ● 話し合いの素地を築く lay the *groundwork for* discussion.

そじ 措辞 wording; diction; phraseology. ● 巧みな措辞 a happy *turn of phrase*; superb *wording*.

*そしき **組織** 名 (系統だった) a system; (有機的な) (an) organization 〘「組織化」の意では 🄤〙; 〘細胞の〙tissue. ● 政治組織 (形態としての) a *system of* government; (団体としての) a political *organization*. ● 政治運動の組織化 the *organization of* a political campaign. ● 犯罪組織 a criminal *syndicate* /síndikət/. ● 上皮[結合; 筋; 神経]組織 epithelial [connective, muscular, nervous] *tissue*. (〖参考〗体の四つの基本的組織)
── **組織的な** 形 systematic; organized. ● 組織的でない unsystematic. ● 組織的な研究をする make a *systematic* study 《*of* it》; study 《it》 *systematically*.
── **組織(化)する** 動 organize; systematize /sístəmətàiz/. ● 生徒会を組織する *organize* a students' association. ● 集められたデータを組織化する *systematize* the collected data.
● 組織改革 an organizational reformation; reorganization. ● 組織図 an organization chart.
● 組織培養 tissue culture. ● 組織労働者 organized labor [workers]. (関連) 未組織労働者 unorganized labor [workers])

そしたら (⇨そうしたら)

そしつ 素質 〖資質〗the makings 《of》;〖適性〗(an) aptitude 《for》;〖才能〗(主に芸術の) (a) talent 《for》;(特別優れた) a genius (! 複数形なし). ● 素質に恵まれた子供 a gifted child. ● 音楽の素質がある have an aptitude [a talent, a genius] for music; have musical aptitude [talent]. ▶彼はい い作家になれる素質がある He has (in him) the makings of a great writer.

そして and.

解説 I (1) and の発音: 文中では通例 /ən(d)/ と弱く発音され, 文頭や, コンマ (,), セミコロン (;)など, 息の休止の後, また, and の後の語を強調する場合は通例 /ænd/ と強く発音される.
(2) 文をつないで段落を構成する場合, 日本語の「そして」と同様, and を繰り返し用いるとくどい文体となるので, besides 〖書〗moreover 〖(その上と)〗, 〖書〗furthermore (さらに)や場合によっては, これらの語を用いずに独立した文を並列させた方がきびきびした文体となり効果が上がる.

(a)〖並列〗

解説 II (1) and の位置とコンマ: 通例, 列挙する要素が二つの場合は'A and B', 三つ以上の場合は'A, B (,) and C'のように最後の要素の前に and を置く. and の前のコンマは厳密には用いない限り省略可. ちなみに《米》ではコンマを置き,《英》では省略する傾向にある. なお, すべての要素を強調するときや会話では'A (,) and B (,) and C'となることもある.
(2) 列挙の順序: (a) 異なる人称の語句を and でつなぐ場合, you, he, and I のように通例二, 三, 一人称の順となる. ただし, 親しい者や目下の者と並列する場合は I が最初に置かれることもある.
(b) その他の語句の場合では音節数の少ない方を前に置く傾向がある: 若くそして美しい young and beautiful. (! 前の語は単音節, 後の語は 3 音節) ただし, 'men, women, and children'のように慣用的に語順が決まっているものもある.
(3) 形容詞の並列と and: (a) 限定用法の場合, and は通例省略される: 多くのそして美しい写真 many (×and) beautiful photographs. ただし, 同類の性質を表す形容詞を並列する場合は and があることもある: 風が強く寒い日 a cold (and) windy day./背が高く, そしてハンサムな男 a tall and handsome man. これに対し, 色や材料を表す形容詞の場合は and は省略しない: 赤と(そして)黄色の入った傘 a red and yellow umbrella./金と(そして)銀でできた時計 a gold and silver watch.
(b) 叙述用法の場合, 文語的な表現を除いて and は省略されない.

▶我々は一晩中飲んで, 歌って, そして踊り明かした We spent the whole night drinking, singing and dancing. (! spend＋目的語＋doing の構文) ▶私は音楽を聞くこと, そして散歩をすることが好きだ I like listening to music and taking [×to take] a walk. (! and は文法的に同種のものをつなぐ) ▶母は読書, そして私は入浴をしていた Mother was reading and [(一方)], while] I was having a bath./I was having a bath and [, while] Mother was reading. (! while は on the other hand と交換可能だが, while は上に書き言葉. また on the other hand は主語を強意的に対照させて Mother was reading. I, on the other hand, was having a bath. のような言い方をすることが多い) ▶彼はたばこは吸わないし, そして酒も飲まない He never smokes or [×and] drinks. (! 二つの要素を両方同時に否定する場合は or)/〖書〗 He neither smokes nor drinks. (⇨又, -も)

(b)〖結果〗▶船は沈んだ. そして 10 人が亡くなった The ship sank, and ten lives were lost. /The ship sank. And /ænd/ ten lives were lost. のように And で文を始めてもよいが, 前文と and に続く文が特に短い場合はこのように 1 文にまとめる方がよい.
(c)〖順序〗▶彼はドアをノックして, そして(＝それから)入って来た He knocked on the door, (and) then came in. (⇨それから)

そしな 粗品 〖ささやかな贈り物〗a small [a little] present. ▶粗品ですがお受け取りください This is just a small present. I hope you like [you'll like] it.

そしゃく 咀嚼 图 (かみくだくこと) mastication; (かむこと) a chew.
── 咀嚼する 動 〖書〗masticate; chew; (考えて理解する) digest /daidʒést, di-/.

そしゃく 租借 图 a lease.
── 租借する 動 lease. ▶99 年の契約で…を租借する have … on a 99-year lease.
● 租借権 a lease. ● 租借地 leased territory.

そしゅう 蘇州〖中国の都市〗Suzhou /súːdʒòu/.

そしょう 訴訟 (通例民事の) (a) suit, (a) lawsuit; (行為, 手続き) (an) action; (訴訟事件) a case. ● 民事[刑事]訴訟 a civil [a criminal] action. ● 訴訟に勝つ[負ける] win [lose] a case. ● 訴訟を取り下げる drop [withdraw] a suit. ● その会社を相手どって損害賠償を求める訴訟を起こす bring [file, start] a suit [a lawsuit] for damages against the company; sue the company for damages; bring an action for damages against the company.
● 離婚訴訟を起こす file a divorce suit; sue for divorce. ▶彼らはそのビルの建設中止を求める訴訟を起こした They brought a suit to have the construction of the building stopped.
● 訴訟手続き legal proceedings. ● 訴訟人 a suitor; (原告) a plaintiff.

そじょう 俎上 ● 俎上に載せる take [bring] up 《a problem》for discussion.
● 俎上の魚(うお) ● 俎上の魚である be quite helpless; be left to one's fate; be at the mercy of《him》. (⇨ まないたの鯉)

そじょう 訴状 (告訴状) a letter of complaint; (請願書) a petition.

そしょく 粗食 图 (質素な食事) a simple diet; (粗末な食べ物) poor food.
── 粗食する live on a plain [a frugal] diet.

そしらぬ 素知らぬ ● 素知らぬ顔をする (無視する) ignore; (知らないふりをする) pretend ignorance. (⇨知らん顔)

そしり 謗 (非難) (a) criticism. ● 大いに世間のそしりを受ける receive [come in for] a lot of criticism from the world 《for》.

そしる 謗る (悪口を言う) say* bad things about 《him》,〖書〗speak* ill of《him》(⇨悪口); (非難する) criticize.

そすい 疎水, 疏水 a (water) channel; a canal; (灌漑用の) an irrigation canal.

そすう 素数〖数学〗a prime number.

そせい 組成 (構成) composition. ● 化学的組成 chemical composition.
● 組成式〖化学〗composition formula.

そせい 蘇生 图 resuscitation /rɪsʌ̀sɪtéɪʃən/; (生き返り) revival. ● 口移し蘇生法を施す practice mouth-to-mouth resuscitation《on him》.
── 蘇生する 動 come* (back) to life; revive; (蘇生させる) bring* 《him》(back) to life,〖書〗 resúscitate; revive.

そぜい 租税 (a) tax.
● 租税回避地 a tax haven. ● 租税収入 (税収) tax

そせいらんぞう 粗製乱造 图 (粗悪な商品の大量生産) mass production of goods of inferior [bad, poor] quality.

—— **粗製乱造する** 動 mass-produce inferior goods; (作品を) churn ... out.

そせき 礎石 (すみ石) a córnerstòne; (定礎) a foundation stone.

そせん 祖先 an áncestor. (⇨先祖) ▶人類の祖先 man's [human] ancestors. ▶オオカミは犬の祖先だ The wolf is an [×the] ancestor of [is ancéstral to] the dog.
・**祖先崇拝** ancestor worship.

そそ 楚々 ▶楚々とした (清らかで美しい) pure and beautiful.

そそう 阻喪 ●意気阻喪する (=意気を喪失する) lose heart.

そそう 粗相 图 ▶この骨董品の扱いにはくれぐれも粗相のない (=注意する) ように Be very careful with this antique.

—— **粗相(を)する** 動 〖へまをする〗 do* a careless thing, be careless; (大へまをする) make* a blunder; 〖失礼な言動をとる〗 be impolite (to him); 《大小便をもらす》 have* a toilet accident.

そぞう 塑像 a clay [a plaster, a plastic] figure. (❢ clay は「粘土」, plaster は「石膏(セッコウ)」, plastic は「可塑性物質」)

***そそぐ 注ぐ ❶**〖流し入れる〗pour 《into》. ▶彼は水差しからコップに水を注いだ He *poured* water *out of* a jug *into* a glass.
❷〖流れ込む〗flow 《into》. ●太平洋に注ぐ利根川 the Pacific-*flowing* Tone River 《米》[River Tone 《英》]. ▶その川は海に注いでいる The river *flows* [*empties*] *into* the sea.
❸〖集中する〗(金・精力などを) devote 《to》; (注意などを) cóncentràte 《on》; (視線などを) fix 《on》. ●息子に深い愛情を注ぐ give [示す] show one's son deep affection; love one's son deeply. ▶彼は研究に全力を注いだ He *devoted* all his energies to [*put* all his energies *into*] his research./He *devoted* himself *to* his research. ▶彼はドアに視線を注いだ He *fixed* his eyes [His eyes *fell*] *on* the door.

そそぐ 雪ぐ (ぬぐい去る) wipe; (取り除く) remove. ●汚名をそそぐ *clear* one's name; *wipe out* the disgrace.

そそくさ(と) hurriedly, in a hurry. ▶彼女は仕事が終わるといつもそそくさと家に帰る She always goes home *hurriedly* after work. / She always *hurries* home after work.

そそっかしい (不注意な) careless; (思慮のない) thoughtless; (軽率な) hasty; (早まった) rash. ▶彼女はそそっかしい She is *careless* [is a *careless* girl, behaves *carelessly*].

そそのかす 唆す 〖誘惑する〗 tempt,《やや話》 egg ... on; 〖扇動する〗 incite. (⇨扇動) ▶彼をそそのかして宝石を盗ませる *tempt* (餌をちらつかせて) *entice*》 him to steal a jewel [*into* stealing a jewel]; 《やや話》 *egg* him *on* to steal a jewel.

そそりたつ そそり立つ ▶イチョウの木が空高くそそり立っている The gingko tree *rises* high [《やや書》 *towers*] into the sky.

そそる (かき立てる) excite; (刺激する) stímulàte; (特に食欲を) whet (-tt-). ●興味をそそる *excite* one's interest; *whet* one's appetite 《for》.

そぞろ ●気もそぞろ (落ち着かない) feel restless. ●そぞろに (何となく) somehow. ●そぞろ歩き a stroll; an amble.

そだ 粗朶 brushwood.

そだいごみ 粗大ゴミ 〖書〗 large-size refuse /réfjuːs/; (人) a cipher (『「無価値な人」の意).

そだち 育ち ❶〖発育, 生育〗 growth. ▶育ち盛りの子供 a *growing* child. ▶今年は稲の育ちがよかった Rice was well *grown* this year.
❷〖養育〗 breeding; upbringing. ▶彼女は育ちのいい女性です She is a woman of (good) *breeding*./She is a well-*bred* [a well *brought-up*] woman. ▶彼はまったく育ちが悪い (=行儀を知らない) He has no *breeding* at all. ▶彼は都会[田舎]育ちだ He *was brought up* [*was raised*] in a city [the country].

***そだつ 育つ** grow*; 〖大人になる〗 grow up; 〖育てられる〗 be brought up, be raised. ▶米は温暖な気候でよく育つ Rice *grows* well [*flourishes*] in a warm climate. ▶彼女は仙台で育った She *grew up* [*was brought up, was raised, ×was grown up*] in Sendai. (❢ 「成人するまで」の意を含むのに「10歳まで仙台に育った」という場合には, She lived [×*grew up*] in Sendai until she was ten (years old). などとする. be grown up は「大人になっている」の意) ▶彼は立派な若者に育った (=成長した) He *grew up* to be [*into*] a fine young man. (❢ to be の場合, grow up は *bring up* より適切不可) ▶妹は母乳[ミルク]で育った My sister was breast-*fed* [bottle-*fed*].

そだてあげる 育て上げる (⇨育てる)
そだてのおや 育ての親 foster parents.
***そだてる 育てる**

WORD CHOICE 育てる

bring ... up 主に親が子供を育て上げること. ▶彼女はカナダで生まれカナダで育った She was born and *brought up* in Canada.

raise 子供を育てたり, 植物を栽培したり, 動物を飼育したりすること. 主に《米》. ●その女性が子供を育てるのを手伝う help the woman *raise* 《up》 her children.

rear 子供を育てたり, 植物を栽培したり, 動物を飼育したりすること. 主に《英》. ●子供を育てるという重荷 the burden of child *rearing*.

頻度チャート

bring ... up
▰▰

raise
▰▰▰▰▰▰▰▰▰▰

rear
▰

   20   40   60   80   100 (%)

❶〖成長させる〗(人を) bring* 《him》up; (人・動物・作物などを) raise; (作物・植物などを) grow*; 〖大事に世話する〗 nurse. ●子供を母乳[ミルク]で育てる breast-*feed* [bottle-*feed*] one's child. ●鉢植えの草花を育てる *grow* [*raise, nurse*] a potted plant. ▶彼女は5人の子供を女手一つで育てた She *brought up* five children by herself [on her own]. (❢ 「我が子として(育てる)」なら ... *as her own*.) ▶彼の給料では子供を3人育てるのは無理だ His salary isn't big enough to *bring up* three children on. ▶お宅のぼたんの見事なこと. どうしたらこんなふうにうまく育てられるのですか I just love your peonies. How do you get them flourish like this?
❷〖養成する〗(人を) train; (感情・思想などを) cultivate,《書》 foster. ●2人の友情を育てる (=はぐくむ) *cultivate* [*foster*] a friendship between the

そち 措置 measures《to do; against》（!通例複数形で）a step. ●青少年の犯罪に対して[を防止するため]必要な措置を取る take necessary *measures against* [*to prevent*] juvenile crimes. ●酔っ払い運転にきびしい措置を取る（=取り締まる）*crack down on* drunken driving.

そちゃ 粗茶 ●粗茶ですがどうぞ Have a cup of tea.

＊そちら ❶[そこ]（over）there;[その方向］that way（⇨そこ❶, こちら❶）;［相手のいる所］your place [country]. ●そちらへ行ってはいけない Don't go (*over*) *there* [*that way*]. ●2,3 分したらそちらへ参ります I'll be coming [✗going] *there* [*to you*] in a few minutes.（!相手の所へ行くときは come（⇨行く）．(2) 単に I'll *be there*…/I'll be with you…ということも多い）

❷［それ，その(人)］that;［あなた］you;（電話で）《米》this,《英》that.（⇨こちら❷❸）●（電話で）そちらはどなたですか Who is *this* [*that*] speaking? ●もしもしこちら初子だけど．そちら健ちゃん？ Hello. This is Hatsuko. Is *this* [《英》*that*] Kenji? ●そちらの今日の天候はいかがですか What's the weather like *in your area* [*part of the country, at your end*] today?（!How… like という人もいるが正式ではない）●そちらはいかがお過ごしですか How are *you* [(ご家族は) *all your family*] getting along?

そつ ●そつのない（=抜け目のない）男 a clever [a smart] man. ●仕事をそつなくこなす（=そつなく）●彼は何事をするにもそつがない（=如才ない）He is *tactful about* [*attentive*] *careful in*] everything he does./He does everything smartly.

そつい 訴追 名《法律》［起訴］prosecution;［弾劾］impeachment.
── **訴追する** 動 prosecute; impeach. ●収賄のかどで裁判官を訴追する *impeach* a judge *for* taking a bribe.

そつう 疎通 ●両者の意思疎通を図る（=相互理解を促進する）promote *mutual understanding* [（意思疎通の断絶を取り除く）break down the *communications* gap] between the two. ●彼らは意思疎通を欠いている They lack *mutual understanding* [*aren't communicating*]. / There is a lack of *understanding* [*communication*] between them. ●本校では先生と生徒の間の意思の疎通はよい Teacher-student *communications* are good at our school.

そつえん 卒園 ── **卒園する** 動（幼稚園を）finish kindergarten;（保育園を）finish nursery school. ●卒園式 a kindergarten [a nursery school] graduation ceremony.

ぞっか 俗化 vulgarization.
── **俗化する** 動 vulgarize. ●俗化した海辺の町 a *vulgarized* seaside town. ●観光開発がなされてからその村は急速に俗化してしまった The village *has* rapidly *been vulgarized* by the flashy hand of the tourist industry.

ぞっかい 俗界 the world;（宗教的立場に対し）secular society.（⇨俗世間）

ぞっかい 続開 ── **続開する** 動（再開する）resume.
そっかん 速乾 ●速乾(性のある)インク *quick-drying* ink.

ぞっかん 続刊 名（続けての刊行）continued publication;（その本）a succeeding book [issue] (of the series).
── **続刊する** 動 continue to issue [publish].

そっき 速記 名 shorthand;《米》stenography. ●速記を習う learn *shorthand*; take lessons in *stenography*. ●速記を普通の文に直す transcribe *shorthand*. ●彼は速記ができる He can take [write (in)] *shorthand*.
── **速記する** 動 write* [take*]…(down) in shorthand; take [make*] shorthand notes 《of》. ●秘書は社長の話を速記した The secretary *wrote down in shorthand* what the president said.
●速記者《米》a stenographer,《英》a shòrthand-týpist. ●速記録 shorthand [stenographic] notes.

ぞっきぼん ぞっき本（説明的に）a new book sold at a very reduced price.

そっきゅう 速球 a fastball. ●豪速球 a flameball, a smoke ball.
●速球投手 a fastballer. ●左腕の速球投手 a fastballing left-hander.

そっきょう 即興 improvisation /ìmprəvəzéɪʃən/. ●即興で演奏する play《jazz》*impromptu*. ●即興で詩[曲]を作る *improvise* a poem [a tune]. ●即興で演説する speak *impromptu* [*off the cuff*]; make an *impromptu* speech.
●即興曲 an impromptu; an improvisation. ●即興詩人 an improvisor.

＊そつぎょう 卒業 名 graduation.（!《米》では大学を含めて各種の学校の卒業をさすが，《英》では通例大学の卒業の意で用いる）●大学卒業者 a college graduate /ɡrǽdʒuət/. ●（大学卒業記念の）写真 one's (college) *graduation* photo. ●彼は T 大学の法科の卒業生だ He is a *graduate in* [a law *graduate*] *of* T University. ●そちらの今日の天候はいかがですか What's the weather like *in your area* ●彼は T 大学の卒業生だ（!(1)《話》では短縮して a grad ともいう. of の代わりに from は用いない. (2) graduate 名 を用いずに「T 大学の卒業生だ」というとき，単に He *went to* T university. で済ませることも多い）●卒業見込みの者も応募可《広告》Final year students may apply.
── **卒業する** 動（大学などを）graduate《from》.（!(1)《英》では通例大学の卒業に限って用いるので，その他の学校では finish [leave*]《school》または complete an educational course《of school》などを用いる. (2) be graduated from は《米れ》，graduate《college》は《非標準》）●苦学して大学を卒業する *work* one's *way through* college. ●大学を卒業させる *put*《him》*through* college. ●来春卒業する見込みである be expected to *graduate* next spring. ●彼は T 大学の言語学科を優等で卒業した He *graduated* with honors *in* linguistics *from* T University. ●彼は昨年春に高校を卒業した He finished [*graduated from*《米》, *left*《英》] senior high school last spring.（!《米》では left は用いると「退学した」の意にもとれるので注意）●どこの大学を卒業しましたか Where [What college, Which college] did you *graduate from*? ●卒業すると学ぶことをやめてしまう人が少なくない Many people stop learning once they *graduate from* school. ●あの子はもういい加減こんないたずらは卒業してもいいころだ It's about time he *outgrew* [*grew out of*] these mischievous ways.
●卒業アルバム《米》a yéarbòok. ●卒業式（hold）a graduation (ceremony) [《米》a commencement].（!《米》でも前の方が普通）●卒業試験（take [pass; fail]）a graduation exam. ●卒業証書（receive [be given,《話》get]）a diploma.（!《英》では大学以外では certificate が普通）●卒業論文 a graduation thesis. ●ジョン・ミルトンの作品についての卒業論文を書く write a *graduation thesis* on the works of John Milton.

ぞっきょく 俗曲（説明的に）a popular song sung

with *samisen* accompaniment.

そっきん 即金 〖現金〗cash; 〖現金支払い〗cash payment. ●100万円を即金で払う pay one million yen *down*. (**!** *down* は「即金で」の意の副詞) ▶買い物はいつも即金で支払う I always pay (*in*) *cash* for anything I buy.

そっきん 側近 (...に近い人々) those close to ...; (補佐役) an aide /éid/. ●大統領の側近たち the *aides to* [xof] the President.

ソックス (a pair of) socks. ●ハイソックス 《a pair of》long [(ひざまでの長さの) knee(-length)] socks; 《和製語》high socks.

***そっくり** ❶〖そっくりそのまま〗just [exactly] as .... ▶その町は10年前とそっくりそのままだ The town is *just as it was* ten years ago. ▶(それらは)そっくりそのままにしておきなさい Leave them *just as they are*. ▶彼女は少女のころとそっくりそのままだ She looks *just as she did* when she was a little girl. ▶その地図をそっくり(=そのまま)写していほしい I want you to draw a copy of the map *exactly as it is*. (**!** copy the map だけでは make a xerox of the map (地図を(ゼロックス)コピーする)ととられる)

❷〖そっくりみんな〗all ..., every ..., everything, the whole .... ▶私はお金をそっくり(=まるごと)とられた *All* the money I had was stolen. (**!** ×The whole money ... とはいわない)/(人主語) I had *all the money* stolen. ▶後の方は「とられた」ところにもなるので注意) ▶長男が父親の仕事をそっくり引き継いだ The oldest son has succeeded his father in the *whole* business. ▶彼はその提案をそっくり受け入れた He accepted the *whole* of the proposals.

❸〖そっくり似ている〗look exactly [just] like ..., resemble completely [perfectly]. ▶彼女は母親そっくりだ She *looks exactly like* her mother./She is *the picture* [*the* (*spitting*) *image*] of her mother. (**!** (1) spitting の他に, very, living も可. (2) 他に a double, a carbon copy, 《話》a look-alike (そっくり似たもの[人])を用いて表すこともできる: 彼女はマリリン・モンローそっくりだ She is *a double* of Marilyn Monroe. (3) 2人を主語にする場合は The mother and daughter *look* [*are*] *very* (*much*) *alike*. で, much を省略するのは《話》) ▶2人はいとこ同士だが双子(=一卵性双生児)のようにそっくりだ They are cousins but *look like identical twins*. ▶その新型車は本の中の未来の車とそっくりです The new model car *completely resembles* a future car in a book.

そっくりかえる 反っくり返る lean* back [backward]. ●ひじかけいすにそっくり返る *sit back arrogantly* [(命令者のような態度で) 《書》*imperiously*] in an arm chair; *lean back* in an armchair.

ぞっけ 俗気 (⇨俗気(ｿﾞｯｷ))

そっけつ 即決 图 (その場での決定) an on-the-spot [《話》a snap] decision.
—— **即決する** 動 decide 《it》 on the spot; (即座に) decide 《it》 promptly [immediately].
●即決裁判〖法律〗a summary judgment.

そっけない 素っ気ない 〖返事などが短いなまでに短い〗curt /kə́ːrt/; 〖不愉快なまでにあからさまな〗blunt /blʌ́nt/; 〖ぶっきらぼうな〗brusque /brʌ́sk/; 〖冷淡な〗cold. ●そっけない返事 《give him》 a *curt* [a *blunt*] answer. ●そっけない態度で in a *brusque* [a *cold*] manner; brusquely; coldly. ▶「ノー」と彼はそっけなく答えた "No," he answered *curtly* [*bluntly*].

そっこう 即効 ▶この薬は頭痛に即効がある This medicine has [takes] an *immediate effect on* a headache.
●即効薬 a quick remedy 《*for*》.

そっこう 速攻 a quick attack; (特にバスケットボールで) a fast break.

そっこう 速効 a quick effect. ▶液体肥料は速効性がある Liquid fertilizers *work* [*act*] *quickly*.
●速効性肥料 a quick-acting fertilizer.

そっこう 側溝 a gutter.

そっこう 続行 图 continuation.
—— **続行する** 動 continue; go* on 《*doing*》. (⇨続ける) ●仕事を続行する *continue* working [*to work*]; *go on* working [*with* the work]. ▶試合は続行された The game (*was*) *continued*.

そっこうじょ 測候所 a weather station, a meteorological /mì:tiərəlɑ́dʒikl/ station [obsérvatòry].

そっこく 即刻 (⇨すぐ) ●即刻それをする do it *immediately* [*at once*, 《話》*right away*]; do it *as soon as possible* [*one can*] (**!** one can の方が「できれば早くしてください」という穏やかな言い方). ●即刻(=猶予なく)出発する leave *without delay*. ●即刻解雇される be *summarily dismissed*. (⇨解雇) ▶詳細が決まりましたら即刻連絡します We'll let you know *as soon as* we've arranged the details.

ぞっこく 属国 (従属国) a dependency; 《書》a subject state (**!** subject は「隷属的な」の意); 〖保護国〗a protéctorate.

ぞっこん (心の底から) heartily, from the bottom of one's heart. ▶そっこんほれている be *madly* [*head over heels*] in love 《*with*》; really love; (一時的に) be infatuated 《*with*》.

そつじ 卒爾 ▶卒爾ながら(=突然で失礼ですが)お尋ねします Excuse me for my abrupt question.

そつじゅ 卒寿 one's 90th year [birthday]. (⇨還暦)

そっせん 率先 ▶率先して(=先頭に立って)計画を実行する *take the lead* [*initiative*] *in* carrying out the plan. ●率先して(=自発的に)その仕事をする do the work *on* one's *own initiative*. ▶彼は率先して(=最初に)救助隊に加わった He *was the first to* join the rescue party.

そつぜん 卒然 ▶彼は卒然として(=突然)悟りを開いた *Suddenly* he was spiritually awakened.

そっち 〖そこ〗there, over there; 〖その方向〗that way. (⇨そちら, こちら)

そっちのけ ●そっちのけにする neglect; ignore; pay no attention 《*to*》; lay ... aside. (⇨無視する)

そっちゅう 卒中 (発作) a stroke. ●ひどい卒中を起こす have a serious [a massive] *stroke*. (**!**「卒中を起こした人」は *a stroke* victim) ▶彼は卒中を起こして口がきけなくなった He had a *stroke* and lost his speech./The *stroke* left him speechless.

***そっちょく** 率直 图 frankness; candidness.
—— **率直な** 形 frank; candid; outspoken; straightforward.

使い分け **frank** 「率直な」の意を表す最も一般的な語。自分の思っていることなどを隠しだてせずに言うこと。
candid 自分に不都合なことなどであっても包み隠しなどせずずけずけと言うこと。
outspoken 隠しておいた方がいいようなことでも無遠慮なほどずけずけ言うこと。
straightforward 正直に単刀直入に言うこと。

▶この件について君の率直な意見を聞きたい I'd like 《to hear》 your *frank* [*candid*, *straightforward*, *honest*] opinion about this matter.
—— **率直に** 副 frankly; candidly; 《話》straight out. ▶率直に言って君の計画はうまくゆかないよ *Frankly* (*speaking*) [*To be frank* (*with you*), *To be quite honest* (*with you*)], your plan will fail. (**!** 476

に不都合・不愉快なことを言うとき表現を和らげる言い方. speaking, with you はしばしば省略される) ▶私には率直に話しなさい Speak to me *frankly*./Be *frank* [*straightforward*, *open*] *with* me. ▶率直に言ってくださりありがとうございます I appreciate your *frankness* [*straightforward opinion*]. ▶彼女は彼に好きではないと率直に言った She told him *straight out* that she didn't love him.
会話「それ好きじゃないの?」「率直に言うとそうなんだ」"Don't you like it?" "I don't, *frankly*."

*そっと ❶ [静かに] quietly; (平穏に) peacefully. ▶彼は引退後田舎にそっと暮らしている He is living *quietly* [*peacefully*] in the country after his retirement. ▶彼女がまだ眠っていたので彼はそっとトイレに行った He went *quietly* to the bathroom because she was still asleep.
❷ [密かに] secretly, in secret; privately, in private. ▶そっと彼の顔色をうかがう look into his face *secretly*; steal a look at him. ▶彼女は私にそっと自分の電話番号を教えてくれた She told me her phone number *in private* [*privately*].
❸ [じゃまをしないで] ▶どうかそっとしておいて(=じゃまをしないで)ください I don't want to *be disturbed*. ▶彼女をしばらくそっとして(=1人にして)おきなさい Leave her *alone* for a while.
❹ [手荒でなく] (軽く) lightly; (穏やかに) gently; (優しく) softly. ▶そっと触れる touch (it) *lightly*. ▶私はその陶器をそっと扱うように言われた I was told to handle the porcelain *gently*. ▶彼女はそっと私の肩をたたいた She patted me *gently* [*softly*] on the shoulder. ▶そっと(=ゆっくり慎重に)やれ, Easy! Easy does it!
❺ [気づかれないように] ▶そっとキスをする steal a kiss. ▶そっと出ていく steal one's way out; slide (quietly) out (of) the door (注意 (米) では door, window のときはしばしば of を省く). ▶彼女は私の手にそのメモをそっと渡して立ち去った She *slipped* [*slid*] the note into my hand and went off. (注意 slip は「敏速に」, slide は「滑るように」上の意)

ぞっと — ぞっとする 動 (怖さなどで震える) shudder, shiver, tremble (*with* fear). ▶ぞっとするような(=おそろしい)話 a *horrifying* [(血も凍るような) a *blood-curdling*, (うす気味の悪い) a *creepy*] story. ▶寒くてぞっとした(=骨の髄まで冷える) be chilled to the bone [*marrow*]. (注意「恐怖でぞっとする」の意で用いるのは文語的) ▶少女は血を見てぞっとした The girl *shuddered* at the sight of blood./It *gave* the girl the shivers [*shudders*] to look at blood. (注意 口語的な慣用句. 後の方が強意的) ▶サービスのひどいあのホテルに泊まらなければいけないと思っただけで彼はぞっとした He *shuddered* just to think he had to stay at the hotel with terrible service. ▶その流血の場面に彼は背筋がぞっとした A shiver [*Shivers*] ran down his back at the sight of the bloody scene. ▶私は体中にぞっと震えがきた I *was trembling* (with fear) all over. ▶走っているネズミを見ると彼女はぞっとした A running rat made her flesh creep [gave her the creeps]. (注意 creep は体に何かはうような強い嫌悪感や恐怖感を表す)
●ぞっとしない ▶君の今日のその服装はぞっとしない(=感心しない)ね The clothes you wear today are *not so pleasing* to me.

そっとう 卒倒 图 a faint /féint/.
—— 卒倒する 動 (気絶する) faint; (倒れる) collapse. ▶彼はショックのあまり(貧血を起こして)卒倒した He *fainted* with shock [*from* an attack of anemia].

そつなく ▶仕事をそつなくこなす be an efficient worker.

そっぱ 反歯 buckteeth. (⇨出っ歯)

そっぽ ●そっぽを向く [別の方を見る] look the other way; [目をそらす] look away; [無視する] ignore. ▶私が話しかけたら彼女はそっぽを向いた She *looked the other way* [*looked away*, (顔を背けて) *turned away*] when I spoke to her. ▶彼らは私の意見にそっぽを向いた They *ignored* [(そんなのでは駄目だと素気ない態度をとった) (話) *turned up* their *noses at*] my remarks.

そつろん 卒論 [『卒業論文』の略] (⇨卒業)

*そで 袖 [衣服の] a sleeve; [舞台の] wings (注意 通例複数形). ●長袖[半袖]のシャツ a long-[a short-]*sleeved* shirt (注意「半袖」は ×half-sleeve とはいわない); a shirt with long [short] *sleeves* (注意 両腕なので複数形). ●袖なしのドレス a *sleeveless* dress. (注意 ×no sleeve とはいわない) ●袖をまくる roll [tuck] up one's *sleeves*. (注意 roll up one's sleeves は比喩的に「仕事にとりかかる」の意にも用いる) ●袖にすがる cling to 《his》 *sleeve*; (助けを求める) beg 《him》 for help. ●舞台の袖で(出番を待つ) wait in the *wings*. ●袖の下を渡す (⇨袖の下) ▶彼の上着は袖が少し長い The *sleeves* of his jacket are a little too long. ▶彼は私の袖を引っ張った He pulled me by the [×a, ×my] *sleeve*. (注意 人に重点を置いた表現)/He pulled my *sleeve*. (注意 引っ張った部分に重点を置いた表現)
●袖にする (冷たく扱う) treat ... coldly [chilly]; give ... the cold shoulder; (ないがしろにする) ignore; (見捨てる) jilt.
●袖振り合うも多生の縁 Even a chance acquaintance is a divine ordinance.
●袖を通す 新しい服に袖を通す put a new piece of clothing on.
●袖を引く pull one's (kimono) sleeve; (そっと注意する) gently hint [remind]; (誘惑する) tempt.
●袖口 a cuff (優 〜s). ●袖ぐり an armhole.
●袖丈 the length of a sleeve; a sleeve length.
●袖だたみ an informal way of folding a *kimono*.
●袖付け (⇨袖付け)

ソテー [〈フランス語〉] (一皿の) a sauté /soutéi/. ●ポークソテー pork sauté. (注意 料理名は U)

そてつ 蘇鉄 [植物] a cycad /sáikæd/.

そでつけ 袖付け ▶袖付けをする sew on a sleeve. ▶シャツに袖付けをする sew a sleeve onto a shirt; *sew a sleeve to* a shirt.

そでのした 袖の下 a bribe; (a) pay-off. ▶政治家に袖の下を渡す *bribe* a politician; (話) *pay* a politition *off*. ▶彼に袖の下を握らそうとしたが彼は受け取らなかった I tried to *pay* him *money under the table*, but he wouldn't take it.

*そと 外 ❶ [外部] (外側) the outside; (戸外) the outdóors (注意 単数扱い). ●家の外 the *outside* of a house. ●外の騒音 *outside* nóises. ●窓から外を見る look *out* (*of*) the window. (注意 (米) では window, door のときはしばしば of を省略する) ●外へ出る go [get] *out* (*of* the house); go *outsíde* [*outdóors*]. ▶このドアは外からは開けられません This door cannot be opened from (the) *outside*. ▶門の外で待っています I'll be waiting for you *outside* [((米)話) *outside of*] the gate. ▶外は寒いが中は暖かい It is cold *óutside* [*óutdoors*], but warm ínside [ìndoors]. (注意 対比によるアクセントの移動に注意) ▶彼は外で庭いじりをしています He is *out* gardening./He is gardening *outside*. (⇨野外)
❷ [家庭外] ▶今晩は外で食事(=外食)をしよう Let's eat [(書) *dine*] *out* this evening.
❸ [外面] ▶彼はめったに感情を外に表さない He

そとあるき 外歩き 〖外出〗an outing;〖外回り〗outside work.

そとう 粗糖 raw [crude] sugar.

そとうみ 外海 the open sea. (⇨外海(がい))

そとおもて 外表 ・外表にたたむ fold 《cloth》with its *right side out*.

そとがけ 外掛け〔相撲〕*sotogake*; outside leg trip.

そとがこい 外囲い an enclosure.

そとがま 外釜 a boiler installed outside the bathroom.

そとがまえ 外構え outward appearances. ●外構えの立派な家 an imposing [a handsome] residence.

そとがわ 外側 the outside, the exterior. (⇨外部, 内側);〖外見〗one's appearance. ▶ドアは外側から鍵がかけられていた The door was locked *on the outside* [*from* (*the*) *outside*]. ▶このドアは外側へ開きます This door opens *outward*. ▶ドアは普通内へ開くので, その場合には open inward という必要はない)

そどく 素読 ── 素読する 動 read* 《a passage of a classical work》aloud (without paying attention to the meaning).

そとぜい 外税 tax excluded [exclusive].

そとづら 外面 ▶夫は外面はいい(が内面は悪い) My husband *is friendly with everyone outside his home*.

そとのり 外法 the outside measurement(s).

そとば 卒塔婆 a *sotoba*;(説明的に)a symbolic stupa of a long thin board to be set up behind a tombstone in memory of the dead (! stupa は「仏舎利塔」の意).

そとびらき 外開き ●外開きのドア a door which *opens outward*.

そとぶろ 外風呂〔屋外にある〕a detached bath.〔他家の〕a neighbor's bath;〔銭湯〕a public bath.

そとぼり 外堀 an outer moat.
●外堀を埋める ▶目的を達成するためにはまず外堀を埋めなさい(=その障害となるものを取り除け) In order to achieve your purpose, you should begin by removing all the obstacles to it.

そとまご 外孫 a child of one's daughter.

そとまた 外股 ●外股で歩く walk *with* one's *toes turned out*.

そとまわり 外回り〖家の回り〗around the house;〖外勤〗outside work;〖環状線の〗the outer track (↔the inside track).

そとみ 外見 (an) appearance. (⇨外見(がい))

そとめ 外目 ❶〖外見(がい)〗(an) appearance. (⇨外見) ❷〖中心よりやや外に寄った〗▶速球が外目に決まった The fastball cut the outside part of the plate.

そとゆ 外湯 a bathhouse built outside the hotel [inn].

そとわく 外枠 ❶〖外側の枠〗an outer frame;(競馬で)an outside racetrack [《英》racecourse]. ❷〖範囲外〗▶予算の外枠で *outside* the budget.

そなえ 備え〖準備〗(物などに対する) preparations 《*for*》;(蓄えなどの)provision 《*against*》(⇨備える❶);〖設備〗equipment;〖防御手段〗a defense. ●備えがある(準備)be prepared [ready]《*for*》;(防備)be armed [be fortified]《*against*》(! 前の方は人, 後の方は場所に用いる). ●備えがない (準備)be unprepared《*for*》;(防備)be defenseless. ●戦闘に対する備え *preparations for* battle. ●攻撃に対する備え a *defense against* an attack. ▶大雪に対する備えは十分だ We *are* well *prepared for* heavy snow. ▶私たちは最悪の場合に備えていなければならない We must *prepare* [*be ready*] *for* the worst. ▶この船はレーダーの備えがない This ship *is not equipped* [*provided*] *with* a radar.

●備えあれば憂いなし (まさかの時に備え貯金せよ) Save (up) for [《古》*against*] a rainy day.;《ことわざ》Providing is preventing.

そなえつけ 備え付け ●備え付けの(=用意して置いてある) 用紙 papers *kept* (*ready*) in the room. ●備え付けの(=作りつけの)食器棚 a *built-in* cupboard [*fixed*]. ●備え付けの(=固定した)座席 *fixed* seats.

そなえつける 備え付ける〖設備などを〗equip (-pp-);〖必要なものを供給する〗provide;〖家具などを〗furnish;〖装置などを取り付ける〗install. (⇨備える) ●ぜいたくな家具を備え付けた部屋 a luxuriously *furnished* room. ●図書館に多くの辞書を備え付ける *provide* [*furnish*] the library *with* a lot of dictionaries. ●エアコンを部屋に備え付けてもらう *have* an air-conditioner *installed* [(しっかり取り付ける) *fixed*] in the room. ▶この工場は10台のベルトコンベアーが備え付けられている This factory *is equipped* [*is provided*] *with* 10 conveyor belts. (! (1) 前の方はある目的のために用意することを強調する. (2) belt conveyors は《まれ》)

そなえもの 供えもの an offering. ●供え物をする make *offerings《to*》.

__そなえる 備える__ ❶〖準備する〗(蓄え・装備などを) provide, make provision《*for, against*》;(前もって必要な用意をする) prepare《*for, against*》. (! いずれも for は「予測して」, against は「対抗して」を含意する) ●老後に備える *provide for* (one's) old age. ●地震に備える *provide* [*prepare*] *against* an earthquake. ●試験に備える *prepare for* an examination. (⇨準備(をする)) ●万一に備えて貯金する *save* money *for* [《古》*against*] a rainy day. ▶納屋には長く寒い冬に備えて干草がいっぱいあった The barn was full of hay *ready for* the long cold winter. ▶私は万一に備えて傘を持って行った I took an umbrella (*just*) *in case*. (! in case の後に it rains, it should rain が省略されている)

❷〖設備する〗equip (-pp-)《*with*》;(家具などを) furnish《*with*》;(必要・便利を予測して) provide《*with*》;(器具・装置などを) install《*with*》. ●その工場に最新の機械を備える *equip* the factory *with* the most modern machinery. ●家に家具を備える *furnish* [*provide*] a house *with* furniture. ▶私は部屋に電話を備えた I had a telephone *installed* in my room. (!「have＋物＋過去分詞」(してもらう)の形に注意)

❸〖有する〗possess (! have の堅い語);(生まれながら恵まれている)《書》be endowed《*with*》. ●彼はすぐれた指導者に必要な要件(=なるべき能力)をすべて備えていた He *possessed* [✕was possessing] all the qualities to be of a good leader. ▶彼は文才を備えている He *is endowed with* literary talent.

そなえる 供える〖供え物を〗offer ... (up);〖置く〗place. ●彼の墓に花を供える *place* flowers before [(up)on] his grave.

ソナタ〖音楽〗a sonata /sənɑ́ːtə/. ●ピアノソナタ a piano *sonata*.
●ソナタ形式 a sonata form.

そなわる 備わる be gifted [《書》endowed /indáud/]《*with*》;(備え付けてある) be equipped《*with*》. (⇨備える)

ソニックブーム sonic boom. (参考 超音速飛行をする航空機の衝撃波が地上に達して生じる騒音)

そねざきしんじゅう 『曾根崎心中』 (The) Love Suicides at Sonezaki. [参考] 近松門左衛門の人形浄瑠璃)

そねみ 妬み envy; jealousy. (⇨妬(ねた)み、嫉妬(しっと))

そねむ 妬む be envious [jealous] 《of》. (⇨妬(ねた)む)

その 形 the; that.

> **解説** the は前に出た名詞や前後関係から何を指すか分かる名詞の前につける。that はど指示の気持ちは強くない。that は指示したり、指し示す気持ちで用いる。複数名詞の前では those になる。代名詞として「そのこと[物・人]」の意でも用いる。

●机の上のその赤鉛筆 that red pencil [(複数)those red pencils] on the desk. ▶行ってその日のうちに(=同じ日に)帰る go and come back the same day. ▶その映画はあまりおもしろくなかった The movie was not very interesting. ▶校門のところで背の高い男の人を見た。その人はサングラスをかけていた I saw a tall man at the school gate. The man [He, ×That man] was wearing sunglasses. ▶そのズボンは君に似合わない Those (particular) pants [trousers] don't look good on you. (❗particular があると「特にそのズボンは」の意) ▶彼は来ないかも知れません。その場合は私が議長をします He may not come. In that case I'll take the chair. (❗He may not come, in which case I'll ... でも可) ▶その日[朝]といえばそれは It was 《a》 nice weather (on) that day [morning]. ▶市長は当時病気でしたが、そのことはだれにも知らされなかった The mayor was then sick, which [but it, but that] was not known to anybody. (❗which, it, that は前の文全体をさす) ▶その点では君と同意見だ I agree with you there [on that point].

その 間 er, erm, uh. ▶ええと、つまり、その(う)、とても難しい問題だってことです Erm I mean, er, it's a very difficult problem.

その 園 (庭園, 菜園) a garden; (果樹園) an orchard; (場所) a place. ●桜の園 a cherry orchard. ●学びの園 a school.

そのう 粗嚢 (鳥・虫類の) a craw; a crop.

* **そのうえ その上** [それに] besides, what is [(話) what's] more, [書] moreover (❗(1) besides は前述の内容を軽く補強する。後の二つはより重要でことを強意的に追加する。(2) besides と moreover は文頭・文中・文尾のいずれにも置くが、what is more は通例文尾には置かない)(⇨又❸);[さらに][書] furthermore (⇨さらに);[それに加えて] on top of that (くだけた言い方。不快なことに用いることが多い), (やや書) in addition (to that). (❗以上の語句はセミコロン(;)や and、ダッシュ(ー)などの後に続けられることも多い) ▶彼女は頭もいいし、その上美人だ She is intelligent; besides, she is good-looking./She is intelligent and good-looking besides./She is intelligent. Besides [(さらによいことに) What is better], she is good-looking. ▶その家は小さかったし、その上値が高すぎた The house was small, and what is more [moreover, on top of that, (さらに悪いことに) what is worse, to make matters worse], (書) to make the matter worse], it was too expensive. (❗what is worse は主文の時制と一致させて what was worse としても可)

そのうち ❶ [間もなく] soon, before long; (近いうちに) one of these days (❗警告にも用いられる (⇨いつか❶)); (いつか) someday, sometime ((英) (こは some day, some time のように 2 語にもつづる); (遅かれ早かれ) sooner or later. ▶彼らの婚約はそのうちに発表されるであろう Their engagement will be announced soon [one of these days]. ▶彼もそ

のうち親の気持ちが分かるでしょう He will appreciate his parents' feelings sooner or later [in time]. ▶その他の細かい事はそのうちに(=やっていくうちに)分かってくるよ The other details you'll figure out as you go along. (❗概要の説明等の直後などは the other details は本来の figure out の後の位置から対比のために文頭に移動する方が自然)

[会話]「君はそれをするつもりかい」「ええ、そのうちに」 "Are you going to do it?" "Yes, sometime in the future."

❷[該当者の中で] ▶10人の先生がその会に出席したが彼もそのうちの1人だった Ten teachers attended the meeting and he was one of them. ▶彼には子供が4人いる。そのうち2人は学生だ He has four children, two of them [whom, ×who] are students.

そのかわり その代わり [代わりに] instead (❗通例文頭・文尾で);[しかし] but;[だから] so. (⇨代わりに) ▶父はお金はくれなかった。その代わり図書券をくれた My father didn't give me money. Instead(,) he gave me book coupons./My father gave me book coupons instead of money. ▶この布は質がよい。その代わり値段が高い This cloth is of good quality, so it's expensive.

そのかん その間 during the time; in the meantime; meanwhile. (⇨間(かん)❶) ▶その間何をしていたのですか What were you doing during the time?

そのき その気 ●その気になったら if I [you] want 《to do》. ▶彼女はおだてられてその気になった She was flattered into doing it. ❗話題の内容を doing it に当てはめるとよい.「そのバイクを買う気になった」 buying the bike など)

そのくせ [それでも] still;[しかし] but, (and) yet (❗(and) yet は but より対照の意味が強い);[それにもかかわらず]《書》 nevertheless (❗but より強い対照を示す。文頭・文中・文尾いずれも可); for all that (❗通例文尾に置く). ▶私が正しいとみんな知っていたが、そのくせだれも賛成してくれなかった Everyone knew I was right; still [nevertheless] nobody supported me. ▶彼女は東京で寂しい思いをしたが、そのくせ故郷に帰る気にはなれなかった She felt lonely in Tokyo, but [(and) yet] she didn't feel like going back home.

そのくらい (⇨それくらい)

そのご その後 (そのあと) after that;(以来) since (then), from then [that time] on;(後で) afterward, later. (❗具体的な数字とともに用いる場合は afterward より later, after の方が普通) ▶その後彼に会っていない I haven't seen him since (then). (❗ since を強めて「その後ずっと」は I haven't seen him ever since. となる (⇨[次例])) /I didn't see him after that. (❗通例 since は現在完了, after that は過去とともに用いる) ▶その後彼らは幸せに暮らした They have lived happily ever since./They lived happily ever after [afterward(s)]. (❗ever は since, after, afterward(s) を強調する) ▶その後5日たって彼は私のもとにやって来た Five days later he came to me. ▶その後いかがお過ごしですか How are you getting along?/How have you been? (❗「その後」は具体的な語(句)ではなく完了形などによって表されることもあるので注意)

そのころ その頃 [その当時] in those days;[その時] at that time, then. ●その頃の学生 students in those days. ▶その頃日本には鉄道はなかった There were no railroads in Japan in those days. ▶私はその頃まだ学校に通っていた I was still at [(米) in] school at that time [then]. ▶その頃には(=その頃までには)大学を卒業しているでしょう I will have

そのじつ その実 actually; in fact. ▶彼は肯越しの金は持たないなくて言いながら、その実がっちりため込んでいる He always says he spends all the money he earns, but *actually* [*in fact*] he has a lot of money in the bank [he's *actually* got fat savings (in the bank).

そのすじ その筋 (その方面) that field; (当該の役所、特に警察) the authorities; (やくざ) gang. ●その筋の専門家 an expert in *that field*. ●その筋の命により by order of *the authorities* [*the police*].

そのせつ その節 ▶その節は大変お世話になりました Thank you very much for your kindness *at that time*. (事情) 米英ではその時に礼を言うのみで後々繰り返して礼を言う習慣はない

そのた その他 (残り全部) the others; the rest (数えられるものをさす場合は複数形) (⇨残り, 他(ﾎｶ)); (列挙の後に) and so on [forth] (⇨など). ●その他のother. ▶生徒のうち 10 人は教室で勉強し、その他の者は外で遊んでいた Ten pupils were studying in the classroom while *the others* [the *other* pupils, *the rest*] were playing outside. (!) (1) the をつけない *other* pupils は「他の生徒」の意で、この場合は不可. (2) ×*the rest* pupils とはいわない

そのため (その理由[目的]で) for that reason [purpose]; (その結果) as a result, 《やや書》consequently (!) 文頭に用い、コンマで区切ることが多い).

そのつど その都度 each time. (!) 接続詞的にも用いる) ▶私は3回その小説を読んだが、その都度何かためになることを学んだ I have read the novel three times, and *each time* I learned something instructive. ▶会えばその都度彼女は文句を言う *Each* [*Every*] *time* I see her, she says something to complain of. (!) 接続詞的に用いたもの)

そのて その手 ❶【策略】that trick. ▶その手は食わないぞ You can't fool me with *that trick* [*your old trick*]./None of *your games*!/(一杯上手(ｼﾞｮｳｽﾞ)の手を知っている) I know a trick worth two of that. **❷**【その種類】that kind. ▶その手の話は聞いたことがあるよ I've heard a story *of that kind*.

そのとおり その通り ˇThat's how. (!) 単に Right. ともいう); ˇThat's it. (!) 「そうそう、そのとおり[調子]」という感じ); (賛成して) I think you're right. (!) I think を省略しないこと) ▶そのとおりにします I'll do *just like that*./(おっしゃるとおりに) I'll do *just as you tell me to*. ▶そのとおり、まったく賛成だ Exactly [*Precisely*, 《話》*Absolutely*]. I quite agree. 会話「ねえ、健さん、そのとおりでしょ」「まったくそのとおりだ」 "*Isn't that right*, Ken?" "*You can say that ／again*./*No doubt about it*./(言われてみれば) *That's certainly true*." (!) 前の二つの応答は強い同意を表し、親しい間柄で用いる) 会話「作家の田中二郎さんではないですか」「ええ、そのとおりです」 "*Aren't you* Jiro Tanaka, the author?" "*Yes, indeed*."

会話「なるほど、その方が街がよく見えるってわけね」「そのとおり(=分かってくれたね)」 "I understand. You got to see more of the city!" "*You got it*." (!) get to do は《米話》で「...することができる(can)」の意)

そのとき その時 then, at that time; 〖その当時〗in those days; 〖その瞬間〗at that moment [instant]; 〖特定の事が起こったその時〗on that occasion. ●その時のアメリカの大統領 the *then* President of the United States. ▶私はその時名古屋に住んでいた I was living in Nagoya *in those days* [*at that time*]. (!) 進行形は「一時的に」を含意) ▶ちょうどその時電話が鳴った The telephone rang just *at that moment* [*then*]./Just *then*, the telephone rang. ▶私が外出しようとしていたちょうどその時彼が訪ねてきた Just *as* [*when*] I was going out, he called on me. (!) just when は話し手にとって迷惑であることを暗示することがある) ▶その時以来彼から一度も便りがない I have never heard from him since *then*. ▶その時までにはこの小説を読み終えているでしょう I will have finished reading this novel by *that time* [by *then*]. ▶その時初めてわが国は真に自由になるであろう *Then*, and not until *then*, this country will [will this country] truly be free. (!) 後の方は副詞句が先行しているのにつられて助動詞 will が主語の前に出た表現で、前の方にくらべ文語的でかつ詠嘆的. 否定語・準否定語を含む語句が先行する場合に多い (⇨否)

そのば その場 ❶【場所】the spot; (場面) the situation; 〖場合〗the occasion. ●その場を救う save *the situation*. ▶その場に居合わせた人たち those (who were) present. ▶たまたまその場に居合わせた I happened to be *there* [(現場に) *on the spot*]. **❷**【即座】●その場で決める decide (it) *on the spot* [*then and there*, *there and then*]; (迅速に[即座に]) decide (it) *promptly* [*immediately*]. ▶その場で飲むように店の人がレモネードのびんを開けてくれた The shopkeeper opened the bottle of lemonade for me to drink *there and then*.

そのばかぎり その場限り ─ その場限りの 形 (一時しのぎの) temporary, stopgap; (口先だけの)《軽蔑的》glib. ●その場限りのことを言う say something *just to suit the occasion*.

そのばしのぎ その場しのぎ (⇨その場限り) ●その場しのぎの解決法 a *stopgap* solution.

そのばのがれ その場逃れ (⇨その場限り) ●その場逃れの言い訳をする make a *makeshift* excuse.

そのひぐらし その日暮らし ●その日暮らしをする live (from) hand to mouth (!) 最近は from を省略する形も用いられる); (将来のことなど考えずに暮らす) live from day to day without thought for the future.

そのへん その辺 ❶【そのあたり】around,《主に英》about; there,《やや話》thereabout (!) 通例 or の後に用いる); (近くに) near there; (どこかに) somewhere. ●どこかその辺に somewhere *around* [*about*] (*there*). ▶その辺(=途中)までごいっしょしましょう I'll come with you *part of the way*. ▶子供は遠くへ行くはずがない. (どこか)その辺にいるに違いない The child couldn't have gone far; he must be (somewhere) *around*. ▶彼は秋田かどこかその辺の出身だ He comes from Akita *or* (somewhere) *thereabout*. ▶正確な金額は分からないがその辺のところだ I don't know how much exactly, it's *there or thereabout*. (!) 具体的な数値とともに用いて、たとえば 1,000 円 *or so* [*thereabout*], *somewhere about* 1,000 yen. のように用いる) **❷**【そういったこと】▶その辺のことはよく分からない I'm not quite sure *about* [*of*] *it*.

そのほか その外 the others. (⇨その他)

そのまま ❶【その状態で】as it is (!) (1) さすものによって as they [you] are などになる. 過去形も可. (2) 通例文尾に置く); (手をつけていない) intact,《やま》as is. ▶古い家をそのまま保存する[買う] keep [buy] an old house *as it is* [*intact*,《米》*as is*]. ▶机の上のものはさわるな、そのままにしておいてくれ Don't touch my things on the desk. Leave them (*just*) *as they are*. (!) just は as を強める) ▶君が思うことをそのまま(=正確に)彼に話しなさい Tell him *exactly* what you think. 会話「このくずかごはどうしましょうか」「それがあったところにそのまま置いておいて」 "What about this waste-

そのみち その道 (その方面・分野) that field; (同業者) that trade; (医師・弁護士・教師などの) that profession; (芸事) that art. ▶その道の達人 the authority in *that field* [*line*] (《!》*line* の方が範囲が狭い); the master of the *art*.

そのむかし その昔 ▶昔々の昔、ドロシーという名の女の子がいた *Once upon a time*, there was a girl named Dorothy. (《!》一般に「昔」は a long time ago を用いる)

そのもの その物 (当の物) the very thing; (それ自体) itself. ▶彼は正直そのものだ He is honesty *itself*./ 《やや話》He is *the* (*very*) *picture* of honesty. ▶その物ずばりだ That's it exactly./That's just right. (⇨ずばり❷)

そのような such. (⇨そんな)

そのように (in) that way, like that; 《書》 thus. (⇨そんな) ▶そのようにじろじろ私を見つめないでください Don't stare at me *like that* [(*in*) *that way*]. ▶そのようにして彼女は英語を修得した *That is the way* she mastered English. ▶彼はチームのキャプテンなのだから、そのように(=それ相応に)ふるまうべきだ He is (the) captain of the team, and should behave *accordingly*.

:**そば 側 ―― そばの** [形] 《近くの》nearby; 《近所の》neighboring (《!》限定的に); 《すぐ近くの》next to …, close to …(《!》close to の方が接近の度合いが高く、「触れるほど近くの」の意. next to は主に順序関係を表す) ●そばの川へ魚釣りに行く go fishing in a *nearby* river [a river *nearby*, a river *in the neighborhood*]. ▶私の家のそばの空き地 a vacant lot *next to* [*close to, by the side of, near*] my house; a vacant lot *in my neighborhood*.

―― **そばに[を]** [副] 《かたわらに》by …; beside …(《!》by は前後・左右・上下関係を表すのに対し、beside は主に左右の位置関係を表す); 《…のそばに》by [at] the side of …, by [at] one's side (《!》by, beside より「わき」を強調した言い方); 《すぐ近くに》near [close] to …; 《近くに》near …, nearby. ▶そばに来る come [go] (up [near]) *to one's side* [*beside …*]. ▶そばについて離れない stay *at one's side* and won't leave. ▶海岸のそばに公園がある There is a park *by* [*near*] the beach. (《!》by は near より近くを表し、near では海は見えなくてもよいが、by では海の見える所に位置していることが含意される) ▶彼は私のそばに座った He sat *beside* [*next to*] me./He sat *by* [*at*] my side. (《!》「あたりに」の意では around を用いる: 皆暖炉のそばに座った Everyone sat *around* the fireplace.) ▶新しい靴のそばに置くと古い靴はひどく形がくずれて見える *Beside* the new shoes, the old ones look very deformed. (《!》deformed は deform (形を損なう)の過去分詞形が形容詞化している) ▶三井住友銀行のそばまで行った I walked *by* [*past*] the Sumitomo Mitsui Bank. (《!》by はそばを通って行くことを表すだけだが、past では通って向こうへ行ったことが含意される) ▶彼の家は道路のそばに[=沿いに]ある His house is *on* the street. ▶彼はいつも辞書をそばに置いておく He always keeps a dictionary *at hand* [《話》*handy*]. ▶そばを離ればだめよ Don't keep away from me./Don't avoid me.

《会話》「そばにいてくれると思っていたのに、あちらへどのくらい行っていることになるの?」「大丈夫だよ、母さん、2,3か月もしたらいつもそばにいるから」 "I thought you would *be around*. How long are you gonna be there?" "You're gonna be fine, Mom. You'll always have me in a couple of months." (《!》gonna は going to の短縮形)

そば 蕎麦 (植物) buckwheat; (食品) buckwheat noodles, *soba*. (《!》日本の麺(ﾒﾝ)類は (Japanese) noodles で表すだけで十分なことが多い) ▶ざるそば *buckwheat noodles* (topped with shredded *nori*) served on a bamboo (work) plate. (《!》「もりそば」と区別する場合には ( ) 内が必要) ▶中華そば Chinese *noodles*.

● そばがき *sobagaki*, (説明的に) buckwheat flour stirred in hot water till it becomes a soft cake, eaten hot with soy. ● そばがら buckwheat chaff. ● そば粉 buckwheat flour /flάuər/. ● そば屋 (店) a *soba* [a noodle] shop; a *soba* [a noodle] restaurant; (屋台) a noodle stand [《主に英》stall].

そばかす a freckle. (《!》通例複数形で) ▶彼女の顔はそばかすだらけだ Her face is covered with *freckles*. (《!》「そばかすだらけの顔」は a *freckled* face)

そばだつ 峙つ (高くそびえる) soar; tower. (⇨そびえる)

そばだてる ▶耳をそばだてる(=音に気づいて聞き耳を立てる) prick up one's ears 《*at*; *when-* 節》.

そばづえ 側杖・側杖を食う (とばっちりを食う) get a by-blow 《*in* their fight》.

ソビエト the Soviet Union; (公式名) the Union of Soviet Socialist Republics (略 USSR, U.S.S.R. ロシア文字表記 СССР). 《[参考] 1991 年解体 (⇨シーアイエス, ロシア)》

そびえる rise (**high**); (そびえ立つ) soar, 《やや書》 tower. ▶私たちの上にそびえる大きな切り立つ great cliffs *towering* [*soaring*] *over* [*above*] us. (《!》over は威圧感を伴う) ▶そびえ立つ山 a lofty [*soaring, towering*] mountain. ▶渓谷の高みにそびえ立つ壮麗な城 a magnificent castle *sitting perched* high above the valley. (《!》高さだけでなく横幅のある建物などが高所にある場合) ▶高層マンションが都心にそびえ立っている High-rise condominiums *rise* [*soar, tower*] *over* the city. (《!》いずれも進行形不可)

そびやかす 聳やかす ▶肩をそびやかす square one's shoulders. ●肩をそびやかして歩く (極端に胸を張って歩く) strut; (肩を左右に振って歩く) swagger.

そびょう 素描 a (rough) sketch. ●人物素描 a character *sketch*, a profile. ▶その俳優の人物素描をする write a *profile* about the actor; profile the actor.

-そびれる (機会を失う) miss a chance 《*to* do》; (…しようと思っていたのにそれを果たさない) fail 《*to* do》. ▶お礼を言いそびれた I *missed the chance* [*I failed*] *to* express my thanks 《*to, for*》. ▶必要なことでうっかり聞きそびれたこともあるでしょう There are just some things you need that you probably *didn't know* to ask.

そひん 粗品 (⇨粗品(ｿｼﾅ))

*そふ 祖父 a grandfather. (⇨おじいさん)

ソファー a sofa. (⇨椅子(ｲｽ))

● ソファーベッド a sofa bed.

ソフィア 〚ブルガリアの首都〛Sofia.

ソフト 名 ❶ 〚ソフトウェア〛〚コンピュータ〛(a piece of) software. ▶ワープロ [表計算] ソフト a word processing [a spreadsheet] *software*. ▶このソフトは私のコンピュータでは動かない This *software* program won't run *on* my computer. ▶我が社はゲームソフト

ト製作に乗り出した Our company started writing video game software.
❷〖ソフト帽〗《米》a soft hat, 《英》a felt hat.

— **ソフトな** 形 〖柔らかい, 軽い〗soft. ●ソフトな(＝人あたりのよい)人 a affable 〖優しい〗gentle, ×a soft〗person. (!(1) affable は主に男性に用いる. (2) soft は「だまされやすい」などの否定的な意味になることが多いので避ける方がよい)
●ソフトコピー 〖スクリーン上に表示される出力情報〗a soft copy. ●ソフトコンタクトレンズ a soft contact lens. ●ソフトテニス soft tennis. ●ソフトフォーカス〖軟焦点〗〖写真〗a soft focus. ●ソフトランディング〖軟着陸〗a soft landing.

ソフトウェア 〖コンピュータ〗(a piece of) software. (⇨ソフト)

ソフトクリーム《米》soft ice cream, 《英》ice cream (cone). (〖具体的な一盛りは〗Ⓒ) (⇨アイスクリーム)

ソフトタッチ — **ソフトタッチの** 形〖手触りが〗soft to the touch; 〖人当たりが〗amiable, gentle, softhearted.

ソフトドリンク a soft drink.
ソフトボール《play》softball.
***そふぼ 祖父母** one's grandparents.

ソプラノ 〖音楽〗soprano /səprǽnou/. ●ソプラノで歌う sing soprano. ●ソプラノ歌手 a soprano (֊ ～s, soprani). ●ソプラノの声 a soprano voice.

そぶり 素振り 〖態度〗a manner, an attitude; 〖様子〗an air; 〖気配〗a sign; 〖顔つき〗a look; 〖身振り〗a gesture; 〖ふるまい〗behavior. ●あいつのそぶりは妙だ There's something odd in his manner./He's behaving oddly. ▶彼は怒って〖私の話を聞いて〗いるそぶりは見せなかった He gave [showed] no sign of anger [listening to me].

***そぼ 祖母** a grandmother. (⇨おばあさん)

そほう 粗放 — 粗放な 形 careless; rough.
●粗放農業 extensive farming.

そぼう 粗暴 名〖乱暴〗roughness /rʌ́fnəs/; 〖暴力を振るうこと〗violence.

— **粗暴な** 形 rough; violent. ●粗暴なふるまい rough [violent] behavior.

そほうか 素封家 a rich family 〖個人〗person].

***そぼく 素朴** 〖純真〗simplicity.
— **素朴な** 形 simple (!人に用いるとは「お人よしの, だまされやすい」の意になることもあるので注意); 〖気取らない〗unaffected; 〖無経験や好みの単純な〗unsophisticated. ●いなかで素朴な生活をする lead a simple life in the country. ●素朴な疑問を持つ have a simple question (about). ▶彼らは皆善良で素朴な人でした They were all good and simple people.

そぼふる そぼ降る 《it を主語にして》drizzle. ●そぼ降る雨 a (light) drizzle; a (slightly) drizzling [drizzly] rain. (! a drizzle は小雨から霧雨ぐらいまでの雨をさすので, 上のように形容詞や副詞を用いて降る様子を調節する)

そぼろ 〖料理〗*soboro*; seasoned fish [chicken] crumbles; powdered fish [chiken].

そま 杣 (⇨杣木(㍲), 杣人(㍲), 杣山(㍲))
そまぎ 杣木 trees grown for lumber 《主に米》[timber 《主に英》].

***そまつ 粗末** — **粗末な** 形〖質が悪い〗poor; 〖質が悪くて粗野な〗coarse; 〖量が少ない〗scanty; 〖手入れをせず古びた〗shabby; 〖質素な〗humble. (⇨貧弱) ●粗末な食事 a poor [〖簡単な〗simple, 〖量の少ない〗a scanty] meal. ●粗末な家 a humble [a shabby(-looking), a shoddy] house. (! shoddy は「作りのずさんな (shoddily-built)」の意) ▶彼女は粗末な服を着ていた She wore poor [coarse, shabby] clothes./She was poorly [shabbily] dressed. ▶お粗末さまでした (食事の後などで) I hope you('ve) enjoyed it. (事情 英語では日本語式に ×I'm sorry it was a poor meal. などとはいわない)/(講演などの後で) Thank you (, I hope you've enjoyed it.).

— **粗末にする** 動〖むとんちゃくである〗be careless about [of]…; 〖むだに使う〗waste; 〖世話などを怠る〗neglect; 〖人をひどく扱う〗treat 《him》shabbily. ●お金を粗末にする waste one's money; spend money carelessly. ●命を粗末にする have no [little] regard for one's (own) life. ▶彼は親を粗末にしている He neglects his parents./He treats his parents shabbily [(不親切に) unkindly]. (! ×He shabbily [unkindly] treats…. は不可)

そまびと 杣人 a woodcutter; a lumberjack, a timberjack.

そまやま 杣山 a timber forest; 《集合的》timberland.

ソマリア 〖国名〗Somalia /soumáːliə/; 《公式名》the Somali Democratic Republic.

そまる 染まる be dyed. (⇨染める) ●青く染まる be dyed blue. ●よく染まる dye well. (! ×be dyed well とはしない) ●血に染まる be stained with blood. (!「血に染まった」は blood-stained) ●悪に染まる sink into vice. ●空は夕日で赤く染まっていた The sky was glowing red with sunset.

そみつ 粗密 sparseness and denseness.
●粗密波〖物理〗a compression wave.

***そむく 背く** 〖人・命令などに〗disobey, go* against …; 〖約束などを破る〗break*; 〖法律などを犯す〗violate; 〖裏切る〗betray. ●社長の命令に背く disobey [go against] the president's order. ●約束に背く break [go back on] one's promise(s). ●法に背く violate 〖(反対の行動をとる) run counter to, act contrary to〗the law. ●国に背く betray 〖(反逆する) rise against, rebel against〗the country. ▶彼女は親の意に背いて彼と結婚した She disobeyed her parents 〖(親の願いに逆らって) went against her parents' wishes] and married him./(親の反対にもかかわらず) She got married to [×with] him in spite of [despite] her parents' disapproval. ▶彼は私たちの期待に背かなかった (＝期待に添った) He met [came up to, lived up to] our expectation(s).

そむける 背ける 〖顔[目など]を〗turn (one's face [eyes]) away 《from》; 〖特に目を〗look away, 《書》avert (one's eyes) 《from》. ▶彼はその光景に耐えられなくて顔を背けた He couldn't stand the sight and looked [turned his face] away.

ソムリエ ＜フランス語＞ 〖レストランなどのワイン係〗a sommelier /sʌ̀məljéi/.

そめ 染め dyeing; 〖色つけ〗coloring. ●染めがよい[悪い] be well [badly] dyed. ●2色染め two-color dyeing; 〖染め物〗two-colored dyed goods.

-ぞめ -初め ●橋の渡り初め the first crossing ceremony of a new bridge. ●書き初め new year's first calligraphy.

そめあがる 染め上がる dye (well [deep blue]).
そめあげる 染め上げる finish dyeing. ▶彼はその綿布を鮮やかな黄色に染め上げた He dyed the cotton cloth (in) bright yellow.

そめいよしの 染井吉野 〖植物〗a Yoshino cherry tree.

そめかえす 染め返す redye (the cloth); dye (the cloth) again.

そめこ 染め粉 (a) dye.
そめつけ 染め付け 〖染めること〗dyeing; (プリントすること) printing; 〖あい色で模様をつけた磁器〗《a piece

そめぬく 染め抜く leave* (a pattern) undyed.
そめもの 染め物 (染め物) dyed goods [(布) cloth]; (染めること) dyeing.
そめもよう 染め模様 a dyed pattern [design].
そめる 染める dye /dái/; color. (❗dye は染料で染めること. color は色つけることで染料によらなくてもよい)
● 布に髪を赤く染める *dye* cloth [one's hair] red. ●手を血に染める *stain* one's hands *with* blood. ▶彼女はつめを赤く染めた(=塗った) She *painted* her (finger)nails red. ▶夕日が空を赤く染めた Sunset *dyed* [*colored*] the sky red. ▶彼女ははおを赤く染めた She *blushed* [*turned red*].

そめわけ 染め分け ━ 染め分けの 形 parti-colored.
● 染め分けの朝顔 a morning glory with *parti-colored* flowers.
そめわける 染め分ける dye in different colors.
そもう 梳毛 (そろえた長い羊毛) carded [combed] long-staple wool; (その糸) worsted /wústid/ yarn.
そもそも ⦅最初の⦆ first; ⦅第一に⦆ first(ly); ⦅まず第一に⦆ to begin [start] with; ⦅根本的には⦆ basically; ⦅いったい⦆ on earth. (⇨一体) ▶そもそも彼を議長に選んだのが間違いだ(=最初に重大な間違いは…) The *first* and fatal mistake is that we chose him as chairman./*Firstly* [*To begin with*], it was a mistake that we chose him as chairman. ▶そもそもなぜ彼女が彼と結婚したのか考えられない I can't think why *on earth* [*in the world*] she married him. (❗on earth, in the world は why を強める) ▶彼女はそもそもどうしてそこへ行かなければならなかったのか分からなかった She had no idea why she had to go there *at all*.

そや 粗野 ━ 粗野な 形 ⦅下品な⦆ vulgar; (言動が性的) coarse; (洗練されていない) unrefined; ⦅無作法な⦆ rude; (言動が荒々しい) rough /rʌ́f/; (無骨で) boorish. ●彼の粗野な話し方 his *coarse* way of speaking.
そよう 素養 ▶彼はフランス語の素養(=一応の心得)がある He has some *knowledge* of French./He knows some French. (⇨知識, 技術)
そよかぜ そよ風 (a) breeze, a soft [a gentle] breeze [wind]. (❗wind より breeze を多用する). (⇨風) ▶そよ風が吹いている It's blowing *gently* [*softly*]./A *gentle breeze* is blowing.
そよぐ (さらさら音を立てる) rustle /rʌ́sl/; (ゆらゆら揺れる) sway. ▶木の葉が風にそよいでいた The leaves *were rustling* [*swaying*] in the wind./The wind *rustled* [*swayed*] the leaves.
そよそよ ▶風がそよそよ吹いている It's blowing *softly* [*gently*]. ▶葉が風にそよそよ揺れている Leaves are moving *gently* in the wind. ▶そよそよ吹く風が快適だった I felt good in the *light* wind.
そよふく そよ吹く ●そよ吹く春風 a *gentle* [a *soft*] spring wind.
:**そら** 空 ❶ ⦅天⦆ the sky; the air.

> 解説　通例 the sky と単数形を用いるが, 広がりを強調して the skies と複数形で用いることがある. また空の状態についての修飾語がつくと通例 a を伴う. the air は空中をさす.

①【〜空】●晴れた[曇った]空 a clear [a cloudy] sky. ●明るい[暗い]空 a bright [a dark] sky. ●星空 a starry sky. ●夏空 the summer sky. ●ロンドンの灰色の空 the gray skies of London. ●女心と秋の空 'Women's mind and the autumn *sky* are changeable.'/⦅ことわざ⦆ Women are as wavering (changeable, inconstant) as the wind.

②【空〜】▶飛行機が空高く飛んでいる A plane is [There is a plane] flying high up in *the sky*. ▶カモメは空高く舞い上がった The seagull flew high [up] into *the sky* [*the air*]. ▶花火は夜空いっぱいに広がった Brilliant flashes of fireworks spread all over the dark *sky*.

③【空は[が]】▶空は青く雲一つなかった *The sky* was blue and cloudless. ▶空が暗くなった[明るくなった] *The sky* has darkened [cleared]. ▶東京には空がないと千恵子は言う Chieko says she cannot see much *sky* in Tokyo.

④【空の】●空の旅を楽しむ enjoy one's *flight* [an air trip, traveling by plane]. ●明るい大西洋の空の下を航海する sail under the bright Atlantic *sky* [*skies*].

⑤【空に】●目を空に向ける look up to *the sky*. ●風船は空に上がった The balloon rose [went up, (ふわふわと) drifted away] into *the sky*. ▶今夜は空に星が出ている There are stars in *the sky* tonight. ▶東の空には星がいっぱいだ The eastern *skies* are full of stars. ▶人工衛星ひまわりは打ち上げられて数秒で空に消えた The satellite *Himawari* disappeared [vanished] into *the sky* a few minutes after it was launched.

⑥【空を】▶私は空を見上げた I looked up at *the sky*.

❷ ⦅その他の表現⦆ ●そらで覚えている know ⦅it⦆ by heart. (⇨暗記) ▶彼はその詩をそらで朗唱した He recited the poem *from memory*.

● 空色 sky blue.

そら there; look. (⇨ほら)
そらおそろしい 空恐ろしい ⦅何となく[非常に]不安に感じる⦆ feel* a vague [a strong] fear ⦅about⦆; ⦅恐ろしいほどの⦆ ⦅話⦆ terrific. ●彼女の空恐ろしいまでの記憶力 her *terrific* memory.
そらごと 空言 (うそ) a lie; (作り事) a made-up story.
そらす 反らす ●体を反らせて(=曲げて)床に手をつく *bend* backward and touch the floor. ●胸を反らす(=突き出す) *stick* [*throw*] out one's chest (❗自慢・自信・反抗を含意); (上体を後ろに傾ける) lean back (❗上方を見る, どっかり座っているときの姿勢).
そらす 逸らす ⦅方向を⦆ turn ... away ⦅aside⦆; ⦅注意などを⦆ distract, divert; ⦅いやなものから目をそむける⦆ look away, ⦅書⦆ avert; ⦅質問などをはぐらかす⦆ ⦅やや書⦆ evade. ●彼の怒りをそらす *turn away* his anger. ●話をそらす(=話題を変える) *change* the subject. ●その仕事から彼の気をそらす *distract* his attention *from* the work. ●人をそらさない(=機転のきく)話しぶり a *tactful* speech. ▶彼女はその恐ろしい光景から目をそらした She *turned* her eyes *away* [*look away, averted* her eyes] *from* the terrible sight. ▶ボールから目をそらすな *Keep* your eye *fixed* on the ball.
そらぞらしい 空々しい obvious. (⇨白々しい)
そらだのみ 空頼み a vain hope. ▶私はそれが空頼みであると分かっていたのだが, それでも万が一にかけたかった I knew it was a *vain hope*, but I still hoped against hope.
そらとぼける 空惚ける (知らないふりをする) pretend ignorance [not to know]. (⇨とぼける)
そらなき 空泣き 空泣きする(=空涙を流す) (⇨空涙)
そらなみだ 空涙 false (不誠実な) insincere] tears, ⦅やや話⦆ crocodile tears. ●空涙を流す shed [weep, cry] *false tears*.
そらに ●他人の空似 an accidental [a chance] resemblance.
そらね 空寝 (たぬき寝入り) a make-believe sleep. (⇨狸)

そらねんぶつ 空念仏 (⇨空(むな)念仏)

そらまめ 空豆 〖植物〗a broad bean.

そらみみ 空耳 ▶私の空耳に違いない I must *be hearing* [*imagining*] *things*. (❗通例進行形で)

そらみろ そら見ろ Dídn't I ＼téll you só?/I told you so, didn't I?

そらもよう 空模様 the look of the sky. ▶空模様が怪しい The *weather* looks threatening./(雨になりそうだ) It's likely to rain [looks like rain]. ▶この空模様だと今夜はひと雨降るかもしれない (*Judging*) *from* [*by*] *the look of the sky*, it may rain [we may have rain] tonight.

そらんじる 諳じる learn ... by heart. (⇨⇨ 暗記する)

そり 反り (板などの) a warp (in a board).
● 反りが合わない (うまくやってゆけない) be not congenial (*to*); can't get along [on] well (*with*).

そり 橇 (馬ぞり) a (horse) sleigh; (運搬用) 〖主に米〗a sled, 〖主に英〗a sledge. (❗小型の a sled, a sledge は「遊び用のそり」もさす) ▶その村へそりで行く go [ride] to the village *on* [*in*] *a sleigh; sleigh* 〖主に米〗*sled*, 〖主に英〗*sledge*] to the village.
● 斜面をそりで滑り降りる slide down the slope *on a sled*.

そりあじ 剃り味 ▶このシェーバーはそり味がいま一つだ This electric razor *doesn't shave well*./This shaver *isn't good enough*.

そりかえる 反り返る (板などが) warp; (人がいすなどに座って) sit* back imperiously (in the chair).

ソリスト [<フランス語] a soloist /sóulouist/. (⇨ソロ)

そりはし 反り橋 an arched bridge.

そりみ 反り身 ▶反り身になる lean backward; (そっくり返る) throw one's shoulders back and stick one's chest out; (胸をぐいと張る) throw one's chest out (❗自信・自惚などのしぐさ).

そりゃ (⇨それは)

そりゃく 粗略, 疎略 ●粗略に扱う (物を) handle roughly; (人・事を) treat lightly; (人を) be not polite (*to* him).

そりゅうし 素粒子 〖物理〗an elementary particle.

ソリューション 〖問題解決〗a solution.

そりん 疎林 a sparse wood.

そる 反る (板などが) warp; (体の一部が) lean* backward. ▶レコードを日の当たる所においておいたら反ってしまった The record *warped* when it was left in the sun.

そる 剃る (顔・頭などを) shave; (ひげなどを切り落とす) shave ... (off). ●頭[鼻の下; 口ひげ]をそる *shave* one's head [under one's nose; one's mustaches].
● きれいにひげをそった顔[男] a clean-*shaven* face [man]. ● ひげをそってもらう have a shave. (❗ have の代わりに get も可) ●男は毎朝ひげをそらなければならないんだ Men need a shave [have to *shave* (*themselves*), have to *shave* their faces] every morning.

ゾル [<ドイツ語] 〖コロイド溶液〗〖化学〗a sol /sɒ(ː)l/.

ソルダム 〖植物〗a soldum. (参考 スモモの一品種)

ソルフェージュ [<フランス語] 〖音楽〗solfège /sɑlféʒ/.

それ 代 ❶【物・人・事を指し示す(気持ちで)】that (複 those). (⇨これ) ▶私が言いたいのはそれです *That's* what I mean. ▶それとこれとは話が違う This is quite different from *that*./This is one thing and *that* is quite another. ▶そのアメリカ製のライフルはすぐにそれとわかった The rifle was immediately identifiable [recognizable] as American [an American product]./I recognized at once that the rifle was an American product.

会話 (写真をのぞいて)「それだれ？」「この男の人のこと？」「ええ、それそれ」"Who is *that* (man) [×he]?" "You mean this gentleman?" "＼*That's* it."

❷【前述の物・事を表す(代)名詞, 文内容を受けて】it. ▶彼は約束があると言ったがそれはうそだった He said he had an appointment, but *it* was a lie. (❗(1)後半は ...*which* was a lie. といえる. この which は前の節を受ける指示代名詞. (2) 指し示す気持ちで it の代わりに that を用いてもよい) ▶彼が大学へ進学しなくても, それはそれでかまわない *It's* all right (even) if he works without going on to university. ▶野菜の花だってそれはそれで(＝それ特有の)風情がある The flowers of vegetable plants have their own charm, too. ▶それがどうした(と言うのだ) So what?

会話 「車を買った」「本当？」「そう, それは何色？」"I bought a car." "Really? What color is *it*?"

解説 日本語では「それ」とわりなくても, 英語では常に形式的な主語として it を用いる表現がある.
(ⅰ) 時間: 12時です *It's* 12 o'clock./1月17日火曜日です *It's* Tuesday, January 17.
(ⅱ) 天候: この部屋は暑い *It's* hot in this room.
(ⅲ) 温度: 摂氏20度です *It's* 20 degrees centigrade.
(ⅳ) 距離: 京都から20キロあります *It's* 20 kilometers from Kyoto.
(ⅴ) 環境: ここはうるさい *It's* noisy in here.
(ⅵ) 現在の状況: 楽しいね *It's* fun.

❸【その時】then, that time. ●それ以来 since *then*. (❗通例現在完了時制とともに用いる (⇨それから❶))

❹【その他の表現】 ▶それ以上近づくと撃つぞ If you come any closer [any further], I'll shoot (you).

翻訳のこころ 錯覚がようやく成功し始めると私はそれからそれへ想像の絵の具を塗りつけてゆく (梶井基次郎『檸檬』) As illusion has finally succeeded in taking over me, I begin to paint with imaginary colors one after another [the other]. (❗(1) 「...が錯覚を起こす」は illusion takes over ... と表す. (2) 「し始める」は has taken ... と現在完了形で表す. (3) 「それからそれへ」は one after another [the other] (次から次へ)と表す)

それ 間 there; look. (⇨それみろ) ▶それごらん, だから言わないことじゃない ＼Told you só!/Dídn't I ＼tell you só?/Whát did I ＼téll you! (❗物事に取りかかるときに気合いを入れて)それっ！ *Hére* ＼*goes*!

*それから ❶【順序】(その後(すぐ)) then; (その後) after that; (後で) afterward, later; (それ以来) since (then), from then on; (次は) next. (⇨その後, これから) ▶彼は夕食を食べて, それからすぐ寝た He had dinner, (*and*) *then* went to bed [and went to bed soon *after that*, and went to bed soon *afterward*]. (❗(1) いずれも過去・未来のある時点を起点にして順序を表す場合に用いる. (2) that を省略した soon after の方が普通) ●我々はまず京都, それから奈良へ行った First we went to Kyoto, *and then* to Nara [and to Nara *next*]. (❗「まず京都, それから奈良, それから大阪へ行った」のように三つ以上の要素についていう場合は First we went to Kyoto, *then* to Nara, *and then* to Osaka.) ▶彼は1年後に上京した He went to Tokyo a year *later* [a year *after that*]. (❗ a year *after* の形は比較的まれ) ▶彼は5月に横浜に行って, それから(というもの)ずっとそこにいる He went to Yokohama in May and has been there ever *since* (*then*). (❗過去のある時点から現在まで継続していることを表し, 通例現在完了形とともに用いる. ever is

「ずっと」の意で since の意味を強める)▶来週大阪に行ってそれからはそこで生活します I'm leaving for Osaka next week and *from then on* will be living there. ❗*from then on* は過去にも未来にも用いる. cf. from now on)
❷【追加】▶我々は京都と奈良,それから大阪にも行った We went to Kyoto, Nara, *and also* Osaka. (❗この順で行ったとは限らない. (⇨そして 解説 Ⅱ (2))
❸ で,それから?(相手の話を促して)Well, ↘*then*?/↗*Yes?*
会話「この家のセールスポイントは何ですか」「ええ,まず場所が申し分ないし,それから値段が手ごろです」"What is the selling [×sales] point of this house?" "Well, first, the location is perfect. *Then* the price is reasonable. (❗しばしば第一要素を導くfirst(ly), in the first place, for a start, to start with などと呼応して) (⇨まず,第一)

『**それから**』*And Then.* [参考]夏目漱石の小説

それきり(⇨それっきり)

それくらい▶私はそれくらいしか知りません I know only *that much.* ▶私だってそれくらいのお金[本]は持っている I have quite *as much* money [*as many* books]. ▶その仕事はそれくらいにしておこう Let's leave the task *at that.*/*So much for the task.* (慣用的な言い方)▶1か月かそれくらいでは速記技術の習得は無理です It is impossible to acquire shorthand skill in a month *or so.* ▶それくらいの(=そんな取るに足りない)ことで腹を立てるな Don't get angry about *such a small [a little] thing.*

それこそ▶それこそ(=それはまさに)私の欲しかった本です That is *the very [just the]* book (that) I wanted. (❗ともに book を強める)▶君がそんなことをしたら,それこそ(=本当に)彼は怒るでしょう If you do so, he will *really* get angry.

それしき それ式 ▶それしきのことで騒ぐな Don't make a fuss over a trifle like that.

それじゃ(それなら) then; (そうか,つまり) so; (なるほど) well; (さて) now; (じゃあね) bye. ▶それじゃ,1時間後に電話するよ *Bye* [*Bye now*]! I'll call you in an hour.

それそうおう それ相応 ▶あんなにお世話になったのだからそれ相応の(=それにふさわしい)お礼はしなければなりません He helped you so much, and you'll have to give him *something suitable* to show your gratitude. ▶それ相応の(=理にかなった)分け前はもらえるものと思っていた I thought I could have a *reasonable* share. ▶あれだけのことをしたのだからそれ相応の覚悟はしているのでしょうな You are prepared to pay for what you've done?

*****それぞれ** each; (述べられた順に) respectively. ▶学生たちはそれぞれ自分の意見を持っている The students *each* have their own opinion [×opinions]. (1) 副詞の each が主語を修飾する場合は,通例一般動詞の前, be 動詞の後, 助動詞の直後・直前に置かれる. (2) 動詞・代名詞は複数呼応するのが原則. (3) 主語は複数の限定された名詞や代名詞に限られる: They [×Students] *each* have their own opinion.)/*Each* student has [×have] their [his] own opinion. (❗「each+単数可算名詞」は通例単数扱いだが,呼応する所有代名詞は今は his より their が一般的. 《書》his or her も可)/*Each* (*one*) *of the students* [×*Each* (*one*) *of students*] has their [his] own opinion [have their own opinion]. (❗(1) each of の後には限定された複数名詞や複数代名詞が続き,動詞はしばしば複数呼応する. (2) 文脈から明らかな場合は of 句は省略可. ただし, each を単独で代名詞として用いるより each one を用いる方が普通: *Each* (*one*) has [their] [his] own opinion.) ▶彼らにそれぞれ 500 円やった I gave *each* of them 500 yen./I gave them 500 yen *each*. ▶健太と航太はそれぞれ 18 歳と 12 歳です Kenta and Kota are 18 and 12 years old *respectively*. (❗*respectively* は通例文尾に置かれる.

それだから so; 《やや書》therefore. (⇨だから)

*****それだけ** ❶【数量,程度】that [so] much; (それほど) so, (話) that; (それだけ一層) the+比較級 (*for, because* 節). ▶それだけあれば間に合う *That* (*much*) will do. ▶1時間早く起きれば,それだけゆったりした気分にひたれますよ If you get up an hour earlier, you will feel *that much more* [*all the more*] relaxed. ▶それだけ勉強すれば,たぶん試験に合格するでしょう If you study *so* [*that*] hard, you will probably pass the exam. ▶彼は欠点があるからそれだけ好きだ I like him (*all*) *the better for* his faults [(*all*) *the better because* he has some faults]. ▶はるばる彼に会いに出かけたのだが,それだけのことは(十分)あった I went out all the way to see him, but it was (well) *worth that*. ▶もし首になれば別の仕事を見つけるよ. それだけのことさ If I get fired, I'll try to find another job. ↘*That's all* (*there is to it*). ▶5万円はあげるけどそれだけだよ I'll give you fifty thousand yen and *no* [*nothing*] *more.* ▶そのチームは今年は絶好調だ. それだけにファンの期待も大きい The team is in top shape this year, so it raises its fans' expectations *all the more.*
❷【そのことだけ】▶それだけが不安である *Only that* [《やや書》*That alone*] makes me uneasy. ▶私が言いたいのはそれだけです *That's all* I want to say.
会話「他に何か?」「いや,それだけです」"Anything else?" "No, ↘*that's it* [↘*that's all*]."

それだま 逸れ弾 a stray bullet [(散弾銃の) shot].

それっ(⇨それ 圓)

それっきり▶それっきり(=それ以来)彼から音沙汰(おとさた)がない I have heard nothing from him *since* (*then*) [*ever since*]. (⇨それから❶)▶審理はそれっきりになっている(=中断している) The trial *has been suspended*. ▶話はそれっきりですか Is that *all* you want to tell me? ▶リンゴはもうそれっきりですか Are they *the last* of the apples? (❗the last は「最後のもの・人」などの意)▶ぼくたちは大げんかして,それっきり(=それを最後に)付き合わなくなった We had a big fight and broke up *for good*.

それぽっち▶それっぽっちのお金しか持っていないの Is it all the money you have? ▶それっぽっちのけがで泣くな Don't cry over such a *slight* bruise /brúːz/.

*****それで** 【だから】 so, so that 《so の方がくだけた言い方》; 《やや書》therefore; [それから] then; [そして] and. (⇨だから) ▶彼は勉強が嫌になった. それで学校をやめた He lost interest in studying. *So* [(その理由で) *For that reason*] he left school./He lost interest in studying, *so* [*so that*] he left school. ▶それで思い出したのだけど,彼女会社をやめたそうよ *Which* ↘*reminds me,* I hear she left the company. (❗*which* は関係詞の非制限用法で,直前の相手の発言内容を *That* reminds me. I. ...よりスムーズに受け継ぐ効果的な言い方)
会話「それで君はそのテニスクラブに行って楽しかったというわけだね」「ええ,だからいつまたか行きたいわ」 "So you enjoyed going to the tennis club." "↘*Yes* and I'd like to go ↘*again,* ↘*sometime.*"
会話「彼に電話をしたよ」「それで彼は何と言った?」 "I called him." "What did he say (, *then*)?"
会話「かつては京都に住んでいました」「それで今はどこに住んでいるの?」 "I used to live in Kyoto." "*And* /ǽnd/ where do you live now?"
会話「それで言うことはおしまいですか」「まあそうだね」 "Is

それでいて (それなのに, それでも) yet.

それでこそ ▶「それでこそ男だ」とコーチははっぱをかけた *That's the boy!* encouraged the coach. (! 《主に米話》). 一般に「それでこそ男だ」は, He was (xa) man enough to do it./What he did is worthy of a man. (それをしたとは彼は男らしい とか, He is worthy of being a man. (一人前の男と言われるに 値するなど文脈によってさまざまに訳出される)
会話「彼の方からあの仕事をしたいとの申し出がありまし た」「それでこそ原此」"He volunteered to do the work." "*That's just* like Hara."

それでなくても ▶また追加の仕事なの？ それでなくても(＝ 現状のままで)十分忙しいのに Another job into [《米》in] the bargain? We are busy enough *as it is.*

それでは [そうすると] then (! 通例文頭・文尾で); so (! 文頭で, 相手の意向を確かめる); [ところで] well; [さて] now. (⇒では) ▶それでは君は今夜来られないね *Then* you can't come tonight./*So* you can't come tonight (*then*). ▶それではぼつぼつ失礼しないと, 明日学校があるから. *Well,* I guess I should be going. I have (to go to) school tomorrow. (! I have school in the morning の方が普通)
会話「申し訳ないんだけど, 私ココアはだめなの」「それでは 紅茶はいかが」"I'm sorry, but I don't care for cocoa." "*Would* you like a cup of tea, *then*?"

それでも [しかし] but; [それにもかかわらず]《話》all [*just*] the same,《やや話》still,《書》nevertheless; [たとえそれでも] even so; [それでもなお] (and) yet. (⇒しかし) ▶疲れていたがそれでも深夜まで働かねば ならなかった I was tired. *Still* [*All the same, Even so*], I had to work till late at night./I was tired, *but* [(*and*) *yet*] I had to work till late at night. ▶わがままなところもあるが, それでも彼女が好きだ With all her selfishness, I'm *still* in love with her. ▶大事な試合が控えているんだ. 君は出られなくなる かもしれないが, それでもいいのか We have a big match coming up. You're not gonna be in it maybe. Is *that* what you want? (! 前文を that で受けて 文意を接続させる言い方.《話》gonna は going to の 短縮形)

それというのも ▶私は山登りには参加しませんでした. それ というのも体力に自信がなかったのです I did not go (mountain) climbing with them, *because* I wasn't sure of my (physical) strength.

それどごろか ▶彼は試合に勝てると思っていたが, それどごろ か大敗した He expected to win the game, but *instead* [*on the contrary*] he lost badly. (! (1) instead は通例文頭または文尾, 時に文中で用いられる. on the contrary は文頭または文中が普通. (2) 上の 表現の代わりに to the contrary, on the other hand を用いるのは誤り (⇒反する)) ▶霧がうすれ晴れ る気配はなかった. それどころかむしろ濃くなってきさえしてい た The mist wasn't showing any sign of lifting (↔rising)―*in fact,* if anything, it was growing thicker. (! 通例否定文の後に用いて先行 文の内容をさらに強調する)
会話「野球はお嫌いなんですね」「(いいえ)それどころか大 好きです」"You don't like baseball, do you?" "*On the contrary* [*Fàr fróm it*]! I like it very much." (! On the contrary!, Far from it! はとも

に通例否定文・疑問文などの後に用いて先行の文とまった く正反対の意味を強調する. 後の方は単独でも用いる)

それとない [間接的に] indirect; [何気ない] casual. ●それとない依頼 an *indirect* request. ▶それとないし ぐさに女らしさを感じる In her *casual* movements, I sometimes find her feminity.

それとなく [間接的に] indirectly; [何気なく] casually. ▶それとなくその事件に触れる make an *indirect* reference to the event. ●それとなく彼の方 に目をやる give him a *casual* glance. ▶彼はそれとな く辞任をほのめかしていた He *hinted* (*to* us) [*gave* (us) *a hint*, *dropped a hint*] that he would resign. (⇒ほのめかす)

それとも or. (⇒または) ▶あの人は君のお父さん？ それとも おじさんなの？ Is that your ╱father *or* your ＼uncle? (! (1)…？ uncle? とすると「父, おじ, それ とも別の人か」の意. (2) 応答は yes, no を用いず He's my father. (父です)のように答える)

それなのに [しかし] but; [それでもなお] (and) yet (! 不 可解な気持ちによる感情的な含みを伴う. (⇒しかし, かかわ らず) ▶彼は試験に落ちた. それなのに満足げな様子だった He failed the exam, *but* [(*and*) *yet*] he looked satisfied. ▶彼にそれをするよう繰り返し言った. それなの にしなかった I repeatedly told him to do it *and* [*but*] he didn't do it. (! この and は対照を表し /ǽnd/ と強く読む)

それなら [そういうことなら] then; [もしそうなら] if so. (⇒それでは) ▶駅まで行くの？ それなら私を車に乗せ Are you going to the station? *If so,* I'll give you a ride 《主に米》[a lift 《主に英》]. ▶それなら事 は簡単だ *That* makes it easier.
会話「あすまた会おうよ」「それならどこで？」"Let's get together again tomorrow." "Where *then*?"
会話「今日は休みです」「それなら映画に行こう」"I have a holiday today." "*Then* let's go to the movies."
会話「すごく疲れたなあ」「それなら早めにお休みなさいよ」 "I feel very tired." "Go to bed earlier, *in that case.*"

それなり ❶[そのまま] as it is [stands]. ▶その計画は それなりになっている The plan has been left *as it is.*/《まだ未決定だ》The plan is *still unsettled.*
❷[それ相応に] ▶それはそれなりに重要だ It is important *in its own way.* ▶大学まで出ているのだからそれ なりの学問(＝知識)はあるのだろう I think he has *a certain amount of* knowledge because he is a college graduate.

それに [その上] besides, what is more,《書》moreover; [加えて] on top of that. ▶行きたくないんだ. それ に時間も遅すぎるし I don't want to go; *besides* [*what's more*] it's too late. (⇒その上)
会話「彼は試合に出たがらないかもしれないよ」「それに彼 が来るかどうかだって分からないじゃないか」"He may not want to play." "*And* (*in any case*) how do you know he'll turn up?" (! and は単独では /ǽnd/ と 強くゆっくり発音する)

それにしては ▶彼は食べ物の好き嫌いが激しい. それにして はとても健康だ He doesn't (want to) eat many kinds of food. He is very healthy, *considering.* ▶彼女は 160 センチはないと言うが, それにしては大 きく見える She says she isn't as tall as 160 centimeters, but she looks much taller *than she really is.*

それにしても [それでも] still; [たとえそうでも] even so; [それにもかかわらず]《やや書》nevertheless. ▶彼はよ く勉強する. それにしても成績があまり向上しないな He studies hard. *Still* [*Even so*] he shows little improvement in his school record. ▶文句は言

それにつけても ▶それにつけても思い出されるのはあの痛ましい事故だ *That reminds me of that tragic accident.*

それにもかかわらず (⇨それなのに)

＊それは ❶ [本当に] really; [非常に] very, extremely. (!後の方が強意的) ▶彼女はそれはいい先生でした *She was a really [a very, an extremely] good teacher.*
❷ [それに対して] ▶それはありがたい *Thank goodness [God] for that.*
❸ [その他の表現] ▶それはないでしょう *That's unfair, isn't it?/That's not fair, is it?*

そればかりか ▶それどころか(＝その上), 彼は私の宿題まで手伝ってくれた *Besides [What is more, 《書》Moreover]*, *he even helped me with my homework.* (⇨その上) ▶今の仕事はおもしろいし, それにばかりか(＝それにまた)将来の見込みもあるのだ *The job is interesting, and again it offers good prospects.*

それはさておき putting that aside. (⇨さておき)

それはそうと [ところで] by the way, incidentally (⇨ところで); [さて] well. ▶それはそうと, 最近の男に会いましたか *By the ＼way [＼Incidentally], have you seen him lately?* ▶それはそうと, 今何時 *＼Well, what's the ＼time?*

それはそれは very, extremely. (⇨それは)
[会話] 「あなたに関する新聞や雑誌の切り抜きを2冊持っているんです」「本当ですか, それはそれは(なんとありがたいことか)」 *"I have two albums of press clippings about you." "Really? How very good of you!"*

それほど so, 《話》that. (⇨そんなに) ▶私はバナナはそれほど好きじゃない *I don't like bananas so [very] much.* ▶リンゴはそれほど高くない *Apples aren't (all) that expensive.* (!all that は否定文・疑問文に用いられ否定を弱める, 主に《話》) ▶それはどおっしゃるならお引き受けいたしましょう *I'll accept your offer if you insist.* (!「仕方なく引き受ける」気持ちを強く暗示)
[会話] 「忙しいですか？」「いや, それほどでもないですね」 *"Are you busy?" "No, not ＼really [very]."*

＊それまで ❶ [そのときまでずっと] until [till] then; up to that time. (⇨まで) ▶それまでここにいます *I'll be here until then.*
❷ [そのときまでに(は)] by then [that time]. ▶それまでには帰って来なさい *Come back by that time.*
❸ [それで終わり] ▶やってみてだめならそれまでだ *If you try but don't succeed, that's that [that's the end of it].* (!あきらめの気持ちを表す慣用表現)

それみたことか それ見たことか (⇨そら見ろ)

それみろ ▶それみろ, 私の言ったとおりだろう *There! I told you [I thought] so./See, didn't I tell you so?*

それゆえ それ故 [やや書] therefore; [書] accordingly (!文頭に用い, 直後にコンマを打つことが多い). (⇨だから)

＊それる 逸れる [弾などがねらいが外れる] miss; [急に針路を変える] swerve; [話などが脱線する] stray《from》, wander《from, off》; [正道からそれる] go* astray; [注意などをそらす] distract. ▶本通りから横道へそれる *turn off the main street into a side street.* ▶論点からそれる *wander [go] off [stray (away) from, 《れている》be beside] the point.* ▶通常の飛行コースからそれる *deviate from the usual flight path.* ●それた sailing throw. ▶投球はそれて打者の頭上を通った *The pitch sailed over the batter's head.* ▶痛烈なゴロは投手のひざに当たってそれた *The hot grounder bounced off the pitcher's knee.* ▶彼のバックホームはそれた *His throw to the plate was wide [off line].* ▶弾丸が的をそれた *The shot missed the target./(大きく) The bullet went wide (of the mark).* ▶その車はトラックを避けようと左にそれた *The car swerved to the left to avoid the truck* 《米》[lorry 《英》]. ▶話題がわき道へそれた *The conversation strayed [wandered] from the subject.* ▶物音で注意が本からそれた *The noise distracted me [distracted my attention, diverted my attention] from the book./I was distracted from the book by the noise.*

ソれん ソ連 (⇨ソビエト, ロシア)

ソロ [独奏, 独唱] a solo /sóulou/. ▶ソロで歌う *sing solo.*
●ソロホームラン a solo home run.

ゾロアスターきょう ゾロアスター教 Zoroastrianism.
●ゾロアスター教徒 a Zoroastrian.

そろい 揃い (一式) a set. (⇨揃(い)い) ▶ディナー用食器一そろい *a set of dinner dishes*; a dinner set. ▶新しい家具一そろい *a new set [suite /swi:t/] of furniture.* ●そろいの服を着ている双子 *twins (dressed) in matching clothes.* ▶皆様おそろいで(＝いっしょに)お出かけですか *Is everybody going out together?* ▶皆さんおそろいでしたら会議を始めます *If everyone is here, we'll start the meeting.*
●揃いも揃って ▶彼らはそろいもそろって初心者ばかりだ *Each and every one of them is [×are] a beginner./They're all a bunch of beginners.* ▶彼女の娘たちはそろいもそろって皆美人だ *Her daughters are all beautiful, every one of them [without a single exception, 《やや古》one and all].*

-ぞろい -揃い ▶三つぞろいの服 *a three-piece suit.* ▶彼の娘たちは美人ぞろいだ *All (of) his daughters are beautiful./His daughters are all beautiful.*

そろいぶみ 揃い踏み ▶3人の内蔵助そろい踏み *Three Kuranosuke performers appear on the stage together.*

＊そろう 揃う ❶ [一か所に集まる] get* together, gather. (⇨前の方がくだけた言い方) (⇨集まる) ▶証拠は十分そろっている *Enough evidence has been gathered.* ▶正月休みは家族全員がそろう *All (the members of) our family get together for the New Year vacation.* ▶ぼくらはそろって(＝いっしょに)出かけた *We went out (all) together.* ▶この図書館には科学の本がわりとそろっている *This library has a large [a good] collection of books on science.* ▶この店にはシャツが豊富にそろっている *This store has a large [a wide] selection of shirts.* (!(1) この selection は「選択の範囲」の意. 図書館などのように収集してある場合は前例のように collection を用いる. (2) 店の人に言う場合は You have.... が自然. (3) 逆に「そろっていない」は have a poor selection of ... という)/They carry [have] almost all kinds of shirts at this store.

❷ [完全になる] be complete [completed]. ▶この1冊で全集がそろう *This volume makes the set complete./This volume makes a complete set./This volume completes the set.*
[会話] 「もうメンバーそろったかい」「今のところ2人足りないんだ」 *"Have you got a full team yet?" "So far, we're two people short."* (!short は「不足して」の意)

❸ [同じになる](数量などが等しい) be equal [even]; (形などが均一である) be uniform. (⇨同じ) ▶そろった歯 *regular* (↔irregular) *teeth.* ▶(スカートなどの)丈がそろうようにすそを直す *adjust the hemline so (that) it's even.* ●そろいもそろって (⇨揃い [成句])
▶それらのひもは長さがそろっている *Those strings are*

equal [*the same*] in length. ▶少女たちはそろって(=すべて)青い目をしていた All (*of*) the girls had blue eyes.

そろう 疎漏 (手落ち) a fault, a mistake; (見落とし) an oversight.

***そろえる** 揃える ❶【一か所に集める】collect, gather, get*... together (**!**前の二つより口語的の); (準備する) prepare. ●論文の資料をそろえる collect material [*gather* material, *get* material *together*] for an essay. ●工作の材料をそろえる *prepare* materials for handicraft. ●ひざをそろえる *put* one's knees *together*. (**!**「ひざをそろえて座っている」は sit with one's knees *together*)

❷【全部整える】●ゴルフクラブを全部そろえている[そろえる(=買う)] *have* [*buy*] a *complete* set of golf clubs. ●数をそろえる *make up* [*complete*] the number.

❸【きちんと整える】arrange; put*... in order. ●棚の本をそろえる *arrange* the books on the shelf. ●靴をそろえる *put* [*place*] one's shoes neatly *side by side*.

❹【調和させる】●声をそろえて読む[答える] read [answer] *in chorus* [*unison*]. ●(彼と)歩調をそろえる *keep* step (*with* him). ●かばんと靴の色をそろえる *match* the bag *with* the shoes in color.

❺【同じにする】●大きさ[長さ]をそろえる make ... all *the same* size [*length*]. ●隣の家と垣の高さをそろえる *make* the fence *as tall as* that of the next door.

そろそろ ❶【ゆっくりと】slowly; (用心深く) gingerly /dʒíndʒərli/. ●丸木橋をそろそろ歩いて渡る walk *slowly* [*gingerly*] across the log bridge.

❷【程なく】soon, 《書》before long. ●お父さんがそろそろ帰ってくる Father will be back *soon* [*before long*]./It won't be long before Father comes back. ●うちの息子はそろそろ独立できる(=独立するのに十分な)年頃だ Our son is old *enough to be* independent.

❸【もう(時間だ)】●そろそろ10時だ It's *almost* [*nearly*] ten o'clock. (almost, nearly については(⇨ 似た [類語]))●そろそろ帰らなければ I think I must be going now. (**!**I think I must go now. ともいえるが, 進行形にして唐突さを避ける方が丁寧)/It's *about* time to go.

ぞろぞろ ❶【多数が続くさま】●子供たちがぞろぞろ学校から出てきた Children *filtered out of* the school. ●スペイン広場界隈には観光客がぞろぞろ歩いている You can see a lot of tourists *milling around* in Piazza di Spagna and its neighborhood.

❷【後に引きずるさま】●そろぞろ引きずる; (重い物を) drag. ●少女たちが長いスカートをぞろぞろ引きずって歩いてきた The girls came *trailing* their long skirts behind them./The girls came with their long skirts *trailing* behind them.

そろばん 算盤 an abacus /ǽbəkəs/ (複 ~es, abaci /-sài/). ●《西洋では子供に数を教えるのにしか用いない》●そろばんで計算する count [*calculate*] *on* an *abacus*.

●そろばんが合う ●その仕事はそろばんが合わない(=もうからない) The job doesn't pay.

●そろばん高い ●そろばん高い(=勘定高い)人 a *calculating* person.

●そろばん尽く ●そろばん尽くの mercenary /mə́ːrsənèri/. ●あの男はそろばん尽くでしか動かない The man is motivated only by a desire for financial gain.

●そろばんをはじく use an abacus; (打算的である) be calculating [mercenary].

ぞろめ ぞろ目 a double. ●ぞろ目を出す throw a *double*.

ソロモンしょとう ソロモン諸島 〖国名〗the Solomon Islands.

ぞろり (⇨ぞろぞろ)

そわせる 添わせる (夫婦にさせる) make* (them) man and wife. ●初子を長男に添わせる marry Hatsuko *to* the eldest son.

そわそわ 副 (落ち着きなく) restlessly; (神経質そうに) nervously. ●間もなく生まれてくる赤ん坊の父親がそわそわと廊下を行ったりきたりしていた An expectant father walked up and down the corridor *nervously*.

—**そわそわする** 動 become* restless;《話》fidget /fídʒit/. (**!**手や足を動かしたり, 座っている人が神経質そうに位置を変えたり, 腰を浮かしたりする動作を示す.) ●彼は舞台に上がる前はいつもそわそわする He always *fidgets* before he goes on stage.

***そん** 損 图 ❶【損失】a loss. (⇨損失)

①【損は】●よい物を買えば損はない(=割に合う) It *pays* (you) to buy good articles.

②【損に】●結局損になる result in a *loss*. ●自分の損になることをする do *against* one's own *interests*.

③【損を】●私は損を承知でそれを売った I sold it *at the sacrifice of* my own *interests*. ●この取り引きでは損さえしなければ(=収支がとんとんならば)よしとせねばなるまい I'll be lucky if I *break even* on this deal.

❷【不利】(a) disadvantage. (⇨不利)●彼は英語を話せないので非常に損をしている His inability to speak English is a great *disadvantage* to him [*puts him at a great disadvantage*]. ●長男は損だと思う I don't think there is *any advantage in* being the oldest son.

❸【むだ】(a) waste. ●やるだけ時間の損だ It is a *waste* of time doing so.

—**損な** 形【もうからない】unprofitable;【不利な】disadvantageous; (好ましくない) unfavorable. ●損な商売[取り引き] an *unprofitable* business [deal]. ●彼は損な立場にいる He is in a *disadvantageous* [an *unfavorable*] position.

—**損(を)する** 動 lose* money. ●彼は商売で大損 [100万円] をした He *made* big *losses* [*made a loss of* one million yen, (失った) *lost* one million yen] in the business. ●親切にして損をすることはなかろう You will *lose* nothing by being kind. ●私は20ドル損をしてそれを売った I sold it *at a loss of* twenty dollars.

●損して得取れ (ことわざ) You must lose a fly to catch a trout.

そんえい 村営 ●村営の village-run. ●このテニスコートは村営です These tennis courts *are run by* the village.

そんえき 損益 profit and [or] loss; gain and [or] loss 《*on, in, from*》. ●経常損益 *profit or loss on* [*from*] ordinary activities.

●損益計算 income determination. ●損益計算書 a profit and loss statement [account]; an income statement; a statement of profit and loss. ●損益分岐点 a break-even point.

そんかい 損壊 —**損壊する** 動 be damaged and destroyed.

***そんがい** 損害【物の破損】damage;【利益の損失】a loss; (死者などの死傷者) a casualty.

①【～損害】●200万円の損害 a *loss* of two million yen; *damage* amounting to two million yen.

②【損害が】●洪水で田畑が流されて農家に莫大な

害が出た The flood washed away fields and caused enormous losses to farmers. ▶洪水による損害は[は] 2 億 5 千万円に達する[見積もられている] The *damage* caused by the flood amounts to [is estimated at] two hundred fifty million yen.

③【損害を[も]】● 商売で大損害をこうむる suffer heavy *losses* in the business. ●その損害を埋め合わせる make up (for) the *loss*. ▶会社は全損害を賠償した The company paid [compensated for] the total *damage*. ▶あらしで作物は大きな損害を受けた The crops suffered great *damage* from the storm./The crops *were* greatly *damaged* by the storm./(与えた) The storm *did* [*caused*, ×*gave*] great *damage* to the crops./The storm *damaged* the crops greatly. ▶きのう地震があったが実際には何の損害もなかった Yesterday we had an earthquake, but there was no real *damage* done.

● 損害額 the cost of damages. ● 損害賠償 compensation for damage [loss]. ● 損害賠償金〘法律〙damages (⚠通例複数形で). ▶彼は不当な解雇に対し会社に 1,000 万円の損害賠償金を要求した He claimed 10 million yen (in) *damages* [×*damage*] against the company for unfair dismissal. ● 損害保険 insurance against damage [loss]；〘保険〙casualty insurance.

ぞんがい 存外 unexpectedly. (⇨囲 案外) ▶やってから存外やさしかった I could do it easier *than I thought*.

そんぎかい 村議会 a village assembly.
● 村議会議員 a member of the village assembly.

そんきょ 蹲踞 — **蹲踞する** 動 squat; take* a squatting position.

*そんけい 尊敬 名 respect《*for*》；(深い敬愛)〘書〙reverence /révərəns/《*for*》. ▶彼はその生物学の教授に深い尊敬の念を抱いている He has (a) great *respect* [great *reverence*] *for* the biology professor./He *respects* the biology professor greatly. (⇨動) ▶彼は教師として皆の尊敬的である(= 皆が尊敬している) Everyone *respects* [*looks up to*] him as a teacher. (⚠日本語にひかれ, ×He is the object of everyone's *respect* as a teacher. のようにはいわない)/(皆の尊敬を集めている) He wins [earns] everyone's *respect* as a teacher./As a teacher, he *is held in great* [*high*] *respect* (⚠《書》で, 慣用的な表現). ▶彼の勇敢な行為は尊敬に値する His brave deed deserves [is worthy of] *respect*.

— **尊敬すべき** 形 (立派な) honorable.〘⚠respectable は「悪くはない」という意で, 通例積極的な尊敬の意味しない。この意での reverend は《古》〙●尊敬すべき行為 an *honorable* deed.

— **尊敬する** 動 respect；(仰ぐ) look up to ... (⚠口語的). ▶彼は近所の人たちから皆尊敬されている He *is respected* [*is looked up to*] by all his neighbors.

● 尊敬語 an honorific.

そんげん 尊厳 dignity. ● 労働の尊厳 the *dignity* of labor. ● 人間の尊厳を傷つける[保つ] impair [maintain] human *dignity*.

● 尊厳死 death with dignity. ● 尊厳死を選ぶ権利 the right to die with *dignity*.

:**そんざい 存在** 名 existence /ɪgzístns/；〘生命・感覚などが存在すること〙being；〘そこにいること〙presence. ● 幽霊の存在を疑う doubt the *existence* of ghosts. ● 神の存在を信じる believe in (the *existence*) of God. (⚠通例( )内は省略する。×believe God とはいわない) ● 存在意義がある[ない] have [don't have] the significance of *existence*. ▶彼は私の存在には気づいていなかった He was not aware of my *presence*. ▶彼は口数は少ないが存在感のある人だった He was a man of few words but of great *presence*. (⚠単独で「存在感のある男」というときは a man with great presence の方が普通) ▶その会社は海外市場でも存在感を強めてきた[無視できない存在になってきた] The company is making its *presence* strongly felt [is becoming a *presence* to be reckoned with] in the overseas market as well. ▶最近彼の存在がいかに大切かが分かってきた Recently I have been realizing how much he means to me. (⚠このように「存在」の意は訳語ではなく文脈で表されることもある)

— **存在する** 動 exist, be in existence；〘存在するようになる〙come* into existence [being]. ● 存在しない be nonexistent. ▶そのようなものは本当に存在するのか Does such a thing really *exist*? ▶この習慣はその地方で今もなお存在している This custom still *exists* [is still *in existence*,（守られている）*is still observed*,（実行されている）*is still practiced*] in the region. ▶人間が地上に存在するようになってからどれくらいたつだろうか How long is it since a human being *came into existence* [*being*] on earth?

● 存在理由 its [one's] reason for being; raison d'être /réizoun détrə/.

ぞんざい — **ぞんざいな** 形〘がさつな〙rough /rʌ́f/；〘失礼な〙rude, impolite；〘不注意な〙careless；（なおざりな）negligent；〘ずさんな〙slipshod, 《話》sloppy.
● 口のきき方がぞんざいである be *rough* in one's speech; speak *rudely*. ▶あんまりぞんざいな口をきかないようだ I'd like you a little more polite. (⚠トーンダウンした言い方の一例)

— **ぞんざいに** 副 ▶彼女は仕事をぞんざいにする She does her work *carelessly* [*negligently*, *in a slipshod way*].

ぞんじあげる 存じ上げる (⇨存じる)

*そんしつ 損失 a loss. (⇨損) ● 500 ドルの損失 a *loss* of 500 dollars. ● ストライキによる損失 strike *losses*. ● 洪水による損失 *losses* from floods. ● 取り返しのつかない損失 an irretrievable *loss*. ● 損失を取り戻す make up (for) a *loss*. ● 2,300 ドルの純損失を計上する record [report] a net *loss* of 2,300 dollars. ▶社長の死は我が社に大きな損失である The president's death is a great *loss* to our company. ▶敵軍は大きな損失を被った The enemy forces suffered heavy *losses*. ▶その会社は株式市場で大きな[巨額の]損失を出した The company made big [huge] *losses* on the stock market.
● 損失補填 loss compensation.

そんしょう 尊称 an honorific title.

そんしょう 損傷 damage. ● 損傷を与える damage (the ship); do damage (*to* the ship). ● 損傷を受ける be 《badly》damaged; receive [suffer]《a lot of》damage.

そんしょく 遜色 ● 遜色がない be in no way inferior《*to*》；《やや書》bear [stand] comparison《*with*》；(can) compare favorably《*with*》.

そんじょそこら ▶この皿は名品ですよ. そんじょそこらにあるものじゃありません This plate is excellent. You cannot find this one *anywhere*. [This is not one of those ordinary plates.]

そんじる 損じる〘体面などを傷つける〙damage, hurt；〘感情を損ねる〙《やや書》offend, 《話》get* on《his》bad [wrong] side；〘壊す〙break*；（部分的に）damage；〘むだに遣う〙waste. ● 兄の機嫌を損じる *offend* [*get on the bad side of*] one's (older)

ぞんじる 存じる brother. ●書き損じる make a mistake in writing; write incorrectly. ▶彼はその不祥事で大いに名声を損じた His reputation *was* greatly *damaged* by the scandal./The scandal *tarnished* his reputation severely. (!) tarnish は「曇らせる, (名誉を)傷つける」の意)

ぞんじる 存じる ❶ [思う] I (would) think* (!) would がある方が丁寧さが増す); (信じる) I believe. (⇨思う) ▶山田さんは 50 歳を超えていると存じます I *think* [*believe*] Mr. Yamada is over fifty. ●英語には特に謙譲表現はないが, Mr. Yamada is, I *think* [*believe*], over fifty./Mr. Yamada is over fifty, I *think* [*believe*]./I *would think* Mr. Yamada is over fifty. のようにいうことによって断定を避けた控えめな気持ちを表すことが可)
❷ [知る] know*. ▶ご存知でしょうがこちらはガーナー先生です I *think* you *know* Mr. Garner. (⇨❶)
会話「彼はいつ帰ってきますか」「存じません」"When will he be back" "I don't *know*./I *have no idea*." (!) 後の方が穏やかな言い方で, 時に質問に対する当惑を暗示する)

ぞんする 存する [存在する] exist; (依然としてある) remain; [本質的にある] consist [lie*] in ...; (選択, 決定などが握られている) rest with .... ▶幸福は満足に存する Happiness *consists* [*lies*] *in* contentment. ▶主権は国民に存する Sovereignty *rests with* the people.

ぞんぞく 存続 图 [保持] retention; [続くこと] (a) continuation, [書] continuance.
―― **存続する** 動 continue (to exist); (持ちこたえる) last; (困難にめげず) endure. (⇨続く)
●**存続期間** the term of existence.

ぞんぞく 尊属 a lineal ascendant.
●**尊属殺人** the killing of one's ascendant; (父親殺し) patricide; (母親殺し) matricide.

そんだい 尊大 ―― **尊大な** 形 árrogant; (もったいぶった) self-important. ●**尊大な態度** an *arrogant attitude* [manner].

そんたく 忖度 ―― **忖度する** 動 ●人の気持ちを忖度する guess [imagine] others' feelings.

*__**そんちょう 尊重** 图 respect 《for》.__ ●個人の権利の尊重は民主主義の基礎である *Respect for* individual rights is the basis of democracy.
―― **尊重する** 動 respect, have* respect 《for》; (高く評価する) value, 《書》 esteem. ●彼の意見を尊重して out of *respect for* [《書》 *deference to*] his opinion. ●長年の交友関係を尊重する *value* a friendship of long standing. ●技術を非常に尊重する *value* [*esteem*] technology highly. ▶彼女は他人のプライバシーを尊重しない She doesn't *value* [*respect, has* no *respect for*] other people's [others'] privacy.

そんちょう 村長 the chief (⑧ ～s) of a village (!) 米英にはその種の長がいない。町長, 市長は a mayor /méiər/ というので, これを借用するのもひとつの考え)

そんどう 村道 a village road.

そんとく 損得 profit and loss (!) 日本語との語順の違いに注意); [利害] an interest. ●損得を計算する calculate the *profit and loss*; (利点を調べてみる) weigh the *advantages* 《of》. ▶損得は問題ではない It does not matter whether I *gain or lose*.

*__**そんな** 形 ❶ [今述べたような] such__ (!) 冠詞 a, an は such の後に); [その ような] ... like that (!) such より口語的); [その] that; [そんな種類の] that kind [sort] of .... ▶私はそんなことを言った覚えはありません I haven't said *such* a thing [×a such thing;《複数》 *such* things]./I said no *such* thing./I didn't say any *such* thing. (!) no や any のように, 形容詞的に用いられた some, all, other, another などの不定代名詞または数詞も such の前に置く。ただし代名詞としての不定代名詞では such some [all, others, another] の語順をとる)/I said nothing of *the kind* [*sort*]. ▶そんな美しい花は見たことない I've never seen a beautiful flower *like that* [*such* a beautiful flower, 《書》 *so* beautiful a flower]./ That's the most beautiful flower (that) I've ever seen. ▶そんな大金を借りることはできません I can't borrow *such* a large amount of money. ▶ハンバーガーとかホットドッグとか何かそんなものが食べたい I want to eat a hamburger, a hot dog or something *like that* [or (some) *such* food]. ▶そんなの気にしないで Don't worry about *that*. ▶彼はいつもそんなふうにふるまった He always acted *that* way [*like that*]./*That*'s the way he always acted. (!) 前の way は副詞的, 後の way は接続詞的な使い方) ▶そんなわけで彼は遅れて来ました *That*'s why he came late. ▶そんな機械はもう使われていない [話] *Those kind* [*sort*] *of* machines are no longer used [in use]. (⇨種類) ▶そんな格好でまさか仕事に行く気じゃないでしょうね You couldn't go to work *in that*.
❷ [その他の表現] ▶あなたのことが嫌いとかそんなことじゃないよ。ただ 1 人になりたいだけなのよ *It's not that* I don't like you. I just want to be alone. (!) It's not that ... (...だからではない) はくだけた言い方で Not that ... ともいう) ▶世の中ってそんなものだ *That*'s *the way* the world is. (!) この That's the way 〈it [he] is〉 の表現型は, 一般に「何故？」と尋ねられて具体的に説明しない場合に用いられる: That's the way it is [comes]. (それはそんなものなんですよ)/That's the way he is. (あの人はそんな男なんですよ))/*That*'s the world for you. (!) for you は文尾につけて相手の注意を引いて「ねえ, そうでしょう」といった感じの感嘆表現) ▶そんなことだろうと思った (= 驚かない) I'm not surprised./(前文の内容を受けて) I thought *as much*. (大ざっぱに言えば) まあそんなところです *That*'s *about it*./You could say *that*. (!) 相手の言った内容にゆるやかに同意する表現)
会話「私たちこの 3 日間口もきかないの」「まあそんなことってあるよね」"We haven't talked to each other for the past three days." "Well, *it happens*."
●**そんなこんな** this and that; this, that and the other. ▶そんなこんなで結局ハワイには行けなかった What with one reason and another [*this and that*], I couldn't go to Hawaii.

―― **そんな** 圃 ▶そんな(こと言わないで)! いっしょに行こうよ Oh, come *on! Let's go together.
会話「首にされたよ」「そんな! 」"They've given me the sack." "They haven't!/Oh, no!/No way!"
会話「ちょっと! 玄関の鍵が開いてるわ」「そんな(はずがない)! 」"Look! The door's unlocked." "How can *that* be?"

*__**そんなに** [それほど(までに)] so, 《話》 *that*; [それほどたくさん] (量が) so__ [《話》 *that*] much; (数が) so [《話》 *that*] many; [そんな風に] like *that* (⇨そんな); [あまり...でない] not very, (計) *not* (all) *that* ... (!) 通例否定文・疑問文で形容詞の前で). ▶どうしてそんなに遅くなったの？ Why were you *so* [*that*] late? ▶つまらない事にそんなに騒ぐな Don't make *so much* fuss [*such* a fuss] about trifles. ▶そんなに魚が釣れたの？ Did you catch *that many* fish? ▶彼女はそんなに歌がうまくない She doesn't sing *very* [*so*] well. ▶トマトはまあまあの値段だけれども, レタスはそんなに安くない Tomatoes are reasonable, but lettuces aren't *all that* cheap.

会話「しまった，奴に言うのを忘れちゃった」「そんなに大事なことなの？」 "Oh, my God! I've forgotten to tell him." "Does it matter *all that much*?" (❗ Oh, my God! はかなり深刻な失敗のときに発する間投詞)

会話「それは 1 万円以上したよ」「あら，そんなに」 "It cost over ten thousand yen." "Oh, my! As much as *that*." (❗(1) Oh, my! (あら，まあ) は女性の好む間投詞. (2) as much as は多さを強調して「…ほども多く」の意)

会話「戻ってきてどのくらいになるの」「そんなに(=あまり)たってないよ」 "How long have you been back?" "Not *very* [*so*] long." (❗ so は女性に好まれる)

そんのう 尊王 royalism.
● 尊皇攘夷(じょうい)(説明的に) a conviction that restoration to the Imperial rule and expulsion of foreigners from Japan are essential to gain political stability.

そんぱい 存廃 ▶ その制度の存廃が議論されている The question whether to *continue* the system *or not* [*or abolish it*] is now made the subject of discussion.

そんぴ 存否 ● その詩人の生家の存否(=存在するのかしないのか)を尋ねる ask if the house where the poet was born exists (or not). ● 祖父の存否(=祖父が健在かどうか)を問う ask if one's grandfather is still alive and well.

ゾンビ (a) zombi(e).
そんぷ 尊父 your father.
ソンブレロ [<スペイン語] a sombrero /sɑmbréərou/ (複)~s).

ぞんぶん 存分 ── 存分に ● 存分にスキーを楽しむ(=心ゆくまで) enjoy skiing *to* one's *heart's content* [(最大限に) *to the full*]; (とことん) *thoroughly* enjoy skiing. ● 存分に食べる(=好きなだけ) eat *as much as* one *likes*; (腹いっぱい)《話》eat *till* one *is full*; 《書》eat one's *fill*.

そんぼ 損保 〖『損害保険』の略〗(⇨損害)
そんぼう 存亡 life or death. ● 存亡の危機 life crisis. ● 国家存亡のとき at national crisis. ● 危急存亡のとき in time of crisis; in a crisis.

そんみん 村民 (全体) the (whole) village (❗ 単・複両扱い); (個人) a villager. (⇨村人)

そんめい 尊名 ▶ ご尊名はかねがね伺っております I have often heard about you.

ぞんめい 存命 ▶ 母の存命中にこの仕事を完成した I completed this work while my mother *was alive* [*living*].

そんもう 損耗 wear; (a) loss. ● 体力の損耗を防ぐために in order not to *lose* our physical strength.

そんゆう 村有 ● 村有の広場 open land *owned by the village*; open land that *belongs to the village*.
● 村有財産 village property.

そんらく 村落 a village.
● 村落共同体 a village community.

そんりつ 村立 continued existence.
そんりつ 村立 ● 村立の village. ● 村立小学校 a *village* elementary 《米》[primary 《主に英》] school.

そんりょう 損料 (使用料) (a) rent.

た

*た 田 a paddy (field), a rice field. (⇨たんぼ)
*た 他 other(s). (⇨外(ほか), その他)
た 多 ▶君の努力を多とします(=感謝する) I greatly [deeply] appreciate your efforts./I appreciate your efforts very much.

-た ❶ [過去の行為・できごと] [過去形] 《did》; [完了形] had 《done》; [現在完了形] have* 《done》.

> 解説 (1) 過去形と現在完了形: 過去の行為・できごとでも、現在とは断ち切られた過去として見る場合は過去形を、現在と関連するできごととして見る場合は現在完了形を用いる。(詳しくは (⇨-(し)ている ❺)
> 解説 (2) 過去形と過去完了形: 二つの過去のできごとの順序関係をはっきりさせようとする場合、基準となる過去には過去形を、さらにさかのぼった過去には過去完了形を用いる。(⇨-(し)ていた ❺)

▶きのう雨が降った It *rained* yesterday. (❗ 過去を明示する副詞とともに過去のできごととして述べている) ▶もう夕食を食べました I've already *had* supper. (❗ 夕食を食べたという過去の行為の影響で、現在は空腹感を感じていないことを暗示) ▶警察が現場にやってきたときにはやくざたちは逃げたあとだった When the police *came* to the scene, the gangsters *had* (already) *run* away. (❗ (1) 過去がある方が、やくざの姿が形もなかったことが強調される。(2)《米》では過去形を用いて ... already ran away. ともいう。ただしこの場合 already を使わないと「警察の到着」と「やくざが逃げた」こととがほぼ同時に起きたことになるので注意。(3) when の代わりに before, by the time など前後関係を明示する接続詞を用いる場合は主節も過去形ですますことも多い) ▶三味線を習い始めたがとても楽しいと分かった I *started* to learn samisen, and *found* it very enjoyable. (❗ 二つの行為やできごとを時間の流れに沿って述べる場合は過去形を用いる)

❷ [結果としての現在の状態] [状態動詞の現在形] 《do》.

> 解説 日本語では「-(し)た」となっていても、英語では状態動詞と呼ばれる動詞を用いるため、現在形のままで現在の状態を表すことができる。(詳しくは (⇨-(し)ている ❷ (a))

▶あら、せりふを忘れたわ Oh, my! I *forget* my lines. (❗ forgot は「忘れていた」の意: "Did you turn off the light?" "Oh, I *forgot*.") ▶分かりました、すぐ対処いたします I *see* [*understand*]. I'll take care of it right now. ▶ああ、思い出したぞ Now I *remember*. (⇨思い出す [第1文例]) ▶試験は終わった The exams *are* over.

❸ [現在目の前のできごとを感嘆的に] [現在形] 《do》. ▶何だ、こんなところにいたのか Oh, there you *are*! ▶ほら来た、バスが来た Here *comes* the bus! ▶やられた You *beat* me. ▶小野のヘディング、抜けた、入った(サッカーの実況で) Ono *heads* it past the goalkeeper and *scores*. (❗ it = the ball)
会話 「さあ、参ったか」「参った」"Now *do* you give up?" "I *give* up."

❹ [軽い命令] ▶すぐに出た出た Get out right away.

-だ ❶ [断定] ▶彼は我がチームの主将だ He *is* (the) captain of our team. (❗ 無冠詞が普通)

❷ [命令] ▶君が行くのだ Yóu *must* go. ▶おい、耳の穴をかっぽじってよく聞くんだ Yóu cock úp your ＼ears./Cock úp your ＼ears, ＼will you? (❗ 肯定の命令文に you をつけて、また will you を下降調でいうといらだちの気持ちを表す)

❸ [述語の内容を省く言い回し] ▶あしたから学校だ(=授業が始まる) School *begins* tomorrow. (❗ (1) 計画表・時刻表などにすでにある確実な未来のできごとをいう場合は単純現在時制を用いる。(2) tomorrow は副詞として用い、× ...from tomorrow としない) ▶ぼくはコーヒーだ(=コーヒーを注文する) I'll *have* coffee.

たあいない (⇨たわいない)

ダーウィン [英国の博物学者] Darwin (Charles (Robert) ～). ▶ダーウィンの進化論 *Darwin's* theory of evolution; Darwinism.

ターキー [七面鳥] (a) turkey; [ボウリングの3連続ストライク] a turkey.

ダークグレー [黒っぽい灰色] dark gray. ●ダークグレーのスーツ a *dark gray* suit.

ダークホース a dark horse; a long shot. (❗ 競馬では後の方がよく用いられる)

ターゲット a target. (⇨的(まと)) ●若者をターゲットにした新型車を発表する show a new model *targeted* at young people.
●ターゲットゾーン [目標相場圏] [経済] a target zone.

タージマハール [インドの墓廟(びょう)] the Taj Mahal /táːdʒ məhɑ́ːl/.

ダージリン [インドの都市] Darjeeling; [紅茶] Darjeeling (tea).

ダース (12 個) a dozen /dʌ́zn/ (略 doz., dz.). (❗ 数詞や many, several の後では単・複同形) ●1[3]ダースの卵 a [three] *dozen* (*of*) eggs. (❗ 今は of を省略して形容詞的に用いるのが普通) ●数ダースの鉛筆 some *dozens* of pencils. ●some の後は複数形。some *dozen* pencils は「およそ1ダース(=10本余り)の鉛筆」の意 ●このグラスを4[半]ダースください Four [Half a, A half] *dozen* of these glasses, please. (❗ 特定のものの数をいう場合 dozen の後の of は省略できない) ●あのハンカチは1[半]ダースいくらですか How much are those handkerchiefs *a dozen* [*a half dozen*, ×half a dozen]? ●卵はダース単位で売られている Eggs are sold *by the dozen* [(1ダースずつで) *in dozens*, ×by a dozen].

タータンチェック [格子縞模様] tartan, 《和製語》tartan check. ●タータンチェックのスカート a *tartan* skirt.

ダーツ [投げ矢遊び] darts (❗ 単数扱い); (ダーツの矢) a dart. ●パブでダーツをして遊ぶ play *darts* in a pub; (1ゲーム) have a game of *darts* in a pub.

ダーティー [汚い] dirty. ●ダーティーなイメージ a corrupt image.

ダート [泥] dirt. ●ダートコース(競馬場の) a dirt track [course].

タートルネック [とっくりえり] 《主に米》a turtleneck, 《主に英》a polo neck. ●タートルネックのセーターを着ている wear [be in] a *turtleneck* [a *polo-neck*] sweater.

ターニングポイント [転換点] a turning point. ●人生のターニングポイント the *turning point* in one's life.

ターバン [<ペルシャ語] a turban. ●ターバンを巻く[巻いている] wrap [wear] a *turban*. ●ターバンを巻いた男 a *turbaned* man.

ダービー ❶【競馬等】(英国の) the Derby. ●日本ダービー the Japan *Derby*. ❷【同市内・同地域内のチーム同士の試合】a derby match.

> **参考** (1) 主なダービーマッチ: オールドファーム・ダービー Old Firm derby (スコットランド・グラスゴウ市のセルティック対レインジャーズ)／マージーサイド・ダービー Merseyside derby (リヴァプール市のリヴァプール対エヴァートン)／ナショナル・ダービー National derby (その国を代表するチーム同士の試合. スペインのレアル・マドリード対バルセロナなど).
> (2) 世界最古のダービーマッチは、イングランドのノッツ・カウンティ対ノッティンガム・フォレスト Nottingham derby だといわれている.

ターピン a turbine. ●水力[圧力]ターピンを回す spin a water [a pressure] *turbine*.

ターボ turbo-. ●ターボエンジン a turboengine. ●ターボ車 a turbocharged car; a turbo. ●ターボジェット機 a turbojet. ●ターボチャージャー a turbocharger; a turbo.

ターミナル〖終着駅〗a terminal. (⇨終点) ●バスターミナル a bus terminal.
●ターミナルアダプター〖コンピュータ〗a terminal adapter (略 TA). ●ターミナルケア〖終末医療〗terminal care. ●ターミナルビル (鉄道の) a railroad [a railway (英)] terminal (building) (which houses a shopping complex, restaurants, or/ and a hotel, etc.); (空港の) a terminal (building), an air terminal. ●ターミナルホテル a hotel at a railroad terminal.

ターミネーター〖終端抵抗〗〖コンピュータ〗a terminator.

ターム〖用語〗a term. ●テクニカルターム〖専門用語〗a technical *term*.

ターメリック（香辛料）turmeric.

ダーリン（呼びかけ）(my) darling. (❗夫婦・恋人同士、親が子に対して用いる)

タール tar. ●くいにタールを塗る *tar* a post.

ターン ❶ a turn. ❷ U ターン (Uターン)
──**ターンする** 動 ●右へターンする *make* [*take*] a *turn* to the right; *turn* (to the) right. ●上手にターンする *make* a good *turn*.
●ターンテーブル a turntable.

ターンオーバー〖サッカー〗(a) turnover. (参考) (1) 攻守が入れ替わること. (2) 出場メンバーを交代制で回転させること (⇨ローテーション)

たい 体 ●落石から体をかわす *dodge* the falling rocks. ▶その計画は徐々に体を成してきた The plan has gradually begun to *take shape* [*form*]. ▶名は体を表す (⇨名(な) ❶)

たい 対 ❶【対等】an equal footing. (⇨対等)
❷【対する】(競技などでの A 対 B) A versus B (略 vs., v.); (A-B 間の関係を示して) between A and B; (B と対立して) A against B; (B に対しての) A to B; (B に向けての) A toward B; (B との関係の中での) A with B. ●日本対アルゼンチンのサッカーの試合 a Japan *versus* Argentina soccer game; a soccer game *between* Japan *and* Argentina. ●貧者対富者の鋭い対立 a sharp confrontation of the poor *against* the rich. ●日本の対アジア(外交)政策 Japan's foreign policy *toward* [*to*] Asia.
❸【比率】to…. (⇨比) ▶第 1 試合は 2 対 1 で我々が勝った We won the first game (by [with] a score of) 2 *to* 1. (❗負けた場合でも We lost…2 *to* 1. で数字の順序は変わらない)

たい 隊 〖目的遂行のための集団〗a party, a team; 〖兵士の集団〗(特殊任務の隊) a corps /kɔ́ːr/ (複 ~ /kɔ́ːrz/); (軍隊) an army; 〖楽団〗a band. ●先発隊 an advance *party*. ●海兵隊 a marine *corps*. ●海軍音楽隊 a marine *band*. ●隊を組んで in a body. ●隊を組む (グループを) form a *party*; (列を) form a *line*, 《主に米》line up. ●隊を解く disband.

たい 鯛 〖魚介〗a sea bream, a red-snapper. (❗通例単・複同形. 肉は ◯. 米英の sushi bar でよく使われるのは後の方) ●鯛焼き (⇨鯛焼き) ▶腐っても鯛 (⇨腐る [成句])

たい 他意 ●別に他意はない I have no *other intentions* [*purpose*]./I don't mean *anything else* by it.

タイ〖国名〗Thailand /táilænd/; (公式名) the Kingdom of Thailand. (首都 Bangkok) ●タイ人 a Thai. ●タイ語 Thai. ●タイ(人[語])の Thai.
●タイ料理 Thai food.

タイ〖同音〗a tie. ●タイをする *make* a *tie*.

タイ〖同点〗a tie. ●5 対 5 のタイ a *tie*, 5 to 5; a 5-5 *tie*. ●タイ記録を出す *tie* the record.

-たい 助 want 《*to* do》; would like 《*to* do》; 《書》wish 《*to* do》; hope 《*to* do》; long 《*to* do》; be anxious [eager] 《*to* do》; (したい気がする) feel* like 《doing》.

> **使い分け** want 欲するままにしたいという欲求を表す.
> would like 控えめに「できれば…したい」という希望を表す.《話》では通例 'd like のように短縮形で、さらに控えめには I could [can] use … を用いる.
> wish to 不定詞を従えて、would like よりさらに丁寧に希望する気持ちを表す.
> hope 実現の可能性があることを望むこと.
> long wish よりさらに強意的で、思い焦がれること.
> be anxious [eager] ほぼ同じ意味だが、anxious は不安の入り混じった気持ちで切望すること、eager は熱烈に切望すること.

▶退職したら静かな山里に住みたいなあと思っています I *want to* [I think it would be nice to] live in a quiet mountain village after I retire from my job. (❗(1) 日本語にひかれて ×I think I want…. としない. (2) 後の方は「住めちゃいなあ」といった控えめな願望表現) ▶日本に帰ってきたらいちばん食べたいものは何ですか What is the food you most *want to* eat [you *want to* eat most] when you come home to Japan? ▶君に今すぐにそこへ行ってもらいたい I *want* [I'd *like*] you *to* go there right away. (⇨頂く ❸) ▶来年は新しい家を建てたい I *hope* to build a new house [*to* have a new house built] next year. (⇨建てる) ▶だれもが平穏無事な生活を送りたいと思っている Everybody *wishes* to lead [*wishes for*] a peaceful and quiet life. ▶あなたの誕生パーティーに出席したいと思っていたのに（できなかった）I *wanted* to come to your birthday party, but I couldn't. (❗次例の含みのある言い方に比べこれが最も普通)/I *had wanted* [*had hoped*] *to* come to your birthday party. (❗I wanted [hoped] to have come… とはあまりいわない)/I'd *like to* have come to your birthday party. ▶今は食べたくない I don't *feel like* eating now. ▶家にいるより釣りに出かけたい I *would rather* go fishing *than* stay home. (⇨むしろ ❶) ▶あのね、こんなこと言いたくないんだけど君との約束だめなんだ Well, I *hate* to have to tell you this [I *don't feel good about* telling you this, I *wish* I didn't *have to* tell you this], but I'm afraid I can't keep my promise. (❗相手を

−たい

失望させるようなことを告げるときの前置き)

会話「勉強のためぜひ海外に行きたい」「私も行きたいけどお金がないので行けないわ」"I *am anxious* [*eager, longing*] *to* go abroad for study." "I *wish I could* go but I can't, because I don't have enough money." (❗ wish は節を伴う場合は実現できない願望を表し, 節中の(助)動詞を仮定法過去形にする)

会話「ああ, たばこが吸いたい(=死ぬほど欲しい)」「だめ! ここは禁煙よ」"I'm *dying for* a cigarette." "We don't smoke here. Forget it."

会話「土曜日, 映画に行くんだけど. いっしょに行かない?」「それは残念. 勉強がんばってね」"I'm going to the movies on Saturday. Would you like to come with me?" "I'd like [*love*] *to* very much, but I have a lot of assignments to do this weekend." (❗ love は主に女性語) "Too bad. Good luck with your work."

−たい −帯〖地理〗the 《frigid [temperate, torrid]》 zone.

*だい 大 ❶〖大きい〗big (-gg-), large, great (⇨大きい); 〖巨大な〗huge; 〖広大な〗vast; 〖重大な〗serious.

①〖〜大〗●卵大の腫瘍(ﾊ) a tumor *as big as* an egg; a tumor *the size of* an egg. ●実物大の像 a statue *as large as* life; a *life-size*(d) statue.

②〖大〜〗●大農場 a *big* [*large*, *huge*] farm. ●大企業《集合的》*big* business (❗ 単数扱い); (個々の) a *large* company. ●大問題 a *big* [a *major*, 《重大な》a *serious*] problem. ●大事業 a *great* enterprise. ●大損害 *great* [*heavy*, *serious*] damage. ●大砂漠 a *vast* desert. ●大手術 a *major* operation. ●大地震 a *major* earthquake. (⇨地震)

❷〖その他の表現〗●彼女は声を大にして安全運転の重要性を説いた She *emphasized* the importance of cautious driving. ●その失敗は彼の怠慢によるところが大である The failure is *largely* due to his laziness.

●大なり小なり だれでも大なり小なりぬぼれはある Everyone is *more or less* conceited /kənsíːtid/.

●大は小を兼ねる Too big is better than too small.

*だい 代 ❶〖世代〗a generation (❗ 約 30 年間をさす); (人生の期間) one's lifetime (⇨一代); 〖時代〗a time (❗ しばしば複数形で); 〖統治期間〗a reign. ●代を経るにつれて as the *generation* goes by. ●代々 from *generation* to *generation*. ●何代も前に *generations* ago. ●彼の 5 代目の子孫 his descendant in the fifth *generation*. ●私の祖父の代に in my grandfather's *time* [*days*]. ●桓武天皇の代に in [during] the *reign* of Emperor Kanmu. ●代が替わる (⇨代替わり) ●彼の一家は何代にもわたってこの町に住んでいる His family has lived in this town *for* (many) *generations*. (⇨代々)

❷〖料金〗(手数料, サービス料) (a) charge; (率で決まる料金) a rate; (乗車賃) a fare; (家賃, 使用料) (a) rent; 〖勘定〗a bill; 〖代金〗a price. (⇨料金) ●電話代 (1 回の通話料) a telephone *charge*; (料金) a telephone *rate*. ●バス代 a bus *fare*.

❸〖代わり(の)〗●代役 a súbstitute. ●代案 an *alternative* /ɔːltə́ːrnətiv/ plan. ●代打 a *pinch* hitter. ●代わりの a *substitute* teacher.

❹〖在職むの順序〗●第 40 代米国大統領ロナルド・レーガン Ronald Reagan, the 40*th* President of the United States. ●11 代目市川海老蔵 Ichikawa Ebizo XI. (❗ XI is the eleventh と読

む) ●ケネディはアメリカの何代目の大統領ですか How many presidents were there before Kennedy in the United States? (❗ 現職についている場合は現在完了形を用いて … have there been before … も可)/ Which [*What*] *number* President of the United States was Kennedy? (❗ (1) what の代わりに which の方が普通. (2) 現職の場合は現在形を用いる)

❺〖10 年単位の年代・年齢区分〗●1960 年代の後半 in *the* late 1960s [*1960's*]. (❗ いずれも nineteen sixties と読む) ●10 代 one's teens. (⇨十代) ●彼はまだ 20 代前半だ He is still *in* his early (⇨ late) *twenties*. (❗ 常に複数形)

*だい 台 ❶〖物をのせる〗a stand (❗ しばしば複合語で), a rest; (支柱) a holder, a support; (彫像などの) a pedestal; (宝石などの) a setting, a mounting; (腰かけ) a stool; (壇) a platform. ●譜面台 a music *stand*. ●指揮台 a podium. ●足のせ台 a footrest; a footstool. ●プラチナの台にダイヤをしつらえる set a diamond in a platinum *mounting*.

❷〖単位〗●5 台の車 five cars.

❸〖区切り〗(到達の段階) a mark. ●英語の成績で 90 点台をとる get [×take] ninety *something* in English. ●我々の 1 か月の売り上げは 100 万円台に達した Our monthly sales have reached 1,000,000 yen *mark* [*level*]. ●9 時台はバスの便がよくない The bus service is not good *between* nine *and* ten.

*だい 題 〖本などの表題〗a title; (本などの章や節の見出し) a heading; 〖主題〗a subject; 〖テーマ〗a theme /θiːm/; 〖話題〗a topic. ●この劇の題は『ハムレット』です The *title* of this play is "Hamlet." ●彼の本の題は何ですか What is the *subject* [*theme*] of his book? ●『ルーツ』という題の本を買った I bought a book *titled* [*entitled*] "Roots."

*だい− 第− ●憲法第 9 条 the 9*th* article [Article 9] of the Constitution. ●第五交響曲 Symphony *No.* 5; the *Fifth* Symphony. (❗ No. のときは名詞の後につけるのが原則) ●第一級の政治指導者 a first-class [a first-rate] political leader.

たいあたり 体当たり ●彼女の体当たりの演技がこの映画をより感動的なものにしている She *put everything she had into her role* to make this movie more impressive.

—体当たりする 動 ●強盗に体当たりする throw oneself [(飛びかかる) hurl oneself] *at* the robber. ●彼はドアに体当たりしたがドアは動かなかった He *threw himself at* [*against*] the door, but it didn't move.

たいあつ 耐圧 —— 耐圧の, 耐圧性の 形 pressure-resistant.

タイアップ 名 a tie-úp. —— タイアップする 動 tie úp (*with*).

ダイアル (⇨ダイヤル)

ダイアローグ (a) dialogue, 《米》(a) dialog. (⇨対話)

たいあん 大安 a *taian* day; a lucky [an auspicious] day; (説明的に) a day set by *in-yo* divination for doing important things, such as weddings, trips, etc. (⇨仏滅) ●大安に結婚式を挙げる hold a wedding (ceremony) on a *taian* day.

たいあん 対案 ●対案を出す offer a counterproposal (*to*).

だいあん 代案 an alternative /ɔːltə́ːrnətiv/ plan.

たいい 大尉 (米軍・英陸軍の) a captain; (英海軍の) a lieutenant; (英空軍の) a flight lieutenant.

たいい 大意 〖要点〗the (main) point; 〖骨子〗the

たいい 体位 ❶【体格】(a) physique; (体力) physical strength. ●日本人の体位の向上を図る aim to improve the *physique* of the Japanese people.
❷【体の位置】a position; (姿勢) (a) posture.

たいい 退位 名 (an) abdication (from [of] the throne).
── 退位する 動 ▶王は王子に位を譲るため退位した The king *abdicated* (*from*) the throne in favor of the prince. (❗ from を省略すると他動詞. 文脈により (from) the throne を省略することも可)

だいい 題意 (題名の) the meaning of a title; (問題の) the meaning of a question.

たいいき 帯域 【電気】a band.
●帯域幅 a band width.

たいいく 体育 【学科】physical education《略 PE》(❗ 通例, 略語を用いる);《話》gym. ●体育系のクラブ an athletic club. ●体育の先生 a *physical education* [a *PE*] teacher. ●体育の授業 a *PE* lesson [class].
●**体育館** a gymnasium /dʒɪmˈneɪziəm/;《話》a gym. ●**体育大会**《主に米》an athletic(s) meet,《主に英》an athletic(s) meeting.(⇨運動会)
●**体育の日** Physical Education Day; (Health) Sports Day; Physical Fitness Day.(※事情 米英にはない)

***だいいち 第一** 名 first.(❗ 通例 the ~) ●NHK 第一 (a program of) NHK *I* /wʌ́n/.
──**第一(の)** 形 first (❗ 通例 the 形); (最も主要な) primary; (先導的な) leading; (先頭に立つ) the foremost; (全体の中で主な) main. ●第 1 課[章] the *first* lesson [chapter]; (見出し) Lesson [Chapter] *I*. ▶もしだれかが首になるとすれば第一候補は君だろう You'll be the *first* to go if anyone has to be fired. (❗ go は「首になる(be fired)」意の婉曲表現) ▶彼の第一の目的はその機械を見ることだった His *prime* objective was to see the machine. ▶これが私が行けない第一の理由です This is my *primary* reason (why, that) I can't go. ●健康が第一だ Health comes *first*./Health is the most important of all.
── **第一(に)** 副 first(ly) (❗ first の方が口語的), in the first place, to begin with; (何よりも先に) first of all. ▶彼はまず第一にその仕事を片付けた He finished the job *first* [*first of all*]. ▶まず第一にそれは値段が高すぎる. 第二に私はそれが気に入らない *First*(*ly*) [*In the first place*], it costs too much. *Second*(*ly*) [*In the second place*], I don't like it. /(以下 third(ly) [in the third place], ..., (最後に) last(ly) [finally] のようにいう) ▶どこか旅行に行きたいが, 暇はないし, 第一(=その上)そんな金がない I'd like to take a trip somewhere, but I'm too busy and *besides* [*what's more*] I don't have any money for it.

■ DISCOURSE
田舎に大型ショッピングセンターを建てることは, さまざまな点で破壊的である. 第一に, 交通渋滞を引き起こすであろう The construction of a large shopping center [mall] in a rural area may be destructive *in many ways*. *First*, they may cause traffic jams. (❗ in many ways (多くの点で)は抽象的内容を述べるディスコースマーカー. first 以降に具体的内容を述べるとよい)

●**第一印象** first [initial] impressions. (⇨印象)
●**第一次産業** a primary industry. ●**第一次世界大戦** World War I /wʌ́n/,《やや書》the First World War.

だいいちぎ 第一義 ▶私は世界平和を第一義と考えている I regard world peace as *most important*. ▶彼の言っていることは第一義的(=根本的)には正しい What he says is *fundamentally right* [(原則として) *right in principle*].

だいいちにんしゃ 第一人者 the leading person.
●心臓病に関する第一人者 a *leading authority on* heart disease; *the foremost* heart disease *specialist*. ▶彼はジャーナリズムの分野では第一人者だ He is one of the *top minds* in (the field of) journalism. (❗ mind は「(知的な面から見た)人」の意)

だいいっしゅ 第一種 first class.
●**第一種運転免許** a first-class driver's license《米》[driving licence《英》]. ●**第一種郵便**《by》first-class mail [《英》post]. (※事情 米国では個人の普通郵便. 英国では翌日配達で日本の速達に当たる)

だいいっせい 第一声 ●駅前で第一声をあげる(=選挙活動を始める) start an election campaign in front of the station.

だいいっせん 第一線 ❶【戦場の最前線】the front. (⇨前線)
❷【最も重要な働きのできる位置】the front line,《やや書》the forefront; (指導的立場) the leading position. ●第一線の作家たち *front-line* [*leading*] writers. ●第一線を退く retire from *the front line*. ●研究の第一線にいる[に立つ, で活躍する] be [stand; be active] *in* [*at*] *the front line of* research. ▶彼女は第一線で活躍している女流ピアニストの中で最も優れている She's the topmost [best] among female pianists *on the front line*. (❗ excellent は「最上」の意を含む語なので the *most excellent* female pianist は避ける)

だいいっぽ 第一歩 the first step《*to, toward*》.
●第一歩を踏み出す ▶両国は和平への第一歩を踏み出した The two countries took *the first step toward* [*to*] peace.

たいいん 退院 ── 退院する 動 ●退院している be out of (the) hospital. (❗《米》では通常 the をつける) ▶患者は退院した The patient *left* [*got out of*] (the) *hospital*. /(退院を許された) The patient *was discharged from* (the) *hospital*.

たいいん 隊員 a member of a party. ●南極探検隊員 a *member of* the Antarctic expedition.

だいいん 代印 ── 代印する 動 (代わりに捺印する) put a [one's] seal 《*to* a document》by proxy; (代わりに署名する) sign for 《him》. (※事情 (1) 米英は通例署名で済ませる. (2) 代理人が署名をする場合, 本人の名前の前に for や p.p. をつけて書く)

たいいんれき 太陰暦 the lunar (⇔solar) calendar /kǽləndər/.

たいえい 退嬰 ●**退嬰的な** 形 (保守的な) conservative; (進取の気性のない) unenterprising.

だいえい 題詠 (行為) composing a poem on a previously given subject; (歌) a poem composed on a previously given subject.

だいえいはくぶつかん 大英博物館 the British Museum.

たいえき 体液 bodily fluids;【生理】humor.

たいえき 退役 ── 退役する 動 retire from active service.
●**退役軍人**《米》a veteran,《主に英》an exserviceman. ●**退役将校** a retired officer.

ダイエタリーファイバー 【食物繊維】dietary fiber.

ダイエット 名 a diet.

たいえん ダイエットする 動 go [(している) be] on a diet. ●ダイエットして体重を減らす reduce one's weight by [through] *dieting*.
会話 「直美, クッキー食べる?」「やめとくわ. 今ダイエット中なの」"How about a cookie [some cookies], Naomi?" "No, thanks. *I'm dieting* [*on a diet*]." (!減量している事を暗示) ●ダイエット飲料 diet drinks. ●ダイエット食品 diet food.

たいえん 耐炎 ── 耐炎性の 形 flame-resistant, flameproof.

だいえん 代演 ── 代演する 動 perform [play, act] instead of 《him》; stand in for 《him》. ●代演者 (代わりの俳優) a substitute actor; (映画の代役) a stand-in, a double.

たいおう 対応 名 còrrespóndence. ●インターネット対応の携帯電話 an Internet-*capable* cellular phone. ●…への対応策を講じる take measures *against* …. (⇨対策)
── **対応する** 動 (相当する) correspond 《to》; (対処する) cope 《with》. ●その英語に対応する日本語 the Japanese *equivalent* of the English word. (! equivalent は「対応する語・句」の意) ▶日本語の「青」は英語の 'blue' に対応する 'Ao' in Japanese *corresponds to* [*is equivalent to*] 'blue' in English. ▶彼はその事態に迅速に対応した He promptly *coped with* the situation.

だいおう 大王 a great king. ●アルフレッド大王 King Alfred *the Great*. ●閻魔(*)大王 Yama, *the Great King of* the (Buddhist) Hades.

だいおう 大黄 〖植物〗rhubarb.

だいおうじょう 大往生 ●大往生をとげる die a *peaceful* [*a natural*] *death* 《*at* the age of 98》.

ダイオード 〖二極管〗〖電子工学〗a diode. ●発光ダイオード a light-emitting *diode* 《略 LED》.

ダイオキシン 〖化学〗dioxin /daiάksin/. ●ダイオキシンを処分する clean up *dioxin*.

たいおん 体温 (one's) temperature. (⇨熱, 温度) ●体温を計る take [×measure] one's *temperature*. (! measure temperature は「気温を測定する」を意味) ●体温を調節する regulate one's *temperature*. ▶彼の体温は普通より高い[低い] His *temperature* is above [below] (the) normal. ▶鳥類は哺乳(ほにゅう)類より体温が高い Birds have higher *temperature* than mammals.
●体温計 a (clinical) thermometer /θərmάmətər/. ●体温計をわきにはさむ[口にくわえる] put a (clinical) *thermometer* under the arm [in the mouth]. (事情 前の方は日本人・イタリア人に, 後の方は米英人に多い計り方) ●体温調節 (×a) regulation of body temperature.

だいおん 大恩 ●大恩がある be greatly indebted 《to him》; owe 《him》a great deal [debt] of gratitude.

だいおんじょう 大音声 《*in*》a very loud [(とどろき渡る) a thunderous] voice. (⇨大声)

たいか 大火 a big [a great] fire. ▶その村は昨年大火に見舞われた A *big fire* hit [(起こった) broke out in] the village last year.

たいか 大家 a (great) master; (芸術の) a maestro /máistou/ (複 ~s) (の巨匠); 〖権威〗an authority 《*on*》; 〖専門家〗an éxpert 《*on, in*》. ●ピアノの大家 a *master* of the piano; a *master* pianist. ●物理学の大家 an *authority* on physics; an *expert* on [in] physics.

たいか 大過 ●大過なく(=大きな失敗もなく)任務を果たす do one's duty *without* 《*making*》 *any serious mistakes* [*blunders*].

たいか 対価 〖書〗a consideration.

たいか 退化 〖生物〗retrogression, degeneration; 〖医学〗(筋肉などの萎縮(いしゅく)) atrophy.
── **退化する** 動 〖生物〗retrogress, degenerate; 〖医学〗atrophy.

たいか 耐火 ── 耐火(性)の 形 ▶この壁は耐火性である This wall is *fireproof* [*proof against damage from fire*]. (! ×This wall is proof against fire. は不可. ただし, アスベストは耐火性だ Asbestos is *proof against* fire. は可) ●耐火建築 a fireproof [a fire-resistant] building. ●耐火れんが (a) firebrick.

たいか 滞貨 〖配達されずにたまった貨物[郵便物]〗an accumulation of undelivered freight [mail]; 〖商品の売れ残り〗goods which remain unsold, unsold goods; (在庫) an unsold inventory.

たいが 大河 a large river.
●大河小説 a saga /sά:gə/ (novel).

だいか 代価 (a) cost; (値段) a price. ▶この勝利に対して我々は大変な代価(=犠牲)を払った We paid a great *cost* for this victory./This victory was won at (a) great *cost*. ▶国民はどんな代価を払っても平和を得たいと望んでいる The people want peace *at all costs* [*at any price*].

たいかい 大会 (多人数の) a big [a mass] meeting; (総会) a general meeting [assembly]; (代表者の) a convention; (政治・宗教的な) a rally; (運動・競技の) 《主に米》a meet, 《主に英》a meeting; a competition, a tournament. (⇨集会, 会) ●党大会 a party *convention*. ●花火大会 a firework(s) *display*. ●トーナメント[勝ち抜き]方式の野球大会 a baseball *tournament*.

たいかい 大海 the ocean. (⇨海) ●大海の一滴(=ごく少量) a drop in the bucket [*ocean*].

たいかい 退会 名 one's withdrawal 《*from*》. ●退会届を出す submit a notice of *withdrawal*.
── **退会する** 動 withdraw 《*from*》; leave. ▶医師会を退会する *withdraw from* the medical society.

たいがい 大概 副 ❶〖だいたい〗(一般に) generally (speaking); (通常) usually; (ほとんどの場合は) mostly, for the most part; (ほとんど) almost, nearly. (⇨大抵 ❶) ▶放課後はたいがいテニスをします I *usually* [*generally, mostly*] play tennis after school. ▶私の仕事はたいがい片づいた My work is *almost* [*mostly*] finished [done].
❷〖多分〗probably. (⇨多分)
❸〖度を越さない程度に〗▶酒はたいがいにしておきなさい(=飲みすぎないようにしなさい) Don't drink *too much*. ▶冗談もたいがいにしろ You mustn't [Don't] *carry* your jokes *too far*! (! carry … far は「度を越す」)
── **大概の** 形 (大部分の) most; (ほとんどの) almost [nearly] all. (⇨ほとんど ❶ [第 1 文例]) ●たいがいの場合は in *most* cases. ▶たいがいの生徒は校則を守る *Most of* [*Almost all* (*of*)] the students observe the school rules.

たいがい 対外 ── 対外的な 形 foreign /fɔ́:rən/; (海外の) óverseas; (国際的な) international. ●対外援助 aid to foreign countries. ●対外関係 international [(外交の) diplomatic] relations. ●対外債務 an external [a foreign] debt; external liabilities. ●対外資産 foreign [overseas] assets. ●対外政策 a foreign policy. ●対外投資 foreign [external, overseas, international] investment. ●対外貿易 external [foreign] trade [commerce].

たいがいじゅせい 体外受精 in vitro /in ví:trou/ [test-tube, external (↔internal)] fertilization 《略 IVF》. (! in vitro はラテン語で「試験管の中での」

意)
● 体外受精児 a test-tube baby.
だいかいてん 大回転 【スキー】 the giant slalom /slá:ləm/.
だいがえ 代替え ⇨代替(だいたい)
*****たいかく 体格** [体の造り] (a) build; (特に男性の)《やや書》(a) physique; [体質] constitution. (⇨体(からだ)❷) ▶ 彼は体格がいい[貧弱だ] He has a good [a poor] *build* [*physique*]./He is a man of [with a] good [poor] *build* [*physique*]./He is a well-[a poorly-]*built* man. (🔒 build は女性にも用いるが, figure の方がよく用いられる) ▶ 君のような体格ではラグビーは無理です With a *build* [a *physique*] like yours, rugby is impossible.
たいがく 退学 ▶ 彼は盗みで退学(処分)になった He *was expelled from* [《話》*was kicked out of*] *school* for stealing.
―― 退学する 動 (通例自主的に) leave [《話》quit] school; (成績不良で) 《主に米語》flunk out of school. ▶ 彼は 17 歳で高校を退学した He *left* [《やや話》*dropped out of*] *high school* at seventeen. (🔒「高校を退学した人」は a high school dropout (⇨中退)) ▶ 彼は家の事情で息子を退学させた He *withdrew* his son *from* [made his son *quit*] *school* for family reasons./For family reasons he *withdrew* his son.
● 退学処分 expulsion from school. ● 退学届 (submit) a notice of withdrawal from school.
*****だいがく 大学** a university 《略 univ.》; a college 《略 col.》.

解説 I (1) **university** は修士以上の学位を与える権限を持つ総合大学, **college** は学部の大学をいう。しかし, 総合大学を特に強調せず広い意味での「大学」を表すときは, たとえ大学名に university が使われていても, college を用いる方が普通。
(2) 建物や場所ではなく機能としての大学教育を表す場合, college は通例無冠詞で, university は通例《主に米》では the をつけるが, 《英》では今では無冠詞で用いる。したがって, 一般に学生または教師が「大学へ通う」は go to college,《主に米》go to the university,《英》go to university のようにいう。ただし, 修飾語を伴ったり特定・不特定の大学をさすときは米英ともに通例冠詞を伴う: いい[その, ある]大学へ行く go to a good [the; a] college [university]. なお, 一般に専門学部, 大学院をさすとき,《米》では大学のことを school ということもある: 看護学部 the *School* of Nursing/法学部 the *School* of Law; the Law *School*./米国では法科大学院, 法学 (law) の他に医学 (medicine), 経営学 (business) も学部ではなく大学院をさす)

① 【〜大学】 ● 教員養成大学 《米》 a teachers *college*,《英》 a teacher(s') training *college*. ● 医科[商科]大学 a medical [a commercial] *college* [*university*]. ● 国立[公立; 私立]大学 a national [a public; a private] *university* [*college*]. ● 短期大学 《米》 a junior *college*. ● 有名[一流; 難関]大学 a famous [a prestigious; a selective] *college*. ● 4 年制大学 a four-year *college*. ● 放送大学 (日本の) the *University* of the Air; (英国の公開大学) the Open *University*. ● 小文字の open university は 《米》では「通信制大学」 ● 市民大学 a citizens *college*.
会話「彼はどこの大学ですか」「同志社です」 "Where does he go to 《《米》the》 *university*?/What [×Where] *university* does he go to?" "(He goes to) Doshisha." (🔒 知名度や状況から明らかな場合は University は省略可)

解説 II (1) 「神戸大学」のように大学名に地名がつく場合, Kobe *University* と the *University* of Kobe の二通りが可能だが, 正式名は大学によってどちらかに決まっているのが普通。一方,「慶応大学」のように地名のつかない大学 (「日本大学」なども同様) の場合は Keio *University* といい, ×the University of Keio とはいわない。
(2) 大学名の例: 川崎医科大学 Kawasaki Medical School. (🔒 A University School of Medicine の形で school of medicine を医学部でなく, 医科大学に用いることも多い)/甲南女子大学 Konan Women's *University*./神戸市外国語大学 Kobe City *University* of Foreign Studies./京都薬科大学 Kyoto Pharmaceutical *University*./東京芸術大学 Tokyo National *University* of Fine Arts and Music./武蔵工業大学 Musashi *Institute* of Technology. (🔒 理工系専門の大学名には institute がよく用いられる)

② 【大学〜】 ▶ 彼は大学時代に京都に住んでいた He had lived in Kyoto when he was a *college* student [while he was in college]. (🔒 in his college days は日常的にはあまり用いられない) ▶ 大学生活はいかがですか How do you like your life *in college*?/How are you doing *in* your *college*?
③ 【大学は】 ▶ 大学はここから遠い The *university* [*college*] is a long way [×far] from here. ▶ 日本の大学は入りにくく出やすいとずっと言われてきた It's been said that Japanese *colleges* [*universities*] are hard to get into but easy to get out of [to graduate from]. (🔒「ずっと」は現在完了形で表す)
④ 【大学の[に]】 ● 大学の友だち a *college* friend. ● 大学に進学する go on to *college*. ● 大学に入る(入学する) get into [《やや書》enter] *college*; (大学で勉強を始める) begin [start] *college*. ▶ 彼は K 大学の英文学の学生[教授]です He is a student [a professor] of English literature at [×of] K *University*. (🔒 後に the *University* of K の形が続く場合は in を用いる (⇨解説 II)) ▶ 彼女は大学に在学している She is in 《米》 [*at* 《主に英》] *college*./She is *at* (the) *university*./She goes to *college* [(the) *university*]. (🔒 *university* の冠詞を省略するのは《英》(⇨解説 I (2)))
⑤ 【大学を[で]】 ● 大学を卒業する graduate from [finish,《英》leave] *college*. ● 大学やから中途退学する drop out of [leave,《話》quit] *college*. (🔒 leave the *college* は「下校する」の意) ● 大学で美術を学ぶ study fine arts *at college*. ▶ 彼は大学を出たばかりです He is fresh from *college*. ▶ 彼は大学で教えています He teaches *at* (the) *university*. (🔒 冠詞を省略するのは《英》(⇨解説 I (2)))
● **大学芋** daigakuimo; (説明的に) deep-fried and candy-coated sweet potatoes. ● **大学教育** university [college, (高等の) higher, tertiary] education. ● **大学教師** a university [《主に米》a college] teacher. ● **大学教授** a university [《主に米》a college] professor. ● **大学公開講座** university extension. ● **大学祭** a college festival. ● **大学進学率** the rate of students going on to college; the college going rate. ● **大学生** a college [a university] student; (大学院生に対して学部学生) an undergraduate (student). (関連)《米》では学年ごとに次のようにいう: 1 年生 freshman/2 年生 sophomore/3 年生 junior/4 年生 senior) ● **大学生活** college [campus] life. ● **大学出**[卒] a college graduate. ● **大学入試**《take》a college

だいがくいん [a university] entrance exam [《書》examination]. (❗「入試でK大学を受ける」は take the entrance exam to [for, of] K University)
● 大学入試センター the National Center for University Entrance Examination. ● 大学ノート a large-sized notebook. ● 大学病院 a university hospital.

だいがくいん 大学院 a graduate《主に米》[a postgraduate《英》] school. ▶彼女はコロンビア大学の大学院で国際関係の研究をしている She is in *graduate school* at Columbia University, studying international relations./She is a graduate student of international relations at Columbia University.
● 大学院課程 《take》the graduate course. ● 大学院生《主に米》a graduate student; 《英》a postgraduate (student). ● 大学院大学 a graduate-course university; (説明的に) a university with no undergraduate courses.

たいかくせん 対角線 【数学】a diagonal /daiǽgənl/ (line). ● 対角線を引く draw a *diagonal*.

ダイカスト 〔鋳造法〕die-casting. (❗その製品は〖C〗)

だいがっこう 大学校 ● 気象大学校 Meteorological College. ● 防衛大学校 National Defense *Academy*.

だいがわり 代替わり ── 代替わりする 動 (継承する) succeed 《one's father's business》; (…の経営権を得る) take* over 《a restaurant》. ▶数か月ぶりにハーブ店へ行ったら代替わりして(=経営者が替わって)いた A few months later, I found the herb shop *had changed hands* [the herb shop *under new management*].

たいかん 体感 a physical feeling.
● 体感温度 sensory temperature;【気象】the wind chill temperature.

たいかん 耐寒 ── 耐寒(性)の 形 ● 耐寒性植物 a *hardy* plant. ● 耐寒訓練 a training in the cold (winter).

たいかん 退官 图 retirement. (⇨退職)
── 退官する 動 ▶桃山教授はこの3月で京都大学を定年退官されます Prof. Momoyama will *retire* (under the age limit) *from* Kyoto University this March.

たいかん 退館 ── 退館する 動 exit [leave] 《a library》.

たいかん 大観 ❶ [広く全体を見渡すこと] a comprehensive survey. (⇨概観) ❷ [壮大な景色] a spectacular view.

たいかん 大鑑 (専門事典) an encyclopedia.

たいかん 大願 ● 大願成就 the fulfillment of one's ambition [*aspiration*]. ▶ついに大願が成就した Our greatest wish *has been realized* [*carried out*] at last.

たいがん 対岸 图 the other [opposite] side 《on the river》. ── 対岸に 副 on the opposite bank [shore]; on the other [opposite] side of the river [lake].
● 対岸の火事 someone else's affairs. (⇨人事(ひとごと))

だいかん 大寒 *daikan*; (説明的に) the coldest period between about January 20 and February 4, the first day of spring.

だいかん 代官 an acting administrator [governor].

だいがん 代願 ── 代願する 動 ▶彼の1日も早い回復を家族のために代願する(=代わりに祈願する) *pray for* his speedy recovery *in place of* his family. ● 彼女の旅券を代願する(=代理で出願する) *apply for* her passport *in her place*.

たいかんしき 戴冠式 《hold [have]》a coronation (ceremony). (⇨戴式)

だいかんみんこく 大韓民国 (⇨韓国)

たいき 大気 图 the atmosphere; the air. (⇨空気)
❶ ── 大気(中)の 形 atmospheric.
● 大気汚染 air [atmospheric] pollution. ● 大気圏 (⇨大気圏)

たいき 大器 ● 大器晩成 Great talents mature late. ▶彼は大器晩成型だ He is a *late bloomer*. (❗「遅咲きの花」の意)

たいき 待機 ── 待機する 動 (備えて待つ) stand by 《for; to do》; (油断なく) be on the alert 《for, against》. ● 紛争に備えて待機する *stand by* [(待機している) *be on standby*] for trouble. ● (すぐ応じられるよう)家で待機している *be on call* [*standby*] at home.

たいぎ 大義 (主義) a cause; (理由) (a) reason.
● 大義名分 ● 平和という大義名分のために働く work *for* [*in the cause of*] peace. ▶戦う大義名分が立たない(=きちんとした理由がない) We don't have a *good reason* to fight.

たいぎ 大儀 (⇨億劫(おっくう)) ▶外は寒いから散歩に出るのは大儀だ I *can't be bothered to* go for a walk because it's cold outside.

たいぎ 体技 martial arts; (説明的に) a kind of sports such as wrestling, judo, sumo, etc. (⇨格闘技)

だいぎいん 代議員 [代表者] a representative;[会議などに派遣する] a delegate. ● (派遣)代議員団 a delegation. (❗単・複同扱い)

だいきぎょう 大企業 a big [a large; (一流の) major] company; a big business; (特に大きな) a giant (firm [corporation]).

たいきけん 大気圏 the (Earth's) atmosphere. ● 大気圏内の核実験 an *atmospheric* nuclear test. ● 大気圏への再突入に成功する make a successful re-entry into *the* (*Earth's*) *atmosphere*.
● 大気圏外 (宇宙空間) outer space.

たいぎご 対義語 an antonym. (⇨反意語)

だいぎし 代議士 [国会議員] a Diet member. (⇨議員) ● 自民党の代議士 a *Diet member* of the Liberal Democratic Party; an LDP *Diet member*.

だいきち 大吉 *daikichi*; great good luck [fortune]. (⇨何籤(おみくじ))

だいきぼ 大規模 ── 大規模な 形 large-scale. ● 大規模捜索 a *large-scale* search 《for》.
── 大規模に 副 on a large scale; (話) in a big way.

たいきゃく 退却 图 (a) retreat. (❗(a) withdrawal でないことに注意 (⇨撤退)) ● 最前線からの退却 the *retreat* from the front. ● 退却を命じる order a *retreat*.
── 退却する 動 retreat [make a retreat] 《from》. ▶軍隊は森の中へ退却した The troops *retreated* [*fell back*] into the forest.

たいぎゃく 大逆 ● 大逆罪 (high) treason;【法律】lese-majesty /líːz mǽdʒəsti/.

たいきゅう 耐久 ● 耐久消費財《米》durable goods;《英》consumer durables. ● 耐久性 durability. ● 耐久性のある durable. ● 耐久レース an endurance race. ● 耐久力 (忍耐力) endurance; (持久力) stamina /stǽmənə/.

だいきゅう 代休 a make-up holiday. ▶私は週末働いたので2日間代休をとった I worked on the weekend, so I *took* two days *off*.

だいきゅうし 大臼歯 a molar.

たいきょ 大挙 ── 大挙して 副 (大勢で) in large [great] numbers. ● 大挙してやってくる come in large numbers. ●大挙して(=群がって)押しかける throng 《*to, toward*》.

たいきょ 退去 图 ●退去命令 an *expulsion* order.
── **退去する** 動 〔去る〕 *leave**; 〔危険地域などから〕 *evacuate*; 〔軍隊が〕 *withdraw**《*from*》.
●退去させる(追放する) *expel*; 〔望ましくない外国人を〕 *deport*. ▶彼はその部屋から退去するように命じられた He was ordered to *leave* [*go out of*] the room. ▶その記者は国外に退去させられた The journalist *was deported* [*expelled from the country*].

たいぎょ 大魚 a *big fish*.
●**大魚を逸する**(大きな利益や成功を逃す) *fail to achieve great gains or success*.

たいきょう 胎教 *prenatal* [*antenatal*] *training*; (胎児に及ぼす影響) *an influence on an unborn baby*. ▶よい音楽が胎教によいというのは本当です It is true that good music *has a good effect on an unborn baby*.

たいぎょう 怠業 《米》《*stage*》 a *slowdown*, 《英》《*go on*》 a *go-slow*.

だいきょう 大凶 *daikyo*; very bad luck [*fortune*].
(⇨御神籤(ᠵᠬ))

たいきょく 大局 ●物事を大局的に見る *see things in perspective*. ●(もっと大局的な視野で立って判断する *judge from a wide*(*r*) [*a broad*(*er*)] *view of things*. ●大局を誤る *take a wrong view of things*.

たいきょく 大曲 a great [(規模の大きい) a *large-scale*, (画期的な) an *epoch-making*] *musical composition*.

たいきょく 対局 图 a game of *shogi* [*go*].
── **対局する** 動 *play* (a game of) *shogi* [*go*] 《*with*》.

たいきょく 対極 *opposite sides*.

たいきょくけん 太極拳 *tai chi* (*chuan*) /táɪ tʃíː (tʃwáːn)/, *taikyokuken*; (説明的に) a Chinese system of exercise, originally a martial art, employing deliberate and smooth movements in time to deep breathing.

だいきらい 大嫌い (⇨嫌い) ●大嫌いな虫 (やや書) a *loathsome* /lóʊðsəm/ *insect*. ●ニンジンが大嫌いだ I *hate* carrots. ▶ニンジンは私の大嫌いなもの 《話》Carrots are my *pet hate* [*pet aversion*]. ▶あんたなんか大嫌い I don't like you a bit. (⚠ I hate you. では関係の修復の余地がなくなる言い方になる)

たいきん 大金 a *large sum of money*; a *lot of money*. ▶100万円というのは私には大金です One million yen is *a lot* (*of money*) to me. ▶彼はその事業に大金を投資した He put *a large sum of money* into the business.

*****だいきん 代金** (値段) a *price*; (費用) (a) *cost*; (料金, 経費) (a) *charge*. ●(電話・荷物などで)代金受取人払いの *collect*. ▶服の代金はいくらですか What's the *price* of the dress?/*How much* do I owe you for the dress? ▶その代金はまだいただいておりません It has not yet *been paid for*. (⚠ You have not yet paid for it. の受け身表現) ▶彼女に車の修理代金として10万円を請求した I asked her to *pay* 100,000 yen *for* repairing the car.
●**代金引換** *cash* 《米》*collect*》 *on delivery* 《略 COD., cod.》. ●代金引換払いで注文する *place a COD order*.

たいく 体躯 ▶彼女はすらりとした体躯の持ち主だ She is slenderly [slightly] *built*./She is a woman of a slender [slight] *build*.

だいく 大工 a *carpenter*; (建具屋) a *joiner*. ●腕のたつ大工(=大工仕事の上手な人) a *good carpenter*.
●日曜大工 (人) a *do-it-yourselfer*; (仕事) *do-it-yourself* 《略 DIY》. ●日曜大工の店 a *do-it-yourself* shop.
●大工仕事 *carpenter's work*; *carpentry*. ●大工道具 *carpenter's tools*; (一そろい) a *carpenter's outfit* [*kit*].

たいくう 対空 ●対空砲火 *antiaircraft fire*. ●対空ミサイル an *antiaircraft missile*.

たいくう 滞空 ●滞空時間 the *duration of flight*; *flight duration*. ●滞空飛行 an *endurance flight*.

*****たいぐう 待遇** 〔人などに対する処遇〕 *treatment*; 〔給料〕 *pay*, (a) *salary*; 〔ホテル・店などの客扱い〕 *service*; 〔接待〕 a *reception*.
① 【待遇~】 ▶彼らは待遇改善を求めてストライキに入った They went on strike for better *treatment* [*pay*, (労働条件) *working conditions*]. (⇨③)
② 【待遇が~】 ▶我々の会社は待遇がよい Our company *treats* [*pays*] us well. ▶パートは正社員より待遇が悪い(=給料が安い)ことが多い Part-timers *are* often *paid* less than regular employees.
③ 【待遇を~】 ●従業員の待遇を改善する *give the employees better treatment*; (給料を上げる) *give the employees a raise* 《米》 [*a rise* 《英》]; (労働条件を改善する) *improve the employees' working conditions*. ▶彼は国賓としての待遇を受けた He *was treated* [*welcomed*] *as a state guest*.

*****たいくつ 退屈** 图 *boredom*. ●退屈しのぎにテレビを見る (=テレビを見て時間をつぶす) *kill time* (*by*) *watching TV*.
── **退屈な** 形 (おもしろくなくて) *boring*; (長たらしくて) *tedious* /tíːdiəs/; (新鮮味のない) *dull*; (単調な) *monótonous*. ●退屈な本 a *boring* [a *tedious*, a *dull*] *book*. ●退屈な田舎の生活 《xa》 *monotonous country life*. ▶午後の英語の授業は退屈だった。退屈で寝てしまった English class this afternoon was *boring*. I fell asleep from the *boredom* [*because I was bored*]. ▶彼はまったく退屈な人だ He is a very *boring* person./He is such a *bore*. ▶退屈だなあ What a *bore*!/How *boring*! ▶彼は退屈そうだ He looks *bored* [×*boring*]. ▶その演説は長すぎて退屈だった The speech was too long and *dull*.
── **退屈する** 動 *get** *bored*. ▶彼女の長話にはひどく退屈する I *am* [*get*] very *bored with* [*by*] her long talk./Her long talk *bores* me to death./She *bores* me to death with her long talk. ▶今夜の上演は失敗だった。観客が退屈していたもの The performance tonight fell flat. The audience *was bored*. ▶ぶらぶらして暮らすのも退屈してきた I'm *getting bored* (*with*) [(飽きてきた) I'm getting tired *of*] living in idleness.

たいぐん 大軍 a *large* [a *great*, a *vast*] *army*.
●大軍を率いて首都を攻撃する *lead a large army against the capital*.

たいぐん 大群 a *large group* [*herd*, *flock*, *swarm*]. (⚠動物によって用いる語が異なる (⇨群れ))
▶アリの大群 a *large swarm* [an *army*] of ants.

たいけ 大家 (金持ちの家) a *wealthy family*; (家柄のいい家) a *good family*. (⇨名家)

*****たいけい 体系** 图 a *system*. ●学問体系 a *system of learning*. ●給与体系 a *wage* [a *pay*] *structure*. ●体系を立てる *formulate* a *system* 《*of*》; *systematize*.
── **体系的な** 形 *systematic*. ▶彼のやり方は体系的でない His methods are not *systematic* [*lack system*].
── **体系的に** 副 *systematically*. ●体系的に研究する *make a systematic study* 《*of*》.

たいけい 大兄 ▶それにつけて大兄のご高見を承りたく存じ

ます Could *you* kindly give me your opinion about it?

たいけい 大系 a series. (🔢 単・複同形) ▶現代生物学大系 a *series on* modern biology.

たいけい 大計 〘大がかりな計画・政策〙(長期の) a long-range plan [policy]; (遠大な) a far-reaching plan [policy]. ▶国家百年の大計を立てる establish a *far-reaching state policy*.

たいけい 大慶 a great pleasure [joy]. ▶この展覧会の開催を宣言するのは私にとって大慶に存じます It is a *great pleasure* for me to declare this exhibition open.

たいけい 体刑 〘懲役〙penal servitude; 〘体罰〙(⇨体罰).

たいけい 体型 (主に女性の) a figure; (主に男性の) (a) physique. ▶(体格) a figure. ▶体型に合った服 clothes fit for one's *figure*. ●体型を保つ keep one's *figure*. ●体型が崩れる lose one's *figure*.

たいけい 隊形 〘軍事〙(battle) formation. ●戦闘隊形を取った敵の軍隊 the enemy army in *battle formation*. ▶隊形が崩れた The *formation* broke.

だいけい 台形 《米》a trapezoid /trǽpəzɔ̀ɪd/, 《英》a trapezium /trəpíːziəm/ (🌐 ~s, trapezia).

だいけい 代稽古 ▶習字の先生が病気なので私が2週間代けいこを務めた Because of the calligraphy teacher's illness I filled the role of a *substitute teacher* for two weeks.

***たいけつ 対決** 图 (a) confrontation 《with》; (決着をつけるための) 《話》 a showdown 《with》. ▶与野党間の対決 a *confrontation between* the ruling party [parties] and the opposition parties.

— **対決する** 動 ▶彼らはテロリストと対決した They *confronted* [had a *showdown* with] the terrorists.

***たいけん 体験** 图 (an) experience. (⇨経験, 初体験)
●貴重な体験をする have a valuable *experience*. ▶私は自分の体験から話しているのです I'm speaking *from* (my own) *experience*. ▶祖父は戦時中の体験を話してくれた My grandfather told me about his *experiences* during the war. (🔢 通例複数形で)

— **体験する** 動 experience; (試練・変化などを)《やや書》undergo*; 〘困難などを経る〙go* through .... ●あらゆる苦労を体験する *experience* [*undergo, go through*] all sorts of difficulties [hardships]. ●初体験する cut one's teeth 《*on, in*》. ●体験学習 learning by [through] experience. ●体験コース (直接参加の) a hands-on course.

たいけん 大圏 a great circle. ●大圏航路 the great circle route.

たいけん 大権 the supreme power; (統治権) the governing power.

たいげん 体現 图 the embodiment 《*of*》.
— **体現する** 動 embody.

だいけん 大検 〘大学入学資格検定〙the University Entrance Qualification Examination.

たいげんそうご 大言壮語 图 big talk.
— **大言壮語する** 動 《話》talk big. ●大言壮語する人 a big talker.

***たいこ 太鼓** 〘楽器〙a drum. ●大太鼓 a bass *drum*.
●小太鼓 a snare [a side] *drum*. ●太鼓をたたく (鳴らす) beat a *drum*; play the *drum*. ●太鼓に合わせて行進する a march to the beat of a *drum*. ▶太鼓が鳴り出した The *drums* began to beat.
●太鼓持ち 〘男芸者〙a professional male entertainer; 〘おべっか使い〙a toady. ●太鼓橋 an arched bridge. ●太鼓腹 (人) a potbelly. ●太鼓判 (⇨太鼓判).

たいこ 太古 — **太古の** 形 (地球のできたころの) prime-val; (原始の) primitive. (⇨原始) ●太古の森 *prime-val* forests.

たいご 隊伍 (⇨隊列)

:たいこう 対抗 图 〘競争〙competition 《*with*》; 〘張り合い〙(競う) rivalry. ●クラス(高校, 大学)対抗試合 an *interclass* [an *inter-high school*; an *intercollegiate*] match. ●日米対抗野球試合 a Japan *versus* [*vs.*] America baseball game; a baseball game *between* Japan *and* America; a Japan-U.S. baseball game. ●対抗意識 rivalry 《*between, among*》.

— **対抗する** 動 match; (匹敵する) equal /íːkwəl/; (抵抗する) counter; (競う) compete /kəmpíːt/ 《*with, against*》. ●A 氏に対抗して立候補する run *against* Mr. A. ▶彼は英語では彼女に対抗できない He can't *match* [*equal*] her *in* English./He is no *match for* her [is not her *equal*] *in* English. ▶力には力で対抗するのが彼の主義です His principle is to *counter* [*meet*] force *with* force. ▶小さな商店は安売りでスーパーに対抗した Small stores *competed with* the supermarket by selling goods cheap. (🔢 cheap は「安く」の意の副詞)
●対抗者 (1 対 1 で戦う) an opponent; (同じ目標をねらう) a rival. ●対抗馬 (⇨対抗馬).

たいこう 大功 meritorious service. ●大功を立てる render *meritorious service* 《*to*》.

たいこう 大綱 〘基本原則〙fundamental principles; (大筋) an outline. ●経済政策の大綱を定める lay down the *fundamental principles* of the economic policy.

たいこう 体腔 the abdominal [body] cavity; the coelom /síːləm/.
●体腔動物 a coelomate.

たいこう 対向 ●対向車 (近づいてくる車) an oncoming car. ●対向車線 the opposite lane; an oncoming lane.

たいこう 退行 图 〘心理〙regression; 〘生物〙retrogression. — **退行する** 動 regress; retrogress.

たいこう 退校 — **退校する** 動 leave school. (⇨退学)

だいこう 代行 图 a representation. ●学長代行 the *acting* president.

— **代行(を)する** 動 ▶校長の代行をする *act for* the principal. ▶ヨーロッパでは当社のエージェントが代行して仕事をしている Our agents *represent* us in Europe.

だいこう 代講 ●石井先生の代講で (=代わりとして) 英語を教える teach English *as a substitute* [《話》a *fill-in*] *for* Mr. Ishii.

だいごう 題号 (⇨表題)

たいこうじあい 対校試合 an interscholastic game.
●S 高とサッカーの対校試合をする *play* a game of soccer *against* S High team.

たいこうば 対抗馬 (競馬の) a rival horse 《*to*》; (スポーツの) a (leading) contender 《*for* the championship》; (選挙の) a rival candidate (*to* Mr. A).

たいこうぼう 太公望 〘釣りをする人〙an angler.

たいこく 大国 〘大きい国〙a large [a big] country; 〘主要国〙a major country; 〘強国〙a big power, (超大国) a superpower; 〘偉大な国〙a great nation [country]. (⇔ 小国) ●世界の経済[軍事]大国 a world economic [military] *power*.

だいこくてん 大黒天 *Daikokuten*; (説明的に) the god of wealth, one of the seven gods of good luck.

だいこくばしら 大黒柱 〘柱〙the central pillar; 〘中心となる人・物〙the mainstay; 〘一家の稼ぎ手〙the breadwinner. (⇨柱)

たいこばん 太鼓判 ● 太鼓判を押す ▶ 彼の人物については私が太鼓判を押します(=完全に保証します) I *fully guarantee* his character./I *fully guarantee* that he has a good character.

だいごみ 醍醐味 a real pleasure. ▶ 旅の醍醐味を味わう feel [experience] the *real pleasure* of travel.

だいこん 大根 〖植物〗a Japanese radish. (❗ radish は二十日大根のこと)
● 大根足 thick legs; beer-barrel legs. ● 大根下ろし (切物) grated radish;(器具) a radish grater.
● 大根役者 a bad [a poor, 《話》a lousy] actor [actress];《話》a ham (actor).

たいさ 大佐 (海軍以外の米軍・英陸軍の) a colonel;(米海軍・英海軍の) a captain;(英空軍の) a group captain.

たいさ 大差 a great [a big] difference, much difference. ● (選挙で)大差で勝つ[負ける] win [be defeated] by a *wide margin*. ▶ 両者の間にはあまり大差がない There is no *great difference* [not *much difference*] between the two./They are not very different from each other. ▶ どちらにしても大差はない It makes very little difference./It doesn't make much difference.

たいざ 対座 ── 対座する動 sit face to face 《with》. ▶ メアリーは私と机をはさんで対座した Mary sat face to face with me across the desk.

たいざ 退座 ── 退座する動 leave one's seat.

だいざ 台座 a pédestal.

たいさい 大祭 (大規模な) a big [a great] festival;(神社の重要な) a grand festival.

*****たいざい 滞在** 图 (a) stay. ● 短い[3週間の]滞在 a short [(a) three weeks'] *stay*. ▶ ロンドン滞在中に彼に会った I met him during my *stay* [while I *was* (*staying*)] in London. ▶ 滞在中は楽しかったですか Did you enjoy your *stay*?

── **滞在する** stay 《at+場所, with+人》. ● 長期滞在する stay for a long period; make a long *stay*. ● 友達の家に滞在する stay at one's friend's (house) [*with* one's friend]. ● 横浜に1か月間滞在する stay (*for*) a month in Yokohama [*for* はしばしば省略される]; *stay in* Yokohama *for* a month;(過ごす) spend a month in Yokohama.
会話「どのぐらいそのホテルに滞在するのですか」「少なくとも週末まではおります」"How long are you going to *stay* at the hotel?" "Until the end of the week at least."
● 滞在客 (ホテルの) a guest;(観光地などの) a visitor.

たいざい 大罪 〖法律上の〗a great [a grave] crime;〖宗教・道徳上の〗(キリスト教で) a deadly sin;(ローマ・カトリック教で) a mortal sin. ● (キリスト教の)七つの大罪 the seven *deadly sins*.

だいざい 題材 〖資料〗material 《*for*》;〖主題となる内容〗the subject matter 《*of*》;〖主題〗a theme /θiːm/. ── 随筆の題材 material *for* [*the subject matter of*] an essay.

たいさいぼう 体細胞 〖生物〗a somatic cell.

たいさく 対策 a measure (❗しばしば複数形で); a step;(対抗策) a countermeasure (❗しばしば複数形で、報復的な意を含むこともある). ▶ 政府は有効な不況対策を講じることを約束した The government has promised to take effective *measures* to counter depression [*against* depression].

たいさく 大作 〖すぐれた作品〗a great work;(傑作) a masterpiece;〖大規模な作品〗(本) a voluminous work;(絵・彫刻) a large-scale work.

だいさく 代作 图 ghostwriting. ── 代作する動 ghostwrite 《an essay》.

● 代作者 a ghostwriter.

たいさつ 大冊 a large volume [book].

たいさん 耐酸 ── 耐酸(性)の形 acid-proof, acid-resistant. ● 耐酸性の食器 *acid-proof* tableware.

たいさん 退散 ── 退散する動 (散る) disperse, be dispersed;(逃げる) run away. ▶ さてそろそろ退散するか I think it's about time to *go*./I think we should *be going* now./I am afraid it is time (that) we were *going*.

たいざん 大山 ● 大山鳴動してねずみ一匹 the mountain in labor [〖『イソップ物語』〗の句から, in labor は「陣痛の苦しみにある」の意];(ことわざ) Much cry and little wool.

たいざん 泰山 Tai Shan /tái ʃáːn/.

*****だいさん 第三** 图 third. (❗通例 the ～)
── 第三(の) 形 third. (❗通例 the ～) ● 第3問 question *number three* [*No. 3*]; the *third* question. (❗後の方が堅い言い方)
── 第三(に) 副 third(ly) (❗ first(ly), second(ly) と並べて用いる); in the third place. (⇨第一(に))
● 第三紀 (地質時代の) the Tertiary (period). ● 第三国 a third power [country]. ● 第三次産業 a tertiary industry. ● 第三者 (⇨第三者) ● 第三世界 the Third World. ● 第三セクター a joint venture of a local government and private businesses;(和製語) a third sector.

だいさんしゃ 第三者 〖契約・事件などの〗〖法律〗third party 《*to*》;〖部外者〗an outsider. (⇨他人) ▶ その契約をするときには第三者の立ち合いがなくてはならない There must be a *third party* present when you make the contract. (❗ present は後置修飾の形容詞)

たいさんぼく 泰山木 〖植物〗an èvergreen magnólia, a bat tree. (⇨木蓮(もくれん))

たいし 大志 〖野心〗(an) ambition;〖強い願望〗(an) aspiration. ● 外交官になるという大志を抱いている have an *ambition* [be *ambitious*] to be a diplomat. ● 少年よ、大志を抱け Boys, be *ambitious*.

たいし 大使 an ambássador (❗しばしば Ambassador),(女性の) an ambássadress. (❗(1) 呼びかけは Mister [Madam] Ambassador, 改まった場合は Your Excellency. (2)「公使(大使の次の位)」は a minister,「領事」は a consul) ● 駐日[東京駐在]英国大使 the British *Ambassador* to Japan [*in* Tokyo]. (❗前置詞の to は用いない) ● 全権大使 an *ambassador* plenipotentiary /plènipəténʃəri/. ● 大使級会談を開く hold talks at *ambassadorial* level; hold *ambassador*-level talks. ● スペイン大使を6年間務める serve six years as *ambassador* to Spain. (❗ as の後では無冠詞)
● 大使館 ⇨大使館

たいし 隊士 (兵士) a soldier;(武士) a warrior.

たいじ 対峙 ── 対峙する動 (向かい合う) face each other;(対決する) confront each other. ● 相対峙する両軍 the two armies *confronting each other*. ▶ 二つの巨峰が谷を隔てて対峙している The two lofty peaks *are facing each other* across the valley.

たいじ 胎児 a baby in the womb;(妊娠9週以後の) a fetus /fíːtəs/;(妊娠8週までの胎芽(たいが)) embryo /émbriòu/ (⊛ ～s).

たいじ 退治 图 〖撲滅〗extermination;〖征服〗conquest.
── **退治する** 動 ● 害虫を退治する root out [get rid of, destroy, 〖書〗exterminate] harmful insects.

だいし 大師 *daishi*, a great teacher; (説明的に) an honorific title given to a Buddhist priest of high virtue. ● 弘法大師 Kobo-*daishi*.

だいし 台紙 (写真の) a mount; a mat. ● 台紙にはる

だいし mount 《a photogragh》.
だいし 台詞 (⇨台詞(%))
だいじ 大事 图 ❶[重大事] an important [a serious] matter, 《やや書》 a matter of great [serious] importance; (危機) a crisis (櫃 crises). ● 国家の大事 a national *crisis*. ▶ 火事は大事に至らず鎮火した The fire was put out before it got *serious*. ▶ 彼は大事(=大変な面倒)を引き起こした He caused *serious* trouble.

❷[大事業] a great undertaking [enterprise]. ▶ 彼は大事を成し遂げた He has achieved *great things*.

● 大事の前の小事 (大事をなすには小事にかまってはいられない) You must make small sacrifices in order to achieve a great thing./(大事をなすには小事にも気をつけなければならない) You must be careful about even a small thing in order to achieve a great thing.

● 大事をとる ▶ 大事をとって彼はすべて書類にしてもらった *To be on the safe side*, he had everything put in writing.

── 大事な 形 ❶[重要な] important; (重大な) serious; (決定的な) crucial. (⇨大切な) ▶ 大事な話がある I have something *important* to tell you. ▶ 交渉は大事な局面を迎えた The negotiation has entered upon a *serious* phase. ▶ 彼は大事な時にミスをしてしまった He made a mistake at the *crucial* moment. ▶ 大事なことはよいレポートを提出することです *It's important* (for you) *to* turn in a good report. / *It's important that you* (《主に英》 *should*) [*The important thing is to*] turn in a good report. ▶ 小野の足の状態ほど大事なことはない Nothing is more *important* than the condition [state] of Ono's foot.

会話 「もう私は大事ではないというのか」「もちろん大事だよ」 "Do you mean I don't *count* any more?" "Of course, you *dó cóunt*." (⚠ do は動詞 count を強調する助動詞)

DISCOURSE
何を言うかよりもどう言うかの方が大事なこともある. 例えば, 冷淡な調子で「ありがとう」と言うことは, うれしくない, さらには腹を立てていることさえ意味するかもしれない What you say is sometimes less *important* than how you say it. **For example**, if you say "Thank you" in a cold way, it may mean that you are not happy, or even annoyed. (⚠ for example (例えば)は具体例に用いるディスコースマーカー)

❷[貴重な] precious, valuable; (いとしい) dear (to), (限定的な) beloved. ● 大事な時間をむだに遣う waste *precious* [*valuable*] time. ▶ 彼は私たちにとってとても大事な人だ He is very *precious* to us.

── 大事に 副 [注意深く] carefully, with care. ▶ (お体) お大事に Take (good) /ˈcare (of yourself). (⚠ 親しい人との別れのあいさつ. 手紙の結びにも用いられる. 通例 of 以下は省略る)/(病人・患者に) I hope you (will) sóon get /ˈbetter./I hope you're [you'll be] /ˈwell.

会話 「それちょっと持ってもいい?」「そうねえ, じゃ大事に扱ってよ」 "May I hold it for a minute?" "Well, *be careful with* it." (⚠ with は「…に関して」の意)

── 大事にする 動 [気を配る] take* (good) care of…; [大切に持ち続ける] 《やや書》 treasure; (愛情深く) 《書》 cherish. ▶ 父は大事にしていた絵を全部手放さねばならなかった My father had to part with all the paintings that he *had treasured* [*had cherished*].

ダイジェスト [[要約]] a digest.

たいしかん 大使館 an embassy. (⚠ しばしば Embassy) ● ロンドンの日本大使館 the Japanese *Embassy* in London.
● 大使館員 (個人) a member of the embassy [staff]; (全体) the embassy (staff).

だいしきょう 大司教 (ローマカトリック教会の) an archbishop /ˈɑːrtʃbɪʃəp/.

だいしぜん 大自然 nature. ● 大自然の神秘 the mysteries of *nature*. ● 大自然の懐に抱かれて生きる live in the bosom of nature [the unspoilt countryside].

***たいした** 大した [[多量の, 重要な]] much*; [[多数の]] many* (以上二つは通例否定文・疑問文で用いる (⇨たくさん)); [[非常に]] very; [[本当に]] really; [[偉大な]] great; [[立派な人[こと]]] something. ▶ 彼女はいたし美人だ She's *very* [*really*] beautiful./She's a *real* beauty. (⚠ 感嘆文で How beautiful she is! ともいえる) ▶ 彼はたいした政治家だ He's a *great* politician. ▶ それは実にたいした経験だったよ It was *quite* an experience. (⚠ 「quite a + 程度を含意しない名詞」は「並はずれてすばらしい」の意) ▶ たいしたものだ (That's) *great* [*wonderful*]!/That's *really something*! ▶ 彼はそのうちたいした人物になるだろう He'll be *something* [*somebody*] one of these days. ▶ まあすごい, 坊ちゃん大したものですね "How nice! You must be proud of your son." (⚠ 日本語との発想の違いに注意)

会話 「たばこやめたよ」「たいしたものですね」「そうだろう」 "I quit smoking." "You're *amazing*!/I admire you for it." "I know." (⚠ I know. は相手に同意してあいづちを打つ言葉. Yes, indeed. に近い)

[たいした…でない] not much, not much of a…; (多くない) not many [much]. ▶ 彼はたいした歌手ではない He's *not much* as a singer./He's *not much of* a singer. ▶ 見た目はたいしたことないが彼は力(=影響力)のある政治家です He may *not* look (like) *much*, but he's an influential politician. ▶ 彼がその責任をとって辞職するかどうかはたいした問題ではない It matters *little* [That's a *small* matter] whether or not he resigns his post taking the blame for it. ▶ 1日2日の仕事だ. たいした仕事じゃないよ That's about one or two day's work. It's *not a big* job. ▶ 電車で5分しかかからないのなら歩いてもいいたことはない If it only takes five minutes by train, it'll be an *easy* walk (↔a good walk).

会話 「なんて気前のよかったこと!」「やあ, でもたいしたこどじゃないさ」 "How generous you've been!" "Oh, but it's *nothing much*."

会話 「あの人, ころんで足の骨を折ったんですって」「たいしたことでなければいいけど」 "He says he fell and broke his leg." "*Nothing ˇserious*, I hope./I hope it won't be *serious*."

たいしつ 体質 [[体の構造]] a constitution; [[病気しやすい]] 《やや書》 (a) disposition; [[傾向]] a tendency; [[集団特有の行動・思考パターン]] culture. ● 弱い [虚弱な] 体質の人 a person with a weak [a feeble] *constitution*. ● 太りやすい体質 a *tendency* to get fat. ● 体質を改善する improve one's *physical condition*. ▶ 彼は風邪をひきやすい体質だ He is *prone* to colds [*to* catch (a) cold]./《やや書》 He *is disposed* to colds./《話》 He *easily* catches cold. ▶ ビールは私の体質に合わない Beer does not agree [Beer disagrees] with me. ▶ この意の agree with は通例否定文で用いる) ▶ まだ古い企業体質を温存している会社は多い Many companies still can't get out of their traditional corporate *culture*.

たいしつ 耐湿 ── 耐湿(性)の 形 damp-proof.

たいしつ 退室 ── **退室する** 動 go out of the room; leave the room. ▶明かりを消してから退室すること Turn off the light before you *leave the room*.

だいしっこう 代執行 execution by a substitute [by proxy].

*****たいして 大して** 〖あまり…でない〗not very [so]; not ... (very) much. (⇨大分) ▶この本はたいして役に立たない *This book is not very* [*so*] *useful*. ▶そんなことはたいして気にしていません *I don't mind it very much*. ▶新しい計画は前のとたいして違わない *The new plan is not very different from the old one*. ▶彼はたいして学のある男ではない *He isn't much of a scholar*. (❗️*much of a ...* は「たいした…」. 否定文で用いる) ▶お時間はたいしてとらせません *I won't take up much of your time.*/*It won't take much time*.

たいして 対して (⇨対する 動)

たいしぼう 体脂肪 body fat.
● 体脂肪率 body fat percentage.

たいしゃ 大赦 (an) amnesty;〖法律〗a general pardon, oblivion. ●大赦を行う grant 《him》 a general pardon; grant 《them》 an amnesty.

たいしゃ 代謝 ●新陳代謝〖生理〗metábolism. (⇨新陳代謝) ●基礎代謝〖生理〗basal metabolism.
● 代謝異常 metabolic disorder.

たいしゃ 退社 ── **退社する** 動 〖出社に対して〗leave the office; (タイムカードを押して) clock out (↔clock in);〖入社に対して〗(辞職) resign (from a company),《話》quit; (通例定年で退職する) retire (from a company). ▶きのうは何時に退社しましたか *What time did you leave the office* [*clock out*] *yesterday*?
● 退社時間 clock-out time.

だいしゃ 台車 〖荷物を運ぶための〗《米》a cart,《英》a trolley; (2輪の) a hánd trùck;〖鉄道車両の〗a truck. ●ペプシのケースを台車で運ぶ wheel cases of Pepsi on a *hand truck*.

だいじゃ 大蛇 a (very) large snake.

たいしゃく 貸借 (簿記の貸方と借方) debit and credit; (貸し借り) borrowing and lending. (❗️いずれも語順に注意)
● 貸借対照表 a balance sheet (略 B/S, b.s.).

たいしゃくてん 帝釈天 *Taishakuten*; (説明的に) one of the twelve Buddhist guardian deities who guards the east.

だいしゃりん 大車輪 ❶〖大きな車輪〗a big wheel. ❷〖体操競技の鉄棒の技〗a giant swing. ❸〖一生懸命に〗《*at*》full capacity;《*at*》full [high] tilt.

たいしゅ 大酒 (⇨大酒(おおざけ))

たいじゅ 大樹 a big tree. ▶寄らば大樹の陰 A *big tree* is a good shelter.

*****たいしゅう 大衆** the (general) public (❗️《米》では単数扱い.《英》では単・複両扱い. ただし呼応する代名詞は they で, it は堅い言い方); the masses (❗️複数扱い); the people (❗️複数扱い).

> **使い分け** **the public** 合理的な判断ができ健全な民主主義を支える人々.
> **the masses** 社会機構が理解できずマスコミに踊らされる人々でしばしば軽蔑的に用いられる.
> **the people** 国家や自治体を構成する一般の人々, 特に選挙民.

● 大衆向けの娯楽 mass [*popular*] entertainment. ● 大衆化したスポーツ a *popularized* sport. ● 大衆性が必要だ need the *common* touch. ▶彼の演説は大衆の支持を得た His speech won *popular* support [the support of *the people*]./(大衆にうけた) His speech appealed to *the* (*general*) *public*. ▶その計画は大衆の抵抗という大きな壁に突き当たった The program struck against a massive wall of *public* resistance. (❗️この public は形容詞) ▶日本の一般大衆は彼の政策を支持しているようだ The *general public* of Japan [The Japanese *public*] seem(s) to favor his policies.
● 大衆運動 a máss mòvement; (草の根運動) a gráss-roots mòvement. ● 大衆課税 mass taxation. ● 大衆芸術 popular art. ● 大衆紙 a popular (↔quality) newspaper. ● 大衆車 an economy car. ● 大衆社会 (a) máss society. ● 大衆食堂 a popular [(安い) a cheap] restaurant; (セルフサービスの) a cafeteria. ● 大衆文化 popular [〖話〗pop] culture. (❗️〖話〗では pop cult (ポップ文化) ともいう) ● 大衆浴場 a public bathhouse.

たいしゅう 体臭 a body odor (略 BO). ●不快な体臭を消す薬 a chemical (スプレー) a spray) to remove unpleasant *body odors*.

*****たいじゅう 体重** (one's) weight. ●はかりで(自分の)体重を計る *weigh oneself* on the scale(s). (❗️×measure one's weight ... とはいわない); (体重計に乗る) step on the bathroom scale. ▶ずいぶん増えた [減った] I have gained [lost] (a lot of) *weight*. (❗️(1)「増えた」は put on *weight* も可. (2)「3キロ増えた [減った]」なら ... gained [lost] 3 kilos. (3)「50キロに増えた [減った]」は My *weight* has increased [decreased] to 50 kilos. ▶私は体重を減らにたい. 相当「少し」オーバーしているから I want to lose some *weight* [reduce (my) *weight*]; I'm much [a little] too heavy. (❗️(1) 単に lose weight では「すべての体重を失う」の意にもなる. (2) reduce weight は大げさな言い方) ▶彼は私と体重が同じだ He is the same *weight* as I am./He and I are the same *in weight*.
会話「体重はどれくらいありますか」「65キロです」"How much do you *weigh*?" "(I *weigh*) 65 kilos."/"What's your *weight*?" "(My *weight* is) 65 kilos." (❗️話し言葉では I *weigh*, My *weight* は通例省略される) **事情** (1) 65 kilos は米英ではポンドを使って 143 pounds ということが多い. (2) 日常的には医師と患者, 家族の間以外では話題としては避ける)
● 体重計 a bath [a bathroom] scale (家庭用の体重計は浴室に置くことから); (和製語) health meter.

たいしゅつ 退出 ── **退出する** 動 leave; (引き下がる) withdraw 《*from*》.

たいしゅつ 帯出 图 ●帯出禁止 (表示) Not to be taken (《主に米》checked) out.
── **帯出る** 動 take (a book) out.

*****たいしょ 対処** ── **対処する** 動 deal 《with》; (うまく) cope 《with》. ●困難な事態に対処する *cope with* a difficult situation; *deal with* a difficult situation *successfully*. ▶この件にはただちに対処しなければならない We have to *deal with* this matter immediately./This matter requires our immediate attention.

たいしょ 大書 ── **大書する** 動 write in large characters [letters].

たいしょ 大暑 *taisho*; (説明的に) the hottest time of the year, around July 23.

たいしょ 対蹠 ── **対蹠的な** 形 〖正反対の〗antipodal; exactly [diametrically] opposite.

だいしょ 代書 ── **代書する** 動 ▶彼は悪筆なので手紙はいつも妻に代書してもらう As his handwriting is very poor, he always asks his wife to *write* letters for him.
● 代書人 a professional letter-writer; a judicial scrivener.

たいしょう 対象 ❶ [行為・思考・感情などの] an object 《of》; [非難などの] a target 《of, for》. ●研究の対象 the *object* [(題目) *subject*] *of* one's studies. ●輸入制限の対象となっている食品 food (which is) *subject to* import restrictions. ▶彼のふるまいはしばしば非難の対象となった His behavior was often came in for the *target of* criticism./His behavior often came in for criticism.
❷ [目標] ▶子供を対象とした本 a book (*intended*) *for* children; a child-oriented book. ▶この歴史書は高校生を対象に書かれている This history book *is written* [*is intended*] *for* high school students.

たいしょう 対照 图 (a) cóntrast. (**!**「対照となるもの」の意は 🅒) ▶彼は二つの(異)文化の対照研究をした He made a *contrastive* study of the two (different) cultures. ▶白い建物は黒い森と鮮やかな対照 (=コントラスト)をなしている The white building makes a sharp *contrast with* [is in sharp *contrast to*] the dark forest./The white building *is sharply contrasted* [*contrasts sharply*] *with* [*against*] the dark forest. ▶次郎とは対照的に三郎はよく勉強する生徒だ *In contrast to* [*with*] Jiro, Saburo is a diligent student. ▶隣りのご夫婦は大変対照的だ. ご主人は背が高く太っていて奥さんは小柄でやせている The couple next door are quite [such] a *contrast*—the husband is tall and stout, and [while] the wife is short and thin.
—— **対照する** 動 cóntrast (A *with* B, A *and* B). ▶それを原文と比較対照しなさい *Contrast* [*Compare*] it *with* [*and*] the original.

たいしょう 大正 Taisho, the Taisho period.

たいしょう 大将 (陸軍) a (full) general, 《米話》a four-star general; (海軍) an admiral, a full admiral; [首領] a head, a chief (圈 ~s), a leader, (政党の) (兄けなして) a boss. ●お山の大将 (⇨お山の大将) ●若大将 (⇨若大将)

たいしょう 大勝 图 a great [(決定的な) a decisive, (圧倒的な) a crushing, a runaway game, (完全な) a perfect] victory; (選挙の地滑り的な勝利) a landslide victory. (⇨圧勝)
—— **大勝する** 動 ▶ジャイアンツに 9 対 1 で大勝する wipe out the Giants, 9-1. ●選挙で大勝する *win* an election *by a landslide* [(大差で) *by a large majority*]. ▶私たちのチームは 10 対 0 で快勝した Our team *won* [(やや書) *gained*] *a great victory* by a score of 10 to 0. (**!** 10 to 0 は ten to nothing と読む)

たいしょう 大賞 a grand prix (⇨グランプリ); (the) first prize.

たいしょう 対称 (左右の釣り合い) sýmmetry (↔ asymmetry). ▶このつぼは完全に左右対称をなしていない This pot is not completely *symmétrical*.

たいしょう 隊商 a caravan.

たいしょう 退場 图 [俳優などの] an exit; [サッカー] sent-off. ▶松井は退場をさせられた [野球] Matsui was ejected [banished, tossed out]./[サッカー] Matsui was given his marching orders. ▶キャンベルは後半 4 分, 2 枚目のイエローで退場になった Campbell was dismissed four minutes into the second half for his second bookable offence.
—— **退場する** 動 [去る] leave*; [抗議して] walk out 《of》; [俳優などが] exit, make* one's exit 《from》. ●急に宣誓して退場する *make a* hasty *exit*. ▶彼らは票決に抗議して退場した They *walked out of* [*left*] the meeting to show their opposition to the vote.

だいしょう 大小 (大きさ) (a) size. ●大小により[かかわらず] according to [regardless of] *size*. ●大小の差んろを vary in *size*. ●大小いろいろの靴 shoes *of* various [different, (すべての) all] *sizes*. ▶その内海には大小合わせて 100 以上島がある There are more than 100 islands, *large and small* [(話) *big and little*], in the inland sea.

だいしょう 代償 [賠償] compensation, 《書》reparation; [代価] (a) cost. ●...の代償として in *compensation* for.... ●いかなる代償を払っても at all *costs*; at any *cost* [*price*]. ●高価な代償を払って勝利を得る gain a victory *at* (a) *great cost*.

たいしょうえび 大正海老 [動物] an oriental [a fleshy] shrimp.

だいじょうかん 太政官 [歴史] the Cabinet (in old Japan).

だいじょうだいじん 太政大臣 [歴史] the Prime Minister (in old Japan).

だいじょうだん 大上段 ●大上段に構える (剣道で) hold a sword above one's head; (威圧する態度) take a high-handed attitude 《*to*》.

だいじょうぶ 大丈夫 ❶ [人・物事が申し分ない] 《話》all right, OK, O.K.; [安全な] safe; [確信している] sure (**!** 叙述的に); [事が可能な] possible. ▶彼に任せておけば大丈夫だ If you leave it to him, it'll be *all right*./(すべてを任せられることができる) You can leave everything to him. ▶この水は飲んでも大丈夫だ This water is *safe* [(適する) *good*] to drink. (**!** 文脈上問わない場合は to 以下を省略して, 例えば Is this water *safe* [*good*] enough? のようにいえる)/It is *safe* to drink this water. ▶大丈夫, 彼は成功するよ He is *sure* to succeed./I'm *sure* (*that*) he will succeed. (**!** ×It is sure that.... とは通例いわない)/*Surely*, he will succeed. (**!** He is sure of success./He is sure that he will succeed. とすれば彼自身が大丈夫と思っていることを表すのでの場合は不可)/(保障するよ) *Let me assure you*, he will succeed./To tell the truth, *I* (*can*) *assure you*.
会話「きっと落ちちゃうよ」「大丈夫よ(=心配するな). 下を見なければまったく大丈夫よ」 "I'm sure I will fall." "*Don't worry!* You'll be *safe* enough if you don't look down."
会話「大丈夫? 救急車呼んであげるよ」「いえ, おかまいなく. 自分でなんとかできますから」「本当に?」「ええ, ありがとう」 "Are you *all right* [*OK*]? Let me call an ambulance for you." "No, please don't bother. I can manage, thank you." (**!** 事典) このような好意的な申し出には断るときにも thank you を添えて応答することが適切) "Are you sure?" "Yes, but thank you just the same."
❷ [その他の表現] ▶時間は大丈夫です(=十分ある) I've got *enough* [*plenty of*] time. ●急げば大丈夫です(=間に合う) If we hurry, we'll *make it*. ●この辞書なら大丈夫だ(=役に立つ) This dictionary *will do*.
会話「先生, 患者の具合はどうですか」「もう大丈夫です(=危険を脱している)」 "How's the patient, doctor?" "He's *out of danger* now./(快方に向かっている)(話) He's gonna *make it*." (**!** gonna /gəna/ は going to の口語発音を反映したつづり. この make it は「回復する」の意)

だいじょうぶっきょう 大乗仏教 the Mahayana /màːhəjáːna/ (↔the Hinayana), Máhayana Búddhism. (参考) サンスクリット語で「大きな方の乗り物」の意)

たいじょうほうしん 帯状疱疹 shingles; [医学] herpes zoster.

だいじょうみゃく 大静脈 the main vein; [解剖] vena cava /víːnə kéivə/.

たいしょうりょうほう 対症療法 (症状に応じた治療) symptomatic therapy [treatment]. ● 対症療法を行う treat the symptoms. (■比喩的にも用いる)

たいしょく 大食 图 gluttony.
— **大食の** gluttonous.
— **大食する** 動 eat a great deal; 《話》eat like a horse.
● 大食漢 a big [a heavy] eater; a glutton (■意地汚なさを含意).

たいしょく 耐食 — **耐食(性)の** 形 anticorrosive.
● 耐食剤 (an) anticorrosive.

たいしょく 退色 — **退色する** 動 fade. (⇨褪(ぁ)せる)

たいしょく 退職 图 (通例定年による) a retirement; (辞職) resignation. ● 早期[希望]退職をする take early [voluntary] retirement.
— **退職する** 動 (定年などで) retire; (辞職する) resign; (仕事をやめる)《話》quit (-tt-) one's job. (⇨辞める)
▶彼は 60 歳でその会社を退職した He retired from the company at (the age of) 60.
会話「あの方そろそろ退職されるのですか」「ええ、この夏で 60 歳ですよ」"Is she retiring soon?" "Yes, I think she'll be sixty this summer."
● 退職金 a retirement allowance; (会社都合による中途退職時の) severance pay. ● 退職者 a retired employee; (英) a retiree /rɪtàɪəríː/.

たいしょこうしょ 大所高所 ● 大所高所(=広い視野)から物を見る take a broad [a macroscopic (↔microscopic)] view (of). ● 問題を大所高所に立って判断する judge a matter from a broad view; 《米話》look at the big picture.

だいじり 台尻 the butt (of a shotgun).

たいしん 耐震 — **耐震の, 耐震性の** 形 (建物が) earthquake-resistant; (免震性の) earthquake-proof (⇨免震); (時計が) shockproof. ● 耐震構造の建物 an éarthquake-proof [a quàke-resistant] building.

たいじん 大人 〚巨人〛 a giant; 〚立派な人〛 a person of high virtue.

たいじん 対人 ● 対人関係 personal relations [relationships]; interpersonal relations. (■単数扱い) ● 対人恐怖症〚医学〛 ànthropophóbia.

たいじん 対陣 — **対陣する** 動 face each other; (野営する) encamp facing each other.

たいじん 退陣 (辞任) (a) resignation; (a) step-down. (⇨辞職) ▶社長の退陣を要求する demand the resignation of the president.

だいしん 代診 图 (医師) a substitute doctor, 《英》a locum.
— **代診する** 動 examine 《patients》in place of 《Dr. H》.

* **だいじん 大臣** 〚日本の〛a minister; 〚米国の〛(長官) a secretary; 〚英国の〛a secretary (of state), a minister (■minister は農水大臣と無任所大臣にのみ用いる); (閣のa cabinet minister. (■以上いずれもしばしば大文字で) ● 大臣級の人 a person of ministerial [《英》Cabinet] rank. ● 行政改革担当大臣 the Minister of State [State Minister] for Administrative Reform. ● 外務大臣になる become 〖(任命される) be appointed〗 (the) Minister of Foreign Affairs. (■補語の位置では通例無冠詞) ● その問題について関係大臣に陳情する lobby the relevant minister over the issue. ▶彼は大臣をやめた (内閣から退いた) He resigned from the Cabinet. / (大臣の座を退いた) He resigned his seat in the Cabinet.
● 大臣政務官 a parliamentary secretary.

だいじん 大尽 a millionaire, a billionaire; a very wealthy person. (⇨富豪)

● 大尽風を吹かせる show off one's wealth.

だいしんさい 大震災 a great earthquake disaster.
● 関東大震災 the Great Kanto Earthquake.

だいしんどちか 大深度地下 deep underground [subterranean] areas.

だいじんぶつ 大人物 a great person [figure]. ● 維新史に残る大人物たち great figures in the history of the Meiji Restoration.

ダイス 〚さいころ〛dice;〚打ち抜き型〛a die (⊕ dies /dáɪz/).

だいず 大豆 〚植物〛《米》 a soybean,《英》a soya bean.

たいすい 耐水 — **耐水(性)の** 形 water-resistant.

たいすう 対数 〚数学〛a logarithm /lɔ́(:)gərìðm/.
● 対数表 a table of logarithms.

だいすう 代数 algebra /ǽldʒəbrə/. ● 代数の問題を解く solve a problem in algebra [an álgebra pròblem].
● 代数式 an àlgebráic expression. ● 代数方程式 an àlgebráic equation.

だいすき 大好き (⇨好き) ▶マドンナは私の大好きな歌手です Madonna is one of my favorite singers. (■favorite は「最も好きな」の意なので ×very [most] favorite は不可)/I'm a great fan of Madonna.
▶リンゴが大好きだ I like apples very much./I am very fond of apples./I love apples. (■いずれも ×an apple は不可) ▶おじちゃん、大好き I love you, Uncle. ▶彼は甘い物が大好きです He has a weakness for sweet things. (■好ましくないもの[こと]が大好きなことを表す)

* **たいする 対する** 動 ❶〚面する〛face. ❷〚応対する〛receive.
— **対して, 対する** 前 ❶〚真向かいに〛opposite (to) ...,《主に米話》across from .... ▶彼は彼女に相対して座った He sat down opposite [across from] her.
❷〚…に向かって〛to ..., toward ...; (反対して) against ..., on ...; (利益・賛成などのために) for ....

> **使い分け** to, toward では方向の意に加えて到着点を, toward は方向を表すが, 心的態度・行為などの対象を表す場合は交換して用いられることが多い.
> **against** 反対・不利益・圧制などの対象を表す.
> **on** 敵意や攻撃の対象を表す.
> **for** 親切・忠告・愛情などの対象を表す.

● 圧制に対して抗議する protest against oppression. ● 学生に対して厳しい先生 Be kind to older people. ▶彼女に対して抱いている感情はどんなものですか What are your feelings like toward her?/How do you feel toward [about] her?
▶彼は詩に対して偏見を持っている He has a prejudice against poetry. ▶私は彼の親切に対して感謝した I thanked him for his kindness. ▶それは彼に対する有益な教訓だ It is a useful lesson for [to] him. (■to は単に対象を示すが, for は useful と呼応してその人のためになることを含意する)

❸ [関して] about ... (⇨関する); [対応して] to ...; [おける] in .... ●その問題に対して意見を述べる express one's opinion *about* [*on*] the matter. ●彼はそれに対して何と言ったの What did he say *to* [(答えて) *in response to*] that? ▶彼は言語学に対して強い関心を示した He showed a strong interest *in* linguistics.
❹ [備えて] against ..., for .... ●地震に対する備え preparations *against* an earthquake. ●老後に備えてお金を蓄える save money *for* one's old age. (⇨備える)
❺ [比較・対照して] to ...; (as) against ...; as opposed to .... (❗後の二つは強意的) (⇨対(5)) ●50に対して200の多数で再選される be reelected by a majority of 200 *to* 50. ●話し言葉に対しての書き言葉 (the) written language *as opposed to* (the) spoken language. ▶今月の売上高は先月の80万円に対して100万円に達する The sales this month amounts to 1,000,000 yen *as against* [*compared with*] 800,000 yen last month. (❗前の方は相当な遠いのあることを表し対照の意が強い) ▶彼は英語が得意なのに対して(=一方)弟は数学が得意だ He is good at English, *while* [*but on the other hand*, ×*on the contrary*] his brother is good at math. (❗*on the other hand* は対照を強調して He is good at English. His brother, *on the other hand*, is good at math. という語順も可)
❻ [交換, 比例] ●その本に対して1,000円支払う pay 1,000 yen *for* the book. ●1,000円に対して(=につき)100円の手数料を取る[出す] get [allow] a commission of one hundred yen *per* thousand.

たいする 体する understand 《his wishes》 clearly [perfectly]. ▶母の意を体して父の隣に埋葬した *In compliance with* her wishes, Mother was buried next to Father.

だいする 題する ●『今日の日本』と題する本 a book *entitled* [*under the title of*] "Japan Now".

*****たいせい 態勢** [態度] an attitude; [準備] preparation(s) (❗通例複数形で); [状態] (a) condition. ●防御の態勢を取る take a defensive *attitude*. ●攻撃の態勢にある *be ready* [*be prepared*] *to* attack. ●新入生の受け入れ態勢を整える make preparations [arrangements] *for* [*to* accept] the new students.

たいせい 大成 ── 大成する 動 ▶彼は学者として大成した He became a great scholar./He was a great success as a scholar.

たいせい 大勢 [全般的状況] the general situation; [一般的傾向] the general tendency; the (general) trend; [時流, 風潮] the tide. ●大勢を把握する grasp [take in] the *general situation*. ●大勢に従う follow the *general trend*; swim [go] with *the tide* [*current* (*of the times*), *stream*]. (❗「大勢に逆らう」は swim *against* ...) ●大勢を決する set the *tide*. ▶会議の大勢は彼と反対の方に傾いた The *tide* of opinion ran against him in the meeting.

たいせい 体制 [組織] a system; [構造] (a) structure; [権力機構] an establishment (❗しばしば the E-. 単・複両扱い). ●政治体制 a political *system*. ●資本主義体制 the capitalist *structure*. ●日本の経済体制 the economic *structure* of Japan. ●救急医療体制 an emergency medical treatment *system*. ●集団指導体制を強化する strengthen the collective guidance *system*. ●現体制を揺るがす upset the present *structure* [*establishment*]. ▶彼は体制側だ He is with [belongs to] *the Establishment*. (⇨反体制)

たいせい 体勢 (体の姿勢) (a) posture; (体の平衡) one's bálance. ●体勢をくずす lose one's *balance*.

たいせい 対生 ●この植物の葉は対生だ The leaves of this plant are in *opposite* pairs.

たいせい 耐性 (許容能力) (a) tolerance; (抵抗力) resistance. ●抗生物質に対する耐性 a *tolerance* to antibiotics. ●ペニシリン耐性菌 penicillin-*resistant* bacteria. (❗複数扱い) ●耐性のある tolerant.

たいせい 胎生 图 『生物』 viviparity /vàivipǽrəti/.
── **胎生の** 形 『生物』 viviparous. (関連) 卵生の oviparous)
●胎生動物 a viviparous animal.

たいせい 退勢 (衰え) (やや書) (a) decline; (衰運) (やや書) one's declining fortune. (⇨挽回)

たいせい 泰西 the Occident; the West. (⇨西洋)

たいせいほうかん 大政奉還 [歴史] the Restoration of the Imperial Rule.

たいせいよう 大西洋 the Atlantic (Ocean). ●大西洋横断飛行 a transatlantic flight. ●北大西洋条約機構 the North *Atlantic* Treaty Organization 《略 NATO /néitou/》.

たいせき 体積 vólume. ▶この箱の体積は3立方メートルです The *volume* of this box is three cubic meters.

たいせき 退席 ── 退席する 動 leave one's seat; (部屋を出る) leave the room. ▶彼は会議中に退席した He *left the room* in the middle of the conference [while we were holding a meeting].

たいせき 堆石 『高く積まれた石』 a pile of stones; 『氷河によって運ばれた岩石』 『地学』 a moraine.

たいせき 堆積 图 (an) accumulation. ●ごみの堆積 an *accumulation* [a *heap*, a *pile*] of rubbish.
── **堆積する** 動 (蓄積する) accumulate; (山積する) pile up.
●堆積岩 sedimentary rock. ●堆積物 sediment.

たいせき 滞積 ── 滞積する 動 accumulate; pile up. (⇨溜まる❷)

:**たいせつ 大切** ── **大切(さ)** 图 importance. ●健康の大切さを知る realize the *importance* of (good) health.

DISCOURSE
私はお金が人生にとって大切という意見に部分的にしか賛成できない **I only partially agree with** the statement that money is *everything* in life. (❗I very much [definitely; only partially] agree with ...(私は非常に[明らかに; 部分的にのみ] ...を支持する)は賛成を表すディスコースマーカー)

── **大切な** 形 [重要な] important; [貴重な] (価値があり有益な) valuable; (価値があり失いたくない) precious; [決定的な] crucial. (⇨大事) ●大切な行事 an *important* event. ●大切な助言 (×a) valuable advice. ●大切な思い出 *precious* memories. ●大切な試合に負ける lose the *crucial* [*key*] game. ▶これは私にはとても大切な問題です This is a very *important* matter [(やや書) a matter *of great importance*] to me. ●後の方では通例 great, much, some, no, little などを伴う)(重要性を持つ) This *means* a lot to me. ▶彼女は私の大切な友達です She and I [×I and she] are very good friends./I value her friendship very much. ▶遊びは子供時代になくてはならない *Play* is a very *important* [a *vital*, (不可欠な) an *indispensable*] element in every child's life. (❗英語では重要性を強調するときは vital や important な

たいせつ 大切 ― [[宝のように大事にする]] treasure, (大事にかわいがる)[書] cherish; [[気を配る]] take* care of .... (⇨大事にする) ▶もっと体を大切にすぐけた方がいい You should take better care of yourself. ▶余暇を大切にしなさい (有効に過ごせ) Make good use of your leisure time./(むだにするな) Don't waste your leisure time.

たいせつ 耐雪 ― **耐雪の** 形 snow-resistant, snowproof.

たいせん 大戦 a great war; (世界戦争) a world war.
● 第一次世界大戦 World War I (⚠ I は one と読む。無冠詞); (やや書)(⇨大戦) the First World War. (⚠ the Great War ともいう)

たいせん 対戦 名 ● ジャイアンツとタイガースの直接対戦シリーズ a head-to-head series between the Giants and the Tigers.
― **対戦する** 動 (試合をする) play; play [have] a game [a match] (with, against) (⇨試合 ③); (競争する) compete /kəmpíːt/ (with, against); (ボクシングなどで戦う) fight (with, against). ▶ヤンキースと対戦する play the Yankees. ● 10 人の打者と対戦する face ten batters.
● 対戦相手 an opponent. ● 対戦成績 the win-loss records [between A and B].

たいせん 対潜 ― **対潜の** 形 [軍事] antisubmarine.

たいぜん 大全 ● 園芸大全 the Complete Collection of Gardening.

たいぜん 泰然 ― **泰然とした** 形 (落ち着いた) calm, self-possessed. ● 泰然自若としている keep one's self-possession; be calm [self-possessed].

だいせんきょく 大選挙区 a large constituency [electoral district].
● 大選挙区制 the large-constituency system.

だいぜんてい 大前提 the major premise.

*__たいそう 体操__ (体育管を行う) gymnastics (⚠ 複数扱い。ただし学科目としては単数扱いで,《話》gym ともいう); (運動) physical exercise, (physical) gymnastic exercises. ●(体育) 準備体操 warm-[warming-]up exercises. ● 美容体操 calisthenics; (健康のための) keep-fit exercises. ● 器械体操をする practice apparatus gymnastics. ● 体操競技に出場する enter a gymnastics competition. ● 世界体操選手権大会 the World Gymnastics Championships. ▶彼は毎朝ラジオ体操をする He does radio (gymnastic) exercises every morning. ▶おばあちゃんは頭の体操のためにニュースをよく聞いている To exercise her brain, Grandma often listens to news programs on the radio. (⚠(1) 身体・脳・心理などの働きを正常に保つためにする体操は exercise. (2)「よく」は often で表す)
● 体操選手 a gýmnast.

たいそう 大葬 an Imperial funeral.

たいそう 大層 [非常に] very, very much, so (⚠ so は主に女性に好まれる); (すごく) terribly,《話》awfully; (極めて) extremely; (大いに) greatly. (⇨非常に) ▶彼はそれをたいそう気に入っている He likes it very [so] much./He is very fond of it./He is very [greatly] pleased with it. ▶今日はたいそう寒い It is very [terribly, awfully, extremely] cold today.

だいそう 代走 (人) a pinch [a substitute] runner.
● 鈴木の代走に出る (go in to) run [pinch-run] for Suzuki.

だいそうじょう 大僧正 (仏教で) an archbíshop.

だいそつ 大卒 a college [a university] graduate.
● 大卒男子[女子] a male [a female] college graduate.

だいそれた 大それた (無謀な) wild; (向こう見ずな) reckless; (恐れを知らぬ) audacious; (思いやりがない,ふとどきな) outrageous; (無思慮な) thoughtless. ▶彼は大それた望みをいだいていた He kept a wild hope. ▶なんと大それたことをしてしまったのか What an audacious thing you have done!

たいだ 怠惰 ― **怠惰な** 形 lazy; [[仕事をしていない]] idle. ● 怠惰な学生 a lazy student. ● 怠惰な生活 (lead) an idle life. (⇨怠ける)

だいだ 代打 (人) a pinch hitter. ● 代打ホームラン a pinch(-hit) homer. ● 田中の代打に出る a pinch-hit for Tanaka; go to bat for Tanaka. ● 2 連続代打二塁打を打つ hit doubles in two consecutive pinch-hit appearances.

*__だいたい 大体__ 名 [[概要]] an outline; [[あらすじ]] a sketch; [[要点]] a gist /dʒɪst/. ▶その計画のだいたいを述べてください Please give me the outline of the plan./Please outline the plan for [to] me.
― **だいたい** 副 ❶ [[おおよそ]] (約) about; (ほとんど) almost, nearly (⇨ほとんど[類語]); (一般に) generally; (全体から見て) on the whole; (大部分は) mostly, for the most part; (大ざっぱに) roughly /rʌfli/. ▶私たちはだいたい同じ年だ We are about the same age. ▶それはだいたい 10 キロメートルです That's about [roughly] ten kilometers. ▶宿題はだいたい終わった I have almost finished my homework. ▶彼らの意見はだいたい好意的であった Their opinion was generally favorable. ▶だいたいにおいて計画はうまくいった On the whole, the plan went well. ▶その村の人たちはだいたい親切だ The villagers are mostly kind./Most of the villagers are kind. (×Most of villagers, ×almost the villagers are kind.) ▶試験はだいたいできた (=ほとんどすべての問題に答えた) I answered almost all (of) the questions [×almost the questions] on the exam.
会話 「待遇はよかったですか」「だいたいね」"Were you treated well?" "More or less."
❷ [[強調]] (絶対的に) absolutely; (本当に) really. ▶だいたい君は間違っている You are absolutely wrong./(最初から) You are wrong from the beginning [the start].
― **大体の** 形 (一般の) general; (大ざっぱな) rough; (ほとんどの) most. (⚠ 通例 the はつけない) ● だいたいの計画 a general plan. ● だいたいの見積もりをする make a rough estimate. ● だいたいのものはスーパーで買います I get most things from the supermarket. ● タクシーの運転手にだいたいの住所(=住所の一部)を告げる I gave [told] the cab [taxi] driver part of the address [(通りの名前だけ) only the street name].

だいたい 大隊 a battalion;(空艇団の)《米》a squadron. ● 大隊長 a battalion [a squadron] commander.

だいたい 大腿 a thigh. ● 大腿部の負傷 a thigh injury; an injury to the thigh.
● 大腿骨 a thighbone /θáɪboʊn/; [解剖] a femur (複 ~s, femora).

だいたい 代替 ― **代替の** 形 alternative /ɔːltɜ́ːrnətɪv/; (代用の) súbstitute.
● 代替医療 alternative medicine. ([参考] 漢方薬・民間療法など). ● 代替エネルギー (太陽熱・風力などを用いた) alternative (sources of) energy. ● 代替バス a substitute bus. ● 代替品 a substitute. ● 代替輸送《米》alternative (×a) transportation,《英》alternative (×a) transport.

だいだい 橙 [色] orange, an orange color; [果物] a bitter orange. ● だいだい色のクレヨン an orange(-colored) crayon.

だいだい 代々 〈世代から世代へと〉from generation to generation; 〈何代にもわたって〉for generations. ▶この絵は代々我が家に伝わっている This painting has been handed down in my family *from generation to generation*. ▶あの家は代々本屋を営んでいる That family has kept [run] a bookstore *for (many) generations*.

だいだいてき 大々的 ── 大々的に 形 ●新車を大々的に(=広く)宣伝する advertise a new car *extensively* [〈大規模に〉*on a large scale*]. ●大々的に報道する give *large* coverage 《to it》.

だいだいひょう 大代表 the main (tele)phone number.

だいたすう 大多数 the [a] majority (↔the [a] minority). (⇒多数) ●国民の大多数 a *majority* of the people. ▶大多数の人はその提案に賛成だ The 〈great〉*majority* is [are] in favor of the proposal. (🔲 一つの集団としてとらえるときは単数扱い, 1 人 1 人を考えるときは複数扱い)

タイタニックごう タイタニック号 the Titánic.

たいだん 対談 图 a talk; 《会見》an interview.

── **対談する** 動 talk 《*with*》; have a talk [an interview] 《*with*》.
● 対談番組 〈有名人どうしの〉《米》a talk show; 《英》a chat show. (⇒トークショー)

たいだん 退団 ── 退団する 動 leave 《the team》. ▶ベルリンフィルハーモニックオーケストラを退団する *leave* the Berlin Philharmonic Orchestra.

だいたん 大胆 ── 大胆(さ) 图 boldness; daring; 《やや書》audacity.

── **大胆な** 形 〈勇敢で度胸のある〉bold; 〈冒険好きな〉daring; 〈豪胆な〉《やや書》audacious; 〈恐れを知らない〉fearless. ●大胆な考えは a *bold* [*daring*] idea. ▶それは本当に大胆な(=思い切った)デザインだ That is a very *bold* [*daring*] design. ▶あんな険しい山を登るとは君もずいぶん大胆だね It's very *bold* [*daring*, *audacious*, *fearless*] of you to [*for*] climb that steep mountain.
●大胆不敵 な 《不敵》●大胆不敵な行動 a *bold* act.

── **大胆に** 副 boldly; 〈恐れずに〉fearlessly. ▶彼は大胆にも大男に戦いを挑んだ He *dared* (to) [《書》*ventured to*] challenge the big man to a fight. (🔲 dare の後の to はしばしば省略される) ▶強盗の手口が年々大胆になってきている Robbery is [Robbers are] getting *bolder* every year.

だいだんえん 大団円 a denouement; 〈出演者総出の大フィナーレ〉a grand finale; a happy ending. ▶物語は大団円で終わっている The story has *a happy ending*.

たいち 対地 ● 地対地の[に] ground-to-ground.
● 対地攻撃 an air raid. ● 対地速度 ground speed.

たいち 対置 图 (a) contraposition.

── **対置する** 動 contrapose; place ... in contraposition 《*to*, *with*》.

だいち 大地 〈空に対しての〉the earth; 〈地表, 地面の〉the ground; 〈土地〉land. ●母なる大地 mother *earth*; Mother Earth. (🔲 無冠詞)

だいち 台地 (高原) a plateau /plætóu/ (⑱ ~s, plateaux /-z/) (しばしば複数形で); 〈高台〉《やや書》a height (🔲 しばしば複数形で単数扱い). ●武蔵野台地 the Musashino Uplands.

だいちのうた『大地の歌』 *The Song of the Earth*. 〈参考〉マーラーの交響曲)

たいちょ 大著 〈内容の優れた〉a great work, 〈傑作〉a masterpiece; 〈分量の多い〉a voluminous work.

たいちょう 体長 length. ●体長 50 センチのコイ a carp 50 centimeters *long*.

たいちょう 体調 〈physical〉 condition, 《話》shape. ●体調がいい[悪い] be in good [bad, poor] *condition* [*shape*]. ●体調をくずす get [go] out of *condition* [*shape*]. ●レースに備えて体調を整える get into 〈good〉 *shape* for the race. ●欠かさずジョギングをして体調を取り戻す get back in *shape* by jogging regularly.

たいちょう 退庁 ── 退庁する 動 leave the (government) office.

たいちょう 退潮 〈衰え〉(a) decline 《*in*》. ●退潮のきざしが見える show a sign of a *decline* 《*in*》.

たいちょう 隊長 a captain, a leader; 〈軍隊などの〉a commander.

だいちょう 大腸 〖解剖〗the large (↔small) intestine /intéstin/.
● 大腸炎 〖医学〗colitis /kəláitis/. ● 大腸カタル catarrh of the colon. ● 大腸菌 a colon bacillus /bəsíləs/ (⑱ bacilli /-lai/). (🔲 colon は「結腸」) ● 病原性大腸菌 O-157 E. coli O-157 /í: kóulai ou-/. ● 大腸ポリープ a colon polyp.

だいちょう 台帳 〈元帳〉a ledger; 〈会計帳〉an account book. ● 販売台帳 a sales *ledger*.

タイツ tights. (🔲 (1) 複数扱い. (2)《英》ではパンスト (panty hose) も含む) ●綿のタイツをはく wear (a pair of) cotton *tights*.

†たいてい 大抵 副 ❶〔だいたい〕〈一般に〉generally; 〈通常〉usually; 〈大部分は〉mostly; 〈ほとんど〉almost, nearly. (⇒ほとんど) ▶たいてい毎朝 6 時に起きる I *usually* [*generally*] get up at six every morning. ▶この部屋の本はたいてい(=ほとんどすべての本を)読みました I read *almost all* 〈*of*〉 the books [×almost the books] in this room. ▶彼の小説はたいていおもしろい His novels are *mostly* interesting./Most of his novels [×His most novels] are interesting. ▶私はたいていここにいるが時々外出することもある I'm here *most of the time*, but I go out now and then.

❷〔たぶん〕probably. ▶あしたはたいてい雨であろう It will *probably* rain tomorrow./It *is likely to* rain tomorrow. (⇒多分)

❸〔ほどほどに〕(⇒大概 ❸)

── **たいていの** 〈大部分の〉most; 〈ほとんどすべての〉almost [nearly] all (⇒圓 ❶). ● 並大抵の (⇒並大抵) ▶たいていの男の子は野球選手にあこがれる *Most* boys [×Most of boys] admire baseball players. (🔲*Most of the boys...* では「特定の男の子の大部分は」ことになり, ここでは不適当) ▶たいていの生徒は自転車で登校する *Most of the students* [×The most students, ×Most of students] come to school by bicycle. (🔲*Most* students come.... では「一般に生徒はたいてい自転車で登校するものだ」の意になり, ここでは不適当)

たいてい 大帝 a great emperor. ● ピョートル大帝 Peter the Great.

たいてい 退廷 ── 退廷する 動 leave the court [courtroom].

たいてき 大敵 a great [a powerful] enemy; 〈最大の敵〉an àrchénemy 〈事情〉米英人はしばしばサタン (Satan) を思い浮かべる). ●油断大敵 (⇒油断 [成句])

たいでん 帯電 图 electrification. ● 帯電防止スプレー an antistatic spray.

── **帯電する** 動 be electrified. ● 帯電させる electrify.

たいと 泰斗 an authority 《*on*》. (⇒権威, 大家)

†たいど 態度 〈心構え〉an áttitude 《*to*, *toward*》; 〈物腰〉a manner; 〈ふるまい〉behavior.

❶ 【〜態度】 ● 立派な態度 a good [an admira-

たいとう

ble] *manner*. ●断固とした態度 a determined *attitude*. ●だらしな態度 (xa) loose *behavior*.

② 【態度が[は]】 ▶私に対する彼の態度はよい His *attitude toward* [*to*, x*against*] me is good. ▶彼の態度が大きい He has a haughty *attitude*. (🔳 x*His attitude is big*. とはいわない) ▶彼の態度が気に入らない I don't like his *attitude* [*manner*]. ▶お前は食事中の態度が実に悪い Your table *manners* [x*manner*] are [Your *behavior* at meals is] really bad. ▶ファンの態度はひどかった The *behavior* of the fans was very bad (↔*good*)./The fans *behaved* very badly (↔*well*). ▶彼は人前では態度が変わる He *behaves* differently in public. 会話 「彼の態度はどう?」「近頃はとても思いやりがあるよ」 "How's he *behaving*?" "Recently he's been very considerate."

③ 【態度に】 ▶彼は感情をすぐ態度に表す He easily shows his feelings in his *attitude*. ▶焦りが彼女の態度に出ていた Impatience was apparent in her *attitude*.

④ 【態度を】 ●態度を改める alter one's *attitude*. ●冷たい態度を示す show a cold *attitude*. ●柔軟な態度を見せる show a flexible *attitude*. ●米国は日本[その問題]に対し強硬な態度をとった America took a strong *attitude toward* Japan [the problem]. ▶態度をはっきりさせろ Make up your *mind*./Tell us *which side you're on*. (🔳直訳的な Determine your *attitude*. では意味がはっきりしない) ▶彼は友人にひどい態度をとった He *behaved* badly *to* [*toward*] his friends./He treated his friends badly. (🔳前の方が堅い言い方)/(無礼なことをした) He *was rude to* his friends. ▶もう態度を決めたか(=決心したか) Have you *decided* yet? ▶先生にそんな態度をとってはいけない You shouldn't *act* like that *toward* your teacher.

⑤ 【態度で】 ●毅然とした態度で *with* a firm *attitude*. ●ぞんざいな態度で *in* a rude *manner*; rudely.

たいとう 台頭 图 (出現) the rise. ●ナチスの台頭 the *rise* of the Nazis /nάːtsiz/.
── **台頭する** 動 rise. ●台頭してきている be 《quickly》 on the *rise*.

たいとう 対等 图 equality; 【対等の人】 an equal /íːkwəl/.
── **対等の** 形 【能力・体力・地位などが匹敵する】 equal 《*to*》; 【互角の】 even 《*with*》. ●対等の立場[条件]で on equal footing [terms] 《*with*》. ●彼らを対等の人間として扱う treat them as one's *equals*. ▶彼女は彼と能力の点で対等だ She *is equal to* [*equals*] him in ability./She is his *equal* in ability.
── **対等に** 副 equally. ●彼を対等に扱う treat him *equally*. ▶君は彼と対等には戦えないだろう。彼は強すぎる You'll never *be even* with him. He's too powerful.

たいどう 胎動 【胎児の動き】 movements of the fetus, fetal movement, quickening; 【社会的な動きの気配】 signs 《*of*, *that* 節》.

たいとう 大刀 a long sword.

だいどうげい 大道芸 a street performance.
●大道芸人 a street performer.

だいどうしょうい 大同小異 (だいたい同じ) almost [much] the same 《*as*》. (⇒同じ)

だいどうだんけつ 大同団結 ── **大同団結する** 動 present a united front 《*against*, *to*》.

だいどうみゃく 大動脈 the main artery, 【解剖】 an aorta /eiɔ́ːrtə/ (優 ~s, aortae); 【主要幹線】 a trunk [a main] road.

だいとうりょう 大統領 a president. ●肩書きや特

ダイナミック

定の大統領に用いる場合には大文字で表す. 呼びかける(大統領閣下) Mr. President, (女性) Madam President. 後の方の場合 Ms. が適切な場合もあろう) ●合衆国大統領にブッシュを大統領に選んだ They elected Bush (to be) *President* of the United States. (🔳補語が役職・身分などを表す場合は冠詞はつけない. 「ブッシュ大統領」は *President* Bush)

── **大統領の** 形 presidential.
●大統領官邸 a presidential mansion; 《米国の》 the White House. ●大統領候補者 a candidate for the presidency; a presidential candidate. ●大統領選挙 the presidential election. ●大統領夫人 the President's wife; the first lady (🔳しばしば F- L-). ●大統領予備選挙 the presidential primaries.

たいとく 体得 ── **体得する** 動 master; learn ... by [from, through] experience.

たいどく 胎毒 【医学】 baby's eczema.

だいどく 代読 ── **代読する** 動 ●市長のメッセージを代読する *read* the message *for* [《やや書》 on behalf *of*] the mayor.

***だいどころ 台所** a kitchen; 【簡易の】 a kitchenet(te). ▶彼女は時々台所で朝食をとる[食事をする] She sometimes has breakfast in the *kitchen* [eats at the *kitchen* table]. (🔳後の方の方が *kitchen* とはあまりいわない)
●台所仕事 (xa) kitchen work. ●台所用品 kitchen utensils;《集合的に》 kitchenware.

タイトスカート (サイドラインが垂直の) a straight skirt; (すそ幅がヒップより狭い) a sheath skirt. (🔳a tight skirt は「体にぴったりしてきついスカート」の意)

タイトル ❶ 【題名】 a title. (⇒題名) ▶その本のタイトル the *title* of the book.
❷ 【選手権】 a title. ●タイトルを防衛する[失う] defend [lose] one's *title*. ▶彼女は「ミス日本」のタイトルを勝ち取った(=に選ばれた) She won the Miss Japan *title*.
❸ 【称号、肩書き】 a title; (学位) a degree.
●タイトルバー『コンピュータ』 a title bar. ●タイトルバック a title background,《和製語》 a title back. ●タイトルページ a title page. ●タイトルホルダー 『選手権保持者』 a titleholder. ●タイトルマッチ a title match [(ボクシングの) fight]. ●タイトルロール a title role.

タイトロープ 【綱渡りの綱】 a tightrope.

たいない 体内 ── **体内の** 形 intérnal.
●体内受精 internal fertilization (↔in vítro fertilization). ●体内時計 a biological [a body, an internal] clock.

たいない 対内 domestic, home, internal. ●対内政策 a *domestic* policy.

たいない 胎内 (子宮内) the inside of a womb /wúːm/. ●胎内で[に] in the womb.
●胎内感染 prenátal [antenátal] infection.

だいなし 台無し ── **台無しにする** 動 (すっかり) ruin; (計画などを) upset,《話》 mess ... up,《話》 make a mess of ... . ●台無しになる be spoiled [spoilt]; (失敗に終わる) come to nothing. ▶悪天候で休暇[計画]が台無しになってしまった The bad weather *spoiled* our holiday [*upset* our plans]. ▶私はコーヒーをこぼして彼女の新しい服を台無しにしてしまった I *ruined* her new dress by spilling my coffee on it.

ダイナマイト ●ダイナマイトで岩を割る shatter [blow up] a rock with *dynamite*; dynamite a rock.

ダイナミック ── **ダイナミックな** 形 【動的な、活動的な】 dynámic; 【精力的な】 energetic.

ダイナモ 〖発電機〗a dynamo (複 ~s).
だいに 第二 图 second. (❗通例 the ~)
── **第二(の)** 形 second. (❗通例 the ~); (別の) a second; (二次的な) secondary. ●第2章 chapter *two*; the *second* chapter. (❗後の方が堅い言い方) ●第二アクセント the *secondary* accent [stress]. ●第二の啄木 *another* [a *second*] Takuboku. ▶彼は定年後作家として第二の人生を歩み出した He started a new life as a writer after he retired.
── **第二(に)** 副 second(ly); first(ly)の後で用いる); in the second place. (⇒第一(に))
●第二次産業 a secondary industry. ●第二次世界大戦 World War Ⅱ /túː/; 《やや書》 the Second World War.

たいにち 対日 ●対日関係[貿易] relations [trade] *with Japan*. ●アメリカの対日政策 America's policy *toward Japan*. ●悪い対日感情を持つ have bad feelings *toward Japan*; (反日的感情) have *anti-Japanese* sentiment.

たいにち 滞日 a [one's] stay in Japan. ●滞日中に during *one's stay in Japan*; while *staying in Japan*.

たいにん 大任 (大役) an important task [(使命) mission; (任務) duty]. ●大任を引き受ける [帯びる] undertake [be charged with] an *important task*.

たいにん 退任 图 (辞職) (a) resignation. (⇒辞職)
── **退任する** 動 resign (one's post). ▶彼は3月末で代表取締役を退任することになっている He is due to *resign* as chief executive at the end of March.

だいにん 代人 a proxy. ●代人を務める be *proxy* [*for him*].

ダイニングカー 〖食堂車〗a dining car.
ダイニングキッチン 〖台所兼食堂〗a kitchen(-cum)-dining room (❗cum /kʌ́m/ は「…兼用の, …付きの」意); a kitchen with a dining area; a dining room-kitchen combination; 《米・婉曲的》 an éat-in kitchen; 〖和製語〗 a dining kitchen.
ダイニングルーム a dining room. (⇒食堂)

たいねつ 耐熱 ── **耐熱(性)の** 形 heatproof; heat-resistant. ●耐熱ガラス heat-resistant glass.

だいの 大の ●大の男 a *grown* [ˣa *big*] man. ●大の(=熱烈な)野球ファン a *great* [an *enthusiastic*] baseball fan. ▶彼と私は大の仲よしだ He and I are *great* [*good*, *close*] friends.

たいのう 滞納 default; (税金・借金の) delinquency.
── **滞納した** 形 (延滞の) overdue (❗通例叙述的); back; (不払いの) unpaid. ●滞納家賃 back rent.
── **滞納する** 動 ▶彼は税金を滞納している He *has not yet paid* taxes./He *has left* taxes *unpaid*./His taxes *are overdue* [*behind in payments*].
●滞納金 arrears /ərɪ́ərz/. ●滞納者 a ⟨tax⟩ defaulter.

だいのう 大脳 〖解剖〗the cerebrum /sərí:brəm/ (複 ~s, cerebra). ●大脳皮質 the cerebral cortex.

だいのう 大農 ●大規模的農業経営 a large-scale farming; 〖豪農〗a wealthy farmer.

だいのう 代納 ── **代納する** 動 〖代理で納める〗pay for ⟨him⟩; 〖物で納める〗pay in kind [goods, produce].

だいのうかい 大納会 the final session of the year.

だいのじ 大の字 ●大の字になって寝そべっている (手足を伸ばして) lie with one's arms and legs spread out; (ぶざまに) sprawl (out).

だいのつき 大の月 a month of 31 days.

たいは 大破 ── **大破する** 動 ●大破させる damage ⟨it⟩ badly, do [ˣgive] a lot of damage ⟨*to* it⟩. ▶機体は大破した The plane *was badly damaged* [*completely wrecked*]. (❗後の方が破損の程度がひどい。The plane was a total wreck. ともいえる)

ダイバー a diver.
たいはい 大敗 图 〖完敗〗a complete [a crushing] defeat.
── **大敗する** 動 ▶私たちの野球チームは10対0で大敗した Our baseball team *was completely defeated* [*beaten*] by a score of 10 to 0./Our team *was routed* 10-0. (❗10-0 は ten to nothing と読む)

たいはい 退廃 图 〖腐敗〗decay; 〖道徳・芸術などの衰退〗décadence; 〖堕落〗corruption. ●道徳の退廃 moral *decay*.
── **退廃的(な)** 形 decadent; corrupt. ●退廃的生活を送る lead a *corrupt* life.
── **退廃する** 動 be corrupted. ●道徳を退廃させる *corrupt* morals.

たいばつ 体罰 physical [《やや書》corporal] punishment. ●生徒にひどい体罰を加える impose severe *corporal punishment* on the student.

だいはっかい 大発会 the first session of the year.
たいはん 大半 (⇒大部分) ●人生の大半を外国で過ごす spend *most* [*the greater part*] of one's life abroad; live in foreign countries *almost all* his life. ▶私は1年の大半をそこで過ごした I lived there for *a large part* of the year.

たいばん 胎盤 图 〖解剖〗a placenta (複 ~s, placentae). ── **胎盤の** 形 placental.
●胎盤剥離 separation of the placenta.

たいひ 対比 图 〖比較〗(a) comparison; 〖対照〗(a) contrast.
── **対比する** 動 (⇒比較する) ●二つの小説を対比する *compare* the two novels; *make* a *comparison between* the two novels. ●都会生活と田舎生活と対比する *compare* [*contrast*] (ˣa) city life *with* country life.

たいひ 待避・待避線 (鉄道) a siding. ●待避場所 (狭い道路での車の) 《米》 a turnout, 《英》 a lay-by.
たいひ 退避 图 shelter. 〖無冠詞に注意〗(⇒避難)
── **退避する** 動 take shelter.
たいひ 堆肥 cómpost. ●堆肥の山 a *compost* heap [pile].

タイピスト a typist. (❗今はコンピュータを打つ人も us)
だいひつ 代筆 ── **代筆する** 動 ●彼の手紙の代筆を write a letter *for* him.

たいびょう 大病 ── **大病する** 動 suffer from a major [a serious] sickness [illness]. (⇒病気)

だいひょう 代表 图 〖行為〗representation; 〖人〗a representative; (会議などに出席する) a délegate; (代表団) a delegation 〖集合的に用い, 単・複両扱い〗; (サッカーなどの) an international. ●比例代表制 proportional *representation*. ●従業員代表 a *representative* of the employees. ●サッカー日本代表(チーム) the Japan(ese) national soccer [《英》football] team. ●元イングランド代表のシェリンガム a former England International Sheringham. ●代表Aマッチ an International A match. ●ワシントン会議への日本代表 Japan's *representatives* [the *delegates from* Japan] to the Washington Conference. ▶彼は私たちのクラスの代表です He is a *representative* of our class./He *represents* our class.
── **代表する** 動 represent; (代理を務める) act for …; (典型である) be typical of …, 《やや書》typify. ▶彼は日本を代表して会議に出席した He *represented* Japan at the conference. ▶彼は委員会を代表している He *is acting for* the committee. ▶彼女は

友を代表して話した She spoke for [on behalf of, 《米》in behalf of] her classmates. (⇨代わり) ▶これは16世紀の英国の教会を代表する建物です This *is typical of* [*typifies*] the 16th century English churches.

—— 代表的な 形 (典型的な) typical. ●代表的なアメリカ人 a *typical* American.

●代表権 the right of a representative. ●代表作 one's most important work; one's masterpiece. ●代表団 a delegation. ●代表取締役 a representative director. (⇨会社) ●代表番号 (電話の) the key number.

ダイビング 名 diving. ([参考] サッカーでは「シミュレーション」の意で diving を用いるのが一般的 (⇨シミュレーション)) ●スカイダイビング skydiving. ●スキューバダイビング scuba *diving*. ●スキンダイビング skin *diving*. ●ダイビングに行く go *diving* (in the sea).

—— ダイビング(を)する 動 dive (*into* water); enjoy diving.

●ダイビングキャッチ (make) a diving catch (*at* a ball); a dive to catch (the ball). ●ダイビングヘッド a diving header.

たいぶ 大部 —— 大部の 形 voluminous (books, documents).

たいぶ 退部 —— 退部する 動 leave* [quit*] the 《tennis》club.

***タイプ** [型] a type; [種類] a kind, a sort. ●新しいタイプの車の型 a new *type* [*model*] of car. (❗(1) 前の方は車種, 後の方は外観やデザインに重点を置いた(年)型 (⇨型③). (2) a の次にくる名詞は通例単数, 無冠詞) ▶君は銀行家タイプではない You are not the banker *type*. ▶彼は私の好きなタイプではない He is not my *type*. ▶[次例よりも口語的)/He is not the *type* [*kind*] of man I like.

[会話] 「彼はどんなタイプの人ですか」「好感の持てるタイプのやつだよ」"What *sort* of man is he?" "He's a likable *sort* of fellow."

[翻訳のこころ] でもどう考えても, ケイシーはそんな大がかりなつまらない冗談を仕組むタイプではなかった (村上春樹『レキシントンの幽霊』) With all my imagination, Casey could not possibly be the type (the kind of person) who would come up with such an elaborate but mundane joke. (❗(1)「どう考えても」は with all my imagination (想像力を大いに膨らませても)と表す. (2)「(のような)タイプ(の人, 人物)」は the type または, the kind of person. (3)「しくむ」は come up with (考えつく, 結果をだす)を用いる)

タイプ [タイプライター] a typewriter. (⇨タイプライター) ●手紙をタイプで打つ *type* (*out*) a letter; write a letter on [×by] a *typewriter*. ●タイプ打ちの手紙」は a *typewritten* letter) ▶彼女はタイプを打つのが速い She *types* fast [well]./She is a fast [a good] *typist*. ▶彼はタイプに向かって仕事をしていた He was working at a *typewriter*.

●タイプミス a mistake in typing; a typing mistake; 《話》a typo; (和製語) mistype.

***だいぶ** 大分 [非常に] very, (やや話) so; (very) much (⇨非常に), [かなり] a great deal, (やや書) greatly; [かなり] rather, quite (❗ 比較の余地のある語とともに用いる), fairly (❗ 以上の3語はこの順に程度が低くなる), 《話》pretty; [相当に] considerably.

[解説] **very** は形容詞・副詞の原級を修飾する. **much** は(ⅰ)比較級, (ⅱ)different など否定の概念を含む形容詞, (ⅲ)afraid のように a- で始まり叙述的に用いられる形容詞, (ⅳ) too + 形容詞・副詞, (ⅴ)動詞(句)を修飾するが, (ⅰ)と(ⅳ)の場合を除き, 肯定文で very, so などの修飾語を伴わず単独で用いるのは堅い言い方. なお, a great deal, a lot, rather, considerably なども比較級を修飾することができる.

▶彼はだいぶ疲れているようだ He seems *very* [*so, rather, quite, pretty*] tired. ▶これは私が予想していたのとだいぶ違う This is *very* [*much*] different from what I expected. ▶君の英語はだいぶ上達したね Your English has improved *very much* [*a lot, considerably, greatly*]. (❗ greatly は通例好ましい意味の動詞・過去分詞を修飾)/Your English has become *much* [*rather, considerably, a great deal, a lot,* ×*fairly*] better. (❗ fairly は通例比較級を修飾しない) ▶この前お目にかかってからだいぶたちますね It's been 《主に米》[It's 《主に英》] *quite* a long time since I saw you last. (❗ ×a quite long time は音調上通例用いられない) ▶昨夜は雪がだいぶ降った It snowed *a lot* [*a great deal, heavily*] last night./We had *a lot* [*a great deal*] of snow last night.

***たいふう** 台風 a typhoon. ([参考] 太平洋西部で発生したものをいう. インド洋で発生したものは cyclone /sáikloun/, 西インド諸島付近で発生したものは húrricàne) ●台風圏内にある be within the *typhoon* area. ▶台風が南シナ海で発生した A *typhoon* formed [was born] in the South China Sea. ▶台風は沖縄に上陸する(=を襲う)だろう The *typhoon* will strike [hit, ×land] Okinawa. ▶台風10号は近畿地方に向かって進んでいる *Typhoon* No. 10 is heading for the Kinki district.

●台風警報 (issue [give]) a typhoon warning. ●台風の目 the center [eye] of a typhoon; 《比喩的》the stórm cènter.

だいぶきん 台布巾 a cloth for wiping the table (clean).

だいふく 大福 *daifuku*; (説明的に) a rice cake stuffed with sweetened bean paste.
●大福帳 (元帳) a ledger. (⇨台帳)

たいぶつ 対物 ●対物訴訟 real action (↔personal action). ●対物レンズ an objective; an object lens [glass].

だいぶつ 大仏 a huge statue of Buddha (usually made of bronze). ●奈良の大仏(殿) (the Hall of) the *Great Buddha* at Nara. ●建て替える [文例]

***だいぶぶん** 大部分 [ほとんど] most (*of*); [大半] the greater part (*of*); [大多数の(人)] the [a] majority. ●人生の大部分(=大半)を新潟で過ごす spend *most* [*the greater part*] of one's life in Niigata. ▶学生の大部分が寮生活をしている *Most* [*The majority, A majority*] of the students live in the dormitory. (❗ most students は漠然と「たいていの学生」をさす)/The students *mostly* live in the dormitory. (⇨副) ▶大部分の近代音楽は難解だ *Most* (×of) modern music [*A large part of* modern music] is difficult to understand.

—— 大部分(は) 副 mostly; [主に] mainly, chiefly. (⇨ほとんど) ▶この雑誌の大部分は広告だ *Most of* this magazine [×*Most this magazine*] is advertisements./This magazine is *mostly* [*for the most part*] advertisements. (❗ for the most part は文頭も可. mostly は文頭では「多くの場合」の意)

タイプライター a typewriter. (⇨タイプ) ●和文タイプライター a Japanese-language *typewriter*.

タイプレーク 《テニス》a tie(-)breaker, 《英》a tiebreak.

たいぶんすう 帯分数〖数学〗a mixed number. (⇨分数)

たいへい 太平 peace. (⇨平和) ▸ 太平の世に in time(s) [a period] of *peace*. ▸ 天下太平 (⇨天下[成句])

たいべい 対米 ▸ 対米感情〖政策〗feelings [a policy] *toward the United States*. ▸ 対米輸出 exports *to the United States*. ▸ 日本の対米貿易は黒字だ Japan's trade *with the U.S.* is operating in the black./Japan has a trade surplus with [×on] *the U.S.*

タイペイ 台北〖台湾の首都〗Taipei, Taipeh.

たいへいき 太平記 *Taiheiki; A Chronicle of Mediaeval Japan*. (参考 室町時代の軍記物語)

たいへいよう 太平洋 the Pacific (Ocean). ▸ 南[北]太平洋 the South [North] *Pacific*. ▸ 太平洋横断飛行 a transpacific flight.
— **太平洋沿岸諸国** the Pacific countries. — **太平洋戦争** the Pacific War; the War in the Pacific.

たいべつ 大別 ▸ これらは二つに大別できる These *can be classified* [(分けられる) *divided*] *roughly into* two groups.

‡**たいへん 大変** 副 (非常に) very (❗形容詞・副詞または形容詞化した現在分詞・過去分詞を修飾する); (大いに) very much (❗動詞または過去分詞を修飾する); (本当に) (すごく) (話) terribly; (極度に) extremely. ▸ 大変申し訳ありません I'm *very* [*terribly, awfully, so*] sorry. (❗最後の2語は特に女性に好まれる) ▸ 彼女はすばらしい女性だ She is a *very* nice [*such a nice*] woman. ▸ 彼は歴史に大変興味があります He is *very* [*highly*] interested in history. (❗highly は very より堅い語で, しばしば動詞派生の形容詞を修飾し, 日常的な単音節の語を修飾しない) ▸ 音楽会は大変楽しかった I *very much* [*really*] enjoyed the concert. (❗very much は文尾も可)/I enjoyed myself *very much* at the concert. (❗very much の位置に注意) ▸ 彼女の社会奉仕は市民に大変感謝された Her social service was *very much* [(やや書) *greatly*, (やや書) *deeply*] appreciated by the citizens. (❗greatly は動詞・過去分詞を, deeply は感情・心理を表す語を修飾する)
会話 「大変ご親切にありがとうございました」「どういたしまして」"It was *most* kind of you." "Don't mention it." (❗この most は very の意の堅い語)

— **大変な** 形 ❶〖程度が〗(ひどい) terrible; (重大な) grave; (深刻な) serious; (困難な) hard; (骨の折れる) tough. ▸ 大変な失敗をする make a *terrible* [a *grave*] mistake. ▸ 大変な努力家 a hard worker. (❗この hard は「熱心な」の意) ▸ 株式市場は今大変な状況にある The stock market is in a *grave* [a *serious*] situation now. ▸ あのがんこおやじを説得するのは大変な仕事だ It's a *big* job [It's *tough* (*work*)] to persuade the stubborn old man. ▸ 十代は多くの点で最も大変な時期です The teens are *the hardest* [*the most difficult*] years in many ways. ▸ 子供の世話をするには大変な忍耐が必要です You need *a lot* [*a great deal*] *of* patience to take care of children. ▸ ちょっと大変なことになったな Oh dear, what have I gotten myself into? (❗get oneself into は「自分である状況に陥ってしまう」の意) ▸ 大変だ(=ああ困った)! いったいどうしたらよいだろうか *Good God* [*My God, Good Heavens*]! What on earth should I do?
会話 「太郎が交通事故にあったって聞いた?」「えっ本当, まあそれは大変な」"Did you hear Taro was in a traffic accident?" "Oh, really? How *terrible*!/That's *too bad*."

❷〖数量が〗(多くの) a lot of ...; (ばく大な) enormous; (数えきれない) countless. ▸ 大変なお金 *a lot* [(話) *lots*] *of* money; an *enormous* sum of money. ▸ 毎冬大変な数のスキーヤーが蔵王を訪れる *A great many* [*A good many, A great number of*] skiers visit [come to] Zao every winter. ▸ 彼は大変な酒飲みだ(たくさん飲む) He drinks *a lot* [*a great deal*]./(大酒飲みだ) He is a *heavy* drinker.

たいべん 胎便〖医学〗meconium.

だいべん 代返 ▸ 代返をしてくれないか Can you answer the roll call for me?

だいべん 大便 (書) feces /ˈfiːsiːz/ (❗複数扱い), (書) excrement (⇨排泄(せつ)); 〖検便用の〗〖医学〗stool(s), (婉曲的) solid waste. ▸ 大便をする (書) defecate /ˈdɛfəkeɪt/; (話) have a BM (❗BM は bowel movement の略); (婉曲的) move [relieve, empty] one's bowels. (⇨便, 検便)

だいべん 代弁 — **代弁する** 動 speak for 〈him〉; act as a spokesman 〈for him〉.
— **代弁者** (男・女) a spokesperson; (男) a spokesman, (女) a spokeswoman (❗複数形は共に -men); (軽蔑的) a mouthpiece.

たいほ 退歩 图〖逆戻り〗retrogression (↔progress); 〖悪化〗deterioration; 〖堕落〗degeneration.
— **退歩する** 動 (書) retrogress; deteriorate; degenerate.

たいほ 逮捕 图 an arrest. ▸ 逮捕状を出す issue an *arrest* warrant; issue a warrant for 〈his〉 *arrest*. ▸ あなたに逮捕状が出ています (警察官や検事が現場で) We have a warrant for your *arrest*./A warrant is out [There is a warrant out] for your *arrest*.
— **逮捕する** 動 arrest, place [put*] 〈him〉 under arrest; (追跡して捕まえる) catch*; (一斉に) round ... up. ▸ 私は飲酒運転で逮捕された I was *arrested* for drunken driving. ▸ 正当な理由なく私を逮捕することはできない You can't *arrest* me without due cause. ▸ 彼は密輸の罪(殺人の容疑)で逮捕された He *was arrested for* smuggling [on suspicion of murder]. ▸ 警官は彼を窃盗の現行犯で逮捕した The police officer *arrested* [*caught*] him in the act of) stealing./The policeman [policewoman] *arrested* [*caught*] him just as he was stealing. (❗(1) caught は「窃盗の現場を見つけた」の意で, 実際に逮捕したかどうかは文脈による. (2) 警察が犯人に対して「現行犯で逮捕する」という場合は *We caught* [×*catch*] *you red-handed.* のように過去形になる) ▸ 待て! 逮捕する! Stop! You're *under arrest*! (❗警察官の言葉) ▸ 犯人はまだ逮捕されずにこの辺にいる The criminal is still *free* [(やや書) *at large, at liberty*] around here.

*****たいほう 大砲** a gun; (旧式の) a cannon, 〖集合的〗cannon. ▸ 大砲の弾 a shell. ▸ 大砲を撃つ fire a *gun*.

たいぼう 待望 — **待望の** 形 long-awaited, long-expected. ▸ 彼女に待望の赤ちゃんができた She had her [a] *long-awaited* baby. ▸ 待望のスキーシーズンがやってきた The *long-awaited* skiing season has come.
— **待望する** 動 look forward 〈to doing〉.

たいぼう 耐乏 austerity. ▸ 耐乏生活をする lead a *hard* [an *austère*] life.

たいぼく 大木 a big tree. (❗「高さ」を強調するときには a tall tree) ▸ カシの大木 a great [(巨大な) a gigantic; (威風堂々とした) a majestic] oak tree.

だいほん 台本 (一般に) a script; (映画の) a screenplay, a scenario (複 ~s); (歌劇の) a libretto

だいほんえい 〜s, libretti). ▶その番組は台本なしだ The show isn't scripted./The show's *unscripted*.

だいほんえい 大本営 the Imperial Headquarters.

だいほんざん 大本山 〔仏教〕〔総本山〕(⇨総本山);〔総本山直下の寺〕the headquarters of a Buddhist sect. (!)headquarters は単･複両形.

たいま 大麻 〔植物〕hemp; 〔麻薬〕(マリファナ)《smoke》marijuana /mǽrəwàːnə/; (インドの) cánnabis.
● 大麻中毒 cannabism.

タイマー a timer, (英) a time switch. ● タイマーつきラジオ a clock radio. ● 炊飯器のタイマーを6時にセットしてよく set the *timer* on the rice cooker *for* six o'clock [*to* have the rice cooked *at* six o'clock]. ● オーブンにタイマーをかける put the oven on the *timer*.

たいまい 大枚 a large sum (of money). ▶たかがスーツ1着に大枚100万円もはたく pay just for a suit *to the tune of* one million yen. ▶to the tune of は〈話〉で「…もの額」の意で法外な高額を含意)

たいまい 瑇瑁 〔動物〕a hawksbill (turtle).

たいまつ 松明 a torch. (!)(英)には「懐中電灯」の意もある)

*** たいまん** 怠慢 ── 怠慢の 图 〔義務などを怠ること〕neglect 《*of*》; 〔だらしなさ, むとんちゃく〕《やや書》negligence 《*of*》 (!)前の方は行為, 後の方は性質・習慣についている); 〔不注意〕carelessness. ● 職務怠慢で解雇される be dismissed for *neglect of* duty; be dismissed for *being negligent* [*neglectful*] *of* one's duties.

── 怠慢な 形 neglectful 《*of*》, negligent 《*of, in*》; 〔不注意な〕careless; 〔怠惰な〕lazy. ▶自転車に鍵もかけずに放っとくなんて君の怠慢だ It's *careless of* [xfor] you *to* leave your bicycle unlocked.

だいみょう 大名 a *daimyo*, a *daimio* (複 〜s); (説明的に) a Japanese feudal lord.
● 大名行列 a *daimyo* procession. ● 大名旅行(ぜいたく旅行) a luxurious trip.

タイミング timing. ● タイミングのよい timely; 《やや書》opportune /ápərt(j)uːn/ (↔inopportune); well-timed (↔ill-timed). ▶いいタイミングだ Good timing!/Right on time! ▶タイミングがすべてだ *Timing* is all. ▶彼の発言はタイミングがよかった The *timing* of his remarks was [xwere] good [perfect]./His remarks were *timely* [*well timed*]./He made *timely* [*opportune, well-timed*] remarks. ▶彼はよく打者のタイミングを外して投げる He often throws a batter off his *timing* [off a batter's *timing*]. ▶その打者のタイミングが合っている The batter is on the pitch.

タイム 〔シソ科のハーブ〕〔植物〕a thyme.

タイム ❶〔[所要]時間〕time. ● ランナーのタイムをとる *time* [*clock*] a runner. ● 5マイル競走を不満足な〔記録的な; 24分5秒の〕タイムで走る run a five-mile race in poor *time* [in record *time*; in a *time* of twenty-four minutes five seconds]. ▶100メートルの私の最高タイムは11秒4だ My best *time* in the 100-meter dash is 11.4 seconds.
❷〔競技の一時中断〕a time(-)out. ● 〔審判が〕タイムを宣する call a *time-out*; 〔話〕call *time*. ● タイムを要求して靴のひもを結ぶ call for a *time-out* to tie [do up] one's shoestrings. ▶タイム! Time out!
● タイムアウト a time(-)out. (⇨❷) ● タイムカプセル a time capsule. ● タイムキーパー a time keeper. ● タイムサービス a limited-time sale; (和製語) time service. ● タイムスイッチ a timer; a time switch. ● タイムスパン a time span. ● タイムテーブル 〔時刻[予定]表, 時間割〕a timetable. ● タイムトライアル (自転車競技などの) a time trial. ● タイムトラベル 〔時間旅行〕(SFでの) time travel. ● タイムトンネル a time corridor; (米国のSFドラマ) *The Time Tunnel*. ● タイムマシーン a time machine. ● タイムラグ 〔時間差〕a time lag. ● タイムリミット 〔set〕a time limit [(締め切り)] a deadline] 《*for*》.

『**タイム**』〔雑誌名〕*Time*. (参考)米国の週刊誌)

タイムアップ Time's [Time is] up. (!)xTime up. は不可)

タイムカード a time card [sheet]. ● タイムカードを押す punch a *time card*; (出社時に) clock in [on], (米) ring in; (退社時に) clock out [off], (米) ring out.

タイムズ 〔新聞名〕*The Times*. (!)*The London Times* ともいう) ● ニューヨークタイムズ *The New York Times*.

タイムスリップ 图 a time warp.
── タイムスリップする 動 ●過去へタイムスリップする slip into the past; slip back in time.

タイムリー ▶彼の到着はタイムリーであった His arrival was *timely*./He arrived *at the right moment* [(ちょうど予定の時刻に)] *just on time*]. ● タイムリーエラー 〔野球〕a run-scoring error; (和製語) timely error. ● タイムリーヒット 〔野球〕 [get [have]] an RBI single [a clutch hit]. (!)(1) RBI は run batted in (打点) の略. (2) a timely hit とはあまりいわない)

タイムレコーダー a time clock [recorder]. ● 出勤したときにタイムレコーダーを押す clock in [on] (↔clock out [off]); ring in (↔ring out). (!)パンチ式の場合は punch in [on] (↔out))

たいめい 待命 ● 待命中である be awaiting further instructions [orders].

だいめい 題名 a title. (⇨題, タイトル)

だいめいし 代名詞 〔文法〕a pronoun; 〔同義語〕a synonym 《*for*》.

たいめん 体面 〔体裁〕appearances; 〔威信〕prestige /prestíːʒ/; 〔名誉〕honor; 〔面目〕face. ● 体面上 for the sake of *appearances*; for *appearance's* sake. ● 体面を重んずる emphasize *appearances*. ▶彼らはされは彼のせいだと主張して体面を保とうとした They tried to *save* (*their*) *face* [xfaces] by saying (that) it was his fault. (!)*their* は通例省略される) ▶それでは私の体面にかかわる That will affect my *prestige* [*honor*]./That will make me lose (xa) *face*. ▶彼の行為は学校の体面を汚した His conduct *disgraced* [*dishonored*] (the name of) the school.

たいめん 対面 图 a meeting.
── 対面する 動 ●30年ぶりで彼と対面する meet [have a *meeting* with] him for the first time in thirty years.
● 対面交通 walking [driving] (on the other side of the street [road]) facing traffic.

たいもう 大望 〔野心〕(an) ambition; 〔強い願望〕(an) aspiration. (⇨野心, 大志) ▶彼はアメリカ大統領になろうという大望を抱いていた He had an *ambition* to become (the) president of the United States. (!)*His ambition* was to become.... のようにもいえる. 無冠詞が普通)

たいもう 体毛 (体の) body hair; 〔陰毛〕pubic hair. ▶体毛が濃い have thick *body hair*.

だいもく 題目 〔表題〕a title; 〔話題〕a topic.

だいもんじ 大文字 ● 大文字で 《write》 with thick [bold] strokes.

たいや 逮夜 〔葬儀[忌日]の前夜〕the eve of 《*his*》 funeral [the anniversary of 《*his*》 death].

タイヤ a tire. ● 自動車のタイヤ an automobile *tire*.

- スペアタイヤ a spare *tire*. ● タイヤの溝 *tire* grooves. ● タイヤに(ポンプで)空気を入れる pump up a *tire*. ● タイヤを取り替える put on [fix] a new *tire*. ● タイヤがパンクした I had [got] a flat *tire*.
- タイヤチェーン tire chains.

ダイヤ ❶ 〖宝石〗(a) diamond. ● 人造ダイヤ an imitation *diamond*. ● ダイヤの指輪 a *diamond* ring. ▶このダイヤは3カラットです This *diamond* weighs three carats./This is a three-carat *diamond*. ❷ 〖トランプ〗a diamond. ● ダイヤのエース [7] the ace [seven] of *diamonds*.

ダイヤ 〖列車の運行表〗《主に米》a (train) schedule, 《主に英》a (train) timetable. ▶大雪でダイヤが乱れた The *train schedule* was disrupted because of the heavy snowfall./《物が主語》The heavy snowfall caused some irregularities in the trains. (⚠ 後の方は堅い言い方). ▶列車はダイヤどおりに運行している The Trains are running *on schedule* [*time*].

たいやき 鯛焼きを a *taiyaki*; (説明的に) a fish-shaped pancake stuffed with sweetened bean paste.

たいやく 大厄 〖災難〗a great calamity; 〖厄年〗the great climacteric.

たいやく 大役 an important task [〖使命〗mission; 〖任務〗duty; 〖配役〗role]. ● 大役を果たす achieve [《やや書》accomplish] one's *important task*.

たいやく 対訳 a translation printed side by side with the original. ● 聖書のギリシャ語原典の英語行間対訳(本) an interlinear English *translation* of the original Greek Scriptures.

だいやく 代役 a súbstitute, 《話》a fíll-in; 〖俳優の〗an understudy; (映画の) a stánd-in. ● 代役を務める (一般に) act as a *substitute* [*for*]; (俳優・役の) understudy; (俳優の) stánd ín [*for*]. ▶彼は私が休暇でいない間私の代役を務めた He *substituted for* me [was my *substitute*, 《話》*filled in for* me] while I was away on vacation.

ダイヤグラム 〖図表〗a diagram (⇨図); 〖列車の運行表〗(⇨ダイヤ).

ダイヤモンド 〖宝石〗(a) diamond (⇨ダイヤ); 〖野球〗the diamond (⚠ 〖内野〗をさすのが普通だが、外野を含めた「グラウンド」の意で用いることもある). ● ダイヤモンドを1周する round the bases.
- ダイヤモンド婚式 〖結婚 60[75]周年〗a diamond wedding. ● ダイヤモンドダスト diamond dust.

***ダイヤル** 图 (電話・ラジオなどの) a dial. ● ダイヤルを回す dial (a telephone number, the radio). ● ラジオのダイヤルを音楽番組に合わせる *dial* [tune in to] a music program.

—— **ダイヤルする** 動 dial. ● 6725 番にダイヤルする *dial* 6725. (⚠ ボタン式電話にも用いる)
- ダイヤル式電話 a dial phone. ● ダイヤルトーン 〖電話の発信音〗《米》a dial tone, 《英》a dialling tone. ● 電話の「呼び出し音」は a call signal [×sign]. ● (⇨ダイヤルアップ, ダイヤルイン)

ダイヤルアップ 〖電話回線を使ったインターネット接続〗〖コンピュータ〗dial-up.
- ダイヤルアップ接続 a dial-up connection.

ダイヤルイン 〖ダイヤル直通電話〗(a) dìrect-dial telephone. (⚠ 方式をさすときは 〖U〗); 〖和製語〗dial-in. ▶この番号はダイヤルインになっています At this number you can reach me directly.

たいよ 貸与 图 lending; (貸付(物)の) a loan.

—— **貸与する** 動 lend; loan. ▶制服は貸与されます They lend you a uniform.
- 貸与コレクション (美術館への) a loan collection. ● 貸与奨学金 a scholastic loan. (関連➡ scholarship (返還しなくてよい)奨学金)

***たいよう** 太陽 the sun. ● 午後[真昼]の太陽 the afternoon [midday] *sun*. ● 燃えるような[灼熱(しゃくねつ)の]太陽 a blazing [a scorching] *sun*. (⚠ 種類を表す場合 a がつくことがある) ▶太陽は東から昇り西に沈む The *sun* rises in [×from] the east and sets in the west. ▶太陽は照っていたが風は冷たかった The *sun* was shining, but the wind was cold. ▶太陽は出ていなくて、山には雨雲がかかっていた There were no *sun*, and rain-clouds hung low over the mountains.

—— **太陽の** 形 solar. ● 太陽の光線 the rays of *the sun*; *the sun's* rays; sunbeams. ▶午前中この部屋には太陽の光がいっぱい差し込む This room gets plenty of *sun* [sunlight, sunshine] in the morning./There is a lot of *sun* in this room in the morning. (⚠「太陽光線, 日光」の意では通例無冠詞)
- 太陽エネルギー solar energy [(太陽の放射を熱や電気に交換した) power]. ● 太陽エネルギー利用設備 (ソーラーシステム) a solar heating system. (⚠ ×a solar system とはいわない) ● 太陽系 〖天文〗the solar system. ● 太陽黒点 〖天文〗a sunspot. ● 太陽電池 a solar cell [(複数の solar cell から成る) battery]. ● 太陽神 a sungod; 〖ギリシャ神話・ローマ神話〗Apollo /əpɑ́lou/. ● 太陽灯 a sun lump. ● 太陽熱 solar heat. ● 太陽熱温水器 a solar water heater; a solar collector. ● 太陽熱発電 solar power (generation). ● 太陽年 a solar year.
- 太陽暦 the solar calendar.

たいよう 大要 〖概略〗an [a broad] outline; 〖要約〗a summary. ● その計画の大要を説明する give the *outline* of the project.

たいよう 大洋 the ocean. (⇨海) ● 大洋を航海する sail *the ocean*.
- 大洋航路 an ocean lane. ● 大洋州 Òceánia. (⇨オセアニア)

***だいよう** 代用 图 substitution.

—— **代用(を)する** 動 (B の代わりに A を使う) súbstitùte A for B, use A for B; (A を B として使う) use A as B. ● ろうそくで懐中電灯の代用をする *substitute* [*use*] a candle *for* a flashlight. ▶この時計はストップウオッチにも代用できる This watch can also *be used* [can also *serve*] *as* a stopwatch.
- 代用血液 〖医学〗a blood substitute. ● 代用教員 《米》a substitute teacher, 《英》a supply teacher. ● 代用品 a súbstitute (*for* butter).

たいようねんすう 耐用年数 (機械・道路などの) (a) life (覆 lives). ▶この冷蔵庫の耐用年数は約8年です The *life* of this refrigerator should *last* about 8 years./This refrigerator should *last* about 8 years.

たいようのきせつ 『太陽の季節』Season of the Sun. (〖参考〗石原慎太郎の小説)

たいよく 大欲 greed, avarice; an extreme desire.
- 大欲は無欲に似たり 《ことわざ》 Grasp all, lose all./All covet, all lose.

だいよん 第四 图 fourth. (⚠ 通例 the ~)

—— **第四(の)** 形 fourth. (⚠ 通例 the ~)

—— **第四(に)** 副 fourth(ly); in the fourth place. (⇨第一(に))
- 第四紀 (地質時代の) the Quaternary (period). ● 第四次産業 a fourth [quaternary] industry.

***たいら** 平ら —— **平らな** 形 flat (-tt-); (凹凸のない) even (↔uneven); (なめらかな) smooth /smúːð/ (↔rough); 〖水平な〗level. ▶平らな道が海岸へと続いている An *even* [A *smooth*, A *flat*] road leads to the coast. ▶テントを平らな場所に張った We pitched our tent on a *level* place [on the *flat*]. ▶サッカ

たいらげる 平らげる [全部食べる] eat*... up, 《話》put*... away; [平定する] [鎮圧する] 《やや書》suppress; [制圧する] 《やや書》subdue. ● 自分の食べ物を全部平らげる eat up [finish off] one's food. ▶ 彼はラーメンを3杯も平らげた He ate three whole [ate up three] bowls of Chinese noodles. ▶ 彼はそのスパゲティを軽く平らげて皿を洗い、それからいつもの仕事に戻った He made short work of the spaghetti, washed up the dishes, then returned to the chores. (🛈 make short work of は「手際よく片づける」の意の慣用表現)

たいらん 大乱 a great rebellion; a great uprising.

だいり 代理 图 [行為] representation; [人] (仕事などの) an agent; (会議などの) a representative; (職権を持つ) a deputy; (投票などの) a proxy. (⇨代理人) ● 議長代理 (副議長) a deputy chair; (臨時の) the acting chair. (⇨代行) ● 課長代理 an assistant manager. ● その大学の学長代理 the acting president of the university. ● 病気の山田氏の代理でここに来ました I am here for [in place of] Mr. Yamada, who is sick. (⇨代わりに❶)

── **代理(を)する** 動 [代表する] rèpresent; [代行する] act for …. (⇨代わりをする) ▶ 私は会議で社長の代理をした(=務めた) I acted for [on behalf of, 《米》in behalf of] the president at the meeting. (🛈 後の方は代名詞が目的語のときは on [in] 〈his〉behalf となる)

● **代理戦争** a war by proxy. ● **代理母** a súrrogate (mother).

だいり 内裏 the Imperial Palace.
● **内裏雛**(びな) emperor and empress dolls.

だいリーガー 大リーガー a major /méidʒər/ leaguer. (⇨メジャーリーガー) ● イチローは大リーグの選手です Ichiro is a major leaguer.

だいリーグ 大リーグ the major /méidʒər/ leagues, the majors. (⇨メジャーリーグ)

だいりき 大力 ● 大力の男 a man of great [matchless] strength. ● 大力無双の Herculean.

たいりく 大陸 a continent. ● 大陸の continental. ● 新[旧]大陸 the New [Old] Continent. ● ヨーロッパ大陸式朝食 continental breakfast. (参考) パンとコーヒー、紅茶だけの軽い朝食) ● アジア[ヨーロッパ]大陸 the Asian [European] Continent.
● **大陸移動説** the continental drift theory. ● **大陸横断旅行** transcontinental travel. ● **大陸間弾道弾** [軍事] an intercontinental ballistic missile 《略 ICBM》. ● **大陸性気候** [気象] a continental climate. ● **大陸棚** a continental shelf.

だいりせき 大理石 marble. ● 大理石の像 a marble statue.

たいりつ 対立 图 [反対] (an) opposition; [意見などの衝突] (a) cónflict. ● 激しい利害[労使間]の対立 a sharp conflict of interests [between labor and management].

── **対立する** 動 [反対している] be opposed 《to》; [衝突する] disagrée 《with》; [意見が一致しない] differ 《with》. ● 対立した意見 opposing [conflicting] opinions. ▶ 愛は憎しみと対立する Love is opposed to hatred. ▶ Love conflicts with hatred. ▶ 新しいダムの建設をめぐって知事は県議会と対立していた The governor was opposed [in opposition] to the prefectural assembly over the construction of a new dam.

● **対立候補** one's opponent; one's rival candidate.

だいりてん 代理店 an agency; an agent. (🛈 前の方は代理業などの業務を行える場所をさし、後の方はその業務を行う人に重点が置かれる) ● **広告代理店** an advertising agency. ● **旅行代理店** a travel agency [agent, 《米》bureau]. ● **輸入代理店** an exporter's selling agent [agency]; an importer's buying agent [agency]. ● **総代理店** (すべての) a general agent. ● (唯一[一手]の) an exclusive [the sole] agent.

だいりにん 代理人 an agent; (代表者) a representative. ● 総代理人 a general agent. ● 代理人を務める act as [an] agent. ▶ 彼は日本における当社の代理人です He is an agent for our company in Japan. / He represents our company in Japan.

たいりゃく 大略 [概略] an outline; [要約] a summary. ● 講義の大略を述べる give [(作る) make] a broad outline of the lecture.

たいりゅう 対流 图 [物理] convection.
── **対流の** 形 convective.
● **対流圏** [気象] the tróposphere. ● **対流式ヒーター** a convection heater; a convector.

たいりゅう 滞留 ── **滞留する** 動 ❶ [滞る] (徐々に) accumulate; (山積みになる) pile up. ● 仕事が滞留する一方である My work is really piling up. ❷ [滞在する] stay. (⇨滞在する)

たいりょう 大量 图 a large quantity.
── **大量(の)** 形 a large quantity of …, large quantities of …; (大規模の) large-scale, mass. ▶ 大量の金(ﾂ)が見つかった A large quantity of [A lot of] gold was found.
── **大量に** in quantity, in large quantities; (大口に) in bulk; (大規模に) on a large scale. ● 大量にアスピリンを飲む take aspirins in quantity. ▶ 彼らは海外の工場から直接大量に輸入し始めた They have started importing directly and in bulk from plants abroad.
● **大量失業** large-scale unemployment. ● **大量生産** (⇨大量生産) ● **大量注文** 《get [take]》 a bulk order.

たいりょう 大漁 a good [a big] catch of fish; (一網分の) a good [a big] haul (of fish). ▶ 今日はサケが大漁だった We had [got] a good [a big] catch of salmon today.
● **大漁旗** a good-catch flag.

たいりょう 退寮 ── **退寮する** 動 leave the dorm [dormitory].

たいりょうせいさん 大量生産 mass [large-scale] production. (⇨マスプロ) ▶ バターを大量生産する màss-prodúce butter.

たいりょく 体力 (physical) strength; (生来の) power(s); (持久力) staying powers, (physical) stamina (⇨スタミナ). ● 体力の限界 the limit of one's physical strength [one's powers]. ● 体力がつく[をつける] gain [build up, develop] one's physical strength. ▶ 彼はあの山に登るだけの十分な体力がある He has enough strength [is strong enough] to climb [xgo up] the mountain. (⇨登る ❶ [第2文例]) ▶ 年とともに体力が衰えていくのが分かる I find my strength [powers] failing with age. ● 手術後彼はまだ体力が回復していない He hasn't got his strength back yet after the operation. ▶ 彼は私よりも体力がある He is physically stronger than I am [《話》than me, 《古·まれ》than I].
● **体力テスト** a physical (strength) test.

たいりん 大輪 (花) a large flower. ● 大輪の朝顔 a large-flowered morning glory.

タイル a tile. ● タイル張りの浴室 a tiled bathroom.

ダイレクト — ダイレクトな 形 [直接的な] direct. — ダイレクトに 副 [直接(に)] directly.
- ダイレクトキャッチ (⇨ダイレクトキャッチ) • ダイレクトプレー [サッカー] a direct play. [参考] できるだけシンプルに，フィニッシュから逆算してプレーを組み立てる考え方 (⇔ ポゼッションプレー) • ダイレクトマーケティング direct marketing. • ダイレクトメール direct mail (略 DM); [軽蔑的に] júnk màil. • ダイレクトメソッド [外国語の直接教授法] the direct method.

ダイレクトキャッチ • ボールをダイレクトキャッチする [野球] catch a ball on the fly [before it hits the ground]. (!) ×make a direct catch とはいわない)

たいれつ 隊列 (縦列) a file, a column; (横列) a rank; [隊形] formation. • 隊列を組む form a rank [a line]. • 隊列を乱す break ranks [formation].

だいれん 大連 [中国の都市] Dalian /dáːljɑːn/.

たいろ 退路 (退却する道) a way of retreat; (退却) retreat. • 敵の退路を断つ cut off the enemy's retreat.

たいろう 大老 tairo; (説明的に) the chief minister of the Tokugawa shogunate.

だいろっかん 第六感 a sixth sénse (!) 常に単数形で); [直感] intuition; [予感] a hunch. • 彼はそんなことに第六感がよく働く He has a keen sixth sense in such matters. ▶女の第六感が働いたのか彼女は不安そうな表情を浮かべた Her face clouded as her feminine intuition went to work.

たいろん 対論 a debate (on, about).

*たいわ **対話** (a) dialogue, (米) a dialog; (話し合い) a talk. • 親子の対話不足 lack of dialogue between parents and children. • 武力によってではなく対話によってこの問題を解決する solve the issue through ＼dialogue, not by ˇforce. • 野党と[労使間の]対話を持つ have a dialogue with the opposition [between labor and management]. (!) a dialogue の代わりに talks (公式の会談) を用いることも可)
— 対話する 動 have a dialogue (with); talk (with).

たいわん 台湾 Taiwan /tàiwáːn/; (旧称) Formosa. • 台湾人 a Taiwanese. (!) 単・複同形) • 台湾語 Taiwanese. • 台湾(人[語])の Taiwanese. • 台湾政府 the Taiwan Government.

たう 多雨 a heavy rainfall; much rainfall.

ダウ • ダウ平均株価 the Dow-Jones average. ▶ダウ平均は 1.4 パーセント上昇した The Dow rose 1.4 percent.

たうえ 田植え rice-planting, (説明的に) transplanting of rice seedlings from the rice nursery to the paddy field. • 田植え時 the rice-planting season. • 田植えをする plant rice; (稲の苗を植える) plant [transplant] rice seedlings.
• 田植え機 a rice-planting machine.

タウリン [生化学] taurine /tɔ́ːriːn/.

タウン a town. (⇨町) • ニュータウン a new town; (新しく造られた) a new housing development.
• ゴーストタウン a ghost town.
• タウンウェア [街着] street clothes. (!) townwear はまれ) • タウン誌 a city news magazine. • タウンハウス a town house. • タウンミーティング a town meeting.

ダウン — ダウンする ❶ [倒れる] • 働き過ぎてダウンする (=病気になる) be made ill by overwork; break down by working too hard. • 風邪でダウン come down [go down, (寝ている) be down] with a cold. ▶彼は第 1 ラウンドでダウンした(=打ち倒された) He was downed [was knocked down, (話) was floored] in the first round. ❷ [下がる] ▶売り上げが今月は 5 パーセントダウンした Sales are down 5 percent this month.

ダウン [鳥の綿毛] down. (⇨羽毛)
• ダウンジャケット a down jacket.

ダウンサイジング [規模縮小] downsizing.

ダウンしょう ダウン症 [医学] (a child with) Down's syndrome.

ダウンタウン [繁華街, 都心] (主に米) dówntòwn, (英) the city center.
— ダウンタウンの 形 dówntówn. • ダウンタウンのレストラン a downtown restaurant.
— ダウンタウンに[へ] 副 dówntówn.

ダウンヒル [滑降競技] [スキー] downhill.

ダウンロード 名 [ホストコンピュータからのデータの転送] [コンピュータ] (a) download (↔upload).
— ダウンロードする 動 download. • 必要な情報はインターネットで自分のパソコンにダウンロードできます The information you need can be downloaded to your personal computer through the Internet.

たえいる 絶え入る die; pass away. • 絶え入るばかりに as if one's heart would break.

たえがたい 堪え難い • 堪え難い(=我慢できない)痛み an unbearable [(やや書) an intolerable] pain. • 堪え難い(=非常に強い)悪臭 an overpowering stink.
• 堪え難い(=抵抗できない)誘惑 (an) irresistible temptation. ▶(接してみて)彼の無礼さは堪え難い I find his rudeness unbearable. (⇨耐える)

たえかねる 堪え兼ねる be unable to bear [stand] (the pain, toothache).

だえき 唾液 saliva /səláivə/.
• 唾液腺 [解剖] sálivary glands.

たえしのぶ 堪え忍ぶ (長い間忍耐強く) (やや書) endure; (苦痛・悲しみなど重みに) bear*. (⇨我慢する)
• つらさを堪え忍ぶ endure the pain.

*たえず **絶えず** [断続的に] (くり返し) continually; (いつも) always, all the time (後の方が口語的) (いつも [解説]); [とぎれないで連続的に] (絶え間なく) continuously; (とぎれなく) without a break; (間断なく) (やや書) incéssantly (⇨ずっと❸); (変わりなく) constantly. • 絶えず努力する make constant [continued] efforts; (日夜努力する) make efforts day and night. ▶彼は絶えず不平を言っている He is always [continually, constantly] making complaints./He is grumbling all the time. (!) いずれも進行形で用いると通例話し手の非難の気持ちを表す) • 彼の言葉が絶えず頭に浮かんでくるのです His words keep (on) coming (back) into my mind.

たえだえ 絶え絶え • 息も絶え絶えである try to catch one's breath; be (all) out of breath. (!) all がある方が強意的)

たえなる 妙なる (絶妙な) exquisite /ikskwízit/; (甘美な) sweet. • 妙なる笛の音 the exquisite tones of a flute.

たえま 絶え間 名 a break.
— 絶え間ない 形 (途切れなく続く) continuous; (やむことなく続く) incessant, (書) ceaseless (!) incessant は通例悪いことに用いるが; (変わることのない) constant. • 絶え間ない努力をする make constant [ceaseless] efforts. • 絶え間なく雨が降り続いた It rained without a break [continuously, incessantly]. (⇨絶えず)

*たえる **耐える. 堪える. 堪える** ❶ [我慢する] (苦痛・悲しみなど重みに) bear* ❶; (ひるまず) stand*; (長い間忍耐強く) (やや書) endure; (大目に見る) (やや書) tolerate; (ちょっとしたことに耐える) (話) put* up with .... (!) 最後は

耐えることよりあきらめを含意. 以上はいずれも can を伴って否定文・疑問文で用いることが多い. bear, stand, endure は肉体的苦痛にも用いる)(⇨我慢する) 彼女の愚痴には堪えられない I can't *put up with* her grumbling.

【会話】「君は耐えられなくなって私を見捨てたのか」「ええ, 神経がまいってしまったの」"Did you run out on me because you *couldn't take it*?" "Yes, I was just a wreck." (*can't take it* は【大変な困難や苦労に】対処しきれない】の意の口語的慣用表現)

❷ 〚持ちこたえる〛(状況・検査に) stand*; (力・行為に) 〚書〛withstand*; (検査・重圧・苦難に) bear*; 〚抵抗する〛resist. ● 厳密な検査に堪える bear [stand] the rigorous examination. ● 酒の誘惑に耐える resist [打ち勝つ) get over] the temptation to drink. ● あらし〔危機〕に耐えた(=切り抜けた) come through a storm [a crisis]. ● そのガラス壺は摂氏(セ)120度の熱に耐えられる The glass-pot can *stand* a heat of 120℃./The glass-pot *is heat-resistant* (up) to 120℃. (⇨摂氏) ● その橋は大人 2~3 人の重さにも耐えられないだろう The bridge could hardly *bear* [〚書〛*sustain*] the weight of 2 or 3 adults at a time. ● 戦争中, 毎日のように耐えたかをお話します I'll tell you how we *got through* every day during the war.

❸ 〚値打ちがある〛be worth [worthy of]《*doing*》; 〚適応力がある〛be equal to [fit for]…. ● 彼なら社長の重責に堪える He is *equal to* [*fit for*] the heavy task of the president [the presidency].

● …に堪えない ● 感謝〔遺憾, 悲しみ〕に堪えない be *very* [*extremely*] grateful [regretful, sorrowful]. ● 人々が飢えに苦しむ見るに堪えない(= 見ていられない) I can't *stand* [*bear, endure*] seeing the people suffering from hunger. ● その小説は 2 度読むに堪えない(= 値打ちがない) The novel is *not worth* reading twice.

たえる 絶える 〚死滅する〛become extinct, die (~d; dying) out (⇨絶滅), 〚止む〛stop (-pp-), 〚書〛cease; 〚終わる〛end, come* to an end; 〚書〛(なくなる) fail; 〚尽きる〛be exhausted; 〚供給がとだえる〛be cut off. ● 息子からの消息〔連絡〕が絶えた I *lost* contact with my son. ● 石油の供給が絶えた The supply of oil *failed* [*was cut off*]. ● 彼は息が絶えた He *died*./《婉曲的》He *passed away*./ 《書》He *breathed* his last. ● あの食料の配給を待つ人の列が絶えるのを見届けるまで私はここを離れるわけにはいかない I will not leave here until I see the *end* of that breadline.

【…が絶えない】 ● 私の母は苦労が絶えない My mother is *never free from* care./(心労が) My mother is *always filled with* anxiety. ● 我が家はけんかが絶えない Some (members) of my family *are always* quarreling. (!進行形を用いて話し手の非難の気持ちを表す) ● この通りなら交通が絶えない There is a *continuous* stream of traffic on this street. ● 富士山の頂上は 1 年中雪が絶えない The top of Mt. Fuji is covered with snow *all the year* (*a*) *round*.

だえん 楕円 图 〚数学〛an ellipse; (卵形) an oval /óʊvl/. ― 楕円(形)の 形 elliptic(al); oval.

:たおす 倒す ❶ 〚転倒させる〛bring*… down, (投げ倒す) throw*… down; (当たって) knock … down [over]; (切り倒す) cut*… down; (引っ張り倒す) pull … down; (破壊する) destroy; (引っくり返す) tip (-pp-) … over. (⇨倒れる ❶) ● 彼を投げ倒す *throw* him *down*. ● 相手を殴り倒す *knock* one's opponent *down*. ● 古家を倒す(= 壊す) *pull down* [*destroy*] an old house. ● 座席を倒す *put* a seat *back*. ● 彼をアッパーカットで倒した I *brought* him *down* with an uppercut. ● 電気スタンドを倒さない(= 倒れてひっくり返さない)ように気をつけなさい Take care not to *knock* [*tip*] the desk lamp *over*.

❷ 〚負かす〛beat*, defeat (後の方が堅い語); (転覆させる) overthrow*, topple, (殺す) kill. ● そのチームを倒す *beat* the team. ● 政府を倒す *overthrow* [*topple*] the government. ● 暴君を倒す(失脚させる) *overthrow* a tyrant; (殺す) *kill* (〚意図的に〛 *murder*, (暗殺する) *assassinate*) a tyrant. ● 独裁者を倒せ *Down with* the dictator! (〚…を倒せ〛の意の慣用表現)(…なんかいらない) We *don't want* the dictator!

たおす 斃す kill 《a lion》. (⇨殺す)

たおやか 嫋やか grace. (⇨優美)

たおやめ 手弱女 a graceful [an elegant] woman.

*タオル a towel /táʊəl/. (!手ぬぐいの意と皿などをふくきんの意も含む); 〚洗面〔浴用〕タオル〛《米》a washcloth, 《英》a facecloth. ● バスタオル a bath *towel*. ● タオルで体をふく dry oneself with a *towel*; towel oneself. ● 手をふくタオルはここにあります Here's a *towel* to wipe [dry] your hands with. (!with に注意)

● タオルを投げる (ボクシングで) throw in the towel (参考) 試合放棄の意思表示); (降参する) give up.

● タオル掛け (浴室の) a towel rack [horse]. ● タオルケット a light cotton blanket. (!×towelket は towel と blanket を結びつけて作られた和製英語) ● タオル地 toweling.

たおる 手折る break [snap] (off) 《a branch》. (⇨折る ❶)

たおれこむ 倒れ込む fall* (down) 《*in*》. ● 庭に電柱が倒れ込んできた The (electricity) utility pole *fell* (*down*) *in* the garden. ● 彼は疲れ切っていて倒れ込んだ He got worn out and *collapsed* [*sank*] *into* a chair.

:たおれる 倒れる ❶ 〚転倒する〛fall* (down [over]); (勢いよく) tumble (ぐらついて) topple (over [down]); (くずれる) collapse; (卒倒する) faint. ● 地面に倒れる *fall* (*down*) *on* [*to*] the ground. (!on は倒れる地点, to は方向に重点がある) ● あお向けに倒れる *fall* backward [*on* one's back]. ● ばったり倒れる *fall* suddenly; (大の字に) *fall* (at) *full length*. ● 倒れた木 a *fallen* tree. ● その子供は木の根につまずいて倒れた The child stumbled over the root of a tree and *fell* (*down*)./The child *tumbled* [*fell*] *over* the root of a tree. ● その老女はよろけて道に倒れた The older [old] woman *toppled over onto* the street. ● 雪の重みで小屋が倒れた The shed *collapsed* [*fell*] under the weight of the snow. ● 村の大部分の家があらしで倒れた Most of the houses in the village were *destroyed* by the storm./The storm *destroyed* most of the houses in the village. ● 少女たちのうち数人が空腹で倒れた Several of the girls *fainted from* hunger. ● 強風でたくさんの木が倒れた(= 吹き倒された) Many trees *were blown down* by the gale./The gale *blew down* a large number of trees. ● 彼は人波に押されて倒れた He *was pushed down* [*over*] by the crowd.

❷ 〚病む, 死ぬ〛〚病気になる〛become* [get*, fall*] sick (⇨病気)(健康を害して倒れる) collapse; (風邪などにかかる)《話》come* down 《*with*》; 〚死ぬ〛die (~d; dying), (殺される) be killed. ● 流感で倒れる *come down with* (the) flu. ● がんで倒れる(= 死ぬ) *die of* [〚書〛*succumb to*] cancer. ● 戦闘で倒れる *be killed* [*die*] *in* battle;《書》*fall* in battle.

▶彼は過労で倒れた He became [got, fell] sick because of overwork. ▶2,3週間休まないと彼は倒れてしまうよ If he doesn't take a couple of weeks' rest, he'll *collapse*. (⚠ a couple of は《話》で「2, 3の」の意.《米話》では of を省略することもある) ▶彼は凶弾に倒れた He *was shot and killed* [*was shot to death, was shot down*] 《by a killer [an assassin, a gang]》.

❸ [滅びる] (崩壊する) fall*; collapse; (破産する) go* bankrupt, fail; (没落する)《やや書》 decline, ruin. ▶労働党は経済政策の失敗で倒れた The Labour Party *fell* (*from power*) [*collapsed*] because of the failure of its economic policy. ▶その不景気の時にいくつかの銀行が倒れた Several banks *went bankrupt* [*failed*] during the depression.

たか 高 (⇨高が)
- たかが知れた • たかが知れた(=ささいな)事 a *trifling* matter; a trifle.
- たかが知れている be nothing great [much].
- たかをくくる (甘く考える) be very optimistic 《about》;(軽く考える) take《it》 lightly;(見くびる) make light of.

たか 鷹 [鳥] a hawk /hɔ́ːk/;(鷹狩り用の) a falcon /fǽlkən/ (⚠この意では通例) /fɔ́ːkən/).
• 鷹狩り falconry. • 鷹狩りをする hunt with a *falcon*. • 鷹匠 a falconer; a hawker. • タカ派 (⇨鷹派)

たか 多寡 the number; the quantity; the amount. (⇨多少)

たが a hoop /húːp/. ▶(たるの)たががゆるんだ The *hoops* of the barrel got loose.
• たががゆるむ (気持ちがゆるむ) slack off; weaken; become lax;(統一が欠ける) lack unity.
• たがを締める tighten the hoop;(気持ちを引き締める) brace oneself《for》.

***だが** (⇨しかし) ▶きつい仕事だが, 楽しくやっています It is 《×a》 hard work, *but* [(*and*) *yet*] I enjoy it./*Though* [*Although*] it is hard work, I enjoy it./It is hard work; *all the same* [《やや書》 *however*,《書》 *nevertheless*], I enjoy it./The work is hard. I enjoy it, *though* [《やや書》 *however*,《書》 *nevertheless*, ×although]. (⚠ though は《話》で文尾で用いる) ▶彼は母親を愛していたが, 父親を憎んだ He loved his mother, but he hated his father./He loved his mother as much as he hated his father. (⚠ 後の方が英語的表現)

ダカーポ [<イタリア語] [[曲の始めに戻って]] [音楽] da capo (略 DC).

ダカール [[セネガルの首都]] Dakar /dɑːkɑ́ːr/.

‡**たかい 高い 形**

(WORD CHOICE) 高い
high 物体・程度・状態などが普通以上に高いこと. しばしば高さに加え, 横幅もある巨大な物体に用いる. • 高い山 a *high* mountain. (⚠ 山は横にも伸びている) • 高レベル[質; 危険性] *high* level [quality; risk].
tall 人・物がたてに細長く, すらりと高いこと. 特に人の身長を言う. • すらっと背の高い女性 a *tall* slender woman. • 高く伸びた芝 *tall* grass.

頻度チャート

high ▬▬▬▬▬▬▬▬▬▬
tall ▬▬▬
　　　20　40　60　80　100 (%)

❶ [高さが] high (↔low); tall (↔short) (⇨[類語]); 《主に書》 lofty. • 高い天井 a *high* ceiling. • 高い塀 a *high* [×a *tall*] wall. • 高いビル a *tall* [a *high*] building;(高層の) a *high-rise* building. (⚠「今 30 階の高さにいる」は We're now 30 stories *high*. という) • 高い鼻 a *long* [a *large*, a *big*] nose. (⚠(1) 米英ではほぼ言葉には用いない. (2) a high nose とすると顔の中での位置が上方にあることをさす (⇨低い ❶ [第3文例])) ▶富士山は日本でいちばん高い山です Mt. Fuji is *the highest* mountain in Japan./The height of Mt. Fuji is greater than any other mountain [《話》any mountain] in Japan. ▶天井が高すぎて部屋がなかなか暖まらない The ceiling is too *high* [×*tall*]. The room is hard to heat. ▶彼女は姉と同じくらい背が高い She is as *tall* as her sister. ▶彼は私より3センチ高い He is three centimeters [one inch] *taller than* I am [《話》*than* me,《古, まれ》*than* I].(⚠ 米英では centimeter の代わりに inch を用いることが多い. 特に《米》ではその方が普通) ▶どのくらい高い所から彼は落ちたのか How *high up* did he fall from?/From what *height* did he fall? ▶もう7時なのに太陽はまだ高かった It was seven in the evening, and the sun *was* still *high* [still *stayed up*, was still *up*].

❷ [金額が] (値段が) high;(品物が) expensive, high-priced,《英やや古》 dear. • 高い値段で売る[買う] sell [buy]《it》at a *high* price. • この牛肉の値段は高すぎる The price of this beef is too *high*. (⚠ すでに金銭の意味を含んでいる語とともに high が一般的だが,《米話》では時に expensive が用いられることがある)/This beef is too *expensive* [*costs too much*, ×is too high]. • 東京は物価が高い Prices are very *high* [×*expensive*] in Tokyo./Things are very *expensive* in Tokyo. (⚠ 文脈があれば Tokyo is very *expensive*. も可) ▶彼女は高い給料をもらっている She gets a *high* (↔a *low*, a *small*) salary./She is well-paid. ▶うわー見事な細工だ. さぞ高かったことでしょう What a superb work! It must have cost a fortune. (⚠(1) a fortune は「多額の金」の意で口語的. (2) 持ち主の社交的な会話の場合, 後半は It is from China? (中国のものですか)など金銭以外に関心を示す方が適切)

会話「5,000円でお分けしましょう」「うわっ, それは高いわ」"You can have it for five thousand yen." "Oh, that's a lot of money."

❸ [地位・希望・程度などが] high;(高遠な) lofty. • 高い理想 *high* [*lofty*] ideals. • 地位の高い人 a person with a *high* position; a person of *high* position. • 程度の高い学校 a *prestigious* [a *high-grade*] school. • 程度の高い(=上級)英語コース an *advanced* course in English. ▶彼は望みが高すぎる His aims are too *high* [*lofty*]./He aims too *high*./(大志を持つ) He is too *ambitious*. ▶彼は高い(=高い水準の)教養を身につけている He has a *high* level of culture. (⚠この場合 ×a high culture とはいわない)/He is a man of culture. ▶この数学の問題は普通の高校生には程度が高すぎる(=難しすぎる) This mathematical problem is too *difficult* [*hard*] for average high school students. (⚠ 後の方が口語的)

❹ [温度・圧力などが] high. ▶この部屋の温度は高すぎる The temperature in this room is too *high*./The temperature is too *high* in this room. ▶母は高い熱を出している My mother has a *high* fever.

❺ [声・音・格調などが] (声・音が大きい) loud;(かん高い) shrill, high-pitched;(洗練された) refined. • 高い声で話す speak in a *loud* [a *shrill*] voice;(大きな声で) speak loudly [《話》loud]. • かん高い叫

たかい 声 a *shrill* [a *high-pitched*] cry. ▶この曲はキーが高すぎて私には歌えない This piece is keyed too *high*. I can't sing it. ▶彼は格調の高い文章を書く He writes in a *refined* [a *lofty*, (威厳のある) a *dignified*] style.

— **高く** 副 high; (評価などで) highly; (犠牲・代償において) dearly. ▶飛行機が空高く飛んでいた The airplane was (flying) *high* [×*highly*] up in the sky. ▶電車より飛行機で行く方が高くつく It is more *expensive* [It *costs* (you) more] to go by airplane than by train. ▶彼の今度の小説は高く評価されている His new novel is valued *highly* [(好意的な批評を受ける) reviewed very *favorably*]./They think *highly* of his new novel. ▶その経験は高くついた That was a *costly* experience./That cost me *dearly* [*dear*]. (❗ cost 《him》 dear は成句)

— **高くする[なる]** 動 (位置・程度などを) "go *up*, *rise*". (⇨高める, 高まる) ▶塀を1メートル高くする raise a wall one meter. ●声を高くする raise one's voice. ▶最近野菜が高くなった Vegetables *have become expensive* [*have gone up in price*] recently. ▶興奮すると血圧が高くなる Excitement will *raise* (↔*lower*) our blood pressure./If we get excited, our blood pressure *goes up*.

たかい 他界 — **他界する** 動 pass away. (❗ die の婉曲表現)

*__たがい 互い__ each other, one another.

> **解説** (1) 2者間には each other, 3者以上では one another が原則だが, 今では2者でも one another が, 3者以上でも each other が用いられる. (2) ともに他動詞または前置詞の目的語(の一部)として用い, 主語としては用いない. (⇨「第6文例」). また「互いに」という日本語に引かれて副詞句として用いないように注意.

●互いに話し合う talk to [×talk] *each other*; talk *together*. ▶この子供たちはお互いにとても仲がよい These children are very friendly with *each other* [*one another*]. ▶彼らは互いに尊敬し合っている They respect *each other* [*one another*]./(相互に尊敬の念を持っている) They have [共有する] share] a *mutual* feeling of respect. ▶彼らはお互いの長所を知っている They know *each other's* [*one another's*, *mutual*] strong points. ▶我々はお互いにプレゼントを交換した We gave *each other* presents. / We exchanged presents [×present] (*with each other*). ▶お互いに頑張ろう *Let's* do our best. (❗ 日本語と異なり, 代名詞のどちらにも for each other や for one another をつけられない. つけると違った意味になるので注意) ▶彼らはお互いに何を考えているのか分かっている They *each* know [*Each* of them knows] what *the other* thinks. (❗ ×They know what each other thinks. とはいわない. なお, 否定文にすると *Neither* of them knows [《話》 know] what *the other* thinks. となる)

だかい 打開 — **打開する** 動 [[打ち破る] break; [突破口を開く] find a *breakthrough* (*in*); [打開策を見つける] find a way out (*of*). ●行き詰まりを打開する *break* the deadlock.

たがいちがい 互い違い — **互い違いに** 副 alternately /ɔ́ːltərnətli/. ●互い違いになる[する] 《やや書》 alternate (*with*). ▶幸福と不幸は互い違いにやって来る Happiness and unhappiness *come alternately* [*one after the other*]./Happiness *alternates with* unhappiness. ▶その鉄塔は白と赤のペンキが互い違いに塗ってあった The steel tower was painted in *alternating* red and white stripes. (❗ 色の順序に注意)

たかいびき 高鼾 a loud snore. ▶彼は高いびきをかいて寝入っていた He was fast asleep, *snoring loudly*.

たがう 違う ●計画にたがわず exactly according to the plan. ▶期待にたがわず彼はやって来た He came (*just*) *as we had expected*.

たがえる 違える ●彼女は約束をたがえない She *never breaks her promise*./She *keeps her promise*./She *is true to her word*.

たかが 高が ▶たかが100円くらいの金 a *small* [(取るに足らない) a *trivial*] *sum* like one hundred yen. ▶たかがゲームだ. そう興起になるな It's *only a game*. Don't get so excited. ▶たかが本一冊のためにわざわざ来たのね You came all the way *just* for a book. (⇨高) ▶たかが知れた (⇨高(た)か) [成句]]

たかく 他覚 ●他覚症状 [医学] objective (↔subjective) symptoms.

たがく 多額 ●多額の金 *a large amount of* money; *a large sum* [*large sums*] *of* money, 《話》 a fotune. ●多額の資金 *a large amount of funds*.

たかくか 多角化 图 diversification. ●事業[経済]の多角化 business [economic] *diversification*. ●積極的な多角化戦略を実行する implement an aggressive *diversification* strategy.

— **多角化する** 動 diversify 《business》; (多角化して…に乗り出す) diversify [branch out] (*into* computer software》. ▶多くの企業が事業活動を多角化している Many companies *are diversifying* their business activities.

たかくけい 多角形 (⇨多角形(たかっけい))

たかくけいえい 多角経営 diversified business (operations), diversified operations [management]. ●多角経営の大会社(＝複合企業) a conglómerate. ●多角経営をする diversify business.

たかくてき 多角的(な) (多種多様な) diversified; (多国間の) multilateral; (全面的な) many-sided. ●多角的な事業[農業] *diversified* business [agriculture].

— **多角的に** 副 ▶問題を多角的に(＝いろいろな角度から)見る view the problem *from different* [*various*] *angles*.

たかくぼうえき 多角貿易 multilateral trade.

たかくもり 高曇り cloudy weather (with thin clouds high up across the sky).

たかげた 高下駄 《a pair of》wooden clogs with longer supports.

*__たかさ 高さ__ ❶ [上下の高さ] (a) height /háit/; (高度) (an) áltitude. ▶1万フィートの高さを飛ぶ fly *at a height* [*an altitude*] *of* 10,000 feet. (❗ 米文ではメートル法よりヤード法の方が日常的) ▶これくらいの高さの像 a statue about this *high* [《まれ》 *height*]. (❗ この this は「これくらいの」の意の副詞で, 形容詞・副詞を修飾する口語表現) ▶この木は10メートル以上の高さになる This tree grows to a *height* of over 10 meters./This tree grows *taller* [×*higher*] than 10 meters. ▶この机は子供に合わせて高さが調節できる You can adjust this desk to the *height* of any child.
会話 「あの塔の高さはどのくらいですか」「333メートルです」"How *high* [*tall*] is that tower?" "It is 333 meters [1,092 feet] *high* [*tall, in height*]." (⇨高い)
❷ [声の高低] a pitch. ●声の高さを変える vary the *pitch* of one's voice.
❸ [値段の高さ] ▶東京の物価の高さに驚く be surprised at the *high* prices in Tokyo.

だがし 駄菓子 《米》 cheap candy, 《英》 cheap

たかしお 高潮 a tidal wave; 《暴風津波》a storm surge. ● 高潮警報《give [issue]》a tidal wave warning.

たかしまだ 高島田 the *takashimada* hairstyle. ● 高島田を結う do up one's hair (in) *takashimada* style.

たかせぶね 高瀬舟 a flat-bottomed boat.

たかせぶね『高瀬舟』 *The Boat on the River Takase*. 〘参考〙森鷗外の小説》

たかだい 高台 《小高い所》a rise;《やや書》a height /háit/ (▲しばしば複数形で);(丘) a hill.

たかだか 高々 ❶ [せいぜい] (多くて) at (the) most, not more than ...;(たった) only;(いちばん高くても) at the highest. ▶ その会合に出たのはたかだか30人くらいだった There were *at most* [*not more than*] 30 people (present) at the meeting.
❷ [高い様子] (空高く) high,《書》aloft;(声高く) loudly, in a loud voice. ● 旗を高々と揚げる hoist [fly] a flag *high*. ● 高々と笑う laugh *loudly*. ● 成功に鼻高々である be proud of one's success.

だかつ 蛇蝎 a serpent and a scorpion. ▶ 当時共産主義者は蛇蝎のごとく嫌われた In those days the communists were loathed like (as if they were) *vipers*. (! viper は「毒ヘビ」の意)

たかつき 高坏 a small one-legged table (for offerings to an altar).

だがっき 打楽器 〘音楽〙a percussion instrument; the percussion 〘集合的に用い単・複両扱い〙. ● 打楽器奏者 a percussionist.

たかっけい 多角形 〘数学〙a pólygòn. ● 多角形の polýgonal.

〘関連〙三角形 a triangle/四角形 (=四辺形) a quadrilateral/五角形 a pentagon/六角形 a hexagon/七角形 a heptagon/八角形 an octagon/九角形 a nonagon/十角形 a decagon

たかどの 高殿 〘高楼〙a lofty [a tall] building, a skyscraper;〘2階[3階]建ての家〙a two-storied [a three-storied] house.

たかとび 高飛び — 高飛びする 動 run away;《主に書》flee; (ひそかにあわてて立ち去る)《話》skip (off, out). (⇨逃げる) ▶ 犯人は海外へ高飛びする寸前に捕えられた The criminal was arrested just before he *ran away* overseas [*fled the country*, *skipped (out of) the country*].

たかとび 高跳び 〘競技〙《do》the high jump.

たかとびこみ 高飛び込み 《do》the high dive.

たかな 高菜 〘植物〙leaf mustard; Indian mustard.

たかなみ 高波 high waves;(高潮のときの) tidal waves. ● 高波にのまれる be swallowed (up) by the *high waves*; be lost in the *high waves*.

たかなる 高鳴る beat*, 〘書〙throb (-bb-). ▶ 興奮で胸が高鳴った My heart *beat* [*leaped up*] with excitement.

たかね 高値 〘高い〙[Xexpensive] price; 《株式で》a high. ● 高値がつく[を呼ぶ] fetch a *high* price; be quoted high. ● 最高値を更新する rally [break] through the old *highs*. ● 土地は結局それほど期待したほどの高値はつかなかった(=高値で売れなかった) The land didn't fetch a *high price* as we were hoping it would. ▶ その会社の株が昨日新高値をつけた The shares of the company hit a new *high* yesterday.

たかねのはな 高嶺の花 《手が届かない》be beyond 《his》reach. ▶ それはしょせん高嶺の花だ It's *out of* [*beyond*] *my reach*, after all.

たかのぞみ 高望み 図 ▶ もうそろそろ高望みはやめるときだ (=人生で自分の分にあった位置につくべき時になった) It's about time to take your place in life.
— 高望みする 動 ask too much; aim too high; be too ambitious. (⇨高い ❸) あまり高望みをするときっと失敗するよ If you *ask too much* [*aim too high*], you're sure to fail.

たかのつめ 高の爪 〘植物〙a cayenne pepper.

たかは 鷹派 the hawks, the hawk side;(タカ派の人) a hawk. (⑰ ハト派) ● タカ派政策 hawkism. ● タカ派的発言 a *hawkish* statement. ● ハト派とタカ派 (軍事面で) doves and *hawks*.

たかばなし 高話 ● 高話をする talk in a loud voice.

たかばりちょうちん 高張り提灯 a paper lantern hung on a pole (at the porch).

たかびしゃ 高飛車 — 高飛車な 形 (高圧的な) high-handed;(支配者などが傲慢(ごうまん)な)《やや書》over-bearing.
— 高飛車に 副 ● 高飛車に出る act *high-handedly*.

たかぶる 高ぶる ❶ 〘緊張する〙● 感情が高ぶる be filled with emotion;(興奮する) get excited;(神経質になる) get nervous. ❷ 〘驕(おご)る〙(⇨驕る)

たかまくら 高枕 ● 高枕で眠る sleep peacefully.

たかまり 高まり (増大) an increase 《of》;(感情・苦痛などの)《やや書》a surge 《of》. ● 緊張の高まり an *increase* of tension. ● 感情の高まり a *surge* of emotion.

*:**たかまる** 高まる 〘向上する, 感情などが強まる〙rise*;〘増大する〙grow*;〘増加する〙increase. ● 高まる疑惑 a *rising* [《やや書》a *mounting*] suspicion. ▶ 彼の名声が高まった He *rose* in fame./His fame *rose* [*got higher*,《書》*was enhanced*] ▶ そこに近づくにつれて緊張が高まっていった Tension *was growing* [*increasing*] as we got near there./We *got more nervous* as we got near there. ▶ そのスキャンダルに国民の関心がますます高まっていった The people *got* [*became*] more and more *interested* in the scandal.

たかみのけんぶつ 高見の見物 ● 高見の見物をしている (=何もしないで傍観する) stand (idly) by and watch; (just) remain an onlooker.

たかめ 高目 ● 内角高めのシュートを投げる pitch a screwball *high* and inside; pitch a *high* and inside screwball. (! 英語では高低を先に, 内外角を後に) ● 高めの球を振る打者 a *high-ball* hitter. ● エアコンの温度を少し高めにセットする set the air conditioner at a little *higher* temperature.

たかめ 田亀 〘昆虫〙a giant water bug.

*:**たかめる** 高める 〘量・質を増す〙incréase;〘水準・程度などを上げる〙raise;〘効果・速度などを強める〙heighten;〘改善する〙improve;〘才能・技能などを養成する〙《やや書》cúltivàte. ● 安全性[能率]を高める *increase* safety [efficiency]. ● 生活水準を高める *raise* the standard of living (in our country); make the standard of living *higher*. ● 後の方が口語的 ● 効果を高める *heighten* an effect. ● 教養を高める *improve* [*heighten* the level of] one's culture; *cultivate* oneself. ▶ これらの写真がこの本の価値を高めている These pictures *increase* [*heighten*] the value of this book.

*:**たがやす** 耕す cúltivàte (!「開墾する」の意も含む);〘すで〙《米》plow /pláu/,《英》plough /pláu/. ● 荒れ地を耕す *cultivate* the wilderness. ● 畑を耕す *cultivate* the field; do the plowing.

*:**たから** 宝 (宝物) (a) treasure;(貴重なもの) a precious [a valuable] thing. ● 家の宝 a family *treasure* (先祖伝来の) *heirloom*. ● 埋もれた宝を探す look for buried *treasure*. ▶ 彼はまさに会社の宝だ He is a real *treasure* [a tremendous *asset*]

to our company. (!修辞的な表現)/(とても大事な人である) He *means a lot* to our company. (!日常的な表現) 宝の海を返せ Bring back the *treasure* of our sea [*a sea of treasure*]. (!a sea of treasure は魚などの海から得られる宝物で, the treasure of our sea は海そのものを宝物と考える)/We want the *treasure* of our sea back! (!標語などに用いる)
- 宝の持ち腐れ (使われていない宝) (a) useless treasure; (才能) (a) wasted talent, (a) waste of talent.
- 宝くじ (⇨宝くじ) ● 宝探し a treasure hunt.
- 宝島 a treasure island; 〖書名〗 *Treasure Island*. ● 宝船 a treasure ship.

:だから ❶【結果を表す節を伴って】so, so that; (そういうわけで) That's why (⇨❷); (やや書) therefore; (当然の結果として)(やや書) consequently; (その状態に合わせて)(書) thus; (その状態に合わせて)(書) accordingly.

〖解説〗 **so** は日常的な接続詞で通例コンマの後または文頭中で用いる。**so that** 節は **so** より堅い言い方。通例前にコンマを置く。**therefore, thus, consequently, accordingly** は接続詞的な副詞で通例セミコロン(;), and の後または文頭中で用いる。ただし, しばしば一般動詞の前, 助動詞・be 動詞の後にも用いられ, その方が改まった感じがやわらぐ。また consequently は通例コンマに置く。

▶ 山田先生は休みです。だから今日は数学の授業はありません Mr. Yamada is absent, (*and*) *so* [*so that, and therefore, and consequently*] we have no math class today./Mr. Yamada is absent. *So* [*Therefore, Consequently*], we have no math class today. ▶ 道路は凍結していた。だから徐行しなければならなかった The road was frozen and *accordingly* we had to drive slow.
〖会話〗「それで中村を待っているのか」「そう。だから彼がやって来たらすぐに部屋に通してくれ」 "So you're expecting Nakamura." "Yes *and* when he arrives, show him in immediately."
〖会話〗「だって彼ははんの子供じゃないの」「だからどうだっていうの」 "After all he's only a child." "*So* what?" (!So what? が慣用的な言い方)
❷【理由を表す節を伴って】because, (やや書) since, (主に英) as.

〖解説〗 **because** 節ではそれが表す理由にその文の重点がある。主節に続けて文尾に置くことが多いが, 文頭に置くと主節と同様重要度が高いという含みがある。**since** 節は既知の事実を理由に表す。文の重点はここにはなく主節にある。通例文頭に置く。**as** 節は(書)で, 付帯状況的に軽く理由をそえる。(⇨-ので [第2文例])

▶ 彼はよく練習した。だから競走に勝った He won the ˇrace(,) *because* he trained ˋhard./*Since* [*As*] he trained hard, he won the race./He trained hard. *That's why* he won the race.
▶ その本にはミスプリントがある。だからといってつまらない本というわけではない The book is nót wórthless *júst* [*simply, mérely*] *because* there are some ˇmisprints in it. (!通例 just, simply, merely を伴い, その直前にコンマや休止を入れない。第1例とのイントネーションの違いに注意 (⇨-から ❸, -ので)。because の代わりに ×since, ×as は不可) ▶ 太郎は奥さんのことをけなしてばかりいる。だからといって奥さんを愛していないわけではない Taro is always running down his wife. But *he doesn't mean* that he doesn't love her. (!(1) 前の文は進行形を用いて話しての不満の気持ちを表す。(2) it は先行文全体をさす) ▶ だから言ったでしょう

I ˋtold you só./Didn't I tell you?
〖会話〗「なぜ彼は今日欠席なの」「病気だからです」 "Why isn't he here in class today?" "*Because* [×Since, ×As] he is sick." (!これは It is because ... の省略表現で Why 文の応答以外では It [The reason] is because .... のようにしか省略できない)
〖会話〗「彼らにはその仕事を仕上げるだけの時間はないよ」「だからって仕事を始めない理由にはならないでしょう」 "They don't have time to finish the job." "*That's* no reason for not starting it."

たからか 高らか ● 声高らかに歌う sing *in a loud voice* [*loudly*, ×aloud] (!aloud は単に「声を出して」の意); (話) belt out. ▶ 聖歌隊は「ハレルヤコーラス」を高らかに歌った The choir *belted out* the "Hallelujah Chorus."

たからがい 宝貝 〖魚介〗 a cowry, a cowrie.

たからくじ 宝くじ a (public) lottery. ● 宝くじ(券)を買う buy *lottery tickets*. ▶ 彼は宝くじで3,000万円を当てた He won thirty million yen in the *public lottery*.

たからもの 宝物 (a) treasure. (⇨宝)

たかり 集り (行為) extortion; (人) an extortioner. (⇨ゆすり)

たかる 集る ❶【群がる】(集まる) gather; (うようよする) swarm; (群がる) flock; (込み合う) crowd. (⇨群がる) ▶ 子供たちが地面に寝ころんでいる男の周りにたかり始めた Children *were gathering around* the man lying on the ground. ▶ その食べ物にハエが真っ黒にたかっている Flies *are* [There are flies] *thick around* the food.
❷【せびり取る】 ● 彼女に金をたかる (無理やり取る) *squeeze* [*extort*] money *from* her; (強要して) *obtain* money *from* her *by extortion*; (吸い取る) (話) *sponge on* her *for* money. ▶ 教師に飲み食いをたかるのは学生の特権と心得ている者もいる Some students take it as one of their privileges to *sponge* their food and drink *from* their teachers.

-たがる want [would like] 《*to* do》 (!後の方が控えめな言い方); (思い焦がれる, 熱望する) long 《*to* do》; (切望する) be anxious [eager] 《*to* do》. (⇨-たい) ▶ 彼女は故郷に帰って平穏に暮らしたがっている She *wants* [*longs*] *to* go back to her hometown and live a peaceful life in her hometown. ▶ 彼は中国に残してきた息子の消息を知りたがっている He *is eager* [*anxious*, (話) *dying*] *to* hear about his son he has left behind in China. ▶ 子供たちは早くプレゼントを見たがった(=見たくてうずうずしていた) The children *were impatient* [*couldn't wait*] *to* see the presents.

たかわらい 高笑い 图 a loud laugh; (連続的な) (×a) (loud) laughter.
—— **高笑いする** 動 laugh loudly; give a loud laugh.

たかん 多感 —— **多感な** 形 (感情的に動かされやすい) susceptible; (過敏に傷つきやすい) sensitive. ● 多感な青年 a *susceptible* [*sensitive*] young man. ▶ 彼は多感で日々心身を消耗している He is extremely *sensitive* and suffers a lot.

だかん 兌換 图 conversion 《*of* dollars *into* euros》.
—— **兌換する** 動 convert 《dollars into euros》. ● 兌換できる[できない] convertible [inconvertible]. ● 兌換紙幣 a convertible note.

たかんしょう 多汗症 〖医〗 hyper(h)idrosis.

***たき 滝** a wáterfall; falls 《固有名詞の場合は後の方を用いるのが普通で通例単数扱い》; (大きい) (やや書) a cátaract; (小さい) (やや書) a cáscade. ● 滝に打たれる stand under a *waterfall* (to purify oneself). (事情 欧米には修行や願かけに滝を使う習慣はない) ▶ あ

の山の向こうに滝がある There is a *waterfall* beyond that mountain. ▶ナイアガラの滝は世界的に有名です (The) Niagara *Falls* is [×are] world-famous. (**!** 著名なものは通例 the を省略する) ▶この滝は数百メートル下に落ちている These [×This] *falls* cascade [×cascades] down a few hundred meters./These *falls* are [×is] a few hundred meters high. ▶雨の滝のように降った The rain fell *in torrents*. ▶汗が顔を滝のように(=川となって)流れた Sweat ran down my face *in rivers*./Sweat poured down my face.
- 滝つぼ the basin of a waterfall.

たき 多岐 ●多岐にわたる (さまざまな) various; (多様な) divérse; (複雑な) cómplicated; complex. ▶彼の活躍の分野は多岐にわたっている He works in *various* fields.

たぎ 多義 〖言語〗polysemy /pάlisi:mi/.
- **多義語** 〖言語〗a polysemous /pàlísí:məs/ word.

唾棄 唾棄すべき detestable, despicable.

だきあう 抱き合う hug (-gg-) [embrace] each other. (**!** 後の方が堅い言い方) (⇨抱き締める) ▶抱き合って泣く cry *in each other's arms*. ▶恋人たちはかたく抱き合った The lovers *hugged* [*embraced*] each other tightly.

だきあがる 炊き上がる ▶ご飯が炊き上がった The rice *is boiled* [*cooked*].

だきあげる 抱き上げる pick ... up. ▶赤ちゃんを抱き上げる *pick up* a baby (in one's arms).

だきあわせ 抱き合わせ ●シャンプーをリンスと抱き合わせて売る tie shampoo in with hair conditioner.
- **抱き合わせ販売** (hold, run) a tíe-in sale. (**!** その商品をa tie-in という)

たきあわせる 炊き合わせる ●魚と野菜を炊き合わせて I cooked fish and vegetables in their respective cuisine and served them in one dish.

だきいぬ 抱き犬 (ペット用小型犬) a lapdog.

だきおこす 抱き起こす ▶1人の青年が転んだおばあさんを抱き起こした A young man put his arms around the fallen old woman and helped her to her feet.

だきかかえる 抱きかかえる hold*... in one's arms.
- けが人を抱きかかえて救急車に運び込む carry an injured person into the ambulance *in one's arms*.

たきぎ 薪 firewood. (⇨薪(§)) ● 薪を拾う gather [collect] *firewood*.
- **薪能** Takigi No(h); (説明的に) an open-air *No(h)* play performed mainly in the precincts of a shrine or temple with light supplied by burning firewood in the evening.

だきぐせ 抱き癖 ●抱き癖がつく form [develop] the *habit of being held in* ⟨his⟩ *arms*; (いつも抱いてほしいと言う) always want to be held in ⟨his⟩ arms.

たきぐち 焚き口 a fire door.

たきこみごはん 炊き込みご飯 (説明的に) boiled rice mixed with meat [fish] and vegetables.

たきこむ 炊き込む (味方に引き入れる) win* [bring*] ⟨him⟩ over [around]; (計画などに巻き込む) involve ⟨him⟩ in ⟨a bank raid attempt⟩.

タキシード a tuxedo (⑱ 〜s), (主に米話) a tux, (英) a dinner jacket.

たきしめる 薫き染める impregnate ⟨clothes⟩ with the perfume by burning incense.

だきしめる 抱き締める (愛情をこめて) hug (-gg-), embrace. (**!** 後の方が堅い語) (⇨抱く) ▶彼女は息子をしっかりと抱き締めた She *hugged* her son tightly./She *gave* her son a tight *hug*.

だきすくめる 抱き竦める hug ⟨him⟩ tight(ly); hold ⟨him⟩ tight(ly) in one's arms; give ⟨him⟩ a bear hug.

たきだし 炊き出し 〘会話〙「私たちは地震の被災者のために炊き出しをしたよ。で、何人分ほどしたの」「100人分とてことかな」 "We *set up a soup kitchen* for earthquake victims." (**!** soup kitchen は「(ホームレスや罹災者のための)スープ接待所」) "Good for you! How many people did you feed?" "As many as 100."

たきたて 炊き立て ●炊き立てのご飯 just-cooked rice.

だきつきすり 抱き付き掏摸 (説明的に) a pickpocket who steals wallets while throwing his arms around victims.

だきつく 抱き付く ●彼に抱きつく (しがみつく) cling to him; (腕の中に飛び込む) throw *oneself into* his arms. ▶子供は母親の首に抱きついた The little boy [girl] *flung* his [her] arms *around* his [her] mother's neck.

たきつけ 焚き付け kindling. ●新聞紙を丸めてたきつけにする make balls of newspaper and use them as *kindling*.

たきつける 焚き付ける ❶〘火をつける〙light [kindle] a fire ⟨in a wood stove⟩.
❷〘そそのかす〙(やや話) egg ... on ⟨to do⟩; (扇動する) stir (-rr-) ... (up) ⟨to do⟩. ●彼をたきつけて盗みをさせる egg him *on* to steal.

だきとめる 抱き留める catch ⟨a child⟩ in one's arms.

だきね 抱き寝 ▶マキは赤ちゃんを抱き寝している Maki is sleeping with her baby in her arms.

たきび 焚き火 a fire; an open-air fire.
── たき火(を)する **動** make [build] a fire (in the open air).

だきゅう 打球 (打ったボール) a batted ball; (ボールを打つこと) batting. ●強い打球 a hard-hit ball; a shot.

たきょう 他郷 a foreign country. (⑱ 異郷)

***だきょう 妥協** 图 (a) compromise /kámprəmàiz/. (**!** 具体的には C. (米) では日本語と同様、弱腰のうしろめたさを伴うこともあるが、〘英〙ではプラスイメージのある語)
- 妥協して by *compromise*. ● 妥協に達する reach [come to, arrive at] a *compromise*. ▶この件に関しては妥協の余地はない There is no room for *compromise* on this matter./(これ以上妥協しない) We're not *making* any more *compromises on* this matter.
── 妥協する **動** compromise, make* a compromise ⟨with⟩; (やや話) meet* ⟨him⟩ halfway. ▶彼らは映画を見に行くことで妥協した They *compromised by* going to the movies.
- **妥協案** a compromise (plan).

たきょくか 多極化 multipolarization. ●多極化した国際情勢 *multipolarized* [(多極(分散)の)] multipolar] international situations.

たぎる (沸騰する) boil. ●怒りで血が煮えたぎる seethe [⟨話⟩ *boil* (*over*)] with rage.

***たく 炊く, 焚く** ❶〘煮る〙boil. (⇨煮る) ●ご飯を炊く *boil* rice; (加熱調理する) cook rice.
❷〘燃やす〙burn*; (火をおこす) make* a fire ⟨in a room⟩; (火を燃やす) light a fire ⟨in a fireplace⟩.
- 香をたく *burn* incense. ●風呂をたく *heat* the bath; (準備をする) prepare the bath; get the bath ready.

たく 宅 〖自宅〗one's house, one's home; 〖夫〗one's husband.

タグ 〖付け札〗a tag.

***だく 抱く** ❶〘両腕で抱える〙hold*... in one's arms;

(愛情をこめて抱き締める) hug (-gg-), embrace. (❗後の方が堅い語). ▶彼女は赤ちゃんを抱いていた She *was holding* her baby *in* her arms. ▶小さいお子さんは必ず抱いて(連れて行って)ください《掲示》Tiny children must *be carried* in your arms. ❷ [鳥が卵を] sit*. ▶めんどりが卵を抱いていた The hen *was sitting* (on its eggs).

だく 諾 (承諾) consent; (受諾) acceptance.

だく 駄句 a trashy haiku.

ダグアウト a dúgout.

たくあん 沢庵 pickled Japanese radish; (説明的に) half dried radishes pickled in a mixture of rice bran and salt in a tub weighted down with heavy stones on the lid. (⇨漬物)

たくいつ 択一 (⇨二者択一)

たぐいまれ 類まれな (比類のない) incómparable; (無類の) mátchless. ● 彼女の類まれな美しさ her *incomparable* [*matchless*] beauty.

たくえつ 卓越 图 excellence.
— **卓越した** 形 (優秀な) excellent; (目立って優れた) prominent; (他に抜きん出た) outstanding; (著名な) distinguished.
— **卓越する** 動《書》excel (*in, at*). ▶彼は雄弁家として卓越している He *excels* [*is outstanding*] *as* an orator.

だくおん 濁音 a voiced sound [consonant].

‡たくさん ❶ [数・量が] a lot of ..., (話) lots of ..., (十分間に合うほど多くの) plenty of ... (❗以上は複数可算名詞・不可算名詞の前で); [数が] many*, 《やや書》 a large number [large numbers, a great number] of ... (❗以上は複数可算名詞の前で); many a+単数名詞 (❗単数扱い); [量が] much*, 《やや書》a great [a good] deal of ... (❗以上は不可算名詞の前で。a good deal of の使用は肯定文に限られる). (⇨多い)

解説 肯定平叙文に many, much を単独で用いるのは堅い言い方で、主に《書》。代わりに a lot of, a great number of, a great deal of などを用いる。否定文・疑問文・条件文では、a lot of, lots of も可だが、many, much の方も最も普通に用いられる。

▶その森にはシカがたくさんいる There are *a lot of* [*lots of*] deer in the forest./There are *a large* [*great*] *number of* deer in the forest. (❗great の方が強意的)/The forest *is full of* 《書》*abounds with*] deer. (❗(米)では in より with の方が普通)
▶きのうはたくさん雪が降った We had *a lot of* [*lots of*, *a great deal of*] snow yesterday. / It snowed *a lot* [*a great deal*] yesterday. (❗後の文では副詞用法). ▶私にはあまりたくさん時間がない I don't have *much* [*a lot of*, *lots of*, ×*plenty of*] time. (❗否定文では a lot of, lots of を用いる方が強意的。plenty of は通例否定文では用いられない) ▶しなければならないことがたくさんある I have *a lot* (*of things* [*work*]) to do./《書》There are *many* things [*is much* (work)] to do. ▶彼女はなんとたくさんの卵を買ったんだろう What *a lot of* [*a number of*] eggs she's bought! (❗感嘆文では ×What many [lots of] eggs ...! は使われない。How many eggs ...! も口語ではまれ) ▶ケーキをたくさん食べすぎた I ate *too many* pieces of cake [*much* cake]. (❗前者は, so の後では肯定文でも many, much は普通に用いる。×too lot of とはいわない) ▶非常にたくさん雨が降ったので外出できませんでした We had *so much* rain [*such a lot of* rain] (that) we couldn't go out. ▶私は彼女よりたくさん本[お金]を持っている I have *more* books [money] than she (does). (❗「ずっとたくさんの本[お金]」なら a lot more books [money], many more books [much more money] となる) ▶彼は 3 人のうちで一番たくさん本[お金]を持っている He has *the most* books [money] of the three. ▶彼女はかなりたくさんの人形を持っている She has *quite a lot of* [*rather a lot of*, *quite a few*, *a good many*, ×*quite many*] dolls. (❗quite a few は「予想以上に」多いことを暗示) / (非常に多くの) She has *a great many* dolls. (❗very many は一般に肯定文では避けられる)

会話 「質問[荷物]はたくさんありますか」「はい,たくさんあります」"Do you have *many* questions [*much* baggage]?" "Yes, *a lot* [*lots*]." (❗(1) Do you have *a lot of* [*lots of*, *plenty of*] questions? のようにa lot of, lots of, plenty of を疑問文で用いるとしばしば肯定の答えを期待していることを暗示。(2) 答えとして ×Yes, many [much]. は不可。ただし否定で答えるときは No, not many [much]. といい, ×No, not a lot [lots]. は不可)

会話 「リンゴをもう一つもらってもいい?」「いいわよ。まだたくさん残っているから」"Can I have another apple?" "Of course. There are *plenty* left." (❗plenty は plenty of apples の意)
❷ [十分] enough, 《やや書》sufficient. (⇨十分)
▶ご忠告はもうたくさんです I've had *enough of* your advice. / (もうごめんだ) I *won't* stand for *any more* of your advice. (❗stand for は「耐え忍ぶ」の意でこのような否定文で用いられる慣用表現)/(うんざりだ)《話》I'm *fed up with* your advice. ▶1,000 円あればたくさんだ One thousand yen will be *enough* [*sufficient*]./(十分間に合う) One thousand yen *will do*.

会話 「もう 1 杯お茶はいかがですか」「もうたくさんいただきました」"How about another cup of tea?" "Thank you. I've had *enough* [*plenty*]." (❗文脈から明らかな enough tea, plenty of tea の tea, of tea を省略したもの)

会話 「今日はテニスはしたくない」「この前は風邪を引いていたね。もうたくさんよ。だれか他の人を見つけてするわ」「お好きなように」"I don't want to play tennis today." "Last time you had a cold. *I've had it.* I'll find someone else to play with." (❗with に注意)/"Suit yourself."

たくしあげる たくし上げる (まくり上げる) tuck ... up; (巻し上げる) roll ... up. ▶そでをたくし上げる *tuck up* one's sleeve(s).

***タクシー** a taxi, a cab, 《書》a taxicab. (⇨車)

参考 外国でタクシーを利用するときの表現と注意点
(1) 呼び止めるとき: Taxi [キャブ]!
(2) 行き先ははっきりと please をつけて: (Could you take me to) the Sheraton Hotel, *please*? (❗( )内は通例省略する).
(3) 降りたいとき: *Please* let me off here./(ここで結構) This is fine, *thank you*.
(4) 支払うときはチップを含めて払うが,お釣りは遠慮せず請求する: ($ 7.00, please. と言われたら) OK. Here's $10.00. Give me $1.50 back, please. (❗チップを $ 1.50 として)
(5) 自動ドアは一般的ではないので特に降りた後,自分でドアを締めることを忘れずに.

① 【~タクシー】 ● 個人タクシー an owner-driven *taxi*. ● 無線タクシー a radio [a radio-dispatched] *taxi*.
② 【タクシーに】 ● タクシーに乗る (乗り込む) get in [into, ×on] a *taxi*; (利用する) take a *taxi*. ▶タクシーに乗って神戸まで行った I took a *taxi* [a *cab*] to Kobe.
③ 【タクシーを】 ● 流しのタクシーを拾う get [《話》

たくしき pick up] a cruising *taxi*. ●タクシーを呼ぶ (電話で) call a *taxi*; (合図して止める) hail [flag (down)] a *taxi*. ▶彼は個人タクシーをしている He drives an owner *taxi*. ●タクシーを呼んでください Can you call [get] me a *taxi*, please?
④【タクシーで】 ●タクシーで行く go by [in a] *taxi*. ▶彼はタクシーで家へ帰った[彼女の会社まで行った] He took a *taxi* home [to the office where she worked]. (⇨②)
●タクシー運転手 a taxi driver; (主に米) a cabdriver. ●タクシー代[料金] a taxi fare. ●タクシー代を払う pay the driver. ●タクシー乗り場 (主に米) a taxi stand, a cabstand; 《英》a taxi rank.

たくしき 卓識 an excellent idea. (⇨卓見)

たくしこむ たくし込む ▶シャツを(ズボンの中に)たくし込みなさい Tuck your shirt into your trousers [pants].

たくじしょ 託児所 a (day) nursery, a day-care center, 《英》a creche [《まれ》a crèche] /kréʃ/. (⇨保育[保育所])

たくじょう 卓上 (机上用の) desk; (コンピュータなどが) desktop.
●卓上カレンダー a desk calendar. ●卓上スタンド a desk lamp.

たくしん 宅診 a consultation at a clinic.

たくす 託す [[任せる]](物・事を)《やや書》entrust, trust (❗ 前の方が普通); (人・物を) leave*. ●将来に望みを託す be hopeful about one's future. ●我々は彼にその仕事を託した We *entrusted* [*trusted*] him *with* the task. / We *entrusted* [《今に比》*trusted*] the task *to* him./I *left* the task *with* him. (❗ leave を用いると信頼感が弱くなる) ▶留守中の家族のことを彼に託した I asked him to look after my family while I was away.

だくすい 濁水 muddy waters, turbid water.

たくする 託する entrust. (⇨託す)

たくぜつ 卓絶 excellence. (⇨卓越)

たくせん 託宣 an oracle. (⇨神託)

たくそう 託送 图 consignment. ●託送販売で[on] consignment. ── **託送する** 動 consign ... 《to》.
●託送品 a consignment.

たくち 宅地 (住宅用地) a building lot.
●宅地造成[開発]業者 a developer. ●宅地分譲 sale of building lots.

だくてん 濁点 (put) a sonant [a voice-sound] mark.

タクト [<ドイツ語] a baton. ●タクトをとる conduct [《主に米》direct,《英》lead] 《an orchestra》.

ダクト [送管] a duct.

たくはい 宅配 图 home [door-to-door] delivery. (⇨宅配便) ▶あのピザ店はネットで宅配用の注文を受けつけている That pizza house takes food orders for *home delivery* by [on] the Net.
── **宅配する** 動 deliver 《goods》to 《his》house.

たくはいびん 宅配便 (a) home [door-to-door] delivery service (❗ 具体的な意では a がつく); courier /kúriər/ service. ●宅配便を取り扱う offer a *home delivery service*. ▶両親がリンゴ1箱宅配便で送ってくれた My parents sent me a box of apples by *home delivery service*.

たくはつ 托鉢 图 (religious) mendicancy.
── **托鉢する** 動 go about asking for alms /áːmz/.
●托鉢僧 a mendicant priest.

たくばつ 卓抜 (抜群の) excellent. (⇨卓越)
●卓抜な着想 an *excellent* idea.

だくひ 諾否 ▶諾否をお知らせください Please let me know *whether* you *accept* it *or not*.

タグボート [引き船] a tugboat, a towboat.

たくほん 拓本 a rubbed copy. ●碑文の拓本をとる make *a rubbing* of an inscription on a tombstone.

***たくましい** 逞しい 形 [[体格が]] (がっしりした) robust /roubʌ́st/, (屈強な) sturdy; [[筋骨が]] muscular; [[精神が]] strong-minded. ●たくましい体格のボディーガード a *robust* [a *sturdy*] bodyguard. ●strong を用いると通例「力持ち」の意) ●たくましい腕 *muscular* arms. ●想像力がたくましい(=活発である) have a *vivid* imagination. ▶彼はたくましい体格をしている He's very *powerfully* built./He has a *large strong* build [*physique*].
── **たくましく** 副 vigorously; powerfully. ▶その話を聞いて私は想像力をたくましくした The story *fired* my imagination.

たくみ 巧み ─ **巧みな** 形 (上手な) good*; (熟練を示す) skillful; (巧妙な) clever. ●巧みな作品 a *good* [a *skillful*] production. ●巧みな運転 *skillful* driving. ●巧みな言い訳をする make a *clever* [《やや書》an *adroit*] excuse.
── **巧みに** 副 skillfully; (如才なく) cleverly. ●巧みに細工した指輪 a *skillfully* crafted ring. ●巧みな人はきわめて巧みに箸(ハシ)を扱う He uses chopsticks very *skillfully*./He is very *skillful* [*good*] at using chopsticks. (❗ He *has* great *skill with* chopsticks. はおおげさで不自然)

たくむ 巧む [[工夫する]] devise; [[たくらむ]] plot.

タクラマカン ●タクラマカン砂漠 [[中国の砂漠]] the Taklamakan /tǽkləmɑkɑːn/ Desert.

たくらみ 企み [[陰謀]] a plot; [[共同謀議]] (a) conspiracy; [[悪だくみ]] a scheme, a design; [[計略]] a trick. (⇨計画, 計略) ●政府転覆のたくらみ a *plot* [a *conspiracy*, a *scheme*, a *design*] *to* overthrow the government.

たくらむ 企む [[陰謀を企てる]]《やや書》plot (-tt-); [[共謀する]]《やや書》conspire; [[悪だくみする]] scheme, design; [[いたずらなどを]]《話》be up to .... (⇨計画) ●政府転覆をたくらむ *plot* [*conspire*, *scheme*] *to* overthrow the government; *plot* [*scheme*] the overthrow of the government. ▶彼は何かよからぬ事をたくらんでいる He *is up to* something.

たぐりこむ 手繰り込む (釣り糸を) reel in《a fishing line》; (地引き網を) draw [pull in]《a dragnet》.

たぐりつ 卓立 excellence. (⇨卓越)

だくりゅう 濁流 a muddy stream.

たぐりよせる 手繰り寄せる (強くぐいぐいと引く) haul ... in. ●網をたぐり寄せる *haul in* a net.

たぐる 手繰る (手元へ寄せる) pull in [(強く) haul in]《a rope》; (記憶をたどる) search《one's memory for...》. ●つり糸を手繰る *reel in* a fishing line.

たくわえ 蓄え [[貯蔵]] a stock, a store; [[貯金]] savings. ●食糧の蓄え a *stock* [a *store*] of food. ●多少の蓄えをしておく keep some *savings*《in a bank》. ▶燃料の蓄えが底をついた *Stocks* of fuel have run out.

***たくわえる** 蓄える ❶ [[ためる]] (貯金する) save ... (up), (貯蔵する) store ... (up); (財産などを蓄積する) accumulate; (増強する) build*... up. ●家を買うためにお金を蓄える *save* (up) money to buy a house. ●サイロに干し草を蓄える *store* hay *in* a silo; *store* a silo *with* hay. (❗ 前の方は「場所」に、後の方は「(蓄える)物」に重点のある言い方) ●知識を蓄える *accumulate* [*store up*] knowledge.
❷ [[とっておく]] save; put* [lay*]... aside [away]. ●その計画に[まさかの時のために]お金を蓄える *save* [*put aside*] some money *for* the plan [a rainy day]. (❗ *against* a rainy day は今は《古》)

❸ [ひげを] ● 口ひげをたくわえる[たくわえている] grow [have, wear] a mustache.

たけ 竹 〖植物〗 bamboo /bæmbúː/ (❗限定用法では通例 bámbo (⇨竹の子)). (1本の竹) a bamboo (tree) (֍ ～s). ● 竹の皮[節] a *bamboo* sheath [joint]. ● 竹のカーテン the *bamboo* curtain [*Bamboo* Curtain]. ▶その家具は竹でできている The furniture is made of *bamboo*.
● 竹を割ったよう ● 竹を割ったような性格の男性 a straightforward [a frank and honest] man.
● 竹垣 a bámboo fénce. ● 竹細工 bámboo wórk [wáre]. ● 竹竿 a bámboo póle. ● 竹筒 a bamboo cylinder. ● 竹とんぼ a *taketombo*; (説明的に) a flying bamboo toy in the shape of a dragonfly. ● 竹ぼうき a bamboo broom. ● 竹やぶ a bamboo thicket [grove]. (参考) 欧米では竹やぶの存在は珍しい ● 竹やり a bamboo spear.

たけ 丈 〖身長〗 height /háit/, 〖書〗 stature; 〖長さ〗 length. (⇨身長, 長さ) ▶スカートの丈を詰める shorten the *length* of one's skirt. ▶(背)丈が伸びる grow *tall(er)*. ▶このズボンは彼女には丈が短すぎる These pants 《米》 [*trousers* 《主に英》] are [*The length* of these pants 《米》 [*trousers* 《主に英》] is] too short for her.

たけ 岳 a high mountain. (⇨高山)
たけ 茸 a mushroom. (⇨茸(きの))
たけ 他家 another family.

-たげ ▶彼は眠たげな顔をしている He *looks* sleepy. ▶彼女は何か話したげにしていた She *seemed* to have something to tell me.

*-**だけ** 《副助詞》 ❶ [限定] (ただ…だけ) only, just (❗後の方が口語的. 修飾される語句の直前に置くのが原則), 《やや書》 alone (❗前記の名詞・代名詞の直後におかれ,直前は不可. 《話》では強意的), (単に) simply, 《やや書》 merely. (⇨のみ ❶, -しか) ▶彼だけがその事実を知っている *Only* he [He *alone*] knows the fact./He is the *only* person that [who] knows the fact./(彼を除いて)だれもその事実を知らない Nobody knows the fact *except* him. ▶彼の頭にあるのは仕事のことだけだ He thinks of *nothing but* his work./《話》He *only* think of his *work*. (❗に言葉では普通 only を動詞の直前, 助動詞でも be 動詞の直後に置き, 音調によって修飾関係を明確にする) ▶このことは母さんに言わないでよ. 心配させるだけだから Don't let Mom know this. It will *only* cause a lot of worry for her. ▶彼はその容疑者と友達だというだけで警察に逮捕されたのですか Was he arrested by the police *just* [*simply*] because he was friends with the suspect? ▶それを食べるかと思っただけで吐き気がした I felt sick *just* to think I had to eat it. (❗次例より口語的)/The *very* [*mere*] thought of eating it sickened me. ▶彼は運がよかっただけだ He was *just* lucky./He was lucky *and nothing more*. (❗後の方が強意的) ▶いつあなたと 2 人だけで会えますか When can I see you *alone*?
会話「お母さん, キャンデー食べてもいい?」「いいけど, 一つだけよ」"May I have some candy, Mom?" "Yes, dear, but *only* one candy." (❗前の方の candy は Ⓤ, 後の方の candy は Ⓒ)
会話「どこに行くの」「手紙を出しに行くだけさ」 "Where are you going?" "*Just* [*Only*] to mail 《主に米》 [post 《主に英》] a letter."
会話「あなたに負けたから彼機嫌が悪かったのよ」「それだけのことかい」 "He was cross because you beat him." "Is that *all* it was?"
【A だけでなく B も】 not only A but (also) B; B as well as A. (❗(1) いずれも B に意味上の重点がある. (2) A, B ならば語, 句なら句のように文法上同類の形式となるのが原則) ▶彼だけでなく私にも責任がある The responsibility lies *not only* with him *but* (*also*) with me. (❗*Not only* he *but* (*also*) I am [×is] responsible for it. のように, この句が主語の位置に来ることは《まれ》)/I am responsible for it *as well as* he [〖話〗him]. (❗(1) 代名詞の場合には I, *as well as* him, an … の語順はあまり用いない. (2) 名詞の場合から The student, *as well as* his parents, is ....となるが, 両端をコンマで区切らない口語的な文脈では as well as が and の意に近づく次いで複数形動詞を用いる傾向がある) ▶旅行は私たちに楽しさを与えてくれるだけでなく視野を広げてくれる Traveling *not only* gives us ＞pleasure, *but* (*also*) broadens our ＼horizons./Traveling enriches our experience *as well as* giving [(×it) gives] us pleasure.

❷ [...に比例して] (...すればするほどそれだけ) the＋比較級, the＋比較級; (...につれて) as, 《英・書》 according as. ▶人は年をとればとるだけ賢くなる *The older* we grow, *the wiser* we become. (❗「the ＋比較級... the＋比較級」構文の場合《いに用は》 *The more ..., the more wise ....* もよく用いる)/*As* we grow older, we become wiser./We gain wisdom *with* age./The more old [The older] we are, the more wise [the wiser] we become. (❗×The more old men は不可)

❸ [差異] (...の差で) ▶彼は父より 2 センチだけ背が高い He is two centimeters taller than his father./He is taller than his father *by* two centimeters. (❗特に後の方で差を強調する場合に用いる. 前の方が普通) ▶バス料金が 30 円だけ値上げになった The bus fare was raised *by* thirty yen. (❗日本語では「...だけ」を表現しない場合も多い)

❹ [程度] (これだけ) so [〖話〗that] much; (...だけ多く) as much [many] as ...; (十分な) enough; (せめて...だけでも) at least. ▶これだけは確かだ. 殺し屋は金目当てではなかった *This much* is certain; the killer was not after money. ▶これだけ言ってもまだ分からないのか Don't you understand me yet after I've told you *so much*? ▶みんながどれだけ君の(健康の)ことを心配しているか分からないだろう You'll never know *how* anxious [concerned] we all are [×we are all] about [for] you. ▶好きなだけ食べなさい Eat *as much as* you like. ▶みんなが座れるだけ椅子がありますか Are there chairs *enough* [*enough* chairs] for everyone to sit on? ▶みそ汁だけでも飲んでから出勤したほうがいいと思うけど Maybe you'd better *at least* have a bowl of *miso* ＼soup before you go to ⁄work. (❗at least を文頭に置いて *At least* you might be better to ... のようにもいえる)
会話「二ついただいていいですか」「お好きなだけどうぞ」 "May I take two?" "Take *as many as* you like."
会話「もうしばらくいてもいいかい」「もちろん. いたいだけいろよ」 "Can I stay a bit longer?" "By all means, stay *as long as* you wish."

❺ [価値, 評価] ▶彼はがんばっただけあって(=おかげで)成績が大いに上がった *Thanks to* his efforts [hard work], his grades improved greatly. ▶さすが留学しただけのことはあるね(=無駄に留学しなかった) You didn't go abroad for study *for nothing*. ▶彼は苦労人だけあって(=だから)思いやりがある *Since* he has seen much of the world, he is considerate. ▶その本は読むだけの価値はある The book is *worth* reading./*It's* worth reading the book. (⇨価値) ▶彼女は大統領夫人だけに(=にふさわしく)なかなかの社交家だ *As may be expected of* the president's

たげい 多芸 图 vèrsatílity.
- 多芸は無芸《ことわざ》Jack of all trades (and master of none). (！「器用貧乏な男」の意 (⇨器用))
── 多芸の 形 vérsatile. ● 多芸多才な役者 a versatile performer.
たけうま 竹馬 《(a pair of)》(bamboo) stilts. ● 竹馬に乗って歩く walk on [×with] stilts.

*だげき 打撃 ❶ [強く打つこと] a blow; [精神的打撃] (a) shock (⇨ショック); [損害] damage. ● 頭にひどい打撃を食らう get [receive] a severe blow on [to] the head. ▶そのスキャンダルは彼の政治生命に致命的な打撃を与えた The scandal was [×gave] a fatal blow to his political career. ▶彼の事業はその地震で大きな打撃を受けた His business was badly hit [was greatly damaged] by the earthquake./His business suffered a great blow [great damage] from the earthquake.
❷ [野球で] batting, hitting. ● 打撃用のヘルメット [手袋] a batting helmet [glove]. ▶そのチームは打撃がかなりいい The team is hitting pretty well./(打率が高い) The team's batting average is pretty high. (⇨バッティング)
● 打撃王 (首位打者) a batting champion [king]. (！シーズンを通した成績については leading hitter とはいわない) ● 打撃コーチ a batting coach. ● 打撃戦 a slugfest. ● 打撃不振 a batting [a hitting] slump. ● 打撃練習 (take) batting practice.

『たけくらべ』Teenagers Vying For Tops. (参考 樋口一葉の小説)
たけだけしい 猛々しい (勇猛な) ferocious; (恥知らずな) shameless.
だけつ 妥結 图 (解決) a settlement; (合意) an agreement.
── 妥結する 動 ▶交渉は妥結した The negotiations came to a settlement [an agreement]. (！ came to の代わりに reached も可)
たけつしつ 多血質 ── 多血質の 形 sanguine.

*だけど(も) (⇨けれど(も), しかし) ▶彼女は美人だけど, 私は好きになれない She is beautiful, but [Though she is beautiful,] I don't like her. ▶なるほど彼はすぐれた学者だけど, 教え方がうまくない It is true [Indeed] he is a good scholar, but he isn't good at teaching [isn't a good teacher]. ▶あのホテルはサービスが悪かった. だけど料金は安かったのよ The service was poor at that hotel. The charge was low, though [《やや書》however, ×although]. (！though は[話]で通例文尾に置く)
会話「やらないって言ってたじゃないか」「だけど今になったらやりたいんだよ」"You said you wouldn't do it." "Well, I want to, now." (！ to に注意)

たけとりものがたり『竹取物語』Taketori Monogatari (The Tale of the Bamboo Cutter); The Bamboo-Cutter and the Moon-Child. (参考 平安時代の物語)
たけなが 丈長 ── 丈長の 形 ● 丈長のスカート a long skirt. (図 丈長)
たけなわ 酣 ── 私がそこに着いたときには宴会はたけなわ(=最高潮)であった The party was in full swing [at its height] when I got there. ▶秋まさにたけなわである(=最中である)We are now in the midst [most pleasant part] of fall. (！「夏の盛りに」なら in the height of summer)
たけのこ 竹の子 a bámboo shoot [×sprout] (！ sprout は bean などの芽. アクセントについては (⇨竹)).

● たけのこ御飯 bamboo shoot rice.
たけみじか 丈短 ── 丈短の 形 ● 丈短のスカート a short skirt. (図 丈長)
たけみつ 竹光 [[竹製の刀]] a bamboo sword; [[切れない刀]] a blunt sword.
たけりたつ 哮り立つ ▶ライオンがたけりたつのが聞こえた I heard lions roar and roar.
たけりたつ 猛り立つ ▶そんなつまらんことでたけりたつな Don't get worked up [work yourself up] over such a trivial matter.
たける 長ける (すぐれる) be good at; excel in; be proficient in. ● 技にたけた職人 a very skillful craftsperson; a craftsperson of great skill. ▶彼は文才にたけている (文章を書くことにすぐれている) He is an excellent writer./(才能がある) He has a talent for writing.
たける 闌ける ● 春たけて in the height of spring.
たける 哮る roar. (⇨哮り立つ)
たける 猛る rage. (⇨猛り立つ)
だけれど(も) though. (⇨けれど(も), しかし)
たけん 他見 ● 他見をはばかる書類 a secret [a confidential] document.
たげん 多元 ── 多元的な 形 pluralistic.
● 多元放送 a broadcast that links multiple locations. ● 多元論 pluralism.
たげん 多言 ▶このことは多言を要しない There is no need to dwell on it.
だけん 駄犬 a mongrel, a mutt; a cur.
たこ [医学] a callus /kǽləs/; (つま先付近の) a corn. ● 足にたこができる [できている] get [have] a callus [a corn] on one's foot. ▶耳にたこができるほどその話を聞かされた (聞くのがいやになった) I am sick and tired of hearing that story./(いやというほど聞いた) I've heard enough.
たこ 凧 a kite. ● たこを揚げる fly a kite. ▶ほら, たこが揚がっているよ Look! A kite is flying [《ふわふわと》floating].
● 凧揚げ kite-flying. (話題) 欧米では, とび・ひし形・リボンなどの形で, 冷たい東風の吹く3月がシーズン ● たこ揚げ大会 a kite-flying contest. ● 凧糸 a (kite) string.
たこ 蛸 [動物] an óctopus (複 ~es, octopi /-pài/). (事情) 米英では気味の悪い生物と考えられている) ● たこ足配線 ▶たこの足は何本ですか How many arms [×legs] does an octopus have?
たこあし 蛸足 ● たこ足配線をする put too many plugs in one [(たった一つの)a single] outlet.
たこう たこう ── 多孔性の 形 porous.
● 多孔性 porosity.
たこう 多幸 ▶ご多幸をお祈りいたします I wish you all the best [every happiness]. (！ 前の方が普通) ▶(手紙で)御多幸を祈りつつ With best wish(es)./Best wishes.
だこう 蛇行 ── 蛇行する 動 (川・道などが) wind /wáind/; meander /miǽndər/. ▶前の車, 蛇行しているよ. 酔っ払い運転じゃないか The car ahead is running in (a) zigzag [《比喩的》(道いっぱいを占めて) is all over the place]. Isn't the driver drunk?
たこく 他国 图 [外国] a foreign country (⇨外国); [同国内の] another province.
── 他国の 形 foreign.
たこく 多国 ● 多国間協定 a multilateral agreement. ● 多国間交渉 multilateral negotiations.
たこくせき 多国籍 multinational.
● 多国籍企業 a multinational corporation. ● 多国籍軍 the multinational forces.
タコス [＜スペイン語] tacos. (参考 メキシコ料理)
たこつぼ 蛸壺 an octopus pot; (1人用の壕)[軍事]

a foxhole.

たこにゅうどう 蛸入道 [[タコ] an octopus (⇨蛸); [坊主頭の人] a man with a close-cropped head.

たこはいとう 蛸配当 a bogus dividend (paid out of fictitious profits).

たこべや 蛸部屋 a labor camp.

たこやき 蛸焼き *takoyaki*; (説明的に) a small, ball-shaped pancake with diced octopus and other ingredients in the center.

たごん 他言 ▶他言は無用 (だれにも言うな) Don't tell (it to) anyone. (❗( )内の語句はしばしば省略される)/(秘密をもらすな) Don't let it out. (秘密にしておけ) Keep it (a) secret./(ここだけの話) (話) Just between us [you and me]./(話) For your ears only.

たさい 多才 ― 多才な 形 ▶多才な作家 a writer of many talents; a *versatile* [a *multi-talented*] writer.

たさい 色彩 ― 多彩な 形 ❶ [色とりどりの] colorful. ❷ [いろいろな] various /véariəs/. ▶多彩な行事 *various* events. ▶多彩な顔ぶれ all kinds of people; people from *all walks of life*.

ださい (やぼったい) unfashionable; (特に女性が) dowdy /dáudi/; (話) (叙述的に) not in. ▶ださい女 a *dowdy* woman. ▶彼はださい服を着ていた He was in [wore] *dowdy* [*dull and unfashionable*] clothes.

たさく 多作 ― 多作な 形 ▶彼は多作な作家だった He was a *productive* [a *prolific*] writer. (❗prolific はほめ言葉に)/He wrote a lot of [*numerous*] books.

ださく 駄作 a poor [a trashy] work, 《話》trash.

たさつ 他殺 (a) murder. ▶他殺死体 the body of a murder victim.

たさん 多産 名 prolificacy. ― 多産の 形 prolific.

ださん 打算 名 calculation. ― 打算的な 形 (金銭面で) mercenary; (抜け目のない) calculating; (利己的な) selfish. ▶打算的でない, 打算抜きの uncalculating.

たざんのいし 他山の石 a lesson to learn from [wisdom to gain through] other people's mistakes. ▶私たちは1986年のチェルノブイリの大惨事を他山の石とすべきである We should learn a lesson from the Chernobyl /tʃəːrnóubil/ disaster in 1986.

たし 足し ▶足しになる help; be of use. ▶足しにする (⇨不足 ❶ ②) ▶何かの足しになるかもしれない It may *be of* some *use* [*help*] (to you). ▶1切れのパンでは腹の足しにならない A piece of bread is not *enough to* satisfy my hunger. ▶そんなはした金では何の足しにもならない Such chicken feed *isn't of any help* [*isn't worth a damn*]. (❗後の方は男性語で通例否定文で用いられる)

たじ 他事 other things; other matters. ▶他事を顧みるいとまがない I have no time to pay any attention to *other things*.

たじ 多事 ▶今年は例年に比べ多事多難の年であった We have had a lot of *incidents and difficulties* particularly this year. (❗an eventful year は「興味深いことが多くあることの年」の意が普通で、ここでは不可)

だし 出し ❶ [煮出し汁] (soup) stock. ▶出しを取る make [prepare] *soup stock*.

❷ [口実] an excuse, a pretext; [手先] a tool. ▶彼を出しに使う use him *as a tool*. ▶彼が出張を出しにして観光に行ったとはけしからん It's a shame (that) he *used* the business trip *as an excuse to* go sightseeing. (❗that は省略されることが多い) ▶彼は私を出しにして(=利用して)その有力な政治家に近づいた He *used* me *to* get to know the political leader.

だし 山車 a *dashi*; (説明的に) a kind of float with a variety of colorful decorations in festival parades.

―だし ▶彼女は美人だし、聡明だし、生涯の伴侶として申し分のない人です She's a perfect partner in life for me; she's beautiful, *and* (*what's more*, *she's*) bright. (❗( )内を省略するときは and /ænd/ と強く読む)

だしあう 出し合う [[資金を]] club (-bb-) together (*to do*); [[共同出資する]] pool. ▶金を出し合ってカメラを買う *club together* [*pool* one's money] *to* buy a camera; 《話》*chip in for* [*chip in to* buy a camera. ▶その費用を出し合う(=共同負担する) *share* [《話》*go halves in*] the expenses. (❗後の方も、2人で半分ずつ出し合う場合にも3人以上の場合にも用いる)

だしいれ 出し入れ ▶このハンドバッグは小さくて物の出し入れに不便だ This handbag is too small to *put* things *in and take* them *out*. (❗語順に注意)

だしおしみ 出し惜しみ ― 出し惜しみする 動 (⇨出し惜しむ)

だしおしむ 出し惜しむ grudge. ▶寄付金を出し惜しむ *grudge* a donation; *be unwilling* [*reluctant*] *to* make a donation.

:たしか 確か ― 確かな 形 ❶ (a) [確信して] (主観的判断に基づいて) sure; (客観的事実に基づいて) certain (❗sure より堅い語); (強く確信して) positive. (⇨確信, きっと) ▶それは確かだよ I'm *sure* [*certain*, *positive*] *of* [*about*] it./That's *for sure*. (疑いの余地はない) (*There's* no *doubt about* it. (❗( )内は省略されることが多い) ▶彼がその車を盗んだのは確かだ I *am sure* [*certain*, *positive*] (*that*) he stole the car./He is *sure* [*certain*] to have stolen the car. (❗確信しているのは主語ではなく話し手であることに注意。次例も同様)/*It is certain* [×*sure*] *that* he stole the car./*Surely* [*Certainly*] he stole the car./*I have* [*There is*, 《話》*It is*] no doubt *that* he stole the car. ▶彼女のことは言えません I can't say *for sure*./(断言はできない) I'm not absolutely *sure*.

[会話] 「確かですか」「もちろん確かだ」"Are you (quite) *sure*?" "*Positively*./(I'm) ábsolutely *positive*." (❗単に *Sure*? とも聞く。応答文は相手が自分のことを疑っているようなときに強い確信を表す)

(b) [確実な] sure, certain; (明確な) positive; (確定的な) definite /défənət/. ▶その病気の確かな治療法 a *sure* [a *certain*] cure for the disease. ▶確かな事実 a *certain* [a *positive*] fact. ▶確かな証拠 *positive* [(疑う余地のない) *undoubted*] evidence. ▶確かな返事 a *definite* answer.

❷ [正確な] accurate /ǽkjərət/; (間違いのない) correct; (厳密に正確な) exact. (⇨正確) ▶数字が確かであ be *accurate at* figures. ▶確かな時間を教えてくれ Tell me the *exact* [*correct*] time.

❸ [信頼できる] reliable; (安心できる) safe; (信用できる) trustworthy. ▶確かな筋からそれを聞く hear it from a *reliable* [a *safe*] source. ▶それは確かな情報です That information is *reliable*. ▶あの医者の腕は確かだ We can trust [put trust in] the (skill of the) doctor./He is a *reliable* [a *trustworthy*] doctor. ▶あの人の射撃の腕は確かなものだ(=上手な射撃手だ) He is a *very good* [a *skillful*] shot [shooter].

❹ [堅実な] sound; (堅固な) firm. ▶確かな投資 a *sound* [a *safe*] investment. ▶(理論などが)確かな基礎の上に立っている be on (a) *firm* ground. ▶彼は気は確か(=正気)かしら I wonder if he is *in* his

たしかめる

—— 確か(に) ● 〖確実に〗 surely, certainly, for sure 〖certain〗 (⇨きっと); 〖疑いなく〗 undoubtedly, without (a) doubt (⇨疑いなく); 〖本当に〗 indeed, truly (⇨本当 ③); 〖記憶では〗 as I remember; (記憶が正しければ) if I remember right(ly).

① 〈確かに…だ〔する〕〉 ▶確かに彼に以前会ったことがある Surely 〖Certainly〗 I have met him somewhere before./(自覚している) I know 〖断言してもいい〗 I could swear〗 I have met him somewhere before. ▶彼は確かに幸せそうだ He surely 〖〖話〗 sure〗 seems happy. (❗certainly は surely より客観的なのでこの文脈で用いるのは不自然 (⇨[次例])) ▶それは確かに彼のカメラだ That is certainly 〖undoubtedly〗 his camera. ▶確かに彼を招待したんだよね You did invite him, didn't you? (❗did は動詞を強調する) ▶原稿確かに受け取りました I surely received your manuscripts.

② 〈確かに…だが〉 ▶確かに彼は若いが分別はある It is true 〖Indeed〗 he is young, but he is wise./(話) He's young, all ／ right, but he ＼is wise. (⇨なるほど)

会話 「このパレードは本当にすごいよ」「確かに面白いけど」 "This parade has to be the wildest ever!" "I must admit it is fun." (❗消極的な容認を示す)

③ 〈(自信はないが)確か〉 ▶彼には確か娘が3人いる He has, I ／ believe, three daughters./He has three daughters, I ＼believe. ▶確か(=私の記憶では)以前はたばこをお吸いでしたね You used to smoke as I remember. ▶確か(=私の記憶が正しければ)彼はその会に出席していた If I remember right [rightly, correctly], he was present at the meeting.

たしかめる 確かめる 〖調べる〗 see; 〖念のために〗 make* sure 〖of; that 節〗; 〖照合や検査により〗 check; 〖真偽を〗 confirm. ▶自分の目で確かめる(see〗 (it) with one's own eyes. ▶単語のつづりを辞書で確かめる check the spelling of a word in a dictionary. ▶彼がもう到着したかどうか確かめてくれますか Will you see 〖check〗 whether he has arrived yet? (❗whether の代わりに if も可) ▶電話をして彼があす来ることを確かめておこう I'll phone and make sure 〖that〗 he comes tomorrow. (❗that 節中はまれに現在時制で)

会話 「そこには入れないよ」「そうかい? 確かめてみよう」 "You can't go in there." "Can't I? We'll see about that."

会話 「彼はすでに知っているよ」「彼に確かめたの?」 "He already knows." "Did you confirm 〖check〗 it with him?"

だしがら 出し殻 (コーヒーの) coffee grounds; (茶の) used tea leaves; (煮出し汁の) the leavings from making soup stock.

タジキスタン 〖国名〗 Tajikistan, Tadzhikistan; (公式名) the Republic of Tajikistan. (首都 Dushanbe) ●タジキスタン人 a Tajik. ●タジキスタン語 Tajik. ●タジキスタン(人〖語〗)の Tajik.

タシケント 〖ウズベキスタンの首都〗 Tashkent /tæʃként/.

だしこんぶ 出し昆布 dashikombu; (説明的に) (dried) kelp [sea tangle] used for soup stock.

たしざん 足し算 addition (↔subtraction). ●足し算をするώ. (⇨足す)

だしじゃこ 出し雑魚 dashijako; (説明的に) small, boiled and dried sardines.

だしじる 出し汁

たしせいせい 多士済々 a large number of talented people. ●多士済々たる知識人 a galaxy of intellectuals.

だじゃれ

たじたじ ●たじたじする〖させる〗 stagger. ●たじたじと後ろへ下がる stagger backward. ▶敗北のニュースに将軍はたじたじとなった The general was staggered to hear the news of defeat. ▶彼は彼女の強い態度にたじたじとなった(=戸惑った) He was confused 〖(圧倒された)〗 overwhelmed〗 by her strong attitude.

たしつ 多湿 high humidity. ▶夏の間はしばしば高温多湿になるので薄手の服が必要となります During the summer, the weather is often hot and humid and requires lightweight clothing.

たじつ 他日 (いつか) someday; (また別の日〖時〗に) some other day 〖time〗, another day. (⇨いつか)

だしっぱなし 出しっ放し ▶水を出しっ放しにしておく Don't leave the water 〖水道の〗 tap〗 running.

だしなげ 出し投げ 〖相撲〗 dashinage; a forward throw.

たしなみ 嗜み 〖趣味〗(嗜好(ミュウ)) (a) taste 〖for〗; (心得) knowledge (⇨心得); 〖礼儀〗(慎み) modesty; (言動のまとまり) decency. ●たしなみのある modest (↔immodest); decent (↔indecent). ●音楽のたしなみ taste in music. ▶彼女には(女性としての)たしなみがない She lacks modesty 〖decency〗.

たしなむ 嗜む ●酒をたしなむ (飲みものが好き) like to drink; (付き合い程度に飲む) drink just to be sociable. ▶彼は俳句をたしなんでいる He likes to compose haiku poems./He has a taste for haiku poetry.

たしなめる (いましめる) 〖書〗 reprove 〈人+for+事〉; (つつしませる) advise 〈him not to do〉.

だしぬく 出し抜く outwit (-tt-); steal* a march 〈on him〉. ▶警察を出し抜いて逃げる outwit the police and escape.

だしぬけ 出し抜け ——出し抜けに 圖 (唐突に) abruptly; (急に) suddenly; (思いがけなく) unexpectedly. (⇨不意に)

だしもの 出し物 (プログラム) a program fare. ●いつもの出し物 the usual fare. (❗食べ物, 番組などについて用いる) ▶国立劇場の今日の出し物は何ですか What's on 〖the program〗 at the National Theater today? (❗前の方が普通. on は「上演されて」の意)

たしゃ 他社 another company (愈 other companies).

たしゃ 他者 another person (愈 other people).

たしゃ 多謝 ❶〖感謝〗 many 〖a thousand〗 thanks. ▶ご厚情多謝 Thanks a lot for your kindness. ❷〖おわび〗 ▶妄言多謝 Please forgive my unreasonable statement.

だしゃ 打者 〖野球〗 a batter, a hitter. (❗ batter は打席に立っている打者をさすことが多く, 「ホームラン打者」「強打者」などという場合は hitter が普通. ⇨バッター) ●強打者 a power hitter; a slugger. ●代打(者) a pinch hitter (⇨ピンチ〖ピンチヒッター〗). ●右〖左〗打者 a right-[a left-]handed batter. ●首位打者 (シーズン途中, または1チーム内の) a leading hitter; (シーズンを通じた) a batting champion 〖king〗 (⇨打撃〖打撃王〗). ●指名打者 a designated hitter 《略 DH》. ●先頭打者 a leadoff man 〖batter〗. ●3割打者 a .300 hitter. (❗ a three hundred hitter と読む) ●初球〖悪球〗打ちの打者 a first-ball [a bad-ball] hitter. ●広角(に打つ)打者 a spray hitter. ▶タイガースは初回に打者一巡した The Tigers batted around in the first inning.

だじゃく 惰弱 ——惰弱な 厖 effeminate 《voices》; effete 《young men》.

だじゃれ 駄洒落 (ごろ合わせ) a pun; (へたな冗談) a bad [a poor] joke. (⇨洒落(ﾒｬ)) ▶彼はだじゃればかり言っている He's always telling poor jokes and

だしゅ 舵手 a helmsman (複 -men), a steersman (複 -men); (ボートの) a coxwain /kάksn, kάkswèin/, a cox.

だじゅう 多重 ── **多重の** 形 multiple. ●音声多重放送 (sound) *multiplex* broadcasting; (放送番組) a (sound) *multiplex* broadcast. ●文字多重放送 (a) télètèxt. (❗(1) television text broadcast(ing) の略. (2) 番組を出す場合は ⓒ)
● **多重衝突** a mass collision; (話)a pileup.

たしゅたよう 多種多様 ── **多種多様な** 形 ●多種多様な話題 *many different kinds of* topics; *various* (*kinds of*) topics; *a wide variety of* topics. (❗ of の後は集合名詞も可) ▶この問題についての意見は多種多様である There is *a diversity of* opinion on the issue. (❗通例 diversity も opinion も単数形で用いる)

たしゅみ 多趣味 ●多趣味な人 a person of *wide* [*varied*] *interests*. ▶あの人は多趣味だ He has *lots of hobbies*.

だじゅん 打順 the batting order; the lineup. ●打順4番 the fourth position [place, spot] in *the batting order*; the cleanup. ▶打順を少しじる make a few changes in the *batting order*. ▶打順が回ってくる get one's turn at bat. ●新庄の後ろの打順になる hit behind [after] Shinjo. ▶打順は何番ですか Where [When] does he bat (in the *order*)? / What number hitter is he? ▶ジョーンズは打順が7番に下がった Jones dropped to seventh in the *batting order*.

たしょ 他所 another place (複 other places).
たしょ 他書 another book (複 other books).

***たしょう** 多少 图 〖数の〗the number; 〖量の〗the quantity; 〖金額などの〗the amount. ▶費用[数]の多少は問題でない The cost [number] doesn't matter. ▶金額の多少にかかわらず当銀行に預金してください Please deposit your money in our bank regardless of its *amount*. ▶多少にかかわらずご寄付願います Your contribution, *large or small*, will be gladly accepted./ *Any amount* of contribution will be gratefully accepted.

── **多少の** 形 〖数が〗a few, some; 〖量が〗a little, some. (⇨少し❶) ▶彼には多少の友人がいる He has *a few* [*some*] friends. ▶私は多少の英語は話せる I can speak *a little* [*some*] English./ I can speak English *a little*.

── **多少(は)** 副 (少し) a little, 《話》a (little) bit; (いくぶん) (やや書) somewhat (⇨少し❷); (かなり) rather, 《話》pretty (⇨かなり). ▶今日は多少気分がよい I'm feeling *a little* [*a little bit*] better today./ I'm feeling *rather* [xpretty] better today. (❗pretty は比較級を修飾しない) ▶彼は多少当惑したようだった He looked *somewhat* [《話》*kind of*] puzzled./ He looked *rather* [*pretty*] puzzled.

たしょう 他生 〖前世〗one's previous life [existence]; 〖来世〗the next life [world].
● **他生の縁** the karma from one's previous life.
たしょう 他称 (第三人称) 〖文法〗the third person.
たじょう 多情 〖感情が豊かな〗passionate; (感じやすい) sensitive; 〖移り気な〗fickle.
● **多情多恨** ●芸術家とは本来多情多恨である Artists are so *sensitive* by nature that they are liable to hold a lot of worries and grudges.
● **多情仏心** ●多情仏心の人 a fickle but very warm-hearted person.

だじょうかん 太政官 〖歴史〗the Cabinet (in the Meiji era).
だじょうだいじん 太政大臣 〖歴史〗the Prime Minister (in the Meiji era).
たしょく 多色 〖in〗many colors. ●多色刷り multicolor(ed) printing. ●多色刷りのマンガ本 a *multicolored* comic book.
たしょくしょう 多食症 〖医学〗bulimia.
たじろぐ (しりごみする) flinch 〔*from*〕, recoil 〔*from*〕. ●激しい抵抗にたじろぐ *flinch from* (a) strong resistance.
だしん 打診 ── **打診する** 動 (意向を探る) sound [《米話》feel] 《him》out 《*about, on*》; 〖医学〗examine ... by percussion.
たしんきょう 多神教 polytheism.

たす 足す ❶〖加える〗add. (⇨加える❶) ●スープにもう少し水を足す *add* some water *to* the soup. ●不足分を足す(=埋め合わせる) *make up for* the deficit. ▶4足す5は9 Four *and* five make(s) [is, are] nine. (▶くだけた言い方) / Four *plus* five equals [is] nine. (❗正式な言い方) / *Add* four *and* five, and you have nine.
❷〖済ます〗●用を足す (⇨用[成句])

だす 出す
INDEX

❶ 外に出す	❷ 取り出す
❸ 見せる	❹ 送る
❺ 選出させる	❻ 提供する
❼ 発表する	❽ 展示する
❾ 提出する	❿ 発する
⓫ 発揮する	⓬ 開始する
⓭ 応答させる	

❶〖外に出す〗put*... out; (突き出す) stick*... out; (手などを前に出す) hold*... out. ●舌を出す *put* [*stick*] *out* one's tongue. ▶ゴミを出すのを忘れないでね Don't forget to *put out* the garbage. ▶草木が新芽を出した The plants *put out* [《書》*forth*] early shoots. ▶窓から顔を出すな Don't *put* [*stick*] *your* head [xface] *out of* the window. (身を乗り出すな) Don't *lean out of* the window. ▶彼は私に手を差し出した He *held out* [*offered*] his hand *to* me. (動作 握手を求めるときの動作)
❷〖取り出す〗take*... out; (しまっている所から) get*... out; (解き放す) let*《him》out. ●水道[ガス]を出す *turn on* the water [gas]. ▶彼はピストルを引き出しから出した He *took out* a pistol *from* the drawer. (❗drawers とすれば〖たんす〗の意) / He *took* a pistol *out of* the drawer. ▶車を出してドライブに行こうよ Let's *get* the car *out* and go for a drive. ▶彼は鳥をかごから出してやった He *let out* the birds *from* the cage. / He let the birds *out of* the cage. ▶私をここから出してくれ Let [*Get*] me *out of* here.
❸〖見せる〗show*; (露出する) bare; (暴露する) expose. ●肩を出す *show* one's shoulders. ●感情をすぐ出す *show* one's feelings easily. ▶彼女はパーティーに顔を出した She *showed* herself [*appeared, turned up*] at the party. ▶彼はついにぼろを出した He *exposed* his shortcomings at last. ▶その子供はお腹を出して寝ていた The child was sleeping with his belly *uncovered*.
❹〖送る〗send*; (手紙などを) 《主に米》mail, 《英》post; (信号などを) give*. ●小包を郵便で出す *send* a parcel by mail. ●コートをクリーニングに出す *send* one's coat to the laundry. ▶私は彼に手紙を出した I *sent* him a letter [*sent* a letter *to* him]./ I *mailed* a letter to him. / (書いた) I *wrote* (a letter) *to* him. (❗a letter は通例省略する) ▶学校へ行くく

中の手紙を忘れずに出してください Remember to mail [post] this letter for me on your way to school. ▶彼らに出発の合図を出した I gave them a signal for departure.
❺【選ぶ】elect; (候補者に指名する) put*... up; (生み出す) produce, turn ... out (❗後の方が口語的). ●代議員の中から議長を出す elect a chair [a chairperson] from among the representatives. ▶私たちは彼を市長候補として出した We put him up as mayor. ▶この大学は多くのすぐれた学者を出した This university has produced [turned out] a lot of great scholars./(この大学の卒業生である) A large number of great scholars are graduates from this university. ▶この学校は毎年約500人の卒業生を送り出す This school graduates about 500 students every year.
❻【提供する】(与える) give*; (支払う) pay*; (供給する) supply, provide; (飲食物を) serve. ●彼に資金を出す supply him with the funds; supply the funds for [to] him. ●新しい事業に金を出す(=投資する) invest one's money in a new business [enterprise]. ●臨時列車を出す(=運行させる) run a special train. ●先生は宿題をたくさん出した Our teacher gave (us) a lot of homework [×homeworks]. ▶彼女はその絵に1万円出した She paid [gave] ten thousand yen for that painting. ▶彼女は私たちにビールを出してくれた She served us beer./She served beer to us.
❼【発表する】 announce; (公にする) make*... public; (話に出す) mention; (発令する) issue; (出版する) publish, bring* [put*] ... out (❗後の方が口語的). ●いくつかの命令を出す issue several orders. ●声明(文)を出す issue a statement. ●その本の改訂版を出す publish [bring out] a revised edition of the book. ●レコードを出す(=発売する) release a CD. ▶彼の死亡通知を数人の友人だけに出した We have announced his death to some friends only. ●お名前を出してもかまいませんか May I mention your name?/May I make your name public? ●この雑誌は毎週出されている This magazine is issued [published] weekly.
❽【展示する】exhibit /iɡzíbit/, display; (掲示する) put*... up; (載せる) put, place. ●新聞に求人広告を出す put [place] a want ad in the paper. ▶彼女は草花品評会にバラを出した She exhibited [displayed] some roses at a flower show. ▶店の前に看板を出した They put up a signboard in front of the store.
❾【提出する】(上位の者に) submit (-tt-); (手渡す) hand ... in; (送付する) send*... in; (書類などを添えて, present /prizént/ (❗公式に出すことをいう), (主に米) turn ... in. ●大学に入学願書を出す send in one's application for admission to a college. ●すばらしい案を出す(=提案する) come up with a good plan; propose [put forward, bring forward] a good plan. ▶このほかに今日の会議に出す議題はない There is nothing else [no other agenda] to be submitted to [to be brought up for] today's conference. ▶宿題は月曜日に出しなさい Hand [Turn] in your homework on Monday. ▶太郎, そこに何を持っているのかな. さあ, 出しなさい Taro, let's see what you've got in there. Come on, fork it out. (❗fork out は「(金など)をしぶしぶ出す」の意の口語表現)
❿【発する】(声などを) give*, (書) utter; (音などを) make*; (におい・煙などを) give ... off, (書) emit (-tt-); (病気で熱を出す) run*. ●大声を出す give [utter] a loud cry. ●声を出して本を読む read a book aloud [×loudly]. (❗loudly は「大きな声で」の意). ●ひどい音を出す make [×give] a terrible noise. ●微熱を出す[出している] run [have] a slight fever. ▶その腐った卵はひどい悪臭を出していた The rotten egg was giving off [emitting] a terrible smell.
⓫【発揮する】▶彼は政治で十分実力を出した He showed his ability fully in the political world./He did himself justice in politics. ▶彼は全力を出して戸を押し開けた Putting out [(使って) Using] all his strength, he pushed the door open./He pushed the door open with all his strength [might]. ▶元気を出せ Cheer up!/Take heart! ▶私は時速80マイルのスピードを出していた I was doing [making] 80 miles per hour.
⓬【開始する】▶彼は渋谷に店を出した(=開店した) He opened a store on [《英》in] Shibuya. ▶その銀行は大阪に支店を出している The bank has a branch (office) in Osaka. ▶雨が降り出した It began [started] to rain.
⓭【応対させる】▶ちょっと待って, 恵美子を電話口に出すからね Hold on. I'll put Emiko on (the phone). (❗hold on は「電話を切らないでおく」の意) ●責任者を出してください Let me meet the person in charge, please!

*たすう 多数 〘多くのもの・人〙 many (❗複数扱い); 〘大多数〙 the [a] majority (❗単数形で); 〘過半数〙 a [the] majority. (⇨大多数, 大部分)
① 〖~多数, 多数~〗 ●絶対多数 the overall majority. ●安定多数 the comfortable majority. ●多数決の原理 majority rule. ●150対20の圧倒的[絶対的]多数で勝つ win by an overwhelming [an absolute] majority of 150 to 20. ▶民主党が多数党である The Democratic Party is the majority [a majority party].
② 〖多数の〗 ●国会で3分の2の多数を占める have [hold] a two-thirds majority in the Diet. ▶その会合では若者が多数を占めた Young people were in [a] majority at the meeting.
── 多数の 形 a lot of, many; (やや書) a large [a great] number of. (⇨たくさん) ▶多数の学生がアルバイトをしている A lot of [(たいていの) Most] students have part-time jobs. (❗many [most] of the students との比較 ⇨多く)
●多数意見 a majority opinion. ●多数派 the majority.
だすう 打数 〘野球〙 an at(-)bat 《略 a.b.》(❗厳密には an official at bat); 〘ゴルフ〙 a stroke. ●4打数3安打である go 3 for 4. ▶彼は333打数100安打で3割を打った He hit .300, with 100 hits in 333 at-bats.
たすうけつ 多数決 ●多数決で決める decide by majority [a majority vote]. ●多数決に従う accept a majority decision.
*たすかる 助かる ❶【救助される】be saved; (切迫した危険から) be rescued; 〘生き残る〙survive; 〘回復する〙recover. ▶その航空機事故で助かったのは彼だけです Only he was saved [was rescued] from the plane accident./Only he survived [He was the only survivor of] the plane accident [crash]. ▶手術で彼女の命は助かった The operation saved [×rescued] her life. (⇨助ける) ❷ ▶その病人は助からないだろう The patient will not recover (from his illness). (❗「助かる見込みのない人」を《話》a goner という) ▶もう助からないと(命を)あきらめた I gave up all hopes of life.
会話 「あっ, 船が来るぞ」「わあ, 助かった」 "Look! Here comes a ╱boat." "Thank God." (❗苦難・

危険などからの解放感を表す)
❷【助けになる】be helpful [useful]《to》, be (of) help《to》; [労力などが省ける] save, be saved. ▶ 彼のおかげでとても助かった He was very *helpful* [a great *help*, 《書》of great *help*] to me./He *saved* me a lot of trouble. (❗(1) a help は「助けになる人・物」. 後の great help は「大きな助け」の意の抽象名詞で, a lot of help ともいえるが肯定文なので ×of much help は不可. (⇨助け) (2)「君がそれをやってくれて助かった」は It's *helpful* of [×for] you [You are *helpful* to] do it. ×It's helpful that you do it は不可) ▶ それで大いに費用が助かった That *saved* me a lot of money. ▶ 本当に助かりました You've been 《a》great *help*.

たすき 襷 *tasuki*, (説明的に) a kind of sash used to hold up tucked *kimono* sleeves; (選挙の候補者の使う) a white sash worn diagonally across the shoulder. ● たすきがけで with one's *kimono* sleeves tucked up.

タスク [作業課題]《やや書》a task.
● タスクフォース [特別作業班] a task force.

*たすけ 助け [助力] help; (公的援助) 《書》aid; (補佐)《やや書》assistance; [救助] rescue; [救援, 救助] relief; [支援] support. ● 助けを求める ask for *help*; (大声で) cry [call] (out) for *help*. ● 助け船を出す (⇨助け船) ▶ 私には君の助けが必要だ I need your *help* [*aid*, *assistance*, *support*]. ▶ 私はそれをだれの助けも借りないでやった I did it without 《any》 *help*. ▶ 彼はちっとも助けにならない He is (of) no *help* [*assistance*] to me./He isn't *helpful* to me at all. (❗「あまり助けにならない」は He isn't much help [very helpful] to me.) ▶ よい辞書は言葉を勉強する上で大きな助けになる Good dictionaries are a great *help* in a study of languages. (❗ help は「助けになる物・人」の意. 主語が複数であっても ×helps とはしない) ▶ 辞典の助けを借りずにその本を読んだ I read the book *without the help* [《恩恵》 *benefit*] of a dictionary.

たすけあい 助け合い mutual help; (共通の目的達成のための協力) cooperation. ● 歳末助け合い運動 a year-end charity drive.

たすけあう 助け合う (2人で) help each other [(3人以上で) one another]. (⇨互い解説) ▶ 人はだれでも助け合いたいと望んでいるものです We all want to *help one another*.

たすけあげる 助け上げる (救助する) rescue《from, out of》; pick《him》up《from, out of》. ● ヘリコプターで助け上げられる be picked up [rescued] by a helicopter.

たすけだす 助け出す (救助する) save; (差し迫った危険から) rescue. ▶ 消防士は彼を火事から助け出した The firefighter *saved* [*rescued*] him *from* the fire./The firefighter *helped* him *out of* [×from] the fire.

たすけぶね 助け船 ● 助け船を出す help《him》out; give《him》assistance [a helping hand]; (ヒントを出す) drop a hint; give《him》a hint.

*たすける 助ける ❶【助力する】help《A to do; A with B》;《書》aid, assist; [救援・救済する]《書》relieve; [支援する] support.

使い分け	help	「助ける」の意の最も一般的で強い語.
	aid	通例団体などに対して「公的な金銭的援助をする」の意.
	assist	「補助的な仕事をする」の意.

● 助け起こす *help*《him》《to》get up (❗ to の省略については (⇨手伝う)); *help*《him》to his feet. ● アフリカ諸国を助ける (=援助する) aid [give aid to] African nations. ● 貧しい(洪水の被災者)を助ける (=救援する) relieve [give relief to] the poor [the flood victims]. ● 消化を助ける help [promote] digestion. ▶ 彼は市長を助けて市政を再建した He *assisted* the mayor in reestablish*ing* [*in* the reestablishment of,《まれ》*to* reestablish] the city government. ▶ あなたには家事を [子育てでは] ずいぶん助けてもらいました I've got a lot of *help from* you *with* the housework [*in* bringing up my children]./You've *helped* me a lot *with* the housework [*to* bring up my children].
❷【救助する】save; (差し迫った危険から) rescue; (手助けする) help (❗この意では ×assist, ×aid は不可); [助命する] spare. (⇨救う) ● 彼の命を助ける (医者などが) save; (命を, ×help) his life [*rescue*, help の目的語は人]; (殺さない) spare him [his life]. ● 彼[船員]を助けに行く go to his *rescue* [the *rescue* of the sailors]. ▶ 助けてくれ (危険, 窮状に直面して) *Help*! [×Aid, ×Assist] [me]!/(強盗などに命乞いして) *Save* me!

たずさえる 携える [持ち歩く] carry《it》《with one》; [連れる]《やや書》be accompanied《by him》. ● 上等のワイン[秘書]を携えて彼のところへ行く go and see him *with* a fine bottle of wine [one's secretary]. ▶ 彼らは手を携えて(=一緒に)ヨーロッパへ出発した They started for Europe *together*.

*たずさわる 携わる [従事する] engage, be engaged《in》. ● 教育に携わる engage [be engaged] in education. ● その辞書の仕事に携わっている be engaged in compiling the dictionary; be engaged [at work] on the dictionary. (❗特別の分野をさす場合は on を用いる) ▶ 彼は広告業に携わっている He *is* [*works*] *in* advertising.

ダスター [ダスターコート]《米》a duster,《英》a dustcoat; [和製語] duster coat; [ぞうきん, はたき] a duster, a dustcloth.

ダストシュート [落下式ごみ収集装置]《米》a garbage [a trash] chute,《英》a rubbish chute.

たずねあてる 尋ね当てる (見つける) find ... out; (人の居所を) locate.

たずねびと 尋ね人 [行方不明者] a missing person, (集合的で) the missing; [新聞の個人消息欄] a personal column,《米》the personals (❗前の方は一般的の広告をさせるが, 後の方は a personal ad ともいい, 友人・恋人募集の個人消息のみを扱う; [英語] an agony column (❗人生相談を含む).

たずねる 訪ねる visit (❗長期の訪問にも用いる最も一般的な語); (特定の目的で) pay a visit《to》(❗ visit より堅い言い方); (職務・儀礼で) call《on+人, at+場所》(❗ちょっと立ち寄ること. 《主に英》で《米》では《やや古》); (親しい人をぶらりと) come* over《to》; (予告なしにひょっこりと) drop (-pp-) in [by]《on+人, at+場所》; (遊びに行く) come* [go*] to see (❗訪問先が話し手または聞き手の場合は come を, 第三者ならば go を用いる); (捜し当てて) look《him》up. ● おばが今日訪ねてくる My aunt is coming to *visit* today. ▶ 訪ねてくださったとき留守にしていてごめんなさい Sorry I was out when you *visited* me.
①【(人)を訪ねる】▶ 我々はきのう高橋氏を訪ねた We *visited* Mr. Takahashi yesterday./We *paid* [*made*] a *visit to* Mr. Takahashi yesterday./《主に英》We *called on* Mr. Takahashi [*at* Mr. Takahashi's house] yesterday. ▶ 彼がゆうべ僕をひょっこり訪ねて来た He *dropped in on* me last night. (⇨② [第 2 文例])
②【(場所)を訪ねる】▶ いつか当地においでになったら, お訪ねください Come and see me [Come over to my

house, *Look* me *up* if you're ever here. (❗come and see は come to see より口語的的. 《米話》では come see ということもある. ただし, come (and) see の型は come が原形のときに限られる: He *came to* [×and] *see* me.) ▶彼が大きい木の家をひょっこり訪ねて来た He *dropped in at* my house last night. (⇨①〔第2文例〕)

③【(人)を(場所)に訪ねる】 ●田中氏を会社に訪ねる *visit* Mr. Tanaka *at* the office.

:**たずねる 尋ねる** ❶【質問する】 *ask*,《やや書》*inquire*; (一連の質問を) *question*. ●案内所で尋ねる *ask* [*inquire*] *at* the information desk.

① 【(人)に尋ねる】 ▶判事は証人に尋ねた The judge *asked* [*inquired of*, *questioned*] the witness.

② 【(物・事)を尋ねる】 ▶彼らは私の名前を尋ねた They *asked* [*inquired*, *wanted to know*] my name [what my name was]. (❗*wanted to know* が最も普通) ●彼女は私たちの健康(のこと)を尋ねた(=私たちに元気かと尋ねた) She *asked* [*inquired*] *about* our health./She *asked* [*inquired*] *after* us [our health]. (❗×She *asked* [*inquired*] our health. とはいえない. She *asked about us*. は健康も含めて近況を尋ねること)

③ 【(人)に(物・事)を尋ねる】 ●彼女に私の旧友の消息を尋ねる *ask* her where an old friend of mine is. ●彼に脱線事故の様子を尋ねる *ask* him how the derailment occurred. ▶私は彼に時間を尋ねた I *asked* him the time. (❗*ask* A B の型は通例 B が question, way, reason, name, time や wh-節・句のときに限られ, それ以外は ask A about B の型を用いる)/I *inquired* [×*asked*] the time *of* him. (❗*ask* A *of* B の型は A が「質問」に類する語に限られる (⇨質問する))/I *asked* him *for* the time. (❗「彼に時間を教えてほしいと頼む」の意で丁寧な尋ね方)/I *asked* [*inquired of*] him what time it was. ▶先生に試験の結果を恐る恐る尋ねた I nervously *asked* my teacher *about* my exam results.

④ 【(人)に…について尋ねる】 ●彼女にその件について尋ねる *ask* [*inquire of*, *question*] her *about* the matter. ●彼に研究結果の詳細について尋ねる *ask* him *about* the details of the research results. ▶主治医に彼の病状についてそっと尋ねた I secretly *asked* his doctor *about* his condition.

⑤ 【((人)に)…かと尋ねる】 ▶支配人はいないかと尋ねた I *asked* for the manager. ▶彼女は私に部屋の掃除をしたかと尋ねた She *asked* me [*inquired of* me, ×*asked* me] *if* I had cleaned my room./She *asked* [*said to*] me, "Have you cleaned your room?" (❗*inquire* の場合は, "Have you cleaned your room?" she *inquired*. のように, 通例 of me はつけずに文尾に置く)

❷ 【捜し求める】*search* (*for*). (⇨捜す) ●幻の魚を尋ねてアマゾン川をさかのぼる *go up* the Amazon *in search of* a fancy fish.

タスマニア [オーストラリアの島・州] Tasmania /tæz-méiniə/(略 Tas(m).).

だする 堕する ●現実離れした考えに堕する *laspe into* a daydream.

たせい 多勢 ●**多勢に無勢**(まず勝目のない闘いである) It is fighting against heavy [all the] odds. (❗odds は「優劣の差」)

だせい 惰性 [習慣] (a) habit (⇨習慣); [慣性] inertia (⇨惰力). ●惰性でコーヒーを飲む drink coffee *out of* [*from*, *by*] (*force of*) *habit*.

だせいせっき 打製石器 [考古学] a chipped [flaked] stone tool. (関連▶ 磨製石器 a ground stone tool)

だせき 打席 ●打席につく be *at* [come (up) to] *bat*; step (up) to the plate. ●4回の打席で2安打する get two hits in four times *at bat*. ●規定打席数 the required number of plate appearances. ▶彼は2打席目にホームランを打った He hit a home run in his second *at bat*.

たせん 他薦 recommendation. ●他薦による候補者 a candidate *recommended by others*.

たせん 多選 ●多選知事[市長] a governor [a mayor] *elected many times*.

だせん 打線 the batting lineup [order]. ●強力打線 a powerful *batting lineup*. ●上位[下位]打線 the top [bottom] of the *batting order*. ●打線を少し組み変える make a few changes in the *batting lineup*.

たそう 多層 ●**多層建築** a multistory building. ●**多層フィルム** A multilayer film.

-たそう ▶彼女はパリに行きたそうだった She *looked as if* she *wanted to* visit Paris./She *acted as if* she *was anxious to* go to Paris.

たそがれ 黄昏 twilight; (暗くなる直前のころ)《やや書》dusk. (⇨日暮れ) ●たそがれ時に at *dusk* [*twilight*]; in the *twilight*; on a dusky evening. ●人生のたそがれ時 one's *twilight* years. ▶たそがれが迫ってきた The evening *twilight* came (on)./*Dusk* fell.

だそく 蛇足 ●蛇足ながら(こう言うのは余計なことだが) although it is superfluous to say so, ….

たそくるい 多足類 [動物] a myriapod.

ただ 多い many; a great many.
●**多々ますます弁ず** The more, the better.

*****ただ 只 — ただの** 形 ❶ [普通の] ordinary (↔extraordinary); (普通によく見られる) common; (通例の) usual (↔unusual). ▶あれはただの女ではない She is no *ordinary* woman./She isn't *just any* woman. ▶ただの風邪だ It's a *common* cold. ●ただならぬことが彼に起きた Something *unusual* [深刻な] *serious*] has happened to him.

❷ [無料の] free. ●ただの切符 a *free* ticket. ▶子供の入場料はただです Admission for children is *free*./There is no admission *charge* for children./《やや書》Children are admitted *free*. ●このシャツはただみたいな値で買った I bought this shirt *for practically nothing* [《話》*dirt cheap*, 《話》*for a song*, 《話》*at a giveaway price*].

❸ [その他の表現] ▶ぼくに口答えをしたらただでは済まないよ(=思い知らせてやる)《話》I'll *teach* you *to* talk back to me. (❗通例未来形で) ▶あいつはただじゃおかない, 私をうそつき呼ばわりしたんだ He *can't get away with* this. He's calling me a liar. (❗*get away with …* は《話》, 「(軽い罰で)済ませる」の意)
●**ただより高いものはない**《ことわざ》(何でもただでは手に入らない) We can't get something for nothing.; (骨折りなしして利得なし) No pains, no gains.

— ただで 副 [無料で] free, free of charge, for nothing.

*****ただ 唯 ❶ [単に] (ただ…だけ) only, merely; (単純にただ) simply; (ほんのただ) just.

使い分け only
only 書き言葉では通例修飾する語(句)の前に置くが, 話し言葉では動詞の直前に置かれるのが普通で, 強調したい部分は強勢で示す. **merely** only のやや堅い語で, 通例修飾する語(句)の前に置く. **simply** only, merely と同意だが「(他の要素を交えず)単に」の意. **just** 「ほんのただ」という軽い意味で, 会話でよく用いられる.

●町でただ一つのホテル the *only* hotel in the town. ▶ただ彼にだけはその話をした I told the story *only to* him. (... to hím only. の語順も可)/《話》I ónly told the story to ˎhim. (書き言葉では音調が出ないので，通例「ただその話をしただけで他のことはいっていない」の意になる)/He is the *only* person I told the story (to). (the *only* は形容詞)/▶そんな薬を飲めばただ病気になるだけだ Such medicine will *only* [*merely*] make you sick. ▶ただ意見が合わないというだけで彼は従業員を解雇した He dismissed his employees *just* [*simply*, *only*, *merely*] because he disagreed with them. ▶ただ犬を見ただけで彼はこわがる *Just* the sight [The *mere* sight] of a dog makes him afraid [scared]. ▶そんなところにただつっ立ってないで手伝って Don't *just* stand there. Help me.

会話「毎日あの丘に登って何をしているのですか」「ただ散歩しているだけだよ。歩くのが好きなんでね」"What do you do up in the hills every day?" "(I) *just* walk. I like to walk."

❷【ひたすら】(...しさえすればよい) have* only to (*do*)(文脈によっては *only* have to *do* となることもある); (...ばかりする) do* nothing but (*do*). ▶君はただ一生懸命勉強しさえすればよい You *only* [*just*] *have to* study hard. (!you have only to... の強調形。次例に近い意味になる)/All you have to do is (to) study hard. (!to はしばしば省略される) ▶彼女はただ泣いてばかりいる She *does nothing but* cry./She *just* [*only*] cries. (⇨しか [第 4 文例])

── ただの 形【単なる】mere; [ただ一つ [1 人] の] single. ▶それはただの偶然にすぎなかった That was *only* [*just*, *merely*] a coincidence./It was a *mere* coincidence. ▶今ポケットにはただの 1 円も入ってない I don't have a *single* penny in my pocket. ▶私はただの一度も参内したことがない I've never *ever* been to (xa) court. (!never を強調する言い方)

── ただ 接 (だがしかし) but, 《話》only. ▶行きたいんだが，ただお金がない I want to go, *but* [*only*] I don't have enough money. (!but の方が強意的)

だだ 駄々 ▶だだをこねる (むずかる) be fretful; (わがままを通そうとする) try to have [get] one's own way; (聞き分けがない) be unreasonable.

ただい 多大 ──多大の[な]形 (量・程度の大きな) great; (重大な) serious. ▶多大の労力を要する require *a great deal of* labor. ▶あらしが作物に多大な損害を与えた The storm did *great* [*serious*, *a lot of*] damage to the crops. ▶それは我が国に多大の利益をもたらすだろう It will *greatly* benefit our country.

ただい 堕胎 (an) abortion. (⇨中絶)

*ただいま 1 間 Hi, Hello; I'm home [back] (now)! 事情 米英では帰宅時に日本語のような決まり文句はない。例えば，新婚夫婦なら I missed you! ということもある)

会話「ただいま，お母さん」「まあ，お帰り。楽しかった？」"Hi, Mom. I'm ˇhome." "Hi, dear. Did you have a good time?"

── ただ今 副 (⇨今) ❶【現在】(目下) now; (将来はともかく今は) at present. ▶ただ今パリに滞在中です I'm [*now* 《主に米》*presently*] staying in Paris. (!「今」は特に副詞で示されにことあもる)

❷【少し前】just (!通例文中で完了形とともに用いる); just now (!通例文末で過去形とともに用いる) ▶ただ今手紙を書き終えたところです I finished a letter *just now*. (!xI have *just* finished a letter just now. とはいわない)/I have *just* finished [《主に米》I *just* finished] a letter.

❸【近い未来】just (!通例文中で進行形や be going [about] to do などに用いる); (すぐに) 《話》right away, in a minute. (⇨すぐ) ▶ただ今参ります I'm (*just*) coming [xgoing]./I'll be there *right away*.

ただえる 称える praise. (⇨褒める, 賞賛する)

ただえる 湛える 〖満たす〗fill 《with》; 〖あふれそうになる〗《やや書》brim (-mm-) 《with》. ●笑みをたたえている wear a smile; 《話》be all smiles. ●満面に笑みをたたえて with smiles all over; smiling all over. ▶貯水池は満々と水をたたえる The reservoir /rézɚrwɑːr/ is *full of* water.

*たたかい 戦い, 闘い 〖戦争〗(a) war, (局地的な) battle (⇨戦争); (格闘, 戦闘) a fight; (争い, 衝突) a cónflict; (奮闘) a struggle. (!いずれの語も比喩的にも用いられる) ●戦い抜く *fight* it out.

❶【~(の)戦い】●貧困との戦い a *war* [a *fight*] *against* poverty. ●暴風雨との戦い a *battle* against the elements. ●麻薬の戦い *war on* drugs; drug *war*. ●差別との戦い a *struggle against* racial discrimination. ●自由を求める戦い a *struggle* [a *fight*] *for* freedom. ●母国を敵から解放するための戦い a *struggle* to free our home country from the enemy. ●良心[愛と憎しみ]との戦い a *conflict with* one's conscience [*between* love and hate]. ▶わなにはまった象の救出は時間との戦いになった Freeing the trapped elephant became a *battle* against time.

❷【戦い方】●戦いは朝早くに始まった The *battle* started early in the morning. ▶彼らの戦いは非常に激しかった Their *fight* was terribly hard [*fierce*].

たたかう 戦う, 闘う ❶【戦闘する】fight 《*against*, *with*》; make* [《やや書》wage] war 《*against*, *on*》; (開戦する) go* to war 《*against*, *with*》. (⇨戦争) ▶その領土をめぐって戦う *fight* over [about] the territory. ▶彼らは夜明けまで激しく敵と戦った They *fought* fiercely [*fought* a fierce battle] *against* their enemies until dawn.

❷【競争する】contend; (争う) fight* 《*with*, *for*》. ●正々堂々と戦う play [*fight*] fair [xfairly]. ▶私は彼と選手権をかけて戦った I *contended with* [《ボクシングなどで》*fought with*] him *for* the title.

❸【困難などと】(奮闘する) struggle 《*with*, *against*》; (格闘する) fight*; (抵抗する) resist. ●困難と闘う *struggle with* [*against*] difficulties. ●誘惑と闘う *fight* 《*against*》 [*resist*] temptation. (!against を用いない fight の他動詞用法では双方向性の直接対決の感じが強くなる) ●自由のために闘う *fight* [*struggle*] *for* freedom. ●世界平和を守るために戦う *struggle* to preserve world peace. ▶彼女はがんと闘っている She *is fighting against* [*struggling with*] cancer.

たたかわす 闘わす ▶彼と激論を闘わす have a heated discussion with him 《*about*, *over*》; argue with him 《*about*, *over*》.

たたき 叩き ●アジのたたき *chopped* (raw) horse mackerel. ●カツオのたたき *lightly-broiled* bonito. ●肩たたき (⇨肩叩き)

たたきあげる 叩き上げる (努力して A から B になる) work one's way up 《*from A to B*》.

たたきうり 叩き売り a sacrifice (sale). (⇨投げ売り) ●冬物のたたき売りをする *bargain away* winter clothes.

たたきおこす 叩き起こす wake* (him) up roughly; throw* [《むりやり》kick] (him) out of bed.

たたきおとす 叩き落とす (たたく) knock, hit*, 《やや書》strike*; (特にハエなどを) swat (-tt-). ●彼の手からそれをたたき落とす *knock* it from his hand.

たたきこむ 叩き込む ●板にくぎをたたき込む drive [《金づ

たたきころす

ちで) *hammer*] a nail *into* the board. ▶ある考えを彼にたたき込む *drum* [*hammer*] an idea *into* his head [*into* him]. ▶さっきははっきりものを言うことの大切さをアメリカ人の子供は小さい頃からたたき込まれている The importance of speaking out promptly *is drummed into* American children from an early age. ▶そのことを頭へたたき込んでおいてくれ Just *get* that *in* your head.

たたきころす 叩き殺す beat*... to death.

たたきだい 叩き台 (試案)(やや書) a tentative plan. ▶たたき台を作る make a plan for discussion; work out a *tentative plan*. ▶それでは,彼の案をたたき台にして議論を進めよう Well, let's take up his plan [proposal] as a *starter* of [a *basis* for] our discussion.

たたきだいく 叩き大工 (下手な大工) an unskillful carpenter.

たたきだす 叩き出す ❶[追い出す] turn [(話) kick] ... out (⇒追い出す);[解雇する](話) fire. ▶ぼくは家賃が払えなくてアパートからたたき出された I *was kicked out of* the apartment because I couldn't pay the rent. ❷[模様などを] emboss.

たたきつける 叩き付ける [物を投げる] throw*; (激しく) fling*; [雨・風が激しく当たる] beat* (*against, on*). ▶コップを壁に[床に]たたきつける *throw* [*fling*] the glass *against* the wall [*to* the floor]. ▶辞表を上司にたたきつける(=突き付ける) *thrust* one's resignation *at* one's boss. ▶たたきつけた打球 (野球) a chopper. ▶たたきつけてゴロを打つ (野球) hit a chop. ▶雨が激しく窓をたたきつけていた The rain *was* (severely) *beating* [*pelting*] *against* the windows.

たたきなおす 叩き直す (徹底的に矯正する)(やや書) remedy ... thoroughly. ▶彼のひねくれた根性をたたき直す *remedy* his crooked nature *thoroughly*.

たたきのめす 叩きのめす knock ... down.

:たたく 叩く ❶[打つ] strike* (⚠ 意味は最も広い。hit より堅い語); (ねらって強く) hit*; (こぶしや固い物で) knock; (続けざまに) beat*; (軽く) tap (-pp-), pat (-tt-); (どんどんと) pound; (どんと) bang; (平手で) slap (-pp-); (手を) clap (-pp-). (⇒打つ)

①《...を~》 ▶太鼓をたたく *beat* a drum. ▶手をたたく(拍手や人を呼ぶために) *clap* one's hands; (神前で) *clap* one's hands in prayer. (⚠「2度叩く」は make two handclaps) ▶彼の背中をぽんとたたく *pat* him [*give* him *a pat, tap* him] *on* the [×his] back. (書評) 賞賛・慰めなどのために手のひらで軽くたたく動作。英語特有の言い方で, 人を中心とし背中のところで彼をたたく感じのこと) ▶ピアノの鍵盤(けんばん)をたたく *press* (そっと) *touch*, (がんがん) *hammer at*] the keys of the piano. ▶彼は私の頭をたたいた He *hit* [*struck*, (こつんと) *knocked*] me *on* the head. (⚠これは of の代わりに one's とすることもある。He *hit* [*struck, knocked*] my head. は体の部分に重点を置いた言い方) ▶だれかが戸をたたいている Someone *is knocking* [(どんどん) *pounding, banging*; (こんこん) *tapping*] at [*on*] the door. (⚠ at はたたく対象, on はその動作に重点がある) ▶彼はいたずらをして尻をたっぷりたたかれた He *was beaten* [*was spanked*] a lot *on* the bottom for his mischief./He got [*was given*] a good *beating* [*spanking*] *on* the bottom for his mischief. ▶9番ホールで10もたいてしまった(ゴルフで) I *took* ten at the ninth hole.

②【(物)で...をたたく》 ▶手で彼をたたく *hit* [*strike*] him with one's hand. ▶平手で彼の顔をたたく *slap* him *on* [*in, across*] the face (⚠ on はその表面を打つこと。in はめ込む感じ。across は表面を横切る感じを伴う); *slap* his face. ▶彼は指先でこつこつと机をたたいた He *tapped* (*on*) [*drummed on*] the desk with his fingers./He *tapped* [*drummed*] his fingers *on* the desk. (⚠いらいらした様子などを表す)

❷[攻撃する] attack; (非難する) criticize. ▶首相の政策は新聞でひどくたたかれた The Prime Minister's policy *was* harshly *attacked* [*was* severely *criticized*] in the newspapers.

❸[値切る] beat*... down. ▶彼は手袋の代金は5,000円ですと言ったが, 私は買いたくて4,000円に値引きさせた He was asking 5,000 yen for the gloves, but I *beat* him *down* to 4,000 yen. (⚠...*beat* the price *down*... ともいえる)

❹[しゃべる] ▶陰口をたたく talk behind (his) back. ▶大きな口をたたくな(=生意気言うな) Don't be so cheeky.

ただごと ただ事 ▶これはただ事ではない(普通の事ではない) This is *something out of the ordinary*./(重大事だ) This is a *serious matter*. ▶先生を殴っただとただ事ではすまんぞ You hit your teacher? You'll get into trouble.

ただし 但し ❶[しかし] but; (やや書) however. (⇒しかし) ▶もう寝てもよい。ただしあしたは早く起きなさい You can go to bed now. *But* get up early tomorrow morning.

❷[もし...ならば] if; (制限・限定を表して) provided 《*that*節》; (条件を表して) on condition 《*that*節》(⚠いずれも if より堅い言い方) ▶私の車を使ってもいいです。ただし5時までに返してくれるならばです You can use my car *if* [*provided* (*that*), *on condition* (*that*)] you give it back by five. (⚠ on condition (that) の場合... you *will* give... となることもあるが, if, provided (that) では不可)

:ただしい 正しい [形] right; correct; proper.

> **使い分け** **right** 事柄が事実・基準・道理に合っており正しいこと, 人が判断・意見などにおいて正しいこと, 行為などが法律・道徳・社会通念上正しいことのほか, 特定の目的に最も適してよう正しいことをいう。
> **correct** 欠点や誤りがなく正確で正しいこと, また礼儀や規則にかなっており正しいこと。
> **proper** 方法などが目的・状況・礼儀にかなっていて正しいことをいうやや堅い語。

▶正しい時間[解答] the *correct* [*right*] time [answer]. ▶正しい箸(はし)の持ち方 the *right* [*proper*] way to hold chopsticks. ▶彼がそうするのは正しい He *is right in* doing [*to* do] it./*It is right of* him *to* do it./*It is right that* he do [《主に英》*should* do] it [*for* him *to* do it]. (⚠should は道徳的判断を示す) ▶君(の言うこと)が正しい You are *right* [*in the right*]. (⚠後の方が意味が強い。(話)では意味を強めて *Right* you are! ともいう) ▶その問題に対する彼の判断はまったく正しかった He was quite *correct* [*right*] in his judgment on the matter. (⚠correct, right は very ではなく quite, absolutely などで強調する) ▶スープを飲むときに音を立てるのは正しくない *It is* not *correct* [*proper*] *to* make a noise when you eat soup. (⚠*It is* not *proper that* you (《主に英》*should*).... といえるが, correct は that 節 はとらない)

— **正しく** [副] right(ly); correctly; properly. ▶正しく行動する act *right* [*rightly*]. (⚠(話) では right の方が好まれる) ▶彼は正しく英語が話せる He can speak English *correctly*./He can speak *correct* [*good*, ×*right*] English.

ただしがき 但し書き (契約・条約などの)(やや書) a proviso /prəváizou/ (優 ~s, ~es). ▶ただし書きをつける add a *proviso*. ▶...というただし書きつきで with the *proviso* that .... (❢ しばしばコンマで区切られて文頭または文尾で)

***ただす 正す** correct, 《書》rectify. ●誤りを正す *correct* errors. ●誤った考えを正す *put* [*set*] 《him》 *right* (in his ideas). ●行いを正す (改善する) *improve* one's behavior; *mend* one's ways [manners]; (改心する) *reform* oneself. ●服装を正す(=きちんとする) *make* oneself *tidy*. ●姿勢を正す (体をまっすぐにする) *straighten up*; (態度や考えを是正する) *rectify* the 《political [diplomatic]》posture. ▶私の英作文の誤りを正してください Please *correct* (the) *mistakes* in my English composition. (❢ の があると必ず誤りがあることを暗示する) ▶悪は正さなければならない Wrongs should *be righted*.

ただす 糾す ●その件の真相をただす(=尋ねて明らかにする) *inquire into* the matter. ●元をただせば (⇨元〔成句〕)

ただす 質す (質問する) ask; (確かめる) make* sure 《of; that 節》. ●彼女に真意をただす *ask* her *about* her (real) intention.

たたずまい 佇まい (an) átmosphère; 《外見》(an) appearance. ●この町のヨーロッパ的なたずまい the European *atmosphere* of this town.

たたずむ 佇む 街角で1人たたずんでいる *keep standing* alone on the street corner.

ただただ (強調して) simply, absolutely. ▶彼女の才能にはただただ I'm *simply* amazed at her talent. ▶ただただ妻に感謝するばかりだ *All I can do is* (to) thank my wife.

ただちに 直ちに (すぐに) at once, right away [off]; (即座に) immediately; (敏速に) promptly. (⇨すぐ〔類語〕) ▶その老婦人は直ちに病院に運ばれた The older [old] woman was taken to (the) hospital *at once* [*without delay*]./The elderly woman was *immediately* taken to (the) hospital. ▶これといった理由もなく体重が減ってきたら直ちに医者に診てもらうべきです If you're losing weight for no particular reason, you should see your doctor *promptly* [*immediately*].

だだっこ 駄々っ子 (甘やかされた子) a spoiled child 《❽ children》; (聞き分けのない子) 《やや書》 a willful child; (むずかる子) a fretful child.

だだっぴろい だだっ広い (広すぎる) too [excessively] large. ●だだっ広いホール an *excessively big* [*a very spacious*] hall. (❢ spacious は「(ほめて)広々としてゆったりした」の意なので不適切) ▶ぼくのおばあちゃんはだだっ広い家に1人で住んでいる My grandma lives alone in a *very big* house.

ただでさえ 只でさえ ▶彼はただでさえ不幸なところへ(=不幸に加えて)恋人に去られた *To add to* his misfortune, he lost his girlfriend. ▶ただでさえ頭痛がするのに(=さらに悪いことに)のどまで痛い I have a headache, and *what's worse*, a sore throat.

ただどり 只取り — 只取りする 動 get 《it》 for free [nothing].

ただなか 只中 (⇨真っ只中)

ただならぬ (普通でない) unusual; (異常な) extraordinary; (変な) strange. ●ただならぬこと something *unusual*. ●ただならぬ気配 an *unusual* sign.

ただのり 只乗り 图 《get》 a free ride. ●ただ乗り客 a free rider; (隠れて乗っている者) a stowaway; 《米話》(優待券による)a deadhead.
— **ただ乗りする** 動 ●電車にただ乗りする *steal a ride* on a train.

ただばたらき 只働き ▶それではただ働き同然だ That's just like *working without pay* [*for nothing*].

たたみ 畳 a tatami (mat); (説明的に) straw mat about 6 feet by 3. ●畳のへり the border of a *tatami*. ●畳を敷く lay 《↔take up, lift》 six *tatami* mats. ●四畳半の畳部屋 a four-and-a-half *mat* room. ●畳の表替えをする (自分で) reface a *tatami* (mat); (人に頼んで) have a *tatami* (mat) refaced.
●**畳の上で死ぬ** die in one's bed.
●**畳表** *tatami* (mat) facing. ●**畳屋** a *tatami* maker.

たたみいわし 畳鰯 *tatami-iwashi*; (説明的に) dried baby sardines flattened like a sheet.

たたみかける 畳み掛ける ●彼にたたみかけて質問する(=彼に質問を浴びせる) *fire* questions *at* him.

たたみこむ 畳み込む (たたんで入れる) fold 《it》 (up) and put 《it in》; (心に留める) keep [bear] 《it》 in mind. ●着物をたたんすたたみ込む *fold* a kimono (*up*) and *put* it in a chest of drawers. ●先生の言葉を胸にたたみ込む *keep* the teacher's words *in mind*. ●たたみ込むように(=次々と[立て続けに])質問する ask questions *one after another* [*in succession*].

*****たたむ 畳む** (折って) fold ... (up); (閉じて) shut*, close. ●シーツをたたむ *fold* the sheets. ●ふとんをたんで片付ける *fold up* the bedding and put it away. ●傘をたたむ (=閉じる) *fold* (*up*) an umbrella. ●店をたたむ (=商売をやめる) go out of business; *close down* one's store. (❢ close one's store とすれば「1日の終わりに店を閉める」の意にもなる)

ただもの 只者 an ordinary [a common] person. (⇨凡人) ▶あの人はただ者ではない He is no *ordinary man*.

*****ただよう 漂う** ❶ 【漂流する】 (風・波などに流されて) drift; (浮かんで) float. ●空を漂う雲 clouds *drifting* [*floating*] *across* the sky. ●流れのままに漂ういかだ a raft *drifting* [*floating*] with the current. ▶小船が湖に漂っている There is a boat *drifting* [*floating*] on the lake. / A boat *is drifting* [*floating*] on the lake. (⇨流れる❸)
❷ 【たちこめる】 ▶花の香りが漂っている The air *is scented with* flowers. / There's a smell of flowers in the air. ▶教室にはなごやかな雰囲気が漂っていた There was a friendly atmosphere in the classroom.

ただよわせる 漂わせる spread 《a smell》. ▶バラは部屋中によい香りを漂わせる Roses *spread* their sweet smell [*perfume*] in the whole room.

たたら 蹈鞴 ●**たたらを踏む** totter.

たたり 祟り 〘のろい〙a curse; 〘悪霊〙an evil spirit. (⇨祟(たた)る) ●この家にはたたりがある This house is possessed by [with] *evil spirits*. ●さわらぬ神にたたりなし 'If you touch deities, *curses* will be called down on you.'/(ことわざ) Let a sleeping dog lie.

たたる 祟る 〘のろう〙curse; 〘悪霊にとりつかれている〙be possessed [be cursed] by an evil /íːvl/ spirit. ▶旅行中は悪天候にたたられた We *were cursed* with bad weather during our trip. ●怠けたことがたって落第した I failed *because of* my laziness [*because* I was lazy].

ただれ 爛れ an inflammation 《of the ear [eye, toe]》; (炎症などによる) a sore.

ただれる 爛れる 〘炎症などで痛む〙become* sore; 〘化膿(かのう)する〙 fester. ●ただれた目[耳] *sore* eyes [ears]. ●ただれた(=放蕩(ほうとう)な)生活をする 《やや書》 lead a *dissipated* life. ●あいた傷口がただれてきた The open wound *has festered*.

たたん 多端 ▶彼は事務多端のため暇がない He has very little free time because of *a lot of*

たち 質 (性質) (a) nature; (体質) (a) constitution. (⇨性質, 体質) ●たちの悪い (悪質な) bad; (邪悪な) evil /íːvl/; (意地の悪い) ill-natured, wicked /wíkid/; (質が劣る) inferior. ●彼は忘れっぽいたちです He's forgetful./He *is apt* [*prone*] *to forget*. ▶彼は賭け事には向かないたちです(=生まれつきついていない) He's not *by nature* a betting man [a gambler]. ▶そんなことをするとは彼もたちが悪い It is *wicked* of [×for] him [《やや古》 He *is wicked* to do such a thing. (⇨悪い)

たち 太刀 a sword. (⇨刀)

-たち -達 (**!**「...たち」に当たる英語はなく, 名詞・代名詞の複数形で表す) ●子供たち children. ●動物たち animals.

たちあい 立ち会い 〖列席〗 presence; 〖証券取引所の〗 a session; 〖監査〗 observation. ▶藤井氏立ち会いのもとで in the *presence* of Mr. Fujii.
● 立ち会い演説 a campaign speech. ● 立ち会い人 a witness; (選挙現場の) a (poll) watcher.
● 立ち会い場 a (trading) floor; a boardroom.

たちあい 立ち合い *tachiai*; the initial (jump-off) charge. ●立ち合いで待ったをする call a wait at [on] the *tachiai*.

たちあう 立ち会う ▶何人かが開票に立ち会った Some people *witnessed* [*were present as witnesses for*] the vote counting.

たちあおい 立ち葵 〖植物〗 a hollyhock; a rose mallow.

たちあがり 立ち上がり ❶〖電子機器の〗 start-up. ●このコンピュータは立ち上がりが早い(遅い) This computer starts quickly [slowly]./This computer is quick [slow] (in) *getting started*.
❷〖野球で〗 ●立ち上がりが悪い get off to a shaky start; have a rough [a rocky] first inning. ▶山田は立ち上がりから 3 連打を打たれた Yamada gave up three hits in a row at the beginning of the game.

たちあがり 裁ち上がり 〖裁縫〗 cutting.

*****たちあがる** 立ち上がる ❶〖起立する〗 stand* up, get* up; rise* [get] to one's feet. (**!** rise は堅い言い方, get は口語的) ●ぱっと(よろよろと; やっと)立ち上がる spring [stagger; struggle] to one's feet. ●いすから立ち上がる stand up [get up] from one's chair. ▶彼は立ち上がって客を迎えた He stood up [got up, rose] to welcome the guest.
❷〖行動を起こす〗 take* action (⇨立つ ❹); (決起する) rise* (up) (against); (始める) start. ●募金に立ち上がる start to collect money. ●戦災から立ち上がる(復興する) recover from the war damage; rise from the ashes of war. ▶彼らは独裁政治〖独裁者〗に対して武装して立ち上がった They rose (up) *in arms* [took up arms] against dictatorship [the dictator]. ▶なぜ立ち上がって闘わないのか Why don't you *stand up* and fight?

たちあげ 立ち上げ (a) start-up. ●立ち上げ費用 *start-up* cost.

たちあげる 立ち上げる 〖事業・計画などを〗 launch; 〖コンピュータを〗 boot (up). ●パソコンを立ち上げる *start up* a personal computer. ▶その新しいプロジェクトを立ち上げるのはやりがいのある仕事だった It was a challenging job to *start up* the new project.

たちいたる 立ち至る ▶不況がこれ以上続けば我が社は倒産の事態に立ち至るであろう If the recession goes on any longer, it *will lead* us to [《いやがおうでも》*drive*] us *into*] bankruptcy.

たちいふるまい 立ち居振る舞い movements. ▶彼女の立ち居振るまいは優雅だ Her *movements* are elegant [graceful]./She moves very elegantly [gracefully].

たちいりきんし 立入禁止 ▶立入禁止 〖掲示〗(入場禁止) No admittance [entrance, entry]./(一般の方立入禁止) Private./(芝生などに) Keep off.../(部屋などに) Keep out.../(土地などへの無断侵入禁止) No trespassing. ▶無用の者立入禁止 〖掲示〗 *No admittance* except on business. ▶芝生へ立入禁止 〖掲示〗 *Keep off* the grass. ▶立入禁止の看板がその所有地のまわりに立てられていた *No trespassing* signs were posted all around the property.

たちいりけんさ 立ち入り検査 ●立ち入り検査をする make an on-the-spot inspection (of)

たちいる 立ち入る ❶〖入る〗 enter; 〖侵入する〗 tréspass (on his land). (⇨入る) ▶この部屋に立ち入るな Don't *enter* [*go into*] this room. ▶芝生に立ち入るべからず 〖掲示〗 *Keep off* the grass.
❷〖人が事に干渉する〗 interfére [meddle] (in). ▶私事に立ち入らないでください Don't *interfere in* [(鼻をつっこむ) 《話》 poke your nose into] private matters. ▶あまり(私事)に立ち入った話はやめよう Let's not *be too personal* [(せんさく的な) *inquisitive*].

たちうお 太刀魚 〖魚介〗 a scábbard fish. (**!** 通例単・複同形, 肉は ⓤ)

たちうち 太刀打ち ●太刀打ちできる《やや書》 bear [stand] comparison 《with him in...》; be a good match (for him in...). ●太刀打ちできない《やや書》 don't bear [stand] comparison 《with him in...》; be no match (for him in...); can hardly compete 《with him in...》. ▶料理では母にとても太刀打ちできない I just *can't compare with* my mother in cooking.

たちうり 立ち売り (人) a street vendor.

たちおうじょう 立ち往生 ― 立ち往生する 動 (⇨渋滞する) ▶車は雪の中で立ち往生した The car *stuck* [*got stuck*] in the snow. ▶彼の質問で私はまったく立ち往生してしまった He really *stumped* me with that question. (**!** stump は《話》で「...をまごつかせる」の意)

たちおくれ 立ち遅れ a late start. ●立ち遅れを取り戻す make up for lost time.

たちおくれる 立ち後れる (⇨後れる ❷) ●スタートで立ち後れる make a slow [a late] start.

たちおよぎ 立ち泳ぎ ― 立ち泳ぎする 動 tread /tréd/ water.

たちかえる 立ち返る come back [return] (to). ●本論に立ち返る *return* to the main point. ●初心に立ち返る *go back* to the initial enthusiasm.

たちかぜ 太刀風 a swish of a sword. ●太刀風鋭く斬りかかる slash at him with a sharp *swish*.

たちがれ 立ち枯れ ●立ち枯れの木立 a *dead* clump of trees. ●立ち枯れる die; (立ち枯れ病で) damp off. (⇨枯れる)
●立ち枯れ病 damping-off.

たちき 立木 A tree.

たちぎえ 立ち消え ●立ち消えになる (計画などが実現に失敗する) fall through; (むだに終わる) come to nothing; (火が) go [die] out. ▶その道路計画は立ち消えになった The plan to build [×make] a road *fell through* [*ended up in smoke*].

たちぎき 立ち聞き ― 立ち聞きする 動 (盗み聞きする) eavesdrop (-pp-) 《on their conversation behind the door》. (**!** overhear は「たまたま聞く」の意)

*****たちきる** 断ち切る cut*... off. ●(人との)関係を断ち切る break off [cut off, 《書》 sever] one's relations 《with》. (⇨切る ❷)

たちきる 裁ち切る cut cloth.
たちぐい 立ち食い ── 立ち食いする 動 (立って食べる) eat (…) standing.
• 立ち食いそば 《a bowl of》 *soba* to eat standing.
• 立ち食いそば屋 a stand-up *soba* bar.
たちぐされ 立ち腐れ • 立ち腐れになる (建物が) fall into (a state of) decay; be dilapidated.
たちくらみ 立ちくらみ • ここのところよく立ちくらみ(が)する These days I often *feel dizzy when I get to my feet*.
たちこめる 立ち込める (霧などが) hang* 《over》; (香りが) fill. ▶空港に霧が立ちこめていた Mist *hung over* the airport./(空港は霧に包まれていた) The airport *was enveloped* [*veiled*, *shrouded*] *in* mist. ▶部屋中に魚を焼くにおいが立ちこめていた The room *was filled with* a smell of grilling fish.
たちさき 太刀先 • the point of a sword.
たちさばき 太刀捌き • 太刀さばきが見事である be good at wielding a sword; be a good swordsman.
たちさる 立ち去る leave*; (行ってしまう) go* away 《from》. • その場所を立ち去る *leave* [*go away from*] the place. • さよならも言わずに立ち去る *leave* [*walk off*] without saying good-by. • 彼に立ち去れと命じる tell him to *leave* [*go away*]; order him *away*.
たちさわぐ 立ち騒ぐ make a lot of noise. (⇨騒ぐ❶) • 立ち騒ぐ群集 an agitated crowd.
たちしごと 立ち仕事 a job in which one has to stand a lot. (!×a standing job とはいわない)
たちしょうべん 立ち小便 ── 立ち小便(を)する 動 urinate /júərənèit/ on [in] the street; (英語) piss outdoors. (⇨小便)
たちすがた 立ち姿 one's standing posture.
たちすくむ 立ち竦む • 恐怖でその場に立ちすくむ stand rooted [(くぎ付けになる) riveted] to the spot in terror; stand there *petrified* with terror.
たちすじ 太刀筋 • 太刀筋がいい be good at wielding a sword; be a good swordsman.
たちせき 立ち席 standing room. (⇨立ち見)
たちつくす 立ち尽くす stand still [motionless]. ▶その眺めのあまりの美しさに時のたつのも忘れてその場に立ち尽くした I was so fascinated by the beauty of the view that I *stood* there losing track of time.
たちっぱなし 立ちっぱなし • 立ちっぱなしである (座れなくて) have to stand all the way; (自分の意志で) keep standing. ▶東京までずっと立ちっぱなしだった I had to *stand* [*remain standing*] all the way to Tokyo.
たちづめ 立ち詰め ⇨立つ❶ [第4文例, 立ちっぱなし]
たちどころに 立ち所に (すぐに) right away, at once (!後の方が堅い言い方); (一瞬のうちに) in a moment [an instant]; (たちまち) in a flash. • たちどころに(=その場で)決心する make up one's mind *on the spot* [*thén and thére, thére and thén*].
***たちどまる** 立ち止まる (足を止める) stop (-pp-); (一時的に) pause. • 急に立ち止まる *stop* suddenly; *come to a* sudden *stop*. ▶彼はびっくりして立ち止まった Startled (by a big sound) he *stopped* suddenly./He *stopped* in amazement. (!前の方は物理的なもので, 後の方は何かに驚嘆したの意) ▶彼は立ち止まってたばこを吸った He *stopped* to smoke. (!stop smoking は「たばこを吸うのをやめる」の意)/He *stopped* and smoked. ▶彼はちょっと立ち止まって, それから歩き出した He *paused* for a moment, and then started to walk [walked] again.
たちなおる 立ち直る get* over …; recover 《from》 (!後の方が堅い語). • そのホームレスの男を立ち直らせる (=自立できるようにする) get the homeless man *on his feet*. ▶彼女はやがて母のショックから立ち直った She soon *got over* [*recovered from*] the shock of her mother's death. ▶エースは3回に立ち直った The ace settled [got settled] down in the third inning.
たちならぶ 立ち並ぶ (一列に) stand* in a row; (通りに沿って) line. ▶大通りにはアパートやオフィスビルが立ち並んでいる The main street *is lined with* apartment houses and office buildings.
たちのき 立ち退き [移転] a move; [法律の力による追い立て] (an) eviction; [危険区域からの退避] (an) evacuation. ▶アパートの立ち退きを迫られた I was told to *move out of* [(立ち去る) *leave*] my apartment.
• 立ち退き通告 a notice of eviction. • 立ち退き料 compensation for eviction.
たちのく 立ち退く [立ち去る] leave*; (すばやく)《話》clear out 《of》; [引っ越して行く] move out 《of》 (⇨立ち退き); [退避・撤退する] evacuate 《from》. ▶私たちは直ちにその地域から立ち退くように命じられた We were ordered to *evacuate* [*leave*] the area at once. ▶警察は暴力団員たちをアパートから立ち退かせた The police *evicted* gangsters *from* their apartments.
たちのぼる 立ち上る go* up, rise*. (!前の方が口語的) • 遠くに煙の立ち上るのが見える I (can) see smoke *going up* [*rising*] in the distance. ▶浴衣姿の女の子から立ちのぼる石けんの香りがいっそう爽やかだった The fragrance of soap *emanating* [*rising*] from the girls wearing *yukata* smelled all the more refreshing. (!香りなど目に見えないものが生じ伝わってくる場合は rise より emanate が適切)
※**たちば** 立場 ❶ [地位, 境遇] (他人との関係で決まる社会的位置) a position; (人の置かれている状況) a situation; (立脚) a footing 《⇨位置, 地位》; [基盤] a ground. • 対等の立場にある[に立つ] be [stand] on an equal *footing* [×*position*]《with》. • 共通の立場を見いだす find a common *ground*. ▶もし君が彼の立場だったらどうしますか What would you do if you were in his *place* [×*position, shoes*]? ▶残念ながらあなたを援助できる立場にありません I'm afraid I'm not in a *position* to help you. (!…, I'm in no *position* to help you. ともいえる) ▶私が今どんな立場にあるのかはよく分かってくれていると思う You know very well *where* I *stand*. ▶立場によって考えも違う One's opinion varies according to one's *position*.

❷ [見地] a point of view; [観点] a standpoint; [見解] a position; [政治的立場] a stand 《on》. • 立場を明らかにする make one's *position* clear; define one's *position*. • お互いの立場を尊重する respect each other's *positions* [*point of views*]. • 立場を変えて見る look at 《it》 from a different *standpoint* [(角度) *angle*]. • その問題に強硬な[現実論の]立場を取る take a strong [a realistic] *stand on* the issue.
• 立場がない ▶そんなことになったら, ぼくの立場がない(=面目がつぶれる) It would put me in an embarrassing *position* [an awkward *situation*]./It would probably cause me some embarrassment.
たちはだかる 立ちはだかる [行く手のじゃまをする] (人・困難などが) stand* in 《his》 way, confrónt; (障害物となって) block. • 私たちの前に立ちはだかる難問 the difficult problems *confronting* us. ▶見知らぬ人が私の前に立ちはだかった A stranger *stood in* my

way./(意味を強めて) A stranger *confronted* me. ▶あの高いビルが立ちはだかって視界をさえぎっている That tall building *blocks* our view.

たちはたらく 立ち働く (かいがいしく働く) work diligently [like a bee].

たちばな 橘【植物】*tachibana*; (説明的に) a kind of citrus fruit native to Japan.

たちばなし 立ち話 ━━ 立ち話をする 動 stand talking [(ぺちゃくちゃと) chatting].

たちはばとび 立ち幅跳び the standing broad jump.

たちばん 立ち番 图 (a) watch, guard; (人) a watch, a guard. ━━ 立ち番(を)する 動 keep a watch 《*over*》; stand guard 《*over*》.

たちふさがる 立ち塞がる (⇒立ちはだかる)

たちまち 忽ち [すぐに] at once, immediately (⇒すぐ [類語]); (すばやく) quickly; (一瞬のうちに) in a moment [an instant, a minute]; (突然に) suddenly, all of a sudden (**!** 後の方が口語的で強意的). ▶彼はたちまちたちまちうちに作り終えた He finished it *in a moment* [*in no time*]. ▶たちまち空が暗くなった The sky darkened *suddenly*. ▶そのニュースはたちまち(=すばやく)社内に広がった The news spread *quickly* through the office./The news got around *fast* in the office.

たちまわり 立ち回り [劇・映画に] a fighting scene; [けんかに] a scuffle; (殴り合い) a fight. ● 犯人の立ち回り先 the criminal's whereabouts.

たちまわる 立ち回る [行動的に] act; (身を処する)《書》 conduct oneself; (策略を用いる) maneuver; (うまくやる)《略》do* well; [歩き回る] go* [walk] around. ▶彼は何事においてもうまく立ち回る He *acts* [*conducts himself, maneuvers*] tactfully in everything./(処理そうまくする)《話》He *plays his cards well* [*right*] in everything.

たちみ 立(ち)見 ━━ 立(ち)見する 動 watch 《a game》 standing.
● 立見客《話》a standee. ● 立見席 (xa) stánding room. ● 立見席のみ《掲示》Standing room only (略 SRO).

たちむかう 立ち向かう (敵・危険などに) confront; (困難などに勇気をもって立ち向かう) face, face up to ... (**!** 後の方は引き下がらないことを含意); (人に抵抗し) stand* up to .... ● 勇敢に敵に立ち向かう *confront* an enemy bravely; (戦う) *fight against* an enemy. ● 危険に立ち向かう *confront* danger. ▶今の若い者は困難に立ち向かう勇気がない Young people today can't *face* anything difficult. ▶彼に立ち向かって行かないと彼はいつまでも君をいじめるよ If you don't *stand up to* him, he's just going to keep on bullying you. (**!** keep on doing は「いつまでも(しつこく)...し続ける」の意)

たちもち 太刀持ち a sword bearer.

たちもの 断ち物 ● 断ち物をする abstain from certain food so that the god may grant one's wish.

たちやく 立ち役 [歌舞伎] a leading male role.

たちゆく 立ち行く (生活していく) live [get along]《*on*》; (収入内で暮らす) make (both) ends meet; (事業・商売をやっていく) manage [operate, run] 《*business*》. ▶私の安月給では暮らしを立ち行くのがやっとだった On my small salary we could barely *get along* [*make ends meet*].

だちょう 駝鳥 [鳥] an óstrich.

たちよみ 立ち読み ━━ 立ち読みする 動 ▶当店では読み物のマンガ本を立ち読みするお客様が多くて困っています The trouble is that many customers spend time reading (through) [xbrowsing through] comic books on sale instead of buying them in our bookstore. (**!** read through は「終わりまで読む」の意. browse /bráuz/ through は「(どんな本なのか)さっと見る」ことで、日本語の「立ち読み」のようなうしろめたい行動ではない)

たちよる 立ち寄る (ひょっこり訪ねる) drop (-pp-) in 《*on*＋人, *at*＋場所》, stop (-pp-) [drop] 《*by*》; (立ち寄る)《主に英》call 《*on, at*》; (旅行の途中で立ち寄る) stop off 《*in, at*》; (飛行機で旅行の途中に立ち寄る) stop over 《*at, in*》. (⇒ストップ **❸**) ▶彼はキオスクに立ち寄って新聞を買った He *stopped by* a kiosk and bought a newspaper.

たちわざ 立ち技 standing techniques.

たちわる 断ち割る split* 《*bamboo*》, (ぶった切る) chop (-pp-).

だちん 駄賃 [謝礼] a reward. ▶お使いに行ってくれたらお駄賃に1,000円あげよう I'll give you a thousand yen as a reward if you go on [do, run] an errand for me.

たちんぼう 立ちん坊 (⇒立ちっぱなし)

・**たつ** 立つ ❶【人や動物が立つ】(立っている) stand* (↔ sit); (立ち上がる) stand (up),《書》rise*, rise [get*] to one's feet (**!** get は口語的). ● 窓の近くに立つ *stand* near [by] the window. (**!** by の方が接近していることを含意する) ● 片足で立つ *stand on* one leg [foot]. (**!** on に注意. xwith は不可) ● 転んだ子供を立たせる *raise* a fallen child *to* his *feet*; *help* a fallen child (*get*) *to* his *feet*. ▶男の子は母親のうしろに立っていた The boy *stood* [*was standing*] behind his mother. (**!** 後の形は一時的状態を強調) ▶先生が教室に入って来ると皆立った Everyone *stood* (*up*) [*got up*] when the teacher came into the classroom. ▶私は彼が来るのを立って待っていた I *stood* waiting for him. ▶私は上野駅までずっと立ち続けだった I had to *stand* all the way to Ueno Station. ▶座ろうと思えば座れたが自分の意志で立ち続けた場合は stand は状態動詞ではなくなり、I *kept* (*on*) *standing*.... ということも可.(⇒続ける)) ▶バスには立っている乗客のためにつり革がある The bus has straps for *standing* passengers (to hold on to). ● 椅子から立った He *stood up* [*got up*] *from* the chair./(離れた) He *left* his seat. ▶ぼうっと立っていないで働け You ought to work instead of *standing around* [*about*]. ● 先生は(罰として)彼をすみに立たせた The teacher *stood* [*put*] him in the corner.

❷【物が立っている】stand*; (存在する) be. ● 学校は町のはずれに立っている Our school *is* [*stands*] *on* the outskirts of the town. (**!** 校舎は動かせない物なので xOur school is standing.... は不可) ● 丘の頂上に天文台が立っている There *is* [*stands*] an astronomical observatory on (the) top of the hill. (**!**(1) 存在・出現などを表す動詞には 構文が可. (2) An astronomical observatory is.... は不自然) ▶たくさんの看板が駅前に立っていた A lot of signboards *were put up* in front of the railroad station. (**!** put up は「(掲示など)を掲げる」の意)

❸【立ちのぼる】rise*. (⇒立ち上る) ▶彼はほこりが立たないように庭に水をまいている He is sprinkling water in the garden to keep the dust from *rising* [to keep the dust down].

❹【行動を起こす】take* action; (反抗する) rise* (up)《*against*》. (⇒立ち上がる) ● 市長選に立つ(=立候補する) *run* for mayor (xa, xthe) [(the) mayoralty]. ● 彼の証人に立つ *stand* witness *for* him. ▶立つべき時が来た The time has come *to take action* [*for action*]./It's time to *act*.

❺【立場・状態にある】● 議論で彼の側に立つ(=彼に味方する) *take sides with* [*side with*] him in the argument. ●人の上に立つ(=人を指導する) lead other people. ●彼は大金を失って苦境に立っている He *is in trouble* [*in difficulties*] because he has lost a large sum of money. (!)後の方は特に金に困っていることだ)

❻ [成り立つ] (論理に合う) be logical; (道理にかなう) be reasonable; (計画などが) be made; (方針などが確立される) be established. ▶君の議論は筋道が立たない(=筋が通らない) Your argument *is illogical* [*not logical*]. ▶計画は立ちましたか Have you *made* your plan? ▶まだ我々の方針は立っていません Our policy *has* not *been established* yet./We haven't decided on our policy yet.

❼ [出発する] leave* (*for*), start 《*from*》. ▶彼女はあす東京へ立つことになっている She *is leaving for* Tokyo tomorrow. ▶彼は日本を立ってアメリカへ向かった He *left* [*started from*] Japan for America.

● 立つ鳥跡を濁さず (去る前に自分の身辺を整理すべきである) You should put your affairs in order before you leave./(どんな悪い鳥にも自分の巣はよごさないものだ)(ことわざ) It is an ill bird that fouls its own nest.

*たつ 建つ [造られる] be built; [像などが] be erected, be set [put] up (!)後の方が口語的). ▶このあたりは新しい家がぞくぞく建っている New houses *are being built* one after another in this neighborhood. (!)自動詞用法の New houses *are building*... は《書》または《古》) ▶公園に記念碑が建った They *erected* [*set up*, *put up*] a monument in the park.

*たつ 経つ [経過する] pass (by [*away*]) (!)しばしば by, away を伴って過去の意を強調); [時間が経つ] go* (通例様態を表す副詞(句)を伴う), go by, go on (!)前の方は時の経過、後の方は時の経過の継続性を強調); [飛ぶように過ぎる] fly*. (⇒過ぎる) ▶時間の経つのを忘れる forget [not notice] the *passage of time* (!)やや堅い表現); 《話》lose track of time. ▶時が経つにつれて彼のことは忘れ去られた As time *passed* [*went by*, *went on*], he was forgotten. ▶象牙(『》)は年月が経つと(=年月とともに)黄色くなる Ivory turns yellow *with age*. ▶今日はなかなか時間が経たなかった Time *passed* [*went*] slowly today. ▶彼が死んで 10 年経った It is [It has been] ten years since he died./Ten years *have* [×has] *passed* since he died./He has been dead (for) ten years. (!)Ten years *has* passed....は不可)/(10 年前に死んだ) He died ten years ago. ▶この家は建ってから少なくとも 30 年は経っている(=30 年の古さだ) This house is at least 30 years *old*. ▶どちらが正しいかは時が経てば分かる Time will tell [show] which is right. (!)単に Time will tell. でもこの意は表せる)

会話 「彼が出かけてからどのくらい経つの」「10 分かそこらよ」"How long *has* he *been gone*?" "Ten minutes or so."

① [...経って[経ったら]] [[未来について]] (現在・過去から見て) in ...; (現在から見て) ... from now; [[過去について]] after ...; ... later, ... after (that). ▶彼は 1 週間経ったら帰って来るだろう He will be back *in* a week('s time) [be back a week *from now*]. (!)*in* a week は「1 週間(以)内に (within a week)」の意にもなる (⇒②)) ▶彼は 1 週間経って帰って来た He came back *after* a week [a week *later*, a week *after* (*that*)]. (!)after a week が単に期間を表すだけなのに対し、後の二つは「(それから)1 週間経って」の意. なお、... after より ... later の方が普通)

② [...経たないうちに] ▶彼は 1 週間も経たないうちに (= 以内に) 帰って来るだろう He will be back *within* [*in* (*less than*)] a week./(帰って来る前に 1 週間いだろう) It will not be a week *before* he comes [×will come] back. ▶3 週間と経たないうちに沖縄は 4 回もひどい台風を経験した *In less than* three weeks, Okinawa went through four terrible typhoons.

たつ 絶つ, 断つ ❶ [断絶する] (関係などを) break... off; (人と) break with .... ▶日本はその国との外交関係を絶った Japan *broke off* [*severed*] diplomatic relations with the country.

❷ [断念する] give*... up; (誓って) swear*... off. (⇒止む) ▶たばこを断つ *give up* [*stop*] smoking; 《話》(誓ってやめる) *swear off* smoking.

❸ [遮断する] cut*... off; [中断する] interrúpt. ▶その町は外部との連絡が断たれてしまった The town has been cut off from all outside communication. ▶列車の運行が脱線のため断たれている Train services *have been interrupted* by the derailment. ▶敵の退路を断つな Don't *close off* the enemy's escape route.

❹ [命を奪う] ▶自らの命を絶つ *take* one's own life; (自殺する) kill oneself, commit suicide. (⇒自殺) ▶彼は交通事故で命を絶った He *was killed in* a traffic accident. ▶彼の政治生命は絶たれた His political career has come to an end [(だめになる)《話》*is done for*].

❺ [根絶する] ●悪の根を絶つ *root out* evils. ●悪習を絶つ *get rid of* a bad habit.

たつ 辰 the Dragon.
● 辰年 [「十二支」] the year of the Dragon. (⇒干支)《関連》

たつ 裁つ cut*. (⇒裁断) ●スカートを作るために生地を裁つ *cut* cloth for a skirt.

だつ 脱— ●脱工業化の *post*-industrial. ●有権者の脱政治化 *depoliticization* of the electorate. ●脱サラする (⇒サラ)

たつい 達意 ●達意の文 lucid [intelligible] writing.

だつい 脱衣 —脱衣する 動 take off one's clothes; undress (oneself).
●脱衣場 a dréssing room, a chánging room; (海水浴場やプールなどの)《米》a bathhouse; (体育施設の) a locker room.

ダッカ [バングラデシュの首都] Dacca /dǽkə/.

だっかい 脱会 —脱会する 動 (やめる) leave. ●医師会を脱会する *leave* [*withdraw from*] the medical association.

だっかい 奪回 —奪回する 動 (取り戻す) win [get] ... back, regain. ▶タイトルを奪回する *win back* the title. ▶政権を奪回する(=返り咲く) *return to* power.

たっかん 達観 图 (悟り) philósophy.
—達観する 動 ●人生を達観する be philosóphical of [《英》on] life; take a *philosophical* view of life. ●達観して philosóphically.

だっかん 奪還 —奪還する 動 recapture, regain.

だっきゃく 脱却 —脱却する 動 get out of ...; (困難な状態から) pull out of ...; (...から自由になる) get rid of .... ●長い不況から脱却する *pull out of* a long depression.

たっきゅう 卓球 ping-pong, táble(-)tènnis. ●卓球のボール a *ping-pong* bàll. ●卓球のラケット a *ping-pong* racket [paddle, bat]. ●卓球をする play *table tennis* [*ping-pong*].
●卓球選手 a táble-tennis [a píng-pong] plàyer. ●卓球台 a píng-pong tàble.

だっきゅう 脱臼 图 (a) dislocation. ●肩の脱臼

たっきゅうびん 宅急便
― **脱臼する** 動 〖医学〗dislocate. ● 肩を脱臼する *dislocate* one's shoulder.

たっきゅうびん 宅急便 〖『宅配便』の商標名〗(⇨宅配)

タック 〖服飾〗(縫いひだ) a tuck. ● そでにタックを取る make *tucks* in the sleeves; put *tucks* in at the sleeve.

ダッグアウト 〖野球〗a dúgòut.

タックス 〖税金〗(a) tax.
● タックスフリー〖免税〗tax free. ● タックスヘイブン〖税金回避地〗a tax haven.

ダックスフント [<ドイツ語]〖動物〗(犬) a dachshund /dάːkshùnt, -hùnd/, 〖英語〗a sáusage dòg.

たづくり 田作り (⇨ごまめ)

タックル 图 a tackle, a challenge.
― **タックルする** 動 tackle; make a tackle.

-たっけ ▶ 高校時代よく勉強したっけ〖回想〗We studied very hard in high school, *didn't we?* ▶ あの人は何て言ったっけ〖質問〗What is his name?/What did he say?

たっけん 卓見 an excellent idea. ● 卓見に富んだ論文 a paper [an academic paper, an essay] full of *excellent ideas*.

だっこ 抱っこ (⇨抱く) ▶ ママ、だっこして Carry me, Mom!

だっこう 脱肛 〖医学〗anal prolapse; proctoptosis /pràktəptóusis/.

だっこう 脱稿 ― **脱稿する** 動 finish (writing)《an article》; complete《a thesis》.

だっこく 脱穀 ― **脱穀する** 動 thresh.
● 脱穀機 a thréshing machine; a thresher.

だつごく 脱獄 图 prison breaking; (1回の行為) a prison break, a jailbreak.
― **脱獄する** 動 escape from prison; break (out of) prison.
● 脱獄囚 a prison [a jail] breaker; (逃亡囚) an escaped convict.

だつサラ 脱サラ ― **脱サラする** 動 quit the company and become self-employed. ● 脱サラしてレストランを開く *quit the company* and open a restaurant.

だつさんしん 奪三振 〖野球〗a strikeout. (❗打者が喫する三振にも用いる) ▶ その投手は9人のバッターから奪三振5の成績だった The pitcher *struck out* five of the nine batters.
● 奪三振王 a strikeout king.

たっし 達し an official notice. ● 達しを出す issue *an official notice*.

だつじ 脱字 an omitted letter.
● 脱字記号 a caret〖記号 ∧〗.

だっしにゅう 脱脂乳 skim [skimmed] milk.

だっしふんにゅう 脱脂粉乳 (powdered) skim [skimmed] milk; non-fat dry milk.

だっしめん 脱脂綿 〖米〗absorbent /əbzɔ́ːrbənt/ cotton, cotton batting; 〖英〗cotton wool.

たっしゃ 達者 ― **達者な** 形 ❶〖壮健〗● 達者な人 a *healthy* person. ▶ 父は年をとっているが達者です My father is old, but he is *healthy* and *active* [《書》 *hale and hearty*].
❷〖上手〗● 口の達者な人 a *good* talker; (軽蔑的) a *glib* talker. ● 腕の達者な外科医 a *skillful* surgeon. ● 達者な(=流ちょうな)英語を話す speak *fluent* English; speak English *fluently*. ▶ 彼女は水泳が達者(=得意)です She is *good* at swimming./She is a *good* swimmer. ▶ 彼は芸達者(=多才な人)だ He is a *versatile* entertainer.

だっしゅ 奪取 图 seizure /síːʒər/.
― **奪取する** 動 (敵地などを) seize /síːz/; (権力・地位などを不法に)《書》usurp. ● 城を奪取する seize [*capture*] a castle. ● 王位を奪取する seize [*capture*, *usurp*] the throne. ● 1試合で15三振を奪取する strike out fifteen batters in a game.

ダッシュ 图 ❶〖符号〗a dash (―); a prime (′) (❗bは /bíːpráim/ と読む). (⇨巻末 [句読法])
❷〖突進〗a dash.
― **ダッシュする** 動 〖突進する〗dash, make a dash《for》.

だっしゅう 脱臭 ― **脱臭する** 動 remove the unpleasant smell; deodorize.
● 脱臭剤 (a) deodorant /dióudərənt/; (a) deodorizer.

だっしゅつ 脱出 (an) escape.
― **脱出する** 動 ● 燃えている家から脱出する *escape from*《外へ出る》*get out of* the burning house. ● 海外に脱出する *escape to* a foreign country. ● 脱出速度 (引力からの)〖物理〗escape velocity.

ダッシュボード a dashboard; 《主に米話》a dash.

だっしょく 脱色 decòlorátion.
― **脱色する** 動 remove the color, decólorize; (漂白する) bleach.

たつじん 達人 〖大家, 名人〗a master (⇨大家〖たいか〗, 名人); 〖専門家〗an éxpert. ● 柔道の達人 a *master* [an *expert*] *at judo*.

だっすい 脱水 图 dehydration /diːhàidréiʃən/. (❗「脱水症」の意でも用いる) ● 脱水症状を起こす become [be] *dehydrated*. ● 脱水症状を起こして死ぬ die of *dehydration*.
― **脱水する**〖させる〗動 (やや書)dehýdrate; (洗濯機で) spin-dry.
● 脱水機 (洗濯機の) a spin-dryer, a spinner.

***たっする** 達する ❶〖行き着く〗reach, get*《to》; (到着する) arrive《at, in》(⇨着く), (伸びる) extend《to》(⇨及ぶ). ● 結論に達する reach [*arrive at*, *come to*] a conclusion. ▶ 彼は時間どおりに目的地に達した He *reached* [*arrived at*, *got to*] his destination on time. ▶ 物音どうやら我々の耳に達しなかった Not a sound *reached* our ears. ▶ 彼女の髪は腰に達している Her hair *reaches down to* [*comes (down) to*] her waist.
❷〖数量が〗(及ぶ) reach; (総計…になる) amount to …, total (up to)…. ▶ 彼の負債は100万円に達した His debts *reached* [*amounted to*, *totaled* (*up to*), *came to*, *ran* (*up*) *to*] one million yen. ▶ 応募者が1,000人に達した The number of (×the) applicants *reached* [*amounted to*] 1,000./The applicants *totaled* 1,000. (❗主語が人の場合は total を用いる) ▶ 彼は90歳に達した He *reached* the age of ninety./He *became* ninety (years old) on his last birthday. (⇨為〖な〗る ❹)
❸〖達成する〗achieve, 《やや書》accomplish; (実現する) realize. ● 目的を達する *achieve* [*accomplish*, *realize*] one's purpose; *reach* [《書》*attain*] one's goal.
❹〖ある状態・基準に〗(到達する) reach, (努力して)《書》attain《to》; (届く) come* up to …; (習得する) master. ● プロの域に達する *reach* the professional level. ● 標準に達する[しない] *come up to* [*fall short of*] the standard. ▶ 劇はここでクライマックスに達する The play *reaches* [*comes to*] its climax here.

だっする 脱する ● 難局を脱する *get out of* a difficult situation. ● 危機を脱する(=乗り越える) *get over* a crisis. ● 生き埋めの危険を脱する(=逃れる) *escape (from* the danger of*)* being buried alive. ● 不況から脱する come out of [《立ち直る》 *recover from*] the recession.

たつせ 立つ瀬 ▶それでは私の立つ瀬がない (苦境に陥る) That would put me in a tight corner./(面子を失わせる) That would make me lose face.

＊たっせい 達成 名 (an) achievement; (並外れた目標の)《書》(an) attainment.
— **達成する** 動 ｜目標を達成する achieve [《書》attain] one's objective [goal].

だつぜい 脱税 名 tax evasion. ▶彼は脱税で告訴された He was accused of *tax evasion*.
— **脱税する** 動 evade (paying) taxes.
● **脱税者** a tax evader.

だっせん 脱線 名 [列車の] (a) derailment; [話の] a sidetrack, 《書》(a) digression 《from》.
— **脱線する** 動 ｜[列車が] go off [leave, jump] the rails 《次の言い方より口語的》; be [get] derailed; [人が話で] be [get] sidetracked 《into doing》; wander [stray, 《書》digréss] 《from the subject》; get off 《the subject》. ▶ちょっと脱線しましたが、話をもとに戻しましょう I've *been sidetracked* for a minute, but I'll get back to what I was talking about.

だっそ 脱疽 名 (⇨壊疽(えそ))

だっそう 脱走 名 (an) escape.
— **脱走する** 動 ｜刑務所を脱走する escape [run away] from prison; break (out of) prison. ▶兵士は軍を集団で脱走した The soldiers *deserted* 《from》 the army in a group.
● **脱走者** a rúnawàу; (脱獄者) an escàpée.
● **脱走兵** a deserter /dizə́ːrtər/.

だつぞく 脱俗 ｜脱俗している keep [hold, remain, stand] aloof from the worldly affairs. ● **脱俗の** unworldly.

＊たった [ただ…だけ] only; [(数・量が)わずか…にすぎない] no more than ...; [ちょうど…だけ] just.

> **使い分け** only 「たった」を意味する最も一般的な語.
> **no more than** only よりやや堅い表現.
> **just** only より正確・厳密さを強調する.「たった今」という意も.

● たった3日間 *only* for three days; for *only* three days. ● たった1分の差で列車に間に合わない miss the train by *just* one minute. ● たった1人で行く go *all alone* [*by oneself*]. ▶彼にはたった一つ弱点がある.ギャンブルである He has *only* one weak point: gambling. ▶彼はたった2時間しか働かなかった He worked *only* [*no more than*] two hours. ▶彼はたった今到着したばかりです He has (*only*) *just* [《主に米語》He *just*] arrived. (!) *only* があると強意的)/He arrived *just now*. (!) *just now* は過去時制とともに用いる)

＊だったい 脱退 名 (会などからの) (a) withdrawal.
— **脱退する** 動 withdraw 《from》; (去る) leave. ● 文学会から脱退する *withdraw from* a literary society. ● 連盟から脱退する《書》*secede from* the federation.

-だったか ｜昨年たぶん彼に会ったことがある It was *probably* last year that I saw [met] him.

たったひとりのはんらん『たった一人の反乱』 *Singular Rebellion*.《参考》丸谷才一の小説

だったら if so. (⇨それなら)

タッチ ❶[触ること] a touch; [野球] a tag ▶野手がベースにタッチする場合と手が触る場合は touch も用いる. ● タッチの差で敗れる be defeated by a *touch*. ● タッチネットする *touch* the net. ▶彼は病院へ急いで駆けつけたが、タッチの差で娘の死に目にあえなかった He rushed to the hospital, but his daughter had died just minutes before he arrived.
❷[芸術的手法、キーや弦の調子] a touch. ● 重い[軽い]タッチのピアノ a piano with a heavy [light] *touch*. ● 生き生きしたタッチで絵をかく paint a picture with a vivid *touch*. ● 彼は軽快なタッチでピアノを弾いた He had a light *touch* on the piano.
— **タッチする** 動 ❶[触る] touch. ● 走者にタッチする *tag* a runner; make a *tag* on a runner.
❷[関係する] ▶私はその問題にタッチしていません I *have nothing to do with* [I *have no connection with*, I'm *not involved in*] the matter.
● **タッチアンドゴー** (do [make]) a touch and go.《参考》飛行機の離着陸訓練 ● **タッチタイピング** touch-typing. (⇨ブラインドタッチ) ● **タッチダウン**[ラグビー・アメフト] a touchdown. ● **タッチダウンする** make a touchdown; touch down. ● **タッチパネル** [コンピュータ] (touch) a touch screen [panel]. ● **タッチプレー** [野球] a tag play.

タッチアウト [野球] a tágoùt; (和製語) a touch out. ▶走者は二塁でタッチアウトになった The runner *was tagged out* at second (base).

タッチアップ 名 [野球] a tág ùp.
— **タッチアップする** 動 tag up. (!) touch up は「帰塁する」

だっちょう 脱腸 (a) hernia. (⇨ヘルニア)

タッチライン [サッカー・ラグビー] a touchline, a side-line. ● タッチラインを割る go over the *touchline*. ● タッチライン際50ヤードのラン 《his》 fifty-yard run down the *touchline*.

ダッチロール [航空] a Dutch roll.

ダッチワイフ a Dutch wife.

たって (=たっても)とおっしゃるなら if you *insist* [*will*]. ▶彼のたっての頼みでその本を彼に貸してやった I lent the book to him *at his earnest* [《重ねての》*repeated*] request.

-たって 《接続助詞》❶[たとえ…しても] even if ..., even though .... (!) 前の方が口語的)(⇨-ても ❶)▶雨が降ったって出発します I'll start, *even if* it rains [×will rain].
❷[どんなに…しても] no matter whát [whére, hów, etc.]. (⇨-ても❶) ▶彼はどんなにたくさん食べったって太らない *No matter how* [*However*] much he eats, he never gets fat [《婉曲的》gain weight, put on weight]. (!) *No matter how* ... の方が However ... より口語的) ▶どこへ行ったって、家はいい所はないと分かるよ *No matter where* [*Wherever*] you go, you will find there is no place like home. (!) 前の方が口語的)

＊だって after áll (!) 通例文頭で、聞き手も知っていると思われる理由を確認する); [なぜなら] because (!) 直接的な原因を表し、新情報を導く); [と言うのは] 《書》for (!) 軽く理由を付け足す). (⇨なぜならば[と言うのは]) ▶その子はまだ歩けない.だってまだ10か月だから The baby can't walk yet. *After all*, he's only ten months old. (!) 次例と異なりこの場合「あなたもご承知のとおり」の意を含む)/The baby can't walk yet, *because* [×since, ×as,《書》*for*] he's only ten months old.
会話 「なぜそんなに楽しそうなの」「だって今日はデートだから」"Why do you look so happy?" "*Because* [×*For*] I have a date today." (!) *Why* ...? に対しては *Because* ... で答える)
会話 「何ぐずぐずしているの」「だって靴が見当たらないのよ」"What are you waiting for?" "I can't find my shoes." (!) このように「だって」にあたる語を入れないこともある)

-だって 《副助詞》❶[…でさえ] even. (⇨-でも) ▶小さい子供だってそんなこと知っている *Even* a little child knows that. ▶彼は何だってできる He can do any-

だって thing [everything]. ▶びた一文だってやるものか I won't give *a single* penny. / *Not a single* penny will I give. (!) 後の方が強調的)
❷ [...もまた] too, as well (!) いずれも通例文尾で); also (!)(1) too より堅い語. (2) 通例動詞は動詞の前, be 動詞・助動詞の後で). (⇒また)
会話 「私はピアノが弾ける」「私だって弾ける」 "I can play the piano." "I can (play the piano), ＼*too.*" (!)(1)「(ある楽器の他に)ピアノだって弾ける」の意では強勢の位置は後ろに: I can play the piano, ＼*too.* (2) 否定文では too を用いず either を用いる: 私だってピアノは弾けない I can't play the piano, *either* (×*too*).)
会話 「じゃあそのことで腹を立てていたのか」「ああ, だれだって腹も立つよ」 "You were angry about it, then." "Well, who wouldn't have been?" (!) 修辞疑問文を用いた言い方)
❸ [聞き返すとき] 会話 「答えは 6 だって？」「それじゃ間違ってる？」 "You say the answer is six?" "Am I wrong then?"
会話 「6 時までにここに来るって彼言ってたわ」「何時までにだって？」 "He'll be here by six, he said." "By what time(, did he say)?" (!) He'll ..., he said は中間話法で, 正確には He said that he would ..., となるところ)
会話 「何だって？」「どうして聞いてないのよ. ばかねぇ」 "What's thát you ／say?/Whát (did you) ／say?" "Why don't you listen, you idiot?"

だっと 脱兎 ●*脱兎の勢いで* at a furious [a terrific] speed.

だっとう 脱党 图 (a) defection《*from*》,《米》a bolt.
— **脱党する** leave [defect from,《米》bolt (from)] a party.
●脱党者 a defector,《米》a bolter.

たづな 手綱 reins. ●手綱を締める[引く; ゆるめる] tighten [pull (on); loosen] the *reins*. (!) 比喩的にも用いる) ●手綱さばきが上手である handle the *reins* skillfully.

たつのおとしご 竜の落とし子 [魚介] a sea horse.

だっぴ 脱皮 图 the shedding of the skin;[生物] an ecdysis [ékdəsis/ékdəsɪs/-si:z/].
— **脱皮する** 動 ●蛇は脱皮する The snake *sheds* [*casts* (*off*)] its *skin*. ●彼女は古い考え方から脱皮した She *shed* [*got rid of*] his old way of thinking.

たっぴつ 達筆 ●彼は達筆だ He *has* (×a) *good handwriting.*/He *writes a good hand.*/He *writes well.*

タップダンス (1回の) a tap dance; (踊ること) tap dancing. ●タップダンスを踊るな a tap dance; tap-dance, tap. ●踊る人は a tap dancer, 靴は tap shoes)

たっぷり ❶ [いっぱい満ちて] [十分に] fully, a lot, plentifully; (気前よく) generously. ▶雨の後で大地はたっぷり水を吸っていた The earth has *fully* soaked up the water after the rain. ●彼は庭にたっぷり水をまいた He watered the garden *plentifully.* ●彼女はトーストにマーマレードをたっぷりぬった She put marmalade *generously* on her toast.
❷ [十分に] enough (⇒十分); (量・程度が十分な) good; (十分旨に合うほど多くの) plenty of .... (たくさん) ●彼らはお金はたっぷりある They have *enough* [*plenty of*, *no lack of*] money. ▶そのシャツは横幅がたっぷりある That shirt is wide [large] enough. ▶我々はたっぷり休んだ We have had a *good* rest. ▶私たちはたっぷり 1 時間は待った We waited for a *good* hour. ▶ここから駅までたっぷり 20 キロは(=20 キロも)ある It is *no less than* twenty kilometers

from here to the station. ▶彼はたっぷり 100 キロはある(=100 キロをかなり超えている) He weighs *well* over one hundred kilos.

ダッフルコート 图 a duffel [a duffle] coat.

だっぷん 脱糞 图 defecation.
— **脱糞する** 動 excrete feces; defecate.

だっぽう 脱帽 — **脱帽する** 動 take off [《米話》tip] one's hat 《*to*》. (!) 比喩的にも用いる) ●彼の勇気に脱帽する *take off* [《米話》*tip*] *one's hat to* him for his courage.

だっぽう 脱法 ●脱法行為をする circumvent [evade] the law.

たつまき 竜巻 [[陸上の]] a tornado /tɔːrnéidou/ (優〜(e)s),《米話》a twister (参考) 主に米国中西部に起こる); [[海上の]] a waterspout.

たつみ 巽 southeast.

だつもう 脱毛 (病気などが原因の) loss of hair; (美容のための) removal of hair.
●脱毛剤 a hair remover; a depilatory. ●脱毛症 [医学] alopecia /ælopí:ʃiə/; (円形脱毛症) alopecia areata /æriéitə/.

＊**だつらく** 脱落 ▶文中に 1 語脱落がある A word *is left out* [《欠けている》 *is missing*] in the sentence.
— **脱落する** 動 (競争などで落後する) drop out 《*of*》; (遅れる) drop [fall] behind (...); (文章などが漏れ落ちている) be omitted, be left out (!) 後の方が口語的). ●レースから脱落する a *drop out of* the race; *drop* [*fall*] *behind* (the others) in the race.
●脱落者 a drópout.

だつりょく 脱力 ●脱力感を覚える feel as if all one's strength were gone.

だつりん 脱輪 — **脱輪する** 動 (車輪が車軸から) come off; (車が道から) run off.

＊**たて** 縦 ❶ [長さ] (a) length; [高さ] (a) height /háit/. (⇒横) ●タオルを縦に折りたたむ fold a towel *lengthways* [*lengthwise*]. ●縦(=垂直)の線を引く draw a *vertical* (↔horizontal) line; draw a line *vertically* (↔horizontally). ●この花壇は縦 7 メートル, 横 4 メートルです This flower bed is seven meters *long* [*in length*] and four (meters) wide [in width]. (!) long, wide の方が口語的. 米英では four meters wide and seven (meters) *long*. というのが普通)/This flower bed is four meters *by* seven. (!) by の前後は横×縦の順が多い) ●子供たちは縦に 1 列に並んだ The children lined up *one behind another* [*behind each other*]./The children stood *in a single file.* (!) file は「列列」)
❷ [その他の表現] ●首を縦に振る(=同意する) agree,《書》assent; nod one's head [×neck]; nod in agreement [《やや書》assent].
●**縦から見ても横から見ても** ▶彼は縦から見ても横から見ても紳士だ(あらゆる点で) He is *every inch* a gentleman./(完全な) He is a *perfect* gentleman.
●**縦の関係** (上下関係)《have》a vertical (↔horizontal) relationship 《*with*》. (⇒上下)
●**縦のものを横にもしない** ▶夫は家ではごろごろするばかりで縦のものを横にもしない My husband wo*n't lift a finger to* do anything but laze around at home. (!) do nothing but (do) 「(...する以外は何もしない)の強調した言い方」

たて 盾 [[a shield; [円形の]] a buckler. ●法律[校則]を盾に on the strength of the law [school rules]. (⇒応用)
●**盾にとる** use (it) as a shield [an excuse]. (!) excuse は「口実」の意)

たて 殺陣 a fighting scene.
●殺陣師 a swordplay instructor.

- **-たて** [［...したばかりの］] fresh 《*from*》, (新しい) new; [新たに] freshly, newly 《以上は2語は通例過去分詞の前に置く》. ● 焼きたてのパン fresh [*freshly* baked] bread; bread *fresh from* the oven. ● 取りたてのイチゴ *freshly* picked strawberries. ● 炊きたてのご飯 *just*-cooked rice. ● 学校出たての社員 an employee *fresh from* [*just out of*] school. ● 結婚したての夫婦 a *newly* married couple; newlyweds.
- **たで** 蓼 [植物] a smartweed.
  - ● たで食う虫も好きずき 'Some insects prefer bitter leaves of knotweeds.'/(好みは説明できない) 《ことわざ》 There's no accounting for taste [《今は古》tastes]./(人はそれぞれ) 《ことわざ》 To each his own. (➪好み)
- **だて** 伊達 ▶彼女はだて眼鏡をかけている She wears glasses *for appearance' sake* [*just for show*]. ▶彼はだてに(= むだに)留学をしたわけではなかった He didn't study abroad *for nothing*. ▶だてや酔狂で(= 単におもしろ半分で)こんなことができるものではない This is something you can't do *just for fun* [(ただの)気まぐれで *just on a whim*].
  - ● だての薄着 ▶彼はだての薄着をして風邪を引いた He caught (a) cold because he *wore thin clothes despite the cold in order to look nice*.
- **-だて -立て** ▶2頭立ての馬車 a two-horse carriage.
- **-だて -建て** ▶3階建ての家 a three-*storied* [a three-*story*] house; a house of three stories. ● 一戸建ての家 a *detached* house. ● 2階建てバス a *double-decker* [ˣa two-story] bus.
- **たてあな** 縦穴, 竪穴 a pit.
  - ● 竪穴式住居 a pit dwelling.
- **たてあみ** 建て網 [漁業] a fish trap.
- **ていた** 立て板 ▶立て板に水 ▶彼女の話し方は立て板に水だ(= 非常に流ちょうに話す) She talks very fluently [with great fluency].
- **たいと** 縦糸 the warp (⇔wept, woof).
- **たてうり** 建て売り —— 建て売りする 動 build and sell a house; sell a ready-built house.
  - ● 建て売り住宅 a ready-built house; 《集合的》ready-built housing; 《米》 a tract home [house] 《参考》各戸がほぼ同じ形態の住宅団地の一軒.
- **たてかえる** 立て替える ▶彼のタクシー代を立て替えた(貸してやった) I *lent* him his taxi fare./(彼に代わって支払った) I *paid* his taxi fare *for* him.
- **たてかえる** 建て替える rebuild*; (再建する) reconstruct. (➪建てる) ▶大仏殿は752年に建てられたが, 1708年に現存のものに建て替えられた The present Hall of the Great Buddha, originally built in 752, *was rebuilt* in 1708.
- **たてがき** 縦書き vertical writing. ● 縦書きにする write 《it》 vertically [in vertical lines, from top to bottom].
- **たてかける** 立てかける put* 《lean*, rest, set*, stand*》... 《against》. ▶彼は壁にはしごを立てかけた He *put* [*leaned, set, stood*] a ladder *against* the wall.
- **たてがみ** (馬・ライオンなどの) a mane. ▶たてがみのあるマネ maned (⇔maneless).
- **たてかんばん** 立て看板 (看板) a signboard; (大きな広告掲示板)《米》a billboard,《英》a hoarding. (➪看板) ▶文化祭の立て看板 a *signboard* for the school festival.
- **たてぎょうじ** 立行司 [相撲] a *tategyoji*; the head sumo referee.
- **たてきる** 立て切る shut [close] 《the door》 tight(ly).
- ***たてぐ** 建具 (移動可能な) fittings; (作り付けの) fixtures. (▶取り付けの照明器具など, 家の機能を果たすのに不可欠なもの)
  - ● 建具屋 《米》a (door) carpenter,《主に英》a joiner.
- **たてぐみ** 縦組み [印刷] vertical typesetting. ● 縦組みにする typeset [set type] vertically.
- **たてこう** 立て坑, 縦坑 a (mine) shaft.
- **たてごと** 竪琴 [楽器] a harp. ● たて琴を弾く play the *harp*.
- **たてこむ** 立て込む [人で混雑する] be crowded 《with》. ▶彼は仕事が立て込んでいる He *is* very *busy* [*is pressed, is tied up*] *with* work.
- **たてこむ** 建て込む [場所が建物で一杯になる] be built up. ▶家が建て込んだ地域 a *built-up* area.
- **たてこもる** 立てこもる (部屋に) shut* oneself (up) in one's room; (城に) hold* the castle 《against》.
- **たてじく** 縦軸 (グラフの) a vertical axis /ǽksɪs/, a y axis; (機械の) a vertical shaft.
- **たてじま** 縦縞 vertical stripes; (細い縞) pinstripes.
- **たてしゃかい** 縦社会 (説明的に) a society in which vertical relationships are regarded as important.
- **たてつく** 盾突く (公然と) defy; (反抗する) disobéy. ▶党のリーダーに盾突く *defy* a party leader.
- **たてつけ** 立て付け, 建て付け ▶この戸はどうにも立て付けが悪い(= なめらかに動かない[開閉できない]) This door won't *move* [*open and close*] smoothly.
- **たてつづけ** 立て続け —— 立て続けに 副 (連続して) in succession, in a row; (間をおかずに) one after another. ▶立て続けに酒を3杯飲む have three drinks *in a row*. ● 立て続けに質問をする ask questions *one after another*. ▶そのことが4回立て続けに起こった It happened four times *in (close) succession*.
- **たてつぼ** 建て坪 (a) floor space. ▶建て坪120平方メートルの住宅は東京では相当大きい方だ Houses that have a *floor space* of 120 square meters are much bigger than the average ones in Tokyo.
- **たてなおす** 立て直す ❶ [正常(の位置)に戻す] put*... back in place; (人・事態を) put... to rights [normal]. ● 倒れた看板を立て直す *put up* a fallen signboard *again*.
  ❷ [作り直す] make* [arrange, shape]... again. ● 計画を立て直す make a plan *again*; make a *renewed* plan.
- **たてなおす** 建て直す rebuild*, reconstruct. (❗いずれも「企業を建て直す」意にも用いる)
- **たてなが** 縦長 —— 縦長の 形 vertically long; (長方形の) oblong (▶「横長」の意にもなる).
- **たてひざ** 立て膝 ● 立てひざする sit with one knee drawn [pulled] up close to the chest.
- **たてぶえ** 立笛 [楽器] a recorder /rɪkɔ́ːdər/. (➪リコーダー)
- **たてふだ** 立て札 《米》a bulletin /búlǝtn/ board, 《英》a notice board. ● 立て札を立てる put up a *bulletin board*.
- ***たてまえ** 建て前 (表向きの原則) one's public principle(s); (公の立場) one's official stand. ● 建て前では in *theory*; in *principle*. ▶入場券がなければ入れないというのは建て前だ *Officially*, you can't enter without a ticket./You can't get in without a ticket. It's a *principle*. ▶建て前と本音があんなに違う人も珍しい I've never met a person like him who *says one thing and means quite another*.
- **だてまき** 伊達巻 (料理) *datemaki*; (説明的に) a rolled omelet mixed with whitefish.
- **たてまし** 建て増し 图 (an) extension. (➪増築)

たてまつる 奉る 〘差し上げる〙offer (⇨差し上げる❷); 〘祭り上げる〙set (him) up (as president).

＊たてもの 建物 a building; a structure (❗後の方が堅い語). ●高い建物 a tall [a high] building. ▶建物全体の重量кによる4本の柱にかかっている These four pillars receive [sustain] the weight of the entire structure (of the building).

たてやくしゃ 立て役者 〘中心人物〙a leader, a leading figure; 〘中心となる俳優〙a leading actor [actress].

たてゆれ 縦揺れ 图 a [the] pitch (↔a [the] roll). (❗複数形にしない)

── 縦揺れする 動 rise and fall; (船が) pitch. (⇨揺れ)

たてよこ 縦横 length and width 〘《書》breadth〙.

-だてら ●女だてらに unlike a woman; although [though] she is a woman. ●子供だてらに大きな口をたたくんじゃない Don't talk big! You're just a kid.

﹡たてる 立てる ❶〘立て起こす〙(立たせる) stand*; (倒れた物を起こす) raise; (定位置に立てる) set*; (掲げる) put*... up; (しっかり立てる) plant. ●テーブルにろうそくを立てる stand candles on a table. ●壁にはしごを立てかける stand [set, put, lean] a ladder against the wall. (⇨掛ける) ●道路標識を立てる put up road signs. ●地面にポールを立てる(=固定させる) fix [set] a pole in the ground. ●尾[耳]をぴんと立てる (⇨尾, ぴんと) ▶通りに旗が立てられた The flags were put up [were set up, (掲揚された) were hoisted] in the streets. ▶最初に K2 の頂上に旗を立てたのはだれでしょう Who first planted a flag on the peak of K2?

❷〘発生させる, 出す〙(ほこりなどを) raise; (音などを) make*. ●大きな音を立てる make a loud [so much] noise. ●うわさを立てる start [広める] spread] a rumor. ▶その車はもうもうとほこりを立てて走り去って行った The car sped away, raising a cloud of dust. ●スープを飲むときは音を立てるな Don't make noise when you eat [have, ✕drink] soup./Don't slurp your soup. ●スープをすする音 slurp は「音を立てながら飲食する」の意で, 欧米ではマナーに反する) ▶声を立てるな(しっ！) Hush!/(静かに) Be quiet!

❸〘計画・理論などを〙(作成する) make*; (打ち立てる) set*... up; (確立する) establish. ●夏休みの[家を買う]計画を立てる make plans for the summer vacation [to buy a house]. ●新しい理論を立てる set up [build, formulate] a new theory. ●新記録を立てる set up [establish, set] a new record. ●政策を立てる establish 〘やや書〙frame] a policy.

❹〘その他の表現〙●彼を私の先輩として立てる(=敬意を持って応対する) be respectful to him as my senior. ●顔を立てる save (↔lose) face. (❗今はone's を付けない) ●医者として身を立てる establish oneself as a doctor. ●大統領候補に立てる(=推薦する) put up a candidate for the presidency.

＊たてる 建てる build*, put*... up; (建設する) construct 〘build より堅い語〙; (...の上に) found (on) (❗しばしば受け身で); (記念碑などを) erect, set* [put]... up [set [put]... up の方が口語的). ●丸太で小屋を建てる build [put up] a cabin from the logs. ▶彼は新しい家を建てた He built a new house./He had a new house built. (❗前の方は「自分でまたは建築業者に命じて家を建てた」の両方の意を表すが, 後の方は「建築業者に建ててもらった」の意. 日常表現では前の方が多く用いられる) ▶家の近くに新しいスーパーが建てられている They are building [con-

structing] a new supermarket near my house. (❗They は漠然と「建築業者」をさす)/A new supermarket is being built [is under construction] near my house. ▶その建物は固い地盤の上に建てられている The building is founded on solid ground. ▶この記念碑はメアリー女王に敬意を表して建てられた This monument was erected [was set up, was put up] in honor of Queen Mary. (❗in honor of の代わりに単に to でもこの意は表される)

たてわり 縦割り ●縦割り行政 a vertical administrative system.

たてん 他店 another store (❸ other stores).

だてん 打点 〘野球〙a run batted in (略 an RBI). ●打点のチャンス an RBI situation. ●打点つきのシングルヒット an RBI single. ▶彼は3打点をあげた He had 3 RBIs./He drove [batted] in 3 runs. ●打点王(タイトル) (win) an RBI title.

だでん 打電 ── 打電する 動 send a telegram 《to》; telegraph.

だと ●そうだといいのですが If (that is) so, I'm happy. ▶目撃者の話だと, 男は中肉中背でやくざ風だそうです According to the witnesses, the man is of medium height and looks like a gangster.

たとう 多投 ── 多投する 動 ▶デイブはカーブを多投する Dave is a curve ball pitcher./Dave's pitching is full of curves.

だとう 打倒 图 ●内閣打倒！ Down with the Government! (❗Down with ... は「...を倒せ」の意のスローガンの決まり文句)

── 打倒する 動 ●政府を打倒する(=転覆させる) overthrow the government. ●敵を打倒する(=負かす) defeat the enemy.

＊だとう 妥当 ── 妥当な 形 (適切な) appropriate, proper; (正当な) valid. (⇨適当) ●妥当な措置をとる take appropriate [proper] measures. ●妥当な結論 a valid [(理にかなった) a reasonable] conclusion. ●妥当な(=手ごろな)値段で at a reasonable price.

たとうかい 多島海 an archipelago /ὰːrkəpéləgòu/ (❸ ～s, ～es); 〘エーゲ海〙the Aegean Sea.

だどうし 他動詞 〘文法〙a transitive verb.

＊たとえ 〘仮に...でも〙even if..., even though... (❗前の方が口語的); 〘いかに...でも〙no matter how [what, who, etc.]..., however [whatever, whoever, etc.].... (❗no matter＋wh-語 の方が口語的) ▶たとえ忙しくてもそれをやります Even if [though] I'm busy, I'll do it. (❗No matter [However] I am 〘《書》may be〙, I'll do it. は不可)/No matter how [However] busy I am 〘《書》may be〙, I'll do it. ▶たとえ彼が何を言おうと,だれも本気にしない No matter what [Whatever] he says 〘《書》may say〙, nobody takes it [him] seriously. (❗him は「彼の言うこと」) ▶彼女はとてもいい人のようだ. たとえそうでも本当には信用してはいない She looks like a very nice person. Even so [✕if, ✕though], I don't really trust her. (❗I don't really ... は部分否定であることに注意) ▶たとえ君が謝ったとしても許してあげない Even if you apologized, I wouldn't forgive you. (❗仮定法を用いて「そんなことはないだろうが」の意を暗示) ▶彼はお金をまず家族のために使い, 自分のために使うことは, たとえあったとしても二の次であった He used his money for the sake of his family first and only secondarily, if at all, for his own sake.

● たとえ火の中水の中 ●あなたのためならたとえ火の中水の中(=どんな苦労も平気だ) Any hardship will be nothing at all to me if it does you good.

たとえ 譬え 〘直喩〙a simile /símali(ː)/; 〘隠喩〙a met-

たとえば aphor; 〚寓喩〛a fable, an allegory; 〚ことわざ〛a proverb, a saying; 〚例〛an example, an instance; 〚例証〛an illustration. ●たとえを引いて理論を説明する explain a theory *by an example*. ●たとえに言うように as the *proverb goes* [*runs, says*]; as the *saying goes*.

●たとえ話 (主に聖書の) a parable; (動物などを擬人化した) a fable 〚参考〛『イソップ物語』(*Aesop's Fables*) など); (登場人物に真実・忍耐・善などの名前をつけた) an allegory.

*たとえば **例えば** 〚典型的には〛for example (!堅い《書》ではしばしば e.g. /fɔrigzǽmpl, 時に i:dʒí:/ と略記する); 〚具体的には〛for instance; (…のような) such as …; (例を挙げれば) (let us) say. ●野菜, 例えばニンジンやキュウリ vegetables, *for example,* [*for instance, e.g.*] carrots and cucumbers; vegetables *such as* [*like*] carrots and cucumbers.

▶数ある都市, 例えば神戸や横浜は港で有名です Some cities, *such as* Kobe and Yokohama, [*Such cities as* Kobe and Yokohama] are famous for their ports. ▶だれでも, 例えば幼稚園児でもそれを知っている Anyone, (*let's*) *say*, a kindergartner, knows it.

〚会話〛「おみやげをたくさん買ってきてあげたよ」「例えばどんな」"I've bought lots of presents for you." "*Like* what?/What, *for example* [*instance*]?"

*たとえる **譬える** compare 〈A to B〉, 《書》liken 〈A to B〉. ●人生をドラマにたとえる *compare* life *to* [*with*] a drama. (!今は with も用いられる) ●心臓はポンプにたとえることができる The heart *can be compared* [*You can compare* the heart] *to* a pump. ▶夕日がたとえようもないほど美しかった The setting sun was beautiful *beyond description*. (⇨筆舌)

たどく 多読 〚名〛extensive reading.
── **多読する** 〚動〛(多く読む) read a lot of books; (広く読む) read widely [extensively].

だとしても even so. ▶そうだとしても君が辞める理由はない *Even so,* there is not any reason for you to quit.

だとすると if so. ▶彼女は忙しすぎるといつもこぼしている. そうだとすると, 他の人を探さないといけない She is always complaining that she is too busy. *If so*, we have to find another man.

たどたどしい (つかえながらの) halting; (やや書) faltering; (よろめいた) tottering. ▶たどたどしい英語で話す speak (in) *halting* [*faltering,* (不完全な) *broken*] English; speak English in a *faltering* way. ●たどたどしい足どりで歩く walk with *tottering* [(不安定な) *unsteady*] steps; walk *unsteadily*.

たどりつく たどり着く ●目的地にたどり着く(=やっと到達する) *finally reach* [*get to*] one's destination.

*たどる **(沿って行く) follow**; (跡をたどる) trace. ●小道をたどって湖まで歩いて行く *follow* the path *to* the lake. ●家路をたどる go home; *make one's way* home. ●その語の語源をたどる *trace* the word (*back*) *to* its origin. ●記憶をたどる(=調べる) search (やや書) *retrace* one's memory. ▶1字1字たどりながら読む *spell out* a sentence. ▶彼女は母親と同じ運命をたどった She *followed* the same fate as her mother. ▶旅行者は地図の上で自分たちの行程をたどった The tourists *traced* their route on a map. ▶旅客機は大型化の道をたどっている(=絶えずより大きくなっている) Airliners *are getting bigger all the time.*

たどん 炭団 a briquet(te).

*たな **棚** a shelf (複 shelves); (網・格子状の) a rack; 〚岩棚〛a ledge; 〚暖炉の上の〛a mantelpiece. (⇨吊(つ)り棚) ●一番上の棚 the top *shelf*. ●棚に置く put [place] (it) on a *shelf*. (!put を用いる方が口語的) ●棚をつる make [put up] a *shelf*; fix a *shelf* (to the wall). ●棚から食器を下ろす get dishes down from the shelf. (!「階段からたんすをおろした」は We got the wardrobe *down* (×from) the stairs.) ●この本箱には棚が8段ある The bookcase has eight *shelves*.

●棚からぼたもち ▶突然の財産相続はまったく棚からぼたもちだった The sudden inheritance was a real *windfall* [an absolute *godsend*]. (⇨棚ぼた)
●棚に上げる ▶自分のことを棚に上げて他人を非難する《ことわざ》The pot calls the kettle black. (!「自分のことを棚に上げてからに」は Speak for yourself. (自分のことだけを言え)〛

たなあげ 棚上げ ── 棚上げする 〚動〛shelve. ▶その計画は2年間棚上げされた The plan *was shelved* for two years.

たなおろし 棚卸し 〚名〛❶〚在庫調べ〛《米》inventory, 《英》stocktaking. ●棚卸しのため出庫を停止する stop shipping for *inventory* [*stocktaking*]. ❷〚あら探し〛(⇨粗(あ)探し)
── **棚卸しする** 〚動〛take inventory 《米》[stocktaking 《英》].
●棚卸し資産 inventories.

たなこ 店子 a tenant (↔a landlord).
たなご 魚 a Japanese bitterling.
たなごころ 掌 (手のひら) the palm of one's hand.
●たなごころの内 ▶すべてはあなたのたなごころの内だ Everything is [You have everything] *in the palm of* your hand.
●たなごころを反(かえ)す (態度を急に変える) change one's attitude suddenly.
●たなごころを指すように 《know …》like the palm of one's hand.

たなざらえ 棚浚え ── 棚浚えする 〚動〛have a clearance sale.

たなざらし 店晒し ── 店晒しの 〚形〛《米》shopworn, 《英》shopsoiled; left on the shelf. (!比喩的にも用いる) ●店晒しになっているバーゲン品 *shopworn* [*shopsoiled*] bargain goods. ▶私たちが出した企画はずっと店ざらしにされている Our project *has been left on the shelf* for a long time.

たなだ 棚田 a rice terrace.

たなばた 七夕 the Star Festival; (織女星と牽牛星の祭り) the Festival of the Weaver Star and the Cowherd Star [Vega /víːɡə/ and Altair /ǽltɛər/]. ▶日本では子供たちは7月7日の夜, 短冊や色紙で飾った竹を立てて七夕を祝います In Japan children celebrate the *Star Festival* on the evening of July 7th, putting up bamboos decorated with poem cards and colored tapes.

たなびく 棚引く ●遠くの方にたなびく煙が見えた I saw *a trail of* smoke in the distance. ▶かすみが山にたなびいていた(=かかっていた) A haze *hung* [*lay*] over the hills.

たなぼた 棚ぼた 〚〚意外な授かり物, 特に遺産・幸運など〛〛a windfall; 〚〚思わぬ幸運・出来事〛〛a godsend. (⇨棚) ●棚ぼた式のもうけ an unexpected *windfall*.

たなん 多難 ●多難である(困難な) be hard; (困難が多い) be full of difficulties. ●多難な年 a *hard* year; a year *full of hardship*. ▶我々の前途は多難 Our future is *full of difficulties.*/(暗たんとしている) We have a dark future before us.

*たに **谷** ❶〚地理上の〛 a valley (!両側を山に囲まれた平地で, しばしばその中を川が流れている); (深く狭く両側が切り立った谷) a gorge, a ravine /rəvíːn/ (!これらより小さいのが a gully); (通例水流のある大規模な)

だに canyon. ●山あいの美しい谷 a beautiful *valley* between the mountains.
❷〘気圧の〙〘気象〙a trough /trɔ(ː)f/ (働 〜s). 気圧の谷が近づいている〘通り過ぎた〙A [An atmospheric] *trough* is approaching [has passed away].

だに 〘虫〙a tick; 〘人〙(人から金銭などを絞り取る者) a leech; (社会に害を与える人々) vermins.

たにおり 谷折り (折り紙で) 《make》a valley fold. (⇨山折り)

たにがわ 谷川 a mountain stream.

たにく 多肉 ── 多肉の 圏 freshy 〘leaves〙; succulent 〘plants〙.
●多肉植物 a succulent.

たにし 田螺 〘魚介〙a pond snail; a freshwater snail; an aquatic snail.

たにぞこ 谷底 the bottom of a ravine /rəvíːn/. (⇨谷) ●谷底に沈む sink to *the bottom of the ravine*.

たにま 谷間 ❶ 〘谷あい〙a valley. (⇨谷) ▶その村は山の谷間にある The village is down in the *valley*.
❷ 〘取り残された所〙a slum. ●社会の谷間に住む人々 slum dwellers.

ダニューブ ●ダニューブ川 〘ドナウ川の英語名〙the Danube /dǽnjuːb/. (⇨ドナウ)

たにょうしょう 多尿症 〘医学〙polyuria.

*__たにん__ 他人 other people, others. (❗(1) 前の方が口語的でよく用いられる。(2) 日本語の「他人」は「身内でない人」や「利害関係などのない人」を意味することが多いが, 上の2語は自分以外のすべての人をさす。(3) 単数形は another 〘person〙; 〘血縁のない人〙an unrelated person; 〘知らない人〙a stranger; 〘部外者〙an outsider. ●他人の手をわずらわす cause trouble to *other people*. ●他人任せにする leave 〘it〙to *other people*. ▶他人の助けは当てにならない You can't count on *other people* to help you [on *other people's* help]. (❗通例 ×others' help とはいわない) ▶私たちは他人同士です We are not *related* to each other./We are *strangers*. ▶他人が横から口をはさむべきではない *Outsiders* should not get a word in edgeways.
●他人の空似 a chance resemblance.

たにんぎょうぎ 他人行儀 ●他人行儀にする be formal 《with him》. ▶他人行儀なことを言わないで Don't be a stranger!

たにんごと 他人事 other people's affairs. (⇨人事)

たにんずう 多人数 many (↔a few) people; a large (↔a small) number of people. (⇨たくさん❶)

たぬき 狸 a raccoon /rækúːn/ dog; 〘ずるい人〙a cunning person, 〘話〙an old fox. 事情 米英の寓話(わ)ではキツネが一般的)▶取らぬたぬきの皮算用〘ことわざ〙(かえらぬうちにひなの数を数えるな) Don't count your chickens before they're hatched./(捕らえぬうちに熊の皮を売るな) Don't sell the bear skin before catching the bear.
●たぬき寝入り a make-believe sleep; 《主に英》a sleep like an opóssum. ●たぬき寝入りをする pretend to be asleep; 〘話〙play possum.
●たぬきうどん tanuki-udon; (説明的に) udon noodles in soup with bits of fried batter.
●たぬきおやじ a foxy man.

‡**たね** 種 ❶ 〘植物の〙a seed (❗集合的にいう場合は Ⓤ); (特にモモ・サクランボなどの堅い) a stone, 《米》a pit (❗stone より堅い); (特にリンゴ・ミカンなどの) a pip.
●種なしブドウ seedless grapes. ●種抜き味つきのプルーン pitted and flavored prunes. ●畑に小麦の種をまく seed [sow] wheat *in* the field; seed [sow] the field *with* wheat. ▶ヒマワリは種が多い Sunflowers are seedy 〘full of seeds〙. ▶植物は花が咲いた後に種ができる A plant produces *seed* 〘seeds〙after it has flowered. ▶庭にレタスの種をまいた I planted lettuce *seeds* in the garden. 事情 plant は「成育を目的として地中に埋める」の意で, 種・苗・木のいずれも目的語にとる) ▶このリンゴは種から育てたものです This apple tree has been grown from *seed*. ▶まいた種は刈らねばならない〘ことわざ〙As you *sow*, so shall you reap. ▶まかぬ種は生えぬ〘ことわざ〙Nothing comes of [from] nothing./〘ことわざ〙You cannot make an omelette without breaking an egg.
❷ 〘動物の〙●良い種 (=品種) の馬 a good *breed* of horse.
❸ 〘原因〙(a) cause; (源) a source. ●けんかの種 the *cause* of a quarrel. ▶彼は両親にとって心配の種だった He was a constant 〘*source*〙of worry to his parents. ▶この庭は私の自慢の種だ This garden is my *pride* 〘and joy〙. ▶残念ながら人の世に争いの種は尽きない Unfortunately there is no end to the *seeds* of discord in the world we live in [〘書〙in which we live].
❹ 〘材料〙(話題) a topic; (題材) a subject (❗前の方より堅い語); (アイデア) an idea; (料理の) an ingredient 〘*of*〙. ▶すぐに話の種が尽きた We soon ran out of *topics* of conversation [*things* to talk about].
❺ 〘秘密〙a secret; (手品などの技術) a trick; (手品の仕掛け) 〘話〙a gimmick. ●種を明かせば, 彼が箱の中にいたのだ *To tell the truth*, he was in the box.
●種が割れる ▶彼の手品の種が割れた (=明らかになった) The secrets of his magic tricks *were revealed*.
●種も仕掛けもない (手品で) I have no tricks up my sleeves.
●種油 rapeseed [colza] oil. ●種牛 a seed bull. ●種馬 a stallion; a studhorse. ●種銭 capital. ●種違い a half brother [sister]. (郷 腹違い) ●種火 (ガスコンロなどの) a pilot light [burner]. ●種本 (原典) a source book.

たねあかし 種明かし ── 種明かしをする 動 〘秘密を明かす〙reveal 〘give away〙secrets 《*to* him》; 〘手品の種を明かす〙show 〘(説明する) explain〙a trick used in magic.

たねがしま 種子島 〘火縄銃〙a matchlock, 《主に米》a harquebus.

たねぎれ 種切れ (⇨種 ❹) ▶もう話は種切れだ I have run out of topics of conversation.

たねつけ 種付け ── 種付けする 動 (交尾する) serve; mate with 《a female》; copulate with 《a female》.
●種付け馬 (種馬) a stallion; a studhorse. ●種付け料 a stud fee.

たねまき 種まき 图 (seed) sowing. (⇨種❶) ●種まき時 seedtime. ▶春は種まきに最適の季節だ Spring is the best season for *sowing*.

── 種まき(を)する 動 plant 〘sow〙seeds.

たねもの 種物 〘種物の種〙a seed (⇨種); 〘具入りうどん〘そば〙〙(説明的に) a bowl of noodles with other ingredients such as meat, tempura and an egg; 〘かき氷〙shaved ice with syrup on the top.

たねをまくひと ●『種をまく人』*The Sower*. (参考 ミレー作の絵画)

たねん 他年 some other time; later in life. (⇨後年, いつか)

たねん 多年 many years. (⇨長年) ▶彼は多年にわたってその問題を調査している He has been looking into the matter *for* 〘many〙 *years*. (❗many を省略するのは 〘話〙)

―だの
- 多年生植物 a perennial (plant).

―だの《副助詞》[物事を並べあげる] and; or; and so on [forth]. (⇒―とか) ・文学的の音楽だの literature, music, *and so on* [*forth*]. ▶あの店では石けんだの歯ブラシだの(=そういった種類の物)を売っている They sell soap, toothpaste *and the like* at that store. (**!** 文脈によっては That store sells .... も可)

たのう 多能 ― 多能な形 ●多能な人物 a versatile person; a many-sided character.

:たのしい 楽しい 形

WORD CHOICE 楽しい

pleasant 場所・時間・体験などが快適で心地よいこと。●楽しい一夜を過ごす have a *pleasant* evening.

delightful 時間・出来事・体験などが華やかで特に心をうきうきさせるほど愉快なこと。通例 pleasant, pleasing よりも強い楽しさを含意する。●楽しい一日 a *delightful* day

pleasing 主に出来事・場所などが人を喜ばせること。

頻度チャート

pleasant
delightful
pleasing

20　40　60　80　100 (%)

(人を楽しませる) enjoyable; (人を満足させる) pleasant, delightful, (書) pleasing (⇒[類語]); (幸せな) happy; (陽気な) merry; (よい) nice, good*. ●楽しい我が家 one's *happy* home. ▶ゴルフはとても楽しい Playing golf is very *enjoyable* [*good fun*, *great fun*]. (**!** playing に注意)/It is (×a) great *fun* to play golf. (**!** fun には不定冠詞をつけない) ▶パーティーは楽しかった We had an *enjoyable* [a *nice*, a *pleasant*, a *good*] time at the party. (⇒楽しむ) ▶彼と話していると楽しい It is *pleasant* to talk with him./He is *pleasant* to talk with. (×I am pleasant to talk with him. とはしない。I を主語にする場合は I like talking with him. のようにはいえる (⇒会話 [第2例])) ▶彼はナイスな人だ [is a *pleasant* person, is (×a) *fun*] to talk with. (**!** 文尾の with に注意)/It's (×a) *fun* to talk [talking] with him. ▶今日はずいぶん楽しそうだね You look very *happy* today, don't you?

会話「楽しい休暇を過ごしてね」「あなたもね!」"Have a *good* [a *nice*] vacation [《主に英》holiday]." "And you, too!"

会話「この大学での勉強は楽しいですか」「ええ」"Do you *enjoy* [*How do you like*] studying here?" "Yes, I do. [I like it./It's all right.]" (**!**(1) How do you like ...? は物事の好き嫌いを尋ねる表現. (2) 実際にその大学にいて「この大学で」というときは at this college とはあまりいわない. (3)「あんまり楽しくない」なら Not ˇreally.)

会話「京都へ1週間行ってきたよ」「そう. で, 楽しかった?」「とってもね」"I've been to Kyoto for a week." "Oh, yes. Did you *have a good time*?" "Yes. A marvelous time."

会話「おやすみなさい. 楽しい夜でしたわ」「来ていただけてよかった」"Góod ˊnight and thanks for a ˋlovely evening." "I'm glad you could come." (**!** パーティーなどでのもてなしに対するお礼の言葉. Good night 以下は やや大げさに「こんな楽しかったことはないわ」 I don't know when I've enjoyed myself so much. などというのも時に効果的)

― 楽しく 副 (幸せに) happily; (愉しく) merrily.

▶余生を楽しく暮らしたい I want to spend the rest of my life *happily*./(×I wish to) I want to enjoy the rest of my life. ▶私は京都で3日間楽しく過ごした I had an *enjoyable* three days in Kyoto. (**!** enjoyable three days をひとまとまりのものと考えて an を付した表現. an を除けば, 1日1日を追想する感じの表現となる)/I had a good time for three days in Kyoto. ▶まだ宵のうちだ. 楽しくやろう It's still early in the evening. Let's *have fun*.

― 楽しさ 名 (⇒喜び, 楽しみ)

たのしませる 楽しませる entertain; [愉快な気持ちにさせる] amuse; [喜ばせる] please, delight (**!** 後の方が強意的). ●目を楽しませる *please* the eyes (*of*). ▶彼は手品をして私たちを楽しませてくれた He *entertained* [*amused*] us *with* magic tricks. ▶彼のみごとな演技は観客を楽しませた His brilliant performance *delighted* the audience./The audience *was* [*were*] *delighted* by his brilliant performance.

:たのしみ 楽しみ ❶ [愉快] (喜び) (a) pleasure; (満ち足りた喜び) (an) enjoyment; (大きな喜び) (a) delight; (気晴らし) a diversion. (⇒喜び) ●田舎暮らしの楽しみ the *pleasures* [*delights*] of country life. ●読書から楽しみを得る get *pleasure* from (reading) books. ▶彼の主な楽しみは庭いじりである His chief *pleasure* [*enjoyment*, *amusement*] is gardening./Gardening is his chief *pleasure*./(楽しみを見出している) He finds *pleasure* [*enjoyment*] chiefly in gardening. ▶音楽を聴くのは彼には大きな楽しみであった Listening to music was a great *pleasure* to him./He *took* great *pleasure in* listening to music. ▶私は楽しみで絵をかいているだけで, まともに取り組もうとはしない I paint pictures only *for pleasure* [《やや話》just *for fun*], and I've never taken it up very seriously. ▶いつの時代も楽しみ(=自分を楽しませるもの)を見つけながら生きてきた All my life, I have found something to entertain myself with.

❷ [望み] hope. ●将来楽しみな(=有望な)若者たち promising [*hopeful*] young people; young people with a *bright future*. ▶あなたの手紙を楽しみにしています (待ち望んでいる) I'm *looking forward to* (receiving) [×receive] your letter./(手紙をもらいたい) I'd love to hear from you. (**!** 主に女性言葉)

:たのしむ 楽しむ enjoy; (喜びを見いだす) find* [take*] pleasure 《in》; [楽しくやる] have* fun; (楽しい時を過ごす) have a good time, enjoy oneself; [遊んで] amuse oneself; [観劇などで] be entertained. ●人生を大いに楽しむ *enjoy* life a great deal; *find* a lot of (書) much] *pleasure* in life. ●ショーを見て楽しむ *be entertained by* a show. ▶パーティーで大いに楽しんだ I *had* a lot of *fun* [*a very good time*] at the party./I *enjoyed myself* very much at the party./I very much *enjoyed* the party. (**!** ×I was very enjoyable at the party. の自動詞用法は不可)/The party *was* full of *fun* [*very enjoyable*]. (**!** ×I was very enjoyable at the party. とはいわない) ▶彼は休日には小説を読むのを楽しむ He *enjoys* reading [×to read] novels on a holiday. (**!** 次例より口語的)/He *takes* pleasure [*enjoyment*, *delight*] in *reading* novels on a holiday. (**!** この順で楽しみの度合いが強くなる) ▶これはだれでも楽しめる本だ This is a book everyone *can enjoy*./This is an *enjoyable* book *for* everyone. ▶少年たちはトランプをして楽しんだ The boys played cards and *had* a lot of *fun* [*a very good time*]. (**!** 次の訳より口語的)/The boys

だのに but, (al)though. (⇨のに)

たのみ 頼み ❶ 【要請】 (a) request; (好意) (a) favor.
● 頼みを聞く(=かなえる)〖書〗grant 〖(応じる〗comply with〗 ⟨his⟩ *request*. ● 頼みを断る refuse 〖(丁寧に〗decline, 〖すげなく〗turn down〗 ⟨his⟩ *request*. ▶君にちょと[たっての; ちょっと]頼みがあるんだ I've got a [a big; a small] *favor* to ask (of) you. (⇨頼り) ▶君の頼みというのは何だ What is it that you /*want*? (*What* do you *want*? の What を強調した構文) ▶父の頼みで大阪に行った I went to Osaka at my father's *request* [*at the request of*] my father. ▶小遣いを上げてほしいという私たちの再三の頼みを(どうしても)父は聞き入れなかった Father wouldn't listen to [turned down, 〖書〗did not grant] our repeated *requests for* a larger allowance.

❷ 【頼り】 (信頼) reliance; (信用) trust; (依存) dependence. ● 頼みになる友 a *reliable* [a *dependable*, a *trustworthy*] friend.
● 頼みの綱 ▶頼みの綱は君だけだ You are my (one and) only *hope*./I have no one but you to *rely* [*depend*] *upon*. (**!** upon に注意)

たのみこむ 頼み込む (熱心に頼む) ask earnestly; (懇願する) plead* ⟨*with* him; *to* do, *for*⟩. ● 彼に考え直してほしいと頼み込む *plead with* him to reconsider [*for* reconsideration].

†たのむ 頼む ❶ 【要請する】 ask; 〖(やや書〗request; beg (-gg-); 〖(やや書〗implore.

┌─────────────────────────────
│ 使い分け ask 人に何かを頼む最も一般的な語.
│ **request** きちんとした形式・手順をふみ, 当然受け入れ
│   られるべき正式な要請を行うこと.
│ **beg** 身を低くして上位の相手にひたすら懇願すること.
│ **implore** 感情をこめて必死に懇願すること.
└─────────────────────────────

● 彼に助言を頼む ask him *for* advice; ask ⟨*for*⟩ his advice. (**!** for を用いると求める気持ちが強くなる) ● 彼に伝言を頼む ask him *to* give a message. ▶太郎に7時に起こしてくれと頼まれた Taro *asked* me *to* wake him at 7 o'clock. (**!** *I was asked by* Taro *to* wake him at 7 o'clock. とはあまりいわない) ▶彼は彼女に助けてくれるよう頼んだ He *asked* [*requested*] her *to* help him./He *requested* [*asked*] that she (〖主に英〗*should*) help him. (**!** ask *that*... の型は堅い言い方)/He *made a request to* her *for* help. ▶あなたに頼みたいことがあるですが Can I *ask* you a favor [*ask a favor of* you]?/Could [Would] you *do me a favor*? (**!** (1) can, will より丁寧. could, can の方が日常的によく用いられる. (2) この直後に頼みたい内容を, and keep an eye on my bag for a little while? (ちょっとこの鞄を見ていてくれますか)のように続けることも多い. (3) ごく親しい間柄では Do me a favor. のようにもいう) ▶彼女に頼まれて来たのです I came *at her request*. ▶妻は私に頼むから勤めをやめないでくれと言った My wife *begged* [*implored*] me *to* give up the idea of quitting the job. ▶頼むから泣くのはやめて *Please* 〖(話〗*For goodness sake*〗 stop ╱*crying*. (**!** 後の方が強いいらだちを表す)/*Do* [*Do please*, 〖(話〗*Please* *do*] stop ╱*crying*. (**!** (1) do は強意の助動詞. いずれも *crying* と下降調になると「いいかげんやめないか」といった強い口調になる. (2) この程度の言い方で効を奏さない場合は Why don't you do me a real favor and…? (本当に頼むから…)のようにもいえる)

会話 「はいどうぞ. 頼まれた図書館の本よ」「これは私が頼んだのじゃないわ」"There you are. Your library book." "This isn't the one I *asked for*." (**!** Your library book. の前に It is を補って考える)

❷ 【任せる】 ▶この荷物を頼みますど(=めんどうを見てください) Please *look after* this baggage. ▶この件は彼に頼もう(=委任しよう) I'll *leave* 〖(やや書〗*entrust*〗 this matter *to* him. ▶彼にこの店を頼むことにした(=管理を任せた) I've decided to *put* him *in charge of* this store.

会話 「これはマイクに渡すものなんだけど, 僕はもう行かなきゃならない. 君に頼めるかい」「あなたの頼みならいつでも頼まれるわ」"This has to go to Mike, but I can't stay any longer. Can I *count on* you?" "You could always *count on* me." (**!** (1) count on は「頼りにする」の意. (2) You could の could に注意)

❸ 【注文する】 order; 〖(予約する〗reserve, book.
● その本屋に新刊本を頼む *order* a new book *from* [×*to*] the bookstore. ● 窓のそばのテーブルを頼む *reserve* a table by the window. ▶タクシーを頼んでくれ Please *call* a taxi for me [*call* me a taxi].

***たのもしい 頼もしい** 〖(頼りになる〗dependable, reliable; 〖(将来有望な〗promising, hopeful. ● 頼もしい父親 a *dependable* [a *reliable*] father. ● 末頼もしい学生 a *promising* [a *hopeful*] student; a student *of promise*. ● 頼もしい(=希望に満ちた)言葉 *hopeful* words.

***たば 束** (同種類の小さな) a bunch ⟨*of*⟩; (束ねた大きな) a bundle ⟨*of*⟩; (穀物などの) a sheaf (֎ sheaves) ⟨*of*⟩. ● 鍵の束 a *bunch of* keys. ● 木切れの束 a *bundle of* sticks. ● 束にして[なって] in a *bunch* [a *bundle*]; (人が) in a *group*. ● 新聞を束にする *bundle* (*up*) newspapers; *tie up* newspapers *in a bundle*. (⇨束ねる)

だは 打破 ── 打破する 【動】 (敵などを負かす) defeat; (悪習などを取り除く) get rid of…. ● 偏見を打破する *get rid of* [*break down*] the prejudice.

だば 駄馬 〖(荷馬〗a packhorse, a cart horse, a draft horse; 〖(下等な馬〗a hack, a jade.

たばかる deceive. (⇨騙(す)す)

***たばこ 煙草** (a) tobácco (֎ ～(e)s) (**!** たばこの総称で, 特に「刻まれたもの」をいうときは〖C〗); (紙巻き) a cigarétte, 〖(米まれ〗cigaret; (葉巻) a cigár; (植物) a tobacco plant; 〖(喫煙〗smoking.

① 【～たばこ】 ▶火のついたたばこ a lighted [lit] *tobacco*. (**!** lit を誤用とする見方もある. 限定用法は lighted) ● かみ[パイプ用]たばこ chéwing [pipe] *tobacco*. ● 寝たばこ (⇨寝たばこ)

② 【たばこは】 ▶たばこは体に悪い Smoking [×*Tobacco*] is bad for our [the] health. ▶おたばこはご遠慮ください Please [Kindly] refrain from *smoking*./〖(提示〗No *smoking*.

③ 【たばこの】 ▶たばこの煙 *cigarette* [*cigar*] smoke. ● たばこの吸い殻 a *cigarette* butt [end]. ● たばこの火をつける light (up) a *cigarette*. ● たばこの火を消す[もみ消す; 先をつぶして消す] put [crush; stub] out one's *cigarette*. ▶その火事の原因は彼のたばこの火の不始末だ The cause of the fire was his (careless handling of) *cigarette* butt./His *cigarette* butt was the cause of the fire.

④ 【たばこを】 ● たばこを立て続けに吸う chain-smoke (*cigarettes*). ● たばこを吸う人 [吸わない人] a smoker [a nonsmoker]. ● たばこを口にくわえる put a *cigarette* in one's mouth [between one's lips]. ● たばこをふかす smoke a *cigarette*. ● たばこを

くゆらせる puff at [on] one's pipe; puff at [on] a *cigarette*. ▶たばこをよく吸lこと吸う He *smokes* a lot [*heavily*]./He is a heavy smoker. ▶父は1日に10本ほどたばこを吸います My father *smokes* about 10 *cigarettes* a day. ▶たばこを1箱ください I'd like a páck (米) [a pácket (英)] of *cigarettes*, please. (!小箱の入った大箱は a carton of cigarettes) ▶叔父はついにたばこをやめた My uncle gave up [stopped, 《話》quitted] *smoking* at last. (!smokingの代わりに tabacco を用いるのはまれ)

DISCOURSE
あらゆる公共の場所を禁煙にすべきだと考える. そもそもたばこの煙は体に悪い In my opinion, smoking should be prohibited in all public places. **To begin with**, *cigarette* smoke is harmful to the body. (!to begin [start] with, (第一に)は複数の要素の列挙に用いるディスコースマーカー)

- たばこ入れ (紙巻き用) a cigarétte càse; (葉巻用) a cigár càse. - たばこ銭 money for cigarettes [tobacco]; (小額の小遣い) a small allowance; (わずかな心付け) a small tip. - たばこ税 a tobacco tax. - たばこ屋 (店) (米) a cigar store; (英) a tobacconist's (shop).

たばた 田畑 (the) fields. ▶田畑で働く work in the *fields*. (⇨野良仕事, 田)

たはつ 多発 图 ▶ここは自動車事故多発地点だ Car accidents *occur frequently* at this spot./Many car accidents *occur* here.
── 多発する 動 occur [happen] frequently.
- 多発性神経炎 [医学] multiple neuritis /njuəráɪtəs/; polyneuritis.

たばねる 束ねる bundle ... (up); tie 〈~d; tying〉 up ... in a bundle. ▶廃品回収業者が出すように新聞を束ねる *bundle* (*up*) newspapers to give to a junk dealer. ▶小枝を三つに束ねる *tie up* sticks in three *bundles* [*in bundles of* three]. ▶家族を一つに束ねる *keep* a family *together*.

*たび 度 ▶私はこの写真を見るたびに父のことを思い出す *Whenever* [*Every time, Each time*] I see this picture, I think of my father. (!後の二つの方が口語的)▶口にする思いは出さずにこの写真は見ない I *never* see this picture *without* thinking of my father./(この写真はいつも私に父のことを思い出させる) This picture always reminds me of my father. (!後の二つはやや堅い表現) ▶彼は呼吸のたびにぜいぜいいう He wheezes *as* he breathes. (!反復を含意する動詞の場合は同時に併用して生じることを表す接続詞 as でこの意味が伝わる) ▶彼は三たび[幾たびか]会ったことがある I've 《×ever》 seen him three [*several*] *times*. (⇨回) ▶彼は日曜日のたびに(=毎日曜日に)家族に手紙を書く He always writes 《主に英》to) his family *every* Sunday [*on* Sundays]. (!複数形に注意) ▶彼は口を開くたびに言うことが違う(=最初に言うことと次に言うことが違う) First he says one thing, then another.

*たび 旅 图 (一般的に) a trip; (比較的長い) a journey; (旅をすること) travel; (周遊の) a tour; (船旅) a voyage. (⇨類語)
①【〜旅】● 船の旅 a *voyage*. ● 空の旅 an air *trip*; air *travel*; *travel* [a *trip*] by air. ● 長い列車の旅 a long train *journey*; a long *journey* by train. ● ヨーロッパへの旅 a *trip* [a *journey*] *to* Europe. (!ヨーロッパに着いてからなら a *trip* in Europe) ● 北海道周遊の旅 a *tour of* [*around*] Hokkaido. ● 一人旅でもこわくない I'm not afraid to *travel* alone.
②【旅(の)〜】● 旅の僧 a *traveling* [(巡礼している)

itinerant /aɪtínərənt/] monk /mʌŋk/. ▶旅慣れている be used to traveling [×journeying]. ▶旅の空で故郷を思った I recalled my hometown *far from home*.
③【旅は[に]】● 旅に出る go on a trip [*journey*]. ▶旅は身軽なのがいいですね I believe in *traveling light*. (!light は副詞) ▶旅は道連れとよく言いますが、ご一緒できて本当に楽しゅうございました As it's often said good company on the road is the shortest cut, I really enjoyed your company. (!good ... cut は「旅の道中は楽しい人と一緒だと短く感じられる」の意)
- 旅の恥はかき捨て Away from home, one feels no shame in doing anything.
── 旅をする 動 travel. (⇨旅行する) ▶かわいい子には旅をさせよ (ことわざ) (むちを惜しめば子供は甘えてだめになる) Spare the rod and spoil the child.

たび 足袋 《a pair of》 *tabi*; (説明的に) traditional Japanese-style socks with pouches that separate the big toe from the four other toes.

だび 荼毘 (火葬) crèmátion. ● だびに付す cremate /krɪméɪt/.

たびかさなる 度重なる ▶彼は度重なる不幸にも屈しなかった He bore up under *repeated* [*a series of*] misfortunes. (⇨回) ②

たびがらす 旅烏 a wanderer. ● しがない旅がらす a petty wanderer.

たびげいにん 旅芸人 an itinerant [a strolling] entertainer. ▶旅芸人の一座 an itinerant theatrical troupe.

たびごころ 旅心 (旅情) a traveler's sentiment; (旅行願望) the desire to travel [for traveling].

たびさき 旅先 ● 旅先で(旅行中に) during [on] one's *trip* [*journey*]; (滞在先で) at the place where one is staying; (見知らぬ土地で) in a strange land. ▶旅先から帰る return from one's *journey*. ▶旅先から手紙を出す write 《to him》 while *traveling* [*during one's journey*].

たびじ 旅路 a journey 《to》.

たびじたく 旅支度 ▶今夜旅支度をしないといけない I have to get ready for the *trip* [*journey*] tonight. ● 旅支度をしては(⇨ならない 解説)

たびだち 旅立ち setting out on a journey 《to》. (⇨旅立つ) ● 新しい人生への旅立ちを始める start a new life. ● 旅立ちの準備をする(=死に支度をする) prepare for one's death.

たびだつ 旅立つ leave* 《for》, set* out 《for》. ● 北海道へ旅立つ *set out on a journey* [*trip*] *to* Hokkaido. ● 天国へ旅立つ(=亡くなる) go to heaven; die; 《婉曲的》pass away.

*たびたび 度々 often; frequently; (何回も) many [《話》lots of] times; 《くり返して》repeatedly; (何度も何度も) again and again.

解説 **(1)** often は異なる場面で, **frequently** は同じ場面での出来事に用いる: 彼はきのうの授業中たびたび居眠りをした He *frequently* [*lots of times*, ×*often*] dozed off yesterday when he was in class.
(2) この2語は主に文中で用いられ, その位置は always に準じるが, 否定語の前に置くことも可能. また文頭, 文尾にも自由に用いるが, often は平叙文の文尾では修飾語を伴うのが普通. (⇨[第2文例]).
(3) frequently は often より堅い語.

▶最近彼をたびたび見かけました I have *often* seen him recently./《話》I have seen *a lot of* him recently. ▶彼はたびたびその丘に登った *Often* he climbed the hill./He *often* climbed the hill.

(!文尾では He climbed the hill *very often*. が普通)●もっとたびたびそこへ行きたい I'd like to go there *more often*. (!*oftener* より今は普通) ●私は授業であてられると何と言ってよいか思いつかないことがたびたびあった I *often* didn't think of what to say when I was called on in class. (!I *didn't often* think .... は「...思いつくことばかった」の意) ●私はもう一度やらせてほしいと父にたびたび頼んだ I asked [begged] my father *repeatedly* [*again and again*] to let me try once more.

タヒチ 〖南太平洋の島〗Tahiti /təhíːtiː/. ●タヒチ人 a Tahitian /təhíːʃən/. ●タヒチの Tahitian.

ダビデ David /déivid/.
●ダビデの星 the Star of David. (参考 ユダヤ教・イスラエル国家の象徴)

ダビデぞう『ダビデ像』*David*. (参考 ミケランジェロ作の彫像)

たびびと 旅人《やや書》a traveler.

たびまわり 旅回り 图 (⇨旅芸人)
── 旅回りする 動 (芸人などが) make a tour 《*of*》.

たびやくしゃ 旅役者 an itinerant [a strolling] actor.

タビュレーター a tabulator. (⇨タブ)

たびょう 多病 ── 多病な 形 sickly, delicate.

ダビング 图 dubbing. ── ダビングする 動 make a copy; copy; dub 《a tape》.

ダ・ビンチ 〖イタリアの画家・科学者〗da Vinci /də víntʃi/ (Leonardo ～).

タフ ── タフな 形〖容易に屈しない〗tough; 〖強い〗strong. ●タフな男 a *tough* guy.

タブ 〖コンピュータ〗a tab (tabulator の略). (参考 事前に設定した位置までカーソルを移動する機能)
●タブキー a tab key.

タブー 〖禁忌, 禁制〗(a) tabóo (複 ～s). ●その話題はタブーだ The subject is (a) *taboo* [*tabooed*]./It's a *taboo* subject.

だぶだぶ 〖大きすぎる〗too large; 〖ゆるい〗loose; 〖袋のようにふくれている〗baggy. ▶この上着は私にはだぶだぶだ This jacket is *too large* [*loose*] for me. (⇨ぶかぶか) ▶彼はだぶだぶのズボンをはくのが大好きだ He likes wearing *baggy* pants 《米》[trousers 《主に英》]. ▶最近彼は太ってだぶだぶしてきた He has gotten fat and *flabby* recently. ▶水を飲みすぎて腹がだぶだぶになった I drank too much water, so I'm *ready to burst*.

だぶつく ❶〖大きくてだぶだぶしている〗(⇨だぶだぶ)
❷〖供給過剰になっている〗be glutted 《*with*》. ▶市場には冬物衣料がだぶついている The market is *glutted with* winter clothes./There is a *glut* of winter clothes on the market.

だふや だふ屋 a (ticket) scalper 《米》[tout 《英》].

たぶらかす (だます) cheat, trick. (!前の方が悪質)
●彼をたぶらかしにせ物をつかませる *cheat* [*trick*] him *into* buying a fake. ●彼をたぶらかして金を取る〖巻き上げる〗*cheat* [*trick*] him *out of* his money.

ダブリン 〖アイルランドの首都〗Dublin.

ダブる 〖部分的に重なる〗òverláp (-pp-); 〖日程が〗fall* together; 〖留年する〗repeat 《the year》. ▶ダブって見えを be seeing double. ●代金を誤ってダブって払う pay for it *twice* by mistake. ●彼の仕事と私の仕事は一部ダブっている His work and mine *overlap*./His work *overlaps with* mine. ▶文化の日と日曜日がダブるので月曜日も休みになる Culture Day *falls on* (a) Sunday, so we have another holiday on Monday.

ダブル double. ●ダブルの上着 a double-breasted jacket. ●ダブルの部屋 a *double* room. ▶スコッチダブルで頼むよ *Double up* on the Scotch, will you?
●ダブルインカム 〖共稼ぎ世帯〗a double-income family. ●ダブルキャスト 〖二重配役〗double casting. ●ダブルスタンダード 〖二重基準〗a double standard. ●ダブルスチール 〖野球〗a double steal. ●ダブルデッカー 〖2 階建てバス〗a double-decker, a double-decked bus. ●ダブルブッキング 〖二重予約〗double-booking. ●ダブルベッド a double bed. ●ダブルボギー 〖ゴルフ〗a double bogey.

ダブルクリック ── ダブルクリックする 動 〖コンピュータ〗double-click. (⇨クリックする)

ダブルス 〖テニス〗doubles /dʌ́blz/ (↔singles). (!単数扱い) ●混合ダブルス mixed *doubles*. ●ダブルスをする play *doubles*. ●ダブルスで破る beat 《them》 in *doubles*.

ダブルスコア ▶うちのチームはダブルスコアで勝った Our team won by *twice the score of* the other team.

ダブルスペース ●ダブルスペースで(= 1 行おきに)打つ double-space.

ダブルチェック ── ダブルチェックする 動 〖再確認する〗double-check.

ダブルパンチ ●あごにダブルパンチを食わせる give 《him》 a one-two punch on 〖×to〗 the jaw. (!×double punch は和製英語) ▶我が社は経済的にダブルパンチを食った Economically we've had a double blow [*one-two punch*]./We have suffered an economic *double whammy*. (!whammy は「悪魔の目」「不運(な目)」の意)

ダブルフォールト 图 〖テニス〗a double fault.
── ダブルフォールトする 動 double-fault.

ダブルプレー 〖野球〗a double play. ●ダブルプレーの打球 a *double-play* ball. ●ダブルプレーにしとめる make [turn, pull off] a *double play*. ●ダブルプレーを食う ground into a *double play*. (!逆に「ダブルプレーを阻止する」は break up a double play) ●(塁を詰めて)ダブルプレーの段取りをする set up a *double play*. ▶彼はゴロを打ってダブルプレーになった He grounded into a *double play*. (!単に「ダブルプレーに倒れる」なら hit into a double play) ▶走者は二塁でダブルプレーの二つ目のアウトになった The runner was doubled up at second.

ダブルヘッダー 〖野球〗a doubleheader. (参考 第 1 試合は an opener, 第 2 試合は a nightcap) ●ダブルヘッダーに連勝〖連敗〗する sweep [lose] a *doubleheader*. ●ダブルヘッダーを 1 勝 1 敗で分ける split a *doubleheader*.

タブレット a tablet.

タブロイド 〖新聞〗a tábloid. ●タブロイド版の tabloid.

***たぶん** 多分 〖十中八九〗probably; 〖おそらく〗likely, maybe, perhaps; 〖ひょっとすると〗possibly.

> 解説 (1) 次のような順で確率が低くなる: probably (80-90%くらい), likely (70% くらい), maybe, perhaps (30-50%くらい), possibly (約 20%)
> (2) 文中での位置: probably は通例文中で, 時に文頭・文尾で用いる。maybe と perhaps は通例文頭で, 時に文中・文尾で用いる。possibly は文頭・文中・文尾のいずれでも普通に用いる。また, いずれも否定語の後では用いない: 「たぶん彼は来ないだろう」He will *probably not* [He *probably* won't, ×He will not probably] come.
> (3) probably, maybe, perhaps, possibly の 4 語は応答として単独でも用いるが, likely は否定文の場合を除き, most, very などの修飾を伴う: 「彼はあす来るだろうか」「たぶん来る[来ない]だろう」"Will he come tomorrow?" "*Probably* [*Probably*

たぶん ... not]./*Most likely* [*Not likely*]."
(4) should が probably ほどの確率を示すことがある. ただし話し手が期待する内容に限られる: 原稿は昨日郵送しましたのでたぶん明日着くはずです I mailed [《主に英》posted] the manuscript yesterday, so it *should* be there tomorrow.

▶彼はたぶん今日電話をしてくるでしょう He'll *probably* [*It's probable that* he'll] call me up today. (**!** 後の方が堅い言い方. ×He is probable to call.... は不可)/*I suppose* (*that*) he'll call me up today. (**!** that はしばしば省略する. He'll call me up today, *I suppose*. の語順も可)/*He is likely to* [*It is likely that* he will] call me up today. (**!** この likely は形容詞.副詞と同じで70%くらいの確率を表す. 後の方が堅い言い方) ▶たぶん彼は病気だろう *Perhaps* he *will* be sick. (**!** Perhaps he *will* be sick. では「病気になるだろう」の意)/《主に英》*I dare say* [*I daresay*] he is ill. /*I dare say* [*daresay*] (*that*) he is ill. He is ill, *I dare say* [*daresay*]. の語順も可) ▶それはたぶん本当かもしれない It may *possibly* be true. (**!** (1) possibly がない方が可能性が高くなる. (2) 反対の意味は It can't *possibly* be true. (絶対に本当ではありえない)で表す. not の位置に注意)

《会話》「彼は生きているだろうか」「たぶんね」"Is he alive?" "I ˇhope so." (**!** (1) この場合 probably や maybe などで答えると,「生きているだろう」とも「生きていないだろう」ともとれるので避ける. (2) hope は話者が望むことに対して用いる. したがって「たぶんだめ(=生きていないでしょう)など望ましくないことに対する懸念を表して I'm afraid not. となる)

《会話》「泳ぎに行くの?」「たぶん行かないわ」"Are you going for a swim?" "*Probably not.* / *Not* ˇ*likely.*" (⇨*解説*(**3**))

《会話》「コンサートのチケットは手に入るかしら」「たぶん大丈夫でしょう」"Would I be able to get a ticket for the concert?" "You *might*."

たぶん 他聞 ▶これは絶対他聞にはばかることですよ This is strictly [*completely*] *confidential*.
だぶん 駄文 poor writing, 《英》waffle.
たべあるき 食べ歩き ▶うまいものの食べ歩きをする make a tour of eating dainty food.
たべあわせ 食べ合わせ ▶スイカと天ぷらは食べ合わせが悪い If you eat watermelon and *tempura* together, you will feel sick.
たべかす 食べ滓 the leavings. (⇨食べ残し)
たべかた 食べ方 ▶私はシカ肉の食べ方(=料理法)を知らない I don't know *how to cook* deer meat. ▶彼は作法にかなった食べ方を知らない He has no *table manners* [×*manner*].
たべごろ 食べ頃 ▶このメロンは今が食べごろです This melon is just *right for eating*. ▶この種の桃は8月が食べごろである(出盛りである) This type of peach *is in season* in August./(熟して食べられるようになる) This kind of peach *is ripe enough to eat* [*is ripe and ready for eating*] in August.
たべざかり 食べ盛り ▶うちには食べ盛り(=成長期)の男の子が2人いる We have two *growing* boys.
たべすぎ 食べ過ぎ overeating; eating too much. ▶食べ過ぎは健康によくない *Eating too much* is not good for the health.
たべずぎらい 食べず嫌い (⇨食わず嫌い)
たべすぎる 食べ過ぎる eat too much; overeat. ▶あめを食べすぎると虫歯になるよ Don't *eat too much* candy or you'll get bad teeth.
タペストリー [《つづれ織り》] (a) *tápestry*.
たべちらす 食べ散らす [《食べかすを散らかす》] (子供などが) litter 《the table》 with pieces of food; [《あれこれ少しずつ食べる》] try a little of every dish on the table.
たべで 食べで ●食べでのある substantial 《breakfasts》; solid 《meals》.
たべのこし 食べ残し (残飯) the leavings of a meal; (料理の手っかずで余ったもの) léftòvers. (⇨残り物) ▶彼は昼食を食べ残した He *left* his lunch *half-eaten*.
たべほうだい 食べ放題 ●食べ放題の店 an all-you-can-eat restaurant. ▶あの喫茶店はたった1,000円でケーキが食べ放題です At that tearoom you can *eat as much* cake *as you want* just for 1,000 yen.

*****たべもの 食べ物** food (**!** 通例種類のときは Ⓒ だが, 《米》では Ⓤ 扱いすることも多い. 食品をさすときは a piece [an article] of 〜); [《内容・栄養から見た食事》] (a) diet; [《皿に盛った料理》] a dish (⇨料理); [《蓄えた食糧》] provisions (⇨食糧).

①【〜な食べ物】 ●動物性の食べ物 animal *food*(*s*). (**!**「動物の餌(ミネ)(food for animals)」ではない) ●植物性の食べ物 vegetable [×plant] *food*(*s*). **!** plant food(s) は「植物の栄養(=肥料)」の意 ●犬の食べ物(=ドッグフード) dog *food*(*s*). ●あっさりした食べ物(低脂肪で消化のよい) light *food*; (香辛料・調味料をあまり加えない) plain *food*. ●こってりした食べ物(栄養の高い) rich *food*; (消化が悪くてしつこい) heavy *food*. ●病人の食べ物 the *diet* of a patient; *food* for a sick person. ●ヘルシーな食べ物 healthy *food*. ▶コロッケは私の好きな食べ物の一つ A croquette is one of my favorite *food*(*s*) [*dishes*].

②【食べ物は[が]】 ●食べ物が偏っている[いない] have an unbalanced [a balanced] *diet*. ▶冷蔵庫の中にはまだ少し食べ物がある There is still some *food* in the refrigerator. ▶その食べ物は体によい The *food* is good for your health [《話》for you]. ▶何か温かい食べ物がほしい I'd like something hot to eat.

③【食べ物に】 ▶夏は食べ物に気をつけなさい Be careful about what you eat [*your food, your diet*] in summer. ▶彼は食べ物に好き嫌いがある He has his likes and dislikes about his *food*. (**!** 対照強勢に注意)/(食べ物の好みがうるさい) He is particular [《話》fussy] about his *food*.

*****たべる 食べる**

WORD CHOICE 食べる

eat 人・動物が食事・食べ物を食べることを表す最も一般的な語. ●朝食にバナナを食べる *eat* a banana for breakfast.

have 人が食事をとること. 具体的な食品を口に入れて食べる場合は eat, 抽象的な食事を取る場合は have が好まれる. 動物に対しては用いない. ●家族と夕食を食べる *have* dinner with the family.

take 人が一定量の食事をとること. 医学・栄養学などの文脈で用いることが多い. ▶彼は食事を取ったが, 十分食べたわけではない He *took* a meal, but didn't have enough.

❶[食べ物を食べる] eat*; have*; take* (⇨[類語]); (主に動物が) feed*.

①【＋食べる】 ●大皿からとって食べる *eat* off [from] the big plate. ●ひと口で食べる *eat* (*it*) in one bite. (**!** take a bite 《out of an apple》は「ひと口食べる」の意) ●たらふく食べる *eat* as much as one wants; *eat* one's fill. ●彼はいつもがつがつしたように食べる He always *eats* greedily./He is a greedy eater. ▶彼はよく食べる人だ He *eats* a lot./(大食家だ) He's a big eater. ▶(レストランで)まだ食べ

ています(から下げないでください) I'm still *working on* it. (❗口語的慣用表現) ▶今朝から何も食べていない I *haven't eaten* anything since this morning. ▶こんなに食べきれない(こんなにたくさんは) I *can't eat* this much./(これ全部は) All of this *is more than* I *can eat* [*take*]. (❗日本語につられて ×...*more than* I *can't eat* [*take*]. としない) ▶よくかんで食べなさい *Chew* (your food) well and swallow it.

会話 「十分食べましたか」「十二分に食べたよ」 "*Have* you *had enough*?" "Yes, I'*ve had* more than enough."

❷【...を食べる】 ●朝食を食べながら議論する *discuss* (*it*) *over* breakfast. ●ピザ[夕食]を食べに行く *go out for* pizza [*to* dinner]. (❗いずれも *eat* は用いない) ●肉ばかり食べる *eat* nothing but meat; *eat* only meat. ●夕食に魚を食べた I *had* [*ate*, ×*took*] fish for supper. ●私は(出された)野菜を全部食べた(=平らげた) I *ate up* my vegetables. (❗*up* は「完全に」の意) ●少年たちは昼食を腹一杯食べた The boys *ate* [*had*] a hearty lunch. ●煮豆をもうひと口食べた I *took* another *bite* [*ate* another *mouthful*] *of* boiled beans. ●彼はずるずる音を立ててうどんを食べ始めた He *dug into* the noodle, slurping noisily. (❗*dig into* ... は《話》で「がつがつ食べ始める」の意. 目的語が省略されると自動詞で *dig in* となる) ▶シカは牧場で草を食べていた The deer *were feeding* [*grazing*] *in* [*on*] the meadow. ▶牛は草を食べる Cows *eat* [*feed on*] grass. (❗「常食とする」の意では進行形不可) ▶今は何も食べたくない I don't want *to eat* now. (❗...*eat* any *food* ...という必要はない)/I don't want *to take* anything now. ▶ナシはもう食べあきた(たくさん食べた) I *had* [*ate*] enough *of* pears. (しばしば食べるので) I'*m tired of eating* pears. ▶こんなにおいしい料理は食べたことがない I've never *tried* [*tasted*, *eaten*] such nice food. (❗*try* は「試しに食べてみる」, *taste* は「味わう」の意)

会話 「母さん, アイスクリームをもう少し食べてもいい?」「もうないよ. あなたがみんな食べてしまったんだもの」 "*May* I *have* some more ice cream, (please,) Mother?" "There isn't any more. You'*ve eaten* it all." 事情 このような場合一般にアメリカの家庭では子供に May I ... とともに please と呼びかけ語(ここではmother)をつけるように教育する

会話 「何か食べようよ. おなかがぺこぺこだ」「そうしよう」 "Let's *get* something to eat. I'm starved 《米》[*starving* 《英》]." "Yes, let's."

会話 「サラダを勝手に取って食べてよろしいですか」「ええ, どうぞ」 "*May* I *help myself to* the salad?" "Sure./Of course./Yes, please./Yes, do./ Please do." (❗(1) *help oneself to* は「自由に取って食べる[飲む]」の意. (2) 単に Yes, または ×please ということについては (⇨どうぞ ❸, ぜひ))

❸【...で食べる】 **(a)**【手段, 場所】 ●ナイフとフォークで食べる *eat with* a knife and fork. (❗×*a* knife and *a* fork とはいわない) ●外で食べる(=外食する) *eat* [《書》 *dine*] *out*. (❗「家で食べる」は *eat in*, *have* (*dinner*) *in*)

(b)【食物の状態】 (❗*eat* +目的語+形容詞・分詞の型で用いられる) ▶この魚は生で[煮て]食べる We *eat* this fish raw [*cooked*]. (❗raw [*cooked*] は「生の[料理にした]状態で」の意の補語)

❷【生活する】(食べて生きている) live 《*on*》. (⇨生活する) ▶年金だけではとても食べていけない I can hardly *live on* [*off*] my pension alone. ▶これで家族を食べさせるのがやっとです This is just enough to make a living and *support* [*feed*] my family.

— **食べられる** 動 ▶この果物は食べられますか Is this fruit *good to eat*?/(やや書) Is this fruit *edible*? (❗*edible* は「無害で食用に適する」の意) ▶この桃は熟しすぎて食べられない This peach is not *eatable* because it is too ripe. (❗*eatable* は味などおどうにか満足できること. しばしば否定文で) ▶トムさん, イカのさしみは食べられますか(=好きですか) Tom, do you *like* raw squid?

翻訳のこころ 料理はもうすぐできます. 十五分とお待たせはいたしません. すぐ食べられます (宮沢賢治『注文の多い料理店』) The meal will be ready soon. We won't keep you waiting for more than fifteen minutes. You can start your meal soon [get to eat right away]. (❗(すぐ)食べられます」はレストランでの言葉遣いとしては ... start your meal soon. の方が ... get to eat right away. より適切)

だべる 駄弁る have* an idle talk 《*with*》, 《話》 gab (-bb-).

たべん 多弁 — **多弁な** 形 tálkative. ●多弁になる become very talkative. ▶酒が少し入ると男は多弁になった A few drinks loosened his tongue. (❗「不用意なことをべらべらしゃべる」の含みが強い)

だほ 拿捕 名 capture.
— **拿捕する** 動 capture. ●日本の漁船を拿捕する *capture* a Japanese fishing boat.

たほう 他方 the other. ●他方では on the other hand. (⇨一方)

***たぼう 多忙** busyness /bízinis/. (❗business /bíznis/ は仕事・商売の意で, 発音も異なる点に注意) (⇨忙しい)
●多忙である be very busy 《*with* one's work; *doing*》; have a lot [《書》much] to do. ▶ご多忙のところおじゃましてすみません I'm sorry to trouble you when you are so *busy*./(別れ際に) I'm sorry to have taken so much of your time.

だほう 打法 『野球』 a batting stance.
だぼう 打棒 batting. (⇨打撃 ❷)
たほうめん 多方面 many [various] directions.
— **多方面の** (いろいろの) various; (多くの) many; (多面的の) many-sided. ●多方面で活躍する be active *in many directions* [(分野) *fields*]. ●多方面にわたる才能の持ち主 a person of *various* [*many*] talents; a *versatile* person. ●多方面にわたる問題 a *many-sided* issue.

だぼく 打撲 【打つこと, たたくこと】 (げんこつ・棒などで) a blow; (武器類で) a stroke. ●頭に打撲を受ける get a *blow* [a *stroke*] on the head.
●打撲傷 a bruise.
だぼはぜ 『魚介』 a goby.
だぼら 駄法螺 big talk. (⇨法螺(⁸ぶ))

***たま 玉, 珠** 『球状のもの』 a ball; 『ガラス玉』 a bead; 『宝石』 a gem; 『眼鏡の』 a lens; 『硬貨』 a (ten-yen) coin; 『うどんなどの』 a small pile (*of* noodles). ●火の玉 a *ball* of fire. ●珠のれん (珠暖簾) a *ball* of wool. ▶彼は顔に玉の汗をかいていた *Beads* of sweat stood on his face.
●玉にきず (唯一の難点) the only trouble 《*with*》; (唯一の欠点) the only fault [*flaw*] 《*in*》; (楽しみや価値をそぐ物事) 《話》 a fly in the ointment. ▶彼は頑固なのが玉にきずだ The only trouble with him is (that) he is stubborn./Stubbornness is his only flaw [the only flaw in his character].

***たま 球** 『球技・玉突きの』 a ball 《投球・打球の種類にも用いる》; (打者への投球) a pitch; (送球) a throw; 『電球』 (a light) bulb. ●いい球 『野球』 a nice *pitch* [*ball*], a good *throw*. ●球足の速い(テニス)コート a fast court. ●球を投げる[捕る; 打つ] throw [catch; hit] a *ball*. ●難しい球を打ち返す 『テニス』

return a difficult shot. ▶今日は球が走っている The pitcher's *got a lot of movement* today. ▶彼は外角への球をセンターへ安打して He hit an outside *pitch* to center for a single. ▶電気の球が切れた The *bulb* has burned out.

*たま 弾 〚銃砲別の弾〛(小銃弾) a bullet; (散弾) a shot; (砲弾) a shell; (空気銃などの) a slug; 〚使用の状態〛(装填(ﾃﾝ)された弾) a charge; (発射された弾) a shot, a gunshot.

❶【弾が】●腕に弾が当たった I got a *shot* [*was shot*] in the arm. ●この銃は弾が入っている[いない] This rifle *is loaded* [*empty*].

❷【弾の】●我々は敵の弾の届く[届かない]所にいた We were within [out of] *gunshot* of the enemy. (🖉この gunshot は「射程距離」の意で Ⓤ)

❸【弾に】●彼は流れ弾に当たって負傷した[死んだ] He was wounded [was killed] by a stray *bullet*.

❹【弾を〖で〗】●銃に弾を込める[抜く] *load* [*unload*] a gun. ●弾を撃ち込む put a *bullet* 《*into*》. ●弾を発射する fire (a *bullet* from) a gun. ●弾で撃ち抜く send [fire] a *bullet* 《*through* a wall》.

●弾傷 a bullet [a gunshot] wound. ●弾よけ a protection against bullets.

たまあし 球足 ●球足の速いテニスコート a *fast court*. ▶彼の打球は速い球足で三遊間を抜けた The ball he hit went quickly through the hole (between third base and shortstop).

たまいし 玉石 a round stone.

たまかざり 玉飾り a thick ring of straw festoon.

たまぐし 玉串 ●玉ぐしを捧げる offer a branch [a sprig] of a sacred tree to a god.
●玉ぐし料 a monetary offering to a god.

たまげる be very surprised; 《話》be flábbergàsted 《*at, by*》. (⇒驚く) ▶芝居は時々行くが実に立派でたまげるばかりだ I go to the theater [see plays] from time to time, and 〖×but〗 marvel at the splendid performances there. (🖉(1)「芝居に行く」は go to the theater の方が see plays より普通. (2) 「…行くが」の前後の文は相反する意ではないので but は不適切)

*たまご 卵, 玉子 ❶〚鳥・虫などの〛an egg (🖉通例鶏卵をさす); (魚介類の) 〖集合的〛spawn.

the white (白身)
the yolk (黄身)
the shell (殻)

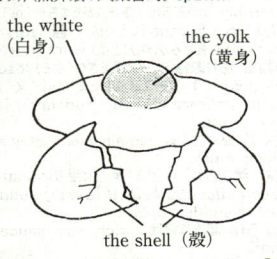

①【～卵】●生みたての卵 a new-laid [a newly laid] *egg*. ●新鮮な[古い]卵 a fresh [a stale] *egg*.
●生卵 a raw *egg*. ●ゆで[落とし]卵 a boiled [a poached] *egg*. ●錦糸卵 golden strings of thin omelets.

②【卵～】●牛肉の卵とじ sliced beef bound together with undercooked *egg*. ●卵形の顔 an *egg-shaped* [an *oval-shaped*] face.

③【卵が】●卵がかえった The *eggs* hatched (out). ▶夏は卵が腐りやすい *Eggs* go bad [rotten] easily in summer. (🖉×Eggs are easy to go bad …. は不可)

④【卵の】●卵の殻 an eggshell. ●卵の白身[黄身] the white [yolk] of an *egg*.

⑤【卵を】●卵を産む lay an *egg*; (魚介類が) shoot *spawn*, spawn. ●卵をかえす hatch an *egg*. ●卵をかき混ぜる beat an *egg*. ●卵を抱く sit on *eggs*. ●卵を焼く〖ゆでる〗fry [boil] an *egg*. ●ボウルに卵を割る break an *egg* in a bowl. ▶彼は朝食で卵を少し食べ残した He had some *egg* left over at breakfast.

🗨「卵をどんなふうに召し上がりますか」「半熟[かたゆで]にしてください」 "How would you like your *eggs*?" "I'd like mine soft-boiled [hard-boiled]."

❷〚未熟者〛●外交官の卵(=駆け出しの外交官) a *fledgling* /flédʒliŋ/ diplomat. ●詩人の卵(新進の詩人) a *budding* poet; (未来の詩人) a *future* poet; (近い未来の詩人) a poet-*to-be*; (将来人志望の人) 《しばしば軽蔑的》a *would-be* poet. ▶彼女はスターの卵だ She's a star *in the making*. (🖉「修業中の」の意)

●卵酒 'hot *sake* mixed with raw eggs'; (エッグノッグ) eggnog (参考 通例ラム酒に卵・牛乳・砂糖・香料を混ぜた飲料). ●卵焼き rolled fried-eggs. (事情 外国では一般的でない)

*たましい 魂 〖精神〗spirit; 〖霊魂〗(a) soul (🖉 spirit より宗教的・道徳的響きを伴う). ●開拓者魂 the frontier [pioneering] *spirit*. ●死者の魂 the *spirits* of the dead. ▶彼の肉体は滅んだが魂は永遠に生き続けている Although his body is in death, he has an eternal *soul*. ▶彼は仕事に魂を打ち込んでいる He puts his *heart and soul* into the work. (⇒全身全霊) ▶彼は彼女の美しさに魂を奪われている(=魅了されている) He *is fascinated* [*is charmed*] *with* her beauty.

●魂を入れ替える (行いを改める) mend one's ways; improve [mend] one's behavior.

だましうち 騙し討ち 〖(闇討ち, 奇襲攻撃) a sneak [a surprise] attack. ━ 騙し討ちする 動 make [launch] a sneak [a surprise] attack 《*on*》.

だましえ 騙し絵 an optical illusion picture.

だましとる 騙し取る cheat [trick] 《him》out of 《his money》. (⇒騙(ﾀ)る)

たまじゃり 玉砂利 gravel. (⇒砂利) ●玉砂利を敷いた道 a *gravel*(ed) path [road, drive].

だます 騙す ❶〚うそをついて〛deceive; 《話》take 《him》in; 〖計略を用いて〗trick (🖉必ずしも悪意を含まない); cheat (🖉計略・不正手段で金品・優位などをだまし取ること). ●彼をだまして…と信じ込ませる deceive [cheat] him *into* believing that …. ●彼をだまして金を取る cheat him 《out》of his money (🖉 out of の方が普通); swindle him *out of* his money; swindle his money *out of* him. (🖉人を目的語にとる方が普通. swindle は cheat よりこみ入った手段を含意する) ▶彼女の無邪気な顔つきにまんまとだまされた I *was* easily *deceived* [〖話〗*taken in*] by her innocent looks. ●彼は彼女をだまし, その書類にサインさせた He *tricked* her *into* signing the papers. ▶彼にだまされないよう気をつけなさい You must be careful (that) he does not *cheat* you [*not to be cheated* by him]. (🖉 that 節内は通例現在時制) ▶あなた, 彼, 絶対だまされているわ(=うそをついている). 話があますぎるもの You must *be lied to*. That sounds too good to be true. ▶だまされたと思って(=私の言葉を信じて)これをやってごらん Just *take* my *word for it* and do this.

❷〚なだめすかす〛(子供などを) coax; (損傷のある機械などを慎重に扱う) nurse. ●子供をだまして寝かせる coax

ダマスカス

a child *to* go to bed [sleep].
●**だましだまし** ▶私はおんぼろ車をだましだまし走らせて国境を越えた I *nursed* my old wreck across the border.
ダマスカス 〖シリアの首都〗Damáscus.
たまたま 〖偶然に〗by chance, by accident; 〖思いがけず〗unexpectedly; 〖たまたま...する〗happen 〖《書》chance〗to do, It happens 〖《古》chances〗that .... ▶私は上野駅で彼にたまたま会った I met him at Ueno Station *by chance* [*by accident*]./I *happened* to meet 〖《書》ran into〗him at Ueno Station./*It (so) happened (that)* I met him at Ueno Station. (❗so は happen の偶然性を強める。強勢を置いて読む)
会話「切符を譲ってあげましょうか」「たまたま(=あいにく)もう買ってしまいました」"Can I sell you a ticket?" "I've already got one, *as it happens*."

たまつき 玉突き billiards. (❗単数扱い) ●玉突きをする play *billiards*.
●**玉突き衝突[事故]** a multiple collision; 《話》a pileup. ▶凍結した路上で 10 台の車が玉突き衝突[事故]をした There was a ten-car *pileup* [*chain (reaction) collision*] on the icy road./Ten cars *piled up* [*collided with each other*] on the icy road. ●**玉突き台** a billiard table. ●**玉突き場** a billiard room. ●**玉突き棒** a cue.
たまてばこ 玉手箱 a casket. ●開けてくやしい玉手箱 Pandora's box; the apple of Sodom; the Dead Sea apple [fruit].
たまに 〖時たま〗occasionally, 〖ほんの時たま〗only occasionally (⇨時々); 〖めったに...しない〗rarely, 《やや書》seldom. ⇨たまに来る客 an *occasional* visitor. ▶彼からたまに便りがある I *occasionally* hear from him./I get an *occasional* letter from him. ▶我々はたまに野球をする We *occasionally* play baseball. (❗sometimes ではやや頻度が高くなる)/We play baseball *once in a while*. ▶このような光景はたまにしか見たことがない I have *rarely* [*seldom*] seen such a sight. ▶*Rarely* [*Seldom*] have I seen .... のような倒置構文は《書》) ▶たまには(=いつもと変えて)外食しよう Let's eat out *for a change*.
会話「彼は大阪に来ることがありますか」「ごくたまにね」"Does he ever come to Osaka?" "*Only very occasionally*./Every *once in a while*."

たまねぎ 玉葱 〖植物〗an onion /ʌ́njən/. ●タマネギの皮 an *onion* skin. ●タマネギスープ ónion sóup. ▶タマネギの皮をむいてください Will you peel the *onions*? (❗the onion skins は不可)
たまの (時々の)occasional; (まれな)rare. ▶たまの休みなのでどこかへ行きたい Since I *rarely* [*don't very often*] have a day off, I'd like to go somewhere. / (久しぶりに休みを取ったので) Since I've taken a day off *for the first time in ages*, I'd like to go somewhere.
たまのこし 玉の輿 ●**玉の輿に乗る** ▶彼女は玉の輿に乗った She married into a family of much higher social position.
たまのり 玉乗り ●玉乗りをする balance oneself on a ball.
たまのれん 珠暖簾 a bead curtain, a curtain (made) of beads.
たまひろい 球拾い a ball boy [girl]; (裏方)a backstage worker. ●打撃練習の球拾いをする shag balls for batting practice. ▶元首相は政治の前面には出ず球拾いに徹したいと言った The ex-prime minister said he would not appear on the political stage but would do what he can *backstage*.

たまる

たまむし 玉虫 〖昆虫〗a (two-striped green) buprestid; a jewel beetle.
たまむしいろ 玉虫色 图 iridescence /ìrədɛ́sns/.
── 玉虫色の 厖 irídescent; (あいまいな) ambíguous.
▶玉虫色の答弁をする give an *ambiguous* reply.
たまもの 賜物 (結果)(a) result; (成果)a fruit. ●天の賜物 a godsend; a gift of Heaven. ●努力の賜物 the *result* [*fruit(s)*, (報酬)*reward*] of one's efforts.
だまらせる 黙らせる 《話》shut*... up; 《やや書》silence; make* (him) hold (his) tongue. (❗その他、黙らせる原因となる動詞に down をそえて, shout (him) down (どなって黙らせる)などのようにいえる)
***たまらない** 堪らない ❶〖耐えられない〗unbearable; 《やや書》intolerable. ●たまらない暑さ *unbearable* [*intolerable*] heat. ●悲しくてたまらない(悲しみのうちひしがれる)be *overcome* [*overwhelmed*] *with* grief. ●心配でたまらない(=死ぬほど心配だ)be worried to death. ●頭が痛くてたまらない(=割れるような頭痛がする)have a splitting headache. ▶暑くてたまらない I *can't stand* [*bear*, 《話》*put up with*] the heat. (⇨耐える)/The heat is *unbearable* [*intolerable*]./(耐えられないほど暑い)It is *unbearably* [*terribly, too*] hot. ▶彼女が気の毒でたまらない I am *deeply* [*extremely*] sorry for her. ▶おかしくてたまらなかった(=笑わざるを得なかった)I *couldn't help laughing* [《米話》couldn't help but laugh]. ●後の方が普通) ▶早起きがいやでいやでたまらない I *detest* [*hate*] having to get up early. ●前の方が意味が強い) ▶そんなことがたまるか(=あり得ない)That's *impossible*./That *can't be true*.

❷〖切望する〗be anxious; 〖熱望する〗be eager 《for; to do》; 〖待ち切れない〗can't wait 《to do》; (うずうずしている)be impatient 《to do》; 〖死ぬほど欲しい〗《話》be dying 《for; to do》. ▶子供たちは外で遊びたくてたまらなかった The children *were impatient* [《話》*had an itch*] *to* play outdoors. ▶(酒を)1 杯飲みたくてたまらない I'm *dying for* [*to have*] *a drink*./I (just) *can't wait to* have a drink. ▶彼に会いたくてたまらない気持ちだ I *very much* want to see him.
── **たまらなく** 副 (耐えられないほどに)unbearably; intolerably; (非常に)very much, 《話》awfully; 《話》terribly. (⇨非常に) ▶それがたまらなく欲しい(欲しくてたまらない)I want it *badly*. (❗badly は主に want, need を強める)/(ぜひ)I *dó* want it. (⇨厖 ❷)
たまりかねる 堪り兼ねる (我慢できなくなる)lose* patience 《with》. ▶彼の無作法にたまりかねて文句を言った *Losing patience with* his rudeness, I complained to him.
だまりこくる 黙りこくる remain silent; stay silent; 《話》keep mum.
だまりこむ 黙り込む (⇨黙る) ●急に黙り込む suddenly *become silent*; *fall silent* [*dumb*] suddenly; *fall into* a sudden *silence*.
だまりじょうゆ 溜まり醤油 rich soy sauce 《for sashimi》.
たまりば 溜まり場 ●画家の溜まり場(=会合の場所)a *rendezvous* /rάːndəvùː/ *for* artists; a *favorite haunt* [《話》*a hangout*] *of* artists. ●暴走族の溜まり場(=集まる場所)a *gathering place for* motor-cycle gangs.
***たまる** 溜まる, 貯まる ❶〖集まる〗(少しずつ)collect, (自然に)gather; (長期にわたり積もる)accumulate, be accumulated; (山積みになる)pile [heap] (up). ▶ほこりが机の上にたまった Dust *collected* [*gathered, accumulated*] on the desk. (❗gather が最も

語的) ▶彼女の目には涙がたまっていた *There were tears in her eyes.*/(あふれていた) *Her eyes were full of* [*swimming with*, 《やや書》*brimming with*] *tears.*
❷[とどこおる] (仕事などをやり残す) have* 《a lot of work》 left [*unfinished*]; (借金などをためる) run* ... up. ▶宿題がたくさんたまっている *I have a lot of homework left* [*to do*]*.*/*A lot of homework has piled up.* ▶あの店にはつけがたまっている *I have run up bills at that store.* ▶家賃が3か月もたまっている *I am three months behind my rent.*
❸[金が残る] be saved. (⇨貯める) ▶とうとう100万円貯まった At last I've *saved* one million yen.

だまる 黙る 動 ❶[話をしない] (静かになる) become* [fall*] silent; become [be] quiet (❗silent は音・声があまりたくないこと。quiet は音・声が少なくて静かなこと。quiet の方が口語的①);(話すのをやめる) stop (-pp-) talking, 《話》 shut* up (❗通例命令形で); (沈黙している) keep* silent [quiet]. ▶怒った顔をして子供たちを黙らせた *shut* the children *up* 《やや書》[*silence* the children] with an angry look. ▶黙りなさい/(静かに) *Be quiet!*/*Quiet!*/*Silence!*/(話をやめろ) *Stop talking!*/《話》 *Shut up!*/《話》 *Zip your lips!*/《米話》 *Button it!* ▶彼はそのことについて黙っていた He *kept silent* [*said nothing*] *about* the matter./(人に話さないでおいた) He *kept* the matter *to himself.*
❷[文句を言わない](我慢する) 《話》 put* up with ...; (大目に見る) overlook, pass ... over. (⇨動❶) ▶もうこれ以上君の文句に黙っていられない *I can't put up with* [《やや書》*endure*] *your complaining any longer.*
── 黙って 副 ❶[静かに] (無言で) in silence, silently; (ひと言もなく) without a word; (不満を言わずに) without (×a) protest. ▶黙って部屋を出て行く leave the room *in silence* [*without (saying) a word, without saying anything*]. ▶黙って屈服する give way *without protest.* ▶黙って彼の誤りを見逃す *overlook* [*pass over*] his mistake. ▶私たちは黙って座っていた We sat *silently* [*in silence*].
❷[無許可・無届けで] ▶親に黙って (=知らせずに) 学校をやめる quit school *without telling* one's parents. ▶黙って (= 無届けで) 学校を休む stay away from school *without* (*previous*) *notice* [*calling in*]. ▶欠席の連絡は通例電話で学校に入れるため Please call in when you're sick. (病気の時は学校に電話してください などという) ▶黙って (=許可なく) 私の車を使ったのだけど Who used my car *without* (*my*) *permission* [*without asking*]?

たまる(もの)か 堪る(もの)か ▶そんなことがあってたまるか *That can't be!/Why, it's impossible!* ▶あんなやつに負けてたまるか *I'll be damned if he beats me.* ▶おれの気持ちがお前に分かってたまるものか *You can never know how I feel.*/*There's no way you can know how I feel.*

たまわる 賜る《書》be granted; (いただく) be given. ●拝謁を賜る *be granted* an audience.

たみ 民 (人民) people; (共和国の) a citizen; (君主国の) a subject. ▶民、信なくば立たず *People* accept nothing or nobody that cannot be trusted.

ダミー a dummy. ●ダミー会社 [架空の会社] a dummy company. (⇨ペーパー [ペーパーカンパニー])

だみごえ 濁声 (耳障りな[しわがれた]声) a harsh [《やや書》a raucous] voice. ●だみ声で話す speak in a harsh [a raucous] voice.

タミフル Tamiflu. [参考] A 型 B 型インフルエンザ感染症治療薬. 一般名はリン酸オセルタミビルカプセル ●一服のタミフル a dose of *Tamiflu*.

だみん 惰眠 ●惰眠をむさぼる idle the time away; spend time in a relaxed way, doing nothing; waste time.

ダム a dam. ●黒部ダム the Kurobe *Dam.* ●多目的ダム a multipurpose *dam.* ●ダム建設用地 a *dam* site. ●ダムを造る build [construct, ×make] a *dam* across a river.

たむけ 手向け [供え物に] an offering; [[はなむけ]] a farewell gift (⇨餞(ば), 餞別).

たむける 手向ける ●祖母の墓前に花をたむける place flowers on one's grandmother's grave.

たむし 田虫 ringworm. ●田虫ができる have (×a) *ringworm.*

たむろする 屯する (たまり場にする) 《話》 hang* out; (集まる) gather; 《やや書》 assemble. ▶高校生が数人駅でたむろしていた Some high school students were *gathering* at the station.

***ため 為 ❶**[目的] (...のために) for ...; (...するために) to 《do》, in order [so as] to 《do》 (❗to 不定詞が目的を表すことを明示する場合、in order [so as] to do が用いられる. so as to do は口語的で、結果を含意することもある); so [《書》in order] 《*that* 節》; (...の目的で) for the purpose of ..., with a view to .... (❗ともに主に《書》で、目的を強調する場合に用いる. 後の方がより堅い言い方). ▶私たちはその切符を買うために3時間並んだ We had to stand in line three hours *for* [*to get*] the tickets. (❗行動や行為をするための目的には ×for getting ... のように動名詞は用いない. ただし物の使用目的をいう場合にはその限りではない: このナイフはチーズを切るためのものです This knife is (used) *for cutting* [*used to cut*] cheese.) ▶君は何のために英語を学ぶのですか Whát do you learn ↘English *for?*/What is your *purpose in* [《まれ》*of*] learning English?/*For* what *purpose* do you learn English? ▶お役に立ててうれしいわ. だってそのための友達ですもの I'm happy to help you. That's what friends are *for.* ▶彼は試験に合格するために最善を尽くした He did his best *to* [×in order to*] pass the exam. (❗do one's best や make efforts の後では to do しか用いることができない) ▶彼女はドイツ語にみがきをかけるためにドイツに行く予定です She is going to Germany *to brush up* [*for the purpose of brushing up*] *her German.*/She is going to Germany *so that* she brushes [*will brush, may brush, can brush*] up her German. (❗ 主節の動詞が過去(完了)の場合には that 節中は通例 could, would, should,《書》might が用いられる (⇨[次例])) ▶彼らは私が入るために道をあけてくれた They stepped aside *so (that)* I *could* get in. (❗《話》ではしばしば that を省略する)/They stepped aside (*in order*) for me to get in. (❗for me は to 不定詞の意味上の主語、この場合 ×so as to は不可) ▶この詩を鑑賞するためには声を出して読むべきです *In order* [×So as] *to* appreciate this poem, you should read it aloud. (❗so as to は通例文頭では用いない) ▶列車に遅れないためにいつもより早く家を出た I left home earlier than usual *so* [*so that, in order that*] I wouldn't miss the train. (❗that 節中が否定の場合 should,《書》might も用いられる ▶×could は不可; 接続詞は後の方はど堅い言い方)/I left home earlier than usual *in order* [*so as*] *not* to miss the train. (❗not の位置に注意.「...しないようにするために」という否定の目的を示す不定詞句は構文上 to do をとる場合 (⇨[第4文例]) 以外では、通例 ×not to do とはいわない) ▶花嫁さんの健康のために乾杯しましょう Let's drink *to the*

health of the bride.
会話「君は謝るべき」「謝るだって？いったい何のためにさ」"You must apologize." "Apologize? *What* on eárth ＼*for?*" (❗on earth は what を強める)
❷ [原因, 理由] (ので) because, (やや書) since, 《主に英・やや書》as (⇨—ので 解説); (理由・原因の) because of ..., 《書》owing to ..., 《書》on account of ..., due to ..., (❗以上の前置詞句はいずれも because　節などを用いるより堅い言い方); from ..., through ..., with ..., for ... (❗以上は4つの前置詞は連語関係で決まっている場合が多い) ▶6か月間病気だったため失業した I lost my job *because* I was sick for six months. (❗I was sick for six months, so I lost my job. の方がくだけた言い方。日常会話ではI lost my job. I was sick for six months. のように接続詞を用いないことも多い)/*Because* [*Since, As*] I was sick for six months, I lost my job. (⇨—ので [第 2 文例]) ▶風邪のため会社を休んだ He stayed away from work *because of* [*owing to, on account of, due to*] a cold. (❗(1) ... because he got a cold. の方が口語的。(2) このように be 動詞の後以外で用いる due to は誤りとする人もあるが, 口ではよく用いられる) ▶彼女は食べすぎたため病気になった She became sick *from* eating too much [*because* she ate too much]. (❗後の方が口語的) ▶彼の不注意のために事故が起きた The accident happened *through* his carelessness./The accident *was due* [*owing*] *to* his carelessness. (❗be 動詞の後では due to が普通) ▶彼の顔は怒りのため赤くなった His face became red [He flushed] *with* anger. ▶彼は金を盗んだために罰せられた He was punished *for* stealing money.
❸ [結果] so, so that; (そういうわけで) That's why .... ▶彼ははっきりと説明しなかった。そのため(=その結果)だれも分からなかった He didn't explain it clearly, so [*so that*] nobody could understand it [why he did it]. (❗so の方が口語的) ▶彼女は果物は何でも好きです。健康なのはそのためです She likes all kinds of fruit. *That's why* she is healthy.
❹ [利益] (...のために) for ...; (...最も一般的な語); (...の利益のために) for the sake [good, benefit] of .... ● 正義のために *for the cause of* justice. ● 祖国のために戦う fight *for* one's own country. ● 彼の父親のために開かれたパーティー a party given *for* [*in honor of*] his father. (❗in honor of は「...に敬意を表して」の意) ▶健康のために毎朝散歩する I take a walk every morning *for* my health. ▶彼のお金はすべて貧しい子供たちのために遣われた All her money was used *for the sake of* poor children. ▶君のためなら何でもするよ I'll do anything *for your sake.*

— ため 图 (有益) good. ▶その旅行は彼女には(とても)ためになった The trip did her (*the world* [*a power*] *of*) *good*. (❗the world [a power] of は「とてもたくさんの」の意。a world of ともいう) ▶彼の授業はたいそうためになった(=教えられるところが多かった) His classes were very *instructive*. ▶おもしろくてためになる(=有益な情報の多い)お話ですね。話してくれてありがとう That's a very interesting and *informative* story. Thank you for sharing it.

*だめ 駄目 — 駄目な 形 ❶ [役に立たない, むだな] useless /júːsləs/, (of) no use /júːs/; (❗後の方は叙述的に, 《話》では通例 of を省略する); no good (❗no use より口語的); (無益な) vain (❗useless より堅い語。通例限定的に); (間に合わない) won't do; (不十分な) not enough. (⇨無駄) ▶彼を説得しようとしてもだめだ It is *useless* [*no use*] to try to persuade him./It is *useless* [*no use, no good*] trying to persuade him./There's *no good* [*no use*] (*in*) trying to persuade him. (❗《話》では通例 in は省略する) ▶一生懸命やったがだめだった I tried hard, but it was *useless* [was *no good*]. (❗次の 2 例より口語的) ▶I tried hard, but *in vain* [*to no purpose*]./(成功しなかった) I tried hard *without* (*much*) *success* [*only to fail*]. (❗この to は結果を表す) ▶私はフランス語は(=ろくでなしだ) He is *good for nothing* [*a good-for-nothing* (guy)]. ▶それくらいの金ではだめだ That isn't *enough* money.
会話「ちょうどいい大きさのネジが見つからないよ」「これじゃだめ？」"I can't find the right sized screw." "*Won't* this one *do*?"
会話「あの教授に頼むよ」「あの教授は頼んでもだめだよ」"I'll ask that professor." "He's *not* the man *to* ask."

❷ [不可能な] impossible; (無能な) incompetent; incapable; 《話》hopeless. ▶この宿題を 1 日で終えるなんてとてもだめだ It *is impossible* (*for* me) *to* [I *can't*, ×I am impossible to] finish this homework in one day. (❗×It is impossible that I finish .... は不可) ▶私はフランス語はさっぱりだめです I'm *hopeless at* French./(全く話せない) I *can't* speak French at all.
会話「もう少しいられるでしょう？」「申し訳ないけどだめなの」"Can't you stay a little longer?" "I'm sorry I *can't*."
会話「月曜はだめなんだ(=都合がつかない)」「どうしてだめなの」「夜バイトしているんだ」"I *can't* make it on Mondays." "Why *not*?" "Every Monday night I work part-time."

❸ [望みがない] hopeless; (間違った) wrong; (...できない) can't*. ▶あの患者はもうだめだ That patient's condition is now *hopeless*. (❗単に That patient is .... とするより普通)/There is *no hope* for that patient now. ▶もうだめだ(=万事休す) It's *all over* [*up*] *with* me./《話》I've had it./《話》I'm done for. ▶その答えはだめだ The answer is *wrong* [*isn't correct*]./You're *wrong*.

❹ [禁止, 義務] (...してはいけない) must not; (...すべきではない) should not; (...できない) can't* (⇨いけない❷); (...しなければならない) must, have* to; (...すべきだ) should (⇨—ならない) ▶泣いてはだめよ You *must* [*should*] *not* cry. (❗後の方が穏やかな言い方)/*Don't* cry. (泣くのをやめる) Stop crying. ▶宿題がすむまでテレビを見ちゃだめだよ You *can't* watch TV until you've done your homework. ▶急がなくてはだめだ You *must* [*have to*, 《話》*have got to*] hurry. (⇨—ならない) ▶英語くらいしゃべれないとだめだ You *should* be able to speak English at least.
会話「この本を持って行こう」「だめよ。それは太郎のよ」"I'll take this book." "You *mustn't* [Oh, *don't*]. That's Taro's."
会話「入っていいですか」「だめよ」"Can I come in?" "No, you *can't*." (⇨いい⓮)
会話「もうこれ以上は食べたくないよ」「だめ, お食べなさい」"I don't want to have another one, thank you." "Yes, you will."
会話「このリンゴをどうぞ」「一つしかだめ？」"Here's an apple for you." "*Can't* you give me [*Can't* I have] more than one?"
会話「ママ, 少しお金をくれない？」「だめだめ」"Mom, can you give me some money?" "*No way!* (❗no way は no の強意表現で, 依頼の返答として間投詞的に用いる。人指し指を立てて横に振る動作を伴うことが多い)/(絶対だめ) The answer is *definitely no*."
会話「たばこを吸ってもいいですか」「申し訳ないけどここではだめです。ロビーならいいですよ」"Can we smoke?"

"Not in here, I'm afraid. Only in the lobby."
❺ 〖その他の表現〗 ● だめでもともと (⇨駄目元) ● 健康でなくてはならない(=健康がいちばん大切だ) Health is everything [the most important thing]. ▶ぼくは血を見るとだめだ(=ひるむ) I cringe at the sight of blood. ▶彼は運転免許の試験だめだったそうよ He failed [didn't pass] his driving test, I hear. ▶またしてもだめか! Just my luck!
● だめを押す check (it) twice, double-check; make doubly sure 《of it; that 節》. (⇨駄目押し)
● だめを出す (⇨駄目出し)

―― 駄目にする[なる] 動 (台なしにする) spoil (❗物・事・子供などに用いるが,機械・道具などには用いない (壊す)); ruin (❗spoil より徹底さを強調する.主に物・機会・前途などに用い,子供に用いるのは(やや話)); (損害を与える) damage; (腐る) go* bad [rotten], spoil; (壊す) break*; (行事などを取り消す) cancel; (計画などを狂わす) upset*. ▶わがままをさせて子供をだめにするな Don't spoil [ruin] your child by [with] indulgence. ▶あらしで作物はだめになった The storm damaged [did damage to] the crops./The storm spoiled [ruined] the crops. ▶牛乳は冷やしておかないとだめになる Milk will go bad [(すっぱくなる) go sour /sáuər/] if you don't keep it cool. (❗牛乳はgo rotten は用いない) ▶資金不足でその計画はだめになった A lack of funds upset the plan./The plan fell through because we were short of funds. ▶雨のため試合はだめになった(=延期された) The game was called off [was canceled] because of (the) rain. (❗雨の方が主口語的) ▶試合の途中であることを暗示の)/(話) The game was rained out 《主に米》《英》.

ためいき 溜め息 a sigh /sái/. ● ため息まじりに言う say with a sigh. ● 深い[ほっとして]ため息をつく sigh deeply [with relief]; give a deep sigh [a sigh of relief].

ためいけ 溜め池 a reservoir /rézərvwà:r/, a pond.

ダメージ 〖被害〗 damage /dǽmidʒ/. ● ひどいダメージを受ける be heavily [badly] damaged. ● ダメージを与える cause (do, ×give) damage 《to》; hit.

だめおし 駄目押し ❶ ● 犠牲フライでだめ押しの1点を加える deliver [add] an insurance run with a sacrifice fly. ● だめ押し点を取るために代打を起用する put in a pinch hitter for an insurance run.

―― 駄目押しする ● 彼にあす来るようにだめ押しする(=念を押す) make doubly sure that he comes tomorrow. (❗that 節中は未来のことも通例現在時制で)

ためがき 為書き a note of dedication; (説明的に)a note on an work of calligraphy which shows who the presentee of the work is.

ためこむ 溜め込む 〖物を蓄える〗 store ... (up); 〖財宝・食料などをひそかに〗 hoard; 〖貯金する〗 save ... up. ▶アリは冬のために食料を溜め込む Ants store up [hoard] food for the winter. ▶彼は老後に備えて金を溜め込んだ He saved (up) money for [《古》against] his old age. (❗money は省略可)

ためし 例し 〖先例〗 a précedent; 〖実例こったためしがない Nothing of that sort has ever happened here before. ▶彼女は怒ったためしがない She has never been angry./I've never known her (to) get angry. (❗to を省略するのは《主に英》)

ためし 試し 試し a trial, a test, a try.

―― 試しに 副 on trial; as a trial [a test, an experiment]. ● 買う前に試しにその機械を使ってみる take the machine on trial before buying it.

● ギリシャ料理を試しに食べてみる try Greek food. ▶彼は試しに新型のパソコンを使ってみた He tried using a new-model personal computer. (❗try doing は実際にやってみることであるが,try to do はしようと努めることで実際にはしないことをある) ▶私はどれがいちばん似合うか試しに帽子をいくつかかぶってみた I tried on several hats to see which one suited me best. (❗try ... on は 「試着する」の意)

ためす 試す 〖試してみる〗 try; 〖性能などを試す〗 try ... (out) (❗try out は 「十分に試す」の意), test; 〖確かめる〗 see. ● 力を試す try [test] one's strength. ▶もう一度試してごらん Try (it) again./Have another try (at it). ● この新しいローションを試してみます I'll try this new lotion./I'll give this new lotion a try. ● どのくらい速く泳げるか試してみよう Let's (try to) see 《(米主に) (英) try》 how fast we can swim. ● 次の計算問題をもっと速くできるかどうか試してごらん See if you can do the next sum more quickly.

だめだし 駄目出し ● だめ出しをする (やり直しを命じる) ask [order] 《him》 to do 《that scene》 again; (批判する) criticize 《him》.

ためつすがめつ 矯めつ眇めつ ● ためつすがめつ見る scrutinize 《the documents》 (closely); look at [examine] ... carefully [thoroughly].

ために 為に (⇨為(ため))

だめもと 駄目元 ● 断られてもだめもとだ I'd be none the worse for being turned down.

ためらい (a) hesitation. ● 何のためらいもなく without any hesitation. ● ためらいがちに hesitatingly; (ためらって) hesitantly.

ためらう hésitàte 《about; to do》; 〖選択に迷う〗 waver 《between》; 〖思案する〗 pause 《on》; 〖気おくれする〗 shy 《away》 《from》; 〖ひるむ〗 flinch, 《主に書》 shrink 《from》; 〖しり込みする〗 (自信がなくて) hold* back 《from》; (いやがって) hang* back. ● 彼に会うのをためらう hesitate to meet him; shy away from meeting him. ● 進むか戻るかためらう hesitate [waver] between going on and turning back. ▶彼はまだその受諾をためらっている He is still hesitating [hesitant] about accepting it./He is still hesitating 《about》 whether to accept it [whether he should accept it]. (❗wh- 節の前では前置詞はしばしば省略される) ▶彼女は少しもためらわずに援助を申し出た Without any hesitation She offered help./She had no hesitation in offering help./She did not hesitate to offer help. ▶ためらっていないで思いつくままどんどんやりなさい Don't hold back. Just go with what you think of.

*ためる 貯める, 溜める ❶ 〖蓄える〗 (金・労力などをとっておく) save ... (up); (食料などを) store ... (up); (少しずつ長期にわたって蓄積する) accumulate. (⇨蓄える) ● まさかの時に備えて金を貯める save (up) [put aside, lay aside] money for [《古》 against] a rainy day. (❗save (up) の場合は money がなくてもこの意になる) ● 貯めた金 one's savings. ● 水槽に水をためておく store water in the reservoir. ● 財産をためる accumulate a fortune. ● 新車を買うためにお金を貯めている I'm saving (up) for [to buy] a new car. ❷ 〖集める〗 collect, gather. (⇨集める, 溜まる) ● 目に涙をためて with tears in one's eyes; with one's eyes filled with tears.
❸ 〖とどこおらせる〗 〖溜まる ❷〗 ● 借金をためる accumulate [run up] a debt /dét/. (❗後の方が口語的.run up は 「(借金などを)急にふやす」 こと) ● ガス代をためる run up a gas bill; (未払いのままにしておく) leave a gas bill unpaid.

ためる 矯める 〖形を整える〗 train 《roses along the wall》; 〖性質・癖を直す〗 break a habit; cure

ためん 他面 (他の面) another side; (二つのうちのもう一方の面) the other side; 「もう一面では」while, on the other hand.

ためんたい 多面体 〖数学〗 a polyhedron (↔複 ~s, -dra).

ためんてき 多面的 ── 多面的な 形 〖興味・才能など〗多方面にわたる] many-sided; 〖多才な〗versatile; 〖いろいろな〗various. ●多面的な質問 a *many-sided* question. ●多面的な才能のある芸術家を *versatile* artist. ●多面的に(=いろいろな角度から)人生を見る view life *from various angles*.

たも(網) たも(網) a landing net.

たもう 多毛 ── 多毛の 形 hairy, hirsute.
●多毛症 〖医学〗hirsutism.

たもうさく 多毛作 multiple cropping.

たもくてき 多目的 ── 多目的な 形 multipurpose; (あらゆる用途にかなう) all-purpose. ●多目的ダム a multipurpose dam. ●多目的ホール a multipurpose [an all-purpose] hall.

***たもつ** 保つ 〖自分の支配下に置いて〗keep*; 〖一定の位置や状態に〗hold*; 〖現状のまま、よい状態に〗keep ... up, 《やや書》maintain (⇨維持); 〖価値あるものの状態を変えずに〗preserve (⇨保存); 〖なくならないように〗《やや書》retain. ●若さを保つ *keep* one's youth. ●秩序を保つ *keep* [*preserve, maintain*] order. ●バランスを保つ *keep* [*retain*] one's balance. (⚠ *keep* one's balance は「平静を保つ」の意にもなる; *maintain* one's equilibrium. ●自車と前方車の間に一定の車間距離を保つ *keep* a certain distance between one's car and the one ahead. ●まっすぐな姿勢を保つ *hold* oneself erect. ●体面を保つ *keep up* [*preserve*] appearances; save (one's) face. (⇨体面). ●高い生活水準を保つ *maintain* a high standard of living. ▶彼は競走で最後まで首位を保った He *held* [*maintained*] the lead until the end of the race.

たもと 袂 〖着物の〗a kimono sleeve. (⇨袖). ●たもとに入れる put (it) in one's *sleeve*. ●橋のたもとで(=そばで)会う see 《him》 *by* a bridge.
●たもとを分かつ ▶我々は彼らとたもとを分かち新しい党を結成した We *broke* [《話》*split* (*up*)] *with* them and formed a new party.

たやす 絶やす ▶ exterminate; kill; get* rid of ..., completely; (家系などを) let*... die out. ●火を絶やさない *keep* the fire burning [*going*]. ▶雑草を全部は絶やすことはできない We cannot *kill* all the weeds. (⚠部分否定に注意) ▶彼女はいつも笑顔を絶やさない She is always smiling.

***たやすい** 形 easy; simple. (⇨易い). ●たやすい問題 an *easy* [a *simple*] question.
── **たやすく** 副 easily; (難なく) without difficulty [trouble]; (すぐに) readily. ●たやすく引き受ける accept it *readily*.

たゆう 太夫 a leading actor in a *No*(h) play; (女形) a female-role actor in *kabuki*; (義太夫語り) a *gidayu* reciter; (最高位の遊女) a courtesan of the highest rank.

たゆたう 〖ゆらゆらする〗sway (from side to side, backward and forward); 〖ためらう〗hesitate (⇨ためらう, 迷う ❸). ●波にたゆたう小舟 a small boat *swaying* on the waves.

たゆむ 弛む ●たゆまぬ(=不断の)努力 《make》a *steady* [(よく知らない) an *untiring*] effort. ●たゆまず働く work *steadily* [*untiringly*].

たよう 多用 ❶〖多忙〗busyness. (⇨多忙)
❷〖多く使うこと〗▶彼は外来語を多用する He *uses too many* loanwords.

たよう 多様 ── 多様な 形 (種類がさまざまな) various; (著しく異なった) diverse. (⇨色々.)
── **多様化する** 動 diversify. ●学生の多様化したニーズに答える answer the *diversified* needs of students.
●**多様性** variety; diversity.

***たより** 便り 〖手紙〗a letter; 〖短信〗a note, 《話》a line; 〖消息〗news, 〖書〗word. (⇨手紙). ●彼から毎月定期的に便りがある I *hear from* him regularly every month. (⚠手紙だけではなく電話やイーメールなどによる連絡を含む) ▶この頃彼らからとんと便りがない(手紙がこない) I have not gotten [received] a *letter* from him lately. (⚠ get を用いる方は口語的)/(消息がない) I've heard nothing [I've had no *news*] at all from him lately.
会話「あすパリへたちます」「着いたらちょっとお便りをください」"I'm off to Paris tomorrow." "Send [Drop] me a *line* when you get there."
●**便りがないのはよい便り** (ことわざ) No news is good news.

***たより** 頼り 〖信頼〗reliance, dependence; 〖物質的依存〗dependence, reliance; 〖助け〗help; 〖人を支える人〗a support. (⇨頼る). ▶この町では君だけが頼りなんだ You are my only *reliance* in this town./I have no one but you to *rely on* [*turn to*] in this town. ▶彼が他人を頼りにしているのは残念なことだ His *dependence* on others is deplorable./It is deplorable that he *depends* [*is dependent*] *on* others. ▶あの男はとても頼りになる He is a very *dependable* (信頼できる) *trustworthy, reliable*〗 man./He is a man you *can depend* [*rely*] *upon* a lot./《話》He is a real *trouper*./《やや書》He is my rock. ▶我々は地図を頼りに宝を探しあてた We found the treasure *with the help of* a map.

-だより -便り ●東京[海外]便り *news from* Tokyo [*abroad*]. ●花便り *news of* cherry blossoms.

たよりがい 頼り甲斐 ●頼りがいがある dependable; reliable (↔unreliable). ▶あの人は頼りがいがない He is not *dependable* [*reliable*]./He can't *be trusted*.

たよりない 頼りない (信頼のおけない) unreliable, undependable; (あいまいな) indefinite; (不十分な) poor. ●頼りないやつ an *unreliable* [an *undependable*] guy.

***たよる** 頼る 〖依存する〗(物質的に) depend [rely] on [upon]... 《for》; (援助・安らぎなどを求めて) turn to ... 《for》; 〖当てにする〗(信頼に) rely [depend] on ...; 〖rely は過去の経験に基づく信頼を暗示》; (計算して) count on [upon]...; 〖最後の手段として頼る〗fall* back on ....

解説 **on** と **upon**: 一般に on より upon の方が堅い語だが、リズムの関係で upon が好まれることが多い。

▶彼女は金銭面で息子に頼っている She *depends* [*is dependent, relies*] *on* her son *for* money. ▶彼には頼る身寄りが1人もいなかった He had no relative to *depend upon* [*turn to*]. (⚠文章では upon が好まれる) ▶彼は気がめいるといつも酒に頼る When he is depressed, he always *turns* [*resorts*] *to* drink. ▶彼は親戚を頼って福岡に来た He came to Fukuoka, *counting on* his relative's help. ▶忙しくて料理できない場合はレトルト食品に頼ることが多い When I'm too busy to cook, I often *fall back on* retort pouches.

たら 〖植物〗a Hercules-club; an angelica tree; a devil's-walking-stick; a prickly ash.

たら 鱈 〖魚介〗a cod(fish). (⚠ 通例単・複同形. 肉は Ⓤ)

-たら 《副助詞》 ❶ 〖仮定, 条件〗 (もし...ならば) if ... (⇨もし); (...するときは) when.... ▶動いたら撃つぞ If you move, I'll shoot you. /Don't move, or (else) I'll shoot you. ▶もしフランス語が話せたら仕事はずっと楽になるんだが If I spoke French, my job would be much [《話》a lot] easier. ▶現在の事実に反する仮定) ▶車が故障しなかったら乗せてあげられたんだが I could have given you a ride if my car had not broken down. (❗過去の事実に反する仮定) ▶困ったら必ず私に連絡しなさい Be sure to [and] let me know if [when] you are in trouble. (❗(1) if では「困るかどうかは分からないが」、when では「たぶん困るだろうから」を含意する. (2) be sure and の方が口語的) ▶何があったのかを聞いたら君は考えを変えるだろうと思うよ After [When] you've heard what happened, you'll change your mind, I think. ▶この箱を開けようとしたら壊れたのです I was simply trying to open this box when it broke. (❗この when is and then (するとそのとき) に近い用法で, 過去の出来事を単純過去形で述べる前に, その背景的状況を過去進行形や be about to (do) などを用いて説明する場合に用いられる)

❷ 〖軽い非難・賞賛の気持ちを表す〗 ▶よせたらよせよ Do stop it. (❗do は強調の助動詞) ▶彼女, もう失礼ったらあらやしないか She's so véry (〖主と英語〗) éver só) ＼rude. ▶花子ったら長電話しているよ That Hanako has been on the phone for a long time again. (❗は無強勢で, 嫌悪, 不賛成の気持ちを表す) ▶そうじゃないんだったら That's not it, I tell you. ▶じれったい気持ちを表す慣用表現)

── **-たら** 《終助詞》 〖提案〗 ▶彼に尋ねてみたら How [What] about asking him?/Why don't you [Why not] ask him? (⇨どう)

たらい 盥 a tub; (洗濯用の) a washtub, a washing tub.

たらいまわし 盥回し ▶その子は親戚(ﾙﾝｾｷ)の間をたらい回しにされた The child was tossed around among his [her] relatives. ▶患者は病院から病院へとたらい回しにされた The patient was passed on like a parcel [was ping-ponged] from one clinic to another.

ダライラマ 〖チベット仏教の教主〗 the Dalai Lama /dáːlai láːmə/.

だらかん だら幹 〖労働組合〗〖政党〗 のだらしない幹部) a corrupt union [party] leader.

だらく 堕落 图 〖政治・道徳的腐敗〗 corruption; 〖ふしだらになること〗 a fall (from grace) (❗常に単数形で); 〖品位を落とすこと〗 degradation; 〖文芸などの退廃〗 decadence. ▶警察の堕落 the corruption of the police; police corruption. ▶人格の堕落 the degradation of character. ▶芸術の堕落 decadence in art.

── **堕落する[させる]** 動 corrupt; (品位を下げる) degrade; (道を踏みはずす) 《書》 go* astray; (堕落する) degenerate 《into a narcotic》. ▶彼は都会の生活で堕落した He was corrupted by city life. ▶権力を持つ人を堕落させる Power corrupts those who hold it. ▶金のために結婚して自分を堕落させるな Don't degrade yourself by marrying for money.

── **堕落した** 形 corrupt. ▶堕落した政治家 a corrupt politician. ▶堕落した女 〖古〗 a fallen woman.

-だらけ 〖...でいっぱいの〗 full of ...; 〖...でおおわれた〗 covered with .... ▶しわだらけのシャツ a shirt full of wrinkles [creases]. ▶血だらけの手 a hand covered with blood; a bloody hand. ▶通りはごみだらけだった The streets were full of litter./(山のようにあった) There were piles of litter on the streets. ▶彼の車は泥だらけだった His car was covered with dirt. ▶デッキは血だらけだった There was blood all over the deck.

だらけた (だらっとしている) be listless; (怠けている) be sluggish. ▶あまりの暑さにみんなだらけている The intense heat has made everybody listless.

たらこ 鱈子 cod roe /róu/; (塩漬けにした) salted cod roe.

-たらしい ▶長ったらしいあいさつを述べる give a lengthy [(長くて退屈な) a tedious] address. ▶あの人のきざったらしいものの言い方にむかむかする The affected way he speaks makes me sick.

たらしこむ 誑し込む 《話》 take ... in completely 《with sweet talk》; 〖誘惑する〗 tempt; (特に若い女性を) seduce.

だらしない 〖服装・態度・言葉などが〗 slovenly /sláv-ənli/, (特に身なりが) 《話》 sloppy; 〖不品行〗 loose /lúːs/, immoral; 〖部屋など整理されていない〗 untidy; 〖無頓着(ﾑﾄﾝﾁｬｸ)な〗 careless. ▶だらしない行為 loose [immoral] conduct. ▶だらしない身なり an untidy [a sloppy] appearance. ▶だらしない生活を送る lead a loose life. ▶彼は生来性格がだらしない He has a loose character by nature. ▶彼は服装がだらしない。もっときちんとするといいのに He dresses too sloppily. He should dress neater. ▶彼女は道徳的に見てだらしない She is morally loose. (❗性的にだらしない意を含む) ▶この机の散らかしようを見てくれ, まったくなんてだらしのないやつだ Look at this messy desk. What a complete slob! (❗slob は「無精でだらしのない人 (slovenly person) 」の意の口語表現) ▶近頃の親は子供にだらしない (=厳格でない) Parents today aren't strict enough with their children.

たらしめる ▶偉大な政治家たらしめる条件 the requirements for a great statesman.

たらす 垂らす ▶床に水を垂らす (=ぼたぽた落とす) drop [(こぼす) spill] water on the floor. ▶鼻水を垂らしている have a runny nose. ▶窓にカーテンを垂らす (=ぶら下げる) hang down a curtain over [on] the window.

-たらず -足らず 〖...より(すこし)少ない〗 (a little) less than ...; 〖以内〗 within ...; 〖ほぼ〗 nearly. ▶1 週間足らずで within [in less than] a week. ▶駅まで1キロ足らずです It is less than [nearly] a kilometer /kəlámətər/ to the station.

ダラス 〖米国の都市〗 Dállas.

たらたら 〖汗・血などが〗 〖垂れる〗 (⇨だらだら ❶). ▶たらたらしず[水滴]になって落ちる drip. ▶たらたら細く流れ落ちる trickle down. ▶彼女のぬれた手から水がたらたら落ちていた Water was dripping from her wet hands. ▶血が彼の額を[その傷口から]たらたら流れた Blood trickled down his forehead [trickled from the wound].

❷ 〖不平・お世辞などを〗 ▶彼は上役にいつもお世辞たらたらだ He is always rolling flattering words to his superiors. (❗進行形を用いて話し手の悲観の気持ちを表す) ▶彼女はいつも不満たらたらです She is always full of complaints./She is always complaining.

だらだら ❶ 〖だらだら流れる〗 (たれるように) drip (-pp-); (細い流れで) trickle; (小さい流れで) stream; (流れる) flow. (❗英語では「ぼたぼた」と「だらだら」との間を区別する語がないので他の語とともに工夫する. flow in drops で 「ぽたぽた[たらたら]」にもなる) (⇨たらたら) ▶私は彼の顔から血がだらだら流れるのを見た I saw blood trickling down his face.

❷ 〖だらだら続く〗 drag on (-gg-). ▶彼の退屈な演説がだらだら2時間も続いた His boring speech dragged on for no less than two hours.

── **だらだらした** 形 (長すぎる) (too) lengthy; (長くて

退屈な) tedious; (延長された) prolonged; (遅い) slow; (人がのろまな) sluggish; (だらしない) slovenly /slʎvənli/; (傾斜が) gentle. ● だらだらした演説 a *tedious* speech. ▶だらだらするんじゃない! Be quick about it! ▶私たちはだらだら坂を降りていった We went down a *gentle* hill [slope].

タラップ [<オランダ語] (飛行機の) a ramp; (船の) a gangplank, a gangway. ▶タラップを降りる go [《やや書》step] down the *ramp*. ▶タラップを登って乗船する walk up the *gangplank* onto a boat.

たらばがに 鱈場蟹〖動物〗a king crab; (特にアラスカ産の) an Alaskan king crab.

たらふく ▶(…を)たらふく食う eat one's fill (of ...); eat (...) as much as one wants.

だらりと ❶〖物が〗● だらりとたれる hang (down) loosely /lɑ́ːsliː/. ▶彼は長い手を横にだらりとたらしていた His long arms were hanging *loosely* at his sides./He had his long arms hanging *loosely* at his sides. ▶若い女が帯を後ろに下げて締めていた A young woman wore her sash with its end hanging *loosely* (on the back).
❷〖気持ちが〗(ものうげに) languidly; (する事もなく) idly.

だらんと loosely. (⇨だらりと)

-たり 《接続助詞》❶〖動作・状態を列挙する〗and (then); (ある時は...またある時は...) now ... now ...; now ... then ...; (...やら...やらで) what with [by] ... and what with [by].... (!! with は理由、by は手段・方法を表す。後の what with [by] は普通省略される) ▶彼は泣いたり笑ったりした He cried *and* (*then*) laughed. ▶寒かったり暑かったりして天候が不順だ The weather is changeable, *now* hot, *now* cold. ▶きのうはテレビを見たり音楽を聞いたりして1日中家にいた *What by* [✗*with*] watching television *and* listening to music, I stayed (at) home all day yesterday./Yesterday I spent the whole day at home, watching television *and* listening to music. ▶健康でいたければたばこを吸ったり食べすぎたりしてはいけません If you want to stay in health, you should not smoke *or* [✗*and*] eat too much. (!! 否定命令の後で and を用いると「喫煙しかつ暴食するのはいけない(どちらか一つはするのはよい)」の意になる) ▶1日中雨が降ったりやんだりしていた It was raining *off and on* 《米》[*on and off* 《英》] all day (long). (!! ✗*for all day* とはいわない)
❷〖例としてあげる〗▶木の枝を折ったりなどしてはいかん Don't break branches off a tree or anything.

ダリ 〖スペインの画家〗Dali /dɑ́ːliː/ (Salvador ～).

-だり (⇨-たり)

ダリア 〖植物〗a dahlia /dǽljə/.

タリウム 〖化学〗thallium.

たりきほんがん 他力本願〖宗教〗the salvation of souls through the benevolence of Buddha.
❷〖他人に頼ること〗relying [depending] on other people [others]; (他人に助けを求める) turning to others for help.

たりつ 他律 图 heteronomy.
—— 他律的な 圏 heteronomous.
—— 他律的に 圖 heteronomously.

だりつ 打率 〖野球〗a batting average. ▶今シーズンの彼の打率は3割5分4厘だった His *batting average* of [for] this season was .354./He had a .354 *batting average* this season./He *batted* [*hit*] .354 this season. (!! .354 は three hundred fifty-four または three fifty-four と読む) ▶彼は3割6分で首位打者のタイトルを獲得した He won the title with a .360 (*batting*) *average*.

-たりとも even. ▶水なしでは1日たりとも過ごせない We can't do without water *even* for a day.

***たりない** 足りない ❶〖十分でない〗be not enough, be insufficient (!! 後の方が堅い言い方 (⇨十分)); (不足している) be short (*of*, *for*...), lack. (!! 通例前の方は具体的なもの、後の方は抽象的なものに用いる); 〖紛失している〗be missing. ▶その服を買うにはお金が足りない I don't have *enough* money to buy the dress. ▶君は努力が足りない You're *not* working hard *enough*./(もっと努力すべきだ) You should work harder. ▶彼のことはいくらほめてもほめ足りない We *cannot* praise him *enough*. ▶生産を上げるには人手が足りない We're *short of* hands *short-handed*] *for* increasing production. ▶小遣いが足りなくなってきたので彼から借金しなければならない《人が主語》I'm running *short of* pocket money and have to borrow some from him./《物が主語》My allowance *is running short*, so I have to borrow some money from him. (!! *run short* は進行形で用いられることが多い) ▶6フィートに2インチ足りない It *is* two inches *short of* six feet. ▶いすが三つ足りない We *are* three chairs *short*. (!! 不足分を強調する場合は We *are short* (*by*) three chairs. といえる)/(もう三つ必要だ) We need three more chairs [〖書〗three chairs more, ✗more three chairs]. ▶彼は経験が足りない He *lacks* [*is lacking in*] experience. (!! *lacks* の方が普通)/He is inexperienced [〖話〗*green*]. ▶この本は4ページ足りない There *are* four pages [Four pages *are*] *missing* in this book. ▶昨年は日照時間が足りなかったので米が不作だった We had a poor rice crop last year because we did*n't have much* [✗we were short *of*] sunshine. ▶彼女は数学の力が足りない(=得意でない) She *is weak in* [*poor at*] mathematics. ▶2,000円では電車賃にも足りない(=をまかなえない) Two thousand yen will *not cover* even the train fare.

会話「君に6箱残しておいたよ」「それじゃ足りないよ」"I've left you six boxes." "That's [✗They are] *not enough*."

❷〖価値がない〗be not worth (*do*ing). (⇨価値) ▶彼の提案は取るに足りない His proposal *is not worth* consider*ing*./His proposal *counts for nothing* [〖書〗*is beneath* our *notice*].
❸〖頭が悪い〗be stupid; be dull; be simple-minded. ▶あの娘は少し頭が足りない(=あまり賢明ではない) She isn't very bright./〖話〗She's *a bit short on* brains.

タリバン [<アラビア語] 〖アフガニスタンのイスラム原理主義組織〗the Taliban [Talibaan] /tɑ́ːləbɑ̀ːn/. ▶タリバンは崩壊した The *Taliban* had come undone.

たりゅう 他流 another school.
● 他流試合 (enter) a contest with another school (*of* karate). ● 他流試合をする try one's skill against a follower of *another school* (*of* karate).

たりょう 多量 —— 多量の 圏 a great [a good] deal of ...; 《やや書》a large quantity [amount] of ... (!! large quantities [amounts] of となることもある). (⇨たくさん ❶) ▶オレンジは多量のビタミンCを含んでいる Oranges contain *a lot of* [*a great deal of*] vitamin C./(ビタミンCに富む) Oranges are *rich in* vitamin C.
—— 多量に 圖 in quantity, in large quantities; (豊富に) 《やや書》in abundance. ▶日本は多量に石油を輸入している Japan imports oil *in large quantities*./Japan imports *a large quantity* of oil. ▶食料が多量に(=十分に)ある We have *plenty of*

だりょく 打力 batting [hitting] ability, bat. ●打力を向上させる improve one's *bat*.

だりょく 惰力 《慣性・惰性》 inertia /ináːrʃə/. ●惰力で動く move on [by, through] *inertia*.

＊た(り)る 足(り)る ❶ 【十分である】 be enough; be sufficient (🎵前の方より堅い言い方)(⇨十分); [間に合う] do*, 〖書〗 serve (⇨間に合う). ●2,000 人の客を収容するに足るホテル a hotel large *enough* to accommodate 2,000 guests. ▶ 数日の旅行なら 5 万円あれば足りる Fifty thousand yen will *be sufficient*, *do*] *for* a few days' trip.
〖翻訳のこころ〗しかしいかに桁を違えて考えてみても，不思議なのは喜助の欲のないこと，足ることを知っていることもう（森鷗外 『高瀬舟』） Considering [Taking] into account the (big) difference between his and my level of life expectations, what's mystifying is that Kisuke is just so selfless and he knows how to be fully satisfied.（🎵(1)「桁」は his and my level of life expectations (喜助と自分(船頭)の人生における期待度, 満足度)を表す.(2)「足ること」は how to be fully satisfied (満足の仕方, どうしたら十分満足できるか)と表す）

❷ 【価値がある】 be worth 《do*ing*》; be worthy 《*of*; *to* do》; deserve. ▶ 彼の理論は考慮するに足る His theory *is worth* [*deserves*] considering./His theory *is worthy of* being [《やや書》 *to* be] considered.

たる 樽 （大だる） a barrel; （小だる） a keg; （酒だる） a cask. ●ビール 1 たる a *barrel* [*cask*] of beer. ●ビールだる a beer *barrel* [*cask*], たる入りビール beer on tap, たるの口をあける tap a *cask* 《*of* sake》. ●たるに詰める put 《beer》 in a *barrel*.
●樽柿 persimmons mellowed in a *sake* cask. ●樽酒 casked *sake*.

だるい 〖人が〗(無気力な)《やや書》 languid; (不活発な) sluggish; 〖手足などが〗 heavy. ●この暑さで体がだるい I feel *languid* [*sluggish*, *listless*] in this heat. ▶ 腕がだるい My arms are *heavy*.

たるき 垂木 a rafter.

タルタルステーキ tartar(e) steak.

タルタルソース tártar(e) sàuce.

タルト a tart. ●リンゴ入りタルト an apple *tart*.

だるま 達磨 〖＜サンスクリット語〗〗 〖【達磨大師】 Bodhidharma /bóudidάːrmə/ (a founder of the Zen sect of Buddhism); 【人形】 a dharma doll. ●達磨に目を入れる paint in [add] one of the eyes on a *dharma* doll (when one's wish is fulfilled). ●雪だるま a snowman. ●火だるま a mas of flames.
●だるまストーブ a potbellied [a potbelly] stove.

たるみ 弛み （ロープなどの）(the) slack; （肌・筋肉の）(a) sag, (the) droop. ●ロープのたるみの箇所をぴんと張る take up the *slack* in a rope; make a rope tighter. ●ズボンのたるみ a *sag* in one's pants 《米》 [trousers《主に英》].

＊たるむ 弛む ❶ 〖ロープなどが〗 slacken; (筋肉などが) get* loose [（太ってぶよぶよの） flabby], (年齢のために) sag (-gg-). ●その老人のたるんだほお the older man's *sagging* [*loose*] cheeks. ▶ そのロープはたるんでいる The rope *is slack*.（↔tight). ●(たるみがある) There *is some slack* in the rope. ▶ 彼の仕事最近はたるんでいるね He's *been slack*. 【怠慢な】 negligent, (怠惰な) lazy] in his work recently. ▶ 君はこのところたるんでいるね You *are losing* your *willpower* these days.

〖翻訳のこころ〗 そのときケイシーは見違えるくらい老けこんでいた．白髪の増えた髪は伸び，目の下が袋のようになって黒くたるんでいた．手の甲の皺まで増えたみたいだ (村上春樹『レキシントンの幽霊』) By then, Casey had gotten so old that I barely recognized him. His hair was grayer and longer. Puffy dark bags sagged under his eyes. He seemed to have more lines even on the back of his hands, too.（🎵(1)「そのとき」は「時が過ぎてある時点で」の意なので, at that time よりby then とする.(2)「見違えるくらい」は I barely recognized him (彼だと認識できなかったくらい)と表す）

ダルメシアン 【動物】(犬) a Dalmatian /dælméiʃən/.

だれ 垂れ ❶ 【だらりと下がったもの】 a flap. (⇨垂れ幕, 垂れ几帳, 垂れ目) ❷ 【料理の】(掛け汁) sauce; (肉汁) gravy.

＊だれ 誰 ❶ 【だれ, だれが】 who. ▶ 誰が君に聞いたら *Who* asked you?（🎵反語的に「君などに聞いていないよ, 黙っていてくれ」の意を表す口語的慣用表現） ▶ 隣の部屋でだれが話しているか *Who* is talking in the next room?（🎵複数の人が予想される場合でも単数で受けるのが普通） ▶ 〖玄関に来た人に〗 だれだか行ってみよ. 帰ってもらうつもりだけど I'll see *who* it is and send them away.（🎵性別が不明なので it, them で受けていることに注意） ▶ だれがこの絵をかいたか知らない I don't know *who* painted this picture. ▶ だれが私たちの担任になると思いますか *Who* do you think will take charge of our class?（🎵⤫Do you think who will... とはいえない） ▶ この会合の出席者はだれだか分からない I don't know *who's who* at this meeting.

〖会話〗 「あらまあ, だれかと思ったら」「やあ, 元気？」"Well, look *who's* here!" "Hi! How's things?"

〖会話〗 「（一体）だれが花びんをこわしたの」「私じゃないわよ」"*Who* (ever) broke the vase?" "＼I didn't./（話）Not ˅me."（🎵(1)「私です」なら "＼I did./(話) ＼Me."(2) ever は who を強める）

〖会話〗 「(ドアのノックをだれ)だれ」「私よ」"*Whó* ↗is it?" "It's me."（🎵(1) *Who* can that be? は内部にいる者同士で「いったい(今どき)だれかしらね」. Who's there? (⇨ 〖会話〗 〖第 1 例 注〗), Who are you? は不審者に「お前はだれだ」「そこにいるのはだれだ」の意で, いずれもここでは不可.(2)一般にはドアをノックされたら黙ってドアを開けるか, または, Come ˅in. というのが普通）

〖会話〗 「あれはだれ」「田中先生よ」「田中先生ってだれ」「私たちの英語の先生よ」"*Whó*'s ＼that?" "It's Ms ＼Tanaka." "＼*Who*'s Ms Tanaka?" "She's our ＼English teacher."

❷ 【だれの】 whose.
〖会話〗 「あれはだれのボールですか」「健のです」"*Whose* ball is that?/*Whose* is that ball?" "It's Ken's."

❸ 【だれに[を, と]】 who, 《書》 whom. ▶ 帰り道でだれに会ったの *Who* [*Whom*] did you see on your way home? ▶ 息子のことをほかにだれに相談したらいいのか私には分からない I really don't know *who* else to talk to about my son. ▶ だれといっしょに行きますか *Who* [*Whom*] are you going *with*?/*With whom* [⤫who] are you going?（🎵Whom with? よりさらに堅い言い方）

〖会話〗 「あなたは監視されているわ」「だれに」"They are watching you." "*Who* ˅is?"（🎵疑問代名詞 who を主語に用いるときは通例単数扱い）

〖会話〗 「彼女, 来月結婚するのよ」「だれと？」"She's getting married next month." "*Who* ˅to?"（🎵Who is she getting married to? の省略表現）

❹ 【だれが[に, を, と]...しようと】 whoever, no matter who.（🎵後の方が口語的） ▶ だれが援助を求めても

だれか

彼女は助けてくれないだろう *No matter who* [*whoever*] asks her for help, she won't help them. (❗動詞は単数で呼応するが, 代名詞が them ではなく him で呼応するのは《書》)

● **だれ言うとなく** ▶だれ言うとなくこの谷を「座頭谷」と呼ぶようになった *I don't know who said it first*, but this valley came to be called "Zado-dani."

● **だれはばからず** ▶だれはばからず(=遠慮せず)意見を述べる state one's opinion *freely*.

:だれか 誰か (肯定文で) **sómeone, sómebody**; (疑問文・否定文・if 節で) **ányone, ánybody**; [[だれかあ る...]] **sóme** /sʌ́m/, xs(ə)m/ 《+単数可算名詞》 (❗ a(n) とほぼ同意.

> 解説 (1) somebody, anybody の方が someone, anyone より口語的で, 呼びかけでは好まれる: だれかここへ来てくれ Come here, *somebody*. しかし, 関係詞が続く場合をはじめ一般的に someone, anyone の方が好まれる傾向がある: だれか英語の話せる人が必要だ We need *someone* who can speak English.
> (2) someone, somebody, anyone, anybody はいずれも単数扱い. 複数が想定される文脈でも xsomeones など s のつく代名詞は堅い文では不可. また, 呼応する代名詞は《書》では he, his, him だが, 《話》または性差別表現を避ける場合では they, their, them が多く用いられ, 特に付加疑問では they が普通: だれかここにかばんを忘れている *Someone* left *their* [*his*] bag here. (❗ their is his or her の意なので xbags と複数にはしない)/だれか私のパソコンをいじったでしょ *Someone* touched my PC, didn't *they*?
> (3) 肯定文でも意味内容が否定であれば anyone, anybody を用いる: だれが我々の救助に来てくれるとは思えない I doubt that *anyone* will come to our rescue. (=I believe no one will come ....)
> (4) 疑問文, if 節でも肯定の答え・肯定の内容を予期する場合は someone, somebody を用いる: だれか彼の居場所を知っていますか Does *someone* know where he is?/だれか彼の居場所を知っていたら教えてください If *someone* knows where he is, please tell me. いずれも「だれか知っていそうだ」と話し手が思っていることを含意する. anyone ではこの含みはない.

▶だれかがドアをノックしている. だれだか見てきてくれ *Someone* is knocking on the door. Go and see who it is. (❗このような場合性別不明なので it で受けるのが普通) ▶彼はだれかと話をしている He is speaking to *someone* [xanyone]. (❗否定文「だれとも話をしていない」は He is not speaking to *anyone* [xsomeone].) ▶今日はだれか欠席していますか Is *anyone* absent today? ▶だれかクロスワードパズルやりたくない? Doesn't *anyone* want to do the crossword? ▶あそこでだれかとても背の高い人を見ました I saw *someone* very tall [xvery tall someone] over there. (❗ someone, somebody, anyone, anybody を修飾する形容詞はその直後に置く) ▶それはだれか他の人のペンです. 私のは持っています That's *someone* else's [xsomeones' else's] pen. I have mine. ▶だれか男の子が走って逃げている *Sóme* boy is running away. (❗ (1) some に強勢がある. (2) Sóme bóys are .... では「何人か男の子が」の意) ▶君たちの中でだれか『マイフェアレディー』という映画を見たことのある人はいますか Has [Have] *any* of you ever seen the movie, *My Fair Lady*? (❗ (1) of 句が続く場合は anyone, someone などは不可. (2) any が

「だれか 1 人でも」(any one of you) の気持ちのときは単数扱い, 「何人か」(some of you) の気持ちのときは複数扱いとなる)

だれかれ 誰彼 ▶彼女はだれかれなしに(=だれにでも)話しかける She speaks to *anyone* (*and everyone*).

たれこみ 垂れ込み a típ-off. ▶コカインの密輸計画について警察に匿名電話の垂れ込みがあった The police received a *tip-off* from [were tipped off by] an anonymous caller about the plan to smuggle in cocaine. (➾密告)

たれこめる 垂れ込める hang* low. ▶暗雲が垂れ込めていた Dark clouds *were hanging low*./The sky *was overcast* with low-hanging dark clouds.

たれさがる 垂れ下がる hang* (down); (だらりと) 《やや書》 **droop** (down). ▶柳が池の上に垂れ下がっている A willow *hangs* [*droops*] over the pond. (➾垂れる❶)

だれしも 誰しも (だれでも) **éveryone, éverybody.** ▶だれしもが詩人になれるわけではない Not *everyone* can be a poet. (➾誰でも〔第 3 文例 注〕)

だれしらぬ 誰知らぬ ●だれ知らぬ者がない Everyone [Everybody] knows ....

だれそれ 誰某 Mr. [Miss, Mrs., Ms] **Só-and-so.** (❗ Mr. — と書き, ― be blank と読む言い方もある)

だれだれ 誰々 ▶誰々が行きましたか *Who* went?

:だれでも 誰でも [[どんな人でも]] 《肯定文で》 **ányone, ánybody**; [[だれもみな]] **éveryone, éverybody**; [[...の人はだれでも]] **whoéver**; [[どんな...でも]] **ány** 《+通例単数可算名詞》.

> 解説 (1) anybody, everybody の方が anyone, everyone より口語的.
> (2) 上の 4 語はいずれも単数扱い. 代名詞は堅い文では he で呼応するが, 《話》または性差別表現を避ける場合は they が多く用いられる. (➾誰か)

▶運転免許のある人ならだれでもそれに応募できる *Anyone* who [*Whoever*] *has* [xhave] a driver's license can apply for it./*Anyone* can apply for it if *they* have [《書》 *he* has] a driver's license. ▶20 歳以上の人はだれ(で)も選挙権がある *Everyone* (of) twenty years or over *has* [xhave] the vote. ▶だれでも作家になれるわけではない Not *everybody* can be a writer./*Everybody* can't be a ˇwriter. (❗いずれも部分否定だが, 後の文は下降調にすると全否定で「だれも作家になれない」の意にもなりあいまいなので, 前の文が普通) ▶学生ならだれでもその仕事をすることができる *Ány* student [*Any* (one) of the students] can do the job. (❗ ány óne は any の強意形. of 句が続く場合は xanyone は不可) ▶来たい人はだれでも招待しなさい Invite *whoever* [xwhomever] wants to come.

たれながし 垂れ流し (失禁) **incóntinence**; (工場の排出) 《書》 **dischárge** (*of* untreated éffluent).

たれながす 垂れ流す ●有毒廃水を川に垂れ流す 《書》 *dischárge* toxic éffluent into the river.

:だれ(に)も 誰にも ❶ [[だれもみな]] **éveryone, éverybody**; [[どんな人も]] **ányone, ánybody** (❗以上すべて単数扱い (➾でも, 誰か 解説 (2))); [[すべての...]] **all** (+(the [one's])+複数名詞) (❗ all は形容詞).

▶だれもなくっすり眠った *Everyone* [*Everybody, All the people*, xAll] slept well. (❗ all は通例単独で「特定の人達が」の意には用いない) ▶クラスの[私たちの]だれもが試験の準備で忙しい *Éveryone* in the class [*Évery óne* of us, xEveryone of us] is busy preparing for the exam. ▶彼はだれにも親切です He is kind to *anyone*.

❷ [[だれ(に)も...ない]] **nóbody** (❗ xno body と 2 語につづらない), **nó òne**; **none** /nʌ́n/; **not anyone** [anybody].

解説 (1) nobody と no one は同意だが, 呼びかけでは nobody が好まれる: だれも立つな *Nobody*, stand up. (=*Don't anybody* stand up.)
(2) nobody, no one はいずれも単数扱い. 代名詞は堅い文では he で呼応するが《話》では they が多い. 特に付加疑問には they が普通: ほかにだれも電話してこなかったね *Nobody* [*No one*] else called me, did *they*?
(3) none は単数扱いが本来の用法だが, none of ... の形を取る場合, 後の複数(代)名詞にひかれて複数扱いが多い.

▶部屋にだれもいない There isn't [×aren't] *anyone* in the room./There's [×There're] *nobody* [*no one*] in the room. ▶彼はだれにも会わなかった He didn't see *anybody* [saw *nobody*]. (**!** 以上 2 例いずれも nobody を用いる方が強意的) ▶だれも来なかった *Nobody* [*No one*, ×Not anybody] came. (**!** (1) 上の 2 例と異なり, 文頭では ×not anybody は不可. (2) 関係詞などの修飾語句が続く場合を除き anybody の後に通例否定語は置けないので ×Anybody didn't come. は不可) ▶それをやりたがる人はだれもいないみたいだ *Nobody* seems anxious to do it. ▶友達はだれも助けてくれなかった *None* [*Not one*] of my friends helped me. (**!** (1) of 句が続く場合は no one, nobody は不可. (2) ×Any of my friends didn't help me. は不可 (⇨第 3 文例)) ▶だれもそれを知らないわけではない It is not that *nobody* knows it./(知っている人が少しだけいる) There are only a few people who know it.

会話「これ君にはやれないよ」「だれもくれなんて頼んでないよ」"I can't give it to you." "*Nobody* [*No one*] asked you to. (**!** to に注意)/*Who* asked you to give it?" (**!** 後の方は修辞疑問文)

会話「だれが誤解してたの」「ぼくたちはだれも」"Who's got it wrong?" "*None* of us (have [has])."

だれひとり 誰一人 〖ただ 1 人も...ない〗 not a single person; 〖1 人も...ない〗 nobody. (⇨誰(にも **❷**)) ▶だれ 1 人遅刻しなかった *Not a single person* [*Nobody*] arrived late. (**!** 前の方が強意的) ▶あいつらだれ 1 人として何の役にも立たなかったよ *None* of them were [was] any good.

たれまく 垂れ幕 (高所より垂らす幕) a banner (**!** a banner は「横断幕」だが,「垂れ幕」と同じ目的で使われる); (説明的に) a long flag vertically hung with a message on it. ▶近日公演のコンサートを宣伝する垂れ幕が劇場の外側につるされていた There was *a long flag hung down* outside the theater to advertise the coming concert.

たれみみ 垂れ耳 drop [lop] ears.
たれめ 垂れ目 downward sloping [slanting] eyes.
*****たれる 垂れる** ❶〖垂れ下がる〗hang; (ぶらりと) dangle; (うなだれるように) droop; (液体がぽたぽたと) drip (-pp-), drop (-pp-); (ちょろちょろと) trickle. ● 恥じて頭を垂れる hang [droop] one's head in shame. ● 頭を垂れて(=うなだれて)立っている stand with one's head *hanging* [*drooping*]. ● 足をだらりと垂れてソファーに寝そべる sprawl on a sofa with one's legs *dangling*. ▶彼女の左目に髪が垂れていた A wisp of hair *fell over* her left eye. ▶水がパイプの継ぎ目から垂れている Water *is dripping* [*dropping*] (*down*) *from* the joint in the pipe./The joint in the pipe *is dripping* [*dropping*] water. (**!** drip の方が普通) ▶血が傷口から垂れた Blood *trickled from* the wound.
❷〖示す〗 ▶教訓を垂れる give 《him》 a lesson. ▶彼は生徒に範を垂れた He *set an example to* his students.

だれる 〖話・パーティーなどが〗become* dull; (だらだらと続く) drag (-gg-); 〖活動・動作などが〗become inactive; 〖人が〗(あきあきして) get* bored; (気分がものうくて)《やや書》feel* languid. ▶この小説は途中でだれる This novel *becomes dull* [*sags*] in the middle.

タレント ● テレビタレント a TV *personality* [*star*, *celebrity*]. 《和製語》a TV talent.
タロいも タロ芋 〖植物〗a taro /táːrou/ (圏 ~s).
:-**だろう** ❶ 〖推量〗〖...と思う〗I think* [suppose, 《米語》guess] (*that*)...; I hope (*that*)...; I am afraid [《書》I fear] (*that*)....

使い分け think 「思う」の意味の一般的な語.
suppose think より意味の軽い語.
guess 何となくそう思うの意.
hope 何かよいこと・望ましいことを期待するの意.
be afraid, **fear** よくないこと・望ましくないことを心配するの意.

▶彼はもうすぐ帰って来るだろう I *think* [*suppose*, *guess*] (*that*) he'll come [get] home soon. ▶彼の乗った列車は遅れないだろう I don't *think* [*suppose*, *guess*] (*that*) his train will be late. (**!** 次例と異なり, 主節を否定するのが普通)/I *hope* (*that*) his train won't be late. (**!** (1) I hope ではそうあってほしいという含みが加わる. また that 節中が未来のことであっても実現可能性を強めて単純現在形が用いられることも多い. (2) 以上いずれの場合の that も通例省略する) ▶真理子は約束どおりには来ないだろう I'*m afraid* [*fear*] Mariko won't come on time.

会話「あすは雨だと思う?」「そうだろうね」"Do you think it will rain tomorrow?" "I *think* so./I'*m afraid* so." (**!** (1) 後の方では特に雨が降ってもらっては困るという含みがある. (2) ×I think [I'm afraid] it.

(b) 〖推量を示す助動詞を用いて〗(でしょう) will; (違いない) must; (かもしれない) may; (はずがない) can't. ▶あしたはたぶん晴れるだろう It *will* probably [It's probably *going to*] be nice weather tomorrow. (**!** will は確信を持った推量を表す. 天候は通例確信を持った推量は不可能なので probably を添える方が自然. be going to は現在の状況から判断した推量を表し, 話し手の意志ではどうにもならないことを暗示する) ▶正午までにはニューヨークに着くだろう We'*ll* get to [be in] New York by noon./We'*re getting to* New York by noon. (**!**「着くことになっている」の意. 進行形の用法に注意) ▶明日の今頃にはこの仕事を終えているだろう I'*ll* have finished this work 〖主に米〗have this work finished] by this time tomorrow. (**!** 未来完了の表現) ▶君は 10 時間以上眠っていたのだから眠くはないだろう You *can't* be sleepy because you have been sleeping (for) more than ten hours. (⇨はず)

会話「電灯が切れた」「ヒューズがとんだのだろう」"The lights have gone out." "The fuse *must* have blown." (⇨違いない)

会話「彼は別のを買うかな」「だろうね」"Will he buy another one?" "He *may* [Maybe]."

(c) 〖推量を示す副詞を用いて〗(たぶん) probably; maybe, perhaps; possibly. (**!** この順に確信度が弱くなる) (⇨たぶん) ▶その船はおそらくしけで沈没したのだろう *Probably* the ship sank in a storm./《やや書》*It's probable that* the ship sank in a storm. ▶たぶん天気はよくなるだろう *Maybe* [*Perhaps*] the weather will get better. (**!** この 2 語はほぼ同じ意味だが, maybe の方が口語的) ▶1 時間に 7 キロ歩くのはとても無理だろう You *can't possibly* [*It is* quite

impossible for you *to*, ×You are quite impossible to] walk 7 kilometers in an hour. ▶(1) possibly が can't の後で用いられると否定を強める働きをする. (2) *It is impossible that* you *should* walk … は「…歩くなんてありえない」の意)
❷【仮定の帰結として】would; could; might. ▶もし母が生きていたら私の結婚をとても喜んでくれただろう If my mother were alive, she *would* be very pleased with my marriage. ▶君が私の忠告に従っていたら成功していただろう If you had followed my advice, you *could* have succeeded. ▶おそらく土曜日まで待った方が賢明だろう It *would* probably be wiser to wait till Saturday. (!=it=to wait に仮定の意が含まれている)
❸【念を押す】(! 付加疑問文で表す) ▶君はいっしょに行かないんだろう？ You *aren't* going ／*together*, ＼*are you*? ▶もっとよく勉強しなければならないと君に言っただろう I told you that you must work harder, *didn't* I?
❹【感嘆】 ▶これはなんと感動的な映画なんだろう What a moving film this is! (! 文脈から明らかな場合, this は通例省略される) ▶今日はなんて寒いのだろう *How* cold it is today!
会話 「サーファーなの？」「うん」「かっこいい！」「だろう！」"Are you a surfer?" "Yes, I am." "Cool!" "You said it!" (! You said it. は「まさにあなたの言うとおり」の意)
❺【思案】wonder（+*wh*-節［句］). ▶彼女はどうして来なかったのだろう I *wonder why* she didn't come. ▶このラジオ番組はどれくらい聴取者がいるのだろう I *wonder how* many listeners this radio program has.

タロット (1組の)《a pack of》tarot /tǽrou/ card, the tarot. [参考] 78 枚 1 組. 占い用)

タワー a tower /táuər/. (⇨塔) ●東京タワーにのぼる go up [×climb] the Tokyo *Tower*. ●タワー型コンピュータ a tower (computer [model]).

たわいない 形 (つまらない) trivial,《書》trifling;（思慮のない）(邪気のない) innocent. ▶たわいないことでけんかをする quarrel over *trivial* [*trifling*] matters.
── **たわいなく** 副 (邪気なく) innocently;（正体なく）dead;（簡単に）easily. ▶たわいなく眠っている be *dead* asleep; be sleeping *like a top*. ▶たわいなく負ける be *easily* beaten.

たわけ 戯け ▶このたわけめ You *fool* [*idiot*]! (! 前方よりも軽蔑的)

たわけた 戯けた ▶たわけたことを言うな Don't talk *nonsense*!

たわごと 戯言 (ばかげた話) nonsense,《俗》balóney; silly [foolish] talk. ▶たわごとを言うな Don't talk *nonsense* [*rubbish*]./*Nonsense*!/*Rubbish*!

たわし 束子 《米》a scrúb brush,《主に英》a scrúbbing brush [事情] 米英では長目の柄付が多い);（ナイロン・金属繊維を丸めた）a scourer (参考)

たわむ 撓む sag (-gg-);（曲がる) bend* (down). ▶雪の重みで屋根がたわんだ The snow *sagged* under the weight of snow./The snow *caused a sag* in the roof.

たわむれ 戯れ (ふざけ, 楽しみ) fun;（冗談）a joke,《書》(a) jest. ▶戯れで(冗談で) as a *joke* [*jest*];（本気でなく）in *fun* [*jest*];（必要からではなく楽しみで）for *fun*.

たわむれる 戯れる (遊ぶ) play 《*with*》(⇨遊ぶ);（冗談を言う）joke 《*with*＋人, *about*＋事》. ●子犬とたわむれる *play with* a puppy.

たわら 俵 a straw (rice) bag.
● **俵を割る**【相撲】be pushed out of the ring;（負ける）be defeated [beaten]; lose (a battle [a game]).

たわわ ●実たわわになった木 trees *heavy* [*loaded*] *with* fruits.

たん 反 【土地の面積の単位】a tan (⑲ 〜) [参考] 約 992m²);【反物の長さの単位】a *tan*; a roll [参考] 幅約 34cm, 長さ約 10.6m).

たん 痰 phlegm /flém/. ●たんがのどにからむ get *phlegm* in one's throat. [事情] 人前でたんを切ろうとせき払いするのは無作法とされる) ▶血痰が出ます I bring up [（せきとともに）cough up] bloody *phlegm*.

たん 端 ●端を発する (…の結果として生じる) result 《*from*》;（…に源を発する) originate 《*in*》. ●つまらない誤解に端を発した口論 a quarrel that *resulted from* a little misunderstanding.

タン 【牛の舌】ox tongue. ●タンシチュー tongue stew.

* **だん 段** ❶【階段】stairs; (1段) a step. ●段を上がる（降りる）(屋内で) go up [down] the *stairs*;（屋外で）go up [down] the *steps*. ●1段ばしに石段を駆け上がる run up the stone *steps*, two at a time. ▶彼ははしごの踏み段に足をかけた He put a foot on the *step* of the ladder.
❷【重なりの一つ】(棚) a shelf (⑲ shelves);（棚・ケーキの層）a tier;（ロケットの) a stage. ●上の段の花びん a flower vase on the upper *shelf*. ● 2 段式ロケット a 2-*stage* rocket. ●二段ベッド (子供用の) a bunk bed.
❸【文章の段落】a paragraph;（新聞の1段）a column. ● 5 段抜きの見出し a five-*column* heading. ▶その新聞は 1 ページが 7 段組みだ The paper has seven *columns* to a page.
❹【段位】a rank, a grade, a degree, a *dan*. ●段が上がる be promoted to a higher *dan* [*degree*] 《*in*》. ●何段ですか What *dan* are you? ●彼は柔道 5 段だ He is a fifth *dan* (holder) at judo./He is a fifth *dan* judoist.
❺【時, 場合】▶英語を話す段になるといつも尻ごむ When it comes to speaking [×speak] English, I always get nervous.
❻【程度】▶彼はテニスにかけては私の数段上だ(=比較にならない) I *am no match for* him in tennis.

だん 暖 ●暖をとる warm oneself 《*at* the fire》.

だん 談 ●車中談 an informal *talk* on a train. ●成功談 a success *story*. ●冒険談 one's adventures. ●その事故の目撃者の談によると according to a witness *account* of the accident.

* **だん 壇** 【地面より一段高い所】a platform, a raised floor;（演壇）a platform;【説教壇】a pulpit /púlpit/. ●壇上に立つ stand on [take] a *platform*.

-だん -団 【集団】a group (⇨集団, 団体);（活動をともにする）a corps /kɔ́ːr/ (⑲ corps /kɔ́ːrz/), a party;（リーダーのいる）a band;【派遣団】(代表) a delegation;（任務を帯びた) a commission. ●記者団 a *corps* [a *party*] of reporters; a press *corps*. ●窃盗団 a *band* [(一味) a *gang*] of thieves. ●代表団の一員 a member of a *delegation*. ●調査団 an inquiry *commission* [*group*]. ●青年団 a youth association [*group*].

だんあつ 弾圧 名 【権力による圧制】oppression;【活動・反乱などの抑制】《やや書》suppression. ●弾圧政策 a policy of *suppression*. ●弾圧的な支配者たち *oppressive* rulers. ●弾圧の下に苦しむ groan under *oppression*.
── **弾圧する** 動 ●反体制グループを弾圧する *oppress* [（取り締まる）*clamp down* 《*on*》] dissident groups. ●思想の自由を弾圧する《やや書》*suppress* freedom of thought.

たんい 単位 ❶〖長さ・熱量・貨幣などの〗a unit;〖貨幣の呼称としての〗(a) denomination. ●貨幣の単位 a unit of money; a monetary *unit*. ●いろいろな単位の硬貨 coins of various *denominations* [*units*]. ▶グラムは重さの単位である The gram is a *unit* of weight. ▶バターはポンド単位で売買される Butter is sold *by the* [ˈxa] pound. ▶それらを5個単位で(=5個ずつ)包装した We packed them *in* fives.
❷〖全体の1構成分子を成す〗a unit. ●家族は社会の小さな単位である The family is a small social *unit* [a small (basic) *unit* of society].
❸〖授業の;(科目の)〗a credit;(科目)a course.〖事情〗米国の大学では学位をとるコースをと単位をとるコースがある) ●必修単位 required *credits* [*courses*]. ▶英語を5単位取った I got five *credits* in [for] English. ▶卒業には最低125単位が必要です A minimum of 125 *credits* is required for graduation [the graduation *requirements*]. ▶単位を落とした(=その科目の試験に落ちた) I failed [《米話》flunked] the *course*.
●単位互換制度 a credit transfer system.
●単位制学校 a credit system school.

だんい 段位 a *dan*, a grade. ▶トムの剣道の段位は3段だ Tom is a third *dan* [*grade*] kendoist.

たんいせいしょく 単為生殖〖生物〗parthenogenesis;(植物の)apogamy.

たんいつ 単一 (たった一つの) single; (まとまった) únitary.
●単一国家 a unitary state. ●単一通貨 single currency (参考) ヨーロッパ連合(EU)のユーロ (euro) など。●単一民族 a single race.

たんいち 単一 a D (size) battery. (⇒電池)

だんいほうしょく 暖衣飽食 ― 暖衣飽食する 動 (ぜいたくに暮らす) live in luxury; lead a life of luxury.

だんいん 団員 a member. (⇒会員, -団) ●合唱[劇]団員 a *member* of a chorus [a theatrical company].

たんおん 単音 a single sound;〖音楽〗a monotone.

たんおん 短音 a short sound.
●短音記号〖音楽〗a breve (記号 ⌣).

たんおんかい 短音階〖音楽〗the minor scale.

たんか 担架 a stretcher; (台車付きの)《米》a gurney /ɡə́:rni/. ●担架で運ぶ carry (him) on a *stretcher*.

たんか 単価 (単位価格) a unit price (原価) cost).
●単価10円で売る sell (them) at 10 yen *each* [*per piece*,《やや書》*apiece*]. ▶この家の坪単価はいくらですか How much does this house *cost per tsubo*?

たんか 炭化 图 carbonization. ― **炭化する** 動 carbonize.
●炭化カルシウム 〖化学〗(calcium) carbide.
●炭化水素 hydrocarbon. ●炭化物 carbide.

たんか 啖呵 ― たんかを切る (盛んにののしる) swear a lot; (投げつけるように言う) shoot (defiant) words (*at*); speak in a clear, caustic way.

たんか 短歌 a tanka (poem); (説明的に) a thirty-one syllable verse. (⇒和歌)

だんか 檀家 a *danka*; (説明的に) a supporting member family of a Buddhist temple.

タンカー a tanker. ●石油タンカー an oil *tanker*. ●10万トンのタンカー a 100,000-ton *tanker*.

***だんかい 段階**〖発展過程の一時期・状態〗a stage, a step;〖能力・難易などの〗a grade. ▶その計画は初期[最終]の段階だ The plan is *in* its early [final] *stages*. (⚠通例複数形で) ▶交渉は重大な段階にあった The negotiations were *at* a crucial *stage*.
― **段階的** 形 gradual.

― **段階的に** 副 gradually. ●従業員を段階的に減らす reduce the work force *gradually*.

だんかい 団塊 ●団塊の世代(第二次世界大戦直後のベビーブームの時に生まれた世代) a baby-boom generation; (人) a baby boomer.
●団塊ジュニア(団塊の世代の子供にたちにあたる世代) a baby-boomer junior.

だんがい 断崖 a cliff (高い ~s), a precipice, a bluff (高い ~s). (⚠詳しい説明は(⇒崖(常)))

だんがい 弾劾 图〖法律〗impeachment.
― **弾劾する** 動〖法律〗impeach《him *for* taking a bribe》.
●弾劾裁判所 a Court of Impeachment.

だんかさね 段重ね ●三段重ねの弁当箱 a triple-decker lunchbox; a three-*tiered* lunchbox.

だんかざり 段飾り ●五段飾りの人形 dolls displayed on a five-*tiered* stand.

たんかだいがく 単科大学 a college. (⇒大学)

たんかん 胆管〖解剖〗the bile duct.

たんがん 単眼 (昆虫・節足動物の) an ocellus; a stemma.

たんがん 単願 ― **単願する** 動 ▶彼は博多高校を単願した He *sent in an application* to Hakata High School *only*.

たんがん 嘆願 图《書》a plea 《*for*》; (請願) a petition. (⇒懇願, 請願)
― **嘆願する** 動 ●彼女の助命を嘆願する beg《him》for her life; beg《him》to spare her life.
●嘆願書 a (written) petition.

だんがん 弾丸 (銃の) a bullet /búlət/; 《米話》a slug; (散弾) a shot;《砲弾》a shell. ●32口径の弾丸を心臓に撃ち込まれて殺される be killed by a .32 *slug* to the heart. (⚠.32 は 32-caliber の略)
●弾丸列車 a bullet train. (参考) 日本の新幹線列車。●弾丸ライナー〖野球〗a hard line drive; a bullet.

たんき 単記 single entry.
●単記投票(制) a single-entry (system).

たんき 短気〖すぐおこる気性だ〗a hot [a quick, a short] temper. ▶短気は損する Don't *lose your temper*./Don't *be impatient*./*Be patient*.
●短気は損気 (ことわざ) Haste makes waste. (⚠「急(せ)いては事を仕損ずる」の意)
― **短気な** 形 hot-[quick-, short-]tempered;〖せっかちな〗impatient. ▶彼は短気だ He is *hot-tempered*./He has a *hot* [a *quick*, a *short*] *temper*./He *easily loses his temper*. (⚠このtemperは「平静な気分」の意)/He *gets angry easily*. (⚠He is easy to get angry. は不可)

たんき 短期 a short period (of time); a short term. (⇒短期, 長期)
― **短期(の)** 形 short; short-term. ●オーストラリアへ短期留学する go to Australia on a *short* study program.
●短期貸付 a short-term loan. ●短期金利 the short-term [short-run] interest rate. ●短期契約 a short-term contract. ●短期講習 a short (-term) course. ●短期国債 a treasury bill《略 TB》. ●短期集中講座 a crash [a intense] course.
●短期大学 a junior college. (⇒大学) ●短期予想 a short-term forecast.

だんき 暖気 warmth; moderate heat; (気候) warm weather. ●暖気団〖気象〗a warm air mass.

だんぎ 談義〖説教〗a sermon, a lecture (⇒説教, 小言); 〖世間話に近い自由な議論〗《*have*》 informal discussions 《*about*》. ▶下手の長談義 《ことわざ》 (簡潔は機知の真髄) Brevity is the soul of wit.

たんきかん 短期間 a short period. (⇒短期) ●短期

たんきゅう 探求 (make) a search 《for》. (⇨追求)

たんきゅう 探究 图 〖研究〗research (❗しばしば複数形で); 〖研究〗 (a) study; 〖調査〗 (an) investigation; (an) inquiry.
— **探究する** 動 do 〖×make〗 research(es) 《into, on》; study; investigate; inquire 《into》.

だんきゅう 段丘 〖地学〗a terrace; a bench.

たんきょり 短距離 a short distance; (射程か) (a) short range. (⇨長距離)
● 短距離競走 a short-distance race; a dash.
● 短距離選手 a sprinter. ● 短距離弾道ミサイル 〖軍事〗 a short-range ballistic missile.

タンク 〖貯蔵用の〗a 《water》 tank; 〖戦車〗a tank.
● タンク車 (タンクローリー) a tanker, 《米》 a tank truck [trailer]; (鉄道の) a tank car; 《和製語》a tank lorry.

ダンクシュート 图 〖バスケ〗a dunk (shot); 《和製語》a dunk shoot. — **ダンクシュートする** 動 dunk.

タングステン 〖化学〗tungsten (元素記号 W).

たんぐつ 短靴 《a pair of》 shoes.

タンクトップ a tank top.

たんクローンせいこうたい 単クローン性抗体 〖生物〗a monoclonal antibody.

たんけい 短径 the minor axis. (⇦ 長径)

だんけい 男系 the male line. (⇦ 女系)

*__だんけつ__ 団結 图 〖結合〗union; 〖一致〗unity; 〖共通の利益・目的による〗solidarity. ● 団結が固い have a strong *solidarity*. ▶団結は力なり(ことわざ) *Unity* is strength. 〖参考〗労働組合のスローガンとしてはこれが普通./*Union* is strength.
— **団結する** 動 ● 彼は反対派に共通の旗のもとに団結するよう訴えた He called upon all opposition groups to *unite* under a common banner. ▶団結すれば立ち,分裂すれば倒れる *United* we stand, divided we fall. 〖参考〗J. Dickinson, "The Liberty Song" より
● 団結権 the right of organization. ● 団結力 the power of unity.

*__たんけん__ 探検 图 (an) exploration (❗具体例をさす場合は ⓒ); an expedition (❗探検など特定の目的を持った長途旅行). ● 南極探検 an Antarctic *exploration*; an *exploration* of the Antarctic. ● 月の探検(旅行)に行く go on an *expedition* to the moon.
— **探検する** 動 explore. ● その島を探検する *explore* [*make an exploration of*] the island.
● 探検家 an explorer. ● 探検隊 an expedition; an expeditionary party.

たんけん 短剣 a dagger. ● 彼を短剣で刺し殺す stab him to death with a *dagger*.

たんげん 単元 (学習の) a unit.

だんげん 断言 图 (an) assertion; (a) declaration; (an) affirmation.
— **断言する** 動 〖自分が正しいと強く主張する〗assert; 〖言明する〗declare, say* positively [definitely]; 〖疑問なしに対して〗(I) affirm; 〖保証する〗assure. ▶囚人は自分は無実だと断言した The prisoner *declared* [*asserted*, *affirmed*] *that* he was innocent. ▶declare は自分を省略できるが, assert, affirm はできない ▶危険はないと断言する I (can) *assure* you [*say positively*, *am positive*, 《話》*swear*] (*that*) there is no danger.

*__たんご__ 単語 〖個々の〗a word; 〖ある言語・個人などの用いる語全体〗(a) vocabulary. (⇨語) ● 英語の単語帳 a notebook for English *words*. ● 英単語をたくさん知っている know a lot of English *words*; 〖語彙(ゐ)が豊かだ〗 have a rich *vocabulary* [×many vocabularies] of English (⇨語彙). ● 単語力をつける increase one's *word* power. ▶単語の意味が分からない場合は辞典で調べなさい If you don't know the meaning of a *word*, look it up in your dictionary. ▶'know'という単語を過去形にしなさい Put the *word* 'know' into the past tense.

たんご 端午 《celebrate》the Boy's Festival.

タンゴ a tango (徴 ~s). (❗通例 the ~) ● タンゴを踊る dance the *tango* (~es; ~ed; ~ing).

だんこ 断固 副 (決定的に) decisively; (固く決心して) résolutely; (ゆるぎなく) firmly; (きっぱりと) flatly.
● 断固拒絶をする refuse *flatly*; give a *flat* refusal.
● 断固(=飽くまで)戦い抜く fight it out. ● 自らの潔白を断固証明する(=固く決心している) be *firmly* determined to prove [on proving] one's innocence.
— **断固とした[たる]** 形 〖決定的な〗〖やや昔〗decisive; 〖決心の固い〗〖書〗resolute; 〖ぐらつかない〗firm; 〖きっぱりした〗flat. ● 断固たる処置をとる take *decisive* [*firm*] measures. ● 彼に断固たる態度をとる take a *resolute* [a *firm*] attitude toward him.

だんご 団子 《a piece of》 *dango*; (説明的に) a kind of dumpling, usually made of rice or wheat flour. ● くし団子 *dumplings* on a stick. ▶花より団子 (⇨花 〖成句〗)
● 団子鼻 a snub nose.

たんこう 炭鉱, 炭坑 a coal mine. (関連) 縦坑 shaft, pit/横坑 gallery) ● 炭鉱で働く work *in* [×at] a *coal mine*.
● 炭鉱夫 a coal miner.

だんこう 団交 〖「団体交渉」の略〗collective bargaining.

だんこう 断交 — **断交する** 動 (国交関係を絶つ) break off diplomatic relations 《with》.

だんこう 断行 — **断行する** 動 carry 《a plan》 out.
● 政治改革を断行する *carry out* political reforms.

だんごう 談合 图 〖不正に入札価格を取り決めること〗(行為) bid-rigging; (事件) a bid-rigging scandal [case]; 〖共謀すること〗collusion on contract bidding, a prebidding agreement. ● 談合入札をする put in a rigged bid. ▶政府は企業の談合を黙認すべきではない The government should not tolerate private-sector *collusion*.
— **談合する** 動 (不正に入札価格を決める) rig; (共謀する) conspire to agree on price, form a ring.

たんこうしき 単項式 〖数学〗a monomial (expression).

たんこうぼん 単行本 a book. ▶彼は新聞や雑誌に書いたエッセイを単行本にした He published his essays he wrote for newspapers and magazines in *book form*./He published a book of essays chosen from his contributions to newspapers and magazines.

たんこぶ (打撲による) a bump; (打撲・病気による) a lump. ● 頭にたんこぶができる[ある] get [have] a *bump* on [one's] head. ▶田中さんは私にとってまさに目の上のたんこぶだ Mr. Tanaka is a real *problem* for me [such a *nuisance* for [to] me]./Mr. Tanaka is very *troublesome* for me.

だんこん 男根 a phallus, a penis.
● 男根崇拝 phallicism.

だんこん 弾痕 a bullet mark.

たんさ 探査 图 a probe /próub/. ● 月[金星]探査機 a lunar [a Venus] *probe*. — **探査する** 動 ● 月面を探査する *probe* the surface of the moon.

たんざ 端座 — **端座する** 動 sit up straight; sit properly.

だんさ 段差 difference in level. ● 段差なし住宅

house with non-uneven floors; a barrier-free house. ▶この先段差あり〔掲示〕Bump ahead.
ダンサー [踊り子] a dancer, a dáncing girl.
たんさい 単彩 ― 単彩の 形 monochromatic.
●単彩画 a monochrome.
たんさい 淡彩 ―(give) light [thin] coloring.
●淡彩画 a wash drawing; a light-colored picture.
たんさい 断裁 名 cutting. ― 断裁する 動 cut.
●断裁機 a cutter; a cutting machine.
だんざい 断罪 ― 断罪する 動 ▶裁判官はその男を死刑と断罪した(= 有罪判決を下した) The judge *passed sentence* of death on him.
たんさいぼう 単細胞 a single cell.
― 単細胞の 形〔生物〕single-celled, ùnicéllular; (考えが単純な) simple, simple-minded.
●単細胞生物 a singlecelled [a unicellular] organism, 〔生物〕a monad.
たんさく 単作 名 a single crop.
― 単作する 動 single-crop.
たんさく 探索 名 (捜索) a search.
― 探索する 動 ▶逃亡者を探索する *search* [*make a search*] *for* a runaway.
たんざく 短冊 a strip of paper (to write a *tanka* or *haiku* on). ▶ニンジンを短冊切りする cut carrots into *rectangular* slices.
タンザニア 〔国名〕Tanzania /tænzəníə/; (公式名) the United Republic of Tanzania. (首都 Dar es Salaam) ●タンザニア人 a Tanzanian ●タンザニア(人)の Tanzanian.
たんさん 単三 (電池) a AA (size) battery. (⇨電池)
たんさん 炭酸〔化学〕carbonic acid.
●炭酸飲料 a carbonated drink. ●炭酸ガス carbonic acid gas; (二酸化炭素) carbon dioxide. ●炭酸カルシウム calcium carbonate. ●炭酸水 carbonated water; (ソーダ水) soda water. ●炭酸ソーダ carbonate of soda. ●炭酸ナトリウム sodium carbonate.
たんし 短詩 a short poem [verse].
たんし 端子〔電気〕a terminal.
だんし 男子〔男〕a man (働 men), a male; [少年] a boy.
●男子学生 a boy [a male] student. ●男子校 a boys' school.
だんじ 男児 a boy; a man. (⇨男子)
タンジェント〔数学〕a tangent (略 tan).
たんじかん 短時間 ●短時間でその問題を解く solve the problem *in* [×for] *a short time*.
たんしき 単式 ― 単式簿記 single entry.
だんじき 断食 名 (宗教上などの理由で断食すること) fasting; (断食期間) a fast; (イスラム教徒の) Ramadan /ræmədɑːn/. (⇨絶食) ― 断食する 動 fast.
たんしきんるい 担子菌類 the basidiomycetes.
たんじつ 短時日 ▶短時日に in a short time; in a few days.
たんじつ 短日 ― 短日性の 形 short-day.
●短日植物 a short-day plant.
たんじつげつ 短日月 ⇨短時日(訳)
だんじて 断じて 副 〔絶対に〕absolutely; (確かに) definitely /défənitli/, 〔決して...ない〕never; 〔書〕by no means (⇨決して [類語]). ▶断じて私は考えを変えません I will *never* [I *absolutely* won't] change my mind. 《やや話》I wouldn't change my mind *for the world*. ▶彼は断じて目的を達成すると言った He swore to achieve his purpose.
会話「彼と付き合ってもいいですか」「断じていかん」"May I go out with him?" "*Absolutely* [*Définitely*] ＼not.*"

たんしゃ 単車 (ride) a motorcycle, 《英》a motorbike; (小型の) 《米》a motorbike. (⇨バイク)
だんしゃく 男爵 a baron. (! 称号: (英国以外で) Baron .... (英国で) Lord ... (⇨貴族 解説))
●男爵イモ a *danshaku* potato; an Irish Cobbler.
●男爵夫人 a baroness.
だんしゅ 断酒 ― 断酒する 動 give up [stop, quit] drinking. (⇨禁酒)
だんしゅ 断種 名 sterilization; (去勢) castration.
― 断種する 動 sterilize; castrate.
たんじゅう 胆汁〔生理〕bile /báil/, 〔古〕gall /gɔ́ːl/.
●胆汁(質)の bilious /bíljəs/. (⇨胆石)
たんじゅう 短銃 a pistol; a gun. (⇨ピストル)
だんしゅう 男囚 a male prisoner [convict]. (⇨囚人)
たんしゅく 短縮 名 〔縮小〕(a) reduction, 〔削減〕〔書〕(a) curtailment.
― 短縮する 動 (時間・長さを短くする) shorten; (切り詰める) cut ... down; (話・時間などを切り上げる) cut ... short; (大きさ・数量を減らす) reduce. ●授業時間を短縮する *shorten* [*reduce*] school hours. ●操業を短縮する *reduce* [*cut down*] operation. ●滞在期間を3日(だけ)[3日に]短縮する *cut short* one's visit *by* [*to*] three days. ●he is を he's と短縮する *contract* 'he is' *to* 'he's'.
●短縮形〔文法〕a contracted form. (参考) do not に対する don't, I will に対する I'll など

*****たんじゅん** 単純 名 simplicity.
― 単純な 形 simple; 〔人について〕(頭・考えが) simple-minded (!悪い意味で用いる). ●単純な消費者 *simple-minded* buyers. ●単純な間違い a *simple case of* mistake. (!a *simple* mistake は「おかしやすい間違い」の意) ●あんなおだてにひっかかるとは君も単純だね It's *simple* [*simple-minded*, (世間知らず) *naive* /nɑːíːv/] *of* you *to* fall for that sort of flattery.
― 単純化する 動 simplify. ●その問題を単純化する *simplify* the question.
●単純平均 a simple average.

*****たんしょ** 短所〔欠点〕a shortcoming (!通例複数形で); 〔弱点〕a weak point, a demerit; (性格上の) a fault. ●その計画の長所と短所 the mérits and démerits /diːmèrits/ of the project. ●対照強勢に注意 (⇨長所) ●短所を補う make up for one's *shortcomings*. ●彼の短所につけ込む take advantage of his *weak points*. ▶彼女の短所には目をつぶってやれよ You should close your eyes to her *faults*.
だんじょ 男女 men and women; both sexes. ●男女の役割 *male* and *female* roles; (男女による役割分担) a sex role. ●男女を問わず regardless of *sex*; without distinction of *sex*. ●男女兼用の服 [ヘアスタイル] *unisex* clothes [haircuts]. (! unisexual は「(動植物が)単性の」の意). ▶20人の男女がその会に出席した Twenty *men and women* attended the meeting. ▶本校では体育の授業は男女別になっています The PE classes are separated *by* [*according to*] *sex* in our school. (! PE は physical education の略)

DISCOURSE
男女平等は原則として、 男性と女性が家庭と職場の両方において権利と役割を担うべきであることを意味する *Gender equality* **means**, in principle, **that** men and women should have equal rights and roles(,) both at home and in the workplace. (! A means that [to]... (A ... を意味する) は定義に用いる表現)

- 男女関係 relations between the sexes.
- 男女共学 coeducation, 《話》 coed. (⇨ 共学)
- 男女共同参画 gender equality. • 男女差別 sex discrimination. • 男女同権 equal rights (for men and women) (**!** for 以下は通例省略される); equality between the sexes; the equality of the sexes. • 男女同権主義 feminism.

たんしょう 単勝 ― 単勝式馬券 a win ticket.

たんしょう 探勝 ― 探勝する 動 visit beauty spots [places of scenic beauty]; take [go on] a sightseeing trip (*to* Nikko).

たんしょう 短小 ― 短小な 形 short and small.

たんしょう 嘆賞 admoration, praise. • 嘆賞に値する admirable, praiseworthy.

― 嘆賞する 動 admire, praise; (激賞する) extol, praise highly.

***たんじょう** 誕生 图 (a) birth. • 子供の誕生に立ち会う be present at the *birth* of a child. • 誕生祝いに彼に時計をプレゼントする give him a watch *for* [*as*] a *birthday* present [gift]; give him a watch *for* [✕as] his *birthday*. ▶ 赤ちゃんの誕生おめでとうございます (手紙で) Congratulations on your new addition.

― 誕生する 動 be born. (⇨ 生まれる)

- 誕生会 a birthday pàrty. (**!** その主役の男性[女性]は a birthday boy [girl] という) • 誕生石 a birthstone. • 誕生日 (⇨ 誕生日)

だんしょう 断章 a fragment 《of poetry [a manuscript]》.

だんしょう 談笑 ― 談笑する 動 have a pleasant talk [chat] 《*with*》; chat 《*with*》.

だんじょう 壇上 • 壇上に on the *platform* [*dais*].

たんしようしょくぶつ 単子葉植物 a monocotyledon; a monocotyledonous plant.

たんじょうび 誕生日 one's birthday. • 彼女の20歳の誕生日を祝う celebrate her twentieth *birthday*. ▶ 誕生日おめでとう Happy *birthday* (to you)! (**!** 最近は Congratulations! ともいうようになってきた)/(これが何度もめぐってきますように)(I wish you) many happy returns (of the day)!

会話 「高雄の誕生日はいつ?」「6月5日だよ」 "When's Takao's *birthday*?" "It's (on) June 5." (**!** 5 は (the) fifth と読む)

たんしょく 単色 a single color; (単色画) (a) mónochrome. ― 単色の 形 monochromátic.

たんしょく 淡色 a light [a pale] color.
― 淡色の 形 light-colored, pale-colored.

だんしょく 男色 sodomy; pederasty.
• 男色家 a sodomite; a pederast.

だんしょく 暖色 a warm color.

たんじる 嘆じる [嘆く] grieve; [感心する] admire.

だんじる 断じる [断定する] conclude 《*that* 節》; [判決を下す] judge 《him guilty》; [断行する] carry ... out resolutely.

だんじる 談じる [話す] talk [speak*] 《*to* [*with*] him *about* it》; [談判する] negotiate, bargain.

たんしん 短針 [時計の] the hour [short] hand [✕needle].

たんしん 単身 ― 単身で 副 alone; by oneself. (⇨ 一人, 単独) • 単身赴任する leave for one's new post *alone* [*without* one's *family*].

たんしん 短信 a (brief) note; 《話》 a line, a short letter; (新聞・雑誌などの) a short report.

たんじん 炭塵 coal dust.
• 炭塵肺(症) black lung disease. • 炭塵爆発 coal dust explosion.

***たんす** 箪笥 [洋服だんす] a wardrobe; [整理だんす] a chest (of drawers), 《米》 a bureau 《徴 ~s, bu-reaux /-z/》; (鏡つきの) 《米》 a dresser; [和dんす] a chest of drawers for kimonos. • たんすのこやしになっている be kept unused in the *wardrobe*. ▶ 彼女はたんす預金をしている She keeps her savings at home instead of in a bank.

ダンス a dance; dancing. (⇨ 踊り, 踊る) • ダンスをする dance 《*with* her》 (**!** do a dance は「うれしくて小踊りする」の意); have a *dance* 《*with*》. • 社交ダンス a social *dance*. (**!** 上流階級の社交ダンスは a ballroom dance ともいう)

会話 「このダンス, お付き合いいただけますか」「喜んで」「なかなかダンスがお上手ですね」 "May I have this *dance* with you?" "With pleasure." "You're really a good *dancer*."

• ダンスパーティー (⇨ ダンスパーティー) • ダンスホール a dance hall.

たんすい 淡水 (live in) fresh water (⇔seawater).
• 海水を淡水化する desalt sea water.
• 淡水魚 a freshwater fish. • 淡水湖 a freshwater lake.

だんすい 断水 图 the suspension of the water supply. • 明朝2時から5時まで断水になります The water supply will *be (cut) off* from 2 a.m. to 5 a.m. tomorrow.

― 断水する 動 (水を止める) cut off the water supply.

たんすいかぶつ 炭水化物 (a) carbohydrate /kɑːrbouháidreit/. • ジャガイモは炭水化物が多い Potatoes contain a lot of *carbohydrate*.

たんすいろ 短水路 a short course.
• 短水路記録 a short-course record.

たんすう 単数 the singular 《略 sing.》.
• 単数形 a singular form. • 単数名詞 a singular noun.

ダンスパーティー 《give, hold》 a dance; (公式の盛大な) a ball. (**!** a dance party はパーティーの種類を特定する場合を除き避けた方がよい) (⇨ 舞踏 [舞踏会]) [参考] 米国の高校・大学で卒業記念行事の一つとして開かれるダンスパーティーを a prom という) • ダンスパーティーに行く go to a *dance*.

たんせい 丹精 (注意) care. • 丹精こめて(=できる限り注意深く) with the utmost *care*. • 丹精こめて育てた花 one's *carefully* nurtured flowers.

たんせい 単性 unisexuality.
• 単性花 a unisexual flower.

たんせい 端正 • 端正な顔立ちの男 a *handsome* man; a man with *regular features*.

***だんせい** 男性 图 a man 《徴 men》, the male (⇔female) sex, 《話》 a guy; (紳士) a gentleman 《徴 -men /-mən/》. • 男性中心の社会 a *male*-dominated society; patriarchy /péitriɑːrki/ (**!** 原義は「父権制」の意だが, 今は「男性上位社会」の意で用いられることが多い).

― 男性的 形 masculine; manly. (⇨ 男らしい)
• 男性的なスポーツ a *manly* [a *masculine*] sport.
• 男性的な声 in a *masculine* voice. (**!** 女性の男声をさすこともある) ▶ 彼女は背が高くて男性的だ She is tall and *masculine*.

• 男性雑誌 a men's magazine. • 男性美 manly [masculine] beauty.

だんせい 男声 a male (⇔female) voice.
• 男声合唱 a male chorus.

だんせい 弾性 图 [物理] elasticity.
― 弾性の(ある) 形 elastic.

たんせき 胆石 [医学] a gallstone /gɔ́ːlstoun/. • 胆石による痛み the *gallstone* pain. (⇨ 胆汁) • 痛みを感じない胆石 a silent *gallstone*.

• 胆石症 [医学] cholelithiasis.

だんぜつ　断絶 名 ●世代間の断絶 the generation gap. ●**断絶する** 動 (国交などを) break off 《diplomatic relations *with* a country》.

たんせん　単線 a single (↔a double) track. ●単線の single-track. ●単線運転する run on a *single track*.

たんぜん　丹前 a quilted Japanese dressing gown.

たんぜん　端然 ── 端然と 副 《sit up》 straight; 《sit》 properly.

だんせん　断線 ── 断線する 動 ▶あちこちで断線した The *wires were broken down* here and there.

だんぜん　断然 ① [はるかに] **by far**, **far and away** (❗比較級・最上級を強める. 前の方は前置・後置ともに可. 後の方は前置のみ.) ② [きっぱりと] **flatly**, **absolutely**. ●断然それを拒否する refuse it *flatly*; give a *flat* refusal to it. ▶彼は身の高さではクラス中断然一番だ He is *by far* [*far and away*] the tallest boy in his class./He is the tallest boy *by far* [ˣ*far and away*] in his class. ▶私は断然行きます (だれが反対しようと) *No matter who opposes* me, I will go./(どんな犠牲を払っても) I will go *at all costs*.

たんそ　炭素 【化学】 **carbon** 〈元素記号 C〉. ●一[二] 酸化炭素 càrbon monóxide [dióxide]. ●炭素化合物 a cárbon còmpound. ●炭素税 a cárbon tàx.

たんそう　炭層 a coal seam; a coal bed.

たんぞう　鍛造 ── 鍛造する 動 **forge**.

だんそう　男装 ●男装している wear [be (disguised) in] men's clothes.

だんそう　断想 fragmentary thoughts.

だんそう　断層 【地学】 a fault; (ずれ) 【地学】 a dislocation. ●活断層 an active *fault*. ●断層写真 a tómogram. ●断層線 a fault line.

だんそう　弾奏 ── 弾奏する 動 play 《the guitar, the koto》.

だんそう　弾倉 (連発銃の) a magazine; (回転式ピストルの) a cylinder.

たんそきん　炭疽菌 【医学】 ánthrax. 〈参考〉生物兵器に用いられる〉

たんそく　探測 名 a probe; sounding. **── 探測する** 動 probe. ●探測機 (宇宙探測の) a (space) probe. ●探測気球 a sounding balloon.

たんそく　短足 short legs. **── 短足の** 形 short-legged. ▶彼は胴長短足だ He has a long trunk [torso] and *short legs*.

たんそく　嘆息 《give》 a sigh. (⇨溜め息, 嘆く)

だんぞく　断続 名 **intermittent**. **── 断続的に** 副 **intermittently**. ▶終日雨は断続的に降った It rained *on and off* all day (long)./We had *intermittent* rain [showers] all day.

たんそびょう　炭疽病 【医学】 anthrax.

だんそんじょひ　男尊女卑 (男性優位) predominance of men over women; (男性優位主義) male chauvinism /ʃóuvənìzm/. 〈⇨ 女尊男卑〉 ●男尊女卑の社会 (= 男性支配の社会) a *male-dominated* society.

たんだ　単打 【野球】 a base hit; a single; a one-base hit.

たんだい　短大 a junior college. (⇨大学) ▶彼女は短大生です She goes to junior college./She's a junior college student.

*****だんたい　団体** a group, a party, a body; 【競技の】 a team; 【組織体の】 an organization.

┌─────────────────────────────
│ 使い分け　**group** 何らかの関係があって現に集まっている集団の意で, 最も一般的な語.
│ **party** 共通目的のための一時的な集団.
│ **body** 計画された方法で一体のように行動する集団.
└─────────────────────────────

┌─────────────────────────────
│ 解説　**group**, **party**, **team** は単数扱いが原則だが, 《英》では個々の構成員をさすときは複数扱い: その団体は大部分が少年です The *party is* 《米》 [*are* 《英》] mostly boys.
└─────────────────────────────

① 【～の団体, 団体～】 ●圧力団体 a pressure group; (院外の) a lobby. (〈参考〉議会のロビーで議員に陳情することから) ●研究[公共]団体 a research [a public] body. ●慈善団体 a charitable *organization*. ●宗教団体 a religious body [*organization*]. ●50名の団体 a *party* of fifty. ●非営利団体 a nonprofit *organization* (略 NPO). ●団体行動をとる act together [as a *group*].
② 【団体が】 ▶小学生の団体が中国へ行く予定です A *party* [A *group*] of schoolchildren is going [(書) is to go] to China.
③ 【団体に[を]】 ●団体を設立[解散]する set up [dissolve] an *organization*. ▶彼はある宗教団体に入っている He is a member of [belongs to] a religious *organization*.

●団体客 (旅行の) a party of tourists. ●団体競技 (団体戦) a team competition; (球技などの試合) a team game; (団体でするスポーツ) a team sport. ●団体交渉 (engage in) collective bargaining. ●団体生活 a group life. ●団体旅行 (make) a group [a package] tour. (❗(1) package を用いる言い方は旅行社提供のセット旅行. (2)「団体旅行をする」は travel in a *group* [a *package*] ともいう) ●団体割引 a group reduction. ●団体割引料金 a group rate; (乗り物の) a reduced fare for a party.

だんだら　段だら ●紅白の段だら幕 a curtain in red and white *stripes*. ●段だら縞 different-colored [multi-colored] *parallel* stripes.

たんたん　坦々 ── 坦々とした 形 ●坦々とした (= 平らな) 道 a *flat* road; (起伏のない) a (stretch of) road *without ups and downs*. ▶彼の坦々とした (= 波乱の少ない) 半生 his *uneventful* earlier life.

たんたん　淡々 ── 淡々とした 形 ●冷静な calm; (動じない) philosophical; (無関心な) indifferent 《to》. **── 淡々と** 副 calmly /káːmli/; (感情を交えず) dispassionately.

*****だんだん　段々** 名 〈階段〉(屋外の) steps; (屋内の) stairs. ●段々になった道 a stepped path. **── 段々** 副 〈徐々に〉 gradually, by degrees (❗後の方が堅い言い方); (少しずつ) little by little, 《話》 bit by bit; (ますます) more and more, increasingly. ●だんだん知識を身につけていく get knowledge *little by little* [(1歩1歩) *step by step*]. ▶彼の健康はだんだん回復していた His health was *gradually* improving [was showing a *gradual* improvement]./He was getting better *little by little* [*bit by bit*]. ▶彼は彼女のことがだんだん好きになった He *gradually* got [came] to like her. (❗ˣHe *gradually* liked her. は不可) ▶麻薬問題はだんだん国際化してきた The drug problem has become *more and more* international [global]. ▶彼は仕事をするにつれてだんだん夢中になっていった As he worked, he grew *increasingly* absorbed. ▶だんだん暖かくなってきた It is getting *warmer* (*and warmer*). (❗比較級で「だんだん」の意が表せる)

●段々畑 terraced fields.

たんち　探知 detection. ●探知機 (⇨探知機) **── 探知する** 動 detect. 〈❗逆探知する〉は trace.

だんち　団地 【アパート団地】 a housing 《米》 an apartment] complex; 【建て売り分譲住宅団地】 《米》 a housing development, 《英》 a housing estate. ●公営団地に住む 《米》 live in a public

housing complex [a housing project]; 《英》live in a council block (of flats). (参考) いずれも主に低所得者向け
- 団地族 residents of a housing complex.

だんち 暖地 a warm place [district, region]; (温帯地方) the temperate regions.

だんちがい 段違い ● 段違いである (並ぶ者がいない) be unmatched, be unequalled; (並はずれて優れている) be by far the better [best] (!) better は2者, best は3者以上の間での比較). ▶このパソコンは古いのに比較すると段違いによい This PC is *far* [*much*, 《話》*a lot*] better than the old one.
- 段違い平行棒 (the) uneven parallel bars.

たんちき 探知機 a detector. ● 魚群探知機 a fishfinder. ● 金属探知機にバッグを通す put one's bag through a metal *detector*.

たんちょう 単調 [翻訳のこころ] 私は島の単調さに驚いた. 歩いても歩いても, こつこつの固い道である (太宰治『猿ヶ島』) I was surprised by the monotonous nature of the island. No matter how far I walked, a hard rocky road stretched before [in front of] me. (!) (1) 「単調」は島の自然をも含んだ環境全体のことを意味しているので, monotony でなく monotonous nature と表す. (2) stretch は目の前から遠くの方へずっと延びている様子を表す
—— 単調な 形 (変化のない) monotonous; (おもしろくない) dull; [色調・絵に] flat (-tt-). ● 単調なリズムで in a *monotonous* rhythm. ● 単調な生活を送る lead [live] a *monotonous* [(決まりきった) a *routine*] life. ▶単調な田舎の生活も初めはなかなかよいと思ったが, やがて飽きてきた I found the *monotonous* country life quite pleasant at first, but soon I grew tired of [×from] it.
—— 単調に 副 monótonously.

たんちょう 探鳥 bird-watching.

たんちょう 短調 【音楽】a minor (key). (⇨長調)

だんちょう 団長 the head [leader] of a party.

だんちょう 断腸 ● 断腸の思い ▶中国を去るのは断腸の思いであった It really *broke* my *heart* to leave China.

たんちょうづる 丹頂鶴 【鳥】a Japanese crane; a red-crested white crane.

たんてい 探偵 (人) a detective; (事) detective work [service]. ● 私立探偵(社) a private *detective* (agency). ● 探偵につけられる be shadowed by a *detective*. ● 探偵をつける set a *detective* ((on him)).
● 探偵ごっこをする play *detectives*.
● 探偵小説 a detective story.

だんてい 断定 名 [結論] (a) conclusion; [決定, 判断] (a) decision.
—— 断定的な 形 (結論づける) conclusive; (変更のない) decided; (強く言い切る) assertive. ▶彼はいつも断定的な口調で意見を述べる He always has a *decided* manner of giving his opinion. (!) decisive manner は決断の早い様子を表す
—— 断定する 動 conclude; decide. ▶その絵にせ物だと断定された They *concluded that* the painting was a forgery./They *concluded* the painting to be a forgery.

たんてき 端的 —— 端的な 形 (明白な) plain; (単刀直入の) straightforward. ● 端的な事実 a *plain* [an *obvious*] fact. ● 端的な表現 *straightforward* expressions. ● 端的に(=率直に)言えば *frankly* speaking; to *be frank* ((with you)).

たんでき 耽溺 名 indulgence.
—— 耽溺する 動 indulge ((oneself)) in ((wine [a woman])).

たんでん 炭田 a coalfield.

*たんとう 担当 charge. ▶君の担当の医者 [先生] は誰ですか Who is *your* doctor [teacher]? (!) 言い方に注意)
—— 担当する 動 ● 彼にそのプロジェクトを担当させる put the project *in* [*under*] his *charge*; put him *in charge of* the project. ● 英語を担当する(= 教える) *teach* English. ● 政権を担当している(= 権力の座にある) be *in power*. ▶私は50人の生徒を担当している I am *in* [《書》*have*] *charge of* fifty students. (⇨担任) ▶だれがその実験 [部門] (の責任)を担当するのか Who will *take charge of* the experiment [department]? ▶その販売員はこの地域を担当している The salesman [saleswoman] *covers* this area.
● 担当者 (管理・責任者) the person in charge ((of)).

たんとう 短刀 a dagger.

だんとう 弾頭 a warhead. ● 核弾頭 a nuclear *warhead*.

だんとう 暖冬 ▶今年は暖冬だった We have had a *mild winter* this year. (!) *mild* は寒暖が「厳しくない」に重点がある. a *warm* winter も場合により可: 暖冬異変 an abnormally warm winter)

だんどう 弾道 【物理】a trajectory.
● 弾道ミサイル [弾] a ballistic míssile. ● 大陸間 [中距離] 弾道弾 an intercontinental [an intermediate range] ballistic missile 《略 ICBM [IRBM]》.

だんとうだい 断頭台 a guillotine /ɡíːlətiːn/. ● 断頭台に登る go to the *guillotine*. (⇨ギロチン)

たんとうちょくにゅう 単刀直入 ● 単刀直入に尋ねる ask ((him)) *point-blank* ((about it)). ▶単刀直入に言いなさい (率直に) Speak *frankly*./(ずばり要点を言いなさい) Come [Get] *right to the point*.

たんどく 丹毒 the rose, 【医学】erysipelas /èrəsípələs/.

たんどく 単独 —— 単独の 形 [たった一つ[1人]の] single; [独立した] independent; [別々の] separate /sépərət/; [独占的な] exclusive; [1人で行う] one-man; [1人で演じる] solo; [独力の] single-handed. ● 単independent action, act ((×an) *independently* ((separately)); (任意の行動をとる) take *arbitrary* action.
● 単独飛行をする make a *solo* flight; fly *solo*.
—— 単独で 副 [1人で] alone, by oneself (!) 後の方は「独力で」の意もある); [独立して] independently; [個々に] individually, separately. ● 単独で北極へ行く go to the Arctic *alone* [*by oneself*]. ▶私たちはめいめい単独でその問題を処理した Each of us dealt with the problem *individually* [*separately*].
● 単独会見 ((have)) an exclusive interview ((with)). ● 単独内閣 a single-party [a one-party] cabinet. (!) 単・複両扱い) ● 単独犯 a one-person [a single-handed] crime.

たんどく 耽読 —— 耽読する 動 be absorbed [be engrossed] in ((reading)) ((a detective story)).

だんトツ (断然トップの) by far the best; (比べ者のない) matchless; (ぶっちぎりの) outright. ▶彼は高校野球でだんトツのホームランバッターだった He was *by far the best* home-run hitter in the high-school baseball world. ▶S選手はロンドンマラソンでだんトツで優勝した S was the *outright* winner of the London marathon.

だんどり 段取り (手配) arrangements; (準備) preparations. (⇨準備) ● 段取りをする[つける] make *arrangements* [*preparations*] ((for)).

タンドリーチキン tandoori /tændúəri/ chiken. 《参考》インド料理）

だんな 旦那 （家・店などの主人）a master, 《話》a boss; (夫) one's husband; (男性への呼びかけ) sir. (**!**「田中の旦那」のような言い方は *Mr.* Tanaka とする) ● 若旦那 (主人の長男) a young *master*; (大家の若者) a young *gentleman*.

たんなる 単なる （ほんの，単純な）simple. ▶単なるうわさにすぎない It's a *mere* [×a simple] rumor. ▶それは単なる計算ミスだ It's a *mere* [a *simple*] miscalculation.

＊たんに 単に only, just (**!** only より口語的), 《やや書》merely; (**!**[単純にただ] simply. (⇒唯(%)) ▶私はただ単に習慣からそれをしただけです I did it *only* [*just, simply*] from habit./I *only* [*just, simply*] did it from habit.

たんに 単二 （電池）a C (size) battery. (⇒電池)

たんにん 担任 图 （= 担当) ● 担任の教師 a *homeroom* [a *home room*] teacher. ▶私たちの学級担任は島田先生です Our class 《米》*homeroom*, 《英》*form* teacher is Mr. Shimada./The teacher *in* (×the) *charge of* our class is Mr. Shimada./(担任している) Mr. Shimada is *in* [《書》*has*] *charge of* our class. ▶相田先生の246担任です [私たちの担任は相田先生です] He is *in* [*under*] Mr. Aida's *charge*./He is *in* [*under*] *the charge of* Mr. Aida. (**!** 後の方では charge に the をつけることに注意)

── 担任する 動 take [(している) be in] charge of.... ● 彼が担任している生徒 the students *in* [*under*] his *charge*.

タンニン 〖化学〗tannin. ● タンニン酸 tannin acid.

だんねつざい 断熱材 ínsulating matèrial, insulation; an insulator.

たんねん 丹念 ── 丹念に 副 (注意して) carefully; (念入りに) eláborately; (綿密に) closely. (⇒念入り)

だんねん 断念 ── 断念する 動 give* (...) up, abandon. (⇒諦(%)) ● 断念させる 動 get [(説得する) persuade] ⟨him⟩ *to* give (...) *up*; (思いとどまらせる) 《やや書》dissuade ⟨him *from* doing⟩. ▶我々は中国旅行を断念した We *gave up*, 《やや書》*threw up* our plan to visit China. (**!** give up [throw up] visiting.... ▶旅行を途中でやめる] 意にとる) ▶父は私に大学進学を断念させた My father *got* [*persuaded*] me *to give up* the idea of going to college./My father *persuaded* me *not to* go to college [*dissuaded* me *from* going to college].

たんねんど 単年度 a single fiscal year, 《英》a single financial year. ● 単年度(= 年次)予算 an annual budget.

たんのう 胆嚢 〖解剖〗a gáll blàdder. (**!** 1語につづることもある) ● 胆嚢炎〖医学〗inflammation of the gall bladder. ● 胆嚢がん gall-bladder cancer.

たんのう 堪能 ── 堪能な 形 (上手な) good*; (熟達した) 《やや書》proficient. ● ピアノに堪能である be a *good* [a *proficient*] pianist; be *good* [*proficient*] *at* (play)ing the piano. ▶彼は英語が堪能だ He is a *good* speaker of English./He speaks *good* English./He is *good* [at *proficient in*] English./He has a *good* command of English.

── 堪能する 動 （満足した) be satisfied ⟨*with*⟩; (楽しむ) enjoy; (料理・飲み物などを) eat* [drink*] (...) to one's heart's contént, 《書》eat [drink] one's fill ⟨*of*...⟩. ● よい音楽を十分堪能できる *be* quite *satisfied with* good music; thoroughly *enjoy* good music.

たんぱ 短波 a short wave, 《書》a high-frequency [an HF] sound wave. 《関連》中波 a medium wave/長波 a long wave. ● 短波で送信する transmit ⟨a message⟩ by *short wave*; shortwave ⟨a message⟩. ● 短波受信機 a short-wave receiver. ● 短波放送 short-wave broadcasting; (番組) a short-wave broadcast. ● 短波ラジオ a short-wave radio.

たんはい 炭肺〖医学〗(炭粉症) anthracosis 《参考》炭鉱夫によく見られるので miner's lung とも呼ばれる); (黒色肺) black lung.

たんぱく 淡泊 ── 淡泊な 形 〖食物が〗(あっさりした) plain; (消化のよい) light; (病人用で刺激の少ない薄味の) bland; 〖人が〗(あっさりした) frank; (無関心な) indifferent ⟨*to*⟩. ● 淡泊な味 a *simple* taste. ● 淡泊な気性 a *frank* disposition.

たんぱく 蛋白 ● 蛋白源 a source of protein(s). ● 蛋白質 (⇒蛋白質) ● 蛋白尿〖医学〗albuminuria.

たんぱくしつ 蛋白質〖生化学〗protein /próuti:n/. (**!** 種類をいうときは ⦗C⦘) ● 動物[植物]性たんぱく質 an animal [a vegetable] *protein*.

だんばしご 段梯子 wooden stairs (without risers).

たんぱつ 単発 ● 単発式ピストル a single-action revolver.

たんぱつ 短髪 short hair; a crop. ● 短髪にする crop one's hair.

だんぱつ 断髪 图 bobbed hair.

── 断髪する 動 have one's hair bobbed. ● 断髪式〖相撲〗(説明的に) a ceremony in which a sumo wrestler's topknot is cut off when he retires.

タンバリン 〖楽器〗a tambourine /tæmbəríːn/.

たんパン 短パン 《a pair of》shorts.

だんぱん 談判 图 (交渉) negotiation(s). (**!** 通例複数形で)

── 談判する 動 negótiàte ⟨*with*⟩; (売買条件のことで) bargain ⟨*with*⟩. (⇒交渉)

たんび 耽美 ── 耽美的な 形 《やや書》aesthetic /esθétik/. ● 耽美主義 æsthéticism. ● 耽美主義者 an áesthete.

たんぴょう 短評 a short [a brief] comment ⟨*on*⟩.

だんびら 段平 （刃の広い刀）a broadsword; (刀) a sword.

たんぴん 単品 ❶[一種類の品物] a (single) kind of article. ● 単品の大量生産 mass manufacturing of *one type of product*. ❷[セットになっている品物の一つ] a piece. ▶絵の具はすべてセットでも単品でもお買いいただけます You can get all the colors *loose* [*separately*] or by the dozen./《店頭標示》(All the colors are) available *by the piece* or case.

ダンピング 图 〖不当廉売〗dumping. ── ダンピングする 動 dump ⟨goods⟩.

ダンプカー 《主に米》a dump truck, 《英》a dumper (truck). (**!** (1)《英》では a tipper truck [lorry] ともいう. (2) a dump car は「鉄道の傾斜台付きの貨車」の意)

タンブラー a tumbler.

タンブリング 〖マット上での宙返り〗〖体操〗tumbling.

たんぶん 単文 a simple sentence.

たんぶん 短文 a short sentence [composition].

たんぺいきゅう 短兵急 ● 短兵急な 形 （にわかな）abrupt; (ひどく急いだ) impetuous; (あわただしい) precipitate.

── 短兵急に 副 （にわかに）abruptly; (ひどく急いで) im-

ダンベル 《a pair of》 dumbbells.
- ダンベル体操 dumbbell exercise.

たんぺん 短辺 the short side of a rectangle. (⇨長辺)

たんぺん 短編 〖小説〗a short story (❗ novel は「長編小説」の意); (小品) a sketch; 〖映画〗a short movie.
- 短編作家 a short-story writer. ● 短編集 a collection of short stories; collected short stories 《of》.

だんぺん 断片 (こわれた) a frágment 《of》; (1片) a scrap 《of》. ● 断片的知識 (×a) fragmentary knowledge 《of》. ● 事故の断片的ニュース scraps of news about the accident.

たんぼ 田んぼ a rice field; (水田) a paddy [paddies] (field). (❗ 通例複数形で) ● 田んぼを耕す plow /pláu/ a rice field. ● 田んぼに水を引く irrigate paddies [a rice field].
- 田んぼ道 a path [a lane] through rice fields.

たんぽ 〖拓本を取るための道具〗a dabber.

たんぽ 担保 (保証) security; (見返り) collateral; pledge. (⇨抵当) ● 借金の担保として in [as] security for a loan. ● …を担保に取る[入れる] get [give, put up] … as security. ▶彼は家を担保にして金を借りた He borrowed money on the security of his house.
- 担保付貸付金 a secured [a collateral] loan. ● 担保物権 a security; a collateral.

『タンホイザー』 Tannhäuser /táːnhɔ̀ɪzər/. (参考) ワグナー作曲のオペラ

たんぼう 探訪 图 ● 奈良へ古寺探訪に行く visit Nara to find out about some historic temples there.
—— 探訪する 動 visit … to find out 《about》 [to investigate 《into》].
- 探訪記事 an investigative report. ● 探訪記者 an investigative reporter.

だんぼう 暖房 heating. ● 暖房を入れる[切る] turn on [off] the heating [heater]. ● 暖房を強める[弱める] turn up [down] the heating [heater]. ● 暖房が入っていない[いない] be well [poorly] heated. ● 暖房の入っていない列車 an unheated train. ▶うちは室内暖房用に石油ストーブを使っている We heat our rooms with kerosene heaters. ▶この部屋は暖房がききすぎている This room is overheated.
- 暖房器具 a heater. ● 暖房装置 a heating apparatus; a heating system. ● 暖房費 heating costs.

だんボール 段ボール 〖紙〗cardboard, còrrugated páper; 〖箱〗a cardboard box.

たんぽぽ 〖植物〗a dandelion /dǽndəlàiən/.

タンポン (生理用) a tampon; (外科の止血用) a surgical pad.

だんまく 弾幕 〖軍事〗a barrage; (大砲による弾幕) an artillery barrage 《on》.

たんまつ 端末 a (computer) terminal.
- 端末装置 a terminal device; a terminal unit.

だんまつま 断末魔 (死の苦しみ) (主にском) death throes. ● 断末魔の叫び a cry of death throes.

たんまり ● たんまりもうける make a large [《話》a tidy] sum of money; make a large [《話》a tidy] profit.

だんまり ● だんまりを決め込む become [keep] silent; 《話》clam up.

たんみ 淡味 —— 淡味の 形 plain 《food》.

たんめい 短命 ▶彼は短命だった He was short-lived./ (若死にした) He died young.

タンメン [<中国語] (説明的に) Chinese noodles served with meat and vegetables in broth.

だんめん 断面 ● 横[縦]断面 a cross [a vertical] section. ● (事件などが)現代社会の一断面を示す show a cross section [a picture] of today's society.

だんめんず 断面図 a cross section 《of a plant stem》; a sectional plan 《of a building》.

だんめんせき 断面積 a cross section.

たんもう 短毛 图 short hair. —— 短毛の 形 short-haired.

たんもの 反物 (一反) a roll of cloth for kimono.

だんやく 弾薬 ammunition.
- 弾薬庫 〖軍事〗a (powder) magazine.

だんゆう 男優 an actor. (⇨役者)

たんらく 短絡 图 (電気のショート) a short circuit, 《話》a short.
—— 短絡的な 形 ● 短絡的な(=単純な)考え simplistic thinking.
—— 短絡する[させる] 動 short-circuit, 《話》short.

だんらく 段落 (文章の) a páragràph.

だんらん 団欒 ●一家だんらんを楽しむ have a good time at home with one's family; (離れていた家族が集って) have a family gathering.

たんり 単利 simple interest.

だんりゅう 暖流 a warm current.

たんりょ 短慮 ● 短慮な (短気な) hot-tempered; (浅慮な) shallow (⇨浅はかな).

たんりょく 胆力 courage. (⇨度胸)

だんりょく(せい) 弾力(性) 图 (伸縮性のある性質) èlasticity; (曲げられる性質) flexibility; (ばねのような性質) spring.
—— 弾力(性)のある, 弾力的な 形 elàstic; flexible; springy. ● 弾力的な規則 an elastic [a flexible] rule. ● 弾力は大変弾力性がある Rubber has a lot of elasticity./ Rubber is very elastic.

たんれい 端麗 —— 端麗な 形 graceful; handsome; beautiful; good-looking. ● 容姿端麗な女性 (⇨容姿)

だんれつ 断裂 〖医学〗rupture. ● アキレス腱断裂 rupture of Achilles tendon.

たんれん 鍛練 图 ● 身体の鍛練 physical training 《for a race》.
—— 鍛練する 動 ● 心身を鍛練する train one's body and mind. ● 足腰を鍛練する build up [harden] one's body 《for rock-climbing》. (❗ body に注意)

だんろ 暖炉 〖壁に取りつけた〗a fireplace; 〖炉辺〗a hearth. ● 暖炉にあたる warm oneself at the fireplace [by the hearth].

だんわ 談話 (a) talk; (所見) (a) comment. ● 増税に関する首相の談話 the Prime Minister's talk on tax increases.
- 談話室 (ホテルなどの) a lounge /láundʒ/; 《古》a parlor.

ち

:ち 血 ❶ [血液] blood /blʌ́d/.
① 【血が[は]】 ▶切り傷から血が出ている *Blood is coming* [(流れ出る) *running*, (にじみ出る) *oozing*, (吹き出る) *pouring*] *from the cut*./ The cut *is bleeding*. ▶血は体内を循環している *Blood circulates through* [*flows around*] *the body*.
② 【血の】 ●血の跡 a bloodstain; (かすかな跡) a trace of *blood*. ●血の海 a sea [pool] of *blood*; seas of *blood*. ●血のかたまり a clot of *blood*. ●血のついたシャツ a *blood*-stained shirt. (⇨血まみれ)
●血の気 (⇨血の気)
③ 【血に】 ▶上着は血に染まっていた The jacket was soaked with *blood*. ▶彼女の手は血にまみれていた Her hand was covered with *blood*.
④ 【血を】 ●血(=出血)を止める stop the *bleeding*. ●血を採る draw *blood* 《*for a test*》. (⇨採血, 献血); ●血を吐く (口から) vomit *blood*, have a bleed; (せきをして肺などから) cough (up) *blood*.
●血を吸う suck *blood*. ▶兵士は祖国のために血を流した The soldiers *bled* [《書》 *shed their blood*, (死んだ) *died*] *for their country*.

❷ [血統] ▶私たちは血がつながっている We are related *by blood*./ (血縁者だ) We are *blood* relatives [relations]. ▶私にはアイルランド人の血が少し流れている I have a little Irish *blood* in me.

❸ [その他の表現] ●血の涙(= 悲痛な涙) bitter tears. ●血も凍るような光景 a *blood*-curdling [(恐ろしい) *a horrible*] sight. ●会社の再建のために新しい血を入れる bring in new [fresh] *blood* to reconstruct the company.

●血が騒ぐ ▶ボクシングの試合を見ると血が騒ぐ Watching a boxing match *gets my blood rushing*.
●血が上(のぼ)る ▶社長の頭に血が上って(かりかりして)いるときは近寄らないに限る It's best to stay away from the boss when his *blood* is up.
●血が沸く ▶大きな船を見て彼の血が沸いた The sight of the great ship *stirred his blood*. (❗made his blood boil は「激怒させた」の意で, 不適切)
●血で血を洗う (血族同士で争う) have a family feud; (悪に悪に報いる) revenge wrong with wrong.
●血と汗の結晶 the fruit of one's blood and sweat [(苦労と努力) labors and efforts].
●血となり肉となる ▶学んだことが血となり肉となる You *get what you learned in your food*.
●血に飢える ▶血に飢えた戦士 a *bloodthirsty* warrior.
●血の通う ▶血の通った(= 人情味のある)政策を求める demand a *humane* /hjuːméɪn/ policy 《*from the government*》.
●血のにじむような ▶血のにじむような努力をする make *strenuous* efforts 《*to do*》.
●血の巡りが悪い ▶あの男は血の巡りが悪い(=理解が遅い) He *is slow in understanding* [*in understanding*]./(話) He *is slow* (↔*quick*) *on the uptake*.
●血は争えない 《ことわざ》 Blood will tell.
●血は水よりも濃し (他人より身内)《ことわざ》Blood is thicker than water.
●血も涙もない ▶血も涙もない男 a *cold-blooded* [a cold and heartless] man.
●血沸き肉躍る ▶血沸き肉躍る試合 a *very exciting*

[*a thrilling*, *a stirring*] game.
●血を吐く思い ▶その気の毒な子供たちを見たとき血を吐く思い(=ひどくつらい思い)だった *My heart bled* when I saw the poor children.
●血を引く ▶彼は王室の血を引いている He is of *royal blood*./(子孫だ) He is a descendant of [is descended from] a royal family.
●血を分ける ▶血を分けた兄弟 one's *blood* brother.

*ち 地 [地球, 大地] the earth; [地面] the ground; [土壌, 国] soil; [場所] a place. ●天と地 heaven and *earth*. (❗通例この語順で無冠詞) ●地の果てに着く reach the end(s) of the *earth*. ●異国の地を踏む set foot [tread] on foreign *soil*. ●安住の地を求めて look for [seek] a *place* where one can live in peace.
●地に足が着く ▶しっかり地に足が着いている have [keep] one's feet firmly on the *ground*. (❗「現実[実際的]である」の意もある)
●地に落ちる ▶彼の信用は地に落ちた(=なくなってしまった) His credit *is gone* [(台なしになった) *is completely ruined*]./(失った) He *has entirely lost* his credit.

ち 知 wisdom. (⇨知恵)
ちあい 血合い the dark-reddish flesh of fish.
チアガール 《主に米》 a cheerleader; 《和製語》 a cheer girl.
チアノーゼ cyanosis /sàiənóusis/.
チアリーダー 《主に米》 a cheerleader.
チアリーディング (説明的に) 《主に米》 a performance of cheerleader; 《和製語》 cheerleading.
ちあん 治安 (社会の平安) the (public) peace; (社会の秩序) (public) order; (法と秩序が保たれている状態) law and order (❗通例単数扱い. 軍事力などの介入を暗示); (保護されし侵されないこと) security. ●治安を乱す disturb *the peace*. ●治安を維持する keep [maintain] *the peace*; keep [maintain] *order*; keep [maintain] *law and order*. ●町の治安を回復する restore the *order* of the city. ▶この地域は夜は治安が悪い This area is not safe [×secure] at night.

:ちい 地位 a place; (他との相対的な) (a) position (❗重要さを含意することもある); [持ち場] a post (❗位置を含意する); [身分] (a) status; [位] (a) rank. (⇨立場, 境遇, 身分) ●地位の高い人 a man [a woman] of *position* [*rank*]. ●社会的な地位の高い人 have a high (↔a low) social *position*. ●社長の地位につく take a *position* [*a post*] as president. (❗as に続く名詞が役職名を表すときは通例無冠詞) ●人事部長の地位についている [任命される] be in [be appointed to] the *position* of personnel /pə̀ːrsənél/ manager. ●女性の社会的地位を向上させる improve [raise] the social *status* of women. ▶彼は私の名声を利用して地位を築いてきた He has been using my good name to get *places*. ▶彼はその会社で重要な地位を占めていた He held an important *position* [*place*, *post*, ×*status*, ×*rank*] in the firm. ▶彼は軍隊で私より地位が低かった He was [ranked] below (↔above) me in the army. ▶地位が人をつくる例はよくある The position often makes the man. ❶(1) 「...(の例)がある」は, 英文では there is (are) で始めるより, 文の主旨だけを述

ちい 地衣 (⇨地衣類)

ちいき 地域 图 an area (❗特定の用途に当てられた境界の不明確な区域. 広い地域も狭い地域もさすが, 通例 district, region より狭い);［地域社会］a (local [regional]) community, a region (❗地理的・社会的にまわりと区別される特徴を持つ地域); a district (❗行政上区別された機能を持つ地域. region より狭い). ●商業地域 a business *area* [*district*]. ●人口過密地域 a densely populated *area* [*region*]. ▶被害は広い地域に及んでいる The damage covers a wide *area*. ▶ワールドカップは開催地域の活性化につながることが多い The World Cup often leads to revitalizing the host *districts*. ▶湖をきれいにするには地域ぐるみの取り組みが必要だ The whole *community* should cooperate to clean the lake. ❗この — community は「地域住民」の意
— **地域(の)** 形 local; regional. (⇨地方) ●地域の代表 a representative of one's *district* [*region*]; one's *local* delegate.
●**地域活動** community activities. ●**地域間隔差** regional differences. ●**地域研究** area studies. ●**地域住民** local residents. ●**地域紛争** a regional dispute.

ちいく 知育 ●知育を偏重する put [lay, place] too much emphasis on *intellectual training*; attach too much importance to *intellectual education*. ▶子供たちに大事なものは知育よりもむしろ徳育である What is needed for children is not so much *intellectual education* as moral education.

チーク(材) teak; (木) a teak (tree). ●チークで作った家具 *teak* furniture.

チーク(カラー) (⇨⑱ 頬紅)

チークダンス ●チークダンスをする dance cheek to cheek;《和製語》do a cheek dance.

:ちいさい 小さい

WORD CHOICE **小さい**

little サイズが小さく, 愛らしくかわいらしいこと. 主観的・感情的な評価を含む. ●小さなぼうや a *little* boy. ●大草原の小さな家 a *little* house on the prairie.

small 物理的・客観的にサイズや規模が小さいこと. 主観的含意は含まれない. ●京都の西の小さな町 a *small* town in the west part of Kyoto.

tiny サイズが驚くほど小さいこと. しばしば tiny little の形で小ささとかわいらしさを強調する. ▶小さなお目々をあけてごらん Open your *tiny* little eyes.

❶［形状が］small (↔large); little* (↔big); tiny. ●小さい家 a *small* [a *little*, a *tiny*] house. (❗後の二つは感情を含意. したがって「かわいい家」は a cute *little* [*tiny*] house で, ×a cute *small* house とは通例いわない) ●世界で一番小さい国 the *smallest* country in the world. ●大根を小さく切る cut a radish into *small* pieces. (❗cut a radish *small* とするのはまれ) ▶小さいころ彼とよく遊んだものだ When (I was) a *small* [a *little*] child, I used to play with him. (❗(1) I was は省略可. (2) 文脈によって small, little はなくても可)/When I was *small* [(まれ) *little*, (幼い) *very young*], I used to play with him. ▶その消しゴムはすぐに小さくなった The eraser became *smaller* soon. ▶古い絵には無数の小さな亀裂(きっ)が入っていた There were a lot of *tiny* cracks in the old painting. ▶服が小さくなってしまったね You've *grown out of* your clothes. (❗成長期の子供の場合の言い方. 大人の場合は日本語の発想に一致する Your clothes are too small for you now. などという).
会話 「自転車に乗りたいな」「まだ小さいからだめだよ」"I want to ride a bike." "No, dear. You're too *young* [×small] (to ride one)."

❷［数・程度・音・声などが］(数・程度・音が) small; (声が) low. ●小さい数 a *small* [×a little]. ●小さなパーティー a *small* party. ●小さい声で話す talk in a *low* [a *small*] voice; (ささやき声で) talk in *whispers* [*a whisper*]. ●ラジオの音[ガスの火]を小さくする *turn down* the radio [gas]. ▶騒音はだんだん小さくなりついにやんだ The noise became *less and less* until it finally died out.

❸［取るに足らない］(小さな) small; (ちょっとした) little; (ささいな) trivial, 《書》trifling; (わずかな) slight. ●小さな過ちを犯す make a *slight* [a *small*, a *trivial*] error (*in*). ●小さなことにくよくよする worry about *little* [*trivial*] things.

❹［気性・人物などが］●気の小さい人 (臆病(おくびょう)な) a *timid* person; (度量の狭い) a *narrow-minded* [a *small-minded*] person. ●小さくなる (肩身の狭い思いをする) feel *small*; (怖くてすくむ) shrink 《*from*》.

ちいさな 小さな (⇨小さい)

ちいさめ 小さめ a little smaller, 《やや話》little on the small side; (小型の) small-size(d). ▶ジーンズは小さめの方がおしゃれですよ As for jeans, a *slightly smaller* pair [those *rather on the small side*] will make you look more attractive. ▶みかんは小さめの方が甘い Small-size mandarin oranges are sweeter (than large-size ones).

チーズ cheese. (❗一定の形に加工したものは Ⓒ) ●粉チーズ grated *cheese*. ●くん製チーズ smoked *cheese*. ●プロセスチーズ processed *cheese*. ●チーズ一切れ［一かけら］a slice [a piece] of *cheese*. ▶はい, チーズ！(写真を写すとき) Say *cheese*!

関連 チーズの種類：ブルー[カマンベール；チェダー]チーズ blue [Camembert; Cheddar] cheese/コテージ[エダム；パルメザン]チーズ cottage [Edam; Parmesan] cheese/ピメント[プロボローネ]チーズ pimento [Provolone] cheese.

●**チーズケーキ** cheesecake. ●**チーズバーガー** (a) cheeseburger. ●**チーズフォンデュ** (a) cheese fondue.

チーター 〖動物〗a cheetah.

チーフ ［主任］a chief (⑱ ~s), a head. ●チーフアンパイア an umpire-in-chief;《和製語》a chief umpire.

チーム a team (❗集合的. 単・複両扱い); a squad; a club (❗ただし, 国際試合ではチーム象徴試合：the England team in the World Cup), a side (❗集合的. 単・複両扱い). ●勝つ[負け]チーム a winning [a losing] *team*. ●首位のチーム the first-place team. ●チームを作る make [form, organize, put together] a *team*. (❗make the team は「チームのメンバーに入る」) ●チームを指揮する run a team [a club]. ●いいチームに育てる build up a good *team*. ●チームのメンバーである, チームに入っている be a member of a *team*; be on 《米》[in 《英》] the *team*. ●**チームカラー** the characteristics of a team. (❗複数形の team colors はチームを象徴するユニフォームや応援旗などの色のこと);《和製語》a team color. ●**チームティーチング** team teaching. ●**チームプレー** team play. ●チームプレーに徹する play hard for the team. ●**チームメイト** one's teammate. ●**チームワーク** teamwork. ▶勝負はチームワークのよしあしで決まる The success depends upon good *teamwork* among the members [staff].

ちいるい 地衣類 〖植物〗 lichen /láikən/.
ちうみ 血膿 bloody pus.
***ちえ** 知恵 (賢明さ)(やや書) wisdom, (理解力, 思考力)《やや書》wits; (頭脳) (a) brain (**!** しばしば複数形で), a head; (知能) intelligence; (思いつき) an idea (⇒考え), (思慮分別) sense.
① 【～(の)知恵, 知恵の～】• 古人の知恵 the *wisdom* of the ancients. • 入れ知恵 (⇒入れ知恵)
• 生活の知恵を身につける acquire *wisdom* for living. • 知恵遅れの子 a (*mentally*) *retarded child*; 《婉曲的》a developmentally challenged [delayed] *child* (**!**「発達的に問題がある[遅れた]子」の意); (学業遅進児) a slow learner. • 知恵のないやり方 a *stupid* [an *unwise*] way. ▶ 三人寄れば文殊(\(もんじゅ\))の知恵 (⇒三人)
② 【知恵が】 • 彼にはそれをするだけの知恵がない He is not *wise* enough [doesn't have the *wisdom*] to do it. ▶ 人は年とともに知恵がつく As we grow older, we become *wiser*./We gain *wisdom* with age. (**!** 前の方が口語的の)• いい知恵がちっとも浮かばない I can't think of any good *idea*.
③ 【知恵を】• 苦境から脱け出しようという知恵を絞る rack one's *brain*(s) [《話》beat one's *brains* out] (trying) to get out of the difculties. • 知恵を出し合う put one's *heads* together. • 知恵を働かせる use one's *brain*(s) [*head, wits*]. ▶ あなたのお知恵をお借りしたいのですが I'd like to ask for your *advice*./《やや話・まれ》Can I pick your *brains*?
• 知恵が回る ▶ 彼はよく知恵が回る He has quick *wits*. (⇒利口)
• 知恵比べ a contest of wits. • 知恵者 (知恵のある人) a wise man [woman]; a person of wisdom. • 知恵熱 teething fever. • 知恵の輪 puzzle rings. • 知恵歯 a wisdom tooth.
知恵袋 the brains.
チェアパーソン a chairperson. (**!** chairman, chairwoman の男女共用語 (⇒議長)
チェアマン a chairman (㊍ -men); 《男女共用》a chairperson, the chair. (⇒議長)
チェーン a chain. • 自転車のチェーン a bicycle *chain*. • タイヤチェーン a tire *chain*. • 車にチェーンを付ける [巻く] put *chains* on the tires of a car. ▶ 家に一人でいるときは(玄関の)ドアにチェーンをかけなさい Put the *chain* on the door when you are alone in the home.
• チェーンストアー[店] a chain [《主に英》a multiple] store. • チェーンスモーカー a chain smoker. • チェーンソー a chain saw. • チェーンメール 〖コンピュータ〗 chain mail.
ちえこしょう『智恵子抄』 *Selection of Poems about Chieko*. [参考] 高村光太郎の詩集
チェコ 〖国名〗 Czech /tʃék/; (公式名) the Czech Republic. (首都 Prague) • チェコ人 a Czech. • チェコ語 Czech. • チェコ(人)[語]の Czech.
チェコスロバキア Czechoslovakia. ([参考] 現在はチェコとスロバキアに分離・独立)
チェジュとう 済州島 〖韓国の島〗 Cheju /tʃédʒú:/ Island, Chejudo.
チェス chess. • チェスのこま a chessman. • チェスをする play *chess*; have a game of *chess*.
• チェス盤 a chessboard.
ちえっ (いら立ち) tut /t/ (**!** tut, tut ともいう), tsk /t/; (不快) phew /pfjú:/; (くそっ) damn [darn] it.
チェッカー 〖ゲーム〗《米》checkers, 《英》draughts.
• チェッカー盤 《主に米》a checkersboard; 《英》a draughtsboard.
チェッカーフラッグ 〖カーレースで使用する市松模様の旗〗 (wave) a checkered flag.
チェック 图 ❶【検査, 点検】a check. • 正しい答えにチェック印をつける Put a *check* 《米》[a *tick*《英》] by the correct answer. ([事情] √印のこと. 英米では日本の○印の代わりにこれを用いる)
❷【格子じま】• チェックの服 a *checked* [a *checkered*] dress. • チェックのはではなスカート a skirt with loud *checks*. • タータンチェックのキルト a *plaid* /plǽd/ [a *tartan*] kilt. ([参考] スコットランドの男性のはく伝統衣装)
❸【小切手】• トラベラーズチェック a traveler's *check*.
── チェックする 動 (検査[点検]する) check; (敵の選手を)《主に英》mark, take on. • その数字をチェック(=点検)する *check* [make a *check* on] the figures.
• チェックポイント 〖国境・長距離レースなどの検問所〗 a chéckpoint; 〖点検個所〗a point to be checked. • チェックリスト 〖照合表〗 a chéck list.
チェックアウト 图 checkout. ▶ チェックアウトは何時ですか What time is *checkout* here?
── チェックアウトする 動 check out 《of [from]》a hotel.
チェックイン 图 checkin.
── チェックインする 動 check in 《at a hotel, for a flight》. (**!**「ホテルにチェックインする」は check *into* a hotel ともいう)
チェリー 〖さくらんぼ〗 a cherry.
チェルノブイリ 〖ウクライナの都市〗 Chernobyl /tʃɜːrnóubl/.
チェロ 〖楽器〗 a cello (㊍ ~s). • チェロ奏者 a cellist.
• チェロを弾く play the *cello*.
ちえん 地縁 regional ties; territorial ties.
ちえん 遅延 图 (a) delay.
── 遅延する 動 be delayed; be late. (⇒遅れる)
• 遅延利息 interest for arrears.
チェンジ • チェンジになる 〖スポーツ〗 (攻撃が終わりになる) be retired. ▶ チェンジになった 〖野球〗 The teams changed sides. • チェンジ (野球の実況放送で) The side has been retired./Side retired.
• チェンジアップ 〖野球〗 a change(-up). • チェンジオブペース a change of pace. • チェンジコート 〖スポーツ〗 a changeover; a change of sides. • チェンジコートをする change sides; change round. • チェンジレバー 〖変速レバー〗《米》a gearshift; 《英》a gear lever.
チェンバロ 〖＜イタリア語〗 〖楽器〗 a harpsichord, 《まれ》a cembalo (㊍ ~s). • チェンバロ奏者 a harpsichordist.
チェンマイ 〖タイの都市〗 Chiang Mai /tʃiáːŋmái/, Chiengmai.
ちおん 地温 (地面の) ground temperature; (地中の) soil temperature.
***ちか** 地下 underground. (**!**「非合法」「秘密」などの比喩的意味にも用いられる) (㊉ 地上) • 地下1階[2階]に on the first [second] *underground* floor; (部屋など) in the first [second] *basement*. • 地下 10メートルのところで at ten meters *underground* [*below ground*].
── 地下の 形 underground; 《やや書》(地中の) subterranean. • 地下の勢力 an *underground* influence. • 地下の水流 a *subterranean* stream.
── 地下に[で] 副 (秘密組織etc)地下にもぐる go *underground*; go into hiding. ▶ 炭坑夫は地下で働く Coal miners work *underground* [*under the ground*].
• 地下街 an underground shopping center [arcade]. • 地下核実験 an underground nuclear test. • 地下活動 underground activities.

- **地下茎** a subterranean [an underground] stem. ●**地下資源** underground resources. ●**地下水** underground [subterranean] water. ●**地下組織** an underground organization.

ちか 地価 the price of land; land prices. ▶このところ地価は上昇[下落]している The *price of land* is going up [coming down] these days.
- **地価税** (a) land value tax; (a) land-holding tax.

ちか 治下 ▶エリザベス女王治下の in [*during*] *the reign* of Queen Elizabeth. ▶英国はビクトリア女王治下時代に繁栄した Britain prospered *under* Victoria *rule*.

:**ちかい 近い** ❶〖距離〗near (↔far) (#副詞・前置詞としても用いる); (ごく近い) close /klóus/. ●目が近い be nearsighted. (#近視) ▶私たちの学校は駅に近い Our school is *near* [*close to*] the station. (#near は前置詞としても用いるので near to の形は避けられる) ▶病院はここから近い The hospital is *near* [✗*near from*] here./(ほんの少し離れている) The hospital is *just a little way(s)* from here. (#(米)ではしばしば ways を用いる)/(遠くない) The hospital isn't *far* from here. (#far の場合は from が必要) ▶窓にいちばん近いところに来て座りなさい Come and sit *nearest* (*to*) the window. (#比較級・最上級の場合は to を伴うことが多い) ▶バス停へはこの道を行くのがいちばん近い This is the *nearest* [*shortest*] way to the bus stop.

❷〖時間〗near; (接近した) close. ▶春は近い Spring is getting *near* [*close*] [*at hand*]. (#at hand を伴うのは《書》)/(すぐそこに来ている) Spring is (*just*) *around the corner*. ▶かれこれ真夜中に近い It is *close to* [*nearly*] midnight. (⇒❹) ▶石油がなくなる日は近い(=やがて来る) The time *will soon come* [The day *is in sight*] when we will run out of oil. (#(1) when は time [day] を先行詞とする関係副詞. (2) when が that に代えることもできる) 【会話】「近いうちに昼ごはんでもいっしょに食べようよ」「それはいいね」 "Let's have lunch together *one of these days* [(まもなく) *soon*, (いつか) *sometime*]." "Good idea." (#A good idea. の A の省略に注意)

❸〖関係, 程度〗close, near. ▶近い親戚(は) a *close* [a *near*] relative. (#close の方が一般的) ▶完成に近い be *near* completion. ▶彼らに対する私の気持は怒りに近いものだった My feeling toward them was *close to* anger. ▶彼の回復は奇跡に近かった His recovery was *almost* a miracle. (#a near miracle とは通例いわない) ▶彼らがやろうとしていることは不可能に近い What they are attempting is *almost* [*next to*] impossible. (#next to は通例否定語の前で用いる) ▶彼女のふるまいは狂気に近い(=狂気と紙一重だ) Her actions *verge* [*border*] *on* madness.

❹〖数値〗(ほとんど) nearly, almost (#almost の方が接近の度合いが強い); (およそ, 約) about, (米) around. (#nearly, almost が「もう少しで達しそうだがそれを越えよう」場合に用いられるのに対し, about はその数量の前後を意味する) ▶クラスには 40 人近い学生がいる There are *nearly* [*about*] 40 students in the class. ▶祖母は 90 に近い Grandmother is *nearly* [*almost*, 《英》*going on* (*for*)] 90. (#go on (for) は通例進行形で用いる)

ちかい 地階 a basement. (⇒地下)
ちかい 誓い (神にかけての) an oath; (公のまたは厳粛な) a vow /váu/; (人との固い) a pledge. (⇒宣誓) ●フランスに対する忠誠の誓い an *oath* of allegiance to France. ●誓いの言葉を交わす (結婚式で) exchange (✗marriage [✗wedding]) *vows*. (#✗marriage [✗wedding] vows は誤り) ●秘密厳守の誓いのもとに under *pledge* [a *vow*] of secrecy. ●誓いを守る [破る] keep [break] one's *vow*. ●誓いをたてる swear an *oath*. (⇒誓う)

*ちがい 違い ❶ difference(*in*); (はっきりした区別) (a) distinction. (#いずれも具体的には C). ●年齢の違い a *difference* in age; an age *difference*. ●意見の違い a *difference* of opinion. ●生まれの違い the *distinctions in* birth. ▶値段はどれくらい違いますか What's the *difference in* price? ▶野球とクリケットの違いが分からない(=区別ができない) I can't tell the *difference* [《やや書》 make a *distinction*] *between* baseball and cricket./I can't *tell* [don't *know*, 《やや書》 can't *distinguish*] baseball *from* cricket. ▶彼とは 3 歳違いです I am three years older [younger] *than* he is [《話》 him, 《古・まれ》 he].

【会話】「タクシーに乗るとしたらどうだろう」「たいして違いはないよ」 "What if we take a taxi?" "It doesn't make any *difference*." (#「大違いだ」は It makes all the difference [a big difference]. (⇒大違い)

*ちがいない 違いない 〖推量〗(現在の) must 《do》 (#do は状態または習慣的行為を表す動詞), have (got) to 《be》; (過去の) must have 《done》; 〖確かに〗surely, certainly; 〖確信している〗I am sure [certain] (*that* too; *of*) (#通例 sure(ly) は主観的な判断に基づく場合に, certain(ly) は確かな根拠があるなど客観的な用いる). ▶彼が犯人に違いない He *must* [has to] be the culprit. (#(1) 後の方が客観的な根拠に基づいた推量で確信の程度は強い. (2) 否定は通例 can't, 《書》 cannot: He *can't* be the culprit. (彼が犯人であるはずがない)) ▶彼はそれを知っていたに違いない He *must have known* it. ▶彼が試合に勝つに違いない He will *surely* [*certainly*] win the game./*I am sure* [*certain*] (*that*) he will win the game./*I am sure* [*certain*] *of* his *winning* the game./*It is certain* [✗*sure*] *that* he will win the game./*He is sure* [*certain*] *to* win the game. (#(1) He *is sure* [*certain*] *of winning* the game. とは話し手はなく主語の確信を表して「彼は(自分が)試合に勝つと確信している」の意. (2) このような未来についての推量には must は用いられない)

ちがいほうけん 治外法権 〖法律〗extraterritorial rights, extraterritoriality.

ちかう 誓う swear, swear [take*] an oath; vow /váu/; 《書》 pledge.

【使い分け】 **swear**, **swear an oath** 正式にまたは宣誓して誓うこと.
vow 公にまたはおごそかに誓うこと.
pledge 特に重責を担う個人・団体・政府機関などが人に固く約束すること.

●忠誠を誓う *pledge* allegiance; *swear* [*take*] *an oath* of allegiance. ▶彼は真実のみを語ることを誓った He *swore* to tell the truth./He *swore* [*took an oath*] *that* he would tell the truth. (#参考 裁判で尋問を受ける者は I *swear to* tell the truth, the whole truth, and nothing but the truth. と最初に宣誓する) ▶彼は禁煙を心に誓った He *vowed* [*made a vow*] *to* give up smoking./He *vowed* (*that*) he would give up smoking./He *resolved* to give up smoking. ▶彼女は二度とそんなことはしないと誓った She *pledged herself* [(約束した) *promised*] *not* to do it again. ▶誓って言いますが, そのことは口外していません I never told anybody about it, I *swear*./I never, *on my oath*, told anybody about it.

ちがう 違う

WORD CHOICE 違う

be different 複数の人・物が根本的・質的に異なること. ▶知能の点で人と動物は違う People *are different* from animals in intelligence.
vary 人・物が何らかの点において部分的に異なり、さまざまであること. ●重要度は違う *vary* in importance
be distinct 複数の人・物が、はっきり区別・区分できるほど明らかに異なること. ▶電子辞書は紙の辞書と顕著に異なる E-dictionaries *are distinct* from paper dictionaries.

頻度チャート
be different ▬▬▬▬▬▬▬▬▬
vary ▬▬▬
be distinct ▬

20　40　60　80　100 (%)

❶ [異なる] be different 《from, 《主に米》than, 《英》to》, differ 《from》; vary 《from》; be distinct 《from》; (似ていない) be not like …, be unlike (…). (⇒異なる) ▶人は皆違った考えを持っている *Different* people have *different* ideas. ▶町に住むのと田舎に住むのとは大いに違う Living in a city is quite *different from* living in the country./(大きな違いがある) There *is a big difference* between living in a city and living in the country. ▶これは私が思っていたのと違う This *is different* [*differs*] *from* what I expected. (❗This is *not* what I expected. ともいえる) /This *is different than* 《主に米》[*to* 《英》] what I expected./This *is different than* I expected. (❗後に節を伴う場合、米英とも場が多い) ▶彼らの性格はあまり違わない They *are* not much *different* in character *from* each other. (❗different には比較の概念が含まれているので、比較級に用いられる修飾語 much, no, any, far なども用いられる) ▶彼は昔の彼とは違う He *is different* [a *different* man] *from* what he used to be. (❗日常会話では He is quite *another* man now./He's changed a lot. などの方が普通) ▶偽物と本物のダイヤはどう違うのですか What [×How] *is* the *difference between* imitation and real diamonds?/How *different* are imitation and real diamonds? ▶これらの靴は大きさは違うが形は違わない These shoes *vary* [*differ*] in size, but not in shape. ▶馬はロバは違う Horses *are distinct from* donkeys. ▶その 2 人の兄弟は風采(ﾌｳｻｲ)がまったく違う The two brothers *are* quite *unlike* (↔ *very* (much) *alike*) in their appearance. ▶姉と違って花子は服装に無関心である *Unlike* [×*Different from*] her (older) sister, Hanako is indifferent to her dresses. (❗Hanako, unlike her sister, is …. の語順も可) ▶この仕事はデスクワークとはぜんぜん違います It's *nothing like* desk work. ▶彼女は他の人とはひと味違う She has something *different* from others./Hers is somewhat *different* from others. ▶知っていることと教えることは違う To know is *one thing*, (and) to teach is *another*./It is *one thing* to know and *another* to teach./Knowing *is different from* teaching. (❗前の二つの方が強意的で日本語に近い)

❷ [一致しない] (人が意見などで) disagree 《with》; (食い違っている) 《書》 be at variance 《with》. ▶その問題に関してはあなたと意見が違います I *disagree* [*don't agree*] *with* you on the matter./My opinion about the matter *is different* [*differs*] *from* yours. (⇒❶) ▶それは話が違う That's *not* what you said. ▶それでは契約と違う That's *against* the contract. ▶もし親が子供に対して責任をもつべきだとするなら、子供を生むかどうかを決める権利を与えられてしかるべきです．違いますか If you expect people to be responsible for their children, you have to give them the right to decide whether or not to have children. Wouldn't you *agree*? (❗I agree.(その通りだ)と相手に言わせようと強く迫る言い方)

❸ [間違っている] be wrong; (思い違いをしている) be mistaken. ●違うバスに乗る take the *wrong* bus. ▶私の言うことが違っていたら訂正してください Correct me, if I *am mistaken* [*wrong*]. ▶この手紙はあて名が違っている This letter *is wrongly* addressed [is addressed *wrong*(*ly*)]. ▶前の方が一般的)/The address on [×of] this letter *is wrong* [(不正確) *not correct, incorrect*].

会話 (電話で)「番号が違っています」「お騒がせしてすみません」 "You have the *wrong* number./(ややふっきらぼうに) *Wrong* number." "Sorry you've been troubled."

会話「あれは君の弟かい?」「いや、違うよ」 "Is that your brother?" "No, it's *not*."

会話「君はあのネクタイが気に入らなかったって太郎が言ってたよ」「それは違うよ、あれはすごく気に入ったよ」 "Taro said you didn't like the tie." "That's *not true*. I liked it very much."

*ちかく 近く

❶ [距離] ①[近くの] nearby. ●近くの店 a *nearby* [×a near, ×a close] store (❗通例 near, close は物を表す名詞の前では用いない．ただし，near は最上級・比較級の場合は普通に用いる: いちばん近くの郵便局 the *nearest* post office); a store *nearby* [*close by*] (❗名詞の後では near をとつるることがある). ▶彼は大阪の近くの小さな町に住んでいる He lives in a small town *near* [*around*] Osaka.

②[近くに[まで]] near (…); nearby, near by; (すぐ近くに) close by; (…の近辺に) 《話》 around …; (近所に) in the neighborhood 《of》. ●この近くに *near* [*around*] here; *in* this *neighborhood*. ▶近くに本屋はありませんか Is there a bookstore *near* [*nearby*]? ▶もっと私の近くにいらっしゃい Come *nearer* (*to*) [*closer to*] me. (⇒近い❶) ▶彼はいつも近くに(= 手元に)辞書を数冊置いている He always keeps [*has*] several dictionaries *near* [*close*] *at hand*. ▶近くまで来たので、ちょっと寄ろうかと思って(寄られた) I was *in the neighborhood* and thought I'd drop in [*by*].

③[近くだ] ▶それはすぐ近くだ It's quite *near* [quite *nearby*, *just around the corner*]. ▶彼の家は駅のすぐ近くだ His house is quite *near* [(very) *close to*] the station.

④[近くから] ▶その絵を近くから(= 近距離で)見てみよう Let's look at the picture *at close* [*short*] *range*.

❷ [時間] (まもなく) soon, 《書》 before long; (じきに) 《話》 (近いうちに) one of these days. ▶彼は近く渡米する He will go to the U.S. *soon* [*before long, one of these days*, (近い将来に) *in the near future*]. ▶彼は 1 時近くに(= 1 時ちょっと前に)来た He came *just* [*shortly*] *before* one o'clock. ▶前の方が口語的)/He came at *nearly* one o'clock. ▶夕方近く雨が降り出した It began to rain *toward* [×*near*] evening.

❸ [ほとんど] (⇒近い❹) ▶父が死んで 10 年近くになる It has been 《主に米》[*is* 《主に英》] *nearly* [*almost*] ten years since my father died.

ちかく 地殻 the (earth's) crust.
●地殻変動 〖地学〗 diastrophism /daiǽstrəfìzm/; (政治的激変) political upheavals.

ちかく 知覚 图 〖〖認知〗〗〖書〗 perception; 〖感覚〗 sensation. (●感覚) ●知覚の鋭い人 a very perceptive man [woman]; a person of great perception.
―― 知覚する 動 ●物をはっきりした対象として知覚する 〖書〗 perceive things as definite objects.
●知覚過敏 〖医学〗 supersensitivity. ●知覚神経 a sensory nerve. ●知覚麻痺 〖医学〗 anesthesia /æ̀nəsíːʒə/; (一般的に) stupor.

ちがく 地学 〖科目〗 earth science. (❗通例複数形で. 地質学・天文学などを含む)

***ちかごろ** 近頃 副 (最近) recently, lately (⇨最近 解説); (このごろ) these days, nowadays.
―― 近頃の 形 recent; (今日の) present-day. ●近頃の出来事 a recent event. ●近頃の教育の傾向 present-day trends in education. ▶近頃の子供は安心して道路で遊べない The children *of today* [*Children today, Present-day children*] can't play safely on the street.

ちかしつ 地下室 (建物の地階) a basement; (ワイン・食糧などの地下貯蔵室) a cellar.

ちかちか ●ちかちか光る flicker; (かすかにとぎれて) glimmer. ▶遠くにちかちかする光を見た I saw a light *flickering* in the distance. ▶車のヘッドライトで目がちかちかした (=痛んだ) My eyes *were irritated by* the car headlights.

ちかぢか 近々 (間もなく) soon,〖書〗 before long; (じきに) shortly.

ちかづき 近付き ●彼と近づきになる (知り合いになる) *get* [*become*] *acquainted with* him; *make* his *acquaintance*; (友人になる) *make* [*become*] *friends with* him. (❗複数形に注意)

***ちかづく** 近付く ❶〖場所などに〗(近くなる) get* near [closer]; (近くへ動く) approach, come* near (❗後の方が口語的); (次第に近づく) draw* near (❗やや文語的); (話し手の方へ歩み寄る) come up, (相手の方へ) go* (*to*). ▶私のうしろから近づいて来る足音 footsteps *coming up* behind me [*approaching* me from behind]. ▶単に「近づいて来る足音」なら approaching footsteps) ▶彼らは私に近づいて来た They *got* [*came*] *near(er)* [*closer*] *to* me. (❗(1) 原級では near me, near to me のどちらもいえるが,前の方が多く用いられる. 比較級・最上級では to を伴う方が多い. (2) close は near より接近度が強い/(懇意になろうとした) He tried to *get acquainted with* me. ▶船は岸へ近づいた The ship *approached* [*drew near*] the shore. (❗日本語の「へ」に引かれて ×approached to, ×drew near to とはいわない) ▶女の子が私に近づいて来てサインを求めた A girl *came* [*walked*] *up* to her and asked for her autograph. ▶カメラがスカーレットに近づいていって彼女の顔が大写しになった The camera *closed in on* Scarlet until her face filled the screen. (❗close in は「徐々に距離を詰める, 忍び寄る」の意) ▶あのグループには近づかない (=離れている) 方が身のためですよ I'd advise you to [You'd better] *keep* [*stay*] *away from* that group./(かかわらない方がいい) You'd better *not get involved with* [*get mixed up with*] that group. ▶私には彼女は近づきがたい (=近寄りがたい) 感じがする (⇨近寄り難い)

❷〖時・行事など〗 approach; come* [get*]; near; (次第に近づく) draw* near; (すぐにやって来る) come soon; (間近に迫っている) just around the corner,〖書〗 be near [close] at hand. ●終わりに近づく draw [come] *to* an end [a close]. ▶出発の時間が近づいている The time *is approaching* when [that] we must leave. (❗when は time を先行詞とする関係副詞, that は we must leave at の at を省略または吸収して成立する副詞的関係代名詞) ▶冬休みが近づいてきた The winter vacation *is coming soon* [*is drawing near, is just around the corner*].

ちかづける 近づける 〖〖近くに移動させる〗〗move (持って来る) bring*, (引く) draw*, (置く) put*; ... near [close]; 〖〖近くへ来るのを許す〗〗 allow ... to come near, let*... near. ●目に本を近づけて見る *hold* a book *close to* one's eyes. ▶机にいすをもっと近づけなさい Move [Draw] the chair *nearer to* the desk. ▶子供たちをその場所に近づけるな Don't *allow* the children to *go near* the place./(遠ざけておけ) *Keep* the children *away from* the place. (❗後の方が普通)

ちがった 違った different; (別の) another; (誤った) wrong. (⇨違う, 異なる) ▶カーテンを替えると部屋が違ったように見える The room looks *different* after I've changed the curtains.

ちかてつ 地下鉄 《米》a subway; 《主に英》an [the] underground,《英話》a [the] tube. (❗ロンドンの地下鉄」の意では the U-, the T- と通例大文字で表す); (パリなどの《話》the metro. ●地下鉄の駅 a *subway* station. ●地下鉄で行く take the *subway* (*to* Umeda); go (*to* Umeda) *by subway*.

ちかどう 地下道 (道路横断用の) an underpass,《英》a subway; (地下の通路) an underground passage.

ちかば 近場 ●近場で in the neighborhood (*of*).

ちかみち 近道 图 a shortcut, a short(er) way. ▶この道を行こう. 学校への近道だ Let's go this way. It's a *shortcut* to the school. ▶これが駅までのいちばんの近道です This is *the shortest* [*quickest*] *way* to the station. ▶成功への近道はない There is no *shortcut* 〖王道〗 royal road〗 to success.
―― 近道(を)する 動 take a shortcut (*to*).

ちかめ 近め ●近めの球 an inside [a tight] pitch. ●打者の近めへ投げる pitch a batter inside [tight].

ちかよりがたい 近寄り難い unapproachable; be difficult to approach. ▶私には彼女は近寄りがたい感じがする She seems *unapproachable* to me.

ちかよる 近寄る approach; come* [get*] near. (⇨近付く ❶) ▶建物に近寄るな (=から離れていろ) Stay [Keep] (right) *away from* the building. (❗right を入れる方が強意的)

***ちから** 力

| WORD CHOICE | 力 |

power 権力・能力・影響力・体力・電力など, 各種の力を意味する最も一般的な語. ●権力闘争 the *power* struggle.
force 実際に相手を攻撃したり, 相手に働きかけたりする強い力. 軍事力・暴力・強制力を意味するほか, 自然界の物理力をさす場合もある. ●経済制裁の力 the *force* of economic sanctions.
energy 実際の仕事などに費やされることになる潜在的な精力・活力・行動力. ●町の再建に力を注ぐ devote one's *energies* to rebuild the city.

頻度チャート

power ▇▇▇▇▇▇▇▇▇▇

force ▇▇▇▇▇▇

energy ▇▇▇▇

| | 20 | 40 | 60 | 80 | 100 (%) |

ちからいっぱい

❶ [体力] (physical) strength; power(s); force; energy.
① 【力～】 ●力自慢する boast of one's *strength*; pride oneself on one's *strength*.
② 【力が】 ●力がつく[出る] gain *strength* [*energy*]; become energetic. ●力が尽きる use up all one's *energy*; (疲れ切る) be tired out, be exhausted. ▶彼にはその手術を乗り切るだけの力(=体力)がない He has no *strength* [isn't *strong* enough] *to* survive the operation. ▶その家具を動かすのに大変な力がいった It took a lot of *energy* to move the furniture. ▶彼は彼女を助ける力がなかった He was *powerless* [*unable*, ×*could not*] to help her. ▶彼は私より力が強い He's *stronger* than I am [《話》than me,《古・まれ》than I]. ▶周囲に期待されるほど力が出る The more people expect from me, the more *power* [*strength*] I can exert. (❗strength はものを支えるなど身体・物理的な力の強さ. power はエネルギーや精神・抽象的な力の強さ)
③ 【力の[で]】 ●力のない声で in a *weak* voice. ●あらん限りの力で(=力いっぱい) with all one's *strength* [*might*, *energy*, *force*]. (⇨全力) ●力の及ぶ限りで to the best of one's *abilities* [*ability*]. ▶彼は知恵の足りない分は力で補った What he lacked in wit, he made up for in *energy*. (❗what 節は made up の目的語で,強調のために前に移動されたもの)
④ 【力を】 ●力を出す put out one's *strength*. ●肩の力を抜く relax one's shoulders.

❷ [精神力] strength; power(s); force; [元気] energy. ●意志の力 the *strength* [*force*] of one's will; one's will *power*. ●力のこもった演説 a *forceful* [a *powerful*] speech. ●力が出る cheer up; get encouraged. (⇨元気) ▶最初から失敗して力が抜けてしまった I *was discouraged* by the failure from the first.

❸ [物理的な力] power; force. ●蒸気の力 the *power* of steam. ●自然の力 the *power* of nature; (攻撃的・破壊的な) the *forces* of nature, natural *forces*. ▶この機械は電気の力で動く This machine works [is powered, ×moves] by electricity.

❹ [行動力] power; energy (❗しばしば複数形で); [能力] ability (❗power, energy は実際の行動力, ability は内に備わった性質としての能力を); [努力] (an) effort (❗しばしば複数形で).
① 【～(の)力】 ●読む力 one's reading *ability*; one's *ability* to read 《*...of* reading はまれ》. ●自分の力で by [for] oneself (❗for は「自分のために」を含意する); by [through] one's own *efforts*. (⇨独力, 自力)
② 【力が[は]】 ▶彼は英語の力がめきめきついてきた He has made rapid progress in English./He has rapidly improved his (*ability to*) English./He has been getting more and more proficient in English. ▶私にはその仕事をひとりで仕上げる力がありません I don't have the *power* to finish the work alone./It isn't *in* [《書》*within*] my *power* to finish the work alone. ▶自分の力が足りないことは十分わかっている I am well aware of my lack of *ability*. ▶彼のフランス語の力はすばらしい He has a very good command of French. (❗command は「言葉を自由に操る力」)
③ 【力の】 ●力のある(=有能な)人 an *able* [a *capable*] person. ●力のない人 an *incapable* person. ●力の及ぶ限り努める do one's best; try as hard as possible [one can];《書》make one's utmost efforts. ▶力の限りその仕事をするつもりだ I will do the job *to the best of* my ability [*power*].
④ 【力に】 ▶その仕事は彼の力に及ばない The task *is too much for* him./He *is* not *equal to* (doing [×do]) the task.
⑤ 【力を】 ●力を発揮する show [display] one's *ability*. ●力を注ぐ concentrate one's *energy* [*efforts*]《*on*》. ▶彼らは力を合わせてそれを仕上げた They worked together to finish it. (⇨協力する)

❺ [効力, 威力] power; [影響力] influence, force; [権力] power; (権威) authority.
① 【～の力】 ●世論の力 the *force* of public opinion. ●親の力で through the *influence* of one's parents. ●政府の力で by the *authority* of the government.
② 【力が】 ▶大統領は法案を拒否する力がある The President has the *power* to veto bills.
③ 【力の】 ●力のある政治家 a *powerful* [an *influential*] politician. ●力のない powerless.
④ 【力を】 ●力を持つ have (great) *power* [*influence*]《*over*+人, *in*+場所》. ●力を振るう exercise one's *power* [(影響力) *influence*]《*over*》.

❻ [助力] help;《書》aid; assistance. (⇨助け, 力添え) ●...の力(添え)で with [《まれ》by] the *help* of .... ●力になる help, assist; (支援する) back 《him》up. ●力にする(=力と頼む) rely [depend] 《*on*》.

❼ [強調, 重視] emphasis; stress.

❽ [資力] means. ▶私には車を買う力がない(=余裕がない) I *can't afford to* buy [×*buying*] a car. (❗to buy は省略可)/《やや書》I don't have the *means* to buy a car.

● 力に余る be beyond [out of] one's *power*; be more than one can do. (❗後の方が口語的)
● 力は正義(なり)《ことわざ》Might is [《英》makes] right.
● 力を入れる ▶彼は美術品の収集に大いに力を入れた He *put* a great deal of *effort* into collecting works of art. ▶その学校は実学に特に力を入れている The school *puts* particular *emphasis* [*stress*] *on* practical learning./The school particularly *emphasizes* [*stresses*] practical learning. (❗習慣的行為を表す文脈なので進行形にはしない)
● 力を落とす (落胆する) be discouraged [frustrated].
● 力を貸す help, assist; (支援する) back 《him》up.
● 力を借りる ask 《his》help; ask 《him》for help.
● 人の力を借りずにする do 《it》without *help* (from another); (まったく独力でする) do 《it》all *by oneself*.
● 力をつける (体力を) build up one's *strength*; (能力を) acquire the power 《*to do*, *of doing*》[the ability 《*to do*》].

ちからいっぱい 力一杯 (力の限り) with all one's strength [《書》might]; (一生懸命に) as hard as one can. (⇨全力)

ちからうどん 力うどん *chikaraudon*; (説明的に) a bowl of *udon* noodles with a rice cake in it.

ちからかんけい 力関係 a power balance. ●労使の力関係 the *power balance between* labor and management. ▶裁判の公正も対立勢力の力関係によって左右されることがある Justice in court can be swayed by the *balance between* (two) opposing forces.

ちからくらべ 力比べ a contest of strength. ●力比べをする see who (人) [which (物)] is the stronger [strongest] (❗stronger は2者の場合, strongest は3者以上の場合に用いる); measure one's strength 《*against*》.

ちからこぶ 力こぶ the biceps /báisèps/. [🔲 単·複同形] ・腕を曲げて力こぶを作る bend [flex] one's arm and make *the biceps* stand out.
・**力こぶを入れる** ・高等教育の充実に力こぶを入れる put special emphasis on the development of higher education.

ちからしごと 力仕事 heavy work; 《肉体労働》manual [physical] labor.

ちからずく 力ずく ── 力ずくで 🔲 by force, forcibly. ・力ずくで戸を開ける *force* the door (open). (🔲 (1) open は形容詞で *force* open the door の語順も可. (2) the door は意志のある生物ではないので ˣ*force* the door *to* open は不可) ▶警察は力ずくでデモ行進を阻止した The police checked the demonstration parade *by force* [*forcibly*]./The police *used force* to check the demonstration parade. ・彼は力ずくで(=無理やり)彼女に署名させた He *forced* her *to* sign [*into* sign*ing*] her name. ▶ほかに手段がなければ力ずくでやろう(=力に訴えよう) If there is no other way, we will resort to [*use*] *violence*.

ちからぞえ 力添え 图 《援助》help, 《書》aid. ・妻の力添えで *with the help of* my wife.
── **力添えする** 動 help; 《書》aid; give 《him》a hand. ・彼の事業に力添えする *help* [《書》*aid*] him *in* the enterprise. (🔲 ˣhelp [aid] his enterprise とはいわない)

ちからだめし 力試し 〖体力〗 a test of one's strength; 〖能力〗 a test of one's ability. ・力試しをする try one's *strength*; test one's *ability* 《in》.

ちからづける 力付ける encourage; cheer ... up. (⇒励ます)

ちからづよい 力強い 〖強力な〗powerful, strong; 〖議論などが〗forceful; 〖心強い〗reassuring, encouraging. ・力強い主張 a *powerful* [a *forceful*] argument. ・力強い文体 a *vigorous* style. ・彼の演説の力強さ the *power* [*force*] of his speech. ・力強く思う feel *reassured* 《*to* do; *that* 節》.

ちからなく 力なく 《弱々しく》weakly; 《生命力の弱った》feebly; 《がっかりして》in a low-spirited way. ・力なく笑う smile *weakly* [*sickly*]. (🔲 後の方は「病人の不健康な笑い」を表す)

ちからまかせ 力任せ ・力任せに with all one's strength [《書》might]. (⇒全力)

ちからまけ 力負け ・完全に力負けする completely beaten 《by a strong opponent》.

ちからみず 力水 《力士(ﾘｷｼ)が土俵で口をすすぐ水》〖相撲〗 *chikaramizu*; the water for strength and refreshment.

ちからもち 力持ち a very strong man [woman]; a person of great strength. 〖前の方が口語的〗
・綿の下の力持ち (⇒綿の下 [成句])

ちからわざ 力業 a feat of strength.

ちかん 痴漢 《さわり魔》《米話》a groper; 《変質者》a pervert. ▶私は地下鉄で何度も痴漢にあいました(=体をさわられました) I was felt [《英》touched] up many times on the metro.

ちき 知己 《知人》an acquaintance (⇒知り合い); 《友人》a friend; 《友達》(⇔友達). ・百年の知己を得る find a true *friend* 《*in* him》.

> 翻訳のこころ 馬車の中では、田舎紳士の饒舌が、早くも人々を五年以来の知己にした《横光利一『蠅』》In the horse carriage, the talkative country gentleman soon made the passengers feel as if they had known *each other* for (as long as) five years. (🔲「知己」は know each other (互いに知り合っている)と訳す)

ちき 稚気 childishness. ・稚気のある childish.

ちぎ 遅疑 ・遅疑逡巡する(ためらう) hesitate.

***ちきゅう** 地球 〖惑星としての〗 earth ▶(1) 通例 the ~. (2) 他の惑星と対比して固有名詞的に (the) Earth と書くこともある. また「惑星」を用いて《on》the [this, our] planet ともいう; 〖人間の生活の場としての〗the globe, the world. ・地球にやさしい earth-friendly. ・地球上のすべての人々 the whole *earth* [*world*] 《🔲 単数扱い》; all the people *on the earth* [*in the world*]. ・地球上でいちばん強い男 the strongest man *on earth* [*in the world*]. (🔲 最上級の後で earth は無冠詞) ・全地球的規模の問題 a *global* issue. ▶彼らは月に行って無事地球(=地上)に帰った They went to the moon and returned to (*the*) *earth* [*Earth*] safely. ・我々は船で地球を一周した We sailed around *the globe* [*the world*].
・**地球温暖化** global warming. ・**地球儀** a (terrestrial) globe. ・**地球人** (SF で宇宙人 (alien) に対して) an earthling. ・**地球物理学** geophysics.
・**地球村** the global village.

ちぎょ 稚魚 《ふ化したばかりの魚》fry; 《幼魚》young fish. (🔲 いずれも集合的, 複数扱い) ▶1 万匹のアユの稚魚をその川に放流する stock the river with ten thousand *ayu fry*.

ちきょう 地峡 an isthmus /ísməs/. ・パナマ地峡 the *Isthmus* of Panama.

ちきょうだい 乳兄弟 a foster brother [sister].

ちぎり 契り 《約束》a promise; 《誓い》a pledge; a vow. ・夫婦の契りを結ぶ 《結婚の約束を取り交わす》 exchange marriage *vows*.

ちぎりえ 千切り絵 (a) collage of scraps of colored paper.

ちぎる 千切る 《紙などを引き裂く》tear* /téər/ (⇒裂く); 《パンなどを》break*; 《摘む》pick; 《もぐ》pluck. ・紙を細かくちぎる *tear* a sheet of paper into pieces.

ちぎる 契る ❶〖約束する〗promise; 《誓う》pledge; vow. ❷〖性交する〗have sex 《*with*》.

ちぎれぐも 千切れ雲 《ばらばらの雲》fragments of clouds.

ちぎれる 千切れる 《破れる》tear*, become* torn; 《とれる》come* off. ▶その和紙は容易にちぎれなかった The Japanese paper didn't *tear* easily. ▶耳がさでちぎれるほど痛かった(=ひりひりと痛んだ) My ears *were tingling* with cold.

チキン chicken. ・フライドチキン fried *chicken*.
・**チキンナゲット** a chicken nugget. ・**チキンライス** chicken pilaf(f) seasoned with tomato ketchup; 《和製語》a chicken rice.

ちぎん 地銀 〖「地方銀行」の略〗a local bank.

ちく 地区 〖境界の不明確な〗an area; 〖特定の用途で区別される〗a zone (⇒地帯); 〖特定の人々が住む〗a quarter; 〖行政上の〗a district (⇒地方, 地域); 〖メジャーリーグの 3 つに分かれた〗Division. ・この地区では in this *area* [*district, region*]. ・文教地区 a school *zone*. ・スペイン人地区 a Spanish *quarter*.
・住宅地区 a residential *quarter* [*district*]. ・農業地区 an agricultural *district*. ・地区の野球大会 a *regional* baseball tournament. ・《メジャーリーグの》地区優勝シリーズ the *Division* Series.

ちく- 築- ▶この家は築 5 年だ It is five years since this house was built./This house was built five years ago.

ちくいち 逐一 《何もかも》everything; 《詳細に》in detail. ・逐一報告する report *in detail*.

ちぐう 知遇 ・知遇を得る be well treated 《by the King》; find favor 《of the Emperor》.

ちくご 逐語 ・逐語的に(=1 語ずつ)校正する read the proof *word by word* [ˣword for word].

ちくごやく 逐語訳 (a) word-for-word [a word-by-

ちぐさ 千草 various (kinds of) plants and flowers.

ちくざい 蓄財 图 ●不正蓄財 ill-gotten *wealth* [*gains*].
— **蓄財する** 動 amass [accumulate] wealth.

ちくさつ 畜殺 图 slaughter.
— **畜殺する** 動 slaughter; butcher.
●畜殺業 butchery. ●畜殺場 a slaughterhouse; an abattoir.

ちくさん 畜産 stockbreeding; stock raising [farming]. ●帯広畜産大学 Obihiro University of Agriculture and Veterinary Medicine.
●畜産科. ●畜産(農業高校の) a livestock breeding course. ●畜産物 stock farm products. ●畜産農家 a stock [a livestock] farmer.

ちくじ 逐次 ●それらを逐次(=1つ1つ)調べる examine them *one by one*. ▶その4巻ものの辞書は逐次(=次々と)刊行される The dictionary in four volumes will be published *one after another*.

ちくしゃ 畜舎 a cattle shed; (羊・豚の) a cote; (豚の) a pigsty; 《米》 a pigpen.

ちくしょう 畜生 [獣][(書)a beast, a brute (⇨動物); [ののしり] Damn (it)! (❗ しばしばばかって d—d, d—n と書かれる), Hell!, Fuck it!, (人に向かって) (God) Damn you!, Go to hell!, You bastard!, Son of a bitch!, Fuck you! (❗ ほぼこの順に強い表現になる。人前で使ってはならないとされる禁句)▶「ちくしょう,おれは行かないぞ」と彼は口汚く言った "*Damn* (it), I won't go!" he swore.

ちくじょう 逐条 ●逐条審議する discuss *article by article* [*clause by clause*, *item by item*]. (❗ article, clause は「条項」, item は「項目」の意)

ちくじょう 築城 — 築城する build a castle; (陣地を作る) fortify (a castle *against* the enemy).

ちくせき 蓄積 图 (長期にわたりためた[たまった]もの) (an) accumulation. (❗「蓄積物」は [C]) ●知識の蓄積 the *accumulation* of knowledge.
— **蓄積する** 動 accumulate; (蓄える) store ... (up).

ちくたく ●時計がちくたくいう音 the *ticking* of a clock. (❗ tick で繰り返し音を表す)▶時計がちくたくいっている The clock is *ticking*./The clock is *going tick tock* [*tick tack*].

ちくちく ●(刺すように)ちくちくする[させる] prick, prickle. ▶とげちくちくした Thorns *pricked* (me). ▶この布はちくちくする This cloth *prickles* (my skin)./ This cloth *feels prickly*. (❗「ちくちく」は痛みが少ないとかゆみに近うので itchy (むずがゆい)も使える)

ちくてい 築堤 (築いた堤) an embankment; (堤を築くこと) building an embankment.

ちくでん 蓄電 the storage of electricity.
●蓄電器 a condenser. ●蓄電池 a storage cell, a secondary cell, a storage battery; 《英》 an accumulator.

ちくねん 逐年 year by year; each year; as the years pass.

ちくのうしょう 蓄膿症 [医学] empyema /èmpaií:miə/.

ちくはぐ — **ちぐはぐな** 形 (つじつまの合わない) inconsistent, incoherent; (相容れない) incompatible (*with*). ●ちぐはぐである (調和してない) do not match [go well] (*with*). ▶この赤いかばんはスーツとはちぐはぐだ This red bag doesn't *match* (*with*) [*go well with*] the suit.

ちくばのとも 竹馬の友 a childhood friend. (⇨幼なじみ)

ちくび 乳首 a nipple; (特に動物の) a teat. ●ほ乳びんの乳首 (米) a nipple, 《英》 a teat.

ちくまがわのスケッチ 『千曲川のスケッチ』 *Chikima River Sketches*. (《参考》島崎藤村の随筆・小品集)

> **古今ことばの系譜『千曲川のスケッチ』**
> 毎年十一月の二十日前後には初雪を見る。ある朝わたしは小諸の住まいで目がさめると、思いがけない大雪が来ていた。（略）赤い毛布で頭を包んだわらじばきの小学生徒の群れ、町屋の軒下にしょんぼりとたたずむ鶏、それから停車場のほとりに貨物を満載した車の上にまで雪の積もったさまなぞを見ると、降った、降った、とそう思う。
> Every year around the twentieth of November, they had the first snow in this district. One morning, I woke up in my house in Komoro and found an unexpectedly heavy snowfall. ... I saw groups of children in straw sandals, going to school, head wrapped in a large red muffler. Roosters were sitting lonely under the houses, and fully-loaded goods wagons, near the station, had got covered with snow. I said to myself, "Good heavens! What a great fall of snow!" (❗ (1)「毛布」は blanket では奇異なので、大きいマフラーとして訳した。(2)「降った、降った」のような感嘆の言葉は直訳せず、そのような場合に言いそうな表現にする。ここでは「おやおや」として訳した）

ちくり ●ちくりと刺す prick; (虫・植物が) sting. (❗「蚊が刺す」は bite) ▶私は針で指をちくりと刺した I *pricked* my finger with a needle. ▶虫がちくりと刺した The bug *stung* me. ▶彼の言葉が私の良心にちくりときた His words *pricked* my conscience. ▶彼女は時々彼にちくりといや味を言う She sometimes says something *sarcastic* [*spiteful*, *catty*] to him.

チグリス ●チグリス川 the Tigris /táigris/.

ちくりん 竹林 a bamboo grove. (⇨竹 [竹やぶ])

ちくる (告げ口する)《話》squeal, rat (*on*); tell ... (*on*). ●おれのことをちくったな You *squealed* [*ratted*] *on* me!

チクロ [化学] cyclamate /sáikləmèit/.

ちくわ 竹輪 a *chikuwa*; (説明的に) a hollow tube-like fish cake, boiled and mostly broiled.

ちくわぶ 竹輪麩 a *chikuwabu*; (説明的に) a tube-shaped cake of flour and fish paste.

ちけい 地形 [地表などの形状] a configuration; [一地方の地勢] topógraphy; [自然の地形] natural features. ●地形学 topography. ●地形図 a topográphical map.

チケット [切符, 券] a ticket.
●チケットショップ (説明的に) a discount shop which sells train or airline tickets, gift certificates, book coupons and so on; 《和製語》 a ticket shop. (❗ a ticket agency はプレイガイドに相当)

ちけん 治験 a clinical trial; a clinical practice.
ちけん 知見 knowledge. (⇨知識)
ちけんしゃ 地権者 the rightful owner of the land.
ちこう 遅効 slow effect.
●遅効性肥料 (a) slow-acting fertilizer.

*****ちこく** 遅刻 图 lateness (*to*), 《主に米》 tardiness. ●遅刻者を調べる check (off) the latecomers [those who have come late].
— **遅刻する** 動 be late [《主に米》 be tardy] (*for*, *to*). (↔be punctual) ●学校[授業, 会社; 1時間目]に(30分)遅刻する be (thirty minutes) *late for* school [class; the office; the first period]. (❗ for の代わりに to も可。ただし「遅刻して来る」は come late to [×for]...) ▶遅刻！学校初日の最初の授業に

遅刻するとはどういうことですか(先生が遅れてきた生徒に対して) Tardiness! What's the idea of *being late for* your first class on your first day of school? ▶3回遅刻すると欠席1回の扱いになります If you *are late* three times, you'll be counted absent once.
【会話】「8時だよ」「ええっ! 遅刻だ」"It's eight o'clock." "Heavens! I'm *late*."
● 遅刻届 a late slip [note]; (主に米) a tardy [(入室許可証)] an admit] slip【事情】米国の高校では遅刻者は学校に届け出てこれを受け取らないと授業を受けられないという方式をとっていることが多い.

ちこつ 恥骨【医学】the pubis; the public bone.
チコリ【植物】chicory.
ちさん 治山 afforestation.
ちし 地誌 a topography. ● 地誌学 topography.
ちし 致死 ── 致死の形 lethal /líːθəl/, fatal.
● 致死量 a lethal dose /dóus/. (*of*)《略 LD》.
ちじ 知事 a (prefectural) governor. ● 佐賀県知事 the *governor* of Saga Prefecture. ● 知事選に出馬する enter the race for *governor*.【!】役職を示すときは無冠詞)

:**ちしき** 知識 (学習・経験による) knowledge; (他から与えられる) information《いずれも数えるときは a piece of ~》; (体験による)《やや書》(an) acquaintance【!】通例myかなな知識をいう; (学び得た学識) learning; (専門的技術)《話》know-how.
①【~知識】▶ 基礎知識 (a) basic *knowledge*. ● 予備知識 (a) preliminary [(a) background] *knowledge*. ● 専門知識 expertise. ● 豆知識 a small piece of *knowledge*. ● 深い[浅い]知識 (a) profound [superficial] *knowledge*. ● 広い知識 (an) extensive *knowledge*. ● 限られた知識 (a) limited *knowledge*. ● 完全な知識 (a) thorough *knowledge*. ● (インターネット上で得られるような)うわべだけの知識 superficial *knowledge*.

DISCOURSE
本で学んだ知識よりも直接体験の方が影響が大きいと思う I would say firsthand experience has a greater *influence* on us than knowledge (learned) from books.【!】I would say ... + 比較級 (...の方がより...と思う)は二者択一を表すディスコースマーカー. I think ...よりも丁寧で, 論説文に適している)

②【知識～】▶彼は知識欲が旺盛(毒)だ He is very thirsty for *knowledge*./He has a great thirst for *knowledge*.
③【知識が[は]】▶彼は法律についてかなりの[十分な]知識がある He *has* a good *knowledge of* law.【!】通例 of の句を従えると a を伴うことができるが, 複数形にはならない)/He *knows* law well./He *knows* quite a lot *about* law./He is very *knowledgeable about* law. ● 私は物理の知識がまったくない I *have* no *knowledge of* physics./I *know* nothing of physics./(まったく無知だ) I *am* totally *ignorant of* [*about*] physics. ● 彼のドイツ語に関する知識はたいしたことはない His *knowledge of* German is rather poor.【!】His *knowledge about* German .... とすると間接的な知識を表し, 運用能力より文法知識などを問題にする)
④【知識を】● 知識を得る get [gain, acquire] *knowledge*《*from* a book》. ● 知識を吸収する absorb *knowledge*. ● 英語の知識を向上させる[生かす; ひけらかす] improve [use; show off] one's *knowledge of* English. ● この本は英国についての役に立つ知識を与えてくれる This book gives us useful (pieces of) *information* [×useful information] *about* [*on*, ×*of*] Britain.【!】about は一般的情報, on は専門的情報を暗示)
● 知識階級 the educated class [classes]; the intelligentsia.【!】ともに単・複両形扱い) ● 知識人 an intellectual; (学のある) a person of knowledge [learning]; (教養豊かな) a (highly) cultured person, an educated [a well-educated] person.

ちじく 地軸 the earth's axis.
ちしつ 地質 (土質) the nature of the soil; (ある地域の) the geology《*of*》.
● 地質学 geology. (⇒地学) ● 地質学者 a geologist. ● 地質図 a geological map. ● 地質調査 a geological survey.
ちしつ 知悉 ── 知悉する 動 (知り尽くす) know everything《*about*》; have a thorough knowledge《*of*》; (詳しく知る) be familiar《*with*》.
ちしま 千島 ● 千島列島 the Kúril(e) Islands; the Kuril(e)s.
ちしゃ 知者 a wise man; a man of great wisdom; a sage.
ちしゃ 萵苣【植物】(a) lettuce.
ちしょう 知将 a resourceful general; a shrewd /ʃrúːd/ general.
*:**ちじょう** 地上 名 【地面】 the ground; 【地表】 the earth's surface.《⇔ 地下》● 地上200メートルの所に at 200 meters *above*《⇔*below*》*ground*. ● 地上10階地下2階のビル a building with ten stories *above ground* and two below. ▶多数の死体が地上に横たわっていた There were a lot of (dead) bodies lying *on the ground*. ▶傷ついた鳥は地上に落ちた The injured bird fell *to* [×*on*] *the ground*. ▶セミは地上に出るまでの数年間を土の中で過ごす Cicadas spend several years below the ground before they *come out*.
── 地上の形 (この世の) earthly; (地上の) surface.
● 地上の楽園 an *earthly* paradise; a paradise *on* [×*of*] *earth*.
● 地上管制 ground control. ● 地上権 surface rights. ● 地上整備員 (空港の) a ground crew.《集合的. 単・複両形扱い) ● 地上戦 land fighting. ● 地上デジタル放送 digital terrestrial broadcasting. ● 地上波 a terrestrial (broadcast) signal.
ちじょう 痴情 blind love; a foolish passion; (のぼせ上がり) an infatuation《*with*, *for*》. ▶彼女は若い男との痴情におぼれていた She *was* infatuated *with* a young man.
ちじょうい 知情意 intellect, emotion, and volition.
ちじょく 恥辱 (a) humiliation. (⇒屈辱)
ちじん 知人 an acquaintance. (⇒知り合い)
ちじん 痴人 a fool; an idiot. (⇒馬鹿)
*:**ちず** 地図 a map; (航海・航空の) a chart; (地図帳) an atlas.
①【~(の)地図】● 世界地図 a *map* of the world; a world *map*. ● 旅行地図 a touring [a tourist] map. ● 東京の市街[道路]地図 a city [a road] *map* of Tokyo. ● 5万分の1の地図 A *map* on [drawn to] a scale of 1:50,000.【!】one to fifty thousand と読む) ▶地下鉄の地図はたいていのホテルでもらえる You can get subway *maps* from most hotels.
②【地図の[を]】● 地図を開く (たたんである地図を) unfold a *map*; (巻いてある地図を) unroll a *map*; (書籍型の地図を) open an atlas. ● 地図を見る(=地図でその場所を探す)《⇒見》 ● 地図をたよりに with the help of a *map*. ● 地図を片手にその町を歩く walk around the town with a *map*. ● その場所を地図の上に載せる put the place on a *map*. ▶彼女は私にこ

ちすい のあたりの地図をかいてくれた She drew [xwrote] a *map* of the area for me. ▶彼は地図の見方が上手だ He is good at reading *maps*. (❗この read は「読み取る」の意)/He is a good *map*-reader.
③《地図で[に]》 ●地図でその場所を捜す look up the place on [xin] a *map*; (見つけるために地図を調べる) look at [《やや書》consult] a *map* to find the place. ▶その小さな町はこの地図に出ていない The little town is not (shown [marked]) on this *map*.

ちすい 治水 (洪水調節) flood /flʌd/ control.
● 治水事業 a flood control project.

ちすじ 血筋 blood, stock, descent, 《書》lineage. (⇨家柄, 血❷) ●日本人の血筋を引くアメリカ人 (日系米人) an American of Japanese *descent*; a Japanese American. ▶前の方が正式な言い方》a line of musicians./He comes from a (good) musical *stock*./(音楽は血の血脈だ) Music is in his *blood*. ▶彼は貴族の血筋を引いている He comes from an aristocratic *stock*./He is a man of aristocratic *stock*.
● 血筋は争えない 《ことわざ》Blood will tell./《ことわざ》Like father, like son.

ちせい 地勢 geographical features; (地形) topógraphy.

ちせい 治世 a reign. (⇨代(ﾀﾞｲ) ❶)

ちせい 知性 图 (感情・意志に対して) íntellect; (知能) intélligence; (良識) sense. ●知性に訴える appeal to one's *intellect*. ●知性に欠ける lack *intelligence*. ●知性の向上する one's *mind* grows.
── 知性的な 形 (⇨知的) ●知性的な人 an in-téllectual [an íntelligent] person; a person of *intellect* [*intelligence*].

ちせいがく 地政学 图 geopolitics. ── 地政学の 形 geopolític(al).

ちせき 地籍 a land register.

ちせき 治績 《great》achievements in administration.

ちせつ 稚拙 ── 稚拙な 形 (未熟な) poor. ●稚拙な作品 a *poor* work.

ちそう 地相 the physiognomy (of land).

ちそう 地層 a stratum /stréitəm/; (覆) strata; a layer. ● 地層学 stratigraphy. ● 地層学者 a stratígrapher.

ちぞめ 血染め ── 血染めの 形 bloodstained (shirts).

チター 【楽器】a zither /zíðər/.

ちたい 地帯 (環状の) a zone (❗特定の目的・用途・特徴によって区分された区域); (細長い) a belt; 《ある区域》an area; [地方] a region. ●[地方, 地域] 安全[危険]地帯 a safety [a danger] *zone*. ●占領[非武装]地帯 an occupation [a demilitarized] *zone*. ●砂漠[森林]地帯 a desert [a forest] *area* [*region*]. ●工業地帯 an industrial *region* [*belt*]. ●戦争地帯 a war *zone*.

ちたい 遅滞 (a) delay; (支払いなどの) arrears. (❗通例複数形で) ●遅滞なく without delay; (ただちに) immediately.
── 遅滞する 動 delay; be overdue; be in arrears 《*with* the rent》.

ちたい 痴態 (a) foolery; foolish conduct; silly behavior. ●痴態を演じる make a fool of oneself; behave foolishly; 《英話》act [play] the goat.

ちだい 地代 (⇨地代(ﾁﾀﾞｲ)).

ちだるま 血だるま ●血だるまになった covered (all over) with blood. (⇨血まみれ).

チタン 【化学】titanium /taitéiniəm/《元素記号 Ti》.
● チタンの titánous.
● チタン合金 a titanous alloy.

ちち 父 ❶ [男親] a father; (父であること) fatherhood. (⇨お父さん) ●妻の父 one's wife's *father*. ●義父 a father-in-law. (⇨義父) ●父の愛 paternal love. ●父(親)らしい fatherly. ●父(親)のない子供 a fatherless child. ●父親としての責任を果たす fulfill the responsibilities of *fatherhood*. ▶スミス氏はジャック[花嫁]の父親だ Mr. Smith is Jack's *father* [the *father* of the bride]. ▶ ×the *father* of Jack とはいわない》私にはよい父親だった He was a good *father* to me. ▶彼は太郎には父親のような人だった He was like a *father* [a *father* figure] to Taro. ▶この父にしてこの子あり《ことわざ》Like *father*, like son.
❷ [開祖] the father. ●アメリカ建国の父たち the founding *fathers* of America. ▶メンデルは遺伝学の父だ Mendel is the *father* of genetics.
● 父の日 Father's Day. ●日米英では6月の第3日曜日、オーストラリア・ニュージーランドは9月の第1日曜日》

ちち 乳 [乳汁] milk; (母乳) mother's milk; (牛乳) cow's milk; [乳房の一方] a breast. ●赤ちゃんに乳を与える (=授乳する) breast-feed one's baby. ●単に *feed* one's baby ともいう》●牛の乳をしぼる *milk* a cow. ▶赤ん坊が母の乳を吸っている The baby is sucking its mother's *milk* [*breast*]. ▶この牛は乳があまり出ない[出なくなった] This cow doesn't *milk* very well [has stopped *giving milk*]./The cow is *running* [has *run*] *dry*. (❗The cow is *going* [has *gone*] *dry* ともいう》
● 乳しぼり milking action. ● 乳しぼり機 a milking machine; a milker.

ちち 遅々 ▶彼の英語は遅々として進歩しない He is making *hardly any* [*almost no*, (*very*) *little*] progress in English./His progress in English is *discouragingly* slow.

ちぢ 千千 various; different. (⇨様々, 色々)

ちちうえ 父上 a father. (⇨父)

ちちかた 父方 one's father's [《やや書》paternal] side. ●父方の祖母 one's grandmother *on* one's *father's side*; one's *paternal* grandmother.

ちぢかむ 縮かむ (自由に動かなくなる) get* stiff; (感覚がなくなる) go numb. ▶寒くて手が縮かんでいる My hands *are numb* with cold.

ちちくさい 乳臭い (幼稚な) childish; (未熟な) green, immature, 《話》 (still) wet behind the ears; 《書》callow. ▶乳臭い赤ちゃん a baby *smelling* of milk. ▶あいつははたち過ぎてもまだ乳臭い(=幼稚だ) He's over twenty and still too *childish*.

ちちくる 乳繰る flirt in secret.

ちぢこまる 縮こまる (寒さ・恐怖で) huddle (up together). (❗主語は複数形) ▶子犬たちは部屋の片隅で縮こまっていた The puppies *huddled up* in a corner of the room.

ちちばなれ 乳離れ (離乳する) be weaned; (自立する) be independent. ▶彼はまだ乳離れできないでいる He is not yet *independent* (of his parents).

ちぢまる 縮まる (縮む) shrink*; (短くなる) be shortened; (せばまる) narrow, be narrowed. (⇨縮む) ▶その政策で貧富の差が縮まるだろう The policy will help *narrow* [*reduce*] the gap between (the) rich and (the) poor. ●対句の場合は無冠詞が普通》●トップのランナーと2位との差はみるみる縮まってきた The second runner *is gaining* rapidly *on* the leader.

ちぢみあがる 縮み上がる [[恐怖・寒さなどで身を縮める]]

shrink*, cower /káuər/; 〖おびえさせる〗scare. ●恐怖で縮み上がる *shrink* [*cower*] in fear. ●強盗に縮み上がって後ずさりする *shrink* [*cower*] *away* from a robber. ▶不気味な音を聞いて彼女は縮み上がった The weird noise *scared* [*frightened*] her stiff./She *was scared* [*was frightened*] *stiff* by the weird noise. (❗stiff は強意語. ほかに to death なども用いられる)

ちぢむ 縮む (布などが) shrink; (筋肉・金属・ゴムなどが) contract; 〖短くなる〗be shortened. ▶ウールはお湯で洗うと縮む Wool *shrinks* when washed in hot water. ▶この金属は冷えても縮まない This metal won't *contract* in cooling. ▶仕事の無理がたたって彼の寿命は 20 年も縮んだ His life *was shortened* by 20 years through the strain of hard work. ▶恥ずかしくて身の縮む思いがした I was so embarrassed that I wished I could disappear.

ちぢめる 縮める 〖長さ・時間を〗(短くする) shorten, (切り上げる) cut... short (今短縮する); 〖話などを〗condense. ●命を縮める *shorten* one's life. ●滞在を 2 日縮める *cut short* one's stay by two days. ●そのドレスを縮める *take in* the dress. (❗take in は「服などを小さくする」の意)

ちちゅう 地中 ●地中の[に] underground. ●それを地中に埋める bury it *in the earth* [*ground*]; bury it *underground*.
●地中寒暖計 an underground thermometer.

ちちゅうかい 地中海 the Mèditerrànean (Sea).

ちぢれげ 縮れ毛 curly (frizzy, crisp] hair. (❗curly は渦巻き状の, frizzy は細かく縮れた, crisp はきちんとカールした)

ちぢれる 縮れる curl (... up). ▶葉が霜で縮れた The frost made the leaves *curl* (*up*)./The frost *curled* the leaves (*up*). ▶彼女は縮れた髪をしている She has *curly* [*frizzy*] hair.

ちつ 帙 a folding case (for a book).

ちつ 膣 〖解剖〗the vagina /vədʒáinə/ (複 ~s, vaginae /-niː/). ●膣の vaginal.
●膣炎 〖医学〗vaginitis /vædʒənáitis/.

チック(しょう) チック(症) 〖医学〗a tic. ▶私は緊張するとチックがでます I develop a tic when I feel nervous.

ちっこう 築港 图 harbor construction.
── 築港する 動 construct a harbor.
●築港工事 harbor construction work.

ちつじょ 秩序 order; (集団の規律) discipline.
① 【～秩序】 ●社会秩序 public [social] *order*. ●法と秩序 law and *order*. (❗通例単数扱い. ×order and law の語順は不可)
② 【秩序～】 ●秩序立った orderly; (組織的な) systematic. ●秩序正しいデモ隊 *orderly* demonstrators. ●秩序正しく行進する march *in an orderly manner* [*in good order*]. ▶彼らは常に何事も秩序立てて行う They always do everything *systematically*./They are always *systematic* about everything.
③ 【秩序が】 ●軍隊の秩序が乱れていた *Discipline* was lost in the army./(規律を欠いていた) The army was lacking in *discipline*.
④ 【秩序を】 ●秩序を確立[回復]する establish [restore] *order*. ●町の秩序を保つ (統治者が命じて) keep [preserve, maintain] *order* in the town; (被治者が) keep good *order* in the town. ●秩序を乱す disturb *order*.

ちっそ 窒素 nitrogen /náitrədʒən/ (元素記号 N). ●二酸化窒素 nitrogen dióxide /daióksaid/.
●窒素酸化物 nìtrogen óxide. ●窒素肥料 (a) nitrogenous fertilizer.

ちっそく 窒息 图 (酸素不足での) suffocation; (首を絞めたり呼吸器官をふさいでの) (a) choke. ●窒息死する die of [be killed by] *suffocation*; suffocate; *choke* to death. ●まくらで赤ん坊を窒息死させる *suffocate* a baby with a pillow. ▶もちがつまってもう少しで窒息死するところだった I nearly *choked to death* on a rice cake.
── 窒息する[させる] 動 súffocàte; choke; (新鮮な空気がなくて) stifle. ▶煙にまかれてもう少しで窒息するところだった I *was* almost *suffocated* [*choked*, *stifled*] *by* the smoke. (❗choke が最も口語的)/I *was suffocating* in the smoke. (❗進行形に注意)

ちっちゃい[な] (小さい) small; (非常に小さい) tiny.
●ちっちゃい[な] *a small* [*little*, *tiny*] house.
●赤ん坊のちっちゃい[な]指 *tiny* fingers of a baby.

ちつづき 血続き blood relationship. (⇨血縁)

ちっとも 【少しも...でない】not (...) at all, not (...) in the least, (話) not (...) a bit; 【決して...しない】 never; 【何も...ない】 nothing. (⇨一向(に)) ▶私はちっとも驚かなかった I wasn't surprised *at all* [*in the least*]. ▶あーあ, 芝生はちっとも刈り終わらないよ Oh, I'll *never* finish mowing the lawn.
会話 「おなかはすいてない?」「いいえ, ちっとも」"Aren't you hungry?" "No, *not at all* [*not in the least*, (話) *not a bit*]."
会話 「あらおかしい! また間違っちゃった」「そんなのちっとも自慢することじゃないわよ」"How funny! I've got it wrong again." "It's *nothing* to be proud of."
会話 「それ, まだお借りしたままですみません」「ちっとも(=まったく)かまいませんよ. 特に急いでいるわけではないですから」"Sorry I haven't returned it." "That's *quite* all right. I'm in no particular hurry for it."

チップ 〖コンピュータの〗a chip. ●マイクロチップ a microchip.

チップ ❶ 〖野球〗a foul tip. ●ボールをファウルチップする *tip* the ball (for a) foul; foul-tip the ball.
❷ 〖心付け〗a tip. ●チップをはずむ tip 〈him〉 generously; give 〈him〉 a generous [a large] *tip*. ▶運転手に 50 ペンスのチップを渡した I *tipped* the taxi driver 50 pence. ▶(これ)チップです Here's your *tip*.

チップイン 〖ゴルフ〗 a chip in.

チップショット 〖ゴルフ〗a chip (shot).

ちっぽけ ── ちっぽけな 形 very small; tiny, (話) teeny.

ちてい 地底 the bowels of the earth.

ちてき 知的 ── 知的な 形 (生まれつき知能のある) intelligent; (知力と錬磨した) intellectual. ●知的な(=知能指数の高い)子 an *intelligent* [×an intellectual] child. (❗通例小児については intellectual は用いられない) ●知的障害の子 a mentally retarded child. (⇨知恵[知恵遅れの子]) ●知的生活を楽しむ enjoy the *intellectual* life. (❗intellectual life は「知能のある生物」の意) ●あの人は知的だ He [She] is an *intellectual* man [woman]./He [She] is a person *of intellect*. ▶彼女の目はとても知的に輝いていた Her eyes were bright and very *intelligent*. (❗×brightly intelligent とはいわない)/(知性を感じさせる輝いた目をしていた) She had bright eyes with a look of great *intelligence* in them.
●知的好奇心 intellectual curiosity. ●知的障害 a mental disability; (軽蔑的) mental retardation. ●知的障害者 a mentally handicapped [retarded] person. (❗今では a person who has learning difficulties などという方が普通) ●知的所有[財産]権 intellectual property rights. (参考) これを保護するための国連の専門機関が World Intellectual Property Organization (世界知的所有

ちてん 地点 〖特定の〗a spot; 〖1点〗a point. ● 出発地点 the stárting *point*. ● 交通に便利な地点 a convenient *spot* 〔場所〕*place*〕for public transportation. ▶この地点で道路は北へ向かう At this *point* the road turns north. ▶ここはあの事故のあった地点です This is the *spot*〔現場〕*scene*〕of the accident. / The accident happened [occurred, xtook place] at this *point* 〔*place*〕.

ちどうせつ 地動説 the heliocéntric 〔Copérnican〕system.

ちとせ 千歳 〖千年〗a thousand years; 〖永遠〗etérnity.

ちとせあめ 千歳飴 *chitoseame*; (説明的に) a long stick of red-and-white candy to celebrate the *shichigosan* festival. (⇨七五三)

ちどめ 血止め (⇨止血)

ちどり 千鳥 a plover /plʌ́vər/. ● 千鳥格子模様のジャケット a *hound's-tooth* check jacket.

ちどりあし 千鳥足 ▶通りを千鳥足で歩く *stagger* [*reel*] (*drunkenly*) along the street.

ちどん 遅鈍 slow and stupid.

ちなまぐさい 血なまぐさい bloody, 〘書〙gory. ● 血なまぐさい戦い a *bloody* battle.

ちなみに 因みに 〔ついでながら〕by the way, incidentally; 〖これに関連して〗〘書〙in this connection. ▶あれはなかなかいい本ですよ。ちなみに値段は1,000円です The book is really good. *By the way*, it's 1,000 yen.

ちなむ 因む be associated 〔*with*〕. ● 未(ぴつじ)年にちなんだ絵 a picture *associated with* the year of the Ram. ▶彼はおじの名にちなんで一郎と名づけられた He was named Ichiro *after* 〔〘主に米〙*for*〕his uncle.

ちにちか 知日家 an expert on Japan; a Japanólogist. ▶彼は知日家ではあるが親日家ではない He is well-informed about Japan but not pro-Japanese.

ちぬき 血抜き —— 血抜きする 動 〘料理〙let blood out from the liver of (a cow, a pig) by dipping in water before cooking.

ちぬる 血塗る (刀剣に血を塗る) smear a sword with blood.

ちねつ 地熱 图 the heat of the earth's interior. —— 地熱の 形 geothérmal. ● 地熱発電 geothermal power generation. ● 地熱発電所 geothermal power station.

ちのあめ 血の雨 (shed) a great deal of blood.

ちのう 知能 intelligence, 〘知力〙intellect, 〘知的能力〙the mental [intellectual] faculties.

> 使い分け **intelligence** 「理解の早さ, 賢さ」などを意味し, 教育とは関係のない生得的能力をさす. **intellect** 「理解力, 思考力」など教育や訓練によって養われるものをいう. 従って「知能」に近いのは intelligence.

● 知能の高い子 a child of high *intelligence*; an *intelligent* child. (❗通例 ×an *intellectual* child とはいわない) ● 彼より知能が優れている be superior to him in *intelligence*; have a higher *IQ* than him. ● 知能を発達させる develop *the mental faculties* [*the intellect*]. ● 知能の遅れた子供たちの世話をする look after (*mentally*) *retarded* children. (⇨知恵〔知恵遅れの子〕) ▶彼は年齢の割に知能が高い He is *intelligent* for his age./He has [shows] high *intelligence* [a high IQ] for his age.

● 知能検査 (give) an intelligence [an IQ] test. ● 知能指数 (⇨知能指数) ● 知能犯 (事) a clever crime; (人) a clever criminal.

ちのうしすう 知能指数 an intelligence quotient 〘略 IQ〙. (戀 感情指数) ● 知能指数130 an *IQ* of 130. ● 知能指数が高い [低い] have a high [low] *IQ*.

ちのうみ 血の海 a sea of blood. (⇨血)

ちのけ 血の気 ● 血の気のある男 a *hot-blooded* [a *hot-tempered*] man. ● 血の気のない顔 a *colorless* (青ざめた) a *pale* face. ▶彼の顔から血の気が引いた He turned [went] pale [white] (*at* the news, *with* fear)./The *color* [*blood*] drained from his face.

チノパン chinos.

ちのみご 乳飲み子 (赤ん坊) a baby.

ちのり 地の利 ● 地の利を得ている be conveniently located [situated]; be in a good location [situation]. ▶病院を建てる場合にはまず地の利(=地勢上の利点)を考慮するべきだ First of all, we should think of the *geographical advantage* when we build a hospital.

ちのり 血糊 gore; a blood clot. ● 血のりのついたシャツ a *bloodstained* shirt.

ちはい 遅配 (a) delay 〔*in*〕. ● 郵便の遅配 a *delay in* postal delivery. ▶給料は10日遅配になった The payment of wages *was delayed* by ten days. / There was a ten-day *delay in* the payment of wages.

ちばしる 血走る get* 〔(血走っている) be〕bloodshot. ● 血走った目 *bloodshot* eyes.

ちばなれ 乳離れ (⇨乳離れ)

ちばらい 遅払い delayed payment 〔*of*〕.

ちばん 地番 a lot number.

ちび (小さい人) a small (背の低い) a short person. ● うちのちび our *little one* [*boy, girl*]; our little *kid*. (⇨ちび子)

ちびちび little by little, bit by bit; (惜しむように) sparingly. ● ちびちび金を貯める save money *little by little* [*bit by bit*]. ▶彼はブランデーをちびちびのむのが好きです He likes *sipping* (at) [(大事に時間をかけて) *nursing*] brandy. ▶ネズミはチーズをちびちびかじる Mice *nibble at* the cheese.

ちびつ 遅筆 ● 遅筆である be a slow writer. (戀 速筆)

ちびっこ ちびっ子 (子供) a little kid, a tiny tot; (かわいい女の子) a moppet; (わるがき) a brat.

ちひょう 地表 the earth's surface; the surface of the earth.

ちびりちびり (⇨ちびちび)

ちびる 小便 [大便] をちびる wet [soil] one's pants.

ちびる 禿びる ● ちびた(=使い古してすり減った)靴 *worn-out* shoes. ● ちびた(=短くなった)鉛筆 a *stubby* pencil. ▶この鉛筆は先がちびている This pencil is *blunt* [*dull*].

ちぶ 恥部 〘陰部〙the private parts, 〘話〙the privates; 〘醜い部分〙(恥ずべき源) a source of embarrassment 〔*for*〕; (けがすもの) a disgrace 〔*to*〕.

ちぶさ 乳房 one's breast(s). (❗通例複数形) ● 乳房の小さい女性 a woman with small *breasts*; a small-*breasted* woman. ▶彼女の小さく高い乳房が好きだ I like her small high *breasts*.

チフス 〘医学〙(腸チフス) typhoid /táifoid/ (fever); (発疹チフス) typhus /táifəs/ (fever); (パラチフス) pàratýphoid (fever).

ちへい 地平 〘大地の平面〙the surface of the earth; 〘地平線〙the horizon.

ちへいせん 地平線 the horizon. (⇨水平線)

チベット 〖中国の自治区〗 Tibet. ●チベット人 a Tibétan. ●チベット語 Tibetan. ●チベット(人[語])の Tibetan.

ちへど 血反吐 ●血へどを吐く vomit [spit] *blood*.

ちば 地歩 (足掛かり) (a) footing, a foothold. ●地歩を築く get [gain] a *footing* [a *foothold*] 《*in the business world*》. ●…としての地歩を固める(=確立する) establish oneself as …. (⇨足場 ❷)

:ちほう 地方 ❶ 〖広い地域〗 a region, a district, an area; 〖部分〗 a part.

> 〖使い分け〗 **region** 地理的・社会的・文化的にまわりの部分からさめられる特徴を持つ地方.
> **district** 行政区分された, ある特色や機能を有する地方.
> **area** 明確な境界のない地方. 広い範囲も狭い範囲も表す.
> **part** 国や一地方の中の一部分の意. 複数形で用いることも多い.

●山岳地方(=地帯) a mountainous *region* [*district*]. ●その国の南部地方 the southern *region* [*part*] of the country. ●沿岸地方(=地域) the coastal *areas* [*regions*]. ▶東北地方の冬は大変厳しい Winter in the Tohoku *district* [*region*, *area*] is very severe. ▶この地方は雨が多い It rains a great deal in this *region* [*district*, *part* of the country]. ▶祭りは地方によって異なる Festivals vary from *region* to *region*.
❷ 〖中央に対して〗(田園地帯) the country; (大都市から離れた田舎) the provinces. ●地方に住む live in *the country* [*the provinces*].
── **地方** 形 〖広い地域の〗(ある1地方に関係のある) local (❗ local は「田舎の」の意はない); (特定地域の) regional (❗ local より広い範囲をさす); 〖中央に対する〗(田園地帯の) country; (田舎の) provincial. ●地方の町 a *country* town. ●地方のなまり a *local* accent. ●地方の習慣を守る a *local* [*regional*] custom. ●地方独特の風習 *provincial* customs.
●地方記事 local news. ●地方行政 local administration. ●地方競馬 horse racing conducted by local government. ●地方検察庁 a district public prosecutors office. ●地方公共団体[自治体] a local public body [government] (❗ 単・複両扱い) ●地方公務員 a local government employee [worker, official]. ●地方裁判所 a district court. ●地方紙 a local newspaper. ●地方自治体 a local government. ●地方税 local color. ●地方税 local [〖英〗 council] taxes. ●地方選挙 a local election. ●地方大学 a regional university. ●地方版 a local edition. ●地方分権 decentralization.

ちほう 痴呆 ●痴呆が出る go senile /sí:nail/. ●痴呆症 〖『認知症』の旧称〗〖医学〗 dementia /dimén∫ə/. ●老人性痴呆症 〖医学〗 senile dementia. 〖参考〗 アルツハイマー病 (Alzheimer's disease) はその一つ)

ちぼう 知謀 (⇨はかりごと)

ちまき 粽 *chimaki*; (説明的に) a steamed rice cake wrapped in a bamboo leaf, traditionally eaten on Children's Day (May 5th).

ちまた 巷 ●巷の声を聞く pay attention to *public* opinion. ●巷のうわさでは… People say 《that》…; It is *rumored* 《that》…. ●歓楽の巷 gay *quarters*. ●戦乱の巷 a battle *field*.

ちまつり 血祭り ●敵を血祭りにあげる (流血の戦いをして負かす) defeat the enemy in bloodshed [a blood-bath]; (殴ったりけったりしてひどい目にあわせる) beat up the enemy viciously.

ちまなこ 血眼 ●血眼になって(必死になって) frantically. ▶彼らは彼女の子供をそこらじゅう血眼になって捜した They looked everywhere for her child *frantically*.

ちまみれ 血まみれ ── **血まみれの** 形 (血痕(ﾁ)の付いた) bloodstained; (血だらけの) bloody. ●血まみれのワイシャツ a *bloodstained* [a *bloody*] shirt. ▶男は血まみれになって倒れていた The man was lying in 《a pool of》 *blood*.

ちまめ 血まめ a blood blister. ●手に血まめができる get *blood blisters* on one's hand.

ちまよう 血迷う (正気を失う[失っている]) go* [be] out of one's mind; (自分を制御できなくなる) lose control of oneself.

ちみ 地味 (the productivity of) the soil. ●地味が肥えている The soil is rich [fertile, productive].

ちみち 血道 ●血道を上げる (異性に) be madly [head over heels] in love 《*with* him [her]》; (道楽などに) be obsessed 《*with* video games》.

ちみつ 緻密 名 〖精密〗 precision; 〖正確〗 accuracy. ── **緻密な** 形 precise; accurate; (綿密な) close; (細心な) minute /main(j)ú:t/; (念入りの) elaborate; (注意深い) careful. ●緻密な観察 a *close* [a *careful*, a *minute*] observation. ●緻密な計画 an *elaborate* plan; (よく考えぬいた) a *carefully thought-out* plan.

ちみどろ 血みどろ ── **血みどろの** 形 (血まみれの) bloody /bládi/. ●血みどろの顔[戦い] a *bloody* face [*battle*].

ちみもうりょう 魑魅魍魎 the evil spirits of mountains, rivers, and forests.

ちめい 地名 a place name, the name of a place. ●地名辞典 a dictionary of place [geographical] names; a geographical dictionary.

ちめいしょう 致命傷 a fatal [a mortal, a deadly] injury; a fatal [a mortal, a deadly] wound. (⇨負傷) ▶彼は事故で致命傷を負った He got a *fatal* [a *mortal*, a *deadly*] *injury* in the accident./He was fatally [mortally, ×deadly] *injured* in the accident./The accident left him *fatally* [*mortally*, ×*deadly*] *injured*. (❗ 結果的に死んだことを含意) ▶彼の失敗は昇進にとって致命傷になった His blunder proved *fatal* [×*mortal*, ×*deadly*] *to* his promotion.

ちめいてき 致命的 ── **致命的な** 形 fatal; mortal. ●致命的な重傷 a *fatal* [a *mortal*] injury; a *fatal* [a *mortal*] wound. ●致命的な失敗をする make a *fatal* [×a mortal] mistake 《*of*, *in*》. ●私は致命的な病気にかかって余命いくばくもない I have a *fatal* disease and I have only a little time to live.

ちめいど 知名度 the degree of name recognition. ●知名度の低い[ない] little known; unknown; obscure. ▶彼は作家として知名度が高い(=よく知られている) He is *famous* [*well-known*] as a writer. ▶ハリー・ポッターシリーズで有名になる前のローリングは知名度がゼロといっていい存在だった Rowling was almost *unknown* before she published the Harry Potter series.

ちもう 恥毛 pubic hair. (⇨陰毛)
ちもく 地目 the classification of land (category).

*ちゃ 茶 ❶ 〖飲料〗 (a) tea. (❗ (1) 種類をいうときは ©. (2) 米英では tea といえば通例紅茶 (black tea) をさす) (⇨お茶) ●抹茶 powdered green *tea*. ●ウーロン茶 oolong. ●ほうじ茶 roasted *tea*. ●麦茶 barley *tea*. ●薄い[濃い]お茶1杯 a cup of weak [strong] *tea*.
❷ 〖色〗 brown. (⇨茶色) ●こげ[薄]茶 dark [light] *brown*.

チャーシュー [＜中国語] roast pork.
● チャーシューメン Chinese noodles with roast pork on the top.

チャーター ── **チャーターする** 動 ● 社内旅行にバスをチャーターする *charter* a bus for their outing.
● チャーター機 a charter(ed) plane; a plane for charter. ● チャーター便 a charter(ed) flight.

チャート [図表] a chart. ● [〈英〉*sheet*]. ▶彼のシングルは6週間連続でヒットチャート第1位だった His single topped the *charts* for six straight weeks.

チャーハン 炒飯 [＜中国語] (Chinese) fried rice.

チャービル [植物] chervil.

チャーミング ── **チャーミングな** 形 (魅力的な) charming; (かわいい) pretty; (外から見て) attractive.

チャームポイント one's best [most attractive] feature; [和製語] a charm point. ● 彼女のチャームポイントはえくぼだ Her best feature is her dimples.

チャイコフスキー [ロシアの作曲家] Tchaikovsky /ʧɑɪkɔ́(ː)fski/ (Pyotr Ilyich ~).

チャイナ [中国] China.
● チャイナタウン [中国人街] (a) Chinatown.

チャイブ [植物] a chive. (!通例複数形で)

チャイム a chime. (!通例複数形で) ▶玄関のチャイムが鳴っている I hear the *chime* of the doorbell./The front door [The doorbell] is chiming.

チャイルドシート a child [baby] car seat; [和製語] a child seat.

ちゃいろ 茶色 brown. ● 茶色がかった brownish. ● 薄[赤]茶色 light [reddish] *brown*. ● 茶色の髪[目] *brown* hair [eyes]. ● 茶色のコートa *brown* coat.

ちゃうす 茶臼 a tea grinding hand mill.

チャウダー (料理) chowder. ● クラムチャウダー clam *chowder*.

ちゃえん 茶園 (茶畑) tea bushes; (農園) a tea plantation [field, garden].

ちゃかい 茶会 a tea-party; (茶道の) a tea ceremony party.

ちゃがし 茶菓子 a cake served with tea. (!(1) 菓子の種類によって *manju*, *higashi* などと適宜変えるとよい. (2) 〈米〉ではクッキー・ビスケット類, 〈英〉ではケーキ類が普通.

ちゃかす 茶化す [冗談にしてしまう] turn 《his words》 into a joke; [からかう] make* fun of 《him》; [ふざけて真意を曲げる] playfully twist 《his》 words.

ちゃかちゃか (落ち着きのない様子) restlessly; (騒々しい様子) noisily. ● ちゃかちゃか動き回る move around [about] *restlessly and noisily*.

ちゃかっしょく 茶褐色 dark brown.

ちゃがま 茶釜 an iron teakettle.

ちゃがゆ 茶粥 *chagayu*, (説明的に) rice gruel made by boiling rice with tea.

ちゃがら 茶殻 used tealeaves [tea-leaves].

ちゃき 茶器 〈a set of〉 tea-things; tea utensils /juː(ː)ténslz/.

ちゃきちゃき (生っ粋の) 〈書〉 trueborn. ● ちゃきちゃきの江戸っ子 a *trueborn* Tokyoite /tóukiouàit/; a Tokyoite *through and through*.

ちゃきん 茶巾 a dishtowel [〈英〉] a tea towel, a tea cloth] for the tea ceremony.
● 茶巾ずし *chakinzushi*, (説明的に) a vinegared rice ball wrapped in a thin omelette.

-ちゃく -着 ❶ [到着] (⇨到着) ● 4日 [4時] 神戸着の船 a ship (which is) *due* at Kobe on the fourth [at four]. ▶この列車の東京着は何時ですか What time does this train *arrive at* [*get to*, *reach*] Tokyo?
❷ [着物] ● ズボン1着 a *pair of* pants 〈米〉[trou-sers 〈英〉]. ● 背広[スーツ] 10着 ten *suits* (of clothes).
❸ [着順] ▶彼はそのレースで1着になった He came in [finished] *first* in [*at*] the race. (!(1) in は参加者, at は結果の立場から. (2) 「何着でしたか」は How did he place [finish] in the race?)

ちゃくい 着衣 ● 着衣のまま with one's clothes on.

ちゃくえき 着駅 an arrival station.

ちゃくがん 着岸 ── **着岸する** 動 get to the shore.

ちゃくがん 着眼 ● 着眼点 (観点) a viewpoint, a point of view; (見地) a standpoint, (話) an angle. (⇨着目) ▶さすが彼だけあって着眼点が独創的だ This is an original [a fresh] *point of view* that could be expected of him alone.

ちゃくし 嫡子 (跡取り息子) one's son and heir /ʃənəɡér/; (嫡出子) one's legitimate (↔illegitimate) child (裁 children).

ちゃくじつ 着実 steadiness.
── **着実な** 形 [堅実な] steady; [健全な] sound.
● 着実な生活水準の向上 a *steady* improvement in [×of] living standards.
── **着実に** 副 steadily; (1歩1歩) step by step. ▶彼は着実に学業が進歩している He is making 〈×a〉 *steady* progress in his studies./He is progréssing *steadily* in his studies. ▶彼は会社で着実に出世コースを歩んできた He has been climbing up the company ladder *step by step*.

ちゃくしゅ 着手 ── **着手する** 動 [始める] start, begin* 《*to* do》; [取りかかる] set* about 《do*ing*》.
● 仕事に着手する *start* [*begin*] to work; *set about* the work. ● 内閣改造に着手する *set about* reshuffling the Cabinet. ● 新しい事業に着手する *start* [*make a start*] *on* a new business.

ちゃくしゅつ 嫡出 名 legitimacy ── 嫡出の 形 legitimate; born in wedlock.
● 嫡出子 a legitimate children.

ちゃくじゅん 着順 (in) the order of arrival.

ちゃくしょう 着床 名 implantation.
── **着床する** 動 be implanted, become attached to and embedded in the uterine lining.
● 着床前診断 pre-implantation diagnosis /dàiəɡnóusis/.

ちゃくしょく 着色 名 coloring. ● 人工着色料 artificial food *coloring*. ── **着色する** 動 color.

ちゃくしん 着信 the receipt 《of a phonecall》.
● 着信音 a sound of the receipt. ● 着信記録 a record of the receipt.

ちゃくすい 着水 名 (a) landing (on the water); (特に宇宙船の) (a) splashdown. (⇨着地)
── **着水する** 動 land on the water; make a splashdown.

ちゃくせき 着席 ● 着席順に in the order of one's seats.
── **着席する** 動 sit down; take [have] a seat.

ちゃくせん 着船 ── **着船する** 動 reach port [the harbor].

ちゃくそう 着想 (a) conception; an idea. (!後の方が一般的な語 (⇨考え❷)) ● 着想の豊かな人 a person of ideas; an idea person. ▶その計画は着想がすばらしい The plan is brilliant in *conception* [*concept*].

ちゃくだつ 着脱 ▶この部品は着脱が簡単だ This part can *be easily attached or detached*.

ちゃくだん 着弾 ● 着弾距離 gunshot; the range of a gun. ● 着弾距離内[外]にある be within [out of] gunshot 《*firing*》 *range*). ▶そのガンの着弾距離は4マイルだ The gun has a *range* of four miles.

ちゃくち 着地 图 〖着陸〗(a) landing, (a) touchdown;〖体操など〗(a) landing. ●着地の失敗で大破する crash on *touchdown [landing]*.
— **着地する** 動〖飛行機が〗land, make a《smooth》landing, touch down.
ちゃくちゃく 着々 ●研究が着々(=着実に)進む make 《a》*steady* progress in one's studies. ●着々と仕事を続ける go on working *steadily*〖(1歩1歩)*step by step*〗.
ちゃくにん 着任 — **着任する** 動 ●神戸に着任する arrive at one's new post in Kobe; come to Kobe to take up one's new post.
ちゃくはつ 着発 departure and arrival.
●着発信管 a percussion fuse.
ちゃくばらい 着払い〖商品に対する支払い〗cash 〖《米》collect〗on delivery《略 COD》. ●このじゅうたんを着払いでお願いします Please send this carpet *COD*.
ちゃくひょう 着氷 — **着氷する** 動 ice (up); be coated with ice. ▶その飛行機は着氷した The airplane *has iced (up)*.
ちゃくふく 着服 — **着服する** 動〖横領する〗embezzle;〖自分のものにする〗pocket.
ちゃくぼう 着帽 — **着帽する** 動 put on a hat [a cap];〖している〗wear a hat [a cap]. ●着帽したまま with one's hat [cap] on. ▶ここでは保安帽を着帽しなければならない You are required to *wear a hard hat* here.
ちゃくメロ 着メロ〖携帯電話の〗a melody signaling; an incoming call.
ちゃくもく 着目 — **着目する** 動〖気づく〗notice,〖観察して〗observe;〖注意を払う〗pay attention to ….(⇨注目, 着眼)
ちゃくよう 着用 — **着用する** 動 ●背広を着用する *put on* a suit;〖着用している〗*wear* a suit, *have* a suit *on*.(⇨着る) ●シートベルトを着用している *wear* a seat belt.
ちゃくりく 着陸 图 (a) landing (↔takeoff);〖特に航空機の〗接地(a) touchdown. ●空港の着陸用滑走路 a *landing* strip at an airport. ●着陸態勢に入るstand by for *landing*. ●月面着陸 a moon *landing*. ●湖に緊急着陸をする make an emergency *landing* on the lake. ●パリから東京まで無着陸飛行をする make a *non-stop flight* from Paris to Tokyo. ▶この飛行場では毎年何百万回という離着陸が行われている There are millions of takeoffs and *landings* at this airport each year.
— **着陸する** 動 land (↔take off), make* a *landing*;〖特に航空機が〗touch down. ●羽田空港に無事着陸する *land* safely at Haneda Airport. ●月面に着陸する *land on* the moon. ●飛行機をパリに着陸させる *land* an airplane *at* Paris. ●飛行機を強制着陸させる *force* a plane *down*.
●着陸場 a lánding field [ground]. ●着陸地点 a landing site; a touchdown point.
ちゃくりゅう 嫡流 the direct line《of the Konishi family》.
チャコール〖木炭〗charcoal.
●チャコールグレー〖濃灰色〗charcoal gray. ●チャコールフィルター a charcoal filter.
ちゃこし 茶漉 a tea strainer.
ちゃさじ 茶匙 a teaspoon. ●紅茶に茶さじ2杯の砂糖を入れる put two *teaspoonful(s)* of sugar in tea.
ちゃしつ 茶室 a tearoom; a tea-ceremony room.
ちゃしぶ 茶渋 tea incrustations. ●茶渋のついた茶わん a tea-stained cup.
ちゃしゃく 茶杓〖抹茶を掬い取るさじ〗a spoon (for powdered tea);〖茶の湯で使うひしゃく〗a tea ladle.

ちゃじん 茶人〖『茶の湯を好む人』〗a lover [a devotee] of tea ceremony;〖『風流人』〗a person of refined taste.
ちゃせき 茶席〖茶室〗a tea-ceremony room.
ちゃせん 茶筅 a (bamboo) tea whisk.
ちゃそば 茶蕎麦 *chasoba*;〖説明的に〗buckwheat noodles blended with powdered tea.
ちゃたく 茶托 a (teacup) saucer.
ちゃだんす 茶箪笥 a tea cupboard /kábərd/;〖説明的に〗a kind of cupboard for storing tea things or tableware.
ちゃち — **ちゃちな** 形〖安っぽい〗cheap;〖貧弱な〗poor;〖みすぼらしい〗shabby;〖見せかけだけの〗shoddy;〖粗雑な〗crude. ●ちゃちな時計 a *cheap* watch. ●ちゃちな家 a *poor* [a *shabby*, a *shoddy*] house. ●ちゃちなモデルガン a *crude* model gun. ●ちゃちな(=浅薄な)議論 *flimsy* arguments. ▶その店は作りがちゃちだ The store is *shoddily* built.
ちゃちゃ 茶々 ●ちゃちゃを入れる interrupt《him》with frivolous comments; make frivolous remarks.
ちゃっか 着火 ignition. (⇨発火)
●着火点 an ignition point.
ちゃっか 着荷 the arrival of goods.
ちゃっかり〖打算的な〗calculating;〖賢い〗clever,《米》smart;〖抜け目のない〗shrewd;〖ずる賢い〗cunning;〖実際的な〗practical. ▶お金の事になると彼はちゃっかりしている He is *calculating* when it comes to money.
チャック a (zip) fastener (❗Chack は商標名. fastener にはホック・スナップなども含まれる);〖主に《米》〗a zipper,《英》a zip. ●かばんのチャックを開ける[閉める] *zip* the bag open [closed, shut]. (❗open は形容詞) ●背中のチャックを上げる[下ろす] *zip [unzip]* the back of one's clothes. ▶このズボンはきつすぎて, チャックがこわれてしまった These pants are too tight and the *zipper on* them has broken.
ちゃづけ 茶漬け (⇨お茶漬け) ●鯛茶漬け *chazuke* with slices of porgy on it.
ちゃっこう 着工 ▶その橋の建設は来年着工の予定です The construction of the bridge will *start* next year.
ちゃづつ 茶筒 a tea caddy; a tea canister.
チャット 图〖コンピュータ〗a chat. ●チャット仲間 a chát gròup. — **チャットする** 動 chat.
チャップリン〖英国の喜劇俳優〗Chaplin (Sir Charles Spencer ~).
チャド〖国名〗Chad;〖公式名〗the Republic of Chad. (首都 N'Djamena) ●チャド人 a Chadian. ●チャド(人)の Chadian.
ちゃどう 茶道 (⇨茶道(さどう))
ちゃどころ 茶所 a tea-producing district.
ちゃのま 茶の間 a dining room-cum-living 〖《英》sitting〗room (❗cum は「…とを兼ねる」の意) (事情) 米英では living room で食事をとる習慣は普通ない; an eat-in family den (❗den は狭くてむさくるしいが居心地のよい部屋をいう.
ちゃのみ 茶飲み ●茶飲み茶わん a teacup. ●茶飲み友達〖親しい仲間〗a good friend; a companion (at the tea table). ●茶飲み話〖have〗a chat over (a cup of) tea. (❗over は「…しながら」の意)
ちゃのゆ 茶の湯 tea ceremony. (⇨茶道(さどう))
ちゃばこ 茶箱 a tea chest; a tea box.
ちゃばしら 茶柱 a tea stalk (in a cup of tea).
ちゃぱつ 茶髪 brown-dyed hair. ▶彼は茶髪にした He *dyed* his hair *brown*.
ちゃばら 茶腹 ●茶腹である have drunk too much tea.

ちゃばん 茶番 (笑劇, ばかげたこと) a farce. ▶会議はとんだ茶番だった The meeting was an absolute farce. ●茶番劇 a farce.

ちゃびん 茶瓶 an earthen teapot.

ちゃぶだい 卓袱台 a low (dining) table; a collapsible [folding] (low) table.

チャペル [礼拝堂] a chapel. ▶チャペル(での礼拝)に遅刻する be late for *chapel*. (❗「礼拝の場」「礼拝」の意での chapel は無冠詞)

ちゃぼ 矮鶏 〖鳥〗 a Japanese bantam.

ちゃぼうず 茶坊主 [権力にへつらう人] a toady.

ちやほや —— **ちやほやする** 動 make* much of ...; (あれこれ機嫌をとる) make a fuss over [〖英〗of]...; (おだて) flatter. ▶子供をいつもちやほやしすぎると困るよ If you *make* such *a fuss over [of]* your child all the time, you'll be in trouble in the future.

ちゃみせ 茶店 a tea stall; a tea booth.

ちゃめ 茶目 ●(a) 茶目な (陽気に戯れる) playful; (いたずら好きな) mischievous. ●茶目な小犬 a *playful* puppy. ▶彼は茶目っ気たっぷりだ He's *full of [a lot of] fun*.

ちゃや 茶屋 (茶販売店) a shop selling tea; (茶店) a tea stall. (⇨茶店)

ちゃら ▶これでちゃら(=貸し借りなし)になったね This has made us *even*./Now we are *even*.

ちゃらちゃら ●ちゃらちゃら音を出す[立てる] (硬貨などが) chink; (鍵などがふれあって) tinkle, jingle (ジャラじゃらも含む). ▶彼が歩くとポケットの中でコインがちゃらちゃらいった The coins *chinked [clinked, jingled]* in his pocket as he walked. ▶彼はときどきちゃらちゃらした格好をする He sometimes shows a *flashy* appearance [behavior].

ちゃらんぽらん (無責任な) irresponsible; (当てにならない) unreliable; (いいかげんな) sloppy. ▶なんてちゃらんぽらんな奴だ How *irresponsible* he is!

チャリティー 〖慈善(行為)〗 charity.
●チャリティーコンサート a charity concert. ●チャリティーショー a charity show.

ちゃりん ●ちゃりんと with a clink [a chink]. ●ちゃりん音をたてる[音をさせる] clink, chink. ▶硬貨が石の床に落ちてちゃりんといった A coin *clinked* when it fell on the stone floor.

チャレンジ 〖名〗 [挑戦] a challenge. ●チャレンジ精神 spirit for challenge.
—— **チャレンジする** 動 (試みる) try; (挑戦する) challenge. (⇨挑戦する, 挑む) ▶この難しい目標の達成にチャレンジしてほしい I'd like you to *challenge* to achieve this difficult goal. (❗ ×challenge this difficult goal は不可)

チャレンジャー [挑戦者] a challenger.

ちゃわん 茶碗 〖湯飲み〗 a teacup, (茶道の) a teabowl; 〖ご飯茶碗〗 a (rice) bowl /bóul/. ●茶わん1杯 a *teacup* (a teacupful) (*of tea*); a *bowl* (a bowlful) (*of rice*). ●茶わんにご飯を盛る serve [put] rice in a *bowl*.
●茶わん蒸し chawan-mushi, (説明的に) a cup-steamed egg custard containing chicken, shrimp, and vegetables.

-ちゃん [-ちゃん] (に当たる英語はなく, 名前を呼び捨てて親愛の情を表す) (⇨-さん)

ちゃんこなべ ちゃんこ鍋 *chankonabe*, (説明的に) a one-pot hot dish containing chunks of vegetables, fish, meat, etc., commonly eaten by sumo wrestlers.

チャンス (an) opportúnity, a chance. (❗ (1) 日本語の「チャンス」は 前の方に相当する場合が多い. (2) 後の方が偶然性が高い) (⇨機会) ●絶好のチャンス a golden *opportunity*; an ideal *chance*. ●一生に一度の[千載一遇の]チャンス the *chance [opportunity]* of a lifetime; a once-in-a-lifetime *chance [opportunity]*. ●チャンスに強い打者 a clutch hitter. ●チャンスがある have a *chance (of; to do)*; have an *opportunity (for, of; to do)*. ●チャンスを作る create a *chance*. ●チャンスをつかむ[得る] seize [get] a *chance*. ●チャンスを逃がす miss a [one's] *chance*. ●チャンスに三振する strike out in a clutch situation. ▶君にもう一度チャンスを与えよう I'll give you another [one more] *opportunity*. ▶チャンスが来たんだ. 見送るわけにはいかない I've got [×I got] an *opportunity*. I can't pass it up. ▶彼はとても才能があるもの, きっといつかチャンスがめぐってくるよ He's so talented. I'm sure he's going to get a (big) *break* someday. (❗ break は「(成功する)機会」の意の口語)
●チャンスメーカー a player who sets up the table, a table-setter; 〖和製語〗 a chance maker.

ちゃんちゃらおかしい Isn't it a laugh?/How ridiculous [absurd]!

***ちゃんと** ❶ 〖社会通念にかなうように〗 (正式に) formally; (上品に) respectably, decently; (きちんと) properly. ●ちゃんと座る sit *properly*; (正座する) sit up straight. ●ちゃんとした人 a *decent* [a *respectable*] person. ●その晩会食にはちゃんとした服装で行かなければいけない You have to be *formally [properly]* dressed to go to the dinner party. ▶ちゃんとした服装でなかったら, 面接はうまくいかないよ Unless you dress yourself *respectably*, you won't be successful with your interview. ●ちゃんと(=行儀よく)しなさい Behave (⇨misbehave) (yourself).
❷ 〖整然と〗 neatly; orderly. ▶ベッドはいつもちゃんと整えておきなさい Always keep your bed *neatly* made [*neat and tidy*]. ▶字はもっとちゃんと書きなさい. あなたの r と s ははぎらわしい Write more *neatly*. Your "r" and "s" are quite confusing.
❸ 〖確実に〗 (間違いなく) without fail; (無事に) safely; (正確に) exactly; (時間どおりに) punctually. ▶彼は家賃を毎月ちゃんと払います He pays his rent *without fail* (規則正しく) *regularly* every month. ▶言われたとおりちゃんとやりなさい Do *exactly* as you are told. ▶彼はちゃんと9時に来ます He comes *punctually* at nine. ▶道はちゃんと分かっているのですか(=確かですか) *Are* you *sure* you know the way?
❹ 〖申し分なく〗 (完全に) perfectly, completely; (正しく) right, correctly (❗ right の方が口語的); (満足に) satisfactorily. ▶彼女はちゃんとその問題が解けます She can solve the problem *perfectly*. ▶彼女はちゃんとフランス語が話せます She can speak French *satisfactorily*. ▶練習しなさい. コンサートまでにちゃんとできるようになるわ Go on practicing. I think you can get it *right* by the concert. (❗ この right は形容詞. 副詞を用いて play it right [correctly] ともいえる)

チャント a chant.
〔参考〕 特にヨーロッパのサッカーファンが愛唱する応援歌の一種. 節のみで特にメロディーらしきものがないものと, 欧米のポピュラーソングのメロディーに独自の歌詞をあてはめた「替え歌」の2種類がある.

チャンネル a channel. ●テレビのチャンネルを変える[回す] change [turn] the *channel* on TV. ●テレビのチャンネルを素早く次々と変える〖話〗 zap between *channels* quickly. ●テレビのチャンネルの取り合いを

ちゃんばら a fight 《with him》for a TV *channel*. ▶10チャンネルに変えていいかい Can I change it to *Channel 10?* ▶2チャンネルで野球をやっている You can see the baseball game on *Channel 2*.

ちゃんばら a sword fight. ●ちゃんばら映画 a *samurai* movie (with a lot of *sword fights*).

チャンピオン a champion, 《話》a champ. (❗個人をさす場合は単数形。チームをさす場合は champions と複数形になる) ●ヘビー級の世界チャンピオンになる become the world heavyweight (boxing) *champion*. ●世界チャンピオンの座を獲得する[失う; 守る; 保持する; 奪還する] win [lose; defend; hold, 《書》retain; regain] the world *championship*. ▶チェルシーは昨シーズンのプレミアリーグチャンピオンである Chelsea is the defending *champions* of English Premiership. ●チャンピオンカップ〘優勝杯〙a championship cup; 《和製語》a champion cup. ●チャンピオンズリーグ〘サッカー〙UEFA Champions League. ●チャンピオンフラッグ〘優勝旗〙a championship flag; 《和製語》a champion flag. ●チャンピオンベルト a championship belt.

ちゃんぽん ❶[ごちゃまぜ] (a) mixture. ●ちゃんぽんにする mix 《A *and* [*with*]》B. ●英語と日本語をちゃんぽんで話す speak in a *mixture* of English and Japanese. ❷[料理名] *champon*; (説明的に) a dish of Chinese noodles topped with stir-fried pork, shrimps and vegetables and served hot in broth.

ちゆ 治癒 图 (傷などの) healing; (病気などの) a cure.
—— **治癒する** 動 heal (up). (⇨治る)

チュアブル〘かめる〙chewable 《foods》.

ちゅう 知友 a bosom [a close, a good] friend.

ちゅう 知勇 wisdom and courage [valor]. ●知勇兼備の名将 a great general renowned for his supreme *wisdom and courage*.

ちゅう 中 〘平均〙an average; 〘中位〙middle, medium; 〘上中下 3 部作の〙the second part (of the three-part series). ●中型 *medium* size. ●中規模の会社 a *medium-sized* firm. ●私の成績は中以上[以下]だ My grade is *above* [*below*] *average*. (⇨平均)

ちゅう 宙 (空中) the air.
●宙に浮く float in the air; (未決定である)《話》be up in the air, 《書》be pending. ▶強い突き上げるような揺れで一瞬体が宙に浮いた(=空中に放り上げられた)ように感じた With a surging jolt in the heart I felt myself tossed *into* the air for a moment. ●その計画は宙に浮いたままだ The plan *is pending*.

ちゅう 注 a note. (⇨注, 注釈)

:‒**ちゅう** ‒中 ❶[期間](…の間に) during …; in …; (やや書) in the course of …; (…の間ずっと) throughout …, all through …; over …; (…の以内に) within …; (…までに) by ….

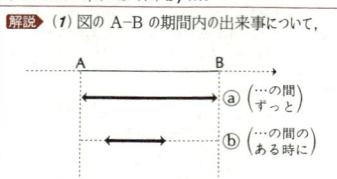

解説▶(1)図の A‒B の期間内の出来事について,

```
       A              B
       ←──────────────→
                    ⓐ (…の間
                       ずっと)
       ←—  —  —  —  —→
                    ⓑ (…の間の
                       ある時に)
```

during, in は ⓐ, ⓑ を, in the course of は ⓑ を, through(out), all through, over は ⓐ を表す.

(2) during と in の違い: (ⅰ) during は特定の期間の継続を強調し, 動詞が状態や習慣を表すときによく用いられる: 戦時中苦しい目にあった We suffered hardships *during* [×in] the war. (cf. He was killed *in* the war. (彼は戦死した))
(ⅱ) stay, visit, meal などしばらく続く出来事を表す名詞につけて「〜中に…した」と行為を述べるときは during で, in は用いない: 滞米中に英語を覚えた I learned English *during* my stay in America [*while* (I was) staying in America]. (❗従節中の主語が主節のそれと同じで be 動詞を従える場合は省略可)
(ⅲ) 不特定の期間の経過(…の内に)を表す場合は in のみを用いる: 数日中に仕上げます I'll finish it *in* a few days. (❗within では「…以内に」の意を表す)
(3) **over** は holiday(s), weekend, vacation など比較的短期間を表す語とともに「その終わりまで」の意を含んで用いられる: クリスマス[休暇]中は家にいます I will stay at home *over* Christmas [the holiday(s)].
(4) 期間を表す名詞が last, next, this などを伴うときは通例 during, in, over などは用いない: 先月中彼女に 5 回会った I saw her five times last [×*during*] last month.

▶午前中に彼がやって来た He came *in* [*during*] the morning. (❗ in の方が普通) ▶旅行中はずっと彼といっしょでした I was with him *throughout* [*all through*] the trip. ▶それは今月中に仕上げてください Please finish it *by* the end of this month [*within* this month]. (❗(1) 前の方が普通. (2)「今日中に」は単に today とするか by tonight などで表す. ×*within* today [this day] とはいわない)
❷[従事, 状態] (a) [前置詞+行為・活動を表す名詞を用いて] ●勤務中 be *on* duty. (❗警官・医者・看護師などで交替制の仕事についている) ●仕事中 be *at* work. (❗以上 2 例は「…している最中」の意) ●工事[がんの治療]中 be *under* construction [treatment for cancer]. ●検討中 be *under* study. ●売出中 be *on* sale. (❗以上 4 例は「…されている最中」の意) ▶授業中は注意を集中せよ Be attentive *in* [*during*] class. ●彼は食事中に眠ってしまった He fell asleep *over* dinner. (❗この over は「食べながら」の意)
(b) [進行形を用いて] ▶彼は今食事中です He *is having* dinner. (❗(a) の型を用いて《書》He is *at the* [《英》*at*] *table*. ともいえる) ▶その本は印刷中だ The book *is being* printed.
(c) [be going on, be under way などを用いて] ▶パーティーは進行中です The party *is* (*going*) *on* [*is under way*]. (❗ going はしばしば省略される)
(d) [while+節, when+節などを用いて] ▶外出中におじが訪ねてきた My uncle came to see me *while* I was out. (❗ while 節は (a) の型を用いて《書》*during* [*in*] my absence ともいえる)
❸[確率] ▶十中八九彼が勝つよ *Probably* [《話》Ten *to* one] he will win. (⇨十中八九) ▶20 人中 5 人が試験に合格した Five *out of* twenty people passed the test.
❹[場所] (中に) in …; (全域にわたって) (all) over …, through(out)… (❗ all over, throughout の方が「すみずみまで」の意を強調する); (通り抜けて) through …. ●空中に浮かぶ気球 a balloon floating *in* the air. ●海中に飛び込む jump *into* [×in] the sea. ●日本中を旅行する travel *all over* [*throughout*] Japan. ●市中を案内する show 《him》*over* [*around*] the city.

:**ちゅうい** 注意 图 ❶[留意] attention;

notice. ●注意を喚起する call [awaken] 《his》 attention 《to》. ●注意をそらす distract 《his》 attention 《from》. ●注意を向ける turn [direct, give] attention 《to》. ▶彼は私の忠告に注意を払わなかった He didn't *pay* any *attention* [*heed*] *to* my advice./He *took* no *notice* [*heed*] *of* my advice. ▶そのおもちゃは彼の注意を引いた The toy attracted [caught, drew,《話》got] his *attention*. (!受身では His *attention* was attracted [was drawn] to the toy./His *attention* was caught by the toy.) ▶あの病院は患者に対する注意がよく行き届いている That hospital *gives* the best *attention to* [(よく世話をする) *takes* good *care of*, (思いやりが深い) *is* most *considerate toward*] its patients. ▶勉強に注意を集中しなさい *Concentrate* 《your *attention*》*on* your study./(全精力を傾けなさい)*Concentrate* all your energies [energy] *on* your study.

❷ [用心] care, caution. (!後の方は用心深さを含意) ▶それには特別な注意が必要だ It needs [《書》 requires] special *care*. ▶彼は要注意人物だ We have (got) to watch out for [《話》keep our eye on] him. (⇨動❷)/(ブラックリストに載っている) He is on the black list (of the police). ▶君はスペリングに注意が足りない You are *careless* about [*of*] your spelling. (!取り扱いを暗示する場合は with も可: 火の扱いに注意が足りない You are *careless with* fire.)

❸ [忠告] advice (!数える場合は a piece [a bit, a word] of ... を用いる). [警告] (a) warning, 《法律》(a) caution. ▶辞書の選択に関してひとこと注意を与えておきます Let me give you a piece of *advice about* [《やや書》*on*] the choice of dictionaries. ▶こうなったのは先生の注意を無視したからですよ This is because you neglected [didn't follow, didn't take] your teacher's *advice*. ▶駐車違反で警官に注意を受けた The police officer gave me a *warning against* [a *caution for*] illegal parking./I *was cautioned for* [I *was warned about*, I *was warned against*] illegal parking by the policeman [policewoman].

── 注意する ● [留意する] pay* [give*] attention 《to》, attend 《to》; [注目する] take* notice 《of》, 《やや書》take note 《of》, 《書》note 《that 節》. ▶先生のおっしゃることをよく注意して聞きなさい You must *pay* close *attention* [Listen very *carefully*] *to* what your teacher says. ▶横断する際には信号によく注意しなさい *Take* particular *notice of* the traffic lights when you cross the street. ▶その単語のつづりに注意しなさい *Note* the spelling of the word [*how to spell* the word].

❷ [用心する] take* care 《of; to do; that 節》, be careful 《of, about; to do; that 節, wh- 節》, be cautious 《of; to do》; 《やや書》beware 《of; that 節, wh- 節》, 《古》mind 《that 節》. (!命令形が不定詞としてのみ用いる). [気をつける] look [watch] out 《for》(主に英) mind 《that 節, wh- 節》(通例命令文で). ▶花びんを割らないように注意しなさい *Take care* [*Be careful*] *not to* break the vase. (!not to の代わりに ×so as [in order] not to とせない)/*Take care* [*Be careful*,《やや書》*Beware*,《英》*Mind*]《*that*》you don't break the vase. (!that 節中には通例未来を表す助動詞を用いない)▶健康に注意しなさい *Be careful of* your health./*Take care of* yourself. (!別れ際のあいさつには単に Take care. ということも多い) ▶彼は彼女の感情を害さないように注意した He *was cautious* of offending [*not to* offend] her. ▶犬

に注意せよ《掲示》Beware of the dog. ▶その通りはよくよく注意して渡りなさい Cross the street *with* extreme *care* [*caution*]./*Be* extremely *careful* 《*in*》crossing the street. (!in は《話》ではしばしば省略される. in の代わりに *when* you cross .... も可) ▶言葉に注意しなさい *Be careful* 《*about*》what you say. (!wh- 語の前では about は通例省略される)/*Be careful in* your speech [*with* your words]. (!in は「...するときに」, with は「...の扱いに」の意) ▶足もと[頭上]に注意しなさい *Watch* your step [head]./《英》*Mind* your step [head]. (!(1) この場合 step は単数形で用いる. (2) この「頭上に」は「頭をぶつけないように」の意. 上から物が落ちてくるかもしれない場合は Danger overhead! のようにいう) ▶冬山ではなだれに注意しなさい *Look* [*Watch*] *out for* avalanches in winter mountaineering.

❸ [忠告する] advise, [警告する] warn, caution. (!warn の方が重大な危険・刑罰を暗示する) ▶医者に酒を飲むなように注意されました The doctor *advised* me *to* stop drinking. (!The doctor *advised* (me) *that* I (《英》should) stop drinking. ともいうが, 不定詞を用いる方が普通) ▶彼は子供たちにその川で泳いではいけないと注意した He *warned* [*cautioned*] the children not *to* swim in the river./He *warned* [*cautioned*] the children *against* swim*ming* in the river. ▶ドアに錠をかけるのを忘れないように注意して[=思い起こさせて]ください *Remind* me *to* lock the door.

●注意書き (説明書き) directions 《for》; (注釈) notes. ●注意を要する matters to be attended to; NB (!書物などでよく用いられる略号). ●注意報 a 《flood [storm]》warning. ●注意力 attention.

ちゅうい 中位 (位置) the middle position; (地位) the middle rank; (品質) medium quality; average quality.

ちゅうい 中尉 《陸軍・米海兵・米空軍》First Lieutenant; 《米海軍》Lieutenant Junior Grade; 《英海軍》Sublieutenant; 《英空軍》Flying Officer.

ちゅういぶかい 注意深い [慎重な] careful, (用心深い) cautious; [油断のない] watchful; [気を配る] attentive. ▶彼は君ほど注意深くない He's not as [so] *careful* [*cautious*] as you are. (!否定文では so を用いることがあるが, 《米》では古風) ▶彼女の運転はとても注意深い She is a very *careful* [*cautious*] driver./She drives very *carefully* [*cautiously*]. ▶注意深い読者ならこの誤植に気がつくであろう An *attentive* reader will notice this misprint.

── 注意深く [慎重に] carefully, (用心して) cautiously; [油断なく] watchfully; [気を配って] attentively. ▶その荷物をもっと注意深く包みなさい Wrap (up) the parcel more *carefully* [*with greater care*].

チューインガム (chéwing) gum. ●チューインガム 1 枚 a stick [a piece] of *chewing gum*. ●チューインガムをかむ chew *gum*.

ちゅうおう 中央 图 [真ん中] the center, the middle (!前の方は middle より厳密な意味をもち, 円などの中心点をいう). [中心部] the heart. ●中央気象台 the *Central* Meteorological /ˌmiːtiəˈrɒlədʒɪkl/ Observatory. ●中央郵便局 the *Central* Post office.

── 中央の 形 central, middle. ●中央の通路 a *central* aisle.

── 中央に 副 ●部屋の中央に立つ stand *in the middle* [*center*] *of* the room. ▶銀行は市の中央にある The bank is *in the center* [*heart*] *of* the city./The bank is *in the central part of* the

city.
- 中央演算処理装置〖コンピュータ〗central processing units《略 CPU》. - 中央官庁 central government agencies. - 中央銀行 a central bank. - 中央競馬 JRA horse racing.（**!** JRA は the *Japan Racing Association* の略）. - 中央集権 centralization of power. - 中央政府 the central (↔ local) government. - 中央分離帯《米》a median /míːdiən/ (strip),《英》a central reserve [reservation].

ちゅうおう 中欧 Central Europe.
ちゅうおうアジア 中央アジア Central Asia.
ちゅうおうアフリカ 中央アフリカ ［地域］ Central Africa
ちゅうおうアフリカ 中央アフリカ ［国名］ Central Africa;（公式名）the Central African Republic.（首都 Bangui）. - 中央アフリカ人 a Central African. - 中央アフリカ(人)の Central African.
ちゅうおうアメリカ 中央アメリカ Central America.
ちゅうおん 中音 〖音楽〗（男性）baritone;（女性）mezzo-soprano.
ちゅうか 中華 - 中華街 (a) Chinatown. - 中華思想 Sinocentrism. - 中華そば Chinese noodles. - 中華丼 *chukadon*,（説明的に）a bowl of rice topped with chop suey. - 中華なべ a wok. - 中華料理 Chinese food [dishes];（料理法）Chinese cooking [cuisine /kwizíːn/]. - 中華料理店 a Chinese restaurant.
ちゅうかい 仲介 ［名］（仲裁）mediation. - 仲介の労をとる［に立つ］ act as a *mediator* [a go-between]《between》.
—— **仲介する** ［動］《やや書》mediate《between》.
- 仲介者 a mediator;（仲立ち）a go-between;（交渉の）《やや書》an intermediary.
ちゅうかい 注解 ［名］(an) annotation.（⇒注釈）
—— **注解する** ［動］ annotate《the works of Shakespeare》.
- 注解者 an annotator.
ちゅうがい 虫害 damage from insects.
ちゅうがえり 宙返り（1回の）a somersault;（飛行機の）a loop. - 2回転返りa double *somersault*. - 宙返りを（連続）2回する turn [do, throw] two *somersaults*; somersault twice. ▶ 飛行機が宙返りをして人々を楽しませた The plane *looped the loop* to entertain the crowd.
ちゅうがえり『宙返り』*Somersault*.［参考］大江健三郎の小説）
ちゅうかく 中核 （中心）the core 《*of*》;（核心）the kernel 《*of*》. - 近代思想の中核 the *core of* modern thought [（政治的な）ideologies].
*ちゅうがく 中学（⇒中学校, 中学生）▶ 彼は中学1年生です He is *in the first year of junior high school*./He is a first-year student at [*of*] *junior high school*./《米》He is *in the seventh grade* [is a *seventh grader*].
ちゅうがくせい 中学生 a junior high school student [（男子）boy;（女子）girl].（⇒生徒）
ちゅうがくねん 中学年 the third and fourth grades 〘《英》forms〙.
ちゅうかじんみんきょうわこく 中華人民共和国（⇒中国）
ちゅうがた 中型, 中形 —— **中型[形]の** medium-sized, middle-sized.
- 中型車 a medium-sized car.
ちゅうがっこう 中学校 a junior high school,《話》a junior high.（⇒学校）- 女子中学校 a girls' *junior high school*.
*ちゅうかん 中間 ［名］〖真ん中〗the middle.

—— **中間の, 中間的な** ［形］〖位置が真ん中の〗middle;〖学期が中間の〗midterm;〖時期が〗(やや書) interim;〖場所・時間などが〗intermediate;〖仲介の〗intermediary;〖中庸の〗moderate. - 進化の中間段階に at an *intermediate* stage of evolution.
- 中間的な（＝穏健・中道的な）意見 a *moderate* [*middle*] opinion.

—— **中間に** ［副］（中途に）halfway, midway. ▶ その市は京都と大阪の中間にある That city is *halfway* [*midway*] *between* Kyoto and Osaka.
- 中間階級 the middle class. - 中間管理職 middle management.（**!** 集合的. 単・複両扱い）.（人）a middle manager. - 中間子〘物理〙a meson. - 中間試験 a midterm exam 〘書〙examination;《米話》a midterm.（**!** しばしば複数形で）. - 中間色 a neutral color. - 中間地点 the halfway point. - 中間報告 an interim report;（経過報告）a progress an interim, a middle] report.（⇒経過）

ちゅうき 中気（⇒中風 (ちゅうふう)）
ちゅうき 中期（中ごろ）the middle. - 江戸時代中期に in the *middle* of the Edo era [period].
ちゅうき 注記 ［名］ a note.（**!** 頭注 (a headnote)・脚注 (a footnote)・傍注 (a side note) などに細分される）
—— **注記する** ［動］ note; give a note 《*on*》.
ちゅうき 駐機 - 駐機場 a hardstand; an apron.
ちゅうぎ 忠義 〖忠節〗loyalty 《*to*》;（忠実）faithfulness 《*to*》.（やや書）fidelity 《*to*》.
—— **忠義な** ［形］ loyal 《*to*》; faithful 《*to*》.
ちゅうきゅう 中級の ［形］ intermediate. - 中級英語講座 an *intermediate* [a *middle*] English course.
ちゅうきょり 中距離 a middle distance.
- 中距離競走 a middle-distance race. - 中距離走者 a middle-distance runner. - 中距離弾道弾[ミサイル] an intermediate-range ballistic missile《略 IRBM》.
ちゅうきん 忠勤 - 忠勤を励む do [perform] one's duty faithfully; serve《one's master》faithfully; be a faithful person [servant, employee]《*to*》.
ちゅうきん 鋳金 metalwork. - 鋳金家 a metalworker. - 鋳金術 metalworking.
ちゅうきんとう 中近東 the Middle (and Near) East.（**!** 現在では（ ）内を省略するのが普通（⇒中東））
ちゅうくう 中空 - 中空に[の] in midair;（空中）in the air;（空洞）hollow《trees》.
ちゅうぐらい 中位 - 中ぐらいの ［形］〖大きさ・質などが並の〗medium;〖背丈などが中程度の〗middle;〖平均の〗average;〖あまりよくない〗(軽蔑的) mediocre;〖程度などが適度の〗moderate. - 中ぐらいの大きさの卵 *medium*-sized eggs. - 中ぐらいの才能の人 a person of *average* [*moderate*] abilities. ▶ 彼は中ぐらいの背の高さです He is of *medium* [*average*] height. ▶ ステーキは中ぐらいに焼いたのが好きだ I like my steak *medium*. ▶ 彼は知能[成績]が中ぐらいです He is about *average* in intelligence [grades]./His intelligence is [His grades are] about *average*.
ちゅうくんあいこく 忠君愛国 loyalty and patriotism.
ちゅうけい 中継 ［名］〖放送〗(a) relay;〖放送局間の〗(a) hookup. - 実況中継 (a) *relay* from the spot. - 生中継 a live *relay* broadcast. - 衛星中継 *transmission* by [via] satellite; a satellite *hookup*《*with*, *between*》. ▶ この番組は中継放送でお届けしています This program comes to you by *relay broadcast*.

—— **中継する** 動 relay, broadcast*《it》by relay.
● 全国にテレビ中継する *broadcast*《it》over a nationwide TV *hookup*; *televise*《it》over a nationwide *network*. ● 中継したボールを一塁へ転送する throw the *relay* to first. ● そのコンサートはロンドンから衛星中継された The concert *was transmitted* [*broadcast*] from London by [via] satellite. (⇨衛星) ▶ 二塁手がライトからの送球を中継した The second baseman *relayed* the ball from the right fielder.
● 中継局 a relay station.

ちゅうけん 中堅 〖中心勢力〗the backbone; 〖大黒柱〗the mainstay. ▶ 彼らは中堅(=中ぐらいの地位の)の社員である They are the *middle-rank* workers [*the backbone*] of the company.
● 中堅手〖野球〗a center fielder.

ちゅうけん 忠犬 a faithful dog.
ちゅうげん 中元 the fifteenth of July; 〖贈り物〗a midsummer gift (⇨お中元).
ちゅうげん 忠言 advice. (⇨忠告)
● 忠言耳に逆らう〖ことわざ〗Good medicine is bitter in the mouth./Good advice sounds harsh in the ear.

ちゅうこ 中古 —— **中古の** 形 used; sécondhánd.
● 中古車を買う buy a *used* [a *secondhand*] car; buy a car *secondhand*.
● 中古品 used [secondhand] goods [articles].

ちゅうこう 中高 ● 中高生 *junior and senior high school* students. ● 中高一貫教育 a six-year *secondary school* system. ● 中高教育の緊密な連携 close cooperation between *lower and upper secondary schools*. (❗以上 2 例は日本の学校制度に対応した言い方)

ちゅうこう 昼光 daylight.
● 昼光色 a daylight color.

ちゅうこうそう 中高層 ● 中高層アパート a *high-and-medium-rise* apartment building.

ちゅうこうねん 中高年 (年齢) middle age (❗通例 40 歳代-60 歳代半ばまで(⇨中年)); (人) people of middle age, middle-aged people.

ちゅうこうねんれいそう 中高年齢層 the middle age group [bracket]. (⇨中高年)

*__ちゅうこく__ 忠告 名 〖助言〗advice /ədváis/ (❗教えるときは a piece [two pieces] of 〜); (専門的な) 〖書〗counsel; 〖警告〗a warning. ● 忠告に従う follow, listen to, ×obey〗〈his〉*advice*; act on 〈his〉*advice*. ▶ 彼は医師の忠告に従って〔働かないで〕働き続けた He kept (on) working *on* [*against*] his doctor's *advice*. (❗前の方の on は継続の観念を強調する副詞)
—— **忠告する** 動 〖助言する〗advise /ədváiz/, give* [offer]《him》advice (❗advise は常に未来の行為について用いる); 〖警告する〗warn. ▶ 彼は私に何も忠告してくれなかった He didn't *give* me any *advice*. (❗通例 ×He didn't *advise* me anything [anything *to* me]. は不可) ▶ 医師は彼に少し休養をとるように忠告した The doctor *advised* him to take some rest [*advised*《him》that (1) to 不定詞の用いるのが普通. that 節中の主語と間接目的語が同じ場合間接目的語はしばしば省略される. (2) だれに忠告したかが文脈から明らかな場合は The doctor *advised* (taking) some rest. も可] ▶ 先生は生徒たちにカンニングをしてはいけないと忠告した The teacher *warned* her class *not* to cheat [*against* cheating] in [on] the exam.

*__ちゅうごく__ 中国 〖国名〗China; (公式名) the People's Republic of China. (首都 Beijing) ● 中国人 (個人) a Chinese (❗単・複同形); 〖集合的〗the Chinese (❗複数扱い). ● 中国語 the Chinese; the Chinese language. ● 中国(人)[語]の Chinese.
● 中国共産党 the Chinese Communist Party.

ちゅうごくちほう 中国地方 the Chugoku district.
ちゅうごし 中腰 (in) a half-rising [a half-sitting] posture.

ちゅうさ 中佐 〖陸軍・米海兵隊・米空軍〗Lieutenant Colonel; 〖海軍〗Commander; 〖英空軍〗Wing Commander. 〖通例連隊長・独立部隊の大隊長〗

ちゅうざ 中座 —— **中座する** 動 ● 会の途中で中座する leave《the room》in the middle of [halfway through] a meeting; *leave* a meeting *in the middle*. ● パーティーを中座させてもらう excuse oneself from a party.

ちゅうさい 仲裁 名 (紛争などの裁定) arbitration; (調停) mediation. ● 争議を仲裁に付する submit [refer] the dispute to *arbitration*. ▶ その労使紛争は彼の仲裁により解決した The labor dispute was settled *through* his *mediation* [*arbitration*]. ▶ その紛争は仲裁に付された The dispute went to *arbitration*. (❗went to の使い方に注意)
—— **仲裁(を)する** 動 ● 紛争を仲裁する *arbitrate* [*mediate*] a dispute. ● 会社と組合の仲裁をする *arbitrate* [*mediate*] between the company and the union.
● 仲裁人 an arbitrator; (調停者を) a mediator.

ちゅうざい 駐在 名 residence. (❗「駐在期間」の意では ⓒ). ● 海外駐在員 an overseas worker [representative]. ▶ ベルリン駐在の特派員 a correspondent *stationed* in Berlin. ▶ 東京での 3 年間の駐在中 during a three-year *residence* [a *residence* of three years] in Tokyo.
—— **駐在する** 動 reside /rizáid/.
● 駐在所 a residential police box.

ちゅうさんかいきゅう 中産階級 (中流階級) the middle class(es); (有産階級) the bourgeoisie /bùərʒwɑːzíː/.

*__ちゅうし__ 中止 名 (継続していたものを) discontinuation; (一時的な) suspension; 〖取り消し〗cancellation. ● 生産中止 *discontinuation* of production. ● 野球の試合の中止 the *cancellation* of a baseball game. ● 降雨中止ゲーム a rain-out (game).
—— **中止する** 動 〖止める〗stop (-pp-); (継続していたものを) discontinue; (一時的に) suspend; 〖取り消す〗cancel, call ... off. ● エアコンの生産を中止する *stop* [*discontinue*, *suspend*] production of air conditioners. ● 野球の試合を中止する *cancel* [*call off*] a baseball game. (❗call a game は「コールドゲームにして中止する」の意) ▶ 彼女はパリ旅行をしぶしぶ中止した She *canceled* her trip to Paris reluctantly.

ちゅうし 注視 名 a (steady) gaze, an intent look.
—— **注視する** 動 (一心に見つめる) gaze《at》; look intently《at》; (注意して見守る) watch ... carefully [closely]; (視線をすえる) keep one's eyes fixed《on》.

ちゅうじえん 中耳炎 inflammation of the middle ear; 〖医学〗otitis media /outátəs míːdiə/.

ちゅうじく 中軸 ❶〖中央を貫く軸〗an axis (複 axes /æksiːz/). ▶ その映画は音楽家としての彼女の成長を中軸として展開する The movie *centers on* her growth as a musician.
❷〖中心となる〗the central figure. ● 中軸(=打順の中心を打つ)打者〖野球〗the meat of the order.

*__ちゅうじつ__ 忠実 名 faithfulness《to》; (忠誠) loyalty. (⇨誠実) ▶ 職務に対する忠実さにかけてはだれにも負けない When it comes to *faithfulness* to duties I am

second to none.

— **忠実な** 形 faithful 《to》; (うそ偽りのない) true 《to》; (忠誠な) loyal 《to》● 忠実な犬 a *faithful* dog. ● 国[主義]に忠実である be *loyal* to one's country [cause]. ▶彼女は約束に忠実である She is *faithful* [*true*] *to* her word. ▶その翻訳は原文に忠実だ The translation is *faithful* [*true*, ×*loyal*] *to* the original.

— **忠実に** 副 faithfully. ▶彼は私の忠告に忠実に従った He followed my advice *faithfully*.

***ちゅうしゃ** 注射 an injection, 《話》a shot. ● 静脈[皮下]注射 (⇨静脈, 皮下) ● 注射をしてもらう get an *injection* [a *shot*]. ● 彼に抗生物質の注射をする give him an antibiotic *injection* [*shot*]; *inject* him with an antibiotic. ● 注射で痛みを止める kill the pain by *injection*. ▶彼は血糖値をコントロールするために毎日インシュリンの注射が欠かせない He can't control his blood sugar levels without daily *injections* of insulin.

● 注射器 a syringe /sɪ́rɪndʒ/, an injection syringe. ● 注射針 a (hypodermic) needle.

ちゅうしゃ 駐車 图 parking. ▶駐車禁止《標識》No *parking*. (🛈 丁寧に Thank you for not parking./Don't even think of parking here, thank you./*Park* your car at your own risk. などということも多い) ▶ここは駐車禁止なんですが We don't *park* here. (🛈 You're not permitted to *park* here. より当たりのやわらかい言い方) / You're in a no-*parking* zone. ▶その通りは狭くて駐車は難しかった The narrow street made *parking* difficult.

— **駐車する** 動 park. ● 駐車してある車 a *parked* [×a *parking*] car. ▶路上にたくさん車が駐車してある Lots of cars *are parked* [×*are parking*] on the street.

● 駐車違反 a parking violation; illegal parking. ● 駐車違反呼び出し状 (get) a parking ticket. ● 駐車場 (⇨駐車場) ● 駐車料金 a parking charge.

ちゅうしゃく 注釈 (注記) a note; 《書》(an) annotation (🛈 音楽や映画の解説文で含む). ● 注釈付きの本 a book with (*explanatory*) *notes*; 《書》an *annotated* book. ● 注釈を加える add *notes* 《to a book》; 《書》annotate 《a book》.

● 注釈者 an annotator.

ちゅうしゃじょう 駐車場《米》a parking lot;《英》a car park; (駐車区域) a párking área. (🛈 白線などで仕切られた駐車スペースまたは駐車場以外で駐車するスペースは a parking space [spot, place], 建物の地下などにある駐車場は《米》a parking garage という (⇨モーター [モータープール])) ▶駐車場はいっぱいだった The *parking lot* was packed [full]. ▶車はホテルの駐車場に止めて[入れて]おいたらいい You can put your car in the hotel *parking garage*《米》[*car park*《英》]. ▶そのデパートは客用の無料駐車場を備えている The department store provides free *parking* for its customers.

ちゅうしゅう 中秋 ▶今夜は中秋の名月だ Tonight is the [a] harvest moon night./We have a harvest moon tonight. (⇨月)

ちゅうしゅつ 抽出 图 (化学的・機械的方法による) extraction《*from*》; (見本の) sampling. ● 無作為抽出 random *sampling*.

— **抽出する** 動 ● エキスを抽出する *extract* essence《*from*》.

ちゅうじゅん 中旬 the middle of the month. (⇨上旬)

***ちゅうしょう** 抽象 图 abstraction.

— **抽象的な** 形 abstract. (⇨ 具体的な) ▶君の説明は抽象的すぎる Your explanation is too *abstract*. ▶この絵は現代社会の不安を抽象的に表現している This picture represents anxieties in present-day society in the *abstract* (↔in the concrete).

● 抽象画 an abstract painting; (抽象的美術作品) an abstract. ● 抽象概念 an abstract idea, an abstraction. ● 抽象名詞〖文法〗an abstract noun.

ちゅうしょう 中傷 图 (言葉による) (a) slander; (文書による) (a) libel /láɪbl/《*on, against*》● 彼についての中傷 *slanders* [*libels*] about him. ▶彼の発言は私への中傷だ What he said is (a) *slander against* me [*on* my good name].

— **中傷する** 動 ▶彼はよく君のことを中傷する He often *slanders* you.

ちゅうじょう 中将〖陸軍・米海兵隊・米空軍〗Lieutenant General;〖海軍〗Vice Admiral (🛈《米》では俗に three-star general という);〖英空軍〗Air Marshal.

ちゅうしょうきぎょう 中小企業 medium-sized and small enterprises [companies, businesses]; (大企業に対し漠然と) small [minor] enterprises. (🛈 ×small sized enterprises とはいわない (⇨企業).

***ちゅうしょく** 昼食, 《書》(a) lunch, 《書》(a) luncheon; (午餐(ごさん)) (an (early) dinner (⇨夕食 [類語]). ● 昼食時に at lunchtime; (勤め先の) in [during] the *lunch* hour [break] ● 昼食会を催す give [hold] a *luncheon*. ▶1時に昼食をとる have *lunch* at one o'clock. ▶商談をしながら昼食をとる, 商談を兼ねての昼食会を開く have a business *lunch*. (🛈 英米の商慣習)

***ちゅうしん** 中心

WORD CHOICE 中心

center 平面・立体・回転運動などの幾何上の中心(部). 通例, 時間の中心には用いない. ● 部屋の中心に in the *center* of the room.

middle 平面・時間などの中心(部). 通例, 立体の中心には用いない. ● 真夜中(＝夜の中心)に in the *middle* of the night.

focus 注意・興味・関心の注がれる中心的対象. ● それは我々の関心の中心だ It is the *focus* of our attention.

頻度チャート

center ████████████
middle ████████
focus ███

20   40   60   80   100 (%)

〖真ん中〗the center, the middle;〖興味・議論などの中心〗the focus (複 〜es, foci /fóʊsaɪ/ (⇨[類語]);〖中心部, 核心〗the heart.

① **〖〜(の)中心〗** ● 円[台風]の中心 the *center* of a circle [a typhoon]. ● 男性中心社会 a male [×men's] society. ● その運動の中心となる(＝中心的役割を演じる) play a *central* [(指導的な) *leading*] role in the movement. ▶パリは世界のファッションの中心だ Paris is the fashion *center* of the world. ▶それが我々の議論の中心だ That is at [×in] our discussion. (🛈 活動の中心は at を用いる) I was educated *at* Kyoto (私は京都で教育を受けた).

② **〖中心〜〗** ● 商業の中心地 a commercial *center*; a center [a *hub*] of commerce. ▶校長は学校の中心的存在だ The principal is the *cen-*

[(かなめ) *pivot*, (推進者) the driving force behind] of the school.
③【中心に】 ● 中心に線を引く draw a line *in the middle*. ▶彼は大阪の中心に住んでいる He lives *in the center [heart] of* Osaka./He lives *in the central part of* Osaka./He lives *in central* Osaka. ▶今度の選挙のことが話題の中心になった The coming election became the *focus of conversation*./(話題が集中した) Conversation *centered on* 〈*around*〉 the coming election. ▶彼女を中心にして新党が結成された A new party was formed *with her as the central figure*. ▶彼は世界は自分を中心に回っていると思っている He thinks the world revolves *around him*.
● 中心角 a central angle. ● 中心人物 a central [a leading] figure; a key figure [person]; a driving force (*behind*). ● 中心線 the central line. ● 中心選手 a key [a leading] player. ● 中心点 the central point. ● 中心部 the central part.
ちゅうしん 中震 a moderate earthquake.
ちゅうしん 忠臣 a loyal [a faithful] retainer [subject].
ちゅうしん 注進 ━━ 注進する 動 report 〈an event *to him*〉 immediately [without delay].
ちゅうしん 衷心 ● 衷心より(心から) from the bottom of one's heart. ▶衷心より哀悼(誌)の意を表します Please accept my *deepest* condolences.
ちゅうすい 注水 ━━ 注水する 動 pour water 〈*into a water tank*〉.
ちゅうすいえん 虫垂炎 (盲腸炎)〖医学〗 appendicitis /əpèndəsáitis/.
ちゅうすう 中枢 ①〖中心〗the center;〖活動の中心〗the hub. ▶産業の中枢 a *center* [*a hub*] of industry. ▶政治の中枢機関 *central organ of* politics.
● 中枢神経 the central nerves. ● 中枢神経系 the central nervous system.
ちゅうせい 中世 medieval times (! 古代・近代と対比して); the Middle Ages (! 500年ごろから1500年ごろまで,時に1100年ごろから1500年ごろまで).
● 中世ヨーロッパ Europe in *medieval times*. ● 中世の建物 *medieval* buildings.
● 中世史 medieval history. (参考) 476年の西ローマ帝国滅亡から1453年の東ローマ帝国滅亡まで)
ちゅうせい 中正 名 fairness; impartiality.
━━ 中正な 形 fair (tricks); impartial 〈judges〉; unbiased 〈advice〉.
━━ 中正に 副 fairly; impartially.
ちゅうせい 中性 ①〖化学上の〗neutrality;〖文法上の〗the neuter (gender). ▶働きアリは中性だ Worker ants are *neuter* [*sexless*].
● 中性子 a neutron. ● 中性子爆弾 a neutron bomb. ● 中性脂肪 neutral fat. ● 中性洗剤 (a) neutral detergent.
ちゅうせい 忠誠 (特に国家・君主に対する) 〈書〉allegiance 〈*to*〉;(忠節) loyalty 〈*to*〉. ▶忠誠を尽くした be *loyal* 〈*to*〉. ▶忠誠の誓い an oath *of allegiance* [*loyalty*]. ▶彼は王に忠誠を誓った He swore (an oath of) [took an oath of] *allegiance to* the king.
ちゅうせき 沖積 ● 沖積世 the alluvial epoch.
● 沖積層 (an) alluvium. ● 沖積土 alluvial soil. ● 沖積平野 an alluvial plain.
ちゅうせつ 忠節 loyalty 〈*to*〉. (⇨忠誠)
ちゅうぜつ 中絶 名 (妊娠の) (an) abortion.
━━ 中絶する 動 ▶彼女は子供は2人しか欲しくなかったので,3人目を妊娠した中絶した She only wanted two children, so she *got* [*had*] *an abortion* when (she was) pregnant for the third time. (! 医師が主語の場合は perform an abortion 〈*on her*〉となる)

*ちゅうせん 抽選 名〖行為〗drawing lots;〖くじ〗a lot, (富くじ) a lottery. (⇨くじ) ▶抽選に当たる draw a winning 〈losing〉 number; win 〈*lose*〉 a *lottery*. ▶この授業を取りたい人が多すぎるので抽選で選ばなければならない So many students want to take this class that we have to choose *by lot* [*by drawing lots*]. ━━ 抽選する 動 draw lots.
● 抽選会 a lottery. ● 抽選券 a lottery ticket. ● 抽選番号 a lottery number.
ちゅうせんきょく 中選挙区 a multiple-seat constituency [electoral district].
● 中選挙区制 the multiple-seat constituency system.
ちゅうそう 中層 (層状のもの) the middle layer; (階級) the middle class. ● 中層のアパート a *medium-rise* apartment building.
ちゅうぞう 鋳造 名 casting.
━━ 鋳造する 動 cast; (貨幣を) coin, mint. ● 青銅で鐘を鋳造する *cast* a bell *in* bronze; *cast* bronze *into* a bell. ● 100円硬貨を鋳造する *coin* [*strike*] 100-yen pieces; *mint* [*strike*] 100-yen coins.
● 鋳造所 a foundry; (貨幣の) a mint.
ちゅうそつ 中卒 (米) a junior high school graduate; (英) a school-leaver (! 義務教育修了後,就職する人をさす).
ちゅうたい 中退 ━━ 中退する 動 (退学する) leave school, dròp óut (of school [college]); (意図的に学校をやめる) quit school. (! (1)(英) では leave school は「卒業する」の意. この school には university を含めない. (2) drop out の理由はさまざまで,成績不良とは限らない) ▶彼女は大学を中退して貿易商社に就職した She *left* [*quit*] *the university* and got a job with [in] a trading company. ▶彼は田中さんと結婚するために卒業を前に中退した He *dropped out* just before graduation to marry Miss. Tanaka.
● 中退者 a 〈high school [college]〉 dropout.
ちゅうたい 中隊 a company. (! 通例単数・複数扱い)
● 中隊長 a company commander. (! 通例中尉・大尉)
ちゅうだん 中段 (階段) the middle of the stairs; (剣道の) 〈*be at*〉 middle guard; (寝台車の) the middle berth. ▶カーブを右スタンドの中段へ打ち込む hit a curve halfway up right field stands.
ちゅうだん 中断 名 (a) stop; (an) interruption; discontinuation; suspension.
━━ 中断する 動 (止める) stop; (妨げる) interrupt; (継続しているものを) discontinue; (一時的に) suspend. ▶その番組は臨時ニュースのために中断された The program *was interrupted* by a special news flash./The program (abruptly) *cut* to a special news flash. (! cut to は「(画面が)別の画面に切り変わる」の意) ▶野球の試合は雨で中断した The ball game was delayed due to rain. ▶子育てのために仕事を中断する女性は多い Many women *take time out* from work to take care of their children.
ちゅうちゅう ● (赤ん坊が)母親のおっぱいをちゅうちゅう吸う *suck* one's mother's milk. ▶ネズミはちゅうちゅう鳴く A mouse *squeaks*. ▶彼女はオレンジジュースをストローでちゅうちゅう吸った She *sucked* orange juice *noisily* through a straw. ▶母親は赤ちゃんのほおにちゅうちゅうキスした The mother *repeatedly* kissed her baby on the cheek *with a smack*.

ちゅうちょ 躊躇 图 (a) hesitation; 〖気乗りしないこと〗 reluctance; 〖良心のとがめ〗(やや書)〖やや書〗(❗ しばしば複数形で)〖遠慮〗 reserve; 〖優柔不断〗 indecision. ● ちゅうちょなく without *hesitation*; 〖いやがらずに〗 without *reluctance*; 〖平気で〗 without *scruple*; 〖遠慮なく〗 without *reserve*.
── 躊躇する 動 hesitate (*about*; *to do*). (⇨ためらう) ▶ 彼女はドアをノックする前に一瞬ちゅうちょした She *hesitated* for a moment before knocking on the door.

ちゅうづり 宙吊り ● 宙吊りになる hang 〖だらりと〗 dangle] in the air [in midair].

ちゅうてつ 鋳鉄 cast iron.

ちゅうと 中途 halfway; midway. ● 中途退学する (⇨中退) ● 中途採用する (年度の途中で) hire ... midway through the year; (経験者を) hire ... in mid-career. ● 旅の中途で引き返す turn back *halfway* [*midway*] through the trip. (⇨途中)

ちゅうとう 中東 the Middle East.
● 中東諸国 Middle Eastern countries; countries in the Middle East. ● 中東和平会談 Middle East peace talks.

ちゅうとう 中等 middle(-class); (中程度の) medium. ● 前期[後期]中等教育 lower [upper] *secondary* education.

ちゅうとう 柱頭 (柱の) the capital; (花の) a stigma.

ちゅうどう 中道 ── 中道の 形 (穏健な) middle-of-the-road (略 MOR).
● 中道主義者 a middle-of-the-roader, 〖政治〗 a centrist. ● 中道政党 a middle-of-the-road [a centrist] party. (❗ その中の左[右]派は the left [right]-of-center faction)

ちゅうどく 中毒 poisoning; (麻薬などの常用) addiction. ● 薬品[カドミウム]中毒 chemical [cadmium] *poisoning*. ● 麻薬[テレビ; 活字]中毒 drúg [télevision; bóok] *áddiction*. ● アルコール中毒 (⇨アルコール). ● 麻薬中毒患者 a drug [a narcotic] *addict*. ● 食中毒にかかる get food *poisoning*. ● ガス中毒になる be [get] *poisoned* by gas. ● 麻薬中毒にかかる[かかっている] *become* [*be*] *addicted* to drugs. ● 中毒死する be *poisoned* to death (*by gas*). ● 彼は仕事中毒だ He is a work *addict* 〖話〗 a workaholic.

ちゅうとはんば 中途半端 ── 中途半端な 形 〖事が〗 (半ばできている) half done, (未完成の) unfinished, (不完全な) halfway; 〖人・答えなどが〗 (どっちつかずの) indecisive, (なまぬるい) lukewarm. ● 中途半端な仕事をする do a *halfway* job. ● 中途半端な態度をとる take a *lukewarm* attitude (*toward*). ▶ 物事を中途半端にしておいてはいけない You should not leave things *half done* [*unfinished*]./You should not do things *by halves*.

ちゅうトロ 中トロ moderately-fatty tuna.

ちゅうとん 駐屯 ── 駐屯する 動 (配置される)(やや書) be stationed; (守備隊が) be garrisoned.
● 駐屯地 〖やや書〗 a station; (特に遠隔地の) a post; (守備隊の) a gárrison. ● 駐屯部隊 a garrison. (❗ 単・複両扱い)

チューナー 〖ラジオなどの同調器〗 a tuner.

ちゅうなんべい 中南米 South and Central America (❗ 語順に注意); (ラテンアメリカ) Latin America.
● 中南米諸国 Latin American countries.

ちゅうにかい 中二階 a mezzanine /ˈmézəniːn/.

ちゅうにくちゅうぜい 中肉中背 ● 中肉中背の人(=中ぐらいの身長と体格の人) a person of *medium height and build*.

ちゅうにち 駐日 ● 駐日米国大使 the U.S. Ambassador *to Japan*.

ちゅうにち 中日 (彼岸の) the day of the spring [autumn] equinox; (なかび) the middle day (*of*).

ちゅうにゅう 注入 图 (an) infusion; (an) injection.
● 公的資金の注入 an *injection* of public funds.
── 注入する 動 (注ぐ)(やや書) infuse; (通例に) inject.

チューニング 〖音合わせ〗 tuning /tʃúːniŋ/.

ちゅうねん 中年 middle age. (❗ 通例 40 歳くらいから 60 歳代半ばくらいまでを漠然とさす (⇨中高年)) ● 中年の男 a man of *middle age*; a *middle-aged* man. ● 中年である be *in middle age*. (❗ ×be [×one's] middle age としない) ● 中年太りになる develop (a) *middle-age(d) spread*. (❗ 冗談めかした言い方, but put on weight in middle age といえば普通の表現となる) ▶ ゴルフをやっていたお陰で私は中年太りをまぬがれた Golf saved me from a *middle-aged spread*.

ちゅうのう 中脳 〖解剖〗 mesencephalon (複 mesencephala, 〜s); the midbrain.

ちゅうは 中波 〖電気〗 (the) medium wave (略 MW); medium frequency (略 MF). (関連 短波 a short wave/長波 a long wave)

ちゅうは 中破 modest [some] damage.

チューバ 〖楽器〗 a tuba. ● チューバを吹く play the *tuba*.

ちゅうハイ 酎ハイ *shochu* and soda.

ちゅうばいか 虫媒花 an entomophilous flower.

ちゅうばん 中盤 (将棋などの) the middle stage [part] of a game. ▶ 選挙は中盤(戦)に入った The election campaign has reached the *middle stage*.

ちゅうび 中火 (中くらいの炎) a medium flame; (中くらいの熱) medium heat. (⇨弱火)

ちゅうぶ 中部 〖中心部〗 the central part; 〖中央部分〗 the middle part. ● 中部地方 the *Chubu* [*Central*] district; (日本の中部) *the central part* of Japan. ● 中部日本 *Central* Japan.

チューブ a tube; (タイヤの) an inner tube. ● チューブ入りの絵の具 *tube* colors. ● 歯磨き入り歯みがき a *tube* of toothpaste. ● チューブから絞り出す squeeze 《paint》 from a *tube*. ▶ タイヤだけでなくチューブも破れている The *tube* is broken as well as the tire.

ちゅうふう 中風 〖医学〗 paralysis /pəræləsis/. ● 中風をわずらっている be paralyzed; have [suffer from] *paralysis*.
● 中風患者 a pàralýtic.

ちゅうふく 中腹 ● 山の中腹で彼にばったり出会う meet him unexpectedly *halfway up* [*down*] the mountain. (❗ up は山を登って行く場合, down は下る場合) ▶ 山の中腹の小屋で休憩した There was a hut *halfway up* [*down*] the mountain, and we took a rest there.

ちゅうぶらりん 宙ぶらりん ▶ 猿は木に宙ぶらりんにぶら下がっている The monkey *is hanging* from the tree. ▶ その件を宙ぶらりん(=未決定)にしておくな Don't leave the matter *unsettled* [*pending*].

チューブレスタイヤ a tubeless tire.

ちゅうべい 中米 (中央アメリカ) Central America.
● 中米の Central American.

ちゅうべい 駐米 ● 駐米(日本)大使 the Japanese Ambassador *to the U.S.*

ちゅうへん 中編 (小説) a novélla (複 〜s). (❗ 複数形 -velle /-liː/ は好まれない) (⇨小説)

ちゅうぼう 厨房 a kitchen. (⇨台所)

＊ちゅうもく 注目 图 notice; (注意) attention. ● 注目に値する本 a noteworthy 〖注目すべき〗 a *notable* book; a book *worthy of note*. ▶ その選手は今や人々の注目の的だ The athlete is now the focus [center] of public *attention*. / The athlete is now *in the limelight* [*public eye*]. ▶彼の新しい小説は一般大衆の注目を集めた His new novel attracted [drew] public *attention*. ▶その作家は今出回っている本を浴びている The writer is *very much in the* public *eye* now.

— 注目する 動 [[注意を払う]] pay* [give*] attention to ...; [[気にとめる, 関心を寄せる]] take* notice of ...; [[注意して見守る]] watch. ●授業中先生に注目する pay (close) *attention to* one's teacher [what one's teacher says] in class. (❗listen carefully [attentively] to ... といってもほぼ同意) ▶当時批評家たちはだれもこの詩人に注目していなかった No critics *took notice of* this poet in those days. (❗×*Any* critic took *no* notice of .... は不可) ▶日本式経営法が今引国から注目されている The Japanese way of management *is now being watched with* (keen) *interest* by the rest of the world. (❗この場合 the rest of を忘れないこと) ▶世間が君に注目している The eyes of the world are *upon* you. ▶私のやることに注目してくれ. 失敗すればいつでもやめる Focus [Pay] *your attention on* what I am doing. I'm always ready to resign if I should fail [If I fail, I will resign anytime]. (❗この文は「やめる意思のあること」に焦点があてられているので, 前の文のように if I fail を文末に置く方が分かりやすい)

ちゅうもん 注文 图 ❶ [[あつらえ]] (an) order 《*for, from*》. (❗「注文品[書]」の意では ◯)

① 【~を注文】 ▶丸善への注文をする make an *order for* a book *from* [×to] Maruzen. ●大口 [小口] の注文 a large [a small] *order*. ●急ぎの注文 a rush [an urgent] *order*. ●追加注文をする make an additional *order*.

② 【注文~】 ●注文仕立て(=オーダーメード)のスーツ a made-*to-order* [a custom-made, a tailor-made] suit; a suit made *to order*. ▶その本は注文中だ I have the book *on order*. / That book is *on order*.

③ 【注文が[は]】 ▶この工場には多数のロボットの注文が来ている The factory has a lot of *orders for* robots. ▶その辞書に注文が殺到している There is a rush *of orders for* the dictionary. ▶ご注文はお決まりでしょうか(レストランで) Are you ready *to order*, sir [ma'am]? (❗sir は男性客, ma'am は女性客に対して)

会話 「ほかにご注文は?」「これで結構です」 "Would you like [Could I get you] anything else, sir [ma'am]?" "No, that's fine."

④ 【注文の】 ▶彼の注文の品を届ける deliver his *order*; deliver the things he *ordered*. (❗×deliver his *ordered* things とはいわない) ▶注文の品(=注文したもの)がまだ届かない What I *ordered* hasn't [haven't] arrived yet. (❗注文したものが単数か複数かによって動詞の単・複が決まる) / My *order* hasn't arrived yet.

会話 「ご注文の本が入りました」「分かりました. 取りに寄ります」 "Your book's arrived, sir [ma'am]." "Right. I'll call in [drop in] for it." (❗drop in は よりくだけた言い方)

翻訳のこころ 当軒は注文の多い料理店ですから, どうかそこはご承知ください(宮沢賢治『注文の多い料理店』) We have many orders at our restaurant. We hope you'd understand (any delays). (❗(1)「(料理などの)注文」は order. (2) 「ご承知ください」は前に「(料理が出来上がる時間の)遅れ(=delay)を」を補うと分かりやすい)

⑤ 【注文に】 ●注文に応じる accept [take up] an *order*.

⑥ 【注文を】 ●注文を取る take 《his》 *order*. ●注文を聞く call for *orders*. ●海外から注文を受ける get [receive] *orders from* abroad. ●電話の注文を受け付ける accept telephone *orders*.

会話 「ご注文をお伺いします」「ローストビーフとビールをください」「私も同じものを」"May I have [take] your *order*, please?" (❗order を用いずに May I get something, sir [ma'am]? のようにも言う) "I'll have roast beef and beer." "I'll have the same, please." (❗客も please を付ける方が礼儀正しい言い方)

❷ [[依頼, 要求]] (要請) a request; (お願い) a favor; (強い要求) a demand; (条件) a condition. ▶彼に無理な注文をするな Don't make an unreasonable *request of* [*demand on*] him. ▶君に一つ注文(=お願い)がある I have a *favor to ask of* you. / Will you do me a favor? ▶それは無理な注文だ That's an unreasonable *demand*. / That's *asking* too much. (❗口語的な言い方) / (難しい要求だ) 《話》 That's a tall [a large] *order*. ▶ぼくに家事をしろというのは無理な注文だ It's too much to *ask of* me to keep house.

● 注文をつける ▶私からは何の注文(=条件)もつけません I'll *make* no *conditions*.

— 注文する 動 ❶ [注文する] order 《*from*》. ●酒屋にビールを1ケース注文する *order* a case of beer *from* [×to] a liquor store (❗×*order* a liquor store a case of beer の語順はとらない); *give* a liquor store an *order for* a case of beer; *place* an *order for* a case of beer *with* a liquor store. (❗最後の例は商用文などで好まれる言い方) ▶ステーキを3人前注文する *order* three portions of steak; *order* steak for three. ▶それを電話で注文する *order* it by telephone. ▶私たちは(店員に)紅茶とコーヒーを注文した We *gave* an *order* (*to* a waiter) *for* tea and coffee.

❷ [[依頼・要求する]] (依頼する) ask; request; (要求する) demand.

● 注文住宅 a custom-built [a custom-made] house. ● 注文書 an order for goods; an order sheet. ● 注文生産 production to order.

ちゅうもんのおおいりょうりてん『注文の多い料理店』 *The Restaurant of Many Orders*. (〖参考〗宮沢賢治の童話)

ちゅうや 昼夜 (⇨日夜) ▶彼らは昼夜交代で働いた They worked in *night and day* shifts. ▶彼女は昼夜を問わず[昼夜の別なく]働いた She worked in *night and day* [*all day and all night without stopping*, (24 時間ぶっ通しで) *around the clock*]. ▶彼は一昼夜[二昼夜]働きつめだった He kept working continuously *for twenty-four hours* [*two days and* (*two*) *nights*].

ちゅうゆ 注油 — 注油する 動 oil; lubricate.

ちゅうよう 中庸 ●中庸を得た(=穏健な)意見の持ち主 a person with *moderate* /mάdərət/ opinions; a moderate. ▶彼は中庸を守ることを旨とした He made it a principle to be *moderate* [(極端に走らない) not to go to extremes].

ちゅうよう 中葉 around [about] the middle 《*of* the Meiji era》.

ちゅうりつ 中立 图 neutrality. ●中立を保つ observe *neutrality*; remain [keep] *neutral*; (どちらの味方もしない) do not take sides. ●その地域を中立化する *neutralize* the territory.

— 中立の 形 neutral. ●その問題に中立の[中立的]態度をとる take a *neutral* attitude toward the

problem; stand *neutral* in the problem. ● 中立主義 neutralism. ● 中立主義者 a neutralist. ● 中立政策 a neutrality [a neutralist] policy. ● 中立国 a neutral nation.
チューリップ 〖植物〗a tulip.
チューリヒ 〖スイスの都市〗Zurich /zúərik/.
ちゅうりゃく 中略 the omission of the middle part 《*of*》. (! …で表す)
ちゅうりゅう 中流 ❶ 〖川の〗the middle reaches (of a river) (⇨上流); (川幅の中ほど) midstream. ▶その川は中流は浅い The river is shallow in *midstream*.
❷ 〖社会の〗▶戦後国が豊かになったということは、今や多くの家族が中流の生活を楽しめるということなのだ In the postwar years the affluence of the country means that many families can now live a *middle-class* existence.
● 中流階級 the middle class(es). ● 中流家庭 a middle-class family.
ちゅうりゅう 駐留 ── 駐留する 動 (配置される) be stationed; (居残る) remain.
● 駐留軍 (占領軍) occupation forces. ● 在日米駐留軍 American forces (*stationed*) in Japan.
ちゅうりん 駐輪 ── 駐輪する 動 park a bicycle.
ちゅうりんじょう 駐輪場 a bicycle parking lot. (! (学校などの)自転車置き場は a bike shed という)
ちゅうれつ 中列 (sit *in*) the middle row.
ちゅうろ 中ロ〖露〗 中ロ〖露〗の 形 Sino-Russian.
ちゅうロ 駐ロ〖露〗 ● 駐ロ(日本)大使 the Japanese ambassador *to* Russia.
ちゅうわ 中和 名 〖化学〗(酸とアルカリの融合による) neutralization; (逆の性質のものの対抗作用による) counteraction.
── 中和する 動 neutralize, counteract; (解毒剤で) antidote. (! 中和剤はそれぞれ a neutralizer, a counteractive, an antidote)
チュニジア 〖国名〗Tunisia /t(j)u(ː)níːʒiə/; (公式名) the Republic of Tunisia. (首都 Tunis) ● チュニジア人 a Tunisian. ● チュニジア(人)の Tunisian.
チュニス 〖チュニジアの首都〗Tunis /t(j)úːnəs/.
ちゅんちゅん ▶スズメが庭でちゅんちゅん鳴いている Sparrows *are chirping* in the garden. (! chirp はスズメだけでなく、小さい鳥や昆虫にも用いる)
ちょ 緒 緒に**つく** (始まる) start; (順調に始める) get under way.
-ちょ -著 (written) by. ● 小西良行著『生態学入門』*An Introduction to Ecology by* Yoshiyuki Konishi. (! 書名は通例イタリック体)
ちよ 千代 (千年) a thousand years.
● 千代に八千代に (いついつまでも) forever.
ちょいちょい sometimes. (⇨時々, ちょくちょく)
ちょいやく ちょい役 ▶ちょい役で映画に出る play a *bit role* in the movie. (⇨端役)
***ちょう** 腸 a bowel /báuəl/. (! a bowel は腸の一部で、通例 the bowels で腸全体を表す); 〖解剖〗the intestines /intéstinz/. (! 通例単数扱い). (! 日常語では stomach を用いる (⇨おなか)) ● 大[小]腸 the large [small] *intestine* [*bowel*]. ▶腸が悪い I have *bowel* [*intestinal*] trouble.
● 腸炎 inflammation of the intestines. ● 腸カタル intestinal catarrh. ● 腸重積 intussusception. ● 腸チフス typhoid (fever). ● 腸捻転 a twist in the intestines; 〖医学〗volvulus. ● 腸閉塞 intestinal obstruction; 〖医学〗ileus /íliəs/.
ちょう 丁 〖さいころの目の偶数〗an even (↔an odd) number.
ちょう 庁 an agency. ● 金融庁 the Financial Services Agency.
ちょう 兆 ❶ 〖数〗● 1 兆 a trillion; 〖英古〗a billion. ● 10 兆円 ten *trillion* yen. ❷ 〖きざし〗● 吉兆 a good (↔an ill) omen [sign].
ちょう 町 (地方公共団体) a town; (市や区の小区画) *cho*; (距離) a *cho* (参考 約109m); (面積) a *cho* (参考 約99アール).
ちょう 長 ❶ 〖かしら〗a head; a chief (働 ~s) (! head より小さい集団の長); (上司) 〖話〗a boss (! 社長などの場合に主任・課長などと上司もさし、日本語の「ボス」の悪い含みはない); (指導者) a leader. ● 一家の長 the *head* [*patriarch*] of a family; (かせぎ手) the *breadwinner* in one's family. ▶彼はグループの長 He's the *head* [*leader*] of the group. ❷ 〖長所〗(a) merit.
ちょう 蝶 〖昆虫〗a butterfly. (事情 日本では春を連想させる優雅な昆虫だが、英国では夏の虫で軽薄さ、気忙しさを連想させる) ▶チョウは花から花へと(ひらひら)飛ぶ *Butterflies* flit [float, flutter] from flower to flower. (! from A to B で AB が同一名詞の場合は通例無冠詞)
● 蝶よ花よと ▶蝶よ花よと育てる bring up 《one's daughter》 with much care and affection; lavish love [affection] on 《one's daughter》. (! lavish は「惜しみなく与える」の意)
ちょう- 超- ● 超大型タンカー a *super*tanker. ● 超自然的な存在 *super*natural beings. ● 超近代的な設備 *ultra*modern equipment. ● 超氷河期 a 'super ice age'. ● 超低金利 rock-bottom [super-low] interest rates. ● 超純水 *ultra*pure water. ● 超かつく (⇨むかつく) ▶超疲れた 〖米話〗I'm *super* tired./〖英話〗I'm *quite* exhausted.
-ちょう -丁 ● はさみ一丁 a pair of scissors. ● 豆腐一丁 a cake of *tofu*.
-ちょう -朝 〖時代〗a period, an age (! period は時の長短に関係なく、期間を表す. age は特定の人物・事件で代表されるような時代を表す); 〖治世〗a reign /réin/; 〖王朝〗a dynasty /dáinəsti/. ● 平安朝 the Heian *period*. ● ビクトリア朝 the Victorian *age*; the *reign* of Queen Victoria. ● 清[チューダー]朝 the Qing /tʃíŋ/ [Tudor] *dynasty*.
-ちょう -調 ● パステル調のスカーフ a pastel-*shaded* scarf. ● ビクトリア調の家屋 a Victorian-*inspired* house.
ちょうあい 寵愛 名 ● 王の寵愛を受ける gain the king's *favor*; gain the *favor* of the king. ● 王の寵愛を失う lose the king's *favor*; lose *favor* with the king.
── 寵愛する 動 ● 多くの女の中で特に彼女を寵愛する *favor* her among many women.
ちょうい 弔意 (哀悼) 《やや堅》condolences; (悔み) sympathies. ● 弔意を表す express (one's) *condolences* 《*to*》.
ちょうい 弔意 condolence(s); sympathy.
── 弔慰する 動 ● condole 《*with* him》; offer [express] one's condolences 《*to* him》; formally express one's sympathy 《*to* him》.
● 弔慰金 condolence money.
ちょうい 潮位 the height of the tide.
ちょういちりゅう 超一流 ── 超一流の 形 extremely fine, ultrafine. ● 超一流のスター a superstar. ● 超一流私立大学 《one of》 the most prestigious private colleges.
ちょういん 調印 (署名) signing. ▶平和条約が両国政府によって署名・調印された The peace treaty *was signed* (*and sealed*) by both governments. (! and sealed は省略されることも多い (⇨印鑑))
● 調印式 a signing ceremony.

ちょうえい 町営 — 町営の ⟨形⟩ municipal. ●町営プール a municipal swímming pool.

ちょうえき 懲役 imprisonment; (強制労働を伴う)《英》[法律] penal servitude. ●無期懲役 life imprisonment. ▶彼は3年の懲役に処せられた He was sentenced to three years *in prison* [*three years' imprisonment*].

ちょうえつ 超越 — 超越する ⟨動⟩ (限界を)《書》transcend; (域を越える) rise above ...; (離れている) stand aloof 《from》. ●人知を超越する *transcend* all human knowledge [*wisdom*]. ●世俗を超越する *rise above* the world.

ちょうえん 腸炎 [医学] enteritis. ●急性腸炎 acute enteritis.

ちょうおん 長音 a long sound; (長母音) a long vowel.
●長音符[声] a macron.

ちょうおん 聴音 — 聴音器 a listening instrument.
●聴音機 a sound locator.

ちょうおんかい 長音階 [音楽] a major scale.

ちょうおんそく 超音速 (a) supersónic spèed. ▶このジェット機は超音速で飛ぶ This jet plane flies *at supersonic speed*.
●超音速航空機 a supersonic aircraft. ●超音速飛行 supersonic flight. ●超音速旅客機 a supersonic transport (略 SST).

ちょうおんぱ 超音波 ⟨名⟩ supersónic wàves; (医療用の) últrasòund /ʌltrə-/.
— 超音波の ⟨形⟩ supersónic; ultrasónic.
●超音波検査 supersonic testing. ●超音波スキャナー an ultrasound scanner.

*__ちょうか 超過__ ⟨名⟩ (an) excess; [余剰] (a) surplus. ●輸入超過(=輸出に対する輸入の超過) an *excess* of imports over exports. ●制限重量超過の手荷物に対して超過料金を払う pay *extra* for one's *excess* baggage. (❗お支払いの超過分はお返しいたします If you pay *more than* necessary, the extra money will be given back to you./Any *excess* in payment [《書》Any *overpayment*] will be returned [《書》*refunded*].
— 超過する ⟨動⟩ (限度などを) exceed; [...以上である] be more than ..., be above .... ●制限時間を超過する *exceed* the time limit. ●費用は予算をはるかに超過した The expense far *exceeded* [*was way above*] our estimate. (❗後の方が口語的)/It cost far *more than* we had estimated. ▶輸出は輸入を10億ドル超過している The exports *exceed* the imports by a billion dollars. ▶その小包は重量が3キロ超過している The parcel is three kilos *overweight* [*overweight* by three kilos]. (❗後の方は超過分を強調する) ▶そのバスは定員を超過している The bus *is overloaded*.
●超過額 a surplus; an excess 《of》. ●超過勤務 overtime work. ●週に12時間の超過勤務をする work *overtime* 12 hours [do 12 hours' *overtime*] a week. ●超過勤務手当 overtime pay; an overtime allowance.

ちょうか 弔花 funeral flowers; (花輪) funeral wreath.

ちょうか 町家 [商人の家] a marchant('s) house; [町中の家] a house in a busy town.

ちょうか 長靴 long boots; (戦闘用ブーツ) combat boots.

ちょうか 釣果 a catch. ▶今日はニシンの釣果に恵まれた I brought in a good [a huge, a large] *catch* of herring today.

ちょうかい 町会 [町議会] a town council; [町内会] (⇨町内).
●町会議員 a member of a town council.

ちょうかい 朝会 a morning meeting.

ちょうかい 懲戒 (処分) disciplinary action [measures]. ●懲戒免職になる be dismissed for *disciplinary reasons*; (悪事がばれて) resign (one's office) in disgrace. ▶会社はその社員を懲戒処分にした The company has taken *disciplinary action* against the employee.

ちょうがい 鳥害 damage caused by birds. ●鳥害を受ける be damaged by birds.

ちょうかく 聴覚 hearing; [医学] an auditory /ɔːdətɔːri/ sense. ●聴覚が鋭い[にぶい] have acute [poor] *hearing*. ●聴覚を失う lose one's *hearing*. ▶彼の聴覚は弱ってきている His *hearing* is getting worse.
●聴覚障害者 a person with a hearing loss;《婉曲的》a hearing-impaired person; an aurally challenged person. ●聴覚テスト a hearing test.

ちょうかん 長官 (官庁などの) a director general; 《米》the Secretary. ●宮内庁長官 the *Director General* of the Imperial Household Agency. ●国務[商務]長官 the *Secretary* of State [*Commerce*]. ●最高裁判所長官 the *Chief Justice* of the Supreme Court;《米》the *Chief Justice* of the United States Supreme Court.

ちょうかん 朝刊 a morning (news)paper. (❗夕刊と区別するときは a morning edition ともいう)

ちょうかんず 鳥瞰図 a bird's-eye view.

ちょうき 弔旗 a flag of mourning. ●弔旗を揚げる [hoist, run up] *a flag draped with black cloth*; (半旗を) fly (a *flag*) *at half-mast*.

ちょうき 長期 ⟨名⟩ a long period (of time); a long term. (⇨期間) ▶その会談は長期に及んだ The talks lasted for a *long* (*period of*) *time*.
— 長期の ⟨形⟩ long-term; (展望期間の長い) long-range. ●(映画などが)長期興行[公演]を続けている be running *long*.
●長期協定 a long-term agreement. ●長期金利 the long-term interest rate. ●長期計画 a long-term [a long-range] plan. ●長期契約 a long-term contract. ●長期欠席 a long absence. (⇨長欠) ●長期戦 a long-drawn(-out) [a prolonged] war. ●長期滞在 an extended [a lengthy] stay. ●長期予報 a long-range [an extended] weather forecast.

ちょうぎかい 町議会 a town council.
●町議会議員 a town council(l)or; a town councilman.

ちょうきょう 調教 ⟨名⟩ (馬などの) training.
— 調教する ⟨動⟩ train 《a horse》.
●調教師 a trainer.

ちょうきょり 長距離 a long distance; (長い射程距離) (a) long range.
●長距離競走 a (long-)distance race. (❗(1) distance の方が普通. (2)《英》では中距離競走も含む) ●長距離選手 a (long-)distance runner. ●長距離打者 a power hitter; a slugger. ●長距離弾道弾 [ミサイル] a lóng-range ballistic missile. ●長距離電話 a long-distance (phone) call;《米》long distance. ●長距離電話をかける call [phone] (him) *long-distance*. (❗この long-distance は副詞) ●長距離電話に金をかける spend a lot on long distance. ●長距離輸送 long (distance) haul. ●長距離列車 a long-distance train.

ちょうきん 彫金 chasing; metal carving. ●彫金を施す chase.
●彫金師 a chaser.

ちょうけい　長径 the major axis /ǽksiːs/. (⇨短径)

ちょうけし　帳消し ── 帳消しにする 動 (相殺する) cancel ... (out); (なくす) wipe ... out. ●借金を帳消しにする *cancel* (*out*) a debt; *write off* a debt. ●ダブルプレーを取ってエラーを帳消しにする turn a double play to erase an error. ▶敷金でこの3か月の家賃の滞納分を帳消しにします Your security deposit will cancel out the rent you haven't paid for the last three months. ▶当社に対する世間の信用は今回の金融不祥事で帳消しになってしまった Our credit with the public has been wiped out by this financial scandal.

ちょうけつ　長欠 a long absence; (無断の) ábsentéeism.
●長欠児童 a child who has been absent from school for a long time. (⚠形容詞の longtime は常に限定的に用いる: a *longtime* friend 長年の友人)

ちょうげんぼう　長元坊 〘鳥〙a kestrel.

ちょうこう　兆候 a sign, (やや書) an indication; (病気や悪いことの) a symptom. ●インフルエンザの兆候が現れる develop *symptoms* [*signs*] of influenza. ▶戦争終結の兆候がはっきり出ている There are sure *signs* [clear *indications*] *that* the war will be over. ▶くしゃみは風邪の兆候であることが多い Sneezes often *indicate* [are often a *sign* of] colds.

ちょうこう　長江 〚長い川〛a long river; 〚揚子江〛the Changjiang, the Yangtze River.

ちょうこう　長考 ── 長考する 動 think about (a problem) for a long time; (熟考する) think (a problem) over for a long time; ponder (*on* [*over, about*] a problem).

ちょうこう　調光 ── 調光する 動 change the brightness of an electric light gradually.
●調光器 a dimmer.

ちょうこう　調香 the blending of perfumes.
●調香師 a perfumer.

ちょうこう　聴講 图 ●聴講を許可する grant (him) permission to *audit* a course.
── 聴講する 動 (講義を聴く) attend (a lecture, a course), sit in on (a seminar); (学生が単位を取らずに)《米》audit (a lecture, a course).
●聴講生《米》an auditor; a non-matriculated student;《英》an occasional student. ●聴講料 a fee for auditing.

ちょうごう　調号 〘音楽〙a key signature.

ちょうごう　調合 ── 調合する 動 prepare [〔書〕compound] (a medicine for the flu). ●薬剤を調合して消化剤を作る *compound* drugs *into* a digestive. ●処方の薬を調合する *make up* [《米》*fill*] a prescription.

ちょうこうぜつ　長広舌 a harangue /həræŋ/. ●長広舌をふるう harangue.

ちょうこうそう　超高層 ●超高層ビル a high-rise building; (数十階の場合) a skyscraper. ●超高層マンション a high-rise apartment building.

***ちょうこく　彫刻 图** 〚彫刻術〛(像を作る) sculpture; (彫る, 彫って作る) carving; (表面に彫る) engraving; 〚彫刻品〛(像) a sculpture ((集合的には 回)); (小像, 装飾品) a carving; (浮き彫り) a relief (⇔ ～s). ●(象牙などの)装飾彫刻 decorative *carving*. ●古代彫刻 《集合的》ancient *sculpture*. ●木[石]の彫刻品 a wood [stone] *carving*.
── 彫刻する 動 sculpture; carve; engrave. ●彫刻してある柱 a *sculptured* [a *carved*] pillar. ▶明彦は石を彫刻して像を作った Akihiko sculptured [carved] a statue *out of* stone. / Akihiko carved stone *into* a statue.

●彫刻家 (像の) a sculptor; (彫り物の) an engraver. ●彫刻刀 a chisel.

ちょうこく　超克 ── 超克する 動 surmount; overcome; get ... over.

:**ちょうさ　調査 图** (an) examination; (an) investigation; (質問などによる) (an) inquiry; (学術的な) research(es) (⇨研究 [類語]); (統計・測量などによる) (a) survey.

使い分け examination 調査・検査の意を表す一般的な語.
investigation 公的機関などによる詳しい事実・原因の調査.

●市場調査 market *research*. ●実地調査 an on-the-spot *investigation*. ●身辺調査(身元調査) a background *check*. (⇨身元) ●実態調査 (⇨実態) ●調査方法 a method of *investigation*. ●その事故[伝染病]の原因調査 an *investigation* into the cause of the accident [epidemic]. ●調査中の事柄 the matter *under investigation* [*examination*]. ▶何人の人がその製品を使用したか調査が行われた A *survey* was conducted to find out how many people used the product.

── 調査する 動 examine; investigate, make* [conduct, carry out] an investigation (*of, into*); inquire (*into*); survey; research (*into, on*). (⇨研究する) ●その殺人事件を調査する *examine* the facts. ●その殺人事件を調査する *investigate* [look into, inquire into] the murder case. ●ヘリコプターからその土地を調査する *survey* the land from a helicopter. ▶警察はその火事の原因を調査している The police *are investigating* [*making an investigation into*] the cause of the fire./The police *are* [×is] *investigating* how the fire broke out. ▶さらに事件を調査した結果, 彼はわいろを受け取ったことが明らかになった Further *investigations into* the case showed [revealed] that he had accepted bribes.

●調査委員会 an investigation [an inquiry] committee. (⇨委員会) ●調査員[官] an investigator, an examiner. ●調査書 (学業成績の) a transcript (of school grades). ●調査報告書 an inquiry report. ●調査用紙 (アンケート用紙) a questionnaire.

ちょうざい　調剤 ── 調剤する 動 prepare medicines; (処方せんどおりに) dispense [make up] a prescription.
●調剤師 a pharmacist. (⇨薬剤師) ●調剤室 a dispensary. ●調剤薬局 a pharmacy. (⇨薬局)

ちょうざめ　蝶鮫 a sturgeon. (通例単・複同形)
〔参考〕この卵の塩漬けがキャビア (caviar) である.

ちょうさんぼし　朝三暮四 (同じ結果) six of one and half a dozen of the other.

:**ちょうし　調子 ❶** 〚状態, 具合〛condition,《話》shape; (運動選手の体調) form; (機械などの正常な状態) 具合 (⇨具合 ❶)
①《調子が[は]》●調子がよい[悪い] be in good [bad, poor] *condition*; be in [out of] *condition* (⚠以上は最も意味が広く, 以下の代わりにも用いる); (体調がよい[悪い]) be in good [bad, poor] *health*; feel well [unwell, sick,《主に英》ill]; (機械が) be in working [be out of] *order*. ●調子が戻る get back (やや書) return, make a return) to one's normal *condition*; be back in form. ●調子がでる get into *condition*; (活動などに慣れて自分のペースでできるようになる) get into [《米》hit] one's *stride*. ▶最近どうも体の調子がよくない I don't *feel* very *well* [《話》*good*] these days. (⚠feel good は

「よい気分である」の意にもなる)/I'm not *myself* these days. ▶そのためにすっかり調子が狂ってしまった That has completely put me out of *condition*. ▶選手たちは最高に調子がよかった The players were in perfect *condition* [《話》in tiptop *shape*]. ▶その投手は調子が戻った The pitcher got his rhythm. ▶その投手は調子がいい[悪い] The pitcher is sharp [shaky]. ▶その打者は調子がいい[悪い] The batter is hot [struggling]. ▶車の調子がおかしい Something is [There's something] wrong with my car./My car isn't running well. (❗後の方は走っている車についていう)

❷【調子が】● 彼の調子はしだいによくなってきた His *health* [*condition*] is gradually improving./He is gradually improving in *health* [his *condition*]. (❗「体調」の意は condition より health の方が明確な言い方) ▶調子はどうですか(体の) How are you (feeling) today?/(暮らし向きなど生活全般の) How's everything?/How are you getting along [on]?/(商売の) How's (your) business? (❗いずれも一種のあいさつ。応答は Okay, I guess. (まあまあですが)などという) ▶機械の調子はどうですか How's the machine? / How does the machine work [run]? ▶高校時代から自分の調子は自分でわかった。悪いときは全部小さくなる Since I was in high school, I have always been able to tell my condition. Whenever I'm in a bad condition [shape], I feel as if all of me has become very small. (❗(1) bad condition は「体の調子が悪い」, bad shape は「練習不足などで調子が悪い」の意。(2) become small は「能力がない、無力である」の意)

【会話】「あの選手の調子はどうですか」「最近調子を落としています」 "What kind of *form* is that player in?" "He's been in bad [out of] *form* recently." (❗逆に「調子がよい」は in (good) form)

【会話】「学校の調子はどう?」「どうも調子がでないわ」 "How's school *going*?" "I don't feel like *I'm doing well*." (❗I feel like *I'm* not *doing well*. とはあまりいわない)

❸【調子を】● 体の調子を崩す lose one's *health*. ● 機械の調子を整える keep the machine in good order. ● その試合に備えて調子を整えておきなさい Get yourself in (good) *condition* [*Condition* yourself] for the game. ▶体の調子をよくしたかったら, もっと運動をしないとだめだよ If you want to *get fit*, you should get more exercise. (❗fit は《話》で, 「元気な, 健康な」の意)

❷【音調, 口調】(音色, 口調) a tone; (音の高低) a tune, a key, a pitch.
①【調子が】● 調子が合って[はずれて]いる be *in* [*out of*] *tune* 《*with*》. ▶彼の演説の調子が突然変わった The *tone* of his speech [His speech tone] has suddenly changed.

②【調子を[に]】● (楽器の)調子を合わせる tune (up). ● 声の調子を上げる[落とす] raise [lower] (the *pitch* of) one's voice. ● 調子を変える (声の) modulate one's voice; (話の) change one's *tone*. ● 音楽に調子を合わせて踊る dance (*in tune*) to the music. ● 調子をはずさずに歌う sing *in tune*; carry a *tune*. ▶その新聞は政府攻撃の調子を和らげた The newspaper *toned down* its attack against [on] the government. ▶彼の声は問いただすような調子になった His voice took on [assumed] an inquiring *tone*.

③【調子の】● 調子の高い[低い] high-[low-]pitched. ● (歌が)調子のよい (音が調和のとれた) harmónious; (律動的な) rhýthmical; (旋律の美しい) melódious.

④【調子で】● 怒ったような[穏やかな; 強い]調子で in an angry [a soft; a forceful] *tone*. ● ふざけた調子で in a jokey *tone*; jokingly. ● 命令するような調子で in a *tone* of command, in a commanding *tone*. ● 一本調子で話す speak in a monotone. ● 調子はずれで歌う sing *out of tune* [*off key*]. ▶同じ(ような)調子で彼の質問が続いた His questions continued the same [a similar] *tone*.

❸【やり方】● a way; a manner. ● いつもの調子で(=いつもやるように) as [《話》like] one always does. ▶こういう調子でそれをやりなさい Do it (*in*) *this way* [*in this manner*, *like this*]. ▶彼はいつもあんな調子だ That's always his *way*.

❹【その他の表現】● この調子ではあすまでに仕事が終らないだろう *At this rate*, we won't be able to finish the work by tomorrow. ▶その調子 That's it./That's the way./You are doing it quite well./(そのまま続けなさい) Keep it up. Keep it up.
● 調子のいい ● 調子のいい(=口先のうまい)セールスマン a *smooth* [a *smooth-talking*] salesperson.
● 調子に乗る ● あら, 調子に乗ってつい余計なことを言ってしまったわ。ごめんなさい Oh, I shouldn't have said that. I *got carried away*. Sorry.
● 調子を合わせる (人と仲よくやっていく) get along [on] (well) 《*with*》 (表面上うまく合わせる) play along 《*with*》.

ちょうし 銚子 a *sake* /sá:ki/ bottle.
ちょうじ 丁字 a clove.
ちょうじ 弔事 an unhappy event; (葬儀) a funeral. (⇔ 慶事)
ちょうじ 弔辞 a message of condólence; a condolences (❗通例複数形で) (通例演説) a memorial address. 【事情】弔辞では We are gathering here not to mourn the death of Mr. A, but to celebrate his life. He lived a full life. (私たちがここに参集いたしましたのは A 氏の死を悼むためではなくその充実した生涯を称えるためであります)のように積極面にふれる傾向がある ● 弔辞を述べる offer 《him》 one's *condolences*; make a *memorial address*. ● 弔辞を送る send 《him》 a *letter* [*message*] *of condolence* (*on his mother's death*).

ちょうじ 寵児 a darling; (花形) a star. ● 文壇の寵児 a *darling* of the literary world; one of the most sought-after writers.

ちょうししゃ 聴視者 (⇔視聴者)
ちょうしぜん 超自然 — 超自然の 形 supernatural.
● 超自然現象 the supernatural.
ちょうじつ 長日 — 長日性の 形 long-day.
● 長日性植物 a long-day plant.
ちょうしゃ 庁舎 a government office building.
ちょうじゃ 長者 a wealthy [a rich] person; (百万長者) a millionaire; (億万長者) a multimillionaire; a billionaire.
● 長者番付 a list of millionaires.
ちょうしゅ 聴取 hearing. ● 彼から事情を聴取する (言い分を聞く) *hear* what he has to say; (尋問する) question him. ▶彼女は警察の事情聴取を受けた模様である She *was* presumably *questioned* by the police.
● 聴取者 (ラジオの) a (radio) listener; 《集合的》an audience, a radio audience.
ちょうじゅ 長寿 long life; 《書》longevity /lɑndʒévɪti/. (⇔長生き) ● 長寿の秘訣(ひけつ) the secret of *longevity*. ● 長寿を保つ live long; enjoy *longevity*. ● 長寿食の macrobiotics.
● 長寿社会 (高齢社会) an aged society. (【参考】総人口の 14 パーセントが 65 歳以上の社会をさす。 その半

ちょうしゅう 徴収 ── 徴収する 動 collect;［課す］《や
　ぎ》levy.▶彼から税金を徴収する collect a tax
　from him; levy a tax *on* him.
ちょうしゅう 聴衆 an audience, (出席者数) an at-
　tendance（■集合名詞で単数扱い. 通例修飾語を伴
　う）;（聞き手）a listener.

> 解説　audience は集合名詞で通例単数扱いだが,
> 《英》では多数の観客を考える場合は複数扱いが普通.
> 通例複数形にはしないが, 複数の観客集団をさす場合
> は複数形.

　● 耳よく肥えた聴衆 a very appreciative *audi-
　ence*. ▶聴衆は彼女の歌に聞きほれた The *audience*
　was［《英》were］charmed by her song［sing-
　ing］. ▶会場には 2,000 人［多く］の聴衆がいた There
　was an *audience* of 2,000［a large *audience*］
　in the hall.（■ ✕ 2,000［many］audiences は不
　可. 例文中の audience は attendance と交換可）
　▶彼の演説は全国各地で多くの聴衆を魅了した His
　speech fascinated a lot of *audiences* all over
　Japan.
ちょうじゅう 鳥獣 birds and beasts; fur and feath-
　er.
　● 鳥獣保護区 a (wildlife) sanctuary.
*__ちょうしょ 長所__ a good［a strong］point;［価値］a
　merit (↔a demerit);［美徳］a virtue;［有利な点］
　an advantage (↔a disadvantage). ▶彼女の長所
　と短所 her mérits and démerits /díːmèrits/ (■対
　照的強勢に注意); her strengths and weaknesses.
　▶［その計画］の長所はどういうところですか What are
　his *good points*［the *merits of* the plan］?（■
　尋ねるときは複数形を用いる. 日本語にひかれて ✕*Where
　are*...? とはしない）▶能弁は政治家としての彼の長所の
　一つだ Eloquence is one of his *merits*［*strong
　points*］as a politician. ▶この機械の長所はほとんど
　修理がいらないことだ The *advantage*［*virtue*］of
　this machine is that it takes so little repair.
ちょうしょ 調書 (訴状, 明細書) a bill; (報告書) a
　report. ● 支払調書 a payment bill. ● 供述調書 a
　witness report. ● 調書を取る draw up a report
　《by questioning him》;《話》book《him for...》
　（■通例 be booked《for》の形で用いる.
ちょうじょ 長女 the［one's］oldest［《主に英》
　eldest］daughter; one's first-born daughter.
　（⇨長男）
ちょうしょう 弔鐘 a funeral bell.
ちょうしょう 嘲笑 名［冷やかし］ridicule（■必ずしも悪
　意はない）;［不信・皮肉をこめた］a scoff（■通例複数
　形で）;（下品な言葉を伴う）a jeer, (皮肉をこめた冷たい)
　a sneer（■あざけり度合いはいちばん強い）. ● 嘲笑
　の的になる become an object of *ridicule*. ● 嘲笑を招く
　ことをしてはいけない You should not do anything
　to bring *ridicule* on yourself.
── 嘲笑する 動　（⇨嘲(*ﾁｮｳ*)る）▶彼は私を嘲笑した He
　laughed *at*［jeered (*at*), sneered *at*］me.
*__ちょうじょう 頂上__ (山の) the top, the summit（■後
　の方が堅い語）;（とがった山の）the peak. ● 山の頂上に
　at［on］the *top* of a mountain; at［on］a
　mountaintop.（■ at は単なる位置を, on は表面との
　接触を示す）▶彼らはついにエベレストの頂上をきわめた
　They scaled the *peak*［(頂上に着いた) reached
　the *summit*］of Mt. Everest at last. ▶頂上は霧
　でおおわれていた The *top* of the mountain was
　covered with mist./Mist *topped*［*crowned*］
　the mountain. ▶彼の人気は今や頂上(=絶頂)だ He

is now *at the peak of* his popularity./His popularity is now *at its peak*.
　● 頂上会談 (首脳会談) a summit (meeting).
ちょうじょう 超常 ● 超常現象 the supernatural.
*__ちょうしょく 朝食__（◯食事, 夕食）a breakfast. ● 朝
　食にベーコンエッグを食べる have bacon and eggs for
　［✕at］*breakfast*. ● 急いで朝食をとる have［eat,
　《書・古》take］*breakfast* quickly; have a hasty
　breakfast.（■(1) take は堅苦しく今はほとんど用いら
　れない. (2) 冠詞の有無に注意）▶朝食はもうおすみですか
　Have you had (your［✕a］) *breakfast* yet? ▶朝
　食は何を食べましたか What did you have［✕eat］
　for *breakfast*?（■ eat は食べる行為そのものを強調す
　るときに用いる. 例: He takes a long time to *eat* a
　substantial breakfast.）
ちょうじり 帳尻 (収支勘定) balance. ● 帳尻を合わせる
　balance (the books［accounts］); (収支を合わせ
　る) make both ends meet. ▶帳尻が合わない The
　books don't *balance*.
ちょうじる 長じる［成長する］grow;［すぐれる］be ex-
　cellent;［年長である］be older.
ちょうしん 長身 (背の高い) tall; (人) a tall person.
ちょうしん 長針 (時計の) the minute［long］hand.
ちょうじん 鳥人 (飛行家) an aviator; a pilot, a
　birdman; (スキージャンプの競技者) a ski jumper; (棒
　高跳びの選手) a pole vaulter.
ちょうじん 超人 a sùperhúman person; (男) a
　súpermàn（⑩ -men）; (女) a superwoman
　（⑩ -men）. ● 超人的な記憶力の持ち主 a person of
　superhuman memory. ● 超人的な努力をする make
　superhuman efforts.
ちょうしんき 聴診器 a stethoscope /stéθəskòup/.
　● 聴診器を当てる apply a *stethoscope*《to him》.
ちょうしんけい 聴神経［解剖］an auditory［an
　acoustic］nerve.
ちょうしんせい 超新星 a sùpernóva.
ちょうしんこつ 彫心鏤骨 ── 彫心鏤骨する 動
　take great pains to write poems［to do one's
　literary work］.
ちょうず 手水 ● 手水を使う wash one's hands and
　face clean.
　● 手水鉢 a washbowl;《英》a washbasin.
ちょうずる 長ずる（⇨長じる）
*__ちょうせい 調整__ 名 (an) adjustment; (a) regula-
　tion.（⇨調節）● (税金の)年末調整 the year-end
　tax *adjustment*.
── 調整する 動［適合させる］adjust /ədʒʌ́st/;［望み状
　態にする］regulate;［楽器・エンジンなどを］tune ...
　(up). ● 時計を調整する (時刻を合わせる) *adjust* a
　watch; (専門家が) *regulate* a watch. ● 意見の違い
　を調整する *adjust*［*iron out*］the differences
　(of opinion).（■ ✕the different opinions とはいわ
　ない）▶車を調整してもらっている I'm having (the
　engine of) the car *tuned up*.
ちょうせい 町勢 the state of the economy of a
　town.
ちょうせい 長征 a long march; (中国共産党軍の大移
　動) the Long March.
ちょうせい 調製 ── 調製する 動 prepare; make《a
　thing》to order; produce《a thing》for a cus-
　tomer.
ちょうせい 徴税 名 tax collection. ── 徴税する 動
　collect a tax《from》.
ちょうせき 潮汐 ebb and flow; a tide.
　● 潮汐点 a tidemark. ● 潮汐表 a tide table.
*__ちょうせつ 調節__ 名 (an) adjustment; (a) regula-
　tion; contról.（⇨調整）● 調節のできる座席 an *ad-
　justable* seat. ● 音声調節つまみ a volume *control*.

ちょうぜつ
- 自動調節のエアコン a self-*regulating* air-conditioner.
— **調節する** 動 [適合させる] adjust; [望む状態にする] regulate; [制御する] contról (-ll-). ・ラジオの音量を調節する *adjust* [*control*] the volume on the radio. ・室温を調節する *regulate* the temperature of a room. ・機械の速さを調節する *regulate* the speed of a machine. ・声を調節する *modulate* one's voice 《*to*》. ・彼は自分の身長に合わせて座席を調節した He *adjusted* the seat to his height.

ちょうぜつ 超絶 — **超絶した** 形 transcendent.
- 超絶した技巧 a *transcendent* technique.

***ちょうせん 挑戦** 名 a challenge; (試み) a try, an attempt. ・挑戦に応じる accept 《*his*》 *challenge* 《*to* a game; *to* do》. ・挑戦状をたたきつける throw down a *challenge* 《*to* him》.
— **挑戦的な** 形 [攻撃的な] aggressive; [権力などに反抗的な] defiant. ・挑戦的態度をとる take a *defiant* attitude 《*toward*》.
— **挑戦する** 動 [試みる] try, attempt; [戦いをいどむ] challenge; [公然と反対する] defy. ・難しい仕事に挑戦する *try* [*attempt*] 《*to* do》 a difficult task. ・世界記録に挑戦する *try* [*attempt*] *to* set the world record. ・チャンピオンに挑戦する *challenge* the champion. ・世論に挑戦する *defy* public opinion. ▶K 大学の入試に再度挑戦します I will *try to* pass the entrance exam of [for, to] K University again. (❗ ×I will challenge.... とはいわない) ▶彼は競走しようと挑戦してきた He *challenged* me *to* (run) a race.
- 挑戦者 (選手権などへの) a challenger (↔defender); (クイズ番組などの) a contestant.

ちょうせん 朝鮮 Koreá. ・北[南]朝鮮 North [South] *Koreá*. (⇒北朝鮮, 韓国) ・朝鮮人 a *Korean*. ・朝鮮語 *Korean*; the *Korean* language. ・朝鮮[人]の *Korean*. ・朝鮮戦争 the *Korean* War. ・朝鮮人参 a ginseng. ・朝鮮半島 the *Korean* Peninsula.

ちょうぜん 超然 — **超然とした** 形 (人と交わらない) aloof; (私情におぼれず冷静な) detached. ・超然とした人 a person of *aloof* character. (❗ 通例 aloof は「人」の前に使わず×an aloof person) ・超然として語る (やや書) talk with a *detached* air. ・他のみんなから離れて超然としている stand [keep, hold oneself] *aloof from* the others. ・世事に超然としている detach oneself from the world.

ちょうそ 彫塑 (彫刻と塑像) carvings and sculptures.

ちょうぞう 彫像 a (carved) statue.

ちょうそく 長足 ・長足の進歩を遂げる make (×a) rapid progress 《*with, in*》.

ちょうぞく 超俗 — **超俗的な** 形 unworldly 《men, outlooks》.

ちょうそん 町村 towns and villages.
- 町村合併 the merger of towns and villages.

ちょうだ 長打 [野球] a long hit; an extra-base hit. ・ライト線に長打を放つ make a *long hit* down the right-field line.
- 長打率 a slúgging average. (参考) 総塁打数を総打数で割った数字) ・長打力 the power (to hit a long ball).

ちょうだ 長蛇 ・長蛇の列をなして in a *long* line [《英》 queue 《kjú:》].

ちょうだい 長大 — **長大な** 形 ・長大な石仏 a *tall*, *huge* stone image of Buddha. ・長大な(=雄大な)山脈 a *grand* mountain range. ・長大な小説 a *long* novel.

ちょうだい 頂戴 ❶ [もらう] receive; get*. ▶きょうお手紙をちょうだいしました I *received* [*got*] your letter today. ▶ご親切なお手紙をちょうだいし，ありがとうございます Thank you very much for your kind letter. ▶あなたがちょうだいと言ったの，このバッグでしょ This is the bag you *asked for*, isn't it ? ▶あちらに着いたらお便りちょうだいね Send me a line [《話》 *Drop* me a note] when you get there.
❷ [食べる, 飲む] have*. ▶ありがとう, もう十分ちょうだいしました I've had enough, thank you. ▶母さん, お水ちょうだい May I *have* [Please *get* me] some water, Mom? (語法) 子供は親に対しては May I ×Can] や Please をつけて言うようにしつけられる)
❸ [...してください] 《どうか》 please; (...してくださいますか) Would you ...? (⇒下さい) ▶ちょっと待ってちょうだい Wait a minute [a moment], *please*. ▶窓を開けてちょうだい Could [Would, Can, Will] you please open the window? (❗ 前の方がご丁寧な言い方)

ちょうたいこく 超大国 a superpower.

ちょうたつ 調達 名 《書》 procurement. ・現地調達 local *procurement*. ・海外調達 (部品などの) outsourcing; offshore *procurement*; (資金の) offshore *funding*. ・資金調達 funding; fund raising.
— **調達する** 動 (必要な物を) get; 《書》 procure; (資金を) raise. ・金を調達する *raise* money 《*for*》; raise funds. ・外部資金を調達する *access* external sources of funding.

ちょうだつ 超脱 — **超脱する** 動 transcend. (⇒超越)

ちょうたん 長短 (長所と短所) mérits and démerits /diːˈmɛrɪts/ (❗ 対照強勢に注意); good and bad points; advantages and disadvantages; strong and weak points.

ちょうたんぱ 超短波 ultrashòrt /ʌltrəˈ-/ wáves; very high frequency (略 VHF). ・極超短波 ultra-high frequency (略 UHF).

ちょうちょう 町長 the mayor (of a town).

ちょうちょう 長調 [音楽] a major (key). ・長調で in a *major* key. ・ホ長調交響曲 a symphony in E *major*.

ちょうちょう 蝶々 a butterfly. (⇒蝶) ・ショパンの『蝶々』 Chopin's *Butterfly*.

ちょうちょうはっし 丁々発止 丁々発止 (刀を交える) cross swords 《*with*》 (❗ 比喩的にも用いる); (激論をする) have a heated [a spirited] discussion.

ちょうちょうふじん『蝶々夫人』 *Madam Butterfly*. (参考) プッチーニ作曲のオペラ

ちょうちん 提灯 a (paper) lantern. ・ちょうちんをつける[消す] light [put out, 《吹き消す》 blow out] a *lantern*.
- ちょうちんに釣り鐘 (ことわざ) A hanging temple bell against a lantern./(不釣合いな) ill-matched (↔well-matched).
- ちょうちん行列 a lantern parade [procession].
- ちょうちん持ち (⇒提灯持ち)

ちょうちんもち 提灯持ち [ちょうちん携帯者] a lantern carrier; [さかんにほめる人] a praiser; 《話》 a booster. ・ちょうちん持ちをする [携帯する] carry a *lantern*; [ほめそやす] sing one's praises; 《話》 boost.
- ちょうちん持ちの記事 a good [a favorable] write-up; a flattering article.

ちょうつがい 蝶番 hinge a door. ▶戸のちょうつがいが外れている[外れた] The door is off its *hinges* [came *unhinged*]. ▶戸はちょうつがいで開閉する The door swings (open and shut) *on its hinges*. (❗ open, shut

ちょうづめ 腸詰め (a) sausage.
ちょうてい 朝廷 the Imperial Court.
ちょうてい 調停 名 mediation; (仲裁) arbitration (!前の語より法的強制力が強い). ●調停に乗り出す undertake *mediation*. ●争いを調停により解決する settle a dispute through [by] *mediation*. ▶調停は不調に終わった *Mediation* ended in failure.
— **調停(を)する** 動 mediate; (仲裁する) arbitrate. ●停戦を調停する *mediate* a cease-fire. (調停が成立したことを含意) ●ストライキの調停をする *mediate in* a strike. ●労使間の調停をする *mediate* [*arbitrate*] *between* the workers and the employers.
●調停案 a mediation plan. ●調停委員会 a mediation committee. (!その委員は全員を ～). ●調停者 a mediator.

ちょうてん 頂点 [三角形などの] the apex /éipeks/; [頂上] the top, the summit, (先端) the peak (!以上3語は比喩的にも用いる); [最高潮] the climax; [名声などの絶頂] the zenith /zí:niθ/. ●三角形の頂点 the *apex* [*vertex*] of a triangle. ●名声の頂点に達する reach the *summit* [*peak*] of fame. ▶彼女はこの分野での頂点をきわめた She achieved [reached] the *zenith* in this field.
ちょうでん 弔電 (send) a telegram of condólence. 〔事情〕米英では弔電で済ますことは礼儀に反するのであまり利用されない
ちょうでんどう 超電導 名 superconductivity.
— **超電導の** 形 superconductive.
●超電導体 a superconductor.

*ちょうど 丁度 ❶ 【きっちり】 (ちょうど, 正確に) just (!否定文には用いない); (正確に) right, exactly, precisely (!前の3語より堅い語). ●ちょうど定刻に来る come *just* [*right*, *exactly*] on time. ▶彼はちょうど7時に起きた He got up at *exactly* seven./He got up at seven *precisely* [[話] *sharp*]. ▶このロープはちょうどいい長さです This rope is *just* long enough. ▶ちょうど今暇です I am free *just* [*right*] now. ▶ちょうど外出しようとしていたとき彼が来た *Just* as [when] I was going out, he came. (!when を用いると話し手が迷惑に思っていることを暗示することがある)/I was *just* going out when he came. ▶この帽子はわたしにちょうどよい(＝ぴったり合う) This hat fits me (*perfectly*) [(見事に) *beautifully*]./This hat is *just* my size. ▶これは私がちょうど読みたいと思っていた本です This is *the very* book that I have wanted to read. (!very は the, this などの限定語を伴って「まさにその」の意を表す)/This book is *just* what I have wanted to read.
〔会話〕「浜田さんのお宅はどちらでしょうか」「ちょうど真向いになります」"Could you tell me where the Hamadas live?" "*Just* [*Right*] across the road."

❷ 【まるで】▶あの男はちょうど猿のように木に登る He climbs a tree *just like* [*as if* he were] a monkey. (⇒まるで)

ちょうど 調度 (家具類) (*a piece of*) *furniture*; (作り付けの備品) a fixture. (!通例複数形で) ▶豪華な調度付きのマンションを借りる rent a gorgeously *furnished* apartment.
ちょうどうけん 聴導犬 a héaring dog.
ちょうとうは 超党派 ●超党派的に on a *suprapartisan* [a *nonpartisan*] basis. (!supra- は「...を越えた」の意の接頭辞)
●超党派外交 suprapartisan [nonpartisan] diplomacy.
ちょうとっきゅう 超特急 a superexpress (train).

●超特急のぞみ the *superexpress* Nozomi.
ちょうない 町内 (地域社会) a community (!これを外から眺めれば a local community); (4つの街路に囲まれた街区) a block; (通り) a street; (区域) an area. (!英語には「町内」を表す語はないので, 以上を場合によって使い分けたり, 説明的に訳す必要がある (⇒町(ﾁｮｳ)))
●町内の人々 community members; (全員) the whole street [*neighborhood*]. ▶私たちは同じ町内です We live on the same *block*./(私の近所の人たちです) They live in my neighborhood.
●町内会 a neighborhood association.
ちょうなん 長男 the [one's] oldest [[主に英] eldest] son (!息子が3人以上の場合に用いる. 2人なら older [[主に英] elder]); one's first-born son. (⇒兄) ▶一郎が長男の一郎です This is Ichiro, my *oldest son* [[話] *boy*].
ちょうにゅう 調乳 — **調乳する** 動 dissolve powdered milk in water for feeding a baby.
ちょうにん 町人 *chonin*; (説明的に) townspeople, that is, merchants, trades people, and artisans who were systematized as forming the lowest social class in the Edo period. (⇒町民)
●町人気質(ｶﾀｷﾞ) the spirit of townspeople. ●町人文化 the culture of [developed by] townspeople.
ちょうネクタイ 蝶ネクタイ a bow /bóu/ tie.
ちょうのうりょく 超能力 (have) supernatural power.
●超能力者 a person with supernatural power.
ちょうは 長波 a long wave (略 LW). (関連) 短波 a short wave/中波 a medium wave)
ちょうば 帳場 (旅館の) a front desk; (商店の) a cash desk.
ちょうば 跳馬 (体操用具) a vaulting horse; (競技) the vault. ●跳馬でけがをする be injured on the *vault*.
ちょうはつ 長髪 long hair. (⇒髪) ▶私たちの学校は長髪は禁止になっている *Long hair* is forbidden [prohibited] in our school.
ちょうはつ 挑発 provocation. ●挑発にのってそれをする do it *under provocation*.
— **挑発的な** 形 ▶彼は彼女の挑発的な態度を無視した He did not respond to her *provocative* attitude [her *come-on*]. (!性的な挑発以外にも用いられる)
— **挑発する** 動 provoke; (女性が男性を) [米話] give[him] the come-on. ▶彼は挑発されて彼らとけんかをした He *was provoked* to fight [*into fighting*] with them.
ちょうはつ 徴発 名 requisition.
— **徴発する** 動 requisition; commandeer.
ちょうはつ 調髪 hairdressing. (⇒理髪)
ちょうばつ 懲罰 名 (罰) punishment; (懲戒) discipline.
— **懲罰する** 動 ▶両議院は院内の秩序を乱した議員を懲罰することができる Each House may *punish* members for disorderly conduct.
●懲罰委員会 a disciplinary committee.
ちょうはん 丁半 *chohan*; (説明的に) odd and even numbers on a dice. ●(丁半)賭博 gambling at dice.
ちょうぶ 町歩 [面積の単位] a *cho*. (参考) 約99アール)
ちょうふく 重複 名 [くり返し] (a) repetition; [部分的に重なること] (an) overlap; [余分] (a) redundancy. ▶この本は重複が多い This book is full of *repetition(s)*.
— **重複する** 動 overlap (-pp-); (くり返す) repeat. ●重複した repeated; overlapping; redundant.

ちょうぶつ 長物 無用の長物 (⇨無用) [成句]
ちょうぶん 長文 (長い1節) a long passage; (長い1文) a long sentence.
・長文読解力 ability to read and understand long passages; long-passage reading comprehension.
ちょうへい 徴兵 图 conscription;《米》the draft.
・徴兵を逃れる evade *the draft*.
── **徴兵する** 動 彼は18歳で徴兵された He *was conscripted* [《米》*was drafted*] *into* the army at eighteen.
・徴兵忌避者《主に米》a draft dodger [evader]; (自己の良心による) a conscientious objector (略 CO). ・徴兵制度 the draft system. (参考)米国ではベトナム戦争以後は志願制)
ちょうへん 長辺 the long side of a rectangle. (⇨短辺)
ちょうへん 長編 (小説) a novel. (! a short novel, a novella (中編小説)に対するときは a long [a full-length] novel という); (映画) a long [a full-length] film.
・長編作家 a novelist.
ちょうぼ 帳簿 a book, an account book; (原簿) ledger. ・帳簿をつける keep *accounts* [*books*]. ・帳簿に記入する make (an entry) in a *book*;《書》enter (an account) in a *book*. ・帳簿を締める(=決算する) close the *books*. ・帳簿をごまかす falsify the *accounts*,《話》cook the *books*.
・帳簿係 a bookkeeper.
ちょうほう 重宝 ── **重宝な** 形 (便利な) convenient; (手ごろな) handy; (有用な) useful. ・重宝な道具 a *handy* tool. ▶ 車はとても重宝なものです A car is a great *convenience*./A car is very *convenient*.
── **重宝する** 動 ▶ その缶切りはとても重宝した The can opener was [came in] *useful* [*handy*]. (! 後の動詞には「いざというときには」という含みがある)
ちょうほう 諜報 (⇨情報)
・諜報活動 espionage. ・諜報機関 an intelligence [《英》a secret] service; (組織) an intelligence organization. ・諜報(部)員 an intelligence [《英》a secret] agent; a spy.
ちょうぼう 眺望 a prospect; 《書》[全景] a panorama. (⇨眺め). ・眺望のよい部屋 a room with a (good [fine, wonderful]) *view*.
ちょうほうき 超法規 ・超法規的措置をとる take measures above the law.
ちょうほうけい 長方形 图 a rectangle, an oblong.
── **長方形の** 形 rectangular, oblong.
ちょうほんにん 張本人 (暴動などの首謀者) a ringleader; (企てなどの;《書》an author. ・そのいたずらの張本人 the *author* of the mischief; the mischief-*maker*. ▶ この暴動の張本人はだれだ Who is the *ringleader* of this riot?/(だれが始めたのか) Who *started* this riot?
ちょうまんいん 超満員 ・超満員である (入りすぎている) be overcrowded (*with*); (話) be jam-packed (*with*). ・観客で超満員のスタジアム a stadium *jam-packed with* spectators.
ちょうみ 調味 ── **調味する** 動 (塩・コショウなどで) season; (香料で) flavor.
ちょうみりょう 調味料 (塩・コショウなど) (a) seasoning, a condiment (! 後の方は通例複数形でも); (香料) (a) flavoring; (香辛料) (a) spice. ・化学(=人工)調味料 artificial *flavoring* [*seasoning*].
ちょうみん 町民〔全体〕the (whole) town (! 単・複両扱い); the townspeople, the townsfolk (! 複数扱い);〔個人〕(男性) a townsman (複 -men), (女性) a townswoman (複 -men), (男女共用) a townsperson. (⇨町人) ▶ 彼はここの町民です He lives in this town.
ちょうむすび 蝶結び a bow /bóu/, a bowknot. ・蝶結びにする tie in a *bow*. ・蝶結びのネクタイ a bow tie.
-ちょうめ -丁目 ・三崎町2丁目 2-*chome*, Misaki-cho. ・栄町6丁目14番地21号 6-14-21 Sakae-machi.
ちょうめい 町名 the name of a town [a street].
ちょうめい 長命 (長生き,《やや書》long life) ▶ カメは長命だ Turtles *are long-lived* [*live long*].
ちょうめん 帳面 (ノート) a notebook (⇨ノート); (帳簿) a book, an account book (⇨帳簿). ・帳面づらを合わせる make the *accounts* balance; (ごまかす) falsify the *accounts*,《話》cook the *books*.
ちょうもん 弔問 图 a condólence càll. ・弔問の記帳をする sign a condolence book.
── **弔問する** 動 call on (him) to express one's condolences (*on* his father's death).
・弔問外交 diplomacy in black; funeral diplomacy. (! in black は「喪服姿での」意) ・弔問客 a caller for condolences.
ちょうもんかい 聴聞会 ・聴聞会を開く hold a *hearing*.
ちょうもんのいっしん 頂門の一針 The sting of a reproach is the truth of it.
ちょうやく 跳躍 a jump; a leap. ・第1回目の跳躍で世界新記録を出す set a world record on his first *jump*.
── **跳躍する** 動 jump; leap. (⇨飛ぶ)
・跳躍競技 jumping. ・跳躍選手 a jumper.
・跳躍台 a springboard.
ちょうゆう 町有 ・町有財産 town property; municipal property. ・町有林 a town-owned forest.
ちょうゆう 釣友 (釣り仲間) a fishing companion.
ちょうよう 長幼 young and old. ・長幼の序 Eldest First.
ちょうよう 徴用 ── **徴用する** 動 commandeer; (徴兵する) conscript,《米》draft.
ちょうらく 凋落 (傾くこと;《やや書》a decline; (倒れること) a fall. (! ともに通例単数形で) ・旧家の凋落 the *decline and fall* of an old family.
── **凋落する** 動 (やや書) decline; fall.
ちょうり 調理 图 cooking; [料理法] cookery.
── **調理する** 動 cook. (⇨料理)
・調理師 a cook. (! cooker は調理器具のこと) ・調理実習 cooking practice. ・調理場 a kitchen. ・調理台 a kitchen table; a counter (! 流し台に続く部分)
ちょうりつ 町立 ── **町立(の)** 形 municipal. ・町立病院 a *municipal* hospital.
ちょうりつ 調律 图 tuning.
── **調律する** 動 ・ピアノを調律する *tune* a piano.
・調律師 a (piano) tuner.
ちょうりゅう 潮流 a (tidal) current, a tide; [時勢の] the stream. ・時代の潮流に逆らう[従う] swim against [with] the *stream* [*current*, *tide*] of the times. ▶ カジュアル着(=カジュアルな服装をすること)が近年の潮流だといわれている Wearing casual clothes has been [said to be] the trend [×*tide*] of recent years. ▶ ファッションの潮流は tide でなく trend で表す

ちょうりょう 跳梁 ── 跳梁する 動 [[のさばる]] have one's own way; domineer 《over》.

ちょうりょく 潮力 tidal power.
・潮力発電 tidal power generation.

ちょうりょく 聴力 hearing. ・右耳の聴力を失う lose one's *hearing* in [×of] the right ear. ▶聴力が衰えてきている My *hearing* is getting poorer [worse].
・聴力検査 a hearing test.

ちょうるい 鳥類 birds.
・鳥類学 òrnithólogy. ・鳥類学者 ornithologist・鳥類保護区 a bird sanctuary.

ちょうれい 朝礼 a morning meeting [assembly].

ちょうろう 長老 (年長者) the elders, the seniors; (政界の) an elder political leader. ▶彼は村の長老だ He is one of the village *elders* [*seniors*].

ちょうろう 嘲弄 图 ridicule; mockery; derision; a scoff; scorn.
── 嘲弄する 動 ridicule; mock 《at》; deride; scoff 《at》; scorn.

ちょうわ 調和 图 (a) harmony; [釣り合い] balance.
①[～(の)調和] ・色の調和 the *harmony* of colors. ・心身の調和 the *harmony* [*balance*] of mind and body. ・人間と自然との調和 the *harmony* between people and nature. ・予定調和 preestablished *harmony*.
②[調和の] ・調和のとれた色の組み合わせ the *harmonious* combinations of colors. ・自然との調和のとれた生活をする live *in harmony with* nature.
③[調和] ・調和を欠く lack *harmony*. ・調和を損なう impair [break] *harmony*.
── 調和する 動 harmonize 《with》; [似合う] match. (⇨合う) ・調和している[いない] be *in* [*out of*] *harmony* 《with》. ・調和させる harmonize 《A with B》; match 《A with B》. ・調和して harmoniously. ▶この絵の色は(互いに)よく調和している The colors in this picture *harmonize* [*match*] nicely 《with each other》. ▶カーテンはじゅうたんとよく調和している The curtains *harmonize* [*match, go*] well *with* the rugs. (❗ match は次例のように自動詞として用いる方が普通)/The curtains and the rugs *match* well [are a good *match*]. (❗ The curtains are a good *match for* the rugs. ともいえる)

チョーク chalk. (❗ (1) 数えるときは a piece [a stick] of chalk のようにいう。(2) 種類を表す場合は ⓒ) ・黄色のチョーク (2本) two pieces of) yellow *chalk*.・何本かの色チョーク colored *chalks*. ・チョークの粉 *chalk* dust. ・チョークで黒板に字を書く write letters with [in] *chalk* on the blackboard; chalk letters on [across] the blackboard.

チョーサー [英国の詩人] Chaucer (Geoffrey ~).

ちよがみ 千代紙 (a piece [a sheet] of) *chiyogami*; (説明的に) colored Japanese paper printed with beautiful patterns (used to make dolls or fold origami).

ちょき (じゃんけんのはさみ) 《show》 scissors. (⇨じゃんけん)

ちょきちょき ▶お父さんが庭で木をちょきちょき切っている Daddy *is clipping* the twigs of a tree in the garden. ❗ snip は「ちょきんと切る」に近い

ちょきん 貯金 图 [貯蓄] savings (❗ 通例複数扱い); [預金] a deposit. (⇨預金) ・郵便貯金 postal *savings*. (❗ 《英》にはこの制度があるが,《米》では1966年に廃止) ▶彼女には郵便貯金にかなりの[多くの]貯金がある She has considerable [much, ×many] *savings* in the post office. (❗ 「少額の貯金」は a little [×a few] savings) ▶なけなしの貯金をはたいて自転車を買った I bought a bicycle with what little *savings* I had. (❗ 「少ないながらも持っているすべての貯金で」の意) ▶タイガースは貯金が3ある The Tigers are three games above .500. (❗ .500 is five hundred と読む)
── 貯金する 動 (蓄える) save (up); deposit. (⇨預金) ・もしもの時[まさかの時]のために貯金する *save up* (money) for [《古》against] a rainy day. ▶彼は車を買うために貯金をしている He *is saving* (up) for [to buy] a car.
・貯金通帳 a passbook; a bankbook. ・貯金箱 a moneybox; a piggy bank (❗ 豚の形をしていることから).

ちょきん(ちょきん) ▶彼ははさみで少女の髪をちょきん(ちょきん)と切った He *clipped* [*snipped*] the girl's hair with scissors. (❗ 1回の行為を表すには clip [snip] (a flower) off とする切り方に力が感じられる)

ちょくえい 直営 direct management [(管理) control]. ・政府直営の事業 an enterprise *under direct government control*. ・セブンイレブンの直営店 a 7-eleven *operated store* [《英》*shop*]. ・このホテルは全日空直営です This hotel is *under the direct management of* ANA.

ちょくおん 直音 [音声] a straight syllable (in Japanese).

ちょくげき 直撃 图 a direct hit. ・地震の直撃(=大打撃)を受ける *be hard hit* by an earthquake. ・フェンス直撃の二塁打を打つ hit a double off the fence.
── 直撃する 動 ・ボールを直撃する hit a ball off the foul pole. ▶落石が彼の頭を直撃した The falling rock *hit* him *directly* [*square, right*] on the head.

ちょくげん 直言 图 unreserved advice.
── 直言する 動 speak (to him) without reserve [reservation]; speak plainly [frankly] 《to him》.

ちょくご 直後 (時間的に) just [right, immediately] after ...; (位置的に) just behind [at the back of, 《米》in back of] .... ▶彼は帰国した直後に亡くなった He passed away *just after* he came back to Japan. ▶バスの直前直後で道路を横断してはいけません Don't cross the street *just before* or *behind* a bus.

ちょくご 勅語 an Imperial edict [rescript]. ・教育勅語 the *Imperial Edict* on Education.

ちょくさい 直截 (⇨直截(ちょくせつ))

ちょくし 直視 ── 直視する 動 ・死を直視する *look death in the face* [×*eye*] (or *face* (up to) death. (❗ (1) 後の方は死は避けられないものとして対処することを。(2)「人を直視する」は look 《him》 in the eye)

ちょくし 勅使 (send) an Imperial envoy [messenger].

ちょくしゃ 直射 图 ▶それは直射日光を受けていた It *was exposed to direct* sunlight [*was directly exposed to* sunlight]./The sun *was shining directly* on it. (⇨日光)
── 直射する 動 (太陽・明かりなどが) shine [fall] directly 《on》.

ちょくじょうけいこう 直情径行 ・直情径行の人 (衝動的に行動する人) a person who *acts on impulse*; an *impulsive* person; (思ったままを言行に移す人) a *straightforward* person.

ちょくしん 直進 ── 直進する 動 go straight (on). ▶光は直進する(=まっすぐ伝わる) Light *travels in a straight line*./Light *travels straight*.

ちょくせつ 直接 ── 直接の, 直接的な 形 direct, immediate; (人に頼らずじじきつで) personal. ● 直接の原因 a direct [an immediate] cause. ▶私はその男性と直接的な接触はなかった I had no direct contact with the man.

── **直接(に)** 副 direct(ly), immediately; (じきじきに) in person, personally; (伝聞でなくじかに) firsthand, at first hand. ▶(どこへも寄らずに)直接ロンドンへ行く go direct(ly) [straight] to London. (!この文脈では directly より direct の方が普通) ▶災害の様子を直接罹災(ﾘｻｲ)者から聞く hear how the disaster was [what the disaster was like] at first hand from the victims. ▶会合のことは彼に直接伝えておきました I told him personally [directly] about the meeting. ▶直接彼に会った方が早い It's quicker to meet him in person. ▶私だって信じられなかったけど, 当の本人から直接聞いたのよ(話) I didn't believe it either, but I got it straight [right] from the horse's mouth. (!1) straight from the horse's mouth は「当の本人から直接に」の意の慣用表現. (2) 再帰代名詞を用いて, ... but he [she] told me himself [herself]. のようにもいえる)

会話 「彼を知ってたのか」「直接では

ないがね。警察にいた頃にいたんだ」 "You knew him?" "Of him. He was around when I first joined the police." (!I knew of him の省略表現で knew him (面識があった)との対比のために of に強勢を置く)

● 直接行動 (take) direct action. ● 直接税 a direct tax. ● 直接請求 (make) a direct demand. ● 直接選挙 a direct election. ● 直接対戦 a head-to-head action. ● 直接民主主義 (a) direct democracy. ● 直接話法 〖文法〗 direct speech.

ちょくせつ 直截 ── **直截な** 形 direct; frank; straightforward. ● 直截簡明な plain and simple.

── **直截に** 副 directly; frankly; straightforwardly.

***ちょくせん 直線** a straight line. ● 直線を引く draw a straight line. ▶直線 A と B が C で交わる Line(s) A and B cross [meet] at C.

● 直線運動 a straight-line motion. ● 直線距離 distance in a straight line. ▶ここから新宿までは直線距離にして 10 キロだ It is ten kilometers in a straight line from here to Shinjuku./From here to Shinjuku is ten kilometers as the crów flies. (!as the crow flies は慣用表現) ● 直線コース (run on) a straight course.

ちょくぜん 直前 (時間的に) just [right, immediately] before ...; (位置的に) just [right] in front of .... ▶試験の直前に just before the exam. ▶私の車の直前にタクシーが割り込んだ A taxi cut in just in front [ahead of] my car.

ちょくそう 直送 名 ● 産地直送のカニ crabs fresh from the fishing port. ● apples なら orchard (果樹園), potatoes なら farm (農園) のように産地を特定するとよい)

── **直送する** 動 send ... straight [directly] 《from, to》.

ちょくぞく 直属 ── **直属の** 形 (直接の監督のもとに) under the direct [immediate] supervision [(管理) control] 《of》. ● 直属の上司 one's direct supervisor; one's boss. (!言い方は日常語) ▶政府直属の機関 an agency under the direct control of the government. ▶彼は K 氏の直属の部下です He is under Mr. K's direct management [control]. (!He is working under Mr. K. が普通)

ちょくちょう 直腸 the rectum. ● 直腸がん 《xa》rectal cancer; 《xa》cancer of the rectum.

ちょくちょく ▶彼はちょくちょく(=しばしば)遊びに来ます He often comes to see me. ▶彼女はちょくちょく(=ときどき)外国に行きます She sometimes goes abroad./She goes abroad from time to time.

ちょくつう 直通 ❶ 〖乗り物〗 a direct 《a through》service. (⇨直行) ▶ここから空港まで直通バスがあります There is a direct bus (service) from here to the airport.

❷ 〖電話〗 ▶彼に直通電話をかける call direct to him; phone him direct. ▶大臣同士は直通電話を持っている The ministers have a direct telephone link with each other./(即時直通電話で結ばれている) The ministers are linked by pickup phone.

── **直通する** 動 ▶この列車は大阪へ直通します This train runs [goes] through to Osaka./This is a through train to Osaka.

● 直通列車 (途中で止まらない) a nonstop train; (乗り換えなしの) a through train.

ちょくどく 直読 ── **直読する** 動 ▶漢文を直読する read classical Chinese writing without applying Japanese word order.

ちょくのう 直納 ── **直納する** 動 deliver goods directly 《to consumers》.

ちょくばい 直売 名 (直接販売) direct sales. ● (農産物の)産地直売所 a farmers' market; a green-market. ▶このリンゴは生産者直売です(=直接売られている) These apples are sold directly by the producers.

── **直売する** 動 ▶この会社は製品を直売している This company sells its products directly to the consumers.

● 直売店 a direct sales store.

ちょくはん 直販 direct sales [selling, marketing]. ● 直販会社 a direct seller.

ちょくほうたい 直方体 〖数学〗 a rectangular parallelepiped.

ちょくめん 直面 ── **直面する** 動 (困難などに) face; 〖書〗 be confronted 《with, by》. ▶我々は新たな問題に直面している We are faced [are confronted] with a new problem./A new problem faces [confronts] us. (!現在形に注意) ▶私たちはいつかこの日かこのような問題に直面しなくてはならない We all have to face this kind of problem sometime or another [sooner or later]. ▶多くの危機に直面して彼の勇気もくじけてしまった His courage weakened in the face of so many dangers.

ちょくやく 直訳 名 a literal (word-for-word) translation. ● 直訳調[的表現] literalism.

── **直訳する** 動 translate 《it》 word for word; translate 《it》 literally [mechanically].

ちょくゆ 直喩 a simile.

ちょくゆにゅう 直輸入 名 direct import.

── **直輸入する** 動 ▶フランスからワインを直輸入する import wine directly from France.

ちょくりつ 直立 名 ● 直立不動(=気をつけ)の姿勢をとる stand at attention.

── **直立した** 形 (垂直の) upright; (まっすぐ立っている) erect; (まっすぐに) straight.

── **直立する** 動 stand upright [erect, straight].

ちょくりゅう 直流 名 direct (↔alternating) current (略 DC, dc). ● 直流の direct-current.

ちょくれつ 直列 (電気の) (a) series (↔parallel). ● 電池を直列につなぐ connect batteries in series. ● 直列回路 a series circuit.

ちょこ 猪口 a sake cup.

ちょこざい 猪口才 ── 猪口才な 形 (こざかしい) smart-alecky; (生意気な) saucy.

ちょこちょこ ●ちょこちょこ歩く (幼児が) toddle; (小またで) walk with short steps. ●小さい子供がちょこちょこ ごぜいてきた A small child came *toddling* (up to me). ▶彼はちょこちょこ(=ちょくちょく)私の家に来ます He *often* comes to my house.

ちょこまか ●(子供が)ちょこまか歩く toddle. (⇨ちょこちょこ) ▶彼女は一日中ちょこまか動き回っていた She was working [running] about *busily* all day long./She *was bustling about* all day long. (**!** bustle /bʌ́sl/ は「せわしく動き回る」の意)

チョゴリ [＜朝鮮語] *chogori* /tʃougɔ́:ri/; (説明的に) a traditional Korean short jacket which is worn with *baji* (= men's baggy trousers) or a *cima* (= women's long wraparound skirt).

チョコレート (a) chocolate. (●種類をいうときは [C]) ●板チョコ a bar of *chocolate*; a *chocolate* bar. ●ビター[ミルク]チョコレート bitter [milk] *chocolate* (s). ●ウイスキー入りのチョコレート a *chocolate* with whisky inside. ●甘い詰め物の入ったチョコレート a *chocolate* with sweet filling.

チョコレートかくめい「チョコレート革命」 *Chocolate Revolution*. (参考) 俵万智の歌集)

ちょこんと ●ちょこんとおじぎする make a little bow 《to》; make just a bow (**!** そんざいな感じのおじぎ). ●小皿のような帽子をちょこんとのせた頭 a head with a plate-like cap *perched* on it. ▶バス停で少年ちょこんと1人立っていた A small boy stood *alone* at the bus stop. ▶バットにちょこんと当てるとサードゴロになった He swung *lightly* for a grounder to third.

ちょさく 著作 [活動] writing; [著書] a book; (作品) a work; (作品集) writings. ●著作で生計をたてる live by one's pen.
── **著作する** 動 write 《a book》.
●著作者 (著者) an author. (⇨著者)

ちょさくけん 著作権 (a) copyright (記号 ©). ●著作権の侵害 a breach [an infringement] of *copyright*; (a) (literary) piracy. ●著作権を侵害する infringe a *copyright*. ●著作権を得る copyright 《a book》. ●その本の著作権を所有している hold the *copyright for* [*on*] the book.
●著作権使用料 a royalty. ●著作権法 the Copyright Law.

ちょしゃ 著者 an author; (執筆者) a writer. ●著者不明の本 a book by an *anonymous writer*; an *anonymous* book. ▶彼女がその物語の著者です She's the *author* of the story./She *wrote* the story.
●著者目録 an author catalogue [index].

ちょじゅつ 著述 (書くこと) writing; (著書) a book. ●著述家 (作家) a writer; (著者) an author. ●著述業 the literary profession.

ちょしょ 著書 (本) a book; (努力・活動の所産としての著作) a work; (著作集) writings (⇨著作). ▶彼には心理学に関する著書が多い He has written a lot of *books* on psychology.

ちょすい 貯水 ●貯水池 a water tank. ●貯水ダム a water-storage dam. ●貯水池 a reservoir /rézərvwà:r/. ●貯水量 (貯水できる量) the capacity of water storage; (貯水されている量) the volume of water in store. ▶草木ダムの水位が危険なまでに低くなっている At the Kusaki Reservoir, the water is running dangerously low.

ちょぞう 貯蔵 图 (備蓄) storage; (保存) preservation. ●冷凍貯蔵 cold *storage*; refrigeration. ●貯蔵状態のよい in a good state of *preservation*.

── **貯蔵する** 動 (蓄える) store; (保存する) preserve. ●納屋に穀物を貯蔵する *store* [*stock*] grain *in* a barn; *store* a barn *with* grain. ●野菜を塩漬けにして貯蔵する *preserve* vegetables *in* salt.
●貯蔵庫 a storehouse. ●貯蔵物 stored goods; (a) stock.

ちょたん 貯炭 a coal supply; a supply [a store, a stock] of coal.

*ちょちく **貯蓄** 图 [金] savings (⇨貯金); a deposit (⇨預金); [行為] saving.
── **貯蓄する** 動 save (up); save money.

ちょっか 直下 ●橋の直下に(=ちょうど下に) *directly* [*right*, *just*] *under* the bridge. ▶私たちの船は今赤道直下にいる(=ちょうど赤道上にいる) Our ship is *just* [*right*] *on* the equator now. ▶訴訟は急転直下(=突然)解決した The lawsuit was *suddenly* settled.
●直下型地震 an earthquake directly above its focus.

ちょっかい ●ちょっかいを出す (干渉する) interfere 《in》; (鼻を突っ込む) (話) poke one's nose 《into》; (女性に) (話) make a pass 《at》; mess around (米話) [about (英話)] 《with》.

ちょっかく 直角 [数学] a right angle. ●直角になる form [make] a *right angle* 《with》. ▶その柱は床と直角になっていない The pillar isn't *square with* [*to*] the floor. ▶その2直線は直角に交わっている The two lines are [*cross*] *at right angles*.
●直角三角形 a right(-angled) triangle. (**!** -angled を省略するのは(米))

ちょっかん 直覚 (⇨直感)

ちょっかつ 直轄 ●財務省直轄の機関 an institution *under the direct control* [*supervision*] of the Ministry of Finance.

ちょっかっこう 直滑降 a straight downhill run; a schuss /ʃús/. ●直滑降で滑り下りる *run straight down* the hill; (make a) schuss.

*ちょっかん **直感** 图 (an) intuition; (直感に基づく考え) 《話》 a hunch. (⇨勘) ●直感で真相をつかむ seize the truth *by intuition* [*intuitively*]. ●直感に頼って行動する play [act on] a *hunch*. ●直感が当たる (=正しくいい当てる) guess right (↔wrong). ▶私は彼が正しいと直感的に思った (My) *intuition* told me that he was right./I had a *hunch* that he was right.
── **直感する** 動 ●危険を直感する(=察知する) *sense* the danger.

ちょっかん 直諫 ── **直諫する** 動 ●主君に直諫する 《書》 remonstrate *with* the lord 《about》.

ちょっかんひりつ 直間比率 the ratio of direct and indirect taxes.

チョッキ [＜ポルトガル語] (米) a vest; (英) a waistcoat /wéskət/, /wéɪskòʊt/. (**!** (英)では vest は肌着のシャツの意) ●防弾チョッキ a bulletproof *vest*.

ちょっきゅう 直球 [野球] 《throw》 a fastball. (**!** a straight ball とはあまりいわない) ●バッターに対し時速155 キロの直球を投げる throw a 155-*kph fastball* on a batter. (**!** kph は kilometers per hour の略) ●バッターに直球で真っ向勝負する challenge a batter with a *fastball*.

ちょっきり ●1 時間ちょっきり *just* an hour. ●ちょっきり1 時に *just* [*exactly*] at one o'clock. 《話》 at one o'clock *sharp*. (⇨ちょうど)

ちょっけい 直系 a direct line [descent]. ●直系の子孫 a direct descendant 《of》.
●直系会社 a directly affiliated company.

ちょっけい 直径 [数学] a diámeter. ●直径10 センチ

の木の幹 a tree trunk (which is) ten centimeters *in diameter*.
会話 「直径はいくらですか」「5センチです」"How wide *across* is it?/How wide is it *in diameter*?/What is its *diameter*?" "It's five centimeters (*across* [*in diameter*])."

ちょっけつ 直結 ●直結している be directly connected 《*with*》.

ちょっこう 直行 ── **直行する** 動 ●彼の所へ直行するつもりだ I'll *go straight* [*direct*] to him.
● **直行便**(飛行機の) a nonstop [a direct] flight 《*to* Paris》.

***ちょっと** ❶[少し](程度が) a little,《話》a bit, a little bit; (数が) a few; (量が) a little; (数・量が) some; (わずかの) slight; (わずかに) slightly; (いくぶん)《やや書》somewhat; (もう少しで...するところだ) nearly, almost. (⇒少し ❶ ❷) ●ちょっと新聞に目を通す *glance at* [*through*] the paper. ●ちょっと見た(=一見した)ところでは at first sight. ●ちょっと私たちのところにお電話ください *Just* give us a call. ●英文学についてちょっと知識がある I have *a little* [*some*] knowledge of English literature. ●この本はちょっと難しすぎる This book is *a little* [*a bit*] too difficult. ●ちょっと風邪をひいている I have a *slight* [《話》*a bit of* a] cold. ●もうちょっとで車にひかれるところだった I *nearly* [*almost*] got run over by a car. ▶私はちょっと見ただけで彼女が泣いていたことが分かった I saw *at a glance* that she'd been crying./A *mere glance* told me that she'd been crying. ▶ちょっと聞いたんだけど君仕事をやめるんだって *Someone* told me [I *hear*(*d*)] *that* you're going to quit your job.
会話 「疲れた？」「ほんのちょっと」"Are you tired?" "*Just a little* [*a bit*]."/《話》"Kind [*Sort*] *of*." (!いずれも前に I'm, 後に tired を省略した言い方)
会話 「会議は上の階の会議室でやります」「あそこじゃちょっと狭くない？」"The meeting's in the upstairs conference room." "That *won't* be big enough, will it?" (!「狭い」を「十分広くない」と裏返いい, かつ will it? と付加疑問で, 表現をやわらげている)

翻訳のこころ ちょっと名高る庭園に行けば, 噴水はさまざまな趣向を凝らして風景の中心になっている (山崎正和『水の東西』) Whenever you visit a garden of a *certain* fame [renown], you'll find a fountain in a variety of designs and styles, occupying the center [central position] of the landscape. (!(1)「ちょっと」は certain (ある程度の). (2)「趣向」には通例 idea や plan を用いるが, ここでは噴水について述べているので design and style とする)

❷[少しの間] a (little) while; (瞬間的) a moment, a minute, a second; (短い時間) a short time. (⇒少し ❸) ▶途中ちょっと京都へ寄るう pay a *short* visit to Kyoto on the way. ▶ちょっとお待ちください Please wait *a moment* [*a minute*, *a second*]./*Just a moment*, please./*One moment*, please. ▶彼はちょっと考えてから答えた He answered after thinking *for a while* [*after a moment's* thought]. ▶町はちょっとの間にだいぶ変わった The town has changed a good deal *in a short time*. ▶ちょっとのところで(=1分の差で)列車に乗り遅れた I missed the train *by a minute*. ▶ちょっと寄ってきませんか Won't you come in *for a moment*? (!for the moment は「当面」の意)

❸[かなり] rather; fairly;《話》pretty;《英》quite. (⇒かなり) ▶今日はちょっと寒い It's *rather* [*fairly*, *quite*] cold today. (!通例 rather は好ましくない意味合い, fairly は好ましい意味合いで用いられる) ▶ちょ

っと時間かかりますが It takes *quite a* [*some*] \time, I'm /afraid.
❹[容易には(...できない)] (not ...) easily. ▶ちょっとやそっとではその仕事はできないよ You can't do that job so *easily*./That's not such an *easy* job. ▶彼の話はちょっと信じられない(信じるのは難しい) It's *hard* to believe his story./(完全には信じない) I can't *quite* believe his story. ▶あの人の名前はちょっと(=まったく)思い出せない I *just* can't remember [recall] his name. (!just can't は「まったく...することができない」意の口語的な言い方)

❺[呼びかけ, 注意喚起](失礼ですが) excuse me; (ねえ, おい)《米話》say,《古》I say. ▶ちょっとすみませんが何時でしょうか *Excuse me*, but could you tell me the time? ▶ちょっとすみません(私にも言わせてください) Could I say some words? (! Could I say a few words? は「ちょっとごあいさつ申し上げます」の意) ▶ちょっと, 君 *Say*, you. ▶ちょっとこれを見てごらん *Just* look at this. (! just は命令文の意味をやわらげる)

会話 「ああ, うるさいなあ」「うるさいだって？ ちょっとそれどういう意味？」"Oh, you're a nuisance." "I'm a nuisance? *Just* what do you mean by that?" (! just は疑問詞を強め話し手のいらだちを表す)
❻[気軽に] ●ちょっと彼のところ[彼の家]に立ち寄る *drop in on* him [*at* his house]. (! drop in は「ちょっと立ち寄る」の意) ▶ちょっとお尋ねしたいのですが May I ask you *something*?
会話 「どこに行くの」「ちょっとそこまで」"Where are you going?" "*Just* over there."

ちょっとした ❶[わずかの] ●ちょっとした風邪 a *slight* cold. ●ちょっとした(=ささやかな)親切 *a little* (act of) kindness. ●ちょっとした(=取るに足らない)ことに腹を立てる get angry about *trifles* [*little things*]. ▶それはほんのちょっとした問題だ It's only a *small* matter [problem]. ▶彼はちょっとした学者だ《話》He is *something of* a scholar. ●彼の話にはちょっとした皮肉があった There was *a touch of* irony in his story. ▶これ, ちょっとしたものですが Here's a *little* something for you./I'd like to give you a *little* something. (!(1) something は名詞化している. (2) プレゼントを手渡すときの控えめな表現で, 日本語の「つまらないものですが(どうぞ)」に相当)
❷[かなりの]《⇒相当な》

ちょっぴり (⇒ちょっと)

チョップ ❶[あばら骨付き厚切り肉] ●ポークチョップ pork *chop*(s). ❷[たたき切るような一撃] ●空手チョップ a karate *chop*.

ちょとつもうしん 猪突猛進 ●猪突猛進する(=まっしぐらに突進する) make a headlong rush《*at*》; rush headlong《*at*》.

ちょびひげ ちょび髭《wear》a small mustache.

ちょぼく 貯木 a stock of lumber [《英》timber].

ちょぼちょぼ (散らばってある) sparsely; (似たりよったりで) mùch the sáme. ●そばかすがちょぼちょぼある be *sparsely* freckled. ▶成績は君とちょぼちょぼだよ Our grades are *much the same*.

ちょめい 著名 ── **著名な** 形 (有名な) famous, noted; (傑出した) distinguished, prominent. (⇒有名)

ちょろい (簡単な) very easy,《話》as easy as pie [a piece of cake]. ●ちょろいこと《話》child's play;《話》a cinch. ▶あんなテストなんてちょろいもんさ The test is *child's play* [*as easy as pie*] to me.

ちょろちょろ ●蛇口から水がちょろちょろ流れている音がする I can hear water *trickling* (*down*) [a constant *trickle* of water] from the tap. ▶キャンプファイアーがまだちょろちょろ燃えている The campfire *is* still

ちょろまかす *burning unsteadily* [*flickering*]. ▶子供はちょろちょろするな Don't *move around*, you kids!

ちょろまかす (小さな[少額の]ものを)《やや話》pilfer, filch. ●店の金をちょろまかす *pilfer* some money *from* the store.

ちょん ●拍子木をちょんと打つ beat clappers.
●ちょんになる〖終わりになる〗end;〖くびになる〗be fired.

チョンガー [<朝鮮語]〖独身男性〗a bachelor.

ちょんぎる cut*［snip（-pp-)］... off. ●糸をはさみでちょん切る *snip off* the thread with scissors. ●首をちょん切る *cut off* the head (*of* the king);(首にする)〈⇨首(句))).

ちょんぼ ●ちょんぼをする make a mess (*of*);《主に米話》make a goof, goof up.

ちょんまげ 丁髷 a topknot. ●ちょんまげを結う[結っている] do up [wear] a *topknot*.

ちらかす 散らかす 〖物を〗scatter;〖場所を〗《話》mess ... up;（ぼらくたなどで）litter. ●おもちゃを部屋中に散らかす *scatter* toys *around* [*all over*] the room. ●机の上を書類で散らかす *litter* a desk *with* papers. ●台所を散らかしを*(=*乱雑にして)おく *leave* the kitchen *untidy* [*in a mess, in disorder*]. ▶部屋を散らかすな Don't *mess up* the room. ●何と言う散らかしようなの、さっさとかたづけなさい What a *mess*! Clean it up quick. (**!** 命令文では quickly はあまり用いない) ▶ごめんなさいね、こんなに散らかしていて I'm sorry everything is *all over* the place.

ちらかる 散らかる 〖まき散らかされている〗be scattered;〖部屋が紙くずなどで〗be littered (*with*);〖部屋などがめちゃくちゃな状態である〗be in a mess, be in disorder. ●散らかった部屋 a *messy* [a *disorderly*] room. ●床には紙くずが散らかっていた Bits of paper *were scattered* on the floor./The floor *was littered* with bits of paper. ▶私の部屋は今ひどく散らかっている My room *is* (in) an awful *mess* right now./My room *is* very *messy* [*untidy*] now.

ちらし 散らし（宣伝・広告・案内用に）a handbill,《もと米》a flier (**!** flyer ともつづる);（折りたたまれた）a leaflet;（新聞の折り込み広告）an (*advertising*) insert. ●リサイクルのちらし a recycling *leaflet*; a *leaflet* about [on] recycling. (**!** on は内容が専門性の高い場合に用いられる) ●ちらしを配る give out [hand out, distribute] *handbills*. ●ちらしを拾う pick up a *leaflet*.
●ちらし広告 a handbill advertisement.

ちらしずし 散らし寿司 *chirashizushi*,（説明的に）vinegared rice topped with sliced raw fish, shrimp, egg, vegetables, and many other ingredients.

ちらす 散らす ●暴徒を散らす(=四散させる) *scatter* [《やや書》*disperse*] the rioters. (**!** disperse の方が徹底的に広範囲に散らに散る) ●はれものを散らす(=消散させる) *resolve* the tumor. ●気を散らす(=そらす) *distract* (*him*) [(*his*) attention] (*from*); *divert* (*his*) attention (*from*).

ちらちら ❶〖花びら・雪などが〗●ちらちら舞う flutter. ▶桜の花びらがちらちらに散り落ちている The petals of cherry blossoms *are fluttering* in the spring breeze.
❷〖光などが〗●ちらちら光る flicker. ▶遠くで赤い光がちらちら光っている A red light *is flickering* in the distance. ▶ヘッドライトの光で目がちらちらした The headlights *dazzled* my eyes.
❸〖人の面影などが〗▶父の怒った顔がちらちら脳裏をよぎった The angry face of my father *flashed* across my mind ［(目に浮かんだ) before my eyes].
❹〖時折見える[聞こえる]様子〗▶彼女は部屋着姿で、その下に赤いネグリジェがちらちら見えた She wore a dressing gown with *glimpse of* a red nightgown beneath. ▶彼のことをちらちら(=時々)耳にする I *sometimes* [*occasionally*] hear of him./I hear of him *now and then* [*from time to time*].

ちらつかせる ●ナイフをちらつかせる *flash* a knife. ●うまい話をちらつかせる *dangle* a carrot *before* [*in front of*] (*him*). ▶上司は昇進をちらつかせながら(=昇進の可能性を目の前にぶらさげて)彼女に余分の仕事を押しつけた *Dangling* the prospects of promotion (*before* her), her boss loaded her with extra work.

ちらつく (光がかすかに) glimmer;（明滅する）flicker. ▶テレビの画面がちらついている The TV screen *is flickering*. ▶昨夜は小雪がちらついていた It was snowing *lightly* last night./We had a *light* snow last night. ▶彼の顔かたちが目の前にちらついて(=私にとりついている) His face still *haunts* me. (**!** 進行形にしないことに注意) ▶彼女に会ったときそのことが頭にちらついた That *passed* [*went*] *through* my *mind* when I saw her.

ちらっと ●ちらっと見る glance 《*at*》, take a glance 《*at*》. ●ちらっと見ただけで *at* a glance. ▶彼女は私の方をちらっと見た She *glanced at* me./She *took a quick look at* me. ▶彼はちらっと見てその家がいい家だと分かった He could tell *at a glance* that the house was in a good condition [it was a good house]. ▶車で通り過ぎるとき彼女の姿がちらっと見えた I *caught a glimpse of* her when I drove past.

ちらばる 散らばる 〖分散している〗be [lie*] scattered;〖紙くずなどが散らかっている〗be littered. ▶テーブルに書類が散らばっていた Papers *were scattered on* [(一面に)(*all*) *over*] the table./The table *was littered with* papers./Papers *littered* the table. ▶私たちの親戚(は)は全国に散らばっている Our relatives *are scattered all over* [*throughout*] the country. ▶足もとに気をつけて、割れたガラスがそこらじゅうに散らばっているから Watch your step. There's ▶a lot of broken glass *all around*.

ちらほら ▶ちらほら(=ここかしこに)桜の花が咲き始めている Cherry blossoms have begun to bloom *here and there*. ▶山腹に新緑がちらほら(=点在するのが)見える You can see new green leaves *dotting* the mountainside. ▶彼女が離婚するかもしれないといううわさはちらほら(=時々)聞きます I *sometimes* [*occasionally*] hear a rumor (that) she may be divorced.

ちらりと (⇨ちらっと)

ちらん 治乱 war and peace.
●治乱興亡 vicissitudes.

*****ちり** 塵 〖ほこり〗dust;〖ごみ〗《米》trash,《英》rubbish;〖汚れ〗dirt. (⇨埃(^{ほこ}), ごみ) ●細かいちり fine *dust*. ●ちりにまみれる be covered with [in] *dust*. ●ちり一つない部屋 a spotless room, a room free of *dust*. ●彼は本箱のちりを払った He *dusted* the bookcase. ▶あの男には誠実さもちりほどもない The man doesn't have an atom [a particle] of sincerity.
●ちりも積もれば山となる 'Heaps of dust often makes a mountain in time.'/(ことわざ) Many a little makes a mickle./(ことわざ) Many drops make a shower. (**!** いずれも /m/ の頭音のくり返しに注意)

*****ちり** 地理 geography. ●この辺の地理に明るい know this area very well; be familiar with this area. ▶ぼくはこの辺の地理に暗い I am a stranger

ちり around here./I don't know my way around here.
— **地理的(な)** 形 geographical. ●地理的条件 *geographical* conditions.
●**地理学** geography. ●人文[自然]地理学 human [physical] *geography*. ●地理学者 a geographer.

ちり 〖鍋料理のひとつ〗(説明的に) a pot of fish and vegetables stew eaten with citrus dipping sauce as it cooks. ●ふぐちり globefish one-pot (stew).

チリ 〖国名〗Chile, Chili /tʃíli/; (公式名) the Republic of Chile. (首都 Santiago) ●チリ人 a Chilean. ●チリ(人)の Chilean.

ちりあくた 塵芥 trash, rubbish; dust. (⇨ごみ)

ちりがみ 塵紙 〖鼻紙〗a tissue, (1 枚) a box of tissues (❗tissue paper は「包装用の薄紙など」の意); 〖トイレ用〗(a roll of) toilet paper [tissue], (巻紙) a toilet roll.
●ちり紙交換 (行為) collection of old newspapers in exchange for toilet rolls; (人) an old-newspaper collector.

チリソース chili sauce.

ちりちり ●ちりちりになる[する] frizzle; shrivel; shrink. (❗ frizzle は音を立てて焦げたり、焼けたり、縮んだりすること、さらに小さく硬い巻き毛状になることもさす。shrivel はしわを巻き毛状に縮む、shrink は様々な条件で縮むことを広くさす) ▶ベーコンがフライパンの中でちりちり焼けている The bacon *is frizzling* in the frying pan. ▶彼女の赤ん坊は頭の毛がちりちりだ Her baby has *frizzy* hair. ▶毛糸が焼けてちりちりに（=巻いて）縮んだ A burnt piece of wool *shrank up in curls [a curl]*.

ちりぢり 散り散り ●ちりぢりの雲 *scattered* clouds. ▶群衆は銃声を聞いてちりぢりに（=ばらばらに）なった The crowd *scattered* [〖やや書〗*dispersed*, *broke up*] at the sound of the gun.

ちりとり 塵取り a dustpan.

ちりのこる 散り残る ▶ブドウの木には最後の一葉だけが散り残っていた There *was* only *one leaf left* on the vine./Only *one leaf was* still on the vine.

ちりばめる 散りばめる a stud (-dd-); (❗通例受身で); 〖はめ込む〗set*; 〖象眼する〗inlay*; 〖まき散らす〗scatter. ●金をちりばめた箱 a box *inlaid [set] with* gold. ●星をちりばめた空 a sky *studded [sprinkled] with* stars; a star-*studded* sky.
▶王冠にはダイヤモンドがちりばめられていた The crown *was studded* [*was set*] *with* diamonds.

ちりはらい 塵払い ●ちり払いをする(=ほこりを払う) dust.

ちりめん 縮緬 silk crepe.
●ちりめん紙 crepe paper. ●ちりめんじゃこ boiled and dried baby sardines. ●ちりめんじわ fine wrinkles.

ちりゃく 知略 a plot; a conspiracy. (⇨はかりごと)

***ちりょう** 治療 〖手当て〗(medical) treatment, medical care (後の方は特に大きな医療機関における); 〖完全治癒〗a cure; 〖治療法〗a treatment, a cure (*for*); (薬や手術によらない) 〖医学〗therapy; (回復に効果のある) 〖やや書〗a remedy. ●外科治療 surgical *treatment*. ●放射線治療 radiation *therapy*. ●集中治療室[病棟] 〖医学〗an intensive *care* unit; an ICU [an I.C.U.]. ●がんの新しい治療法 a new *treatment* [*cure*, *remedy*] *for* cancer. ●治療を受けている be under *medical treatment*. ●患者に治療を施す give a patient *treatment* (*for*). ●その医者の治療で回復する recover under the doctor's *treatment* [*care*]. ▶彼女は 2 年前に胃がんの治療を受けた She received [underwent] *treatment for* stomach cancer two years ago. ▶彼は治療のために入院した He entered (《主に米》the) hospital for *treatment*.
— **治療する** 動 treat; 〖完全に治す〗cure. (❗(1) いずれも目的語には患者・病気の両方が可。(2) 後の方はけがには用いない) (⇨治す) ▶彼の病気[けが]を治療する a *treat* his illness [injury]; *treat* him *for* his illness [injury]. ▶その患者の心臓病を治療する a *cure* the patient *of* his heart disease. ▶虫歯の治療をしてもらう have one's decayed tooth *treated*.
●**治療費** the cost of (medical) treatment, a doctor's fee.

ちりょく 地力 the fertility of the soil.

ちりょく 知力 mental [intellectual] power(s); (知性) intellect, (a) mind; (知能) intelligence; (理解力) wit(s); (頭脳) a brain (❗しばしば複数形で).

ちりれんげ 散蓮華 (⇨蓮華)

ちりんちりん ●ちりんちりんと音を出す tinkle; jingle. ●風鈴のちりんちりんという音 the *tinkle [jingle]* of a wind bell. ▶後ろから自転車のベルがちりんちりんと鳴るのが聞こえた I heard (the sound of) a bike('s) bell coming behind me.

***ちる** 散る ❶ 〖花・葉などが〗(落ちる) fall*; (散在する) scatter; (ひらひらと) flutter (down). ▶風で桜の花が散った The wind made the cherry blossoms *fall [scatter]*./The wind *scattered* the cherry blossoms.
❷ [群衆などが分散する] 〖解散する〗break* up; (四方に散る) scatter, 〖やや書〗disperse (⇨散らす); 〖雲などが消散する〗break away, 〖やや書〗disperse. ▶デモ隊は警察が到着すると散っていった The demonstrators *broke up* [*scattered*, *dispersed*] when the police arrived.
❸ [気が] (人の注意をそらす) distract, divert (*from*). ▶騒音のために気が散って本が読めなかった The noise *distracted* me *from* my reading./I *was distracted from* my reading by the noise.

チルド (冷蔵の) chilled. (❗関連 (冷凍の) frozen)
●チルド食品 chilled foods. ●チルドビーフ chilled beef.

ちれい 地霊 a spirit living in the ground.

ちれき 地歴 geography and history.

ちろちろ ▶炎がちろちろ(と)燃えている The flames *are flickering*. ▶沢の水がちろちろ(と)流れていた The water in the mountain stream *was trickling*.

チロル ●チロル地方 the Tyrol [Tirol] /tírouɫ, táirouɫ/. ●チロル地方の Tyrolean, Tyrolese.

ちわ 痴話 ●痴話げんか a lovers' quarrel.

チワワ 〖動物〗(犬) a chihuahua.

ちん 狆 〖動物〗(犬) a Japanese spaniel.

ちん 朕 we.

チン 图 (鈴の音) ting, tinkle.
— **チンする** 動 (食べ物を) heat [cook] (it) in a microwave; (鼻を) blow one's nose. ▶チンして食べる食品 microwavable foods. ▶彼女はその子供の鼻にハンカチを当てて「さあ、チンして」と言った She held her handkerchief to the child's nose and said, "Here (you) *blow*!"

ちん 珍 (まれな) rare; (奇妙な) strange. ●珍種のラン a *rare* kind of orchid. ●珍獣 a *rare* animal. ●珍問 a *strange* [(見当違いの) an *off-key*] question.

-ちん -賃 ●運賃 (旅客の) ⟨a bus [a train, an air]⟩ fare; (貨物の) freight. ●家賃 (a) rent. ●駄賃 (a) reward; a tip. ●工賃 (=手間賃) wages.

ちんあげ 賃上げ 图 a pay raise 《米》 [rise 《英》], a

ちんあつ 鎮圧 图 suppression.
― 鎮圧する 動 suppress, put ... down. (❗後の方が口語的む)▶反乱はすぐに鎮圧された The revolt *was* quickly *suppressed* [*put down*].

ちんうつ 沈鬱 ― 沈鬱な 形 (気分を滅入らせる) depressing; (憂うつな) gloomy. ▶沈うつな雰囲気な *gloomy* [a *depressing*] atmosphere. ▶彼は沈うつな面持ちで私を見上げた He looked up at me with a *depressed* [*gloomy*] expression.

ちんか 鎮火 ― 鎮火する 動 ▶火事はすぐに鎮火した The fire *was* quickly *put out* [*was quickly brought under control*]. (⇨火事)

ちんか 沈下 ▶地盤沈下 ground *subsidence*.
― 沈下する 動 (一般に沈む) sink; (土地・建物などが)《やや書》 subside. ▶その建物は基礎が弱いために徐々に沈下している The building *is* gradually *sinking* [*subsiding*] because of weak foundations.

ちんがい 鎮咳 ▶鎮咳薬 (せき止め) a cough medicine.

ちんがし 賃貸し ― 賃貸しする 動 (長期間土地・家などを) rent [《英》 let] ... (out); (短期間車・ボートなどを) rent 《米》 [hire 《英》] ... (out); (リース契約で)《やや書》 lease ... (out). (❗ lend は「無料で貸す」の意 (⇨貸す)

ちんがり 賃借り ― 賃借りする 動 (長期間土地・家などを) rent; (短期間車・ボートなどを)《米》 rent, 《英》 hire; (バスなどを団体で) charter; (リース契約で)《やや書》 lease. (❗ borrow は「無料で借りる」の意 (⇨借りる)

ちんき 珍奇 ― 珍奇な 形 (奇妙な) strange; (珍しい) rare; (新奇な) novel; (奇妙な) queer, odd.

チンギスハーン (⇨ジンギスカン)

ちんきゃく 珍客 an unexpected visitor [ˣguest]. (❗ guest は通例招待された客)

ちんきん 沈金 ▶沈金彫り lacquer ware inlaid with gold.

*__ちんぎん__ 賃金 (労賃) wages. (⇨給料)
① 【~賃金】 ▶最低[基本]賃金 a minimum [a basic] *wage*. ▶高[低]賃金で働く work at high [low] *wages*.
② 【賃金~】 ▶男女の賃金格差は大きい There is wide inequality [a big difference] in *wages* between men and women. (❗《主に英》 では同一会社内での同種の仕事における労働者間の「賃金格差」は通例複数形で *wage* differentials という) ▶賃金交渉で組合は1万円の賃上げを獲得した The union won a 10,000 yen raise at the *wage* talks [*negotiations*]. ▶この産業の賃金水準は高い There is a high *wage* level [standard] in this industry./This *wage* level [standard] of this industry is high.
③ 【賃金が[は]~】 ▶今年は賃金がずいぶん上がった *Wages* have increased [risen, gone up] a lot this year. ▶我々の賃金が下がった Our *wages* have fallen [gone down]. ▶賃金は消費者物価にスライドすることになっている *Wages* are to vary with consumer prices.
● 賃金カット a cut in wages; a wage cut [cutback]. ● 賃金体系 a wage system. ● 賃金凍結 a wage freeze; a freeze on wages. ● 賃金労働者 a wage earner; 《主に米》 a wageworker. (⇨サラリーマン)

ちんしゃ 狆しゃ (醜い顔) an ugly face.

ちんけ ▶ちんけ(=最低)な男 the meanest man; a worthless man; a good-for-nothing.

ちんげい 珍芸 an unusual [an uncommon] and droll [amusing] trick [performance]. (❗ trick はイヌ・サルなどの芸, performance は人間の芸)

ちんけいざい 鎮痙剤 an antispasmodic; an anticonvulsant.

ちんげんさい 青梗菜 【植物】 bok choy; (説明的に) a variety of Chinese cabbage.

ちんこう 沈降 (地盤などの沈下) subsidence; (沈澱作用) sedimentation. ▶赤血球沈降速度 the erythrocyte *sedimentation* rate; the *sedimentation* rate of red blood cell.

ちんこん 鎮魂 ▶鎮魂曲 a requiem /rékwiəm/. ▶鎮魂祭 a requiem (mass).

ちんざ 鎮座 ― 鎮座する 動 be enshrined.

ちんさげ 賃下げ a pay [a wage] cut.

ちんじ 椿事, 珍事 an unexpected [a rare] event; an accident.

ちんしごと 賃仕事 piecework. (⇨内職)

ちんしもっこう 沈思黙考 图 meditation.
― 沈思黙考する 動 (深く考える)《やや書》 meditate (*on*); think deeply (*about*); (深く物思いに沈んでいる) be (deep) in meditation; be deep in thought.

ちんしゃ 陳謝 ― 陳謝する 動 apólogize; an apology. (⇨詫(ゎ)びる, 謝る) ▶彼に遅れたことを陳謝する *apologize* [*make an apology*] to him *for* being late.

ちんしゃく 賃借 ― 賃借する 動 (⇨賃借りする)
● 賃借権 a right of lease. ● 賃借人 a lessee (↔ lessor).

ちんしゅ 珍種 ▶珍種のバラ a rare kind [*variety*] of rose.

ちんじゅ 鎮守 a village shrine. ▶鎮守の森 the grove of a *village shrine*.

ちんじゅう 珍獣 a rare beast [animal].

ちんじゅつ 陳述 a statement. ▶陳述を取り消す withdraw one's *statement*. ▶虚偽の陳述をする make a false *statement*. ▶陳述書を提出する hand in a (written) *statement*.

ちんしょ 珍書 (⇨珍本)

ちんじょう 陳情 a petition. ▶政府に陳情書を提出する present a *petition* to the government. ▶都立託児所増設の陳情書には5万人が署名していた The *petition* for more metropolitan nurseries had 50,000 names.
― 陳情する 動 petition. ▶我々は市長に新しい道路を造ってほしいと陳情した We *petitioned* the mayor *for* a new road [*to* build a new road, *that* a new road (《主に英》 *should*) be built].
● 陳情者 a petitioner. ● 陳情団 (議会の) a lobby.

ちんせい 沈静 ― 沈静(化)する 動 die down. ▶地価の上昇が沈静化してきた The rise in land prices has begun to *die* [*slow*] *down*.

ちんせいざい 鎮静剤 a sedative /sédətiv/; (精神安定剤) a tranquilizer.

ちんせつ 珍説 (珍しい話[意見, 説]) a strange story [opinion, theory].

ちんせん 沈船 a sunken ship.

ちんせん 沈潜 ― 沈潜する 動 【水中深く沈む】 sink deep into the water; 【没頭する】 be lost in (thought); be absorbed in 《one's book》.

ちんたい 沈滞 图 stagnation; 【不活発】 inactivity. ▶連戦連敗でチームには沈滞ムードが漂っている Our team has lost every game and is in a *depressed mood* [《話》 in the doldrums].

ちんたい 沈滞した 形 stagnant; [活気のない] inactive, dull.
— 沈滞する 動 stagnate, become stagnant [dull].
ちんたい 賃貸 名 ● 不動産の賃貸で収入を得る have an income from property *rentals*.
— 賃貸する 動 (⇨賃貸しする)
● 賃貸契約[期間] a lease. ● 5年間の賃貸契約で家を借りる rent a house on a five-year *lease*; take a five-year *lease* on a house. ● 賃貸人 a lessor (↔a lessee). ● 賃貸マンション a rental apartment. ● 単に an apartment だけでもよい ● 賃貸料 (土地・建物などの) (a) rent (*for*); a rental.

チンタオ 青島 [中国の都市] Qingdao /tʃíŋdáu/.
ちんたら ● 彼はちんたらちんたら取り散らかした後かたづけをした He *unwillingly* cleaned up the mess *in an inefficient way*.
ちんちくりん [人] [軽蔑的] a dwarf, a shorty. ● この着物はちんちくりんだ (=短すぎる) This *kimono* is *too short* for me.
ちんちゃく 沈着 名 [平静] calmness, [やや書] composure.
— 沈着な 形 calm, composed. ● 彼の沈着な顔に composed face. ● 彼の沈着な行動のおかげでその子の命は助かった His *calm* act saved the child's life.
ちんちょう 沈丁 — 珍重する 動 [大事にする] treasure; [高く評価する] value ... highly. ● そのつぼを珍重する *treasure* the vase.
ちんちょう 珍鳥 a rare bird.
ちんちょうげ 沈丁花 [植物] a daphne /dǽfni/.
チンチラ [動物] a chinchilla. (! 毛皮は U)
● チンチラウサギ a chinchilla rabbit.
ちんちん ● [鐘や嘴子(ﾔｶﾝ)の音] ● ちんちん音がするtinkle, jingle. ● 路面電車がちんちん音を出しながら走っていた A streetcar ran along making *tinkling* sounds.
❷ [湯沸かしが鳴る音] ● やかんがちんちん沸いている The kettle *is singing*.
❸ [犬の芸] ● ちんちんする stand on its hind legs.
● (犬に命じて)ちんちん Beg!/Sit up!
ちんちんでんしゃ ちんちん電車 (路面電車) [米] a street car, a trolley; [英] a tram, a tramcar.
ちんつう 沈痛 — 沈痛な 形 [悲しい] sad (-dd-); [悲嘆に暮れる] sorrowful [! sad より激しく長続的]; [深刻な] grave; [死を悼む] mournful. ● 彼女は沈痛な面持ちだった She looked *sad* [*sorrowful*, *grave*, *mournful*].
ちんつうざい 鎮痛剤 a painkiller, an analgesic /ænldʒí:zɪk/. ● 鎮痛剤を飲む take [×drink] a *painkiller*.
ちんてい 鎮定 — 鎮定する 動 quell [put down] a revolt.
ちんでん 沈澱 — 沈澱する 動 settle; (沈澱している) be deposited. ● コップの中に何か柔らかいものが沈澱している Something soft *is deposited* in the glass.
— 沈澱物 (a) deposit; (a) sediment.
ちんとう 珍答 a strange [an offbeat] answer; (とっぴな) an unpredictable answer.
ちんどんや ちんどん屋 a *chindon'ya*; (説明的に) a street (musical) band hired to advertise special sales, the opening of new stores, and so on.
ちんにゅうしゃ 闖入者 (乱入者) an intruder.
チンパンジー a chimpanzée; [話] a chimp.
ちんぴら a hooligan, a hoodlum; (不良少年) [米] a punk. ● ちんぴらにからまれた Some *punks* tried to pick a quarrel with me.
ちんぴん 珍品 a rarity; a rare article.
ちんぶ 鎮撫 — 鎮撫する 動 (鎮圧する) suppress 《a riot》; (静める) pacify 《a riot》.
ちんぷ 陳腐 — 陳腐な 形 (使い古した) hackneyed, trite; (ありふれた) commonplace; (古くさい) stale.
● 陳腐な表現 a *hackneyed* [*trite*] expression; a cliché /kli:féi/. ● 陳腐な冗談 a *stale* [*a stock*] joke. ● 陳腐なことばかり言っている政治演説 a political speech full of *commonplaces*.
ちんぶん 珍聞 a strange [a curious] story.
ちんぷんかんぷん ● 物理学は私にはちんぷんかんぷんだ (=まったく理解できない) I can't understand physics *at all*./Physics is (《英》all) Greek to me.
ちんべん 陳弁 (弁明) (an) explanation; (弁解) (an) excuse.
ちんぽ(こ) a penis; 《俗》a cock.
ちんぼつ 沈没 名 ● タイタニック号の沈没 the sinking of the *Titánic*.
— 沈没する 動 sink, go down. (⇨沈む❶) ● 漁船が根室沖で沈没した The fishing boat *sank* [*went down*] off Nemuro. ● 我が軍は敵軍の艦船を多数沈没させた We *sank* a number of enemy ships.
— 沈没船 a sunken ship.
ちんぽん 珍本 a rare book.
ちんまり ● ちんまりした 形 (小さいながらも整った) compact; (小さいが居心地のいい) snug. ● ちんまりしたゲーム室 a *snug* game room. ● 彼女のちんまりした鼻 her *small charming* nose.
ちんみ 珍味 [おいしい物] 形 a delicacy; [風味のよい食物] a dainty (food); [ごちそう] a feast. ● 季節ごとの珍味 the *delicacies* [*dainties*] of the season. ● 山海の珍味 all sorts of *delicacies*.
ちんみょう 珍妙 — 珍妙な 形 (odd and) funny; (相当変わった) eccentric; (古) queer. ● 珍妙ないでたちで in an *eccentric* outfit.
ちんむるい 珍無類 — 珍無類な 形 queerest; strangest.
****ちんもく** 沈黙 名 (a) silence. (! 沈黙の期間をいうときは C) ● 私は彼女の沈黙を承諾にとった I interpret her *silence* as (her) consent. ● 2人の間に長い[気まずい]沈黙が続いた A long [An awkward] *silence* hung between the two.
● 沈黙は金 (ことわざ) Silence is golden.
● 沈黙を守る maintain silence; keep [remain] silent; hold one's tongue.
● 沈黙を破る break (the) silence.
— 沈黙する 動 fall silent [into silence]. ● 沈黙した silent. ● 沈黙して in *silence*. ● (議論などでやりこめて)沈黙させる reduce 《him》 to *silence*; silence 《him》.
ちんもく 『沈黙』 Silence. (参考) 遠藤周作の小説
ちんもん 珍問 a strange [an offbeat] question; (とっぴな) an unpredictable question.
ちんれつ 陳列 名 (a) displáy; (an) exhibition /èksəbíʃən/.
— 陳列する 動 [はっきり見えるように並べる] displáy; [一般の人に公開する] exhibit /ɪgzíbɪt/. (⇨展示する)
● ショウインドーに商品を陳列する *display* [*exhibit*] goods in a show window. ● 店頭に新刊書を陳列してある New books *are displayed* [*on display*] in the bookstore.
● 陳列室 a showroom; an exhibition room.
● 陳列台 a display stand [counter]. ● 陳列棚 a showcase. ● 陳列品 an exhibit; an article on display [exhibition].

つ

ツアー ❶[旅行] (観光旅行) a sightseeing tour; (団体旅行) a group [an organized] tour; (パック旅行) a package [×a pack] tour. (⇨旅行) ●スキーツアー a ski tour. ●ガイド付きツアー a guided tour. ▶ツアーコンダクター a tour conductor. ▶アルプスへはヨーロッパのツアーで行きました I went to the Swiss Alps *on a group tour* of Europe.
❷[巡業] a tour. ●全国ツアーをする go on a nationwide [a national] *tour*; tour the country. ▶ツアーに出ている(=遠征中の)ドジャーズ the Dodgers *on tour*. (❗「遠征試合」は an away (game [match]).

***つい ❶**[時間・距離について] (ほんの) only; (ちょうど) just (❗通例文中で完了形と用いるが, 《主に話》では過去形とも用いる); (たった今) just now (❗通例文尾で過去形と用いる (⇨第 2 文例]). 現在時制では「ただ今は」「今のところ」の意となる). ▶ついさっき着いたばかりだ He's *just* arrived./He arrived *just now* [*recently*]. (⇨さっき) ▶彼らが引っ越して来たのは 3 日前[最近]のことだ It was *only* three days ago [*only recently*] that they moved in. (❗強調構文) ▶つい今しがた彼女から手紙を受け取った I've *just* got (《主に米語》I *just* got] a letter from her./I received a letter from her *just now*. (⇨❶[注]) ▶つい先日彼のお父さんに会った I saw his father *just* the other day. ▶学校はついそこ(=目と鼻の先)です The school is *just* around the corner. (❗(1) The school is a stone's throw from here. のような言い方は余り使わない. (2) just around the corner は文脈によって「つい角を曲がったところ」の意になる)/The school is *very* near [×near from] here. ▶つい最近まで京都に住んでいた I lived in Kyoto until *quite* recently. (⇨最近)
❷[うっかりして] (不注意に) carelessly; (間違って) by mistake; (思わず) in spite of oneself; (偶然) by chance, by accident; (意図せずに) unintentionally. (⇨ついつい) ▶ついうっかりして彼のかばんを持って行ってしまった I've taken his bag *by mistake* [*carelessly*]. ▶つい腹を立ててしまった I got angry *in spite of myself*. ▶とてもいらいらしていたのでそのことをつい忘れてしまった I was so irritated that I *just* forgot about it. ▶彼に言うつもりはなかったが, つい口を滑らしてしまった I didn't mean to tell him, but let it slip out.

つい 対 a pair. ●対になる make [form] a *pair*. ●一対の本棚 a *pair* of bookshelves (❗単・複両扱い); (同形の二つの) twin bookshelves. ●対になっている (=そろいの)ネックレスとブレスレット a *matching* necklace and bracelet; a necklace with a bracelet *to match*. ▶それは対になっている. 彼が片方を, 私のもう片方を持っている It's a *pair*. He has one, and I have the other.

つい 終 the last. (⇨最後) ●ついの別れ(=死) (a) death.

ツイード (生地) tweed. ●ツイードのスーツを着た男 a man (dressed) in *tweeds*; a man who is wearing *tweeds* [a *tweed* suit]. (❗tweeds で上着とズボン[スカート]をさす) ▶ツイードのジャケット a *tweed* jacket; a jacket in *tweed*.

ついえる 費える ▶貯蓄が費えた(=減った) The savings *dwindled* (*away*). ▶つまらない事に時間が費えた(=ただに使われた) Time *was* wasted on trifles.

ついえる 潰える (負けて総崩れになる) be routed; be completely defeated 《*in* a battle》; (計画, 希望などがだめになる) collapse, break down, fall through.

ついおく 追憶 (書) reminíscence. ●個々の思い出 ℂ. しばしば複数形で用いる ●追憶にふける(書) remínisce 《*about* the good old days》.

***ついか 追加** 图 [つけ足すこと] (an) addition; [補足] a supplement (❗完成されたものにつけ足してよりよくすること). ●職員の 5 名追加 the addition [×supplement] of five men *to* the staff. ●人の追加は supplement は不可) ●条文の追加 the *supplement* of an article. ▶コーヒーを三つ追加注文した I ordered three *more* coffees.
── 追加する 動 [A を B に] add 《A *to* B》(⇨加える); supplement 《B *with* A》(⇨補う) ●表に欄を一つ追加する add a space to the list; *supplement* the list *with* a space.
●追加条項 a rider. ●追加予算 a supplementary budget. ●追加料金 an additional [(余分の) an] extra] charge; (特別のサービスに対する) a supplement.

ついかんばん 椎間板 [解剖] an intervértebral disk. ●椎間板ヘルニア [医学] hernia /hə́ːrniə/ of the *intervertebral disk*; a herniated disk. (⇨ぎっくり腰)

ついき 追記 图 (後記) a póstscript.
── 追記する 動 add a postscript; (...と書き足す) add that ....

ついきそ 追起訴 《bring》a supplementary indictment [suit] 《*against*》.

ついきゅう 追及 图 [調査] (an) investigation; [[詰問] questioning. **── 追及する** 動 (非難する) accuse 《A *of* B》; (調査する) investigate; (詰問する) question; (激しく尋問する)《話》grill. ●犯人の行方を追及する(=捜査する) *search for* a criminal. ●追及をかわす[たくみにそらす] evade [(ごまかす) dodge, (受け流す) parry, ×avoid] one's *question*(s). (❗avoid は「近付かない」ことで, この場合は使えない) ▶彼らはその事故に対する責任を追及した They *accused* him of responsibility for the accident.

ついきゅう 追求 图 pursuit /pərsúːt/. ●富の追求 the *pursuit* of wealth.
── 追求する 動 ●幸福[利潤]を追求する *pursue* /pərsúː/ [(書) *seek*] happiness [profit].

ついきゅう 追究 ── 追究する 動 ●真理を追究する *pursue* /pərsúː/ [(書) *seek*] (the) truth. ●「真理の追究」 is the *pursuit of* (the) truth)

ついく 対句 [修辞] an antíthesis /æntíθəsis/. (複 antítheses /-sìːz/); (対語) ●「人生は短く, 芸術は長し」のように対をなす語句) ●対句をなす form an *antíthesis*.

ついげき 追撃 图 (素早い) a chase /tʃéis/; (しつこい) pursuit /pərsúːt/.
── 追撃する 動 chase; pursue /pərsúː/. ●敵機を追撃する *chase* the enemy plane.

ついご 対語 a pair of words; (反対語) an antonym.
ついこつ 椎骨 『解剖』a vertebra (穆 vertebrae, ~s). — 椎骨の 形 vertebral.
ついし 追試 (⇨追試験)
ついしけん 追試験 (米) a makeup (exam [test]) (!「再試験」の意もある); (英) a resit /rí:sít/. ▸追試験を受ける 《米》make up an exam 《in math》; 《英》resit /rí:sít/ an exam (he failed).
ついじゅう 追従 — **追従する** 動 follow ... (blindly); (まねる) imitate, copy.
ついしょう 追従 名 sycophancy /síkəfənsi/. (!⇨おべっか) — **追従する** 動 fawn /fɔ́:n/ 《on, upon》.
● 追従者 a sýcophant. ● 追従笑い a sycophántic smile.
ついしん 追伸 a póstscript. (!通例 P.S. [PS] という略語を用いる.「再追伸」は P.P.S.) ▸手紙に追伸をつける add a *postscript* to a letter.
ついずい 追随 名 — **追随を許さない** 他の追随を許さない (並ぶ者はない) have no equal [be second to none] 《in》; (群を抜いている) far ahead of all others 《in》.
— **追随する** 動 ▸ ...に追随する (...の例にならう) follow in 《his, its》 footsteps.
ツイスト the twist. ▸ツイストを踊る twist; dance [do] the *twist*.
ついせき 追跡 名 『捕らえようとして』(素早い) a chase; (しつこい) pursuit. ▸追跡の手を逃れる escape from *pursuit*.
— **追跡する** 動 chase; pursue; (足跡を追う) track. (⇨追跡 ❶ ● 泥棒を追跡する *chase* (after) [*pursue*, (あとを追う) *run after*] a thief. ▸スピード違反の車を追跡する *chase* [*pursue*] a speeding car. (!speeding は「違反速度で走る」の意. 単に「速い」の意もある) ▸銀行強盗を追跡中である [追跡して捕える] *be in pursuit of* [*track down*] a bank robber.
● 追跡者 a pursuer. ● 追跡調査 a follow-up survey [check].
ついぜん 追善 — **追善供養** 《hold》a memorial service 《for a dead person》. ● 追善興行 a memorial performance in honor of 《Mr. A》.
ついぞ never; not ... ever. ▸ついぞ京都に行ったことがありません I've *never* been to Kyoto.
ついそう 追送 ▸追送書類 supplementary documents to *be sent* [*mailed*] *later*.
ついそう 追想 reminiscence. (⇨追憶)
ついぞう 追贈 — **追贈する** 動 confer a title [a degree, an honor] posthumously 《on, upon》. ▸その大学は彼に名誉学位を追贈した An honorary degree *was conferred on* him *posthumously* by the university.
ついたいけん 追体験 — **追体験する** 動 《後で自分でも経験する》experience personally.
ついたち 一日 《on》the first day of a month. ● 1月1日 January 1(*st*). (⇨日付)
ついたて 衝立て a (movable) partition. ▸台所とダイニング部分を衝立てで仕切る *partition off* the dining area *from* the kitchen.
ついちょう 追徴 名 『追加の徴収』an additional collection [請求] charge].
— **追徴する** 動 make* an additional collection [charge] [charge] ... in addition.
▸税を追徴する *collect* taxes *in addition*; *collect more* taxes. ▸彼は100万円追徴された He *was charged an additional* one million yen.
● 追徴金 money collected [paid] in addition; (的罰の) a forfeit; a penalty. ● 追徴税 a penalty tax.

ついつい ▸このドレスは赤札でたったの 4,800 円だったので，ついつい買ってしまった (= どうしても我慢できなかった) This dress was only 4,800 yen on sale, so I just couldn't resist.

：ついて 前 ❶【関して】about ...; on ...; of ...; over ...; concerning ...; as to ...; as for ....

[使い分け] **about** 最も一般的な語.
on 内容が専門的で高度な場合に用いる: 日本についての本 a book *about* [*on*] Japan. (!*about* では一般的内容, *on* では専門的内容を暗示)/社会福祉についての論文 a paper *on* [x*about*] social welfare. (!論文は専門的なので通例 *on* を用いる)
of *about* としばしば交換できるが, *about* が詳しくふれるのに対し, *of* は (全般的に) 軽くふれる場合に用いられる. たとえば think *about* it では「そのことについて長くいろいろと考える」ことが, think *of* it では「ちょっと思い浮かべる」ことを含意する.
over「...をめぐって」の意で, しばしば意見の対立・不一致を含意する.
concerning *about*, *on* の堅い語で限定的なことに用いる.
as to は《主に英・やや書》で wh-節が続く場合に好まれるがそれ以外では *about*, *on* が普通.
as for すでに出た話題に関連して別のことを述べる場合に用いる. 通例次の文または節の初めに置かれる (*as to* にもこの用法がある). 時に軽蔑や無関心を含意する.

● その事故について話をする talk *about* [*of*] the accident. ● 税制改革について意見を述べる express an opinion *about* [*on*, *concerning*, 《書》*with regard to*] tax reform. ▸この件について質問はありませんか Do you have any questions *about* this matter? ▸それについてよく知ってるよ I know all *about* it. ▸それについてどう思いますか What [x*How*] do you think *of* [*about*] that?/(それについてご意見はどうですか) What is your opinion *of* that?/What do you say *to* that? (!*to* は「...に関連して, 対して」の意で, ある程度決まった連語や慣用的な言い方に限られる) ▸彼は鳥についての話をした [講演をした] He spoke *about* [*on*] birds. ▸彼らはささいなことについて議論した They argued *about* [*over*] trifles. (!... discussed 《x*about*, x*over*》 trifles. ともいえる) ▸彼は英語はできないが, 数学について言えばクラスで一番です He is not good at English, but *as for* [*as to*, (...ということになると) *when it comes to*] math 《米》 [*maths*《英》], he is at the top of the class.
❷【ごとに】a; 《書》per .... (⇨-に付き)
❸【ともに】with .... (⇨一緒に)
❹【後に】after .... (⇨後(あと))
❺【下(もと)で】under .... (⇨下(もと))

— **ついては** 接 (and) so; 《やや書》therefore. ▸車が故障してしまいました．ついては駅まで乗せてくれませんか My car broke down, (*and*) *so* could you give me a ride to the station?

ついで 名 返すのはついでの折で結構です Please give it back *at your convenience* [when you have a chance to come this way]. (!前の方は「都合のよい時」, 後の方は「このあたりに来る機会があったとき」の意)

— **ついでに** 副 by the way; incidentally, (途中で) on the way 《to》. ▸ついでにその件について一言申し上げます *By the way*, let me tell you something about the matter. ▸事のついでにもう一つお願いを聞いていただきたいのですが ˇ*Incidéntally* [*By the wáy*], I'd like to ask another favor. (!後の方が口語的) ▸駅へ行くついでに (=途中で) 花を買った I bought some flowers *on my way to* the station. ▸彼に電話したついでに (=ともに) 彼女のことを聞いてみた When I talked with him on [over] the phone, I asked about her. ▶アイロンをかけているついでにジーンズも頼むね You can iron my jeans *while you are at it.* (**!**(1) You can は穏やかな命令を表す. (2) Can you …? としてもほとんど意味は変わらないが, これは依頼も表す.) ▶(ほんの)話についでに彼は家族のことにふれた He mentioned his family (only) *in passing.*

ついで 次いで (and) then [next]. (⇒次に) ▶我々のクラスで次郎は太郎に次いで足が速い Jiro runs fastest *after* [*next to*] Taro in our class. ▶英語に次いで私の好きな学科は物理だ *After* [*Next to*] English, my favorite subject is physics. ▶彼に次いで(=引き続いて)私が立ち上がった *Following* him, I stood up.

ついていく ついて行く (後に続く) follow; (いっしょに行く) go* [come*] (together) (*with*) (**!** come は聞き手に同伴する場合に用いる (⇒行く)); (同伴する)《やや書》accompany; (ぴったりと, 呼ばれないのに)《話》tag (-gg-) along (*behind*, *with*); (…に遅れないように) keep* up with…. ● 外角球について行く〔野球〕catch up with an outside pitch. ▶その子は父親の後について行った The kid *followed* [*tagged along behind*] his father. ▶彼が東京へ行くときには私がついて行きます I'll [I am going to] *accompany* him when he goes to Tokyo. ▶彼女は非常に速く走ったので行けなかった She ran so fast (that) I couldn't *keep up* [*to keep*] with her. ▶その授業はついて行くのが大変ですか Is it tough *keeping up with* that class?

ついている lucky (↔unlucky). (⇒運, 幸運) ▶彼はすることなすことみなついている He is *lucky* [*has good* (↔*bad*) *luck*] *in* whatever he does. ▶私はついていた I was *lucky.*/*Luck was* [《米話》*The breaks were*] *with* (↔*against*) me. (**!** break は「幸運」の意.「ついてきた」は *Luck is coming my way.*/(《через通じて》ついていたのさ) I had all the *luck.*/I feel I'm *in* (↔*out of*) *luck* now. ▶あなたついてないね Tough *luck* [《米話》*break*] (for you)! ▶今日はついてないよ Today is not my (*lucky*) day.

会話「君が1等賞をとったぞ」「信じられないぐらいついてるわ」"You've won (the) first prize." "What an incredible bit of *luck*!" (**!** luck は Ⓤ なので ×What an incredible luck! とはいわない)

ついてくる ついて来る (後に続く) follow; (いっしょに来る) come* (along) (*with*, *to*), come together (*with*) (⇒来る); (ぴったりと, 呼ばれないのに)《話》tag (-gg-) along (*behind*, *with*); (…に遅れないように) keep* up with…. ▶俺についてこい Come along with me./Follow me. ▶その子は私について来た The kid *followed* [*came along with*, *tagged along behind*] me. ▶ついて来られるように一生懸命勉強しなさい You should study hard to *keep up with* us.

ついでに (⇒ついで)

ついてまわる 付いて回る follow around [about]. (⇒付き纏(まと)う) ▶どこへ行こうが例の悪いうわさが影のように彼に付いて回った That bad rumor *followed* him *like a shadow* [*dogged* him] wherever he went. ▶学歴は一生付いて[回る]一生の間ずっと重大な役割を果たすと考えるのは妄想である It's a delusion to think that one's educational background *plays a crucial part* throughout one's life.

ついとう 追討 ── 追討する 動 hunt … down.

ついとう 追悼 图〔哀悼〕mourning. ▶故田中氏の追悼会(=追悼の式)を催す hold a *memorial* service for [a ceremony *in memory of*] the late Mr. Tanaka. ● 故人の霊に追悼の辞を述べる give a *me-*

morial address for the dead person [《やや書》deceased].
── **追悼する 動** mourn 《*for*》. ● 死んだ友を追悼する *mourn for* one's dead friend.

ついとつ 追突 图 a rear-end collision.
── **追突する 動** ● 車に追突する crash into [collide with, (どんと) bump into] the rear [back] of a car. ▶私の車はトラックに追突された My car *was struck from behind* [《話》*was rear-ended*] by a truck. (**!**「追突された車」は a rear-ended car)

*__**ついに 遂に**__ at last, at long last,《書》at length; after all; finally; eventually; in the end.

使い分け at last, at long last, at length いずれもあることが実現することを表すが, at last はけれど待ち望んでいたこと, 努力の末であることに重点があり, at long last はその強意表現. at length は通例文頭に置かれ時間的な経過に重点を置く.
after all 結果が期待を・意図に反するものであることを表す. 通例文尾, 時に文頭に置く. (⇒結局)
finally 動詞の前や文頭に置き,「長時間経過した後で最終的に」または文頭に置いて「列挙したり, 一連の話題を締めくくって最後に」の意.
eventually「度重なる遅れや多くの問題・議論などを経て最後には」の意.
in the end 通例文頭・文尾で,「試行錯誤のあと最後には」の意. 通例文頭・文尾に置く.
after all 以外は否定文では用いない.

▶彼は何度か試験を受けて, ついに合格した He took the exam several times, and *at last* he passed it [he *finally* passed it, he passed it *in the end*]. (**!** at last の代わりに after all を用いることはできない)/He took the exam several times, *until* (*at last*) he passed it. (**!** 前の言い方より合格するまでの期間を強調する. at last がある方が強意的) ▶ついに春が来た *At last* [×Finally, ×In the end] spring has come. (**!** finally, in the end を用いると春の次に季節が来ることになるので不可) ▶ついにその計画は失敗した The plan failed *after all* [*in the end*, ×at last]. (**!** at last は失敗のために努力したことになるので不可)/(失敗に終わった) The plan *ended in failure.* ▶ついに彼はその会に姿を見せなかった *After all* [×At last] he didn't come to the meeting. (**!** after all は話し手の待ちかねた気持ちを表す)

ついにん 追認 ── 追認する 動 (後から承認する) 《やや書》approve (↔disapprove). ● 現状を追認する *approve* the existing state of affairs.

ついのう 追納 ── 追納する 動 make an additional [an extra] payment; pay extra.

ついばむ 啄む 〔鳥が物を〕pick (*at* …). ▶おんどりが穀物をついばんだ A cock *picked* (*at*) [(くちばしでつついた) *pecked* (*at*)] the grain.

ついひ 追肥 〔spend〕 additional fertilizer [manure]; top-dressing. ● 追肥を施す top-dress 《*on*》.

ついび 追尾 ── 追尾する 動 chase; pursue. (⇒追跡する)

ついぼ 追慕 ── 追慕する 動 cherish the memory 《*of* one's dead mother》.

*__**ついほう 追放 图**__ 〔国外への〕(刑罰としての) banishment; (政治的理由による) exile /égzail/; (不法外国人などの) deportation; 〔党・宗派などからの〕 a purge; 〔排除〕 elimination. ● 貧困追放 the *elimination* of poverty. ● 覚醒剤追放運動《carry out》a campaign *against* stimulant drugs. ● 追放の身である[となる] be in [go into] *exile.*
── **追放する 動** banish; exile; deport; purge; (地位・職場などから)《書》oust. ● 大統領を追放する *oust*

the president. ▶この通りから車を追放する(=締め出す) shut out cars from this street. ▶彼は大逆罪で本国から追放された He *was banished* [*was exiled*] *from his country for* high treason. ▶多数の不法入国者が追放された A lot of illegal immigrants have *been deported*.

ついやす 費やす 〚金・時などを遣う〛spend (*on*+图; (*in*) doing), 《書》expend; (むだに) waste, squander; 〚人に費やさせる〛take*; cost* (**!** cost はしばしば負担の重さを含意する). ●たくさんの金を本に費やす *spend* [*expend*] a lot of money *on* books. ●つまらないことに時間を費やす *waste* one's time *on* trifles. ▶彼は1日3時間ローマ史の研究に費やしている He *spends* three hours a day (*in*) study*ing* Roman history. (**!** in は通例省略される) ▶彼はこの辞書の完成させるのに 20 年を費やした It *took* him [He *took*] twenty years *to* complete this dictionary. (⇨掛ける, 掛かる ❾)/He *spent* 20 years *for* the completion of this dictionary. ▶彼はその寺院を建てるのに 10 億円費やした It *cost* him [×He *cost*] one billion yen *to* build the temple. ▶チャーチルは人生の最良の年月を即興の演説の準備に費やした Winston Churchill *spent* the best years of his life preparing to give impromptu speeches. (**!** impromptu speech は「(原稿などの)あらかじめの準備なしにするスピーチ」の意)

ついらく 墜落 图 〚飛行機などの〛a crash; (落下) a fall. ▶飛行機の墜落で死ぬ be killed in a plane *crash*.

── 墜落する 動 crash; fall*; (急に落下する) drop (-pp-). ▶ヘリコプターが山中[海上]に墜落した A helicopter *crashed* into the mountains [*went down* over the sea].
●墜落現場 a crash site.

ついろく 追録 a supplement; an addendum (榎 addenda).

ツイン twin.
●ツインベッド (片方) a twin bed, (両方) twin beds.
●ツインルーム a twin bedroom; (英) a twin-bedded room; (俗に) a twin (room).

つう 通 (権威者) an authority 《*on*》; (専門家) an expert (*in*, *on*, *at*); (物知り) a well-informed person, 〚話〛a person in the know.
●財政通である 《やや書》 be *very well-informed in* finance; be an *authority on* finance; be a financial *expert*. ▶彼は中国通として知られている He is known as China hand.

-つう -通 ▶手紙3通 *three* letters. ▶この契約書を3通作成してください Please make three *copies* of this contract.

ついん 痛飲 ── 痛飲する 動 drink heavily; booze; drink like a fish.

つういん 痛院 ── 痛院する 動 go to ((米) the) hospital; (医院に) go to the doctor's office ((米) [doctor's (英)]. ⇨ 病院. 解説

つううん 通運 transport, transportation.
●通運会社 a transportation company; an express company.

ツーエー Double A. ●ツーエーでプレーする play Double-A ball.

つうか 通貨 (a) currency; 〚金(銭)〛money. ●外国通貨 foreign *currency* [*currencies*]. ●基軸通貨 a key *currency*. ●現地通貨 local *currency*. ●国際通貨 international [world] *currency*. ●国際通貨基金 the International Monetary Fund (略 IMF). ●主要通貨 a big [a major] *currency*. ●単一[統一された]通貨 a single [a common] *currency*. ●強い[弱い; 安定した]通貨 a strong [a weak; a stable] *currency*. ▶ドル紙幣は米国通貨の一つです Dollar bills are among the US America's *currency* [*currencies*]. (**!** among に注意)
●通貨危機 a monetary crisis. ●通貨切り上げ currency revaluation. ●通貨切り下げ currency devaluation. ●通貨スワップ a currency swap.
●通貨制度 a monetary system.

つうか 通過 图 (a) passage. (⇨通行) ●法案の通過 (=可決) the *passage* of a bill.
── 通過する 動 pass. (⇨通る ❶) ▶京都の上空を通過する fly [*pass*] over Kyoto. ▶急行が間もなく当駅を通過します An express train will *pass* (*through*) this station shortly. ▶予算案は議会を通過した The budget *has passed* the Diet./The Diet *has passed* the budget.
●通過駅 a nonstop station. ●通過儀礼 a rite of passage.

つうかあ ▶彼とはつうかあの仲です We understand and communicate each other perfectly well./(お互いに波長が合っている) We are on the same wavelength./He is on my wavelength.

つうかい 痛快 ── 痛快な 形 (たいそう愉快な) very enjoyable [pleasant]. ▶相手チームがこてんこてんにやっつけられるのを見て痛快だった It was very *enjoyable* [喜びを与え] It gave us *great pleasure*] to see our rival team beaten thoroughly.

つうかく 痛覚 a sense of pain. ●無痛覚(症)〚医学〛analgesia.

つうがく 通学 图 ●自宅通学の学生 a student *commuting* from his [her, his or her] home.
── 通学する 動 go* to [attend] school (**!** 前の方が口語的); (交通機関を使って) commute to school.
●徒歩で通学する walk to school; go to school by foot 〚話〛[on foot 《主に英》]. (**!** 前の方が普通. 後の方は「他の通学手段ではなく歩いて」というときに用いる. 次例も同様) ●自転車で通学する cycle to school; go to school by bicycle. ●通学途中で on the way to (*and from*) school. ▶何で通学しているの How do you go [*come*] *to* school?
●通学区域 a school district.

つうかん 通巻 ●通巻 30 巻からなる百科事典 an encyclopedia in 30 volumes.

つうかん 痛感 ── 痛感する 動 feel keenly; keenly [fully] realize. ▶英語を習得する難しさを痛感する *keenly realize* the difficulty of learning English. ▶私は毎日練習する必要性を痛感した I *felt keenly* the necessity to practice every day [of daily practice].

つうかん 通関 customs clearance.
── 通関する 動 (通関手続きを済ます) go through (the) customs.
●通関業者 a customs broker. ●通関士 a registered customs specialist. ●通関申告書 a bill of entry. ●通関手続き customs procedure [formalities].

つうかん 通観 图 a comprehensive survey 《*of*》.
── 通観する 動 survey 《the whole state of the economy》.

つうき 通気 ●通気性がよい(部屋などが) be well-ventilated (⟷poorly-ventilated); (衣類が) breathe well.
●通気孔 a vent, an air vent.

つうき 通期(の) 形 full-year. ●通期の売上高[営業利益] *full-year* sales [operating profit].
●通期決算 full-year results.

つうぎょう 通暁 ── 通暁する 動 (⇨精通する) ●英文

学に通暁している be well versed in English literature.

つうきん 通勤 图 a work-trip; (定期券による通勤) a commuter trip, (米) commutation. ●通勤ラッシュに during [in] the rush hour(s). ▶私の通勤時間は約 1 時間です I spend about an hour (in) *commuting* to work. (🔢(1) in は通例省略される。(2) この work は「職場」の意)/It takes me about an hour to get to the office./My *commúting* time is about an hour.

── **通勤する** 動 〖定期券で通う〗commute; 〖仕事に行く[来る]〗go* [come*] to the [one's] office, go [come] to work; 〖店員などが通う〗live out (🔢live in (住み込み)に対して). ▶彼は浦和から東京へ電車で通勤している He *commutes* from Urawa to Tokyo [between Urawa and Tokyo] by train./He *comes* [*goes*] *to* work *from* Urawa *to* Tokyo by train. ▶彼らは自転車で通勤する They *cycle to* work [*go to* work *by bicycle*]. (🔢前の方が普通 (⇨通学))

● **通勤者[客]** a commuter. ● **通勤手当** a commutation allowance. ● **通勤定期券** (米) a commutation ticket; (英) a season ticket. (⇨定期券) ● **通勤電車** a commuter train.

つうげき 痛撃 (ひどい打撃) ((deal [deliver, strike])) a severe [a hard, a heavy] blow; (厳しい攻撃) ((carry out [make])) a scathing [a violent] attack.

***つうこう 通行** passage; 〖乗り物の往来〗traffic. ●一方通行の道路 a one-way street. ▶この道路は車両の通行が禁止されている The *passage* of vehicles is [×are] prohibited on this road. ▶ここは車の通行がほとんどない There's almost [×nearly] no *traffic* here. ▶この通りは通行量が多い There's a lot of [heavy] *traffic* on this street./The *traffic* is heavy [×busy] on this street. (🔢「人通りの多い通り」は a *busy* street) ▶その橋は補修のため通行止めになっています The bridge is *closed* [*is blocked*] *to traffic* for repairs. ▶左側通行《掲示》Keep (to the) left./Walk left. (🔢前の方は車に対して,後の方は人に対して) ▶通行止め No *entry*./《掲示》No *thoroughfare*./(Road) Closed./(これより先) No *passage* this way.

● **通行禁止区域** a non-passing zone. ● **通行証** letters of transit. (🔢letters は「公式文書」で通例複数形) ● **通行人** a passerby (復 passersby); (歩行者) a pedestrian. ● **通行料** (車の) a toll. ● **通行料金所** a toll booth; a toll station. (🔢前の方は個々の,後の方は総称として)

つうこう 通航 ── **通航する** 動 navigate; sail.
つうこく 通告 图 (書) (a) notification; (通知) (a) notice. (⇨通知) ▶最後通告はしばしば 48 時間という期限がつけられる An ultimatum is often issued with a 48-hour deadline for compliance. (🔢 deadline for complicance は「(通告)に従うまでの期限」の意)

── **通告する** 動 notify ((A of B; A that 節)). ▶5 か月間の一時解雇を通告された I *was notified* [I received *notice*] of my five months' layoff. (🔢 of 以下は that they would lay me off for five months ともいえる)

つうこく 痛哭 ── **痛哭する** 動 (ひどく嘆き悲しむ) lament; grieve ((at, over, about)).
つうこん 痛恨 ●…は痛恨の極みである《やや書》It is most [deeply] regrettable that ....; It is to be greatly regretted that ....
つうさん 通算 图 a total. ●通算して 20 年この市に住む live in this city for a *total* of twenty years. ●通算して 5 度目の優勝をする win five victories *in all* [*total*]. ●通算の通算記録を持っている hold the career record for stolen bases. ▶彼の通算打率は 2 割 9 分だ He has a lifetime batting average of .290.

── **通算する** 動 total; sum [add]... up.
つうし 通史 a complete history ((of Japan)).
つうじ 通じ ((have)) a (bowel) movement. (⇨便通)
ツーシームファストボール 〖野球〗a two-seam fastball; a two-seamer. (🔢沈む速球. 人差し指と中指を 2 本の縫い目の上に沿わせて投げる)

つうじて 通じて ❶ [...中] (...の間中) throughout .... ● 1 年を通じて *throughout* the year; *all* the year (*around*). ●一生を通じて *throughout* [*all through*] one's life; *all* one's life. ▶年間を通じて (=四季の中で)私は夏がいちばん好きだ I like summer best *of all* the seasons.

❷ 〖仲介〗(...を通じて) through .... ●ラジオを通じて講演する talk *on* [*over*, *through*] the radio. ●あらゆる機会を通じて *on* every occasion. ▶私は彼を通じて彼女を知った I got to know her *through* him. ▶あらゆる機会を通じて(=利用して)彼に会った I took every opportunity to see him.

つうしゃく 通釈 ((make)) a comprehensive interpretation ((of the law)).
つうしょう 通称 ●通称名 a commonly used name. ●寅次郎, 通称トラ Torajiro, *commonly called* Tora.
つうしょう 通商 trade; (大規模な) commerce. ●日米通商交渉 Japan-US *trade* talks. (🔢米国では US-Japan ...の語順をとる)

● **通商協定** an agreement of commerce; a trade agreement. ● **通商航海条約** a treaty of commerce and navigation. ● **通商条約** a commercial treaty.

つうじょう 通常 ── **通常(の)** 形 〖いつもの〗usual; 〖ありふれた〗common; 〖並みの〗ordinary; 〖規則に合った〗regular; 〖一般的な〗general.

── **通常** 副 〖習慣的にいつも〗usually; 〖普通程度に〗ordinarily; 〖一般に〗generally, in general; 〖概して〗as a rule. (⇨普通, いつも, 普段) ▶営業時間は通常 9 時から 5 時までです We are *usually* [*generally*] open from nine to five.

● **通常会員** an ordinary [a regular] member. ● **通常国会** an ordinary [a regular] (session of the) Diet. ● **通常兵器** (在来型の兵器) a conventional weapon /wépən/. (🔢 a nuclear weapon (核兵器)に対していう) ● **通常郵便** ordinary mail.

ツーショット ●彼[彼女]とのツーショット a photograph of him [her] and me. (🔢英語の a two-shot は「2 人の俳優が演じる(映画・テレビの) 1 シーン」)

***つうじる 通じる** ❶ 〖道路・交通機関などが〗(道路などが) lead*, go*, run* (*to*); (乗り物が運行する) run; (ドア・部屋などが) open ((*into*, *onto*)); (鉄道などが敷設される) be laid [built]; (開通する) be opened. ●海岸に通じている道路 a road *leading* [*going*, *running*] *to* the seashore. ●庭に通じているドア A door that *opens* [*leads*] *into* a garden. ▶すべての道はローマに通ず(ことわざ) All roads *lead to* Rome. ▶この道はどこへ通じているのですか Where does this road *go* [*lead* us *to*]? ▶伊東から下田まで鉄道が通じている A railroad [A train] *runs* from Ito to Shimoda./ There is a railroad [a train] service from Ito to Shimoda. /(鉄道が伊東と下田をつないでいる) A railroad *connects* [*joins*] Ito *with* Shimoda./ Ito and Shimoda *are connected* [*are joined*, *are linked*] *by* a railroad. ▶両市間に高速道路がまもなく通じるだろう An expressway *will be built* [*be*

ツーラン 《slam》a two-run homer [homerun].

ツーリスト a tourist.

ツーリング touring (by car).

ツール 〖道具, 手段〗a tool.
- ツールバー『コンピュータ』a tool bar. • ツールボックス『コンピュータ』a tool box.

つうれい 通例 〖一般に〗generally; 〖通常は〗usually; 〖概して〗as a rule. (⇨普通, 通常) ▶通例仕事は5時に終わる We *generally* [*usually*] finish the work at 5 o'clock.

つうれつ 痛烈 — 痛烈な 形 〖言葉などが辛らつな〗bitter; 〖打撃などが〗hard. ▶痛烈な皮肉 (a) *bitter* irony. ▶痛烈なびんたを1発食らう get a *hard* slap on the cheek.

— 痛烈に bitterly; severely. ▶痛烈にその劇を批判する criticize the drama *bitterly* [*severely*].

つうろ 通路 a passage (《英》では主に「廊下(ろうか)」のこと); (道) a way; (バス・劇場などの) an aisle /áil/.
- 〖列車・劇場などの〗通路側の席 an *aisle* seat; a seat *on the aisle*. (関連)窓側の席 a window seat; a seat by the window. • 通路をあける〖ふさぐ〗 (⇨道③) ▶その二軒の間には狭い通路が通っている There's a narrow *passage* between the two houses.

(会話)「セロテープはどこにありますか」「3番通路の左側にあります。ずっと奥の方です」「どうも」"Where is the Scotch tape?" "Third *aisle* on the left, all the way to the back." "Thanks a lot."

つうろん 通論 (概論) an outline 《*of*》.

つうわ 通話 a (telephone [phone]) call. (⇨電話)
- 市内通話 a city [a local] *call*. • 市外通話 a long-distance *call*. • ダイヤル即時[国際ダイヤル]通話 a direct [an international subscriber] dialing càll. • 指名[番号]通話 a person-to-person [a station-to-station] *call*. • コレクトコール • 料金受信人払い通話 (make) a collect 《米》 [a reverse(d)-charge 《英》] *call*. ▶1通話3分間の料金は10円です The charge is ten yen for each three-minute *call*./(市内通話が3分間で) Local *calls* are ten yen for three minutes. ▶今通話中です The line *is busy* 《英》 [*is engaged*] now.
- 通話料 telephone charges; (1回の) a charge for a call.

***つえ 杖** a cane, 《主に英》a (wálking) stick. • 魔法の杖 a magic *wand*. • 杖を携える carry [take] a *cane*. • 杖にすがる lean (heavily) on one's *cane*. • 杖をついて歩く walk with (the help of) a *cane*. ▶転ばぬ先の杖 (=よく見てから跳べ) 《ことわざ》 Look before you leap.
- 杖とも柱とも頼む ▶彼女は杖とも柱とも頼む(=頼りにする)一人息子に先立たれた She lost her only son, who was her only support. (!)*who* の非制限[継続]用法に注意)
- 杖をひく (散歩する) take a walk (with a cane); (旅をする) travel, take a trip.

つか 束 (本, 紙の厚み) the bulk 《*of* a book [paper, cardboard]》.
- 束柱 a short support.

つか 柄 (刀の) a hilt. (⇨柄(え))

つか 塚 a mound /máund/. • 貝塚 a shell-*mound*. • アリ塚 an ant hill. • 一里塚 a milestone.

つが 栂 〖植物〗a hemlock fir [spruce]. (!)単にhemlock ともいうが, 文脈によっては毒ニンジンと混同されるおそれがある)

つかい 使 ❶〖用件〗an errand. • 子供を(郵便局まで)使いにやる send a child (to the post office) *on an errand*. ▶使いに行ってくれませんか Will you go *on [run] an errand* for me?

❷〖人〗(使者) a messenger; (持参人) 〖書〗a bearer; (会社などが雇う) an errand [a messenger] boy [girl] (⇨使い走り). ▶使いの者を送る send a *messenger* 《*to*》. ▶この使いの者にご返事をください Please send back [let me have] your answer by the *bearer* of this note. ▶忘れ物を取りにだれか使いの人を事務所までよこしてくださいませんか Will you *send* someone *to* the office for what you've left here? ▶彼女への伝言を持たせて彼を使いに出した I *sent* him *off* with a message for her.

❸〖用いる人〗• ライオン使い (=調教師) a lion trainer [tamer]. • 蛇使い (a snake) charmer.

つがい 番 a pair. • 3組のつがいの白鳥 three *pairs* [*couples*] of swans. • つがいになる form a matching *pair*.

つかいかけ 使いかけ • 使いかけの(=一部使用された)ノート a *partially used* notebook.

つかいかた 使い方 • 動詞 make の使い方(=用い方) the *use* [〖語法〗*usage*] of the verb 'make'. ▶余暇の賢明な使い方を知っている人は少ない Very few people know the wise *use* of their time. ▶この機械の使い方を知っていますか Do you know how to *use* [〖動かす〗*work, run*] this machine? ▶この掃除機の使い方を教えてください Could you show me *how to use* this vacuum cleaner? (!)*how this vacuum cleaner works* では意味合いが異なるので注意)

つかいがって 使い勝手 • 使い勝手のいい(=使いやすい)辞書 a dictionary *easy* (⇨*hard*) *to use*; (利用者に役立つ) a *user-friendly* dictionary.

つかいきる 使い切る use ... up. (⇨使い果たす)

つかいこなす 使いこなす 〖物を〗(うまく取り扱う) handle, manage; (十分に利用する) make* full use of ...; 〖言語を〗have* (a) good command of 《English》.

つかいこむ 使い込む • 使い込んだペン a *well-used* pen; a pen one *has used for a long time*.

つかいこむ 遣い込む (公金などを横領する) embezzle; (他人の金を) 〖書〗misappropriate. ▶彼は会社の金1,000万円を使い込んで解雇された He was dismissed for *embezzling* [*having embezzled*] ten million yen from the company.

つかいすて 使い捨て • 使い捨ての紙コップ[かみそり] a *disposable* [a *throwaway*] paper cup [razor]. (!)後の方が口語的)
- 使い捨てカメラ a disposable [a throwaway] camera. • 使い捨て社会 the throwaway society.

つかいすてる 使い捨てる throw (it) away after use.

つかいだて 使い立て ▶お使い立てしてすみませんが... (I'm) sorry to trouble you, but ....

つかいて 使い手 (使う人) a user; (達人) an expert, a master. • 剣の使い手 a master swordsman.

つかいで 遣いで ▶当時1万円は遣いではあった Ten thousand yen *went a long way* [*went far*, (長く持った) *lasted* (us) *a long time*] in those days. (!)*go far* は否定文では *go a long way* より普通)/(たくさん物が買えた) We *were able to* [*could*] *buy a lot* for ten thousand yen in those days. (!)*in those days* という過去のある期間を示す語があるので *could* も可)

つかいなれる 使い慣れる get* used [accustomed] to 《it; doing》. ▶私の使い慣れたペン a pen I'*m used* [*accustomed*] *to using*; (愛用の) my *favorite* pen.

つかいにくい 使い難い (⇨—難い) ▶このデジカメは使いに

つかいはしり 使い走り 〖用事〗an errand; 〖人〗an errand boy [girl] (*for*) 〖!〗大人についてもいう); (職場の雑用係) 〘話〙a gofer (〖!〗go for からの造語. gopher ともつづる). (⇨使い) ▶彼の使い走りをする go on [run] errands [an errand] *for* him; be a *gofer for* him.

つかいはたす 使い果たす, 遣い果たす 〖資金・精力などを〗use ... up; 〘書〙exhaust. ▶彼女はその金をすっかり使い果たした She *used up* [*exhausted, ran through*] the money. / (すべての金を遣った) She *spent all* the money.

つかいふるし 使い古し ●使い古しの靴 *much*(-)*used* shoes. ●使い古しのパソコン a *much used* personal computer.

つかいふるす 使い古す wear* ... out. ●使い古した生地 *worn-out* material. ●使い古された(=古くておもしろくない)冗談 a *stale* joke. ●使い古された文句 a *cliché* /kliːʃéɪ/; (使い過ぎた) an *overworked* phrase.

つかいみち 使い道, 遣い道 〖用途, 使用法〗a use /júːs/. ●使い道が多い have many *uses*; (多くの目的に使用される) can be used widely [in many ways]. ●使い道が限られている have limited *uses*. ▶この辞書はもう使い道がない(=役に立たない) This dictionary *is useless* [*of no use, no good*] now. ▶正しいお金の遣い道を知らなければならない You must learn the proper *use* of your money./You must learn *how to use* your money properly.

つかいもの 使い物 ●使い物になる be useful, be of some use. ●使い物にならない be useless, be of no use.

つかいやすい 使い易い (⇨易い) ▶その新しいパソコンは使いやすい The new PC is *easy to operate* [*user-friendly*].

つかいわける 使い分ける 〖正しく〗use ... properly; 〖必要に応じて〗use ... according to one's needs. ●3か国語を使い分ける have (*a*) *good command of* three languages. ●時と場合によって言葉を使い分ける *suit* one's words *to* the occasion; *use* right words at the right time.

:つかう 使う, 遣う

WORD CHOICE 使う

use ある意図を持って, 道具・機器・施設・原材料・能力などを使用すること. ▶想像力を使ってごらんなさい *Use* your imagination.

handle 自らの手先を使って, 道具・機器・武器などを器用に使いこなすこと. ●小さい鍋を巧みに使う *handle* a sauce pan skillfully.

employ 雇用契約に基づき, 使用者が使用人を使うこと. あるいは, 特定の技術・方法などを採用して使用すること. ▶本論文では歴史的アプローチを使った We *employed* historical approaches in this paper.

頻度チャート

use ████████
handle ████
employ ██
 20 40 60 80 100 (%)

❶〖物を〗use /júːz/, (物や機会などをうまく利用する) make* use /júːs/ of ... (〖!〗通例 use の前に形容詞を伴う); (道具や施設を役立てる) put* ... to use /júːs/ (〖!〗use の前に形容詞を伴うことが多い); employ; handle. (⇨使える) ●のこぎりを上手に使う *use* [*handle*] a saw skillfully. ●スプーンを使ってスープを飲む have [×drink] one's soup *with* [*using*] a spoon (〖!〗後の方が堅い言い方); *use* a spoon to eat [for eating] one's soup. ●つぼを花びん代わりに使う *use* [*employ*] a pot *as* a vase. (⇨代用) ●土地をうまく[最大限に]使う *make* good [the best] *use of* the land; *put* the land *to* good [the best] *use*. ●台所を共同で使う *share* the kitchen 《with him》. ▶その紙切れ何に使うのですか What do you *use* the paper *for*? ▶石油を全部使ってしまった We *have used* (*up*) all the oil. (〖!〗up を入れると「使い尽くす」感じが強まる) ▶地下室はよく食料や燃料を貯えるのに使われる A cellar *is* often *used for* storing food and fuel. ▶羅針盤はいつごろから使われるようになりましたか When did the compass *come into use* [*to be used*]? ▶この型のバスは今はもう使われていない This type of bus *is out of* (↔in) *use* now. ▶その砂糖あんまり使うなよ. それだけしかないんだから 〘話〙*Go easy on* [*with*] the sugar. That's all we have. (〖!〗go easy on ... は「...を手加減して用いる」の意)

会話「君の自転車を使っていいかい」「パンクしてしまっていて今使えない(=利用できない)んだ」"Can I *use* [(借りる) *borrow*] your bike?" "I've had a flat tire and it's not *available* now."

❷〖金・時間を〗(費やす) spend*; (むだに使う) waste; (有効に利用する) use, make* use of .... ●多くのお金を本に遣う *spend* a lot of money *on* 〖主に米 *for*〗books. ●余暇をピアノの練習に遣う *spend* one's spare time (*in*) practicing [×to practice] the piano. (〖!〗動名詞の前の in は通例省略する) ●時間を有効に遣う *use* one's time effectively; *make* good [full] *use* of one's time. ▶どのようにお金を遣うか決めなさい Decide how you will *spend* [*use*] the money. ▶つまらない物にお金を遣ってはいけません Don't *waste* your money *on* useless things.

❸〖人を〗(雇う) employ; (利用する) use (⇨利用); (うまく扱う) manage. ●人を使うのがうまい be good at *handling* [*managing*] people. (〖!〗manage は扱いにくい人を扱うこと) ▶あの会社は多くの外国人を使っている That company *employs* a lot of foreigners. ▶おたく(の会社)で私を使ってもらえませんか How would you like me to work for you? (〖!〗もっとだけ直接的な言い方では Why not *try* me? などともいう)

❹〖気を〗▶彼はまわりの人に気を遣った He *was attentive* to those around him. (〖!〗those は「人々」の意) ▶(私のことで)そんなに気を遣わないでください Don't *bother about* me so much. (〖!〗Please don't *bother*. は「どうぞおかまいなく」/Don't *go to* so much *trouble for* me. (〖!〗Don't *go to* any *trouble* on my account. などともいう. on my account は「私のために」の意味)

❺〖言葉を〗use; 〖言語を〗(話す) speak*; (自由に使いこなす) have* (a) good command of 《English》. ●丁寧な言葉を遣う *use* polite language; *speak* politely.

❻〖策を〗●きたない手を使う *use* a dirty trick. ●二枚舌を使う tell lies; say one thing but mean another.

❼〖乗り物を〗use; (乗って行く) take*. (⇨利用)

つがう 番う (動物が交尾する) mate 《with》; couple; copulate 《with》; (種馬が交尾する) cover; (一対になる) pair up 《with》.

つかえ 痞え mental pressure. ●胸のつかえがおりる be relieved.

*つかえる 支える ❶〖人・物が多い〗▶道[入り口]は車がつかえていてなかなか進めない There are so many cars

つかえる on the street [at the entrance] that I can hardly move forward. (⇨渋滞) ▶私は仕事かかえている I *have too much* work (to do)./My hands are full. (⇨塞(ふさ)がる❷)

❷ [引っ掛かる] (大きすぎて入らない) be too big to go into …; (刺さる) stick 《in》. ▶そのたんすはドアにつかえて部屋に入らない The wardrobe *is too big to go into* the room through the door. ▶彼は魚の骨がのどにつかえた A fish bone *stuck in* his throat./(のどにつかえて息苦しくなる) He *choked on* a fish bone. ▶その部屋は天井が低かったので頭がつかえた The room had such a low ceiling that my head *touched* it [I couldn't stand up straight]. ▶言葉がつかえて出て来なかった Words *stuck in* my throat./I *was choked up for* words./(驚き・怒りなどで) Words failed me.

❸ [塞(ふさ)がる] be blocked (⇨塞がる❶); be stopped (up). (⇨詰まる)

つかえる 仕える serve, be in 《his》 service; work 《for, under》; [仕えて世話する] wait [attend] 《on》. ▶神に仕える *serve* God [one's master]. ▶王に仕える *wait on* a king. ▶ワンマン社長に長年仕える *work for* [*under*] the despotic president for many years.

つかえる 使える (使うことができる) usable, available (⇨使う); (役に立つ) useful; (有能な) capable. ▶使える(=便利な)ガイドブック *a handy* guidebook. ▶使える(=役に立つ)ホームページ *a useful* site. ▶デートに使える(=おすすめの)レストラン *recommended* restaurants for couples. ▶このクリーナーは銀食器にも使えますか Can this cleaner *be used with* silver (ware)? ▶トラベラーズチェックは使えますか (店での買い物に) Do you *take* [*accept*] traveler's checks? ▶この自動販売機は1万円札が使えます This vending machine *takes* 10,000-yen bills. ▶それは古いけどまだ使える That's old, but it's still *usable* [(通用する) *good*]. ▶彼は使える(=有能な)男だ He is a *capable* man.

つかえる 痞える ▶胸がつかえる lie heavy on one's stomach. (❗食物が主語) ▶悲しみで胸がつかえた I *was filled* with sorrow./Sorrow *filled* my heart. ▶彼のやさしいひと言で胸につかえていたものが(=心から重荷が)取れた His kind words took a load off my mind.

つがえる 番える set [fix] an arrow on the bow (string).

つかさどる 司る (担当する) take charge of 《a store》, be in charge of 《pupils》; (管理する) manage 《economy》; (支配する) preside over 《a meeting》.

つかずはなれず 付かず離れず ▶課長とは付かず離れずの関係にある With my section manager I maintain relations which are *neither too close nor too distant*. (❗簡単に I keep *a proper distance* with my boss. (適当な距離を保っている)などといった方がよい場合もある)

つかつか ▶つかつかと歩み寄る walk *straight* [*right*] up 《to him》.

つかぬこと 付かぬ事 ▶つかぬ事をお尋ねしますが (唐突な質問で失礼ですが) Excuse my abrupt question, but …; (話題を転換して) By the way, ….

つかねる 束ねる bundle … up. (⇨束(たば)ねる)

つかのま 束の間 图 [瞬間] a moment. ▶束の間もくつろげない I can't relax (myself) *even for a moment*. ▶我々の幸福な生活も束の間だった Our happy life *lasted only a short time* [*while*]. (❗ while は名詞で「時間」の意)./ Our happy life came to an end too soon.

—— **束の間の** 形 momentary; (短い) brief; (すばやく過ぎる) passing, 《書》 transient; (はかない) fleeting; (短命の) short-lived /-láivd, -lívd/; (一時的な) temporary. ▶束の間の平和 a *brief* peace. ▶束の間の幸せ *momentary* [*transient, fleeting, short-lived, temporary*] happiness. ▶束の間のうちに in a *moment*.

***つかまえる 捕まえる, 掴まえる** ❶ [捕らえる] (追跡・わななどで) catch*; 《話》 get*; (力・策略などで) 《やや書》 capture; (不意打ち・追跡などで) take*; (逮捕する) arrest (⇨逮捕). ▶網でチョウを捕まえる *catch* a butterfly with [in] an insect net. (❗with は道具を示すだけだが、in は包み込む感じを伴う) ▶私の猫はネズミを2匹捕まえた My cat *caught* two mice. ▶警官はそのどろぼうを捕まえた The police *caught* [*took*, (逮捕した) *arrested*] the thief. ▶その囚人は刑務所から脱走しようとしたところを捕まえられた The convict *was caught* [×*captured*] (in the act of) trying to [just as he was trying to] escape from prison. (❗「見つかった」の意にもなる (⇨捕まる❸))
▶そいつを捕まえろ！財布をとられたんだ *Seize* [*Stop*] him! He stole my wallet!

❷ [握る] (動くものを急に) catch*; (力を入れて急に) seize /síːz/; (自分の手で) take* ; (目的語が物のときは持ち去ることを暗示); (しっかりと) take [get*, catch] hold of …; (婉曲表現). (⇨掴(つか)む) ▶彼女は私の腕をつかまえた She *caught* [*took, seized*] my arm./She *caught* [*took, seized*] me by the arm. (❗前の方は「腕」に重点を置くのに対して、後の方は「人」に重点を置き感情のこもった表現) ▶彼は私をつかまえて放そうとはしなかった He *took* [*got, caught, seized*] *hold of* me and would not let me go.

❸ [呼び止める] ▶タクシーをつかまえる (呼び止める) *hail* a taxi; (つかまえる) *get* [*catch*] a taxi.

❹ [居所をつかむ] (タイミングよく会う) catch*; (連絡する) 《話》 get* (hold of …). ▶彼が帰宅するところをうまくつかまえた I *caught* him just as he was going home.

❺ [相手にする] ▶事もあろうに親をつかまえて「おい」とは何だ Of all things, how dare you say "Hey" *to* your own father?

つかませる 掴ませる ❶ [わいろを] slip (-pp-) 《some money》 into 《his》 hand; bribe 《him to do [into doing]》. ▶彼女に100ドルつかませて彼らの関係を探らせる *bribe* her *with* a $100 bill *to* find out their relationship.

❷ [にせものを] palm … off 《on》. ▶にせのシャネルのバッグをつかませられた I had a fake Chanel bag *palmed off as* genuine./They *palmed* a fake Chanel bag *off on* me.

つかまる 捕まる, 掴まる ❶ [捕らえられる] (一般に) be caught; (逮捕される) be arrested. (⇨逮捕、捕まえる❶) ▶彼は何もしていないのに捕まった He *was arrested* [They *got* him *in jail*] *for* something he didn't do. (❗この方は口語的) ▶その車はスピード違反でパトカーに捕まった(=停止させられた) The car *was stopped* by a patrol car for speeding. (❗この場合 be caught は接触を暗示して不自然)

❷ [しっかりつかむ] (状態) hold* (on) to …, keep* hold of …; (動作) take [get*, catch*] hold of …. (⇨掴(つか)む) ▶私は手すりにしっかりつかまっていた I *held* (*on*) to the handrail tightly. (❗on がある方が強意的)/I *was hanging onto* the handrail. (❗後の方が口語的. 何につかまるのかいう必要がないときは hold on tight(ly), hang on.) ▶このロープにつかまれ、引っ張り上げるから *Catch hold of* this rope and I'll pull you up.

❸【見つかる】catch*. (⇒捕まえる❸❹) ▶彼は自転車を盗んでいるところを捕まった He *was caught* steal*ing* the bicycle. (⇒捕まえる❶)

❹【引き止める】▶中田さんに2時間もつかまってしまった I *was detained* [*was held up*] by Mr. Nakata for two hours./(話) Mr. Nakata *buttonholed* me for two hours.

つかみ 掴み a grip; a hold; a grasp. ●ひとつかみの a handful ⟨of salt⟩.

つかみあい 掴み合い grips, a grapple (! 取っ組み合いも含めて); (取っ組み合い) a scuffle (! 少々小競りを含む). ●彼とつかみ合いをする come to grips with him; *grapple* [*scuffle*] *with* him.

つかみかかる 掴み掛かる grapple, (飛びかかる) fly* [lunge] *at*. ▶彼は突然怒り狂って私につかみかかってきた He suddenly *flew* at me in a violent temper.

つかみがね 掴み金 (大ざっぱな額の金) a rough sum of money.

つかみどころ 掴み所 ●つかみどころがない difficult to catch; (分かりにくい) ⟨文書⟩ elusive; (あいまいな) vague. ●つかみどころのない質問 a *vague* [!要領を得ない] a pointless question.

つかみどり 掴み取り ●コインのつかみ取りをする grab *a hand of* coins. ●魚のつかみ取りをする catch fish *with* one's *hands*.

:**つかむ** 掴む ❶【手でつかむ】catch*; take*; hold*, take [get*] hold of …; seize /síːz/; grasp; grip (-pp-); clutch; grab (-bb-).

> 使い分け catch 動くものや動物・人などを(追って)つかまえる.
> take 動かないものを手に取る.
> hold, take [get] hold of 手・腕などで支えて持つ.
> seize 突然力を入れてつかむ.
> grasp しっかりつかむ.
> grip grasp よりさらに強くつかむ.
> clutch しっかりとつかんで離さない.
> grab 荒っぽく無遠慮につかむ.

▶彼女は私の手をつかんだ She *caught* [*took*, (ぐいっと) *seized*] me by the hand./She *caught* [*took*, (ぐいっと) *seized*] my hand. (! (1) by は「…によって」ではなく「…を掴んで[引っ張って]の意. (2) 前の言い方は me, 後の言い方は hand に重点がある) ●この魚はぬるぬるしていてつかめない This fish is too slippery to *hold* ⟨*it*⟩. ●おぼれる者はわらをもつかむ⟨ことわざ⟩ A drowning man will *grasp* [*clutch*] *at* a straw. (! grasp [clutch] at…は「…をつかもうとする」の意. will は「…するものだ」という習性の意を表す. 今では catch at … より普通) ●彼は落ちないようにロープをつかんだ He *grasped* [*took hold of*, *clutched*] the rope so as not to fall down. ●彼は私のかばんをつかんで逃げた He *seized* [*grabbed*] my bag and ran away. ●強盗は私のかばんをつかんだ手を離そうとしなかった The robber would not let go his *grip on* my bag.

❷【入手する】get*; (発見する) find*. ●大金をつかむ *get* a lot of money. ●機会をつかむ *get* [*grasp*, *seize*] an opportunity [a chance]. ●手がかりをつかむ *find* a clue ⟨*to*⟩.

❸【理解する】understand*, make*… out (! 後の方は通例否定文・疑問文で); (把握する) grasp. ●話の要点をつかむ[つかみそこなう] *grasp* [*miss*] the (main) point of the speech. ●彼は早口でしゃべるので話の内容がつかめない He speaks so fast that I can't *understand* him [what he's saying]. (! understand のほかに catch, get も可)

つかる 漬かる 〖水浸しになる〗 be flooded; (水中に沈む) be submerged (in the water); 〖漬物が〗 be pickled. ●熱いふろに漬かる(=体を浸す) soak ⟨*oneself*⟩ *in* a hot bath. ▶運動場は洪水で漬かっていた The playground *was flooded*./The playground *was submerged* by flood. ●彼はひざまで水に漬かって立っていた He stood knee-deep *in* (*the*) *water*. ●このキュウリはよく漬かっている These cucumbers *are well pickled*.

つかれ 疲れ 〖過労・運動などによる〗fatigue /fətíːg/; 〖体力・意欲のなくなった〗weariness; 〖極度の〗exhaustion. (⇒疲労)

①【〜疲れ】●肉体的[精神的]な疲れ physical [mental] *fatigue*. ●ひどい疲れのために倒れる collapse *from* [*with*] *exhaustion*; fall down *because* ⟨*one*⟩ *is tired* [*is worn*] *out*.

②【疲れが】●彼は疲れがたまって病気になった He got [became] sick because of an excess of *fatigue*. ●長旅の疲れが出た I'm [*got*, *felt*] *tired from* [*after*] the long trip. ●疲れが取れない I can't get over [get rid of] my *fatigue*./(疲れたままである) I'm still tired [exhausted].

③【疲れを】●疲れを感じる feel *tired* [*weary*, *fatigue*d]. ●疲れを知らない男 a *tireless* man. ●眠って疲れを取る sleep off one's *fatigue*. ●旅の疲れをいやす relieve one's *fatigue from* a journey. (! quite の次の二つの用法に注意. I'm *quite* tired (かなり疲れた). I'm *quite* exhausted [tired out] (全く疲れ果てた).)

つかれはてる 疲れ果てる be tired out, ⟨話⟩ be dead tired; ⟨やや書⟩ be completely [absolutely] exhausted. ●飛行機の旅で疲れ果てる be *tired out from* [×*of*] *the* plane trip. ●身も心も疲れ果てた I'm *quite* [*completely*] *exhausted* [I'm *tired out*] *in* mind and body.

つかれめ 疲れ目 (目の疲れ) éyestràin; (疲れた目) tired eyes. ●長時間コンピュータ画面を見ていて疲れ目になる get *eyestrain* from watching the display of a computer for a long time. ●この目薬は疲れ目に効きます These eyedrops are good *for tired eyes*.

:**つかれる** 疲れる get* tired, get weary /wíəri/, ⟨*from*⟩ (! 後の方が堅い言い方); 〖極度の〗⟨やや書⟩ get exhausted /ɪɡzɔ́ːstɪd/ ⟨*from*⟩, get tired out, get worn out. (! 以上いずれも「疲れている」状態を示すときは get に代えて be を用いる) (⇒疲れ, 疲労) ●疲れる仕事 *tiring* [*fatiguing*] work. ▶彼は最近年のせいか疲れやすい He easily *gets tired* these days perhaps because of his age. ●彼は仕事で[長く歩いたので]非常に疲れていた He *was* very *tired from* his work [*after* his long walk]./His work [His long walk] *took* a lot *out of* him. (! (1) after は「…の後だから」「…したのだから」の意で因果関係を表す. (2) take it out of … は「(体力や労力が要るために)疲れさせる」の意) ●家の掃除で疲れた I *got tired* ⟨*from*⟩ cleaning the house. (! 後に動名詞がくるときには from が省略されることがある) ●まったくくたくたに疲れた I'm completely [absolutely, ×very] *exhausted*./I'm really *tired* [*worn*] *out*./(話) I'm dead *tired*. ●1日中あの子たちのお守りをしたなんてさぞかし疲れたことでしょうね It must *have been* terribly *tiring* [×*tired*], minding the children all day. (! it is minding 以下を指す. minding の前にコンマが必要)/(話) You must *have been all in*, taking care of the kids all day. ●be all in は「(ひどく疲れる」の意) ▶アフガン国民は戦争に疲れ, 平和を切望している The people of Afghanistan *are weary* of war and anxious for peace. (⟨参考⟩ アフガニスタンの憲法起草の経過説明)

── **疲れた** 形 tired; weary. ▶疲れた顔をしている look *tired* [*weary*]; have a *tired* [*weary*] look (on one's face). ▶疲れた足取りで階段を上る go up the stairs with *weary* steps.

つかれる 憑かれる ▶悪霊につかれる be possessed by [with] an evil spirit. ▶つかれたように勉強する study like one *possessed*. (⚠ 名詞に後置する)

つかわす 遣わす 〖派遣する〗send;〖与える〗give; (授ける) bestow (a thing *on* him).

***つき 月** 名 ❶〖空の〗the moon. (⚠ (1) 特定の時期・状態の月をいうときには ... 構文中では冠詞は a を用いる. (2) 色は, 欧米では通例 the silver moon, 青白い感じの月は the pale moon とよぶ)

①【~月, 月~】▶明るい月 a bright moon. ▶月旅行をする travel [take a trip] to the *moon*.

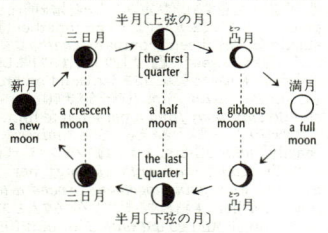

半月［上弦の月］
三日月 → the first quarter → 凸月
新月 ↑   ↓ 満月
a new moon
a crescent moon / a half moon / a gibbous moon / a full moon
                the last quarter
                三日月
                十六夜
半月［下弦の月］

②【月が】▶月が出た［沈んだ］The *moon* has risen [set]./The moon is up [down]. ▶月は日ごとに満ち［欠け］る The *moon* is waxing [waning] day by day. ▶月が明るく輝いている The *moon* is shining bright(ly). (⚠ brightly は副詞で輝く動作に, bright は形容詞で輝いている状態に重点がある) ▶月が雲間から現れた［雲に隠れた］The *moon* appeared from behind [disappeared behind] the clouds. ▶今夜は月が出ている［出ていない］There's a [no] *moon* tonight.

③【月の】lunar. ▶月の軌道 the *lunar* orbit. ▶月のない夜 a moonless [a *dark*] night. (⚠ 前の方が詩的な表現) ▶月の光を浴びて(= 月に照らされて) in the *moonlight*. ▶月のうさぎを見る《婉曲的に》look at the man [《比喩的》]the face] in the *moon*. (⚠ (1) on でなくは in であることに注意. (2) the man in the moon は「月面の人影に煮た斑点模様」の意で「知らないこと, ありそうもないこと」を含意する)

❷〖暦の〗a month (略《米》mo《略》mos);《英》mth (略 mths)). (⚠ 1–12月のうちのひと月も, 不特定の約30日間も示す) (⇒月 ❶)

①【~月】▶ひと月前に(=from now) a *month* ago; (過去のある時から) a *month* before. ▶ひと月で(=今からひと月後に) [以内に] in [within] a *month*. ▶来る月も来る月も a *month* after *month*. ▶2月はいちばん短い月だ February is the shortest *month*.

②【月~】▶月々の平均収入 one's average *monthly* income. ▶月遅れの雑誌 a back number (of a magazine). (⇒月遅れ) ▶月いくらで借りる rent (it) by the [×a] *month*. ▶月極め(⇒月極め)

③【月に】▶月に1[2; 3] 度 once [twice; three times] a *month*. ▶月1度の会合 a *monthly* meeting. ▶月に20万円かせぐ earn 200,000 yen a [per] *month*.

● 月とすっぽん ▶彼は兄と比べると月とすっぽんだ He is (as) different from his brother *as night and day*《米》[*chalk and cheese*《英》].

● 月に叢雲花に風 Just as dense clouds hide the moon, so winds blow off the blossoms./(楽しみを台無しにするものは常にある) There is always something to spoil our pleasure.

● 月着陸船 a lunar module [lander]. ● 月の入り (a) moonset. ● 月の出 (a) moonrise. ● 月ロケット a moon rocket.

つき 付き ❶〖付着〗● 付きのよい(= 強力な)接着剤 a *strong* adhesive. ▶この紙はインクの付きがよい［悪い］ This paper *takes* ink well [badly]. ▶この木は火の付きがよい［悪い］ This wood is quick [slow] to *kindle*.

❷〖運〗luck. ▶つきが続く［落ちた; 回ってきた］One's *luck* lasts [has run out; has turned in].

❸〖付属〗▶社長付きの秘書 a secretary *to* [×of] the president. ▶大使館付き通訳 an interpreter *attached to* an embassy. ▶3食付きの部屋代 the charge for a room *with* three meals. ▶時計付き(= 時計が組み込まれた)ラジオ a radio *with* a clock *built in*. (⚠ built in は「(家具などを)作り付けにする」の意) ▶家具付きのアパート a *furnished* (↔ an unfurnished) apartment.

つき 尽き ▶彼の運が尽きた His luck *has run out*./He *has run out of* luck.

つき 突き〖突き刺すこと〗a thrust;〖フェンシング〗(突きの動作) a lunge, (得点になる突き) a touch (⚠ かすって得点にならない突きは a pass). ▶剣で一突きする make a *thrust* with a sword.

つき 搗き polishing brown rice.

*** つぎ 次** 名 (次の物を) next. ▶次はいよいよ私の番だ Finally I'm (the) *next*. ▶次はどなたですか Who's *next*? ▶次の方(どうぞ) *Next*(, please). ▶次は(=次回は)何をしましょうか What shall we do *next* [*next time*]? ▶次は大阪です(地図などを見ながら) The *next* station is Osaka./(乗客へ案内) We are now *approaching* [*arriving at*] Osaka./We will soon be arriving at Osaka.

● 次から次へ ▶不幸が彼の身に次から次へと起こった Misfortunes happened to him *one after another*./He had *one* misfortune *after another*. (⇒次々)

── **次の** 形 (時間・順序の点で) next; (現在から見て) coming; (後に続く) following. ▶その次の日の夕方に (on [×in]) the *following* [*next*] evening. (⚠ 現在以外の特定の時を基準にする場合は通例 the を伴い前置詞は省略可) ▶(京都の)次の駅［次の次の駅］で降りてください Get off at the *next* station (*to* Kyoto) [the station after the *next* one, 《英》the *next* station but one]. (⚠ but は前置詞で first, next, last の後で「... をも含まないで」の意) ▶次の土曜日に来てください Please come *next* Saturday [《英まれ》on Saturday *next*]. (⚠ (1) ×on *next* Saturday とはいわない. (2) 一般にこれからやって来るいちばん近い土曜日をさすが, 今週の土曜日か来週の土曜日かのあいまいになることがある. 今週の土曜日は Please come *this* (*coming*) Saturday. 来週の土曜日は Please come on Saturday *next week* [《米》a *week from* Saturday]. のようにいえば明確になる) ▶次の世代の人たちはいったい何を考えているのだろうか I wonder what the *coming* generation is [×are] thinking about. ▶次の二つの章を声に出して読みなさい Read aloud the *following* [*next*] two chapters. ▶私は次のような手紙を受け取った I have received the *following* letter. ▶規則は次のとおりです The rules are *as follows* [×follow]: .... ▶この町に来て, 次の日彼女の両親に会った I got to this town, and (on) the *next* day I saw her parents. (⚠ day を修飾する場合は(話)では the も省略されることがある)/(=この町へ来た次の日に) I saw her parents the day *after* I got to this town.

── **次に** 副 next; (それから) then; (2 番目に) second;

(後に) after ....　▶次に到着する列車は大阪行きです The *next* train to arrive [The train which arrives *next*] is bound for Osaka. (❗列車の発着で確実な未来の予定には現在形を用いる)　▶いちばんいい行き方は車、次は電車です The best way is by car; the *next* [*second*] best is by train. ▶英語の次に好きな科目は何ですか What subject do you like best *next to* English? ▶さて、次に行きましょう Let's now move on to the *next*. ▶赤ん坊ははずははうようになり、次に歩けるようになる A baby first learns to crawl, (and) *then* [*next*] it learns to walk. (❗baby は性別を問題にしない場合は it で受ける)　▶まず第一に値が高すぎる。次にその色が気に入らない First(ly), it costs too much, and second(ly), I don't like its color. (❗*In the first place* ..., and *in the second place*, ... のようにもいえる)　▶小説、あなたの次に読ませていただけるかしら Can I read that novel *after* you? ▶次に会ったとき彼は大学生でした He was a college student *next time* I [*when I next*] saw him. (❗next time は接続詞に使われている)

つぎ 継ぎ a patch. ●継ぎだらけの[かかとに継ぎの当たった]靴下 socks full of *patches* [with *patches* on the heels]. ●彼のズボンに継ぎを当てる *patch* (*up*) his pants 《米》[trousers 《英》]; put [sew] a *patch on* his pants.

つきあい 付き合い ❶【交際】《やや書》(an) association (❗仕事・友情・愛情のいずれの関係にも用いる); (友達の) (a) friendship; (仲間の) fellowship; (知人の)《やや書》(an) acquaintance;【人間関係】a relationship.

①【～つきあい】●長い間の付き合い a *friendship* of long standing. ●わずかなつきあいで結婚する get married 《*to* her》*on* (a) brief *acquaintance*. ●付き合いが狭い[広い] have few [a lot of] *acquaintances*.　▶太郎とは10年来のつきあいです I have known Taro for ten years./I *have been friends* [《やや書》*have been acquainted*] with Taro for ten years. ▶太郎と私は10年来のつきあいです Taro and I have had a *friendship* of ten years. ▶我々は会ったら話をする程度のつきあいです We have only a speaking *acquaintance* (*with* each other)./We are *on* speaking *terms with* each other. (❗後の方が口語的)

②【つきあいが】●(人)つきあいがよい[悪い] (社交的である[ない]) sociable [unsociable]; ((複数の人)にうまくとけ込む[とけ込まない]) mix [do not mix] well (*with*). ▶彼はつきあいが広い He has a wide *acquaintance*(ship) [(多くの知人がある)] plenty of *acquaintances*]. ▶当方は暴力団とのつきあいはない We have no *relationship*(s) [*association*] *with* the gang. /(暴力団に知人[友人]はいない) We have no *acquaintances* [friends] among gangsters. ▶彼女とのつきあいは長くは続かなかった My *association with* her did not last long. ▶田舎はつきあいが難しい *Human relationships* are difficult [(わずらわしい) troublesome, (複雑だ) complex] in the country. (❗annoying も可だが「腹立たしい」の意味合いが強くここでは不適)/(田舎の人たちはつきあいにくい) Country people are difficult to *get along with*. (⇨付き合う)

③【つきあいを】●つきあいをやめる (⇨付き合う❶)
▶我が家は近所の人と親しいつきあいをしています My family is in close *association with* the neighbors./My family enjoys friendly *relationships* [good *fellowship*] *with* the neighbors. ▶君は人とのつきあいをもっとよくすべきです You should try to be more *friendly* [*sociable*,《話》*social*,

(外向的) *outgoing*].

④【つきあいで】▶つきあいで彼女と酒を飲みに行った I went drinking with her *sociably* [(*just*) *to be sociable*]. (❗「つきあいで飲む人」は a social drinker)

❷【いっしょにいること】company. ▶彼とのつきあいはうんざりだ。人の悪口ばかり言うんだもの I'm tired of being with him [*of his company*]. He only says bad things about other people. ▶(演説で)みなさん、最後までおつきあいください Stay *with* me, ladies and gentlemen.

つきあう 付き合う ❶【社交として】go* [《米》hang*] around, go about 《*with*》(❗hang は長期間にわたることを暗示),《やや書》associate 《*with*》; (複数の人にとけ込む) mix 《*with*》;【男女間で】go 《*with*》(❗性的関係を含意する); (特定の1人と結婚を前提として) go out 《*with*》,《2 人が主語》go together (❗go steady 《*with*》, keep* company 《*with*》は《古》); (しばしば会って) see*. ▶以上の go はいずれもしばしば進行形で)　▶ああいうやつとつきあうな Don't *go around* [*associate*] *with* him./(近づくべきではない) You should *stay away from* a person like him. ▶彼女は他のみんなとうまくつきあえる She *mixes* well [easily] *with* others. ▶ぼくは彼女とつきあっています《話》I'm *going* (*out*) *with* [*seeing*] her./《話》She and I *are going together*./I *spend a lot of time with* her. ▶結婚するまでにいろいろな人とつきあうべきだ You should *go out with* a lot of different people [《話》*play the field*] before you get married. ▶彼女とつきあうのをやめました (= 絶交した) I *broke up with* her. ▶彼はつきあっているうちに(= 親しくなるにつれて)いい人だということが分かってきた I'm finding that he's a good man as I *get to know* him better [《やや書》we *get better acquainted*]. 会話「その人、どんな人なの？」「つきあい(= 仲よくやってゆきやすい[にくい]感じよ」"What's he like?" "He seems like an easy [a hard, a difficult] person to *get along with*." ❗He seems easy [hard, difficult] *to* ... のようにもいえる)

❷【相手をする】keep 《him》company. ▶太郎の勉強につきあって図書館にいました I was in the library *keeping* Taro *company* while he was studying. ▶今晩食事を[1杯]つきあって(= 同伴して)くださいませんか Would you please have (×a) dinner [a drink] *with* me this evening?/I was wondering if you'd like to *meet* me for dinner [a drink] this evening? ▶デパートに行くところなんだけどつきあって(= いっしょに来て)くれない？ I'm going to the department store. Do you want to *come with* me? (❗Do you want to ...? は Will you please ...? に近く、単に Please ... と言うより丁寧ないい方)

つきあかり 月明かり moonlight. ●月明かりの下を散歩する walk *in* [×*under*] *the moonlight*. ●月明かりでその寺を見る see the temple *by moonlight*. ●月明かりの夜に on [×*in*] *a moonlight* [*a moonlit*] night.

つきあげ 突き上げ (圧力) pressure 《*from*》. ●突き上げを食う be put under *pressure* 《*by*》. ●下部組織からの突き上げ *pressure from* the subordinate organization. (⇨突き上げる)

つきあげる 突き上げる (圧力をかける)《主に米》pressure,《主に英》pressurize; put* pressure 《*on*》. ●組合の幹部から突き上げを食らう *pressure* [*put pressure on*] the leaders of a union 《*to do*》.

つきあたり 突き当たり the end. ●廊下の突き当たりの部屋 the room at *the end* of the corridor. ●私の家はこの道の突き当たりです My house is at *the* of this road.

つきあたる 突き当たる ❶[衝突する] run* 《into, against》; bump 《into, against》. (⇨ぶつかる❶)
❷[行き止まる] come* to the end 《of a street》; (行き詰まる) reach [end in] 《a》 deadlock; (行き詰まっている) be at a deadlock. ▶その交渉は厚い壁に突き当たった The negotiations have reached (a) complete [(an) utter] deadlock.

つきあわせる 突き合わせる (照合する) check ... 《against, with》; (比較する) compare ... 《with, to》. ▶コピーを原文と突き合わせる check the copy against [with] the original.

つきうごかす 突き動かす (人の心を強く動かす) move [touch, afffect] 《him》 deeply. ▶突き動かされる be moved [affected, touched] deeply.

つきおくれ 月遅れ ▶月遅れの雑誌 (1か月前の雑誌) a month-old magazine. ▶月遅れ(=旧暦)の正月 the lunar New Year; the New Year on the lunar calendar.

つきおとし 突き落とし [相撲] tsukiotoshi; thrust down.

つきおとす 突き落とす ▶がけから岩を突き落とす push a rock over the cliff. ▶彼女を列車から突き落とす push [shove] her off the train. (‼ shove /ʃʌv/ は「乱暴に押す」の意) ▶絶望のふちに突き落とされる be plunged into the depths of despair. (‼ the depths は最も深い[強烈な、耐えられない]部分の意)

つきかえす 突き返す (受け取りを拒む) refuse to receive [accept]; (送り返す) send*... back. ▶書類を突き返す refuse to receive the papers.

つきかげ 月影 moonlight. ▶月影さやかな夜 《on, ×at》 a bright moonlight [moonlit] night.

つきがけ 月掛け ▶月掛け貯金 monthly savings.

つきがわり 月替わり ▶その映画館の上映作品は月替わりだ The movie theater changes its program monthly. ▶彼は月替わりで東京と福岡を勤務している His work alternates between Tokyo and Fukuoka every month.

つぎき 接ぎ木 图 grafting.
―― **接ぎ木する** 動 graft. ▶バラの木を病気に強い台木に接ぎ木する graft a rose on [upon, onto] a disease-resistant rootstock.

つききず 突き傷 a stab; a stab wound.

つききめ 月極め monthly. ▶月極めの購読者 a monthly subscriber. ▶私は月ぎめで給料をもらっている I'm paid monthly [by the month].

つききり 付き切り ▶彼女はつききりで息子を看病している She is in constant attendance on her son. (‼次例の方が口語的)/She is sitting right by her son's bedside [stays right by her sick son] every minute. (‼ right は「ちょうど」「すぐ」の意)

つきぐち 注ぎ口 (急須・ポットなどの) a spout.

つぎこむ 注ぎ込む 【流し込む】 pour 《in, into》; 【金・時間・精力などを】 put* 《in, into》; (利益をもくろんで) invest 《in》; (やたらと) pour 《into》; (費やす) spend* 《on》. ▶魔法びんに暖かい湯をつぎ込む pour hot water into a Thermos (《米》bottle, 《英》flask). ▶彼は自分の事業に全財産をつぎ込んだ He put [invested] all his fortune in his business.

つぎざお 継ぎ竿 a jointed fish rod.

つきささる 突き刺さる stick* 《in, into, through》 (‼ into は中へ刺さる、through は突き通る); [突き詰す] pierce. ▶とげが指に突き刺さった A splinter stuck in my finger. (‼ A splinter stuck me in the finger. ともいえる/I got a splinter in my finger.) ▶くぎが自転車のタイヤに突き刺さった A nail pierced the tire of my bicycle. ▶彼女が私たちに最後に言った言葉がぐさりと胸に突き刺さった The last thing she said to us hit home with me. (‼成句表現)

つきさす 突き刺す (槍・フォークなどで) stick*; (刃物などで) stab (-bb-), (ぐさりと) thrust. (⇨刺す) ▶針刺しに針を突き刺す stick a needle into a pincushion. ▶肉をフォークで突き刺す stick the meat with a fork; stick a fork into the meat. ▶その強盗は被害者の背中をナイフで突き刺した The robber stabbed [thrust] a knife into the victim's back./The robber stabbed [thrust] the victim's back [the victim in the back] with a knife.

つきしたがう 付き従う (ついて行く) follow; accompany; (服従する) obey.

つきずえ 月末 the end of the month. (⇨月末(げつまつ))

つきすすむ 突き進む (押し分けて) push one's way 《through》. ▶破滅に向かって突き進む head straight for disaster; rush to ruin. ▶彼は人込みの中を突き進んだ He pushed his way through the crowd.

つきそい 付き添い [行為] attendance 《on》; [人] an attendant 《for a sick person》; (護衛人) an escort. (⇨付き添う) ▶患者の付き添いをする(=世話をする) look after [take care of, attend 《on》] a patient. ▶前の二つの方が口語的) ▶よくなるまで彼女が私の付き添いをします She is my attendant until I get well.
● **付き添い看護師** an attendant nurse; a nurse in attendance 《on》. (関連 担当医 an attendant doctor; a doctor in attendance)

つきそう 付き添う [世話をする] look after..., take* care of..., attend 《on ...》 (‼前の二つの方が口語的) 《付き添う》; [同行する] accompany, go* with ...; [護衛する] escort. ▶花嫁に付き添う attend a bride. (事情 花嫁の付き添い人 (attendant) には、既婚女性の a matron of honor と未婚女性の a bridesmaid の区別がある) ▶彼女には2人の看護師が付き添っていた She had two nurses attending [in attendance on] her.

つきたおし 突き倒し [相撲] tsukitaoshi; frontal thrust down.

つきたおす 突き倒す push 《him》 over [down].

つきだし 突き出し ❶[酒のさかな] a snack served with alcoholic drinks; hors d'oeuve; an appetizer. ❷[相撲] tsukidashi; frontal thrust out.

つきだす 突き出す (身体などの一部を) stick*... out; (引き渡す) hand ... over 《to》. ▶窓から顔を突き出す stick one's head out (of) the window. (‼《米》ではしばしば of を省略する) ▶彼を警察に突き出す turn him over [《話》in] to the police.

つぎたす 継ぎ足す 【加える】 add 《to》; 【広げる】 enlarge. ▶そのスカートを継ぎ足して大きくする enlarge the skirt. ▶書斎を新しく継ぎ足して家を広げる enlarge one's house by adding a new study.

つきたてる 突き立てる thrust 《a spear into the ceiling》; (しっかりと立てる) plant 《a pole in the snow》.

つきたらず 月足らず ▶月足らずで生まれる be born prèmaturely [before its time].

つきづき 月々 [毎月] every [each] month. ▶うちはアパートの賃貸で月々100万円の上がりがある We get a million yen monthly [every month] by renting apartments. ▶自動車の月々の支払い金は5万円ですA monthly installment on my car is fifty thousand yen.

*つぎつぎ(に) 次々(に)** one after another; (連続して) in succession. (⇨次々に) ▶少年たちは次々と水中に飛び込んだ The boys jumped into the water one after another./One boy after another jumped into the water. (‼主語 One boy after another は単数扱い) ▶不幸が次々起こった Misfor-

つきっきり 付きっ切り (⇨付き切り)

つきつける 突き付ける ●ピストルを彼に突き付ける point a gun *at* him. ●被疑人に新しい証拠を突き付ける *confront* the accused *with* new evidence. ●辞表を上司に突き付ける *thrust* one's resignation *at* one's boss.

つきつめる 突き詰める ●突き詰めて(=徹底的に)論じる discuss 〖取り扱う〗deal with 《the matter》*fully* 〖*thoroughly, exhaustively*〗. ●そのことをそんなに突き詰めて考える(=思い詰める)な Don't take it so seriously!/Don't take it to 《your》heart! (⚠決まり文句)

つきて 継ぎ手 a coupling; a joint.

つきでる 突き出る stick* out; 《鋭い角度で》jut (-tt-) out, 《やや書》project. ●くぎが板から突き出ていた There was a nail *sticking out* of the board. ●巨大な岩が岸から川に突き出ていた A huge rock stuck out 〖*jutted out*, *projected*〗 from the bank *into* the river. ●彼は腹が突き出ている His stomach sticks out 〖*xjuts out*〗. (⚠「あご」の場合は通例 a jutting chin 〖jaw〗 という) ●クロッカスが雪の下から突き出ている Crocuses *thrust out of* 〖*up through*〗 the snow.

つきとおす 吐き通す ●その件については彼はうそをつき通した Regarding 〖For〗 that incident, he's lied from the beginning to the (very) end.

つきとおす 突き通す 《貫く》pierce. ●彼の体に剣を突き通す(=刺し通す) *thrust* 〖*run*〗 a sword *through* him.

つきとばす 突き飛ばす ●彼を突き飛ばす push 〖《手荒く》*shove*, 《突然激しく》*thrust*〗 him *away*. ●彼を突き飛ばして倒す *knock* him *over* 〖*down*〗; 《ぶつかって》 *bowl* him *over*.

つきとめる 突き止める 〖見つけ出す〗find*... out; 〖跡をたどって〗trace; 〖場所·場面などを〗locate. ●真相を突き止める *find out* the truth. ●そのうわさの出所を突き止める *trace* the source of the rumor; *trace* the rumor *to* its source. ●犯人の所在を突き止める *locate* a criminal. ●問題のありかを突き止める *locate* the source of the problem.

つきなみ 月並み ── 月並みな 形 《ありふれた》commonplace; 《因習的な》conventional; 《語句などが陳腐な》《やや書》trite. ●月並みな文句を避ける avoid trite 〖*hackneyed*〗 phrases; avoid clichés /kliːˈʃeɪz/.

つきにほえる『月に吠える』 *Howling at the Moon*. (参考) 萩原朔太郎の詩集)

つきぬける 突き抜ける pierce; penetrate; go* through .... (⇨❶)

つきのま 次の間 《隣の部屋》the adjoining 〖next〗 room; 《控えの間》an anteroom; an antechamber.

つきのわぐま 月の輪熊 『動物』a moon bear; an Asiatic black bear.

つきば 継歯 a pivot tooth; 《英》a pivot crown.

つきはぎ 継ぎはぎ 《継ぎ》a patch. ●継ぎはぎの(寄せ集めの)patchy; 《継ぎをあてた》patched. ●継ぎはぎだらけのズボン much-*patched* pants. ●継ぎはぎ細工 (a) patchwork.

つきはじめ 月初め the beginning of the month. (⇨上旬)

つきはなす 突き放す 《押しのける》push ... away; 《強く》thrust ... away; 《見捨てる》leave, desert, forsake, abandon; 《離す》detach oneself 《*from*》.

▶彼が破産したのを知ると彼女は急に突き放した態度を取るようになった When she knew his bankruptcy, she suddenly began to behave as if she had nothing to do with him. ▶カーブは追いすがるジャイアンツを緒方の満塁ホームランで再び突き放した Ogata's grand slam brought in another big lead for the Carp over the Giants who had been coming closer. ▶この時点で我々のプロジェクトを突き放した目で見てみることも必要だ We need to look at our project *objectively* at this point./We must *detach ourselves from* our project for a moment so that we can see it rightly.

つきばらい 月払い ●月払いで by monthly payment 〖《日》 monthly installments〗. ●月払いにする pay 《the rent》monthly 〖each month〗.

つきばん 月番 《*on*》monthly duty.

つきひ 月日 《年月》years; 《時》time. ●寂しい月日(=生活)を送る lead 〖live〗 a lonely *life*. ▶月日がたつにつれて彼の怒りはやわらいだ As *years* 〖*time*〗 went by, his anger cooled (off). (⚠人を主語にすると he cooled down となる) ▶月日のたつのは早いものだ *Time* passes 〖*goes by*〗 quickly./*Time* flies. (⇨光陰)

つきびと 付き人 an attendant.

つきべつ 月別 ●月別支払い a *monthly* payment 〖income〗.

つぎほ 接ぎ穂 《接ぎ木の》a graft; a scion. (⇨接ぎ木) ●接ぎ穂をする graft 《*on, onto*》. (⇨接ぐ) ●《話の》接ぎ穂を失う be unable to keep up the conversation 〖keep the ball rolling〗.

つきまぜる 搗き交ぜる 〖ついて交ぜ合せる〗 pound together; 〖異質なものを一緒にする〗 mix together.

つきまとう 付きまとう 〖想念が心から離れない〗 haunt (⚠通例受身で、悪い意味で用いる); 〖人·動物などが人を〗 《つけ追い》まわる) follow 《him》 around 〖*about*〗, 《くっついて行く》《やや話》 tag (-gg-) along, 《まといつく》 hang* around. ●死の恐怖につきまとわれる be haunted by the fear of death. ●ストーカーにつきまとわれる be stalked; be harassed by a stalker. ▶彼女がどこに行っても子供がつきまとう No matter where she goes, her kids *follow* her *about* 〖*tag along* (*with* her)〗. ▶どんな勝利にも悲しみがつきまとう No victory is free from sorrow. (⚠No victory と主語に否定すると強い主張になる)

つきみ 月見 moon viewing. 事情 米英人は月に対して狂気や夢想といったマイナスのイメージを持つ傾向があり、日本人のように、詩的な感情や寂しさを込めて月を眺めることはあまりない) ●9月の中ごろに月見をする enjoy the full moon 〖月見の宴を開く〗 have a *moon-viewing* party〗 around the middle of September.

つきみうどん 月見うどん 《説明的に》(a bowl of) *udon* noodles in hot soup with a raw egg yolk on top.

つきみそう 月見草 『植物』an evening primrose.

つきみそば 月見そば 《説明的に》(a bowl of) buckwheat noodles in hot soup with a raw egg yolk on top.

つぎめ 継ぎ目 a joint; 《板·布の》a seam. ●パイプの継ぎ目の漏れ a leak at the *joint* in a pipe. ●継ぎ目のないテーブルの天板 the *seamless* top of a table.

つきもの 付き物 go with; 《... を伴う》 be accompanied 《*by*》. (⚠後の方が堅い表現) ▶お祝いに酒は付き物だ *Sake* will *go with* a Japanese feast./《必須である》 *Sake* is *essential to* a Japanese feast.

つきもの 憑き物 ●つき物に取りつかれる be possessed (by *the devil*, by an *evil spirit*). ▶彼の戦いぶりは

つきやぶる 突き破る (突破する) break* through ...; (強行突破する) crash through ...; (突き進む) thrust through .... ▶敵の防御線を突き破る *break through* the enemy defenses.

つきやま 築山 a miniature [a small] hill in a Japanese-style garden.

つきゆび 突き指 a sprained finger [(足の指) toe].
● ボールで突き指をする *sprain* a *finger with* a ball; *have* a *finger sprained with* a ball.

つきよ 月夜 a moonlight [a moonlit] night. ▶月夜にかられた夜行 on a moonlight [a moonlit] night. ▶なんて美しい月夜だ What a beautiful *moonlight night* (it is)!
● 月夜に釜を抜かれる 'A cauldron is stolen on a moonlight night.'/(常に油断をしてはいけない) Always be on your guard.
● 月夜にちょうちん 'a paper lantern on a moonlight night'; (無用なもの) a useless thing.

つきる 尽きる ［無くなる］ run* out; ［使い尽くされる］ be used up; （資源・体力などが） be exhausted /igz5:stid/; ［終わる］ end. ▶我々の食料が尽きた 《人が主語》 We *have run out of* food./《物が主語》 Our food *has run out*. ▶紙が尽きた All the paper *has been used* (*up*). ▶力が尽きた My strength *is exhausted* [*gave out*]. (! 後の方が口語的) ▶いつまでも話は尽きなかった We talked *endlessly*. ▶精根尽き果てた I *am* completely [*absolutely*] *exhausted*./I *am exhausted and tired out*. (! 同意の語を重ねて強調している (⇨果てる [第2文例])) ▶この本には尽きない魅力がある This book has *inexhaustible* appeal. ▶道はここで尽きる The path *ends* there. ▶それはばかばかしいの一言に尽きる(＝まったくばかばかしい) It's a *sheer* [*(a) complete, an utter*] nonsense.

つきわり 月割り ● 月割りで (1か月当たりの平均で) per [a] month; (月賦で)《pay》 in monthly installments (⇨月賦).

:つく 付く, 点く ❶ ［付着する］ (粘着する) stick* ⟨*to*⟩; (べったりつく) cling* ⟨*to*⟩ (⇨くっつく); (しみがつく) be stained ⟨*with*⟩; (油などで汚れる) be smeared ⟨*with*⟩. ● 血のついたワイシャツ a shirt *stained* [*smeared*] *with* blood; a blood*stained* shirt. ▶ぬれたドレスが彼女の体にぴったりついていた The wet dress *stuck* [*clung*] *to* her body.

❷ ［付属する］ (持っている) have*; (持って歩く) carry; (付属している) be attached ⟨*to*⟩; (備わっている) be provided ⟨*with*⟩; ［備えつけられている］(器具・装置などが) be equipped ⟨*with*⟩; (家具が) be furnished ⟨*with*⟩. ▶ポケットのついた［ついていない］コート a coat *with* [*without*] pockets. ▶この列車には寝台車がついている This train *has a sleeping car*./A sleeping car *is attached to* this train. ▶やっと家に電話がつきました We've finally *had* a telephone *in* our house./(備えつけてもらった) We've finally *had* a telephone *installed* in our house. (! have＋物＋過去分詞の構文) ▶この本には索引がついている The book *has* [*is provided with*] an index. ▶その自動車にはスノータイヤがついている The car *is equipped with* snow tires. ▶そのアパートは家具がついています *Is* the apartment *furnished*? ▶そのダイニングセットにはいすが四つついている The dining set *comes with* four chairs.

❸ ［随従する］ (看護する, 付き添う, 仕える) attend ⟨*on*...⟩; (給仕する) wait ⟨*on*⟩; (同伴する) accompany; (いっしょに行く［来る］) go* [come*] with...; (後について行く) follow. ▶二人の看護師が患者についている Two nurses *attend* ⟨*on*⟩ [(世話をする) *look after, take care of*] the patient. (! 後の方が口語的)/The patient is being *cared for* by two nurses. ▶彼は両親について旅行した He went on a trip *accompanying* [*with*] his parents. ▶君が先に行ってくれれば私は後からついて行きます I'll *follow* you if you go ahead of me. ▶他の学生について行くために一生懸命勉強しなければならなかった I had to work hard to *keep up with* the other students. (! keep up with ... は「...に遅れずについて行く」)

❹ ［所属する］ belong ⟨*to*⟩; ［味方する］ side [take* sides] ⟨*with*⟩; (他の派に転向する) go* over ⟨*to*⟩. ▶敵側につく *go over to* the enemy. ▶そのふたはあのジャーについている The lid *belongs* [×is belonging] *to* that jar. ▶彼は経営者側についた He *took the side of* the management. ▶彼はいつも貧しい者や弱い者の側についている He *is always on the side of* poor and weak people./He always *sides with* poor and weak people.

❺ ［生じる］ (実を結ぶ) bear*; (収穫・利子などを生む) yield; (根がつく) take* root. ● (病後)体力がつく(＝増す) gain strength. ● ぜい肉がつく(＝体重が増える) *gain* [*put on*] weight. ● 悪い癖がつく *form* [(簡単に) *acquire*, (だんだんと)(やや書) *develop*] a bad habit. ● 英語の力がつく *make* ⟨×a⟩ *progress in* English; *improve* one's English. ▶この木はたくさん実がつきますか Does this tree *bear* much fruit? (! 肯定文では a lot of [much, ×many] fruit が普通) ▶その債券は 6 分の利子がつく The bonds *yield* [*bear*] six percent [×percents] interest.

❻ ［火・電気がつく］ (火がつく) catch* fire (! 物が主語); (マッチがつく) strike*; (明かりがつく) go* on, come* on. ▶日本の木造家屋は火がつきやすい Japanese wooden houses easily *catch fire*. (! ×Japanese wooden houses *are easy to* catch fire. は不可) ▶どうしても火がつかない The fire won't *light*./(マッチが) The match won't *strike*. ▶明かりがついた［ていた］ The lights *came* [*were*] *on*. ▶火のついたたばこを捨てるな Don't throw away *lighted* [*lit*] cigarettes. ▶車のライト［テレビ］がつかない My car lights don't [The TV doesn't] *work*.

❼ ［値がつく］ (費用がかかる) cost*; (値段がつけられている) be priced ⟨*at*⟩. ▶カメラは日本で買う方が高く［安く］つく Cameras *cost* more [less] in Japan. ▶あの失敗は我々には高くついた That mistake really *cost* us [《書》*cost* us dearly]. ▶そのコートは高い［10 万円の］値段がついていた The coat *was priced high* [*at* 100,000 yen].

❽ ［決まる］ 話はついた That *settles* it!/The problem *is settled*.

:つく 着く ❶ ［到着する］ arrive ⟨*at*, *in*, *on*⟩, get* ⟨*to*⟩, reach; (列車が駅・プラットホームに入ってくる) pull ⟨*into*⟩; (人・乗り物が到着予定である) be due ⟨*at*, *in*⟩. (⇨到着する)

使い分け arrive 「到着する」の意の最も一般的な語. 前置詞としては, 通例狭い場所や単なる到達地点は at, 広い場所や滞在の場合は in, 場所の表面が意識されると on が用いられる.
get to arrive at より口語的で, しばしば努力して着くことを含意する.
reach やや堅い語で, 通例何らかの努力をして到達することを含意する. 人類が月に着いた Man *reached* [*got to*] the moon.

① 【場所に】［から］着く ● 家に着く *get* [*arrive*, *reach*] *home*. (! home は「家に」という副詞. したがって ×*get to home* や ×*arrive at home* は不可) ● 東

京から着く arrive [×reach] from Tokyo. ▶1時間ほど歩いたら小さな村に着いた After about an hour's walk I got to a small village./(やや書) About an hour's walk took [brought] me to a small village. ▶さあ,上野駅に着きましたよ Here we are [×were] at Ueno Station.
会話「彼らはこの前の金曜日にシドニーを発ったんだよ」「じゃあああしたにならなければここに着かないでしょうね」"They left Sydney last Friday." "So they won't be here until tomorrow, will they?"
②〖(人・物)が〖に〗着く〗 ▶スミスさんはいつ着きますか When will Mr. Smith arrive [×reach, ×get to]? ▶reach, get to は目的語が必要)/What time is Mr. Smith due in [due to arrive]? ▶この列車は何時にパリに着きますか What time does this train get to [arrive at, reach (×to)] Paris? (❗列車の発着など確実な未来の予定には現在形を用いる)/What time is the train due in Paris? ▶あなたの手紙は今日着きましたよ Your letter got here today./(受け取った) I got [received] your letter today. ▶あら,もう飛行機着いたの？ すぐ迎えに行くわ Oh, is your flight in already? I'll be right over to pick you up. (❗right over は「すぐそちらに」の意)
会話「(私たちは)間に合うように着くかしら」「時間前に着くだろうよ」"Will we be in time?" "We'll be ahead of time."
❷〖届いて触れる〗(届く) reach; (触れる) touch. ▶天井が低いので私の頭は天井につきそうだった The ceiling was so low that my head almost reached [touched] it.
❸〖身を置く〗(座る) sit*. ● 食卓につく[ついている] sit [be] at table. ● 正餐(ﾃﾞ)の卓につく sit down to dinner. ● 席について(=着席して)ください Sit down [Take a seat, Have a seat], please./Please be seated. (❗後の方が形式ばった言い方になる. Do you want to sit down? ともいう Please sit down. などより丁寧な言い方)

つく 就く ❶〖地位などに〗take; 〖職業に〗《やや書》enter, (従事する) follow. ● 職につく get a job. ● 法律関係の職につく go into (×the) law; enter [follow] the law profession. ● 王位につく come to [mount,《書》ascend] the throne. ▶彼は会社でいい地位についている He has [holds] a good position in the company. (❗「ついた」なら took, has taken)
❷〖始める〗〖床につく(=寝る) go to bed. ● 帰途につく leave for home. ● 席につく take [have] a seat; (座る) sit down. ▶彼は流感でここ1週間床についている He's been laid up for a week with (the) flu.
❸〖師事する〗(指導のもとで研究する) study ... under 《professor K》; (レッスンを受ける) take* lessons 《from him》.

つく 吐く ● うそをつく tell a lie. ▶「じゃあ,彼女が来るのを待つよ」と彼はため息をつきながら言った "I'll wait for her, then," he said with a sigh.

つく 突く ❶〖突き刺す〗(刃物で) stab (-bb-), (ぐさりと) thrust; (針で) prick, (槍(ﾔﾘ)で) spear; (ヤギなどが頭で) butt; (動物が角・牙(ｷﾊﾞ)で) gore; (突き通す) pierce. ● 彼の心臓をナイフで突く stab [thrust] a knife into his heart; stab [thrust] his heart with a knife. ▶彼は短刀で背中を突かれた He was stabbed in [×on] the back with a dagger. ▶針で指を突いてしまった I pricked my finger with [on] a needle. (❗on は「誤って」「不注意で」を含意)
❷〖押す〗push, (急に強く) thrust, (棒で) poke, (ひじで) elbow, (軽く) nudge. ● 彼の胸を突く push [thrust] him on the chest; give him a push [a thrust] on the chest. ● 彼をひじで突いて押しのける elbow him aside.
❸〖地面などに当てる〗● 机の上に両ひじをついて座る sit with one's elbows on the desk. (❗「机にひじをつく」は rest one's elbows on the desk) ● 両ひざをついて哀れみを請う fall on one's knees [kneel down] and beg for mercy.
❹〖打ち当てる〗strike*; (ボールをはずませる) bounce. ● 鐘をつく strike a bell; (鳴らす) ring a bell; (晩鐘・弔鐘をゆっくり鳴らす) toll a bell. ● バスケットボールをつく bounce a basketball. ▶彼は球をつくのが上手だ(玉突きなどで) He is good at knocking balls.

つく 突く,衝く ❶〖攻める〗attack. ● 敵の背後をつく attack the enemy in the rear. ● 不意をつく take 《him》by surprise; (すきをつく) catch 《him》off (his) guard. ● 彼の弱点をつく(=つけ込む) take advantage of 〖指摘する〗point out] his weak point; (痛い所を)《叩》hit [get] him where it hurts. ▶君の言ったことは核心をついている[いない] What you have said is to [beside] the point.
❷〖ものともしない〗● あらしをついて出発する start in spite of [in the face of] the storm. ● やみをついて進む advance through the darkness.
❸〖感覚を強く刺激する〗● 鼻をつく(=不快な)におい an offensive [刺激性のある] a sharp] smell. ▶ドアを開けたとたん,悪臭が鼻をついた Just as I opened the door, a bad smell hit me [assailed my nostrils].

つく 搗く ● もちをつく pound steamed rice into cake.

つく 憑く (想念が) obsess, possess; (悪霊が) possess. (❗いずれも通例受身で用いる (⇒憑かれる, 取り付く❷)) ▶あなたには悪霊がついている You're possessed (by [with]) an evil spirit)./(乗り移っている) The devil has got into you.

つぐ 継ぐ ❶〖受け継ぐ〗succeed 《人; to＋職務・称号・財産など》;〖仕事・責任などを〗take (...) over;〖伝統などを〗follow;〖相続する〗inherit. ● 父の仕事を継ぐ take over [succeed to] one's father's business (❗前の方が口語的); take over the business from one's father; succeed one's father in one's business. ● 家の伝統を継ぐ follow one's family tradition. ▶彼は安倍氏のあとを継いで会長になった He succeeded Mr. Abe as president [to the presidency]./He took over as president when Mr. Abe retired. (❗as に続く1人しかいない役職名は無冠詞) ▶彼は父親の志を継いで医師になった He followed in his father's footsteps and became a doctor.
❷〖継ぎ足す〗add; (言葉を) continue. ● 炉に炭を継ぐ add some charcoal to the fire. ▶「それに楽しかったよ」と彼は言葉を継いだ "And I had a good time," he continued [added].

つぐ 次ぐ ❶〖次に位する〗▶横浜は東京に次ぐ大都市です Yokohama is the largest city next to [after, ×next] Tokyo./(人口が) Yokohama is the next [second] largest city to Tokyo in population. ▶英語に次いで私の好きな学科は物理だ Next to [After] English, my favorite subject is physics. ▶このトンネルは長さでは六甲トンネルに次ぐものだ This tunnel comes next [second] to the Rokko Tunnel in length.
❷〖次に続く〗▶彼は成功に次ぐ成功に得意だった He was elated at [by] one success after another. (⇒続く)

つぐ 注ぐ (流し入れる) pour 《into》; (満たす) fill 《with》. ● コップにミルクを注ぐ pour milk into a

glass; fill a glass *with* milk. ▶ビールを注ぎましょうか Shall I *pour* [*fill*] you a glass of beer?/Shall I *pour* [*fill*] a glass of beer *for* you?
- **つぐ 接ぐ** (接ぎ木をする) graft (*on, onto*); (骨を) set; (木材を) splice.
- ***つくえ 机** a desk. ▶彼は机に向かって[勉強[仕事]をして]いる He is (working) at the [his] *desk*.
- **つくし 土筆** 『植物』a horsetail.
- **ーづくし ―尽くし** ・国[花]づくし enumeration of names of countries [flowers].
- ***つくす 尽くす** ❶ [ある限り出す] ・食べ尽くす eat *up* the food; eat *all* the food. ・手(=手段)を尽くす try *every* means; (何でもやってみる) try *everything*. ・論議を尽くす discuss 《it》*completely* [(あらゆる角度から) *from every angle*]. ・彼は全力を尽くして私を助けた He helped me *with all* his strength./(最善を尽くした) He *did* his *best* to help me./(できる限りのことをした) He *did all* he *could* to help me. ▶私はその事件を知り尽くしている I *know everything* about the incident. ・その意味はひと言では言い尽くせない The meaning *cannot be expressed* in a word. ・何はあれ, 自分の力のありったけを尽くしたい I'll *do the best* I can for [about] anything and everything I do. (❗ anything and everything は「あらゆること」を強調する表現)
❷ [ささげる] devote (*to*); [奉仕する] serve. ・障害者のためによく尽くす(=多くのことをする) *do a lot for* (helping) handicapped people. ・国家に尽くす *serve* one's country. ▶彼は世界平和の促進のために尽くした(=一生をささげた) He *devoted* his life *to* promoting [the promotion of] world peace.
- **つくだに 佃煮** *tsukudani*, (説明的に) preserved small fish, shellfish, *konbu*, etc. boiled down in soy sauce and sugar.
- **つくづく** [まったく] quite, completely, utterly; [心から] heartily; [念入りに] closely; [熱心に] intently; [痛切に] keenly. ・その絵をつくづくと眺めるa look at the picture *closely* [*intently*]. ・試験勉強がつくづく(=心底から)いやになる get *heartily* sick [tired] of studying for exams. ▶健康のありがたさがつくづく身にしみる I *keenly* [*fully*] realize the value of good health. ・私は彼女の親切をつくづく(=心の底から)ありがたく思った I thanked her for her kindness *from* (*the bottom of*) *my heart*./(大いに) I *greatly* appreciated her kindness.
- **つくつくぼうし** 『昆虫』a fall cicada.
- **つぐない 償い** compensation, 《書》reparation; [贖罪(ﾉﾞ)の] 《書》atonement. ・…の償いとして in compensation for …. (⇨賠償) ・過去の過ちの償いをする *make up* for a previous wrong. (⇨償う)
- **つぐなう 償う** [埋め合わせする] make* up for …; [罪を] 《書》atone (*for*); [補償する] 《書》compensate (*for*); [賠償する] 《書》make reparation (*for*). ・損失を償う *make up for* [*compensate for*] the loss. ・損害を償う *pay* [*make reparation*] *for* the damage. ・出費を償う *cover* the cost (expenses). ▶彼は自分の罪を償った 《書》He *atoned for* his sin.
- **つくね 捏ね** a meat ball.
- **つくねいも 捏ね芋** 『植物』a Chinese yam.
- **つくねる 捏ねる** (こねる) knead. ・練り粉をつくねて球形にする *knead* the dough *into* a ball.
- **つくねんと** (ぼんやりと) vacantly; absent-mindedly; (何もせず) idly; (ひとりで) alone.
- **つくばい 蹲い** *tsukubai*, (説明的に) a (stone) washbasin (in a Japanese garden).
- **つくばしゅう** 『菟玖波集』 *Tsukuba Collection of Linked Poetry*. (参考) 室町時代の最初の連歌撰集)

- **つくばね 衝羽根** a shuttlecock.
- **つぐみ 鶫** 『鳥』a thrush.
- **つぐみ** 『TUGUMI』 *Goodbye Tsugumi*. (参考) 吉本ばななの小説)
- **つぐむ 噤む** [口を閉じる] shut* [close] one's mouth; [口を控える] hold* one's tongue; [意図的に人と口をきかない] keep* silent. ▶彼は突然口をつぐんだ He suddenly *shut* [*closed*] his *mouth*. ・しばらくの間口をつぐんでくれよ *Keep* your *mouth shut* [(静かにしている) *Keep quiet*] for a while, will you? ▶彼はその政治的に不穏な事件について口をつぐんでいた He *kept silent* [*remained mute*] *about* the political scandal.
- **つくり 作り, 造り** [構造] (組み立て方) construction; (構成) structure; (型) make (❗ 製品の良否を問題にする). ・頑丈な作り(=体格)の男 a strongly-built man; a man of strong *build*. ・最高級の作りのバイオリン a violin of the finest [first-class] *make*. ・造りがしっかりとした家 a (very) solidly *built* house; a house of solid *structure*. ・レンガ造りの建物 a brick building; a building (*made*) *of* brick. ・オランダ風の造りの家 a Dutch-*style* house; a house in the Dutch *style*. ・モダンな造りの(=現代風建築の)家 a modern architectural house. ・鯛の造り thin slices of raw sea bream.
- **つくり 旁** the right-hand radical of a Chinese character.
- **つくりおき 作り置き** ・作り置きの食べ物 the food *cooked* [*prepared*] *in advance*.
- **つくりかえる 作り替える, 作り変える** [作り直す] make*… over; (最も口語的に); (服・建物などを) remodel; (建物を) rebuild*; [転換する] convert; [脚色する] adapt. ・その物語を子供向けに作り変える *adapt* the story *for children* [*to the needs of children*]. ▶物置小屋は大きな遊び部屋に作り替えられた The shed *has been made over* [*been remodeled, been converted*] *into* a big playroom.
- **つくりかた 作り方** how to make 《a doll, a chocolate cake》. (⇨作る)
- **つくりごえ 作り声** a disguised [a feigned] voice. ・作り声で話す speak in a *disguised voice*. ・女声の作り声をする *disguise* a woman's *voice*.
- **つくりごと 作り事** (an) invention; (虚構) (a) fiction; [作り話] a made-up story. (⇨作り話)
- **つくりざかや 造り酒屋** (醸造元) a *sake* brewery.
- **つくりだす 作り出す** (生み出す) produce; (創造する) create; (考え出す) invent; (作る) make*. ・流行を作り出す *create* [*set, start*] a fashion.
- **つくりつけ 作り付け** ▶私の書斎の壁には本棚が作り付けになっている The bookshelves *are built into* the walls of my study.
- **つくりばなし 作り話** [でっちあげ話] a made-up story; [作り事] (an) invention; (虚構) (a) fiction; (ごっこ遊び・芝居など) make-believe. ・作り話をする *make up* [*invent*] a story 《*about*》. ▶前の方が口語的) ▶それはまったくの作り話だ That's a pure *invention* [a complete *fiction*].
- **つくりもの 作り物** ▶そのろう人形館の人形はどれも実に見事な出来で, とても作り物とは思えない Every wax figure in the museum is quite excellent and hardly looks *artificial*.
- **つくりわらい 作り笑い** a forced smile [laugh]. (⇨笑い) ・作り笑いをする force a smile [a laugh]; give [put on] a *forced smile* [*laugh*] 《*at*》. ▶政治家の方はつくり笑いをなさるんですよ Politicians put on *forced smiles*.

つくる 作る, 造る

WORD CHOICE 作る

make 具体的な物品の製作, 食料の生産・製造, 芸術作品や抽象的価値の創造などを幅広く指す最も一般的な語. ● 牛乳からチーズを作る *make* cheese from milk.

produce 主に販売目的で, 商品・製品を大量に工場生産すること. また, 映画作品・テレビ番組などを製作すること. ● DVDプレーヤーを作っている工場 a plant *producing* DVD players.

manufacture 商品・製品を大量に工場生産すること. produce 以上に機械生産・大量生産の含意が強い. ● 車を大量に作る *manufacture* the large amount of cars.

頻度チャート

make ▬▬▬▬▬▬▬▬▬▬
produce ▬▬▬
manufacture ▬

20　40　60　80　100 (%)

❶ [製造・加工する] make*; manufacture; produce.
① [...を作る] ● 卵を使ってケーキを作る *make* a cake *with* eggs. (❗ with は材料の一部分を示す) ▶彼女は私にスカートを作ってくれた She *made* me a skirt./She *made* a skirt *for* me. (❗ 前の方は「何を」, 後の方は「だれに」作ったのかに重点がある言い方) ▶スーツを作りたいのですが I'd like to háve a suit *made*. (❗ 人に作ってもらう場合) ▶あの会社は何を作っているのですか What does that company *produce* [*manufacture*]?
② [...で[から]作る] ▶パンは小麦から作る Bread *is made from* wheat. (❗ 原則として原料と製品の質が変わる場合は from. 質が変わらない場合は of. また, 廃物利用の場合には from, out of が好まれる) ▶この箱はガラスで作られている This box *is made of* glass.
会話「取っ手は何で作るつもりなの」「木でさ」 "What are you going to *make* the handle *of*?" "*Of* wood."

❷ [建造する] build*, 《やや話》put*... up, 《やや話》construct; [創造する] create. ● 家を造る *build* [*put up, construct*, ×*make*] a house. ● 船[鉄道; 道路]を造る *build* [×*make*] a ship [a railroad; a road]. ▶この橋は石で丈夫に造られている This bridge *is* solidly *built of* stone. ▶神が世界を造ったと彼は信じている He believes that God *created* the world. ▶自然は曲線を作り, 人間は直線を作る Nature *creates* curves [×*curve line*] and men *create* straight lines.

❸ [組織する] organize; (設立する) found, establish, set*... up; (形作る) form. ● 大学を作る *found* [*establish, set up*] a college. ● 列を作る *get into* line; *form* a line; line up. ▶そのコーチは15人で野球チームを作った The coach *organized* [*formed*] a baseball team of fifteen members. ● 人間は社会を作る Human beings [People] *form* a society. ▶私はこの会社を一から作り上げた I *built* this company *up* from nothing.

❹ [創作する] make*; (文・詩・曲などを書く) write*, compose; (映画などを) produce. ● 映画を作る *make* [*produce*] a film. ● 詩を作る *write* [*compose*] a poem. (❗ くだけた口語では *make* a poem ともいう) ● 文学作品を作る *produce* literary works. ● (先発投手起用)試合を作る 《野球》keep the team in the game. (参考 リードを許しても 1, 2 点までに抑えることをさす)

❺ [栽培する] grow*, raise. ▶彼は趣味としてトマトを作っている He *grows* [*raises*] tomatoes as a hobby.

❻ [作成する] (文書などを) make*, draw*... up; (書類・請求書・表などを) make... out; (草稿などを) prepare. ● 請求書[志願者リスト]を作る *make out* the bill [a list of applicants]. ● 演説の原稿[試験の問題]を作る *prepare* a speech [an examination]. ▶私たちは契約書を作らねばならない We must *make* [*draw up*] a contract.

❼ [形成する] make*; (形作る) form, 《やや書》shape. ▶スポーツは青年の人格をつくる Sports *form* [*shape*] the character of young people. ▶若い間によい習慣を作っておきなさい Try to *form* [*develop*] good habits while (you are) young. ▶立派な先生は子供が性格をだんだん作りあげる手助けをする A good teacher helps (to) *build up* a child's character.

❽ [虚構する] (でっちあげる) make*... up, invent (❗ 前の方が口語的); 《やや書》fabricate. ● うまい口実を作りあげる *make up* [*invent*] a good excuse.
会話「もっともな理由がないんだよ」「じゃあ一つ作りなさいよ」"I have no real excuse /ikskjúːs/." "*Invent* one, then."

❾ [調理する] make*; (用意する) prepare, 《主に米》fix; (加熱して) cook. ● サラダを作る *make* [*prepare, fix*, ×*cook*] salad. ● スープを作る *make* [×*cook*] soup. ▶母は朝食を作ってくれた Mother *got* breakfast *ready* for us./Mother *cooked* [*prepared*] breakfast for us./Mother *cooked* [*prepared*] us breakfast.

❿ [苦心して用意する] (金を調達する) raise; (集める) collect; (時間をさく) spare. ● その事業の資金を作る *raise* funds for the undertaking. ▶私のために5分時間を作ってくれますか Can you *spare* me five minutes?/Can you *spare* five minutes *for* me?

つくろう 繕う ❶ [修理する] mend, fix (⇒修理する); (かがって) darn; (当て布をして) patch... (up). ● 靴下を繕う *mend* [*darn*] (a hole in) a sock. ● 上着のほころびを繕う *patch* [*mend*] a tear /téər/ in a coat. ● ほころびた縫い目を繕う (=縫う) *stitch up* a torn seam.
❷ [取り繕う] ● 体裁を繕う *keep up* [*save*] appearances. ● その場を取り繕う *patch* things *up* for the moment. (⇒取り繕う)

つけ 付け ❶ [勘定書] a bill; (食堂などの)《米》a check; [掛け売り] credit, an account. ● つけを払う pay a [one's] *bill*. ● つけで買う buy (it) *on credit*; charge (it) *to* [*against*] (me, my account). (⇒つける❼ [第2文例]) ▶私のつけにしておいてくれ Put it on my *bill* [*account*, 《主に米話》*tab*]. (❗ tab は主に飲食店の支払い時に用いる) ▶あの店はつけがきく That store gives us *credit*./I have an *account* at that store.
会話「お支払いはどのようになさいますか」「つけにしておいてください」"How would you like to pay?" "(I'll) *charge* it (to me)."
● つけが回ってくる ▶今しっかり働かないと, 後でつけが回ってくる If you don't work hard now, you will have to *pay for* it later.

つげ 黄楊 【植物】a box (tree); (つげ材) boxwood. ● つげのくし a *boxwood* comb. ● つげの垣根 a *box* hedge.

ーづけ 付け ● 3月5日付けの手紙 a letter *of* [*dated*] March 5. ● 4月1日付けの転任(命令) transfer *effective on* April 1. (❗ effective は全

-づけ -漬け ぬか漬け vegetables pickled in rice-bran paste. ●牛肉のみそ漬け beef preserved in *miso*. ●キュウリの浅漬け a lightly-pickled cucumber. ▶今週はアルコール漬けだ I have drunk too much almost every day this week.

つけあがる 付け上がる 〚うぬぼれる〛get* conceited; 〚厚かましくなる〛grow* impudent; 〚付け込む〛take* advantage of ....

つけあわせ 付け合わせ 〚料理の添え物〛(a) garnish. ●付け合わせにニンジンとトマトを使う use carrots and tomatoes as a [for] *garnish*. ●パセリを付け合わせたステーキ a steak *garnished with* parsley.

つけいる 付け入る take* advantage of .... (⇨付け込む) ▶彼には付け入るすきがない(＝常に警戒を怠らない) He's always *on* his guard.

つけうま 付け馬 (説明的に) a person who goes with a customer to his house to collect his bill.

つけおとし 付け落とし (an) omission (*in* a book). ▶彼はよく勘定の付け落としをする He often *forgets to* enter accounts.

つけおび 付け帯 *tsukeobi*; (説明的に) simple *obi* for light dressing.

つけかえる 付け替える 〚取り替える〛replace 《A *with* B》, (交換する) change 《A *for* B》; 〚新しくする〛renew; 〚表紙を付け替える〛re-cover. ▶タイヤが磨り減ったから新しいのと付け替えなければならない I have to *replace* the worn tire *with* a new one./I have to *change* the worn tire *for* a new one. ▶オーバーのボタンを付け替えてもらった I hád my buttons *replaced* on my overcoat. (❗*replaced* の後にwith other ones を省略した言い方)

つけぐすり 付け薬 an external medicine; (軟膏) (an) ointment.

つげぐち 告げ口 图 ●告げ口をする人 (話) a telltale. **—告げ口する** 動 ●彼らのことを先生に告げ口する *tell* the teacher *on* them. (❗go to the teacher and *tell on* them ともいえるが, ✕tell on them *to* the teacher とはいわない) ▶ぼくが遅刻したってだれかがボスに告げ口したんだ Who *told* [*reported to*] the boss (that) I was late? (❗子供が先生に告げ口するような場合には report は用いない)

つけくわえる 付け加える add. ●その文に1語付け加える *add* a word *to* the sentence. ●その語の前に冠詞を付け加える *put* [✕add] an article *before* the word. ●「つまり, 詐欺師なんですよ」と彼は付け加えた "In short, he's an impostor," he *added* [(と言って言葉を結んだ) *concluded*].

つけげ 付け毛 a hair piece; (美容用) hair extensions; (男性用) a hair toupee.

つけこむ 付け込む take* advantage of .... ●彼の弱味[人のよさ]に付け込む *take advantage of* his weakness [good nature].

つけこむ 漬け込む pickle 《cucumber》.

つけじる 付け汁 (a) dip.

つけだし 付け出し 〚相撲〛*tsukedashi*; (説明的に) being promoted to the *makushita* division by skipping the ranks at the bottom.

つけたす 付け足す add. (⇨付け加える)

つけたり 付けたり (付録) a supplement (⇨付録); (口実) an excuse.

つけどころ 付け所 ▶きみはすがに目の付け所が違うね I admire your point of view./Your aim is perfectly right./Your aim is very much to the point.

つけとどけ 付け届け (贈り物) a present, a gift.

つけね 付け根 〚舌・耳・つめ・毛などの〛the root; 〚つめ・耳・鼻などの〛the base; 〚関節〛a joint. ●耳の付け根まで赤くなる blush *to the roots* of one's hair [✕ears]. ●私の肩の付け根 my shoulder *joint*. ▶彼女の茶髪は付け根のあたりが黒かった Her dyed light brown hair was black at the *roots*.

つけねらう 付け狙う 〚あとをつける〛follow; (尾行する) shadow, 《話》tail; 〚命をねらう〛seek* 《his》life.

つけひげ 付け髭 ●付けひげをしている wear a *false mustache* [(あごひげ) *beard*].

つけびと 付け人 an attendant; (衣装係) a dresser.

つけふだ 付け札 a label; a tag. (⇨荷札)

つけまつげ 付け睫 ●付けまつげをしている wear *false eyelashes*.

つけまわす 付け回す (ついて回る) follow ... around [about]; (つきまとう) tag (-gg-) along; (跡をつける) tail; (自分の姿を隠して付け回す) stalk. ▶私の跡を付け回すのはやめて Stop *following* me about./Don't *tag along* behind me.

つけめ 付け目 (目当て) an aim; (利用できる点) an advantage. ▶彼の人のよさがこちらの付け目だ His good nature is to our *advantage*. ▶そこが彼の付け目だ That's *what he's aiming at*. (❗通例進行形で)/That's his aim.

つけめん 付け麺 (説明的に) noodles and soup served separately to dip them in.

つけもの 漬物 pickles; (説明的に) vegetables pickled in salt, rice bran, *miso* or *sake* lees. ●ナスの漬物 a *pickled* Japanese eggplant.

つけやき 付け焼き (⇨照り焼き)

つけやきば 付け焼き刃 (見せかけ) a (thin) veneer /vəníər/ (❗通例単数形で); (借り物の知識) (やや書) borrowed wisdom.

つける 付ける, 点ける ❶ (a) 〚取り付ける〛put; (固定する) fix; (付属品を本体に付ける) attach; (装置などを備え付ける) install. ●シャツにボタンをつける *put* [(縫いつける) *sew*] buttons *on* a shirt. ●壁に鏡を(取り)つける *fix* a mirror *to* the wall. ●商品に一つずつ値札をつける *attach* a price tag *to* [*put* a price tag *on*] each article. ●彼女はジャケットにバラの造花をつけていた(＝ピンで留めていた) She wore an artificial rose *pinned* to her jacket. ▶新居に水道とガスをつけてもらった We had water and gas *installed* in our new house. (❗「have＋物＋過去分詞」の構文)

(b) 〚接合する〛put* 〚(位置を定めて) set*〛(*to*). ●荷車に馬をつける *put* a horse *to* a cart. ●本箱を壁につける(＝壁によせて置く) *put* [*set*] a bookcase (*up*) *against* the wall. (❗up は「...に向かってしっかりと」の意) ▶彼はジョッキに口をつけると一気に飲みほした He *set* the mug *to* his lips and drained it in a single gulp.

❷ 〚塗る〛(一面に塗る) spread*; (薬品など塗布する) apply; (上にのせる) put* 《*on*》; (油・ペンキなどを塗る) smear; (しみをつける) stain; (身につけている) wear*. ●タオルに石けんをつける *apply* soap *to* a towel. ●髪に香水[油]をつける *put* perfume [oil] *on* one's hair; *perfume* [oil] one's hair. (❗「身につけている」は wear perfume (⇨着ける)) ▶彼はパンにバターをつけた He *spread* butter *on* his bread./He *spread* his bread *with* butter. ●後の方はパン一面にバターを塗ることを暗示. 「いすにジャムをつけて汚す」なら *smear* jam *on* the chair; *smear* the chair *with* jam という) ▶彼は傷口に薬をつけた He *applied* the medicine *to* [*put* the medicine *on*] the wound. ▶彼女はアイシャドーをつけすぎている She *wears* too much eye(-)shadow.

❸ 〚付け加える〛add 《*to*》. ●その本に注をつける *add* [(《書》) *append*] notes *to* the book. ●条件をつける *set* a condition 《*on*》. ●利子をつけて金を返す pay

back the money *with* (5%) *interest*. ● そのメロディーに歌詞をつける *put* [*set*] *words to the melody*.
❹ [備えさせる] ● 知恵をつける (獲得する) *acquire intelligence*; (入れ知恵をする) *put an idea into* ((his)) *head*. ● 体力をつける (=増す) *gain strength*. ▶彼はずいぶん英語の力をつけた He *has made* (×a) *great progress in* English./He *has greatly improved his* English./His English *has greatly improved*.
❺ [付き添わせる] ● その男に見張りをつける *set a watch on the man*. ▶病気の父に看護師をつけた I *had my sick father attended by a nurse*. ▶君のお供に彼をつけよう I'll *send him with you*.
❻ [跡をつける] (後ろからついて行く) *follow*; (跡をたどる) *trace*; (尾行する) *shadow*,《話》*tail*. ●トラの足跡をつける *follow* [*trace*] *the tracks of a tiger*. ▶私たちは跡をつけられているように思う I *feel someone is following* [*shadowing*, *tailing*] *us*./I *feel we are being followed* [*shadowed*, *tailed*].
❼ [記入する] (日記・帳簿などを続けてつける) *keep**; (書き留める) *write** [*put**]... *down*; (書く) *write*; (名前・金額などを記載する)《書》*enter*. ●日記をつける *keep a diary*. ●出納簿をつける *keep an account book*. ●会計簿にその金額をつける *enter the sum in the account book*. ▶注文した品目に✓印をつけなさい *Put a check next to the items you want to order*. ▶今は払いません. つけて(=つけにして)おいてください I *won't pay now*; *put it down to me* [*charge it to my account*]. (⇨付け)
❽ [価格を決める] (売り手が値をつける) *price* (🚨しばしば受身で(⇨付け❼)), *put** [*set**] *a price* ((*on*)); (競売などで買い手が値をつける) *bid**; (価格を提示する) *offer*. ●その商品に安い値をつける *put a low price on the goods*. (🚨《話》では *put a cheap price* ... も可だが避けた方が無難 (⇨安い 解説)) ●その本に5,000円の値段をつける *put* [*set*] *the book at five thousand yen*; *put* [*set*] (*a price of*) 5,000 *yen on the book*. ▶彼はその花びんに100ポンドの買い値をつけた He *bid* [*offered*] 100 *pounds for the vase*.
❾ [点火・点灯する] *light**; (ラジオ・明かりなどを) *put**... *on* (↔*put*... *out*); (スイッチをひねって明かり・ラジオ・テレビなどを) *turn* [*switch*]... *on* (↔*turn* [*switch*]... *off*); [放火する] *set** *fire* ((*to*)), *set*... *on fire*. ●たばこ[ローソク]に火をつける *light a cigarette* [*a candle*]. ●マッチで火をつける *light* [*kindle*] *a fire with a match*; (マッチをする) *strike a match*. ▶電灯をつけてください Please *put* [*turn*, *switch*] *on the light*. ▶だれかが家に火をつけた Someone *set fire to the house* [*set the house on fire*]. (🚨 ×...*lit the house* とはいわない) ▶ラジオをつけても[つけていても]かまいませんか Do you *mind if* I *turn on the radio* [*have the radio on*]? ▶テレビをつけたままにしておくな Don't *leave the television on*. ▶ラジオをつけたまま眠るな Don't *sleep with the radio on*.

つける 着ける ❶ [身につける] *put**... *on* (🚨動作を表す); (身につけている) *wear**, *have**... *on*. (🚨状態を表す) (⇨着る) ●ドレスを身に着ける *put on* (↔*take off*) *one's dress*; *put one's dress on*. ●制服をつけた警官 *police officers* [(男の) *policemen*, (女の) *policewomen*] *in* (×a) *uniform* [*wearing uniforms*]. (🚨 *in* は「着用」を表す. この場合 ×*in uniforms* とはならない) ●彼女は髪にリボンをつけていた She *wore* [*was wearing*, ×*was putting on*] *a ribbon in her hair*./She *had* [×*was having*] *a ribbon on in her hair*. ▶彼は魔よけのためにそのお守りを身につけていた He *wore the charm to ward off evil spirits*. ▶この犬は首輪をつけていない This dog *has no collar around its neck*. ▶彼女は上着に花をつけて部屋に入ってきた She *came into the room with a flower on her jacket*. (🚨 *with* は「...を身につけた状態で」の意)
❷ [船・車などを] (岸に上げる) *put**... *ashore*; (横付けにする) *bring** ((a ship)) *alongside* ...; (寄せて止める) *draw** [*pull*] ((a car)) *up*. ●ボートを岸に着ける *put* [*bring*] *a boat ashore*. ▶彼は船を岸壁に着けた He *brought the ship alongside the wharf*. ▶運転手は車を門の前に着けた The *driver drew* [*pulled*] *up his car in front of the gate*.

つける 漬ける [物を液体に浸す] *soak*, *steep*; [漬物にする] *pickle*. ●パンをミルクに漬ける *soak* [*steep*] *bread in milk*. ●石けん水に汚れたシャツをつけておく *soak* [*steep*] *a dirty shirt in soap water*. (🚨前の方は布に石けん水をたっぷり吸わせることに, 後の方は石けん水の中で汚れの成分を抽出することに意味の重点がある. したがって steep tea in hot water (茶葉をお湯につける) で soak を用いるのは不適切) ●牛肉を塩に漬ける *pickle* [*preserve*] *beef in salt*; *salt beef*. ●足を水たまりにちょっとつける *dip one's foot into the pool*.

***つげる 告げる** ❶ [知らせる] *tell**, 《書》*inform*; [公表する] *announce*. ●別れを告げる *say* [×*tell*] *good-by* ((*to him*)). (🚨 *tell* は (言葉を目的語にとらない) ●それをだれにも告げないでおく (=自分の胸にしまっておく) *keep it to oneself*. ▶この情報はだれにも告げないでくれたまえ Don't *tell this news to anybody*. ▶召し使いが一行の到着を告げた The *servant announced the arrival of the party*. ▶彼女は名前を告げずに立ち去った She *left without giving her name*.
❷ [示す] ●時計が5時を告げた The clock *struck* [×*hit*] *five*. ●*o'clock* をつけることはまれ) ▶厚い雲が嵐の接近を告げていた The *heavy clouds warned us of an approaching storm*. (🚨日英両文とも擬人的用法)

***つごう 都合** 图 ❶ [便宜] *convenience*. (🚨この語自体は「好都合」の意. 「不都合」は *inconvenience* (⇨好都合, 不都合) ●都合よく *conveniently*. (🚨「運よく」の意なら(⇨❸)) ●都合悪く *inconveniently*.

① [都合が] ●都合がよい[悪い] (⇨[成句]) ●都合がつき次第 *as soon as it is convenient for you* (🚨 *as soon as possible* は「今すぐ」の感じが強く, 失礼な場合もあるので *as soon as you can*, *at any time convenient for you* の方が好まれる); 《書》*at one's earliest convenience*. ●仕事[スケジュール]の都合がつき次第 *as soon as one's work* [*schedule*] *allows*. ▶明日は都合がつかないので来られません I *cannot* (*manage to*) *come tomorrow*. (🚨 *manage to* を入れる方が丁寧)

② [都合を] ●先方の都合を聞く *ask his convenience*. ●彼に今夜の都合を聞く *ask him if tonight is convenient* [《話》*OK*] (*for him*); (体があくかを) *ask him if he is free* [《やや書》*available*] *tonight*. ▶ご都合をお知らせください Please *let me know if that's all right with you*.

③ [都合で] *for* (*the sake of*) *convenience*. ▶こちらの都合で君には辞めてもらうことになった We've *decided to dismiss you because of our situation* [×*for our convenience*]. (🚨後の方は *dismiss you* との関係では実際的ではない使えない)
❷ [場合, 事情] *circumstances*; [理由] *a reason*. ●都合により *for certain reasons*. ●一身上の都合で *for personal reasons*. ●仕事の都合で *because of* [*due to*, *on account of*] *one's work*. ▶都合次第では, 式は延期になるかもしれない *Depending on circumstances*, *the ceremony may be*

つごもり

put off. ▶彼の都合で我々の出発が遅れた Our departure was delayed *for reasons of his own*.
❸ [首尾] ●都合よく fortunately; luckily. ●都合悪く unfortunately; unluckily. ▶都合よく列車は混んでいなかった *Fortunately*, the train was not crowded./It was *fortunate* that the train was not crowded. ▶万事都合よく行っています Everything *is going well* [*moving smoothly*] (*with* me).
❹ [やりくり] (手配, 準備) arrangements. ●都合をつける (⇨動) ▶5 時に出発できるよう都合をつけられますか Can you *arrange* [*manage*] *to* start at five? ▶1 時間ほど都合をつけて(=時間を割いて)いただけないでしょうか Could you spare me about one hour?
❺ [全部で] in all, all told. (⇨合計)
●都合のよい convenient (*for* [*to*] +人, *for*+事) (❗日常会話ではやや堅い言い方. 主語は物・場所・日時で, 人を用いることは不可); (話) be all right [O.K.] (*with* [*by*] +人); (ふさわしい) be suitable (*for, to*); (有利な) be favorable (*for*+事, *to*+人). ●テントを張るのに都合のよい場所 a convenient [a *suitable*, (よい) *a good*] place *for* pitching a tent. (❗convenient は「水などが近くにあり便利な」, suitable は「場所がそれに適した」の意) ▶あなたの都合のよいときに when (it is) *convenient for* [*to*] you (❗×when *you are convenient* は不可. when you are free [have (free) time] の方がくだけた言い方); when it suits you; (書) at your *convenience*. ▶何時がいちばん都合がよろしいですか What time would be most *convenient* [(話) *best*] *for* you? ▶その件はご都合のよいようにしてください Arrange the matter at your own *convenience* [*in* your own *favor*]. ▶彼は子供のころアメリカに住んでいたので, 英語の勉強には大変都合がよかった(=有利だった) He lived in the United States when he was a child, and it was a great *advantage* (役立った) *was very helpful*, *was a big help*, ×was very convenient] *in* learning English.

会話「月曜日にお越しいただきたいのですがご都合はよろしいですか」「ええ, 結構ですよ」"Would it be *convenient for* [*to*] you *to* come on Monday?" "Yes, it'll *be all right with* me." (❗には … convenient to you for you to come …? (あなたの…来るのはあなたにとって都合がよいか)の to you か for you のいずれかを省略した表現. したがってポーズを置く場合は for you の前, to you の後が適切)

会話「今日は都合が悪い. 明日にしてくれないか」「いいよ. 明日何時ならいい?」「君の都合のいいときなら何時でもいいよ」"It is *inconvenient* today [I can't *manage* today, Today is impossible, ×I'm inconvenient today]. Can't you make it tomorrow?" "That's fine. What time tomorrow?" "Any time that *suits* you *best*."

●都合が悪い ▶都合の悪いときに客が来た We had a visitor at a *bad* time [an *unwelcomed* hour, an *awkward* time].

—— 都合する 動 arrange, make arrangements (*for; to do*), (何とかやりくりする) (話) manage (＋图; *to do*), (話) make it (❗慣用句でしばしば can, could を伴う); (金を貸す) lend; (調達する) raise. ▶お困りなら少しは(金を)ご都合できます I could *lend* you some money if you're hard up [pressed].

つごもり 晦 the last day of the month. (⇨晦日(ﾐｿｶ))
つじ 辻 [四つ辻] a crossing, a crossroads (❗単数扱い); [街角] a corner of a street, a street corner; [街路] a street.
つじうら 辻占 a slip of paper telling one's fortune; (吉凶の前兆) an omen of one's (good or bad) luck.
つじぎり 辻斬り street murder; (人) a street murderer.
つじごうとう 辻強盗 a holdup; (人) a holdup man, a footpad; (馬に乗った強盗) a highwayman.
つじせっぽう 辻説法 图 street preaching.
—— 辻説法する 動 preach 《*to* large crowds》 on the street.
つじつま 辻褄 ●つじつまの合った (首尾一貫した)《書》consistent; (論理的に)《書》coherent (*kouhiərənt*/. ●つじつまの合わない説明 an *incoherent* [an *inconsistent*] explanation. ▶信条とつじつまの合わない(=一致しない)行動 actions that *are inconsistent with* one's principles. (❗この意味では限定的には用いない)
つた 蔦 [植物] ivy. ▶ツタのからまった塀 a fence covered with [in] *ivy*; an *ivy*-covered fence.
-づたい -伝い ●土手[線路]伝いに歩く walk *along* the bank [railroad tracks].
つたいあるく 伝い歩く ▶赤ん坊がよちよち壁を伝い歩き始めた The baby began toddling along using the wall for stability.
つたう 伝う ●ロープを伝って上がる[降りる] climb [×go] *up* [*down*] a rope. ●川を伝って(=伝いに)進む go *along* a river.
つたえきく 伝え聞く hear* [learn*] from others. ▶それを伝え聞いて知っているだけだ I know it only *from* [*by*] (×a) hearsay.
***つたえる** **伝える** ❶ [告げる] tell*; [知らせる]《書》inform; [伝達する]《やや書》convey, communicate; [(正式に)通知する]《やや書》notify; [報道する] report. (⇨知らせる) ▶彼はぼくが言ったとおり伝えてくれ *Tell* him just as I said. ▶我々は彼の知らせをただちに伝えた We *told* him the news [*told* the news *to* him] immediately. ▶彼にそう(=それを)伝えます I'll *tell* him that. ▶何か彼に伝えることはありませんか Do you want me to *tell* him anything for you?/(伝言がある) Do you *have* a *message* for him? ▶その会合のことは彼に直接伝えておきました I *told* him personally *about* the meeting. ▶彼に折り返し電話をするようお伝えください Will you *tell* him *to* call me back? ▶1 時間たったら戻ると彼に伝えてくれ *Tell* him (*that*) I'll be back in an hour (×an hour *later*). ▶母親の死をまだ彼女に伝えていないんですか Haven't you *informed* her *of* her mother's death [*that* her mother is dead]? (❗is dead は direct にくらべ結果に重点を置いた表現) ▶自分の気持ちは言葉では伝えられない My feelings can't *be conveyed* by [in] words. (❗以下の言い方のほうが日常的) / I can't put my feelings into words./Words cannot express how I really feel. ▶会議は 2 週間延期すると彼らに伝えてくれたまえ *Notify* them *that* the meeting will be postponed for two weeks./*Notify* them *of* a two-week postponement of the meeting. ▶伝言は忘れずに彼に伝えます I'll never forget to *give* your message *to* him. ▶新聞の伝えるところによれば首相は内閣改造を行うらしい It is *reported* in the newspapers that [According to the newspapers], the Prime Minister will reshuffle his cabinet. (❗ともに堅い言い方で, 日常会話では The newspapers *say* [*report*, ×*tell*] that .... の方が普通)

❷ [伝授する] teach*; [後世に残す] hand [pass] ... down; [導入する] introduce. ▶その陶芸家は技術を息子に伝えた The potter *taught* the art *to* his son. ▶これらの習慣は何百年も前から父から子へと伝えられてきたものである These customs *have been*

handed [been passed] down from father to son through [over] the centuries. (!(1) 用例は受身で用いる. (2) from father to son は father と son が対句で用いられているので無冠詞) ▶1543年にポルトガル人が鉄砲を日本に初めて伝えた Portuguese people [《やや書》The Portuguese] *introduced* guns *into* Japan in 1543./The Portuguese *brought* guns *with* them *into* Japan in 1543. ▶その発がん性の物質は人のDNAに入り込むこともあり、そうなると病気を子供に伝えることになる That cancer-causing substance can get into your DNA, and you'll be *passing* the disease *to* your child(ren).
❸【送る】send*; (光・音などを) conduct, transmit (-tt-). ▶金属は熱をよく伝える Metal *conducts* [*transmits*] heat well./Metal is a good conductor of heat. ▶その情報はすべての営業所へファクスで伝えられた The information *was sent* [*was transmitted*] *to* every office by fax [《書》facsimile].

つたない 拙い (へたな) poor; (未熟な) unskillful. ● つたない英語で話す speak (in) poor English. ● つたない弁解 (make) a *poor* [a *clumsy*] apology [excuse]. ● つたない芸 《xan》*unskillful* performance.

つたわる 伝わる ❶【(うわさなどが)広まる】spread, travel; (巡り伝わる) circulate, go* around; 【(意図・考えなどが)理解される】get* across 《to the audience》. ▶悪い知らせはすぐに伝わる《ことわざ》(悪事千里を走る) Bad news travels quickly [fast]. ▶殺人事件のニュースはすぐに町中に伝わった The news about the murder *spread* rapidly [*traveled* fast, *circulated*] quickly] throughout the town [among the townspeople]. ▶著者の意図がはっきりと伝わってこない The writer's intention does not *come across* too clearly. (!(伝わる) come across は「(読者の側から見て)理解される」の意) ▶そのことは会長に伝わってると思っていたよ I thought the chairperson *had been told about* it. (⇨伝える ❶)
❷【後世に残る】come* down, be handed down; 【導入される】come, be brought, be introduced. ▶これは200年前から我が家に伝わる宝物である This treasure *has come* [*has been handed*] *down* in my family for two centuries. ▶鉄砲は1543年に日本に伝わった Guns *came to* Japan in 1543./Guns *were introduced into*] Japan in 1543.
❸【光・音などが)進む】travel; 【電気などが)送られる】be conducted, be transmitted. ▶光は音より速く伝わる Light *travels* faster than sound.

ツタンカーメン 【古代エジプトの王】Tutankhamen /tùːtɑːŋkáːmən/.

*つち 土 ❶【土壌】(地層の一部としての) earth; (植物生育のための) soil; (靴などについたばらばらの) dirt; (粘土) mud; (粘土) clay; 【地面】the ground. ● やせた土 poor *soil*; barren *earth*. ● 土臭い(=田舎びた) rustic. ● 土のにおい smell of *earth*; 《やや話》an *earthy* smell. ● 土のついた指 *earthy* fingers. ● 土に埋める bury 《it》in the *ground*. ● 土を耕す cultivate the *earth* [*soil*, *ground*]. ● 土を払い落とす turn (up) the *soil*. ● コートの土を払い落とす brush the *dirt* from one's coat. ▶小麦栽培によい土が必要です Wheat farming requires good [《肥沃(ひよく)な》fertile, rich] *soil*.
❷【国土】soil, land. ● 土一升(しょう)金(きん)一升 このあたりの土地は土一升金一升(=非常に高い) The land around here is *very expensive* [《話》*worth its weight in gold*]. ● 土がつく ▶横綱に初めて土がついた The Yokozuna lost [《話》*hit the dirt*] for the first time.
● 土となる ● 異国の土となる(=外国で死ぬ) die on [be buried in] 《xa》foreign *soil* [*land*].
● 土に帰る return to the soil; (死ぬ) die.
● 土を踏む ▶彼は10年ぶりに母国の土を踏んだ He set foot in [(戻った) returned to] his home country for the first time in ten years.

つち『土』*The Soil*. (《参考》長塚節の小説)
つち 槌 【金づち】a hammer; (岩石を割る大づち) a slédgehàmmer; 【木づち】a wooden hammer; (小づち) a mallet; (杭(くい)を打つ大づち) a maul; (議長が使う) a gavel /gǽvl/.

つちいじり 土いじり (子供の) playing in the mud; (園芸) gardening.
つちいろ 土色 ― 土色の 形 muddy brown;【皮ふの色が】(黄色がかった) sallow; (青白い) pale. ▶彼の顔は疲労で土色だった His face was *pale* [*sallow*] with fatigue.
つちかう 培う (養う) 《やや書》cultivate, (育成する) 《書》foster. ● 健全な精神を培う *cultivate* a sound mind.
つちぐも 土蜘蛛 【動物】a ground spider.
つちけいろ 土気色 muddy brown; pale; gray. (⇨土色)
つちけむり 土煙 《raise》a cloud of dust.
つちふまず 土踏まず the arch of the foot.

*つつ 筒 (円筒) a cylinder /sílindər/; (導管) a pipe; (管, くだ) a tube; (銃身) a barrel. ● 竹筒 a bamboo *cylinder*. ● 筒茶わん a *cylindrical* teabowl.

―つつ ❶【...しながら】(⇨ながら) ▶母が持ち直してくれることを祈りつつ病院に急いだ I rushed to the hospital hop*ing* that my mother would pick up. ▶おじは喫煙は体に悪いと分かりつつ(=分かっているけれども)どうしてもやめられない My uncle just can't quit smoking *though* he knows it's bad for his [the] health.
❷【進行中の動作】▶彼女は回復しつつある She's getting better. ▶私たちは勝利に近づきつつある We *are well on* our *way* to winning 《xto win》. (!be well on one's [the] way to ... は「ほぼ...に達している」の意) ▶その法案を阻止する動きが進みつつある A move *is under way* to block the bill.

つづいて 続いて next; then. (⇨次 ❸)
つづうらうら(で) 津々浦々(で) throughout [all over] the country; 《米》from coast to coast; (広く) far and wide.
つっかいぼう 突っかい棒 (支柱) a prop. (!比喩的にも用いる) ● 突っかい棒をあてる place a *prop* 《against, under》; prop ... up. ▶戸が開かないように何か突っかい棒をしよう Let's *prop* the door shut with something. (!shut は過去分詞で補語)
つっかえる 突っかえる be blocked. (⇨支(つか)える)
つっかかる 突っ掛かる (毒舌をあびせる) lash out 《at, against》; (食ってかかる) turn on 《him》. ● だれにでもつっかかる *lash out at* everyone.
つっかけ 突っ掛け 《a pair of》clogs. (!もとはぬかるむ道を歩くための木底靴)
つっかける 突っ掛ける slip 《one's shoes》 on.
つつがなく 恙無く safely, in safety. ● つつがなく暮らす live *in peace and quiet*.
つつがむし 恙虫 【動物】a tsutsugamushi mite; a chigger; a harvest mite.
● 恙虫病 tsutsugamushi disease; 【医学】scrub typhus.

つづき 続き 【継続】(続く[続ける]こと, 中断後の再開) (a) continuation, 《書》continuance (!継続の状態を表す);【連続】(a) succession; (一連) a series

(❶単・複同形); [一続きの期間] a spell. (⇨連続)
●物語の続き a *continuation* of a story; (続編) a *sequel* to a story. ▶不作続きで米の値段が上がった A *series* [A *succession*, A *sequence*] of bad harvests caused a rise in the price of rice. ▶長い間日照り続きです We have had a long *spell* of dry weather. ▶話の続き(=残り)を聞こう Let's listen to the *rest* of the story. (❗the *rest* の使い方に注意)

●続き柄 (family) relationship. ●続き部屋 a suite/swíːt/ (of rooms). ●続き物 a serial (story).

つつぎり 筒切り round slices (*of* a mackerel). ●筒切りにする cut 《a mackerel》 in [into] round slices.

つつきる 突っ切る cross; go* [run*, cut*] across ...; (スピードを上げて) speed across .... ▶原っぱを突っ切って行った先にある小さな教会 a small church *across* the field. ▶赤信号の交差点を突っ切る *speed across* the intersection against the red light.

つつく (棒・指などで) poke; (とがった物で) pick; (鳥がくちばしで) peck (at ...). ▶氷をついて穴をあける *pick* a hole in the ice. ▶なべをみんなでつつく *eat together from a single pot heated at the table*. ▶彼は私のわき腹をひじでつついた He *poked* me [*gave me a poke*] in the ribs with his elbow./(軽く) He *nudged* me [*gave me a nudge*] in the ribs with his elbow. (❗合図や注意を引くために) ▶小鳥は穀物をつついていた The bird *was pecking* [*picking*] (*at*) grain. ▶食べ物を(いやそうに)つつくのをやめてちゃんと食べなさい Stop *picking* [《話》*pecking*] *at* your food and eat! ▶人につつかれない(=文句を言われない)ようにしなさい Be careful not to *be picked at* [*be found fault with*].

*❖**つづく 続く**

WORD CHOICE 続く, 続ける

continue 一貫して行われてきたことを引き続いて継続すること, または一時中断されていたことを再開して継続すること. 動名詞, to 不定詞が続く. ▶英語の学習を続ける We *continue* to study English.
go on 行為・状態などが変化せずに継続すること. 動名詞, with+名詞などが後に続く. ▶彼はさらに3年間働き続けた He *went on* working for another three years. ▶それにもかかわらず, 人生は続いてゆく. Nevertheless, the life still *goes on*.
last ある状態が変化せずに続くこと. しばしば継続期間が明示される. ▶会議は6時まで続いた The meeting *lasted* until six o'clock.

頻度チャート
continue ▇▇▇▇▇▇▇▇▇▇
go on   ▇▇▇▇
last   ▇▇
         20 40 60 80 100 (%)

❶ [単一の出来事などが] (継続する) continue, 《やや話》 go* on; (持続する) last. (❗いずれも進行形にしない)

① 《...が[は]続く》 ▶晴天が1週間続いた The nice weather *continued* [*lasted*, *went on*] (for) a week. (❗強調のため for 句を文頭に置く場合は for の省略が不可) ▶その番組はニュースの後も続いた The program *continued* [*went on*, ×*lasted*] after the news. ▶会合は夕方まで続いた The meeting *continued* until [into] the evening. (❗until で

は「夕方には会合は終わっていた」, into では「終わったのは夕方でした」. 「6時まで」のように時点を示す文脈では until (×into) six) ▶その慣習は今日も続いている The custom *continues* [×*is continuing*] today. ▶演説は何時間も延々と続いた The speeches *went* [*ran*] *on and on* for hours. (❗on の反復は継続的の意を強める) ▶10月の中旬にひとしきり晴天が続いた We had a *spell* [a *run*] of nice weather about the middle of October. (❗fine weather も可だが, 《米》では nice が普通) ▶雨は3日間降り続いている It's been raining [It has rained] for three days *running* [*three consecutive days*]. ▶何事も永遠には続かない Nothing *lasts* forever.

会話「ストはいつまで続くのだろうか」「そう長くは続くまい」"How long will the strike *last*?" "It won't *last* (long)." (❗Until when ...? より How long ...? の方が普通)

② 《...に続く》 ▶5ページに[より]続く Continued on [from] page 5. ▶裏面に続く (P.)T.O. (❗*p*lease *t*urn *o*ver. の略)/《米》Over. ▶(次号に)続く To *be continued*. (❗The story [article] is to be continued in the next month's issue. の略)

❷ [土地などが] continue; (延びる) extend; (通じる) lead* (*to*). (❗いずれも進行形は不可) ▶彼の農場は川まで続いている His farm *extends* as far as the river. ▶この廊下は会議室に続いている This hall *leads* to the conference room.

会話「この道はどこまで[どれくらい]続いているのですか」「国境線で [50キロ] 続いています」"How far does this road *continue*?" "It *continues* to the border [(for) 50 kilometers]."

❸ [連続する] ▶ひっきりなしに続く訪問客[交通の流れ] a steady *stream* of visitors [traffic]. ▶最近自動車事故が続く There has been [We have had] *a series of* car accidents recently./(次々と起る) Car accidents have happened *one after another* recently.

❹ [類似の物が並ぶ] ▶その道には車の長い列が続いていた There was *a long line* of cars along the road./A lot of cars *lined* the road.

❺ [後に続く] follow. ▶彼の言葉のあとに気まずい沈黙が続いた An awkward silence *followed* [(やや話) *came after*] his words. ▶柩(ʰ²)の後には会葬者の長い列が続いた The cóffin [《米》cásket] *was followed* by a long line of mourners. (❗casket は婉曲語法)

❻ [隣接する] be next to ..., 《やや書》 adjoin. ▶我々の庭は彼らの庭と続いている Our garden *is next* [*adjacent*] *to* theirs.

つづけざま(に) 続け様に (次々と) one after another; (続けて) in succession, 《話》 in a row. ▶彼は続けざまにヒット曲を出した He had hit songs *one after another* [*in* (quick) *succession*, *in a row*]./He had *a string of* hit songs. ▶続けざまに3日間雪が降った It snowed for three *straight* [*successive*, *consecutive*] days. (❗consecutive には中断のないことを強調)

つづけじ 続け字 a cursive character. ●続け字を書く write in a *cursive style* [*hand*].

*❖**つづける 続ける** continue, 《やや話》 go* on; keep* (on ...)/《doing を従え「休みなく...し続ける」と「くり返し...し続ける」の意を表す. on を伴うと反復の意味が強調されてしばしば執ようさを暗示する》. (⇨続く [類語])

① 《...を続ける》 ▶努力を続ける *continue* [*keep up*] one's efforts. ▶沈黙を続ける *continue* (*to be*) *silent* [×*silence*] (❗*continue silently* は「黙って続ける」); *keep* silent [silence]; *remain* silent

[×silence]. ▶中断の後彼は続けてその話をした He went on with the story [to tell the story] after the break. (!on は副詞なので ×...he went on telling the story. は不可 (⇨[類語]))
②[~続ける] ▶火を燃やし続ける keep [×keep on] the fire burning. ▶図書館に通い続ける continue to visit the library. (!断続的な反復行為) ▶仕事を続けなさい Go on with your work. (!前置詞の使い方に注意) ▶彼は雪をものともせずに運転し続けた He continued to drive [continued driving] in spite of the snow./He went on [kept on] driving in spite of the snow. ▶物価が上がり続けている Prices keep [on] [continue] going up. (!進行形を用いて Prices are going up. ともいえる) ▶電車でずっと立ち続けていた(=立っていなければならなかった)のでとても疲れた I was really tired because I had to stand [×kept on] standing] all the way on the train. (!自分の意志で立ち続けた場合は kept (on) standing は可 (⇨立つ❶)) ▶彼は5時間続けて勉強をした He studied for five hours straight [on end, (休憩しないで) without a break]. (⇨連続, ぶっ通し)

つっけんどん ―― つっけんどんな 形 (言葉少なく丁寧でない) curt; (直截すぎる) blunt; (そう言う[する]時間さえ惜しいといわんばかりの) brusque.
―― **つっけんどんに** 副 curtly; bluntly; brusquely.

つっこみ 突っ込み ▶この論文は突っ込みが足りない This thesis lacks depth [is not deep enough]./This thesis should have treated the subject deeper. ▶これ全部いただきます. 突っ込みでいくらですか I'll take all of these. How much does it make altogether? ▶「明日がある, 明日がある, 明日があるさ」と口ずさんだあとで, 「ほんまにあるんかい」とツッコミを入れずにはいられない Whenever I croon, "There's another day. There's another day. There's another day," I can't help but ridicule myself and say, "Is there really?" (!ここでは自分にツッコミを入れているので「自分自身を嘲笑する」と表

*つっこむ **突っ込む** ❶[激しい勢いで進む] (突進する) dash 《for》, rush 《at》; (突入・衝突する) run* [go*] 《into》; (激突する) crash 《into》; (水中などに) plunge 《into》; (落ちる) fall* 《into》. ▶敵陣(の中)に突っ込む dash [rush, run] into the enemy lines. ▶頭から堀割りに突っ込む fall headfirst into a ditch. ▶車が登校中の子供の列に突っ込んだ A car ran [went] into the children walking in single file to school. ▶バスが川に突っ込んだ The bus plunged [(転がり落ちた) tumbled] into the river. ▶打者は(投球に)突っ込んだ [野球] The batter got out in front of (the pitch).

❷[中に入れる] put*; (ぐいと) thrust; (無造作に荒々しく) shove /ʃʌv/; (先のとがったものなどを) stick*; (押し込む) push. (!以上いずれも into 句を伴う) ▶彼はポケットに手を突っ込んで鍵(ぎ)を取り出した He put [thrust, shoved, stuck] his hand into his pocket and took out a key.

❸[問題の詳細に迫る] ▶突っ込んだ(=徹底した)研究 thorough [in-depth] research 《into》. ▶その件についてもっと突っ込んだ話し合いをする discuss 《×about》 that matter in more detail [more closely]; talk further 《×farther》 about that matter. (!far の比較級で「なおいっそう」の意. 程度を表す場合は farther はまれ) ▶彼は知ったかぶりをしたが, いくつか突っ込んだ(=鋭い)質問をされてぼろを出した He talked knowingly, but exposed his ignorance when (he was) asked a few pointed questions.

❹[関わる] ▶他人の事に首を突っ込むな《話》Don't poke [stick] your nose into other people's affairs.

つつさき 筒先 (銃・砲の) a muzzle; (ホースなどの) a nozzle.

つつじ [植物] an azalea /əzéiliə/. (!サツキなども含む)

つつしみ 慎み (控えめ) modesty; (遠慮) reserve.
● 慎み深い (控えめな) modest; (遠慮した) reserved (attitude).

*つつしむ **慎む** ❶[用心する] be careful 《about, of》; [分別がある] be prudent. ▶言葉[口]を慎め Be careful about your language [what you say]./Watch your words.
❷[控える][書] refrain 《from》; keep*... off; (やめる) stop (-pp-), give*... up (!後の方が口語的); (量を減らす) cut* down 《on...》. ▶医者は彼にたばこを慎むように言った The doctor advised him to refrain from [stop, give up] smoking. (!×stop to smoke や ×give up to smoke は不可. 必ず動名詞が後に来る)/The doctor advised him not to smoke. ▶私の父はアルコールを慎むようにしている My father tries to keep off alcohol.

つつしんで 謹んで respectfully. (!直訳しない場合が多い) ▶ご逝去に対し謹んでお悔やみ申し上げます Please accept my sincere [deepest] sympathy on his [her] death.

つつそで 筒袖 a tight sleeve. ●筒袖の着物 a tight-sleeved kimono.

つったつ 突っ立つ (ただ立っている) just stand*. ▶どうしてこんな所に突っ立っているの Why are you standing around [about] doing nothing?

つつどり 筒鳥 [鳥] a Himalayan cuckoo; an Oriental cuckoo.

つつぬけ 筒抜け ●筒抜けになっている (秘密などが漏れる) leak out 《to》. ▶隣の部屋の音が筒抜けに聞こえる We can hear all the noises from the next room.

つっぱしる 突っ走る (突進する) dash 《for》; (まっすぐに) rush headlong 《into》. ●ゴールめがけて突っ走る dash for the finish line [(サッカーなどの) the goal].

つっぱねる 突っぱねる (強い態度で拒絶する) reject; turn ... down flat(ly). (!後の方が口語的) ▶援助の申し出を突っぱねる reject one's offer of help; turn down the offer of help flatly.

つっぱる 突っ張る ●屋根を木の柱で突っ張る(=支える) prop up the roof with a wooden post. ●自分の意見を突っ張る(=固執する) persist in [stick to] one's opinion. ▶あの生徒はちょっとつっぱっている(=反抗的な)ところがある That student is a little defiant. ▶He's something of a defiant student. とすると, something が「いくぶん」から「かなり」まで幅広く解釈されるので文脈をよく見て用いる必要がある)/(不良少年のような行動をする) That student acts somewhat like a hooligan.

つっぷす 突っ伏す lie face down [lie on one's face, fall flat on one's back] suddenly.

つつましい 慎ましい [控えめな] modest; [質素な] simple (⇨つましい). ●つつましい食事 (have) a simple meal. ●つつましく暮らす live simply; lead a simple life. ▶彼女はとてもつつましい女性だ She is a very modest woman.

つつみ 包み ▶しっかり包装した物, 郵送用の小包》 a package, 《主に英》 a parcel (!《英》では郵送用の小包に package は用いない); [人や馬の背に乗せる荷] a pack; [束ねたもの] a bundle. (⇨[荷物]) ●本の包みa large package of books. ●ひと包みの種子 a pack 《米》 [a packet 《英》] of seeds. (⇨袋, 包)
●包みをあける open a package. ●プレゼントの包みを

解く unpack [unwrap] a present. ▶彼女は買い物袋をいっぱい抱えて店を出た She left the shop with an armful of *packages* [*parcels*]. ▶ひと包みの毛布が罹(り)地に送られた A *bundle* of blankets was sent to the stricken area.
● 包み紙 wrápping pàper; a wrapper.

つつみ 堤 a bank. (⇨土手)

つつみ 鼓 a *tsuzumi* (drum); (説明的に) a small shoulder drum which they tap with the fingertips.

つつみかくす 包み隠す hide*, 《やや硬》 conceal; (悪事などをおおい隠す) cover ... up; (秘密にしておく) keep* ❨it❩ secret ❨from him❩. ▶身分を包み隠す hide [conceal] one's identity. ▶自分の罪を包み隠す *cover up* one's guilt. ▶警察に自分の罪を包み隠さず述べる(=白状する) *confess* one's crime *to* the police; *make a clean breast of* one's crime *to* the police. ▶包み隠さず(=率直に) 彼にすべてを打ち明ける tell him everything *frankly*.

つつみちゅうなごんものがたり 『堤中納言物語』 *The Riverside Counselor's Stories*. ❨[参考] 平安時代の短編物語集❩

つつみやき 包み焼き ●シャケの包み焼き salmon wrapped in foil and broiled.

*__つつむ 包む__ (紙・布などで包みくるむ) wrap (-pp-) ... (up); (すっぽり覆う) envelop. ▶それを風呂敷に包む *wrap* [*fold*] it in a *furoshiki*. ▶彼女はプレゼントを赤い包装紙で包んだ She *wrapped* (*up*) the present in red wrapping paper. ▶このかばんを贈り物用に包んでください Will you *gift-wrap* this bag? ▶山の頂上は霧に包まれていた The mountaintop *was wrapped* [*was enveloped*, *was shrouded*] *in* mist. ▶その事件はなぞに包まれている The affair *is veiled* [*is enveloped*, *is shrouded*] *in* mystery. ▶スタンドは熱気に包まれていた(=満たされた) The stands *were filled with* excitement. ▶その家は炎に包まれていた The house *was in flames* [*on fire*].

【翻訳のこころ】 雨は、羅生門を包んで、遠くから、ざあっという音を集めてくる(芥川龍之介『羅生門』) The rain has enveloped Rashoumon, and gathered all the sounds of downpour from far away. (❗「包む」は envelope (すっぽり覆う)を用いる. cover (上からカバーをかける)より完全に覆ってしまう状態を表す)

つづら 葛籠 a wicker trunk.

つづらおり 葛折り ●つづら折りの(=曲がりくねっている)山道 a *winding* [*zigzag*] mountain path.

つづり 綴り ❨❨単語の❩❩ (a) spelling (❗「つづり字」では C, 「つづり方」では U); ❨❨正字法❩❩ orthógraphy; ❨❨書類の❩❩ a file. ▶つづりの間違いだらけの手紙 a letter full of spélling mistakes [misspellings]. ●つづりを間違える misspell ❨❨a word❩❩; spell ❨❨a word❩❩ wrong. ▶「ウエンズデー」のつづりを覚える learn how to spell "Wednesday". ▶彼のつづりは正確だ His *spelling* [×spell] *is correct* [*good*].

つづりかた 綴り方 ❨❨単語の❩❩ spelling; ❨❨作文❩❩ (a) composition. ●その単語のつづり方 how *to spell* the word; the *spelling* of the word.

つづる 綴る ❨❨文字を❩❩ spell; ❨❨文章を❩❩ write*. ▶お名前はどうつづるのですか How do you *spell* your name?/What is the *spelling* [×spell] of your name?/(つづりをお願いします) Could you *spell* your name, please? ▶「フォウ」という語はエフ・オー・イーとつづります The word "foe" is *spelled* f-o-e. ▶彼は正しく字をつづれない He cannot *spell* correctly./He is a poor speller. (❗「つづりの正確な人」は a good speller) ▶彼らの歴史は血と涙でつづられてきた Their history *has been written* in blood and tears.

つづれ 綴れ (ぼろ着) rags. (⇨ぼろ)
● つづれ織り[錦] hand-woven brocade; (a) tapestry.

つて ❨❨縁故❩❩ connections, contacts, 《話》 pull (❗時に a ～); ❨❨人に対する影響力❩❩ influence; ❨❨仲介者❩❩ an intermediary. ▶つてで就職する get a job *through connections* [*contacts, pull*]; get a job by *using* (*his*) *influence*. ▶つてを探す hunt for *connections*; hunt [look] for an *intermediary*. ▶彼は有力なつてがあってその地位を得た He had powerful *connections* [*contacts, pull*] and got his position.

つど 都度 ▶私は何度も食事に誘われたがそのつど(=毎回)丁寧に断わった I was asked to dinner many times, but I declined politely *every* [*each*] *time*. (⇨度(ど))

つどい 集い (集まり) a (social) gathering; (集会) a meeting. ●青少年の集い a *gathering* of young people.

つどう 集う (集団で) gather; (会に) meet*.

つとに 夙に (朝早く) early in the morining; (ずっと以前に) long ago; (幼い時に) in one's childhood; (幼い時から) from childhood.

つとまる 務まる (力量がある) be equal 《*to; to doing*; x*to*》; (資格がある) be qualified 《*for; to do*》. ●議長の役が務まる *be equal to* the functions of a chairman [a chairwoman]. ▶それでよく仕事が務まるものだ I wonder why people don't criticize you about your way of working.

‡**つとめ 勤め** ❨❨仕事❩❩ work; a job. (⇨仕事, 勤務) ● 勤めに出る go to work [the office]. (❗work は無冠詞で「職場」の意) ● 勤めから帰る come back [home] from *work*. ● 勤めを変える change one's *job*. ● 勤め(=仕事)を辞める leave [《話》 quit] one's *job*. (⇨辞める)
【会話】「お勤めはどちらですか」「ABC 銀行です」「そこでどんなお仕事をしていらっしゃるのですか」「出納(すい)係です」"Who do you work for?" "(For) ABC Bank." "What do you do there?" "I'm a teller ❨❨米❩❩ [cashier ❨❨英❩❩]." ❨❨事情❩❩ 米英では通例職種を尋ね, 勤め先だけを尋ねることは普通しない)
● 勤め口 a ❨❨仕事❩❩ job; ❨❨書❩❩ a position. ● 勤め先 (勤務先) one's office. (⇨勤務)
● 勤め人 an office worker; (事務職員) a white-collar worker.

つとめ 務め ❨❨義務, 本分❩❩ duty; ❨❨任務, 職務❩❩ a duty (❗通例複数形で). ▶子孫に対する我々の務めを果たす do our *duty* to our posterity. ▶務めを怠る neglect one's *duty*. ▶医師の[としての]務めは the *duties* of [as] a doctor. ▶市民を守るのが警察官の務めだ It's a police officer's *duty* to protect citizens. ▶彼は任された困難な務めを立派に果たした He successfully carried out the difficult *duties* left [entrusted] to him.

つとめあげる 勤め上げる ▶父は昨年銀行員として 40 年間を無事勤め上げて退職した My father worked for the bank for forty years and retired last year. (❗「無事」を強調するには without a hitch とか without any problems を bank の後に添える)

つとめて 努めて (できるだけ) as ... as possible [one can*]; (最大限努力する) do* one's best. ●努めて運動するようにしている try to get as much exercise *as possible*. ●努めて平静を保とうとする *try* (*hard*) [*make an effort*] to keep one's composure.

*__つとめる 勤める__ work ❨*in, at, for*❩; (雇われている) be employed ❨*in*❩; (仕える) serve ❨*in, with*❩. ●その会

社で秘書として勤める work [have a job] as a secretary in the company. ●官庁に勤める serve in a government office; (公務員として) serve as a government employee. ●A家にお手伝いとして勤めている be in service [be working as a helper] with Mrs. A. ●学校に勤める teach in [at] a school; 《米》teach school; be employed as a teacher. ●彼は石油会社に勤めています He works in [at, for] an oil company. (!建物または組織の一員であることが意識される場合には in、単に場所が意識される場合には at、雇われて働く気持ちを表す場合は for を用いる。対応する質問文は in, at では Where does he work?、for では Who does he work for?(⇨関))
▶その会社に勤めてどれくらいになりますか How long have you been with the company?

*つとめる 務める 〖職などの任務を果たす〗 serve; 〖役目を果たす〗(…として) act 《as》; play. ●議長を務める serve as chairperson. (!一つの団体に1人しかいない役職は無冠詞) ●代議士[スペイン大使]を務める serve ten years in Parliament [as ambassador to Spain]. ●委員を務める serve on a committee. ●パーティーの主人役を務める act as host at a party. (!このように資格を表すときは無冠詞) ●劇で主役を務める play the leading part [role, character] in a play.

つとめる 努める 〖やってみる〗try 《to do》; 〖努力する〗make* an effort 《to do》 (!try より堅い言い方)、《やや堅》endeavor 《to do》. ●努力する、努めて)
▶期日までにそれを完成するよう努めます I'll try to finish it by the deadline. ●全力をあげて宿泊客のサービスに努めました We made every effort [did our best] to provide the guests with acceptable service. ●彼女は息子の看病に努めた(=専念した) She devoted herself to attending her sick son.

*つな 綱 (a) rope (!最も一般的な語. cord より太い); (a) cord (!「1本の綱」は時には a (piece of) rope [cord]); a line (!thread (糸)、cord, rope など広くひも状のものを表す語). (⇨紐❶) ●命綱 a lifeline. ●綱をぴんと張る stretch a rope tight 《between》. ●綱を引っ張る pull [draw, (強く) haul (away)] a rope. ●綱を伝って降りる climb down a rope. ●洗濯物を干し綱にかける hang the clothes on the line. (!語法 米英では通例ロープにかけ、物干しざおとにかけない)

ツナ tuna.

つながり 繋がり a connection, a link; 〖関係〗(a) relation, (a) relationship. ●血のつながり blood relationship [ties]. (⇨血縁) ●つながりがある be related 《to》; be connected 《with》. (⇨関係)

*つながる 繋がる ❶〖結びつく〗(連結する) connect 《with》 (!何かの中間媒体で連結する); link 〖結び付きが connect より強い〗; 〖結合・接合する〗join (!じかに密着している). ▶この部屋は廊下で食堂とつながっている This room connects [links] with a dining room by a hallway./This room is connected with [is linked with, is joined to] a dining room by a hallway./This room and a dining room are connected [are linked] by a hallway. ▶この道はずっと先で 16 号線につながっている This road joins 《×to》 Route 16 far ahead. ▶ガンがつながって(=列をなして)飛んでいく Wild geese are flying in a line [a file]. (!ガンは通例 V 字型になって (in a V formation) 飛ぶ)
❷〖関係する〗▶彼は私の家と血のつながっている(血縁がある) He is related to my family by blood./(親戚《しんせき》だ) He is a blood relative of my family. ▶貧困は犯罪と密接につながっている Poverty is closely related to [connected with, linked up with] crime. ▶この二つの事実はどこかでつながっているに違いない These two facts must somehow be correlated with each other. (!correlate は「相互に関係させる[する]」の意)
❸〖電話が〗▶やっと電話が彼につながった I finally got through to him (on the phone)./(通じた) I finally got [reached] him. (!get の方が口語的)
▶ニューヨークにつながっています You are connected with New York.

つなぎ 繋ぎ 〖連絡〗a connection; a link; 〖一時しのぎ〗a stopgap. ●次の幕までのつなぎに(=幕間に)手品をする do magic tricks during [in] the intermission 〖(主に英) interval〗 before the next curtain rises. ●つなぎに卵を少々加える add a little egg to bind.
●つなぎ予算 a stopgap budget.

つなぎとめる 繋ぎ止める keep*; (船を) moor. ●かろうじて命をつなぎ止める barely keep 《him》 alive; (死をまぬがれる) narrowly escape death. ●そんな安給料では彼をつなぎ止めておけない You won't be able to keep him on such a small salary.

つなぎめ 繋ぎ目 〖ひもなどの結び目〗a knot; 〖接合所〗a joint. ●ガス管のつなぎ目を締める tighten up the joints in the gas pipes. ▶ロープのつなぎ目がゆるんできた The knot in the rope has loosened.

*つなぐ 繋ぐ ❶〖結びつける〗(ひも・ロープなどで) tie 《~d, tying》; (しっかりと) fasten; (しっかりくくりつける) lash; (犬などを(革)ひもでつなぐ)《米》leash; (鎖で) chain; (馬などの綱を杭などにひっかける) hitch; (船を) moor. ●犬を木につなぐ tie [fasten, lash] a dog to a tree. ●犬を(革)ひもでつなぐ《米》leash a dog; put a dog on a leash《米》[a lead《英》]. ●馬を柱になぐ hitch a horse to a pole. ●ブイにつながれたボート a boat moored [fastened] to a buoy. ▶その犬を恐がらなくてよい。つないであるから Don't be afraid of the dog, it is on a leash [a chain].
❷〖連結する〗connect; link; join. (!connect は何かの連結物によってつなぎ合わせる。link はしっかりと強く connect する。join は直接接触させてつなぐ) ●ホースを蛇口につなぐ connect [join] a hose /hóuz/ to a faucet. ●2 枚の板をつなぐ join two boards together. ●手をつないで歩く walk hand in hand. ●トースターをコンセントにつなぐ plug in the toaster. ▶この道路は A 市と B 市をつないでいる This road connects A City with [and] B City. ▶この橋はその島と本土をつないでいる This bridge joins [links] the island to the mainland.
❸〖電話〗▶山田さんにつないでください Please connect me with [put me through to] Mr. Yamada. (!応答として「つながりました」は You are connected.)
会話 (電話で)「山田さんをお願いします」「はい、今おつなぎします」"(I'd like to talk to) Mr. Yamada, please." "Oh, yes. (I'm) putting you through."
❹〖かろうじて保ち続ける〗(⇨繋ぎ止める)

つなとり 綱取り (説明的に) ozeki's endeavor to get promoted to yokozuna by getting results.

つなひき 綱引き (have [play at]) a tug-of-war.

つなみ 津波 a tsunami (wave); a tidal wave. ●津波を引き起こす cause [set up] a tsunami. ▶津波がその海岸を襲った A tidal wave hit [struck] the coast.

つなわたり 綱渡り tightrope walking. ●綱渡り師 a tightrope walker. ●綱渡りをする walk a tightrope. (!(1) 比喩的に「危険を冒す」(take a risk [risks])の意でも用いられる. (2) walk on a tightrope とは通例いわない)

つね 常 (⇨いつも、通例、必ず、普段) ▶彼は早起きを常と

している He *makes a point of getting* [*makes it a rule to get*] up early in the morning. 朝の方については (⇨必ず❷))/(通例早く起きる) He *usually* [(いつも) *always*] *gets up early in the morning*. (1) usually の代わりに文頭または文末に as a rule を用いるのは《書》. (2) 過去の習慣的行為を表し, 現在はそうでないことを示す場合は He *used to get up early in the morning.* とする) ▶若者の常として(=若者が普通そうするように)彼も冒険好きである He is adventurous, *as is usual with* young people [*as young people usually are*]. ▶それは世の常だ That's the *way of the world*.

つねづね 常々 (いつも) *always*; (かねづねから) *for a long time*.

***つねに** 常に *always*. (⇨いつも) ・常になく *unusually*.

つねひごろ 常日頃 *usually*; *normally*. (⇨普段)

つねる 抓る *pinch*, *give*《him》*a pinch*; (きつく) *nip* (-pp-). ▶夢でないことを確かめるために自分[ほお]をつねってみた I *pinched* myself [*my cheek*] *to make sure I wasn't dreaming*.

***つの** 角 (牛・ヤギ・羊・サイなどの) *a horn*; (シカの) *an antler*; (触角) *an antenna* /ænténə/ (*pl* antennae /-ni:/), *a feeler.* ・角のある[ない]動物 a *horned* [*hornless*] animal. ・角で突く *butt*《him》with its *horns*; horn [gore]《him》. ・雄羊には角がある[生えている] A ram has [*grows*] *horns*. ▶カタツムリが角を出した[引っ込めた] The snail has put out [has drawn in] its *antennae.*
・角突き合わせる ▶近所同士で角突き合わせている(=いがみ合っている)なんて嘆かわしいことだ It's a shame (that) the neighbors are at each other's throats.
・角を出す ▶帰りが遅いと女房が角を出す(=怒る) My wife *gets angry* [《話》*gets her back up*] if I stay out late.
・角を矯(た)めて牛を殺す (小さな欠点を直そうとして全体をだめにする) ruin the whole in an attempt to correct a minor fault; (治療の方が病気より悪い) The remedy is worse than the disease.
・角細工 horn carving; antler work. ・角笛 a horn.

つのかくし 角隠し a *tsunokakushi*; (説明的に) a bride's hood [*headdress*] (at a wedding).

つのだる 角樽 a two-handled *sake* keg.

つのつきあい 角突き合い *quarrel*《with him about a thing》. ・角突き合わせる ⇨角 [成句]

つのぶえ 角笛 a horn. (⇨角)

つのらす 募らす ・不安を募らす *deepen* one's uneasiness. ・恐怖の念を募らす *kindle* fear. ・緊張を募らす *heighten* [*increase*] tension.

つのる 募る ❶[高じる] *grow**; [増す] *increase*, (次第に) *gather*. ・つのる不満 *growing* discontent. ▶彼は彼女への思いをつのらせた His love for her *grew* [×*increased*]. ・それに対する私の好奇心はつのる一方だった I was getting *more and more* curious about it. ▶彼の心に不安がつのってきた Anxiety *has gathered* [*grown*] in his mind. ▶風が吹きつのってきた The wind began to *blow harder* [*rise*].
❷[募集する] (事務員などを) *look for*《clerks》; (寄付金などを) *collect*《contributions》. (⇨募集する)

***つば** 唾 [唾液(ミ)] *saliva* /səláɪvə/; [吐いたつば] *spit*.
・手をつばでぬらす *wet* one's hand *with saliva* [*spit*]. ・彼の顔[彼]につばをかける *spit* in his face [*at him*]. (! いわゆる「軽蔑」「怒り」を表す行い) ・道路につばを吐く *spit* on the road. ▶レモンのにおいでつばが出てきた The smell of a lemon has made my mouth *water*.
・つばをつける (自分のものになるよう仕組む) set up a claim《*to* it》; (主に子供が)《米話》have dibs《*on* it》.

つば 鍔 [刀の] a sword guard; [帽子の] a brim. ・つばの広い婦人帽 a broad-*brimmed* women's hat.

つばき 椿 [植物] a camellia /kəmíːliə/.
・椿油 camellia oil.

***つばさ** 翼 a wing. ・翼のある天使 a *winged* angel.
・翼を広げる[はたたかせる] spread [flap] its *wings*.

つばぜりあい 鍔迫り合い ・つばぜり合いを演じる(接戦をする) have a close race [game]《*with*》; (負けず劣らずの戦いをする) have a neck-and-neck race《*with*》, run neck and neck《*with*》.

つばめ 燕 [鳥] a swallow /swálou/. ・イワツバメ a martin. ▶ツバメが三匹来たからといって夏にはならない(ことわざ) One *swallow* does not make a *summer*. (!「早合点してはいけない」の意)
・燕返し[剣術] a quickly reversed cut; [柔道] a swallow flight reversal.

ツバル [国名] Tuvalu (! 公式名も同じ). (首都 Funafuti) ・ツバル人 a Tuvaluan. ・ツバル(人)の Tuvaluan.

***つぶ** 粒 [穀物・砂・塩などの] a grain; [水の一滴] a drop. ・一粒の米 a *grain* of rice. ・大粒の雨 large [great] *drops* of rain. ・粒のあらい[細かい]砂 coarse-*grained* [fine-*grained*] sand. ・粒状の薬 granulated [granular] medicine. ▶大粒の雨が降り始めた The rain began to fall in large *drops*.
・粒がそろっている ▶生徒の粒がそろっている(=一様によい) All of the pupils *are uniformly good* [*the crème de la crème*]. (! 後の方は慣用句) ▶このミカンは粒がそろっている(=大きさが同じだ) These oranges *are all of a size* [*all the same size*] (↔ vary in size).

つぶあん 粒餡 sweetened bean paste containing beans intact.

つぶさに ・つぶさに(=注意深く)観察する observe(…) *carefully*. ・計画を(=詳しく)説明する explain the plan *in detail*; give a *detailed* explanation of the plan. ・つぶさに(=いろいろ)世の辛酸をなめる experience [go through] many hardships.

つぶし 潰し ・つぶしがきく ▶学校の先生の多くはつぶしがきかない Many school teachers are not *fit for* other types of work.

つぶしあん 潰し餡 mashed sweetened bean paste.

***つぶす** 潰す ❶[外部からの力で](押しつぶす) crush; (ぺちゃんこに) squash; (乱暴に壊す) break*; (粉々に) smash; (いもなどをすりつぶす) mash. ・飛び乗ってボール箱をつぶす *crush* [*squash*, *break*, ×*smash*] a cardboard box by jumping on it. (! break はかたい箱の場合). ・靴をはきつぶす *wear out* one's shoes. ・にきびをつぶす *squeeze* a pimple. ▶彼の車はトラックに押しつぶされてぺちゃんこになった His car *was squashed* flat by the truck [《英》lorry].
❷[失う] ・身代をつぶす *lose* one's fortune; (破産する) go bankrupt. ・チャンスをつぶす *lose* [*miss*] a chance. (! 後の方が普通) ▶彼は私の顔をつぶした (面目を失わせた) He *made me lose* (×*my*) *face*./(面食らわせた) He *embarrassed* me.
❸[空いた時間をつぶす] kill time; (時間をむだにする) waste time. ・テレビを見て時間をつぶす *kill* time (by) watching TV. ・我々は車中での時間をつぶすために小説を何冊か求めた We got several novels to *kill* [*pass*] the time in the train. (! *the time* に注意)

つぶぞろい 粒揃い ▶粒揃いの picked; choice(st). (⇒粒, 粒選)

つぶだつ 粒立つ (泡立つ) foam; froth.

つぶつぶ 粒々 ▶粒々(=果肉)の入っているオレンジジュース orange juice with *pulp*. ▶このねり粉はまだ粒々(=かたまり)がある This batter is still *lumpy*.

つぶて 礫 a stone; a pebble. ▶つぶてを打つ(=小石を投げる) throw a *stone* ⟨*at*⟩. ▶紙つぶて a spitball. ▶梨のつぶて (⇒梨[成句])

つぶやき 呟き a murmur; a mutter. (⇒呟く)

つぶやく 呟く [低い声で言う] murmur; [不平や侮辱の言葉を低い声で言う] mutter; [ぶつぶつ文句を言う] grumble. ▶ひとりつぶやく *murmur* [*mutter*] to oneself. ▶彼の名をつぶやく *murmur* his name.

つぶより 粒選り ── 粒選りの 形 [食物など極上の] choice; [精選した] picked, handpicked. ▶粒選りのリンゴ the choicest [最高の the best] apples; apples of *the best quality*. ▶粒選りの登山家 picked [handpicked] alpinists /ǽlpɪnɪsts/.

つぶら ▶つぶらな瞳(ひとみ) lovely round eyes.

つぶる [閉じる] close, shut*. ▶目をつぶって音楽を聴く listen to music with one's eyes *closed* [*shut*]. ▶彼の無作法に目をつぶる(=大目に見る) *overlook* [見て見ぬふりをする] *pretend not to see*, *close one's eyes to*⟩ his misbehavior.

***つぶれる 潰れる** ❶ [壊れる] (強く押されて) crush, be crushed; (ぺちゃんこになる) squash, be squashed; (ばらばらに壊れる) break*, be broken; (粉々になる) smash, be smashed; (建物などが破壊される) be destroyed; (崩壊する) collapse. (⇒つぶす) ▶彼の重みでつぶれた The box *crushed* [*got crushed*] under his weight. ▶卵はすぐつぶれる Eggs *break* [*are broken*] easily.

❷ [役に立たなくなる] ▶目がつぶれる(視力を失う) lose one's (eye)sight; (盲目になる) go blind. ▶顔がつぶれる(=面目を失う) lose (↔save) face. ▶あまり大声で叫んだため声がつぶれてしまった I *lost my voice* from yelling too much./(声をからした) Too much yelling *made* me [my voice] *hoarse*. ▶雨のために我々の計画はつぶれた The rain *ruined* [*canceled*] our plan. ▶その会社はつぶれてしまった(廃業した) The firm *went out of business*./(倒産した) The firm *went bankrupt*. ▶客の入りが悪くなったためその店はつぶれてしまった(=閉鎖した) There wasn't any more business, so the shop *closed down*.

❸ [むだに使われる] ▶くだらない仕事で多くの時間 [1日の大半] がつぶれた(=取られた) The silly job *has taken up* a lot of time [the better part of the day].

つべこべ ▶つべこべ言う (理屈を並べる) argue; (文句を言う) complain. ▶つべこべ言わずに私の言うとおりにしろ Don't *argue* (with me). Just do as I tell you. ▶つべこべ言わずに仕事にかかれ Get down to your work without *complaining*.

ツベルクリン [<ドイツ語] tuberculin /t(j)u(ː)bə́ːrkjələn/. ●ツベルクリン検査 a tuberculin test. ツベルクリン反応 a tuberculin reaction.

***つぼ 壺** ❶ [容器] a pot; (広口で取っ手のない) a jar; (花びん) a vase. ▶ジャムを壺に入れて保存する *pot* jam. (保存したジャムは *potted* jam)

❷ [図星] ▶思うつぼにはまる (自分の) turn out just as one wished [wanted]; (相手の) play into ⟨his⟩ hands.

❸ [指圧・針灸での] (指圧の) a designated [a meridian] point for *Shiatsu*; (鍼灸の) an acupoint. ●つぼを押さえる (論点をはずさない) keep to the *point*.

つぼ 坪 a *tsubo* (単・複同形); (説明的に) a (former) Japanese unit of area equal to about 3.3 square meters.

つぼざら 壺皿 (ばくち用の) a dice cup; (小さくて深い皿) a small dish.

***つぼみ 蕾** a bud. (花だけでなく葉のつぼみにも用いる) ▶ふくらんだバラのつぼみ a swollen [a fat] rose *bud*. ▶つぼみのうちに摘み取る nip ... in the *bud*. (通例比喩的に「...を未然に防ぐ」の意に用いる (⇒摘む)) ▶桜のつぼみはまだ固い The *buds* of the cherry trees are still young [tight]. ▶つぼみがほころびかけている The *buds* are bursting [⟨やや書⟩ bursting]. ▶木々に(花の)つぼみがふくらんでいる [出始めた] The trees *are in (full) bud* [*are budding, are putting out buds*]. ▶後の方は Buds are appearing on the trees. ともいえる

つぼむ [花が閉じる] close; [つぼみを持つ] put* out buds.

つぼめる (⇒すぼめる)

つぼやき 壺焼き ▶サザエのつぼ焼き a turban shell broiled in its own shell.

:**つま 妻** a wife (複 wives).

① 【~妻】 ▶新妻 a bride; ⟨やや話⟩ a newlywed (「夫」にも用いる。×a new wife とはいわない). ▶前の妻(=先妻) (別れた) one's ex-*wife*, ⟨やや書⟩ one's former *wife*; (亡くなった) one's late *wife*. (「one's first wife は両者の意を含む」) ▶正式の妻(=正妻) a lawful *wife*. ▶内縁の妻 a common-law *wife*. ▶人妻 a married woman. ▶幼な妻 a childwife.

② 【妻を[は]】 ▶私には妻がいる I'm married. (通例 × I have a wife. とはいわない. ただし, I have a wife, a daughter, and two sons. などのようにいう場合は可)

③ 【妻の】 ▶妻(として)の⟨書⟩ wifely. ▶妻のつとめ *wifely* duties. ▶妻の[らしい]気遣い *wifely* concern. ▶妻の実家 one's *wife*'s parents' home [house]. (⇒実家)

④ 【妻に[で]】 ▶美穂を妻にする(=結婚する) *marry* [*get married to*] Miho. ▶彼女は彼のよい妻になった She made him a good *wife*./She made him a good *wife* to [⟨今はやや古⟩ for] him. (She became a good *wife* to him. と異なり, 素質を暗示する) ▶2年前に彼女に死別れた(=妻を亡くした) He lost his *wife* two years ago. (×He had his *wife* die.... とすると「殺し屋を雇って妻を殺させた」の意にとられる恐れがある) ▶私は妻であり母親であることに喜びを感じている I enjoy being a *wife* and (×a) mother.

⑤ 【妻を】 ▶妻(となる人)を捜す look for a *wife*. ▶妻をめとる(=結婚する) marry, get married. ▶妻を亡くす(=妻に死なれる) (⇒④ [第2文例])

つま ❶ [刺身の] a garnish; (説明的に) shredded vegetables or seaweed served with raw fish. ❷ [添えもの] ▶どうせ私は刺身のつまだ(=主役ではない) I am always playing second fiddle.

つまさき 爪先 a tiptoe. ▶つま先が冷える one's toes are cold. ▶つま先で歩く walk *on tiptoe*(s); tiptoe. (on tiptoe と単数の方が普通) ▶つま先上がり [下がり] の道 a gently uphill [downhill] road. ▶その靴は堅くて私はつま先を痛めた The shoes were stiff and pinching my toes.

つまさきだつ 爪先立つ stand on tiptoe(s). (on tiptoe と単数の方が普通)

つまされる ▶彼女の話を聞いて身につまされた I *felt really sad at* [*was deeply moved by*] her story.

つましい 倹しい frugal; thrifty. (倹の方が倹約の意が強い) ▶つましい主婦 a *frugal* [a *thrifty*] housewife. ▶つましい生活をする lead a *frugal* life; live *frugally*. (⇒質素) ▶彼らはわずかな年金でつましく暮ら

している They are scraping by on their small pension.

つまずき 躓き（失敗）(a) failure《*in*》; (後退) a setback《*in*》. ●仕事上のつまずき《×a》*failure in* one's business.

つまずく 躓く ❶［物に］stumble; trip (-pp-). ●石につまずいて倒れる *stumble* [*trip*] *on* [*over*] a stone and fall. ▶つまずかないようにしてね(=足もとに気をつけて). 道がでこぼこしているから Watch [Mind] your step. The road is bumpy. (❗steps でないことに注意)

❷［失敗する］fail《*in*》; (人が計画などで) have* [suffer] a setback《*in*》. ●人生につまずく take [make] a false step in life.

つまだち 爪立ち standing on tiptoe. ●爪立ちで歩く walk on tiptoe.

つまだてる 爪立てる stand on tiptoe.

つまはじき 爪弾き（のけ者）an óutcàst. ●社会のつまはじき a social *outcast*. ●つまはじきにする（無視して仲間に入れない）leave《him》out; (村八分にする) ostracize; (嫌って受け入れない) (hate and) reject. ▶ぼくは時々家でつまはじきにあっているように感じる I sometimes feel *left out* of my family. (❗この left は過去分詞)/I sometimes feel as if I *were* [was] *left out* of my family.

つまびく 爪弾く (ギターなどの弦を) pluck,《米》pick; (ギターなどを) strum (-mm-)《on》《a guitar》.

つまびらか 詳らか ──詳らかに detail. (⇨詳しい) ●つまびらかにする make ... clear. (⇨明らかにする)

つままれる ⇨つまむ ❷)

つまみ［取っ手］a knob;［スイッチ］a switch;［レバー］a lever;［酒の］(前菜) an hors d'oeuvre /ɑːrdˈɜːrv/ (❗日本語のおつまみにぴったりする英語はない);［ひとつまみ］a pinch 《*of* salt》.

つまみぐい つまみ食い ❶［指でつまんで］●つまみ食いをする eat with one's fingers.

❷［盗む］●シュークリームをつまみ食いする(=こっそりとって食べる) sneak a cream puff. ●政党の資金をつまみ食いする(=着服する) pocket the party funds.

つまみだす つまみ出す (力ずくで) throw*... out; (追い出す) turn ... out. ▶彼は飲み屋からつまみ出された He *was thrown out* of the pub.

つまむ ❶［はさむ］(はさんで拾う) pick ... (up); (指でまむ) pinch. ●ピンセット[指]でガラスの破片をつまむ *pick* (*up*) bits of glass with tweezers [one's fingers]. ●鼻柱をつまむ *pinch* the bridge of one's nose. ●(悪臭のため)鼻をつまむ *hold* one's nose. ▶このクッキーおいしいよ. どうぞつまんでちょうだい These cookies are good. Please hélp yoursèlf.

❷［ばかす］bewitch. ●きつねにつままれる *be bewitched* by a fox. ●きつねにつままれたような顔をする look *puzzled* [*bewitched*, (ぼかんとした) *blank*].

つまようじ 爪楊枝 ●つまようじを使う use a *toothpick*; pick one's teeth. (事情) 米英では人前で使わないのがよいとされる)

つまらない ❶［おもしろくない］uninteresting; dull; boring.

> 使い分け **uninteresting** 特別な特徴や興味をそそるものがないこと.
> **dull** 単調で刺激がなくつまらないこと: 長く退屈でつまらない晩 a long and *dull* evening.
> **boring** 人や活動が退屈でうんざりさせること: つまらないパーティー a *boring* party.

●つまらない本 an *uninteresting* [a *dull*, a *boring*] book. ▶昨夜見た劇はつまらなかった The play I saw last night was *dull* [*boring*]. ▶とてもつまらなそうですね You look so *bored* [×*boring*]. ▶1 人で酒を飲んでもつまらない(=楽しくない) It's no *fun* drink*ing* [*to* drink] alone.

❷［取るに足らない］(重要でない) unimportant, insignificant; (ささいな) trivial,《書》trifling; (価値のない) worthless; (愚かな) silly. ▶彼はつまらないことを気にしすぎる He worries too much about *unimportant* [*little*, *trivial*, *trifling*] things./《米話》He sweats the *small stuff* too much. ▶つまらないことにいったいなに騒ぐんだ What a fuss about *nothing* at all! ▶彼はつまらない間違いをして首になった He was fired for a *silly* [a *stupid*, (小さな) a *small*] mistake. ▶つまらないものですがどうぞ Here's a *small* present [*gift*] for you./Here's a *little* something for you. I hope you like it. などと続ける. 日本語に引かれて It's nothing but .... などといわない. (⇨さしあげる)

つまり ❶［すなわち］that is (to say); namely (❗堅い《書》ではしばしば前の方は i.e. /ðætiz, 時に áiíː/ と, 後の方は viz /néimli, 時に viz/ と省略);［分かりやすく言えば］or;［言い換えれば］in other words.

> 解説 (1) **that is (to say)** と **namely** の違い
> (ⅰ) 後により具体的なものが続く場合は両方とも可能だが namely の方が普通: 私のいちばんの親友, つまり山田君がきのう遊びに来た My best friend, *namely* [*that is (to say)*] Yamada, came to see me yesterday.
> (ⅱ) 後により抽象的なものが続く場合や完全な文をなす説明が続く場合は that is (to say) を用いる: Yamada, *that is (to say)* [×namely] my best friend, came to ....
> (ⅲ) that is (to say) は言い換えた語句の後に置くこともできるが namely および i.e., viz は通例不可: My best friend, Yamada, *that is (to say)* [×namely, ×i.e., ×viz] came to ....
> (2) 特定の語句を用いず同格のコンマでも表現できる: My best friend, Yamada, [Yamada, my best friend,] came to ....

●獣医, つまり動物の医師を a veterinarian, *that is* [*or*] a doctor for animals. ▶私のふるさとは日本の首都つまり東京です My hometown is the capital of Japan, *namely* Tokyo. ▶彼は財布を落とした. つまり無一文になった He lost his wallet, *that is* [×*namely*] he has no money at all./He lost his wallet—*in other words*, [*I mean* /əmiːn/] he has no money at all. (❗I mean は補足説明や訂正する場合に会話でよく用いられる)

会話 「版権って?」「ええ, つまりこういうことです」 "Copyright?" "Yes. It's like this./Let me put it this way." (❗この後に比較的長い説明が続く)

❷［要するに］in short; in brief《後の方が堅い言い方》;《話》to cut [make] a long story short; (ひと言で言えば) in a word《書》to sum up;［実際には］in fact. ▶つまりその事故は君の責任だ *In short* [*To cut a long story short*, *In a word*] you are responsible for the accident. ▶彼は自分は人道主義者だと言っているがつまりは偽善者にすぎない He says he is a humanitarian, but *in fact* he is only a hypocrite /hípəkrɪt/.

つまる 詰まる ❶［いっぱいである］be full 《*of*》; be filled《*with*》; be packed《*with*》. (⇨詰める, 詰め込む) ●お札のいっぱい詰まった財布 a wallet *full of* [(はみ出るほど) *stuffed with*] bills. ▶この百科辞典には有用な情報が詰まっている This encyclopedia *is packed with*《×a》useful information. ▶今週は予定が詰まっている My schedule *is full* [*tight*] this week./I have a *full* [a *tight*, a *heavy*]

つまるところ

schedule this week. (**!** ×a hard schedule は和製英語)

❷ 【つかえて通じなくなる】(小さな穴などが) be stopped up; (鼻などが) be stuffed up; (管・煙突などが) be clogged [blocked] up; (息が部分的または完全に) choke. ● もちがのどに詰まって死ぬ choke to death on (one's) *mochi*, a kind of rice cake.) ▶風邪で鼻が詰まった My nose *is stuffed* [*is stopped*] *up* with [because of] a cold. (**!** I've got a stuffy nose. もよく用いる) ▶流しによく炊事のごみが詰まる The sink often *gets stopped* [*clogged*, *blocked*] (*up*) *with* kitchen waste. (**!** becomes clogged [blocked] も可) ● 彼は涙で声が詰まった His voice *was choked* with tears.

❸ 【窮する】(⇨困る) ▶返事に詰まる do not know how to answer; be lost [be stuck, be at a loss] for an answer. ● 金に詰まる 《話》 be hard up; be pressed for money. ● 言葉に詰まる be *lost for* words; *stumble over* ones words.

❹ 【縮まる】 ▶先頭走者と2位集団との差がじりじり詰まってきた The distance between the leading runner and the second group is *shrinking* [*narrowing*] inch by inch./(じりじり追い上げてきた) The second group of runners are edging up behind the leading runner.

❺ 【野球で】 hit off the fists; get jammed. ● 詰まった当たり a handle hit. ● 打者を詰まらせる jam a batter.

つまるところ 詰まる所 in short. (⇨つまり)

:**つみ 罪** 〖宗教・道徳上の〗(a) sin; 〖具体例は C〗; 〖法律上の〗 a crime; 〖規則違反などに対する〗 an offense; 〖失敗などに対する責め〗 blame 《for》; 〖有罪〗 guilt.

① 【~罪】 ● 重大な罪 a grave *sin*; a serious [a grave] *crime* (**!** grave の方が強意的); 〖法律〗 a felony.

② 【罪が[は]】 ▶彼には罪がない(=無実である) He is innocent [not *guilty*]. ▶それは事故だったのだから,だれにも罪はない It was an accident, so no one *is to blame* [*is to be blamed*, *is responsible*] (for it).

③ 【罪(の)】 ● 罪のある(罪深い) sinful; (有罪の) guilty. ● 罪のない(= 無邪気な子供の寝顔 the child's *innocent* sleeping face. ● 罪のないそ a *white* [《無害な》a *harmless*] lie. ● 罪の意識(=罪悪感)を持つ have a *guilty* conscience; feel *guilt* [*guilty*] 《about》. ▶彼には罪の意識がない He has no sense of *guilt* [*sin*].

④ 【罪に】 ▶彼は殺人の罪に問われた He *was accused of* [*was charged with*, ×was blamed for] murder. ● blame は総称的な名詞をとらない。特定化した the murder なら可。blame は accuse, charge より非難の度合が弱く「彼のせいにされた」の意) ▶私は無実の罪に問われている I am *accused of* a *crime* I did not commit. ▶夜間ライトをつけずに運転するのは罪になりますか Is driving without lights at night an *offense* [*against the law*]?/Is it an offense to drive without lights at night?

⑤ 【罪を】 ● 罪を犯す commit a *crime* [a *sin*]; sin. ● 罪を重ねる commit *crimes* one after another. ● 窃盗の罪を犯している be guilty of a *crime* [×a *stealing*]. ● 警察に罪を自白すると confess one's *crime* to the police. ● 罪を許す (主語は神) forgive (him) (his) *sin*; (主語は人) forgive (him) for (his) *crime*. ● 罪(= 有罪)を認める admit one's *guilt*; (被告が法廷で) plead *guilty*. ● 彼に罪を着せる(無実の罪を負わせる) make a false *charge against* him; (不当な責任を負わせる) put [lay] the *blame on* him 《for》. ▶彼は恋人の罪をかぶった He *took* the *blame for* his girlfriend. ▶罪を犯す子供の年齢はますます低下している Young people are committing *crimes* [×*sins*] at much younger ages than before.

⑥ 【罪だ】 ▶うそをつくのは罪だ It is a *sin* [×a *crime*] to tell [×*say*] lies [a lie].

つみ 詰み (将棋・チェスの) a checkmate. (⇨詰む)

—つみ -積み ▶5トン積みのトラック a five-ton truck. (**!** ×a five-tons truck とはしない)

つみあげる 積み上げる pile ... up. (⇨積む) ● テーブルに皿を高く積み上げる *pile up* dishes high on the table; *pile* the table high *with* dishes.

つみおろし 積み降ろし ▶積み降ろしをする load and únload 《goods》. (**!** 対照強勢に注意)

つみかえ 積み換え tran(s)shipment.

つみかえる 積み換える tran(s)ship.

つみかさね 積み重ね (蓄積)(an) accumulation. ● 努力の積み重ねる the *accumulation* of one's efforts; (たゆまぬ努力) (a) steady effort.

つみかさねる 積み重ねる pile [(山のように) heap]... (up). (⇨積む ❶, 重ねる ❶) ● 知識を積み重ねる(=蓄積する) *accumulate* knowledge. ● 実験を積み重ねる perform [condúct] *a series of* experiments.

つみき 積み木 a building block; 《米》 a block, 《英》 a brick.

つみくさ 摘み草 gathering herbs.

つみこみ 積み込み (船へ) shipping, shipment, loading.

つみこむ 積み込む load. ● 車(トラック)に荷物を積み込む load [put] goods *into* a car [onto a truck]. (**!** load では多量の積み荷の含みがある。onto は列車・飛行機・船などにも用いる) *load* (*up*) a car [a truck] *with* goods. (**!** load up は「満載する」の意) ▶船は小麦を積み込むためにバンクーバーに寄港した The ship called at Vancouver to *load* [*take on*] a cargo of wheat.

つみだし 積み出し sending, 《書》 forwarding; shipment (**!** 《米》では輸送機関は何でもよいが,《英》は主に船で).

● 積み出し港 a port of shipment.

つみだす 積み出す send*... off 《to》, 《書》 forward 《to》; ship (-pp-) ... off 《to》 (**!** 《英》では主に船で).

つみたて 積み立て (お金をためること) (an) accumulation.

● 積立準備金 (会社の) accumulated reserves.
● 積立定期預金 an accumulative deposit.

つみたてる 積み立てる 〖貯金する〗 save ... (up); 〖金をたくわえる〗 put* [lay*] ... aside; 〖預金する〗 depósit. ● 月々3万円を積み立てる *put* [*lay*] *aside* 30,000 yen each month. ● 銀行に金を積み立てる *deposit* some money *in* a bank. ▶彼女は給料の3分の1を海外旅行のために積み立てている She *is saving up* a third of her salary for traveling abroad.

つみつくり 罪作り —— 罪作りな 形 cruel; wicked; heartless. ▶そんなことを言うなんて君は罪作りな人だ It is *wicked* of you to say such a thing.

つみとばつ 『罪と罰』 *Crime and Punishment*. (参考 ドストエフスキーの小説)

つみとる 摘み取る (一つ一つ摘む) pick, 《書》 pluck; (はさみ取る) nip (-pp-) ... (off). (⇨摘む) ● 綿花を摘み取る *pick* cotton. ● しぼんだ花を摘み取る *nip off* a dead flower.

つみに 積み荷 a load (**!** 一般的な語); (大量に遠距離を運ぶ貨物) freight /freít/, (a) cargo. (⇨荷) ● 積み荷をおろす unload the *cargo*. ▶トラックから積み荷が落ちた The *load* fell off the truck.

つみのこし 積み残し ● 積み残しが出る leave 《passengers, goods, cargo》 (behind).

つみびと 罪人 (⇨罪人(ざいにん))

つみぶかい 罪深い sinful.

つみほろぼし 罪滅ぼし atonement for one's sins. ● 罪滅ぼしに in *atonement* for .... ● 罪滅ぼしをする atone [make *atonement*] for ...; (埋め合わせをする) make up for .... ● 私は妻をヨーロッパ旅行に連れて行った。海外勤務で長年家を留守にしている間独りで子供たちを育ててくれた妻への罪滅ぼしになると思ったのだ I took my wife with me to Europe. I thought I'd make up [spend *a little conscience money* on her] for her raising our children by herself while I was away on my overseas assignment for many years. (❗(1) make up for は「…の埋め合わせをする」の意. (2) conscience money は本来, 脱税者などが罪滅ぼしに納める匿名の献金のこと)

つみれ 摘入れ a fish cake; a fish ball.

***つむ 摘む** (一つ一つ) pick, 《書》 pluck; (はさみ取る) nip (-pp-) ... (off); 〚集める〛 《主に書》 gather. ● 花を摘む pick [pluck] flowers. ● イチゴを摘む pick [gather] strawberries. ▶ 私たちはその陰謀の芽を摘んだ We nipped the plot *in the bud*. (❗慣用句) ▶ 花が吹く前の芽を摘んしまったのだ You nipped the buds before they could bloom. (❗could は「咲く可能性があったのに」を含意)

***つむ 積む** ❶ 〚上に重ねる〛〚積み上げる〛 (一つ一つきちんと) pile ... (up); (雑然と山のように) heap ... (up); (干し草・紙などを形を整えて積んだり) stack ... (up); 〚敷く〛 lay*. ● れんがを積む (積み重ねる) *pile* (*up*) bricks; (雑然的) *heap* (*up*) bricks; (きちんと敷く) *lay* bricks. ● 干し草を高く積む *stack* hay high. (❗「干し草の山」は a haystack) ● 机の上には山のように積んである There's *a pile* [*a heap*] *of books* on the desk. ▶ どんなに金を積んでも幸福は買えない *No amount of money* can buy happiness. ❷ 〚荷を載せる〛load. (⇨積み込む) ● トラック[車]に本を積む load a truck [a car] *with* books; load books *onto* a truck [*into* a car]. ● 船は鉄鉱石を積んでいた The ship was *loaded with* iron ores. ❸ 〚蓄積する〛 ▶ もっと練習を積む practice harder. ● 経験を積む *gain* experience; become experienced 《in》.

つむ 錘 a spindle.

つむ 詰む ● 字の詰んだ(=間隔が密集した)印刷 close [fine] printing. ▶ あと 5 手で詰むよ I'll *checkmate* [*mate*] you in five moves.

つむぎ 紬 pongee /pɑndʒíː/.

つむぐ 紡ぐ spin*. ● 糸を紡ぐ *spin* (thread). ● 綿を紡いで糸を作る *spin* cotton into thread.

つむじ a hair whorl [the whorl of hair] on the head.
● つむじを曲げる ▶ 彼女は彼の言葉につむじを曲げた(=機嫌を損ねた) She *got cross at* his remarks.
● つむじ曲がり(人) a *perverse* (へそ曲がりの) [*con-trary*] person (米話) a crank. ● 彼は生まれつきつむじ曲がりだ He is *perverse* by nature./He was born *perverse* (米話) *cranky*].

つむじかぜ つむじ風 a whirlwind.

つむる (閉じる) close, shut*. (⇨つぶる)

***つめ 爪** ❶ 〚手の指の〛 a nail. ● 手の指のつめは fingernail, 足の指のつめは toenail という) ● つめを短く切っておく keep one's *nails* clipped. (❗clipped は過去分詞で補語) ● つめをかむ bite one's *nails*. (❗比喩的に「いらいらする」「悔しがる」の意も表す) ● つめの手入れをする do [manicure] one's *nails*. ▶ つめを切らなければいけない You must cut [clip, 切りそろえる) trim] your *nails*./Your *nails* need cutting [clipping, trimming]. ● 彼のつめは長く伸びていた He let his *fingernails* grow long./He had long *fingernails*. (❗自分の意志で長く伸ばしている場合は He wore [was growing] his *fingernails* long. という)
❷ 〚鳥や獣などの〛a claw, (ワシなどの猛鳥の) a talon. (❗2 語とも通例複数形で) ● つめを立てる fasten [bury] 《its》 claws 《into》. ● つめを隠す(=ひっこめる) draw in 《its》 *claws*. ● つめをとぐ sharpen 《its》 *claws*. (❗比喩的に人にも用いる) ● つめで穴を掘る *claw* a hole. ▶ 能ある鷹(たか)はつめを隠す 'A wise hawk does not show his *talons* [×claws]'./(ことわざ) (静かな川は深い; ずる)賢い人はあまりしゃべらない) Still waters run deep. (事情 米英では無口であることはマイナスのイメージを伴う傾向の方が強い)
❸ 〚琴・ギターなどの〛 a plectrum 《徴 ~s, plectra》, 《話》 a pick.
● つめに火をともす ▶ 一家はつめに火をともすような暮らしをしていた They lived a *miserly* /máizərli/ [a *stingy*] life./(その日暮らしをしていた) They lived from hand to mouth. (❗後の方は「備えをせずに暮らす」という意もある)

つめ 詰め (将棋の) checkmating; (最終段階での行動) one's actions at the final stage. ▶ 詰めが甘かった (=最終段階で慎重でなかった) I was not prudent [careful] enough at the final stage.

─づめ -詰め ❶ 〚…に詰め込まれた〛 ● ワインをびん詰めにする *bottle* wine. ● クッキーを箱詰めにする *pack* cookies *in a box*. ● 箱詰めのリンゴ apples *packed in a case* [*a carton*]. ● 400 字詰めの原稿用紙 a sheet of 400-character manuscript paper.
❷ 〚(継続して)...し通し〛 ● 働きづめる keep [go on] working. ● 満員バスで立ちづめだった I had to *stand* [×keep *standing*] *all the way* in a jampacked bus.
❸ 〚…勤務の〛 ● 国会詰めの記者 a newsperson *assigned to* the Diet. ▶ 彼は本社詰めだ[になった] He *works at* [*has been transferred to*] the head office.

つめあと 爪跡 (つめを立てた跡) a nail [a claw] mark; (ひっかいた跡) a scratch. ● 戦争の爪跡 the *scars of war*. (❗a scar は切り傷ややけどの跡などいつまでも残るもの) ▶ 彼女の腕に猫の爪跡が残っている She has a *scratch* on her arm from a cat. ▶ 10 月の洪水の爪跡がまだ残っている There are still *traces of the damage* from the October flood.

つめあわせ 詰め合わせ 图 (各種取り合わせたもの) an assortment. ● チョコレートの詰め合わせを 1 箱彼に送る send him a box of *assorted* chocolates.
── 詰め合わせる 形 assorted.

つめいん 爪印 a thumbprint. (⇨拇印(ぼいん))

つめえり 詰め襟 (立ち襟) a stand-up (↔turn-down) collar /kάlər/.

つめかえる 詰め替える (再び満たす) refill; (詰め直す) repack.

つめかける 詰め掛ける 〚大勢の人が押しかける〛 crowd, throng; 〚取り囲む〛 besiege. ▶ 数万人の観客がスタジアムに詰めかけた Tens of thousands of spectators *crowded* the stadium. ▶ その女優に報道陣が詰めかけた Reporters *crowded around* [*besieged*] the actress.

つめきり 爪切り nail clippers; (はさみ式) nail scissors. (❗いずれも複数扱い. 数えるときは a pair [two pairs] of で動詞は pair を受ける数に呼応する)

つめきる 詰め切る (患者に詰めきる(=常に付き添う) *attend* a patient all the time.

つめご 詰め碁 a go problem.

つめこみ 詰め込み ●詰め込み教育 the cramming system of education. ●詰め込み教育[勉強]をする cram 《him》[cram]《for an exam》. ●詰め込み主義 cramming.

つめこむ 詰め込む pack; (無理やり) cram (-mm-); (急いで乱雑に) stuff; (ぎっしり) jam (-mm-); [押し込む] crowd. (⇨詰める, 押し込む) ●食物を腹いっぱい詰め込む stuff oneself with food; gorge (oneself) on [with] food. ●頭に知識を詰め込む cram knowledge; force knowledge into one's head. ▶彼はスーツケースに衣類を詰め込んだ He packed clothes into [in] his suitcase [packed his suitcase with his clothes]. ▶50名の生徒が小教室に詰め込まれた Fifty pupils were crammed [were jammed, were packed, were crowded] into the small classroom./The small classroom was crammed [was jammed, was packed, was crowded] with fifty pupils. ▶徹夜で詰めこんだ知識は大脳に刻み込まれることなく, 数日のうちに消えてしまう Knowledge crammed in overnight is not instilled in the cerebrum and vanishes in a few days.

つめしょ 詰所 (衛兵の) a guardroom; a guardhouse; (守衛の) a lodge; (沿岸警備隊の) a coast-guard station.

つめしょうぎ 詰め将棋 a *shogi* problem.

:つめたい 冷たい [形] ❶[温度の] cold (↔hot); (快く冷たい) cool (↔warm); (不快に冷たい) chilly; (凍りつくほど) freezing; (氷のように) icy. ●冷たい水 cold water. ●冷たいレモネード cool lemonade. ●冷たいコーヒー cold [ice(d)] coffee. ●氷のように冷たい風 an icy wind. ▶北風は身を切るように冷たい The north wind is cutting [biting] cold. (❗ cutting, biting は副詞的に cold を修飾する) ●冷たいものでもどうですか How [What] about something cold to drink?/How about a cold drink? ❷[態度などが] (冷淡な) cold; (平然とした) cool; (心の冷たい) cold-hearted. ●冷たい歓迎を受ける receive a cool [a chilly] welcome. ●冷たい目で冷たい目で見る look at 《him》coldly; (氷のように冷たいなざしでにらむ) give 《him》an ice cold stare. ▶彼は心の冷たい人だ He is a cold-hearted man./He has a cold heart. ▶なんて冷たいことを言うの！ What a heartless thing to say! ▶彼女は初めて出会ったとき私にとても冷たかった She was very cold to me [treated me very coldly] when we first met. (❗ 前の方は態度の, 後の方は行為の冷たさをいう)

── **冷たくなる** [動] [熱が冷める] get* cold; [愛情がなくなる] cool off (⇨冷める); [死ぬ] die (～d; dying), be dead (and cold). ▶彼女は私に冷たくなってきた She has cooled off toward me.

『つめたいよるに』 On a Cold Night. (参考) 江國香織の小説)

つめのあか 爪の垢 ▶彼にはつめのあかほども(=少しも)誠意がない He doesn't have an atom of sincerity. ●つめのあかをせんじて飲む ▶彼のつめのあかをせんじて飲んで(=教訓を得て), もっと分別をわきまえなさい You should take a lesson from him [(見習う) learn from his example] and know better.

つめばら 詰め腹 ●詰め腹を切らされる (無理に辞職させられる) be forced to resign.

つめもの 詰め物 (包装用) padding; (当てもの) packing; (歯の) a filling; (料理用の鳥などの) (a) stuffing. ●詰め物をする a pad; fill; stuff. ▶彼らはガラス食器を保護するためにたくさん詰め物をした They used a lot of padding to protect the glassware. ▶彼はサンタクロースらしくおなかに詰め物をした He padded his stomach so that he

would look (more) like Santa Claus /sǽntə klɔ̀ːz/.

翻訳のこころ 少し前に続けていた治療の際の詰物がとれて, そこに何かの繊維がきつくい込んだらしい(竹西寛子『蘭』) The filling, that was put in his tooth for the treatment he received a while ago, came off. And in its place, some kind of fiber seems to have gotten tightly lodged. (❗ filling には「(もちのあんなどの)詰め物」の意もあるので, ここでは in his tooth と限定するとよい)

つめやすり 爪鑢 a nail file.

つめよる 詰め寄る ●返事しろと彼に詰め寄る(=返事を迫る) press him for an answer.

:つめる 詰める ❶[容器・空所を] pack; (満たす) fill; (急いで乱雑に) stuff; (狭い場所にぎっしり) jam (-mm-); (狭い場所に無理やり) cram (-mm-); [穴などをふさぐ] stop (-pp-) ... (up); (栓で) plug (-gg-) ... (up). (⇨詰め込む) ●弁当を詰めてもらう pack 《his》lunch. ●虫歯を詰めてもらう have one's cavity [a tooth] filled 《with gold》. ●冷蔵庫に食物を詰めすぎる jam too much food into a refrigerator. ●壁の割れ目にしっくいを詰める stop (up) [fill in] a crack in the wall with plaster. ▶彼は箱にリンゴを詰めた He packed [put] apples in [into] the box./He packed the box with apples. ▶男はかばんに紙幣を(あふれるほど)詰めて逃げた The man crammed [stuffed] the bank notes into his bag and ran off. ▶ドアで指を詰めた(=はさんだ) I got my finger caught [pinched] in the door./The door caught [pinched] my finger./I pinched my finger in the door. (❗ 後の二つの方が普通)

❷[間隔を] (席などを詰める) move over [up]; (列などで間を詰める) move 《座る sit*, 《立つ》stand*》closer together; (乗り物などで入り口から奥に進む) move [pass] along [down] (a bus) (❗ pass の方が move よりも「ずっと奥に」を含意する); step (-pp-) (well) back into the car (❗ エレベーターの場合). ●詰めて書く write close(ly) (together). ●外野手間を詰める[野球] bunch the outfielders. (参考) 右中間・左中間を詰めた守備を取ること) ●二遊間を詰める play a batter up the middle. ▶詰めてくださってありがとう Thank you for moving over for me. (❗ move over は「席を詰める」の意) ▶列の前の方へ詰めてください Move [Step] up to the front of the line.

❸[休みなく続ける] ●根を詰めて(=休憩をとらずに)働く work without taking a break; (仕事に集中する) concentrate on one's work.

❹[短くする] (丈を) take* ... up, shorten (↔let down); (幅を) take ... in (↔let ... out). ▶スカートのウエストを少し [2 センチ] 詰めてもらった I hád the waist of my skirt taken in a little [2 centimeters]./I hád my skirt taken in a little [2 centimeters] at the waist.

❺[出費を減らす] cut* back on 《expenditure》. (⇨切り詰める)

❻[出かけて勤務する] ▶夜でも常に 2 人の医師が詰めています(=任務についている) There are always two doctors on duty even at night.

❼[議論などを] ●問題をもっと詰める(=より詳しく論じる) discuss the matter in more detail [further, more thoroughly].

:つもり ❶[意図] (an) intention; (目的) a purpose. ①[～のつもり] ▶それは冗談のつもりだった I meant /mént/ it as [for] a joke./It was meant [was intended] as a joke. (❗ この用法の intend は通例受身) ▶この絵は私を描いたつもりですか Is this picture

つもる

meant [intended] to be me? ▶遊びのつもりでたばこを吸い始めたがやめられなくなった I started smoking (*just*) *for fun* [*for the fun of it*], but never gave it up.

❷【つもりで】 ▶彼は君を手伝うつもりでここへ来た He came here *to help* [*for the purpose of* helping, *with the intention of* helping] you. (!後の二つは堅い言い方) ▶どういうつもりでそんなことを言うのか What do you *mean by* (saying) that? (!しばしば挑戦的な意味を含む)

❸【…するつもりである】 be going to do; be doing; be planning to do, be thinking of doing; mean to do, intend to do.

> 使い分け **be going to** do すでに決定済みの計画・予定を表すが、それほど確実性は高くなく比較的先のことにも使える。通例動作動詞を従え、くだけた会話ではしばしば be gonna /gə(:)nə/ do となる。
> **be doing** 通例時の副詞を伴い、すでに取り決められた近い未来の確実な予定を表す。心理的・実質的に準備段階に入っていることを暗示する。
> **be planning to do, be thinking of** doing 計画・考慮の途中でまだ確実には決めていないことを表す。
> **mean to** do 本来の意図を実際の結果と対比するときに用いることが多い。
> **intend to** do 強い意志を暗示するやや堅い語。《話》で用いると強意的に響く。

▶来年イギリスに行くつもりです I'm *going to go* [*I'm going*] to Britain next year. (!go, come を用いる場合は、be going to go [come] より be going [coming] を用いる方が普通)/I'm *thinking of going* [*planning to go*, 《話》 *planning on going*, 《主に米話》 *figuring on going*] to Britain next year./I *intend* [*mean*] *to* go to Britain next year. ▶今晩は外で食事するつもりです I'm *going to eat* [*I'm eating*] out this evening. (!(1) 現在進行形は「進行中」の意と区別するために未来を示す副詞を伴うのが普通だが、×I'm *meeting* him next year [some time]. のように違い、または漠然とした未来のことには用いない. (2) will を用いると話の最中に外で食事をする決心をしたことになり、「…しよう」に近くなる) ▶彼は大きくなったら教師になるつもりです He *is going to* [×*will*] be a teacher when he grows up. (!(1) be going to が遠い将来のことを表すときは通例、未来をある副詞(句)が必要. (2) will では話し手の未来に関する推量を表すので、ここは不可) ▶彼は彼女に会うつもりだった He *was going to* see her. (!厳密には会ったかどうかは不明だが、会わなかったことを表す文脈で用いられることが多い(⇨会話))/He *had meant* [*had intended*] *to* see her./He *meant* [*intended*] *to* have seen her. (!後2例のように過去完了形・完了不定詞を用いると通例実現しなかった過去の意図を表す) ▶あなたの感情を傷つけるつもりはなかった I didn't *mean* [*intend*] *to* hurt you./I had no *intention of* hurting you. (!前の方が普通)

▶もしごいっしょしてくださるおつもりでしたらお宅へお迎えにあがります If you *are going to* [*will*] join us, we'll pick you up at your place. (!この will は未来に従属節で条件節可も)

> 会話「今日先生から電話があったのよ」「何で？」「太郎君とけんかしたんだって。本当なの」「うん。話すつもりだったんだけど忘れてたんだ」"Your teacher called today." "Oh, what did he say?" "You got into a fight with Taro. Is this true?" "Yeah. I *was going to* tell you about it, but I forgot."

❷【思い込み】 ▶彼女は自分では美人のつもりでいる She *thinks* [(信じている) *believes*] (*that*) she is beautiful./《書》 She *thinks* herself (*to be*) [*believes* herself *to be*] beautiful. (!think では to be を通例省略することもあるが、信念を強く表す場合は省略しない) ▶あの子は怪物のつもりだ(＝ふりをしている) That child *is making believe* (that) he is a monster.

❸【心構え】 ▶来春ニューヨーク支店に転勤してもらうことになったので、そのつもりでいてくれ We decided that you would be transferred to the New York branch next spring, so prepare yourself [*get ready*] for it.

*つもる **積もる** ❶【雪・ほこり・借金などが】 (…の状態にある) lie*; (積み重なる) pile up; (堆積する) accumulate; (総計…になる) add up [amount] to .... ▶雪が2メートルほど積もった The snow *lay* about two meters deep on the ground./The snow *piled* [*heaped*] *up* about two meters high. ▶この雪は積もるでしょう The snow will *stay*. ▶床にほこりが厚く積もっていた Dust *lay* thick on the floor./The floor *was* thickly *covered* with dust. ▶彼の借金は積もり積もって100万円を越えた His debts *ran up to* over one million yen.

❷【話・恨みなどが】 ▶彼に積もる(＝根深い)恨みがある I have a *deep-rooted* hatred toward him./(うっ積した憤り) I have *pent-up* resentment at [against] him.

❸【見積もる】 estimate. (⇨見積もる)

●積もる話 ▶積もる話がある have a lot [a great deal] to talk about; have quite a story to tell.

*つや **艶** ❶【光沢】 (a) gloss; (a) luster; (a) polish; (a) sheen. (⇨光沢)

> 使い分け **gloss** 化粧品、光沢剤の塗布、研磨、特別な仕上げなどによる表面的なつや。
> **luster** 光の反射によってできるつや。
> **polish** 家具・つめなどを磨いて出したつや。
> **sheen** 布・羽毛・鉱物などの表面のつや。

●つやのない色 a *dull* color. ●つやを出す (磨いて) polish 《it》 (up); (光沢剤を塗って) put polish on 《it》. ▶彼女の髪には美しいつやがある Her hair has a lovely *gloss* [*luster*, *sheen*]./She has *glossy* [《主に書》*lustrous*] hair./Her hair is *glossy*. ▶真鍮(ﾁｭｳ)はよく磨くとつやが出る Good polishing gives brass a *luster*./Brass gets a *luster* if you polish it up. ▶うちの体は病気になると毛のつやがなくなる When our cat is sick, her fur loses its *luster*.

❷【若々しさ】 ●つやのある(＝豊かで美しい)声 a *mellow* voice. ●つやのない(＝血色の悪い)顔 a *sallow* (↔a *glowing*) face.

❸【おもしろ味】 ●話につやをつける(＝粉飾する) dress a story up; (《やや書》) embellish a story.

つや 通夜 ●通夜を営む keep an all-night watch [keep vigil] over a dead body. ▶A 氏の通夜は月曜日今後 7 時から祥雲寺にて執り行われます *All-night wakes* [*A vigil*] *for* Mr. A will be held at the Shoun-ji Temple at [×*from*] 7 p.m. Monday.

つやけし 艶消し matting; (ガラス・金属の) frosting; [一座の興をそぐ人]《話》 a wet blanket. ●つや消しなことを言う spoil [kill] the *interest* of a story. ●つや消しガラス frosted glass. ●つや消し写真 a mat(ted) photograph; a photograph with a mat finish. ●つや消し塗料 flat paint.

つやだし 艶出し polishing; (金属の) burnishing; (光沢) polish.

つやっぽい 艶っぽい ●つやっぽい話 a *love* story. ●つやっぽい目つき an *amorous* look. ●つやっぽいしぐさ a *coquettish* manner. ▶浴衣を着た幸子はとてもつやっぽかった Sachiko was very *sexy* in her *yukata*.

つやつや　(光沢のある様子) luster. ●新車のつやつや the *luster* of a new car. ●つやつやした絹[髪] *glossy* silk [hair]. ●つやつやした肌の色[顔色]をしている have a *glowing* complexion.

つやぶきん　艶布巾　a polishing cloth.

つやぼくろ　艶黒子　a woman's mole beside her lips.

つやめく　艶めく　(つやつやして見える) glossy; shiny; (色気がある) sexy, sexually attractive.

つややか　艶やか　── 艶やかな 形　glossy; sleek; shiny; lustrous.

*__つゆ__　露　(a) dew; (露のしずく) a dewdrop. ●今朝牧草地にたくさん降りた　We had [There was] a heavy *dew* all over the meadow this morning. (!) A heavy *dew* fell [formed] on…. のようにもいえる) ●草[芝]にはまだ露でぬれている The grass is still *dewy* [*wet with dew*]. (!) (1) 後の方が普通. (2)「露を含んできらきら光っている」なら … is glittering with dew.) ●それについては露ほども(＝少しも)知らなかった I did *not* know anything *at all* [*in the least*] about it.

*__つゆ__　梅雨　the rainy [wet] season. ●空梅雨 a dry *rainy season*. ●梅雨はいつ始まりますか When will the *rainy season* set in? ●日本列島はそろそろ梅雨に入ってきた The Japanese islands are gradually entering *the rainy season*./We're gradually entering *the rainy season* in the Japanese islands. ●梅雨が明けた The *rainy season* is over. ●梅雨明けしたとみられる The rainy season appears to be over now.
●梅雨明け the end of the rainy season. ●梅雨入り the start of the rainy season. ●梅雨晴れ a spell of (xa) nice weather during the rainy season.

つゆ　汁　soup (⇨汁(⅙)); (水分) moisture. ●そばつゆ sauce dip for *soba*.

つゆくさ　露草〖植物〗a dayflower; (ムラサキツユクサ) a spiderwort.

つゆはらい　露払い　❶［先駆け］a forerunner; a herald. ❷［前座］a curtain raiser; a minor performer. ❸［相撲］a *tsuyuharai*; (説明的に) a *sumo* wrestler who leads a *yokozuna* at a ring-entering ceremony.

:**つよい**　強い 形　strong; powerful; tough.

　WORD CHOICE　強い

　strong　人や物事の持つ力・程度の強さを指す最も一般的な語．体力・精神力・影響力・経済力・軍事力ほか，色彩・光・感情・味覚などの程度の強さもさす．●強い国家[チーム; 意志; 信念; 臭い] a *strong* country [team; will; belief; smell]

　powerful　他のものに比べて，際立って影響力が強大なこと．しばしば，社会的権力・権威を含意する．●強い軍隊[リーダー; 影響力] a *powerful* force [leader; influence].

　tough　人が肉体的・精神的にたくましく，簡単には屈しないこと，または，物が丈夫で壊れないこと．●たくましき女性 a *tough* woman.

　▆ 頻度チャート ▆
　strong ████████████████████
　powerful ████████
　tough ██████
　　　　20　40　60　80　100 (%)

①【強い～】●強い国 a *strong* [a *powerful*] nation. ●強いロープ a *strong* [a *tough*] rope. ●強い風 a *strong*［(並以上の) a *high*,（凶暴な）a *violent*］wind. ●強い光 *strong*［(強烈な) *intense*］light. ●強い酒 *hard* [*strong*] liquor. ●強い信念 a *strong*［(固い) a *firm*］belief. ●強い布地 (xa) *strong*［(持ちがいい) (xa) *durable*］cloth. ●強い地震 a *strong*［a *big*,（激しい）a *severe*］earthquake. ●強いドイツなまりで speak with a *strong*［a *thick*］German accent.

②【…が[の]強い】●責任感が強い have a *strong* sense of responsibility. ●君の相手は腕っぷしがとても強そうだ Your opponent looks very *strong* [*powerful*]. ●彼は意志の強い人だ He is a *strong*-willed man / a man of *strong* will. (!) A *strong*-minded man は「気の強い人」の意) / He has a *strong* [an *iron*] will. ●今夜は風が強いThere is a *strong* wind (blowing) tonight./The wind [It] is blowing *hard* [xstrongly] tonight./It is very windy tonight. ●彼はひどい近眼なので度の強い眼鏡をかけている He wears (eye) glasses of heavy corrective lenses, because he's very short-sighted. ●君は運が強い You are very fortunate. ●小泉氏は改革者という印象が強い We have a *strong* impression that Mr. Koizumi is a reformer. ●最近の若者は利己主義の傾向が強い Young people today have [show] a *strong* tendency to be egoistic.

③【…に強い】●歴史に強い(＝歴史が得意だ) be *strong in* [*good at*] history. ●機械に強い be *good with* (xa) machinery. (!) with では扱うのが上手の意) ●寒さに強い(＝抵抗力がある) have good *resistance* to cold. ●さびに強い金属 a metal that *resists* rust; a *rùst-resistant*[*-proof*] métal. ●彼は酒に強い(＝大酒飲み) He is a *heavy* [xa *strong*] drinker./(すぐには酔わない) He doesn't get drunk easily. (!) He has a high (⇔a low) tolerance for liquor. ともいえる) ●この建物は地震に強い(＝耐震だ) This building is earthquake-*resistant*. (!) earthquake-proof は「免震の」の意)

── **強く** 副　strongly; powerfully;［激しく］hard;［強固に］firmly;［強調して］emphatically. ●強く殴る人[物] *hard* [xhardly]. ●彼らは強くその計画を支持したに反対した] They *strongly* supported [opposed] the plan.

── **強くなる** 動　get* [grow*, become*] strong(er), strengthen; intensify. (⇨強まる) ●風が強くなった The wind *became stronger* [*strengthened*].

── **強くする** 動　make*《it, him》strong(er), strengthen (!) with は口語的);intensify;［つまみなどをひねって］turn … up. (⇨強める) ●運動は筋肉を強くする Exercise *makes* muscles *stronger* [*strengthens* muscles]. ●エアコンを強くしてください Please *turn up* the air conditioner.

つよがり　強がり　［虚勢］(an act [a show] of) bravado;［はったり］(a) bluff (複～s);［負け惜しみ］sour /sáuər/ grapes (!) イソップ物語から. ●強がりを言う say with *bravado*; be a lot of *bravado* 《about》; bluff; cry *sour grapes*. ●彼女の切り出した別れ話はただの強がり(＝おどし)だと彼は思った When she said she was going to leave him, he thought it was only a *bluff*.

つよがる　強がる　(⇨強がり [強がりを言う])

つよき　強き　●強きをくじき弱きを助ける crush the strong and help the weak.

つよき　強気　── 強気の 形　［積極的な, 攻撃的な］aggressive;［強硬な］strong, firm;［くじけない］not discouraged, undaunted;［楽天的な］optimis-

つよく ▶彼は何事にも[自分の発言に]強気だ He is *optimistic about* everything [*in his statements*].
- **強気相場**〖経済〗a bull [a bullish] market.

つよく 強く (⇨強い[強く])

つよごし 強腰 ●強腰に出る assume [strike, take] an aggressive [a determined] attitude 《*about*, *to*, *toward*》; take a firm [a resolute, a strong] stand 《*on*》. ▶政府は今回の税制改革問題では強腰に出た The government *took a resolute stand on* the issue of the tax reform.

つよさ 強さ 〖力・権力・能力などの〗power (❗ 体力・精神力についていう場合は複数形でも用いられる); 〖肉体・精神・物の〗strength; 〖色・光・調子・感情などの〗intensity. ● 筋肉の強さ muscle *power*. ▶アメリカ経済の強さ the economic *power* [*strength*] of the U.S.A. ▶日差しの強さ the *intensity* [*strength*] of the sunlight. ▶ロープの強さを調べる test the *strength* of the rope. ▶非常時に冷静でいられる精神の強さを持つ have the *strength* of mind to remain calm during an emergency. ▶力の強さでは彼の右に出る者はいない No one can match him in *strength*. (❗ He is (the) *strongest*. でもその意は表せる)

つよび 強火 〖強い炎〗a high flame; 〖強い熱〗high heat. ●強火にかける put [cook] over a *high flame*. (⇨弱火)

つよふくみ 強含み 〖〖相場が値上がりする気配にあること〗a strong tone.

:つよまる 強まる 〖強くなる〗become* [grow*, get*] strong(er), strengthen; 〖暑さ・痛みなどが〗intensify, become intense; 〖勢いを強める〗gather strength [force]. ▶北風が午後から強まった The north wind *became stronger* [*strengthened*, *gathered strength*] in the afternoon. ▶暑さが日ごとに強まってきた The heat *is getting more and more intense* day by day./It *is getting hotter* (*and hotter*) day by day. ▶彼に対する嫌悪の情がだんだん強まってきた The hatred for him *grew on* [*upon*] me./I came to hate him *more and more*.

つよみ 強み a strong point, (a) strength; 〖利点〗an advantage. ▶ …という強みがある have the *advantage* of…. ▶英語が彼の強みだ English is his *strong point*.

:つよめる 強める 〖強化する〗strengthen; 〖程度を〗intensify; 〖信念を〗confirm; 〖強調する〗emphasize. ●故郷へのあこがれを強める *intensify* one's longing for home. ●語気を強めて命令を繰り返す repeat an order *emphatically* [〖力強く〗*forcefully*]. ▶石油ストーブの火を少し強める *turn up* the kerosene heater a little. ▶私たちは労働組合との結びつきを強めたい We want to *strengthen* our ties with the labor union.

つら 面 a face. (⇨面構え, 面の皮, 面汚し) ▶今さらどの面さげて親元へ帰ろうか How can I *have the face to* return home to my parents?/How can I return home and *face* my parents?

つらあて 面当て ●面当てを言う say spiteful things. ▶彼女は私への面当てに別の男と結婚した She married another man to *spite* me.

***つらい** 辛い 形 〖困難な〗hard, 〖話〗tough /tʌf/ (⇨苦しい); 〖苦痛な〗painful; 〖むごい〗bitter; 〖耐えがたい〗unbearable; 〖胸が張り裂けそうな〗heartbreaking.
① 【つらい～】 ●つらい生活を送る lead a *hard* [a *tough*] life. ▶こんなつらいことは生まれて初めてだ I have never had such a *hard* time [a *bitter* experience] in my life./This is the *bitterest* [the most *painful*] experience I have ever had in my life.
② 【…はつらい】 ●早起きはつらい It's *hard* [xI am hard] to get up early./〖いやだ〗I hate to get up early. ▶彼女と別れるのはつらかった It was *hard* [*painful*, *heartbreaking*] to separate from her./〖残念だった〗I was very sorry to separate [part] from her. (❗ separate は結婚などして別れる. part は物理的に離れる) ▶貧乏はつらい(=耐えがたい) Poverty is *hard to bear*./*I can't stand* poverty./Poverty is *painful*. ▶男はつらいよ It's ↘*tough* being a ↗ *man*.
会話 「それでどっちとデートするつもりなの?」「迷ってるのよ」「まったくつらいところね(=最高につらい選択だ)」"So which of the two are you going to go out with?" "I'm not sure." "(That's) the *toughest* choice, really."

— **つらく** 副 ●つらく当たる be hard 《*on* him》; 〖厳しく扱う〗treat 《him》 harshly.

-づらい (⇨-にくい)

つらがまえ 面構え 〖顔付き〗a look. ●不敵な面構え 《have》a fearless [a daring] *look*.

つらさ 辛さ pain; bitterness. ●別れのつらさ the *pain* [〖悲しみ〗*sorrow*] of parting [separation].

つらだましい 面魂 ●不屈の面魂をしている look invincible.

つらつら fully. (⇨つくづく, よくよく)

つらなる 連なる 〖遠く連なる山々〗a distant *range* of mountains. ▶山脈が南北に連なっている(=延びている) The mountains *range* [*run*, *stretch*, *extend*] north and south.

つらにくい 面憎い hateful [detestable, abominable] 《children》.

***つらぬく** 貫く ❶〖貫通する〗pénetràte; 〖とがった先で穴をあける〗pierce; 〖通り抜ける〗go* through…. ▶弾丸が彼の胸を貫いた A bullet *penetrated* [*pierced*, *went through*] his chest. ▶1本の川がその町を貫いて流れている A river *runs* [*flows*] *through* the town. (❗ 進行形にしない)
❷〖貫徹する〗●意志を貫く *carry out* one's intention. ●主義を貫く(=固守する) *stick to* one's principles.

つらねる 連ねる 〖沿って並ぶ〗line; 〖名を載せられている〗be (put) on the list 《*of*》. ▶有名店が通りに軒を連ねている The street *is lined with* famous shops./Famous shops *line* the street. (❗ 前の方が普通)

つらのかわ 面の皮 ▶いい面の皮だ It serves [〖話〗Serve(s)] him [you, them] right!
●**面の皮が厚い** ▶彼は面の皮が厚い He is thick-skinned. (⇨厚かましい)
●**面の皮をはぐ** ●奴の面の皮をはぐ(=恥をかかせる) humiliate (⇨鼻っ柱); 〖犯罪者などの正体を暴く〗expose [unmask] him.

つらよごし 面汚し 〖不名誉となる人〗a disgrace 《*to*》; 〖書〗a dishonor 《*to*》. (❗ ともに単数形でのみ用いる) ▶彼らは学校の面汚しだ They're a *disgrace to* our school.

つらら 氷柱 an icicle /áisikl/. (❗ 通例複数形で) ▶冬になると軒先につららができる Icicles hang from the roof in the winter. (❗ 物理学的表現では, 動詞は form)

つられる 釣られる 〖その気にさせられる〗be tempted 《*to do*》. ▶値段の安さにつられてその服を買った I *was tempted to* buy the dress because it was so inexpensive./The low price *tempted* me to buy the dress. (❗ 前の方が普通)

***つり** 釣り ❶〖魚釣り〗fishing; 〖釣りざおによる〗angling.
① 【～釣り】 ●沖[海; 川]釣り offshore [sea;

つり [river] fishing. (⇨磯釣り) ・夜釣り night fishing. ・アユ釣りに出かける go ayu fishing [fishing for ayu].

②【釣りが】▶彼は釣りがうまい He is good at fishing./He is a good angler. ▶彼は釣りが趣味です He is fond of [likes] fishing./Fishing is his favorite amusement. (❗Fishing is his hobby. ともいえるが幼稚な言い方)

③【釣りに[から]】▶釣りから帰る return home from a fishing trip. ▶川に釣りに行こう Let's go fishing in [at, ×to] the river./Let's go to the river to fish [go fishing].

④【釣りを】▶1日中川でマス釣りをしたが1匹も釣れなかった I fished for trout in the river [fished the river for trout] all day and caught nothing. (❗(1)「10匹釣った」は I caught [×fished] ten trout. で, 今は fish は用いない. (2) trout は単・複同形)

❷ [釣り銭] change. (⇨釣り銭) ▶お釣りを100円ごまかす(=少なく渡す) shortchange 100 yen. ▶このお釣り, まちがっているみたい I think you've given me the wrong change.

・釣り糸 a fishline; a (fishing) line. ・釣り具 (集合的) fishing tackle. ・釣りざお a fishing ròd [pòle]. (❗単に rod ともいう) ・釣り仲間 a fishing compànion; a fellow angler. (⇨仲間) ・釣り場 a fishing plàce [spòt]. ・釣り針 a fishhook. (❗単に hook ともいう) ・釣り人 an angler, a fisherman (🅱 -men). (❗(1) fisherman は「漁師」の意もある. (2) fisher は女性以外では廃語) ・釣り舟 a fishing boat. (❗「漁船」の意もある) ・釣り堀 a fishing pònd.

つり 吊り 〖相撲〗 tsuri, (説明的に) lifting up one's opponent.

*つりあい 釣り合い balance; proportion. (❗前の方は主に二つ以上の物の重さ・位置・力などが釣り合うこと. 後の方は全体から見て大きさの割合, 位置などが適切で美しいこと) (⇨調和, バランス) ・栄養面で釣り合いのとれた食事 a (well-)balanced diet. ・体の釣り合いを保つ[失う] keep [lose] one's balance. ・力の釣り合いを崩す upset [disturb, destroy] the balance of power. ・つま先で立って体の釣り合いをとる balance (oneself) on one's toes.

*つりあう 釣り合う 〖平衡を保つ〗 balance 《with》; 〖比例している〗 be in proportion 《to, with》; 〖似合う〗 match (⇨調和する, 合う). ▶今月の出費は収入と釣り合った Our expenditure for this month has balanced with our income./Our expenditure and income has balanced (with each other) this month. ▶その犬の短い足は長い胴体と釣り合っていなかった The dog's short legs were not in [were out of] proportion to its long body. ▶そのシャンデリアとロココ風の家具はよく釣り合っている The chandelier and the rococo furniture match well [are a good match]./The chandelier goes well with the rococo furniture. ▶彼女はうちの息子とは釣り合わない She is not a good match for our son. (❗この match は堅いやや古風な語で「結婚相手」の意)

つりあげる 吊り上げる (上げる) lift; (まゆなどを) raise (one's eyebrows); (価格などを) raise (the prices) by manipulation; 《話》 jack ... up. ▶石油の価格を不当につり上げる jack up oil prices unfairly.

つりあげる 釣り上げる land. ・サケを釣り上げる land [(リールで引き上げる) reel in] salmon /sǽmən/.

つりおとし 釣り落とし 〖相撲〗 tsuriotoshi; lifting body slam.

つりおとす 釣り落とす fail to land a fish.

つりがき 釣り書き (説明的に) a brief account of one's personal history and family background.

つりがね 釣り鐘 a suspended temple bell.

つりがねそう 釣り鐘草 〖植物〗 a (dotted) bellflower.

つりかわ 釣り革 a strap. ・つり革につかまる hold (onto) a strap; (ぶら下がる) hang onto a strap.

つりこむ 釣り込む ・話に釣り込まれる be charmed [carried away] by one's story [speech].

つりさがる 吊り下がる hang* (down) 《from》; (ぶら下がる) dangle 《from》.

つりさげる 吊り下げる (吊るす) hang*; (ぶら下げる) dangle.

つり(せん) 釣り(銭) change. (⇨釣り ❷) ▶彼に500円釣り銭を出した I gave him 500 yen change. ▶釣り銭おことわり(=出是ません)《掲示》 No change given./(釣り銭なしで願います) Exact fare, please.

つりだし 釣り出し 〖相撲〗 tsuridashi; lift out.

つりだな 吊り棚 (天井からつり下げた棚) a shelf hung from the ceiling; (ぶら下がった棚) a hanging shelf (🅱 shelves).

つりだま 釣り球 〖野球〗 a bait pitch. ・釣り球に手を出す go for a bait pitch. ・釣り球で打者を釣る bait a batter.

つりて 吊り手 (蚊帳の) a hanger; (吊り革) a strap.

つりどこ 釣り床 a hammock. (⇨ハンモック)

つりばし 吊り橋 (山あいの) a rope bridge; (比較的大規模の) a suspension bridge.

つりひも 吊り紐 (上げ下げ窓の) a sash cord [line].

つりめ 吊り目 图 slant eyes. ── 吊り目の 圏 slant-eyed.

つりわ 吊り輪 〖体操〗 the rings.

つる 蔓 〖植物〗 (巻きひげ状の) a tendril; (サツマイモなど地面をはう) a runner; 〖眼鏡の〗 bows.

・つる植物 a vine; (地面・壁などをはう) a creeper.

つる 釣る ❶ 〖魚を〗 catch; (...を求めて釣りをする) fish 《for》. (⇨釣り ❶ ⑤) ▶この湖ではマスがよく釣れる There is good trout fishing in the lake.

[会話]「釣れますか」「釣れませんな」 "Do you catch [have] any?" "None." (❗釣り仲間では Any? だけで済ますことも多い)

[会話]「釣れたかい」「たくさん釣れたよ」 "Have you caught any (fish)?" "Yes. I've had a big catch."

❷ 〖さそう〗 tempt. ▶広告に釣られてそれを買った The advertisement tempted me to buy it. (⇨釣られる)

つる 弦 (弓の) a bowstring /bóustrìŋ/.

つる 鶴 〖鳥〗 a crane.

・鶴の一声 The king's word is more than another man's oath. ▶彼の鶴の一声で計画は中止された One word from him and the project was stopped.

・鶴は千年亀は万年 'A crane lives a thousand (years) and a tortoise ten thousand years.'/(鶴は長寿と幸運の象徴である) A crane and a tortoise are symbols of longevity and good fortune.

つる 吊る hang*, suspend (❗hang より堅い語); 〖ぶらぶらさせる〗 swing*; (ひもでつるす) string. ・ランプを鎖で天井からつる hang a lamp on [×to] a chain from the ceiling; suspend a lamp by a chain from the ceiling. ・クリスマスツリーにつられた飾り物 ornaments hung on a Christmas tree. ・木の間にハンモックをつる hang [swing, string] a hammock between the trees. ・棚をつる(=壁に取りつける) fix a shelf to [×on] the wall. ・首をつる hang oneself. (❗この hang の過去・過去分詞は

hanged)

つる 攣る (こむら返りを起こす) get* [have*] (a) cramp 《in one's leg》.

つるかめ 鶴亀 〖縁起直しに言う言葉〗● 二度と戦争が起こりませんように, 鶴亀, 鶴亀 God [Heaven] forbid 《that》 another war should break out.

つるくさ 蔓草 a vine /váin/; (表面をはうもの) a creeper; (はい上がるもの) a climber.

つるし 吊るし ●つるしの(=既製の)スーツ a ready-made suit. ●つるしで買う buy 《a suit》 off the rack.

つるしあげ 吊るし上げ (いんちき裁判) a kangaroo court. ●つるし上げを食う be subjected to a kangaroo court.

つるしあげる 吊るし上げる set up [hold] a kangaroo court to try 《him》; (厳しく詰問する) cross-examine 《him》 《about》.

つるしがき 吊るし柿 a persimmon peeled and hung up to dry.

つるす 吊るす hang*. (⇨吊〈つ〉る)

つるつる ❶ [滑りやすい] slippery. ▶床はつるつるだから気をつけて Be careful. The floor is very slippery.
❷ 〖表面がすべすべしている〗 smooth; (柔らかくてつやのある) silky. ●石をつるつるになるまで磨く grind a stone until its surface is smooth. ▶彼女の肌はつるつるしている She has silky [smooth] skin.
❸ 〖油っこく〗 oily, well-oiled; (ワックスを塗って) waxed. ●滑る前にスキーを(ワックスで)つるつるにする Skis are waxed before they are used.
❹ 〖はげで〗 bald /bɔ́ːld/. ▶彼は頭がつるつるだ He has a bald head./He is bald [bald-headed].
❺ 〖うどんなどを飲み込む音〗 ▶日本ではうどんをつるつる音を立てて食べるのは許される In Japan one is allowed to eat one's noodles with a slurping sound./〚話〛 It's OK in Japan to slurp one's noodle soup.

つるはし 鶴嘴 a pickax, 〚話〛 a pick.

つるばら 蔓薔薇 〖植物〗 a climbing [a rambling] rose; a rambler.

つるべ 釣瓶 a well bucket.

つるべうち 釣瓶撃ち ●鉄砲を釣瓶撃ちにする(=続けざまに撃つ) blaze away 《at》; fire continuously with guns.

つるべおとし 釣瓶落とし ●秋の日は釣瓶落とし(=沈むのが早い) (秋) 〚成句〛

つるむ 〖交尾する〗 mate 《with》; copulate 《with》; 〖一緒に行動する〗 hang out 《with》; spend a lot of time 《with》.

つるりと ❶ 〖滑るさま〗 ●つるりと滑べる slip 《on the floor》. (❗ slip の中に「あっという間に」「思いがけなく」という意が含まれている) ●コメディアンはバナナの皮を踏んでつるりと滑べっておどけてみせた The comedian tried to be funny by slipping on a banana skin.
❷ 〖皮などが大きくむけるさま〗 ▶トマトの皮はゆでるとつるりと (楽に)むける Tomato skins peel (off) easily after [when] they are boiled.

つれ 連れ ❶ 〖人〗 a companion; 〖集合的〗 company; 〖状態〗 company. (⇨仲間) ●連れになる fall into company 《with him》. (⇨一緒) ▶お連れ様は何人ですか (一行の人数を尋ねて) How many are there in your party, sir?
–づれ –連れ (同伴して) with .... ▶夫婦 2 人連れの married couple. ●子供連れで旅行する travel with one's children.

つれあい 連れ合い one's spouse. (⇨配偶者)

つれこ 連れ子 one's son [daughter] by one's previous marriage.

つれこむ 連れ込む (連れて行く[来る]) take* [bring*] 《to a hotel, into a room》.

つれさる 連れ去る take*... away [off]; (誘拐する) kidnap 《-pp-》, carry ... off.

つれそう 連れ添う (夫婦になって共に生活する) be married 《to》. ●30年連れ添った妻 one's wife of thirty years. ▶私たちは連れ添って 30 年になります We have been married for thirty years.

つれだす 連れ出す take*... out. ●散歩[昼食]に連れ出す take him out for a walk [to lunch]. ▶馬を馬小屋から連れ出しなさい Take the horses out of the stable.

つれだつ 連れ立つ ●連れ立って (...といっしょに) with ...; (いっしょに) together. (⇨一緒に)

つれない 徒然 ●つれないを慰める kill time.

つれづれぐさ『徒然草』*Essays in Idleness*. (参考 兼好法師の随筆)

〚古今ことばの系譜〛**『徒然草』**
師のいはく、「初心の人、二つの矢を持つことなかれ. 後(のち)の矢を頼みて、初めの矢に等閑(なほざり)の心あり. 毎度ただ得失なく、この一矢に定むべしと思へ」と言ふ. His teacher said, "A beginner should not hold two arrows. It will make him rely on the second arrow and be careless with the first. Each time you shoot you should think not of hitting or missing the target but of making this one the decisive arrow." (Donald Keene) (❗(1)「得失」はこの場合 profit and loss であるが「的に当たるか外れるか」という意味なので, その文脈上の具体的な意味を訳している. (2) decisive は「それでもって勝負を決める」の意)

–つれて as ...; with .... (⇨従って) ●春が近づくにつれて as spring approaches; with the approach of spring. (❗前の方が口語的) ●月日がたつにつれて (時間) with the passage of time; (年月) as the years go by; with the years. ▶彼は年をとるにつれて優しくなった As he got older, he became kinder [he's got mellower]./The older he got, the kinder he became.

つれていく 連れて行く take*; (聞き手の所へ) bring*; 〖連れ去る〗 take ... away 《to》; 〖案内する〗(先に立って) lead*, (同行して) guide. ●彼を急いで病院に連れて行く rush him to the hospital. ▶太郎をいっしょにコンサート[ピクニック;ドライブ]に連れて行ってはどうですか Why don't you take Taro to the concert [on a picnic; for a drive] with you)? ▶彼は私たちを旅行に連れて行ってくれた He led [took, guided] us on a trip. ▶パーティーには彼を連れて行っていいですか(電話で) Can I bring [take] my boyfriend along to your party [to your party with me]? (⇨行く) ●強盗はつかまって警察へ連れて行かれた The robber was caught and taken away to the police.

つれてかえる 連れて帰る (連れて帰って来る[行く]) bring* [take*] ... home [back] (❗ home では「自宅・自国に」; (行って連れて帰って来る) (go* and) get*, 《主に英》 fetch. ▶今手がはなせないので, あなた保育所へ行って子供を連れて帰ってくれないかしら I'm tied up right now. Could you go and get [fetch] the kid from the day nursery?

つれてくる 連れて来る bring*; (行って連れて来る) (go* and) get* (❗〚話〛では go to ... の代わりに go and ... を用い, it がしばしば省略される), 《主に英》 fetch. ▶ぜひ奥さんもパーティーに連れて来てください Please dó bring your wife to the party with you./Please dó bring your wife along [around] to the party. (❗ do は強意の助動詞) ▶私は大急ぎで医者を連れて来た I ran and got [《主に英》fetched] a doctor.

つれない 〖不親切な〗 unkind, unfriendly; 〖冷淡な〗

cold, cold-hearted. ◦つれなくする treat 《him》 *unkindly* [*coldly*]. ◦つれない女 a *cold-hearted* woman. ▶彼がメリーにデートを申し込んだとき彼女はつれなく(=そっけなく)断わった When he asked Mary for a date, she refused *bluntly* [*flatly*]. (❗she 以下は, 口語で she *gave* him *the cold shoulder*. ともいえる.「つれなく扱った」の意)

つれにいく 連れに行く ▶子供を学校に連れに行った I *went to get* [*collected*,《主に英》*fetched*] my child *from* school. (❗*went to get* の代わりに *went and got* も可能だが, 前の方は目的が達成されたかどうかは不明であるのに対して後の方は「行ってその結果連れて帰った」ことが暗示される)

つれにくる 連れに来る ▶父が5時に連れに来てくれることになっている My father *is coming to get* [《主に英》*is fetching*] me at five.

つれもどす 連れ戻す (こちらへ) bring* [take*]... back; (あちらへ) take ... back.

つれる 連れる (いっしょである) be with ...; (同伴している)《やや書》be accompanied by .... ▶彼女はだれか連れていましたか, それとも1人でしたか *Was* (there) anyone *with* him or was he alone? ▶その子は母親に連れられて公園に行った The child went to the park *accompanied by* [*with*] his mother. (⇨①)/The mother *took* her child *to* the park./The child went to the park *with* his mother. (❗第1例では公園へ行くのが子供の意思によったことが, 第2例では母親の主導によったことが, 第3例では両者の活動・楽しみであったことが含意される)

つれる 釣れる catch*. (⇨釣る)
つれる 攣れる (⇨攣る)
つわぶき 石蕗【植物】a Japanese silverleaf.
つわもの (武士) a warrior; (猛者) a tough guy.
つわり ◦つわりがひどい have bad *morning sickness*.
つんざく (音・声を) pierce, earsplit*, rend*. ▶朝の空気をつんざく銃声がした A gunshot *rent* [*pierced*] the morning air. ▶耳をつんざくような悲鳴が聞こえた I heard a *piercing* [an *earsplitting*] scream.
つんつるてん ❶[衣服が] much too short. ▶去年あの子に買ったセーターがつんつるてんになってしまった The sweáter I bought for him last year has become *much too short*./He *has outgrown* the sweater I bought last year. (❗outgrow「(衣服の大きさ)を超えて大きくなる」の意)

❷[頭がはげて] completely bald. ▶(頭が)つんつるてんだ He has a *very bald* head./(おどけて) He's *as bald as a coot*. (❗coot /kúːt/ は水鳥の一種)

つんつん ◦つんつんしている (お高くとまった)《話》stuck-up; (よそよそしい)《話》stándòffish; (不機嫌な) cross; (いらいらして)《話》edgy. ◦(においが)つんつんする (⇨つんと❷) ◦つんつんしている女性 a *stuck-up* woman. ▶そんなにつんつんするなよ Don't be so *edgy*.

つんと ❶[つんとすました]《話》stándòffish; (お高くとまった)《話》stuck-up; (うぬぼれて) conceited. (⇨澄ます❷) ▶彼女はつんとした様子で話しにくい She looks too *standoffish* [*stuck-up*] to be communicative.

❷[においなどがきつい] (刺すように刺激する) sharp, pungent; (悪臭で鼻をつく) rank. ◦(わさびなどが)鼻につんとくる *sting* the nose. ▶実験室はつんとする薬品のにおいがした The laboratory had a *sharp* [a *pungent*] smell of chemicals. ▶その場所はつんと鼻にくる腐った魚のにおいで満ちていた The place was filled with the *rank* smell of rotten fish.

つんどく 積ん読 (説明的に) buying books and just piling them up without reading.
ツンドラ [凍土帯] the tundra /tʌ́ndrə/.
つんのめる ◦前につんのめる (ほとんど前に転びそうになる) almost fall forward; (前に傾く) lean forward. ▶彼は歩道を走っていき, 四つ角でつんのめるようにして立ち止まった He ran down the sidewalk and came to a *hard* stop at a street intersection. ▶目の前にあることにつんのめっている(=それだけに集中する)と, 今度は自分の命を粗末にしたり疲れすぎたりしてしまう If you *get* too *focused on* what's immediately in front of [right before] you, you'll end up not taking your life seriously or getting exhausted. (❗「自分の命を粗末にする」は「真剣に生きない」と表す)

て

て 手
INDEX

❶ 人間・動物の手　❷ 物の(取っ手)
❸ 人手　❹ 手間, 手数
❺ 手段, 方法　❻ 将棋・相撲などの
❼ 種類　❽ 方向
❾ 所有

WORD CHOICE 手

hand 手のひらと手首からなる部分のこと. 日本語の「手」と異なり, 手首(wrist)や腕(arm)は含まない. ●手を握る[伸ばす, つかむ] shake [extend, hold] one's hand.

arm 肩から手首にあたる腕のこと. 時に肩から ひじまでを upper arm (上腕), ひじから手首までを forearm (前腕)と区別する. ●腕を骨折する broke one's arm. ●腕を組む cross [fold] one's arms.

palm hand を構成する一部分としての手のひらのこと. 意味を明確にするため, 時に of the [one's] hand が後続する. ●手の中にすくった水 water in the cup of the *palm* of my hand.

頻度チャート
hand
arm
palm

20　40　60　80　100 (%)

❶ 【人間・動物の手】a hand; an arm; a palm /pá:m/ (⇨[類語]); (手の指) a finger (⇨指); (猫などのかぎづめのある) a paw.

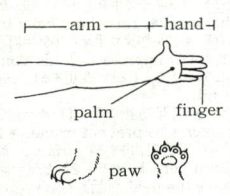

── arm ──── hand ──
palm　finger
paw

① 【~手】●優雅な手 a delicate *hand*. ●ほっそりした手 a slender *hand*. ●短くてずんぐりとした手 a pudgy *hand*. ●節くれ立った手 a gnarled *hand*. ●かさかさした手 a coarse *hand*. ●がさがさの手 a rough *hand*. ●つるつるした手 a smooth *hand*. ▶(犬に)ローバー, お手! Give me your *paw* [(握手!) Shake *hands*], Rover.

② 【手が】●左手が痛い I have a pain in my left *hand* [*arm*]./My left *hand* [*arm*] hurts. ▶あそこになっているリンゴに手が届きますか Can you *reach* that apple on the tree?

③ 【手の】●手の甲 (⇨手の甲) ●薬は子供たちの手の届かない所に置いておきなさい Keep all medicines *out of* (↔*within*) *reach of* children. (❗ reach は「手の届く距離」の意)

④ 【手に】●彼はその本を手に取った[持っていた] He took [had] the book in his *hand*(s). (❗ hands は両手であることを示す) ▶何か冷たいものが私の手に触れた Something cold touched my *hand*.

⑤ 【手を】●手を上げる (降伏して) hold up one's *hands*; (宣誓するときに右手を) lift one's *hand*; (攻撃・おどしのために) lift [raise] one's *hand* 《*against, to*》. (⇨[第 1, 2 文例]) ●両手をポケットに入れて with one's *hands* in the pockets; hands in pockets. (❗ 後の方は《書》) ●両手をしっかり握りしめて with one's *hands* clasped together tight. (❗ 祈り・感動・不安のしぐさ) ●手を取り合って歩く walk *hand in hand* 《*with*》. ●手をつなぐ(=取り合う) hold *hands* 《*with*》. ●彼の手をひっこめる draw back one's *hand*. ●彼の手を取る take his *hand*; take him by the *hand*. (❗ 前の方は「手」, 後の方は「人」に焦点を当てた言い方) ●老女の手をひいて通りを渡る lead an old woman *by the hand* across the street. ●手を合わせる(=合掌する) join one's *hands* [*palms*] together. (❗ 欧米人の祈りの動作は「手を組む」 fold one's hands) ●額に手をかざす (⇨額) ▶生徒たちは手を上げて「はい(田中)先生」と言った The students put their *hand*(s) up [raised their *hand*(s)] and said, "Please, Miss Tanaka." (❗ (1) 片手を上げるので主語が複数でも通例単数形で用いる. (2) 日本語では単に「先生」とも言うが, 英語では Miss [Mr.] Tanaka のように言う. 単に Miss だけでは失礼) ▶彼はたたみの上に手をついて深くお辞儀をした He put his *hands* on the *tatami* floor and made a deep bow. ▶彼はつまずいて手をついた He stumbled and fell on his *hand*. ▶彼らは歌に合わせて手をたたいた They clapped their *hands* in time to the song. ▶その箱に手を触れるな Don't *touch* the box./Keep your *hands* off the box. ▶彼は棚の上の箱を取ろうと手を伸ばした He *reached for* a box on the shelf. ▶彼は友達にさよならと手を振った He *waved* good-by [《書》 waved his *hand* in farewell] *to* his friends. ▶私のコートから手を離せ *Let go of* my coat. ▶彼は食事に手をつけなかった He left his food *untouched*.

⑥ 【手で】●衣類を手で洗う wash the clothes with one's *hands*. ●肉を手でつまんで食べる eat the meat with one's *fingers*. ▶猫がネズミを手で引っ掛けた The cat caught a mouse with its *paw*.

❷ 【物の】(取っ手) a handle. ▶水差しの手が取れた[欠けた] The *handle* of the pitcher has come off [broken off].

❸ 【人手】a hand; (助力) help.
① 【手が】●手が足りない We are *short-handed* [*short of hands*, (職union不足) be *understaffed*]. (❗「手は足りている」なら We have a full staff.) ▶もっと手が欲しい We want more *hands* [*help*]. ▶今日は手があいています(=何もすることがない) I have nothing [*no work*] *to do* today./I am *free* today.
② 【手を】●子供たちはそのテーブルを運ぶのに手を貸してくれた The children *gave* [*lent*] me a (*helping*) *hand* to carry the table. とも言える)/The children *helped* me (*to*) carry the table. (❗ to のある方は間接的な援助か, to のない方は直接的な援助を含意する)/(子供たちの手を借りた) I *got help from* [*had the*

[手間, 手数] trouble; (世話) care.

① 【手が】 ▶ そうすれば手が大いに省けるだろう That will save us a lot of *trouble*. ▶ 時間がなくて細かいところまで手が回らなかった(=気配りできなかった) I was too pressed for time to give my attention to the details.

② 【手の】 ▶ 手のかかる(=骨の折れる)仕事 a *laborious* [(面倒な) *troublesome*] task. ● 手のこんだ細工(=作品) an *elaborate* piece of work; (技) *sophisticated* workmanship.

③ 【手を】 ▶ 手をかけたごちそう an *elaborate* dinner. ● 親の手を離れる(=独立する) *become independent of* [×from] one's parents. ● 手を抜く(=手抜き) ▶ 父は手をかけてバラを育てた My father took *great care* to grow the roses.

❺ [手段, 方法] (手段) a means (**!** 単・複同形); (方法) a way; (術策) a trick.

① 【手は[が]】 ▶ その手は食わない(=だまされない) I won't fall for that *trick*. ▶ 今となってはもう打つ手がない There is nothing more we can do now. (**!**「打つべき手はみな打ってある」なら We've done everything necessary for success. となる)

② 【手の】 ▶ この情勢では手のつけようがない(絶望的だ) This is a *hopeless* situation./(何もできない) *Nothing can be done about* this situation./(どう扱ってよいのか分からない) We don't know [are at a loss] what to do with this situation.

③ 【手に】 ▶ 彼の手にまんまと乗せられた(=だまされた) I *was* completely *taken in* by him.

④ 【手を】 ▶ きたない手を使う use a dirty *trick*. ▶ 彼は前にもその手を使おうとしたことがあるのよ. だから気をつけて He tried that *trick* before. So beware.

❻ [将棋・相撲などの] (将棋の) a move; (相撲の) a trick; (トランプの) a hand. ● いい手 a good (↔bad) *move*. ● 相撲の 48 手 all the *tricks* in sumo wrestling.

❼ [種類] a kind, a sort. ▶ その手の音楽[人]は好きでない I don't like that *kind* of music [those *kind*(s) of people]. (⇨種類)

❽ [方向] ▶ 舞台の手前から登場する appear from the *left* of the stage. (参考 英語は日本語と異なり舞台から見ていうので, 客席の方に向かって左が上手になる) ▶ 流れはその地点でふたつに分かれる The stream branches off at that point. ▶ 大きな岩が行く手を遮っている A big rock *stands in* our *way*.

❾ [所有] (所有権) hands. ▶ その土地は彼の手に渡った The land fell into his *hands*./The land came into his *possession*. ▶ その家は人の手から手へと渡った The house has changed *hands* several times [(短期間に) quickly]. (**!** 複数形に注意. この場合 ×The house passed from hand to hand. とはしない)

● 手が後ろに回る (逮捕される) be [(話) get] arrested.

● 手がつけられない ▶ その暴動は手がつけられなくなった The riot *has got out of hand*./The riot *has got out of control*.

● 手が出ない ▶ そんな高級車にはとても手が出ない(=買う余裕がない) I *can't afford* (*to buy*) such a luxury car. ▶ その打者は外角の直球に手が出なかった The batter froze on the fastball on the outside./The fastball on the outside froze the batter.

● 手が止まる ▶ ラジオから好きな音楽が流れてくるという仕事の手が止まってしまう When I hear my favorite music on the radio, I often pose in my work.

● 手が入る ▶ その件に警察の手が入った(=捜査が始まった) The police have begun their investigation into the matter.

● 手が離せない ▶ 今仕事で手が離せない(=拘束されている) I *am tied up* [*have my hands tied*, (手がふさがっている) *have my hands full*, (とても忙しい) *am very busy*] with the work right now.

● 手が回る ▶ 彼には警察の手が回っている(=警察が追跡している) The police *are* already *on his track*. ▶ その仕事に手が回りかねる(=時間の余裕を見つけられない) I *can't get around to* [*find time for*] the work.

● 手に汗を握る ● 手に汗を握って breathtakingly. (**!** with one's own hands in sweat は「額に汗して」に相当する. (⇨額)) ● 手に汗を握るような試合 a *breathtaking* [a *very exciting*] game. ● 手に汗を握って見る watch (it) *with breathless interest* [*in excitement*]. (⇨汗 ❹)

● 手に余る ▶ その仕事は私の手に余る The work is *beyond* [*above*] me./The work is *beyond* my *ability*.

● 手に入れる ▶ 彼は賭(か)け事で大金を手に入れた(=獲得した) He *won* a lot of money in gambling.

● 手に負えない ▶ その火事は私たちの手に負えなかった We couldn't *bring* [*get*] the fire *under control*.

● 手につかない ▶ 心配で心配で仕事が手につかない(=仕事をする気がしない) I'm so worried that I don't *feel like* working. ▶ 二塁手はボールが手につかなかった The second baseman couldn't find the handle on the ball.

● 手に取るように ▶ その報告書を読むと事故の様子が手に取るように分かる The report gives us a *clear* picture of the accident.

● 手に入る ▶ その本は手に入りにくい The book is hard to *get* [*come by*, (書) *obtain*]. ▶ その演奏会の切符はこの窓口で手に入ります The tickets for the performance are *available* at this window.

● 手の裏を返す (⇨手の裏)

● 手の施しようがない ▶ もう手の施しようがない There's nothing to be done.

● 手も足も出ない ▶ その難問に手も足も出なかった(=能力をはるかに超えていた) The difficult question *was far beyond my ability*.

● 手を上げる ▶ あの子に手を上げた(=殴った)ことは一度もない I have never raised my *hand* to the boy.

● 手を入れる ▶ 彼の作文に手を入れる(=訂正する) *correct* [(改善する) *improve on*] his composition. ● 彼の案に少々手を入れる(=変更する) *change* his plans a bit.

● 手を打つ ● 犯罪防止の手を打つ(=対策を講じる) take *measures* to prevent crime. ● 1,000 万円で手を打つ(=売買契約をする) *strike a bargain* at ten million yen. ▶ それで手を打とう(=話は決まった) 《話》 That's the deal./《話》 You've got a deal./《話》 That settles it [the matter]. (⇨決まり)

● 手を替え品を替え ● 手を替え品を替え彼女を説得しようとする try every possible *means* to persuade her.

● 手を切る ● 彼と手を切る(関係を絶つ) cut [break off] the *connection* with him; (絶交する) *break with* him.

● 手を下す ▶ 彼女は自分は手を下さずに(=手を汚さずに)浮浪児たちにスリをさせていた She never got her *hands* dirty [(面倒なことに巻き込まれないようにした) always tried to keep her nose clean] by getting street urchins to be pickpockets.

● 手を組む ● 彼と手を組む (提携する) join *hands* with him; (味方する) *side with* him.

● 手をこまぬく ● 手をこまぬいて見ている(=傍観して何もしない) sit back and do nothing.

●**手を染める** ▶相場に手を染める(=始める) go *in for* speculation; *speculate in* stocks.
●**手を出す** ▶事業に手を出す(=始める) start [乗り出す] *embark on*] a business. ▶株に手を出す(=投機する) *speculate in* stocks. ▶その問題に手を出して失敗した I failed when I tried *to settle the matter*.
●**手を尽くす** ▶その問題の解決に八方手を尽くす(=あらゆる手段を試みる) try [take, 《書》exhaust] *every (possible) means* to settle the matter.
●**手をつける** ▶この問題は難しくてどこから手をつけたら(=始めたら)いいか分からない This problem is so difficult that I don't know where to *begin*.
●**手を引く** ▶かかわりたくなかったので手を引いた I didn't want to be involved, so I *washed my hands of* it.
●**手を広げる** ▶関西地方に営業の手を広げる *extend* [*expand*] one's *business into* the Kansai area.
●**手を焼く** ▶そのいたずらっ子[彼のいたずら]にまったく手を焼いている The naughty boy [His mischief] *gives* me a lot of *trouble*./The naughty boy [His mischief] is quite a *handful*. (!*a handful* は《話》で「やっかいな子[事]」の意)
●**手を汚す** (⇨手を汚す)

-て ❶[そして] and. ▶彼らは一晩中飲んで歌って踊った They drank, sang, *and* danced all night.
❷[その後] (以来) since; (あと) after. ▶日本にいらっしゃって何年になりますか How many years has it been《米》[is it《英》] *since* you came to Japan? ▶出火して10分後に消防車が到着した Fire engines came ten minutes (×later) *after* the fire started.
❸[原因・理由] ▶働きすぎて病気になる become sick *from* [*through*, 《やや書》*because of*] overwork; work too hard *and* get sick (!この and は結果を表す). ▶寒くて震える shiver *with* cold. ▶いろいろお世話になりありがとうございました Thank you *for* everything you did to me. ▶ごいっしょしてきて楽しかったです I've enjoyed your company.
❹[にもかかわらず] but. ▶彼はフランスにいても日本食ばかり食べている He is in France, *but* he eats only Japanese food.
❺[付加] ▶あの店は野菜が安くて新鮮だ Vegetables are inexpensive *and* [*are not only* inexpensive *but*] fresh at that store.

で (それで) and; yes. (!いずれも上昇調で、相手の話を促す) ▶で、どうしたの *And*, what did you do?

で 出 ❶[出身] (血統) origins; (前歴) (a) background. ▶大学出の人 a university [a college] graduate; a person of college *background*.
●東京の出である *be* [*come*] *from* Tokyo. ▶出がいい *come from* a good family. ▶彼は貴族の出だ He *comes from* [《英》*of*] a noble family./He is a man of noble *origins*.
❷[出具合] ▶人の出 (⇨出足) ▶出がよい (品物が) sell well; (水などが) come out well; (茶などが) draw well.
❸[出現] ▶[出番] one's turn. ●月の出に at the moonrise. ●(役者が)出を待つ wait for one's *turn* to appear on the stage.
▶リンゴの出が早い Apples *have come in* earlier. (!*come in* は「(季節になって)出回る」の意)

:-で《格助詞》
INDEX
❶ 場所 　　　　 ❷ 時間
❸ 手段, 方法 　　❹ 原因, 理由
❺ 材料, 成分 　　❻ 基準, 割合, 金額
❼ 事情, 状態 　　❽ 話題, 論題

❶[場所] at ...; in ...; on .... (⇨-に)

【使い分け】**at** 比較的狭い地点に用いる.
in 比較的広い場所に用いる.
ただし、この「広い」「狭い」は絶対的なものではなく、狭い所でも広がりをもつ「場所の中」に意識がある場合は in を、広い所でも到着[乗り換え, 通過]など単なる地点となるような場合には at を用いる: 軽井沢で夏休みを過ごす spend the summer vacation *in* Karuizawa./大阪で列車を乗り換える change trains *at* Osaka.
on 表面との接触を表し、「...の上で[に]」の意.

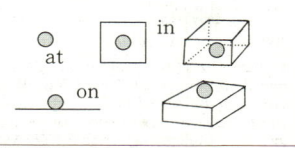

▶駅で彼女を待っていた I was waiting for her *at* [*in*] the station. (!at は駅の構内、プラットホーム、駅前広場などの1地点をさす. in は特に駅の構内の意)
▶その事故は交差点で起こった The accident occurred [happened] *at* [×*in*] the crossing.
▶パーティーで[バスで]彼女に会った I met her *at* the party [*on* the bus]. ▶私は小さな村で1人暮らしをしている I live alone *in* [×*at*] a small village. (!自分の住んでいる所は小さな場所でも in で表す) ▶子供が何人か公園で[通りで；外で]遊んでいた Some children were playing *in* the park [*on* the street; *outside*]. (!×at the park は不可. in the street は《主に英》). ▶彼は箱根の宿で静養しているおじを訪ねた He visited his uncle who was taking a rest *at* an inn *in* Hakone. ▶彼らは結婚後農場で働く予定です They are going to work *on* [×*in*, ×*at*] a farm after they get married. (!一時的に働く場合には at も可)

❷[時間] at ...; on ...; in ... (⇨-に); (...までに) by (⇨まで); (以内に) within ....

【使い分け】**at** 時の一点・時刻を表し、時間とともに用いる: *at* five (o'clock).
on 特定の日・機会を表し、日にち・曜日などと、また特定の日の朝・午後・晩に用いる: *on* Sunday/*on* April 4/*on* the morning of 23rd.
in 比較的長い時間を示し、月・年・季節・世紀などとともに用いる. また、時間的な経過による現時点からの時の経過をさす: *in* April/*in* 2008/*in* spring/*in* the 21st century.

【解説】時を表す「で」はある範囲の時を示すことが多く、日本語では「では、でも」という形になる場合が多い.

▶そのデパートは8時で閉まる The department store closes *at* eight (o'clock). ▶おばは昨年74歳で亡くなった My aunt died last year, *at* (the age of) 74. /《英》My aunt died last year, aged seventy-four. ▶彼らは1時間で空港に到着します They will arrive at the airport *in* [*within*] an hour. (!*in* は「...たてば」の意で「時の経過」を示し、通例その期間の終わりのときをさす. within はその時間[期間]内ならいつでもよい) /(今から1時間後に) An hour *from* now [×After an hour, ×An hour later] they will arrive at the airport. (!*after*, *later* は過去の文脈で用いる) ▶今度の4月でこの会社に勤めて6年になります I will have been working for this company for six years next April [×*in* next April]. (!前に next, last, this などを伴った時を表す語句は副詞的に用いるので前置詞は不要)/By next April I will have been working for this company for six years. ▶たった1週間で私たちは大の仲よしになった After only a week, we've become the best of friends. ●ここ10年間でいちばん寒い日だった It was the coldest day for [《米》*in*] ten years.

❸ [手段, 方法] (道具) with ...; (手段) in ...; (交通・通信などの手段) by ...; (支え, 依存) on ...; (仲介的な手段) through ....

> 使い分け **with** 道具を示して「…を用いて」の意を表す: *with* a key.
> **in** 手段・材料を示す: *in* black ink/鉛筆で書く write *in* pencil [*with* a pencil].

● ハンカチでそれを包む wrap it *in* [《まれ》*with*] a handkerchief. ● 低い声で話す speak *in* a low voice. ● 手紙をワープロで書く type a letter *on* [*with*, ×*by*] a word processor. ● 手紙[電報]で by letter [telegram]. ● 徒歩で学校へ行く go to school *by* [話] [*on*《主に英》] foot; walk to school. (❗後の方が普通. 前の方は他の通学手段との対比で用いられる) ● 電話で彼と話をする talk with him *on* [*over*] the telephone. (❗「(他の方法ではなく)電話でそれをキャンセルする」は cancel it *by* telephone) ● 顕微鏡でそれを調べる examine it *under* [(通して) *through*] a microscope. ▶だれかが石で窓ガラスを割った Someone broke the window (×*glass*) [windowpane] *with* a stone. ▶彼は列車で旅行するのが好きです He likes traveling *by* train [*in* a train, 《米》*on* a train]. (❗*by* は手段としての交通機関を示し, 無冠詞・単数が原則. *on* は「列車に乗って」, *in* は「列車の中で, 車中で」という感じが強い. *on* と *in* では通例冠詞を伴うことに注意. ただし形容詞がつく場合は *by* も冠詞を伴う: *by* the 9:10 train; *by a* slow train) ▶彼は安月給で生活している He lives *on* [×*with*] a small salary.

会話 「この花は英語で何と言うの?」「sunflower です」 "What do you call [×*say*] this flower *in* English? / What is the English for this flower?" "Sunflower."

会話 「ここへは何でこられたのですか」「タクシーでです」 "*How* did you come here?" "*By* taxi."

会話 「何で切ったの」「ナイフでさ」 "*How* did you cut yourself?" "*On* my knife." (❗*with* my knife とすれば自分の意志でわざと切ったことになる)

会話 「お支払いは現金でなさいますか, それともカードでなさいますか」「ビザで払います」 "Are you paying *in* cash or *by* credit card?" "I'll pay *with* Visa."

❹ [原因, 理由] for ...; from ...; through ...; with ... (❗以上の前置詞は結びつく語との関係で決まっていることが多い); (…の理由[原因]で) because of ..., 《書》owing to ..., 《書》on account of ....

▶ローマは史跡で有名です Rome is famous *for* its historic spots. ▶その運転手はスピード違反で逮捕された The driver was arrested *for* (over-)speeding. ▶彼は肺がん[過労]で死んだ He died *of* lung cancer [*from* overwork]. (❗die of は死因が病気・飢え・老衰など直接的な原因の場合, die from は負傷・året・不注意・衰弱など間接的な原因の場合に用いるのが原則 (⇒死ぬ)) ▶その事故は彼の不注意で起こった The accident happened *through* his carelessness./(彼の不注意がその事故を引き起こした) His carelessness caused the accident. ▶その少年は飢えと寒さで震えていた The boy was shivering *with* cold and hunger. ▶彼女は風邪で寝ていた She was in bed *with* a cold. ▶「病気で寝ている」は be sick in bed, 「病気で入院している」なら単に be in the hospital でよい) ▶長い病気で彼はすっかりやつれてしまった Because of [Owing to, On account of] his long sickness, he has become very thin and feeble. (❗*Because* he has been sick for a long time, ... や He has been sick for a long time, *so* he can't .... の方が口語的) ▶建物の大半は昨夜の地震で破壊された Most of the buildings were destroyed *by* [*in*] the earthquake last night. ▶彼女は同情心[親切心; 悪意]でそれをした She did it *out of* pity [kindness; spite]. (❗out of は心理的動機を表す)

❺ [材料, 原料] of ...; from ...; with ....

> 使い分け **of** 通例材料のもとの形が変化しない場合に用いる: そのボールは革でできている The ball is made *of* leather.
> **from** 原料と製品の質が変化する場合に用いる: 炭は木から作られる Charcoal is made *from* wood.
> **with** 成分の一部を示す: 生地は小麦粉と水で作られる A paste is made *with* flower and water.

▶それは何でできていますか What is it made *of* [*from*]? ▶この家は木でできている This house is built [made] *of* [×*from*] wood. ▶パンは小麦粉で作る Bread is made *from* [*of*] flour./Flour is made into bread. (❗後の方は「小麦粉はパンになる」の意で into は変化を示す) ▶子供たちは砂で山を作った The children made a mountain (*out*) *of* [×*from*] sand.

❻ [基準, 割合, 金額] (基準) by ...; (割合) at ...; (交換) for ....

> 使い分け **by** 計量・判断の基準を表す: ものは見かけで判断できない You can't judge a book *by* its cover.
> **at** 単価・割合・計器類の表示する値を表す: シャトルは14度の傾斜で大気圏に再突入した The shuttle reentered the atmosphere *at* 14-degree slope.
> **for** 「…と引き換えに」という交換, または売買・取引の金額を表す際に用いる: 私はその子供たちのために無償で働いた I worked for the children *for* free.

▶肉はグラム単位で売られる Meat is sold *by* the gram. (❗by the+数量の単位の形をとる) ▶給料は1時間[1日]いくらでもらっている I am paid *by* the hour [the day]. (❗×*by* an hour [a day] とはいわない) ▶その鉛筆は1ダース 1,000 円で売られている The pencils are sold *at* 1,000 yen a dozen. ▶その本を 5,000 円で買った I bought the book *at* [*for*] 5,000 yen./(本に 5,000 円支払った) I paid 5,000 yen *for* the book. ▶車は全速力で走っていた The car was running (*at*) full speed. (❗at を省略するのが《話》) ▶私はこれまで(ずっと)ワイン3杯でやめることにしてきました I've always stopped *at* three glasses of wine. (❗「現在完了形+always」の使い方に注意) ▶他人を外見で判断するのは危険です It's dangerous to judge other people *by* their appearances.

❼ [事情, 状態] at ...; in ...; with .... (❗いずれも一定の語と結びついて慣用的なものが多い) ▶彼はすっかりくつろいでいた He was completely *at* ease. ▶大急ぎで仕事を終えた I finished my work *in* a great hurry [《やや書》 *in* great haste]. ▶そういう事情でそこには行けません *In* [*Under*] the circumstances I can't go there. (❗under の方が「そういう事情」の影響が強い) ▶彼は腕を組んで座っていた He sat *with* his arms folded. (❗with は付帯状況を表す. 以下2例も同様) ▶食べ物を口にほおばったままでしゃべってはいけません Don't speak *with* your mouth full. ▶電灯をつけたままで外出してはいけません Don't go out *with* the lights on. (!on は継続の意を表す副詞)

❽ 〖話題, 論題〗about ...; on .... (!about は一般的内容に, on は専門的内容に用いられる (⇨ついて〖類語〗)) ▶会社じゅうそのうわさでもちきりだ The whole office is talking *about* it. ▶つまらないことで文句をいったりけんかしたりするものではありません You should not complain *about* or quarrel *over* small things. (!quarrel *about* も用いられる. over は「...をめぐって」の意で *about* より関心の度合いが強い) ▶彼はスペイン革命」という題で講演した He gave a lecture *on* the Spanish Revolution. ▶投資[妻への贈り物]のことで相談にのってください Please give me some advice *on* my investments [*about* a present for my wife].

−で (接続助詞) 〖そして〗and; (一方) while. ▶あれが学校で, こちらが町役場です That is a school, *and* this is the town hall. ▶この小説を読んで感想を書きなさい Read this novel *and* (then) write your impressions of it. (!*After* reading this novel, write... ともいえる) ▶彼は政治家で, 弟は芸術家だ He is a statesman, *while* his brother is an artist.

であい 手合い 〖a fellow, a guy. ▶あんな手合いとは付き合うな Don't mix with such a person [such people]. 〖碁・将棋などの試合〗a game; a match.

であい 出会い a meeting; (突然の, 危険なものとの)〖書〗an encounter. (⇨出合う) ●出会い系サイト a *dating* site; (正確に) an Internet *dating*-service site. ▶私と真知子との出会いはこんな具合でした My first *meeting* with Machiko [The way I first met Machiko] was like this. ▶この本との(偶然の)出会いが私の人生を変えた Coming [Running] *across* that book changed my life. ▶外国旅行をすると興味深い人々との出会いがあるものだ Foreign travel will give us chances to *meet* interesting people.

であいがしら 出会い頭 ▶2台の乗用車が交差点で出会いがしらに(=交差点に入ったとたんに)衝突した Two cars collided (with each other) *the moment* they entered the intersection. ▶2人は出会いがしらに(=すれ違いざまに)どんとぶつかった The two bumped into each other in *passing*.

であう 出会う 〖人・物などに〗meet; (偶然に) come* [run*] across ...; 〖困難・不幸などに〗meet with ..., 〖書〗encounter. (⇨合う) ▶困難に出会う *meet with* [*encounter*] difficulties. ▶駅で先生にばったり出会った I *happened to meet* my teacher [*met* my teacher *by chance*] at the station./I *came across* [*ran across, ran into, bumped into*] my teacher at the station. ▶多くの分からない単語に出会った I *met* [*came across*] lots of words I didn't understand.

であか 手垢 finger marks. ●手垢をつける put *finger marks* (*on*). ●手垢のついた(=よく使いこんだ)辞書 a *well-thumbed* dictionary.

てあし 手足 〖腕と脚〗arms and legs, 〖書〗limbs; 〖手と足〗hands and feet. ●手足のない死体 a body without *limbs*. ●手足の長い猿 a long-*limbed* monkey. ●手足がぶるぶると震える tremble in every *limb*. ●彼の手足を縛る bind [tie] him *hand and foot*. ●手足を伸ばす stretch out one's *limbs*; (ゆっくり休む) relax. ●手足となって上司に仕える work hard for one's boss.
●手足口病 hand-foot-and-mouth disease. (参考 子供のウイルス感染症)

であし 出足 〖スタート〗a start; 〖人の出〗a turnout. ●出足のよい車 a fast-*starting* car; (米) a car with good pickup. ▶彼の商売の出足は快調だった His business made [got off to] a good *start*. ▶選挙の出足は悪かった There was a bad [poor, a low] *turnout* at the polls./The *turnout* of voters was bad [poor, low]. (!よい出足の場合は good, high)

てあたりしだい 手当たり次第 (無計画に) at random. ●その試合の切符を手当たり次第に買いあさった buy up *all available* tickets for the match. ▶彼は手当たり次第本を読む He reads *at random*.

てあつい 手厚い 〖温かい〗warm; 〖真心のこもった〗cordial; 〖もてなしのよい〗hospitable. ●手厚いもてなしを受ける be given a *warm* [a *cordial*, a *hospitable*] reception; be treated with *warm* [*great*] hospitality. ●手厚い(=ていうやうやしく)遺体を葬る bury the dead body *respectfully* [*with respect*]. ▶彼女は病気の友人を手厚く(=優しく)看病した She looked after her sick friend *tenderly* [(注意深く) *carefully*]. ▶日本の農業は政府によって手厚く保護されている Japan's farm industry is *well* protected by the government.

てあて 手当て 〖通例医師による直接の〗(a) treatment; 〖病院の〗medical care. ●彼に応急手当てを施す give him first aid; give (x the) first aid to him; give him first-aid *treatment*. ▶彼女は病院で脚の骨折の手当てを受けた She received *treatment* for a broken leg in the hospital./She *was treated for* a broken leg in the hospital. ▶彼はその病院で手厚い手当てを受けている He is receiving excellent *medical care* in that hospital. ▶母親は子供の傷[やけど]の手当てをした The mother *treated* [(薬を塗った)包帯をして) *dressed*] her child's injury [burn].

てあて 手当 〖給与〗(xa) pay; 〖定期的に一定額が支給される金〗an allowance; 〖臨時の一時金〗a bonus; 〖保険・年金などの給付金〗(a) benefit (!しばしば複数形で). ●家族[住宅]手当 a family [a housing] *allowance*. ●年末手当 a year-end *bonus*. ●失業手当 unemployment *benefit*(*s*). ▶私は月2万円の扶養手当をもらっている I get a monthly *allowance* of 20,000 yen for dependents.

てあぶり 手焙り a small(-size) brazier for warming hands.

てあみ 手編み 图 ▶彼女は手編みの帽子をかぶっていた She wore [was wearing] a *hand-knitted* cap./She wore a cap *knitted by hand*.
── 手編みする 動 hand-knit; knit*... by hand.

てあら 手荒 ── 手荒い 服 rough; (暴力的な) violent. ●手荒く取り扱う handle ... *roughly*. ▶絶対手荒なまねはするなよ Be sure not to do anything *violent*. ▶新人投手はプロの手荒い洗礼を受けた The rookie pitcher was viciously taught what it is to be a professional./The rookie pitcher underwent a real baptism of fire.

てあらい 手洗い 〖個人の家の便所〗a bathroom, a washroom; (ホテル・劇場などの) a rest room; (公園などの) a comfort station. (⇨便所)

*−である ❶ 〖断定・指定などを表す〗be. (⇨です) ▶彼は大阪大学の学生である He *is* a student at Osaka University.
❷ 〖同格を表す〗●作家である私の父 my father, a writer; my father, who is a writer.

であるく 出歩く (外出する) go* out; (歩き回る) walk about [around]. ▶夜は1人で出歩くな Don't *walk about* [*around*] alone at night. ▶彼女はいつも出歩いている. いつ電話をしても家にいたためしがない She's always *out*. Every time I call her up she isn't in. (!このような人を《話》a gádabòut という)

−であれ 〖何であれ〗whatever, no matter what; 〖だれ

てあわせ

であれ] whoever, no matter who (■いずれも no matter ... の方が口語的); [...であろうと～であろうと] whether ... or ～ (■..., ～は це・句・節). ▶それが何であれ開けないでくれ Don't open it, *whatever* [*no matter what*] it is. ▶犬であれ猫であれ動物をいじめてはいけない You shouldn't abuse any animal, *whether* it is a dog or a cat.

てあわせ 手合わせ a game; a match. (⇨試合) ▶彼は初手合わせだった I played against him for the first time.

てい 体 ●ほうほうの体で逃げ出す scramble to get away. (⇨体よく) ▶彼は疲労困憊(蕊)の体だった He *looked* [*appeared*] exhausted [tired out]. ▶彼の奥さんは体のよい(=名目だけ体裁のよい)お手伝いです His wife is just a *glorified* maid.

てい 低- low (⇔high). ●低価格 a *low* [×a cheap] price. ●低レベルの *low*-level. ●低年齢層 a *lower* age group [bracket]. ●低脂肪牛乳 *low*-fat milk. ●低排出ガス車 a *low* emission vehicle. ●低インシュリンダイエット insulin *resistance* diet.

-てい 《書》a residence. ●官邸 an official *residence*. ●矢野邸 Mr. Yano's [the Yano] *residence*.

-てい 帝 an emperor; an empress. ●ピョートル大帝 Peter *the Great*. (■ the great emperor の略)

ていあつ 低圧 (低い圧力) low pressure; (低い電圧) low voltage.

***ていあん 提案** 图 (控えめな) (a) suggestion; (積極的な) (a) proposal. ▶その川に橋をかけようという提案があった There was a *proposal* [a *suggestion*] *that* we (《主に英》should) build a bridge over the river./There was a *proposal* [×a *suggestion*] *to* build a bridge over the river. ▶それをするために多くの提案がなされた Many *proposals* were made [put forward] for doing it.
── 提案する 動 suggest 《*doing*; *that* 節》; propose 《*doing*; *that* 節》 (■後の方が堅い語で積極的提案を含意する); [動議として] move. ●積極案を委員会に提案する *propose* an aggressive plan *to* the committee. ▶彼は私にその家を買ってはどうかと提案した He *suggested* (to me) *that* I (《主に英》should) buy the house./He *suggested* my buying the house. (■×He suggested me *to* buy .... のように不定詞は用いない) ▶私は朝に出発することを提案します I *propose leaving* [*that* we (《主に英》should) *leave*] in the morning. (■(1) propose の代わりに suggest も可. (2) I *propose to leave* .... は通例「私は出発するつもりである」の意)

■ **DISCOURSE**
高校卒業者の英語力改善のために, 私は以下の対策を提案したい In order to improve the English (language) skills of high school graduates, I would like to *suggest* the **following** measures. (■ following (以下の)は抽象的内容を述べるディスコースマーカー. 続けて具体的内容を述べる)

ティー [茶] tea. ●アイスティー iced *tea*. ▶レモンティーを二つください Two *teas* with lemon, please. (■ lemon tea はレモンで香りをつけた紅茶)
●ティーカップ a teacup. ●ティースプーン a teaspoon. ●ティーブレイク (take) a coffee [《主に英》tea] break (*at* three). ●ティーポット a teapot.

ティー [ゴルフ・野球の] [ゴルフ] a tee; [野球] a (batting) tee. ●ティーアップする tee up. ●ティーオフするtee off.
●ティーグランド a teeing [×tee] ground. ●ティーショット a tee shot.

ていい 低位 a low position [rank].

てい 帝位 the Imperial throne. (⇨王位)

ディーエイチ [『指名打者』『野球』] a DH 《*d*esignated *h*itter の略》.

ディーエヌエー [『デオキシリボ核酸』] DNA 《*d*eoxyribo*n*ucleic *a*cid /dí:ə̀ksəìbou(j)u:klí:ik ǽsid/の略》.

ディーケー DK ●3DKのマンション a *three-room* apartment *with a big kitchen* [*a kitchen and a dining room*, ×*a dining kitchen*]. (■ a big [a large] kitchen は通例 dining room を含む)

ティーケーオー a TKO 《*t*echnical *k*nockout の略》.

ディージェー a DJ 《*d*isk *j*ockey の略》.

ティーシャツ a T-shirt, a tee shirt.

ディーゼル ●ディーゼルエンジン a diesel (engine [motor]). ●ディーゼルカー (車両一般) a diesel; (鉄道) a rail diesel car.

ていいち 定位置 one's (regular) position. ●ショートの定位置を獲得する get the *position* of a regular shortstop. ●定位置で守る play (a batter) straightaway [straight up].

ティーチングマシーン a teaching machine.

ティーバッグ a tea bag.

ディーピーイー film [photo] processing, 《和製語》DPE 《*d*eveloping, *p*rinting and *e*nlarging (現像, 焼き付け, 引き伸ばし)の略》.

ティーピーオー (the time, the place and) the occasion; 《和製語》TPO. ●ティーピーオーにふさわしい服装をする dress suitably [properly] for the *occasion*.

ディーブイ [『家庭内暴力』] domestic violence.; 《和製語》DV. (■主に夫婦間・恋人間の暴力をさす)

ディーブイディー a DVD 《*d*igital *v*ersatile [*v*ideo] *d*isc の略》.

ディープキス a deep kiss, a French kiss. (⇨フレンチキス)

ディーラー a dealer. ●自動車のディーラー a car *dealer*; a *dealer* in cars.

ティールーム [『喫茶店』] a tearoom.

ていいん 定員 ❶[規定の人数] a fixed [a prescribed] number; [制限人数] the number limit. ▶志願者の数は定員に達した[を超えた] The number of applicants reached [exceeded] the *fixed number*.
❷[収容力] (seating) capacity. (■時に a ～) ●定員(=座席数)300名の劇場 a theater with a *seating capacity* of 300. ▶その列車の定員は500名です The train has a (*seating*) *capacity* of 500./The train's *capacity* [The (*seating*) *capacity* of the train] is 500. (■ seating を用いる文では「座席数が500」の意) ▶そのバスは定員以上[定員の2倍も]乗せていた The bus was packed beyond [to twice] its *capacity*.

ティーンエージャー a teenager; 《主に米話》a teen. (■ 13–19歳ごろまでの少年[少女]をいう《十代》). ●ティーンエージャー向きの雑誌 a *teenage* [《主に米話》*teen*] magazine. ▶彼女はティーンエージャーだ She is a *teenager* [a *teenage*(*d*) *girl*, *in* her *teens*].

ていえん 低塩 ──低塩の 形 low-salt.
●低塩醤油 a *low-salt* soy sauce. ●低塩食 a *low-salt* diet. ●低塩食品 foods with a *low-salt* content.

ていえん 庭園 a garden; (大邸宅の) a park. (⇨庭)
●屋上[山水式]庭園 a roof [a landscape] *garden*.

ていおう 帝王 (君主) a monarch; (皇帝) an emperor. ●帝王学を学ぶ be taught the duties of the *King* [*Queen*, *Emperor*]. ●暗黒街の帝王 the *king* of the 《Chicago》 underworld.

ていおうせっかい 帝王切開 (a) Caesarean /sizéəriən/ section [birth, operation]; 《do》a Caesarean.

- 帝王切開で子を産ませる deliver ((her *of*)) a child by *Caesarean* ((*section*)). ● 帝王切開で産まれる be born by *Caesarean* ((*section*)); ((話)) be born *Caesarean*.

ていおん 低音 ━━ 〖音〗a low (a deep) sound; (調子に) a low-pitched sound, a low tone; 〖声〗〖音楽〗bass /béis/ 〖男声最低音〗. ● 低音で歌う sing *bass* [in a *low voice*].

ていおん 低温 a low temperature. ● 低温で保存する preserve ((it)) at a *low temperature*.
●低温殺菌 (low-temperature) pasteurization. ●低温やけど a *low-temperature* burn. ●低温輸送 refrigerated transport. ●低温療法 cryotherapy; refrigeration.

ていおん 定温 a constant [a fixed] temperature.
●定温動物 a warm-blooded [a homeothermic] animal.

*ていか 低下 图 〖下がること〗a fall, (急に) a drop; 〖衰え〗(やや書) a decline; 〖質の劣化〗(a) deterioration. ● 人気の低下 a *decline* in popularity. ● 品物の質の著しい低下 a marked *deterioration* in the quality of goods.
━━ 低下する 動 (下がる) fall*, (急に) drop (-pp-); (衰える) (やや書) decline; (悪化する) (やや書) deteriorate; (健康などが衰える) fail; (程度などを落とす) lower; (量が減る) decrease; (価値などが減る) lessen. ▶温度が急に低下した The temperature *fell* [*dropped*] suddenly./There was a sudden *fall* [*drop*] *in* temperature. ▶学生の学力が低下した The students' scholastic attainments *have declined* [*dropped*]. ▶視力がめっきり低下した My eyesight *has failed* badly.

■■■ DISCOURSE
このようにして、日本の出生率は低下した In this way, the birth rate has *dropped* in Japan. (⚠ In this way (このようにして)は結論に用いるディスコースマーカー)

ていか 定価 a fixed price; (表示価格) a list price; (正規の価格) a regular price. (⚠ 単に price だけでよいことも多い) ▶それを定価で売る sell it *at a fixed price*. ▶私はその品を定価の1割引で買った I bought the article at a 10% discount off the *price*.
●定価表 a priced catalog.

ていかいはつ 低開発 ━━ 低開発の 形 underdeveloped ((areas)). ●⚪ 国には developing (開発途上の) を用いるのが普通

ていがく 低額 a small sum [amount] of money.
●低額所得者 a person with a low income. ●低額所得者層 the low income bracket.

ていがく 定額 a fixed sum [amount]. ●月額定額(料金) fixed charge per month.
●定額貯金 fixed amount postal savings. ●定額法 the straight line method. ●定額預金 a fixed (saving) deposit. ●定額料金 a flat rate.

ていがく 停学 suspension from school ((*for* bad conduct)). ▶カンニングで1週間停学させられた I *was suspended* for a week *from school for* cheating./I was put on a week's *suspension* (from school) *for* cheating.

ていがくねん 低学年 the lower grades ((米)) [forms ((英))]. (⇒学年)

ていかん 定款 the statutes of a company ((an institution)).

ていかん 停刊 图 suspension of publication.
━━ 停刊する 動 suspend publication ((*of*)).

ていかん 諦観 图 resignation.
━━ 諦観する 動 resign oneself ((*to* fate)); accept ((one's fate)) with resignation.

でいがん 泥岩 (a) mudstone.

ていかんし 定冠詞 〖文法〗a definite /défənit/ (↔an indefinite) article.

ていき 定期 ━━ 定期(的な) 形 (規則正しい) regular; (周期的な) pèriòdic(al). (⚠ 前者は定められたとか [に]期間をあけて]起こること。後の方は通例同じ間隔でくり返し行われること。いずれも通例限定的に用いる)
━━ 定期(的に) 副 regularly; pèriòdically. ●機械を定期的に検査する inspect a machine *regularly*. ●定期的に報告書を出す make a report *at regular intervals*; make a *periodic* report ((*to*)). (⚠ 後の方が「一定の間隔をあけて」の意が強い) ▶朝会は月1回定期的に開かれる We have our morning assembly *regularly* once a month.
●定期入れ a pass holder. ●定期刊行物 a periodical (publication). ●定期券 (⇒定期券). ●定期検診 ((have)) a periodic [a regular] medical checkup. ●定期購読 subscription. ●定期試験 ((take)) a regular exam. ●定期昇給 ((get)) a periodic [a regular] (pay) raise ((米)) [rise ((英))]. ●定期便 (飛行機) an airliner; (船, 飛行機) a liner. ●定期預金 ((make)) a time [a fixed] deposit.

ていき 提起 ━━ 提起する 動 (持ち出す) bring ... up; (出す) raise. ▶いくつかの問題を提起する *bring up* some problems.

ていぎ 定義 图 (a) definition. ▶鯨は定義上哺乳(ほにゅう)類は A whale is a mammal *by definition*.
━━ 定義する 動 define. ▶犬を「人間の最良の友達」と定義する *define* a dog *as* "man's best friend". ▶きみは犬をどう定義しますか How do you *define* a dog?/What's your *definition* of a dog?

ていぎ 提議 图 (a) proposal.
━━ 提議する 動 propose. (⇒提案)

ていきあつ 低気圧 〖気象〗low (atmospheric) pressure (⇒気圧); a depression; a cyclone. ●熱帯性低気圧 a tropical *low*; (インド洋の) a cyclone.

ていきけん 定期券 ((米)) a commuter('s) [a commutation] ticket; ((英)) a season ticket, ((英話)) a season. (⚠ 日常会話では a train [a bus] pass などの方が普通) ●3か月のバス通勤定期券 a three-month *bus pass* (for work). ●定期券で通勤する commute ((*from* A *to* B, *between* A *and* B)). ●定期券を更新する renew one's *commuter's ticket*. ●定期券通勤者 a commuter.

ていきじょうしゃけん 定期乗車券 (⇒定期券)

ていきせん 定期船 a liner.

ていきゅう 低級 a low class; low quality. ●低級な(下品な) vulgar. ●低級な趣味 a *low* taste. ●低級な番組 a *vulgar* [(知的でない) a *lowbrow*, ((話)) (くだらない) a *trashy*] program.

ていきゅう 庭球 〖テニス〗(lawn) tennis.

ていきゅうび 定休日 a regular holiday. ▶このスーパーは月曜日が定休日だ This supermarket is closed on Mondays. (⚠ Mondays と複数形になることに注意)

*ていきょう 提供 图 an offer. ●食料の提供 an *offer* of food. ●(商品の)特別提供 a special *offer*. ●情報提供者 an informant; (警察などへの) an informer; (臓器の) a ((kidney)) donor. ●窃盗犯に関する情報提供者には1,000ドルの賞金を出します We will give a reward of 1,000 dollars to anyone with information about the thieves. ▶全商品割引価格でご提供中です All items *are being offered* at reduced prices.
━━ 提供する 動 offer; 〖供給する〗(足りないものを) supply; (必要な物を) provide; 〖与える〗give*. ●労力を提供する *offer* one's services ((*to*)). ●腎臓を

テイクアウト a takeout, a carryout; 《英》a takeaway. (⇨持ち帰る) ▶テイクアウトで寿司(ｼ)2人前お願いします Two orders of sushi *to tàke óut* [*of tákeòut* sushi], please.

ていくう 低空 a low-altitude. ●低空飛行をする fly low; fly at a *low altitude*; (落第すれすれの及第) barely pass the exam; squeeze by [through] the exam.

テイクオーバー 〖企業の買収, 乗っ取り〗a takeover.
テイクオフ 〖離陸〗(a) takeoff.
ディクテーション 〖書き取り〗(a) dictation. ●英語のディクテーションをさせる give 《him》 an English *dictation*. ●英語のディクテーションの試験を受ける have a test in English *dictation*.

テイクバック ― **テイクバックする** 動 (ゴルフ, テニスで) move the club [racket] back.

デイケア (adult) day care. (!単なる day care は〖就学前児童の〗昼間保育〗をさすのが普通)
●デイケアセンター an adult day-care center; a day-care center for the elderly.

ていけい 定形 (標準の大きさ) a standard size; (一定の形) a fixed form.
●定形郵便物 standard-sized (↔nonstandard-sized) mail.

ていけい 提携 图 (タイアップ) a tie-ùp; (協力) cooperation. ●技術提携 a technical *tie-up*; technical *cooperation*. ●業務提携 a business tie-up. ●資本提携 a capital *tie-up*. ●戦略的提携 a strategic *alliance*.
― **提携する** 動 tie (～d; tying) up 《with》; (協力する) cooperate 《with》. ▶我が社はアメリカの会社と提携している Our company *is tied up with* an American firm.
●提携先 one's business partner.

ていけい 定型 (決まった型) a fixed form, a regular pattern.
●定型詩 poetry with a fixed form [a regular pattern].

ていけつ 締結 图 conclusion. ●平和条約の締結 the *conclusion* of a peace treaty.
― **締結する** 動 ●米国と〖3国間で〗条約を締結する *conclude* a treaty *with* the United States [*between* the three nations].

ていけつあつ 低血圧 low blood pressure (↔high blood pressure).
●低血圧症 hypotension /hàipouténʃən/ (↔hypertension).

ていけん 定見 ●定見(=ゆるがない意見)がない have no firm [(定まった) fixed, (明確な) definite] *opinion* 《of oneself》.

ていげん 低減 图 (大幅な減少) (a) reduction; (a) cutback; (徐々な減少) (a) décrease, (a) diminution, (a) fall-off.
― **低減する** 動 reduce; cut(...) back; décrease, diminish, fall off.

ていげん 逓減 图 (a) décrease, (a) diminution. ●収穫逓減の法則〖経済〗the law of *diminishing returns*.
― **逓減する** 動 décrease; diminish.

ていげん 提言 图 (⇨提案)
ディケンズ 〖英国の小説家〗Dickens (Charles ～).

ていこ 艇庫 a boathouse.
ていこう 抵抗 图 (a) resistance 《to》.
①〖～抵抗〗 ●空気抵抗 air *resistance*; the *resistance* of the air. ▶銅は鉛より電気抵抗が少ない Copper has less electric *resistance* than lead (has).
②〖抵抗～〗 ●その子は病気への抵抗力がほとんどない The child has almost no *resistance* to disease [*power to resist* disease]. ▶これらのネズミは毒に対して抵抗力がついている These rats are *resistant to* poison.
③〖抵抗に〗 ●敵の激しい抵抗にあう meet with (a) strong *resistance* from the enemy.
④〖抵抗を[も]〗 ●この計画を提案するのに抵抗を感じた(=気乗りがしなかった) I was *unwilling* [(ためらいを覚えた) I felt *hesitant*] to propose this plan. ▶I was *reluctant*... では「気が進まないまま提案した」の意) ▶彼の計画は強い抵抗を受けた There has been a lot of *resistance* to his plan. ▶彼は私の提案を何の抵抗もなく(=無条件に[喜んで])受け入れた He accepted my proposal *unconditionally* [*willingly*].
― **抵抗する** 動 resist; (耐えて屈しない) 《書》withstand*. ▶我が軍は敵の攻撃に頑強に抵抗した Our troops *resisted* 《xto》 an enemy attack stubbornly./Our troops *put up* [*made*, 《やや書》*offered*] *a* stubborn *resistance to* an enemy attack. ▶彼は警察に逮捕されまいと抵抗した He *resisted* being arrested by the police. (!×resisted to be arrested は不可)
●抵抗運動 a resistance movement. ●抵抗者 a resister (! resistor は〖(電気の抵抗器)〗; a resistant. ●抵抗勢力 resistance forces; (守旧派) the old guard.

ていこく 定刻 (予定の時刻) the scheduled time; (約束の時刻) the appointed time; (一定の時刻) a fixed time. ▶会議は定刻に開かれた The meeting opened at [xon, xin] *the scheduled time*./(時間を厳守には守った) The meeting started *punctually*. ▶列車は定刻に着いた The train arrived *on time* [*schedule*]. ▶バスは定刻より5分遅れて[早く]出た The bus left five minutes *behind* [*ahead of*] *schedule*. ▶彼女は定刻にやって来た She came at *the appointed time*. ▶私は毎日定刻に家を出る I leave home at the *fixed time* every day.

ていこく 帝国 an empire. ●大英[ローマ]帝国 the British [Roman] *Empire*.
●**帝国の** 形 imperial; of an empire.
●帝国主義 imperialism. (関連) 反帝国主義 anti-imperialism) ●帝国主義的(な) imperialistic. ●帝国主義者 an imperialist. (関連) 反帝国主義者 an anti-imperialist) ●帝国大学 an imperial university.

ていさ 艇差 a distance between boats. ●艇差半艇身で勝つ win *by* a half length. (⇨艇身)
でいさ 泥砂 muddy soil, mud.
デイサービス 〖老人のための日帰り介護〗 adult day-care; 《和製語》day service.

ていさい 体裁 图 〖外見〗(an) appearance; 〖体面, 世間体〗appearances (!この意では常に複数形); 〖見苦しくないこと〗decency, respectability; 〖形式〗a form, (本の) a format.
①〖体裁～〗 ●体裁上 for *appearance's* [*decency's*] sake. ●体裁よく着飾る dress *decently*.
②〖体裁が〗 ▶この飾りは体裁がよい This ornament *looks good* [*decent*]. ▶彼に謝るのは体裁が悪かった(=ばつが悪かった) I felt *awkward* [*embarrassed*] to apologize to him. ▶そのパーティーに呼

味があったのだが, 体裁があって行けなかった I wanted to go to the party, but I didn't go *for appearance' sake*.

③【体裁の】 ●体裁のよい服装で in *decent* [*presentable*] clothes. ●体裁のよい (=もっともらしい) 言い訳をする make a *plausible* excuse /ɪkskjúːs/.

④【体裁を】 ●体裁を繕う keep up [save] *appearances*. ●お体裁を言う talk *glibly* [*smoothly*]. ▶あの先生は体裁を気にしない That teacher doesn't care about his *appearance* [(about) *how he looks*]. ▶この本は論文集という体裁を取っている This book takes a *form* of a collection of theses.

—— 体裁ぶる 動 ［見えを張る］show* off; ［気取る］put* on [assume] airs. ▶そんなに体裁ぶるのはよせよ Oh, stop *showing off* [*putting on airs*]!

ていさつ 偵察 名 ［敵状の］scouting; ［書］［軍事］(a) reconnaissance /rikάnəzəns/.

—— 偵察する 動 scout; ［書］［軍事］reconnoiter /riːkənɔ́itər/.

●偵察員 a scout. ●偵察機 a scout; a spy [a reconnaissance] plane.

ていざん 低山 a low mountain.

***ていし 停止** 名 (a) stoppage, a stop; (一時的に) suspension. ●生産停止 the *stoppage* of production. ●営業［発行］停止 *suspension* of business [publication]. ●一時停止標識 a *stop* sign. ▶一時停止《標識》Stop.

—— 停止する 動 (動いているもの・活動が［を］) stop (-pp-), pause; (続いている動作・状態形式が) cease ［siːs］; (一時的に) suspend. (⇨止まる, 止(と)める) ●小切手の支払いを停止する *stop* (payment of) a check. ●戦闘を停止する *cease* fire. ●ガスの供給を停止する *suspend* [*cut off*] the gas supply. ●信号でいったん停止する *stop* ［車が］*pull up*, *come to a full stop*] at the traffic lights. ●30日間運転免許を停止される *have* one's driver's license *suspended* for 30 days. ▶エンジンが停止した The engine *has stopped* [×ceased]. ▶私はビデオを停止した I *paused* the video. ●彼の心拍はだんだん弱くなりつつに停止した His heartbeat got weaker and weaker and then it *ceased*. ▶彼は出場を停止されている He *is suspended* [*under suspension*] from the game. (❗アクセントに注意)

●停止信号 (交通の赤信号) a red light.

***ていじ 提示** 名 presentation; (価格) an offer.

—— 提示する 動 (見せる) show*, (取り出して) produce; (差し出す) present. ●パスポートを提示する *show* [*produce, present*] one's passport.

ていじ 丁字 ―― 丁字形の 形 T-shaped.

●丁字帯 a T bandage. ●丁字路 a T-junction; a T-intersection.

ていじ 定時 a fixed time; (予定の時間) the scheduled time. ●定時に(=時間通りに) on schedule [time]. ▶彼はしばらくぶりに定時に退社した He left the office at the *fixed time*, which he couldn't do for some time.

ていしき 定式 a formula (複 -lae /-liː/, ～s), an established form. ●定式化される be formularized [established] (*as*).

●定式化 formularization.

ていじげん 低次元 ―― 低次元の 形 （レベルの低い) low-level; low-grade; (低俗な) vulgar. ●低次元の議論 a *low-level* argument.

ていしせい 低姿勢 a low profile /próufail/. ●低姿勢をとる adopt [keep, (ややる) maintain] a *low profile*. ●低姿勢の政治家 a *low-profile* politician.

ていじせい 定時制 a part-time course.

●定時制高校 a part-time high school. (❗a night school は「夜間学校」)

ていしつ 低湿 ●低湿な土地 low and damp land [ground], (⇨湿)

ていしゃ 停車 名 a stop. ●各駅停車の列車(=普通列車) a local ［《米》a way] train. ●停車中の列車 a *standing* [×a stopping] train. ●停車する予定の列車 a *stopping* train は「止まりかけている列車」のこと) ▶停車禁止《標識》No *standing* [*stopping*].

—— 停車する 動 stop (-pp-), come* to a stop. (⇨止まる) ●各駅に停車する *stop* at all stations. ●急停車する *stop* short. ▶この列車は当駅で3分間停車します This train *makes* a three-minute *stop* [*stops* for three minutes] at this station. ▶次に停車するのはどこですか What [Where] is the next *stop*?/Where *does* the train *stop* next? ▶彼の車は信号で一時停車した His car *stopped* [*pulled up*] at the traffic lights.

—— 停車させる 動 stop (-pp-) ［a car]. (⇨止める)

●停車時間 stoppage time.

ていしゃじょう 停車場 a station. (⇨駅)

ていしゅ 亭主 ❶【夫】one's husband. (⇨夫) ●亭主をしりに敷く rule ［話] henpeck] one's *husband*. ▶彼は亭主関白(=妻に対し独裁的にふるまう夫)だ He is a *tyrant* [an *autocrat*] over his wife. (❗tyrant は「専制君主」, autocrat は「独裁者」の意)/(家庭の実権を握っている) He rules the roost at home. (❗roost は本来は「(鳥の)とまり木, ねぐら」の意)/He wears the pants 《米》[*trousers*《英》] in the family. (⇨かかあ天下)

❷【客に対する】a host. (⇨主人)

●亭主持ち a married woman.

ていしゅ 艇首 the bow /báu/.

ていしゅう 定収 a fixed income.

ていじゅう 定住 名 settlement.

—— 定住する 動 ●パリに定住する settle (down) in Paris; reside in Paris permanently.

●定住地 one's fixed [permanent] dwelling (place).

ていしゅうは 低周波 名 a low (↔high) frequency.

●低周波の 形 low-frequency.

ていしゅく 貞淑 ―― 貞淑な 形 chaste; faithful. (❗両語とも男にも用いる)

***ていしゅつ 提出** 名 presentation (*of*). ●委員会への新たな資料の提出 the *presentation* of new data to the committee.

—— 提出する 動 ［書類・答案などを］(上位の者に) submit (-tt-); (手渡す) hand ［《主に米》turn]... in; (改まって) present; ［議案などを] introduce, present; ［抗議・異議などを]《法律》file, lodge; ［問題を] pose; ［証拠を] produce, bring*... forward. ●請願書を市長に提出する *present* a petition *to* the Mayor; *present* the Mayor (*with*) a petition. (❗アクセントに注意) ●辞表を上司に提出する *submit* one's resignation to one's boss. ●法案を議会に提出する *introduce* a bill *in* Congress. ▶授業の終わりに宿題を提出しなさい Hand [Turn] your homework *in* at the end of the class. ▶学期末レポートは火曜日の朝提出しないといけない My term paper has to *be in* on Tuesday morning.

ていじょ 貞女 a chaste [a faithful] woman.

ていしょう 低床 ●低床バス a low-platform bus.

ていしょう 提唱 名 (提案) (a) proposal; (支持)《書》advocacy.

—— 提唱する 動 (公に)《書》advocate 《*doing*; *that* 節》; (提案する) propose, 《書》advance. ●死刑の廃止を提唱する *advocate* the abolition of capital

ていじょう 呈上 图 presentation. — 呈上する 動 present. (⇨進呈)
・提唱者 an advocate 《*of*》.

ていじょう 泥状 ― 泥状の 形 muddy.

ていしょく 定食 a set meal;（高級レストランなどの）a table d'hôte /táːbl dóut/. ・焼き肉定食 a *set meal* with broiled meat.

ていしょく 定職 (決まった) a regular [(安定した) a steady] job. ・定職に就く get a *steady job*. ・定職がない have no *steady job*.

ていしょく 抵触 ❶[法などに触れること] ・法に抵触する (＝反する) be *against* [*contrary to*] the law. ❷[矛盾すること] conflict 《*with*》.

ていしょく 停職 suspension from one's job. ・1 か月間停職になる be suspended for a month from office.

ていしょとく 低所得 ・低所得者 a person with low income;（集合的）a low-income group. ・低所得者層 the low income bracket.

ていしん 挺身 ― 挺身する 動 volunteer 《*for*; *to do*》, offer oneself 《*for*》, come forward.
・挺身隊 a volunteer corps /kɔ́ːr/ (複 ～ corps /kɔ́ːrz/).

ていしん 艇身 a boat's length. ・半艇身差で勝つ win the race by a half [(英) half a] *length*.

ていすい 泥酔 泥酔している be really drunk;《話》be blind drunk;《話》be plastered.

ていすう 定数 ❶[一定の数] a fixed number;（定足数）a quorum. ・定数に満たない fall short of the *quorum*. ❷[数学］a constant (↔a variable).

ディスカウント 割引 (a) discount. ・ディスカウントストア a *discount* [(米) a *cut-rate*,《英》a *cut-price*] store.

ディスカッション (a) discussion. (❗debate よりくだけた「討論」)

ディスク a disc, a disk. (❗CD や DVD には disc を用いることが多い)

[関連] いろいろなディスク: 起動ディスク a startup [a boot] *disk*/光磁気ディスク a magneto-optical [an MO] *disk*/磁気ディスク a magnetic *disk*/システムディスク a system *disk*/デジタルビデオディスク a digital video*disk*/光ディスク an optical *disk*/ミニディスク《商標》Mini *Disk*《略 MD》/両面(フロッピー)ディスク a double-sided (floppy) *disk*.

・ディスクジョッキー a disk jockey《略 D.J.》. ・ディスクドライブ a disk drive.

ディスクロージャー [[情報開示]] disclosure.

ディスコ a disco (複 ～s),《今は古》a discotheque.
・ディスコで夜通し踊る (dance at a) *disco* all night. ・ディスコ音楽 disco music.

ディストリビューター [[特定地域内の販売代理店]] a distributor.

ディズニー [[米国のアニメ映画製作者]] Disney (Walt(er Elias) 〜). ・ディズニーランド Disneyland.

ディスプレー [[展示]] (a) display;[[コンピュータの]] a monitor, a display. ・フラットパネルディスプレー a flat-panel *display*.
・ディスプレー画面 display screen.

ディスポーザー [[生ごみ処理機]] a (garbage) disposer.

ていする 呈する ・深刻な様相を呈する (＝帯びる) *take on* a serious aspect. ・活況を呈する (株式市場などが) be very active.

ていする 挺する ・身を挺して (＝命がけで)危機を乗り切る *risk one's life* to get over the difficulty.

ていせい 帝政 imperialism;（特に旧ロシアの）czarism /záːrizm/.
・帝政ロシア Czarist Russia.

ていせい 訂正 图 (a) correction. ▶訂正は赤インクで願います *Corrections* should be *made* in red ink. (参考) 米英では訂正に青インクを用いる. cf. blue-pencil) ▶その翌日に訂正記事を載せたよ. その写しを送ってきいます We ran a *We Were Wrong* the next day. I can send you a copy. (❗We Were Wrong は「訂正記事」のことなので a をつけることに注意)

― **訂正する** 動 correct, make* a correction;（正す）put*... right. (⇨正す) ▶つづりが間違っていれば訂正してください *Correct* my spelling if it's wrong./*Correct* my misspellings [errors in my spelling] if any. ▶その誤植は次の刷りで訂正された The misprint *was put right* in the next printing.

ていせいぶんせき 定性分析 [化学] qualitative analysis.

ていせつ 定説 [学問的な] an established theory [belief];[一般に認められた意見] an generally accepted opinion. ・定説をくつがえす overturn the *established theory*.

ていせつ 貞節 图 《やや古》faithfulness,《やや書》fidélity (↔infidelity). ― **貞節な** 形 faithful 《*to*》.

ていせん 停船 图 order a ship to stop.

ていせん 停戦 图 [軍事] a cease-fire;（通例一時的な）a truce, an armistice.

― **停戦する** 動 cease fire; make a truce [an armistice]《*with*》.
・停戦会議 a cease-fire conference. ・停戦協定 a cease-fire agreement; a truce.

ていそ 定礎 laying of a cornerstone. ・定礎式を行う hold a *cornerstone* laying ceremony.

ていそ 提訴 ― **提訴する** 動 (裁判にかける) bring ... before the court;（告訴する）sue;（訴える）appeal to .... ・その事件を提訴する bring the case *before the court*; present the case *to the court*. ▶労働省は ILO に提訴した The labor *appealed* to the ILO.

ていそう 低層 ・低層住宅地 a low-rise housing development.

ていそう 貞操 chastity;《今はまれ》virtue (❗chastity の婉曲語). ・貞操を守る[失う] defend [lose] one's *chastity*.

ていぞう 逓増 图 (an) increase. ― **逓増する** 動 incréase.

ていそく 低速 (a) low (↔(a) high) speed. ・低速で運転する drive at *low speed*.

ていぞく 低俗 图 (a) vulgarity.
― **低俗な** 形 ・低俗なテレビ番組 a *vulgar* [(低級な) a *lowbrow*] TV program.

ていそくすう 定足数 《やや書》a quorum /kwɔ́ːrəm/. ・定足数に達する achieve a *quorum*. ▶会議は定足数に足りず延期された The meeting was adjourned since there was no *quorum* [we didn't have a *quorum*].

***ていたい** 停滞 ― **停滞している** 動 (止まっている) be at a standstill;（遅れている）be delayed;（沈滞している）be stagnant. ▶豪雪のため交通は完全に停滞した The heavy snow brought traffic to a *standstill*./Traffic came to a *standstill* in the heavy snow. ▶景気が停滞している Business *is stagnant* [*slow*, *slack*]. ▶秋雨前線が日本列島の上に停滞している(＝居すわっている) The autumnal rain front *is settling in* [(なかなか去らない) *lingering*] over the Japanese Islands.

・停滞前線 a stationary front.

ていたい 手痛い 《厳しい》severe; 《深刻な》serious; 《多大の犠牲を払った》costly. ● 手痛い打撃を与える give a *painful* [a *hard*, a *severe*, a *serious*] blow 《to him》. ● 手痛い失敗をする make a *serious* [a *costly*] error. ● 彼女から手痛い(=手厳しい)批判を受ける draw *severe* [*痛烈な* *sharp*] criticism from her; be *severely* [*sharply*] criticized by her.

ていだい 帝大 [『帝国大学』の略] (⇒帝国) ● 旧帝大 a former imperial university.

ていたいおん 低体温 low temperature. ● 低体温症 〖医学〗 hypothermia. ● 低体温麻酔 〖医学〗 low-temperature [hypothermic] anesthesia.

ていたく 邸宅 a mansion (❗ 豪壮でしばしば古い大邸宅); a residence (❗ a house より高級感を伴う); a villa (❗ 保養地や郊外の広い家つきのもの).

ていたらく 《みっともない, 情けない》shameful; miserable. ▶ 何というていたらく(=みっともない)! Shame on you!/(情けない) What a shame!/(みじめな) What a *miserable* condition you are in!

ていだん 鼎談 a three-person talk. (⇒対談)

でいたん 泥炭 peat.

ていち 低地 lowlands.

ていち 定置 ● 定置網 a fixed shore net. ● 定置網漁業 fixed shore net fishing.

ていちゃく 定着 图 ● 従業員の定着(=安定)を図る improve the *stability* of the work force.
── **定着する** 動 《確立される》be established; 〖根付く〗take* root; 〖一般に受け入れられるようになる〗《話》be here [have come] to stay. ▶ その習慣は私たちの間に定着した The custom *has been established* [*has taken root, has come to stay*] among us. ▶ 資本主義はその国に深く定着した Capitalism *has planted* its *roots* deeply in that country.

でいちゅう 泥中 ● 泥中の蓮(葉) 'a lotus flower in a muddy pond'; 《ことわざ》'A myrtle among thorns is a myrtle still.'

ていちょう 丁重 〖礼儀正しさ〗politeness; 〖礼儀正しく思いやりがあること〗courtesy.
── **丁重な** 形 polite; courteous; 《敬意を表す》respectful. ▶ 丁重な手紙 a *polite* [a *courteous*] letter. ▶ 彼は目上の人に丁重だ He is *polite* [*courteous*] *to* his superiors.
── **丁重に** 副 politely; courteously; 《敬意を表して》respectfully. ● 客を丁重に扱う treat one's guest *politely* [*courteously*, *respectfully*]. ● その申し出を丁重に断わる *decline* the offer 《*politely*》(❗ 丁重に断わる は「丁寧に断わる」の意 ⇒断わる)

ていちょう 低調 ─ **低調な** 形 《活気がない》dull; 《不振な》sluggish; 《不活発な》inactive. ● 低調な市況 a *dull* [a *sluggish*, a *不景気な* *slack*] market. ▶ 彼女の成績は低調だ(=低い) She has *poor* grades at school./Her grades are *poor*. ▶ 彼は打撃が低調だ(=スランプに陥っている) He is *in a batting slump*.

ていちょう 艇長 [小型船の長] a captain.

ていちんぎん 低賃金 low wages [pay]. (⇒賃金)

ティッシュ(ペーパー) a tissue; 〖商標〗a Kleenex (❗ 単複同形). ● ティッシュペーパー 〖包装用の薄い紙〗tissue paper ● ティッシュ 1 箱 a box of *tissues*.

ていっぱい 手一杯 ● 《手がふさがっている》have one's hands full 《*with*》; 《とても忙しい》be very busy 《*with*》. ▶ 宿題で手一杯だ I *have* (got) *my hands full with* homework.

ていてつ 蹄鉄 a horseshoe. ● 蹄鉄を打つ shoe a horse.

ていてん 定点 a fixed point.

● 定点観測 《×a》 fixed point observation. ● 定点観測船 a ship weather station; an ocean station vessel.

ていでん 停電 图 《電気が消えること》a blackout; 《電力供給の停止》a power failure [cut] 《後の方は意図的な場合もある》; 《米》a power outage. ▶ あす午後 8 時から 10 時まで停電になります(=電気(の供給)が止まる) The *electricity* (supply) *will be* (cut) *off* [There will be a *blackout*] from 8 p.m. to 10 p.m. tomorrow.
── **停電する** 動 ▶ 台風のため停電した The typhoon caused a *power failure* [*suspension*]./*Power service was suspended* because of the typhoon. ▶ ショートして停電した An electrical short-circuit led to a *blackout*.

ていど 程度 ❶ 〖度合い〗〖程度の段階〗(a) degree (❗ 具体的には Ⓒ); 〖能力・許容量などの範囲・限度〗(an) extent (❗ 通例 to ... extent という句で用いる). ● 程度の問題 a matter [a question] of *degree*. ● それぞれの程度の差はあっても満足しうる be satisfied *in* varying *degrees*. ▶ そのことについてどの程度ご存知ですか *How much* [*To what degree*, *To what extent*] do you know about it? (❗ how much が最も口語的的) ▶ 教育の程度に応じが, 大部分のアメリカ人は 1 万語から 2 万語の単語を知っている *Depending on* education, most Americans know 10,000 to 20,000 words.
【ある程度】▶ その報告はある程度本当だ The report is true *to some* [*a certain*] *extent*./There is *some* [*a certain amount of*] truth in the report. ▶ 彼はそのことについてある程度知識がある He has *some* knowledge of the subject. ▶ 君が言いたいことはある程度分かる I see what you mean *in a way*.
❷ [水準] 〖知的・道徳的・社会的水準〗a level; 〖比較・評価の基準〗a standard. ● 大学程度の学生 a student at a college *level*; a college-*level* student. ● 日本の高い教育の程度 Japan's high *level* of education. ● 程度の低い番組 a vulgar [a low-*level*] program. ▶ この動物たちは知能の程度がかなり高い These animals have a rather high *level* of intelligence. ▶ この問題は君には程度が高[低]すぎる The *level* of this question is too high [low] for you. ▶ 彼の知能程度は私と同じだ His mentality [《話》(知能指数) IQ] *is on a level with* mine. ▶ その国は生活程度が高い The country has a high *standard* of living.
❸ [限度] a limit. ▶ なんでもものには程度がある There is a *limit to* everything./Everything has its *limit*(s).
❹ [およそ] ● 5,000 円程度の損をする lose *about* five thousand yen.

でいど 泥土 mud; dirt; 〖書〗mire.

ていとう 低糖 《have》a low sugar content.

ていとう 抵当 《通例不動産の》(a) mortgage /mɔ́ːrɡɪdʒ/; 〖担保〗security. ● 家が抵当に入っている a house *in mortgage*. ● 財産を抵当に入れて銀行から 500 万円借りる *mortgage* one's property *to* a bank *for* five million yen. ● その土地は 5,000 万円の抵当に入っている There is a *mortgage of* fifty million yen *on* the land. / The land *is mortgaged for* fifty million yen. ▶ 彼は家を抵当に入れて金を借りた He borrowed the money *on* (*the security of*) his house. / He *offered* his house *as security* [*mortgaged* his house, *placed a mortgage* on his house] to borrow the money.

● 抵当権 a mortgage. ● 抵当証券 a mortgage

ていとく 提督 (司令長官) an ádmiral.

ていとん 頓挫 ―頓挫する[している] 動 come* to [beat] a standstill; (交渉が) reach [beat] (a) deadlock. ▶作業が停頓している Work *is making no* [*is not making any*] *progress.*

ディナー (a) dinner. (⇨夕飯)
• ディナークルーズ a dinner cruise. • ディナーショー a dinner and floor show 《*at a hotel*》《和製語》 a dinner show. • ディナーセット dinner set.

ていない 邸内 • 邸内で on the *premises.* (⚠常に複数扱い) ▶邸内での飲酒はご遠慮下さい No alcohol is allowed on these [×*this*] *premises.*

ていない 庭内 • 庭内の[で, を] in the *garden.* • 庭内をひと巡りする take a turn [a stroll, a walk] *around the garden.*

‡ていねい 丁寧 名 〖礼儀正しさ〗 politeness; courtesy; 〖注意〗 care.

― **丁寧な** 形 ❶ 〖礼儀正しい〗 polite; (礼儀正しくて思いやりのある) courteous; (無作法にならない程度に礼儀正しい) civil; (敬意を表する) respectful. • 丁寧な返事 a *polite* [a *courteous*] reply. ▶彼は丁寧な言葉遣いをする He uses *polite* language [has a *polite* way of speaking]./He speaks *politely.* ▶そんなに早く返事をくれるとは彼はなんて丁寧な人なんでしょう How [*courteous*] (it is) of him to write back so soon! (⚠it is は通例省略する) ▶彼は丁寧だが親しめない He is *civil* but not friendly. (⚠*civil* はよそよそしさを暗示)

❷ 〖注意深い〗 careful; (綿密な) close; (徹底的な) thorough. • 丁寧な字(=きちんとした字体) *neat* handwriting. ▶その大工は仕事が丁寧だ The Carpenter is *careful* with his work [《話》does a *neat* job].

― **丁寧に** 副 ❶ 〖礼儀正しく〗 politely; courteously; (うやうやしく) respectfully. • 彼に丁寧におじぎするbow /báu/ to him *politely* [*respectfully*]. • 老人に丁寧に接する deal *respectfully* with older people; be *respectful* to [*toward*] older people.

会話「結果をメールでお知らせしましょう」「それはご丁寧に(=ご親切に)どうも」"I'll let you know the results by [via] e-mail." "Oh, that's very *kind* of you."

❷ 〖注意深く〗 carefully; (綿密に) closely; (徹底的に) thoroughly. • 高価な花びんを丁寧に扱う handle the expensive vase *carefully* [*with care*]. • 彼の歯を丁寧に診察する examine his teeth *closely* [*thoroughly*]; make a *close* [a *thorough*] examination of his teeth.
• 丁寧語 (総称的) polite language; (個々の語) a polite word.

ていねい 泥濘 (⇨ぬかるみ)

ていねん 定年 (the) retirement áge, the age of retirement; (年齢制限) (the) áge limit. • 定年になる reach *retirement age.* • 定年前に辞める take early *retirement.* • 60歳で定年退職する *retire* (at the age of) 60. ▶あの会社の定年は何歳ですか What is the *retirement age* in that company?/At what age do they have to retire in that firm?
• 定年制 an age-limit system; a mandatory retirement system.

ていのう 低能 imbecility; weak-mindedness; (人) a weak-minded person.

ていはく 停泊 名 anchoring. • 停泊中の船 a ship (lying [riding]) *at anchor* 《*in* Kobe Port》.

― **停泊する** 動 anchor, come* to anchor. ▶我々は湾内に停泊した Our ship *anchored* [We *anchored* (our ship)] in the bay. ▶横浜港には今大きな船が2隻停泊している Two large ships *are* now *in* Yokohama Port.
• 停泊所 an anchorage.

ていはつ 剃髪 • 剃髪を施してもらう have one's head shaved 〖修道士が〗 tonsured.

デイパック 〖小型のリュックサック〗 a daypack.

ていばん 定番 • 就職活動のための定番のスーツ a *standard* suit [dress] for job-hunting.
• 定番商品 regular assortment.

ていひょう 定評 an established reputation (⚠文脈により established は省略できる); a (good) name. (⇨評判) • 業界で一番との定評のある会社 a firm with an *established reputation* as being the best in that industry. ▶その出版社はすぐれた辞書の出版で定評がある The publisher has a *name* [a *reputation*] for publishing good dictionaries.

ディフェンス 〖守備〗《米》 defense, 《英》 defence.
• ゾーン[ライン]ディフェンス zone [line] defense. • 相手のディフェンスを突破する break through their *defensive line.* • ディフェンスラインの裏を突く over the top of opponent's *defensive line.* • 彼はディフェンスの選手です He plays 《on》 *defense* 《米》 [《in》 *defence* 《英》, 《as》 a *defender*]. (⚠( )内の前置詞はしばしば省略される)

ディフェンダー 〖守備選手〗〖競技〗 a defender.

ディベート 《hold [get into]》 a debate 《on, about, over》. (⇨ディスカッション)

ディベロッパー 〖宅地開発業者〗 a developer.

ていへん 底辺 〖三角形などの〗 a base. • 社会の底辺にいる人々 people at the *bottom* of society; people at the *bottom rung* of the ladder.

*****ていぼう 堤防** a bank; (人工の) an embankment; (通例土手・土でできた防潮堤) a dike. ▶川は増水し堤防を越えてはんらんした The river swelled and overflowed its *banks.*

ていぼく 低木 shrub, 《集合的に》 shrubbery; a bush.

ていほん 定本 〖標準となる本〗 a standard text; 〖決定版〗 a definitive version.

ていほん 底本 〖土台となる本〗 the original text; 〖種本〗 a source book.

ていほんかえる『定本蛙』 *Frogs: The Standard Edition.* (参考) 草野心平の詩集)

ていまい 弟妹 one's younger brother(s) and sister(s).

ていめい 低迷 名 • 経済の低迷 economic *weakness* [*slowdown*].

― **低迷している** 動 〖雲が低くたれこめる〗 hang low; 〖悪い状態のままである〗(成績などが) do not improve; (株価などが) do not rally; (市況などが) be sluggish, be dull.

ていめん 底面 〖数学〗 the base.

ていめんせき 底面積 the area of the base.

ていやく 定訳 (標準訳) a standard translation; (定評のある訳) an accepted translation.

ていやく 締約 (⇨締結)

ていよう 提要 (⇨概論)

ていよく 体よく (丁寧に) politely; (如才なく) tactfully; (遠回しに) in a roundabout way.

ていらく 低落 (下落) a fall 《*in*》, 《やや書》(a) decline. ▶彼の人気は低落傾向にある His popularity *is going down* [*is falling*, *is on the decline*].

ていらず 手入らず ― **手入らずの** 形 unused; untouched; (自然の) wild. (⇨手つかず)

ティラノザウルス 〖古生物〗 a tyrannosaur /tiránəsɔːr/.

ていり 低利 low interest. ●低利で金を借りる borrow money at *low interest*.
●低利融資 a low-interest loan.

ていり 定理 〖数学〗a theorem.

でいり 出入り 图 ❶〖出たり入ったり〗going [coming] in and out (❗日本語では語順が逆になる点に注意. go は外から come は内から見ている場合);《書》entrance and exit. ●裏口から出入りする use the back door. ▶無数の蜂がせわしげに巣箱を出入りしている Countless bees *are* busily *going in and out of* the beehive.
❷〖訪問〗うちの出入りの洗濯屋 a laundry keeper [worker] serving my family;《話》our laundry keeper. (❗laundryman は男以外を避ける) ▶あの家は出入り(=客)が多い The family has a lot of *visitors*. ▶彼らはその博物館に出入りを許されている They *have* [*are given*] *the run of* the museum. (❗the run は「出入り[使用]の自由」の意) /(使用する権利を持つ)They *have access to* the museum.
❸〖収支〗●金の出入りを記録しておく keep a record of *income and outgo*.
── 出入りする 動 ●窓から出入りするな Don't *go* [*come*] *in and out* through the window. ▶彼が私の家に出入りする(=訪れる)ことを禁じた I told him not to *visit* [*come to*] my house.

でいりぐち 出入り口 〖建物・部屋の〗a doorway; 〖戸口〗a door; 〖塀・囲いの〗a gateway. ●出入り口に立つ stand in the doorway; stand at the door.

ていりつ 低率 a low rate. ▶当校の中途退学者はきわめて低率にとどまっている Our school has a very *low* dropout *rate* so far.

ていりつ 定率 a fixed rate [percentage]. ●5 パーセントの定率で at a *fixed rate* of 5 percent.
●定率減税 fixed rate tax reduction. ●定率法 the fixed percentage method.

ていりつ 鼎立 ── 鼎立する 動 ●党内には3派が鼎立している There are three powers *opposing one another in the party*./Three powers *are vying with* one another for intraparty supremacy.

ていりゅう 底流 an undercurrent. ▶この問題の底流には人種的偏見がある(=人種的偏見が根底にある)(ややき)Racial prejudice is the root cause of [〖書〗*underlies*] this problem.

でいりゅう 泥流 a mudflow.

ていりゅうじょ 停留所 a (bus) stop. (⇨駅)

ていりょう 定量 a fixed quantity.
●定量分析〖化学〗quantitative analysis.

ディル 〖植物〗a dill.

*ていれ 手入れ 图 ❶〖修繕, 世話〗(修理) repair (❗「修理作業, 修理の意」の意では通例複数形で); (主に衣類の) mending; 〖世話〗care; (草木などの) trimming; 〖整備〗maintenance. ▶この家は手入れが必要だ This house needs *repairing* [*to be repaired*]. ▶その庭は手入れが行き届いている The garden *is well kept*. (❗「手入れの行き届いた庭」は a *well-kept* garden) ▶君の髪の手入れは行き届いているよ Your hair *is well taken care of* [*is well trimmed*].
❷〖警察の〗(急襲) a raid; (検挙) a róundùp. ●賭博(とばく)場の手入れを行う raid [*make a raid on*] a gámbling hòuse.
── 手入れする 動 〖修繕する〗repair, mend,《話》fix (❗mend は《米》では主に布製品の修繕に用いる (⇨修繕する, 修理する)); 〖世話する〗take* care of ...; (刈り込む) trim (-mm-); 〖保全する〗maintain. ●投網(とあみ)を手入れする mend [*fix*] a cásting nèt. ▶バ

ラの木を手入れする trim [*take care of*] rose-bushes. ▶古城はよく手入れされていた The old castle *was kept in* good *condition* [(維持されていた) *was kept up* very well, *was maintained* very well]. ▶公園はずっと手入れされていない The park *has been neglected* [*been uncared for*].

ていれい 定例 (定期的な) regular.
●定例会 a regular meeting.

ディレードスチール 〖野球〗a delayed steal.

ディレクター 〖演出家, 映画監督〗a director; 〖放送番組の制作統括者〗a producer.

ディレクトリー 〖コンピュータ〗a directory.
●ディレクトリー型検索エンジン search engines and directories. ●ディレクトリーサービス a directory service.

ていれつ 低劣 ── 低劣な 形 (下等な) low; (いやしい) mean, base; (無価値な) worthless. ●低劣な読み物 *worthless* 〖話〗*trashy*] reading.

ディレッタント 〖好事家〗a dilettánte.

ていれん 低廉 ── 低廉な 形 inexpensive; cheap

ディンクス 〖子供のいない共働き夫婦〗《話》dinks 《double income no kids couple の略》. (❗(1) 若くて yuppie より裕福なエリート層. (2) 夫婦の片方を言う時は a dink》

ティンパニー 〖楽器〗〖集合的〗timpani (❗単・複両扱い); (個々の) a kettledrum. ●ティンパニー奏者 a tímpanist.

てうえ 手植え ●祖母が手植えした樫(かし)の木 an oak tree *planted* by Grandma.

てうす 手薄 ●会場の警備は手薄だった(=不十分だった) The meeting place was *insufficiently* guarded. ▶営業部は今手薄になっている The sales department *is now understaffed*. ▶豚肉の在庫が手薄=品薄になってきていた Pork in stock *was running short*.

てうち 手打ち 手打ちうどん hàndmáde noodles.
●(商談を)手打ちにする strike a bargain.

てうち 手討ち 手討ちにする 《書》put 《him》 to the sword; kill 《him》 with a sword.

デーゲーム 〖競技〗a day game (↔a night game).

デージー 〖植物〗a daisy.

テーゼ 〖<ドイツ語〗〖命題〗〖論理学〗a thesis.

データ data (❗本来は複数形だが, 集合的に単数扱いすることが多い. 動 (情報) information. ●データをとる take *data* (on). ●すべてのデータをコンピュータに入れる feed all the *data* into a computer. ▶このデータは手に入る These *data* are [This *data* is] available.
●データ圧縮 data compression. ●データ回路 a data circuit. ●データ項目 a data item. ●データ収集 data capture [collection]. ●データ処理 data [information] processing. ●データセンター a datacenter. ●データ通信 data communications [com(m)s]. ●データディスク a data disk. ●データ入力 data entry. ●データバンク a data bank. ●データベース (⇨データベース). ●データ変換 data conversion. ●データ放送 data broadcasting. ●データリンク a data link (略 D/L).

データベース 〖コンピュータ〗a database, a data bank.
●画像データベース an image *database*. ●オンラインデータベース an online *database*. ●リレーショナルデータベース a relational *database* (略 RDB). ●データベースからデータを取り出す take data out of the *database*. ●...のデータベースを作る[構築する] make a *database* of ....
●データベース管理 a database management.

デート 图 《話》a date. ●デートに出かける[中である] go out [be] on a *date*《with》. ●デートを申し込む ask

《her》for a *date*; ask 《her》out. ▶今夜のデートのお相手はだれなの Who are you going out with tonight?/《米話》Who is your *date* for tonight? ▶円山公園は人気のあるデートコースです Maruyama Park is a popular place with [among] *dating* couples. (!× ... a popular date course is)
——デートする 動 ●彼女とデートする have a *date with* her; go out with her; 《主に米話》*date* her; (誘い出す)*take* her out.

テーピング ●ふとももにテーピングする 《スポーツ》*tape* one's thigh.

テープ a tape; (接着用の)(adhesive) tape (! しばしば商標の《米》Scotch tape, 《英》Sellotape も用いる); (磁気テープ) (a) (magnetic) tape (!録音・録画済みのものは a tape (recording)); (見送り・装飾用の) a (paper) streamer.

① 【～テープ, テープ～】●45分テープ(録音用) a forty-five-minute spool of *tape*. ●テープ1巻a roll of *tape*. ●絶縁テープ a insulating tape. ●絶縁用テープ a friction tape.

② 【テープ】● ●テープをかける(=再生する) play (back) a *tape* 《on a deck》. ●テープを早送りする[巻戻す] fast forward [rewind] a *tape* (! forward は動詞); wind forward [back] a *tape*. ●テープをはる tape; 《米》Scotch-tape; 《英》Sellotape. ●テープを切る(陸上競技で)break [breast] the *tape* (! breast は女性の乳房を連想させるのでこの意で用いるのを好まない人もいる); (開通式などで) cut [snip] the *ribbon*. ●《テープカット》●歌手にテープを投げる throw a *streamer* at a singer.

③ 《テープに[で]》●テープに録音[録画]する record 《a program》on tape; tape 《a program》. ●包みをテープでくくる put *tape* around a parcel; tie a parcel with (a piece of) *tape*; *tape* a parcel. ●荷物に配達伝票をテープでとめる *tape* a delivery tag *to* a package.
●テープデッキ a tape deck.

テープカット 图《儀式》a ribbon-cutting ceremony.
——テープカットする 動 cut the ribbon.

テーブル a table. (⇨食卓) ●テーブルを囲んで座る sit around a *table*. ●テーブルに皿を置く put plates on the *table*. ●テーブルを予約する reserve [《英》book] a *table*. ●交渉のテーブルにつく sit at the negotiating *table*. ●テーブルについている人々が皆笑った The whole *table* laughed. (!「テーブルについている人々」の意では単・複両扱い)
●テーブルウェア tableware. ●テーブルクロス a tablecloth. ●テーブルスピーチ an after-dinner speech; a speech at dinner; (昼食会での) a luncheon speech; (和製語) a table speech. ●テーブルスプーン a tablespoon. ●テーブルセンター (テーブル中央の)a centerpiece; (帯状の) a table runner (参考)コーヒーテーブルなどに置く装飾用の長い布); (和製語) a table center. ●テーブルチャージ a cover charge; (和製語) a table charge. ●テーブルナイフ a table knife. ●テーブルマット (熱い料理の皿に敷く) a table mat; (一人分の食器をセットするための) a place mat. ●テーブルマナー table manners, manners at table. ●テーブルワイン table wine. (参考)ふだんの食事で飲むワイン)

テープレコーダー a tape recorder. ●テープレコーダーで録音する record 《music》 on a *tape recorder*; tape-record 《music》.

テーマ[<ドイツ語] 〘主題〙(a) a subject, (著作などの基本テーマ) a theme /θiːm/; 〘話題〙a topic. ●私の研究テーマ the *theme* [*subject*] of my study.
●テーマ曲 a theme song [tune]; (番組の)《米》a signature tune (!《米》では a theme song). ●テーマソング a theme song. ●テーマパーク a theme park.

テーラー 〘仕立て屋〙 a tailor. ●テーラーメイドの背広 a *tailor-made* suit.

テールエンド 〘最後尾,最下位〙 the tail end.

テールライト 〘尾灯〙 a taillight; a tail lamp.

ておい 手負い ●手負い(の)クマ a *wounded* bear. (!この意では ×injured としない)

デオキシリボかくさん デオキシリボ核酸 deóxyribo-nucléic ácid (略 DNA).

ておくれ 手後れ ●手後れである(人が) be beyond help; (事が) be too late. ▶手後れにならないうちに彼に手術を施した We operated on him before it *was too late*. ▶がんと分かったときには手後れだった They did not discover the cancer until *too late*. (!この they は病院側[医師]をさす)

でおくれる 出遅れる (始めるのが遅れる) get* a late start 《on》; (走者が) get off to a bad start. ▶当社は中国市場に出遅れた (参入が遅れた) We entered the Chinese market rather late./(他に遅れを取った) We fell behind in entering the Chinese market.

ておけ 手桶 a bucket, 《主に米》a pail. (⇨桶(おけ))

ておしぐるま 手押し車 a pushcart; (一輪車) a wheelbarrow.

ておしポンプ 手押しポンプ (消火用の) a *hand-operated* water pump; a stirrup pump.

ておち 手落ち 〘過失〙a fault; 〘誤り〙a mistake. (⇨手抜かり)▶これは当方の手落ちでした.申し訳ありません This is our *fault*. We apologize for it.

デオドラント 〘体臭止め〙(a) deodorant.

ておの 手斧 (小型の斧) a hatchet; (ちょうな) an adz.

ており 手織り ——手織りの 形 handwoven.

デカ 〘『刑事』の隠語〙《俗》a dick. (⇨刑事)

でかい (お高くとまった) haughty; (ごう慢な) arrogant; (大きい) big. (⇨大きい) ●態度ででかいやつ a *haughty* [*arrogant*] man. ●(世間をあっと言わせるような)でかいことをやってのける set the world [《英》Thames] on fire; do something very remarkable. ▶あいつはいつもでっかいことばかり言ってやがる He always *talks big* 《話》*through his hat*]./《俗》He's a lot of hot air.

てかがみ 手鏡 a hand mirror.

てがかり 手掛かり 〘事件などの糸口〙a clue; 〘解決のかぎ〙a key; 〘犯人などの痕跡(こんせき)〙a track; 〘臭跡〙a scent. ▶警察は彼の居所の手がかりをつかんだ The police found a *clue* to his whereabouts. ▶犯人は何も手がかりを残さなかった The criminal didn't leave any *clues* [*tracks*]. ▶問題解決の手がかりはない There is no *key* [*clue*] *to* (*solving*) the problem. ▶ついに我々はその事件の手がかりを得た At last we are *on the track* [*scent*] *of* the case.

てがき 手書き 图 handwriting.
——手書きの 形 handwritten. ●手紙や日記などの手書きの資料 *handwritten* materials such as letters and diaries.
——手書きする 動 write by hand.

てがき 手描き ——手描きの 形 handdrawn. ●手描きの友禅 *yuzen* fabric with decorative patterns drawn by hand.

てかぎ 手鉤 a hook.

でがけ 出掛け ▶出がけに田中君から電話がかかってきた I had a (phone) call from Mr. Tanaka (*just*) *as* [*when*] *I was going out* [*I was leaving home*].

てがける 手掛ける (扱う,処理する) deal* with ..., handle; (着手する) put* one's hand to .... ●失業問題を手掛ける *deal with* the problem of unem-

でかける ployment. ●その仕事を手掛ける *put* one's *hand to the work.*

***でかける 出掛ける** 〖外出する〗*go* * *out*; 〖出発する〗*leave* *, *start*, *be off*. (⇨出発する) ●散歩に出かける *go out* for a walk. ●旅行に出かける *start* (*out* [*off*]) on a trip. ●我々は夕方地元のカラオケバーへ好んで出かけます We like *going out* to the local *karaoke* parlor in the evening. ●父は8時過ぎに出かけました(=家を出ました) Father *left* home after eight. ▶私がそこに着いたときにはもう彼は出かけたあとだった By the time I got there he *had gone*. ▶彼女は買い物に出かけています She *has gone* [*is out*] shopping. ▶私は家族が出かけている間に家の掃除をした I cleaned the house while my family *was away* [*out*]. (❗ away は遠方へ, out は比較的近い所への外出を含意)
会話「彼女傘を持っていくのを忘れたわ」「そうね, すごく急いで出かけていったもの」"She's forgotten her umbrella." "Yes, she *left* in such a hurry."
会話「どこに出かけるの」「医者に行くんだ. すぐに戻るよ」"Where *are you off* to?" "To see the doctor. I won't be long."

てかげん 手加減 ●手加減をする(=大目に見る) make allowances (for). (⇨手心)

てかご 手籠 a (hand) basket.

てかず 手数 (⇨手数(てすう))

でかす ●でかした! Well done!/I'm proud of you! (❗ ×Bravo! /brá:vou/ は主に役者·歌手などにかける讃辞でここでは不適)

てかせ 手枷 a manacles. ●手かせ足かせをかけられている be (kept) in fetters; be fettered 《by》. (❗ fetters は「足かせ」, 比喩的に「束縛」の意)

でかせぎ 出稼ぎ 图 ●東京に出稼ぎに行く go to Tokyo to *work*.
—— **出稼ぎする** 動 work away from home.
●出稼ぎ労働者 (季節労働者) a seasonal worker; (外国への) a migrant worker.

てがた 手形 ❶〖為替手形〗a draft; a bill (of exchange). (❗ draft は内国為替, bill は外国為替を表すとされるが, 実際には区別なく用いられることが多い) ●不渡り手形 a dishonored *bill* [*draft*]. ●約束手形 a promissory *bill* [*note*]. ●手形に裏書きする endorce a *bill* [a *draft*]. ●手形を振り出す draw a *bill* [a *draft*] (*for* 100,000 yen *on* him). ●手形を割り引く[落とす] discount [honor] a *bill* [a *draft*]. ●手形を現金に替えてもらう get [have] a *bill* [a *draft*] cashed. ●手形で支払う pay *by draft*. ●無冠詞に注意
❷〖手の押し形〗a handprint. ●赤ん坊の手形をとる take the *handprint* of a baby.
●手形交換所 a clearing house.

でかた 出方 ●彼の出方をうかがう watch what move he will make. ▶相手の出方一つだ It depends on how they approach us.

てがたい 手堅い (確実な) sure; (堅実な) sound; (信頼できる) reliable. ●手堅い方法 a *sure* method. ●手堅い人 a *reliable* person.

てがたな 手刀 〖空手〗a karate chop. ▶力士は懸賞を受けるとき手刀を切った〖相撲〗The sumo-wrestler made a thankful gesture of *hand-chopping* three times over the prize before he received it.

デカダンス 〖退廃派〗decadence.

てかてか ●以前は頭をポマードでてかてかしている人がよくいた There used to be many people who had their hair *shining* [*glistening*] with pomade. ▶彼のズボンのおしりはてかてかしている The seat of his pants is *shiny* [*glossy*]. (❗ 布などがすれててかてかしている場合)

でかでか ●彼らの結婚のニュースは1面にでかでかと書き立てられた(=はでに扱われた)〖話〗The story of their marriage *was splashed* [*plastered*] across [all over] the front page.

てがみ 手紙 a letter; (短い) a note, 《話》a line; (郵便物) mail. (⇨郵便, 巻末【手紙の書き方】)
❶【~手紙】 ●置き手紙 a *message* [a *note*] *left behind.* ●いやがらせの手紙 hate *mail*. (❗ この場合 a hate *letter* は未) ●4月8日付けの手紙 one's *letter* dated [of] April 8.
❷【手紙が[は]】 ▶彼女から手紙が来ましたか Have you gotten [received] a *letter* from her? (❗ get を用いる方が口語的なり)/Have you *heard from* her? (❗ 電話などによる連絡も含む) ▶今朝私に手紙(=郵便)は来ていませんでしたか Is there any *mail* for me this morning? ▶催しの詳細を問い合わせる手紙がたくさんきた A lot of people *have written in* (asking) about details of the meeting. (❗ write in は「(会社·組織などに)問い合わせ[投書]の手紙を出す」の意)/There were a lot of *letters* asking for details of the meeting. ▶手紙は心の手渡しなんです Writing a letter is like offering your heart in your hands to another person. (❗「手紙」は文の後半のoffering a heart に合わせて the letter でなく writing a letter と表す)
会話「彼の手紙はどこへ(あてて)出せばいいのですか」「原宿へ出せばいい」「それはご自宅の住所ですか」"Do you know where I can *write to* him?" "(*Write to* him) at Harajuku." "Is it his home address?"
❸【手紙の】 ▶私はすぐに手紙の返事を書いた I answered [replied to] the *letter* immediately. (⇨返事) ▶この手紙の送料はいくらですか What's the postage on [for, ✗of] this *letter*?
❹【手紙に】 ▶手紙によると彼は近くアメリカに発つということだ He says *in* his *letter* [His *letter* says] that he is leaving for America soon. (❗ According to his letter, ... とはあまりいわない)
❺【手紙を】 ▶私は彼に長い手紙を書いた I wrote him a long *letter* [a long *letter* to him]. (❗ 単に「手紙を」なら I wrote (to) him. ⇨【第4文例】) ▶ロンドンへ手紙を出した I sent a *letter* to London. (❗ (1) ✗I *sent* London a letter. は不可. (2)「家へ」なら I wrote (✗to) home.) ▶着いたら簡単な手紙をください Please drop me a *note* [a *line*] when you get there. ▶お手紙をありがとうございます Thank you for your *letter* [for *writing* (*to*) me]. (❗ 後の方で to を省略するのは《主に米》)/It's nice to hear from you. ▶私は人に手紙を書くのも人から手紙をもらうのも大好きだ I love writing *letters* to others and receiving *letters* from them as well. (❗ as well は「両方とも, どちらも」の意を強調する)
会話「お手紙を出しておきましょうか」「ええ, よろしかったらお願いします」"Shall I mail these *letters* for you?" "Yes, ⁄please, if you dón't ˅mind."
❻【手紙で】 ●お返事は手紙で(=書面で)お願いします Please answer [reply] *by letter*. ▶彼は手紙でいつ来るかと尋ねてきた He *has written* and asked (me) when I will come./He *has written* asking [to ask] (me) when I will come. ▶彼女はまもなく結婚すると手紙で知らせてきた She *wrote* (*to*) me *that* she was going to get married soon. (❗ (to) me は文頭の方が明らかな場合 *省略可*)

てがら 手柄 (功績) a great achievement; 《書》a meritorious deed; (それによる信用) credit. ▶私はそれをすべて自分の手柄としない(=手柄を一人占めしない) I won't take [have] all the *credit* for it to

でがらし 出涸らし weak and flavorless tea.

てかる (てかてか光る) shine; glisten. ▶(てかてか光り)彼の顔は脂でてかっていた His face *was shiny* [*was glistening*] with oil.

てがる **手軽** 图 (手軽さ) easiness; convenience.
── **手軽な** 形 〚容易な〛easy;〚簡単な〛simple;〚便利な〛convenient.
── **手軽に** 副 〚容易に〛easily. ●パンとコーヒーで手軽に朝食をすませる take a *simple* [*light*] breakfast of bread and coffee. ●手軽に買い物のできる店 a store *convenient* for shopping. ▶「手軽な店」は a *convenient* store. ●カードのおかげで海外で手軽に買い物できるようになった (Credit) cards have made it *easier* to do shopping overseas.

デカルト 〚フランスの哲学者〛Descartes /deɪkɑ́ːrt/ (René /rənéɪ/ ~).

デカンター 〚卓上用のガラス製酒瓶〛a decanter /dɪkǽntər/.

:てき **敵** an enemy,《書》a foe;〚競技などの相手に〛an opponent (⇨相手 ❸);〚敵軍, 敵艦隊〛the enemy (! 前者は用い単・複両両表).
① 〖~(の)敵〗 ●共通の敵 a common *enemy*. ●政敵 a political *enemy* [*opponent*]. ●核兵器は人類の敵だ Nuclear weapons are an *enemy of* [*to*] human beings.
② 〖敵~〗 ●敵側 the *enemy*'s side. ●味方と敵に分かれる(戦争などで) be divided (up) into friends and *enemies* [*foes*] (! foe は文語的な語だがこの連語では普通に用いる); (試合などで) divide (up) into *opposing* teams.
③ 〖敵が[は]〗 ●彼は敵が多い[ない] He has a lot of [no] *enemies*. ●敵(軍)は敗れた The *enemy was* [*were*] defeated.
④ 〖敵の〗 ●敵の攻撃 an *enemy* attack. ●敵のピッチャー the pitcher of the *opposing* [*rival*] team.
⑤ 〖敵に〗 ●敵に立ち向かう fight against [advance to meet] the *enemy*. ●敵につく(寝返る) go over [defect] to the *enemy*; (味方する) take sides with the *enemy* (*against* us). ●彼を敵に回したくない I hate making [to make] an *enemy of* him./(議論などで) I don't want him as my *opponent*. ●あの男は味方にすれば頼もしいが, 敵に回せば恐ろしいやつだ The chap is a good friend but a bad *enemy*.
⑥ 〖敵を〗 ●彼の高圧的な態度は多くの敵を作った He made a lot of *enemies* by his high-handed manner./His high-handed manner made [earned] him many *enemies*.
⑦ 〖敵なしだ〗 ▶彼は向かうところ敵なしだ He *carries all* [*everything*] before him. ▶彼は将棋では敵なしだ Nobody is his *match* [can match him] in *shogi*.
● **敵艦** an enemy ship. **敵兵** an enemy (soldier); 《総称》 the enemy.

-てき -滴 a drop. (⇨一滴) ●1滴の水 a *drop* of water. ●2, 3滴たらす let fall a few [two or /ə/ three] *drops*. ●ミルクを最後の1滴まで飲む drink the milk *to the last drop*.

でき **出来** ❶ 〚試験・競技などの結果・成績〛a result. (! 通例複数形で) ●出来のよい[悪い]学生 a *bright* [a *dull*] student. ●彼は英語の出来がよい[悪い] He *is doing well* [*poorly, badly*] *in* English. ●試験の出来不出来は運にもよる Success (or failure) in [The *results* of] exams may depend on luck. ▶上出来! Well done!/Very good!/Good job!/《米俗》Hot dog! ▶彼はクラスでいちばん出来が悪い He's the slowest [worst] student in the class. (! 前者の方は単に「成績が悪い」意だが, worst は品行も含むので, 場合によって適当でない)
〖会話〗 「試験の出来はどうだった」「あまりよくなかったよ」 "How did you *do* [*make out*] on the exam?/How was the exam?" "I didn't do very well."
❷ 〚出来ばえ〛〚製品の〛workmanship. (⇨出来栄え) ▶このテーブルの出来はすばらしい This table is very well made.
〖会話〗 「ハムレットを見たよ」「すばらしい出来だったでしょ」 "I saw *Hamlet*." "Wasn't it a splendid *production*?"
❸ 〚(収穫)〛a crop, a yield. ▶今年の米は出来はよい We have a good [a big] *crop* of rice this year. ▶作物の出来不出来(=作柄)は天候によるところが大きい The crop depends largely on the weather.

できあい **出来合い** ── 出来合いの 形 ready-made; (服の) ready-to-wear. (⇨既製) ●出来あいのサイズ a stock size.

■ **DISCOURSE**
出来あいの食品のなかには化学物質を含むものもあり、それらをとり過ぎると疲れたりイライラしたりする Some *ready-made* food contains chemicals, **which** causes you to feel [be] tired or frustrated if eaten too much. (!, which ... (そしてそれは...)は因果関係を述べるときに用いるディスコースマーカー)

できあい **溺愛** ── 溺愛する 動 ●孫を溺愛する dote on one's grandchild; (盲目的に愛する) love one's grandchild *blindly*.

できあがり **出来上がり** ❶ 〚完成〛●出来上がり寸前である be near *completion*; be almost finished.
❷ 〚出来ばえ〛(⇨出来栄え)

*できあがる **出来上がる** ❶ 〚仕上がる〛be finished; 〚完成される〛be completed; 〚用意できる〛be ready. ▶その記事の原稿は来週出来上がる I will *finish* (writing) the manuscript of the article next week. ▶服はいつ出来上がりますか When will my suit *be ready*?
❷ 〚その他の表現〛 ▶彼らは宿につく前に出来上がっていた They *were happily drunk* before they reached the hotel. (! be merry in one's cups (楽しく酔う)は少し古い表現)

てきい **敵意** hostility, 《書》enmity. ●あらわな[隠れた]敵意 open [hidden] *hostility*. ●敵意のある態度をとる take a *hostile* attitude. ●彼に敵意を抱く have [feel] *hostility toward* him; be [feel] *hostile to* him.

テキーラ 〚メキシコ産の蒸留酒〛tequila /təkíːlə/.

てきえい **敵影** the enemy (troops). ▶敵影を見ず The *enemy* is not to be seen.

*てきおう **適応** 图 adaptation. ●適応性に富む be adaptable (*to*); be rich in adaptability.
── **適応する** 動 〚環境などに〛(積極的かつ柔軟に) adapt (oneself) (*to*); (努力して) adjust (oneself) (*to*); (曲がりなりに)《書》 accommodate oneself (*to*); 〚体制・規則などに〛conform (*to*). (⇨順応する) ▶恐竜は気候の急激な変化に適応できなかったので絶滅した Dinosaurs died out because they could not *adapt* [*adjust*] *themselves to* rapid changes in climate. ▶彼は何とか新しい生活に適応した He *has* somehow *accommodated himself to* his new life.
● **適応症** 〚医学〛indication.

てきおん **適温** ●適温に保つ keep《foods》at a *suita-*

てきがいしん 敵愾心 hostility, 《書》(an) antagonism; a hostile [《書》an antagonistic] feeling. ●敵愾心を燃やす be hostile [antagonistic] ((to, toward)); have hostility [(an) antagonism] ((to, toward)).

てきかく 的確 ── 的確な 形 ●的確な(=正確な)描写をする give an accurate [a precise] description ((of it)); describe ((it)) accurately [precisely]; describe ((it)) with accuracy [precision]. (⇒正確) ●的確な(=適切な)答え an apt answer.

てきかく 適格 ── 適格な 形 (資格のある) qualified; (選ばれるのにふさわしい) eligible. ▶彼はその地位に適格だ He is qualified [eligible, the right man] for the position. ▶彼は教師に適格だ He is qualified to be a teacher.
● 適格者 a qualified [an eligible] person.

*てきぎ 適宜 (自分の判断で) at one's discretion; (随意に) freely. ●適宜帰宅する go home at one's discretion.

てきごう 適合 图 ●技術開発は急ぎ, 社会への適合はゆっくりと We must hurry the technological development, but we must [need to] go slow with its actual application to society.
── **適合する** 動 (ぴったり合う) fit; (要件を満たす) conform ((to)); (資格などを満たす) meet. ●安全規定に適合する conform to the safety regulations. ●求められている資格に完全に適合する meet the requirements perfectly. ▶君の理論は事実に適合していない Your theory doesn't fit the facts.

てきこく 敵国 an enemy [《やや書》a hostile] country; 《集合的》the enemy.

できごころ 出来心 (衝動) impulse. ●出来心でそれを盗んだ I stole it on (a sudden) impulse.

*できごと 出来事 an occurrence; a happening (!通例複数形で); (重大な) an event; (付随的な) an incident (!event より小さい); (世間に知られた) an affair; (偶発的で好ましくない) an accident. ●よくある[日常の]出来事 a common [an everyday] occurrence. ●世の中の出来事 the happenings of the world. ●2006年の主な出来事 the major [main] events [affairs] of 2006. ●ちょっとした出来事 an incident of little importance; a trivial incident. ▶彼は日々の出来事を日記に書いている He writes daily occurrences [happenings] in his diary. ●月面着陸は歴史的な出来事です Landing on the moon was a historic event. ●あの列車事故はおそろしい出来事でした The train accident was a terrible affair. ▶それは一瞬の出来事だった(=一瞬に起こった) It all happened in a flash.

てきざい 適材 ▶その仕事には彼が適材だ He is the right [a suitable] person for the job./He is fit for [is suited to] the job.
● 適材適所 ▶私たちは適材適所に人員を配置する We put the right men in the right places. (!上の文ではしばしば複数形が用いられる)

テキサス 《米国の州》Texas 《略 Tex. 郵便略 TX》.

テキサスヒット 『野球』a Texas leaguer ((hit)); a Texas league single; a bloop((er)). (!和製語》 a Texas hit.

てきし 敵視 ── **敵視する** 動 ●彼を敵視する (敵と見なす) look upon him as an enemy; (敵意を抱いている) be hostile to [have hostility toward] him. (⇒敵意)

てきじ 適時 ── 適時の 形 timely.
● 適時打 『野球』a clutch hit. (!a timely hit とはあまりいわない)

できし 溺死 图 drowning.
── **溺死する** 動 drown. (⇒溺れる❶)
● 溺死体 a drowned body.

てきしつ 敵失 『野球』an error by one's opponent fielder; an opposing fielder's error. ●敵失で2点を得る score [get] two runs on an (opposing fielder's) error. (!このような状況ではエラーは相手によるものであることが明らかなので on an error とするほうが普通)

てきしゃせいぞん 適者生存 ●適者生存の世界[原理] the world [principle] of the survival of the fittest.

てきしゅつ 摘出 图 ●腫瘍(ﾘｭｳ)の摘出手術 an operation to remove the tumor.
── **摘出する** 動 remove; (困難を伴って) 《やや書》extract.

てきしゅう 敵襲 an enemy attack; (予期しない攻撃) raid. ●敵襲にあう be attacked [raided] by the enemy.

てきしょ 適所 the right place. ●適材適所 (⇒適材 [成句])

てきじょう 敵情 ●敵情を探る reconnoiter enemy movements.

てきしょく 適職 (find) a good [a suitable] job ((for him)). ●多くの人が適職を探している Lots of people search a suitable job for themselves.

てきじん 敵陣 the enemy('s) camp.

てきず 手傷 ●手傷を負う get a wound.

できすぎ 出来過ぎ be too good ((for)). ●それは話ができすぎる The story is too good to be true.

*テキスト 『教科書』a textbook (!text は通例「本文」「原文」の意); 『コンピューター』a text.
● テキスト入力 text entry. ● テキストファイル a text file. ● テキストフォーマット a text format.

*てきする 適する be suitable, be fit (-tt-) ((for)); suit, fit (-tt-) ((を適当 [類語])); 『地位などに適格である』be qualified ((for)).

①【(人)に適する】●病人に適した食事 meals fit for a sick person. ▶ここの湿度の高い気候はぼくに適していない The wet climate here doesn't suit [(体質に合わない) doesn't agree with] me. (!agree with は否定文で用いることが多い)

②【(事)に適する】●結婚式に適した服 a suitable dress for the wedding; a dress suitable for the wedding. (!前の方は永続的で, 後の方はその場限りのことについて用いる) ●釣りに適した日 a good ((うってつけの)) a perfect] day for fishing. ▶彼はその仕事には適していない He is not fit for [to do] the job. (!「彼は医者には適していない」では He's not fit to be a doctor [xfor a doctor].)/(生まれつき向いていない) He's just not cut out for [to do] the job. (!通例否定文で用いられる) ●この水は飲用には適していない This water is not fit [good] to drink. ●このやせた土地においしいジャガイモの生育に最も適している This poor land is fittest [most suitable, best] for growing good potatoes.

てきせい 適正 ── 適正な 形 (正しい) right; (本来あるべき) proper; (公正な) just; (公正な) fair; (理にかなった) reasonable. ●適正な分配 a fair share. ●適正な処置をする take adequate mesures. ●適正な判断をする pass a just [a fair] judgment ((on it)).
● 適正価格 a reasonable price. ● 適正利潤 a reasonable profit.

てきせい 適性 (an) áptitùde. (⇒素質) ●適性がある[ない] have an [no] aptitude ((for)).
● 適性検査 an aptitude test.

てきせい 敵性 ●敵性行為 a hostile act; an act of hostility. ● 敵性国家 a hostile country.

てきぜい 敵勢 [敵の力] the enemy's strength; [敵の軍勢] the enemy's army [troops].

＊てきせつ 適切 ── **適切な** 形 (必要を満たした) suitable 《for, to》; (好ましい) good* 《for; to do》; (能力のある) fit (-tt-) 《for; to do》; (その場によく調和した)《やや書》 appropriate 《for, to》; (本来そうあるべき) proper 《for, to; to do》; (時を得た) timely; (直接関連があり妥当な) relevant 《to》; (やるだけの能力がある) adequate 《to》. (⇨適当 [類語], ふさわしい) ● 適切な助言をする give good [timely, relevant] advice. ▶ 彼の演説はその場に適切なものではなかった His speech wasn't suitable [good, fit, appropriate, proper] for the occasion. ▶ 彼は適切な答えをした He made a good [an appropriate, a proper] answer./(適切に答えた) He answered appropriately [properly]./(的を射た) His answer was to the point. ▶ 彼らはその事故のあと適切な(= 正しい)処置を取った They did the right thing after the accident.

会話「おいおい，ジョージと呼べよ」「職務中にそのように呼ぶのは適切ではないと思いますがね，警部」"Oh, come on! Just call me George." "It would not be proper to refer to you as such while we are on duty, Captain."

てきぜん 敵前 ● **敵前上陸** landing in the face of the enemy. ● **敵前逃亡** (a) desertion /dɪzə́ːrʃən/ under enemy's fire. ● **敵前逃亡者** a deserter under enemy's fire.

できそこない 出来損ない 图 (失敗作) a failure; (役立たず) a good-for-nothing.
── **出来損ないの** 形 (出来ばえの悪い) poorly-made.

てきたい 敵対 图 (敵意) hostility. ● アメリカに敵対行為をとる take hostile action against America.
── **敵対する** 動 be hostile 《to, toward》; (反する) oppose; (手向う) rise 《against》. ▶ なぜその子は親と敵対するのだろう Why does the child turn against [oppose] his parents?
● **敵対関係** an adversarial relationship 《between A and B》.

できだか 出来高 ● (仕事などの) a piece; (産出高) a yield; (通例複数形で); (株などの) a volume; (a) turnover.
● 出来高払い payment by the piece.

できたて 出来立て ── **出来立ての** 形 (食べ物が) fresh, (あつあつの) hot; (服などが) brand-new. ● できたてのパン bread fresh [hot] from the oven /ʌ́vn/; oven-fresh bread.

てきだんとう 擲弾筒 a grenade launcher.

てきち 適地 ● ぶどう栽培の適地 land suitable for growing grapes.

てきち 敵地 enemy land [territory]. ● 敵地にスパイを送り込む infiltrate a spy into enemy territory.

できちゃった(けっ)こん 出来ちゃった(結)婚 a shotgun wedding.

てきちゅう 的中 ── **的中する** 動 (的に当たる) hit the target; [(的の中心)] bull's-eye; (正しいと分かる) prove right; (実現する) come true. ▶ 水雷が的中した The torpedo hit the target. ▶ 彼の経済予測が的中した His forecasts about economy proved right.

てきど 適度 ── **適度の** 形 [節度があってほどよい] moderate (⇔excessive); [目的・状況などにかなって適切な] proper. ● 適度の運動をする get [《英》take, ×do] moderate [proper] exercise; exercise moderately [in moderation]. (!) (1) do は特殊な運動に限り用いられる. (2) 後の方は堅い言い方》
● 適度に暖かい部屋 a moderately warm room.

＊てきとう 適当 ── **適当な** 形 ❶ [適切な] suitable 《for, to》; good* 《for; to do》; fit (-tt-) 《for; to do》; appropriate 《for, to》; proper 《for, to; to do》 (!) proper は比較変化しない); adequate 《for》. (⇨ふさわしい, 適切)

使い分け ▶ **suitable** 特定の目的・状況・人などの必要条件にうまく合うことを表す.
good 特定の目的・人に一般的に好ましいと考えられていること，また有益でふさわしいことを表す.
fit 特定の状況に適応するために必要な能力・資格・準備などが備わっていることを表す.
appropriate 特定の状況から必要とされているものと適合する特徴が備わっていることを表す. しばしば優雅さ・魅力・礼儀正しさを暗示する.
proper やや堅い語で，本来そうあるべきこと，または理性的判断・習慣・礼儀などの点からふさわしいことを表す.
adequate 特定の要求を満たすのに質的または量的に必要なだけはあることを表す.

● 適当な(= 妥当な)値段で売る sell at a reasonable price. ▶ この役に適当な人を捜しているんです I'm looking for someone good [suitable, fit, appropriate] for this role./(ぴったりの) I'm looking for the right person for this role. ▶ 本当に彼はあんまり適当じゃないね He's not good enough, I (can) tell you. (!) I (can) tell you は let me tell you とも いい, 自分の発言に対する確信を表す慣用表現) ▶ こういった服装は正式の結婚式には適当でない Such clothes are not suitable [appropriate, proper] for a formal wedding./It is not suitable [appropriate, proper] to wear such clothes at a formal wedding. ▶ 最も適当と思うものを選びなさい Choose which you feel most appropriate. ▶ この家は6人家族には適当だ This house is adequate for a family of six. ▶ 君は適当に(= 少し)運動が必要だ You have to get [《英》take] some exercise./(適度な) You have to get proper [moderate] exercise.

❷ [いいかげんな] (無責任な) irresponsible; (あいまいな) vague. ▶ 彼は本当に適当な男だ He's a really irresponsible guy.
── **適当に** 副 ▶ お任せしますから, 適当にやってください I'm going to leave it to you. I hope you'll do (it) as you see [think] fit. ▶ 二言三言適当に答えておいたよ I made a few vague [どっちつかずの) non-committal] replies. ▶ 適当に(= 好きなように)やっていただいて結構です You can do it as you like [(いつでも好きなときに) whenever you like]. ▶ 彼はそのセールスマンを適当に(= 如才なく)あしらった He treated the salesman [saleswoman] diplomatically.

てきにん 適任 ── **適任の** 形 (ぴったりの) right, perfect (!) 前の語は通例限定的に); (必要条件を満たした) suitable. (⇨ふさわしい) ▶ 彼は その役に適任だ He is the right man [is perfect] for the role./He is suitable [(十分力量がある) competent enough, (よい選択) a very good choice] for the role.

できばえ 出来栄え (製品の) workmanship; (仕事などの) performance. ▶ 見事な出来栄えの品々 articles of fine workmanship. ● 出来栄えによる支払い performance-related pay. ▶ その映画はすばらしい出来栄えだった The movie was very good [well produced]. ▶ 出来栄えはともかく仕事が期限に間に合ってよかった I'm happy I could finish the work before the deadline. The quality is the next question.

てきぱき ❶ [活発に] briskly, actively. ▶ 魚市場では人々がてきぱき働いている You can see people working briskly in the fish market.

❷ [[効率よく]] efficiently. ● てきぱきした秘書 a quick, efficient [(事務能力がすぐれている) a businesslike] secretary. ● 難局をてきぱきと(=見事に)処理する handle a difficult situation capably. ▶彼女はいつも物ごとをてきぱきと片付ける She always gets things done promptly and efficiently [in a businesslike way].
❸ [[素早く]] quickly; (迅速に) promptly. ▶てきぱきしないと遅れるよ Be quick about it or you will be late.

てきはつ 摘発 图 exposure.
── **摘発する** 動 expose. ● 汚職を摘発する expose corruption.

てきひ 適否 ● 適否を問う ask if it [he, she] is right 《for》 [suitable 《for, to》, appropriate 《for, to》].

てきびしい 手厳しい severe. (⇨厳しい) ● 手厳しい批判 severe [(痛烈な) bitter] criticism. ● 手厳しく批判される be severely criticized.

てきひょう 適評 《make [pass]》 an appropriate [(適切な) a fitting; (妥当な) a relevant] comment 《on》.

てきふてき 適不適 suitability; fitness; (生来の) (an) aptitude; (行動の正しさ) propriety. ▶彼のとった行動の適不適が問題になっている The propriety of his behavior is called in question./They question the propriety of his having done so.

できふでき 出来不出来 (⇨出来 ❸) ● ワインの良し悪しはその年のぶどうの出来不出来による The quality of wine depends much on how good the year's grapes are [is influenced by the quality of the year's grapes]. ▶どんなに優れた作家の作品にも出来不出来はある(=良いとは限らない) Even the works of best writers are not always good.

てきほう 適法 ── **適法の** 形 legal (↔illegal); (合法の) lawful (↔unlawful); (正当な) 《書》 legitimate (↔illegitimate).
● 適法行為 a legal act.

てきめん ● 効果てきめんである (すぐ効く) have an immediate effect 《on》; work immediately.

できもの 出来物 a swelling (❗はれもの全般をさす), (でき) a boil, (吹き出もの) a pimple; (腫瘍(しゅよう)) a tumor. ▶赤ん坊の首の後ろにできものができている The baby has a boil on [x in] the back of its neck.

てきや 的屋 (安物売り) a cheapjack; (安物のおもちゃ, 飾り物などを売る人) a sidewalk vendor; 《米話》 a pitchman.

てきやく 適役 ── **適役の** 形 (適している) suitable, suited; (ふさわしい) right. ▶彼女はこの仕事には適役でない She is not suitable [not the right person] for this job.

てきやく 適訳 a good [a proper] translation. ▶英語の適訳が見出せない日本語が多い Many Japanese words and phrases have no exact equivalents [proper expressions] in English.

*****てきよう 適用** 图 application. ● 法律の適用 the application of the law (to the case). ▶彼は失業保険の適用を受けている He is covered by [x with] unemployment insurance.
── **適用する** 動 apply /əpláɪ/ 《A to B》. ● 適用できる applicable. ▶この規則は外国人には適用できない We cannot apply this rule to foreigners./(当てはまらない) This rule cannot be applied [be applicable] to foreigners. ❗This rule cannot apply to foreigners. とするより cannot be applied to とする方がよい)

てきよう 摘要 图 (要約) a summary, 《書》 recapitulation; (概略) an outline; (講義などの骨組) a syllabus; [[抜粋]] an ábstract.
── **摘要する** 動 summarize.

てきりょう 適量 a proper quantity; (薬の) a proper dose /dóus/. ● 適量を超す take too much; (飲酒で) drink too much.

:**できる 出来る** 動 [[能力がある]] can*; be able to ⟨do⟩; be capable of ⟨doing⟩; [[可能である]] be possible (↔be impossible) (❗It is possible (for+人) to do で用いる); [[可能にする]] 《書》 enable (＋人＋to do).

> **解説** (1) be able to は「実際にできる」ことに, be capable of は「(潜在的)能力がある」ことに重点がある. can はこの両方を含みこの中で最も一般的.
> (2) be able to は通例「人を主語にでなない: そのホテルは800人収容できる The hotel can [×is able to] accommodate 800 people.
> (3) be able to は受身には用いない: 彼は容易に救出できない He cannot be [×is not able to be] rescued easily.
> (4) can の否定は can't または 《書》 cannot が普通 (⇨[上例]). can not は特に堅い言い方や, 修辞疑問文, 肯定文との対照を示す場合に限られる.
> (5) can と be able to. 一般に be able to の方が堅い語で, 能力を強調する.
> (a) 現在時制ではどちらも可能だが, can の方が普通. (⇨① [第1文例])
> (b) 未来時制では can は用いず will be able to を用いる. ただし未来についての現在の判断を示す場合 (⇨① [第2,3文例]) や if 節では can を用いる: あす彼に会うことができたらその本を渡しておきます If I can [×will be able to] meet him tomorrow, I'll give him the book.
> (c) 過去時制では原則として次のような使いわけである: (i) (肯定文で) 過去の一般的能力を表す場合は could, was able to のいずれも可: 彼は若いときはフランス語を話すことができた He could [was able to, used to be able to] speak French when he was young. (❗used to … は現在はできないことを暗示) しかし過去の一回限りの行為については could ではなく was able to を用いる. ついに彼は試験に合格することができた At last he was able to [×could] pass the exam. この場合, At last he managed to pass [succeeded in (passing)] the exam. あるいは単に At last he passed the exam. ということも多い. なお次のような場合 could は可. He could hardly speak French. (彼はほとんどフランス語を話すことができなかった)のように hardly, only, just などの修飾語句を伴う場合. I could (＝was able to) see him through the window. (窓から彼が見えた)のように知覚動詞 (see, hear, smell, feel など)とともに用いる場合. He said he could (＝was [would be] able to) finish it by tonight. のように従節中で用いる場合. (ii) 《否定文で》couldn't, was not able to のいずれも可: 彼女はセーターを編むことができなかった She couldn't [wasn't able to, was unable to] knit a sweater. (❗後の二つは試みたができなかったことを含意)
> (iii) 《疑問文で》could, was able to のいずれも可: 彼はその質問に答えることができましたか Could he answer the question? は Yes, he managed to [×could]./No, he couldn't.)
> (d) 現在[過去]完了では can は用いず have [had] been able to を用いる: 彼はその問題を解くことができなかった He hasn't been able to [×hasn't could] solve the problem.

できるだけ

❶ 【...が[は]できる】 ▶彼はスキーができる He *can* ski./He *is able to* ski [*is capable of* skiing]. ▶私は1週間でその仕事をすることができる I *can* do the work in a week./*It is possible for* me to do [×I am possible to do, ×It is possible that I will do] the work in a week. (❗×The work *is possible* for me to do.... は不可だが, 否定詞・準否定語が入ると可: The work *is impossible* [*hardly possible*] for me to do ....) ▶このゲームは幼い子供でもできる This game *can* be played by young children. (❗日本語との対応にも注意) ▶のこぎりがあればそれは簡単にできるのだが I *could* do it if I had a saw. (❗仮定法の表現. 「のこぎりがあればそれは簡単にできたのだが」のように過去のことについていうときは I *could have* done it if I had had a saw. となる) ▶彼女はスケートができるようになった She *has learned* [*become able*, ×*become*] *to* skate. ▶絶対ミス[遅刻]はできない We *can't afford to* make a mistake [*to* be late]. ▶彼にはその仕事はできない He *is unequal* [*not equal*] *to* the job./The job *is beyond* him [his *power*, his *ability*]. ❗He *can't* do the job. は能力がないのか, 何かの事情でできないのかあいまい)

会話 「やっとちゃんとできたよ」「よくやったね!」"At last I *managed to* [×*could*] do it *right*./At last I've got it *right*." "Well done!"

❷ 【...することが[は]できる】 ▶私はいいプレゼントを見つけることができなかった I *couldn't find* [*failed to* find] a good present. ▶そんな高い本を買うことはできません(=買う余裕はありません) I *can't afford* (*to* buy, ×buying) such an expensive book. ▶その事実を否定することはできない *There is no* denying [*It is impossible to* deny, ×It is impossible that we deny] the fact. (❗前の言い方は口語的)

❸ 【...できる】 ▶私はあしたの会合に出席できるでしょう I'll *be able to* go [×*be capable of* going] to the meeting tomorrow. (❗*be capable of* は継続的な能力について用いるのでここでは不可) I *can* go to the meeting tomorrow. ▶彼の講義は難しすぎて私には理解できない His lecture is so difficult (that) I *can't* understand it./His lecture is too difficult for me to understand (it). (❗*to* 不定詞の意味上の主語である for 句がない場合は通例 it は省略する)

―― 出来る 動 ❶ 【上手である】 be good* at [in]... (↔be poor at [in]...) (❗通例 at は技能, in は分野を示す); (熟練している) be skillful in [at].... ●できる生徒 (利口な) a *bright* (↔a dull) student; (理解の早い) a *quick* (↔a slow) student; (有能な) an *able* student. ●よくできた人(=人格者) a person of (great) *character*; a *good* person. ▶彼は英語ができる He *is good at* [*in*] English. (❗at では運用面, in では学科の成績を示す) ▶He *does well* (↔*poorly*) *in* English./(話すのがうまい) He speaks good English.

会話 「試験はどうだったの」「今度は前よりよくできたよ」"How did you do *on* the exam?" "I *did better* this time." (❗前置詞 on に注意)

❷ 【作られる】 be made (*of*, *from*, *with*) (❗通例 of は材料が原形をとどめている場合, from はとどめていない場合, with は成分を示す); (建造される) be built, be constructed (❗後の方が堅い語); (設立される) be formed, (組織される) be organized. ▶丈夫にできている箱 a strongly made box. ▶たくさんの卵からできたケーキ a cake *made with* lots of eggs. ▶新しくできた委員会 a newly *formed* [*organized*] committee. ▶この机はオーク材でできている This desk *is made of* [×from] oak. ▶ワインはブドウからできる Wine *is made from* grapes./《ブドウを主語にして》Grapes *are made into* wine. ▶そのビルは5年前にできた The building *was built* [*was constructed*, (完成した) *was completed*] five years ago.

❸ 【仕上がる】 be finished; (完成する) be completed (❗前より堅い言い方. 長い時間[期間]を要するものに用いることが多い); 【用意が】 be ready. ▶絵はすばらしくよくできている[まだ半分しかできていない] The painting *is beautifully finished* [*is still only half-finished*]. ▶論文はできましたか *Have* you *finished* [*completed*] (writing) your paper? (❗×...finished [completed] to write... は不可) ▶夕食(の用意)ができました Dinner's *ready*.

会話 「車は今修理しているところです」「分かりました. それでは, いつ取りに行けばいいですか」「4時にお立ち寄りください. その頃には確実にできていますから」"The car is being repaired right now./We're still working on the car." "I see. Tell me, when can I pick it up?" "Come by at four o'clock. I'm sure it'll *be ready* by then."

❹ 【生まれる】 be born; 【発生する】(現れる) appear, (でき物などが) have*. ▶彼女に赤ちゃんができた (産まれた) A baby *was born* to her./(妊娠している) She *is* expecting [*pregnant*]. (❗婉曲表現の後者の言い方の方が好まれる) ▶太郎がお腹にできたとき, 夫は大変喜んでくれました When I *started* Taro, my husband was very happy. (❗start は《話》で「(赤ん坊)を妊娠する」の意) ▶顔に湿疹(しっしん)ができた I*'ve got a* rash [A rash *has broken out*] on my face. (❗a rash は「一群の湿疹」の意) ▶君は胃にかいようができている You *have an* ulcer in your stomach [a stomach ulcer]. ▶用事ができたので出かけないといけない Something *has* just *come up* so I must go now. ▶学生時代にたくさんの友達ができた I *was able to make* a lot of friends while I was a student.

❺ 【育つ】 grow*; 【産出する】 produce; 【(作物ができる)】 crop (-pp-). ▶今年できた(=収穫された)米 the rice *harvested* this year. ▶北海道ではジャガイモができる Potatoes *grow* [They *grow* potatoes] in Hokkaido./Hokkaido *produces* potatoes. ▶今年はリンゴがよくできた The apples *cropped* well this year./(収穫が多かった) There was *a good crop of* apples this year.

❻ 【その他の表現】 ▶4名をそちらに回せばこちらがひどく人手不足になります. 2名で何とかできませんか(=何とかやっていけませんか) If I give you four people, I'll be terribly short-handed. Couldn't you *get along with* two? ▶ココアできますか(喫茶店で) Do you have hot chocolate [《英》cocoa]?

できるだけ 出来るだけ as ... as possible [one can]. (❗...は形容詞・副詞, または形容詞を伴う名詞. 後の方が口語的) ●できるだけ早く as soon as you can ▶できるだけ早くここへ来なさい Come here *as soon as possible* [*you can*]. (❗as soon as possible の略語 ASAP はメールなどでよく用いられる: できるだけ早く連絡して Let me know *ASAP*.) ▶私はできるだけ多くの時間[助手]が必要なのです I need *as much time* [*as many assistants*] *as possible*. (❗(1) much の後には不可算名詞, many の後には可算名詞の複数形が続く. (2) ×I need time as much [×I need assistants as many] as possible. は不可) ▶試験に合格するようできるだけのことはしなさい Do everything you can (do) (《最善を尽くせ》Do your best, (できる限りの努力をしなさい) Make every possible effort) to pass the exam. ▶できるだけのことはやってみましょう I'll do what I can./I'll try to do my very best.

てきれい 適例 a good example; a case in point.

てきれいき 適齢期 a marriageable age. ●適齢期の娘 a daughter of *marriageable age*; a *marriageable* daughter.

できレース 出来レース ▶学級委員を選ぶ選挙は, 最初から出来レースのようなものだった(=結果は初めから決まっていた) The result of the class officers election *was determined from the beginning*.

てぎれきん 手切れ金 severance money.

できれば 出来れば if (at all) possible (!*at all* がある方が強意的で「万一」の意); (希望を言えば) preferably. ▶できれば電話してもらいたい I want you to call me up *if* (it is) *possible* [×if you can]. (!*if* you can は「あなたにその能力があれば」という失礼な言い方)/*Perhaps* you would [could] call me up. (!後の文は婉曲的で丁寧な依頼表現. could の方が more *would* よりさらに丁寧)▶できれば(=せずにすむのなら)その仕事はしたくない I don't want to do the work *if I can help it*. ▶英語圏の国で英語を学びたいものだ, できればイギリスで I'd like to study [learn] English in an English-speaking country, *preferably* in Britain.

会話「物理の宿題手伝ってほしいのだけど, 力学のところをやってるの」「本当に, できれば手伝ってあげたいのだけれど, 物理は全く分からないわ」"Can you help me with my physics homework? We're learning about dynamics." "Believe me, I would *if I could*, but I don't know the first thing about physics."

てぎわ 手際 〖能率〗efficiency; 〖腕前〗(a) skill. ●手際のよい efficient; skillful. ●手際よい be efficient [skillful] 《in doing》. ●手際よく efficiently; skillfully; with *efficiency* [*skill*]. ●手際よく物ごとを片付ける get things done *efficiently*.

てきん 手金 a deposit. (⇨手付(金))

テグ 大邱 〖韓国の都市〗Taegu /tάɪɡuː/.

でく 木偶 〖木彫りの人形〗a wooden doll; 〖操り人形〗a puppet; 〖役立たず〗⇨木偶の坊.

てぐす 天蚕糸 (釣り糸用の) (fishing) gut.

てぐすね 手ぐすね ●**手ぐすね引く** ▶交通巡査はかなりの速度オーバーで走っている車をあげようと手ぐすねひいて待っていた The speed cops *were all ready* [*all set*] *for* the cars that were coming with speed well over the limit.

てくせ 手癖 手癖が悪い (盗癖がある) have a habit of stealing things; (すりを働く) be light-fingered; (異性関係がだらしない) be (sexually) promiscuous; be loose 〖《話》easy〗 in one's morals.

てくだ 手管 (⇨手練(ホムェ)手管)

てぐち 手口 (犯罪の)〖書〗a modus operándi; (方法) a method; (策略) a trick. ●巧妙な手口 a clever *modus operandi*.

*でぐち 出口** an exit /éksit, éɡzit/,《英》a way out. ●劇場の出口 the *exit from* the theater; the *way out of* the theater. ▶出口がふさがっている The *exit* is blocked.

●**出口調査** 〖take [conduct]〗 an exit poll.

てくてく ▶果てしなく続く田舎道をてくてく(=ひたすら)歩く walk on along the endless country road. (!「てくてく」が自然体の歩き方をさすかぎり, trek は「苦労して」, hoof it は「仕方なく」の意が加わるので, ここでは不適切)

テクニカラー 《商標》Technicolor. ●テクニカラー映画 a film in *Technicolor*; a *Technicolor* film.

テクニカルターム 〖専門用語〗a technical term.

テクニカルノックアウト a technical knockout 《略 TKO》.

テクニカルライター a technical writer.

テクニック 〖技術〗(a) technique /tekníːk/.

テクノクラシー 〖技術万能主義〗〖経済〗technocracy.

テクノストレス téchnostrèss. (参考) コンピュータ業務などに伴うストレス

でくのぼう 木偶の坊 (役立たずの人) a good-for-nothing (fellow); (自主性のまったくない人) a dummy; (あやつり人形) a puppet.

テクノポリス 〖技術支配社会〗a technopolis /teknάpəlis/; 〖高度技術集積地域〗an area of high-tech industries.

テクノロジー 〖科学技術〗technólogy.

てくび 手首 a wrist. ●手首を捕える catch 《him》 by the *wrist*; take 《his》 *wrist*. ▶バッティングでは手首の使い方が重要だ It is the *wrist* action which is important in batting.

てくらがり 手暗がり ▶手暗がりになって字が書きにくい A dark spot made by my own hand interferes with my writing./I can't write well because my own hand throws a shadow on the paper.

てぐるま 手車 ❶〖手押し車〗a handcart; a pushcart. (⇨手押し車) ❷〖遊戯〗a teguruma; (説明的に) a game of carrying a child on two other children's crossed arms.

でくわす 出くわす happen to meet. (⇨会う❷, ❹)

でげいこ 出稽古 出稽古をする give lessons at one's pupil's home.

てこ 梃 a lever. ●てこで持ち上げる[動かす] lever 《a rock》 up [out]; raise [move] 《a rock》 with a *lever*. ●てこの原理を応用する use *leverage*.

●**てこでも動かない** ▶彼はこう言い出したらてこでも動かない Once he has expressed his opinion, he persists in it. (! persist in ... は「...をあくまで主張する」の意)/Once he has made up his mind, you can't budge him (from it). (! budge は「わずかに動かす, 意見を変えさせる」の意)

てこいれ 梃入れ — 梃入れ(を)する 動 (補強する) shore [prop]... up. ●衰退ぎみの経済にてこ入れをする *shore up* the declining economy.

デコーダー 〖解読ソフト〗〖コンピュータ〗a decoder.

てごころ 手心 手心を加える (大目に見る) make allowance(s) for 《it, him》; (手加減する) pull one's punches; go easy on 《him》. ▶彼女は議論するとき一切手心を加えないので, 彼女と議論することを嫌がる人もいます She doesn't *pull any punches* in argument, so there are some people who don't like to argue with her.

てこずる 手古ずる (手を焼く) have* trouble 《with, doing》. ▶彼のわがままにさんざんてこずった I had a lot of *trouble with* his selfishness./His selfishness gave me a lot of *trouble*. ▶打者は彼のカーブにてこずった The batter couldn't handle his curve balls./The batter had trouble with his curves.

てごたえ 手応え 〖反応〗(a) response (!「返事」の意では Ⓒ); 〖効果〗(an) effect. ●手応えのある学生たち *responsive* students. ●我々の発言に対して積極的な手応え(=反応)は今のところない We've got no positive *response* to our remarks. ▶今日の彼の演説は聴衆に相当手応え(=効果)があった His speech today *had* quite an *effect* [an *impact*] *on* [*upon*] the audience.

でこぼこ 凸凹 ⇨ ─凹凸の 形 rough; (ごつごつした) rugged /rάɡid/; (こぶだらけの) bumpy. ●でこぼこのゲレンデ a *rough* [a *bumpy*] ski run; a ski run full of *bumps*. ▶その道はでこぼこだった The road was *rough*.

デコレーション [飾り] (a) decoration. ●クリスマスのデコレーション Christmas *decorations*.
●デコレーションケーキ a large-sized fancy [×a decoration] cake. (!普通のケーキは a fancy cake または単に a cake)

てごろ 手頃 ―― 手頃な 形 (扱いやすい) handy; (便利な) convenient; (必要条件を満たした) suitable; (妥当な) reasonable; (適度の) (やや書) moderate.
●手ごろな大きさの箱 a *handy*-sized box; a *convenient*-sized box; a box of *handy* [*convenient*] size. ▶この手帳は持ち歩くのに手ごろだ This notebook is *handy* to carry about. ▶会合のための手ごろな場所を探しています We are looking for a place *suitable* [a *suitable* place] *for* our meeting. (⇒ふさわしい) ▶値段が手ごろだったのでそれを買った The price was *right*, so I bought it./I bought it because the price was *reasonable*. ▶(家賃の)手ごろなマンションを探しています We've been looking for an apartment we *can afford* [where the rent is *affordable* [×*moderate*]]. (!家賃が moderate であっても借り手に affordable とは限らない)

てごわい 手強い (扱いにくい) tough, stiff; (恐るべき) (やや書) formidable. ●あんな手強い交渉相手とやりあったのは初めてだ He is the *toughest* negotiator I've ever been up against. ▶あの子の今度のボーイフレンドは太郎にとって手強い相手だなあと思う I think her new boyfriend is (×a) *stiff* competition to Taro.

テコンドー [<朝鮮語] [競技] taekwondo /tàikwándou/; (説明的に) a Korean martial art of self-defense using violent kicks.

デザート (a) dessert /dizə́ːrt/; (英語) afters. ●デザートを出す serve *dessert* 《to him》. ▶デザートにアイスクリームを食べた I had ice cream for *dessert*.
●デザートワイン dessert wine. (参考) 食後または食間に出される通例甘口のワイン)

てざいく 手細工 handiwork.
●手細工品 a handiwork, handicrafts.

デザイナー a designer. ●工業[商業]デザイナー an industrial [a commercial] *designer*. ▶彼女はその店の(服飾)デザイナーをしている She is a (dress) *designer* [designs (dresses)] for the shop.
●デザイナーブランド a designer label. ●デザイナーブランドのコート a *designer* coat.

デザイン 名 (a) design. ▶この家具はデザインがとても現代的だ This piece of furniture [×This furniture] is very modern in *design*.
―― **デザインする** 動 design 《a dress》.

でさかり 出盛り be in (↔out of) season. ▶果物は出盛りが安い Fruit is cheap (*when it is*) *in season*.

でざかる 出盛る ▶栗は秋に出盛る Chestnuts *are in season* in the fall.

てさき 手先 ❶ [指先] (手) one's hands; (指) one's fingers. ▶彼は手先が器用だ He is good [clever, skillful] (↔clumsy) with his *hands* [*fingers*]. (⇒不器用)
❷ [手下] a pawn, a tool, 《話》a cat's-paw. ▶彼は警察の手先だ He is a *pawn* [a *tool*] (in the hands) of the police. ▶彼は私を手先に使った He *used* me *as a pawn* [a *tool*]./He made a *pawn* [a *cat's paw*] of me.

できき 出先 [これから行く所] where one is going; [行っている所] where one has gone [(滞在している) is staying]. ●出先で風邪をひく catch a cold *at the place where one is staying*.
●出先機関 (官庁の) a local agency of the government; (会社の支店) a branch office (of a company).

てさぎょう 手作業 (手作業での仕事) handiwork.

てさぐり 手探り ●手探りで捜す grope [feel] for 《the light switch》. ●手探りでドアの方に進む grope [feel] one's way *to* the door.

てさげ 手提げ (婦人用) a handbag, 《米》a purse; (革製書類用) a briefcase; (角型書類用) an attaché /ætəʃéi/ case. (⇒鞄(かばん))

てさばき 手捌き handling; (手の動き) the movement of the hand(s). ●手さばきもあざやかにカードを一気に切る shuffle the cards *quickly and skillfully*. ▶巡査は見事な手さばきで交通整理をしていた The police officer controlled the traffic with smart [neat, wonderful, skillful] *movements of the hands*.

てざわり 手触り a [the] touch; a [the] feel. ▶この布は手触りがいい(＝なめらかだ) This cloth *feels* smooth. ▶この布は絹のような手触りがあります This cloth is silky *to the touch* [*feel*]./This cloth has a silky *touch* [*feel*]./This cloth *feels* silky [like silk].

でし 弟子 (個人指導の) a pupil; (学生) a student; (学説・教義などの信奉者) a follower, a disciple /disáipl/; (見習い工) an apprentice 《to》. ●まな弟子 one's favorite *pupil*. ●弟子入りする become one's *pupil*; be apprenticed 《to》. ●弟子をとる take a *pupil*. ▶彼は中西教授の弟子だ He is a *student under* [*of*] Prof. Nakanishi./He is Prof. Nakanishi's *student*.

てしお 手塩 ―― <u>手塩にかける</u> ●手塩にかけて育てる raise [(人を) bring up, (植物を) grow]... with *tender* [*loving*] *care*.

てしお 出潮 a tide coming in at around the moonrise.

デジカメ [[デジタルカメラ]の略] (⇒デジタル)

てしごと 手仕事 handiwork. ●手仕事が得意である make things skillfully with one's hands.

てした 手下 (手先) a pawn; (政界・やくざのボスの子分) one's henchman.

デジタル 名 digital /dídʒətl/. (® アナログ) ▶デジタル技術は高度情報化社会に不可欠だ *Digital* technology is vital [indispensable] to our highly developed information society. (!vital の方が indispensable より「不可欠」の意が強い)
―― **デジタル化する** 動 digitize; go digital. ●写真をスキャナーで読み取ってデジタル化する *digitize* a photo by a scanner.
●デジタルオーディオテープ a digital audio tape 《略 DAT》. ●デジタル家電 digital home appliances. ●デジタルカメラ a digital camera. ●デジタル計算機 a digital computer. ●デジタル通信 digital communications. ●デジタルデバイド [情報格差] a digital divide. ●デジタルテレビ a digital television. ●デジタル時計 a digital watch [clock]. ●デジタルビデオディスク a digital videodisc 《略 DVD》. ●デジタル放送 digital broadcasting. ●デジタル録音 digital recording.

てじな 手品 (総称) magic, conjuring /kʌ́ndʒəriŋ/; (個々の手品の芸) a (magic [conjuring]) trick. ●トランプの手品をする do [play, perform] a card *trick* [*card tricks*]; do [show] some *magic* (*tricks*) with cards. ●手品で帽子からウサギを出す *conjure* a rabbit out of a hat (↔*conjure* (*it*) *away*); *produce* a rabbit from [*pull a rabbit out of*] a hat *by magic*.
●手品師 a magician; a conjurer.

でしな 出しな (⇒出掛け)

デシベル 〚物理学〛 a decibel 《略 dB》.

てじめ 手締め (説明的に) clapping of the hands [handclapping] to celebrate a successful close 《of a bargain, a party》. ▶手締めをする celebrate with *handclapping*.

てじゃく 手酌 ●手酌で酒を飲む help oneself to *sake* /sάːki/.

でしゃばり ── でしゃばりな 形 (干渉好きな) meddlesome; (差し出がましい)《やや書》intrusive; (遠慮がなさすぎる)《話》pushy. ●でしゃばりな人 a meddler; a busybody.

でしゃばる 〚干渉する〛interfere [meddle]《*in*》;《話》poke [stick] one's nose《*into*》;〚じゃまをする〛《やや書》intrude;〚無遠慮で生意気である〛be forward,《話》be pushy《⇨出過ぎる ❶》. ▶私のことにでしゃばらないでくれ Don't *interfere in* [《話》*poke your nose into*] my affairs./(口出ししないでくれ)《話》Don't *butt* [《話》*horn*] *in on* my affairs./(自分のことをしっかりやれ) Mind your own business. ▶でしゃばるつもりはないが言いたいことがある I don't want to *intrude*, but I have something to say. ▶年長者に対してでしゃばった態度をとってはいけない You must not *be too forward with* your elders.

*__**てじゅん 手順**__ (物事をする手続き) (a) procedure《*for*》;〚工程〛a process. ▶彼は何事も手順を踏んで処理する(=正しい手順に従う)ように心がけている He tries to follow the right *procedure* in everything he does.

てじょう 手錠 《a pair of》 handcuffs,《話》cuffs. ●彼に手錠をかける put *handcuffs* on him; handcuff him. ●手錠をはずす put *handcuffs* off《him》.

-でしょう I think [suppose,《米話》guess].《⇨-だろう》

-でしょうか I wonder if ....《冊 相手に遠慮がちに尋ねる〚依頼する〛時に用いる。主に女性に好まれる表現》●少しお時間をいただけないでしょうか(=私のために割いてくれないでしょうか) *I wonder if* you could spare me a little time.《冊 I *am wondering* if ..., I *wondered* if ..., I *was wondering* if ... とすると、より丁寧な言い方となる》

てしょく 手燭 a portable candlestick.

*__**-です** 「-だ」の丁寧体だが、英語では必ずしも形式上の丁寧体があるわけではない__》 ▶彼女はとても活発な人です She *is* very active. ▶それ結構です That'*ll* be fine. (冊 断定調のを避けた言い方) ▶ご協力いただければ幸いです I *would* appreciate it [I would be happy] if you would cooperate with us. (冊 仮定法による控えめな言い方)

てすう 手数 〚面倒, 迷惑〛trouble.《⇨手間》▶その機械で我々の手数がずいぶん省けるだろう The machine will save us a lot of *trouble*. ▶これは手数のかかる(=面倒な)仕事です This is *troublesome* work.
●**手数をかける** trouble. ▶お手数をかけてみませんが、その写真を送っていただけますか I am sorry to *trouble* [*bother*] you, but will you send me the picture?/May I *trouble* you to send me the picture? ▶あなたにそんなに手数をおかけしたくありません I don't like *putting* you *to* [*giving* you] so much *trouble*.

てすうりょう 手数料 (サービス料) a (service) charge; (委託料) (a) commission. ●銀行手数料 a bank(ing) *charge*; bank *commission*. ●仲介手数料 an intermediation [an intermediary, a brokerage] *fee* [*charge*]. ●手数料込みは includes [be inclusive of] *charges* [*fees*]. ●取り扱い手数料 a handling *fee* [*charge*]. ●5 ドルの手数料を払

う pay a five dollar *service charge*. ▶住民票交付の手数料は 200 円です The *charge* for giving [issuing] a resident card is 200 yen./They charge you 200 yen to give a resident card.《冊 後の文例のように charge (請求する) を用いる方が自然》▶彼女は売上高に対してすべて 1 割の手数料(=歩合)を取っている She gets a *commission* of 10 percent [a ten percent *commission*] on all the sales she makes. ▶彼は手数料(=手間賃)として 1 万円請求した He charged me 10,000 yen for the *trouble*.
会話 「手数料はどのくらいですか」「15 パーセントいただきます」"How much *commission* do you charge?" "We take fifteen percent."

ですが but.《⇨けれど(も), だが》

てずから 手ずから (自分の手から) personally; in person; (自分の力で) by oneself; (自分自身で) oneself. ▶総理が優勝杯を手ずから優勝者に渡した The Prime Minister *himself* gave the championship cup to the winner.

ですから so; therefore.《⇨だから》

てすき 手漉き ── 手漉きの 形 handmade 《Japanese paper》.

てすき 手隙 ●あなたのお手すきの折に at your free time; when you are free; when you have time.

でずき 出好き《話・やや古》a gadabout. ▶直美は出好き(=外出するのが好き)だ Naomi *likes to go out*./ Naomi *is fond of going out*.

てすぎる 出過ぎる ❶〚出しゃばる〛▶出過ぎたまねをするな Don't *be too forward* [《話》*pushy*].《冊 pushy は通例けなして「強引な」の意)/(自分のことをしっかりやれ) Mind your own business.
❷〚程度を超える〛▶彼の腹は出過ぎている His stomach *sticks out too much*./He is too fat [thick] around the middle.《冊 middle は《話》で「胴, おなかのあたり」の意》▶このお茶は出過ぎている(=濃過ぎる) This tea *is too strong*.

デスク 〚机〛a desk;〚新聞の編集部〛a newspaper desk,《米》the desk;〚新聞編集次長〛a sub-editor,《米》a deskman 《圈 -men》.
●デスクトップ《⇨デスクトップ》●デスクプラン〚机上の計画〛an impractical plan; a paper plan, a plan on paper. ●デスクワーク (do) deskwork.《冊 事務・研究・文筆など。しばしば비較的》

デスクトップ 名 〚卓上〛a desktop.
── **デスクトップの** 形 desktop.
●デスクトップコンピュータ a desktop (computer). ●デスクトップパブリッシング desktop publishing《略 DTP》.

ですけど but.《⇨だけど, けれど(も)》

てすさび 手遊び ●手遊びに絵を描く (暇つぶしに) paint pictures *just to kill time*; (楽しみのために) paint pictures *just for fun* [*just for the fun of it*].

てすじ 手筋 ❶〚芸事などへの適性〛(have) a natural aptitude《*for*》.《⇨筋❻》
❷〚囲碁・将棋などの〛(最善の手順) the best move (s). ▶手筋を読む try to find the *best moves*.

でずっぱり 出突っ張り ▶その女優は舞台[芝居]に出ずっぱりだ(=終始出演している) The actress is on the stage all through the show [the play].

*__**テスト** 名 ❶〚学校などの試験〛a test; an exam;《主に米》(簡単な) a quiz.《⇨試験[類語]》●学力テスト an achievement *test*. ●実力テスト an (academic) ability *test*. ●ペーパーテスト(=筆記試験) a written *test* [*exam*].《冊 ×a paper test とはいわない》●多肢選択テスト a multiple-choice *test*. ●テストを受ける take a *test*.

テストステロン

❷【実験】▶あー、あー、あー、ただいまマイクのテスト中 Testing, testing, one, two, three [A, B, C].
—— **テスト(を)する** 動 give 《students》 a test 《in English》.
● テストケース〖先例となるもの〗 a test case. ● テストパイロット a test pilot. ● テストパターン〖画像調整用図形〗 a test pattern. ● テスト飛行 a test [a trial] flight. ● テストマッチ〖クリケット・ラグビー〗 a test match.

テストステロン〖生化学〗testósteróne.

デスマスク a death mask.

デスマッチ〖プロレス〗a fight to the finish [the death];《和製語》a death match.

てすり 手摺り （階段・エスカレーターなどの）a handrail (⚠横木に重点がある); （階段の） bannisters (⚠柱も含む全構造をさす); （船・橋の）a guardrail; a railing (⚠縦欄に重点がある. 複数形は柵全体をさす). ● 手すりにつかまって階段を下りる go downstairs holding onto the handrail [bannisters].

てずり 手刷り 名 hand printing. —— **手刷りの** 形 hand-printed.
● 手刷り印刷機 a handpress.

てずれ 手擦れ —— **手擦れする** 動 be damaged [worn] by repeated handling. ● 手ずれした本 a book worn by repeated use [handling].

てせい 手製 —— **手製の** 形 （機械を使わずに手で作った）handmade (⚠服飾品など); （自家製など）homemade (⚠食物・服飾品など). (⇨手編み)

てせい 手勢 soldiers under one's command.

てぜま 手狭 —— **手狭な** 形 （狭い）small; （窮屈な）cramped. ● 手狭な部屋 a small [a cramped] room. ● 手狭になる become cramped 《for space》.

てそう 手相 the lines on one's palm. 関連 感情線 the heart line/頭脳線 the head line/運命線 the Saturn line/生命線 the life line. ● 手相を見る read 《his》 palm. ● 手相がいい have lucky lines on one's palm.
● 手相占い palmistry. ● 手相見 a palmist.

でぞめしき 出初め式 the New Year parade of fire brigades.

てそろう 手揃う （出席者が）be all present; （若葉など）be in full leaf. (⇨出尽くす)▶意見が出そろう All opinions are given.

てだし 手出し 名 （かかわり合い）(an) involvement.
—— **手出し(を)する** 動 （かかわる）be involved 《in》; involve oneself 《in》; （干渉する）meddle 《in》; （殴る）hit 《him》. ▶私はその件には手出しはしたくなかった I didn't want to involve myself in the matter. ▶あの子に手出ししたら承知しないぞ If you lay a finger on her, you'll be sorry for it. (⚠「(人に)指一本でも触れる」が原義で, 否定文, if 節で用いられる)

でだし 出だし a start. ● 出だしが好調である make [get off to] a good (↔a bad) start. ● 出だしでつまずく make a false start. ● 歌の出だしが分からない can't sing the first part of the song.

てだすけ 手助け help. (⇨助け, 手伝う)

てだて 手立て （方法） a way, a means; （手段）a measure. ● 手立てがない there is no way [means]《of》. ● 手立てを講じる take measures 《to do》.

でたて 出たて ● 大学を出たての若い人たち young people fresh from [out of] college. ● 出たての本 a book just out; a book just put on sale.

でたとこしょうぶ 出たとこ勝負 take pot luck; 勝負でやる deal with it as it comes; （臨機応変にする）《話》play it by ear; （即興でする）《話》ad-lib. (⇨アドリブ)

てだま 手玉 ● <u>手玉に取る</u> （自由に操る）《話》twist 《him》around one's little finger; （扱い方を心得ている）know how to handle 《him》.

でたらめ 名〖意味のないこと〗 nonsense. ● でたらめをいう talk nonsense.
—— **でたらめな** 形 （なりゆき任せの） random; haphazard (⚠random より意味が強く時に非難の意がこもる); （無責任な） irresponsible; （信頼できない） unreliable. ● でたらめな(=でまかせの)返答 a random answer. ● でたらめな人間 an irresponsible [an unreliable] person. ● でたらめに(=手当たり次第に)選ぶ make a random choice; choose at random. ▶彼の話はまったくでたらめだ What he says is absolute nonsense. (⚠nonsense を強める語には他に complete, pure, sheer, utter などがある)/(でっちだ) His whole story is made up [is invented]. ▶彼の仕事ぶりはまったくでたらめだ He works in a very haphazard way.

デタント [<フランス語]〖緊張緩和〗(a) détente /deitɑ́ːnt/.

てぢか 手近 —— **手近な** 形 （よく知られた） familiar; （すぐそばの）nearby,《話》handy. ● 手近な例をあげる give a familiar example. ● 手近なレストラン a nearby [《話》a handy] restaurant; a restaurant nearby. ● ペンと手帳を手近に(=手元に)置いておく keep a pen and a notebook near [close] at hand [(すぐに手の届く範囲に) within easy reach,《話》handy].

てちがい 手違い a mistake; （混乱を招くような間違い）《話》a mix-up. (⇨過失, 誤って)▶計画に手違いが生じた The plan went wrong. ▶手違いでコンサートの入場券が二重発券されていた The concert ticket was double-booked by mistake [accident]./There was a mix-up over the ticket reservations and the concert ticket was double-booked.

てちょう 手帳 a (small) notebook;《英》a pocketbook;（ポケットダイアリー）a diary.
会話「来週の金曜空いてる？」「ちょっと待ってね, 手帳見てるから」"Are you free on Friday next week?" "Just a moment. I'll have a look in my diary."

てつ 鉄 iron /áiərn/;《元素記号 Fe》; （鋼鉄）steel. ● 酸化鉄 iron oxide. ● くず鉄 iron scrap (iron). ● 粗鉄 crude iron. ● 鋳鉄 cast iron. ● 鉄(製)のなべ an iron pot; a pot made of iron. ● そのなべは鉄でできている The pot is made of iron. ▶彼の意志は鉄のように固い He has a will of iron [an iron will]./He is a man of iron.
● 鉄は熱いうちに打て（ことわざ）（好機を逃すな）Strike while the iron is hot./(矯めるなら若木のうち) You cannot teach an old dog new tricks.
● 鉄亜鈴 (a pair of) iron dumbbells. ● ダンベル
● 鉄格子 iron bars; (窓) an iron-barred window. ● 鉄材 iron [steel] material.

てつ 轍 a rut (⇨わだち) ● 前車の轍を踏む (⇨前車[成句])

ていろ 鉄色 a steely blue; a greenish dark blue.

てっか 鉄火 ● 鉄火な(=気性の激しい)女 a fierce woman; a woman with a violent temper.
● 鉄火丼 tekkadon; (説明的に) rice served in a bowl topped with raw tuna slices and nori flakes. ● 鉄火場 (ばくち場) a gambling den.

てっかい 撤回 名 (a) withdráwal.
—— **撤回する** 動 辞表を撤回する withdraw one's resignation. ● 前言を撤回する withdraw [take back] one's previous remarks.

でっかい (⇨でかい)

てっかく 的確 (⇨的確[てきかく])

てっかく 適格 (⇨適格[てきかく])

てつがく 哲学 philosophy. (!個人の哲学大系・人生観を表すときは ⓒ). ●カント哲学 the *philosophy of* Kant. ●ギリシャ哲学 Greek *philosophy*. ●道徳哲学 moral *philosophy*. ●経験[実践]哲学 empirical [practical] *philosophy*. ▶「控えめに考えていれば失望することもない」というのが彼の(人生)哲学です His *philosophy* is, "Think small, so you won't be disappointed."
●哲学者 a philosopher. ●哲学書 a philosophy book. ●哲学博士 a Doctor of Philosophy 《略 Ph.D.》. (⇨博士)

てつかず 手つかず (手を触れていない) untouched; (未使用の) unused. ●手つかずのボーナス one's *untouched* bonus; the bonus *one hasn't spent a penny yet*. ▶例の翻訳は手つかずのままだ. その前に片付けなくてはならない雑用が多くて I *haven't started on* the translation *yet*. I have many odd jobs to take care of before that.

てつかぶと 鉄兜 a steel helmet.

てづかみ 手づかみ ▶魚を手づかみにする catch a fish *with* one's *hands*. ●いちごを手づかみで食べる eat strawberries *with* one's *fingers*.

てっかん 鉄管 an iron pipe [tube].

てつき 手つき ●器用な手つきで skillfully, 《やや書》 dexterously. ●無器用な手つきで clumsily. ●慣れた手つきで魚をさばく dress a fish with a practiced *hand*.

てっき 鉄器 ironware; (金物類) hardware.
●鉄器時代 the Iron Age.

てっき 敵機 an enemy plane;《総称》enemy [《やや書》hostile] aircraft.

デッキ [《船の》] a deck; [《列車の》] 《米》 a platform (!《英》ではバスの乗降口). ▶彼はデッキで日光浴を楽しんでいた He was *on* (×the) deck, basking in the sun.
●デッキチェア a déckchàir.

てっきょ 撤去
── **撤去する 動** remove. ●バリケードを撤去する *remove* barricades.

てっきょう 鉄橋 (鉄道の)《米》a ráilroad bridge;《主に英》a ráilway bridge; (鉄製の) an iron bridge. (⇨橋)

てっきり [確かに] surely, certainly; [疑いなく] without doubt, undoubtedly. ▶てっきり(=きっと)彼は成功すると思っていた I thought he would *surely* succeed./I *was sure* (that) he would succeed. ▶てっきり彼女は有罪だと思った(=確信した) I *was convinced* that she was guilty. ▶てっきり(=当然)君がその事を知っていると思った I *took it for granted that* you knew the matter.

てっきん 鉄琴 a glockenspiel.

てっきん 鉄筋 a reinforcing bar [rod].
●鉄筋コンクリート reinforced concrete; ferroconcrete. ●鉄筋コンクリートの建物 a reinforced concrete [a ferroconcrete] building.

でつくす 出尽くす ▶話題が出尽くす run out of the topics of conversation. ▶ご意見も出尽くしたようですから, 議案の採決に移ります There seems (to be) *nothing left unsaid*, so we'll be taking a vote on the subject./*All opinions seem to have been given* on the bill, so we'll put it to the vote, shall we?

てづくり 手作り ── **手作りの 形** (手製の) handmade; (自家製の) homemade. (⇨手製) ●手作りのケーキ a *homemade* cake.

てつけ(きん) 手付(金) a deposit (!「敷金」の意もある);『法律』earnest money. ▶彼女は毛皮のコートに 5 万円の手付(金)を払った She *made a deposit of* [*deposited*, (頭金として払う)《話》*put down*] 50,000 yen *on* her fur coat.

てっけつ 鉄血 (軍備) arms (複数扱い); weapons.
●鉄血宰相 the Iron Chancellor (参考 ドイツの政治家ビスマルクの異名)

てっけん 鉄拳 (固く握ったげんこつ) a hard [a clenched] fist. ●鉄拳制裁を加える(=罰としてげんこつで殴る) hit 《him》 with one's fists as a punishment.

てっこう 鉄鉱 (石) iron ore.

てっこう 鉄鋼 (iron and) steel.
●鉄鋼業 the steel industry.

てっこうじょ 鉄工所 an ironworks. (!単・複同形, 通例単数扱い) ●鉄工所で働く work at an *ironworks*.

てっこく 敵国 (⇨敵国(てきこく))

てっこつ 鉄骨 (鉄材) iron, steel; (骨組み) an iron [steel] framework. ●鉄骨プレハブ住宅 a prefabricated house on a *steel framework*.

てざい 鉄剤 an iron medicine;『薬学』a chalybeate.

てっさく 鉄柵 an iron fence.

デッサン [<フランス語] [下絵] a sketch; [略画] a rough drawing. (⇨絵)

てつじ 綴字 (a) spelling. (⇨綴(つづり))

てっしゅう 撤収 withdrawal; removal.
── **撤収する 動** withdraw; remove. ●軍隊を撤収する *withdraw* the army 《*from*》; *pull* the army 《*out of*》. ●テントを撤収する *strike* a tent.

てつじょうもう 鉄条網 a barbed-wire fence; (barbed-wire) entanglements.

てつじん 哲人 [『哲学者』] a philosopher; [『賢人』] a person of wisdom, a wise person; a sage.

てつじん 鉄人 an iron man.
●鉄人レース [『トライアスロン』の別名] an iron man race, a triathlon.

てっする [専念する] devote oneself to …; put* one's heart and soul into …; [忠実に守る] be true to 《one's principle》. ●金もうけに徹する *devote oneself* [*give oneself up*] *to* making money. ●安全第一に徹する be (always) *true to* the principle of "Safety first." ●夜を徹して働く work *all night* (*long*) [*through the night*].

てっせい 鉄製 ── **鉄製の 形** iron 《bridges》; 《鉄製品》made of iron.
●鉄製品 (家庭用) ironware; (装飾的なもの) ironwork.

てっせん 鉄線 [鉄の針金] steel wire. ●有刺鉄線 barbed *wire*.

てっせん 鉄線 [植物] a clematis.

てっそく 鉄則 a hard-and-fast [an ironclad] rule.
●鉄則を守る follow a *hard-and-fast rule*.

てったい 撤退 图 (a) withdrawal (!(a) retreat でないことに注意 (⇨退却)); a pullout; (占領地などからの) (an) evacuation. ●軍隊の撤退 the *withdrawal* [*pullout, evacuation*] of troops 《*from* a place》.
── **撤退する 動** withdraw; pull … out; evacuate. ▶軍隊はその地域から撤退した The army *withdrew from* [*pulled out of, evacuated*] the area.

てつだい 手伝い [『行為』] help, (補佐)《やや書》assistance (⇨助け); [『人』] a helper, (助手) an assistant 《*to*》. ●左官手伝い a plasterer's *helper*. ●お手伝いさん (⇨お手伝い(さん)) ▶あなたは家の手伝いをよくしますか Do you often *help* (your mother) at home? (⇨手伝う)

てつだう 手伝う help, give* [lend*] 《him》 a (helping) hand 《*with; to do*》; [補助する]《書》assist. (⇨助ける❶) ●彼の仕事を手伝う *help* him *with* [(*to*) *do*] his work (!to のない方は直接的な援助か,

to のある方は間接的な援助を表すと言われるが, 実際には意味構造があいまいにならない場合は to は省略されるのが一般的); 《書》 assist him in [in doing] his work. (❗ ×help [assist] his work は不可) ● 彼がコートを着るのを手伝う help him into [on with] his coat. ▶何を手伝うの What can I help you with? ▶私は彼女が指輪を探すのを手伝った(=手伝って見つけた) I helped her (to) find her ring. (❗ 受身では о も必要: She was helped to find her ring.) ▶(ちょっと)君たち, たんすを動かすのを手伝ってくれ Help (me) move the chest, boys!/Come on, boys! Give (me) a hand with [to move] the chest! (❗(1)目的語が自明の場合や特定の人でない場合, 目的語は通例省略される. (2) ×give [lend] your hand とはいわない) ▶母に少し手伝ってもらってこの服を作りました I made this dress with a little help from my mother.

会話 「手伝おうか」「いや, 大丈夫」 "You need a hand with that?" "No. I got it." (❗ it は a hand を指す)

会話 「何か手伝いしましょうか」「ええ, おさしつかえなければその食料品の袋を上へ運んでいただけませんか」「いいですとも, 喜んで手伝わせていただきます」 "(Is there) anything I can help you with [can do for you]?/(困っている知らぬ人に) Can I be of any help (to you)?" "Sure. Would you carry those grocery bags upstairs, if you don't ˇmind?" "Certainly. I'd be glad to give you a hand."

でっち 丁稚 an apprentice. ●大工として丁稚奉公をする serve an [one's] apprenticeship as a carpenter. (⇨年季)

でっちあげ でっち上げ (人を罪に陥れる)《話》a frame-up; (容疑の) a trumped-up charge; (話の) a made-up story; an invention.

でっちあげる でっち上げる (人を犯人などに)《話》frame ... up; (容疑などを) trump ... up; (話・アリバイなどを) make* ... up, invent. (❗ 前の方が口語的) ●話をでっち上げる make up [invent, 《話》cook up] a story. ● 彼を逮捕するために窃盗の容疑をでっち上げる frame him for theft [trump up a charge of theft] to arrest him. (❗ いずれも通例受身で用いられる)

てっちゅう 鉄柱 an iron pillar [(円柱) column].

てっつい 鉄槌 ● **鉄槌を下す** (厳しく処する) punish 《them》severely.

***てつづき 手続き** 〖手順〗 procedure; (法律などに基づく正式な) formalities; (訴訟の) proceedings; (要件) requirements. ●正規の手続きを踏まずにビザを取得する get a visa without (following) the regular procedure [due process]. ●輸出手続きを済ませる go through the export formalities [procedures]. ● 彼に対して離婚訴訟の手続きを取る take [start, 《書》file] proceedings for divorce against him. ● 形式的な手続きを省く cut the formal proceedings [〖書〗the red tape]. ▶ 彼女は要件を満たしていなかったので選考から漏れた She was screened out because she failed to meet the requirements.

***てってい 徹底** 图 thoroughness.

── **徹底する** 動 ❶〖中途半端でない〗be thorough /θə́ːrou/. ▶彼は何事においても徹底している He is thorough in [about] everything. ● 彼女の仕事は徹底している Her work is thorough./She is a thorough worker.

❷〖十分に行き届く〗● 交通ルールを子供たちに徹底させる drive the traffic rules home to the children; drive home to the children that the traffic rules must be observed. ▶その命令は下部組織に徹底しなかった The order did not reach the smallest unit.

── **徹底的な, 徹底した** 形 〖完全な〗thorough, complete; 〖完璧(𝑘𝑎𝑛𝑝𝑒𝑘𝑖)な〗perfect; 〖余すところのない〗exhaustive; 〖根本的な〗radical; 〖手段などが思い切った〗drastic. ● 徹底した反戦主義者 a thorough [complete] pacifist. ● 徹底したうそつき an out-and-out liar. (❗ 好ましくない人・事に用いる) ● 徹底的な改革を行う make a radical [a drastic] reform.

── **徹底的に** 副 thoroughly, completely (❗ 動詞によっては《do》out [up] の形で行為の徹底さを示すこともできる); perfectly; exhaustively; radically; drastically. ● 徹底的に打ち負かす beat 《him》completely. ● 徹底的に戦う fight it out; (最後まで) fight it to the end. ● 部屋を徹底的に掃除する clean out a room; clean a room all up (❗ all は up を強調する). ▶ 警察は事件を徹底的に調査した The police investigated the case thoroughly [through and through]./The police made a thorough investigation into the case. ▶ この案件は徹底的に話し合われてから採決された This proposal was talked out before it was voted upon.

てっとう 鉄塔 a steel tower; (高圧線用の) a pylon /páilɑn/.

***てつどう 鉄道** 《米》a railroad, 《英》a railway.
① 〖～鉄道〗● 私営[国営]鉄道 a private [a government, a state-run] railroad. ●登山鉄道 a mountain railway. ● 高架鉄道 《米》an elevated railroad, 《米話》an el /él/ [an L]; 《英》an elevated [an overhead] railway
② 〖鉄道〜〗● 鉄道会社で働く work on [for] the railroad; work for a railroad company. (❗ 会社名には ... Rail(road)s と複数形を用いる. ただし単数扱い) ▶ その国は鉄道網が高度に発達している The railroad network [A network of railroads] is highly developed in the country.
③ 〖鉄道が[を]〗● 鉄道を敷く construct [lay, build] a railroad. ● 通勤に鉄道を利用する take the railroad to one's office; commute by rail [on the railroad]. (❗「交通手段」としての鉄道をさす時は通例 ×a railroad は用いない) ▶ 大雨のため鉄道が一部不通になった Part of the railroad service was suspended [was crippled] because of the heavy rain.
● **鉄道員** a railroad worker [employee]; 《米》a railroader, 《英》a railwayman. (❗ 特に運転手以外の) ● **鉄道運賃** a railroad fare; (貨物の) railroad freight rates. ● **鉄道公安官** a railroad police officer; 《集合的》the railroad police. ● **鉄道工事** (修理) railroad repairing; (建設) railroad construction [building, works]. ● **鉄道事故** (have [meet with]) a railroad accident. ● **鉄道ストライキ** a railroad strike. ● **鉄道輸送** rail [railroad] transportation; transportation by rail [train].

てっとうてつび 徹頭徹尾 (初めから終わりまで) from beginning to end, from start to finish; (徹底的に) thoroughly; (あくまで) firmly. ▶ 彼はその案には徹頭徹尾反対した He objected to the plan from start to finish. ▶ 戦争には徹頭徹尾反対する I oppose war, through and through. (❗ through and through は強い強調)

デッドエンド 〖道の行き止まり〗a dead end.
デッドストック 〖売れ残り品〗dead stock.
デッドスペース 〖死角, 家の中などの使えない空間〗(a) dead space.
デッドヒート ● デッドヒートを演じる have a close race

デッドボール [game, contest] 《with him》. (!) a dead heat は「同点, 同着」のこと.

デッドボール (⇨死球) ● デッドボールで一塁に出る be hit by a pitch and take first (base). (!) a dead ball はファウルグラウンドなどに落ちたインプレーではないボールのこと. 打者が「(今の)デッドボールだ」というときは "I got hit." などという)

デッドライン 天国 The top; (山頂) the summit. ● 木のてっぺんに at [on] the top [✕summit] of a tree; at [on] a treetop. (⇨頂上) ● 塔のてっぺんまで登る climb to the top of the tower. ● 私の頭のてっぺんから足のつま先までじろじろ見る stare at me from top [head] to toe; stare me up and down.

てっぽう 鉄棒 (鉄の棒) an iron bar; (体操用の) a horizontal bar (!) 競技種目は the 〜). ● 鉄棒を練習する practice [work out] on the bar. ● 鉄棒にぶらさがって体を振る hang from a bar and swing.

てっぽう 鉄砲 a gun,《集合的》firearms. (⇨銃) ● 鉄砲を撃つ shoot [fire] a gun. ● 鉄砲の狙いを定める point [aim] a gun (at).
● 鉄砲肩 a strong [a rifle] arm. ● 鉄砲肩の外野手 a strong-armed outfielder. ● 鉄砲玉 (銃弾) a bullet. ● 鉄砲水 a flash flood.

てっぽうゆり 鉄砲百合 【植物】an Easter lily.

てづまり 手詰まり (行き詰まり) (a) deadlock, (a) stalemate. ● 八方手詰まりである[になる] be in [reach, come to] a complete deadlock.

てつめんぴ 鉄面皮 ── 鉄面皮の brazen; utterly shameless.

***てつや** 徹夜 図 ● 徹夜で勉強する study all night; stay [sit] up all night studying. ● 徹夜で会議をする have an all-night [an overnight] conference.
── 徹夜する 動 stay [sit, be] up all night. ● 徹夜して=屋外で寝てまでして)切符を買う sleep out for tickets. ● 彼と徹夜してその問題を議論した I stayed [sat] up all night with him, discussing the matter.

てつよい 手強い (⇨手厳しい, 手強(ごわ)い)

てつり 哲理 philosophy; philosophical principles.

てづり 手釣り ── 手釣りする 動 fish with a handline. (!) handline は「手釣り用の糸」.

てづる 手づる (つて)《話》(a) pull; (縁故) connections; (影響力) influence. (⇨コネ)

てつろ 鉄路 (鉄道線路) a railroad; 《英》a railway. (!) 鉄道も意味する)

てつわん 鉄腕 ● 鉄腕投手 a iron arm; a workhorse.

テディベア (ぬいぐるみのクマ) a téddy bèar.

ててなしご 父無し子 a fatherless child.

でどころ 出所 (源) a source. ● そのうわさの出所 the source of the rumor. ▶ 金の出所 (=だれが金を出したか)が分からない I don't know who supplied the money [(どこからその金が出たか) where the money came from].

テトラパック [三角すい型の紙容器]《商標》Tetra Pak.

テトラポッド [波消しブロック] a tetrapod.

てどり 手取り take-home pay; after-tax (←before-tax, pretax) earnings. ▶ 税金を引くと彼の手取りは少なかった His take-home pay was small after taxes. ▶ 月収は手取りで20万円だ I earn 200,000 yen net [after tax] a month. (!) この net は形容詞の後置用法で「税引(後の)」「掛け値なしの」の意)

とりもたしとり 手取り足取り ▶ 彼は手取り足取り泳ぎ方をおしえてくれた He taught me step by step how to swim.
[会話] 「まだ答えを教えてもらってないよ」「いつも手取り足取り教えなくちゃいけないのかい」"You haven't told me the answer." "Must I always spoonfeed you?" (!) spoonfeed は通例けなして過度に甘やかすことを含意)

デトロイト [米国の都市] Détroit.

テトロン pólyester (fiber). (!) Tetoron は日本での商標名)

テナー [音楽] tenor; (声) a tenor (voice); (人) a tenor. (⇨テノール) ● テナーサックス [楽器] a tenor saxophone《話》sax).

てないしょく 手内職 ● 手内職で収入を補う supplement one's income by doing easy manual

てなおし 手直し 图 (修正) modification; (改良) improvement; (原稿などの) revision; (微調整) readjustment.
── 手直しする 動 modify; improve; revise; readjust.

でなおす 出直す 〖再び来る〗come* again, be back here; 〖再出発する〗start (all) over again, make* a fresh start. ▶頭を冷やして出直して来い You'd better cool off and *come back later*.

てながざる 手長猿 a long-armed ape; a gibbon.

てなぐさみ 手慰み ❶〖もてあそぶこと〗 ▶手慰みに鉛筆を転がす roll a pencil just to relieve the idle moments. ❷〖ばくち〗(⇨博打(₆ょぅ))

てなげだん 手投げ弾 a (hand) grenade.

てなずける 手なずける 〖飼いならす〗tame; 〖説得して味方に引き入れる〗win*... over (to one's side); 〖親しくなる〗make* friends 《with》. ▶ライオンを手なずけるには忍耐がいる It takes patience to *tame* lions. ▶あの委員会を手なずけるのは大変だよ We will have much difficulty in (in) *winning over* the committee. (🅛 in は通例省略する)

てなべ 手鍋 a pan.
● **手鍋提(**ᵴ**)げても** ▶手鍋提げても(＝どんなに貧乏でも)彼と一緒になりたい I want to marry him though he is very poor.

てなみ 手並み (⇨お手並み)

てならい 手習い (学習) learning; (習字) calligraphy. ▶六十の手習い《ことわざ》Never too late to *learn*.

てならし 手馴らし ── 手馴らしに by way of practice ── 手馴らしをする 動 practice; get into practice.

てなれた 手慣れた 〖熟練している〗skillful. ▶手慣れた手つきでタマネギをスライスする slice an onion with a *practiced* hand. ▶彼女は教えることは手慣れている She is *skillful* 〖十分経験を積んでいる〗is *very experienced*〗*in* teaching./(慣れている) She is *used* [*accustomed*] *to* teaching.

テナント 〖商業が目的の賃借人〗a tenant. (🅛 英語の tenant にはアパートや土地の借り手なども含まれる) ▶テナント募集〖掲示〗《米》For rent./《英》To let.

*テニス (lawn) tennis. ●軟式テニス softball *tennis*.
〖参考〗日本で考案された競技. 単に tennis といえば硬式テニスのこと) ●テニス選手 a *tennis*(-)player. ●テニスの試合 a *tennis* match [*tournament*]. ●テニス部員 a member of the *tennis* club. ●テニスをする play (a game of) *tennis*. ▶彼女はテニスがとても上手です He is a very good *tennis* player./He is very good at (playing) *tennis*./He plays *tennis* very well. ▶軽井沢にいるときはよくテニスをします I play a lot of *tennis* while I'm staying in Karuizawa.
● テニスコート a *tennis* court. ●テニスラケット a *tennis* racket.

てにてに 手に手に ▶多くの市民が手に手に小旗をもってチャンピオンの帰郷を祝った Many citizens, *each with* a small paper flag *in* their 〖《書》*his or her*〗 *hand*, welcomed the return of the champion [the champion back] to his hometown. (🅛 their hand に注意)

デニム dénim. ●デニムのジーンズ denims. ●デニムのスカート a *denim* skirt.

てにもつ 手荷物 baggage, (hand) luggage. (🅛 (1) いずれも数えるときは a piece [two pieces] of ～. (2) イギリス起源の luggage はアメリカでは高級感を伴う) (⇨荷物) ●フロントに手荷物を預ける leave one's *baggage* 〖持ち物〗 *things*〗 at the front desk. ▶この手荷物をしばらく預かってください Please hold [keep] this *baggage* for a while.
● **手荷物預(り)所**(ホテル・劇場などの) a cloakroom; 《主に米》a checkroom; (特に駅の) 《米》a baggage room, 《主に米》a checkroom; 《英》a left-luggage (office). ● **手荷物預り証**《米》a baggage check; 《英》a luggage ticket. ● **手荷物受取所** (空港の) a baggage claim (area).

てにをは 〖文法〗(助詞) (Japanese) postpositional particles. ▶彼はてにをはの使い方さえ知らない He doesn't know grammar at all.

てぬい 手縫い ── 手縫いの 形 handmade. ● 手縫いのシャツ a *handmade* shirt; a shirt *sewn by hand*.

てぬかり 手抜かり (誤り) a mistake, an error; (見落とし) 〖やや書〗an oversight. ▶調査にいくつか手抜かりがあった There were some *errors* [*oversights*] in the investigation. ▶これが最後のチャンスだ. 手抜かりがないか確かめなさい This is our last chance. Make sure everything goes right.

てぬき 手抜き 图 ●手抜き工事をする *cut corners* in the construction work.
── 手抜きする 動 (仕事をぞんざいにする) skimp [scamp] one's work; (経費・時間・手間を切り詰める) 《話》cut corners.

てぬぐい 手拭い (ぬれた手をふく) a (hand) towel; 〖洗面【浴用】タオル〗《米》a washcloth, 《英》a facecloth, a (face) flannel. (⇨タオル)

てぬるい 手ぬるい (厳格さのない) 〖やや書〗lenient /líːniənt/. ●手ぬるい処罰 a *lenient* punishment.

テネシー 〖米国の州〗Tennessée (略 Tenn. 郵便略 TN).

てのうち 手の内 ●手の内を見せる show one's hand [cards]; put [lay] one's cards on the table. ● 手の内を見せない keep [hold] one's cards close to one's chest.

てのうら 手の裏 (⇨掌(ᵗᵉ))
● **手の裏を返す** (すっかり態度を変える) change one's attitude completely.

テノール 〖音楽〗tenor /ténər/. (⇨テナー) ●テノールを歌う sing *tenor*. ●テノール歌手 a *tenor*.

てのこう 手の甲 the back of one's hand.

てのひら 掌 the palm [flat] of one's hand; a palm. ●コインをてのひらに隠す *palm* a coin.
● **掌を返す** ●てのひらを返すように(＝急激に)考えを変える change one's opinion *abruptly* [(完全に) *completely*]; 《話》change one's tune. (🅛 (1) 「態度」にも用いる. (2) sing another tune ともいう)

デノミ 〖通貨の単位切り下げ〗devaluation (🅛 英語の denomination は「通貨の種類」のこと); 〖通貨の名称変更〗redenomination. ●デノミを実施する devalue (the dollar).

てのもの 手の者 one's men.

-ては (接続助詞) ▶そうおだてられては君の申し出を断われない I cannot turn down your offer *after* you flattered me that way.

てば 手羽 a chicken wing.
● **手羽焼き** a grilled wing stick.

*では 〖話題を変えて〗(ところで) well; (よろしい次は) áll right, 《話》OK, okay; 〖注意を促して〗(さて) now (🅛 以上通例文頭で. いずれも大きな下降調でいう); 〖話題を引きついで〗(それでは) then (🅛 通例文頭・文尾で); 〖別れの言葉とともに〗then. (⇨それでは) ▶では今日はここまで *Well*, that's all for today. (🅛 授業終了時の先生の言葉) ▶では本題に入りましょう *All right* [*Now*], let's move on to the main subject.
会話 「田中に頼んでもむだだよ」「では大塚さんの方がよいでしょうか」"It's no good asking Tanaka." "*Well*, would Mr. Otsuka be a better choice?" (🅛 この well は譲歩を表す. 平板に近い下降調でいう)

会話「スポーツは好きではないんだ」「では何が好きなの．音楽かい」"I don't like sports." "What do you like, *then*? Music?"
会話「いいえ，私が欲しいのはそれではありません」「ほう，ではあなたが思っていたのはこれですか」"No, that's not the one I want." "*Well then*, is this the one you had in mind?" (**!** well then の連語で用いることが多い)

***では** ❶[関して] (…ということになると) when it comes* to …; (…に関する限り) as far as … be concerned; (…において) in … ▶英語では彼がクラスで一番です *When it comes to* English [*As far as* English *is concerned*], he is the best in the class. ▶この点では私が間違っていました I was wrong *in* this respect.
❷[判断] (…から判断して) (judging) from …; (…の考えでは) in one's opinion; (…によれば) according to …; [基準] by …. ▶この空模様ではまもなく雨だろう *From* the look of [*Judging from*] the sky, it will rain soon. ▶時刻表では列車は5時30分に出る *According to* the time schedule, the train leaves at 5:30. (**!** The time schedule *says* (*that*) the train …. のようにもいえる) ▶私の考えでは君は大学に進学すべきだ *In* my *opinion* [*view*], you should go on to college. (**!** ごく普通に I think you should …. でもよいが，×According to *my opinion*…. とはいえない (⇒意見)) ▶私の時計ではちょうど6時です It's exactly six o'clock *by* my watch. ▶この雨ではバスも遅れるだろう The bus will come late *in* this rain. ▶その制度では生徒は学年ごとに必要な単位を取得するようになっている The system *is* (*such*) *that* [*Under* the system] students are expected to obtain all credits required in each grade. (**!** such は日常的には通例省略される)
❸[対比，強調] (場所) in …; at …; (**!** 両語の違いは (⇒で)); (手段) by …; (時) in ….

解説 日本語では「…を対比・強調すると「…では」になることがある：ペンで書く write *with* a pen./ペンでは書かない do not write *with* a pen.

▶きのうの静岡では晴れだったが大阪は雨だった It was a nice [*fine*] *day in* Shizuoka, but it rained in Osaka yesterday. (**!** It was fine. とはあまりいわない) ▶バスでは時間に間に合わない You won't get there in time *by* bus. ▶修理には1週間かかります．3日ではできません It takes a week to fix it. We can't do *in* three days. (**!** in は「…の期間以内に」の意) ▶これでは足りない(=十分でない) This is not enough.
① [A ではなく B] not A but B. (**!** A と B は対等の関係にある語・句・節) ▶その案に反対したのは私ではなく中村だ It was *not* ˇme *but* ˏNakamura who opposed the ∕plan./The plan was opposed *not* by ˇme *but* by ˏNakamura. (**!** ×by not me but Nakamura や ×not by me but Nakamura は不可)/The plan was opposed by ˏNakamura, *not* by ˇme. ▶人間は四つんばいではなくまっすぐ立って歩く Human beings walk upright *rather than* on all fours.
② [… ではないのに] ▶彼はどうしてあんなに女の子にもてるのかしら．別にいい男というわけではないのに I wonder why he's so popular with girls. *It isn't as if* he's really a good-looking man. (**!** 慣用表現)

***デパート** a department store. (**!** 単に ×depart, ×department とはいえない) ▶彼女はそのデパートに買い物に行った [で買い物をした] She went shopping [did some shopping] at [in, ×to] *that* *department store*.

てはい 手配 图 ❶[準備，用意] (組織的にする準備) arrangements 《*for*》; (将来に向けての準備) preparations 《*for*》. ▶結婚式の手配は万端整っています All the *arrangements* [*preparations*] *for* the wedding have been made.
❷[警察の](捜索) (a) search 《*for*》. ●犯人の手配をする start a *search for* a criminal.
── 手配する 圗 arrange [make* arrangements] 《*for*》; (準備する) prepare 《*for*》. ●車を手配する get the car ready. ▶彼があなたを空港に出迎えるよう手配します I *arrange for* him to meet [*that* he ((英)*should*) *meet*] you at the airport. ▶その旅行社は私たちのヨーロッパ旅行の手配を一から十までやってくれた The travel agency *arranged* everything *for* our trip to Europe. ▶君が仕事に就けるよう手配しよう I'll *see* (*to it*) *that* you get [will get] a job. (**!** get が本来の言い方だが will get も徐々に用いられるようになってきた)
●手配師 a day labor agent.

てはいり 出入り going in and out. (⇒出入(ᵢᵣ)り)
てばかめ 出歯亀 [のぞき見の常習者] a Peeping Tom; a voyeur /vwɑːjɜːr/.
てばこ 手箱 a small box (in which small things are stored).
てはじめ 手始め ── 手始めに 圗 (まず最初に) first of all. ▶手始めにこの小説を読もう *First of all*, I'll read this novel./I'll *begin with* [*by* reading] this novel.
てはず 手はず arrangements 《*for*》; (計画) a plan; (予定) a program. ▶パーティーの手はずを整える *arrange* [*make arrangements*] *for* the party [*to* have the party]. ▶式の手はずはついている The *arrangements have been made for* the ceremony. ▶君が支配人に会えるよう手はずを整えよう I'll *arrange for* you *to* meet the manager. ▶部長は手はずが狂ったことに大変怒っている The manager is in a fury over a *plan* that went wrong.

ではずれる 出外れる ▶町を出外れたところに古刹(ᵢ)があった We came to an old temple *at the end of* the town./There was an old temple *on the outskirts of* the town.
てばた 手旗 a small 《*paper*》 flag; (通信用の) a semaphore flag. ●手旗信号をする signal with flags; send a message by *semaphore*.
デバッガー [コンピュータ] a debugger (program).
デバッグ ── デバッグする 圗 [コンピュータ] debug.
てばな 手鼻 ●手鼻をかむ blow one's nose with one's fingers.
ではな 出端 (⇒出端(ᵢ)))
ではな 出花 ●番茶も出花 (⇒番茶 [成句])
ではな 出端, 出鼻 (=出たとたん) ▶山田さんに呼び止められた Mrs. Yamada called to me to stop *just when* I left home.
●出端をくじく ▶彼の一言で私は出端(= 初めの意気込み)をくじかれた His single remark killed [dampened] my *enthusiasm at* the start.
てばなし 手放し ●手放しでほめる give *unreserved* praise 《*to* him》; praise 《him》 *unreservedly*. ●その知らせに手放しで喜ぶ be *overjoyed at* [*to* hear] the news.
てばなす 手放す part with …. (**!** part from … は「(人)と別れる」の意); (売る) sell*. ●家を手放す *part with* one's house; *sell* one's house. ▶彼は息子を手放したく(= 遠くへやりたく)なかった He hated *sending away* his son. ▶作文にはこの辞書は手放せない (必需品である) This dictionary is a *must* in writing a composition./(…なしですませない) We *can't do without* this dictionary in writing a com-

position. 翻訳のこころ 祖母の遺言だと言うと,父はいつか店を手放すからお前に継がせてやる,そうなったらそこで花屋をやるといい,と許してくれた(吉本ばなな『みどりのゆび』) I told my father that was my grandmother's will. Then, he said (that) he would eventually sell his business and let me have his shop, and I could [might] open a flower shop there. (⚠(1)「店を手放す」は「商売を止める。店を(他の人に)売る」と考え,sell one's business と表す. (2)「許してくれた」は主語に許可を与えることを表す can, may を用いる. (3) he said (that) 以下は,時制の一致で過去形になっていることに注意)

でばぼうちょう 出刃包丁 a kitchen knife for cutting fish or chicken bones.

てばやい 手早い 形 quick. ・仕事が手早い do one's work *quickly*; be *quick* about one's work.
—— 手早く 副 quickly. ・食卓を手早く片付ける clear the table *quickly*.

ではらう 出払う be all out. ・家族の者は皆出払っています All the family are *out*. (⚠ all のような明白な複数概念の語を伴う場合は米文らも複数扱い)

でばん 出番 (順番) one's turn; (好機での) time. ・出番を待つ wait (for [until it is]) one's *turn*. ▶君の出番だよ It's your *turn*./(芝居などで) You're on *stage* next./(自分を売り込むチャンスだ) This is your *chance*. ▶私の出番はなかった I had no *part to play*. ▶新庄の出番だ It's Shinjo *time*. ▶そこは私の出番(=私が分担する所)だ,まかせておけ That's *where I come in*. Leave it to me.

てびかえる 手控える (⇨控える)

てびき 手引き 图 [指導,案内] guidance, lead; [紹介] introduction; [案内者] a guide. ・彼の手引き(=つて)でこの職を得る get this position *through* him.
—— 手引きする 動 guide; lead. (⇨導く)
・手引書 a guide(book) (*to*); (入門書) a handbook; (指導書) a manual.

デビスカップ [テニス] the Davis Cup.

デビットカード a debit card.

てひどい 手ひどい (きびしい) severe; (容赦のない) merciless. ・手ひどい批判を浴びる be *severely* criticized; meet (with) *severe* criticism. ▶今度の台風で手ひどい打撃(=多大の損害)を受けた We suffered *severe* [*heavy*, *a lot of*] damage [xdamages] by the typhoon.

デビュー [<フランス語] 图 a debut /déibju:/.
—— デビューする 動 ・歌手としてデビューする *make* one's *debut* [*get* one's *start*] as a singer.

てびょうし 手拍子 ・手拍子を取る beat time with one's hands; keep time by clapping (one's hands).

デビル [悪魔] a devil.

てびろい 手広い (⇨広い) ・手広く(=大規模に)商売している do business *on a large scale*.

でぶ (話) a fatty; (呼びかけ) Fatty.

デフォルト [初期設定] [コンピュータ] a default; [債務不履行] [経済] default.

デフォルメ [<フランス語] 图 [美術] deformation.
—— デフォルメする 動 deform.

てふき 手拭き (タオル) a hand towel; (ハンカチ) a handkerchief.

*****てぶくろ** 手袋 (各指が分かれた) gloves /gl*ʌ*vz/; (親指だけ分かれた) mittens. (⚠片方だけをいうときは単数形: 右手の手袋 one's right *glove* [*mitten*]) ・暖かい手袋一対 a warm pair of *gloves*. ・白い毛糸の手袋一対 a pair of white woolen *gloves*. ・手袋をはめる [脱ぐ] put on [take off] one's *gloves*. ・[はめている] 状態は wear *gloves*; have on *gloves* [*gloves on*] (⇨着る)) ・手袋をはめて[はめたままで] with one's *gloved* hand; with one's *gloved* hands. ▶手袋を片方失った I lost one of my *gloves*.

でぶしょう 出無精 (人) (話) a stay-at-home, (主に米話) a homebody.

てぶそく 手不足 ・手不足である be short of hands, be shorthanded; (職員が不足している) be understaffed.

てふだ 手札 ・手札がいい have good cards in one's hand; have a good hand.
・手札判[型] a cardsize photograph. (参考 約105mm×80mm)

でぶね 出船 [出港する船] a ship leaving port; [出港] departure from a port.

てぶら 手ぶら ・手ぶらで(=手みやげを持たないで)彼の家に行く visit his house *without a present* (in one's hand). ▶「今夜はごちそうだよ」といって彼は釣りに出かけたが,手ぶらで(=何の収穫もなく)帰ってきた He went fishing, saying "We'll have a feast tonight," but came home *empty-handed*.
会話 「パーティーに何か飲み物を持っていくわ」「ありがとう,でも本当に気を遣わないで.手ぶらで来てちょうだい」"I'll bring something to drink to your party." "That's very nice of you, but don't bother. *Just bring yourself*." (⚠慣用表現)

てぶり 手振り (手の動き) a movement of the hand; (しぐさ) a gesture. ・大げさな身振り手振りで with exaggerated *gestures*.

てぶれ 手ぶれ camera shake. ▶シャッターを切るとき手ぶれしない(=カメラをぐらつかせない)ように気をつけてね Be careful not to *shake* the camera when you press the shutter. ▶この写真は手ぶれしている(=カメラの動きを示す) This picture shows *movement of the camera*.

デフレ(ーション) deflation (↔inflation). ・デフレ効果 a *deflationary* effect. ・デフレ対策を実施する implement anti-*deflation* measures.
・デフレスパイラル [経済] a deflationary spiral.

デフロスター [霜取り装置] a defroster.

テフロン [商標] Teflon.

てぶんこ 手文庫 (説明的に) a small box for keeping letters, papers, and the like.

でべそ 出臍 a protruding navel /néivl/.

テヘラン [イランの首都] Teheran /terá:n/.

デベロッパー (⇨ディベロッパー)

てべんとう 手弁当 ・手弁当で(自費で) at one's own expense; (無報酬で) without pay.

てぼうき 手箒 a short-handled broom.

でほうだい 出放題 ❶ [水などが] be left running; be running freely. ▶水道管が破裂して水が出放題になって(=吹き出して)いる The waterpipe broke and water *is squirting out*.
❷ [出任せ] (⇨出任せ)

デポジット [預かり金] a deposit.
・デポジット方式 a deposit formula (to recover empty cans and bottles).

てほどき 手解き (秘伝などの) (やや書) initiation (*into*). ・彼に商売の手ほどきをする give him the first lessons in (successful) business; teach him how to do business successfully.

てぼり 手彫り hand-carving. ・手彫りの盆 a *hand-carved* tray.

*****てほん** 手本 [模範] a model, a pattern; [例] an example; [習字の] a copybook. ・彼によい手本を示す set him a good *example*; set a good *exam*-

ple to [for] him. (!set の代わりに give を用いると「よい実例である」の意となる) ▶これは彼らが見習うべきいい手本になる This serves as a good model [pattern, example] for them to follow. ▶ N 氏は若い弁護士の手本となる人物です Mr. N is a role model for young lawyers. (!role model は「役割として模範となる人」の意) ●彼女は母親の行儀を手本にした She modeled her manners after [on] her mother's. (⇨模範) ●この手本どおりに書くようにしなさい Try to write after this model writing.

*てま 手間 〖時間〗time;〖手数〗trouble;〖努力〗(an) effort;〖労力〗labor. (!time and trouble [effort, labor] と合わせて用いると「手間ひま」の感じを表す) ●手間取る (⇨手間取る) ▶この機械のおかげでずいぶん手間が省ける This machine saves (us) a lot of time [trouble]. ▶お手間を取らせてすみません Thank you for your time [your trouble, the trouble you have taken for me]. (!用件が終わって去るときのお礼の表現)/(申し訳ありません I'm sorry to trouble you.)/(!これから何か頼むときの前置きの表現) ▶彼は手間ひまをかけてその絵を描いた He put in a lot of time and effort to paint the picture. (!put in は「(労力など)をつぎ込む」の意)

デマ〔<ドイツ語〕〖うそのうわさ〗a false 〖(根拠のない)〗groundless, an unfounded rumor;〖虚報〗〖婉曲的〗misinformation. (⇨噂(うわさ)) ●デマを飛ばす start [spread, circulate] a false rumor. ●…というデマが飛んでいる There is a groundless rumor (going around) that…. ●それはとんでもないデマだ The rumor is completely unfounded.

*てまえ 手前 ❶ 〖こちら側, 前の方〗●仙台より一つ手前 (=前)の駅で降りる get off the train (at) one station before Sendai. ●銀行の手前を右に回る turn right just before one comes to the bank. ▶その公園は川の手前にある The park is on [×in] this (↔the other) side of the river. ▶写真(=最前列に)に立っているその女の人の奥さんです(写真などで) The woman standing in the foreground is his wife. ▶私たちは目的地の手前数マイルのところにいた We were some miles short of our destination. ▶私は終点の1つ手前でバスを降りた I got off the bus at one stop before the end of the line. ❷ 〖体面〗●世間の手前(=体裁上)for appearance's [decency's] sake. ●子供の手前(=前では)in front of [〖書〗in the presence of] one's children.

てまえ 点前 (⇨お点前)

てまえ 出前 图 delivery. (!a delivery は1回の出前, または出前の食べ物) ▶あの店は出前をしている That restaurant has a home delivery service.
— する 動 (注文により食事[料理]を配達する) deliver meals [dishes] to order;(宴会などの料理とサービスを提供する) cater 《for a party》. ▶そばを出前してもらった I had soba delivered./I got a delivery of soba.
●出前持ち a delivery boy [girl].

てまえがって 手前勝手 — 手前勝手な 形 selfish; self-centered.

てまえみそ 手前味噌 self-praise. ●手前みそをいう praise oneself;《軽蔑的》blow one's own trumpet [horn].

でまかせ 出任せ ●出任せの(=行き当たりばったりの)発言 a random remark. ●出任せの(=無責任な)返事をする give an irresponsible answer;(考えずに答えず) answer without thinking.

てまき 手巻き ●手巻き寿司 a hand-rolled sushi.
●手巻きたばこ a hand-rolled cigarette. ●手巻き時計 a windup clock [watch].

てまくら 手枕 ●手枕をする rest one's head on one's hands [arm]; sleep with one's arm [hands] for a pillow.

デマゴーグ 〖扇動(せんどう)政治家〗a demagogue.

てまちん 手間賃 (賃金) wages;(一般に給料) pay. (⇨賃金)

でまど 出窓 a bay window;(弓形張り出し窓) a bow /bóu/ window.

てまどる 手間取る ▶その仕事にはずいぶん手間取った(=時間を取った) The work took me a lot of time (to do)./It took a lot of time for me [me a lot of time] to do the work. ▶こんなに遅れてすみません. 途中交通渋滞で手間取った(=遅れた)のです I'm sorry to be so late. I was delayed by a traffic jam on my way here.

てまね 手真似 a gesture.

てまねき 手招き 图 beckoning.
— 手招きする 動 ●もっと近くに来るよう[中に入るよう]彼に手招きする beckon him (to come) nearer [in].

てまひま 手間暇 ●手間ひまをかける use [put in] a lot of time.

てまめ 手まめ — 手まめな 形 ●手まめな(=手先が器用な)人 a skillful person. (⇨器用, 手先) ▶彼女は手まめに部屋の片付けをした(面倒がらずにする) She didn't bother to put the room in order./(てきぱきと) She tidied up the room efficiently.

てまり 手鞠 a temari,(説明的に) a traditional Japanese ball, the size of a baseball, decorated by colorful threads artistically wound around it.

てまわし 手回し (用意) preparations 《for》;(手配) arrangements 《for》. ●何事にも手回しがいい be clever at making preparations for everything.

てまわりひん 手回り品 〖持ち物〗one's things;〖(やや書)〗belongings;〖身の回り品〗one's personal effects (化粧用具・衣類など);〖手荷物〗baggage, luggage. (⇨手荷物)

でまわる 出回る 〖市場に出る〗(出ている) be on the market;(出るようになる) appear [arrive] on the market;(売られている) be sold (everywhere), be around;〖出盛りだ〗be in season. ▶この地方では10月にリンゴが出回る In this district, apples are on the market [in season] in October. ▶模造真珠が出回っている(=売られている) Imitation pearls are around.
会話 「ところで果物はどうしよう」「そうねえ, 今のところナシがかなり出回っている(=豊富にある)わ」"And now what about fruit?" "Well, pears are plentiful at the moment."

てみじか 手短 — 手短な 形 brief.
— 手短に 副 briefly. ●手短に言えば in short. (⇨つまり ❷) ●筋を手短にまとめる outline the plot briefly; give a brief [short] summary of the plot.

でみせ 出店 〖支店〗a branch (store);〖露店〗a stand.

デミタス (カップ) a démitàsse (cup);(コーヒー) demitasse.

てみやげ 手土産 ●手土産を持っていく visit [《主に英》call on] 《him》 with a present [a gift].

むかう 手向かう (立ち向かう) stand* up 《to, against》;(敵対する) turn 《against》. (⇨刃向かう)

でむかえ 出迎え (⇨出迎える) ▶姉が京都駅まで出迎えに来てくれた My sister came to meet [×see] me at Kyoto Station. ▶see は「見送る」の意)

でむかえる 出迎える (出向いて会う) meet* (↔see); (歓迎する) welcome; (言葉・動作とともに歓迎する) greet. ▶彼女は玄関で客を出迎えた She greeted her

でむく guests at the door.

でむく 出向く go* [come*] to ...; (訪問する) visit.

テムズ ●テムズ川 the Thames /témz/.

でめ 出目 protruding eyes.

でめきん 出目金 〖魚介〗 a pop-eyed goldfish.

デメリット a disadvantage; (短所) a demerit.

*-ても (接続助詞) ❶〖たとえ...としても〗even if ..., even though ..., (!前の方が口語的)▶君が倍の速さで走っても彼には追いつけないだろう *Even if* [*Even though*] you run twice as fast, you won't be able to catch up with him. ▶今さら彼にそう言ってもしょうがない There's no use say*ing* it to him now.

❷〖どんなに〗...であっても〗no matter how [what, who, when, where, which]...; however [whatever, whoever, wherever, whichever].... (!「no matter＋wh-語」の方がwh-ever 語より口語的) ▶いくら疲れていても授業中に居眠りをしてはいけない *No matter how* [*However*] tired you are, you must not doze off in class. (!*However* tired you *may* be, ... のように 'may' を用いるのは〘書〙) ▶だれが言っても結果は同じだろう *No matter who* [*Whoever*] says [×will say] so, the result will be the same. (!「no matter wh- 節」内の動詞は現在形を用いる) ▶彼は何をやってもうまくやるだろう I think he'll succeed in *whatever* [×no matter what] he tries. (!「no matter＋wh-節」は文の主語や, 動詞・前置詞の目的語にならない)

❸〖...してもいい〗▶少し個人的な質問をしてもいいですか It is all right *if* I ask [*Can* I ask] some personal questions? (⇔いい⓮)

❹〖けれども〗, though, although. (!前の方が口語的) ▶彼に声をかけてもしらん顔だった *Though* [*Although*] I called (out) to him, he pretended not to recognize [hear] me.

*でも ❶〖しかし〗but; 〖しかしながら〗(やや書) however; (それにもかかわらず)〘書〙nevertheless; (けれど)〘話〙though. (⇔しかし, けれど(も)) ▶私はそのパーティーに出席したいのです. でも行けません I'd like to go to the party, *but* I can't. ▶私はそのことはあまりよく知らない. でも, 彼の言ったことは信じられない I don't know much about it. *However*, I can't believe what he said./I don't know much about it. I can't believe what he said, *however* [*though*, ×*although*].

*デモ a dèmonstrátion, 〘話〙a demo /démou/. (複 ～s). ●学生デモ a student *demonstration*. ●デモ参加者 a démonstrator. ●消費税反対〘賃上げ〙のデモをする demonstrate [hold a demonstration] *against* consumption taxes [*for* a pay raise].

-でも (副助詞) ❶ ▶どんなに健康でも暴飲暴食は慎むべきだ *No matter how* [*However*] healthy you are, you should refrain from intemperance. (⇔ても❷) ❷ ▶これは日本語でも(=ですら)うまく表現できない I can't express this well *even* in Japanese. ▶お茶でも(=か何か)いかが Would you like tea *or something*? (!この「でも」は一種のぼかし表現. Would you like some tea? との違いに注意)

デモクラシー 〖民主主義〗démócracy.

てもち 手持ち ●手持ちの商品 goods *in stock* [*store*], (⇔在庫) ▶手持ちの金がなくなった I spent all the money I *had on* [*with*] me. ●金などの小物には on が普通だ/I ran out of cash *in* [*on*] hand.

てもちぶさた 手持ち無沙汰 ▶今は手持ち無沙汰だ(何もすることがない) I have nothing to do now./(時間をもて余している) I *have* time *on* my *hands*.

デモテープ 〖試聴用テープ〗〘話〙a demo (tape).

てもと 手元 図 ▶手元が狂って当たらなかった I missed my *mark* [*aim*]. ── 手元に 副〖手近に〗(near) at hand; 〖持ち合わせて〗on [in] hand; 〖家に〗at home. ▶彼はいつもその辞書を手元に置いている He always keeps the dictionary *at hand* [*nearby*, 〘話〙*handy*]. ▶私は手元に現金がない I have no cash *in* [*on*] *hand*. (!次の方が普通だ/I have no cash *on* me. ▶彼女は一人息子を手元に置いておきたかった She wanted to keep her only son *at home* [(そばに) *by* her *side*]. ▶それを手元に置いておくの, それとも売るの? Would you *keep* it or sell it?

●手元不如意 ●手元不如意である be short of money; be in financial difficulties.
●手元金 ready money; cash in hand.

でもどり 出戻り a divorced woman (living with her parents).

てもなく 手もなく (簡単に) easily. ●手もなく勝つ win *easily* [*hands down*].

でもの 出物 〖普通より安い処分品〗goods disposed at a bargain price; (お買い得もの) a bargain, a good buy; 〖おなら〗a fart. (!出物の原義は「できもの」(a boil)) ▶芦屋に格安の宅地の出物があります There is a building lot, a real *good buy*, in Ashiya.
●出物腫れ物所きらわず 'Boils and farts do not choose the place or time when they come out.'/(ことわざ) Necessity knows no law.

デモンストレーション 〖実演, 示威運動〗(a) demonstration. ●新型機械のデモンストレーション(＝実演説明)をする give a *demonstration* of a new machine; demonstrate a new machine. (⇔デモ)

てやき 手焼き ●手焼きせんべい hand-grilled Japanese rice crackers. (!baked は直火(じかび)を当てずに焼くことなのでここでは不適)

デュアル 〖二重の〗dual. ●デュアルスラローム〖スキー〗a dual slalom.

デュエット a duet. ●デュエットをする sing a *duet*.

デュッセルドルフ 〖ドイツの都市〗Düsseldorf /d(j)úsaldɔ̀ːrf/.

でよう 出様 (⇔出方)

*てら 寺 a (Buddhist) temple. (!通例 temple だけでよい. 「長谷寺」は the Hasedera *Temple* が普通だが, the Hase Temple も可. Hasedera だけでもよい) ●寺の鐘 the bell of a *temple*; a *temple* bell. ●寺参りをする go to [visit] a *temple*. (!参拝の意を明確に表すには go to the temple to worship などとする)

てらい 衒い (気取り) (an) affectation, 〘話〙show-off; (見せかけ) a pretension (!しばしば複数形で). ●何のてらいもなく without any *affectation*.

てらう 衒う (気取る) affect, 〘話〙show* off; (見せかける) pretend. ●奇をてらう make a display of one's originality; *show off* one's originality.

デラウェア 〖米国の州〗Délaware (略 Del. 郵便略 DE).

てらこや 寺子屋 a *terakoya* school; (説明的に) a kind of primary school for children of the uneducated class, where they taught the three Rs before the *Meiji* Restoration. (!the three Rs は *r*eading, *w*riting, and *a*rithmetic のこと)

てらしあわせる 照らし合わせる (符合する) check 《A *against* [*with*] B》; (比較する) compare 《A *with* [*to*] B》. ●原文と翻訳を照らし合わせる *compare* [*check*] the translation *with* the original.

てらす 照らす ❶〖光などが〗(照らす) shine (*on*, *over*); (光をあてる) light*... (up); (照明する) illuminate; (明るくする) lighten. ●ぼんやりと照らされた廊下 a dimly *lit* [*illuminated*] corridor. ▶日の光が

女の髪を照らした The sun *lit* [*lighted*] *up* her hair. ▶月が水面[野原]を照らしている The moon *is shining on* the water [*over* the field]. ▶多くの電球がステージを照らした A lot of electric lamps *illuminated* the stage.
❷ [比較する] compare 《*with*》; [照合する] check 《*with*》. (⇨照らし合わせる) ▶規則に照らしてその件を処置すべきだ We should decide the case *according to* the rule. ▶過去に照らして現在を研究しなければならない We must study the present *in the light of* the past.

テラス a terrace. ●テラスに出る go out onto the *terrace*.
●テラスハウス (1 戸分)《米》a row house;《英》a terrace(d) house.

てらせん 寺銭 (ばくちで) a house commission [《話》cut].

デラックス ── デラックスな 形 [高級な] deluxe (❗)
(1)《英》で de luxe と 2 語にもつづる. (2) 主に宣伝文句に用いられる); luxurious /lʌɡʒúəriəs/. (⇨豪華な)
●デラックスなホテル a *deluxe* [*a luxurious*] hotel.

てらてら ── てらてらした 形 shiny; (てかてかの) glossy. ●てらてらしたはげ頭 a *shiny* bald head.

テラマイシン [薬剤][商標] Terramycin.

てり 照り [晴天][(the) sunshine; [干ばつ] (a) drought; [光沢] (布地などの) (a) gloss; [料理の] a glaze. ▶照りのある風艷 *glossy* [*shiny*] material.
●卵黄を塗ってパイに照りを付ける *glaze* a pie with yolk. ●みりん醤油で魚に照りを出す *glaze* a fish with *mirin* and soy sauce [sweetened soy sauce].

テリア [動物] (犬) a terrier.

デリート 名 [削除] (a) deletion. **── デリートする** 動 delete.
●デリートキー a delete key.

テリーヌ [<フランス語] (料理) (a) terrine /tərí:n/.

てりかえし 照り返し (光[熱]の反射) the reflection of light [heat].

てりかえす 照り返す reflect (light [heat]).

デリカシー delicacy; [感受性の鋭さ] sensitivity.
●デリカシーに欠ける人 a person lacking in *delicacy*; an *insensitive* person.

デリカテッセン [<ドイツ語] [洋風惣菜店] a delicatessen;《話》a deli.

デリケート ── デリケートな 形 ●デリケートな肌 (a) *sensitive* [(a) *delicate* /délikət/] skin. (❗ 前の方は敏感で弱い肌、後の方はきめの細かい肌のこと) ●デリケートな神経 a *sensitive* heart. ●デリケートな(=微妙な)問題 a *delicate* problem.

てりつける 照り付ける ▶太陽が容赦なく照りつけた The sun *beat* [(かあっと) *blazed*] *down* mercilessly (*on* us).

テリトリー [領域] a territory; [勢力範囲] one's domain. ▶台所は女房のテリトリーだからぼくは余計な手出しはしない The kitchen is my wife's *domain*, so I don't interfere in her work there.

てりはえる 照り映える ●夕日に美しく照り映えるもみじ autumn(al) colors *shining* [*glowing*] *beautifully* in the late setting sun.

デリバティブ [金融派生商品] derivatives.
●デリバティブ取引 a derivative transaction.

デリバリー [配達] delivery.

てりやき 照り焼き (a) *teriyáki*; (説明的に) fish [meat] broiled after being marinated in soy sauce, sweet *sake* and sugar.

てりゅうだん 手榴弾 a (hand) grenade /ɡrənéid/.

てりょうり 手料理 (自家製の) a homemade [a home-cooked] dish. ▶彼女は手料理でぼくをもてなした She entertained him with *dishes* she *cooked* [*prepared*].

***てる 照る** [輝く] shine*; [天気が晴れる] clear up. ▶太陽がさんさんと照り輝いていた The sun *was shining* bright(ly) above us.

:でる 出る
INDEX

❶ 外へ出る	❷ 出発する
❸ 現れる	❹ 突き出る
❺ 流れ出る	
❻ 出版・掲載・発表される	
❼ 出席する	❽ 由来する
❾ 生じる	❿ 与えられる
⓫ 卒業する	⓬ 売れる
⓭ 生み出される	⓮ 至る
⓯ 超過する	⓰ 電話・玄関に応対する
⓱ 熱・せきなどが	⓲ 茶がせんじ出される
⓳ 提出される	

● WORD CHOICE ● 出る
get out 人・物が、主に強い意思によって内部から外部へ出ること. しばしば閉鎖的・束縛的な内部空間から、抵抗などを乗り越えて、自由な外部の解放・脱出・逃避することを含意する. ▶(部屋の)外へ出て新鮮な空気を吸ってはいかが? Why don't you *get out* (*of* the room) and enjoy fresh air?
come out 人・物が、自然に内部から外部へ出ること. しばしば物事の出現・露見・終了を含意する. ▶その会見で新事実が出てきた A new facts *came out* at the interview.
go out 主に人が外に出ること. しばしば息抜きなどのために戸外へ出ることを含意. ▶バーに飲みに出かけよう Let's *go out* drinking [to drink, for a drink] to the bar.

● 頻度チャート ●
get out
come out
go out
20 40 60 80 100 (%)

❶ [外へ出る] (出て行く) go* out 《*of*》; (出てくる) come* out 《*of*》; (去る) leave*; (場所から出る) get* out 《*of*》; (転居して行く) move (out) (⇨引っ越す).
●庭に出る[出てくる; 出ている] go out into [come out into; be out in] the garden. (❗ ×go [come] out in the garden は不可) ●買い物に出る *go* (*out*) shopping. ●散歩に出る *go* (*out*) *for a walk*. ●前へ出る(=進み出る) *step forward*. ▶彼は黙って部屋を出た He *went out of* [*left*] the room without (saying) a word. ▶主人は勤めに出ました(=行きました) My husband *has gone* [*left*] *to work*. ▶出て行け *Get out* (*of here*)!/*Go away* (from here)! ▶彼は昼食に出ています He *is out* to lunch. ▶地下鉄の駅を出たところで彼女は新聞売りに道を聞いた *Outside* the subway station, she asked a newspaper seller the way.

会話 「つまんない映画だな」「じゃあ出ましょうよ」 "This is a rather boring movie." "Let's *go*, then."

❷ [出発する] (場所を去る) leave*; (動き出す) start 《*from*》; (列車が動く) pull out. (⇨出発) ▶旅行に出る *go* [*start*, *set out*] *on* a trip. ▶彼は東京を出てパリに向かった He *left* [*started from*] Tokyo *for* Paris. ▶私はいつも5時に会社を出る I always *leave* [*get away from*] the office at five o'clock. ▶こ

でる

の列車は8時15分に出る This train *leaves* [《書》*departs*] at 8:15. (!*eight fifteen* と読む. 列車・飛行機などの時刻表による出発には start を用いない)
▶電車はちょうど出るところだった The train *was just pulling out* [was about to *start*]. ▶船は航海に出て10日たっていた The ship *was out* at sea for ten days.
❸ [現れる] (現れる, 出演する) appear; (出てくる) come* out; (隠れていたものが) emerge 《*from*》 (!come out より堅い語); (物が偶然見つかる) turn up; (見える) show*. ●人前に出る *appear* in public [before the audience]. ●ジョン・ウェインの出ている西部劇 a Western *with* John Wayne. ▶このごろ彼女はめったにテレビ[舞台]に出ない She seldom *appears on* television [*on* the stage] these days. ▶その映画にはだれが出ていますか Who *is* (*starring*) *in* the film? / *star in …* は「…に主演する」の意) ▶星が出た[出ている] The stars *came out* [*are out*]. ▶太陽が出た(=昇った) The sun *has come up* [*risen*]. /(雲間などから) The sun *has come out*. ▶クマがほら穴から出てきた A bear *came out* [*emerged*] *from* its cave. ▶心配するな. 指輪はきっと出てくる Don't worry. Your missing ring is bound to *turn up*. ▶スリップが出ているよ Your slip *is showing*. (!進行形で用いる) ▶はしかが彼の体中に出た The measles *broke out* all over his body. ▶この城には幽霊が出るそうだ I hear this castle *is haunted* (by a ghost)./A ghost is said to *haunt* this castle. (!*haunt* は「幽霊などが(場所に)出没する」の意) ▶イチゴがそろそろ出るころだ (⇒出回る) Strawberries will soon *be in season*. (⇨出回る)
❹ [突き出る] (突出する) stick* out, 《書》 protrude; (伸びる) reach*. ▶彼は前歯が出ている His front teeth *stick out* [*protrude*]. ▶枝が塀の外に出すぎている The branches *reach out* far beyond the fence.
❺ [流れ出る] (鼻水が) run*; (血が) bleed*; (涙などが) flow. ▶鼻血[鼻]が出ているよ Your nose's *bleeding* [*running*]./You're *bleeding* [*running*] *at* the nose./You've got a *bleeding* [*runny*] nose. (!a running nose はあまり用いない. 不可とする人もいる) (⇨鼻血) ▶彼女の目から涙が出た Tears *flowed* [*ran*] *from* her eyes./Her eyes *ran* with tears. ▶水道管が凍ってしまって水が出ない The water pipes have been frozen, and the water won't *come out*.
❻ [出版・掲載・発表される] appear; (出版される) come*; be published (!前の方が口語的); (発行される) be issued; (表・名簿に) be listed. ▶そのニュースはどの新聞にも出ている The news *is* [*appears*, *is reported*] in every newspaper./Every newspaper *carries* the news. (!*carries* の代わりに has は通例用いない) ▶彼の本は来春出るでしょう His book will *come out* [*be published*, *appear*] next spring. ▶この語はこの辞書には出ていない This word *isn't listed* [*isn't given*, *isn't found*] in this dictionary. ▶まもなく新しい切手が出ます New stamps will *be issued* shortly. ▶試験の結果はいつ出る(=発表される)のですか When are the results of the exam *announced*?
❼ [出席する] be present 《*at*》 (!be 動詞だけでも存在を表す (⇨[第1文例])), 《やや書》 attend; (参加する) take* part 《*in*》, 《やや書》 participate 《*in*》; (試合・劇などに) play 《*in*》 (競技などに) enter, enter (oneself) for …. ▶あなたはその式に出ましたか Did you *go to* the ceremony? (!次例より口語的)/ *Were* you (*present*) *at* [Did you *attend*] the ceremony? ▶彼は100メートル競走に出る決心をした

He decided to *take part in* [*enter*] the 100-meter dash. ▶彼女はテニスの決勝戦に出た She *was in* the tennis final. ▶彼は知事選に出る(=立候補する)ことにした He decided to *run for* [《英》 *stand for*] governor.
❽ [由来する] come* 《*from*》; (やや書) derive [be derived] 《*from*》. ▶この語はラテン語から出ている This word *comes* [*derives*] *from* Latin./This is a word *of* Latin *origin*. ▶彼の家は平家から出ている His family *comes* [(子孫である) *is descended*] *from* the Heike clan. ▶その習慣は異教徒の祭りから出てきたものである The custom *comes* [×*came*] *from* a pagan festival./The custom *originated in* [*from*] a pagan festival.
❾ [生じる] (結果として生じる) come* 《*from*》; (突発的に) break* out; (偶発的に) occur (-rr-). ▶憎悪はしばしば誤解から出てくる Hatred often *comes from* [*is often caused by*] misunderstanding. ▶火は台所から出た The fire *broke out* [*started*] *in* the kitchen. (!in の代わりに from も可) ▶近所にコレラ患者が出た A case of cholera *has occurred* [*broken out*] in the neighborhood. ▶強い風が出てきた A strong wind *is rising* [*getting up*]./ There is a strong wind *rising* [*getting up*].
❿ [与えられる] be given; (食卓に供される) be served. ▶それをする許可が出た I *was given* permission to do it./I was permitted to do it. ▶お昼にサンドイッチが出た Sandwiches *were served* at lunch. ▶この前の試験にどんな問題が出ましたか What (kind of) questions *were given* [*were asked*, *came up*] in the last exam? ▶ボーナスはいつ出ますか When do we *get* our bonus?
⓫ [卒業する] graduate 《*from*》. ●東京大学の法学部を出る *graduate in* law *from* Tokyo University. (!学部[学科] は from でなく in を用いる) ●大学を出たばかりの女性 a woman *fresh from* [*out of*] college; a woman *just* [*straight*] *out of* college. ▶彼は去年高校を出た He finished [《米》 *graduated from*, 《英》 *left*] high school last year.
⓬ [売れる] sell*. ▶この車はとてもよく出る This car *sells* well./This car is a good [*a big*] *seller*./ (需要が多い) This car *is in* great *demand*.
⓭ [生み出される] (産出される) be produced; (利益などが) be yielded. ▶この県からは政治家がたくさん出た This prefecture *has produced* [*has turned out*] a lot of statesmen and stateswomen./(この県の出身である) A large number of political leaders *come* [×*came*] *from* this prefecture. ▶この地域には銅が出る This area *produces* copper. ▶あらゆる努力をしてみたがよい結果は出なかった All my efforts did not *yield* a good result.
⓮ [至る] (ある場所にやってくる) come* 《*to*》; (道が通じる) lead* 《*to*》. ▶まもなく湖に出た We soon *came to* a lake. ▶この道を行くと海に出る This road *leads* [*goes*] to the ocean.
⓯ [超過する] exceed. ▶費用は3万円を出ないでしょう The cost will not *exceed* [*be more than*] thirty thousand yen. ▶彼は60歳を出ている He *is over* (↔*under*) sixty.
⓰ [電話・玄関に応対する] answer, get*. ●玄関に出る *answer* [*get*] the door. ▶彼は今電話に出ています He *is on* the phone now. ▶(相手の方が)お出になります. 今おつなぎします Your party *is on* (the line). I'll put you through. ▶申し訳ありませんがお出になりません (交換手の発話) I'm sorry, I'm not getting any reply. ▶彼に電話をしたがだれも出なかった I called him (up), but

there *was* no *answer*.
- 会話「電話が鳴っていますよ」「私が出ましょう」 "The phone is ringing." "I'll *answer* [*get*] it." (! この場合 will の代わりに be going to は用いられない)

⑰【熱・せきなどが】▶高い熱が出た I *had* a high fever. ▶ひどいせきが出て困った I *was troubled with* [*by*] a bad cough. ▶彼の額に玉のような汗が出ていた Drops of sweat *stood* [There were drops of sweat] on his forehead.

⑱【茶がせんじ出される】▶このお茶はよく出る This tea *draws* well. ▶お茶が出すぎないうちにつぎなさい Pour out the cups before the tea *gets too strong and bitter* [《英やや語》the tea *is stewed*].

⑲【提出される】be handed in, be turned in; (問題が持ち出される) be brought up, come* up. ▶彼の辞表はまだ出されていない His resignation is not yet *handed* [*turned, sent*] *in*. ▶これらの問題が委員会に出た These matters *came up* [*were brought up*] in the committee. ▶きのうの会合では事故のことは話に出なかった The accident *was not mentioned* [We didn't talk about the accident] at yesterday's meeting. (! 後の方が口語的)

● 出る杭は打たれる 《ことわざ》A protruding nail will be hammered down. (!事情 集団主義と同一性 (collectivism and conformity) は日本人の典型だが、その例にこのことわざがよく引用される)

● 出る所に出る ▶そこまで言うなら出る所に出て(=法廷で)決着をつけようじゃないか If you insist, let's settle the matter in court.

● 出る幕ではない ▶お前の出る幕じゃない(=知ったことではない) That's no business of yours [none of your business]./(関係がない) This has nothing to do with you.

テルアビブ 〖イスラエルの都市〗Tel Aviv /tèl əvíːv/.
デルタ ●デルタ地帯 a delta (region).
てるてるぼうず 照る照る坊主 ▶天気がよくなるよう男の子は軒下に照る照る坊主をつるした The boy hung a shiny-shiny bonze, a small handmade doll, under the eaves and prayed to it for fine weather [prayed that it would bring nice weather]. (!事情 米英にはこの習慣はないが、次のような歌を歌うことはある: Rain, rain, go away. Come again another day. Little Johny wants to play.)

てれかくし 照れ隠し ●照れ隠しに笑う hide [cover (up)] one's embarrassment with a smile. (!事情 米英人は照れ隠しに笑うことはあまりない)

てれくさい 照れ臭い (きまりが悪い) feel* embarrassed [(恥ずかしい) bashful]. ▶彼女は照れくさそうに笑った She smiled *shyly*./She gave a *shy* smile. ▶若い女性と話をするのは照れくさい I'm *shy* [*bashful*] *about* talking to a young girl. ▶授業中先生にとてもほめられて照れくさかった I *felt* [*was*] *embarrassed* when I was highly praised by the teacher in class.

テレクラ a *terekura*; a telephone club; a party-phone line.
テレコミュニケーション 〖遠距離通信〗telecommunications, 《話》telecoms.
テレコム 〖『テレコミュニケーション』の略〗《話》telecoms.
てれしょう 照れ性 ●照れ性である be shy; be bashful.
テレタイプ a teleprinter;《米》a teletypewriter;《商標》Teletype. ● テレタイプで送信する send a message *by teleprinter*.
テレックス (a) telex. ● テレックスで送る send *by telex* (!無冠詞); telex.

でれでれ ● でれでれした (だらしない) slovenly; (怠惰な) idle; (女性に甘い) be soft (*on*). ▶この夏休みはでれでれと過ごしてしまった I've spent this summer vacation *idly* [*without doing anything worthwhile*]. ▶人前でデレデレするのはやめてちょうだい、いやね Don't *show too much affection* in public, right?

テレパシー telepathy.
:テレビ 〖放送〗television,《話》TV (! いずれも通例無冠詞); 〖受像機〗a television [《話》a TV] (set) (! 《話》ではしばしば省略する).

①【〜テレビ】● カラー [白黒]テレビ a color [a black and white] *television*. (!白黒の場合の語順に注意) ● ケーブル [有線]テレビ cable *television*. ● 37インチテレビ a 37-inch *television*. ● 液晶テレビ a liquid crystal (display) *television*. ● 高品位テレビ high-definition *television*.

②【テレビ(の)〜】● テレビの映像 a *TV* image. ● テレビの画面 a *television* [a *TV*] screen; a telescreen. ● テレビっ子 a video boy [girl].

③【テレビは】▶このテレビは映りがよい The picture is clear on this *TV* (set)./This *TV* gets good reception [works well, works fine]. (!特定のチャンネルに言及する場合は ... gets [picks up] channel 6 very well. などとする)

④【テレビの[に]】● テレビの音を小さく[大きく]する turn down [up] the *television* [*TV*]. (!受像機そのものをさすのが冠詞をつける) ● テレビに出る appear on *television* [*TV*]. ●《ゲストで》make a guest appearance on *TV*. ● テレビにかじりつく be glued to the *TV*; sit glued to the *television* screen.

⑤【テレビを】● テレビを見る watch (×the) *television* [*TV*]. ● テレビをつける[消す] turn on [off] the *television*. ● テレビをつけっ放しにしておく leave the *television* on. ▶毎日何時間テレビを見ますか How many hours do you spend watching *TV* [sitting in front of a *TV set*] every day?

⑥【テレビで】● 私はきのうテレビで「ミュージック・オブ・ハート」を見た Yesterday I watched [saw] the movie "Music of the Heart" *on television* [*TV*]. ● look at お類推・混交で *at* television ということもあるが (非標準) ● そのテニスの試合は来週テレビで放送されるだろう The tennis match will *be televised* [be broadcast *on television*] next week. (cf. on the radio)

● テレビ映画 a television [a TV] film; a telefilm.
● テレビカメラ a television [a TV] camera; a telecamera. ● テレビ業界 the world of television. ● テレビ局 a television [a TV] station. ● テレビゲーム (play) a video game. ● テレビ視聴者 a viewer;《集合的》a television audience. (⇒視聴者) ● テレビショッピング television shopping; teleshopping. ● テレビタレント a TV personality [star]. ● テレビ伝道師 a tèlevángelist. ● テレビ電話 a videophone. (! ×TV telephone とはいわない) ● テレビドラマ a television play; a teleplay. ● テレビ番組 a television [a TV] program; (長時間の慈善番組) a telethon. ● テレビ放送 a television [a TV] broadcast; a telecast. ● テレビ放送網 a television [a TV] network.

テレビゆ テレビ油 turpentine.
テレポート 〖通信〗a teleport.
テレホン a (tele)phone.
● テレホンカード a phone [a telephone] card. ● テレホンサービス (a) telephone information service. (! telephone service は「電話による業務」の意) ● テレホンショッピング telephone shopping. ● テレホンバンキング telephone banking. ● テレホンマ

テレマーク 〖スキー〗a telemark.
テレマーケティング telemarketing.
てれや 照れ屋 a shy [a bashful] person. ● 照れ屋の shy, bashful.
てれる 照れる 〚恥ずかしがる〛be shy; (特に子供・女性が) be bashful; 〚きまりが悪い〛feel* awkward, feel embarrassed. ● 照れたようにちょっと笑う give an *embarrassed* [a *bashful*, a *shy*] little smile.
てれわらい 照れ笑い an embarrassed laugh [smile]; (はにかんだ笑い) a bashful laugh [smile]. (⇨照れる)
てんてくだ 手練手管 〖書〗wiles. ● 恋の手練手管 love's *wiles*. ● 手練手管を弄する[にたけている] use [know] *every trick in the book*. ▮ in the book (「物の本に載っている」の意: every crime in the book ありとあらゆる犯罪)
テロ terror, térrorism. ● 爆弾テロ *terrorism* using bombs. ● 自爆テロ suicide bombing. ● 政治的目段としてテロ行為を行う use *terrorism* as a political tool. ▶ 我々はテロには屈しない We're not going to bow to *terrorism*.
‣ テロ攻撃 a terrorist attack. ‣ テロ組織 a terrorist organization.
テロップ a telop. (参考 元は商品名 television opaque projector の略) ● テロップを流す run a *telop*.
テロリスト a terrorist.
テロリズム térrorism. (⇨テロ)
てわけ 手分け — 手分けする 動 ▶ 私たちは手分けして仕事をした(=仕事を分けた) We *divided* the work among [between] us. ▶ 彼らは手分けしてその男を捜した They went out *separately* [*in several parties*] to search for the man. (▮ 前の方は「ばらばらに分かれて」の意, 後の方は「数組に分かれて」の意で, They *separated into groups* and searched for the man. ともいえる) ▶ 私たちは手分けして部屋を掃除した We cleaned the room, *each doing their part*.
てわたす 手渡す hand; (引き渡す) hand ... over 《*to*》.
会話 「彼にこの手紙を手渡してくれませんか」「自分で手渡したらどう」"Could you *hand* him this letter?" "Why don't you *give it to* him *yourself*?"

:てん 点 ❶ 〖印・記号としての〗(小さな点) a dot; (小数点) a (decimal) point; (句読点) a punctuation mark; (斑点(は)) a speck. ● 点線を引く draw a *dotted* line; dot a line. ● j に点を打つ dot [put a *dot* over] a 'j'. ● 3.15 three *point* one five. ● 0.01 (naught) *point* naught one. (▮(1) naught を省略しない方がよい. (2) zero または oh を用いることもある) ▶ 飛行機は遠くて点のように見えた The airplane looked like a *dot* in the distance. ▶ 空には一点の雲もなかった There wasn't a *speck* of cloud in the sky.

❷ 〖評価〗(得点) a mark, 《米》a grade; (評価点) a grade, a mark (参考 通例 A (Excellent, 優), B (Good, 良), C (Fair, Passing, Average, 可), D (Below Average, 可), F (Failure, Failing, 不可) の 5 段階評価. E (Conditionally passed 条件付合格) を設けるところもある); (試験の得点) a score. ● いい点を取る get [×take] good [↔poor] *marks* [*grades*]; get high [↔low] *marks* [*grades*]. ● 彼の数学に満点を与える give him full *marks* [a full *mark*, a perfect score, ×full grades] for math. ▶ 君の物理の点はCだ. 結果ではなく努力に対して点をつける(=評価する)のが私の方針なんだからね Your *grade* in physics is C. It's my policy to *grade* you on the effort, not on the result. ▶ 私たちの英語の先生は点が甘い Our English teacher is an easy [↔a hard, a strict] *grader* [*marker*].
会話 「英語の試験で何点取ったの」「80 点だった」"What mark [What, How much] did you get on [in] the English test?" "I got a *grade* of 80 《米》[80 *marks* 《英》, a *score* of 80] (out of 100) on it." (▮(1)《米》では a mark of 80 も用いる. (2) 答えの文は単に I got 80 percent on it. ということが多い)
会話 「テイラー先生, すみません. 宿題を持ってきました」「どうして期限内に提出しなかったの. もう点はあげられませんよ」"Sorry, Miss Taylor. This is my assignment." "Why didn't you hand it in on time? I'm not going to *mark* it now."

❸ 〖競技の〗(得点) a point; (総得点) a score; (クリケット・野球などの) a run ● 打点 a run batted in/自責点 an earned run/失点 a run allowed/得点 a run scored (▮ 失点か得点かを明らかにする場合は allowed, scored をつける); (サッカーなどの) a goal. ● 6 点リードしている be ahead by six *points* [*runs*]. ▶ 1 回表にシングルヒット 3 本で 2 点をあげる score two *runs* on three singles in the top of the first inning.
会話 「いま点はどうなっているの」「5 対 2 で勝っています」"What's the *score* now?" "We are leading by five to two."

❹ 〖問題点, 観点〗a point; (見地) a viewpoint, a standpoint; (様相) an aspect; (箇所, 細目) a respect; (方面) a way. ▶ その点で彼は間違っていた On that *point* [In that *respect*] he was mistaken. ▶ 私たちはその問題を純粋科学の点(=観点)から議論した We discussed the question from a *viewpoint* [a *standpoint*] of pure science. ▶ あらゆる点からその問題を考えると, この方法が最善のようだ If we consider the problem from every *aspect* [(角度) *angle*], this method seems to be the best. ▶ 品質の点ではこの品物があれよりもすぐれている In quality [As far as quality is concerned] this article is superior to that one. ▶ 多くの科目の選択がより自由にできるという点で大学は高校とは異なっている College is different from high school *in that* you have more freedom in choosing courses you want to take. ▶ そこが問題の点です That's where the question lies. ▶ 彼の行動には遺憾な点が多い His conduct leaves much to be desired.
会話 「それで刺身はひどくまずかったのか」「そうなんだよ. でもその他の点ではまあまあだったよ」"So the *sashimi* was terrible." "Yes, but *in other respects*, it was a fairly good meal."

❺ 〖品物の数〗a piece. ● 陶器 5 点 five *pieces* of pottery. ▶ 昨夜宝石類を 15 点盗まれた I had fifteen *pieces* [*articles*] of jewelry stolen last night.

*てん 天 ❶ 〖空〗the sky. (⇨空) ▶ 変な物が天から降ってきた Some strange things fell from *the sky*.
❷ 〖神〗God, Heaven 《の代用語》; (天国) heaven (▮ しばしば大文字で). ● 天の声 the voice of *God* [*Heaven*]. ● 天にましますわれらの父 our *heavenly* Father; our Father who is in *Heaven*. ● 天の助けをこう call upon *Heaven* for help. ● すべてを天に任せる leave all to chance. ▶ 天(地神明)に誓って私は彼に会ったこともない I swear to *God* that I have never met him. ▶ 私は成功を天に祈った I prayed to *God* for success. ▶ 天は人の上に人をつくらず, 人の下に人をつくらずといへり It is said that *Heaven* creates no man, either above or below another (man).
● 天高く馬肥ゆる秋 'The autumn sky is clear

てん 典 a (solemn) ceremony.

- 天にも昇る心地 ▶ 私はその競走に勝って天にも昇る心地だった《話》I was in (seventh) *heaven* [was walking on air] when I won the race.
- 天は自ら助くるものを助く《ことわざ》*Heaven* helps those who help themselves.

てん 貂 〘動物〙a marten. (✍ 黒テン a sable, 白テン an ermine などの種類に分かれる. いずれも毛皮の場合は〘U〙扱い)

-てん -展(展覧会) an exhibition /èksəbíʃən/; (展示会) a show. ● 現代彫刻展 an *exhibition* [a *show*] of modern sculptures. ● ゴッホ展 a Gogh *exhibition*. ● 洋ラン展 an orchid *show*. ● 手塚治虫回顧展 a retrospective *show* of Tezuka Osamu's work.

-でん -伝 ● リンカーン伝(=伝記) a *life* [a *biography*] of Lincoln. ● 偉人伝 *lives* of great people.

-でん -殿 〘立派な建物〙a hall. ● 拝殿 a *hall* of worship. ● 大仏殿 the *Hall* of the Great Buddha.

でんあつ 電圧 voltage /vóultɪdʒ/. ● 電圧を上げる[下げる] increase [step up] (↔decrease, step down) (the) *voltage*. ▶ 電圧が高い[低い] The *voltage* is high [low].
- 電圧計 a vóltmèter.

てんあんもんひろば 天安門広場 Tiananmen /tjá:nənmèn/ Square.

てんい 天意 the will of God [Heaven].

てんい 転移 〖変化〗a change; 〘がんなどの〙spread, 〘医学〗metástasis. ● がんの転移 the *spread* [*metastasis*] of cancer.
— **転移する** 動 spread (by metastasis) (to); metastasize (to).

でんい 電位 electric potential.
- 電位計 an electrometer /ɪlèktrámətər/. ● 電位差 potential difference.

てんいむほう 天衣無縫 (⇨回 天真爛漫(らんまん))

てんいん 店員 〖米〗a clerk, a salesclerk; 〖英〗a shop assistant (✍ 以上すべて性別に関係なく用いる); (男の) a salesman, (女の) a saleswoman (✍ 優 は共に -men); (ともに〖外交員〗の意と区別したいときは at a store を直後に加える. 最近は男女の区別なく a salesperson (優 salespeople) が普通.

てんいん 転院 图 (a) transfer.
— **転院する** 動 transfer [change] (*from* A hospital) to (B hospital). ● 転院してきた患者 a transfer.

てんうん 天運 one's destiny; one's fate.

でんえん 田園 (田舎) the country. ● 田園生活を楽しむ enjoy the pleasures of *country* [*rural*,《書》*pastoral*] life; enjoy life in the *country*.
- 田園地帯 a rural area [district]; the countryside. ● 田園都市 a garden [a rural] city.
- 田園風景 a rural [《書》a pastoral] landscape.

でんえんこうきょうきょく 『田園交響曲』 *Pastoral Symphony*. (參考 ベートーベン作曲の交響曲)

でんえんにしす 『田園に死す』 *Pastoral: To Die in the Country*. (参考 寺山修司の歌集)

でんえんのゆううつ 『田園の憂鬱』 *Rural Melancholy*; *Gloom in the Country*. (參考 佐藤春夫の小説)

てんか 天下 ❶〖世の中〗(世界) the world; (全国) the whole country; (世間) the public. ● 天下を取る(政権を握る) come into power; (政権を握っている) be in power; (全国を征服する) conquer *the whole country*. ● 天下一品 (⇨天下一品) ● 彼の発明品は天下に知れ渡っている His inventions are world-famous [well-known *all over the world*]. ▶ 金は天下の回りもの (ことわざ) Money is a great traveler *in the world*./(ことわざ) Money changes hands./(ことわざ) Money will come and go.
❷〖思うままにふるまうこと〗▶ 夏の海辺はかっぱたちの天下だ(=海辺で思う存分楽しめる) Good swimmers are able to enjoy themselves to the full at the seaside in summer.
- 天下太平 ▶ 天下太平だ All the world is *at peace*./"All's right with the world." (參考 R. Browning の詩から)
- 天下晴れて ▶ 彼らは天下晴れて(=法律上正式に)夫婦になった They were *legally* married.
- 天下分け目 ▶ 天下分け目の(=決定的な)戦い a *crucial* battle.

てんか 点火 图 ignition. ● 点火スイッチを入れる turn [switch] on (↔off) the *ignition*.
— **点火する** 動 ignite; (火をつける) light; (花火などを)set...off.

てんか 添加 图 addition (to). ● 食品添加物 food additives. ● ビタミンC添加スポーツドリンク a vitamin C-added sports drink; a sports drink *fortified with* vitamin C. (✍ fortify は 〖アルコール, ビタミンなどで強化する〗の意) ● アルコール添加酒 *fortified* wine. (參考 sherry, martini など) ● 無添加食品 additive-free foods.
— **添加する** 動 add... (to).

てんか 転化 图 (a) change. — **転化する** 動 change (⇨変化する); (なる) turn (⇨なる).

てんか 転科 图 a change of department.
— **転科する** 動 change (*from* the English department) to (the French department).

てんか 転嫁 — **転嫁する** 動 責任を他人に転嫁する *shift* the responsibility [(失敗などに対する責任) the blame] *onto* other people; (責めを負わせる) *lay* [*put*] the blame *on* other people. (⇨擦(なす)り付ける)

てんか 転訛 〘言語〗corruption.
- 転訛語 a corruption.

でんか 殿下 His (Imperial) Highness. (✍ 呼びかけや you の代わりに用いるときは His の代わりに Your を使う. いずれの場合も三人称単数扱い) ● 皇太子殿下 *His Imperial Highness* the Crown Prince. (✍ 「浩宮殿下」は Prince Hiro) ● 三笠宮殿下 *His Imperial Highness* Prince Mikasa.

でんか 電化 electrification.
— **電化する** 動 electrify. ▶ 数年前にその鉄道は電化された The railroad *was electrified* some years ago.
- 電化製品 (電気器具) electrical appliances [goods].

*__てんかい 展開__ 图 〖進展〗(a) development; 〖拡大〗expansion. ▶ 事件は新たな展開を見せている The case shows a new *development*.
— **展開する** 動 〖進展する[させる]〗develop; 〖徐々に明らかになる[する]〗unfold; 〖やや専門的〗develop [expand] the theory. (✍ expand は 「内容を充実させる」の意) ▶ 物語は意外な結末へと展開した The story *developed into* an unexpected ending. ▶ 雄大な景色が眼下に展開し始めた A magnificent landscape began to *unfold* [*spread out*] below our eyes. (✍ 前の方は「徐々に開ける」, 後の方は「一面に広がる」の意)
- 展開図 a development.

てんかい 転回 图 a turn. ● 言語理論におけるコペルニクス的転回 a Copérnican *revolution* in linguistic theory.
— **転回する** 動 turn; make [take] a turn.

てんがい 天涯 ● **天涯孤独** ▶彼は天涯孤独の身である He is *all alone, with no one to depend on*.
てんがい 天蓋 a canopy /kǽnəpi/.
でんかい 電界 【物理】an electric field.
でんかい 電解 图 【化学】electrolysis.
— **電解する** 動 electrolyze.
● **電解液** an electrolytic solution. ● **電解質** an electrolyte. ● **電解質** electrolyty.
てんかいっぴん 天下一品 — **天下一品の** 形 (比べるもののない)(書) beyond compare; (ずば抜けた)(書) òut of this wórld; (競うもののない) unrivaled; (並ぶもののない) unequaled. ▶ポリーニのベートーベンは天下一品だと私は思う I think Pollini's piano performance of Beethoven is *beyond compare* [*out of this world*].
てんがく 転学 (⇨転校)
でんがく 田楽 ❶【舞楽の】 *dengaku*, (説明的に) dancing and music performed at agricultural observances and festivals in medieval Japan. ❷【料理の】 *dengaku*, (説明的に) skewered materials roasted and then coated with *miso*.
でんかのほうとう 伝家の宝刀 — **伝家の宝刀を抜く**《話》play one's trump card.
てんかぶつ 添加物 an additive. ● **食品添加物** food *additives*. ● **添加物の入っていない食品** *additive*-free foods.
てんかふん 天花粉 talcum powder.
てんから 天から ● **天から…しない** (最初から) not ... at all. ▶彼女はおれの言うことなんか天から問題にしなかった《話》She did*n't give me a hang* [*a hoot, two hoots*] *about* what I said.
てんかん 転換 图 (a) change; (急な) a switch. ● 車の方向転換をする do [make] a *U-turn*; turn a [one's] car around. ● 180度の転換をする do an about-face 《主に米》[an *about-turn* 《主に英》]. ● 配置転換 job *rotation*.
— **転換する** 動 ● 発想を転換する *change* [*make a change in*] one's way of thinking; *switch* (*over*) *to* a different way of thinking.
● **転換期** (転換点) a turning point (*in*); (過渡期) a transition period. ● **転換期の大学** the university *in transition*. ● **転換社債** a convertible (corporate) bond.
てんかん 癲癇 【医学】épilèpsy. ● **てんかんの人** an *epileptic* person. ● **てんかんの発作を起こす** have an *epileptic* fit.
てんがん 点眼 — **点眼する** 動 apply eye lotion; use eye drops.
● **点眼剤** eye drops.
てんがんきょう 天眼鏡 a magnifying glass (used by physiognomists).
:**てんき 天気** weather. (❗通例 the ~. ただし good weather のように形容詞がつく場合は無冠詞)(⇨天候, 空模様)

①【〜天気】 ▶いい天気ですね It's a *nice* [*a beautiful, a lovely*] *day*, isn't it?/It's *nice* [*good*] *weather*, isn't it? (❗いずれもくだけた言い方ではしばしば It's を省略する) ▶山の天気は変わりやすい The *weather* in the mountains is changeable. ● 散歩するにはもってこいの[=申し分のない]天気だ The *weather* is perfect [It's perfect *weather*] for a walk. ▶このいやな天気はいつまで続くのだろうか How long will this nasty [terrible, miserable] *weather* last [stay]?
会話「あすの天気はどうですか」「テレビでは晴れだって」"What's the *weather* like tomorrow?/How's the *weather* tomorrow?" "The TV says it's nice." (❗前の尋ね方が普通. What ... like は「どのよ

うなものか」とおおよそのことを尋ねる慣用表現)
②【天気が】 ▶あした天気がよければこの町を見物しよう If it's *nice* [(天候が許せば) If the *weather* permits] tomorrow, I'll see the sights of this town. ▶天気は相変わらずぐずぐずついている The *weather* remains [stays] as unsettled as ever. ▶まもなく天気がくずれるだろう The *weather* will break soon. (❗「天気がもつ」は The *weather* holds.) ▶天気が次第によくなってきた The *weather* is improving [changing for the better, 《話》looking up]. (❗「悪くなる」は change for the worse)
③【天気の】 ▶こんなに天気のよい日には外で遊びなさい Play outdoors on a *nice* [a *fine*] *day* like this./《やや書》Play outdoors on such a *nice day* [in such *nice weather*].
④【天気に[で]】 ▶どんな天気であろうとあした出発します I'll start tomorrow in all kinds of *weather* [*in all weathers*]. (❗前の方が普通)/(晴雨にかかわらず) I'll start tomorrow, *rain or shine*. (❗語順に注意) ▶体育大会は幸いよい天気に恵まれた We were lucky to have good *weather* at the athletic meet《米》[*meeting*《英》]. ▶雨が降りそうだと思ったが, 結局よい天気になった I thought it was going to rain, but it turned out nice [it cleared up after all]. (❗clear up は「晴れ上がる」)
⑤【天気を】 ● 天気を予報する forecast [foretell, predict] the *weather*.
● **天気雨** a shower while the sun shines. ● **天気概況** general weather conditions. ● **天気図** a weather map [chart]. ● **天気相談所** the Weather Information Bureau.
てんき 転記 — **転記する** 動 copy; 【簿記】post. ● 記載事項をすべて元帳に転記する *post* all the items in the ledger.
てんき 転機 a turning(-)point. (⇨分かれ道, 分かれ目) ● **転機に立つ** be at a *turning point* (*in*). ▶この出来事が彼の人生の転機になった This event marked a *turning point* in his life. ▶彼女は人生の転機が訪れていると思った She felt a *change* was coming into her life.
てんぎ 転義 图 a transferred [a figurative] meaning. — **転義の** 形 figurative.
:**でんき 電気** electricity; (電流) (an) electric current, (a) current; (電灯) a light, an electric light; (電力) (electric) power.

①【電気が】 ▶その電線には電気が通じていなかった The wire wasn't charged with *electricity*./The wire was*n't live* /láiv/ [was *dead*]. ▶電気がびりっときた I got an *electric* shock. ▶ヒマラヤのこの村には電気が来ていない There is no *electricity* in this Himalayan village. ▶ゆうべからずっと彼の部屋の電気がついている The *light* has been on (↔off) in his room since last night.
②【電気を】 ● 電気を起こす generate *electricity*. ● 電気(=電灯)をつける[消す] turn on [off] the *light*. ● 電気を入れる[切る] turn on [cut off] the *electricity*. ● 家に電気を引く install *electricity* in a house. ● 電気を節約[むだ遣い]する save [waste] *electricity*. ● 電気(=電灯)をつけたまま寝る sleep with the *light* on. ▶プラスチックは電気を通さない Plastic doesn't conduct *electricity*. ▶彼らは電気代を払わなかったので電気を止められた They didn't pay their bills, so the *electricity* was cut off.
③【電気で】 ● 電気で開閉する窓 *electrically* operated windows. ▶この機械はすべて電気で動いている These machines all run *on* [are all worked by] *electricity*.

— 電気の 形 electric; electrical.

> **使い分け** electric 通例「電気を伝える」や「(特定の物が)電気で動く」の意で、後の場合他の動力源でも動くことを暗示する。
> **electrical** 「(人・仕事が)電気に関する」や「(一般的分類として)電動の」の意で用いられる。

- 電気あんか an electric foot warmer. • 電気椅子 an electric chair; 《話》a hot seat. • 電気いすによる処刑 electrocution. • 電気回路 an electric circuit. • 電気がま〔炊飯器〕 an electric rice cooker. • 電気かみそり an electric shaver [razor]. • 電気機関車 an electric locomotive.
- 電気器具 electric(al) appliances; 《集合的》 electric(al) apparatus. • 電気技師 an electrical engineer; an electrician. • 電気工学 electrical engineering. • 電気自動車 an electric car. • 電気スタンド 〔卓上〕a desk lamp; 〔床上〕a floor lamp. • 電気洗濯機 a washing machine; 《英式・米》a washer. • 電気掃除機 a vacuum cleaner.
- 電気抵抗 electric resistance. • 電気店 an electrical appliance store. • 電気ドリル a power drill. • 電気のこぎり a power saw. • 電気分解 (an) eléctrólysis (複 -ses /-siːz/). (⇨分解する)
- 電気メス an electric scalpel. • 電気毛布 an electric blanket. • 電気料金 the electricity charge. • 電気冷蔵庫 an electric refrigerator.

でんき 伝奇 • 伝奇小説〔物語〕a romance. (■その作者は a romancer, a writer of romance(s))

でんき 伝記 a biography, a life (複 lives). (■伝記は書名などに多い) • A 氏の伝記を読む read the biography [life] of Mr. A.
- 伝記作家 a biographer.

テンキーパッド 〔コンピュータ〕a numeric keypad. (■時に a ten-key pad ともいう)

でんきくらげ 電気水母 〔動物〕a Portuguese man-of-war.

てんきゅう 天球 (天空) the vault of heaven; 〔天文学〕 the celestial sphere.
- 天球儀 a celestial globe.

でんきゅう 電球 an electric (light) bulb, a (light) bulb. • 裸電球 a naked light bulb. • 100 ワットの電球 a 100-watt bulb. • 電球を取り替える〔つける〕 change [put in, screw in] a light bulb. ▶電球が切れた The light bulb has gone [burned out, blown out]. (■「切れた電球」は a burnt-out bulb)

てんきょ 典拠 〔出典〕a source; 〔権威のある〕an authority. • 聖書を典拠にして cite on the authority of the Bible. • すべての引用文の典拠を示す cite the sources [authorities for] all the quotations.

てんきょ 転居 图 〔引っ越し〕(a) move, (a) removal (■後の方が堅い語); 〔住所を変えること〕a change of address. • 転居を通知する give a notice of one's change of address; give a removal [ˣa move] notice; (転居通知を送る) send a change-of-address card.
— 転居する 動 move (to, into) (⇨引っ越す) • ニューヨークへ転居する move 〔《書》remove〕 to New York. (⇨移転) • 下記に転居しました We have moved to the following address.
- 転居先 (新しい住所) one's new address. • 転居通知 a change-of-address card.

てんぎょう 転業 — 転業する 動 change one's occupation [business].

でんきょく 電極 an eléctrode. (関連 陽極 the positive pole/陰極 the negative pole).

てんきよほう 天気予報 the weather forecast, 《話》 the weather; (テレビ・ラジオの) a weather report; 《米》 weather information. • 長期天気予報 a long-range weather forecast. • ラジオの天気予報を聞く listen to the weather forecast on the radio;《話》listen to the weather. • ニュースの後に天気予報を見る watch the weather (forecast) after the news. ▶京都のあしたの天気予報は晴れのち曇りだ The weather (forecast) [The weather forecaster] says it will be fair and later cloudy in Kyoto tomorrow. (■According to the weather (forecast) [the weather forecaster], it will be... より普通.)
- 天気予報官 (気象予報士) a weather forecaster. (⇨気象)

てんきん 天金 • 天金の本 a book with a gilt top.

てんきん 転勤 图 a transfer /trænsfər/. • 転勤希望 one's transfer request.
— 転勤する 動 • 彼は神戸支店に転勤した He (was [got]) transferred /trænsfə́ːrd/ to the Kobe branch (office). (■受身は他人の意志で転勤させられた感じを伴う) ▶松井一男さんをご紹介いたします。このたび名古屋支社から転勤してこられました I'd like to introduce Mr. Kazuo Matsui. He's just joined us from the Nagoya office.

てんぐ 天狗 a tengu; (説明的に) an imaginary red-faced human figure with a protruding long nose, who flies through the air with two angel-like wings; 〔自慢家〕a boaster, a conceited person. • 天狗の面で人を脅かす scare 《him》 with a mask of a Japanese long-nosed goblin.
- 天狗になる get conceited; be puffed [《話》stuck] up.

てんくう 天空 the open [broad] sky. • 天空の下で under the broad sky 《of the countryside》.
- 天空にそそり立つ天守閣 the castle tower rising to a majestic height [high into the open sky].

てんぐさ 天草 〔植物〕àgar-ágar.

てんぐだけ 天狗茸 a death cap.

デングねつ デング熱 〔医学〕dengue (fever).

でんぐりがえし でんぐり返し • でんぐり返しをする (⇨でんぐり返る)

でんぐりがえす でんぐり返す (形勢を逆転させる) turn the tables 《on him》; reverse the situation.

でんぐりがえる でんぐり返る (頭と両手で前転〔後転〕する) do a forward [a backward] roll on one's head.

てんけい 天恵 a gift of nature; (天然資源) natural resources. • 天恵が豊かである be blessed with natural resources; be favored by nature.

てんけい 天啓 a heavenly revelation; (神のお告げ) (divine) revelation.

てんけい 典型 〔タイプ〕a type; 〔模範〕a model; 〔見本〕a specimen.
— 典型的な 形 typical; model. • 彼は典型的な日本人だ He is a typical Japanese./He is the very type of a Japanese.

てんけい 点景 (説明的に) people or animals that enhance the value of a landscape painting [photograph].

でんげき 電撃 ❶ 〔電気ショック〕an electric shock. ❷ 〔電光石火の攻撃〕a lightning attack. • 電撃的な速度で with lightning speed.
- 電撃結婚 a sudden marriage. • 電撃戦 a blitz.
- 電撃療法 electroshock [electroconvulsive] therapy.

*てんけん 点検 图 a check; (an) inspection. (⇨検査)
— 点検する 動 • 車を総点検する give the car a

でんげん 電源 〖電力の源泉〗a power source; 〖電力の供給〗a power supply; 〖スイッチ〗a switch; 〖電気プラグの差し込み口〗a plug; 〖米〗an outlet, 〈英〉a socket. ●電源を切る cut [shut] off the *power supply*; (プラグをはずす) pull out the *plug*. ●ミシンを電源につなぐ(=電源をコンセントにつなぐ) plug in (the cord of) the sewing machine. ▶照明の電源を入れてください Please turn on (↔off) the light *switch*. ▶点検する前には電源が切ってあるか確認してください Just before you check on it, you have to make sure (that) the *power* is (turned) off.
●**電源開発** development of power sources.

てんこ 点呼 a roll call. ●点呼をとる have [take, do] a *roll call* 《of the students》; call the *roll*.

*てんこう 天候** weather. (⇨天気) ●悪天候 bad *weather*. ●不順な天候 unsettled [(季節はずれの) unseasonable, (変わりやすい) changeable] *weather*. ▶天候が許せばいつでも出発します We are ready to start at any moment, *weather* permitting [if the *weather* permits, (天気がよければ) if the *weather* is good (enough)]. (⚠ good の代わりに fine も可)

てんこう 転向 图 (主義などの)〈やや書〉conversion.
— **転向する 動** 〈やや書〉convert 《to》; (…になる) turn. ●社会主義者に転向する convert to socialism. ●プロ(ゴルファー)に転向する become a professional (golfer); *turn* professional. (⚠ turn の後の名詞は無冠詞) ●リリーフから先発に転向する be converted [shifted] from a relief pitcher to a starter. ●外野から三塁へ転向する shift [switch] from the outfield to third base.

てんこう 転校 图 changing schools.
— **転校する 動** change one's school; change [transfer] to another school. (⇨移る❶)
●**転校生** a transfer (student).

でんこう 電光 〖電気の光〗electric light; 〖稲妻〗lightning.
●**電光石火**(^{せっか})**の** ●電光石火のように like (a streak of) *lightning*. ●電光石火の速さで with *lightning* speed; (as) quick as *lightning*.
●**電光掲示板** an electric bulletin board [(得点板) scoreboard]. ●**電光ニュース** an illuminated news display.

てんこく 篆刻 图 a seal carving.
— **篆刻する 動** carve a seal (with one's name in *tensho* script). (⇨篆書)
●**篆刻家** a seal carver.

てんごく 天国 heaven (↔hell). (⚠ しばしば Heaven); (天国のようなすばらしい場所・状態) (a) heaven; (楽園) (a) paradise. ●天国の〖のような〗heavenly. ●歩行者天国 a pedestrians' *paradise* [*mall*]. ●天国に行く[召される] go to *heaven*. ▶おじいさんは天国にいると彼は信じている He believes that his grandfather is in *heaven*. ▶アフリカは野生動物の天国だ Africa is a *paradise* for wild animals.

でんごん 伝言 〖ことづけ〗a message 《that him》. ●彼女にすぐ家に帰るようにという伝言を残す leave her a *message* to come home soon. ●伝言をうけたまわりましょうか(電話で) May I take a *message*?/Would you like to leave a *message*?/Can I give 《him》 a *message*? ▶伝言をお願いしたいのですが(電話で) I'd like to leave a *message* with you./Could you give 《him》 a *message* for me? ▶あなたに伝言を彼に伝えます I'll give your *message* to him. ▶彼からあなたに伝言があります I have [There's] a *message* for you from him.
●**伝言板** a message board.

てんさ 点差 the difference in points 〖野球〗runs〗. ●1点差の勝負に泣く lose a game [a match] by one point; 〖野球〗lose a one-run game. ●点差を広げる[縮める] widen [narrow] the lead.

てんさい 天才 〖人〗a genius 《in, at》; 〖才能〗genius 《for》. (⚠ 通例 a 〜). ●数学の天才 a mathematical *genius*; a genius in mathematics; (話) a wizard at math. ●まれにみる天才的な選手 an exceptionally *talented* player. ●彼は友達をつくることにかけては天才だ He has a *genius for* [is a *genius at*] making friends. ▶彼女は天才(=生まれながらの)ピアニストだ She is a *born* pianist.
●**天才教育** genius education. ●**天才児** a child [an infant] prodigy 《on the violin》.

てんさい 天災 a natural disaster. (⇨災害)
●天災は忘れたころにやってくる A natural disaster will occur [happen, hit us] when we least expect it.

てんさい 甜菜 a (sugar) beet.

てんさい 転載 图 ▶本書の無断転載を禁ず《表示》No part of this book may *be reproduced* without the prior permission of the publishers. (⚠ prior は「前もって」の意で冗語的だが, 慣用的に用いられる)
— **転載する 動** (複製する) reproduce.

てんざい 点在 — **点在する 動** 《物が主語》dot (-tt-) 《with》; 《場所が主語》be dotted 《with》. ▶丘の斜面に春の花が点在していた Spring flowers *dotted* the hillside./The hillside *was dotted* [(散らし模様のように) *was studded*] with spring flowers.

てんさく 添削 图 correction.
— **添削する 動** correct. ▶私は先生に作文を添削してもらった I *had* my composition *corrected* by the teacher. (⚠「have＋目的語＋過去分詞」の構文)

てんさく 転作 — **転作する 動** change crops.

でんさん 電算 電算化する computerize.
●**電算機** a computer. (⇨コンピュータ(ー)) ●**電算機で処理する** computerize. ●**電算機論** computer science.

てんさんぶつ 天産物 natural products.

てんし 天子 an emperor.

てんし 天使 an angel. ▶その子供は天使のようだった(=ように見えた) The child looked *angelic* [looked like an *angel*].

*てんじ 展示** 图 (an) exhibition /èksibíʃən/; (a) displáy; (a) show. ●展示会を開く hold a *show* [an *exhibition*, (米) an *exhibit*].
— **展示する 動** 〖公開する〗exhibit /iɡzíbit/; 〖陳列する〗displáy; 〖見せる〗show*. (⚠ それぞれ put*…on exhibition [display, show, (米) exhibit] でも表せる. 自分の作品についていうときは控えめに show を用いることが多い(⇨陳列する)) ●生徒の作品を教室に展示する *exhibit* [*display*] the students' works in a classroom. ▶その美術館には彼の絵が展示されている His paintings *are on exhibition* [*on display*, *on view*, (米) *on exhibit*] at the gallery.
●**展示場** an exhibition hall [room]. ●**展示即売会** an exhibition and sale 《of dolls》. ●**展示品** an exhibit.

てんじ 点字 braille /bréil/. (⚠ しばしば B-) ●点字の本 a book in *braille*. ●点字を読む read *braille*. ●点字で書く write in *braille*. ●点字で打つ braille (a story).
●**点字印刷物** (郵便物の上書きで) literature for the blind. ●**点字ブロック** a tactile /tǽktl/ tile.

***でんし** 電子 图 an electron. ━ 電子の 形 electronic.
- 電子オルガン an electronic organ [keyboard]. (!Electone は商品名) ● 電子音 an electronic sound. ● 電子音楽 electronic [synthetic] music. ● 電子楽器 an electronic (musical) instrument. ● 電子機器 an electronic machine;《集合的》electronic equipment. ● 電子計算機 a computer. (⇒コンピュータ(-)) ● 電子決済 electronic (account) settlement;『経済』electronic funds transfer《略 EFT》. ● 電子顕微鏡 an electron microscope. ● 電子工学 electronics. (!単数扱い) ● 電子コマース『商取引』electronic commerce《略 e-commerce》. ● 電子辞書 an electronic [a computerized] dictionary. ● 電子出版 electronic publishing《略 e-publishing》. ● 電子手帳 an electronic diary [organizer]. ● 電子投票 electronic voting. ● 電子図書館 a digital library. ● 電子認証 electronic certification. ● 電子ブック《商標》Electronic Book. ● 電子マネー electronic money. ● 電子メール electronic mail《略 e(-)mail》(⇒イーメール) ● 電子レンジ a microwave oven,《話》a microwave.

でんじ 電磁《電磁気》elèctromágnetism.
- 電磁石 an electromagnet. ● 電磁調理器 an elèctromagnétic cooker. ● 電磁波 an electromagnetic wáve. ● 電磁場 an electromagnetic field. ● 電磁ロック an electrónic lock. (!ドアロックの場合には lock の前に door を入れる)

てんじく 天竺 [インドの古い呼称] India.
- 天竺もめん coarse cotton cloth. ● 天竺浪人 an unemployed;《浮浪者》a tramp.

てんじくあおい 天竺葵『植物』a geranium.

てんじくねずみ 天竺鼠『動物』《モルモット》a guinea pig.

てんじつえん 天日塩 (⇒天日塩 (てんぴ))

てんしゃ 転写 图『書』transcription.
━ 転写する 動『書』transcribe.

*__でんしゃ__ 電車 图 a train, an electric train (!汽車などと区別する場合以外には単に train でよい); [市街電車]《米》a streetcar, a trolley (car);《英》a tram (car). ● 通勤電車 a commuter train. ● 満員電車 a jam-packed train. ● 電車の駅 a railroad [a train] station; (市街電車の停留所) a streetcar stop.
- 電車賃 a train fare.

てんしゃく 転借 图 又借り.

てんしゅ 天主 God; the Lord.
- 天主教 (カトリック教) Roman Catholicism. ● 天主堂 a Roman Catholic church.

てんしゅ 店主《米》a storekeeper,《英》a shopkeeper; (店の所有者) the owner of a store.

てんじゅ 天寿 ● 天寿を全うする live out one's natural life span. (!live out は「…の終わりまで生きる」の意)

でんじゅ 伝授 图 (手ほどき)《やや書》initiation (into).
━ 伝授する 動 ● 彼に秘伝を伝授する《やや書》initiate him into the secret (of).

てんしゅかく 天守閣 a castle tower.

てんしゅつ 転出 ━ 転出する 動 move out (⇔move to [into]).

てんしょ 添書 [添えた手紙] a letter [a note] one attaches to one's gift; [紹介状] a letter of introduction (of 紹介).

てんしょ 篆書 a tensho; (説明的に) an archaic form of Chinese characters, now chiefly used when engraving a seal with one's name.

*__てんじょう__ 天井 [部屋の] a ceiling; [屋根の内側の] a roof《檐》~s). ● 天井の高い[低い]部屋 a high-[low-]ceilinged room; a room with a high [a low] ceiling. ▶ 天井にハエがとまっている There is a fly on the ceiling. (!前置詞 on に注意) ▶ 天井裏で変な音がした I heard a strange noise under the roof.
- 天井知らず《話》The sky's the limit.
- 天井画 a painting on the ceiling. ● 天井桟敷 an upper gallery.

てんじょう 天上 heaven. ● 天上の音楽 heavenly music.
- 天上天下唯我独尊 Holy am I alone throughout heaven and earth.

てんじょう 添乗 ━ 添乗する 動 accompany and take care of a group of tourists; conduct a tour.

てんしょう 伝承 图 (言い伝え) (a) tradition; (民間伝承) folklore.
━ 伝承する 動 be handed down.
- 伝承文学 oral literature.

てんじょういん 添乗員 a tour conductor. ● 添乗員つきの旅行 a conducted tour. ▶ 彼女はそのアメリカ旅行の添乗員をつとめた She conducted the American tour./She acted as (a) conductor on the American tour.

てんしょく 天職 a [one's] vocation. ▶ 教えることは私の天職だ。単なる仕事ではない Teaching is my vocation, not a job.

てんしょく 転職 图 a change of job [occupation]. (⇒DISCOURSE)

> **DISCOURSE**
> 企業は終身雇用を保証できないため, 労働者は転職を考える Since many companies can not guarantee lifetime employment for their employees, they think about *changing their jobs*. (!since … (…なので)は理由に用いるディスコースマーカー)

━ 転職する 動 change one's job; (取り替える) change jobs [careers]; (新しい職につく) get a new job; (別の仕事を見つける) find another job. ▶ 彼は建築家から転職してシェフになった人です He is an architect-turned chef.

でんしょく 電飾 illumination. (⇒イルミネーション)

でんしょばと 伝書鳩 a carrier [a homing] pigeon.

テンション [緊張] tension.

てんじる 転じる (変える) change; (向ける) turn. ● 攻勢に転じる change to the offensive. ● 話題を転じる change the subject. ● 海の方に目を転じる turn one's eyes [look away] toward the sea.

てんしん 点心 (禅家の) refreshments or a snack before lunch; (茶会の) sweets served at a tea ceremony; (中華料理の) Chinese snacks.

テンシン 天津『中国の都市』Tianjin /tjɑːnˈdʒɪn/.

てんしん 転身 ━ 転身する 動 ▶ 彼はサラリーマンから小説家に転身した He is a former office worker turned novelist.

てんしん 転進 图 (軍隊の) shifting of one's position; (撤退) a pullback. (!「退却」((a) retreat) の婉曲語) ━ 転進する 動 shift one's position; pull back; retreat.

てんじん 天神 god in heaven; 『神社』a Tenjin shrine; (説明的に) a shrine dedicated to the memory of Sugawara no Michizane, who is deified as a symbol of learning.

でんしん 電信 telegraph. (⇒電報) ● 電信で by telegraph. ▶ 被災地との電信は不通になっている Telegraphic communications with the stricken area are suspended [are cut off]. (⇒通信 ③)

- 電信機 a telegraph (apparatus); a telegraphic apparatus. ● 電信術 telegraphy. ● 電信柱 a utility pole. (⇨電柱) ● 電信符号 a telegraphic code. (⇨モールス符号 (Morse code))

てんしんらんまん 天真爛漫 图 (無邪気) innocence; (うぶ) naiveté. (⇨純真) ― 天真爛漫な 形 innocent; naive; (子供のように) childlike.

テンス 『時制』『文法』a tense.

てんすい 天水 rainwater.
● 天水桶 a rainwater tank.

てんすう 点数 『成績』a mark, 《米》a grade; 『競技の』a point. (⇨点)
● 点数をかせぐ (⇨取り入る)

てんせい 天性 nature. (⇨性質) ● 天性の画家 a natural [(生来の) a born] painter. ● 天性の怠け者 be lazy by nature; be born lazy. ● ピアノを弾くことは今や彼にとって第二の天性となっている Playing the piano is now [comes as] second nature to him. (参考 習い性となる (ことわざ) Habit is turned into nature.)

てんせい 展性 malleability /mæliəbɪləti/. ● 展性のある malleable.

てんせい 転生 transmigration of the soul; (a) metèmpsychósis (獨 -ses /-si:z/). ― 転生する 動 transmigrate; undergo metempsychosis.

てんせき 転籍 ― 転籍する 動 transfer one's permanent domicile (from Kyoto to Sendai).

*__でんせつ__ 伝説 图 (a) legend (一般的には Ⓤ); (言い伝え) (a) tradition; (民間伝承) (集合的に) folklore. ▶伝説によればこの湖には竜が住んでいたそうだ According to (a local) legend [Legend says that, There is a legend that] a dragon lived in this lake.
― 伝説(上)の 形 ● 伝説上の英雄 a legendary [(書) a fabulous] hero; a hero in legend.

てんせん 点線 a dotted line; 『ミシン目の入った』a perforated line. ● 点線を引く draw a dotted line. ▶点線のところで切り取りなさい Cut along the dotted line./(用紙の指示書き) To be detached along the perforated line.

てんせん 転戦 ― 転戦する 動 move from one battlefield to another; fight in various battles.

てんぜん 恬然 ● 恬然として恥じない be devoid of the sense of shame; be quite shameless. (⇨平気, 平然)

*__でんせん__ 伝染 图 (空気・水・昆虫などを介する) infection; (接触による) contagion. ● 水による伝染 infection from water. ● 伝染を防ぐ prevent infection.
― 伝染性の 形 infectious; contagious. (❗いずれも比喩的な意味でも使われる) ● 法定伝染病 an infectious disease designated by law; a legal epidemic. (⇨感染症)
― 伝染する 動 ▶あくびは伝染する Yawning is infectious [contagious].

でんせん 伝線 (主に《米》) a run; 《英》a ladder. ● 新しいストッキングが伝線する have a run in a new stocking.

でんせん 電線 an electric wire; (電話線) a telephone wire [line]. ● 新築の家に電線を引く put up electric wires in a new house; wire a new house (for electricity).

てんそう 転送 图 forwarding.
― 転送する 動 ● その手紙を彼[彼の新居]に転送する forward the letter to him [his new home].
● 転送先 a forwarding address.

でんそう 電送 ― 電送する 動 transmit [send] 《a message》 electronically; telex; fax.
● 電送写真 a fax, a facsimile. ● 電送文 (テレックスによる) a telex; (ファックスによる) a fax, a facsimile.

てんそく 天測 『天文学』(an) astronomical observation.

てんそく 纏足 『中国の昔の風習』foot-binding; (その足) bound feet; (矮小(ゎぃしょぅ)化した足) dwarfed feet.

テンダーロイン (牛ヒレ肉) téndərlòin.

てんたい 天体 heavenly [celestial] bodies.
● 天体観測 an astronomical observation.
● 天体図 a celestial map. ● 天体物理学 astrophysics. ● 天体望遠鏡 an astronomical telescope.

てんたい 転貸 (⇨又貸し)

てんたく 転宅 (引っ越し, 転居)

でんたく 電卓 a (pocket [desk]) calculator.

でんたつ 伝達 图 communication. ● 言語[ジェスチャー]による意思の伝達 the communication of one's ideas through language [by gestures].
― 伝達する 動 (やや書) convey [communicate] (information to him). (⇨伝える)
● 伝達事項 a message.

デンタルフロス 『歯科』a dental floss.

てんたん 恬淡 ― 恬淡とした 形 indifferent (to).
● 金に恬淡としている(=こだわらない) be indifferent to money.

てんち 天地 ❶ [天と地] heaven and earth (❗無冠詞で); (宇宙) the universe. ● ハイドンの『天地創造』Haydn's The Creation. ▶神は天地を創造した God created heaven and earth [the universe]. ▶天地神明に誓って私は彼に会ったこともない (⇨天 ❷)
❷ [人間の住む世界] (世界) a world; (国土) a land. ▶人々は新天地[自由の天地]を求めて大西洋を渡った People crossed the Atlantic in search of a new world [a free world, a land of freedom]. ▶ここはまったく別天地だ This is indeed a different world.
❸ [上下] ▶天地無用 (掲示) This side up./Do not turn over.
● 天地の差 ▶両国間には生活水準に天地の差がある There is a world of difference in the standard of living between the two countries.

てんち 転地 ● 熱海へ転地(療養)に行く go to Atami for a change (of air); go to Atami for one's health.

でんち 田地 (⇨田, 田んぼ)

でんち 電池 a battery, a cell. (❗前の方は cell の連結体) ● 電池を充電する charge a battery. ▶このおもちゃは電池で動く This toy works [runs] on [by] batteries. (❗「電池で動くおもちゃ」は a battery-powered toy) ▶電池が切れている The batteries are dead (are finished, have run down, 《英》have gone flat).

> 関連 いろいろな電池: アルカリ電池 an alkaline battery/乾電池 a (dry) battery, a dry cell/太陽電池 a solar battery/蓄電池 a storage battery/ニッケルカドミウム電池 a nickel-cadmium battery/リチウムイオン電池 an lithium-ion battery/単1 [単2; 単3; 単4]電池 a "D" [a "C"; a "AA"; a "AAA"] size battery [cell].

てんちうじょう 『天地有情』 Heaven, Earth and Sentient Beings. (参考) 土井晩翠の詩集

てんちゃ 点茶 tencha; (説明的に) making tea by whisking powdered green tea in hot water.

てんちゅう 天誅 《書》(divine) retribution. ● 天誅を加える[下す] execute 《him》 in retribution for

でんちゅう 殿中 ▶殿中で in the palace [court].

でんちゅう 電柱 《米》a utility pole; (電灯線用の) an electric [a light] pole; (電話線用の) a telephone pole; (電信用の) a telegraph pole.

てんちょう 天頂 the zenith /zíːnəθ/ ● 天頂距離 the zenith distance.

てんちょう 店長 a manager. ▶新しい店の店長 the *manager* of a new store.

てんちょう 転調 名 『音楽』(a) modulation; a change of keys.
── **転調する** 動 ▶ハ長調からト短調に転調する *modulate* from C major to G minor.

てんつゆ 天つゆ dipping sauce for *tempura*.

てんで 【てんで…ない】(全く) not … at all. ▶彼の話はてんで信用できない We cannot believe his story *at all*./What he says is *absolutely un*believable [*by no means*] believable].

てんてき 天敵 a natural enemy.

てんてき 点滴 『医学』a drip, an intravénous drip (⚠ 単に an intravénous, 略して an IV ともいう). ● 点滴中 be *on an intravenous bottle*. ▶点滴を受ける[施す] get [give ⟨him⟩] a *drip*; be put [put ⟨him⟩] *on an intravenous bottle*; be fed [feed ⟨him⟩] *intravenously*. ● 移動式点滴スタンドを動かしてうろうろする walk around with a rolling *IV* stand. ▶点滴の針を何度も打ったので腕にあざができて(=針あとを残して) 青黒くなってしまった I've gotten an IV many times and the needles left black and blue spots on my arm. (⚠「青黒い」は black and blue で白と逆になることに注意) ● 点滴剤 drops. ● 点滴注射器 an instillator.

てんてこまい てんてこ舞い ── **てんてこ舞いの** 形 very busy, hectic. (⇨忙しい). ▶てんてこ舞いの決算期 a *hectic* accounting period. ▶子供が5人もいるので毎日てんてこ舞いです I have five children, and they keep me *very busy* every day.

でんてつ 電鉄 (電気鉄道(会社)) 《米》an electric railroad (company); 《英》an electric railway (company). ▶阪神電鉄 Hanshin *Electric Railway* Co., Ltd.

てんてつき 転轍器 a (railway) switch, switches; 《英》points.

てんでに ▶子供たちはてんでに(=各自で) 遊んでいる Each child is playing *in their own way*. ▶彼らはてんでに(=別々に) 家へ帰った They *separated* and went home./They returned to their *respective* homes.

てんてんと 点々と (あちこちに) here and there. ▶公園の中に点々と桜が植えられている The park *is dotted with* cherry trees./Cherry trees *dot* the park. ▶血がその傷口から点々と落ちていた Blood *was dripping* from the wound.

てんてんと 転々と ● 職を転々と変える change jobs many times; drift from job to job. ● 各地を転々とする move around from one place to another. ▶ボールがバックネットの方へ転々とする間に二者が生還した The two runners got home while the ball was *rolling* to the backstop.

てんでんばらばら (無秩序な) disorderly; (やや書) (さまざまな) various. ● てんでんばらばらな意見 *various* opinions. ● てんでんばらばらなことをする(=好きかってなことをする) do only what they like. ▶一家はてんでんばらばらになった(=違う所に住むようになった) All (the members) of my family have come to live in different places.

てんてんはんそく 輾転反側 ── **輾転反側する** 動 toss and turn in one's sleepless bed. (⇨寝返り).

でんでんむし でんでん虫 『「カタツムリ」の別称』a snail.

テント a tent; (サーカスの)《話》a big top. ● テント生活 camping (in tents). ● テントを張る pitch [put up, set up] a *tent*. ● テントをたたむ fold [take down, pull down] a *tent*. ● 酸素テントをベッドの上に組み立てる(医療で) construct an oxygen *tent* over a bed. ● テント村 a tent(ed) [a camp] village.

でんと (不動に) immovably; (堂々と) imposingly, 《まれ》stately; (ひるまずに) unflinchingly. ▶山頂に巨大な石がでんと座っていた A huge stone sat *immovably* on the mountaintop.

てんとう 店頭 ● 店頭に並ぶ[並んでいる] (=販売されて[されている]) go [be] on sale. ● 店頭で売られるを sold at *the store* (薬が処方箋なしで) *over the counter*]. ● 店頭株 an over-the-counter stock.

てんとう 転倒 ── **転倒する** 動 『転ぶ』fall (down [over]), (勢いよく) tumble (⇨転ぶ, 倒れる ❶); 『気持ちが』 be upset (⇨動転); 『立場などが』 be reversed. (⇨逆転).

てんとう 点灯 ── **点灯する** 動 turn [switch] on (↔off) the light.

***でんとう** 伝統 名 (慣習) (a) tradition (⚠ この語は、主に先祖伝来の社会的伝統を意味するだけなので、日本語の「伝統」とずれる場合には文脈に応じて訳す必要がある); (歴史) history.
① 《伝統が》● 我が校の野球部は長い伝統がある(=歴史が長い) Our school baseball team has a long *history* [*tradition*].
② 《伝統の》● 彼は伝統のある(=創立の古い) 大学を卒業した He graduated from an *old-established* university. ▶彼の作品には伝統の重みが感じられる I feel the weight of *tradition* in his work.
③ 《伝統を》● 古い日本の伝統を受け継ぐ[重んじる; 守る] inherit [value; follow] old Japanese *tradition*. ▶我が校の偉大な伝統(=名声) を守ってゆくつもりです We will keep up our school's great *reputation*.

■ **DISCOURSE**
日本の伝統行事をひとつ挙げるとしたら, 正月行事を挙げたい **If I were to** name one typical [special] *traditional* Japanese *event*, **I would** choose the New Year celebrations. (⚠「条件→帰結」のパターン. 序論でよく用いられる)

── **伝統的な** 形 traditional. ● 伝統的な中国の祭り a *traditional* Chinese festival. ● 人々は伝統的な衣装をまとっていた People were [were dressed in] *traditional* costumes.
── **伝統的に** 副 traditionally. ▶花嫁は伝統的に白い衣装をまとう The bride *traditionally* [*by tradition*] wears white.
● 伝統芸能 traditional performance art.

***でんとう** 電灯 an electric light [lamp]. (⚠ 前の方はしばしば a light と略される) (⇨電気) ● 電灯をつける turn [swich] on (↔off) *the light*. ● 電灯をつけっぱなしにする leave *the light* on. ▶この部屋にはもっと明るい電灯が必要だ We need a brighter *light* in this room. ▶暗くなると電灯が自動的につく The *light* comes on automatically as it gets dark.

でんどう 伝道 名 『伝道の仕事』 mission, missionary work; 『説教』 preaching. ● 伝道に従事する be engaged in *mission* [*missionary work*].
── **伝道する** 動 ● キリスト教を伝道する preach Christianity; evangelize. ▶日本にキリスト教を伝道する *evangelize* Japan.
● 伝道師 (宣教師) a missionary; (説教師) a

preacher.
でんどう 伝導 图〖物理〗conduction.
― **伝導する** 動 condúct; transit (electricity).
- 伝導性［率］〖物理〗conductívity. • 伝導性のある condúctive. • 伝導体〖物理〗a conductor.

でんどう 殿堂 (聖域) a sanctuary; (会館) a hall.
- 学問の殿堂 a *sanctuary* of learning. • 野球殿堂入りする make [be elected to] the Baseball *Hall of Fame*.

でんどう 電動 ― **電動(の)** 形 eléctric(-powered).
- 電動歯ブラシ an electric toothbrush.

てんどうせつ 天動説 the geocéntric [Ptolemaic /tàləméiik/] system.

てんとうむし 天道虫 《米》a ladybug, 《英》a ladybird.

てんとして 恬として ● 恬として(=恬然として)恥じない (⇨恬然(だん))

てんとせん 『点と線』Points & Lines. (〖参考〗松本清張の小説)

てんとりむし 点取り虫 (ガリ勉家)《米語》a grind /gráind/,《英話》a swot.

デンドロビウム〖植物〗a dendrobium.

てんどん 天丼 *tendon*; (説明的に) a bowl of rice topped with shrimp *tempura*.

てんない 店内 店内の in the store [〖英〗shop]
- 店内紹介 store information. • 店内放送 an announcement on [over] the (store's) PA system. • 店内メニュー eat in menu.

てんにゅう 転入 ― **転入する** 動 • 大阪から東京に転入する *move to* [*into*] Tokyo from Osaka.
- 転入生 a transfer (student). • 転入届 a moving-in notification.

てんにょ 天女 a celestial nymph.
てんにん 天人 a heavenly being.
てんにん 転任 a tránsfer. (⇨転勤)
てんねつ 電熱 • 電熱で by electric *heat*.
- 電熱器 an electric stove《米》[cooker《英》].

てんねん 天然 图〖自然〗nature. (⇨自然)
― **天然の** 形 natural; (手を加えていない) unartificial; (金属などが) native; (野生の) wild. • 天然芝(球場)で試合をする play a game on grass. ▶ 彼女は天然ボケだ She does or says stupid [funny] things without any intention.
- 天然ガス natural gas. • 天然現象 a natural phenomenon. • 天然資源 natural resources. ▶ その国は天然資源が豊かです The country has lots of [is rich in] *natural* resources. • 天然色 a natural color. • 天然パーマ (have) naturally curly hair.

てんねんきねんぶつ 天然記念物 a natural monument [treasure]. • 天然記念物に指定する desígnate 《the bird》 as a *precious natural treasure*.

てんねんとう 天然痘 (have [suffer from]) (x a) smallpox. ▶ 天然痘は前世紀中に根絶された *Smallpox* was eradicated in the last century.

てんのう 天皇 an emperor. • 天皇の Imperial. • 明治天皇 the *Emperor* Meiji. • 天皇ご一家 the Imperial family.
- 天皇制 the Emperor System of Japan. • 天皇誕生日 the Emperor's Birthday. • 天皇杯 the Emperor's Trophy. • 天皇陛下 His Majesty the Emperor;《呼びかけ》Your Majesty.

でんのう 電脳 (⇨コンピュータ(-))

てんのうざん 天王山 ▶ 交渉は今夜天王山を迎える(=重大な決定がされる)The negotiations will come to a *crucial stage* this evening. (⇨山場)

てんのうせい 天王星 Uranus /júərənəs/.

てんば 天馬 (古代中国の話) the Creator's flying horse;〖ギリシャ神話〗Pegasus.
- 天馬空(を)行く ● 彼の天馬空を行くがごとき(=自由奔放な)演奏にすっかり魅了された I was utterly fascinated by his freewheeling performance.

でんば 電場〖物理〗an electric field.

***でんぱ** 電波 a radio wave. • 電波に乗る be broadcast; go on the air.
- 電波障害 radio interference. • 電波探知機 a radar. • 電波望遠鏡 a radio telescope. • 電波妨害 jamming.

でんぱ 伝播 图 (普及)〖書〗propagation; (広まり) spread. • 新しい思想の伝播 the *propagation* of new thoughts.
― **伝播する** 動 〖書〗propagate; spread.

てんばい 転売 图 (a) résale. ― **転売する** 動 resell.

てんばつ 天罰 〖書〗(divine) retribution 《for+悪事》. ▶ 彼らには今に天罰が下ります *Retribution* swiftly overtakes them. / 〖話〗They'll get their *comeuppance* /kˈʌmpəs/ before long.
- 天罰てきめん ▶ 天罰てきめんだ(=当然の報いだ、ざまあ見ろ)(It) serves you [him, her, them] right. (❗ 悪いことをしたら仕返しがきた時にあざけっていう)/〖ことわざ〗Every sin brings its punishment with it. (❗ 悪いことをしたら、それが何であれ罰(ば)が当たる)

てんばん 天板 the top 《of a table》.〖the table top ともいう〗

てんぴ 天日 the sun, sunshine. • 天日で乾かす dry (it) *in the sun* [*sunshine*].

てんぴ 天火 an oven. (⇨オーブン)

てんびき 天引き 图 (控除)《やや書》deduction.
― **天引きする** 動 • 給料から天引きする *deduct* from the salary.

てんびじお 天日塩 solar [bay] salt.

てんびょう 点描 a sketch. • 人物点描 a character *sketch*.
- 点描画法 pointillism.

でんぴょう 伝票 〖商取引の〗a slip; 〖レストランなどの勘定書〗《米》a check,《英》a bill. • 売上伝票 a sales *slip*. • 注文伝票 an order *slip*. • 入金[支払]伝票 a recéiving [a páyment] *slip*. • 引き出し[預け入れ]伝票 a withdrawal [a deposit] *slip*.
- 伝票を切る issue a *slip*.

てんぴょうのいらか 『天平の甍』 The Roof Tile of *Tempyo*. (〖参考〗井上靖の小説)

てんびん 天秤 a balance, scales. (⇨はかり) • 両天秤 (⇨両天秤)
- 天秤にかける ● その手術の効果と危険性を天秤にかける *weigh* the benefits *against* the possible dangers of the operation.

てんびんざ 天秤座〖占星・天文〗Libra (❗ the はつけない); (天秤宮)〖占星〗the Balance [Scales]. (⇨乙女座) • 天秤座(生まれ)の人 a Libra, a Libran. (❗ 後の方は形容詞としても用いる)

てんぶ 転部 图 (学部[クラブ]の) changing schools [clubs].
― **転部する** 動 • 理学部から文学部へ転部する *change* from the school of science to the school of literature. • テニス部からバスケット部へ転部する *change from* the tennis club *to* the basketball club.

てんぷ 天賦 • 天賦の才 a gift《for》(❗ divine などの形容詞を必要としない); (生まれながらの才能) a natural [an inborn, an innate] talent《for》. • 音楽に天賦の才がある have a *gift* [*a natural talent*] *for* music.

てんぷ 添付 ― **添付する** 動 attach; (張る)《書》affix. • 注文用紙に小切手を添付する *attach* a check *to* the order form.

●添付書類 an attached document. ●添付ファイル an attachment.

てんぷ 貼付 ▶写真を出願用紙に貼付のこと *Affix* [*Attach*] your photo *to* the application form.

てんぷ 田麩 *dembu*; (説明的に) mashed whitemeat fish seasoned and then dried.

でんぶ 臀部 (人間の) the buttocks; (けもの・鳥などの) the rump.

てんぷく 転覆 图 (乗り物の) a turnover; (政府などの) an óverthròw. ●政府の転覆 the overthrow of the government.
── 転覆する 動 ●政府を転覆させる òverthrów [òvertúrn] the government. (⚠前の方が普通) ▶ボートは風で転覆した The boat *overturned* [*capsized*] in the wind. (⚠(1) 後の方は特に船についていう. (2) 受身形として「懸命の努力にもかかわらず」などの言外の意味が強く感じられる. 受身形では in は by となる) (⇨引っくり返る)

てんぶくろ 天袋 a *tembukuro*; (説明的に) a smaller closet built on the ordinary closet in a Japanese-style room.

てんぷら 天ぷら *tempura*; (説明的に) a Japanese dish of deep-fried fish and vegetables.

テンプレート 〖コンピュータ〗 a template.

てんぶん 天分 a gift; (努力によって伸びる) (a) tálent. ●天分のある人 a *gifted* [a *talented*] man. ●音楽の天分に恵まれる have a *gift* [a *talent*] *for* music; (書) be endowed with músical tálent.

でんぶん 伝聞 (また聞き) héarsay. ▶伝聞は法廷では証拠として採用されない *Hearsay* is not adopted as evidence in a court of law.

でんぶん 電文 a telegram, (英) a telemessage.

でんぷん 澱粉 starch. ●でんぷん質の食べ物 *starchy* foods; starches.

テンペラ → テンペラ画 (a) tempera (painting).

てんぺんちい 天変地異 a natural disaster.

てんぽ 店舗 《主に米》 a store, 《主に英》 a shop. (⇨店) ●仮店舗 a temporary *store*.

テンポ a tempo (複 ~s; 〖音楽〗 tempi /témpi:/); (拍子) time; (歩調) a pace; (速度) a speed. (⇨歩調) ●速いテンポの曲を演奏する play a *fast* tune; play a tune in [*with* a] quick tempo. (⚠「速いテンポで弾く」なら play ... at a quick tempo) ●都会生活の速いテンポ the fast *pace* of city life. ●生産のテンポを上げる pick up (↔slow down) the *speed* [*tempo*] of production. ●片足でテンポを取る beat *time* with one's foot. ●(投手が)テンポよく投げる work fast. ●彼女のテンポについていけなかった I couldn't *keep pace* [*keep up*] *with* her. ●彼はいつもワンテンポおくれている He's always one *step* behind others in doing anything.

***てんぼう** 展望 图 [眺め] a view; [将来の見通し] prospects 《*for*》, an outlook 《*for*》. (⚠後の方がより客観的な見通し) ●長期的展望に立ったエネルギー政策 a *far-seeing* energy policy. ●丘の頂上からの町の展望はすばらしい There is [We have a] wonderful *view* in [(全景) *panorama*] of the town from the hilltop./The hilltop has [(やや書) commands] a fine *view* of the town. ●経済の展望は暗い The *prospects for* the economy are [The *outlook for* the economy is] poor. (⚠... not good. ともいえる) ●思い切った改革を行わない限り新しい展望[=成功の可能性]は開けない Unless we make some [ˣany] drastic changes, new *prospects* for success won't open up [be opened]. (⚠some に注意)
── 展望する 動 survey, make* a survey 《*of*》. ●政治情勢を展望する *survey* [*make a survey of*] the political situation.
●展望車 an observation car. ●展望台 an obsérvatòry.

***でんぽう** 電報 〖電文〗 a telegram, a telegraphic message, 《主に米語》 a wire; 〖海外電報〗 a cable, (書) a cablegram; 〖通信方式・機構〗 telegraph; 〖通信〗 telegraphic communication.
① 【電報を】 ▶お母さんに電報を打ちましたか Have you *sent* a *telegram* to your mother?/Have you *telegraphed* [《主に米語》 *wired*] 《*to*》 your mother? ▶母から父が重病だという電報を受け取った I got a *telegram* from my mother saying (that) my father was very sick. ▶兄にすぐ帰るよう電報を打った I *telegraphed* [*wired*] my brother to come back as soon as possible.
② 【電報で】 ▶結果は電報で知らせてください Please let me know the results *by telegram* [*telegraph*, *wire*]. (⚠無冠詞) / Please *telegraph* [*wire*] me the results. (⚠後の文では ... the results to me. の語順も可)
●電報為替 telegraph money order 《略 TMO》; (銀行的電信扱い) cable [《英》 telegraphic] transfer. ●電報業務 the cable and telegraph services. ●電報用紙 a telegraph form. ●電報料(金) a telegraph charge.

でんぼう 伝法 a bravado (複 ~(e)s).

てんま 天馬 a winged horse (ペガ).

デンマーク 〖国名〗 Denmark /dénmɑːrk/; (公式名) the Kingdom of Denmark. (首都 Copenhagen) ●デンマーク人 a Dane; 《総称》 the Danish /déiniʃ/. ●デンマーク語 Danish. ●デンマーク(人[語])の Danish.

てんまく 天幕 a tent. (⇨テント)

てんません 伝馬船 (はしけ) a lighter; (平底大型荷船) a barge.

てんまつ 顛末 (一部始終) everything, the whole story; (詳細) all the details. ●事件の顛末を話す tell *everything* about the event.

てんまど 天窓 a skylight. ●天窓のある部屋 a room with a *skylight*.

てんまんぐう 天満宮 a *Temmangu* shrine. (⇨天神)

てんめい 天命 (運命) fate; (神の配慮) 〖宗教〗 (a) providence. (⇨人命❷) ▶天命に従う resign oneself *to fate*. ▶人事を尽くして天命を待つ (⇨人事 [成句])

てんめつ 点滅 ── 点滅する 图 flash on and off; (遠くの明かりが) blink. ●点滅させる turn [switch] 《a light》 on and off. ▶ほとんどの対向車がヘッドライトを点滅させて行く手にねずみ取りがいるぞと警告してくれた Most oncoming cars warned us of a speed trap ahead of us with their headlights *flashing on and off*.

てんもう 天網. ●天網恢恢(かいかい)疎にして漏らさず (小さな悪事でも天罰をまぬがれることはできない) 'Heaven's net may seem to have too coarse meshes but it never allows any evils to pass through.'/《ことわざ》 God's mill grinds slow but sure./《ことわざ》 Heaven's vengeance is slow but sure.

てんもんがく 天文学 图 astrónomy.
── 天文学の, 天文学的な 形 astronómic(al). ●天文学的な数字 *astronomical* figures.
●天文学者 an astrónomer.

てんもんだい 天文台 an astronomical observatory.

てんやく 点訳 ── 点訳する 動 braille /bréil/ 《a story》, transliterate [transcribe] 《a book》 in braille.

てんやく 点薬 (⇨点眼)

てんやもの 店屋物 ● 店屋物をとる have a meal delivered 《*from* a local restaurant [food shop]》; get [order for] a take-out 《*from* a Chinese restaurant》.

てんやわんや ● てんやわんやの大騒動になる be thrown into *utter confusion* [*chaos*]. ▶燃える劇場から逃げ出す人々であたりはてんやわんやの様相を呈した People, each trying to run away from the burning theater, presented a sight of *utter confusion*. ▶ここ何日か仕事は忙しいし、子供は熱を出すしでてんやわんやだった I had a *hectic* few days. I had to deal with a rush of work and, to make things worse, my child ran a fever.

てんゆうしんじょ 天佑神助 God's [divine] help.

てんよ 天与 ● 天与の才 (⇨天賦)

てんよう 転用 图 a diversion.
— **転用する** 動 divert 《*to*》. ● その金を他の目的に転用する *divert* the money *to* some other purposes.

てんらい 天来 — 天来の 形 providential; heavenly. ● 天来の啓示 *divine* revelation.

でんらい 伝来 图 (伝承) transmission; (渡来) (an) introduction; ● 先祖伝来の財産 an heirloom /éərlùːm/; a family heirloom. ▶この刀は先祖伝来のものだ This sword *has been handed down* [*been transmitted*] *from* my ancestors.
— **伝来する** 動 ▶仏教は6世紀に朝鮮から日本に伝来した Buddhism *was introduced into* Japan *from* Korea in the sixth century.

てんらく 転落 图 〖落下〗 a fall; 〖破滅(の原因)〗 a downfall. ▶彼は出世するのが早すぎた. それが転落のもとになった He was a success too soon. It was his *downfall*.
— **転落する** 動 ▶馬から転落する *fall off* a horse. ▶男は崖から悲鳴を上げて転落していった The man *fell over* the cliff letting out a scream of terror. ▶タイガースは最下位に転落した The Tigers *dropped* to the last place.

てんらん 天覧 ● 天覧に供する be submitted to his Majesty for inspection.
● 天覧試合 a match [a game] honored by the presence of [held before] the Emperor.

てんらんかい 展覧会 ● an exhibition; (話) a show. ● 美術展覧会を開く hold [put on, stage, mount] an art *exhibition*. ● 展覧会に出品する show [display] (one's work) at [in] an *exhibition*.
● 展覧会場 an exhibition gallery [hall].

でんりそう 電離層 the ionosphere /aiάnəsfìər/.

でんりゅう 電流 電離層 an electric current, (a) current.
● 高[低]圧電流 a high-[a low-]tension *current*.
● 電流の通じている[いない]電線 a live /láiv/ [a dead] wire. ● 電流を通す[通ず] turn off [on] the *current*. ▶この電線には強い電流が流れている There is a powerful *electric current* running through this wire.
● 電流計 (アンペア計) an ammeter.

でんりょく 電力 ● (electric) power, electricity. ▶あちらでは電力事情が悪くて停電は日常茶飯事です The *electric power* situation is so bad there that power failures are all too common.
● 電力会社 an electric power company. ● 電力供給 the supply of electric power [electricity]; the power supply. ● 電力計 a wattmeter; (家庭に取り付ける) an electric meter. ● 電力消費(量) power consumption. ● 電力料金 (electric) power rates.

てんれい 典礼 a ceremony; (儀式, 祭式) a ritual. (⚠ キリスト教の洗礼など)

てんれい 典麗 — 典麗な 形 elegant; (きわめて美しい) exquisite. ● 典麗な花嫁姿 her *exquisite* beauty in bridal costume.

でんれい 伝令 a message; 〖人〗a messanger; (軍軍の) an orderly. ● 伝令を出す send *a messenger* [*an orderly*].

でんわ 電話 图 (a) telephone, (a) phone; (通話) a call, a (tele)phone call, 《主に英》 a ring; (回線) a line.

【解説】 telephone, phone は「通信方式[業務]としての電話 (telephone system [service])」の意では U, 「電話機 (telephone set)」の意では C. telephone と phone は通例交換可能だが、phone の方がくだけた言い方. また、複合語では phone を用いることが多い.

①【電話が】 ▶電話が鳴っている The *phone* is ringing. ▶君にお母さんから電話がかかっているよ There's a (*phone*) *call* for you from your mother./Your mother wants you *on the phone*. (⚠単に「お電話ですよ」は You're wanted *on the phone*.) ▶山田から電話があったとお伝えください Please tell him [her] (that) Yamada *called*. ▶話し中に電話が切れた I got cut off [The *phone* went dead] in the middle of a call. ▶うちの事務所には2台しか電話がない Our office has only two *telephones* [*lines*]. ▶ロンドンに電話が通じない I can't *get through to* London./(話し中) The *line* to London is busy 《米》*engaged*《英》.
会話 「ぼくに電話なかった？」「ええ、だれからも」"Did anybody call me?" "No, nobody."
②【電話の】 ▶電話の調子がとても悪いわ. もっと大きな声で話してくれ It's a terrible line [The *line* is very bad]. Can you speak up [louder]?
③【電話に】 ▶電話に出てくれませんか Can you answer [get] the *phone* for me? ▶彼は別の電話に出ています He is (talking) *on* another [the other] *phone*. (⚠ 後の方は2台のうちの1台をさす) ▶彼は今電話に出られません He can't come to the *phone* now. ▶彼を電話に出してくれませんか Will you please get him *on the phone*?/Please call him *to the phone*.
④【電話を】 ▶電話をする (⇨動) ● 電話をとる pick up the receiver; get the *phone*; take the call.
● 電話を切り換える[取り次ぐ] transfer the *call*.
● 電話をしてタクシーを呼ぶ *telephone* [*phone*] *for* a taxi. ▶お電話を(有りがとう Thank you for *calling* (me) [your *call to* me]. (⚠電話を切る前に言う決まり文句) ▶電話をお借りしてよろしいでしょうか May I use your *phone*? (⚠移動可能な電話の場合、use の代わりに borrow も可 (⇨借りる)) ▶数日前彼から電話をもらった I *got a call* (*from*) from him a few days ago. ▶今電話を待っているところです I'm expecting a *call*. ▶引っ越して来たばかりでまだ電話を引いていません We've just moved in and we haven't had the *phone* installed yet. ▶うん、分かった. じゃあ、もう電話を切るよ Oh, OK, I'll hang up [《主に英》*ring off*]. (⚠相手がまだ話している途中で切る場合は I *hung up on* him./I *hung up* while he was talking. のように言う. 立場を変えて「電話を切られた」というときは He *hung up on* me. となる. on は不利益を表す) ▶しばらく電話を切らずにお待ちください Will you *hold the phone* [*line*] for a minute?/*Hold* [*Hang*] *on* a minute, please. ▶「電話を切ってお待ちください」は *Hang up* (*the phone*) and wait, please.) ▶後で折り返し電話をします I'll *call* (you) *back* later. ▶だれが彼からの電話を受けたんだ Who took his *call*? ▶内線23の田中さんに電話をつないでください Could you *put* me *through to* Mr.

Tanaka [*connect* me *with* Mr. Tanaka] on extension 23, please? ▶ さっき病欠の電話を入れた I've just *called in* sick. (❗ 電話を受けた人が上司などに告げるときには He *told* [*informed*] us *by phone that* he was sick. より He *called* (us) *and said* he was sick. などというのが普通)

会話 「あす 10 時にそちらに着きます」「着いたら電話をください」 "I'll be going to be there at ten tomorrow." "When you arrive, just give me a *call*."

⑤ 【電話で】● 電話で注文する order (it) *by phone*; 《米》 call in an order (*for* it). ● 電話で問い合わせる 《書》 inquire [make inquiries] *by phone*. ▶ 昨夜彼と電話で話した I spoke to him *on the phone* [*over the phone*, *by phone*] last night. (❗ by は単に通信の手段を表すが, on, over は通信の媒体として途中いろいろな処理を経ることを暗示する)

— **電話する** 動 call, 《主に米》 call ... (up), 《主に英》 ring*... (up); phone ... (up), telephone; make* a (phone) call (❗ call が最も口語的で一般的で. telephone, phone は改まった感じを与え, telephone の方が堅い語); (特定の番号・案内に) dial. ● 202-1422 [案内係; 日本] に電話する *dial* 202-1422 [the operator; Japan]. (❗ dial はプッシュホンにも用いる. 番号の読み方は (⇒電話番号)) ▶ お話しできてうれしかった. お電話してくれてありがとう It was good to talk to you. Thanks for *calling* [*phoning*]. (電話を終えるときの決まり文句) ▶ あす会社に電話してください Please *call* [*phone*] (me at) the office tomorrow./Please *give me a call* [×a phone] at the office tomorrow. (❗ いずれも at の代わりに ×to は不可) ▶ 会社から彼に電話したが留守だったので留守電に伝言を入れておいた I *called* [*phoned*] him (*up*) from the office, but he was out. So I left my message on the answering machine. (❗ 過去形は実際に相手と話をした場合にもしない場合にも用いられるので, 相手が留守であったことを明確にするために try を添えて I *tried* to call him (up)..... ということもある) ▶ 私は(彼に)数分遅れるかもしれないと電話した I *called* [*phoned*] (him) to say (that) I might be a few minutes late. (❗ 自分の職場などに報告のため電話を入れる場合は called him のかわりに called in とする (⇒図 ⑤ [最終文例]))

会話 「手紙じゃ間に合わないよ」「それなら彼に電話してみたら」 "A letter wouldn't be quick enough." "Try *getting* him *on the phone*, in that case."

● 電話局 a telephone exchange. ● 電話嫌い a telephone hater. ● 電話交換手 an [a telephone] operator. ● 電話交換台 a switchboard. ● 電話セールス telephone selling; telesales. ● 電話線 (set up) a telephone line. ● 電話ボックス 《主に米》 a (tele)phone booth; 《主に英》 a (tele)phone box; 《英》 a call box. ● 電話魔 a telephone addict. ● 電話料金 telephone rates.

でんわちょう 電話帳 a (tele)phone book [《書》 directory]. (参考) 「個人別電話帳」 the General Directory, 《通称》 the White Pages と 「職業別電話帳」 the Classified Directory, 《通称》 the Yellow Pages がある. ● 電話帳を見る look in [×at] *the phone book*. ● 電話帳で医師を探す look up a doctor *in the telephone book* [*the Yellow Pages*].

でんわばんごう 電話番号 a (tele)phone number. ● 電話番号案内に電話する dial Directory Assistance 《米》 [Enquiries 《英》]. ● 電話(番号) 570-1938 内線 610 《表示》 *Phone* [*telephone*, 《英》 *Tel*]: *570-1938 ext. 610*. (❗ ext. は extension の略) ▶ 電話番号は何番ですか What is your *phone* [*telephone*] *number*?/(電話番号を教えてください) Tell [Give, ×Teach] me your *phone number*. (❗ (1) 文脈から明らかな場合 phone は省略可. (2) 答えは, Oh, it's 103-4567. とか My phone number is .... で, 数字は one-oh /ou/ - three のように一つずつ読む. また, 同じ数字が続くときは, たとえば - 33 - では double three と読む)

会話 「ジムの新しい電話番号が分からないんだ. 引っ越したばかりでね」「(電話)番号案内に聞けば分かると思うよ」 "I don't know Jim's new *number*—he's just moved." "Well, you could get his new *number* from *Directory Assistance*."

と

*と 戸 a door; (引き戸) a sliding door; (観音開きのガラス戸) French windows [《主に米》doors] (❗主に庭やバルコニーに通じる; (雨戸) shutters. (⇨玄関)

> **解説** door は一般に建物・部屋・乗り物・家具などの扉をさすが、広義では戸口の手前にある空間をも含めた「玄関・出入り口 (doorway)」の意でも用いる。通例 the を伴う。なお米英では男性が戸を開けて女性を先に通すのが習慣。

① 【～の戸】● 表[裏]の戸 the front [back] door. ● 車[戸棚]の戸 the car [closet《米》, cupboard /kʌ́bərd/《英》] door.
② 【戸が】● 戸が少し開いている The door is slightly [a little] open. ● 戸がひとりでに閉まった The door closed [shut] by itself. ● 地震がきて、戸がたがたと揺れた When an earthquake happned, the sliding doors rattled.
③ 【戸を】● 戸を開ける open the door; (押して) push open the door (❗(1) push the door open は開いた結果を強調する言い方. (2) 欧米の戸は通例内側に開くので、push in the door ともいえる。逆に内部から外へ出るときは pull open the door となる. (3) 引き戸の場合は draw open (↔shut) the door); (鍵で) unlock (↔lock) the door. ● 戸を閉める close [shut] the door (❗close の方がゆっくりした動作を表す); (ばたんと) bang [slam] the door. ● 彼は戸を閉めて出ていった[入ってきた] He closed the door after he got out of [got into] the room./He closed the door behind him (❗behind him は「出ていった」の意にも「入ってきた」の意にもなる) ● だれかが戸をノックしています There's a knock on [at] the door./I can hear someone knocking on [at] the door.

と 斗 〖容積の単位〗a to. (❗約 18 リットル)
と 徒 〖同類の人〗a [the] set. (❗集合的) ● 芸術の徒 an arty set. ● 無頼の徒 a gang of outlaws. ● 忘恩の徒 (one of) those ungrateful people. ● 学問の徒 scholars.
と 途 帰国の途につく start on one's way home.
と 都 (東京都) Tokyo (Prefecture); (住所や日常語としては単に Tokyo だけで表すのが普通), Tokyo Metropolis /mətrɑ́pəlɪs/, the Metropolis of Tokyo (❗Metropolis は主に新聞用語); (周辺地を含めた行政区画として) Greater Tokyo.
● 都政 the administration of Tokyo; the Metropolitan government. ● 都知事 the Governor of Tokyo (Metropolis). ● 都知事選挙 the Tokyo gubernatorial /g(j)uːbərnətɔ́ːriəl/ election. ● 都バス a Tokyo Metropolitan bus.

:-と 〖格助詞〗❶【随伴】with .... ● ぼくはガールフレンドと映画を見に行った I went to the movies with my girlfriend./My girlfriend and I went to the movies. (❗×I and my girlfriend の語順は非常にくだけた言い方の場合を除いてとらない)

❷【対象, 対立】(...と) with ...; (...に対して) against .... ● 敵と戦う fight against [with] the enemy. (❗against では対立関係がよりはっきり示される) ● A と組んで B の組とテニスをする play tennis with A against the B couple [pair]. ● 彼は店の入口で友達と話をしていた He was talking to [《主に米》 with] a friend at the entrance of the store. (❗to では一方的で短い話のこと, with は相互に長い間話すことが多い) ● 将来は多くの困難と戦わねばならないだろう We will have to struggle against many difficulties in the future. (❗against は立ち向かう感じ) ● 悪いけどこのあと健さんと会うことになってるのよ Ken's meeting (×with) me later, I'm afraid. /I'm meeting Ken .... (と異なり約束の主導権は健の方にあることを示す言い方)

❸【比較】● この辞書をあの辞書と比較してみたが、あまり違いは認められなかった Though I compared this dictionary with that one, there wasn't much difference. ● 私は数学では正彦とは比べものにならない I am no match for Masahiko [I am not clever enough to compete with Masahiko] in math (ematics).

❹【結果】to ..., into .... (⇨以❽) ● 夜半から雨は雪となった The rain changed to [into] snow at [×from] midnight. ● 彼は 3 年後立派な選手となった He became a good player after three years.

❺【思考の内容, 引用】(...ということ) that. ● あすは雨じゃないかと思う I'm afraid (that) it'll rain tomorrow. (❗that は通例省略される. It'll rain tomorrow, I'm afraid. のように文尾も可) ● きっと事態は好転すると思う I'm sure (that) things will improve [get better]. ● 掲示には「試験が午前 9 時開始」と書いてある The notice says, "The examination starts at nine a.m." (⇨言う) ● 彼のエッセイに正直は最悪の策とある(=という話だ) He writes in his essey that 'honesty is the worst policy'.

❻【動作が行われる様子】● 遊覧船はゆっくりと方向転換をした The sightseeing boat turned around slowly. ● 子供たちが次から次へと行進していった Children were marching off one after another.

❼【並置】and. ● そして (a)) ● 輸入と輸出 import and export. (❗対照強勢に注意) ● 私たちは田中さんと中村さんと鈴木さんにお礼を言いたい We want to thank Mr. Tanaka, Mr. Nakamura, and Mr. Suzuki.

❽【以上】● 私の家は駅から歩いて 10 分とかからないところにある My house is not more than [《以内》within] ten minutes' walk from the station.

-と 〖接続助詞〗❶【...するとき】when ... (⇨時 ❷); (...するやいなや) as soon as ... (⇨すぐ ❶); (...につれて) as ...; (...するまで必ず) whenever .... ● 制服に着替えると彼は全然違って見えた He looked quite different when he changed into a uniform. ● 戸を開けると(そこに)かわいい女の子が笑顔で立っていた I opened the door to find a pretty girl smiling at me. (❗この to は「結果」を表す不定詞を導く. したがって and を用いて I opened the door and found ... のようにもいえる) ● 彼女は私を見るとわっと泣き出した As soon as [The instant, The moment] she saw me, she burst out crying. (❗後の二つの方が強意的)/《やや書》On seeing me, she burst into tears. ● 年を取ると記憶力が悪くなってくる As we grow older, our memory becomes poorer. ● 私は酒を飲むと気分が悪くなります Whenever [Every time] I drink, I feel sick. (❗この方が口語的. When I drink, I always.... ともいえる. (⇨いつも ❷))

❷【もし...ならば】if .... ● 5 時までには家を出ないとコン

サートに遅れるよ *If you don't leave home by five, you'll be late for the concert.* ▶次の角を右へ曲がると郵便局があります *If you turn to the right at the next corner, you will find [xthere is] the post office.* (!日本語につられて there is とすると英語の表現としてはきわめて不自然. 曲がろうと曲がるまいと郵便局は存在しているので) ▶このバスに乗ると空港に行けます *This bus will take you to the airport.* (!If you take this bus, you'll be able to get to the airport. は簡潔でよく用いられる言い方) ▶眼鏡をかけないと黒板の字が見えません *I can't see what (is) written on the board without glasses.*

❸ 〚たとえ…でも〛 **even if** [*though*]…; (…だろうとかろうと) **whether … or not.** ▶たとえ音楽は嫌いだろうとこのコンサートは楽しめるだろう *Even if you don't like music, you will enjoy this concert.* ▶雨が降ろうと降るまいと出発しよう *Whether it rains or not, let's get started.* (!whether が長い場合は or not は whether の直後に置かれる傾向が強い. or not の代わりに or no を用いるのは堅い言い方. また, whether 節中に они を用いるのは文語的) ▶Let's start [〚話〛get started], *rain or shine.* (!慣用表現) ▶どこへ行こうと親切な人はいる *No matter where* [*Wherever*] *you go, you'll find kind people.* (!前の方が口語的)

*ど **度** ❶ 〚温度・角度などの〛 **a degree;** (酒の) **proof.** ●30度の角度をなして at an angle of 30 *degrees*. ●180度の転換をする make a 180-*degree* turn [turnaround]. ●気温が摂氏35度に上昇した The temperature went up [rose] to 35℃. (!thirty-five *degrees* centigrade [Celsius] と読む. 0度の場合も zero *degrees* と degree は複数形) ●このブランデーのアルコール度数は40度だ This brandy is 80 *proof* [40 *percent* alcohol]. (!proof は「アルコール標準強度」.〚米〛では100プルーフが50パーセントに相当する)

❷ 〚眼鏡の〛 ●度の強い眼鏡 *thick* glasses; glasses with *thick* lenses. ●15度の眼鏡 glasses of 15 *degrees*. ●眼鏡の度を合わせてもらうため眼科医院に行ってきた I've been to the eye doctor's to get my glasses fitted.

❸ 〚程度, 節度〛(程度) (a) **degree;** (限度) **a limit;** (節度) (a) **moderation.** ●酒の度を過ごさない(=適度に飲む) be *moderate* in drinking; drink *in moderation*. ●その問題に対する関心度は人によってさまざまだ The *degree* of concern over the problem varies from person to person. ●冗談も度が過ぎるよ You *carry* your joke *too far*./You go *too far in* your joke. ▶日光浴も度を越すと危険だ Sunbathing can be dangerous if (it *is*) *overdone*.

❹ 〚回数〛 **a time.** (⇨回) ●1度 **once.** (⇨一度) ●2度 **twice.** ●3〚4〛度 **three** [*four*] *times*. ●3度に1度は *once in* (every) *three times*. ▶1週間に2度〚2週間に1度〛映画を見に行きます I go to the movies *twice a week* [*every two weeks*]. ▶来日するのは今回が3度目です This is my *third* visit to Japan.

●度を失う lose one's presence of mind [one's composure]; (あわてる) be [get] upset.

ど- ❶ 〚名詞・形容詞について意味を強調する語で, 英語に対応する語がないため, その適宜意訳する〛 ●どけち[あほ] 〚英語の absolute skinflint [fool]. ●どえらい(=ひどい)事件 a *terrible* incident. ●ど根性(=気力)のある男 a man with *guts*. ●大都会のど真中(=ちょうど真中) *right* in the center of a big city.

*ドア **a door.** (⇨戸) ●アコーディオン〚回転; 自動〛ドア an accordion [a revolving; an automatic] *door*. ●ドアチェーン **a door chain.** ●ドアポケット **a door pocket.** (〚参考〛冷蔵庫のドアについた入れ物) ●ドアホン **an intercom.** ●ドアホンで名前を告げる give one's name through [over] the intercom. ●ドアマン **a doorkeeper.** (男の) **a doorman** (複 -men).

どあい **度合い** (程度) **a degree;** (広がり) **a measure.** (⇨程度) ●彼らの親密さの度合いは the *degree* [*measure*] of their intimacy. ●対立の度合いを深める intensify the *degree* of their conflict.

とあみ **投網** **a cast(ing) net.** ●投網を打つ **cast a** (*fishing*) *net*.

とある ●とある(=ある)寺 **a certain temple.**

とい **樋** 〚縦の〛**a drainpipe, a rainwater pipe;** 〚水平の〛**a gutter.**

とい **問い** **a question;** 〚書〛**an inquiry.** (⇨質問, 問題)

といあわせ **問い合わせ** (an) **inquiry;** (情報) **information;** (照会) (a) **reference.** ●問い合わせの手紙 a letter of *inquiry*. ●問い合わせをする(⇨問い合わせる) ▶お問い合わせは 001-0001 へ *For inquiries, please call* (us *on*) 001-0001./*Call* [*Dial*] 001-0001 *for information.*/*Inquiries* 《*about*…》 *should be directed to* 《*Kyoto*》 001-0001.

といあわせる **問い合わせる** (尋ねる) **ask** 《*about*》; **inquire** 《*of*+人, *about*+物・事; *if* [*wh*-]節》 (!ask より堅い語), **make* inquiries** 《*about*》 (!常に複数形に注意); (照会する) **refer** (-rr-) 《*apply, write** 》 《*to him for information*》. (⇨尋ねる) ●案内係で航空運賃のことを問い合わせる ask [*inquire, make inquiries*] at the information counter *about* the air fare. ●その本はないかと本屋に問い合わせる *inquire for* the book in [〚to〛] a bookstore. ▶列車の時刻表のことで〚何時に列車が出たか〛旅行代理店に問い合わせた I *inquired of* the travel agency *about* the train schedule [what time the train had left]. ▶詳細は総務部へお問い合わせください For particulars, *apply to* the general affairs department.

–といい –と言い ▶彼女は人格といい能力といい申し分ない *Both* her personality *and* ability are [Her ability *as well as* her personality is] completely satisfactory.

–という –と言う ▶小田さんという男の人 *a* Mr. Oda; a man *named* [*called*] Oda. ●タケシという名で通っている go by the name *of* Takeshi. (!of は同格を表す) ●宇宙飛行士になりたいという彼の夢 his dream *of* becoming [his ambition *to* be] an astronaut. ●100万円という(=のような)大金 *such* a large sum *as* one million yen. ●窓という窓は壊された *Every single* [*Each and every*] window was broken. ●彼女が結婚したということ[ニュース]を聞きました I heard *that* [the news *that*] she got married. ●次の日曜に遊びに行くという手紙がいとこから来た My cousin wrote me a letter *saying* (*that*) he would come to see me the next Sunday. (!(1) xa letter that he would come … とはしない. (2) My cousin wrote (to me) that …., ともいえる) ●若いということはすばらしい *Being young is wonderful.*

〚会話〛「君の案は大変おもしろいと思うよ」「ということは採用していただけるのでしょうか」 "I think (*that*) your idea is very interesting." "*Does that mean* you're going to adopt it?" (!対話文では相手の発言を関係詞で受けて Which means …? と上昇調でいうと日本語により近い緊密な応じ方になる)

〚会話〛「彼はすてきな人なんでしょ」「というううわさだわ」 "He's nice, isn't he?" "*So they* [*people*] *say*."

翻訳のこころ 病院というところは，玄関から入った瞬間には居心地が悪くもぞもぞして早く帰りたいと思うが，しばらくいると慣れる〈吉本ばなな『みどりのゆび』〉Hospitals often make us feel uncomfortable the minute we enter, and we want to leave as soon as possible. After a while, however, you somewhat get used to there [their atmosphere]. (❗(1) a place called ... (...という(ところ))は特別・特殊な場所についてのみ用いるので，病院のような一般的な場所には必要ない．(2) their atmosphere は「病院の雰囲気」の意)

-というと -と言うと ▶某元横綱というと(=というのは)若乃花のことですか By 'a former certain *yokozuna*' do you mean Wakanohana? ▶パリというと(=といえば必ず)エッフェル塔をまず最初に想い出す I remember the Eiffel Tower first of all *when* I hear the word Paris.

-というのに -と言うのに (けれども) though; (しかし) yet. (⇨が ❶, しかし) ▶彼は病気だというのに仕事に行った *Though* [*Although*] he was sick, he went to work.

-というのは -と言うのは (なぜなら) because; (という訳は)《書》for. (⇨なぜならば) ▶もう失礼しなくては，というのは明日はいつもより朝早いものですから I must be going now, because [for] I have to get up earlier than usual tomorrow morning.

-というのも -と言うのも (⇨-と言うのは)

-といえども -と言えども (でも) even; (けれども) though. (⇨いえども)

-といえば -と言えば talking [《やや書》speaking] of [about] .... (❗口語表現で通例文頭に置く) ▶京子といえば，最近結婚したらしい *Speaking* [《英》*Talking*] *of* Kyoko, I've heard that she got married recently.

といかえす 問い返す (聞き返す) ask again; (反問する) ask back.

といかける 問い掛ける ask; ask 《him》 a question; put* a question to 《him》. (⇨問う)

といき 吐息 (ため息) a sigh /sái/. ●青息吐息である (⇨青息吐息)

といし 砥石 a whetstone; (回転式の) a grindstone. ●きめの細かい砥石でかみそりをとぐ sharpen a razor *on* a fine-grained *whetstone*.

といた 戸板 a wooden shutter (to protect a house from rain).

といただす 問い質す 〖質問する〗ask 《him》 a question; 〖尋問する〗question 《him about [on, as to] it》. (⇨尋問)

***ドイツ** 〖国名〗 Germany; (公式名) the Federal Republic of Germany. (首都) Berlin ●ドイツ人 a German; (総称) German people, 《やや書》the Germans. ●ドイツ語 German, 《書》the German language. ●ドイツ(人[語])の German. ●ドイツの統一 the unification of Germany; *German* unification.

どいつ (物) which; (人) who.
●どいつもこいつも ▶どいつもこいつも役立たずだ They are *all* useless./*All* of them are useless.

-といった -と言った ▶ジャガイモとかニンジンといった根菜(類) root vegetables *such as* [*like*] potatoes and carrots. ●これといった (⇨これといった)

-といって -と言って ▶どこといって悪いところはないのだが体が疲れやすい I have no *particular* ailments, but somehow I get tired easily. ▶だからといって金で解決できるものでもない *But* [*Nevertheless*(,)] it's not something you can settle with money. (⇨だから ❷)

-といっても -と言っても ▶彼らの別荘といっても古い田舎家です Their villa is, *in fact,* an old farmhouse. ▶安いといっても 1 万円はします *Though I say* it's inexpensive, it costs ten thousand yen. ▶社長といっても名ばかりで実権は専務が握っている He is the president *only in name*. The executive director has control of the company.

といつめる 問い詰める question 《him》 closely; press 《him》 for an answer; (厳しく尋問する) 《話》grill 《him》.

ドイル 〖英国の小説家〗 Doyle (Sir Arthur Conan /kóunan/ ～).

トイレ(ット) 《米》a bathroom, 《英》a toilet; (レストラン・劇場などの) 《米》a rest room. (便所) ▶トイレが近い(=頻尿である) have frequent needs to urinate. ●トイレの水を流す flush a toilet. ▶トイレをお借りできますか May I use [×borrow] your *bathroom*? ▶備え付けの紙以外はトイレに流さないでください Please don't flush anything but the tissue provided here down the *toilet*. ▶トイレはどちらですか (レストランなどで) Where can I wash my hands?/《米》 Can you tell me where the *rest room* is?

トイレットペーパー toilet paper [tissue]; a toilet roll; (婉曲的) bathroom tissue [roll]. ▶トイレットペーパー 2 個 two rolls of *toilet paper* [*toilet tissue*].

-といわず -と言わず ▶あすといわず(=いわなくて)今すぐ仕事にかかりましょう We'll set to work right now. There's no point in putting it off till tomorrow. (❗「あすまで延ばしてもメリットはない」の意) ▶赤ん坊は顔といわず背中といわず(=全身に)発疹が出ている The baby has a rash in the face, in the back — all over his body.

***とう 塔** a tower; (教会などの尖塔(ﾂﾞ)) a steeple (❗その先端は a spire); (東洋風の多層の塔) a pagóda; (記念塔) a monument. ●テレビ塔[給水塔] a television [a water] *tower*. ●エッフェル塔 the Eiffel /áifl/ *Tower*. ●五重の塔 a five-storied *pagoda*. ●象牙(ｹﾞ)の塔 an ivory *tower*.

***とう 等** ❶ 〖等級〗a class; (段階) a grade; 〖質〗quality; 〖賞〗prize. ●1 等船室[車] a first-*class* cabin [railroad car]. ●特等席 a special seat. ▶私はコンテストで 1 等になった I won (the) first *prize* in the contest. (❗は通例省略される)
[会話] 「何等で旅行しますか」「2 等です」 "What *class* will you travel?" "(I'll travel) (by) second *class*." (❗この場合，*class* を省略するのが普通。by はしばしば，class も時に省略される)
❷ [...など] 《話》 and so on [forth]; etc. (⇨など)
❸ 〖等しい〗even, regular, equal. ●等間隔に at *even* [*regular*] intervals.

***とう 問う** ❶ 〖尋ねる〗ask; 《やや書》inquire. (⇨尋ねる, 質問する). ●彼の安否を問う ask [inquire] *after* his safety. ●その案の賛否を問う put the proposal *to* the vote. ●...を世に問う(=世間に判断を求める) ask the public *for* judgment on .... ▶いま彼の力量が問われている His ability *is* now *in question*.
❷ [問題にする] (気にかける) care 《about》 (❗通例否定文・疑問文で．〜しない」にしばしば); (重要である) matter (❗仮主語 it とともにしばしば否定文で). ●男女を問わず *regardless* [《やや書》*irrespective*] *of* sex. (⇨問わず) ▶事の成否は問わない I don't *care about* success or failure./It doesn't *matter* [I don't *care*] whether you will succeed or fail.
❸ 〖追及する〗▶彼は贈賄の罪に問われている He *is charged with* [*is accused of*] bribery. ▶彼は事故の責任を問われた He *was accused of* causing [responsibility] for the accident. (❗前の undefined

直接的)
● 問うに落ちず語るに落ちる When questioned by others, we never fail to keep our secret, but talking voluntarily, we inadvertently reveal our secret.

とう 当 ●当(=我々の[この]ホテル our [this] hotel. ●当不当 right or wrong. ●当確(⇨当確). ●当の本人に尋ねる ⇨当の.
●**当を得た** (ふさわしい) proper 《for》; (目的にぴったりの) appropriate /əpróupriət/ 《for, to》; (理にかなった) sensible. ▶彼のスピーチは当を得た(=その場に適したものだった) His speech was appropriate [proper] for the occasion. ▶彼は当を得た助言をした He gave sensible advice./(要を得た) His advice was to the point.

とう 党 a party. (⇨政党, 与党, 野党, 保守, 革新) ●党を結成する form a party. ●党に入る join a party. ●党を脱退する leave [withdraw from] a party. ▶その党の党員数は3,000だ The party has 3,000 members (a membership of 3,000).
●**党員** a member of a party, a party member.
●**党首** a party leader. ●**党大会** 《米》a party convention;《英》a party conference.
●**党役員** a party officer.

とう 唐 [中国の王朝] the Tang /tá:ŋ/ (dynasty).

とう 棟 a (large) concrete building. ●2号棟5階に住んでいる live on the fifth floor of the apartmenthouse No. 2;《英》live on the fourth floor of a block of flats No. 2.

とう 糖 (糖分) sugar. ●尿に糖が出る have an excess of sugar in the urine /júərin/.

とう 薹 (花の軸) a flower stalk.
●**薹が立つ** (種ができる) go [run] to seed; (いちばんよい時期を過ぎる) pass one's prime; (婚期を過ぎる) pass the right age to marry.

とう 籐 [植物] cane, rattan.
●**籐いす** a cane chair.

-とう -島 Island; Isle /áil/. ▶マン島 the Isle of Man.

-とう -頭 a head. (❗単·複同形) ●牛40頭 forty head [×heads] of cattle. (❗forty cattle ともいう. ×forty cattles は不可) ●3頭の馬 three horses.

:どう ❶[方法] how. ▶どうしたら児童虐待の問題は解決できるのだろうか How is it possible for us to solve the problem of child abuse? (❗文章での問題提起の表現. 口頭では How can we solve ...? が普通) ▶どう答えてよいか分からなかった I didn't know how [what] I should answer. (❗how は答え方を, what は答える内容を問題にする. I didn't know how [what] to answer. より口語的)

❷[意見・好みなど] (どのような) how; (何) what. (❗通例 how は形容詞·副詞, what は名詞に対応する) ▶この計画をどう思いますか What [×How] do you think about [of] this project?/(君の意見はどうか) What's your opinion about this project? ▶もし彼が来なかったらどうする[なる] What if he doesn't come? (❗what if の後は通例好ましくないこと) ▶でどうなったと思う? And do you know what?
会話「映画どうだった」「よかったよ」"How was the movie?" "Great!"/"How did you like the movie?" "I liked it very much." (❗(1)前の方がくだけた言い方. (2)相手の説明·批評を尋ねるときは What was the movie like? などという)
会話「最初の授業はどうだった?」「なかなかおもしろかったよ. 君のほうはどうだった?」「こっちもおもしろかった」"How did your first class go?/How did you find your first class?" "Pretty interesting. How [What] about yours?" "Mine, too."

❸[体調·暮らしぶりなど] how, what. ▶どうしているの? お元気? How are you doing [getting along]?/(親しい人に) How's it going?/What's new [up, happening]? (❗返事は実情とは関係なく前の方には Just fine, thanks./Oh, not bad. (まあまあね), 後の方には Nothing special. (別に変わりないわ) などというのが普通) ▶どうなさいました (医者が患者に) What can I do for you?/What seems to be the trouble [problem]? ▶どう[手はどう]したんですか What's the matter (with you)? [with your hand?] (❗Is there anything the matter ...? の方が控えめな言い方になる) ▶宿題はどうしたの (先生が生徒に) Where's your homework? ▶君と花子とはいったいどうなっているの? 仲がいいと思っていたのに What's wrong [《米語》What's the deal] with you and Hanako? I thought you were good friends.
会話「かぜの具合はどうですか」「たいしたことありません[だいぶいいです]」"How's your cold?" "Not too bad [Much better], thank you."

❹[勧誘·提案] (...しないか) Would you like [care for]...? (❗以下の言い方より丁寧); (❗) How [What] about ...? (⇨❷ 会話 [第2例]); 《話》What do you say to ...? (❗この to は前置詞);《話》Why don't we 《do》?; (...してはどうか);《話》Why don't you 《do》?; (提案する) suggest. ▶次の日曜日いっしょにピクニックに行くってのはどうだろう How about [What do you say to] going on a picnic next Sunday? (❗(1) 2文に分けて Let's go on a picnic next Sunday. Hòw abóut it [What do you say]? も可. (2)節を用いて How about (if) [What do you say] we go on a picnic next Sunday? のようにもいえる)/Why don't we go on a picnic next Sunday?/Would you like to go on a picnic with me next Sunday? (❗控えめに提案する場合は Would you (by any chance) be interested in going ...?/(主に女性表現) I was just wondering if you'd like to go .... などとなる) ▶明日もう一度やってはどうですか I suggest (that) you (《主に英》should) try again tomorrow. (❗that は《話》ではしばしば省略される)/I suggest trying [×to try] again tomorrow. ▶5万円でどうですか How's fifty thousand yen sound? (❗'s は does の短縮形)
会話「ケーキをもう一つどうですか」「いただきます[いえ結構です]」"Would you like another piece of cake?" "Yés, ↗please [Nó ↘thank you]." (❗Wouldn't you like ...? は非常に丁寧な言い方)
会話「それはいけないね. 薬を飲んだらどう?」「もう飲んだわ. でも効果がないの」「じゃあ, すぐ医者にみてもらったらどうだろう」「ええ, それがよさそうね. そうするわ」"That's a shame. Why don't you take some [×any] medicine?" (❗any を用いると「なぜ薬を飲まないの」の意になる) "I already tried it. But it didn't help." "Well, maybe you should see a doctor right away." (❗「...するなら~がいいけど」というこの控えめな忠告) "Yes, that sounds like good advice. I will."

❺[その他の表現] ▶どうなさいましたか (道や買い物などの選択に迷っているとき) May I help you? (❗店などでは「(いらっしゃいませ)何にいたしましょうか」の意) ▶それがどうした. 私には関係ないよ《話》So ↘what [Whát ↘óf it]? It doesn't concern me. ▶失敗したってどうってことないよ It doesn't matter [doesn't make any difference] at all if you fail. ▶そんな損害くらい金持ちにはどうってことはない Such damage doesn't mean anything to rich people.
会話「それは名案だと思わない?」「さあどうでしょうかね」

"Don't you think it's a good idea?" "Well, I'm not sure [I don't know] about that./(そこまで言う気shiはない) I wouldn't go as far as (to say) that." (❗いずれも不賛成を表す婉曲的な表現)

*どう 胴 ❶ a trunk, a torso (⑳ ~s); (人・動物の) a body; [衣服の] a body, (婦人服の) a bodice; [船の] a hull. ● 胴回りが 80 センチ be 80 cm around the *waist* [in *girth*]. ● 彼は胴が長い [太い] He has a long [a big] *trunk* [*torso*]. ● 胴回りはいくらか *What's* your *waist measurement?*

*どう 銅 copper (元素記号 Cu).
● 銅貨 (⇨銅貨) ● 銅メダル a bronze medal.

どう 堂 [神仏を祭る建物] a temple; a shrine; a hall.
● 堂に入(い)る ● 彼の結婚式でのスピーチは堂に入ったものだった(=見事だった) His speech at the wedding reception was *excellent* [*superb*, *masterly*, *very good*].

どう 道 [行政区] a prefecture. (❗北海道は普通 Hokkaido と表記する) (⇨同)

どう- 同- ●同日(=同じ日)に on *the same* day. ●同(=前述の)証人 the witness (*mentioned*) *above*, the *above-mentioned* witness; 《書》the *said* witness.

とうあ 東亜 （東アジア）East Asia; (極東) the Far East. ●東亜の East Asian; Far Eastern.

どうあげ 胴上げ ●監督を胴上げする *toss* the [their] manager *into the air*.

とうあつせん 等圧線 [気象] an isobar /áisəbɑːr/.

とうあん 答案 [用紙] an exam [(小テストの) a quiz] paper, (解答用紙) an answer sheet; [解答] an answer. ●答案を出す hand 《米》turn) in one's (*exam*) *paper*. ●英語の答案を添削する [採点する] *correct* [*mark*, 《米》*grade*] (*exam*) *papers* in English.

とうい 糖衣 sugarcoating.
● 糖衣錠 a sugar-coated tablet.

*どうい 同意 [名] (話し合い・説得による) agreement; (熟慮の上での)《書》assent; [目下の者の申し出や要求などに応じること]《やや書》consent; [やや書] approval. ●うなずいて同意を示す nod *in agreement* [*consent*, *approval*]. ●同意を求める ask [《書》seek] (his) *agreement* [*consent*]. ●同意を得る get [obtain] 《書》(his) *consent* [*approval*]. ▶彼は両親の同意を得て彼女と結婚した He married her *with* his parents' *consent* [*approval*].

── 同意する 動 agree (*to*+事, *with*+人・意見, *on*+決定条件); [書] assent (*to*; *to do*);《やや書》consent (*to*; *to do*); [よいと認める] approve (*of*). (⇨賛成する) ● その提案に[示された条件に]同意する *agree to* the proposal [*on* the asked terms]. ● 彼の意見に同意する *agree with* him [his opinion]. ▶彼らは彼を援助することに同意した They agreed [*consented*] *to* help him. ▶父は私の外国留学にどうしても同意してくれなかった My father would not *agree* [*consent*, *give*] his *consent*] *to* my studying [study] abroad.

どうい 同位 （同じ位置[位]）the same position [rank].
● 同位角 [数学] the corresponding angles.
● 同位元素 [物理] an isotope. ● 同位体 [物理] an isotope. ● 放射性同位体 a radioactive *isotope*, a radioisotope.

どうい 胴衣 ●救命胴衣 a life jacket; 《米》a life preserver. (❗《英》では「護身用のこん棒」のことなので注意)

どういう [何(の)] what; [どんな方法で] how. (⇨どんな)
▶君の言う「愛」とはどういう意味か? *What* do you mean by the word "love"? ▶どういうわけか私は彼が信用できない *Somehow*(,) I can't trust him./I can't trust him(,) *somehow*.
会話 「健、私のことは忘れて」「それはどういうことなんだい」 "Ken, you can get me out of your mind." "*What* do you mean by (saying) that?/*What* does that mean?" (❗「怒り・抗議」の表現)

どういご 同意語 a synonym /sínənim/ (↔an antonym). ▶big is large の同意語です "Big" is a *synonym for* [*of*] "large."/"Big" and "large" are *synonyms*./"Big" *is synonymous with* "large."

とういそくみょう 当意即妙 ●当意即妙の答えは a repartee /rèpɑːrtíː/. (❗そのやりとりの意では U) ▶彼の応答は当意即妙だった(=すばやく気転がきいた) His answer was *quick and witty*. ▶彼らは食卓を囲んで当意即妙の受け答えを楽しんだ They enjoyed exchanging *witty repartee* over dinner.

*どういたしまして ❶ [「ありがとう」に答えて] That's all right [《話》OK]./Sure./《主に米》You're welcome. (❗米国では最も一般的. 強調して You're very [quite] welcome. とも)/(おやすいことです) It's nothing./《話》No problem. (❗よく用いられるが目上の人には避けた方がよい)/(とんでもない) Not at all./(こちらこそ) It's a pleasure./Mý ˋpleasure. (❗目上の人にも用いる丁寧な言い方)/(礼にはおよばない) Don't mention it./(いつでもどうぞ) Anytime. (⇨ありがとう 会話 [第 1 例])
会話 「迎えに来てくれてありがとう」「どういたしまして. ご旅行はいかがでしたか」"Thank you for coming to meet us." "*It's a pleasure* [*My pleasure*]. How was the trip?" (❗ちょっとしたことでは何も言わないことも多い: "Here's your bag." "Thanks." (「はい, かばん」「ありがとう」))
❷ [「すみません」に答えて] That's all right [《話》OK].; (気にしないでください) Never mind. (⇨すみません 解説 (1))

:とういつ 統一 [名] [単一性, まとまり] unity; [一つにまとめること] unification; [一様であること] uniformity; [標準化, 画一化] (a) standardization; [首尾一貫性] consistency; [集中] (a) concentration.
● 国家の統一 national *unity*. ● アラブ諸国の統一 the *unification* of the Arab nations. ● 精神統一 mental *concentration*. ● 多様の中に統一を見いだす find *unity* in variety [*diversification*]. ▶彼の考えは統一を欠く His ideas lack *unity* [*uniformity, consistency*].

── 統一する 動 unify (⇨統合する); [標準に合わせる] standardize. ● 国家を統一する *unify* the nation.
● 価格を統一する *standardize* the prices.
● 統一行動 (団結した行動) a united action. ● 統一国家 a unified (↔a divided) country. ● 統一試験 a unified test. ● 統一戦線 (present [form]) a united front (*against*).

どういつ 同一 ●同一の 形 the same (❗強調すると the very same, one and the same という形で用いることもある); (寸分違わぬ) identical. (❗same より堅い語. 例) the ~) (⇨同じ 類語) ●まったく同一の人物 one and the same person; the *identical* person. ● 自分を映画の主人公と同一視する *identify* oneself with the hero of the film. ● 同一労働に対する同一賃金 *equal* pay for *equal* work.
● 同一性 identity.

とういん 党員 a member of a political party; a political party member. ● 党員になる join a political party.

とういん 登院 ── 登院する 動 attend (a session of) the Diet.

とういん 頭韻 ● 頭韻を踏む alliterate. ● 頭韻を踏んでいる alliterative (*poems*).

どういん 動因 (直接の原因) a direct cause; (動機) a motive. (⇨動機)

どういん 動員 图 (a) mobilization. ● 総動員 the full *mobilization* 《*of*》.
— **動員する 動** (軍隊などを) 《やや書》mobilize; (出動させる) call ... out; (集める) 《やや書》assemble. ● 新しい橋の建設に反対するために住民を動員する *mobilize* residents to oppose the construction of a new bridge. ▶ あの映画は 20 万人もの観客を動員したんですってね It's said that the film drew an *audience* of two hundred thousand.
— 動員令 mobilization orders.

とうえい 投影 — 投影する (⇨反映).
— 投影する 動 《やや書》project.
● 投影図 a projection. ● 投影図法 the method of projection.

とうえん 登園 — 登園する 動 (幼稚園へ) go to kindergarten; (保育園へ) go to nursery school. (❗いずれも この場合は無冠詞)

とうおう 東欧 East Europe. ● 東欧の East European. ● 東欧諸国 East European countries.

とうおん 唐音 the Japanese version of Tang pronunciation of a Chinese character.

どうおんいぎご 同音異義語 homónym. ● 同音異義語では a hómonym; a hómophòne. (❗前の方は bill (請求書/くちばし) のように同じつづりの, 後の方は sun (太陽) と son (息子) のようにつづりが異なるもの)

とうおんせん 等温線〖気象〗an isotherm.

とうか 灯火 a light; (灯火の明かり) lamplight. ● 灯火の下で読書する read *by lamplight*.
● 灯火親しむべき候(⑤) ▶ 灯火親しむべき候となった The best season for reading has come [is on].
● 灯火管制 《carry out》a blackout.

とうか 投下 — 投下する 動 ▶ その都市に爆弾を投下する *drop* bombs on the city; bomb the city. ▶ 多くな資本を新しい事業に投下する *invest* a huge amount of capital *in* a new enterprise.
● 投下資本 invested capital.

とうか 透過 — 透過する 動〖物理〗transmit;〖生物〗permeate 《*into*; *through*》.
● 透過性の permeable.

とうか 等価 equal value; (同等) equivalence 《*to*》. ● 土地 A と等価のオフィスビルを交換する exchange land A for an office building of *equal* value.

とうか 糖化 saccharification. ● でんぷんを糖化する *saccharify* starch.

とうが 陶画 a picture on ceramic ware [(磁器) porcelain /pɔ́ːrsəlin/].

*どうか ❶〖要請〗please, kindly. (⇨どうぞ)

> 使い分け **please** 相手の意思や都合を考慮しつつ依頼・命令をする時に用いる. 決定権が相手にあることを暗示するので丁寧な依頼や嘆願となり, 日本語の「どうか」に近い.
>
> **if you please** please より丁寧で堅い表現. 相手に好都合な場合にのみ依頼・命令を承諾すればよいことを表す.
>
> **kindly** please より堅い語で, 相手の意思や都合に関係なく依頼・命令をする時に用いる. しばしば話し手の怒りやいらだちを暗示し, 時に押しつけがましく響くので目上の人には避けた方がよい.

▶ どうかこの手紙を出してください *Please* [*Kindly*] mail this letter for me./Will you *please* [*kindly*] mail this letter for me? (❗いずれも kindly より please を用いる方が普通) ▶ どうかそんなとは言わないでください *Please* don't say that. (❗ Don't say that, *please*. も可. Don't *please* say that. は避ける) ▶ どうか行儀よく願いますよ *Kindly* behave yourself. (❗ ×Behave yourself *kindly*. は不可 (⇨〖類語〗)) ▶ どうかよろしく How do you do? (❗初対面のあいさつ)

❷〖変だと不審そる様子〗▶ 君は最近どうかしているよ Something is wrong [the matter] with you these days./(君らしくない) You're not yourself these days. ▶ ごめんなさい. 私どうかしていたみたいで I'm sorry. I don't know what got into me. (❗ get into は《話》で「(人に) ある態度をとらせる」の意) ▶ どうかしましたか Is (there) anything wrong [the matter] (with you)?/What's wrong [the matter, the problem] (with you)?/What happened (to you)? ▶「安ければよい」という考えはどうかと思う I don't like the idea [《やや書》I doubt the wisdom] of "the cheaper, the better."

どうか 同化 assimilation.
— 同化する 動 《やや書》assímilate 《*into* French culture》. ▶ アメリカは多くの国からの移民という同化してきた The United States *has* [×have] *assimilated* immigrants from a considerable number of nations. ▶ その釣り人の姿は風景と同化していた The angler seemed to *be part of* the scenery.

どうか 銅貨 a copper (coin).

どうが 動画〖人形や物が動く映画〗an animation; an animated cartoon. (❗後の方は「漫画映画」の意もある)

どうが 童画 (子供向けの絵) a picture for children.

とうかい 倒壊 图 (a) collapse. ● 倒壊寸前である be on the verge of *collapse*.
— 倒壊する 動 (つぶれる) collapse; (倒れる) fall* down; (破壊される) be destroyed. ▶ 地震でそのビルが倒壊した The building *collapsed* in [*fell down* in, *was destroyed* by] the earthquake.
● 倒壊家屋 a collapsed house.

とうがい 当該 — 当該(の) 形 (関係ある) concerned. (❗通例名詞の後に置く) ● 当該官庁 the authorities *concerned*; the *competent* authorities. (❗competent は「管轄権のある」の意. 官庁・裁判所などに使う) ● 当該人物 the *said* person; the person *concerned*.

とうがい 凍害 frost damage. ● 凍害を受ける suffer *frost damage*; be damaged by frost.

とうがい 等外 图 also-ran. ● 等外に落ちる (=一定の等級の外になる) be not placed; fail to win a prize.
— 等外の 形 (品物が) off-grade (apples).
● 等外品 an off-grade (product).

とうかいどう 東海道 ● 東海道五十三次 fifty-three stages along the Tokaido Road.

とうかいどうちゅうひざくりげ『東海道中膝栗毛』*Travels on Foot on the Tokaido*. (〖参考〗十返舎一九の滑稽本)

とうかく 当確 (=当選確実) Mr. Kita (*is*) *sure to win*. (⇨当選)

とうかく 倒閣 图 the óverthròw of the Cabinet. — 倒閣する 動 óverthrow the Cabinet.

とうかく 頭角 ● 頭角を現す〖きわだっている〗stand out; (異彩を放つ) cut [make] a conspicuous [a brilliant] figure 《*in*》; (目立つ) distinguish oneself 《*in*》. ▶ 彼は政治家として頭角を現し始めた He began to *stand out* [*distinguish himself*] as a politician.

どうかく 同格 ● 同格である rank equally 《*with*》, be of the same rank 《*as*》;〖文法〗be in apposition 《*to*》. ● 同格語 an appósitive.

どうがく 同学 ● 同学の士 one's school friend; (専門分野が同じである人) a companion in one's studies.

どうがく 同額 (同じ金額) the same amount of money; (同じ値段) the same price. ●同額の寄付をする contribute *as much money as* 〈him〉. ▶うちの会社の給料は男女同額です Both sexes are paid *equally* in our company./(差別はない) There is no wage discrimination between men and women in our company.

どうがく 道学 〘道徳学〙 moral philosophy; ethics; 〘道教〙 Taoism /dáuɪzm/.

どうかしている (⇨どうか❷)

どうかすると (⇨ともすると)

どうかせん 導火線 (火薬の) a fuse; (事件などの誘因) a cause. ●導火線に点火する light a *fuse*. ▶それが反乱の導火線となった It *caused* [*sparked* 《英》*off*] the revolt.

とうかつ 統合 图 unification.
―― **統合する** 動 unify. ●いろいろな考えを統括する *unify* various ideas *into* one.

とうかつ 統轄 图 〘監督〙 supervision; 〘管理〙 control. ●ベル氏の統轄のもとに *under the supervision* [*control*] of Mr. Bell.
―― **統轄する** 動 supervise. ●計画を統轄する *supervise* [*control*] the project.

どうかつ 恫喝 图 (a) threat; 《書》(an) intimidation. ―― **恫喝する** 動 threaten; 《書》intimidate.

とうがらし 唐辛子 a red pepper; a cayenne /kaién/ (pepper). ●薬味としては Ⓤ.

とうかん 投函 ―― **投函する** 動 (主に米) mail, 《主に英》post. ●手紙を投函する *mail* a letter. (!) put [drop] a letter in [into] a mailbox より普通 [会話]「報告書を一部送ってください」「了解．今夜投函します」"Will you send me a copy of the report?" "OK. It will *be in the mail* [I'll *send* it *by mail*] tonight."

とうかん 等閑 ●等閑視する (⇨[等閑に付する])
●等閑に付する (おろそかにする) neglect; (軽んじる) make light of...; (無視する) disregard.

とうがん 冬瓜 〘植物〙 a wax gourd; a gourd melon.

どうかん 同感 ▶私はあなたと同感です I *agree with* you./《書》I *am of the same opinion as* you./《書》I *am of your opinion*./(同感する) I *sympathize with* your opinion./I feel the same way (*as* you do). [会話]「実にけしからん」「まったく同感です」"It's all very disgusting." "I *couldn't agree* more." (!) I couldn't agree more. は「まったく賛成だ」の意の成句表現．反対は I couldn't agree less.

どうかん 動感 ●動感にあふれている be full of *movement*.

どうかん 導管 (ガス・液体などの) a duct; (動物・植物の) a vessel; (導水管) a conduit.

どうがん 童顔 〘子供らしい顔〙 a childish [〘少年のような〙 a boyish] face; 〘赤ん坊みたいな顔〙 a baby face. ●童顔の青年 a *boyish-looking* [a *baby-faced*] youth.

***とうき 陶器** 〘磁器を除く焼き物の総称〙 pottery, (素焼き, 土器) earthenware (!) 以上は狭義の「陶器」; 〘磁器〙 porcelain /pɔ́ːrsəlɪn/, (一般に) china (!) 以上はいずれも集合的で，数えるときは a piece [two pieces] of ... のようにいう); cerámics (!) 以上のものを総称した陶磁器類．複数扱い). ●陶器の花びん a *china* vase. ●陶器の作り方を習う learn how to make *pottery*. ▶あの店は陶器類を売っている They sell *ceramics* at that store./That store sells *ceramics*.
●陶器商 (店) a china shop; (人) a china dealer.
●陶器職人 a potter. ●陶器製造所 a pottery.

とうき 冬期, 冬季 winter (season), wintertime.
●冬季オリンピック the Olympic Winter Games; the Winter Olympics.

とうき 当期 (今期) the current year [period]; (今年度) the current fiscal year. ●当期純利益 net income for the *current year*; *current* (*year's*) net income.

とうき 投棄 ―― **投棄する** 動 (投げ捨てる) throw [cast] ... away; (ごみなどをどさっと) dump. ●有毒物質を海洋に投棄することを禁じる forbid the *dumping* of toxic substances into the sea. ●ごみを不法に投棄する *dump* refuse /réfjuːs/ illegally; *make* an illegal *dumping* of refuse.

とうき 投機 图 speculation. ●土地投機を抑制する curb *speculation* [〘投機的投資〙 *speculative* investment] *in* land. ●投機的な動きを規制する regulate *speculative* activity. ●不動産[為替]投機 real estate [exchange] *speculation*.
●投機する 動 ●株に投機する *speculate in* stocks.
●投機家〘筋〙 a speculator 《*in* real estate》.

とうき 党紀 ●党紀を乱す disrupt [〘破る〙 break] party discipline.

とうき 党規 party rules. (⇨党則)

とうき 登記 图 registration. ―― **登記する** 動 register.
●登記所 (不動産の) a real property registration office. (◆欧米では a registry office) は出生・結婚・死亡など戸籍関係を扱う所) ●登記簿 a register.
●登記料 a registration fee.

とうき 騰貴 图 〘値段の〙 a rise (↔a fall); 〘不動産・株などの〙 (an) appreciation. ●物価の騰貴 a *rise* in prices; a price *rise*. ●土地の騰貴 《a 《50 percent》 *appreciation* of land; an *appreciation* 《of 50 percent》 *in* land values.
―― **騰貴する** 動 rise; appreciate. ▶地価が騰貴している Land prices are *rising* [*on the rise*]./(急騰している) Land prices *are soaring*.

とうぎ 党議 (党内での会議) a party conference [〘公式の〙 convention]; (党の決定) a party decision. ●党議に従う abide by the *party decision*. ●問題を党議にかける bring up the question at the *party conference*.

とうぎ 討議 图 〘議論〙 (a) discussion; (賛否対立の正式な) (a) debate; 〘議会などの〙 (a) deliberation.
―― **討議する** 動 discuss 〈the matter〉; debate 〈about [on]〉 〈the matter〉; (細部にわたり慎重に) 《書》 deliberate 〈on [about, over]〉 〈the matter〉. ▶その問題は上院で熱心に討議された The question *was* hotly *debated* in the Senate.

とうぎ 闘技 (sporting) competition; a (sporting) contest.
●闘技者 a competitor; a contestant. ●闘技場 an [a sporting] arena; a ring; a ground; a field.

***どうき 動機** a motive 《*for*》. ●卑劣[利己的; 個人的] な動機から from a low [a selfish; a personal] *motive*. ▶研究を始められた動機は何ですか What is your *motive* [*reason*] *for* starting your studies?/What made you start your studies? ▶彼には犯行の動機がない He has no *motive* to commit [*for*] the crime. ▶子供たちがこれを学びたくなるように動機付けをしなければならない We have to *motivate* the children *to* (want to) learn this. (!) 名詞は motivation)

どうき 同期 ❶〘同じ年度〙 ▶私たちは同期です (同級だった) We were *in the same class* [We were *classmates*] *in school*./(同期卒業生だ) We are *graduates in the same year*./(同年の入社だ) We joined

どうき *the company in the same year*.
❷ [同じ時期] ● 前年同期比で売上げを20パーセント伸ばす boost sales by 20 percent *year on year* [*over last year*]. ▶昨年の同期と比べると暖かい Compared with the same [それに相応する] For the *corresponding* period of last year, it's warmer.
● 同recreation会 (学校の) a class reunion. (⇨同窓会)

どうき 動悸 [医学] palpitation. (❗しばしば複数形で) ●動悸がする get *palpitations*; throb. ▶心臓が激しく動悸を打った My heart *throbbed* heavily [[医学] *palpitated* violently, (どきどき鼓動した) *beat fast*].

どうぎ 胴着 a padded sleeveless undergarment.

どうぎ 動議 a motion. ●緊急動議 an urgent *motion*. ●休会の動議を出す propose a motion to adjourn the meeting [*that* the meeting (《主に英》 should) *adjourn*]; *move* (*for*) an adjournment. ●動議を採択[否決]する adopt [reject] the *motion*.
会話「議長, 即時採決を動議します」「動議に賛成の方はおられますか」"Mr. Chairman (男性) [Ms. Chairwoman (女性)], I *move that* we (《主に英》 should) take an immediate vote." "Would anyone like to second the *motion*?"

どうぎ 道義 morality. ●道義心の強い人 a person of strong *moral* fiber. ●道義上の責任がある have a *moral* responsibility [*for*]; be *morally* responsible [*for*]. ▶彼の行為は道義的に許せない His conduct cannot be excused [is inexcusable] from a *moral* point of view. ▶それは道義に反する That is against *morality*.

どうぎご 同義語 a synonym (*for, of*). (⇨同意語)

とうきん 唐黍 (⇨とうもろこし)

***とうきゅう** 等級 a class; (段階) a grade; (程度) a degree. ●等級別で売られる be sold *in grades*. ●卵を大きさで等級に分ける *grade* eggs according to size.

とうきゅう 投球 [名] a pitch; [投球法] (a) delivery.
●ワンバウンド投球 a *pitch* in the dirt; a dirt ball.
●うまく緩急をつけた投球をする make a good combination of fast and slow *pitches*. ●投球フォームがよい have a good *pitching* form; (いい投球をする) have a fine *delivery*; make a good *pitch*. ●投球の動作に[構えに]入る get set for the *pitch*. ●投球を腕に受ける take a *pitch* on the arm. ●中4日の(投球間隔)で投げる *pitch* on four days' rest.
── 投球する 動 pitch (a ball). (❗ pitch は投球のみに用いる. throw は主に送球に用いるが, 投球に用いることもある)
●投球イニング数 innings pitched. ●投球数 a pitch-count; the number of pitches.

とうぎゅう 闘牛 bullfighting; (1試合) a bullfight.
●闘牛士 a bullfighter; (牛にとどめを刺す主役) a matador; (騎馬闘牛士) a picador. ●闘牛場 a bullring.

どうきゅう 同級 ●和子と私は同級です (同じクラスにいる) Kazuko and I are *in the same class*./(私の同級生だ) Kazuko is one of my *classmates*.
会話「どのように知り合ったの?」「高校で同級生でした」「それ以来ずっと付き合っていわけ?」「そうよ. ずっと仲良しだったの」"How did you get to know each other?" "We *went to high school together*." (❗ We went to the same school. では学校が同じであっても学年が同じとは限らない) "And you've been in touch ever since?" "Yes. We've been good friends."

どうきゅう 撞球 (⇨ビリヤード)

とうぎょ 統御 [名] (統制) control; (命令) (a) command (❗複数形なし); (支配) rule.
── 統御する 動 control, take control (*of*); take [have] command (*of*). ●全軍を統御する *take control of* the whole army.

どうきょ 同居 [名] 同居人を置く take in [have] a roomer [《米》 [a lodger 《英》].
── 同居する 動 ▶息子一家は私たちと同居している Our son and his family *live with* us./We have our son and his family *living under the same roof*.

とうきょう 東京 ●東京外国為替市場 the Tokyo foreign exchange market. ●東京証券取引所 the Tokyo Stock Exchange. (⇨東証)

どうきょう 同郷 ●同郷の人 a person from the same city [town, village]. ▶彼は私と同郷です He comes from *my hometown*.

どうきょう 道教 Taoism /dáuizm/. ── 道教の 形 Taoist.

どうぎょう 同行 [[巡礼に] a fellow pilgrim; [[修行者] an ascetic of the same religion.

どうぎょうしゃ 同業者 [商人・職人などの] the trade; [医者・弁護士などの] the profession. (❗いずれも集合的に用い単・複両形扱い. 個人をさす場合は a man in the same trade [profession] という) ●同業者の (=同業である)浅野さん Mr. Asano, who *is in the same trade* [*line of business*].
●同業者組合 a trade association.

どうぎょうたしゃ 同業他社 (競合会社) a competing company; a competitor; a rival. ●同業他社より優位に立つ hold a competitive advantage over one's *competitors* [*rivals*].

とうきょく 当局 the authorities. (❗複数扱い) ●関係当局[当局者] the *authorities* concerned. ●学校[市]当局 the school [municipal] *authorities*.

とうきより 等距離 ●等距離にある be equally distant (*from*); be equidistant (*from*). ▶東京から等距離にある3都市をあげられますか Can you name three cities which are *equidistant from* Tokyo?
●等距離外交 equidistance diplomacy.

どうきん 同衾 ── 同衾する 動 sleep together; go to bed with (*her*); sleep with (*him*). (❗いずれもセックスをする意にもなる)

***どうぐ** 道具 ❶ [用具] a tool; an implement; an instrument; a utensil; (用具一式) a outfit; (舞台の大道具) scenery; (舞台の小道具) props, 《書》 properties.

> 使い分け tool 片手に持ち単純な作業を行うための道具. ハンマーやドリルなど, 特に職人などの道具をさす.
> implement tool より大きく, 単純な構造の道具. 特にくわ・すきなど.
> instrument 精密で学術的な仕事に使う道具. 医療用メス・温度計など.
> utensil 料理・掃除などに用いる家庭用の道具. やや堅い語.
> kit, outfit ある目的のために必要な道具一式.

●大工道具 a carpenter's *tools* [*outfit, kit*]. ●園芸用具 gardening *tools* [*implements*]. ●台所道具 kitchen *utensils*. ●修理道具一式 a repair *kit* [*outfit*]. ●ひげそり道具 a shaving *kit*. ●道具を使う use a *tool*.
❷ [手段] a tool. (⇨手段) ●他人を道具のように使う use other people as a *tool*. ▶教科書は教師の商売道具だ Textbooks are *tools* of the teacher.
●道具方 (特に大道具の) a scenershifter; (一般に裏方) a stagehand. ●道具箱 a toolbox. ●道具屋 [古道具屋] (店) a secondhand store; (人)

dealer in secondhand articles.
とうぐう 東宮 the Crown Prince.
● 東宮御所 the Crown Prince's Palace.
とうくつ 盗掘 ― 盗掘する 動 rob (-bb-) a tomb 《of its treasures》.
どうくつ 洞窟 a cave; (大規模な) a cavern.
とうけ 当家 ● 当家(=私たちの家)の主人 the head of our family. ● ご当家(=相手の家)の皆様 all of your family. ▶ 当家に何かご用ですか What has brought you to this house?

*とうげ 峠 ❶ 〖山道の〗 a (mountain) pass; (頂上) a peak. ● 大菩薩峠 the Daibosatsu Pass. ● 峠を越える cross (over) a (mountain) pass [peak].
❷ 〖絶頂〗 a peak; 〖危機〗 a crisis 《複 crises /-si:z/》. ▶ 夏の暑さも峠を越した The heat of the summer has passed its peak. ▶ その患者の病気は峠を越して快方に向かっている The patient has passed the crisis and is getting better. ▶ この仕事も峠を越した We've got over the most difficult part of [《話》the hump with] this work.

どうけ 道化 〖人〗(道化師) a buffoon; (サーカスなどの) a clown; (昔の王侯・貴族にかかえられた) a fool; 〖事〗 buffoonery; clowning.
● 道化芝居 a farce.

*とうけい 統計 名 statistics. (**!**複数扱い. 個々の統計値は a statistic) ● 人口統計 population [vital] statistics. ● 去年の自殺の統計(数値) the statistics on suicides for last year. ● 統計をとる collect [take] statistics 《on》. ▶ その統計によると, 年々軽自動車の数が増加している According to the statistics, [The statistics show that] the number of subcompact cars is increasing year by year. (**!**特定の統計に言及しない場合は Statistics show .... と無冠詞で用いる)
― 統計(上)の 形 statistical.
― 統計上, 統計的に 副 statistically. ▶ 統計的に見ると statistically (speaking). ● 統計(学)上意味のある差異 a statistically significant variation.
● 統計学 statistics. (**!**この意では単数扱い) ● 統計学者 a statistician. ● 統計資料 statistical data 《on》. ● 統計図 a statistical graph. ● 統計表 a statistical table.

とうけい 東経 east longitude. ● 東経135度10分にある be (located) at longitude 135 degrees 10 minutes east. (**!**(1) 通例 Long. 135°10′E と略す. (2) longitude を最後に置いていることが多い)

とうけい 闘鶏 〖闘い〗 a cockfight; 〖鶏〗 a fighting cock. ● 闘鶏場 a cockpit.

とうげい 陶芸 ceramics (**!**単数扱い); ceramic art; (焼き物作り) pottery.
● 陶芸家 a ceramist, a ceramic artist; a potter. ● 陶芸教室 a pottery class.

どうけい 同形 ― 同形の 形 of the same shape. ● 左右同形 symmetry. (**!**形容詞は symmetrical) ● これと同型の船 a ship of the same model as this (one).

どうけい 同系 ― 同系(の) 形 〖血統などが同じ〗 of the same stock; 〖同血族の, 同性質の〗〖書〗cognate; 〖(会社などが)同系列下の〗 affiliated; 〖同じような〗 similar. ● 王家と同系の家族 a family cognate with [to] the royal family. ● 多くの同系会社を経営する run a lot of affiliated companies. ● これらの民族はすべて同系です All these races are of the same stock.
● 同系色 a similar color.

どうけい 同慶 ▶ご子息のご結婚がお決まりとの由ご同慶の至り(=とても喜ばしい)でございます How happy I am to hear that your son has become engaged./I'd like to offer my heartfelt congratulations on your son's engagement.

どうけい 憧憬 ● 外国に憧憬を抱く(=あこがれる) yearn [have a yearning] for foreign countries. (⇨憧(ﾋﾟ)れ)
― 憧憬する 動 ● リンカーンを憧憬する(=賛美する) admire Lincoln.

とうけつ 凍結 名 〖水・財産などの〗 a freeze, freezing; 〖返済などの一時的な〗 a moratorium 《複 -ria》. ● 賃金と物価の凍結を解除する lift a freeze on wages and prices [a wage and price freeze]. ● 債務返済の3年凍結を宣言する declare a three year moratorium on one's debt.
― 凍結する 動 freeze. ● 凍結した道 a frozen [an icy] road. ▶川は凍結した[していた] The river froze [was frozen]. ▶地代は凍結すべきだ Land rents should be frozen.
● 凍結財産 frozen assets.

とうげつ 当月 this month. (⇨今月)
どうけつ 洞穴 (⇨洞窟(ﾄﾞｳｸﾂ))
どうげつ 同月 the same month. ● 前年同月比 as compared with that of the same month of the previous year.

どうける 道化る clown around 《with》; play the clown; act silly 《with》. ● 彼は道化て犬のまねをしてみせた He played the clown pretending to be a dog.

とうけん 刀剣 a sword.
とうけん 闘犬 〖犬のけんか〗 a dogfight; 〖犬〗 a fighting dog.
どうけん 同権 equal rights. ● 男女同権 (⇨男女)
とうげんきょう 桃源郷 (地上の楽園) an earthly paradise; a paradise on earth 〖×on the earth〗.
とうご 統語 ― 統語的な 形 syntactic.
― 統語的に 副 syntactically.
● 統語論 〖文法〗 syntax.

とうご 頭語 (手紙の書き出し) a salutation. (**!**Dear Mr. Smith, Dear Sir など)

とうこう 刀工 a sword-maker.
とうこう 投光 ― 投光する 動 floodlight.
● 投光器 a floodlight. ● 投光照明 floodlights; 《話》floods.

とうこう 投降 ― 投降する 動 surrender (oneself) 《to》, give oneself up 《to》. (**!**後の方が口語的)
● 投降者 a person who surrenders [has surrendered].

とうこう 投稿 名 (a) contribútion. (**!**「原稿」は ⓒ)
● おもしろい投稿が満載されている雑誌 a magazine full of interesting contributions.
― 投稿する 動 ● 雑誌に俳句を投稿する contribute /kəntríbju:t/ haiku to a magazine. ▶彼はその新聞によく投稿する He often contributes [He is a frequent contributor] to that newspaper./He often sends contributions to that newspaper.
● 投稿者 a contributor /kəntríbjutər/. ● 投稿欄 the reader's column.

とうこう 陶工 a potter; a cerámist.
とうこう 登校 名 ▶登校拒否児童が増え続けている A growing number of children refuse to go to school./School-phobic pupils are steadily increasing. ▶登校の途中で彼女は交通事故にあった She had a traffic accident on her [the] way to school.
― 登校する 動 go to school.
● 登校拒否(症) refusal to go to school [to attend school]; (学校恐怖症) school phobia.

*とうごう 統合 名 〖部分・要素などの全体への〗integration; 〖結合して一体にすること〗 unity; 〖統一〗 uni-

とうごう fication; 〖会社などの合併整理〗 consolidation.
● いろいろな企画の統合 the *integration* of various projects. ● 民族の統合 the *unity* [*unification*] of the people [race]. ● 統合の象徴 a symbol of the *unity*. ● 二つの会社の統合 the *consolidation* of two companies *into* one.

── **統合する** 動 íntegrate; unite; unify; consolidate; 《いっしょにする》put*... together. ● A を統合して B にする *integrate* A *into* B. ● A と B を統合する *integrate* A *with* B. ● 負債を統合する *consolidate* debts. ● 村の二つの小学校を一つに統合する *put together* [*combine*] two elementary schools in the village *into* one.
● 統合失調症 〖医学〗 schizophrenia /skìtsoufríːniə/. ● 統合幕僚会議 the Joint Staff Council.

とうごう 投合 (⇨意気投合)
とうごう 等号 〖数学〗 an equal sign [mark].
どうこう (どうこうの) this or that. (⇨とやかく) ● どうこう言える立場ではない be not in a position to say *this or that*.
どうこう 同行 ── **同行する** 動 go* [come*] with ..., 《やや書》accompany.
会話「今パスポートは持っていないのですが」「それでは、署まで同行願います」"I don't think I have my passport on me at the moment." "In that case, I'll have to ask you to *come to* the police station *with* me [to *accompany* me to the police station]."
● 同行者 a (traveling) companion.

どうこう 同好 ● 同好会 (⇨同好会) ● 同好の士 (同じ趣味を持っている人たち) people with [分かち合う] sharing] the same interest.
どうこう 動向 ● 〖傾向〗 a trend; 〖事態の成り行き〗 movement. ● 金利動向 the *trend in* interest rate; interest rate *movements*. ● 経済の動向 economic *trends*. ● 世論の動向 the *trend* of public opinion. ● 時代の動向 the *movement* of the times.
どうこう 瞳孔 〖解剖〗 the pupil (of the eye).
● 瞳孔反射 a pupillary reflex.
どうこういきょく 同工異曲 ▶最近の演歌は同工異曲のものが多い(=似たり寄ったりである) There is *not much difference among* present-day [current] *enka* songs.
どうこうかい 同好会 a club. ● テニス同好会 a tennis *club*; an amateur tennis *club*. (❗後の方は特にプロと区別した言い方) ● 音楽同好会を作る form [organize] a music-lovers' *club*.
とうこうせいてい 東高西低 ● 東高西低の気圧配置 a distribution of atomospheric pressure in which the high pressure area lies to the east and the low pressure area (lies) to the west.
とうこうせん 等高線 〖地理〗 a contour /kántuər/ (line).
● 等高線地図 a contour map.
とうごく 投獄 imprisonment.
── **投獄する** 動 imprison 《him》; jail 《him》; put [throw] in prison. (⇨刑務所)
どうこく 慟哭 图 (大声をあげて泣く) a wail; a bitter weep [cry].
── **慟哭する** 動 wail; weep [cry] bitterly.
どうこくじん 同国人 a fellow countryman [countrywoman];《書》a compatriot.
とうこつ 頭骨 a skull;〖解剖〗cranial bones.
とうこん 当今 ── **当今の** 形 today's 《young people》; 《the young people》 of today; present-day. ● 当今の政治情勢 the political situation *at present*.
とうこん 闘魂 fighting spirit; fight. ● 不屈の闘魂 an indomitable [an unyielding] *fighting spirit*.
どうこん 同根 ▶この二つの問題は同根である These two problems come [derive] from the same root.
どうこん 同梱 ── **同梱する** 動 pack together 《with》. ● 機械に同梱されている説明書 a manual *packed together with* the machine.
どうこんしき 銅婚式 ● 銅婚式を祝う celebrate a [one's] *bronze wedding* (*anniversary*). (❗《米》で bronze anniversary ともいう)
とうさ 等差 (等しい差) (an) equal difference.
● 等差級数 〖数学〗 an arithmetic(al) series. ● 等差数列 〖数学〗 an arithmetic(al) progression.
とうさ 踏査 图 〖正式の詳細な調査〗a súrvey;〖探検,実地踏査〗(an) exploration;〖徹底的な調査・研究〗(an) investigation.
── **踏査する** 動 survey; explore; investigate. ● その島を実地踏査する make an on-the-spot *survey* of the island; *explore* the island.
とうざ 当座 ❶ 〖差し当たり〗 for the present, for the moment; (当分の間) for the time being; (仮に) temporarily. ● 当座のしのぎに(=仮の手段として) as *temporary* measures; as a makeshift [a stop-gap];《やや書》a *temporary* expedient. ▶10万円あれば当座は間に合う One hundred thousand yen will be enough *for the present* [(当座の費用に) *for the immediate expenses*]. (❗文頭では 100,000 yen と数字で書かない方がよい)
❷ 〖しばらくの間〗▶ここへ来た当座は何を見ても珍しかった I found everything strange *for some time* [*for a while*] after I came here.
● 当座貸越[借越] an overdraft; a bank overdraft. ● 当座資産 quick assets. ● 当座比率 the quick ratio. ● 当座預金 a checking 《米》[a current《英》] account. ● 100 万円当座預金にする deposit one million yen in a *checking account*.

:**どうさ** 動作 a movement (⇨動き); (身ぶり) a gesture. ● 驚いた動作をする make a *movement* [a *gesture*] of surprise. ● 彼は動作(=身のこなし)が実に素早い His *movements* are very quick [agile]./ He can move very quickly. ▶ 彼は我々に部屋から出るよう動作で示した He *gestured* to us *to go* out of the room.
とうさい 当歳 ── **当歳の** 形 one-year-old.
● 当歳馬 a yearling.
とうさい 搭載 ── **搭載する** 動 (持っている) have; (積んでいる) carry; (装備している) be equipped 《with》. ▶この車は新型エンジンを搭載している This car *has* [*is equipped with*] a new (type of) engine.
とうさい 登載 (⇨掲載)
とうざい 東西 ❶ 〖東と西〗 east and west. ● 東西南北 north, south, *east and west* (❗通例この語順;《羅針盤の 4 方位》the four points of a compass. ▶その島は東西に横たわっていた The island lay *east and west*. ● 川は東西に(=東から西へ)流れている The river runs [flows] *from east to west*.
❷ 〖東洋と西洋〗 the East and the West. ● 東西間の緊張[関係] *East-West* tensions [relations]. ● 古今東西の歌 songs of *all ages and countries*. ● 洋の東西を問わず(=世界中どこでも) all over the world.
どうざい 同罪 ● 同罪である be equally bad [guilty, (責任のある) responsible]. ▶君も同罪だよ You *are equally to blame*. (❗be to blame は「責任を負う

されるべきである」の意)
とうさく 倒錯 图 《やや書》(a) perversion. ●倒錯した愛情 *perverted* affection. ●性的倒錯者 a (sexual) *pérvert*.
とうさく 盗作 图 (a) plagiarism /pléɪdʒərɪzm/ (❗ 作品は C, 行為は U), 《話》a crib. (⇨盗用)
── **盗作する** 動 plagiarize [《話》crib] 《his novel》. ●盗作者 a plagiarist.
どうさつ 洞察 图 (an) insight 《into》, penetration 《into》. ●洞察力のある人 a person of *insight* [*penetration*]. ●深い洞察力がある have a deep *insight*. ▶彼の講演は私にこの問題に対する洞察を与えてくれた His lecture gave me an *insight* into the matter.
── **洞察する** 動 (見通す) see into 《the future》.
とうさん 父さん 图 (⇨父)
とうさん 倒産 图 (a) bankruptcy /bǽŋkrʌptsi/; (破綻) a failure. ●倒産寸前に追い込まれる be nearly *bankrupt*; be on the brink of *bankruptcy*; almost go *out of business*. ▶中小企業の倒産が相次いだ Many medium-sized and small enterprises *went bankrupt* one after another./There was a succession of *bankruptcies* of medium-sized and small enterprises. (❗ ×small-sized は不可)
── **倒産する** 動 go bankrupt; 《話》gò bróke [únder].
どうさん 動産 图 movable property; 【法律】movables.
●動産保険 property insurance.
どうざん 銅山 图 a copper mine.
とうざんさい 唐三彩 图 Tang three-color ware.
*__とうし 投資__ 图 (an) investment. (❗「投資金額」の意では C) ●個人[外国]投資家 an individual [a foreign] investor. ●公共[民間]投資 public [private] *investment*. ●国債への投資 *investment* in national bonds. ●設備投資 *investment* in (plant and) equipment; capital *investment*; equipment spending. ●直接[間接]投資 direct [indirect] *investment*. ▶君が受けている教育は将来への投資だ Your education is an *investment* in your future.
── **投資する** 動 invest 《in》. ▶彼はその会社に100万円投資した He *invested* [made an *investment* of, 《やや話》*sank*] one million yen *in* the company. (❗ sink はしばしば回収が困難な場合)

■ DISCOURSE
上記の理由より，政府は宇宙旅行に投資するより，地球環境保護にお金を投じるべきだと私は結論づける Based on the reasons stated above, I conclude that the government should spend money on preserving the earth's environment rather than investing on space travel. ●Based on the reasons stated above, I conclude that ... (上記で述べた理由に基づき，私は…と結論する)は結論に用いるディスコースマーカー)

●投資環境 an investment environment [climate]. ●投資収益 returns on investment; income [revenues] from investment. ●投資信託 (an) investment trust.
とうし 凍死 图 death from (exposure to) cold.
── **凍死する** 動 freeze [be frozen] to death; (寒さで) die from [of] cold.
とうし 唐詩 图 poems of the Tang period.
とうし 透視 图 ── **透視する** 動 (X線透視装置で見る) look 《at the chest》 through a fluoroscope /flúərəskòup/; (透かして見る) see through ....
●透視画法 perspective. ●透視検査 【医学】(レントゲンの) an X-ray examination. ●透視図[画] a perspective drawing.
とうし 闘士 图 a fighter; (活動家) an activist; 【人・主義のために戦う】a champion; (擁護(ﾖｳｺﾞ)者) a defender. ●組合活動の闘士 a *fighter* in union activities; (活動家) a union *activist*. ●女性の権利の(擁護を求める)闘士 a *champion* [a *defender*] of women's rights.
とうし 闘志 图 【闘う元気】fighting spirit, fight; 【軍隊などの士気】fighting morale /mərǽl/. ●闘志がない [を失う] lack [lose one's] *fighting spirit* [*fight*]. ●闘志を見せる show *fight*. ▶彼はまだ闘志満々だ He still has plenty of *fight* in him./He is still full of *fight*.
*__とうじ 当時__ 图 [その時]then (❗ この意では文尾に置く), at that time, back then 《❗ なつかしく昔を振り返る気持ちを暗示》, at the time 《of》; [その時代に] in those days. ▶当時パリに滞在中だった I stayed [was] in Paris *then* [*at that time*, *in those days*]. ▶終戦当時生活はきびしかった Life was hard *when* the war ended [*at the end of the war*].
── **当時の** 形 ●当時の首相 the *then* Prime Minister. ●当時の思い出にふける be lost in one's memories *of those days*.
とうじ 冬至 the winter solstice.
とうじ 杜氏 图 a (chief) brewer of sake /sáːki/.
とうじ 湯治 a hot-spring cure. (⇨温泉) ▶彼は湯沢に湯治に行った He went to Yuzawa *for a hotspring cure*./He took the cure at Yuzawa (hot springs).
●湯治客 a visitor at hot springs; a visitor to a hot-spring resort.
とうじ 答辞 an address in reply. ●彼女は卒業式で答辞を述べた(=卒業生総代だった) She was the valedictorian /vǽlədɪktɔ́ːriən/. (❗ 《米》では make an *address in reply* at the graduation ceremony や《米》make a *valedictory speech* [a *valedictory*] at the commencement などの言い方より一般的)
どうし 同志 图 【労組・政党などの】a comrade /kámræd/ (❗ 呼び掛けにも用いる); (仲間) a fellow member; 【仲間】a companion; 【志を同じくする人たち】like-minded people. ●同志宮本 Comrade Miyamoto.
どうし 動詞 图 a verb. ●規則[不規則]動詞 a regular [an irregular] *verb*.
── **動詞の** 形 verbal.
●動詞句 a verbal phrase.
どうし 導師 图 【法会(ﾎﾞ)】, 葬式を執り行う僧】an officiating priest 《at a Buddhist [a funeral] service》.
-どうし 一同士 ●同国人同士 fellow countrymen. ●敵(ﾃｷ)同士 mutual enemies. ●親戚(ｾｷ)同士のもめごと trouble *between* relatives. ▶彼らは仲間同士で言い争った They argued *among* themselves. ▶彼らは長年の友達同士です(=お互いに仲がよい) They have been friends *with each other* for (many) years. (❗ friends の複数形に注意) ▶あの2人はれっきとした同士だ They are lovers./They love each other.
*__どうじ 同時__ ── **同時の** 形 simultaneous.
── **同時に** 副 at the same time, at once; (まったく同時に) simultaneously; (偶然同時に) coincidently; (いっさいに) together. ▶同時に話さないでくれ Don't talk *at the same time* [*at once*, *together*]. ▶大相撲は BS1 と1チャンネルで同時に放送された The grand sumo tournament was telecast *simultaneously* [was a *simultaneous* telecast] on BS1 and Channel 1 in those days.

── 同時に 腰 ❶ [...とともに] (B だけでなく A も) A as well as B (！A, B は対等の語句 (⇨[第 1 文例])); (...だがまた同時に) at the same time; (他方) on the other hand; (...の一方で) while .... ▶それは彼にとっては有利である と同時に また 不利でもある It is to his disadvantage *as well as* to his advantage. ▶山登りは楽しい、だが同時に危険である Mountain-climbing is fun, but *at the same time* [《主に書》 *on the other hand*] it is dangerous./《主に書》 *While* mountain-climbing is fun, it is dangerous.

DISCOURSE

自動車の普及は公害など多くの問題の大きな要因だが、同時に多くの恩恵の主因でもある **Although** the increased use of automobiles is a major cause for many problems such as (air) pollution, it has brought many benefits *as well*. (！Although..., ~ (...だが~)は逆接を表すディスコースマーカー. ...の部分に譲歩、~の部分に主張となる内容がくる)

❷ [ちょうどその時に] just as ...; the moment ...; (...するとすぐに) as soon as ...; (...の後すぐに) soon [shortly]; after .... ▶外へ出ると同時に雨が降りはじめた *Just as* [*The moment*, *As soon as*] I went out, it began to rain. (！前の二つの方が強意的)/《書》I had *no sooner* gone out *than* [I had *hardly* gone out *when*] it began to rain. (！simultaneous(ly)は使えない (⇨すぐ❶)) ▶彼は卒業と同時に就職した *Just after* he graduated, he got a job./《やや書》 *On* graduation, he obtained a job.

● 同時録音 a simultaneous recording 《of》. ● 同時録音する record (it) simultaneously; make a simultaneous recording.

どうじ 童子 (幼い子供) a young child (複 children).
とうしき 等式 [数学] an equality.
とうじき 陶磁器 cerámics ❶ (1) 複数扱い. (2) 磁器・陶器のほか煉瓦にも含む広い意味); (食器類の) china(ware). (！いずれも集合的 (⇨陶器))

どうじく 同軸 ● 同軸ケーブル coaxial cable.
とうじご 頭字語 an acronym. (！UNESCO /juː(ː)néskou/ (= *U*nited *N*ations *E*ducational, *S*cientific and *C*ultural *O*rganization) のように頭文字を合わせて 1 語として発音するもので、WHO (= *W*orld *H*ealth *O*rganization) のように 1 文字ごとアルファベット読みするものは普通含めない)

とうじこく 当事国 the country [countries] concerned.
とうじしゃ 当事者 (関係者) the person concerned [involved], the party concerned [involved]; (利害関係者) the interested party. (！いずれも party は法律用語) ● 訴訟 [事故] の当事者 a *party to* a suit [an accident]. ● 当事者同士の話し合い the talks [conference] between *the persons* [*parties*] *concerned*.

どうじだい 同時代 名 the same age [period].
── 同時代の 形 contemporary. ▶ 我々と同時代の人々 our contemporaries. ▶ 夏目漱石は森鷗外と同時代の人だった Soseki Natsume was *contemporary with* [was *a contemporary of*] Ogai Mori.

とうしつ 等質 [同質] (⇨同質); [均質] equality; uniformity.
とうしつ 糖質 (蛋白質・脂質に対して) [生化学] glucide; (炭水化物) carbohydrate.
とうじつ 当日 [その日] that day; [まさにその日] the very day 《of》; [定められた日] the appointed day.

▶当日はひどい雪だった It snowed heavily (*on*) *that day*. ▶試験の当日病気にした I got sick *on the very day of the exam*. ▶通用当日 (= 発行日) 限り Valid [Good] *for the day of issue only*. (！切符の表示)

● 当日券 (公演の日に売られる券) a ticket sold on the day of performance; 《英》 a day ticket.

どうしつ 同室 ── 同室する 動 share a room 《with》; room 《with》.
● 同室者 a roommate.
どうしつ 同質 [同じ品質] the same quality; [同種] homogeneity /hòumədʒəníːəti/. ● 同質の文明 a *homogeneous* /hòumədʒíːniəs/ civilization.
どうじつ 同日 《occur on》 the same day.
● 同日の談ではない (同じ基準では比べられない) 《A and B》 cannot compare; There is no comparison 《between A and B》.
● 同日選挙 a simultaneous election.
どうじつうやく 同時通訳 (事) (a) simultaneous /sàiməltéiniəs/ translation; (人) a simultaneous interpreter. (⇨通訳) ● 同時通訳をする act as *simultaneous interpreter*; do [make] a *simultaneous translation*. ▶あの月面着陸の歴史的瞬間は日本語の同時通訳付きで生中継された That historic [×historical] moment of the moon landing was televised live with *simultaneous* Japanese *translation*.

とうしつせい 透湿性 moisture permeability.

***どうして** 副 ❶ [どんなふうにして] how; in what way [manner]; [どうしたの (⇨ど❸)] ▶そんな少ない収入でどうして暮らしていたの *How* have you been getting along on such a small income? ▶針治療がどうして効くのかだれにも分からない No one knows *how* acupuncture might work.

❷ [なぜ] why, 《話》what... fòr?, 《話》Hów còme...? (！最後は話し手の驚きを含意; 《どういういきさつで》 how. (⇨なぜ)) ▶今日はどうして遅くなったの *Why* are you late today?/*How come* you are late today? (！語順に注意) / *What* kept you [made you late] today?

[会話] 「彼女はフランスにいるんだと思ってたよ」「どうしてそんなふうに考えたの」 "I thought she was in France." "*Where* did you get that idea *from*?/*What* made you think so?"

[会話] 「彼は機嫌が悪いよ」「どうして？」「パーティーに招かれなかったんだ」「どうしてなの？」 "He's in a bad mood." "*Why*?" "He hasn't been invited to the party." "*Why* ╲*not*?" (！否定文に対しては not を落とさないこと)

── どうして 副 ❶ [それどころか] on the contrary. (！前言を強く否定する)
[会話] 「外は寒いよ」「どうして、寒いどころか暑いよ」 "It's cold outside." "*On the* ╲*contrary*, it's hot./It's *far from* cold; it's hot."

❷ [いやはや] indeed. ▶どうして、彼はたいしたやつだよ *Indeed*, he is a great man.

***どうしても** ❶ [どんな犠牲を払っても] at all costs, 《否定文で》 at any cost; [何があっても] no matter what; [どんなことをしても必ず] one way or another [the other], if it is the last thing 《one》 do (！かなり強い決意を表すときの言い方); [まったく] simply, 《話》 just (！ともに否定語の前に置いて意味を強める). ▶どうしても核戦争だけは防止しなければならない We must prevent (a) nuclear war *at all costs* [*no matter what it costs*, 《書》*whatever the cost*]. ▶この計画はどうしてもやりとげてみせる I'll carry this plan through *no matter what* [*one way or another*, *if it's the last thing I do*]. ▶どう

しても彼の名前が思い出せない I can't *possibly* [《話》*just* can't, 《話》can't *for the life of me*] remember [recall] his name. (!) just, possibly, for the life of me は の意味を強める.

❷ [その他の表現] ▶ 彼はどうしても自分の思うようにやろうとする He *will* have his own way. (!) この will は強い意志を表す. 通例強勢が置かれ, 'll のように短縮形にしない. ただし, 否定文では必ずしも強勢は置かれず短縮形も可. 次例参照) ▶ 彼女はどうしてもそうしようとはしない She *will nót* [*nòt*] do it. ▶ ドアがどうしても開かなかった The door *refused to* [*wouldn't*] open.
▶ そのお金がどうしても必要だ(というわけではない)I (don't) *badly* need the money. (!) badly は need, be in need of, want とともに用いる口語的な強意副詞. 否定文では ×badly don't... の語順は不可) ▶ 息子はどうしても行くと言ってきかない My son *insists on* going [×insists to go]./My son *insists that* he (《主に英》*should*) go.

《会話》「これいただいてもいい?」「どうしてもっていうんならいいよ」"Can I take this one?" "You can if you *insist*."

《会話》「火曜日はどうしてもだめなんだ」「そんな! どうしてもうんとは言ってくれないの?」"I can't manage Tuesday./Tuesday's impossible [hopeless]." "Oh, come ⌐on! *There's nothing I can do to* persuade you?"

【翻訳のこころ】ケイシーは珍しく, 仕事の都合でどうしても一週間はロンドンに行かなくてはならなかった (村上春樹『レキシントンの幽霊』) It was unusual [for] Casey, but [×and] he *had to* go to London on business for a week. (!) (1)「珍しく」は unusual (通常とは異なって)で表す. (2)「どうしても...しなくてはならない」は have to ... で表す)

とうしゃ 当社 our [this] company. ▶ 当社はあらゆる種類の貨物を扱っております We handle all types of cargoes.

とうしゃ 投射 图 projection.
── 投射する 動 project. ▶ 大スクリーンに投射する *project* 〈it〉 on a large screen.

とうしゃ 透写 图 tracing. ── 透写する 動 trace.
● 透写紙 tracing paper.

とうしゃばん 謄写版 a mimeograph. ● 謄写版で刷る mimeograph.

とうしゅ 当主 the present head of the family; the present master of the house.

とうしゅ 投手 (野球の) a pitcher, 《米話》a hurler.
▶ ジャイアンツの投手陣 the Giants' pitching staff [corps /kɔ́ːr/]. ● 層の厚い控え投手陣 a deep bullpen. ● 投手を務める pitch [be (a) *pitcher*] 《for one's team》; (登板する) take the mound; come in to pitch. ● 投手を降板させる knock out a *pitcher*; knock a *pitcher* out of the box.

【関連】いろいろな投手: 先発投手 a starting *pitcher*; a starter/救援[リリーフ]投手 a relief *pitcher*; a reliever/中継ぎ投手 a middle reliever [man]; a setup man/抑えの投手 a closer/敗戦処理投手 a mop-up man/勝利投手 a winning *pitcher*; a winner/敗戦投手 a losing *pitcher*; a loser/最多勝投手 the winningest *pitcher*/右腕投手 a right-handed *pitcher*; a righty/左腕投手 a left-handed *pitcher*; a lefty; a southpaw/主戦投手 an ace (*pitcher*)/速球投手 a fastball *pitcher*; a fastballer/剛速球投手 a hard-throwing *pitcher*; a flamethrower/火の玉投手 a fireballer/鉄腕投手 an iron man; a workhorse/技巧派投手 a finesse /finés/ *pitcher*/20勝投手 a twenty-game winner.

● 投手交代 a pitching change. ● 投手戦 a pitcher's battle; a pitching duel. ● 投手板 a pitcher's plate; the rubber. ● 投手力 pitching [mound] strength.

とうしゅ 党首 a party leader [head]; the leader [head] of a political party. ● 四党首会談 a conference of *the heads of four political parties*.

どうしゅ 同種 (⇨種類) ● 同種のリンゴ apples *of the same kind* [*sort*]; *the same kind* [*sort*] *of* apples.

とうしゅう 踏襲 ── 踏襲する 動 [従う] follow. (⇨継ぐ) ● 前例を踏襲する *follow* a precedent.

トゥシューズ [バレエ] toe shoes.

とうしゅく 投宿 ── 投宿する 動 [宿に泊まる] put up [stay] at a hotel [an inn].
● 投宿者 a guest of a hotel [an inn].

どうしゅく 同宿 ● 同宿の人 (宿での) a person who spends in the same hotel; (下宿での) a fellow lodger [《食事付きの》boarder]; a roommate.

とうしょ 当初 ● 当初の計画 the *original* plan. ● 当初から (*right*) from the *beginning* [*start*]. (!) right 图 is from 句を強める. from the *very* beginning も別の強め方)

とうしょ 当所 (この所) this place [town; city]; (当地) here (⇨当地). ● ご当所力士 a *sumo* wrestler who is a native of *your place*.

とうしょ 投書 图 a letter (to the editor).
── 投書する 動 ● 新聞に投書する *write* 〈*a letter*〉 *to* a newspaper.
● 投書箱 a suggestion box. ● 投書欄 the readers' column.

とうしょ 島嶼 islands. (⇨島)

とうしょ 頭書 ● 頭書の通り as mentioned above.

どうしょ 同書 (同じ本) the same book; (前に述べた本) the book (previously mentioned). ● 同書に ibid. (!) ラテン語 ibidem の略.「直前に引用されたのと同じ本[章, 節, ページ]などに」の意)

とうしょう 刀匠 a sword-maker.

とうしょう 東証 [『東京証券取引所』の略] the Tokyo Stock Exchange 《略 TSE》. ● 東証一部に上場する listing on the *Tokyo Stock Exchange* 1st section.
● 東証株価指数 the Tokyo Stock Exchange (stock) Price Index 《略 TOPIX》. ● 東証平均株価 the Tokyo Stock Exchange (stock) price average.

とうしょう 凍傷 frostbite (!) 最悪の場合, 患部の切断が必要); chilblains (!) 通例かゆみの程度が軽いもの, しもやけ, 通例, 複数形で広がりのある部分をさす). ● 重度の凍傷 deadly *frostbite*. ▶ 彼の指は凍傷にかかっていた[かかった] He was suffering from *frostbite in* [He got *chilblains on*] his fingers./His fingers were [got] *frostbitten*. (!) 「凍傷にかかった指」は frostbitten fingers)

とうしょう 闘将 (大将) a brave general; (闘士) a fighter.

*****とうじょう** 登場 图 appearance (on the stage).
● 新製品の登場 the *appearance* of a new product. ▶ ロメオ登場 (脚本のト書で) *Enter* Romeo./Romeo *enters*. (!) 前の方は Let Romeo enter. という*演劇的命令*)
── 登場する 動 (現れる) appear; (舞台に) appear on the stage, come*on. ▶ 彼女は第1幕で登場する She *appears* [*comes on*] in the first act.
● 登場人物 a character; (配役) a cast (!) 集合的に用い単・複両扱い).

とうじょう 搭乗 ── 搭乗する 動 (an) embarkation. ▶ JAL551便にご搭乗のお客様は12番ゲートからお入りください

どうしょう

Passengers for JAL 541 should now proceed to Gate (No.) 12 (for *boarding*). ▶BA079 便ご搭乗のお客様へ最終のご案内を申し上げます Ladies and gentlemen, this is the final (*boarding*) call for Flight BA 079.

── 搭乗する 動 ● 福岡行きボーイング 747 に搭乗する *board* [*go on board, go aboard, get on* (*board*)] Boeing 747 for Fukuoka.
- 搭乗員 (1 人) a crew member; (全体) the crew.
- 搭乗券 a boarding card [pass]. ● 搭乗者名簿 a passenger list. ● 搭乗手続き check-in. ● そのためのカウンターは a check-in (counter)) ● 搭乗手続きをする check in (*at the airport*).

どうしょう 銅賞 a bronze (award [《メダル》medal]).
- 水彩画展で銅賞を受賞する get [win, be given] a *bronze* at a watercolor exhibition.

:どうしょう 同情 sympathy (*for*); pity (*for*); compassion (*for*). (⇨情け)

┌─ 使い分け ─ **sympathy** 他人の悲しみや苦しみなどに共感し、ともに分かち合う気持ち。
pity 苦境にある人をあわれみ、時には見下す気持ち。
compassion 事情を察し、助けになるよう振る舞おうとする深い思いやりの気持ち。 ┘

- 同情心をそそる arouse ⟨his⟩ *sympathy* [*pity*]. ● 彼に同情の意を表す express one's *sympathy* for him. ● 同情を寄せる extend one's *sympathy* ⟨*to*⟩. ▶彼は同情より援助を必要としていた He needed help more than *sympathy*. ▶同情の気持ちから彼に金を貸してやった I lent him some money *out of sympathy* [*pity, compassion*]. ▶同情などほしくない I don't want any of your *pity*./Don't *pity* me. (⇨恵む) ▶彼には同情心がない He has no *pity* [lacks *compassion*].

── 同情的な 形 sympathetic; compassionate. (! 後の方が堅い語。) ● 同情的なまなざし [言葉] *sympathetic* looks [words]. ▶彼は彼女の不幸に同情的だった He was *sympathetic* [*compassionate*] to her misfortune.

── 同情する 動 sympathize (*with*+人・事, *over* [*about*]+事); (あわれむ) pity. ▶すぐ同情する人 a person of ready *sympathies*. ● 同情すべき状態 a *pitiable* condition. ▶彼女はその孤児に同情した She *sympathized with* the orphan./She felt sorry [*sympathy, pity, compassion*] *for* the orphan. ▶私は彼らにまったく同情しません。自業自得だから I feel no *pity* for them at all. They got what they deserved.
- 同情者 a sympathizer. ● 同情票 a sympathy vote.

どうじょう 同上 ── [上と同じ] the same as (stated) above; a ditto (略 do., d°) (⊚ ~s) (! 同じ語句の省略を表す。文中には使用されない。表などでは a ditto mark (〃)をつける)。 ● 同上の(= 上記の)目的で for the *above-mentioned* purposes.

どうじょう 同乗 ── **同乗する** 動 ride ⟨*with* him⟩. (⇨相乗り)
- 同乗者 a fellow passenger.

どうじょう 道場 a *dojo* (⊚ ~s); (説明的に) a room or a hall where *judo* or *kendo* is practiced.
- 柔道の道場 a *judo dojo* [*school*]. ● 道場破りをする offer a challenge at a *kendo* [*judo*] school and defeat its members.

どうしょういむ 同床異夢 'sleep together and have different dreams'; (説明的に) have different opinions [objectives] though they are allied on the surface.

とうじょうか 頭状花 〖植物〗 a compound flower.

どうしょうもない どう仕様もない (⇨仕様 ❶)

どうしょくぶつ 動植物 plants and animals; 《書》(ラテン語) flora and fauna. (! いずれについても、日本語と同じ語順でいう場合もある)
- 動植物界 the plant and animal kingdoms.

とうじる 投じる ❶ [投げる] throw*. (⇨投げる) ● 湖水に身を[石]を投じる *throw* oneself [a stone] *into* the lake.
❷ [費やす] spend*; (支払う) pay*; (投資する) invest. ● 巨額為投じる *at* huge cost. ● 大金を骨董[品]に投じる *spend* a great deal of money *on* antiques; *pay* a great deal of money *for* antiques. ● 全財産をその計画に投じる *invest* all one's fortune *in* the project. ● 仕事に身を投じる(= 専念する) *devote* oneself *to* the job.
❸ [票を] cast*. ● 彼に 1 票を投じる *cast* one's vote *for* [*give* one's vote *to*, *vote* (*for*)] him.
❹ [仲間に入る] join. ● 過激派に身を投じる *join* the radicals.

どうじる 動じる (動転する) get* upset ⟨*by*⟩. ● 動じやすい get easily upset [confused]. ▶彼はものに動じない〖話〗 He is unflappable./He is always calm and never *gets upset* and angry.

とうしん 刀身 the blade of a sword; a sword blade.

とうしん 灯心 a wick.

とうしん 東進 ── **東進する** 動 move east(ward).

とうしん 答申 名 (報告) a report.
── 答申する 動 (...に) A について答申する submit a *report* on A ⟨*to*⟩.
- 答申案 a draft of a report. ● 答申書 a report.

-とうしん -等親 (⇨親等)
-とうしん -頭身 ● 8 頭身の well-propotioned.

とうしん 党人 a (dyed-in-the-wool) party member. (! 「糸にする前に染めた(= 最初から政党人として育った)」の意)

とうじん 蕩尽 ● 全財産をたった数年で蕩尽する(= 使い果たす) go [run] through one's entire fortune in a few years.

どうしん 童心 a child's mind [heart]. ● 童心を傷つける(感情を害する) hurt a *child's feelings*; (無邪気さを砕く) destroy the *innocence of a child*. ▶彼は童心に帰って(= また子供になり)、子供たちといっしょに遊んだ He became a child again [無邪気になって] became as innocent as a child] and played with the children.

どうじん 同人 (趣味などが同じ仲間に)《書》a coterie /kóutəri/. (! 集合的に用い、単・複両扱い) ● 文学同人 a literary *coterie* [*group*].
- 同人誌 a literary coterie magazine.

どうしんえん 同心円 〖数学〗 a concéntric circle.

とうしんじさつ 投身自殺 ● 投身自殺する kill oneself [commit suicide] ⟨*by jumping off* the cliff [*by throwing oneself into a river*]⟩.

とうしんせん 等深線 〖地学〗 an isobath.

とうしんだい 等身大 ● 等身大の肖像画 a *life-size* [*life-sized*] portrait. ● 等身大に引き伸ばす enlarge to *life size*.

とうすい 透水 water permeability. ▶この道路は透水性舗装がされている This road is paved with materials *permeable* to water.

とうすい 陶酔 intoxication. ● 自己陶酔 (ひどい自己満足) complacency; (ナルシズム) narcissism.
── 陶酔する 動 ● 彼は勝利の喜びに陶酔していた(= 酔いを忘れた) He *was carried away by* [《酔いしれた》《書》*was intoxicated with*] the joy of victory.

とうすい 統帥 ── **統帥する** 動 command.
- 統帥権 (最高指揮権) 〈have〉 the supreme com-

どうすいかん 導水管 an aqueduct.

とうすう 頭数 《集合的》a head. ▶《単・複同形》▶乳牛の飼育頭数は 20 を超える We have more than twenty milk cows [twenty *head* of dairy /déəri/ cattle]. (! *head* と結びつくのは cattle (飼育牛の総称で複数扱い)のみ. dairy cattle は肉牛 (beef cattle)に対し酪農場の牛の意で乳牛をさす)

どうすう 同数 the same number. (⇨同じ) ▶梨と同数のリンゴ *as many* apples *as* pears. ▶勝ちが同数の場合にはプレイオフが行われる There will be a play-off when the two teams [competitors] got *the same number* of wins.

とうぜ 党是 (政党の根本方針) party principles; (選挙公約) a party. (! ふつう複数にしない)

***どうぜ** (! ぴったりの訳語がないので適宜意訳が必要) ▶どうせだめだ(=どういうふうにしてもできない) I can't do it *anyway*./There's no way to do [of doing] it. ▶彼はどうせ(=きっと)失敗するよ I'*m sure* (*that*) he will fail. (⇨きっと)/(最終的には) He will *finally* fail [fail *in the end*, ×fail after all]. (! *after all* は結果が意図・予想に反することを含意するので不可 (⇨結局)) ▶どうせ(=少なくとも)その本は読まなくてはならない I have to read that book *at least* [*at least* that book]. (! 前の方では least に, 後の方では book に強勢がある)/(別の理由 [目的] で) I have to read that book *for another reason* [*purpose*]. ▶そのことは後で彼と話そう. どうせ(=だって)彼もそこへ行くんだろう Let's talk about it with him later. *After áll*, he is going to go there, too, isn't he? (! *after áll* は通例文頭に置き, 聞き手と話し手の共通の知識を確認する)

会話 「彼は君の誕生会には来れないかもしれないよ」「どうせ(=どっちみち)来るとは思ってなかったわ」"He may not be able to come to your birthday party." "I didn't expect him to come *anyway* [*anyhow*, *in any case*]." (! 前の文脈の内容が自分とは関わりがないかのようにいうことで, 自分を慰めてあきらめの気持ちを表す. 通例休止をはさまずに文尾に置く)

会話 「君もそそっかしいなあ」「どうせおれはそそっかしいよ」"You are so careless." "Yes. You are right. I'm careless."

会話 「ごめん, 君を疑ったりして」「どうせ僕は信用されてないんだから」"Sorry I suspected you." "*I should have known* you don't trust me." (! すねた気持ちを表す)

① 【どうせ…なら】 (もし…なら) if …; (仮にも…なら) if … at all (! 強意的). ▶どうせ買うのならいちばん高いのにしなよ *If* you buy it [(買わなければならない) have to buy it, (買うつもり) are going to buy it], you should choose the most expensive one./*If* you buy it *at all*, you should choose the most expensive one. ▶どうせ直らないのなら手術は受けない *If* there's no hope of recovery, I won't have an operation.

② 【どうせ…しても】 (たとえ…しても) even if …. ▶どうせ彼の家へ行っても彼はいないよ *Even if* you go to his house, I'm sure he is out.

***とうせい 統制** 图 [権力などによる管理] (a) control (! 「統制手段」の意のときは通例複数形で); [規則などによる取り締まり] (a) regulation. ●思想統制 thought *control*. ●物価統制を課す(緩和する; 強化する) impose [relax; tighten] price *controls*. ●貿易に対する政府の統制を撤廃する lift government *controls on* [*over*] trade. ▶その国は現在軍の統制下にある The country is now *under* [*in*] *the control of* the military.

―― **統制する** 動 control (-ll-); (規制する) regulate. ●生産をきびしく統制する strictly *control* production; *place* production *under* strict *control*; *exercise* [*exert*] a strict *control over* production. ●産業を統制する *regulate* industries.

●統制経済 a controlled economy. ●統制品 controlled articles; goods under government control.

とうせい 当世 (今日) (こんにち) today; (現代) the present day. ●当世の女の子 girls *today*; *today*'s girls; *present-day* girls. ●当世風の(=最新式の)ホテル an *up-to-date* [現代的な] a *modern*] hotel.

とうせい 党勢 ●党勢を拡張する extend the *party power*.

どうせい 同姓 (同じ姓) the same family name, the same surname. ▶私は彼女と同姓です I have *the same family name* as hers [she has]. ▶彼は同姓同名の営業部の同僚とよく混同される He is often confused with his *namesake*, a co-worker in the sales department.

どうせい 同性 the same sex. ▶同性なのでみなさんの気持ちはよく分かります I quite understand how you feel because we are *of the same sex* [you are those *of my own sex*].

どうせい 同棲 图 《書》cohabitation. ●同棲の相手 one's *live-in* partner.

―― **同棲する** 動 ●彼女と同棲する live with her without being married; 《書》cohabit with her; (やや古・おどけて) live in sin with her.

どうせい 動勢 [美術] (ムーブマン) movement.

どうせい 動静 [動き] movements; [様子] a situation; (現状) how things are; [推移] a development. ●敵の動静をうかがう [探る] watch [spy on] the *movements* of the enemy.

どうぜい 同勢 ▶我々は同勢 10 人です Our *party* [*group*] is made up of ten people./Ten people make up our *party* [*group*].

どうせいあい 同性愛 图 homosexuality (↔heterosexuality); (女性の) lesbianism /lézbiənɪzm/.

―― **同性愛の** 形 homosexual (↔heterosexual); lesbian. ●同性愛の人 a homosexual; 《話・けなして》a homo (複 ～s), 《話》a gay, 《けなして》queer; (女性) a lésbian. (⇨ホモ)

とうせいしょせいきたぎ 『当世書生気質』 *Temperament of Students of Nowadays*. (参考 坪内逍遥の小説)

とうせき 投石 ―― **投石する** 動 ▶暴徒たちは警官に投石した The mob *threw* [*hurled*] *stones* [《米》 *rocks*] *at* the police officers.

とうせき 党籍 party membership. ●党籍を離脱する leave [secede from] the party. ●党籍を剥奪(はくだつ)される be deprived of one's *party membership*.

とうせき 透析 [医学] dialysis /daɪǽləsɪs/. ●人工透析 artificial *dialysis*. ●透析為を受ける undergo *dialysis*. ▶私はもう何年も透析を受けている I have been on *dialysis* for years.

●透析器 a dialyzer; 《英》a dialyser. ●透析療法 dialysis.

どうせき 同席 ―― **同席する** 動 (出席する) attend; be present (*at*); (⇨出席する); (…と座る) sit* with …. ▶山岸氏もその会に同席していた Mr. Yamagishi *attended* the meeting, too./(出席者の 1 人だった) Mr. Yamagishi was one of those *present at* the meeting.

どうせだい 同世代 (*of*) the same generation. ▶そう思うのは同世代だからです We think so because we belong to *the same generation*.

とうせつ 当節 (⇨当今)

*とうせん 当選 名 [選挙での] one's election 《*to*》; [懸賞などでの] winning a prize. (⇨入選) ● 当選の(= 当選する) have a (good) chance of *winning* [be likely to *win*] the *election* (↔have no chance [be unlikely] to *be elected*). ▶彼女の大統領当選は確実だ She will surely *be elected* President./She is sure to *win* the presidential *election*./Her *election* to the Presidency is secure.

── **当選する** 動 [選挙で] be elected; (選挙に勝つ) win* an election; [懸賞などで] win a prize. (⇨入選する). ● (S 県代表の)国会議員に当選する *be elected to* the Diet (as member for [from] S Prefecture). ● 宝くじで 1 等に当選する *win* (the) first *prize* in a public lottery.

● **当選券** a lucky [a winning] ticket. ● **当選者** (選挙の) a successful candidate; (懸賞などの) a prize winner. ● **当選番号** a lucky [a winning] number.

*とうぜん 当然 副 (もちろん) of course; (不思議ではない) no wonder; (当然のこととして) as a matter of course; (自然の成り行きとして) naturally; (正当に) rightly. ▶彼が中村と絶交するのは当然だ (*It's*) *no wonder* (*that*) he breaks with Nakamura. (❗ that は通例省略する。以下の言い方より口語的) / *It is natural* [*right*] *for* him *to break with Nakamura.* / *It is natural* [*right*] *that* he should [《米》would] *break* [《話》he *breaks*] *with* Nakamura./*Naturally* [*Rightly*], he breaks with Nakamura. ▶あいつは首になって当然だ(=首に値する) He *deserves to* be fired 《話》[sacked 《英話》].

会話「木村は運転免許の試験だめだったよ」「当然だわ」 "Kimura failed his driving test." "*No wonder*."(驚かないわ) I'm not surprised."

会話「失礼なことをしてほんとうに申し訳なく思っています」「謝らなければならないのは私の方です。あなたが腹を立てるのはしごく当然ですよ」"I'm so sorry I was rude." "*No*. I'm the one who should be sorry. You have *every right* to be angry." (❗この right は「権利」の意。なお、人にぶつかったときなど謝る相手に「あなたが悪いんじゃないですよ」というのには "You're *right*." がよく用いられる)

── **当然の** 形 natural. ● 怠慢の当然の結果 the *natural* result [consequence] of negligence. ▶それは当然なことだ It is *a matter of course*. ▶私たちは言論の自由を当然のことと思っている We *take* freedom of speech *for granted* [*as a matter of course*]. (❗ ×We are taking ... は不可) ▶彼は当然の報いを受けた He got what he *deserved*./It *served* him *right*.

とうぜん 陶然 (⇨うっとり)
どうせん 同船 ── **同船する** 動 be in the same boat [ship].
● **同船者** a fellow passenger.
どうせん 動線 a line of flow; a traffic line.
● **動線計画** flow planning. ● **動線図** a flow [a traffic] diagram.
どうせん 導線 [物理]a conductor; a conducting wire.
どうぜん 同前 (⇨同上)
どうぜん 同然 as good as .... (❗形容詞・動詞に先行して、副詞的に用いる) ▶彼は死んだも同然だ He is *as good as* [(ほとんど)*almost*] *dead.*/(実質的には) He is *practically* [*virtually*] *dead.* ▶我々は仕事を終えたも同然だ(=ほとんど終えた) We have *almost* fin-

ished our work. ▶その家はウサギ小屋も同然だった The house was *little* [*no*] *better than* a rabbit hutch.

*どうぞ ❶ [要請] please, if you please; kindly. (⇨

❷ [勧誘, 提供, 希望] ▶コーヒーをどうぞ Here's your ╲coffee. (Enjoy!) (❗《米語》では「どうぞ」の意を込めて "Enjoy!" と付け加えることも多い)/Here's a cup of ╲coffee *for you*. (❗目の前に差し出していう場合。プレゼントなどを渡すときも Here's something [This is] for you. のようにいう) ▶どうぞよいご旅行を Have a nice trip. (❗(1) 丁寧には I hope you have a nice trip. といい、×Please have a nice trip. は不可. (2) 応答は Thank you, I will. など) ▶どうぞ(お入りください) Cóme ╲in. (❗強く促すときは *Dó* come ╲in, (話) Cóme *on* ╲in. ともいう (⇨会話 [第 1 例 注]))/*Pléase* come ╱in. (❗(1) 第 1 例より丁寧な言い方。単に ×Please. はいえない. (2) 通例 please を文頭に添えると話し手が聞き手の行為に恩義を感じることを暗示する。 一方、 ╲Come in, ╱please. のように文尾に please を置くと話し手が、責任者や主催者など、その場を取り仕切る立場にあることを暗示する。 ただし、╲plee-ease と母音を長く発音すると逆に弱者が強者に「お願いだから」と頼むう言い方になるので注意) ▶こちらヒューストン、ロケット切り離し準備、どうぞ (無線で) This is Houston. Stand by for staging. *Over*. (❗応答の「了解」は *Roger*.)

会話「なんておいしいケーキだこと」「もう 1 切れどうぞ」 "What a delicious cake!" "*Have another piece*./*Let me give you* another piece." (❗(1) 話し手が相手の利益になると確信している場合は please は用いない。したがって ×Have another piece, please. はいえない。(2) Another piece, *please*. は通例「もう 1 切れください」の意。(3) のその方が丁寧な言い方)

会話「ちょっとライターを貸してください」「はいどうぞ」 "Please lend me your lighter." "╲*Here it ╱is.*/╲*Here you ╱are* [*go*]." (❗前の方は物に、後の方は人に重点がある。単に ╲Here. ともいう. 単に Sure. や Go ╲ahead. ともいうが ×(Yes,) please. は不可)

❸ [承諾, 許可] of course, certainly, surely; 《書》by all means. (⇨是非)

会話「ここに座っていいですか」「どうぞ」 "Can I sit here?" "(Yes,) *of course* [*certainly*, *surely*, 《話》 *sure*]./*Go ahead*./*Why not*?/*By all means*." (❗単に ×Please. はいえないで Please do. Do please. という。単に Yes というのも無礼。Yes, do. は可)/"Do [Would, ×Will] you mind if I sit here?" "*No, not at all*." (❗mind は「反対する」の意なのでどうぞは No. で答えるのが普通だが、《話》では Yes, certainly. のように答えることもある。×Please. は不可)

会話「もう一つ質問があるのですが」「どうぞ」「引き続きどうぞ」 "I've one more question to ask." "*Go on*."

会話「クッキーを食べていいですか」「どうぞ」 "May I have some cookies?" "(どうぞご自由に) *Help yourself.* / (はいどうぞ) *Here you are*." (❗この場合 "Please." は不可)

とうそう 逃走 名 (an) escape;《話》(a) getaway.
● **逃走用の車** a getaway car. ▶その犯人はまだ逃走中だ The criminal *is still at large* [《やや話》*on the run*].

── **逃走する** 動 escape; get [run] away; make one's escape [getaway]. (⇨逃げる❶)
● **逃走経路** an escape route. ● **逃走者** a runaway; (主に警察などからの) 《やや書》a fugitive.

とうそう 闘争 [闘い] a fight; (苦闘) a struggle; (衝突) (a) conflict; [ストライキ] a strike. ● 激しい権

とうそう 闘争 a fierce *struggle* [*fight*] *for* power; a fierce power *struggle* [×*fight*]. ●階級闘争 the class *struggle*. ●武力闘争 an armed *conflict*. ●闘争心をかきたてる arouse *fight* [*fighting spirit*]. ●会社に対して賃上げ闘争を行う carry on a *struggle with* the company *for* higher wages.

とうぞう 頭像 a sculpture of one's head. (! 胸像 a bust)

どうそう 同窓 ▶私たちは同窓です(=同じ学校に通った) We went to [attended] the same school./(同じ学校の)卒業生だ) We are graduates of [×*from*] the same school. ●(⇨同窓会, 同窓生)

どうぞう 銅像 a bronze statue.

どうそうかい 同窓会 〖組織〗《米》an alumni /əlʌ́mnaɪ/ [an alumnae /-niː/] association,《英》an old boys' [girls'] association;〖会合〗《米》a home-coming party,《米》an alumni [an alumnae] reunion,《英》an old boys' [girls'] reunion;〖話〗a class [a college] reunion. ▶エール大学90年度卒業生同窓会を開く hold a Yale's *Class* of '90 *reunion* [a *reunion for* Yale's *Class* of 1990].

どうそうせい 同窓生 〖男性〗《主に米》an alumnus (複 alumni /-naɪ/)(!複数形で女性を含めて用いるのは性差別の観点から避ける傾向がある),《英》《主にパブリックスクールの》 an old boy (略 OB);〖女性〗《主に米》an alumna (複 alumnae /-niː/),《英》an old girl (! 略称の ×OG は用いられない).

とうぞく 党則 ●党則に違反する violate [break] *party regulations* [*rules*].

とうぞく 盗賊 (こっそり盗む人) a thief (複 thieves); (強盗) a robber; (屋内に侵入して盗む) a burglar.

どうぞく 同族 (同じ部族[家族]の) (of) the same tribe [family].
●同族会社 a family company. ●同族結婚〖人類学〗endógamy. ●同族目的語〖文法〗a cognate object.

どうそじん 道祖神 a *dosojin*; (説明的に) a travelers' guardian deity /díːəti/.

とうそつ 統率 图 command (! 強制的な力で人に命令し動かすこと); leadership (! さまざまな指導的立場で人を動かすこと). ▶彼は統率力がある He has good *leadership* [*ability to command*]./He is a good *leader*.
── 統率する 動 command; lead.

とうた 淘汰 图 selection. ●自然[人為]淘汰 natural [artificial] *selection*.
── 淘汰する 動 select;〖取り除く〗get* rid of; (好ましくないものを) weed [pick]... out. ▶時代の変化についていけず淘汰される企業も少なくない Not a few companies *are got rid of* as unfit competitors for the changing world. (! unfit competitor は「競争に不適なもの」)

とうだ 投打 pitching and batting. ▶投打がうまくかみ合っている Our *pitching and batting* come together nicely.

とうだい 灯台 a lighthouse (複 -houses /-zɪz/,《米》-sɪz/);〖古〗a candlestand. (⇨灯明)
●灯台もと暗し (ことわざ) At the base of the candle [candlestand] it is dark. ●灯台守 a lighthouse keeper.

とうだい 当代 〖現代〗the present age. ●当代の(=当今の)作家 contemporary [present-day] writers; writers of today. ▶彼は当代随一の作曲家だ He is the greatest composer *of today* [*in the present age*]./He is the greatest *contemporary* composer.
●当代語 (現代の言葉) the present day language.

どうたい 同体 ●雌雄(しゆう)同体〖生物〗hermaphroditism. ●同体で倒れる〖相撲〗fall to the ground *at the same instant*. ●一心同体 (⇨一心)

どうたい 動体〖物理〗a body in motion; a moving body.

どうたい 動態〖物理〗movement. ●人口動態統計 vital statistics. (! 時に単数扱い) ●種族の動態(=動き)を調査する investigate [look into] the *movement* of races.

どうたい 胴体 〖人の〗a trunk, a torso (複 ~s); (人・動物の) a body;〖飛行機などの〗a body, a fuselage; (機体の下側) a belly. ●男の胴体と手足 a man's *trunk* [*torso*] and limbs. ●胴体着陸する make a *belly* [a *crash*] landing; *belly*-land; *crash*-land. (! 後の二は他動詞として「胴体着陸させる」の意でも用いられる)

どうたい 導体〖物理〗a conductor. ●良[不良]導体 a good [a poor] *condúctor*.

どうたく 銅鐸 a *dotaku*; (説明的に) a bell shaped bronze utensil which was supposedly used in the Yayoi period.

とうたつ 到達 图 (到着) (an) arrival;〖達成〗《書》attainment.
── 到達する 動 reach; arrive《at》; (努力の末)《書》attain. ●ある結論に到達する reach [arrive at, come to] a conclusion. ●山頂に到達する reach the top of the mountain. ●完成の域に到達する come to [reach, attain] perfection.

とうたん 東端 the eastern tip. ●最東端の町 the easternmost town (*of* the country).

とうだん 登壇 ── 登壇する 動 get up on [mount] the platform.

どうだん 同断 ▶以下同断 The rest is *the same*.

とうち 当地 here;〖この場所〗this place [(町) town; (市) city, (国) country]; ●ご当地 your place [town, city, country]; your part of the country. ▶当地は雪の降ることはめったにありません We rarely have snow *here*.

とうち 倒置〖文法〗inversion.
●倒置法 inversion;〖修辞〗anástrophe.

とうち 統治 图 (権力による支配) rule; (政治的な支配) government. (⇨支配)
── 統治する 動 rule; govern. (⇨治める ❶)
●統治者 a ruler.

* **とうちゃく** 到着 图 arrival (↔departure). ●到着順に in order of *arrival*. ●到着次第 on one's *arrival*; as soon as one *arrives*. (!後の方が口語的) ▶悪天候のため飛行機の到着が遅れた The plane *arrived* late because of the bad weather./The bad weather delayed the plane's *arrival*. (⇨延着)
── 到着する 動 arrive《at, in》, get*《to》, reach. (⇨着く ❶) ▶列車は午後1時に駅に到着します The train *arrives at* [*gets to*, ×*reaches*, (予定である)*is due at*] the station at 1:00 p.m. ▶昨夜遅くそこに到着した We *got* [×*got to*] there late last night. ▶何年も苦闘した後、彼らは南極に到達した After some trying years, they *reached* [*got to*] the South Pole. (! reach は通例、goal などには「努力して到達する」ことを含意. この場合 arrive at は不自然)
●到着時刻 the arrival time; the time of《his》arrival. ●到着ホーム an arrival platform.

どうちゃく 同着 ●同着3位 finish in a *dead heat* for third; share the third place《*with*》.

どうちゃく 撞着 ●自家撞着 (⇨自家)

とうちゅう 頭注 a headnote (↔a footnote).

どうちゅう 道中 (旅) a trip; a journey; (旅の途中で)

とうちょう during the journey 《to》; on the way 《to》.▶道中ご無事を Have a good trip./Safe journey./Bon voyage /bɑ̀n vwɑiɑ́ːʒ/! 〖！フランス語で good journey の意. Farewell と似た感じで用いられる〗▶道中の暑気にはまいった The heat *on the way* was terrible.
● 道中記 a traveler's journal.

とうちょう 盗聴 图 (wire)tapping, a (wire)tap.
── 盗聴する 動 tap 〖(米) wiretap〗 《a telephone》; listen in 《on 〔to〕a conversation》. ● 私は電話が盗聴されているように思う I think my phone has *been tapped*.
● 盗聴器 (会話の) a concealed microphone,《話》 a bug; (電話の) a wiretapping device, a wiretap.

とうちょう 登庁 ── 登庁する 動 go [come] to the (government) office.

とうちょう 登頂 图 ● 冬のエベレスト登頂に成功する make a successful winter *ascent of* Mount Everest.
── 登頂する 動 ● モンブランに登頂する reach [*get to*, ×*go up*] *the summit* [*top*] *of* Mont Blanc.

どうちょう 同調 ── 同調する 動 〘共感する〙 sýmpathize 《with+人・事》; 〘同じようにする〙 follow suit. ● 彼の考えに同調する *sympathize with* him [his idea]; (本来の意見を変えて) *come around to* his idea; (しぶしぶ) yield to his idea. ▶ K 社がコーヒーの値下げに踏み切るならば, 我が社も同調せざるを得ないだろう If K Company lowers the prices of coffee, we'll have to *follow suit*. 〖！follow suit は「右にならう」の意〗
● 同調者 a sympathizer.

どうちょう 道庁 Hokkaido government office. (⇨県庁)

とうちょく 当直 ▶今夜は当直だ I am *on duty* tonight./I must *stay over on night duty* today.
● 当直医 a doctor on night duty; a night doctor.

ずきずき 痛み (ずきずきする痛み) a throbbing pain; a throb of pain. ● 疼痛を覚える feel a *throbbing pain* 《on the tip of the middle finger》.

*とうてい 到底 〘どうしても…できない〙 can't possibly 〖！possibly は can't を強調する〗; 〘少しも…ない〙 not (…) at all; (断じて…ない) not (…) by any means, by no means 〖！前の方が否定の意味が強い〗; 〘まったく〙 quite. ▶君の夢はとうてい実現できないだろう Your dream *can't possibly* [《話》*just can't*] be realized./It's *quite* impossible to realize your dream. ▶その結果はとうてい満足できるものではなかった The results were *not at all* [*by no means*, 〘ほど遠い〙《やや書》*far from*] satisfactory. (⇨決して) ▶それはとうてい私の力ではできない It is *far* [*quite*] beyond my power./《話》It's *by far* too much for me.
 会話 「今日中にはとうていそこには着けないよ」「君が考えてるほど遠くはないよ」"There's no way we can get there today." "It's not as far as you think."

どうてい 同定 图 identification.
── 同定する 動 identify 《A as B》.

どうてい 童貞 virginity;（人）a virgin.（⇨処女）● 童貞を失う lose (←keep) one's *virginity*.

どうてい 道程 (⇨道のり)

どうてい 『道程』 The Road Ahead.〖参考〗高村光太郎の詩集〗

どうていこ 洞庭湖 〘中国の湖〙 Dongting Hu /dùntíŋ húː/.

とうてき 投擲 图 a throw 《of 50 meters》.
── 投擲する 動 throw.

● 投擲競技 a throwing event.〖！砲丸投げなど〗

どうてき 動的 ── 動的な 形 dynamic /daináɛmik/.

とうてつ 透徹 ── 透徹した 形 〘筋道のよく通った〙 clear, lucid. ● 透徹した論理 clear logic. ● 透徹した議論 a *lucid* argument.

どうでもよい 〘気にしない〙 do* not care 《about; wh-節》; 〘重要でない〙 it doesn't matter 《wh-節》. ● そんなことはどうでもよい I *don't care about* 〘無関心だ〙 *am indifferent to*〕that. ▶人が何と思おうと私にはどうでもよい I *don't care* 〘*couldn't care less*〕*what* (other) people think of me. ● 後の言い方の方が強意的〗▶彼が勝っても負けても私にはどうでもよい It *doesn't matter* 〘*it doesn't make any difference*,《話》*It's all the same*〕to me *whether* he wins or loses.

とうてん 当店 our [this] shop 〖(米) store〗. ● 当店自慢のロールキャベツ our special cabbage rolls. ● 当店価格 our price: 《$24.95》. ● 当店オリジナル商品 our original product(s).

とうてん 読点 《put》 a comma 《to show a short puase in a sentence》.

どうてん 同点 〘得点・得票などの〙 a tie; 〘同点引き分け〙 a draw. ● 同点ゴール〖サッカー〗 equalizer, 〘まれ〙 leveller. ● 同点ホームランを打つ hit a (game-) *tying* homer. ● 彼と同点で首位を分け合う *tie* him for (the) first place. ● 同点になる点を阻止する save the *tying* run. ● 同点の均衡を破る得点 a *tiebreaker*; a *tiebreaking* run. ● 2 対 2 の同点に追いつく *tie* the score at two. ▶ドラゴンズはジャイアンツに 9 回裏で同点に追いついた The Dragons *tied* the Giants in the bottom of the ninth inning. ▶その得点で同点になった That point *tied* the score. ▶ point はバレーボール・バスケットボールなどの得点〕▶ソフトボールの試合の結果は 1 対 1 の同点だった The softball game ended in a *tie* [a *draw*], 1 to 1.
● 同点決勝戦 a play-off.

どうてん 動転 图 upset.
── 動転する 動 be upset. ▶その悲しい知らせに彼女はすっかり動転した The sad news *upset* her very much./She *was* very [terribly] *upset by* the sad news.

とうてんこう 東天紅 〖鳥〗 a totenko; (説明的に) a brown fowl 〘雄〕rooster》with a long tail.〖参考〗ニワトリの一種〗

とうど 凍土 frozen soil. ● 永久凍土地帯 (the) tundra /tʌ́ndrə/.

とうど 陶土 potter's clay; kaolin(e). 〖！後の方は磁器用の土〗

とうど 糖度 《a high》 sugar cóntent. 〖！content は「含有量」の意〗▶このリンゴの糖度は 16 パーセントです This apple has a *sugar content* of 16 percent./This apple contains 16 percent (natural) sugar.

とうとい 貴い, 尊い (貴重な) precious;（価値のある）valuable;（高貴な）noble;（神聖な）holy, sacred. ▶人の命は何よりも貴い Human life is the most *precious* thing./《やや書》Nothing is more *precious* than human life.

*とうとう（ついに）at last, 《書》at length;（最終的に）finally;（最後には）in the end 〖！以上の語は否定文では用いない〕;（結局）after all. 〖→遂に〕〖類語〕

とうとう 等々 and so on.（⇨など❶）

とうとう 滔々 ● とうとうと〘よどみなく〙述べる speak eloquently [*fluently*]. ▶その川はとうとうと〘＝勢いよく〕流れている The river flows *swiftly*.

どうとう 同等 图 equality.
── 同等の 形 equal 《to》;（相当の）equivalent 《to》.

どうとう

- 同等の人 one's equal. ● 同等のもの an equivalent. ● 同等の条件で on *equal* terms《with》. ● 高校卒業またはそれと同等の学歴を持っている者 those who have a high school diploma or its *equivalent*.

— 同等に 副 ● 彼らを同等に扱う treat them *equally* [as *equals*].

どうとう 堂塔 ● 堂塔伽藍(がらん) the main hall, pagoda, and other buildings of a Buddhist temple.

どうどう 堂々 — 堂々とした 形 [立派な] (雄大な) grand; (威圧するような) imposing; (威厳のある) dignified, stately. ● 堂々とした大邸宅 a *grand* [an *imposing*, a *stately*] mansion. (⇨マンション) ▶彼は堂々とした老紳士だ He is a *dignified* old gentleman. ▶顔を上げて堂々としていなさい Lift up your head and be *proud*.

— 堂々と 副 ❶ [立派に] grandly; (威風堂々と) majestically. ▶日本選手は堂々と入場行進した The Japanese players marched *grandly* onto the field. ▶何百年もの年月を経た歴史的建造物が夜明けの空に堂々とそびえている A historic building, hundreds of years old, stands *majestically* against a dawn sky.
❷ [恐れずに] (勇敢に) bravely; (公正に) fair (and square); (自信を持って) confidently. ▶彼は敵と堂々と戦った He fought the enemy *bravely* [(雄々しく) *heroically*]. ▶堂々と自分の意見は述べなさい Express your opinion *confidently* [*with* *confidence*].

どうどうめぐり 堂々巡り ▶我々はその問題で堂々巡りの議論をしているばかりだ We are only discussing *in* *circles*. ▶彼の頭の中では同じ考えが堂々巡りするばかりだった His mind *was going around in circles*./The same thought kept coming back in his mind.

****どうとく 道徳** 名 (社会的行動・慣習の基準) morals (❗ しばしば男女間の品行をさす); (道義) morality; (特定の集団・職業の) ethics (❗ 複数形による (⇨倫理)).
● 不道徳 immorality. ● 交通道徳 traffic *manners*. ● 公衆道徳を守る conform to public morals [*morality*]. ▶彼は道徳観念がない He has no *morals* [*moral sense*]./He is *amoral* /eɪmɔ́(:)rəl/. ▶このごろでは商道徳が特に低下している Business *morals* especially are low these days. ▶道徳は時代とともに変化する *Morality* changes with the times.

— 道徳的(な) 形 moral; (倫理的な) ethical. ● 道徳的退廃 *moral* decay. ▶あなたの行為は道徳的観点からすれば[道徳的に]正しくない Your action is wrong from a *moral* point of view./Your action is *immoral* [*morally* wrong]. (❗ immoral は男女間の不品行を暗示するため、職業倫理をさすときは代わりに unethical を用いることも多い)

● 道徳家 (時に軽蔑的) ▶ a moralist. ● 道徳教育 moral education. ● 道徳律 the moral standard [code].

とうとさ 貴さ, 尊さ ● 命の尊さ(=大切さ) the *preciousness* of life. ▶子供たちは農作業を体験することを通して労働の尊さを学びます Children learn the *value* of labor through exposure to farm work.

とうとつ 唐突 — 唐突な 形 (不意の) sudden; unexpected. ● 唐突な質問 an *unexpected* [a *sudden*] question.

— 唐突に 副 ● 唐突に(=不意に)その話を切り出す bring up the subject (quite) *unexpectedly* [*suddenly*].

とうとぶ 貴ぶ, 尊ぶ [[尊敬する]] respect; (尊敬して仰ぎ見る) look up to ...; [[尊重する]] respect; value.

とうどり 頭取 a president.

とうない 党内 ● 党内の争い *intraparty* squabbles [conflicts, strife].
● 党内右派 the rightist faction in the party.
● 党内左派 the leftist faction in the party.
● 党内事情 an intraparty situation; a political situation in the party. ● 党内派閥 intraparty factions.

どうなが 胴長 — 胴長の 形 long-torsoed. (⇨胴)
● 胴長で短足の犬 a dog with a *long body* and short legs.

とうなす 唐茄子 (⇨南瓜(かぼちゃ))

とうなん 東南 the southeast (略 SE). (❗語順に注意) (⇨東, 北西)

とうなん 盗難 [[窃盗]] (a) theft; [[不法目的侵入]] (a) burglary; [[強奪]] (a) robbery. (❗3 語とも盗難事件の意では C). ● 警察に車の盗難を届ける report to the police the *theft* of one's car. ● 盗難にあう (物が) be stolen; (人・場所が) be robbed (*of* one's money); (場所が)《米》be burglarized, 《主に英》be burgled.
● 盗難品 a (case of) theft [burglary, robbery]. ● 盗難被害者 a victim of theft. ● 盗難品 a stolen [×a taken] article;《集合的》stolen goods. (⇨盗品)

とうなんアジア 東南アジア Southeast Asia.
● 東南アジア諸国連合 the Association of Southeast Asian Nations (略 ASEAN).

とうなんとう 東南東 the east-southeast (略 ESE).

とうに a long time ago. (❗ とっく(に))

> **翻訳のこころ** 下人は、さっきまで、自分が、盗人になる気でいたことなぞは、とうに忘れているのである (芥川龍之介『羅生門』) *By now* the man has *already* forgotten that he was thinking about becoming a burglar until a little while ago. (❗ (1) 「とうに」は by now ... already (早くも...する)と表す。(2) a man には「下人, 召使い」の意がある)

どうにいる 堂に入る ▶彼女のフランス語は堂に入ったものだ(=実にうまい) She *has* an impressive [*a perfect*] *command* of French./She *is* quite at *home in* French.

どうにか (なんらかの方法で) somehow (or other), in some way (or other), 《米話》someway, (in) one way or another (⇨なんとか); (かろうじて) barely. ▶どうにか(して)あすまでにそこへ行こう I'll *get* there *somehow* (*or* *other*) [*manage to* get there (*somehow*)] by tomorrow. (❗ manage to taと「困難なことをうまくやりとげる」の意だが、manage 単独でも用いられる:「手伝いましょうか」「いいですよ, どうにかやれますから」"Do you want me to help you?" "No, thanks. I can *manage* (it).") ▶どうにか家に帰る金はある I have *barely* enough money to get [go] home. ▶100 万円ほどどうにかなりませんか(=何とか貸していただけませんか) Could you (*possibly*) lend me one million yen? (❗ possibly を用いるとさらに丁寧さが加わる)

どうにも ▶私はどうにも(=まったく)それが理解できない I *can't* understand it *at all*./I *simply* [《話》*just*] *can't* understand it. (❗ simply, just は否定語の前に置く) ▶こう暑くてはどうにもやりきれない This heat is *far* [《話》*way*] too much for me.
● どうにもならない ▶人間の力ではどうにもならない It's *beyond* human *control*./*There's no help for* it. ▶彼の病気はどうにもならない (治す方法がない) *There's no way to* cure his illness./(どうしようもない) Noth-

ing can be done about his illness./(治る見込みがない) He is *hopelessly* ill.
翻訳のこころ どうにもならないことを、どうにかするためには、手段を選んでいるいとまはない(芥川龍之介『羅生門』) This is no time to be choosing a method [a way] to manage to do what normally cannot be done. (**!**「…はどうにもならない[できない]」は … cannot normally be done (通常の方法では不可能である)と表す)

とうにゅう 投入 ── 投入する **動** •その事業に多額の資金を投入する *invest* a lot of money *in* the enterprise; *put* [*sink*] a lot of money *into* the enterprise. •紛争地域に軍隊を投入する《書》*commit* troops to the conflicting area.

とうにゅう 豆乳 soybean milk.

どうにゅう 導入 **名** introduction. •数学教育へのコンピュータの導入 the *introduction of* computers *into* math teaching.
── 導入する **動** •農業に新しい科学技術を導入する *introduce* new technology *into* farming. ▶鉄道会社は女性を痴漢から守るために女性専用列車を導入している To protect women from gropers, railroad companies have *introduced* [*allocated*] "women only" coaches [cars] in their trains. (**!**電車の個々の車両は train でなく coach や car) (**事myg*女性専用車両は米英ではあまり例がない)

| DISCOURSE |
LED はさまざまな製品に急速に導入された. 例えば信号機, 照明, 指示器などである LEDs have promptly begun to be *used* in a wide variety of products, **such as** traffic lights, illumination lights, indicator lights, and so on. (**!** such as (例えば)は具体例に用いるディスコースマーカー)

とうにょうびょう 糖尿病 **名** 〖医学〗diabetes /dàiəbíːtiːz/. (**!**単数扱い)
── 糖尿病の **形** diabetic.
•糖尿病患者 a diabetic; a person with *diabetes*. •糖尿病性網膜症〖医学〗diabetic retinopathy.

とうにん 当人 •当人(=彼ら, 当事者)同士で話し合う talk *about* the matter) between them (the *persons concerned* (**!**法律的な語)). •当人の(=その人自身の)意向を尊重する respect his [her] *own* wishes. ▶彼が問題の当人です He is the *person in question*. ▶当人(=同一人物)にまちがいないか Are you sure he [she] is the *same person*?

とうねん 当年 (今年) this year; (その頃) at that time. ▶彼女は当年とって二十歳(はたち)、もう一人前です She is twenty years old *this year*. She is an adult now.

どうねん 同年 the same year; (同じ年齢) the same age. (⇨同(どう)い年) •同年4月に in April of *the same year*.

どうねんぱい 同年配 •同年配の人 a person of the same age; (《話》around) one's age. ▶私たちは同年配です We are (*of*) *the same age*.

とうの 当の •当の本人(=問題になっている人)に尋ねる ask *the person in question*; (本人に) ask the person *himself* [*herself*]; ask him [her] *in person*. ▶当の本人(=彼[彼女])自身は気にしていない He *himself* [She *herself*] doesn't care.

どうの ▶彼女は彼の学歴がどうの収入がどうのと批判する She finds fault with his academic background and his income.

どうのこうの •彼の作品にどうのこうのとケチをつける *pick holes in* his work; *find fault with* his work.

翻訳のこころ うちの家族はアロエがどうのこうの言っている場合ではなくなってしまった(吉本ばなな『みどりのゆび』) The situation changed so that our family could no longer [not] be talking about *what we should do with the aloe*. (**!**「(アロエが)どうのこうの」は what we should do with the aloe (アロエをどうするか、どう処分するか)と表す)

とうのむかし 疾うの昔 ▶そのことはとうの昔に決着をつけたつもりだ I think we settled the matter *long ago*.

とうは 党派 (政党) a party; (派閥) a faction,《軽蔑的》a clique. •党派を組む establish a *party*; form a *faction* [a *clique*]. •党派に分かれる split into *factions*. •超党派外交 supra-party [nonpartisan] diplomacy.

とうは 踏破 ── 踏破する **動** •アフリカ大陸を踏破する *travel through* the continent of Africa *on foot*.

とうば 塔婆 ⇨卒塔婆(そとば).

どうはい 同輩 (同僚) a cólleague; (同等の人) one's equal;《書》(**!**通例複数形で).

とうはいごう 統廃合 **名** integration and closure.
── 統廃合する **動** •中央省庁を統廃合する *streamline* the central government offices.

とうばく 倒幕 ── 倒幕する **動** overthrow the Shogunate (government).

とうはつ 頭髪 hair (on the head). (**!**(1) 文脈があれば単に hair でよい. (2) 1本が問題のときは ⓒ)

とうばつ 討伐 **名** suppression;《書》subjugation. (**!**前の方は討伐の過程に, 後の方は結果に重点があある)
── 討伐する **動** suppress, subdue;《書》subjugate. •反乱軍を討伐する *suppress* [*subdue*] the rebellion.

とうばつ 盗伐 ── 盗伐する **動** cut down and steel trees [bamboos].

とうはん 登坂 ── 登坂する **動** climb a hill; walk [(車で) drive] uphill; go up a《steep》gradient [《米》grade].
•登坂車線 a (climbing) lane for slower traffic.
•登坂力 gradability.

とうはん 登攀 **名** climbing; (壁なの) scaling.
── 登攀する **動** climb (up) (Mt. Mckinley); scale (the south wall).
•登攀者 a climber. •登攀隊 a climbing party.

*****とうばん** 当番 (順番) one's turn; (義務) (a) duty (*to* do). •当番制で炊事をする *take turns* (*at* [*in*]) cooking; *take it in turns* to cook. •当番についている (警官・看護師などが当直で) be *on duty* (↔off duty). ▶私は炊事当番を忘れていた I forgot my *duty* to cook. ▶あした私は戸締まりの当番だ It's my *turn* to lock up the house tomorrow.
•当番表 a (duty) roster;《英》a rota.

とうばん 登板 **名** a mound appearance. ▶彼は20回の登板で7勝5敗だった He was 7-5 [seven-and-five] in 20 *appearances*.
── 登板する **動** pitch (a game); take* [go* up to] the mound; make a mound appearance. •救援投手を登板させる send a reliever to the rubber (**!**the rubber は「投手板」); put a reliever to pitch. ▶彼は30試合に登板した He *has pitched* [*hurled*, *tossed*] 30 games.

どうはん 同伴 •夫人同伴で *with* [*accompanied by*] one's wife. ▶子供は大人同伴のときのみ入場を許される Children are admitted on condition that they *are accompanied by* adults. (**!**映画入場者指定表示は《米》R (Restricted),《英》PG (Parental Guidance))
── 同伴する **動** 《やや書》accompany. ▶彼女は彼に

同伴して東京に行った She went to Tokyo *with him*./She *accompanied* him to Tokyo.
- 同伴者 one's companion [partner]; one's accompanying person.

どうばん 銅版, 銅板 a cópperpláte.
- 銅版画 a copperplate print. (⚠ plate に彫ったものは a copperplate engraving)

とうひ 当否 (正しいか否か) right or wrong; (適切さ) fitness,《書》propriety /prəpráiəti/. ▶ その措置の当否は疑問だ I doubt the *propriety* [*fitness*] of the measure./I doubt whether the measure is *proper or not*.

とうひ 逃避 图 (an) escape. ● 現実逃避者 an escapist.
— 逃避する 動 ● 不快な現実から逃避する *escape from* unpleasant reality.
- 逃避行 an escape journey. ● 逃避主義 escapism. ● 逃避文学 escapist literature.

とうひ 党費 (党の経費) party expenses; (党への納入金) a party membership fee.

とうひ 等比 (等しい比) (an) equal ratio. ● 等比級数《数学》a geometric(al) series. ● 等比数列《数学》a geometric(al) progression.

とうひ 頭皮 the scalp.
- 頭皮マッサージ scalp massage; friction.

とうひ 掉尾 ▶ 巨匠のピアノ演奏会がコンサートの掉尾を飾った The maestro brought the concert to successful *end* with his performance on the piano.

*とうひょう 投票 图 (a) vote; (無記名の) (a) ballot; (選挙での) poll (⚠ 通例 the 〜. 投票数の意では a 〜).

① 【〜投票】● 記名[無記名]投票 an open [a secret] *vote*. ● 無効投票 an invalid *vote*. ● 信任 [不信任]投票 a *vote* of confidence [nonconfidence]. ● 不在者投票 an absentee *vote* [*ballot*].

② 【投票〜】● 女性の投票権 the *vote* [*ballot*] *for* women; the woman's *voting* right. ▶ 総選挙の投票率は高かった[低かった] The *voter turnout* was high [low] in the general election./There was a heavy [a light] *poll* in the general election. ▶ 投票結果は真夜中までには判明するだろう The result of the *poll* will be known by the middle of the night. (⇨真夜中)

③ 【投票に[は, を, で]】● 第1回目の投票で on the first *ballot*. ● 投票に行く(＝投票所に行く) go to the *polls*; go to *vote*. ▶ もう投票はすみましたか Have you been to *vote* yet? ▶ その議案は投票に付された The bill came [went, was put] to the *vote*. ▶ 彼らは新しいキャプテンを選ぶために投票を行った They held a *ballot* to choose a new captain. ▶ その問題は投票で決められるだろう The matter will be decided *by vote* [*ballot*]./A *vote* will be taken *on* [*to decide*] the matter.

— 投票する 動 vote, ballot, give* one's vote [ballot]. ● 議案について投票する vote [take a vote] *on* a bill. ● 動議に賛成投票する vote [ballot] *for* (↔against) a motion. ● 投票してその決議案を否決する *vote down* the proposal. ▶ 彼はK氏に投票した He *voted* (*for*) Mr. K./彼は棄権した《話》/He *gave* his *vote* to [《やや書》*cast* his *vote for*] Mr. K./His *vote went to* Mr. K. ▶ 彼らは投票して会議の延期を決定した They *voted* to postpone the meeting./They *voted that* the meeting (《主に英》*should*) be postponed.

- 投票所 the polls;《米》a pólling plàce;《英》a pólling stàtion. ● 投票箱 a bállot bòx. ● 投票日 the vóting [pólling, eléction] dày. ● 投票用紙 a bállot (pàper). ● 投票用紙記入所 a vóting [《英》a pólling] bòoth.

とうひょう 灯標 〖航路標識の総称〗a light beacon [navigator].

とうびょう 投錨 图 (錨を)下ろす) anchoring.
— 投錨する 動 anchor; drop [cast, come to] (the, [ˈæn]) anchor.
- 投錨地 an anchorage.

とうびょう 闘病 ● 闘病生活を送る fight [battle] a disease; live under medical treatment.

どうひょう 道標 (案内標識) a signpost. (⚠ a guidepost は《古》)

どうびょう 同病 the same disease.
- 同病相憐(ｱﾜ)れむ Misery makes strange bedfellows.

とうひん 盗品 《集合的》stolen goods; (一つの) a stolen article.

とうふ 豆腐 *tofu* /tóufu:/, bean curd. ● 豆腐1丁 a block [a cake] of *tofu*. ● 湯[焼き; 揚げ]豆腐 boiled [broiled; deep-fried] *bean curd*. ● 高野豆腐 freeze-dried *bean curd*.
- 豆腐にかすがい like water off a duck's back; (効果がない) have no effect 《*on*》.
- 豆腐屋 a *tofu* maker [seller].

とうぶ 東部 the east; (東の地方) the eastern part; (米国の) the East. (⇨南部)
- 東部諸州 (米国の) the Eastern States.

とうぶ 頭部 頭部にけがをする be injured in [on] *the head*.

どうふう 同封 图 ● 同封の写真 an *enclosed* photo. ▶ 詳細については同封のパンフレットをご覧ください For further information, please refer the brochure *enclosed*.

— 同封する 動 enclose. ▶ 写真を1枚同封します I'm sending you a photo *with* this letter./ I *enclose* [I'm *enclosing*] a photo (*with* this letter). (⚠ (1)進行形にするとややくだけた言い方になる. (2) *Enclosed*, please find a photo./Please find *enclosed* a photo. は《英》でも今は特に堅い言い方に限られる)

- 同封物 an enclosure.

どうふく 同腹 ● 同腹の兄 a brother born of the same mother ● (父親の違う) a half brother.

*どうぶつ 動物 图 an animal; a beast; a brute.

<blockquote>
【使い分け】**animal** 広義で植物に対する動物をさすが, 日常語では狭義に人間に対する動物や哺乳(ﾎﾆｭｳ)類としての動物をさすことが多い.
beast, brute 人間以外の高等哺乳類を表すが, beast は文語的な語で, 大きく危険な動物, 特に四足獣をいうのに対して, brute は単に大きな動物をいい, 同情の意を込めて用いることが多い.
</blockquote>

- 愛玩(ｱｲｶﾞﾝ)動物 a pet (*animal*). ● 肉食[草食]動物 a carnivorous [a herbivorous] *animal*. ● 野生動物 wild *animals*. ● 下等[高等]動物 the lower [higher] *animals*. ▶ 人間は言葉を遣う唯一の動物だ Man is the only *animal* that talks.

— 動物の, 動物的な 形 animal. ● 動物の習性 *animal* behavior. ● 動物的本能 an *animal* instinct. ● 動物的な欲望(＝肉欲) *animal* desires.
- 動物愛好者 a zoophilia. ● 動物園 (⇨動物園)
- 動物学 zoology /zouíləʤi/. ● 動物学者 a zoologist. ● 動物虐待 zoosadism. ● 動物恐怖症 a zoophobia. ● 動物質 animal matter. (⚠「(食品が)動物質を含まない」は animal-free) ● 動物性食品 animal food. ● 動物病院 a veterinary /vétərənèri/ clinic; an animal medical center.

どうぶつえん 動物園 a zoo /zúː/ 《⊕ ~s》(!) zoological /zòuəládʒikəl/ gardens は今では動物園の名前に用いられている以外は《古》;《米》(ニューヨークの) the Wildlife Conservation Park;《英》(ロンドンの) the Zoo. ● 上野動物園 Ueno Zoo. ● 動物園へ行く go to the *zoo*.

***とうぶん** 当分 〖当分の間〗for the time being; 〖今のところは〗for the present; 〖しばらくの間〗for some time, for a while. ● 当分は働かなくても食っていける I can get along without working *for the time being* [*for the present*]. ● 当分雪は降るまい It won't snow *for some time*.

── 等分する 動 divide ... equally [into equal parts]. ● 利益を等分する *divide* [*share*] the profits *equally*. ● 財産を 2 等分する *divide* the fortune *into two equal parts* [*into halves*].

とうぶん 糖分 sugar. ● 糖分を控える(=糖の量を減らす) cut down (on) *sugar*;《やや書》reduce one's intake of *sugar*. ● 糖分抜きのダイエットをしている be on a *sugar*-free [a no-*sugar*] diet. ● 糖分の取りすぎはよくない It's not good to take too much *sugar*.

どうぶん 同文 the same sentence(s). ▶ 以下同文 (賞状を読むとき) The same message.

とうへき 盗癖 〖心理学〗kleptomania /klèptəméiniə/. ● 盗癖のある人〖心理学〗a klèptomániàc,《話》a klepto 《⊕ ~s》. ● 彼は盗癖がある He is a *kleptomaniac*./He has *kleptomaniac* tendencies./《米話》He has sticky fingers.

とうべん 答弁 an answer, a reply (!) 前の方が口語的);(説明) an explanation. ● 答弁を求める demand an *answer* 《of [*from*] him》; ask 《him》 for an *answer*. ● 答弁に窮する《やや書》be at a loss for an *answer* 〖(どう答弁するか) how to *answer*〗.

── 答弁する 動 answer; reply.

とうへんぼく 唐変木 (にぶい人への) a blockhead; (偏屈な人) a bigot. (!) ののしり言葉として用いる)

とうほう 当方 (!) 一人称代名詞で表す) ▶ 当方には(= 私どもに関する限り)異存はない As for us [For our part], we have no objection./(私どもの側に) There's no objection *on our part*.

とうほう 東方 the east.(⇨東) ▶ 彼は京都の東方およそ 10 キロの所に住んでいる He lives about ten kilometers *east of* [*to the east of*] Kyoto. (!) 前の方が口語的)

とうぼう 逃亡 图 (an) escape. ● 逃亡中の脱獄囚 an escaped prisoner *on the run*.

── 逃亡する 動 ● 刑務所から逃亡する escape [make an escape, run away] from prison. ● 西側へ逃亡する(=亡命する) defect to the West. ● 戦線から逃亡する desert from the front line.

● 逃亡者 a rúnawàoy; (脱獄後の) an escàpèe. ● 逃亡犯人 a fugitive from justice.

どうほう 同胞 (同国民) a (fellow) countryman [countrywoman] 《⊕ -men》;(同国人)《書》a compatriot /kəmpéitriət/. ● 海外の同胞 countrymen and countrywomen overseas [abroad].

とうほうけんぶんろく 『東方見聞録』 The Travels of Marco Polo. (参考) マルコ・ポーロの旅行記)

とうほく 東北 the northeast《略 NE》. (!) 語順に注意)(⇨東, 西東)

● 東北地方 the Tohoku district.

● 倒木 a fallen tree.

とうほくとう 東北東 the east-northeast《略 ENE》.

どうほこ 銅鉾 〖考古学〗a *dohoko*; (説明的に) a bronze pike in the *Yayoi* period.

とうほん 謄本 a certified copy. ● 戸籍謄本 a *full copy* of one's *family register*.

とうほんせいそう 東奔西走 ── 東奔西走する 動 (忙しく働く) busy oneself 《*doing*》; with》; (始終動いている) be always on the move.

どうまき 胴巻き a money belt.

どうまごえ 胴間声 ● 胴間声で in a thick, raucous voice.

どうまわり 胴回り a waist /wéist/. (⇨ウエスト)

とうみつ 糖蜜 《米》molasses 《単数扱い》;《英》treacle 《シロップ》syrup.

どうみても どう見ても ▶ 彼女は 30 歳だと言うが, どう見てもそうは思えない She says she is thirty, but, to [by, from], *áll appéarances*, she is not [can't be] so young [old]. (!) (1) 通例文頭または動詞の直後に置く. (2) but 以下は簡単に she *never looks so*. でもよい) ▶ どう見ても(=あらゆる観点から)彼の主張は正しい What he says is right *from all points of view*. ● 彼はどう見ても(=せいぜい)二流の作家だ He is a second-rate writer *at best*.

どうみゃく 動脈 〖解剖〗an artery /άːrtəri/. ● 大動脈 the main *artery*. (!) 比喩的にも用いる)

● 動脈血 arterial blood. ● 動脈硬化(症)《suffer from》hardening of the arteries;〖医学〗artèriosclerósis. ● 動脈瘤 (りゅう) 〖医学〗an aneurism /ænjərizm/. (!) aneurysm ともつづる) ● 脳動脈瘤が破裂して死ぬ die after rupture of a brain *aneurism*.

とうみょう 灯明 ● 灯明をそなえる offer [light] a votive candle.

● 灯台

とうみん 冬眠 图 hibernation /hàibərnéiʃən/. ● 冬眠からさめる awake from *hibernation*.

── 冬眠する 動 hibernàte (during the winter); (冬眠に入る) go into hibernation.

● 冬眠動物 a hibernant animal.

とうみん 島民 an islander; (島の人々) island people.

どうみん 道民 a citizen of Hokkaido; (全体) the citizens [people] of Hokkaido.

とうむ 党務 party affairs [duties].

***とうめい** 透明 图 transparency.

── 透明の 形 transparent《⇔opaque /oupéik/》;(澄んだ) clear. ● 半透明の translucent. ● 透明なガラス *transparent* glass. ● 透明な水 *clear* water.

● 透明度 (the degree of) transparency. ● 経済政策決定過程の透明度を高める promote *transparency* in economic policy making. ● 透明人間 an invisible person.

***どうめい** 同盟 an alliance. ● 日英同盟 the Anglo-Japanese *Alliance*. ● 2国 [3国]同盟 a dual [a triple] *alliance*. ● 同盟を結ぶ allý (oneself) [be allied] 《with, to》; form [enter into] an *alliance* 《with》.

● 同盟国 an ally /ǽlai/; an allíed country. (関連) 非同盟国 a non-allied country)

どうめい 同名 ● 同名の人 a person with *the same name*; (his) namesake.

どうめいし 動名詞 〖文法〗a gerund.

とうめん 当面 〖差し当たって〗for the present; for the time being. (⇨当分)

── 当面の 形 ● 当面の(=現在の)問題 the *present* problem; the problem *at hand*; the question *of the moment* [《書》*hour*]; (我々の直面している問題) the question (that) *we face* [《やや書》*are confronted with*]. ● 当面の(=差し迫った)仕事 urgent [pressing] business.

***どうも** ❶ 〖非常に〗very; very much; (本当に) really; (まったく) quite.

解説 時間に遅れたときなど、「どうもどうも」と日本語ではあとを言わないこともあるが、英語では I'm really sorry I've kept you waiting so long. などあとを補うことが必要. あるいは発想を変えて、(米・英人式に) Thank you very much for waiting so long. も可.

▶どうもすみません I'm *very* [*so*, 《話》*terribly*] sorry. (❗so は主に女性語) ▶どうもご親切さま How kind of you!/It's *very* kind of you! ▶どうもあきれたやつだ He's *really* [*quite*] a fool. ▶どうも困った I'm *really* [*quite*] in trouble./《話》I'm in a *real* [a *nice*] fix. (❗nice は反語的) ▶本当にどうもありがとう (ありがとう) I can't thank you more.

会話 「うちのパーティーにいらっしゃいませんか」「それはどうも. 喜んでお伺いします」"Would you like to come to our party?" "Oh [Why], thank you *very much*. We'd be delighted [glad] to."

会話 「すてきなお宅ですね」「どうも(=気に入っていただいてうれしいです)」"What a nice house!" "I'm glad you like it."

会話 「郵便局ですか. よく分からないんです. すみません」「いや、どうも」"The post office? Sorry, I'm not really sure." "Well, *thanks* anyway."

❷【なんとなく】▶どうも時計の調子がよくない *Something* is wrong [There is *something* wrong] with the watch. ▶どうも彼にはおかしなところがある There is *something* strange [×strange *something*] about him. ▶どうも雨になりそうだ (おそらく) It's *likely* to rain./It *looks like* rain. ▶(いずれも単に予想を表す)/*I'm afraid* it will rain. (❗I'm afraid はよくないことを述べる際に発言を和らげるのに用いられる) (⇨【次例】)

会話 「私たちは遅刻でしょうか」「どうもそのようです」"Are we (going to be) late?" "*I'm afraid* so./I *suppose* so." (❗suppose は think より意味が弱い. I suppose so. はしぶしぶ同意を示す)

会話 「学校はどう?」「どうもあまり調子がよくないわ」"How's school going?" "I don't *feel like* I'm doing well." (❗feel like は「…のような気がする」の意で feel as if に対する《米話》)

❸【どういうわけか】somehow. ▶どうも彼女が好きになれない *Somehow* I don't like her./(あまり好きではない) I don't *really* like her. ▶どうもそのことについては自信がありません I'm *not so* [*quite*] sure about it. ▶どうも行く気がしない I'd *rather* not go.

❹【どうしても】▶どうもしかたがない It can't be helped. ▶どうもうまくできない (いかに努力しても) However hard I (may) try, I can't do it well. (❗may を用いるのは文語的)/(まったく) I *just* can't do it well. (❗just は否定語の前に置いてこれを強調)

どうもう 獰猛 图 (獰猛さ) ferocity; fierceness.
— **獰猛な** (荒々しい) fierce; (血に飢えたような) ferocious; (残忍な) savage. ● 獰猛なトラ a *fierce* [a *ferocious*, a *savage*] tiger.

とうもく 頭目 a leader; a boss; (首謀者) a ringleader.

どうもと 胴元 a banker; a bookmaker, 《話》a bookie.

とうもろこし 《米》 corn (❗《英》でも sweetcorn という品種に人気があるよ), (英) maize. ● トウモロコシ 1 本 [2 本] an ear [two ears] of *corn*; (軸つきトウモロコシ) a *corn* on the cob [two *corn* on the cobs]. ● トウモロコシの皮をむく shuck *corn*.

どうもん 同門 ● 同一の弟子 a fellow student [pupil]. ● 同門のよしみ (やや古) fellowship.

とうや 当夜 (その夜) that evening [night]; 《on》that particular evening [night]; (今夜) this evening; tonight. (❗evening と night を含む)

とうや 陶冶 — **陶冶する** 動 ● 人格を陶冶する *build up* [*develop, improve, train*] one's character.

とうやく 投薬 — **投薬する** 動 give [《書》administer] medicine 《to a patient》; (処方する) prescribe medicine (for a patient).

どうやら ❶【どうにかして】somehow (or other). ▶どうやら間に合った I *somehow* got there in time./(やっと間に合った) I *managed to* get there in time.
❷【様子を見ていると】なんとなく ▶どうやら君は私を仕事の鬼としか思っていないようだが、私だって家庭は大事にしているよ *Apparently*, [*It appears that*] you think of me only as a demon worker. Well, I am also a family man. ▶どうやら(=どうも)雨になりそうだ (⇨どうも❷) ▶その顔つきからすると、どうやら試合に負けたようだね(=推察する) I *gather*, from your looks, you lost the game.

とうゆ 灯油 kérosene, 《英》páraffin (oil).

どうゆう 同憂 ● 同憂の士 (同じように心配している人) those who are concerned about 《falling standards in education》.

とうよ 投与 (⇨投薬) ● 薬の大量投与 a massive *dose* /dóus/ of medicine.

*****とうよう** 東洋 图 the East (❗「東欧」「米国東部」の意もあるので注意); 《書》the Orient.
— **東洋の, 東洋的な** 形 Eastern; Oriental. ● 東洋の風俗 the *Eastern* manners. ● 東洋の神秘 the mystery of the *Orient*. ● 東洋的な考え方 an *Oriental* way of thinking.
● 東洋医学 Oriental medicine. ● 東洋史 Oriental history. ● 東洋諸国 the Eastern [Oriental] countries. ● 東洋人 (軽蔑的・やや古) an Oriental (❗特に日本人・中国人をさす); (総称) the Orientals. ● 東洋美術 Oriental art(s). ● 東洋風[趣味] Orientalism. ● 東洋文明 Oriental civilization.

とうよう 当用 (日常的に使う) for daily use, daily.
● 当用漢字 *toyokanji*, (説明的に) Chinese characters selected for daily use. ● 当用日記 (日付のある日記) a jotter's diary.

とうよう 盗用 图 《文章・アイディアなどの》(a) plagiarism. (⇨盗作) ▶彼の論文の一部は私の論文からの盗用だ He *plagiarized* [*stole*] part of his thesis *from* my thesis.
— **盗用する** 動 plagiarize; steal.

とうよう 登用 (任用) (an) appointment.
— **登用する** 動 ▶彼を支配人に登用する *appoint* him manager; (昇進させる) *promote* him to manager. (❗後の言い方は通例受身で用いる) ▶若い人材を登用する(=雇う) *employ* young talents.

*****どうよう** 同様 — **同様の** 形 (同一の) the same; (似ている) similar. (⇨同じ)

①【同様の〜】● 同様の仕方で in a *similar* manner [*way*]. ● 同様の境遇にいる be in a *similar* situation; be similarly situated. ▶同様のことが多くの他の学生についてもいえる *The same* (thing) can be said of many other students.

②【…と[も] 同様に】▶病人(の容体)は 1 週間前とほとんど同様です The patient is *almost the same as* (he was) a week ago. ▶私も同様です It's *the same with* me. (❗with は「…に関しても」の意)/《話》*Same* here. ▶父はスポーツが好きですが、私も同様です My father is fond of sports, *and so am* I [*and I am, tóo*]. (⇨又) ▶彼は酒もたばこもやりません. 私も同様です He *neither* drinks *nor* smokes, *and neither* do I [*and I don't, either*]. ▶彼は兄たちと同様頭がよい He is *as* bright *as* his brothers./*Like* his brothers he is a bright boy./(劣らず同様) He is *no less* bright *than* his brothers.

▶私はお前と同様ばかでない I am *no more* foolish *than* you are. ▶家内も私も同様がとても気に入ってます My wife likes it *as* much *as* I do. ▶まだ1,000キロしか走っていないからその車は新品同様(=実質的には新品)です With only 1,000 kilometers on it, the car is *practically* [*as good as*] new. 会話「イタリアでは職業を持つ女性が増えています」「日本でも同様です」"More and more women are having jobs [are working] in Italy." "*The same* in Japan."

── 同様に 副 (同じように) similarly; (…のように) like …; (等しく) equally; (同じ方法で) in the same way. ▶外国語を学ぶのは容易ではない。同様に外国の風習になじむのには時間がかかる Learning a foreign language is not easy. *Similarly*, getting familiar with the customs of another country takes time. ▶彼はその孤児を自分の子供同様に世話した He looked after the orphan *just like* his own child./(まるで自分の子みたいに) He took care of the orphan *as if* he were [《話》was] a child of his own.

*どうよう 動揺 图 (社会・心をかき乱すこと) (a) disturbance; (不満足・怒りなどによる) unrest. ●政治的動揺を招く produce political *unrest* [a political *disturbance*]. ●心の動揺を静める calm [《やや書》compose] oneself.

── 動揺する 動 (突然心の平静を失う) be shaken (up); (平安を乱される) be disturbed; (取り乱す) be upset. ▶彼はその知らせにひどく動揺した He was badly shaken (up) by [at, with] the news. (【】byが最も普通)/He was very disturbed by [at, to hear] the news./He was very upset by [to hear] the news.

── 動揺させる 動 shake*; disturb; upset*.

どうよう 童謡 (子供向けの歌) a children's song; (英米の伝承的な) a núrsery [《主に米》a Mòther Góose] rhỳme. (【】「童謡集」の意では(a book of) nursery rhymes,《集合的》Mother Goose が用いられる)

とうらい 到来 〖来ること〗coming;〖到着〗arrival;〖特に重要な事柄・人などの〗the advent (*of*). ●春の到来 the *coming* [*arrival, advent*] of spring. ●新時代の到来 the *coming* [*advent*] of a new age. ●時節の到来を待つ wait (for) one's chance. (【】wait のみを用いたときは「好機・時などが来るのに備えて待機する」の意) ▶好機到来だ A good chance *has come*./Here's our chance.

── 到来物 (もらい物) a present [a gift] (received from Mr. Tanaka).

とうらく 当落 ▶当落(=選挙の結果)はすぐ判明するでしょう The *results of the election* [The *election results*] will be known soon. ▶彼の当落(=当選か落選か)はまだ分かっていない His *success or failure in the election* is not yet known. ▶彼女は当落線上にある She is *straddling the thin line between victory and defeat*./(選ばれる率が五分五分である) She has *a fifty-fifty chance of being elected*./She is *a borderline* candidate.

とうらく 騰落 〖物価の騰貴と下落〗rise and fall; fluctuations.

どうらく 道楽 ❶〖放蕩(ホッ)〗《書》dissipation. ●道楽をする(放蕩の生活をする) lead a *loose and dissolute* life; (若気の至りで)《話》sow one's (wild) oats.

❷〖趣味〗a hobby; (時間つぶしの娯楽) a pastime. ●道楽に切手収集をする collect stamps *as a pastime* [*at leisure*]. ▶私の道楽は料理と魚釣りです My *hobbies* are cooking and fishing.

●道楽息子《書》a profligate /práfligət/ son. (⇨ど ら息子) ●道楽者《やや書》a libertine; a loose [a fast] liver.

どうらん 胴乱 a vasculum.

どうらん 動乱 (平和の乱れ) (a) disturbance; (激変) (an) upheaval. ●イランの動乱 the *disturbance* [*upheaval*] in Iran. ●動乱のアジア war-[strife-] torn Asia.

とうり 党利 party interests. ●党利党略に走る put *party interests* first; (特定の主義にかたよった政治をする) play partisan politics.

:どうり 道理 图 〖理屈〗reason,《話》logic (⇨理屈); 〖思慮分別〗sense.

①【道理に】●道理に合った reasonable; sensible. ●道理に合う be reasonable; stand to *reason*. ●道理に反した unreasonable; senseless. ●道理に反する be unreasonable; be against [contrary to] *reason*. ▶彼の言ったことはある意味で道理にかなっている What he said, in a sense, *makes sense*.

②【道理を】●道理を聞き分ける listen to *reason*. (【】助言などに従うこと) ▶彼は物の道理をわきまえている(何が大切であるか分かっている) He knows what's what. /(道理をわきまえた人) He's a *reasonable* [a *sensible*] person. ▶少しは道理をわきまえなさい ╲Have some ╱ *sense*.╱Now be *reasonable*.╱Don't be so *unreasonable*.╱Why don't you be *reasonable*? (【】いら立った表現)

③【道理だ】▶彼女が怒るのも道理だ (十分な理由がある) She *has every* [(a) *good*] *reason to be angry* [*of getting* angry, *that* she got angry]./(もっともだ) She *may well* get [be] angry.

── 道理で ▶どうりで彼は忙しいわけだ(それが理由を説明する) That explains why he is so busy. (【】会話では2文に分けて That explains it. He's so busy. ということも多い)/(それで理由が分かった) Now I see why he is so busy. ▶どうりで(=当然)テレビがつらいはずだ。電源が入ってないんだもの *No wonder* the TV doesn't work; it hasn't been plugged in. (【】(It's) no wonder (that)… の(　)内が省略されたもの)

とうりつ 倒立 图 a handstand; (頭と両手をつけてする倒立) a headstand.

── 倒立する 動 do a handstand [a headstand]; stand on one's hands [head].

どうりつ 同率 the same percentage [rate]. ●同率で首位に立つ rise to the top with *the same* winning *percentage*.

どうりつ 道立 ●道立 A 高等学校 Hokkaido Prefectural A High School.

とうりゃく 党略 (⇨党利)

とうりゅう 逗留 图 (滞在) a stay.

── 逗留する 動 stay (*at*). ●伊豆の宿屋に長逗留する make a *long stay* at a hotel in Izu.

とうりゅうもん 登竜門 a gateway to success. ▶芥川賞は日本の文壇への登竜門だ The Akutagawa Prize is the *gateway* to the literary world in Japan.

とうりょう 投了 ── 投了する 動 admit (-tt-) oneself beaten [defeated]; admit (one's) defeat; (碁・将棋で) give up the game.

とうりょう 棟梁 a master carpenter.

とうりょう 等量 an equal amount [quantity]. ●等量に分ける share *the same amount* each.

とうりょう 頭領 a leader; a head; a boss.

どうりょう 同僚 a co-worker, a fellow worker; (主に専門職の) one's colleague. (⇨仕事, 仲間) ▶こちらが同僚の磯崎でございます This is Miss Isozaki, a *colleague from work*. (❗) .... She *works with*

どうりょく 動力 (motive) power. ●太陽電池を動力として使う use solar batteries for *power*.
● 動力芝刈機 a power(-driven) mower; an engine-powered mower. ●動力車 (機関車) a railroad engine. (⇨機関車) ●動力炉 a power reactor.

どうりん 動輪 a driving wheel.

とうるい 盗塁 图 〖野球〗a steal; a stolen base; base-stealing. ●盗塁を15回試みて10回成功する be successful on ten of fifteen *steal* attempts.
── 盗塁する 動 steal (a base). ●二塁 [本塁]へ盗塁する *steal* second [home]. ●200盗塁する *steal* 200 *bases*. ●盗塁に失敗する be caught *stealing*. ●盗塁王 a stolen base king [champion]. ●盗塁死 caught stealing.

どうるい 同類 〖同じ種類〗the same kind [class]; 〖仲間〗an associate, (共謀者) an accomplice. ●同類項〖数学〗a similar [a like] term.

とうれい 答礼 图 a return salute. ●彼を答礼訪問する make a return call on him.
── 答礼する 動 return [answer] the salute. ▶私がおじぎをすると，彼は帽子を傾けて答礼した When I bowed, he tipped his hat *in return*.

どうれつ 同列 (同じ等級) the same rank [level]. ▶私をあんなやつらと同列に考えないでくれ Don't *rank* me among the lot of them. (❗ The lot of them は all of them の意の口語的慣用句)

どうろ 道路 a road; (街路) a street; (都市を結ぶ幹線道路) 《主に米》a highway. (⇨道❶) ●舗装道路 a paved road. (❗舗装されていない道路は an unpaved *road*, 《米》 a dirt *road*.) ●有料道路 a toll road. ●合流[交差]する道路 merging [intersecting] roads. ●道路沿いの建物 a building *on* the *road* [*street*]. (❗on の代わりに along を用いると長く伸びている建物を暗示する．複数の建物が並んでいる場合は along の方が好まれる) ●道路を作る[建設する] make [build] a *road*. ●道路を横断する cross a *road* [a *street*]; walk across a *road* [a *street*]. ●道路の右側を歩く walk on the right side of the *road*. ▶道路が開通した[閉鎖された] The *road* was opened [was blocked] to traffic. ▶最新の道路網が主要工業地帯を結んでいる A network [A mesh] of modern *highways* connects [×is connecting] all major industrial centers.
● 道路工事 (修理) road repairing; (建設) road construction [works]. ●道路工夫 a roadman. ●道路情報 traffic [route] information. ●道路地図 a road map (本になったものは a road atlas); (市街地図) a city map. ●道路標識 a road sign.

とうろう 灯籠 a lantern; (特に庭などの) a garden lantern. ●石灯籠 a stone *lantern*. ●つり灯籠 a hanging *lantern*.
● 灯籠流し *toronagashi*; (説明的に) the custom of floating paper lanterns lighted with candles on a river or the sea at the end of the *Bon* festival.

とうろう 蟷螂 (⇨かまきり)
● 蟷螂の斧を振るう (自分の非力を顧みずに強い相手に歯向かう) fight against the stronger regardless of one's poor ability; (むだ骨を折る) throw straws against the wind.

***とうろく** 登録 图 (a) registration; 〖帳簿・表などへの記入〗(a) register, (an) entry. ●住民登録 resident *registration*. ●商標登録 the *registration* of a trademark. (❗「商標登録する」は *register* a trademark) ●クラスの登録 the enrollment for [×of] a class. ●住所氏名の登録が必要です The *register* of your name and address is required. ▶登録済み (標示) Registered.
── 登録する 動 register (for, with). ●特許局に登録する *register* (it) *with* the Patent Office. ▶履修する科目を登録しなければなりません You must *register* 〖《米》*sign up*〗 *for* the courses you are going to take. ▶彼は医者として登録されている He *is registered as* a doctor.
● 登録者 a registrant. ●登録商標 a registered trademark (記号 ®). ●登録制 a registration system. ●登録選手名簿 a roster. ●登録番号 a registration number. ●登録簿 a register. ●登録料 a registration fee.

***とうろん** 討論 图 (賛否対立の正式な) (a) debate; (議論) (a) discussion. (⇨議論) ●テレビ討論会 a TV *debate*. ●パネル討論会 a panel *discussion*. ●公開討論会を打ち切る close a *forum*. ●討論 (会) を have [hold] a *debate* (on politics). ▶新空港を建設すべきか否かをめぐって激しい討論が戦わされた Whether to build a new airport or not was hotly [heatedly] *debated*.
── 討論する 動 debate (on [about]…); discuss. ●その問題について彼と討論する *debate* (*about*) the question *with* him; *discuss* 〖×discuss about〗 the question *with* him.

どうわ 同和 ●同和教育 social integration education; education for removing [getting rid of] social discrimination.

どうわ 童話 (おとぎ話) a fairy tale [story]; (子供向きの話) a children's story.
● 童話作家 a writer of children's stories.

とうわく 当惑 图 puzzlement, 《書》perplexity; (a) confusion; bewilderment; embarrassment. ●当惑の種 a perplexity; an embarrassment. ●当惑の表情を浮かべている have a puzzled [a bewildered] expression on one's face (❗a puzzling [a bewildering] expression は他の人を当惑させるような表情); look puzzled [bewildered].
── 当惑する 動 (理解できなくて) be puzzled [《書》perplexed] (by, about); (考えが混乱して) be confused (by, at); be bewildered (by, at) (❗後の方が強意的); (気まずくて，恥ずかしくて) be embarrassed (at, by). ▶私はいくぶん当惑して彼を見た I looked at him in some *puzzlement* [*bewilderment*]. ▶彼女は彼の態度にひどく当惑していた She *was* very *puzzled* [*confused, embarrassed*] *by* his attitude. (❗受身的な意味が強いときは (very) much で修飾される)/His attitude was very *puzzling* [*confusing, embarrassing*] *to* her. ▶どう答えてよいか当惑した I *was at a loss* for an answer./I *was puzzled* (*about*) [I *was at a loss*] *what to* answer. (❗ puzzle を用いる方が口語的)

とえい 都営 ── 都営の 形 (Tokyo) Metrópolitan.
● 都営地下鉄 a Tokyo Metropolitan subway. ●都営バス a Tokyo Metropolitan bus.

とえはたえ 十重二十重 ●十重二十重に取り囲む crowd closely together around 《a star player》.

どえらい ど偉い (ものすごい) tremendous; (驚くほどの量 [額]) staggering; (信じられないほど) fabulous; (とてつもない) stupendous. (❗以上いずれも 《話》) ●どえらいスピードで at a *tremendous* speed. ●どえらい間違いをする make a *stupendous* mistake. ●どえらい美人 a *stunning* beauty.

とお 十 ten. (⇨三つ)

とおあさ 遠浅 ▶海は遠浅になっている(=岸から相当の距離まで浅い) The sea is *shallow* for a *good* [*for some*] *distance* from the shore.

とおい 遠い far*; a long way (off [away]); distant, far-off, faraway; remote.

> 使い分け far 漠然と遠く離れていることを表す。通例否定文・疑問文で用いるが, too, so, as, very, away, off などを伴うときは肯定文でも用いられる.
> **a long way (off [away])** ある場所でかなりの距離あることを表す。肯定文で用いる.
> **distant** 簡単に到達できない非常に大きな空間の隔たりを表す.
> **far-off, faraway** far を強めた形で限定的に用いられるやや堅い語.
> **remote** 地理または生活空間の視点から隔たりが大きいことを表す.

● **[距離が]** ▶遠い国 a *far-off* [a *distant*, a *remote*] country (!今日では ×a far country とはいわない; a country *a long way off* [*far away*]). ▶私の家は駅から遠い My house is *a long way* (*off* [*away*]) *from* the station. (!My house is *far* [*distant*] *from* the station. とはしない)/It's *a long way to* my house *from* the station. ▶「to+場所」が続くときは off, away をつけない/My house is *a great* [*a long*] *distance* from the station. ▶月は地球から遠い The moon is *distant from* the earth. (!このように絶対的遠方を表す場合は distant を用いる) ▶東京は京都より遠い Tokyo is *farther* [《主に英》 *further*] *away* than Kyoto.

会話 「事務所はここから遠いのですか」「いいえ遠くはありません」 "Is the office *far from* here?" "No, it's not *far*."

❷ **[時間]** distant; remote. ● 遠い過去に in the *distant* [*far-off*, *remote*] past; *far* in the past. ▶彼が大統領に選ばれるのもそう遠いことではないでしょう 《主に書》 It won't be so *long before* he is [×will be] elected president./(近い将来に) He will be elected president *in the near future*.

❸ **[関係, 程度]** ▶彼女は私の遠い親戚(ﾘｭｳ)だ She is a *distant* [a *remote*] relative of mine. (!×my distant relative は不可) ▶彼は幸福からほど遠い He is *far from* (*being*) happy. (=being は通例省略する)/(まったく幸福でない) He is *not* happy *at all*. (⇨少しも) ▶彼の説明は真実にはほど遠い His explanation is *far* [*a long way*] *from* the truth.

トーイック [[国際コミュニケーション英語能力テスト]]《商標》TOEIC /tóuik/《*T*est *o*f *E*nglish for *I*nternational *C*ommunication の略》.

とおえん 遠縁 a distant relationship. ▶彼女は私の遠縁に当たる She is *distantly* related to [*connected with*] me./She is a *distant* [a *remote*] *relative* of mine.

とおか 十日 ▶十日間 for *ten* days. ● 十日間の休暇 a *ten-day* vacation. ● 5月10日に on May *10*(*th*). (⇨日付)

とおからず 遠からず （間もなく） soon, before long, shortly. （⇨間もなく） ▶新しい幹線道路は遠からず完成するでしょう The new highway will be completed *soon* [(近い将来に) *in the near future*]./《主に書》 It will not be *long before* the new highway is completed.

トーキー a talkie (↔silent film).

*__**とおく 遠く**__ ❶ **[距離が]** **a** (great [a long]) distance. (⇨遠い [類語])

① **【遠く(の)】** （場所が） distant; far-off, 《やや書》 faraway. ● 遠くの村 a *far-off* [a *distant*] vil-

lage; a village *a long way off* [*far away*]. ▶私は眼鏡がないと遠くの物が見えない I can't see *distant* objects without glasses.

② **【遠くに[へ, で, まで]】** ▶両親は遠くに住んでいます My parents live *a long way off* [*far away*, *far off*]. (!×live far [*in the distance*] は不可) ▶(はるか)遠くに明かりが見えた I saw a light *in the* (*far*) *distance*. (!in the distance は漠然と見える[聞こえる]範囲に用いる) ▶彼はできるだけ遠くへ逃げた He fled as *far away* as possible. (!この例のように遠さを強調するときは away は省略不可) ▶どこか遠くで犬の鳴き声がしていた Somewhere *far off* [*in the distance*], a dog was barking. ▶その子はどれくらい遠くまで行きましたか How *far* did the child go? (!単に距離を問う場合は Hòw fár...?, 遠くへ行ったことが前提にあってその距離を問う場合は Hów fàr...? のように発話される) ▶私は健二より遠くまで泳げる I can swim *farther* [《英》 *further*] than Kenji.

③ **【遠くから】** ▶遠くからいらしたのですか Have you come *a long way*? ▶塔は遠くから見えた The tower could be seen *from a long way off* [*from a distance*, *from far* (*away* [*off*])], 《書》 *from afar*].

❷ **[程度が]** ▶テニスでは彼に遠く及ばない He is *much* [*far*, *even*] better at tennis than I am [《話》 than me, 《古・書》 than I]. (!いずれも比較級を強める)

● 遠くの親戚(ﾘｭｳ)より近くの他人 ▶いざという時に頼りになるのは遠くの親戚より近くの他人である It's a near neighbor rather than a relative living *a long way off* who I can rely on for help when I need. (!「It ... who」節の強調構文)

トークショー 《米》 a talk show; 《英》 a chat show.

トーゴ [[国名]] Togo /tóugou/; 《公式名》 the Republic of Togo. (首都 Lome) ● トーゴ人 a Togolese /tòugouliːz/. ● トーゴ(人)の Togolese.

とおざかる 遠ざかる ❶ **[離れていく]** go* away; （船が） sail away; （車が） drive* away; （音が） die (～d; dying) [fade] away. ▶その人の姿は暗やみの中へ遠ざかっていった She *went away* [姿を消した) *disappeared*] into the darkness. ▶車の音は遠ざかって聞こえなくなった The sound of the car *died* (*away*) *in the distance*.

❷ **[近寄らない]** keep* [stay] away 《*from*》; (かかわりを持たないでいる) stay out 《*of*》. ● 悪友から遠ざかっている keep *away from* [(避ける) *avoid*] 《×a) bad company. ● けがで2か月間試合から遠ざかっている *be out of* games for two months through injury. ▶私はここしばらく数学から遠ざかっている I've been *away from* math 《米》 [maths 《英》] for a while.

とおざける 遠ざける [[近寄らせない]] keep* 《him》 away. ● 人を遠ざけて(=秘密で)話をする have a talk *behind closed* [*locked*] *doors*; have a *private* [×a closed-door] *talk*. ● 彼を都会生活から遠ざける (=疎遠にさせる) *estrange* /istréindʒ/ him *from* city life. ▶あの連中を遠ざけておきなさい *Keep* them *away* 《*from* you》./*Keep* them *at a distance*./(避けよ) *Avoid* them.

とおし 通し ● 通し切符 a through ticket. ● 通し番号 a serial [a consecutive] number. (⇨連番) ▶...に 1 から 50 まで通し番号をふる *number*... *consecutively* from 1 to 50.

-どおし -通し [[...し続ける]] keep* (on) doing (動作の継続を表す); [いつも...してばかりいる] be always doing (!習慣的行為を表し, 通例非難の意を含む). ● 夜通し看護する nurse 《him》 *all night* [*all through the night*, *throughout the night*]. (!単

の二つの方が強意的)▶彼は死ぬまで働き通しだった He *kept* (*on*) *working* till the end of his life. ▶電車がとても混んでいたので3時間立ち通しでした The train was so crowded that I *had to stand* [I *stood*] for three hours. (**!** 日本語につられて …I (was) kept standing という言い方は不自然 (⇒立つ❶))
▶彼女は愚痴の言い通しだった She *was always* complaining.

:**とおす 通す, 透す** ❶ [通らせる] (通過させる) let*... pass; (穴・門などを) pass [let]... through; (道をあける) make* way 《*for*》. ●針(の穴)に糸を通す *pass* [*draw*] *a thread through* (*the eye of*) *a needle*; *thread a needle*. ●上着のそでに手を通す *put one's arms* [×*hands*] *through the sleeves of a jacket*. ●カードを磁気読み取り機に通す *pass a card through a swipe*; (*a plastic*) *card*. ▶通してください *Let me pass* [*through*], *please*./May I *get through* (*me*, *please*?/Make *way*, *please*./Excuse *me* (私が人の前を通るときのあいさつ). ▶群衆は救急車を通すために道をあけた The crowd *made way for the ambulance*.
❷ [通わせる] ● A-B間にバスを通す(= 運行を開始する) *start a bus service between A and B*. ●床下にパイプを通す(= 伸ばす) *run pipes under the floor*. ●森に新しい道を通す *build* [*open*, ×*make*] *a new road through a forest*.
❸ [無事に通過させる] pass. ●議案を通す *pass the bill*; (反対などにもかかわらず) *get the bill through*. ▶試験官は応募者全員を通した The examiners *passed* all the applicants.
❹ [案内する] show*... in. (**!** 単に「中に入れる」なら let*... in (⇒入れる)) ▶お客様をお通ししなさい *Show the guests in*. ▶彼は居間へ通された He *was shown* [*let*] *into the living room*.
❺ [入り込ませる] let*... through [in]; (熱・電気などを伝える) conduct. ●部屋に風を通す *let air into a room*; (換気する) *air* [*ventilate*] *a room*. ▶この布は水を通さない This cloth *does not let* water *through*; (防水加工してある) *is waterproof*]. (⇒通る)/This cloth will *keep out* water. ▶この窓は十分な光を透す This window *lets enough light through*./This window *lets in* [*admits*] *enough light*. ▶銅は電気を通す Copper *conducts* [*transmits*] *electricity*./Copper *is a conductor* of *electricity*.
❻ [終わりまで続ける] (...のままでいる) keep*, remain. (⇒通し) ●会議中沈黙を通す *keep* [*remain*] *silent during a meeting*. ●書類に目を通す *look through* [*over*] *the paper*. (**!** through は終わりまでとわたり見る, over はざっと見ること) ●仕事をやり通す *carry the work through*. (**!** 困難さを暗示) ▶彼は30代まで独身で通した He *remained single* [*unmarried*] *until he was in his thirties*. ▶私はその本を読み通した I *read the book through*.
❼ [思いどおりにする] ●我を通す(= 自分の思うようにする) *have* [*get*] *one's* (*own*) *way*. ●意見を通す(= に固執する) *stick to* [頑固に] *persist in*] *one's opinion* ▶君は行動に筋を通さねばならない You must *be consistent in* your actions.
❽ [手段・道具などを介して] through (**!** through などの前置詞によって表される) ●英語を通して理解し合う *understand each other through English*. ●望遠鏡を通して月を見る *look at the moon through a telescope*. ●弁護士を通して彼と交渉する *talk to him through a lawyer*; *have a lawyer negotiate with him* 《*for me*》. ▶その音は壁を通してかすかに私

の耳に届いた The sound came to me faintly *through* the wall. ▶彼はテレビを通して国民に訴えた He appealed to the nation *on* TV.

トースター a toaster. ●オーブントースター《米》a *toaster* oven. (**!** 語順に注意) ●トースターでパンを焼く bake (×a) toast in a *toaster*; toast bread.

トースト toast. ●トーストになる *toast* (*bread*). ●バターをつけた[何もつけない]トースト toast buttered [dry] *toast*. ▶朝食はトーストを2枚食べた I had two pieces [slices] *of toast* for breakfast. (**!** ×two *toasts* は不可)

とおせんぼう 通せん坊 ●両手を広げて通せん坊する *stand in* [*block*]《*his*》*way spreading one's arms*.

トータル [合計] the total, the sum. (⇒合計) ●トータルなとらえ方をする see《the problem》*from all angles* [*directions*]; look at (it) *as a whole*.
●トータルファッション an ensemble.

トーチ (たいまつ) a torch; (聖火) the Olympic torch.
●トーチランプ (携帯用バーナー)《米》a blowtorch, a torch;《英》a blowlamp.

トーチカ [<ロシア語][小要塞][軍事] a pillbox.

とおで 遠出 图 an outing. (**!** しばしば家族・団体など集団によるものをいう)
── **遠出する** 動 go on an outing.

トーテム a totem.
●トーテム信仰 totemism. ●トーテムポール a totem pole.

トートバッグ a tote bag.

トートロジー [同語反復] (a) tautology.

ドーナ(ッ)ツ a doughnut /dóunʌt/,《米》a donut.
●ドーナツ現象 (都市人口の) a 'doughnut phenomenon', flight of residents from the central part of a city to the spreading suburbs.
●ドーナツ盤 (EP 盤レコード) an EP record.

トーナメント a《golf》tournament. ●トーナメントで優勝する win [take first place in] *a tournament*.

とおなり 遠鳴り a distant sound [(とどろき) roar, (ごろごろ) rumble]. ●潮(しお)の遠鳴り the *distant sound* of the sea; the *distant roars* of the waves.

とおのく 遠のく ●(遠ざかる) (音などが) die (〜d; dying) [fade] away; (危険などが)《やや堅》recede. ▶凍てついた道を行く足音が遠のいていった Footsteps on the frozen road *died away* (in the distance). ●このところ4連敗でそのチームの優勝の可能性は遠のいた(= いっそう少なくなった) Their recent four consecutive losses *have reduced* the chances of the team's winning the pennant./The chances of the team winning the pennant are now *remote* after their recent four consecutive losses. ▶「慎一さんは死んだのね」私は遠のいていく意識の中で聞いた "Shinichi is dead, then?" I asked as I was *losing consciousness*.
❷ [疎遠になる] ▶彼の足が遠のいた His visits have become less frequent./His visits became rarer.

とおのり 遠乗り a long ride. ●自転車で遠乗りを楽しむ enjoy a *long ride* on the bicycle. ●自動車で遠乗りをする take [have] *a long drive*; drive a long distance.

ドーバー ●ドーバー海峡 the Straits of Dover.

ドーパミン [生化学] dopamine.《参考》脳神経の興奮を伝達する物質)

トーバンジャン 豆板醤 [<中国語] (説明的に) Chinese bean paste made of fermented mixture of broad beans and red peppers.

とおび 遠火 ▶魚をおいしく焼くには、焼きあみをうまく遠火にセットしなさい To grill fish nicely, adjust the

ドーピング [薬物使用]doping. ▶彼はドーピングでレースの出場資格を失った He was disqualified from the race because he failed a *dope* test.
- ドーピング検査 a dope test; a drug test.

トーフル [米国留学のための英語学力テスト][商標] TOEFL /tóufl/ 《*T*est *o*f *E*nglish as a *F*oreign *L*anguage の略》.

ドーベルマン(ピンシェル) [動物] a Doberman pinscher.

とおぼえ 遠吠え 图 (鳴き声) a howl /hául/. ▶負け犬の遠吠え a beaten dog's barking from a safe distance.
— **遠吠えする** 動 howl. ▶隣の犬の遠吠えが耳ざわりで昨夜はなかなか寝つけなかった Disturbed by the *howls* the neigbor's dog gave out, I couldn't get to sleep easily last night.

とおまき 遠巻き ●その男を遠巻きにする(=距離を置いて囲む) surround the man at a distance.

とおまわし 遠回し ●遠回しに言う say 《it》 *in a roundabout way* 《*indirectly*》; (それとなく言う) make an *allusion* 《*to* it》; hint 《*at* it》; (なかなか要点に触れない) beat around 《米》[about《英》] the bush. (!通例否定文で用いる) ▶彼は彼女がうそをついていると遠回しに言った He *hinted* [*suggested*] that she was telling lies.

とおまわり 遠回り ● a roundabout way [route, course]; a detour /dí:tuər/. ●遠回りして帰る go home by a *roundabout* [a *longer*] way. ▶彼は繁華街を避けて遠回り(=回り道)した He *took a roundabout way* [*made a detour*] to avoid the busy street. ▶大学に入るまでに少し遠回りをしてきた(=年月をかけてきた)人だったので, 同じ学年でも彼は三つ上だった Although we were in the same year, he was three years older than me, because he had *taken some time* before enrolling in college.

ドーム a dome. ●東京ドーム the Tokyo *Dome* (Stadium).
● ドーム球場 a dome field [stadium].

とおめ 遠目 ▶島は遠目には(=遠方から見ると)平和そのものに見えた The island looked very peaceful *from a distance*.
● 遠目が利く can see a long distance.

ドーラン greasepaint. (参考)ドイツ Dohran 社の製品名から) ●ドーランで化粧する make up with *greasepaint*.

*****とおり 通り** ❶[街路] a street; (大通り) an avenue, a boulevard /búləvɑːrd/; (本通り) a thoroughfare /θɔ́ːrou fèər, θɛ́ːrə-/; (車道) a road. (⇒道) ▶名称としては St., Ave., Blvd., Rd. のように略記し, St. は無強勢(Dóver St.), 他は強勢を伴って発音する (Pàrk Áve.) (⇒街) ▶混雑した[人気のない]通り a crowded [a deserted] *street*. ▶通りを歩く walk along the *street*. ▶住宅街の通りでは女の子たちがきゃっきゃっ言いながらドッジボールをしていた *In a street* of the residential area, a group of girls were playing dodge ball shouting and laughing. (!前置詞は《米》on,《英》in の傾向があるが, このような住宅に囲まれた空間が意識される場合には米英を問わず in が普通) ▶彼の家にはにぎやかな通りに面している His house faces [is *on*] a busy *street*. ▶その店は通りの向こう側にある The store is across [on the other side of] the *street*. ▶ヒルトンホテルは何通りにありますか What *street* is the Hilton Hotel *on* [*in*]?
会話「それはワシントン通りのどこにありますか」「ワシントン通り 214 番地にあります」"Where *on* Washington *Street* is it?" "It's at 214 Washington *St.*" (!(1) 英語では番地を先にいい, 前置詞は at. (2) 214 は twó fóurteen と読む)

❷[人・車の往来] traffic. (⇒往来) ▶車の通りが激しい There is heavy *traffic.*/*Traffic* is heavy.

❸[水・空気などの流通] ▶下水の通りをよくする clear [improve] the drain. ▶この排水管は通りが悪い This drainpipe does not run well./This pipe does not drain well. ▶この部屋は風の通りがよい This room is airy [(換気がよい) is well ventilated].

❹[声の] ▶彼女の声は通りがいい Her voice carries very far [very well].

❺[評判, 通用] ▶彼は世間の通りがよい[悪い] He has a good [a bad] *reputation*. ▶そう言った方が通りがよい It sounds better to say so.

*****-とおり -通り** ❶[…のように] as [《話》like], 《+節》; […に従って] according to .... (⇒のとおり) ●計画のとおりにそれを行う do it *as* planned [*according to* (the) plan]. ▶思ったとおり彼は来なかった He didn't come as [*like*] I (had) expected. ▶言われたとおりにしなさい(目下の者へ) Do *as* you are told [I say]. ▶ね? 言ったとおりでしょ See whát I ╱mean?/╱See, whát did I ╲tell you! (!後の方は「それごらん」と非難する言い方にもなる)
会話「彼はきっぱりと断わったよ」「私が言ったとおりでしょう」"He refused point-blank." "Isn't that just what I said he'd do?"

❷[種類, 方法] ▶それには二通りのやり方がある There are two *ways* of doing it./(二通りのやり方ですることができる) You can do it in two *ways*.

*****-とおり -通り** ❶[…のように] as 《+節》; […に従って] according to .... (⇒-通り(訓り)) ●約束どおりに時計を買ってやる buy him a watch *as* promised. ●計画どおりに進んでいる be going on *according to* plan. (!慣用句)

❷[…程度] ▶建物は九分通りできた The Building has almost been completed./The Building is ninety percent done.

とおりあめ 通り雨 (にわか雨) a shower; a passing rain. ▶通り雨だからもう少しここにお帰りになっては? It's only a *shower*. Can't you stay here a little longer?

とおりあわせる 通り合わせる (たまたま通りかかる) happen to be passing by. ●事故現場に通り合わせる *happen to be* at the scene of the accident.

とおりいっぺん 通り一遍 — 通り一遍の 形 [皮相的な] superficial; [形式的な] formal; [何気ない] casual; [おきまりの] conventional; [(言動などが)おざなりの][書] perfunctory. ●通り一遍のあいさつを交わす exchange *formal* [*conventional*] greetings. ●通り一遍の返事をする give a *casual* [a *perfunctory*] reply. ●通り一遍のことを言う make *conventional* remarks. ▶航海については通り一遍の知識しかない I have only a *superficial* knowledge of navigation.

とおりがかり 通り掛かり ●通りがかりの人(=通行人) a passer-by (®passers-by). ●通りがかりのタクシーを拾う pick up a *passing* taxi; (呼び止める) hail a taxi. ▶通りがかりに(=途中で)この手紙を忘れずに出してください《米》Please remember to mail this letter *on the way*./《英》Please remember to post this letter *on the way*. ▶通りがかりの節は(=こちらに来られたときはお立ち寄りください Please drop in if you *come this way*.

とおりかかる 通り掛かる (そばを通る) pass by 《...》. ▶彼は通りかかった村人に助けられた He was saved by

とおりこす 通り越す 〖通り過ぎる〗**go*** **past** ..., **pass**; 〖越えて行く〗**go over** ...; 〖範囲を越える〗**go beyond** .... ●駅を通り越す *go past* [*pass*] the station. ●危機を通り越す *pass* [*get through*] (脱する), *overcome*, *ride out*] a crisis. ▶彼の言葉は冗談を通り越している His remarks *are beyond* a joke. ▶ヘリコプターが頭上を通り越していった A helicopter *went* [*flew*] *over* our heads [us, overhead].

とおりすがり 通りすがり ●通りすがりの人に道を尋ねる ask a *passer-by* for directions.

とおりすぎる 通り過ぎる 〖通過する〗**go*** **past** [**by**] (...), **pass** (**by**), (車で) **drive*** **past**(...). ▶車で田中さんのそばを通り過ぎた I *passed* (*by*) Mr. Tanaka on the street. ▶彼は急いで通り過ぎていった He *passed by* [*went past, went by*] hurriedly./He *hurried by*. ▶私は彼女が門の前を走って通り過ぎるのを見た I saw her *run past* [*by*] the gate.

とおりな 通り名 (通称) a commonly used name; (一般的な名前) an ordinary name.

とおりぬけ 通り抜け ●通り抜け禁止《掲示》No Thoroughfare /θəːroufèər, θʌ́rə-/.

とおりぬける 通り抜ける go* [**pass**] **through** .... (!**walk**, **run*** などの動きが用いられる); (苦労して) **get*** **through** .... ●町を通り抜ける *go* [*pass*, (車で) *drive*] *through* a town. ●トンネルを通り抜ける *go* [(走って) *run*] *through* a tunnel. ▶私たちはからみ合った下ばえの中をなんとか通り抜けた We *got through* the tangled underbrush.

とおりま 通り魔 (殺人者) a random killer (!「(幻影のように)さっと姿を消す犯罪者」の意を前面に出すと *phantom* killer となる; (刃物を使った) a (street) slasher. ▶彼の犯行は通り魔的なものだった(=特に理由なく犯罪を犯した) He committed the crime for no particular reasons.

とおりみち 通り道 (道筋) the way; (通過する道) a passage. ▶倒木がほこらへの通り道をふさいでいた A fallen tree blocked *the way* to the small shrine. ▶九州は台風の通り道だ(=台風がよく襲う) Typhoons hit Kyushu very often.

＊とおる 通る, 透る 〖通行する〗**go*** (**by**, **past**, **through**), (!運動によって walk, drive*, run* などが用いられる); (通り過ぎる) **pass***. ●郵便局のそばを通る *go by* [通り過ぎる] *go past, pass* (*by*)] the post office. ●門を通る(=通り抜ける) *go through* [*pass* (*through*)] the gate. ●野原を通って森へ駆けて行く *run through* [*across*] the field (and) *to* the woods. (!through は「通り抜けて」, across は「横切って」の意) ●私の後[前]を通る *pass behind* [*in front of*] me. ●本通りを通って行こう Let's *go along* [*go down, go by, take*] the main road. (!後の二つは目的地に行く手段としてその道を通ること) ●この道は車がよく通る A lot of cars *pass along* this road./(交通量が多い) There is a lot of [heavy] traffic on this road. ▶トラックが通る(=通り過ぎる)たびに少年たちは道をあけた The boys stepped aside every time a truck *passed by*. ▶その道路は通れない(=通行止めだ) The road *is closed to traffic*. ▶車を移動してくれますか. 通れないものですから Can you move your car? It's *blocking* my way. ▶右側を通りなさい *Keep* to the right. ▶ハワイを通って(=経由して)ロサンゼルスに行った We went to Los Angeles *via* /váiə/ [*by way of*] Hawaii. (!後の方が堅い言い方)

❷〖交通機関が運行する, 道が通じている〗**run***; 〖道・路線が開通する〗**open, be opened**. (⇨開通) ▶ここは 30 分ごとにバスが通っている Buses *run* [There is a bus *service*] every thirty minutes here. ▶この道は森を通っている This road *runs* [*passes*] *through* the woods.

❸〖無事に通過する〗**pass**. ●試験に通る *pass* an examination. (!学科目の場合は pass in English. pass (an exam) in English (英語(の試験)に通る)の目的語が省略された表現で, in が必要) ●検閲[税関]を通る *pass* the censor [the Customs]. ▶法案は議会を通った The bill *has passed* the Diet./The Diet *has passed* the bill.

❹〖…で通る〗**pass** (*as, for*) (!実際にはそうではないという含みがある), (知られる) **be known** (*as, for*); (評判である) **have*** **a reputation** (*for*); (受け入れられる) **be accepted**. ●変人で通っている *be known as* [*go for*] an odd person. ●名の通った(=有名な)画家 a *well-known* [*famous*] painter. ▶彼は中国語がとても上手なので中国人といっても通るだろう He speaks Chinese so well that he could *pass for* [*as*] a Chinese. ▶彼は長年ブラウンという名で通っていた He *went by* [*under*] the name of Brown for years. ▶彼女はけちで通っている She *has a reputation for* being stingy [*for* stinginess]./She *has the reputation of* being stingy [×*of* stinginess]. ▶そんな言い訳は通らない We can't *accept* such an excuse./That's no excuse. ▶この文章は意味が通らない This sentence doesn't *make* (*any*) *sense*.

❺〖声・熱などが届く〗▶彼女の声はよくとおる Her voice *carries* quite *far* [*penetrates*]. (!...carries very well. ともいう)/She has a *clear* [a *penetrating*] voice. ▶この肉はよく火が通っている[いない] This meat *is well done* [*is underdone*].

❻〖水・空気・電気などが流れる〗(⇨通り❸) ▶この電線には高圧電流が通っている This wire is charged with a high-tension current./There *is* a high-tension current *running through* this wire. ▶この薬を飲むと詰まった鼻が通りやすくなります This medicine will help to clear up your stuffy nose.

ドール 〖人形〗a doll.
●ドールハウス 〖人形の家〗《米》a dollhouse, 《英》a doll's house.

トーン 〖調子〗a tone. ●トーンを上げる[下げる] tone 《one's voice》up [down].

トーンダウン ── トーンダウンする 動 (語気などを和らげる) tone down.

とか 都下 ●都下に《live》in Greater Tokyo [the Greater Tokyo area].

とか 渡河 图 crossing a wide river. ●敵前渡河 a forced crossing of the river (in the face of the enemy).

── **渡河する** 動 go across [cross] a (wide) river.

-とか (副助詞) 〖例として並べて示す〗▶バナナとかオレンジのような果物が好きだ I like fruit(,) *such as* bananas *and* oranges. (!I like *such* fruit *as* bananas and oranges. のようにもいえる) ▶キャンプに行くときは地図とかランプとかを持って行きなさい (You'd better) take a map, a lamp, *and such* [《話》*suchlike*] when you go camping.

とが 咎 (過失・失敗の責任) a fault; blame. (!後の方は責めを負うべきものという意味合いが強い) ▶誰のとがでも(=過失)でもない Nobody *is to blame* 《for》this. (!be to blame (責めを負うべきである)は成句)

とかい 都会 图 a city; a town (!田舎 (the country) に対して都会というときは通例 the をつけるが, 近くの町や住んでいる町をいうときは無冠詞が普通). (⇨都市,

どがいし 都外紙 —— 都外視する 動 (考慮に入れない) take* no account 《of》; leave "... out of consideration; (無視する) ignore; (軽視する) disregard. ▶彼らは採算(=利益)を度外視してその鉄道工事を始めた They took no account of [ignored] the profit when they started the railroad construction. ▶費用を度外視して(=費用にかまわずに)作ってみましょう I'll make it regardless of the expense [no matter how much it costs]. (!後の方が口語的)

とがき ト書き a stage direction.

とかく ❶ [ややもすれば] (...する傾向がある) be apt to 《do》; be liable to 《do》; tend to 《do》; (...するものである) will* 《do》.

> **使い分け** apt 通例よくない生来的・習慣的な性質や傾向を表す。
> liable 望ましくないことを招きやすい人の傾向をしばしば警告をこめて表す。
> tend to 同じ展開が反復して起こること、時によくない傾向を表す。
> will 習慣や習性を表す。

▶我々はとかく過ちをしがちである We are all apt [liable] to make mistakes. ▶過度の飲酒はとかく肝臓障害を引き起こす Excessive drinking tends to cause liver trouble. ▶世間はとかくうるさいものだ People will talk.
❷ [あれこれ] ▶彼にはとかくのうわさがある There are various rumors about him. ▶彼はとかくするうちに戻ってきた In the meantime [Meanwhile] he came back.

とかげ 蜥蜴 [動物] a lizard. (!皮は Ⓤ)
● とかげのしっぽ切り a lizard's casting off its tail when it escapes; (自分の身を守るために下位の者に責任をかぶせること) putting all the blame on one's subordinate(s) to protect oneself.

*__とかす__ 溶かす, 解かす [固体を熱で] melt; [固体を液体の中で] dissolve /dɪzɔ́lv/; [金属などを] fuse; (液化する)〔書〕liquefy. (⇒溶ける) ▶砂糖を紅茶に溶かす dissolve [melt] sugar in tea. ▶湯をかけて凍結した水道管を解かす thaw (out) a water pipe with hot water.

とかす 梳かす ・髪を丁寧に[きちんと]とかす comb one's hair carefully [neatly].

どかす 退かす (⇒どける)

どかた 土方 a construciton laborer [worker].

どかっと ❶ [重そうに] heavily. ▶屋根から雪がどかっと落ちた Snow fell off the roof with a heavy [(こわいような音をさす) a frightening] thump.
❷ [一度に大量に] ▶キャベツをどかっと入荷した Cabbages came in in great amount.

どかどか ❶ [うるさい足音を立てて] with loud footsteps. ▶大勢の警官がどかどかと部屋に入ってきた A number of police officers trod into the room with loud footsteps [poured into the room noisily]. (!pour は「なだれ込む」の意で主語は多人数の場合に限られる)/A lot of policemen stamped into the room. (!stamp は「足を踏み鳴らして歩

く」の意)
❷ [急にたくさん] ▶昼食時にはお客さんがどかどか来る They have a sudden swarm of customers around lunchtime. (!they は店の人をさす)

とがめ 咎め ❶ [責める] blame. ・良心のとがめ(=呵責(ホ゛ン)) the pangs [pricks] of conscience.

*__とがめる__ 咎める ❶ [責める] (責任があるとして) blame 《(for)》; (怒りよりも失望して) reproach 《(for)》; (怒ったり非難して)〔書〕reprove 《(for)》. ▶彼の不注意をとがめる reproach him with his carelessness [for being careless]. (!×reproach his carlessness は不可) ▶私は君が遅れたことをとがめないよ I don't blame [reproach] you for coming late.
❷ [問いただす] ▶警官にとがめられる be questioned by a policeman.
❸ [心が] ▶私は良心がとがめる(=良心が痛む) My conscience pricks [is pricking] me./I feel the prick of conscience. ▶彼に本を返していないので気がとがめる(=やましく思う) I feel guilty about [at] not returning the book to him. (!I have a guilty [a bad] conscience about.... ともいえる)

どかゆき どか雪 a (concentrated) heavy snow.

とがらす 尖らす ・棒の先をとがらす sharpen the point of the stick. ▶彼女はすぐに口をとがらす She is quick to pout /páʊt/. (ふくれたり、すねる表情) ▶私は彼女の行動に神経をとがらせた I got nervous about her action.

とがりごえ 尖り声 (⇒とげとげしい)

__とがる__ 尖る (鋭くなる) become sharp. ● 先のとがった棒 a pointed stick. ▶鉛筆の先がとがりすぎた The point of the pencil has become too sharp. ▶「君の名前は何ていうの」私は腹が立っていたので声もとがっていた "What's your name, please?" I was angry and my voice was brittle.

どかん 土管 ・土管を埋める lay an earthen [a clay] pipe.

どかんと ・どかんという音を立てて with a bang [a crash]. ・どかんという音を立てる(爆発して) explode; (激しく打って) bang; (落雷など) 《it が主語》 thunder; (激突して) crash 《(into, against)》. ▶花火が夏の夜空にどかんと何度も鳴った Fireworks banged [went off with a bang] many times in the summer night sky.

*__とき__ 時 名 ❶ [時間] time; (経験としての) a time (!形容詞を伴って); (時刻) an hour.
① [時が[は]] ▶時がたつのは早い Time passes [goes by] quickly./Time flies. (⇒光陰) ▶時がたつにつれて彼の決意は固くなった As time went on [passed], his resolution became firmer. ▶時がたてば彼の無実が分かるでしょう Time will tell [show] that he is innocent. ▶時はあらゆる傷をいやす Time heals all wounds./Time is the best healer.
② [時の] ▶彼は読書に夢中になっていて時のたつのを忘れた He was completely absorbed in reading and lost (×the) track of time [was unconscious of the passage of time]. (!(1) 前の方の lose (↔keep) track of は「...の(足跡)を見失う」の意の成句。(2) 後の方の形を用いる)
③ [時を] ▶彼は時をたがえず(=時間通りにやって来た He came on time [punctually]. ▶私たちはパーティーで楽しい時を過ごした We had a good time [had fun, enjoyed ourselves, ×enjoyed] at the party. ▶不幸は時を選ばずやって来る Misfortunes come at all hours. ▶時かせぎのため彼はあいまいな返答をした In order to gain time, he gave an ambiguous answer.
❷ [時期, 場合] (特定の時) time; (ある過程における一

とき

定の時) a moment; (出来事などの) an occasion; (場合) a case.
① 【～時】 ▶そのころが私の人生の最良の時でした It was the happiest *time* of [in] my life. ▶その時あなたは何をしていましたか What were you doing *then* [*at that time, at that moment, on that occasion*]? ▶その時以来彼から便りがない I haven't heard from him since *then*. (❗主節は現在完了形になる) ▶月曜日は私がいちばん忙しい時(= 日)です Monday is the *day* (*when* [*that*]) I am busiest. (❗(話) では通例 when, that を省略するり) I'm the (×the) busiest on Monday. ▶どんな時でも希望を失うな Don't give up hope *at any time*.
② 【時に[は]】 ▶私に感謝する時が来るでしょう *Someday* you will thank me./(書) The *time* will come *when* you (will) thank me. (❗The *time* when ... will come. の語順より普通。後の will は繰り返しを避けるためしばしば省略される) ▶どうしたらいいのか分からなくなる時がある There are *times* [*occasions, moments*] *when* I don't know what to do./(時々) I *sometimes* don't know what to do. ▶私はジャズに夢中になっていた時があった There was a *time when* I was crazy about jazz./I *used to be* crazy about jazz. (⇨昔) ▶あの時は物価はもっと安かった Prices were lower *at that time* [((話) *back*) *then*, (当時) *in those days*]. ▶私たちはある時は励まし合い，またある時はけんかもしました *Sometimes* we encouraged each other, *and sometimes* we had an argument. ▶なすべき[しかるべき]時が来ればやりますよ We'll cross the bridge when we come to it. (⇨取り越し苦労) ▶時が時だけに空港の警備を強化しなければならない *Under the circumstances*, we must beef up security in the airport.
③ 【時の】 ▶時の(=いま話題の)人 the man [the woman] *of the hour* [((話) *in the news*]. ●時の (=その当時の)政府 the *then* government; the government *in those days*. ▶私たちが初めて会った時のことを覚えていますか Do you remember the first *time* [*occasion*] we met?
④ 【時に(は)】 ▶彼の結婚式の時に *at the time* [*on the occasion*] *of* his wedding. ●彼が死ぬ時に *at the moment of* his death. ▶彼はちょうどよい時に来た He came just *at the right time* [*moment*]. ▶火事の時にはこのレバーを引きなさい Pull this lever *in case of* fire. ●うちでは特別な時にだけ上等の器を使います We only use the good china [*dishes*] *on special occasions*. ●忙しい時に限って次から次へと電話がかかってくる I have one call after another *only when* I am busy.
(会話) 「でもあの映画もう見ちゃったよ」「そういう時には見てないという顔をしてろよ」"But I've already seen that movie." "Pretend you haven't *in* [×at] that *case*."
⑤ 【時と】 ▶それは時と場合による That (all) depends./It all depends.
❸ 【好機】 (適した時) (a) time; (機会) a chance, (an) opportunity. (⇨機会) ▶今晩はその秘密を彼女に打ち明けるよい時だ This evening is a good *time* [*chance, occasion*] to tell her the secret. ▶今こそ行動すべき時です Now is the *time to act* [*for action*]./The *time* for action is now. ▶そろそろその問題について話し合う時だ *It is about time* we discussed the problem [(for us) to discuss the problem]. ▶前の方が口語的で，節内の動詞は今は直説法過去形が普通 ▶時を見てそのことを彼と相談しましょう I'll talk it over with him when the time is right. ▶彼の警告は時を得ていた His warning was *timely*./He gave a *timely* warning.

ときあかす

❹ 【時代】 a time. (❗しばしば複数形で) ●時の流れに逆らう go against the currents of the *times*. ●明治天皇の時に in the *time*(*s*) *of* the Emperor Meiji. (❗the Emperor ... に注意)
●時は金なり (ことわざ) Time is money.
●時を移さず ▶警察は時を移さず彼らの救援に向かった The police *lost no time* (*in*) setting [(ただちに) *immediately* set] out to rescue them. (❗in を省略するのは (話). lost の代わりに wasted も可)
●時の記念日 Time Day.
── ...する時 接 when ...; as ...; while ....

解説 (1) when は二つの出来事が(ほぼ)同時に起こる場合や, ある出来事が起こっているときに他の出来事が起こる場合に用いる. as は二つの行為が平行して行われる場合やある行為が終わらないうちに別の出来事が起こる場合に用いる. 3 語の中で同時性が最も強く, 節中には通例動作動詞がくる. while は「...する間(に)」の意で, 節中には通例継続を表す動詞または進行形がくる.
(2) 他に「...する[の]時(に)」は分詞構文で表されることもあるが, 主に書き言葉.

▶私は通りを歩いている時先生に出会った I met my teacher *when* [*as, while*] I was walking down the street. (❗when [as, while] 節を主節の前に置いてもよい) ▶私の犬は道を横切っている時にひき殺された My dog was run over and killed *when* [*while*, ×as] crossing the road. (❗when, while 節中では主節と同じ主語と be 動詞はしばしば省略される) ▶私がそこへ着いた時にはすでに彼は出発していた *When* [×As] I arrived there, (I found) he had already left./(主に書) *On arriving* [*Arriving*] there, I found he had already left. ▶彼は子供の時京都に住んでいた *When* (he was) a child [*As* a child, (書) *In* his childhood, ×As he was a child], he lived in Kyoto. (❗as a child は ×は文尾にも置ける) ▶彼女がテレビを見ている時, 私は新聞を読んでいた *While* she was watching TV, I was reading a newspaper. (❗二つの動作が同時に進行している場合は while を用いる) ▶私がちょうど出ようとしている時に彼が来た He came *just as* [*just when*] I was going out. (❗just as は単に時間的偶然の一致を表すが, just when は「よりによってその時に」のように迷惑であることを暗示することがある)/(するとその時) I was just going out *when* he came. (❗「彼が(突然)来た」ことに焦点を当てて後の話を続けたい場合で, when は and then に近い意味になる) ▶彼がそこへ行くときはいつも雨が降る *When* he goes there, it (always) rains. (❗現在時制の場合 always は省略可)/*Every time* [*Whenever*] he goes there, it rains. ▶当日彼が行けない時は(=とすれば)私が代わりに行きます *If* he can't go on that day, I'll go instead. ▶今度やる時はもっと注意しなさい Be more careful (*the*) *next time* you do [×will do] it. (❗Be more careful *when* you do it *next time*. より普通. 同様に次の時は初めて...する時には), the last time (この前...した時には)なども接続詞的に用いる) ▶あなたが帰宅する時までにはこの仕事を終えておきましょう I'll have finished this work *by the time* [*before*, ×*until*] you come home. (⇨-まで)

とき 鴇, 朱鷺 〖鳥〗 a Japanese crested ibis /áibis/ (⑱ ~, ~es).
とき 土器 《集合的》earthenware. ●土器のつぼ an *earthenware* pot [(容器) *vessel*].
どき 怒気 anger. ●怒気を顔に表す show one's *anger*. ●怒気を含んで抗議する protest in an *angry tone*.
ときあかす 解き明かす make ... clear [plain]; clear

ときいろ 鴇色 light [pale] pink.

ときおこす 説き起こす ▶その事件の遠因から説き起こす(=説明を始める) begin one's lecture on the incident by talking about [explaining] its remote cause; give one's lecture on the incident starting from its underlying cause.

ときおよぶ 説き及ぶ refer (-rr-) to ...; touch upon 《the future of Japan》.

ときおり 時折 occasionally. (⇒時々)

とぎいん 都議会 the (Tokyo) Metropolitan Assembly.
● 都議会議員 a member of the (Tokyo) Metropolitan Assembly. ● 都議会議員選挙 a (Tokyo) Metropolitan Assembly election.

とぎじる 研ぎ汁 water in which rice was washed.

とぎすます 研ぎ澄ます 《刀などを》《鋭利にする》sharpen ... (to perfection); 《磨き上げる》polish ... up; 〖神経などを〗keen. ● 研ぎ澄ました知性 keen intellect.

トキソプラズマ《住血原虫》a toxoplasma.

とぎだし 研ぎ出し polishing. ▶みかげ石の研ぎ出し polishing of a granite slab.

ときたま 時たま occasionally. (⇒時々)

-ときたら -と来たら ▶息子はいつも部屋をきちんとしているが, 娘ときたら(=はどうかというと)もう散らかしっぱなしです My son always keeps his room neat and tidy, but *as for* my daughter she [that daughter of mine] leaves her room an awful mess. (❗ that には軽蔑的な含みがある (⇒たら))

どきっ — **どきっとする** 動 be given a start; be startled. ▶どきっとするじゃない, ノックもしないで部屋に入ってくるなんて What a *start* you *gave* me coming into the room without knocking. ▶今入ったばかりのドアが開かなくなっているのを知って彼はどきっとした With a *start* he realized (that) the door behind him was locked. ▶知らない人に名前を呼ばれてどきっとした I *was startled* when I was called my name by a stranger.

どぎつい 《色・衣服などが》《はでな》loud; 《いやにぎらぎらする》garish /ɡéəriʃ/; 《けばけばしい》gaudy; 〖音などが〗ひどく不快な〗harsh; 〖化粧などが〗heavy. ▶どぎつい色 a *loud* [a *garish*, a *gaudy*] color. ●どぎついことを言う use *harsh* [《ひどい》*shocking*] language. ●どぎつい化粧をしている wear *heavy* [*too much*] make-up.

ときつける 説き付ける persuade《him *to* obey his mother》.

‡ときどき 時々 〖ときには〗sometimes; 〖ときたま〗occasionally; 《折々に》from time to time, 《そんなにしょっちゅうではないが》(every) now and then [again]; 《断続的に》on and off [off and on]; 《たまには》(every) once in a while.

解説 (1) *sometimes* は「ときどき…する」という肯定的な含みを持つのに対し, *occasionally* はそれより頻度が低く, 「たまにしか…しない」という否定的な含みがある. (2) この 2 語は主に文中で用い, 位置は always に準ずるが, 否定語の前に置き, 直後には用いない. また文頭, 文尾にも用いる. (⇒いつも)

▶ときどき彼は我々を訪ねてくれる ✓*Sometimes* he visits 《主に英》 calls on] us. (❗ 頻度副詞と対比して *Usually* we visit him, but の後に続くような場合に好まれる (⇒[第 5 文例])) / He *sometimes* visits us. ▶私はときどき将棋で勝てることがある I can *sometimes* beat my uncle at *shogi* [Japanese chess]. ▶ときどきどうしてよいかわからないことがある I don't know what to do. (❗×I don't *sometimes* know .... は不可)/I am *sometimes* at a loss (as to) what to do. ▶専門家だってときどきミスをするEven experts *sometimes* make mistakes. (❗ sometimes の代わりに can を用いて言き換え可) ▶ときどきはテレビを見ますよ. でもたいていはあまりに忙しすぎてねえ I *occasionally* watch television. But usually, I'm far too busy. ▶彼はときどき自分の行く道を地図で確かめた *From time to time* he checked his route on the map. ▶2 年前にけがをして, それが今でもときどきひどく痛くなる I have this injury two years ago and it still flares up (*every*) *now and again* [*once in a while*]. (❗ every のつく方が強意的. 文頭でも用いる) ▶曇りときどき雨 《日記など》で Cloudy with *occasional* rain./Cloudy, *sometimes* rain. ▶天気予報では Cloudy with a *chance of* rain. のようにもいうが, 雨の降る確率は前の 2 文より低い

会話 「彼にはときどき会うの」「はい, ときどき」"Do you *ever* see him?/Do you see him *at all*?" "Yes, I *sometimes* do." (❗ (1) 普通の疑問文では通例 sometimes の代わりに ever, at all を用いる. cf. Do you *sometimes* see him or do you never see him? (❗ 選択疑問文の場合) (2) Do you *sometimes* see him? というと肯定的な答えを期待していることを暗示する. (3) 答えは Yes, *sometimes*. ともいえる

どきどき — **どきどきする** 動 《心臓などが》beat* fast, 《やや書》throb (-bb-); 〖人が わくわくする〗be thrilled. ▶彼女は外国に行けると思っただけでどきどきした She *was thrilled* just to think she could go abroad./Her heart *throbbed* [*pounded*] with excitement at the thought that she could go abroad. ▶舞台に上がるとどきどきしてしまって《=ひどくあがって》, せりふを忘れそうになる When I'm on stage, I *get all nervous* and nearly forget my lines. ▶結果を待っている間私は心臓がどきどきしていた I felt my heart *beating fast* [*throbbing*] while I was waiting for the result.

ときとして 時として 《ときたま》occasionally (⇒時々); 《ある場合には》in some cases. ▶時として困難な問題にぶつかる We *occasionally* run into difficulties.

ときならぬ 時ならぬ ● 時ならぬ《=季節はずれの》雪 an *unseasonable* snowfall. ▶我々は彼の時ならぬ《=不意の》訪問に驚いた We were surprised at his *unexpected* [*(突然の) sudden*] visit.

ときに 時に 〖ときには〗sometimes (⇒時々); 〖ところで〗now; by the way, incidentally. ▶時に彼の名前を思い出せないことがある *Sometimes* I can't remember his name. ▶時に皆よく聞いてくれ *Now* listen to me, you all. ▶時にその映画はごらんになりましたか *By the way* [*Incidentally*], have you seen the film? ▶化学はおもしろく, 美しく, 時に役立つ Chemistry is interesting and beautiful, and can be useful *at times* [*sometimes*]. (❗「時に」は「役立つ」だけにかかるので, ... interesting, beautiful and useful at times としない)

ときには 時には sometimes; 《ときたま》occasionally. (⇒時々) ▶時には東京へ出ることもあります. せいぜい月一度ぐらいです I'm in Tokyo *occasionally*—once a month or so. ▶私は時には自炊し, また時には外食する I *sometimes* cook for myself and *sometimes* [*at other times*] eat out. (❗ *occasionally* にはこのような対照的に用いる用法はない)

ときのこえ 鬨の声 a war [a battle] cry. ● ときの声を揚げる 《やや書》raise] a *war cry*.

ときはなす 解き放す release; set ... free. ● 鳥をかごから解き放つ *release* a bird from the cage.

ときふせる 説き伏せる persuade. (⇒説得する)

ときほぐす 溶きほぐす ●卵を溶きほぐす beat an egg.
ときほぐす 解きほぐす ●［からまったものを］（糸などを）untangle;（謎を）unravel. ●糸のもつれを解きほぐす *untangle* the knots in the string. ●謎を一つ一つ解きほぐす *unravel* a mystery step by step.
❷［凝り固まったものを］（筋肉のこりを）massage;（心の緊張などを）relax; reduce [relieve]《the stress》;（不信感などを）remove, get* rid of ... ▶彼からの1通の手紙で彼に対する不信感は解きほぐされた A letter from him *removed* my distrust of him.

どぎまぎ ── **どぎまぎする 動** ［心が混乱する］be confused;（あわてふためく）be flustered; ［気が動転する］be upset;［きまり悪く思う］be embarrassed, ［おどおどする］be nervous. ▶彼女はその金のことを聞かれてどぎまぎした She *got confused* [*upset, flustered*] when (she was) questioned about the money. ▶人前で話をするといつもどぎまぎする I always *feel embarrassed* [*nervous*] when I make a speech in public.

ときめき ［心臓の鼓動］(a) beating; ［興奮］excitement. ●幼かったころのわくわくするようなときめき the joyful *excitement* I felt as a small boy [girl]. ●胸のときめきを感じる feel one's heart *beating fast*; feel *excitement* 《over》.

ときめく ▶私の胸は喜びでときめいた（＝鼓動した） My heart *beat fast* [《やや堅》*throbbed*] with joy.

ときめく 時めく ●flourish.（!その後の衰退を暗示する）▶あの方も平成の初めに時めいた政治家の1人でした He was one of those politicians who *had flourished* in the early period of Heisei.

どぎも 度胆・度肝を抜く ▶子供はフランケンシュタインの仮装にただただ度肝を抜かれた The boy was startled *out of* his *wits* when he saw Frankenstein's disguise.（!startle は「驚く」の意が最も強い語の一つ. out of one's wits は「正気を失って」の意）

ドキュメンタリー a dòcuméntary.
● ドキュメンタリー映画 a documentary (film).
ドキュメンテーション ［文書化］［コンピュータ］documentation.
ドキュメント ［記録］a dócument.
どきょう 度胸 ［勇気］courage,［決断］《話》pluck,［強い神経, 剛気］nerve,［根性］《話》guts. ●度胸を試す test one's *courage* [*nerve*]; put one's *courage* [*nerve*] to the test. ●度胸をすえる pluck up one's *courage*. ▶彼は度胸のある［ない］男だ He has a lot of [no] *guts*./He is a *bold* [a *timid*] man. ▶私はそれをやってみるだけの度胸がない I don't have the *courage* [*nerve*, *guts*] to try it./I am not *bold* [*brave*] enough to try it.
どきょう 読経 图 sutra /súːtrə/ recitation.
── **読経する 動** recite a sutra.
ときょうそう 徒競走 a footrace. ●徒競走をする run a race.
どきり （⇒どきっ）
とぎれとぎれ 途切れ途切れ ── **途切れ途切れの** 形 broken; intermittent. ●とぎれとぎれの眠り *broken* [*intermittent*] sleep.
── **途切れ途切れに 副** ●とぎれとぎれに話す talk *brokenly* [*intermittently*]. ▶彼らの会話がとぎれとぎれに聞こえた（＝会話の断片が聞こえた） We heard *bits* [*fragments*] of their conversation.
とぎれる 途切れる ●途切れることなく続く車の列 an *unbroken* line of cars; cars lined up *without a break*. ▶彼の声は感情が高まって途切れがちであった His voice *was breaking* with emotion. ▶彼の演説はしばしば野次で途切れた（＝中断された） His speech *was often interrupted* with jeering. ▶話が途切れた（＝間があいた） There *was a pause* [*a break*] in the conversation. ▶突然音楽が途切れた The music *cut off* suddenly. ▶ここで家並みが途切れている（＝終わっている） A row of houses *ends* here.

ときわぎ 常盤木 an evergreen tree.
ときん 鍍金 （⇒めっき）
ときん 都銀 ［［「都市銀行」の略］（⇒都市）
どきん （⇒どきっ）▶胸がどきんとした My heart *pounded* [*thumped*] violently.

*****とく 解く** ❶［ほどく］（結んだものを）undo*, untie（～d; -tying）;（縛ったものを）unbind*;（包み・荷物などを解いて中身を出す）unpack;（ほどく）loosen. ●ロープの結び目を解く undo [*untie, loosen*] the knot in a rope. ●ロープを解く *untie* [*unbind*] a rope. ▶彼はその包みを解いた He *undid* [*untied, unpacked*] the package.
❷［解決する］（問題・なぞなどを解明する）solve, work ... out（!後の方が口語的）;（なぞ・疑いなどを明らかにする）clear ...up;（疑い・誤解などを追い払う）dispel（-ll-）,（取り除く）remove;（怒りなどを静める）appease. ●方程式を解く *solve* [*work out*] an equation. ●なぞを解く *solve* [*clear up*] a mystery. ▶彼の疑いを解く *dispel* [*remove, clear up*] his doubts.
会話 「それ自分で解けないの？」「ねえ, 答えはどうなるのさ」"Can't you *work* it *out* for yourself?" "Oh, come on. What's the answer?"
❸［解除する］（封鎖・包囲などを）lift, raise;（職務・重荷などから解放する）release《from》,《書》relieve《of》;（解среть）dismiss《from》. ●包囲を解く *lift* [*raise*] a siege /siːdʒ/. ●戒厳令を解く *lift* martial law. ●彼の任務を解く *release* him *from* [《書》*relieve* him *of*] his duty. ▶彼は職を解かれた He *was relieved of* his post.（!《書》だが次例に比べて婉曲的な言い方）/He *was dismissed* [*was discharged*] *from* his post.

*****とく 得** 图 ［利益］(a) profit;［恩恵］benefit;［有利］(an) advantage;［有利］use /júːs/, good（!use の意 益］）（⇔不利益）
① 【得が】▶そこ行って何の得があるのか What's the *use* [*good*] of going there?（!反語的な表現で, It's no *use* [*good*] going there.（そこへ行ってもむだだ）と同じ意味）
② 【得に】▶そんなことをしても少しも得にならない You will not *gain* anything out of doing such a thing./You'll have nothing to *gain* by doing that.
③ 【得を】▶彼女はその取り引きでかなり得をした She *made* a considerable *profit on* the deal. ▶将来そのことで得をするでしょう You will *benefit from* [*by*] it in the future./You will *get benefit from* it in the future. ▶それで10ドル得をする（＝節約できる） That saves you ten dollars. ▶特売！スキー用品が2割お得《広告》 Sale! *Save* 20% on skiing equipment. ▶正直は得をする（＝割に合う） It *pays to* be *better off* selling your house now.（!better off doing は「...する方がよい［賢明だ］」の意の慣用句）▶それが1万円なら得な買い物だ It's a *good bargain* [《話》*buy*] at ten thousand yen. ▶彼は得な性分だ He has a *lucky* nature./He is *lucky* by nature.

── **得な 形** ［もうかる］profitable;［有利な］advantageous;［幸運な］lucky. ●得な商売 a *profitable* business. ●英語をしっかり勉強しておくと得です It would be *advantageous to* you [*to* your *advantage*] to study English hard. ●今家を売った方が得でしょう You would be *better off* selling your house now.（!better off doing は「...する方がよい［賢明だ］」の意の慣用句）▶それが1万円なら得な買い物だ It's a *good bargain* [《話》*buy*] at ten thousand yen. ▶彼は得な性分だ He has a *lucky* nature./He is *lucky* by nature.

とく 徳 (a) virtue（↔(a) vice）. ●徳を養う cultivate

とく *virtue*. ▶徳の高い人 a person of high [great] *virtue*; a virtuous person. ▶徳とする appreciate《the way he dealt with it》. ▶正直は徳(目の一つ)だ Honesty is a *virtue*. ▶私は今日までずっと人間の徳というものを厳しく追及してきた Until this day I have pursued *virtue* with rigor.

とく 都区 ●都区内に in [inside, within the limits of] (the 23 wards of) Tokyo. (■ロンドンやニューヨークの区は borough /bə́ːrou, 《英》bʌ́rə/と呼ばれる)

とく 梳く comb /kóum/ one's hair.

とく 溶く dissolve /dizʌ́lv/; (混合する) mix《A *with* B》; (玉子をかきまぜる) beat*(⇨溶かす). ▶砂糖を酒でとく *dissolve* sugar *in* sake /sáːki/. ▶粉を水でとく mix the powder *with* water.

とく 説く ［［説明する］］ explain; ［［説教する］］ preach; ［［提唱する］］ advocate; ［［説得する］］ persuade.
▶仏教[倹約]を説く *preach*《us》Buddhism [frugality]. ▶新説を説く *advocate* a new doctrine. ▶彼に道理を説いて誤りをさとす reason *with* him *about* his mistake. ▶読書の価値を熱心に説く (=力説する) *emphasize* [*put emphasis on*] the value of reading. ▶彼を説いて(=説得して)それをさせた I *persuaded* him *to* do it./I *persuaded* him *into* doing it. ▶彼は教育の重要性を説いた He *explained* (*to* us) *how* important education is. (■このように節を従える場合は to us は前に来る)/(指摘した) He *pointed out* the importance of education.

***とく** 研ぐ ❶［［刃物を］］ grind*, whet (-tt-); (鋭くする) sharpen; (特に, かみそりを) hone. ●砥石(ﾄ)でナイフを研ぐ *grind* [*whet, sharpen*] a knife on a whetstone [a stone]. (■動詞 whet のときには a stone が好ましい)
❷［［米を］］ wash; (すすぐ) rinse.
❸［［鏡・レンズを］］ polish. (⇨磨く)

***どく** 毒 ❶［［有害物］］ (a) poison /pɔ́izn/; (ヘビ・サソリなどの) venom.
①【毒～】●毒入りチョコ a *poisoned* chocolate.
②【毒が】●毒が回った The *poison* took effect. ▶このキノコは毒がある This mushroom is *poisonous*.
③【毒に】▶彼はキノコを食べて毒にあたって死んだ He ate a toadstool and died of *poisoning*./He was killed by the *poison* of a toadstool.
④【毒を】●毒を消す counteract the effect of *poison*. ●毒を飲んで自殺する poison oneself; kill oneself by taking [×drinking] *poison*. ▶彼は彼女の飲み物に毒を入れた[盛った] He *poisoned* her drink.
❷［［悪影響］］ ▶食べ過ぎは体に毒だ(=有害だ) Eating too much is *harmful to* [*bad for*] your health.
●毒にも薬にもならない ▶この本は毒にも薬にもならない(=よくも悪くもない) This book is neither good nor bad. (■語順に注意)
●毒を食らわば皿まで If you eat poison, you must lick even the plate./(ことわざ) You may [might] as well be hanged for a sheep as for a lamb.
●毒をもって毒を制す 'Counteract *poison* with *poison*.'/(ことわざ) Fight fire with fire.

どく 退く ▶どいてくれ (じゃまにならないようによける) Get out of the [my] *way*./(行く手をふさぐな) Don't stand in my *way*./(場所をあけてくれ) Make room for me./Step [Move] *aside*.

***とくい** 得意 ❶［［自慢］］ (誇り, 自負) pride; (勝ち誇った) triumph /tráiəmf/. ●自分の庭をたいそう得意に眺める look *with* great *pride* [*very proudly*] at one's garden. ▶彼は数学で満点をとって得意顔で家に帰ってきた He got full marks in math《米》[maths《英》] and came home *triumphantly* [*in triumph*].
❷［［上手］］ ●得意である be (very) *good*《*at*》; be strong《*in*》. ●歴史はあまり得意ではない be not very *good at* history [(得意分野でない)《話》be not in one's department].
会話 「君の得意科目は？」「数学と物理. 君は？」 "What are your *best* [*strongest*, (×most) *favorite*] subjects?" "(My *best* [*strongest, favorite*] subjects are) math and physics. What are yours?" (■(1) 複数形で尋ねていることに注意. (2) 一般に何が得意かを尋ねる場合は What are you *good at* [*strong in*]?)
❸［［顧客］］ (店のお客) a customer; (レストランなどの常連) a patron /péitrən/; ［［取引先］］ a connection.
●上［常］得意 a good [a regular] *customer*. ●長年のお得意 an old *customer*. ●新しいお得意ができる gain [get] new *customers*. ●そのレストランのお得意たち the *patrons* of the restaurant. ▶あの会社はアメリカにお得意が多い That firm *has* a large number of *connections* in America.
●得意満面 ▶彼は得意満面であった He is *beaming with triumph*.

—— **得意な** 形 ❶［［誇りに満ちた］］ proud; (勝ち誇った) triumphant. ●彼の得意な顔を見る look at his *proud* [*triumphant*] face.
❷［［上手な］］ good*; (有能な) strong; ［［気に入りの］］ favorite. (⇨名 ❷)
❸［［繁栄した］］ palmy; (栄光ある) glorious. ●得意な(=全盛)時代に in one's *palmy* days. ▶だれにも得意な時があるものだ《ことわざ》 Every dog has his day.

—— **得意がる** 動 (誇る) be proud《*of; that* 節》, take* pride《*in*》, pride oneself《*on; that* 節》; (うぬぼれる) get* conceited《*about*》. ▶彼は息子が成功したので得意っている He is *proud of* [*takes pride in, prides himself on*] his son's success./He is *proud that* his son has succeeded. ▶彼は成功してもけっして得意がったりしなかった He never *got conceited about* [(やや話) *got puffed up* (*with pride*) *over*] his success./His success didn't *go to* his *head* at all.
●得意な good customer. ●得意先 (⇨得意先)

とくい 特異 —— **特異な** 形 ●特異な(=比類のない)存在 a *unique* [*peculiar*] being.
●特異性 peculiarity. ●特異体質 ［医学］(an) idiosyncrasy. ▶彼は豚肉に対する特異体質(=アレルギー体質)がある He *is allergic* [*has an allergy*] *to* pork. ●特異日 ［気象］ a singularity; (説明的に) a calendar day that has a statistically high probability of particular weather, such as rain or sunshine.

とくいく 徳育 ●徳育に重きを置く put emphasis on *moral education* [(修養) *moral culture*].

とくいさき 得意先 a customer. (⇨得意 ❸) ●得意先を回る do the rounds of one's *customers*. ▶あの店は得意先が多い That store has a lot of *customers*./They have a lot of *customers* at that store.

どぐう 土偶 a clay image [figure, doll] (made in the Stone Age).

どくえい 独泳 —— **独泳する** 動 swim alone. ▶300メートルを過ぎると彼女の独泳となっていた She *was swimming far ahead* of other swimmers when she passed the 300-meter point./The *gap* between her and other swimmers *was beginning to widen* more and more after the 300-meter

どくえん 独演 图 ●独演会を開く (演芸などの) hold a one-man show.
— **独演する** 動 give a solo performance; perform alone.
どくが 毒牙 ●…の毒牙にかかる fall victim [《やや書》prey] to…; become a victim of…; be preyed upon [on] by….
どくが 毒蛾 〖昆虫〗a poisonous moth; (マイマイガ) a gypsy moth.
とくがく 篤学 ●篤学の士 an ardent [an avid, an enthusiastic, a devoted] student.
どくがく 独学 ●独学で得た知識 self-taught knowledge. ●独学で学者になった人 a self-taught scholar. ▶彼はほとんど独学で植物学者になった As a botanist, he is largely self-taught [self-educated].
— **独学する** 動 learn (it) by oneself; teach oneself.
どくガス 毒ガス poison gas. ●毒ガス攻撃を受けた場合に in the event of a poison gas attack. ●毒ガスでやられる be gassed. ●毒ガスを吸い込む breathe poison [poisonous] gas; gas oneself.
どくがん 独眼 形 one-eyed.
とくぎ 特技 (⇒才能) ▶彼女の特技はジャム作りだ Her specialty is making jam.
とくぎ 徳義 morality; morals. ●徳義を守る observe a code of ethics. ●徳義のある人 a man of honor. (⇒道義)
どくきのこ 毒茸 a poisonous mushroom; a toadstool.
どくぎょ 毒魚 a poisonous fish (複 ~, ~s).
どくけ 毒気 (⇒毒気(ど゙く))
どくけし 毒消し an antidote. ●サソリにかまれたときの毒消しを用意しておく prepare an antidote for [to] scorpion bite.
どくご 独語 ❶〖独(ひと)り言〗(a) soliloquy. (⇒独り言) ❷〖ドイツ語〗German. (⇒ドイツ)
どくご 読後 ●その本の読後感を記す write down one's impressions of the book.
どくさ 木賊 〖植物〗a scouring rush; a shave grass.
どくさい 独裁 图 (独裁政治) dictatorship; autocracy /ɔːtɒkrəsi/. (いずれも軽蔑的. 国家の意では [C])
— **独裁的な** 形 dictatorial /dɪktətɔːriəl/; autocratic.
●**独裁者** a dictator; an autocrat.
とくさく 得策 a wise [a good*] policy. ▶黙っている方が得策だろう(=賢いだろう) It would be wiser [more advisable, more diplomatic] for us to remain silent.
とくさつ 特撮 图 〖「特殊撮影」の略〗special effects.
— **特撮する** 動 use special effects.
どくさつ 毒殺 — **毒殺する** 動 ▶敵は多くの罪のない人々を毒殺した The enemy killed many innocent people with poison. ●The enemy poisoned many innocent people (to death).
とくさんぶつ 特産物 a specialty, a special product. (⇒名産)
とくし 特使 a special envoy. ●首相の特使として彼を中国に派遣する send [(特派)する] dispatch] him to China as the Prime Minister's special envoy.
どくし 毒死 death caused by poison. (⇒毒 ❶ ❸)
*__どくじ 独自__ — **独自の** 形 (⇒独特) ●彼独自の理由で for reasons of his own. ●独自の見解を発表する express one's own [personal] views. ●独自の(=他に類のない)文体で書く write in a unique style. ▶我々はその事件を独自に調査した We made

an independent investigation into the incident.
●**独自性** (個性) individuality; (独創性) originality.
とくしか 篤志家 (慈善心のある人) a charitable person; (博愛家) a philanthropist; (奉仕活動家) a volunteer.
とくしつ 特質 a characteristic (⇒特徴); (物の) a property; (その人[物]であるための) a quality. ▶強いのが鋼鉄の(一つの)特質です Strength is a property of steel.
とくしつ 得失 《書》profit and loss, profits and losses; (功罪) mérits and démerits; (長所と短所) advántages and disadvántages. (❗以上2例は対照強勢に注意) ●その問題の得失を論ずる debate the merits and demerits [(是非) the pros and cons] of the issue.
とくじつ 篤実 — **篤実な** 形 sincere; kind. ●温厚篤実な人柄(He is known to be) a true gentleman.
とくしってんさ 得失点差 〖サッカー〗the goal difference.
とくしゃ 特写 an exclusive photograph.
とくしゃ 特赦 (個人の) a special pardon; (政治犯などの) (an) amnesty 《for, to》. ●政治犯に特赦を行って grant (an) amnesty for [to] political criminals. ●特赦を発表する declare an amnesty 《for》. ●特赦で釈放される be released from prison under an amnesty.
どくしゃ 読者 a reader (❗最も一般的な語); (新聞・雑誌の定期購読者) a subscriber; (読書界) the reading public. ●一般の[熱心な]読者 a general [an avid] reader. ▶この新聞は多くの読者を持っている(=広く読まれている) This newspaper is widely read. / (発行部数が多い) This newspaper has a large circulation.
●**読者数[層]** (新聞・雑誌などの) a readership (❗常に単数形で); the number [a class] of readers.
●**読者欄** the readers' column.
どくじゃ 毒蛇 a poisonous snake; a viper.
どくしゃく 独酌 — **独酌する** 動 〖1人で飲む〗drink sake alone [by oneself, in solitude]; 〖手酌する〗help oneself to sake.
*__とくしゅ 特殊__ — **特殊な** 形 〖特別な, 普通でない〗special (↔ordinary, common); 〖特定の〗particular (↔general); 〖風変わりで特有の〗peculiar; 〖比類のない〗unique. (⇒特別) ●特殊訓練を受けた警官 a specially trained police officer. ●単語の一般的な意味と特殊な意味 the general and particular meanings of a word. ●真実をゆがめてしまう特殊(=特異)な才能を持っている have a peculiar talent for distorting the truth. ●特殊な経験をする have a unique experience.
●**特殊学級** a special class; (説明的に) a class for the handicapped. ●**特殊教育** special education; education for the disabled. ●**特殊鋼** special steel. ●**特殊講義** a special lecture 《on》. ●**特殊撮影** (⇒特撮) ●**特殊法人** (政府の) a governmental corporation.
とくしゅ 特種 a special kind 《of》. (⇒種類)
とくしゅ 特需 special procurement.
どくしゅ 毒手 ●毒手にかかる fall victim [prey] 《to》. (❗ victim, prey に冠詞をつけない)
とくしゅう 特集 — **特集する** 動 (雑誌・新聞が) feature. ▶この雑誌は政界の汚職事件を特集している This magazine features payoff scandals in political circles. ▶NHKは南極大陸を特集した(=特別番組を放映した) The NHK broadcast

[broadcasted] a feature [a special] program on the Antarctic Continent. ● 特集記事 a feature (article); (雑誌の) a cover story (❗表紙絵に対応する記事). ● 特集号 a special issue. ●オリンピック特集号を出す publish a *special issue* on the Olympic Games. ● 特集番組 a feature (program).

どくしゅう 独習 ── **独習する** 動 ●英語を独習する *study* [*learn*] English *by oneself*; *teach oneself* English.
● 独習書 a teach yoursélf book; (とらの巻)《話》a crib, 《米》a trot.

*__どくしょ 読書__ reading. ●熱心な読書家 an avid /ǽvid/ [a great] *reader*; (多読の) a well-read /-réd/ person; 《軽蔑的》(読書狂) a bookworm.
● 読書力を養う improve one's *reading* ability.
● 私は読書が好きだ I like [am fond of] *reading*.
● 読書百遍(ひゃくぺん)意(い)おのずから通ず Repeated reading makes the meaning clear.
── **読書する** 動 read* (books). (❗通例 books は省略される) ●読書しながらうたた寝してしまう *read* oneself into a nap. ●今どきの子供はあまり読書しない Children today don't *read* a lot [never *do* a lot of *reading*]./(多くの時間を使わない) Children today don't spend much time (in) *reading*.
● 読書会 a reading circle; a book club. ● 読書界 the reading public. ● 読書感想文 a book report. ▶この本を読み終わったら, 読書感想文を(=読んだ本の感想を)書いてください When you are through with this book, I'd like you to write your impressions of it. ● 読書感想文コンクール a book report contest. ● 読書室 (図書閲覧室) a reading room.

とくしょう 特賞 (1等賞の上の大賞) the grand [best] prize (❗the special prize は, 特別賞で1等賞より下); the highest prize. ●彼の絵は展覧会で特賞を取った[受けた(=与えられた)] His painting won [was awarded] the *grand prize* at the exhibition. (❗後の方は「主題(審査委員会)+ awarded his painting the grand prize」の受身の一つ)

とくじょう 特上 ── **特上(の)** 形 [(食物などが)極上の] the choicest; [とびきり立派な] supérb; [(品物などが)極上の] superfine. ● 特上の果物 the *choicest* fruits; fruits of *superb* quality. ● 特上小麦粉 *superfine* flour. ● 特上肉 *prime* beef. (❗「上肉」は choice beef, 「中肉」は good beef, 「並肉」は standard beef)

どくしょう 独唱 動 a (vocal) sólo (働~s). ●ソプラノ独唱 a sopráno *solo*.
── **独唱する** 動 sing a solo; solo.
● 独唱会 a recital. ● 独唱者 (ソリスト) a soloist.

*__とくしょく 特色__ [一般に] a characteristic, [目立った特徴] a feature; [独特の性質] a peculiarity; [固有の性質]《書》a property; [区別] (a) distinction. (⇨区別) ●特色のある(=すぐれた特徴を持つ)学校 a school with (some) distinguished *features*. ● 本来の特色を失う[失わない] lose [preserve] the original *characteristic*(s). ▶日本の景色の特色は何ですか What are the *characteristics* of Japanese scenery? ▶金(きん)には多くの優れた特色がある Gold has lots of distinguished *properties*.

とくしん 特進 ●2階級特進する get [be given] a two-rank *promotion* 《to》; be promoted two ranks 《to》.

とくしん 得心 [納得] (a) conviction; [満足] (a) satisfaction. (⇨納得)

とくしん 篤信 ● 篤信家 (信仰の念のあつい人) a firm [an ardent] believer 《in Catholicism》.

どくしん 独身 ● 独身(の) 形 single; (現在法律上の結婚をしていない) unmarried. ●独身生活を送る live *single*; lead a *single* life. ●一生独身で過ごす remain *single* [*unmarried*] all one's life; live and die *single*.
● 独身貴族 'a single aristocrat'; a swinging [an aristocratic] bachelor (❗後の方は後の概念も言葉もないという母語話者が多い). ● 独身者 a single [an unmarried] man [woman]; (男性) a bachelor; (女性) a fille /fíːɪ/; 《軽蔑的》an òld máid, a spinster, 《和製語》an old miss. ● 独身寮 (会社などの) a dormitory for single [unmarried] employees; (特に男子の) a bachelor apartment.

どくじん 毒刃 ●毒刃に倒れる be put to the sword; be killed with a dagger.

どくしんじゅつ 読心術 mind reading. ▶彼女は読心術にたけている She is good at *reading* other people's *mind*.

どくしんじゅつ 読唇術 lip reading. ●読唇術を心得ている be able to lip-read; be able to understand what a person is speaking by watching his lips move.

どくず 読図 ── **読図する** 動 read a map [a diagram].

とくする 得する (⇨得③)

どくする 毒する poison. ▶彼は都会の生活に毒されていた He *has been poisoned* by city life.

とくせい 特性 (特徴) a characteristic; (物質や植物の特性) a property. ▶自然への執着はこの民族の特性である The love of nature is *a characteristic* of [is *characteristic* of] this race./This race *is characterized* by the love of nature. ▶ソーダには汚れを落とす特性がある Soda has the *property* [(性質) *quality*] of removing dirt.

とくせい 特製 ── **特製(の)** 特別に作った specially made; ... of special make. ▶これはその会社特製の旅行かばんです This is a traveling bag *specially made* by that company./(その会社だけが作っている) This is a traveling bag *made only by* that company./Only that company *makes* this kind of traveling bag.
● 特製品 a specially made article. ● 特製本 a specially bound book.

とくせい 徳性 morality; virtue. ●徳性の高い人 a man [a woman] of great *virtue*; a very *virtuous* man [woman].

どくせい 毒性 toxicity. ●毒性のある poisonous, 《やや書》tóxic. ●毒性の強いガス toxic gas. ▶このキノコは毒性がある This toadstool is *poisonous*.

とくせつ 特設 ── **特設(の)** 形 special; (臨時の) temporary. ▶…のための特設ステージ a stage *specially prepared* [*made*] *for*....
── **特設する** 動 ●構内に電話ボックス数基を特設する *set up* some telephone booths *temporarily* on the premises.

どくぜつ 毒舌 [悪く言うこと] a barbed /báːɪbd/ [a sharp] tongue; [悪口の言葉] a barbed [a biting] remark. (❗barbed は「批判的で思いやりのない(=とげのある)」の意) ●毒舌を吐く make *barbed remarks* 《about》. ●あの男は毒舌家だ He has a *barbed* [*biting*, a *sharp*] tongue.

とくせん 特選 [極上の] メロン the *choicest* melon. ▶彼は美術展で特選(=特賞)になった He won the *grand* [*best*] *prize* at the art exhibition. (⇨特賞)
● 特選品 (えり抜きの品) choice articles [goods].

どくせん 毒腺 a poison gland.
どくせん 独占 图 a monopoly. ▶その会社は石油販売の独占権を持っている(=独占している) The firm has a *monopoly on* oil sales. ▶我々は同社と独占契約を結んだ We signed an *exclusive* agreement with the company.
── 独占する 動 monopolize, make* a monopoly of ...; 〖専有する〗have* [keep*] (it) to oneself.
● 権力[彼の愛]を独占する *monopolize* power [his love]. ▶彼はその部屋を独占していた He *had* the room *(all) to himself*.
● 独占インタビュー an exclusive interview. ● 独占価格 a monopoly [a monòpolístic] price. ● 独占企業 a monopoly [a monopolistic] enterprise [firm]. ● 独占禁止法 the Antitrust [Antimonopoly] Law. ● 独占資本 monopoly capital. ● 独占販売権 an exclusive marketing right.
どくぜんてき 独善的 ── 独善的な 形 〖一人よがりの〗self-righteous. ▶彼はとても独善的だ He is a very *self-righteous* person.
どくそ 毒素 a toxin; a poisonous substance.
とくそう 特捜 〖「特別捜査」の略〗a special investigation.
● 特捜部 the special investigation department.
とくそう 特装 ● 特装本 a specially bound book.
どくそう 毒草 a poisonous plant [herb].
どくそう 独走 图 ▶巨人は早くも独走態勢に入った The Giants *are* already *running far [way] ahead of the other teams* in the pennant race.
── 独走する 動 〖他を引き離す〗leave the rest [the others] far behind, run way ahead of the rest [the others] (! way は〖話〗で ahead を強めて「ずっと先に」の意); 〖自分勝手に行動する〗have one's own way.
どくそう 独奏 a solo (複 ~s). ▶彼はピアノの独奏をした He played [performed] a piano *solo*.
● 独奏会 (give) a (piano) recital. ● 独奏者 a soloist.
どくそう 独創 图 originality, 〖創造性〗creativity.
▶彼の作品は独創性にあふれている His works show great *originality*.
── 独創的な 形 original; 〖創造的な〗creative; 〖発明の才のある〗inventive, ingénious. ● 独創的な考え[作家] an *original* idea [writer]. ▶独創的なアイデアにはみんなが反対する Everyone comes out against *creative* ideas.
とくそく 督促 ── 督促する 動 ▶借金の返済を私に督促する〖催促する〗urge me to pay back my debt; 〖しつこくせがむ〗〖やや話〗press me for payment of my debt.
● 督促状 a demand letter; 〖主に英〗a reminder.
ドクター 〖医師〗a (medical) doctor; 〖博士〗a doctor. ● ドクターストップがかかっている have the *doctor's* order to stop 《doing》. (! ×doctor stop は和製英語)
● ドクターコース a doctoral program; 〖和製語〗doctor('s) course.
とくだい 特大 ── 特大(の) 形 〖特に衣服が〗outsize(d), oversize(d); 〖話〗king-size(d); 〖話〗extra-large [-big]. ● 特大の衣服 *outsize* [*extra-large*] clothes. ● 特大サイズコーナー an *outsize* (clothing) counter. ● 特大の帽子 an *oversize* [a *king-size*], an *extra-big* cap. ● 特大のホームラン a *tape-measure* home run.
● 特大号 an enlarged special issue. ● 特大品 an outsize.

とくたいせい 特待生 a student on a scholarship. (! an honor student は成績の良い学生を選んでこう呼ぶが奨学金は与えられていない) ▶彼はエール大学で特待生になった He got [won] a *scholarship* at Yale University. (! at を to に代えば, 入学前に特別の団体から奨学金を得たことになる。なお, two scholarships は 2 か所からの奨学金)
どくたけ 毒茸 a poisonous mushroom; a toadstool.
とくだね 特種 〖記事〗《やや話》a scoop; 〖独占記事〗an exclusive (article [report]); 〖材料〗material for a scoop. ▶これは我が社(=新聞)の特ダネだ This is the *scoop* for our paper.
どくだみ 〖植物〗(a) *dokudami*.
どくだん 独断 图 〖自分勝手な決断〗an arbitrary decision; 〖独断的態度〗a dogmatic manner; dógmatism. ● 独断で決める decide (it) *arbitrarily* 〖1 人で〗*for oneself*, (自分自身の判断で) on one's *own judgment*, 〖独断専行している〗act on one's *own authority* 〖相談せずに〗*without consultation*〗.
── 独断的な 形 〖勝手な〗arbitrary; 〖自説を押しつける〗〖書〗dogmatic.
どくだんじょう 独壇場 ▶リストの演奏にかけては彼の独壇場だった(=競争相手がいなかった) He *was unequaled* [*was unrivaled*] as a Liszt player.
とぐち 戸口 a door, a doorway. ● 戸口から戸口へ from *door* to *door*. ▶彼は戸口に立っていた He stood *at the door* [*in the doorway*].
とくちゅう 特注 ── 特注する 動 order ... specially 《from》.
● 特注品 a made-to-order [a custom-made] article, a special order.
*とくちょう 特長 〖長所〗a strong [a good] point; 〖取り柄〗a merit. ● 特長を十分生かす make full use of one's *strong* point [*merit*]. ▶この新型車の最大の特長は燃費効率がよいことです The *strongest point* of this new model is *in* good gas mileage /máilidʒ/.
*とくちょう 特徴 a chàracterístic. (! 他との区別の手がかりとなる性質のことで最も一般的な語); 〖特に目立ったところ〗a feature; 〖特に人格の〗a trait /tréit, 〖英〗tréi/; 〖一風変わった独特の〗a peculiarity; 〖固有の性質〗a quality. ▶彼の声には特徴がある He has a *characteristic* [*a typical*, *a peculiar*] voice.
会話「男の顔に何か特徴(=目印となるもの)はありましたか」「そうですねぇ, めがねをかけていたと思いますが」"Were there any *marks* on his face?" "Well, he had glasses on, I ∕ suppose." (! have ... on は wear と同じ意味で, 「...を身につける」の意)
【〜の特徴】● この辞典の特徴 the *characteristics* of this dictionary. ● その地方の気候の特徴 the climatic *features* of the district. ● その男[車]の特徴を言う describe the man [(the *features* of) the car]. (! describe the man's features とすると「その男の顔だちを詳しく説明する」の意となる) ▶寛容さは彼の特徴の一つである Generosity is one of his *characteristics* [*traits*]. ▶長い鼻が象の特徴だ The long nose is a *peculiarity* of the elephant. ▶そういった行動は今日の学生の特徴だ That kind of behavior *is characteristic of* the students of today. ∕ (受動うけられる) The students of today *are characterized* by that kind of behavior.
── 特徴的な 形 characteristic, (一風変わった) peculiar; (典型的な) typical; (目立つ) striking.
どくづく 毒づく use abusive language 《at》. (⇒悪態)
とくてい 特定 ── 特定(の) 形 specific; (特別の)

とくてん special; (決まった) particular, specified.
— **特定する** specify; (位置を) pinpoint. ●その船の位置を特定する *pinpoint* the position of the ship.
●**特定保健用食品** designated health food; food for special health use. ●**特定郵便局** a special post office.

とくてん 特典 [特権] a privilege; [恩典] a benefit. ●良い会社の(給与外の)特典 the *benefits* of a good company. ▶運動設備利用の特典は会員に限られます Only members have the *privilege* [*利点*) *advantage*] of using the sports facilities.

とくてん 得点 ❶ [競技の] (総得点) a score (⇨スコア); (野球など) a run; (サッカー・ホッケーなど) a goal; (その他) a point. ●相手チームを無得点に抑える hold the other team *scoreless*; shut out the opposing team. ●得点圏にランナーを置いて with runners in *scoring* position. ●得点をあげる score a *run*. ●得点をあげる 2 塁打を打つ hit a *run*-scoring double. ●得点のチャンスを逃す miss a *scoring* chance. ▶地元チームは 4 対 3 (の得点)で勝った The home team won the game by a *score* of 4 to 3. ▶今得点はどうなっている? What's the *score* now? ▶バレーの試合の最終得点はいくつでしたか What was the final *score* at the volleyball match? ▶彼は 6 点の得点をあげた He scored six *runs* [*goals*, *points*]. ▶日本の体操選手たちは平均 9.6 という高得点をあげた The Japanese gymnasts earned a good average *score* of 9.6.
❷ [試験の] (得点) a mark, (米) a grade. (⇨点) ●このテストで最高得点をとる get [ˣtake] the highest *mark* [*score*, *grade*] on the test.
●**得点王** [サッカー] the top scorer, the leading scorer. ●**得点圏打率** [野球] one's batting average with runners [men] in scoring position. ●**得点差** (⇨得失点差) ●**得点率** [サッカー] the goal average.

とくと 篤と (注意深く) carefully; (十分に) thoroughly /θˈɜːrouli, θάːrə/.

とくど 得度 — 得度する 動 [仏教] become a Buddhist priest [(尼) nun]; enter the Buddhist priesthood.

とくとう 特等 [特賞] the grand prize (⇨特賞); [特別の等級] a special class. ●福引きで特等を当てる draw the *grand* [*highest*] *prize* in the lottery.
●**特等室** a special(-class) room. ●**特等席** (劇場などの) a box (seat).

とくとくびょう 禿頭病 loss of hair; baldness; [医学] alopecia /ˌæləpˈiːʃiə/.

どくどく ●とくとくと注がれるウイスキーの音 the *gurgling* sound of whiskey pouring out of the bottle.

とくとく 得々 — 得々と 副 (誇らしげに) proudly; (意気揚々と) triúmphantly, in triumph. (⇨得意, 意気揚々)

*__どくとく 独特 — 独特の 形__ [特有の] (やや書) peculiar; [類のない] unique; [独創的な] original; [特別による] special (↔general); [独自の] one's own, of one's own; [特質を示す] characteristic. ●ヘミングウェイ独特の文体 a style *peculiar* [(書) *proper*] *to* Hemingway. ●彼独特のやり方で問題を解く solve the problem in his *own* way. ●彼女独特の笑みをたたえて with her *characteristic* smile. ●彼独特の才能を発達させるように努めなさい Try to develop your *special* ability. ●そのような事柄には彼独特のやり方がある He has a way of his *own* in such matters. ●彼は独特の歌い方をする He has a *unique* singing style.

どくどく ▶傷から血がどくどく流れ出た Blood flowed

(out) *heavily* from the wound. (▲gush は「急にたくさんあふれ出る」の意で,「どくどく」には当たらない)/ Much blood ran from the wound.

どくどくしい 毒々しい garish /ɡéərɪʃ/; (けばけばしくて下品な) gaudy /ɡɔ́ːdi/. ●毒々しいメークをしている wear *gaudy* makeup. ●毒々しい(=悪意のある)言葉を使う use *malicious* [*spiteful*] language.

ドクトリン [原則] (a) doctrine.

どくとるマンボウこうかいき『どくとるマンボウ航海記』 *Doctor Manbo at Sea*. (▲参考▼ 北杜夫の小説)

*__とくに 特に__ especially; specially; particularly; in particular; specifically.

┌─────────────────────────────────────┐
│ **使い分け** **especially, specially** 互いに交換して │
│ 用いられるが一般に前の方は (書) に,後の方は (話) で │
│ 好まれる. 本来の使い分けについては (⇨特別(に)). │
│ **particularly** especially とほぼ同意で,個別化・ │
│ 特殊化に重点がある. │
│ **in particular** particularly と同意だが,通例名 │
│ 詞や nothing, anyone などの直後に置く. また次の │
│ ように一般的なことを述べた後で最重要例を導入する │
│ のに使われる: このクラスの生徒はみんな背が高い. 特に太 │
│ 郎は 190 センチもある The students in this class │
│ are all tall. *In particular* [ˣEspecially, │
│ ˣSpecially], Taro is no less than 190 centi- │
│ meters tall. │
│ **specifically** 「同種のものの中から特に指定して」の │
│ 意. │
└─────────────────────────────────────┘

●私の特に仲のいい友達 a *special* [a *particular*] friend of mine. ●その問題に特に注意をはらう pay *special* [*particular*] attention to the problem. ▶私は京都が好きだ. 特に春がいい I like Kyoto, *especially* [*particularly*] in the springtime. ●この本は特におもしろいというわけでもない This book isn't *particularly* [*especially*, *specially*] interesting./This book isn't of *particular* [*special*, (書・まれ) *especial*] interest. ▶特にその作家を批判に敏感だ The writer, *especially*, is sensitive to criticism. (▲主語を修飾する最上級はその直後に置く) ▶これは特に重要な問題だ This is an *especially* important matter. ▶今日特にすることはありません I have nothing *special* [(*in*) *particular*] to do today. ▶私は特に招かれてはいない I'm not (*specifically*) invited. (▲この「特に」は英語ではあまり意味がない)

とくのうか 篤農家 a good [an efficient] farmer.

どくは — 読破する 動 ▶1日1冊を読破する *read through* a book a day.

とくはい 特配 图 (特別の配当) a special dividend; (特別の配給) an extra [a special] ration. ●特配を受ける (⇨動)
— **特配する 動** give [get] extra rations.

とくばい 特売 a (special [bargain]) sale. (▲通例単に a sale という) ●特売価格で買う buy (it) at a special [a sale, a bargain] price. ●下着の特売品あさりをする hunt *bargains in* underwear. ●特売日 (掲示) *Sale today*. ▶あの店は今カメラの特売をやっている They are having [holding, (話) running] a *sale on* cameras at that store./ There is a *sale* of cameras going on at that store. ▶このかばんは特売で安く買ったのです I got this bag cheap in a *sale* [*at a sale*, (米) *on sale*].
●**特売場** a bargain floor [(台) counter, (地階) basement]. (▲最後の言い方は米英のデパートでは地階に特売場があることから)

とくはいん 特派員 a (special) correspondent (*for The Times*). ●我が社のシドニー特派員からの報告 a report from our Sydney *correspondent*.

- NHK ロンドン特派員 an NHK *correspondent* in London.

どくはく 独白 图 (a) monolog, (a) soliloquy /səlíləkwi/.
— **独白する** 動 deliver (in) a soliloquy.

とくはつ 特発 ● 特発列車 an extra train. ● 繁忙期には1日数本特発する run a few *extra trains* a day in season.

とくばん 特番 〔「特別番組」の略〕a special. ● テレビの夜の選挙特番 an election night *special* on television.

とくひつ 特筆 special mention. ● 特筆すべき出来事 an event worthy of *special mention*; a *noteworthy* event. ● 特筆大書 (⇨特筆大書)

とくひつたいしょ 特筆大書 —— 特筆大書する 動 write (it) in large [red] letters. ● 特筆大書すべき (きわめて重要な) vitally important.

とくひょう 得票 the number of votes polled; (票を)vote. ● 法定得票数 the legally required (minimum *number of) votes*. ▶ その候補者の得票数は2,000票だった The candidate got [gained, polled] 2,000 *votes*.

どくふ 毒婦 (男をだます悪い女) a wicked /wíkid/ woman.

どくふ 読譜 —— 読譜する 動 (楽譜を見て理解する)read music.

どくぶつ 毒物 (a) poison /pɔ́izn/. (❗個々の毒物は C)
● 毒物を検出する find out [detect] *a poisonous substance*. ● 砒素(ひそ)はよく知られた毒物である Arsenic is *a known poison*.
● 毒物学 toxicology.

:とくべつ 特別 图 ● 彼は特別(＝例外)だ He is an *exception*.
—— **特別(の)** 形 special,《書・まれ》especial; particular; specific; 〔例外的な〕exceptional; 〔異常な〕extraordinary; 〔余分の〕extra; 〔固有の〕peculiar.

> **使い分け** special 領域や範囲が限定されていることを表す. 時に高度な専門性を表すこともある.
> especial 一般とは極端にかけ離れることを表す. 堅い文体の書き言葉で用いられる.
> particular 特定の要素が本来は同種・同質であるはずの他の要素と大きく異なっていることを表す.
> specific 抽象的・流動的ではなく具体的・特定的であることを表す. 堅い文体の書き言葉で用いられることが多い.

● 彼に特別の注意を払う pay *special* [*particular*] attention to him. ● 特別な場合を除いて except on *special* occasions. ● 特別な目的のためにそれをする do it for a *special* [a *particular*] purpose. ● 特別の理由もなく for no *particular* [*special*] reason. ● 特別な事例を引用する cite *specific* cases.

—— **特別(に)** 副 especially; specially; 〔格別に〕particularly, in particular; 〔異常に〕extraordinarily; 〔例外的に〕exceptionally.

> **解説** specially と especially: 原則として specially は「特定の目的のために、特別な方法で」の意で、especially は「非常に、とりわけ」の意で用いるが、口語では especially の代わりに specially が用いられることも多い. especially は堅い文体に多く、特に前置詞や接続詞の前で好まれる. (⇨特に〔類語〕)

● 特別製のカメラ a *specially*-made camera. ● 特別才能のある少年 a boy of *exceptional* talent; an *exceptionally* talented boy. ● 特別に興味ある問題 a matter of *special* interest; a *specially* interesting matter. ● 特別上等のワイン extra good wine. ▶ 彼女は私のため特別に歌ってくれた She sang *especially* [*specially*] for me. (❗ 前の方は「他の人ではなくとりわけ私のために (for me above all)」の意を、後の方は「私のために特別の目的で (for a particular purpose for me)」の意を含む. ただし、後の方は「私のために特別な方法で歌ってくれた」の意にもなる) ▶ その庭は特別大きかった It was a *particularly* large garden. ▶ 今日は特別暑い It is *specially* [*especially*] hot today./(例外的に) It is *exceptionally* [(いつもなく)*unusually*] hot today. ▶ どうして君だけを特別扱いしなくてはならないのか What makes you so *special*?

● 特別会計 a special account. ● 特別機 a special [particular] plane. ● 特別急行列車 a special [limited] express train. ● 特別区 (東京都の区) a special ward; (特別な目的の区) a special zone. ● コロンビア特別区 the *District* of Columbia 《略 DC》. ● 特別号 (増刊号) an extra number. ● 特別講義 a special lecture 《*on*》. ● 特別講習 a special class [course] 《*in* modern Greek》. ● 特別国会 a special session of the Diet. ● 特別職 (特別な公職) special public office [service]. ● 特別番組 a special. (⇨特番) ● 特別養護老人ホーム a nursing home for the aged.

どくへび 毒蛇 a poisonous snake.
とくほう 特報 图 special news. (⇨速報)
—— **特報する** 動 announce [give] special news 《*about*》; flash.

どくぼう 独房 a (solitary) cell. ● 独房に監禁される be placed in *solitary confinement* [《話》*in solitary*].

とくほん 読本 (教科書) a textbook; (リーダー) a reader.

ドグマ 〔教義〕(a) dogma.

どくみ 毒味 —— 毒見する 動 (味見をする) taste 《soup》; (毒の混入をみる) have ... in one's mouth to see if the food is poisoned.

とくむ 特務 ● 特務(＝特別の任務)を帯びている be on *special duty*.
● 特務機関 an intelligence [a secret] organization.

どくむし 毒虫 a poisonous [a venomous] insect.
とくめい 特命 ● 特命(＝特別の使命)を帯びて派遣される《やや書》be sent on a *special mission*.
● 特命全権大使 an ambassador extraordinary and plenipotentiary.

とくめい 匿名 anonymity /ænənímətɪ/. ▶ 私は匿名の手紙を受け取った I received an *anonymous* [a *nameless*] letter. ▶ 彼女は匿名で記事を書いた She wrote an article *anonymously*./(匿名が条件で) She wrote an article on condition of *anonymity*.

とくもく 徳目 ● 徳目を並べる list [《やや書》enumerate] virtues.

どくや 毒矢 a poisoned arrow.
とくやく 特約 ● 特約を結ぶ make a *special contract* [*arrangement*]. ● …との特約により by *special arrangement* with ....
● 特約店 (特別代理店) a special agency; (チェーン店) a chain store; a multistore,《英》a multiple shop.

どくやく 毒薬 (a) poison. (⇨毒) ● 毒薬を飲んで自殺する kill oneself by taking some *poison*; poison oneself.

とくゆう 特有 —— 特有の 形 〔固有の〕《書》proper; 〔独特の〕《やや書》peculiar; 〔特性を示す〕characteristic; 〔独自の〕of one's own; 〔他と区別できる〕distinctive. ● 特有の癖 a habit *peculiar*

とくよう [*proper*] to him. ●人間特有の本能 an instinct *characteristic of* [*proper to*] human beings. ▶日本の文物は特有の美を備えている Things Japanese have a beauty *of their own*. (! things Japanese は日本的な物質的な特有のもの。Japanese things と異なることに注意) ▶その美しさは彼の作品に特有のものです The beauty is *specific* [*peculiar*] *to* his works. ▶彼女はイギリス人ではないと思う。フランス語特有のなまりがあるから She can't be English [an Englishwoman]. She's got a *distinctive* French accent.

とくよう 特養 〘「特別養護老人ホーム」の略〙(⇒特別)

とくよう 徳用 ── 徳用(の) 形 economical.
●徳用な an economical article. ●徳用びん an economy(-sized) bottle.

どくりつ 独立 名 independence; 〘自活〙 self-support. ●独立を宣言する declare *independence*.
●独立心に欠ける lack the spirit of *independence*.
●独立心のある女性 an *independently*-minded woman.
── 独立の 形 independent; (自立の, 自活の) self-supporting.
── 独立する 動 become* [be] independent 《*of*》; (自活する) support oneself. (⇒自立する) ●独立して independently; (自分の力で) for oneself; (人の助力を借りないで) on one's own. ▶インドは1947年英国から独立した India *became independent of* [*from*] Britain in 1947. (! 独立が多く用いられるようになった)/India *won* [*gained*] *independence from* [×of] Britain in 1947. ▶彼はまだ若いので独立して生計を立てることができない He is still too young to *support himself* [*earn his own living*]. ▶彼は独立して商売を始めた He started an *independent* [his *own*] business./(独力で店を開いた) He opened a store *for himself* [*on his own, of his own*]. (! of his own は「自分自身の」の意で a store に直結する)
●独立独歩 ▶彼は独立独歩の人だ He is very *independent* [*self-reliant*].
●独立運動 an independence movement; a movement for independence. (! 特定の国のものは the independence movement of India, the movement for Indian independence のようにいう) ●独立記念日 Independence Day. (! 米国では 7月4日に当たるので, the Fourth of July ともいう) ●独立行政法人 an independent administrative corporation [agency]. ●独立国 an independent country; a sovereign state. ●独立採算制 the self-supporting accounting system. ▶彼は独立採算制でホテルチェーンを経営している He runs a chain of hotels on a *self-paying* basis. ●独立戦争 a war of independence. (! the War of Independence は米国の独立戦争をさす. 《英》では the War of American Independence という)

どくりょう 読了 ── 読了する 動 ●小説を読了する finish *reading* a novel; (始めから終わりまで読む) read a novel *through*.

どくりょく 独力 ── 独力で 副 by oneself, on one's own. (! 後のが口語的); (自分のためになるように) for oneself. ▶彼はそれをまったく独力でやった He did it all *by himself* [*on his own*]. ▶彼女独力での世界一周の航海を計画している She plans *single-handed* voyage around the world.

とぐるま 戸車 a roller fitted on a sliding door; (窓枠に取り付けた車) a sash roller.

とくれい 特例 (例外) an exception, (特別の場合) a special case. ●規則に特例を設ける make an *exception* of a rule.

とくれい 督励 名 encouragement.
── 督励する 動 ●計画を遂行するように彼を督励する(=激励する) encourage [(刺激する) spur; (促す) urge] him to carry out the plan.

とぐろ ▶蛇がとぐろを巻いた[巻いていた] The snake coiled (*itself*) up [*lay in a coil*].
●とぐろを巻く ▶あいつらはよくこの喫茶店でとぐろを巻いている(=いつまでもねばっている) They *are* often *sitting around* in this coffee shop *for a long time*. (! I often see them sitting ... の方が口語的)

どくろ 髑髏 a skull.

どくわ 独和 ── 独和辞典 a German-Japanese dictionary.

*******とげ** 刺 (植物の茎にある) a thorn; (動物・植物などの) a prickle, a spine; (木などの破片) a splinter. ●とげのある thorny, prickly; (言葉などが) cutting, stinging. ●バラのとげ the *thorns* on the roses. ●指のとげを抜く pick [pull] a *thorn* out of one's finger; remove a *thorn* from one's finger. ▶手のひらにとげが刺さった I got a *splinter in* [*into*] my palm./ A *thorn* ran into my palm. ▶彼の言葉にはとげがある He has a very sharp tongue. ▶彼女はとげを含んだ声でまた尋ねた She asked again *with an edge to* her voice.

とけあう 溶け合う ▶これらの二つの色は溶け合って青になる These two colors *blend* [*merge, melt*] into blue. ▶この緑と青が溶け合う(=色を混ぜていくうちにお互いが他の一部となる)かどうかは私には分からない I can't tell if this green *merges in with* [*into*] blue. ▶ニューヨークは人種のるつぼと言われるが, 実際には人種は少しも溶け合っていない New York is often said to be a 'melting pot,' but actually different races are not *mixing together* at all (there).

とけあう 解け合う (⇒打ち解ける)

*******とけい** 時計 (掛け時計, 置き時計) a clock; (腕時計, 懐中時計) a watch. ●区別する場合は a wall [a table] clock (掛け[置き]時計), a wrist-watch (腕時計), a pocket watch (懐中時計) のようにいう)
① 〜 [〜から 〜] ●目覚まし時計 an alarm (*clock*). (⇒目覚まし) ●自動巻き時計 a self-winding *watch*. ●デジタル[アナログ]時計 a digital [an analog] *watch* [*clock*]. ●振子, 電波[電波]時計 a pendulum (an electric; a radio) *clock*. (! a clock radio は「ラジオ時計」)
② [〜部で 〜] ● 時 計 仕 掛 け(の) clockwork. ●時計回りの[に] clockwise. ●時計と逆回りの[に] 《米》counterclockwise, 《英》anticlockwise. ●時計のバンド 《米》a watchband, 《英》a watch-strap. ●時計の(かちかち[ちくたく]という)音 the ticking of a *watch* [a *clock*].
③ [時計が[は]] ●君の時計は何時ですか What time is it by your *watch*? ▶その時計は正確だ The *clock* is correct [right]./The *clock* keeps good [right] time. ▶その時計は狂っている The *clock* is wrong [(正確に動かない) isn't running right, (故障している) is out of order]. ▶この時計は5分進んでいる[遅れている] This *watch* is five minutes fast [slow, 《米・スコット》 behind, ×late]. ▶私の時計は1日に10分進む[遅れる] My *watch* gains [loses] ten minutes a day. ▶この時計は動かない This *watch* doesn't work [×move]. ▶時計が2時を打った[指していった] The *clock* struck [showed] two (o'clock). (! o'clock はない方が普通)
④ [時計を[と]] ●時計をはめる put on (↔take off) a *watch*. (! 「はめている」状態をいうときは wear a watch) ●時計を巻く wind (up) a *clock* [a *watch*]. (! wind の発音は /wáind/) ▶テレビの時報など

とけこむ

時計を合わせる set one's *watch* by the TV time signal [the time-signal on TV]. ● 目覚まし時計を6時に合わせる set the alarm *clock* for six. ▶彼は時計を10分遅らせた[進めた] He put [set] his *watch* ten minutes back [ahead]. ▶その仕事を終えることにとらわれっこでやっている I'm working *against the clock* to finish the job. (❗against the clock は「時間に追われて」の意の口語的表現)
● **時計皿**〖化学〗a watch glass. ● **時計数字**（ローマ数字）Roman numerals. ● **時計台** a clock tower. ● **時計屋**（人）a watchmaker,《米》a jeweler;（店）a watchmaker's,《米》a jeweler's.

とけこむ 溶け込む ❶〖溶けて入り込む〗melt (*into*). (⇨溶ける)
❷〖なじんで一体となる〗fit (-tt-) (*into*);（順応する）adapt (oneself) (*to*). ● 地元の人たちに溶け込む *fit in* with the local people. ● 都会の生活に溶け込めない can't *fit into* city life (❗「都会の生活に上手に溶け込む」なら *fit in* well *to* city life となる). ▶彼はすぐにその新しい環境に溶け込んだ He adapted (himself) quickly [(容易に) easily] *to* the new environments.

どげざ 土下座 图（ひれ伏すこと）prostration.
— **土下座する** 動 throw oneself on the ground,《やや書》prostrate oneself. ● 土下座して謝る fall [go down] on one's knees to ask for pardon.

どけち (⇨どけち)

とけつ 吐血 图〖医学〗hematemesis.
— **吐血する** 動 vomit blood (from one's stomach).

とげとげしい ● とげとげしい（＝辛らつな）言葉 *sharp* [*biting*,（心に突き刺さる）*stinging*] words. ● とげとげしい（＝荒々しい）態度で in a *harsh*〖敵意のある〗a *hostile*] manner.

とげぬき とげ抜き〘a pair of〙tweezers.

*** とける 溶ける 解ける**（固体が熱で）melt;（固体が液体の中で）dissolve;（凍結した物が）thaw;（金属などが）fuse (❗専門的な語). ● 解けてなくなる *melt* away. ● 解けて水になる *melt into* water. ▶太陽が出ると雪は解けはじめた The snow began to *melt* [*thaw*] when the sun came out. ▶導管の凍結が解けた The pipe *thawed*. ▶雪は夜中ごろやんだ.そして朝にはすっかり解けてしまっていた The snow stopped around midnight. And in the morning it had all *gone*. ▶塩は水に溶ける Salt *dissolves* in water./Salt *is soluble* (↔*insoluble*) in water. ▶銅と錫(すず)が溶けてブロンズができる Copper and tin *fuse together* to make bronze.

*** とける 解ける**（なぞ・問題などが解明される）be solved, be worked out（後の方が口語的）;（結ばれた物がほどける）come* untied [undone];（疑いなどが晴れる）be cleared, be dispelled;（封鎖・禁令などが撤廃される）be lifted. (⇨ほど・溶ける)▶この数学の問題はどうしても解けない I can't for the life of me *solve* [*work out*] this math problem. ▶靴ひもが解けた My shoelace *has come untied* [*undone*,（ゆるんだ）*loose*]. ▶誤解は解けた The misunderstanding *was cleared up*. ▶彼の怒りは解けた（＝消え去った）His anger *disappeared* [*was gone*,（和らいだ）*melted away*].

*** とげる 遂げる** ❶〖高い目標に到達する〗attain;〖苦難の末獲得する〗achieve;〖努力の末成就する〗accomplish. ● 目的を遂げる *attain* [*achieve*] one's goal; *accomplish* one's purpose. (❗前の方が最終目的を達成する感じが強い) ● 思いを遂げる *attain*〖実現させる〗*realize*] one's wish.
❷〖結果となる〗● 自殺を遂げる *commit* suicide. (❗日常語としては kill oneself の方が普通) ● 著しい[長

足の]進歩を遂げる *make* (×a) remarkable [rapid] progress (*in*).

■ **DISCOURSE**
日本はこの10年間、さまざまな変化を遂げてきた．しかし人口の減少は、この10年間で経験した変化の中でも最大級のものだ Japan has *undergone* many changes in the past ten years. *Yet* the decrease of its population is one of the greatest changes it has experienced during this period. (❗yet（しかし）は逆接を表すディスコースマーカー. 文頭で用いると「しかし」の意になる)

どける 退ける（他の場所に移す）remove;（現在地から移す）move;（邪魔にならないようにする）get (a chair) out of the way. ● 庭からの石をどける（＝取り除く）*take* the stone *out of* the garden; *remove* the stone *from* the garden. ● 雪をどける *get rid of* the snow (❗get rid of は「(好ましくないものを)排除する」の意) ▶そのオートバイをどけてくれ *Get* the motorcycle *out of the way*.

どけん 土建 ● **土建会社** a construction company. ● **土建業** civil engineering and construction. ● **土建業者** a civil engineering and building contractor.

とこ 床 [a] bed. (⇨ベッド) ● 子供を床に寝かしつける put [get] a child to *bed*. ● 床を整える make a [the, one's] *bed*. (❗ベッドをいつでも寝られる状態に整えることであるが、「ふとんを敷く」の意でも用いられる) ● 床を上げる put away the bedding [bedclothes]. ● 床を離れる get up (from *bed*);（床から出る）get out of *bed*;（病床から）leave one's *bed* [sickbed].
● **床につく** go to bed (❗×go to a [the] bed は不可);（病気で）take to one's bed. ● **床についている**（寝ている）be in bed;（病気で）be sick in bed. ● 風邪で床についている *be in bed* with a cold,《話》be laid up with a cold.
● **床に伏す**（病気で）take to one's bed;（床に身を伏せる）lie face down on the floor.

‡**どこ** ❶〖場所〗where;〖どの方向〗which direction [way]. ▶市役所はどこですか *Where*'s the city hall?/（教えてください）Can you tell [×teach] me *where* the city hall is?/*Which direction* [*way*] is the city hall? ▶ここは東京のどこですか *Where* in Tokyo am I [×is here]? (⇨**会話**〔第2問〕) ▶いちばん近い地下鉄の駅はどこですか *Which* is the nearest subway station? ▶あの列車はどこ行きかしら Do you know *where* that train goes [is bound for]?

会話「エジプトの首都はどこですか」「カイロです」"*What* [×*Where*] is the capital of Egypt?" "Cairo (is) [（古）It's Cairo]."

会話（写真を見て）「まあすてき．（ここは）どこですか」「インドのどこ？」"Oh, that's nice. *Where's* this?" "It's India." "*Where*(*abouts*) in [*What part of*] India?"

会話「その時計はどこ製ですか」「日本製です」"*Where* was the clock made?" "It was made in Japan."/"*What* make is the clock?" "It is a Japanese make."

翻訳のこころ どこをどう歩いたのだろう，私が最後に立ったのは丸善の前だった（梶井基次郎『檸檬』）I don't remember [can't recall] *where* and how I walked. In the end, I found myself (standing) in front of Maruzen. (❗(1)「どこ」は which place でなく where で表す．(2)「…にいる（ことに自分自身が気づく）」は find oneself in …)

① 【どこが】where;【何が】what. ▶その種をまくのは

どこか一番いいだろう *Where's* the best place to plant the seeds? ▶その機械のどこが故障ですか *What's* [×*Where's*] wrong with the machine?
【会話】「それはとてもできないよ」「どこがそんなに難しいの」 "I can't possibly [《話》 just can't] do that." "*What's* so difficult about it?/*What* is it (that) troubles you so much about it?"
【会話】「どことどこが試合をやっていたの」「ドラゴンズとジャイアンツよ」"*Who* [×*Which*] was playing *who*?" "The Dragons and the Giants."

② 【どこの】 where; 【何】 what; 【どちらの】 which; (どこ(＝だれ)の家の) whose. ▶どこの出身ですか *Where* are you [do you come] from? ▶(どこで生まれたか) *Where* were you born?/(何高校卒業) *Where* did you go to high school?/*What* high school did you graduate from? ▶どこの劇場でやってるの *Which* theater is it playing at? (❗*is playing* は「上演されている」の意) ▶だれも彼がどこのだれだか知らない Nobody knows *where* he comes from or who he is.
【会話】「それどこの犬？」「知らない。僕にずっとついて来たんだ」"*Whose* dog is it?" "I don't know. He has tagged along behind me all the way."

③ 【どこに[へ, で]】 where. ▶彼らはどこにいるの *Where* are they now? ▶どこに花びんを置けばいいか彼に聞いてください Ask him *where* to put [you should put] the vase. (❗後の方が口語的) ▶それをどこで見つけたの *Where* did you find it?
【会話】「どこにお勤めですか」「ソニーです」"*Who* [×*Where*] do you work for?" "(I work for) Sony." ▶*Where* do you work? は勤務地を聞く言い方/"*What* [*Which*] company do you work for?" "(I work for) Sony." (❗*which* を用いるとすでに職種は知っていることを暗示)
【会話】「ミラー先生は授業中机に座っているんだよ」「どこにですって」"Mr. Miller sits on his desk while teaching." "On *what*?"
【会話】「どこへ行くの」「大阪へ」"*Where* are you going (to) [*Where* ×to]?" "(To) Osaka." (⇨⑥; どちら❷)

④ 【どこから】 where ... from. ▶どこから電話しているの *Where* are you calling *from*? ▶どこからか(＝どこかある所から)ひどいにおいがしてきた There came a bad smell *from somewhere*. ▶夜明けとともにどこからもなく何百という露店が現れて広場を埋めつくす At the break of dawn hundreds of stalls appear *from* [*out of*] *nowhere*, filling [and fill] the whole square. ▶どこから始めていいものやら I wonder *where* to begin [(何から) *what* to begin *with*].

⑤ 【どこまで】 how far. (❗程度にも用いる) ▶彼はどこまで信用できるのか分からない I don't know *how far* I can trust him. ▶神戸のことならどこからどこまでも知っている I know *every* part of Kobe [(すべてのこと) *everything* about Kobe].
【会話】「どこまで新幹線で行くのですか」「京都までです」"*How far* are you going (to go) on the Shinkansen?" "(I'm going) as far as Kyoto." (❗このように距離を問題にするのではなく、駅の切符売り場の係員やタクシーの運転手が「どこまで」と目的地を聞く場合は *Where to*, sir [ma'am]? (やまで))
【会話】「この前の授業ではどこまでやりましたか」「30 ページの 7 行目で終わりました」 "*Where* were we [*How far* did we go] (in the) last class?" "We left off at line 7 on page 30." (❗この問いかけはいずれも話を中断や脱線の後再開するときに「どこまで話しましたっけ」の意で用いることができる)

⑥ 【どこへ[に]...しても】 【...の所どこでも】 *wherev*-

er; 【どの場所でも】 anywhere. ▶どこへ行っても親切な人はいます *Wherever* [*No matter where*] you go, you'll find kind people. (❗後の方が口語的. *Wherever* you *may* go, ... は文語的) ▶彼はどこへ行くにもカメラをもって行った He took his camera *wherever* he went. ▶それをこの部屋のどこに置いてもよい You can put it *anywhere* in this room.

⑦ 【どこに[へ]も...以】 not ... anywhere, nowhere. ▶休み中特にどこへも行かなかった I didn't go *anywhere* [went *nowhere*] in particular during the vacation. ▶彼の財布はどこにも見当たらなかった His wallet was *nowhere* to be found./He could *not* find his wallet *anywhere*.

❷ 【どの点】 what. ▶その本のどこが(＝どの部分が)おもしろかったですか *What part* of the book did you find interesting? ▶彼はどこにいい所がない There is *nothing* good about him. ▶ラバと馬はどこがどう違うのか私には分からない I have no idea *what* the *difference* between a mule and a horse is.
【会話】「それじゃあまりに大きすぎるよ」「大きすぎる？どこが？」 "It's much too [×*too much*] big." "Too big? In *what* respect?"

とこあげ 床上げ ── **床上げする** 動 (病気が治る) recover from one's illness.

とこいり 床入り ── **床入りする** 動 (寝る) go to bed; (新婚夫婦が) consummate one's marriage.

とこう 渡航 图 〖船・飛行機で〗a voyage; 〖船で〗a passage. ● 渡航手続きをする go through the formalities for *going abroad*.
── **渡航する** 動 ▶ハワイに渡航する go on [*make*] *a voyage to* Hawaii; *go over to* Hawaii. ● 海外渡航する *make a* foreign *voyage*; go abroad.
● 渡航者 a passenger.

どごう 怒号 图 a roar (of anger); a howl /hául/ (of rage).
── **怒号する** 動 roar (in anger); (怒りでわめく) howl with rage.

どこか ❶ 【場所】 somewhere, 《米話》someplace; (どこかある...) sóme (❗以上 3 語は通例肯定文および yes の答えを予想する疑問文で用いる); anywhere, 《米話》anyplace; (どこかある...) any. (❗以上 3 語は通例疑問文で用いる) ▶どこかこの辺[他の場所]で彼の帽子を見た I saw his hat *somewhere* near here [*somewhere* else, elsewhere, 《米話》*someplace* else]. (❗elsewhere は somewhere else より堅い語) ▶ここは寒い。どこか暖かい所へ行こう It's cold here. Let's go (×to) *somewhere* warm [×*warm somewhere*]. (❗(1) 形容詞は somewhere, anywhere の後に置く. (2) Let's go to *some* warm place. ともいえる. この場合 place は名詞なので to が必要. これに対し somewhere も形容詞も修飾されている臨時的名詞であるが、本来は副詞なので前置詞は不要) ▶どこか(＝どこでもいいから)景色のよい所へ行きたい I want to visit *any* scenic spot. ▶どこか具合が悪いの。しんどそうだよ Is there *something* wrong? You look very tired [don't look too well].

【どこかへ[に, で, の]】 ▶あすどこかへ行きますか Are you going *anywhere* [*somewhere*] tomorrow? (❗(1) somewhere ではどこかへ行くということを前提とした尋ね方. (2) Are you going out tomorrow? (あす外出しますか)の方が普通) ▶私はその本を本箱のどこかに入れた I put the book *somewhere* [×*anywhere*] in the bookcase. ▶彼は東京のどこか[東京かどこか]に住んでいるのですか Does he live (×in) *anywhere* in Tokyo [in Tokyo or *anywhere*]? ▶どこかにいいレストランはないでしょうか Do you know *where* there's a good restaurant? ▶どこかのばかがこんなところに自転車を置きやがって

Some fool left a bike [a bicycle] here.
会話 「どこかで お目にかかったような気がするのですが」「さあ、そうでしたかしら」 "I think we've met you *somewhere*." "I'm not sure. Do you?"

❷ 【どことなく】 (⇨どことなく) ▶彼はどこか人を引きつけるところがある There's *something* attractive about him.

とこかざり 床飾り a *tokokazari*; (説明的に) a work of art for decorating a *tokonoma*.

ドコサヘキサエンさん ドコサヘキサエン酸 【生化学】DHA ((*do*cosa*h*exa*e*noic /dɑ̀kəsəhèksəinóuik/ *a*cid の略)).

とこしえ 永え eternity. (⇨永遠, 永久)

とこずれ 床擦れ 《get [have; (防ぐ) prevent]》a bedsore.

どこそこ 何処其処 ▶どこそこの人と聞いたがよく思い出せない I can't exactly remember *where he came from*.

とこつち 床土 seedbed soil [earth].

どこでも 【どの1か所でも】anywhere, 《米話》anyplace; 【どこもすべて】everywhere; 【...する所はどこも】wherever. ▶どこでも好きな所に座りなさい Sit down *anywhere* [*wherever*] you like. ▶どこでも君といっしょに行くよ I'll come [go] with you *everywhere* [*wherever*] you 《×will》 go. ▶その本はどこでも買える You can buy the book *everywhere* [《この本屋でも》at *any* bookstore]. ▶どこでもいつでも勉強するようにしよう Try to study whenever and *wherever* you can. (! 英語の語順は「時→場所」)
会話 「どこへ行きたい」「どこでもいいよ」"Where do you want to go?" "*Anywhere* [×*Wherever*] will do." (! *wherever* は接続詞で名詞的には使えない)

とことこ ▶とことこ歩く walk with short, steady steps. (! *toddle* は「よちよち[ちょこちょこ]歩く」の意で不安定な歩き方なので, ここは不適)

どことなく 【どういうわけか】somehow; 【何らかの点で】in some way. ▶どことなく彼は虫が好かない *Somehow* I don't like him. ▶彼女はどことなく私の母に似ている She looks like my mother *in some way.*/《諧》She has [bears] *some* resemblance to my mother. ▶彼はどことなく変わったところがある There is *something* strange about him.

とことん ▶とことんまで戦う fight it out; fight *to the bitter end*. ▶そのこと, 急がないから, とことん調べてもらえませんか Would you go into the matter *exhaustively*? I'm not in a hurry.

とこなつ 常夏 《an island of》everlasting summer.

とこのま 床の間 a *tokonoma*; (説明的に) an alcove in a guest room of a Japanese-style house where flowers, a hanging scroll, and other decorative objects are displayed.

とこばしら 床柱 a (decorative) *tokonoma* post.

とこばなれ 床離れ ●床離れ(=寝起き)がよい get up promptly. ▶(病気が)日々よくなっていますから床離れももうすぐですよ You're getting better, and you'll be able to *get out of bed* soon.

どこまで 〖どこまで〗 how far. (⇨どこ❻)

どこまでも 〖果てなく〗endlessly. ●どこまでも論争する dispute *endlessly* [(徹底的に) *thoroughly*]. ●どこまでも続く砂漠 an *endless* desert. ●彼を尊敬したらどこまでもついて行く(=忠実に従う) respect him and *faithfully* follow him. ▶彼はどこまでも潔白だと言い張った He *insisted that* he was innocent./He *insisted on* his innocence.

どこも 〖いたる所〗everywhere; 〖どの〗every; 〖すべての〗all. ▶家の中はどこも(かしこも)きれいでした The house was clean [《米話》spic-and-span] *everywhere.*/*Everywhere* [*Every place*] was clean in the house. (! *everywhere* は前の文では副詞, 後の文では名詞) ▶店はどこも閉まっていた *Every* store was [*All* (the) *stores* were] closed. ▶この車はどこも故障していない Nothing is [There is nothing] wrong with this car.

とこや 床屋 (店) 《主に米》a barbershop, 《英》a barber's (! 複数形は barbers または barbers'); (人) a barber.

とこやま 床山 a professional 《sumo [actor]》hairdresser.

どこやら 何処やら (ばくぜんとした場所を示して) somewhere. ▶どこやらで人の声がした I heard someone's voice *somewhere* [(この辺りで) *around here*].

とこよのくに 常世の国 (海の向こうの遠い国) a faraway land across the sea; (不老不死の国) the land of eternal life; (死者の国) the land of the spirits of the dead.

ところ 所 図

INDEX

❶ 場所	❷ 余地
❸ 家	❹ 場合, 時
❺ 点, 部分, 関係	❻ 事
❼ 範囲, 程度	❽ ...するところだ

❶ 【場所】a place (! 最も一般的な語); (特定の地点) a spot; (都市・建物などのあった跡, 建築予定地) a site; (事故などの現場) a scene; (活動の所在地・中心地) a seat. ●古い城のあった所 the *site* of an old castle. ●魚のよく釣れる所 a good fishing *spot*. ▶京都には見る所がたくさんある There are a lot of *places* to see in Kyoto. ▶交通の便利な所に住みたい I want to live in a *place* (which [×where] is) convenient to public transport. ▶我が家にまさる所はない There is no *place* like home. ▶ここは私たちが最初に会った所です This is (the *place*) *where* we first met. (! the place は通例省略する) ▶どこへでも好きな所に行ってよい You may [can] go *wherever* you like. (! *may* は先生など目上の人が用いる) ▶所もあろうに(=数ある場所の中で), こんな所に住もうなどとは思わなかった I never expected to live here, of all *places*. ▶その本を元の所に戻しなさい Put the book back in its *place* [*where* it was, *where* you found it]. ▶それをあそこの空いている所に置きなさい Put it on the empty *spot* over there. ▶ここが事故のあった所です This is the *scene* of the accident [*where* the accident happened]. ▶大学は学問をする所だ A university is a *place* [《ややまれ》a *seat*] of learning [*where* we learn]. ▶駅は歩いて20分の所にある The station is twenty minutes' walk from my house./It is twenty minutes' walk from my house to the station.
会話 「花子はどこ?」「めぐみの所かも」"Where's Hanako?" "She may be Megumi's *place*." (! この *place* は部屋などをさすが, 別の家 (⇨❸) をさすこともある)

> 解説 特定の場所は前置詞で表されることもある: 角を曲がったところにスーパーがある There's a supermarket *around* the corner. 入り口のところで太郎に会った I met Taro *at* the door.

❷ 【余地】(人・物が入れるだけの場所) room; (空間, 余白) space. ▶我が家の裏庭には車を止めておく所がない There is no *room* [*space*] to park a car in our backyard.

❸ 【家】(建物としての) a house (複 houses /-ziz/

―どころ

《米》-siz/); (家庭生活の場としての) a home (■《米》では home を house で置き換え同義に用いることもある); 《話》one's [a] place (■one's または a をつけて home, house の意で用いる); [住所] an address. ● 封筒に所書きを書く address an envelope. ▶私の所は郵便局の近くです My *house* [《米》*home*] is near the post office. ▶彼は住む所がない He has no *house* to live in [*no place* to live (in), 《話》*nowhere* to live]. (■place の場合は in を省略する方が普通) ▶今彼はおじの所にいる He is staying at his uncle's (*house*) [*with* his uncle] now. ▶帰りにあなたの所に寄りますよ I'll drop in at your *place* on my way home. ▶彼の所と名前を教えてください Tell [*Give*] me his name and *address*. (■語順に注意)

❹ [場合, 時] (ふさわしい時機・場合) an occasion; (瞬間) a moment. ▶ここは君が音頭をとるべきところだ This is an *occasion* for you to take the lead. ▶彼女はちょうどよいところへやって来た She has come at the right *moment*. ▶ちょうど私が外出しようとしたところへ彼が到着した He arrived *just as* I was going out./I was just about to go out *when* he arrived. ▶今日のところはそれでおしまい That's *all for* today. (■授業の終わりなどに先生がいう言葉) ▶彼はよく君のいないところで悪口を言っている He often says something bad about you *when* you are not around [*陰で*) *behind your back*]. ▶母のいるところで(=面前で)その話をしないでくれ Don't talk about it *in* my mother's *presence* [*in the presence of* my mother]. (■日常会話では Don't talk about it *when* my mother's around [*present*]. の方が普通)

❺ [点, 部分, 関係] (点) a point; (部分) a part; (文の1節) a passage. ▶これが彼のよい[悪い]所だ This is his good [bad] *point*./(長[短]所だ) This is his strong [weak] *point*. ▶彼の中国に関する論説はあちこち間違っている所がある *Parts* of his article on China are mistaken./His article on China is mistaken *here and there* [*in places*]. ▶この小説には難しい所がたくさんある This novel has a lot of difficult *passages* (in it)./There are a lot of difficult *passages* in this novel. ▶彼はいい奴なんだがちょっと意地っぱりな所がある He is a nice guy but there's an obstinate [*streak* of obstinacy] in him. (■streak は「性格の一部」) ▶彼の言葉にはちょっと辛らつな所がある He has [There is] a *touch* of bitterness in his words. ▶この本を読むと教えられる(=学ぶべき)所が多い There is *a lot* to learn from this book./We can learn *a lot* from this book.

❻ [事] ▶彼の言うところから判断すると, 仕事がかなりついようだ Judging from *what* he says, the work seems (to be) pretty hard for him. [会話]「もし健が手伝ってくれれば簡単さ」「でも手伝ってくれるの? そこがはっきりしないところなのよ」"It'll be easy if Ken helps." "Will he, though? That's *what* we're not sure of."

❼ [範囲, 程度] ▶私の知るところでは彼は無罪だ *As far as* I know [*To the best of* my knowledge] he is innocent. ▶私の聞いたところでは, 彼は外国にいるということだ The way [(限りでは) *As far as*] I heard it, he is abroad. (■The way ... は「…(ところ)から判断して」という接続詞的用法) /He is abroad, or so I've heard. ▶今までのところ私たちはうまくいっている So far [*Up to now, Until now*] we have been successful. (■現在完了形とともに用いる) ▶新聞の伝えるところによれば新潟に大雪が降ったそうです *According to* the paper, [The paper says

(*that*)] there was a heavy snow in Niigata. ▶まあまんなところでしょう(=ほぼ正しい) I'd say that's about right.

[会話]「彼女にできるのはせいぜいこんなところだろう」「もう少しうまくやるような気がするよ」 "She'll *never* do *any better*." "I have a feeling she will."

❽ [...するところだ] (心づもりとして) be going to do (■前もって決めていることを含意する); (約束などあって) be doing; [...したところだとする] have* (just) done; (行って帰って来たところだ) have (just) been to ...; [もう少しで...のところだ] almost, nearly; [...している最中だ] be doing. ▶買い物に行くところだ I'*m going to* do some shopping. (■be going to よりさらに近接の意味を表す言い方に be about to do, be on the point of doing などがある) ▶例の新刊の旅行記を読んだところです I've *just read* [《米・英話》 *I just read*] that new travel book. ▶公園へ花見に行ってきたところです I've (*just*) *been* to the park to see the cherry blossoms. ▶実家の母に会いに行って戻ってきたところです I'*m just back* from seeing my mother at my parents' home. ▶今仕事を探しているところです I'*m looking for* a job. ▶あやうく溺れ死ぬところだった I (was) *almost* [*nearly*] drowned./I *came near* (*to*) being drowned. (■《堅》ではしばしば to を省略する) ▶彼女がカーテンの陰で泣いているところを見た I saw her *weep*ing behind the curtain. (■「感覚動詞+目的語+現在分詞」の構文)

[会話]「荷物を取ってきてくださってありがとう」「気にしないで, どっちみち駅へ行くところだったんですもの」 "Thank you for getting my parcel." "Think nothing of it. I *was going to* the station anyway."

● **所変われば品変わる** 《ことわざ》 So many countries, so many customs.

── ところ [*接*] (...してみたら) when. ▶担任の先生に進路の相談をしたところ, S 大学に出願するよう勧められた *When* I talked to my class teacher about my future course, he advised me to apply to S University.

-どころ ▶当時はとても生活が苦しくて海外旅行どころではなかった(=思いもしなかった) I was so hard up at that time that I *never thought of* traveling abroad. ▶彼はばかどころではない(=決してばかなんかではない) He is *no* fool./He is *not* a fool *at all*./He is *anything but* [*far from*] foolish.

[会話]「彼女はあまり具合がよくないんだって?」「あまりどころじゃないよ, 昨日もまた心臓発作を起こしたんだ」"She's not so well, is she?" "*Not* so well *at all*. She had another heart attack yesterday." (■相手の発言をそのまま引き継いでさらに強めて応答する言い方)

ところが (しかし) but; (しかしながら) however; (やや書) however; (…だけれども) though ..., although ...; (だ一方) while ... (⇒[しかし, けれど(も)]) ▶彼女を訪ねた. ところが留守だった I visited (■[主に英] called on] her, *but* she was out [xabsent]./I went to her house. *However*, she was not at home. ▶うちは天然資源に富む. ところが君の国は乏しい This country is rich in natural resources, *but* [*while*] yours is poor. (■(1) this country については (⇒[国]). (2) while は主に《書》)

-どころか 《副助詞》 **❶ [...とは反対に]** ▶彼は金持ちどころか, まったく貧乏だ *Far from* (being) rich, he is quite poor. (■far from (being) の後は名詞・形容詞. being は通例省略する) (彼は金持ちではない. それどころかまったく貧乏だ) He isn't rich; *on the contrary*, he is quite poor. ▶その家具は役に立たないどころかじゃまになった The furniture was *worse than* useless.

ところかまわず

会話「今度の仕事は楽しいですか」「それどころか、まったくつまらん」"Are you happy with your new job?" "*On the contrary*, it's very dull."

❷ […は言うまでもなく] ▶彼は車どころか、軽飛行機も持っている He has a lightplane, *not to speak of [to say nothing of, not to mention]* a car. (❗これらの表現は肯定・否定のいずれの後にも用いる)/(車がなくでなく軽飛行機も持っている) He has *not only* a car *but* (*also*) a lightplane. (⇨のみならず) ▶彼は英字新聞どころかやさしい英語で書かれた教科書も読むことができない He can't read a textbook written in easy English, *let alone* [(まして新聞を読むことはできない) *much less*, 《やや堅》*still less*] an English newspaper. (❗(1) いずれも上例のように not などの否定語や difficult などを含んだ否定的文脈の後で用いる. (2) これらのậ句の後では前文と同じ部分は省略、通例名詞・形容詞・副詞・動詞などの否定したい語句だけが来る)(⇨ましで)

ところかまわず 所構わず ▶あの人は所構わず(=どこにいても)大声で話す He speaks too loudly *wherever [no matter where]* he is. ▶彼の方が口調が悪い) ▶彼はその犬を所構わず(=至る所)棒でたたいた He beat the dog *all over* with a stick.

ところせましと 所狭しと ▶この部屋には骨董(とう)品が所狭しと置いてあった The room *was crowded [filled, packed] with* antiques.

ところで ❶[話は変わるが] (さて) ↘*now*; (では) 《話》↘*well*; (ねえ) ↘*tell me* (❗相手に意気込んで尋ねる前置き); [話はそれるが] 《話》*by the* ↘*way*, ↘*incidentally*. (❗(1) 上記の通例文頭で. (2) 最後の二つは余談的な話題やまた重要なことをさりげなく切り出すときによく用いる) ▶ところでもう一つ質問があります *Now* [*Well*], I have one more question to ask you. ▶うん、元気だよ。ところでこの週末はどうするつもり? Just fine, thanks. *Tell me*, what are you going to do this weekend? (❗このように最初の話題を切り出すときには by the way, incidentally は用いない)

会話「さて行きましょうか」「ところで道はちゃんと分かっているの」"Shall we go now?" "*Well*, are you sure you know the way?"

会話「すばらしい結婚式ですね」「ええ、花子さんはきれいな花嫁さんね」「ところで、太郎君と花子さんとはどんなふうにして知り合ったの」"It's a lovely wedding, isn't it?" "Yes, Hanako is a beautiful bride." "*By the way* [*Incidentally*], how did Taro and Hanako get to know each other?"

-ところで 〔接続助詞〕[[たとえ…でも] (even) *if* … (❗even がある方が強意的); [だれが…しても] *no matter who* …, *whoever* … (❗前の方が口語的). 文脈に応じて who の代わりに what, where, how, when を用いる). (⇨しても) ▶先生が言ったところで彼は聞きはしまい *Even if* [*Even though*] the teacher warns him, he won't listen. ▶どこへ行ったところで人生は厳しい *No matter where* [*Wherever*] you go, life is hard. ▶それについて不平を言ったところで仕方がない It's [There's] no use complaining [xto complain] about it.

ところてん ところ天 *tokoroten* jelly; (説明的に) semi-transparent, short-cut noodlelike jelly made of agar /ɑ́:gər/, eaten cold with sweetened vinegar sauce, and so on.
●ところ天式に (自動的に) automatically; (機械的に) mechanically; (順送りに) successively.

ところどころ 所々 *in places*; [[あちこち] *here and there*. ▶白壁のところどころはげていた The white wall was off *in places*. ▶雪がところどころ残っている The snow remains *here and there*.

ところにより 所により *in* (some) *places*. ▶関東地方は所により雨でが暖かいでしょう In the Kanto district it will be *partly* rainy but warm. ▶だいたいは曇りでしょう. 所により日の差すこともあるでしょう In general it should be cloudy and it is likely that *some of you* will have a little sunshine. (❗「所により」の部分を予報を聞いている人に直接話しかける手法を表現した例)

どこんじょう ど根性 (不屈の精神) an indomitable spirit; (度胸・気力) a lot of guts. ▶浪花のど根性 the *indomitable spirit* of Osaka people.

とざい 吐剤 an emetic (medicine).

どざえもん 土佐衛門 a drowned person; (水死体) a drowned body.

とさか 鶏冠 a cockscomb /kákskòum/.
●とさかにくる (頭にくる) get mad; 《事が主語》drive ⟨me⟩ mad. (⇨頭 [成句])

どさくさ [[混乱] confusion; [[騒ぎ] (a) trouble.
●どさくさに紛れる ▶どさくさに紛れていろいろことをする fish in troubled waters. ▶「漁夫の利を占める」という成句から) ▶彼はどさくさに紛れて店の主人の金を持ち逃げした He ran away with the storekeeper's money *in the confusion* [《話》 *in the mess*]./(混乱を利用して) He took advantage of the confusion *to* make off [away] with the storekeeper's money.

とざす 閉ざす ❶[閉める, 閉じる] close, shut*. (⇨める) ▶門戸を閉ざす *close* [*shut*] the gates (*to* immigrants). ▶口を堅く閉ざしている *keep* one's mouth *shut* tight [*tightly shut*]. ▶この子は心を閉ざしているから、それを開いてくれる人間が必要だ This boy is so *defensive* that he needs someone who can get through to him.
❷[閉じ込められる] (雪で) be snowed in [*up*]; (氷で) be icebound. ●氷に閉ざされた港 an *icebound* port. ▶その村は1週間雪に閉ざされていた The village *was snowed in* [*up*] for a week.

とさつ 屠殺 ⑧ slaughter; butchery.
── 屠殺する ⑩ slaughter; butcher.
● 屠殺場 a slaughterhouse 《覆 -houses [-ziz/, 《米》-siz)》; an abattoir /æbətwɑ́:r/.

どさっと ❶[重い物が立てる音] with a thud. ▶彼は重い袋を床の上にどさっと置いた He put down the heavy sack *with a thud* on the floor./He *dumped* the heavy sack on the floor. ▶彼はいすにどさっと座った He sat down *heavily* in the chair./(音を立てて) He *flopped* (*down*) in [into] the chair. (▶ flop は thud よりやや軽い音で、sit down with a flop のように名詞にも用いられる)
❷[一時にたくさん] ▶注文がどさっときて多忙をきわめている Orders *poured* [*flooded*] *in*, and we are very busy./A *rush* (*for* the toy) [A *flood* of orders] keeps us very busy.

とさにっき 『土佐日記』 *The Tosa Diary*. (【参考】紀貫之の仮名日記)

とざま 外様 [よそ者] an outsider.
● 外様大名 an outside *daimyo* [feudal lord]; (説明的に) a *daimyo* who was not a hereditary vassal of the Tokugawa family.

どさまわり どさ回り (地方興行) a road show. ●どさ回りをする (地方巡業中である) be on the road; 《主に米》barnstorm. ●どさ回りの一座 a theatrical company *on the road*; 《米》a *barnstorming* troupe. (❗ともに単・複両扱い)

どさりと with a thud. (⇨どさっと)

とざん 登山 ⑧ [[山に登ること] mountain climbing; [[スポーツとしての登山] mountaineering. ●絶好の登山日和 good *climbing* weather. ●登山に行く go *climbing* 《*in* the Alps》. — **登山する** 動 climb [go up] a mountain. ● 登山家 a mountaineer; an alpinist (⚠ 高山の登山家). ● 登山靴 《a pair of》 mountain-climbing boots. ● 登山クラブ a mountaineering club. ● 登山者 a (mountain) climber (⚠ 登山家も含む). ● 登山口 a mountaineering entrance. ● 登山鉄道 a mountain railway. ● 登山熱 a craze for mountaineering.

どさんこ 道産子 《馬》 a horse native to Hokkaido; 《人》 a native of Hokkaido. (⚠ 上例の to を of に, of を to に換えることはできない)

とし 年 ❶ 【年齢】 an age, year(s) (⚠ a [one] *year* old のような例を除いて常に複数形で用いる) (⇨年齢, -歳); 〖老齢〗 (old) age (⚠ 無冠詞).
① 《～年》 ▶彼らは同い年だ They are (of) the same *age* [《古》 of an *age*]. (⚠ (1) 《話》 では通例 of を省略する. (2) 年の代わりに year は用いない) ▶彼はまだ学校に行く年ではない He is *too young* [*not old enough*] *to* go to school.
② 【年～】 ▶年相応にふるまう act [be] one's *age*. ⚠ 命令形で用いることが多い)
③ 【年が[は]～】 ● 年は 30 くらいの女性 a woman (who looks) about 30 *years* old ▶次の 2 例より口語的》; a woman of about 30 (*years*) (⚠ (1) years はない方が普通. (2) ×a woman of about 30 years old とはいわない); a woman *aged* about 30 (⚠ *aged* の発音は /éidʒd/). ▶私たちはずいぶん年が違う We are far apart in our *ages*. ▶年齢の上下が明らかなら You are much *older* [*younger*] *than* I am [《話》 *than* me]. のようにもいえる) ▶彼はかなり年がいっている He is well along [in, 《書》 advanced] in *years*. (⚠ He is old. の婉曲的な表現)/ He is rather *old*.
会話 「彼の年はいくつですか」「25 です」 "How *old* is he?" "He is 25 (*years old*)." (⚠ ×He is 25 years. は不可)/"What [×How many] is his *age*?" "He is 25 (*years of age*)." (⇨-歳)
④ 【年の】 ● 君ぐらいの年の少年 a boy (of) your *age* [*years*]. (⚠ 《話》 では of を省略する (⇨年頃)) ● 年の功 (⇨年の功) ▶君ぐらいの年にはたくさん本を読んだものだ When I was (at) your *age*, I used to read a lot. ▶年のせいで物忘れがひどくなった My memory has failed *with age*./*Age* has dimmed my memory. ▶体が弱ってきた. 年(のせい)だね I have grown weak. I feel my *age* [*years*]. (⚠ I feel *I'm old*. ともいえる)
⑤ 【年に】 ● 15 の年に at (the *age*) of) 15; when (he) is 15 (*years old*). ▶この年になって at one's *age*. ▶彼は年に似合わず現実的だ He is realistic *beyond* his *years* [×*age*]. ▶この年になってやっと親のありがたさが分かった I appreciated how much I owed my parents only *when* I was *this age*.
⑥ 【年を】 ● いい年をしてそんなばかなことはするものではない(=君の年ならもっと分別があるべきだ) You should know better at your *age*./You are *old enough to* know better.
⑦ 【年に[で]】 ▶もう年だよ I'm *getting on*.
会話 「首にされたよ」「そのお年で！」 "They've fired me [《英語》 given me the sack]." "At your *time of life*!"

❷ 【暦年】 a year. (⇨年/月) ● 年の始め[暮れ]に at the beginning [end] of the year. ▶後の方は at the *year*-end も可》 ● 来る年も来る年も *year* after *year*. ● 年がたつにつれて as *years* go [pass] by. ● 年とともに変わる change with (the) *years*. ▶年が明けた The new *year* has begun. ▶年が改まると同時に寒くなった It got colder as soon as the *year* changed [at the turn of the *year*]. ▶彼がアメリカにいた年に父親が死んだ His father died *the year* [*in the year*] he was in America. (⚠ 前の方の year は接続詞的) ▶我々は借金なしで何とか年を越した We managed to get through the *year* without a debt.

会話 「どうぞよいお年を」「あなたもね」 "(A) Happy New *Year*!" "(The) same to you." (⚠ (1) 《話》 では通例 a を省略する. (2) 前に I wish you をつけると, a をつけた場合と同様に少し堅い表現になる)

● 年には勝てない (年に逆らえない) One can't fight (against) old age./(年をとることについては何もできない) One can't do anything about getting old.
● 年を取る get [become, grow] old. (⇨年取る)
● 一つ年を取るる become a year *older*. ▶彼は見かけよりも年を取っている He is *older than* he looks./(年の割に若く見える) He looks young *for* his *age*./(実際より若く見える) He looks *younger than* he (really [actually]) is. ▶彼女は年を取らない. いつ会っても同じだ She is *ageless*, the same every time I see her.

とし 都市 图 a city; a town.

解説 city は一般に town より多少とも人口が多く重要性のある大きな町を指す. 《米》 では自治体として公称されている市をいう. 《英》 では city の資格があっても town を用いることが多く, city を用いると少し堅い言い方になる.

● 学園都市 a college [a university] *city* [*town*]. ● 田園都市 a garden *city* [×town]. ● 近代[現代]都市 a modern [a provincial] *city*. ● 工業[商業; 観光]都市 an industrial [a business; a tourist] *city*. ● 国際[過密; 衛星]都市 a cosmopolitan [an overpopulated; a satellite] *city*. ● 姉妹都市 《米》 a sister *city*; 《英》 a twin *town*. ● 主要都市 a metrópolis. (⚠ 通例複数形にしない) ▶神戸は人口が 100 万を越える大都市 Kobe is a big [a large] *city* with a population of more than one million.

— **都市の** 形 urban /ə́ːrbən/. (⚠ 通例限定的に) ● 都市化 urbanization. (⚠ 「都市化する」は urbanize) ● 都市開発 urban development. ● 都市ガス (city [town]) gas. (⚠ ( )内は通例省略する) ● 都市銀行 a city bank. ● 都市空間 urban space. ● 都市計画 city 《米》 [town 《英》] planning. ● 都市景観 a cityscape. ● 都市交通 city [urban] transportation 《主に米》 [transport 《主に英》]. ● 都市国家 (古代ギリシャの) a city state; (ポリス) a polis. ● 都市再開発 urban renewal. ● 都市生活 city [town, urban] life. ● 都市部 an urban district. ● 都市問題 an urban problem.

とじ 綴じ ● 綴じが緩んだ本 a book whose *binding* got loose. ● 綴じのしっかりした本 a well-*bound* book.
● 綴じ糸 (本の) (a) binding thread; (衣服の) (a) basting thread.

-どし -年 会話 「あなたは何年生まれですか」「戌年(いぬどし)です」 "*What year of the zodiac* /zóudiæk/ were you born in?" "The *year* of the dog."

どじ 图 ● どじを踏む (a) make a silly [a foolish] mistake; (とんでもないことをやらかす) make a blunder; (へまをやる) 《話》 make a mess of it; mess (...) up 《*on*》.
— **どじな** 形 ● どじな(=ばかな)奴 a stupid person; (大ばか者) an idiot.

としあけ 年明け ● 年明けに at the beginning of the new year; (正月早々に) early in the New Year.

としうえ 年上 〖年長者, 先輩〗 one's senior (↔one's junior). ▶彼は私より3歳年上です He is three years *older than* I am 〖話〗 me, 《書・まれ》]./He is three years my *senior* [〖書・まれ〗 *senior to* me]. (❗(1) 前の方が普通の言い方。(2) 特に年齢差を強調する場合には by three years の形で文尾に置かれる) ▶あなたとジョンとではどちらが年上ですか Who [Which] is *older*, you or John? ▶お兄さんはあなたより何歳年上ですか How *much older* [×How *older*] is your brother than you are?

としおいる 年老いる grow [get] old; age. ●年老いた父 one's *old* [〖書〗 *aged*] father.

としおとこ 年男 (説明的に) a man whose *eto* (sign of the Chinese zodiac) is the same as that of the current year. (⇒干支〖え〗)

としおんな 年女 (説明的に) a woman whose *eto* (sign of the Chinese zodiac) is the same as that of the current year. (⇒干支〖え〗)

としがい 年甲斐 ─ 年甲斐もない ▶うちのおばあちゃん, ピアノを習い始めたんだ。年甲斐もなく My grandma has begun to take piano lessons, *at her age*. (❗コンマ以下をあきれたという感じでいう。forgetting her age も可) ▶妹をいじめるのはやめなさい。年甲斐もない(＝年相応に行動しなさい) Don't tease your sister. *Act your age*.

としかさ 年嵩 ─ 年嵩の 圏 (年上の) older. ●かなり年かさの〖英〗の紳士 an *elderly* gentleman. (❗old, aged より心遣いのある言い方)

どしがたい 度し難い (救いがたい) incurable, incorrigible; (先に希望が持てない) hopeless; (とんでもない) impossible. ●度しがたいお調子者 an *incurably* light-minded person.

としかっこう 年格好, 年恰好 会話 「その男の年格好は?」「そうね, 30歳ぐらいかな」"How old do you think the man is?" "Well, let me see. About thirty, I think."/"He looked about thirty."

としご 年子 ▶その姉妹は年子だ The sisters were born within a year of each other [in two successive years]. ▶ぼくと兄とは年子だ I am only one year younger than my brother.

としこしそば 年越し蕎麦 (説明的に) buckwheat noodles customarily eaten on New Year's Eve.

としごと 年毎 ─ 年毎に 副 every year; year after year. ▶年ごとに体力の衰えを感じる I feel I get weaker *every year*.

とじこみ 綴じ込み a file. ●とじ込みの付録 a *bound-in* supplement (to a magazine).

とじこむ 綴じ込む file 《a letter》, put* 《papers》 in a file; keep* 《letters》 on file.

とじこめる 閉じ込める shut* [〖錠を掛けて〗 lock]...(up) 《in》; confine... 《to, in》; (雪で) snow... in [up] 《通例受身で》. ●丸5日間雪に閉じ込められる be snowed in for five whole days. ▶彼は子供を納戸に閉じ込めた He *shut* [*locked*] his child 《up》 *in* the closet. ▶誘拐された子供は1週間その家に閉じ込められていた The kidnapped child *was shut up* [*was confined*] *in* the house for a week.

とじこもる 閉じ籠もる shut* [〖錠を掛けて〗 lock] oneself (up) 《in》. ●彼は部屋に閉じこもって考えた He *shut himself* 《up》 *in* [*confined himself to*] his room to think. ▶彼女は自分の殻に閉じこもって人と話さなかった She *went* [*retired*] *into* her shell and did not speak to other people.

としごろ 年頃 [年齢] an age (⇒年〖と〗, 年齢); [結婚適齢期]〖書〗 marriageable age. ●年ごろの娘 a daughter of *marriageable age*; a *marriageable* daughter. ▶適齢期の概念は崩れているので, このような表現を好まない人も多い ▶私には君と同じ年ごろの息子がある I have a son (about) the same *age* as you./I have a son (of) your *age*. ▶中学生は難しい年ごろである Junior high school students are in the difficult *stage of life*.

としした 年下 〖年下の者, 後輩〗 one's junior (↔senior). (⇒年上) ▶彼は私より3歳年下だ He is three years *younger than* I am 〖話〗 me, 《古・書》]./He is three years my *junior*. (❗前の方が普通の言い方)

としゅん『杜子春』 Toshishun. (参考) 芥川龍之介の小説

とじしろ 綴じ代 an edge [a margin] 《of two centimeters》 left for binding.

-としたことが (...ともあろう者が) of all people. (❗「すべての人の中から」の意) ▶あんな失敗をするなんて Why must I, *of all people*, make such a blunder?/I can't think how I made such a blunder. (❗the how は理由を表す)

どしつ 土質 the quality of the soil; soil quality. ●土質を改良する improve *the quality of the soil*. ●土質力学〖土木〗 soil mechanics. (❗単・複両扱い)

としつき 年月 years; (時) time. (⇒年月〖ねん〗)

-として ❶〖立場, 資格, 機能〗as ...; 〖代金・報酬など〗for .... ●作家として有名である be famous *as* a writer. ●たるをいすとして使う use a barrel *as* a stool. ▶彼は善良な人として通っている He passes *as* [*for*] a good man. ▶彼は知事として発言した He spoke 《*in this capacity*》 *as* governor. (❗as の後に1人だけの職名がくる場合通例冠詞をつけない) ▶ぼくは高校生なんだから高校生として扱ってほしい I'm a high school student, so I want to be treated *like one* 〖それなりに〗 *as such*]. ▶彼は本の代金として1,000円払った He paid a thousand yen *for* the book. (❗for は「交換」の意を表す)
❷〖強調〗▶1人としてその誤りに気づかなかった Not a single person noticed the mistake. (❗単に「1人も気づかなかった」は No one noticed ....)

-としては 〖関して〗as for ... (❗既述のことに関して新しい話題を導入する。通例文頭で用いる); 〖関する限り〗as far as ...; 〖...の割には〗for .... ▶私としてはとても満足です *As for* me [*As far as I am concerned*, 《書》 *For* my *part*], I am very satisfied./I *for one* [I, *for one*,] am very satisfied. ▶ぼくとしてはそう思うけど I *should* think so. (❗should は控えめな気持ちを表す) ▶彼女は女性としては背が高い She is tall [×taller] *for* a woman.
会話「ごたついてしまってごめんなさい」「あなたとしてはどうしようもなかったわよ」"I'm sorry for the mess." "♡You cóuldn't hélp it." (❗you の音調に注意)

-としても (たとえ...でも) even if. (⇒-しても)

としどし 年年 every year. (⇒毎年)

どしどし ❶〖遠慮せずに〗without reserve [reservation], unreservedly; (ためらいなしに) without hesitation; (自由に) freely. (⇒どんどん) ●どしどし(＝次から次へと)逮捕する arrest 《them》 *one after another*. ●どしどし[＝「好きなだけ」]やる do *as much as* 《one》 *likes*. ▶記者たちはどしどし大統領に質問した Reporters asked the President questions *unreservedly*. (❗この unreservedly は「ずけずけと無遠慮に」の意にとられることもある)
❷〖足音〗(荒々しい音を立てて) tramp; (立腹して) stomp; (地響きを立てて歩く) lumber. ▶彼女はどしどし2階へ上がっていって子供たちを大声でどなりつけた She *tramped* up the stairs and shouted angrily at her children.

としとる 年取る 動 [年を取る] grow*, become*, get* old, age;《書》advance in years. ▶年取って忘れっぽくなった I've become forgetful with *age*. ▶年取ってからでないとできない(=年をとった時にだけ楽しむことができる)面白いことがいろいろある There are certain things you can enjoy doing only *in your old age*.

— **年取った** 形 old;《やや書》aged (！old より高齢をさす). ▶年取った男の人 an *old* [an *aged*] man. (！(1) 婉曲的には older を用いることが多い. (2) aged は限定的に用いた場合, 発音は /éidʒid/)

としなみ 年波 ●寄る年波に腰が曲がっている be bent with *age*. ▶だれも寄る年波には勝てない Nobody can struggle against (their) *advancing age*.

としのいち 年の市 (正月用品を売る市) a year-end fair for new year's decorations and other necessaries; (年末の売り出し) a year-end sale.

としのこう 年の功 the wisdom of age. ▶さすが長年の功だ(=経験がものを言う) Experience will tell./He is experienced and wise.
会話 「あなたのとった処置が適切だったと医者が言っていたよ」「それは年の功ってやつさ」"The doctor said you did the right thing." "That's the kind of *wisdom that comes with age*."

としのせ 年の瀬 the end of the year. ●年の瀬も押し詰まりまして when we are at the very *end of the year*; when the new year is just around the corner.

としは 年端・年端も行かぬ ▶年端も行かない子 a child of *tender years*; a small child.

としま 年増 a youngish woman.

とじまり 戸締まり 名 ▶外出の前に戸締まりを確かめよ Make sure (that) you *lock* [will lock] (the house) *up* before going out. (！make sure (that)... の節内では現在時制を用いるのが原則だが, 今は未来形も用いられるようになってきた)

— **戸締まりする** 動 lock (…) up.

としまわり 年回り ▶今年は年回り(=運勢)がいい[悪い] It has been predicted (that) I *am in a lucky* [*an unlucky*] *year*.

とじめ 綴じ目 ▶この本はとじ目が緩んでいる This book is loose at the *seam*.

としゃ 吐瀉 [医学] vomiting and diarrhea. ●吐瀉物 a (patient's) vomit and excreta.

どしゃ 土砂 earth (and sand); earth and rock.

どしゃくずれ 土砂崩れ a landslide. ▶土砂くずれでぼくの家が埋まった My house was buried by a *landslide*.

どしゃぶり 土砂降り [大雨] (a) heavy [(a) pouring] rain; [豪雨] (a) torrential rain; [ざあざあ降り] a downpour. ▶土砂降りだ It's *pouring* (down)./It's raining very hard [very heavily]./The rain is very heavy./[話] It's *raining cats and dogs*. ▶降れば土砂降り (⇨降る [成句])

としゅ 斗酒 ●斗酒なお辞せず ▶彼は斗酒なお辞せずだ(=大酒飲みだ) He will drink ten bottles of *sake* without saying "I've had enough."/He is a heavy drinker.

としゅくうけん 徒手空拳 — **徒手空拳で** 副 [武器を持たずに] unarmed; without weapons; [資本なしで] without capital. ▶彼は徒手空拳で今の仕事を始めた He started his business *on a shoestring*. (！on a shoestring は「ほとんど無一文で」の意)

としゅたいそう 徒手体操 (美容体操) calisthenics (⚠単・複両扱い); (器械を使用しない) gymnastics without apparatus.

***としょ 図書** (総合的に) books. (⇨本) ●参考図書 reference *books*. (！辞書, 地図なども含む) ●推薦図書 recommended [suggested] *books*. ●図書閲覧室 a reading room. ●図書カード a *tosho* card; (図書券)《英》a book token. ●図書館 (⇨図書館) ●図書室 a library. ●図書目録 a catalog of books; (図書館の) a library catalog. (！書名としては Longman Catalogue (ロングマン社図書目録), 2005 Books in Print (2005 年出版図書目録)のような形をとることが多い)

としょ 屠所 ⇨屠殺 [屠殺場]

とじょう 途上 (⇨途中) ●発展途上にある(=繁盛している)事業 a *prosperous* [*expanding*] business.

●途上国 a developing country [nation]. (！a backward [an underdeveloped] country [nation] は後進国 [低開発国] の婉曲表現)

とじょう 登城 — 登城する go to castle.

どじょう 土壌 soil. ●肥沃な土壌 rich [fertile] (↔ poor) *soil*. ●土壌を改良する improve the *soil*. (！ the をつける)

●土壌汚染 soil pollution.

どじょう 泥鰌 [魚介] a loach /lóʊtʃ/. ▶ドジョウすくい scooping loaches; (踊り) a loach-scooping dance. ●ドジョウひげ a thin mustache.

どしょうぼね 土性骨 ⇨背骨.

***としょかん 図書館** a library. (！図書室の意も含む)
●公立[学校]図書館 a public [a school] *library*. ●国会図書館 the National Diet *Library*; (米国の) the *Library* of Congress. ●移動図書館《米》a bookmobile;《英》(= 《主に英》a traveling) library. ▶図書館から数冊本を借りる borrow several books from the *library*. ▶本を借りに[返しに]図書館に行った I went to the *library* to borrow [return] books. ▶これは図書館の本です This is a *library* book./This book belongs to the *library*.

●図書館員 (司書) a librarian. ●図書館学 library science. ●図書館長 the chief librarian; the curator [director] of a library.

としょく 徒食 — 徒食する 動 [仕事もせずに暮らす] lead [live] an idle life; live idly.

***としより 年寄り** [老人] (男性) an older [an old, an elderly] man (複 men); (女性) an older [an old, an elderly] woman (複 women /wímin/), an old [an elderly] lady; (総称) old people, aged people;《やや書》the old,《やや書》the aged. (⇨老人) ▶年寄りじみている be old before one's time. ▶あの男は十年でもないのに年寄りじみた歩き方をする He walks like an *old man*, though he is not that old.

●年寄りの冷や水 an old person's indiscretion. ▶それは年寄りの冷や水というものだよ That's *an old person's indiscretion*./That's something an old person shouldn't say or do.

***とじる 閉じる** close (↔ open), shut*. ●閉まる, 閉める) ●窓を閉じる *close* [*shut*] the window. ●口を閉じなさい *Close* your mouth. (！Shut your mouth! は「黙れ」という意で, この場合 close は用いられない) ●会を閉じる *close* [×shut] the meeting. ▶彼は目を閉じてその音に神経を集中した He *closed* his eyes as he concentrated on listening to the sounds. ▶私は読んでいた本を閉じた I *closed* the book I was reading.

***とじる 綴じる** [とじ込んで整理する] file; [本を] bind*. ▶手紙をとじる *file* (away) the letters. ●雑誌をとじておく *keep* the magazines *on file* [*in a file*].

どじる (⇨どじ [どじを踏む])

としわすれ 年忘れ a year-end party. (⇨忘年会)

としん 都心 the center [heart] of a city (！東京

とじん

場合は ... of Tokyo となる); 〖商業地区〗《米》a downtown; 《英》the city center. ● 都心に行く go *downtown*; go to *downtown* Tokyo. ▶彼は都心に住んでいる He lives in *the center* [*central part*] *of the city*.

とじん 都塵 ● 都塵(=都会のごみごみしたところ)を離れて away from the *dirt and noise of the city*.

どしんと (⇨どすんと)

トス ❶〖コイン投げ〗a toss, a tossup. ▶トスで先攻を決めよう Let's toss a coin and see who bats first./Let's decide who bats first by a *tossup*. ❷〖至近距離からの軽い送球〗a toss.(⚠下手からだけではなく上手からのこともある) ● ボールを彼にトスする *toss* him the ball; toss the ball *to* him. ❸〖バレーボール・テニスの〗a set, a setup. ● 正確なジャンピングトスを上げる give an accurate jump *set* (*to* the spiker).(⚠トスを上げる人は a setter) ● トスバッティング〖野球〗pepper; a pepper game. ● トスバッティングをする play pepper.

どす (短刀) a dagger; (ナイフ) a knife.
● **どすの利いた** ● どすの利いた声で in a *threatening* voice.
● **どすを利かす** threaten; say [do] ... threateningly.

どすう 度数 (回数) the number of times; (頻度) frequency; (温度・角度の) a degree. ● 度数制 (電話の) the message-rate [call-rate] system. ● 度数料金 (電話の) message [call] rates.

『トスカ』 Tosca. (⚠プッチーニのオペラ)

ドスキン 〖めすジカの皮〗doeskin.

どすぐろい どす黒い ● どす黒い血 *dark red* blood; *blackish* blood. ● どす黒い肌をしている have (a) *dusky* [(a) *swarthy* /swɔːrðɪ/] skin.

ドストエフスキー 〖ロシアの小説家〗Dostoevski /dàstəjéfski/ (Feodor Mikhailovich ~).

とする 賭する stake 《one's life *on* the outcome》; risk 《one's life, do*ing*》. ● 職を賭してやる *risk* los*ing* one's job.

-とすれば (⇨する ⑩ (b), もし)

どすんと (重い物が落下して) with a thud, with a flop (⚠thud よりやや軽い音); (衝突して) with a bump. ▶彼は重いかばんをどすんと置いた He put down his heavy bag *with a thud*./He *dumped* his heavy bag. ▶彼は床にどすんとしりもちをついた He *flopped down* on the floor, bottom first./He fell on the floor on his bottom *with a flop*. ▶ボートはどすんと川岸にぶつかった The boat *bumped into* the bank of the river.

とせい 渡世 (大ばくちを打つ人)《俗》a high roller. ▶彼は大工を渡世(=職業)にしている He makes a living as a carpenter./He is a carpenter by trade.
● 渡世人(にん) a gambler.

どせい 土星 〖天文〗Sáturn. ● 土星の環 *Saturn's* rings.

どせい 怒声 an angry voice. ● 怒声を浴びせる vent one's anger 《*on* one's men》.

どせきりゅう 土石流 a mudflow, a flood of rocks and mud; (火山爆発による) a volcanic mudflow.

とぜつ 途絶 图 〖停止〗(a) stoppage; 〖一時中止〗(a) suspension; 〖中断〗(an) interruption. ● 輸出の途絶 the *stoppage* of exports.
—途絶する 動 be suspended; be interrupted; (断たれる) be cut off. (⇨途絶える)

とせん 渡船 a ferry; a ferryboat.
● 渡船場 a ferry; (列車などとしての) a transfer.

とそ 屠蘇 *toso*; (説明的に) *sake* with seven special herbs immersed in it, drunk ceremoniously on the festive new-year days to keep away the evil spirit throughout the year.

とそう 塗装 图 〖ペンキなどを塗ること〗painting; 〖ペンキなどの上塗り〗coating; 〖塗料〗paint. ▶板塀(いた)の塗装がはげ始めた The *paint* on the wooden fence began to peel off.
—塗装する 動 ● 門を白く塗装する *paint* the gate white.
● 塗装工 a painter. ● 塗装工事 painting. ● 塗装材料 cóating matèrials.

どそう 土葬 (埋葬) (a) burial /bérɪəl/.
—土葬する 動 ● 死体を土葬する *bury* /béri/ a dead body.

どぞう 土蔵 (説明的に) a white-washed storehouse with a super-thick mud wall.

どそく 土足 ● 土足で (くつをはいたまま) with one's shoes on. ● 土足厳禁 〖掲示〗Shoes off./Please take off your shoes before entering. ▶互いのプライバシーには土足で踏み込まない(=無遠慮に入らない) We shouldn't *bluntly intrude into* [*enter*] the privacy of each other.(⚠米英では室内で靴を脱ぐ習慣がないので with one's shoes on では日本語と同じ意が伝わらない)

どぞく 土俗 traditional local customs; folkways.
● 土俗学 〖『民俗学, 民族学』の旧称〗(民俗学) folklore; (民族学) ethnology.

***どだい 土台** a base, a basis 《*for* ~》. base は文字どおり土台の意. basis は比喩的な意味で用いられることが多いが; 〖建物の〗a foundation.(⚠比喩的にも用いられる) ● 将来の生活の土台を築く establish the *base for* one's future life; lay the *foundations* of one's future life. ● 長い経験を土台にした知識 (a) knowledge *based on* long experiences. ▶この建物は土台がしっかりしている This building has [is built on] solid *foundations*.

どだい ● どだい(=まったく)無理な要求 an *utterly* unreasonable demand. ▶君はどだい(=根本的に)間違っている You are *fundamentally* [*essentially*] wrong. ▶あいつはどだい(=始めから)借金を返す気なんかなかったんだ He *never* thought of returning the money *from the start*.

とだえる 途絶える ▶衛星通信はしばらく途絶えた(=中断された) The satellite communications *were interrupted* [*断たれた*] *were cut off*] for a while. ▶このところ彼女からの便りが途絶えている(=こない) I haven't *heard from* her lately. ▶通りはすっかり人通りが途絶えた(=なくなった) The streets *were* completely *deserted*.

どたキャン 图 〖直前になってキャンセルすること〗a last-minute cancelation.
—どたキャンする 動 cancel 《the meeting》 at the last minute.

どだんす (⇨どたばた)

とだな 戸棚 (食器・衣服などの)《米》a closet /klázət/, 《英》a cupboard /kʌ́bərd/. ● 食器戸棚 a (kitchen) *cupboard*; (食卓のそばに置く背の低い) a sideboard.

どたばた ― どたばた(と) 副 (騒々しく) noisily. ● 足を踏み鳴らして)どたばた歩く pound 《*along*, *down*, *up*》. ▶彼女はどたばたと階段を上がった(降りた) She *pounded up* [*down*] the stairs.
―どたばたする 動 (騒ぎたてる) make 《much, a great》 fuss; (子供がはね回る) romp around [*about*]. ▶子供たちはどたばたしてしかられた The children were scolded for *making too much noise*.
● どたばた喜劇 a slapstick (comedy).

とたん 途端 (⇨すぐ❶) ▶家を出たとたんに雨が降り出した It started to rain *just as* [*as soon as*] we left home. ▶見たとたん彼と分かった *The moment* [*The minute, The instant*] (*that*) I saw him, I recognized him. (!) *that* は省略されることが多い ▶そのとたん爆弾が爆発した *Just then* [*At that very moment*] the bomb exploded.

とたん 塗炭 ▶塗炭の苦しみ ▶高進するインフレで人々は塗炭の苦しみ(=非常な苦しみ)を味わった People *suffered greatly* [*terribly*] when the inflation was rampant.

トタン [<ポルトガル語] (亜鉛めっき鉄) galvanized iron; (波形の) corrugated iron.
• トタン屋根 a tin roof;《建築》a galvanized sheet iron roof; a corrugated-iron roof.

どたんば 土壇場 [最後の瞬間]《*at*》the last minute [moment]; [もうこれ以上待てないぎりぎりの時間]《やや話》《*at*》the eleventh hour; [食うか食われるかの状況] a do-or-die situation. ▶土壇場に追い込まれる be driven into a *do-or-die situation*; (窮地に) be driven into a *corner*. ▶土壇場で逃げる make a *last-minute* exit [*escape*]; (危ないところで逃げる) *escape by the skin of* one's *teeth*. ▶その計画は土壇場で変更になった The plan was changed *at the last minute* [*the eleventh hour*].

どたんばたん noisily, with loud noises. (⇨どたばた) ▶上の階の子供たちがどたんばたん騒いでいる The children *are romping around* [*about*] upstairs.

*****とち** 土地 ❶ [地所] land (!) 数えるときは a piece of land; (所有地) a property; (書) an estate; (小区画地) a plot; (土地の1区画) a lot.
①【~土地, 土地~】▶有効な土地利用 an effective use of *land*; an effective land use. ▶300平方メートルの土地付きの家を買う buy a house with a three hundred square meters of *land*. ▶どうです, なかなかいい土地でしょう What do you think? It's a good piece of *land*, isn't it?
②【土地が】▶家は高くないが土地が高い The house is not expensive, but the *land* is. (!) expensive を繰り返さないことに注意
③【土地の】▶土地の値段 the price of *land*; *land* prices. ▶この土地の広さはどのぐらいですか How large is this *land* [(一区画) *lot*]?
④【土地に】▶土地に投資する invest in *land*.
⑤【土地を】▶土地を遊ばせておく keep [leave] *land* idle. (!) 前の方は意図的, 後のはそうでない場合 ▶土地を買う buy (a piece of) *land*; buy a *plot* [a *lot*]. (!) 「その土地(全部)を買い上げる」では buy up the *land*) ▶その土地を安い値段で売る sell the *land* [the *property*] at a low price. ▶その土地を借りる lease the *land*. ▶彼は田舎に広大な土地を持っている He owns a large *estate* [a vast tract of *land*] in the country.
❷ [耕作地] land; ground; (土壌) soil. ▶やせた[肥えた]土地 poor [rich, fertile] *soil*. ▶土地を耕す cultivate [《古》till] the *land* (*ground*). ▶そこにはあまり耕作できる土地がない There isn't much arable *land* there.
❸ [場所] a place; (地域) (やや書) a locality. ▶初めての土地 a strange *place*. (!) 「この土地は初めてです」は I'm a stranger here [in this *place*]. などという ▶その土地の人々 local *people*;《話》the locals. ▶何かその土地の名物を買う buy some *local* specialties.
• 土地改革 land reform. • 土地開発 land development. • 土地改良 land improvement. • 土地家屋 land and buildings; (不動産) real estate. • 土地転がし land-rolling. • 土地収用 land

expropriation of land. (!) 「買い上げ」「取り上げ」のいずれも含む • 土地所有者 a landowner. • 土地っ子 a native 《*of*+地名》. (!) 単独では軽蔑的に響くことがあるのでは

とち 栃 (⇨栃の木) • 栃の実 a horse chestnut;《英》a conker.

とちがら 土地柄 (土地の気風) the genius of the place; the nature of the locality. • 古い土地柄 the old-fashioned *genius of the place*.

とちのき 栃の木 《植物》a horse chestnut.

とちめんぼう 栃麺棒 ▶栃麺棒を食う[振る] (面食らう) be flustered, get in a fluster.

どちゃく 土着 ――土着(の) 圏 native. • 土着の人 a native 《*of*》.
• 土着民 natives; native people.

*****とちゅう** 途中 ❶ [行き帰りの] on the [one's] way 《*to, from*》; halfway. ▶途中で[家へ帰る途中で]雨に降られる be caught in the rain *on the way* [*on* one's *way*] home. ▶学校へ行く途中で彼女に会った I met her *on the* [*my*] *way* to school. ▶東京から帰る途中, 名古屋に寄った I stopped off at Nagoya *on the* [*my*] *way* back *from* Tokyo. ▶彼らは映画を見に行く途中だった They were *on their way* [×*ways*] *to* see a movie. ▶途中まで君と行こう I'll come *halfway* [*part of the way*, (話) *part*(-)*way*] with you. (!) come に注意 ▶彼は途中で引き返した He turned back *halfway*. ▶どこか途中で鍵(𝑘)をなくした I lost my keys somewhere *along the way*.
❷ [旅などの] ▶(飛行機で)旅行の途中ロンドンに立ち寄る *stop over* [*make a stopover*] in [*at*] London. ▶京都で途中1泊した I *stopped* overnight [*made an overnight stop*] in Kyoto. ▶散歩の途中で(=散歩をしている間に)これを見つけた I found this *while* I was having a walk [*during* my walk]. (!) 前の方が口語的. I was の省略も
❸ [ものごとの] (半ば) halfway; (中程で[に]) midway; (最中に) in the middle (*of*); (中途半端に) by halves. (!) 通例否定文で ▶途中で学問[研究]をやめるな Don't give up the study [the research] *halfway*. ▶彼女は話の途中で言葉を詰まらせた She paused *in the middle of* her talk./She paused *midway* through her talk. ▶仕事を途中でほったらかして(=中途半端にして)はいけません Don't do the work *by halves*./Don't leave the work *half done* [*unfinished*]. ▶映画は途中から見たくない I hate to see a movie *from the middle*. ▶お話の途中で(=お話中)申し訳ありませんが, 今何時か教えてください Excuse me for *interrupting* you, but please tell me what time it is now. (!) 電話が途中で切れた We *were cut off* (while talking on the phone). (!) The telephone was cut off. では「(料金未納で)電話を止められた」の意

とちょう 都庁 the (Tokyo) Metropolitan Government (Office). • 庁 Office を添えると建物を表す

どちょう 怒張 ▶怒張静脈《医学》varicose vein.

*****どちら** ❶ [どれ] which;[二つのうちの一つ] either;(どちらも...ない) neither;[両方] both;[どちらを...しよう と] whichever.

解説 (1) **either** と **neither** は (i) 形容詞, (ii) 代名詞, (iii) 接続詞の用法がある. (i) 形容詞としては either [neither] +単数名詞の形で用いる. (ii) 代名詞としては either, neither をそれぞれ単独で用いる場合と either [neither] of+the [one's]+複数名詞, either [neither] of+複数代名詞の形で用いる場合がある. いずれも単数扱いが原則だが《話》では特に否定文・疑問文で複数扱いが多い. (iii) 接続

詞としては either A or B, neither A nor B の形で用いる. A, B は文法的に対等の関係にある語・節がくる. 後に動詞が続いた場合は B に呼応するのが原則だが,《話》では B が単数でも複数扱いになることが多い.

(2) **both** は both＋複数名詞, both of＋the [one's]＋複数名詞, both A and B の形で用いる. いずれも複数扱い. A, B は通例対等の関係にある語・句・節がくる.

① 【どちら(の...)が】 which. ▶どちらが君のバッグ[手袋]ですか *Which* is your bag [are your gloves]?/*Which* bag is [*which* gloves are] yours? ▶どちらが正しいのか分からない I don't know *which* is right [the right one]. ▶君たちのどちらが窓を壊したんだ *Which* [×*Who*] of you has broken the window?
【会話】「私と彼とではどちらがその仕事に向いているかしら」「どっちもちょっと言えないよ」 "*Who* [×*Which*] do you think is fit for the job, him or me [《書》he or I]?" "That's a tough [difficult] decision [choice]." (!) tough が口語的)

② 【どちら(の...)を】 which; [【どちらを...しようとも】 whichever. ▶どちら(の服)を着るか決めないといけない You have to decide *which* (dress) to wear [*which* (dress) you should wear]. (!) 後の方が口語的) ▶あなたがどちらを選んでも私はかまいません *No matter which* [*Whichever*] (one) you choose, it doesn't matter to me. (!) 前の方が口語的. *Whichever* (one) you *may* choose, ... は文語的)

③ 【どちらか】 either ... or .... ▶その責任は彼か私かのどちらかにある *Either* he *or* I am responsible for it. (!) 呼応のわずらわしさをさけて *Either* he is responsible for it *or* I am. ともいう. am の後に responsible for it が省略されている) ▶彼は遅れて来るかもう来ないかのどちらかだ *Either* he's late *or* he's not coming.
【会話】「どちらに聞いてもむだだよ」「いや, どちらかが答えを知ってるに違いない」 "It's no good asking *either* of them." "Well, *one* of them must know the answer."

④ 【どちら(の...)も...だ】 both; either. ▶その川はどちらの岸にも木が植えてあった There were trees on *both* sides [on *either* side] of the river. (!) side, end, hand などの語の前では either は「両方の」の意になる) ▶私たちどちらも釣りが好きです We *both* like fishing. (!) 同格の both の位置は一般動詞の前, be 動詞・助動詞の後)/*Both of* us like fishing. ▶彼はピアノもギターもどちらも弾けます He plays *both* the piano *and* the guitar. ▶2 人の子供はどちらも泳ぐのがうまい *Either of* the children is [×are] good at swimming./*Both* children [*Both* (*of*) the children, ×*Both of* children, ×*The both* children] are good at swimming.

⑤ 【どちら(の...)も...ない】 neither; not either. ▶どちらの話も本当ではない *Neither* story [×*stories*] is true. (!)×*Either* story is *not* true. とはいわない) ▶私の両親はどちらもコーヒーを飲まない *Neither of* my parents drinks [×*drink*] coffee. (!)*Both of* my parents d*on't* drink ˇcoffee. は, coffee の下降調を下降上昇調にすると部分否定の意味になる. したがって《書》では全否定との区別がつかなくなるため避けた方がよい) ▶彼も彼のお父さんもどちらも家にいなかった *Neither* he *nor* his father was [《話》were] at home.
【会話】「どちらが好きですか」「どちらも好きじゃない」 "*Which* do you like better [prefer, 《話》like best]?" "*Neither*./I like *neither* (of them)./I don't like *either* (of them)."

⑥ 【どちら(の...)でも】 either; [...するものはどちらでも] whichever. ▶火曜日か水曜日に来なさい. どちらの日でもよい Come Tuesday or Wednesday. *Either* will be fine. [*Either* day is [×*are*] OK.] ▶どちらでも君のすすめる方を買います I'll buy *whichever* [×*no matter which*] (one) you recommend.

❷ 【どこ】 where; 【どの方向】 which way. (⇒どこ ❶) ▶どちらでこれを買いましたか *Where* did you buy this? ▶警察署はどちらですか *Where* [*Which way*] is the police station? ▶あなたの自宅の住所はどちらですか *What's* [×*Where's*] your home address?
【会話】(空港で)「やあこんにちは. どちらまで(ご旅行)ですか」「週末をちょっと北海道で. で君はどちらへ?」「ぼくは沖縄です」 "Hello. *Where* are you traveling to?" "I'm off to Hokkaido for the weekend. And *where* are you off to [《米》*where* are you headed]?" "I'm going to Okinawa." (!) 米英では意味もなく「どちらへ」とか「お出かけですか」とは尋ねない. もしあいさつとして用いるなら How far are you going? ぐらいが適当)

❸ 【どなた】 who. (⇒どなた) ▶どちら様でしょうか May I have [ask] your name, please?/(電話で) *Who's* calling [speaking], please?
【会話】(電話で)「どなた」「三郎だよ」「三郎さん? どちらの」「もちろん森三郎だよ」 "Who's this [《英》that]?" "It's Saburo." "Saburo? Saburo *who*?" "(!)*...who*? に注意) "Saburo Mori, of course."

どちらかといえば **どちらかと言えば** if anything; [むしろ...したい] would [had] rather .... (!) would の方が普通. 《話》では 'd rather) ▶どちらかと言えば彼は以前より幸福そうだ *If anything*, he seems happier than before. ▶どちらかと言えば家でテレビを見ていたい I'd *rather* watch television at home. (!) 否定は I'd *rather not* watch .... となる) ▶あの人は親切というよりどちらかと言えば交際上手なのです He is sociable *rather than* kind.
【会話】「7 歳にしてはやや小柄じゃないですか」「どちらかと言うとそうですな」 "Isn't he rather small for seven?" "He ˇis, ╱*rather*."

どちらにしても 【なんにせよ】 in any case, 《話》anyway; 【2 者のうちどちらの場合でも】 in either case. (⇒どっちみち) ▶どちらにしても, 君はその会に出席しなければならない *In any* [*either*] *case* you have to go to the meeting.

とちる (間違える) make* a mistake. ● せりふをとちる *muff* [《米》*blow*] one's lines.

とおいつ — **とおいつおうつ** 動 (思案する) be still undecided; hesitate. (⇒迷う ❸, ためらう)

とっか **特化** 图 specialization.
— **特化する** 動 specialize 《in》. ● 鉄道模型に特化した商店 a store that specialized in model trains.

とっか **特価** (特別価格) a special price; (値引き値段) a reduced price; (安売り値段) a bargain price. ● 特価でカメラを買う buy a camera *at a special* [*a reduced*, *a bargain*] *price*; buy a camera *on sale* 《米》[*on* (special) *offer* 《英》]. (⇒特売)

とっか **特科** (自衛隊の砲兵部門) the artillery; (講義など) a special course.

トッカータ 【音楽】 a toccata.

どっかい **読解** ● 生徒の読解力をつける improve the students' *reading comprehension* [*ability to read and understand*]. ● その生徒の読解力をテストする give the student a *reading comprehension* test.

とっかえひっかえ **取っかえ引っかえ** ▶彼女は青山のブティックで取っかえ引っかえオーバーを試着した She tried on *one* overcoat *after another* at a boutique in

Aoyama.
とっかかり 取っ掛かり ▶まだ問題解決の取っ掛かり(=どこから…を始めるか)が見つからない We still can't find *where to start* solving [解決の糸口] *a clue to* the problem.
どっかと (⇨どっかり)
どっかり ●顔のまん中にどっかりあぐらをかいている鼻 a big nose *settled* in the center of one's face. ▶大男がどっかり(=重々しく)ひじ掛けいすに座った The big man sat down *heavily* into an armchair. ▶売り上げがどっかり減った Sales have decreased *enormously*.

とっかんこうじ 突貫工事 rush work. ●突貫工事で(=短期間で)家を建てる build a house *in a short time*; run up a house. (! run up は「短時間[期間]で作る」の意. run up a dress (あっという間に服を縫い上げる)/run up a debt (みるみる借金をためる))
とっき 突起 图 (突き出たもの) a projection. ●骨にある突起物 a *projection* on a bone.
—— 突起する stick out, 《やや書》 projéct. ●突起している projecting.
とっき 特記 图 ▶特記事項なし Nothing to report./ Nothing in particular. ▶この事実は特記に値する This fact deserves [is worth] *special mention*.
—— 特記する mention specially, make special mention of ….
どつき 度付き ●度付きサングラス sunglasses *with lenses*.
どっき 毒気 (⇨毒気(ビン))
とつぎさき 嫁ぎ先 (夫の家族) the family a woman marries into; (娘の夫) one's daughter's husband.
とっきゅう 特急 (座席指定の) 《米》a limited express (train). ●特急券 a limited express ticket.
とっきゅう 特級 [[最高の品質]] the highest quality. (⇨極上)
●特級酒 the highest [(最もよい) the best] quality sake; sake of the highest [the best] quality. ●特級品 the highest quality article [goods].
とっきょ 特許 (発明・考案の) a patent /pǽtnt, péit-/. ●特許を取った機械 a *patent* machine. ●特許を申請する apply for a *patent*. ●発明品の特許を取る take out [get, obtain] a *patent for* an invention; patent an invention. ●特許出願中 《表示》 Patent pending. (! The patent is pending. より)
●特許権 a patent (right). ●特許権侵害で訴える sue 《him》 for infringement of a *patent* [*patent* infringement]. ●特許使用料 royalties 《on AIDS drugs》. ●特許所有者 a pàtentée. ●特許庁 the Patent Office. ●特許品 a patent; a patented article.
どっきょ 独居 —— 独居する 動 live alone.
●独居老人 an old man [woman, person] living alone; a lone old man [woman, person].
どっきりカメラ [[番組名]] Candid Camera. (! 小文字で普通名詞として「隠し撮り用小型カメラ」の意で用いられる)
ドッキング docking.
—— ドッキングする 動 dock. ●二つの意見をドッキングさせる *put* [*join*] two opinions *together*. ▶ソユーズはサリュートとうまくドッキングした Soyuz was successfully *docked with* Salyut.
どっきんほう 独禁法 [[「独占禁止法」の略]] (⇨独占)
とっく 特区 (特別区) a special zone. ●経済特区 a *special* economic *zone*.

とつぐ 嫁ぐ (結婚する) marry 《him》; get* [be] married 《to him》. (形は状態を表す). ●山田家へ嫁ぐ *marry into* the Yamada family. ●娘を嫁がせる *marry (off)* one's daughter 《to him》.
どつく 匚 突く 動 hit; (繰り返し殴る) beat. ●殴る
ドック [[船舶の修理・建造用施設]] a (dry) dock. ●乾 [湿; 浮き] ドック a dry [a wet; a floating] *dock*. ●船をドックに入れる put a ship into *dock*; dock a ship. ▶船はドックに入っている[入った] The ship is in [has gone into] *dock*. (! 無冠詞に注意)
ドッグ [[犬]] a dog.
●ドッグフード dog food. ●ドッグレース a dog racing [race].
とっくに [[ずっと以前に]] a long time ago, long ago, 《話》 ages ago; [[すでに]] already; [[かなり]] well (! past, over などの前置詞を修飾). ▶彼はその大学をとっくに卒業しました He graduated from the college *a long time ago* [*long ago*]. ▶昼食の時間はとっくに過ぎている It's long after [past] lunchtime. ▶彼女はとっくに 30 を過ぎている She is *well over* [*past*] thirty. ▶宿題はとっくに(=すでに)終わったよ I have *already* finished my homework.
とっくみあい 取っ組み合い (つかみ合い) a grapple; (激しい) a scuffle.
とっくみあう 取っ組み合う grapple [scuffle, wrestle] 《with》; come to grips 《with》.
とっくり 徳利 a *sake* bottle. ●とっくり首のセーター (主に米) a turtleneck (sweater); 《主に英》 a poloneck (sweater).
とっくん 特訓 [[特別な訓練]] special training; (集中的な) intensive training; [[特別な授業]] a special lesson; (集中的な) an intensive lesson; [[(学習者のための)集中訓練コース]] an intensive course. ●英語の特訓を受ける go through *special* [*intensive*] *training* in English; take *intensive lessons* [*courses*] in English. ▶あの予備校では今受験生を特訓中です They *are giving intensive lessons to* the students preparing for (entrance) exams at that preparatory school.
—— 特訓する 動 ●水泳選手を特訓する *give* swimmers *special* [*intensive*] *training*; *train* swimmers *specially* [*intensively*].
どっけ 毒気 (悪意) 《やや書》 málice; (意地悪) spite.
●毒気を含んだ批評 *malicious* [*spiteful*] criticism.
●毒気に当てられる (相手の強い態度に気持ちがなえる) be discouraged [《書》 be dispirited] (by counterattack).
●毒気を抜かれる (あぜんとさせられる) be taken aback 《at [by]》 his lack of …; be struck dumb.
とっけい 特恵 —— 特恵の 形 [[経済]] preferential.
●特恵関税 preferential duties; a preferential (treatment) tariff. ●特恵待遇 preference [preferential] treatment.
とつげき 突撃 图 a charge; [[突進]] a dash. ●突撃らっぱを鳴らす sound the *charge*. ●突撃隊は全滅した(=1 人残らず戦死した) The *shock troops* were killed to a man.
—— 突撃する 動 ●敵をめがけて突撃する make a *charge* [a *dash*] at the enemy; charge (at) the enemy.
とっけん 特権 (a) privilege. ●特権を行使[乱用; 停止]する exercise [abuse; suspend] a *privilege*. ●特権を与える give [grant] a *privilege*. ●特権意識が強い have a strong consciousness of social *privilege*. ▶彼にはそれをする特権がある He has the (special) *privilege of* doing [*to* do] that.
●特権階級 the privileged class(es).

どっこい ▶どっこい, そうは問屋がおろさない No, you are expecting too much. (!相手の行動をさえぎるときにいう)

どっこいしょ 〘どすんと〙with a plump. (!腰をおろすとき) ▶いすにどっこいしょと腰をおろす sit down on a chair *with a plump*; *plump* (*oneself*) *down* on a chair; (ほら, どっこいしょと言って座る) sit down on a chair, saying, "*Here we are.*" ●重い買い物バッグをどっこいしょと床に置く *plump down* a heavy shopping bag on the floor. ●どっこいしょと(=全力を尽くして)かごを持ち上げて棚に上げる lift the basket up to the shelf *with all* one's *might*.

どっこいどっこい (⇨似たり寄ったり) ▶A と B はどっこいどっこいである A is almost 〘(量的に)about, (質的に)much〙 the same as B.

とっこう 特攻・特攻隊 〘「特別攻撃隊」の略〙 a special [a suicide] attack corps /kɔ́ːr/, (● /kɔ́ːrː/) [unit].

とっこう 特高 〘「特別高等警察」の略〙 the Special Political Police.

とっこう 徳行 a good [a virtuous] act.

どっこうせん 独航船 a catcher (boat).

とっこうやく 特効薬 a wonder drug (!驚くほどよく効く薬); a miracle drug (!特に新薬に関するジャーナリズム用語); a specific medicine [remedy] (*for* AIDS). ●青少年非行に対する特効薬 a *special cure* [*remedy*] *for* juvenile delinquency. ▶この薬は結核の特効薬だ That is a *specific medicine for* tubèrculósis [TB]./The drug *is* highly *specific for* tuberculosis.

とっさ 咄嗟 ― 咄嗟の 〘(迅速な)quick, prompt; (予期しない)unexpected; (即時の)〙〘やや書〙instantaneous. ▶とっさの機転で by one's *quick* wits. ▶とっさの質問に答えられなかった I couldn't answer an *unexpected* question./The question was *quite unexpected*, so I couldn't answer it. ▶それはとっさの出来事だった It happened *in an instant* [*suddenly, all at once*]. (⇨副)

― 咄嗟に 副 〘(素早く)quickly; (一瞬に)in an instant; (突然)suddenly, all at once. ●とっさに(=反射的に)身をかわして落石をよける dodge a falling rock by reflex action. ●「それは私ではない」と彼はとっさに答えた "It wasn't me [〘書〙I]," he was *quick* to react [*explain*].

どっさり (⇨たくさん) ▶非常時に備えて缶詰をどっさり買い込む lay in *a lot of* [*plenty of*] canned food for emergencies. ▶彼の机の上には書類がどっさり積み上げられていた There were documents piled up *so high* on his desk.

ドッジボール 〘球技〙 dodge ball. ●ドッジボールをする play (a game of) *dodge ball*.

とっしゅつ 突出 名 (突き出ること)projection; (目立つこと)prominence.
― 突出する 動 stick out,〘やや書〙projèct; (張り出す)jut out. ●突出した projecting; prominent. ▶岬が湾内に突出している The headland *juts out* into the bay.

とつじょ 突如 (突然)suddenly. (⇨突然)

どっしり 〘堂々と〙imposingly; (重々しく)heavily; (威厳をもって)dignifiedly. ●どっしりした建物 an *imposing* [〘がっしりした〙a *solid*] building. ●どっしりした人 a *dignified* person. ▶広場の中心にどっしりした記念碑が建っていた A *massive* monument stood in the center of the square.

とっしん 突進 名 a rush; a dash.
― 突進する 動 rush; dash. (!後の方が勢いが感じられる) ▶彼は席を取ろうと突進した He *rushed* [*made a rush*] for a seat.

とつぜん 突然 副 suddenly, all of a sudden, all at once; unexpectedly; abruptly.

〘使い分け〙 **suddenly** 急に予期せぬ事が起こること.
all of a sudden, all at once suddenly とほぼ同意で用いるが, all of a sudden の方が口語的でより強意的.
unexpectedly 思いがけぬ事が起こること. 備えが十分でないことを暗示する.
abruptly 何の予告もなく不意に変化が起こること. しばしば不快〘不利〙な結果を暗示する.

▶突然そのドアが開いた *Suddenly* [*All of a sudden, All at once*] the door opened. ▶私は突然自分の過ちに気がついた I *suddenly* realized my mistake. ▶私の息子は7歳の時に突然原因不明の病気で死んだ My son, who was seven year olds, died *unexpectedly* of unknown causes. ▶そのグループは突然コンサートツアーの残りをキャンセルした The group *abruptly* canceled the rest of the concert tour.

― 突然の 形 sudden; (思いがけない)unexpected; (不意の)abrupt. ▶我々は彼の突然の死に驚いた We were surprised at his *sudden* [*unexpected*] death./We were surprised that he died *suddenly* [*unexpectedly*]./(青天の霹靂(へきれき)だった) The news of his death was (*like*) *a bolt from* [*out of*] *the blue*. (!通例好ましくないことに用いる) ▶彼の辞職はまったく突然のことだった His resignation was very *sudden*./He resigned *all of a sudden*.
●突然変異 mutation (!具体例・変異種は 〚C〛); (異変)a mutant.

とったん 突端 ●岬の突端 the *tip* [(とがった端)the *point*] of a cape.

どっち 〘どれ〙which; 〘どこ〙where. (⇨どちら)

どっちつかず ― どっちつかずの 形 〘当たりさわりのない〙nòncommíttal; 〘中立的な〙neutral; 〘両意に取れる〙equivocal /ikwívəkəl/; 〘逃げ口上の〙evasive; 〘あいまいな〙ambiguous. ●どっちつかずの返事をする give a *noncommittal* [an *equivocal*, an *evasive*, an *ambiguous*] answer. ●どっちつかずの態度をとる take a *neutral* [(決定的でない)an *indecisive*] stand. ▶彼の態度はどっちつかずだ His attitude is *equivocal* [*neutral*, (決まっていない)*undecided*].

どっちみち 〘とにかく〙(どんな場合でも)in ány càse, 〘話〙anyway, 〘話〙anyhow; (2者のうちどちらの場合でも)in either case, 〘話〙either way; 〘結局〙after all. ▶君はどっちみち間に合わないよ You will not be in time (for it) *anyway* [*anyhow*]. ▶どっちみちそんなことは私にとって大した問題ではないよ It doesn't make much difference to me *in any case* [*anyway, either way*]. ▶どっちみち彼は事業に失敗するでしょう He will fail in business *after all*. ▶どっちみち(=遅かれ早かれ)何もかも元どおりに収まるでしょう *Sooner or later* everything will come right again.

〘会話〙 「かばんを取ってきてくださってありがとう」「気にしないで. どっちみちもう一度教室に行くところだったんですもの」"Thank you for getting me my bag." "Think nothing of it. I was going back to the classroom *anyway*."

とっちめる (強くしかる)tell* 〘him〙 off severely 〘*for*〙, 〘話〙give* 〘him〙 a good talking-to 〘*for*〙. ▶トシは遅刻ばかりしているよ. 一度とっちめてやらなくては Toshi is always late. I'll have to *give him a good talking-to*.

とっちゃんぼうや 父ちゃん坊や a fine gentleman with a childish side to his character; (童顔の人)a baby-face man.

とっつかまえる 取っ捕まえる catch; 〘話〙nab (-bb-).

《話》nail. (⇨捕まえる)

とっつき 取っ付き ● 取っ付き(=初め)から from *the beginning* [*start*]. ● 取っ付き(=初め)は at first. ● 右側の取っ付き(=一番手前)の部屋 *the first* room on the right side. ● 取っ付きにくい人 a person who is *difficult* (↔*easy*) *to approach* [*talk to*]; an *unapproachable* (↔an approachable, a friendly) person.

とって 取っ手 〖握り〗a handle, a grip; 〖ドア・引き出しなどのつまみ〗a knob; 〖引き手〗a pull (⚠通例複合語で); 〖水差しなどの〗an ear.

-とって 〖には〗to ...; 〖ためには〗for .... (⚠to か for か前にくる形容詞・名詞によって決まることが多い) ● 彼にとって大きな驚き a great surprise *to* him. ● その数学の試験は私にとってはやさしかった[難しかった] The math was easy [difficult] *for* me. ● 炭鉱の閉山はその町の人々にとって死活問題であった Closing the coal mine was a matter of life and death *to* [*for*] people in the town. (⚠ (1) この例のように to と for の両方がつく場合、単に対象・方向を示すときは to が、「…のために」と目的を示すときは for が好まれる。(2) 強調のために文頭位に移される場合は for の方が普通)

とってい 突堤 a bréakwàter; (小規模な) a jetty.

とっておき 取って置き — 取って置きの 形 〖最もよい〗best; 〖取っておいた〗kept; reserved; 〖貴重な〗valuable. ● 取って置きの服を着て出かける go out in one's *best* clothes 〖晴れ着〗one's *Sunday best*〗. ▶彼は取って置きのワインを開けた He opened a bottle of his *best* wine. / He opened a bottle of the wine *kept for* a special occasion. ▶彼は彼女に取って置きの笑顔を見せた He smiled at her with a smile *reserved* [×*kept*] *especially for* her. (⚠ kept は抽象名詞には用いない)

とっておく 取って置く ❶ 〖保持・保管する〗keep*; (腐らないように) preserve; 〖(ホテルなど)予約する〗reserve. ● 魚を塩漬けにして取っておく *preserve* [*keep*] fish in salt. ● 彼のために座席を取っておく *reserve* 〖(主に英)*book*〗a seat for him; (確保する) *save* 〖(努力して) *secure*〗him a seat; *save* [*secure*] a seat *for* him. ▶おつりは取っておいていいよ *Keep* the change. ▶この肉はあしたまで取っておけますか(=もちますか) Will this meat *keep* till tomorrow? (⚠ keep は「長持ちするもつ」の意の口語表現) ❷ 〖別にしておく〗(金や品物などを取っておく) put*... aside; (金などを特別の目的に) set*... aside; (金などをたくわえる) save. ● そのケーキの残りをあした食べようと取っておく *put* the rest of the cake *aside* for tomorrow. ● 万一に備えて金を取っておく *save* 〖残しておく〗 *keep* money for a rainy day. ● 昼食に 1 時間取っておく *allow* [*set aside*] an hour for lunch. (⚠ allow は「余裕をみておく」の意) 会話 「このプリンとってもおいしいわね」「少しは私に取っておいて」"What a tasty [a delicious] pudding!" "*Save* [*Leave*] some of it for me."

とってかえす 取って返す (戻る) get* back, return (⚠前の方が口語的); 〖引き返す〗turn [double] back. ● 急いで取って返す hurry back; *turn back* in a hurry.

とってかわる 取って代わる 〖…の代わりをする〗take* the place of ...; 〖入れ替える〗replace. ▶この市ではバスが市電に取って代わった Buses *have taken the place of* [*have replaced*] streetcars in this city.

とってくる 取って来る get*, bring*; 《話》go* (and) get; 《主に英》fetch. ▶(犬に)取って来い Go and *fetch*! / 《米話》Go *fetch*! ▶彼にいすを取ってきてあげなさい *Get* [*Bring*] him a chair. / *Get* [*Bring*] a chair for him. / Go and get [《米話》Go get] him a chair. (⚠ go (and) get の形は go が原形の場合にのみ用い、goes, going, went, gone の場合には用いない) / *Fetch* him a chair [a chair *for* him].

とってつけた 取って付けた (不自然な) unnatural; (わざとらしい) àrtificial; (うわべだけの) false. ● 取って付けたような笑い方をする(=作り笑いをする) *force* a smile; (ぎこちなく) smile *stiffly*; put on an *artificial* [a *false*] smile. ▶彼は彼女に料理がうまいと取って付けたようなお世辞を言った He complimented (her on) her cooking, but it sounded *unnatural* [*false*].

とっても so, very. (⇨とても)

どっと ❶ 〖勢いよく起こる様子〗 ▶聴衆はどっと笑った The audience *burst into* laughter [*burst out* laugh*ing*]. ▶〖後の方が口語的〗▶少年たちはどっと走り出した The boys *broke into* a run. ▶人々がどっと部屋に入ってきた People *burst into* the room. ▶彼女の目に涙がどっとあふれてきた Tears *welled up* in her eyes.
❷ 〖多くの物・人がいっせいに押し寄せる様子〗 (群がる) throng, crowd; (殺到する) flood. ▶野球場にその試合を見るためどっと押し寄せた People *thronged* to the ballpark to see the game. ▶問い合わせの手紙がどっときた Letters of inquiry *flooded* [*poured*] *in*. / There was a *flood* of letters of inquiry.
❸ 〖状態が急激に変化する様子〗 ▶彼はその仕事を終えるとどっと寝こんだ He *suddenly* fell sick after he had completed the work. ▶彼は長くきつかった 1 日の仕事の後どっと疲れを感じた A *surge of* tiredness caught up with him after the long hard day's work.

ドット 〖点〗a dot. ● ドットコム 〖インターネット関連企業〗a dot-com. ● ドットプリンター a dot(-matrix) printer. ● ドットマップ 〖物の分布地図〗a dot map.

とつとつ 訥々 ● とつとつと(=口ごもりながら)話す speak [talk] *falteringly*. ● とつとつと説明する *falter* [*stammer*] *out* an explanation.

とっとと ▶とっとと出て行け! Get out of here! / You go away right now!

とつにゅう 突入 — 突入する 動 ● 敵陣に突入する(=勢いよく突っ込む) *dash into* the enemy; (突撃する) *rush* [*charge*] *at* the enemy. ● ストに突入する *go* (*out*) *on* strike; *plunge into* a strike. ▶彼らは首相官邸に突入した They *stormed* (*into*) the prime minister's office.

***とっぱ** 突破 名 (妨害・難関の) a breakthrough.
— **突破する** 動 break* through ...; 〖困難などを乗り切る〗get* over ...; overcome*; 〖超過する〗rise* above ...; exceed. ● 敵陣を突破する *break through* the enemy's line 〖防御線〗defenses〗. ● 赤信号を突破する *run through* a red signal. ● 多くの苦難を突破する *get over* [*overcome*] a lot of difficulties. ● 入試の難関を突破する *overcome* [*get over*] the hurdle of an entrance exam; (難しい入試に合格する) *pass* a difficult entrance exam. ▶この大学の志願者は 10 万人を突破した The number of applicants for entrance to this university *rose above* [*exceeded*, (超えた) *passed*] 100,000.
● 突破口 a breakthrough; (城壁などの) a breach.

とっぱつ 突発 名 an outbreak; (暴力などの) an outburst.
— **突発的な** 形 ● 突発的な(=予期せぬ)事件 an *unexpected* occurrence [*incident*].
— **突発的に** 副 unexpectedly; suddenly.
— **突発する** 動 break [burst] out; (突然起こる)

とっぱん 凸版 ●凸版印刷 letterpress; relief printing.

とっぴ 突飛 ━ **突飛な** 形 (現実離れした) fantastic; (向こう見ずな) reckless, wild; (異常な) extraordinary, unusual; (常軌を逸した) eccentric; (過度な) extravagant /ɪkstrǽvəgənt/.

とっぴょうし 突拍子 ● **突拍子もない** 突拍子もない(=無謀な)考え a *wild* [(現実離れした) a *fantastic*, (ばかげた) a *crazy*] idea. ● 突拍子もない(=異常な)事を言う say *extraordinary* [(途方もない) *monstrous*] things.

トッピング (料理の) (a) topping.

トップ 〖首位〗the top. (⇨先頭) ●トップクラスのホテル a *first-class* [a *first-rate*, a *leading*] hotel. (⚠ ×top-class は和製英語) ●トップの座を守る stay *on top*. ●トップに立つ come out (on) top (in the race). ▶彼女は成績はいつもクラスのトップだ She is always *at the top* of the class. (⚠「トップクラスにいる」なら She is *one of the best* students in the class.) ▶彼はその競走でトップを切ってゴールした He came in [finished] *first* in the race.
● **トップ会談** a top-level [a summit] conference. ● **トップ下** 〖サッカー〗a behind-the-front man. ● **トップスピン** 〖前回転〗〖球技〗topspin. ●トップスピンをかける put *topspin* (on a ball). ● **トップニュース** 〖記事〗the lead (story). (⚠新聞では第 1 面 (the front page) の右上欄に (on the upper right) 配置される) ● **トップバッター** a leadoff (batter [man]); the first batter. (⚠「最優秀打者」の意) ● **トップマネージメント** 〖企業の最高幹部〗top management. ● **トップモード** 〖最新流行〗the latest fashion; (特に上流階級の) high fashion; 《和製語》top mode. ● **トップライト** 〖天窓採光〗a top light. ● **トップランナー** (リレー競走の第 1 走者) the first runner; (競走の先頭の走者) the first [leading] runner; (一流の走者) a top [a leading] runner. ● **トップレディー** (ある分野・職業の) the first lady 《*of*》.

とっぷう 突風 a gust [a blast] (of wind). (⇨風)

トップダウン 名 〖上意下達〗(管理) top-down management; (意思決定) top-down decision-making.
━ **トップダウンの** 形 top-down (↔bottom-up). ●トップダウン方式 a top-down management style.

とっぷり ▶その小屋にたどりつかぬうちに日がとっぷり暮れた It got *quite* [*completely*] dark before I reached the cottage. (⚠修飾語なしで十分な意味の出る場合もある: 日はとっぷり暮れた It has fallen dark.)

どっぷり (深く) deep(ly). ▶彼女は肉片をどっぷりソースの中に浸した She *dipped* pieces of meat *deep into* the sauce./She *soaked* pieces of meat in the sauce. ▶彼はどっぷりその陰謀にかかわっていた He was *deeply* involved in the conspiracy.

トップレス ━ **トップレスの** 形 〖胸部を露出した〗topless. ● **トップレスの水着** [女性] a *topless* swimsuit [woman].

トップレベル 〖最高水準〗the highest level 《of》; 〖最高幹部〗a top-level executive. ●トップレベルの会談 *top-level* talks; (首脳会談) *summit* talks. ●トップレベルに近づく approach the *highest level*.

とつべん 訥弁 ●訥弁である(=しゃべり方がへただ) be a poor [an awkward] speaker.

どっぽ 独歩 ●独立独歩(=自立) independence. (⇨独立) ●古今独歩(=無比)の名作 a *peerless* masterpiece.

とつめんきょう 凸面鏡 a convex mirror.

とつレンズ 凸レンズ a convex lens (↔a concave lens).

-とて 《副助詞》〖であっても〗even. ▶君とてそうするだろう *Even* you would do so. ▶子供とてそうすることは許されるはずがない *Even* a child cannot be allowed to do so.

━ **とて** 《接続助詞》〖...としても〗even if [though].... ▶金があるからとて何でも買えるわけではない *Even if* you are rich, you cannot buy everything.

どて 土手 (川・湖の a bank) 〖天然・人工いずれも含み、小道や畑などの境界となる土盛りもさす〗; (堤防) an embankment (⚠道路や鉄道の土手もさす); (土手道) a causeway.

とてい 徒弟 an apprentice. (⇨弟子)
● **徒弟期間** one's apprenticeship. ● **徒弟制度** the apprentice system.

どてっぱら 土手っ腹 《俗》guts. ▶土手っ腹に風穴をあけてやるから覚えていろ Remember, I'm going to drill a hole in your dirty *guts*.

とてつもない unreasonable. (⇨途方もない)

*とても **❶** 〖非常に〗very, very much, so (⚠ very は原級の形容詞・副詞を修飾. very much は動詞を修飾. so は very の代用語として女性に好んで用いられる); (ひどく) terribly, (話) awfully; (本当に) really (⚠動詞も修飾可); (この上なく) extremely, (やや書) highly; (たいそう) badly (⚠ need, want などを修飾する). ▶けさはとても寒い It's *very* [*so*, *terribly*, *awfully*, *extremely*] cold this morning. ▶彼の講義はとても興味深い His lectures are *véry* [*réally*, 《米》*quíte*] interesting to me. (⚠ quite は「予想外に」を暗示. 《英》では quite interesting となり「まあまあだ」の意)/I am *very* interested in his lectures./I have a *great* interest in his lectures./His lectures interest me *very* [*so*] *much*. ▶パーティーはとても楽しかった I enjoyed the party *very much*. (⚠ I (*very*) *much* enjoyed the party. の語順では very の省略も可. ×I enjoyed the party much. は不可)/I *really* enjoyed the party./The party was *very* [*really*, *highly*] enjoyable./I had a *very* [*quite* a] good time at the party. ▶彼はその金がとても欲しかった He *badly* wanted the money./He wanted the money *badly*. ▶彼女はとても親切なので級友に大変好かれている She is *so* kind [*such* a *kind girl*] (*that*) she is liked very much by her classmates. (⚠《話》では that がしばしば省略される)

❷ 〖どうしても...ない〗(まったく...ない) not(...) at all; (とうてい...できない) can't [《書》cannot] possibly, 《話》just can't, 《話》can't for the life of me. (⚠ possibly, just, for the life of me は can't を強める (⇨どうしても)) ▶彼はとても勉強しているとは言えない He's *not* diligent *at all*. (⚠ He is *far from* (being) diligent./He is *anything but* diligent. はやや堅い言い方) ▶とても成功の望みはない There is *no* hope (*at all*) of my success. ▶とてもじゃないが、妻にお前は死ぬなんて私の口からは言えないよ *For the life of me*, I *can't* tell my wife she's going to die. ▶そんなことはとても(=絶対)無理だ It is *absolutely* [《全く》*quite*] impossible. ▶彼女はとても病人のようには見えない She *hardly* looks like she's sick.
会話「彼女、本当に婚約したんだよ」「とても信じられないよ」"She's actually engaged." "Wóuld you \believe it!"

どてら a (wide-sleeved) padded *kimono* robe.

とでん 都電 a Toei streetcar. (⇨路面 [路面電車])

とど 〖動物〗a (Steller's) sea lion.

どどいつ 都々逸 a *dodoitsu*; (説明的に) a traditional popular love song sung to (a) *samisen* accompaniment.

とう 徒党 (悪人などの群れ) a gang; (派閥) a faction; (陰謀者) conspirators.
- **徒党を組む** form a gang [a faction];《やや書》conspire. ● 徒党を組んで労働者を襲う assault laborers *in a gang*; 《話》gang up *on* [*against*] laborers.

どとう 怒濤 (荒れ狂う波) angry [furious, violent, wild,《やや書》turbulent] waves. ● 怒濤のように押し寄せる (群衆などが) 《やや書》surge (*forward*) *into* the square, *toward* the Bastille; (感情などが) surge (up).

とどうふけん 都道府県 the administrative division of Japan: Tokyo, Hokkaido and prefectures.

トトカルチョ [<イタリア語]【サッカー賭博】totocálcio; a soccer pool;《英》the pools.

:とどく 届く ❶[着く] (到着する) arrive (*at*); (到達する) reach, get* (*to*). (⇨着く ❶) ▶ 小包はきのう届いた The parcel *arrived* [came, ×reached] yesterday./(配達された) The parcel *was delivered* (to me) yesterday. ▶ 今朝彼から手紙が届いた (=手紙を受け取った) I *got* [*received*, *had*] a letter *from* him this morning./I *got* [*received*] his letter this morning./His letter *reached* me this morning. ▶ 今朝書類かばんを電車に置き忘れたんですが、届いていないでしょうか I left [×forgot] my briefcase on the train this morning. I wonder if it *has been handed in* [《米》*turned in*]. (! hand in, turn in は「(だれかが拾った物を)差し出す」の意)

❷[達する] (手が届く) reach (! 人が主語); (物が届く) reach; (音・弾丸などが) carry. ● …の手の届く[届かない]ところに within [out of] (the) reach of …. ● すぐ手の届くところに (=手元に) near [close] at hand. ▶ 彼は背が高いので天井に手が届く He is so tall that he can reach the ceiling. ▶ そのはしごは窓まで届かない The ladder doesn't *reach* the window. ▶ その薬は子供の手の届かない所に置いておきなさい Keep the medicine *out of the reach of* [*away from*] the children./Keep the medicine where the children can't *get at* it. (! get at は「…に手を伸ばして取る」の意) ▶ その車は私の給料ではとうてい手が届かない That car *is* completely *out of* (×the) *reach* with my salary. ▶ その女優の声は劇場の後列まではっきりと届いた The actress' voice *carried* clear *to* the back rows of the theater. ▶ 彼はもう50に手が届く(=ほぼ 50 歳だ) He is *almost* [*nearly*] 50 years old. ▶ 弾丸は的に届かなかった The shot *fell short of* the mark.

とどけ 届け [報告書](a) report; [通知] (a) notice (! 通知書は[C]); [登録] registration. ● 欠席届を出す send in a *notice* [a *report*] of absence. ● 警察に被害届を出す *report* the damage *to* the police. ● 出生[死亡]届を出す *register* a birth [a death]. ● 届け先 (受取人の住所) the receiver's address.

とどけで 届け出 [通知]《書》(a) notification. ● 知事選挙の届け出をする (=立候補の登録をする) *file for* the gubernatorial election. ● 2 週間以内に届け出をしなければならない *Notification* must be made within fourteen days.

とどけでる 届け出る (⇨届ける ❷)

*とどける 届ける ❶[渡す]**(送る) send*;(配達する) deliver; (持って行く) take*; (持って来る, 相手のところへ持って行く) bring*. ● 小包を郵便で届ける *send* a parcel by mail [《主に米》post《主に英》]. ● 品物を客に届ける *deliver* goods *to* a customer. ▶ この伝言を彼に届けてくれませんか Will you *send* [*take*] this message *to* him? ▶ 彼らはそのお金を警察に届けた (=引き渡した) They *handed in* [《米》*turned in*] the money *to* the police.
会話「スコッチをワンケース届けてほしいの」「すぐにお届けします」 "A case of Scotch, please. I need a *delivery*." "I'll *bring* it *to* you right away./(参ります) I'll be right with you."

❷[報告する] report; (正式に通知する)《書》notify; (登録する) register. ● 彼の失踪(そう)を警察に届ける *report* [*notify*] his disappearance *to* the police; *notify* the police *of* his disappearance. ▶ 彼は赤ん坊の出生を区役所に届けた He *registered* the birth of his baby at the ward office.

とどこおりなく 滞りなく ● 滞りなく(=遅れずに)支払う pay (it) *without delay* [(期日どおりに) *on time*,《書》*duly*]. ● 会合は滞りなく(=すらすらと)終わった The meeting went off *smoothly* [(支障なく) *without a hitch*, *without accident*].

とどこおる 滞る ● 滞った back (! 限定的に); (期限の過ぎた) overdue (! 通例叙述的に); (未払いの) unpaid. ● 滞った家賃 *back* rent. ▶ 彼は 3 か月も家賃が滞っている He *is* (three months) *behind with* [*behind in*, *in arrears with*] his rent./His rent *is* (three months) *overdue* [*in arrears*]. ▶ 事務が滞っている The office work *is not getting on smoothly*./We *have a delay* in the office work.

*ととのう 整う, 調う 動 [用意ができる]** be ready [prepared] (*for*) (⇨用意); (完了する) be completed; [まとまる] be arranged. ▶ 準備はすべて整った Everything *is ready*./All preparations *are complete* (d). ▶ 2 人の縁談が調った (第三者によって) A marriage *has been arranged* between the two./(当人同士で) The two *are engaged*.

― **整った 形** [きちんとした] tidy; [こざっぱりした] neat; [服装などがまともな] decent /díːsnt/. ● 整った部屋 a *tidy* [a *neat*] room. ● よく(設備が)整った台所 an excellent [a well-fitted] kitchen. ● 服装が整っている be *neatly* [*decently*] dressed. ● 整った顔をしている be *good-looking*; (目鼻立ちの) have *regular features*; (横顔の輪郭がはっきりした) have a good and strong profile /próufail/.

:ととのえる 整える, 調える ❶[きちんとする] tidy ...(up), (並べる) arrange. ● 部屋を整える *tidy* (*up*) a room. ● 髪を整える *tidy* [*arrange*,《主に米》*fix*] one's hair. ● 起床してシーツを整える(=しわを伸ばす) get out of bed and *smooth out* one's sheet. ▶ 彼女は外出の前に身なりを整えた She *got dressed* before going out.

❷[用意する] get* ... ready, prepare (*for*); (手配して) arrange (*for*) (⇨用意); (準備をする); (配置する) set*. ● 旅の準備を整える(出発直前に) *get ready for* the journey; (前もって) *prepare* [*make preparations*] *for* the journey. ● 葬儀の手はずをすべて整える *arrange* everything [*make all arrangements*] *for* the funeral. ● 来客用にテーブルを整えるset a table for the guests.

❸[とりそろえる] (買う) buy*; (設備を) equip (-pp-) (⇨設備); (資金を) raise《funds, money》. (⇨調達する)

とどのつまり (最後には) in the end. ▶ 彼はギャンブルにのめり込んでとどのつまり会社を首になった He fell into gambling and lost his job *in the end* [and *came down to losing* his job]. (⇨結局)

とどまつ 椴松 【植物】a (kind of) fir.

*とどまる 止まる ❶[残る]** stay;《書》remain. ● 現職にとどまる *stay* [*remain*] in one's present office. ▶ 彼は家にとどまった He *stayed* [*remained*] (at) home. (! remain は他人が去った後に取り残さ

とどめ ❷[限定される] be limited 《*to*》. ▶損害は100万円程度にとどまった The loss *was limited to* about a million yen./The loss was *only* about a million yen. (!後の方は「意外に少なかった」を含意する) ▶その計画に反対しているのは彼だけにとどまらない He is not *the only* person who is opposed to the plan.

● **とどまる所を知らない** ▶原油価格の高騰はとどまる所を知らない There is *no limit* [*end*] *to* the rise in crude oil prices.

とどめ 止め ● **止めを刺す** [[完全に殺す]] [一突き] give 《him》 a final thrust [[一発]] shot], finish 《a wounded animal》 off; (比喩的) put an end to ..., give 《him》 a finishing [a fatal] blow; [[一番である]] be the best. ▶花は吉野にとどめを刺す(=桜の花は(なんといっても)吉野が一番だ) The cherry blossoms in Yoshino are (*the*) *most beautiful*./There is *no place like* Yoshino *to* enjoy the beauty of cherry blossoms.

どどめ 土留め (a) sheathing; (木材による) (a) timbering; 《build》a retaining wall.

***とどめる 止める** ❶[残す] (そのまま残す) retain; (後に残す) leave*; (元の場所にいさせる) make*... stay. ● 彼を現職にとどめる(=辞めないように説得する) *persuade* him *not to leave* his office. ● 歴史にその名をとどめる *leave* its [his, her] name in history. ● 記憶にとどめる memorize; *fix*... in one's memory. ● 記録にとどめる *leave*... on record. ▶新会社は元の会社の特色をほとんどとどめていない The new company *retains* almost no features of the old one.

❷[限定する] limit; (保つ) keep*. ● 被害を最小限にとどめる *keep* [*limit*, *reduce*] the damage *to a minimum*; *minimize* the damage. ▶今日の勉強は第3章だけにとどめておこう We'll study *only* Chapter 3 today./We'll *limit* our study *to* Chapter 3 today. ▶この話はこの場にとどめてほしい *Keep* this story *to yourself* [within you].

とどろかす 轟かす ▶飛行機が爆音をとどろかせて飛び去った A plane *roared* away. ● 彼は天下に名をとどろかせた He *made* [*won*] *a name for himself* in the world.

とどろき 轟き ❶(轟音(ごうおん)) a roar; (雷などの) a rumble, a peal; (うなり) a rumble. (! rumble はごろごろ鳴る音, peal は繰り返し鳴る雷の大きな音) ● 大砲[波]のとどろき the *roar* of the gun [waves]. ● 雷のとどろき a *rumble* [a *peal*] of thunder. ● 胸のとどろき the *pounding* [*fast beating*] of the heart.

とどろく ❶[大砲・雷鳴・海などが] roar. ▶稲妻が光ってすぐ雷鳴がとどろいた Just after lightning flashed, the thunder *roared*./The thunder *roared* [*rolled*] soon after a flash of lightning.

❷[広く知られる] (⇨響く❹)

トナー toner. ● トナーを交換する change a toner.

ドナー [臓器提供者] a donor /dóʊnər/.
● ドナーカード a donor card.

とない 都内 ● 都内に(=首都(の)地域に)住む live in the (*Tokyo*) *Metropolitan area*.

ドナウ ▶ドナウ川 the Danube /dǽnjuːb/.

となえる 称える call [name]《the building the Garden-in-the-Air》.

となえる 唱える ❶[くり返し言う] (祈とう文などを) chant; (暗唱する) recite. ● 呪文(じゅもん)を唱える *recite* a spell. ▶修道士たちは祈りの言葉を唱えていた The monks *were chanting* [*saying*] their prayers /préərz/.

❷[主張する] (意見などを出정する)《やや書》advance; (反対などを持ち出す) raise. ▶ダーウィンは新しい進化論を唱えた Darwin *advanced* a new theory of evolution. ▶彼はその計画に異議を唱えた He *raised* [*made*] *an objection to* the plan./He *made an objection to* the plan.

トナカイ [動物] a reindeer /réindiər/. (!単・複同形)

-となく ● 昼となく夜となく(=昼も夜も)働く work day *and* night [night *and* day].

どなた who. (⇨だれ❶) ▶どなたですか (名前を尋ねて) May I have your name, please?/What's your name, please? (!前の方が丁寧な言い方. Who are you? は「お前はだれだ」に相当する失礼な尋ね方)/(電話で) Who's this [《英》that], please? (!(1) Who ＼is this? は詰問調で「一体だれなの」, Who ＼was it? は「今の電話だれなの」の意. (2) May I ask *who* I'm speaking to? ともいえる. この方が丁寧)/(ドアのノックなどに) Who ／is it?/Who's there?

どなべ 土鍋 an earthen pot.

となり 隣 ●[隣の家] the next house (複 houses /-ziz/, 《米》-siz/), the house next door; (隣の家の人) one's next-door neighbor, one's neighbor next door (!単に neighbor だけだと「隣の家の人」だけでなく「近所の人」の意にもなる); (隣の席) the next seat. ● 私たちは隣同士です We are *next-door neighbors*. ● カナダと合衆国は隣同士です Canada and the United States are *neighbors* [are *neighboring* countries]. (! 建物では必ずしも next-door は用いない) ▶お隣へ行って砂糖を借りてきます I'm going [I'll run] *next door* and borrow some sugar. ▶うちの右[左]隣は郵便局です The *next building* on the *right* [*left*] is a post office.

━ **隣の 形** ● 隣の家の女の子 the girl *next door*. ● 隣の町まで車で行く drive to a *neighboring* city. ▶隣の部屋の声が聞こえる I can hear the voices in the *next* room. ● 私の隣の席は空いていた The *next* seat to mine [×Next to my seat] was vacant. ▶すぐ隣の家に泥棒が入った There was a robbery (in the house) right *next door*. ▶隣の人とおしゃべりするのをやめなさい (先生が生徒に) Stop talking to your *neighbor*.

会話 「彼らの店はどこですか」「駅のすぐ隣です」 "Where is their store?" "It's right *next door to* the station."

━ **隣に 副** ▶彼は私の家の隣に住んでいる He lives in the house *next to* mine./He lives *next door to* me [×my house]./He is my *next-door neighbor*.

● **隣の芝生は青い** 《ことわざ》 The grass is always greener on the other side of the fence.

● **隣近所** (隣人たち) the [one's] neighbors; (付近) the [one's] neighborhood (!集合的に「付近の人々」の意であるが, a は不定冠詞は単・複両扱い).

となりあう 隣り合う (⇨隣接する) ● 隣り合って住む live *next door to each other*. ● 隣り合って座る sit *side by side* [*next to each other*]. ● 隣り合う家 *adjoining* houses.

となりあわせ 隣り合わせ ▶私たちは隣り合わせに座った We sat *side by side*. (!(1) 席などで「右[左]隣に座る」は sit on one's right [left] side でよい. (2)「私の席は彼と隣り合わせです」は My seat is *next to* his.)

どなりつける 怒鳴りつける shout [yell] 《*at* him》. (⇨怒鳴る)

どなる 怒鳴る ❶[大声で叫ぶ] shout 《*at*》; (鋭く耳ざわりな声で) bark 《*at*》; [怒号する] roar 《*at*》; [わめく] yell 《*at*》. ● 怒ってどなる *roar* with anger. ● 遅刻して上司にどなられる *be shouted* [*yelled*] *at* by the boss for being late. ▶そうどなるな Don't *shout* [*bark*, *roar, yell*] *at me.* ▶ああいうふうに人の前でどなるのはよくない *Shouting* like that [that way] is not a proper thing to do in a public place. ▶彼らは列車が遅れたといって駅長室にどなり込んだ(＝怒って突入した) They *stormed into* the station manager's [stationmaster's] office to complain about the delay of the train.

となると ❶ [その事実を踏まえると] in that case; if it is so. (**!** 文頭に用いる)
会話 「健は足の骨を折ったそうだ」「となると今シーズンはもう出場できないだろう」"I hear [heard] (that) Ken broke his leg." "*In that case* he won't be able to play this season."
❷ [そうした状況の場合には] ▶あの子が音大へ進むとなると相当お金がかかる *If* she goes to music school, I'll have to pay [it will cost] a lot of money. ▶いざ外出となると彼女はお化粧に時間がかかる *When* it is decided to go out, she spends a lot of time making up her face.

ドニエプル ●ドニエプル川 the Dnieper /dníːpər/.
とにかく anyway. (⇨ともかく)
どにち 土日 Saturday and Sunday; the weekend. (⇨週末)
とにもかくにも 兎にも角にも at any rate; in any case; putting this and that aside. (⇨ともかく)
▶とにもかくにも(＝いろいろな事情はさておき)、会社の存続にはリストラは避けられない *At any rate*, we have to reorganize the structure and cut down the staff, if we want to go on. (**!** この場合の at any rate は english 言えば) (結論を言えば) に近い)
とにゅう 吐乳 ──吐乳する 動 (赤ん坊が) spit up milk.
とねりこ [植物] an ash (tree).
との 殿 (主君) a lord. (**!** 呼びかけは My Lord)
:どの which; [何の] what; [だれ] who. (**!** which は選択の数が限られているがwhat, who は限られていない) (⇨どちら) ▶どの季節が一番好きですか *Which* [×*What*] season do you like best? ▶どのテレビ番組が見たいの *Which* [*What*] TV program do you want to watch? ▶どの男の子がぼくの妹をたたいたの *Which* boy [*Who*] hit my sister?
【どの...も】(＋単数可算名詞); (すべての) all (＋(the [one's]＋複数名詞); (それぞれの) each (＋単数可算名詞); [どんな...も] any; [どの...も...ない] none (*of*＋the [one's]＋単数・複数名詞).

解説 三つ [3 人] 以上の個々に注目しながら全体として例外がないことを強調するのが every. あるまとまりを全体として取り上げるのが all, every の方が語調が強い。二つ [2 人] 以上からなる集団のうちの個々を別々に取り上げるのが each, 「どれをとっても」の意で用いるのが any.

▶どの生徒も個性を持っている *Each* [*Every*] student has [×*have*] their [(やや書)*his*] own personality./*Each* [*Every one*, ×*Every*] of the students has [have] their [(やや書)*his*] own personality./*All* (of) the students (生徒は一般に) *All* students have their own personality. (⇨皆)
▶ほとんどの車もゆっくりと走っていた Almost *every* [×*each*] car was driving slowly. (**!** ×Almost car was... とはいわない) ▶どの本を読んでもよろしい You can read *any* book(s). (**!** book では「1 冊」、books では「何冊でも」の意) ▶彼の本はどの本も読んでいない I haven't read *any* of [I've read *none* of] his books. ▶どの先生も今日は試験をしないでしょう *None* of our teachers are [(やや書) is] going to give us a test today. (**!** (1) 堅い (書)を除いて通例複数扱い。(2) *Every* teacher is nót going...

↘*today.* ともいえるが、下降上昇調で ... ↗*today.* とすると下記の先生は試験をするかどうかあいまいなのが避けられる。(3) ×*Any* of our teachers is *not*... は不可) ▶彼はクラスのどの男の子よりも力が強い He's stronger than *any* other boy [(やや書) *any* boy] in his class. (**!** He's the strongest boy in his class. の方が普通) / *No* (other) boy in his class is as strong as he is [(書・まれ) as he].
–どの -殿 [事務的・公的敬称] (男性に) Mr. ; (女性に) Mrs. [Ms., Miss]. (⇨–様)
どのう 土嚢 a sandbag. ▶川の土手に土のうを積む *sandbag* [put *sandbags* on] the riverbanks.
とのがた 殿方 a gentleman (複 -men /-mən/). ●殿方用手袋 *men's* gloves.
:どのくらい how (＋下数・量・高さなどを表す形容詞・副詞). (**!** 強勢は形容詞・副詞の方に置く)
❶ [数] how many; [量] how much. ▶どのくらい蔵書をお持ちですか *How many* books do you have?/*How large* is your library? ▶この市の人口はどのくらいですか *What* [*How large*, ×*How many*] is the population of this city? ▶彼はあなたよりどのくらい年上ですか *How much* older [×*How older*] is he than you are? ▶給料はどのくらいお望みですか *What* salary do you expect to get?
会話 「あなたの体重はどのくらいですか」「50 キロです」 "*How much* do you weigh?" "I weigh 50 kilos."/"*What* is your weight?" "It's 50 kilograms."
会話 「3 メートルの差をつけて勝ったよ」「どのくらいの差ですって」 "I won by three meters." "By *how much*?"
❷ [距離] hòw fár; [頻度] how often.
会話 「ここから君の学校までどのくらいありますか」「歩いて約 10 分です [約 2 キロです]」 "*How far* [×*distant*] is it from here to your school?" "It's about a ten-minute walk [about two kilometers] from here."
会話 「じゃあどのくらいの頻度で図書館へ行くの」「できるだけ頻繁に」 "Well, *how often* do you go to the library?" "As often as I can." (**!** 「月にどのくらい ...」なら How many times a month ...? という)
❸ [期間, 時間] hòw lóng.
会話 「日本に来てどのくらいになりますか」「かれこれ 10 年です」 "*How long* have you been in Japan?" "Nearly ten years." (**!** (1) 日本にいて尋ねる場合は in Japan よりhere の方が普通。(2) Have you been here long? (もうこちらには長くいらっしゃるのですか)は How long より当たりのやわらかい、期間を尋ねる言い方)
会話 「新潟から上野までどのくらいかかりますか」「上越新幹線を使えばわずか 2 時間です」 "*How long* [*many hours*] does it take (you) to go from Niigata to Ueno?" "It takes only two hours on the Joetsu Shinkansen."
会話 「休暇はどのくらい取れるの」「3 週間だと思うよ」 "*How much* vacation (米) [holiday (英)] time can you take?/*How long* a vacation [a holiday] can you take?" "Three weeks, I hope."
会話 「あとどのくらいしたら劇が始まりますか」「あと 2–3 分よ」 "*How soon* [×*early*] will the play begin?" "In a couple of minutes."
会話 「待っててくれる?」「どのくらいで戻るの」 "Wait for me, won't you?" "*How long* will you be?"
❹ [高さ] hòw táll [high] (**!** tall は人または細長い物について、high は通例幅広く(大きい物に使われる); [大きさ] how big [large] (**!** big は単に形の大きさではなく、主観的に「大きい、重要な」と感じられるときに、large

は客観的に「広さ,長さ,分量」の大きさを表すときに用いられる); [幅] how wide; [年齢] how old. ▶運動場の広さはどのくらいですか *How large* [×*wide*] is the playground?

会話「あなたの身長はどのくらいありますか」「170センチあります」 "*How tall* [×*high*] are you?" "I'm 170 centimeters (tall)." (!! 話 ではしばしば応答文の tall を省略する) "*What* is your height?" "It's 170 centimeters."

会話「今高度はどのくらいですか」「3万8,000フィートです」 "*How high* are we (flying)?" "At (an altitude [a height] of) 38,000 feet."

会話「彼女と住むには狭すぎるって? 君のアパートはどのくらいの広さなの」「ほんの1部屋のアパートです」 "Too small to live with her? *How small* [×*narrow*] is your apartment?" "It's only a one-room apartment." (!! hòw lárge が広いか狭いかに関係なく広さの程度を尋ねる言い方であるのに対して, hów small は狭いとあらかじめ分かっていて, その狭さを尋ねる場合に使う)

❺ [程度] ▶あなたの車はどのくらい損傷を受けていますか *How badly* damaged is your car? ▶彼女はどのくらいピアノが弾けますか[英語が話せますか] *How well* [×*How much*] can she play the piano [speak English]? ▶彼がどのくらい一生懸命勉強したかあなたは知っていますか Do you know *how hard* he studied? ▶その番組はどのくらい(=どれほど)人気があってもすぐ中止すべきだ The program, *however* popular (it is), should be stopped right now.

会話「君が森君と試合をするんだってね」「彼はどのくらいの腕なの」 "I hear you're playing Mori." "*How* good is he?" (!! good は「熟達した」「巧みな」の意)

とのさま 殿様 [封建君主] a (feudal) lord. ●殿様のようにふるまう act like a *lord*; lord it (over).

とのさまがえる 殿様蛙 [動物] a Japanese meadow frog.

とのさまばった 殿様ばった [昆虫] a migratory locust.

どのへん どの辺 ▶その店は渋谷のどの辺にある *What part of* Shibuya is the store located?

会話「背中のどの辺が痛いのですか」「どの辺って言えないんです. ちょこちょこ場所が変わるんです」 "*Where* do you feel pain in your back?" (!! Where in your back? でも通じる) "I can't *spot* [*locate*] it *exactly*. The pain changes its place very often."

どのみち どの道 (⇨どっちみち)

-とは 《副助詞》 ❶ [ある物事を取り立てて] ▶青春とは生命の爆発である Youth is an explosion of life.

❷ [意外なことを表して] ▶彼女が夜1人で外出するとは愚かだった It was foolish of her [She was foolish (enough)] *to* go out alone at night./How foolish she was *to* go out alone at night! ▶はるばる君がやってくるとは It is surprising [a great surprise] *that* you *should* have come all the way. (!! should は当然・意外・遺憾などの話し手の感情を表す (⇨-なんて))

とば 賭場 a gambling den; a gaming house (⑱-houses /-ziz, (米)-siz/); (賭博(⒨)宿) a joint.

どば 駑馬 [のろい馬] a slow horse; [才能のない者]an untalented person.

トパーズ (a) topaz /tóupæz/. (|参考| 11月の誕生石)

とはいうものの とは言うものの but; though (...). (⇨とは言えど)

とはいえ とは言え [しかし] but; [けれども] although ..., though (...). (!! although より口語的. (⇨けれども))

会話「彼自転車を何台も持っているんだよ」「とはいえ彼貸してくれる気があるのかしらね」 "He has plenty of bikes." "Will he be willing to lend them, *though* [×*although*]?" (!! although には副詞の用法はない)

とばく 賭博 gambling. (⇨賭(&)け) ●とばくをする gamble 《*on* horses》. ●野球とばくをする bet *on* baseball games.

● 賭博師 a gambler. 賭博場 a gámbling hòuse; a casino /kəsí:nou/.

とばくち とば口 (入り口) an entrance; (物事の始め) the beginnings; the first stage.

とばし 飛ばし [株式] stock shuffling. (|参考| 決算対策のために含み損を抱えた株式などを一時的に他社に転売すること)

どばし 土橋 a wooden bridge paved with earth.

とばす 飛ばす ❶ [空中へ上げる] (飛行機などを空中へ) fly*; (ロケットなどを打ち上げる) launch; (弾丸・矢などを発射する) shoot*; (吹き飛ばす) blow*...off (⇨吹き飛ばす); (水などをまき散らす) splash. ▶ハトを飛ばす *fly* [解き放す] *let loose* a pigeon. ●人工衛星を飛ばす *launch* [*send up*] an artificial satellite. ●的をめがけて矢を飛ばす *shoot* an arrow *at* the target. ▶ライト兄弟は史上最初に飛行機を飛ばした The Wright brothers first *flew* [were the first to *fly*] an airplane in history. ▶風で帽子を(吹き)飛ばされた My hat *blew off* (in the wind)./I had my hat *blown off* (by the wind). (!! ×I was blown off my hat. とはいわない)/The wind *blew* my hat *off*. ▶私に水を飛ばすな(=はね散らすな) Don't *splash* water *on* me./Don't *splash* me *with* water.

❷ [速く走らせる] (車・馬などを) speed*; (馬を) gallop; [速く走る] (車で) drive* fast; (馬に乗って) gallop. ●馬に乗って野原を飛ばして行く *gallop across* the field. ▶時間がなかったので駅までかなりの速さ[全速力]で車を飛ばした I *drove* to the station *at high* [*full*] *speed* because I was pressed for time.

❸ [途中を抜かして進む] skip (-pp-) (*over* ...). ●数ページを飛ばして読む *skip* (*over*) a few pages. ●雑誌を飛ばして読む *skip through* a magazine. ●コマーシャルを(早送りで)飛ばしてビデオを見る (話) watch a video, *zapping through* the ads in it. ▶この課は飛ばしてもよい This lesson can *be skipped* [(省略される) *be omitted*]. ▶出席をとるとき先生は私の名前を飛ばした The teacher *skipped* my name when he called the roll.

会話「私の発言は飛ばしてください」「それはあなたの自由です」 "May I *pass* it?" "There's [It's] your privilege."

❹ [言葉・情報を発する] ●デマを飛ばす(=広める) *spread* [*circulate*] a false rumor. ●冗談を飛ばす (話) *crack* a joke.

❺ [左遷する] demote ... 《*to*》. (⇨左遷)

どはずれ 度外れ —度外れの 形 extraordinary; unusual; (げしない) excessive. ●度外れに大きな声 an *extraordinarily* big voice. (⇨桁外れ)

どはつ 怒髪 —怒髪天を衝(°)く One's hair bristles [stands on end] with anger. (⇨激怒)

とばっちり ▶私は彼らのけんかのとばっちりを食った(=けんかに巻き込まれた) I *was* [*got*] *involved in* their quarrel.

どばと 土鳩 a (common) pigeon. (!! pigeon は鳩の総称)

とばり 帳 a curtain. ▶夜のとばりが下りる(=夜になる) Night falls.

とはん 登坂 (⇨登坂(⒨))

とび 鳶 ❶ [鳥] a (black) kite. (⇨鳶(⒨)) ❷ [とび職]

a construction worker [laborer]; a scaffolding builder.

とびあがる 飛び上がる, 跳び上がる ❶ 〘はね上がる〙 jump (up); 〘大きく〙 leap* (up); 〘勢いよく〙 spring* (up). ●その知らせに跳び上がって喜ぶ *jump* [*leap*] *for joy at the news*. ●テーブルの上に跳び上がった He *jumped* [*sprang*] *out of the chair*. ❷ 〘空中に〙 fly* [soar] up ⟨*into* the sky⟩.

とびあるく 飛び歩く run* around. (⇨駆け回る)

とびいし 飛び石 ⟨a garden path made by arranging⟩ stepping stones. ●飛び石連休 〘断続的な休日〙 a series of holidays with one or two intervening workdays.

とびいた 飛び板 a springboard. ●飛び板飛び込み springboard diving. ●飛び板飛び込みの選手 a springboard diver.

とびいり 飛び入り 〘自由参加の〙 open. ▶このテニスの試合は飛び入りは自由です(=アマを問わず飛び入り参加できる) This tennis match *is open to* all./This is an *open* tennis match. ▶彼はその競技に飛び入り(=エントリーしないで)参加した He took part in the game *without submitting his entry beforehand* [*as an unofficial entrant*].

とびいろ 鳶色 ⟨茶褐色⟩ dark brown.

とびうお 飛び魚 【魚介】a flying fish. (❗通例単・複同形).

とびうつる 飛び移る ●枝から枝へと飛び移る(鳥が) *fly from* branch *to* branch. ●船から船に飛び移る *jump from* one boat *into* another.

とびおきる 飛び起きる, 跳び起きる 〘ベッドから〙jump [spring*] out of bed; 〘あわてて立ち上がる〙jump to one's feet.

とびおりじさつ 飛び降り自殺 ●橋から飛び降り自殺をする kill oneself by *jumping from* [*off*] a bridge.

とびおりる 飛び降りる jump [leap*] down ⟨*from*⟩. (⇨飛ぶ) ●電車から地面へ飛び降りる a *jump from* [*off*] the train onto the ground. ●2階の窓から飛び降りる *jump out* ⟨*of*⟩ the upstairs window. (❗ *of* を省略するのは〘主に米〙)

とびかう 飛び交う ⟨鳥などが⟩ fly* 〘すいすい〘ひらひら〙と〙flutter, flit (-tt-) about. ●花から花へと飛び交うチョウ butterflies *fluttering* from flower to flower. ▶怒声が飛び交った Angry voices *flew about* 〘あちこちに飛んだ〙 *flew back and forth*.

とびかかる 飛び掛かる jump 〘勢いよく〙spring*, 〘大きく〙leap*〙 at [on]...; 〘急に〙 pounce on [upon]...; 〘獲物などに〙fly* at ...; 〘急に襲いかかる〙turn on ...; 〘身を投げつける〙throw* 〘力強く〙hurl, 〘激しく〙fling*〙 oneself at [on].... ●その犬は彼ののどをめがけて飛びかかった The dog *jumped* [*sprang, leapt*] *at* his throat. ▶少年たちは泥棒に飛びかかった The boys *jumped* [*sprang*] *on* the thief./The boys *threw* [*hurled, flung*] *themselves on* the thief. ▶猫はいすから犬に飛びかかった The cat *pounced on* the dog from the chair. ▶ライオンは調教師に飛びかかった The Lion *turned on* its tamer.

とびきゅう 飛び級 skipping. ●昔は高等学校へは中学から飛び級で入ることができた In the old school system ⟨of Japan⟩, one was able to *skip* the fifth year of the middle school to enter a high school.

とびきり 飛び切り 〘例外的に〙exceptionally; 〘並外れて〙 extraordinarily; 〘断然〙 〘最上級の前に置いて〙 by far, much, the very. ●飛び切り上等のワインの中の飛び切り上等の *the very best* wine; wine *of the very best* [*the highest*] quality. ▶彼は飛び切りの秀才だ He is *exceptionally* [*extraordinarily*] bright./He is *by far* [*much*] *the brightest*.

とびぐち 鳶口 a fire hook.

とびこえる 飛び越える, 跳び越える jump ⟨over ...⟩. (⇨飛び越す)

とびこす 飛び越す, 跳び越す ●垣根(の上)を跳び越す *jump* [*leap*] ⟨*over*⟩ a fence; 〘少しも触れずに〙 *clear* a fence. ●水たまりを跳び越す *jump across* [*over*] a puddle. (❗*across* は「横切って」, *over* は「上を跳び越えて渡ること」) ▶跳び越すには小川の幅が広すぎた The stream was too broad to *jump over*.

とびこみ 飛び込み 〘水泳の〙a dive; diving. ●優雅な飛び込みを披露する show a graceful *dive*. ●飛び込み自殺をする kill oneself by *jumping* in front of a train. ▶彼女は飛び込みが上手だ She is good at *diving*./She is a good *diver*. ●飛び込み競技 a díving èvent. ●飛び込み台(板) a díving bòard, ⟨高飛び込みの⟩ a díving plàtform.

とびこむ 飛び込む ❶ 〘水の中へ〙 dive* [jump, plunge] ⟨*into, in*⟩ ●dive は通例「頭から飛び込む」の意; 〘部屋などの中へ〙 burst [rush] ⟨*into*⟩; 〘鳥・石などが飛んで入る〙 fly* ⟨*into, in*⟩. ●彼女を救おうとその川に飛び込む dive [jump, plunge] *into* the river to save her. ●頭から水に飛び込む *dive into* the water head first. (❗足から飛び込む は *jump* [*plunge*] *into* the water feet first) ▶ここは浅すぎて飛び込めない This water is too shallow to *dive* [or *plunge*] *into*. ▶その少年は部屋に飛び込んできた The boy *burst* [*rushed, dashed*] *into* the room.

❷ 〘飛び込み自殺する〙 ●電車[川]に飛び込む *throw oneself in front of* a train [*into* a river].

とびさる 飛び去る fly* away.

とびしょく 鳶職 a construction worker [laborer]; a scaffolding builder.

とびだし 飛び出し (⇨飛び出す) ●飛び出しナイフ 〘米〙 a switchblade; 〘英〙 a flick knife.

とびだす 飛び出す 〘飛んで出る〙 jump 〘大きく〙leap*, 〘勢いよく〙spring*〙 out; 〘走り出る〙 run* 〘大急ぎで〙 rush〙 out; 〘破って出る〙 break* out. ●ベッドから飛び出す *jump* [*leap*] *out of* bed. ●家を飛び出す(=家出する) *run away from* home. ▶彼は〘教室から〙運動場へ飛び出した He *ran* [*rushed*] *out of* his classroom〙 *into* the schoolground. ▶ウサギが茂みから飛び出すのを見た I saw a rabbit *jump* [*spring*] *out of* the bushes.

とびたつ 飛び立つ 〘鳥が〙 〘飛び去る〙 fly* away; 〘飛び上がる〙 fly up; 〘飛行機が〙 take* off; 〘ロケットなどが〙 lift off. (⇨離陸) ▶ツバメが巣から飛び立った The swallows *have flown away from* their nest.

とびち 飛び地 〘囲っている国から見ての〙an enclave; 〘囲われている国から見ての〙 an exclave; 〘広義に, 行政区分上の〙 a detached piece of land.

とびちる 飛び散る ⟨火花・破片などが⟩ fly*; ⟨水などが⟩ splash, spatter ⟨*on, over*⟩. ●血の飛び散った衣類 blood-*spattered* clothes. ▶飛行機が着陸するとき車輪から火花が飛び散った A lot of sparks *flew up* from the wheels when the plane landed. ▶水が床に飛び散った The water *splashed on* [*onto*, 〘一面に〙*over*] the floor.

とびつく 飛び付く jump [spring*] at ...; 〘獲物などに急に襲いかかる〙 pounce /páuns/ on [upon].... ●鉄棒に飛びつく *jump* [*spring*] (*up*) *at* a horizontal bar. (❗上の方が *jump* より身軽さと勢いのよさを含意する) ●申し出〘チャンス〙に飛びつく *jump at* an offer [a chance] ⟨*to do*⟩.

トピック 【話題】 a topic. ●今週のトピックス the

week's *topics*.
とびでる 飛び出る (⇨飛び出す) ● 目玉が飛び出るような値段 (⇨目玉)
とびどうぐ 飛び道具 [遠方から敵を撃つ道具] a firearm; a missile. ●〖弓・矢・鉄砲など〗
とびとび 飛び飛び (あちこちに) here and there; (間をあけて) at intervals. ●雑誌を飛び飛びに読む read a magazine *here and there* [in places, (無作為に) *at random*]; *skip through* a magazine.
とびにゅうがく 飛び入学 early college entrance; (制度) an acceleration system [「飛び級制度」は a skípping sýstem という] ▶彼は千葉大学に飛び入学した学生です He is one of the students who skipped the third year of high school and went on to Chiba University.
とびぬけて 飛び抜けて ▶彼はクラスで飛び抜けて背が高い He is *by far* [*much*, *far and away*] the tallest boy in his class. (❗いずれも最上級を強める副詞語句) ▶彼は飛び抜けて音楽が上手だ He is *outstandingly* good at music./He *stands out from* [《書》*far excels*] the others in music.
とびのく 飛び退く (後ろに) jump [leap*] back;(横に) jump [leap] aside.
とびのる 飛び乗る (⇨又る❶) ●馬[バス]に飛び乗る *jump on* [*onto*] a horse [a bus]. ●タクシーに飛び乗る *jump into* a taxi.
とびばこ 跳び箱 (跳馬) a (vaulting) horse. ●跳び箱を跳ぶ vault a *horse*.
とびはなれる 飛び離れる ❶【距離が】▶本土から飛び離れている孤島 an isolated island *far (away)* [*many miles distant*] from the mainland.
❷【能力が】▶彼女の詩は飛び離れてうまい Her poems are *by far the best*./Her poems are *much* [*far*] *better than* those of the rest.
❸【飛びのく】(⇨飛び退く)
とびはねる 跳び跳ねる jump [bounce, spring*] up and down (*for joy*); (水などが) splash. ●【跳ねる】▶水があたりに跳びはねた Water *splashed* around [*about*].
とびひ 飛び火 ❶【飛び散る火の粉】flying sparks; (飛び移る炎) leaping flames. ▶花火の飛び火で出火した *Flying sparks* from (the) fireworks started the fire. ▶火事が川向こうに飛び火した The flames [fire] *leaped across* the river. ▶汚職事件は数人の閣僚にも飛び火した[=巻き込んだ] The scandal *involved* some of the cabinet ministers.
❷【皮膚病の】【医学】impetigo /impətáigou/.
とびまわる 飛び回る, 跳び回る ❶【空中を】 fly* around [《主に英》about]; (羽ばたいて) flutter around [《主に英》about].
❷【跳ね回る】jump around. (⇨跳ね回る)
❸【奔走する】run* about [《主に英》about]. (⇨駆け回る❷)
どひょう 土俵 the (sumo wrestling) ring.
●土俵際で at [right on] the edge of the ring; (時間ぎりぎりに) at the last moment.
●土俵に上がる go on the ring; (話し合いの共通の場につく) sit at the table for a talk; 《議題が主語》be put on the table.
●土俵を割る (相撲で) be pushed out of the ring; (人に屈する) give in.
●土俵入り a ring-entering ceremony of sumo wrestlers.
とびら 扉 a door (⇨戸); 〖門〗 a gate; 〖本の〗 a title page; the front page.
どびん 土瓶 an earthenware teapot.
●土瓶敷き a teapot mat. ●土瓶蒸し *dobinmushi*; (説明的に) steamed *matsutake* mushrooms,

fish and vegetables in clear broth served in an earthenware teapot.
とふ 塗布 ── 塗布する 動 apply 《ointment *to* the wound》; spread 《ointment *on* the wound》.
●塗布剤 an application; (軟膏の類) (an) ointment; (a) salve; (液状の薬) (a) liniment.
:とぶ 飛ぶ, 跳ぶ ❶【空中を飛ぶ】(鳥・飛行機などが) fly*, (滑るように) glide, (表面をすれすれに) skim (-mm-), (高く舞い上がる) 《主に書》soar; (鳥・チョウなどがすいすいと) flit (-tt-); (羽をばたつかせて) flutter; (吹き飛ぶ) blow* off.
①【...を飛ぶ】●空を[空中をすうっと, 波間を]飛んでいるカモメ seagulls *flying in* the sky [*gliding through* the air; *skimming* the waves]. ▶たくさんの風船が空中を飛んでいた There *were* lots of balloons [Lots of balloons *were*] *flying through* the air. (❗前の方は風船の存在に, 後の方は飛んでいる場所に重点がある言い方. ×There were flying lots of balloons .... の語順は不可) ▶彼は太平洋を飛行機で飛んだ He *flew* (横断して) *across*, (上空を) *over*) the Pacific. (❗(1) He は乗客, 乗員のいずれでもよい. (2) *fly (by* [*with*]) Japan Airlines は「JAL(日本航空)で旅行する」の意)
②【...へ[で]飛ぶ】 ▶私たちの飛行機はモスクワへ直通で飛んだ Our plane *flew* direct *to* Moscow. ▶チョウがひらひらと花から花へ飛んでいる A butterfly *is* [There is a butterfly] *fluttering* [*flitting*] from flower to flower. ▶書類は風で飛んだ The papers *blew off* (in the wind)./The wind blew the papers *off*.
❷【飛ぶように行く】(飛ぶように走る) fly*; (急いで行く) hurry, hasten (❗hurry より堅い語), (大急ぎで) rush. ▶家で飛んで帰る *fly* [*hurry*] home. ▶彼を助けに飛んで行く *hurry* to help him. ▶現場に飛んで行く *rush* [*dash*, *hurry*] *to* the scene. ▶彼はにこにこして私のところへ飛んで来た He *flew at* me with a smile. (❗at は「...を目がけて」の意) ▶休暇は飛ぶように過ぎる The vacation *flies by*. ▶犯人は国外へ飛んだ[=逃亡した] The criminal *fled* [*ran away from*] the country. ▶新製品は飛ぶように[=ものすごく]売れている The new product is selling [going] *like hot cakes*.
❸【跳ねる】jump; spring*; hop (-pp-); (大きく跳んで移動する) leap* (❗jump より堅い語); (足を交互にけりながら) skip (-pp-). (⇨跳ねる)

WORD CHOICE 跳ぶ
hop 人・動物・昆虫などが, 足で地面を蹴って跳躍すること. ▶溝を跳び越える *hop* across the gap.
spring 人・物などが, ばねのように, すばやく勢いよく跳ねること. やや改まった文脈で用いることが多い. ▶ライオンはその男に飛びかかった The lion *sprang* at the man.
jump 人などが, 地面から離れ, 空中のある方向に向かって勢いよく跳ぶこと. ▶どれだけ高く跳べますか How high can you *jump*?

頻度チャート

hop
spring
jump

20 40 60 80 100 (%)

●上下に跳ぶ *jump* [×leap] up and down. ●2メートル跳ぶ (垂直・水平方向に) *jump* two meters; (走り高跳びで) *clear* the bar at two meters. ●溝を跳んで渡る *jump* [*leap*, *hop*] *across* a ditch. (⇨飛び

越す) ▶縄跳びで何回跳べますか How many times can you *jump* [*skip*] rope?
❹〖途中が抜ける〗●話題があちこち飛ぶ *jump* [*skip*] from one topic to another. ▶この本は 8 ページ飛んでいる(=抜けている)There are eight pages [Eight pages *are*] *missing* from this book.
● 飛んで火に入る夏の虫 《ことわざ》(愚か者は不幸をさがし求める)A fool hunts for misfortune.

どぶ 溝 a (muddy) ditch; (排水溝) a drain, (道路沿いの) a gutter. ● どぶをさらう clear (out) a *ditch*. ▶それは金をどぶへ捨てるようなものだ That was like (a case of) throwing [pouring] money down the *drain*.
● どぶ板 a ditch cover. ● どぶ川 a narrow river with dirty, stagnant ditchwater.

どぶくろ 戸袋 a shutter case [box].

どぶねずみ 溝鼠〖動物〗a brown [water] rat.

どぶろく unrefined *sake*.

どぶん (⇨どぼん) ▶橋の上から川へどぶんと飛び込む jump into the river *with a splash* from the bridge.

とべい 渡米 図 ● 渡米中である be on a visit to the United States [America].
── 渡米する 動 go to [visit] the United States [America]; (出発する) leave for the United States [America].

どべい 土塀 a mud [《やや書》an earthen] wall.

とほ 徒歩 ● 徒歩で on foot. ● 徒歩旅行に出かける go on a *walking* tour; go hiking [on a hike]. ▶私は毎日徒歩通学する I *walk* to school [*go to school on foot*] every day. (⚠前の方が普通)

とほう 途方 ● 途方に暮れる ▶彼はどうすべきか途方に暮れた He *didn't know* what he should do. (⚠次例より口語的)/He *was at a loss* (as to) what to do. (⚠as to は省略する方が普通)/(いろいろ試みたあげくに)《話》He *was at his wits' [wit's, wits] end* about what to do.
● 途方もない 〖並外れた〗extraordinary (↔ordinary);〖ばかばかしい〗(理屈に合わず) absurd; (こっけいで) ridiculous, ludicrous;〖値段・要求などが法外な〗unreasonable;〖とてもありえない〗impossible;〖信じられない〗incredible. ▶途方もない天才 a person of *extraordinary* [《またみる》*rare*] genius. ● 途方もないことを言う say *absurd* [*ridiculous*] things. ● 途方もない値段をふっかける charge an *unreasonable* [an *extraordinary*] price. ● 途方もない旅行(奴)an *impossible* journey [*fellow*]. ▶彼の足は途方もなく大きい He has *extraordinarily* [*incredibly*] big feet./His feet are *extraordinarily* [*incredibly*] big.
会話「彼女の衣装はかなり風変わりだったね」「途方もなかったわよ」"Her costume was rather odd, wasn't it?" "It was *incredible* [*ludicrous*]."

どぼく 土木 (工事) public [engineering] works.
● 土木技師 a civil engineer. ● 土木工学 civil engineering.

とぼける 〖知らぬふりをする〗pretend ignorance [not to know];《話》play dumb; (無実のふりをする) play innocent (⇨しらをきる);〖おどける〗play the fool.
● とぼけた表情 =無表情な顔つき》(have) a blank look;《make》a poker face.

***とぼしい** 乏しい 〖数・量・貯えなどが不十分な〗poor (↔rich), (in);〖供給が十分でない〗scarce (↔plentiful);〖必要な数・量などがまったく不十分な〗scanty;〖貧弱な〗《やや書》meager;〖大事なものが欠けている〗deficient (*in*);〖不足している〗short (*of*). ● 乏しい収穫 a *poor* [a *scanty*] harvest. ● 乏しい収入 a *meager* [a *scanty*] income. ▶日本は天然資源に乏しい Japan is *poor* in natural resources. ▶戦時中バターは乏しかった Butter was *scarce* [*scanty*] in wartime. ▶彼は知力が乏しい He doesn't have *enough* intellect [intelligence]. (⚠しばしば後に to 不定詞が続くことを暗示)/《やや書》He is *deficient in* [*lacks*] intellect. (⚠通例 run short (of) が具体的物質に用いるのに対して(⇨〖次例〗), lack は抽象的事柄に用いる) ▶彼は資金が乏しくなってきた He *is running short of* funds./His funds *are running short*. ▶彼は英語を教えた経験が乏しい He has *very little* [《書》has *little*] experience in teaching English.

とぼしさ 乏しさ ● 資源の乏しさ the *scarcity* of resources.

とぼとぼ ● とぼとぼ歩く (のろのろと) plod; (つらそうに) trudge. ▶おばあさんが 1 人雨後のぬかるんだ道をとぼとぼ歩いている An older [an old] woman *is plodding* along the muddy road after the rain. ▶子供たちはみな山道をとぼとぼ下りて行った All the children *trudged* down the mountain path.

とほほ ▶仕事が忙しく、土曜は休日出勤になりそうです。とほほ… I'm so busy with my work that I'll have to go to work even on Saturday. *Woe is me!*

ドボルザーク 〖チェコの作曲家〗Dvořák /dəvɔ́ːrʒɑːk/ (Antonín ～).

トポロジー 〖位相幾何学〗〖数学〗topology.

どぼん with a splash [a plop]. ▶前の方は比較的小さなものがあまりしぶきを上げずに液体の中に入る〖落ちる〗,後の方は音も軽いので、「どぼん」では with a *loud* plop と音の大きさを暗示する場合もある) (⇨どぶん) ▶鯉は勢いよくはねて、池の中へどぶんと落ちた The carp sprang into the pond *with a splash* [*a loud plop*]. (⚠… sprang and splashed [plopped] back into the pond のように動詞に使うこともできる)

どま 土間 an earth [《米》a dirt] floor.

トマト 〖植物〗a tomato /təméɪtoʊ/ (《復》～es). ● ミニトマト a cherry tomato. ● トマトケチャップ tomato ketchup. ● トマトジュース tomato juice. ● トマトスープ tomato soup. ● トマトソース tomato sauce. ● トマトピューレ tomato purée.

とまどい 戸惑い (困惑) (a) confusion; (まごつき) embarrassment. ● とまどいを感じる be confused; be embarrassed. ● とまどいを見せる〖隠す〗show [hide,《やや書》conceal] one's *confusion*.

とまどう 戸惑う (当惑する) be at a loss; (困惑する) be puzzled (*by*); (まごつく) be confused (*by*). ▶私はどうしたものかとまどってしまった I *was at a loss* (分からなかった) I *didn't know*, I had no idea] what to do. ▶彼は彼女の態度にとまどった He *was puzzled by* her attitude.

トマホーク 〖米国の巡航ミサイル〗〖軍事〗a Tomahawk. ●トマホーク〖北米インディアンの手斧〗

とまや 苫屋 a grass-thatched hut (*on the beach*).

とまり 泊まり 〖宿泊〗(a) lodging (⇨宿泊);〖滞在〗a stay;〖宿直〗night duty. ▶一晩泊まりで日光へ行く go on [make] an overnight trip to Nikko. ▶今晩は泊まり(=宿直)です I'm *on duty* tonight. ▶彼は泊まりがけで遊びに来た He came to *stay overnight with* us.
● 泊まり客 a guest, a visitor.

−どまり 止まり ●この電車は大阪止まりだ This train *goes only as far as* [*terminates at*] Osaka. ▶彼は課長止まりだろう He will *not be promoted higher than* a section manager. ▶セーターなら高くてもせいぜい 5 万円止まりだろう I don't think a sweater'll [I think a sweater *won't*] *cost more than* fifty thousand yen at the highest. (⚠後の方はあま

とまりぎ 止まり木 (鳥の) a perch. ▶鳥が止まり木にとまっていた A bird sat [was] on the *perch*.

とまりこむ 泊まり込む stay (overnight) 《*at*》. ●月内に仕事を完成させるため会社に何日も泊まり込む *stay at* the office for days to finish the work by the end of the month. ▶彼らはホテルに一晩泊まり込んで戦略会議を続けることにした They chose to *stay overnight at* the hotel and continue the discussion about their strategy.

＊とまる 止まる, 留まる ❶【停止する】(動いているものが) stop (-pp-), come* to a stop; (車などが) pull up; (駐車している) be parked. ●急に[すうっと; 完全に]止まる *stop* suddenly [smoothly; completely]; *come to a sudden* [*a smooth*; *a complete*] *stop*. ▶信号で車が止まった A car *stopped* [*pulled up*, *drew up*] at the traffic light(s). ▶この列車は各駅に止まります[盛岡まで止まりません] This train *stops* at all stations [goes nonstop to Morioka]. ▶次は明石に止まります [列車内で] We will soon be *making a* brief *stop* at Akashi. ▶バスが停留所に止まっている The bus *is* (*standing*) [×*stopping*] at the bus stop. (**!** *be stopping* は「止まりかけている」の意) ▶工場の生産が止まった[止まっていた] Production at the factory *was brought to* [*was at*] *a standstill*. ▶噴水は今日は止まっていた The fountain *did not play* today.
❷【やむ】(続いていたものが) stop (-pp-). ▶腕の痛みが止まった The pain in my arm *has stopped* [(なくなった) *has gone*]. ▶心臓が止まるほどびっくりした I was so scared (that) my heart almost *stopped* beating. ▶彼は笑いが止まらなかった He couldn't *stop* laughing.
❸【中断する】 stop (-pp-); (一時的に) be suspended. ▶水道が止まった The water supply *has stopped* [(止められた) *has been cut off*]. ▶大雪のためすべての交通が止まった All the traffic *was suspended* because of the heavy snow. / The heavy snow *stopped* [*blocked*, (まひさせた) *paralyzed*] all the traffic.
❹【鳥などが】(止まり木に) perch 《*on*》, sit* 《*on*》; (降りて留まる) alight, settle 《*on*》. ●スズメは枝に留まった[留まっていた] The sparrow *perched* [*sat, was sitting*] *on* the branch. ▶ハエが天井に留まっている There is a fly *on* [×*in*] the ceiling. (**!** *on* は表面の接触を表す)
❺【その他の表現】▶彼の作文は先生の目に留まった His composition *attracted* his teacher's interest. (⇨目)

＊とまる 泊まる stay; (主に英) put* up; (話) stop (-pp-); (書) lodge.

> 使い分け **stay** ある場所に宿泊することを表す最も一般的な語.
> **put up** stay とほぼ同義だが, 特別な客としてホテルなどに宿泊することを表すこともある.
> **stop** 特に短期間宿泊する場合に用いる.
> **lodge** 部屋代を払って短期間または一定期間宿泊すること.

●ホテルに泊まる *stay at* [*in*] a hotel, (記帳して泊まる) check into a hotel. ●友達の家に泊まる *stay with* a friend; *stay at* a friend's (house). ●一晩泊まる *stop* for the night (**!** for は「…を過ごすのに」の意); *stay* overnight; (外泊する) sleep over 《*at*》. ●日曜まで[日曜1日]泊まる *stay over* till Sunday [*over* Sunday]. (⇨〜まで) ▶どこに泊まるのですか Where are you going to *stay* [(話) *stay at*]? (**!** What [Which, ×Where] hotel are you going to *stay at* [*in*]? では(どこのホテルに泊まるのですか)では at, in になる) ●昨夜は終電車に間に合わなかったので, 友人の家に泊まった Last night I was not in time for the last [×*final*] train, so I *slept over at* my friend's home. ●そのホテルには 500 人泊まれる Five hundred people can *stay at* the hotel. / (収容できる) The hotel *has accommodation*(*s*) *for* [《米》can *accommodate*] 500 people. (**!** s をつけるのは《米》)

どまんじゅう 土饅頭 『土をまるく盛り上げた墓』a grave mound; 『考古学』a barrow.

どまんなか ど真ん中 ●東京のど真ん中に住む live *in the middle* [*center*, *heart*] of Tokyo. ●的(t)のど真ん中に当たる hit the bull's-eye [the *center* of a target]. (**!** いずれの場合も強い right で強調する必要はない) ●ど真ん中へ速球を投げる pitch a fastball down the *middle* [*pipe*].

とみ 富 『財産』wealth; (a) fortune; (書) riches (**!** 複数扱い) (⇨財産); 『資源』resources. ●海の富と資源 resources of the sea. ●富を作る make a [one's] *fortune*. ●巨万の富を築く build [heap] up an enormous [a vast] *fortune*. ●彼の富は意欲と勤勉の結果だった His *wealth* was a product of ambition and hard work.

とみくじ 富くじ a lottery. (⇨宝くじ)

とみに (にわかに) suddenly; (顕著に) remarkably. ▶彼女は近ごろとみに美しくなった She has *suddenly* become beautiful recently.

ドミニカ『ドミニカ国』(dàmini:ka/; (公式名) the Commonwealth of Dominica (首都 Roseau); 『ドミニカ共和国』the Dominican Republic. (首都 Santo Domingo) ●ドミニカ人 a Dominican. ●ドミニカ(人)の Dominican.

ドミノ (ゲーム) dominoes (**!** 単数扱い); a domino. ●ドミノ移植 『医学』a domino transplant. ●ドミノ現象 a domino phenomenon. ●ドミノ効果 a domino effect. ●ドミノ倒し a domino toppling. ●ドミノ理論 the domino theory.

とみん 都民 a citizen of Tokyo; a Tokyoite /tóukiouàit/. (**!** 主に新聞用語) (⇨市民)

とむ 富む ❶【財産が多い】be rich; be wealthy. (⇨金持ち, 裕福)
❷【豊富である】(場所が) be rich 《*in*》; (…でいっぱいである) be full 《*of*》 (**!** abundant より口語的); be abundant 《*in*》. ●経験に富む人 an experienced person. ●示唆に富む意見 a suggestive comment; a comment *full of* suggestions. ▶この国は天然資源に富む This country *is rich in* natural resources. / This country has a lot of natural resources. (**!** This country については (⇨国)) ▶この湖は魚に富む This lake *is full of* fish. / (書) This lake *abounds in* [*with*] fish. / Fish *are abundant* 《*in*》 Fish *abound*] in this lake.

トムソーヤのぼうけん『トムソーヤの冒険』 The Adventures of Tom Sawyer. (参考) マーク・トウェーンの小説)

とむらい 弔い a funeral. ●弔いの鐘 a *funeral* bell. ●弔い合戦 (fight) an avenging battle.

＊とむらう 弔う 『死者を悼む』grieve 《*for*》, (書) mourn 《*for*》; 『冥福(ホシン)を祈る』pray 《*for*》. ●死者を弔う grieve [pray] for dead people [(やや書) the dead].

ドメイン 『コンピュータ』a domain.

とめおき 留め置き ●留め置きを食う(＝拘束される) be kept [held] in custody. ●原級留め置きとなる be kept in the same grade. ▶郵便局留め置きに To be left till called for. (**!** 指定の文句)
●留め置き郵便 (局留め郵便)《米》general deliv-

ery, 《英》poste restante.
とめおく 留め置く ●郵便局に手紙を留め置く hold his mail at the post office. ●警察署に留め置く keep him in custody [detain].
とめがね 留め金 (かばん・ネックレスなどの) a clasp; (ドアなどの) a catch.
とめぐ 留め具 (⇨留め金)
ドメスティックバイオレンス 〚夫・恋人などから受ける暴力〛 domestic violence.
とめそで 留袖 a *tomesode*; (説明的に) a women's black *kimono* with family crests at the top and a beautiful design at the bottom worn ceremonially at happy occasions.
とめだて 留め立て ▶いらぬ留め立てをするな(=引き止めるな) Don't try to stop me.
とめどなく 止めどなく (際限なく) endlessly; (ひっきりなしに) incessantly. ▶止めどなくしゃべる talk *endlessly* [*incessantly*]. ▶止めどなく涙が出た(=流れ落ちた) Tears streamed down my face *incessantly*.
:**とめる** 止める, 留める ❶ 〖停止させる〗(動いているものを) stop (-pp-); (駐車させる) park. ▶彼は信号で車を止めた He *stopped* his car [*pulled up* (his car)] at the traffic light(s). ▶警官はその車をスピード違反で止めた The police officer *stopped* the car for speeding. ▶車をどこに止める(=駐車する)ことができますか Where can I *park* the car? (▲一時停止する場合は stop も可) ▶彼はブレーキをかけて車を止めた He braked his car *to a stop*. ▶彼はタクシーを呼び止め，それに乗って行った He *hailed* a taxi [《主に米》a cab] and left. (▲hail は「大声で呼ぶ」ことで，それだけではタクシーが止まったかどうか分からない)
❷ 〖出なくする〗 stop (-pp-); 〖こらえる〗(あくびなどを) (やや書) suppress; (涙などを) hold*... back; (息を) hold; 〖除く〗(痛みなどを) relieve, stop. ●ひどい出血を止める *stop* heavy bleeding. ●あくびを止める(=かみ殺す) *stifle* [*suppress*] a yawn. ●息を止める (水中などで) *hold* [*stop*] one's breath. (❗前の方は驚きなどで「息を殺す[のむ]」の意である場合もある) ●痛みを止める *relieve* [*stop*, *kill*] the pain. ●せきを止める *relieve* [*suppress*] a cough. ●大きく息を吸って，そして止めて Please take a deep breath and *hold* it.
❸ 〖消す〗(テレビなどを) switch [turn] ... off; (水・ガスなどを) turn ... off; (エンジンなどを) stop (-pp-). ●ラジオを止める *switch* [*turn*] *off* the radio. ●ガスを止める *turn* [*shut*] *off* the gas. ●後の方は元栓などに用いるが，(料金未納で) *cut off* [*stop*] the gas. ●エンジンを止める *stop* [*cut*] the engine. ●ベルを止める *silence* the bell. ●彼は寝ている間に目覚まし時計を止める癖があって，しょっちゅう仕事に遅れていた He was late for work all the time because he used to *turn* the alarm clock *off* in his sleep.
❹ 〖中止・断念させる〗 stop (-pp-); (説得して) (やや書) dissuade 〈him *from* doing〉; 〖禁止する〗(公的に) 〈書〉 prohibit; (私的に) (やや書) forbid*. ●私は彼らのけんかを止めた I *stopped* [*put a stop to*] their quarrel. ●私は彼が映画に行くのを(引き)止めた I *stopped* him *from* going to the movies. (❗I stopped him going .... とするのは《英話》/(説得して) I *dissuaded* him *from* going to the movies. (❗I *persuaded* him *not* to go to the movies. という方が口語的) ●医者は彼の酒を止めた The doctor *forbade* him *to* drink [*forbade* him *drinking*, *forbade* his *drinking*]./(やめるよう助言した) The doctor *advised* [(命じた) *ordered*] him *to* give up drinking. (❗(1) The doctor *advised* (him) [*ordered*, ×*ordered* him] *that* he (《主に英》should) give up .... のように that 節も用いるが，to 不定詞を用いる方が口語的. (2) 強制的には The doctor *made* him *to* give up ....) ▶このテニスコートの使用は止められている The use of this tennis court *is prohibited*./We *are prohibited from* using this tennis court./(許されていない) We *are not allowed* [*permitted*] *to* use this tennis court.
❺ 〖抑える〗 stop (-pp-); 〖防ぐ〗 prevent. ●経済成長を止める 〚《軍》*arrest*〛 economic growth. ●破裂したパイプの水もれを止める *stop* [*check*] the flow of water from the burst pipe. ●さびを止める *prevent* rust; *keep ... from* rusting.
❻ 〖固定する〗 fasten; (びょうで) tack; (ピンで) pin (-nn-) ... (up); (くぎで) nail; (テープで) tape; (ボタンで) button ... (up). ●ピン[びょう]で絵を壁に留める *fasten* a picture *to* the wall *with* pins [tacks]; *pin* [*tack*] a picture *to* [*on*] the wall. ▶彼女は髪をヘアバンドで留めている She *holds* her hair in place with a hair band.
❼ 〖注意する〗 ●気にも留めない pay no attention 〈*to*〉. ●新聞の小さなコラムに目を留める(=気づく) *notice* [(注視する) *fix* one's *eyes on*] a small newspaper column. ●それを心に留めておきましょう I'll *keep* [*bear*] it *in mind*.
❽ 〖野球〗 ●(野手が)痛烈なゴロを止める *block* [*stop*] a hard-hit grounder. ●スイングを途中で止める *check* one's *swing*. ●止めたバットに当たったゴロ a checked-swing grounder.

__とめる__ 泊める (宿泊させる) put... up; (短期間有料で) lodge (⇨泊まる[類語]); 〖収容する〗 accommodate. ●一晩彼女を *put* (him) *up* for the night; *give* (him) *a* night's *lodging*; *lodge* (him) *overnight*. ▶その民宿は週末我々を泊めてくれた The tourist home *put us up* for [*let us stay* (for)] the weekend.

とも 友 a friend. (⇨友達, 仲間)
とも 供 (付添人) an attendant. (⇨御供)
とも 艫 (船尾) a stern (↔a bow /báu/).

*__とも__ (副助詞) ❶ 〖両方とも〗 both (❗主語の同格として用いる場合は通例 be動詞・(最初の)助動詞の後，一般動詞の前に置く(⇨[第1文例])); (A, B とも) both A and B; (A, B とも...ない) neither A nor B. ▶その包みは二つとも私のです *Both* (*of*) *the* packages are mine. (❗「包み」であることが明らかな文脈では *Both* are mine. といえる)/The packages are *both* mine./The packages *both* belong to me. ▶男女がテニスに優勝した *Both* men *and* women won the tennis championship. ▶彼には娘が 2 人いて，2 人とも 10 代初めです He has two daughters, *both* in their early teens. ▶彼も私も両方ともその事故に責任はない *Neither* he nor I am [(話) are] responsible for the accident./He is *not* responsible for the accident, *nor* am I. ▶店は 5 軒とも休んだった *All* the five stores were closed./*None* of the five stores were open.
会話 「和男が私の髪を引っ張ったの」「まあ 2 人ともおよしなさい」 "Kazuo's been pulling my hair." "Now, stop it, you two."
❷ 〖...を含めて〗 including ..., inclusive of .... (⇨込み) ▶これは税金とも値段ですか Is this the price *including* [*inclusive of*] taxes? ▶私ともで(=を入れて) 10 人がその行事に参加した Ten people, *including* me, took part in the event.

――とも (接続助詞) ❶ 〖たとえ...だとしても〗 even if [though]...; (どんなに...であろうとも) no matter (*wh-* 節). (❗次の言い方より口語的に however [whatever, whoever, wherever, etc.]) (⇨ても) ▶天候がたとえ荒れていようとも私は行きます I will go, *even if* the weather is rough. ▶どんなことが

ろうとも動いてはいけません No matter what [Whatever] happens, you must not move.
❷【断言】(もちろん) of course; (結構です) certainly, surely, 《話》 sure. ▶もちろん行きますとも Of course, I ╲will go. (❗意志を強調する. ✕I'll go. のように短縮形は用いない)

会話「電話を借りてもいいですか」「ええ、いいですとも」"May I use your telephone?" "Yes, of course./Certainly./Sure(ly)." (❗Yes, you can. とも答えてよい)

会話「ごいっしょしてもかまいませんか」「いいですとも」"Do you mind if I join you?" "Not at all./Certainly not." (❗Yes では not で受けることが正しい. ただし《話》では文意を汲んで Yes, certainly./Sure(ly). などと答えることもよくある)

会話「山田正和を知っていますか」「知ってますとも. 彼は義理の兄ですもの」"Do you know Masakazu Yamada?" "╲Oh yes./╲Indeed I dó. He's my brother-in-law."

会話「長くはかからなかったでしょ」「かかりましたとも」"It didn't take you long." "Actually, it ╲did, you know." (❗Actually は「予想に反して実は」の意)

❸【およその限界】(遅くとも) at the latest; (少なくとも) at least. ▶遅くとも10時までには帰ります I'll be back by [✕until] ten (o'clock) at the latest.
▶少なくとも 1,000 円はかかるだろう It'll cost at least [not less than] 1,000 yen.

━ども《接続助詞》(けれども) though …; but. ▶彼は大男にlike気が小さい Though he is a big man [《書》As big a man as he is], he is timid. ▶行けども行けども雪野原だ You go on and on, but you cannot see anything [there is nothing] but snow.

ともあれ anyway. (⇨ともかく ❶❷)
━ともあろうものが━ともあろう者が【人もあろうに】of all people. ▶総理大臣ともあろう者が汚職事件に関係していたとは We can't possibly [《話》just can't] believe that the prime minister, of all people, was involved in the corruption case./(他でもない総理大臣が) How surprising it was that no less a person than the prime minister should have been involved in the corruption case!

ともえ 巴 a tomoe; (説明的に) a circular design of swirling water used as a family crest. ▶三つ巴 (⇨三つ巴)
• 巴戦 a three-way playoff. • 巴投げ【柔道】tomoe-nage; a circle throw.

*ともかく ❶【いずれにしても】anyway, anyhow (❗いずれも口語的に); at ány ràte (❗at ány ráte では「どんな割合でも」の意. この3語はしばしば文頭で「それはさておくとして」という気持ちで本題を切り出すのに用いられる); (どんな事情にせよ) in ány càse. ▶ともかく計画を進めよう Anyway [Anyhow, At any rate], let's go ahead with our plans. ▶雨かもしれないがともかく行きます It may rain, but I will go anyway [anyhow, in any case, ✕at any rate]. (❗この文尾の anyway, anyhow は「たとえそうでも」ぐらいの意)
❷【別として】apart from …. ▶冗談はともかく、それをどうするつもりですか Apart from joking [Joking aside], what are you going to do with it?
❸【まだしも】▶謝るならともかく(=大目に見てもらえるだろうが)彼は反省している様子もない It would be overlooked if he apologized. But he does not show any signs of regret. ▶ほかの人にならともかく(=人もあろうに)私にうそをつくなんてひどいよ How mean (it is) of you to tell a lie to me of all people! ▶彼の外見はともかく(=結構だが),

性格が気に入らない He looks all right, but I don't like his character.
❹【どうであろうとも】whether (…) or not. ▶勝ち負けはともかく正々堂々と戦わねばならない Whether you win or not [win or lose], you must play fair.
▶結果はともかく精一杯努力することが大切だ It's important to do your best no matter how the result turns out to be.

ともかせぎ 共稼ぎ (⇨共働き)
ともぎれ 共切れ • 共ぎれでベルトを作る make a belt with the same cloth used for the dress.
ともぐい 共食い 【動物の】cannibalism /kǽnəblizm/; 【人間の】(相互に害を及ぼす競争) (a) mutually harmful competition; (食うか食われるかの) (a) dog-eat-dog competition. ▶ピラニアは貪欲な魚だが共食いはしない Piranhas /pərǽːnjəz/ are greedy fish but they are not cannibals [they won't eat each other]. (❗cannibal は「共食いする動物」の意)

ともしび 灯火、灯 a light; (ランプの) a lamplight. • 谷間の灯火 lights burning in the valley. • 風前の灯 (風前の灯) • 平和ី運動の灯火を掲げる (=推進する) carry the peace movement forward.

ともしらが 共白髪 • 共白髪の夫婦 a couple grown old together; (高齢になるまで生きた) a couple lived to a great [a good old, a ripe old] age.

ともす 灯す • 明かりをともす (ランプを) light a lamp; (電灯を) turn [switch] on a light. • 一晩中明かりをともしておく keep the light burning all through the night. (⇨ともる)

ともすると (しがちである) be apt (to do); (時々) sometimes. ▶子供はともするといたずらをする Children are apt to get into mischief./Children can be mischievous /místʃɪvəs/. ▶彼はともすると家に帰らないことがあった He sometimes didn't come home. (❗否定文では sometimes は通例否定語の前に置く)

ともだおれ 共倒れ 图 ▶このままでは私たちは共倒れになってしまう We may go down together [(ともにだめになる) be ruined together] the way we are. ▶建築会社が数社共倒れになった Several construction companies went under together.
━ 共倒れする 動 go down [fall] together; cut one another's throats; (会社が倒産する) go under together.

*ともだち 友達 a friend; 《話》 a pal. (⇨仲間)

> 解説 (1) 日本では少し親しくなると「友達」という friend はよく理解し合い好ましく思う相手にのみ用いる. 単なる知り合いとしては acquaintance を用いる (⇨知り合い). また companion は友情の有無は問題にせず単に行動をともにする人の意であるから注意.
> (2) friend など、普通2人以上の可能性が高い語を所有格とともに用いて、例えば「私[父]の友達」という場合, 次の三つの言い方がある.
> (i) a friend of mine [my father('s)] は複数の友達の中から初めて話題に登場する不特定の「ある友達」の意. (❗✕a friend of me は不可) また this, that など指示形容詞を伴う場合にはこの形を用いる: この私の友達 this friend of mine. (❗✕this my friend は不可)
> (ii) one of my [my father's] friends は (i) とほぼ同意で、複数の友人の中の1人であることを強調する言い方.
> (iii) my [my father's] friend は前後関係からだれのことか明らかな「その友達」の意で, the friend に相当する. したがって, 紹介の場では下の ② の例文のようにいうことができる. 話題の初めにいきなり用いると友達が1人しかいないことを暗示する.

①【～(の)友達】 ●親しい[仲のいい]友達 a close [a good, a great] *friend*. (⇨親友) ●男[女]友達 a *boyfriend* [a *girlfriend*]; a male [a female] *friend*. (❗前者は女性の男友達、男性の女友達をさす場合は性的関係を含むので、単なる友人関係には *friend* だけでよい) ●幼(ホッホ)友達 a childhood *friend*. ●昔からの友達(=旧友) an old *friend*. ●いざというときに頼りにならない友達(=友達がいのない人) a fair-weather *friend*. ●仕事上の友達 a business *associate*. ●クラスの友達 a classmate. (❗《米》では it a boy [a girl] (who is) in the same (homeroom) class as me などという方が普通) ●飲み友達《話》a drinking *pal*. ●日常会話では I often drink with him. ということも多い

②【友達(の)～】 ●彼女と友達づきあいをしている be *friends* [have a *friendship*] with her. ●彼との友達づきあいをやめる break (off one's *friendship*) *with* him. ●こちらは友達の田中太郎君です This is my *friend* Taro Tanaka./This is Taro Tanaka, a *friend* of mine./This is my *friend*(,) Taro Tanaka. (❗友達の姓名には Mr. などの敬称をつけない) ●姉と私は友達のように仲がいい My sister and I are getting along well with each other like *friends*.

③【友達が】 ●彼は友達が多い He has a lot of *friends*. ●彼はすぐ友達ができる He *makes friends* easily.

④【友達に】 ●彼と友達になった I *have* become [*have made*] *friends* with him./He and I *have* become [*have made*] *friends*. (❗*friends* は常に複数形) ●友達になってください(=仲よくしましょう) Will you be *friends with* me? ●Will you be *my friend*? は「私の味方になってください」の意/Let's be *friends*. ●彼らは子供の友達になるよう犬を買ってやった They bought the child a dog for *companionship*.

⑤【友達と】 ●友達とスキーに行った I went skiing with a *friend* [some *friends*]. (❗特定の友達でなければ my *friend*(s) としない)

⑥【友達だ】 ●彼とは高校時代からの友達だ I went to high school with him and we've been in friends ever since. (❗次例はより日常的な言い方/ I've been *friends* [been *on friendly terms*] *with* him since we were in high school./He's a *friend* from high school. ●彼は ぼくの友達では[なんかでは]ない He is not a [no] *friend* of mine.

ともづな 纜 a hawser /hɔ́ːzər/; a mooring line. ●ともづなを解く free (a ship) from moorings; (いかりを上げる) weigh (the) anchor.

ともづり 友釣り ●友釣りをする use a live *ayu* as a decoy to fish for *ayu*.

ともども(に) together. (⇨一緒に)

*****ともなう 伴う** **❶【共に起こる・存在する】** go* (hand in hand) 《*with*》, go together; (必ず伴う) involve; (変化などを引き起こす) bring*... about. ●貧困には くく犯罪が伴う Crime often *goes* (hand in hand) *with* poverty./Crime and poverty often *go together* [hand in hand]./Crime often *accompanies* poverty. ●その手術には多少の危険が伴うう The operation *is not without risk*./There is some risk (*involved*) in the operation./The operation *is accompanied by* [《まれ》 *with*] some risk. ●物価上昇に伴って(=つれて)生活が苦しくなってきた With prices going up [*As* prices are going up], life is becoming harder.

❷【いっしょに連れて行く】 take*; (同行する)《やや書》 accompany. (❗go with の方が口語的) ●社長は秘書を伴って出張した The boss *took* his secretary *with* him on a business trip./The boss went on a business trip (*together*) *with* [*accompanied by*, ×accompanied with] his secretary.

-ともなく ●聞くともなく(=ぼんやりと)ラジオを聞く listen *idly* to the radio.

ともに 共に **❶【いっしょに】** together; (...といっしょに) (together, along) *with* .... (⇨一緒に) ●食事をともにする eat [《書》dine] *together*. ●運命[喜び]をともにする share (in) one's fate [joy]《*with*》. ●利害をともにする(=共通の利害を持つ) have common interests《*with*》. ●私は彼とともに働いた I worked *with* him./(協力して) I worked *hand in hand with* him.

❷【両方とも】 both《A and B》; (否定) neither ... nor; [また同時に]) also. (⇨両方、共) ●母子ともに健康な Mother and child are *both* doing well. (❗ mother and child が対句的に用いられると通例無冠詞であることに注意) ●君も彼もともに正しくない Neither you *nor* he are [《書》is] right. (❗ (1) 主語 neither A nor B に続く動詞・代名詞は B に一致させるのが原則であるが,《書》以外では複数呼応の方が普通. (2) 次例の最初の言い方が最も口語的) / You aren't right, and he *isn't either* [《やや書》(and) *nor* is hé], (and)《書》(and) *neither* is hé]. ●うれしく感じるとともに光栄にも思う I feel happy, and I *also* feel honored. (❗後半を強調して I feel *not only* happy *but* (also) honored. ともいえる) ●公害は貧困とともに現代の重要問題の一つである Along with poverty, pollution [Pollution, *as well as* poverty,] is one of the major problems of the times.

❸【同時に】 when ...; (つれて) as ...; (...のあとまもなく) soon after .... ●バブル経済の崩壊とともに日本は厳しい不況に見舞われた Japan was hit by severe depression *when* the bubble economy ended. ●彼は年とともに慈悲深くなった *As* he grew older, he became more merciful. ●ぼくらの友情は卒業とともに終わると君はいつも言っていた You used to say our friendship would end *soon after* we graduated.

とものかい 友の会 ●鉄道友の会 a railfan club. ●友の会に入会する join an association《*of*》.

ともばたらき 共働き ●共働き家庭 a *two-pay-check* [a *two-income*, a *double-income*] family; a *dual-career* [a *two-career*] family. (❗厳密には「共働き」に当たる英語はないので、普通は次のようにいう: 彼の両親は共働きだ(=両方とも仕事を持っている) Both (of) his parents have jobs./His parents both work.) ●最近は共働きの世帯が増えてきた The number of *double-income* households has been increasing recently.

ともびき 友引 a *tomobiki* day; (説明的に) a day of no wins and no losses by *in-yo* divination, and popularly believed to be a bad day for holding funerals because the Chinese characters read 'dragging one's friends into ...'.

どもり 吃り 〖どもること〗(興奮などで一時的に) stammering; (習慣的に) stuttering; 〖人〗 a stammerer; a stutterer. (⇨吃る)

ともる 灯る be lit. ●彼の部屋に明かりがともっている A light *is on* [*burning*] in his room. /彼の部屋はうそくなどに限らず電灯にも用いる)/His room *is lit* [*is lighted*] (*up*).

どもる 吃る stammer; (特に習慣的に) stutter. ●どもりながらあやまる *stammer* (*out*) an apology. ●どもりながら答える answer *stammeringly* [*stutteringly*]. ●彼はひどく[少し]どもる He *has a* bad [*a* slight] *stammer*.

とや

とや 鳥屋 (小屋) a birds' cage [coop, pen].
- **鳥屋に就く** (換羽期に入る) be in molt 《米》[moult 《英》].

どやがい どや街 a flophouse (複 -houses /-ziz, 《米》-sez/) [a dosshouse] district; 《米》 a skid row.

とやかく ▶とやかく言う(=あれこれ言う) say this and that 《about》; say things 《about》. ▶他人事にとやかく口を出すな(=干渉するな) Don't *interfere* [*meddle*] *in* other people's affairs. ▶彼女の服装をとやかく言うな(=あら探しをするな) Don't *be so critical about* what she wears. ▶とやかく言わずに(=不平を言わずに)仕事をしろ Do your job without *making complaints*.

どやす blow up 《at》《米》; blow ... up 《英》; (こっぴどくしかる) dress ... down. ▶車を壁にぶつけておやじにえらくどやされた I got *a good dressing-down* from my dad for bumping his car against the wall.

どやどや ▶人々がどやどやと部屋に入ってきた People came into the room *noisily*, /in a *(群がって)* crowded/ into the room. ▶(ホテルの)廊下をどやどやと通る人の声で目がさめた The *babblings* of people going along the corridor woke me up. (! babbling は「内容不明のべちゃくちゃしゃべり」) ▶食堂へ行く人たちがどやどやとエレベーターを降りていった A crowd of people *tumbled out of* the elevator 《主に米》 [lift 《英》] to the restaurant.

ーとやら 何とやらいう人 Mr. [Mrs.] what's-his [her]-name. ▶安藤さんとやらから電話だよ There's a phone call for you from *a* Ms. Ando./Ms. Ando, *I think she said so*, wants you on the phone.

どよう 土用 the dog days (! 英語の意味は「1年のうちで暑い期間」); (盛夏) the height of summer.
- **土用波** high waves in [during] the dog days. **土用の丑の日** the Midsummer [midsummer] Day of the Ox. **土用干し** summer airing. (!「土用干しする」は air 《clothes》)

*__どようび__ 土曜(日)__ Saturday 《略 Sat.》. (⇨日曜(日))

どよめき 〘騒ぎ〙 a stir; 〘大騒動〙 (a) commotion; 〘興奮〙 excitement. ▶心のどよめきを静める calm one's *excitement* [*apprehension*]. ▶その知らせを聞いて群衆にどよめきが起こった There was a *stir* among the crowd when they heard the news./The news caused a *stir* among the crowd.

どよめく 〘響き渡る〙《場所が主語》resound /rizáund/ 《with a thunder of applause, loud boos》/ 〘人々がざわめく〙(⇨どよめき).

とら 虎 a tiger; (雌) a tigress.
- **虎になる** (ひどく酔う) get dead [blind] drunk.
- **虎の威を借るきつね** (ことわざ) (ライオンの皮をかぶったロバ) an ass in a lion's skin.
- **虎の尾を踏む** (きわめて危険なことをする) do something very dangerous; (大変な危険を冒す) take a great risk.
- **虎を野に放つ** let a tiger (run) loose in a field; (行動の自由を与える) give (him) a free hand.

とら 寅 the Tiger.
- **寅年**〘十二支〙the year of the Tiger. (⇨干支(え)関連表)

どら 銅鑼 a gong. ▶どらを鳴らす beat [sound] a *gong*.

とらい 渡来 图 (訪問) a visit 《to, from》; (導入) introduction (from abroad). (⇨伝来)
—**渡来する** 動 (やって来る) come (over) 《to Nagasaki》; visit; (導入される) be introduced 《into, from》.

- **渡来人** a *toraijin*; (説明的に) Chinese or Korean immigrants in ancient times (approximately between fourth and eighth century) who introduced their high-level culture into Japan.

トライ 〘ラグビー〙a try. ▶トライをあげる score a *try*.

ドライ —**ドライな** 形 (事務的な) businesslike; (実際的な) practical; (打算的な) calculating; (感情的でない) unemotional.
- **ドライアイス** 〘医学〙dry ice. **ドライアイス** dry ice.
- **ドライイースト** 〘乾燥酵母〙dry yeast. **ドライカレー** curried rice [pilaf]; (和製語) dry curry.
- **ドライクリーニング** dry cleaning. (⇨クリーニング)
- **ドライクリーニングする** dry-clean 《clothes》. **ドライビール** 〘辛口のビール〙dry beer. **ドライフラワー** a dried flower. **ドライフルーツ** dried fruit. **ドライマティーニ** a dry martini. **ドライミルク** 〘粉乳〙dried milk, dry milk, powdered milk.

トライアスロン 〘競技〙a triathlon /traiǽθlɑn/.

トライアルアンドエラー 〘試行錯誤〙trial and error.

トライアングル 〘楽器〙a triangle /tráiæŋgl/. ▶トライアングルを鳴らす play the *triangle*.

ドライバー ❶〘運転者〙a driver, (特に自家用車の) a motorist.
❷〘ねじ回し〙a screwdriver. ▶プラスドライバー a Phillips head *screwdriver*. ▶マイナスドライバー a slotted head *screwdriver*.
❸〘ゴルフ用具〙a driver, the number 1 wood.
❹〘コンピュータの〙a driver. ▶プリンタードライバー a printer *driver*.

ドライブ ❶〘車での〙a drive (for pleasure). ▶神戸まで[を]ドライブする go for a *drive* to [in] Kobe; drive to [in] Kobe. ▶彼女をドライブに連れていった I took her (out) for a *drive*.
❷〘打球の回転〙topspin. ▶ドライブをかける put *topspin* on the ball.
❸〘コンピュータの〙a disk drive. ▶ディスクドライブ a disk *drive*. ▶仮想ドライブ a virtual disk *drive*. ▶24倍速ドライブ 24-speed *drive*.
- **ドライブマップ** a road map.

ドライブイン a drive-in; (食堂) a drive-in [(街道沿いの) a roadside] restaurant. (! 前の方は車に乗ったまま食事ができるものをいい, 日本語の「ドライブイン」は通例後の方にあたる)
- **ドライブインシアター** a drive-in theater.

ドライブウェー (ドライブ用観光道路) a scenic drive [highway]; (高速道路) 《米》 an expressway; 《英》 a motorway. (! driveway は (私邸の)車道)

ドライブスルー 《米》a drive-through.

ドライヤー (髪の) a hair-dryer, a blow-dryer; (衣類の) a (clothes) dryer. (! dryer は drier ともつづる)
- ▶ドライヤーで髪を乾かす blow-dry one's hair.

トラウマ 〘心的外傷〙trauma.

とらえどころ 捕らえ所 ▶捕らえ所のない(=当てにならない)奴 a *slippery* [(ずるい) a *tricky*] customer. ▶捕らえ所のない(=あいまいな)話 a *vague* [an *ambiguous*] talk.

__とらえる__ 捕らえる ❶〘捕まえる, 握る〙catch. (⇨捕まえる ❶❷)

❷〘抽象的事項を〙(五感・知性で) catch*; (把握する) grasp; (魅了する) charm; (見つける) catch sight of .... ▶意味をとらえる *grasp* [*catch*] the meaning. (! catch は通例進行形, 受身, 命令文では用いない)
- **機会をとらえる** take [seize (on)] a chance (*to do*). **真相をとらえる** *get at* the truth. ▶彼の心をとらえる (勝ち取る) win his heart; (知らぬ間にさらう) *steal* his heart. ▶この絵は彼の特徴をよくとらえている This picture *has caught* his dis-

とらがり 虎刈り ▶彼はとら刈りにされた He had his hair cropped uneven.
とらかん 虎巻 (⇨虎の巻)
ドラキュラ (吸血鬼) Dracula.
トラクター a tractor.
どらごえ どら声 ●どら声を張り上げて話す speak in a *loud thick voice*.
トラコーマ [医学] trachoma /trəkóumə/.
ドラゴン [竜] a dragon.
ドラスティック ── ドラスティックな 形 [過激で思い切った] drastic. ●ドラスティックな税制改革を行う carry out a *drastic* tax reform.
トラスト [企業összeg] a trust. ●トラスト禁止法 an antitrust law.

***トラック** [貨物自動車] a truck, 《英》 a lorry; (小型の) a pickup; (大型の) 《米》 a rig. ●長距離トラック a long-distance *truck*. ●2トントラック a two-ton *truck*. ●トラック運送(業) 《米》 trucking (business [industry]). ●トラック運転手 a *truck* 《米》 [a lorry 《英》] driver, 《米》 a trucker. ●トラック 1台分の土 a truckload of dirt. ●トラックで品物を運ぶ carry goods *by truck* [*on a truck*].

トラック [競走路] a (running) track. ●トラック競技 a track event [race]. ●トラック競技の選手 a *track* athlete.

ドラッグ [薬物] a drug.
ドラッグ ── ドラッグする 動 [コンピュータ] drag. ●アイコンをドラッグしてデスクトップに移す *drag* an icon (and drop it) onto the desktop. ●思いの位置にドラッグする *drag* to the position wanted. ●ドラッグアンドドロップする drag-and-drop.

ドラッグストア 《主に米》 a drugstore; 《英》 a pharmacy, a chemist('s shop).
トラックパッド [コンピュータ] a track pad.
ドラッグバント [野球] a drag bunt. ●ドラッグバントをする make [attempt] a drag bunt; drag a bunt.
トラックポイント [コンピュータ] 〔商標〕 a track point. (! pointing stick ともいう)
トラックボール [コンピュータ] a trackball, a control ball.
とらつぐみ 虎鶫 [鳥] a golden mouse.
トラップ [排水管の防臭弁, クレー放出機, わな] a trap; [サッカー] trapping. ●胸でボールをトラップする take the ball on one's chest.
とらねこ 虎猫 a brown tabby.
どらねこ どら猫 a bossy alley cat.
とらのこ 虎の子 a tiger cub; (貴重な貯金) (precious) savings; (話) a nest egg (! 将来に備えた貯金).
とらのまき 虎の巻 [語学書などの] a key; (話) a crib; (米話・まれ) a pony. ●英語教科書の虎の巻 a *key* [a *crib*] *to* an English textbook. (! to の代わりに of も)
トラバーユ [<フランス語] [転職] a change of job.
トラフ [舟状海盆] [地学] a trough.
とらふ 虎斑 [虎編模様] tiger-like stripes.
トラファルガー ●トラファルガーの海戦 the Battle of Trafalgar /trəfælgər/. ●トラファルガー広場 Trafálgar Squáre.
とらふぐ 虎ふぐ [魚介] a tiger globefish.
ドラフト ●タイガースのドラフト1位の選手 the Tigers' first-round pick *in the draft*; the No. 1 draft pick of the Tigers. ●ドラフト1位に指名される be drafted first; be picked first in the *draft*. ●ドラフト会議 a dráfting sèssion. ●ドラフト制 the draft system.
ドラフトビール 《米》 draft beer, 《英》 draught beer.
トラブる (問題を起こす) get into trouble; (故障する) break down. ▶昨日仕事でトラブってしまった I *got into trouble* over my work yesterday.
トラブル [[問題]] (a) trouble (⇨問題(%)); [[機械の不調]] [コンピュータ] a malfunction; (突然の) a glitch; (欠陥) an error. ●女性[金銭]問題でトラブルに巻き込まれる get into *trouble with* women [*over a money matter*]. ●コンピュータのトラブルで due to a computer *malfunction*. ▶何かトラブルでも? What seems to be the *trouble*? (! 出すぎないよう気づかいながらの質問)
●トラブルメーカー a troublemaker.
トラベラーズチェック 《米》 a traveler's check; 《英》 a traveller's cheque.
〔会話〕「このトラベラーズチェックは 1,000 ドルあります。どのように現金にされますか」「50ドル16枚, 20ドル10枚でお願いします」"These *traveler's checks* are worth $1,000. How do you want it?" "Sixteen fifties and ten twenties, please." (! it は $1,000 を一つの単位として受けている)

トラホーム (⇨囲 トラコーマ)
ドラマ a play; a drama. (⇨劇) ●ラジオドラマ a radio *play*. ●テレビドラマ a television *play*; a *drama* for TV. ●(テレビやラジオの)連続ドラマ a serial; (一話完結の) a series. ●ホームドラマ a soap opera, (話) a soap. ●小説をテレビドラマ化する dramatize a novel for television.

ドラマー a drummer.
ドラマチック ── ドラマチックな 形 [[劇的な]] dramatic. (⇨劇的)
ドラム [楽器] a drum. (⇨太鼓) ●ドラム奏者 a drummer. ●ドラムをたたく beat a *drum*.
ドラムかん ドラム缶 a drum; an oil drum.
どらむすこ どら息子 [道楽息子] 〔書〕 a profligate /prɑ́fligət/ son; (聖書の中で悔い改めた) the prodigal son; (甘やかされた) a spoiled son.
どらやき 銅鑼焼き a *dorayaki*, (説明的に) a sandwich of two small pancakes with a filling of sweetened bean paste.

とられる 取られる, 盗られる (⇨取る) ●あっけに取られる be dumbfounded. ▶彼はロープに足をとられてころんだ He *caught* his foot in the ropes and fell. ▶私は財布を盗られた (こっそり) I *had* my wallet *stolen*. (! これは事後に「あの時は困った」といったニュアンスでいうときで, 直後の発言は能動文を用いて Someone stole my wallet. とする方が自然)/My wallet *was stolen*. (! ×I was stolen my wallet. は不可)/(力ずくで) I was robbed *of* my wallet. (! 後の二つの受身文は被害を客観的に報告する言い方)

とらわれ 捕らわれ ●捕らわれの身である be a captive [a prisoner]; be in captivity [prison].

***とらわれる 捕らわれる** ❶ [捕まえられる] be caught; (抵抗して捕らえられる) be captured; (捕虜になる) be made [taken] (ˣa) prisoner; (逮捕される) be arrested. ▶その泥棒は警察に捕らわれた The thief *was caught* [*was arrested*] by the police. ▶彼は敵に捕らわれた He *was captured* [*was made prisoner*] by the enemy.
❷ [とりこになる] (恐怖などに取り付かれる) be seized (*with*); (…の奴隷になる) be a slave (*to*, *of*); (執着する) stick* [adhere] (*to*); (左右される) be swayed [influenced] (*by*). ●恐怖に取られる *be seized with* fear [panic]. ●目先の利益に捕らわれる *be swayed by* the thought of [*目がくらむ*] *blinded by*] a quick profit. ▶彼は因習に捕らわれている He *is a slave to* old customs./(縛り付けられ

いる) He *is tied to* [*is bound by*] old customs./(執着している) He *sticks to* old customs. ▶情にはよく感情に捕らわれる We *are often swayed* [*influenced*] *by* sentiment. ▶捕らわれた(=因習的な)考えは捨てよ Give up a *conventional* idea [(偏見のある意見) a *prejudiced* opinion]. ▶彼は何事にも捕らわれない心を持っている He *has* [*keeps*] *an open mind*./He *is open-minded*./(しきたりに捕らわれない) He *is free from convention*./(偏見がない) He *is free from prejudice*.

トランキライザー〔精神安定剤〕〔薬剤〕a tránquilizer.

トランク(かばん)(大型の) a trunk; (小型の) a suitcase; 〔車の〕《米》a trunk, 《英》a boot.
●トランクルーム〔家財保管庫〕a rental storage room. (❗a trunk room は通じるが一般的ではない)

トランクス(a pair of) trunks (❗水泳用の体に密着した男性用パンツ); (ボクサーパンツ) boxer shorts, boxers (❗後の方は日常語。ボクサーなどのはく競技用短パンまたはそれに似たゆったりした男性用下着).

トランシーバー a transceiver.
トランジスター a transistor.
●トランジスターラジオ a transistor radio.

トランス〔変圧器〕a (power) transformer.
トランプ(トランプの札) a (playing) card; (トランプ遊び) (playing) cards. (❗通例複数扱い) 〔参考〕日本語の「トランプ」は英語では trump (切り札という)から) — of cards. (❗単数扱い) ▶トランプをする play *cards*; have a game of *cards*. (❗×do [play] trumps は不可) ▶トランプを切る shuffle [cut] the *cards* [deck, pack].
●トランプを配る deal (out) the *cards* [deck, pack] (*to*).

トランペット〔楽器〕a trumpet. (⇨喇叭(らっぱ)) ▶トランペットを吹く blow a trumpet; play the trumpet.
●トランペット奏者 a trumpeter; (楽団の) a trumpet.

トランポリン a trampoline.
:**とり** 鳥 a bird; a fowl /fául/; (⿃ 〜s, 〈集合的〉〜); 〔鶏〕a chicken; (雌) a hen; (雄) a cock, 《主に米》a rooster.

> 使い分け bird 「鳥」を表す最も一般的な語.
> fowl 鶏・アヒル・七面鳥などの家禽(きん)をさすが、修飾語を伴って集合的に鳥類の意でも用いる: 水鳥 waterfowl. (❗water birds ともいう)

●鳥の鳴き声〔さえずり声〕a bird call [a birdsong].
●鳥の一群 a flock of *birds*. (❗「鳥が群れをなす」は *Birds* flock together.) ●鳥の肉 (⇨鳥肉) ●鳥を飼う(小鳥を) have [《主に英》keep] a (pet) *bird*; (鶏・アヒルなどを) keep *fowls*. (❗を飼う) ▶林の中で鳥が鳴いている *Birds* are singing [chirping, twittering] among the trees. ●冬には南へ飛んで行きます The *birds* fly south in 《主に米》the) winter.
●鳥インフルエンザ bird [avian] flu. ●鳥インフルエンザの大流行 a *bird flu* pandemic.

とり 取り (最後の出演者[番組]) the last performer [program]. ▶彼女は伝統の年末の歌の祭典で取りを取った(=番組中最後に歌う名誉を持った) She *had the honor to sing the last song on the program* at the traditional year-end music festival.

とり 酉 the Rooster.
●酉年〔十二支〕the year of the Rooster. (⇨干支(し)) 関連)

ドリア〔＜フランス語〕〔料理〕doria.
トリアージ〔＜フランス語〕〔災害医療での治療優先順序の選別〕triage /tríːɑːʒ/.

とりあい 取り合い a scramble. ●席の取り合いをする *scramble* (必死になって) *struggle*] *for* seats.

とりあう 取り合う ❶〔互いに取る〕●手を取り合う join hands. ●手を取り合って泣く take each other's hands and weep. ●手を取り合って(=協力して)仕事をする do a job *hand in hand*.
❷〔奪い合う〕scramble 《*for*》. ●選手はボールを取り合った The players *scrambled* [(争って) *struggled*] *for* the ball.
❸〔相手にする〕●取り合わない(無視する) ignore; 《やや書》disregard; (注意を払わない) pay no attention to ...; take no notice of ...; (耳を貸さない) turn a deaf ear to ... ▶彼は私の警告に取り合わなかった He *ignored* [*paid no attention to, turned a deaf ear to*] my warnings.

***とりあえず** ❶〔直ちに〕at once, right away; immediately; (...するとすぐに) as soon as [the moment] (＋節); (すぐに) (急いで) in a hurry, 《書》in haste (急いで). ▶とりあえず彼に礼状を出した I sent a thank-you letter *at once* [*right away*]. ▶その知らせを受けると彼は(取るものも)とりあえず東京へ向かった *As soon as* [*The moment*] he got the news, he started for Tokyo. ▶彼女はとりあえず夫のところに駆けつけた She *hurried to* her husband./She went to her husband *in a hurry*.
❷〔当分の間〕for the time being, for now (❗次の句より口語的), for the present. ▶とりあえず彼との部屋を使うことにした I decided to share the room with him *for the time being*.
❸〔第一に〕first (of all). ▶とりあえずもっと英語を勉強しなさい You should study English harder *first (of all)*.

***とりあげる** 取り上げる ❶〔手に取る〕pick ... up 《*from*》. ●受話器を取り上げる *pick up* (↔put down) a receiver.
❷〔奪う〕take*... away 《*from*》; (私有物を権限により) confiscate; (権利・財産などを) 《やや書》deprive (《人＋*of*＋物》; (資格を) disqualify; (免許などを無効にする) cancel. ▶彼からナイフを取り上げる *take* the knife (*away*) *from* him. ▶彼から財産を取り上げる *take* his property *away from* him; *confiscate* his property; *deprive* him of his property. ▶判事の資格を取り上げられる *be disqualified* as a judge. ▶先生は私が授業中に漫画を読んでいるのを見つけて取り上げた The teacher caught me (in the act of) reading a comic in class and *took* it *away* [*confiscated* it]. ▶スピード違反で運転免許を取り上げられた My driver's license was *canceled* [was *taken* away] for speeding. (⇨-れる)
❸〔採用する〕adopt; 〔受け入れる〕accept; 〔議題にして論じる〕take*... up; 〔書物などで論じる〕deal* with ..., treat; 〔報道する〕report, cover; (大々的に) feature. ●その本で取り上げられた(=扱われた)問題 the subject *dealt with* in the book. ▶私の提案は取り上げられなかった My suggestion *was not adopted* [*accepted*]./(拒否された) My suggestion *was turned down* [*was rejected*]. ▶この問題はたびたび国会で取り上げられた This matter *has often been taken up* in the Diet. ▶その汚職事件は新聞で大々的に取り上げられた The bribery case *was featured* [*was given* a lot of *coverage*, (大げさに) *was played up*] in [×by] the newspapers.
❹〔助産する〕deliver. ●五つ子を無事取り上げる *deliver* the quintuplets safely.

とりあつかい 取り扱い 〔物の〕handling; 〔人・物の〕treatment; 〔客の〕service. ●手荒い〔親切な〕取り扱いを受ける receive rough [kind] *treatment*.

とりあつかう

▶彼は機械の取り扱いがうまい He is good [excellent] at *handling* machines. ▶このホテルは客の扱いが悪い They give poor *service* at this hotel./The *service* is poor at this hotel. ▶取り扱い注意《表示》(*Handle*) *with care*./《破壊注意》Fragile /frǽdʒəl/.
● 取り扱い時間 service hours. ● 取り扱い店 a dealer; (代理店) an agency. ● 取り扱い人 an agent.

****とりあつかう 取り扱う** 〚待遇する〛treat; 〚扱う〛handle; 〚処理する, 扱う〛deal* with ...; 〚商品を売買する〛deal in ...; 〚電報などを受け付ける〛accept. (⇨扱う) ▶ガラスを注意して取り扱う *handle* glass carefully. ▶彼はよく子供を手荒に取り扱う He often *treats* [*handles, deals with*] his children roughly. ▶この本はこの前の戦争を取り扱っている This book *treats* [*deals with*] the last war.

とりあわせ 取り合わせ (a) combination; (an) arrangement; (取りそろえたもの) an assortment. ▶この生け花は色の取り合わせがすばらしい The *combination* of colors is wonderful in this flower arrangement.

とりあわせる 取り合わせる combine; (並べる) arrange.

ドリアン 〚植物〛a durian. 〘参考〙果物の王様といわれる)

とりい 鳥居 a *torii*; (説明的に) a gateway commonly built at the entrance to a Shinto shrine.

とりいそぎ 取り急ぎ 〚取り急ぎ…する〛hasten to 《do》. ▶新規事業に関するお手紙をいただき取り急ぎお礼申し上げます I *hasten* to thank you for your letter about a new business.

トリートメント 〚髪の手入れ〛hair treatment.

ドリーム 〚夢〛a dream. ● ドリームチーム a dream team. ● ドリームランド a dreamland.

とりいる 取り入る 〚人の機嫌を取って好かれるようになる〛gain favor with ...; 〚気に入られるようにする〛curry favor with ..., 《書》ingratiate oneself with ...; 〚へつらう〛《話》make* [play] up to ..... ▶贈り物をして先生に取り入ろうとする try to *curry favor with* [*ingratiate oneself with*] the teacher by giving him [her] presents. ▶彼は政治家に取り入るのがうまい He is clever in *gaining favor with* [*支持*] *support of*》 political leaders. ▶あの男はいつも上役に取り入ろうとしている He is always trying to *make* [*play*] *up to* his boss.

とりいれ 取り入れ (a) harvest; harvesting. (⇨収穫)

とりいれる 取り入れる ❶ 〚中に入れる〛take* ... in. ● 洗濯物を取り入れる *take in* the washing [wash].

❷ 〚収穫する〛harvest; gather ... in (〘!〙文語的); (摘む) pick. ● 畑の作物を取り入れる *harvest* the fields. ● リンゴを取り入れる *pick* apples. ▶農民たちは作物を取り入れた The farmers *harvested* [*got in, gathered in*] their crops.

❸ 〚採用する〛adopt; (受け入れる) accept; (導入する) introduce ... 《into》; (考えなどを組み入れる) incorporate ... 《into》. ▶新説を取り入れる *adopt* [*accept*] a new theory. ▶ここはあらゆる最新技術を取り入れた日本で最も進んだ遊園地です This is the most advanced amusement park in Japan, *introducing* [*incorporating*] all the latest technologies.

とりえ 取り柄 a merit (↔a demerit); 〚すぐれた点〛a good [a strong] point; 〚欠点を補うよい点〛a saving grace. (⇨長所) ▶彼 [この方法] にはこれといった取り柄がない He [This method] has no particular *merits* [*good points*]. ▶彼は丈夫なのだけが取り柄だ He has the (only) *merit* of being healthy./His (single) *saving grace* is being healthy.

トリオ a trio /tríou/ (⧼複⧽ ~s).

とりおこなう 取り行う (催す) hold*; (公式に行う) perform. ● 国葬を執り行う *hold* a state funeral. ● 進水式を執り行う *perform* [*hold*] a launching ceremony.

とりおさえる 取り押さえる catch*; (逮捕する) arrest. ● 泥棒を取り押さえる *catch* a thief.

とりおとす 取り落とす 〚手から落とす〛drop (-pp-); let ... fall; 〚うっかり抜かす〛omit (-tt-) [leave ... out] by mistake.

とりがい 鳥貝 〚魚介〛a Japanese cockle; an egg cockle.

とりかえ 取り替え (an) exchange. (⇨交換)

とりかえし 取り返し recovery.
● 取り返しのつかない 〚取り戻せない〛《書》irrecoverable; 《書》irretrievable; (償えない)《書》irreparable. ▶取り返しのつかない(= 致命的な)失敗をする make a *fatal* mistake [error]. ▶彼はその言葉を口走ったことを後悔したが, もう取り返しがつかなかった He regretted the words, but they *were* already *past* [*beyond*] *recall*. ▶済んだことは取り返しがつかない(ことわざ) What is done cannot be undone.

とりかえす 取り返す get* ... back, regain; (損失などを) recover, make* ... up 《for》 (〘!〙受身では for を省略する); (仕事などの遅れを) catch* up on [with] 《one's work》. ● 借金を取り戻す ▶彼から金を取り返す *get the money back* from him.

****とりかえる 取り替える, 取り換える** 〚交換する〛(新しいものを) change, replace; (やり取りする) exchange (⇨交換する); 〚新しくする〛renew. ● 花びんの水を取り替える *renew* the water in a vase.
〘会話〙「このセーター, 取り換えてもらえませんか」「どうしてですか. どこかお気に召さないところでも」「いえ, サイズが違うんです」"Can I *exchange* this sweater, please?" "Why? What's wrong with it?" "Well, it's the wrong size." (〘!〙the に注意)

とりかかる 取り掛かる set* about ...; (熱心に) get* down [set] to ... (〘!〙set to ... はやや古い感じの語); 〚始める〛start; begin*. (⇨掛ける❿) ● 必要なデータの収集に取りかかる *set about* gathering the necessary data. ● 建設工事に取りかかる *start* construction work.

とりかご 鳥籠 a (bird) cage.

とりかこむ 取り囲む surround. (⇨囲む)

とりかじ 取り舵 《号令》Port!/《米》Left! ▶取り舵いっぱい《号令》Hard aport!

とりかたづける 取り片付ける clear ... away. (⇨片付ける❶)

とりかぶと 鳥兜 〚植物〛an aconite; a monkshood.

とりかわす 取り交わす exchange. (⇨交換する)

とりきめ 取り決め (協定) an agreement; (手はず) (an) arrangement; (約束) a promise; (決定) (a) decision. ● 取り決めを守る[破る] obey [break] *the agreement*.

とりきめる 取り決める (日取りなどを定める) fix; (打ち合わせる) arrange; (合意の上決定する) agree on ...; (締結する) conclude. ▶次の会の時間と場所を取り決める *fix* [*arrange, agree on*] a time and place for the next meeting.

とりくずす 取り崩す 〚建物などを〛(⇨取り壊す); 〚定期預金などを〛(転用する) divert 《the reserve fund》 to other purposes; (解約して使う) cancel 《the time deposit》and use the money 《for》.

とりくち 取り口 〚相撲〛the way of *sumo*.

とりくみ 取組 (試合) a match; (相撲・ボクシングなどの) a bout /báut/. ● 好取組 a good [an interesting]

***とりくむ 取り組む** [[問題に対処する]] work 《on》; [[格闘する]] wrestle 《with》. ● 難問に取り組む work on [wrestle with, (正面からまともに取り組む) come to grips with, (真剣に取りかかる) tackle, (立ち向かう) face] a difficult problem. ▶彼は回顧録の執筆に取り組んでいる(=従事している) He *is engaged in [working on]* writing his memoirs /mémwɑːrz/.

とりけし 取り消し (約束・行事などの) (a) cancellation; (免許・命令などの) (a) revocation; (言・訴訟などの) (a) withdrawal. ● 運転免許の取り消し the *revocation* of a driver's license. ● 取り消しのできない決定 an *irrevocable* /irévəkəbl/ decision. ● 前言の取り消しを要求する demand the *withdrawal* of 《his》previous remarks. ▶注文の取り消しをしてもよいですか May I *cancel* the order?

***とりけす 取り消す** [[予約・注文・約束などを]] cancel; [[許可・命令などを]] revoke; [[言などを]] take* ... back, withdraw* (**!** 前の方が口語的). ● 予約[注文]を取り消す *cancel* an appointment [an order]. ● 前言を取り消す *take back* [*withdraw*] one's previous remarks. ▶私は運転免許を取り消された My driver's license *was revoked*.

とりこ 虜 [[捕虜]] a prisoner, a captive. (⇨捕虜) ● 恋のとりこ a *prisoner* [a *captive*] of love. ▶男の子はみんな彼女の美しさのとりこになった(=魅惑された) All the boys *were fascinated* [*were charmed*, (やや書) *were captivated*] by her beauty./(夢中にさせた) (話) Her beauty *drove* all the boys *crazy*.

とりこしぐろう 取り越し苦労 ── 取り越し苦労(を)する 動 (将来について心配する) worry; (くよくよする) fret} about the future; (心配しすぎる) be overanxious 《about》; worry unduly 《about》. ▶取り越し苦労するな Don't *worry* [*fret*] *about the future*./(先のことは成り行きに任せておけ) Let the future take care of itself./(ことわざ) Don't cross your bridges before you come to them. (「橋のたもとに着くまでは橋を渡るな」の意) ▶取り越し苦労かもしれないが, また世界大戦が起きるような気がする I may *be overanxious* [*be worrying unduly*], but I'm afraid another world war may break out.

とりこぼす 取り零す [[相撲]] give away one's good chance to win; be defeated unexpectedly.

とりこみ 取り込み ▶今取り込み中なので(=忙しくしておりますから), 後で電話します I'm very busy now. I'll call you (up) later. (⇨取り込む❷)
● 取り込み詐欺 《operate》 a confidence [(話) a con] game (米) [trick (英)]. ● 取り込み詐欺師 a confidence man [woman] (英) a confidence trickster.

とりこむ 取り込む ❶ [[取り入れる]] take* ... in. ▶風が強く吹かないうちに洗濯物を取り込んでください Please *take* [*get*] the washing *in* before it begins to blow hard.
❷ [[ごたごたしている]] (忙しい) be busy; (混乱している) be in confusion. ▶今は取り込んでいますので, あす来てください I'm *very busy* [*tied up*] now, so please come tomorrow. ▶家の中は取り込んでいる My house *is in confusion*./(家族のもめ事がある) I have some *family trouble*(s) [*strife*].

トリコモナス ⇨トリコモナス症 [医学] trichomoniasis.
とりごや 鳥小屋 (小鳥の) a birdhouse (複) ~s /-ziz, (米) -siz/; (鶏の) a henhouse.
とりころす 取り殺す possess and kill.
とりこわし 取り壊し 《やや書》(a) demolition. (⇨取り壊す) ● 建築物取り壊し業者 (米) a wreck. (英) a demolition worker. ● 取り壊し作業 demolition work. ▶古い博物館の取り壊し(=取り壊しの計画)を中止した They gave up the idea of *pulling down* [*demolishing*] the old museum.

とりこわす 取り壊す (人や建物を) pull [tear*] ... down; demolish. [[前の二つより堅い語]] ▶新築するために古い家が取り壊された The old house *was pulled* [*was torn, was knocked*] *down* to build a new one./The old house *was demolished* to build a new one.

とりさげる 取り下げる withdraw*; drop (-pp-). ● 彼女の告訴を取り下げる *withdraw* [*drop*] a charge against her. ● 辞表を取り下げる *withdraw* [(撤回する)《書》 *retract*] one's resignation.

とりざた 取り沙汰 (うわさ) (a) rumor, 《やや話》 talk. ▶そのことは世間でいろいろ取り沙汰されている(=広まっている) There are a lot of *rumors* about it./It is much *talked about*.

とりざら 取り皿 a (small) plate.
とりさる 取り去る ● 不純物を取り去る remove [get rid of] impurities. ● 不必要な語を取り去る(=除く) *get rid of* [《やや書》 *eliminate*] unnecessary words.

とりしきる 取り仕切る manage, control (-ll-). ● 自分の担任のクラスも取り仕切れないダメ教師 a bad teacher who can't *manage* [*control*] his class.
● 店を1人で取り仕切る *run* a store *all by oneself*.

とりしずめる 取り鎮める 《書》quell [quiet down, put down] 《a riot [a disturbance]》.

とりしまり 取り締まり [[規制による]] (a) regulation; [[権力による]] (a) control; [[管理による]] management; [[監督による]] supervision; (違法行為に対する) a crackdown 《on》. ● 賭博(なく)の一斉取り締まり a *crackdown on* gambling. ● 暴力に対する取り締まりを強化する strengthen *regulation*(s) [*control*] *against* violence.
● 取り締まり規則 regulations.

とりしまりやく 取締役 a director, an executive. ● 代表取締役 a representative *director*. ● 専務取締役 a senior managing *director*. ● 常務取締役 a managing *director*. (**!** 役職名は会社によって言い方が異なることがある) ● 取締役を務める sit on the *boards*. ● 取締役に就任する assume the office of *director*.
● 取締役会 a board of directors. ● 取締役会(議)を開く have a board meeting. (**!**「取締役会議室」は a boardroom) ● 取締役会長 a chairman [chairwoman]. ● 取締役社長 a president. ● 取締役副会長 a vice chairman [chairwoman]. ● 取締役副社長 a vice president.

***とりしまる 取り締まる** [[統制する]] control (-ll-); [[規制する]] regulate; [[管理する]] manage; [[監督する]] supervise; [[調べる]] check; [[違法行為(者)に断固とした処置をとる]] crack down 《on》. ● 過激派を厳重に取り締まる keep radicals *under* strict *control*. ● 酔っ払い運転を取り締まる *crack down on* drunk(en) driving [drivers].

とりしらべ 取り調べ [[警察の捜査]] (an) investigation; [[問い合わせ, 調査]] (an) inquiry; [[尋問]] questioning; (長時間にわたる徹底的な) (an) interrogation. ▶その殺人事件は目下取り調べ中だ The murder *is under investigation*. ▶彼は数時間にわたって警察の厳しい取り調べを受けた He *was severely questioned* [(長時間徹底的に) *interrogated*, (話) *grilled*] for several hours by the police.
● 取り調べ室 (警察の) an interrogation room.

とりしらべる 取り調べる [[調査する]] investigate; [[尋

とりすがる 取りすがる ❶[離れまいとする] hold [cling, hang] onto 《his arm》; (哀願する) appeal 《to him to do》. (⇨哀願)

とりすます 取り澄ます look prim. (⇨澄ます❷)

とりそろえる 取り揃える ▶その店には婦人靴が各種取り揃えてある The store has a wide [a large] choice of ladies' shoes./They have a wide variety of ladies' shoes in stock.

とりだす 取り出す ❶[中から外へ出す] take*... out.
●かばんから本を取り出す take out a book from one's bag; take a book out of one's bag.
❷[抽出する] ●その岩石から金を取り出す extract gold from the rocks.
❸[選び出す] ▶彼女は気に入ったドレスを1着取り出した She picked out [selected] one dress that she liked.

とりたて 取り立て 图 ●税金の取り立て the collection of the taxes.

—— **取り立ての** 形 [新鮮な] fresh; [新しく摘んだ] freshly picked. ●取り立ての野菜 fresh [freshly picked] vegetables; vegetables fresh from the field [garden]. ●取り立てのサケ1匹 a fresh-caught salmon; a salmon fresh from the sea [river]. ●この桃は取り立てだ These peaches are fresh from the orchard.
●取り立て金 money collected.

とりたてて 取り立てて (特に) particularly; especially. ▶取り立てて言うほどの手柄ではない His achievement is not particularly [especially] remarkable./His achievement is not something worth mentioning [nothing to speak of].

とりたてる 取り立てる ❶[金などを] [強制的に] 《書》 exact; (集金する) collect; (政府が税金などを) levy. ●彼から税金を取り立てる exact [collect] taxes from him.
❷[よい地位に] (任命する) appoint; (昇進させる) promote. ▶彼はマネージャーに取り立てられた They appointed 《him》 (xa, ×the) manager.

***とりちがえる 取り違える** [別のものと間違える] mistake* [take*] 《A for B》; (混同する) confuse 《A with B》 (⇨混同する); [誤解する] misunderstand*. ▶彼は私が言った意味を取り違えた He got me wrong. (!次例より口語的)/He misunderstood me [what I said].

とりちらかす 取り散らかす scatter... about. (⇨散らかす)

とりつ 都立 (⇨公立, 県立) ●都立病院 a metropolitan hospital.

とりつぎ 取り次ぎ [仲介・代理をすること] agency; [代理店, 取り次ぎ店] an agency; [配給会社] a distributor; [代理人, 代理店] an agent (!agency は代理業務の行われる場所, agent は人に重点がある); [玄関番] a doorkeeper. ●朝日新聞の取り次ぎ店 an agency [an agent] for the Asahi Shimbun.
●海外旅行の取り次ぎをする act as (an) agent for foreign travel. ●玄関へ取り次ぎに(=応対に)出る answer the door [bell].

とりつく 取り付く ❶[すがる] cling* to ...; hold* on to .... ●窓の出っぱりに取り付く cling to the ledge of a window.
❷[悪霊などが付く] ●野心[悪魔]に取り付かれる be possessed 《by》. ●野心[悪魔]に取り付かれている be possessed by ambition [a devil]. ●恐ろしい病気に取り付かれている(=犠牲になる) fall victim to [(かかる) 《書》 contract] a deadly disease. ▶彼はあやしげな考えに取り付かれていた He was possessed by a strange idea./A strange idea took hold of him.
●取り付く島もない be left (utterly) helpless; be thrown upon one's own resources.

トリック a trick. (⇨計略) ●まんまとトリックに引っ掛かる be completely tricked; 《話》 be easily taken in.
●トリック [だまし絵] an optical illusion.
●トリック映画 a trick film. ●トリック写真 a trick picture. ●トリックプレー [競技] a trick play. (!参考 野球の隠し球 (a hidden-ball trick) など) ●トリックレーヤー a tricky player, a free flicker.

とりつぐ 取り次ぐ ❶[伝える] tell*. ▶私は田中さんから電話があったことを彼に取り次いだ I told him that there was a call for him from Mr. Tanaka.
❷[仲介する] mediate; (代理人をする) act as (an) agent 《for》. (⇨取り次ぎ) ●K社は全国の書店に本を取り次いでいる K Company distributes books to the bookstores all over the country. (!distribute は「配る」)

とりつくろう 取り繕う [うまくごまかす] gloss over ...; (機嫌に対処して) smooth... over; [修繕する] repair, mend; (継ぎを当てて) patch... up (!けんかなどを「一時的に取り繕う」の意もある). ●失敗を取り繕う gloss [smooth] over one's faults. ●人前を取り繕う keep up appearances. ▶彼はその場を何とか取り繕った He managed to save the situation [patch things up] for the moment.

とりつけ 取り付け ❶[銀行の] a run. ▶その銀行が取り付けにあった There was a run on [xat] the bank.
❷[据(す)え付け] installation. (⇨取り付ける❶)
❸[買い付け] ●取り付けの酒屋 one's usual [(ひいきの) favorite] liquor store.

とりつける 取り付ける ❶[備え付ける] (固定させる) fix; (正しい位置に) set*... out; (ぴったり合うように) fit (-tt-); (装置などを) install; (水道・ガスなどを) lay*... on. (⇨備え付ける) ●棚を壁に取り付ける fix a shelf to [on] the wall. ●レストランの外に看板を取り付ける set out a signboard outside a restaurant. ●暖房装置を部屋に取り付ける install a heating system in the room; furnish the room with a heating system. ●新しい錠をドアに取り付けてもらった We had a new lock fitted on the door.
❷[同意などを得る] ●彼の同意を取り付ける get [obtain] his agreement. (!後の方が堅い語)

ドリップコーヒー drip cóffee.

とりて 取り手 ❶[受け取る人] a receiver. ▶父の遺品のバイオリンの取り手がいない Nobody wants to have the violin which our father left us.
❷[相撲] (技のうまい人) a sumo wrestler with good technique; a technically advanced sumo wrestler.

とりで 砦 (人工的に築造された) a fort; (要塞(ようさい)の) a fortress (!fort より大きいもの); [主義・思想などの] a stronghold. (!本来の意味の砦は《古》) ▶農村部は保守党の最後のとりでだった The rural district was the last stronghold of the conservative party.

とりとめのない 取り留めのない (筋の通らない) incoherent; (まとまりのない) rambling; (要領を得ない) pointless. ●とりとめのないことを言う say incoherent things; make pointless remarks. ●とりとめのない会話 a rambling conversation. ●昔のことをとりとめもなく話す ramble (on) about the past.

とりとめる 取り留める ▶彼は命を取り留めた(=危うく死を免れた) He narrowly escaped death./He had a narrow [a hair's-breadth] escape from death.

とりどり 取り取り —— **取り取りの** 形 (いろいろの) vari-

ous; diverse; different. (❗最後は相違を強調する)
● 色とりどりのバラ roses of *various colors*; roses *in different* [*a variety of*] *colors*.

とりなおす 取り直す ● 気を取り直す cheer up; 《話》buck up. ● 相撲を取り直す wrestle a second bout.

とりなし 執り成し (仲裁・調停) mediation 《*between, in*》; intercession 《*with*》.

とりなす 執り成す ● 2 国間をとりなす(=調停する) 《やや書》 *mediate* /míːdièit/ *between the two countries*. ● 彼は社長に私のことを上手にとりなしてくれた 《やや書》 He *interceded* /ìntərsíːdid/ *with the president for me* [*on my behalf*].

とりにいく 取りに行く go to [and] get 《a book》 (❗ and を用いる方が口語的); (取って戻ってくる) fetch. ● ハイデンは妹のためにコートを走って取りに行った Hayden ran over to *fetch* a coat for his sister.

とりにがす 取り逃がす (つかまえそこなう) fail to catch; (機会などを逃す) miss 《a chance》. (⇨逃[が]す) ● 犯人を取り逃がす *fail to catch* [*arrest*] *a criminal*; *let* a *criminal slip away*.

とりにく 鳥肉 (鶏の肉) chicken; fowl; (家禽(きん)の肉) poultry. (❗具体的には turkey (七面鳥の肉)などで表す)

トリニダード・トバゴ 〚国名〛 Trinidad and Tobago /trinídæd-(ə)n-təbéigou/; (公式名) the Republic of Trinidad and Tobago. (首都 Port-of-Spain)

トリノ 〚イタリアの都市〛 Turin /t(j)úərin/.

とりのいち 酉の市 the festival of the rooster; (説明的に) the fairs held in November at Shinto shrines.

とりのける 取り除ける remove. (⇨取り除く)

とりのこす 取り残す leave*... (behind). ● ひとり取り残される be *left* (all) *alone*. ● 時代の進歩に取り残される *fall* [be *left*] *behind the times*.

*****とりのぞく 取り除く** remove, take*... away (❗後の方が口語的); (取り除いてきれいにする) clear ... (away); (いやなものを除く, 脱する) get* rid of .... ● 道路から雪を取り除く *remove* snow *from the road*; *clear* snow *from the road*; *clear the road of* snow. ● 彼の苦痛を取り除く *remove* [*get rid of, relieve*] *his pain*. ● いかなる聖人といえども性欲を取り除くことはできないと思う I don't think any saint can *get rid of* [*shake off, free*] *their mind of* sexual desire.

とりはからい 取り計らい (手はず) (an) arrangement; (裁量) 《やや書》 discretion. (⇨取り計らう) ▶ 彼女の取り計らいで万事うまく運んだ Everything went well *through* her *arrangement* [《やりくりで》 by her *management*].

とりはからう 取り計らう 〚処理する〛 deal* with ...; 〚手はずを整える〛 arrange; 〚配慮する〛 see* 《(to it) that 節》 (❗ to it はしばしば省略される). ▶ その件は適当に取り計らってください Please *deal with* [*settle*] the matter as you think fit. ▶ 旅行社が我々のオーストラリア旅行のすべてを取り計らってくれた The travel agent *arranged* everything *for* our trip to Australia. ▶ そんなことが二度と起こらないように取り計らってください *See to it that* this never happens [will never happen] again. (❗前の方が本来の言い方で普通)

とりはぐれる 取りはぐれる (貸した金を) fail to get back the money 《I lent him》.

とりはこぶ 取り運ぶ make things go on smoothly. ▶ 株主総会は混乱もなく取り運ばれた The general meeting of stockholders [《英》 shareholders] *went on* [*was carried on*] *without a hitch*. (❗ without a hitch は「障害・遅延もなく」の意)

とりばし 取り箸 《a pair of》 serving chopsticks.

とりはずし 取り外し ● 取り外しのできるフード *a detachable* [*a removable*] hood. (⇨取り外す) ▶ この棚は取り外しができます This shelf *is removable* [*movable*] (↔fixed)./This shelf *can be removed*.

とりはずす 取り外す 〚取り去る〛 remove, take*... away [off] (❗後の方が口語的); (設備などを) 《書》 dismantle. ● びんのふたを取り外す *take* the bottle cap *off*. ● その古い家から屋根と壁を取り外す *dismantle* the old house *of* its roofs and walls. ● テントを取り外す *lift* a tent. ▶ この 2 部屋を仕切っている障子を取り外すと広いワンルームになります When you *take away* [*remove*] the sliding doors dividing these two rooms, you can get one spacious room.

とりはだ 鳥肌 góoseflèsh, góose pìmples [bùmps].
● 鳥肌が立つ ▶ その蛇を見たとき体中に鳥肌が立った I got *gooseflesh* [I felt *gooseflesh* break out] all over when I saw the snake. (❗体の部分を指定する場合は *on* 《one's arms》)/《話》 I've got 《米》 [gone 《英》] all goosey when I saw the snake.

とりはらう 取り払う (取り除く) remove, take*... away (⇨取り除く); (取り壊す) pull ... down, 《やや書》 demolish. ▶ その古い建物は取り払われてその跡にオフィスビルが建つことになっている The old building is going to *be pulled down* [*be demolished*] to make way [space] for an office building.

トリハロメタン 〚化学〛 trihálométhane.

とりひき 取り引き ❶ 〚商行為〛 (売買) a deal, 《書》 a transaction; (商売) business; (取り引き関係) dealings; (貿易) trade; (売買契約) a bargain; (不正売買) traffic.

① 【~取り引き】 ● インサイダー取り引き insider *trading*. ● 現金[信用]取り引き cash [credit] *transactions*. ● 国内取り引き domestic [home] *trade*. ● スワップ取り引き swap *transactions*. ● 先物取り引き forward [futures] *transactions*. ● 麻薬取り引き drug *traffic*; the *traffic* in drugs. ● カードを盗まれましたので, このカードのいっさいの取り引き要件を停止してください My credit card was just stolen. Please stop all *transactions* on this card.

② 【取り引き~】 ● 取り引き契約を結ぶ close a *deal*. ▶ その店と取り引き関係がある We have *dealings* [*business relations*, *trade connections*] *with* the store.

③ 【取り引きが】 ▶ その会社との取り引きがまとまった We have made [struck] *a bargain with* the firm. ▶ その銀行とは取り引きがあります(=口座を持っている) I have an *account* with the bank.

④ 【取り引きを】 ● 取り引きをする (取り引き関係がある) deal [get a deal] 《with+人・会社》 (⇨②); trade 《with+人・国》; (契約を交わす) make 《英》 do) a deal 《with+人・会社》. ● 取り引きを始める [停止する] enter into [break off] *business relations* [*connections*] 《with》. ● あの会社と穀物の取り引きをしている We do *business* [We *deal*] *with* that company *in* grains.

⑤ 【取り引きで】 ▶ 彼はその取り引きでかなりの利益をあげた He made a large profit *on the deal*.

❷ (駆け引き) a deal. ▶ その法案をめぐって自民党は民主党と取り引きしようとしている The Liberal Democrats are trying to *make* [《英》 *do*] *a deal* with the Democratic Party over the bill.

● 取引価格 the market price. ● 取引銀行 one's bank; (主要取引銀行) one's (main) bank. ● 取引先 (顧客) a customer; (商売の関係者) a business

connection. ●取引所 (証券や商品の) an exchange. ●証券[商品]取引所 a stock [a commodity] exchange. ●取引条件 the terms of business [trade]. ●取引高 a turnover.

トリプシン 〖生化学〗trypsin.

とりふだ 取り札 (説明的に) a card to be picked up in a game of *karuta*.

トリプル triple.
● トリプルアクセル 〖フィギュアスケート〗a triple axel. ● トリプル A 〖株式〗triple-A [AAA] rating; 〖野球〗Triple A; Class AAA. ● トリプル A の企業 a *triple*-A rated company. ● トリプルクラウン 〖三冠王〗the Triple Crown. ● トリプルプレー 〖野球〗《pull [make]》a triple play. ●単独トリプルプレー an unassisted *triple play*. 〖参考〗1人の野手が捕殺なしで単独で行う珍しいプレー. ● トリプル安 〖株価・円相場・債券価格が同時に安い状態〗a *triple* decline; (説明的に) simultaneous price down of three financial assets.

ドリブル 图 a dribble. ● ドリブルでディフェンダーを抜く *dribble* past a defender. ▶オーウェン, ドリブルで3人抜き！ Owen *dribbled* past three players!
── ドリブルする 動 dribble.

とりぶん 取り分 (利益などの) one's share [〈話〉cut] 《*in [of]* the profits》; (歳入などの割り当て) a portion.

トリポリ 〖リビアの首都〗Tripoli /trípəli/.

トリマー 〖ペット美容師〗a (pet) trimmer. (❗️今は pet を省略するのが普通)

とりまき 取り巻き a hanger-on 《hangers-on》; 〖政治家・やくざなどの子分〗a henchman 《-men》(以上2語は軽蔑的); 〖信奉者〗a follower.

とりまぎれる 取り紛れる ▶忙しさに取り紛れて(=あまりに忙しかったので)彼女の返事を忘れていた I was *so busy that* I forgot to answer her letter.

*****とりまく** 取り巻く (周りを囲む) surround 《⇨囲む》; (包囲する) besiege; (周りに群がる) cluster [gather] around ... ▶群衆はバスの事故現場を取り巻いた The crowd *surrounded* [*clustered around, gathered around*] the scene of the bus accident. ▶彼を取り巻く状況はすべて彼に不利であった All of the circumstances *surrounding* him were unfavorable (to him).

とりまぜる 取り混ぜる 〖混ぜ合わせる〗mix ... together; 〖各種取りそろえる〗assort. ●オレンジを大小取り混ぜて売る sell large and small oranges 《*all*》 *mixed together*; (いろいろの大きさの) sell oranges *of various sizes*. ●いろいろ取り混ぜたキャンディーassorted candy. ●100円玉、10円玉取り混ぜて300円 three hundred yen *in* 100-yen and 10-yen coins. (❗️in は「...の形で」の意)

とりまとめる 取り纏める 《⇨纏(2)める》▶私たちの辞表を取りまとめる collect [gather] our resignations.

とりみだす 取り乱す 〖気が動転する〗be upset 《*about, by*》; 〈話〉go* (all) to pieces; 〖平静を失う〗break* down, 〈書〉lose* one's composure [〖自制心を〗self-control]. ●事故のことで[妻の突然の死を聞いて]取り乱す be *upset about* the accident [*by* the news of one's wife's sudden death]. ▶取り乱すことなく(=冷静に)ふるまう behave *with composure* [*calmly*].

トリミング 〖写真〗trimming.
── トリミングする 動 trim 《a picture》away [off].

とりむすぶ 取り結ぶ ❶ 〖約束を〗●条約を取り結ぶ conclude a treaty. ●正式の契約を取り結ぶ *make* a formal contract. 《⇨結ぶ, 締結》
❷ 〖機嫌を〗●機嫌を取り結ぶ(=取る)(...の気に入るようにする) humor; please; 《...にへつらう》 curry favor with .... 《⇨機嫌 ❶》
❸ 〖間を持つ〗▶若い人の間を取り結ぶ help young people *to* get engaged [married].

とりめ 鳥目 night blindness.

とりもち 取り持ち 〖仲介役〗a go-between; an intermediary; 〖尽力〗〈書〉good offices. ▶大塚君の取り持ちで A 社とのビジネス関係ができた Thanks to Mr. Otsuka's *good offices*, I could establish business relationship with A Company.

とりもち 鳥もち birdlime.

とりもつ 取り持つ (仲を) act as a mediator [a go-between]; (客を) entertain.

とりもどす 取り戻す regain; (取り返す) get* ... back; (回復する) recover; (元に戻す) restore. ●意識を取り戻す *recover* [*regain*] one's consciousness (❗️regain の方が書き言葉的); còme tó. ●社会の秩序を取り戻す *restore* public order. ●勉強の遅れ[睡眠不足]を取り戻す *catch up on* one's study [one's sleep]. ●彼女は彼に貸した金を取り戻した She *got back* [*recovered*] the money she had lent him. (❗️前の方が口語的) ▶彼は仕事のピッチをあげて遅れを取り戻した(=むだに過ごした時間を埋め合わせた) He *made up for* lost time by working at a faster pace.

とりもなおさず 取りも直さず ●彼の釈放は取りも直さず民主主義の勝利である(=を意味する) His release means [〖外ならない〗*is nothing but*] the victory of democracy.

とりもの 捕り物 (逮捕連行) an arrest; (身柄の拘束) a capture.
●捕物帳 a detective story (in the Edo period).

とりやめ 取り止め cancellation. 《⇨中止》

とりやめる 取り止める 《⇨止(*)める》●会議を取り止める cancel [〈話〉*call off*] the meeting.

トリュフ [<フランス語] 〖キノコの一種、チョコレート〗a truffle /trʌ́fl/.

とりょう 塗料 paint. (❗️paints は「絵の具」の意)《⇨ペンキ》●塗料を塗る paint 《the fence》.
●塗料店 a paint store.

どりょう 度量 broad-mindedness. ●度量の大きい[広い] broad-minded 《↔narrow-minded》.

どりょうこう 度量衡 weights and measures.
●度量衡器 méasuring instruments.

どりょく 努力 图 (an) effort (❗️しばしば複数形で); 〖頑張り〗hard work; 〖骨折り〗pains; 〖大きな努力〗〈やや書〉(an) endeavor. ●努力の賜物 the result [fruit(s)] of one's *efforts*. ●努力を惜しまない spare no *effort* [〈書〉*pains*] 《*to do*》●それをするには多くの時間と努力を要するだろう It will take a lot of time and *effort* to do it. ▶彼はそれを自分自身の努力でやった He did it *by* [*through*] his own *efforts*. ▶私たちは彼を助けようとあらゆる努力をした We made every (possible) *effort* to help him. ▶彼を更正させようとする我々の努力はうまくいかなかった Our *efforts* to reform [*at* reform*ing*] him were unsuccessful.

── 努力する 動 make* an effort 《*to do*》(❗️try より堅い言い方); (懸命に) strive* 《*for; to do*》; 〖やってみる〗try 《*to do*》, 〖一生懸命に〗work hard 《*to do*》; 〖骨を折る〗take* pains 《*to do*》, 〈やや書〉endeavor 《*to do*》. ▶私は月末までにその仕事を終えようと非常に努力した I *made* great *efforts* [*strove*] to finish the work by the end of the month. ●締め切りに間に合うよう努力します I'll *try to* [〈話〉*try and*] meet the deadline./(最善を尽くす) I'll do [*try*] *my best* to meet the deadline. (❗️しばしば「期待にそえないかもしれないが」の意を暗示)
●努力家 a hard worker.

とりよせる 取り寄せる (注文する) order. ● 見本を取り寄せる send for a sample. ▶もしその本の在庫がないなら東京から取り寄せます If the book is not in stock, we can *order* it from Tokyo.

ドリル ❶ [きり] a drill. ● ドリルで板に穴をあける *drill* (a hole *in*) a board.
❷ [練習] (give) a drill 《*in* typing》.

とりわけ [[特に]] especially; [[格別に]] particularly, in particular; [[何にもまして]] above all, most of all; [[その中でも特に]] among other things. (⇨特に,殊に) ▶私はハイキングに行くのが好きだ,とりわけ秋がよい I like going hiking, *especially* [*particularly*] in the fall. ▶彼は強く, 勇敢で, とりわけ正直だ He is strong, brave and, *above all*, honest. ▶あのレストランの天ぷらがとりわけ好きです I like the *tempura* at that restaurant *best of all*. ▶日当たりのいい南斜面はとりわけ果樹の栽培に適していた The sunny south slope was suitable for growing fruit trees *among other things*.

とりわける 取り分ける ❶ [選別する] séparàte. ● 不良品を取り分ける *separate* defective products *from* good ones.
❷ [分けて取る] (食事で) serve; (盛り分ける) dish ... out; (分配する) deal*... out. ▶サラダを取り分けるのを手伝ってください Please help me *serve* [*dish out*, *deal out*] the salad.

ドリンク (ドリンク剤) a nóurishing drink; a health drink; (飲み物) something to drink.

とる 取る, 捕る, 採る, 執る INDEX

❶ 手で取る・つかむ ❷ 奪う
❸ 取り除く ❹ 得る
❺ 買う ❻ 採取する
❼ 採用する ❽ 記録をとる
❾ 摂取する ❿ 解する
⓫ 要する ⓬ 要求する
⓭ 取っておく ⓮ 執り行う

WORD CHOICE 取る
take 物などを手にすること. ● テーブルの上のグラスを取る *take* a glass on the table.
get 物・地位・順位・賞などを取ること. ● 数学のテストで満点を取る *get* the full mark in the math test.
have 食事・休暇・睡眠などを取ること. ● 昼食を取る *have* lunch.

❶ [手で取る・つかむ] take*; (取ってくる) get*; (行って取ってくる) go* to get, (話) go and get, (《主に英》) fetch (⇨取って来る); (手を伸ばして) reach; (手に取って渡す) hand; (取って人に回す) pass. ● 彼女の手を取る (=つかむ) *take* [(突然力を入れて) *seize*, (乱暴に) *grab*] her *by* the hand; *take* [*seize*, *grab*] her hand. ● 棚から [戸棚から] コップを取る *take* a glass *from* the shelf [*out of* the cupboard]. ● ボールを捕る *catch* [*take*] a ball. ● フライを捕る *catch* a fly; make a catch of a fly. ● ゴロを捕る *take* a grounder. ● 片手で [両手で] ボールを取る (=受けとめる) *catch* the ball *in* one hand [*with* both hands]. ▶彼は受話器を手に取った He *took* the receiver (in his hand)./(取り上げた) He *took* [*picked*] *up* the receiver. ▶彼は帽子を取りに帰った He went back *for* [*to get*] his hat. ● 前置詞の for でも表せることに注意) ▶私が取ります (電話・ベルなどに応答するとき) I'll *answer* [*get*, ×*take*] it. (❗この場合 to get を用いて ×I'm going to answer [get] it. とはいわない) ▶棚の花びんを取ってください Can you *hand* me the vase on the shelf [the vase on the shelf *to*

me]?/Can you *reach* me the vase on the shelf [the vase on the shelf *for* me]? (❗この意では hand, reach の代わりに take は用いられないことに注意)/(取ろうと手を伸ばす) Can you *reach* (*out*) *for* the vase on the shelf?/Can you *get* the vase *down* from the shelf for me? ▶ボールを投げろ, ぼくが取る (=捕らえる) から Throw the ball, and I'll *catch* it.

会話「サラダをテーブルの真ん中に置きます. お取りしましょうか」「いえ, いいです. 自分で取りますから」 "I'll put the salad in the middle of the table. Do you want me to [《英》 Shall I] *serve* you?" "No, that's all right. We can *help ourselves* (*to* it)."
会話「チケットはいつ取りに行けばよろしいですか」「水曜日にお立ち寄りください」 "When can I *pick up* the tickets?" "Come by on Wednesday."
会話「ご注文の本が入りました」「分かりました. 取りに寄ります」"Your book's arrived, sir." "Right. I'll call (in) *for* it."
会話 (食卓で)「塩を取って (=回して) くださいませんか」「はいはい, どうぞ」「ありがとう」 "Could you *pass* [×*take*] (me) the salt, please?" "Of course, ＼here you ／are [it ／s]." "Thanks."

❷ [奪う] take*... (away) 《*from*》; (こっそり盗む) steal*; (力ずくで奪う) rob (-bb-), (《やや書》) deprive (A *of* B). ● 子供からおもちゃを取る *take* a toy (*away*) *from* a child. (❗away を用いると持ち去る感じが出る) ● 老女から金を取る *steal money from* an older woman; *rob* an older woman *of* her money; (だまし取る) *cheat* an older woman *out of* her money.

❸ [取り除く] (身につけているものなどを取り去る) take*... off; (取り出す) take ... out; (除去する) remove; (いやなものを取る, 脱ぐで) get* rid of ...; (省く) leave*... out, omit (-tt-) (❗前の方が口語的に); (削除する) (《やや書》) delete. ● じゅうたんのしみを取る *take* a stain *out of* the carpet; *remove* a stain *from* the carpet. (❗後の方が堅い言い方) ● 芝生の雑草を取る (=引抜く) *pull* some weeds *out of* the lawn. ● 寝て疲れを取る *sleep away* one's fatigue. ▶帽子を取りなさい *Take off* your hat./*Take* your hat *off*. (❗前の方は (例えば部屋に入ったりしたときに) 単に帽子を取られっているにすぎないが, 後の方は部屋の中でもまだ帽子をかぶっている男に対して「何だその帽子は」といった感じである) ▶この語は取ってしまった方がよい This word should *be left out* [*be omitted, be deleted*, (線を引いて消される) *be crossed out*]. ▶彼は熱がとれた His fever *is gone*./He *is rid of* the fever.

❹ [得る] (所有するようになる) get*, (努力・計画して) (《やや書》) obtain; [賞などを獲得する] take*, (勝ち取る) win*; [受け取る] take; (差し出されて) receive (❗take より堅い語); (喜んで) accept. ● 学位を取る *get* [*obtain*] a degree. (❗この場合通例 take は使わない) ● 彼らからわいろを取る *take* [*receive, accept*] a bribe *from* them. ● 1 等賞を取る *win* [*take*] (the) first prize. ● 運転免許を取る *get* [×*take*] a driver's license. ● 1 日 [1 か月] 休暇を取る *take* a day *off* [*a month's vacation*]. ▶彼はその英語のテストで満点を取った He *got* [*received, won, scored*, ×*took*] full marks in the English test. ▶彼は 40 万円の月給を取っている He *gets* [*receives, takes, draws*] a monthly salary of 400,000 yen.

会話「あの仕事取れたよ」「それはよくやった」 "I've *got* the job." "Well done!"
会話「休暇はどのくらい取れるの」「3 週間だと思うよ」 "How much vacation will you *get*?" "Three

weeks, I hope."
❺ [買う] buy*, get* (❗ get の方が意味が広く口語的); [注文する] order (⇨取り寄せる); [定期的に購読する] take*, get, subscribe *to*... (❗ 前の2語の方が口語的). take. ▶私はあの店からしょう油をとっている(=買う) I buy [get] soy sauce *from that store*./(配達してもらう) I have soy sauce *delivered from* that store.
会話「何新聞をとっていますか」「朝日新聞です」"What newspaper do you take [get, subscribe *to*]?" "I take [get, subscribe *to*] the Asahi."
❻ [採取する] (摘む) pick, (集める) (主に書) gather; (エキスなどを抽出する) (やや書) extract 《*from*》; [捕獲する] catch*; (抵抗・困難を克服して) capture.
● 花を取る pick [gather] flowers. ● ブドウから汁を採る squeeze [extract] juice *from* grapes. ● 川へ魚を捕りに[山へキノコを取りに]行く go fishing in the river [mushroom-gathering on the hill]. (❗ ×...*to* the river [hill] は不可) ▶きのう何匹魚を捕りましたか How many fish did you catch yesterday? (✔ ×fishes は不可)
❼ [採用する] (人・手段・態度などを) take*; (方針などを) adopt; (態度を) (やや書) assume; [選ぶ] choose*; (選んでとる) take; (より好む) prefer (-rr-) 《*to*》. ● 新しい方法を採る take [adopt] a new method. ● 彼女に対して誠実な態度をとる take [assume] a sincere attitude toward her. ● 新卒を5人採る take [正式に雇う] employ, 《米》 hire; (一時的に雇う) 《英》 hire] five new graduates. ▶仕事か子供を取るか選択を迫られる女性が多い Many women have to choose between career and family. (❗ career は「生涯の職業」の意) ▶私は今年六つの科目[フランス語]を取っている(=履修している) I'm taking six courses [French] this year. ▶この行は聖書から取られている(=引用されている) This line is taken [is quoted] *from* the Bible. ▶彼はおじいさんの名をとってジョンと名づけられた He was named John *after* [《米》*for*] his grandfather.
会話「二つ取っていいですか」「好きなだけお取りなさい」"May I take two?" "*Take* as many as you like."
❽ [記録をとる] (書き留める) write* [put*, take*]... down, record; (計る, 測る) take. ● 彼の脈をとる take [feel] his pulse. ▶私は教授の話をノートに取った I wrote [put, took] down what the professor said (in my notebook)./(書) I made [took] a note of what the professor said.
❾ [摂取する] (食べる) have*, eat* (❗ 前の方が口語的); (薬・飲食物を体内に取り入れる) take*. ● 朝食をとる have [eat, 《古・まれ》 take] breakfast. ● 睡眠を十分とる have [get] enough sleep.
❿ [解する] (受け取る) take*; (解釈する) interpret; (理解する) understand*; (なんとか) 《通例疑問文・否定文で》 make*... out. ● 彼の冗談をまじめにtake his joke seriously; (みなす) regard his joke *as* serious. ▶こっちが何を言ってもあいつは悪い方にとる Every time I say something to him, he takes it badly [wrong, in the wrong way]. (❗ 逆に「よい方にとる」は take it well [in good part]) ▶この文章の意味がとれますか Can you understand [make out] what this sentence means? ▶ぼくが君のことを怒っているとはとらないで(=思わないで)ほしい I do hope you don't *think* I'm angry with you.
⓫ [要する] (費やす) spend*; (場所・時間を) take*... up; (占める) occupy; (割く) spare. ▶彼は夕食に多くの時間を取る He spends a lot of time for dinner [(*in*) hav*ing* dinner]. (❗ in は通例省略する) ▶このテーブルは場所を取り過ぎる This table takes (*up*) [*occupies*] too much space. (❗ 前の方が口語的) ▶その仕事に時間の大半を取られている Most of my time *is taken up* with [by] the work. ▶忙しくて読書する時間が取れない I am too busy to spare time for reading.
⓬ [要求する] (料金を) charge; (費用を要す) cost*; (罰金を科する) fine. ● スピード違反で10ドルの罰金を取られる be fined ten dollars *for* speeding. ▶この店では配達料を(500円)取られる This store charges (us) (five hundred yen) *for* delivery. ▶この帽子に1万円取られた This hat cost me ten thousand yen./I paid [gave] ten thousand yen *for* this hat.
⓭ [取っておく] (蓄える) save; (ある目的のためにのけておく) put* [set*]... aside; (ずっと持っている) keep*; (目的のために) reserve; (予約する) reserve, 《主に英》 book; (努力して確保する) (書) secure; (余裕をみておく) allow. (⇨取って置く) ● ホテルに部屋を取る re*serve* [book] a room at a hotel; make 《×take》 *a reservation for* a room at a hotel. (⇨予約) ▶雨の日用にお金に少し取ってある I have a little money put [set] aside *for* [《古》against] a rainy day. ▶私は今までの日記を全部取ってある I keep all my diaries.
⓮ [執り行う] do*, perform (❗ 後の方が堅い語); (労を) take*. ● 事務を執る do office work. ● 職務を執る perform duties. ● 仲介の労を取る take the trouble to mediate; act as a mediator. ▶彼女はこの会社で事務を執っている She is a secretary of this company. (✔ She is an office worker....のような漠然とした言い方はあまりしない)

● 捕らぬたぬきの皮用 'Catch the raccoon dog before you sell his skin.' 《ことわざ》(かえらないうちからひなの数を数えるな) Don't count your chickens before they're hatched.
● 取るに足りない (重要でない) unimportant; (つまらない, 意味のない) insignificant; (ささいな) minor, small; (無視できる) negligible; (どうでもいい, ごくわずかな) trivial, (書) trifling. ● 取るに足りないささいなこと *insignificant* details. ● 取るに足りない問題[お金] a *trivial* matter [sum of money]. ▶これは取るに足りない問題だ This is just a *minor* [a *small*] problem. ▶確かに損害は受けたが取るに足りない程度だ The damage was done, but it is *negligible*.
● 取るものも取りあえず ▶取るものも取りあえず(=大急ぎで)病院に駆けつけた I hastened to the hospital *without a moment's delay*.

とる 撮る [写真を] take*; photograph; (スナップ写真を) take a snapshot 《*of*》, 《話》 snap (-pp-); [映画を] film, shoot*. (⇨録音) ▶その風景の写真を何枚も撮る take a lot of pictures of the landscape. ▶写真を撮ってもらった I had my picture *taken*.

とる 録る record. (⇨録音)

ドル a dollar (記号) (参考) アメリカ・カナダ・オーストラリアなどの国の貨幣単位. 1ドル=100セント(cent); [ドル値] the dollar. ● ドルが上昇[下落, 反発]すると予想する expect the *dollar* to appreciate [depreciate, rally]. ● 5[10]ドル紙幣 a five-[ten-]*dollar* bill. (❗ (1) 《話》では単に a five, a ten ともいう. (2) a $5 [$10] bill とも書く) ▶この本は5ドル50セントで This book costs five *dollars* and fifty. $5.50 とも書く. また《話》では通例 five fifty のようにいう) ▶1ドルは117円です One *dollar* has a present value of 117 yen. ▶5ドル札を5枚, 5ドル札を10枚ください (両替するとき) Five tens, ten fives, please. ▶円高ドル安が続いている The yen has continued to strengthen against *the dollar*.
● ドル売り dollar-selling. ● ドル化 dollarization

トルエン 〖化学〗 toluene /tάljuːn/.

トルク 〖回転モーメント〗 torque /tɔ́ːrk/.
- トルクコンバーター(自動車の) a torque converter.
- トルクモーター a torque motor.

トルクメニスタン 〖国名〗 Turkmenistan /tɜːrkmenəstǽn/. (公式名も同じ) (首都 Ashkhabad) • トルクメン人 a Turkmen. • トルクメン語 Turkmen. • トルクメン(人)(語)の Turkmen.

トルコ 〖国名〗 Turkey /tɜ́ːrki/; (公式名) the Republic of Turkey. (首都 Ankara) • トルコ人 a Turk, (総称) the Turkish. • トルコ語 Turkish. • トルコ(人)(語)の Turkish.
- トルコ石 turquoise /tɜ́ːrkɔɪz/. (❗個々の宝石は [C])
(参考) 12 月の誕生石)

トルコこうしんきょく 『トルコ行進曲』 *Turkish March*.
(参考) モーツァルトの行進曲)

トルストイ 〖ロシアの小説家〗 Tólstoy (Leo Nikolayevich ~).

トルソー 〖胴体だけの彫像〗 a torso.

トルネード a tornado /tɔːrnéɪdoʊ/ (複 ~es).

トルメン 〖巨石墳墓の一種〗〖考古学〗 a dolmen.

ドルばこ ドル箱 〖観光客がこの町のドル箱である Tourism is a *moneymaker* [*a gold mine*] *for* the city.

ドルフィン a dolphin.
- ドルフィンキック 〖水泳〗 a dolphin kick.

ドルマリン (a) tourmaline. (参考) 10 月の誕生石)

‡**どれ** which. • どれでも (⇨どのでも) ▶どれが君[君の車]ですか *Which* is yours [your car]? ▶きのうどれ[服はどれ]を着たの *Which* (one) [*Which* dress] did you wear yesterday? ▶どれを買えばよいか決められない I can't decide *which* to buy [*which* I should buy]. (❗後の方が口語的)

[会話]「母はそのグリーンの壁紙が好きなの」「あなたはどれが好みなの」"Mother likes the green wallpaper." "*Which one* do you prefer?"

[会話]「どれがどれやら」「その青いのがあなたのよ」"*Which* is *which*?" "The blue one's yours."

[会話]「その缶を開けてください」「どれ(=何)で」"Open that can, please." "*What* ＼with?" (❗With what? ともいうが (参考) では この語順が普通)

トレアドールパンツ 〖闘牛士風の女性用ズボン〗 toreador pants.

どれい 土鈴 an earthenware bell.

どれい 奴隷 a slave; (身分) slavery. • 奴隷のように働く work like a *slave*. ▶リンカーンは奴隷を解放した Lincoln freed [(やや書) emancipated] the *slaves*.
- 奴隷解放 the freedom [(やや書) emancipation] of slaves. • 奴隷制度廃止 the abolition of slavery. • 廃止論者 an abolitionist)

トレー a tray.

トレーサビリティー 〖履歴管理〗 traceability.

トレーシングペーパー tracing paper.

トレード • トレードする 〖一塁手をタイガースにトレードし、交換にその投手を採る *trade* the first baseman *for* the Tigers *in exchange for* the pitcher. ▶その投手はトレードに出されている The pitcher is on the (trading) block [up for trade].
- トレードオフ 〖二律背反の関係〗 a trade-off 《between》. • トレードマーク 〖商標, (人・物の特徴)〗 a trademark. • トレードマネー (プロ野球で) the money paid in trading a player; (主にプロサッカーで) a transfer fee; (和製語) trade money.

トレーナー 〖上下そろいの運動着〗 a sweat suit, (話) exercise sweats; (和製語) a trainer; (体操者) a gym suit; (指導者の指導法に関する) a trainer; (馬・犬などの調教師, 運動選手の応急医療士などにも用いる).

トレーニング (a) training. (⇨練習, 訓練)
- トレーニングウェア a sweat suit, a tracksuit; (和製語) training wear. • トレーニングパンツ sweatpants. (❗今では日本でもスエットパンツが普通), (米) tracksuit bottoms. (❗上着 (sweatshirt, tracksuit top) と合わせて a sweat suit, a tracksuit となる). training pants はおしめがとれる時期の幼児用のパンツ)

トレーラー a trailer.
- トレーラーハウス (米) a (hóuse) tràiler; (英) a (mótor) càravan. (❗その駐車指定区域は (米) a trailer park [camp], (英) a caravan site という)

どれくらい どれ位 how many [much, long, old]. (⇨どのくらい) ▶あとどれぐらいで終わりますか *How soon* [*close*] are you finishing the work? (❗特に終わる時期に関心がある場合にこのような言い方を用いる)

ドレス a dress. (⇨洋服)
- ドレスメーカー (人) a dressmaker; (店) a dressmaker's (shop).

ドレスアップ ── ドレスアップする 動 dress [deck] (oneself) up 《for》. ▶彼女はパーティーに行くのを目一杯ドレスアップしている She is all *dressed up* [*dressed up* to the nines] *for* the party.

ドレスデン 〖ドイツの都市〗 Dresden /drézdən/.

とれだか 取れ高 〖捕獲高〗 a catch, a take; 〖収穫高〗 a crop. (⇨収穫 ❶)

どれだけ 〖ガソリンはあとどれだけあるの *How much* gas is there left? (⇨どのくらい) ▶どれだけ金がかかっても, おれは天に届く塔をつくるのだ I will build a tower that reaches the sky, *however* [*no matter how*] much it costs. (⇨どんなに)

とれたて 取れたて (⇨取り立ての) • 取れたての果物 (a) fruit *fresh from* the orchard. • 取れたての魚 a fish *fresh from* the sea.

トレッキング 名 〖徒歩旅行〗 a trek.
── **トレッキングする** 動 trek, go trekking 《in, through》.
- トレッキングシューズ (a pair of) trekking shoes.

ドレッサー 〖化粧台〗 a dresser, a dressing table.

ドレッシー ── ドレッシーな 形 elegant, (話) dressy.

ドレッシング (a) dressing. • ドレッシングをかける put *dressing* 《on the salad》.

どれでも 〖どんな…でも〗 (三つ以上) any 〖肯定文で. /éni/ と強勢を置いて読む〗; 〖…はどれも〗 whichever. ▶どれでも好きなおもちゃを買ってよろしい You can buy *any* [*whichever*] toy(s) you like. (❗(1) toy では「一つ」, toys では「いくつでも」の意. (2) toy(s) が明らかな場合は省略して …*any* [*whichever*] you like. といえる)

どれどれ well. ▶どれどれ, ちょっと見せてごらん *Well*, let me have a look at it.

トレパン 〖「トレーニングパンツ」の略〗 sweatpants. (⇨トレーニング)

どれひとつ どれ一つ ▶バーゲン品にはどれ一つとしていいものがない *None* of the bargain goods are [is] worth buying. (❗(話) では複数形で受けることが多い)

どれほど どれ程 〖どのくらい〗 how; 〖どんなに…でも〗 however. (⇨どのくらい, どんなに) ▶彼女がどれほど君を愛しているか君は分かっていない You don't know *how* much she loves you.

ドレミファ [<イタリア語] (音階) a (musical) scale.

どれも [すべて] all; [どの一つも] every óne (!否定語より 1 語につらない); (否定文で) ány (!否定語より後に置く). ▶彼の作品はどれもすばらしい *All* (of) his works *are* [His works are *all*, *Every one* of his works is] wonderful. ▶彼の小説はどれも読みたくない I *don't* want to read *any* of his novels. (!…*any* of his ~ novels の音調では「どれでも読みたいわけではない」と部分否定になる) ▶これらの本はどれもおもしろくない *None* of these books *are* [《やや書》 is] interesting. (!✕*Any* of these books is *not* interesting. は不可)/*Not one* of these books is interesting. (!この方が強意的)

トレモロ 〖音楽〗a trémolo.
● トレモロアーム (エレキギターの) a tremolo arm.

トレリス 〖格子垣〗a trellis.

*__とれる__ **取れる, 撮れる** ❶ [得られる] (獲得される) be obtained [got]; (生産される) be produced; (捕えられる) be caught; (見いだされる) be found. ▶海草から沃素(ﾖｳｿ)が取れる Iodine *is obtained* from seaweed. ▶このあたりはジャガイモがたくさん取れる A lot of potatoes *are produced* [*are grown*] around here.

❷ [はずれる] (ボタン・柄などが取れる) come* off (…).
▶背広のボタンが取れた A button *has come off* [*fallen off*] my business suit. ▶ワイシャツのボタンが一つ取れている One of the buttons on my shirt *is off* [*is missing*].

❸ [除去される] be removed; (痛みなどが去る) go*; (しみなどが) come* off [out]. ▶このインクのしみは取れないと思う I don't think these ink stains will *come off* [*out*]. ▶その痛みはもう取れましたか Has the pain *gone* yet? ▶前夜の疲れがすかり取れた I *was* completely *recovered* [(さわやかな気分になった) *refreshed*] from the fatigue the night before.

❹ [解釈される] be interpreted [be taken] as. ▶彼の沈黙はいやだという意味に取れる His silence can *be interpreted* [*be taken*] *as* dislike.

とれる 撮れる ▶この写真はよく撮れている This picture *has come out* well./(人が主語) You *have come out* well in this picture./You *look* really [*very*] *good* in this picture.

トレンチ(コート) a trench coat.
トレンディ trendy; fashionable.
トレンド [傾向] trend. ● トレンド情報 trend information.

とろ 〖マグロなど魚のあぶら身〗fatty meat (of tuna).

とろ 吐露 = 吐露する 動 真情を吐露する (考えを正面きって述べる) speak one's mind; (ぶちまける) lay bare one's thoughts [heart]; give vent to one's inmost feelings.

*__どろ__ **泥** mud (!最も一般的な語); dirt (!泥だけでなくほこり (dust) など汚れ全般を指す); 〖土〗soil, earth. ▶泥のこびりついたタイヤ a *mud*-caked tire; a tire caked with (dry) *mud*. ▶彼の靴は泥だらけだった His shoes were covered with [in] *mud*./His shoes were (very) *muddy*. (⇨泥まみれ) ▶あの車が私[私のズボン]に泥をはねかけた The car splashed *mud* over me [my pants 《米》 [trousers 《英》]]. ▶象は泥に足をとられて動けなかった The elephant got stuck in the *mud*.
● 泥のように眠る sleep like a log [a top]; (熟睡する) sleep soundly [deeply].
● 泥をかぶる take the blame (for him).
● 泥を塗る ▶親の顔に泥を塗るようなことをしてはいけない You should not *disgrace* your parents.
● 泥を吐く (罪を自白する) confess [《やや話》 own up to] one's crime; 《話》 come clean.

● 泥足 muddy [dirty] feet. ● 泥足で座敷に上がる enter [come into, go into] the tatami-floored room with muddy feet. ● 泥水 muddy water.
● 泥よけ (車・自転車などの) a mudguard.

とろい [頭の鈍い] dull, slow; (愚かな) stupid; [勢いが弱い] low. (⇨とろ火)

トロイ Troy.
● トロイ戦争 the Trojan /tróudʒən/ War. ● トロイの木馬 the Tròjan hórse.

トロイカ [<ロシア語] a troika.

とろう 徒労 ▶私たちの努力は徒労に終わった (何にもならなかった) Our efforts *came to nothing*./(むだだった) Our efforts were *fruitless* [*futile, a waste*].

どろうみ 泥海 a muddy sea.

どろえのぐ 泥絵の具 color wash; 《英》 distemper.

ドロー ❶ [引き分け] a draw.
❷ [抽選によって決められた対戦カード] a draw.
● FA カップ 3 回戦のドロー the *draw* of the FA Cup third round.

トローチ 〖薬学〗a troche /tróuki/; (せき止め用ドロップ) a lozenge /lázindʒ/.

トロール 〖底引き網〗a trawl (net).
● トロール船 a trawler (!「トロール漁する人」の意にもなる); a trawl-boat.

どろくさい 泥臭い [洗練されていない] unrefined; (粗野な) crude. ▶泥臭いが誠実な男だ He's *unrefined* but honest [sincere]. (!sincere は言行一致であることをいう)

とろける 蕩ける ❶ [溶ける] melt. ▶チョコレートが口の中でとろけた The chocolate *melted* on the tongue [in the mouth].
❷ [うっとりする] (魅惑される) be charmed [《やや書》 enchanted] 《by, with》; (魂を奪われる) be fascinated 《by, with》. ▶青年は彼女のえも言われぬ美しさに身も心もとろける思いがした The young man *was* completely *fascinated by* her exquisite beauty.

どろじあい 泥仕合 ● 泥仕合(=醜い中傷合戦)をする [演じる] sling [throw, fling] mud at each other; engage in *mudslinging* [a *mudslinging contest*].

トロッコ a truck.

『**トロッコ**』 *The Truck*. (参考) 芥川龍之介の小説

どろっとした どろっとした液体 thick liquid.

ドロップ [菓子] a drop; [野球] a drop; a dropball.

ドロップアウト 名 [脱落者] a dropout.
— **ドロップアウトする 動** drop out (of).

ドロップキック 名 [ラグビー・アメフト] a drop-kick.
— **ドロップキックする 動** drop-kick.

とろとろ ● とろとろ眠る doze (off); have a doze. (⇨とうとう) ● 弱火でとろとろ煮る simmer (it) over a low flame [heat]. ● ふかひれをとろとろになるまで煮る stew shark's fins till they are *pulpy* [*very tender*]. ● 仕事をとろとろと(=しんどそうにのろのろと)する do one's job *sluggishly*. ▶道が渋滞してとろとろとした走りかたで The traffic jam on the road forced us to *crawl* by [(じわじわと進む) *edge* forward].

どろどろ (泥状の) muddy; (濃くて) thick; (パルプ状で) pulpy; (糊(のり)状で) starchy; (コロイド状で) colloidal.
● どろどろの道 a *muddy* road. ● どろどろのスープ *thick* soup. ● どろどろになったごはん *starchy* boiled rice.
● トマトをどろどろになるまで煮なさい Boil your tomatoes till they get *pulpy*.

どろなわ 泥縄 [「泥棒を見て縄をなう」の略] 《ことわざ》 It is too late to shut the stable door when the horse is stolen. (!馬が盗まれてから馬小屋の戸を閉めてももう遅いの意) ● 泥縄式で(=土壇場になって) 受験勉強をしたってむだですよ It is no use trying to cram for the entrance exam *at the last minute* [*moment*].

どろぬま 泥沼 a bog; (ぬかるみ) mud. ●泥沼にはまり身動きがとれなくなる be stuck [caught] in the *mud*; get bogged down in the *mud*. ●借金の泥沼 a quagmire of debts. ▶交渉は泥沼に陥った[泥沼化した] The negotiation *got bogged down* [*began to drag on*].

とろび とろ火 (very) low heat, a (very) low fire. (!) 電熱による場合が多くなった後の言い方は少なくなった) ●なべをとろ火にかける put the pan over *low heat*. ●とろ火で煮る (沸騰点ぎりぎりで) simmer 《soup》; (くつくつと) boil 《stew》 gently [slowly].

トロピカル tropical.
●トロピカルフルーツ tropical fruit(s).

トロフィー (win) a trophy.

*****どろぼう 泥棒** 【人】a thief (徂 thieves) (!最も一般的な語); a robber; a burglar; a housebreaker; (万引き) a shoplifter; 〖行為〗(a) theft; (a) robbery; (a) burglary.

> 使い分け **thief** 特に暴力を用いずこっそり持ち去る「こそ泥」「かっぱらい」をさす。
> **robber** 武器による脅しや暴力によって金品を強奪する「強盗」をさす。
> **burglar** 民家や会社の建物の玄関や窓の鍵を壊し無理に押し入ってものを盗む人。通例夜に忍び込む「夜盗」をさす。
> **housebreaker** burglar とほぼ同意だが, 特に昼間の「押し込み強盗」をさす。

●自動車泥棒 a car *thief*. ●火事場泥棒 a *thief* at a fire. ●泥棒をつかまえる catch [(逮捕する) arrest] a *thief*. ●泥棒を働く commit (a) *theft* [(a) *robbery*, (a) *burglary*]; (盗む) steal (it *from* him); (奪い取る) rob (*him of* it). (⇒盗む) ●泥棒! (逃げる泥棒に対して) Stop, *thief*!/(他の人に助けを求めて) Stop *thief*!/(待て！ 泥棒だ!) Stop, he's a *robber*! ▶泥棒にあいました (警察署で) I'd like to report a *theft*./I was just robbed [×*stolen*]. ▶昨夜私の家に泥棒が入った A *thief* [A *burglar*] broke into my house last night./My house was broken into [was robbed] last night.
●泥棒に追い銭 (ことわざ) That's throwing good money after bad.
●泥棒を捕らえて縄をなう (ことわざ) That's like locking the stable door after the horse has been stolen.

どろまみれ 泥まみれ ●泥まみれの長靴 *muddy* boots; boots *covered with mud*. ▶彼らは雨の日にラグビーをして全身泥まみれになった They *got muddy* all over (by) playing rugby on a rainy day.

とろみ ●とろみのある(=濃い)スープ thick (↔thin) soup. ●スープに小麦粉を加えてとろみをつける thicken soup *with* flour.

とろり 〖液体が〗thick; (クリーミーな) creamy; 〖眠そうな状態〗sleepy [drowsy /dráuzi/, heavy] (eyes). (⇒とろん) ●とろりと溶けるチーズ cheese that *melts easily*. ●とろりと甘い声で in a *melting* voice. ▶私は壁によりかかったまままとろりとしてしまった I *dozed off* a little with my back against the wall.

トロリーバス a trolley bus. ●トロリーバスで by *trolleybus*.

とろろ 薯蕷 grated yam.
●とろろ芋(り) a yam.

とろろこんぶ とろろ昆布 very thin tangle shavings. (!(1) 常に複数形で. (2) 通例 tangle は「糸などがもつれて始末におえない状態」をさす語として用いるので, この場合は説明が必要: tangle＝large and thick seaweed used as food in many ways)

とろん とろん (眠そうな) (目を開けていられない) drowsy /dráuzi/; (まぶたが付きそうな) heavy; (生気のない, 鈍い) dull. ▶あの子の目はいつもとろんしている The boy's eyes are always *dull*.

どろん 〖名〗 sudden disappearance.
── **どろんする** 〖動〗(姿を消す) disappear suddenly; (逃げ出す) run [get] away; (持ち逃げする) make off [away] (*with*). ▶集金した金を持ってどろんというのはどうかね How do you like my idea (that) we *make off* with the money we collect?

ドロンゲーム a drawn game, a draw. (⇒引き分け)

どろんこ 泥んこ ●泥んこ道 a *muddy* road. ▶昔は子供たちが道で泥んこ遊びをしたものだ The children used to *play with mud* in the street.

トロント 〖カナダの都市〗 Toronto /tərántou/.

トロンボーン 〖楽器〗 a trombone. ●トロンボーンを吹く play the trombone. ●トロンボーン奏者 a trombonist.

とわ 永久 ── **永久の** 〖形〗 eternal; everlasting. ▶あの時が彼との永久の別れになろうとは I never thought that was the last time I saw him.
●永久の眠りにつく go to one's eternal [last] sleep.

とわず 問わず ●男女を問わず *regardless* [(やや書) *irrespective*] *of* sex. ▶協会は金額の多少を問わず寄付を募った The association requested contributions, *large or small*. ▶晴雨を問わず私は行きます I'll go, *rain or shine* [×*shine or rain*]./I'll go, *whether* it rains *or not*. (⇒後の方が口語的) ●─と (接続助詞) ❸ 〖第2文例〗 ▶彼は行き先を問わず(＝どこへ行こうと)いつもカメラを持って行く He always carries a camera with him *no matter where* [*wherever*] he goes. (!前の方が口語的) ▶経験は問わず(＝不要)《広告》 No experience necessary.

どわすれ 度忘れ ── **度忘れする** 〖動〗 ▶彼の名前を度忘れしてしまった. でもすぐ思い出せると思う I *have forgotten* his name *for the moment*. I'll remember it soon. (⇒忘れる)/I *can't remember* [*think of*] his name *right now*. It'll come back in a moment.

トン a ton (⑧ ～s, ～). (船・船荷の) tonnage /tánidʒ/.
●5トン積みのトラック a five-*ton* [×- tons] truck. ●砂糖10トン ten *ton*(*s*) of sugar. ●総トン数 gross *tonnage*. ●5,000 総トンの船 a ship of 5,000 gross tons [5,000 tons *gross*]. ●その船のトン数は1万5,000トンだ The ship has a *tonnage* of 15,000.

どん bang; bump; thump; thud. (!いずれの語も名詞・動詞に使える.「どん」にかぎらず, いろいろの音を表す) (⇒どんと) ▶重い扉がどんと閉まった The heavy door *banged* shut. ▶彼女は扉をどんと閉めた She slammed the door *with a bang*. (⇒ばたん, がちゃん) ▶自動車どうしがどんと大きな音をたてて衝突した The cars crashed into each other *with a bang*. (!比較的軽い衝突音は bump で表す (⇒[次例])) ▶パーキングのとき隣の車にどんと当てってしまった When I was parking my car, I *bumped* the car beside me. (!類例: 前の車にぶつかったが, 軽くどんと当たった程度だった I hit the car in front of me, but it was just a *bump*.) ▶彼にどんとばかりに背中をたたかれたので倒れそうになった He *thumped* my shoulder rather hard, nearly knocking me over. (!thump は bang ほど強くないので, 副詞で強さを補うとよい. thump だけだと「とん(とん), こつこつ」などに似てくる. 他の方法で音を強める例: 彼は重い箱をどんとばかりに床に置いた He *thumped* a heavy box down on the floor. heavy で音を補強しているが, thud を用いると逆に heavy をつけなくても箱が重いことを示す. 類例:

put down a box *with a thud*.) ▶彼は怒って机をどんとたたいた He *banged* angrily on the desk with his fist./He *banged* his fist angrily *on* the desk.

どん 鈍 (切れ味の悪いこと) dullness (↔sharpness).

ドン [親分] a leader; 《話》a boss. (⚠ don はイタリア語で貴族・高僧の称号)

ドン [ドン川] the Don.

トンガ [国名] Tonga /táŋə/; (公式名) the Kingdom of Tonga. (首都) Nuku'alofa • トンガ人 a Tongan. • トンガ(人)の Tongan.

どんか 鈍化 —**鈍化する** 動 slow (down). ▶経済成長の勢いが鈍化した The rate of economic growth *has slowed (down)*.

どんかく 鈍角 [数学] an obtuse angle.
• 鈍角三角形 an obtuse-angled triangle.

とんかち (⇨金槌(がな))

とんカツ 豚カツ a deep-fried (breaded) pork cutlet. (⇨カツレツ)

とんがる 尖る (⇨尖(とが)る)

どんかん 鈍感 —**鈍感な** 形 [頭・感覚が] dull; [感受性が] insensitive; [評判などに] thick-skinned. • 耳が鈍感だ be *dull of* hearing. • 美に鈍感である be *insensitive to* beauty. • 鈍感でうぬぼれの強い男 a *thick-skinned*, conceited man.

どんき 鈍器 (凶器となる堅いもの) a blunt and heavy weapon /wépn/. (⚠ a brick, a club などと具体的にいうのが普通)

『ドンキホーテ』 *Don Quixote* /-kwíksət, -kihóuti/. [参考] セルバンテスの小説 • ドンキホーテ流の quixotic /kwiksátik/. • ドンキホーテの現代版 *a modern Don Quixote*.

とんきょう 頓狂 (⇨素っ頓狂)

どんぐり an acorn /éikɔːrn/. • どんぐりまなこの 《話》 goggle-eyed.
• どんぐりの背比べ There's nothing [little, not much] to choose between them.

どんぐりとやまねこ 『どんぐりと山猫』 *Judge Wildcat and the Acorn*. [参考] 宮沢賢治の童話

> 古今ことばの系譜 『どんぐりと山猫』
> おかしなはがきが、ある土曜日の夕がた、一郎のうちにきました。
>
> かねた一郎さま　　　九月十九日
> あなたは、ごきげんよろしいほで、けつこうです。
> あした、めんどなさいばんしますから、おいでなさい。とびどぐもたないでくなさい
>
> 　　　　　　　　　　　　　　　　　山ねこ拝
>
> One Saturday evening, a most peculiar postcard arrived at Ichiro's house. This is what it said:
>
> *September 19*
>
> *Mr. Ichiro Kaneta*:
> *Pleased to know as how you're well. Tomorrow I've got a difficult case to judge, so please come. Please don't bring no firearms.*
>
> *Yours respectfully,*
> *Wildcat*
> (John Bester)
>
> (⚠ (1) as how は that の俗語・方言形. 山猫の手紙をまねた人の書いた調子であるので用いられている. (2) 「めんどうな」は「裁くのが難しい」の意) (⇨鞄(かばん))

とんこう 敦煌 [[中国の都市]] Dunhuang /dúnhwá:ŋ/.

どんこう 鈍行 • 鈍行列車 'a slow train'; (各駅停車の普通列車) a local train. (⚠《主に米話》で単に a local ともいうが, この場合同種のバスなどをさす)

とんこつ 豚骨 pig bones.

• 豚骨スープ pig bone soup. • 豚骨ラーメン ramen [Chinese noodles] in pig bone soup.

とんざ 頓挫 —**頓挫する** 動 come* to a deadlock.

どんさい 鈍才 名 a dull person.
—**鈍才の** 形 dull-witted, slow-witted; dull.

とんし 頓死 名 sudden death. —**頓死する** 動 die suddenly.

とんしゅ 頓首 (手紙の結び) (Very) sincerely yours./ 《英》 Yours sincerely [truly]. (⇨敬具)

どんしゅう 呑舟 • 呑舟の魚 a big fish [shot]; a man of the highest caliber. • 大物のたとえ

どんじゅう 鈍重 —**鈍重な** 形 slow; 《書》(鈍くてのろい) bovine. • 鈍重な男 a *bovine* man.

とんしょ 屯所 [兵士などが詰めている所] a (military) post; a camp; quarters.

どんじり どん尻 the tail end (*of*). ▶私は小学校のときクラスのどん尻にいた I was (*at the*) *bottom of* the class in my primary school days. ▶列のどん尻に並んでいたのでコンサートの券は買えないと思った I was at *the tail* (*end*) *of* the line 《米》 (queue /kjúː/《英》) and I thought I couldn't get the concert tickets.

どんじる 豚汁 *tonjiru*; (説明的に) miso soup with pork and vegetables.

どんす 緞子 thickly-woven satin damask. • 金襴(きんらん)緞子 gold brocade.

とんずら —**とんずらする** [している] 動 take* it [be] on the lam. (⚠ on the lam 《話》は「警察の目から逃走中で」の意)

とんせい 遁世 —**遁世する** 動 (仏門に入る) enter the Buddhist priesthood (⇨仏門); (隠居する) live a quiet life of seclusion from the world; live a secluded life.

とんそう 遁走 —**遁走する** 動 take* flight; run* away; 《書》 flee*.
• 遁走曲 [音楽] a fugue /fjúːg/.

どんそく 鈍足 • 鈍足の走者 a slow [a flat-footed] runner. ▶彼は鈍足だ He is a slow runner./He lacks foot speed.

どんぞこ どん底 (一番深い所) the depths. • どん底生活を送る live in *extreme* [*abject*] *poverty*. (⚠ abject の方が意味が強い. 次例に用いて, in abject misery ともいえる) ▶彼は不幸のどん底だった[に落ちた] He was in [fell into] *the depths of* misery.

とんだ (大変な, ひどい) terrible, 《話》 awful; (思いもよらない) unexpected; (重大な) serious; (取り返しのつかない) fatal. (⇨とんでもない) ▶とんだ目にあう have a *terrible* experience. • とんだ災難を受ける suffer an *unexpected* misfortune. • とんだ間違いをする make a *serious* [a *terrible*, a *gross*, a *fatal*] mistake. ▶君はとんだことをしてくれたね What have you done! • とんだ見当違いだ(＝まったく間違っている) You're *completely* [*quite*] *mistaken* [*wrong*].

ドンタク [<オランダ語] • 博多ドンタク the Dontaku Festival.

とんち 頓智 • とんちがきく have a ready [a quick, a sharp] wit.

とんちゃく 頓着 —**頓着する** 動 (⇨無頓着) ▶彼は金には頓着しない(＝無関心だ) He *is indifferent to* money./He *is not interested in* (making) money. ▶私は人のうわさなどに頓着しない(＝気にしない) I *don't care* (*about*) what others say (about me). (⚠ wh-節の前では about は通例省略される) ▶彼は人の気持ちなどに頓着しない(＝気配がない) He *has no regard for* other people's feelings./(気づかいを示さない) He *doesn't show any concern for* other people.

どんちゃんさわぎ どんちゃん騒ぎ • どんちゃん騒ぎをする

どんちょう 緞帳 a drop curtain.

とんちんかん ― **とんちんかんな** 形 (ばかげた) absurd; (的外れの) off [beside] the point; (無関係の) irrelevant. ●とんちんかんな質問をする ask 《him》 an *absurd* question. ●とんちんかんなことを言う say something *off the point*; make *irrelevant* remarks.

どんつう 鈍痛 a dull pain [ache].

どんづまり どん詰まり (最後の段階) the final stage; (行き詰まり) a deadlock; (行き止まり) a dead end, an end. ▶うちは袋小路のどん詰まりにある We live at the *end* of a cul-de-sac /kʌ́ldəsæ̀k/. (❗cul-de-sacは しばしば「行き詰まり」の意でも用いられる)

とんで 飛んで ●千としで20 (=1,020) one thousand and twenty; one oh two oh.

***とんでもない** ❶[思いがけない] unexpected; (取り返しのつかない) irreparable; (途方もない) outrageous; (ひどい) terrible. (⇨とんだ) ●とんでもない誤解[誤り] a *gross* misunderstanding [mistake]. ●とんでもない失敗 an *irreparable* failure. ▶とんでもない事故が起こった A *terrible* accident happened.

> 翻訳のこころ 考えてみれば，こんなとんでもない時刻にどこの誰かがパーティーなんか開くだろう (村上春樹『レキシントンの幽霊』) To be serious (about it), who on earth would give a party at such an *odd* time of the day as this? (❗(1)「とんでもない」は odd (妙な，通常でない)で表す．(2)「どこの誰かが」は who の後に on earth を置いて意味を強める)

❷[強い否定] ▶歩くのもやっとなんだから走るなんてとんでもない I can hardly bear to walk, *let alone* run. (❗通例否定文の後で用い，「…は言うまでもなく」の意)

会話「あなた，彼のことそうそっけないって言ったの？」「とんでもない．言うもんか」"Did you call him a liar?" "*Good heavens* [*Goodness*] no!/I *most certainly* didn't."

会話「ホウレンソウは好きじゃないと思ってたわ」「とんでもない．大好きだよ」"I thought you didn't like spinach." "*On the contrary*, I love it." (❗相手の言葉を否定して，「それどころか」の意．文頭で用いる)

会話「手伝ってくれてありがとう」「とんでもない (=たいしたことじゃない)」 "Thank you for your help." "*It was nothing.*/(どういたしまして) *Don't mention it.*"

会話「あなたを本会の名誉幹事に任命しようと考えています」「とんでもない話だ」"We're going to nominate you the honorary secretary of our society." "*That'll be the ˇday!*" (❗「その日が楽しみだ」の意であるが，このように皮肉に用いられることが多い)

どんてん 曇天 a cloudy [an overcast] sky; (曇った天気) cloudy weather. (⇨曇り)

どんでんがえし どんでん返し ●どんでん返し (=意外な結末)のある物語 a story with an *unexpected* [a *surprise*] *ending*.

とんと (完全に) completely; (否定形で) (まったく…ない) not ... at all. ▶そのことはとんと忘れていた I *completely* [(やや話) *clean*] forgot about it./I forgot *all* about it. ▶彼の言いたいことがとんと分からない I have *no* idea [I don't have *the slightest* idea] (of) what he means. (❗wh- 節の前の of は《話》では通例省略される)

どんと ❶[思いきり] ▶さあ，どんと来い Come on!
❷[十分，どっさり] ▶この事業が当たれば，どんと金が入ってくるぞ If we succeed in this business, we'll get a *huge sum* of money. (❗《話》で we'll make *a load* [*a pot, loads, pots*] *of* money. など)

とんとん ❶[とんとん(という音)] a knock; (激しくすばやい) a tap; (軽い) a rap. ●とんとんとたたく knock 《*on, at*》; (すばやく) tap, (軽く) rap 《*on, at*》. ▶ドアをとんとんたたく音がした There was a *knock* [a *rap*] *on* the door. ▶だれかがドアをとんとんたたく音を聞いた I heard someone *knocking on* [*at*] the door. ▶父親が息子にこった肩をとんとんたたくよう頼んだ The father asked his son to *tap* his stiff shoulders.

❷[同じ程度であること] ●とんとん (=五分五分)である be even; be equal 《*to*》; be the same 《*with*》; be on a par 《*with*》. ▶2人の選手の実力はとんとんだ The two contestants *are the same* in (their) power. ▶昨年は収支はとんとんだった The gains and losses were *on a par* last year.

***どんどん** ❶[どんどん打つ] (どんと音を立てて) bang; (続けざまに) beat*. ▶彼はバスのドアをどんどんたたいたが，バスは彼の叫び声を無視してごう音を立てて走り去った He *banged on* [*against*] the door, but the bus driver ignored his cries and roared away. (❗against の方が on より激しく打つ様子を伝える) ▶花火が夏の夜空にどんどん鳴り続けた Fireworks kept (on) *banging* in the summer night sky. ▶彼は太鼓をどんどん (=激しく)たたいた He *beat* the drum *loudly* [《猛烈に》 *violently*]. ▶聴衆は床をどんどん踏み鳴らした The audience *stamped* the floor. (❗アンコールの要請・怒りの抗議の動作)

❷[勢いよく] (早く) rapidly; (急速に) quickly; (活発に) briskly. ▶都市部の人口がどんどん増えている The urban population is increasing *rapidly* [*quickly*]. ▶彼は後も振り返らずにどんどん歩いていった He walked *quickly* [(歩き続けた) *kept on* walking, walked *on and on*] without looking back. ▶夏になると彼は午前中にどんどん仕事をした In (the) summer he worked *briskly* in the morning.

❸[遠慮せずに] unreservedly, without reserve; (ためらわずに) without hesitation; (自由に) freely. ▶彼は年上の人にも (自由に)どんどん言いたい事を言う He says what he has to say *unreservedly* to his seniors. ▶彼女は母親のお金をどんどん服に遣った She spent her mother's money *without hesitation* on her clothes. ▶どんどんこの部屋をお使いください Please use this room *freely*.

❹[次から次と] one after another; (ひっきりなしに) continuously, in succession. ▶彼女はイチゴをどんどん食べた She ate strawberries *one after another*. ▶彼についての苦情がどんどんきた We had complaints about him *continuously*. ▶港には船がどんどん入ってきた Ships sailed into the harbor *in succession*.

❺[ますます] ▶状況はどんどんひどくなる The situation is getting *worse and worse*. (❗比較級＋比較級の形で漸次的変化を表す) ▶コンピュータはどんどん (=絶えず)安くなってきている The price of computers is going down *all the time*.

とんとんびょうし とんとん拍子 ― **とんとん拍子に** 副 (速く) quickly, rapidly; (支障なく) without a hitch. ●とんとん拍子に出世する rise *rapidly* in the world; (昇進する) be promoted *very quickly*. ▶すべてとんとん拍子に進んだ Everything went (on) *very smoothly* [*without a hitch*].

***どんな** ❶[どのような] (何，何の) what; (どんな種類の) what kind [sort] of ... (❗後に単数名詞がきても通例 a, an はつけないが《話》ではつけることもある); (どんな特徴の) what ... like; [どのように して] how. ▶どんなご用件でしょうか (電話で) May I ask *what* it is [you are calling] about? ▶孤独がどんなものかご存知ですか Do you know *what* it is to be lonely? ▶どんな車を持っているの *What kind* [*sort*] *of* car do

どんなに you have?/*What* car do you have? (**!** 後の方は車名など具体的に聞く場合だが《まれ》) ▶彼はどんな人？ *What* [×*How*] is he *like*? (**!** 外見・性格などを聞く場合で, 応答は He's wet and dark. (背が高くて色黒です). He's a very nice man. (とてもいい人です)など。外見だけを聞く場合は What does he look like?) ▶どんなふうにしてその問題を解いたの *How* did you solve the problem? ▶どんな理由で(=なぜ)遅れたんだ *Why* did you come late?/《話》*How come* you came [are] late?

❷ 〖いかなる〗(どんな…も) any; (どの…も) every (**!** 以上2語は通例強勢を受ける); (すべての) all. (⇨どの❷ 解説) ▶ /*Any* [*Every*] child knows ↗ that! (**!** any の方が強意的) ▶彼はどんなスポーツも好きです He likes *all* kinds of sports. ▶どんなことをしても彼に会いたい I want to see him *at all costs* [*no matter what* (it *costs*)]. ▶宇宙飛行士はどんな時でも(=常に)冷静でなければならない Astronauts must be calm *at all times*.

❸ 〖たとえ…でも〗no matter what, whatever. (**!** 前の方が口語的。譲歩節中に may を用いるのは文語的) ▶どんなことがあっても私はそこへ定刻に行きます *No matter what* [*Whatever*] happens, I'll be there on time./*Come what may*, I'll be there on time. (**!** come what may は慣用的な言い方) ▶どんな反対があろうとあなたと結婚します I'll marry you, *no matter what* [*whatever*] opposition we get. ▶どんなことがあっても絶対にそれを手放すんじゃないよ *Whatever* you do, don't part with it. (**!** 命令文の文頭・文尾に用いる慣用表現)

どんなに ▶健康にはどんなに注意してもしすぎることはない We *can't* be *too* careful of our health. ▶どんなに忙しくても故郷の両親に月に1回は手紙を出した方がよい *However* [*No matter how*] busy you are, you should write home to your parents at least once a month. (**!** 後の方が口語的. *However* busy you *may* be, …. は文語的) ▶彼女がどんなに喜んでいるかあなたには分からないでしょう You'll have no idea *how* happy she is. ▶みなさんどんなにほっとなさってることでしょうねえ！ *How* relieved you all must be!

****トンネル** ❶ 〖山・地下・海底を貫く〗a tunnel /tʌ́nl/. ●海底トンネル an underwater *tunnel*. ●恵那山トンネル the Enasan *Tunnel*. ●山にトンネルを掘る cut [dig, bore] a *tunnel* through a mountain. ▶列車はトンネルを通り抜けた [抜け出た] The train passed through [came out of] a *tunnel*.

❷ 〖野球で〗●トンネルをする let a grounder go [pass, roll] through [between] one's legs; let a ball go through the wickets.

❸ 〖その他の表現〗▶景気はトンネルを抜けた(=上昇基調に転じた) Business *is* finally *picking* [*looking*] *up* after the recession.

●トンネル会社 a dummy company.

とんび 鳶 〖鳥〗a kite.
●とんびが鷹(たか)を生む(ことわざ)A black hen lays a white egg. (**!**「ブルネットの子供からブロンドの子供が生まれた」などの意)/A genius is born to ordinary parents.
●とんびに油揚げをさらわれる have something nice snatched away when we least expect it. ●とんびに油揚げをさらわれたような顔をして with a stupid [a vacant] look of surprise.

どんぴしゃ(Just) right. ▶私の予感はどんぴしゃりだった My hunch proved *right*./《話》(的を射た) I *hit the bull's eye*. (**!** 慣用句) ▶費用の計算は1回でどんぴしゃり=正確だった We calculated the cost *accurately* at the first trial.

ドンファン 〖女たらし〗a Don Juan /dɑ̀n hwáːn/; 《話》a lady-killer.

とんぷく(やく) 頓服(薬) a one-shot-medicine; (解熱剤) an antifebrile (drug).

どんぶり 丼 a (china) bowl /bóul/. ●親子どんぶり rice served in a bowl with chicken and egg on it.
●どんぶり勘定 spending money with no attention to the balance of earnings and expenses.
●どんぶり飯 rice served in a bowl.

とんぼ 蜻蛉 〖昆虫〗a dragonfly. (**事情** 米英では悪魔の使いで, 災いをもたらす存在と考えられている) ●赤トンボ a red *dragonfly*.

とんぼがえり 蜻蛉返り 〖宙返り〗a somersault. ●連続2回 [3回]のとんぼ返り a double [a treble] *somersault*.
── 蜻蛉返りする 動 do [make, turn] a somersault; (水泳で) do a somersault turn; (急いでもどる) make a quick turn 《to Osaka》.

とんま 〖間抜け〗a blockhead, an ass; a dunce, an idiot. ▶なんてとんまな Don't be so *stupid*.

ドンマイ Never mind./Don't worry. (大したことではありません) It doesn't matter. (参考 日本語の「ドンマイ」は Don't mind. の略。ただし, 英語では Don't mind. はあまり用いない)

とんや 問屋 〖人〗a wholesale dealer 《in》, a wholesaler; 〖店〗a wholesale store; 〖商売〗wholesale business. (⇨卸) ●食料雑貨問屋 (人) a *wholesale* grocer.
●問屋がおろさない ▶そうは問屋がおろさない You're asking [expecting] too much./(そう思うちは君の勝手だが, そうはいかない) That's what you think.
●問屋街 a wholesale district.

どんよく 貪欲 〖名〗greed(iness),《書》avarice 《for》.
── 貪欲な 〖形〗●貪欲な人 a greedy [an avaricious] person. ●真理を貪欲に探求する pursue truth *greedily*; be *greedy for* truth.

どんより ── どんよりした 〖形〗(鉛色をした) leaden /lédn/; (暗い) dark; (灰色の) gray; (陰うつな) gloomy, dull; (一面曇った) overcast (通例 dull, gray などの意が含まれる). ●どんよりした(=輝きのない) 目 dull [lackluster] eyes. ●どんよりした空 [日] an *overcast* sky [day]. ●その日の午後はずっとどんよりしていた It was *overcast* all that afternoon.

どんらん 貪婪 〖非常に欲が深い〗《書》avarice; 《書》rapacity. ── 貪婪な 〖形〗《書》avaricious; 《書》rapacious.

な

な 名 ❶ [名前] (人・動物・物などの) a name. (⇨名前)
▶彼の名はチャールズだがチャーリーという名で通っている His *name* is Charles but he goes *by the name of* Charlie. ▶彼は私の名を呼んだ He called my *name* [me *by name*]. ▶彼女は庭の花の名を全部言った She *named* [*mentioned*] all the flowers in the garden.

❷ [名声] fame; (評判) (a) reputation, a name.
• 名もない作家 a *nameless* writer. ▶彼は画家として名が高い [名が通っている] (有名だ) He is *famous* [is *well-known*, *has a name*] as an artist. ▶彼は当校の名を汚した He blotted [*disgraced*] the good *reputation* of our school./He was a disgrace to our school. ▶名に恥じないように行動しなさい You should live up to your *reputation* [*name*].

❸ [名目] 彼は名ばかりの医者です He is a doctor *in name only* [(いいかげんな) *of a kind*]./He is a *nominal* doctor.

❹ [口実] ▶彼は社会奉仕の名のもとに私腹を肥やした He made his own profit *on* [*under*] *the pretext of* doing social service. (⇨名目)

• 名は体を表す A name [A label] reflects [embodies] the bearer's character [personality]./(名前と性質はしばしば一致する)《ことわざ》 Names and natures do often agree.
• 名をあげる (⇨[名を成す])
• 名を売る ▶彼はその小説で名を売った He *won fame* by the novel. ▶彼はマスコミに名を売ろうとして (=知名度を得るために) あらゆることをした He did everything he could to *get publicity* [*make* himself *well known*] in the mass media.
• 名を捨てて実を取る《ことわざ》Pudding rather than praise./Honor buys no beef in the market.
• 名を留(ど)める ▶彼の勇気は歴史に名をとどめた (=記録された) His courage *went down* in history.
• 名をなす ▶彼は歌手として名をなした [あげた] He *won fame* [*made a name for himself*, *made his name*] as a singer./He *became famous* as a singer.

な 菜 greens; vegetables. •菜の花 rape blossoms. ▶お菜もみんな食べなさいね Eat up your *greens*. (🛈食卓にのせる菜っ葉の類)

-な《終助詞》❶ [禁止, 命令] ▶騒ぐな *Don't* be noisy!/(静かにしろ) Be quiet. ▶決して最後まであきらめるな *Never* give up to the very end. (🛈*Don't* give up ... より強意的) ▶彼は私にそんなことはするなと言った He told me *not* to do that. ▶そんなと心配するなよ You *shouldn't* worry about it.
〚会話〛「そんなやり方をするなよ」「じゃあどうやるの」"You won't do it that way." "Well, how then?"
❷ [確認] ▶君はそれあんまり上手じゃないよな You're nót very ↘good at it, ↘are you?
❸ [願望, 思案] ▶もっと英語が上手になりたいな *I wish* I could speak English better.
〚会話〛「サーモンステーキにしようっと. おいしそうだから」「私もそれにしようかな」"I'm going to try the salmon /sǽmən/ steak. It sounds delicious." "*Maybe* I'll try that too."

なあ listen; look (here);《米話》say,《古》I say. (⇨ねえ 〚圀〛)

-なあ《終助詞》❶ [願望] I wish; I hope. ▶金持ちだったらなあ *I wish* I were [《話》was] rich. (🛈現在の実現不可能な願望)/*How I wish* I were rich! ▶彼が来るといいのになあ (可能性は薄いが) *I wish* he would come./*If only* he ✓*comes* [would ✓*come*]. (🛈 (1) if only の後は直説法または仮定法. (2) I wish より感情的で強い願望を表す) (可能性はある) *I hope* he will come [he comes]. (🛈 comes の方が will come より実現可能性を強調する)
❷ [感嘆] what; how. ▶かわいい娘だなあ *What* a pretty girl (she is)!/*How* pretty she is!

ナース [看護師] a nurse.
• ナースコール calling a nurse; (ボタン) a nurses' call button. • ナースステーション a nurses' station;《和製語》a nurse station.

なあて 名宛 (⇨宛名)
• 名宛て人 (手紙などの) an addressee /ædresí:/; (手形の) a drawee.

なあなあ [妥協] (a) compromise; (なれ合い) a cozy《米》[a cosy《英》] relationship; collusion. ▶なあなあで済ませる (難しいことは避けて通関係者の相互の利益をはかる) avoid challenge; do not offer difficulty; (関係者の相互の利益をはかる) work to the mutual advantage of those concerned. (🛈 work to は「…の線に沿って行動する」の意)
• なあなあ主義 a compromising practice.

なあに what. (⇨何[だ])〚代〛〚圀〛
〚会話〛「遅くなってすみません」「なあに, いいんですよ」"I'm sorry I'm late." "Oh, that's all right."

ナーバス — ナーバスな 〚形〛[神経質な] nervous. (⇨神経質)

ない 無い ❶ [打ち消し] not; no.

〚解説〛(1) not を含む否定文の作り方:
(a) be 動詞と助動詞を否定する場合はその後に not を置く: He is *not* at home./I can't [《書》can*not*] swim.
(b) 一般動詞の否定は「do, does, did+not+原形」: He does *not* work./I did *not* go there.
(c) 話し言葉やくだけた書き言葉では通例 isn't, doesn't, didn't のような短縮形が用いられる.
(2) no を含む否定文の作り方:
no は形容詞. 主語や目的語の前に置いて「no+名詞」の形で否定を表す: 彼には友達 [母] がいない He has *no* friends [mother]./学生はだれ 1 人としてその問題が解けなかった *No* [×*No the*] students could solve the problem. not を用いる場合と異なり, それぞれ「友達 [母親] がいない」「学生はその問題が解ける」というような前提がある場合に用いられることが多く, 一般には He doesn't have *any* friends [a mother]./*None* of the students [*Not* a student] could solve the problem. より堅い言い方で強意的.

▶そのうわさは本当ではない The rumor *isn't* true. ▶彼はその娘と結婚したいと思っていない He doesn't want to get married to the girl. (🛈「…したいと思わない」を ×He doesn't think he wants ... とは言わない) ▶人々はもはやその事実に目をつぶることはできない People can't [《書》cannot] close their eyes to the fact *any longer*./People can *no longer* close their eyes to the fact. (🛈 not ... any longer,

no longer は「もはや…ない」の意)(⇒できる 動 解説)
▶遅れないようにと彼女に言った I told her *not* to be late. (! to 不定詞を否定する場合は not をその前に置く) ▶そんなに怒るな。ほんの冗談だ *Don't* be [get] so angry. It's just a joke. (! 否定命令文は be 動詞・一般動詞とも肯定命令文の文頭に Don't を置く) ▶彼女は1日中家にいたわけではない He *wasn't* at hóme for the whole ˇday. (! (1) 部分否定。この後に He was out for a while in the afternoon. (午後しばらくは出かけていた)などの補足説明を続けることが多い。(2) He *wasn't* at ⁄home for the whole ˎday. と読むと「1日中家にいなかった」(全部否定)の意になるため、это場合は For the whole ˇday, he wasn't at ˎhome. の語順が好まれる(⇒必ず ❷ (2))) ▶だれもそんなこと言えないよ No one can say that. / Who can say that? (! 反語的に) ▶私の車はここからあまり遠くない所に駐車してあります My car is *not* parked far from here.

会話「あす彼女は来ますか」「いや、来ないと思う」"Is she coming tomorrow?" "I do*n't* think so./I think *not*." (! 後の方が堅い言い方)
会話「次郎に頼んだらどう」「彼はとても頼む気にはなれないね」"How about asking Jiro?" "He is *the* very *last* man to ask."

①【…(で)もないし、…(で)もない】 ▶その野菜はおいしくもないし栄養もない That vegetable is *not* tasty *or* [×and] nutritious. (! 次例の方が標準的)/That vegetable is *neither* tasty *nor* [《話》*or*] nutritious.

②【…ではなく、…である】 not … but …. ▶彼は私の父ではない。兄です He's *not* my ⁄father, *but* my ˎbrother. ▶私はそれが欲しくないのではない。買えないのです *It's not that* I don't want it, *but that* I can't afford it. ▶彼はけちではないにしてもとても締まり屋であることは確かだ He's surely very thrifty *if not* stingy. (! if not は「…とまではいかないかもしれないが」の意で形容詞・副詞・数量詞の前に置く)

❷【存在しない】 ▶今朝はあなたの手紙はなかった There were *no* letters [We did*n't* have *any* letters] for you this morning. (! ×There were not any letters…。のように not と any を連続して用いるのは通例避ける) ▶それはなかったことにしよう Let's act as though it *never* happened. ▶あー、困った。パスポートが gone. Oh, my God! My passport *is gone*. ▶その時ソ連とはもはやなくなっていた The Soviet Union was *no more* at that time. ▶君は私の妻に一度も会ったことがあるよね I don't think you've ever met my wife. ▶人を紹介するときの常套句に「…ではないと思う」という日本語に引かれて I think you've *never* met my wife. のようには普通しない。believe, suppose, imagine, expect などについても同様/(記憶にない) I *don't* remember you ever meeting my wife.

会話「まああなた！ 私、へまをしてしまったわ」「うろたえることはないよ」"Oh dear! I have made a mess of it." "There's *nothing* to get upset about."

【…ほどよいものはない】 ▶寒い夜の温かいふろほどよいものはない There's *nothing like* a warm bath on a cold night.

❸【欠けている】lack. ▶彼は常識がない He *lacks* [*is lacking in, has no*] common sense. ▶その家には電気も水道もなかった The house was *without* electricity or running water.

❹【願望】▶ I wish …. (! wish に続く節内の(助)動詞は仮定法) ▶はやく晴れないかなあ *I wish* it would clear up soon. (! なかなか晴れそうもないという気持ちを表す)

❺【依頼、命令、禁止】(⇒-ないか)

●無い袖は振れぬ 'A man who wears a sleeveless dress cannot wave his sleeves.'/《ことわざ》A man cannot give what he hasn't got.

●無くて七癖 We all have our little foibles.

ない 亡い dead. (⇒亡き) ▶あの人は今や亡い He is *dead and gone*./He is *no more*.

-ない -内 (…以内)《時に》, 《話》inside (of) …. (⇒以内) ●建物内に *in* [*within, inside*, 《主に米》*inside of*] a building. ●2時間内で[に]*within* [*in*, 《話》*inside (of)*] two hours. (! 「(今から) 2 時間したら」の方が普通(⇒以内 [第3文例])) ●予算内で *within* [×*in*] the budget. ▶政府内にはいろいろと反対意見がある There are many opposing opinions *within* the government.

ナイアガラ ▶ナイアガラの滝 Niágara Fálls. (! 単・複両扱い。《英》では the をつけて複数に扱うのが普通)

ないあつ 内圧 internal pressure.

ないい 内意 ●内意を受けて by *private instructions (of)*. ▶彼に内意を伝えた I revealed my *intention* to him./I made my *intention* known to him./I told him what I had in mind.

ナイーブ [<フランス語] ── ナイーブな 形 (純真な) innocent; (感じやすい) sensitive; (素朴な) simple; (幼稚な) childish.

ないいん 内因 an internal cause.

●内因性うつ病〘医学〙endogenous depression.

ないえん 内苑 ▶神宮内苑 the Meiji Shrine *inner garden*.

ないえん 内縁 ●内縁の妻[夫] one's *common-law wife* [*husband*]. ●内縁関係を結ぶ make a *common-law marriage*.

ないか 内科 〘病院の〙the internal medicine department; 〘内科学〙internal medicine.

●内科医 《米》an internist, 《米書》a physician. (! ともに 《英》では 《古・俗》で、単に doctor という)

-ないか ❶【依頼】 ▶少しお金を貸してくれないか *Will* [*Can*] *you please* lend me some money? (⇒ください ❷ ③)

❷【命令・禁止】 ▶食事中にテーブルにひじをつくのはやめないか *Stop* resting [*Don't* rest] your elbow on the table while eating.

❸【勧誘】 ▶映画を見に行かないか *Why don't we* go [*Why not go, Let's go, How about* going, *What do you say to* going] to the movies? (! いずれも親しい間柄で用いるくだけた言い方)

❹【同意を求めて】 ▶なかなかいい本じゃないか It's a good book, *is*n*'t it*?/*Isn't it* a ˎgood book! (! 感嘆文の一種(⇒何と)) ▶やあ太郎じゃないか Well, if it isn't Taro! (! I'm surprised などの帰結節を省略した形)

ないかい 内海 an inland sea.

ないかい 内界 the inner world; the mind.

ないがい 内外 ❶【内部と外部】●家の内外をきれいにする clean the *inside and óutside* of a house. ●空港の内外を巡視する patrol *in and around* [*inside and óutside*] the airport. ▶その建物は内外ともぼろぼろになっている The building is rotten *inside and out* [*within and without*]. (! 後の方は箱など比較的小さい物には用いない)

❷【国内と国外】●内外の事情 *internal and external* affairs. ●内外のニュース *domestic* [*home*] *and foreign* news. ▶その作家は国の内外で有名である The writer is famous both *at home and abroad* [*overseas*].

❸【およそ】▶それは 10 ドル内外ははするでしょう It will cost *about* [*around*] ten dollars./It will cost ten dollars *or so*.

ないかく 内角 ❶ 〘数学〙an interior angle. ▶三角形

ないかく 三角形の内角の和は何度ですか How many degrees is the sum of a triangle's *interior angles*? ❷〖野球〗the inside (corner). ●内角低めの球 a low, *inside* ball; a ball low *on the inside*. (！英語では高低を先に, 内外角を後にいう) ●速球で内角をつく throw a fastball on *the inside (corner)*; come *inside* with a fastball.

ないかく 内閣 a cabinet. (！しばしば C-. 個々の閣僚を考えるときは複数扱い) ●単独[連立]内閣 a single-party [a coalition] *cabinet*. ●小泉内閣 the Koizumi *Administration* 《米》[*Cabinet*《英》]. (！単・複両扱い) ●新内閣を組織する organize [form] a new *cabinet*. ●内閣改造 a cabinet reshuffle. (！「内閣を改造する」は reshuffle a cabinet) ●内閣官房長官 the Chief Cabinet Secretary. ●内閣総辞職 a general resignation of the Cabinet. (⇨総辞職) ●内閣総理大臣 the Prime Minister; (フランス・イタリア・中国などの) the Premier; (ドイツなどの) the Chancellor. (⇨首相) ●内閣府 the Cabinet Office.

ないがしろ ●ないがしろにする (軽視する) make light of ...; (無視する) ignore. (⇨軽んじる)

ないき 内規 (会社などの) a bylaw; (団体内の) a rule, a regulation. ●会社の内規によって under the company *bylaws*. ▶これは会社の内規に定められている This is laid down in the *bylaws* [*rules*] of the company.

ないきょく 内局 an intra-ministerial bureau.

ないきん 内勤 图 office work; desk work. (⇔外勤) ── **内勤する** 動 work in the office. ●内勤社員 an office [desk] worker; a clerk.

ないくう 内宮 the Inner Shrine of Ise.

ないけい 内径 the inside diameter; (口径) the caliber. (⇨口径)

ないけん 内見 (⇨内覧)

ないげんかん 内玄関 (⇨内(2)玄関)

ないこう 内攻 图〖医学〗a retrocession. ── **内攻する** 動 retrocede; strike inward.

ないこう 内項〖数学〗internal terms.

ないごうがいじゅう 内剛外柔 an iron hand [fist] in a velvet glove. ▶彼は内剛外柔だ He looks [appears to be] gentle, but in fact he is strong willed [unyielding, bold, aggressive].

ないこうてき 内向的 ── **内向的な** 形 introverted (↔éxtroverted). ▶彼は内向的だ He is *introverted*./(内向的な人だ) He is an *introvert* (↔an extrovert).

ないこく 内国 ── **内国の** 形 domestic; inland. ●内国為替 domestic exchange. ●内国貿易 domestic [inland, home] trade.

ないさい 内妻 (⇨内縁)

ないさい 内債 a domestic loan. (⇔外債)

ないざい 内在 ── **内在する** 動 ínherent (*in*),〖書〗ímmanent (*in*). ●現在の教育制度に内在する不公平 inequalities *inherent in* the present educational system. ▶神は人間の心に内在する God is *immanent in* our mind.

ないし 〖または〗or; 〖...から...まで〗from ... to ...; 〖...と...の間〗between ... and .... ●月に3回ないし4回映画を見に行く I go to the movies three *or* four times a month. ●参加者は30人ないし40人でしょう The number of (×the) participants will be *from* thirty *to* forty [*between* thirty *and* forty].

ないじ 内示 (an) unofficial announcement [〖書〗notification]. ▶新工場の工場長に昇進するとの内示があった I *was unofficially told* that I would be promoted to manager of the new plant.

ナイジェリア 〖国名〗Nigeria /naidʒíəriə/; (公式名) the Federal Republic of Nigeria. (首都 Abuja) ●ナイジェリア人 a Nigerian. ●ナイジェリア(人)の Nigerian.

ないじえん 内耳炎〖医学〗otitis /outáitis/ interna.

ないじかく 内耳核〖医学〗internal hemorrhoids [〖英〗haemorrhoids].

ないしきょう 内視鏡〖医学〗an éndoscòpe. ●内視鏡検査 endoscopy.

ないじつ 内実 ●内実は in fact; (実際は) in reality. (⇨実(5)①)

ないじゅ 内需 domestic demand; (国内消費) home consumption. (⇔外需) ●経済は輸出主導型から内需主導型へと移行した The driving force of the economy has shifted from exports to *domestic demand*. ●内需拡大 the expansion of [(増加)an increase in] domestic demand. ●内需関連株 domestic demand-related stocks.

ないしゅう 内周 the internal circumference 《of》.

ないじゅうがいごう 内柔外剛 ●内柔外剛の人 a person who looks [appears to be] strong [brave, unyielding], but in fact is weak-hearted [diffident, timid].

ないしゅっけつ 内出血 图 internal bleeding;〖医学〗internal hemorrhage /hémərɪdʒ/. ── **内出血する** 動 bleed [hemorrhage] internally; have (an) internal hemorrhage.

＊**ないしょ** 内緒 形 (a) (秘密の). (⇨秘密) ●彼に内緒にする keep (it) *secret* [*a secret*] from him. ▶みんなには内緒にしておきましょう Let's keep it *secret* [*to ourselves*]./(だれにも言わないでおきましょう) Let's not tell anybody.

会話「その人にはどこで会えるの」「これがその住所だ。ただし僕から聞いたことは内緒にしておいてくれ」"Where can I see him?" "Here's his address. But you *didn't* hear it from me." (！実際に口に出したあとで「あなたは聞かなかった(ことにしてくれ)」という言い方で, しばしば最後に OK, right? (いいね, 分かったね)などをつけて念を押す)

── **内緒の** 形 (秘密の) secret; (内密に語られる・書かれる・行われる) confidential. ●内緒(の)の話をする have a *confidential* [*a private*] talk 《*with*》(！前の方は「打ち明け話」, 後の方は「密談」の意); (ひそひそ話をする) talk in whispers 《*with*》. ▶これは内緒の話だよ(＝ここだけの話だよ) This is *between you and me* [*between ourselves*], you know.

── **内緒で** 副 (こっそりと) in secret, secretly; (知らせずに) without letting 《him》know; (隠れて) behind 《his》back. ▶彼は奥さんに内緒で彼女と付き合っているらしい They say he's seeing her *behind the back of* his wife. ●内緒事 a secret. ▶私たちには内緒事は何もない We have no *secrets* from each other. ●内緒話 a confidential [a private] talk. (⇨形)

ないじょう 内情 the inside facts [story]. (⇨内幕) ●経済界の内情に通じている know the *inside facts* [*story*] of the economic world; be familiar with the *inside* of the economic world. ●内情に詳しい者の犯行 an inside job. ▶その国の内情(＝実情)はだれにも分からない No one knows the *real state of affairs* in the country.

ないしょく 内職〖副業〗a job on the side (⇨アルバイト);〖出来高仕事〗piecework. ▶彼の妻は彼の収入を補うために内職をしている His wife *is doing* some *work at home* to supplement his income.

ないじょのこう 内助の功 ▶彼は妻の内助の功によって出

世した Thanks to his *wife*'s *help*, he succeeded in life./His success in life is due to his *wife*'s *help*.

ないしん 内心 名 ❶ [心の中] (心中) one's inner [inward] thoughts; (心) one's heart; (真意) one's real intention [感情] feelings. ▶政治家は決して内心を見せない Politicians never tell us their *inner thoughts* [their (*innermost*) *hearts*]./Politicians never tell us what they are really thinking in their *hearts*.
❷ [数学] the inner center.
── 内心(は) 副 (心の中で) in one's heart, inwardly, 《やや強》 deep down. ▶彼女はうわべは全く平静だったが内心は怒っていた She was quite calm on the surface but angry *inside* [*deep down*].

ないしん 内申 (⇨内申書)

ないしん 内診 (婦人科の) an internal examination; a gynecological test [examination].

ないじん 内陣 an inner sanctum (of a temple [a shrine, a church]). (⇔ 外陣)

ないしんしょ 内申書 an official school report on the record of a student, 《米》 a transcript (of grades); [推薦状] a letter of recommendation. (!) 日本式内申書制度はない

ないしんのう 内親王 an Imperial princess. (⇔ 親王) ▶愛子内親王殿下 Her Imperial Highness Princess Aiko.

ナイス nice; good. (!) nice は感じがいい, good は本質的にいい
●ナイスガイ a nice guy. ●ナイスショット a nice [good] shot.

ないせい 内政 (内情) internal [domestic] affairs. ▶その国は日本の内政に干渉した The country interfered in the *internal affairs* of Japan.
●内政干渉 interference in the internal [domestic] affairs of other countries. ●内政問題 an internal affair.

ないせい 内省 名 introspection.
── 内省的 形 introspective.
── 内省する 動 introspect; look into one's mind.

ないせき 内戚 (父方の親類) a paternal relative; a relation on one's father's side. (⇔ 外戚)

ないせん 内戦 a civil war.

ないせん 内線 (電話の) an extension 《略 ext.》. ●内線 120 番をお願いします *Extension* [Give me *extension*] 120, please. (!) 120 は one-two-o /oʊ/ または one-twenty のように読む
●内線電話 an extension telephone; (会社・飛行機などの) an intercom. ●内線番号 an extension (number).

ないそう 内装 interior decoration.

***ないぞう** 内臓 internal organs; (生命に不可欠の器官) vital organs. ▶どこか内臓の具合が悪い I have something wrong with my *internal organs* [(おなか)《話》*insides*].
●内臓疾患 an internal disease.

ないぞう 内蔵 ●コンピュータを内蔵した[=組み込んだ]カメラ a camera with a *built-in* computer.

ナイター a night game. (!) nighter は《俗》▶今日のナイターは雨で流れた Today's *night game* was rained out.
●ナイタースキー night skiing.

ないだく 内諾 ── 内諾する 動 give one's informal [private] consent 《to》.

ないだん 内談 (have) a private [a secret] talk 《with》. (⇨密談)

ないち 内地 名 [本国] one's home country; [本土] the mainland. (⇔ 外地)

── 内地の 形 (国内の) home; domestic.
●内地勤務 home service.

ナイチンゲール [鳥] a nightingale.

ナイチンゲール [英国の看護師] Nightingale (Florence ～).

ないつう 内通 名 secret communication 《with》; (裏切り) betrayal; [男女間の] (an) adultery.
── 内通する 動 communicate secretly with the enemy; betray (us) to the enemy; (男女が) commit adultery 《with》.

ないてい 内定 (非公式の決定) an unofficial [an informal] decision. ●就職の内定を取り消す renege /rinɪɡ/ [go back] on one's *promise* of employment.
── 内定する 動 ●就職が内定する get a *promise* [an *unofficial decision*] of employment. ▶彼は昇進が内定している It has been unofficially *decided* that he (《主に英》should) be promoted./An *unofficial decision* has been made *for* his promotion.

ないてい 内偵 a secret investigation.
── 内偵する 動 investigate ... secretly [in secret].

ないてき 内的 ❶ [内部の] internal; (本質的な) intrinsic. ❷ [精神面の] inner; spiritual.
●内的葛藤 (かっとう) (overcome) a mental [an inner] conflict. ●内的生活 inner [spiritual] life.

ナイト [騎士] a knight. (!) 男性は Sir, 女性は Dame の称号を受けるが一代限りで貴族ではない (⇨ 貴族 解説)

ナイト [夜間] night.
●ナイトガウン [寝巻きの上にはおる部屋着] 《米》 a bathrobe; 《英》 a dréssing gòwn. (!) nightgown は《主に米》で「寝巻き, ネグリジェ」の意) ●ナイトキャップ [就寝用帽子]《wear》 a nightcap; [寝酒] (have) a nightcap. ●ナイトクラブ a nightclub. ●ナイトケア [医学] night care. (参考) 高齢者・障害者を夜間のみ福祉施設に預かり介護を行うこと) ●ナイトゲーム [夜間試合] a night game (↔a day game). ●ナイトショー a midnight show;《和製語》a night show.

ないない 内々 ── 内々の 形 secret; private; informal, unofficial. ●彼女と内々の話をする have a *private* [(打ち明けた) a *confidential*] talk with her; talk with her *in private* [*privately*]. ●内々の訪問をする make an *informal* [an *unofficial*] visit.
── 内々に 副 (秘密に) secretly, in secret; (内密に) privately, in private; (非公式に) informally, unofficially; (オフレコで)《話》off the record. ●内々に彼と会う meet him *secretly* [*privately, informally*]. ▶このことは内々にしてください Please keep this matter *secret* [(人に話さないで) *to yourself*].

ないないづくし 無い無い尽くし ●無い無い尽くしの生活を余儀なくされる be forced to lead a life *with* (*absolutely*) *nothing*.

ないねんきかん 内燃機関 an internal combustion engine.

ないはんそく 内反足 [医学] a clubfoot.

***ナイフ** a knife (複 knives); (折りたたみ式の小型ナイフ) a pocketknife (複 -knives); a penknife (複 -knives); (折りたたみ式の) a clasp knife; (食卓用の) a table knife. ●飛び出しナイフ (押しボタン式の)《米》a switchblade (knife);《英》a flick-knife. ●ペーパーナイフ a paper knife. ●ジャックナイフ a jack-knife. ●果物[パン切り; 登山]ナイフ a páring [a bréad; a húnting] knife. ●ナイフを研ぐ sharpen [whet, grind] a knife. ●ナイフを開く[畳む] open

ないぶ [close] (the blade of) a *knife*. ● ナイフとフォークで食べる eat with (a) *knife* and fork. (❗対句なのでaは通例省略し, and /ən/ と読む) ▶ このナイフはあまり切れない This *knife* won't cut well./(刃が鈍い) This *knife* has a dull [a blunt] edge. (❗dull は使い込んだ結果, blunt はもともと切れないことを示す) (⇒鈍い) ▶ そのナイフには刃が 4 枚と栓抜きがついている The *pocketknife* has four blades and a bottle opener.

ないぶ 内部 〖内側〗the inside, the interior; 〖内輪〗the inside. ● 建物の内部 the *inside* [*interior*] of a building. ● 内部の者 people on the *inside*; insiders. ▶ 彼は内部事情に通じている He has a lot of *inside* information. ▶ これは内部の者の仕業に違いない This must have been an *inside* (↔an óutside) [an insider's] job./This must have been done by an insider (↔an outsider).
● 内部監査 an internal audit. ● 内部工作 internal maneuvering. ● 内部抗争 an internal strife [conflict]; 《話》infighting. ● 内部告発 whistle-blowing. ▶ だれかが会社の脱税を内部告発したに違いない Someone must have blown the *whistle on* the company's tax evasion. ● 内部告発者 a whistle-blower. ● 内部者取引き (インサイダー取り引き) insider trading [dealing]. ● 内部情報 inside information. ● 内部調査 an internal investigation. ● 内部留保 internal reserve; retained earnings.

ないふくやく 内服薬 (an) oral [ˣinternal] medicine. ● 内用 internal medicine は「内科」 ▶ この薬は内服薬ではありません This medicine should not be taken *internally*.

ないふん 内紛 (内部のいざこざ) (an) internal trouble [やや書 conflict]; (政党の) (a) trouble [やや書 strife] within the party, intraparty strife.

ないぶん 内分, 内聞 ▶ このことは何とぞ内聞に(=あなたの内に留めておくように)お願い申します Please *keep* this story [information] *to yourself*.

ないぶんぴつ 内分泌 〖医学〗internal secretion. ● 内分泌腺 an endocrine gland. ● 内分泌障害 endocrinopathy.

ないへき 内壁 an inside [an inner] wall.

ないほう 内包 图 (暗示的意味) (a) connotation. ── 内包する 動 connote; (必然的に含む) involve. ▶ spinster という語は否定的な意味を内包する The word 'spinster' has negative *connotations*.

ないまく 内膜 〖医学〗an internal membrane.

ないまぜ 綯い交ぜ ● 糸をない交ぜにする interweave [weave] threads of different colors. ● うそとまことをない交ぜにして作り話をする 《比喩的》 weave [mix] truth and falsehood into a story; put facts and fiction together to make a story.

ないみつ 内密 (a) secret. (⇒内緒, 秘密)

ないむ 内務 ● 内務省 《米》the Department of the Interior;《英》the Home Office. ● 内務大臣《英》the Home Secretary. ● 内務長官《米》the Secretary of the Interior.

ないめい 内命 ● 内命を受ける be given [receive] a *secret order* [*instruction*]. ● 上司の内命を受けて under *secret* [*informal*] *orders* from one's boss.

ないめん 内面 the inner side; (内部) the interior. ▶ 人は外面ではなく内面によって価値を計られるべきだ We [《書》One] should be valued by *what we are* [《書》one *is*], not by what we look [《書》one looks]. (❗主語 one を受ける代名詞は he or she, they とすることもある) ▶ あなた方 2 人は外見はよく似ているが内面はずいぶん違っている You two look

alike but you're very different *inside*.
── 内面的な 圏 inner; internal. ● 内面的な葛藤(かっとう) the *inner* conflict.

ないものねだり 無い物ねだり ▶ その子はいつも無い物ねだりしている The child is always asking for the impossible [what is impossible to get].

ないや 内野 the infield; the diamond. ● 前進守備の内野を抜くヒットを打つ hit a single past the drawn-in *infield*.
● 内野安打 an infield single [hit]. ● 内野ゴロ an infield grounder. ● 内野ゴロを打つ[に打ちとる] hit [get a batter on] an *infield grounder*. ● 内野手 an infielder. ● 内野守備 infielding. ● 内野守備(陣)を固める solidify the *infield*. ● 内野席 the infield stands. ● 内野フライ an infield fly. (❗「インフィールドフライ」の意もある)

ないやく 内約 ● 内約にこぎつける reach an *informal* [(仮の) a *provisional*, (当事者間での) a *private*] *agreement* (*with*).

ないゆう 内憂 ● 内憂外患 内憂外患こもごも至る be beset with *difficult problems arising from abroad as well as at home*.

:**ないよう** 内容 〖容器などの中身〗cóntents; 〖意味内容〗cóntent; 〖実質〗substance; 〖質〗quality.
①【～内容】● 箱の内容 the *contents* of a box. ● 形式と内容 form and *substance* [*content*]. ▶ 彼はその計画に反対だという内容の手紙をよこした He wrote me a letter *saying that* [《書》*to the effect that*] he was against the plan.
②【内容が[の]】● 内容の充実した[乏しい] 話 a speech of much [little] *substance*. ● 内容が豊富[貧弱]だ be rich [poor] in *content*. ▶ 彼の演説には内容がない His speech says nothing. /《以下の言い方より口語的》/There is no *substance* [nothing *substantial*] in his speech. /His speech has no *substance*.
③【内容を[に]】● 教育の内容を改善する improve the *quality* of education. ▶ 会議の内容を教えてください Tell me what you discussed [talked about] at the meeting. ▶ なるほどこの論文の形式は結構だが内容は賛成しかねる Indeed the form of the article is good, but I don't approve of its *content*.

ないよう 内用 ── 内用する 動 take medicine. (❗液体の薬を飲むときは drink も可)
● 内用薬 medicines for internal use; internal medicines.

ないようせき 内容積 (冷蔵庫などの) internal cubic volume.

ないらん 内乱 (内戦) a civil war; (反乱) (a) rebellion, (a) revolt. (⇒反乱)

ないらん 内覧 a preview 《of Sharaku's woodblock prints exhibition》. ● 結婚式場の内覧会 a bridal fair.

ないりく 内陸 inland.
● 内陸国 a landlocked country. ● 内陸性気候 (大陸性気候) a continental climate. ● 内陸地方 an inland area.

ないりんざん 内輪山 the inner rim of a volcanic crater.

ナイル ● ナイル川 the Nile. (❗the River Nile, the Nile River も頻度は低いが可)

ないれ 名入れ ● 名入れタオル a towel *with one's (company's) name printed on it*.

ナイロビ 〖ケニアの首都〗Nairobi /naɪróubi/.

ナイロン nylon. ▶ ナイロンは合成繊維です *Nylon* is a synthetic textile [fiber].
● ナイロンストッキング 《a pair of》 nylons [nylon

stockings]. ●ナイロン製品 nylon goods.
ナイン [[九]] nine; [[野球]] the nine, a baseball team.
なう 綯う ●縄をなう make [《やや書》twine] (a) rope. ●わら縄をなう twist [《やや書》twine] straw into a rope.
なうて 名うて ── 名うての [形] well-known; (著名の) famous 《for one's valor, as a winter resort》; (悪名の高い) notorious 《for, as》; infamous /ínfəməs/《for》. ●名うての詐欺師 a well-known [a notorious] impostor.
ナウル [[国名]] Nauru /nɑːúːruː/; (公式名) the Republic of Nauru. (首都 Yaren) ●ナウル人 a Nauruan. ●ナウル(人)の Nauruan.
なえ 苗 a seedling; [[樹木の]] a sapling /sǽpliŋ/. ●稲の苗 young rice plants. ●苗を植える plant a seedling. ●苗木 a young plant [tree], a sapling. ●苗床 a seedbed.
なえる 萎える [[しおれる]] wither (⇒しおれる); [[力を失う]] lose* strength; (弱くなる) become* weak, weaken. ●足が萎えてきた have become weak in the legs.

* **なお** 尚 [副] ❶[[いまだ]] still, yet. (**!** 後の方が強意的(⇒まだ ❶[類語])) ●私の祖父は今もなお健在です My grandfather is *still* healthy. ●あの痛ましい事件から 10 年たった今もなお被害者の中にはトラウマに苦しんでいる人がいる Ten years now after the tragic incident, some of the victims are *yet* suffering from its trauma.
❷[[一層]] (さらに多く) more; (さらに一層) much, even, far, still [[いずれも比較級を強める]]; (さらに進んで) further. (⇒なおさら) ●なお一層悪いことには what is worse (*still*); (and) to make (×the) matters worse. ●なお一層健康に注意しなさい (Be) *more* careful of your health. ▶彼は背が高いが, 兄はなお高い He is tall, but his brother is *much* [*even, still*] taller. ▶あなたはなおよくこの件を調べなければならない You must look into the matter *further* [×farther]. ▶この仕事には英語がなお絶対必要です. スペイン語も少し分かればなお有利です(=それだけっそうよい) The knowledge of English is essential; if you know some Spanish, *all the better* [*so much the better*] for this job.
── なお [接] (さらにつけ加えると) moreover. ▶なお, 詳細は追ってお知らせします *Let me add that* I'll let you know the details later.

なおかつ 尚且つ ❶[[その上]] what is more; besides; not only ... but also .... ▶恵子は美人でなおかつ気立てもいい Keiko is beautiful, and *what is more,* [(and) *besides,*] she is good-natured./Keiko is *not only* beautiful *but (also)* good-natured.
❷[[それでもまだ]] still; yet; however. ▶みんなに見放されても彼はなおかつ(=それでもまだ)がんばっている Though all his friends have left him, he is *still* holding his own. (**!** hold one's own は「自分の立場を守り通す」の意)

なおさら 尚更 (...のためなおさら) (all) the more for [because]... (**!** all を用いる方が強意的); [なおさら...でない] much [still] less (**!** 否定文に続けて. 肯定文に続けて though much [still] more (なおさら...だ) は《今はまれ》). ▶その子には短所があるためなおさらかわいい I love the child *all the more for* his faults [*because* he has some faults]. ▶その患者は薬を飲んだためになおさら悪くなった The patient got *still worse from* taking medicine. ▶彼女は自転車にも乗れない, オートバイはなおさらだ She can't even ride a bicycle, *much less* [《言うまでもなく》*let alone*] a motorcycle. (**!** let alone は通例否定文の後で用い

る) ▶人は持てば持つほどなおさら欲しくなる The more we have, *the more we want*.
なおざり ●なおざりにする (捨ておく) neglect; (軽視する) make light of .... ▶家族[仕事]をなおざりにすべきではない We should not *neglect* our family [duties].
なおし 直し (修正) (a) correction; (修理) repair; (主に衣類の) mending. ●直しのいっぱい入った原稿 a manuscript full of *corrections*. ●服を寸法直しに出す take one's suit to the shop for *alteration* [to have it altered]. (**!**「かぎ裂きの直しに」なら to have its tear /téər/ mended とする)

:なおす 直す ❶[[修理する]] repair; mend; fix. (⇒修理する, 修繕する)

> [使い分け] **repair** 車や構造が比較的複雑なものの修理や破損した建物・器物・布製品の修繕を表す.
> **mend** 《米》では主に布製品の修繕, 《英》では構造が比較的単純なものの修理や修繕を表す.
> **fix** 口語的な語で repair, mend の代わりに用いられる.

●車を直す *repair* [*fix*] a car. ●上着のひじが薄くなってきたよ. 直さなくてはね Your jacket is wearing thin at the elbows. They need *mending* [(当て布をして) *patching*]. ▶私は時計を直してもらった I had my watch *repaired* [《英》*mended*]./《話》I got my watch *fixed*.
❷[[矯正する]] correct; (悪癖などを直す) cure; (除く) get* rid of .... ●欠点を直す *correct* [*get rid of*] one's shortcomings. ●子供の悪癖を直す cure a child of his bad habits. ●自分の悪癖なら *get rid of* one's bad habits となる) ●行儀を直す *improve* [《やや書》*mend*] one's manners. ▶彼女は子供のはしの持ち方を直そうとした She tried to *correct* her boy who was holding his chopsticks wrong.
❸[[訂正する]] correct. ▶この文章を直してくれませんか Will you *correct* this sentence for me? ▶間違えたらその場で直してください Please *correct* me immediately if I make a mistake.
❹[[作り変える]] (衣服などを) alter, 《主に米》make* ... over. ▶この服を私に合うよう(仕立て)直してくれませんか Will you *alter* this dress [*make* this dress *over*] to fit me?
❺[[換算する]] change, 《やや書》convert. ●ドルを円に直す *change* [*convert*] dollars into yen. ▶1 マイルをメートル法に直すといくらですか How many meters are there in a mile [does a mile *make*]?
❻[[翻訳する]] translate [put*]... (*into*). (**!** 後の方が口語的) ●その文を日本語から英語に直す *translate* the sentence from Japanese into [《まれ》*to*] English. ▶どうぞこれを英語に直してください Please *put* [*turn*] this *into* English.
❼[[調整する]] adjust; [整える] (服装・髪などを) fix; (整理する) put*... in order. ●髪[化粧]を直す *fix* one's hair [makeup]. ▶彼は鏡の前に立ち止まってネクタイを直した He stopped before the mirror to *adjust* his tie. ▶絵の位置を直しなさい. 傾いているよ *Fix* the painting, it isn't straight.
❽[[片付ける]] (元に戻す) put*... back; (しまう) put ... away. ▶彼女は服をたんすに直した She *has put* [*laid*] the clothes *away* in the chest of drawers.
❾[[再びする]] ●...し直す (*do*) over again. (**!** 各々の複合動詞の項を参照)

* **なおす** 治す [[治療(%)]] (病気を) cure 《him *of* a disease》; (傷を) heal; [[治療を施す]] treat (**!** 必ずしも治ることを含意しない); [[取り除く]] get* rid of .... ▶傷

治す heal a wound. ▶その医者[薬]は彼の病気を治した The doctor [medicine] *cured* (him *of*) his disease. ▶彼は頭痛を治すのにアスピリンを飲んだ He took some [an] aspirin to *get rid of* [《やわらげる》*ease*] his headache. (❗ 頭痛には通例錠剤を飲むので, an は普通ではない)

なおのこと 尚のこと (⇨尚更)

なおも 尚も ▶風はなおも吹き荒れた (さらに継続して) The wind *continued* to blow hard./(さらにいっそう) The wind blew *much* [*still*] harder.

‡**なおる 直る** [[癖・故障など]]《取り除く》get* rid of …; 《修理される》be repaired, be mended, be fixed. (⇨直す) ▶悪い癖が直る *get rid of* [《大きくなって脱する》*outgrow*, 《克服する》*overcome*] a bad habit. ▶その時計はもう直らない The watch can't *be repaired* [*be mended*, *be fixed*]. ● キちんなる. 直れ 《号令》Right, dress!; Eyes front! [As you were!]

*なおる 治る [[病気・けがなどが]] recover 《*from* an illness》; get* over 《a cold》 (❗ 通例軽い病気); be cured 《*of* a disease》; 《よくなる》get well; [[病気が]] be cured; [[傷が]] heal (up). (⇨治す) ▶治りかけの傷 a *healing* cut. ▶治りにくい皮膚病 a *stubborn* skin disease. ▶病人はすぐに治った The patient *recovered* quickly [*made* a quick *recovery*]. ▶風邪はもう治りました I've got over [《抜け出す》*got rid of*, ×*recovered from*] my cold now. (❗ recover from … は風邪などよりもっと重い病気に用いる) ▶病気は一向に治りそうにもない I don't seem to *be getting* any *better*. ▶その病気は治らない That disease is *incurable*.(↔curable)./(治療法がない) *There is no cure for* that disease.

会話 「そのおでこどうしたの. 血が出てるわ」「ほんのかすり傷だ. 2～3日もすれば治るよ」"What happened to your forehead? It's bleeding." "Just scratches and they'll *heal up*, and I'll *get over* them, I'll *be all right*] in a few days."

会話「彼のがんは治る見込みがあるのか」「まだ分からない, さらに検査しないといけないそうだ」"Can they *cure* his cancer?" "They don't know … they have to run more tests." (❗ they は《病院の》医師をさす. Can his cancer be *cured*? より口語化する)

なおれ 名折れ disgrace. (❗ 不名誉をもたらす人[事柄]をさす場合は a がつく. 複数形しない(⇨不名誉)) ▶彼女は一家の名折れだ She is a *disgrace* to our family. ▶彼の昨日の行動は会社の名折れになる What he did yesterday will bring *disgrace* on the company.

‡**なか 中 ❶** [[物の内側]] the inside (↔outside); 《内部》the interior (↔exterior). ● 自動車の中の *inside* [*interior*] of a car. ▶家の中は暗かった The *inside* of the house was dark./It was dark *inside* [*in*] the house. (❗ inside は外との対比を合意する)

① 【中に[で, へ, を]】 in …; into …; 《内部に》inside …; within ….

解説 (1) in は内部を表す最も一般的な語. inside と within は外部との対比を合意し, 特定の範囲内を強調する. within の方が堅い語.
(2) into と in は移動を表す動詞とともに用いて内部への移動を表すが, into は移動に, in は移動の結果生じた状態・状況に重点がある.

● 部屋の中で遊ぶ play in the room. ▶封筒の中を確かめる see what is *in* [*inside*] the envelope; check the contents of the envelope. ▶中へ入ろう Let's go *in* [*inside*, ×*into*]. (❗ 目的語がない場合 into は不可) ▶彼女は部屋の中に入り, 明かりを全部 つけた She stepped *into* [*inside*, *in*] the room and turned on all the lights. ▶彼はそれをくずかごの中に投げ捨てた He threw it *into* [《《話》 *in*] the wastebasket. ▶彼女はあらしの間家の中にいた She stayed *inside* (the house) [*indoors*, *in* the house] during the storm. ▶時々電車の中で彼に出会うよ Occasionally I run into him *on* [《英》*in*] the train. 「電車に乗っていて」の意)

② 【中から】 out of …. ● 部屋の中から出て行く go *out of* a room. ▶彼はケースの中から時計を取り出した He *took* a watch *out of* the case. ▶ドアは中から(=内側から)鍵(ぎ)がかかっていた The door was locked *from inside* [*from within*, ×*from* in].

❷ 【真ん中】 the middle; the center. (⇨真ん中) ▶中 3 日おいて(=3 日経って)彼を訪ねる call on him *after an interval of* three days. ▶中の(=2 番目の)兄 one's *second* oldest brother. ▶湖の中ほどに小島がある There is an islet about in the *middle* [*center*] of the lake. ▶その投手は中 5 日で登板する The pitcher pitches on five days' rest [with five days of rest].

❸ 【範囲内】 in …; of …; among ….

解説 (1) 形容詞の最上級とともに用いる場合, in は family, class, world のような集合体を示す名詞と用いてその範囲を示し, of は all や the four boys のような複数名詞と用いて部分を表す.
(2) among は同種の三つ以上の中に入り混じっていることを表し, 複数名詞か集合名詞を伴う.

● 三つの中から一つを選ぶ choose one *out of* [*from* ⟨*among*⟩] the three. ▶群衆の中に彼女を見つけた I found her *among* [*in*] the crowd. ▶彼は家族[みんな]の中でいちばん早起きだ He gets up earliest *in* his family [*of* all of us]. ▶四季の中で夏がいちばん好きだ I like summer best *of* [×*of* all] the four seasons. (❗ 数詞がつくと all は用いられない) ▶中には[学生の中には]読書好きの者もいる *Sóme* people [*Sóme* students, *Sóme of* the students] like reading books. (❗ この用法の some は通例強勢が置かれ, …, but others do not (しかしそうでない者もいる)を含意する) ▶これはこれまでに見た中でいちばんいい映画 This is the best movie I've ever seen.

❹ 【最中】 in …; (…のさなかに) in the middle of ….
● 豪雨の中を歩く walk *in* [(…について) *through*] the heavy rain. ▶あらしの中で道に迷った I got lost *in the middle of* [《古》 *in the midst of*] the storm.

なか 仲 [[交際上の]] terms; [[関係]] (a) relationship, (a) relation. ● 《間柄》 ▶仲のよい夫婦 a *loving* [a *devoted*] couple. ▶仲のよい友達 a *close* [a *good*, a *great*] friend. ❗ an intimate friend はしばしば性関係をも含意するので, 異性間では避けた方が無難 ▶仲を取りもつ mediate 《*between* them》; (男女間の) fix 《her》 up with 《him》. ▶彼女は智子と仲がよい She and Tomoko are *close friends*./She *gets along* [*on*] *with* Tomoko./She is *on friendly* [*good*] *terms with* Tomoko. (❗ 最後は堅い言い方) ▶あの 2 人の少年は全く仲が悪い The two boys don't *get along* [*on*] at all 《*with* each other》. ▶彼らは恋仲になった They *fell in love with* each other. ▶戦争が 2 人の仲を引き裂いた The war separated the two. ▶両家は犬猿の仲である The two families are always fighting like cats and dogs.

ながあめ 長雨 a long [《降り続く》a continuous] rain; a long spell of 《×a》 rainy weather.

なかい 仲居 a waitress.

ながい 長い

WORD CHOICE 長い

long 時間・距離・物体などが長いこと。▶長い沈黙が続いた There was a *long* silence.

lengthy 時間・物などが長いこと。また、演説・講義・本・書類などが長々しくどいこと、後の方の意味では、しばしば否定的意を持つ。● 長い演説 a *lengthy* speech.

頻度チャート

long ████████████████████
lengthy ██
　　　20　40　60　80　100 (%)

[[時間・距離などが]] long (↔short); (長たらしい)《しばしば軽蔑的に》lengthy. (⇨[類語])●長い旅 a *long* journey. ●長い説教 a *lengthy* sermon. ▶この橋はあの橋より10メートル長い This bridge is ten meters *longer* than that one./This bridge is *longer* than that one by ten meters. (!前の方が普通)

① [[長い間[こと]、長く]] for a long time, long; for (very) long.

解説 long, for (very) long は通例否定文・疑問文で用いる。ただし次の場合は肯定文でも可: (i) so, as, too, enough などで修飾されるか比較級で用いられる場合: 雨はもっと長く続くだろう The rain will last *longer*. (ii) 「have long +信念・想定・態度などを表す動詞」の形で用いられる場合: 私は長い間それをしようと考えてきた I have *long* thought of doing that. ただし、I've been thinking of doing that *for a long time*. の方が口語的.

● 長い間の苦労 long [many] years of hardships. ▶長い間行方不明になっている妻 one's *long*-lost wife. ▶彼は長い間そこにいる He has been there (for) *a long time*. (!for は継続・状態を示す動詞の後では省略可. 文脈では通例省略されない) ▶長い間大変お世話になりました Thank you very much for everything you've done for me *over the years*. ▶本を長い間ありがとうございました Thank you very much for the book. I'm afraid I've kept it *longer* than I should. (!相手に不便をかけるほど長く借りていたのではないかと懸念しつつ述べている) ▶ここには長くいられません. 長くても3時間です I can't stay here (for) *long*. I'll be here for three hours *at the longest*. ▶彼は長くは働かなかった He didn't work *for long*. (!He didn't work *for a long time*. は「長い間失業していた」の意)(ほんの短期間働いた) He only worked for a short time. ▶できるだけ長くここにいたい I want to stay here as *long as* I can. ▶彼女の幸せは長くは続かなかった Her happiness did not *last* (long).

会話「チェスやれる?」「かつてはやれたよ. でももう長いことやってないんだ」"Can you play chess?" "Once I could. But I haven't played (for) *ages* [*an age*]." (!誇張表現)

会話「ぼくはもうあまり長くないかもしれない」「何てことを言うの」"I may not live much *longer* [*be long for this world*]./I may not be *very long* [*have a very long time*] to live." "That's no way to talk."

② [[長くする[なる]]] ▶ズボンを2センチ長くする make one's pants two centimeters *longer*; *lengthen* one's pants [*let* one's pants *down*] (by) two centimeters. ▶だいぶ日が長くなってきた The days *are getting* considerably *longer*.

③ [[長くかかる]] ▶図書館ができるまでには長くかかるでしょう It will *be a long time* [x*till*] the library is [x*will be*] built. (!この構文では主節の動詞は未来か過去時制. 以下の否定文でも同様) ▶長くかかりますか Will (!it は省略するのが普通) *it be long*? (!it を省略するのが文法にくだけた表現) ▶長くはかかりません(=すぐ戻ります) I won't *be long* (*before* I come back [(*in*) com*ing back*]). (!( )内は省略する方が普通) ▶その仕事を終えるのにそう長くはかからなかった It didn't *take* very *long* to finish the work./It *wasn't* so *long before* [*till*] we finished the work. (⇨[解説])

● 長い目で見る ▶長い目で彼の将来を見るべきだ You should *take a long*(-*range*) *view of* his future. ▶長い目で見れば君は大学に行く方がよいだろう It will be better *in the long run* for you to go to college.

● 長いものには巻かれろ (目上の人と争ってもむだだ) It is useless to argue with our elders./(勝てないなら仲間になれ)《ことわざ》If you can't beat them, join them.

● 長いわらじをはく (長旅に出る) go on a long journey.

ながい 長居 图 a long stay [visit].
── **長居する** 動 stay (too) long; (他の客よりも) outstay, overstay.
会話「長居いたしまして御迷惑ではなかったでしょうか」「とんでもありません」"I hope we didn't *outstay* [*overstay, wear out*] our *welcome*." "Not at all." (いずれも「長居して嫌われる」の意)

ながいき 長生き (長寿) longevity /lɑndʒévəti/. ▶彼女は長生き(=長寿)の家系だ She comes from a *long-lived* family./Her family is noted for its *longevity*.
── **長生きする** 動 ▶女はたいてい男より長生きする Most women [(平均して) On average, women] *live longer* than men. ▶君は私より10年は長生きするだろう You will *outlive* [*survive*] me by ten years. (!survive は身内同士だけに用いる語)

ながいす 長椅子 (背もたれ・ひじかけ付きの) a sofa /sóufə/, a couch /káutʃ/; (背もたれ・ひじかけのない) a divan (!しばしばベッドとしても用いられる). (⇨椅子(ザ))

ながいも 長芋 (植物) a Chinese yam.

なかいり 中入り an intermission; 《英》 an interval.
● 中入り後の取組 *sumo* matches after the *intermission*.

ながうた 長唄 a *nagauta*; (説明的に) a refined traditional song sung with *samisen* accompaniment, which has developed along with *kabuki*.

ながえ 長柄 ● 長柄のパラソル a *long*-handled sunshade [parasol]; a sunshade [a parasol] *with a long handle*.

なかおもて 中表 ▶生地を中表にたたむ fold down material so that the right side is turned in.

なかおれ 中折れ [[帽子]] a fedora /fidó:rə/; 《英》 a trilby.

なかがい 仲買 (仲買業務) brokerage. ● 株の仲買をする act as (a) *stockbroker*.
● 仲買手数料 (やや書) brokerage, brokerage fees. ● 仲買人 a broker. ● 株式仲買人 a stockbroker.

なかがわ 中側 the inside. (⇨内側)

ながき 長き ▶その裁判は20年の長きにわたった It took *as long as* twenty years before the case was settled.

ながく 長く (⇨長い)

ながぐつ 長靴 boots, 《英》 high boots; [[ひざに達する]] top boots (!乗馬・狩猟用); (太ももまでおおう)

waders (!釣り人用). (⇨靴) ●長靴をはく[脱ぐ] pull on [off] one's *boots*.
なかぐろ 中黒 〚点〛a centered dot.
なかごろ 中頃 about [around] the middle of .... (⇨中旬)
***なかさ** 長さ (物・時間の) (a) length. (!特定の長さは ⓒ) ●長さ100メートルの船 a ship 100 meters *long* [*in length*]; a 100-meter-*long* ship. (⇨幅❶) ●そのテープを5センチの長さに切る cut the tape to a *length* of five centimeters. ●このボートとあのボートは同じ長さです This boat is *as long as* [is (*of*) *the same length as*, has *the same length as*] that one.
会話「そのロープの長さはどのくらいですか」「20メートルです」 "How *long* is the rope?" "It is 20 meters (*long*)."/(やや書) "What is the *length* of the rope?" "Twenty meters."
なかされる 泣かされる (⇨泣かせる)
ながされる 流される ●〚もって行かれる〛be carried away; (さっと) be swept away; 〚流水・波に〛be washed away; 〚吹き流される〛be driven away. ●情に流される be swayed by sentiment. ●時流に流される be carried [be swept] *away* by the current of the times. ●洪水で橋が流された The bridge *was washed* [*was carried, was swept*] *away* by the flood.
ながし 流し ❶〚洗う場所〛(台所の) a (kitchen) sink; (風呂場の) a draining floor. ❷〚客を求めて移動すること〛●流しのタクシー a *cruising* taxi. ●流しの芸人 a *strolling* musician. (⇨❺)
ながしあみ 流し網 a drift net.
● 流し網漁法 drift-net fishing.
ながしうち 流し打ち 图 ●流し打ちの打者 an *opposite-field* [a *slice*] hitter. ●流し打ちのホームラン an *opposite-field* home run.
── 流し打ちする 動 go [hit] the other way; (右[左]打者が) slice (a ball) to right [left]. ●カーブを流し打ちする inside out a curve to right.
ながじ 中敷き (部屋の敷物) a rug; (靴の) an insole.
ながじきり 中仕切り a partition; (つい立) a screen.
ながしこむ 流し込む ●パンを紅茶で流し込む *wash* bread *down* with tea. ●作業員は生コンを枠組みに流し込んだ The men *poured* fresh concrete *into* the forms.
ながしどり 流し撮り ── 流し撮りする 動 take a panning shot 《*of* a moving object》.
ながしめ 流し目 ●流し目で見る (横目で) cast a *sidelong glance* 《at him》, give [throw] 《him》 a *sidelong glance*, look [glance] *sidelong* 《at him》; (色目で) look 《at him》 *flirtatiously* [*amorously*], (やや書) cast *flirtatious* [*amorous*] *glances* 《at him》.
なかす 中州 a sandbank; (船の航行を妨げる中洲) a sandbar (!時にa bar ともいう); (三角州) a delta.
なかす 泣かす make*... cry. (⇨泣かせる)
なかす 鳴かす make*... sing.
:**ながす** 流す ❶〚水などを〛run*; (勢いよく) flush; (排水する) drain 《*out, away, off*》. ●下水[溝]に水を流す *run* the water *down* the waste pipe [*into* the ditch]. ●トイレの水を流す *flush* a toilet. ●水を流しっぱなしにするな Don't leave the water *running*. ●入浴後湯を流しておきなさい *Drain* the water *out* [*Run* the water *off*] after taking a [your] bath. (⇨前の方が普通)
❷〚血・涙を〛(書) shed*; (血を) bleed*. ●血を流す (=死ぬ, 負傷する) *bleed* (書) *shed* one's blood 《*for* one's country》. ●彼女は涙を流した She *shed* tears. (!tears を主語にして, Tears *ran down* her cheeks [*face*]. のようにいう方が普通) ●彼は額から血を流して地面に倒れた He fell to the ground, (with) blood *streaming from* his forehead.
❸〚浮かべて流す〛float; 〚水の力で押し流す〛*wash*... *away* [*out, off*]. ●丸太を川に流す *float* a log *down* a river. (!通例 down のような方向・到着点を示す副詞(句)を伴う. なければ「浮かべる」の意) ●背中を流す *wash* [(にすって) *scrub*] 《his》 back. ●汗を流す (汗をかく) *sweat* 《婉曲的に》*perspire*; (ふろなどで) *wash off* one's sweat.
❹〚音楽を〛play; 〚放送を〛broadcast*; 〚うわさを〛spread*, circulate. ●FM 放送局はよい音楽だけでなくニュースも流している The FM station not only *plays* good music but *broadcasts* news.
❺〚客を求めて移動する〛(タクシーが) cruise /krúːz/ 《streets》; (芸人が) stroll 《*from* bar *to* bar》.
ながすくじら 長須鯨 〚動物〛a finback, a fin whale.
● シロナガスクジラ a blue whale.
なかずとばず 鳴かず飛ばず ●彼は最初のアルバムを出して以来鳴かず飛ばずだ He hasn't been well known or has been forgotten since his first album was released.
-ながせ -泣かせ ●乗客泣かせのストライキ (やや書) a passenger-*hampering* strike. ●あの子は親泣かせだ (親を悲嘆にくれさせる) He is really *breaking* his *parents' heart*./(やっかい者だ) He is *really* a *nuisance* (話) a *pest*] to his parents./(米話) He's a *pain in the neck* to his parents. (!慣用句)
なかせる 泣かせる make*... cry; 〚感動させる〛move [touch]... to tears. ●泣かせる (=感動的な) 話 a *touching* [a *moving*] story. (!後の方がより感動的) ●だれがその子を泣かせたの Who *made* the boy *cry*? ●その映画には泣かされた The movie *moved* me *to tears*./I *was moved to tears* by the movie. ●彼女は結構男を泣かせるんじゃないの I think she has broken so many hearts. ●break one's heart は「悲しい思いをさせる」の意) ●あいつにはずいぶん泣かされた (=ずいぶん迷惑をこうむった) He *gave* me a lot of *trouble*.
ながそで 長袖 long sleeves. ●長袖のシャツ a *long-sleeved* shirt; a shirt *with* long sleeves.
なかぞら 中空 (⇨中空)
なかだか 中高 ── 中高の 形 convex.
なかたがい 仲違い 图 〚口論〛a quarrel 《with》; 〚不和〛(書) (a) discord; 〚疎遠〛estrangement.
── 仲違いする 動 quarrel 《話》fall out, 《話》have a falling-out 《*with*+人, *over*+事》. ●彼らは仲たがいしている They are on bad terms [(口もきかない間柄だ) They are *not on speaking terms*] with each other./They *are estranged from* each other. (!be estranged from each other は夫婦について用いると別居していることを含意)
なかだち 仲立ち 〚調停〛mediation /miːdiéiʃən/; (調停人) a mediator; 〚仲介〛intermediation; (仲介人) (やや書) an intermediary; (仲人) a go-between. ●...の仲立ちをする (やや書) *mediate* between ...; (やや書) act as (an) *intermediary* for ...; act as (a) *go-between* for ....
ながたらしい 長たらしい lengthy. ●長たらしい演説 a *lengthy* [(くどい) a *long-winded* /-windəd/] speech. (⇨長々と)
なかだるみ 中弛み ●シーズン中の中だるみ (米) a mid-season *slump*. ●下半期に入ると景気が中だるみになった Business *went* [*fell*] *into a slump* [(落ち込んだ) *slackened off*] after the first half year. ●会議は途中で中だるみになった (不活発になった) The meeting became *dull* halfway through./(だれた) The meeting *sagged in the middle*.

ながだんぎ 長談義 a lengthy talk; a long tedious speech.

ながちょうば 長丁場 ●長丁場の仕事 a *time-consuming* work. ▶長丁場になる It will *take a long time* (*to* do).

なかつぎ 中継ぎ [[仲介]] intermediation; [[代替]] a relay. ●中継ぎをする《やや書》act as (an) *intermediary* (*for*); relay. ●**中継ぎ投手**《野球》a middle reliever [man]; (抑えの投手の直前の) a setup man, 《和製語》a set-upper. ●**中継ぎ部隊** a *middle-relief* corps. ●**中継ぎ貿易** transit trade.

ながつき 長月 [9月] September; (陰暦の) the ninth month of the lunar calendar.

-なかったら [[...でなければ]] if ... not; [[今...がないならば]]《書》if it were not for ...; (現在の事実に反する仮定); [[あの時...がなかったならば]]《書》if it had not been for ... (! 過去の事実に反する仮定). ▶君の助けがなかったら私はその仕事ができないだろう If you *didn't* help me, I couldn't do the work. */Without* [《書》*If it were not for*, 《書・古》*But for*] your help, I couldn't [×can't] do the work. (!(1) いずれも「助けがあるのでその仕事ができる」の意. (2)「助けてくれるかどうか分からないが, もし助けてくれないなら」の意では *If you don't* help me [*Without* your help, ×*But for* your help], I can't do the work. but for は仮定法で用いるのでここでは不可) ▶彼のアドバイスがなかったら大損するところだった *If* he *had not given* me some advice, I would have lost a lot of money./《書》*If it had not been for* his advice, I would have suffered a great loss. (! 以上いずれも「実際は大損しなかった」ことを含意)

ながっちり 長っ尻 ▶彼は来るといつも長っ尻だ He stays for a long time whenever he comes to see us. (! ... stays too long とか outstays his welcome などとも いう)

ながつづき 長続き ──**長続きする** 動 last (for) a long time. ▶このよい天気は長続きしないだろう This fine weather won't *last* (*long*). (⇨持つ❼) ▶彼は何をしてもあまり長続きしない (= 最後までやり通すことができない) He never *sticks at* [*to*] anything very *long*./(一つの職に) He can't *keep* a job very *long*.

なかづり 中吊り ●**中吊り広告** an ádvertising pòster hung along the aisle of a train.

なかでも 中でも [[とりわけ]] [[ほかにもいろいろある中で特に]] among others, among other things. (! things は people, places などとすることもある) ▶彼は中でも音楽が好きだ He likes music *above all* [*among others*, *among other subjects*].

ながでんわ 長電話 a long telephone conversation [call]. ▶長電話をする talk for a long time on the phone.

なかなおり 仲直り 图 (a) reconciliation /rèkənsiliéiʃən/ 《*between*, *with*》.

──**仲直りする** 動 become [make] friends 《*with* him》 again; make* (it) up 《*with*》; be reconciled 《*with*》 (! 後の方が堅い語); (けんかを一時的におさめる) patch up the quarrel. ▶A と B が仲直りさせる *reconcile* A *with* B; *get* A *and* B *back together*. (! 後の方が口語的) ▶彼と仲直りしたらどうですか Why don't you *make* (*it*) *up with* him? / Why don't you *be reconciled with* him? ▶どうも 2 人は仲直りしそうにない There is no sign of them *making up* [*becoming friends again*].

会話 「たぶんあなたが彼に謝った方がいいわ. そうすれば仲直りできるかもしれないわよ」「なるほどね. ありがとう」 "Maybe you ought to apologize to him. That might help *patch things up* between you two." "Good idea. Thanks."

***なかなか 中々** ❶ [[たいへん]] (非常に) very; (かなり) rather, quite, fairly (⇨かなり), 《話》pretty; (相当に) considerably (! 通例動詞・比較級を修飾する (⇨だいぶ 解説)). (⇨相当(に)) ●なかなかかわいい少女 a *very* pretty girl; *quite* [*rather*] a pretty girl. ▶今日はなかなか暖かい It is *fairly* [*pretty*] warm today. ▶彼はなかなかの詩人だ《話》He's *some* poet. (! some に強勢を置く)

会話 「彼の作品どう思う?」「なかなかいいよ」 "What do you think of his work?" "(It's) *quite* góod [*not* too bad]." (! quìte gòod は「まあまあよい」の意. 後の方は控えめな表現で, より口語的)

❷ [[なかなか...しない]] (すぐに[容易に]...しない) not readily [easily] (do); (どうしても...しない) will* not (do), refuse (*to* do) (! will は習性を表す. 通例強勢を受ける); (...どころではない) far from 《*do*ing》. (⇨まだまだ) ▶その問題はなかなか解けなかった I couldn't *readily* [*easily*] solve the problem./(解くのに長く時間がかかった) The problem *took* me *a lot of time to* solve./(解くのに難儀した) I *had difficulty* (*in*) *solv*ing the problem. (! 通例 in を省略する) / It was very *difficult* to solve the problem. ▶このドアはなかなか開かない This door *won't* [*refuses to*] open. ▶彼はなかなか借金を払わなかった He was *slow in* mak*ing* his payments. ▶パラシュートはなかなか開かなかった The parachute had a *delayed* opening. (! delayed は「遅れた」の意) ▶彼女ほどの美人はなかなかいないよ She's *about the most* beautiful girl I've ever seen.

ながながと 長々と ❶ [[長い間]] for a long time; [[くどく]] at (great) length; (話し方が) long-windedly /-wíndədli/. ▶彼は長々と演説した He made a speech *for a long time*./(長たらしい演説をした) He made a *lengthy* [a *long-winded*] speech. ▶彼は私たちに長々と身の上話をした He told us the story of his life *at* (*great*) *length*.

❷ [[手足を伸ばして]] ●長々と芝生の上に寝そべる lie *at full length* on the grass; *spread oneself* [*stretch* (*oneself*) *out*] on the grass.

なかには 中には ●中にはとてもおもしろい本もある Some (of the) books are very interesting. (! 通例 some に強勢を置く (⇨中 ❸))

なかにわ 中庭 a court, a courtyard; (スペイン風住宅の) a patio /pǽtiou/ (複 ~s).

ながねん 長年 for (many) years (! many を省略するのは《話》); (長い間) for a long time. ▶長年の研究 *long* [*many*] *years* of research (! 《話》では long, many はしばしば省かれる); a *long-time* research. ▶長年の (= 古くからの) 友人 an *old* [*long-time*] friend. ▶彼女は教師としては長年の経験がある She has (×a) *long* experience as a teacher [in teaching]. ▶長年ここに住んできました I've lived here (*for*) *a long time*. (! 《話》では for はしばしば省略される)

ながの 永の ▶あれが彼との永の(= 永遠の)別れとなった That was the last time I saw him (alive).

ながの 長の ▶長の患いでやせこけている be gaunt from one's long illness.

なかば 半ば ❶ [[半分]] half; (中途で) halfway. (⇨半分) ▶私の仕事は半ば終わった *Half* (*of*) my work is finished./My work is *half* done [finished]./I am *halfway* through the work now. ▶彼は半ば口を閉ざしたまま言っていた He was saying with his mouth *half*-open. ▶半ば無意識にそう言った I said so *half* unconsciously.

❷ [[真ん中あたり]] in the middle 《*of*》. ●通りの半ば

in the middle [×center] *of* the street. ●6月の半ばに *in the middle of* June; in *mid-*June. ●週[1年]の半ばに *at midweek* [*midyear*]. ●学期半ばで退学する leave school *in midterm*. ●開発半ばの国 a *semi-developed* country. ●彼女は彼の演説の半ばで(=最中に)席を立った She left her seat *in the middle of* [*during*] his speech. ●彼女は40歳の半ばで死んだ She died *in her mid-forties* [*middle forties*].

❸【一部分】(一部分は) partly, 《やや書》in part; (部分的に) partially. ●頭が半ばはげた男 a *partially* bald man. ●彼の成功は半ば我々の援助のおかげだ He succeeded *partly* because we helped him./His success was due *in part* to our help [assistance].

ながばなし 長話 a long talk [《雑談》chat]. ●彼と長話をする talk [chat] with him *for a long time*; *have a long talk* [*chat*] with him.

なかび 中日 (相撲・芝居などの) the middle day 《*of* a sumo tournament [a public performance]》.

ながびく 長引く take* a long time; (だらだら続く) drag (-gg-) on. ●交渉は思ったより長引いた The negotiations *took longer* than (we) expected. ●風邪はいつまでも長引いた I couldn't get rid of the cold *for an unusually long time*. ●戦争がおわってすでに2年になる。この分だとあと2年ぐらい長引きそうだ The war has already been fought for two years, and it could *drag on* for two more years or so. ●彼は3日でできる仕事を1週間に長引かせた He *drew out* [*prolonged*] three days' work *to* a week.

なかぶた 中蓋 an inner [an inside] lid.

ながぼそい 長細い (⇨細長い)

なかほど 中程 ⑳ 教会は私の家とあなたの家の中程にあります The church stands *halfway between* my house *and* yours. ●中程へお進みください (列車・バスの乗客に対して) *Move along* [*Step forward*], please.

── 中程で ⑳ [[中間・中途で]] halfway; [[位置・時間の真ん中で]] in the middle 《*of*》. ●討論の中程で about *halfway through* a discussion; *in the middle of* a discussion. ●丘の中程で彼にばったり会う come across him *halfway up* [*down*] the hill. (❗ up と down の違いは自分が登って行くか下って行くかによる)

*なかま 仲間 a friend; a fellow; a partner; a companion; company; a group; a circle. (⇨友達)

> 使い分け friend 友情で結ばれた仲間.
> fellow 仕事・会社・国籍などの共通点に注目した仲間. しばしば名詞の前で形容詞的に用いる.
> partner 対等の関係で活動をともにする相棒, 共同事業者.
> companion 文語的で, 友情の有無は問わず単に行動をともにする仲間.
> company 一緒に時間を過ごす通例複数の人.
> group さまざまな種類の集団.
> circle 同じことに興味を持つ人の形式ばらない集まり. 後の3語はいずれも単・複両扱い.

①【~の(仲間】 ●楽しい仲間 pleasant *company*. ●仕事仲間 (同じ職場で類似の仕事の) a co-worker; (同じ職場の) a *fellow* worker; (専門職・役員などの) a colleague; (共同出資の) an associate, a partner. ●文学仲間 a literary *circle* [*coterie* /kóutərì/]. ●後の酒はしばしば軽蔑的) 音楽愛好者仲間 a *fellow* music-lover. ●犯罪者仲間 *fellows* [*partners*] in crime. ●あの人たちは釣り仲間です I often go fishing with them. (❗次の訳より普通)/They are my fishing *companions* [《話》*buddies*]. ●彼は会社の仲間です He works with me at the office./He is one of my *co-workers* [*fellow workers*]. ●1頭の猿が危険が近きつつあるのに気づいてキーと鋭い鳴き声を発して仲間に知らせた A monkey spotted some danger on the way and screeched, letting (*the*) *other monkeys* know. (❗he をつけると「群れのすべて」の意になる)

②【仲間~】 ●仲間意識 (have) a *fellow* feeling 《*for* him》; (a feeling of) fellowship. ●仲間入りする(=仲間に入る) (⇨③) ●彼は仲間はずれにされた He was [got] left out (in the cold)./He was left out of [excluded from] the *group*. ●彼らは仲間うちでは口論を始めた They started arguing *among* them. (❗ ... *among* themselves. は「他人はかまわず自分たちだけで」の意)

③【仲間の】 ●彼らの仲間に入る join them. ●ゲームの仲間に入る join [take part] in a game. ●悪い仲間に入っている[入る] be in [get *into*] bad *company*. ●仲間に入れる (許可で) let 《*him*》in; (強制) draw 《*him*》 in. ●仲間に入らない stay out of the *group*. ●彼は仲間に人気がある He is popular with his *friends* [*group*, *circle*].

④【仲間だ】 ●彼もその仲間だ He is one of them [the *group*]. ●オオカミ犬の仲間だ The wolf is a *member* of [《属する》belongs to] the dog family.

なかまわれ 仲間割れ a split 《*in* a group, *between* A and B》. ●仲間割れをする (be) split (up) [be divided] 《*into* two groups *over* the issue》. ●ちょっと, 仲間割れをしないで (けんかはやめなさい) Come on, stop quarreling among yourselves./(団結しない) You guys, stick together!

なかみ 中身 cónents. (⇨内容) ●中身のない男 a *hollow* man. ●引き出しの中身を床にぶちまける empty the *contents* of a drawer onto the floor. (❗通例《 》内は省略される) ●かばんの中身はがらくたばかりだった The *contents* of the bag were a lot of junk.

なかみせ 仲見世 *Nakamise*; (説明的に) a store which is on the premises of a temple or a shrine. ●浅草仲見世 Asakusa *Nakamise*.

ながめ 眺め a view; a sight; 《書》a prospect; [景色]((個々のまとまった) a scene, 《集合的》(ある土地全体の) scenery. (⇨風景)

> 使い分け view 特定の場所で目に映る景色や, 視界に入ってくる眺め・見晴らし.
> sight 人の注意を引き付ける景色・光景.
> prospect 遠くを望むような場所から見た広がりのある眺め・見晴らし. 通例単数形で用いる.

●眺め(=見晴らし)のよい部屋 a room with a (fine) *view*. ●美しい日没の眺め a beautiful sunset *sight* [*scene*]. ●山頂からの海の眺め(=見晴らし)がいい You can get a fine *view* of the sea from the mountaintop./The mountaintop has [gives, 《見渡す》《書》commands] a fine *view* of the sea. (⇨見晴らし) ●ビルのために眺めが妨げられている The *view* is cut off by the building./The building blocks the *view*.

ながめ 長目 ●髪を長めに刈る have one's hair cut *a little long*, ●longish hair is fairly long hair (かなり長い髪の毛の意で不適)

ながめる 眺める [[見る]] look at...; [[凝視する]] (集中して) gaze at...; (じろじろと) stare at...; [[景色などを見渡す]] get [have*] a view 《*of*》.(⇨見る, 見晴らす) ●星を眺める look (up) at [《じっと》gaze at] the stars. ●彼の顔をじっと眺める gaze at his face. ●妻

ながもち 長持ち ── **長持ちする** 動 (もちがよい) be durable; (長くもつ) last [keep, hold] (for) a long time; (長い使用に耐える) stand long use; (食べ物に) keep (for) a long time. (⇨持ち, 持つ ❼) ▶木綿の靴下はあまり長持ちしない Cotton socks *aren't* very *durable* [don't *wear well*].

ながや 長屋 a row (《英》a terrace(d)) house; (婉曲的に) a town house. ●三軒長屋 a *row house* devided into three units.

なかやすみ 中休み 图 ●仕事の中休み a coffee [a tea] *break*.
── **中休みする** 動 take [have] a rest; take [have] a break. (⇨休憩)

ながゆ 長湯 動 ●私は長湯だ I like to *take* [《英》*have*] *a long bath*.

なかゆび 中指 the [one's] middle finger. (⇨指)

なかよく 仲良く 副 [[楽しく]] happily; [[平穏に]] peacefully. ▶彼らは仲よく暮らしている They live together *happily* [*peacefully, in harmony*]./(仲よくやっている) They *are getting along* [*on*] *well* with each other.
── **仲良くする** 動 (仲良くしている) be friendly 《with》; be [keep*] good friends 《with》; get* along [on] 《with》; (友達になる) become* [make*] friends [ˣa friend] 《with》; (親しい関係を保つ) keep close [friendly] relations 《with》. ▶隣人と仲よくしなさい Try to *be friendly* [*on good terms*] *with* your neighbors. (**!** 後の方は堅い言い方) ▶パーティーでアルゼンチンの少女と仲よくなった I *became* [*made*] *friends with* an Argentine girl at the party. ▶いつもけんかばかりして, 仲良くできないの? You are always arguing. Can't you *be friends* [*get along*]?

なかよし 仲良し a good [a close] friend. (⇨親友) ●大の仲良し be *great friends* (=友達)になる become [make] *friends* 《with him》. ▶あの子供たちは仲良しだ The children are *good friends* [*get along well, get on just fine*].

:─ながら 《接続助詞》❶ [...しつつ] as ...; while ...; over ....

> **使い分け** as 二つの動作が平行して行われている感じが強い.
> **while** 「...しながら」の意の接続詞. 比較的長く継続する時間を表す. (⇨時 圏)
> **over** 「...しながら」の意の前置詞. 「話す, 眠る」などの動詞とともに用いる.

▶彼はご機嫌で口笛を吹きながら歩いていた He walked along *as* he whistled cheerfully. (**!** この後に, 例えば The tune was something familiar to me. (その調べは聞き覚えがあった)が続くような場合はこの構成でよいが, His pace was slow. (ゆっくりとした足どりであった)のように続く場合は He whistled cheerfully *as* he walked along. の順序が適切) ▶彼らはコーヒーを飲みながら休暇中の旅行のことを話し合った They talked about their trip during the vacation *over* (a cup of) coffee [*while* (they were) drinking a cup of coffee]. (**!** (1) over の後は動名詞は続かない. (2) 主節の主語と従節の主語が同一の場合, 従節の主語と be 動詞は省略可) ▶しばらくの間ふるえながら立っていた For a while I stood trembling. (**!** 現在分詞が補語の例) ▶心からほほえみながら彼女は客を迎えた *Smiling* heartily, she welcomed the guests. (**!** 分詞構文の例. ..., *smiling* heartily. のように文末でも可)

❷ [...にもかかわらず] in spite of ...; 《書》despite; (...ではあるが) though ..., although .... (**!** 後の方が堅い語). ▶彼は重い病気でありながらその会合に出席した *Though* [*Although*] he was seriously ill, he went to the meeting./He was seriously sick, *but* [《やや書》*yet*] he went to the meeting./He went to the meeting *in spite of* [*despite*] his serious sickness [illness]. (**!** 以上の中で 2 番目の文を用いるのが最も堅い言い方)

ながらえる 長らえる live long; survive. ●政治生命を長らえる be a politician for a long time.

ながらく 長らく ▶彼と長らく会っていない I haven't seen him (*for*) *a long time* [(*for*) *long*]. (⇨長く, 長い) ▶長らくお世話になりました You've *been* very kind to me. Thank you very much.

なかれ 莫れ ▶君死にたまうことなかれ You *shall never die*. ▶驚くなかれ. 宝くじで 100 万円も当たってしまったよ *Don't be surprised!* I won a million yen in the lottery.

*ながれ 流れ ❶ [気体・水などの] a flow (**!** 複数形にしない); a stream; a current.

> **使い分け** flow なめらかで安定した流れ.
> **stream** 絶え間のない継続した流れ. 水道や水源などから почему流れを暗示する.
> **current** 絶え間のない継続した流れ. 流れの強さや方向を強調する.

●水の流れ the *flow* [*stream*] of water. ●流れの速い川 a fast-*running* river. ●流れにさからって[そって]泳ぐ swim against [with] the *stream*; swim upstream [downstream]. (**!** 前の方が口語的で, 比喩的に「時勢にさからう[従う]」の意もある) ●流れを上る[下る] go up [down] the *stream* [*river*]. ▶その川は流れが速い The river runs [flows] fast 〈=slow〉./The river has a strong *current*.

❷ [人・車・言葉などの] a stream; a flow. ▶ひっきりなしに続く車の流れ a steady *stream* [*flow*] of traffic. ●車の流れに(注意深く)割り込む edge out into the *stream* of traffic. ▶車の流れが速くなってきた The traffic *is moving faster*. ▶早朝からその寺の参拝者の流れが絶えない There has been a *flow* [a *stream*] of visitors to the temple since early morning.

❸ [血統] descent; [流派] a school. ●名門の流れをくむ come from [《主に英》of] a good family. ●ロマン派の流れをくむ belong to the Romantic school.

❹ [推移・動向] ●時の流れ the *passage* [*lapse*] of time. ●(試合の)流れをつかむ control the game; grasp the flaw of the game. ●(試合の)流れを読む read the game. ●(試合の)流れに乗る take charge of the game. ▶その事件が歴史の流れを変えた The event changed the *course* of history. ▶彼のホームランが試合の流れ(=形勢)を変えた His homerun changed (the situation of) the game.

> **翻訳のこころ** 水の流れなのか, 時の流れなのか, 「鹿おどし」は我々に流れるものを感じさせる (山崎正和『水の東西』) *Shishiodoshi* makes us aware [conscious] of something that flows, be it the running of water or the passage of time. (**!** 「(水が)流れる」は run, 「(時が)流れる」は passes)

- 流れにさおさす (時流に乗る) go [swim] with the tide. ▶君の意見は流れにさおさすものだ(=時流に逆らう) Your opinion *is against* the tide. (参考) この日本語の使い方には誤用であるが多く使われている)

ながれあるく 流れ歩く wander /wɑ́ndər/ from place to place. (⇨渡り歩く, 流れ者)

ながれこむ 流れ込む flow [(どっと) pour; (群がって) crowd; (流れるように) stream] *(into)*. ▶この川は日本海に流れ込んでいる This river *flows* [*empties*] *into* the Sea of Japan. (! このように川の常態をいう場合は，×*is flowing* …と進行形にはしないことに注意) ▶難民がどっとその都市に流れ込んだ Refugees *flooded* /flʌ́did/ [*crowded into*] the city.

ながれさぎょう 流れ作業 an assembly line. ●流れ作業のラインにつく work *on an* assembly line.

ながれず 流れ図 a flow chart [diagram].

ながれだす 流れ出す (流れ始める) begin to flow; (流れて外へ出る) flow [run] out.

ながれだま 流れ弾 ●流れ弾に当たる be hit by a *stray bullet*.

ながれつく 流れ着く ▶岸[島]に流れ着く *drift* ashore [to an island]. ▶ヤシの実が潮流に乗って北国の海岸に流れ着いた The current brought a coconut to the shore of a northern country.

ながれぼし 流れ星 a shooting [a falling] star (! 前の方が日常語); (流星，隕石(ぃんせき)) a meteor /míːtiər/. ▶あっ，流れ星だ Oh, there goes [I see] a *shooting star*.

ながれもの 流れ者 [放浪者] a drifter, a wanderer (! a vagabond は(古); よそ者] a stranger; [一時滞在者] a transient (! 通例複数形で).

＊ながれる 流れる

WORD CHOICE 流れる
flow 水・川・涙・気体などが絶えず滑らかに一定の速さで流れること．比喩的に交通の流れなども用いる．▶涙が彼のほほを流れた Tears *flowed* down his cheek.
run 水・川・涙などが流れること．比喩的に感情の流れなどにも用いる．▶川がその地域を流れている The river *runs* through the area.
stream 液体などが勢いよく流れること．比喩的に人の流れなどにも用いる．▶彼の顔を滝のように汗が流れ落ちた Sweats *streamed* down his face.

頻度チャート
flow ━━━━━━━━━━━
run ━━━━━━
stream ━━
      20   40   60   80   100 (%)

❶[川・水などが] flow, run* (! flow の方がとうとうと流れることを強調); [液体が] run; (なめらかに絶え間なく) flow; (速く勢いよく) stream (⇨類語); (一度にどっと) pour; (少しずつ) trickle. (! 以上は流れの方向・様態を表す副詞(句)を後に伴う) ▶流れる水の音 the noise of *running* water. ▶信濃川は北に流れて日本海に注いでいる The Shinano River *flows* [*runs*] north into [to] the Sea of Japan. (! 日本語につられて進行形にしない．進行形は一時的な状態を表す: 今日は川の流れが速い The river *is flowing* [*running*] fast today.) ▶桂川は京都を流れている The Katsura River *flows* [*runs*] through [xin] Kyoto. (! 「貫流する」の意なので in は不可) ▶彼女の目から涙が流れた Tears *ran* [*flowed*, *streamed*] from her eyes./Her eyes *ran* [*flowed*, *streamed*] with tears. (! stream は「と

めどなく流れる」の意) ▶パイプが詰まって水が流れなかった The pipe was choked up and (so) the water didn't *go through* [*drain* (*off*)].

❷[人々・物事が] flow; (続々と) stream; (どっと) pour; [時が] pass. (⇨経う) ▶会話[車]はスムーズに流れた Conversation [The traffic] *flowed* freely [smoothly]. ▶試合後球場から人が続々と流れ出てきた The people *streamed* [Streams of people came] out of the stadium after the game. ▶星が流れた A star *shot* across the sky. ▶田舎では都会と違って時間がゆっくり流れる In the country, unlike in a city, time *passes* [*goes*] slowly. ▶恩師の還暦祝いをホテルで開き，そのあとで銀座に流れた(=行った) We celebrated *kanreki*, the sixtieth birthday, of our former teacher at a hotel and then we all *went to* Ginza.

❸[浮かび漂う] float (! 通例方向・到着点を示す副詞(句)を伴う); drift; [押し流される] be washed [be carried, be swept] away. (⇨流す ❸) ▶ボールが川を流れている A ball *is floating* down the river./There is a ball *floating* down the river. ▶流木が潮に乗って流れていった Driftwood *floated* away on the tide. (! 方向を示す away がなければ「潮に浮かんだ」の意となる)

❹[伝わる] ▶音楽がホールから流れてきた Music came *floating* up from the hall to our ears. ▶町中にうわさが流れた The rumor *spread* [*ran*, *circulated*] all over (the) town. ▶「自分の住んでいる町」の場合は the をつけない) ▶その一家には学者の血が流れている(=学者の血筋だ) Learning *runs* in the family./There *have been the generations of* scholars in the family.

❺[中止になる] be canceled, be called off; (試合などが雨で) be rained out (米) [*off* (英)]. (⇨中止) ▶雨で試合が流れた The game was *canceled* [*called off*] because of (the) rain./Rain *wrecked* the game.

ながれる『流れる』*Flowing*. (参考) 幸田文の小説)

ながわずらい 長患い 图 a long [慢性化した) a chronic, (だらだらと続く) a lingering] illness [disease].
── **長患いする** 動 suffer from a long disease; be sick for a long time.

なかんずく 就中 (特に) especially; (とりわけ) above all; among other things.

なき 亡き dead; (最近死んだ) late, (書) deceased /disíːst/. ▶亡き父 my *dead* [*late*, *deceased*] father. ▶今は亡き田中氏 the *late* Mr. Tanaka. (! 人名・職名・関係を表す語などにつけるときは the を伴う) ▶亡き後 after one's *death*.

なき 泣き ●泣きを入れる (泣きついて頼む) implore 《him to do》; beg 《his pardon》 in tears; beg 《him》 for 《help》.
●泣きを見る ▶そんなことを言うと泣きを見る(=つらい目にあうよ) You will pay for your words.

なぎ 凪 a calm /kɑːm/. ●朝[夕]凪 a morning [an evening] *calm*.

なきあかす 泣き明かす weep* [cry] all night.

なきおとし 泣き落とし ●泣き落としにかかる use tears 《for getting …》; *to* win him over》 try to win 《him》 over by tearful entreaties.

なきおとす 泣き落とす win* 《him》 over by piteous [tearful] entreaties.

なきがお 泣き顔 a tearful face, a tear-stained face. ●泣き顔を隠す hide one's tears.

なきがら 亡骸 a (dead) body.

なきかわす 鳴き交わす sing* [chirp, twitter] to each other.

なきくずれる 泣き崩れる (取り乱して泣く) break* down (crying [in tears]); burst* out crying, burst into tears.

なきくらす 泣き暮らす (1日中泣いている)cry [weep*] all day [long]; (毎日を泣いて暮らす) spend* one's days in tears [sorrow]; lead a tearful [《書》a sorrowful] life.

なきごえ 泣き声 [《泣く声》]a cry, 《やや書》a weep (■ 複数形にしない); (すすり泣き, むせび泣きの) a sob; [涙声] a tearful voice. ● 少年の泣き声 a boy's *cry*; a boy's *sobs*. ● 泣き声で話す speak *in a tearful* [《震え声で》*a shaky*] *voice*; speak *with tears in* one's *voice*.

なきごえ 鳴き声 a cry; [鳥・虫の短い] a chirp; [鳥のさえずり] a song; a twitter (⇨声❷); (からすの) a caw /kɔ́ː/; [犬の] a bark; (きかんきゃん鳴く声) a yelp; [猫の] a meow. (⇨鳴く) ● 早朝のカラスの鳴き声はことのほかうるさい The *cawing* of crows is especially noisy early in the morning.

なきごと 泣き言 (不平) a (useless) complaint. ▶彼はいつも給料が安いと泣き言ばかり言っている He *is always complaining* [*grumbling*, 《俗》*moaning*] *about* his low salary.

なぎさ 渚 (波打ち際) a beach; (岸) (a) shore; (水辺) the waterside.

なきさけぶ 泣き叫ぶ cry; (泣きわめく) cry dramatically; (金切り声で) scream. (⇨泣く)

なきじゃくる 泣きじゃくる [『すすり泣く』]sob (-bb-); [子供などがおいおい泣く] blubber; [鼻をすすって泣く] sniffle. ● 泣きじゃくりながら悩みを語る sob [*blubber*] *out* one's trouble. ▶かわいそうにその少女は泣きじゃくりながら寝てしまった The poor girl *sobbed herself to sleep*. (■ sleepは名詞) ▶彼女は泣きじゃくりながら頼んだ She asked *with a sob* [*between her sobs*].

なきじょうご 泣き上戸 a maudlin drinker.

なきすがる 泣き縋る cling* to (him) in tears.

なきすな 鳴き砂 singing [whistling, squeaking, musical] sand.

なぎたおす なぎ倒す mow [cut*] (the grass) down. ▶彼はチェスでみいる強豪をなぎ倒した(=打ち負かした) He *defeated* [《徹底的にやっつけた》《話》*licked*] *one* strong opponent *after another* at chess.

***なきだす 泣き出す** start to cry [《書》weep]. ● わっと泣き出す burst [*break*] *into* tears /tíɚz/; burst out crying (■ この方が口語的だ); break down (and cry). ▶彼女は今にも泣き出しそうだった She was *on the verge of* [*close to*] *tears*.

なきつく 泣きつく [『懇願する』]beg (-gg-), 《書》entreat; [『嘆願する』]《書》implore. ▶彼は先生に助けてくださいと泣きついた He *begged* [*entreated*, *implored*, (訴えた) *appealed to*] his teacher *for* help [*to* help him].

なきつら 泣きっ面 [泣いている顔] a crying [《書》a weeping] face; [涙ぐんだ顔] a tearful face.
 ●**泣きっ面に蜂**(½) (ことわざ) Misfortunes never come singly./It never rains but it pours. (■ 昔はよい事にも用いたが, 今は「不幸・災害は重なる」の意で日本語のことわざに対応する)/One mischief comes on the neck [tail] of another. ▶泣きっ面に蜂(=さらに悪いことには)夫も病気になった To make matters worse, my husband got sick too.

なきどころ 泣き所 [『弱点』]one's weak [《やや書》vulnerable] point; [アキレス腱(½)] one's Achilles(') /əkíliːz/ heel. (参考) アキレスはただ一か所を除けば不死身であったとされることから. ● 人の泣き所を突く seize on [*upon*] other people's *weak points*. ▶彼は実力のある政治家だが学歴のないのが泣き所だ He is a powerful political leader, but lack of education is his *Achilles' heel*.

なきなき 泣き泣き 《say good-by》in tears;《The couple parted》tearfully. ▶彼女は泣き泣き自分の過去を話した She *sobbed out* her past life./She told her past life *between sobs*.

なぎなた 薙刀 a *naginata*; (説明的に) a short sword fixed to the end of a long shaft, which was used as a weapon.

なきにしもあらず 無きにしもあらず ▶まだ望みはなきにしもあらずだ(=ないわけではない, 少しはある) There is *a little* hope left. ▶勝ち目はなきにしもあらずだ(=勝つチャンスはあまりないが可能性はある) There is *a possibility* for us to win, *though the chance is very small*.

なきぬれる 泣き濡れる be covered in tears; be in a flood of tears; (涙でよごれた) be tear-stained.

なきねいり 泣き寝入り ━ 泣き寝入りする 動 [泣きながら寝入る] cry [sob (-bb-)] oneself to sleep; [やむを得ず受け入れる] be compelled to accept; (屈辱などを甘んじて受ける)《話》take ... lying down (■ 通例否定文で). ▶その会社は倒産したので債権者は泣き寝入りするしかなかった The company went bankrupt, so the creditors *had to* [*were compelled to*] *accept* their fate [(損失) losses]. ▶このような不当な処置に泣き寝入りしてはいけない We must not *take* such an injustice *lying down*.

なきのなみだ 泣きの涙 ●泣きの涙で with tears in one's eyes, with tearful eyes; tearfully.

なぎはらう なぎ払う mow ... down.

なきはらす 泣き腫らす cry one's eyes out. ▶彼女は泣きはらした目をしていた Her eyes *were swollen from crying*.

なきふす 泣き伏す break* down crying.

なきべそ 泣きべそ ●**泣きべそをかく** (子供が) whimper; (今にも泣きそう) almost [half] cry. ●泣きべそをかいている be *almost in tears*; be *close* [*near*] *to tears*.

なきぼくろ 泣き黒子 a mole under the eye.

なきまね 泣き真似 (そら涙) crocodile tears; (にせの涙) false tears. ●泣き真似をする shed [《書》weep] *crocodile tears*; pretend to be crying [weeping];《書》feign tears.

なきむし 泣き虫 a crybaby.

なきやむ 泣き止む stop (-pp-) crying [sobbing].

なきりぼうちょう 菜切り包丁 a kitchen knife for cutting vegetables.

なきわかれる 泣き別れる part in tears 《from him》.

なきわらい 泣き笑い 图 ▶人生は泣き笑いだ (Our) life is checkered with *joy and sorrow*.
 ━ 泣き笑いする 動 smile through one's tears; (声を立てて) cry and chuckle.

‡なく 泣く
> **WORD CHOICE** 泣く
>
> **cry** 感情的・生理的理由により, 声を上げて泣くこと. しばしば泣き声の大きさ・様子などを示す副詞とともに用いる. ▶赤ん坊がミルクを欲しがって大泣きしている A baby is crying furiously for milk.
> [cry＋副] quietly/loudly/aloud
> **weep** 悲しみのために, 主に静かに涙を流して泣くこと. 改まった文脈で多く用いられる. ▶女性が狂乱状態で泣いていた A woman was weeping hysterically.
> [weep＋副] silently/softly/quietly/bitterly
> **sob** 小刻みに息を詰まらせながらすすり泣くこと. 声を上げて泣きじゃくるときから静かにすすり泣くことまで, 幅広く表す. ▶悲しみにむせび泣く sob with grief.
> [sob＋副] uncontrollably/hysterically/quietly/silently

なく

頻度チャート

cry					
weep					
sob					
20	40	60	80	100 (%)	

cry; 《書》weep* (!前の方は声を上げて泣くことに, 後の方は涙を流すことに重点があるが, 区別なく用いることも多い);[すすり泣く] sob (-bb-); [涙を流す]《主に書》shed* tears /tíərz/; [子供などがしくしくと] whimper; [泣き叫ぶ]《書》(しばしば軽蔑的に) wail. ●泣きたくなる feel like *crying*. ●涙をこらえる hold [keep] back one's tears. ▶手を振って別れを告げたとき彼女は泣いていた She was *in tears* when I waved good-by to her.

① [〜(という様子で)泣く] ● 大きな声で泣く *cry* loudly. ● 思い切り[おいおい]と泣く have a good *cry*; [胸かきむしるほど] *cry* [*sob*] one's heart out. ● むせび泣く be choked with tears.

翻訳のこころ メロスは川岸にうずくまり, 男泣きに泣きながら両腕に手を上げて哀願した(太宰治『走れメロス』) Crouching (down) by the river and raising [lifting] his arms [hands], Melos shed tears [cried (out); let out a warrior's cry] and entreated to Zeus. (!let out a warrior's cry は「男泣きに泣く」の言い慣用表現)

② [〜(という理由・原因)で泣く] ● 痛くて泣く *cry* [*wail*] with [in] pain. ● うれしくて泣く *cry* [*weep*] for [with] joy; *shed tears* of joy. ● 同情して泣く(=もらい泣きする) *cry* [*weep*] in sympathy (*with* him). ● 悲報を聞いて泣く *cry* [*weep*] at the sad news. ● 彼の死を悲しんで泣く *cry* [*weep*] *over* his death. (!泣く原因が具体的でない場合は cry about を用いる: 彼のことで泣く *cry about* him) ▶赤ん坊はミルクを欲しがって泣いている The baby *is crying* [×weeping] *for* milk.

③ [泣きながら...する] 《do》with sobs [[目に涙をためて]with tears in one's eyes]. ● 泣きながら寝入る *cry* [*weep, sob*] oneself to sleep. (!この sleep は名詞) ● 彼女は泣きながら自分の過去を語った She *sobbed out* her past life./She told her past life *between sobs*.

● 泣いても笑っても ▶泣いても笑っても試験まであと3日しかない No matter how hard you try, you have *only* [《話》*only* have] three days left before the exam.

● 泣く子と地頭には勝てぬ 'There is no persuading a crying child or government officials.'/(聞き分けのない人に理を説いてもむだだ) There's no use reasoning with an unreasonable person./(体制には従わざるを得ない) You can't beat the system.

● 泣く子も黙る ▶彼は泣く子も黙る鬼監督だ(=恐怖におののかせる厳しい監督だ) He is a very strict coach who is enough to *strike fear in* anyone's *heart*.

:なく 鳴く ▶ [鳥・虫が] (歌うように) sing*; (ちいちいと) chirp; [鳥がさえずる] twitter; [犬が] (わんわんと) bark; (くんくんと) whine; [猫が] me(o)w /miáu/, go* miaow ["miaow"].

解説 日本語では「わんわん[にゃあにゃあ]と鳴く」のように「鳴く」に擬声語を添えて鳴き方を表すが, 英語では bark, me(o)w など動詞1語で表すのが普通.

▶小鳥が木々の間で鳴いている Birds *are singing* [*chirping, twittering*] in the trees. ▶子犬は腹をすかして[ミルクをねだって]くんくん鳴いた The puppy *whined from* hunger [*for* milk].

会話 「ひなはどんな鳴き声なの」「チッチッ[ピーピー]って鳴くよ」"What do the baby birds sound like?" "They go '*tweet, tweet* [*peep, peep*]'."

関連 上記以外の主な鳴き声
[獣類] [牛] (雄) bellow, (雌) moo /múː/; [馬] (ひんと) neigh /néi/, (低くやさしく) whinny; [猿] chatter; [ネズミ] squeak; [羊, ヤギ, 子牛] bleat; [豚] grunt, go "oink, oink".
[鳥類] [雄鶏] (こけこっこうと) crow; [雌鶏] (こっこっと) cluck; [ひよこ] peep; [アヒル] quack; [カラス] caw; [ハト] coo; [フクロウ] hoot.
[その他] [カエル] croak; [コオロギ, キリギリス, スズムシ, マツムシ] chirp; [ハチ] hum, (うなる) buzz.

なぐ 凪ぐ [海が] become calm [quiet]; [風が] die (〜d; dying) down, go* down. ▶海が[風が] (一時的に)ないだ The sea [The wind] (*was*) *lulled*.

なぐ 薙ぐ cut* down 《long grass》by swinging a sickle; mow*.

なぐさみ 慰み (楽しみ) fun, (an) amusement (!前の方が口語的), (気晴らし) a diversion; (娯楽) a pastime. ●慰みにギターを弾く play the guitar *for fun* [*amusement*]. ▶彼女は詩を作ることに慰みを見いだした She found *amusement* in writing poems. ▶テニスは私の唯一の慰みです Tennis is my only *diversion*.

なぐさむ 慰む ❶ [気持ちが晴れる] feel* cheerful [refreshed]; enjoy [amuse] oneself 《*by*》. ● 心が慰まない feel depressed; be in low spirits. ❷ [もてあそぶ] trifle 《*with*》. ● 女を慰む *fool around with* a woman.

なぐさめ 慰め (a) comfort; (a) consolation (!後の方が堅い語). ● 彼女にちょっと慰めの言葉をかける say a few words of *comfort* [*consolatory* words] to her. ● 音楽に慰めを見いだす find *consolation* in music. ● 彼女がいてくれるのが彼には大きな慰めであった Her presence was a great *comfort* [*consolation*] to him.

*なぐさめる 慰める comfort; console (!comfort より堅い語); (元気づける) cheer ... up. ● 彼女は泣いているその子の肩に両腕を回して慰めるように抱きついた She put her arms around the crying boy's shoulders and gave him a *comforting* [(なだめるように) a *soothing*] hug. ▶私は彼女が私を愛していたのだと考えて自分を慰めた I *consoled myself* thinking [*with* the thought] that she had loved me.

なくしもの 無くし物 a lost article; (遺失物) 《集合的》lost property. ▶何か無くし物でもしましたか Did you *lose* something?

なくす(る) 亡くす(る) [失う] lose. (⇨死ぬ) ● 夫を亡くした妻 a wife whose husband *has died* [*is dead*]; 《書》a *bereaved* wife. ● がんで妻を亡くす *lose* one's wife to cancer. ▶彼は交通事故で息子を亡くした He *lost* his son in a car accident./(奪われて)《書》He *was deprived* [*was bereaved*] of his son in a traffic accident. (!bereaved の方がさらに堅い語で, 近親者・友人にのみ用いる) ▶両親を亡くしたのは大きな痛手だった The *loss* of my parents was a great *blow* [*shock*] to me.

なくす(る) 無くす(る) [失う] lose (⇨失う, 紛失する); [望ましくないものを除く・捨てる] get* rid of ...; [制度などを廃止する] abolish, do* away with .... (!後の方が口語的) ● 死刑をなくする *abolish* [*do away with*] the death penalty. ▶彼はそれに対してすっか

り興味をなくしてしまった He *has lost* all interest in it. ▶なまりをなくすのは難しい It's difficult to *get rid of* an accent. ▶私は借金をなくすのに苦労した I had a hard time (in) *getting out of* debt. ▶警察は犯罪をなくそうと努めている The police are trying to *do away with*〔終らせる〕*put an end to* crime. 【…なくして〜(なし)】 No…, no〜. ▶骨折りなくして利益なし〔ことわざ〕*No pain(s), no gains.* ▶改革なくして成長なし *No* reform, *no* growth.

―なくて 〚…なしで〛without…;〚…の欠乏のため〛for lack [want] of …;〚A でなくて B だ〛not A but B. ▶田舎に住んでいると車がなくてはやっていけません Since we live in the country, we can't do *without* a car./〔車は不可欠である〕A car is *indispensable* [必需品] a *necessity*] in our country life. (⇨ 一無して) ▶この花は水がなくて枯れた These flowers died *for lack [want] of* water. ▶あの方は博士なくて教授です He is *not* a doctor *but* a professor. (🔳(1)このような短い文では He is not a doctor. He is a professor. というのが普通. (2)アメリカでは助手・講師を含め大学の先生はたいてい博士号〔a doctor's degree〕を持っており, 身分のよく分からないときは Dr. A と呼ぶことが多い) ▶こんにちな天気の日は家にいるのではなくてどこかへ行きたい I'd like to go somewhere *instead of* staying (at) home on a nice day like this.

なくてはならない indispensable; essential; absolutely necessary.(⇨必要な) ▶それは私にはなくてはならない物です It is *indispensable* to me./〔それがなくてはやっていけない〕I *cannot* do *without* it.

なくなく 泣く泣く reluctantly.(⇨嫌々) ▶泣く泣く不利な条件をのむ *have to* accept the disadvantageous terms.

***なくなる** 無くなる ❶〚消え去る〛be gone (🔳結果の状態を強調);〚消える〛disappear (⇨消える);〚紛失する〛lose*;〔行方不明である〕be missing. ▶戻ってみると自転車がなくなっていた When I came back, my bicycle *was gone [had disappeared].* ▶ぼくの時計がなくなった My watch *disappeared [is missing, is gone].*/〔失った〕I *lost* my watch. ▶頭痛がなくなった My headache *is gone [has gone].*(🔳後の方は「どこかへ行ってしまった」という移動の感じが強い) ▶1時間捜したあげく, それもなくなったものとあきらめた After an hour's search we gave it up *for lost.* ▶やがてこの町から公害がなくなるだろう There will be *no* pollution in this city before long./This city will soon *be free from* pollution. ❷〚尽きる〛run* out;〔不足する〕run short. (⇨尽きる) ▶時間がなくなってきた We *are running out of* time./Time *is running out* 〔時間切れ寸前だ〕*is almost up*]. ▶借金はもうなくなった I'm now *out of* debt. ▶口をきく元気もなくなった I *no longer* have the energy to talk. ▶もう *no longer* は「もはや…ない」の意) ▶一度にそんなにチョコレートを食べてはだめよ. すぐになくなってしまうわよ Don't eat that much chocolate at a time. Soon you *won't have* any *left.* ▶11時を過ぎるとバスがなくなる(=止まる) The bus *stops* running [*There is no* bus service] after 11 o'clock. ▶いよいよという時になって彼は勇気がなくなった His courage *failed* him at the last [crucial] moment. (🔳fail は「(いざという時に)…の役に立たない」の意)

なくなる 亡くなる die (〜d; dying);〔婉曲的〕pass away. (⇨死ぬ)

なくもがな 無くもがな be better left out;〔不必要だ〕be unnecessary. ▶君のあの一言は無くもがなだった(=言わないでおいた方がよかった) That remark of yours *was better left unsaid.*

なぐりあい 殴り合い 〔殴打の応酬〕an exchange of blows;〔けんか〕a fight;〔素手での殴り合い〕a fistfight. ▶彼と殴り合いになった I *began fighting [to fight]* with him./I came to blows with him.

なぐりかかる 殴りかかる hit* 〔《やや書》strike*〕《at him)》. ▶彼は突然殴りかかってきたが, 私はうまくかわした He suddenly hit [took a swing] *at* me, but I warded off his blows. (🔳 at は「…を目がけて」の意. at がない場合は実際に殴ったことになるので, この文脈では tried to hit [strike] me, …の方がよい)

なぐりがき 殴り書き a scribble. 〔《やや話》a scrawl. ●なぐり書きのメモ a *scribbled [a scrawled]* note. ▶このなぐり書きは何と書いてあるのか分からない I can't make out what this *scribble [scrawl]* says.

なぐりこみ 殴り込み ●殴り込みをかける raid; make a raid *(on*).

なぐりたおす 殴り倒す knock [《やや書》strike*, ×hit]…down;《米》〔こぶしで〕punch… out. ●彼を一発で殴り倒す *knock [strike]* him *down* at one blow.

なぐりつける 殴りつける hit, strike. (⇨殴る)

***なぐる** 殴る hit*, strike* 〔🔳hit は「ねらいを定めて強く打つ」の意. この方が口語的;〔こぶしや固い物で〕knock;〔続けざまに〕beat*;〔こぶしで〕punch;〔平手で〕slap (-pp-). (⇨打つ, 叩〈たた〉く) ●彼を棒でひどく殴る *hit [strike]* him hard with a stick; 〔ひどく殴って傷を負わす〕*beat* him *up* with a stick. ●彼の頭を殴る *hit him on* the head; *hit* his head. (🔳前の方は「人」, 後の方は「頭」に焦点を当てた言い方) ●彼を殴り殺す *beat* him *to* death. ●彼を殴って気絶させる *knock [beat]* him unconscious. ●平手で彼女の顔を殴る *slap* her *on [in, across]* the face. (🔳 on, in, across の違いは ⇨叩〈たた〉く) ▶彼が先に殴ったんです. ぼくは殴り返したわけです He *hit* me first. I was only *hitting* back. (🔳 この進行形は行為の反復を表す) ▶その少年はあざができるほど殴られた The boy *was beaten* (until he was) black and blue. ▶鼻面を一発殴ってやった I gave him *a punch on [in]* the nose. (🔳「1発殴られた」は I *got* a punch …). (⇨パンチ) ▶殴られて彼は頭にこぶができた The *blow* raised a bump on his head.

なげ 投げ ❶〔相撲・柔道の〕a throw. ●投げをうつ *throw* one's opponent (*down*). ❷〔投了〕〔碁・将棋〕giving up halfway.

なげいれ 投げ入れ 〔華道〕*nageire*; 〔説明的に〕free style flower arrangement.

なげいれる 投げ入れる throw*… into〜. (⇨投げる)

なげうつ 擲つ 〔〔地位などを放棄する〕give*… up;〔公職などを正式に辞する〕resign;〔仕事などをやめる〕《話》quit*;〔突然〕《話》throw*… up. ●大臣の地位をなげうつ *give up [resign]* one's position as (a) minister. ●命をなげうって(=犠牲にして) *at the sacrifice [cost] of* one's life. ●私財をなげうって孤児院を設立する *spend all* one's fortune setting up an orphan home. ▶彼は仕事をなげうって病人を救うためアフリカに行った He *gave up [quit, 《話》threw up]* his job and went to Africa to save sick people.

なげうり 投げ売り 图 a sacrifice (sale);〔海外市場での〕a dumping.
―― 投げ売り(を)する 動 ●夏物の投げ売りをする *sell* summer wear *at a sacrifice* 〔〔損で〕*at a loss*〕. ●石油を市場に投げ売りする(=ダンピングする) *dump* petroleum *on* the market.

なげおろし 投げ下ろし ●投げ下ろし投球 〔野球〕a round arm delivery. ●投げ下ろしで投げる throw over the top; throw straight overhand.

なげかける 投げ掛ける throw*…*at, on*);〔問題を

なげかつ 起する) pose, cause. ▶その問題に疑問を投げかける *throw* [*cast*] doubt *on* the problem. (⚠ throw の方が口語的) ▶彼に軽蔑のまなざしを投げかける *throw* [*投げつける*] *fling* a scornful look at him.

なげかつ 投げ勝つ outpitch. ▶山田は中村に投げ勝った Yamada *outpitched* Nakamura.

なげかわしい 嘆かわしい 〘遺憾に思う〙regrettable; 〘書〙deplorable (⚠ 不正などに対する強い遺憾を表す). ▶嘆かわしい事態 a *deplorable* [*悲しむべき*] a *sad*] situation. ▶警察官たる者がそんなばかなことをしたとは嘆かわしい限りだ It's most *regrettable* that a police officer committed such a folly.

なげき 嘆き (a) grief; (a) sorrow. (⇨悲しみ)

なげキス 投げキス ▶投げキスをする throw (*her*) a kiss.

なげく 嘆く 〘悲しむ〙feel* sad 《*about, over*》; (深く) grieve 《*about, over*》; 〘残念に思う〙regret 《*it; doing*》; (不正などに) 〘書〙deplore 《*it; his* [*him*] *doing*》. ▶彼の死を嘆く grieve over [*mourn*] his death. ▶彼が麻薬をやっていたことを嘆く deplore his tak*ing* drugs. ▶起こってしまったことを嘆いても仕方がない. 元気を出せよ. 明日という日があるじゃないか It's no use regretting what has happened. Cheer up! Tomorrow is another day, you know.

なげこむ 投げ込む ▶石を池に投げ込む *throw* a stone *into* a pond. ▶大量のごみを川に(どさっと)投げ込む *dump* a lot of trash *into* a river.

なげし 長押 〘建築〙*nageshi*, (説明的に) a decorative horizontal timber put over the usual *kamoi* timber in order to make a Japanese room look formal.

なげすてる 投げ捨てる throw* [fling*, cast*]... away. (⇨捨てる ❶, 投げる)

なげだす 投げ出す 〘放り出す〙(外へ) throw*... out; (下へ) throw... down; 〘放棄する〙give*... up, abandon (⚠ 前の方が口語的). ▶テーブルに鍵をぽんと投げ出して椅子に座る *toss* one's keys on the table and sit down. (⇨出す❶) ▶馬から投げ出される *be thrown* from a horse. ▶足を床に投げ出す *stretch out* one's legs on the floor. ▶自由のために命を投げ出す(=犠牲にする) *sacrifice* [*lay down*] one's life for freedom. ▶彼らはかばんを地べたに投げ出して殴り合いのけんかを始めた They *threw* their schoolbags on 〘to〙 the ground and began fighting each other. ▶仕事を途中で投げ出すな Don't *give up* your work halfway.

なげつける 投げつける 〘目がけて投げる〙throw* [(乱暴に) fling*, (力を入れて) hurl*] (*at*); 〘投げ倒す〙throw (*him*) (*down*). (⇨投げる *fling*) ▶バットを地面に投げつける *fling* a bat *on* the ground.

なげづり 投げ釣り surf-casting. ▶投げ釣りをする fish by casting a line into the sea from the shore.

なげとばす 投げ飛ばす throw* [fling*, hurl*]... away [down]. (⚠ away は「遠くへ」, down は「下へ, 地面へ」) ▶彼はその爆発で空中に投げ飛ばされた He *was thrown* [*was hurled*] (*up*) *into* the air by the explosion.

なげなし ▶なけなしの金(=持っているわずかな金)をはたいて彼女にあげる誕生日のプレゼントを買った I *spent what little money I had* on a birthday present for my girlfriend.

なげなわ 投げ縄 a lasso (極 ~(e)s).

なげやり 投げ遣り (怠慢) neglect, 《やや書》négligence; (無責任) irresponsibility. ▶仕事を投げやりにする be *neglectful* [*negligent*] of one's work; be *irresponsible about* one's work; (ちゃらんぽらんな仕事をする) do *slipshod* [*sloppy*] work.

なける 泣ける ▶彼女の話を聞くと泣けてしかたなかった(=感動のあまり泣いてしまった) I *was moved to tears* by her story./Her story *brought tears* to my eyes.

:なげる 投げる ❶ 〘(主に)手で物を投げる〙throw*; fling*; hurl; 《話》chuck; toss; pitch; 〘人を投げ倒す〙throw (*him*) (*down*); 〘身を投げる〙throw oneself.

> **使い分け** throw 「投げる」の意の最も一般的な語.
> fling, hurl 激しく強く投げるの意だが, fling は時に感情的に乱暴に投げ捨てることを含意する. hurl は大きくて重い物を速く遠くまで飛ばす猛烈な力を強調する.
> **chuck** 口語的な語で物をぽいと投げる.
> **toss** 軽い物を無造作に上に向けて投げる.
> **pitch** 主にボールを目標めがけて(野球では打者に向けて)投げる.

▶犬に石を投げる *throw* a stone *at* [*to*] a dog. (⚠ at は「…を目がけて」, to は「…の方向へ」の意) ▶打者にカーブを投げる *throw* [*pitch*] a curve to a batter. (⚠ to を at とすると打者めがけて(デッドボールを)投げることになる) ▶炒り豆を投げ散らかす *throw* [*fling, chuck*] roasted soybeans *around*. ▶ボールを投げ返す *throw back* a ball. ▶そのタオルを投げて(=放っ)てくれない *Throw* [*Toss, Chuck*] me that towel, please. ▶彼女は怒って手紙をくずかごに投げ入れた She angrily *threw* [*flung, chucked,* ×*hurled*] the letter *into* the wastebasket. ▶彼女はがけから海に身を投げた She *threw herself* into the ocean from a cliff.

❷ 〘視線・疑問などを投げる〙cast*. ▶私に一瞥(いちべつ)を投げる *cast* a glance *at* me. ▶疑問を投げる *cast* doubt 《*on, upon*》. ▶影を投げる *cast* [*throw*] a shadow 《*on*》.

❸ 〘あきらめる〙give*... up. ▶試合を投げる *give up* a game; *give up* [*lose*] all hope of winning a game. (⚠ throw a game は《話》で「わざと試合に負ける」の意)

-なければ 〘…なしでは〙without...; 〘もし…でなければ〙if... not; 〘…でない限り〙unless..., (⚠ unless の方が強意的で, 通例仮定法過去(完了)には用いない); 〘もし…がないならば〙〘書〙if it were [×was] not for..., 《書・古》but for.... (⚠ 現在の事実と反対の仮定を表す) (⇨なかったら, もし) ▶水がなければ生きられない We can't live *without* water. ▶必要でなければタクシーは使わない I won't use taxis *if* (it is) *not* necessary [*unless* (it is) necessary]. ▶あなたの援助がなければ私たちは何もできないだろう *Without* [〘書〙*If it were not for*, 〘書・古〙*But for*] your help, we couldn't do anything./If you *didn't* help us, we couldn't do anything. ▶彼でなければ(=彼以外のだれも)この問題は解けない No one *but* [*except*] him can solve this problem. ▶たばこをやめなければ死んでしまうよ You have to quit smoking *or* you'll die.

-なければならない must. (⇨-ならない ❶)

なこうど 仲人 a go-between; a matchmaker. ▶頼まれ仲人 an invited [a ceremonial] *go-between*. ▶仲人をする act as (a) *go-between* [(a) *matchmaker*] (⚠ a の後ろにはしば無冠詞); arrange a marriage 《*between* A *and* B》. ▶彼らは青山夫妻の仲人で結婚した (青山夫妻による引き合わせをへて) *Through the good offices* of Mr. and Mrs. Aoyama, they met and got married afterwards./(青山夫妻を媒酌人として) Their wedding was held with Mr. and Mrs. Aoyama as *go-between*./Mr. and Mrs. Aoyama acted *as go-between* at their wedding [for their marriage]. (⚠ 前の方は結婚式の媒酌だけだが, 後の方は

なごむ 和む その子供たちの幸せそうな姿を見て心がなごんだ It was *heart-warming* to see the happiness of the children. ▶彼のジョークで会場の雰囲気がなごんだ(=緊張がほぐれた) His joke *relaxed* [*eased*] the tense atmosphere in the hall.

***なごやか 和やか** ——**和やかな** 形 (友好的な) friendly, amicable; (温和な) genial /dʒíːnjəl/; (愛想のよい) amiable. ●なごやかな表情 a *genial* look. ●なごやかな集い a *friendly* [an *amicable*] gathering. ▶会談は終始なごやかなムードで行われた The talks went on in a *friendly* atmosphere./The negotiations were conducted *peacefully*.

なごり 名残 ❶ [痕跡(こんせき)] a trace,《書》a vestige; [遺物]《書》a relic; [戦争・天災などの] an aftermath. (⇨余波) ●昔の風習の名残 *relics* of old customs. ▶この町は少しも昔の名残をとどめていない The town retains no *traces* [*nothing to remind us*] of its former days.
❷ [別離] ●名残の言葉 *parting* [*farewell*] words. ●名残惜しそうに reluctantly. ●名残を惜しむ be reluctant [《書》feel loath /lóʊθ/] to leave 〈him, a place〉. ▶これでお別れとはお名残惜しい I'm sorry to leave you./I hate to (have to) leave you.

ナサ [《米》航空宇宙局] NASA 《the *N*ational *A*eronautics and *S*pace *A*dministration の略》.

ーなさい [命令] ▶答えは鉛筆ではっきりと書きなさい *Write* your answers clearly with a pencil. ▶君たち、静かにしなさい "*Boys, be* quiet!/(いらだって) Yóu be quíet! ▶行ってもいいが夕食前に帰って来なさい You may go, but you *must* [*have to*] come back before supper. (!*must* は話し手の主観的感情を含意し、強い命令を表す. *have to* は話し手以外の客観的事情に基づく命令を表す)

***なさけ 情け** [同情] sympathy; [哀れみ] pity (!しばしば相手を見下す気持ちを含む); [深い思いやり] compassion (!前の2語より堅い語); [慈悲] charity, mercy (!後の語は王様とか裁判官など力を持った人が与える慈悲); [親切] kindness; [愛情] (a) love. ●その人の情けにすがる throw oneself on his *mercy* [*charity*]. ▶シャイロックはアントニオに情けをかけなかった Shylock had no *mercy* on [showed no *mercy* to] Antonio. ▶困っているときは人の情けが身にしみる When we are in trouble, we really feel grateful for other people's *kindness* [*warm heart*]. ▶彼は先生のお情けで試験に及第した His teacher helped him pass the exam *out of pity*./Thanks to his teacher's *mercy*, he passed the exam.
●情けがあだとなる (親切[善意]が相手に害になることもある) Your kindness [good intentions] may turn out to be harmful to the other person.
●情けは人のためならず《ことわざ》(一つ善行をすれば別の善行を受けるに値する) One good turn deserves another./(人助けに施しをする人は神に貸しをつくることになる) He who gives to the poor, lends to the Lord.

なさけしらず 情け知らず (無慈悲な) merciless, 《やや書》pitiless; (残酷な) cruel; (無情な) heartless; [冷淡な] cold-hearted. ●情け知らずの暴君 a *merciless* [a *pitiless*] tyrant. ●情け知らずの仕打ち *cruel* [*heartless, cold-hearted*] treatment.

なさけない 情けない [みじめな] miserable,《書》wretched (!後の方が程度が強い); [哀れを誘う] pitiful,《やや書》pitiable (!軽蔑の感情を含む); [恥ずべき] shameful; [嘆かわしい] deplorable. ●情けない奴 a *miserable* fellow. ●情けない行為 shameful conduct. ●情けない境地にいる be in *pitiable* [*miserable*] circumstances. ▶どうしてそんな情けない顔をしているの Why are you looking so *miserable* [*wretched*]? (!この look の進行形は一時的な状態を表す) ▶そんなことをしたとは情けない It is *deplorable* [《不名誉だ》*disgraceful*, 《残念だ》a *pity*] that he should have done this. ▶なんと情けない What a *shame*!/What a *pity*! ▶約束を破るなんて情けない(=恥じるべきだ) You should *be ashamed of* yourself *for* breaking [having broken] your promise.

なさけぶかい 情け深い [思いやりのある] compassionate; [慈悲深い] charitable, merciful; [心の優しい] kindhearted. ●情け深い人 a *compassionate* [a *kindhearted*] person. ●情け深い判事 a *merciful* [《寛大な》a *lenient*] judge.

なさけようしゃ 情け容赦 ▶情け容赦もなく彼を罰する punish him without *pity* [*mercy*]; punish him pitilessly [*mercilessly*]. ▶兵隊たちは捕虜に情け容赦をしなかった The soldiers *had* [*showed*] *no mercy on* the prisoners.

なざし 名指し ●名指しで批判する criticize 《him》by name.

なさぬなか 生さぬ仲 ▶あの子と花子さんはなさぬ仲(=血縁関係のない親子)です The boy is *not Hanako's own son* [*is Hanako's stepson*].

なし 無し ●なしの干しブドウ *seedless* raisins. ▶何も言うことなし *No* comment. (!アンケートなどの回答) ▶彼の演奏は文句なしだった His musical performance *was perfect* [*left nothing to be desired*].
会話「首になったの」「それはどういうわけ」「説明なし、話し合いも何もなしよ.『あしたから来なくていいよ、さよなら』って、それだけ」"I'm fired." "Hòw's thát?" "*No* explanation, *no* discussion, *no* anything. 'You don't have to come after today. Bye.' That 'was it." (!*no anything* は *not anything* や *nothing* より強意的)

なし 梨 [植物] a Japanese pear /péər/. (!*pear* はしもぶくれの形をした西洋ナシをいう) ●ナシの木 a *pear* tree. ●ナシ畑 a *pear* orchard.
●梨のつぶて ▶連絡してみたがこれまでのところ彼からは梨のつぶてだ(=音沙汰は)I tried to get in touch with him, but I've heard nothing from him so far.

なしくずし 済し崩し ●なしくずしに(=少しずつ)借金を返す pay one's debts *little by little* [*bit by bit*].

ーなして ー無しで without.... ▶彼は彼女なしでは生きていけない He can't live *without* her. ▶車を買うだけの金がなければ車なしで済まさなければならないよ If you don't have enough money to buy a car, you'll have to *do* [*go*] *without* (one). (!(1) 目的語は文脈から明らかなときは省略可. (2) 省略の場合はアクセントは dò [gò] withóut)
会話「チーズバーガーを二つください」「タマネギは入れますか、入れませんか」「なしで結構です」"Two cheeseburgers, please." "Do you want them with or without onions?" "*Without*."

なしとげる 成し遂げる [努力の末成就する]《書》accomplish; [苦難の末獲得する] achieve (!前の方の意でも用いられる); [実行する] carry ... out. (⇨遣り遂げる) ▶努力なしでは何事も成し遂げられない You cannot *accomplish* [*achieve, do*,《実現させる》*realize*] anything without effort.

なしのつぶて 梨のつぶて (⇨梨)

なじみ 馴染み ——**馴染みの** 形 (よく知っている) familiar; (好みの) favorite; (常連の) regular. ●なじみの店 one's *favorite* store. ●なじみの客 a *regular* customer. (⇨常連) ●なじみのない顔 an *unfamiliar* face; 《見知らぬ人》a stranger. ● 私にはなじみが薄い[深い] be less [very] *familiar* to him.

なじむ 馴染む ❶ 〖慣れる〗get* used [accustomed] 《to》;《順応する》adapt [adjust] (oneself) 《to》(❗ adjust は積極的に順応する); 《慣れ親しむ》become* familiar 《with》;《愛着を持つ》become attached 《to》. ▶ 彼はなじみやすい(=仲よくしやすい)人だ He is easy to *make friends with*. ▶ 彼は新しい生活にすぐなじんだ He soon *got used* [*adapted himself*], *adjusted* (*himself*)] to his new life. ▶ 生徒たちはすぐ先生になじんだ(=なついた) The pupils *became attached* [*used*] *to* the teacher soon.
❷ 〖合う〗▶ この上着は着ているうちになじんできた This coat got to *fit better* [(着心地がよくなった) *became more comfortable*] as I wore it. ▶ その壁紙の色は床の色とはなじまない(=合わない) The color of the wallpaper doesn't *match* that of the floor.

ナショナリスト〖民族主義者〗a nationalist.
ナショナリズム〖民族主義〗nationalism.
ナショナル〖国の, 全国的な〗national.
● ナショナルチーム〖国の代表チーム〗the national team [side]. ● ナショナルトラスト〖観光資源保護団体〗the National Trust. ● ナショナルブランド〖製造業者ブランド〗a national brand 《略 NB》. ● ナショナルプロジェクト〖国家的規模の事業〗a national project. ● ナショナルミニマム〖必要最低限の生活水準〗a national minimum standard of living. ● ナショナルリーグ〖野球〗the National League《略 NL》.
(関連) アメリカンリーグ the American League)

なじる 詰る (責任の所在を問題にして) blame; (欠点を指摘して) criticize; (悲嘆・失望しても) (書) reproach.
▶ 彼の怠慢をなじる *blame* him *for* his negligence.

なす 茄子〖米〗an eggplant;〖英〗an aubergine /óubərʒiːn/. (❗ 料理されたものは Ⓤ)

なす 成す ❶ 〖やり遂げる〗achieve; (作る) make*.
▶ 大事をなす *achieve* greatness. ▶ 彼は石油産業で財をなした He *made* a fortune in the oil industry. ▶ 彼女は小説で名をなした She *won* fame by her novels.
❷ 〖形作る〗form; make*. ● 意味をなさない do not *make* sense. ▶ この随筆は彼の本の一部をなしている This essay *forms* part of his book.

なす 為す〖行う〗do*. (⇨(ˀ)る) ● なすべきことをなす *do* what one has to *do*; (義務を果たす) *do* [*perform*] one's duty. ● 彼のなすに任せる let him *do* as he likes. ● 益[害]をなす *do*《the crops》*good* [*harm*]. ▶ 私はなすすべを知らなかった I didn't know [I was at a loss] what to *do*. ▶ 自然に対してなすすべもなかった We were *helpless* against nature.
▶ 老女は犯人のなすがままだった The old woman was *at the mercy of* the criminal. ▶ その暴動は群集心理のなせるわざだった The riot was sparked (off) by the mounting heat of the mob. ● なせば成る, なさねば成らぬ何事も, 成さぬは人のなさぬなりけり You can accomplish anything, if you'll do it. Nothing will be accomplished unless you do it. If something wasn't accomplished, that's because you didn't do it.

なすこん 茄子紺 dusky purple.
ナスダック〖全米証券業者協会相場報道システム〗NASDAQ 《*N*ational *A*ssociation of *S*ecurities *D*ealers *A*utomated *Q*uotations の略》.
なずな 薺〖植物〗a shepherd's purse.
なすび 茄子(⇨茄子(ᴮ))
なずむ 泥む ❶ 〖こだわる〗▶ 旧習になずむ *adhere* [*stick*] *to* old customs.
❷ 〖すんなりと進まない様子〗(⇨暮れ泥む)
なすりあい 擦り合い〖責任・罪の〗recrimination(s) 《*against*》. ● 責任のなすり合いをして時間を浪費する waste time on mutual *recriminations*. (⇨擦り付ける)

なすりつける 擦り付ける ❶ 〖こすりつける〗rub (-bb-); 〖塗りつける〗(油などを) smear; (塗料のどを) daub /dɔːb/. ● クリームを顔になすりつける *rub* cream *into* [*smear* cream *on*] one's face. ● カンバスに絵の具をなすりつける *daub* a canvas *with* paint; *daub* paint *on* a canvas.
❷ 〖責任・罪を〗▶ 彼は自分の失敗の責任を私になすりつけた He *laid* [*put*] the blame for his mistake *on* me./He *blamed* his mistake *on* me./(転嫁した) He *shifted* the blame for his mistake *onto* me.

なする 擦る (⇨擦り付ける)

‡**なぜ 何故**〖理由を尋ねて〗why,《話》whát… fòr?,《話》hów còme…? (❗ 後者は話し手の驚きを含意する); (どういうきさつで) how. (⇨どうして) ▶ なぜそこへ行ったのですか Why did you go there? (❗(1) 答えるときは, 理由を表す節 *Because* I wanted to see him. (彼に会いたかったんです) または目的を表す不定詞句 *To* see him. だけでも可. (2) 原因を主語にして *What made* you *go* there? ともいえる. この方が why 文の詰問の響きがやわらげられ, 丁寧な尋ね方になる. (3) 「一体なぜ…」のように強調するときは *Why ever* [《話》*on earth*,《話》*in the world*] did you go there? のようにいう/*Whát* did you ╲go there *for*?《for に強勢を置くと「何の目的で」の意となる. ×For what…? の語順は不可》/*How come* you went there? (❗ ×How come did you go there? は不可)/Why [How] *is* it *that* you went there? (❗「そこへ行ったのはどうして[どういう訳]だ」と理由を強調する言い方. it は that 節を受ける) ▶ なぜその本を買うべきなのかを知りたい I want to know *why* I should [×why to] buy the book. (❗ 他の疑問副詞と異なり to 不定詞を続けることは不可. why 節の内容が明らかなときは省略可: I want to know *why*. (なぜだか知りたい)) ▶ なぜそんなことをしたかというと, 彼に頼まれたからなんだ *The reason* (*that*) I did it *is that* [《話》*because*] he asked me to. ▶ なぜ彼を招待するの. 彼は来ないよ *Why* invite him? He'll never come. (❗「why＋動詞の原形」はその行為が不必要・むだであることを暗示する) ▶ なぜそんなばかなことが言えるの *How* (*ever*) *can* you say such a silly thing? (❗ 言外に「そんなばかなことは言えないはずだ」という意を含んだ修辞疑問文. however は how ever ともつづり how よりも意味が強い)

〖会話〗「きのう富山に行ったんだ」「なぜ」 "I went to Toyama yesterday." "*Why?*/*What for?*/*How come?*" (❗ I didn't go to Toyama yesterday. のような否定文に対しては *Why* ╲not? となるが, この場合日本語につられて not を忘れないこと. *How come* でもいえるが ×What for? は不可)

〖会話〗「このじゅうたんは好きじゃないんだ」「じゃあなぜ替えないのよ」 "I don't like this carpet." "Then *why don't you* change it?"

〖会話〗「まゆ子の電話番号は何番」「なぜぼくが知ってるんだい」 "What's Mayuko's phone number?" "*How* [*Why*] *should* I know?" (❗ Why [How] should…? は話し手の怒り・いらだちを表す)

なぜか somehow, for some reason (or other). (⇨なんとなく) ▶ なぜか彼は黙っていた *Somehow* [*I don't know why, but*] he was silent 《*about, on*》.

なぜなら(ば) because (❗ 直接の原因・理由を表す); 〖…なので〗since; as (❗ 以上 2 語は通例文頭で用いる. since は相手も承知の理由を表す. as は《主に英》の《書》で付帯状況の理由を表す);〖と言うのは〗for (❗ 文語的で, 主節の後で理由を付け加える.《話》では because で代用する). (⇨だから) ❷ ▶ 私は今日はバスで

なせる 勤しました. なぜなら鉄道がストだったからです I went to the office by bus today, *because* there was a railroad strike. (🛈 日本語と同じにして … today. ×Because … と二つの文に分けるのは不可)/Since [As] there was a railroad strike today, I went to the office by bus. (🛈 前の文では従節(ストライキがあったこと)に重点があり, 後の文では主節(バスで行ったこと)に重点がある)
会話「どうして行ってはいけないの」「なぜならまだ小さすぎるからよ」 "Why can't I go?" "*Because* [×For, ×Since, ×As] you're still too young."

なせる 為せる (⇒為(ﾅ)す)

なせる 撫ぜる (⇒撫でる)

なぞ 謎 图 ❶ [不可解な事] a mystery (🛈「神秘」の意では Ⓤ); [不可解な事・出来事・人] a riddle, (やや書) an enígma. ● よく solve [clear up] a *mystery*. 謎を解く手がかりを見つける find a clue [a key] to the *mystery*. ▶彼の死は謎に包まれている His death is wrapped [shrouded] in *mystery*./(依然として謎である) His death still remains a *mystery* [an enigma]. ▶彼がどのようにしてその情報を手に入れたかは謎だ How he got the information is a *mystery* [a riddle] (*to* me)./It is a *mystery* [a riddle] (*to* me) how he got the information.

❷ [なぞなぞ] a riddle; (パズル) a puzzle. ● 謎を解く solve a *riddle* [a *puzzle*]. ▶彼がなぞ(謎)を出したが答えられなかった He asked a *riddle*, but I couldn't answer it.

❸ [ほのめかし] a hint. ● 謎をかける drop [give (him)] a *hint* (*that* 節).

── **謎の, 謎めいた** 形 mysterious. ● 謎の人物 a *mysterious* [a *mystery*] person (🛈 後の方は強意的に人を驚かせる意図があることを暗示する); an enigma. ● 謎めいたことを言う say something *mysterious*; (謎をかけるように話す) speak in riddles. ● 謎めいた微笑 a *mysterious* [an *enigmatic*] smile. ▶彼は謎の失踪(ｼｯｿｳ)をとげた He *mysteriously* disappeared.

なぞなぞ 謎々 a riddle. ▶このなぞなぞ分かるかな Can you solve this *riddle*? ▶なぞなぞ遊びをしよう Let's play (×at) *riddles*. (🛈 play at … は「…ごっこをする」意. at の後にははねられる人・事柄がくる: play at soldiers (兵隊ごっこをする))

なぞらえる 準える (たとえる) compare (*to*); (似せる) model [copy] (*after*). ▶人生はよく旅になぞらえられる(＝たとえられる) Life is often *compared to* a journey. ▶この寺の庭は宇宙になぞらえて造られている The garden of this temple is made *after* [*from*] *the image of* the universe.

なぞる trace. ● 手本をなぞって字の練習をする practice penmanship *tracing* the model.

なた 鉈 a hatchet.

なだ 灘 (荒れている外洋) a rough open sea. ● 玄海(ｹﾞﾝｶｲ)灘 the Sea of Genkai.

なだい 名代 ── **名代の** 形 (有名な) well-known; famous. ● 名代の塩まんじゅう a *well-known* salty *manju*.

なだかい 名高い (よい事で有名な) famous; (やや書) noted; (悪い事で有名な) notorious (*for*); (よく知られた) well-known. (⇒ 有名) ▶彼女は世界的に名高い生物学者だ She is a world-*famous* biologist. (🛈 通例 She is a famous biologist in the world. (とは言わない)/She is a biologist of worldwide *fame* [(やや書) *reputation*]. ▶シカゴはギャングで名高い Chicago is *notorious* [×*famous*] *for* its gangsters.

なだたる 名だたる well-known; famous; (際立った) distinguished. ● 世界に名だたるピアニスト a world-*famous* pianist; a pianist who *is famous all over the world*.

なたね 菜種 rapeseed.
● 菜種油 rape-seed oil; rape-oil. ● 菜種梅雨 (説明的に) a long spell of rainy weather around the Vernal Equinox week.

なたまめ 鉈豆 〖植物〗a sword bean.

*なだめる 宥める (怒り・興奮・心配などを和らげる) soothe (🛈 calm より堅い語); 〖落ち着かせる〗calm …(down); 〖静かにさせる〗《米》quiet …(down), 《英》quieten …(down); (うまい言葉で説得する) coax; (相手に譲歩して) appease. ▶彼をなだめすかして入院させる *coax* him *into* going [*to* go] to the hospital. ▶彼女は泣いている子供にあめをやってなだめた She *soothed* [*quieted*] the crying child by giving him candy. ▶彼女は彼の怒りをなだめようとした She tried to *soothe* [*calm*, *appease*] his anger. ▶何とかして彼をなだめなくちゃならない Somehow I've got to *calm* him *down*.

なだらか ── **なだらかな** 形 (ゆるやかな) gentle. ● なだらかな坂を降りる go down a *gentle* slope [hill].

なだれ 雪崩 an ávalànche, a snowslide. (🛈 前の方が普通) ● 表層なだれ a surface *avalanche*. ▶なだれにあう be hit [struck] by an *avalanche*; be caught in an avalanche. ▶なだれにあって死ぬ be killed in an *avalanche*.
● 雪崩を打つ ▶中国製品がなだれを打って欧州市場に入ってきた Chinese products *have surged* into the European market.

なだれこむ 雪崩込む 群衆が会場へ[グラウンドに]なだれ込んだ A crowd *rushed into* the hall [*onto* the field]. ▶戸を開けると, やかましいセミの声が部屋になだれ込んできた(＝部屋がいっぱいになった) When I opened the window, the noisy sound of cicadas *filled* the room.

ナチ(ス) 〖政党〗the Nazis; 〖主義〗Nazism. ● ナチス党員 a Nazi.

ナチュラルチーズ natural cheese.

*なつ 夏 summer (🛈《主に米》では 夏の~); (the) súmmertime. (Equinox ⏎ 北半球では 6～8月, 南半球では 12～2月) (⇒春) ● 暑い[長い]夏 a hot [a long] *summer*. ● 高校2年の夏に in the *summer* of one's second year of (senior) high school. ● 夏の盛りに in mid*summer*; in the height [middle] of *summer*. ● 夏負けする get, fall; 夏やせする (夏痩せ) ▶夏は当地はとても暑い It is very hot here in (*the*) *summer* [in (the) *summertime*]. ▶今年の夏はどこへ行く予定ですか Where are you going (×in) this *summer*? ▶京都の夏は祇園祭りとともに始まる *Summer* in Kyoto begins with the Gion Festival. ● 特に冬などと対比していう場合は *The summer in Kyoto* ….と the をつける)

なついん 捺印 图 a seal.
── **捺印する** 書類に捺印する put [set] one's *seal to* papers; *seal* papers. (事情) 米英には朱肉を使って捺印する慣習はない)

なつかけ 夏掛け a light summer quilt; a summer blanket.

*なつかしい 懐かしい 形 〖昔なつかしい〗good old; 〖いとしい〗dear; 〖見[聞き]慣れた〗familiar. ● 懐かしい昔 the *good old* days. ● 懐かしい故郷 one's *dear old* home(town). ● 懐かしい歌を歌う sing some *sweet old* songs. ▶祖母になつかる懐かしい思い出がある I have *good old* [*fond*, *sweet*] memories of my grandmother.

── **懐かしむ** 動 (思い焦がれる)《主に書》yearn (*for*); (あこがれる) long (*for*); (人がいなくて[ものがなくて]寂しい) miss. ▶学生時代を懐かしむ(＝懐古の情で)思い出す *miss* one's student days; look back on one's student days *with nostalgia*. ▶だれでも故郷を懐かしく思う Everyone *longs* [*yearns*] *for* his home (town). ▶小学校の先生のことが懐かしい I *miss* my elementary school teachers. (!) yearn [long] for は人に用いるとしばしば性的欲望を暗示する)

> **翻訳のこころ** プールの人工的な青も，カルキのにおいも，反響する水音も，わたしにはとても懐かしかった (江國香織『チューク』) The artificial blue of the pool water, the smell of chlorine and the echoing of water sounds *were* all very *familiar to* me. (!)「懐かしい」は be familiar to ...(...が見たり聞き慣れている)

なつかしむ 懐かしむ (⇨懐かしい)
なつかぜ 夏風邪 a summer cold [flu]. ▶夏風邪は治りにくい It is not easy to shake off *a summer cold*.
なつがれ 夏枯れ (商売の不振) a summer slump [decline]; (閑散期) the slack summer season.
なつく 懐く 『好きになる』take* to ...; come* to love; (愛着を抱く) become* attached to .... ▶この子はおばにとてもなついている This child *is very attached to* [*fond of*] his [her] aunt. ▶虎は人になつかない Tigers cannot be tamed.
なつくさ 夏草 summer grass.
なつぐも 夏雲 summer clouds; 『気象』(積乱雲) cumulonimbus.
ナックルボール 『野球』a knuckleball. ●ナックルボール(を投げる)投手 a knuckleballer.
なづけおや 名付け親 『代父』one's godfather; 『代母』one's godmother; 『代父母』one's godparents. ●子供の名付け親になってやる be [stand] a child's *godfather* [*godmother*]; be [stand] *godfather* [*godmother*] *to* a child. (!) 役目を示すときは無冠詞)
なづける 名付ける name; (呼ぶ) call. ▶彼はその子犬をコロと名付けた He *named* [*called*] the puppy (×as) Koro. (!)×as をつけるのは不可) ▶ハドソン川は英国の探険家ヘンリー・ハドソンの名をとって名付けられた The Hudson River *was named after* [『米』*for*] the English explorer Henry Hudson.
なつさく 夏作 crops planted in summer (and harvested in fall or early winter).
なつじかん 夏時間 daylight(-saving) time; 《英》summer time.
なっせん 捺染 图 textile printing. ─ 捺染する 動 print.
●捺染のり printing paste.
ナッツ 『木の実』a nut. ●ナッツ入りのパン a (bread) roll with nuts.
なっていない (だめだ) be no good; (役に立たない) be useless; (価値がない) be worthless; (失敗者[作]だ) be a failure. (○駄目な) ▶あの子のしつけはなっていない (きちんと訓練されていない) The child is not well disciplined./(礼儀を知らない) The child has no manners.
なっている (⇨なる❾) ▶来月商用でインドに行くことになっています I *am* [*will be*] *going to* India on business next month.
なってない (⇨なっていない)
ナット 『工具』a nut.
なっとう 納豆 *natto*, fermented soybeans; (説明的に) sticky steamed soybeans fermented in rice straw.
***なっとく** 納得 图 『了解』understanding; 『同意』consent; 『満足』satisfaction; 『確信』conviction. ●双方納得ずくで with mutual *understanding* [*consent*]. ▶納得がいくよう説明しましょう I will explain *to your satisfaction*. (!) to your satisfaction は「君が満足するまで[するように]」の意)/I will give you a *sàtisfáctory* explanation. ▶演説を聞いて納得がいけば (=説得力があれば) 支援しましょう If your speech is *convincing* [*carries conviction*] we will support you. ▶それは納得がいかない That I *can't understand*. /(それはフェアじゃない) That's *unfair* [*not fair*]. (それは❸) ▶お茶くみが女性職員の役割だなんて納得できない I strongly *disagree* that serving tea is (a role [×a job]) for female members in the office to perform.
─ **納得する** 動 『了解する』understand*; 『満足する』be satisfied 《*with*》; 『確信する』be convinced 《*of*; *that* 節》; 『説得される』be persuaded 《*of*; *that* 節》. ▶その説明では納得できない I *am not satisfied with* [*by*] the explanation./The explanation doesn't *satisfy* [*convince*] me. (!) 日常会話では単に That's not good enough. などともいう) ▶それが真実であることを納得した I *was satisfied* [*was convinced*, *was persuaded*] *that* it was true. ▶私は彼女に自動車でなく電車で行くよう納得させた I *persuaded* [『主に米』*convinced*] her *to go* by train rather than by car. (!)実際に電車で行ったことを含意する)
なつのはな 夏の花 *Summer Flowers*. (参考) 原民喜の小説)
なつば 夏場 summer. ●夏場は観光客で混む be crowded with tourists *in* (*the*) *summer* [*in* (*the*) *summertime*].
なつば 菜っ葉 green vegetables; greens. (⇨菜)
なつばしょ 夏場所 『相撲』the summer grand (*sumo*) tournament.
なつばて 夏ばて 图 『夏の無気力』summer lethargy /léθərdʒi/.
─ **夏ばてする** 動 suffer from the summer heat. ▶夏ばてしない (=夏の暑さに勝つ) ためにはしっかり食べてよく眠ることがいちばんです Eat well and sleep well. That'll be the best way to beat the *summer heat*.
なつび 夏日 (強烈な夏の太陽) blazing summer sun; (最高気温が 25℃ 以上の日) a day when the temperature rises above 25℃.
なつびらき 夏開き (説明的に) the beginning of summer recreations, such as mountaineering and sea-bathing.
なつふく 夏服 summer clothes.
ナップザック a knapsack.
なつまけ 夏負け (⇨夏ばて)
なつまつり 夏祭り a summer festival.
なつみかん 夏蜜柑 『植物』a Chinese citron.
なつめ 棗 『植物』(木) a jujube /dʒúːdʒuːb/ (tree); a Chinese date (tree); (実) a jujube; a Chinese date.
●ナツメヤシ (木) a date (palm); (実) a date.
ナツメグ (香辛料) nutmeg.
なつメロ 夏メロ a popular song from good old days; 『話』a golden oldie. (!) 今も人気のある歌だけでなく音楽一般・映画などをさす. 単に an oldie ともいう)
なつもの 夏物 (衣料) summer wear; (帽子・靴などの) summer clothing.
なつやすみ 夏休み 《米》(the) summer vacation. (!) 《英》でも大学の休暇はこのようにいう; 《英》(the) summer holiday(s). (⇨休暇) [類語] ●夏休みの宿題 one's homework *for* (*the*) *summer vacation*. ▶学校は今夏休みです Our school is closed for *the summer vacation*. ▶夏休みに北海道へ行った We went to Hokkaido for the *summer vacation*. (!) for は「過ごすために」の意で to spend ... と置き換

なつやせ

えても同じ)/We took a trip to Hokkaido during *the summer vacation.*「夏休みの間に」参照)

なつやせ 夏痩 ── 夏痩せする 動 lose weight in (the) summer.

なつやま 夏山 ●夏山シーズン the summer mountaineering season. ●夏山登山をする climb a mountain in the summertime.

なであげる 撫で上げる (ブラシで) brush ... up; (くしで) comb ... up. ●髪を左右に上げる (後ろに) *comb* one's hair *back*.

なでおろす 撫で下ろす ●胸をなでおろす(=安心する) give a sigh of relief, be (greatly) relieved.

なでがた 撫で肩 ●なで肩の with sloping shoulders.

なでぎり 撫で斬り ── 撫で斬りする 動 (片っ端から斬る) mow 《them》 down like grass.

なでしこ 撫子 〔植物〕a (fringed) pink.

なでつける 撫で付ける plaster 《one's hair》 down 《with grease》. ●髪の毛をなでつける smooth down one's hair.

***なでる** 撫でる (やさしく) stroke; (やさしく繰り返し) pat (-tt-); [こする] rub (-bb-). ●あごひげをなでる *stroke* one's beard. ●あごをなでる *rub* [*stroke*] one's chin. (❗ものを考えるときの動作) ●彼女は子猫をなでていた She *was stroking* [(愛情をこめて) *fondling, petting*] the kitten. ●彼は子供の頭をなでた He *patted* his child *on* the head./He *patted* his child's head. (❗前の方は「子供に」、後の方は「頭」に重点のある言い方) ●涼しい風がほおをなでた A cool breeze *touched* my cheeks.

***など** 《副助詞》 ❶〔例として示す〕(...など) and so on [forth]; etc. (❗簡略を重んじる文で用いる。通例 and so on [forth] と読む。ラテン語読みは /étsétərə/); (...の類) ... and the like; (たとえば...のような) such as ...; (たとえば) for example, for instance. ●本や辞書など books, dictionaries, *and so on* [*and the like*]; books, dictionaries, *etc.* (❗あとには or and をつけない) ●時計・カメラなどの精密機械 precision instruments(,) *such as* [《話》*like,* 《やや書》*including*] watches and cameras; precision instruments—watches and cameras, *for example*; watches, cameras *and other* precision instruments. ●彼は私に名前、年齢、住所などを聞いた He asked me her name, my age, my address, *and so on*.

❷〔否定の意味を強調〕(...など) (⇨–なんか ❹) ●今日は雨の心配など少しもありません You *don't* have to worry about rain *at all* today. ●この本を1週間で読み終えることなど私にはとてもできそうにない It *would not be possible* for me [I *would be quite unable*] to read through this book in a week. ●人々が皆政治のことなど知らなくても済む(=知る必要がない)ようになれば、それが最もよいと思う I think it best if *nobody needs to know anything* about politics.

❸〔謙遜(けんそん)・軽蔑・非断定調表現として〕(❗英語では特にそれに当たる語句に置き換えられないことも多い) ●彼は私などには見向きもしない He doesn't care for the *likes* of me. (⇨–なんか ❸) ●(仕事の)休みの日などはどのようにお過ごしですか How do you spend your days off? (❗「など」に相当する訳語はない)

会話「父にあげるちょっとしたもの〔ネクタイ〕をさがしています。何〔どれ〕がいいかしら」「そうですね、ネクタイ〔これ〕などいかがでしょう」"I'm looking for a small present [a tie] for my father. What [Which] would you recommend?" "Well, how about a tie *or something* [this one]?" (❗or something (...か何か)のような断定を避けた丁寧表現は、英語では「]内のような特定のものを自信をもってすすめたり提案する文脈では不適)

ナトー 〔北大西洋条約機構〕NATO /néitou/ 《the North Atlantic Treaty Organization の略》.

なとり 名取 a teacher with a professional name; a master [(女性の) a mistress] 《*of* traditional Japanese dance [music]》.

ナトリウム 〔化学〕sodium 《元素記号 Na》. ●炭酸ナトリウム *sodium* carbonate.

***なな** 七 seven; [7 番目の] the seventh. (⇨三)

ななえ 七重 ●七重のひざを八重に折って「七重のひざを八重に折って...を請う go down on one's [bended] knees to beg ...; beg ... most humbly.

ななかいき 七回忌 the sixth anniversary of 《his》 death.

ななかまど 七竈 〔植物〕a mountain ash.

ななくさ 七草 (春の) the seven (edible) spring herbs; (秋の) the seven (flowering) autumn herbs.
●七草粥 rice porridge containing the *seven spring herbs*.

ななころびやおき 七転び八起き ●人生は七転び八起きだ Life is full of *ups and downs*. (❗ups and downs は「(人生の)浮き沈み」の意)

ななし 名無し ── 名無しの 形 nameless. ●名無しの権兵衛 a Mr. What's-his name.

***ななじゅう** 七十 seventy; [70 番目の] the seventieth. (⇨二十, 五十)

ななしゅきょうぎ 七種競技 the heptathlon. ●七種競技の選手 a heptatheletе.

なな つ 七つ seven. ●七つの海 the *seven* seas. ●七つ目の階段 the *seventh* stair.
●七つ道具 paraphernalia (❗通例複数扱い); a set of tools.

ななはん 七半 a 750cc motorcycle.

ななひかり 七光り ●父親の七光り(=影響力)でいい仕事につく get a good job *through the influence of* one's father [(名声・力に便乗して) *by riding on* one's father's *coattails*].

ななふしぎ 七不思議 ●世界の七不思議 the Seven Wonders of the World.

***ななめ** 斜め 图 ●斜め45度 an angle of 45 degrees *diagonally*. ●斜め向かいの家 《筋向かい》 ●ご機嫌斜め 《⇨ご機嫌斜め》 ●彼女の斜め前(後ろ)に座る sit *diagonally in front of* [*behind*] her.
── 斜めの 形 (傾斜している) slanting, 《書》oblique; [対角に斜めの] diagonal 《斜め線》. ●斜めの線を引く draw a *slanting* [an *oblique,* a *diagonal*] line; draw a line *slantwise* [*diagonally, at an angle*]. ●(道路上に)斜め駐車をする [make] (an) *angle* parking.
── 斜めに 副 ●板を斜めに(=はすかいに)置く put a plank *on* [*at*] a *slant*; put a plank *slantwise*; (傾斜させる) *slant* a plank. ●野原を斜めに歩いて行く walk *diagonally* across the field. ●斜めになった床 a *slanted* floor. ●明るい月の光がカーテンのすき間から斜めにさし込んでいた A brilliant moonbeam was *slanting* through a gap in the curtains. ●壁に絵が斜めに掛かっている The picture is (hanging) *askew* on the wall. (❗askew は「(本来まっすぐだべきものが)斜めに」)

ななめよみ 斜め読み ── 斜め読みする 動 read diagonally; (さっと読む) read cursorily.

***なに** 何 ● トーフルで、それ何？ TOEFL? *What* ∖is it? (❗指をさすなどして「これ〔それ, あれ〕は何ですか」の場合は *What's* ∖*this* [∖*that,* ⨯*it*]?)

❶〔何が〕what; [何が...しようと] no matter what, whatever. (❗前の方が口語的) ●箱の中には何が入っていますか *What* is [are] 《主に米話》there) in the box? (❗複数のものが入っていることを

予想して尋ねるときは are を用いる) ▶何が起ころうと考えは変えるな Don't change your mind, no matter what [whatever] happens. (🔳 ...whatever may happen. は文語的)

②【何に】 what; [[何にでも]] everything. ▶あの電話は何についてだった What was that telephone call about? ▶(注文は)何になさいますか What would you like to have? ▶そんな大金を何に使ったんだ What did you spend so much money on? ▶空き缶を集めて何になる(=役に立たない) There's no use [no good, no point] (in) collecting empty cans./(反語的に) What's the use [good, point] of collecting empty cans? (⇨無駄)

③【何を】 what; [[何を...しようと]] no matter what, whatever (⇨①). ▶何を見ているの What are you looking at? ▶何を(ぐずぐず)している何 What áre you doing? (🔳 are に強勢を置き非難を表す. doing に強勢を置けば好奇心を示す) ▶彼女の誕生日プレゼントに何を買おうかな I wonder what to buy [I should buy] for her birthday present. (🔳 後の方が口語的) ▶私が何を言っても彼は聞こうとしません He won't listen to me, no matter what [whatever] I say. ▶何(を)言ってるんだ(ばかなことを言うな) Don't be silly./(ばかを言うのはやめろ) None of your nonsense./Nonsense!

会話 「仕事は何をしてるの?」「秘書をしています」 "What do you do?" "I'm a secretary." ▶職業を尋ねる言い方. What are you doing? は「今何をしているのか」の意)

会話 「町へ何をしに行っていたの?」「銀行に用があったんです」 "What have you been to town for?" "I've just been to the bank."

④【何で】 what; [[どのように]] how. ▶何で書けばよろしいですか What should I write with? (🔳 With what...? は《書》)

会話 「何で通学しているの」「自転車です」 "How do you go to school?" "(I go) by bicycle [《話》 bike]."

⑤【何から】 what. ▶何から始めればよいか(=最初にすべきか)言ってください Tell me what to do first. ▶我々は何から何まで(=すべてに)反対だ We're against everything [the whole thing].

── 何 形 what 《+名》. (⇨何(?)-形)

会話 「君の傘は何色?」「赤です」 "What color is your umbrella?" "It's red."

── 何 感 [聞き返して] what; [[驚き・怒りを表して]] (主に米) why. ▶何? 何と言ったの? What? Whát did you ﾉsay? (⇨何と 感) ▶何, もう(夜の) 12 時だ Why, it's midnight. ▶うわぁ, 何それ[この散らかしようは] Wow! Look at that [the mess].

会話 「何とも奇妙な帽子をかぶっているわね」「何よ!」 "What a very peculiar hat you've got on!" "ヽPlease!" (🔳 please の音調に注意)

*なにか 何か something; (何かある...) some /sʌm, ×səm/《+単数可算名詞》 (🔳 以上 2 語は通例肯定文および yes の答えを予想する疑問文, 肯定の内容を示す if 節で用いる); anything; any. (🔳 以上 2 語は通例疑問文・if 節で用いる) ● 何かの拍子に by some chance. ▶ドアのそばに何かがある There is [×are] something [×anything] by the door. (🔳 (1) 否定文 「...に何もない」は There is not anything [×something]..... (⇨何も). (2) something, anything は単数扱い) ▶ 何か(暖かい)飲み物が欲しい I want something (hot) to drink. ▶何か変なものが飛んでいる Something strange [×Strange something, ×some strange thing] is flying. (🔳 形容詞は something, anything の後に置く) ▶もし何か必要ならば言ってください If you need anything [something], please tell me. (🔳 (1) something では「必要だろうから遠慮なく」の意を含意. anything ではその含意はない. (2)「何か困ったことがあれば」のように好ましくない前提の場合は If you have any [×some] trouble, ... となり, some は不適切)

会話 「何かご質問は(ありますか)」「いや私からはありません」 "(Do you have) any questions?" "No, not from me."

会話 「ほかに何かやることありますか」「それでおしまいよ」 "Do you have any other jobs [anything else] to be done?" "That's all."

会話 「すみません」「はい, 何か」(受付などで) "Excuse me, miss." "Yes, can I help you?"

会話 「何かあったの?」「なんでもないわ」 "What happened?/What's up?" "Nothing."

【...か何か】 ▶ここにいてください. 雑誌か何かを買ってきますから Stay here. I'll get you a magazine or something [some magazine or other]. (🔳 ×a magazine or other とはいわない) ▶彼は銀行の頭取か何かで大変な金持ちです He is a bank president or something like that, very rich. (🔳 この very rich は and he is very rich の縮約した形で会話ではよく用いられる) ▶酒かビールか何か飲みませんか (⇨か (副助詞) ②)

なにがし 何がし ● 何がしという人 (a) Mr. [Mrs., Miss] So and so. ● 何の何がしだったかよく覚えてはいませんが... I don't remember his [her] name exactly, but .... ● チャールズ何がしという名の学生 a student whose name is Charles something. (⇨何とか ②) ● 何がしか(=いくらか)の金 some money; (ある金額の) a certain amount [sum] of money. ● 1 万何がし(か)の金 《話》 ten thousand-odd yen.

なにかしら 何かしら ● 何かしら something. ● いつも何かしら花の咲いている庭 a garden where some kinds of flowers are always in bloom. ▶何かしら胸騒ぎがする I feel something ominous is going to happen./Somehow I feel uneasy.

なにかと 何かと (あれやこれやで) one thing or another; (いろいろな点で) in many [various] ways. ▶何かと忙しい be busy with one thing or another. ▶外国での一人暮らしは何かと不自由であろう It will be inconvenient in many ways to live alone in a foreign country.

なにかというと 何かと言うと ▶聡は何かと言うとすぐに文句を言う Satoshi never opens his mouth without grumbling.

なにがなんだか 何が何だか ▶何が何だかさっぱり分かりません I don't know what the hell's going on. (🔳 「一体何がどうなっているのか」の意)

なにがなんでも 何が何でも at áll cósts. (⇨何としても) ▶何が何でもそこへ行きたい I want to go there no matter what.

会話 「君にはこれまで何度もちがうまくいったためしがない」「よし分かった, 今度は何が何でもうまくやってみせるよ」 "You've tried it many times before. And it's never worked." "All right. Nothing's going to stop me from succeeding this time." (🔳 この be going to は二人称・三人称の主語に用いて話し手の強い意志を表す)

なにかにつけ 何かにつけ (いろいろな点で) in various [many] ways. (⇨何かと) ▶彼女は何かにつけ(=機会あるたびに)彼の古傷を持ち出す She opens [reopens] his old wounds whenever there is a chance. ▶私たちは何かにつけ(=ほんのちょっとしたことがあると)彼女の家に集まっては彼女がピアノを弾いて歌った On the slightest occasion we got together at her place and sang as she played the piano. ▶彼は何かにつけ(=あれこれ口実を見つけて

なにからなにまで 何から何まで all kinds [sorts] of things; everything. ▶彼は仕事のことなら何から何まで心得ている He knows *everything* about his job. /《話》He knows his job *inside out* [*inside and out*]. ▶あなたは何から何まで(=すべての点で)彼と違っている You're different from him *in every way*.

なにくそ 何くそ (⇨くそ 囲) ●何くそという気持ちで働く(=全力を尽くして働く) work *with all* one's *might*; 《話》*go all out for* one's work. ▶何くそ,くそっ,こんなざまで負けるもんか Damn [Darn, Hang] it! I'll never give in to it.

なにくれとなく 何呉と無く in many ways; (あれこれと) in one way or another. ▶北京滞在中は彼が何くれとなく世話をしてくれた He took good care of me *in many ways* during my stay in Beijing.

なにくわぬかお 何食わぬ顔 [罪を犯していない様子] an innocent look; [何も知らない様子] a look of ignorance. ●何食わぬ顔をする(=何食わぬふりをする) play innocent [ignorant]; (!次の言い方より口語的); pretend to be innocent [ignorant]; (書) feign innocence [ignorance]; 《やや書》assume an air of innocence [ignorance]. ▶それから彼は何食わぬ顔をして会に出た Then he went to the meeting *with an innocent look* [まるで何事もなかったかのように] *as if nothing had happened*].

なにげない 何気無い 形 [気まぐれな] casual; [何も気にかけない] unconcerned 《with》; (無関心の) indifferent 《to》. ●そのことに何気ないさまを装う pretend to be *unconcerned with* [*indifferent to*] it. ▶彼の何気ない一言が彼女のプライドを傷つけた His *casual* remark hurt her pride.
── **なにげなく** 副 casually; [故意でなく] unintentionally. ●何気なく雑誌を開く open the magazine *casually*. ●何気なく彼らの話を立ち聞きしてしまう *unintentionally* overhear them talking. (偶然) *happen to* overhear them talking.

なにごと 何事 ❶[何] what; [[何かあること]] [肯定文で] something; [否定文・疑問文・if 節で] anything. (⇨何か,何も) ▶何事が(=何が起こったのか) What happened?/What's the matter?/What's up? ▶彼は何事かささやいた He whispered *something*. (!否定文は He didn't whisper *anything* [×something].) ●文化祭は何事もなく終わった[=順調にいった] The school festival went smoothly [[障害なく終わった]] ended without a hitch].
❷[[すべて]] everything; [[どんな事でも]] anything. ●何事にも最善を尽くす do one's best in *everything*.
❸[とがめて] うそをつくとは何事だ(=いったいなぜそうをついたか) *Why* on earth [*in the world*] did you tell a lie? (!on earth, in the world は疑問文を強める)

なにさま 何様 ▶つべこべ指図するとは(一体)何様のつもりなんだ *Who* (on earth) do you think you are to order me around?

なにしろ 何しろ [とにかく] anyway, anyhow; at any rate; [なぜなら] because (!直後の理由を表す); [だって…だから] after all; [ご承知のように] as you know. ▶なにしろ今日は暑い *Anyway*, it's hot today. ▶あの子のいたずらは許してやれない,なにしろまだ小さいのだから You should overlook his mischief, *because* he is still too young./(なんといっても) You should overlook his mischief. *After all*, he is still too young. (!前文の理由付けを行う.通例文頭で用いる) ▶なにしろ今は景気が悪いのでね Times are bad [hard] now, (*as*) *you know*.

なにせ 何せ (⇨何しろ)

なにとぞ 何とぞ please, if you please. (⇨どうぞ❶)

なになに 何々 ❶[漠然と対象を指して] something; so-and-so. ▶当日は何々を持参すればよろしいでしょうか Could you tell me *what* [*the thing*] I bring with me on that day?
❷[驚き,疑念] (驚き)＼Oh!; /Eh!; (強い驚き) /What! ▶なになに,そんなに心配することはない *No*, you don't have to worry so much.

なににもまして 何にも増して (⇨何より)
なにはさておき 何はさておき (⇨さておき)
なにはともあれ 何はともあれ (⇨さておき)
なにはなくとも 何は無くとも 何はなくともまずビールを 1 杯 Let's have a cup of beer, *though there is nothing else* to refresh us with.

なにびと 何人 ●何人も生まれながら平等である *All men are created equal*. (!リンカーンの有名な言葉.今ではAll people…. という方が適切) ▶何人も人を殴る権利はない *No one* has [×have] the right to hit others.

なにひとつ 何一つ (⇨何も❶)
なにふじゅうなく 何不自由無く ▶夫の死後も彼女は何不自由なく暮らしている She is *well off* [*lives in comfort, is well provided for*] after the death of her husband.

なにぶん 何分 [[どうか]] please; [[ともかく]] anyway, anyhow; [[ご承知[ご覧]のように]] as you know [see]; (!何しろ) ▶その件はなにぶんよろしくお願いいたします I leave it entirely to your discretion.

なにほど 何程 (⇨たいした,どれだけ)

なにも 何も ❶[ひとつも…ない] not anything; nothing (!後の方が強意的). ▶その事について彼は何も言わなかった He *didn't* say *anything* [×something] about it./He said *nothing* about it. ▶新聞には目新しいことは何も出ていない There isn't *anything* [is *nothing*] new in the paper. (!(1) anything, nothing は単数扱い. (2) 形容詞は anything, nothing の後に置く. ×new anything [nothing] は不可) ▶君が留守の間何も変わったことはなかった *Nothing* [×Not anything] *happened* while you were out. (!(1) not anything は文頭に来ない. (2) ×Anything didn't happen …. も不可) ▶驚いて何も言えなかった I was too surprised to say *anything* [×something]. (!内容的に否定文なので anything を用いる) ▶父は何もしていないのに警察に捕まった They [The police] put my father in jail for *something* he didn't do. ▶正夫からは何も言ってこないよ *Not* a word from Masao. ▶その山荘には今時の便利な設備も水道も何もない The cottage has no modern conveniences, no running water, *no nothing*.
会話「あなた,それ私にくれるって言ったわよ」「そんなこと何も言わなかったよ」"You said you'd give it to me." "I said *nothing* of the sort."
会話「それについて何か疑念を抱いているのか」「何に(も). まったく何に(も)」"Do you have any doubts about it?" "*None. None* whatsoever." (!whatever, whatsoever は no+名詞, none, nothing などの後で用いて否定を強める)
❷[反駁(はつ)] ▶何もなぐらなくてもいいだろう(=なぐる理由[必要]はない) You have no reason [need] to hit me. ▶彼が間違っていると言っているのではない I'm not saying [I don't mean] (that) he's wrong.

なにもかも 何も彼も [どれもみな] everything; [すべての物] all. (!後に関係詞節が続いて) ▶彼は何もかも失った He lost *everything* (he owned)./He lost *all* he owned [×all]. ▶何もかもうまくいった *Everything*

なにもの went well. ▶まったく何もかも思いどおりに行かなかった *Nothing* went at all right. (❗ at all は *nothing* を強める)

なにもの 何物 ▶弥生が壮一に抱いていた感情は愛以外の何物でもなかった Yayoi's feelings toward [for] Soichi was *nothing but* love.

なにもの 何者 《だれ》who;《ある人》someone;《どの人も》anyone. ▶何者だ *Who* are you?/*Who* is he [she]?

なにやかや 何や彼や 《あれやこれや》one thing or another,《やや書》this and that;《何かかんか》something or other. ▶何やかやで忙しい I am busy with *one thing or another* [*this and that*]. ▶彼女はいつも何やかや文句を言っている She is always complaining about *something or other*. ▶何やかや(の理由で)東京へは月に2-3回行きます *What with one thing and another*, I go to Tokyo two or three times a month. ▶登山帽と登山靴その他何やかや(=いろいろ)買った I bought an alpine hat, mountain-climbing boots, *and whatnot* [《話》*and have what you*].

なにやら 何やら 《[何か]》something. ▶何やら焦げるにおいがする I can smell *something* burning.

なにゆえ 何故 (⇨何故(ᅗ))

なにより 何より ▶私はアイスクリームが何よりも好きだ I like ice cream *better than anything else* [(とりわけ) *most of all*, *among other things*]. ▶健康が何より(=最も大切)だ Health is *everything* [is *the most important*]. ▶暑い日には冷たいビールが何よりだ *There is nothing like* cold beer [*Nothing is as good as* cold beer] on a hot day. ▶何よりの(=すばらしい)贈り物をありがとう Thank you for your *beautiful* [*wonderful*] present. ▶皆さまお元気で何よりです(=聞いてとてもうれしい) *I'm very glad* [*happy*] *to* hear (that) you are all well. ▶何よりもまず(=まず第一に)十分に休養をとることだ *First of all* you should take a good rest.

> **DISCOURSE**
> 携帯電話を使うことの利点は以下の通りであろう。 第一に、そして何より、場所に関係なく人とつながることができる点がある Some advantages of using a cellular phone would be **as follows**: *first and foremost*, it enables you to connect with people regardless of their location. (❗ as follows: (以下の通りである)は抽象的内容を述べるディスコースマーカー。「何より」以降でその具体的内容を述べる)

なにわぶし 浪花節 (a) *naniwabushi*; 《説明的に》popular story-telling with intermittent songs to the accompaniment of the *samisen* music. ▶彼は浪花節的な人生を生きている(=義理人情を重んじている) He lives in a world where loyalties to other people around him are thought to be very important.

なにをか 何をか ▶何をか言わんや(=もう何も言うことはない) I have nothing more to say./《反語的》*What can I say*?

なぬし 名主 the chief of a village (in the Edo period).《村長》

ナノ 《10億分の1》nano- (略 n).
 ●ナノグラム a nanogram (略 ng). ●ナノテクノロジー 《超微細技術》nánotechnólogy. ●ナノ秒 a nanosecond (略 ns). ●ナノメートル a nanometer (略 nm).

なのか 七日 ▶7日間 for *seven* days. ▶7月7日に on July *7*(*th*). (⇨日付)

-(な)のだ (❗一種の強調語の「...なのだ」に相当する英語はない。《話》ではイントネーションと強勢で表すことができる。例えば、「彼は正直なのだ」は He ˋis honest のように、is を強く下降調でいえばよい。一般に be動詞をbe動詞で強調することによって、「...なのだ」の意を表する。《書》では文脈から文末で表現しなければならない) ▶事態は急を要するのだ(= 本当に切迫している) The situation is *really* urgent. ▶彼の企てはすべて失敗したのだ(=完全に失敗した) All his attempts *completely* failed.

-なので because...;《やや書》since...;《書》as....
(⇨-ので) ▶クリスマスなので彼は実家へ帰った He went home for Christmas *as a matter of course*. (❗斜体字部分は「当然のことながら、社会の慣習にならって」の意)

-なのに but. (⇨それなのに、-のに ❶ ❷)

なのはな 菜の花 〚植物〛rape blossoms.

なのり 名乗り ●名乗りをあげる (立候補する) run《主に米》[stand《英》] for...; (本人だと申し出る) (⇨名乗り出る). ●市長選に名乗りをあげる announce one's *candidacy* for mayor.

なのりでる 名乗り出る ▶彼はその犯人と知り合いだと名乗り出た He *claimed* (that he was an) acquaintance with the criminal. (❗ claim は「...を自分のものとして要求する」で普通は目的語に「物」が来るが、ここは「事」である、「知り合いであることを主張する」の意)

なのる 名乗る ❶《名前を告げる》give* [tell*] one's name《as》. ▶彼は阿部と名乗った He *called himself* Abe.《阿部と自己紹介した》He *introduced himself as* Abe.
❷《名前を使う》▶彼は妻の姓を名乗った He *used* [*adopted*] his wife's family name. (❗ use は「利用する」の意にもなる)
❸《称する》▶「オレはアイヌだ」と名乗る(=公に身分を明らかにする)時代に変わった The time has come when I can *publicly identify myself* as Ainu.

ナパームだん ナパーム弾 〚軍事〛a napalm /népɑːm/ bomb.

なびかせる ❶《草木・旗などを》《曲げる》bend*; 《はためかせる》fly*, flutter; 《波動させる》wave. ▶彼はバスに乗ろうとレインコートをなびかせて走った He ran *flying* his raincoat to catch the bus. / His raincoat *fluttered* as he ran to catch the bus.
❷《人の心を》win* one's heart;《征服する》conquer. ●金の力で彼女をなびかせようとする try to *win* her *heart* [*conquer* her] with money.

なびく ❶《草木・旗などが》《曲がる》bend*;《おじぎをする》bow;《はためく》flutter;《波動する》wave. ▶稲が風になびいていた The rice plants *were bending* [*bowing*] in the wind. ▶旗が微風になびいている A flag *is fluttering* [*flying*, *waving*] in the breeze.
❷《人の心などが》《屈服する》yield,《話》give* in 《to》. ●金の力になびく *yield to*《his》money;《買収される》be bribed, be bought. ▶彼はついに彼女になびいた He finally *gave in to* her./《誘惑に負けた》He finally *gave way to* her temptation.

ナビゲーション 〚航空[航海]術〛navigation; (特にラリーでの方向・速度指示) rally navigation.
 ●ナビゲーションシステム navigation systems.

ナビゲーター a návigàtor.

ナプキン 〚食卓用〛a (table) napkin,《英》a serviette;〚生理用〛《wear》a sanitary napkin《米》[towel《英》]. ●紙ナプキン a paper *napkin*. ▶ひざにナプキンを掛ける lay [spread] one's *napkin* across one's lap. ●ナプキンで口をふく wipe one's mouth *on* [*with*] one's *napkin*.

ナフサ 〚化学〛naphtha.

ナフタ 〚北米自由貿易協定〛NAFTA《the *N*orth

America *Free* **Trade** *Agreement* の略).

なふだ 名札 ● [名前を付ける] a námepláte, a name card; [表札] a nameplate, (戸口の) a doorplate; [席の] a place card; [荷物の] a (baggage) tag; [迷子の] an ID [an identification] tag; [病院のベッドの] a name sheet. ● 胸に名札を attach [pin] one's *nameplate* to one's coat. ● 胸に名札をつけている wear [have] one's *nameplate* on one's lapel (**!** lapel /léipəl/ は上着のえりの折り返し)

ナフタリン [化学] naphthalene /ˈnæfθəliːn/, naphthalin(e); (虫よけ玉) a mothball (**!** 通例複数形で).

なぶりごろし なぶり殺し ● 敵兵をなぶり殺しにする *torture* an enemy soldier *to death*.

なぶりもの なぶり物 ● 人前でなぶりものにされる *be made fun of* in public. (⇨なぶる)

なぶる (笑い物にする) make* fun of ...; (ばかにして笑う) mock at ....

***なべ** 鍋 [浅い] a pan; [深い] a pot, (長い柄のついた) a saucepan. ● シチューなべ a stewpot; (圧力なべ) a Dutch oven /ʌvn/. (**!** 〈米〉では stewpot はあまり使わない) ● 中華なべ a wok. ● なべかま類 *pots* and *pans*. ● なべをこんろにかける put a *pot* on the stove. ● なべで煮る boil 《fish》 in a *pan*. ● 鍋つかみ a potholder. ● 鍋づる a pot bail. ● 鍋奉行 (説明的に) a person who gives one direction or another about how to cook, when to add the ingredients or when to eat best in case of *nabe* cooking. ● 鍋ぶた a pot lid. ● 鍋物 a dish cooked in an earthen pot at the table usually by the diners themselves. ● 鍋焼きうどん *nabeyakiudon*; (説明的に) *udon* noodles and various ingredients in soup, cooked and served hot individually in the casserole.

なべぞこ 鍋底 the bottom of a pot [pan]. ● 鍋底景気 (長引く不景気) a lingering [a prolonged] recession.

ナホトカ [ロシアの都市] Nakhodka /nɑːˈkɔːtkə/.

ナポリ [イタリアの都市] Naples /néɪplz/, [イタリア語名] Napoli /náːpoli/. ● ナポリの Neapolitan /niːəˈpɑlətn/.
● ナポリを見てから死ね See Naples and die. (**!** ナポリが風光明媚の地として有名なことから)

ナポリタン [<フランス語] ● スパゲッティナポリタン spaghetti Napolitana. (⇨スパゲッティ)

ナポレオン [フランスの皇帝] Napoleon /nəpóulɪən/ (~ Bonaparte).

***なま** 生 ━ 生の 形 ❶ [煮ていない] (自然のままの) raw; (調理していない) uncooked; (生煮えの) half-cooked; (沸かしていない) unboiled; (冷凍でない) fresh; (保healthcare処理をしていない) uncured. ● 日本人は魚を生で食べる Japanese people [《やや書》 The Japanese] eat fish *raw*.
❷ [ありのままの, 直接の] (録音・録画でない) live /láɪv/. ● 生の (= 現実に使われている) 英語 *real* English. ▶ 彼は住民の生の (=率直な) 声を聞いた He listened to the *candid* opinions of the local people.
● 生演奏 a live performance. ● 生クリーム fresh cream; (ケーキなどに使う) whipped cream. ● 生コンクリート freshly mixed concrete. ● 生魚 raw fish. ● 生酒 natural *sake*. ● 生卵 a raw egg. ● 生ハム (生食用の) an unused roll of film. ● 生野菜 raw [fresh] vegetables.

なまあくび 生あくび ● 生あくびをかみ殺す stop [stifle, suppress] a yawn (**!** stop yawning ともいう).

なまあげ 生揚げ deep-fried bean curd. (⇨ 厚揚げ)

なまあたたかい 生暖かい uncomfortably warm.
● 生暖かい風 an *uncomfortably warm* wind.

なまいき 生意気な cheekiness; sauciness; impertinence; impudence.
━ 生意気な 形 (子供などが) cheeky, saucy, 《米話》 sassy; (目上・年配者などに対して) impertinent, impudent (**!** 後の方が無礼で, 知らずの意が強い). ● 生意気な子供 a *cheeky* [a *saucy*] child. ● 生意気なことを言うな (= 出しゃばるな) Excuse me for being *forward*, but .... ▶ 彼の生意気な態度には頭に来た I got mad at his *impertinent* [*impudent*] attitude. ▶ そんな事を言うとはおまえは生意気だ It's *impertinent* [*impudent*] of you to say so./ You're *impertinent* [*impudent*] to say so. ▶ 彼は生意気にも私にあんな口のきき方をした He was *impudent* enough [He *had the impudence*] to speak to me like that.
会話 「そんなに飲んじゃいけないよ」「お前こそ父親に向かって生意気な口をきくんじゃない」 "You shouldn't drink too much." "And you shouldn't be so *cheeky* [*saucy*] to your father."

***なまえ** 名前 (人・動物・物などの) a name. (⇨名)

解説 **(1) 米英人の名前の表し方:** (a) 米英では個人名が John Stuart Mill のように三つあることも多いが, 最初の John は個人名で first [Christian, 《米》given] name, 真ん中の Stuart は middle name, 最後の Mill は姓で family [last] name, または surname という. また最初の二つは J. S. Mill のように頭文字で表されることも多いが, 頭文字を使わない正式な氏名を full name という. 姓を目立たせる場合は Mill, J. S. や Mill, John Stuart, また MILL, John Stuart のように書かれることがある.
(b) Mr. の敬称をつけるときは *Mr.* John Stuart Mill, *Mr.* Mill とはいうが ×Mr. John とは通例いわない.

(2) 日本人の名前の表し方: (a) 日本人の名前を表すにはローマ字を用いることになるが, 英語では姓名を日本語とは逆の「名 (first name)＋姓 (last name)」の順でいうので, たとえば鈴木太郎であれば, 英語流に一般に Taro Suzuki ということになる. 日本語と異なり, 少しでも親しくなると, first name で呼び合うようになる.
(b) 自分の名前を書くときは, Taro Suzuki のように氏名を省略せずに書く場合 (full name) と, T. Suzuki のように名をイニシャルにしたり, 場合によってはT. S. のように姓名ともイニシャルにする場合がある. また, Taro SUZUKI のように姓であることを強調するために姓の方をすべて大文字で書くこともある. さらに, 正式の書類などでは, Suzuki, Taro や Suzuki, T. のように姓を先に書いてコンマを置き, その後に名や名のイニシャルを添えることも少なくない.
(c) 日本の歴史上の人物の名前は, 通例, 姓と名を逆にせずに表される: 徳川家康 Tokugawa Ieyasu.

▶ あの花の名前は何ですか (何と呼びますか) What do you *call* that flower?/What is the *name* of that flower? (**!** 後の方は単なる質問だが, 人がきく前の方は親近感を与え, より普通に用いられる) ▶ 私は彼のことは名前しか知らない I know him only *by name* [*by name* only]. (**!** 「顔は知っているが名前は知らない」 は I know him by sight, but not *by name*.)
▶ きのう幸子という名前の女の人が訪ねてみえましたよ A lady [a woman] *named* [*called, by the name of*] Sachiko came to see you yesterday. (**!** 前の二つの方が普通) ▶ 彼の名前でホテルの予約をした I made a hotel reservation in his *name*. ▶ 野生の草花の名前を何種類言えますか How many kinds of wild flower can you *name*?
会話 「お名前を聞かせていただけますか」「小西良行です」

なまがし

"May I have [ask] your /*name*, pléase?/ Would you mind telling me your *name*?" "(My *name* is) Yoshiyuki Konishi." (❗(1) 前の方は最も一般的な名前の聞き方. 後の方が丁寧な尋ね方. (2) 答える場合は最初に姓をいう. くだけた雰囲気のときには名前だけですこともある多い. My name is はよく省略される. 女性の場合は未婚・既婚を示すために自分の名前に Miss, Mrs. をつけることがある.(⇨さん) (3) 名前の聞き方で What is your \name?/What's your /name?/What's your \name, /please? はいずれも目下の者に対して用いるくだけた言い方でこの順に丁寧になる. また Who are you? は「おまえはだれだ」という意で, 失礼な物言. Your name, please. は事務的な言い方. 間接的に人に名前を伝えるような状況では (⇨[次例]))

会話「ピーター・マーチンさんとお目にかかる約束をしています」「お見えになったことをお伝えしますが, (失礼ですが) お名前を伺わせてください」"I have an appointment to see Mr. Peter Martin." "I'll tell him you are here. What *name* shall I say?"

会話「失礼ですが, もう一度お名前を?」「ペインです. ジョン・ペインと申します」"Sorry, what's [what was] your *name* again?/(お名前は何とおっしゃいましたけ) What did you say your *name* was?" "It's Paine, John Paine."

会話「赤ちゃん産まれたら何て名前にするの」「とも子よ, もし女の子だったらね」"What are you going to *name* [*call*] the baby?" "Tomoko, if it's a girl."

会話「最初の子供にどんな名前をつけましたか」「私のおばにちなんで美紀子という名前をつけました」"What did you *name* your first child?" "We *named* her Mikiko *after* my aunt."

● **名前負け** ▶彼は名前負けしている He *is unworthy of his name*./He *does not live up to his name*.

なまがし 生菓子 soft and moist Japanese sweets; (洋菓子) fresh sweets.

なまかじり 生齧り ●なまかじりの学問 a little learning. ▶フランス語はなまかじりの知識 (=限られた知識) しかない I've got only a *limited* knowledge [(わずかな知識) a *slight* knowledge, a *smattering*, (表面的な浅い知識) a *superficial* knowledge] of French. (❗ smattering は名詞で主に「言葉」の知識について用いる)

なまかわ 生皮 (a) rawhide; (a) pelt.

なまがわき 生乾き ―― **生乾きの** 形 (生干しの) *half-dried*; (木材などが未乾燥の) *green*. ●生乾きのイカ *half-dried* cuttlefish. ●生乾きの木材 *green* lumber [*wood*]; (乾燥していない) *unseasoned* lumber [*wood*]. ▶このシャツは生乾きだ (=まだ湿っている) This shirt is *still damp*.

なまき 生木 (立ち木) a live /láiv/ tree; (未乾燥の木) unseasoned wood, green wood ▶後の方は普通たきぎについていう). ●生木を裂く wrench 《lovers, a mother *from* her child》.

なまきず 生傷 (打撲傷) a bruise /brú:z/; (切り傷) a cut. ▶彼は生傷が絶えない He always has some *cuts and bruises* on his body.

なまぐさい 生臭い (魚臭い) *fishy*; (血なまぐさい) *bloody* /blʌ́di/. (⇨血なまぐさい) ▶この食品は生臭い This food *smells of fish*./This food has a *fishy smell*. ▶この美談の裏には生臭い (=うさん臭い) ものが感じられる 〘話〙 I feel something *fishy* behind this moving story.

なまぐさぼうず 生臭坊主 (道徳的に腐った坊主) a corrupt priest.

なまくび 生首 a human head just severed; a severed head. ●生首を切る (⇨解雇する)

なまつば

なまくら 鈍ら 〘刃物が〙 blunt; dull; 〘人が〙 (怠け者の) lazy; (意気地ない) weak-hearted; spineless. (❗人について dull というのは「頭が鈍い」の意)

なまけもの 〘動物〙 a sloth.

なまけもの 怠け者 a lazy person; 〘話〙 a lazybones (複 〜s). (❗ 無冠詞で呼びかけにも用いる) ▶彼はクラスでいちばん怠け者だ He is the *laziest* (boy) in the class.

***なまける 怠ける** be lazy; be idle; (怠る) neglect.

使い分け lazy 仕事などを自分の意志でしようとしないことで非難の意を含む.
idle 仕事がなくてぶらぶらしていることで, 必ずしも非難の意を含まない.

● 勉強を怠ける *neglect* one's studies; *be lazy* [*xidle*] *about* studying [*in* study]. ● 学校を怠ける (=ずる休みする) *play truant* [《米》 *hooky*] *from* school. ● 怠けて時間を過ごす *idle* one's time *away*; *idle away* one's time. ● 怠け癖がつく *fall into an idle habit*. ▶怠けるな Don't *be lazy*./(一生懸命働け [勉強せよ]) Work [Study] hard. ▶私は怠けてなんかいられない I can't be [(余裕がない) afford to *live*] *idle*.

なまこ 〘動物〙 a sea cucumber.

なまごみ 生ごみ 《主に米》 (kitchen) garbage; 《主に英》 (kitchen) rubbish.

● 生ごみ処理機 a garbage 《米》 [a waste 《英》] disposer; a garbage 《米》 [a waste 《英》] disposal (unit). (❗家庭用の生ごみ粉砕機)

なまごろし 生殺し ❶ (⇨半殺し) ❷ 〘相手が困るような中途半端な状態にしておくこと〙 ● 生殺しにする keep 《him》 in an uneasy state. ▶彼は新作のリリースを延期してファンを生殺しの状態にしておいた He *has kept* his fans *very worried* by putting off the release of his new album.

なまじ (⇨なまじっか)

なまじっか ❶ 〘中途半端 [に]〙 (生半可に) not seriously, 《やや話》 by halves (❗通例否定文で (⇨半可)); (上辺だけの) *superficial*; (身の入らない) *half-hearted*; (軽率なこと) *thoughtless*(ly), *rash*(ly). ▶そんななまじっかなことではその試験には通れない You can't pass the exam if you go on studying *half-heartedly* [*in such a half-hearted way*]. ▶なまじっか知っていたのが彼にとって仇 (ẫた) となった His *superficial* knowledge about it worked against him.

❷ 〘いっそのこと〙 ▶なまじっか彼に会わなければよかった I should *never* have met him.

なましょく 生食 ● 生食用のかき oysters that to be eaten raw; "eat raw" oysters.

なます 膾 *namasu*; (説明的に) finely-chopped vegetables or fish, soaked in vinegar.

なまず 鯰 〘魚介〙 a catfish.

なまちゅうけい 生中継 a live relay broadcast. (⇨生, 放送) ▶このレポートはオリンピック会場から衛星生中継でお伝えしております We are reporting *live* by satellite from the Olympic Stadium.

なまっちょろい 生っちょろい ▶そんな生っちょろいやり方ではだめだ (厳しさに欠けている) You should *be more serious* [*enthusiastic*]./(徹底的にやらない) You have to *be thoroughgoing*.

なまっちろい 生っ白い *pale*(-*looking*) 《city boys》; 《look》 pale.

なまつば 生つば saliva /səláivə/. ▶梅干しを見たら生つばが出た I felt a lot of *saliva* filling in my mouth at the sight of a sour plum.

● 生つばを飲み込む (比喩的の) make one's mouth water. (❗ 形容詞で mouth-watering (よだれが出そ

なまづめ 生爪 • 生爪をはがす have one's nail torn off.

なまなましい 生々しい 〖鮮明な〗vivid; 〖新鮮な〗fresh. ● 記憶に生々しい be vivid [fresh] in one's memory. ▶殴られた跡は生々しく腫れ上がっていた The bruise was very livid and swollen. (❗ livid は「青黒い」の意)

なまにえ 生煮え ── 生煮えの 形 half-cooked, half-done, underdone. ● 生煮えのニンジン half-cooked [half-done, underdone] carrots.

なまぬるい 生温い 〖温度が〗lukewarm, tepid; 〖低温を適温とする飲食物が〗warm 〖少温い〗; 〖手ぬるい〗mild, lenient; 〖中途半端な〗halfway. ● なまぬるい湯 lukewarm [tepid] water. ● なまぬるい処置 a halfway [a lukewarm] measure. ▶そこで出されたスープはなまぬるかった The soup served there was lukewarm. ▶さあ座って飲まないか、なまぬるくなるといけないからね Well, will you sit down and have a drink? We won't let it get warm.

なまハム 生ハム unboiled ham.

なまはんか 生半可 ─ 生半可な 形 〖うわべの〗superficial; 〖浅薄な〗shallow; 〖計画・考えなどがあまい〗〘話〙half-baked; 〖気乗りのしない〗half-hearted. ● 生半可な知識 a superficial knowledge; a little knowledge [learning]. ● 生半可な議論 a shallow argument. ● 生半可な試み a half-hearted attempt. ● 彼は生半可な人生観しかない He has only a superficial [a shallow] view of life. ▶そんな生半可な計画では実行に移せない Such a half-baked [(不完全な) an incomplete] plan can't be put into practice. ▶何事も生半可に(=中途半端にしては)いけない You must not do anything by halves [do a halfway job].

なまビール 生ビール draft 〘英〙draught /dræft/; beer; beer on tap. (❗ 注ぎれたものをいうときは 形)

なまびょうほう 生兵法 • 生兵法は大けがのもと《ことわざ》A little learning [knowledge] is a dangerous thing.

なまへんじ 生返事 〖気乗りのしない〗a half-hearted [a reluctant] reply; 〖あいまいな〗a vague answer. ● 生返事をする reply half-heartedly [vaguely].

なまほうそう 生放送 名 a live /laɪv/ bróadcàst. ▶私たちはBS7でワールドシリーズを生放送で見た We watched a live broadcast of the World Series [the World Series going out live] on BS Channel 7. (❗ go out live は「生放送される」の意)

── 生放送する 動 broadcast 《a boxing match》live.

なまぼし 生干し • 生干しのいわし a half-dried sardine.

なまみ 生身 ❶〖生きている体〗a living being; 〖血の通った人間〗flesh and blood. ▶魔法使いの呪文が解けるとみんなそれぞれもとの生身の人間に戻った The spell of the wizard lifted and they each turned back into flesh and blood. ▶これまでに多くの過ちを犯してきた。所詮(=)おれも生身の(=ただの)人間ですよ I have made a lot of mistakes. I'm only human [flesh and blood].
❷〖魚などの〗raw flesh. (⇒生(なま) ❶) ● 鮭の生身 raw salmon /sǽmən/.

なまみず 生水 unboiled water. ▶パリで生水(=水道の水)を飲んだら下痢をした I drank tap water and got severe diarrhea /dàɪəríːə/ in Paris.

なまめかしい 艶めかしい 〖異性を引きつける〗sexy; 〖女性が肉感的な〗〘やや書〙voluptuous; 〖目付きなどが〗〘書〙amorous. ● なまめかしい目つきで throw a sexy [an amorous] look 《at him》; look 《at him》 amorously.

▶翻訳のこころ 研ぎあげられたステンレスの刃は、僕の手の中でなめかしくリアルに光った(村上春樹『レキシントンの幽霊』) The meticulously [well] polished stainless blade shined real and "sexy" in my hand. (❗〘米〙には The gun looks "sexy"(= appealing [attractive]). という gun を女性に見立てた比喩的な慣用表現がある)

なまめく 艶めく look sexy [amorous, bewitching].

なまもの 生物 〖食品〗uncooked [〖腐りやすい〗perishable] food; 〖魚〗raw fish.

なまやき 生焼け ── 生焼けの 形 〖肉などが〗underdone, half-roasted; 〖イモなどが〗half-baked.

なまやさしい 生易しい 〖容易な〗easy; 〖簡単な〗simple. ▶映画スターになるのは生易しいことではない It's not so easy [no easy thing] to be a movie star.

なまゆで 生茹で ── 生茹での 形 not well [properly] boiled; half-boiled.

なまよい 生酔い 名 • 生酔い本性違(たが)わず《ことわざ》Wine shows the man. ── 生酔いの 形 tipsy; a little drunk; intoxicated.

なまり 訛り 〖訛る〗speak* with an accent (⇔訛り); 〖方言〗a dialect. ● 地方なまりをおとす(=取り除く) get rid of one's local accent. ● なまりのない〖ひどい日本語なまりの〗英語を話す speak English without an [with a strong Japanese] accent. ● 彼女の言葉にはなまり〖関西なまり〗がある She has an [a Kansai] accent./She speaks with an [a Kansai] accent./I noticed an [a Kansai] accent in her speech.

なまり 鉛 lead /léd/. ● 鉛色の lead-colored, leaden /lédn/. ● (体などが)鉛のように重い be as heavy as lead.

なまりぶし 生り節 boiled and half-dried bonito.

なまる 訛る speak* with an accent (⇔訛り); 〖転訛(てんか)する〗be [get*] corrupted. ▶サボンがなまってシャボンになる "Savon" is [gets] corrupted [distorted, changed] into "Shabon."/"Shabon" is a corruption [a distortion] of "Savon."

なまる 鈍る 〖刃物などが〗become* dull [blunt]; 〖腕前が〗get* one's hand out; 〖活発でなくなる〗get less active, lose* one's former activeness [vigor].

なまワクチン 生ワクチン 〖生きたままで使うワクチン〗live vaccine /vǽksiːn/.

***なみ 並** ── 並の 形 〖普通の〗ordinary (⇔special); 〖平凡な〗common; 〖平均的な〗average; 〖大きさ・程度などが中間の〗medium. ● 並の人間 an ordinary [an average] person. ● 並の大きさの男 a man of medium size. ● 並のホテル a middle-class hotel. ▶今年の小麦の収穫は並でした The wheat crop was about average this year. ▶彼は並外れた才能の持ち主だ He's exceptionally talented. (並外れた)

***なみ 波** ❶〖水の動き〗a wave; a sea (❗ しばしば (the) ~s, 単・複両扱い. 直前に形容詞を伴う); 〖大波〗a (very) large wave, 〘書〙a billow; 〖うねる大波〗a swell (❗ 複数形にはしない); 〖砕ける波〗a breaker; 〖さざ波〗a ripple; 〖寄せる白波〗surf.
①〖波(の)~〗● 波の音 the sound [〖怒号〗roar] of the waves.
②〖波が〗● 波が高い The waves are (running) high. ● 波が静まった The waves have calmed down./〖海が〗The sea has become quiet [calm]. ▶波が岸に打ち寄せた The waves rolled (in) to [〖激しく〗beat on, 〖砕けた〗broke against] the shore. ▶日没とともに波が立ち始めた The waves

−なみ

began to rise as the sun set. ▶さざ波がひたひたと浜辺を洗っていた Ripples were lapping on the beach.
③【波に】● 波にもてあそばれる be at the mercy of the waves; be tossed about by the waves. ● 波に揺れる[漂う] rock [float] on the waves. ● 波に洗われる be washed by gentle waves. ● 子供が押し寄せた波にさらわれた A child has been washed away [been carried away] by the surging waves.
④【波を】● 荒波をけたてて進む plow /pláu/ [strive through] the angry waves [heavy seas].
❷【人・物事の】● 移民の波 a wave 《主に英》(多数) a spate] of immigrants. ● 人の波にまぎれて見えなくなる disappear [be lost] in a crowd of people. ● 仕事に波がある(=むらがある). (⇨斑(ﾏﾀﾞﾗ))
● 波に乗る ● 人気の波に乗る ride on the wave of popularity. ● 時代の波に乗る go with (↔against) the tide of the times. ● 好景気の波に乗る ride the crest of the boom.
● 波頭 the crest of a wave.

−なみ 並み ● 世間並みの(=普通の)生活 an ordinary life; (生活水準) the usual standard of living. ● 彼を家族並みに(=のように)扱うこと him like [(として) as] a member of the family. ● 人並みの(=平均の)知能 average intelligence. ▶彼女はアメリカ人並みに(=であるかのように)流暢(ﾘｭｳﾁｮｳ)に英語を話す She speaks English as fluently as if she were [《話》was] American.

なみいた 波板 a corrugated sheet.
なみいる 並み居る ● なみいるお歴々を前に before the dignitaries present. ▶そのチームはなみいる強豪を倒して優勝した The team won the championship by defeating these strong teams one after another.
なみうちぎわ 波打ち際 ● 波打ち際で at the shoreline [water's edge].
なみうつ 波打つ wave; (大きく) roll; 〖水面が〗(さざ波で) ripple; (三角波で) 波打つ(=並立つ)海 a choppy sea. (⇨波立つ) ● 稲田が風に波打った The rice field waved [rolled] in the wind.
なみかぜ 波風 〖風波〗 the wind and waves; 〖もめごと〗(a) trouble. ● 激しい波風 strong winds and high waves. ▶そんなことをしたら家庭に波風が立つぞ You'll make [cause] trouble in your family if you do such things.
なみがた 波形 ● 波形記号 a swung dash 《記号 ~》. ● 波形鉄板 corrugated iron.
なみき 並木 a row of trees, roadside trees. ● ポプラ並木の(=で縁どられた)道 a road bordered by a line of poplars. ● 並木道 a tree-lined road; (並木のある大通り) an avenue.
なみしぶき 波しぶき sea spray; spray blown from the surf [sea].
なみせい 並製 ── 並製の 形 common; ordinary.
***なみだ** 涙 a tear. (🗓 通例複数形で)
①【涙~】● 涙一滴 a tear; 《書》a teardrop. ● 涙声で in a tearful voice. ▶彼女に別れを告げると say a tearful good-bye 《to him》. ▶彼は悲しくて涙声になった His voice broke with sadness. ▶彼女は涙もろい(=すぐ心を動かされて涙を流す) She's easily moved to tears./(非常に感傷的だ) She's really sentimental.
②【涙が】● 彼の目に涙が浮かんだ Tears came into [formed in] his eyes. ● 彼女の目は涙がにじんでいた There were tears in her eyes./She had tears in her eyes. ● その煙は目から涙が出た My

なみはずれた

eyes watered in the smoke./The smoke made my eyes water. ▶涙が彼女の目にあふれた(=わきだした) Tears welled up in her eyes./Her eyes filled [brimmed] with tears. ▶涙が彼女のほおを伝って流れた Tears ran [streamed, (ぽろぽろと) trickled, (ころがって) rolled] down her cheeks./Her cheeks were running with tears. ▶これといった理由もないのに涙が止まらなかった(=絶え間なく流れた) The tears flowed ceaselessly for no apparent reason.
③【涙に】● 涙にぬれた顔 a tear-stained face. ▶彼の顔は涙にぬれていた His face was wet [moist] with tears.
④【涙を】● 涙を流す《書》shed tears; (泣く) cry; (しくしく泣く) weep. ● 涙をふく wipe (away) [dry] one's tears 《with a handkerchief》. (🗓 wipe [dry] one's eyes ともいうが「泣くのをやめる」の意で用いられるのが普通) ● 目に涙を浮かべて(=涙ぐんで)身の上話をする tell the story of one's life with tears in one's eyes [with tearful eyes].
● 涙に暮れる ▶彼女は息子の死で涙に暮れた(=ひどく悲しんだ) She broke her heart over her son's death./Her son's death broke her heart./(毎日泣いてばかりいた) She did nothing but weep day and night over her son's death.
● 涙にむせぶ be choked with tears.
● 涙を抑える ▶その光景を見て涙を抑えることができなかった I couldn't hold [keep, fight] back my tears at the sight.
● 涙を飲む bear back one's tears.
● 涙を催す ▶その悲しい話に私は涙を催した(=涙ぐんだ) I was moved to tears by the sad story./The sad story moved me to tears.
● 涙金 a (mere) pittance.

なみたいてい 並大抵 ● 司法試験に合格するのは並大抵のことではない It is no easy matter [task] to pass the bar exam./(大変な勉強が必要だ) It takes a great deal of study to pass the bar exam. ▶彼の才能は並大抵のものではない He is uncommonly [《例外的に》exceptionally] gifted.
なみだぐましい 涙ぐましい ● 涙ぐましい(=感動的な)光景 a touching [a moving, (涙をさそう) a pathetic] sight. ● 涙ぐましい(=苦しくつらい)努力をする make painful efforts (to do).
なみだぐむ 涙ぐむ (涙を催す) (⇨涙 [成句]) ● 涙ぐんだ目で with tearful eyes. ▶彼の目は涙ぐんでいた His eyes were filled [ぬれていた wet] with tears.
なみだつ 波立つ ● 波立つ海 a broken sea; (三角波が立つ) a choppy sea. ▶海は波立っていた The sea was running high./The sea was choppy.
なみなみ ── なみなみと 副 (ふちまで) to the brim; (あふれるほど) overflowingly. ● 酒をグラスになみなみとつぐ pour sake to the brim of the glass; (一杯に満たす) fill the glass up with sake.
なみなみならぬ 並々ならぬ (並外れた) extraordinary; (非凡な) uncommon. ● 並々ならぬ才能の女性 a woman of extraordinary [uncommon, (例外的な) exceptional] talent. ● 並々ならぬ(=大きな)努力をする make utmost [utmost, strenuous] efforts.
なみにく 並肉 regular-grade meat.
なみのり 波乗り 〈enjoy〉 surfing. (⇨サーフィン)
なみはずれた 並外れた 形 extraordinary; (非凡な) uncommon; (普通でない) unusual.
── 並外れて 副 extraordinarily; 《書》 uncommonly; unusually. ● (異常) 並外れて背の高い男 an extraordinarily [an unusually] tall man. ▶彼は並外れて手先が器用だ He's extraordinarily skillful with his hands./He has a great

なみはば 並幅 ordinary width cloth.

ナミビア 〖国名〗Namibia; (公式名) the Republic of Namibia. (首都 Windhoek) ●ナミビア人 a Namibian. ●ナミビア(人)の Namibian.

なみま 波間 ●波間に漂う drift *on the waves*. ●波間に見え隠れする(船などが) now appear *on the waves* and then drop out of sight *behind the waves*.

なめくじ 〖動物〗a slug.

なめこ 滑子 *nameko* mushrooms.

なめしがわ 鞣し革 leather; tanned hide. (⇨革)

なめす 鞣す ●子牛の皮をなめす *tan* [*dress*] calfskin.

なめつくす なめ尽くす ●火は森林500ヘクタールをなめ尽くしてやっと下火になった The fire *burned down* [〘書〙*consumed*] five hundred hectares of forest before it was put under control.

なめとこやまのくま『なめとこ山の熊』*The Bears of Mt. Nametoko*. 〔参考〕宮沢賢治の童話

*__なめらか__ 滑らか ―― 滑らかな 形 ❶ [物の表面が] smooth; (凹凸がない) even; (平らな) flat (-tt-); (柔らかい) soft. ●絹のように滑らかである be as *smooth* as silk. ●彼女の肌は滑らかです She has *soft* [*smooth*] skin. ●木材の表面を滑らかにするのにサンドペーパーを使った We used sandpaper to make the wood *smooth*./We sandpapered the wood *smooth*. ●このリップクリームをつけると唇が滑らかになります This lip balm will *lubricate* your lips. (❗ lubricate は「(油分を与えて)滑らかにする」の意)
❷ [動きなどが] smooth; (流暢(りゅうちょう)な) fluent. ●滑らかな手の動き *smooth* movement of one's arms. ●彼はスペイン語を滑らかに話した He spoke Spanish *fluently*./He spoke *fluent* Spanish./He was *fluent* in Spanish.

なめる ❶ [舌で] lick; (動物がぴちゃぴちゃなめて飲む) lap (-pp-); (味わう) taste. ●唇をなめる(=湿らせる) *moisten* one's lips. ●犬は彼の顔をなめた The dog *licked* his face. ●彼女は指についたジャムをなめて取った She *licked* the jam *off* her fingers. ●子猫は皿のミルクをみんななめて飲んでしまった The kitten *licked up* all the milk in [*lapped* (*up*)] milk from] the saucer.
❷ [経験する] experience; (味わう) taste. ●世の中の辛酸をなめる *experience* [*go through*] the hardships of life;〘やや書〙*taste* the bitters of life. (❗ taste the sweets and bitters of life は「人生の苦楽を経験する」の意の成句的表現)
❸ [みくびる] underestimate. ●試験をなめてかかる do *not take* the exam *seriously*. ●相手をなめてかかるな Don't *underestimate* your opponent./(簡単に打ち負かせると思うな) Don't think you can beat your opponent easily.

なや 納屋 a barn; (物置小屋) a shed.

なやましい 悩ましい sexy; (肉感的な) 〘やや書〙voluptuous; (色っぽい) 〘書〙amorous; (挑発する) suggestive; provocative. ●胸元の開いた悩ましいドレス a *sexy* low-front dress. ●彼女の悩ましい肢体は her *sexy* [*voluptuous*] figure. ●彼女の歩き方はとても悩ましい She has a very *sexy* walk.

*__なやます__ 悩ます worry; annoy; bother.

| 使い分け **trouble** 精神的・心理的な負担をかけて困らせることを表す。
worry 人を不安にさせたり気をもませたりすることを表す。受身で用いられることが多い。(⇨悩む)
annoy, bother 繰り返しじゃまなどをして人の心を乱すことを表す。annoy はその結果腹を立てさせるが、bother には必ずしもその含みはなく、その程度がもっと軽い場合に用いる。 |

●不平を言って悩ます *trouble* [*annoy*] 《him》 *with* complaints. ●質問をして悩ます *annoy* [*bother, worry*] 《him》 *with* questions. ●頭を悩ます(=知恵を絞る) rack one's brains 《*over* a problem》.
●心を悩ます (⇨悩む) ●今日のこの暑さに悩まされている I have *been bothered* by the heat today./The heat has *been bothering* me today. ●騒音に悩まされて一晩じゅう眠れなかった I was so much *annoyed* by the noise [The noise was so *annoying*] that I couldn't sleep all night. (❗ annoying は形容詞)/The noise kept me awake all night.

*__なやみ__ 悩み 〖気をもむこと〗(a) worry; 〖困ること〗(a) trouble; 〖苦悩〗(a) distress (❗ いずれの語も「悩み事、悩みの種」の意では ⒞); 〖迷惑〗(an) annoyance; 〖問題〗a problem. ●悩み(=心配)がない be free from *care*. ●あなたの悩みは何ですか What is your *trouble* [*worry, problem*]?/(何があなたを悩ませているのですか) What *is troubling* [*worrying, annoying, bothering*] you?/(何について悩んでいるのですか) What *are you worried* [*troubled, annoyed, bothered*] *about*? ●人生には悩みが多い Life is full of *worries* [*troubles*]. ●あの子供は両親にとって悩みの種だ That child is a constant (source of) *worry* [*trouble, pain*] to his parents./〘話〙That child is *a pain in the neck* to his parents.

*__なやむ__ 悩む 慣用句 (明確な原因・理由なしに) worry, be worried 《about, over》(❗ 状態をいうときは be worried の方が普通; (病気なる特定の原因・理由で) be troubled, trouble 《about, over, with》(❗ 後の方は通例疑問文・否定文で用いる); be annoyed [bothered] 《about》(⇨悩ます); [病気・悪状況などで苦しむ] suffer 《from》. ●悩むことは何もない There's nothing to *worry* [*trouble*] *about*. ●将来のことでとても悩んでいる I'm *very* [*much, very much*] *worried about* the future. (❗〘話〙では worried を形容詞と考えて very を用いることが多い) ●悩んでいる様子ですね、どうかしたんですか You look *worried* [*troubled, annoyed, bothered*] —is something [×*anything*] *wrong*? (⇨何か) ●彼は長年リューマチで悩んでいる He has been *troubled* [*bothered*] *with* rheumatism for years./He *has suffered from* rheumatism for years. ●目下、食糧不足に悩んでいる国は多い A lot of countries *are troubled by* [*are suffering from*] the food shortage at the moment.

なよなよ ●なよなよした(=ほっそりした)姿 a *slender* figure. ●柳の枝がなよなよと(=ゆるやかに)風になびいていた The willow branches were swaying *gently* in the breeze.

なよやか ―― なよやかな 形 (ほっそりしていて、かつ弱々しい) slender; slim; (しなやかな) supple; lithe /láið/; 〘書〙lissome.

なら 楢 〖植物〗a Japanese oak.

!―なら 〘副助詞〙(…に関しては) as for …; (…と言えば) talking [speaking] of …. ●私なら彼の提案に全面的に賛成です *As for* me, I quite agree to his proposal. (❗ as for は通例文頭に置き、他の人はどうか分からないが私に関して言えばという気持ち) ●野球なら三度の飯より好きだ *Talking* [*Speaking*] *of* baseball, I like it better than anything else. ●山田君とは気が合わないん。でも彼の妹ならすごく好きだよ ˇYamada I dón't get ˇon with, but his ˇsister I like *enormously* [*very much*]. (❗ Yamada と his sister はいずれも目的語であるが対比のために文頭に出して強調した形)

会話 「たばこを吸ってもいいですか」「廊下でなら(=に限

ってい)いですよ」"Can we smoke?" "*Only* in the hall."

▌ DISCOURSE
私なら間違いなく前者を選ぶ I *would definitely* choose the former. (!! *definitely* (間違いなく)は主張を表すディスコースマーカー)

── -**なら**〖接続助詞〗〖仮定，条件〗 if ...; (...の条件で) on condition 《*that* 節》. (⇨もし) ▶気分が悪いのならすぐ帰りなさい If you feel sick, (you may) go home at once. ▶銀座が東京の中心なら，大阪の中心はどこですか If Ginza is the center of Tokyo, what is the center of Osaka? ▶私が君なら仕事を変えるのだが If I were [〖話〗was] you, I would change my do. ▶田中，君らどうする What *would* you do, Tanaka? ▶逃げないからなら放してやってもよい I will let you go *on condition that* you don't try to escape.

ならい 習い (個人の習慣) a habit; (慣習) a custom.
● 世の習い(= 世間のやり方) the way of the world.
● **習い性**(ﾞ)**となる** 《ことわざ》 Habit is second nature.

ならいごと 習い事 (習得した技術・芸事) an accomplishment. 《!! しばしば複数形で》 ▶娘に何か習い事をさせたい I want my girl to learn something in addition to schoolwork. (⇨習う)

*__**ならう 習う** 〖学んで身につける〗 learn* (↔teach); 〖個人レッスンを受ける〗 take* lessons 《*in*》; 〖勉強する〗 study. ▶私はA先生に英語を習っています I'm *learning* [*studying*] English *from* [×to] Mr. A. (!! (1) learn は必ずしも努力を伴わないが完全に身につくことをいい，初心者であることを暗示する。study は積極的に勉強[研究]することをいうが必ずしも身につくとは限らない。(2) I've *learned* English. は習得を完了したことを含意する） ▶彼女にピアノを習っています I'm *taking* piano *lessons from* her./I'm taking *lessons in* piano *from* her./I'm *learning* (how) to play the piano *from* her. (!! 「柔道[空手]を習う」は learn judo [karate]) ▶今学校でフランス革命を習っている We *are learning about* the French Revolution at school now. ▶今日授業でサルが人間の祖先であるということを習った Today we *learned* [×studied] in our class *that* apes were [are] the ancestors of humans. (!! 現在形 are は内容が永遠の真理として解される場合) ▶だれに英語を習っていますか Who *teaches* you English?/Who is your English teacher? ▶静かに過ごすことを習え Study to be quiet./Let it be your ambition to keep calm.
● **習うより慣れよ** 《ことわざ》 Practice makes perfect.

ならう 倣う ❶〖そっくりまねる〗 copy; 〖従う〗 follow; 〖倣って作る〗 model 《it, oneself》 on 《*after*》.... ▶人の例にならう *follow* 《his》 example; (仕事などを継ぐ) *follow* in 《his》 footsteps. ▶パリにならって都市を設計する *model* [*base*] a plan of the city *on* that of Paris.
❷〖整列する〗 ▶右へならえ！ 〖軍事〗 *Dress* right./*Right, dress*.

ならく 奈落 ❶〖地獄〗 Hell; (どん底) (a) hell; the abyss. ❷〖舞台の床下〗 a trap cellar.
● **奈落の底** ▶奈落の底(= 失意の極)に突き落される be plunged [thrown] into the *abyss of despondency*.

*__**ならす 鳴らす** ❶〖鐘・警笛・警報などを〗 sound; 〖ベル・鈴などを〗 ring*; 〖笛・汽笛・サイレンなどを〗 blow*. ▶どらを鳴らす *sound* [*clang*] a gong. ▶ラッパを鳴らす *blow* a trumpet. ▶小銭をじゃらじゃら鳴らす

tinkle [*jingle*] coins. ● 舌をちょっと鳴らす *click* [*clack*] one's tongue. (⇨舌) ▶指をぱちんと鳴らす *snap* one's fingers. (⇨指) ▶用があったらベルを鳴らしてください *Ring* the bell [*Ring for me*] if you want something. ▶後の方は目的語 (the bell) を省略した言い方) ▶クラクションをしつこく鳴らすな Don't keep on (*sounding* [*blowing*]) your horn. (!! on は継続を強調する副詞) ▶だれかが玄関でベルを鳴らしている Someone *is ringing* the doorbell./There is a *ring* at the door.
❷〖評判になる〗 ▶彼は高校時代，名選手として鳴らした He *was well-known* as a good player when he was a high school student.

ならす 馴らす (飼いならす) tame 《a lion》; (家畜化する) domesticate.

ならす 慣らす accustom (⇨慣れる); (訓練する) train. ▶暗やみに目を慣らす *accustom* one's eyes *to* the darkness. ▶耳を英語に慣らす *train* one's ear to understand spoken English; *accustom oneself to* the sound of English. ▶新しい靴をはき慣らす *break in* new shoes.

ならす 均す 〖平らにする〗 level ... (*off*); make*... level [*even*]; 〖平均する〗 average. ▶地面をローラーでならす *level* the ground with a roller; *roll* the ground.

ならずもの ならず者 (やくざ) a gangster; (悪党) a rogue; (ごろつき) a hooligan, a hoodlum.

ならたけ 楢茸 〖植物〗 a honey fungus.

ならづけ 奈良漬け *narazuke*; (説明的に) vegetables preserved in *sake* lees.

-**ならでは** ▶それは彼らならでは(=彼ら以外だれも)できないことだ No one *but* him can do it./(できる唯一の人だ) He is the *only* man that [who] can do it./(彼だけしかできないだろう) *Only* he could do it. (!! could は仮定法過去形で「やろうと思えばできる」の意)

:-**ならない ❶**〖義務，必要〗(...しなければならない) must; have* to /hǽftə/; have got to; (...すべきである) should; ought to; (...ということになっている) be supposed to.

▌ 使い分け **must** 話し手の主観による強い義務を表す．したがって他者に対して用いると命令・強力な助言になる．

have to 話し手以外の，例えば規則・約束・別の人の意志などによる客観的な義務を表し，must にくらべ柔らかな言い方になることが多い．ただし区別なく用いることもある．

have got to have to の口語的表現．

should, ought to は上二つに比べ意味は強くなく，「...すべき」という話し手の望ましさ・忠告などを表し，実際にするかしないかはその人が決めるという含みがある．両者はほぼ同意であるが ought to の方がやや強意的，また道徳・規則などに基づいた客観的な義務には ought to が好まれる．過去形は **should** [**ought to**] **have** 《done》で，「実際にはしなかった」ことを意味する．

be supposed to 控えめな言い方で，規則・話し手の期待などを述べることによってその人が自発的に行うことを促す．

▌ 解説 (1) must は過去・未来・完了の形がないので had to, will have to, have had to を用いる．ただし従節中の過去は must も用いられる: 彼はすぐ家に帰らなければならないと思った He thought (that) he *must* [*had to*] go home immediately.
(2) have got to /əv/ と弱く発音され，I've got to ... のように縮約形で用いることが多い．くだけた表現では 've も落ちて I got to ... のようになるこ

ともある. また have to と異なり通例過去形にできず, 助動詞とともに用いることもできない: ×had got to; ×will have got to は不可. また次のような形でも用いない: ×to have got to; ×having got to.

▶あなたは 9 時までに来なければならない You *must* [*have* (*got*) *to*, *should*, *ought to*, *are supposed to*, (来るよう求められている) *are required to*] come by nine. ▶応募者は 30 歳未満でなければならない Applicants *must* be under thirty years old. (❶「未満」は「以下」でないことに注意) ▶私はいつも朝早く起きなければならない I *have to* [*must*] get up early every morning. (❶(1) I が主語の場合, 習慣的なことには must より have to が好まれる. (2)《英》では have to と have got to の用法に違いがあり, 通例上のように習慣的または繰り返し行われる行為には have to を用い, 次のように習慣的でない行為には have got to を用いる: あした早く起きなければならない I've got to get up early tomorrow.) ▶もう帰らなければならないですか *Must* you [Do you *have to*,《話》*Have* you *got to*] leave now? ▶あした彼に謝らなければならない I will *have to* [×*will have to*] apologize to him tomorrow. (❶未来形にせず I *must* [*have* (*got*) *to*] apologize …. といえる) ▶きのうは東京へ行かなければならなかった I *had to* [×*must*] go to Tokyo yesterday. ▶花に水をやらなければならない We *must* [必要がある] water the flowers./The flowers *need* watering [*to be watered*]. (⇨必要) ▶だれかが残って手伝わなくちゃならない Somebody *has to* [《話》*has got to*] stay behind and help. ▶きのう君は彼に電話をかけなければならなかったのに(しなかった) You *should* [*ought to*] *have called* him up yesterday. (❶*must have called* … は「電話をかけたに違いない」の意) ▶やらなきゃならないことがこんなにたくさんあるんだ I have so many things *to do*. (❶I *have to do* so many things. との違いに注意)

会話「彼に会わなければなりませんか」「ええ, そうしなさい [いいえ, その必要はありません]」"*Must* I see him?" "Yes, you *must* [Yes, you don't *have to*, No, you need not]." (❶(1) Must I …? は相手の意向を聞く言い方. (2) need not の代わりに must not では「会ってはならない」の意 (⇨❷))

会話「君はすぐに謝らなくちゃならないよ」「どうして謝らなくちゃならないのか分からないね」"You *must* apologize at once." "I don't see why I *should*."

❷ [禁止] (してはならない) must* not (❶must は過去形がないので be not allowed to (許可されていない),《やや書》be forbidden to (禁じられている)などで代用する; (すべきでない) should not; ought not to (❶×ought to not としない). ▶あなたはそんなにたばこを吸ってはならない You mustn't /mʌsnt/ [*shouldn't*, *oughtn't to*, *had better not*] smoke so much. (❶must not が最も強い禁止を表す)/*Don't* smoke so much.

❸ [仕方がない] can't help 《*doing*》. ▶私はそのことが心配でならない I *can't help* [*stop*] worrying about the matter./(とても心配) I'm *very* worried about the matter.

ーならば (⇨ば)

ならび 並び (通例横の) a row /róu/; (縦の) a line; (同じ側) a side. ● 本屋の並びにあるカメラ屋 the camera shop *on the side of* the bookstore.

ならびしょうする 並び称する ▶松井はイチローと並び称される (=肩を並べる) 看板選手だ Matsui *ranks with* Ichiro as a star baseball player.

ならびたつ 並び立つ ▶松が道路沿いに並び立っていた The pine trees *stood in a row* along the road. ●音楽家として彼に並び立つ (=匹敵する) 人を見たことが

ない I have never seen his *equal* as a musician. (⇨並ぶ ❷)

ならびに 並びに ▶コンサートは東京ならびに大阪で(=東京と大阪の両方で)行われた The concert was held (*both*) in Tokyo *and* in Osaka (東京そして大阪でも) in Tokyo *and also* in Osaka, (東京だけでなく大阪でも) in Osaka *as well as* in Tokyo]. (⇨そして (a), 及び, 両方, 又 ❸)

*ならぶ 並ぶ ❶ [列を作る] (列を作ってずらっと並ぶ) line up,《英》queue /kjúː/ (*up*); (1 列に並ぶ) stand* in line [《英》a queue], (横 1 列) a row]; (列を作る) form a line [《英》a queue]; (…に沿って並ぶ) line. ●並んで歩く (横に) walk *side by side*; (縦に) walk *one behind the other* [*another*]. (❶the other は 2 人または 3 人以上の特定数, another は不特定数に用いる) ● 3 列に並ぶ stand in [form, get into] three *lines*. ●彼女と並んで座る sit (*side by side*) *with* her; (隣に) sit *next to* her. ▶多くの人がバスを待って並んでいた A lot of people were waiting *in line* for [to get on] the bus./A lot of people were *lining* [《英》*queuing*] *up* for [to get on] the bus. ▶女王を見ようと群衆が舗道に並んだ Crowds *lined* the pavement to see the queen. ▶図書館の壁には本棚が並んでいる The walls of the library *are lined with* bookcases. ▶あそこにロッカーが並んでいるだろう. どれでも使っていいよ There's a *row* of lockers over there. You can use any of them. ▶この通りには有名店がずらりと並んでいる The street *is lined with* famous shops.

❷ [匹敵する] match; (比肩する) rival; (同等である) equal, be equal (*to*). (⇨匹敵する) ▶英語では彼に並ぶ者はいない No one can *match* [*equal*] him *in* English./He *has no equal in* English. (❶この *equal* は「同等の者」)/He is second to none in English.

ならべたてる 並べ立てる (⇨並べる ❷)

ならべる 並べる ❶ [配列する] (配列よく並べる) arrange; (1 列に並ぶ) line … up; (物を 1 列に置く) put [(位置を定めて) set*, (正しい位置に) place]; … in a line [(横 1 列に) in a row]; (隣り合わせに置く) put … side by side; (陳列する) display; (展示する) exhibit. ● 棚に本をきちんと並べる *arrange* books on the shelf. (❶「棚の上の本を整とんする」の意にもなる) ● 名前をアルファベット順に並べる *arrange* [*put*] their names in alphabetical order. ●少年たちを点呼のために 1 列に並べる *line up* the boys [*line the boys up*] for roll call. ●机を 2 列に[丸く]並べる *put* [*arrange*] the desks in two rows [*in a circle*]. ●食卓に料理を並べる *set* [*spread*] dishes *on* the table; *set* [*spread*] the table (*with* dishes). ●いすを並べ替える *rearrange* the chairs; (並べ方を変える) change the arrangement of the chairs. ▶商品がショーウインドーに並べられている The goods *are displayed* [*are on display*] in the (store) windows.

❷ [列挙する] (例をあげる) cite, quote (❶quote はそのまま引用すること); (列挙する)《書》enumerate; (箇条書きにする) itemize. ●例を多数並べ立てる *cite* a large number of instances. ●私の誤りを並べ立てる *enumerate* my mistakes. ●愚痴を並べる *make* [《やや書》*voice*] *a series of complaints*.

ならやまぶしこう『楢山節考』 *The Song of Oak Mountains*. [参考] 深沢七郎の小説)

ならわし 習わし (慣習) (a) custom; (しきたり) (a) convention; (伝統) (a) tradition. ●地元の習わしに従う[を破る] follow [break] a local *custom* [*convention, tradition*]. ▶アメリカやイギリスではクリスマスに七面鳥を食べるのが習わしである They usually

[《やや書》 *habitually*] eat roast turkey on Christmas day in America and Britain./It is *traditional* [《やや書》 *customary*] to eat roast turkey on Christmas day in America and Britain.

なり 生り ● ナスの一番なり the first eggplant *to appear*. ▶今年は柿のなりがいい Persimmon trees have a lot of *fruit* this year./There's much *fruit* on persimmon trees this year.

なり 鳴り ▶この三味線は鳴り(=鳴る音)がよくない This *samisen* doesn't *sound* all right.
● 鳴りを潜(ヒホ)める (活動していない) be inactive; (特に火山が) be dormant; (静かにしている) remain quiet.

なり 形 ❶ [かっこう](外見) (an) appearance; (服装) dress. ▶なりをかまわない don't care about one's *clothes* [one's *appearance*, *how* one *looks*]. ▶ひどいなりをしている be poorly *dressed*. ▶男のなりをしていて in the *disguise* of a man; in a man's *disguise*.
❷ [体つき] ▶年の割には大きななりをしている be big for one's age.

ーなり ❶ [自己流のやり方で] in one's own way. ▶君なりのやり方でしなさい Do your work *in your own way*. ▶だれにもその人(《やや書》 *his*) *own way* of doing things.
❷ [...とすぐ] as soon as .... ▶夜が明けるなり私たちは出発した *As soon as* the day broke we started.
❸ [...まま] ▶帽子をかぶったなりで人にあいさつするのは失礼だ It's rude of you to greet other people *with* your hat on. (⚠ with は付帯状況を表す)
❹ [A, B のいずれも] either A or B. ▶電話なり手紙なりで結果を知らせてください Please let me know the result *either* by phone *or* by letter.

なりあがり 成り上がり an upstart; [成り金] a new rich (⇨成り金).

なりあがる 成り上がる (権力を得る) rise suddenly to power; (金持ちになる) suddenly get rich; rise suddenly to wealth.

なりかわる 成り代わる take the place of .... ●...に成り代わって behalf of ...; in (his) place.

なりきる 成りきる ▶役になりきる get into one's role; be natural in one's role. ▶いくら借金取りでもそこまで冷酷にはなりきれまい I don't think even a debt collector *can be* that cruel [*heartless*].

なりきん 成り金 [成り上がり者] a new rich; [にわか成り金] a nouveau riche /núːvou riːʃ/ ((複)nouveaux riches /~/), a new rich, 《集合的》 the new rich 《複数扱い》. (⚠ new rich には軽蔑的な含みはない)
●戦争[土地]成り金(=不当利得者) a war [a land] *profiteer*. ●成り金になる suddenly get rich; 《話》 get rich quick.

なりさがる 成り下がる (落ちぶれる) come* down in the world. (⇨成り下る).

なりすまし 成り済まし [コンピュータ] spoofing. 《参考》他人のアドレスなどを不正に利用し、別人のふりをしてネットワーク上で活動すること.

なりすます 成り済ます disguise oneself 《as》; pretend 《to be》. ▶男は探偵に成りすましていたが殺人犯だったのだ The man (*had*) *pretended to be* a detective, but he was the murderer himself.

なりたち 成り立ち [起源] (an) origin; [歴史] history; [組織] formation; [構造] structure. ●近代日本の成り立ち the *history* of modern Japan. ●文の成り立ち the *structure* of a sentence.

***なりたつ 成り立つ** ❶ [構成される] be made up of ..., consist of ... (⚠ ×be consisted of としないこと); be composed of .... (⚠順に堅い表現) ▶野球のチームは 9 人から成り立つ A baseball team *is made up of* [*consists of*] nine players. ▶水は酸素と水素とから成り立つ Water *consists* [*is composed*] *of* [×*from*] oxygen and hydrogen.
❷ [存立する] ▶このインフレでは商売も成り立たない(=やっていけない) With this inflation we can't *manage* [*carry on*] our business. ▶君の言い分は成り立たない(=妥当でない) Your claim *is not valid*.

なりて 為り手 ▶このごろは家政婦のなり手がない(=だれもなりたくない) No one wants to be a domestic help these days.

なりどし 生り年 ▶今年のうちの柿はなり年だった Our persimmon tree has produced much [a lot of] fruit this year.

なりと(も) [副助詞] ❶ [せめて...ぐらいは] ▶彼は母親が生きている間にひと目なりとも会いたいと思った He wished to see his mother *just* [*at least*] once while she was alive. ▶彼は電話なりともかけてくれればいいのに He should *at least* give us a phone call.
❷ [...でも] ▶どこへなりとも行ってしまえ Get out of here [my sight]!/Get lost!

なりはてる 成り果てる ●浮浪者に成り果てる be reduced to vagrancy /véigrənsi/; become a vagrant.

なりひびく 鳴り響く [高らかに響く] ring* (out); [反響する] echo; resound /rizáund/. (⇨響く ❷) ▶教会の鐘の音が町中に鳴り響いた The church bells *rang* (*out*) throughout the town. ▶蘭学者としての彼の名声は国中に鳴り響いていた He *was well known* throughout the country as one of the top Dutch scholars.

なりふり 形振り ▶彼女はなりふりはあまりかまわない She doesn't care much *how she looks* [*about her appearance*, 《服装は》 about her *clothes*]. ▶この業界ではなりふりかまわぬ生き残り作戦が展開されている In this business, it's *dog eat dog*, every one of them aiming at their survival. (⚠(1) dog eat dog は 形容詞で「食うか食われるかの戦いをして」の意. dog-eat-dog ともつづる. (2) it は全体の状況を表す. (3) 「生き残りをかけた戦い」は a cutthroat competition ともいう)

なりものいり 鳴り物入り ●鳴り物入りで新車を宣伝する advertise a new model car *with a great deal of fanfare*.

なりゆき 成り行き [経過] the course 《of nature》; [進展] the development 《of events》; [進行] the progress 《of ～》; [結果] the result 《of a matter》. ●事の成り行き次第では according to the *course* [*development*] of events. ●事の成り行きを見守る watch the *course* of things; (結果を待つ) wait for the *result* of things; (静観する) wait and see how things will *turn out*. ●成り行きに任せる (自然の成り行きに) let nature take [follow, run] its (own) *course*; (事の成り行き) let things [matters] take their (own) *course*. ▶彼は事態の成り行きに満足していなかった He was not satisfied with *the way things were going*. ▶今は手の打ちようがない. 成り行きを見るほかないだろう There's nothing we can do. We'll just have to *wait and see*.
●成り行き注文 a market order.

なりわい 生業 an occupation; a profession; a trade; a job. (⇨職業) ▶物書きをなりわいとする earn a living as a writer.

なりわたる 鳴り渡る ring* (out). (⇨鳴り響く)

は「避ける」の意)
❷ 〖できるなら〗if (it is) possible. ▶私はヨ担なるべくタクシーに乗らないようにしている I usually try not to take a taxi *if possible*. (⚠ ×... not ... as often as possible ではこの意にならない) ▶なるべくならここにいたい *If possible*, I'd like to stay here. ▶なるべく外食しないことにしている I don't eat out *if I can help it*.

***なるほど** 成る程 〖副〗〖本当に〗indeed; really; 〖まったく〗quite. ▶なるほどこの本はおもしろい This book is *really* interesting./This book is very interesting *indeed*. (⚠ indeed は very を伴う形容詞・副詞を修飾する. したがって ×This book is interesting indeed. は不可) ▶なるほど君の言うとおりです You're *quite* right./I *quite* agree with you. ▶なるほど君がそう考えるのももっともだ You may (*quite*) well think so./It is *quite* natural that you (《主に英》should) think so.
〖なるほど…だがしかし〗 (it is) true (that)..., but ...; to be sure, but ...; indeed ..., but .... (⚠ 最後はやや堅い言い方) ▶なるほどそれはよい計画だが, 実行は難しい *It is true that* it's a good plan, [It is a good plan, *to be sure*,] *but* it's hard to put it into practice.

——**なるほど** 〖副〗〖あいづち〗
〖会話〗「交通渋滞にひっかかって遅くなってしまいました」「なるほど」"I came late because we were caught in a traffic jam." "*I see*./*Oh, you ＼were*." (⚠ 前の方は「分かりました」, 後の方は「そうでしたかね」の意)
〖会話〗「彼女ったらちっとも決断しようとしないのよ」「なるほど. じゃあ君が決めてやりなさいよ」"She just won't make a decision." "*Uh- ／huh* /ʌ̀hʌ́/! You decide for her, then."
〖会話〗「ペンギンは飛べないけれど, その代わりに泳げます」「なるほどね(=いい所に気がついた)」"Penguins can't fly, but they can swim." "*You've got a good point there*." (⚠ 自分では気づかなかったことを指摘されたときに親しい間柄の人に対して用いる)

なれ 慣れ 〖いつもやっていること〗practice; 〖経験〗(an) experience. ▶慣れでこれが分かる I know this *by practice* [*from experience*]. ▶こういう仕事は理屈より慣れですよ A lot of *practice* is more important than theory to do this job well./You need a lot of *practice* rather than theory to do this job well.

なれあい 馴れ合い 〖結託〗《書》collusion; conspiracy; 〖心地よい関係〗a cozy relationship; 〖相互依存〗interdependence. ● 当局となれ合いで *in conspiracy* [*collusion*] *with* the authorities; by *cozy arrangement with* the authorities. ●なれ合いの(=共謀になる)協定 a *collusive* agreement. ●なれ合いの(=八百長になる)試合 《話》a *fixed* match [*game*]; 《話》a put-up job.

なれあう 馴れ合う 《やや話》have a cozy relationship 《with》; (違法を承知で) conspire 《書》collude》《with》.

ナレーション narration.
ナレーター a narrator.
なれそめ 馴れ初め ▶そもそものなれそめは？ How did you meet?/How did you come to know each other?
なれっこ 慣れっこ (⇨慣れる) ▶苦労には慣れっこになっている I am used to hardship.
なれなれしい 馴れ馴れしい (too) familiar; too friendly; 〖無遠慮すぎる〗too free. ●なれなれしい態度で見知らぬ人に話しかける speak to a stranger in a (*too*) *familiar* manner. ▶彼は先輩になれなれしすぎ

る He is *too familiar* [*friendly, free*] *with* his seniors. ▶なれなれしくしないでよ You're getting *too familiar*./Don't *take* any *liberties with* me. (⚠ 後の方は少し古風な言い方)

なれのはて 成れの果て 《やや話》a wreck of one's former self. (⚠ wreck は「肉体的・精神的に破壊された人 (ruined person)」の意) ▶彼は百万長者のなれの果てだ He is a *wreck* of the millionaire he once was./He is a *ruined* millionaire.

***なれる** 慣れる 〖動〗get* used [accustomed] 《*to*》 (⚠ (1) get used のみ口語的に. (2) get 以外に become, grow も可); (順応する) adjust (oneself) 《*to*》. ▶彼女はすぐに新しい環境に慣れた She soon *got used* [*accustomed*] *to* the new circumstances./She soon *adjusted* (*herself*) [*adapted* (*herself*)] *to* the new circumstances. ▶父は朝早く起きるのに慣れている My father *is used* [*accustomed*] *to getting* up early. ▶彼女はそのことにすっかり[よく]慣れている She is quite [very well] *used to* it. ▶私は東京の満員電車に慣れることができない I can't *accustom* myself *to* the crowded trains of Tokyo. ▶私はこの種の商売には慣れていない(=未経験である) I am *new on* [*to*] this kind of business./I am *not experienced* [*am inexperienced*] *in* this kind of business./(あまり経験がない) I *don't have much experience in* this kind of business. ▶ジーンズが慣れて履き心地がよくなった The jeans fit me comfortably after a lot of wear./I feel comfortable in the jeans now that I've put them on many times.
〖会話〗「新しい職場に慣れてきましたか」「ええ, なんとか. まだ慣れないこともありますけど」"*Are* you *settling in all right*?/(順応する) How are you *adjusting to* your new place of work?" "Yes, fine. I'm still finding my feet, though." (⚠ settle in は「(新しい家・環境などに)落ち着く」の意. settle down ともいう. find one's feet は「独りで歩けるようになる」からの転義)

——**慣れた** 〖形〗(いつもの) usual; (経験を積んだ) experienced (↔inexperienced); (練習を積んだ) practiced. ▶彼は慣れた[慣れない]手つきではしを使った He used chopsticks with a *practiced* hand (ぎこちなく) awkwardly.

なれる 馴れる (人になれる) become* [get*] tame; (飼いならされる) become tamed [(家畜として)domesticated]. ●よくなれている be quite [(とてもよく) really] *tame*. ▶よくなれた犬 a *tame* [a *tamed*] dog. ▶スズメはなかなか人になれない Sparrows won't become *tame*.

なれる 熟れる ▶すし飯は少しおくとなれる(=食べごろになる) The *sushi* rice will *mature* if you leave it for a while.

***なわ** 縄 (太い) (a) rope; (細い) (a) cord. (⇨綱[類語]) ●縄をかける put a *rope* around 《it》; tie 《it》 with 《a》 *rope*; (逮捕רる) arrest 《him》. ●縄をほどく untie the rope(s); (解放する) set 《him》 free, release 《him》 (⚠ 前の方が口語的に). ▶私たちは彼を縄で木に縛りつけた We tied him to the tree with (a) *rope*./We roped him to the tree. ▶警察は殺人現場を縄で囲った The police *roped off* the scene of the murder. (⚠ *rope ... off* は「仕切って入れない」の意)

●縄を打つ (縄をかけてしばる) bind 《him》 with (a) rope; (測量する) survey.
●縄ばしご a rope ladder.
なわしろ 苗代 a rice plant nursery.
なわとび 縄跳び (遊び, 運動)《米》júmp rópe, 《英》(rope) skipping; (縄)《米》a jump [a skip] rope,

なわのれん

《英》a skipping rópe. ● 縄跳びをする《米》skip [jùmp] rópe;《英》skip. ● 縄跳び遊びをする play with a *jump rope*. (❗この遊びに伴う歌の一つ: How many boys can you kiss, one, two, three, ...)

なわのれん 縄暖簾 (のれん) a rope curtain (hanging at the entrance of a drinking place);(飲み屋》a bar;《英》a pub.

なわばり 縄張り (人・動物などの) (a) territory;(官庁などの管轄範囲) jurisdiction; (勢力範囲) a range of influence;(やくざなどの)《米話》turf. ● 縄張り争いをする quarrel 《with him》 about the ownership of the *territory*; fight a *turf* battle 《against》. ● 縄張りを荒らす enter [intrude into] 《his》*territory*; invade 《their》*turf*. ▶動物は本能的に自分の縄張りを守る Animals instinctively defend their *territory*. ▶あの新顔のセールスマンが私の縄張りに割り込んできた The new salesperson cut into my *territory*.

なわめ 縄目 (縄の結び目) a knot;(縄の編み模様) a pattern. ● 縄目をほどく untie a knot [a rope]
● 縄目にかかる (逮捕される) be arrested.

:なに 何 [[なに]] what. (⇨何(⁵) 代) ▶彼は君に何と言ったの *What* did he say to you? ▶何のためにその箱を買ったの (なぜ) *Why* did you buy the box?/(何の目的で)(話) *What* did you buy the box for?/ ×For what did you buy the box? は不可)▶彼らが何と言おうと君は正しい You are right, *no matter what* [*whatever*] they say. (❗前の方が口語的)
▶私の口から言うのも何ですが、妻は頭のいい女です My wife is, *if I may say so*, an intelligent woman.
会話「お髪は何に。高校生のする格好か」「うるさいなぁ、パーマぐらいで」"*What* is your hairstyle *for*? Is that the way a high school student should look?" "It's none of your business. I just got a permanent."
会話「ちょっと君に用があるんだ」「何でしょう」"I want to talk to you for a minute." "*Yes*?"

なん- 難 ❶ [困難] (a) difficulty;(面倒) (a) trouble; (不足) a shortage. ● 就職難 the *difficulty* of getting a job; a job *shortage*. ● 住宅難に悩む suffer from a housing *shortage*. ● 難なくそのホテルを見つけた I found the hotel *without (any) difficulty*./I *had no difficulty* [*trouble*] (*in*) finding the hotel. (❗では通例 in を省略する)

❷ [災難] an accident;(危険) danger. ● 路上で難にあう have [meet with] an *accident* on the street. ● 彼の所に難を逃れる seek *refuge* /réfju:dʒ/ with him. ● 小屋 [木陰]に難を逃れる take *refuge in the hut* [*behind the tree*]. (❗後の2例は「避難する」の意) ▶危うい所で難を免れた I narrowly escaped *danger*./I had a narrow escape.

❸ [欠点] a fault. ▶彼には性格的に難がある He has a *fault* [a *defect*] in his character.

なん- 何- ❶ [なに] what (+名). (⇨何時, 日(゜), 月, 年, 曜日) ▶彼は何日に来ますか *What* date will he come? ▶一番短い月は何月ですか *What* [(どの月) *Which*] month has the shortest days? ▶今年は何年ですか *What* year is this? ▶何曜日にピアノのレッスンを受けていますか *What* day (of the week) do you take piano lessons? ▶何曜日が一番いいと思いますか *Which* day is the best, do you think?/ Which day do you think is the best? (❗×Do you think which day is his character.
会話「今日は何日ですか」「5月20日です」"*What's* the date today?" "(It's) May 20(th)."

❷ [どれくらい] how many 《+複数名詞》. ▶あなたのクラスの生徒は何人ですか *How many* (students [people]) are there in your class? ▶毎日何時間

勉強しますか *How many* hours [(どれくらいの長さ) *How long*] do you study every day? ▶何日から何日まで閉店ですか *What* days are you closed?/ From *what* day to *what* day are you closed? (❗前の方が慣用的な言い方)
会話「11番よ」「何番だって?」"It's number eleven." "*What* number (is it)?"

❸ [ある数の] (数個・数人の) several; (少数の) a few; (いくつかの, 何人かの) some /səm/; [[...より少し多くの]] odd; [[...何とか]] something.

使い分け	several a few (2～3個) より多い数量を漠然と表し,「やや多い」という話し手の気持ちを表す。
a few「少ないがないわけではない」という話し手の気持ちに重点がある.
some 不特定な数量を漠然とさす.
ただし，以上はいずれも相対的表現で，話し手の感じ方や文脈によって同じ数量をさすこともある.
odd, something 数字に添えて、ある数量の端数をぼかして言うのに用いる。

● 10 何年か前 ten and *several* [ten-odd, (10年以上) *more than* ten] years ago. ● 1900 何年に in nineteen *something*. (❗通例19ーと書く) ▶先月は何日か雨の日があった We had *several* rainy days last month. ▶テストは難しかったが何人かの学生は合格した The test was difficult, but *a few* students passed it. (❗*a few* の代わりに very few [(書) few] では「ほとんど合格しなかった」の意(⇨ほとんど❷))▶机の上に英語の本が置いてあった There were *some* English books on the desk.

❹ [多数の] many; a lot of .... (❗通例肯定文では a lot of. 否定文・疑問文では many を用いる. 肯定文で特に主語を修飾する場合以外に many を用いるのは通例(書)) ▶何時間もの間 for (*many*) hours; (長い間) for a long time. ● 何十[何百; 何千; 何万]通もの手紙 dozens [hundreds; thousands; tens of thousands] of letters. ▶彼は何年も前に名古屋に引っ越した He moved to Nagoya *many years* [(話)years] ago. ▶もう何日もふろに入っていない I haven't taken a bath *for* (*many*) days./It's been days since I took a bath. ▶試験までにはまだ何日もある We have *many* [(話) a lot] *more* days before the exam. ▶その事故で何人もの人が死んだ A *lot of* [*Many*] people were killed in the accident.
会話「長いこと待たなきゃならなかったの?」「何週間もだよ」"Did you have to wait long?" "*Weeks*." (❗For weeks. の for が省略されたもの)

なんい 何位 (⇨順位❶)

なんい 南緯 south latitude《略 S.Lat.》. ● 南緯20度15分くらいの所に at about *lat*. 20°15′ *S* (❗at about latitude twenty degrees fifteen minutes south と読む); at about 20°15′ *south latitude* [*S. Lat.*].

なんい 難易 (難しさ) difficulty. ● 仕事の難易により according to the *difficulty* of work [a job]; depending on *how difficult* [*hard*] a job is.

なんおう 南欧 Southern Europe.

なんか 南下 ── 南下する 動 go south(ward); go down; move 《×down》 south.

なんか 軟化 名 [[態度の]] softening; [[相場の]] weakening.

── 軟化する 動 (態度が) soften,《やや書》become conciliatory; (相場が) weaken, become weak. ▶私に対する彼女の態度が軟化し始めた Her attitude toward me began to *soften* (↔harden).

● 軟化剤 a softener.

なんか 何か what. (⇒何(に), など)
-なんか 《副助詞》(⇒など)
❶ [同類のものが他にもあるとの含みを持たせる] ▶ 食料品なんか(＝その他の日常必要とするものは近くの店でそろいます I can get food *and other daily necessaries* at local stores.
❷ [断定調を避けて] ▶ リンゴなんかあげたら喜ばれるかな They'd like apples, *don't you think*? (!「…と思いませんか」と同意を求める言い方で断定を避ける. 比較: Do you think like apples?) ▶ いつも遊んでなんかいないで母さんのお手伝いをしたら Why don't you help Mother instead of playing around all the time? (!日本語の「-なんか」に相当する英語訳はない)
❸ [謙遜(けんそん)・軽蔑を表す] ▶ 彼は私なんかには見向きもしない He doesn't care for *the likes of me*. (!単に me というより謙遜の気持ちを表す. 自分以外に対して軽蔑の気持ちを表す) ▶ あんな男なんかとは口をききたくない I will never speak to *that sort of* man. (!that には this と異なり軽蔑の感情が含まれることがある)/He is the last person I want to speak to.
❹ [打ち消しを強調] ▶ そんな話になんか信じるものか Who would believe that story? (!修辞疑問文で, 普通の否定より強く感情的に訴える言い方. 比較: I won't believe that story.)
会話 「さっきから君たち何を言い合っていたの」「何も言い合いなんかしていないよ」"What have you been arguing about all this while?" "We ＼haven't been arguing." (!異議を唱える場合には be 動詞や助動詞を強く読む)
なんが 南画 the Southern /sʌ́ðərn/ School of Chinese painting.
なんかい 何回 (!回数を尋ねて) how often [many times]; [!肯定文でも普通に用いる]; [!何回も繰り返して] again and again, over and over again, repeatedly. ▶ 京都へ何回も行ったことがあります I have been to [have visited] Kyoto many [*a lot of*] *times*./I have *often* been to Kyoto. ▶ 何回やってみても彼は英語の合格点が取れなかった He tried *again and again*, but he failed English./*No matter how* [(やや書) *However*] *often* he tried, he couldn't succeed in English. ▶ 彼は注意を引こうとして何回も大声で呼んだ He *repeatedly* called in a loud voice, hoping to attract attention.
会話「何回そこへ行きましたか」「1[3]回行きました」"*How often* [*many times*] have you been there?" "I've been there once [three times]."
会話「彼には何回か頼んだわよ」「何回」"I've asked him *several times*." "*How many times*?"
なんかい 南海 the southern sea; (南洋) the South Seas.
なんかい 難解 ▶ この本はとても難解だ This book is very *difficult* [(話) *hard*] to understand.
なんかん 難関 (困難なこと) (a) difficulty; (乗り越えるべき障壁) a hurdle. ▶ 難局にぶつかる meet with a *difficulty*. ▶ 入試の難関を突破する overcome the *difficulty* of the entrance examination; get over [clear] the entrance exam *hurdle*. ▶ 彼は入試で競争率が10倍の難関に挑んだ He took the fiercely competitive entrance examination which only one applicant out of ten could pass. (!could は仮定法過去)
なんがん 南岸 the southern coast.
なんぎ 難儀 名 [困難] (a) difficulty; [苦労, 面倒] (a) trouble; [苦難] (a) hardship. (⇒苦労, 苦しむ)
── **難儀な 形** ▶ 難儀な(＝困難な)仕事 a *hard* [a *difficult*, (骨の折れる) a *laborious*, (やっかいな) a *trou*blesome] job.
── **難儀する 動** have trouble [difficulty] 《*with*; do*ing*》(⇒困る); (つらい目にあう) have a hard time 《do*ing*》, suffer hardship(s); (患っている) suffer from [be troubled with, have trouble with] 《(gout)》.
なんきつ 難詰 ── **難詰する 動** reprimand.
なんきゅう 軟球 a rubber ball. (翻 硬球)
なんぎょうくぎょう 難行苦行 ▶ 難行苦行の末(＝とても苦労して)その計画を達成する carry out the plan with *great* [*much*] *difficulty*.
なんきょく 南極 名 the South [Antarctic] Pole. (翻 北極) ── **南極の 形** antarctic.
● **南極海** the Antarctic Ocean. ● **南極圏** the Antarctic Circle. ● **南極大陸** the Antarctic Continent; Antarctica. ● **南極点** the geographical south pole.
なんきょく 難曲 a difficult piece of music.
なんきょく 難局 [困難な状況] a difficult situation; [困難] (a) difficulty, (財政的な) difficulties; [危機] a crisis 《pl. crises /-si:z/》. ▶ 難局に立つ be in a *difficult situation* [*difficulties*, ✗a crisis]. ▶ 難局に直面している[当たる] be faced with [deal with] a *difficult situation* [*difficulties*, a *crisis*]. ● その難局を乗り切る get over the *difficulty* [*crisis*].
ナンキン 南京 [中国の都市] Nanjing /náːndʒiŋ/.
なんきん 軟禁 (非公式の監禁) informal confinement; (自宅拘束) house arrest. ▶ 彼は自宅に軟禁されている He *is confined* to his house./He is under *house arrest*.
なんきんじょう 南京錠 a padlock.
なんきんむし 南京虫 [昆虫] a bedbug.
なんくせ 難癖 ▶ 彼女はいつも夫に難癖をつけている She is always *finding fault with* [批判している] *criticizing*, (けなしている) 《話》*running down*] her husband.
なんげん 南限 the southern limit 《*of* larch trees》.
なんご 喃語 (乳児の) babbling; (夫婦の寝室での) soft nothings.
● **喃語期** the pre-speech period.
なんご 難語 a difficult word.
なんこう 軟膏 (an) ointment, (a) salve; [筋肉痛などに用いる] (a) liniment. ▶ 傷口に軟膏を塗る put some *ointment* [*salve*] on a cut.
なんこう 難航 ❶ [荒天の中の航海] a rough [a difficult] voyage.
❷ [交渉などがはかどらないこと] ▶ 和平交渉は難航している (進み具合が遅い) The peace negotiations *are making slow progress* [(円滑に進まない) *aren't going on smoothly*]./(厳しい進行状況だ) The peace negotiations *face rough going* [(行き詰まっている) *have been deadlocked*].
なんこうがい 軟口蓋 [解剖] the soft palate; the velum (拉 vela).
● **軟口蓋子音** [音声] velar consonants.
なんこうふらく 難攻不落 ── **難攻不落の 形** impregnable 《fortresses》; invulnerable 《*to*》.
なんごく 南国 (国) a southern /sʌ́ðərn/ country; (地方) a southern district. ▶ 南国情緒豊かな町 a town with a great deal of *southern atmosphere*. ● **南国的の**(＝に特有の)風景 scenery peculiar to [typical of] a *southern province*.
なんこつ 軟骨 [解剖] (a) cartilage /káːrtəlidʒ/; (食肉中の) gristle.
● **軟骨魚類** cartilaginous fish. (! サメ・エイなど) ● **軟骨組織** cartilage tissue.
なんさしょとう 南沙諸島 the Spratly Islands.

なんざん 難産 [難しいお産] a difficult delivery [labor]. ▶長男の時は難産だった I had *great difficulty* when I gave birth to my first son. ▶この会社の設立は思わぬ難産だった He had unexpected difficulty (*in*) establishing this company. (⚠ 動名詞の前の in は通例省略される)

なんじ 何時 what time; when (⚠「いつ」と漠然と時を尋ねる言い方. 正確な時刻を尋ねる場合は what time を使う). ▶今何時ですか *Whát time* [ˣWhen] ˋis it (now)? (⚠ ゆっくりという時は, is it を省略していうときは What ˋtime (ˋis it)? となる. 特に「今」を強調するとき以外は now が省略される)／*What is the time?*／(米) *What time* do you have? (時計を持っていると思われる人に向かって) Do you have *the time* (on you)? (⚠ 通例 Yes, it's twelve by my watch. のような形式で答える)／Could you tell me *the time*? ▶何時に学校へ行きますか *What time* do you go to school? ▶何時に出発したらよいか教えてください Tell me *what time* [*when*] to start. ▶何時までにレポートを提出しなければいけませんか *By what time* [ˣWhen] do I have to hand in my papers? ▶何時の飛行機にしましょうか *What* [*Which*] flight shall we take? (⚠ この take は「利用する」の意)

会話「(閉店時間を気にして)何時まで開いてるかしら」「そうね, 8 時までだと思うわ」"Do you know how long [late] it's open?" "I think it stays open until eight (o'clock)." (⚠ ... until *what time* it's open? より普通)

会話「開館時間は何時から何時までですか」「9 時から 5 時です」「週末も同じですか」「まったく同じです」"(Between) *what hours* are you open?" "What are your *hours*?" (⚠ hours は開館[営業, 就業]時間で, 日本語的な From *what hour* to *what hour* are you open? より慣用的的)／"We're open from 9 a.m. to 5 p.m." "And does that go for the weekends too?" "Yes. Our weekend *hours* are exactly the same as weekdays."

なんじ 汝 (汝は[が]) you, 《古》thou (⚠ you); (汝の) your, 《古》thy (⚠ your); (汝を[に]) you, 《古》thee (⚠ you). ▶汝自身を知れ Know *yourself* [《古》 *thyself*].

なんじ 難字 a difficult Chinese character.

なんじ 難事 a difficulty. ●難事にあたる grapple [deal] with a *difficulty*. (⚠ cope with は「成功」を暗示する場合には可)

なんじ 難治 ●難治性疾患 an intractable disease; a disease that is hard to cure.

なんしき 軟式 ●軟式テニス softball tennis. ●軟式野球 rubberball baseball. (⚠ いずれも日本特有の式)

なんしつ 軟質 ── 軟質の 形 soft 《plastic》.

なんじゃく 軟弱 ── 軟弱な 形 weak; [柔らかい] soft; [めめしい]《書》effeminate,《話》sissy. ●軟弱な性格 a *weak* character. ●軟弱な地盤 *soft* ground.
●軟弱外交 weak-kneed diplomacy.

なんじゅう 難渋 ── 難渋な 形 difficult; troublesome. ●難渋な文章 (⇨難文)

なんしょ 難所 (危険な場所[峠]) a dangerous spot [pass]. ●この山の最大の難所 the most *dangerous spot* [*pass*] of this mountain. ▶架橋工事は最大の難所にさしかかっている The construction of the bridge is approaching its most *difficult stage*.

なんしょく 難色 ●その計画に難色を示す(=認めない) *disapprove of* [(反対している) *be opposed to*] the plan. ▶彼の顔にあらわれた難色を見て, 今は頼み事を ひっこめるのが無難だと思った I thought it wise to take back my request when I saw *a sign of refusal* on his face.

なんしん 南進 ── 南進する 動 move south(ward).

なんすい 軟水 soft water. ●硬水を軟水にする *soften* hard water.

なんせい 南西 the southwest 《略 SW》. (⇨東, 北西)

なんせい 軟性 soft; elastic.
●軟性下疳(かん)【医学】a soft chancre; a chancroid.

なんせん 難船 (難破船) a wrecked ship; (難破) (a) shipwreck. (⇨難破)
●難船信号《send [put out]》an SOS; a distress signal.

ナンセンス nonsense. ▶彼の提案はまったくナンセンスに思える His proposal sounds like complete *nonsense* [sounds completely *nonsensical*].

なんそうさとみはっけんでん『南総里見八犬伝』 *Legend of the Eight Samurai — Satomi Hakkenden*. (⇨参考) 滝沢馬琴の読本(どくほん)

なんだ 何だ [驚き・失望など] oh; (主に米) why [気にしない] do* not care (*about*). ▶何だ, 健二, お前か Oh [*Why*]! It's you, Kenji. ▶雨ぐらい何だ I *don't care about* rain at all. ▶何だ, どうした (=何か起こったのだ) What's up?／What happened?／What's the matter (with you)? ▶何だと, もう一度言ってみろ I beg your ˋpardon?／ˋExcúse me? (⚠ 下降調に注意 (⇨何と 題))

なんだい 難題 (難問) a difficult problem. ●難題(=不当な要求)をふっかける make *an unreasonable demand* 《on him》; ask [demand] too much 《of him》.

なんたいどうぶつ 軟体動物 a mollusk /mάləsk/.

なんだか 何だか ❶【何であるか】what. ▶それが何だか分からない I don't know *what* it is.
❷【どういうわけか】somehow, for some reason (or other) (⚠ 前の方が口語的); (理由は分からないが) I don't know why, but .... ▶何だかその考えは気にいらない *Somehow* [*I don't know why, but*] the idea doesn't appeal to me. ▶何だかエンジン変だぞ (=エンジンに異常なところがある) There's *something* wrong with the engine.／*Something's* wrong with the engine. ▶何だかすごくうれしそうですね You seem very happy *about something*.

なんだか(ん)だ 何だか(ん)だ ●何だかんだ (=あれこれ) 理屈を並べ立てる chop logic; argue *this and that*. ●何だかんだと言って仕事を引き受けない do not take on the job *on one pretext or another*. ▶何だかんだ言ってもまだ習い始めたばかりだから *After all*, he is just a beginner. (⚠ note after all は文尾に置いてもよい)

なんだったら 何だったら if you like. (⇨何なら)

なんたって 何たって (何と言っても) whatever you say. ▶何たって安いよ, 買っておこう It's *very* cheap (*indeed*). [It's cheap *without comparison*.] Let's get it. ▶彼女は何たって口がうまいから She has *such* a glib tongue. (⚠ 非難していう)

なんたって 何たって why. (=なぜ)
会話「学校をやめようと思ってるんだ」「何たって, 合格したばかりじゃないの」「信じられないでしょうが, もう決めてしまったんだ」"I'm going to quit school." "*Say what*? You've just been accepted." "You may not believe it. I've already made up my mind."

なんたる 何たる ●人生の何たるか(=何であるか)を悟る realize what life is. ▶何たることか (やや古) This is a pretty [fine] kettle of fish.／What a mess!

なんたん 南端 (最も南の所) the southernmost part;

なんちゃくりく the southern end [(先端) tip]. ▶彼はこの市の南端に住んでいる He lives *in the southernmost part* of this city.

なんちゃくりく 軟着陸 图 a soft-landing.
── 軟着陸する 動 make a soft-landing (*on*).

なんちゅう 南中 [天文] culmination. ● 太陽が南中する culminate; be on the meridian.

なんちょう 軟調 softness, weakness. ● 景気の軟調 *softness in* economic activity; economic *softness*.
── 軟調市況 a soft market.

なんちょう 難聴 ▶あの子は難聴だ That child is *hard of hearing*./That child's *hearing is* (*very*) *weak* [*poor*]./The child has *hearing trouble*.

なんて 何て [[何という]] what; [[何と]] how; what. (!感嘆を表す) ▶何てことだ What's all this!/Oh, look at this! (!ひどい状況を見て)/Oh my God! (1)意外な状況に驚いたときに主に男性が用いる. (2)強い表現なので特に女性は用い My!/Oh, my! などという) ▶何てうまいんだろう How delicious!/It's *absolutely* delicious. (!delicious=very tasty (たいへんおいしい)なので, very 以上に意味の強い副詞で修飾する)

会話「お久しぶりですね」「しかもまあByりによってこんな所でお会いするなんて!」"I haven't seen you for ages." "And *imagine* us meeting [*Fancy* meeting you] here of all places!"

なんで 何で why. (⇨なぜ)

なんであれ 何であれ whatever. ▶結果は何であれこの計画は実行しよう Let's carry out this project *whatever* the result (may be).

なんてき 難敵 a formidable [one's worst] enemy (試合の)opponent].

*✱ **なんでも 何でも** ❶ [[どれでも]] anything; [[どれもみな]] everything; [[...は何でも]] whatever; [[全部]] all; [[どんな…も]] any. ▶知っていることは何でも話します I'll tell you *anything* [*everything, all, whatever*] I know. ▶いさかかとなれば何でもありだ In case of a quarrel *anything* goes. ▶彼は野球のことなら何でも知っている He knows *everything* about baseball./He has an *all-around* [(英) an *all-round*] knowledge of baseball. ▶音楽なら何でも興味があります I am interested in *all* [*any*, ×*every*] music. (!every は不可算名詞とともには用いない)

会話「どんな映画が好きなの」「何でもいいけど, 特に西部劇が好きです」"What kind of movies do you like?" "*All kinds*, but especially Westerns."

会話「デザートは何がいい? ケーキ, アイスクリーム, プディング, 果物とか, 何て言って」「アイスクリームにするわ」「はい, どうぞ」"What would you like for dessert? ↗Cake, ↗ice cream, ↗pudding or ↘fruit. (You) ↘*name it*." (!列挙したあと「まだほかにもある」という含みで選択を求める言い方. 列挙項目はすべて上昇調で発音) "I'll have ice cream." "OK. You got it."

❷ [[どうやら]] (...とうわさに聞いている) I hear(d) ((*that*)節); (...と一般に言われている) people [they] say

((*that*)節). ▶何でも彼は近く結婚するそうだ I hear(d) [(I don't know for sure but) *they say*] *that* he'll get married soon.

【何でもない】[[とるに足りないこと]] nothing; [[苦しくない]] think nothing of .... ▶あなたのに比べると私の苦労など何でもありません My sufferings are *nothing* (compared) to yours. ▶徹夜の仕事など何でもありません I *think nothing* [*little*] *of* working all night.

会話「でもどうやってそれをやってのけたんだい」「何でもなかったさ. 実に簡単だったよ」"But how did you manage it?" "There was *nothing* to it. It couldn't have been simpler."

会話「また手をわずらわせてすまないね」「かまわないよ. 何でもないもの」"Sorry to trouble you again." "I don't mind. (It's) *no trouble* (at all)."

会話「どうしたの」「何でもない」「何でもないようには見えないけど」"What's wrong?" "(It's) *nothing*." "It doesn't look like *nothing*."

● **何でもかんでも** ▶彼女は何でもかんでも(=すべて)他人のせいにする She blames other people for *everything*.

なんでもみてやろう『何でも見てやろう』 *I'll Go Everywhere and See Everything*. (参考)小田実の紀行文)

なんでもや 何でも屋 a jack-of-all-trades. (!「どれも一流でない」を含意することが多い)

なんてん 何点 (⇨点 ❷❸❺) ▶この前の試験より何点上がりましたか How many more points did you get than the last exam?

なんてん 南天 [植物] a nandina /nǽndinə/.

なんてん 難点 (欠点, 欠陥) a fault, a defect; (短所) a weak point; (難しい点) a difficult point.

*✱ **なんと 何と** 副 what. (!通例 what に強勢を置き, 文は下降調で終わるが, 上昇調は親しみをこめた言い方になる) ▶この魚は何と言いますか What do you call this fish?/*What* is the name of this fish? ▶英語で「さようなら」は何と言いますか How [×What] do you say "sayonara" in English?/*What* is the English for "sayonara"? (!定冠詞に注意) ▶人が何と思おうとかまわない *No matter what* [*Whatever*] others [*people*] (may) think, I don't care. (!〈話〉では通例 may を省略する. ×will は可) ▶何と言っても彼は君の弟なのだから *After áll*, he is your brother. (!通例文頭, 時に文尾で)

会話「どこにお住まいなの」「何と言ったの」「お住まいはどこかと言ったの」"Whére do you ↗ live?" "↗*What* did you sáy?" (!丁寧に聞き返す表現は I bég your ↗*párdon*? というが (Beg) ↗*párdon*? などと省略していうこともある) "I sáid whére do you ↘live?" (!聞き返しに対する応答は最初にいったとおりを反復し, 下降調でいい切るのが普通)

── **何と** 副 what, how. (!いずれも強勢を受けないことが多く, 文は下降調で終わる)

解説 感嘆文には一般に次の型がある.

(ⅰ) **What**+**a**+形容詞+単数可算名詞(+主語+動詞)! (i) 〈書〉では How+形容詞+a+名詞+主語+動詞! の型も用いるが, 比較的まれで, 不定冠詞がある場合に限られる.

(ⅱ) What の後に形容詞+複数可算名詞[不可算名詞]が続くことがあるが, その場合 how とは交換不可.

(ⅲ) what の後に程度を表す名詞が続くときは形容詞がないことがある: 何という うるさこ *What* a *nuisance*!/何と彼らはばかげた *What fools* they are!/何とばかばかしい *What* nonsense! 一方, 程度

を表さない名詞の場合は, *What a game!* (何という〔いい〔ひどい〕試合だ)のように程度の両極端を表すが, 批判的に用いることが多い.
(2) *How*＋形容詞・副詞・分詞(＋主語＋動詞)!
「主語＋動詞」は文脈から明らかな場合, 通例省略される.
(3) 会話ではこれらの型以外に *a lot, really, very, such* などの語が添えられたり, *oh, ah, wow,*《主に米》*boy* などの間投詞や音調などで感嘆を表現することも多い.

▶彼は何と足が速いんだろう *What* a fást ↘rúnner he ís!/*How* ↘fast he rúns!/《書・まれ》*How* fast a runner he is! ▶何と暑いこと *How* hot it is!/《米話》Ís it ↘hot! ▶何と多くの人だ *What* a lot of [《話》*What* crowds of, ˣ*How* many] people! (■「何と多くの...」は ˣ*How* many [much]... の代わりに通例 *What* a lot of ... を用いる) ▶そんなことをするなんて彼は何とばかなんだ *How* stupid [foolish] (it is) of him to do that! (■'it is＋形容詞＋of＋人＋to do'の型の感嘆文では通例 it is は省略する) ▶何と大きくなったのだろう *How* you've grown! (■*How* の後に程度を表す動詞表現が続くと, 形容詞・副詞を伴わず程度のはなはだしさを表す)/You've grown *a lot!*/Háve yóu ↘grown! (■Yes/No 疑問文の形で下降調に言うと感嘆を表す. 聞き手に同意を求める場合は否定疑問文の形にする: Hásn't she ↘grown! さらに ↘Hásn't she grówn!/↗Hásn't she grówn!の順で感嘆の意が強くなる) ▶何ということを言う You shouldn't say that./Do you know what you're saying?

なんど 何度 ❶〖回数を尋ねて〗(何回) how many times; how often. (■*how* many が具体的に数字を要求するのに対して, how often は漠然と頻度を聞く言い方. ˣ*how* frequently は不可) (⇨回数) ▶何度言えば分かるんだ *How many times* do I have to tell you?

❷〖幾度も繰り返して〗over and over again, again and again, repeatedly; (何度も) many times; (しばしば) often, frequently (■*often* より堅く強意的な語). (⇨何回) ▶何度も失敗した後 after repeated [a series of] failures. ▶私は京都に何度も行きました I visited Kyoto *very often* [*frequently, a lot of times*]./I made *frequent* visits to Kyoto./I have been to kyoto *many times*. ▶彼には何度か会ったことがある I've met him *several times*.

❸〖度数を尋ねて〗▶何度ありますか (体温) What's your *temperature?*/(気温) What's the *temperature?* (■特に暑いときには Hów hòt is it?, 寒いときには Hów còld is it? とも) ▶寒暖計は何度ですか *What temperature* is it by [on] the thermometer?/(■単に *What*'s the temperature? ということが多い)/*What* does the thermometer *read* [*say*]? ▶ロンドンの緯度は何度ですか *What* is the latitude of London?
会話▶「この角は何度ですか」「30 度です」"*How many degrees* is this angle?" "It's 30°." (■thirty degrees と読む)

なんど 納戸 〖物置〗a storeroom; 〖衣類・道具類などを入れておく収納室〗a closet;《英》a cupboard /kʌ́bərd/.

なんど 難度 degree of difficulty. ●フィギュアスケートで難度(＝一番難しい技の達成)を競う compete [vie] 《*with* him》 for achievement of the most difficult technique in figure skating.

なんという 何という what. (⇨何, 何と)
なんとう 南東 the southeast (略 SE). (⇨東, 北西)
***なんとか** 何とか ❶〖どうにか...する〗manage 《*to* do》;

(やっていく) manage 《*on*＋収入など, *with* [*without*]＋物・道具など》; 〖どうにかして〗somehow. (■何とかして) ▶何とか正午までに戻って来ます I'll (*somehow*) *manage to* come back before noon./I'll come back before noon *somehow*. ▶父の給料で何とかやっていますが, 楽ではありません We *manage* [*get by*] *on* our father's salary, but it's not easy. ▶1 万円ほどが何とかならないだろうか I need ten thousand yen. Can you *manage* the money for me? (■この *manage* は通例 can, could, be able to とともに用いる) ▶愛情があれば何とかなるものだ Love will find a way. ▶(貯金がなくても)なんとかなる Without my saving, we'll survive.
会話▶「この箱重いや」「一人で何とかできる？」"This box is heavy." "Can you *manage* without help?"
会話▶「火曜日, 何とか都合つけてもらえないかな」「悪いなあ, 火曜日はだめなんだよ. その日は人と会う約束があるんだ」"Could you *manage* Tuesday?" "I'm sorry I can't make Tuesday. I have to meet somebody on that day."
会話▶「すぐそこのハンバーガー店が店じまいしたよ」「昼食はどこへ行こうか」「もうちょっと先のうどん屋で何とかすまそう」"The hamburger house around the corner has closed down." "Where do we go for lunch?" "We'll have to *make do with* the udon place in the next block." (■*make* do with は「(不十分だが)...で妥協する」の意)

❷〖...なにがし〗《話》something; 〖何とか言う人〗(Mr. [Miss, Mrs.]) so-and-so (■軽蔑的にも扱い);《話》what's-his-[her-]name. ●何とかいう老人 [男の人]と話をする talk with the old *so-and-so* [*Mr. So-and-so, what's-his-name*]. ▶彼の名前は山田何とかです His name is Yamada *something*. (■... is Yamada or something. では「山田か何かです」の意) ▶あの何とかさん, まだそこにお勤めですか Is *what's-his-*[*her-*]*name* still working there?

❸〖...何とかという物〗《話》what's-its-name;《英》its-thing, whatsit, thingy,《主に米》what-you-call-it. ▶あの何とかいう物, 何と言うの What do you call that *whatsit* [*thingy*]?

なんとかして 何とかして 〖何らかの方法で〗somehow (or other); some way or other. ▶何とかして 8 時までにそこへ参ります I'll be there by eight *somehow* (*or other*) [*one way or another*]./(どうにかして) I'll *manage to* be there by eight. ▶何とかして(＝何らかの方法で)それを月曜日までに仕上げなくてはならない I have to finish it by Monday *some way or other*. ▶何とかして留学したい I'd like to study abroad *by some means or other* [(どんな手段に訴えても) *by fair means or foul*]./(熱望している) I'm *very eager to* study abroad.

なんとかする 何とかする 〖どうにかやってゆく〗manage; 〖引き受ける〗see* to ...; 〖何か手を打つ〗do* something about.... ●援助なしで何とかする *manage without* 《(なしですます)》《*his*》 help. ▶その件は私が何とかしましょう I'll *see to* the matter./(私に任せてください) You can *leave* the matter *to* me. ▶あなたちょっと太りすぎ. 何とかしたら You're a bit too heavy. Why don't you *do something about* it?

なんどき 何時 (⇨いつ何時)
なんどく 難読 ●難読人名 a person's name *difficult to read*. ●難読字 Chinese characters of *difficult reading*.

●難読症〖医学〗dyslexia. ●難読症の人 a dyslexic.

なんとしても 何としても 〖いくら犠牲を払っても〗at all

なんとなく costs, 《否定文で》at any cost; 〖どんな危険を冒しても〗at any risk; 〖何があっても〗no matter what. ▶何としてもそれを手に入れなければならない I have to get it *at all costs* [*no matter what it costs*, 《書》 *whatever the cost*, ×by all means]. ▶彼は何としてもそこへ行きます I *will* go there *no matter what* [〖どんなことをしてでも〗 *one way or another*]. (!強い意志を表すのが*will* [*shall*] としない) ▶何としても彼に同意させるわ I'm going to get him to agree *if it's the last thing I do*.

なんとなく 何となく 〖どういうわけか〗somehow, for sóme reason (or other); 〖漠然と〗vaguely /véigli/. ▶その部屋は何となく居心地が悪かった *Somehow* [理由は分からないが] *I didn't know why, but* I felt uncomfortable in the room. ▶そのことを何となく覚えている I have a *vague* memory of it. ▶何となくあとをつけられているような感じがする I *have a feeling (that)* I'm being followed [*someone's stalking me*]. ▶あの男は何となく(=どこか)変わったところがある There is *something strange about* him.

会話 「うわぁ，チョコレートキャンディーだ. どうして！ バレンタインデーはまだなのに」「うん，とくに理由なんかないよ. ただ何となく」"Wow! A box of chocolate candy! Why! It's not Valentine's Day yet." "Well, for no special reason. Just *because*."

なんとなれば 何となれば because. (⇨なぜなら(ば))
なんとはなしに 何とはなしに somehow. (⇨なんとなく)
*なんとも 何とも ❶〖強調〗(とても) very; extremely (!*very* より強調的); (実に) really. ▶何とも美しい花 *very* beautiful flowers. ▶何とも申し訳ありません I'm *very* [*really*, *so*, *awfully*] sorry. (!後の方の2語は特に女性に好まれる) ▶何とも難しい状況ですね The situation is *extremely* difficult./*What* a difficult situation!

❷〖否定〗❶〖何とも(…)ない〗 ▶何でも〖何でもない〗 ▶私はころんだけど何ともないよ(=大丈夫だ) I fell down, but I'm *all right* [〖話〗*OK*]. ▶彼は一晩に10万円遣うのを何とも思っていない He thinks *nothing* [*little*] *of* spending 100,000 yen a night. ②〖何とも(…)できない〗 ▶それは何ともできない I *can't manage* it. ▶ちょっと何とも約束できないよ I *can't promise anything*, I'm afraid.

③〖何とも言えない〗 ▶あすそこへ行けるかどうか何とも言えない(=分からない) I'm *not sure* [*I don't know*] whether or not I can go there tomorrow. (!*or not* を文尾に置くこともできるが whether 節が長い場合はこの例のように前に置くことが多い) ▶だれが優勝するかだれにも何とも言えない *Nobody can tell* [〖話〗 *There is no telling*] who will win the championship.

会話 「先生，この人の記憶はそのうち戻りますか」「今のところ何とも言えません」"Will his memory return in time, Doctor?" "I *can't say anything* [*Nobody can say*] at this moment." (!後の方はさらに Who can say …? とも言える)

なんとなく 難なく (⇨難❶)
なんなら 何なら 〖それでは〗then; 〖よかったら〗if you like [*want*] (!*want* は小さくねだった口調になり，目上の人に使わない方がよい); 〖いやでなければ〗if you don't mind; 〖できれば〗if possible, 〖必要なら〗if necessary. ▶何ならおいでください Please come here, *if you like* [*if you don't mind*, *if possible*, (都合がよければ) *if it's convenient for* [*to*] *you*]. ▶何ならうちの者に彼を出席させましょう Let him go to the meeting *if necessary*.

なんなり(と) 何なり(と) 〖何でも❶〗 ▶何か好きなものを注文しなさい Order *anything* you like.

なんなんせい 南南西 the south-southwest (略 SSW).
なんなんとう 南南東 the south-southeast (略 SSE).
なんなんとする 垂んなんとする ▶3,000 になんなんとする(=程度の)聴衆 an audience *close on* [*almost*] 3,000. (!×as many as ... は「...もの数の」の意)
なんにち 何日 (⇨何(なに)❹)
なんにも 何にも (⇨何も) ▶君が来ても何にもならない (=役に立たない) It's [*There's*] *no use* your coming./Your coming *wouldn't be any good*. ▶私たちの努力は結局何にもならなかった Our efforts turned out (to be) *fruitless*./Our efforts *came to nothing*.
なんねん 何年 (⇨何(なに)❹, 年(ねん)❷)
なんねん 難燃 —— 難燃性の 形 fireproof《curtains》; noncombustible.

*なんの 何の ❶〖疑問〗what; (どんな種類の) what kind of ▶これは何の花ですか *What (kind of) flower* is this?/(名前は何ですか) *What's* the name of this flower? ▶これは何の薬ですか *What* is this medicine *for*? (!What kind of medicine is this? より普通) ▶何の(=何について)話をしているのですか *What* are you talking *about*? ▶何のご用ですか (店員などが客に) *What* can I do for you?/Can [May] I help you? ▶何のためにそうしたのですか *What* did you do that *for*?

❷〖否定文で〗(どんな…も) any; (まったく) at all; (少しも) in the least. ▶何の苦労もなく育つ grow up without (undergoing) *any* hardship. ▶何のお手伝いもできずすみません I'm sorry I can't help you *at all*. ▶彼は音楽には何の興味もない He is not *in the least* [*at all*] interested in music. ▶彼に援助をしても何の役にも立たない It is no use [*good*] offering him help. ▶友子からはまだ何の音沙汰(さた)もない *Not a word* from Tomoko yet. (!*Not a word have I heard* .... という強調のための倒置文の省略表現) ▶彼は何の役にも立たない He is *good for nothing*./He is *utterly useless*.

会話 「何か変な音聞こえなかった？」「全然何の音もしなかったよ」"Didn't you hear any strange noises?" "I didn't hear *the slightest* sound."

❸〖その他の表現〗寒かったの何のって It was terribly [*awfully*] cold./*Wás it* ˎcold! (!感嘆文の一種 (⇨と))

なんのかの(と) 何の彼の(と) (あれやこれやで) one thing or another. ●何のかのと言って仕事を怠ける avoid work *on one excuse or another* [*some excuse or other*]. ●何のかのと文句を言う complain about *this and that*.

なんのその 何のその ▶寒さなんて何のその(=平気だ) I do not mind the cold *in the least*.

なんぱ 軟派 图 (男) a playboy; (女) a playgirl.
—— ナンパする 動 (異性をひっかける) pick up a girl [a boy]; (異性と遊び回る) play [〖話〗 run] around with a girl [a boy].
なんぱ 難破 图 (a) (ship)wreck.
—— 難破船 動 ▶我々の船[我々]は四国沖で難破した *Our ship was wrecked* [*We were wrecked*] off the coast of Shikoku.
● 難破船 a wrecked ship, a wreck.
ナンバー a number (略 No., no. 記号《主に米》#) (⇨番号); 〖自動車の〗a registration [〖米〗 license] number. ▶大阪ナンバーの車 a car with an Osaka *license plate*. ●雑誌のバックナンバー a back *number* [*issue*] of a magazine. ●ナンバーツー a *number two*. ▶あなたの車のナンバーは？ What's

your license (plate) *number*?
- **ナンバーエイト** 〘ラグビー〙 a number eight [a no. 8] forward. (参考) 背番号は 8)
- **ナンバーカード** a number cloth. (❗特にマラソンなどに使う番号を書いた布. この意では通例 a number card とはいわない)
- **ナンバーディスプレー** 〘相手方の電話番号表示サービス〙 caller ID display.
- **ナンバープレート** (米) a license plate; (英) a numberplate.

ナンバーズ 〘数字当て宝くじ〙 the numbers. (参考) 米国では違法な数当て賭博で the numbers game [pool] ともいう)

ナンバーワン ● チームでナンバーワンの選手 the *top* [the *number one*] player of the team.

ナンバリング 〘番号をつけること〙 numbering; 〘自動番号器〙 a numbering machine.

なんばん 何番 (⇒番 ❶❹) ● 何番目 (⇒番 ❶)

なんばん 南蛮 〘南洋諸国〙 the South Sea countries.
- 南蛮渡来の品 things imported from *South Sea countries* (such as Siam, Luzon /luːzán/, and Java). ● 鴨南蛮 noodles with duck (chicken) and green onions in soup.
- **南蛮人** (スペイン人) a Spaniard; (ポルトガル人) a Portuguese. ● **南蛮船** a Spanish [a Portuguese] merchant ship. ● **南蛮漬け** *nambanzuke*; (説明的に) deep-fried small fish preserved in seasoned vinegar with sliced onions and chopped red peppers.

なんびと 何人 (⇒何人(๊))
なんびと 何人 (⇒何人(๊))

なんびょう 難病 (難しい病気) a serious disease, a disease difficult to be cured; (治すことのできない病気) an incurable disease; (治し方のまだ分からない病気) 〘書〙 an intractable disease. ● 難病にかかる fall victim to an *intractable disease*. ● 難病を克服する get over [(やや書) overcome, conquer] a *serious disease*.

なんびょうよう 南氷洋 the Antarctic Ocean.

なんぶ 南部 the south; (南の地方) the southern part; (米国の) the South. ▶その一家は東京の南部に住んでいる The family lives in the *southern part* of [in *southern*, in *the south* of] Tokyo. (❗前の二つは《主に米》,最後は《主に英》)
● **南部諸州** (米国の) the Southern States.

なんぷう 南風 a south wind; a wind (blowing) from the south.

なんぷう 軟風 〘気象〙 a gentle breeze.

なんぶつ 難物 (扱いにくい人・事) a difficult person [thing] to deal with; 《話》 a hard [a tough] nut to crack. ▶この問題には参る. 実に難物と言うべきだね This problem is getting me down. This is a *hard nut to crack*.

ナンプラー [<タイ語] nam pla; fish sauce.

なんぶん 難文 a difficult sentence; difficult writing; a sentence difficult to understand.

なんべい 南米 图 South America. ── 南米の 形 South American.

なんべん 軟便 〘医学〙 loose stools.

なんぼ 何程 (⇒幾(𛂦)ら)

なんぽう 南方 图 the south. (⇒❼ 北方)
── 南方の 形 south; southern.
── 南方に 副 ● 南方に行く go (*to the*) *south*. ● インドの南方にある島 an island (*to the*) *south of* India.

なんぼく 南北 north and south. (❗語順に注意) ▶幹線道路が南北に走っている The highway runs *north and south* 〔北から南へ〕 *from north to south*〕.
● **南北戦争** (アメリカの) the Civil War. ● **南北問題** the North-South problem.

なんみん 難民 (避難者) a rèfugée; (故国を追われた) a displaced pérson (略 DP). ● 海上難民 boat people.
● **難民キャンプ** a réfugee càmp. (❗アクセントが移動) ● **難民救済** refugee relief.

なんめん 南面 图 ● 家の南面 the south side of a house. ● 富士山の南面 the south slope of Mt. Fuji.
── 南面する 動 face south.

なんもん 難問 a difficult [a hard, a knotty, 《話》 a tricky] problem [question]. ● 難問に取り組む tackle a *difficult problem*. ● 難問を出す put a *difficult question* (*to him*).

なんよう 南洋 the South Seas.
● **南洋諸島** the South Sea Islands.

なんら 何ら (何も…でない) nothing; (少しも…でない) not ... at all. ▶君はそのことについて何ら心配する必要はない You *don't* have to worry about it *at all*.

なんらか 何らか ── 何らかの 形 some /sʌm/. ● 何らかのテロ対策を講じる take *some* measures against terrorism; do *something* to prevent terrorism. ▶何らかの形で意思表示をするべきです You should express your intentions in *some* way (*or other*). (❗or other を加える方が強意的)

なんろ 難路 [〘でこぼこの〙 rough, bumpy, (岩の突き出た) rugged /rʌ́gɪd/] road [path, track]; a road full of obstacles.

に

に 二 two; 《2番目(の)》the second.

に 荷 ❶ [積み荷] a load (⚠一般的な語. 運ぶ手段・距離を問わない); [大量に遠距離を運ぶ貨物] freight /fréit/, (主に船・飛行機の) (a) cargo (働 ~(e)s) (《英》では鉄道・トラックで運ぶ貨物は goods が普通).
● 軽い[重い]荷 a light [a heavy] *load*. ● 10トンの荷 a ten-ton *load*; ten tons of *freight*. ● 船荷 ship *freight* [*cargo*]. ▶本の荷を解く unpack the books. ▶荷を積む load a *cargo*. ▶船に荷を積む *load* a ship. ▶肩に重い荷をかつぐ carry [bear] a heavy *load* on one's shoulders. ▶そのトラックは荷を満載していた The truck was filled with *cargo*.

❷ [負担・責任] ▶この仕事は彼には荷が重すぎる This work is too much for [(負担が重すぎる) is too heavy a *burden* to] him. ▶これでやっと肩の荷が降りた That's certainly a *load* off my mind [shoulders].
● 荷主 (荷送り人) a consigner; (積み出し人) a shipper.

-に [格助詞]　　　　　　　　　　　　**INDEX**

❶ 場所　　　　　　　❷ 方向
❸ 時間　　　　　　　❹ 目的
❺ 動作の対象　　　　❻ 動作主
❼ 原因　　　　　　　❽ 変化の結果

❶ [場所] at ...; in ...; on ...; into .... (⇨-で)

使い分け at 一点を示す狭い場所に用いるのが原則.
in 比較的広い場所に用いるのが原則.
on 「…の上に」という表面との接触を表す.
into ものに対し「…の中へ」の意の運動を表す.

▶ようやく成田空港[東京]に着いた Finally we arrived *at* Narita Airport [*in* Tokyo]. (⚠広い場所でも自分になじみのない所や中継地などを表す場合は *at* Tokyo とすることもある)/Finally we got *to* Narita Airport [*to* Tokyo]. (⚠前の例より口語的) ▶彼はロンドンのオックスフォード通り102番地に住んでいる He lives *at* 102 Oxford Street in London. (⚠番地は at で示す) ▶彼女は空き地に車を駐車した She parked her car in a vacant lot. ▶1人の少女が戸口に立っていた A girl was standing *at* the door [*in* the doorway]. ▶通りには人がたくさん出ていた There were a lot of people *on* (《主に米》) [*in* (《主に英》)] the street. ▶天井[壁]にハエがとまっている There is a fly *on* the ceiling [wall]. (⚠*on* は接触を示し, 接触していれば位置関係は上でも下でも横でもよい) ▶彼は川に飛び込んだ He jumped *into* [*in*] the river. ▶彼女の髪が私の顔にかかった Her hair was *in* my face. (⚠「彼の顔には(ひげなどの)毛が生えていない」は He has no hair *on* his face. となる. 前置詞の違いに注意)

❷ [方向] to ...; toward ...; for ...; at .... (⇨-へ)

使い分け to 主に到達点を表すが, 時に到達点を暗示せず方向のみを表す場合がある.
toward 「…の方へ」という方向を表わすので, 到達は暗示しない.
for 標的的に用いるのに表す. 目的地やあて先の場合が多い.
at 目標を表す. 一点に向けて意図的な働きかけが起こる状況で用いる.

● ドアの方に歩いて行く walk *to* [*toward*] the door; (近づく) approach (×*to*) the door. ▶次の角を右に曲がりなさい Turn the next corner *to* the right./Turn (*to* the) right at the next corner. (⚠《話》では turn right が普通) ▶少年が犬に石を投げていた A boy was throwing stones *at* [*to*] the dog. (⚠at ではねらいを定めて投げただけで実際に当たったかどうかは不明だが, to では当たったことが含意される) ▶一行は関空をたってロンドンに向かった The party left Kansai Airport *for* [×*to*] London.

❸ [時間] (a) [時点] at ...; on ...; in .... (⇨-で, -から)

使い分け at 時刻を表す.
on 日・曜日や特定の朝・昼などを表す.
in 午前・午後など比較的短い期間から年・季節・世紀など長い期間まで, 範囲としての時間を表す.

▶7時に朝食をとった I had breakfast *at* seven. ▶彼は平成2年1月15日に生まれた He was born *on* January 15 [《やや書》*on* the 15th of January], 1990. (⚠年号は通例西暦を用いる (⇨平成)) ▶5月5日の朝に彼と会う予定だ I'm going to meet him *on* [×*in*] the morning of May 5. ▶次の月曜日に本をお返しします I will give the book back to you (×*on*) next Monday. (⚠last, next, every, this, that などがつくと前置詞はつけない) ▶彼は1980年の5月[春]にローマへ行った He went to Rome *in* May, 1980 [the spring of 1980]. ▶多くの大事業が21世紀に完成される Many big projects will be completed *in* the 21st century.

(b) [期間] during ...; in ...; for .... (⇨間(ｶﾝ)) ▶夏休みに北海道へ行った I went to Hokkaido *in* [*during*, *for*] the summer vacation. (⚠*in* は「夏休み中のある時期に」, *during* は *in* と同意または「夏休みの間中ずっと」, *for* は目的 (⇨❹) を表し, 「夏休みを過ごすために」この意) ▶過去3年間に10回彼と会った I met him ten times *in* [*during*, ×*for*] the last three years. (⚠継続を表す for は回数を表す語句とは用いない. I haven't met him *for* three years. (3年間彼に会っていない) のような場合は可)

❹ [目的] to (*do*); for ...; .... (⚠to は動作の対象 ❶) ▶彼は川へ泳ぎに行った He went to the river to swim [*for* a swim]./He went swimming *in* [×*to*] the river. ▶子供のころよく忘れ物を取りに帰ったものだ When I was a child, I often used to go back home *to* get my things.

❺ [動作の対象] to ...; for .... (⚠to は動作の対象を, for は利益を受けるものの対象を表す) ● 世論に訴える appeal *to* public opinion. ▶君に手紙がきているよ There's a letter *for* you. ▶この花を君にあげよう I'll give you this flower [this flower *to* you]./This flower is *for* you. ▶彼は娘に新しい洋服を作ってやった He made his daughter a new dress [a new dress *for* his daughter].

解説 (1) give A B [B to A] の文型をとる主な動詞: bring, give, grant, hand, leave, lend, offer, owe, pass, pay, play, post, promise, read, recommend, sell, send, serve, show, sing, take, teach, tell, throw, write. (⇨与える)

(2) make A B [B for A] の文型をとる主な動詞: bring, buy, build, call, catch, change, choose, cook, cut, do, fetch, find, fix, get, keep, leave, make, order, prepare, reach, reserve, save, sing. bring と sing は to と for のいずれも可. (⇨買う)

(3) 次のような場合には give [make] A B の構文より give B to A または make B for A の構文が用いられることが多い: (ⅰ) B より A に意味上の焦点がある場合. (ⅱ) A が B より長い場合: 京都に住んでいるめいにプレゼントを買った I bought a present *for* my niece who lives in Kyoto.

❻【動作主】 by ...; from .... ▶彼は級友によくいじめられた He was often bullied *by* his classmates./His classmates often bullied him. ▶老人に昔話を聞くのが好きだ I like hearing old tales *from* old people.

❼【原因】 from ...; with ...; for .... ⚠ from は結果を引き起こす源泉を, with は付随する原因を表す. for は sorrow, pity などの感情を表す語とともに用いる. いずれも成句で用いることが多い) ▶彼は今でもリューマチに苦しんでいる He is still suffering *from* rheumatism. ▶かわいそうに少年たちは恐ろしさに震えていた The poor boys were shivering *with* fear. ▶彼女はあまりのうれしさに泣き出した She felt so happy that she began to cry./She began to cry *for* joy.

❽【変化の結果】 to ...; into .... ▶水が氷に変わる Water changes *into* ice. ▶豆をひいて粉にする Beans are made *into* flour. ⚠ into は著しく質的な変化を伴う場合に用いる) ▶信号が黄から赤に変わった The (traffic) lights changed from yellow *to* red.

❾【割合】 a; in ...; for .... ▶彼は月に 1, 2 度私に会いに来る He comes to see me once or twice *a* month. (⚠「1 週間 [1 年] (につき)」など基準の数字が 1 の場合は, for はつかない) ▶彼は 3 日に一度しかふろに入らない He takes a bath only once *in* three days [every three days, every third day]. (⚠ every は「…ごとに」の意で次に基数＋複数名詞, 序数＋単数名詞を置く) ▶男子 4 人に女子 3 人の割合で進学した Three girls went to college *for* every four boys. ▶本校では 10 人に 1 人の生徒が自転車通学しています One *out of* ten students comes to school by bicycle at our school.

-に-似 ▶お母さん似ですね You *look like* your mother. (⇨似る)

にあい 似合い ▶あの夫婦は似合いのカップルだ They are a *well-matched* couple. ▶彼らは似合いの夫婦になるだろう They'll make [×become] a *nice* [a *good*] couple. ▶あなたがたお 2 人はお似合いですよ You two *deserve* each other. (⚠皮肉としても用いる)

*** にあう 似合う ❶【服装などが】** suit, 《書》become*; (色・柄が調和する) match, go* with .... (⚠これらはいずれも人を目的語にとらない) (⇨合う) ▶その青いドレスはあなたにとてもよく似合っている That blue dress suits [*becomes*, ×*matches*] you very well. (⚠日本語の「…ている」にひかれて進行形にしないこと. 次の 2 文の方が口語的) /That blue dress looks very *good* [*nice*] on you./You look very *good* [*nice*] in that blue dress. ▶彼女には長い髪がいちばん似合う She *looks best with* long hair./Long hair *suits* her best. ▶このセーターに似合うスカーフを探しているの

です I'm looking for a scarf to *go* (*well*) *with* [*match*] this sweater. ▶彼女の短いドレスが長い脚によく似合っていた Her short dress *looked good* over long legs.

翻訳のこころ 五月生まれのせいか, デュークは初夏によく似合っていた (江國香織『デューク』) Duke was at [looked] his best in early summer, probably because he was born in May. ▶ (1)「初夏が似合う」は look one's best [be at one's best] in early summer (初夏に最高の状態であった) を表す. (2) 英語では, 文の主要部が先に述べられる. 日本語と順序が異なっていることに注意)

❷【行動などが】 ▶君には似合わないことをする It *is not like* [*is unlike*] you to do such a thing./《書》It does not *become* you to do such a thing. ▶彼は年に似合わず(=の割りには)体が柔らかい He has a supple body for his age.

にあがる 煮上がる (よく煮える) be well cooked; (沸騰する) come to a 《米》[the 《英》] boil.

にあげ 荷揚げ 图 unloading; (船の) discharge.
── **荷揚げする** 動 unload [discharge] 《a ship》.
● 荷揚げ場 a port of discharge. ● 荷揚げ料 lánding chàrges [ràtes].

-にあたって[あたり] -に当たって[当たり] ● 本を選ぶに当たって(=際して) in choosing [in the choice of] books. ▶本校創立 100 周年記念に当たり大音楽会が催された A great concert was held *on* the centennial of the founding of our school.

にあつかい 荷扱い handling of freight [《英》goods]; freight [《英》goods] handling. ● 荷扱いを丁寧に[手荒く]する handle freight carefully [roughly].
● 荷扱い所 a fréight òffice. ● 荷扱い人 a fréight àgent.

ニアポスト 【サッカー】 a near post.

ニアミス 【航空機の異常接近】 a near miss, 《英》an airmiss, 《米書》 a near midair collision (略 NMAC). ▶自衛隊機とのニアミスがあった We had a *near miss* with a Self-Defense Forces plane./There was a *near miss* between us and a Self-Defense Forces plane.

にい 二位 second place. ▶ (競技などで) 2 位の人[チーム] a runner-up (複 runners-up). ● 競走で 2 位になる come in [finish, be] *second* in the race; be (the) *runner-up* in the race. ▶彼は弁論大会で 2 位になった He won (the) *second* prize in the speech contest.

にい 二尉 (陸尉・空尉) First Lieutenant /lu:ténənt/; (海尉) Lieutenant Junior Grade.

にいさん 兄さん one's older [《米書・英》elder, 《話》big] brother. (⇨兄)

ニース 【フランスの都市】 Nice /ni:s/.

ニーズ needs. ● ニーズに合う商品 products to suit the *needs*. ● ニーズを満たす[に応える] meet the *needs* [(強い要求) *demands*] 《*of*》.

ニーチェ 【ドイツの哲学者】 Nietzsche /ní:tʃə/ (Friedrich ~).

にいづま 新妻 (新婦) a bride; (結婚間もない妻) a newly married woman.

ニート 【無職の若者】 NEET, neet 《*N*ot in *E*ducation, *E*mployment or *T*raining の略》.

にいにいぜみ にいにい蝉 【昆虫】 a kaempher cicada.

にぼん 新盆 the first *Bon* festival after 《one's father's》 death.

にいんせいど 二院制度 a bicameral [a two-chamber] system.

にうけ 荷受け receipt of goods.

- **にうけにん 荷受け人** a consignee.
- **にうごき 荷動き** the 《slow, brisk》 movement of freight [《英》goods].
- **にえきらない 煮え切らない** 《優柔不断な》indecisive; 《はっきりしない》uncertain; 《どっちつかずの》non-committal. ●煮え切らないやつ an *indecisive* fellow. ●政府の煮え切らない(=不確かな)態度 the government's *uncertain* posture 《on》.
- **にえくりかえる 煮え繰り返る** 《湯・やかんなどが》boil hard; 《怒りで》boil with rage; seethe (with rage). (! 以上いずれも通例 be 〜ing の形で用いられる) ●はらわたが煮えくり返る (⇨腸[ガムホ]) [成句]
- **にえたぎる 煮えたぎる** ●煮えたぎっている be boiling (hard); be on the boil.
- **にえたつ 煮え立つ** come to a《米》[the《英》] boil. ▶やかんが煮えたっている The kettle is boiling hard [is on a boil].
- **にえゆ 煮え湯** boiling water.
  ●煮え湯を飲まされる 《裏切られてひどい目にあう》be betrayed cold-heartedly; be terribly hurt by 《his》betrayal.
- **にえる 煮える** boil. ▶豆[やかんの湯]が煮えている The beans *are* [The kettle *is*] *boiling*.
- ***におい 匂い, 臭い** 图 (a) smell, 《やや書》an odor; (a) scent; 《よい》(a) fragrance, 《やや書》(a) perfume; 《悪臭》a stink.

  > **使い分け** smell 「におい」を表す最も一般的な語. よいにおいからいやなにおいまで広く表すが, 形容詞を伴わない場合は悪臭を表すことが多い.
  > **odor** smell の婉曲語で, 不快なにおいをさすことが多い.
  > **scent** そのものに特有のかすかなにおい. 通例よいにおいをさす.
  > **fragrance** 甘く新鮮な草花の香り.
  > **perfume** 濃厚な香水や花のにおい. (⇨香り)
  > **stink** 強い悪臭. (⇨悪臭)

  ●いい[悪い, 強い]におい a good [a bad; a strong] *smell*. ●料理のにおい a cooking *smell* [*odor*]; the *smell* [*odor*] of cooking. ●バラのかすかなにおい a *scent* [a faint *fragrance*] of roses. ●いいにおいのユリ a plant [a *sweet-smelling*] lily. ●腐った肉のいやなにおい the *stink* [unpleasant *smell*, vile *odor*] of rotten meat. ●スープのにおいをかぐ *smell* [くんくん鼻を鳴らして] *sniff* 《at》the soup; *take* [*have*] *a smell* [*a sniff*] *of* the soup.

  ── **匂い[臭い]がする** 動 《物が主語》smell* 《形, of +名》《悪臭を放つ》stink* 《of》;《人が主語》《においを感じる》(can) smell. (! 以上いずれも進行形不可 (⇨匂う)) ▶この花はいいにおいがする This flower *smells* sweet [*sweetly*]./This flower *has a* sweet *smell* [*scent*, *fragrance*, *perfume*]. ▶部屋は薬のにおいがぷんぷんしている The room *smells* [×is smelling] strongly of medicine. (! of を省略して ×The room smells medicine strongly. とはいわない)/There's a strong *smell* [*odor*] of medicine in the room. ▶台所でガスの[何かが焦げる]においがした I could *smell* gas [something burn*ing*] in the kitchen. ●この事件には犯罪のにおいがする There is a *smell* of crime [《話》something *fishy*] about this case./This case *smells* [*stinks*] of crime.

  会話「腐った卵はどんなにおいがしましたか」「ひどいにおいがしました」"How did the rotten eggs *smell*?" "They *smelled* bad [×badly]./They *stank*."

  会話「それはどんなにおいがしますか」「生ごみのようなにおいです」"What does it *smell* like?" "It *smells* like garbage." (! 比喩的の直接関係にないものにおいを

いう場合は of の代わりに like を用いる)
  ●におい消し 《部屋用の》(a) deodorant; [部屋用の] (a) room deodorant. ●におい袋 a scént bàg; a sachet.

- ***におう 匂う, 臭う** 〚悪臭を放つ〛smell* (! 進行形不可);《ひどく》stink*;〚においを感じる〛(can) smell. (匂い) ▶この魚はにおい始めた This fish started to *smell* [*stink*]. ▶何かにおわないか Can't [*Don't*] *you smell* something? (! においてくる前提がある場合の確認のための問いかけ. cf. Can [Do] you smell anything?(何かにおうのですか))
- **におう 仁王** the two Deva Kings; 《説明的に》the guardian gods of Buddhism who stand at the entrance gate of a Buddhist temple.
- **におうだち 仁王立ち** ●仁王立ちになる stand firm, dignified and forbidding.
- **におくり 荷送り** shipment (of goods); 《委託品の》consignment.
  ●荷送り人 a shipper; a consigner. (! 前の方が普通)
- **におわす 匂わす** ❶〚においを発する〛give* off an odor [a scent] (! 主語は主に臭気, scent は香気に用いる);《芳香で満たす》perfume. ▶彼はニンニクのにおいを匂わせていた He *gave off* the odor of garlic./He *smelled of* garlic.
  ❷〚ほのめかす〛hint 《at》; 《暗示する》suggest. ●彼に対する疑いをそれとなく匂わす hint [*to* me] a suspicion against him. ▶彼は辞職を匂わせた He *hinted at* his resignation./He *hinted* [*gave a hint*, 《やや書》*insinuated*] *that* he might resign. ▶彼女の口ぶりは何か不吉な事を匂わせていた Her tone *suggested* [*implied*] something ominous.

- ***にかい 二階** 《米》the second floor, 《英》the first floor; 《2階建ての建物の》the upstairs. (! 単数扱い) (⇨階 [解説]) ●2階建ての家 a *two-story* [*two-storied*] house; a house of *two stories*. (! ×floor は不可 (⇨階 [類語])) ●2階の部屋 an *upstairs* room; a room *on the second*《米》[*first*《英》] *floor*. ●2階に上がる[から下りる] go *upstairs* [*downstairs*]. ▶彼の事務所はそのビルの2階にあります His office is on the *second*《米》[*first*《英》] *floor* of the building. (! 「地下 2 階に」は米英ともin the second basement (⇨地下)) ▶彼は 2 階にいます He is *upstairs*. (! He is up. は「起きている」の意)
  ●二階から目薬《回りくどくて効果がない》be roundabout and inefficient.
  ●2階建てバス a double-decker (bus).

- **にかい 二回** twice, 《回数を強調して》two times; 〚2回目〛the second time. (⇨二度) ●1日に2回この薬を飲む take the medicine *twice* a day. ●ピューリツァー賞を2回も受賞した人 a two-time《米》[two-times《英》] winner of Pulitzer Prize. ▶以前 1-2 回彼に会ったことがある I've seen him once or /ə/ *twice* before. ▶月に 2 回か 3 回は図書館へ行きます I go to the library *two* [×twice] *or* /ɔːr/ *three times* a month. (! (1) or を /ə/ と読むと「2-3 回」とぼかした言い方になる. (2) twice or thrice は 《今は古》) ▶私が中国へ来たのはこれが 2 回目です This is the *second* time I've come to China./This is my *second* visit to China.

- ***にがい 苦い** bitter; 《つらい》bitter, hard; 《気難しい》sour. ●苦い茶 *bitter* tea. ●苦い経験をする have a *bitter* [a *hard*, a *trying*, a *painful*] experience. ●苦い顔をする make a (sour) face; *frown* with displeasure. ▶この方がそれよりも苦い This is more *bitter* than that. ●良薬は口に苦し (⇨良薬) [成句]
- **にがうり 苦瓜** 〚植物〛a balsam pear.

にかえす 煮返す（熱を通しなおす）reheat. ●汁物などを「温めなおす」は heat up, warm up とすることが多い》

にがおえ 似顔絵（肖像画）a portrait.（やや古）a likeness. ●似顔絵を描く paint [draw] 《his》 *portrait*.（❗paint は絵の具で, draw は線で描く場合に用いる）
● 似顔絵画家 a portrait painter;（街頭の）a street [《米》a sidewalk,《英》a pavement] artist.

にかご 荷籠（自転車の）a basket.

にかこくご 二か国語 二か国語による[が自由にしゃべれる] bilingual. ● 二か国語表示の道案内 *bilingual* road signs. ● 二か国語による取扱い説明書 a *bilingual* instruction manual. ▶彼は子供のころフランスで暮らしたのでフランス語と日本語の二か国語が自由にしゃべれる He is *bilingual* in French and Japanese [He has a good command of French as well as Japanese], because he lived in France as a child.

*****にがす 逃がす** ●鳥を逃がす（自由にしてやる）set a bird *free*;（してやる）let a bird go. ●みんな, あいつを追いかけろ. 逃がすな（=逃げさせる）な After him, men, don't *let* him *get away*. 《⇨取り逃がす》
● 逃がした魚は大きい（ことわざ）Every fish that escapes appears greater than it is./The thing you failed to get seems the most valuable.

*****にがつ 二月** February《略 Feb.》.《⇨一月》

にがて 苦手な―苦手な《形》;《不得手な》weak 《in, at》;《へたな》bad* 《at》, poor;《困難な》tough. ●苦手な科目 one's *weak* subject. ▶料理は苦手です I am *weak in* [*at*] cooking./I'm a *poor* cook. ▶悪いけどココアは苦手なんです（=あまり好きではありません）I'm sorry, but I don't care for cocoa very much. 《❗Cocoa is a *weakness* of mine. は逆に「大好物だ」の意 ⇨大好き》▶彼女は暗算が苦手だ（=得意ではない）Mental arithmetic *isn't* her *strong point*.

にがにがしい 苦々しい《形》〔いやな〕disgusting;〔恥ずべき〕shameful.
―**苦々しく**《副》disgustedly; in disgust. ●商道徳の低下を苦々しく思う（=遺憾に思う）*deplore* the moral decay of businesspeople. ▶彼女はちっとも勉強しない息子をいつも苦々しげに見ているばかりで小言一ついわない She looks at her "all play and no work" son *disgustedly*, but she never says anything to him. ▶親を親とも思わなかった若いころの自分を苦々しく思い起こすのだ I'm *ashamed of* my young days when I had no respect for my parents.

にがみ 苦み bitterness;〔苦い味〕a bitter taste. ●苦みのある薬 a slightly *bitter* medicine. ●苦み走ったいい男 a handsome, serious-looking gentleman.

にがむし 苦虫●苦虫をかみつぶしたような顔 ●私に苦虫をかみつぶしたような顔をする make a *sour* /sáuər/ [a *wry* /rái/] face at me;〔しかめ面をする〕*frown at* me.

にがよる 似通う resemble; be alike. ▶神話の中には洋の東西を問わず似通ったものがある There are some myths both in western and eastern worlds, which《closely》*resemble each other*.

ニカラグア〖国名〗Nicaragua /nikɑ́rəɡwə/;（公式名）the Republic of Nicaragua.（首都 Managua）
● ニカラグア人 a Nicaraguan. ● ニカラグア(人)の a Nicaraguan.

にがり 苦汁〖化学〗bittern.

にがりきる 苦り切る look disgusted《at》.

にかわ 膠（gelatinous）glue. ●にかわでつける glue... together, fasten... with glue.

にがわらい 苦笑い〖名〗a wry /rái/ smile [grin].

―**苦笑いする**《動》give a wry smile; smile wryly《at》.《❗smile wryly には「憎しみ・悲しみ・不愉快などで苦々しく笑う」の意》

にき 二期 two periods; two terms. ●選挙で二期連続当選する be elected in *two consecutive terms* [for *two terms* in succession].
● 二期作 double-cropping《of rice》. ● 二期制 a two-term [a two-semester] system. 《⇨学期》

にぎにぎしい 賑々しい《⇨賑やか》

にきび a pimple;〖医学〗acne /ǽkni/;〖参考〗にきびなどの皮膚病の総称》. ●にきびだらけの a pimpled [face [boy]]. ●にきびをつぶす squeeze one's *pimples*. ●顔中にきびだらけである have *pimples* [*acne*] all over one's face. ●大人にきび adult *acne*. ●顔ににきびができた I got *pimples* [*Pimples* came out] on my face.

*****にぎやか 賑やか**―賑やかな《形》❶〔人出が多く活気のある〕busy, bustling 《❗bustling は騒々しさを含意》;〔混み合った〕crowded. ●にぎやかな通り a *busy* [a *bustling*] street. ●街は観光客でにぎやかだった The streets were *busy* [*crowded*] *with* tourists.《⇨賑(ﾆｷﾞ)わう》▶花屋の店先にカーネーションがにぎやかに並んでいた（=あふれんばかりであった）The flower shop was *overflowing with* carnations.
❷〔繁盛する〕prosperous, flourishing, thriving. ▶このあたりも昔はにぎやかだった The place around here used to be *prosperous*.
❸〖陽気な〗《書》merry;〔快活な〕cheerful, lively /láivli/;〔騒がしい〕noisy. ●にぎやかな人 a *cheerful* person. ●にぎやかな会 a *lively* [*merry*] party. ▶小さな子供たちのにぎやかな笑い声が聞こえた We heard the *merry* laughter of young children./We heard young children laughing *merrily*. ▶彼らはにぎやかに飲み食いしていた They were eating and drinking *joyfully* [*with enjoyment*].《❗「飲み食い」の英語の語順に注意》

にきょく 二極―二極の《形》bipolar.
●二極真空管 a diode. ●二極分化 bipolarization; a bipolar division. ●富裕層と貧困層のはっきりとした二極分化 a sharply *bipolar division* of the affluent and impoverished classes.

にぎらせる 握らせる（金を）〔話〕oil [grease] the palm [hand] of《him》; bribe.

にぎり 握り〔取っ手〕a grip; a handle. 《⇨取っ手》
● 一握りの砂 a handful of sand.
● 握り鮨(ｽﾞｼ) hand-shaped sushi. ● 握り飯 a rice ball.

にぎりこぶし 握り拳 a fist. ●握りこぶしを作る clench one's *fist*.

にぎりしめる 握り締める hold*... tightly;（ぎゅっと握る）grasp, grip (-pp-), squeeze 《❗後の方ほど握る力が強い》;〔こぶしを〕clench. ●ペンを握りしめる *hold* a pen *tightly*. ●彼女の手をぎゅっと握りしめる *hold* her hand *tightly*; *grasp* [*grip*, *squeeze*] her hand.
● こぶしを握りしめる *clench* one's fist.

にぎりつぶす 握り潰す❶ crush... in one's hand;（提案などを）squash /skwɑ́/;〔法案などを否決する〕kill《a bill》. ●我々の要望を握りつぶす *squash* our request.

にぎる 握る❶〔つかむ〕（しっかりと）grip (-pp-), clasp, grasp《❗前の方ほど握る力が強い》;（突然に力を込めて）seize /síːz/;〔ぐいとつかんで離さない〕clutch;〔手に持って〕hold*, take* hold of.... 《⇨掴(ﾂｶ)む》〖類語〗●ロープを両手で握る *grasp* a rope with one's hands. ▶彼女はこわがって私の手をぎゅっと握った She *gripped* [*clutched*] my hand in fear. ▶彼女は私の両手をしっかり握って会えてよかったと言った She *clasped* my hands and said she was glad to see me./"I'm

にぎわい

very glad to see you," she said *clasping* my hands. ▶二人は手を握り合ってベンチに座っていた They sat on a bench *holding* hands.
❷〖支配する〗control (-ll-). (⇨牛耳る) ●政権を握る *come into* power; *get* [*seize*] power. (!) (1) seize は「力ずくでとる」. (2)「政権を握っている」は be in power)
❸〖その他の表現〗 ●秘密を握っている[握る] *know* [*get*] ⟨*his*⟩ *secret*. ●寿司を握る *make* sushi. ▶私たちはその試合に手に汗を握った(=興奮した) We *were very excited* at the game./We *were on edge* [⦅米話⦆ *on pins and needles*] during the game.

にぎわい 賑わい ⦅活気⦆ a bustle /bʌ́sl/; ⦅人出⦆ a turnout. (!) いずれも通例複数形にしない) (⇨賑わう) ●にぎわいのある通り *bustling* streets. ▶国際見本市は大変な［かなりの］にぎわいだった There was a large [a good] *turnout* [*crowd*] at the international trade fair.

にぎわう 賑わう ❶〖人出が多い〗be crowded; ⦅活気がある⦆ be alive [lively]. ▶商店街は買い物客でにぎわっていた The shopping streets *were crowded* [*busy*, (ごった返して) *bustling*] *with* shoppers.
▶町中がお祭り気分でにぎわっている The whole town is in festive mood.
❷〖繁盛する〗prosper; flourish /flə́ːrɪʃ/. ●あの店はいつでもにぎわっている That store *is prosperous* [*doing well*] all the time./(客で混雑している) That store *is crowded with* [*is full of*] customers all the time.

にぎわす 賑わす 〖活気づける〗liven ... up, enliven; 〖新聞などで大きく報じられる〗hit* [make*] the headlines; (事件などが) be splashed ⦅*across*, *on*⦆. ▶彼はとても陽気で面白いパーティーではおもしろいことを言って座をにぎわしてくれた He was such a jolly fellow that he *livened up* the atmosphere of a party by saying funny things. ▶彼はノーベル賞の受賞で新聞の一面をにぎわした He *hit* [*made*] the front-page *headlines* when he won the Nobel prize.

にく 肉 ❶〖人間・動物の〗flesh. ▶彼はどちらかといえば肉づきのいい方だ He is, if anything, *on the fleshy side*.
①〖～肉〗 ●腹の肉 the *flesh* of the stomach. ●豚の肉はポークという Pig(')s' *flesh* [The *flesh* of pigs] is called pork.
②〖肉が〗 ▶彼はうんと肉がついてきた (体重が増えた) He *has gained* [*put on*] a lot of *weight*./(特にやせていた人が) He *has filled out* a lot.
③〖肉の〗 ●肉の無い(=やせた)腕 a *thin* [a *skinny*] (↔a *fleshy*) arm. ●肉のしまった男 a *muscular* [a *brawny*] man.
④〖肉に〗 ●ひもが肉にくいこんだ The rope cut into the *flesh*.
❷〖食用の〗meat. (!) いろいろな肉類をいう場合 Ⓒ 扱いにすることがある)
①〖～肉〗 ●鶏肉 chicken. ●牛肉 beef. ●魚肉 fish; the *flesh* of fish. ●羊肉 mutton; (子羊の) lamb. ●ひき肉 ground [minced] *meat*. ●細切れの肉 small pieces of *meat*.
②〖肉を〗[は]〗 ▶肉はどのように焼きましょうか How do you like your *meat* done? ▶この肉は堅い[柔らかい] This meat is tough [tender]. (!) tender の代わりに ×soft とはいわない)
③〖肉を〗 ●肉をきつね色に焼く brown the *meat*. (⇨焼く) ●肉を薄く切る slice *meat*. ●客に肉を切り分ける carve *meat* for the guests. ●いろいろな肉を売っている sell different *meats*.
❸〖植物の果肉〗flesh; (柔らかい) pulp. ●肉の多い果実 *pulpy* fruit.

❹〖印肉〗(⇨印肉)
●肉を切らせて骨を断つ[切る] accept a strategic defeat to win an ultimate victory.
●肉汁 meat juice(s); gravy. ●肉屋 (人) a butcher; (店) a butcher's shop. (!) ⦅米⦆ では a meat market, ⦅英⦆ では the butcher's という. a meatman とはあまりいわない) ●肉料理 meat cooking [dishes].

にくあつ 肉厚 ── 肉厚の 形 (厚い) thick; (肉付きがよい) plump; fleshy; meaty.

*   **にくい** 憎い hateful; (ひどく憎い) detestable. ●憎いやつ a *hateful* guy. ●憎い(=気のきいた)ことを言う say smart [*clever*] things. ●犯人が憎い I *hate* [*detest*] the criminal. ▶彼は彼女のことを憎からず思っているようだ (⇨憎からず [成句])

*   **-にくい** ❶〖困難である〗hard; difficult. ▶その質問には答えにくい The question is *difficult* [*hard*] *to* answer./This is a *difficult* [a *hard*] question *to* answer./*It is difficult* [*hard*] *to* answer the question. ▶ちょっと賛成しにくい I *wouldn't* agree./Oh, I don't know if I *agree* with you. (!) I *don't* agree. では単刀直入に「賛成できません」の意) ▶彼の字は読みにくい His handwriting is *illegible* [*hard* to read]. ▶予約はとりにくいかもしれませんよ You may *have* some *trouble* [*difficulty*] *getting* a reservation.
❷〖その他の表現〗 ▶言いにくいことだが君は間違っていると思う I *hate* to say, but I think you are wrong.
▶このシャツはよごれにくい This shirt *doesn't get* dirty [*soil*] *easily*. (!) soil はしばしば「排泄(⽀)物で汚れる」の意がある)

にくが 肉芽 〖医学〗(a) granulation. ●肉芽腫 a granuloma.

にくからず 憎からず ●憎からず思う (かわいいと思う) love; care for; have a tender feeling ⦅*for*⦆. ▶彼は彼女のことを憎からず思っているようだ I think he *loves* her.

にくがん 肉眼 the naked /néɪkɪd/ eye. (!) ×...eyes と複数形にはしない) ▶それは肉眼で見えない We can't see it *with the* [×our] *naked eye*./It is invisible *to the naked eye*.

にくかんてき 肉感的 ── 肉感的な 形 sexy, sensual. ●肉感的な女性 a *sexually* attractive woman.

にくぎゅう 肉牛 beef cattle. (!) 複数扱い)

にくきりぼうちょう 肉切り包丁 (食卓用) a carving knife (⦅複⦆ knives); (業務用) a cleaver.

にくしつ 肉質 ❶〖体質〗 ●肉質の人[体] a fleshy [⦅書⦆ a corpulent] person [body].
❷〖肉に似た性質〗fleshy ⦅*leaves*⦆.
❸〖品質〗quality of meat. ⦅果物の⦆ *flesh*.

にくしみ 憎しみ (a) hatred, (a) hate. ●憎しみを買う incur [⦅やや弱⦆ excite] *hatred*. ●愛と憎しみ love and *hate*. ▶彼は親に憎しみを抱いている He *has a hatred for* [*of*] his parents./He *hates* his parents.

にくジャガ 肉ジャガ *nikujaga*; (説明的に) meat and potatoes cooked with soy sauce and sugar.

にくしゅ 肉腫 〖医学〗a sarcoma /sɑːrkóʊmə/ (⦅複⦆ ~s, sarcomata).

にくじゅう 肉汁 〖肉から出る汁〗meat juice; gravy; 〖スープ〗meat broth.

にくしょく 肉食 图 (肉の食事) a meat diet. ●肉食の人[主義者] a meat eating person, (婉曲的) a non-vegetarian. (⇨菜食 [菜食主義者])
── 肉食する 動 (人が) eat meat; (動物が) eat flesh.
●肉食動物 a carnívorous [a flesh-eating] animal; a cárnivòre.

にくしん 肉親 a blood relation [relative] (⚠日本語より意味が広く，単に血族の意でも用いる); one's (own) flesh and blood (⚠単・複印形); one's immediate family [kin] (⚠親子，配偶者，兄弟). ●肉親の情 the affection between *blood relations*. ●肉親をさがす look for one's *relatives* [(家族) *family*]. (⇨親戚(しんせき), 近親)

にくずく 【植物】 a nutmeg tree; (香料) nutmeg.

にくせい 肉声 a (natural) voice. (⚠機械を通した声と対比する時以外は，漏例 natural を省略する) ▶電話の声は肉声とだいぶ違う His voice on the phone sounds quite different from his *natural voice*.

*****にくたい** 肉体 图 a body, (書) the flesh. (⚠いずれも精神 (mind)・魂 (soul) と対比して用いる. 後の方は肉体的欲望を暗示) ●健全なる精神は健全なる肉体(＝身体)に宿る (⇨健全 (成句))

── 肉体(の), 肉体的(な) 形 bodily; physical. (⚠後の方がより間接的に肉体に言及する語) ●肉体的の欠陥を *bodily* [a *physical*] defect. ●肉体関係がある have *sexual* relations 《*with*》. ●肉体的の危害を加える do *bodily* harm 《*to* him》.
●肉体美 the beauty of the body; bodily [physical] beauty. ●肉体労働 physical [(手でする) manual] labor. ●肉体労働者 a manual worker [laborer]; a blue-collar (⇔a white-collar) worker.

にくたらしい 憎たらしい 〘憎むべき〙 hateful; 〘悪意に満ちた〙 spiteful; 〘しゃくにさわる〙 provoking. ●憎たらしい顔つき a *hateful* [a *spiteful*] look. ●憎たらしい事を言う say *provoking* [*spiteful*, (生意気な) *cheeky*] things

にくだん 肉弾 a human bullet.
●肉弾戦 a hand-to-hand combat [fight].

にくだんご 肉団子 (ミートボール) a meatball.

にくづき 肉付き ●肉付きのよい (＝太った) 顔 a *fleshy* [(丸々と太った) a *plump*] face. ●肉付きのよい牛 a *well-fattened* cow.

にくづけ 肉付け ── 肉付け(を)する 動 flesh ... out.
●まず大筋を決め，その後細部の肉付けをする first make an outline and then *flesh* it *out*.

にくにくしい 憎々しい hateful. ●互いに憎々しげに相手を見る look at each other *with bitter hatred*.

にくはく 肉薄 ── 肉薄する 動 (包囲の輪を縮める) close in 《*on, upon*》; (近くまで押し進む) run 〘軍隊〙 press 〙 ... hard. ●敵軍がわが(我々に)肉薄してきた The enemy army began to *close in* 《*on us*》.

にくばなれ 肉離れ a torn muscle. ●右のふくらはぎが肉離れを起こした have a *torn muscle* in one's right calf.

にくひつ 肉筆 one's own handwriting.

にくぶと 肉太 ── 肉太の 形 thick; (活字が) bold.
●肉太の文字で書かれたメモ a memo written in a *thick* hand.

にくぼそ 肉細 ── 肉細の 形 thin; (活字が) light.
●肉細の文字で書かれた手紙 a letter written in a *thin* hand.

にくまれぐち 憎まれ口 〘悪意に満ちた言葉〙 spiteful [malicious] remarks. ▶彼はよく憎まれ口をたたく He often says *spiteful* [〘しゃくにさわる〙 *provoking*] *things*./He often makes *spiteful* [*malicious*] *remarks*.

にくまれっこ 憎まれっ子 a bad [(いたずら好きな) naughty] child (複 children); (嫌われている) a hated child.
●憎まれっ子世にはばかる (皮肉にも嫌われている人は世間で幅を利かすものだ) Ironically, hated people will thrive in the world. (⚠will は「習性」を表し，強勢を受ける)

にくまれやく 憎まれ役 ●憎まれ役になる play the part of the villain. (⚠男性については 〘米話〙 では play a bad guy ともいう)

*****にくむ** 憎む hate; detest; 《やや強》 loathe /lóuð/; 《やや書》 abhor /æbhɔ́ːr/ (-rr-). ●後の方ほど意味が強くなる (⇨嫌う) ●この世の不正を憎む hate [loathe, abhor] injustices in this world. ●憎むべき犯罪 a hateful [a detestable] crime. ●彼の父を憎むあまり彼を殺す kill him *out of hatred for* his father. ▶彼は約束を破ったことで私を憎んでいる He *hates* me *for* having broken my promise. ▶憎んではいけない，愛されない者だけが憎むのだ You don't *hate*. Only the unloved *hate*.

にくめない 憎めない ▶彼によく利用されるんだけどなぜか憎めない He often takes advantage of me, but I *can't dislike* him somehow.

にくよく 肉欲 carnal desires; sexual appetite; (過度の) lust. ●肉欲におぼれる indulge in *carnal pleasures*; be a slave to *lust*.

*****にくらしい** 憎らしい 形 hateful; (腹の立つ) provoking. ●憎らしい態度 a *hateful* [a *provoking*] attitude. ●憎らしい男 a *hateful* man. ●憎らしいほど落ち着いている be *provokingly* calm.

── 憎らしげに 副 hatefully; (悪意に満ちて) spitefully.

にぐるま 荷車 a cart. ●荷車を押す[引く] push [pull, draw] a *cart*.

ニクロム 《商標》 Nichrome /náikròum/.
●ニクロム線 Nichrome wire.

にぐん 二軍 (野球の) a farm team [club]. ●二軍に回される[落とされる] be farmed out.

ニケ 〘勝利の女神〙 〘ギリシャ神話〙 Nike /náikiː/.

にげ 逃げ (責任のがれ) the evasion of responsibility, 〘話〙 the runaround.
●逃げを打つ give 《him》 the runaround; (手を引く) try to back out 《*of*》.

にげあし 逃げ足 ●逃げ足になる be ready to run away [fly]. (⇨逃げ腰) ●逃げ足が速い be quick to run away (take flight).

にげうせる 逃げ失せる run away 《*from*》; (うまく逃げおせる) make good one's escape; (姿を消す) get out of sight; disappear.

にげおくれる 逃げ遅れる fail to escape. ▶火事のときもう少しで逃げ遅れるところだった I *narrowly escaped* [*had a narrow escape*] from the burning house. (⚠narrowly は「やっとのことで」の意)

にげかくれ 逃げ隠れ ▶今さら逃げ隠れはしない I won't try to *escape* [*run away*] any longer.

にげきる 逃げ切る make good one's escape; get away 《*from*》; (最後までリードを保つ) keep* [hold] the lead to the end (of the game).

にげこうじょう 逃げ口上 (口実) an excuse /ikskjúːs/; (言い逃れ) an evasion. ●逃げ口上を使う employ *evasions*; give [make] *excuses*.

にげごし 逃げ腰 ●逃げ腰になる (逃げる用意をする) be ready to run away [flee]; (主に米) flee, turn tail and flee]. ●その新しい事業から逃げ腰になる[＝手を引こうとする] try to back out of [(しり込みする) shrink from, (後ずさりする) back away from] the new enterprise.

にげこむ 逃げ込む run* [(急いで) flee*] 《*into*》; (難を避けて) take* refuge (*in* the embassy).

にげじたく 逃げ支度 ●逃げ支度をする prepare for flight; get ready to flee (from ...).

にげだす 逃げ出す escape 《*from out of*》; get* out 《*of*》; run* away 《*from*》; take* to one's heels; (手を引く) back out 《*of, from*》. (⇨逃げる) ▶彼らは燃えさかる家から逃げ出した They *escaped out of*

にげのびる 逃げ延びる (高飛びする) escape arrest by running away to 《a distant place》; (無事に逃げる) escape [run away] safely; (うまく逃げおおせる) make* good one's escape. (⇨逃げる)

にげば 逃げ場 ● 火災で逃げ場を失う (=逃げ道を断たれる) have one's *escape* cut off in the fire; (閉じ込められる) be *trapped* in the fire.

にげまどう 逃げ惑う try to escape 《from the fire》 running this way and that.

にげまわる 逃げ回る run* around [from place to place] trying to escape. ▶ 彼はその仕事を引き受けるのがいやで逃げ回っている He is trying to avoid taking on the job.

にげみず 逃げ水 a mirage /mərá:ʒ/ of water 《on a hot road》.

にげみち 逃げ道 an escape; (逃げる手段) a means of escape. ● 逃げ道を絶たれる have one's *escape* [退路] *retreat* cut off. ▶ 彼の追及からの逃げ道はちゃんと作ってある I have all the answers ready to dodge his questions. (❗ dodge は「巧みに言い抜ける」の意)

*‡**にげる** 逃げる ❶ [逃亡する] (逃げ去る) run* away; (鳥が) fly* away; (人に用いる場合は「飛ぶように急で」,「飛行機に乗って」を含意); (車が[で]) drive* away; (小舟が[で]) row away; (現場からあるいはうまく捕らえずに) get* away 《from》; (逮捕・束縛などから) escape 《from》; (逃げ出す) get out 《of》; (急いで逃げる)《主に書》flee*. ● 一目散に逃げる run away at full speed; 《書》take to one's heels. ● 逃げおおせる succeed in 《書》make good》 one's escape. ▶ 犬が逃げちゃう。捕まえて My dog's running away. Catch him. ▶ 支配人は大金を持って逃げた The manager got away [made away] with a lot of money. ▶ 私は彼に捕まえられて逃げられなかった He got hold of me and I couldn't *break away*. (❗ break away は「束縛などから逃れる」の意)

①《...から逃げる》● 刑務所から逃げる (=脱獄する) *escape from* prison. ● 寮からこっそり逃げる slip [sneak] *away from* the dormitory. ▶ 運転手は事故現場から逃げた The driver drove *away from* the accident. ▶ 彼女は過去から逃げられないことは知っていた She knew she could never *escape* the past.

②《...へ逃げる》● 国外へ逃げる run *away* overseas; (亡命する) flee the country. ▶ 人々は洪水を避けて高い所へ逃げた The people ran [fled] *to* the high ground to escape the flood.

❷ [回避する] (巧みに逃げる) evade; (避けて通る) avoid. ▶ 彼は私の質問をうまく逃げた He deftly *evaded* [*avoided*] my questions.

❸ [その他の表現] ▶ 彼は妻に逃げられた (見捨てられた) His wife *left* him [《話》*walked out on* him]. (❗ 後の方は walked away from him でもよいが, walk out on him の方が「彼を捨てて」の意が強く出る)

● 逃げるが勝ち (ことわざ) (慎重さが勇気の大半) Discretion is the better part of valor.

にげん 二元 ― 二元的な 形 dualistic.
● 二元論 dualism.

にげんきん 二弦琴 a two-string *koto*. (❗ 単・複同形)《琴》● 二弦琴を弾く play the *two-string koto*.

にこう 二項 ― 二項定理 [数学] the binomial theorem /θí:ərəm/. ● 二項分布 [統計] the binomial distribution.

にごう(さん) 二号(さん) a kept woman [mistress], 《婉曲的》a demimondaine /dèmimondéin/.

にこく 二国 ― 二国間協定 a bilateral agreement. ● 二国語 二か国語

にこごり 煮凝り ● 魚の煮こごり (煮こごりそのもの) jellied juice of boiled fish; (魚料理の) jellied fish.

にごす 濁す (泥で水などを) make*... muddy; (液体を) make ... cloudy. (⇨濁る) ▶ 彼女は言葉を濁した (あいまいな返事をした) She *gave* a *vague* /véig/ *answer*./(言質を与えなかった) She *didn't commit herself*.

ニコチン [化学] nicotine /níkəti:n/.
● ニコチン中毒 nicotinism.

にこにこ ● にこにこ笑う smile broadly [brightly] (❗ 前の方は口を大きく開けて, 後の方は晴れやかに笑うこと); beam (❗「太陽の光がさす」を比喩的に用い,「顔つきがうれしさでいっぱい」の意). ▶ 彼女はにこにこしながらウイニングランをした She *smiled broadly* (満面笑みをたたえていた) *was all smiles* as she did a victory lap./She did a victory lap *with a big* [*a broad*] *smile* (on her face). ▶ 「よくやったね」と彼女はにこにこして言った "You did a good job," she *smiled* [*beamed*]. ▶ 彼女は幸せでにこにこしていた She *was beaming* [*smiling brightly*] with happiness.

にこぼれる 煮零れる boil over.

にこみ 煮込み (a) mixed stew. ● 煮込みが足りない be not stewed well; be not boiled long enough.
● 煮込みうどん noodles simmered in broth.

にこむ 煮込む (いっしょに煮る) boil 《them》 together; (よく煮る) boil 《it》 well; (とろ火でゆっくりと) stew. ● 肉を煮込む stew the meat.

にこやか ● にこやかにあいさつする greet 《him》 with a big [a broad, 《晴れやかな》a bright] smile. ● にこやかな顔 one's *bright* [*beaming*] face. ● にこやかに笑う (⇨にこにこ)

にごらす 濁らす (⇨濁す)

にこり ▶ 私の冗談に彼はにこりともしなかった He didn't so much as *smile* [《話》didn't even *crack a smile*] at my joke.

にごり 濁り uncleanness; (泥などによる) muddiness; (透明でないこと) cloudiness; (純粋でないこと) impurity.
● 濁り酒 unrefined *sake*. ● 濁り水 muddy water.

*‡**にごる** 濁る (水が泥で) get* [become*] muddy; (液体が) get [become] cloudy; (空気などが) become foul [polluted]. ▶ 目の濁った (=目の輝きのない) 青年たち young people with *dull* [*lackluster*] eyes. ▶ 台風のあとで川が濁っていた The river *was muddy* after the typhoon.

にさ 二佐 (陸佐, 空佐) lieutenant /lu:ténənt/ colonel /kə́:rnl/; (海佐) commander.

にざかな 煮魚 (説明的に) fish boiled with soy, sugar, and other condiments. (参考 単に boiled fish というのは水煮しただけの魚をさすことが多い. これに好みのソースをかけて食べる)

にさん 二三 ● 2–3 日したら in *a few* [*two or three*, 《話》*a couple* (*of*)] *days*. (❗ of を省略するのは《米話》. ただし「あと 2–3 日したら」なら米英とも in a couple more days が普通) ● 2–3 人の少年たち *a few* [*some*] *boys*. ● some は「漠然といくつか」の意) ● 2–3 度 *two* [×*twice*] *or three times*.

にさんかたんそ 二酸化炭素 carbon dioxide /daiáksaid/ (略 CO₂). (❗ 英文中では通例 CO₂ とは書かない)
● 二酸化炭素排出(量)規制 control of carbon dioxide emissions.

*‡**にし** 西 名 west, West. (⇨通例 the ～)(⇨東)

にじ

— 西(の) 形 west; western; westerly.
— 西に 副 (西方に) (to the) west; (西部に) in the west; (西側に接して) on the west (side); 〖西へ(向かって)〗west; to [toward] the west; westward. ▶日は西に沈んだ The sun has set *in* [xto] *the west*.
● 西も東も分からない (地理に不案内である) be a complete [a total] stranger; (ものの道理が分からない) unreasonable 《child》.
● 西海岸 (米国の) the West Coast. ● 西日本 the western part of Japan.

にじ 虹 a rainbow. ● 虹の七色 the seven colors of [in] *the rainbow*. ● 雨上がりの空に美しい虹がかかった A beautiful *rainbow* appeared in the sky (just) after the rain.

にじ 二次 — 二次(の) 形 〖2番目の〗second; 〖二次的な〗secondary. ● 第二次世界大戦 World War II (Ⅱ は two と読む); the *Second* World War. ● 二次災害の恐れ (some) fear of a *secondary* disaster. ● 二次的な問題 a *secondary* matter.
● 二次会 a second party; (説明的に) a smaller party held after the main party. ● 二次産業 secondary industry. ● 二次試験 a final (→a preliminary) (exam). ● 二次方程式 〖数学〗 a quadratic equation.

ニジェール 〖国名〗Niger /náidʒɚr/; (公式名) the Republic of Niger. (首都 Niamey) ● ニジェール人 a Nigerien /naiʒiəriən/. ● ニジェール(人)の Nigerien.

にしかぜ 西風 a west wind. 類語 英国では乾いた土を湿らせる慈雨をもたらす暖かい春の風] (⇒東風)

にしがわ 西側 the west [western] side; (共産圏諸国に対して) the West.
● 西側陣営〖諸国〗 the Western bloc [nations].

にしき 錦 (織物) Japanese brocade.
● 錦の御旗 平和維持を錦の御旗に for the (*righteous*) *cause* of maintaining the peace.
● 錦を飾る 故郷に錦を飾る return to one's hometown as a successful man [woman].
● 錦絵 a color-printed *ukiyoe*. (⇒浮世絵)

にしきごい 錦鯉 〖魚介〗 a varicolored carp.
にしきへび 錦蛇 〖動物〗a python.
にじげん 二次元 ▷ two dimensions.
— 二次元の 形 two-dimensional.

-にしては 〖…の割には〗for …; 〖考慮すると〗considering 《*that* 節》. ● 5月にしては暑い It is hot [xhotter] *for* May. ▶初心者にしては彼はスキーがうまい He skies well *for* a beginner./He skies well(,) *considering* (*that*) he's a beginner.
会話 「これが太郎の絵よ」「6歳にしてはけっこう上手だね」"This is Taro's drawing." "You know it's rather good for a six-year-old."

-にしても even if … (⇒-しても)

にしび 西日 ● 西日のさす部屋 a room exposed to the *afternoon* [*setting*] sun. ● 西日を避ける (さえぎる) block out *the afternoon* sun.

にします 虹鱒 〖魚介〗a rainbow trout. (!通例単・複同形)

にじみでる 滲み出る ❶ 〖液体などが〗ooze 《*out of, from*》; seep (out) 《*though, from*》. ● 汗がにじみ出ている be oozing (with) sweat. ● 傷口から血がにじみ出ている Blood *is oozing out of* [*from*] the wound.
❷ 〖人柄などその人に備わったものが〗ooze; reveal (itself). ▶彼女の苦心の跡が行間ににじみ出ている Her effort *shows* between the lines of her work. ▶この絵には彼の温かい人柄がにじみ出ている This picture *reveals* his warm personality.

*****にじむ** 滲む 〖色・染料・インクなどが〗run*, spread*; 〖血が〗ooze; 〖汗が〗break* out. ▶この便箋(びんせん)はインクがひどくにじむ Ink *runs* [*spreads*] terribly on this letter paper. ● 傷口から血がにじみ出ている (滲み出る) ▶涙でにじんでよく見えなかった My eyes (*were*) *blurred with* tears./Tears *blurred* my eyes. ▶彼女の手紙には彼女対する競争心がにじみ出ている Her letter *gives away* her competitive spirit toward him. (!*give away* は「本人にはそのつもりがないのに…がつい出てしまう」の意)

にしめ 煮染め 〖しょうゆなどでじっくり煮込んだ料理〗simmered food. ● 鳥肉と野菜の煮しめ chicken and vegetables simmered in a little highly soy-flavored broth until the liquid is almost gone.

にしゃたくいつ 二者択一 a choice between the two [A and B]; the alternative 《*of* A or B》. (⇒選択) ▶彼女は家族か仕事かの二者択一を迫られた She was forced to make *a choice between* family *and* career.

にしゅ 二種 ● 第二種郵便物 the second class mail.

*****にじゅう** 二十 twenty; 〖20番目の〗the twentieth.
● 20代の青年 a young man in *his twenties*. ● 20世紀に in *the twentieth* [*the 20th*] century. ● 20年代の初期[後半; 半ば]に書かれた本 a book written *in the* early [late; mid] *twenties*. (! *twenties* は 1920s [1920's] とも書き, その場合 nineteen twenties と読む)

*****にじゅう** 二重 — 二重(の) 形 〖二つが重なった〗double, 《書》twofold; 〖二つの部分から成る〗dual.
● 二重の生活をする lead a *double* life. ▶彼の言葉には二重の意味がある(=意味がある) His remarks have a *double* [*a dual*] meaning. ● ドアは二重ロックにすべきだ The door should be *double* locked. (⇒鍵)
— 二重に 副 (2度) twice; (二つに) doubly. ▶その小包を二重に包む wrap the parcel *twice*. ● その勘定を二重に払う pay the bill *twice*. ▶ものが二重に見えるので医者に行った I was seeing *double*, so I went to the doctor('s).
● 二重あご a double chin. ● 二重写し (重なり合うこと) overlap, overlapping; (二重露出) double exposure. ● 二重価格 dual prices. ● 二重国籍 (have) dual nationality [citizenship]. ● 二重人格者 a person with a dual [a double] personality; a Jekyll and Hyde. ● 二重唱[奏] a duet; a duo (together ~s). ● 二重帳簿 dual bookkeeping. ● 二重帳簿をつける keep dual accounts (for tax evasion [illegal] purposes). ● 二重橋 (皇居の) the Double Bridge. ● 二重母音 〖音声〗a diphthong. ● 二重窓 a double window. ● 二重丸 a double circle.

にじゅうおくこうねんのこどく 『二十億光年の孤独』 *Two Billion Light — Years of Solitude*. (参考 谷川俊太郎の詩集)

にじゅうしのひとみ 『二十四の瞳』 *Twenty-four Eyes*. (参考 壺井栄の小説)

にじゅうよじかん 二十四時間 ● 24時間体制で on an *around-the-clock* basis. ▶当方の温泉は24時間ご利用いただけます This hot spring is available *24 hours a day* [*around the clock*].

にじょう 二乗 a square. (⇒自乗)
にしょく 二色 two colors.
● 2色刷り two-color(ed) printing.

にじりぐち 躙り口 〖茶室の出入り口〗(説明的に) a very low and narrow entrance to a tea-ceremony room 〖room〗.

にじりよる にじり寄る edge up 《*to*》; approach (…) inch by inch.

にじる 煮汁 〖魚・野菜などを煮た汁〗broth.

-にしろ ▶行くにしろ行かないにしろ金は払います Whether

にしん 鰊 〔魚介〕 a herring. (**!** 通例単・複同形. 肉は Ⓤ) ● ニシンの燻製 (a) kipper, (a) kippered herring.

にしん 二伸 (⇨追伸)

にしん 二審 〔法律〕 the second instance.

にしんとう 二親等 (⇨-親等)

にしんほう 二進法 〔数学〕 the binary system [scale], binary. ● 二進法で計算する count [calculate] in binary.

ニス 〔<オランダ語〕 varnish. ● 机にニスを塗る put (a coat of) varnish on a desk; give a desk a coat of varnish; varnish a desk. ● ニスを塗ったテーブル a varnished table.

-にすぎない -に過ぎない 〔〔ただ単に〕〕 only; just (**!** only より口語的); 〔〔…以上の何ものでもない〕〕 nothing but …; 〔〔…以上のものではない〕〕 no more than …. ▶それは作り話に過ぎない It's only [just,《書》merely, nothing but, no more than] a fiction./It's a mere fiction. ▶私は一介の銀行員に過ぎない I'm no more [better] than a bank clerk.

*****にせ** 偽 图 〔〔模造品〕〕an imitation; 〔〔偽造品[者]〕〕a fake; 〔〔怪しげな物[者]〕〕《話》a phony. (⇨偽物)
—— 偽(の) 形 〔〔本物でない〕〕 false; 〔〔見せかけの〕〕 sham; 〔〔偽造の〕〕 counterfeit /káunṭərfɪt/; fake. ● にせ情報 false data. ● にせダイヤ a fake [a sham] diamond. ● にせ手紙 〔=捏造(ﾈﾂｿﾞｳ)した〕 a forged letter. ▶彼はにせ医者だ He is a fake doctor. (**!** 文脈から明らかな場合は He is a fake [a faker, a phony]. のようにもいえる)
● 偽札 a ounterfeit [a fake] bill.

にせアカシア 偽アカシア 〔植物〕 a false [a black] acacia.

にせい 二世 ❶ 〔日系米人〕 a Nisei (優 〜(s)), a first-generation Japanese American (**!** 「一世」の意でも用いられる (⇨-せ, 三世))
❷ 〔二代目〕 ● チャールズ 2 世 (国王) Charles Ⅱ. (**!** the second と読む) ● ジャック・ジョーンズ 2 世 (一般人) Jack Jones, Jr. 〔参考〕 米英では父親や祖父の名を息子につけることがあり, 両者が存命中には区別するため息子を junior《略 Jr.》と呼ぶ

にせもの 偽物, 偽者, 〔貨幣などの〕 a counterfeit /káunṭərfɪt/; 〔まやかし物〕 a fake, 《話》 a phony; 〔文書・芸術品の〕 a forgery; 〔〔模造品〕〕 an imitation; 〔まがい物〕 a sham; 〔〔人〕〕 a faker. ▶ルイトンのかばんのにせ物 counterfeits of Louis Vuitton /lùːiːs vjúːiṭən/ bags. ▶にせ物は〔=質の悪い模造品に〕ご注意 〔広告・掲示〕 Beware of poor imitations. (〔参考〕 imitation だと断わって売る場合も多い) ▶この絵はにせ物だ This painting is a forgery [a fake].

-にせよ (⇨にしろ)

にせる 似せる 〔〔B にならって A を作る〕〕 model A on [after] B; 〔〔模範としてまねる〕〕 imitate; 〔〔正確にまねる〕〕 copy; 〔〔偽造する〕〕 forge. ● 父親の筆跡に似せる imitate [copy] one's father's handwriting. ● 署名を似せて forge [counterfeit] (his) signature. ● 絹に似せて作った化学繊維 a synthetic made to imitate [in imitation of] silk. ▶この町はパリに似せて作られた This town was modeled on [after] Paris.

にそう 二曹 〔陸曹〕 sergeant second class; 〔海曹〕 petty officer second class; 〔空曹〕 technical sergeant.

にそう 尼僧 a nun; (カトリックの) a sister; (キリスト教以外の) a priestess.
● 尼僧院 a convent, 《やや古》 a nunnery.

にそくさんもん 二束三文 ● 二束三文の[で] very cheap; 《話》 dirt-cheap; 《話》 for a song. ▶彼は本を二束三文で売った He sold his books very cheap(ly) [dirt-cheap].

にそくのわらじ 二足の草鞋 ● 二足の草鞋をはく〔二つの職業についている〕《書》be engaged in two trades. ▶彼は教師と画家の二足のわらじをはいている〔=教師と画家をして生計を立てている〕He makes a living by teaching and (by) painting.

にだい 荷台 (自転車などの) a carrier; (トラックなどの) a load-carrying platform, (車の屋根に付ける)《米》a luggage rack, 《英》a roof rack.

にたき 煮炊き 图 cooking. (⇨料理)
● 煮炊き(を)する 動 cook.

にだしじる 煮出し汁 soup stock.

にだす 煮出す cook [boil] in order to get flavors of the ingredients; make soup stock.

にたつ 煮立つ boil (up); come* to the 〔〔主に米〕〕a boil. ▶やかんの湯が煮立っている The kettle is boiling [is on the boil]. ▶それが煮たったら塩を少々加えなさい When it comes to the boil, add a pinch of salt to it.

にたてる 煮立てる ● 湯を煮たてる boil (up) water [xhot water]; bring water to the 〔〔主に米〕〕a boil. (⇨煮立つ)

にだな 荷棚 a baggage rack.

にたにた ● にたにた笑う smirk; give a smirk. (⇨にやにや)

にたもの 似た者 ▶あの 2 人は似た者同士だ〔=共通点が多い〕They have a lot in common.
● 似た者夫婦〔夫婦はだんだん似てくるものだ〕The longer they are married, the more they are resembling each other./〔ことわざ〕Like husband, like wife.

にたり (⇨にやり)

にたりよったり 似たり寄ったり ▶その兄弟が学校の成績が似たり寄ったりです〔=ほぼ互角だ〕The brothers' school records nearly match. ▶両者は似たり寄ったりだ〔=あまり差がない〕There's not much difference 〔(優劣はあまり) not much to choose〕between the two. ▶政治家ってみな似たり寄ったりだ〔=同じだ〕Politicians are very (much) alike.

にだんがまえ 二段構え ● 二段構えで対処する have another plan in reserve if the first one fails to work.

にだんベッド 二段ベッド bunk beds, bunks. (**!** 単数で用いると上段か下段のいずれか一つをさす)

*****-にち** -日 a day. (⇨-日) ▶彼は 2-3 日で回復するでしょう He will get well in a few 〔《話》 a couple of〕 days. ▶今日は何日ですか What's the date today?/What's today's date?/What day of the month is it today? ▶これを縮めて What day is (it) today? とすると, 週単位での生活が基本の米英では,「きょうは何曜日ですか」の意となるのが普通》 ▶5 月は何日ありますか How many days are there in May? ▶この何日間か彼女に会っていない I haven't seen her for the past [last] few days. (**!** … these few days は《古》) ▶4 月 16 日の土曜日は出社しなければならない I have to go to work on Saturday, 16th of April.

にちえい 日英 Japan and Britain. ● 日英(間)の友好関係を促進する promote good relations between Japan and Britain.
● 日英協会 the Japan-British Society. ● 日英通商 Anglo-Japanese commerce; commerce between Japan and Britain.

にちがく 日額 daily pay.

にちぎん 日銀 〔〔「日本銀行」の略〕〕 the Bank of Japan.

にちげん

- **日銀券** a Bank of Japan note. ● **日銀総裁** the Governor of the Bank of Japan. ● **日銀短観** the Short-term Economic Survey of Enterprises in Japan; *Tankan*. (参考) 日銀が行う「企業短期経済観測調査」の略) ● **日銀特融** a special loan by the Bank of Japan.

にちげん 日限 a deadline 《*for*》. (⇨期日)

にちじ 日時 the time and date 《*for*, *of*》. ▶次の会合の日時を決める fix *the time and date for* [*of*] *the next meeting*. ▶ご都合のよい日時をお知らせ下さい Please inform us when you are available [when it is convenient for you].

にちじょう 日常 〖毎日〗(どの日もみな) every day 《副詞的に用いる。形容詞は everyday と 1 語につづる》; (1 日単位で) daily; 〖通常〗usually; 〖常に〗always. (⇨普段, 毎日, 通例, いつも) ▶日常の仕事 one's *daily* (通常の) *ordinary*) work; (お決まりの退屈な) one's *routine* jobs. ● 日常卑近な(=ありふれた)例 a *common* [《よく知られた》a *familiar*] example.
▶平穏な日常を送る live in peace *every day*; lead a peaceful life *every day*. (❗後の方はやや堅い言い方)

● **日常茶飯事** ▶今日の日本では交通事故は日常茶飯事だ In Japan today traffic accidents are an *everyday* [a *daily*] occurrence. 《... are *all too common*. ともいえる》

● **日常言語** everyday language. ● **日常生活** one's daily [everyday, ×every day] life.

にちどく 日独 图 Japan and Germany.
—— 日独(間)の 形 Japanese-German.

にちぶ 日舞 〖「日本舞踊」の略〗Japanese dancing.

にちふつ 日仏 Japan and France. ● **日仏関係** relations between Japan and France; Franco-Japanese relations.

にちべい 日米 图 Japan and America [the United States (of America)].
—— 日米(間)の 形 Japanese-American; Japan-U.S. ● 日米貿易を促進する promote trade between *Japan and America*; promote *Japanese-American* [*Japan-U.S.*] trade.
● **日米安全保障条約** the Japan-U.S. Security Treaty.

にちぼつ 日没 (a) sunset 《↔(a) sunrise》. (❗日没時刻は 〖C〗, その光景・空の意では 〖C〗) ▶美しい日没 a beautiful *sunset*. ▶我々は日没時[前]ごろにそこに到着するだろう We'll arrive there at [before; about] *sunset*.

にちや 日夜 〖昼も夜も〗night and day, 《やや話》day and night; 〖24 時間休みなく〗around the clock; 〖常に〗always. (⇨いつも) ▶彼は日夜勉学に励んでいる He is studying very hard *day and night*.

にちゃく 二着 ▶二着になる finish [come in] second 《*in the 100 meter dash*》; be a runner-up.

にちゃにちゃ ▶にちゃにちゃする be sticky; 《くっつく》be gummy, 《話》gooey. ▶ガムをにちゃにちゃかむ chew gum *audibly*.

*に**ちよう(び)** 日曜(日) Sunday 《略 Sun.》. (参考) 伝統的には日曜日は週の第 1 日目とされているが, 今日では週の最後の日と考えられている) ▶日曜日に on *Sunday*. (❗(1) 文脈により, 次の日曜, 前の日曜, いつもの日曜のいずれも表す. (2) on Sunday*s*, *every* Sunday は「日曜日にはいつも」, on *the* Sunday は「その日曜日に」, on *a* Sunday は「ある日曜日に」の意. (3) 《話》ではしばしば on を省略する) ▶ある晴れた日曜日の朝に on a fine *Sunday* morning; on the morning of a fine *Sunday*. ▶この前[次]の日曜日に (×on) last [next] *Sunday*. (⇨この前, 今度の) ● 先週[来週]の日曜日に on *Sunday* last [next]

にっき

week. (❗「来週の日曜日」は《英やや話》では (on) *Sunday* week ともいう. ⇨先週, 来週) ▶日曜日は洗濯をする On *Sunday*(s) I do the washing. (❗複数形にすると習慣の観念が強くなる) ▶日曜日にアルバイトをすれば小遣いに困らない If I have a *Sunday* job, I can pay my way.

会話 「1 月 12 日はどこにいたの」「1 月 12 日？」「ええ, 日曜日だったわよ」"Where were you on January 12?" "January 12?" "Yeah. It was a *Sunday*." (❗不定冠詞 a は「他の曜日でなくて」を含意)

● **日曜画家** a Sunday painter. ● **日曜学校** a Sunday school. ● **日曜大工** (人) a Sunday carpenter; a do-it-yourselfer; (仕事) do-it-yourself. (関連) 日曜大工の店 a do-it-yourself store) ● **日曜版** (新聞の) a Sunday supplement.

にちようひん 日用品 daily necessities.

にちりん 日輪 the sun. (⇨太陽)

にちろ 日露, 日ロ Japan and Russia. ● 日ロ間の友好的な関係 friendly relations *between Japan and Russia*.
● **日露交流協会** the Japan-Russia Exchange Society. ● **日露戦争** 〖歴史〗the Russo-Japanese War of 1904-05.

-について 《関して》about ..., of ..., on .... (⇨ついて)

にっか 日課 〖学業, 授業〗a daily lesson; 〖仕事〗one's daily work. ▶生徒に日課を課す impose *daily lessons* [*work*] on the students. ▶日課を終える finish one's *daily work* [*routines*]. ▶散歩を日課にする (=必ず散歩をするように心がけている) *make a point of* taking a walk. ▶通例 take a walk every day などのようにいう) ▶私は少なくとも 1 日に 10 語は英単語を覚えることを日課としている I'm trying to memorize at least ten English words a day.

ニッカーボッカー knickerbockers. (❗単に knickers ともいう)

にっかい 肉塊 a lump of flesh [meat]; 〖肉体〗a body; the flesh.

ニッカでんち ニッカ電池 a nickel-cadmium [a Ni-Cd] battery [cell].

にっかわしい 似つかわしい suitable. (⇨ふさわしい)

にっかん 日刊 —— 日刊(の) 形 daily.
● **日刊紙** a daily (newspaper).

にっかん 日韓 Japan and Korea.
—— 日韓の 形 Japan-Korea; Japanese-Korean. ● 日韓のあつれき friction *between Japan and Korea*; *Japan-Korea* friction.

にっかんてき 肉感的 (⇨肉感(にっかん)的)

-につき 日記 ❶ 〖単位〗(...ごとに) a; per (❗per は主に商業英語. 日常英語では a が好まれる); (...に対して) for ... (❗each, every や数詞の前で) ▶1 日につき 50 ドルを支払う pay fifty dollars a [*per*] day.
▶間違い 1 点につき 3 点減点する I'll subtract three points *for* each mistake.

❷ 〖理由〗because of .... ▶雨天につきテニスの試合はとりやめます We are going to call off the tennis match *because of* [*owing to*] the rain.

❸ 〖関して〗about ..., on .... (⇨関して) ▶その件につき君と話し合いたい I'd like to talk with you *about the matter*.

*に**っき** 日記 a diary /dáiəri/. (❗dairy (酪農場) /déəri/ と混同しないこと); 〖書〗a journal. ● それを日記に書いておく write it (down) [record it, ×keep it] in one's *diary*. ▶英語で日記を書く write a *diary* in English. ▶私は日記をつけている I keep a *diary* [a *journal*]./(毎日日記帳に書く) I write in my *diary* every day.

- 日記帳 a diary.

にっきゅう 日給 daily wages. (⇨週給) ● 日給いくらで働く work *by the day*.

にっきょうそ 日教組 〖『日本教職員組合』の略〗the Japan Teachers' Union.

にっきん 日勤 ● a work on the day shift.

ニックネーム 〖あだ名〗a nickname.

にづくり 荷造り 名 packing. ▶荷造りはできましたか (出発の準備として) Are you packed yet?/Have you finished packing up?/(搬送用に) Have you done your *packing*? (❗最初が最も口語的)
──荷造りする 動 ● 本を荷造りする *pack* the books.

につけ 煮付け ● 魚の煮付け (説明的に) fish boiled and seasoned with sugar and soy sauce.

にっけい 日系 ● 日系一世 an Issei. (⇨一世❶)
● 日系企業 a Japanese company 《*in* Singapore》. ● 日系二世 a Nisei. (⇨二世❶) ● 日系米人 a Japanese-American; an American of Japanese descent [ancestry].

にっけい 日経 ● 日経株価指数 300 the *Nikkei* Stock Index 300. ● 日経平均株価 the *Nikkei* Stock Average; the *Nikkei* stock index. ● 日経平均株価の急落 a drastic decline in the *Nikkei*.

にっけい 肉桂 〖木〗a cinnamon tree; 《香辛料》cinnamon.

ニッケル 名 〖化学〗nickel /níkl/ 〈元素記号 Ni〉.
──ニッケルの 形 nickel; 《めっきの》nickel-plated.
● ニッケルカドミウム電池 (⇨ニッカド電池)

****にっこう** 日光 sunlight; sun, sunshine; a sunbeam.

> **使い分け** sunlight 太陽から届く光を表す. 不可算名詞.
> sun, sunshine 太陽から届く光および熱を表す. 不可算名詞.
> sunbeam 太陽光線を表すやや文語的な語. 可算名詞で複数形で用いることが多い.

● 焼けつくような日光 a [the] blazing *sun*. (❗形容詞を伴うときはしばしば a 〜) ● ふとんを日光消毒する disinfect the bedding with [by] *sunlight* [in the *sun*(*shine*)]. ● 日光浴をする bask 《英》bathe /béiθ/ in the *sun*(*shine*); sunbathe; do (some) *sunbathing* (❗通例 take [have] a sunbath とはいわない. ● 日光のよく当たる部屋 a *sunny* room; a room having a lot of *sun* [*sunshine*]. ● 日光を入れる[さえぎる] let in [shut out] the *sun* [*sunshine*]. ● シャツを日光で乾かす dry the shirt in the *sun* [*sunshine*]. ▶この薬を直射日光に当てはいけない Don't put this medicine in [expose this medicine to] the direct *sun* [*sunlight*, *sunshine*]. ▶木々の間から日光が差し込んできた Shafts of *sunlight* [Beams of *sunlight*, *Sunbeams*] came through the branches.

にっこり ▶少女は私を見てにっこり笑った. 私も彼女ににっこりほほえみかえした The girl gave me a *broad smile*. I gave a *big smile* back at [《まれに》to] her. (❗ a broad [a big] smile で大きく一つほほえむ感じが出る. 第 2 文ごでは it に置き換えることは不可)/The girl *smiled broadly* at me. I *smiled broadly* back at her. ▶いくわよ，カメラに向かってにっこりして Are you ready? *Smile* for [at] the camera.

にっさん 日参 ──日参する 動 come here [go there] every day [daily]; 《書》pay a daily visit 《to》.

にっさん 日産 daily output [production].

にっし 日誌 a diary; 《書》a journal. (❗diary は個人的, journal は公的記録の性格を持つ) ● 学級日誌 a *daily record* of one's class. ● 航海日誌 a logbook. ● 日誌をつける (習慣として) keep a *diary* [a *journal*]; (1 回ごとに) write in one's *diary* [*journal*].

にっしゃびょう 日射病 sunstroke; 〖医学〗(熱射病) heatstroke. ● 日射病にかかる suffer from [get] *sunstroke*. (❗「日光にかかっている」は have [be suffering from] sunstroke)

にっしょう 日照 sunshine.
● 日照権 the right to sunshine; 《英》the right of light. ● 日照時間 the daylight hours.

にっしょうき 日章旗 (the flag of) the Rising Sun; the national flag of Japan.

にっしょく 日食 〖天文〗a solar eclipse; an eclipse of the sun. ● 皆既[部分]日食 a total [a partial] *eclipse of the sun*.

にっしんげっぽ 日進月歩 (x a) steady [rapid] progress /prágres/. (❗steady は「着実な」, rapid は「急速な」進歩を表す. ×steady and rapid progress と二つを併用することはできない) (⇨進歩) ▶科学の発展は日進月歩である Science *is making steady* [*rapid*] *progress*.

にっしんせんそう 日清戦争 the Sino-Japanese War.

にっすう 日数 (the number of) days; 〖期間〗(a) time. ▶その仕事は日数がかかった It took (me) *a long time* [*so many days*] to do the work.

ニッチ ● ニッチ産業 〖すき間産業〗niche industry.
● ニッチマーケット a niche market.

にっちもさっちも ▶交渉にはにっちもさっちもいかなくなっている(=行き詰まっている) The negotiations are *in a deadlock* [*at a standstill*]. ▶株が暴落して彼にはにっちもさっちもいかない(=窮地に陥っている)《話》He's *in a fix* [He's *got himself into a fix*] because the market slumped.

にっちゅう 日中 〖昼間〗daytime, day. (⇨昼❷) ▶森の中は日中でさえ暗かった It was dark in the woods even *in the daytime*. ▶彼らは日中休まず働いた They worked without taking a break *during the day*.

にっちゅう 日中 〖日本と中国〗Japan and China.
● 日中国交正常化 the resumption of diplomatic ties [relations] between Japan and China.
● 日中戦争 the Japanese-Chinese War; the Sino-Japanese War. ● 日中平和友好条約 the Japan-China [Sino-Japanese] Treaty of Peace and Friendship; 《正式名称》Treaty of Peace and Friendship between Japan and the People's Republic of China.

にっちょう 日朝 Japan and North Korea.
● 日朝関係 Japan-North Korea relations. ● 日朝国交正常化交渉 normalization talks between Japan and North Korea.

にっちょく 日直 day duty. ● 日直である be on [have] *day duty*.

にってい 日程 〖仕事などの〗a (day's) schedule [program], (⇨予定); 〖旅の〗a trável plàn, 《書》an itinerary /aitínərèri/; 〖議事の〗the agenda /ədʒéndə/. ● 旅の日程を立てる make [plan] out an *itinerary*. ● 議事日程に上げる place [put] 《the item》 *on the agenda*. ● 試合の日程を変更する *reschedule* the match 《from Monday to Friday》. (❗reschédule は「…の日程[予定]を(…から…に)変更する」の意) ▶今日は日程が詰まっている I have a full [a heavy, a tight] *schedule* today./My *schedule* today is filled./《話》I'm booked up today. ▶今日の日程は? What's your *schedule* [*program*, (計画) *plan*] for today? (⇨スケジュール)

にっ ●にっと笑う grin; give a toothy smile.

ニット 图 knitwear. ── ニットの 圈 knitted 《skirt》.

にっとう 日当 [1日の手当] a daily allowance; [日給] a daily wage (❗通例後置修飾で). ▶日当をもらう receive a *daily allowance*. ▶日当1万円出します We'll give you *wages* of 10,000 yen *a day* [*a daily wage* of 10,000 yen]./We'll *pay* 10,000 yen *a day*.

ニッパー (工具)《a pair of》nippers.

にっぽう 日報 (日ごとの報告) a daily report; [印刷配布されるもの] a daily bulletin; (新聞名として) a daily (newspaper). ▶日報を提出する submit a *daily report*. ▶売り上げ日報 a *daily* sales *report*.

にっぽん 日本 Japan. (⇨日本(にほん))

にっぽんえいたいぐら 『日本永代蔵』 *The Japanese Family Storehouse*. (参考) 井原西鶴の浮世草子.

にっぽんじん 日本人 a Japanese. (⇨日本(にほん)人)

にっぽんばれ 日本晴れ (⇨日本(にほん)晴れ).

につまる 煮詰まる boil down (❗比喩的には「結局は...になる, 煎(じ)つめれば...だ」の意); (結論 [解決] に近づく) get* close to a conclusion [a solution]; (最終段階に達する) come* to the final stage 《of》. ▶労使交渉は煮詰まってきた The negotiations between labor and management *are coming to a* successful *conclusion*.

につめる 煮詰める boil ... down (⇨煮詰まる); (結論に近づける) bring*... to a conclusion. ▶ソースがとろっとなるまで煮詰める *boil* the sauce *down* until it is really thick [it thickens].

にてひなる 似て非なる completely different from each other; 《英話》like chalk and cheese.

にても(に)つかない 似ても(似)つかない (⇨似る [成句])

にてん 二転 ●二転三転する(=情勢が何度も変わる) change again and again. (❗xfrom time to time, xevery so often は「時々」の意で不適)

にと 二兎 ●二兎を追う者は一兎をも得ず (ことわざ) If you run after two hares, you will catch neither.

***にど** 二度 [二回] twice; [二度目] the second time; [再度] again. ▶1-2度 once or /ə/ twice. ●2-3度 two or /ə/ three *times*. (❗twice or thrice は今は《古》) ●二度続けて *twice* over. ▶この雑誌は月に二度発行されます This magazine is published *twice* a month./This is a *twice*-monthly magazine. ▶二度見る必要はない You don't need to look *twice*./(一度見れば十分) One look is enough. ●二度に(分けて)やれ《話》Do it *at* [*in*] *twice*.

①【二度と】 ▶よく聞いて, 二度と言いませんから Listen now, I won't say it *again* [*twice*]. ▶あんな所へは二度と行かない I'll *never* [I won't *ever*] go there *again*. (❗強調して I *never* will go there *again*. ともいう. さらに *Never* will I go there *again*. も文語的, 詠嘆的だが) ▶二度といたしません (以後気をつけます) I'll never do it *again*. (⇨[上例])/(目的語を主語にして) It won't happen *again*. ▶彼は二度とない機会を逸した He missed the opportunity [chance] of a lifetime.

②【二度目の[に]】 ▶彼の二度目の留学 his *second* study abroad. ▶彼は二度目に試験に合格した He passed the exam on his *second* try [in his *second* attempt]. ▶ここへ来たのはこれで二度目だ This is the *second* time (that) I've been here. ●二度あることは三度ある What happens twice [two times] will happen thrice [three times]. (❗回数が他と対照されるときは two times がよく用い

られる. それ以外は twice が普通)/(悪い事は) Misfortunes never come alone. / Bad things (always) come in threes. (❗in threes は「三つずつ」の意)

にとう 二等 [乗り物の] (the) second class; (客船などの特別2等) a cabin class; [競技などでの] second place (⇨二位). ●2等 second-class. ●2等で行く travel *second class*; 《話》go *second*.

にとうしん 二等親 →親等.

にとうだて 二頭立て ●二頭立ての馬車 a carriage drawn by two horses; a carriage and pair.

にとうぶん 二等分 ●二等分する 働 (等しく分ける) divide 《it》 into two equal parts [portions]. ▶リンゴを二等分する(=半分に切る) *cut* the apple *in half* [*into halves*]. ●円を二等分する〖数学〗bisect /báisɛkt/ the circle. ●二等分線 〖数学〗a bisector.

にとうへんさんかくけい 二等辺三角形 〖数学〗an isosceles /aɪsɑ́səliːz/ triangle.

にとうりゅう 二刀流 〖剣術〗fencing with a sword in each hand. ▶彼は二刀流だ(=酒も甘いものも好む) He likes both sweet things and alcoholic drinks./He drinks and has a sweet tooth as well.

-にとって (に対して) to ...; (には) for .... (⇨-とって).

にどでま 二度手間 ●二度手間になる have to do 《it》 over again.

にどね 二度寝 ▶今朝は二度寝してしまった I woke up rather early this morning. I felt sleepy and went to sleep again.

ニトログリセリン 〖化学〗nitroglycerin(e) /nàɪtroʊglísərɪn/.

ニトロセルロース 〖化学〗cellulose nitrate.

ニトロベンゼン 〖化学〗nitrobenzene.

にないて 担い手 ●一家の担い手 the breadwinner in one's family.

***になう** 担う ❶ [引き受ける] accept; take*. ●重要な役割を担う assume [take 《on》] an important role. (❗後の方が口語的) ▶日本は国際的な責任を担うべきだ Japan should *accept* [*take*] international responsibilities. ▶日本の将来は君たちが担っている Japan's future *rests* [*depends*] *on* [*upon*] you. ▶彼は私たちの期待を担っている Our hopes *are placed* [*are pinned*] *on* him.

❷ [背負う] carry 《it》 on one's shoulder [back].

ににんさんきゃく 二人三脚 (競技)《run》a three-legged race. ●二人三脚で...する work together 《to do》; coóperate 《with him to do [in doing]》.

にぬき 荷抜き pilferage. ●輸送中に荷抜きされる be stolen [pilfered] in transit.

にぬし 荷主 [[積み出し人]] a shipper (❗輸送手段は空, 陸のこともある); [[荷送り人]] a consignor; [[持ち主]] the owner of the goods.

にねんせい 二年生 ❶ [[生徒]] a second-year student [(小学生)] pupil 《in high school, at Asahi High School》; [(米)] (大学・4年制高校の) a sophomore, (短大の) a senior, (3年制高校の) a junior, (小[中; 高等]学校の) a second [an eighth; an eleventh] grader. (⇨一年生, 学年)

❷ [[植物]] a biennial (plant).

にのあし 二の足 ●二の足を踏む ▶彼女はそのパーティーに参加することに二の足を踏んでいる She *is hesitating* [*hesitant*] *about going* to the party. (⇨ためらう)

にのうで 二の腕 the upper arm. ●二の腕を出す show (all of) one's *arm*(s).

にのく 二の句 ●二の句が継(つ)げない ●あきれて二の句が

にのつぎ 二の次 〖第2位の〗secondary;〖2次的に重要な〗of secondary importance. ▶それは二の次 That's a *secondary* matter./That matter is *of secondary importance.*/(延期できる) That matter *can wait*. ▶彼女は自分の時間をまず育児と家事に使い,自分の楽しみのために使うことはあったとしても二の次になってしまう She is using [spending] her time for child care and house chores first and only *secondarily*, if at all, for her own pleasure.

にのまい 二の舞い (同じ失敗) the same mistake.
● 二の舞を演じる ▶彼の二の舞いを演じた I made *the same mistake* as he did./(繰り返した) I repeated his mistake.

にのや 二の矢 the second arrow.
● 二の矢が継げない fail to make the second [another] attempt (*to do; at doing*).

—には 〖〖基準を表して〗…としては; …にとっては〗for …;〖…に対して〗to …;〖…の時には〗on …, in …, at …;〖…の場所には〗on …, in …, at …

解説 日本語の「…には」は上記の前置詞を用いて表せることが多いが,主語や目的語を強調することによっても可能なことがある.

▶休暇にはどこに行くの Where are you going *for* your vacation? (❗*for* は「…を過ごすために」の意)
▶野球をするには寒すぎる It's too cold *for* baseball.
▶ダブルスをやるには 1 人足りない We're one short *for* doubles. ▶この本を読むのに私には難しい This book is difficult *for* me to read./It is difficult *for* me to read this book. ▶彼は老人には親切だ He is kind *to* old people. ▶雨の日には野球の試合は中止されます Baseball games are canceled *on* a rainy day. ▶太郎は 7 時には家に戻ってきます Taro will be home *at* [*by*] seven o'clock (*at the latest*). (❗(1) *by* は「…までに」の意で期限までに完了すると限度を表し, *at the latest* は「遅くとも」の意. (2) Taro *will have been* home … のように未来完了形を用いると,特定の未来時点で家に戻っていることを明示する言い方となるが,日常英語では上例のように単なる未来形で表すことが多い) ▶運動場には子供たちが元気よく走り回る姿があった *On* [*In*] the playground, children were seen running around with good spirits. (❗校舎内などと対比する場合は文頭に移動させて強調する) ▶おじさんにはいくつか欠点があるがそれでも私は彼が好きだ My uncle has a few faults, but I still like him./《やや書》With his few faults, I still like my uncle.

会話「それはすぐにはできないな」「それには好きなだけ時間をかけろよ」"It can't be done quickly." "Take as long as you like *over* it." (❗「…について」の意)

にばい 二倍 twice; two-fold; double. (⇨倍)
にばん 二番 the second; number two (《略 No.2》).
●(競技・競争で) 2番の人 a runner-up. ▶右から2番目の少年 *the second* boy from the right. ● 日本で2番目の大都市 *the second* largest city in Japan; the largest city in Japan *but one*. ● 2番目の妹 one's *second* oldest [《米書・英》eldest] sister. ●下から2番目の弟 one's *second* youngest brother;《主に英》one's youngest brother *but one*. ▶彼は2番目に来た He was *the second* (man) to come./He came *second*. ▶そのマラソンで2番だった He was *second* [*runner-up*] in the marathon. (❗この場合通例 second, runner-up は冠詞を省略する)/(2 着で入った) He came in

[finished] *second* in the marathon. ▶彼女は3年生の中で2番です She is *the second best* [*is second*] of the third-year students./(2 位を占める) She ranks *second* among the third graders. (❗third graders は「小学3年生」)

にばんせんじ 二番煎じ 〖お茶の〗a second brew of tea;〖意見・作品などの〗a rehash /rɪ́hæʃ/ (*of*).
にびいろ 鈍色 dark gray. ● 鈍色の dark gray.
にひゃくとおか 二百十日 〖立春から 210 日目〗(説明的に) the 210th day from the beginning of spring (according to the lunar calendar), which approximately falls on the first day of September.
ニヒリスト 〖虚無主義者〗a nihilist /náiəlɪst/.
ニヒリズム 〖虚無主義〗nihilism /náiəlɪzm/.
ニヒル — ニヒルな 形〖虚無的な〗nihilistic /naiəlístɪk/.
にぶ 二部 〖二つの部分〗two parts; (第 2 の部分) the second part;〖刊行物等の部数〗two copies;〖夜間部〗the evening division (*of* a university). ● 二部合唱 (⇨二部合唱)
● 二部作 a series of two books [plays]. (関連 三部作 a trilogy)

*****にぶい** 鈍い dull;〖刃先などが〗blunt (-mm-);〖動作などが〗slow;〖感性が〗insensitive, not perceptive. ● 切れ味の鈍いナイフ a *blunt* [a *dull*] knife. (❗blunt はもともと切れ味が悪いこと, dull は使用の末に切れ味が悪くなったことを表す) ● 鈍い音を立てて with a *dull* [a *thick*] sound. ● 頭の鈍い子 a *dull* [《話》a *dim*] child. ▶ランプが鈍い光を放っていた The lamp gave a *dim* [a *dull*] light. (❗前の方が普通) ▶胃に鈍い痛みを感じます I feel [have] a *dull* pain in the stomach.

にぶおんぷ 二分音符〖音楽〗《米》a half note,《英》a minim.
にぶがっしょう 二部合唱 a chorus in two parts.
● ホワイトクリスマスを二部合唱する *chorus* [*sing*] "White Christmas" *in two parts*.
にふくめる 煮含める simmer in broth until well seasoned.
にふだ 荷札 a label /léɪbl/, a tag. (⇨札(ふだ)) ● 旅行かばんに荷札を付ける put a *label* on [attach a *label* to] one's suitcase; label [tag] one's suitcase.

*****にぶる** 鈍る 〖刃物などが〗get* dull;〖弱まる〗weaken. ▶このナイフは切れ味が鈍ってきた This knife has gotten *dull* [*×blunt*]. (❗blunt はもともと切れないことを表すのでここでは不可 (⇨鈍い[第 1 句例])) ▶彼女は年のせいで聴覚が鈍ってしまった Her hearing *was dulled* by age. ▶その手紙を読んだら決心が鈍った My resolution *weakened* [*was shaken*] when I read the letter./The letter *shook* my resolution. ▶疲れると筆が鈍る. そんなときには海へ散歩に行くことにしている When I'm tired, I can't go on writing smoothly. Then, I go for a walk on the beach. ▶雨のために選挙の出足が鈍ってしまった The rain *put a brake on* the voters' turnout.

にぶん 二分 名 〖二つの部分に分けること〗a division into two parts;〖2 分の 1〗(a) half (複 halves). ▶10 の 2 分の 1 は 5 *Half* [*The half*] of ten is five.
— 二分する 動 divide《it》into two parts [in two, in half]. ● 仕事を二分する *divide* the work *into two parts; halve* the work.
にぶんおんぷ 二分音符 (⇨二分(ぶ)音符)
にべもない にべもなく (=そっけない)返事をする give a *curt* answer. ▶にべもなく(=きっぱりと)断られた I was *flatly* [(ぶっきらぼうに) *bluntly*] refused./(あからさまに) I was refused *point-blank*./I was given

にぼし 煮干し small boiled and dried fish (for making stock).

にほん 日本 Japan /dʒəpǽn/. ●日本(人[語])の Jàpanése. ●日本式 (*in*) a Japanese style [fashion]. ●日本化する Jápanìze. ●日本の文物 things Jàpanése (❗) Jápanèse thíngs は「おみやげ」などの物質的なもの) ●純日本風の家 a house in a purely *Japanese style*. ●日本初のプロバレーボール選手 *the first* professional volleyball player *in Japan*. ▶日本の経済は急激な円高に苦しんでいる *Japan's* economy is suffering from the sharp appreciation of the yen. (❗) *Japan's* はジャーナリズムでよく用いられ, *Japan* economy とするより普通) ▶日本は景色の美しい国です *Japan* is a country of scenic beauty./The scenery of *Japan* is beautiful.

① 【日本＋社会的・文化的な語】●日本画 a Japanese painting. (❗ 画法そのものをさす場合は無冠詞) ●日本学 Japanology. ●日本学者［研究家］ a Japanologist. ●日本髪 the traditional Japanese hairstyle (for women). ●日本嫌い a Japánophòbe. ●日本三景 the three most famous scenic places in Japan. ●日本史 Japanese history; the history of Japan. ●日本時間 (*at* 13:00) Japan time. ●日本酒 *sake*. ●日本製品 Japanese products; products made in Japan [of Japanese make]. ●日本たたき Japan bashing. ●日本茶 Japanese tea. ●日本刀 a Japanese sword. ●日本脳炎 [医学] Japanese encephalitis. ●日本びいき（人） a Jápánophile. ●日本舞踊 Japanese dancing. ●日本間 a Japanese-style room. ●日本料理 Japanese food [dishes, cooking].

② 【日本＋地理名・組織名】●日本アルプス the Japan Alps. ●日本医師会 the Japan Medical Association. ●日本海流 the Japan Current. ●日本教職員組合 the Japan Teachers' Union. ●日本銀行 the Bank of Japan 《略 BOJ》. ●日本芸術院 the Japan Art Academy. ●日本経団連 the Japan Business Federation 《略 JBF》. ●日本工業規格 Japanese Industrial Standards 《略 JIS》. ●日本放送協会 Japan Broadcasting Corporation; the NHK. ●日本農林規格 Japanese Agricultural Standards 《略 JAS》. ●日本列島 the Japanese Archipelago /ɑːrkəpéləgòu/ [Islands].

にほんかい 日本海 the Sea of Japan. (❗ the Japan Sea ともいうが the Sea of Japan の方が正式. 韓国では the Eastern Sea という)

にほんご 日本語 Japanese, 《書》 the Japanese language; (学科) Japanese language.

DISCOURSE
日本語がいかに複雑か, 例を示そう. 第一に, 日本語には三種類の文字がある. …第二に, 日本語には敬語, すなわち敬意を示す言語がある Let me give you some examples of how complicated *the Japanese language* is. **First**, there are three different kinds of letters. … **Second**, it has Keigo, or honorific expressions … (❗ first(ly)～, second(ly)～(第一に…第二に～)は列挙に用いるディスコースマーカー. First, Second は必ずしも組み合わせて用いる必要はない)

にほんしょき 『日本書記』 *Chronicles of Japan*. (参考 舎人親王らによる日本最初の勅撰の歴史書)

にほんじん 日本人 (1人) a Japanese (❗ 単・複同形); (全体) the Japanese (❗ 複数扱い). ●日本人らしい Japanese. ▶彼の名前は日本人にはなじみ深い His name is familiar to *Japanese* (people). (❗ people を添える方が客観的な言い方. 日本語が「我々日本人」となっている場合でも, 特に他民族と対比する場合を除いて … *to us* Japanese. はやや不自然) ▶この町には日本人がたくさん住んでいる A lot of [《やや書》 Many] *Japanese* live in this town. ▶日本人は平和を愛する国民です Japanese people love peace./*The Japanese* are a peace-loving people. (❗ the Japanese は主に日本人以外が用いる客観的なやや堅い言い方だが, 話し手が「日本人とは〈みんな〉こういうものだ」といった固定観念を持っていることを暗示することがある) ▶私は彼が日本人だとは知らなかった I didn't know that he was (a) *Japanese*. (❗ be 動詞の後では国籍を強調する場合を除いて形容詞を用いるのが普通)

にほんだて 二本立て (興行などの) a double bill; (映画の) a double feature, 《米話》 a twin bill. ▶あの劇場でチャップリンの2本立てをやっている They are showing a Chaplin *double feature* [a *double feature* of Chaplin's movies] at the theater.

にほんのしめったふうどについて 『日本の湿った風土について』 *On the Damp Climate of Japan*. (参考 真壁仁の詩集)

にほんばれ 日本晴れ ideal [very nice] weather; a clear and cloudless sky. (⇒快晴) ▶今日は日本晴れだ. 空には雲一つない Today is a *fine* day. There's no clouds in the sky. (❗ (1) 全文で日本晴れの感じが出る. (2) There are…. と複数呼応をしないのは〈話〉)

にほんぶんかしかん 『日本文化私観』 *A Personal View of Japanese Culture*. (参考 坂口安吾の評論)

にまいがい 二枚貝 【魚介】 a bivalve.

にまいかんばん 二枚看板 (中心となる2人の出演者) the two star actors [actresses]; (代表的な二つのもの) the two distinctive features 《*of*》.

にまいごし 二枚腰 【相撲】 【比喩的】 one's last-minute strength to turn the tables on one's opponent.

にまいじた 二枚舌 ▶私は二枚舌を使うやつには我慢できない I can't stand a *fork-tongued* fellow [(二心のあるうそつき) a *double-dealing* liar].

にまいめ 二枚目 (役) a lover's part; (美男) a good-looking [a handsome] (young) man 《men》; 《米俗》a hunk (of a man) (❗ 顔も体も魅力的な男).

-にも (⇒-も)

にもうさく 二毛作 double-cropping; two crops a year. ●二毛作をする double-crop.

にもかかわらず though. (⇒かかわらず)

にもつ 荷物 ❶【手荷物】 《主に米》 baggage, 《主に英》 luggage (❗ いずれも集合的に用い単数扱い. 数えるときは a piece [two pieces] of … のようにいう); 〖(personal) 〗 one's (personal) belongings, one's things (❗ 後の方が口語的); 〖積み荷〗 a load; (貨物) freight /fréit/, (a) cargo 《複 ～(e)s》 (⇒荷); 〖包み〗 a package. ●荷物がある pack one's *belongings* [*things*] (*in* a suitcase). ●荷物をまとめて出て行く pack up [pack one's bag(s)] and leave. ●荷物を解く undo a *package*; unpack a *package*. ●重い荷物を肩にかついで運ぶ carry a heavy *load* on one's shoulders. ●荷物をしっかり口をかける tie a *package* tightly. ▶税関で徹底的に荷物を調べられた I had my *baggage* [(スーツケース) *suitcase*] thoroughly examined at the customs. ▶お荷物はどのくらいありますか How much [How many pieces of] *baggage* do you have? (❗ ×How many baggages…? とはいわない) ▶荷物は散逸しないように

1か所にまとめておきなさい Keep your *things* [《話》*stuff*] together so that they won't be scattered and lost.
❷[負担]《お荷物》

にもの 煮物 (説明的に) vegetables [fish] cooked with soy, sugar, and other condiments. ● 豆の煮物 boiled beans.

にゃあ(お) (猫の鳴き声) a mew /mjúː/, 《米》 a miaow /miáu/.

にゃあにゃあ ● にゃあにゃあ鳴く mew /mjúː/, 《米》 meow /miáu/. (❗mew はカモメなどの鳴き声に用いられることもある) ▶ 猫はおなかがへるとにゃあにゃあ鳴く Cats *mew* [*meow*] when they are hungry. ▶ 彼は猫が戸の外でにゃあにゃあと鳴く声を聞いた He heard a cat *mewing* [the *mew* of a cat] outside the door.

にやく 荷役 (船荷のあげおろし) loading and unloading; (人) a docker, 《米》 a longshoreman (-men).

にやけた (男が変にしゃれた) foppish; (女々しい)《やや書》effeminate. ● にやけた若者 a *foppish* young man, a young fop; an *effeminate* young man.

にやっかい 荷厄介 名 ● 荷厄介になる be a burden (*to*); be encumbered (*with*).
── 荷厄介な 形 burdensome; (かさばって) cumbersome; (面倒な) troublesome.

にやにや ── 副 grin (-nn-) (*at, to* oneself); smirk (*at*). (❗grin は声を立てずに口を歯が見える程大きく開く笑い方で、喜び、軽蔑のいずれの気持ちにも用いられる. smirk は自分の成功や人の失敗を喜ぶような不快な笑いをさす) ▶ 彼は私が個人的な質問にとまどうのを見てにやにやした He *grinned* [*smirked*] *at* my embarrassment of not being able to answer some personal questions. ▶ 彼は初孫の写真を見ながら1人でにやにやしていた He *was grinning to* himself as he looked at the pictures of his first grandchild. ▶「あなた、頭にめがねをのっけて何を探しているの」と彼女はにやにやして言った "Darling, what are you trying to find with your glasses on top of your head?" she *smirked* [said *with a smirk*]. ▶ おい、君、何がおかしいんだ. にやにやするな Hey, man, it's not funny! Take [Wipe] the *grin* off your face. (❗that grin にすると「そのようなにやにや笑い」といったさらに強い怒りが込められる)
(事情) 叱責されたときなどの日本人の困惑の笑いは相手を小馬鹿にしていると誤解されやすい

にやり ● にやりとする (⇨にやにや、ほくそ笑む) ● 彼ににやりと笑ってオーケーの合図をする give him a thumbs-up sign *with a* (*big*) *grin*; give him a (*big*) *grin* and make a thumbs-up sign. (❗thumbs-up は両手の親指の腹を相手の方に向けて立てる身ぶりで了解、賛成などを表す. a big [a broad] smile と交換可)

ニュアンス [＜フランス語]〖語の微妙な違い〗a nuance /n(j)úːɑːns/, a shade of meaning;〖言葉の含み〗overtones. ▶ 彼は演説の微妙なニュアンスは分からなかった He missed the delicate *nuances* of the speech. ▶ この二つの語はニュアンスが少し違う These two words are slightly different in *nuance* [have slightly different *nuances*]. ▶ 彼の言ったことは私の言ったこととはややニュアンスが異なる What he said has some *overtones* different from what I said.

にゅういき 入域 ● 緊急入域 emergency entry.

にゅういん 入院 hospitalization. ● 入院生活に入る apply for *admission to the hospital* 《米》 [*to* hospital 《英》]. ▶ 彼は入院と退院を繰り返していた He *had been in* and *out of* (*the*) *hospital*.
── 入院する 動 go* to [go into, 《やや書》enter] (*the*) *hospital*. (❗通例《米》では冠詞なしではつかない)(⇨病院) ▶ 彼女をすぐ入院させた We *sent* [*took*] her *to* (*the*) *hospital* at once./(入院させられた) She *was hospitalized* at once.
(会話)「彼は脚を折って入院しているのよ」「まあ本当! 大変ね. どれくらい入院することになりそうなの」「あと2, 3週間と言われているの」"He *is in* (*the*) *hospital* with a broken leg." "Oh, really? How awful! How long does he have to stay there?" "A couple more weeks, they say."
● 入院加療 hospital treatment. ● 入院患者 an inpatient. (❗outpatient (外来患者)に対する語. 通例 patient でよい) ● 入院費 hospital charges.

にゅういんりょう 乳飲料 lactic drinks.

にゅうえき 乳液 (化粧用の) milky lotion.

にゅうえん 入園 ── 入園する 動 enter [be admitted to]....
● 入園料 (植物園などの) an admission charge [fee]; (幼稚園などの) an entrance fee.

ニューオーリンズ〖米国の都市〗New Orleans /n(j)úː ɔːrliːənz/.

にゅうか 入荷 名 arrival of goods. ── 入荷する 動 arrive, come in.

にゅうか 乳化 emulsification.
● 乳化剤 an emulsifier.

にゅうか 乳菓 a sweet made from milk; lactic candy.

にゅうかい 入会 (仲間に加わること) joining; (入ることと) entrance (*to*); (入会許可) admission (*to*). ● クラブの入会を申し込む apply for *admission to* [*membership of*] a club.
── 入会する 動 (加わる) join; (入会を許可される) be admitted (*to, into*); (会員になる) become* a member (*of*). ▶ 彼は去年英語研究会に入会した He joined [became a member of, was admitted to, entered] an English society last year.
● 入会金 an entrance [an admission] fee (*to*). ● 入会者 (会員) a member (*of*); (新しく入った会員) an entrant (*to*).

にゅうかく 入閣 ── 入閣する 動 join [《やや書》enter] the Cabinet; become a member of the Cabinet [a Cabinet member].

***にゅうがく 入学** 名 entrance (*into*); (入学許可) admission (*to*); (登録) enrollment (*at, in*). ● 大学入学 *entrance* into college. ● 入学手続きをする go through the *entrance* formalities. ● 入学を志願する apply for *admission* (*to*). ▶ あなたはニューヨーク大学の法学部に入学を許可されたことをお知らせいたします《合格通知》I am pleased to inform you that you *have been admitted* [*accepted*] *to* the School of Law of New York University. (❗不合格通知では I am truly sorry to inform you that we are not offering you admission to .... などという)
── 入学する 動 (学校に入る) get* into [《やや書》enter] ((a) school); (入学を許可される) be admitted (*to*); (小学校に) start school; (登録される) enroll (*in, at*). (❗以上の表現に続く school などの語句は通例冠詞を省略する) ▶ 彼は昨年9月にこの学校に入学した He *got into* [《やや書》*entered*, *was admitted to*, ˣ*entered into*] this school in September last year./He *started* [(*was*) *enrolled*] *in* [*at*] this school in September last year. (❗(1) start [enroll] *at* Harvard (University) などのように大学の場合には通例 at を用いる. (2) enroll は「入学などを許可される」というニュアンスの文脈では通例受身形) ▶ 今日ではどの学校にも女子が入学できる Every school is now *open* to women.

- **入学願書** an application form. **入学金**《pay》an entrance fee. **入学志願者数** the number of applicants for admission to [into] school. **入学式**《have [hold]》an entrance ceremony. (⚠ 日常会話では … a welcoming ceremony の方が普通) 〖事情〗 米英の入学式は通例 9 月) **入学試験** (⇨入学試験)

にゅうがくしけん **入学試験** an entrance exam [《書》examination]《for, of, to》. ▶彼は T 大学の入学試験を受けた[に合格した, に落ちた] He took [passed; failed] the entrance exam for T University.

ニューカレドニア 〖オーストラリア東方のフランス領の島〗 New Caledonia /n(j)ùː kælədóuniə/.

にゅうかん **二遊間** **二遊間コンビ** a middle-infield combination. **二遊間を抜くヒットを打つ** hit a single up [through] the middle.

にゅうかん **入管** 〖『(出)入国管理』の略〗 immigration (control). **空港で入管手続きをする** pass [get] through immigration at the airport.

にゅうかん **入館** **入館自由**《掲示》Open to all. ▶**入館無料**《掲示》Admission free.
— **入館する** 動 enter《a library》.
入館者 a visitor. **入館料** an admission charge《of 2,000 yen》.

にゅうがん **乳癌** 〖医学〗 breast cancer, cancer of the breast;《書》mastocarcinoma. ▶**乳がんにかかっている** have [be suffering from] breast cancer.
乳癌摘出手術 mastectomy.

にゅうぎゅう **乳牛** a milk(ing) cow.

にゅうきょ **入居** 图 (占有) occupation.
— **入居する** 動 (住んでいる) occupy; (引っ越して来る) move《in, into》.
入居者 (居住者) an occupant; (借家人) a tenant. ▶**入居者募集中**《掲示》《米》For rent./《英》To let.

にゅうぎょ **入漁** — **入漁する** 動 fish in other's water(s).
入漁権 the right to fish in other's water(s). **入漁料** fishing fee [charges].

にゅうぎょう **乳業** (産業) the dairy industry; (商売) the dairy business.

にゅうきん **入金** 图 (お金の受け取り) receipt /risíːt/ of money; (支払い) payment. (⇔ 出金)
— **入金する** 動 (受け取る) receive money; (支払う) pay; (振り込む) deposit. ▶**彼の当座預金に 100 ドル入金する** pay [deposit] 100 dollars into his current account. ▶**まだご入金いただいておりません** No payments have been received from you.
入金伝票 a deposit slip.

にゅうこ **入庫** — **入庫する** 動 put《goods》in a warehouse; [車庫などに] (自動車を) put* a car in the garage; (電車を) put a train in the shed; (ボートを) put a boat in the boathouse.

にゅうこう **入坑** — **入坑する** 動 go down into [enter] the mine.

にゅうこう **入港** 图 arrival of a ship) at [in] (a) port. **入港中の船** a ship in port [harbor].
— **入港する** 動 enter (a) port; arrive at [in] (a) port; (寄港する) call at (a) port. ▶**船はあす神戸港に入港の予定だ** The ship is scheduled to arrive at [come into, enter, call at] Kobe Port tomorrow.
入港料 port charges.

にゅうこう **入稿** — **入稿する** 動 send* a manuscript to a printer.

にゅうこう **乳香** (植物) a frankincense tree; (香料, 薬剤) frankincense; olibanum.

にゅうこく **入国** 图 〖国に入ること〗 (an) entry《into, to》; 〖外国からの移住〗 (an) immigration. (⇔ 出国)
不法入国 illegal entry. **不法入国者** an illegal entrant.
〖会話〗「入国の目的は何ですか」「観光です」 "What's the purpose of your visit, sir [ma'am]?" "Sightseeing."
— **入国する** 動 ▶**彼はアメリカに入国した** He entered America. /(入国を認められた) He was admitted into [to] America. /(移住した) He immigrated into [to] America.
入国カード a disembarkation card. **入国管理局** the immigration bureau. **入国許可** entry permission. **入国許可書** an entry permit. **入国審査** immigration (control). **入国審査官** an immigration officer. **入国手続き** entry formalities. **入国ビザ** an entry visa.

にゅうごく **入獄** — **入獄する** 動 go* [be sent] to prison.

にゅうこん **入魂** 图 ▶**あの作品は彼女の入魂の(＝精神を注いだ)作といえよう** I believe she wrote that piece of writing with all her heart and soul.
— **入魂する** 動 consecrate.
入魂式 a consecration ceremony.

にゅうざい **乳剤** (an) emulsion. (⚠ 種類は ⓒ)

にゅうさつ **入札** 图 a bid; a tender. **指名[一般]競争入札** designed [open, public] (competitive) bidding. **入札を行う** call for bids《for, on》. **入札を募る** invite bids [tenders]《for》. ▶**入札は 1 億円から始まった** Bids [Tenders] started at one hundred million yen. ▶**その土地は競争入札にかけられた** The land was put out to competitive bidding [tender].
— **入札する** 動 bid*[tender]《for》; offer one's bid [tender]《for》. **新空港の建設に入札する** bid for [《米》on] a new airport.
入札価格 a bidding price. **入札期間** the bidding [tender] period. **入札者** a bidder, a tenderer.

にゅうさん **乳酸** 〖化学〗 lactic acid.
乳酸飲料 a lactic acid drink [《書》beverage]. **乳酸菌** lactic acid bacteria.

にゅうし **入試** an entrance exam. (⇨入学試験)
DISCOURSE
もし首相になったら, 私は入試をなくしたい If I were to become the prime minister, I would abolish entrance exams. (⚠「条件→帰結」のパターン. 序論でよく用いられる)

にゅうし **乳歯** a milk [a baby] tooth (複 teeth).

にゅうじ **乳児** 〖赤ん坊〗a baby; (乳飲み子)《書・古》a suckling.
乳児死亡率 an infant mortality rate《略 IMR》. **乳児食** baby food.

ニュージーランド 〖国名〗 New Zealand /n(j)uː ziːlənd/. (首都 Wellington) **ニュージーランド人** a New Zealander. **ニュージーランド(人)の** New Zealand.

にゅうしつ **入室** — **入室する** 動 enter the room.

にゅうしつ **乳質** the quality of milk.

にゅうしぼう **乳脂肪** butterfat.

にゅうしゃ **入射** 〖物理〗 incidence.
入射角 the angle of incidence. **入射光線** incident light; an incident ray.

にゅうしゃ **入社** ▶**入社希望者全員が面接を受けられるとは限りません** Not everyone who applies for the job can be invited to the interview.

ニュージャージー

━━ 入社する 動 join [《英書・やや古》enter] a company.
● **入社式** a ceremony on entry into the company. ● **入社試験** (take) an employment exam [an exam for employment]; (面接の)(have) a job interview [an interview for a job]. ▶その会社の入社試験(=勤め口)に応募する apply for a job with the company. ● **入社年度** the year of entry (into the company). ● **入社日** the date of entry (into the company).

ニュージャージー [米国の州] New Jersey (略 N.J. 郵便略 NJ).

にゅうじゃく 柔弱 ━━ 柔弱な 形 weak; (精神的に) weakminded; weak-kneed; effeminate. ▶彼は子供のころは豪傑だったのにいつの間にか柔弱な男になってしまった He was strong and courageous as a boy, but he has grown into a man of *weak* personality.

にゅうしゅ 入手 名 acquisition. ▶願書の入手および提出について問い合わせる ask about how to *get* an application form and send it in.
━━ 入手する 動 get; (長期間かけて自分の力で) acquire; (努力して) obtain. (🔳 後の2語は get より堅い語) ● 情報を入手する *get* [*obtain*] some information (*from*). ▶彼が例の稀購(きっ)本をどのような経路で入手したかは伏せられている It's not open how he came to *obtain* the rare book. ▶この雑誌は大きな書店ならどこででも入手できます This magazine is *available* at any big bookstore.

にゅうしょ 入所 ━━ 入所する 動 enter 《an institute, an office》; (刑務所に) be imprisoned.

にゅうしょう 入賞 ━━ 入賞する 動 win a prize. ▶彼はそのレースで2位に入賞した He *won* (the) *second prize* in the race. (🔳 the は通例省略する)
● **入賞者** a prizewinner.

にゅうじょう 入場 名 [ある場所に入ること] (an) entrance 《into》; [入場の許可] admission 《to, into》. ● 有料[無料]入場者 paying [free] visitors. ● 入場料 a fee [*obtain*] some information (*from*). ● 入場無料《掲示》Admission free. ▶彼は博物館への入場を許可された He was allowed [was permitted] to enter the museum./He was admitted [was granted admission] into the museum.
━━ 入場する 動 (入る) enter; [許可される] be admitted 《to, into》. ▶我がチームは堂々競技場に入場した Our team *entered* [*went into*, *came into*] the field proudly. (🔳 後の二つの言い方の方が口語的) ▶この券で2人入場できる This ticket admits two people.
● **入場券** an admission ticket 《*for*》; (駅の) a platform ticket. ● 入場券のない方は入場お断り《掲示》*Admission* [*Entrance*] by ticket only. (🔳 日本語との発想の違いに注意) ● **入場券売場** (劇場・競技場の) a box office. (⇨切符) ● **入場行進** an entrance march [procession]. ● **入場式** an entrance [an opening] ceremony. ● **入場者** a visitor; (観客) a spectator; (聴衆) an audience; (入場者総数) an attendance.

にゅうじょう 乳状 ━━ 乳状の 形 milky; emulsified.

にゅうじょうりょう 入場料 an entrance [an admission] fee 《*of* 1,000 yen》; admission. ▶入場料はお払いするのですか[必要ですか] Is there an *admission fee*?/Do I have to pay *admission*? ▶その劇場の入場料はいくらですか What is *the admission* [×*admittance*] *fee* to the theater?

にゅうしょく 入植 名 (開拓地での定住) settlement; (外国からの移民) immigration.
━━ 入植する 動 ▶ブラジルに入植する *settle in* Brazil;

immigrate to Brazil.
● **入植者** a settler; an immigrant. ● **入植地** a settlement.

にゅうしん 入信 ━━ 入信する 動 become a believer 《*in* Christianity》.

にゅうしん 入神 ● **入神の技**(*) divine skill. ▶彼女の演奏はまさに入神の技というにふさわしいものであった Her performance was, if I am allowed to choose a word, just *divine*.

***ニュース** [情報] news /n(j)úːz/ 《*of*, *about*; *that* 節》(🔳 単数扱い, 数えるときは a piece [a bit, an item] of news の形になる); [放送] a newscast.
① 【～ニュース】 ● 海外ニュース foreign [overseas] *news*. ● 国内[ローカル; スポーツ; 経済]ニュース domestic [local; sports; financial] *news*. ● 十大ニュース ten big items of *news*.
② 【ニュースが[は]】 ▶今日はいいニュースがあまりなかった There wasn't [×weren't] much good *news* today. ▶1面のニュースは何ですか What is the front-page *news*?/What made the front page? ▶A氏死亡のニュースが流れた The *news* of the death of Mr. A was announced.
③ 【ニュースを[に, で]】 ● ニュース(の種)になる make the *news*. ▶その地震のニュースを聞きましたか Have you heard the *news about* the earthquake? ▶10時のテレビのニュースを見ましたか Did you see the 10 o'clock *news on* TV? ▶ラジオのニュースは Did you hear ... *on* (the) *radio*? となる (⇨テレビ, ラジオ)) ▶ワシントンからの最新のニュースをお伝えいたします Here is the latest *news from* Washington. ▶そのことは昨夜ニュースで知った I learned of it in the *newscast* [*on the news*] last night.
● **ニュース映画** a newsreel. ● **ニュース解説** a news commentary. ● **ニュース解説者** a news commentator. ● **ニュース記事** a news story. ● **ニュースキャスター** a newscaster; 《英》a newsreader. (🔳 ともに単に「ニュースを読む人」の意. 何人かの放送記者・解説者が出る場合の総合司会者は an anchor, (男の) an ánchor màn という) ● **ニュースショー** a news show. ● **ニュースソース** a (news) source. ● **ニュース速報** a (news) flash. (⇨速報) ● **ニュースバリュー** (news) value. ● 「ニュースバリューのある」は newsworthy.

にゅうすい 入水 ━━ 入水する 動 plunge [jump] into the water [river]. ● **入水自殺** 入水(じゅ)する.

にゅうせいひん 乳製品 dairy /déəri/ products.

にゅうせき 入籍 名 registration of marriage.
━━ 入籍する 動 register one's marriage.

にゅうせん 入選 ━━ 入選する 動 win* a prize. ●(作品が)展覧会で入選する be accepted [selected] for an exhibition. ▶彼女の絵はコンクールで1等に入選した Her painting *was selected* for the first prize in the contest./She *won* (the) *first prize* with her painting in the contest. (🔳 通例 the は省略する)
● **入選作品** a (prize-)winning work. ● **入選者** a (prize) winner.

にゅうせん 乳腺 [解剖] the mammary gland.
● **乳腺炎** [医学] mastitis /mæstáitis/. ● **乳腺症** [医学] mastopathy.

にゅうたい 入隊 名 enlistment.
━━ 入隊する 動 (志願して) join [enlist in] the army [(海軍) navy; (空軍) air force]; (徴兵されて) be conscripted [《米》be drafted] into the army [navy; air force].

にゅうたいいん 入退院 ● 入退院を繰り返す go into and out of (the) hospital repeatedly.

ニュータウン a new town. ● 千里ニュータウン Senri *New Town*.

にゅうだん　入団 —— **入団する** 動 ▶彼はボーイスカウトに入団した He *joined* [*was*) *enrolled in*] the Boy Scouts. (⚠enroll は「登録する」の意)

にゅうちょう　入超 〖「輸入超過」の略〗(⇨輸入).

にゅうてい　入廷 —— **入廷する** 動 enter the courtroom.

にゅうでん　入電 (受けた電報) a telegram received 《*from* Nairobi》; (電報を受け取ること) the receipt of a telegram. (⇨電報)

にゅうとう　入党 —— **入党する** 動 ▶彼は日本共産党に入党した He *joined* [*became a member of*] the Japanese Communist Party.

にゅうとう　入湯 —— **入湯する** 動 take《米》[have《英》] a bath. ●**入湯税** a bath tax.

にゅうとう　乳糖 milk sugar; lactose.

にゅうとう　乳頭 a nipple; 〖医学〗a mammilla.

にゅうどう　入道 〖仏教に入った人〗a monk; 〖坊主頭の人〗a man with a skin head; (坊主頭の化け物) a skin-headed monster. ●**大入道** a giant monster.

●**入道雲**〖気象〗a thunderhead. (⚠雷雲や入道雲を含む気象用語. a cumulonimbus /kjùːmjəlounímbəs/《積乱雲》とも呼ばれる)

ニュートラル neutral. ●(車のギヤをニュートラルにする) shift (gears) into *neutral*. ●ニュートラルな(＝中立の)立場をとる remain *neutral*; (どちらかの側につくこと)do not take sides 《*in a struggle*》.

ニュートリノ 〖中性微子〗〖物理〗a neutrino /n(j)uːtríːnou/.

ニュートロン 〖中性子〗〖物理〗a neutron.

ニュートン 〖英国の物理学者・数学者〗Newton (Sir Isaac ～).

にゅうねん　入念 —— **入念な** 形 (注意深い) careful; (綿密な) close; (精巧な) elaborate. (⇨念入り) ●その機械の入念な検査 a *careful* [〖徹底的な〗a *thorough*] examination of the machine. ●入念な準備をする do *elaborate* preparation(s)《*for*》.

—— **入念に** 副 ●入念に練った計画 a *carefully* worked-out plan.

にゅうばい　入梅 the beginning of the rainy season. (⇨梅雨(3))

にゅうはくしょく　乳白色 ●乳白色の milky-white; opal /óupəl/.

にゅうはち　乳鉢 a mortar.

ニューハンプシャー 〖米国の州〗New Hampshire 《略 N.H. 郵便略 NH》.

にゅうぶ　入部 —— **入部する** 動 ▶野球部に入部する join [*enter*, (一員になる) *become a member of*] a baseball club.

ニューフェース (芸能界での) a new star. (⚠new face は「新顔,新参者」で芸能界の新人の意では不適)

にゅうぼう　乳棒 a pestle. ●**乳棒**ですりつぶす pestle.

ニューメキシコ 〖米国の州〗New Mexico《略 N.Mex. 郵便略 NM》.

にゅうめつ　入滅 (釈迦, 聖者の死) the death of Buddha [a high priest].

にゅうもん　入門 ❶〖弟子入り〗▶彼は有名な音楽の先生のところに入門した(＝弟子になった) He *became a pupil of* the famous musician.
❷〖初歩〗●言語学の入門書 a *first book* [a *beginner's book*] *in* linguistics. (⚠a primer は古風な語)

にゅうよう　入用 need. (⇨必要)

にゅうようじ　乳幼児 babies and little children.

ニューヨーク 〖米国の都市〗New York /n(j)uː jɔ́ːrk/ (City)《略 N.Y.C.》; 〖米国の州〗New York《略 N.Y. 郵便略 NY》, (市と区別して) New York State. ●**ニューヨークタイムズ** 〖新聞名〗The New York Times.

***にゅうよく　入浴** 名 a bath; bathing. ●入浴中である be in the *bath*.

—— **入浴する** 動 take《米》[have《英》] a bath (⚠赤ん坊のように人に入れてもらう場合は米英ともに have a bath); 《米》bathe /béið/, 《英》bath. (⚠初めの名詞表現の方が普通) ●赤ん坊を入浴させる give a baby a *bath*; bathe《米》[bath《英》] a baby.

にゅうりょう　入寮 —— **入寮する** 動 enter [be admitted to] the dormitory; (寮生になる) become *a boarder*.

にゅうりょく　入力 名 (コンピュータの) input; (電気の) power input.
—— **入力する** 動 ●コンピュータにデータを入力する *input* data *to* a computer; *type* data *in* [*into* computer].

ニューロコンピュータ a neurocomputer.

ニューロン 〖神経細胞〗〖解剖〗a neuron.

にゅうわ　柔和 gentleness; mildness.
—— **柔和な** 形 (優しい) gentle; (おとなしい) meek. ●柔和な目 *gentle* eyes. ▶彼は柔和な人だ He is a *quiet and gentle* person.

にゅっと (突然) suddenly; (突き出ている様) sticking out. ●フェンスの陰からにゅっと出る appear *suddenly* [*quite unexpectedly*] from behind the fence. ▶生け垣の間からにゅっと棒が突き出てた A long stick *shot out* through the hedge. ▶彼女は戸の脇からにゅっと顔を出して「ではまた」と言った She *stuck* her *head around* the door and said, "See you tomorrow."

ニュルンベルク 〖ドイツの都市〗Nuremburg /n(j)úərəmbɜ̀ːrg/.

にょう　尿 〖医学〗urine /júərin/. ●尿をする urinate; discharge urine.
●**尿管** 〖解剖〗the ureter. ●**尿器** (しびん) a urinal; a bed pan. ●**尿検査** (⇨検尿) ●**尿酸** 〖生化学〗uric acid. ●**尿失禁** incontinence of urine.

にょうい　尿意 a micturition desire. ●尿意を催す have a desire to urinate; want to urineate (frequently).

にょうそ　尿素 〖化学〗urea /juərí:ə/.
●**尿素樹脂** urea resin.

にょうどう　尿道 〖解剖〗the urethra.
●**尿道炎** 〖医学〗urethritis /juriθráitis/; (尿道の炎症) inflammation of the urethra.

にょうどくしょう　尿毒症 〖医学〗uremia; urine poisoning.

にょうぼう　女房 one's wife (複 wives), 《話》one's woman (⚠「恋人」「情婦」の意もあり, 時に女性蔑視の語).
●**女房役** (片腕となる人) one's right hand; (男の) one's right-hand man.

にょうろ　尿路 the urinary tract.
●**尿路結石** 〖医学〗a urinary calculus.

によきによき ●にょきにょきと立つ (急に現れる) spring up; (キノコのように次々出てくる) mushroom.

にょじつ　如実 —— **如実に** 副 truly; (正確に) accurately; (忠実に) faithfully; (生き生きと) vividly; (写実的に) graphically; realistically; (A をあるがままに) as A be. ▶彼のこの作品には戦後の闇市が如実に描かれている This work of his *vividly* describes [*gives a vivid description of*] black markets just after the war./In this work of his, black markets just after the war are described *as they* really *were*.

にょたい　女体 the body of a woman.

にょにん　女人 a woman. (複 women) ▶高野山は女人禁制 《掲示》No Admittance to *Women*. ●**高野山**

にょろにょろ ▶蛇にょろにょろと草むらの中へ入っていった A snake *slithered* its way into the grass.

にら 韮 〖植物〗a leek.

にらみ 睨み 〖権威〗authority; 〖影響力〗(an) influence; (特に政治的な)《話》clout. ●にらみがきかなくなる lose one's *authority*. ▶その先生は生徒ににらみがきく[きかない] The teacher *has authority* [*no authority*] over his students. ▶あの実業家は政界ににらみがきく That businessman *has* (*a*) *great influence* [*has a lot of clout*] in the political circles.

にらみあい 睨み合い ▶にらみ合いの状態にある be glaring at each other; (反目している) be at daggers drawn (with each other). (!後の方は慣用表現) (⇒睨む❶)

にらみあう 睨み合う glare at each other;《話》get in each other's face; (対立する) be at odds 《with》.

にらみつける 睨み付ける glare 《at》; (いまいましげに) scowl 《at》; (相手が目をそらすまで) stare 《him》 down. ▶彼は少年をにらみつけて黙らせた He *stared* the boy in silence.

にらむ 睨む ❶ [見つめる] (怒って) glare 《at》, look angrily 《at, on》, 《話》get* in 《his》 face (!状態を表すには get be be にする); (じっと) stare 《at》, 《話》eyeball. ▶彼は少年をこわい眼でにらんだ He *glared* fiercely (怒りを込めて) *glared* anger] at the boy./(短くきっと)《話》He *shot* the boy *a dirty look*.

❷ [疑う] suspect. ▶警察は彼を殺人犯だとにらんだ The police *suspected* him *of being the murderer*./The police *suspected that* he was the murderer.

❸ [目をつける] keep* an eye on …; (監視する) watch. ▶私は先生ににらまれている The teacher *is keeping an eye on* me./(ブラックリストに載っている) I *am on* [ˣ*in*] the teacher's *blacklist*.

❹ [考慮に入れる] ▶データをにらみ合わせて *in consideration of* [《やや書》*in* 《《英》*the*》*light of*] the data; *taking* the data *into consideration* [*account*].

にらめっこ 睨めっこ 《play [have]》a staring [an outstaring] game. ▶時計とにらめっこで朝食を用意する prepare breakfast *against* the clock.

にらんせい 二卵性 ●二卵性双生児 biovular [fraternal] twins.

にりつはいはん 二律背反 图 antinomy /ǽntinəmi/.
── 二律背反の 形 àntinómic.

にりゅう 二流 ●二流のホテル a *second-rate* [*second-class*] hotel. (!前の方が同じ二流でも下の感じが強い)

にりゅうかたんそ 二硫化炭素 〖化学〗carbon disulfide.

にりんしゃ 二輪車 a two-wheeled vehicle, a two-wheeler; (自転車) a bicycle.

*__**にる**__ 似る 〖性質・外観が〗be like …, be alike; (親など血縁者と) take* after …; (部分的に) be similar 《to》(!like, alike より類似の度合いが低い); 〖外観が〗look like …, look alike, 《やや書》resemble (! 以上はいずれも「似ている」の意で命令形・受身形・進行形は通例不可).

❶ 【…に似る】▶彼は父親と容貌(ようぼう)がよく似ている He *is* very (much) *like* [*really takes after*, really *resembles*] his father *in* appearance./He *looks* just [《話》*a lot*] *like* his father./He

and his father *look* very much *alike* [ˣ*like*]. (! (1)《話》では much はしばしば省略する. (2) 最後の例で like を用いるときは … very (much) like *each other*. とする) ▶彼らは好みが似ている They *are alike* (↔*different*) in their tastes.

❷ 【…に[と]似る】▶君はお母さんよりお父さんに似ているね You *look more like* your father than your mother. ▶この岩は何に似ていますか What *does* this rock *look like*? ▶彼女のドレスは色が私のと似ている Her dress *is similar* in color to [ˣ*with*] mine. ▶これらのよく似た 2 枚の絵を注意して見てください Please look carefully at these two *similar* [ˣ*alike*] paintings. ▶彼女は母親に似て美人だ She is beautiful *like* her mother. ▶兄に似ず私は英語が得意でない *Unlike* [ˣ*Different from*] my brother, I'm not good at English. ▶彼と私は似たところがある(=共通点がある) He and I *have something in common*./He *has some resemblance to* me.

●似ても似つかない ▶彼は父親とは似ても似つかない人だ He *doesn't look like* [*resemble*, ˣ*resembles to*] his father *at all*. (!否定文の場合《話》では not … at all の代わりに not … anything [a thing] like his father. のようにもいえる)/(まったく異なる) He *is quite different from* [*completely unlike*, 《話》*nothing like*] his father.

*__**にる**__ 煮る boil; (とろ火で沸騰寸前までぐつぐつと) simmer; (加熱して料理する) cook. (⇒料理 解説) ▶野菜を煮すぎる *boil* vegetables too much [*long*]. ▶シチューを煮込む *simmer* the stew. ▶砂糖水を半分の量になるまで煮つめる *boil down* the sugar and water to half the volume. ▶スープを 30 分ほどごとこと煮なさい Let the soup *simmer* [*boil gently*] for about thirty minutes.

●煮ても焼いても食えない ▶煮ても焼いても食えない(=したたかで手に負えない)やつ a tough person to deal with.

にるい 二塁 second (base). ●二塁打を打つ make a two-base hit; hit a double; double. ●二塁を守る[に盗塁する] play [steal] *second* (*base*). ●二塁で封殺される be forced out at *second*. ●バントで走者を二塁へ送る bunt a runner to *second*; advance a runner to *second* on a bunt.

●二塁手 a second base player [(男の) baseman]. ●二塁審 a second base umpire.

にれ 楡 〖植物〗an elm (tree).
●楡材 elm.

にれけのひとびと 『楡家の人びと』 *The House of Nire*. (!参考 北杜夫の小説)

にれつ 二列 ●2 列になって (横に) *in two rows*; (縦に) *in a double file*. ●2 列に並ぶ form *two rows* [*a double file*]. ●2 列になって進む walk *two abreast* [*double file*].

にれん 二連 ●2 連の真珠のネックレス (1 本を二重にしたもの) a pearl necklace [a strand of pearls] *folded double*; (加工前から 2 本に分かれているもの) a *double-strand* pearl necklace.
●二連銃 a double-barreled gun.

*__**にわ**__ 庭 a yard; a garden.

> 使い分け **yard**《米》では芝生などを植えた家の周囲の土地全体をさすが,《英》では通例舗装された裏庭をさす.
> **garden**《米》では家のわきや周囲にあり,花・果物・野菜などを育てるための土地をいうが,《英》では芝生や花壇などの部分をいう.

❶ 【～庭】▶前庭 a front *yard*《米》[*garden*《英》]. ●裏庭 (芝生を植えた)《米》a bàckyárd

にわか (《英》ではコンクリート舗装されたものをさす);《英》a back *garden*.
② 【庭の〜】 庭の草むしりをする weed a *garden*. • 庭の手入れをする(芝生を刈り込む) trim a *garden*; (手入れして維持する) maintain a *garden*. ▶ お宅の庭の広さはどのくらいですか How much *garden* do you have? (『*garden* は広さをいう場合は Ⓤ)/How large is your *garden*? (⇨面積)
③ 【庭を】 庭を造る make [(設計する) lay out] a *garden*.
④ 【庭に[で]】 庭に野菜を植える plant vegetables in the *garden*; plant the *garden* with vegetables. (⇨いろいろ) ▶ 彼女は自分の裏庭で野菜を栽培している She grows vegetables in her back *garden*.
• **庭石** a garden rock. • **庭いじり** gardening.
• **庭木** a garden tree. • **庭師** a gardener.

にわか 俄か 形 (突然の) sudden; (唐突な) abrupt; (予期しない) unexpected. ▶ にわか作りの舞台 an *improvised* [a *makeshift*] stage. (『前の方は「寄せ集めの材料で作った」,後の方は「間に合わせの」の意)
• にわか作りのチーム a *scratch* team. • にわか仕込みの知識は実際上何の役にも立たない A *hastily acquired* [A *hastily crammed*] knowledge is of no practical use.
── **俄かに** 副 suddenly; unexpectedly. (⇨突然 [類語]) ▶ にわかに天気が変わった The weather changed *suddenly*. / The weather made a *sudden* [an *abrupt*] change. ▶ にわかには(=今すぐには)決められない I can't decide *right now*.
• **にわか雨** a shower; a sudden rain.

にわさき 庭先 (庭から見て)《*in*》the garden just outside a house; (建物から見て)《*at*》the far end of a garden.

にわとこ 接骨木 【植物】a red-berried elder (tree); (実) an elderberry.

***にわとり** 鶏 a chicken (『特にひよこ (chick) より成長した若い鶏をいう。雌は a hen); (成長した鶏(雄)《主に米》a rooster,《英》a cock (『米 では cock は避ける); (雌) a hen, (家禽(きん)としての) a fowl /fául/; (ひな) a chick. • 鶏の肉 chicken; fowl. (『後の方は鶏肉を含めた鳥肉をさす) • 鶏を飼う keep *chickens* [*fowl*(s)]. ▶ 鶏が鳴いた A *rooster* [A *cock*] crowed /króud/. (『鳴き声は cock-a-doodle-doo)/(雌の鶏が) A *hen* clucked. (『鳴き声は cluck) ▶ それは鶏が先か卵が先かを聞くようなものだ It's like asking which came first, the *chicken* or the *egg*./It's a kind of *chicken*-and-*egg* question. (『a kind of (...のようなもの)の後は無冠詞が標準用法)
• **鶏小屋** a hénhòuse.

にん 任 【職】office;【地位】a post, a position;【任務】a task, a job, a duty;【責任】a responsibility. • 任にある be in *office*; hold the *post* 《*of*》. • 任を果たす carry out [《書》fulfill] one's *duty*. • その任にあらず be not equal to the *task* [*job*]. ▶ 社長は私の任ではない I am unfit for the *position* of president. (『の後の職名は無冠詞)

-にん -人 • 数人 a few *people*; several *people*. (⇨ いくつか [類語]) • 2 人分の仕事をこなす do the work of two *people*. • 何人 (⇨(たー)) • 5 人で連れ立ってショッピングに出かけた They, *five in all*, went shopping. ▶ 3 人の英語の先生が交替で教えに来る Three English tèachers come to our class in turn. (『特に「人」を表す言葉にはつけない)

にんい 任意 ── **任意(の)** 形 (選択自由の) optional; (自発的な) voluntary /vάləntèri/; (独断的な)《しばしば軽蔑的に》arbitrary /ά:rbətrèri/. • 任意の寄付 *voluntary* [*optional*] contributions. • 任意の解釈 (an) *arbitrary* interpretation. ▶ 出席は任意です Attendance is *optional*.
── **任意に** 副 optionally; voluntarily; arbitrarily; (好きなように) as one likes [*pleases*,《書》*wishes*]. • 任意に選ぶ make an *arbitrary* choice; choose *arbitrarily*.
• **任意出頭** (make) a voluntary appearance.
• **任意捜査** a police investigation on a voluntary basis; (宅家捜査) a house search with《the owner's [one's]》consent. • **任意保険** optional insurance.

にんか 認可 图 【承認】approval;【許可】permission;【公認】《やや書》authorization;《話》the green light;【権威筋による認可】《書》sanction. (⇨承認, 許可) • 無認可保育所 an *unauthorized* nursery. • 財務省から認可を得る get [obtain] *autholization* from the Ministry of Finance. ▶ そのビル建設に関する市長の認可が下りた The construction of the building *was authorized by* the mayor./The mayor *gave sanction to* the construction of the building. ▶ これらの製品を売る認可を得ている We *have been licensed* to sell these products.
── **認可する** 動 approve; permit; authorize. • その橋の建設計画を認可する *approve* the plan for building the bridge.

にんかん 任官 图 appointment; (将校への) commission. ── **任官する** 動 be appointed 《*as*》professor, *to* the post of professor》; be commissioned 《*as*》captain》.

***にんき** 人気 popularity.
① 【人気〜】 • 人気絶頂にある be at the height of one's *popularity*. (⇨絶頂) • 人気上昇中のスター a *rising* (↔a fading) star. • 人気取り政策 a *vote-catching* policy. • 人気取りをする seek *popularity*; (大向こう受けをねらった行為をする)《話》*grandstand*. ▶ 彼はクラスの人気者(の 1 人)だ He is a *favorite* [one of the most *popular* students] in the class.
② 【人気の[が]】 ▶ 彼はあまり人気がない He is not very *popular*./His *popularity* is thin. ▶ 青木教授は学生に人気がある Professor Aoki is very *popular with* [*among*, ×to] his students. (『with は「(少数の人)に対して」, among は「(多くの人)の中で」という意を表すが, この場合は with が普通。特に少人数と考えられるときは among は不可: 彼女は友達[クラスメート]に人気がある She is *popular with* [×*among*] her friends [classmates].) ▶ フェンシングはヨーロッパで大変人気のあるスポーツです Fencing is a very *popular* sport in Europe./Fencing enjoys great *popularity* in Europe. ▶ その CD は最近人気が出てきた The CD is becoming *popular* [*winning popularity*, *rising in popularity*] these days. (『「人気が落ちてきた」は ... is losing *popularity*/... is failing in *popularity* といい, × ... is becoming unpopular とは通例いわない)/The *popularity* of the record is beginning to grow these days. ▶ 50 年代のロックに再び人気が出てきた (=流行しだした) Fifties' rock-and-roll music *has come into fashion* [*vogue*] again.
③ 【人気に[を]】 • (スターなどが)人気におぼれる become drunk with success. • 人気を博する win [gain] *popularity*; (一般の人に受ける) catch the public's fancy [eye]. ▶ その転校生はクラスの女の子の人気をさらった(=注目の的になった) The transfer student became *the focus of attention* of all the girl students in the class.

にんき

- **にんき** 人気歌手 a popular singer; a pop idol. (関連) a pop singer 流行(歌)の歌手 • 人気商売 an occupation heavily dependent on popularity. • 人気投票 a popularity contest. • 人気番組 a popular (a hit, 人気抜群の) a breakout] program [show].

にんき 任期 a term of office [service]. • 4年の任期を務める serve a four-year *term* (*as* mayor). • 大統領として(2回目の)任期中に during his (second) *term* as President. • 任期終了前に before the *term* expires. • 大統領の任期は4年である The President's *term of office* is four years.

にんぎょ 人魚 (女性の) a mermaid; (男性の) a merman.

にんきょう 任侠 名 chivalry. • 任侠心に富む男 a man of *chivalry*; a man with a *chivalrous spirit*.
── 任侠の 形 chivalrous.
• 任侠映画 a *yakuza* movie.

*にんぎょう** 人形 ❶ a doll; (あやつり人形) a puppet (比喩的にも用いる), a marionette. • 縫いぐるみ人形 a rag *doll*. • ろう人形 a wax *doll*; (等身大で有名人をかたどった) a waxwork. • 指人形 a (glove) *puppet*. • 人形ごっこをする play *dolls*. • 人形をあやつる move [manipulate, operate] a *puppet*.
• 人形劇 a puppet show [play]. • 人形遣い a puppeteer; a marionette player.

にんく 忍苦 endurance. • 忍苦の(= 苦しみを耐え忍ぶ)一生を送る live a life of *endurance* [*endless patience*].

*にんげん** 人間 ❶ 【人】 a human being, a human, (a) man (豐 men); 【人類】 man, mankind /mǽnkáind/. (人, 人類)

> **使い分け human being, human** 機械や人間以外の動物と対比して人間をさす. a human being の方が一般的.
> **man** 男女を問わず一般に人をさす. 通例無冠詞. ただし1人の人を通して人間全体を表す場合は不定冠詞 a が用いられることがある. また mankind の意で人類全体をさす. この場合は単数無冠詞.
> **mankind** 集合的に人類全体をさす. 通例単数扱いで, 代名詞は it で受ける.
> 最近では男性中心となるのを避けて (a) man, mankind の代わりに, human beings, a human (being), a human person, we, the human race (単数扱い)を用いる傾向がある.

①【人間～】• 人間らしく生きる live *humanly*. • 人間味のある人 (⇨ 人間味) ▶ それは人間わざとは思えない That seems beyond *human* power./That seems *humanly* impossible. ▶ 彼は人間嫌いで He hate *people* [*humans*]./《書》《軽蔑的》He is a *misanthrope* /mísənθròup/.
②【人間は】▶ 人間はだれでも自由に生きる権利がある All *human beings* have [All *men* have, Everyone has] a right to live free. • 人間は環境に適応してきた The *human race* [*Mankind*] has been adjusting itself to its surroundings. ▶ 人間が好奇心がなくなったらおしまいです If *human beings* lose their (sense of) curiosity, it's all over.
③【人間に似た】• 人間に似た動物 a *man-like* animal. ▶ このことは人間にも当てはまる This is also true of *human beings*.

❷【人格】character. (⇨ 人物, 人格, 人柄, 人) • 人間のできた人 (人格者) a man [a woman] of *character*; (いい人) a good person. • 人間(=心)の大きい[小さい]人 a *broad-minded* [a *narrow-minded*] person. • 人間的に成長する grow *in personal*

にんしき

stature; build up one's *character*.
• 人間万事塞翁が馬 《ことわざ》Inscrutable are the ways of Heaven./A joyful evening may follow a sorrowful morning.

── 人間の 形 (人間に備わる, 人間の性質を持つ) human; (人間全体の) man's, ... of mankind. • 人間の体[脳] a *human* body [brain]. • 人間の尊厳 *human* [*man's*] dignity. • 人間の姿をした神 a god in *human* shape. • 人間の歴史 the history of *human beings* [*of mankind*, *of man*]. • そうすることが人間の義務だ It's a *person's* [a *man's*] duty to do that. (! 不定冠詞に注意) ▶ 警察といえども人間だ. クリスマスぐらいゆっくりしなくては Police officers are only *human*. They should let their hair down at Christmas. (! (1) この human は形容詞. (2) let one's hair down は《話》「(よく働いたあとに)くつろぐ」の意) • 守ろう人間の尊厳を Protecting human dignity.
• 人間関係 human relations. • 人間工学 human engineering. • 人間国宝 a living national treasure. • 人間性 (人間としての性質) human nature; (人間としての徳性) humanity (!「動物性」「神性」に対して用いる). • 人間性に反する be against *humanity*. • 人間不信 (⇨ 人間ドック) • 人間不信 (a) distrust of other people. • 人間模様 complex patterns of human relationships.

にんげんしっかく 『人間失格』 *No Longer Human*. (参考) 太宰治の小説

にんげんドック 人間ドック • 人間ドックに入る go into 《米》the) hospital for a *complete* (*medical*) *checkup* [*examination*].

にんげんみ 人間味 • 人間味のある人 a humane [a *warmhearted*] person. (! humane /hju:méin/ は「慈悲深く思いやりのある」の意) • 人間味あふれる「人間味のない」話 a story with a lot of [with no] *heart*.

にんさんぷ 妊産婦 pregnant women and nursing mothers.

*にんしき** 認識 名 【理解】understanding; (気づくこと) realization; (認めること) recognition; (洞察) perception; 【知識】knowledge. • 我々の認識を深める deepen [promote] our *understanding* (*of*).
• 認識の差 a *perception* gap 《*between* A *and* B》. ▶ この問題については彼は認識不足だ He has very little *understanding* [*knowledge*] of this matter./He doesn't *understand* [*know*] anything about what it is. ▶ 婦人解放運動に対する認識を新たにした (新たな観点で見た) I saw the Women's Liberation Movement in a new [a fresh] light./(新しい意味を見いだした) I found a new meaning in the Women's Liberation Movement.

── 認識する 動 【理解する】understand*; (はっきりと) realize (⇨ 分かる ❶); (事実として) recognize; 【知っている】know*. (⇨ 認める) • 実態を正しく認識する *understand* the true situation correctly; have a correct *understanding* of the true situation. ▶ 政府はその問題の重要性を認識し始めた The government is beginning to *realize* the importance of the problem.

■ DISCOURSE
環境危機を人々はもっと認識すべきだと思う I think people should *be more aware of* the environmental crisis. (! I (do) not think ... (...と思う)は主張を表すディスコースマーカー. 単に個人的な意向を述べるときは用いない. ×I think I want to study Chinese.)

にんじゃ 忍者 a *ninja*; (説明的に) an old-time spy (sometimes a killer) who mastered the special technique of stealing into the enemy's territory [house, etc.] in order to carry out his mission.

にんじゅう 忍従 submission; endurance. ▶多くの女性が一種の忍従を強いられた時代があった There were times when many women were forced to *be* completely *submissive* to their husbands.

にんじゅつ 忍術 *ninjutsu*; the art of *ninja* (⇨忍者).

にんしょう 人称 〖文法〗the person. ●一[二; 三]人称 the first [second; third] person.
● 人称代名詞 a personal pronoun.

にんしょう 認証 图《書》attestation. ── **認証する** 動《書》attest.
● 認証官 a high-ranking official whose appointment is made by the Emperor. ● 認証式 an Imperial attestation ceremony.

***にんじょう 人情** 图〖親愛の情〗heart; 〖人間的感情〗human feelings; 〖人間性〗human nature, humanity. ● 人情の機微が分かる see the secrets [subtleties] of *human nature*. ● 人情(=思いやり)を持って捕虜に接する take care of the prisoners *with humanity*. ▶だれでも出世したいと思うのは人情(=自然のこと)だ It's only *natural* for everyone to [It's only *natural* that everyone should] want to get ahead in the world. ▶そのような行為は人情にもとる(=非人情的だ) Such conduct is *inhuman*.
── **人情の(ある)** 形（親切な）kind; (人間味のある) humane /hjuːméɪn/ (❗human (人間的)と混同しないこと); (心が優しい) kindhearted; (心が暖かい) warmhearted. ▶彼は人情の厚い人です He is very kind [*humane*, *kindhearted*]. ▶彼女は人情の薄い[ない]人だ She is unkind [*cold-hearted*, *heartless*]./She has no heart.
● 人情家 a man [a woman] of heart; a person who has a lot of heart; a kindhearted person.
● 人情話 (人情味のある話) a story full of human feelings [(人間的暖かみ) human warmth].
● 人情味 a human touch.

にんじょうざた 刃傷沙汰 ▶ささいなことで始まったけんかは刃傷沙汰(=流血の惨事)になった The quarrel that started over a trifle matter ended in [developed into, led to] *bloodshed* [(切り合い) a *sword fight*].

にんじる 任じる ❶〖任命する〗appoint. ▶彼を会長に任じる *appoint* him chairman.
❷〖自任する〗think* oneself 《*to be*》; (自称する) claim, profess 《*to be*》. ▶彼は専門家をもって任じている He *thinks himself* [*claims*] *to be* an expert.

にんしん 妊娠 图 pregnancy. ● 妊娠中にひどい風邪を引く catch a bad cold during *pregnancy*. ● 望まない妊娠 unexpected pregnancy. ▶妻は妊娠4か月です My wife is three months *pregnant* [*along*]./My wife is in the third month of *pregnancy*.《事情》米英では日本の数え方と1か月ずれる) ▶妊娠おめでとう Congratulations on your pregnancy.
── **妊娠する** 動 become* [get*] pregnant;《婉曲的》be in the family way. ● 妊娠させる put 《her》 pregnant;《婉曲的》put 《her》 *in the family way*. ▶彼女は妊娠しています She *is pregnant*./She is carrying a baby (in her womb). ▶赤ちゃんができていた。とはいえ、周りの事情は妊娠するには今一つだった She was starting a baby, but circumstances were not ideal for *pregnancy*.

● 妊娠中絶 an abortion. (⇨中絶) ● 妊娠中毒症 〖医学〗toxemia (of pregnancy); gestosis.

にんじん 人参 a carrot. ● 朝鮮[高麗]ニンジン a ginseng (❗強壮薬の意では Ⓤ)

にんずう 人数 the number of people [〖書〗persons]. (⇨数(ǂ)) ● 多[少]人数 many [a few] people; a large [a small] *number of people*. ● 野球に必要な人数をそろえる gather enough [necessary *number of*] people to play baseball. ● 会場の人数をかぞえる count *the number of* (×the) attendance in the hall;《話》count *heads* [*noses*] in the hall. ▶その仕事をするには人数が足りない(=もっと多くの人が必要だ) We need more *people* to do the work. ▶私たちのクラスは人数が多すぎる Our class are overcrowded./The *number* of our class is too great [large, ×many].

にんずる 任ずる (⇨任じる)

にんそう 人相 〖顔つき〗a look; (容貌(ᵇぅ), 美貌) one's looks;〖目鼻立ち〗one's features. ● 人相の悪い男 an *evil-looking* man. ● 人相を見る judge 《his》 character by examining 《his》 *features* [〖書〗 *physiógnomy*]. ● 容疑者は新聞記事にある人相書きに一致する The suspect answers to the *description* given in the paper.

にんそうみ 人相見 a physiognomist /fɪziá(g)nəmɪst/.

にんそく 人足 a laborer;《英》a navvy.

***にんたい 忍耐** patience; (長期の苦痛・困難に対する) endurance (⇨我慢, 辛抱);〖積極的な努力〗perseverance. (⇨根気) ● 忍耐強い人 a *patient* person. ● 忍耐と寛容をもって with *patience* and tolerance. ● 忍耐力を養う develop (one's) *perseverance* [*patience*]. ▶その仕事には大変な忍耐がいる The work takes a lot of *patience*. ▶彼女には赤ん坊の世話をするだけの忍耐力がない She doesn't have enough *patience* [*patience* enough] *to* take care of her baby. (❗前の方が強意的) ▶それは彼の忍耐の限度を越えている It's beyond his *endurance* [*patience*].

にんち 任地 one's (new) post; one's place of appointment. (⇨赴任地(ʰ))

にんち 認知 图 recognition /rèkəgnɪʃən/.
── **認知する** 動 ● その子を認知する *récognize* [*acknówledge*] the child as one's own.
● 認知症〖医学〗dementia. (⇨痴呆)

にんてい 人体 ● あやしい人体の男 a suspicious-looking man.

にんてい 認定 ── **認定する** 動〖正式に認可する〗authorize; (資格を与え) qualify;〖承認する〗recognize;〖評点を下す〗〖法律〗find. ● この教科書は文部科学省から認定された This textbook *was authorized* by the Education Ministry. ▶彼は水俣病患者として公式に認定された He *was officially recognized* as a Minamata patient [victim]./He was an officially *recognized* patient of [〖婉曲的〗person (living) with] Minamata disease. ▶陪審員は彼を無罪と認定した The jury *found* him innocent.
● 認定証 (免許状) a certificate /sərtɪfɪkət/; a qualification.

にんにく 大蒜 (球根, 香辛料)〖植物〗garlic. ● ニンニクの1片 a clove /klóʊv/ of *garlic*.

にんぴ 認否 ● 罪状の認否を問う arraign /əréɪn/《him》for a crime; hold an arraignment for a crime.

にんぴにん 人非人 a wretch, an ungrateful wretch; a brute (of a man).

ニンフ 〖ギリシア・ローマ神話〗a nymph.

にんぷ 人夫 a laborer; (荷物運び人) a carrier.

にんぷ 妊婦 a pregnant woman.
● 妊婦服 a maternity dress.
にんぽう 忍法 (⇨忍術)
にんまり ● にんまり(=満足そうに)笑う smile *satisfactorily* [*happily*]; give a *satisfied* [a *happy*] smile.

にんむ 任務 〚義務〛(a) duty (**!** しばしば複数形で); 〚課せられた仕事〛a task (**!** 特につらくて困難な仕事); 〚目的のために派遣されてする仕事〛a mission.

① 【～の任務】 ● 国会議員の任務 the *duties* of a Dietman [a Dietwoman]. ▶ 秘書の任務の一つは手紙をタイプすることだ One of the *duties* of a secretary is to type letters. ▶ 諸君の任務は山の遭難者を救出することだ Your *mission* is to rescue the climbers in distress.

② 【任務を[に]】 ● 任務を果たす do [perform] one's *duty* (**!** 後の方が堅い語); carry out one's *task* [*mission*]. ● 任務に就く set about one's *task*. ● 特別な任務を帯びて米国へ派遣される be sent to the U.S. on a special *mission*. ▶ 首相は彼にインフレを抑える(= と戦う)という任務を与えた The Prime Minister set [gave] him the *task* of fighting inflation. ▶ (上役に)任務を無事完了いたしました *Mission* accomplished, sir [ma'am]. (**!** *My* [*Our*] mission *has been* accomplished ... の略)

にんめい 任命 图 (任用) (an) appointment; (指名) (a) nomination.
— **任命する** 動 appoint; (公式に) nominate. ▶ 首相は彼を自分の後任に任命した The Prime Minister *appointed* [*nominated*, *named*] him (as [to be]) his successor. (**!** 通例 as, to be は省略する) ▶ 彼は校長に任命された He *was appointed* (as [*to be*]) principal. (**!** 補語に1人だけの身分・官職を表す名詞がくる場合は通例無冠詞)/He *was appointed to* the position of principal.

にんめんけん 任免権 ● 任免権がある have *the power* [*right*] *to appoint and dismiss* 《Cabinet ministers》.

ぬ

ぬい 縫い 〘縫うこと〙 sewing; 〘刺繍(しゅう)〙 embroidery. (⇨刺繍)
ぬいあがる 縫い上がる be sewed [stitched] up.
ぬいあわせる 縫い合わせる sew* /sóu/ 〘(ひと針ずつ) stitch〙 ... together. (⇨縫う) ●布切れを縫い合わせる *sew* [*stitch*] pieces of cloth *together*. ●傷口を縫い合わせる *sew up* [*stitch (up)*] a wound.
ぬいいと 縫い糸 séwing thréad; (手術用の) a suture /súːtʃər/.
ぬいぐるみ 縫い包み 〘綿など詰め込んだおもちゃ〙 a stuffed toy; 〘着ぐるみ〙 a costume. ●縫いぐるみ人形 a rág dóll. ●クマの縫いぐるみ a *stuffed (toy) bear*; a *teddy bear*. ●犬の縫いぐるみを着る put on a dog *costume*.
ぬいこむ 縫い込む ●お守りを服に縫い込む *sew* a lucky charm *into* one's clothes.
ぬいしろ 縫い代 ●縫いしろを2センチとる leave a *margin* of two centimeters to *sew up*.
ぬいとり 縫い取り (刺繍(しゅう)) embroidery. (⇨刺繍)
ぬいばり 縫い針 a (séwing) nèedle.
ぬいめ 縫い目 a seam; 〘傷口の〙 a suture /súːtʃər/. ●縫い目をほどく undo [〘引きはがす〙 rip up] a *seam*. ●ほころんだ縫い目をつくろう *stitch up* the torn *seam*. ▶ドレスの縫い目がほころびた The *seam* of my dress has come apart [has come undone]./My dress has come apart at the *seams*.
ぬいもの 縫い物 sewing, needlework. (⇨裁縫)
***ぬう** 縫う ❶ 〘糸で布をつづる〙 sew* /sóu/ ... (up), stitch ... (up). (❗ up を用いると「完全に縫い上げる」の意となる)

> 使い分け **sew** 布地などを縫い合わせたり、衣服などを縫って作ること。
> **stitch** ひと針ずつ縫い合わせる[付ける]こと。

●上手に縫う *sew* (it) well. ●スカートをミシンで[手で]縫う *sew* a skirt on a sewing machine [by hand]. ●スカートのほころびを縫う *sew up* [*stitch (up)*] a rip in the skirt. ●シャツにボタンを縫いつける *sew* [*stitch*] a button *on* a shirt. (❗単に「ボタンを縫いつける」は *sew on* a button) ●上着の内ポケットに名前を縫い込む *sew* one's name *into* [*in*] the inside pocket of one's jacket. ●傷口を5針縫う *put* five *stitches in* a wound; *sew up* a wound *with* five *stitches*. ▶彼女は私にドレスを縫ってくれた She *sewed* [*made*, ×stitched] a dress *for* me./She *sewed* [*made*] me a dress.
❷ 〘その他の表現〙 ●人込みを縫って進む *thread* [*weave*] one's *way through* the crowd. ●家事の合間を縫って *in the intervals of* one's household chores.
ぬうっと (⇨ぬっと)
ヌーディスト 〘裸体主義者〙 a nudist.
●ヌーディストビーチ a nudist beach.
ヌード 图 〘裸〙 a nude. ── ヌード(の) 厖 nude; in the nude. (❗通例芸術的なものをいう)
●ヌード写真 a nude picture [〘話〙 photo]. ●ヌードショー (ストリップ) a stríptèase. ●ヌードダンサー a stríptèaser. 〘話〙 a stripper. ●ヌードモデル a nude model. ●その仕事は nude modeling.
ヌートリア 〘動物〙 a nutria.
ヌードル 〘麺(めん)〙 a noodle. (❗通例複数形で)

ヌーベルキュイジーヌ [<フランス語] 〘新傾向のフランス料理〙 nouvelle cuisine.
ヌーベルバーグ [<フランス語] 〘芸術・政治の革新的動向〙 nouvelle vague /nuːvél váːg/, a new wave. (❗1960年前後のフランスの映画製作の前衛運動をいう場合は大文字で Nouvelle Vague, the New Wave)
ぬえ 鵺 ●ぬえ的人物 (正体不明の人) a person of unknown character; (謎めいた人) an enigmatic [a mysterious] person.
ぬか 糠 rice bran. ●ぬかみそ (⇨糠味噌(なか))
●糠に釘 ▶そんなことをしたらぬかにくぎだ (ことわざ) (砂地を耕すようまったくむだだ) It is like plowing /pláuiŋ/ the sand(s). ●先生の忠告も彼にはぬかにくぎだった(=何の効果もなかった) The teacher's advice *had no effect on* him.
ヌガー [<フランス語] 〘洋風の白い飴〙 a nougat /núː-gət/.
ぬかあめ 糠雨 a drizzle. (⇨小糠(ぬか)雨)
ぬかす 抜かす 〘わざと〙〘うっかり〙省略する〙 omit (-tt-), leave* ... out, miss ... out (❗後の2語の方が口語的); 〘飛ばす〙 skip (-pp-). ●その章を抜かす *omit* [*skip*] the chapter. ●朝食を抜かす *skip* [〘食べそこねる〙 *miss*] breakfast. ●文の中のコンマを抜かす *leave out* a comma in the sentence.
ぬかずく 額ずく prostrate oneself 《before a shrine》; (丁寧に礼をする) bow low.
ぬがせる 脱がせる ●服を脱がせる undress 《a baby》; 〘無理に〙 strip 《him》 *of* 《his》 clothes. ▶妻は私に手を貸してオーバーを脱がせた My wife *helped* me *off* with [*out of*] my overcoat.
ぬかどこ 糠床
ぬかばたらき 糠働き (むだな骨折り) (⇨ 徒労)
ぬかみそ 糠味噌 salted rice-bran paste for pickling végetables. ●キュウリのぬかみそ漬け a cucumber preserved in *salted rice-bran paste*.
●ぬかみそが腐る ▶私が歌うとぬかみそが腐るかもしれないよ My singing might turn the milk (sour).
ぬかよろこび 糠喜び a short-lived joy. ▶彼にぬか喜びさせる(=あらぬ期待をさせる)ようなことは言っていけない You should not say anything to give him *false hopes*.
ぬかり 抜かり ●抜かりなく 〘注意深く〙cautiously; 〘抜け目なく〙 shrewdly; 〘必ず〙 without fail (❗通例約束・命令を強調して (⇨必ず❶))。●彼の仕事はぬかりなく(=完璧(かぺき)で) His work is *perfect*. ▶彼女はやることに抜かりがない She does everything very carefully./(自分のやっていることを心得ている) She knows what she is doing.
ぬかる (地面が泥で) be muddy; (雪が解けて) be slushy.
ぬかる 抜かる (油断して失敗する) be not careful enough. ▶抜かるな Look sharp!/Watch [Look] out!
ぬかるみ mud; (雪解けの) slush. (⇨泥沼) ●ぬかるみの道 a *muddy* [a *slushy*] road.
ぬき 抜き ❶ [...を除くこと] ●...抜きで without .... ●朝食抜きで *without* breakfast. ●そんな難しい話は抜きにして[=脇に置いて] *putting aside* such a difficult problem. ▶カフェイン抜きのコーヒーでもけっこういける Coffee *without* caffeine /kǽfiːn/ is (still)

ぬきあし 抜き足 ・そっと(差し足)でその部屋に忍びこむ get into the room *stealthily* [*on tiptoe*]; steal [tiptoe] into the room.

ぬきうち 抜き打ち (突然の)*surprise*; (事前通知なしで) *without notice*. ・抜き打ちの立入検査をする carry out a *surprise* inspection (*of* an office); inspect 《an office》 *without notice*. ・抜き打ちテスト a surprise test; (米) a pop quiz.

ぬきがき 抜き書き 图 an *éxtract*. (⇨抜粋)
── **抜き書きする** 動 extráct 《passages *from* a book》.

ぬきがたい 抜き難い ・抜きがたい不信感を抱く harbor [have] a deep-rooted [a lingering, a lurking] suspicion 《*about*; *that* 節》.

ぬきさし 抜き差し ・抜き差しならない 抜き差しならない状態にある[陥る] be in [fall into, be caught in] a dilemma, 《話》 be in [get oneself into] a fix.

ぬきさる 抜き去る ・一気に抜き去る pass [go ahead of] 《him》in a spurt.

ぬぎすてる 脱ぎ捨てる [[投げるように脱ぐ]] throw* [cast*]... off; [[靴などをけって]] kick ... off. (⇨脱ぐ)
・長靴を脱ぎ捨てる a *kick off* one's boots. ▶彼は服を脱ぎ捨て川に飛び込んだ He *threw* [*cast*] *off* his clothes and jumped into the river.

ぬきずり 抜き刷り an *offprint*.
ぬきだす 抜き出す (選ぶ) pick ... out, choose*.
・カードを1枚抜き出す *pick out* [×pick up] a card.

ぬきて 抜き手 [[水泳]] an *overarm* [an *overhand*] stroke. ・抜き手を切って泳ぐ swim with *overarm strokes*; swim *overarm*.

ぬきとりけんさ 抜き取り検査 a spot check 《*on*》; a sámpling inspéction. ・抜き取り検査をする spot-check; carry out a sampling check.

ぬきとる 抜き取る [[引っぱり出す]] pull ... out, [[書]] extract; [[引き抜く]] pull ... up; [[選び出す]] pick ... out; [[盗む]] steal*. ・雑草を抜き取る pull [root] up the weeds. ・ポケットから財布を抜き取られた Someone *stole* my wallet out of my pocket./(【注】特に現場でいう場合)/The wallet *was stolen* [《話》*was lifted*] out of my pocket./I had my wallet *stolen* [*lifted*] from my pocket./(すりにあった) I had my pocket *picked*.

ぬきはなつ 抜き放つ ・ぱっと刀を抜き放つ *draw* [*unsheathe*] a sword in a flash.

ぬきみ 抜き身 ・抜き身の刀をぶらさげて with a *naked* [a *drawn*, a *bare*] *sword* in one hand; carrying a *naked sword*.

ぬきんでる 抜きん出る (きわ立つ) stand* out 《*from*, *among*》; (まさる) 《書》 excél (-ll-); (越える) 《書》 surpass. ・数学では他のどの生徒よりも抜きん出ている *stand out from* [*excel*, *surpass*] all other students in mathematics.

‡ぬく 抜く ❶[[引いて抜く]] pull 《*out of*》; (滑らかにそっと) draw* 《*from*, *out of*》; (取り除く) remove 《*from*》. ・彼の指のとげを抜く *pull* [*draw*] a splinter *out of* his finger. ・虫歯を抜いてもらう have one's bad tooth *pulled out* [《やや書》*extracted*]. ・くぎ抜きで釘を抜く *pull out* [*remove*] a nail with pincers. ・さやから剣を抜く *draw* [《書》*unsheathe*] a sword/ひと組のトランプから1枚抜く *pick* [*draw*] a card *from* a pack. (【注】前の方が普通) ・ワインのコルク栓を抜く *uncork* a wine bottle. ・彼のためにもう1本ビールの栓を抜く open [*uncap*] another bottle of beer for him. ・庭の雑草を抜く *weed* a garden; *pull* weeds *out of* a garden; *pull up* weeds in a garden.
❷[[中の気体・液体などを出す, 取り除く]] ・タイヤの空気を抜く *let* the air *out of* a tire; *let out* the air *from* a tire; *let* a tire *down*. ・ふろの水を抜く *empty* [*drain*] a bath(tub). ・ワイシャツのしみを抜く 《get》[*take*] the stain *out of* a shirt; *remove* the stain *from* a shirt.
❸[[無しで済ませる]] ・朝食を抜く *go* [*do*] *without* breakfast; 《話》 *skip* breakfast. ・(仕事などで)手を抜く 《話》 cut corners.
❹[[追い抜く]] (人・車などを) pass, overtake*; (人を走って) outrun*; (事業・競争などで) outstrip (-pp-). ・先頭の走者を抜く pass [*overtake*], (直前に出る) *get ahead of*, (ずっと前に出る) *outstrip* the front-runner. ・発行部数で競合紙[誌]を抜く *outstrip* [*overtake*, *get ahead of*] its rivals *in* circulation. (【注】outstrip は後の2語より意味が強く優秀で他紙[誌]をずっと凌駕（ｶﾘｭｳｶﾞ）することを含意する) ・ドリブルでディフェンダーを抜く dribble past a defender.
❺[[徹底的にする]] ・それを最後までやり抜く *carry* it *through* to the end; *accomplish* it. ・最後まで戦い抜く *fight* it *out*. ・その問題を考え抜く *think* the matter *out* [*through*]. ▶彼は二つの世界大戦を生き抜いた He lived *through* [*survived*] the two world wars.
❻[[抜きん出る]] ▶みんな泳ぎがうまいの中でも健は群を抜いている They are all good swimmers, but Ken is *by far the best* (of them all). (【注】by far は最上級を強める)
❼[[野球で]] ・(投球の)抜いたボール an off-speed pitch; a change(up). ・三塁線を抜くヒットを打って hit a single past the third baseman.

‡ぬぐ 脱ぐ [[身につける物全般を]] take*... off (⇔put ... on), [[書]] remove; (脱ぎ捨てる) throw*... off, cast*... off (【注】throw ... off には「急いで」の意が含まれる); (引っ張って) pull ... off (【注】特にきつい衣服や靴, 手袋などに用いられる); [[衣服を]] get* undressed, undress. (【注】前の方が一般的) ・服も脱がずに眠り込む fall asleep without *undressing* [*undressed*] [*着たままで*] *with* one's clothes *on*. ・帽子を脱ぎなさい *Take* *óff* your `hat./*Táke* your `hat *off*. (【注】(1) 後の方は your hat に話し手の関心が強くあり, 前の方より口調がきつくなる. (2) *Remove* your hat. は堅い言い方) ・服を脱いでパジャマを着た I *took off* my clothes [*took* my clothes *off*] and put on my pajamas./I *got undressed* [*undressed*] and put on my pajamas. ▶おぼれている少年を救うために彼は上着を脱いで川に飛び込んだ *Throwing* [*Casting*] *off* his jacket, he jumped into the river to save the drowning boy. ▶彼女がコートを脱ぐのを手伝った I *helped* her *off with* her coat./I helped her *take* her coat *off*.

ぬくい 温い warm (⇨温かい)
‡ぬぐう 拭う [[軽くこすってふく]] wipe, (ふいて取る) wipe ... off [*out*]; (乾かす) dry. (⇨拭(ﾌ)く) ・額の汗をぬぐう *wipe* the sweat *off* [*from*] one's forehead. ・涙を手の甲で急いでぬぐう *wipe* one's eyes quickly with the back of one's hand. ・不公平の印象をぬぐいきれない can't *wipe out* [(取り除く) *remove*, *get rid of*] the impression that it is unfair.

ぬくぬく (居心地よく) *comfortably*; (雨風の心配なく) *snugly*, (暖かく) *warmly*; (安心して) *safely*. ▶猫は暖炉のそばでぬくぬくと寝ていた The cat was lying *snug*(*ly*) [*snug and warm*] by the fireside.
ぬくまる 温まる get* *warm*. (⇨温(ｱﾀﾀ)まる)
ぬくもり 温もり warmth. ▶ふとんの中にはまだ彼の肌の

ぬくもりが少し残っていた There was still a slight *warmth* from his body in the bed./The bed was still slightly *warm* from his body.

ぬけ 抜け 〔落ち〕an omission; 〔手落ち〕an oversight. ▶この名簿には少し抜けがある Some *omissions* are found in this list of names.

ぬけあな 抜け穴 〔秘密の通路〕a secret passage; 〔法規などの抜け穴〕a loophole 《*in*》. ●抜け穴をふさぐ block (up) a *secret passage*. ●法の抜け穴を見つけ出す find a *loophole* in the law.

ぬけがけ 抜け駆け 图 彼は抜け駆けで競争相手を抑えて契約を取った He got the contract by *stealing a march* on his competitors.

── **抜け駆けする** 動 steal a march 《*on* him》. (⑫「素早い行動で競争相手を抑える」の意で,軽蔑的な含みはない)

ぬけがら 抜け殻 〔セミなどの脱皮〕a cast-off skin [shell]; 〔ヘビなどの〕a slough /slʌ́f/. ▶彼は抜け殻のようになってしまった He is just a *shadow* of his former self.

ぬけかわる 抜け替わる 〔乳歯が〕be replaced by a permanent set (of teeth); 〔毛・羽毛・角が〕molt; 〔ヘビなどの皮が〕slough. ▶猫の毛が抜け替わり始めた Our cats have begun to *shed* their hair.

ぬけげ 抜け毛 (xa) fallen hair; 〔くしですき取った抜け毛〕combings /kóumiŋz/. ▶抜け毛がひどくなってきた My hair *has been falling out* terribly.

ぬけだす 抜け出す 〔こっそり出る〕slip [sneak, steal*] out of 《the room》; 〔職場・仕事などから〕get* away from 《the office》; 〔他より一歩前へ出る〕get ahead of .... ●経済危機から抜け出す come through [〔立ち直る〕recover from] an economic crisis. ▶彼女は32キロ地点で先頭集団から抜け出した She got [〔さっと〕shot] *ahead of* the leading runners at the 32-kilometer mark (in the marathon).

ぬけでる 抜け出る (⇒抜け出す, 抜きん出る)

ぬけぬけと 〔厚かましくも〕impudently; 〔恥知らずにも〕brazenly, shamelessly. ●前の方が強意的》●抜けぬけとうそをつく tell a *barefaced* lie. ▶彼はぬけぬけとそのパーティーに顔を出した He showed up at the party *impudently* [*brazenly*]./He *had the impudence* [〔話〕*cheek*] to appear at the party. ▶よくまあぬけぬけとそんなことが言えるね *How dare* you say such a thing to me?

ぬけみち 抜け道 〔通路〕〔間道, わき道〕a byway; 〔近道〕a shortcut; 〔逃げ道〕an escape route; 〔秘密の通路〕a secret path [passage]; 〔法律などの〕a loophole 《*in*》; 〔口実〕an excuse.

ぬけめ 抜け目・抜け目のない 〔利にさとい〕shrewd; 〔目ざとい〕alert; 〔用心深い〕careful; 〔ずる賢い〕clever (⑫文脈によっては頭のよさを示す); 〔打算的な〕calculating. ●金もうけに抜け目がない be *shrewd* at making money; be *alert* to the chance of making money. ●抜け目のない返答をする make a *clever* [a *careful*] answer. ▶あの人は抜け目のない商売人だ He's a *shrewd* businessman./He's *shrewd* in business.

***ぬける 抜ける** ❶ 〔離れて取れる〕〔髪・歯などが〕fall* out; 〔歯・くぎなどが〕come* out; 〔底が〕drop (-pp-) out; 〔崩れ落ちる〕give* way, collapse. ▶歯が抜けた My tooth *fell out* [*came out*]. ▶前の方がゆるんで,後の方は固い物を混ぜたりすると抜ける) ▶ダンボールの底が抜けた The bottom *has dropped* [*fallen*] *out* of the cardboard box. ●The bottom of the cardboard box has .... の語順より自然》 ▶床が抜けた The floor *has given way* [*fallen in, collapsed*]. ▶彼女は腰が抜けた Her knees *gave way* [*gave* 《*under* her》]./She *collapsed* [*dropped to her knees*].

❷ 〔あったものが無くなる・消える〕〔しみなどが〕come* off [out]; 〔風邪・悪習などが〕〔人が主語〕get* rid of ..., shake*... off. ●悪習から抜ける get out of [*shake off*, 〔話〕*kick*] a bad habit. ●疲労が抜けない(=まだ疲労を感じる) be still feeling tired. ▶風邪がまだ抜けない I just can't (seem to) *get rid of* [*shake off, get over*] my cold. ▶風船の空気が抜けた The balloon *has gone flat* [《書》 *has deflated*]. ●このビールは気が抜けている This beer *is* [*has gone*] *flat*. ▶腕がまひして力が抜けていくのを感じた I felt my arm going numb and *losing* all *its strength*.

❸ 〔あるべきものが無い〕be missing. ●この本は8ページ抜けている Eight pages *are missing from* this book./This book *is missing* eight pages./ This book has eight *missing* pages [eight pages *missing*]. ▶彼の名前が名簿から抜けている His name *has been left off* the list.

❹ 〔愚鈍である〕be stupid [foolish]. ▶あの男は少し抜けている He's rather *stupid*.

❺ 〔組織などから離れる〕leave*. ●会合の途中で抜ける *leave* in the middle of a meeting. ▶部員が数名チームから抜けた Several members *left* [*dropped out of*] the team.

❻ 〔通り抜ける〕●森を抜ける pass [〔歩いて〕*walk*, 〔車で〕*drive*] *through* a wood. ●公園を抜けて(=横切って)近道をする take a short cut *across* a park. ●〔車で〕町を抜けて郊外に(=町から外へ)出る *drive out of* the town. ▶トンネルを抜けると海が見えてきた When I *went out of* the tunnel, the sea came into view.

❼ 〔透き通る〕●抜けるような青空 a *clear* blue sky. ●肌の色が抜けるように白い have a *very fair* complexion.

ぬげる 脱げる 〔はずれる〕come* off; 〔するっと〕slip (-pp-) off. ▶走ったとたんにハイヒールが脱げてしまった Her high-heels *came* [*slipped*] *off* when she broke into a run. ▶このゴム手袋はなかなか脱げない These rubber gloves won't *come off*./〔容易に脱げない〕 I can't *take off* these rubber gloves easily.

ぬし 主 〔主人〕a master; 〔所有者〕an owner, a proprietor. ●その家の主 the *head* of the family. ●電話の主 the caller; the man [woman] at the other end of the line. ●この沼の主 the guardian spirit of this pond. ●主のいない犬 an *ownerless* dog.

ぬすっと 盗人 a thief (國 thieves). (⇒泥棒) ●盗人たけだけしい do wrong and declare brazenfacedly that one is not wrong (by giving self-righteous reason for one's being). ●盗人に追い銭 〔失った金を取り戻すためにさらに金を注ぎ込む〕throw good money after bad; 〔損の上塗りをする〕throw the helve after the hatchet. ●盗人にも三分の理 Even a thief has his reasons. (⑫「何にでも理屈はつけられるものだ」の意)

ぬすびと 盗人 a thief (國 thieves). (⇒泥棒)

ぬすみ 盗み (a) theft; 〔窃盗〕〔法律〕(a) larceny. ●盗みを働く steal; commit *theft*. (⇒盗む)

ぬすみぎき 盗み聞き ── 盗み聞きする 動 彼らの話を盗み聞きする *eavesdrop on* [*listen in on*] their conversation. (⇒盗聴)

ぬすみぐい 盗み食い ── 盗み食い 動 〔こっそり食べる〕eat secretly [on the sly].

ぬすみみ 盗み見 ── 盗み見する 動 steal a look [a glance] 《*at*》; 〔やや書〕look furtively 《*at*》.

ぬすみみる 盗み見る (⇨盗み見する)
ぬすみよみ 盗み読み ― 盗み読みする 動 (こっそりと) read 《his diary》secretly; (肩越しに) read 《his newspaper》over his shoulder.

ぬすむ 盗む ❶ [窃盗する] steal; (ささいな金品を) pilfer. (❗目的語は常に「物」で,文脈から明らかな場合は省略可) ●彼《金庫》から金を盗む *steal* money *from* him [a safe]. ●盗んだ物 a *stolen* [×a taken] thing. ●彼が喫茶店から盗んできたスプーン the spoons he *pilfered from* a tearoom. ▶私はカメラを盗まれた Someone *stole* [*took*] my camera. (❗take は「持ち去る」の意で steal の婉曲語)/My camera *was stolen*. (❗×I was stolen my camera. とはいわない)

❷ [強奪する] rob (-bb-) 《him [a place] *of* a thing》. ▶私は泥棒に財布を盗まれた I *was robbed of* my wallet by the thief./The thief *robbed* me *of* my wallet. (❗×My wallet was robbed./×I had my wallet robbed of by the thief. とはいわない)

❸ [盗作する] (やや書) plagiarize; 《話》crib (-bb-). (⇨盗作) ●彼からアイデアを盗む *steal* [*plagiarize, crib*] an idea *from* [*off*] him.

❹ [その他の表現] ●人目を盗んで(=こっそりと)デートをする go out on dates *secretly* [*in secret*, 《話》*on the sly*]. ●暇を盗んで釣りに行く go fishing *in* one's spare time [*moments*]. ●三塁を3回盗む steal third base three times. ▶彼は先生の目を盗んで(=先生に見られずに)カンニングした He cheated in the exam without the teacher seeing [*noticing*] him. ●昔は仕事は盗んで覚えろと言われ,先輩たちは何一つ教えてくれなかった We used to be told that we must learn [acquire] skills *by observation*, but our senior apprentices taught us nothing.

ぬた *nuta*; (説明的に) Japanese salad of green onions and shellfish seasoned with vinegared-*miso* dressing.

ぬたくる (ペンキ・絵の具などを) daub 《*on* the wall; *with* paint》. (下手な字などを) scrawl.

ぬっと (不意に) suddenly; (思いもよらず) quite unexpectedly. ●暗い所で大男がぬっと現れた A big fellow appeared *quite unexpectedly* out of the darkness./*Suddenly*, a tall figure of a man loomed into view out of the darkness. (❗loom は相手の顔がはっきりせずに不気味さを伴う)

:ぬの 布 (a) cloth. (❗(1) 材料をさすときは ⓤ. 複数形は《two》pieces of cloth で表す.《two》cloths /klɔ(ː)ðz/ は複数枚の「ふきん,ぞうきん,包み布」の意. (2) 衣料の材料としての布には material, fabric を使うことが多い (⇨布地)) ●布で包む wrap [cover] 《it》with 《a》cloth. (⇨包む) ●布(製)の帽子 a *cloth* cap. ●布装の本 a *cloth*-cover book.

ぬのきれ 布切れ a piece of cloth.
ぬのじ 布地 cloth; (織地) (a) fabric; (素材) material. (⇨布)
ぬのめ 布目 texture. ●ざっくりとした[荒い]布目 loose [coarse; close] *texture*.

*ぬま 沼 [沼地] (泥沼地) (a) marsh; (低湿地) (a) swamp; [湖] a lake; (天然の池) a (small) pond. ●尾瀬沼 *Lake* Oze

ぬまじり 沼尻 the head of a lake 《湿地帯》 a swamp, a marsh》.

ぬめぬめ ― ぬめぬめとした 形 (wet and) slimy /sláimi/; slippery. ●なめくじの通ったぬめぬめとした跡 *slimy* trails [trails *of slime*] where slugs had moved.

ぬめり slime /sláim/. ●ぬめりのある (カタツムリ,ヘビなど) slimy; (食材などが) slippery.

ぬらす 濡らす wet*, wet*... wet; (ちょっと湿らせる) dampen; (ちょっと浸す) dip (-pp-). ▶彼女は髪をぬらしてシャンプーを振りかけた She *wet* her hair [*got* her hair *wet*] and then put shampoo on it.

ぬらぬら slippery; slimy /sláimi/. (⇨ぬるぬる)
ぬらりくらり (⇨のらりくらり)

ぬり 塗り a coat. ●ペンキ[ニス]の塗り a *coat* of paint [varnish]; painting [varnishing]. ●ペンキを2度塗りする apply two *coats* of paint. ●机にペンキの下[中; 上]塗りをする give the desk the first [second; last] *coat* of paint. ▶このテーブルはニス[漆]の塗りがよい(=よくニス[漆]が塗られている) This table is well varnished [*lacquered*].

ぬりえ 塗り絵 coloring; a black and white to color in. ●塗り絵帳 a cóloring bòok.
ぬりかえる 塗り替える paint 《a wall》again, repaint; [記録を] break* 《the record》.
ぬりかためる 塗り固める ●壁をしっくいで塗り固める *cover* walls thickly with plaster; *plaster* walls *over*.
ぬりぐすり 塗り薬 [軟こう] (an) ointment. [液状の薬] (a) liniment. ●塗り薬をすり傷につける apply some *ointment* to the scrape; put [(すり込む) rub] some *ointment* on the scrape.
ぬりこめる 塗り込める ●壁に金貨を塗り込める put in gold coins in the wall and *cover* them with plaster; hide [conceal] gold coins in the wall.
ぬりたくる 塗りたくる ●塀にべたべたとペンキを塗りたくる *daub* /dɔ́ːb/ [*smear*] the wall *with* paint; *daub* [*smear*] paint *on* the wall. ●おしろいを塗りたくる *daub* one's face *with* thick makeup; *plaster* one's face *with* makeup.
ぬりたて 塗り立て ●ペンキ塗り立てのドア a *freshpainted* [a *freshly-painted*] door. ●塗り立ての壁 a *fresh(ly)-plastered* wall. ●ペンキ塗り立て [掲示] 《米》*Wet paint*./《英》*Fresh paint*.
ぬりたてる 塗り立てる ❶ [塗って飾る] ●美しく塗り立てた店 a store painted beautifully; a beautifully painted store.

❷ [厚化粧をする] paint 《one's face》thickly [heavily]. (⇨ぬりたくる [第2項])
ぬりつぶす 塗り潰す ●落書きを白く塗りつぶす *cover* the graffiti with white; *paint out* the graffiti; *white out* the graffiti.
ぬりばし 塗り箸 《a pair *of*》lacquered chopsticks.
ぬりもの 塗り物 (うるし細工) lacquer ware.
●塗り物師 a lacquer-ware artist.

:ぬる 塗る (ペンキ・絵の具で) paint; (クレヨン・色鉛筆で) color; (バター・ジャムなどを) spread*; (油などとつくものを) smear; (あまりきれいに塗られていないことを暗に); (薬などを) put*, 《やや書》apply; (おしろいを) powder; (紅を) rouge; (うるしを) lacquer; (ニスを) varnish; (しっくいを) plaster; (ワックスを) wax. ●天井にペンキを塗る *paint* the ceiling; (上塗りする) *coat* the ceiling with paint. ●塀を白く[明るい色に]塗る *paint* the fence white [a bright color]. (❗人に塗ってもらう場合は have the fence painted ... のようにいう) ●クレヨンでさし絵を塗る *color* the illustration with crayons. ●トーストにジャムを塗る *spread* [*smear*] jam *on* the toast; *spread* [*smear*] the toast *with* jam. (❗spread [smear] A with B の構文では,A が B で限定される場合は一面に塗りつけることを暗示) ●傷口にヨードチンキを塗る *put* some iodine [aiədàin] *on* a cut; *apply* iodine *to* a cut. ●顔にクリームを塗る *rub* cream *on* one's face; (すり込む) *rub* cream *into* one's face. ●車にワックスを塗る *wax* a car. ●ほおにおしろいを塗る *powder* one's

ぬるい 温い　lukewarm /lúːkwɔ́ːrm/; tepid. (❗ warm, lukewarm, tepid の順に温度は低くなる (⇒生温い)) ▶ぬるいふろにゆっくり入る take a long, *mildly warm* bath. (❗ lukewarm は「なまぬるい」の意でここでは不適切) ●(冷めて)ぬるくなってしまったお茶 *tepid* [*lukewarm*] tea. ▶赤ちゃんの入浴はぬるいお湯を使いなさい Use *tepid* water to bathe your baby.

ぬるぬる ── ぬるぬるした 形 (滑りやすい) slippery; (何かぬるぬるしたものがついている) slimy /sláimi/; (油がついて) greasy. ▶ぬるぬるした魚をつかまえるのは難しい It's not easy to grasp a *slippery* fish. ▶床が油引きされたばかりでぬるぬるしていた The fresh-greased floor was (*dangerously*) *slippery*.

ぬるまゆ ぬるま湯　lukewarm /lúːkwɔ́ːrm/ [tepid] water. (❗ 後の方が温度は低い) ●ぬるま湯で顔を洗う wash one's face with *lukewarm* water.
● ぬるま湯につかる　▶公務員はぬるま湯につかっているとよく非難される Government employees are often criticized for their *lukewarm* attitude toward work.

ぬるむ 温む　warm. ▶水がぬるんだ The water *got a little warm*./The water began to *warm a little*.

ぬるゆ 温湯　(⇒ぬるま湯)

ぬるりと (⇒ぬるぬる) ▶うなぎは手からぬるりと逃げた The eel *wiggled slimily* [*slipped*] out of my hand(s).

ぬれえん 濡れ縁　an open veranda(h).

ぬれぎぬ 濡れ衣　[間違った非難] a false accusation [charge]. ●濡れ衣を着せる (無実の罪を負わせる) make a false charge 《against》 him) (不当な責任を負わせる) put [lay] the blame 《on him for》. ▶彼は殺人のぬれぎぬを着せられた He *was* falsely *charged with* [*wrongly accused of*] murder. (❗ 前の方が堅い言い方)/《話》 He *was framed for* murder.

ぬれごと 濡れ事　(情事) a (secret) love affair.
●濡れ事師 (芝居) an actor who is good at playing the men's part in a love scene.

ぬれそぼつ 濡れそぼつ　be drenched to the skin; be soaking (wet). (⇒びしょ濡れ)

ぬれて 濡れ手　a wet hand.
●ぬれ手で粟(あわ) (苦労せずにもうける) make a lot of money with little effort; make easy money [profits].

ぬれねずみ 濡れ鼠　●ぬれねずみ(＝びしょぬれ)である be wet through; be dripping wet;《おどけて》 be like [as wet as] a drowned rat. (⇒びしょ濡れ)

ぬれば 濡れ場　a love scene.

ぬればいろ 濡れ羽色　glossy black. ▶髪はからすのぬれ羽色 Her hair is *raven black*.

ぬれる 濡れる　get* wet; (湿る) get damp [moist] (❗ damp は不快な感じを伴う). ●びしょびしょにぬれる *get wet through*. (⇒びしょ濡れ) ▶雨にあてっ放しだったので洗濯物はまだぬれている The washing is still *wet* [*damp*] *from being left in the rain*. (❗ 前の方がぬれ方がひどい) ▶紙袋はぬれるとすぐに破れる Paper bags break easily when they are *wet*. ▶彼女の目は涙でぬれていた(＝うるんでいた) Her eyes were *wet* [*moist*] *with* tears. ▶雨にぬれるからお入りなさい Come in out of the rain!

ぬんちゃく (a pair of) nunchakus; karate sticks.

ね

ね 根 ❶【植物の】a root.
①【～根】● 花の根 the roots of a flower.
②【根が】● そのバラはすぐに根がついた The roses rooted easily./The roses took [struck] root easily. (! 成句のとき root は無冠詞単数. 比喩的にも用いる) ● この雑草は根が深い These weeds have spread deep roots [have rooted deep].
③【根を】● 根を張る send out roots. ● 根を抜く pull 《a plant》 up by the [its] roots.
❷【根元】the root. ● 歯[毛髪; 舌; 耳]のつけ根 the root of a tooth [a hair; a tongue; an ear]. ● 根の深い偏見 deep-rooted prejudice. ● 犯罪の根を絶つ root out the causes of crime.
❸【根源】(根拠) (a) foundation; (本質) heart. (⇒ねっから) ● 彼は根はいい人です (外見と違って) He's very nice at heart [bottom]./(基本的には) He's basically a nice guy.
● **根が生える** ● 彼は根が生えたように動かなかった He didn't move as if he were [《話》was] rooted to the ground.
● **根に持つ** ● 彼は私に対してそのことをまだ根に持っている (=恨んでいる) He still has a grudge against me over the matter.
● **根も葉もない** ● 根も葉もないうわさ a completely groundless [untrue] rumor; a rumor without any foundation.
● **根を下ろす** put down roots 《in》. ● その木はすっかり根を下ろした The tree has taken root firmly. ● 新しい考え方が根を下ろす(=定着する)にはいつも時間がかかる It always takes a long time for new ideas to take root.

ね 子 the rat.
● **子年**【十二支】the year of the Rat. (⇒十二支関連)

ね 音 〖鐘などの〗a sound; 〖楽器の〗a tone; 〖虫などの〗a chirp. ● 澄んだ鐘の音 the clear sound of a bell. ● 美しい笛の音 the sweet tone of a flute. ● 虫の音に耳を澄まして listen intently to the chirps of insects. (事情) 米英人は通例日本人のように虫の音に特別な情感を覚えない)
● **音を上げる** ● 彼はついに音を上げた He gave up in the end.

ね 値 (値段) a price; (費用) (a) cost. (⇒値段)
①【～値】● やみ値の black market price. ● 底値 a rock-bottom price. ● べらぼうな高値 an exorbitant 《書》[a stiff 《話》] price. ● 買い値 a búying [a púrchase] price.
②【値が】● その絵は将来値が出るだろう The picture will rise in price in the future./The price of the picture will rise in the future.
③【値を】● 値をつける price; put [set] a price 《on it》. ● 値をつり上げる drive up prices; force prices higher. ● 値を下げる (値下がりする) drop [go down] in price. (⇒値下がり)
会話「お望みの額は？」「値をつけてください」"How much do you want for it?" "Make me an offer." (! offer は「付け値」のこと)
④【値で】● その中古のカメラをいい値で売れた I got a good price for the old camera./I sold the old camera at a high price.
● **値が張る** ● あちらのコートはこちらのより値が張ります That coat is more expensive [higher in price, ×higher] than this one.

-ね you know. (⇒ねえ《終助詞》)
ねあか 根明 ● ねあかである(性格が明るい) be a cheerful type; (楽天家だ) be an óptimist.

ねあがり 値上がり an increase [a rise] in price, a price increase [rise, 《主に米話》hike]. ● 石油はまた値上がりした There has been another rise [hike] in oil prices. ● ガソリンが 10 円値上がりした (The price of) gasoline has risen [gone up] by 10 yen.

ねあげ 値上げ 图 a raise [an increase] in price, a price raise [《主に米話》hike]. ● 食料品[電気代]の値上げ a raise in food prices [power rates].
──**値上げする** 動 ● 家賃を値上げする raise [×raise] the rent. ● 鋼鉄を 3～5 パーセント値上げする raise [increase] the prices of steel 3 percent to 5 percent; a 3 percent to 5 percent raise [increase] of steel. ● 郵便料金が値上げになった Postal rates were raised [were increased].

ねあせ 寝汗 (a) night sweat. ● 寝汗をかく sweat in one's sleep; sweat at night.

ネアンデルタールじん ネアンデルタール人 (a) Neanderthal man.

ねいき 寝息 ● ベビーベッドで知子の静かな寝息がしていた I heard the quiet [peaceful] breathing of Tomoko in the crib./I heard Tomoko breathing quietly [peacefully] in her crib.
● **寝息をうかがう** see if 《one》 is asleep; make sure (that) 《one》 is asleep.

ねいす 寝椅子 a couch; a sofa.

ネイティブ 〖ネイティブスピーカー〗a native speaker 《of English》.
● **ネイティブアメリカン** a Native American. (! American Indian の現在定着されている呼び名) ● **ネイティブチェック** native speaker's check; 《和製語》native check.

ネイビーブルー 〖濃紺〗navy blue. ● ネイビーブルーの navy blue.

ねいりばな 寝入り端 ● 寝入りばなに地震で起こされた I was awakened by the earthquake just as I had fallen asleep.

ねいる 寝入る fall* asleep; go* [get*] to sleep. (! get to sleep は通例否定文で. この sleep は名詞) ● 赤ん坊はぐっすり寝入っている The baby is fast [sound] asleep.

ネイル 〖つめ〗a nail.
● ネイルアート nail art. ● ネイルアーティスト a nail artist. ● ネイルエナメル 《米》nail enamel; 《英》nail polish [varnish]. ● ネイルサロン a nail salon.

ねいろ 音色 a tone. (⇒音(ⁿ))

ねうごき 値動き price movement; movement (of prices); (株価の) rising and falling of stock prices. ● 小幅な値動き small [modest] fluctuation in prices.

ねうち 値打ち value; worth. (! value は主に実際的な有用性から見た価値をさすのに対し, worth は精神的な価値をさすことが多い (⇒価値))
①【～(の)値打ち】● お金の値打ち the value of money. ● それは一文の値打ちもない It's not worth a penny [a straw]./It's worth nothing. ● この本

読む値打ちがある This book is *worth* [×worth while] read*ing*. (とはいわない)/It is *worth* while to read [*worth* (*while*) *reading*] this book.

会話「この指輪はいくらぐらいの値打ちのものでしょうか」「100 万円ほどのものです」"How much is this ring *worth*?/What's the *value* of this ring?" "It's *worth* [*valued at*] about one million yen."

❷ [値打ちが[は, も, を]] ▶彼にとってそれは大変な値打ちがある[ほとんど値打ちがない; 何の値打ちもない] It is of great [little; no] *value* to him. ▶それは将来きっと値打ちが出るだろう This will certainly increase in *value* in the future./This book will be *worth* more [×more *worth*] in the future than it is today. ▶50 ドルでお買いなさいよ. それだけの値打ちは十分ありますよ Take it for fifty dollars. It's well worth every penny [*it*]. ❶ worth every penny は「50 ドルのどの 1 ペニーをとってみてもそれだけの価値がある」の意. worth it は「それだけの値打ちがある」の意の慣用表現. it は前文の内容を受ける) ▶彼がその値打ちを本当に分かっていると思いますか Do you think he really *appreciates* that? ▶そんなことを言うと君の値打ちが下がる I think you *degrade* yourself by saying that.

ねえ 間 [注意喚起] listen; look (here); [呼びかけ] [米話] say, 《英やや古》I say; [懇願] please, come on (❶ しばしば /kmɔːn/ と発音) [表現をやわらげて] you know (❶ 平叙文の文頭に置き, やや上昇調で読む). ▶ねえ, あんな口のきき方はないだろ Look [*Now look*], you can't say such a thing to me. ▶ねえ, いったいどうしたの Say, what's the matter with you? ▶ねえ[お願い], やめてよ *Please* [*Come on*], stop it. ▶ねえ, 医者に見てもらわないと *You know*, I think you ought to see a doctor. ▶ねえ, 泳ぎに行こうか *I'll téll you whát*—let's go swimming. ▶これから話すことが価値のあることを表す) ▶ねえあなた[君] (夫婦間などで) Darling!/Honey!

―**ねえ**(終助詞) ❶ [相手の同意を求めて] ..., isn't it [is it]? (❶ 通例下降調で読む (⇒解説)); you know /jənóu/ (❶ 平叙文の文尾に置き, 上昇調で読む

> [解説] 付加疑問の形式　人称・数・時制により種々の形をとる. 前が肯定文なら「助動詞+n't+人称代名詞(または there)」, 前が否定なら「助動詞+人称代名詞(または there)」となる. ここで用いられる助動詞は疑問文や否定文を作るときと同じく, 次の 24 個である: am, is, are, was, were; have, has, had; do, does, did; shall, should; will, would; can, could; may, might; must, ought, need, dare, used (ただし最後の used は 《話》では代わりに did を用いる)

▶それはおもしろい It's ＼*fun*, *isn't it*?/Isn't it ＼*fun*! (❶ 後の方は感嘆文の一種 (⇒なんと 間)) ▶今日は学校へ行かなかったよね You didn't go to schóol ＼*today*, ＼*did you*? (❶ 本文の音調が「＼」「／」「＼／」で終わる場合は, ＼did you? のように大幅に下げて読む. ... ＼today, did you? では「行かないとは言わせない」という強い調子になる) ▶それで彼はあなたに電話したんだね(=そうだろう?) So he called you up, *you* ／*know*./いうことならば, So he cálled you ＼*up*, ／*did he*? ❶ 上昇調で肯定文に肯定文の(または否定文に否定の)付加疑問に添えると, このほかに驚き・いらだち・不信などの気持ちを表すこともある) ▶そのことはあなたに言ったわね That's what I ＼*told you*, ／*huh* /hʌ/? (❶ 非難を込めて同意をうながす言い方)

❷ [相手に確かめて] ..., isn't it [is it]? (❶ 上昇調で読む (⇒❶)); (そう思うのですが) I believe [suppose], (そうですね) right. (❶ いずれも文尾に置き上昇調で読む) ▶彼はトムの弟ですね He is Tóm's ＼ *brother*, ／*isn't he*? [I ／*believe*, ／*right*]. ▶ジョージさん, ですよね George, ／*is it* (what your name is)? (❶ 呼びかけたものの自信がない場合で (　) 内はいわないのが普通) ▶昔ここに城がありましたね There used to be a castle here, *didn't* [[英書] *use(d)n't*] *there*? ▶規子に会うのは初めてでしたね I don't think you've met Noriko, *have you*? (❶ 1 人を紹介するときの前置き. (2) この文は I think you haven't met.... と同意で, I think は表現をやわらげるために添えられている. したがって ×..., do I? とはならないことに注意) ▶お便り待ち焦がれていました. 試験勉強でお忙しかったのですね 《手紙で》I've been dying to hear from you. *I understand* you've been busy studying for the exams.

会話「この仕事にはずいぶん時間がかかったのでしょうね」「いやそんなことありませんでした」"You must have taken a lot of time to do this job, *mustn't* /mʌ́snt/ *you*?" "No, I ／*didn't*." (❶ 応答文が mustn't でないことに注意. 応答文の音調については (⇒–か ❶ (b)))

ねえさん 姉さん one's older [《話》big, 《米書・英》elder] sister. (❶ 呼びかけには Sarah などとファーストが普通) (⇒姉)

ネーブル [植物] a navel /néivl/ (orange).

ネーム [名前] one's name; [イラストなどの説明] a caption. ▶彼らは作家としてのネームバリューがある(=名が通っている) He is *famous* [*well-known*] as a writer./He has *a name* as a writer. (❶ ×name value は和製英語)
● **ネームカード** [名札] a name tag; 《和製語》a name card. (⇒名札) ● **ネームプレート** [標札] a nameplate.

ネール (⇒ネイル)

ねおい 根生い (⇒生え抜き)

ねおき 寝起き ―― 一つ屋根の下で寝起きを共にする live under the same roof. ▶彼は寝起きがよい[悪い] (=気分よく[悪く]目覚める) He *wakes* up in a good [*bad*] *mood*.

ねおし 寝押し ―― 寝押しする 動 press 《a pleated skirt》 by putting 《it》 underneath one's sleeping mattress.

ネオン [化学] neon /níːɑn/; 《元素記号 Ne》; (ネオンサイン) a neon (sign).
● **ネオン灯** a neon (light [*lamp*]).

ネガ a negative. (⇒写真 ❺)

*ねがい **願い** ❶ [願望] a wish 《*for*; *to* do; *that* 節》; 《欲望》a desire 《*for*; *to* do》; (希望) (a) hope 《*of*, *for*; *that* 節》. (⇒希望)
① [願いが] ▶願いがかないましたか Did you *get* [*have*] your *wish*?/Did your *wish* come true? ▶ありがとうございました. もう一つお願いがあるんですが Thank you very much. Could you help me with another *problem*?
② [願いを] ● 願いを実現する realize one's *wish* [夢] *dream*). ▶彼は田舎に住みたいという願いを持っている He has a *wish* [a *desire*] *to* live in the country./He has a *hope* of living in the country. ▶彼は名声を得たいという願いを持っている He has a *wish* [a *desire*] *for* fame./He *wishes for* [*hopes for, desires*] fame. (⇒願う ❶)
❷ [要請] a request 《*for*》. (⇒依頼) ▶彼は本人の願いにより他の部署に転属された He was transferred to another post *at his request*. ▶市長は私たちの願いを聞き入れてくれた 《書》The mayor granted

[complied with] our *request*. ▶彼は私の名古屋支店への転勤願いを退けた He turned down my transfer *request* to the Nagoya branch office.
❸ [祈願] a prayer /préər/; [懇願] (an) entreaty. ▶神は彼の願いにこたえた God answered [heard] his *prayers*.
❹ [申請] (an) application. (⇨申請)

ねがいあげる 願い上げる earnestly request; entreat. ▶格別のご配慮を賜りますよう願い上げます I *earnestly request* that you (should) pay special attention to this matter.

ねがいごと 願い事 ●願いの井戸に硬貨を投げ入れて息子のことで願い事をする drop a coin in a wishing well and make a *wish about* one's son.

ねがいさげ 願い下げ ▶そんなことは願い下げだ I *won't do* such a thing *if I'm asked*./I'd rather *be excused from* (doing) such a thing. (❗もっと強い意味で用いる人もいる。その時には(⇨こめびら))

ねがいでる 願い出る ask *(for)*; (正式に, 書類を整えて) apply 《*to* him *for* it》; make* [file in, 《やや書》 submit] an application 《*for*》. ●上司に3日の休暇を願い出る(=求める) *ask* one's boss *for* a three-day leave [three days off]. ●校長に辞職を願い出る(=辞表を提出する) send in [hand in, 《主に米》 turn in, submit] one's resignation to the principal.

***ねがう 願う** ❶ [願望する] wish; 《書》 desire; hope (⇨希望する); want (⇨望む); [強く切望している] be anxious [eager] 《*to* do》.

> **使い分け wish** 基本的には実現が不可能または困難なことに対する願望を表す。
> **desire** wish より強い願望を表し, 願望の実現に対する積極性が示される。
> **hope** 将来などへの期待を表し, wish より実現の可能性が高い。
> **want** hope と同様実現可能な願いであるが, hope より意味が強く, 欠乏・必要からどうしてもそれを満たそうという直接的欲求を表す。

▶我々は彼の成功を願っている We *wish for* [*hope for, desire*] his success. (❗hope は進行形可。wish, desire は通例不可) We *wish* him success [×his success]. ▶あなたが来られることを願っています I *hope (that)* you can come. (❗来られる望みがある。《話》 では that は通例省略する)/I *wish (that)* you could come. (❗来られそうにない。that 節内に仮定法過去。that は通例省略する) ▶私は一刻も早く両親に出会えることを願っています I *dó wish* [*hòpe, desíre] to* meet my parents as soon as possible./I'm very *anxious* [*eager*] *to* meet my parents as soon as possible. ▶彼にすぐに来てほしいと彼女は願っている She *desires* [has the *desire*] that he (《主に英》 should) come at once./She *wants* [*desires, wishes*, ×hopes] him to come at once. (❗desire, wish は要求・命令に近い。want の方がストレートな願望) ▶お静かに願います I *wish* you *would* be quiet. (❗Be quiet, please. などより控えめに要求する言い方)

❷ [依頼する] ask 《A *to* B; A *to* do》; request 《A *to* do》 (❗ask より堅い語)。(⇨頼む); [懇願する] beg (-gg-) 《for ...》 (⇨懇願する). ▶お手伝い願いたいのですが I'd like to *ask* you *for* help [*ask* your help]./I'*d like* you to help me. ▶あすの会議に出席願います You *are requested to* attend the meeting tomorrow.

❸ [祈願する] pray 《(*to* A) *for* B》.

ねがえり 寝返り ●寝返りを打つ turn over in bed; (何度も) roll over [toss about] in bed; (裏切る)(⇨寝返る).

ねがえる 寝返る (寝返りを打つ) turn over in bed; (裏切る) betray; (敵方につく) go* over to the enemy.

ねがお 寝顔 one's sleeping face. ▶彼女の寝顔は美しい She looks beautiful when she is asleep [《(や書》 in her sleep].

ねがさ 根嵩 ●根嵩株 a high-priced stock.

ねかす ❶ [眠らせる] ▶10時に子供を寝かす(=寝つかせる) *put* a child *to bed* [*sleep*] at ten. (❗×... *to the* [*a*] *bed*. とはいわない。sleep は名詞) ●歌をうたって寝かす sing 《*a baby*》*to sleep*.
❷ [横にする] lay*... (down). ●負傷した兵士を担架に寝かす *lay (down)* the wounded soldier on the stretcher. ●箱を寝かす *lay* a box *on its side*. ▶もう10分寝かせておいてくれよ Let me *stay in bed* for ten more minutes [《まれ》 ten minutes more].
❸ [金・商品などを] let* (money, goods) lie idle. ●土地[資本]を使わないで寝かしておく *keep* land [capital] *idle*.
❹ [酒・こうじなどを] age 《wine》; ferment 《rice malt》.

ねかせる 寝かせる put* (him) to bed. (⇨寝かす) ●パン生地を3時間寝かせておく leave the dough to *stand* for three hours.

ねがったりかなったり 願ったり叶ったり ▶それは願ったりかなったりだ (まさに自分が欲していることです) It's just what I want [have in mind]./(願いがかなったかのようだ) It's like a dream come true. (❗慣用句。that has come true の意)

ねがってもない 願ってもない ▶願ってもないことだ I couldn't ask for anything better. (❗could は仮定法過去形で「やろうと思えばできる」の意)/That's just what I want. ▶それは願ってもないお話です I can't thank you enough for your kind offer./《反語的》I don't see how I can refuse such an offer.

ネガティブ ― ネガティブな 形 [消極的な] negative. (⇔ ポジティブな) ●ネガティブな評価 *negative* evaluation.
●ネガティブアプローチ a negative approach. ●ネガティブキャンペーン a negative campaign. ●ネガティブリスト the negative list.

ねかぶ 根株 (⇨切り株)

ねがわくは 願わくは ▶願わくは君に祝福あらんことを *I hope* God may bless you.

ねがわしい 願わしい desirable. (⇨望ましい)

ねかん 寝棺 a coffin (long enough to lay a dead person).

ねぎ 葱 [植物] 《米》 a scallion, 《英》 a spring onion; (アサツキ) a chive. (❗いずれも日本のネギに似ているが同じものではない)
●葱坊主 an onion head. ●葱鮪 /ねぎま/ (なべ料理) a one-pot dish of leeks and tuna.

ねぎらう ▶彼は従業員の労をねぎらった(=礼を言った) He *thanked* [*expressed thanks to*] his employees *for* their efforts. ▶彼は彼女の功労をねぎらった(=ほうびを与えて) ねぎらった He *rewarded* her *for* her services.

ねきりむし 根切り虫 a cutworm.

ねぎる 値切る 《話》 beat* 《the price, him》 down 《*to*》. ●値切るために彼と交渉する bargain with him for a lower price; (値段について) bargain [(やりあう) haggle] with him about [over] the price.
▶私はじゅうたんを1万円に値切った I *beat* the price of the carpet *down to* 10,000 yen. (❗... by 10,000 yen では「1万円だけ値切った」の意) のみの市では値切るのがおもしろいのです The fun is in the *bargaining* at a flea market.

ネクストバッターズサークル [野球] an on-deck

circle; 《和製語》next batter's circle. ●ネクストバッターサークルで(打席を)待つ wait in the *on-deck circle*; be on deck.

ねくずれ 値崩れ a sharp drop in price(s). ▶コンピュータは出て半年もすると値崩れを起こす The price of computers *drops sharply* in six months after they are put on the market.

ねごぜ 寝言 ●寝癖が悪い(=寝ている間に転げ回る) toss about in one's sleep. (⇨寝相(芯))▶髪に寝癖がついた My hair curled the wrong way [My hair got messed up] in my sleep.

ネクター 〖果実飲料〗nectar.

ネクタイ a tie, 《主に米》a necktie. (❗現在では前の方が普通)●蝶(☆)ネクタイ a bow /bóu/ *tie*. ●ネクタイを締める put on a *tie*. ●ネクタイを結ぶ〖ゆるめる; はずす〗knot [loosen; take off] one's *tie*. ●曲がったネクタイをまっすぐにする straighten one's crooked *tie*. ▶彼はスーツを着てネクタイをしている He wears [is wearing] a suit and *tie*. (❗後の方は一時的な行為をさす)

●ネクタイ留め a tie clasp. ●ネクタイピン a tiepin, 《米》a stickpin; (刺し込み式)a tie-tack;《和製語》a necktie pin.

ネクタリン〖椿桃(芋)〗〖植物〗a nectarine.

ねくび 寝首 寝首をかく kill (him) in (his) sleep;《比喩的》(油断につけ込む) catch (him) off (his) guard.

ねぐら 根暗 ●ねくらである(性格が暗い) be a gloomy type; (物事を悲観的に見る人だ) be a péssimist.

ねぐら 〖木の枝など鳥が夜眠る所〗a roost; (巣) a nest;〖家〗one's home. ●ねぐらにつく roost. ●ねぐらに帰る; 離れる leave the *roost*. (❗home は副詞) ●ねぐらを離れる leave the *roost*. ▶カラスはもうねぐらに帰るころだ Crows are *at roost* [*in their nests*].

ネグリジェ 《米》a nightgown, 《英》a nightdress;《話》a nightie. (❗英語の negligee /nèglidʒéi/ は通例寝巻きなどの上にはおる婦人用の薄手の部屋着)

ネグる 〖ネグレクトする〗neglect. (⇨ネグレクト)

ねぐるしい 寝苦しい ▶昨夜はむし暑くて寝苦しかった(=よく眠れなかった) It was so muggy last night that I *couldn't sleep well*.

ネグレクト 〖無視, 怠慢, 育児放棄〗(a) neglect.

*__ねこ 猫__ a cat; (愛称) a puss /pús/, a pussy (cat) (❗いずれも主に小児語); (雄猫) a male cat, a tomcat, 《やや話》a tom; (雌猫) a female cat, a she-cat, a tabby (cat); (子猫) a kitten, a kitty (❗kitty は小児語). (関連) lead a cat-and-dog life (けんかばかりして暮らす) (英語は猫と犬と仲が悪い動物と考えられていることから)) ●三毛猫 a tortoise-shell *cat*. ●黒猫 a black *cat*. ●猫を飼う have [keep] a *cat*. (❗商売などご飼うのでなければ keep は大げさな感じを伴う) ▶外で猫の鳴き声が聞こえた I heard the mew of a *cat* [*cat* mewing] outside. (❗交尾期に鳴くのは caterwaul /kǽtərwɔ̀ːl/ という) ▶我が家の猫はネズミをとるのがうまい Our *cat* is good at catching mice. ▶猫ののどをごろごろ鳴らす A *cat* purrs. ▶彼は借りてきた猫のようだ He is (as) *meek as a lamb* [*a kitten*]. (❗lamb は「小羊」)

●猫にかつお節 ●(キツネにガチョウ[オオカミにヒツジ]の番をさせるようなものだ) It is setting a fox to keep the geese [setting a wolf to guard the sheep].

●猫に小判 ▶それは猫に小判だ〈ことわざ〉It is *like casting pearls before swine*. (❗「ブタに真珠を投げてやるようなものだ」の意)

●猫の手も借りたい ▶猫の手も借りたいほど忙しい I'm very busy and short-handed./I am (as) busy as a bee.

●猫の額 ●猫の額ほどの土地 a *tiny little* strip of land. (❗同義語を重ねて意味を強める)

●猫の目 ●猫の目のように変わる(=風見(ぎ)鶏のように移り気である) His mind is (as) *fickle as a weathercock* (in the wind).

●猫も杓子も(い) ▶どうして猫も杓子も大学に入ろうとするのだろうか Why does *every Tom, Dick and Harry* rush to get into [enter] university? /everybody or the other.

●猫をかぶる ▶その女の子は父親の前では猫をかぶっている《話》The girl *is putting it on* in front of her father. (❗通例進行形で.「芝居をしている」の意)/《米話》She is a good girl in front of her father. It's just a *put-on*.

●猫恐怖症 〖医学〗ailurophobia.

ねこあし 猫足 a carved furniture leg.

ねこいらず 猫いらず rat poison; ratsbane.

ねこかわいがり 猫かわいがり ▶父は末っ子の友美を猫かわいがりにかわいがっている(=溺愛している) Father *dotes on* Yumi, the youngest daughter.

ねこぐるま 猫車 a wheelbarrow.

ねごこち 寝心地 ●このふとんは寝心地がよい[悪い] This futon is *comfortable* [*uncomfortable*] *to sleep in*. (❗in に注意) ▶そのベッドは寝心地はいかがですか *How* do you like [*feel* in] the bed?

ねこじた 猫舌 ●私は猫舌です(熱いものが食べられない) I can't eat hot things [food]. /(舌が熱に敏感だ) My tongue is very *sensitive to* heat.

ねこじゃらし 猫じゃらし 〖植物〗a foxtail (grass); a pussgrass.

ねこぜ 猫背 〈have〉 a (slight) stoop. ●猫背の人 a *stoop-shouldered* [a *round-shouldered*] person; a person with a *stoop* [with *round shoulders*]. ▶彼の猫背はひどくなった His stoop has grown worse.

ねこそぎ 根こそぎ ●雑草を根こそぎにする *pull up* weeds *by the roots*; root up [*uproot*] weeds. ▶多くの家が洪水で根こそぎ流された A lot of houses were *completely* washed away [were swept away] by the flood.

ねごと 寝言 ●寝言を言う talk in one's sleep; talk while (one is) sleeping. ▶寝言(=たわ言)を言うな Don't *talk nonsense*.

ねこなでごえ 猫撫で声 ●猫なで声で(ご機嫌とりの声で) in a *coaxing* voice.

ねこのめ 猫の目 ●猫の目のように変わる(移り気である) be (as) fickle as a weathercock; (意見)《人が主語》say something different every minute.

ねこばば 猫糞 ── 猫糞する 動 ▶彼は道で拾った財布を猫ばばした He *pocketed* the wallet he picked up on the street.

ねこみ 寝込み ▶警察は彼らの寝込みを襲った The police made an attack on them *while they were asleep* [*were sleeping*]./《やや書》The police surprised them *in their sleep*.

ねこむ 寝込む 〖寝入る〗go* to sleep, fall* asleep;〈漫画で〉catch some zzz [z'z];〖熟睡している〗be fast [sound] asleep;〖病床につく・ついている〗take* to [keep*, be confined to] one's bed; be laid up (❗通例受身形で). ▶本を読んでいる間に寝込んでしまう *read* oneself *to sleep* [❗この sleep は名詞]; *fall asleep* while (he is) reading. ▶彼女は先週から病気で寝込んでいる She *has been* sick *in bed* [*been laid up*] since last week. ▶be laid up with sickness は不要.「風邪で寝込んでいる」は She has been in bed [been laid up, been down] with a cold since last week.) ▶彼は事故の後寝込んでいる He *has been bedridden* after the accident. (❗bedridden は「(病気・老齢などで)寝た

きりの」の意)
ねこめいし 猫目石 [地学] a cat's-eye.
ねこやなぎ 猫柳 [植物] a pussy willow.
ねごろ 値頃 ━値頃な 形 reasonable. ●値ごろな[値ごろ感のある]価格 reasonable pricing.
ねころぶ 寝転ぶ lie* (down) 《on》. (⇨横たわる)
ねさがり 値下がり 名 a fall [a drop] in price.
━━ 動 値下がりする 動 ●野菜が大幅に値下がりした There has been a drastic fall [drop] in the prices of vegetables./The prices of vegetables have fallen [dropped, gone down] drastically. ●激しい競争によってパソコンが値下がりした The strong competition pushed down the PC prices.
*ねさげ 値下げ 名 a price reduction [cut], a reduction [cut] in price. (!cut の方が口語的); a markdown. ▶冬物は 30 パーセント値下げになった Winter clothes were reduced in price [were marked down] by 30 percent./Winter clothes were discounted 30 percent.
━━ 値下げする 動 ●衣類を大幅に値下げする give [make, allow] a great [considerable] reduction in the prices of clothes; reduce [lower] the prices of clothes greatly. ●そのかばんを 5,000 円に値下げする reduce [lower] the price of the bag to 5,000 yen.
●値下げ競争 a príce wàr.
ねざけ 寝酒 ━寝酒(を)する 動 have a nightcap.
ねざす 根差す [根をはる] take* (strong) root, root (deeply); [起因する] develop (arise*] 《from》; be rooted 《in》; be at the root 《of》.
ねざめ 寝覚め ●寝覚めがちな夜 (spend) a fitful night.
●寝覚めが悪い ▶2 人でめやたらと飲んだあとの事故死だろう, 寝覚めが悪いといったらありゃしない(=気分がひどくよくない) He died [was killed in an accident] after we had drunk a lot together. I feel awful about it. (⇨後味 [後味の悪い])
*ねじ a screw. ●ねじで留める screw down [up] 《the lid》; ●ねじの頭 a scréw hèad. ●ねじを締める[ゆるめる; 回す] tighten [loosen; turn] a screw. ●ねじを巻く(時計の) wind (up) 《a watch》; (奮起させる) give (him) a good shaking; (主に米) light a fire under (him). ▶ねじがゆるんでいる The screw is loose. (!比喩的に《話》He has a screw loose. (あの男はどこかねじがゆるんでいる)という)
●ねじキャップ a scréw càp. ●ねじ回し(プラスの) a (Phillips) scréwdriver.
ねじあげる 捩じ上げる twist; (ぐいと) wrench. ●腕を捩じ上げる twist 《his》 arm.
ねじきる 捩じ切る twist ... off.
ねじくぎ ねじ釘 [ねじ] a screw; [締めくぎ] a bolt.
●ドライバーでねじ釘を締める tighten (↔loosen) a screw [a bolt] with a screwdriver. ●箱のふたをねじ釘で留める fasten the lid of a box with a screw; screw down the lid of a box.
ねじける 拗ける (心がゆがめられる) be twisted [warped]; (ひねくれる) become* crooked [(やや書) perverse]. ●心のねじけた子 a crooked [a perverse, (やや書) perverted] child. ●あの人は性格がねじけている His personality is twisted [warped]./He has a twisted [a warped] personality.
ねじこむ 捩じ込む ❶ [突っ込む] thrust* 《into》. ●彼のポケットにチップをねじ込む thrust a tip into his pocket.
❷ [強く抗議する] strongly protest 《about》.
ねしずまる 寝静まる be fast [sound] asleep. ▶皆が寝静まる真夜中で私は待った I waited until midnight, when everyone was (fast) asleep.
ねじふせる 捩じ伏せる ●泥棒をねじふせて(腕をねじって押し倒す) hold down the thief by twisting [wrenching] his arm; (押さえつける) press the thief down.
ねじまきどりクロニクル 『ねじまき鳥クロニクル』 The Wind-Up Bird Chronicle. (参考) 村上春樹の小説)
ねじまげる 捩じ曲げる twist; [曲解する] twist. ●針金をねじ曲げる twist a wire; bend a wire by twisting. 《彼の言葉をねじ曲げて(=悪い方に)取る twist [《書》 pervert] his remarks. ▶彼は車の後ろの席から体をねじ曲げて私に手を振った He twisted around in the back of the car to wave to me.
ねしょうがつ 寝正月 ●寝正月をする(=どこへも出かけずに家でゆっくり休養する) spend the New Year's holidays taking a good rest at home without going out anywhere.
ねしょうべん 寝小便 bed-wetting.
━━ 寝小便(を)する 動 wet one's bed. ●寝小便をする人 a bed-wetter.
ねじりはちまき 捩じり鉢巻き ●ねじり鉢巻きで勉強する work energetically [very hard]. ●ねじり鉢巻きをしたいなせな若い衆 a dashing young man with a twisted towel around his head.
*ねじる 捩じる [[よじる]] twist; (強力に) wrench; [[回す]] screw. ●彼の腕をねじる twist [wrench] his arm. ●びんのふたをねじって開ける [閉める] screw the cap off [on, onto] a bottle; screw a bottle open [shut].
ねじれる 捩じれる be twisted. (⇨曲がる)
ねじろ 根城 one's base camp; one's home base.
▶私たちはケイトのアパートを根城にしてヨーロッパ各地を旅行した We used Kate's apartment as our home base from which we traveled extensively in Europe.
ネス ━ネス湖 Loch /lák, láx/ Ness. (⇨ネッシー)
ねすがた 寝姿 how one looks while sleeping. ▶人に寝姿を見られるのはいやだ I hate to be seen while sleeping.
ねすごす 寝過ごす oversleep*. ▶また寝過ごして学校に遅れた I was late for school because I overslept again.
ねずのばん 寝ずの番 ●寝ずの番をする keep an all-night watch [《やや書》 vigil] 《against》. ●寝ずの番をする人 a night watch [《男の》 watchman].
*ねずみ 鼠 [動物] a rat (!ドブネズミの類で mouse より大きい); (ハツカネズミ) a mouse 《mice》 (!米英の家ネズミはこれに当たる。 ●どぶねずみ a brown rat. ●野ねずみ a field mouse. ●袋のねずみ (⇨袋 [成句]) ●ねずみ算式にふえる multiply rapidly like rabbits [×mice]. ▶ねずみはちゅうちゅう鳴く Mice squeak. ●ねずみ講 pyramid selling; a pyramid scheme. ●ねずみ捕り (わな) (set) a rattrap, a mousetrap; (薬) rat poison; (スピード取り締まりの) a speed trap.
ねずみいろ 鼠色 (dark) gray. ●ねずみ色の帽子 a dark-gray hat.
ねぞう 寝相 ▶彼は寝相が悪い(寝ている間に転げ回る) He rolls [tosses] about while (he is) sleeping [in his sleep]. (!while 節を用いる方が口語的)/(だらしなく眠る人だ) He is an untidy sleeper. (!「寝相がいい」は sleep quietly, be a tidy sleeper など)
ねそびれる 寝そびれる ▶昨夜は寝そびれてしまった(寝つくことができなかった) I couldn't get to sleep last night./(目が覚めていた) I lay awake last night.
ねそべる 寝そべる [[横たわる]] lie* (down) 《on》; (大の字になって) stretch (oneself) out, lie (at) full length 《on the floor》 (!《話》ではしばしば at で

ネタ [材料] (新聞などの) a news item; (小説などの) material (⇨種❹); [証拠] evidence, proof; [料理の] material. ●小説のネタを集める collect *material* for a novel. ▶その話をネタにして小説を書く write a novel *out of* the story. ▶お前のネタは上がっているんだ We have found [got] 《×an》 *evidence against* you. ▶この種の事件は週刊誌のいいネタになる 《話》 These kind of incidents make *good copy* for weeklies. (❗慣用句. 新聞・小説などにも用いられる)

ねだ 根太 the joists. ▶根太が抜けた The floor gave way.

ねたきり 寝たきり ▶彼はそれ以来ずっと寝たきりです He *has been kept in* [*has been confined to*, 《婉曲的》 *has stayed in*] bed since then./He *has been bedridden* since then.
● 寝たきり老人 a bedridden old man [woman]; old people confined to bed.

ねたば 寝刃 (切れ味の悪い刃) a dull blade.
● 寝刃を合わせる (刀の刃を研ぐ) sharpen the blade (of a sword).

ねたばこ 寝たばこ ▶寝たばこする smoke in bed. ▶火事の原因は寝たばこだった The fire started from the *cigarette smoked in bed*.

ねたましい 妬ましい [うらやましがる] envious (⤴(う)ましい); (反感を持って) jealous (⇨妬(ね)む); (人をうらやましがらせるような) enviable. ●ねたましいほどの財産 an *enviable* fortune. ▶彼女の才能がわたましい I *am envious* [*jealous*] of her talent.

ねたみ 妬み [美望(ぼう)] envy; [しっと] jealousy. (❗後の語は個人的な感情で根底に「悪意」「反感」がある) (⇨妬む) ●ねたみからそうする do it out of *envy* [*jealousy*]. ●ねたみ深い女 an *envious* [a *jealous*] woman.

****ねたむ 妬む** be envious [jealous] 《*of*》. (❗*jealous* は反感や憎悪の気持ちを含む) ▶彼の成功をねたむ *envy* (him) his success; *envy* him *for* his success; be *envious* [*jealous*] *of* (him) *for* his success. ▶ねたんで彼の悪口を言うな Don't say bad things about him *out of envy* [*jealousy*].

ねだめ 寝溜め ── 寝溜めする 動 (説明的に) get as much sleep as possible to make up for one's lack of sleep.

ねたやし 根絶やし ●根絶やしにする root out, 《書》 eradicate. (⇨撲滅)

ねだる (しきりに) press, keep* asking; (うるさく) pester; (へりくだって) beg (-gg-); (へつらって) wheedle. ▶彼は母親に小遣いをねだった He *pressed* [*pestered*, *begged*] his mother for pocket money. (❗*for* 句の代わりに *to give him* pocket money も可) ▶彼は父にねだって1万円もらった He *wheedled* his father *into* giving 《×to give》 him 10,000 yen./He *wheedled* 10,000 yen *out of* his father.

****ねだん 値段** [価格] a price. [代価] (a) cost. (❗*price* は商品についている価格, *cost* は買うときなどに実際に支払う代金); [金銭的価値] (a) value. (⇨値段)
❶【～値段】●法外な値段 an exorbitant [《話》 an astronomical] *price*. ▶卵は高い[安い; 割引; 手ごろな]値段で売られている Eggs are selling at high [low; reduced; reasonable] *prices*. ▶そんな値段では買わない I won't buy it at that *price*. 《…at such a price. より口語的》 ▶ジャガイモがいい値段じゃないか！ Aren't potatoes a (good) *price*! (❗at a price は「かなりの値段で」)
❷【値段(の)～】●値段の高い時計 an expensive [a high-*priced*] watch. (❗×a high watch とはいわない) ▶それは値段の質は値段の割により The quality of the product is good, considering its *price*. ▶それは値段次第だ It depends on the *price*.
❸【値段が[は]～】●それは値段が高すぎる The *price* is too high/It's too expensive. (❗値段が高い場合は high, 物が高い場合は expensive を用いる) ▶その外車はエンジンの性能がいい、少々値段ははるが The foreign car has a powerful engine. The *price* is rather high, though. (⇨値) ▶この店の肉の値段は他より高い[安い; 手ごろだ] The *price* of meat is higher [lower; more reasonable] at this store./(高い[安い; 手ごろな]値段が付いている) The meat *is priced* higher [lower; more reasonably] at this store. ▶リンゴの値段が上がった The *price* of apples has gone up [risen] (⇔gone down [fallen]). ▶値段が何とかなりませんか Can you give me a special *price*?/(負けておくれ) Won't you take *less*?
【会話】「このスーツの値段はいくらですか」「7万円です」 "What's the *price* of this suit?/*How much* is this suit?" "It's 70,000 yen." (❗(1) ×How much is the price of this suit? は不可. (2) What is the cost of this suit? だと「代金はいくらですか」の意 (⇨いくら))
【会話】「値段なら相談に乗りますよ. いくらならいいのですか」「5,000円にしてよ」 "I might be able to work with you on the *price*. What will you give me for it?" "Make it 5,000 yen."
❹【値段を】●値段を上げる[下げる] raise [lower, reduce, cut] *the price*. ▶全部の商品に値段を付けた I *have put* [*marked*] *prices on* all the articles. /I *have priced* all the articles. ▶値段を比較していちばん安いのを買うつもりだ I'll compare *prices* and buy the most inexpensive [the cheapest].
●値段表 a price list.

ねちがえる 寝違える ▶どうもゆうべ寝違えてしまったみたいだ I must *have got crick in* [*must've twisted*] my *neck while* (I was) *sleeping* last night. (❗ *twisted* の代わりに *switched* もよく用いられる)

ネチケット netiquette. (❗net と etiquette の混成語)

ネチズン a netizen. (❗net と citizen の混成語)

ねちっこい persistent.

ねちねち 副 ●歯にねちねちくっつく *stick to* one's teeth.
── **ねちねちした 形** (粘着性のある) sticky; (糊(のり)のように) glutinous; (しつこい) persistent. ▶この樹脂は長い間ねちねちしている This resin remains (soft and) *sticky* for a long time. ▶彼女はねちねちしている人が好きでない She doesn't like a *persistent* person.

:**ねつ 熱** ❶【物理的な】heat. ●太陽の熱 the *heat* of the sun; solar heat. ▶太陽は我々に熱と光を与えてくれる The sun gives us *heat* and light. ▶熱はたいていの金属を溶かす *Heat* melts most metals.
❷【体温】(a) temperature (❗具体的には ⓒ); [病熱] (a) fever (❗複数形なし)
①【～(の)熱】●彼女は高い熱があった[出た] She had [ran, developed, 《米話》 came down with] a high *fever*./She had [ran] a high *temperature*. ▶私の子供は39度5分の熱を出していた My child was running a *fever* that reached 39.5℃.
②【熱が[は]～】●彼は少し熱があるようだ He seems to have a slight *fever*./He seems (to be) a bit *feverish*. ▶彼女は熱が出て[熱がとれるまで]寝ていた She was in bed with a *fever* [*until her fever* broke]. ▶彼の熱は今朝になって(平熱に)下がった [(*His*

熱より上がった] His *temperature* [*fever*] came down [went up] this morning. ▶熱がないか計ってごらんなさい Take your *temperature* [×*fever*] to see if it's normal. ▶熱が上がった[なかなか下がらない] My *fever* went up [won't go down]. ▶熱はすっかり引いた The *fever* has completely left me [disappeared, gone].

❸〖熱中〗enthusiasm /ɪnθ(j)úːziæzm/ 《*for*》; 〖情熱〗(a) passion 《*for*》; 〖熱烈さ〗heat; 〖熱狂〗a mania /méɪniə/ 《*for*》, (一時的な)a craze 《*for*》. ▶日本の少年たちの間では野球熱が盛んだ There is a lot of *enthusiasm for* baseball among Japanese boys. ▶最近の学生たちは勉学に熱が入らないようだ The students (of) today seem to have no *enthusiasm for* study. ▶彼らは教育問題について熱のこもった議論をした They had a *heated* discussion on [*about*] educational problems. ▶彼は熱をこめて生徒たちに話しかけた He spoke to the students with great *heat* [*energy*, *enthusiasm*]. ●熱が冷める ▶恋人に対する彼の熱が冷めてしまった His *passion for* his girlfriend has cooled off./He has cooled off toward his girlfriend.
●熱に浮かされる ▶ほとんどの子供たちはゲーム熱に浮かされている Most children have a *mania for* (三度の飯より好き) eat, sleep and breathe video games.
●熱を上げる ▶彼女は今の歌手に熱を上げている She is *enthusiastic over* [*about*] the singer./《話》She is *crazy* [*mad*] *about* the singer.

── 熱の 形 thermal.

ねつあい 熱愛 ── 熱愛する 動 《妻[子供]を熱愛している love one's wife [children] *dearly*; adore one's wife [children]. (!ともに通例進行形不可)

ねつい 熱意 (熱狂) enthusiasm 《*for*》, (熱心) eagerness. ●熱意をもって仕事をする work with *enthusiasm*《書》*zeal*.(! *zeal* は宗教的(といえるほど)の信念に基づく熱意をいう) ▶彼は歴史の研究に大変な熱意を示している He shows great *enthusiasm for* [is very *enthusiastic about*] the study of history./He is very *eager* to study history.

ねつえん 熱演 ── 熱演する 動 play one's part enthusiastically [*with enthusiasm*,《書》*with ardor*].

ねつかく 熱核 ── 熱核の 形 thermonuclear.
●熱核兵器 a thermonuclear weapon.

ネッカチーフ a neckerchief (複 〜s, -chieves).

ねっから 根っから ●根っからの(=生まれながらの)商人 a *born* merchant. ●根っからの(=徹頭徹尾)紳士 a gentleman *through and through* [*to the core*]. ●根っからも(=まったく)知らない know *nothing at all*《*about*》. (⇨全く) ▶彼は根っからの(=生まれつきの)善人だ He's *born* good./He's a good man *by nature*./(昔からずっとそうだ) He's a good man, he *always has been*.

ねつかん 熱感 (⇨熱気(ねっき))

ねつがん 熱願 《have》a fervent [切なる] an earnest] wish.

ねつき 寝つき ●寝つきがいい go to sleep [fall asleep] easily. ▶寝つきが悪い can't get to sleep easily. (⇨寝つく)

ねっき 熱気 〖高い温度〗heat; (乾いた空気) hot air; 〖意気込み〗enthúsiasm; (熱烈) heat; (興奮) excitement; (激高) heat. ●熱気でむんむんする(場所が主語) be hot and stifling. ▶彼の話に振りはしだいに熱(= 情熱)を帯びてきた His speech became more and more *enthusiastic*《やや書》*fervent*, (興奮した) *excited*, (激した) *heated*》. ▶サッカーのワールドカップへの熱気が高まってきた There is in-

creased *enthusiasm* for World Cup soccer.

ねつききゅう 熱気球 《*in*》 a hot-air balloon.

ねっきょう 熱狂 〖熱中〗enthusiasm 《*for*》; 〖興奮〗excitement.

── 熱狂的な 形 enthusiastic,《話》wild; (狂信的な) fanatical; (興奮した) excited. ●熱狂的なジャズファン a *fanatical* jazz fan; a *jazz* enthusiast. ●熱狂的な女性解放運動家 a *fanatical* women's libber. ●熱狂的な声援を送る cheer *enthusiastically* [*wildly*].

── 熱狂する 動 become* enthusiastic [《話》go* mad,《話》go crazy] 《*about*》; get* very excited 《*at*, *by*》. (以上「熱狂している」という状態を用いて表す) ▶彼はスキーに熱狂している He *is very enthusiastic about* skiing./《話》He *is mad* [*crazy*, *wild*] *about* skiing. ▶イチローがサードに滑り込んで盗塁に成功すると、観衆は熱狂した When Ichiro slid into third and stole it, the crowd *went wild* [*he drove the crowd wild*].

ネッキング 〖首から上にする愛撫〗《話》necking.

ねつく 寝つく 〖寝入る〗go* to sleep, fall* asleep; 〖病気で〗take* to one's bed. ▶その子はすぐ寝ついた The child *went to sleep* easily. ▶朝の4時ごろまで寝つけなかった I couldn't *get to sleep* till almost four in the morning. (! *get to sleep* は否定文または否定的文脈で用いる: テレビの音を小さくしてくれ。眠りたいんだ Turn down the TV. I'm trying to get to sleep.「そうしてくれないと眠れない」の含みで言っている) ▶小川のせせらぎを聞きながら寝ついた The murmur of a brook lulled me to sleep.

ネック 〖首〗a neck. ▶ネックのセーター a sweater with a V-*neck*, a V-*neck* sweater.
●ネックライン a neckline.

ネック 〖障害・隘路(ないろ)〗a bottleneck (!「交通渋滞を起こす狭い道」の意もある), an obstruction (⇨障害). ▶その開発計画の最大のネックは市民の反対運動なのである The most serious *bottleneck* in the development project is the citizens movement against it.

ねづく 根付く take* root, root. ▶バラは根付きやすいですか Do roses *take root* [*root*] easily?

ネックレス a necklace. ▶真珠のネックレスをしている[する] wear [put on] a pearl *necklace*.

ねつけ 熱気 ●何だか熱気がする I feel sort of feverish.

ねっけつかん 熱血漢 (血気にはやる人) a hot-blooded person; (情熱的な人) a passionate person.

ねつげん 熱源 a source of heat.

ねっこ 根っ子 〖「根」のくだけた言い方〗a root; 〖切り株〗a stump. ●首根っこ the back [nape] of the neck. ●(バットの)根っ子で打つ hit off the fists.

ねっさ 熱砂 hot sand.

ねつさまし 熱冷まし 〖薬剤〗an antifebrile /ǽntɪfiːbrəl/; an antipyretic /ǽntɪpaɪrétɪk/; (説明的に) a medicine for reducing the fever.

ネッシー Nessie; (公式名) Loch Ness Monster. (⇨ネス)

ねっしゃびょう 熱射病 〖医学〗heatstroke. (⇨®®日射病)

ねっしょう 熱唱 ── 熱唱する 動 sing with deep emotion.

ねつじょう 熱情 《書》ardor, (a) passion. (⇨情熱) ●愛国の熱情に燃える burn with patriotic *ardor*. ●宗教的熱情にあふれている be full of religious *fervor*. ●ベートーベンの「熱情」ソナタ Beethoven's *Appassionata* sonata.

‡**ねっしん** 熱心 名・形 〖ひたむきな熱意〗eagerness,《書》zeal (! 後の語は主に仕事, 宗教, 政治について用いている)

［真剣な心］earnestness;［熱狂］enthusiasm;［異常なる熱烈さ］《書》ardor.
── **熱心な** 形 eager;《書》zealous /zéləs/; earnest; enthusiastic; ardent;［勤勉な］hardworking;［注意深い］attentive;［献身的な］《やや書》devoted;［敬虔(ｹｲｹﾝ)な］devout /diváut/.

① 【熱心な〜】● 熱心な学生 an *eager* [an *earnest*, an *enthusiastic*] student; a *hardworking* student. ● 熱心なクリスチャン a *devout* Christian. ● 熱心な支持者 an *ardent* [an *enthusiastic*, a *devoted*] supporter. ● 熱心な聴衆 an *attentive* [an *enthusiastic*] audience. ● 彼の熱心な(＝精力的な)指導の下に under his *energetic* guidance.

② 【熱心である】● スポーツに熱心である be *enthusiastic about* sports;《やや書》be *keen on* sports. ● 研究熱心である be *eager* [《書》*zealous*] *in* one's studies; be *earnest about* one's studies. ▶彼は切手収集に熱心である He is an *eager* [an *ardent*] collector of stamps./《やや書》He is *keen on* collecting stamps.

── **熱心に** 副 ［一生懸命に］hard;［真剣に］eagerly, earnestly;［注意深く］attentively;［一心に］intently;［熱烈に］enthusiastically. ● 演説を熱心に聴く listen *attentively* [*intently*, *eagerly*,(非常に注意深く) *very carefully*] to the speech. ▶彼は熱心に勉強する He studies very *hard* [*in earnest*]./(勉強に没頭する) He *applies himself to* his work. ▶彼らは私を熱心に支持してくれた They supported me *enthusiastically* [*heartily*]./They gave me *enthusiastic* [*hearty*] support. ▶君が熱心にそう言うから一晩よく考えてみよう Since you *insist*, I'll sleep on it.

ねっする 熱する 動 [熱くする] heat ... (up);[熱くなる] heat (up); become* hot;[熱中する] become [get*] enthusiastic;[興奮する] get excited. ▶その水を 90 度まで *heated* (up) the water to 90 degrees [×degree].

ねっせん 熱戦 (激しい競争) a bitter [《話》a hot] contest; (接戦) a close game [race, contest]; (興奮させるような試合) an exciting game [race]; (格闘技の激しい試合) a fierce fight. (⇨激戦, 接戦) ▶私は彼とテニスの熱戦を展開した I had a *close* tennis *match* with him.

ねっせん 熱線 (激しい金属線) a heated wire;[光線] (赤外線) infrared (rays); (熱い光線) thermic rays.

ねつぞう 捏造 图［偽造］forgery;［でっち上げ］invention,《やや書》fabrication.
── **捏造する** 動 ● 文書を捏造する *forge* [《やや書》*fabricate*] the document.

ねったい 熱帯 the tropical [《やや書》torrid] zone (! 後の語は学術用語. 温帯などのように両半球に一つつあるわけではないから zones としない); the tropics (! 複数扱い).

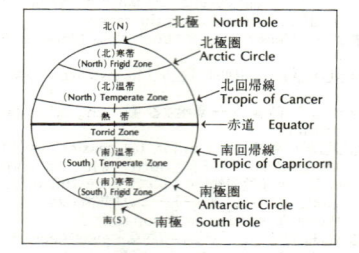

── **熱帯の** 形 tropical.
● 熱帯雨林 tropical rain forests. ● 熱帯魚 tropical fish. ● 熱帯植物 tropical plants. ● 熱帯性気候 a tropical climate. ● 熱帯性低気圧『気象』a tropical cyclone [storm]. (！この中で最も弱いものを a tropical depression という) ● 熱帯地方 the tropics; tropical regions. ● 熱帯夜 a tropical night.

ねっちゅう 熱中 absorption 《in》;［熱狂］enthusiasm 《for》.
── **熱中する** 動 ❶ ［心を奪われている］be absorbed 《in》,《話》be (really) into.... (⇨夢中, 病み付き) ▶彼はチェスに熱中していて彼女が出て行くのに気づかなかった He *was so absorbed in* playing chess that he didn't notice her leave. (！notice は see などと同じく原形不定詞を伴う)/《話》He *was really into* chess, so he didn't notice her leave.
❷ ［情熱を傾けている］be enthusiastic 《about, over》;［夢中になっている］《話》be crazy [mad, wild] 《about》;［献身する］devote oneself 《to》. ▶彼は新しい薬品の開発に熱中している He *is enthusiastic about* [*is devoted to*] the development of a new chemical. ▶あのころロックンロールに熱中していた I *was crazy* [*mad, wild*] *about* rock'n'roll at that time.

ねっちゅうしょう 熱中症『医学』a heat attack.

ねつっぽい 熱っぽい ❶ ［熱っぽい議論］a heated argument. ▶彼女は風邪で熱っぽかった She was *feverish* from her cold./She had a *feverish* cold. ▶ちょっと熱っぽい感じがする I feel *feverish* [hot].
── **熱っぽく** 副 (熱心に) enthusiastically; (情熱的に) passionately, (熱烈に) fervently; ardently. ● 熱っぽく語る talk *enthusiastically* 《about》.

ネッティング ［相殺決済, 差額決済］『経済』netting (balance clearing).

ねつでんどう 熱伝導『物理』thermal conduction.
● 熱伝導率 thermal conductivity.

ネット ［網］a net. ● ネットを張る put up a *net* 《on a court》. ● 髪にネットをしている wear a *hair* net; wear a *net* over one's hair. ● ネット裏から野球を見る see a baseball game from behind the *backstop* [*screen*]. ▶彼はボールをネットに当てた He *netted* the ball.
● ネットプレー net play; playing close to the net.

ネット ［正味］net. ● ネットで 1 万円 ¥10,000 *net* (←gross). ● ネットで 300 グラム 300g *net* weight.
● ネットスコア『ゴルフ』a net score.

ネット ［インターネット］the Internet, the Net [net]. (⇨インターネット) ● ネット利用者 a *net* user.
● ネットオークション online auction. ● ネットカフェ a cybercafe, a net cafe. ● ネットサーファー a Net surfer. ● ネットサーフィン Nét sùrfing. ● ネットサーフィンする surf (the Net). ● ネット自殺 online suicide pact; group suicides arranged on the Internet. ● ネットショッピング Internet shopping, online shopping. ● ネット通販 net trade. ● ネット取り引き online trading. ● ネットバンキング Internet banking, online banking. ● ネット犯罪 (a) cybercrime.

ネット ［ネットワーク］a network. (⇨ネットワーク) ● 首都圏をネットする(＝支店網を築く) cover the Metropolitan area with a *network* of branch offices [(直営店) of outlets]. ● 全国ネットで on the national *network*.

ネットイン ── **ネットインする** 動 (ボールが) touch the net and fall in [fall into the opponent's net]. (！ネットインしたボールは a nét bàll という)

ねっとう 熱湯 boiling (hot) water. (！hot water だ

けでは必ずしも熱湯の意にはならない)(⇨湯). ●熱湯消毒する sterilize (it) in *boiling water*.

ねっとう 熱闘 a fierce struggle; a heated contest.

ネットスケープナビゲーター《商標》Netscape Navigator.

ネットタッチ —— **ネットタッチする** 動《選手が》touch [hit] the net.

ネットボール［競技名］netball;［テニス・バレーボールの］a net ball.

ねっとり —— **ねっとりしている** 形《くっつく》sticky;《糊(%)のような》gluey. ●ねっとりした樹液 sticky sap. ▶ねっとりするまで小麦粉と水を練りなさい Mix and knead the flour /fláuər/ and water till it *thickens*.

ネットワーク a network. ●テレビ［ラジオ］のネットワーク a TV [a radio] *network*. ●パソコンのネットワーク a *network* of personal computers; a personal computer *network*. ●広域ネットワーク a wide area *network*《略 WAN》.

ねっぱ 熱波［気象］a heat wave.

ねつびょう 熱病 (a) fever. ●熱病にかかる have an attack of *fever*. ▶彼女は熱病で死んだ She died of a *fever*.

ねっぷう 熱風 a hot wind;《強い一吹き》a blast of hot air.

ねつべん 熱弁［情熱を込めた演説］an impassioned［熱烈な］a fiery] speech. ●国会で熱弁をふるう make an *impassioned* [a *fiery*,《強い印象を与える》an *impressive*] *speech* at the Diet.

ねつぼう 熱望 an earnest [an ardent] desire.
—— **熱望する** 動 long (*for; to do*); be eager (*for; to do*);《実現について不安を覚えながら》be anxious (*for; to do*). ▶我々は平和と自由を熱望した We *long* [*are longing*] *for* peace and freedom./We *want* peace and freedom *desperately*. ▶多くの学生は中山教授の指導を熱望している A lot of students *are eager to* study under Professor Nakayama.

ねづよい 根強い 形 deep-rooted; firm; strong. ●根強い偏見 a *deep-rooted* prejudice (*against*). ▶ハンセン病患者に対する差別と偏見は世界中で根強いものがあった Hansen's disease patients have suffered *deep-rooted* [*deep-seated*] discrimination and prejudice all over the world.
—— **根強く** firmly;〘書〙tenaciously.

ねつらい 熱雷［気象］a thunderstorm in the heat of summer.

ねつりょう 熱量 the quantity [amount] of heat;［単位］a calorie《略 Cal.》.

ねつれつ 熱烈 —— **熱烈な** 形［燃えるような］ardent;［情熱的な］passionate;［熱狂的な］enthusiastic;［火のような］fiery /fáiəri/. ●文学の熱烈な愛好家である be an *ardent* lover of literature; be *passionately* fond of literature. ●熱烈な演説をする make a *fiery* [a *passionate*] speech.
—— **熱烈に** ▶彼らは我々を熱烈に歓迎してくれた They welcomed us *enthusiastically*./They gave us an *enthusiastic* welcome.

ねてもさめても 寝ても覚めても ▶あなたを寝ても覚めても考えている *Awake or asleep* [*Waking or sleeping*], he thinks of you./He thinks of nothing but you.

ねどこ 寝床［ベッド,床(∮)］(a) bed;《船や列車の》a berth, a bunk;［寝室］a bedroom. ●寝床に入る go to *bed*;《もぐり込む》get into *bed*. ●寝床を整える make a [the, one's] *bed*.

ねとねと —— **ねとねとした** 形《物にくっつくように》sticky. ▶体が汗でねとねとする I'm *sticky* with sweat.

ねとまり 寝泊まり —— **寝泊まりする** 動 stay at night. ●おじの家に寝泊まりする stay [live] with one's uncle; stay at one's uncle's.

ねとる 寝取る ▶彼は自分の上司に妻を寝取られたのを知ってやけっぱちになった He got disgusted to know that his wife *slept with* his boss.

ねなしぐさ 根無し草［浮き草の一種］duckweed;［人］a drifter. ●根無し草の生活 a *rootless* [a *wandering*] life.

ネパール［国名］Nepal /nəpɔ́:l/;《公式名》the Kingdom of Nepal.（首都 Katmandu）●ネパール人 a Nepalese. ●ネパール語 Nepali. ●ネパール(人[語])の Nepalese.

ネバダ［米国の州］Nevada /nəvǽdə/《略 Nev. 郵便略 NV》.

ねばつく 粘つく be sticky;《のりのように》gluey].

ねばっこい 粘っこい ●［物が］sticky;《のりのように》gluey;［粘り強い］tenacious. ▶彼の言葉には関西特有の粘っこいアクセントがある He has a strong *drawling* Kansai accent, particular to that area.

ねばならない must*, have* to.（⇨ーならない）

ねばねば —— **ねばねばした** 形《くっつく》sticky;《のりのように》gluey. ▶ねばねばした手でさわるな Don't touch it with your *sticky* hands.

ねはば 値幅 a price range.

ねばり 粘り ❶［粘着性］stickiness; adhesiveness. ●粘りのある sticky;《粘着性の》adhesive.
❷［粘り強さ］tenacity. ▶英語の勉強には粘り強さが必要です You need *tenacity* [must *be tenacious*] when it comes to learning English.

ねばりけ 粘り気 ●粘り気のある sticky;《のりのような》gluey.（⇨粘り）

ねばりごし 粘り腰 tenacity. ●粘り腰で交渉に臨む negotiate *tenaciously*.

ねばりづよい 粘り強い ●［忍耐強い］patient, persevering;［不屈の］persistent;［着実な］steady;［頑強な］stubborn;［執拗(╮)な］tenacious. ●粘り強い患者 a *patient* [a *persevering*] person. ●粘り強い努力をする make *persistent* [*steady*] efforts. ●粘り強い抵抗にあう meet with *stubborn* [*tenacious*] resistance.

***ねばる** 粘る ❶［ねばねばする］be sticky（▮主に液状でねばねばすることをいう）;《粘着性がある》be gluey; be adhesive (*to*);《くっつく》stick* (*to*).
❷［根気よく続ける］（仕事などを）stick* (*to, at*);（交渉・勝負事などで）hold* out. ●しつこく粘る打者 a pesky hitter; a tough out. ●粘って四球を得る coax a pass. ▶粘って最後までその仕事をした I *stuck to* [*at*] the work until it was finished. ▶労働者たちは賃上げを要求して粘っている The workers *are holding out* for higher wages. ▶中には１杯のコーヒーでいつまでも粘っている人たちがいる Some of them stay in the restaurant *forever* over a cup of coffee. ▶打者は７球ファウルで粘った The batter fought off seven pitches for fouls.

ねはん 涅槃［仏教］Nirvana; the Buddhist Heaven.
●涅槃会(ᵉ) the anniversary of the death of Buddha.

ねびえ 寝冷え —— **寝冷えする** 動 catch a cold [a chill] in one's sleep [while (one is) asleep].

ねびき 値引き 图 a discount; a price reduction; a markdown.（圖 値下げ,《割引》） ●全商品値引き特価で提供中 All items are being offered *at reduced* [*cut*] *prices*. ▶これ以上の値引きは無理です This is our best price (the limit).
—— **値引きする** 動 ●10 パーセント値引きする reduce

the price by 10 percent; give a 10 percent *discount* [a *discount* of 10 percent]; discóunt 10 percent. ●定価から 1,000 円値引きする give [make, allow] a *discount* of 1,000 yen off the fixed price.

ねびく 値引く discount. (⇨値引きする)

ねぶかい 根深い (信念・感情などが) deep-rooted; (態度・状況・考えなどが) deep-seated. ●根深い不信感〈have〉(a) *deep-rooted* distrust 《of》.

ねぶくろ 寝袋 a sléeping bàg.

ねぶそく 寝不足 (a) lack [want] of sleep. ●寝不足で病気になる become sick for *want* [(短さ) shortness] of sleep. (⇨睡眠①)

ねぶだ 値札 a price tàg. (⇨正札)

ねぶと 根太 (腫れ物) a boil.

ねぶみ 値踏み (価格をつけること) valuation; (価値を見積もること) appraisal. ●その家を 1 億円と値踏みする *value* [*set a price on*, 《書》*appraise*] the house *at* one hundred million yen.

ネブライザー 〘医療用噴霧器〙〘医学〙 a nebulizer.

ネブラスカ 〘米国の州〙 Nebraska /nəbrǽskə/ 《略 Neb(r). 郵便略 NE》.

ネフローゼ 〘< ドイツ語〙〘医学〙 nephrosis /nəfróusɪs/.

ねぼう 寝坊 图 a late riser, (特に子供の) 《話》 a sleepyhead. (⇨朝寝坊)
── **寝坊する** 動 (寝過ごす) oversleep, (遅く起きる) get up late.

ねぼけがお 寝惚け顔 ●寝ぼけ顔で with a *sleepy* look.

ねぼけまなこ 寝惚け眼 ●寝ぼけまなこで with *sleepy* eyes.

ねぼける 寝惚ける ●寝ぼけている (目覚めたばかりで頭がぼんやりしている) be stupid from sleep; (半分眠っている) be half asleep. ▶寝ぼけたこと (= ばかげたこと) を言うな Stop *talking nonsense!*

ねぼすけ 寝坊助 ▶ねぼすけ, 起きなさい Get up, *lazybones!* (🔎「怠け者」の意で, 人を起こすときに与えられる親しみを込めた呼びかけ語. 相手が 1 人でも複数形で用いる)

ねほりはほり 根掘り葉掘り ●根掘り葉掘り (= 詳細のすべてを) 聞く ask about every (single) detail 《of》. ▶近所の人は私たちのことを根掘り葉掘り知りたがる Our neighbors *are* very *inquisitive about* everything that we do. (🔎 執拗〈しつよう〉に質問して知りたがること)

ねまき 寝巻き (総称的) night clothes;〘パジャマ〙pajamas,《英》pyjamas (🔎 複数扱い) (⇨パジャマ);〘ネグリジェ〙《米》a nightgown,《英》a nightdress;〘長シャツ型で男(の子)用の〙 a nightshirt.

ねまわし 根回し ── **根回しする** 動 ●〖木を〗 dig around the roots 《of a tree》; 〖事前工作する〗(説明的に) (try to) get a consensus on the matter before it is officially brought up to discussion.

ねまわり 根回り 〘木の根の周囲〙 the circumference of the roots of a tree; 〘高地の周囲に沿った低地〙 the lowlands surrounding (the base of) a highland.

ねみみにみず 寝耳に水 ●その知らせは寝耳に水だった (= あまりに突然のことでひどく驚いた) The news was (like) *a bolt from the blue*. (🔎 a bolt from the blue は「青空に突然走った一条の稲妻 = まったく予想せぬ出来事」の意)

*ねむい 眠い sleepy; (うとうとして) drowsy /dráuzi/. ●食後はしばしば心地よさを暗示する) ▶今朝は早く起きたので眠い I'm [I feel] *sleepy* because I got up early this morning. ▶彼女は眠そうな声で [眠い目をこ

すりながら] 返事をした He answered in a *sleepy* voice 《rubbing his *sleepy* eyes》. (🔎 sleepy の代わりに drowsy も可) ▶その映画を見ていたら眠くなった I got *sleepy* [*drowsy*] while I was seeing that movie./That movie made me (feel) *sleepy* [*drowsy*].

ねむけ 眠気 sleepiness; (快い) drowsiness. ●眠気を催す feel [become] *sleepy*. (⇨眠い) ●眠気と戦う fight *sleep* ●眠気を誘うような天気 *drowsy* weather. ▶眠気ざましにコーヒーを 1 杯飲んだ I drank a cup of coffee to get rid of my *sleepiness*.

ねむのき 〘植物〙 a silk tree.

ねむらせる 眠らせる put* 《a baby》 to sleep. (🔎 婉曲的に「殺す」の意にもなる) ▶その赤ん坊は私を一晩中眠らせてくれなかった The baby *kept* me *awake* all night.

ねむり 眠り (a) sleep; (快い) 《書》 (a) slumber (🔎 しばしば複数形で); 〘うたた寝〙 a doze, (昼間の) a nap. (⇨睡眠, 眠る) ●深い [浅い, ひと] 眠り a deep [a light, a little] *sleep*. ●「眠りの深い [浅い] 人」 は a heavy [a light] sleeper) ●眠りにつく go to *sleep*; fall asleep. ●すぐやかに眠りに落ちる fall into a sound *sleep* [a peaceful *slumber*]. ●永遠の眠りにつく go to *sleep* forever. (🔎 die の婉曲表現) ▶その悲鳴で眠りから覚めた The shriek woke me up from my *sleep*./I *woke up* by the shriek. ●眠り薬 a sleeping pill.

ねむりこける 眠りこける sleep* like a top [a log]. (🔎 top は「(おもちゃの) こま」の意. よく回っていることが動かないように見えることから. log は「丸太」)

ねむりこむ 眠り込む ▶電車で眠り込んで乗り過ごすことがある I sometimes *fall asleep* [(ついうとうとと) *doze off*] on a train and doze past my stop.

:ねむる 眠る ❶〖睡眠をとる〗sleep*, have* [get*] a sleep; 〖寝入る〗go* to sleep, fall* asleep; (寝つく) get to sleep (🔎 通例否定文・疑問文で).

> **解説** (1) sleep, have a sleep は睡眠をとるの意. go to sleep, fall asleep は目の覚めた状態から眠った状態に移ることをいう. 以上のうち sleep は生理現象として自然に眠る場合だけでなく, 自発的に眠ろうとして眠ることも表すが, その場合 have a sleep は **get a sleep** を, go to sleep は **get to sleep** を代わりに用いる方が明確.
> (2) 日本語で「眠れる」という場合でも can を伴わないことも多い.

●10 時間眠る *sleep* (for) ten hours; have ten hours' *sleep*; have ten hours of *sleep* (🔎 通例 a sleep of ten hours とはいわない). ●まだ半分眠っているを引き *half asleep*. ●頭痛を直す *sleep off* a headache. ●地震に気づかず眠る *sleep through* an earthquake. ▶二郎, おはよう. 眠れましたか Good morning, Jiro! How did [×could] you *sleep*? ▶昨晩はよく眠れた I *slept* well [*soundly*] last night./I *had* a good [a sound] *sleep* last night. ▶彼女はぐっすり眠っていた She *was* fast [sound,《話》dead] *asleep*. ▶眠っている子供を起してはいけません Don't wake up a *sleeping* [×asleep] child. (🔎 asleep は限定的には用いない) ▶車の往来の音が耳について眠れなかった I couldn't *sleep* [〖寝つく〗*get to sleep*] because of the traffic noises. (🔎 couldn't のかわりに didn't も可)/The traffic noises kept me awake [made me lie awake]. ▶そのことが心配でまったく眠れなかった I couldn't [didn't] *sleep* a wink worrying about it. ▶私は眠ろうとしている時に音がすると眠れない Noise bothers me when I'm trying to *sleep* [*get to sleep*]. ▶本を読んでいる間に眠ってしまった

went to sleep [*fell asleep*, ×*fell into sleep*] while (I was) reading. ❷ [永眠する] fall* asleep, (永眠している) sleep*; rest (in peace). (▮いずれも婉曲表現) ▶彼は故郷の墓地に眠っている He *sleeps* in a cemetery in his hometown. ▶彼の魂が安らかに眠りますように May he *rest in peace*! (参考 RIP と略し墓碑に刻まれる) ❸ [使われないままである] (設備などが) lie* idle [unused]. ● 眠っている機械 *idle* machines. ● 難破船内に眠っている(=手つかずに放置されている)財宝 treasure *left untouched* in the wreck. ● 大量の原油が海底下に眠っている(=開発されずにそのままある) A great amount of petroleum *lies unexploited* under the seabed.

ねむれる 眠れる ● 眠れる獅子 a *sleeping* lion; (潜在的な危険性に) potential danger.

ねむれるもりのびじょ 眠れる森の美女 *The Sleeping Beauty*. (参考 チャイコフスキーのバレエ音楽)

ねもと 根元 (通例複数形で) a root. ● 木を根元に肥料をまく give fertilizer around a tree. ● 木を根元から切り倒す cut down the tree close *at the roots*.

ねものがたり 寝物語 ● 寝物語をする talk in bed; (ベッドで愛の語らいを交わす) have pillow-talk.

ねゆき 根雪 [冬中地面にとどまっている雪] (説明的に) snow staying on the ground throughout the winter.

ねらい 狙い ❶ [銃や弓でねらうこと] aim; (標的的) a target, a mark. (的) ▶彼のねらいがひどく狂ったので的を10インチ外れた His *aim* was so poor that he missed the target by ten inches. ▶彼はそのトラにしっかりねらいを定めた He *took* good [*careful*] *aim at* the tiger with a gun./He *pointed* his gun very carefully *at* the tiger. (⇨狙う) ❷ [目的] (はっきりとした具体的な) an aim, (確固たる) a purpose, (個人の願望・必要性によって決められた) an object; (意図) an intention; (目標) a target, (要点) a point. ● この会のねらいは the *aim* of this meeting. ● 彼の上京のねらいは the *purpose* of his coming to Tokyo. ▶君のねらいはいいんだが Your *intentions* are good, but…. ▶君のねらいは何ですか What *are* you *aiming at*?/What is your *point*? (何を言おうとしているのか) What are you trying to say [(話) getting at, (話) driving at]? (▮この意の get [drive] at は「意図する(mean)」の意で通例進行形で用い, 受身は不可)

DISCOURSE
この論文は, 日本語における一人称のさまざまな用法の説明をしようとする **This paper aims to** *describe* **the different usages of the first person in the Japanese language.** (▮This paper aims to describe (analyze; outline; present; examine)… (この論文は…の説明[分析; 概説; 紹介; 検証]をねらいとする)は論文の目的を紹介する表現. 序論でよく用いられる.

ねらいうち 狙い撃ち ― 狙い撃ちする 動 snipe 《at a soldier》.

ねらいめ 狙い目 ▶海外旅行をするなら2月がねらい目だ If you want to travel abroad, February is *the best time*. ▶あのレースにかけるなら, この馬がねらい目だ If you want to bet the race, this horse is *the one*.

‡**ねらう 狙う** ❶ [的に向かって構える] aim 《at》. ● よくねらう take good [careful] *aim* 《*at*》. ▶彼はトラを銃でねらった He *aimed at* the tiger with his gun./He *took aim at* the tiger with his gun. ▶彼は獲物をねらった He *aimed at* his prey. ▶彼は私をねらって(=目がけて)石を投げつけた He *threw* [*aimed*] a stone *at* me. (▮命中したかどうかは不明. 命中を含意する場合は He threw me a stone. のようにいう)

❷ [目標とする] (人・本・会社などが) aim 《at, for; to do》. ▶彼は優勝をねらった He *aimed at* (*winning*) the victory [*for* the victory, *to* win the victory]. (▮winning を用いない場合, the victory を主語にして受身可)

❸ [得ようとする] be after …, (書) seek*. ● 金をねらって(=を目当てに)彼女と結婚する marry her *for* money. ▶君は警察からねらわれている(=追われている) The police *are after* you. ▶彼が本当にねらっているのは彼女の遺産だ What he *is* really *after* is her inheritance. ▶彼はふと自分の命がねらわれていると思った He suddenly realized his life *was being sought*.

❹ [うかがう] (機会など) watch for …, (書) seek*. ▶彼は私を殺す機会をねらっている He *is watching for* a chance to kill me.

ねりあげる 練り上げる (⇨練る)

ねりあるく 練り歩く parade; march. ● 町中を練り歩く *parade* (*through*) [*march through*] the streets.

ねりいと 練り糸 (説明的に) a silk thread softened after being processed.

ねりえ 練り餌 (小鳥用の) paste feed; (釣り用の) paste bait.

ねりぎぬ 練り絹 processed and softened silk.

ねりせいひん 練り製品 proccessed fishpaste(s) (▮種類を強調するときは複数形), (説明的に) boiled fish paste, such as *kamaboko*, *chikuwa*, *hampen* and so on.

ねりなおす 練り直す ● 案を練り直す(=みがきをかける) *polish up* [(再考する)《やや書》*reconsider*] the plan.

ねりはみがき 練り歯磨き toothpaste.

ねりもの 練り物 [食品] (練り菓子) cakes made of sweetened bean paste; (練り製品) (⇨練り製品); [[練り固められて作られた宝石[ボタン]] synthetic jewelry [buttons]; [祭の山車] a float (in a parade).

‡**ねる 寝る** ❶ [眠る] sleep*; (寝入る) gò* to sléep, fall* aslèep; (寝つく) get* to sleep (▮否定文・否定的文脈で用いる), (ついうとうとと) doze off. (▮go [get] to sleep の sleep は名詞(⇨sleep)) ● 新しいベッドで寝る *sleep* on a new bed. ● 寝ている be sleeping; be asleep; be in bed. (▮通例 ×be sleeping in bed とはいわない) ● 寝て頭痛[二日酔い]を治す *sleep off* a headache [a hangover]. ▶私は毎晩8時間寝る I *sleep* eight hours every night. ▶テレビを見ているうちいすに座ったまま寝てしまった I *fell asleep* [*went to sleep*, 《話》*dropped off*] in my chair while (I was) watching TV. ▶昨晩は頭が痛くてよく寝られなかった I couldn't *get to sleep* last night because of a headache./A headache *kept* me *awake* [*sleepless*] last night. ▶その日は午前中ずっと寝て過ごした I *slept away* the whole morning that day. ▶このベッドにはだれかが寝ていた形跡がある This bed seems to *have been slept in*. (▮この よう な受身では主語は特定のものに限る) ▶彼は寝ているの起きているの Is he *asleep* or *awake*?

❷ [床につく] gò* to béd. (▮❶ との違いに注意) ● 早く[遅く]寝る *go to bed* early [late]. ● 寝る前にウイスキーを1杯飲む drink a glass of whiskey *before* (one *goes to*) *bed*; (寝酒を飲む) sip a nightcap of whiskey. ▶寝る時間だよ It's time *for bed*./It's time (for you) to *go to bed*./It's time (that) you *went to bed*. (▮最後の文は「

は過ぎているのにまだ床についていない」ことを含意する. that 節の動詞は過去形では通例省略する）▶12時過ぎまであなたの帰りを寝ないで待っていた I *waited* [*sat*] *up for* you till after twelve.
会話「あなたはいつも何時に寝ますか」「12 時です」"What time [When] do you usually *go to bed* [×*sleep*]?" "At twelve (o'clock)."
会話「ぼく，もう寝なさい」「お休みなさい，ママ」"*Off to bed*, dear." "Good night, Mom."

❸ 〖病気で寝ている〗be ill（〖米〗sick）in bed（❗〖米〗では ill は堅い言い方でしばしば病気がひどい場合に用いる）; be laid up 《*with*》. ▶彼は風邪を引いて寝ている He *is in bed* with a cold./〖家で寝ている〗He's *at home in bed with* …./He *is laid up* [*is down*] *with* a cold./He *is lying in bed with* a cold. （❗be lying on one's [the] bed は「ベッドの上で横になっている」の意）

❹ 〖横たわる〗lie*（down）. ▶芝生の上に寝る *lie (down)* on the grass. （❗動作を表す場合は，通例 down を伴う）▶彼はあおむけに〖うつぶせに; ひじをついて〗寝てブドウを食べていた He *was lying on* his back [*on* his stomach; *on* his side] eating grapes.

❺ 〖商品などが〗▶倉庫に寝ている商品 goods *sitting* [×*sleeping*] in a warehouse. ▶土地〖資本〗を使わないで寝かしておく *keep* land [*capital*] *idle*.

❻ 〖セックスをする〗《婉曲的》sleep《*with*》; make love（*to, with*）.

● 寝た子を起こす　寝ている子を起こすな（=寝ている犬はそのままにしておけ）Let sleeping dogs lie.

*ねる 練る　〖粉・粘土などを〗knead /ni:d/; 〖文体などを〗polish; 〖計画・案を〗（考え出す）work ... out; （入念に）elaborate 《*on* one's idea》. ▶練り粉〖粘土〗を練る *knead* dough /dóu/ [clay]. ▶英文を練る *polish* (*up*) one's English style; *make improvements on* one's English sentences. ▶計画の細部を練る *work out* the details of the plan.

ネルー　〖インドの初代首相〗Nehru/néiru:/(Jawaharlal 〜).

ねれる 練れる　▶彼は年とともに人物が練れて（=円熟して）きた He has become more *mellow and tolerant* [He *has mellowed*] over the years.

ネロ　〖ローマの皇帝〗Nero /ni:rou/.

ねわざ 寝業, 寝技　tricky dealings behind the scene; underhanded dealings. ▶寝業師 an underhanded [a scheming] person.

:ねん 年　❶ 〖1 年〗a year. （⇒一年）
① 〖年〜〗● 年内に完成する [by] the end of the *year*; within the *year*. （❗前の方が口語的）
② 〖数詞＋年〗● 5 か年計画 a five-*year* [×five-*years*] plan. ● 20 年の研究の成果 the fruit of twenty *years* of study [research]; the fruit of a twenty-*year* study. （❗×the fruit of study of twenty *years* は不可）● 4 年前に（今から）four *years* ago; （過去のある点から）four *years* before. ● ここ 3 年間 *for* the past [last] three *years*. （❗現在完了とともに用いる）（更に）10 年たてば in (another) ten *years* [*years*' time]. （❗後の方が堅い言い方）● 5 年ぶりに for the first time in five *years*; 〖書〗 after five *years*' interval [absence]. ▶ここへ引っ越してきて 3 年になる It's been [It's] three *years* since we moved here./Three *years* have [×*has*] passed since we moved here./We moved here three *years* ago. ● 20 年は長い Twenty *years* is [×are] a long time. （❗20 年をひとまとまりの時間と考える）▶ 2–3 年前まで京都支店は駅前にありました The Kyoto branch was in front of the station until two or three *years* ago. ▶あなたは何年式のこの車を買ったの

ですか What *year* [*When*] did you buy the car? （❗*In what year* did you buy the car? というのは堅い言い方．「何年前に…」なら How many years ago…? となる）

③ 〖年に〗● 年に 2 回 [2–3 回] twice [two or three times] a *year*. ● 2 年に 1 度 once every [in] two *years*. ● 年に 1 度の行事 an *annual* [a *yearly*] event. （⇒週 [最後の文例]）

❷ 〖年号〗● 1999 年に in (the *year*) 1999. （❗(1) the *year* は通例省略する．ただし年号が主語に来る場合は The *year* 1999 is …. のように the *year* をつける．(2) ×in the *year* of 1999, ×in 1999 *year* は不可．(3) 読み方は nineteen ninety-nine, 2006 年なら two thousand and six となる）● 平成 19 年に in the nineteenth *year* of Heisei. （❗西暦で，または西暦と併記して in the nineteenth year of Heisei (2007) のようにいうのが普通）▶これは 89 年物のバーガンディとボルドーです These are 1989's from Burgundy and Bordeaux. （❗一つをいう場合は an '89 Burgundy）

❸ 〖学年〗a year, 《米》a grade, 《英》a form. （⇒学年, -年生）

*ねん 念　❶ 〖感じ〗a sense, （気持ち）a feeling. ● 深い感謝の念を表す express a deep *sense* of gratitude. ● 不快の念（=感情）を示す show one's displeased *feelings*. ▶彼に尊敬の念を抱く have *respect* for him; *respect* him. ▶自責の念に駆られる suffer from a guilty *conscience*. ▶彼女は不安の念に駆られた She was seized with an uneasy *feeling*.

❷ 〖配慮〗care. （⇒注意）● 念を入れて *carefully*. （⇒念入り）● 念の入った careful; （手の込んだ）elaborate. ▶彼女の化粧は念が入っている She *takes* special *care* of her make-up./She wears *elaborate* make-up.

● 念には念を入れる　▶ドアに鍵をかけたか念には念を入れなさい You must *make doubly sure* (*that*) you've locked the door.

● 念を押す　▶ホテルに予約の念を押す（= 再確認する）*reconfirm* the reservation with the hotel. ▶彼にそうしないよう念を押す（=繰り返し言う）tell him *repeatedly* not to do it. ▶彼にあす来るように念を押したか Did you *make sure* he came tomorrow?/（思い出させたか）Did you *remind* him *to* come tomorrow?

ねんあけ 年明け　〖年季奉公の修了〗the completion of one's apprenticeship; 〖年頭〗the beginning of the new year.

ねんいちねん 年一年　— 年一年と 副 year by year; from year to year; （月日がたつにつれて）as the years go by. （⇒年々）

ねんいり 念入り　— 念入りな 形 （注意深い）careful; （綿密な）close; （精巧な）elaborate. ▶念入りな作品 an *elaborate* piece of work. ● 念入りに調べると on *close* examination.

ねんえき 粘液　〖生理〗mucus /mjú:kəs/. ● 粘液の mucous. ● （性格などが）粘液質の phlegmatic /flegmǽtik/.

ねんおし 念押し　— 念押しする 動（念を押す）（⇒念 [成句]）

ねんが 年賀　（⇒新年, 年始）● 年賀のあいさつを交わす exchange *New Year*('s) greetings. （❗'s の改まった方は最近の言い方）● お年賀 a New Year('s) present. ● お年賀に行く pay a *New Year*('s) call [visit].
● 年賀郵便　New Year's mail.

ねんかい 年会　an annual meeting [convention]. （❗後の方は「代表者の大会」の意）

ねんがく 年額　the annual sum [amount]. ● 年額

100万円を支払う pay one million yen *a year* [*every year*].

ねんがじょう 年賀状 ●年賀状を書く[出す; もらう] write [send; get] *a New Year's card*. 《事情》米英ではクリスマスカードを(I wish you) a Happy New Year. (どうぞよいお年をお迎えください)またはくだけた書き方では、単に Happy New Year. (おめでとう)と書き加えられる程度》▶年賀状はなるべくこの日までにお出しください Recommended last posting date for *New Year's cards* [for New Year].

ねんがっぴ 年月日 the date.

ねんがらねんじゅう 年がら年中 year in and year out; (1年中ずっと) all (the) year around, throughout the year; (いつも) all the time, always.

ねんかん 年刊 图 an annual publication.
—— **年刊で** 副 annually, yearly. ▶この雑誌は年刊です This magazine is published *annually* [*yearly*].

ねんかん 年間 图 〖1年間〗(…年間) for … years; (1年につき) a [per] year; (1年間ずっと) all year around, throughout the year; 〖ある年号の間〗during the … period [era]. ●大正年間に *during* the Taisho *period* [*era*]. 《西暦を用いる方が普通 (⇨[次例])》 ▶2000年から2004年の5年間に *during* [*in*] *the* five *years* between 2000 and 2004 〖×from 2000 to 2004〗. 《では2000年までを省略して単に from 2000 to 2004, between 2000 and 2004 という方が普通》 ▶彼は2年間ロンドンに滞在した He stayed in London *for two years*. ▶年間100万人もの人がそこを訪れる No less than one million people visit there *in a year*./No less than one million people *a* [*per*] *year* visit there. (✍ a [per] year は数量表現の後に用いる) ▶物価は過去30年間上がり続けている Prices have been rising *for* [*during*, *in*] *the past* [*last*] *thirty years*. (✍ Prices will rise *for* [*in*, *during*] the next thirty *years*. のような未来表現の場合、for は「むこう30年間には(先は分からない)」、in は「30年もすれば」, during は「30年間のうちにいずれ」の意)
—— **年間の** 形 (1年間の) annual. ●年間の予定 a schedule *for the year*. ●年間の収入 an *annual* income. ●年収

ねんかん 年鑑 a yearbook; (主に子供のための) an annual; 《英古・米》an almanac /ɔ́ːlmənæk/. ●統計[科学]年鑑 a statistical [scientific] *yearbook*.

ねんがん 念願 〖心からの願い〗one's heart's desire, one's dearest wish; 〖長年の望み〗one's long-cherished desire [wish]; 〖夢〗one's dream. ▶念願がついにかなった My *dream* has come 〖×become〗 true at last. 《口語的》/ My *long-cherished desire* has been fulfilled [realized] at last.

ねんき 年忌 (⇨回 —回忌)

ねんき 年季 ●年季が明ける finish (serving) one's apprenticeship 《as a carpenter; with a local firm》.
● **年季が入っている** ▶彼は年季の入った(=経験を積んだ)外交官です He is an *experienced* [*熟達した*] *a seasoned*] diplomat./He has had a lot of experience as a diplomat.
● **年季奉公** (an) apprenticeship. ●年季奉公に出す 《やや書》apprentice 《one's son》to 《a carpenter》.

ねんきゅう 年休 〖「年次休暇」の略〗an annual (paid) vacation 《米》[holidays 《英》].

ねんきゅう 年給 (⇨年俸)

ねんきん 年金 〖政府・会社などが支給する〗a pension 《事情》米英では通例週・月単位でもらう); an annuity (✍通例年単位で終生にわたってもらう). ●国民[厚生]年金 an employee's *pension*. ●老齢[養老]年金 an old-age [a retirement] *pension*. (✍(1) 前の方は OAP と略されることもある. (2) 《英》では今は後の方が普通》●終身年金 a life annuity. ▶我々は60歳から年金がもらえる We are entitled to (receive) a *pension* at the age of 60. ▶彼は65歳で退職し年金生活に入った He retired on a *pension* at the age of 65. ▶彼は年金で暮らしている He lives on a [his] *pension*./(年金受給者だ) He is a *pensioner*.
● **年金制度** the pension plan.

ねんぐ 年貢 (土地に課す税) land tax.
● **年貢の納め時** ▶年貢の納め時だ《話》The game is up.
● **年貢米** rice collected as farm rent from peasants.

ねんげつ 年月 years; 《時》time. ●苦難の年月を過ごす spend the *years* of hardship. ▶年月がたった *Years* have passed [gone by]./*Time* has passed [gone by]. ▶その仕事を完成するのに多くの年月を要した It took us many *years* [*a long time*] to complete the work.

ねんげん 年限 a term. ●4年間の在職[修業; 契約]年限 the four-year *term* of office [study; a contract].

ねんこう 年功 (長い経験) long experience. ●年功を積む have many *years of experience*. ▶この会社は年功ではなく功績によって昇進する Promotions in this company are based on merit rather than *seniority*.
● **年功序列** a seniority /siːnjɔ́ːrəti/ system. ●**年功序列賃金制度** the wage system based on seniority.

ねんごう 年号 ▶年号が平成と改まった The name of an era was changed to Heisei.

ねんごろ 懇ろ ── **懇ろに** 副 ❶ 〖丁重に〗(心からの) heartily, 《書》cordially; (温かい) warmly; (丁寧に) politely, courteously; (親切に) kindly. ▶彼の亡骸(なきがら)はねんごろに(=彼にふさわしい儀式をもって)葬られた His body was buried with appropriate [(うやうやしい)《やや書》reverent] ceremony.
❷ 〖仲よくなる〗 ▶彼女とねんごろ(=男女の関係)になる become intimate with her.

ねんざ 捻挫 图 a sprain /spréin/.
—— **捻挫する** 動 ●足首をねんざする sprain [twist] one's ankle.

-ねんさい -年祭 an anniversary. ●50年祭 the 50th *anniversary*; the golden jubilee /dʒúːbəliː/ (✍25年は golden の代わりに silver, 60年は diamond を用いる). ▶シュヴァイツァー生誕100年祭を執り行う celebrate the hundredth *anniversary* [《米》the centennial, 《英》the centenary] of the birth of Schweitzer. 《関連》200年祭 a bicentennial, a bicentenary / 300年祭 a tercentennial, a tercentenary / 500年祭 a quincentennial, a quincentenary / 1,000年祭 a millennium》

ねんさん 年産 an annual [a yearly] output. ▶この工場は70万台のテレビを年産する This factory produces [has an *output* of] 700,000 TVs *a year*. (✍「1年につき」の意)

ねんし 年始 the New Year. (⇨年賀) ●年始に回る make a *New Year's* call 《on》.
● **年始客** a New Year's caller.

ねんじ 年次 ── **年次(の)** 形 〖1 年の，年 1 回の〗annual; yearly. ▶我々は 2007 会計年度の年次計画を立てた We've made a program for the fiscal 2007.
- **年次総会** an annual [a yearly] general meeting. ● **年次報告** an annual report. ● **年次(有給)休暇** an annual (paid) leave 〖《米》vacation, 《英》holiday〗.

ねんしき 年式 a model. ▶78 年式の車 a 1978 model (of a) car.

ねんしゅう 年収 an annual [a yearly] income. ▶彼は年収が 1,000 万ある He earns [makes] ten million yen *a year*./He has an *income* of ten million yen *a year*./His *annual* [*yearly*] *income* is ten million yen.

ねんじゅう 年中 (1 年中) all (the) year around, throughout the year; (年がら年中) year in and year out; (いつも) all the time, always. ● **年中行事**▶ここは年中天気がいい The weather is good here *all* (*the*) *year around* [*throughout the year*]. ▶彼女は年中愚痴をこぼしている She is *always* [*forever*] grumbling. (❗後の方が強意的) ▶彼女は 2 人の子供の世話で年中暇なしだ Her two children *keep* her pretty busy *all the time*. ▶年中無休〖掲示〗Open *throughout the year*./Always open./We never close (for business). 〖最近は 24 hours─7 days.─(❗)Open 24 hours a day─7 days a week. なども見られる〗

ねんじゅうぎょうじ 年中行事 〖毎年の行事〗 an annual [a yearly] event [〖儀式〗function]. ▶私たちの市では市民陸上大会が年中行事となった The citizen's track meet has become an *annual event* [*one of chief events of the year*] in our city.

ねんしゅつ 捻出 ── **捻出する** 動 (なんとか準備する) manage to get... ready. ● **旅費を捻出する** *manage to get* traveling expenses *ready*.

ねんしょ 年初 (⇨⍟ 年頭)

ねんしょ 念書 ● **念書をとる** get a *written memorandum of* 《on》.

ねんしょう 年少 ── **年少の** 形 (より年下の) younger 《than》; junior 《to》. (⇨下) ▶彼はその仕事の志願者の中で最年少だ He is *the youngest* of all the applicants for the job.
- **年少組** (幼稚園の) a junior class. ● **年少者** (年下の者) one's junior; a younger one.

ねんしょう 年商 〖年間総売上高〗an annual turnover 《of》; the gross yearly sales.

ねんしょう 燃焼 名 combustion. ● **燃焼時間** *burning* time. ● **完全[不完全]燃焼** perfect [imperfect] *combustion*.
── **燃焼する** 動 burn. (⇨燃える)

ねんじる 念じる 〖念仏などを唱える〗chant 《one's prayers》; 〖願う〗wish 《for》; (祈願する) pray 《for》.

ねんすう 年数 (the number of) years.

-ねんせい -年生 ❶〖学校の〗(小学校の) a ... pupil (中学・高校・大学の) student〗. (❗今は《英》でも student が高校生にも用いられる) 〖関連〗《米》では 4 年制高校・大学の 1 年生を a freshman, 2 年生を a sophomore, 3 年生を a junior, 4 年生を a senior ともいう. 詳しくは (⇨学年)) ▶彼は 10 歳の時 5 年生に編入した He entered the fifth *grade* 《米》[*year*] at ten.
〖会話〗「君何年生?」「高校 3 年生です」"What *grade* 《米》[*year*] are you in?" "I'm a twelfth *grader* 《米》[*twelfth-year* student]./I'm in the third *year* of high school." (❗後の方は日本の制度に合わせた言い方)
❷〖植物の〗 ▶─[二; 多]年生植物 an annual [a biennial; a perennial] plant.

ねんだい 年代 ❶〖世代〗a generation (⇨世代); 〖年齢〗age (⇨年(1)). ▶私の年代の人々 people of my *generation*. ▶30 年代 the thirties [30s, 30's]. ▶彼は私とほぼ同年代だ He is about my *age* [the same *age* as me].
❷〖時代〗▶1980 年代前半に in the early (↔late) 1980's. ▶nineteen eighties と読む.《話》では 1980s もよく用いる ● **年代順に** in *chronological* order; in chronology. ● **年代物のシャンパン** *vintage* [*old*] champagne. (❗vintage はワイン類についてのみ用いる) ● **年代物のエレベーター** an *ancient* elevator (❗old の誇張した語) ▶その壁画の制作年代はおよそ 3000 年前と特定されている The mural is *dated to* almost three thousand years old.
● **年代記** a chronicle.

ねんちゃく 粘着 adhesion.
● **粘着テープ** (an) adhesive tape.

ねんちょう 年長 ── **年長の** 形 (より年上の) older 《than》; senior 《to》. (⇨上) ▶彼はその中ではいちばんの年長者(=最年長者)だ He is *the oldest* in the group [of them all].
● **年長組** (幼稚園の) a senior class. ● **年長者** one's senior.

ねんてん 捻転 〖医学〗twisting; torsion. ● **腸捻転** (a) torsion of the bowel; (a) volvulus.

ねんど 年度 〖会計年度〗the fiscal [《英》financial] year 〖参考〗日本・英国では 4 月 1 日, 米国では前年の 10 月 1 日からの 1 年; 〖学校の〗the school year 〖事情〗米英では通例 9 月から 6 月まで). ● **2008 会計年度** 2008 *fiscal year*; *fiscal* 2008. ● **学年度末** the end of the *school year*. ● **会計年度末に** at the end of the *fiscal year*. ● **来年度予算案** the budget bill for the next *fiscal year*. ▶2007 年度の芥川賞受賞者 the winner(s) of the 2007 Akutagawa Award.

ねんど 粘土 clay. ▶粘土質のclayey /kléii/. ▶粘土で人形を作る make a doll out of *clay*.
● **粘土細工** (a piece of) claywork.

ねんとう 年頭 〖年の初め〗the beginning of the year; 〖新年〗the New Year.
● **年頭教書** (米国大統領の) (the President's annual) State of the Union Message (to Congress).

ねんとう 念頭 ▶その事故が彼の念頭を去らなかった The accident *was always on* [xin] his *mind*. (❗つきまとって離れない場合は on, 単に頭にある場合は in で, ここでは on が適当)/(忘れることができなかった) He *couldn't forget* the accident. ▶もしかしたらという気持ちが念頭から離れなかった The possibility *haunted* my *mind*. (❗haunt は「(考えなどが)つきまとう」の意)
● **念頭に置く** ▶その言葉を念頭に置く(=心の中に留めておく) *keep* [*bear*, *have*] the words *in mind*.
● **念頭に無い** ▶彼は自分の安全など念頭になかった(=気にかけなかった) He *didn't care about* his safety.

ねんない 年内 ● **年内に** 〖年の終わる前に〗before the end of the year; within the year.

ねんね ❶〖眠る〗▶坊や, ねんねの時間ですよ It's time for bed, dear./It's time you went to bed, dear. 〖❗節内は通例直説法過去形 (⇨寝る ❷)〗
❷〖まったくの世間知らず〗▶彼女はもう二十なのにまるきりねんねだ She is still just a child even though she's already twenty. (❗She is so childish though …. ともいえる)

ねんねこ a *nenneko*; (説明的に) an overcoat worn when carrying a baby on the back.

ねんねん 年々 every year. ●年々歳々(=毎年)同じことを繰り返す do the same *every year* [(来る年も来る年も) *year after year*, *year in and year out*]. ●後の二つは継続を強調》 ▶その店は年々(=毎年)大きくなる The store gets bigger *every year* [(年ごとに) *year by year*, *from year to year*]. 《!後の二つは変化を強調》

ねんのため 念の為 ❶ [確認のため] for confirmation; just to be [make] sure. ●念のため確かめる confirm; make sure. ▶念のため契約を文書にした We put the contract in writing *for confirmation*. ▶念のため数えてください *Just to make sure*, please count them.

❷ [用心のため] (just) in case. ▶念のため傘を持って行けよ Take an umbrella with you *just in case*. 《!「雨が降るといけないので念のため…」は …(*just*) *in case* it rains [*should* rain] のようにいう. *should* がつく場合は実現性が低いという話し手の気持ちを表す》

会話「いすは 40 で足りないかい」「念のため(= 余裕をもって)もう一つ二つ持って行ってくれ」"Won't forty chairs be enough?" "*To be on the safe side*, take one or two more."

❸ [注意しておくが] ▶動物園は月曜が休園だよ, 念のため Please *note* that the zoo is closed on Monday. ▶念のためお知らせします (放送・掲示) A *note*. ▶この後に知らせる内容が続く》

ねんぱい 年配 图 〖年齢〗 age. ▶彼は私とほぼ同年配だ He is about my *age* [the same *age* as me]. ▶彼は私より五つ年配だ(=年上)だ He is five years *older than* I am [(話) me, (書・まれ) I].
—— 年配の 形 〖old〗 elderly. ●〖old の代わりに丁重な響きの語〗●年配の方(=かなり高齢の)紳士 an *elderly* gentleman.

ねんばらい 年払い 〖毎年1回の〗 yearly payment; 〖1 年分一括の〗 a year's worth of payment in a lump sum.

ねんぴ 燃費 fuel efficiency; (走行距離) mileage /máilidʒ/ (*per* liter). 事情 米英では多くの場合miles per gallon (略 mpg) で示される》●燃費のいい車 a car with good *mileage*; (低燃費車) a gas-efficient car, (米話) a gas-sipper (↔a gas-guzzler). ▶君のこの車の燃費はどれぐらいですか How many *miles* can you get *per gallon* with this car?

ねんぴょう 年表 ●日本史年表 a *chronological table* of Japanese history.

ねんぷ 年賦 annual [yearly] payment.

ねんぷ 年譜 a chronological record of one's career.

ねんぶつ 念仏 ●念仏を唱える say [chant] a *prayer to the Buddha*; pray to the Buddha. 《!Buddha のつづり字に h をそえたさないように》

ねんぽう 年俸 an annual [a yearly] salary. ●年俸3億円の野球選手 a 300 million-yen baseball player. ●年俸…である earn 《12 million yen》 a year 《!a は「…につき」の意》; one's *annual salary* is 《12 million yen》. (⇨いくら ❶) ▶彼らの給料は年俸制です They are paid *on an annual basis* [*by the year*].

ねんぽう 年報 〖年次報告(書)〗 an annual (report).

ねんまく 粘膜 〖解剖〗 a mucous /mjúːkəs/ membrane.

ねんまつ 年末 the end of the year. (⇨暮れ) ▶年末年始も休まずに営業します We will open at the beginning and the end of the year. ●年末賞与 a year-end bonus. ●年末セール a year-end sale. ●年末調整 a year-end tax adjustment.

ねんよ 年余 more than a year. ●1 年余の交渉 a debate that goes on (for) over a year.

ねんらい 年来 ●年来の(=長年未決定の)懸案 a *long-pending* question. ●年来の(=長い間望んでいた)望 [夢] one's *long-cherished* hope [dream]. ▶私の年来の友 my *old* friend. ▶10 年来の大雪だ This is the heaviest snowfall *in* ten years./This is the heaviest snowfall (that) we have had *for the past* [*last*] *ten years*.

ねんり 年利 annual interest. (⇨利子) ●年利 5 パーセントで銀行から 100 万円借りる borrow one million yen from the bank at an *annual interest* of 5 percent [at 5 percent *interest a year*].

ねんりき 念力 psychokinesis /sàikoukiníːsis/. ●念力で(=精神力で)戸を開ける open the door by one's *mental power* [*force*].

ねんりつ 年率 annual rate.

***ねんりょう** 燃料 fuel. 《!種類をいうときは [C]》 ●固形 [液体; 気体] 燃料 solid [liquid; gaseous] *fuel*. ●核燃料 nuclear *fuel*. ▶燃料が切れかかっている We are running out of *fuel*. ▶石炭やまきは安い燃料だ Coal and wood are cheap *fuels*. ▶飛行機はロンドンに立ち寄って燃料を補給した The plane stopped over at London and (*was*) *refueled*. 《!不足分の補充でなく, 単に「給油する, 燃料を積み込む」の意では fuel を用いる》▶故障は燃料系統だ The trouble is in the *fuel* line.
●燃料計[メーター] a fúel [ə gás] gàuge /geidʒ/. ●燃料タンク a fúel tànk. ●燃料電池車 a fuel-cell-powered vehicle. (参考)「究極のエコカー (an eco-friendly car)」と呼ばれる》●燃料費 fúel expènses, the cost of fuel. ●燃料油 fúel òil.

ねんりん 年輪 (木の) annual [tree] rings. ●年輪を重ねた芸 the art attained by one's efforts over the years. ▶祖母の話の端々に人生の年輪を感じる When I talk with my grandmother, I feel *something deep that comes from her long experience*.

***ねんれい** 年齢 (an) age. 《!通例個々の年齢をいう以外は無冠詞》(⇨年(ﾄ), —歳) ●年齢による差別 agism, (英) ageism; prejudice against middle-aged and elderly people.

① 【~年齢】●本当の年齢 one's true *age*. ●骨年齢 bone *age*. ●対象年齢: 3 歳以上 3 years old and over. ●同年齢の友達 a friend of one's own *age*. ▶彼女は私と同年齢だ She is the same *age* as me. ▶最近結婚する女性の平均年齢が上がってきた The average *age* of women's first marriage is getting higher these days. ▶彼の精神年齢は 10 歳以上だ He has a mental *age* of more than ten. 《!正確には more than ten は 10 歳をも含まないので more than nine と書くべきだが, このように漠然という場合はこのままでよい》

② 【年齢】●年齢制限をもうける set the *age* limit (*at* 40). ●20 から 30 歳の年齢層 the *age* group between 20 and 30; the 20-30 *age* bracket. 《!いずれも単・複両形に, ハイフン (-) を主と読む》●年齢別に分ける classify (*them*) *by age*. ●年齢詐称 misrepresentation of one's *age*. ▶彼らの年齢差は 10 歳です The difference in their *ages* is ten years./There is an *age* difference of ten years between them./There is a ten year age gap between them. ▶あの女優は年齢不詳だ I could never tell how old that actress is. ▶それは年齢不相応な行為だ That's not suitable behavior for someone your *age*.

③【年齢は[が]】▶私の年齢は16歳です I am sixteen years old. (❗×My age is sixteen years old. や ×I am at the age of 16. とはいわない) ▶私たちは年齢が近い Our *ages* are close. ▶彼は私とは年齢が離れている(=私よりずいぶん年が上[下]だ) He's a lot older [younger] than me. (❗a lot of は比較級を強める) ▶お父さんが亡くなられた時年齢はいくつでしたか What age were you [What was your age] when your father died? (❗What age are you [What is your age]? と単独で用いることはない. この場合は How old are you? (⇨-歳 [第1文例]))
④【年齢の】▶どの年齢の子供も漫画が好きだ Children of all *ages* like comics. ▶彼は年齢の割に若く見える He looks young for his *age* [younger than his *age*].
⑤【年齢に】▶年齢・性別に関係なくその仕事に応募できる Anyone, regardless of *age* or sex, can apply for the job.
• **年齢不問** All ages admitted.

の

の 野 a field; (牧草地) a meadow; (荒野) the wilds; (平原) a plain (🚨 しばしば複数形で). ●野に咲く花 a wildflower; a flower in the *field*. ●野(良)に出て働く work in the *field* [on the farm]. ●野べ狩りに行く go hunting *in* [*on*, ×*to*] the *field*. ▶あとは野となれ山となれ (⇨後(㊟) [成句])

の

INDEX

《格助詞》
❶ 所有, 所属
❷ 場所
❸ 時間
❹ 部分
❺ 分量
❻ 材料, 手段
❼ 同格
❽ 動作の主体
❾ 動作の目的
❿ 動作の対象
⓫ …に関する

《終助詞》
❶ 質問
❷ 命令
❸ 周知のこと

──**の**《格助詞》❶ [所有, 所属] 's, of …; to ….

> **解説** (1) 生物の場合 's をつけ, 無生物の場合は of を用いて所有格を作るのが原則. しかし無生物の場合でも, 時間・距離・重量・価格・地名などを表す語については慣用的に 's をつけて表すことがある: 今日の新聞 today's newspaper. / 日本の将来 Japan's future. ただし「今日の日本の情勢」は ×today's Japan's situation のように 's を二つ続けることはできず Japan's situation (*of*) today のようにする.
> (2) 一般に of を用いる方が客観的かつ正確で堅い言い方となるが, 情報の焦点という観点から 's と of の選択が行われる場合がある. the title of the novel, the novel's title のいずれも可能だが, 前の方は novel に, 後の方は title に焦点を当てた言い方.

●私の息子の写真 (特定の) my son's picture; (不特定の) a picture *of* my son ▶後の方は「息子を写した写真」の意だが, 前の方は「息子の持っている写真」「息子が写した写真」「息子を写した写真」のいずれの意にもなる. a picture *of* my son's は「息子が持っている [息子が写した] 写真のうちの一枚」の意) ●彼の両親の車 his parents' car. (🚨 s をつけて複数形にするときはアポストロフィー (') を s の後につける) ●その子供たちのおもちゃ those children's toys. (🚨 不規則な複数形には 's をつける) ●トムとボブの部屋 Tom and Bob's room. (🚨 二人共有の部屋. Tom's and Bob's rooms は二人別々の部屋) ●鳥の卵 a bird's egg; the egg *of* a bird. ●家の窓 the windows *of* the house [×the house's windows]. ●私の何人かの友人 some friends *of mine*; some *of* my friends (🚨 ×*my* some friends は不可. 所有格は a, some, any, no, this, that などとともに用いることはできない) ●だれか他の人の車 somebody else's [×somebody else's] car. ●社長の秘書 a secretary *to* [×*of*] the president. (🚨 慣用的に特定の前置詞が用いられることがある) ●表玄関の鍵 the key *to* [*for*] the front door. ●あの茶色の髪の女の子 that girl *with* brown hair; that brown-haired girl. ▶彼はその会社の社長です He is (the) president *of* the company. (🚨 一人によって占められる役職の場合は通例無冠詞) ▶彼は京都大学の経済学の講師です He is a lecturer *in* economics at [×*of*] Kyoto University. (🚨「教授 [先生, 専攻学生] です」なら …a professor [a teacher, a student] of economics at …. となる) ▶もしもし, IBM のトム・スミスと申します Hello. This is Tom Smith *from* IBM. ▶こちらは NHK ソウル支局の阿部です This is Abe *for* NHK Seoul. (🚨 報道員の場合. カメラマンなら通例 with)

会話「あれはだれのバッグですか」「私 [私の姉] のです」"*Whose* bag is that?/Who does that bag *belong to*?" "It's *mine* [my sister's]./It *belongs to* me [my sister]."

❷ [場所] at …, in …, on …. (⇨-に) ●劇場の切符売り場 the ticket office *at* a theater; a theater ticket office. ●ロンドンの通り the streets *in* London; London streets. ●山の天気 the weather *in* the mountains. ●壁の絵 the pictures *on* the wall. ●顔の傷跡 a scar *on* [×*in*] one's face. ●農場の小屋 a cottage *on* a farm. ●海辺の別荘 a villa *by* the seaside; a seaside villa.

❸ [時間] at …, on …, in …. (⇨-に); (…を過ごすための) for …; (特定の日時・出来事を指定して) for …. ●8時15分の列車 the 8:15 train. ●9時のニュース the nine o'clock news; the news *at* nine. ●日曜日の買い物 shopping *on* Sunday; Sunday shopping. ●朝の散歩 a walk *in* the morning; a morning walk. ●2日間の旅行 a two-day trip; a trip *for* two days. ●夏休みの計画 one's plans *for* the summer vacation. ●19世紀のフランス the France *of* the 19th century. (🚨 France の the に注意) ●2002年度のノーベル物理学賞 the Nobel prize in physics *for* 2002. (🚨 the 2002 Nobel prize in physics ともいえる) ●5時の約束に遅れる be late for the appointment *for* five o'clock.

❹ [部分] of …. ●その少年たちの多く many *of* the boys. ●その問題の一部 (a) part *of* the problem. ▶生徒 [彼ら] の半数がその試験に落ちた Half (*of*) the students [Half *of* them] failed the exam.

❺ [分量] of …. (🚨「a + 分量名詞 + of + 物質名詞」の型で用いるのが普通) ●コップ1杯のミルク a glass *of* milk. ●さじ1杯の塩 a spoonful *of* salt. ●1ポンドのバター a pound *of* butter. ●ひとつかみの米 a handful *of* rice. ●3足の靴下 three pairs *of* socks.

❻ [材料, 手段] (…で作った) of …, from …; (…を使って) in …. (⇨-から) ●スチール製の机 a steel desk; a desk made *of* steel. ●大理石の建物 a marble building; a building *of* [*in*] marble. ●フランス語の手紙 a letter *in* French.

❼ [同格] (A という B) the B *of* A. ●古い都のローマ the old city *of* Rome. ●私の友人のナンシー my friend Nancy; Nancy, a friend of mine. ●英文学教授の金子氏 Mr. Kaneko, professor of English Literature. ●病院長の山田先生 Dr. Yamada, director of the hospital.

❽ [動作の主体] ●彼の両親の同意 his parents' consent. ●政府の決定 the government's decision; the decision *of* [*by*] the government. ●列車の到着 the train's arrival; the arrival *of* the train. ●ディケンズの作品 Dickens'(s)

/díkinz(iz)/ works; the works *of* [*by*] Dickens.
▶君が読んでいた漱石のあの本の名前は何ですか What's the name of that book *by* Soseki you were reading?
❾ [動作の目的] ・子供の教育 children's education; education *for* [*of*] children. ・家族の扶養 the support *of* the family.
❿ [動作の対象] (…のための) *for* …; (…へ) *to* …. ・女子の大学 a women's college; a college *for* women. ・子供の病院 a children's hospital; a hospital *for* children. ・遺産の相続 succession *to* property. ・成功の鍵(産) the key *to* success.
⓫ […に関すること] *about* …, *on* …, *of* …, *in* …. ・料理の本 a book *on* [*about*] cooking. (❗ *on* では専門的, *about* では一般的な内容を暗示) ・政治学の権威 an authority *on* politics. ・世界史の試験 an exam *on* [*in*] world history.

—— の 《終助詞》 ❶ [質問] ▶どこへ行くの Where are you going (to)? (❗ *to* をつけると def は疑問代名詞, つけないと疑問副詞) ▶あの本が読みたいの？ Do you want to read that book?
❷ [命令] ▶静かにするの！ Be quiet!
❸ [周知のこと] ▶そんなことしないの Everyone knows *that* one doesn't do things like that.

ノア ・ノアの箱舟 Noah's Ark.
ノイズ [雑音] (a) noise.
のいちご 野苺 〖植物〗a wild strawberry.
ノイローゼ 〖医学〗neurosis /n(j)uəróusis/; a nervous breakdown. ▶彼はノイローゼだ He has [suffers from] *neurosis*./He is *neurotic*./He is a neurotic.
・ノイローゼ患者 a neurotic.

***のう** 脳 [脳髄] a brain; 〖知力〗(a) brain (❗ 通例複数形で ⇨頭脳). ・脳の手術を行う operate on ⟨*his*⟩ *brain*. ・脳が弱い have no brains; be weak in the head.
・脳圧 intracranial pressure; (説明的に) the pressure of fluids inside the brain. ・脳溢血(いっ) (⇨脳出血) ・脳下垂体 the pituitary (gland); the hypophysis. ・脳外科 brain [cerebral] surgery. ・脳外科医 a brain surgeon. ・脳血栓 cerebràl thrombósis /θrɑmbóusəs/ (❗ thromboses). (❗ 文脈があれば cerebral は省略されることが多い) ・脳梗塞 cerebràl infárction. ・脳細胞 a brain cell. ・脳挫傷 brain contusion. ・脳室 a cerebral ventricle. ・脳出血 (a) cerébral hémorrhage /héməridʒ/. ・脳卒中 a stroke. ・脳腫瘍 a bráin túmor. ・脳性(小児)麻痺 cerébral pálsy /pɔ́ːlzi/. ・脳脊髄(せき)炎 encèphalomyelítis; ・脳塞栓(そく) cerebral embolism. ・脳卒中 (have) a stroke, (やや古) (cerebral) apoplexy (⟨*épəplèksi*/. ・脳軟化症 encèphalomalácia; (俗に) softening of the brain. ・脳波 brain waves. ・脳膜炎 meningitis; cephalomeningitis.

のう 能 [能力] (an) ability. (⇨能力) ▶彼は働く以外能がない(=働いてばかりいる) He's working all the time./He's a compulsive worker. (❗「時間があれば働かずにはいられない人」の意)
▶…のう ▶一生懸命勉強するだけが能ではない(=すべてではない) Working hard is not everything.
▶能ある鷹(たか)は爪(つめ)を隠す 'A wise falcon hides its talons.'; (ことわざ) Still waters run deep.

のう 能 [能楽] a *No*(*h*) play (❗ 単・複同形), a *No*(*h*) play [drama]; (説明的に) a classical Japanese dance-drama employing highly stylized dances, accompanied by a flute, two or three drums, and dramatic chants.
・能狂言 (⇨能狂言) ・能面 a *No*(*h*) mask. ・能面のような顔 an expressionless [an unemotional] face.

のうえん 脳炎 〖医学〗encephalitis of the brain. ・日本脳炎 Japanese encephalitis.
のうえん 農園 a farm. (⇨農場)
のうえん 濃艶 —— 濃艶な 形 voluptuous; bewitching.
のうか 農家 [家] a farmer's house (複 houses /-ziz, 《米》-siz/), (大きい農場主の) a farmhouse; [家庭] a farming family, a farmer's family (❗ 前の方は家族全員で, 後の方は世帯主が農業に従事している家族). ▶米作農家は今いちばん忙しい時期です Now is the busiest season for rice *farmers*.
のうかい 納会 a year-end meeting; (取引所の) the last session of the month (❗「大納会」は … of the year)
のうがき 能書き (薬などの) a statement of virtues.
・能書きを並べ立てる enumerate one's own merits. (⇨手前味噌)
のうがく 能楽 a *No*(*h*) play [dance]. (⇨能)
のうがくぶ 農学部 the department [《米》 college, 《主に英》 faculty] of agriculture.
のうかん 納棺 —— 納棺する 動 place ⟨his⟩ body in a coffin.
のうかん 脳幹 〖解剖〗the brain stem.
・脳幹死 〖医学〗brain-stem death.
のうかんき 農閑期 the farmer's slack season; the slack season on the farm.
のうき 納期 (金銭の) the fixed date for payment; (物品の) the appointed date of delivery; (税金の) the date of tax payment. ▶納期は約1か月です The *delivery time* is about a month.
のうきぐ 農機具 agricultural [farm] machines and implements; agricultural [farm] machinery; [農具一式] farm [farming] implements.
のうきょう 農協 [「農業協同組合」の略] an agricultural cooperative (association).
***のうぎょう** 農業 〖広〗àgrículture, fàrming (❗ 前の方はやや専門的で, その活動・方法・技術面に重点があり, 後の方は産業としての作物栽培・動物飼育に重点がある); the farming industry. ・集約農業 intensive *agriculture*. ・集団農業 collective *farming*. ▶あの人は農業をやっています That man is a farmer. (❗ That man is engaged in *farming* [*agriculture*]. より普通)
—— 農業の 形 àgricúltural. (❗ 名詞の前では通例 /ˈ/ のアクセントになる (⇨農業大学))
・農業協同組合 an agricultural cooperative association. ・農業国 a farming [an agricultural] country. ・農業試験場 an experimental farm, an agricultural experimental station. ・農業大学 an àgricúltural [an àgricúlture] cóllege. (❗ 後の方は主に新聞用語) ・農業用地 fármlànd.
のうきょうげん 能狂言 〖能楽と狂言〗*No*(*h*) and *kyogen*; 〖能狂言〗a *No*(*h*) farce. (⇨@狂言 ❶)
のうきん 納金 payment.
のうぐ 農具 (⇨農機具)
のうげい 農芸 farming and gardening.
・農芸化学 agricultural chemistry. ・農芸高校 an agricultural (and horticultural) high school.
のうこう 農工 agriculture and industry.
のうこう 農耕 [農業] àgricùlture; [農場経営] fàrming; [耕作] cultivation. ・農耕に適した土地 land suitable for *farming*.
・農耕儀礼 agricultural rites. ・農耕生活 an

のうこう agricultural life. (⚠アクセント移動に注意) ●**農耕民族** an agricultural people.

のうこう 濃厚 ── 濃厚な 形 (味・色など) rich; (気体・液体など) thick; (密度が) dense. (⇨濃い) ●濃厚な牛乳 rich milk. ●濃厚なスープ thick soup. ●濃厚な(=熱烈な)ラブシーン a *passionate* love scene. ▶我がチームの敗色は濃厚だ[になってきた] Our team *is very likely* [*is getting more likely*] *to* lose the game.

のうこつ 納骨 ── 納骨する 動 place 《his》 ashes in a tomb.
●納骨堂 a charnel house.

のうこん 濃紺 dark [navy] blue. (⚠単に navy ともいう) ●濃紺のズボン navy trousers.

のうさい 納采 ●納采の儀 (皇室の結納(ゆいのう)) the ceremony of exchange of betrothal gifts within the Imperial Family.

のうさぎ 野兎 a hare /héər/. 《関連》a rabbit 飼いうさぎ)

のうさぎょう 農作業 farmwork. ●農作業をする work on the farm.

のうさくぶつ 農作物 ágricultural [fárm] pròducts; 《集合的》agricultural [farm] produce; (作物) a crop (⚠しばしば複数形で).

のうさつ 悩殺する 動 (うっとりさせる) bewitch; (話) knock 《him》out with one's sex appeal.

のうさんぶつ 農産物 farm products. (⇨回 農作物)

のうし 脳死 〖医学〗bráin dèath. ●脳死状態である be brain-dead.

のうじ 農事 farming, agriculture.
●農事試験場 an experimental farm, an agricultural experimental station. ●農事番組 a fárming prògram.

のうしゅ 嚢腫 a cystoma, 〖医学〗a cyst.

のうしゅく 濃縮 còncentrátion.
── 濃縮する 動 cóncentràte; condense.
●濃縮ウラン enriched uranium. ●濃縮(還元)ジュース concentrated juice.

のうしょ 能書 (⇨回 能筆, 回 達筆)

のうしょう 脳症 〖医学〗brain fever. ●肝性脳症をおこす get hepatic brain fever.

のうじょう 農場 a farm; 〖大規模な〗(通例単一作物の) a 《cotton》plantation; (特定の家畜や果樹の) 《米》a 《chicken》ranch. ●酪農場 a dairy farm. ●農場を経営する run a *farm*. ●農場で働く[生計を立てる] work [live] on [×in] a *farm*.
●農場主 a farmer. ●農場労働者 a farm laborer; (一時的な) a farmhand. (⇨農夫)

のうしんとう 脳振盪 a concussion of the brain, a brain concussion. ●軽い脳振とうを起こす have a mild *concussion*.

のうせい 農政 agricultural administration.

のうぜい 納税 tax payment, the payment of tax.
●納税申告をする file a tax return. ▶私たちは納税の義務がある We must *pay our taxes*./*Paying taxes* is every citizen's obligation./We have the *tax obligation*. ▶今年の納税額はどれぐらいですか How much *tax* do you *pay* this year? (⚠名詞で「納税額」は the amount of one's taxes) ▶納税期限は3月15日です The *tax* deadline is March 15.
●納税者 a 《high》taxpayer.

のうぜんかずら 〖植物〗a trumpet creeper.

のうそん 農村 a farm [a farming] village; (地域社会) a rural community; (田園地帯) a rural area [district].
●農村地帯 a farm [a farming] area.

のうたん 濃淡 (明るい部分と影の部分) light and shade. ●絵に濃淡をつける *shade* a picture.

のうち 農地 farmland, agricultural land. ●農地の開発 the development of *farmland*. ●農地を開拓する cultivate *farmland*.
●農地改革 agricultural reform.

のうてん 脳天 the top of the head; the crown (of one's head).

のうてんき 脳天気 ── 脳天気な 形 (あきれるほど屈託がない) ridiculously carefree; (あまりにも気楽な) too easygoing.

のうど 農奴 a serf; (農奴の身分) serfdom. (⚠「農奴制」の意にもなる)
●農奴解放 release from serfdom.

のうど 濃度 〖液体などの〗〖化学〗concentration; 〖物理〗density. ●その海水中の塩分の濃度 the *concentration* of salt in the sea water. ●高い濃度の塩分を含んでいる contain high *concentrations* of salt. (⚠この場合は通例複数形で用いる) ●現在大気中の二酸化炭素の濃度が高くなってきている The *concentration* of atmospheric carbon dioxide is now higher (than before).
●濃度規制 density regulation.

のうどう 能動 ── 能動的な 形 active.
── 能動的に 副 ●環境保護運動に能動的に関わる be *actively* involved in a movement for environmental conservation.
●能動態 〖文法〗the active voice.

のうどう 農道 a road [(小道) a path] between the fields.

のうなし 能無し ▶彼は能なしだ(=何の役にも立たない) He is *good-for-nothing* [(無能だ) *incompetent*].

のうにゅう 納入 图 〖支払い〗payment; 〖配達〗delivery; 〖供給〗supply.
── 納入する 動 pay 《tax》; deliver 《goods *to* him》; supply 《the army *with* goods; goods *to* the army》.

のうのう ▶他の人は皆職探しに走り回っているというのにあなたはよくものうのうと(=のんきに)していられるわね How could you *be free and easy* when everybody else is running around hunting for a job? (⇨呑気な)

ノウハウ (話) know-how; expertise /èkspəːrtíːz/. ●その経営のノウハウをしっかり身につける learn a lot of *know-how* to manage it [*about* the management]. ▶コンピュータを操作するのにたいしたノウハウは必要としない It doesn't take much *know-how* to operate a computer.

のうはんき 農繁期 the farmer's busy season; a busy season on the farm.

のうひつ 能筆 elegant handwriting; precise penmanship. (回 能書)

のうひん 納品 图 (納めた品物) delivered goods; (品物を納めること) delivery of goods.
── 納品する 動 deliver goods 《*to*》.
●納品書 a statement of delivery.

のうひんけつ 脳貧血 ●脳貧血を起こす have an attack of *cerebral anemia* /əníːmiə/.

のうふ 納付 图 (金の支払い) payment. ●税金の納付 *payment* of one's taxes.
── 納付する 動 pay 《one's taxes》.

のうふ 農夫, 農婦 a farmer; 〖小作農〗a tenant farmer, (昔の・発展途上国の) a peasant; 〖作男〗a farm laborer; (一時的な農場労働者) a farmhand. (⇨回 農民)

のうほう 膿疱 〖医学〗a pustule /pʌ́stʃuːl/.

のうぼく 農牧 agriculture and stock farming.

のうほん 納本 图 delivery of a publication.
── 納本する 動 ●新刊書を2部納本する deliver

のうほんしゅぎ 農本主義 an agriculture-based economic system.

のうみそ 脳味噌 〖頭脳〗brains; 〖脳髄〗a brain. ▶金がないなら脳みそを使え Use your *brains* when you don't have money enough.

のうみつ 濃密 ——濃密な 形〖色合い・音色・味が〗rich; 〖関係などが〗close; 〖描写が〗detailed. ●濃密な風味のチーズ *rich* cheese. ●濃密に結びついた政財界 *closely*-tied political and business circles. ●その場面の濃密な描写 a *detailed* [a *minute*] description of the scene.

*の**うみん 農民** a farmer (通例農場労働者 (farm workers) を雇って農場を経営する人をさし, 日本の一般的な農民とイメージが異なる); 〖自作農〗a landed farmer, (小規模の) a smallholder; 〖小作農〗a tenant farmer; (昔の・発展途上国の) a peasant, (全体) the peasantry (!集合的に用い, 単・複両扱い). ●農民一揆 a peasants' uprising. ●農民運動 a peasant movement.

のうむ 濃霧 a thick [a dense] fog. (⇨霧) ●濃霧警報 a dense fog warning.

のうやく 農薬 agricultural chemicals; (殺虫剤) pesticide; (除草剤) herbicide. ●田に農薬を散布する dust [spray] rice paddies with *agricultural chemicals*. ●農薬(空中)散布 cróp(-)dùsting [spráying].

のうよう 膿瘍 〖医学〗an abscess.

のうり 能吏 (腕利きの役人) an efficient bureaucrat; a talented official.

のうり 脳裏 (心) one's mind; (記憶) one's memory. ●脳裏に焼き付く be printed in one's *mind*. ●脳裏をかすめる come into [cross] one's *mind*; (心に浮かぶ) occur ⟨to him⟩. (!いずれも事柄が主語)

*の**うりつ 能率** 名 efficiency. ●作業能率 work *efficiency*. ●仕事の能率を上げる promote [develop] the *efficiency in* [*at*] one's work. ▶彼がいないと我々の仕事の能率が上がらない(＝仕事がはかどらない) We can't get much work done without him.
——能率的な 形 efficient ▶この機械は我々の目的には能率的でない This machine is *inefficient* [not *efficient*] for our purpose. ▶読書は語彙(ξ)を増やす能率的な方法です Reading is an *efficient* [(効果的な) an *effective*] way of increasing your vocabulary.
——能率的に, 能率よく 副 efficiently. ●非常に能率的に[能率よく]仕事をする work very *efficiently*; work *with* great *efficiency*. ●能率給 efficiency wages.

のうりょう 納涼 ●納涼客 people going [coming] out to enjoy the cool evening breeze [air]. ●納涼船 a summer evening pleasure boat. ●納涼大会 a summer evening festival. ●納涼花火大会 a fireworks display on a summer evening.

*の**うりょく 能力** (an) ability ⟨*to* do; *for* doing⟩; (a) capacity ⟨*to* do; *for* doing; *for*, *of*⟩; a faculty ⟨*for* [*of*] doing; *for*, *of*⟩; (a) capability ⟨*of* doing; *to* do; *for*⟩; competence ⟨*to* do; *for*, *in*⟩; (a) talent ⟨*for*⟩.

> 使い分け **ability** 最も一般的な語で, 実際に物事を成し遂げるための先天的または後天的な知的・肉体的な能力.
> **capacity** 生得的に備わっている何かを受け入れる能力.
> **faculty** 生得的・後天的な特殊な才能. 主に《米》では行政・事務など実務的な才能についても用いる.
> **capability** 事に応じる潜在的能力.
> **competence** 特定の仕事などをするのに必要な適性・資格.
> **talent** 特に芸術的な分野でのもって生まれた才能.

①【〜能力】 ●身体能力 physical *ability*. ●運動能力 athletic *ability*. ●計算能力 mathematical *ability*. ●潜在能力 latent *ability* [*talent*]. ●創造的な能力 creative *ability*. ●生産能力 productive *capacity*. ●収容能力 a seating *capacity*. ●言語[視覚]能力 the *faculty* of speech [sight]. ●教師としての能力 one's *competence* as a teacher. ●超能力 supernatural *power*.
②【能力〜】 ●能力不足 a lack of *ability*. ●能力別クラス編成 *ability* grouping, grouping students by *ability*; 《米》tracking; 《英》streaming.
③【能力が[は]】 ▶彼にはその仕事をする能力がある He has the *ability* [*capacity*] to do the job. (!(1) 最近では the ability *of doing* の型もときに用いられるが避ける傾向. (2) capacity は He has the *capacity for* (doing) the job. の型も可. (3)「能力がない」は He has no *ability to* do the job. のほかThis job is *beyond* his *ability* [*capacity*]. ともいえる)/He *can* do [*is able to* do, *is capable of doing*] the job. (!後の二つの方が堅い言い方)/(耐える力量がある) He *is equal to* [the job]. (⇨できる) ▶我々の能力は不断の努力によってのみ発達する Our *ability* will only grow [develop] by constant efforts. ▶その試験では彼らの論理的な文章を書く能力が問われる Their *ability* to write logically is required in the exam.
④【能力の】 ●能力のある男 an *able* man; a man *of ability*. (!後の方が堅い言い方)
⑤【能力を】 ●能力を伸ばす[引き出す] develop [draw out] ⟨his⟩ *ability*. ●能力を身につける[失う] gain [lose] the *ability* ⟨*to* do⟩. ▶彼女は音楽に非常な能力を発揮した She showed great *talent for* music./She showed great musical *talent*. ●能力給 performance-related pay; performance-based wages. ●能力主義(社会)(the) meritocracy /mèrətákrəsi/.

のうりんすいさん 農林水産 ●農林水産省 the Ministry of Agriculture, Forestry and Fisheries. ●農林水産大臣 the Minister of Agriculture, Forestry and Fisheries.

ノー 〖否定〗no. ▶断わる時ははっきりノーと言うべきです Say *no* clearly when you want to refuse. ▶私の答えはノーです I answer *no*./My answer is *negative*.

ノー 〖ない, 不要の〗〖名詞につけて〗no; non-; -less; (…からはずれた) off-; 〖…されていない〗(動詞の過去分詞につけて) un-. ●ノーカットの映画 a *full-length* [(検閲などで) an *uncut*, (無検閲の) an *uncensored*] film. ●ノーアイロンのワイシャツ a drip-dry [a wash-and-wear, 《英》a *non*-iron] shirt. ▶ぼくはノーマネーだ I have *no* money./I'm penni*less*. ▶広島・阪神戦は雨のためノーゲームになった(＝雨で流れた) The Carp vs. Tigers game was rained out 《米》[off 《英》]. ▶私はその計画にはノータッチです(＝関与していない) I'm *not* concerned with [*don't* have a hand in] the plan.
●ノーカーボン紙 non-carbon paper. ●ノークラッチ(装置) an automatic transmission; (車) an automatic (car); 《和製語》no clutch. ●ノーシード選手 an unseeded player. ●ノースリーブ(服) a sleeveless dress; 《和製語》no sleeve.

ノーアウト 〖野球〗 no out(s); none [nobody] out.
ノーカウント ● 今のはノーカウントだ That does *not count*./(野球で) That's a no-pitch./《和製語》(That's) no count.
ノーコメント No comment.
ノーコン(トロール) 〖野球〗 no control. ▶今日のピッチャーはノーコンだ The pitcher has *no control* today./The pitcher lacks *control* today./The pitcher is wild around the plate today.
ノーサイド 〖試合終了〗〖ラグビー〗 no-side.
ノースカロライナ 〖米国の州〗 Nòrth Carolína 《略 N.C. 郵便略 NC》.
ノースダコタ 〖米国の州〗 Nòrth Dakóta 《略 N.D. 郵便略 ND》.
ノースモーキング no smoking. ●ノースモーキングエリア a *no smoking* [a *nonsmoking*] area.
ノーダ(ウ)ン no out;《和製語》no down.
ノータッチエース (⇨サービス[サービスエース])
‡**ノート** ❶〖帳面〗a notebook. ●この意では note は不可 ・ルーズリーフのノート a loose-leaf /lúːsliːf/ *notebook*. ●ノートに自分の名前を書く write one's name in a *notebook*.
❷〖筆記すること〗 a note. ●講義のノートを取る make *notes* [a *note*] of a lecture; take *notes* of [《米》on] a lecture; write [note, put] down a lecture.
●ノートパソコン a nótebook [a láptop] (computer).
ノートルダム ●ノートルダム寺院 Notre Dame /nòutərdéim/.
ノーハウ 〖話〗know-how. (⇨ノウハウ)
ノーパン wearing no panties.
ノーバウンド ●ボールをノーバウンドで捕る catch a ball on the fly [before it hits the ground]. ●ノーバウンドでバックホームする throw a ball to the plate on the fly.
ノーヒット no hit. ▶我がチームは5回までノーヒットであった Our team made *no hit* [didn't make a hit] until the fifth inning./The opposing pitcher didn't allow us a hit until the fifth inning.
●ノーヒットゲーム a no-hit game; a no-hitter. ●ノーヒットゲームを達成する pitch [throw] a *no-hitter*. ●ノーヒットノーラン a no-hit, no-run game. 〖参考〗日本と異なり、米国ではノーヒットゲームを記録とする〗
ノーブラ braless;《和製語》no bra.
ノーブランド 图 a generic brand; generic-branded 《goods》; off-brand;《和製語》no brand.
●ノーブランドの 圏 off-brand.
ノーベルしょう ノーベル賞 a Nobel prize. ●ノーベル賞受賞者 a Nobel *prize* winner《in physics》;《やや書》a Nobel laureate /lɔ́ːriət/. ●ノーベル物理学賞が彼に与えられた The *Nobel prize for* [*in*] physics was awarded to him./He was awarded the *Nobel prize for* [*in*] physics.
ノーマーク ●ノーマークの選手 an *uncovered* [《主に英》an *unmarked*] player. ▶こっちだ、おれはノーマークだぞ(バスケットボールの試合で) Here, I'm *open*!
ノーマライゼーション 〖等生化、等しく生きる社会の実現〗(a) normalization.
ノーマル 〖正常な〗normal (↔abnormal).
●ノーマルヒル〖スキー〗the normal hill.
ノーモア ▶ノーモアヒロシマ〖標語〗 *No more* Hiroshimas!
ノーラン 〖無得点〗no run. (⇨ノーヒット)
ノーワインドアップ no windup. ●ノーワインドアップで投げる pitch [work] out of the stretch.
のがす 逃す ●好機を逃す miss [lose, give away] a good chance; *let* a good opportunity *slip* (*by*)

[*go*]. ●優勝を逃す miss winning the championship. ▶ぼくの番を逃しちゃったよ I've *missed* my turn. ▶鈴木が決定的なシュートチャンスを逃した Suzuki *missed* a clear chance to shoot.

のがれる 逃れる ❶〖逃げる〗(束縛・苦境などから脱出する) escape 《*from*》; (逃げ去る) run* [get*] away,《主に書》flee*; (逃げ出す) get out 《*of*》. (⇨逃げる❶). ●追っ手から逃れる *escape from* one's pursuers. (⇨❷) ●都会の喧騒(¾)から逃れる run [get] *away from* the bustle of the city. ●もめごと[借金]から逃れる *get out of* one's trouble [debt]. ▶彼らは戦火を逃れて来た They *fled from* the fires of war.
❷〖免れる〗(危険・災難などを未然に免れる) escape; (責任などをいやがって回避する) shirk; (巧みにかわす) evade; ●彼は危うく死を逃れた He narrowly *escaped* [×escaped from] *death* [being killed]./He *had* a narrow *escape from* death. ▶彼はやっと責任を逃れた He managed to *shirk* [*evade*, *get out of*] his responsibility.

のき 軒 eaves. ●軒下に[で] under the *eaves*. ▶つらら が家の軒から下がっていた Icicles hung from the *eaves* of the house. ●映画館が軒を連ねている Movie theaters stand *in a row* [*side by side*].
のぎ 芒 〖植物〗an awn.
のぎく 野菊 〖植物〗a wild chrysanthemum.
のぎくのはか 野菊の墓 *A Tomb of Wild Chrysanthemums*. 〖伊藤左千夫の小説〗
のきさき 軒先 ●軒先に巣を作っている鳥 birds nesting *under the eaves*.
のきなみ 軒並み 〖家の並び〗a row of houses. ▶列車は風雨のため軒並み(=すべて)遅れた *All* the trains were delayed because of the storm.
のく 退く get out of the way. (⇨退(ど)く)
のぐそ 野糞 ― **野糞する** 動 defecate outdoors.
ノクターン 〖音楽〗a nocturne.
のけぞる bend* backward. ●ぼくはボールを避けるためにのけぞって倒れた I *bent backward* to avoid the ball and fell down.
のけもの 除け者 an outcast,《話》an odd man [woman] out. ▶私は近所の人からのけ者にされた I *was shunned* [*was shut out*] by the neighbors.
のける 退ける、除ける 〖除く〗remove; (有害なものを) get* rid of …; 〖じゃまにならないように〗get … out of the way; 〖片づける〗put*… away; 〖省く〗omit (-tt-), leave*… out. ●その障害物をのける *get rid of* [*remove*] the obstacle; *get* the obstacle *out of the way*. ●そのいすをのけてくれ *Put* the chairs *away*./(わきへ寄せる) *Move* the chairs *aside*.
のこぎり 鋸 a saw; 〖手鋸〗a handsaw; 〖丸鋸〗a circular saw; 〖金のこ〗a hacksaw. ●のこぎりの目立てをする sharpen the teeth of a *saw*. ●のこぎりで板をひく *saw* a board; cut a board with a *saw*.
●のこぎりくず sawdust. ●のこぎり歯 the tooth of a saw; a sawtooth.
のこぎりざめ 鋸鮫 〖魚介〗a saw shark.
‡**のこす 残す** ❶〖去ったあとに〗leave*… (behind); (遺産・伝統などを) hand … down. ●借金を残して死ぬ *leave* a debt *behind* 《one》. ●後世に名を残す *leave* one's name to posterity. ●妻を残して死ぬ *leave* one's wife. (〖!〗「妻を残して去る」の意では *leave* one's wife *behind* とすることも多い) ●彼に書き置きを残す *leave* a note *for* him; *leave* him a note. ●母が残してくれた指輪 the ring *handed down to* me *from* my mother. ●彼は息子一人財産残して死んだ When he died, he *left* his son a fortune [a fortune *to* his son]. (〖!〗❷と異なり、この意では to の代わりに for は不可 (⇨与える))

❷【余す】leave*; (節約して) save; (予備に) reserve, put* [set*] (money) aside. ●仕事を残しておく *leave* the work unfinished [half-finished]. ●あすのために精力を残しておく *reserve* one's energy *for* tomorrow. ▶旅行のためにいくらかお金を残す *put* [*set*] some money *aside* for a trip. ▶ケーキを少し残しておいてください *Leave* me some cake. / *Leave* some cake *for* [×to] me. (❗ ❶と異なりこの意では to は不可)

会話「でもそのチーズは好きじゃないんだもん」「いいこと,残さず(=すっかり)食べなさいよ」"But I don't like the cheese." "Eat it *up*, I say."

❸【残留させる】(罰として) keep*... in. ▶彼は放課後1時間残された He *was kept in* an extra hour after school.

❹【その他の表現】▶土俵際でよく残し(=踏ん張り)ました【相撲】He did a fine job of *standing firm* at the edge of the ring.

のこった 残った【相撲】*Nokotta*; (説明的に) Still in!

のこのこ (まったくむとんじゃくに) nonchalantly; (知らぬが仏で) innocently; (ずうずうしくも) brazenly; (恥ずかしげもなく) shamelessly. ●彼は上司に首だと怒鳴られてもある朝этのこのこ出社してくるタイプの男だ He is the kind of man to come to work *nonchalantly* the morning after his boss shouts that he is fired. ●彼は招待もされていないのにパーティーにのこのこやって来た Although he was not invited, he *brazenly* showed up at the party.

のこらず 残らず (⇨全部) ●その魚を残らず食べる eat the *whole* fish. ●金を残らず遣う spend *all* the [×the whole] money. ▶それについて知っていることは残らず(=すべて)彼に話した I have told him *everything* I knew about it. ▶彼らは一人残らずその提案に同意した They *all* [*All* of them] agreed to the proposal. (❗ They agreed to the proposal *to a man*. ともいう硬い表現)

***のこり 残り** the rest; the remainder (❗ 単・複両扱い); (残ったもの) what is left (over); 〚余剰〛 the súrplus; 〚残金〛 the balance; 〚数学〛 (引き算の) (the) remainder.

① 【～の残り】 ●借金の残り the *remainder* [*balance*] of one's debt. ●夕飯の残り (⇨残り物) ●試合の残り時間はあと3分じゃない There's only three minutes *to go* in the game. (❗ to go は時間や距離を示す名詞(句)を修飾する不定詞で「後に残っている」の意の成句的表現) / We have only three minutes *left* before the game is over.

② 【残りは】 ▶ほしいものを取って残りは全部捨てなさい Take what you want and throw all *the rest* away. ▶その事故で5人が死亡,残りは重傷を負った Five people were killed and the *rest* [the *others*] were [×was] seriously injured in the accident. ▶残り(の金)(=釣り銭)はとっておきなさい Keep your [the] *change*. ▶20から5を引けば残りは15だ Five from twenty *leaves* fifteen. (⇨引く)

③ 【残りの】 remaining; (余剰の) surplus. ●残りの半分 the *other* half. ●残りの仕事を片付ける finish the *remaining* work. ▶残りのバナナ[肉]は全部腐っていた *The rest* of the bananas were [The *rest* of the meat was] all rotten. (❗ the rest of+複数名詞「～の残り全部」は(単数)扱い) ▶彼は彼女が眠っている間にウオッカのボトルを見つけ残りの酒を流しに捨てた While she was asleep, he found a vodka bottle and poured the *remains* down the sink.

のこりが 残り香 a lingering scent.
のこりすくない 残り少ない ▶砂糖が残り少なくなってきた Our sugar *is running short*. / We're running *short of* sugar. ▶今年も残り少なくなった The year *is coming* [*drawing*] *to an end*.

のこりび 残り火 embers.
のこりもの 残り物 (食べ残し) leftovers, leftover food. (⇨売れ残り) ●夕食の残り物 the *leftovers* of dinner. ●残り物でシチューを作る make a stew out of *leftovers*. ●残り物を昼に食べる eat [have] *leftovers* for lunch.

：のこる 残る ❶ 【とどまる】stay, 《やや書》remain; (人の去ったあとに) stay behind (❗ この意ではいずれも進行形可) ●卒業後大学に残る stay on [remain] at the college after graduation. ●彼に質問をするためにあとに残る stay *behind* to ask him a question. ▶私たちはロンドンに向かったが彼はまだパリに残っていた We left for London, but he *was* still *staying* [*remaining*] in Paris.

❷ 【余る】be left (over), remain. (❗ 後の方が堅い語) ●売れ残る *be left* [end up] on the shelf; *remain* unsold. ●冷蔵庫にはほとんど食料が残っていない There is [We have] almost no food *left* (over) in the refrigerator. ▶お金はいくら残っていますか How much money *is left*? ▶彼には選択の余地が残っていなかった No choice *was left* (to) him. / He *was left* (with) no choice. ▶10から3を引けば7が残る Three from ten *leaves* seven. (❗ 受身不可) / Ten minus three *equals* seven. / If you take 3 from 10, 7 *remains*.

❸ 【残存する】remain; (まだ消えずに) linger (on). (❗ この意ではともに進行形不可) ●その問題についてはまだ言うことがたくさん残っている Much *remains* to be said on the subject. / (付け加えることがたくさんある) Much *needs to be added* on the subject. ▶彼の言葉はまだ耳に残っている His words still *linger* in my ears. ▶その風習はいくつかの国では今も残っている The custom still *remains* [(細々と) *endures*, (耐えて) *survives*] in some countries. ▶たくさんの土地が開墾されたためにパンダは残っている地域に押し込められたまま餓死している As so much land has been cultivated, pandas are confined to [driven into] the *remaining* areas and starve to death. ▶私はわたくし大変な借金をした(=国に大変な借金を負わせた)大臣として歴史に残るだろう I will probably *go down in* [×on] history as a Minister of Treasury who got the nation into massive debt. (❗ go down in history は「歴史に名を残す,記録される」の意)

のさばる 【思いどおりにする】have* one's own way; 〚威張ってふるまう〛act high-handedly; (偉ぶる) act important; (権力などをふるまわす) 《話》throw* one's weight around. ▶もうこれ以上やくざののさばらせておくわけにはいかない We can't let the gang *have* their *own way* anymore.

のざらし 野晒し — **野晒しの** 形 weather-beaten 《old bicycles》. ●野ざらしにする leave 《it》 out in the open; expose 《it》 to the weather.

のし 熨斗 *noshi*; (説明的に) a small piece of red-and-white paper folding glued onto a wrapped gift at the upper right-hand corner, showing gratitude or respect. ●のしをつける attach *noshi* 《to it》; (進呈する) present 《it *to* him》.

●のし紙 a *noshi* wrapper. ●のし袋 a *noshi* envelope.

のしあがる 伸し上がる ●役員にのし上がる push one's *way* [*rise*] to the position of director; (昇進する) be promoted to director. ▶日本は自動車王国にのし上がった Japan *has grown* [*has developed*]

のしあるく 伸し歩く swagger; strut.
のしかかる 伸し掛かる ▶その問題が彼に重くのしかかった The problem *weighed* [*sat*] heavily *on* him.
のしもち のし餅 (のした餅) flattened rice cake.
のじゅく 野宿 ── 野宿する sleep in the open [out of doors]; (テントを張って) camp (out).
のす 伸す ❶ [勢いが強まる] ▶先般のテロ攻撃事件以来, 米国国民の間でタカ派的風潮がじわじわのしてきている The hawkish tendency has *been* gradually *picking up* strength among the US citizens since the last terrorist attack.
❷ [打ち延ばす] flatten; (金属などを) beat* ... out; (人を打ちのめす) beat ... up, 《話》 flatten.
ノスタルジア [郷愁] 《書》 (feel) nostálgia 《for》.
ノズル [筒口] a nozzle.

:**のせる** 乗せる ❶ [人・物を積む] (車に同乗させる) give* ... a ride [《主に英》 a lift]; (乗り物が乗客を乗せる, 人を車で迎えに行って乗せる, 途中で乗せる) pick ... up; (荷物・客を積む) load; (運ぶ) carry. ▶馬に乗せる 《him》 in the saddle. ▶彼を肩に乗せる give him a ride [*ride* him] on my shoulders. ▶母の自転車に乗せてもらう *ride on* my mother's bicycle. ▶10 人以上乗せたエレベーター an elevator *carrying* more than 10 people. ▶車に荷物を乗せる *load* the baggage *into* a car; *load* a car *with* the baggage (🛈 load A with B の構文で, A が車で限定されている場合は車が荷物でいっぱいであることを暗示). ▶彼に手を貸してタクシーに乗せてやる *help* him *get in* a taxi; *help* [*hand*] him *into* a taxi. ▶彼女を町まで乗せてやった I *gave* her *a ride to* town./I *drove* her *to* town. ▶彼女に駅まで乗せてもらった She *gave* me *a ride to* the station./I *got a ride from* [*with*] her to the station. ▶だれか乗せてってほしい人る? (Does) anybody want a *ride*? ▶バスは止まって乗客を乗せた The bus stopped to *pick* [*take*] *up* passengers. ▶そのけが人は担架で救急車に乗せられた They *loaded* the injured man on a stretcher *into* the ambulance. ▶その船はたくさんの客を乗せていた The ship *had* a lot of passengers *on board*./The ship *was carrying* a lot of passengers. ▶そのバスは 50 人の乗客を乗せられる (= 収容できる) The bus can hold [*accommodate*] fifty passengers.
❷ [欺く] deceive, 《やや話》 take* ... in. ▶ずる賢い政治家に乗せられてはいけない Don't let yourself *be taken in* by crafty politicians.
❸ [調子づかせる] (興奮させる) excite 《the audience》; (うっとりさせる) get 《the audience》 carried away. ▶彼女は観衆の割れるような拍手と声援に乗せられて情熱的に踊った She danced passionately, *carried along with* the roar of applause and cheering from the audience. (🛈 carry ... along は「(人)を激励する」の意)
❹ [その他の表現] ▶歌詞をメロディーに乗せる *match* the words (of a song) *to* the melody.

***のせる** 載せる ❶ [上に置く] put* [place] 《on》 (⇨置く); (A (テーブル・容器など) に B をどっさり載せる・積む) load 《A with B》. ▶花びんを棚にのせる [*place*] a vase *on* a shelf. (🛈 place の方が堅い語) ▶子供をひざにのせる *hold* a child *in* [*on*] one's lap. ▶コップを盆にのせて運ぶ *carry* glasses *on* a tray. ▶クリスマスのごちそうが(いっぱい)のせられたテーブル the table *loaded* [*covered*] *with* a Christmas dinner. (⇨乗せる ❶;車に荷物を乗せる 注).
❷ [掲載する] (新聞などが記事などを) carry; (新聞などに) run*; (発表する) publish. ▶新聞に広告を載せる *put* [*run*] an ad in a newspaper. ▶雑誌に小説を載せる *publish* [*print*] a novel *in* a magazine. ▶その新聞は米国の外交政策に批判的な社説を載せていた The newspaper *carried* [*ran*] a critical editorial about US foreign policy. ▶この辞書は何語載せていますか How many (entry) words [entries] *are there* in this dictionary? (🛈 entry は「見出し語」の意)

のぞかせる 覗かせる let* 《it》 keep out 《from》; (見せる) show*. (⇨ 覗く ❸) ▶この本は古代ギリシアの生活の一端をのぞかせてくれる This book gives us *some* idea of life in ancient Greece.
のぞき 覗き a peep. ▶のぞきをやる play Peeping Tom 《with a telescope》. ▶ a Peeping Tom は「のぞき魔」. この用法での無冠詞に注意
●**のぞき趣味** Peeping Tomism. ●**のぞき窓** [穴] (look through) the peephole 《in the front door》.
のぞきこむ 覗き込む look in. (⇨覗く ❶)
のぞきみ 覗き見 ── 覗き見する peep 《at》, take a peep 《at》. ▶生け垣のすきまから覗き見する *peep through* a gap in the hedge.

:**のぞく** 除く 動 [取り除く] (除去する) remove; (有害なものを除く, 脱ぐ) get* rid of ...; (不要な要素・部分を) eliminate; (除外する) 《やや堅》 exclude; [苦痛・不安などを軽減する] relieve; [削除する] 《やや書》 delete; [省略する] leave* ... out, 《やや書》 omit (-tt-). ▶心配の原因を除く *get rid of* [*remove*] the cause of anxiety. ▶名簿から彼の名前を除く *leave* his name *out* of the list; *remove* [*eliminate, exclude, delete, omit*] his name from the list. ▶我々は彼の負担を除いてやった We *relieved* him *of* his burden. (🛈 ×We relieved his burden from him. とはいわない)
[会話] 「田中家を除きたくないわ」「招待しなくちゃならないと思うんなら, じゃあそうしてもいいよ」"I don't like *leaving* the Tanakas [Tanaka family] *out*." "Well, go ahead and invite them, if you feel you must."

── ...を除いて[除けば] 前 except ...; but ...; (...は別として) except for ..., but for ...; apart [《米》 aside] from .... (⇨ほか ❷ 解説) ▶彼を除いてはだれもその問題が解けなかった No one *except* [*but*] him could solve the problem. ▶彼女は午前中(買い物に行っているとき)を除いていつも家にいる *Except* in the morning [when she is out shopping] she is always (at) home. ▶つづりの間違いが少しあることを除けば君の作文はよくできている Your composition is good [well written] *except for* [*apart from*, ×except] a few spelling mistakes. ▶あの人に関しては英語の先生であることを除けば何も知らない I know nothing about him *except for* the fact that [*except that*] he is an English teacher. ▶バスには運転手を除いて 10 人の人がいた There were ten people in [on] the bus, *excluding* (← including) the driver.

***のぞく** 覗く ❶ [穴・高所などから見る] look [(こっそり) peep, 《話》 peek] 《*into*, *at*, *through*》. ▶谷底[井戸]をのぞく *look down into* a valley [a well]. ▶冷蔵庫をのぞく *look in* a refrigerator. ▶彼女の目[顔]をのぞき込む *look into* her eyes [face]. ▶顕微鏡をのぞいて植物細胞を見る *look through* a microscope *at* plant cells. ▶鍵穴から中(にいる彼)をのぞき見る *look* [*peep, peek*] *in* 《at him》 *through* a keyhole. ▶窓からのぞく *look out* 《of》 a window (🛈 of を省略は 《主に米》); (顔を出して見る) *put* [*stick*] one's head out of a window *and look*. ▶彼の日記をのぞく *peep at* his diary. ▶彼女はよく鏡をのぞく She often *looks* 《at herself》 *in* the

のそだち 野育ち a wild youth; a child brought up on a let-alone principle.

のそのそ ●のそのそ(=ゆっくり, ぎこちなく)動く move slowly (and awkwardly); (ものぐさそうに) move sluggishly 《書》 lazily. ▶1匹の熊がのそのそ川に向かうのを見た I saw a bear lumbering [moving slowly] toward the river. ▶彼女の例のそのそした動きが私の気にさわる Her usual sluggish movement gets on my nerves.

のぞましい 望ましい desirable; 〖勧められる〗advisable; 〖よい〗good. 〖好ましい〗日米関係 desirable relationships between Japan and the United States. ●望ましくない人 an undesirable person. ●あすは制服で来ることが望ましい It is required [to be desired] that you 《主に英》should) come in school uniform tomorrow. ▶子供がテレビを見過ぎるのは望ましくない It is not good for children to watch too much TV.

のぞみ 望み ●〖願望〗(実現困難な望み) (a) wish 《for; to do; that 節》(❗しばしば普通の望みにも用いて控えめな気持ちを表す); (強い願望) (a) desire 《for; to do》; 〖希望〗(a) hope 《of, for; that 節》; 〖夢〗a dream; 〖意志〗(a) will. (⇨希望)

① 〖~望み〗 ● たっての望み an earnest hope. ▶私は生きる望みを失った I have lost my desire [the will] to live.

② 〖望み~〗 ▶何もかも私の望みどおりになった Everything turned out as I had hoped. ▶行くもとどまるも君の望み次第だ You may go or stay as you want (to) [like, 《書》wish].

③ 〖望みが[は]〗 ▶とうとう私の長年の望み(=希望)がかなった (⇨希望 ②) ▶私の望みは世界旅行をすることだ My wish [dream] is to travel around the world. ▶父の会社が倒産したとき, 彼の望みは断たれた When his father's company went bankrupt, he saw the end of his hope. ▶君は望みが高すぎる(=要求しすぎる) You're asking too much.

④ 〖望みを〗 ●彼女の望みをかなえてやる fulfill her wish; (望むものを与える) give her [let her get] what she wants. ▶救助されるという望みを捨てるな Don't give up hope of being rescued [that you will be rescued]. ▶彼女はかつては高い望みを抱いていたに違いない She must have had high hopes once. ▶彼は医者になりたいという望みを持っている He has a desire [an ambition] to become a doctor./He hopes to be a doctor.

❷ 〖見込み〗(a) chance; 〖期待〗(a) hope; 〖展望〗a prospect; 〖可能性〗(a) likelihood. (⇨見込み)

① 〖望みが[は]〗 ▶我々には勝てる望みが十分ある We have a good chance of winning. ▶彼が回復する望みは十分ある[まったくない] There is every [no] hope of [《米》for] his recovery. (❗× ... hope for him to recover. とはいわない) ▶最後の望みは絶たれた My last hope is gone. ▶君の成功の望みは薄い[ほとんどない] The chance of your success is very slim./There's very little [not much] chance of your success./You are very unlikely to succeed. (❗《話》では最後に I'm afraid を添えて語調をやわらげることが多い)

② 〖望みを〗 ●決勝進出に望みをつなぐ hang one's hope on the final. ▶彼は最終レースに望みをかけた He placed his last hope on the final race.

❸ 〖選択〗(a) choice. ▶望みのものを選びなさい Take your choice [pick].

のぞみうす 望み薄 (⇨望み ❷ ①)

のぞむ 望む ❶ 〖欲する〗want, 《書》desire; 〖希望する〗hope; 〖願う〗wish; 〖期待する〗expect; 〖楽しみに待つ〗look forward to .... (⇨欲しい[類語]) ▶君が全力を尽くすことを望みます I hope [×want] (that) you (will) do your best. (❗(1) は《話》では通例省略する. (2) will のない方が実現性を強く表す)/I want [×hope] you to do your best. ▶我々は幸福を望む We want [hope for, wish (for)] happiness. (❗後には実現の困難さが強くなる. wish より wish for の方が普通. hope for の代わりに hope は用いない) ▶私は世界旅行ができることを望む I wish I could [×can] travel around the world. (❗hope と異なり実現が不可能に近いことを願望するので, 節中の (助) 動詞は過去形になる) ▶それは彼が望んだようにうまくはいかなかった It didn't work out the way he wanted it to. ▶これ以上望むべきことは何もない (=申し分ない) There is nothing more we want [《書》left) to be desired]./〖反語的〗Who could wish for [《米》ask for] anything more? ▶いい仕事の口など望むべくもない (=期待できない) You can't expect a good job. ▶日本人はもっと国際感覚を身につけることが望まれている Japanese people are expected to acquire a more international way of thinking. ▶彼にこれ以上何を望むのですか What more do you expect from him?

会話「テニスしないか」「望むところだ」 "How about playing tennis?" "Sure."

❷ 〖見晴らす〗overlook; (人が) get* a view 《of》; (場所が) command. ▶その丘から港が望める We can see [get a view of, overlook] the port from the hill./The hill overlooks [《書》commands] a view of the port.

❸ 〖好む〗like. (⇨好む)

のぞむ 臨む ❶ 〖出席する〗attend. ●開会式に臨んであいさつする attend the opening ceremony and make a speech; (開会式において) make a speech at the opening ceremony.

❷ 〖面する〗face; (見おろす) overlook. ▶そのホテルは海に臨んでいる The hotel faces [overlooks, (隣接する) borders on] the sea.

❸ 〖事に当たる〗● 厳しい態度で臨む(=態度をとる) take a firm attitude 《toward him》. ▶彼は難局に臨んでも(=直面しても)冷静だった He was calm in the face of difficulties./(冷静に立ち向かった) He faced [met] difficulties calmly.

のそりのそり (⇨のっそり)

のたうちまわる のた打ち回る toss and tumble [(やや書)writhe /ráið/ (about)]; (in pain).

のたくる (ミミズなどが体をくねらせて動く) turn and wriggle about.

のだて 野点 〖野外で抹茶を立てること〗an outdoor tea ceremony.

のたりのたり (ゆっくりと) slowly; (悠長に) leisurely.

のたれじに 野垂れ死に ── 野垂れ死にする 動 (惨めな死に方をする) die a dog's death [like a dog]; (行き倒れになる) die by the roadside.

のち(に) 後(に) ❶ 〖あと〗(その後) later, afterward;

のちのち (…の後に) after ...; (今から) in ... (⇨後(゚)); (以来今までずっと) since .... ● 数日後に after a few days; (その時から) a few days *later* [*after* (that)] (**!** 具体的な数字の後では later の方が普通); (これから) in a few days, (in) a few days *from now*. ● 朝食の後に散歩に行く go out for a walk *after* breakfast. ▶ 今行けば, 君は後に後悔するでしょう If you go now, you'll regret [be sorry] (about it) *later* [*afterward*, ×*after*]. ▶ (天気予報で)晴のち雨 Fair *to* [*later*] rainy. (関連) 天気予報では clear (快晴) も含めて fair という) ▶ その後 10 年にわたって彼と文通している I've been exchanging letters with him for ten years *since then*.
❷【将来】後の世 the *future* [*next*] world. ● 後後のため for the sake of *the future*.

のちのち 後後 (⇨後(゚)❷)

のちほど 後程 later (on). ● 後ではお目にかかりましょう I'll see you *later*. (関連) それじゃまた See you later [soon]./Be seeing you.//それじゃ(=さようなら) See you.) ▶ 後はどれをあなたにあげるか I'll explain it to you *later on*.

ノッカー (玄関の) a knocker.

ノッキング【エンジンの異常爆発】knocking.

ノック【叩くこと】a knock. ▶ ドアを激しく [そっと] ノックする音がした There was a violent [a quiet] *knock* on the door. ▶ 彼はドアをノックした He *knocked* on [at] the door./He *gave* a *knock* on [at] the door.

ノック【野球】a fungo (**!** 通例守備練習用に打つ外野フライをさす) 【和製語】a knock. ● ノックを捕る練習をする field *fungoes*. ▶ グラウンドでノックをする hit *fungoes* on the field.

ノックアウト 【名】【ボクシング】a knóckòut (略 KO, K.O.). ● ノックアウト勝ちする win 《the fight》a *knockout* 《話》a *KO*. ● 投手をノックアウトする knock out a pitcher; knock a pitcher out of the box. ● テクニカルノックアウト (⇨ティーケーオー)
— **ノックアウトする** 【動】 knock 《him》 out; 《話》KO 《him》. (**!** 活用形は KO's; KO'd; KO'ing)
● ノックアウトパンチ a knockout punch.

ノックダウン 【名】【ボクシング; 部品の組立て】a knock-down.
— **ノックダウンする** 【動】 knock 《him》down.
● ノックダウン方式 a knock-down system. ● ノックダウン輸出 knock-down export.

のっけから from the (very) start [beginning]. ▶ のっけからお前はうそつきだと言うのでこちらもむっとなった The first thing he said was that I was a liar, which offended me a lot.

のっしのっし ● のっしのっし歩く walk *heavily*; walk with *heavy* strides.

のっそり — **のっそりと** 【副】(ゆっくり) slowly; (物ぐさそうに) lazily, sluggishly. ● のっそりと立ち上がる rise *slowly* to one's feet. ● のっそりと歩いていく make one's way *sluggishly*. ▶ 戸を開けると背の高い男がのっそりと立っていた I opened the door to find a tall man standing there *impassively*. (**!** impassively は「感情のない人のように」の意)

ノット a knot 《kn., kt., k.》. ● 20 ノットの船 a ship with a speed of 20 *knots*. (**!** a ship of 20 knots とは通例いわない) ● 時速 30 ノットで進む do [make] 30 *knots* an hour.

のっとり 乗っ取り 【ハイジャック】 (飛行機などの) a hijack; (飛行機の) a skyjack; 【会社などの】a takeover.
● 乗っ取り犯 a hijacker; a skyjacker.

のっとる 乗っ取る ❶【会社などを】● 会社を乗っ取る *take over* a company.
❷【乗り物などを】hijack; (特に飛行機を) skyjack; (船を) seajack.

のっとる 則る 【従う】follow; (規則などに) conform 《*to*》. ● 会の規則にのっとって *in conformity* 《書》 [*accordance*] 《やや書》 with the rules of the club; *conforming* [《やや書》 *according*] *to* the rules of the club. ▶ 判事は先例にのっとりその事件に判決を下した The judge decided the case, *following* [《やや書》 *according to*] the precedents.

のっぴきならぬ (避けられない) unavoidable. ● のっぴきならぬ用事で on *unavoidable* business. ● のっぴきならぬ事情で owing to *unavoidable* circumstances.

のっぺらぼう ● のっぺらぼうの顔 (凹凸がなく表情にも乏しい顔) a flat, expressionless face; (目も鼻も口もない顔) a flat face without eyes, mouth, or nose.

のっぺり ● のっぺりした顔 a smooth, expressionless face; (整ってはいるがしまりのない顔) a good-looking face that doesn't look intelligent.

のっぽ a tall [(ひょろ長い) a lanky] person; 《ふざけて》《話》a beanpole. ● のっぽのジョー *Long* Joe.

のづみ 野積み ● 建築資材を野積みにしておく leave a heap [a pile] of building materials in the open.

のづり 野釣り fishing in the wild.

*-ので 【接続助詞】 because; 《やや書》 since; 《主に英書》as. (⇨から❸, だから)

> **解説** (1) **because** は 3 語のうちで最も因果関係が強く聞き手にとって新しい内容なので, because 節が通例最も注目される文尾におかれるが, 主節も同様注目させたい場合は because 節を文頭に移動される (⇨ [第 2 文例]). **since** は聞き手がすでに知っていると思われる事実を理由として述べ, **as** は付帯状況的に軽く理由を添える言い方. これらの 2 語では, 最も注目させたい主節の方を通例文尾におく.
> (2) **as** は時を表す用法と紛らわしいことがあるので注意. 次の例では as は when/while の意味なのか because の意味なのかあいまい: 彼は道路で遊んでいて車にはねられた *As* he was playing on the road, he was hit by a car.

▶ 雨が降り出したので出かけなかった I didn't go ╱out, *because* it began to ╲rain. *because* it began to ╲rain. (**!** I didn't go óut *because* it began to ˅rain. だと, because 節は否定の作用域の中にあり, 「雨が降り出したので出かけたのではない(別の理由があった)」の意となる)/I didn't go out *because* of rain. (**!** because 節を用いる方が口語的)/It began to rain, *so* I didn't go out. (**!** くだけた言い方. 日常会話では I didn't go out. It began to rain. のような接続詞無しの文も多い) ▶ 彼は父親の財産を引き継いだので今は大変な金持ちです *Because* [*Since, As*] he inherited his father's fortune, he is now very rich. (**!** (1) He is now very rich *because* he inherited his father's fortune. の語順も可. (2) 原因・理由を表す since 節や as 節は主節の後にくる場合は He is now very rich, *since* [*as*] he inherited his father's fortune. のように前にコンマがおかれることが多い)/Having inherited his father's fortune, he is now very rich. (**!** このように分詞構文も可能だが, 意味があいまいになることも多く, 避ける方が無難) ▶ 彼は非常に疲れていたのでそれ以上歩けなかった He was so tired (*that*) he couldn't walk any further. (**!**《話》ではしばしば that を省略する)/He was *too* tired *to* walk any further.

のてん 野天 the open-air; the outdoors. (同 露天)
● 野天風呂 an open-air bath.

*のど 喉 ❶【器官】a throat.

①【のどの】●ビールでのどの渇きをいやす quench [(和らげる) relieve] one's *thirst* with beer.
②【のどが】▶風邪でのどが痛い I have a sore *throat* from a cold. ●のどがかわいた I'm [I feel] *thirsty*./(ひどく) I'm dying of *thirst*.
③【のどに】▶骨がのどに引っかかった A bone stuck [I got a bone stuck] in my *throat*. (■身体の一部に刺さる意では into は用いない) ▶その老人はもちがのどに詰まった The rice cake *choked* the older man./The old man *choked on* the rice cake.
④【のどを】● 彼女ののどを絞める squeeze her *throat*; (絞め殺す) *strangle* her to death. ● 感極まってのどを詰まらせる be choked up with emotion; gulp emotionally. ▶心配のあまり食事がのどを通らなかった(＝食欲をなくした) I was so worried that I lost my *appetite* [(ほとんど何も食べられなかった) I could hardly eat anything]. ●猫ののどをごろごろ鳴らした The cat *purred*.
❷【歌う声】●のど自慢大会に出る sing in an amateur singing contest. ▶彼はいいのどを聞かせてくれた He sang to us in a sweet *voice*.

● 喉が鳴る ▶そのうまそうな匂いにのどが鳴った The delicious smell *made* my *mouth water*./My *mouth watered* at the delicious smell.
● 喉から手が出る ▶のどから手が出るほどそのオルゴールが欲しい I *want* the music box *so badly*. (■ *badly* は *want* を強める. 「非常に」の意)/(他のどんなものよりも) I *want* the music box *more than anything else* (in the world). (⇨喉元)
● 喉まで ▶彼の名前がのどまで(＝舌の先まで)出かかっていた I had his name [His name was] *on the tip of my tongue*. ▶のどまで出かかっていた怒りのことばをぐっとこらえた I drove back angry words which rose to my lips.

● のどあめ a cough drop. ● のどちんこ the úvula (⑱ ～s, -lae /-liː/). ● のど笛 a windpipe. ● のど仏 an Adam's apple.

*のどか ── のどかな 形 (平和な) peaceful; (うららかな) mild. ▶のどかな田園風景 a *peaceful* rural landscape. ● のどかな春の日 a *mild* [(静かな) a *quiet*, a *calm*] spring day.

のどくび 喉首 the throat. ● のどくびを絞める take [grip] 《him》 by the throat.

のどごし 喉越し ▶のど越しのよい食べ物 food that goes down easily [pleasantly]. ▶ぐいっとひと息にあおるビールののど越しの味(＝のどをいやすような感触)を楽しむものだ When you drink a glass of beer in one gulp, you enjoy that *soothing feeling* [*taste*] *in your throat*.

のどもと 喉元 the throat. (⇨喉(㊀)) ▶彼は男ののど元にナイフを突きつけた He held the knife to [on] the man's *throat*. (■ *to* は方向, *on* は接触を表す)
● 喉元過ぎれば熱さを忘る 'Hot food eaten with much trouble is soon forgotten.'/(危険が去ると神は忘れられる)《ことわざ》The danger past, God forgotten./Once on shore, we pray no more.

のなか 野中 the middle of a field.

:**-のに ❶【にもかかわらず】** although ..., though ..., (■ 前より口語的) in spite of ..., despite ... (■ 前より堅い語); for [with] all ... (■ in spite of より口語的); 《しかし》but. ▶彼はよく練習したのに試合に負けた *Although* [*Though*] he trained hard, (×but) he lost the game./*In spite of* [*Despite, For all, With all*] his hard training, he lost the game./He trained hard *but* lost the game. ▶だめだと言ったのに彼は私の車を使った He used my car *even though* I told him not to. (■ *even* は *though* を強める. ×*even although* とはいわない) ▶彼は息子に厳しいのに娘には甘すぎる He is strict with his son *but* (he is) too soft with his daughter.
会話 「彼, あのソナタをけっこう上手に弾いたね」「きっとちをよと思ってたのにねえ」"He played the sonata rather well." "*And* I felt sure he'd make a mess of it."
❷【なのに】when ...; 〖一方〗while .... ▶十分な給料があるのになぜ残業をするのですか Why do you work overtime *when* you get an enough salary? ▶彼女は活発で話し好きなのに, 妹は物静かで控えめだ She is lively and talkative, *but* 〖(やや書) *while*, (書) *whereas*〗her (younger) sister is quiet and reserved.
会話 「彼, 何て言ってるの」「あなたがそんなに大騒ぎしているのに聞こえるわけないでしょう」"What's he saying?" "How can I hear *when* you're making so much noise?"
❸【ために】to 《*do*》; for .... ▶インドへ行くのにビザを申請する apply for a visa *to* go to India. ▶私は旅行するのに金が必要だ I need money *to* travel [*for* traveling].
❹【希望】(...だとよいのに) I wish ... (■ 実現不可能なことを含意. cf. hope); (すぐに) should (*do*) (■ 過去形は should have (*done*)). ▶雨がやめばいいのに I *wish* [*If only*] it stopped raining. (■ 後の方が感情的(強意的)) ▶もう5分待っていたらあなたは彼女に会えたのに If you had waited another five minutes, you'd have seen her. ▶よせばいいのに彼は競馬に夢中だ He is crazy about horse races. He *should* give it up. ▶その本を買っておけばよかったのに You *should* [*ought to*] *have bought* the book. (■ 買わなかったことを含意)

のねずみ 野鼠 【動物】a field mouse (⑱ mice).

ののしる 罵る 〖悪態をつく〗swear* 《*at*》; 〖悪態をついてののしる〗curse; 〖侮辱するような暴言を吐く〗abuse. ▶彼女は夫の(無能力)をののしった She *swore at* (the incompetence of) her husband. ▶彼は態度が横柄だと店員をののしった He *cursed* [*swore at*] the clerk *for being* arrogant.

-のは ❶【述部・文の主題化】▶雨に濡れるのは風邪のもとです *Getting* wet in the rain is the cause of catching a cold./It's certainly the cause of catching a cold to get wet in the rain. (■ it は to 以下を受ける形式主語) ▶彼がアメリカ生まれだというのは本当ではない It's not true *that* he was born in America. (■ it は that 節を受ける形式主語) ▶君がその問題を解くのはたやすいことだ It's easy *for* you to solve the problem. (■ ×It is easy that you solve .... は不可)
❷【文の強調部分以外の主題化】it is ... 《that [wh-]節》(■ ...は強調される名詞, 代名詞, 副詞(句, 節). 通例ящее書き言葉で用いられる) ▶彼らに本当に必要なのは精神的な支えです *What* they really ˇneed is moral ˋsupport. (■ 物質的支援 (material support)との対比では ... ˋmoral ˋsupport. の音調になる)/*It is* moral ˋsupport *that* they really ↗need. ▶悪いのは私の方で, あなたではない I am to ↗blame, not ˇyou./*It's* ˇme *that* is to ↗blame, not ˇyou. (■(1)改まった言い方では It is not you but I who am to blame. となる. (2)×Who is to blame is me, not you. とはいわない) ▶京都がいちばん美しいのは秋です ˇFall is (the time) when Kyoto is most ↗beautiful. (■ When Kyoto is most beautiful is in (the) fall. とあまりいわない)/*It is* in 《(主に米) the》 fall *that* Kyoto is most beautiful. ▶私が事故にあったのはちょうどこです This is exactly where I had an accident.

(🔲口語的な言い方)/It was on this very spot that I met with an accident. (🔲過去時制の文の一部分が強調される場合は is より was が普通) ▶列車が大幅に遅れたのは大雨のためでした It was because of the heavy rain [because it rained heavily] that the train was considerably delayed. (🔲この場合には because 節の代わりに since 節, as 節が用いられない)

*のばす 伸ばす, 延ばす ❶ [長さ・距離などを] (ある点まで) extend; (引っ張って) stretch ... (out); (長さを) lengthen; (幅を) widen. (⇨伸長) ▶鉄道を国境まで延ばす extend the railroad to the border. ●ゴムをいっぱいに伸ばす stretch (out) the rubber to its fullest extent. ●そでを2センチ伸ばす make one's sleeves two centimeters longer; lengthen one's sleeves (by) two centimeters. ●寿命を延ばす extend the length of one's life. ▶彼は足を伸ばして(=旅行を延ばして)京都まで行った He extended his trip to Kyoto. ▶彼は髪を(長く)伸ばしている He wears his hair long./(伸ばしている途中だ) He's growing his hair (long)./(伸ばし放しだ) He's letting his hair grow (long).

❷ [時間・期間を] extend, prolong (🔲ともにある時点を超えて期間を延ばすこと. prolong は限界以上に長びかせる意が強い); (延期を) put* ... off, postpone (⇨延期); (遅らせる) delay. ●滞在期間を2週間延ばす extend one's stay two weeks longer; prolong one's stay by two weeks. ▶ローンの返済をもう1か月延ばしていただけませんか Would you extend the loan for another month? ▶彼は痛くて我慢できなくなるまで歯医者へ行くのを延ばした He put off [postponed, delayed] going [×to go] to the dentist until the pain was unbearable.

❸ [まっすぐにする] (手足・体・たるんだものを) stretch; (曲がったものを) straighten; (しわを) smooth ... (out). ●手を伸ばす stretch (out) one's arm. (🔲 hand を用いると「手のひらを広げる」の意) ▶棚の[から]本を取ろうと手を伸ばす reach (out) for the book on the shelf. ▶芝生の上で体を思い切り伸ばす stretch (oneself) out on the grass. ●背筋を伸ばす straighten one's back. ●コートのしわを伸ばす smooth out the wrinkles in the coat. (🔲アイロンをかけて伸ばす場合は iron [press] out the wrinkles ...) ▶それは君が手を伸ばせば届くところにある It is within (easy) reach of your hand.

❹ [能力などを] (発達させる) develop; (向上させる) improve; (養う) cultivate; (よりよくする) 《書》 better. ●子供の能力を伸ばす develop [improve] the child's ability. ●個性を伸ばす develop [cultivate] one's individuality. ●売り上げを伸ばす(=増やす) increase [boost] sales.

❺ [広げる] (一面に) spread*; (引っ張って) stretch; (勢力を) extend; (写真を) enlarge. (⇨拡大, 拡張) ●バターをパンの上に伸ばす spread butter on the bread; spread the bread with butter. (🔲後の方は「パン一面に」を暗示) ▶彼は連勝記録を12に伸ばした He extended [raised] his unbroken string of victories to twelve.

のばなし 野放し ●家畜を野放しにする(=放牧する) pasture cattle. ●犬を野放しにしておく let a dog (run) loose. ●不法入国を野放しにする(=取り締まらないでおく) leave illegal entry uncontrolled; let illegal entry go unchecked.

のはら 野原 a field; (牧草地) a meadow; (平原) a plain. ●野(=野)と原 ●広々とした野原 an open field [meadow].

のばら 野薔薇 【植物】 a wild rose.

のび 伸び, 延び ❶ [成長] growth; (増加) an in-crease; a rise. (⇨成長, 増加) ●経済の伸び the growth of the economy; the economic growth. ●伸び率 the rate of growth. (⇨伸び率) ●記録的な伸び record growth [high]. ▶日本の人口の伸びがゆるやかになった Japan's population growth [increase] has slowed down.

❷ [手足を伸ばすこと] ▶日の光を浴びながら伸びをするのは気持ちがいい It's good to stretch (out) in the sun.

❸ [塗料などの] spread. ▶このファンデーションは伸びがいい This foundation cream spreads [goes on] well.

のび 野火 grass fires set in the early spring on mountainsides. (➡野焼き).

のび 『野火』 Fires on the Plane. (参考) 大岡昇平の小説)

のびあがる 伸び上がる ●伸び上がって(=首を長くして)よく見ようとする crane one's neck to see better; (つま先で立って) stand on tiptoe to see better. ▶伸び上がって(=上方へ手を伸ばして)棚の本を取る reach up for a book on the shelf.

のびざかり 伸び盛り ━━ 伸び盛りの 形 (成長が著しい) (fast) growing. ●伸び盛りの子供たち growing children. ▶息子は今伸び盛りですよ My son is growing very fast [《話》 is shooting up].

のびちぢみ 伸び縮み 名 (伸縮性) elasticity.
━━ 伸び縮みする 動 be elastic; expand and contract.

のびなやむ 伸び悩む make* little progress; (停滞する) reach a plateau /plætóu/; (横ばいになる) level off. ▶アフリカへの輸出が伸び悩んでいる Exports to Africa have reached a plateau [made little progress].

のびのび 伸び伸び (自由に) freely. ▶若馬が牧場をのびのびと駆け回っている Young horses are running freely in the pasture. ▶夫が家にいないとのびのびとした気持ちになる(=ほっとする) I feel at ease while my husband is not at home. ▶子供たちはのびのびと(=苦労知らずで)育った The children have grown up free from cares. ▶彼女はのびのびとした字を書く She writes a free and easy hand.

のびのび 延び延び ▶会議が延び延びになった(繰り返し延期された) The meeting was repeatedly put off [postponed]./(長時間遅れた) The meeting was delayed for a long time. ▶ご返事が延び延びになって申し訳ありません I must apologize to you for not answering sooner.

のびやか 伸びやか (⇨伸び伸び)

のびりつ 伸び率 the rate of growth [(増加) increase]. ●経済の伸び率 the rate of economic growth; the growth rate of the economy.

‡のびる 伸びる, 延びる ❶ [長さが長くなる] stretch; extend; lengthen; grow*; spread*.

【使い分け】 stretch 引っ張って長さ・幅が伸びること. 特に弾力性のあるものが伸びる場合に用いる.
extend 長さ・期間などについてある点まで, またはそれを越えて延びること.
lengthen 長さ・期間が延びること.
grow 草木・毛髪などが成長すること.
spread 平面的なものが一面に広がること.

▶このゴムはよく延びる This rubber stretches well [is very elastic]. ▶このセーターは伸びてすっかり型くずれしている This sweater is all stretched out of shape. ▶砂浜が遠くまで延びている A sandy beach stretches [extends, ×spreads] far into the distance. (🔲線的な延び方でなく広がりを示す文脈では spread も可: A sandy beach spreads (out) for miles.) ▶この道路は海岸まで延びている This road *extends* to [*as far as*] the coast. ▶日本人の平均寿命が延びている The average life span of Japanese people [《やや書》 the Japanese] *is lengthening* [*is being extended, is getting longer*]. (!)最後の言い方が最も口語的) ▶彼は今年3センチ背が伸びた He *has grown* three centimeters (taller) this year./He *has grown* ten *taller* this year by three centimeters. ▶彼女は金髪に染めていたが髪のつけ根から黒髪が少し伸びているのが見えた Her hair was dyed blonde except where you could see the black bits *growing out* from the roots. ▶山脈は東西に連なって延びている The mountains *range* [*running*] east and west.

❷ [期間が延長される] extend; (長引く) be prolonged; [延期される] be put off, be postponed (⇒延期); [遅れる] be delayed. ▶私の大阪滞在は5月まで延びた My stay in Osaka *has been extended* to May./My stay in Osaka *has been prolonged* until May. (!)後の方は「不都合なことだが」の意を含む) ▶試合は来週まで延びた The game *was put off* [*postponed*] till next week. ▶彼の病気のため出発が1か月延びた Our departure *was delayed* for a month because he was sick.

❸ [能力などが] (進歩する) 《人が主語》 make* progress; (向上する) improve. ▶英語の力が大いに伸びたね You *have made* (×a) great *progress* [*have improved* greatly] in English./Your English (ability) *has greatly improved*. ▶その会社は大いに伸びるだろう(=将来性がある) The company *has* great *possibilities*./The company has a brilliant future.

❹ [疲れ切る] be exhausted; [気を失う](特に頭を打って) be stunned; (気絶する) pass out. ▶頭に一撃くらって彼は伸びてしまった He *was stunned* by a blow on the head./A blow on the head *stunned* him.

❺ [まっすぐになる] be straightened; [しわが] be smoothed out.

のびる 野蒜 〖植物〗 *nobiru*; a wild rocambole.
ノブ [取っ手] a knob 《*of* a door》.
のぶこ 『伸子』 *Nobuko*. 〖参考〗宮本百合子の小説
のぶし 野武士, 野伏し a wandering, masterless soldier.
のぶとい 野太い [図太い] (⇒図太い, ふてぶてしい); [声が太い] deep. ▶野太い声 a (thick), deep voice.
のべ 延べ the total number. ●延べ床面積 the *total floor space* 《*of* a house》. (!)of のあとに数値がくる場合は the でなく不定冠詞 a を用いる) ▶卒業生は延べ10万人に達した The *total number* of graduates came to 100,000.
のべ 野辺 (⇒野); (⇒野辺送り)
のべいた 延べ板 ●金の延べ板 a gold *plate*.
のべおくり 野辺送り ●野辺送り(=埋葬式)をする hold 《his》 burial service.
のべがね 延べ金 (金の) a gold; (銀の) a silver.
のべつ ●のべつ幕なしに (ひっきりなしに) incessantly; (終わりなく) endlessly; (止まらずに) nonstop; (休みなく) without a break. ▶彼はのべつ幕なしに(=どんどん続けて)しゃべった He talked *on and on*. (!)*on* は継続の意を表す副詞)/(しゃべるのをやめなかった) He never stopped talking.
のべつぼ 延べ坪, 延べ坪 (総床面積) the total floor space 《*of* a house》. (!)建て坪) ▶この建物の延べ坪はいくらですか What is *the total floor space of* this building?
のべばらい 延払い deferred payment.

●延払い契約 deferred payment contract. ●延払い輸出 export on a deferred payment basis; deferred [installment] payment export.
のべぼう 延べ棒 ●金の延べ棒 a gold *bar*; gold bullion (!)bullion は特に金・銀の場合に用いる)
*****のべる** 述べる [言い表す] express; [話す] say*, tell*; [陳述する] state (!)say より堅い語); [記述する] describe; [言及する] mention. ▶先に述べたとおり《書》 as *stated* [*mentioned*] above. ●自分の考えを述べる *express* [*give, state*] one's opinion 《*on*》 (!)state は正式にはっきり述べること); *express* oneself (!)言葉だけでなく身振りでも, また考えだけでなく感情を表してもよい). ●礼を述べる *express* [×say] one's thanks 《*to*》; *give* thanks 《*to*》 (!)「神に(食前などに)感謝を捧げる」意にも用いる). ●真実を述べる *tell* [×say] the truth. (⇒正直 ❸) ●事故の様子を詳しく述べる *describe* the accident in detail; *give* a full *description of* the accident. ▶彼は自分がそれをしたと述べた He *said* (that) [*stated that*] he had done it. (!)state は形式ばった言い方)
のべる 伸べる, 延べる (⇒伸ばす) ●援助の手を伸べる(=差し伸べる) (⇒差し伸べる).
のほうず 野放図 ●野放図な(=始末におえない)奴 an *unruly* [(乱暴な) a *wild*; (横柄な) an *arrogant*] person. ▶彼は野放図に(=果てしなく)金を使った He spent money *endlessly* [(むやみやたらと) *extravagantly*].
のぼせあがる のぼせ上がる (⇒のぼせる)
のぼせる [上気してくらくらする] feel* dizzy; [夢中になる] 《話》 be crazy 《*about*》, 《話》 have* a crush 《*on*》; [思い上がる] be conceited. ▶彼のお世辞に彼女はのぼせあがった His compliments *turned* [*went to*] her *head*. ▶当時多くの若者がビートルズにのぼせあがっていた Many young people *were crazy about* the Beatles in those days.
*****のぼり** 上り, 登り 图 [上ること] going [coming] up, 《やや書》 (an) ascent (↔(a) descent); [上り坂, 勾配(ミス)]《書》 an ascent (↔a descent), an upward slope (⇒上り坂); [登ること] a climb; [上りの列車・エレベーターなど] an up. ▶その道は5度の上り勾配である The road has an *ascent* of five degrees./The road rises with a slope of five degrees. ▶険しい登りで4時間かかった The steep *upward* climb took four hours.

── 上り(の) 形 [列車などの] 《主に英》 up (↔down). 〖事情〗《米》では「北方面行の」の意になる); [上り坂の] uphill; [上向きの] upward. ●上り列車 an *up* (train). ●上り線ホーム an *up* platform.
のぼり 幟 (旗) a flag; (吹き流し, 長旗) a streamer. (⇒旗)
のぼりおり 上り下り ●階段を上り下りする go [(走って) run] up and down the stairs.
のぼりざか 上り坂 an uphill road; an upward slope; an uphill; 《やや書》 an ascent. (↔下り坂) ●急な上り坂 a steep (↔a gentle, a gradual) *uphill road* [*upward slope*]; a steep uphill [*ascent*]. ●数分上り坂を歩く walk *uphill* for several minutes. ▶上り坂のところは自転車を押して上がった I walked my bicycle *uphill*. ▶道はここからずっと上り坂だ The road *is* [*runs*] *uphill* all the way from here. ▶上り坂にさしかかった We came to a *rise in the road* [an *upward slope*].
のぼりちょうし 上り調子 ▶その国の経済は上り調子だ The country's economy is *on the rise*.
のぼりつめる 上り詰める, 登り詰める (頂上まで登る) reach the top [summit] of a mountain. ●官僚の最高の地位まで上り詰める rise [climb] to the highest [top] rank in bureaucracy.

のぼる 上る，登る，昇る ❶ 【高い所へ行く】 go* up, climb (ℹ 前の方が口語的),《書》ascend;（手足を使って努力する）climb (up) (⇨上がる);（段を）step (-pp-) up,《書》mount. ▶丘には go up [climb] a hill. ▶山頂へ登る climb to the top of the mountain. ▶木に登る[登っている] climb (up) [be up in] a tree. ▶壇に登る step up onto [mount] a platform. ▶階段を駆け上る run up the stairs. ▶川を上る（泳いで）swim [（船で）sail, （ボートで）row] up the river. ▶高く登れば登るほど寒くなってきた The higher we went up [climbed], the colder it grew. ▶ケーブルカーで六甲山に登った We went up [×climbed] Mt. Rokko by cable car. ▶丘を上ったところに湖がある There is a lake up [（頂上に）at the top of] the hill. ▶この道を上ると湖に出る(=湖まで上り坂になっている) This path goes up all the way to the lake./This path ascends to the lake.

❷ 【上昇する】 go* up; rise*. (ℹ 前の方が口語的) ▶太陽は東から昇る The sun rises [comes up] in [×from] the east. ▶気温が30度に上った The temperature went up [rose] to 30℃. (ℹ 30℃ is thirty degrees Centigrade [Celsius] と読む) ▶煙が煙突からもくもくと立ち上った Smoke went up [rose,《書》ascended] in thick clouds from the chimney.

❸ 【ある数量に達する】(...に及ぶ) reach;（総計...となる）amount to ...;（...になる）come* to .... (⇨合計) ▶海外からの観光客の数は200万に上るものとみられた The number of tourists from abroad was [×were] expected to reach two million. ▶彼の借金は1,000万円に上った His debts amounted [came, ran up] to ten million yen./His debts totaled (to) ten million yen.

❹ 【昇進する】(出世する) rise*;（昇進する）be promoted (⇨昇進する);（...になる）become*. ▶王位に上る become king;《書》ascend the throne.

❺ 【話題・うわさなどに】 ▶彼の家族がうわさに上った（話題にされた）His family was talked [gossiped] about./（世間の人々がうわさした）People talked about his family. ▶伊勢エビの蒸し焼きがタルタルソースを添えて上った(=出された) Boiled lobster was served with tartar sauce.

のませる 飲ませる ● 【与える】 give*;【動物に水を】water. ▶その薬を病人に飲ませる give the medicine to a sick person. ▶馬に水を飲ませる water a horse. ▶自家製ビールを飲ませてくれる(=出してくれる) レストラン a restaurant that serves home-made beer. ▶冷たい水を1杯飲ませてください Could I have a glass of cold water? ▶ああ，うまい．（この酒）なかなか飲ませるな Oh, it's nice—very drinkable./（まった文で）This sake is really drinking beautifully. ▶うまい地酒を飲ませる(=用意している)店へ案内しよう Let me show you to a place that serves good local sake.

のまれる 飲まれる，呑まれる ● ▶波に飲まれる be swallowed up by the waves. ▶雰囲気に呑まれては(=圧倒されては)いけない Don't be overcome [be overwhelmed] by the atmosphere.

のみ 蚤 〖動物〗a flea. ▶小男の夫婦 a small man with a big wife. (ℹ 慣用表現) ▶ノミに食われる get [be] bitten by a flea. ▶互いのノミ取りをして親愛の情を示す Monkeys show affection by ridding each other of fleas.

● **蚤取り**（薬剤）flea powder. ● **蚤の市** a flea market.

のみ 鑿 〖工具〗a chisel /tʃízl/.

-のみ（副助詞）only, alone. (⇨だけ) ▶医者のみそうすることができる Only a doctor [A doctor alone] can do so. (ℹ only は修飾語の直前にまたがその原則. alone は名詞・代名詞の直後におく) ▶金のみが人生の目的ではない Money is not the only aim [thing] in life. ▶この用紙には氏名の記入のこと Nothing should be written but your name on this form. (ℹ but は except (...を除いて)の意)

のみあかす 飲み明かす drink* all night; spend* all night drinking.

のみあるく 飲み歩く drink* at one place after another;《米》bar-hop (-pp-),《英》pub-crawl.

のみかい 飲み会 a drinking pàrty.

のみくい 飲み食い eating and drinking. (ℹ 語順に注意)

のみぐすり 飲み薬 (a) medicine (to be taken orally).

のみくだす 飲み下す ● ▶水といっしょに錠剤を飲み下す swallow [take] the pill with a gulp of water.

のみくち 飲み口 〖杯などの口に当てる部分〗the lip of a cup; 〖酒の好きな人〗a person fond of drinking; 〖樽などの口の部分〗a tap. ▶これはとても飲み口(=口当たり)がいいカクテルだ This is a very smooth cocktail.

のみこうい 呑み行為 underground bookmaking.

のみごたえ 飲みごたえ (⇨飲みで)

のみこみ 飲み込み ● ▶飲み込みが早い[悪い] be quick [slow] to understand; be quick [slow] at understanding. (⇨分かり) ▶飲み込みの早い(=物覚えのいい)人 a fast [a quick] learner.

のみこむ 飲み込む ❶ 【液体・固形物を】（飲みおろす）swallow;（一気に飲む）gulp. ● 食べ物を飲み込む swallow one's food;（あわてて）gulp (down) one's food. ▶蛇がそのカエルを飲み込んだ A snake swallowed the frog.

❷ 【理解する】 understand*;（把握する）grasp, take*... in. ▶一目で状況を飲み込む take in the situation at a glance. ▶あなたの言うことが飲み込めない I can't understand [make out, grasp] what you mean. (ℹ make out は通例 can を伴い否定文・疑問文で用いる)

❸ 【その他の表現】 ▶「犯人はお前か」と思わず言いかけた言葉を彼は飲み込んだ(=口に出かけた言葉を元に戻した) He was about to say, "So, you did it," but he swallowed back the words.

のみしろ 飲み代 an money for drinking (alcohol).

のみたおす 飲み倒す avoid paying for one's drinks.

のみち 野道 a path through [across] a field.

のみつぶす 飲み潰す drink away one's fortune.

のみつぶれる 飲み潰れる (⇨酔い潰れる)

のみで 飲みで ▶わが社のカートン箱入りワインは従来の瓶詰めワインより飲みでがある(=長くもつ) Our wine in cartons lasts longer than conventional bottled wine.

のみともだち 飲み友達 a drinking compànion.

のみならず ❶ 【A だけでなく B もまた】 not only A but (also) B, B as well as A. (ℹ (1) 前の方が強意的. (2) しばしば also が省略されるが，既も省略されることがある. また，only の代わりに just, merely, simply が, but also B の代わりに but B too [as well] も用いられる. (3), また B は原則として文法的に同等の語句(句,節)がつく. いずれも B を強調する表現で，A, B が主語のとき動詞は通例 B に一致させる) (⇨だけ，又 ❸) ▶彼は日本のみならず香港でも働いた He worked in Hong Kong as well as (in) Japan. ▶彼はその映画を主演のみならず監督もした He not only starred in the film, but (he) (also) directed it [, but he directed it as well]./He is not only the leading actor but (also) the director of the film. (ℹ 通例 isn't only のように短縮しない)

ノミネート ❷ [その上] 彼は私を励ましてくれた. のみならずお金まで貸してくれた He cheered me up; *what is more* [[書] *moreover*], he (even) lent me some money. (⇨その上, 又 ❸)

ノミネート ― ノミネートする 動 nominate 《*him for* the Presidency [the Oscar]》.

のみほす 飲み干す drink*... down [off]; (一気に) gulp ... down, [話] down. ● ミルクを飲み干す *drink* the milk *off*. ● グラスを飲み干す *drink* a glass *dry* [*empty*]. ▶彼は1リットルのビールを一気に飲み干した He *drank off* a liter of beer in [at] one gulp. ▶彼は残りのコーヒーを飲み干して席を立った He *gulped down* the rest of his coffee and left the table.

のみみず 飲み水 drinking [(飲める) drinkable] water. ● 飲み水に困る(=が不足する) be short of *drinking water*. ● その水は飲み水に適している The water is *good to drink* [*fit for drinking*].

*のみもの 飲み物** something to drink, (a) drink; [書] a beverage. (❗ beverageはコーヒー・ビールなど水以外の飲み物) ▶冷たい飲み物をいただけますか Could I have *something* [×*anything*] *cold to drink*? (❗ 疑問文だが,「…いただきたい」とほぼ同意なので anythingは用いない) ▶何かお飲み物はいかが? (Would you) care for a *drink*?/What would you like to drink?

のみや 飲み屋 (酒場) a bar; (英) a pub. (⇨バー)
● 飲み屋街 a (busy) street full of bars.

*のむ 飲む**

WORD CHOICE 飲む

drink 各種の飲料を飲むこと. 自動詞用法では「酒を飲む」ことを含意する. ● 大酒を飲む *drink* a lot (of alcohol).

have 「have＋飲料名 (beer, a drink, a cup of tea [coffee]など)」の形で, それらを飲むことをさす. 何かを飲むという客観的事実そのものをさし, 飲むという行為の詳細(量・程度)は問題としない. ▶お茶でも飲みに行こう Let's go and *have* a cup of tea.

take 薬などを摂取すること. 客観的事実をさし, 行為の詳細は問題としない. ▶食後にこの薬を飲みなさい *Take* this medicine after meal.

❶ [液体を] drink*, take*, have*.

解説 いろいろな飲み方: ちびちび飲む, すする sip./ぐいっと飲む gulp./飲み下す, ごくりと飲む swallow. (⇨飲み込む)/がぶがぶ飲む (やや話・軽蔑的) guzzle./(主に酒を)ぐいぐい飲む [話] swig./(主に動物が)舌でぴちゃぴちゃと飲む lap. (⇨なめる)

● お茶を飲みながら話す talk *over* (a cup of) tea. (❗ 主語が複数の人であっても ×cups of ... にはしない) ● 飲んで憂さを忘れる *drink away* one's worries. ▶父は夕ごはんの前にいつもビールを1本飲む My father usually *drinks* [*has*] a bottle of beer before dinner. ● ミルクを飲んでしまいなさい *Drink* (*up*) your milk. (❗ drink up は通例命令形で用いる) ▶彼女はいつもミルクを熱くして飲む She always *drinks* her milk hot. ▶彼はスープを飲むときいつもずるずると音を立てる When he *eats* [*has*] soup, he always makes slurping sounds. (❗ スープを皿からスプーンで飲むときは通例 eat or have を用いるが, カップなどに直接口をつけて飲む場合は drink も可) ▶コーヒーをもう一杯飲みませんか Won't you *have* [How about] another cup of coffee? (❗ この場合 drinkより have が普通) ▶どこかで一杯飲もうよ Let's *have a drink* somewhere.

会話 「頭がとても痛いの」「だったらアスピリンを少し飲んだら」 "I have a terrible headache." "Why don't you *take* [×*drink*] some aspirin?" (❗「薬を飲む」は通例 take medicine というが, 液体の薬の場合は *drink* medicine も可)

会話 「何を飲みますか」「コーヒーにでもしようかな」 "What do you *drink*?"/(少し丁寧に) What will you *have*?/(気軽な調子で) What *are* you *drinking*?" "A coffee, maybe."

会話 「コーヒーでも飲みに行こう」「うん, 行こう」 "Let's go out for (a cup of) coffee." "Yes, let's."

❷ [たばこを] smoke; have*. ▶私はたばこも酒ものみません I don't *smoke* or [×*and*] drink./I neither *smoke* nor drink. (❗ 前の方が口語的) ▶彼は1日にたばこを20本のむ He *smokes* [*has*] 20 cigarettes a day. 事情 米国では1日のたばこの量は何箱で表すことが多い: He smokes three *packs* (of cigarettes) a day. 1日たばこ3箱のむ)

のむ 呑む ❶ [受け入れる] accept; [同意する] agree 《*to*》. ● 条件をのむ *accept* [*agree to*] the terms. ▶賃上げ要求はのめない We can't *accept* the demand for higher wages.

❷ [軽く見る] ▶彼は最初から相手をのんでかかっていた He *underestimated* his opponent from the start.

❸ [押しこらえる] ● 涙をのむ *suppress* one's tears.

のめのめ ―のめのめと 副 (⇨おめおめと)

のめりこむ のめり込む (夢中になる) be (entirely [completely, thoroughly]) absorbed 《*in*》, [話] get* into .... (⇨夢中) ▶彼女はフラメンコにすっかりのめり込んでいる She *is completely absorbed in* [[話] *is heavily into*] dancing the flamenco.

のめる (前へ倒れる) fall* forward; fall on one's face; (つまずいて) stumble. (⇨つまずく)

のめる (飲用に適する) be good [fit] to drink; be drinkable; (人が酒を) drink; (酒などがうまい) be drinkable (⇨飲ませる [第2文例]). ▶この水は飲めますか Is this water *good to drink*?

のやき 野焼き burning dead grass in early spring. (⑱ 野火)

のやま 野山 hills and fields.

―のような (⇨―様(*よ*) ❸)

のら 野良 (畑) a field; (農園) a farm. ● 野良仕事 (⇨野良仕事)

のらいぬ 野良犬 a stray [an ownerless] dog.

のらくら ―のらくらと 副 (目的なく) idly; (目標もなく) aimlessly; (仕事がきらいで) lazily. ▶彼は普通週末のらくらと過ごす He usually spends his weekends *idly* [*lazily*]. / (何もしないで過ごす) He usually spends his weekends (in) *doing nothing* [*fooling around*]. (❗ in は通例省略する)

― のらくらする 動 ▶彼は若いときのらくらしたのを後悔する He was sorry to have *idled away* his young days.

のらしごと 野良仕事 farm work; work in the fields. ● 野良仕事をする work on the farm; work in the fields.

のらねこ 野良猫 a stray [an alley] cat.

のらむすこ のら息子 a lazy son; a good-for-nothing son. (⑱ どら息子)

のらりくらり idly, lazily; (言質など捕らえどころがなく) elusively; (言質を与えずに) noncommittally. (⇨のらくら) ● のらりくらりと時間を過ごす *idle away* one's time. ▶その政治家は質問にのらりくらり応じた The politician responded to the questions *elusively* [*noncommittally*].

*のり 糊** ❶ [接着用] (小麦粉と水でできた) paste; (合成糊) glue. ● それぞれの隅にのりをつける put some [[話] a dab of] *paste* on each corner. ● そのドアにステッカーをのりで張る *paste* a sticker *on* [*to*] the

door. (⚠ 一面に張る場合は over も可)
❷[洗濯用] ▶ のりのきいたシャツ a well-*starched* [a stiffly *starched*] shirt. ● 衣服をのり付けする *starch* clothes; stiffen clothes with *starch*. ▶ 私のシャツののりの利いた[あまり利いていない]シャツがいい I like a lot of [very little] *starch* in my shirts.

のり 乗り ❶[化粧などの] ▶ 今日は化粧の乗りがいい The powder *spreads well* [*beautifully*] today.
❷[調子づくこと] ▶ 聴衆のノリがいま一つだ(=あまり熱くなってくれない) The crowd *aren't* really *psyched about* our music. ▶ この曲はリズムのノリが軽い The rhythm of this music is *easy to get into* [*is very catchy*].

のり 海苔 *nori*, (アマノリ) laver /léɪvər/; (食品)《a sheet of》 dried laver. ● 味つけ[焼き]海苔 seasoned [toasted] *dried laver*.
● 海苔巻き sushi [(おにぎり) a riceball] rolled in *nori* [dried laver].

-のり -乗り ▶ 500人乗りのエアバス a 500-*seat* [-*passenger*] airbus. ▶ 彼のスポーツカーは2人乗りです His sportscar is a two-*seater* [carries two people]. (⚠ -seater は「…人乗りの乗り物」)

のりあい 乗り合い ● 乗り合い自動車 (路線バス) a route bus.

のりあげる 乗り上げる ● (船が)浅瀬に乗り上げる run ashore [aground]. ● (船が)暗礁に乗り上げる *hit* [*run on*] *a rock*. ● 浜に乗り上げたクジラ a *beached* whale. (⇨座礁。《A whale was beached [beached itself].》より) ▶ 計画が暗礁に乗り上げた(=行き詰まった) The plan *reached deadlock* [*was deadlocked*].

のりあわせる 乗り合わせる ● 電車に乗り合わせる *happen to ride on* [*in*] the same train.

のりいれる 乗り入れる (車を) drive* 《*into*》; (馬を) ride* 《*into*》; (線路などを延長する) extend 《*into*》. ▶ 車を歩道に乗り入れてはならない You must not *drive* your car *onto* the sidewalk. ▶ 阪急神戸線は山陽電鉄と一部相互乗り入れをしている The Kobe Line of Hankyu Railway partly shares tracks with Sanyo Electric Railway.

のりうつる 乗り移る ❶[乗り換える] change 《*to*》. (⇨乗り換える)
❷[霊が] get* into …; 《人が主語》 be possessed 《*by*》. ▶ 彼女は悪魔が乗り移っているようだ The devil seems to *have got into* her./She seemed to *be possessed by* a demon.

のりおくれる 乗り遅れる ❶[乗り物に] miss. ▶ 私は1分違いで終電車に乗り遅れた I *missed* [*failed to catch*] the last train by one minute./I *was* one minute *late for* the last train.
❷[時流などに] ● 時代に乗り遅れる(=ついていけない) *fail to keep up with* the times.

のりおり 乗り降り ▶ この小さい駅では乗り降りの客は日に50人足らずだ Less than fifty people *get on and off* daily at this small station.

のりかえ 乗り換え (a) transfer /trǽnsfəːr/. (⇨乗り換える) ▶ この電車が遅れたら、大阪での乗り換えに間に合わない If this train is delayed, we'll miss our connection at Osaka. (⚠ one's connection は「乗る予定の連絡列車[バス]など」の意) ▶ ここからは地下鉄乗り換えなしに(=直接)家まで帰れます I can take the subway *directly* home from here.
● 乗り換え駅 a transfer station, a station for changing trains; (連絡駅) a junction. ● 乗り換え切符《主に米》a transfer.

***のりかえる 乗り換える** change 《trains》 (⚠ 目的語は複数形), transfer /trǽnsfəːr/ (-rr-) 《*to*》. ▶ 芦屋駅で(急行から)普通列車に乗り換える *change* [*transfer*] 《*from* an express》 *to* a local *at* Ashiya Station. (⚠ 副詞句の語順に注意. at 句はこの位置かまたは文頭) ● 中野駅で中央線[三鷹行き]に乗り換える *change* (trains) [*transfer*] *at* Nakano Station *to* the Chuo Line [*for* Mitaka]. (⚠ 副詞句は逆の語順も可)

┌─翻訳のこころ─ わたしの降りた駅で少年も降り、わたしの乗り換えた電車に少年も乗り、終点の渋谷まで一緒だった (江國香織『デューク』) The boy *changed trains* at the same station to the same line and was with me all the way to Shibuya Terminal. (⚠ 降りる電車と乗りかえる電車の両方をさすので trains になることに注意)

のりかかる 乗りかかる [乗ろうとする] be going [about] to get on 《a train》; [着手する] start [begin*] to do.
● 乗りかかった船 ▶ 乗りかかった船だ. 今さら後へは引けない(=こんなに遠くまで来たのだからもう戻れない) We've come this far. We can't go back now./We've come too far to go back.

のりき 乗り気 (熱意) enthusiasm 《*for*》; (興味) (an) interest 《*in*》. ▶ 彼はその新しい計画にあまり乗り気でなかった He didn't *show* much *enthusiasm for* [*wasn't* very *enthusiastic about*] the new plan./He didn't *show* much *interest in* [*wasn't* very *interested in*, *wasn't* very *keen on*] the new plan.

のりきる 乗り切る [乗り越える] get* over …; (人に困難な時期を乗り切らせる) tide 《him》 over; [切り抜ける] get through …. ● 難局を乗り切る *get over* [*打ち勝つ*) *overcome*] difficulties. ● 嵐を乗り切る (船が) *ride out* a storm. ▶ これだけの食糧があれば冬を乗り切るのに十分だろう This much food would be sufficient to *tide* us *over* the winter.

のりくみいん 乗組員 a crewman ((複) -men), a crew member; (集合的) the crew ▶ 全体を一つの単位と考えるときは単数扱い, 一人一人を問題にするときは複数扱い. ▶ 乗組員は全員救出された All the *crew* [*crew members*] were saved. ▶ その船には乗組員が多い[100人いる] The ship has a large *crew* [a *crew* of 100].

のりくむ 乗り組む get* on board 《a ship [a space shuttle]》.

のりこえる 乗り越える ● 塀を乗り越える *get* [(よじ登って) *climb*] *over* a fence. (⚠「乗り越えて飛び降りる」なら drop down over … のようにいう) ● 多くの困難を乗り越える *get over* [(打ち勝つ) *overcome*] many difficulties.

のりごこち 乗り心地 ▶ この車は乗り心地がいい This car is *comfortable to ride in*./This car *rides well* [*comfortably*].

のりこし 乗り越し ● 乗り越し切符 (運賃精算票) a fare adjustment slip. ● 乗り越し料金 (超過料金) an excess [an extra] fare.

のりこす 乗り越す go* [ride*] past …. ● 二駅[自分の降りるべき駅を]乗り越す *go* [*ride*] *past* two stops [one's stop]. ● 大阪から神戸まで乗り越す *ride past* Osaka *to* Kobe. ▶ 話に夢中になっていて次の駅まで乗り越した(=連れて行かれた) I was absorbed in talking and *was taken on to* the next station.

のりこむ 乗り込む ❶[乗り物に] (乗用車などに) get* into [in] …; (列車・バス・船・飛行機などに) get onto [on, on board, aboard] …. (⚠ into, onto では「乗り込む」行為自身に, in, on では「乗って行く」ことに重点がある (⇨乗る)) ▶ 彼はタクシーに乗り込んだ He *got into* [*in*] a taxi.
❷[威勢よく行く] (到着する) arrive 《*in, at*》; (軍隊を

のりしろ 糊代 an edge 《of paper》left for applying glue.
のりすごす 乗り過ごす (⇨乗り越す)
のりすてる 乗り捨てる (降りる) get* off ...; (放っておく) leave*; (捨て去る) abandon. ● タクシーを街角で乗り捨てる *get off* a taxi on the street corner. ● 自転車を駅で乗り捨てる *leave* one's bicycle [《話》bike] at the station.
のりそこねる 乗り損ねる miss 《the [one's] train》. (⇨乗り遅れる)
のりだす 乗り出す ❶【着手する】(始める) start, begin* (*to do*; *do*ing); (取りかかる) set* about ...; (活動・計画などに) launch; (新[難]事業などに) embark on.... ● 新しい事業に乗り出す *start* [*set about*] a new business; *launch* [*embark on*] a new enterprise. ● 政界に乗り出す(=入る) *go into* [*enter*] politics; *begin* [《書》*enter on*] a political career. ▶ 我々は彼らの説得に乗り出した We *began* [*set about*] persuading them.
❷【身を乗り出す】● 窓[欄干]から身を乗り出す *lean out of* the window [*over* the rail]. ● テーブルに身を乗り出す *lean forward across* the table.
❸【出帆する】sail, set* sail. ● 荒海に乗り出す *sail* [*go*] *out* on rough seas.
のりつぎ 乗り継ぎ a transfer. (⇨乗り換え)
● 乗り継ぎ客 (主に空路の) a tránsfer pàssenger.
● 乗り継ぎ時間 connécting time.
のりつぐ 乗り継ぐ (連絡する) make* a connection 《with》. (⇨乗り換える) ▶ その駅で待ち時間なしで列車を乗り継ぐことができます We can *make* train *connections* [(乗り換える) *change trains*] at the station without waiting.
のりづけ 糊付け ── **糊付けする** 動 (のりで張り付ける) paste; stick ... with glue; (洗濯物などに) starch. (⇨糊)
のりつける 乗り付ける ● 玄関先に車を乗りつける *drive* [*ride*, *pull*] *up* to the front door. ● タクシー[バイク]で乗りつける *come* in a taxi [*on* a motor-bike]. ▶ 車に乗りつけると電車やバスでの通勤がおっくうになる Once you *get used to* traveling in a car, you feel it troublesome to go to work by train or by bus.
のりつぶす 乗り潰す (車を) drive* [use] 《a car》to scrap.
のりて 乗り手 〖自転車・バイク・馬などの〗a rider; 〖乗客〗a passenger.
のりと 祝詞 *norito*, Shinto ritual prayers. ● 祝詞をあげる recite *norito* [*Shinto ritual prayers*].
のりにげ 乗り逃げ ▶ だれかがうちの子の自転車を乗り逃げした Someone *rode away* with my son's [daughter's] bicycle [《話》bike]. ▶ 彼はタクシーを乗り逃げした(=料金を払わずに逃げた) He *ran away without paying* the taxi *driver*.
のりば 乗り場 (バス発着所) a bus station [depot, terminal]; (バス停) a bus stop; (タクシーの) a taxi stand [station, 《英》rank]; (船の) a landing (place).
のりまわす 乗り回す drive* [ride*] around. (❗ drive は自転車・バイク・馬などには用いない (⇨乗る))
● 馬を乗り回す *ride around* on a horse. ● 車で市内を乗り回す *drive* 《a car》*around* the city.
のりもの 乗り物 a 《public》vehicle /víːɪkl/ (❗ 特に陸上のもの. 空の乗り物は an aircraft (⇨航空機)), 《書》a 《public》conveyance; 〖輸送手段〗《public》means of transportation 《主に米》[transport 《英》] (❗ 空・海の乗り物も含む); 〖遊園地の〗a ride. ● 乗り物酔いをする (車や列車に) get

---

1400

---

carsick; (飛行機に) get airsick; (船に) get seasick.
会話「どの乗り物にまず乗ってみたいの？」「ジェットコースターはどう？」"Which *ride* would you like to try first?" "How about the roller coaster?"

:のる 乗る

WORD CHOICE 乗る

get on [in] 乗り物などに乗り込むこと. 馬・自転車などの無蓋の乗り物, またはバス・列車・船舶・飛行機などの大型公共交通機関に乗り込む場合は on を, 乗用車・タクシー・小型ボートなどの有蓋で小型の乗り物に乗り込む場合は in を用いる. ● 自転車に乗る *get on* the bike.
take 乗用車・バス・列車・飛行機などに乗ること. 乗り込むという動作ではなく, 乗る[利用する]という行為自体をさす. ● タクシー[バス]に乗る *take* a taxi [the bus].
board バス・列車・飛行機などの大型公共交通機関に乗り込むこと. 改まった文脈で用いることが多い. ● 飛行機に乗る *board* a plane.

❶【乗り物に】take*; (列車・バスなどに) get* on ... (↔get off); (車・タクシーなどに) get in ... (↔get out of) (⇨〖類語〗); (自転車・バイク・馬などに) ride*, (やや書) mount; (船・飛行機などに) go* [get] on board, board; (車を運転する) drive*; (車を拾う) catch*, get; (エレベーターなどに) step (-pp-) [go] into 《an elevator》.

|解説| 乗り物の手段を強調すれば by が用いられる: He came *by* train [bus, car]. この場合無冠詞だが形容詞で修飾される場合は冠詞がつく: *by a* fast train; *by the* 2:20 train. 「...に乗って」という感じを強調するとon あるいは in が用いられるが, 冠詞をとることに注意: Do you go to school *on* [*in*] a bus?

● 飛行機に乗ってパリへ行く *fly to* Paris; *go to* Paris *by* plane. ● 船に乗る *go* [*get*] *on board* a ship; *board* a ship; *take* ship (❗ 無冠詞に注意). ▶ きのうのバスに乗って公園へ行った I *took* [*rode*] a bus to the park yesterday. / I went to the park *on* [*in*] a bus yesterday. ▶ 銀座に行くにはどの地下鉄に乗ればよいのですか Which subway do I *take* [*ride*, xget on] for Ginza?/Which subway goes [takes us] to Ginza? (❗ 相手が銀座で待っている場合は take の代わりに bring を用いる)/Which is the subway for Ginza? ▶ タクシーに乗って帰ろうよ Let's *take* a taxi home. ▶ 私はいつも大阪駅から電車に乗ります I always *get on* 《a train》at [xfrom] Osaka Station. (❗乗り物が自明の場合は省略するのが普通) ▶ 彼女が車に乗ってエンジンをかけた She *got in* [*into*] the car and started the engine. ▶ 彼は馬に乗り走り去った He *got on* [《やや書》*mounted*] his horse and rode off. (❗ この ride は「乗って行く」の意) ▶ (彼女が乗っているはずの)バスが来たが, 彼女は乗っていなかった The bus came but she wasn't *on* it. ▶ 9 時の飛行機に乗らなくてはならない I must be *on* the 9 o'clock flight. ▶ その船には 50 人が乗っていた There *were* fifty people *aboard* [*on board*] the ship. ▶ 7 時の電車に乗るために今朝は早く起きた This morning I got up early to *catch* [*get*] the 7:00 train. ▶ 君の乗るバスは新宿から出るよ Your bus goes from Shinjuku. ▶ このエレベーターには何人乗れますか How many people will this elevator *hold*? (❗自動車なら ... this car *seat*? となる (⇨一乗り))
会話「このバスは京都駅に行きますか」「ええ行きますよ. 乗ってください」"Does this bus go to Kyoto Station?" "Yes, it does. *Step in*, please."
会話「(私の車に)乗りませんか」「いや歩きますから, 乗

りがとう」"Would you like (to take) a ride [《主に英》a lift] (in my car)?" "Well, I can walk. Thanks anyway." (!この ride, lift は「車に乗せてもらうこと」の意 (⇨乗せる))

❷ [物の上に] (上に上がる) get* on ...; (上を足で踏む) step (-pp-) on ...; (飛び乗る) jump on ...; (上に座る) sit* on .... ▶踏み台に乗る get [step] on the stool.

❸ [加わる] ▶そんな愚かな計画に乗るな(=参加するな) Don't take part in such a foolish scheme. ▶この問題について相談に乗って[=助言を与えて]くれませんか Will you give me some advice [×advices] on this problem? ▶彼はその話に乗ってこなかった He didn't show any interest in the offer./He wasn't keen about the offer.

会話「問題はキャシーが彼にキスさせるかどうかだ」「させる方に 1,000 円賭けるよ」「よし、乗った」"The question is whether Cathy lets him kiss him." "(I bet) 1,000 yen she lets him." "OK! You're on."
(!賭けに応じるときに用いる慣用表現)

❹ [だまされる] be deceived,《話》be taken in.
▶私は彼女の甘言に乗ってしまった I was deceived [was taken in] by her honeyed words. ▶その手には乗りませんよ(=効き目がない) That trick won't work on me./(わなに陥ることはない) I won't fall into such a trap. ▶彼はおだて[調子]に乗りやすい He is easily flattered [carried away].

❺ [ともに運ばれる] ▶電波に乗る be broadcast; go on the air. ●軌道に乗る (⇨軌道 [成句])

❻ [その他の表現] ▶リズムに乗って(=合わせて)踊る dance to the rhythm. ●占有率が 6 割台に乗る(=を超える) achieve an occupation [an ownership] rate of over sixty percent. ●打球にスピードが乗る (勢いが加わる) a (struck) ball picking up pace [speed]. ●一般道路から高速道路に乗る(=入る) get on the expressway. ▶今日は仕事に気分が乗らない I don't feel like working [(専念できない) can't concentrate on] my work today.

のる 載る ❶[上に位置する] ▶ 1 冊の本がテーブルの上に載っていた There was a book on the table.
❷[掲載される] (雑誌などに出る) appear; (新聞などが記事を載せる) carry; (報じる) report; (含む) contain. ●地図に載っている be on a map. ▶彼の名がその新聞[名簿]に載っている His name appears in the paper [on the list]. ▶この辞書にはこの語は載っていない This dictionary doesn't carry [give, enter] the word. ▶この本には役立つ情報がたくさん載っている This book contains [gives] a lot of useful information. ▶すべての新聞にその飛行機事故のことが載っていた All the newspapers reported the plane crash. ▶交通事故は当たり前すぎて、新聞にあまり載らなくなってしまった Traffic accidents have become so common that newspapers rarely [×hardly] report them. (!hardly を用いると「新聞に取り上げるが、詳しいことを述べない」の意になる)

ノルウェイのもり『ノルウェイの森』Norwegian Wood. [参考] 村上春樹の小説

ノルウェー [国名] Nórwày; (公式名) the Kingdom of Norway. (首都 Oslo) ●ノルウェー人 a Norwegian /nɔːrwiːdʒən/. ●ノルウェー語 Norwegian. ●ノルウェー(人[語])の Norwegian.

のるかそるか 伸るか反るか sink or swim; hit or miss; win or lose. (⇨一か八か) ▶のるかそるか彼はそのレースに全財産をかけた Win or lose, he bet all his fortune on the race.

ノルディック ●ノルディック種目 Nordic events. ●ノルディック複合 Nordic combined.

ノルマ [＜ロシア語] (仕事の割当量) an assignment; one's assigned work; (生産・販売などの割当量) a quota. ●ノルマを達成する fill [meet] one's assignment; (割当量を売る) sell [meet] one's quota.
▶今日のノルマは終わった I've done my quota of work for the day.

ノルマンディー [フランス北西部] Nórmandy.

のれん 暖簾 a noren, (説明的に) (店にかける) a shop curtain with its emblem and name hung at the entrance; (評判) (a) reputation (of a shop). ●店ののれんを傷つける(=汚す) stain the reputation of a store.
● **のれんに腕押し** ▶それはのれんに腕押しだ(= 努力[時間]のむだだ) It's a waste of effort [labor; time].
● **のれん分けする** (店の独立を助ける) help《him》to set up another shop with the same name.

のろい slow. ●足[話し方]がのろい be slow on one's feet [in (one's) speech];《書》be slow of foot [speech]. ▶彼は計算がのろい He is slow at (calculating) figures.

のろい 呪い a curse. ●彼に呪いをかける put a curse on him; put him under a curse. ●敵に呪いの言葉を吐く utter a curse against an enemy.

のろう 呪う curse. ●呪われた人 a person (who is) cursed [under a curse]. (!この意では通例叙述的に用い、×a cursed person とはいわない)

のろけ 惚気 ●のろけ話 a boasting story《about one's lover》. (⇨惚気る)

のろける 惚気る (自慢そうに話す) talk too proudly 《about》; (愛情を込めて語る) speak* fondly 《of》.
▶彼は恋人のことよくのろける He often talks too proudly about his girlfriend.

のろし 狼煙 [合図の火] a signal fire, [かがり火] a beacon fire.
● **のろしを上げる** light a signal fire [a beacon].
▶女性が禁酒運動ののろしを上げた(=始めた) Women started [launched into] a campaign against alcohol.

のろのろ (ゆっくりと) slowly; (非常にゆっくりと) at a snail's pace; (だらだらと) sluggishly. ●のろのろ歩く walk slowly, (しぶしぶ) walk reluctantly, (疲れ果てて) trudge, plod. (⇨とぼとぼ) ▶支配人は部下ののろのろ働くのをいやがった The manager hated to see his men work sluggishly. ▶夕方のラッシュで車はのろのろ運転だった(=はうように進んだ) The cars crawled along [moved as slowly as a snail, moved at a snail's pace] in the evening rush hours.

のろま (ばかなやつ) a stupid [(頭の鈍い) a dull] fellow,《話》a blockhead. (⇨のろい)

のろわしい 呪わしい ●呪わしい出来事 an unfortunate happening; a disaster.

*__のんき__ 呑気 ── **呑気な** 形 (気楽な) easy; (楽天的な) optimistic; (うるさくない) easygoing; (心配のない) carefree; (成り行きまかせの) hàppy-go-lúcky. ▶彼はのんきな人 He's an easygoing [an optimistic, a happy-go-lucky] man. ▶He takes things [it] easy. ● **のんきにやる** の意の慣用表現

── **呑気に** 副 ▶彼はのんきに暮らしている He leads a carefree [an easy] life. ▶彼はどんな場合でものんきにしている He's free and easy in any situation.

ノンステップバス [無段差バス] a stepless [a stepfree] bus; [和製語] a non-step bus.

ノンストップ nonstop. ▶この列車は大阪までノンストップです This train goes nonstop to Osaka. (!この nonstop は[副詞]/This is a nonstop (train) to Osaka.

のんだくれ 飲んだくれ [大酒飲み] [軽蔑的] a drunkard; [酔っ払い] a drunken person,《話》a drunk.

のんだくれる 飲んだくれる get dead [blind] drunk.

のんでかかる 呑んでかかる (⇨呑む❷)

ノンバンク 〖融資専門の金融機関〗a nonbank.

***のんびり** (平穏に) quietly; (悠然と) in a leisurely way, leisurely; (ゆっくり) slowly. ● のんびり旅行する take a *leisurely* trip. ● のんびり過ごす spend time *in a pleasant lazy way*. ▶退職後は田舎でのんびり暮らしたい I'd like to lead a *quiet* [(気楽に) an *easy*] life in the country after retirement. ▶その当時は何事ものんびりしていた Everything moved *slowly* in those days. ▶休暇をとってしばらくのんびりしたらどうかしら Maybe you should take a vacation and just *relax* [《話》*take it easy*] for a while.
● のんびり屋 (あくせくしない人) an easygoing person.

ノンフィクション 《集合的》nonfiction.
● ノンフィクション作家 a nonfiction writer.

ノンプロ ── ノンプロの 形 nonprofessional.
● ノンプロ選手 a nonprofessional player. ● ノンプロ野球 nonprofessional baseball.

のんべえ 呑ん兵衛 a drunkard. (⇨飲んだくれ)

のんべんだらり ● のんべんだらりと暮らす (＝怠惰な生活を送る) lead an *idle* [a *sluggish*] life; (時間を空費する) *idle away* one's time; (何もしないで暮らす) live *doing nothing*.

ノンポリ (非政治的な) nonpolitical; (政治に無関心な) apolitical. ● ノンポリの学生 an *apolitical* student.

ノンレムすいみん ノンレム睡眠 non-REM sleep 《non-rapid eye movement の略》, NREM /énrèm/ sleep, (徐波睡眠) slow wave sleep. (＊レム睡眠)

は

は 葉 [[1枚の]] a leaf (働 leaves); (平たく細長い) a blade; [[木全体の]] leaf, [[植物]] foliage /fóuliidʒ/. (関連) 特別な言い方のあるもの: 松, モミ a needle / シダ, シュロ, ヤシ a frond / 蓮 a pad) ●木の葉 the leaves of a tree. ●レタスの葉 lettuce leaves. ●草の葉 the blades [[1枚の]] of grass. ●四つ葉のクローバー a four-leaf [×-leaves] clover. ●葉の茂った[ない] leafy [leafless, bare]. ▶木々に葉が出た[出ている] The trees have come into [are in] leaf. ●木の葉がすっかり落ちた The leaves have all gone off the trees./The trees are bare of leaves. ▶秋になってモミジの葉が色づいた [赤くなった] The maple leaves turned color [red] in the fall.

は 歯 ❶ [[人間などの]] a tooth (働 teeth).

> (関連) いろいろな歯: 義歯 a false tooth (⇨入れ歯)／犬歯 a canine tooth; (糸切り歯) a cutter tooth／知恵歯 a wisdom tooth (⇨親知らず)／前[奥]歯 a front [a back] tooth／乳歯 a baby [[英]] (milk] tooth／永久歯 a permanent tooth.

①【歯〜】 ●歯ぎしりする grind one's teeth. (⇨歯軋り) ●彼は歯並びが悪い He has an irregular [uneven] set of teeth. (! an と set of はしばしば省略される.「歯並びのよい歯」は even [well-placed] teeth) ●彼女がにっこりすると白いきれいな歯並びが見えた She showed [revealed] her beautiful white teeth in a smile [grin]. (! grin の方が smile より口を大きく開ける. cf. a toothy grin 歯が見える(くらいの)微笑) ●この手焼きせんべいはばりばりした歯当たりだ This hand-grilled rice cracker is crunchy.

②【歯の】 ●歯が痛い I have [am suffering from] (a) toothache./My tooth aches [(ずきずきする) throbs]. ▶彼は歯がいい[悪い] He has good [bad] teeth. ●前歯が[欠]抜け落ちた My upper tooth came [fell] out [×off]. (! 前の方は固い物をかんだりして, 後の方はゆるんで抜ける) ▶前歯が1本折れた[欠けた] One of my front teeth broke [was chipped]. ▶この子は歯が生えだした This baby is teething /tíːðiŋ/ [is cutting his teeth]./This baby's teeth are coming through. ●歯が浮いている(ぐらぐらしている) My teeth feel [are] loose. ●その赤ちゃんはまだ歯がない The baby is toothless.

③【歯の】 ●dental. ●歯の治療 dental treatment. ●歯の抜けた老人 a toothless elderly person. ●犬に手をかまれて歯の跡がついた The dog bit me on the hand and left a bite mark on it. (! a tooth mark とは通例いわない)

④【歯に[を]】 ●歯をみがく brush [clean] one's teeth. ●歯を矯正する correct the irregularities of teeth. ●歯を折る break a [one's] tooth. ●歯に矯正具をつける[つけている] put [wear] braces on one's teeth. ●冷たい水を飲むと歯にしみます The tooth smarts when I drink chilled water. ●歯医者に行って奥歯を1本抜いてもらった I went to a dentist and had a tooth out [pulled out]. ▶この歯に大きな穴があいているので詰めないといけません You have a large cavity in this tooth and it must be filled. ▶猿は怒って歯をむいた(むき出した) The monkey bared [showed] its teeth in a rage.

❷ [[器具などの]] a tooth (働 teeth); (歯車の) a cog; (げたの) a support. ●くしの歯 the teeth of a comb. ●歯が数本欠けている古いくし an old comb with some of the teeth out. ▶このこぎりは歯が何本か欠けている Several teeth of this saw are missing [are gone].

●歯が浮く 私はぎしぎしこする音を聞くと歯が浮く(=不快になる) Scraping sound sets my teeth on edge.

●歯が立たない この問題は私には歯が立たない(=難しすぎる) This problem is too hard [difficult, much] for me./This problem is above me [beyond my power]. ▶テニスでは彼には歯が立たない(競争相手にならない) I'm no match for him in tennis.

●歯に衣(きぬ)着せぬ 彼は歯に衣を着せない He does not mince matters [his words]. (! 通例否定文で用いる)/(ずけずけ物を言う) He is outspoken in his remarks. (! outspoken is an outspoken newscaster (歯に衣着せぬニュースキャスター)のように限定的にも用いる)

●歯の根が合わない 恐ろしさで歯の根が合わなかった I shuddered with horror.

●歯を食いしばる 彼は歯をくいしばって仕事をやり続けた He gritted [clenched] his teeth and carried on with the work. ●君は歯をくいしばって我慢しなければならない You must endure it. (!通例 must, have to とともに用いる)

●歯医者 a dentist. (⇨歯医者) ●歯ぐき the [one's] gums. ●歯ブラシ a toothbrush. ●歯磨き (練り) toothpaste; (粉) tooth powder.

は 刃 [[刃先]] an edge; [[刀身]] a blade. ●鈍い刃 a dull [a blunt] edge. ●鋭い刃 a keen [a sharp] edge. ●かみそりの刃を取り換える change razor blades. ●刃をとぐ sharpen the edge 《of》.

は (⇨は(あ))

は 派 [[グループ]] a group, a party; [[学派, 流派]] a school; [[分派]](派閥) a faction; (教派) a denomination, 《時にけなして》 a sect. ●白樺派の文学 the literature of the Shirakaba group. ●賛成[反対]派 a supporting [an opposition] group. ●ロマン派の詩人 a poet of the Romantic school; a Romantic poet. ●自民党の主流派 the major faction of the Liberal Democratic Party. ●新教諸派 the Protestant denominations. ●真宗大谷派 the Otani sect of Shinshu. ●戦後[前]派(世代) the postwar [prewar] generation.

は 覇 ●覇を競う compete [vie] for the championship.
●覇を唱える rule 《over》 by force; hold sway 《over》 by force.

‐は 《副助詞》 ❶ [[話題の中心]]

> 解説 (1) 話題の中心となる名詞相当語句は英語では主語の位置に置かれるのが一般的であるが, 日本語の「は」は通例聞き手が既に知っているかまたは文脈の上で前提となっている事柄に添えられるので, 英語では the, this, that, his などの限定語を添えたり (⇨[第1文例]), 総称表現を用いる (⇨(2), (3)) などの工夫を要することが多い.
> (2) 可算名詞の総称表現は (1) 無冠詞複数可算名詞, (2) 不定冠詞＋単数可算名詞, (3) the ＋単数可算名詞で表すことができる. (1) が最も普通で, (3) は

厳密な定義などを行う場合に用いる.
(3) 不可算名詞の総称表現は必ず無冠詞単数形を用いる: ワインはブドウから作る Wine is made from grapes.

▶この絵は田中氏がかいたものです *This* picture was painted by Mr. Tanaka. (**!**(1) 能動態の Mr. Tanaka painted this picture. は Mr. Tanaka を話題の中心として「田中氏がこの絵をかいた」の意. (2) 不定冠詞を伴った A picture was painted by Mr. Tanaka. は「1 枚の絵が田中氏によってかかれた」の意)/It was Mr. ↘Tanaka *that* [*who*] páinted this ↗picture. (**!**Mr. Tanaka を強調して「この絵をかいたのは他のだれでもない田中氏だ」の意) ▶京都がいちばん美しいのは秋です It is in the ↘fall *that* Kyoto is most ↗beautiful. (**!**これは書き言葉で好まれる強調構文で, 話し言葉では次例が適切) /↘Fall is (the time) when Kyoto is most ↗beautiful. (**!**When Kyoto is most ↘beautiful is in the ↘fall. とはあまりいわない) ▶彼がアメリカ生まれだというのは本当ではない *It*'s not true *that* he was born in America. ▶君がこの問題を解くのはたやすいことだ *It*'s easy *for* you *to* solve the problem. (**!**×It is easy that you solve .... は不可)

❷ [対照的に示す] ▶紅茶は飲んでもよいがコーヒーはだめだ You can [may] drink tea, *but* not coffee. ▶彼は体は大きいが力は弱い Though [Although] he is big, he is weak. (**!**although の方が堅い語); He is big, *but* [*yet*] he is weak. (**!**(1) yet の方が意味が強い. (2) but の方が口語的)

会話「ゴルフはなさいますか?」「以前はやっていました(が最近はしません)」"Do you play golf?" "I ↘used to(, *but* I ↘don't these days)."

❸ [確かさを表して] **会話**「テニスはお好きですか」「え, 好きですとも. 週に一度はやります」"Do you like [enjoy] playing tennis?" "Yes, very much. In fact I play *at least* once a week." (**!**「一度は」の「は」は at least (少なくとも)で表す)

ば 場 ❶ [場所] a place, (特定の)a spot; [余地] room, (a) space. ●よい釣り場 a good fishing *spot*; a good *spot* for fishing. ●公の場で in a public *place*. ●場を取る (場所を占める)take up [occupy] a lot of *space*. ●負けた人はその場で金を払わないといけなかった The losers had to pay *on the spot*.

❷ [場合] an occasion (⇨場合); [場面, 状況] a situation; [機会] a chance, an opportunity. ●彼に活動の場を与える give him an *opportunity* [a *chance*] to play an active role. ●場を踏む(経験を積む) gain experience. (⇨場数) ●その場をつくろう patch up the *situation*. ▶彼の話はその場にふさわしくなかった His speech was not suitable for the *occasion*. ▶冗談を言ってその場を持たせた(=その場の雰囲気をなごませた) I managed to keep *the atmosphere* comfortable by telling jokes. ▶当社は若者の出会いの場を提供します We offer young people a *chance* to meet. ▶私はたまたまその場に居合わせた I happened to be *there* [*on the scene*].

❸ [分野] a field. ●政治の場に出る go into (the *field* of) politics.

❹ [劇などの場面] a scene. ●『ハムレット』の第 1 幕第 2 場の主人公は the main character in Act I, *Scene* ii [the second *scene* of Act I] of *Hamlet*.

*-**ば** [接続助詞] **❶** [仮定, 条件] if .... (⇨もし, -なら, -たら) ▶あした雨が降ればピクニックは中止です *If* it rains tomorrow, the picnic will be canceled./*If* it rained tomorrow, the picnic would be canceled. (**!**前の方は直説法で, 雨が降る可能性については明言していないが, 後の方は仮定法で, おそらく雨は降らないであろうという前提に立って述べたもの) ▶君はやる気があればできるのに You could *if* you would.

❷ [...すると] when .... ▶このボタンを押せばふたが開きます *When* you push this button you can open the lid.

❸ [勧め] Why not ...?, Why don't you ...?. **会話**「頭がひどく痛むんだ」「お医者さんに行けば」"I have a terrible headache." "*Why don't you* go (and) see the doctor?" (**!**and を省略するのは《主に米語》)

は(あ) [肯定の返事, 相づち] yes (⇨はい); uh-húh (**!**電話では Yes と自然); (そうね) well; (なるほど) I see; [笑い, 疑い] ha(h), ahá. ▶はあ, そうですか Yes, indeed./*Oh*, I see. ▶は, かしこまりました Yes [*Certainly*], sir. ▶は, 何とおっしゃいました I bég your ↗pardon, sir? (⇨えっ)

ばあ (人, 特に子供を驚かすとき) Bo(h)! /bóu/; Boo! /búː/. ▶いないいないばあ Peekaboo!

バー ❶ [酒場] a bar [参考] もと酒類を出すカウンターのこと), 《米》a barroom, 《米古》a saloon; (高級酒場) 《英》a saloon [a lounge] bar; (大衆酒場) 《英》a pub, 《英書》a public house; (ホテル・空港などの) a cocktail lounge.

❷ [カウンター式軽食堂] a bar. ●寿司(í)バー a *sushi bar*.

❸ [運動競技の横木] a (cross)bar. ▶現在バーの高さは 2 メートルです The *bar* is now at 2 meters. (**!**at に注意) ▶コールのシュートがバーを叩いた 《サッカー》Cole's shot hit the *crossbar*.

ぱあ ❶ [金がなくなる] ▶マージャンに負けてこの前の時もうけた 1 万円がぱあになった I *lost* (all) the 10,000 yen at mah-jongg that I won the time before. (**!**I lost *all* the money I had のように「全部」を強調する場合もある)

❷ [知能が足りない] ▶あいつ少しぱあじゃない He's a bit *stupid*, isn't he?/(正気でない)《話》He *isn't quite áll thére*, is he? (**!**通例否定文・疑問文で用いる)

❸ [ご破算になる] ▶計画がぱあになった The plan *went up in smoke*. ▶事業の中止でぼくたちが練り上げた販売戦略はぱあになってしまった The sales plan we had worked out so carefully *went down the drain* [*fell through*] when the whole business was stopped. (**!**go down the drain は「(下水に流されるように)むだになる」の意の口語表現)

❹ [じゃんけんの紙] 《show》the paper. (⇨じゃんけん)

パー [基準打数] 《ゴルフ》par. ●イーブンパー *par*. ▶10 番ホールはパー 4 だ The tenth hole is a *par* 4. ▶彼はこのホールをパーで終えた He played this hole *in par*./He got a *par* at [on] this hole.

ばあい 場合 [事例] a case; [事情] circumstances; [時機] an occasion; [時] time. ●そのような場合には in that *case*; in such a *case*;《話》in cases like that;《話》then. ●場合によっては according to *circumstances*; as the *case* may be. ▶努力が報われない場合がある There are *cases* where [《書》in which] our efforts are not rewarded. ▶時と場合による That (all) depends./It all depends. (**!**後の方は on circumstances が省略された決まり文句) ▶このような場合はどうしたらいいだろうか What shall I do *in this case* [《話》*in cases like this*]? ▶どのような場合にもお金の貸し借りはいけない *Under* [*In*] *no circumstances* should you borrow or [×and] lend money. (**!**文頭で用いると倒置構文となり文語的・詠嘆的になる) ▶笑っている場合(=笑い事)ではない It's *no laughing matter*.

パーカッション 【...する[の, な]場合】 （もし...なら）if ...,《主に米》in case ...; （...のとき）when ...; （⇨もし, 場合）▶もし火事の場合には消防署に電話しなさい If [*In case*] there is a fire, telephone the fire station. (**!** 掲示などでは通例 *In case of* fire, ... の形を用いる) ▶万一雨の場合はタクシーで帰ります If it *should* rain, we'll take a taxi home. (**!**「万一」を強調したいときは if 節中に should を用いるが, これは堅い言い方で日常会話では単に *If* it rains [×will rain], ... とするのが普通) ▶必要な場合はすぐそこへ行くべきだ You should go there right away *if* (*it is*) *necessary* [*if the occasion arises*]. (**!** it is は通例省略される) ▶学校を欠席の場合はご連絡ください Please let us know *when* you stay away from school. ▶由紀彦の場合には事情が違う It's different in Yukihiko's *case* [*in the case of* Yukihiko]./It is not the *case with* Yukihiko.

パーカッション （打楽器の一つ）a percussion instrument; （集合的）percussion. ●パーカッションを演奏する play *percussion instruments*; be on *percussion*.

パーキング parking. （⇨ 駐車）
●パーキングメーター a parking meter.

パーキンソンびょう　パーキンソン病 【医学】Párkinson's (disèase); Párkinsonism.

*__はあく　把握__ 图 ▶我々は情報の把握に努めた We tried to *grasp* the information.
── **把握する** 動 （理解する）understand; （しっかりと）grasp; （聞き取る）catch. （⇨理解）●その意味を把握する *understand* [*grasp*, *catch*] the meaning.

ハーグ 【オランダの都市】The Hague /héig/.
●ハーグ裁判所 the Hague Court.

パークアンドライド 【途中まで車で来てバスに乗り換え(市内に入る)こと】park and (bus) ride.

『パークライフ』 *Park Life*. (参考 吉田修一の小説)

ハーケン [<ドイツ語]【登山】a piton /píːtɑn/.

バーゲン （⇨バーゲンセール）

ハーケンクロイツ 【鉤(ｶｷﾞ)十字】a Hakenkreuz; a swastika (ﾁ). (参考 ナチスドイツの紋章)

バーゲンセール 【特売】a sale; 《和製語》a bargain sale. （囧 特売）

バーコード a bar code. ●バーコード読み取り装置 a *bar code* reader [scanner].

パーゴラ 【つる植物を絡ませた棚】a pergola.

パーコレータ （ ）a percolator.

パーサー a purser.

ばあさん （⇨おばあさん）

バージニア 【米国の州】Virginia /vərdʒínjə/《略 Va. 郵便略 VA》.

バージョン 【版】a version.

バージョンアップ 图 an upgrade /ʌ́pgrèid/;《和製語》a version up.
── **バージョンアップする** 動 upgrade /ʌpgréid/.

バージン 图 【処女】a virgin.
── **バージンの** 形 virgin.

バージンロード ●バージンロードを祭壇へと進む walk up the aisle (of the church) to the altar. (参考 (1) この際の音楽は the Wédding Màrch. (2) ×virgin road は和製英語)

バースコントロール 【産児制限】birth control.

バースデー 【誕生日】one's birthday.
●バースデーケーキ a birthday càke. ●バースデーパーティー a bírthday pàrty. ●バースデープレゼント a bírthday prèsent [gìft].

パーセンテージ a 《small [large]》 percentage. （⇨ パーセント）

パーセント a percént,《英》a per cént. (**!** 単・複同形);【百分率】(a) percéntage.

ハート

解説 (1) 通例前に数詞がくるときは **percent** を, what や high, low, large, small などの形容詞がくるときは **percentage** を用いるが, 《話》では percentage の代わりに percent を用いることもある. 記号の%は商業・技術関係の文書以外は避ける.
(2) 通例 25 パーセントより a quarter が, 50 パーセントより (a) half が好まれる.
(3) 0.5 パーセントを point five percent と読むのは堅い言い方. half of one percent,《話》half a percent の方が普通.

●現金払いには 10 パーセント割引する discount 10 *percent* [make a 10 *percent* discount] for cash. ▶私の給料の 15 パーセントが所得税にとられる Fifteen *percent* [×percentage] of my salary is deducted for income tax. (**!** percent of A が主語の場合, 動詞の数は A の数に一致するのが普通) ▶貴校では何パーセントの学生が大学に進みますか What [×How many, ×How much] *percentage* of your students go [×goes] on to college? ▶収入が 10 パーセント減った[増えた] My income has gone down [up] (by) 10 *percent*. ▶この織物はウール 50 パーセントです This fabric is half [50 percent] wool.

パーソナリティー （テレビタレント）a TV personality; （ディスクジョッキー担当者）a disk jockey, 《話》a D.J.; （テレビなどの司会者）a host (**!** 女性はhostess).

パーソナル 【個人の】personal.
●パーソナルコール 【指名通話】a person-to-person call; 《主に英》a personal call. ●パーソナルコンピュータ a personal computer 《略 PC》. （⇨パソコン）●パーソナルチェック【個人用小切手】a personal check.

バーター 【物々交換】barter.
●バーター取り引き barter transactions [trade].

はあたり　歯当たり （⇨歯触り）

ばあたり　場当たり 图 ●場当たり(＝大衆の受け)をねらう play to the gallery.
── **場当たりの** 形 （行き当たりばったりの）haphazard /hæphǽzərd/. ●場当たりな政策 a *haphazard* policy.
── **場当たり的に** 副 in a haphazard way [《やや書》fashion].

バーチャル virtual /vɚ́ːrtʃuəl/.
●バーチャルモール【電子商店街】a virtual mall. ●バーチャルリアリティ【仮想現実, 人工現実感】virtual reality.

パーツ 【部品】a part. (**!** 通例複数形で)

バーディー 【ゴルフ】a birdie. ●バーディーをとる get a *birdie*; birdie.
●バーディーパット a putt for a birdie, a birdie putt.

パーティー ❶【会合, 集まり】a party; （歓迎・祝賀の公的な）a reception. ●誕生[カクテル]パーティー a birthday [a cocktail] *party*. ●パーティーを開く give [hold, have,《話》throw] a *party*; give [hold] a *reception*. ●パーティーに出席する go to [《やや書》attend] a *party*. ●彼をパーティーに招待する invite [ask] him to the *party*. ▶昨晩のパーティーは楽しかった I enjoyed the *party* last night./I enjoyed myself at the *party* last night.
❷【【登山などの)一行】a party. (**!** 集合的に. 個々の構成員をさすときは複数扱い) ●パーティーを組む form a *party*.

バーテン(ダー) 《主に米》a bartender, a barkeep(er); 《主に英》a barman (龺 -men).

ハート 【心臓】a heart. ●ハート型のチョコレート a *heart*-shaped chocolate. ●（トランプの)ハートの 10 [クイー

ハード ── **ハードな** 形 〖厳しい,大変な〗hard ● ハードな人 a very *tough* person. ● ハードな(=激しい)運動をする get [《英》take] *strenuous* [*vigorous*] exercise. (! hard exercise は通例「困難な運動[練習]」の意)

ハード 〖「ハードウェア」の略〗hardware.

パート ❶〖部分〗● 三つのパートに分かれた小説 a novel in [(から成る)] consisting of] three *parts*. ❷〖音楽の〗● ソプラノのパート the soprano *part*. ❸〖パートタイム〗(勤務制度)part-time (↔full-time) (! 形容詞・副詞として用いる); (仕事をする人) part-timer. ● パートの仕事 a *part-time* job. ▶彼女はその店でパートで働いている She works *part-time* [as a *part-timer*] at the store.

バードウィーク 〖愛鳥週間〗Bird Week. (参考) 日本では5月10日から1週間)

ハードウエア hardware (↔software).

バードウオッチング 图 bird watching.
── **バードウオッチングをする** 動 watch wild birds (*in their natural environment*); bird-watch. (! 「バードウオッチングをする人」は a birdwatcher).

ハードカバー a hardcover (book); a hardback.

ハードカレンシー 〖国際的に交換可能な通貨〗〖経済〗 hard currency.

ハードコア 〖露骨なポルノ〗a hard-core pornography; 〖話〗a hard porn.

ハードコピー 〖データを紙などに印刷したもの〗〖コンピュータ〗a hard copy (↔soft copy).

ハードスケジュール 〖a full [a tight, a heavy] schedule;《和製語》a hard schedule.

パートタイマー a part-timer, a part-time worker. (⇨パート ❸)

パートタイム part-time. (⇨パート ❸)

ハードディスク a hard disk. ● 160 ギガ(バイト)のハードディスク a 160-gigabyte *hard disk* (drive). ● フロッピーからハードディスクにデータを移す transfer the data from floppy disk to *hard disk*.

ハードトップ 〖自動車の型の一つ〗a hardtop (convertible).

パートナー a partner. ● パートナーになる become a *partner*. ● パートナーを組む[組んでいる] go into [be in] partnership (*with* him).
● パートナーシップ〖協力関係〗partnership.

ハードボイルド hard-boiled《detective stories》.

ハードル 〖障害物〗a hurdle; 〖競技〗a hurdle race; the《100-meter》hurdles. ● ハードル選手 a hurdler. ● ハードルを跳び越す clear [leap] a *hurdle*.

ハードロック 〖音楽〗hard rock.

ハードワーカー 〖働き者,勉強家〗a hard worker.

ハードワーク 〖きつい仕事〗hard work; (特に罰としての重労働) hard labor.

バーナー 〖燃焼器〗a burner.

ハーネス 〖安全ベルト; 馬・犬の引き具〗a harness.

はあはあ ● はあはあという〖激しい動きなどの〗pant; (大きく) gasp. ▶彼ははあはあ言って駆け戻ってきた He ran back *breathing heavily* [*panting*《*heavily*》]./He ran back *breathless*. ▶勝った力士ははあはあ激しい息づかいでレポーターの質問に答えた The victorious *sumo*-wrestler *gasped out* his answers to the reporter's questions.

バービー ● バービー人形〖商標〗a Barbie Doll [doll].

ハーフ ▶彼は中国人とアメリカ人のハーフだ He is *half* Chinese and *half* American.

ハーブ 〖薬用植物〗a [《米》an] herb /ə́ːrb, há:rb/. ● ハーブ園 a herb garden. ● ハーブティー hérbal tèa;《和製語》herb tea.

ハープ 〖楽器〗a harp. ● ハープ奏者 a harpist. ● ハープを弾く play the *harp*.

ハーフウェーライン 〖サッカー〗a halfway line.

パーフェクトゲーム a perfect game. (⇨完全試合)

ハーフコート a half-length coat;《和製語》a half coat.

ハーフサイズ ● ハーフサイズカメラ a half-frame camera;《和製語》a half-size camera.

ハープシコード 〖楽器〗a harpsichord.

ハーフスイング 〖野球〗a half [a check(ed)] swing.

ハーフタイム 〖中間の休み〗half time; 〖話〗the break. ▶アンリがハーフタイム直前にゴールを決めた〖サッカー〗Henry scored just before *the break*.

ハーフバウンド 〖野球〗an in-between hop. ● ハーフバウンドでボールを捕る take a ball on the *in-between hop*.

ハーフバック 〖中衛〗〖競技〗a halfback《略 HB, H》.

ハーフマラソン a hàlf-márathon.

ハーフミラー a one-way mirror. (@ マジックミラー)

ハーフメード 〖半既製品〗〖服飾〗semi ready-made clothes.

バーベキュー a barbecue《略 BBQ》,《英話》a barbie. (! 装置,料理,パーティーのいずれの意でも用いる. 料理の意では通例 〖U〗) ● バーベキューを食べる eat *barbecue*. ▶私たちは日曜日に庭でバーベキューパーティーを開いた We had a *barbecue* in the garden on Sunday.

バーベナ 〖植物〗a vervain.

バーベル (lift) a barbell.

バーボン 〖バーボンウイスキー〗bourbon.

パーマ 〖話〗a perm,《米話・英》a perm,《古》a permanent wave. ● パーマをかける get [have] a *permanent*; have one's hair *permed*. ● 彼女の髪は天然パーマです Her hair has a *natural curl*./She has a *kink* in her hair.

パーマネント (⇨パーマ)

バーミューダ ● バーミューダショーツ《a pair of》Bermuda shorts. (参考 ひざ上までの半ズボン) ● バーミューダ諸島 Bermúda.

バーミンガム 〖英国・米国の都市〗Birmingham /bə́ːrmiŋəm/.

パーム ● パーム油 palm oil.

パームトップ(コンピュータ) a palm-top (computer).

パームボール 〖野球〗a palm ball.

ハーモナイゼーション 〖協調, 調整〗harmonization.

ハーモニー (a) harmony.

ハーモニカ 〖楽器〗a harmónica, a mouth organ. ● ハーモニカを吹く play the *harmónica*.

バーモント 〖米国の州〗Vermont /vəːrmɑ́nt/《略 Vt. 郵便略 VT》.

パーラー (特殊な業種の店) a parlor. (! 主に《米》である特定の店について用いられる) ● アイスクリームパーラー an ice-cream *parlor*. (! 日本のフルーツパーラーに近い. ただし ×a fruit parlor は和製英語)

ハーラーダービー 〖野球〗the pitchers' race for wins; 《和製語》a hurler derby.

はあり 羽蟻 〖動物〗a winged ant.

パール 〖真珠〗a pearl.

バーレーン 〖国名〗Bahrain, Bahrein /bɑːréin/; (公式名) the State of Bahrain. (首都 Manama) ● バーレーン人 a Bahraini. ● バーレーン(人)の Bahraini.

ハーレム a harem.

ばーん (銃声, 爆発音, 衝突音) bang, blam. ▶これでも食らえ,ばーん,ばーん! Take that, *bang, bang*! (! 子供のピストルごっこでの発声)

はい

‡はい 感 ❶ [質問に対して] yes (↔no); (否定疑問文に対して) no.

> 解説 (1) yes (\) は肯定または否定の答えを求めるいわゆる Yes/No 疑問文に対して肯定文の答えが続く場合に用いる。答えの文では疑問文の主語と助動詞に対応する代名詞と助動詞を伴って短く答えるのが普通で、完全文を繰り返すと不自然に響く。逆に yes だけで終わってしまうとぶっきらぼうに響くことが多い。
> (2) 特に軽く答えたりする場合やくだけた会話では **yeah** /jéə/ (\), **uh-huh** /ʌhʌ́/ (/) などを代わりに用いることが多い。

会話 「あれは太郎ですか」「はい、そうです」 "Is that Taro?" "*Yes, it is./Yeah./Uh-huh.*" (❗ (1) 後に続く be 動詞や助動詞を短縮して ×Yes, it's [I'm, he's]. などとはいわない (⇨いえる). (2) いろいろな助動詞を使って答えの確信度の違いを表すことがある: はい, ひょっとしてそうかもしれません [そうに違いありません] *Yes, it might [must] be.*)

会話 「泳がないんですか」「はい」 "Can't you swim?" "*No* [×*Yes*], I can't./*Uh-huh* /ʌhʌ́/." (❗日本語では「はい」となるが、英語では疑問文が否定疑問かどうかに関わりなく、答えに否定が続く場合は no となる。この場合 *Uh-huh* は鼻にかかった発音をすることに注意)

会話 「あなたの予約は来週の月曜日でしたね」「はい、そうです」 "Your appointment is for next Monday?" "(*Yes./Yeah./Uh-huh.*) That's right."

会話 「コーヒーでもいかが」「はい、いただきます」 "Would you like some coffee?" "*Yes,* /*please.*" (❗ "\\Yes." と下降上昇調でいうと「いただきますけど(他のものがよい)」と言外に反対の意を伝わす)

❷ [承諾して] yes, certainly, 《主に米》surely, 《主に米》sure; 《話》all right, OK [O.K., okay]. ▶はい、承知しました *Yes, certainly* [*with pleasure, of course*]./(客や上位の人に) *Yes* [*Certainly*], *sir*. (❗このように sir, ma'am や Mr. [Mrs.] Jones のような呼びかけの敬称をつけるのが普通.

会話 「この原稿、ファックスしてくれない」「はい」 "Can you fax this copy?" "*All right./Sure.*"

会話 「忘れずに手紙を投函してね」「はい」 "Don't forget to mail the letter." "*No* [×*Yes*], I won't."

❸ [返事] Yes; (出欠の) Here, Present, Yes.

会話 「太郎」「はい」 "Taro!" "*Yes.*" (❗語調によって単なる返事ではなく、「何か用ですか」と呼ばれた理由を聞くことになる)

会話 「中村君」「はい」 "Nakamura." "*Here*(, /*sir* [*ma'am*])." (❗ (1) sir [ma'am] は目上の男性(女性)に対する敬意をこめた返事. (2) Here は I'm here の省略表現)

❹ [相づち] üh-húh; (それで) /*yes,* /*yeah.* (❗相手の話を聞いていることを伝える場合は *yes* [*yeah*] やろなずく動作は ❷の承諾の意と解されるので注意)

❺ [相手の注意を引く] ▶はい、これ *Here* you áre./\\'*Here it is.* (❗ (1) 人に物を渡すとき、前の方は人に、後の方は物に重点がある。(2) 複数の物の場合は *Here* they are. となる。(3) 主語が名詞の場合は *Here's* your change and your order. (はい、お釣りとご注文の品です)の語順をとる。複数の主語でも Here's とする)/《話》\\'*Here* [*There*] you [we] gó. ▶はい、始めましょう *Here* /*goes./Here* we /*go.*

— はい 图 Yes. ▶彼女は「はい」と答えた She answered *yes* [*in the affirmative*]. (❗後の方は堅い言い方)

はい 灰 ash. (❗しばしば複数形で) ▶たばこの灰 cigarette *ash*(*es*). ▶火山灰 volcanic *ash*. ▶死の灰(= 放射性降下物) (radioactive) fallout.

● **灰になる** ▶手紙は燃えて灰になった The letters (were) burned to *ashes*. ▶父は灰になった(= 火葬された) My father was cremated.

はい 拝 ▶中村一郎拝 (手紙で) *Sincerely yours, Nakamura Ichiro.*

はい 胚 〖生物〗(動植物の) an émbryo (優 〜s); (動物の) a fóetus.
● **胚形成** an embryonic formatin. ● **胚珠** (⇨胚珠) ● **胚分化** embryonic differentiation.

はい 肺 图 〖解剖〗 a lung /lʌŋ/. (❗通例複数形で) ▶肺が悪い have (×a) *lung* [*pulmonary*] trouble; have a *lung* complaint; have a weak *chest*. ▶喫煙は肺に悪い Smoking is bad for the *lungs*.
— **肺の** 形 pulmonary /pʌ́lmənèri/.
● **肺機能(検査)** a pulmonary function (test).
● **肺動脈** a pulmonary artery.

—はい 杯 ▶ビール 2 杯 two glasses [mugs] of beer. (❗「2 杯分」を明確にいうときは two *glassfuls* of beer) ▶お茶を 2 杯飲む drink two *cups* of tea. (⇨一杯)

—はい 敗 ▶ 10 勝 2 敗 ten wins and two *losses*; ten victories and two *defeats*. (優 -勝)

***ばい 倍** ❶ [2 倍] twice; double. ▶人の倍働く do *double* work. ▶table 料金の倍額を払う pay *double* the usual fare. ▶ [×*the usual double*] fare. (❗「double ＋限定詞＋名詞」の語順に注意); (2 倍にする) *double* the usual fare. ▶ 4 の倍は 8 である *Twice* four is [are] eight./*Two fours are eight./Eight is double* [*is the double* of] *four*. ▶今朝はいつもより倍近くも時間がかかった It took nearly *twice* as much time as [×*twice longer than*] usual this morning. ▶物価は 5 年前に比べて倍になっている Prices are *twice* as high as [×*twice higher than*] (they were) five years ago./Prices are *twice* [*double*] what they were five years ago. ▶彼の収入は 5 年で倍になった His income *doubled* in five years.

❷ [...倍] ... times.

> 解説 「2 倍」は通例 **twice** で表し、それ以外は ... **times** を用いる。「3 倍」の意で thrice を用いるのは《古》. 0.5 単位の端数がつく場合は one and a half *times* (1.5 倍のように)いい、それ以外の場合は 1.6 *times* (1.6 倍)のようになり、one point six *times* という。

▶この箱はあの箱の 3 倍の大きさだ This box is three *times* as big as [three *times* the size of] that one. (❗比較級を用いた three times bigger than ... は「3 倍」の大きさなのか、もとの大きさに 3 倍を加えた「4 倍」の大きさなのかがあいまいなので避ける方がよい。だし何倍かを問うには比較級が普通 (⇨ 会話)) ▶彼女は私の 10 倍多く英単語を知っている She knows ten *times* as many English words as I do [《話》as me, 《書・まれ》as I].

会話 「ロンドンの人口はパリの何倍ですか」「約 3 倍です」 "How many *times* is the population of London larger [×*more*] than that of Paris?" "It's about three *times* as large."

パイ 〖マージャンの牌(ハイ)〗 a (mah-jong) tile /táil/ [piece].

パイ 〖料理〗(a) pie. (❗ (1) 全体を ©, 切り分けたものは Ⓤ でひと切れは a piece of *pie* という) ▶ミートパイ a meat *pie*. ▶アップルパイを焼く bake an ápple *pie*.

パイ 〖円周率〗pi /pái/ (記号 π).

はいあがる 這い上がる crawl [creep*] up; (よじ登る) climb up. ▶急斜面をはい上がる (手をついて上がる) *crawl* [*creep*] *up* a steep slope. ▶どん底から頂点にはい上がる *climb up* from the bottom to the top

バイアグラ 〖性的不能治療薬〗《商標》Viagra.

バイアスロン biathlon /baiǽθlən/. 《参考》クロスカントリースキーと射撃を合わせた競技》

はいあん 廃案 a rejected bill. ▶その法案は廃案になった The bill *was rejected* [*was dropped*].

はいい 廃位 图 dethronement; deposition.
—— 廃位する 動 dethrone; depose.

***はいいろ** 灰色 图 (a) gray. (▮種類をいうときは [C])
—— 灰色の 形 ❶ [色が] gray. ●灰色の目 *gray* eyes. ●灰色の空 a *gray* [a *cloudy*] sky. ●灰色がかった色 [コート] a *grayish* color [coat].
❷ [比喩的に] (暗い) gray; (わびしい) dreary; (陰気な) dismal. ●灰色の人生 a *gray* [a *dreary*, a *dismal*] life.

はいいん 敗因 the cause of (one's) defeat. ▶練習不足がわが チームの敗因だ Lack of practice is *the cause of our defeat.* / We lost the game *because* we didn't practice enough.

ばいう 梅雨 the rainy [wet] season. (⇨ 梅雨(ツㇼ))
●梅雨前線 a seasonal rain front.

ハイウエー (高速道路) 《米》a freeway, an expressway; 《英》a motorway. (▮a highway は「幹線道路」の意だが,たとえば an interstate highway は州と州を結ぶ高速道路をさす)

はいえい 背泳 (the) backstroke. (▮競技は the 〜)
●背泳をする do (the) *backstroke*; swim *on* one's *back*. ●背泳選手 a backstroke swimmer.

はいえき 廃液 waste fluid; liquid waste. ▶その化学工場は以前は大量の廃液を海に流していた The chemical plant used to discharge a lot of *liquid waste* into the ocean [sea].

はいそ 肺壊疽 〖医学〗pulmonary gangrene; necropneumonia.

はいえつ 拝謁 图 ▶国王は彼に拝謁を賜った The King granted him an *audience.* / 《受身》He was granted an *audience* with the King.
—— 拝謁する 動 《やや書》have an audience 《with》.

ハイエナ 〖動物〗a hyena /háiinə/. (▮hyaena ともつづる)

はいえん 肺炎 〖医学〗pneumonia /n(j)u:móuniə/.
●急性肺炎 acute pneumonia. ●肺炎になる catch [《書》contract] *pneumonia*. ▶赤ん坊は風邪がこじれて肺炎になった The baby's cold developed into *pneumonia*.

はいえん 排煙 —— 排煙する 動 exhaust smoke.
●排煙装置 an exhaust (system).

ばいえん 梅園 an *ume* [a plum] (果実用) orchard [(観賞用) garden].

ばいえん 煤煙 smoke; (すす) soot; (スモッグ) smog. ●工場の煤煙 industrial *smoke*; *smoke* from factories. ●煤煙の多い都市 a *smoky* city.

バイオ 〖生物の〗bio; 〖生物工学〗biotechnology.
●バイオエシックス〖生命倫理〗bioethics. (▮単数扱い) ●バイオガス〖生物ガス〗biogas. ●バイオセラミックス〖生体用陶材〗bioceramics. ●バイオテクノロジー〖生物工学〗biotechnology. ●バイオテロ〖生物テロリズム〗bioterrorism. ●バイオテロリスト a bioterrorist.
●バイオハザード〖生物危害〗a biohazard. ●バイオマス〖生物体量〗biomass.

はいおく 廃屋 a dilapidated house; (人が住まなくなった家) a deserted [an abandoned] house.

ハイオク (ハイオクタンのガソリン) high-octane /ǽktein/ gasoline《米》[petrol《英》].

パイオニア 〖先駆者〗a pioneer /pàiəníər/ 《of modern medicine, in the field》.

バイオリズム biorhythms. ▶彼女は自分のバイオリズムにいつも気を遣っている She always pays attention to her *biorhythms*.

バイオリニスト a violinist. (⇨ バイオリン)

バイオリン 〖楽器〗a violin; 《話》(しばしば軽蔑的な) a fiddle. ●バイオリン奏者 a violinist; 《話》a fiddler.
●バイオリン協奏曲〖ソナタ〗a *violin* concerto [sonata]. ●バイオリンを弾く play the *violin*. (⇨ ピアノ) ▶彼はその管弦楽団の第 1 バイオリンです He plays the first *violin* in the orchestra. ▶それをバイオリンで弾けますか Can you play that *on the violin*?

バイオレンス 〖暴力〗violence.

はいか 配下 (支持者) a follower; (部下) a man 《men》. ●彼の配下となって働く serve [work] under him.

はいか 廃家 (⇨ 廃屋(ツㇼ))

はいが 胚芽 〖動物・植物〗an embryo /émbriòu/ 《〜s》. (⇨ 胚芽米)

はいが 俳画 a simple *sumie* with a poetic charm.

ばいか 売価 a selling [sales] price.

ばいか 倍加 —— 倍加する 動 (2 倍 になる) double; (増大する) multiply; redouble.

ばいか 買価 a buying [purchase] price.

はいかい 徘徊 —— 徘徊する 動 ●通りを徘徊する (歩き回る) wander [walk, (盗人が) prowl /prául/] 《around, 《主に英》about》.
●徘徊症〖医学〗fugue /fjú:g/. 《参考》記憶喪失期間に家を出て徘徊する病癖》●徘徊老人 an old person who abnormally wanders away from home.

はいかい 俳諧 *haikai*; (俳諧連歌) an amusing linked poem; (俳句) (a) *haiku*. (⇨ 俳句)

はいがい 拝外 —— 拝外的な 形 pro-alien; pro-foreign.

はいがい 排外 —— 排外的な 形 antiforeign.
●排外運動 an antiforeign movement.

***ばいかい** 媒介 图 《書》agency; 〖仲介〗mediation; 〖斡旋〗good offices. ▶音は空気の媒介により伝わる Sound travels through the *medium* [*agency*] of air. (▮前の方が普通) ▶不純な飲料水は病気の媒介となりうる Impure drinking water can be a *carrier* [a *vehicle*] of diseases.
—— 媒介する 動 (仲介する) mediate, act as 《an》 intermediary 《between》; 〖伝染病を〗carry 《germs》. ●蚊はマラリアを媒介する Mosquitoes *carry* malaria /məláriə/.
●媒介者 (仲介者) a mediator; (周旋人) an agent; (仲人) a go-between. ●媒介物 (媒体)《書》a medium (複 media); (伝達手段)《書》a vehicle; (病原菌の) a carrier.

はいかぐら 灰神楽 a cloud of ashes.

はいガス 排ガス exhaust gas.
●排ガス規制 emission control. ●排ガス規制車 a low-emission vehicle [car, truck].

はいかつりょう 肺活量 (have a large) lung capacity. ▶あなたの肺活量はどのくらいですか What is your *lung capacity*?

はいがまい 胚芽米 rice with the germ part unremoved.

ハイカラ 〖当世風の〗fashionable; [いきな] stylish. (▮この意で ×high collar は和製英語)

バイカル ●バイカル湖 〖ロシア東部の湖〗Lake Baikal /baiká:l/.

はいかん 拝観 —— 拝観する 動 (見る) see, look at ...; (眺める) view; (参拝する) visit. ●大聖堂を拝観する *visit* the cathedral. ▶この寺は拝観できない This temple *is closed* (↔open) *to visitors*.

はいかん 廃刊

ハイカー 〖ハイキングをする人〗a hiker.

はいかん
- 拝観者 a visitor. ● 拝観料 an admission fee.

はいかん 配管 ⓝ piping; plumbing /plǽmɪŋ/; (!集合的に配管系統[設備]をさす).
—— 配管する ⓥ lay a pipe.
- 配管工 a plumber. ● 配管工事 plumbing.

はいかん 廃刊 ⓝ discontinuance of publication. ▶その雑誌は廃刊になった The magazine *ceased publication* [*was published*]./They *ceased to publish* [*ceased publishing*] the magazine.
—— 廃刊する ⓥ stop [《やや書》*discontinue*] the publication 《*of a newspaper*》.

はいがん 拝顔 ● 拝顔の栄に浴する have the honor [pleasure] of *meeting* [*seeing*] 《*him*》.

はいがん 肺癌 〖医学〗lung cancer.

はいき 排気 exhaust. ● 排気量の大きい車 a large-volume car.
- 排気ガス (⇨ガス) ● 排気管 an exhaust (pipe).
- 排気孔 a vent. ● 排気装置 an exhaust (system). ● 排気弁 (内燃機関などの) a cutout.

はいき 廃棄 ⓝ 〖廃止〗(制度・慣習などの) abolition; (法律などの正式の) repeal; (条約などの) (an) abrogation; 〖放棄〗abandonment. ● 廃棄物 ⇨廃棄物.
—— 廃棄する ⓥ 〖不用品などを〗scrap (-pp-); 〖徹底的する〗abolish; 〖法律などを〗repeal; 〖書〗abrogate. (⇨廃止する) ▶古い車を廃棄して新しいのを買った I *scrapped* my old car and bought a new one.

はいきしゅ 肺気腫 〖医学〗pulmonary emphysema /ɛmfəsíːmə/.

はいきぶつ 廃棄物 (a) waste. (!しばしば複数形で)
- 工場廃棄物 factory *waste*. ● 産業廃棄物 industrial *waste*. ● 放射性廃棄物 radioactive *waste*.
- 核廃棄物 nuclear *waste*. ● 有毒廃棄物 toxic *waste*.
- 廃棄物処理 waste disposal; the disposal of waste. ● 廃棄物処理業者 a disposal firm.

ばいきゃく 売却 —— 売却する ⓥ (⇨売る) ▶彼は伊豆の別邸を売却した He *sold* [処分した] *disposed of*] his villa in Izu. (⇨売る)
- 売却益 (土地・株などの) cápital gàins. ● 売却価格 a sélling prìce.

はいきゅう 配球 ● チェンジアップ, カーブ, ストレートを交えた配球 with a *combination* of changeups, curves, and fastballs.

はいきゅう 配給 ⓝ 〖統制品などの〗rationing; 〖供給〗supply; 〖配布〗distribution. ● 砂糖の配給分 a *ration* of sugar. ● 水害被災者への食料の配給 the *distribution* [*supply*] of food *to* the flood victims. ▶戦時中米は配給だった People *were rationed* rice during the war./Rice *was rationed* (*out*) to people during the war.
—— 配給する ⓥ 〖統制などで一定の量を〗ration (⇨ⓝ); 〖供給する〗supply; 〖配る〗distribute. ▶彼らは被災者に毛布を配給した They *distributed* [*supplied*] blankets *to* the stricken [disaster] people.
- 配給会社 (映画などの) a distributor; a distributing agency.

ばいきゅう 倍旧 ▶倍旧(=いっそう)のお引き立てのほどを願い上げます We solicit [look forward to] your *increased* patronage.

はいきょ 廃墟 ▶廃墟となった城 a *ruined* castle; a castle *in ruins*. ▶その地震でかつてにぎわったその町も廃墟と化した The once-bustling town was [lay] *in ruins* after the earthquake./The once-bustling town *was ruined* by the earthquake.

はいきょう 背教 〖宗教〗apostasy.
- 背教者 an apostate; a renegade.

はいぎょう 廃業 —— 廃業する ⓥ (商売をやめる) give up [close] one's business, go out of business; (店・工場などを閉じる) close down one's store [factory]; (医師などが) give up one's practice; (力士や役者が) retire from [《話》quit] the ring [stage].

はいきりょう 排気量 displacement. ▶排気量2,000ccの車 a car of 2,000 cc *displacement*.

はいきん 背筋 〖解剖〗(a) back muscle. ● 背筋力が強い (⇨背筋力)

はいきん 拝金 ● 拝金主義 mammonism; worship of money.

***ばいきん** 黴菌 a germ, bacteria /bæktíəriə/ (⓵ bacterium). (⇨細菌) ▶傷口にばい菌が入った The cut became infected [septic].

ハイキング a hike; hiking. ▶週末はよく六甲山にハイキングに出かける I often *go on a hike to* [*go hiking in*] Mt. Rokko at [《米》on] the weekend(s). (!×go on a hiking としない)
- ハイキングコース a híking tràil [ròute, còurse].

バイキング ⓝ 〖料理〗(北欧料理) smorgasbord /smɔ́ːrɡəsbɔ̀ːrd/ (⓵種類は [C]), 《和製語》Viking; (一般に立食式の) a buffet /bʌféi/ (meal). ❷〖北欧の海賊〗(1人の) a Viking; (全体) the Vikings.

はいきんりょく 背筋力 back strength. ● 背筋力が強い have a strong back. ● 背筋力をつける strengthen one's back muscles.

はいく 俳句 (a) *haiku*; (説明的に) a (Japanese) seventeen-syllable short poem written in a five-seven-five pattern [meter]. ● 俳句を作る write [compose] a *haiku*.

はいぐ 拝具 ⓝ 敬具

バイク a motorcycle, 《英》a motorbike. (!a bike は通例「自転車」をさす) ● オートバイ) ● ミニバイク (motor) scooter; (ペダル付きの) a moped; (より小型の) a minibike. ● スポーツジムなどのエアロバイク a stationary bícycle [bìke].

はいぐうしゃ 配偶者 (夫) one's husband; (妻) one's wife (⓵ wives); (夫または妻) 〖書〗one's spouse /spaus, spauz/. ● 配偶者の有無 one's marital status. ▶彼女はよい配偶者を得た She got a good *husband*./She married a good man.
- 配偶者控除 tax deduction for one's spouse. (!控除額は a 〜)

ハイクラス high-class 《restaurants》.

はいぐん 敗軍 (敗戦) a defeat; (敗れた軍隊) a defeated army.
- 敗軍の将, 兵を語らず A defeated general should not talk of his battles [excuse himself].

***はいけい** 背景 ❶〖後景〗a background. ▶写真の背景に木が写っている There are trees in the *background* of the picture. ▶青空を背景に富士山がくっきり見える Mt. Fuji is seen clearly *against* the blue sky.
❷〖舞台の〗scenery; a setting; a scene. ● 背景を描く paint *scenery*. ● 背景を変える change the *scene* [*setting*].
❸〖背景的事情〗a background. ▶その事件の社会的〖歴史的〗背景 the social [historical] *background* of the event. ▶この犯罪の背景には何があったのだろうか What was the *background to* this crime?
- 背景幕 a backdrop.

はいけい 拝啓 ❶〖個人あて〗Dear Sir [Madam]; Dear Mr. [Mrs., Miss, Ms.] 《Suzuki》; Dear [My dear] 《Ichiro》.

解説 (1) **Dear Sir [Madam]** は改まったときや，未知の人あてまたは商業文に用いられ，性別不明の場合は **Dear Sir or Madam** も用いられる．
(2)「**Dear Mr. [Mrs., Miss]** ＋姓」は親しい目上の人あてとそれほど親しくない人に対して用いる．昔は既婚・未婚を問わない敬称で，1973年に国連でも正式に採用された．(!)「**Dear Mr. [Mrs., Miss]** ＋名＋姓」のようには用いない：×Dear Mr. John Black)
(3)「**Dear** ＋姓」は目上の人から目下の者へ，「**Dear** ＋名」，「**My dear** ＋名」は親しい間柄で用いる．(!)《米》では Dear ... の方が親密さを表し，My dear ... の方が形式的.《英》ではその逆）(➪巻末〔手紙の書き方〕)

❷〔会社・団体あて〕《米》Gentlemen (!)(1) 最近では Ladies and Gentlemen も用いられる．(2) 結びは Very truly yours が普通．《英》Dear Sirs (!) 結びは Yours faithfully が普通）(➪敬具);〔女性の団体あて〕Ladies, Mesdames /meidǽ:m/.

はいげき 排撃 ── 排撃する 動 denounce《him, it》《as》.

ばいけつ 売血 ── 売血する 動 sell blood.

はいけっかく 肺結核 〔医学〕(pulmonary) tubérculósis (複 -ses)〔略 TB, t.b.〕(古) consumption. ● 肺結核にかかる[かかっている] contract [suffer from, have] *tuberculosis*.

はいけつしょう 敗血症 blood poisoning;〔医学〕septicemia /sèptəsí:miə/; sepsis.

はいけん 拝見 ── 拝見する 動〔「見る」の意の謙譲語〕（手に取って見る）see;（見る）look [have a look] at ... .（➪見る）▶切符を拝見します（車掌が）Tickets, please. ▶免許証を拝見させてください（警官が）Let me *see* [(見せを) *Show* me] your driver's license. ▶お手紙とても楽しく拝見しました（読みました）I really enjoyed *reading* your letter.（お手紙ありがとう）Thank you very much for your letter.

はいご 背後 〔後部〕the back, the rear. ● 敵の背後をつく attack the enemy *from the back [from behind, in the rear]*.
── 背後に 副〔後方に〕behind ..., at the back of ...,《米》in back of ....（➪後ろ）▶彼の背後には政治家がいる He has a politician *behind* him [*at his back*]./ 私の背後には，政治的な野心も党派的な情熱もありません I have *behind* me neither political ambition nor sectarian passion.
● 背後関係 the background. ● 事件の背後関係を調べる investigate [inquire into] *the background* of a case.

はいご 廃語 an obsolete [a disused] word.（➪死語）● 廃語になりかかっている言葉 an òbsolésent word.

はいこう 廃坑 an abandoned gallery.

はいこう 廃校 the closure [closing] of a school. ▶その学校は生徒減のため廃校になった The school *was closed* (*down*) because of a decline in enrollments.

はいごう 俳号 the pseudonym [the pen name] of a *haiku* poet.

はいごう 配合 名〔組み合わせ〕(a) combination;〔配合されたもの〕mixture;〔配列〕a scheme /skí:m/;〔薬の調合〕compounding.（➪調合）● 色の配合 a color *combination*; the *combination* of colors.（➪配色）
── 配合する 動《書》compound; mix. ▶この薬はビタミン A とビタミン B₁₂ が〔いろいろな成分が〕配合されている This medicine *is compounded of* vitamin A and vitamin B₁₂ [*from* various ingredients]. ● 配合飼料 compound feed. ● 配合肥料 compound fertilizer.

はいごう 廃合 abolition and merger.

ばいこく 売国 ● 売国行為 an act of treason /trí:zn/. ● 売国奴 a traitor to one's country.（➪売る）

はいざい 配剤 名 ● 天の配剤 a dispensation.
── 配剤する 動（薬を）dispense medicine.

はいざい 廃材 scrap wood.

はいさつ 拝察 ── 拝察する 動 《I can》imagine.（➪察する）

はいざら 灰皿 an ashtray;（スタンドつきの）a smóking stànd.

はいざん 敗残 ● 敗残者 a failure [a loser] (in life). ● 敗残兵 remnants of a defeated army.

はいざん 廃山 名（➪⇒廃坑）.
── 廃山する 動 close down a mine.

*はいし 廃止 名〔制度・習慣などの〕abolition;〔法令の〕repeal. ● 奴隷制度の廃止 the *abolition* of slavery.
── 廃止する 動〔公的にやめる〕abolish, do* away with ... (!) 後の方が口語的);〔終わらせる〕discontinue, put* an end to ...;〔法令を〕repeal. ● 制服を廃止する abolish [*do away with*] uniforms. ▶死刑を廃止せよ *Abolish* [*Put an end to*] the death penalty. ▶そのバス路線は廃止された The bus route *was discontinued*./ They *stopped* [*discontinued*] bus service on that route.

はいし 拝辞 〔「辞退」の謙譲語〕(➪辞退).

はいジストマ 肺ジストマ（吸虫）a lung fluke;（病気）〔医学〕pulmonary distomatosis [distomiasis].

はいしつ 廃疾 (a) disability.（➪障害 ❷）

はいじつせい 背日性 〔植物〕negative heliotropism.（⇔向日性）● 背日性の植物 a negative heliotropic [apheliotropic] plant.

はいしゃ 配車（車の割当て）allocation of cars. ● 配車係 a dispatcher.

はいしゃ 拝謝 ── 拝謝する 動〔「礼を言う」の意の謙譲語〕▶ご親切に対して拝謝します I express my *cordial* thanks [I am *heartily* grateful to you] for your kindness./ I really *appreciate* your kindness.（➪⇒感謝する）

はいしゃ 敗者 a loser. ● その試合の敗者 the *loser of* [*in*] the game.
● 敗者復活戦 a consolation match.

はいしゃ 廃車 put a car out of service;（解体する）scrap a car.

はいしゃ 歯医者 a dentist;（歯列矯正の）an orthodontist. ● 歯医者へ行く go to [〔診察してもらう〕see] the *dentist*; go to the *dentist's* office [clinic]. ● 11時に歯医者を予約する make an appointment with *one's dentist* for eleven. (! one's は「かかりつけの」の意); make a dental appointment for eleven.

はいしゃく 拝借 ── 拝借する 動 borrow.（➪借りる）▶傘〔電話〕を拝借できますか Could I *borrow* your umbrella [*use* your telephone]? ▶ちょっとお耳を拝借 Just a word for your ear.
会話「どなたか10円玉を一つ拝借できますか（＝貸してくれますか）」「はいどうぞ」"Who will *lend* me a 10-yen coin?" "＼I will."

ばいしゃく 媒酌 名 matchmaking. ● 木村夫妻の媒酌で《書》through the *good offices* of Mr. and Mrs. Kimura.
── 媒酌する 動 make [arrange] a match (*between*);（仲人する）act as (a) go-between 《*for*》.
● 媒酌人 a matchmaker.

ハイジャック

ハイジャック 名 hijacking. (❗個々の事件では [C])
― **ハイジャックする** 動 飛行機をハイジャックする *hijack* [*skyjack*] an airplane.
● ハイジャック犯 a hijacker.

ハイジャンプ 『走り高跳び』『競技』 the high jump.
● ハイジャンプの選手 a high jumper.

はいしゅ 胚珠 〖植物の〗an ovule.

はいじゅ 拝受 ― **拝受する** 動 〖「受け取る」の謙譲語〗 receive respectfully. (⇒受け取る❶)

ばいしゅう 買収 名 〖土地などの〗purchase; 〖株式の買占めによる経営権の取得〗a takeover, a buyout; 〖国などによる土地の強制的な〗expropriation; 〖贈賄〗 bribery; 〖賄賂〗payoff. ● 買収にのる (わいろを受け取る) take [accept] a bribe.
― **買収する** 動 ❶〖買い取る〗buy*, purchase; 〖国などが土地を〗expropriate. ● 企業の合併 [買収] mergers and *acquisition* (略 M&A). ● 彼の店を買収する *take over* [*buy out*] his business. ▶ 同社はこの土地を現金15億円で買収した The company *bought* [*purchased*] the land for 1.5 billion yen in cash.
❷〖贈賄する〗bribe, 《話》buy* [pay*] 《him》 off. ● 金で買収する *bribe* 《him》 with money. ● 彼を買収して黙らせる *bribe* him *to* be silent [*into* silence].
● 買収会社 an acquíring còmpany. (関連) 被買収会社 an acquired company ● 買収戦略 acquisition strategy.

はいしゅつ 排出 名 〖放出〗〖書〗(a) discharge, (an) emission; 〖排泄(せつ)〗〖書〗excretion. ● 二酸化炭素の排出量 *emissions* of carbon dioxide. ● 年間総排出量の削減に努力する make efforts to reduce absolute tons of annual *emission*.
― **排出する** 動 discharge, emit; 〖液体を〗drain; 〖老廃物を〗excrete. ● 有毒ガスを *discharge* [*emit*] toxic fumes. ▶ そのパイプで廃物を川に排出する The pipe *drains* [*discharges*] waste into the river.
● 排出基準 emíssion stàndard. ● 排出権 (an) aemíssion crèdit. ● 排出口 an outlet.

はいしゅつ 輩出 ― **輩出する** 動 appear in great numbers; produce [turn out] a number of ....
▶ イギリスは多くの分野でノーベル賞受賞者を輩出した Great Britain *has produced* a large number of Nobel Prize winners in many fields.

ばいしゅん 売春 prostitution.
― **売春する** 動 prostitute oneself; (生業として) work as a prostitute.
● 売春婦 a prostitute, 《米話》a hooker; 《軽蔑的》 a whore /hɔ́ːr/. ● 売春防止法 Antiprostitution Law.

はいじょ 排除 名 exclusion; removal; elimination; (不法占拠などの) eviction.
― **排除する** 動 〖締め出す〗 exclude; 〖取り除く〗 remove; (不法占拠者などを) evict; (有害物・不要物を) get* rid of ...; (不要物を完全に) 《やや書》eliminate; (じゃまなものを場所から) clear ... (away) 《*from*》. ● この町から暴力を排除する *exclude* [*remove*, *get rid of*, *eliminate*] violence *from* this town. (❗exclude はこれから入るのを防ぐこと、他の3語はすでにあるのを取り除くこと) ● あらゆる障害を排除する (進路からなどを) *clear* all obstacles *out of* the way; (打ち勝つ) *overcome* all obstacles.
▶ ホームレスの人たちはその駅の構内から排除された Homeless people *were evicted* [*were cleared away*] *from* the station precincts.

ばいしょう 賠償 名 compensation, 《書》reparation. ▶ 彼はけがの賠償として多額の金を受け取った He received a large sum of money *in* [*as a*, *by way of*] *compensation* for his injury. ▶ 我々は政府に対して被害の賠償を請求した We demanded that the government (should) *make compensation* [*reparation*] *for* our losses. / We claimed *damages* from the government.
― **賠償(を)する** 動 ● 損害の賠償をする compensate 《him》 for the damage; make reparation for the damage; pay for the damage. ▶ 彼は損害を賠償すると申し出た [賠償してもらいたいと請求した] He offered to *pay* [*made a claim*] for the damage.
● 賠償金 (損害・けがなどの) (a) compensation; 〖法律〗damages; (戦争の) reparations. ● 賠償責任 a liability for reparation.

はいしょく 配色 (色の取り合わせ) the combination of colors; (色彩計画) a color scheme. ▶ この絵は配色が悪いし、空間の使い方がなってない This picture has a poor *color scheme* [(色彩構成) *color composition*] and a lousy use of space.

はいしょく 配食 高齢者配食サービス a *meal-delivery* service for the elderly.

はいしょく 敗色 signs of defeat. ▶ 我がチームは敗色が濃い (勝ち目がない) The odds are against our team. / (たぶん試合に負ける) We will probably lose the game [match].

はいしん 背信 (信頼に背くこと) 《やや書》(a) breach of faith; (裏切り) (a) betrayal. ● 私に背信行為をする (誓いを破る) break faith with me; (私の信頼を裏切る) 《やや書》betray my confidence.

はいしん 配信 ― **配信する** 動 ニュースを配信する supply news 《*to* newspapers》.

はいじん 俳人 a *haiku* poet. (⇒詩人)

はいじん 廃人 a disabled person.

ばいしん 陪審 ▶ 陪審は無罪の評決をした The *jury* reached a verdict of not guilty.
● 陪審員 a jury member, a juror; 〖集合的〗a jury (❗単・複両扱い). ● 陪審裁判 a trial by jury, a jury trial. ● 陪審制度 the jury system.

はいしんじゅん 肺浸潤 〖医学〗infiltration of the lungs.

はいすい 配水 名 water supply. ― **配水する** 動 supply water.
● 配水管 a water pipe.

はいすい 排水 名 〖水はけ〗drainage, a drain; 〖排水設備〗drainage; 〖下水設備〗sewerage /súːəridʒ/.
● その宅地の排水設備 the *sewerage* [*sewage*] arrangements at the housing site. ● この土地は排水がよい[悪い] The *drainage* of this land is good [bad]. / This land *drains* well [badly]. ▶ その船は排水量5,000トンである The ship *has a displacement* of 5,000 tons. / The ship *displaces* 5,000 tons.
― **排水する** 動 drain; (ポンプで) pump ... out. ● 排水するため溝を掘る dig trenches to *drain* the water *away* [*off*]; dig trenches for *drainage*.
● 排水管 a drainpipe; (下水管) a drain; (下水本管) a sewer /súːər/. ● 排水溝 a drain; (下水) a sewer. ● 排水工事 drainage work.

はいすい 廃水 waste water. ● 工場廃水 *waste water* from factories.

はいすいしゅ 肺水腫 〖医学〗an edema /idíːmə/ 《～s, -ta /-tə/》of the lungs.

はいすいのじん 背水の陣 背水の陣を敷く fight with [have] one's back to the wall; fight desperately [for one's life]; make a last-ditch effort.

ばいすう 倍数 〖数学〗a multiple. ● 10は5の倍数だ 10 is a multiple of 5.

ハイスクール 〖高校〗a high school.

ハイスピード ●ハイスピードで at high [full, top] speed.

はいする 拝する 〖頭を下げて拝む〗pray with a bow; 〖受ける〗receive 《an Imperial order》; 〖見る〗 see.

はいする 配する 〖配置する〗《人を部署に》post 《at, on; 《転勤させる》to》, station (❗後の方はしばしば受身で); 《物と物をとり合わせる》arrange. ●適材を適所に配する put the right person in the right place. ●池に松を配する plant a pine tree beside the pond (to set it off).

はいする 排する overcome 《difficulties》. ●万難を排して in the face of [despite] all difficulties; (どんな犠牲を払っても) at all cost(s). (⇨万難)

はいする 這いする crawl 《across the floor》; crawl (along).

ばいする 倍する (⇨倍加する)

はいせい 敗勢 signs of defeat. (⇨⓾ 敗色)

はいせき 排斥 图 expulsion.

── **排斥する** 動 〖人などを追放する〗drive*... out, expel (-ll-) (❗後の方が堅い語); 〖拒絶する〗reject; 〖集団で製品などを〗boycott. ●軍国思想を排斥する reject militarism. ●異端者を教会から排斥する drive heretics out of church; expel heretics from church. ▶その国では日本製品を排斥する運動が起こっている There is a movement against [to boycott] Japanese goods in that country.

ばいせき 陪席 ── **陪席する** 動 《身分の高い人と同席する》sit with one's superiors.
●陪席裁判官 an associate judge.

はいせつ 排泄 图 《老廃物の》《書》excretion; 《ガスなどの》(a) discharge.

── **排泄する** 動 《書》excrete; discharge; void.
●排泄器官 an excretory organ. ●排泄物 (糞便(ﾆﾜ)・尿・汗など) 《書》excreta (❗複数扱い); (特に大便) 《書》excrement; discharges; bodily wastes.

はいぜつ 廃絶 图 《核兵器などの》abolition. ●核兵器の廃絶 the abolition of nuclear weapons.

── **廃絶する** 動 ●核兵器を廃絶する abolish nuclear weapons.

はいせん 肺尖 〖解剖〗the pulmonary apex.
●肺尖カタル 〖医学〗catarrh of the pulmonary apex.

はいせん 配船 ── **配船する** 動 place a ship [put a vessel] on the route.

はいせん 配線 wiring. ●欠陥配線 faulty wiring. ●たこ足配線 (⇨蛸(ﾀｺ)) ●家の電気の配線をやりなおす rewire the house. ▶この古い配線を取り換えねばならない We must have this old wiring replaced.
●配線工事 wíring wòrk. ▶その家はもう配線工事がすんでいますか Is the house wired up yet? ●配線図 a wiring diagram.

はいせん 敗戦 the loss of a war [a battle]; (敗北) (a) defeat.
●敗戦国 a defeated nation [country]. ●敗戦処理 a mop-up duty. ●最終回に敗戦処理登板する mop up in the last inning. ●敗戦処理投手 〖野球〗a mop-up man. ●敗戦投手 〖野球〗a losing pitcher; a loser.

はいせん 廃船 an out-of-service ship. ●廃船にする put a ship out of service; (解体する) scrap a ship.

はいせん 廃線 a discontinued railroad line.

はいぜん 沛然 ●沛然たる驟雨 a torrential downpour; very heavy rain; rain pouring down in torrents; rain coming down [falling] in buckets.

はいぜん 配膳 ── **配膳する** 動 set 〖《英》lay〗a table 《for dinner》; serve 《dinner》.
●配膳室 a servery.

ばいせん 焙煎 图 roasting. ── **焙煎する** 動 roast 《coffee beans》.

ハイセンス refined [excellent] taste; 《和製語》 high sense. (⇨センス)

はいそ 敗訴 a losing (↔a winning) suit. ▶その事件は君の敗訴になるかもしれません You may lose the suit [case]./The case may go against you.

ハイソ (⇨ハイソサエティー)

はいそう 配送 图 delivery. ── **配送する** 動 deliver 《goods to the office》.
●配送車 a delivery van; 《米》a delivery [a panel] truck. ●配送センター a delivery center.

はいそう 敗走 (a) rout /ráut/, 《やや書》(a) flight. ── **敗走する** 動 ●敵を敗走させる put the enemy to rout [flight]; 《やや書》put the enemy. ▶敵は敗走した The enemy was routed./The enemy fled.

ばいぞう 倍増 ── **倍増する** 動 double. ▶所得[志願者数]が倍増した My income [The number of applicants] has doubled.

はいぞく 配属 ── **配属する** 動 assign 〖(特殊任務で一時的に) attach〗《him to a department》. (❗通例受身で)

はいそく 倍速 double-speed. ●倍速 CD-ROM ドライブ a double-speed [a 2×] CD-ROM drive. ●16 倍速 CD-ROM ドライブ a sixteen-speed [a 16×] CD-ROM drive.

ハイソサエティー 〖上流社会〗high society. (❗a society ball (ハイソサエティーの舞踏会)のように限定形容詞として用いるときには high の省略可)

ハイソックス 《a pair of》long 〖(ひざまでの長さの)knee (-length)〗socks; 《和製語》high socks.

はいた 歯痛 (a) toothache. ●歯痛である have (a) toothache. (⇨歯)

はいたい 胚胎 ── **胚胎する** 動 《発生する》originate 《in, from》; (考え・発想が芽生える) germinate.

はいたい 敗退 图 (a) defeat.
── **敗退する** 動 be defeated. ●初戦で敗退する be defeated [be beat(en)] in the first game. (❗後の方が口語的)

ばいたい 媒体 a medium 《穆 ~s, media》. ●広告媒体 advertising media. ●新聞を媒体として through the medium of newspapers. ●空気は音を伝える媒体である The air is a medium for sound.

はいだす 這い出す creep [crawl] out 《of, from》.

***はいたつ 配達** 图 delivery. ●商品配達 the delivery of goods 《to》. ●郵便[無料]配達 mail [free] delivery. ●新聞配達をして金を稼ぐ earn money by delivering papers; (担当区域を) have [run] a paper route and earn money. ▶配達うけたまわります〖掲示〗We deliver. (❗×We accept delivery. とはいわない)

── **配達する** 動 deliver, make* a delivery 《of》. ●手紙[商品]を彼のところに配達する deliver letters [goods] to him. ●無料で配達してもらう have (it) delivered free (of charge). ●配達していただけますか Do [Can] you deliver it?/Do you have a delivery service?

会話 「配達をお願いしたいの。このビールとこのワインを一箱ずつ」「承知しました。すぐお届けします」"I need a delivery. A case each of this beer and that wine." "All right, ma'am. I'll be right with you."

ハイタッチ 《主に米》a high five. (⇨ハイファイブ) ● 彼とハイタッチをする high-five [do a *high five* with] him. (《参考》腰のあたりで手を打ち合う動作は a low five という)

はいたてき 排他的 ── **排他的な** 形 (組織・制度などが) exclusive. ● 排他的な集団 an *exclusive* group. ● よそ者に排他的な態度をとる (不親切にする) be *unfriendly* to [toward] strangers.
● 排他的経済水域 an *exclusive economic zone* (略 EEZ).

バイタリティー (活力) vitality; (生気) life; (元気) vigor. ● バイタリティーにあふれる青年 a young man [woman] full of *vitality* [*life*, *vigor*]. ▶ 彼はバイタリティーがない He has no [lacks] *vitality*.

バイタルエリア 〖サッカー〗 vital area.

はいだん 俳壇 the world of *haiku* poets.

***はいち 配置** 名 〖配列, 整えん〗 (an) arrangement; 〖所定の位置〗 a position; 〖部署〗 a station, a post. ● 居間の家具の配置を変える change the *arrangement* of furniture in the living room; *rearrange* the furniture in the living room. ● 社員の配置転換を行う (人事異動) make a *reshuffle* of the personnel. ▶ ダンサーが配置につくと幕が上がった When the dancers took their *positions*, the curtain rose.
── **配置する** 動 arrange; 〖特定の場所に置く〗 place; 〖部署につかせる〗 station, post; 〖軍隊・核兵器などを〗 〖軍事〗 deploy. ● 机を教室に配置する *arrange* [*place*] the desks in the classroom. ● ヨーロッパにミサイルを配置する *deploy* missiles in Europe. ▶ すべての出口に見張り番が 2 人ずつ配置されている Two guards *are stationed* [*posted*] at every exit.

はいち 背馳 ── **背馳する** 動 (反対になる) go against; disobey. (⇨ 背反する)

ハイチ 〖国名〗 Haiti /héiti/; (公式名) the Republic of Haiti. (首都 Port-au-Prince /pɔ́ːrtoupríns/) ● ハイチ人 a Haitian. ● ハイチ(人)の Haitian.

ばいち 培地 (培養基) a culture medium.

はいちせい 背地性 〖植物の〗 negative geotropism. (⇨ 向地性)

はいちょう 拝聴 ── **拝聴する** 動 listen 《*to*》. ▶ ご意見を拝聴したい Would you please *let me hear* your opinion?

はいちょう 蠅帳 a screened food cupboard.

ハイツ 〖高台〗 heights; 〖アパート〗 an apartment building [house].

はいつくばる 這いつくばる grovel; lie flat on one's hands and knees.

ハイティーン ● ハイティーンの少女 a girl *in her late* (↔ *early*) *teens*. (《!》(1) 16–19 歳の年齢をさすが, 16–17 歳を mid teens として区別することもある. (2) ×high teen は和製英語)

ハイテク 名 high téch, 《話》 hi-téch, high technólogy. ── **ハイテクの** 形 high tech, hi-tech. ● ハイテク関連株 a technology stock [share]. ● ハイテク企業 high-tech firms. ● ハイテク産業 the high-tech(nology) industry. ● ハイテク商品 a high-tech product.

ハイデルベルグ 〖ドイツの都市〗 Heidelberg /háidlbə̀ːrg/.

はいてん 配点 名 the allotment [allocation] of marks.
── **配点する** 動 allot [allocate, give] marks 《*to*》.

はいてん 配転 名 (人事異動) (a) (personnel) transfer; (a) change in personnel. (⇨ 異動) ● 配転を希望する hope for a *transfer* 《*to*》.
── **配転される** 動 ● 支店へ配転される be *transferred* to a branch office.

ハイテン 《主に米》 a high ten. (⇨ ハイファイブ)

はいでん 配電 electric supply.
── **配電する** 動 supply electricity 〖(電力) electric power〗.
● 配電線 a power line. ● 配電盤 a switchboard.

はいでん 拝殿 a house for worship.

ばいてん 売店 a stand, 《主に英》 a stall (《!》 ともにしばしば複合語で); (新聞・軽食などの) a kiosk; (縁日などの屋台店) a booth, a store. ● 駅の売店 a *kiosk* (at a station). ● 新聞の売店 a newspaper *stand*, a newsstand. (《!》 後の方は時に雑誌や本も扱う) ● 学校の売店 a school *store*.

ハイテンポ a fast tempo; 《和製語》 a high tempo.
● ハイテンポな曲 a tune with a *fast tempo*.

バイト 〖アルバイト〗 a part-time job. ● 夏のバイト a summer job.

バイト 〖コンピュータの〗 a byte. ● キロバイト a kilobyte (記号 KB). ● メガバイト a megabyte 《記号 MB》. ● ギガバイト a gigabyte 《記号 GB》. ● テラバイト a terabyte 《記号 TB》. ● 2 バイト文字 a two-*byte* character.

はいとう 配当 〖割り当て〗 allotment; 〖株式の〗 a dividend; 〖分け前〗 a share. ● 現金[株式]配当 a cash [a stock] dividend. ● 1 株年 5 円の配当(金)を受ける get an annual *dividend* of 5 yen per share. ● 利益の配当にあずかる *share* in the profits.
● 配当落ち dividend off; 《英》 ex dividend, ex-dividend; without dividend. ● 配当所得 dividend income. ● 配当性向 the pay(-)out ratio. ● 配当付き dividend on; 《英》 cum dividend, cum-dividend; with dividend. ● 配当率 the dividend rate. ● 配当利回り the dividend yield.

はいとく 背徳 (不道徳) immorality.
● 背徳行為 《書》 immoral conduct; an immoral act.

はいどく 拝読 ── **拝読する** 動 〖〖読む〗の謙譲語〗 read. (⇨ 読む)

ばいどく 梅毒 〖医学〗 syphilis /sífəlis/. ● 梅毒にかかる suffer from *syphilis*.
● 梅毒患者 a sỳphilític.

ハイドン 〖オーストリアの作曲家〗 Haydn /háidn/ (Franz Joseph 〜).

パイナップル (a) pineapple. (《!》 木・実は ⓒ, 果肉は ⓤ)

バイナリー (2 進法) 〖コンピュータ〗 binary.
● バイナリーフォーマット a binary format.

はいにち 排日 ── **排日の** 形 anti-Japanese. ● 排日運動を起こす start an *anti-Japanese* movement. ● 排日感情を起こさせる stir up 〖《やや書》 arouse〗 *anti-Japanese* feelings.

はいにょう 排尿 urination.
── **排尿する** 動 urinate; pass urine.
● 排尿障害 〖医学〗 urination trouble; dysuria.

はいにん 背任 (背信) (a) breach of trust; (公務員の不正行為) 〖法律〗 malfeasance /mælfíːzəns/. ● (特別)背任罪に問われる be charged with (special) *breach of trust* [*malfeasance in office*].

ばいにん 売人 a 《drug》dealer; a pusher; 《麻薬の》a 《drug》peddler 《話》pusher.

ハイネック ●ハイネックのセーター a high-necked sweater.

ハイパー ●ハイパーインフレ(ーション) hyper(-)inflation. ●ハイパーテキスト〖コンピュータ〗a hypertext. ●ハイパーマーケット〖巨大スーパー〗《英》a hypermarket. ●ハイパーリンク〖コンピュータ〗a hyperlink.

はいはい 這い這い 图 a baby's crawl.
── **這い這いする** 動 crawl.

*****ばいばい 売買** 图 buying and selling (❗語順に注意); 〖取り引き〗trade. ●売買契約を結ぶ make [strike] a bargain 《with him, about [over] goods》(⇨契約)
── **売買(を)する** 動 trade 《in》; deal 《in》; 《不正に》traffic 《in》. ▶彼は株の売買をしている《扱っている》He deals in stocks and shares. ▶おれは盗品の売買はしない I don't buy or sell stolen articles. (❗否定語の後では and でなく or を用いる)
●売買益 tráding pròfits. ●売買価格 a tráde [sélling] price. ●売買高 (出来高) a sales amount; trading value [volume]; a turnover. ●売買単位 the unit of trading; a round lot. ●売買手数料 sales [(仲介) broker's] commission; brokerage.

ばいばい 倍倍 ▶倍倍ゲームで(=急激に)売り上げが伸びた The sales increased very rapidly.

バイバイ 《話》bye-bye. ●(1)大人が使うと子供っぽく響く. (2)正式には Good-bye. (3)《話》Bye (now)./See you. などは親しい者同士で用いるのが普通) ▶バイバイ, じゃあまた木曜日 Bye! See you on Thursday!

バイパス a bypass. ●バイパスを通る take the bypass. ●心臓のバイパス手術を受ける undergo a heart bypass (operation); have heart bypass surgery.

はいはん 背反 ── **背反する** 動 go against…; disobey. (⑧ 背(く), 背馳(ち))

はいばん 廃盤 图 廃盤になる〔なっている〕go [be] out of press. ▶そのCDは廃盤となった They stopped producing the CD.

はいはんちけん 廃藩置県 〖歴史〗the abolition of domains and establishment of prefectures.

はいび 配備 (軍の)deployment.
── **配備する** 動 ▶軍隊をベルリンに配備する deploy [(部署につかせる)《やや書》station] troops in Berlin.

はいび 拝眉 (⇨ 拝顔)

ハイヒール high heels, high-heeled shoes; 《和製語》high heel.

ハイビジョン a high-definition television (略 HDTV). (参考) Hi-Vision は日本での商標名)

ハイビスカス 〖植物〗a hibiscus.

ハイピッチ a fast pace; 《ボートをこぐときの》a fast stroke; 《和製語》a high pitch. ▶新しい道路の工事がハイピッチで進んでいる Work on the new road is progressing at a fast pace.

はいびょう 肺病 〖古〗consumption. (⇨結核)

はいひん 廃品 waste [useless] articles; (がらくた) junk. (⇨ 屑(くず), ごみ) ●廃品を回収〔再生利用〕する collect [recycle] waste articles.
●廃品回収業者 a junk dealer.
●廃品 an article for sale; 《揭示》For Sale. (⑳ 非売品)

はいふ 肺腑 ❶〖肺臓〗a lung. (⇨肺)
❷〖心の奥底〗▶肺腑をえぐるような悲痛な叫び a heartbreaking grievous cry.
●肺腑を衝(つ)く 《深く感動させる》move [touch, impress] 《him》deeply; 《非常に驚かす》astonish 《him》; surprise 《him》greatly.

はいふ 配布, 配付 图 《やや書》a distribution.
── **配布〔配付〕する** 動 《手渡す》hand … out; 《配る》give … out; 《分け与える》distribute 《to, among》. ●解答用紙をクラスの全生徒に配布する hand 〔《米》pass〕out answer sheets to all the students in the class.
●配布資料 a handout.

パイプ 〖管〗a pipe; 〖たばこの〗(刻みたばこの) a (tobacco) pipe; (紙巻きたばこの) a cigarette holder. ●パイプにたばこをつめる fill one's pipe. ●パイプに火をつける light one's pipe. ●パイプをくわえて with a pipe in one's mouth [between one's teeth]. ●パイプをふかす smoke a pipe. ●石油をパイプ輸送する pipe petroleum 《to a port》. ▶排水パイプが詰まった The drain pipe was stopped [clogged] up. ▶彼は労使間のパイプ役(=仲介役)を果たした He acted as (a) go-between [acted as (an) intermediary, played an intermediary role] between management and labor.
●パイプ椅子 a steel chair.

ハイファイ hi-fi 《high-fidelity の略》.
●ハイファイ装置 a hi-fi. ▶彼女の歌がハイファイ装置から流れている She's singing on the hi-fi. ●ハイファイビデオ a hi-fi video.

ハイファイブ 《主に米》a high five. (参考)(1) スポーツで得点したときなどに手を上げてパチンと打ち合わせて祝福する. (2) 日本語ではハイタッチともいう. (3) 両手を上げるのは a high ten)

パイプオルガン 〖楽器〗a pipe organ.

ハイフォン 〖ベトナムの都市〗Haiphong.

パイプカット 〖精管切除〗〖医学〗a vaséctomy. ●パイプカットをしている〔してもらう〕have a vasectomy; 《話》have one's tubes cut.

はいふく 拝復 (❗この語に相当する英語はない. 拝啓と同じく Dear を用いる.「7月10日付のお手紙の返事として」in answer [reply, response] to your letter of July 10th などの書き出しでその気持ちを表すことができる) (⇨拝啓)

はいぶつ 廃物 waste materials [articles]; (a) waste ▶しばしば複数形で用. (⇨廃品)
●廃物利用 the recycling of waste materials.

はいぶつきしゃく 廃仏毀釈 〖歴史〗the anti-Buddhist movement in the early Meiji era.

パイプライン 〖油送管〗a pipeline.

ハイブリッド 〖混種の〗hybrid.
●ハイブリッドカー a (gas(oline)-electric) hybrid [a two-powered] car. ●ハイブリッドコンピュータ a hybrid computer.

バイブル 〖聖書〗the Bible ●〖特定分野の権威書〗a bible. ▶これは釣り人のバイブルだ This is the angler's bible.

バイブレーション 〖振動〗(a) vibrátion.

バイブレーター 〖電気マッサージ器〗a víbrator.

ハイブロー 图 〖知識人ぶる人〗《しばしば軽蔑的》a highbrow /háibràu/. (⑳ インテリ)
── **ハイブローの** 形 highbrow.

ハイフン a hyphen. 《巻末 〖句読法〗》●ハイフンでつなぐ join [connect] 《words》with a hyphen [hyphens]; hyphenate. ●ハイフンでつながれた語 a hyphenated word. ●ハイフンで分綴(ぶんてつ)する devide 《a word》with a hyphen. (❗行末で chil-dren と区切るなど)

*****はいぶん 配分** 图 《やや書》(an) allocation, 《やや書》(a) distribution, a division, a share. 《いずれの語も「配分量」の意で C. 複数形なし) (⇨ 動) ●利益の配分にあずかる have one's share in [of] the profits. ▶走者はペース配分を誤った The runner

could not control his [her] pace well.
— **配分する** 動 (権ληνα者が分配量を決めて)(やや書) állocate; (分散したものに) distribute; (分割する) divide, share. ●難民に食物や衣料を配分する *distribute [allocate]* food and clothes *to* the refugees. ●利益を均等に配分する *divide [share]* the profits equally.

ばいぶん 売文 图
●売文の徒 a hack writer; a (literary) hack.

ハイペース 《*at*》a fast pace;《和製語》a high pace. ▶彼は 30 キロ地点までハイペースで快調に飛ばした He ran *fast [at a fast pace]* and in good form as far as the 30 kilometer mark.

はいべん 排便 图《書》(have) a bowel movement; (an) evacuation.
— **排便する** 動 move one's bowels;《書》evacuate the bowels.

はいほう 肺胞 〖解剖〗pulmonary alveoli (単 alveolus). (❗通例複数形で)

ハイボール a whiskey and /ən/ soda; (主に米) a highball.

*****はいぼく 敗北** 图 (a) defeat; (a) loss. ●敗北を認める admit (one's) *defeat*. ▶戦いは彼らの敗北に終わった The battle ended in their *defeat*.
— **敗北する** 動 ▶彼は選挙で敗北した He *suffered* (a) *defeat [was defeated,* ×*defeated]* in the election./He *lost* 《*to* the rival candidate in》the election.
●敗北者 a loser. ●敗北宣言 a public concession of defeat. ●敗北宣言をする concede defeat《*in* an election》. (❗concede は「不本意ながら認める」の意)

はいほん 配本 图 distribution of books. ●漱石全集の第 1 回配本 the first volume *to be distributed* of the Complete Works of Soseki.
— **配本する** 動 distribute books《*to* him [bookstores]》.

ハイミス an unmarried [a single] woman;《和製語》a high Miss. (⇨オールドミス)

はいめい 拝命 — **拝命する** 動 〖「命令を受ける」の意の謙譲語〗 ▶藤原氏は国連日本代表を拝命した(＝任命を受けた) Mr. Fujiwara *was appointed* a Japanese delegate to the United Nations.

ばいめい 売名 (自己宣伝) self-advertisement; (知名度を高めること) publicity. ▶彼は売名のために老人ホームに 1,000 万円を寄付した He contributed ten million yen to the nursing home to *attract the public's attention [seek publicity].*
●売名行為 (do) a publicity stunt.

はいめん 背面 the back; the rear. (⇨背後)
●背面攻撃 a rear attack. ●背面跳び (走り高跳びの) a Fosbury flop.

はいもん 肺門 〖解剖〗the hilum /háiləm/ of a lung. ●肺門リンパ腺炎〖医学〗hilar lymphadenitis.

ハイヤー a hired car. (❗解説 米英にはハイヤー制度はない) ●ハイヤーを雇う (運転手つきで車を借りる) hire a car [高級車] a limousine》with a chauffeur; (タクシーを頼む) hire a taxi. (❗車だけを借りるなら rent a car)

バイヤー 〖買い手〗a buyer.

はいやく 配役 the cast (❗集合的に用い単・複両扱い); (配役をする) casting. ▶劇の配役を決める decide the *cast* of a play; cast a play. ▶配役はプログラムに載っている The *cast* is [are] listed on the program. ▶その映画は配役がまずい[よい] The movie is miscast [well cast].

はいやく 売約 ▶売約済み〖掲示〗Sold.

ばいやく 売薬 a patent /pǽtnt/ médicine; (処方箋(ｾﾝ)なしで売買できる) an over-the-còunter médicine.

*****はいゆう 俳優** (男, 女) an actor, (女) an actress. (⇨役者[類語]) ●映画俳優 a movie *actor [actress]*. ●舞台俳優 a stage *actor [actress]*. ●俳優養成所 a school of acting.

ばいよう 培養 图 (微生物や組織の) culture; cultivation.
— **培養する** 動 culture [cultivate] 《bacteria》.
●培養液 a cúlture sòlution ●培養基 a cúlture mèdium. ●培養土 compost.

ハイライト 〖ひときわ目だつ部分〗a highlight ●今週のニュースハイライト the news *highlights* of this week.

はいらん 排卵 图 ovulation. ●無排卵 〖医学〗 anovulation.
— **排卵する** 動 ovulate.
●排卵期 an ovulatory phase. ●排卵誘発剤 an ovulation inducer; 《俗に》a fertility drug [pill].

はいり 背理 图 irrationality; illogicality.
— **背理の** 形 irrational; illogical.

はいりこむ 入り込む get* in [into ...]; (こっそりと) sneak in [into ...]. (⇨入る❶)

ハイリスク 〖危険率の高い〗high-risk. ●ハイリスクハイリターン high-risk, high-return.

ばいりつ 倍率 ❶〖レンズなどの〗〖光学〗 a magnification; magnifying power. ●倍率 200 倍の望遠鏡 a 200-*power* telescope; a telescope with a magnification of two hundred. (❗記号としては × 200 と表し, by two hundred と読む) ▶このレンズの倍率はいくらですか What is the *power* of this lens?
❷〖競争率〗 ▶その大学の入試は毎年倍率が高い There's a lot of *competition* for admission to the college every year.

*****はいりょ 配慮** 图 〖思いやり〗thoughtfulness, consideration《*for*》; 〖心遣い〗《書》regard; 〖注意〗 attention; 〖骨折り〗 trouble. ▶彼は病気болеの妻への配慮が欠けている He lacks *thoughtfulness [regard] for* his sickly wife./He *is not attentive to* his sickly wife. ▶いろいろご配慮いただきありがとうございます Thank you very much for all the *trouble* you've taken for me. ▶上記の件につきご配慮のほどお願いいたします Thank you for your *attention* to this matter.
— **配慮する** 動 〖思いやる〗 be thoughtful《*of*》; 〖考慮に入れる〗consider, take*... into consideration [account]; 〖手配する〗arrange; 〖気をつける, 取り計らう〗(やや書) see* (to it) that ... 〖(話) では to it または that を省略する〗;〖骨を折る〗take trouble. ●彼の気持ちを配慮する *be thoughtful of [consider]* his feelings. ▶判決を下す際に彼の若さに配慮する *take* his youth *into consideration [take into consideration* (the fact) *that* he is young] in passing sentence. ▶迎えの車が来るよう配慮ください Please *arrange [make arrangements]* for a car to come for me./Please *see to it that* a car comes for me. (❗that 節に未来を示す助動詞を用いるのはまれ)

はいりょう 拝領 — **拝領する** 動 ▶これは彼が主君から拝領した刀だ This is the sword the lord *bestowed on* him.

ばいりん 梅林 an *ume* grove.

バイリンガル ▶うちの孫は日本語とフランス語のバイリンガルです Our grandson is *bilingual* in Japanese and French.
— **バイリンガルの** 形 bilingual.

はいる 入る

INDEX

❶ 中へ
❷ 着く
❸ 会などに
❹ 収容できる
❺ 中に持っている
❻ ある時期・状態になる
❼ 手に入る
❽ 取り付ける
❾ その他の表現

WORD CHOICE 入る

enter 人・乗り物などが, 特定の建物・場所などの内部に入ること。書き言葉で多く用いる。●私はその建物に入った I *entered* the building.

come in 人・物が内部に入ること。内部にいる人の視点に基づく表現。●彼がドアから入ってきた He *came in* by the door. ▶お入りなさい *Come in*. (!) 中にいる人が外にいる人を部屋などに呼び入れられる)

go in 人・物が内部に入ること。外部にいる人の視点に基づく表現。●彼らは部屋の中に入った They *went in* [*into*] the room. ▶中に入りましょうか Shall we *go in*?

頻度チャート

enter ████████████████████
come in █████████
go in ████

  20 40 60 80 100 (%)

❶【中へ】come* in [into ...]; go* in [into ...]; (歩いて) walk in [into ...];《やや書》enter (!) come [go] into ... のいずれの意にも用いられる [⇒類語]; (入り込む) get* in [into ...]. ▶どうぞお入りください *Come* (*on*) ╲*in*, ╱*please*. (!) *on* は強調を表す) ▶ここから入らないでください〔掲示〕Use another door. (!) 日本語との発想の違いに注意 (⇒① [第7文例]))

① 【...に[へ]入る】 ▶彼が部屋に入ってきた He *came into* [*entered*, ×entered into] the room. (!) enter は他動詞なので into は不要) ▶だれもそこには入れないよ No one can *go in* there. ▶列車はトンネルに入った The train *went into* [*went in*, *entered*] the tunnel. ▶彼は窓から中へ入った He *went in* [*went inside*, *got in*, *entered*] through the window. (!) 目的語がないので ×... went [got] *into* は不可) ▶彼はこっそり部屋に入った He *walked* [*stepped*] *into* the room stealthily./He *stole* [*slipped*, *sneaked*] *into* the room. ▶靴に水が入った Some water *got into* [*in*] my shoes. ▶芝生に入るべからず〔掲示〕*Keep off* the grass. (!) 通例 ×Don't enter [step on] the grass. とはいわない。(「(公園に) 犬を連れて入らないでください」は *Keep* the dog *out*.)

② 【...が入る】 ▶泥棒が裏口から入った (押し入った) A burglar *broke into* my house by [×from] the back door. ▶泥棒が入ってこないように部屋には鍵をしておきなさい Lock your room in order to *keep* burglars *out* [*from breaking in*]. ▶この窓からは私の部屋に十分な日光が入らない This window doesn't *let in* [《やや書》*admit*] enough sunlight to my room. ▶新鮮な空気が入るように窓を開けておいた I kept the window open to *get* some fresh air (*in*). (!) ... so that some fresh air would *come in*. より普通)

❷【着く】arrive; (駅・港などに) come* in. ▶列車が3番ホームに入ってきた The train *arrived* [*came in*, *pulled in*] at track 3./The train *came* [*pulled*] *into* track 3. ▶あす2隻の船がこの港に入る Two ships will *arrive at* [*come into*, *enter*] this port tomorrow. ▶注文していた部品は入りましたか Did the part I ordered *come in* [*arrive*]?/Did you get the part I ordered in?

❸【会などに】get* in [into ...],《やや書》enter; (許可されて)《やや書》be admitted to ...; (受け入れられる) be accepted; (手続きをして) enroll; (参加する) join; (職業などにつく) go* into .... ●実業界 [政界] に入る *go into* business [politics]. ▶彼はハーバード大学に入った He *got into* [*entered*, *was admitted to*, *was accepted to*] Harvard University./He *enrolled in* Harvard University. ▶この券で2人美術館に入れます This ticket *admits* two people *to* the museum. ▶どんなクラブ[会社]に入るつもりですか What club [company] are you going to *join* [*enter*]? ▶ぼくはテニス部に入っている I *am a member of* [*am in*] the tennis club./I *belong* [×*am belonging*] *to* the tennis club.

❹【収容できる】(場所・容器が) (can) hold*; (場所・乗り物が)《やや書》(can) accommodate; (座席を持つ) seat; (...の余地がある)《やや書》admit (-tt-). ▶このホールは 1,000 人入る This hall *can hold* [*can accommodate*, *seats*, *admits*] one thousand people. (!) *holds*, *accommodates* も可だが, holds は「実際に入っている」の意にもなりあいまい) ▶スペースが小さすぎて本箱が入らない(収まらない) The space is too small, and the bookcase won't *go in*./ The space is *too* small *for* the bookcase. ▶荷物は座席の下に入らなかった The baggage didn't *fit* under my seat. (!) fit は「大きさが合う」こと)

❺【中に持っている】have*; contain; (全体の一部として含む) include. (!) 以下いずれも進行形不可) ▶ポケットに何が入っているの What do you *have* in your pocket?/What is in your pocket? ▶ぼくの下着はどの引き出しに入っているの Which drawer *has* my underwear? ▶このタンクにはどのくらい水が入っていますか How much water does this tank *contain*? ▶その料金にはサービス料が入っている The service charge *is included in* the price. ▶それらは同じ部類に入る They are *included* [They *come*] *under* the same category. ▶そのビルの地階にエスニック料理の店がいくつか入っている The underground floor of the building *houses* several ethnic restaurants.

❻【ある時期・状態になる】●新しい局面に入る *enter upon* a new phase. ●宇宙時代に入る *enter* the space age. ▶例年より早く梅雨に入った The rainy season *has set in* earlier than usual. (!) set in は通例好ましくない季節などが始まることをいう) ▶当地は今雨季に入っている We *are* now *in* the rainy season. ▶もう10月に入ろうとしていた It was almost the *beginning* of October. ▶今イチゴは最盛期に入っている[入った] Strawberries are now *in* [*has just come into*] season. ▶我々はすぐ討論に入った(始めた) We soon *began to* discuss it [*began* our discussion,《書》*enter into* our discussion].

❼【手に入れる】come* into one's hands; (手に入れる) get*,《やや書》obtain; (差し出されて受け取る) receive (!) get より堅い語). ▶結局その宝石は我々の手に入った The jewel *came into* our hands after all./We *got* [*obtained*] the jewel after all. ▶彼は月に 3,000 ドル入ります He *gets* [*receives*, (収入がある) *has an income of*] 3,000 dollars a month.

❽【取り付ける】install. ▶その家にはいつ電話が入りますか When will the telephone *be installed* in this house?/《人が主語》When can we *get* the telephone *installed* in this house?

❾ [その他の表現] ・競走で3位に入る *come in third* [*take third*] *in the race.* ・火災保険に入る *take out* [《米》 *buy, get*] *fire insurance.* ▶私の傘にお入りなさい *Get under* [×*in,* ×*into*] *my umbrella.* ▶早くお入りなさい Hurry (up) and *take a bath.* (❗「浴槽に入る」は *get into the bathtub*) ▶入ってます(トイレで)Wait [Just] a moment, please. / It's taken [occupied]. ▶私の家はその通りを少し入ったところです My house *is a little way from the street.* ▶あの家は今だれも人が入っていない(=空いている)The house *is vacant* [*empty*]. ▶我がチームは最終回に5点入った(=得点した) Our team *scored* five runs in the last inning. ❗私の run は野球・クリケットなどの得点(⇨点)▶仏教は朝鮮から日本に入った(=伝わった) Buddhism *was introduced into* Japan from Korea. ▶目に何か入ってI've got something in my eye. ▶彼は酒が入るとけんかっぱやくなる He gets quarrelsome when he *drinks*. ▶お茶が入りました I've made (the) tea. /(お茶の用意ができました) Tea *is ready.*

パイル [けば立てた布地] (a) pile.
・パイル織り (a) pile weave.
はいれい 拝礼 — **拝礼する** 動 pray; worship. (⇨拝む, 礼拝)
ハイレグ ・ハイレグの水着 a *high-cut* swimsuit.
*****はいれつ 配列** 图 (an) arrangement. ・机の配列を変える change the *arrangement* of desks.
— **配列する** 動 ・コインを大きさの順に配列する *arrange* coins according to [in order of] *size*.
ハイレベル ・ハイレベルの問題 (レベルの高い) a *high-level* question. (⇨レベル)
はいろ 廃炉 the decommissioning of a nuclear reactor. ・廃炉にする decommission.
パイロット a pilot. ・ジェット機のパイロット a jet *pilot*.
・パイロットプラント [試験的生産工場] a pilot plant.
・パイロットランプ [表示灯] a pilot lamp [light]. (❗後の方は「(ガス器具の)口火」の意でも用いられる)
パイロン (飛行場の目標塔, 高圧線の鉄塔) a pylon; (道路の標識塔) a pylon, a (traffic) cone.
パイン [パイナップル] (a) pineapple. ・パインジュース pineapple juice;《和製語》pine juice.
バインダー [紙ばさみ, 農機] a binder.
*****はう 這う ❶** [虫・動物・人が] creep*; crawl.

> **使い分け creep** 主に足のある動物や人間がこっそりと進むこと. 水や影などが地面をはうように動く様子を表すことも多い.
> **crawl** 蛇などが腹をすって進むこと. 虫や人間に用いると, 身体を地面に近づけ手足を使って進むことを表す.

・四つんばいではう *crawl on* all fours [one's hands and knees]. ▶蛇ははって動く Snakes *crawl*. ▶赤ん坊は部屋の中をはい回った The baby *crawled* [*crept*] *around* in the room. ▶私のアパートはゴキブリがはい回っている(うようよしている) My apartment *is crawling with* cockroaches. ▶壊れた自動車からけがをした男がはい出してきた The injured man *crawled* [*struggled*, ×*crept*] *out of* the damaged car.
❷ [ツタなどが] creep*, 《やや書》 trail 《*along, over*》. ▶ツタが柵(%)をはい始めた The vines are beginning to *creep* [*trail*] *over* the fence.
ハウス [家] a house (懇 houses /-zɪz, 《米》-sɪz/); [温室に] a greenhouse. (懇 大きい) a hothouse. ・ハウス栽培のトマト *hothouse* tomatoes.
・ハウスキーパー [家政婦] a housekeeper. ・ハウスクリーニング [清掃代行業] a housecleaning sèrvice. ・ハウスダスト [室内のほこり] house dust. ・ハウスマヌカン [ブティックの店員] a boutique salesclerk; a

salesclerk [《英》a shop assistant] in a boutique;《和製語》a house mannequin.
はうた 端唄 *hauta*;(説明的に) a short Japanese traditional song sung to the samisen.
パウダー powder.
・パウダースノー [粉雪] powder (snow).
ハウツーもの a how-to book [video] 《*on*》.
バウンド (a) bounce, a bound. ・前の方が普通
・イレギュラーバウンド a bad hop [bounce]. ・ワンバウンドでボールを捕る catch the ball on the first [on one] *bounce*. ・ノーバウンドでライナーを捕る catch a liner on the fly. ▶ライトから三塁へツーバウンドでボールが返ってきた The right fielder threw a two-hopper to third base.
— **バウンドする** 動 bounce; bound. (⇨弾む) ・ボールがフェンスを越えた [フェンスから返って来た] The ball *bounced over* the fence [*back from the wall*]. ▶ボールはショートの前でイレギュラーバウンドした The ball took a bad *bounce* [*hop*] in front of the shortstop.
パウンドケーキ (a) pound cake.
*****はえ 蝿** [昆虫] a fly. ・ハエをたたく flap [swat] a *fly*.
・ハエを取る catch a *fly*. ▶その部屋にはハエがぶんぶん飛び回っていた *Flies* were buzzing around in the room. ▶ハエがごみの山にいっぱいたかっていた There was a cloud [a swarm] of *flies* on the heap of garbage.
・ハエたたき a flyswatter, a flapper. ・ハエ取り紙 (a) flypaper.
はえ 栄え 图 (an) honor. (⇨光栄)
・栄えある 形 glorious; honorable.
はえかわる 生え変わる (永久歯に) get* one's permanent teeth;(羽毛・毛・角が) molt.
はえぎわ 生え際 a hairline. ▶彼は生え際が少し後退している His *hairline* is receding a bit.
はえなわ 延縄 a longline.
・延縄漁業 longline fishing. ・延縄漁船 a longline fishing boat;《主に米》a longliner.
はえぬき 生え抜き 形 ・生え抜きの(=最初から外交を職業としている)外交官 a career /kəríər/ *diplomat*. ・生え抜きの(=(生(ᵏ)っ粋の)江戸っ子 (書) a *trueborn* Tokyoite /tóukiouàɪt/. (⇨生っ粋)
パエリヤ [<スペイン語] [サフランで香りをつけた煮込みご飯] a paella /pɑːélə/.
*****はえる 生える** [成育する] grow*; [芽を出す] sprout,(急に) spring* up; [歯が] come* in. (↔come [fall] out) (⇨歯 ❶ ❷) ▶雑草はどこにでも生える Weeds *grow* [*sprout*] everywhere. ▶うちの子は最初の歯が生えた Our baby *has grown* [*has cut*] his [her] first teeth. ▶雑草が家の庭一面に生えている Our garden *is covered* [*is overgrown*] *with* weeds.
はえる 映える, 栄える ❶ [輝く](輝く) shine*;(照り輝く) glow. ・夕日に映える山々 the mountains *shining* [*glowing*] in the setting sun.
❷ [引き立つ] be shown to (good) advantage;(よく似合っている) look attractive [very nice]. ▶京子がそのドレスを着ると栄える(=きれいに見える) Kyoko *looks beautiful* [*nice*] in that dress. /That dress *looks nice* [*good*] on Kyoko.
はおう 覇王 a powerful king.
パオズ 包子 [<中国語] (説明的に) a Chinese-style bun stuffed with bean jum or meat.
はおと 羽音 (虫の) the buzz [the hum] 《*of bees*》;(鳥の) the flap [the flutter] 《*of wings*》. ・羽音を立てる (虫が) buzz, hum;(鳥が) flap, flutter.
はおり 羽織 a *haori* (coat);(説明的に) a half-length

はおる 羽織る ●コートを羽織る(着る) put on [ぱっと羽織る] fling on] a coat. ●羽織袴を着た新郎 a bridegroom dressed in *haori* and *hakama* [in a formal Japanese *kimono*].

はか 墓 a grave (!遺体を埋葬するために地中に掘られた穴. 広義で墓所をさす); a tomb /túːm/ (!特に墓石のあるものや, 埋葬室のある大きな墓). ●一族の墓 a family *tomb*. ●墓を掘る dig a *grave*. ●墓を作る build a *tomb*. ●古代の王の墓を発掘する excavate the *tomb* of an ancient king. ●墓参りをする visit ⟨his⟩ *grave* [*tomb*]. ▶彼の遺体はこの墓に眠って[埋葬されて]いる His remains rest [are buried] in this *grave*. (!remains は複数扱い).
●墓石 a gravestone; a tombstone. ●墓場 a graveyard.

はか ●はかが行く(仕事が順調に進む) (⇨捗(はかど)る)

***ばか** 馬鹿 名 ❶ [愚かな人] a fool; 《話》a stupid (!呼びかけにも用いる); an idiot;《話》a blockhead; (うすばか) a half-wit.

【使い分け】fool 最も一般的な語. 特に, 知力はあっても常識的な判断ができない人をさすことが多い.
idiot もともと「白痴」の意だが《話》では fool より強い意味で用いる.
blockhead 「頭が悪い」というニュアンスがあり, 男が男に面と向かって喧嘩腰に呼ばれすることが多い.

●ばかみたいに安い家賃で at an *absurdly* low rent.
▶彼はばかではない(利口ともかぎらない) He isn't a *fool*./(はかどころか利口だ) He is no *fool*. (!前の方も He is nót a *fool*. とすると後のほぼ同意になる).
▶このばかめ You *fool* [*idiot, blockhead*]! (!呼びかけのときは無冠詞) ●そんな間違いをするなんて彼はなんてばかなんだ What a *fool* he is to make such a mistake!/How *foolish* he is [(it is) of him] to make a mistake like that! (!感嘆文では it は通例省略する (⇨形)) ●私はそんなふうに金を浪費するようなばかではない I'm not so *foolish* as [I know better than] to waste my money on such trifles. ▶どこのばかがこんなことをしたのか What [×Where] *fool* has done this?

❷ [愚かなこと] foolishness, stupidity; (まったく意味をなさないこと) nonsense. ●ばかを言う (⇨形) ●彼のばかさかげんにあきれる be amazed at his *foolishness* [*stupidity*].

❸ [その他の表現] ▶このねじはばかになっている This screw doesn't *work*!/The threads on this screw *are stripped*.
●馬鹿とはさみは使いよう 《ことわざ》 Praise a fool, and you may make him useful.
●馬鹿につける薬はない There's no cure for a fool.
●馬鹿の一つ覚え 《ことわざ》 He that knows little often repeats it. ▶カラオケではばかの一つ覚えみたいに例の歌をうたった I sang the only song I knew like a cuckoo at the karaoke party. (!「かっこうのように」は「いつも同じ歌をうたう」の意)
●馬鹿を見る ▶彼を信じてばかを見た I *felt like a fool* trusting him.
──馬鹿な 形 foolish; stupid; silly; absurd; ridiculous. (⇨馬鹿馬鹿しい, 馬鹿げた, 馬鹿らしい)

【使い分け】foolish 常識・判断力のないこと.
stupid 生まれつき知能の低いこと. foolish より意味の強い語として用いることも多い.
silly 愚かで軽蔑されるほどばかげたこと. foolish より意味が弱く主観的な語.
absurd 途方もないほど不合理なこと.
ridiculous 嘲笑(ちょうしょう)をさそうほどばかげていること.

●ばかな男 a *foolish* [a *stupid*, a *silly*, an *absurd*, a *brainless*] man. ●ばかな考え a *stupid* [an *absurd*, a *ridiculous*] idea. ●ばかなことをする do a *foolish* [a *stupid*, a *silly*, an *absurd*] thing; play [act] the *fool*; make a *fool* of oneself; commit a *folly*. ▶ばかなことを言うな Don't say *silly* things!/Don't be *foolish* [*stupid, silly, absurd, ridiculous*]. (!(1) ridiculous には「ばかなことをするな」の意にもなる. (2) 肯定文で Be [Get] serious! のようにも言える)/(無意味なことをいうな) Don't talk *nonsense*. ▶二重にお金を払うなんて彼はばかだ It's *foolish* of him to pay for it again./He's *foolish* [a *fool*] to pay [(話)(by) pay*ing*] for it again. (!(1) stupid, silly, absurd, ridiculous もこの型可. (2) 一般に形式主語 it を用いる型の方が普通. その際, 音声上の休止を置くとすれば「of+人」の後. また「of+人」は文脈から myらのそれも省略可)/It's *ridiculous* that he *should* pay [It's *ridiculous for* him *to* pay] for it again. (!(1) 同様の型は silly も可. foolish, stupid は後の不定詞の型は可能だが, that 節を従える型は foolish は通例不可, stupid はまれ. (2) 不定詞が続く場合, 音声上の休止を置くとすれば ridiculous の後)

【会話】「彼は君のせいだと言ってるよ」「そんなばかな」"He says it's your fault." "How *ridiculous*!/What *nonsense*!"

【会話】「首にされたよ」「そんなばかな」"They've fired me." "They haven't!/(信じられない) I can't believe you [it]./(ひどい) That's too much."

──馬鹿に 副 (⇨馬鹿に)
──馬鹿にする 動 (笑いものにする) make* a fool 《of》; (虚仮(こけ)にする) play games 《with》. ▶ばかにするな Don't *make a fool of* me. ●彼はみんなにばかにされたくなかった He didn't like to *be made a fool of* [(笑われる) *be laughed at*, (軽蔑される) *be looked down on*] by everyone. ●おれをばかにしたらあとで後悔することになるぞ You *play games with* me and you'll be sorry for it.

ばか- 馬鹿- ●ばか力 enormous strength. ●ばか丁寧 excessive politeness. ●ばか話《話》chit-chat.
●ばかでかいバスケットボールの選手 a *really huge* basketball player. ●ばか笑いする laugh [《書》 guffaw /gʌfɔ́ː/] loudly; laugh oneself silly.

ばかあたり 馬鹿当たり 名 (大当たり) a (huge [hot]) box-office; a smash [a big] hit.
──馬鹿当たりする 動 《米》 go over with a bang; 《英》 go (off) with a bang. ▶その映画はばか当たりした The film *went with a bang*./The film was a *smash hit* [*a box-office success*].

***はかい** 破壊 名 destruction. ●環境破壊 the *destruction* of the environment; environmental *destruction*.
──破壊的な 形 destructive.
──破壊する 動 (完全に破壊する) destroy; (部分的に壊す) damage; (使いものにならなくする) ruin; (めちゃくちゃにする) wreck. (⇨形) ●ビルを破壊する *destroy* a building; (古い建物などを取り壊す) demolish [*tear down, pull down*] a building. ●開発という名のもとに自然を破壊する *destroy* [*ruin*, ×*damage*, ×*wreck*] nature under the pretext of development. ▶アフガニスタンのバーミヤンの大仏像が破壊された Giant [Great] Statues of Buddha at Bamiyan in Afghanistan *were destroyed*.
●破壊力 destructive power.

はかい 破戒 【仏教】 transgression of a commandment.
●破戒僧 a sinful priest.

はかい 『破戒』 *The Broken Commandment*. 【参考】

島崎藤村の小説

はがいじめ 羽交い絞め ●羽交いにする get a full nelson 《on him》.

ばかがい 馬鹿貝 〖魚介〗a surf clam. 【参考】肉はアオヤギ

***はがき 葉書** a postcard, a card (**!**ともに《英》では主に私製はがきの意でしばしば絵はがきをさす.《米》では官製・私製の両方に用いられる).《官製はがき》《米》a postal card,《米話》a postal. ●往復はがき a reply-paid 《postal》card; a double postal card.【事情】米英にはない）●はがきを書く write a postcard. ●はがきを出す send 〖《話》drop〗《him》a postcard. ●はがきをもらう get [receive] a postcard《from him》.

はかく 破格 ── 破格の 形 extraordinary; （前例のない）unprécedented;（例外的な）exceptional;（特別の）special. ●破格の昇進をする get [obtain] an unprecedented [an exceptional] promotion. ●破格の待遇を受ける receive [enjoy] exceptionally good treatment. ●破格の安値で買う buy《it》at a specially low [reduced] price.

ばかくさい 馬鹿臭い absurd.（⇨馬鹿らしい）

はがくれ 葉隠れ hiding among the leaves.

はかげ 葉陰 ●葉陰で under the leaves.

ばかげた 馬鹿げた foolish.（⇨馬鹿な）

ばかさわぎ 馬鹿騒ぎ 名 high jinks; horseplay;（飲酒で）a drinking spree.
── 馬鹿騒ぎの 形 horseplayful.
── 馬鹿騒ぎする 動 have a wild party (**!**wild は「無礼講の」の意);《話》horse around. ▶今夜は飲んでばか騒ぎしよう Let's go out on the spree [《主に英話》razzle] tonight.

ばかしょうじき 馬鹿正直 simple-minded honesty. ▶彼ははか正直だ He's extremely honest (and simple)./He's too honest.

はかす 捌かす （水を）drain water 《out of the mine》;（商品を売り尽くす）sell out 《of》. ▶シャツは全部捌かした We've sold out of all the shirts.

***はがす 剥がす** take*... off, remove;（裂くように）tear* /téər/,（むき取るように）peel 《off, from》;（こすって）scrape 《off》.（⇨剥（は）ぐ）●切手をそっとはがす take off [remove] the postage stamp carefully. ●壁のペンキをはがす scrape the paint off the wall; strip the paint [off] the wall.

ばかす 化かす bewitch. ●キツネに化かされる be bewitched by a fox.

ばかず 場数 ▶彼は場数を踏んでいる（長い実地経験がある）He has a lot of experience./He is rich in experience./（困難な経験を重ねている）He has gone through a lot.

はかせ 博士 a doctor (**!**肩書きのときは Dr. を氏名の前にづける);〖物知り〗a well-informed person (⇨物知り). ●文学博士 a Doctor of Literature [Letters].（**!**肩書きは D.Lit. [Litt.]）●医学博士 a Doctor of Medicine.（**!**肩書きは M.D., MD）●理学博士 a Doctor of Science.（**!**肩書きは Sc.D., ScD）●湯川(秀樹)博士 Dr.（Hideki）Yukawa. ●K 大学から〖で〗法学の博士号を取る take [get, obtain, receive] a doctor's degree [a Ph.D.] in law from [at] K University. ●博士課程を終える complete a doctoral program [xa doctor's course]《in》.（⇨ドクター〖ドクターコース〗）●博士号 a degree of doctor; a doctor's [a doctoral] degree; a doctrate; a Ph.D. /pi:eɪtʃdi:/;《Doctor of Philosophy の略》(**!**(1) 文系理系ともに用いる. (2) 肩書きのときは K. Abe, Ph.D. のように氏名の後につける). ●博士論文 a doctoral dissertation [《英》thesis].

はがた 歯形 (かみ跡) a toothprint; a tooth mark.

はがた 歯型 （歯科治療用）a die; an impression.

はかたおび 博多帯 ●博多織の帯 an obi traditionally woven on the loom at Hakata.

はかたにんぎょう 博多人形 a Hakata doll.

ばかでかい 馬鹿でかい huge (great); enormous (great); great big (**!**以上の great は「いずれも大きさの強調語で口語表現」); gigantic;（衣服などが特大の）outsize(d).

***はかどる 捗る** ●いっこうにはかどらない make no [little] progress 《with, in》,（何の成果も得られない）get nowhere 《with, in》. ▶仕事ははかどっていますか How are you getting along [on] with your work?/Are you making (good) progress with your work?/Is your work getting along [on] nicely?

はかない 〖空しい〗empty, vain; 〖つかの間の〗fleeting, transient; 〖短命の〗short-lived. ●はかない夢 an empty dream. ●はかない人生 transient life. ●はかないつかの間の青春 fleeting youth. ●はかない幸福 short-lived happiness. ●人生にはかない望みを持つ have vain hopes of life.

はかなむ ●世をはかなんで自殺する（生きている上での希望を失って）lose all hope in life and kill oneself;（絶望して）kill oneself in despair. ▶世をはかなんで（＝絶望して）出家した I despaired of [(いやけがさして) got sick of] this world and entered a monastery [became a priest]. (**!**前の方は世間から離れて隠遁生活を送るのに対し, 後の方は主に一般社会の中で活動する)

ばかに 馬鹿に 〖ひどく〗terribly, awfully;（とても）very; 〖法外に〗unreasonably;（ばからしいまで）ridiculously. ●ばかにならない（＝相当な額のお金 a considerable sum of money. ▶ばかに疲れた I'm terribly [very] tired./I'm tired out./I'm completely exhausted. ▶値段がばかに高い The price is unreasonably high./It's an unreasonable price.

はがね 鋼 steel.
●はがね色 steel blue.

ぱかぱか （馬の歩く音）a clip-clop.

ばかばかしい 捗捗しい 〖急速な〗rapid, quick; 〖満足のいく〗satisfactory. ▶状況にはかばかしい進展がない There is no rapid improvement in the situation./（あまり進展がない）There isn't much improvement in the situation. ▶彼ははかばかしい返事をしなかった His answer was not [（とても…でない） far from] satisfactory. ▶商売ははかばかしくない（順調でない）The business is not doing well./（振るわない）The business is dull [slack].

ばかばかしい 馬鹿馬鹿しい （常識はずれで）absurd;（思慮不足で）silly;（こっけいな）ridiculous. ●ばかばかしい話 a silly talk. ●ばかばかしい高値 an absurdly high price. ▶ばかばかしい（What）nonsense!/How ridiculous!/Rubbish! ▶つまらないことをするのはばかばかしい It's silly to quarrel over trifles.
【会話】「オウムじゃあるまいし，彼のあとについて読むなんてばかばかしくて」「分かるか」"I feel silly [ridiculous] reading after him just like a parrot." "I know."

はかぶ 端株 〖株式〗an odd [a fractional,《米》broken] lot; a fractional stock [share].

はかま 袴 a hakama;（説明的に）a long pleated skirt-like garment worn over a kimono mainly on ceremonial occasions. ●はかまをはいている put on [wear] a hakama.

はがみ 歯噛み（⇨䵩 歯軋（ぎし）り）

ばかやろう 馬鹿野郎 You fool! (⇨馬鹿)
はがゆい be impatient.《口》じれったい、いらいら
はからい 計らい《尽力》《書》good offices. ▶彼の計らいでこの仕事を得た I've got this job through his *good offices*.
はからう 計らう 《...するよう気をつける》see* (to it) that ...; 《手はずをととのえる》arrange. (⇨取り計らう)
▶いいように計らいなさい See (to it) that everything is all right. (🛈(1) to it を省略する方が口語的. (2) 今では that 節に will などの未来を表す助動詞も用いられるようになってきている)
はからずも 図らずも 《思いがけなく》unexpectedly; 《偶然に》by chance, by accident. ▶図らずも私は役員に昇進した *Unexpectedly* I was promoted to be director. ▶図らずも（=偶然）彼に会った I *happened to see* him on the street./I *came across* [*ran into, bumped into*] him on the street.
*はかり 秤《米》a scale, 《英》scales (🛈単数扱い); 《てんびん》a balance, 《a pair of》scales; 《浴室用の体重計》《米》a bathroom scale, 《英》《a pair of》bathroom scales (🛈×a health meter). ●さお[台; ばね; 台所用]ばかり a beam [a platform; a spring; a kitchen] *scale*. ●はかりにかける《重さを計る》weigh 《meat》on the *scales* [*in the balance*]; 《比較する》*weigh* 《the costs》against [*compare* 《the costs》*with*] 《the profits》.
:–ばかり《副助詞》❶ 《およそ》《約》about, 《主に米》around, some (🛈some は数詞の前に限る); 《おおざっぱに》roughly, 《やや書》approximately; 《...かそこら》... or so. (⇨ほど) ▶風邪で3日ばかり学校を休みました I was absent from school for *about* [*around*] three days because of a cold. ▶この大学には5,000人ばかりの学生がいる There are *about* [*some*] 5,000 students in this college./This college has *roughly* 5,000 students.
❷ 《...のみ》《唯一の》only, 《やや書》sole; 《ほんの、単なる》mere 《以上はいずれも通例限定的です》; 《ただ...だけ》only, 《やや書》alone. (⇨–だけ) ▶女の子ばかりのバンド an *all-girl* band. ▶彼らは彼女にばかりつらく当たった They were hard on *only* her [*her alone*]. (🛈alone を用いる方が強意的) ▶その子は泣くばかりで何も言わなかった The child *only* cried and said nothing. ▶彼の語ることは昔の話ばかりだ The *only* thing he talks about is the past stories. 《話》He *ónly* talks about the old ╲days. ▶私に頼ってばかりいないで自分のことは自分でするようにしなさい You should not *keep* turning to me but try to take care of yourself. ▶計画はできた。後は実行に移すばかりだ Now that the plan is completed, *nothing remains but* to put it into practice. ▶その戦争は罪のない人々の命を奪ったばかりでなく、彼らが長い間守りきてきたりとあらゆるものをも破壊してしまった The war destroyed not only innocent people but also everything they had cherished for a long time. (🛈のみならず) ▶それだけじゃないよ、えらく費用がかかるんだ And that's *not all*. It's terribly expensive. ▶子供たちと遊んでばかりはいられない I *can't* play with my children *all the time* 《話》*forever*]. ▶日本は米国追随ばかりが能ではない(=すべてではない) For Japan only following in the footsteps of the U.S. *is not everything*.
❸ 《...して間もない、...したて》《ちょうど今》just; just now (🛈通例 just は現在完了形, just now は過去形と用いる); 《新たに》newly; 《...から出たばかりの》fresh 《from, out of》 (⇨ ❷) ▶いたばかりの Junji has *just* [《米》Junji *just*] arrived here./Junji arrived [×has arrived] here *just now*./《話》Junji has arrived *just this minute*. ▶あれは最近建ったばかりの家です That is a *newly* built house. (🛈newly は通例過去分詞の前で用いる) ▶あの先生は大学を出たばかりです The teacher is *fresh from* [*is just out of*] college. ▶この帽子は去年買ったばかりです I bought this hat *only* last year.
❹ 《もっぱら》《常に》always; 《たえず》constantly. (🛈通例進行形と用いて話し手のいら立ち・不快なと非難の意を表すことが多い) ▶彼女は私のことにおせっかいばかりしている She is *always* [*constantly, continually, forever*] poking her nose into my affairs. ▶彼は毎日毎日本ばかり読んでいる He *does nothing but* read [×to read] day after day. ▶こう毎日雨ばかりではいやになる *All* this rain every day makes me sick.
❺ 《原因, 理由》《ただ...のために》just [*simply*] because ... 《前の方が口語的》 ▶彼らの脅迫にノーと言ったばかりにひどい目にあった I had a bitter experience *just* [*simply*] *because* I said no to their threat.
❻ 《今にも...しそうな》be going 《about》《to do》 (🛈be about to の方が差し迫った未来を表し、be going to より堅い言い方); be on the point of 《doing》. ▶飛行機は離陸せんばかりであった The 《air》plane *was just going to* [*was about to*] take off./The plane *was on the point of* taking off. ▶今にも雨が降り出さんばかりだ It may rain 《at》*any minute* [*moment*].
❼ 《用意ができて》be ready 《to do》. ▶温かい料理を出すばかりにしておいた I got warm food *ready to* serve. ▶彼らは荷作りもして旅行に出かけるばかりとなっている They've packed and they're *ready to* go on a trip.
❽ 《まるで...のように》as if [*though*] .... (⇨まるで) ▶彼は出て行けと言わんばかりにドアを指さした He pointed to the door *as if* [*as much as*] *to say*, "Get out of here."
❾ 《まったく》会話「勝夫の番ですからね」「ぼくの番だとばかり思っていたよ」"It's Katsuo's turn, you know." "I *just* thought it was mine."
はかりうり 量り売り ── 量り売りする 動 sell 《salt》by weight.
はかりかねる 計り兼ねる ▶彼の真意を計り兼ねる《見当がつかない》It is *hard to guess* [*tell*] what he is thinking.
はかりごと 《計画》a plan; 《もくろみ》a scheme /skiːm/, a design (⇨計画); 《計略》a trick, a trap; 《陰謀》a plot, 《陰》 a conspiracy. (⇨計略)
はかりしれない 計り知れない 《計算できない》《やや書》immeasurable; 《不可解な》《やや書》inscrutable. ▶損失は計り知れない The loss is *immeasurable* [*beyond measure*]. ▶近代美術に対する彼の影響は計り知れない His influence on modern art *can't be measured*.
:はかる 計る, 測る, 量る ❶ 《測定する》《長さ・大きさなどを》measure, take*; 《重さを》weigh; 《水深などを》sound; 《所要時間》time; 《計測する》gauge /géidʒ/. ●私の息子の身長を測る *measure* [*take*] my son's height. ●服を作るために彼の寸法を測る *measure* him [*take his measurements*] for a suit. ●体重計で体重を量る *weigh* oneself [*take one's weight*] on the scale. ●体温を計る *take one's temperature*. ●山の高さを測る *gauge*

はかる [measure] the height of a mountain. ●海の深さを正確に[誤って]測る sound [measure] the depth of the sea accurately [wrongly]. ▶時間は時・分・秒で計る Time is measured by the hour, minute and second. ●彼はマラソンでの彼女のタイムを計った He timed her in the marathon race.
❷ [推定する] ▶己をもって[財産によって]他人を計ってはいけない You must not judge other people by yourself [by their wealth]. ▶未来の事は測りがたい We can't tell [There is no telling] what will happen in the future.

はかる 図る ❶ [企てる] (計画する) plan (-nn-); (陰謀を) conspire, plot (-tt-); (試みる) try, attempt (❗try より堅い語でしばしば失敗を暗示する); [求める] [書] seek*; (ねらう) aim ⟨at⟩; [努める] labor [work] ⟨for⟩. ●両国の和睦(ぼく)を図る plan the reconciliation between the two countries. ●政府の転覆を図る plot to overthrow the government. ●再起を図る try to make a comeback. ●自殺を図る attempt suicide; try to kill oneself. ●私利を図る seek one's own interest. ●会社の発展を図る aim to develop [at the development of] the company. ●公益を図る labor [work] for the good of the public.
❷ [取り図る] (⇨便宜 ③)
❸ [考える] ●あに図らんや (案に相違して) (⇨案 ③)

はかる 諮る (相談する) consult ⟨with⟩ [confer with] ⟨the members about it⟩; (審議に付す) submit (-tt-) ⟨the plan to the conference⟩.

はがれる 剥がれる come* [peel] off.
はがんいっしょう 破顔一笑 ●破顔一笑して (にっこりと笑う) with a (broad) smile (on one's face). ●破顔一笑する grin; smile broadly; break into a smile. (❗場合によっては単に smile でよいこともある)
バカンス [<フランス語] ⟪主に米⟫ vacation; ⟪主に英⟫ holidays. (⇨休暇)
はき 破棄 名 [[契約・法令などの]] ⟪書⟫ (an) abrogation; [[法律・契約などの無効]] ⟪やや書⟫ (an) annulment; [[契約などの取り消し]] ⟪日常的な語⟫ (a) cancellation (❗日常的な語); [[約束などの違反]] (a) breach; [[判決などの逆転]] (a) reversal. ●契約破棄で彼を告訴する sue him for a breach of the contract.
── 破棄する 動 ⟪書⟫ abrogate; ⟪やや書⟫ annul (-ll-); cancel; break*; reverse. ●条約を破棄する abrogate [終了させる] terminate, [終了通告をする] denounce] a treaty. ●契約を破棄する (取り消す) cancel [annul] a contract. ●一審の判決を破棄する reverse the decision in the first trial. ●文書を破棄する (破り捨てる, 燃やす) destroy a document; (処分する) get rid of a document.

はき 覇気 (元気) spirit, ⟪やや書⟫ vigor; (積極性) drive; (野心) (an) ambition. ▶あの男には(まるで)覇気がない He lacks spirit [vigor, drive]. ▶あの男は覇気がある He has great spirit [drive]./He is full of energy [ambition].
はぎ 萩 ⟪植物⟫ a Japanese bush clover.
はきけ 吐き気 ⟪書⟫ nausea /nɔ́ːziə, nɔ́ːsiə/. ▶吐き気のするようなにおい a disgusting [a sickening, a nauseating] smell. ●吐き気がする feel like vomiting [⟪話⟫ throwing up]; ⟪書⟫ feel nauseous; ⟪米⟫ feel [be] sick to [at] one's stomach. (❗feel sick to は ⟪英⟫ではこの意になるが, ⟪米⟫ では単に「気分が悪い」の意) ▶その景色を見て吐き気を催した The sight made me feel sick./The sight sickened [nauseated] me./I felt sick [was sickened] at the sight. The sight turned my stomach.
はきごこち 履き心地 ▶このソックスははき心地がよい These socks are comfortable to wear.

はぎしり 歯軋り ── 歯軋りする 動 grind* one's teeth; gnash /nǽʃ/ one's teeth. (❗前の方より比喩的に用いられることが多い. 聖書より). ●寝ていて歯ぎしりをする grind one's teeth in one's sleep. ▶刑事は泥棒を捕り逃して歯ぎしりしてくやしがった The police officer gnashed [ground] his teeth with frustration when he failed to catch the thief.
パキスタン [国名] Pakistan /pǽkistæn/; (公式名) the Islamic Republic of Pakistan. (首都 Islamabad) ●パキスタン人 a Pakistáni (複 ~, ~s). ●パキスタン(人)の Pakistáni.
はきすてる 吐き捨てる spit*... out. ●彼は私に向かって吐き捨てるようにこう言った He spat [⟪主に米⟫ spit] (out) the words at me.
はきそうじ 掃き掃除 ── 掃き掃除(を)する sweep ⟨a room⟩. (⇨掃除(をする))
はきだしまど 掃き出し窓 an opening to sweep dust out.
はきだす 吐き出す [[食べたものなどを]] vomit, ⟪話⟫ throw*... up; [[つば・たんなどを]] spit*... (out); [[煙などを]] belch... (out). ●食べたものを吐き出す vomit [throw up] what one has eaten. ●怒りを吐き出す spit out one's anger ⟨at him⟩. ▶彼はたんをペっと路上に吐き出した He spat (out) phlegm on the street. ▶彼は私に向かってののしりの言葉を吐き出すように言った He spat (out) curses at me. ▶煙突が黒い煙をもくもくと吐き出していた The chimney was belching (out) [vomiting (out)] black smoke.
はきだめ 掃き溜め ⟪米⟫ a garbage heap [mound]; ⟪英⟫ a rubbish heap [mound]. ●掃き溜めに鶴 a jewel in a dunghill.
はきちがえる 履き違える ❶ [履物を] (他人のものと) put* on ⟨his shoes⟩ by mistake; (左右を) put ⟨one's shoes⟩ on the wrong feet.
❷ [考え違いをする] misunderstand*; (取り違えをする) take* [mistake*] one thing for another. ●自由(の意味)をはき違える have a mistaken idea about the meaning of freedom.
はきつぶす 履き潰す wear* ⟨a pair of shoes⟩ out.
はぎとる 剥ぎ取る (ものを無理に) tear* /téər/... ⟨from, out of⟩; (ペンキなどを) strip (-pp-)... ⟨away, off⟩. (⇨剥(は)ぐ) ●本からそのページをはぎ取る tear ⟨off⟩ the page out of a book. ▶(泥棒に)身ぐるみはぎ取られた I was robbed [stripped] of everything I had on.
バギナ [腟] [解剖] a vagina /vədʒáinə/.
はきはき (はっきりした) clear; (あいまいでない) decisive; (意見をはっきり述べる) outspoken; (活発な) active, brisk. ▶先生が生徒にはきはき返答するように注意した The teacher told his pupils to answer clearly (in ⟨簡潔に⟩ concisely). (❗... answer clearly and concisely. ともいえる)/The teacher told his pupils to be decisive in their answers. ●あの人ははきはきものを言う人だ He is an outspoken person.

*****はきもの** 履物 ⟪集合的⟫ footwear (❗靴だけでなくスリッパ, 靴下とも含む), ⟪古・まれ⟫ footgear. ●ちゃんと合った履物をはく wear the correct footwear. ●上がる前に履物を脱ぎください Please take off your shoes [footwear] before you come in.

> 翻訳のこころ お客様がた, ここで髪をきちんとして, それから, 履き物の泥を落としてください (宮沢賢治『注文の多い料理店』) Dear guests, please straighten your hair and get the mud off your shoes [footwear] here. (❗straighten your hair は ⟨くしや手で髪を整えることを表す⟩ 一般的な表現. comb your hair は「くしを使って髪を整える」の意)

ばきゃく 馬脚 ▲馬脚を現す show one's true colors; give oneself away ((by doing)), ((悪人が)) show one's cloven hoof (⬛ 悪魔 (Satan) の足のひづめは割れていて、それが現してしまうの意).

はきゅう 波及 ── 波及する 動 〖及ぶ〗 spread ((to)), extend ((to)); 〖影響する〗 (間接に) influence; (直接に) affect. ▶その運動は一部の大学にも波及した The movement spread to some universities.
● 波及効果 ((have)) a ripple effect ((on)).

バキュームカー a céssspool cleaner trùck; ((婉曲的)) a honey wagon; (説明的に) a tank truck to collect night soil; (和製語) a vacuum car.

はきょう 破鏡 〖壊れた鏡〗 a broken mirror; 〖離婚〗 (a) divorce.
● 破鏡の嘆き ▲破鏡の嘆きを見る (離婚を経験する) go through a divorce; (離婚する) get divorce.

はぎょう 覇業 ▲覇業を成しとげる dominate [conquer] the world. (⇨制覇)

はきょく 破局 (悲劇的結末) a catastrophe /kətǽstrəfi/; (崩壊) a collapse, a breakup. ▶破局を食い止める prevent a catastrophe. ▶その事件は結婚生活の破局(= 崩壊)を招いた The incident brought about the collapse of their married life.

はぎれ 歯切れ ▲歯切れの悪い答弁をする (言い逃れを) give an evasive answer. ▶彼女は歯切れのいい話し方をする She has a crisp and clear manner of speaking./Her speech is articulate /ɑːrtíkjələt/.

はぎれ 端切れ a strap of cloth; a remnant.

***はく 吐く** ❶ 〖吐き出す〗(口の中のものを) spit*; (胃の中のものを) vomit, (話) throw*(...) up, (英) be sick. ● 地面につばを吐く spit on the ground. ●スイカの種を吐く spit out watermelon seeds. ●大量の血を吐く vomit [spit] a lot of blood. ▶吐きそうだ I feel like vomiting [throwing up]./(米) I feel sick to [at] my stomach./(英) I'm going to be [feel] sick. (⬛ (米)では be sick は「病気である」、feel sick は「気分が悪い」の意が普通) ▶彼女は食べたものを全部吐いてしまった She has vomited [thrown up] everything she ate.

❷ 〖煙などを〗 (送り出す) send*... out, (書) emit (-tt-); (息を) breathe... out, (やや書) exhale. ●たばこの煙を吐く blow the cigarette smoke out. ▶あの山は昔は煙を吐いていた That mountain used to send out [emit, (大量に激しく)] belch] clouds of smoke. ▶大きく息を吸ってゆっくり吐きなさい Inhale [Breathe in] deeply and exhale [breathe out] slowly.

❸ 〖言葉・意見を〗 give*; (吐き出すように言う) spit*.
●正論を吐く make [put forth] a sound argument. ●のろいの言葉を吐く utter curses; spit (out) curses ((at him)). ▶泥を吐け ((話)) Spit it out.

***はく** 〖掃く〗(ほうき・はけなどで) sweep*. ●床をほうきで掃く sweep the floor with a broom. ●部屋をきれいに掃く sweep a room clean; give a room a good sweep. ●枯れ葉を掃いて集める sweep dead leaves up; (熊手で) rake dead leaves up. ●掃いてほこりを取る (取り去る) sweep the dirt away.

***はく** 〖履く、穿く〗 〖動作〗 put*... on, (引っ張って) pull on; 〖状態〗 wear*, have*... on. (⇨着る) ▶彼女はブーツをはいた She put on her boots [put her boots on]./She pulled on her boots [pulled her boots on]./(急いで) She slipped on her boots [slipped her boots on]. ▶彼は赤いズボンをはいていた He wore [was wearing] red pants./He had red pants on [had on red pants]./He was (dressed) in red pants. ▶新しいジーンズを買ったけれどなんだけどはいてみると、きつすぎるのよ I just bought

some [a pair of] new jeans, and I can't put [get] them on. They're too tight. (⬛ a pair of jeans を them, They と複数で受けることに注意) ▶彼は白い靴をはいて出かけた He went out in white shoes [with white shoes on, wearing white shoes]. (⬛ with white shoes もだが、with には「持って」の意もあるのでこの場合は避けた方がよい) ▶この靴を試しにはいてみなさい Try these shoes on./Try on these shoes. ▶靴ははき慣らさないとはき心地がよくならない You have to break in shoes before they are comfortable.

はく 拍 〖音楽〗 a beat.

はく 箔 ❶ 〖金属の薄片〗 foil; (金銀などの極薄の) leaf.
● 金箔 gold leaf.
❷ 〖貫禄〗 (権威) prestige; (名声) a reputation, luster. ●はくをつける add prestige ((to his name)); (物に) add value ((to)). ●はくがつく gain prestige [a reputation] ((as a scholar)).

-はく -泊 ●1泊・一泊 ▶2泊3日の旅に出る go on a three-day trip ((to)). ●1泊10,000円のホテル a 10,000-yen-a-night hotel. (⬛ ハイフンの付いていないことも多い) ▶京都で3泊した I spent three nights in Kyoto./I had a three-night stay in Kyoto.

はぐ 剥ぐ (無理に引き裂く) tear* /téər/ ...((off, from)); (むき取る) peel ...((off, from)); (人・物から服やおおいなどをすっかり取る) strip (-pp-) ...((of)); (動物の皮をむく) skin (-nn-) ((a fox)). ●ポスターを壁からはぐ tear ((off)) [手荒に)) rip, (丁寧に) peel] a poster off [from] the wall. ●木の皮をはぐ strip a tree of its bark; bark a tree. ●毛布をはぐ (めくる) pull back ((his)) blanket. ▶彼はサラ金に身ぐるみはがされた He was stripped of all his possessions by loan sharks.

はぐ 接ぐ (紙や布を) patch; sew small pieces together.

ばく 漠 ▲漠とした 形 vague ((ideas)); indistinct ((impressions)).

ばく 獏 〖動物〗 a tapir.

ばく 馬具 harness. ●馬具をつける put a harness on ((a horse)); harness ((a horse)). ●馬具をつけた子馬 a colt in harness.

バグ 〖コンピュータ〗 a bug. ▶バグを取り除く debug ((a program)).

パグ 〖動物〗(小形犬) a pug.

はくあ 白亜 chalk; 〖白色〗 white. ●白亜質の chalky. ●白亜の殿堂 a white hall.
● 白亜紀 〖考古学〗 the Cretaceous (period).

はくあい 博愛 图 〖書〗 philanthropy; 〖慈善〗 charity. ── 博愛(主義)の 形 〖書〗 philanthropic; charitable.
● 博愛行為 a philanthropic act. ● 博愛主義 philanthropy; philanthropism. ● 博愛主義者 a philanthropist.

はくい 白衣 a white robe [dress]; 〖医師などの〗 a white coat. ●白衣を着た医師 a doctor in a white coat; a white-coated doctor.
● 白衣の天使 (看護師) a nurse in white; (ほめて) an angel. (⬛ 天使は白衣をまとっているものなので in white は不要).

ばくおん 爆音 〖爆発音〗 an explosion; 〖飛行機などのごう音〗 a roar. ●飛行機の爆音 the roar of a plane. ▶トンネルの中で大きな爆音がした There was a loud explosion in the tunnel. ▶飛行機は爆音を立てて飛び去った The airplane flew away with a roar.

はくが 博雅 an extensive, accurate knowledge.
● 博雅の士 an accomplished person.

ばくが 麦芽 malt /mɔ́ːlt/.
● 麦芽糖 maltose; malt sugar.

はくがい 迫害 图 〖宗教的・政治上の〗 persecution; 〖権力による圧迫〗 oppression. ● 迫害を受けた[受けている]人 a victim of *persecution*. ● 正義をつらぬくために迫害に耐える suffer *persecution* for the sake of justice.
— **迫害する** 動 pérsecute; oppress.
● **迫害者** a persecutor; an oppressor.

はくがく 博学 (大変な学識) great learning;《書》erudition. ● 博学な人 a person of *great* [(広範な) *extensive*] *learning*; a person who has *wide* [(百科事典的な) *encyclopedic*] *knowledge*; a *widely learned* /lə́ːrnid/ person;《書》an *erudite* /érjədàit/ person.

はくがんし 白眼視 — **白眼視する** 動 (非難を込めて…を見る) look disapprovingly 《*at*》; (冷たい目で見る) look coldly 《*on*》; (偏見を抱く) be prejudiced 《*against*》.

はぐき 歯茎 gums /ɡʌ́mz/. ● 歯茎を部分に分けて考えるので, 歯茎全体は複数形で表す.

はくぎん 白銀 (銀) silver (⇨銀); (雪) snow (⇨雪).

はぐくむ 育む (育てる) bring*...up; (品性・精神などを養う) (やや書) cultivate; (才能などを)《書》foster. ● 道徳心を育む *cultivate* the moral sense. ▶ウィーンが彼女の音楽的才能を育んだ Vienna *fostered* her musical ability. ▶その本が学生の批判精神を育んだ(促進した) The book encouraged students to *develop* a critical mind.

ばくげき 爆撃 图 (aerial) bombing /bɑ́miŋ/. ▶東京は何回かひどい爆撃を受けた Tokyo *was* heavily *bombed* several times./Several heavy *bombing raids* were made on Tokyo.
— **爆撃する** 動 bomb; drop bombs; make a bómbing ràid 《*on*》.
● **爆撃機** a bomber.

ばくげきほう 迫撃砲 〖軍事〗 a trench mortar [gun].

はくさい 白菜 〖植物〗 a Chinese cabbage. (⚠料理したものは Ⓤ)

ばくさい 博才 ▶彼には博才(=ばくちの才能)がある He is *good at gambling*./He is a shrewd gambler.

はくし 白紙 (何も書いてない紙) blank [white] paper; a blank [(未使用の) a clean] sheet of paper. ● 白紙委任する give《him》carte blanche /kɑ̀ːrt blɑ́ːnʃ/. ● 白紙の投票をする cast a *blank* ballot. ▶彼の答案用紙は白紙だった His exam paper was *blank*. ▶それはまだ白紙の状態で Nothing has been decided about it yet.
● **白紙に戻す** start afresh; start all over again.
● **白紙撤回** (取り消し) (a) cancelation. ● ダムの建設計画を白紙撤回する *cancel* the dam construction plan.

はくし 博士 a doctor. (⇨博士(は^か))

はくじ 白磁 white porcelain.

ばくし 爆死 — **爆死する** 動 be killed with a bomb [with an explosive].

はくしき 博識 (extensive) knowledge;《書》a well-informed man [woman]; (博学な人) a widely learned /lə́ːrnid/ person;《書》an erudite /érjədàit/ person. (⇨博学)

はくしじゃっこう 薄志弱行 ▶太郎は薄志弱行だ Taro is *weak-willed and indecisive*./Taro has a weak will and lacks decision.

はくじつ 白日 (真昼の太陽) the midday sun; 〖昼〗 《*in*》broad daylight. ● 白日夢 (⇨白昼夢)
● **白日の下にさらされる** (すっかり明らかになる) be brought to light.

はくしゃ 白砂 white sand.
● **白砂青松** 白砂青松の地 a beautiful beach [place] with sands and green pines. (⚠複数形の場合は「砂浜」の意)

はくしゃ 拍車 a spur. ● 馬に拍車をかける put *spurs* to a horse; spur a horse.
● **拍車をかける** ▶彼に拍車をかけて一層努力させる *spur* him *to* make greater efforts; *spur* him 《*on*》 *to* greater efforts. ▶その国の産業発展に拍車がかかった The country's industrial progress *was speeded up*.

はくしゅ 薄謝 a small token of《my》gratitude [appreciation]. ● 薄謝を呈する offer a *reward*.

はくしゃく 伯爵 (英国の) an earl; (英国以外の) a count. (⇨公爵)
● **伯爵夫人** a countess.

はくじゃく 薄弱 — **薄弱な** 形 weak, feeble (⚠後の方が意味が強い); (根拠が) flimsy. ● 薄弱な理由 a *flimsy* reason. ● 意志薄弱である have a *weak* will.

*はくしゅ 拍手 图 a clap, (拍手をおくる) applause. ● 万雷の拍手 thunderous [(鳴り響く) resounding] applause. ▶観客は彼の演技に盛大な拍手をおくった The audience *applauded* his performance loudly./The audience gave his performance loud *applause*. ▶さあ彼らに大きな拍手をおくりましょう Let's give them a *big hand*. (⚠a big [a good] hand の連語で) ▶そのピアニストは演奏が終わるとあらしのような[総立ちの]拍手かっさいを受けた The pianist got thunderous *applause* [a standing *ovation*] at the end of his performance. (⚠a round of... は「ひとしきりの...」の意) ▶講演が終わると一斉に拍手が起こった There was a round of *applause* as he ended his speech.
— **拍手する** 動 clap (-pp-)《one's hands》(⚠clap one's hands は手をたたくことで, 必ずしも拍手とは限らない (⇨叩(^たた)く)); applaud (⚠大きな拍手をして賞賛を表すこと). ▶聴衆は熱狂的に拍手した The audience *applauded* [*clapped*] enthusiastically.

はくじゅ 白寿 one's 99th year. (⇨還暦) ▶曾祖母は来年白寿を迎える My great-grandmother will be ninety-nine years old next year.

ばくしゅう 麦秋 (麦の取り入れどきで初夏) 《*in*》early summer.

はくしょ 白書 《米》a white book;《英》a white paper. ● 経済白書 an economic *white book*; a *white book* on economy.

はくじょう 白状 图 (a) confession; (an) admission; acknowledgment.
— **白状する** 動 confess; (ついに認める) admit (-tt-); (しぶしぶ認める) acknowledge. ● 自分の罪をすっかり警察に白状する *confess* one's crime fully [*make a full confession of* one's crime] to the police; *confess* fully to the police *that* one committed the crime. ▶彼は金を盗んだことを白状した He *confessed* (*that*) he had stolen [to having stolen, ×to have stolen] the money. (⚠後の方が堅い表現)/He *admitted* [*acknowledged*] (*that*) he had stolen [having stolen, ×to have stolen] the money.
会話「白状することがあるんだ」「まあ何をしでかしたの」"I have a *confession* to make." "Now what have you done?"

はくじょう 薄情 — **薄情な** 形 〖冷淡な〗 cold-hearted; 〖無情な〗 heartless; (容赦しない) pitiless; 〖残酷な〗 cruel; 〖不親切な〗 unkind. ● 薄情な男 a *cold-hearted* [a *heartless*, a *pitiless*] man. ● 薄情なことを言う make *heartless* remarks. ● 彼に薄情なことをする be *cruel* [*unkind*] *to* him; (つらく当たる) be *hard on* him; *treat*《him》 *pitilessly*.

ばくしょう 爆笑 a burst [a roar] of laughter.

はくしょく 爆笑する 動 burst into [roar with] laughter; burst out laughing.
はくしょく 白色 white. ●白色の white.
●白色人種 the white race(s); the Caucasians.
はくしょん 《米》Ahchoo /ɑːtʃúː/!, 《英》Atishoo /ətíʃúː/! 事情 これに対して「お大事に」「どうも」"(God) bless you /bléʃu/!" "Thank you." というやりとりをする習慣がある)
はくしん 迫真 ●迫真の演技 (現実味のある) realistic acting; a realistic performance. ●彼の演技は迫真力に欠けている His acting is not realistic [lacks reality].
はくじん 白人 a white, a white man (複 men) [woman (複 women)]; a Caucasian; [人種] the white race(s). ●白人支配に終止符を打つ put an end to white rule [domination]. ●白人だけの学校 a white school; a school only for whites.
はくじん 白刃 (さやから抜いた刀) a drawn sword; a naked sword. ●白刃の下をくぐる (危険な目にあう) expose oneself to danger.
はくしん 幕臣 〘歴史〙 the retainers [vassals] of the shogunate.
ばくしん 驀進 图 (突進) a dash; a rush.
── 驀進する 動 ●…に向かって驀進する dash [make a dash] for .... ●彼は出世街道を驀進している He continues to rise rapidly in the world [climb the ladder of success].
ばくしんち 爆心地 the center of an explosion; (原爆の) the ground zero, the hypocenter.
ばくすい 爆睡 ── 爆睡する 動 drop off to a dead sleep.
はくする 博する (勝ち得る) earn; (勝ち取る) win*. (⇨得る) ●世界的名声を博する win [earn, gain] a world-wide reputation. ▶その小説は大好評を博した The novel won great popularity [(大当たりした) was a big hit].
はくせい 剥製 stuffing; mounting. ●ライオンの剥製 a stuffed lion.
●剥製標本 a stuffed specimen.
はくせき 白皙 ▶彼は白皙の若者だ (色白の) He is a youth with a fair skin [a fair-skinned young man].
はくせきれい 白鶺鴒 〘鳥〙 a white wagtail.
はくせん 白線 a white line. (⇨線❶)
はくせん 白癬 〘医学〙 trichophytosis.
ばくぜん 漠然 ── 漠然とした 形 (はっきりしない) vague; (意味不明瞭{めいりょう}な) obscure; (意味のあいまいな) ambiguous. (⇨曖昧{あいまい})
── 漠然と 副 vaguely; obscurely; 〘目的なしに〙 aimlessly. ●漠然と本を読む read a book aimlessly [without purpose]. ●彼のことは漠然としか覚えていない I remember him only vaguely [dimly]./I have only a vague [a dim] memory of him.
はくそ 歯屎 plaque. (⇨歯垢{しこう})
ばくそう 爆走 roaring (on a motorbike); driving with a roar.
ばくだい 莫大 ── 莫大な 形 〘非常に大きい〙 huge, vast; 〘異常に大きい〙 enormous. ●莫大な金額 a huge [an enormous, a vast] sum of money. ●莫大な財産を作る make an enormous [〘驚くべき〙《書》a fabulous] fortune.
はくだく 白濁 ●角膜の白濁〘医学〙 a nebula in the cornea. (⇨白などにも用いられる)
はくだつ 剥奪 图《やや書》deprivation. ●公民権の剥奪 deprivation of one's civil rights [one's citizenship].
── 剥奪する 動 ▶彼は公民権を剥奪された His civil rights were taken away./《やや書》He was deprived of his civil rights.
バグダッド 〘イラクの首都〙Baghdad /bǽɡdæd/. (! Bagdad ともつづる)
***ばくだん** 爆弾 ❶〘兵器〙a bomb /bɑ́m/. ●時限爆弾 a time bomb. ●橋に爆弾を仕掛ける plant a bomb on the bridge. ▶昨夜その町に多数の爆弾が落とされた A lot of bombs were dropped on the city last night./The city was heavily bombed last night.
❷〘その他の表現〙 ●爆弾発言をする drop [explode] a bombshell; make a bombshell statement [announcement].
●爆弾を抱える ●心臓に爆弾を抱えている one's heart is a bomb that may explode any time.
はくち 白痴 (状態) idiocy; (人) an idiot.
── 白痴の 形 idiotic.
ばくち 博打 gambling. ●ばくちを打つ gamble. ●ひどいばくち打ちな heavy gambler. ●ばくちで身上をつぶす gamble away one's fortune. ●大ばくちを打つ (大きな危険を冒す) run [take] great risks.
ばくちく 爆竹 a firecracker, a cracker. ●爆竹を鳴らす explode [set off] firecrackers.
はくちず 白地図 a blank map.
はくちゅう 白昼 ▶白昼堂々と現金輸送車が襲われた A bank transport truck was attacked in broad daylight.
はくちゅう 伯仲 ── 伯仲する 動 be almost [nearly] equal (in); be well [evenly] matched (in). ●両者は実力[勢力]伯仲だ The two are almost equal in ability [influence].
はくちゅうむ 白昼夢 a daydream. ●白昼夢を見る daydream (about).
はくちょう 白鳥 a swan; (ひな) a cygnet.
●白鳥座〘天文〙the Swan; Cygnus.
はくちょうのみずうみ『白鳥の湖』Swan Lake. (参考 チャイコフスキー作曲のバレエ曲)
ばくちん 爆沈 ── 爆沈する 動 (沈める) blow* up and sink* (a ship); (沈む) be blown up and sunk.
ばくつく ●黒パンをばくつく (むさぼり食う) devour [take big bites of] brown bread.
ぱくっと ●ぱくっと開いた傷 (裂けている) a gaping /ɡéipiŋ/ [a wide-open] wound. (⇨ぱくり)
バクテリア bacteria /bæktíəriə/ (! 《単》bacterium) (! 通例複数形で)
はくどう 拍動 图 pulsation. ── 拍動する 動 pulsate.
はくとうゆ 白灯油 《米》kerosene, kerosine; 《英》paraffin.
はくないしょう 白内障 ●白内障になる get a cataract.
はくねつ 白熱 图〘高温発光〙 white heat; incandescence.
── 白熱した 形 heated; exciting. ●白熱した議論 a heated discussion. ▶野球の試合はだんだん白熱してきた The baseball game is getting more and more exciting.
●白熱電球 an incandescent lamp.
はくば 白馬 a white horse.
ばくは 爆破 图 a blówùp; (岩石などの) a blast. ▶その爆破事件で10人の死者が出た Ten people were killed in the (bomb) blast.
── 爆破する 動 〘人が爆発物で〙blow*... up; blast. ●彼らは列車を爆破した They blew up [exploded] the train. (! explode は火薬・ボイラー・タンクなどを爆発させる場合に用いる)
はくばい 白梅 (木) a white-blossom ume tree;

white *ume* blossoms.

バグパイプ bagpipes. ▶バグパイプで演奏する音楽 *bagpipe music*. ▶バグパイプを吹く play the *bagpipes*.

ばくばく 漠漠 ── 漠漠たる 形 (広漠たる) vast; extensive; (漠然とした) vague; obscure; indistinct. (⇨漠然)

ぱくぱく ●ぱくぱく食べる (むさぼる) devour; (音を立て口を大きく動かして) munch; (ぱくりとかみつく) snap 《*at*》. ▶犬がぱくぱくえさを食べた The dog *munched (on)* its food. ▶金魚がときどき口をぱくぱくさせた The goldfish *opened and shut its mouth* now and then.

はくはつ 白髪 white hair. (⇨白髪(しらが))

* **ばくはつ** 爆発 图 (an) explosion, a blówùp; (火山の) (an) eruption. ●ダイナマイトの爆発 the *explosion* of the dynamite. ●怒りの爆発 explosions [an *explosion*] of anger. ●火山の爆発 a volcanic *eruption*. ●人口の爆発的増加 a population *explosion*. ●炭鉱でガス爆発が起こった There was a gas *explosion* in the coal mine.
── 爆発する[させる] 動 (爆発物などが[を]) explode, blow* (...) up; (火山が) erupt. ▶ガスタンクが爆発した The gas tank *exploded* [*blew up*]. ▶飛行機に仕掛けられた爆弾が爆発した A bomb set in the plane *exploded* [*blew up*, *went off*]. ▶彼らは列車に仕掛けた爆弾を爆発させた They *exploded* [*blew up*, *set off*] the bomb placed in the train. ▶その火山は去年また爆発した The volcano *erupted* [*blew up*] again last year. ▶ついに彼の怒りが爆発した His anger *exploded* at last./He *exploded (with anger)* at last.
● 爆発物 an explosive (substance). ● 爆発力 explosive force.

はくはん 白斑 〖白い斑点〗a white spot; (太陽の) 〖天文〗a facula; 〖医学〗vitiligo.

はくび 白眉 the best 《*of*》; (傑作) a masterpiece. ●ダ・ビンチの『モナリザ』はルネッサンス芸術の白眉に数えられる Da Vinci's *the Mona Lisa* is counted among the *masterpieces* of [the *best works* of art in] the Renaissance.

はくびしん 白鼻心 〖動物〗a palm civet.

はくひょう 白票 (賛成投票に使う白い票) a white ballot; (㋺ 青票) a white ballot; (白紙に) cast a *blank vote*.

はくひょう 薄氷 thin ice. ●薄氷を踏むような交渉 a very delicate negotiations.
● 薄氷を踏む思い ▶薄氷を踏む思いだ I feel as if I were [《話》I feel like] skating on (very) *thin ice*.

ばくふ 幕府 shogunate. ●徳川幕府 the Tokugawa *Shogunate*.

ばくふ 瀑布 (滝) a waterfall. (⇨滝)

ばくふう 爆風 blast. ●原爆の爆風で死亡する die in the atomic *blast*.

はくぶつがく 博物学 natural history.

* **はくぶつかん** 博物館 a muséum. ●科学 [歴史; 交通; 民族]博物館 a science [a history; a transportation; an ethnographic] *museum*. ▶大英博物館でミイラを見た I saw mummies in the British *Museum*.

はくぶつし 博物誌 a natural history.

はくへいせん 白兵戦 a hand-to-hand fight; a close combat.

はくぼ 薄暮 (たそがれ) 《*at*》twilight; (夕やみ) 《*at*》dusk.
● 薄暮ゲーム a twilight game.

はくぼく 白墨 《a piece of》chalk. (㋺ チョーク) ●白墨で書[描]く write [draw] in *chalk*.

はくまい 白米 polished rice.

ばくまつ 幕末 《in》the last days of the Tokugawa Shogunate.

はくめい 薄命 an early death; a sad fate. ▶佳人[美人]薄命 'Beautiful women die young.'/(ことわざ) Whom the gods love die young.

はくめい 薄明 twilight; dim light. (⇨薄明かり)

はくめん 白面 ── 白面の 形 (色白の) fair-complexioned 《young men》; (未熟な) inexperienced 《students》.

はくもくれん 白木蓮 〖植物〗a white magnolia.

はくや 白夜 (⇨白夜(びゃくや))

ばくやく 爆薬 (an) explosive, blasting powder.
● 爆薬を仕掛ける plant [lay] an *explosive*.

はくらい 舶来 ── 舶来の 形 foreign; (外国製の) foreign-made; (輸入した) imported.
● 舶来品 a foreign-made [an imported] article; 《集合的》foreign-made [imported] goods.

ばくらい 爆雷 a depth charge; a depth bomb.

はぐらかす ●質問をはぐらかす (うまく逃げる) dodge [sidestep (to avoid)], 《書》evade, 《やや話》skirt around] a question. (❗はぐらかす giving an answer も可)
会話 「ゆうべ遅かったわね。会社で仕事していたの？」「どうだ、今夜はフランス料理でも食べに行こうか」「はぐらかさないでよ (=質問の答えになっていないわよ)」"You were late coming home last night. Did you work late at the office?" "How about eating out at a French restaurant tonight?" "You're not answering my question."

はくらく 伯楽 (馬の名鑑定家) a good judge of horses. ●名伯楽 a person with special ability to find an able young person and develop his or her ability.

はくらく 剥落 ── 剥落する 動 peel (off). ▶壁紙が剥落し始めた The wallpaper has begun to *peel*.

はくらん 博覧 ── 博覧の 形 well-read /-réd/; (学識豊かな) erudite /érjədàit/.
● 博覧強記 ● 博覧強記の人 a well-read person with a retentive memory.

* **はくらんかい** 博覧会 an exposition, 《話》an expo (㋺ 〜s); 《しばしば Expo》a fair. ●万国博覧会を開く hold an international *exposition* [a world's fair].
● 博覧会場 an exposition ground; a fairground. (❗いずれもしばしば複数形で)

はくり 剥離 图 exfoliation; 〖医学〗avulsion; detachment. ●網膜剥離 〖医学〗retinal *detachment*.
── 剥離する 動 exfoliate.

はくり 薄利 a narrow [a small] profit margin.
● 薄利で on a *narrow profit margin*.
● 薄利多売 small profits and quick returns 《略 S.P.Q.R.》.

ぱくり 图 (盗用) plagiarizing. ●歌のパクリで訴えられる be accused of *plagiarizing* the song.

ぱくり 副 ●ぱくりと食べる (勢いよく) snap ... up; (がつがつと) gobble... up. ●(傷などが)ぱくりと口を開く split wide open. ●ぱくりと (音を立てて) with a snap. ▶犬は肉片をぱくりと食べた The dog *ate up* [*gobbled up*] a piece of meat in one gulp.

はくりきこ 薄力粉 weak flour.

ばくりゅうしゅ 麦粒腫 〖医学〗a sty /stái/, (㋺ sties, styes), (㋺ 物言い ❷)

ばくりょう 幕僚 《集合的》the staff; (個々の人) a staff officer.
● 幕僚監部 the Staff Office. ●陸上幕僚監部 the Ground *Staff Office* 《略 GSO》. ● 幕僚長 a chief

はくりょく

はくりょく 迫力 名 power; 《話》punch.
— **迫力のある** 形 powerful. ●迫力のある演奏 a *powerful* [《強い印象を与える》an *impressive*] performance. ●彼の演説は迫力がなかった His speech was not *powerful* [《説得力がある》*convincing*] enough./His speech lacked *power*./There wasn't much *punch* in his speech.

ぱくる 〔〖盗む〗《くすねる》pick and steal; 《ひったくる》snatch; 《だます》cheat; 〖逮捕する〗nab (-bb-), pick 《a thief》up. (🔁前の方がくだけた語)

はぐるま 歯車 a cogwheel; a gear(wheel). ●歯車の歯の一つ a cog; 《組織の一部に組み込まれた人》《話》a cog in the machine [wheel]. ●歯車がかみ合う mesh 《with》. (🔁比喩的な意味でも用いる) ▶歯車がうまくかみ合わない The cogs do not *mesh* correctly. (🔁「かみ合っていない」は ... are out of *mesh*.) ●歯車が狂う《比喩的》be out of joint.

はぐるま『歯車』 *Cogwheels*. 〔参考〕芥川龍之介の小説〕

ばくれつ 爆裂 an explosion.
●爆裂弾 a bomb; a bombshell.

はぐれる 逸れる 《連れから離れから》stray 《from》; 《見失う》lose* sight of ...; 《迷子になる》get* lost. (🔁前者が普通) ▶その女の子は人込みの中で母親とはぐれた The girl *strayed from* [*lost sight of*] her mother in the crowd.

はくろ 白露 (露) dew; 《秋分の15日前の日》fifteen days before the autumnal equinox.

ばくろ 暴露 名 (an) exposure; muckraking; 《やや書》a disclosure; 《やや書》a revelation. ●新聞による彼の私生活の暴露 the newspaper's *exposure* [*disclosure*] of his private life.
— **暴露する** 動 〖人の正体・悪事などを〗expose; 〖秘密などを〗uncover, disclose; 《明るみに出す》bring* ... to light; 《自然に、うっかり》reveal. ●脱税行為を暴露する *expose* a tax evasion. ●陰謀を暴露する *expose* [*uncover*] a plot. ●警察に彼の名前を暴露する *disclose* his name to the police.
●暴露記事 an exposé /èkspouzéi/.

はくろう 白蝋 white wax; refined wax.
●白蝋病 《医学》《話》(vibration) white finger disease; 《書》Raynaud's disease [syndrome]. 〔参考〕林業労働者の職業病

はけ 捌け 《排水》drainage; 《売れ行き》sale. ●はけがよい 《水が》drain well (🔁場所が主語); 《商品が》sell well; be in good demand.

はけ 刷毛 a brush. 《⇨ブラシ》●ペンキ用のはけ a paintbrush. ●幅の広いはけでペンキを塗る paint with a broad brush.

はげ 禿げ baldness; 《はげた部分》a bald spot; 〖人〗a bald(-headed) person. 《⇨禿げる》●はげの治療 a cure for *baldness*. ●はげがかかった頭〖男性〗a *balding* head [man]. ●はげ山 《⇨禿げ山》

はげあがる 禿げ上がる ▶彼はだいぶ禿げ上がっている His hair has *receded* considerably.

はげあたま 禿げ頭 《have》a bald head.

はけい 波形 一波形の 形 wavy 《lines》.

はげいとう 葉鶏頭 〖植物〗āmarànth.

はけぐち 捌け口 〖水・感情の〗an outlet; 〖商品の〗a market. ●はけ口のない池 a pond without an *outlet* 《for water》. ●感情のはけ口を見つける find an *outlet* [a *vent*] *for* one's feelings 《in》. ●製品のはけ口を探す look for a *market* for the products. ▶彼はうっ憤のはけ口をスポーツに求めた He used sports as an *outlet* for his frustrations.

はげしい 激しい 形 violent; severe; heavy; intense; bitter; stormy.

〖使い分け〗 **violent** 議論・出来事・感覚・感情・変化・天候などが極端に力や活力にあふれていること．しばしばその突発的で破壊的な性質を暗示する．
severe 害・苦痛・心配・不快などを引き起こすほど程度がはなはだしくどういうこと．
heavy 並はずれて力・量・程度などがはなはだしいこと．主に不快なものに用いる．
intense 力・量・程度・感覚などがはなはだしいこと，感情が強いことをいう．
bitter 議論・争いなどが敵意・怒りがこめられて激しく辛らつであること．
stormy 議論や性質などが強烈な感情に支配されること，有害・不快の含みはない．

---

① 〖激しい〜〗 ●激しい風 a *violent* [a *strong*] wind. ●激しい雨 a *heavy* [a *violent*] rain; 《どしゃ降りの》a downpour. ●激しい音 a *violent* sound. ●激しいせき a *violent* cough. (🔁「激しくせきをする」は cough *violently*). ●激しい地震 a *severe* [a *violent*] earthquake. ●激しい訓練 *intense* [*heavy*, 《集中的な》*intensive*] training. ●激しい感情 an *intense* [a *strong*] feeling; (a) *violent* passion. ●激しい恋 a *stormy* love affair; *passionate* love. ●激しい運動 *strenuous* [*vigorous*] exercise. ▶胃に激しい痛みを感じた I felt a *severe* [a *violent*, 《鋭い》a *sharp*, an *acute*] pain in my stomach./I had a *severe* stomachache.

② 〖...が激しい〗 ▶彼女は気性が激しい She has a *violent* [a *stormy*] temper./《激しやすい》She is a *fiery* /fáiəri/ woman. ●動悸が激しい My heart beats [pounds] *violently*. ▶貧富の差が激しい There is a *wide* disparity between rich and poor. ▶映画界では各社の競争が激しい There is *keen* [*severe*] competition among the companies in the movie industry. ▶この道路は交通が激しい The traffic is *very heavy* (⇔light) on this road. (🔁今は busy も用いられる)/There is a lot of traffic on this road.

— **激しく** 副 violently; severely; bitterly; 〖すごい力で，強く〗hard (🔁押したり移動したりするとき以外は，かなり長時間続くことを除き). ●激しく攻撃をする attack 《him》 *violently*. ●激しくたたく hit 《it》 *hard*. ●激しく(=激しい口調で)非難する criticize 《him》 *severely* [*bitterly*, *harshly*, 《痛烈に》*sharply*]. ●激しく議論をする have a *heated* [a *stormy*, a *violent*] discussion 《about》. ▶雨が激しく降った It rained *heavily* [*hard*]. (🔁「雪」についても用いる)/《どしゃ降りだった》It poured down. ▶気温が激しく(=急激に)変わった The temperature changed *drastically*./There was a *drastic* change in temperature.

— **激しくなる** 動 get* [become*] violent [severe, intense]. ▶風が激しくなった The wind became *stronger*./It began to blow *harder*.

— **激しさ** 名 violence; severity; intensity.

はげたか 禿げ鷹 a vulture. (🔁「禿げ鷲」の俗称．「《弱みにつけこむ》禿げ鷹商法」など比喩的にも用いられる)
●ハゲタカファンド 〖経済〗a vulture fund.

***バケツ** a bucket, 《主に米》a pail. ●バケツ1杯の水を *bucket(ful)* [a *pail(ful)*] of water. ●バケツに水をくむ fill a *bucket* [a *pail*] with water. ▶外はバケツをひっくり返したような雨だ 《話》It's raining [The rain is coming down] *in buckets* outside.

バゲット 〖細長いフランスパン〗a baguette.

バケツリレー (列) a bucket brigade. ●バケツリレーをする form a *bucket brigade*.

ばけねこ 化け猫 a goblin cat.

ばけのかわ 化けの皮 ●化けの皮がはがれる ▶その政治家はとうとう化けの皮がはがれた 《本性をあらわした》The

はけば politician *betrayed himself* [*showed* his *true colors*] at last. ▶ あの詐欺師の化けの皮をはがしたい I'll *rip away* the swindler's *mask*. / (やや書) I'll *unmask* [(暴露する) *expose*] the swindler. (関連) その政治家は実はスパイであることを暴露する *unmask* the politician *as a spy*)

はけば 捌け場 ▶ 子供たちにはエネルギーのはけ場が必要だ Children need an *outlet* for their energy.

はげまし 励まし encouragement. (⇨激励)

*****はげます 励ます** [勇気づける] (現在していることに) encourage 《him *to* do》; (これからするように) encourage 《him *to* do》; [元気づける] cheer ... up; [支援する] support ▶ 病人を励ます *cheer up* a sick person. ▶ もう一度やってみるよう彼を励ました I *encouraged* him *to* have another try.

はげみ 励み (an) encouragement 《*to*; *to* do》; [刺激] a stimulus (複 stimuli /stímjəlai/) 《*to*; *to* do》; [誘因] (やや書) an incentive 《*to*; *to* do》. ▶ 彼女が事務次官になれたことは多くの働く女性の励みになるだろう Her promotion to administrative vice-minister will *encourage* [*be an encouragement to*] many other working women.

*****はげむ 励む** [一生懸命働く] work hard 《*to* do; *at*》; [努力を集中する] concentrate 《*on*》; [傾注する] apply oneself [one's energies] 《*to* doing》; [努力する] make* an effort [efforts] 《*to* do》; [懸命にやってみる] try hard 《*to* do》. ▶ 勉学に励みなさい Work [Study] *hard*. / *Concentrate on* [*Apply yourself to*] your studies.

ばけもの 化け物 ❶ [怪物] a monster; [小鬼] a goblin; [幽霊] a ghost, (話) (おどけて) a spook. ▶ 彼は化け物に追いかけられている夢を見た He had a dream that *monsters* were chasing him.
❷ [特異な能力の人] (異才の人) a prodigy; (超人) a demon, (男) a superman (複 -men). ▶ 彼女は化け物みたいに力がある He has *superhuman* power. ▶ 彼女は90歳なのにまだ舞台に立っている. あの人は化け物だよ She's still on the stage at ninety. She's *very special*.
● 化け物屋敷 a haunted house.

はげやま 禿げ山 a bald mountain.

はける 捌ける ❶ [水が流れる] drain 《off [away]》.
❷ [よく売れる] sell* well. ▶ その品物はよくはけている The goods *are selling well*.

はげる 剥げる go* [become*] bald, (婉曲的) (毛が) get* thin. ▶ 頭が禿げた人 a *bald* man [woman]. (⇨禿げ頭) ● 禿げ上がった額 [はえぎわ] a *receding* forehead [hairline]. ▶ 彼は頭のてっぺんがだんだん禿げてきた(=薄くなってきた) His hair *is getting thin* [*is thinning out*] on top. / He is a little *thinner* on top. (!いずれも婉曲的な言い方. 特に目の前にいる人に向かって You *are going bald*. などというのは失礼)

はげる 剥げる [塗料などが] peel off [away]; [塗料・化粧が] come* off; [色あせる] fade 《⇨褪(*)せる》 ▶ 壁[壁紙]がはげかかっている The wall [wallpaper] *is peeling off*. ▶ ラッカーの上塗りがすっかりはげて(=すり減って)しまった The lacquer coating *has all worn away*.

ばける 化ける (別の姿になる) turn [transform] oneself 《*into*》; take* [assume] the form [shape] 《*of*》; (変装する) disguise oneself 《*as*》. (⇨変装) ▶ こんなとこで死ぬはめになったら君のこと呪って化けて出てやる If I had to die in such a place like this, I'll curse [hold a grudge against] you and *haunt* you. (!(1) had to と仮定法過去形になることに注意. (2) haunt は「幽霊が(ある場所に)現れる」の意だが, 「(ある人に)現れる」という口語表現もある)

はげわし 禿げ鷲 [鳥] a vulture.

*****はけん 派遣** 图 (軍隊·使者などの) dispatch. ● 使者の派遣 the *dispatch* of a messenger.
—— 派遣する 動 send; (やや書) dispatch 《(a messenger)》《*to*》; (代表として) delegate ... 《*to* the conference》. ▶ 政府は文化使節団をフランスに派遣した The government *sent* [*dispatched*] a cultural mission *to* France.
● 派遣軍 an expeditionary force. ● 派遣社員 a worker from a temporary employment agency; 《話》 a temp. ● 派遣労働 (臨時の労働) temporary labor. ● 派遣労働者 a (dispatched) temporary worker.

はけん 覇権 [他国に対する指導権] (a) hegemony /hədʒémənɪ/; (支配権) supremacy, dominance, power 《*over*》; [選手権に] 《win [hold]》 a championship. ▶ それらの国に対して覇権を握る[握っている] establish [hold, have] (one's) *hegemony* over the countries.

ばけん 馬券 a bétting tícket (on a horse).
● 馬券売り場 a bétting (tícket) òffice; [(窓口) window]. ● 場外馬券売り場 an off-track bétting pàrlor.

‡はこ 箱

● **WORD CHOICE** ● 箱

case 各種の物品や商品を保管·運搬するための, ある程度頑丈な入れ物. 形状はさまざま. ● 筆箱 a pencil *case*.

box 主に立方体または直方体のふた付きの箱. ● 段ボール[弁当]箱 a cardboard [lunch] *box*.

chest 通例木製でふた付きの, 大きくて頑丈な箱. ● 大きな木箱 a large wooden *chest*.

● 頻度チャート

case ████████████████████
box ████
chest ██

20   40   60   80   100 (%)

a box; a case; a chest (⇨類語); (商品などの小さな包み箱) a packet, 《主に米》 a pack; (商品包装用の厚紙·合成樹脂などでのわく箱) a carton; (果物·びんなどの保管·運搬用のわく箱) a crate. ● マッチ箱 a matchbox. ● 弁当箱 a lúnch bòx. ● 宝石箱 a jéwelry bòx. ● マッチ1箱 a *box* of matches. ● たばこ 1 箱 a *pack(age)* of cigarettes. (!これを 10 箱とか 12 箱とかまとめたのが a carton) ● 本を箱に入れる put books in a *box* (箱に入った状態を強調する場合は put books *in its case*) (!後の方は購入時に付いてくる箱の場合)
● トマトを箱で買う buy tomatoes *by the case* [*crate*]. ● 箱入り娘 a rim lock.

はごいた 羽子板 a Japanese battledore.

はこいりむすめ 箱入り娘 a well-protected daughter of a respectable family.

はこう 跛行 图 (不自由な足どりで歩くこと) a limp; (不均衡) (an) imbalance.
—— 跛行する 動 limp.

はこがき 箱書き (説明的に) a note of authentication on a box containing a work of art.

はこじょう 箱錠 a rim lock.

パゴダ [寺院の塔] a pagoda.

はごたえ 歯応え ● 歯応えのある[ない]肉 *tough* [*too tender*] meat. ● 歯応えのあるスパゲッティ spaghetti *al dente* /æl déntɪ/. ● 歯応えのあるレタス (ぱりっとした) *crisp* lettuce. ● 歯応えのある本 (読む価値(のある)) a *rewarding* book; a book *worth reading*. ▶ この仕

はこづめ 事は歯応えがある This job is *challenging* [*tough*].
はこづめ 箱詰め ●リンゴを箱詰めにする *pack* apples *in a box*. ●箱詰めの魚 *boxed* [*cased*] *fish*; *fish packed in a box* [*a case*].
はにわ 埴輪 a miniature garden.
はこび 運び 〖進行〗progress; 〖段階〗a stage. ▶体育館は6月15日開館の運びになっている The gym is going to be opened on June 15.
はこびこむ 運び込む carry [bring*]... in. (❗運び込む場所が示されるときは into) (⇒運ぶ)
はこぶ 運ぶ

WORD CHOICE 運ぶ

carry 人や物品を運搬したり、移動させたりすることを示す最も一般的な語。▶この飛行機は一度に250人を運べる This plane *carries* 250 people at a time.
transport 特に交通機関や輸送機関が、物品や人を大量に長距離にわたって運搬・輸送すること。●乗客を空港まで運ぶ *transport* passengers to the airport.
convey 特に乗り物等を使って物品などを運送すること。広義で、音・においなどを運んだり、ニュース・情報などを伝達したりすることもさす。主に〖書〗で用いる。●その国まで麻薬を運ぶ *convey* the drug to that country.

頻度チャート

carry	████████████
transport	██████
convey	███
	20 40 60 80 100 (%)

❶〖物を移動させる〗carry; 〈やや書〉convéy; transpórt. (⇒〖類語〗) ▶テーブルを2階に[部屋の中に; 家の外へ]運ぶ *carry* a table upstairs [*into the room*; *out of the house*]. ▶箱を肩にかついで運ぶ *carry* a box on one's shoulder. ●箱を車のところまで運ぶ *carry a box* (*over*) *to the car*. ❗over は距離を強調する) ▶彼らはけが人を病院まで車で運んだ They *carried* [*took*] the injured man by car *to the hospital.*/They *drove* the injured man *to the hospital*. ▶バスが乗客を駅まで運んだ A bus *carried* [*conveyed*, *transported*] the passengers *to the station*. ▶そよ風がバラの香りを運んでくる A breeze *carries* [*conveys*] the scent of roses. ▶この病気はハエによって運ばれる The disease *is carried* [*is transmitted*] by flies.

❷〖物事が進む〗go* (❗通例態の副詞を伴う); 〖進歩する〗progréss; 〖進行する〗proceed; 〖手はずを整える〗arrange. ▶事はうまく運んだ Everything *went* well. ▶事は順調に運んでいる Things *are going* [*progressing*, *proceeding*] smoothly [*without a hitch*]. ▶このように事を運んだらよいだろうか How should we *arrange* things [*取りかかる*] *go about* this]?

❸〖その他の表現〗▶彼女はわざわざ私の家まで足を運んでくれた She took the trouble to *come* to my house. (⇒行く, 来る)

はこぶね 箱舟 ●ノアの箱舟 Noah's ark.
はこぶねさくらまる『方舟さくら丸』The Ark Sakura. (〔参考〕安部公房の小説)
はこべ 〖植物〗chickweed.
はこぼれ 刃毀れ nicks 《*in a knife*》. ▶刃こぼれした刀 a sword with a *nicked* edge [*blade*].
はこまくら 箱枕 a pillow supported by a (wooden) box; a pillow with a box.
はこみや 箱宮 a miniature *Shinto* shrine.
はこもの 箱物 ●箱物(＝公共施設)の建設に無駄な金を遣う waste money on the construction of *public facilities*.
はこやなぎ 箱柳 〖植物〗a Japanese aspen; a white poplar.
はごろも 羽衣 a robe of feathers. ●天女の羽衣 the celestial *robe* of an angel.
バザー 《hold》a bazaar /bəzá:r/. ●チャリティーバザー a charity *bazaar*.
ハザード 〖ゴルフ〗a hazard.
ハザードマップ 〖災害予測地図〗a hazard map.
ハザードランプ 〖非常用警告灯〗a hazard (warning) light. (❗(1) 通例複数形で. (2) hazard lamps も可だがまれ)
はさい 破砕 ─ 破砕する 動 break ... (into pieces). (⇒砕く)
はざかいき 端境期 〖収穫前の品薄のころ〗the lean [pre-harvest] month(s); 〖閑散期〗the off-season.
はざくら 葉桜 ▶ここ2-3日のうちにすっかり葉桜になってしまった Most of the cherry trees *have sprouted young leaves* in the past few days, shedding their fading blossoms quickly.
ばさつく dry and brittle 《hair》.
ばさばさ ●ばさばさの髪 *dry and unkempt* hair. ●ばさばさにしたしゅろぼうき a *frazzled-up* palmleaf broom.
ぱさぱさ ●ぱさぱさのパン *dry* (*and crumbly*) bread.
はざま 狭間 ▶二つのビルの狭間を通り抜ける (二つのビルにはさまれた狭い所を) go through *the narrow space between* two office buildings.

*****はさまる** 挟まる (はさまれる) be [get*] caught 《*in*》; 〖間に入る〗get 《*between*》. (⇒挟む) ▶車のドアにスカートがはさまった My skirt *got caught in* the car door. ▶食べかすがよく歯にはさまります Food particles often *get* [*are often*] *stuck between* my teeth. (❗後の方は「はさまって取れない」の意)

*****はさみ** 鋏 scissors /sízərz/; 〖大型の〗shears (❗植木・羊毛の刈り込み用); 〖木・針金・つめなどを切る〗clippers; 〖カニの〗a claw; 〖切符を切る〗a punch.

〔解説〕**scissors, shears, clippers** は通例複数扱いで、数えるときは a pair [two pairs] of scissors の形で用いる. a pair of scissors の場合は単数扱い. 漠然と「はさみ1丁」と言うときは a pair of scissors の代わりに some scissors と言う.

●植木ばさみ gárdening shèars. ●はさみをとぐ[使う] sharpen [use] *scissors*. ●このはさみはよく切れない These [×This] *scissors* don't cut well./These *scissors* are not sharp. (❗these scissors では、はさみが1丁なのか2丁 以上なのかは不明. 1丁であることをはっきりと表すには this pair of scissors を用いる). 〔会話〕「はさみがいるんだけど」「はいどうぞ」"I need some *scissors*." "Here you are [×it is]."
●はさみを入れる (はさみで切る) cut 《*it*》(off) with (some) scissors (❗off があれば「切り離す」の意); (庭木に) trim 《a tree》; (切符などに) punch 《a ticket》.

はさみうち 挟み打ち ●敵をはさみ打ちにする attack the enemy *on* [*from*] both sides.
はさみしょうぎ 挟み将棋 *hasami shogi*; (説明的に) a piece-capturing board game played with 18 pawns (*shogi* pieces) on the *shogi* board.
はさみむし 鋏虫 〖昆虫〗an earwing. (❗そのはさみは forceps)

*****はさむ** 挟む ❶〖間に置く〗put* ; 〈やや話〉sandwich... 《*between*》. (❗後の方は通例受身で用いられ、狭苦しさ、圧迫感を伴う) ▶彼は本にしおりをはさんだ He *put* a bookmark *between* the pages of

はざわり

the book [*in* the book]. ▶私の町は山と山の間にはさまれている My hometown *is sandwiched between* the two mountains. ▶バスで2人の太った男性にはさまれてほとんど身動きできなかった I *was sandwiched* [*sandwiched myself*] *between* two fat men on the bus and could hardly move. ▶スイスはフランス、イタリア、オーストリアとドイツにはさまれている (間に横たわる) Switzerland *lies between* [×*among*] France, Italy, Austria and Germany. (❢ それぞれ個別の関係を示すので between を用いる) ▶彼らは机をはさんで (=間に置いて) 向かい合って座った They sat face to face *with* a table *between* them./They sat opposite each other *across* [《主に米》 *across from*] each other at] a table. ▶彼は耳にたばこをはさんで立っていた He was standing *with* a cigarette *behind* his ear.

❷ 【指などをつめる】catch*; (体の一部を) pinch. ● 彼はドアに指をはさまれた He *caught* [*pinched*] his finger *in* the door./He *had* [*got*] his finger *caught* [*pinched*] *in* the door. (❢(1) 前の言い方が普通. (2) ドアを主語にして The door *caught* [*pinched*] his finger. も可) ▶スーツケースを閉めるさきに太郎の指をはさんでしまった I shut the suitcase *on* Taro's fingers. ▶彼は二三塁間ではさまれてタッチアウトになった He was *trapped* and tagged out [(挟殺された)] *between* second and third.

❸ 【落ちないようにつかむ】hold*; (カニなどがはさむ) nip (-pp-). ● クリップボードにはさんだ書類 some papers *on* a clipboard. ▶はしでそれをはさめますか Can you *hold* it with your chopsticks? ▶カニに指をはさまれた I *had* my finger *nipped* by a crab./A crab *had a hold on* my finger.

❹ 【途中に割り込ませる】cut* [break*] in (*on*); interrupt. ▶彼は私たちの話に口をはさんだ He *cut in on* [*interrupted*] our talk. ▶彼のその事に異議をはさんだ (=唱えた) He *made* [*raised*] *an objection to* it. ▶それには疑いをはさむ余地がない There is no *room for doubt about* it.

❺ 【耳に】▶彼は彼女のうわさを小耳にはさんだ (たまたま聞いた) He *happened to hear* a rumor about her.

はざわり 歯触り ● 新鮮で歯触りのいいきゅうり a fresh, *crunchy* [*crisp*] cucumber. (❢ crunchy はかんだ時に出る音に、crisp はぱりっとした食感に焦点がある)

はさん 破産 图 bankruptcy /bǽŋkrʌptsi/; [返済不能]《法律》insolvency. ● 自己破産を申告する file for voluntary [personal] *bankruptcy*. ● 破産の危機にひんする be on the brink of *bankruptcy*. ● 破産を宣告する declare *bankruptcy*. ● 破産宣告を受ける be declared *bankrupt*. ● 事実上の破産 practical *bankruptcy*.

── 破産する 動 go bankrupt, go into bankruptcy. ▶店が火事になり彼は破産した He *went bankrupt* [*was ruined*,《話》*went broke*] after the fire in his shop. (❢ become bankrupt も可) (⇨倒産)
● 破産管財人 a bankruptcy trustee. ● 破産者《法律》a bankrupt; an insolvent (debter). ● 破産申し立て a bankruptcy petition; a petition in [for, of] bankruptcy.

‡はし 端 [[末端]] an end; [[先端]] a tip; [[縁]] an edge, [[書]] a margin; (わき) a side; [[すみ]] a corner. ● 橋の向こうの端 the *other end* of a bridge. ● 島の北の端に at the northern *tip* [*end*] of the island. ● 道路の端に by the *side* of the road. ● テーブルの端に座る (端の席に) sit at the *end* of the table; (表面の端に) sit on the *edge* of the table. ● ページの端を折る turn down the *corner* of a page; make a dog-ear on a page. ● 本を端から端まで読む read a

はじ

book *from cover to cover*; (読み通す) read a book *through*. ▶彼はその通りの端から端まで本屋を探したが一軒もなかった He looked for a bookstore *all along* the street, but he couldn't find one. (❢ all で「端から端まで」の意が出る)

‡はし 橋 ❶ [[建築物]] a bridge.

> **関連** いろいろな橋: アーチ橋 an arch(ed) *bridge*/石橋 a stone *bridge*/旋回橋 a swing *bridge*/吊り橋 a rope *bridge*; (比較的大規模な) a suspension *bridge*/鉄橋 an iron *bridge*; (鉄道の) a railroad *bridge*/はね橋 a bascule *bridge*.

① 【橋の〜】● 橋の欄干 a *bridge* rail; *bridge* railings. ● 橋の上 [下] に over [under] a *bridge*. ● 「おおわれるようにして (真) 上 [下] に」の意) ▶橋のたもと (=そば) で彼女に会った I met her *by* the *bridge*.

② 【橋が】▶その川にはたくさん橋がかかっている There are a lot of *bridges across* [*over*, ×*on*] the river. ● 新しい橋がきのう開通した A new *bridge* opened yesterday.

③ 【橋を】● 川に橋をかける build [construct, (急設する) throw, ×*make*] a *bridge* across a river; bridge a river. ● 橋を渡る cross a *bridge*.

会話 「どこか紳士靴のいい店はないでしょうか」「バリーなんかどうでしょうか. 橋を渡って左側の最初の店です」"Can you recommend me somewhere good for men's shoes?" "Try Bally's. They are just *over* the *bridge*, first left. (❢ somewhere は some place ともいい名詞用法)

❷ 【その他の表現】● 危ない橋を渡る (薄氷を踏む) skate on (very) thin ice. (⇨薄氷) ● 両国間のかけ橋となる act as an *intermediary* [a *bridge*] *between* the two countries. ▶願わくばわれ太平洋の橋とならん My wish is to become a *bridge* over the Pacific. [[参考]] 新渡戸稲造の言葉)
● 橋げた a bridge girder.

はし 箸 chopsticks. ● はし1ぜん a pair of *chopsticks*. ● はしをつける touch 《a dish》; start eating 《the food》. ● はしをつけないで残す leave 《the food》 untouched. ● はしを置く stop eating. ▶彼ははしを上手に使う He's skillful at using *chopsticks*.

> **翻訳のこころ** 父親はちょっと箸をつけただけで専ら酒をふくみ、ひさしの食欲を満足そうにながめていた (竹西寛子『蘭』) My [His] father had only a few bites of the food but mostly drank sake, and happily watched [watched with satisfaction] how much I [Hisashi] was enjoying my [his] meal. (❢ この文を「ひさし」本人が語っている場合には My father, I, my meal となり、第三者が語っている場合には His father, Hisashi, his meal となる)

● 箸が進む ▶食べ物がとてもおいしくてついついはしが進んだ The food was delicious, so I couldn't resist *eating a lot*.
● 箸にも棒にもかからない ▶彼ははしにも棒にもかからないやつだ (役立たずだ) He is a *good-for-nothing*./(所詮やっても改心の見込みはない) He's past praying for.
● 箸の上げ下ろし ▶夫は私のはしの上げ下ろしにまで (=何事にも) 文句を言う My husband *finds fault with everything* I do.
● はし置き a chopstick rest. ● はし立て a chopstick stand. ● はし箱 a chopstick case.

‡はじ 恥 (a) shame; [[屈辱]] (a) humiliation; [[不名誉]] (a) disgrace; [[ばつが悪いこと]] (an) embarrassment. (⇨はずかしい) [[類語]] ▶貧乏はけっして恥ではない Being poor is no *disgrace*./There is no *shame* in being poor. ▶彼は一家の恥 (さらし) だ He is a *disgrace* [a *shame*] to the family. (❢ 「恥と

はじいる

なる人・物」の意では a がつく）▶私は恥を忍んで彼に金を請うた I swallowed my *pride* and asked him for money. ▶こんなことくらい知らないと恥だぞ（こんなことは当然知っておくべきだ）You *ought to* know this. ▶聞くは一時の恥（道に迷うより道を聞くほうがよい）(It's) better to ask the way than go astray.

- 恥の上塗り ▶彼は恥の上塗りをしないようにとても気をつけていた He was very careful not to *add to his shame*.
- 恥も外聞もなく （世間体を顧みずに）《書》without regard for appearances [respectability].
- 恥をかく ▶試験が０点で恥をかいた I *was ashamed* when I got zero on the test. ▶皆に笑われて恥をかいた Everyone laughed at me and I *was humiliated*.
- 恥をさらす （自分の面目をつぶす）bring shame on oneself; （人前で面目をつぶす）disgrace oneself in public.
- 恥を知れ ▶そんなうそをつくとは恥を知れ You should *be ashamed to* tell such a lie./*Shame on you for* telling such a lie. (**!** 単に「恥を知れ」なら *Shame on you* か *For shame!* となる. 後の方が堅い表現で意味が強い. ×*Know shame!* とはいわない）
- 恥をすすぐ[そそぐ]（汚名をぬぐい去る）wipe off a disgrace.

はじいる 恥じ入る be [feel] bitterly [deeply] ashamed (*of*). (⇨@ 恥じる)

はしか 麻疹 〖医学〗measles. (**!** 単数扱い）●はしかにかかる catch [get, have] *measles*.

はしがかり 橋懸かり （能楽）an elevated passage-way with railings leading to the *Noh* stage.

はしがき 端書き a foreword. (⇨序文)

はじき 弾き ❶〖弾くこと〗▶このコートは水のはじきがいい This coat *repels* [*sheds*] moisture *well*.
❷〖ピストル〗《米俗》a piece.

はじきだす 弾き出す ❶〖はじく〗（つめ先などでポンと）flip;（電荷などを）repel. ●陽子をはじき出す *repel* protons.
❷〖排斥する〗《書》ostracize. ●集団から彼をはじき出す *ostracize* him from the community.
❸〖算出する〗calculate;（費用などを）work ... out. ●学校の建設費をはじき出す *calculate* [*work out*] the construction cost of the school.
❹〖ひねり出す〗squeeze (*out of*). ▶家計から１万円をはじき出さないといけない We have to *squeeze* 10,000 yen *out of* the household expenses.

*__はじく__ 弾く ❶〖指・つめではね飛ばす〗flip (-pp-). ●硬貨を指ではじく *flip* [（はじいて回す）*spin*] a coin.
❷〖はね返す〗repel (-ll-). ▶この布地は水をはじく This fabric *repels* water [is water-*repellent*].
❸〖ボールをはじく〗（サッカー）（手のひらで）punch;（こぶしで）fist. ●ゴロをはじく〖野球〗fumble [bobble; juggle] a grounder. ●シュートをはじく〖サッカー〗*punch off* the shot. ▶打球は三塁手のグローブをはじいた〖野球〗The ball bounced [glanced] off the third baseman's glove.

はしくれ 端くれ ▶私だって音楽家の端くれです I'm *a bit of* a musician./I'm a musician, though I'm not a great one.

はしけ a barge, a lighter. ●はしけの船頭（男の）《文》a bargeman;《英》a bargee.

はじける 弾ける（ぱっと開く）burst* open;（音を立てて開く）crack [pop] open;（割れて開く）split* open. ▶コーンがフライパンの中ではじけている The corn is *popping* in the frying pan. (**!** *corn* は集合名詞）▶若い笑い声が廊下を伝って社長室まではじけていった Young people's laughter *rang through* the corridor to the president's office.

はじまる

*__はしご__ 梯子 ❶〖道具〗a ladder;〖脚立〗a stepladder. ●縄ばしご a rópe *ladder*. ●避難ばしご an emergency *ladder*. ●はしごの段 a round of a *ladder*. ●はしごを塀に掛ける put [lean] a *ladder* against the wall. ●はしごを上る〖登る〗climb (up) [go up] a *ladder*. ●はしごを降りる come down a *ladder*. ●はしごを支える steady a *ladder*.
❷〖転々とすること〗▶はしご酒をする have drinks at one bar after another;《米話》go *bar-hopping*;《英話》go on a *pub-crawl*. ▶原因不明の頭痛で何人の医者をはしごしたことか I went to see so many doctors one after another because I suffered from headaches of unknown origin.
- はしご車《米》a (hook and) ladder;《米》a ladder truck.

はじさらし 恥曝し a disgrace; a shame 《*to*》. ●恥さらしをする bring *disgrace* [*shame*]《*on*》one's family. ▶この恥さらしめが *Shame on you!*

ハシシュ 〖インド産の大麻〗hashish.

はじしらず 恥知らず ▶彼は恥知らずだ He is *shameless* [*without shame*]./He *has no* (*sense of*) *shame*. (⇨@)

はしたがね はした金 an insignificant sum of money,《話》peanuts,《話》chícken fèed.

はしたない （みっともない）improper;（慎みのない）immodest;（下品な）vulgar;（不名誉な）disgraceful.
▶はしたないふるまいをするな Don't behave *improperly*.

はしっこい quick; swift. (⇨@ 素早い, すばし(っ)こい)

ばじとうふう 馬耳東風 ●彼の忠告を馬耳東風と聞き流す *turn a deaf ear* [*be deaf*] *to* his advice.

はしなく(も) 端なく(も) unexpectedly. (⇨@ 図らず)

はしのないかわ 『橋のない川』 *The River with No Bridge*. 《参考》住井すゑの小説

はしばし 端々 ●彼の言葉〖動作〗のはしばしからにじみ出る彼のやさしさ his thoughtfulness radiating from [out of] *every word* [*movement*] of his.

はしばみ 〖植物〗（木）a hazel (tree);（実）a hazel, a hazelnut.

パシフィックリーグ 〖野球〗the Pacific League.

はしぶとがらす 嘴太鴉〖鳥〗a jungle crow.

はしぼそがらす 嘴細鴉〖鳥〗a carrion crow.

はじまらない 始まらない ▶今さら何を言っても始まらない（もう遅い）It's *too late* to make complaints./（何の効果・意味もない）There's *no point* in making complaints now./（いいことは何もない）It *won't do any good* making complaints now. ▶今さらくやんでも始まらない（ことわざ）It's *no use* crying over spilt milk. ▶前向きに物事を考えようの意）

はじまり 始まり（開始）a beginning, a start;（原因）a cause;（起源）(an) origin. ●地球上の生命の始まり the *origins* of life on earth. ▶うそつきは泥棒の始まり 'Lying is the *beginning* of stealing.'/（ことわざ）それがこのようなすべての事の始まりだった That's what *kicked* this whole thing *off*.

*__はじまる__ 始まる

WORD CHOICE 始まる

begin 行事・出来事・行動などが始まること. 特に事象が開始され, 時々刻々と変化する段階のごく初期にあることを含意する. ▶その研究は 1987 年に始まった The study *began* in 1987.
start 行事などが始まること. 特に静止状態からの活動の開始・再開を含意する. ▶野球のシーズンが今年はおよそ3週間早く始まった The baseball season *started* about three weeks earlier this year.

はじめ / はじめまして

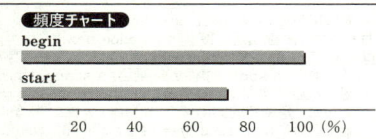

頻度チャート
- begin
- start
- 20　40　60　80　100 (%)

❶ **[開始される]** begin* (↔end); start (⇨[類語]); (会などが) open (閉じられていたものが開かれ始めるの意); (好ましくない季節などが) set* in; (戦争などが) break* out. (⇨始める [類語]) ● 5月1日から始まる1週間のスケジュール one's schedule for the week from May 1. ▶学校は9時 [4月1日; 4月] から始まる School *begins* [*starts*] *at* nine [*on* April 1; *in* April]. (前置詞は from でないことに注意。April 1 は通例 April the first と読む) ▶私たちが会場に着いたときコンサートはもう始まっていた When we got to the hall, the concert *had* already *begun*. ▶朝の礼拝は賛美歌で始まった The morning service *began* [*started, opened*] *with* a hymn. ▶会議は午前10時に始まる The meeting *opens* [*begins, starts*] at 10 a.m. ▶音楽祭の1週間が始まるとこの静かな湖畔の保養地はとても活気のある町になる When the week of the music festival *comes* [*starts*], this quiet lakeside resort becomes a very lively town. ▶雨季が始まった The rainy season *has set in*. ▶第二次世界大戦は1939年に始まった World War Ⅱ *broke out* [*started*] in 1939. ▶その計画はすでに始まっている The project *is under way* already.

翻訳のこころ わたしはそこに立ちつくし, いつまでもクリスマスソングを聴いていた。銀座に, ゆっくりと夜が始まっていた (江國香織『デューク』) I stood there, listening to Christmas songs [carols] for a long time. The night *began* to fall slowly in Ginza. (■ (1)「(夜が)始まっていた」は (the night) began to fall ((夜が)生じ, 起こり始めていた)と表す。この表現は日本語の「夜のとばりが下り始めた」に通じる。(2) Christmas carol は「宗教的なクリスマスソング」の意)

❷ **[起源がある]** start; 《やや書》 originate 《*in*+場所, *with*+人》; [時期が] (...から始まる) date 《*from*》; (...にさかのぼる) date [go*] back 《*to*》. ▶文芸復興はイタリアで始まった The Renaissance *started* [*originated*] *in* Italy. ▶日本の農耕は弥生時代に始まる Agriculture in Japan *dates from* [*dates back to, starts in*] the Yayoi period.

❸ **[その他の表現]** ▶それは今に始まったことではない (古い話だ) That's *an old story*./That's *nothing new*.

*はじめ 初め, 始め ❶ **[始めること] [時]** a beginning, a start (■ beginning は目的を遂げる過程の初めいい, しばしば middle (中ごろ) や end (終わり)と対照的に用いる。start は単に動作の初めをいう); (冒頭) an opening (⇨冒頭); (起源) (an) origin; [いちばん初めのもの] the first.

① **[〜初め]** ● 新学期の初めに at [in] the *beginning* (↔end) of a new term (■ in の方が時間的な広がりを含む); (初日に) on the *opening* day of a new term. ● 昭和の初めに (早い時期に) *early* in the Showa era; at [in] the *early part* of the Showa era.

② **[初めが]** ▶何事も初めが大事 A good *beginning* is always important [makes a good ending].

③ **[初めは [の]]** ● 初めの2ページ the *first* two pages. ● 初めの計画 (元の) the *original* plan. ▶初め(のうち)は彼がきらいでした I didn't like him *at first* [×*for the first time*]. ▶その物語は初め(のうち)は (=初めの部分は)退屈だ The story is boring *at* [*in*] *the beginning*.

④ **[初めに]** (まっ先に) first (of all); (第一に) first (-ly). (⇨まず❶)

⑤ **[初めから]** ▶もう一度初めから読みなさい Read it once more *from the* (*very*) *beginning*. (■ very を添える方が強意的)/(読み直しなさい) Read it *all over again*. ▶私の心は初めから決まっていた My mind was made up *from the beginning*. ▶私は彼の話を初めから終わりまで聞いた I listened to his speech *from beginning to end* [*from first to last*]. (■ 本の場合は I read the book *from cover to cover*. ともいえる。いずれも対句的に用いるので定冠詞 the は省略する) ▶高志がそれをやったのだと初めから分かっていた I knew *from the* (*very*) *start* [*from the* (*very*) *first*, 《話》 *all along*] (that) Takashi did it. (■ that 節でなく普通の名詞句が目的語の場合は I knew *the fact from the* (*very*) *start*. のような語順になる)

❷ **[その他の表現]** ▶ガイドを初め(=含めて) 7 人が死んだ Seven people were killed, *including* the guide.

● 初めよければ終わりよし 《ことわざ》 A good beginning makes a good ending.

*はじめて 初めて first, for the first time.

使い分け first あることが初めて起こって以来の経過を暗示する。通例文中で置く。
for the first time 初めて起こった出来事自体を強調する。

▶富山に来たのはこれが初めてです This is *the first time* (*that*) I've [×*the first time*] come to Toyama. (■ (1) 現在のことを述べる文脈では, that 節中は通例現在完了形になる。(2)「富山に来たのはそのときが初めてでした」のように過去のことは That *was the first time* (*that*) I *had come* [I *came*] to Toyama. のように通例過去完了, 時に過去を用いる)/This is *my first* time in [*my first* visit to] Toyama./I've come to Toyama *for the first time*. ▶初めて京都に行ったとき, 金閣寺を訪れた *The first time* I went to Kyoto [When I went to Kyoto *for the first time*], I visited the Kinkakuji Temple. (■ 前の言い方は the first time が接続詞の働きをし, 後の言い方より普通) ▶私は生まれて初めて富士山を見た I saw Mt. Fuji *for the first time* in my life. ▶君があんなに怒ったのを初めて見た (今まで一度も見たことがない) I've *never* seen you so angry. ▶彼は初めてその体験をした The experience was *new* to him. ▶私は昨日になって初めてそれを知った I knew it *only yesterday*./*It was not until* [*till*] *yesterday that* I knew it. (■ I didn't know it *until* [*till*] yesterday. を強調した言い方。《書》ではしばしば強調のため *Not until* [*till*] *yesterday did* I know it. のように倒置構文を用いる)

会話「ご主人に初めてお会いになったのはいつですか」「3年前です」"When did you *first* meet your husband?/When did you meet your husband *for the first time*?" "Three years ago." (■ 疑問文では最初の言い方の方が普通)

はじめね 初め値 an opening price. (⇨ 終わり値)

*はじめまして 初めまして (It's very) nice [How nice, (I'm very) glad] to ＼meet you./《丁寧》 It's a great pleasure [What a pleasure, (I'm very) pleased] to meet you. (■ (1) How do you do, Mr. A? を交換し合う言い方は古めかしい感じがするので今はまれ。(2) 日本語式に ×This is the first time I

はじめる

have seen you. とはいわない．(3) これに対する応答は (It's) nice [(I'm) pleased] to meet you, too. とか，↘My pleasure. となる．

はじめる 始める begin* (↔end); start (↔finish); 『会などを』open (↔close); 『取りかかる』set* about ....

> **使い分け** **begin** 物事の展開の初期段階を強調する．
> **start** 静止状態からの活動の開始や再開を強調する．
> **open** 主に営業や事業などの開始を表す．

▶みなさん，おはようございます．では始めましょうか (会議などで) Good morning, everyone. Shall we get started (on work)? (❗ get started は start より口語的)/Let's get down to business, shall we?

❶《...を始める》●その仕事を始める start [begin] the work; set about the work (❗ set about は「取りかかる」の意が強い． 特定の仕事ではなく一般に仕事を始める場合は get (down) [set] to work). ●交渉を始める open [begin, 《書》enter into] negotiations 《with》．▶子供に手がかからなくなったので彼女は料理学校を始めた When her children were old enough to take care of themselves, she opened (up) a cookery school. ▶いつチェスを始めたのですか When did you take up chess? (❗ take up は趣味や習慣などを始めること)

❷《...から始める》▶簡単な事 [10 ページ；前の授業の復習] から始めよう Let's begin [start] with something simple [at page 10; by reviewing the last lesson]. (❗ 前置詞の扱いに注意)

❸《～(し)始める》▶雨が降り始めた It began [started] to rain./It began [started] raining. (❗ begin, start は不定詞・動名詞の両方が用いられるが，不定詞は行為・運動の開始自体を，動名詞は開始後に引き続く行為の継続的遂行を強調する)▶先生が話し始めると皆おしゃべりをやめた The teacher started to speak, and everyone stopped talking.

はしゃ 覇者 『征服者』a conqueror; 『優勝者』a champion; 『勝利者』a winner.

ばしゃ 馬車 『乗用の』a carriage (❗ 主に自家用); a coach (❗ 大型で屋根・ドア付き); 『荷馬車』a (horse and) wagon [cart] (❗ 4 輪で 2 頭立ての馬が引く), a cart (❗ 通例 2 輪で 1 頭立て). ●2 頭 [4 頭] 立ての馬車 a carriage and pair [four]. ▶駅馬車 a stagecoach.
●馬車馬のように ▶馬車馬のように働く work like a horse [a slave].

はしゃぐ (子供などが飛び回る) romp (about [around]), frolic (-icked; -icking) (about) ▶その子供はやたらはしゃいでいた (うれしくて興奮していた) The child was wild with excitement.

はしやすめ 箸休め (説明的に) a side dish served between the main dishes.

ばしゃばしゃ ●ばしゃばしゃと浅瀬を渡って向こう岸に行く splash across the shallows to the opposite bank. ▶walk across the shallows with splashes... ともいうが前の方が普通．

ばしゃばしゃ ●ばしゃばしゃする splash water.

パジャマ pajamas /pədʒáːməz/, 《英》**pyjamas**. (❗ 複数形で複数扱い) ●パジャマ 1 着 a pair [a suit] of pajamas. ●パジャマのポケット [上着] a pajama pocket [top]. (❗ ×a pajamas pocket [top] とはいわない) ▶パジャマ姿の男がひじ掛け椅子に腰をかけていた A man in pajamas was sitting in an armchair.

ばしゅ 馬主 the owner of a horse.

ばしゅ 馬首 ●馬首をめぐらす (向きを変える) turn a horse around.

ばじゅつ 馬術 horsemanship; (the art of) riding.

はじらい

●馬術競技 an equestrian event.

はしゅつじょ 派出所 (警察の) a police box.

ばしょ 場所 ❶『所』a place (❗ 最も意味の広い語); (特定の地点) a spot; (事件などの現場) a scene. (⇨項目 ❶) ●次から次へと場所を変える move from place to place. (❗ 対句的に用いるのが無冠詞) ●絶えず紛争の起こる場所 a trouble spot. ▶ここはあの事故のあった場所です This is (the place [spot]) where the accident occurred. (❗《話》では ( ) 内はしばしば省略される)/This is the scene of the accident. ▶この場所は座り心地がよい This place is comfortable to sit in. (❗ in に注意) ▶ここは若者に人気のある場所です This is a popular place [spot] for young people.

| 会話 | 「ごらん，衛兵の交代をやっているよ」「早く！いい場所を取ろう」"Look, they're changing the guard!" "Quick! Let's get a good place."

❷『位置』a location; (位置関係) a position. ●新しい工場にふさわしい場所 a suitable location [用地 site] for a new factory. ●行方不明の息子がいる場所を突き止める locate one's missing son. ▶そのホテルは海を見渡すばらしい場所にある The hotel has a fine location overlooking the sea. ▶警官は地図で学校の場所を教えてくれた The police officer showed me the position of the school on [×with] the map.

❸『余地』room; (空間) space. (⇨項目 ❷)▶私の家にはグランドピアノを置く十分な場所がありません There isn't enough room for a grand piano in my house. ▶私の席は場所をあけてください Please make room for me (to sit on). ▶この家具は場所を取りすぎる This furniture takes up too much room [space].

❹『座席』a seat. ●列車の場所を取っておく (席を予約する) reserve [book] a seat on a train. ▶場所を替わってくださいませんか Could you change seats [places] with me? (❗ この場合 seat, place は常に複数形)

❺『相撲』●春 [九州] 場所 the Spring [Kyushu] Sumo Tournament. ●大相撲初場所 the New Year's Grand Sumo Tournament.

ばしょう 芭蕉 『植物』a plantain; a Japanese banana plant.

はしょうふう 破傷風 『医学』tetanus /tétənəs/, 《話》lockjaw.

ばしょがら 場所柄 ●場所柄(=自分がどこにいるか)をわきまえない don't know where one is. ▶場所柄外国人客が多い As is expected from the place, they have a lot of foreign customers.

はしょる 『すそを折る』tuck ... in [up]; 『短縮する』cut*... short, make*... short. ●長い説明をはしょる cut [make] a long explanation short. ●その本の 2, 3 章をはしょって読む (飛ばし読みをする) skip (over) a few chapters of the book. ●はしょって話せば to make a long story short; in short.

はしら 柱 ❶『支える材』a pillar (❗ 柱全般を表す一般的な語); (支柱) a post; (円柱) a column; (テント・電柱などの) a pole. ●火柱 a pillar of fire [flames]. ●柱を立てると say a pillar. ▶屋根は多くの柱で支えられている The roof is supported by a large number of pillars.

❷『中心的な存在』▶彼らは一家の柱(=大黒柱)を失った They lost their (chief) breadwinner./They lost the chief [sole] support of the family.
●柱時計 a wall clock.

はじらい 恥じらい shyness, bashfulness; 『はつが悪いこと』embarrassment; 『赤面』a blush. ▶彼の言葉に彼女は恥じらいを示した (赤面した) She blushed

はじらう **恥じらう** be ashamed [(特定の原因がなく) bashful]. (⇨恥ずかしい) ●花も恥じらう乙女 a girl as beautiful as any flower; a beautiful girl in the bloom of youth「今が盛りの美少女」の訳) *at* his words.

はしらせる **走らせる** ❶[乗り物などを] run*; (車を drive*. (⇨走る) ●車を走らせる run [*drive*] a car. ▶AとBの間に1日10本の急行を走らせることは難しい It's hard to *run* ten express trains between A and B in a day.
❷[急いで行かせる] (人を) hurry [rush]《*him*》to ...; (使者を) send《a messenger》without delay; (車・馬を) 飛ばす.
❸[すばやく動かす][ペンを] (走り書きする) scribble《the phone number》; (すらすら書く) write ... smoothly; [目を] scan《the newspaper》.
❹[敵を敗走させる] put the enemy to rout [to flight].

はしり **走り** ❶[走ること] running. ●あの車いい走りしてるねえ That car *is running* beautifully.
❷[初物] ●マツタケの走り the *first matsutake* of the season; the *first matsutake* to come on the market. ●走りの果物 early fruit.

はしりがき **走り書き** 图 a hurried note; a scribble. ▶走り書きで記者たちは彼の話をメモした The reporters *scribbled* as he spoke.
―― **走り書きする** 動 2-3行走り書きする write a note *hurriedly*; *scribble* a few lines.

バジリコ [<イタリア語] (⇨バジル)

はしりこむ **走り込む** ❶[走って中に入る] run into. ▶彼女は部屋に走り込んで大声で助けを求めた She *ran into* the room and cried for help.
❷[十分走る] run a lot; (トレーニングとして) do a hard training run. ▶野球選手はシーズンオフに十分走り込んで足腰を鍛えておく必要がある Baseball players need to toughen their bodies by *running* a lot during the off-season.

はしりたかとび **走り高跳び** the high jùmp. ●走り高跳びの選手 a high jùmper.

はしりつかい **走り使い** (用事) an errand; (人) an errand boy. ●走り使いをする go on [run] *errands*《for him》.

はしりつゆ **走り梅雨** (梅雨入り前のぐずついた天気) a spell of unstable weather before the rainy season.

はしりはばとび **走り幅跳び** the lóng [《米》bróad] jùmp. ●オリンピックでの競技名は Long Jump ●走り幅跳びの選手 a lóng jùmper.

はしりまわる **走り回る** run around. ▶教室の中を走り回ってはいけない You should not *run around* in the classroom. ▶彼らは寄付のお金集めに神戸を走り回った They *ran around* Kobe trying to raise money for charity.

はしりよみ **走り読み** ―― **走り読みする** 動 (ざっと読む) read《a report》hurriedly, (やや話) skim through [skim over, 《米》skip through]《a report》; (さっと目を走らせる) run one's éye(s)《over the page》; scan《the newspaper》.

はしる **走る**
  ━━━ WORD CHOICE ━━━ **走る** ━━━
run 人・動物などが急いで走ること. しばしば from, out of, to, toward など, 移動の起点・終点を表す前置詞を伴う. ▶彼はその部屋から走り出てきた He *ran out of* the room. ▶電車は定刻どおり走っている The trains are *running* on time.
jog 人が無理のない緩やかな速度で走ること. 特に健康のためにジョギングをすること. ▶よく川沿いを走ったものだった I used to *jog* along the river.

move 自動車・船などが移動すること. 時に ahead, off, along などの副詞・前置詞を伴う. なお, 自動車の走行には drive, 船舶の走行には sail などを自動詞として用いる場合もある. ●車の走行中はシートベルトをしめてください Fasten your seat belt while the vehicle is *moving*.

❶[人・動物が] run*.

〔解説〕英語の **run** は日本語の「走る」にだいたい当たるが,「急いで行く」という意もあるので注意: 急いで戸を開けてきておくれ *Run* to [and] open the door.

▶家から走り出る *run out of* the house. (!out of は into に対して家の「中から外へ」の意) ●全速力で走る *run* as fast as one can. ▶彼は走るのが速い He *runs* fast./He is a fast runner. (⇨速い 形 ❷)
▶彼は駅から走ってきた He came *running* from the station. (!(1) from は到着点 to に対して出発点を示す. (2) ×He ran and came from the station. とはしない) ●先生のところへ走って行きなさい *Run* (*up*) *to* your teacher. (!「急いで行け」ともとれる) ▶彼は道路を走って渡った He *ran* across the street. ▶私はバスに乗ろうとして走った I *ran for* [*to* catch] the bus./(懸命に走った) I *dashed* [*made a dash*] *for* the bus. ▶彼は100メートルを12秒で走った He *ran* [*covered*] 100 meters in 12 seconds. ▶バス停まで走って3分です It's three minutes' [a three-minute] *run* to the bus-stop. ▶馬はおびえて急に走り出した The startled horse broke into a run [a gallop].

❷[乗り物などが] run*; move (⇨[類語]); (主に車が) drive*; (船が) sail. ▶列車はとてもゆっくり走っていますね The train *is running* [*moving*] very slowly./We *are running* very slowly. (!話し手が乗っている場合は後の方が好まれる) ▶ヨットが速く走っている The yacht *is sailing* [*running*] fast.
▶黒いベンツが止まり1人の男を降ろして走り去った A black Mercedes /mərséidiz/ pulled up, dropped off a man and *drove off*. ▶車は時速50キロで走った The car *ran* (*at*) [*made*] about 30 miles an hour. (!(1) make は「(ある速度で)進む」の意. (2) 米英では ... 50 kilometers とするのが普通) ▶このバスは東京–大阪間を走っている This bus *runs between* Tokyo *and* Osaka [*from* Tokyo *to* Osaka]. (!進行形は通例不可. ただし, 一時的な場合は進行形も可: 今日は列車が走っていない The trains *aren't running* today.) ▶道は川沿いに走っていた The road *ran* [×was running] along [down] the river.
▶そこの空気の抜けたタイヤで走ってる車, 車をわきに寄せなさい You're *driving* on a flat tire. Pull over (your car).

❸[その他の表現] ▶酔わずに生きていられるか, と酒に走りたい = 頼りたい気持ちは分からないではない I somewhat understand your resorting to drinking because life is too difficult to live without getting drunk.

はじる **恥じる** be [feel*] ashamed《*of*; *that*節》. (⇨恥, 恥ずかしい) ●恥ずべき行為 shameful conduct. ●無知を恥じる *be ashamed of* one's ignorance. ●良心に恥じない[恥じる] have a clear [a guilty] conscience. ●名声に恥じない(名声にこたえる) live up to one's reputation; (名に値する) be worthy of the name. ▶私はうそをついたことを恥じた I *was ashamed of* having told a lie./I *was ashamed that* I had told a lie. ▶彼は紳士名に恥じない(紳士たる名に値する) He *is worthy of* a gentleman.

バジル [植物] a basil.

はしれメロス『走れメロス』 *Run, Melos!*; *Melos, Run!* [参考] 太宰治の小説

はしわたし 橋渡し 图 [[仲介]] mediation /miːdiéiʃən/; [[仲介者]] a mediator. (⇨仲介)

—— 橋渡し(を)する 動 (仲介する) (やや書) mediate (*between*); act as a go-between (*for*). ● 二つの文明の橋渡しをする (ギャップを埋める) *bridge the gap between* the two different civilizations.

-ばしん -馬身 a length. ● 2馬身の差で勝つ win by two *lengths*.

はす 斜 ● はすに (=斜めに)ベレー帽をかぶっている wear one's beret *askew* [*at a slant*]. (⇨斜め) ● はす向かい (⇨斜向かい)

はす 蓮 [植物] a lotus. ● 蓮の花[葉] a *lotus* flower [pad]. ● 蓮池 a lotus pond. (⇨睡蓮)

:はず [当然] should ((do)); ought to ((do)); must ((do)); (必ず…するに違いない) be bound (*to* do); [予定] (…することになっている) be supposed (*to* do) (❗ supposed は /səpóustə/ と読む); (書) be due ((to) do); (予定・時間などで決まっている) be due (*to* do).

> **解説** should と ought to は話し手が期待する結果を推量していう言い方だが, should の方が主観的でよく用いられる. must は「…に違いない」という話し手の強い確信を表す.〔話〕では have (got) to が用いられることもある. should, ought, must は通例強勢を受ける.

① 【…である[する]はずだ】 ▶ 今たてば正午までにはそこへ着くはずだ If we leave now, we *should* [*ought to*, ×*must*] arrive there by noon. (❗ *ought to* の後には状態動詞, 特に be 動詞が続く. *must* は通例現在の事に関する話し手の確信を表し, 未来についての推量には be bound to even 用いる (⇨[次例])/If we leave now, we *should* [*ought to*] be there by noon. ▶ 彼はもうすぐ来るはずだ He *should* [*is supposed to, is bound to*] come in a few minutes./He *must* be coming [*is coming,* ×*must come*] in a few minutes. (❗ *must* の後には通例状態動詞がくる. 未来を示す副詞(句)を伴う進行形は現在の時点ですでに取り決められている未来の予定を表す) ▶ バスは10時に到着するはずだ The bus *is due* (*to* arrive) at 10:00. ▶ 彼女は今ごろはもう仕事を終えているはずだ She *should* [*ought to, must*] have finished her job by now. (❗ 彼女がまだ仕事を終えていないことを知っていてこういうと,「終えるはずだったのに終わらなかった」のように結果が予想に反していたことを表す) ▶ 彼らは8時30分に到着するはずだった They *should* [*ought to*] *have* arrived at 8:30. (❗ 実際は到着しなかったことを含意. at 8:30 がない場合は「もう到着しているはずだ」という完了の意にもなる)/They *were supposed to* arrive at 8:30. ▶ そこでノートパソコンを安く買うことができるはずだ You *ought to* be able to [((きっと)) can *surely*] buy a notebook computer at a low price there. ▶ 君は両親に対してもっと敬意を表してもいいはずだ You *should* [*ought to*] be more respectful to your parents. ▶ やつはどこからか来たはずなんだよ. どこからともなくわに出かせずがないもの He *must* [×*has to*] have come from somewhere. He can't have come from nowhere. (❗ 過去の推量を示す場合は have to は不可)

会話 「太郎は部屋にいますか」「いるはずです」"Is Taro in his room?" "Yes, he *múst* [*shóuld*] be." (❗ (1) be は省略不可. (2) must と異なり should には否定の余地はあるので「いるはずなのにいない」では He *should* [×*must*] be, but actually he isn't. となる)

② 【…である[する]はずない】 can't ((be)); (…であったはずがない) can't ((have done)). (❗ 通例 cannot とはせず, mustn't も用いない) ▶ そんなはずはない That *can't* be so [*true*]!/(書き言葉) It *can* [×*Can't*] that be so [*true*]?/That's impossible! ▶ あの店はそんなに込んでいるはずがない That store *can't* [*won't, shouldn't*] be so crowded. (❗ この順に話し手の確信の程度が弱くなる) ▶ その子はまだ幼いのでそんなことをするはずがない He is still very young, so *I'm sure* (*that*) he doesn't [×so he can't] do that. (❗ 後の方は「そんなことはできない」の意なら可)

▶ずっと前から存じ上げていたような気がするのですが. そんなはずはないですよね I feel as if I'd known you all the time. But I *couldn't*, could I? (❗ I couldn't have known … の短縮形 can't にすると確信度は増すが, 丁寧度は減る) ▶ こんなはずではなかった This isn't the way I *expected* it *to* be./It *wasn't supposed to* be like this.

会話 「手伝ってくださる?」「断わるはずがないだろう」"Will you help?" "How *could* I *possibly* refuse?"

会話 「洗うと色落ちするでしょうか」「そんなはずはありません」"Does the color come off (the shirt) when it's washed?" "It's *not supposed to*." (❗ It は the color をさす. to の後の come off を省略した言い方)

▶バス [乗合自動車] a bus (阀 ~es, (米) (時に) ~ses).

① 【~バス】 ● 観光バス a síghtsèeing [a tóur] *bùs*. ● 市内バス a cíty *bùs*. ● スクールバス a schóol *bùs*. ● 長距離バス a long-distance *bus*; (英) a coach. ● 通勤バス a commúter *bùs*. ● 2階建てバス (英) a double-decker. ● 空港バス an airport limousine. ● 東京行きのバス the bus to Tokyo, the Tokyo bus.

② 【バス(の)~】 ● バスの事故 a *bus* accident [crash]. (❗ crash は主に衝突事故) ● バス旅行をする take a *bus* trip [tour] (*to, around*). ▶ ここはバスの便がよい There's a good *bus* service here./This place is convenient for taking *buses*. ▶ きのうのバスの中で田中君に会った I saw Tanaka in [on] the *bus* yesterday. (❗ in は「車内で」, on は「車上で, 乗って」の意)

③ 【バスが[は]】 ▶ ほら, バスが来たよ ↘Here's [Here comes] the [our] ╱*bus*. (❗ (1) この場合 ×Here came …. とはいわない. (2) our bus は「自分たちの乗るバス」の意) ▶ 彼は次のバスはいつ来るかと尋ねた He asked when the next *bus* was due. ▶ 駅から大学まではバスが15分ごとに通っている There is [They have] a *bus* service every fifteen minutes from the station to the college./The *buses* run every fifteen minutes between the station and the college. (❗ 何分ごとか尋ねる場合は How often do the *buses* run? のように言う) ▶ このバスは大阪駅に行きますか Does this *bus* go to Osaka Station?/(話) Is this the Osaka (Station) *bus*? (❗ 話し手がバスに乗っている場合は Am I on the right *bus* to Osaka Station? のように人を主語にしていうことも多い. 運転手などに聞くときは Do you go to Osaka Station? ともいう)

会話 「このバスはどこ行きですか」「東京駅(行き)です」"Where is this *bus* for?" "It's for Tokyo Station."

会話 「次のバスはあと何分くらいで来ますか」「あと15分くらいで来ます」"How soon will the next *bus* be here?" "It'll be along in about fifteen minutes." (❗ will be along は「やって来る」の意の慣用表現)

④ 【バスに[から, を]】 ● バスに乗る[から降りる] get on [off] a *bus* (*at* Umeda). (❗ (1) 列車・船・飛行機などにも通じ, 主に乗[下]車地点をさす文脈に用いる. (2) 乗り込む[降りる]動作・過程に関心がある場合は

例 get onto [out of] a bus を用いる) ● バスに乗り遅れる miss the bus; (時流に取り残される) fail to keep up with the times. ● 8時30分のバスに間に合う be in time for [catch,《話》make] the 8:30 [《主に英》8.30] bus. (■ catch, make は時とかぎりぎり間に合うことを含意) ● バスを待つ wait for a bus.
● バスを乗り違える[違えている] take [be on] the wrong bus. ● 今朝はバスに乗り遅れた I missed [was late for] my bus this morning. (■ my bus は「私がいつも乗るある特定の時刻のバス」の意)
▶ 市バスの36番に乗って次のバス停で降りて5番のバスに乗り換えなさい Take City bus No. 36, get off at the next stop and transfer to a No. 5 bus. ▶ 私たちはバスに揺られながら山道を上がって行った We went up the mountain path on a jolting bus./Our bus jolted along up the mountain path.
⑤【バスで】● バスで学校へ行く go to school by [on a] bus (■ by は「手段」を表し, on は「乗って」の意); take [ride] a bus to school (■ take は「利用する」の意). ▶ ここからその町までバスで3時間ですIt takes three hours to go to the town from here by [on a] bus./It is a three-hour bus ride from here to the town.
● バスガイド a (bus) conductress;《和製語》a bus guide. (■《米》では性差別の匂いを避け a bus conductor が好まれる) ● バスターミナル(大規模な) a bus terminal; a bus station;《米》a depot /díːpou/. ● バス代 a bus fare. ● バス停(留所) a bus stop. ● バスレーン《米》a busway,《英》a bus lane. ● バス路線 a bus route.

バス [<ドイツ語]【低い声】【音楽】bass /béis/. ● バスで[で]歌う sing bass. ● バス歌手 a bass.

バス【ふろ】a bath. (⇨風呂) ● (ホテルの予約などで)その部屋はバス・トイレ付きですか Is the room with a (private) bath?/Does the room have a (private) bath? (■ ホテルでは通例バスとトイレがセットになっているので, トイレは訳さなくてよい)
● バスタブ a bathtub. ● バスローブ a bathrobe. (■ a drèssing gówn ともいう)

バス【伝送路】【コンピュータ】a bus.
● バスマウス a bus mouse.

パス图 ❶ 【無料入場・乗車券】a pass, a free pass;【定期券】a commutation《米》[a season《英》] ticket.
❷ 【ボールの】a pass. ● スルーパス a through-pass. ● バックパス a back-pass. ● 横パス a lateral pass. ● ラストパス the final pass; the last pass. ● パスが通る complete a pass. ● パスを出す make a pass.
❸ 【トランプの】a pass.
── パスする 動 pass. (⇨通る) ● ボールをパスする pass [throw] a ball (to him). ● 試験にパスする pass the examination [test]. ▶ パスします(トランプで) I pass./(意見などを求められて) I'll pass it on.

はすい 破水 ── 破水する 動 ▶ 長男は破水してからすぐに生まれた My first son was born just after I broke the water. ● 彼女は午前1時に破水した Her water broke at 1 a.m.

はすう 端数 【数学】a fraction. ● 端数を切り捨てる round off [《やや俗》omit] fractions. ● その靴2足とも買ってくださるなら端数の430円を値引きしますI'll knock off the odd 430 yen if you'll take both pairs of shoes. ● 端数なしの100 ドルにしましょう Let's make it an even hundred dollars. (■ make it は「…に決める」の意)

● バズーカ バズーカ砲【軍事】a bazooka.
ばすえ 場末 ▶ 彼女は場末の(=中心地区から外れた活気のない通りにある)飲み屋で働いている She works at a bar on a dull street off the downtown area.

はすかい 斜交い askew. (⇨斜(サ))
‡**はずかしい** 恥ずかしい【罪の意識から】be ashamed; be embarrassed; be self-conscious; be shy, (特定の原因なしに) be bashful; be humiliated;【恥ずべき】shameful. (⇨恥い)

[使い分け] **ashamed** 道徳的な過ちや失敗, 愚行について自身に罪悪感や責任があって恥ずかしいと思う気持ち.
embarrassed きまり悪いときや当惑などの気持ち.
self-conscious 人目を気にして落ち着かない[あがる]ときの気持ち.
shy 内気や引っ込み思案で照れくさい気持ち.
bashful 子供特有の恥ずかしさで, 大人に用いたときは極端な内気.
humiliated 屈辱感.

[解説] **ashamed** は人を主語とし叙述的な用法のみに, **shameful** は叙述的にも限定的にも用いる: He is ashamed because he did a shameful [×an ashamed] thing./His attitude is shameful [×ashamed].

● 恥ずかしくて顔を赤らめる blush with shame [embarrassment]. ● 恥ずかしそうな顔をする look shy [abashed]. ● 恥ずかしそうに話す talk shyly [bashfully]. ● 恥ずかしげもなく unashamedly; without shame. ● 彼は恥ずかしがり屋だ He's bashful./He is very shy. (■ 文脈によって「勉強ぎらいな子供」をさすこともある) ▶ 私はうそをついたことをとても恥ずかしく思う I'm much [《話》very] ashamed of having told a lie [that I told a lie]. (■ 恥ずかしさの対象は of 句や that 節で表し, 不定詞を用いて × ... to have told a lie. とはしない) ● それは何も恥ずかしいことではない There is nothing to be ashamed of. ● お恥ずかしい(= 恥ずかしくて言いにくい話)ですが私はスピード違反で捕まったので す I'm ashamed to say [admit] it, but I was caught for speeding. (■ ... say [admit] (that) I was.... も可) ▶ 人前で話すのは恥ずかしい I'm embarrassed [shy] about speaking in public./It's embarrassing for me to speak in public.
▶ 道路で転んでほんとうに恥ずかしかった I was [felt] really embarrassed when I fell on the street.
▶ 恥ずかしくて人前でそんなことはできない I'm too embarrassed to do such a thing in public. ● 恥ずかしがらずに話しなさい Don't be shy of [bashful about] speaking to me. ● 出席者で女性は私1人だったので恥ずかしかった I was the only woman to be present and I was self-conscious. ● 彼女はいつも恥ずかしくない(=きちんとした)身なりをしている She is always decently dressed.

はずかしめる 辱める (面目を傷つける) disgrace; (恥じ入らせる) put* ... to shame; (侮辱する) insult. ▶ 彼の悪行が学校の名[家名]を辱めた His bad conduct disgraced the school [family] name./His bad conduct brought disgrace [shame] on the school [family]./(汚された) The school [family] name was stained with [by] his bad conduct.

パスカル【フランスの哲学者・数学者・物理学者】Pascal /pæskǽl/ (Blaise /bléiz/ ～).

ハスキー husky. ● ハスキーな声で話す speak in a husky voice.

バスケット【かご】a basket. ● バスケット1杯のリンゴ a basket(ful) of apples.

バスケットボール【球技】basketball; (ボール) a basketball. ● バスケットボールをする play basketball. ● バスケットボール選手 a basketball player.

‡**はずす** 外す ❶ 【取り外す】(取り去る) take* ... off,

remove (❗前の方が口語的); (かんぬき・ボタンなどを) undo*; (鎖から) unchain. ●カーテンを外す undo down a curtain. ●上着のボタンを外す unbutton one's coat; undo the buttons on one's coat. ●その門の錠を外して押し開ける unlock the gate and push it open. ●入れ歯を外す(取り出す) take out one's false teeth. ▶サングラスを外しなさい Take off your sunglasses./Take your sunglasses off. (⇒取る❸)

❷[避ける] avoid, (さっと) dodge; (巧みに) evade; [除外する] leave*... out, 《やや書》exclude 《from》; (数に入れない) 《話》count ... out. ●攻撃[質問]を外す dodge an attack [a question]. ●選手を出場メンバーから外す exclude [pull] a player from the lineup. ▶彼はチームから外された He was excluded [removed] from the team. (❗この言い方は「そのチームに入るのを拒まれた」の意にもなる) He was left out of the team. ▶集まっておしゃべりするときは私を外さないで Don't leave [count] me out when you get together and have a chat. (❗後の方は Count me in when .... (数に入れてね)ともいえる

❸[席を離れる] leave* one's seat. ▶彼はしばしば席を外した He left his seat [(机を) desk] frequently. ▶彼は今席を外しています He is not at his desk now./(外出中です) He is out right now. ▶ちょっと席を外してもよいでしょうか May I be excused? (❗子供が授業中にトイレに行くときなど) ▶彼は打席を外した He stepped out of the batter's box.

❹[逃す] miss. ●的を外す miss (↔hit) the target. ▶投手は1球外した The pitcher threw a waste ball [wasted a pitch].

バスストップ a bus stop.
バズセッション [《小グループごとの討論》] a buzz session.
パスタ [<イタリア語] pasta. (参考 マカロニ・スパゲティなど小麦粉で作る麺) ●パスタを食べる have [eat] pasta.
●パスタ料理 a pasta.
バスタオル a bath towel.
はすっぱ 蓮っ葉 ― 蓮っ葉な 形 flippant; frivolous.
パステル (a) pastel. ●パステルで描く draw 《it》 with pastels [in pastel(s)].
●パステル画 a pastel (drawing). ●パステルカラー a pastel (color); pastel shades.
バスト a bust. ●胸の小さい女性 a woman with small breasts; a small-busted woman. ▶彼女のバストは84センチです Her bust measurement is 84 centimeters.
はずべき 恥ずべき disgraceful 《behavior》; shameful 《conduct》.
パスポート [旅券] a pássport. ●日本政府発行のパスポートを使って旅行する travel on a Japanese passport.
会話 「パスポートを見せてください」「はい、これです」 "Your passport, please." "Here you are."
パスボール [野球] a passed [a pass] ball. ●その捕手は昨夜パスボールを二つした The catcher allowed two passed balls last night. ●そのパスボールで2走者進塁した The two baserunners advanced on the passed ball.
バスマット a (bath) mat.
はずみ 弾み ❶[勢い] momentum (複 momenta, ~s); (an) impetus 《to》 (❗複数形なし). (❗(1) いずれも物が運動するときにつく勢いのことをいう. (2) impetus は「勢いの推進力、刺激」の意で用いられることが多い) ●はずみがつく gain [gather] momentum; move increasingly fast. ▶その条約は東洋と西洋の文化交流にはずみをつけるだろう The treaty will give an impetus [(拍車をかける) put spurs] to cultural interchange between the East and the West. ▶バスをよけようとしたはずみに転んだ I tumbled just in trying to avoid the bus.

❷[成り行き] ●何かのはずみで (思いがけなく) by (sòme) chánce. ▶もののはずみでそう言ってしまった I said so by mere chance [(衝動的に) on (an) impulse, (その時のはずみで) on the spur of the moment].

●弾みを食(ら)う ▶乗客たちは急停車のはずみを食って前のめりになった The passengers were plunged forward by a sudden stop.

*はずむ 弾む ❶[はね返る] bounce, bound. (❗人や動物が跳ねる場合にもよく用いられる) ●このボールはよくはずむ This ball bounces [bounds] well. ▶ボールははずんで柵(?)を越えた [部屋から飛び出した] The ball bounced [bounded] over the fence [out of the room].

❷[活気づく] (心が) bound; (話が) become* lively. ●はずんだ(=興奮した)声で in an excited [⨯an exciting] voice. ▶彼女はうれしくて心がはずんだ Her heart bounded [(書) leaped, ⨯bounced] with joy. (❗bounce は比喩的には用いない) ▶話がはずんだ We had a lively conversation./The conversation became lively [went fine].

❸[その他の表現] ▶彼は速く走った後で息をはずませていた He was panting [out of breath, breathless] after he ran fast. (❗前の方ははあはあと大きな息をつくこと、後の方は息切れすること) ▶彼にチップをはずんだ I gave him a big [a generous] tip.

はすむかい 斜向かい ●私の家のま向かいの家 the house diagonally opposite mine. (類 筋向かい)
パズル 《solve》a puzzle. ●ジグソー[クロスワード]パズルをする do a jigsaw [a crossword] (puzzle).
バスルーム a bathroom. (❗通例ふろのほかに洗面所とトイレ付き(⇨便所))
はずれ 外れ ❶[端] ●村の外れに at the edge of a village. ▶彼はその町の外れ(=郊外)に住んでいる He lives in a suburb of [(市外に) outside] the city./He lives on the outskirts of the city.

❷[当たらないこと] ●外れのくじを引く draw a blank. ▶あの寿司屋はは仕入れがきちんとしているから何を食べても外れがない(=期待に反しない) The sushi shop gets their fish from good markets. So, you won't be disappointed whichever sushi you (may) choose.

はずれる 外れる ❶[離れる] (ふた・取っ手などが) come off《...》; (管などが) slip 《-pp-》 off the sill; (関節などが) be dislocated; be put out of joint. ▶なべの柄が外れた[外れかかっている; 外れている] The handle of a pan has come off [is coming off; is off]./The handle has come [is coming; is] off the pan. ▶障子がいつも外れてはがみる The paper sliding door is always slipping off the sill. ❗always を進行形と用いるとしばしば話し手のいらだちを暗示) ▶滑ってひざの関節が外れた I put my knee out of joint [I dislocated my knee] when I slipped./The slip put my knee out of joint. (❗前の方が口語的) ▶第1ボタンがどうしても外れない The top button won't come undone. ▶受話器が外れているのかもしれない The receiver may be off the cradle. ▶ドアのちょうつがいが外れた The door came [⨯went] unhinged. ▶彼は先発メンバーから外れている He is out of the starting lineup. ▶スライダーは外れた The slider was off the plate.

❷[それる] (声の調子などが) be out of tune, (軌道などを) go* out of 《orbit》; [逸脱する] move away 《from》. ▶彼の歌は調子が外れている His singing is *out of* (↔in) *tune.*/He's singing *off key.* ▶宇宙船は月を回る軌道を外れている The spaceship *is out of orbit* around the moon. ▶飛行機は針路を外れて飛んだ The plane flew *off* (↔on) *course.* ▶彼は自分の主義からはずれることはなかった He *never moved away* [《やや書》*deviated*] *from* his principle.

❸[当たらない] (的などを) miss; (予報などが) prove wrong. ▶矢が的を外れた The arrow *missed* the target. ▶今日の天気予報は外れた Today's weather forecast *proved wrong.* ▶当て [=期待] が外れた (がっかりした) I *was disappointed* in my expectation. ▶目算が外れた (期待以下だった) It *fell short of* my *expectations.*

❹[そむく, 反する] ●規則に外れている *be against* [*contrary to*] the rules.

パスワード a password. ▶パスワードを入れてください Please enter your *password.*

はぜ 沙魚 [魚介] a goby 《●～, gobies).

はぜ 黄櫨 [植物] a (Japanese) wax tree.

はせい 派生 图 (a) derivation.
── **派生的な** 形 derivative; (二次的な) secondary.
── **派生する** 動 ▶多くの英語の単語はラテン語とギリシャ語から派生している A large number of English words *are derived*, *derive*] *from* Latin and Greek words.
• **派生語** a derivative. • **派生商品** [経済] a derivative product.

ばせい 罵声 ● **罵声を浴びせる** jeer 《*at*》 shout jeers 《*at*》 boo. 《●罵(ののし)る》 ▶彼は聴衆に罵声を浴びせられても演説を続けた He continued his speech *amid boos and jeers* from the audience.

バセドーびょう バセドー病 [医学] Basedow's /bá:zədòuz/ disease.

パセリ [植物] parsley /pá:rsli/.

はせる 馳せる ❶[早く走らせる] (馬を) gallop 《a horse》. (車を) drive fast [at high speed] (⇨飛ばす); [思いを] think fondly about 《one's home town》; [名声を] achieve 《great renown [world-wide fame]》.

はぜる burst* open; pop (-pp-). (*!*前の方ははぜることに, 後の方はその時の音に重点がある) ▶栗が大きな音をたててはぜた The chestnut *exploded with a* loud *pop.*

はせん 波線 (波上の線) a wavy line.

はせん 破線 (切れ目の入った線) a broken line.

ばぞく 馬賊 a mounted bandit [brigand].

パソコン a personal computer (略 PC). ●ノートパソコン a notebook (*computer*). ●サブノートパソコン a subnotebook (*computer*). ●IBM 互換パソコン an IBM-compatible *personal computer.*

はそん 破損 图 damage; (a) break, (a) breakage. ▶水道管の破損箇所 [a break [a *breakage*] in the water pipe. ▶車の破損箇所を修理する repair the *damage* to [✕*of*] the car.
── **破損する** 動 (物が被害を受ける) be damaged; (二つ以上に割れる) be broken. (⇨壊れる) ▶その車は事故でひどく破損した The car *was* badly *damaged* [✕*broken*] in the accident.

*****はた** 旗 ❶[布などで作ったしるし] a flag; an ensign; a standard; a banner; colors; a pennant, bunting.

使い分け **flag** 最も一般的な語.
ensign 国籍を明示する旗で, 特に船舶用.
standard 国家・団体・組織などを表す旗.
banner 行列の先頭に掲げるスローガンの横断幕をいい, flag の意で用いるのは《書》.

colors 国籍を表す国旗で, 主に軍事的活動を示す軍旗・船旗の意.
pennant 細長い三角旗で,《米》では優勝旗の意にも用いられる.
bunting 行事などの装飾用にひもにつけられた一連の小旗たち.

①[～旗, 旗～] ●白 [赤] 旗 a white [a red] *flag.* ▶彼らは自由の旗のもとに戦った They fought *under the flag* [*banner*] *of* freedom.
②[旗を] ●旗を揚げる (上に) hoist [raise, put up] a *flag;* (旗ざおに) run a flag up a flagpole; (窓や戸口から出す) display [fly, hang out] a *flag.* ●旗を下ろす take down [lower] a *flag.* ●旗を振る wave a *flag.* ▶その船は米国の旗を揚げていた The ship carried the *flag* of the United States.
③[旗が] ●旗が風にはためいていた The *flag* was flying [(小刻みに早く) fluttering, (大きく) flapping] in the wind.
❷[その他の表現] ▶彼は一旗揚げようとアメリカへ行った He went to America to *make* [《主に書》*seek*] his *fortune.*
●**旗を巻く** (降参する) surrender 《*to*》; (手を引く) back out 《*of*》; (撤退する) withdraw 《*from*》.
●**旗ざお** a flagpole; a flagstaff. ●**旗日** (国民の祝日) a national holiday.

はた 傍 (局外者) an outsider; (周りの人) others. ▶花屋の商売ははたで見るほど楽ではない To keep a flower shop is not as easy as outsiders think. ▶彼の優柔不断にははたの者もやきもきしている *People around him* are very irritated by his lack of decision. (*!*斜体部分は Those who are around him ともいえるが《やや書》)

はた 機 a loom. ●機でテーブルクロスを織る make a tablecloth on a *loom;* weave [loom] a tablecloth.

*****はだ** 肌 ❶[皮膚] skin. (⇨皮膚) ●肌をこする rub one's [the] *skin.* ●肌を刺すような寒さ biting [stinging, piercing] cold. ●肌を脱ぐ strip oneself to the waist; bare [expose] one's shoulders. ●柔らかい [敏感な; 褐色の] 肌をしている have (a) soft [(a) tender; (a) brown] *skin.* ●肌ざわりがよい [悪い] (⇨肌触り) ▶この洗顔クリームを使うとお肌が大しくきれいになり, 決してつっぱったりかさつくことはありません This facial cleansing cream makes your *skin* fresh and clean—never taut or dry. ▶肌の色のためにプレーできないコースが, この国にはまだたくさんある Because of the color of my *skin*, I still cannot play golf in many courses in this country.
❷[物の表面] a surface (⇨山肌); (木や石などの木目) grain, texture. (⇨木目)
❸[気質] ▶彼は学者肌 [芸術家肌] である He is a scholarly [an artistic] *type.*/He has a scholarly [an artistic] *turn of mind.* ▶あなたは彼とは肌合いが違うようね He's not my *type of personality*).
●**肌が合わない** ▶私は彼とは肌が合わない (= うまくやっていけない) I can't *get along* [*get on*] *well with* him.
●**肌で感じる** ▶私はその雰囲気を肌で(=じかに)感じた I realized the atmosphere *firsthand* [*at first hand*].

*****バター** butter. (⇨マーガリン) ●バター 1 箱 a stick of *butter.* (*!*stick は「棒状のもの」) ●バター付きのパン bread and *butter* /brèdnbʌ́tɚ/. (*!*単数扱い) ●無塩バター unsalted [*sweet*] *butter.* ●パンにバターを塗る spread [put] *butter* on bread; spread bread with *butter.* ▶トーストにはバターをつけますか Would you like some *butter* for your toast?

●バター入れ a butter dish. ●バターナイフ a butter knife [spreader]. ●バターロール a butter-enriched roll.

パター 〖ゴルフ〛a putter. ●パターゴルフ putting.

はたあげ 旗揚げ — 旗揚げする 動〖挙兵する〗(兵を集める) raise an army; (挙兵する) rise in arms 《against》; 〖事業を始める〗start up 〖launch 《into》〗 a new business.

ばたあし ばた足 the swimming kick for freestyle. ●ばた足で泳ぐ swim with the flutter kick.

はだあれ 肌荒れ ●肌荒れになる suffer from [have] (rough) dry skin. ●肌荒れを防ぐ protect one's skin from going dry.

パターン a páttern. ●行動パターン a behavioral pattern. ●一定のパターンに従う follow a fixed [a set] pattern. ●ワンパターン (⇨ワンパターン(─)) ▶彼は新しい生活のパターン(=型)に慣れた He has got used [accustomed] to the new pattern of life. ●パタープラクティス〖文型練習〗pattern practice.

はたいろ 旗色 (勝算) the chances (of win or defeat); (見通し) the outlook; (形勢) the situation. ▶こちらの旗色が悪い The chances are against us.

はだいろ 肌色 flesh color. ●肌色の flesh-colored.

はたおさめ 旗納め a year-end party 《of a labor union》.

はたおり 機織り weaving; (人) a weaver.

***はだか** 裸 〖裸体〗a naked body. (⇨②)〖❗a nude は通例〖美術作品・写真などの〗裸体』の意〗●裸同然(=ほとんど裸)で almost [nearly, virtually] naked.

—— 裸の 形 naked /néikid/ 〖見る方も見られる方も困惑することを暗示〗; nude 〖裸が上品な上品な芸術、またその裸が芸術と関わりあることを暗示することが多い〗; (むき出しの) bare. ●裸の乞食 a naked beggar. ●裸の海水浴客 a nude swimmer. ●裸の王様 the emperor who has no clothes on. ●裸のまま寝る(何も身につけないで) sleep with nothing on [without any clothes on]. ●情熱的に裸の彼女を抱きしめる passionately embrace her nakedness.

① 〖裸に〗 ●上半身裸になる strip (oneself) to the waist. ●裸にする strip 《him》 naked. (⇨丸裸) ▶医者は私に裸になって(=衣服を脱いでください)と言った The doctor told me to undress [take my clothes off]. ●公園の木々は一晩で(丸)裸になった The trees in the park became (completely) bare in one night.

② 〖裸で〗●(素っ)裸である be (completely) [《話》stark]) naked. ●裸で泳ぐ swim in the nude; (子供が) swim naked. ▶火事になったとき彼は裸だった He had nothing on when the fire started.

●裸一貫 ●裸一貫からたたき上げた男 a self-made man. ●裸一貫から財を成す (ゼロから) make a fortune from nothing [scratch].

●裸の付き合い ●裸のつき合いをする have a close relationship 《with》.

●裸馬 an unsaddled horse. 裸電球 a naked [a bare] bulb.

はたがしら 旗頭 a leader; a chief.

はだかのおうさま 『裸の王様』 The Emperor's New Clothes. (〖参考〗アンデルセンの童話)

はたき 叩き a duster. ●はたきをかける dust 《the shelves》; use a duster.

はだぎ 肌着 〖下着〗underwear; 〖アンダーシャツ〗(米) an undershirt, (英) a vest (❗通例そでなし).

はたく 叩く 〖平手で〗slap (-pp-); 〖ほこりを〗dust ... (down [off]). ●コートのほこりをはたく dust (off) a coat. ●さいふの底をはたいてそれを買う empty one's purse (to the last penny) to buy it. ●有り金をはたいて自転車を買う spend all the money one has [all one's money] on a bike.

バタくさい バタ臭い (西洋かぶれした) (over-)westernized; (unduly) Européanized; (西洋風の) Western, European.

***はたけ** 畑 ❶〖耕作地〗a field; (花・野菜などの) a garden; (単一作物の小区画) a patch. ●小麦畑 a wheat field; a field of wheat. ●段々畑 a terraced field. ●花畑 (花園) a flower garden. ●コーヒー畑 a coffee plantation. (⇨農場) ●リンゴ畑 an apple orchard. ●野菜[キャベツ; イチゴ]畑 a vegetable (a cabbage; a strawberry) patch. (❗比較的小区画の畑に用い) ●ミカン畑 a tangerine grove. ●茶畑 tea bushes. ●ブドウ畑 a vineyard /vínjərd/. ●畑でとれたもの farm products. ●畑仕事をする work (out) in the fields. ●畑へ出る go (out) into the fields. ●畑を耕す plow /pláu/ a field (❗トラクターの引くくすきで耕すこと); (土を耕す) work [cultivate] the soil. ●畑に小麦の種をまく sow wheat in a field; sow a field with wheat. ▶この野菜は畑から取ったばかりです These vegetables are fresh from the garden.

❷〖専門の分野〗a field; 〖得意な分野〗a line. ●実業畑の人 a person in business. ▶それは畑違いです That is out of [not in] my line./That is outside my field.

はたけ 〖皮膚病の一つ〗〖医学〗scabies /skéibiːz/. (❗単数扱い)

はだける ●胸をはだける(=露出する) bare [expose] one's chest [breast(s)]. ●胸をはだけて寝る sleep with one's chest bared.

はたご 旅籠 an inn. (⇨宿屋, 旅館)

パタゴニア 〖アルゼンチンとチリの南部地方〗 Patagonia /pætəgóuniə/.

はたざお 旗竿 a flagpole; a flagstaff.

はたさく 畑作 farming; (作物) crops.

はだざむい 肌寒い chilly. (⇨寒い)

はだざわり 肌触り ❶〖感触〗a [the] touch; a [the] feel. ●肌ざわりがよい[悪い] be smooth [rough] to the touch. ❷〖感じ〗●肌ざわりのよい人 an affable [an agreeable] person.

はだし 裸足 a bare foot (複 feet). ●はだしの少年 a barefoot [barefooted] boy. ●はだして海岸を歩く walk barefoot [barefooted] on the beach. ▶彼らはいつもはだしでいる They always go barefoot [barefooted]. (❗ go barefoot [barefooted] は「はだしで行く」の意もある)

はたしあい 果たし合い 《fight》a duel 《with》. (⇨⑱)

はたしじょう 果たし状 (挑戦状) a (letter of) challenge; (決闘状) a challenge to (fight) a duel.

はたして 果たして 〖予想どおりに〗(just) as one (had) expected, as (was) expected; (確かに) sure enough; 〖本当に〗really; ever 〖疑問文で〗. ▶果たして彼は現れなかった He didn't appear as I (had) expected [心配していたとおり feared]. ▶雨が降ると思っていたが, 果たしてそのとおりになった I thought it would rain, and sure enough it did. ▶果たしてそれは本当ですか Can it really be true? ▶果たしてまた会えるだろうか Will we ever meet again?

はたじるし 旗印 a flag (mark). ●旗印にかかげる carry the banner [flag, slogan] 《of》. ●…の旗印の下に under the banner [flag, slogan] of ....

***はたす** 果たす 〖成し遂げる〗accomplish; 〖苦難の末成し遂げる, 勝ち取る〗achieve; 〖遂行する〗fulfill,

はたせるかな

carry ... out (🛈 後の方が口語的); [行う] perform. ●目的を果たす accomplish [achieve, attain] one's aim; carry out one's purpose. ●義務を果たす do [fulfill] one's duty. ●望みを果たす achieve [realize, fulfill] one's hopes. ●約束を果たす fulfill [carry out, (守る) keep] one's promise. ▶心臓は重要な機能を果たす The heart *performs* an important function.

はたせるかな 果たせるかな (⇨はたして) ▶果たせるかなパーティーは大成功だった The party was a great success, *as we had expected* [*thought*]./*Sure enough*, the party was very successful.

はたち 畑地 farmland.

はたち 二十(歳) ▶彼は二十だ He is *twenty* (years old). (🛈 ×He is twenty years. とはいわない) ▶彼はまだ二十前だ(十代だ) He is still in his *teens*.

ばたっと ●ばたっと倒れる fall with a thud; flop down. ●ばたっと本を閉じる *snap* shut the book. (⇨ばたん)

はたと ❶ [打ち当たる音] ●はたとひざを打つ *slap* one's knee.

❷ [考えなどが急に浮かぶ] ▶彼はある考えをはたと思いついた He *suddenly hit upon* an idea./An idea *flashed* into his mind./He *struck on* an idea. (🛈 flash, strike は「急に早く」の意を含むので suddenly などをつけなくてよい)

❸ [急に行き詰まる] ▶彼ははたと言葉に詰まった He was *really* [(まったく) *quite*] at a loss what to say.

❹ [にらみつける] ▶彼女は私をはたとにらみつけた She *glared at* me. (🛈 glare は「怒ったりした激しい顔つきで見る」の意)/She *stared at* me *fiercely*.

はたばこ 葉煙草 leaf tobacco.

はたはた 【魚介】 a sandfish.

はたはた ▶旗が風ではたはた(=ばたばた)なびいている (⇨ばたばた❶).

ばたばた ❶ [ばたばた音を立てる] (大きく上下または左右に) flap; (小刻みに早く) flutter. ▶旗が風ではたばたなびいている The flag is *flapping* [*fluttering*] in the wind. ▶タカが誇らしげに羽をはたばたさせた The hawk *flapped* its wings proudly. ▶捕まえられた鶏が羽をはたはたいわせた The captive rooster *fluttered* its wings. ▶彼は押さえ込まれてどうしようもなく手足をばたばたさせた He was held down and *flailed* helplessly.

❷ [足音などを)ばたばたさせる] ▶彼はいつもばたばた足音を立てて歩いてくる He always *patters* along. ▶彼はばたばたと二階から降りて来てコートをひっつかんで家を飛び出していった He came *rattling* down the stairs, snatched up his coat and rushed out of the house.

❸ [あわただしく...する] (あわてて急ぐ) scurry; (急いで行く) rush off; (忙しい) be busy. ▶1日中ばたばたする have a *busy* [(てんてこまいの) a *hectic*] day. ▶にわか雨で歩行者は軒先にばたばた駆けていった A sudden shower *set* pedestrians *scurrying* for shelter. ▶その問題はばたばたと解決した The matter was *quickly* settled.

《会話》「もう行かないと遅れるんだ。こんなにばたばたして悪いなあ」「いいんだよ。あとで電話するよ」"I really must be going now or I'll be late. Sorry I have to *rush off* like this." "That's okay. I'll give you a call later."

❹ [次から次へと] one after another. ▶彼ははたはたと相手を倒していった He knocked down his opponents *one after another*.

ばたばた (⇨ばたばた❶❷❹)

はたびらき 旗開き a New Year's party (*of* a labor

はたらきかける

union).

バタフライ [蝶] a butterfly; [泳法] (the) butterfly, the butterfly stroke. ●バタフライで泳ぐ do (*the*) *butterfly*; swim the *butterfly stroke*. ●バタフライ泳者 a *butterfly* swimmer.

はたふり 旗振り (交通整理係) a flagman; (出発合図係) a starter; (運動などの中心人物) a leader.

はだみ 肌身 ▶彼女は運転免許証を肌身離さず持っている(持ち歩く) She *always carries* her driver's license (*with* [*on*] her). (🛈 ( )内は強調のために追加したもの)

はため 傍目 (他人) others, other people; (世間) the world; (部外者) outsiders; (傍観者) bystanders. ●傍目には幸せそうだ(見える) look happy; (思われる) seem (to be) happy. ▶彼は何をするにも傍目を気にしすぎる He is too sensitive to *others* [*the world*] in everything he does.

はためいわく 傍迷惑 (他人に迷惑なこと) a nuisance [a bother] to others. ▶彼女はいつも近所の人のゴシップをまき散らしている。なんとはた迷惑な She is always gossiping about her neighbors. *What a nuisance*! ▶彼は好き勝手なことをして、はた迷惑だ He *bothers* [*annoys*] *others* by getting his own way.

はためく wave [flap (-pp-), flutter] (*in* the wind). (🛈 wave は波打つように大きく, flap はばたばたと音を立てて, flutter はひらひらと速く揺れ動く)

はたもと 旗本 [歴史] *hatamoto*, (説明的に) a direct [an immediate] vassal [retainer] of a *shogun*.

はたらかせる 働かせる (⇨働く)

***はたらき 働き** [仕事] work; [機能] a function; [作用] operation; (活動) workings; [役目] a role.

①【〜の働き】●心臓の働き the *function* [*action*] of the heart. ●心の働き the *workings* of the mind. ▶彼は頭の働きが少し鈍い He hasn't got much (of a) *brain*./He has a *dull mind*.

②【働き〜】●働き者 a hard worker; a hardworking person. ●働きぶり the way one works. ●働き過ぎ overwork. ●働き詰めである(休みなく働く) work without a break (=絶え間なく) incessantly. (🛈 後の方は少し非難の意を含む) ▶伸二は今が働き盛りだ Shinji is now in the *prime of life* [in his *prime*]. (🛈 prime は「最良の時期」の意)

③【働きが[の]】●働きのある人 (能力) an able person, a person of ability; (稼ぎ) a good (⇔a poor) provider. ▶彼女は夫の働きが悪いく(=かせぎが少ない)といつも文句を言っている She is always nagging at her husband for *not earning enough money*.

④【働きに[を]】●働きに出る (出勤する) go to work [the office]; (就職する) get a job. ●働きに応じて《be paid》in accordance with performance [the work one did]. (🛈 前の方は仕事の実績に, 後の方は仕事そのものに重点を置く) ▶コンピュータは日常生活において重要な働きをしている Computers play [×are playing] an important *role* in our daily life.

●働き口 a job; 《書》 a position. ●働き手 a worker; (一家の) the breadwinner 《of the family》.

はたらきあり 働き蟻 [昆虫] a worker ant.

はたらきかける 働き掛ける ▶そのプロジェクトの推進を社長に働きかけてくれないか Can you *work on* [(訴える) *appeal to*] the president *to* promote the project? ▶彼は辞職するように働きかけられた(圧力をかけられた) He *was pressured* [*was pressurized*] into

はたらきばち 働き蜂 [昆虫] a worker bee (！単に worker ともいう); [よく働く勤め人] a workaholic.

はたらく 働く

WORD CHOICE 働く
work 労働・勤労を表す最も一般的な語。通例, 報酬と引き換えの労働を含意する。しばしば for や at が後続するが, for は業務内容, at は場所を特に含意する。▶ 父は銀行で働いています My father is *working for* [*at*] a bank.
labor 精魂をこめて, 懸命に努力・精励して働くこと。報酬を前提としない奉仕労働などにも用いる。▶ 彼らは 1 日中工場で働いていた They *labored* all day in the factory.

頻度チャート
work ████████████████████
labor ██

20 40 60 80 100 (%)

❶ [労働する] work; labor. (⇨[類語]) ▶ 働いている be *working*; be *at work*. ▶ 働き過ぎる *work* too hard [*much*]; 《やや書》overwork; 《古》overwork oneself. ▶ 朝から晩まで[1 日中; 昼も夜も]働く *work* from morning till night [all day (long); day and night]. ▶ 働きながら大学を出る *work* one's way through college. ▶ 彼の(指揮の)もとで働く *work* under him. ▶ その辞書の仕事に 10 年間せっせと働く *labor* for ten years *over* [*at*] the dictionary. ▶ この工場の労働者は 1 日 8 時間働く The workers in this factory *work* eight hours a day. ▶ 彼らは身を粉にして働く They *work* very hard [《話》like a horse, ×very much]. ▶ ここ何年も働きについてきた I've *worked and worked* all these years.
❷ [勤務する] work (*in, at, for*). (⇨勤める)
❸ [機能する] work; 《やや書》function; 《やや書》operate. (！work は成功・効果を, function は目的・任務の達成を, operate は成功および効果を暗示) ▶ 頭がうまく働かなかった My brain didn't *work* well. ▶ 心臓は眠っている間も働いている The heart *operates* [*functions*] continuously even when you are asleep. ▶ その形容詞は副詞として働く The adjective *functions as* an adverb.
❹ [悪事を行う] commit (-tt-); 《やや書》▶ 盗みを働く steal; *commit* (a) theft. (！後の方が堅い言い方)

── 働かせる 動 [人を](無理に) make* 《him》work, work 《him》; [物・能力を] use, 《書》employ; [機械などを] operate. ▶ 頭を働かせる *use* one's head [brain(s)]. ▶ 想像力[分別; 勘]を働かせる *use* one's imagination [discretion; intuition]. ▶ なぜ彼らは彼をそんなに働かせるのか Why do they *make* him *work* [*work* him] so hard? (！後の他動詞的の work は通例様態の副詞を伴う)

ばたり with a thud. (⇨ばたり)

ばたりと ▶ ばたりと倒れる fall *with a flop*. ▶ ばたりと雨がやんだ It stopped raining *suddenly*.

はたん 破綻 图 [計画・事業などの失敗] failure; [破産] bankruptcy; [人間関係の] breaking-up.

── 破綻する 動 ▶ 破綻した外交政策 a *bankrupt* foreign policy. ▶ 事業に破綻をきたした We *failed* in business. ▶ 練りに練った計画でも破綻することがある (Even) the best-laid plan can *fall through*. ▶ 彼らの結婚は 1 年で破綻した Their marriage *was broken up* in a year.

はだん 破談 ● 縁談を破談にする (関係を絶つ) *break off* [(取り消す) *cancel*] *the engagement*.

ばたんきゅう ▶ いやあ疲れたなあ。この分じゃばたんきゅうだよ I'm very tired. I think I'll *fall asleep the moment my head touches the pillow*.

ばたん(と) ● ばたんと音を立てて with a bang; (にぶく重い感じ) with a thud. ▶ 戸をばたんと閉める shut the door *with a bang*; *bang* the door (shut); *slam* the door (shut). ▶ 彼女は床にばたんと倒れた She fell on the floor *with a thud*. ▶ 窓が風でばたんばたん鳴り続けた The window kept on *banging* in the wind.

ばたんと (⇨ばたん(と)) ▶ 机のふたをばたんと閉じる *snap* [*bang*] down the top of a desk. ▶ ドアがばたんと閉まった The door *snapped* shut. ▶ 子供が床にばたんと倒れた The child *fell flat* on the floor.

*はち 八 eight; [8 番目の] the eighth /éitθ/. (⇨三)
● 8 時間労働 *eight*-hour labor. ▶ 額に八の字を寄せる frown; 《書》knit one's brows.

はち 鉢 (どんぶり) a bowl; (植木鉢) a (flower) pot; (水盤) a basin. ▶ バラを鉢に植える plant a rose in a (flower) *pot*; *pot* a rose. (⇨鉢植え)

*はち 蜂 [ミツバチ] a bee, hóneybèe; [スズメバチ] a wasp, (大形の) a hornet. ● 女王[働き]バチ a queen [a worker] (*bee*). ● (ミツバチの)雄バチ a drone. ● ハチの巣 (→蜂の巣) ▶ ハチがぶんぶんいっている *Bees* are buzzing [*humming*]. ▶ 数人の子がハチに刺された Some children were stung by *bees* [*wasps*].

ばち 罰 [天罰] a judgment; [懲罰] (a) punishment. (⇨罰(ば)) ▶ 彼の失敗はあんなに怠けた罰だ His failure is a *judgment on* him for being so lazy./(失敗したのは当然だ) He deserves his failure because he had been so lazy. ▶ そんなものに金を浪費していては罰が当たるよ You'll *be punished* [《話》*get it*] if you waste your money on such a thing.

ばち 撥 (ギター・三味線などの) a pléctrum (圈 -tra, ~s), (話) pick; (太鼓の) a drumstick.

ばちあたり 罰当たり ▶ この罰当たりめ Hang you! / Be hanged (to you)!

はちあわせ 鉢合わせ ── 鉢合わせする 動 (頭と頭を) bump one's heads together; (偶然出会う) run into ..., bump into .... ▶ 街角で旧友と鉢合わせした I *ran into* [*bumped into*] an old friend of mine at the street corner.

はちうえ 鉢植え a potted plant. ● 鉢植えのシュロ a *potted* palm.

ばちがい 場違い ● 場違いな発言 (その場にふさわしくない) a remark *unsuitable* [*improper*] *for the occasion*; a remark which is *out of place*. ▶ その高級レストランではしわだらけのジャケットを着ている彼は少し場違いな感じがした In the exclusive restaurant, he looked slightly *out of place* in his wrinkled jacket.

*はちがつ 八月 August《略 Aug.》. ▶ 8 月に in *August*. (⇨一月)

バチカン [ローマ教皇庁] Vatican. (！単・複両扱い)
● バチカン宮殿 the Vatican Palace. ● バチカン市国 (公式) the State of the City of Vatican; (俗) the Vatican City.

はちきれる はち切れる (いっぱいになる) burst* 《*with*》. (！通例進行形で用いる) ▶ 食べ過ぎておなかがはち切れそうだ I've eaten too much. I'm *bursting*. ▶ ここの娘たちは若さではち切れんばかりだ These girls *are full of* youth. /These girls are *bursting with* youth. ▶ 彼のかばんには本がはち切れんばかりに詰め込んであった His bag was crammed with books *until almost burst*. /His bag *was bursting with*

books.
はちくのいきおい 破竹の勢い irresistible force. ▶ の若い会社破竹の勢いであった The young company *swept* all [*everything*] *before* it.
ぱちくり ●目をぱちくりさせる blink (one's eyes)《in surprise》.
*はちじゅう 八十 eighty;〖80番目の〗the eightieth.（⇨二十, 五十）
はちどり 蜂鳥〖鳥〗a hummingbird.
はちのじ 八の字 ●八の字を寄せる〖額に八の字を寄せる（難しい顔をする）〗frown; knit one's brows.
はちのす 蜂の巣 a honeycomb /-kóum/;〖巣箱〗a beehive. (!単に a comb, a hive ともいう)
● 蜂の巣をつついたよう（ハチの巣をつついたような騒ぎになる（人々・催し物などが）be thrown into utter confusion;〖人が〗stir up a hornets' [ˣa bees'] nest;〖場所が〗〖話〗turn into a madhouse.
ぱちぱち ❶〖しきりに拍手をする〗clap (-pp-). ▶ 聴衆の女優が現れるとぱちぱち拍手をした The audience *clapped* (their hands) when the actress appeared.
❷〖小さめの音が続けてぱちぱちする〗crackle. ▶ 乾いた小枝がぱちぱち音を立てて燃えた Dry twigs *crackled* as they burned.
❸〖目をぱちぱちさせる〗blink (one's eyes).
はちぶおんぷ 八分音符〖音楽〗〖米〗an eighth note;〖英〗a quaver.
はちぶどおり 八分通り ▶ この地域の災害予測図は八分通りでき上がった The hazard map of this area is *eighty percent* completed.
はちぶんめ 八分目（10分の8）eight-tenths (割)eighty percent.
——八分目の〖控え目の〗moderate.
はちまき 鉢巻き a headband, a *hachimaki*;〖説明的に〗a Japanese towel or cloth worn around one's head just like a headband. ● 鉢巻きをする〖している〗put on [wear] a *headband*.
はちみつ 蜂蜜 honey.
はちみり ハチミリ〖映画〗an 8 mm movie;〖映写機〗an 8 mm movie projector;〖カメラ〗an 8 mm movie camera. (!以上 mm は míllimèter と読む)
はちめんたい 八面体〖数学〗an octahedron /ɑ̀ktəhíːdrən/.
はちめんろっぴ 八面六臂 ●八面六臂の大活躍をする（あらゆる方面で）make oneself distinguished [show great ability] in many fields.
はちもの 鉢物（鉢植え）a potted plant(⇨鉢植え);（料理）food served in a bowl.
ばちゃばちゃ ● ばちゃばちゃと水を飛ばす splash. ● ばちゃばちゃさせて with splashes. ▶ 子供たちが水たまりをばちゃばちゃ駆け抜けた The children ran through the pool *splashing about.* / The children *splashed* across the pool.
はちゃめちゃ（支離滅裂な）incoherent;（筋の通らない）unreasonable;（混乱した）topsy-turvy;（文法に反した）broken;（とんでもない）wild. ● はちゃめちゃなストーリー展開 *incoherent* story development. ● はちゃめちゃな値段 an *unreasonable* price. ● はちゃめちゃな生活をする lead a *topsy-turvy* life. ● はちゃめちゃな英語 *broken* English. ● はちゃめちゃに（=支離滅裂に）行動する act *incoherently* / (=ひどく)忙しい be *wildly* busy.
ばちゃん ▶ 水の中に飛び込む jump into the water *with a splash*; *splash* into the water.
はちゅうるい 爬虫類 reptiles.
● 爬虫類時代 the age of reptiles; the reptilian age.

はちょう 波長 a wavelength. ▶ BBCの放送に波長を合わせる *tune in* to the BBC program.
● 波長が合う ▶ 我々は波長が合わない We're not on the same *wavelength*. (!I'm not on his [her] *wavelength*. のようにもいう)
はちょう 破調（調子はずれで）out of tune;（リズムを破る）broken meter.
はちろう 蜂蝋 propolis; beeswax. (圈 プロポリス)
ぱちん ● ぱちんと音を立てて with a snap [a crack, a flick]. (!上の名詞にいずれも動詞としても用いることもできる) ● ぱちんとテレビを消す *flick* off (↔on) the TV. ▶ 彼女はスーツケースをぱちんとさせて閉じた She closed her suitcase *with a snap*./She *snapped* her suitcase shut. ▶ そのふたはぱちんと閉まった The lid *snapped* shut. ▶ クルミをぱちんと割れた The walnut split *with a crack*. / The walnut *cracked* open.
ぱちんこ〖石などを飛ばす玩具〗〖米〗a slingshot,《英》a catapult. ● ぱちんこで小石を飛ばす shoot small stones with a *slingshot*〖米〗[a *catapult*《英》].
パチンコ〖ゲーム〗*pachinko* /pɑtʃíŋkou/;（説明的に）a Japanese upright pinball (game). ● パチンコをする play *pachinko*.
● パチンコ玉 a pachinko ball. ● パチンコ店 a pachinko parlor.
はつ 初（最初の）first. (⇨初めて)
-はつ -発 ▶ 7時20分上野発の青森行き特急 a limited-express (*starting*) *from* Ueno for Aomori at 7:20. ▶ パリ発通信 a Paris *datelined* message; a message *datelined* Paris. ▶ 午前10時30分発の列車に乗る予定だ I'm taking the 10:30 a.m. train. ▶ その手紙はロンドン発3月20日の日付になっている The letter *dates from* London, March 20.
*ばつ 罰 punishment. (!刑罰の意では Ⓒ);（刑罰）a penalty. (!後の語は競技などの罰則にも用いる) ● 重い[軽い]罰 a heavy [light] *punishment*. ● 厳罰 a severe [a harsh] *punishment*. ● 罰をのがれる escape *punishment* [a *penalty*]. (!ˣescape from... といわないことに注意) ● 罰を受ける be [get] punished (*for*). ● 罰を受けずにすむ go unpunished (*for*). (⇨する) ● カンニングをした罰として彼は停学になった He was suspended from school *as* (*a*) *punishment for* cheating. ▶ この罪に対する罰は懲役5年である The *punishment* [*penalty*] *for* [ˣof] this crime is 5 years in prison.
ばつ〖×印〗a cross, an × /éks/. ● その場所にばつ印をつける mark the place with a *cross* [an ×]. (!*cross* は「十字」の意にも用いる)〖事情〗米英ではテストの誤答には何も印をつけないことが多い ● 大きなばつ印をつける make a big ×.
ばつ ● ばつが悪い（気恥ずかしい）be [feel] embarrassed;（気まずく思う）feel awkward /ɔ́ːkwərd/. ● ばつの悪い沈黙（ひと時）(an) *awkward* silence. (!時間の経過を暗に表せる) ● 彼にほめられるばつが悪かった I was embarrassed by his compliments.
ばつ 閥（排他的な集まり）a clique;（大グループの1派）a faction. (⇨派閥) ● 学閥 an academic *clique*.
はつあん 発案 图（提案）(a) suggestion. ● 彼の発案で at his *suggestion*. ● その計画の発案者はだれですか Who *suggested* the plan? ● それは彼の発案による The idea *originates with* him. /（彼の考えだ）That is his *idea*.
——発案する 動（提案する）suggest;（考案する）originate.
はつい 発意 图 (a) suggestion. (⇨発案)
はついく 発育 图〖成長〗growth;〖発達〗develop-

ment.

①[発育〜] ●発育不全の子供たち undergrown [underdeveloped] children. ▶発育盛りの子供が3人いる I have three *growing* children.
②[発育が] ●発育が早い[遅い] *grow* fast [slowly]. ▶この子は発育がよい[悪い] This child is well *grown* [is *undergrown*].
③[発育を] ●この種の遊びは子供の発育を助けるだろう This sort of play will promote (↔retard) the *growth* [*development*] of a child.
── 発育する 動 grow*; develop. (⇨育つ)

バツイチ ●彼女はバツイチです She's single again./ She's a divorced woman.

はつえき 発駅 a terminal. (㊧ 着駅)

はつえん 発煙 ●発煙弾 a smoke bomb. ●発煙筒 a smoke pot.

*__はつおん__ 発音 图 (a) pronunciation /prənʌnsiéiʃən/. (❶個々の具体的な発音は a 〜. ✕pronunciation とつうらないこと) ●英語の発音 English *pronunciation*; the *pronunciation* of English. ▶君の発音はとてもよい[よくなってきた] Your *pronunciation* is very good [is improving]. ▶この語には二つの発音がある This word has two *pronunciations*. ▶彼は発音が不明瞭(りょう)だ His way of *pronouncing* words is not clear./He doesn't have (×a) good *articulation*.
── 発音する 動 pronounce /prənáuns/; (はっきりと〈書〉) articulate. ●単語を間違って発音する *pronounce* a word wrongly; mispronounce a word. ●その語を強く発音する *stress* [*accent*] the word. ●発音しにくい音 a sound difficult to *pronounce*. ▶この単語はどう発音しますか How do you *pronounce* this word?/What is the *pronunciation* of this word? ● "doubt" は /dáut/ と発音される The word "doubt" *is pronounced* /dáut/.
●発音器官 a vócal [a spéech] òrgan. ●発音記号(個々の) a phonetic symbol [sign]; (全体)the phonetic alphabet. ●発音辞典 a pronóuncing dictionary.

はつおん 撥音 【音声】 a syllabic nasal (in Japanese).

はつか 二十日 ●二十日間旅をする travel for *twenty* days; take a *twenty-day* trip. ●5月20日にon May *20(th)* [(the) *twentieth*].

はっか 発火 图 ignition;【化学】(燃焼) combustion. ▶その火事は自然発火による The fire began by spontaneous *combustion*.
── 発火する 動 《書》ignite; (火がつく) catch* fire; (燃え始める) start to burn.
●発火点 the ignition point.

はっか 薄荷 【植物】peppermint. ●ハッカ入りのガム *peppermint* [*spearmint*] gum.

はつが 発芽 ●(種子の) germination.
── 発芽する 動 germinate; (地下茎などが) sprout.

ハッカー a hacker, 〈話〉a cracker. (❶前の方では今は通例よい意味で「コンピュータ専門家」の意に用い、「他人のシステムやホームページに侵入する人」には後の方を用いる) ▶ハッカーがホームページに侵入した A *cracker* attacked [broke] the website. (❶The website was illegally accessed. といってもよい)

はっかい 発会 (会の発足) inauguration. (⇨発足)
●発会式 the inauguration (*of*); an inaugural meeting.

はつかおあわせ 初顔合わせ 【【最初の】the first meeting; 【【組み合わせ】(試合の) the first match [game]; (相撲の) the first bout; (共演の) the first co-starring. (⇨顔合わせ)

はっかく 八角 (形) an octagon. ●八角形の octagonal.

はっかく 発覚 图 detection.
── 発覚する 動 (人の正体)などが) be found out, be detected; (陰謀などが) be uncovered; (明るみに出る) come to light. ▶どの事件も発覚しなかった No case *came* [was brought] *to light*.

はつかだいこん 二十日大根 【植物】a radish.

はつがつお 初鰹 the first bonito of the season.

はつかねずみ 二十日鼠 【動物】a mouse (複 mice).

はつがま 初釜 the first tea ceremony of the new year.

はつがん 初雁 the first wild geese migrating to Japan in early autumn.

はっかん 発刊 图 publication; issue. (⇨出版) ●新しい雑誌の発刊 the *publication* of a new magazine.
── 発刊する 動 publish; issue.

はっかん 発汗 图 【生理】perspiration. ●発汗作用を促す stimulate *perspiration*.
── 発汗する 動 【生理】perspire.
●発汗剤 a diaphoretic.

はっかん 発艦 ── 発艦する 動 ▶2機の飛行機が空母から発艦した Two airplanes *took off* from the carrier.

はつがん 発癌 图 【医学】càrcinogénesis; the production of cancer.
── 発癌性の 形 cancer-causing [-producing]; càrcinogénic.
●発癌物質 a cancer-causing agent; a carcinogen; a carcinogenic substance.

*__はっき__ 発揮 ── 発揮する 動 show; display. ●才能を発揮する show [*display*] one's ability; 〈話〉*do* one's stuff. ▶君たちが力を発揮すれば勝てると思う If you *do* your *stuff* [*bring* your forces *into play*], I think you can win. (❶bring ... into play は〈やや書〉で「...を活用する」の意)

はつぎ 発議 图 (a) propósal; (a) suggestion. (⇨提案) ▶父の発議で at the *suggestion* of one's father.
── 発議する 動 propose; suggest. (⇨提案する)

はづき 葉月 the 8th month [August] by the lunar calendar.

はっきゅう 白球 a white ball.

はっきゅう 発給 ── 発給する 動 issue 《a passport [a visa]》.

はっきゅう 薄給 a low [a small] salary; (×a) low [(×a) small] pay; low [small] wages. (⇨給料)

はっきょう 発狂 ── 発狂する 動 go mad [crazy, insane]. ▶彼は恐怖で発狂せんばかりであった He seemed almost *mad* with fear./Fear seemed to *drive* him *mad*. (❶drive ... mad は「...を発狂させる」の意)

*__はっきり__ ❶ [形・音・記憶などが] clear; vivid; distinct.

> 使い分け clear 形や音、記憶や思考の明瞭さを表す。
> vivid 記憶・描写などが鮮明であることや、色・光などが目に強烈に映ることを表す。
> distinct 視覚や嗅覚などによってはっきりと認識できる状態を表す。

●はっきりした映像 a *distinct* [a *clear*] image. ▶窓から四国の山々がはっきり見えた I could see the mountains of Shikoku *clearly* [I got a *clear* view of the mountains of Shikoku] from the window. ▶うるさくて彼の声がはっきり聞き取れなかった I couldn't hear him [his voice] *clearly* because there was a lot of noise there. ▶今でも

はっきん のときのことをはっきり覚えている I still remember what happened then *clearly* [*vividly*]./I still have a *clear* [a *vivid*] memory of what happened then.

❷ [事実などが] (明らかな) clear; (疑いの余地のないほど明白な) óbvious; (単純で分かりやすい) plain; (他と際立てはっきりした) distinct; (確定的で明らかな) definite /définit/; (正確な) exact. ▶太郎が窓を割ったのははっきりしている It is *clear* [*obvious*] *(that)* Taro broke the window./*Clearly* [*Obviously*] (,) Taro broke the window. (❗(1) Taro *clearly* [*obviously*] broke the window. の語順も可. 文尾に置く場合は, Taro broke the window, *clearly* [*obviously*]. のようにコンマが必要. (2) ×It is clear [obvious] for Taro to have broken .... は不可) ▶そのことを読者が分かるようにはっきり書くべきだ You should write it *clearly* [*plainly*, *definitely*] so (that) the readers can understand you. (❗(話) では that をしばしば省略する) ▶彼の住所をはっきりとは知らない I don't know his address *for certain* [*for certain* where he lives]. (❗(話) では for certain の代わりに for sure も用いられる)/I don't know his *exact* address [*exactly* where he lives]. (❗ *exactly* の前に休止を置くと *where* にかかり「正確な住所を知らない」, *exactly* の後に休止を置くと *don't know* を修飾して「住所をよくは知らない」の意) ▶彼が無実だということははっきりさせる必要がある We have to make it *clear* (証明する) to *prove*) that he is innocent. ▶彼からはっきりした返事はもらえなかった I couldn't get a *definite* answer from him./He didn't answer me [my question] *definitely*. ▶それら二つの単語にはっきりした意味の違いがありますか Are there any *distinct* differences in meaning between those two words? ▶朝から天気がはっきりしない (定まらない) The weather *has been unsettled* [(何度も変わった) *has changed over and over* (*again*)] since the morning. ▶はっきりさせておこう. これは週末の休暇旅行なんかじゃなくて, まじめな視察旅行なんだ. いいね Let's get this straight. This is not a weekend excursion but a serious inspection tour. Right? (❗ 会話や会議ではっきりさせたい点を確認する慣用表現)

❸ [態度などが] (率直な) frank; (ずけずけものを言う) outspoken. ▶はっきり言ってこれは彼の責任です To be *frank* (*with you*) [*Frankly* (*speaking*), *If I may be frank*], it's his fault. (❗(1) To be frank (with you) は強意的に To be *pérfectly* fránk (with you) ともいう. (2) (話) では frank の代わりに honest がよく用いられる (⇒会話). (3) 最後の言い方は婉曲的) ▶彼は何でもはっきりとものを言う人 He gives his *frank* opinion [He *frankly* gives his opinion] about everything./He's really *outspoken about* everything./He's a really *outspoken* person.

(会話)「垣根を刈り終わったよ, どうだい」「そうね. はっきり言うならちょっとすすぎったいなるといいのだけど」「じゃもうちょっと刈るよ」"I've finished trimming the hedge. How does it look?" "Well, to be *honest* with you, you could have done a neater job." "Then, I'll work on it a little more."

はっきん 白金 [化学] platinum (元素記号 Pt).
はっきん 発禁 prohibition of sale; a ban on sale. (⇒発売) ▶この雑誌は発禁になった This magazine *was banned*.
── 発禁する 動 ban the sale (*of*).
● 発禁本 a prohibited [a banned] book.

ばっきん 罰金 [料金] a fine; [反則金] a penalty. ▶彼に罰金を科す impose a *fine* on him. ●スピード違反で (1万円の) 罰金を払う pay a (10,000 yen) *fine* for speeding. ▶彼は駐車違反で1万円の罰金を取られた He *was fined* 10,000 yen *for* illegal parking. ▶遅刻したら1,000円の罰金だ *The penalty for* being late is 1,000 yen./You'll have to pay a *penalty* of 1,000 yen for being late.

バッキンガム ●バッキンガム宮殿 Buckingham Palace /bákɪŋəm pǽləs/.
パッキング [荷造り] packing; [管の継ぎ目の漏れ止め] a gasket.

*■ **バック** 图 [うしろ] the back; [背景] a background; [後援者] a supporter; (金銭面での) a backer; [後衛] a back; [テニスなどの逆手打ち] a backhand (stroke); [背泳] (the) backstroke. ●バックで泳ぐ do (the) *backstroke*. ●車をバックさせる *back* (*up*) a car; back up. ●もうちょいバック *Back up* a little more. ▶投手はバックに助けられた The pitcher was comforted by his fielders.
── バックする 動 ●(野手が) バックする go [get, move] back; race [chase] back; go out.

バッグ a bag. (⇒包み, 袋)
パック 图 [1包み] a pack. 真空パックのコーヒー豆 vacuum-*packed* coffee beans. ●牛乳ワンパック a *carton* [×pack] of milk. (❗ 牛乳・ジュースの紙パックは carton という (⇒包み)) ●美顔パック a face-*pack*; a facial *pack*.
── パックする 動 apply a pack to one's face.
●パックツアー [旅行] 《go on》 a package tour; 《和製語》 a pack tour. ●パックツアーで旅をする travel on a *package* tour.

バックアップ 图 ❶ [支援] support, báckùp. (⇒支援) ❷ [控え (要員), 予備(品)] (a) backup. ❸ [コンピュータ] ●そのファイルのバックアップをとる make a *backup* of the file.
── バックアップする 動 support; back ... (up). ▶彼らはその計画をバックアップしてくれた They *supported* [*backed* (*up*)] the plan. ▶ぼくはすべてのファイルを MO にバックアップしている I *back up* all my files on [*onto*] MO disks. (❗自動詞用法もある) ▶ショートがサードのバックアップをした The shortstop *backed up* the third baseman.
●バックアップシステム a backup system.

バックオーダー [受注残] a back order.
バックオフィス [事務管理部門] a back office.
バックギャモン [西洋すごろく] a backgammon /bǽkgæmən/.
バックグラウンド [背景] a background.
●バックグラウンドミュージック background music.
バックスイング [競技] a backswing.
バックスキン buckskin.
バックスクリーン [野球] the batter's eye (screen). (❗ a back screen というと「バックネット」(back stop, screen) と解される) ●ホームランをバックスクリーンに打ち込む hit a home run over *the center field fence*; hit a home run straightaway to center field.
バックステージ [楽屋] a dressing room. (❗ 英語の backstage は副詞・形容詞として用いられる (⇒楽屋)) ●バックステージに行く go to the *dressing room*; go *backstage*.
バックストレッチ (競走路の) the backstretch.
バックストローク [背泳] 《do [swim]》 the backstroke.
バックスピン [ゴルフ] backspin.
バックスペースキー [コンピュータ] a backspace key.
バックチャージ 图 [競技] a charge in the back (of an opponent); 《和製語》 a back charge.
── バックチャージする 動 charge 《an opponent》 in

はっくつ 発掘 名 (an) excavation, 《話》a dig.
— 発掘する 動 dig ... up, excavate;（人材などを）find. ● 古代の都市の遺跡を発掘する excavate the ruins of an ancient city.
● 発掘現場《work on》an excavation site [《話》a dig (site)].
バックトス 〖野球〗 a back-hand flip.
バックナンバー 〖雑誌などの〗 a back number [issue];〖背番号〗 a uniform number (❗この意では a back number は用いない).
バックネット 〖野球〗 the backstop, the screen;《和製語》backnet. ▶ボールはバックネットに当たった The ball hit the *backstop*.
バックパス a back-pass.
バックパッカー a backpacker.
バックパック a rucksack;《主に米》a backpack. (❗アルミ製の枠につけたものが多い) ● バックパックを背負ってハイキング[旅行]をする backpack [go backpacking] (*in, around*).
バックハンド 〖テニス・卓球〗 a báckhand (↔forehand). ● バックハンドストローク a backhand stroke. ● バックハンドで打つ hit (the ball) *backhand*. ● ライナーをバックハンドで捕る catch a liner backhand [backhanded]; backhand a liner.
バックホーム 〖野球〗 a throw to the plate; throwing a ball home [to the catcher]. ● ワンバウンドでバックホームをする make a one-hop throw to the catcher [plate].
バックボーン the backbone.
バックミラー a rear-view mirror;《和製語》a back mirror.
ぱっくり ● ぱっくり開く[開ける] gape. ● ぱっくり開いた傷口 a *gaping* wound. ▶少年は口をぱっくり開けて私を見た The boy looked at me *with his mouth wide open*./The boy *gaped at* me. (❗gape 1 語で口を開けて驚き見ることをさす)
バックル a buckle. ● 簡単なバックルのついたベルトwith a simple *buckle*. ● バックルをぎゅっと締める *buckle up* a belt.
はづくろい 羽繕い ▶鳥が羽繕いをしていた A bird was *preening itself*.
ばつぐん 抜群 — 抜群の 形 〖傑出した〗 outstanding;〖すぐれた〗excellent;〖匹敵するものがない〗〖書〗 unrivaled. ▶彼の成績は抜群だった His school record was *outstanding* [*excellent*]. ▶彼女はスポーツが抜群だ She is *unrivaled* in sports./She far *excels* others *at* [*in*] sports. ● 彼はクラスの中では抜群に英語がうまい He is *by far* the best English speaker in his class. (❗最上級を強める場合は (by) far, much を用いる)
はっけ 八卦 fortune telling; divination. ● 八卦を見て告げる tell (his) *fortune*. ● 当たるも八卦, 当たらぬも八卦 *Fortune telling* is a hit-or-miss business.
● 八卦見（易者）a fortune-teller.
はっけい 白系 ● 白系ロシア人 a White Russian.
パッケージ 名 〖包装, 包装用容器〗 a package. ● 店のパッケージから肉を取り出す remove meat from store *package*.
— パッケージする 動 pack.
● パッケージソフト〖市販ソフト〗〖コンピュータ〗 a software package. (❗a package(d) software も可 だが a software package が普通) ● パッケージツアー a package tour.
はっけっきゅう 白血球 〖生理〗 a white corpuscle /kɔ́ːrpəsl/, a white (blood) cell. ▶血液検査の結果をみるとあなたの白血球数は多い[正常; 少ない]ですね The blood test has shown that your white count is high [normal; low].
はっけつびょう 白血病 〖医学〗 leukemia /luːkíːmiə/.

:はっけん 発見 名 (a) discovery (❗「発見物」の意ではⒸ); a find. ● コロンブスのアメリカ発見 Columbus'(s) *discovery* of America; the *discovery* of America *by* Columbus. ● 科学上の発見をする make a scientific *discovery*; make a *discovery in* science. ▶その文書はとても貴重な発見だ The document is an invaluable *find*.
— 発見する 動 〖存在が知られていなかった場所・事実などを〗 discover;〖紛失物などを偶然または捜して〗 find*;〖見つけ出す〗 find ... out (❗偶然見つける場合には用いない);〖悪事・凶器などを慎重な調査によって〗《やや書》detect. ● その病気の治療法を発見する find [discover] a cure for the disease. ● テロリストのアパートで爆弾を発見する *detect* [*find*] a bomb in the terrorists' apartment. ● 彼らはその病気が蚊によって伝染することを発見した They *discovered* [*found out*] (*that*) the disease was [is] carried by mosquitoes. (❗was は話し手がこの事実をただ伝えただけだが, found out には真理と信じる気持ちが強い) ▶彼は森の中で死体で[無事] 発見された He *was found* dead [safe and sound] in the woods.
● 発見者 a discoverer.
はっけん 白鍵 （ピアノなどの）a natural; a white key. (⊗ 黒鍵)
はっけん 発券 a banknote issue.
● 発券銀行 the bank of issue.
*はつげん 発言 名 〖意見〗 an opinion;〖所見〗 a remark;〖陳述, 声明〗〖匹敵し立て〗 a statement;〖論評〗 a comment. ● 誤った発言をする make a false *remark* [*statement*]. ▶公的な集まりであのような個人的な発言は不適切だった Such personal *remarks* were out of place at a formal gathering. ● 彼の発言は無視された What he *said* [*mentioned*] was ignored. ● 田中氏の発言を許可します（議長の発言）I'd like to give the *floor* to Mr. Tanaka.

DISCOURSE
だから私は, 学校生活に体操は欠かせないとの発言に賛成する **This is why** I agree with the *statement* that physical exercise is a necessary part of school life. (❗This is why ... (だから)は結論に用いるディスコースマーカー. 複数の理由を挙げた場合でも This why でよい)

— 発言する 動 〖話す〗 speak*;〖言う〗 say*. (⇨言う❶) ● その件に関して発言する *speak* about the matter;（意見を述べる） express [state] one's *opinion* about the matter;（論評する） make a *comment* on the matter. ▶彼は会議で何度も発言したが彼らは耳を貸さなかった He *spoke up* again and again in the meeting, but they didn't listen. ▶彼は会議で一言も発言しなかった He didn't *say* a (single) word [黙っていた] kept silent] at the meeting. (❗single を添えると強意的)
● 発言権 a voice,《話》a say; the right to say;（議場での）the floor. ● その決定に発言権がある[ない] have a [no] *voice* in the decision. ● 発言者 a speaker.
はつげん 発現 名 (a) manifestation.
— 発現する 動 （病気・性質などが）manifest itself (*as, in*).
バッケンレコード 〖ジャンプ台の最長不倒記録〗 the record for [in] the ski jump, the hill record.
はつご 初子 one's first child.
ばっこ 跋扈 — 跋扈する 動 be rampant. (⇨横行する)
はつこい 初恋 ● 初恋に破れる lose one's *first love*.

- 初恋の人 one's *first love*.

はっこう 発行 图; (出版) publication. ● 新札[債券]の発行 an *issue* of new bank bills [bonds]. ● この新聞は発行部数が多い[300万部である] This newspaper has a large *circulation* [a *circulation* of three million].
— **発行する** 動 [切手・通貨・雑誌などを] issue; [書物・雑誌を] publish (⇨出版する); [印刷して] print. ▶ 新しい紙幣は近々発行される The new bills will *be printed, be put in circulation*] soon. ▶ その雑誌は週1回発行される The magazine *is published* [*is issued, comes out*] weekly.
● 発行所 a públishing hòuse; a publisher (後の方は「発行者」の意にもなる). ● 発行日 the day of issue. ● 発行物 an issue; (出版物) a publication.

はっこう 白光 white light; (コロナ) a corona.
はっこう 発光 (放出) 《書》 emission of light; (放射) radiation of light.
— **発光する** 動 send out [《やや書》radiate,《書》emit (-tt-)] light.
● 発光体 a luminous [light-emitting] body. ● 発光ダイオード a light-emitting diode (略 LED). ● 発光塗料 luminous paint.

はっこう 発効 — **発効する** 動 come* into [take*] effect, become effective.
はっこう 発酵 图 fermentation. — **発酵する** 動 ferment.
はっこう 薄幸 — **薄幸な** 形 unfortunate; unhappy. (⇨不幸な)
はつこうかい 初公開 ● 初公開される be open to the public for the first time. (⇨公開)
はつごおり 初氷 the first freeze (of the season). ▶ 不忍池に初氷がはった Shinobazunoike pond *froze* partly *for the first time* this winter.
はっこつ 白骨 bleached bones; (がい骨) a skeleton. ▶ 死体は白骨化していた The body was found in a state of a *skeleton*./The body was found *skeletonized*.
ばっさい 伐採 图 felling; 《主に米》lumbering; (大森林の) deforestation.
— **伐採する** 動 (樹木を) cut*... down, fell; (大森林を) deforest. ▶ 無計画に木を伐採することは禁じられている It is prohibited to *cut down* [*fell*] the trees too freely.

DISCOURSE
木が伐採されると、山の保水力が落ちるため、洪水がより頻繁に起きる可能性がある If trees are *cut down*, mountains can not hold water, **and so** that may cause floods more frequently. (⚠ and so (よって)は結論に用いるディスコースマーカー)

はっさく 八朔 〚植物〛 a thick-skinned grapefruit-like fruit.
ばっさり(と) (抜本的に) drastically; (それっきりで) once and for all; (ばっさり音を立てて) with a thud. ● ばっさり切り倒す chop (a tree) down. ▶ 庭師は枯れた枝をばっさり切り落とした The gardener *chopped off* the withered branches. ▶ 今年は教育援助費がばっさり削られている Educational subsidies *have been drastically* cut down [《話》*been chopped*] this year.
はっさん 発散 图 (熱・光・においなどの) emission; (熱・光などの) radiation; (気体・液体などの) diffusion; (蒸気の) evaporation.
— **発散する** 動 《書》 emit (-tt-); (主ににおい・香り・熱を) give*... off; (主に光・熱を) send*... out; (放射する) radiate. ▶ この腐った卵はひどいにおいを発散している This rotten egg *is emitting* [*giving off*] a terrible smell. ▶ 彼は猛烈に太鼓をたたいてエネルギーを発散させた《話》He *let* [*blew*] *off steam* by beating a drum like crazy. (⚠*let* [*blow*] *off steam* は「(悩み・精力などを)発散させる」の意の成句)

ばっし 抜糸 — **抜糸する** 動 remove [take out] the stitches.
ばっし 抜歯 图 〚医学〛(an) extraction of a tooth.
— **抜歯する** 動 ● 2本抜歯する必要がある need two *extractions*. ● 1本抜歯する *pull out* [〚医学〛*extract*] a tooth.
バッジ (wear) a badge; [《米》a button]. (⚠後の方は比較的大きな円形のもの) ● 「ブッシュに投票を」と標語を書いたバッジを買う buy a "Vote for Bush" *button*.
はっしと 発止と ● はっしと打つ whack; hit... hard. ▶ ボールをはっしと受け止める catch a ball *without fail*. ▶ 彼はボールをはっしと打った He gave the ball a *terrific whack* [*a hard smack*].
はつしも 初霜 the first frost of the year.
はっしゃ 発車 图 (a) departure. ▶ 発車のベルが鳴っていますよ There goes the *starting* [*departure*] bell.
— **発車する** 動 [出発する] leave* (*from*),《書》depart (*from*); start (*from*) (出発する); (列車が駅を出る) pull out (*of*) (↔pull in). ● 7番線から発車する leave [*start, depart*] *from* Track 7. ▶ 東京行きの列車は当駅を10分ごとに発車します The train for Tokyo *leaves* [*pulls out of*] this station every ten minutes. ▶ 列車は今発車したところです The train *has* just *started* [*left*]. ▶ 発車いたします (駅のアナウンス) All aboard! (⚠「全員乗車」の意)
● 発車時刻 the depárture tìme. ● 発車ホーム a depárture plàtform.

はっしゃ 発射 图 a shot,《やや書》(a) discharge.
— **発射する** 動 (弾丸などを) fire, shoot*,《やや書》discharge; (ロケットなどを) launch. ● ライフルを彼に向けて発射する *fire* [*shoot, discharge*] a rifle *at* him. ● 弾を2発発射する *fire* two bullets [shots]. ● 月ロケットを発射する *launch* [*shoot*] a moon rocket; *fire* a moon shot. ● ミサイルを発射する *launch* [*discharge, project*] a missile.
● 発射台 a launch(ing) pad [site].

はっしょう 発症 ● 虫垂炎を発症する *present symptoms* of appendicitis.
はっしょう 発祥 (an) origin. (⇨起源) ▶ ニューオリンズはジャズ発祥の地だ New Orleans is the *birthplace* [*home*] of jazz.
はつじょう 発情 sexual excitement. ● 発情中である be in 《米》[on 《英》] heat; (特に雄の鹿・羊などが) be rutting.
● 発情期 the máting sèason; (雌の) estrus. ● 発情ホルモン (男性の) androgenic hormone; (女性の) estrogenic hormone.
はっしょう 跋渉 — **跋渉する** 動 go* up hill and down dale; walk over hill and dale.
はっしょく 発色 ● 発色現象 color development.
● 発色剤 a coupler.
パッション 〚情熱〛 (a) passion.
パッションフルーツ 〚クダモノトケイソウ〛〚植物〛(a) passion fruit. (⚠単・複同形)
はっしん 発信 图 dispatch.
— **発信する** 動 ● 危険信号を発信する send a danger signal (out) (↔receive).
● 発信音 (電話の)《米》a díal tòne;《英》a díaling tòne; (ピーという電子音) a beep. ● 発信局 the sénding (↔recéiving) òffice. ● 発信地 the place of dispatch. ● 発信人 (差出人) a sender.

はっしん 発振 —— **発振する** 動 〖物理〗oscillate /ásəlèit/.
● 発振器 an oscillator /ásəlèitər/.
はっしん 発疹 a rash. (⇨湿疹)
● 発疹チフス〖医学〗typhus.
はっしん 発進 —— **発進する** 動 (飛行機が) take off; (自動車が) start. ▶彼女が車を急発進させたので, 私はよけるひまがなかった She *started* the car so abruptly that I had no time to sidestep its onrush. (!*ónrùsh* は「突入, 突進」の意)
-バッシング ● ジャパンバッシング(の) Japán-bàshing.
はっすい 撥水 ● 撥水加工を施した水着 a *water-repellent* swimsuit. ▶そのレインコートは撥水性がいい The raincoat *sheds water well*. (⇨はじく)
ばっすい 抜粋 图 an éxtract, an éxcerpt 《*from*》; (要点の) (やや書) an ábstract 《*of*》; 〖選集〗a seléction 《*from*》. ● 本からの抜粋 *extracts* [*excerpts*] *from* a book.
—— **抜粋する** 動 ▶その本から数箇所抜粋する *extract* some passages *from* the book. ● 論文の要点を抜粋する *abstract* [make an *ábstract of*] a thesis; (要約する) *sum up* [*make a summary of*] a thesis.
はっする 発する ❶ [におい・光・熱などを] 《書》emit (-tt-); (主に光・熱を) send*... out; (主ににおい・香り・熱を) give*... off; (光・熱を放射する) radiate. ▶太陽は光と熱を発する The sun *sends out* [*radiates*] light and heat. ▶バラはよい香りを発する Roses *give off* [*emit*] a sweet smell.
❷ [音・声などを] give* 《a cry》; (叫び声・言葉などを) 《書》utter; (発令する) issue. ● 彼らに警告を発する *issue* a warning *to* them; *give* them a warning. ● 問いを発する *utter* [*pose*] a question. (!*utter* は一般的な問いに, *pose* は理論的な問いを発する場合) ▶彼は苦痛の叫びを発した He *gave* a cry of pain. ▶彼は驚いて一言も発することができなかった He couldn't *utter* a word in surprise./(物音などにぎょっとして) *Startled*, he couldn't utter a word.
❸ [起こる] (川などが源を発する) rise* 《*in, from*》; (事が) 《書》originate 《*in, from*》; (事故などが) occur (-rr-). ▶ライン川はスイスに源を発する The Rhine *rises in* Switzerland. ▶その戦争は両国間の競争に端を発した The war *started because of* [*originated in*] rivalry between the two countries.
ハッスル —— **ハッスルする** 動 〖頑張る〗work [try] hard 《*to do*》, try [*do**] one's best, 《米話》hustle.
ばっする 罰する punish; (罰を科する) 《書》inflict (a) punishment 《*on*+人, *for*+悪事》; 〖規律のために〗discipline; 〖競技で〗penalize. ▶彼はうそをついた息子を罰した He *punished* [*disciplined*] his son *for* telling a lie. ▶彼は厳しく罰せられた He *was* [*got*] *punished* severely./He *suffered* a severe punishment./A severe *punishment was inflicted* [*was imposed*] *on* him.
*__はっせい 発生__ 图 〖事件などの〗 (やや書) an occúrrence; (戦争・災害などの) an outbreak; 〖誕生の〗 《書》the génesis. ● 事件の発生 the *occúrrence* of an accident. ● マラリアの発生 an *outbreak* of malaria. ● 文明の発生 the *birth* [*dawn*, 《書》*genesis*] *of* civilization.
—— **発生する** 動 〖事件などが〗happen, occur (-rr-); (!後の方が堅い語); (突然に) break* out; (問題などが) arise* 《*from*》 (⇨生じる); 〖生物が〗grow*; (動物が) breed*; 〖霧などが〗rise*; 〖電気・熱などが〗be generated; ▶昨夜ひどい列車事故が発生した A terrible train accident *happened* [*occurred*] last night./There was a terrible train accident last night. ▶火災が発生したときだれもが建物から外へ飛び出した Everyone rushed out of the building when the fire *started* [*broke out, occurred*].

はっせい 発声 úttrance; (発声法) vocalization.
● 発声器官〖集合的〗the vócal òrgans. ● 発声練習 vócal éxercises [(訓練)] tràining).
はつぜっく 初節句 (説明的に) the first Girls' [Boys'] Festival in the life of a baby girl [boy].
はっそう 発走 —— **発走する** 動 ▶第1レースは午後1時に発走する The first race *starts* at 1 p.m.
● 発走時刻 the póst tìme. ● 発走標 a stárting pòst.
はっそう 発送 图 (荷物などの) shipment (!船ばかりでなくトラック・鉄道・飛行機による場合にも用いられる); (荷物・手紙などの) 《書》dispatch.
—— **発送する** 動 send... (off), 《書》dispatch; (船などの交通機関で) ship; (行荷物で複数の場所に) send... out; (郵便で) 《主に米》mail, 《主に英》post. ● 招待状を発送する *send out* invitations 《*to* them》. ▶その小包はあすの午後発送します I'll *send* (*off*) the parcel tomorrow afternoon.
● 発送先 a fórwarding àddress. ● 発送者 a forwarder; a sender.
はっそう 発想 an idea. ▶...からおもしろい発想を得る get an interesting *idea from* .... ● 発想が豊かである be full of *ideas*. ● 日本人的発想 (考え方) a [the] Japanese *way of thinking*. (⇨考え ❶)
ばっそく 罰則 penal /píːnl/ regulations; (競技の) a penalty.
ばった 〖昆虫〗a grasshopper. (!群れをなして飛ぶ種は《a swarm of》locusts, その大発生は a plague /pléig/ of locusts という)
バッター 〖打者〗〖野球〗a batter, a hitter. (!batter と hitter の違いは (⇨打者); ▶トップバッター a léadòff (batter [man]); the first [a number-one] *batter*. ● バッターボックス a *batter*'s box. ● 右バッター a right-handed *batter*. ● ホームランバッター a home run *hitter*. ● バッターボックスに立つ be at [come (up) to] bat; step (up) to the plate. ▶彼は4番バッターです He *bats fourth* (in the lineup)./He's a cléanùp (hitter). ▶バッターアウト！ Strike three. You're out!
● バッターランナー a batter-runner.
はつたいけん 初体験 (have) the first experience 《*of*》; (セックスの) one's first sex (experience).
● 初体験をする cut one's teeth 《*on, in*》.
*__はったつ 発達__ 图 (a) development (!発達したもの・状態をいうときは ［C］); 〖成長〗growth; 〖進歩〗prógress, (an) advance. (⇨進歩) ● 身体の発達 physical (↔mental) *development* [*growth*]. (!*growth* は自然に発達して完成した状態をさす) ● 科学知識の発達 the *development* [*growth*] of scientific knowledge. ● バイオテクノロジーにおける最近の発達 recent *development in* biotechnology. ▶わが国の産業の発達は大変著しい The country's industrial *development* [*advance*] is really remarkable.
—— **発達する** 動 develop; (進歩する) make* prógress, (やや書) advance; (成長する) grow*. ● よく発達した鉄道網 a highly-*developed* network of railroads. ▶科学技術はここ20年間で著しく発達した Technology *has* (*been*) *developed* remarkably [*has made* remarkable *progress*] during the last [past] 20 years./There have been great *advances in* technology during the last 20 years. ▶熱帯低気圧は台風に発達した The

tropical low atmospheric pressure *has developed into* a typhoon.
—— 発達させる 動 develop; 《やや書》advance. ●筋肉を発達させる *develop* a muscle /mʌsl/.
●発達心理学 developmental psychology.

ばったばった ▶彼女は自分よりはるかに大きな相手をばったばったと投げ倒した She threw down her opponents (who were) much taller than her *one after another*.

ばったや バッタ屋 a cash-and-carry wholesaler.

はったり (a) bluff. ▶それはただのはったりさ It's only a *bluff*. ▶彼は我々にはったりをかけて自分が富豪であると信じ込ませた He *bluffed* us *into* believing (that) he was a millionaire.
●はったり屋 a bluffer.

ばったり (急に) suddenly; (思いがけなく) unexpectedly. ●ばったり倒れる fall *suddenly*; fall over; (どさっと音を立てて) fall *with a thud*; (平らに伏して) fall *flat*. ●「うわ、いかん」という叫び声を最後に飛行機からの交信はばったり途絶えた Just after the voice cried, "Oh, no!" transmission from the plane was *suddenly* cut off. ●私はばったり彼に出会った I *came* [*ran*] *across* him. (! come [run] across は偶然[思いがけず]出会うの意。同じ意味は run [bump] into ... でも表せる) ▶彼はばったり(=これを最後にきっぱりと)たばこを吸わなくなった He stopped smoking *once and for all*.

ばったり (⇨ったり)

ハッチ (船の甲板の昇降口, 航空機の出入り口) a hatch
●ハッチを開ける open a *hatch*.

バッチ ●バッチ処理［コンピュータ］ batch processing.
●バッチファイル a batch file.

パッチ (継ぎ布) [put] a patch (*on*); [一部修正] [コンピュータ] (make) a patch.
●パッチテスト (アレルギーの貼布検査)(conduct [perform]) a patch test.

ハッチバック a hatchback. (参考) 乗用車の形式の一つ)

はっちゃく 発着 名 ●列車の発着 the *arrival and departure* [*coming and going*] of trains. (! 語順に注意) ●列車発着時刻表 a train *schedule*; 《英》a train *timetable*.
—— 発着する 動 come and go; arrive and depart. (! それぞれ語順に注意)

はっちゅう 発注 名 order placement. (⇔受注)
—— 発注する 動 order; place an order (*for*; *with*).
●その本を本屋に発注する *order* the book from [×to] a bookstore; *place* [*make*] *an order for* the book with a bookstore.
●発注書 (購入申込書) a purchase requisition.

ばっちり ❶ [見事に, うまく] ▶今日の試験はばっちりだ I did *very well* on the exam today. ▶彼女の服装はばっちり決まっている The dress looks *perfect* [*very nice*] on her./The dress suits her *very well*.
❷ [十分に] ▶バイトで旅行の費用もばっちり稼いだ I earned *enough* money [《書》*money enough*] for the trip, working part-time. ▶5年もロンドンに勤務するのだから, 英語はばっちり身につけてくるよ I'll *master* English because I'm to stay in London on business for five years.
❸ [抜け目なく] ▶この不況を逆手にとってばっちりもうけている奴もいる Some people are *shrewd enough to* make a lot of money [are making pots of money *shrewdly*] taking advantage of the hard times.

ぱっちり ●目をぱっちり開けて見る stare at 〈him〉*with* one's *eyes wide open* [*with eyes wide*]. ●ぱっちりした(=大きな丸い)目 one's *big round* eyes. (! round に代えて bright [sparkling] 〈きらきら光る〉も可) ●赤ん坊は目をぱっちり開けた The baby opened its eyes *wide*.

パッチワーク 《do》patchwork. (! 作品は C)

バッティング ❶ [野球の] batting, hitting. ●バッティングの練習をする take [have] *batting* practice. ▶彼はバッティングがうまい He is a good *hitter* [*batter*].
❷ [ボクシングの] a butting.
●バッティングアベレージ [打率] a batting average. ●バッティングオーダー a batting order [lineup]. ●バッティングケージ a batting cage. ●バッティングコーチ a batting [a hitting] coach. ●バッティングセンター a batting practice center. ●バッティングティー a batting tee. ●バッティングピッチャー a batting-practice pitcher;《和製語》a batting pitcher. ●バッティングマシーン a pitching machine.

パッティング [ゴルフ] putting.

ばってき 抜擢 名 (a) selection; (a) choice.
—— 抜擢する 動 select; choose; pick ... out 《as [for, to be] vice-president》. (! 受身では as [for, to be] はしばしば省略される). ▶彼女はチームの一員に抜擢された She was picked out for the team.

バッテリー ❶ [電池] a battery. ▶車のバッテリーが上がっている Our car *battery* is dead [has run down, 《英》has gone flat]. (! ×The car has run out of the battery. とはいわない)
❷ [野球の] a battery. ●小田と田中のバッテリーで with a *battery* of Oda and Tanaka. ●バッテリーを組む form a *battery* 《with》.
●バッテリーパック a battery pack.

はってん 発展 名 [発達, 進展] (a) development (! 発展したもの・状態をいうときは C); [成長] growth; [進歩] prógress, (an) advance (⇨進歩); [拡大] expansion. (⇨拡大, 拡張) ●日本の経済の発展 Japan's economic *development* [*growth*]. ●めざましい発展を遂げる achieve [《書》attain] an amazing *development*.
●発展的解消 ▶ヨーロッパ共同体は発展的解消を遂げて1993年11月にヨーロッパ連合となった The European Community *was dissolved in favor of* the European Union in November, 1993. ▶そのいくつかの政府機関は新しい組織に発展的解消した The several government organizations *were dissolved and absorbed into* a new one.
—— 発展する 動 develop; [進歩する] make* progress; [成長する] grow*; [拡大する] expand. ●発展させる develop; [拡大させる] expand. ●事業[考え]を発展させる *develop* one's business [an idea]. ▶その町は大都市に発展した The town *developed* [*grew*] *into* a large city. ▶中国の工業は著しく発展している China's industry *is making* 《×a》remarkable *progress* [×*development*]./China *is making* remarkable *progress* in industry. ▶議論は新しい方向に発展した The discussion *took a new turn*. (! take a turn は「転換する」の意)
●発展途上国 a developing country [nation]. (関連) 先進国 an advanced [a developed] country)

はつでん 発電 名 《やや書》power generation, generation of electricity.
—— 発電する 動 《やや書》generate electricity. ●10万キロワット発電する generate 100,000 kilowatts of power.
●発電機 a dynamo (機〜s), a generator. ●発電所 a pówer stàtion [《主に米》plànt], an electricity generating station. ●水力[火力; 原子力]発電所 a hydroelectric [a thermal; a nuclear] *power plant*.

ばってん 罰点 〚試験での不合格点〛a failing mark 〘(米)grade〙《in》;〚汚点, 黒星〛a black mark (!通例単数形で). ●罰点をつけられる get a failing mark 《in math》;（規則違反などで）《米》get a demerit 《for speeding》. ▶君のミスは上司の罰点になりかねない Your mistakes can be a black mark against your boss.

はっと ❶〚急に〛suddenly, all of a sudden. ▶その時私ははっと約束を思い出した Then suddenly [all of a sudden,] I remembered my appointment. **❷**〚はっと驚かす〛startle. ●はっとするような美人 a stunning [an amazing, ×a startling] beauty. ▶彼が私の肩を急にたたいたので, 私ははっとした I was startled by his sudden tap on my shoulder./He startled me by tapping my shoulder. ▶彼女はその物音にはっとして立ち上がった She started up from her seat at the noise. **❸**〚はっと息をはく〛puff. ▶彼女ははっと息を吹いてろうそくを消した She puffed out the candle. **❹**〚はっと息をのむ〛▶恐ろしさにはっと息をのんだ The terror took my breath away./I caught my breath at the terror.（⇨息 ③）

はっと 法度（a）prohibition.（⇨禁止, 御法度）

バット 〚球を打つ棒〛a bat. ●握りの細いバット a thin-handled bat. ▶バットを振る swing one's bat. ●バットでボールを打つ hit a ball with a bat; bat a ball. ●バットを長く持つ hold one's bat at the knob. ●バットを短かめに持つ choke up one's bat.

バット 〚料理・写真現像用の平たい容器〛a vat.

ぱっと ❶〚突然に〛suddenly, all of a sudden. ▶部屋がぱっと暗くなった The room suddenly went dark./All of a sudden, the room went dark. **❷**〚素早く〛quickly;（即座に）in a flash. ▶その知らせは国中にぱっと広がった The news spread quickly throughout the country. ▶彼はぱっと後ろへ下がってHe stepped back in an instant [a flash]. ▶私がオフィスに入っていくと彼はぱっと自分の席から立ち上がって「さあこっちへ」と言った As I was walking into the office, he jumped up from his desk and said, "Hi, come on in!" **❸**〚急にある状態に変わる〛(!種々の動詞(句)などで表す) ▶少年は母親の手からぱっと離れていった The boy burst free from his mother's hand. ▶火がぱっと燃え上がった The fire flared up. ▶名案がぱっと彼の心に浮かんできた A good idea flashed [(ひょいと) popped] into his mind.
── **ぱっとしない** 形 ▶あの選手は最近ぱっとしない The player is not doing well these days. ▶商売がぱっとしない Business is slack [dull, slow].

パット 〚服の肩などに入れる〛a pad. ●彼女のジャケットには肩パットが入っている Her jacket has shoulder pads.

パット 〚ゴルフの〛a (three-meter) putt /pʌt/. ●パーパットを決める[外す] drop [miss] a par putt; drop [miss] one's putt for a par.

はつどう 発動 動（法律などに訴える）《書》invoke;（権力などを行使する）exercise. ●拒否権を発動する invoke [exercise] one's (power of) veto. ●強権を発動する (強硬手段をとる) take strong measures 《against》.
●**発動機**（モーター）a motor,（エンジン）an engine.

ばっとう 抜刀 ── **抜刀する** 動 draw one's sword. ●抜刀して with a drawn sword.

はっとうしん 八頭身 ▶八頭身の美人 a beautiful, well-proportioned woman; a beautiful woman with a good figure [of good proportions].

ハットトリック 〚サッカー・ホッケー〛a hat trick.（〘参考〙1 試合に同一プレーヤーが 3 ゴールを決めること）(⇨サイクルヒット])▶柳沢はその試合でハットトリックを達成した Yanagisawa scored a hat trick in the game.

ぱっとみ ぱっと見《at》a single glance. ▶そのサイトはぱっと見どてもよく見えるかもしれません The site may look quite good at a first glance.

はつなぎ 端繋ぎ chitchat [small talk] to fill in the time with.

はつなり 初成り the first (fruit(s)) of the season.

はつに 初荷 the first cargo of the New Year.

はつね 初音 the first song《of a bush warbler》of the year.

はつね 初値 〚経済〛the opening [initial] price; the opening quote.

はつねつ 発熱 名 (an attack of) fever. ●発熱で床についているを be in bed with a fever.
── **発熱する** 動 get* [develop] a fever; become* feverish.

はつのり 初乗り 〚have [take]〛 one's first ride 《in a new car; on a train [a bicycle, a horse]》.
●**初乗り運賃** a base fare; the base [a minimum] fare.

はっぱ 発破 (a) blast. ●発破をかけて巨岩を砕く blast a huge rock with dynamite.
●**発破をかける** ▶彼に発破をかける(=強い口調で励ます) spur [urge] him 《to do; into doing; to+行為》.

バッハ 〚ドイツの作曲家〛Bach /bɑ́ːk, bɑ́ːx/ (Johann Sebastian ~).

はつばい 発売 名 (a) sale,〚切手・通貨などの〛issue;〚CD などの〛release. ●その本の発売を禁止する ban the sale [release] of the book. ▶前売券発売中《掲示》Tickets available [on sale] 《for A's concert》. ▶この辞書は 10 月に発売になる(=出版される) The dictionary will be published [come out] in October.
── **発売する** 動 〚市場に出す〛put ... on the market;〚発行する〛issue;〚CD などを〛release. ▶トヨタは今秋新車を発売する Toyota is bringing out a new car this fall. ▶100 インチ液晶テレビが近々発売される 100-inch L.C.D. TV sets will be (put) on sale [on the market] soon.
●**発売元** a sales agency.

はつばしょ 初場所 〚相撲〛the New Year's Grand Sumo Tournament.

はつはな 初花 the first flower(s) [blossom(s)] of the season [in the spring].

はつはる 初春（早春）early spring;（新年）the New Year.

はっぴ 法被 a happi coat;（説明的に）a loose outer garment, with a trademark printed white on the back, worn traditionally by some tradespeople or craftsmen.

ハッピーエンド a happy ending;〚和製語〛a happy end. ●ハッピーエンドで終わる小説 a novel with a happy ending. ●ハッピーエンドになる have [come to] a happy ending.

はつひので 初日の出 the sunrise on New Year's Day; the first sunrise of the year.

はつびょう 発病 動（病気になる）《書》be taken [fall] ill; get [《やや書》become] ill [《主に米》sick];（症状が現れる）show symptoms 《of》.（⇨病気）

はっぴょう 発表 名 (an) announcement,《書》publication;（公開・上演などによる）presentation. ●ニューモデルの発表 the presentation of a new model. ●その件に関する重大[正式]発表をする make an important [a formal] announcement about the matter.

ばっぴょう

— **発表する** 動 (ニュース性のあるものを公式に) announce;(公にする)make*(it)public;(活字にして)publish;(言葉で表現して)express;(論文を口頭で)read*《a paper》. ● 結果[婚約]を発表する announce the results [one's engagement]; make the results [one's engagement] public. ● その雑誌に小説を発表する publish a novel in the magazine. ● 政見を発表する express one's political views. ● 研究発表する read [deliver] a paper. ▶ 岡氏が後任だと発表された Mr. Oka was announced as [⋈to be] the successor. / It was announced that Mr. Oka was the successor. ▶ ノーベル賞受賞者が新聞に発表された Newspapers announced [⋈published] the Nobel Prize winners.(❗publishは発表する媒体を主語にしない)
● **発表者** a presenter.

ばつびょう 抜錨 — **抜錨する** 動 weigh anchor; sail 《from》; set* sail 《from》.

はっぷ 発布 图《書》promulgation. ● 新憲法の発布 the promulgation of a new constitution.
— **発布する** 動 ● 法律を発布する issue [《書》promulgate] a law.

はつぶたい 初舞台 one's first appearance on the stage;(デビュー)one's(stage)debut /deibjú:, déibju:/. ▶ 彼は日比谷劇場で初舞台を踏んだ He made his first appearance [his debut] at the Hibiya Theater.

ハッブル ● ハッブル宇宙望遠鏡 the Hubble (Space) Telescope.

はっぷん 発奮 — **発奮する** 動 (鼓舞される)be inspired;(刺激を受ける)be stimulated [spurred];(感情をかき立てられる)be roused /ráuzd/. ▶ 少年はノーベル賞受賞者の講演を聞いて大いに発奮した The boy was greatly inspired by a speech given by the Nobel prize winner. ▶「T大は無理や, やめとけ」と先生が言ったのは実はぼくを発奮させるための手だった "Probably you can't get to T University. Let me advise you not to try it." This remark of my teacher was a psychological encouragement to me.

はつほ 初穂 (稲の)the first ears of rice of the year;(稲以外の作物の初物)(⇨初物)

はっぽう 八方 ●《すべての方向に》in all directions [every direction];《すべての方面に》on all sides [every side];《至る所で》everywhere.(⇨四方 [四方八方])▶ 鉄道はここから八方に伸びている The railroads run from here in all directions.
● **八方ふさがり** ▶ 八方ふさがりだ I feel myself shut in on every side./(すべてが私に不利になる)Everything goes against me.
● **八方破れ** ▶ 彼の八方破れの(=自由奔放な)私生活 his freewheeling private life. ● 八方破れの(=慣例にとらわれない)芸術家 an unconventional artist.
● **八方美人** everybody's friend.

はっぽう 発泡 — **発泡性の** 形 foamy; fizzy; sparkling. — **発泡する** 動(飲み物が)fizz.
● **発泡酒** low-malt beer. ● **発泡スチロール** styrene /stáiəri:n/ foam;《商標》Styrofoam /stáirəfòum/. ● **発泡性断熱材** styrofoam insulation. ● **発泡性飲料水** fizzy mineral water. ● **発泡性ワイン** sparkling wine.

はっぽう 発砲 图 gunfire, a shot.
— **発砲する** 動 fire [shoot,《やや書》discharge] (a gun). ● 強盗に向けて発砲する fire a gun [a shot] at〘⋈against〙 the robber.
● **発砲事件** a shooting incident.

はっぽうさい 八宝菜 (説明的に) a Chinese dish consisting of vegetables, pork, shrimp, cuttle-fish, etc. sautéed together and thickened with katakuriko.

はつぼし 初星 《相撲》one's first victory [win].

ばっぽんてき 抜本的 — **抜本的(な)** 形 (思い切った)(やや書)drastic;(根本的な)radical;(徹底的な)sweeping. ● 抜本的の処置をする take drastic measures. ● 抜本的改革を行う carry out radical [sweeping] reforms.

はつまご 初孫 one's first grandchild.

はつみみ 初耳 ▶ それは私には初耳だ I've never heard of it before./《話》That's(new)news to me.

***はつめい** 発明 图 (an) invention. ● 蓄音機はエジソンの最も重要な発明の一つであった The phonograph was one of Edison's most important inventions. ▶ 宇宙ロケットの発明に多くの年月を要した The invention of a space rocket took many years./ It took many years to invent a space rocket. ▶ 必要は発明の母 (⇨母 ❷)
— **発明する** 動 invent. ▶ だれが電話を発明したのですか Who invented the telephone?
● **発明家[者]** an inventor. ● **発明品** an invention.

はつもう 発毛 (promote) (new) hair growth. ● 発毛促進に効果がある be effective in the promotion of new hair growth.
● **発毛剤** a hair growth stimulant.

はつもうで 初詣で (pay) the first visit of the year to a shrine;(元旦の)《公》(pay) a visit to a shrine on New Year's Day.

はつもの 初物 the first ... of the season. ▶ 初物のイチゴを食べた I ate the first strawberries of the season.

はつゆき 初雪 the first snow [snowfall] (of the season), the first snow this winter. (⇨降る)

はつゆめ 初夢 one's first dream on the second (or sometimes the first) night of the New Year. ● 初夢を見る have one's first dream.

はつよう 発揚 — **発揚する** 動 enhance 《the reputation》.

はつらつ 潑剌 图 liveliness.
— **はつらつとした** 形 (生き生きとした) lively;(活力にあふれた)vigorous;(活動的な)active. ▶ 彼は元気はつらつとしている He is full of life 《vigor, vitality》.

はつれい 発令 图 (公式発表) official announcement. (⇨布告)
— **発令する** 動 announce;(命令などを)issue. ● 人事異動を発令する announce personnel changes. ● 暴風警報を発令する issue storm warnings.

はつろ 発露 ▶ それは彼らの愛国心の発露(=表れ)であった It was an expression [《書》a manifestation] of their patriotism.

はて 果て ● (端;終わり) an end;(限界) a limit. ● 地の果ての the ends of the earth. ▶ (この意では常に複数形で) 北の果ての the northernmost parts 《of》. ▶ 見渡す限り (彼の欲望には) 果てがない There is no end in sight [no limit(s) to his desire]. ▶ 議論の果ては殴り合いだった Their argument ended in a fight [came to blows].

***はで** 派手 图 ● showiness,(下品さを示して)gaudiness;(ぜいたく)luxury. ▶ その車ははでではないが信頼性は高い The car is not showy [fancy] but very trustworthy.
— **派手な** 形 ❶【衣服・色などが】(人目を引く)showy;(色・柄が下品で)loud; gaudy;(安びかの)flashy;(装飾的な)fancy;(あざやかな)bright. ●fancy, bright以外は通例軽蔑的なニュアンスも. ● はでなドレス[柄] a showy dress [pattern]. ● はでな人 a showy person. ● はでな色 loud [bright] colors.

(❗「はでな色のスカーフ」は a *brightly*-colored scarf)
❷《生活など》(ぜいたくな) luxurious. ▶はでな生活をする lead a *luxurious* life; live *in luxury*.
── 派手に 副 (大げさに) showily; (ぜいたくに) luxuriously; (気前よく) lavishly. ▶はでに金を遣う (豪遊する) live it up. ▶彼ははでに金を遣う He's a big spender.

パテ 〚料理〛(a) pâté /pɑːtéɪ/. (参考) 肉・魚などをすりつぶしてねり固めた料理) ● ガチョウのレバーのパテ goose-liver *pâté*.

パテ 〚接合剤〛putty.

ばてい 馬丁 a groom; a stableman (複 stablemen).

ばてい 馬蹄 a horse's hoof.
── 馬蹄形の 形 U-shaped; horseshoe-shaped. ● 馬蹄形アーチ a horseshoe arch. ● 馬蹄形磁石 a horseshoe magnet.

パティオ 〚<スペイン語〛〚スペイン風中庭〛a patio; an inner court.

はてさて Oh dear!; Dear me!; Dear oh dear!; Dear dear! ▶はてさて, かわいそうなやつだ *Oh dear!* You poor thing!

はてしない 果てしない 形 〚終わりのない〛endless; 〚際限のない〛limitless; 〚広大な〛boundless. ● 果てしない彼の野望 his *limitless* ambition. ● 果てしない要求をする make *limitless* [*unlimited*] demands 《on him》. ▶私たちはそれについて果てしない論議をした We had *endless* discussions about it./We discussed it *endlessly*.
── 果てしなく 副 endlessly; limitlessly. ▶ニューヨークとは異なって東京は市域を広げていく Unlike New York, Tokyo stretches out and out, almost *endlessly*.

はて(な) 〚驚き, 疑い〛what!; why!; 〚思案〛well; (well,) let me see. ▶はてな, 眼鏡をどこへ置いたかな *Let me see*, where did I put my glasses?/I wonder where I put my glasses. ▶はて妙な *How odd* [*strange*]!

はてる 果てる 〚終わる〛end, come* to an end; 〚死ぬ〛die (~d; dying). ▶宴はいつ果てるともしれなかった There was no telling when the feast would *come to an end*. ▶もう疲れ果てた I'm *tired out* [話] *dead tired, completely exhausted*]. (⇨尽きる)

ばてる ▶けさ仕事ですっかりばててしまった (疲れ果てて) I was really *tired* [*worn*] *out* from the heavy work./[話] I *was done in* after the heavy work. (❗do in は受身で用いることが多い).

はてんこう 破天荒 破天荒の 形 (並ぶもののない)《書》unparalleled; (並み外れた)《通例ほめて》phenómenal.

パテント 〚特許〛a patent.

*はと 鳩 a pigeon, 《集合的》pigeon; a dove /dʌv/.

解説 (1)《米》では **pigeon** は通例飼われているハト, **dove** は通例野生のハトに用いるが,《英》では pigeon をどちらにも用い, 特に区別しないことが多い. (2) 平和の象徴としてのハトは dove. (⇨[第1文例])

● 伝書バト a carrier *pigeon*. ● ハトを飼う keep [have] *pigeons*. (❗keep は通例大規模に, have は趣味で数羽飼う場合) (⇨飼い) ▶ハトは平和の象徴だ The *dove* [xpigeon] is a symbol of peace. ▶森の中でハトがクークー鳴いている I hear *doves* cooing in the woods.
● はとが豆鉄砲を食らったよう ▶はとが豆鉄砲を食らったよう (=ぽかんした) 顔をしている look blank [(物も言えないほど驚いた) *dumbfounded*].
● 鳩小屋 a pigeon house. ● 鳩時計 a cuckoo clock. (❗a cuckoo /kúːkuː/ は「カッコウ」の意)

はとう 波頭 (なみがしら) a crest (of a wave); the top of a wave.

はとう 波濤 (大波) billows; a surge; a large wave.

はどう 波動 ② undulation; a wavelike motion.
── 波動する 動 undulate.
● 波動力学 wave mechanics.

ばとう 罵倒 (公然の非難) (a) denunciation; (悪口) abuse /əbjúːs/. ● 彼を罵倒する hurl (a stream of) abuse at him; abuse /əbjúːz/ [《書》denounce] him; call him names.

パトカー a patrol car. (⇨パトロールカー)

はとこ (またいとこ) a second cousin. (⇨いとこ)

ハドソン ハドソン川 the Hudson (River).

はとは 鳩派 the doves (↔the hawks); (人) a dove. (⇨鳩派)

はとば 波止場 a wharf (複 ~s, wharves); (桟橋) a pier. ▶船が波止場に停泊している A ship lies alongside the *wharf*.

バドミントン 〚スポーツ〛badminton /bǽdmɪntən/. ● バドミントンをする play *badminton*. ● バドミントン選手 a badminton player.

はとむぎ 鳩麦 〚植物〛Job's tears; tear grass.

はとむね 鳩胸 ② a pigeon breast; a chicken breast.
── 鳩胸の 形 pigeon-breasted; chiken-breasted.

はとめ 鳩目 an eyelet; a grommet.

はどめ 歯止め (ブレーキ) a brake. ▶際限のない防衛費のふくらみに歯止めをかけるべきだ We should *put a brake on* [*put a stop to, put an end to*] the ever rising defense costs.

バトル 〚戦い〛(a) battle. ● 壮絶なバトルを繰り広げる fight a heroic *battle* 《against, with》.

パトローネ 〚<ドイツ語〛a (film) cartridge [cassette].

パトロール ② patról. ● パトロール中の警官 a police officer *on patrol* (duty) [*on the beat*]. (❗後の方は受け持ち地域を徒歩で巡回中のとき)
── パトロールする 動 ▶警察が(街を)パトロールしている The police *are patrolling* (the street).

パトロールカー a (police) patrol car; a police car; 《米》a squad car;《米》(無線付きの) a (police) cruiser, 《米やや古》a prowl car, 《英》a panda car.

パトロン 〚〚財政〛支援者〛(男性) a patron /péɪtrən/; (女性) a patroness (❗(1)「芸者などのだんな」の意はない. (2) 今は次の言い方が好まれる); (援助者) a supporter, a sponsor.

ハトロンし ハトロン紙 〚<ドイツ語〛brown paper.

バトン a baton /bətɑ́n/. ● 次の走者 [後任者] にバトンを渡す pass [hand over] the *baton* to the next runner [one's successor].
● バトンガール [トワラー] a baton twirler. ● バトンタッチ (⇨バトンタッチ)

バトンタッチ ② a baton pass; 《和製語》a baton touch.
── バトンタッチする 動 (リレーで) pass the baton《to him》; (仕事などを) have《him》take over《one's job》; pass [turn over]《one's job》to《him》.

*はな 花
WORD CHOICE 花
flower 草木が咲かせる各種の花をさす最も一般的な語.
● 赤い花束 a bouquet [bunch] of red *flowers*.
bloom 切花として飾ったり, 花束にしたりするような, 通例, 大ぶりの観賞用の花のこと. しばしば複数形で用いる.
● 星の形をした花 the star-shaped *blooms*.
blossom 開花の後に実をつける, 主に果樹に咲く花のこと. ● リンゴの花 the apple *blossom*.

はな

頻度チャート

flower	████████████████████
bloom	████
blossom	███

20　　40　　60　　80　　100 (%)

❶【植物】 a flower; a blossom; a bloom. (⇨[類語])
①【花が[の, は]】 ● 花の咲くころ the *flower* season. ● 花の咲く草木 a *flowering* plant. ● 満開の桜の花の下で花見をする enjoy cherry-blossom viewing under the cherry *blossoms* in full bloom. ▶ 花が散った The *flowers* are gone. ▶ 桜の花は今が盛りだ The cherry *blossoms* are now at their best [in full bloom]. ▶ 晴天続きで花はしおれてしまった The *flowers* have faded [drooped] due to a spell of sunny weather.
②【花に[を]】 ● 花に水をやる water *flowers*. ● 花を植える[育てる] plant [grow] *flowers*. ● 花を摘む pick [《主に書》gather] *flowers*. ● 花瓶に花を飾る(=生ける) arrange *flowers* in a vase.
❷【生け花】 flower arrangement. ● 花を生けるarrange *flowers*. ● お花を習う take lessons in *flower* arrangement.
❸【精華】 flower. ● 社交界の花 the *queen* of society; a society *beauty*. ▶ 彼女は職場の花だ She is a *beauty* in our office. ● 若いうちが花だ Youth is the best time in your life. ▶ 彼もあのころが花だった Those were his best days./He was in his *prime* at that time. (**!** prime は「全盛」の意)
❹【その他の表現】 ● 言わぬが花 《ことわざ》 Better leave it unsaid./The less said (about) it the better.
● 花が咲く (⇨[動]) ▶ そのことで話に花が咲いた We talked a lot about it./We had a long and animated chat about it.
● 花より団子 'Dumplings rather than flowers.'/《ことわざ》 Pudding before praise./《ことわざ》 Bread is better than the song of the birds. (**!** デンマーク語の訳訳)
● 花を添える ▶ その歌手の出席はそのパーティーに花を添えた The singer's presence added to the *gaiety* of the party.
● 花を持たせる ▶ 彼に花を持たせてやった We let him have (the) *credit* for it.
── 花の [形] floral. (⇨①)
── 花が咲く [動] flower, come* into flower; 《やや書》 bloom, 《果樹に》 《やや書》 blossom. ▶ この植物の花が咲き始めた This plant is beginning to *flower*. ▶ 庭にチューリップの花が咲いている The tulips *are in flower* [*bloom*] in the garden. ▶ リンゴの木の花が咲いている The apple trees *are in blossom* now. ▶ うちの庭は春になるとたくさんの花が咲く We have a lot of *flowers* [Many *flowers* come out] in our garden in the spring.
● 花売り娘 a flower girl. ● 花かご a flower basket. ● 花柄 a floral pattern [design]. (**!** 前者は模様の繰り返しがあるもの. 後者は繰り返しがないもの) ● 花言葉 flower language; the language of flowers. ● 花畑 a flower garden [field]. (**!** field の方が大規模) ● 花屋 (店) a flower shop; (人) a florist.

はな 鼻 ● a nose; (犬・猫・馬などの) a muzzle; (象の) a trunk; (豚の) a snout.
①【～鼻】 ● 低い鼻 a short [(小さい) a small, (ぺちゃんこの) a flat, (低くて上向きの) a snub] *nose*. (**!** ×a low nose とはいわない) ● 赤鼻 (風邪などによる) a red *nose*; (酒飲みの) a strawberry *nose*. ● 鼻筋の通った鼻 a straight *nose*. ● わし[かぎ]鼻 an aquiline *nose*; a Roman *nose*. ● 上を向いた鼻 a turned-up *nose*. ▶ 彼は高い鼻をしている He has a long [a big, a large] *nose*. (**!** high は上下の位置関係で上にあることを示す語で, この場合には用いない. long はピノキオのように鼻梁が長い鼻. big, large は全体として大きいという意で, 米英ではほめ言葉にはならない)
②【鼻(の)～】 ● 鼻の穴 a nostril. ● 鼻の穴をふくらませる swell one's *nose*. (**!** 興奮した表情) ● 鼻めがねをかける place one's glasses on the tip of one's *nose* ● 鼻の下にひげをはやしている wear a mustache. (**!** mustache は「鼻の下のひげ」の意. 日本語につられて *under one's nose* を添えないこと) ▶ 電車に駆け込もうとしたがドアが鼻先で閉まった I tried to dash onto a train but the doors closed *in my face*.
③【鼻が】 ● 鼻 (=鼻水) が出ている (⇨鼻水) ▶ 風邪にかかって鼻がつまっている My nose is stuffed up by a cold./I have a stuffy *nose* with a cold.
④【鼻で】 ● 鼻にかかった声で話す speak [talk] *through* one's *nose*; speak *with a twang*. ▶ 彼女はほんの少し鼻にかかった魅力的な声をしていた She had a slightly *twangy* attractive voice.
⑤【鼻を】 ● ティッシュで鼻をかむ blow one's *nose* with a tissue. (**!** 事情 米英では人前で鼻をすする (sniffle) のはマナーに反するが, 音を立てて鼻をかくのは自然な行為) ● 鼻をきつくつまむ hold [pinch] one's *nose* tight. ● 指で鼻をほじる pick one's *nose* with a finger. ● 鼻をふくらます inflate one's *nose*. ● 鼻をひくひくさせる twitch one's *nose*. ▶「ほら, 鼻をふきなさい」と言って彼女は子供にティッシュを渡した "Here, wipe your *nose*," she said, handing the child a tissue. ▶ 彼女は人指し指で自分の鼻を指した She pointed at her (own) *nose* with a [her] finger./She pointed a finger at her (own) *nose*. (**!** 事情 自分の事を意味して鼻を指すのは日本人のジェスチャー. 米英人は胸を指す) ▶ 実験室に入るとアンモニアのにおいが鼻をついた Ammonia hit [assailed] my *nose* as I entered the laboratory. ▶ その犬は鼻をくんくんいわせて見知らぬ人のにおいをかいだ The dog *sniffed* at the stranger. (**!** 主語が人の場合は「(ばかにして)ふんと鼻であしらう」の意で用いられる) ▶ その犬は私に鼻をすりつけて来た The dog *nuzzled against* me.
● 鼻が利く ● 鼻がきく[きかない] have a good [a bad] *nose* (*for*); have a good [a bad] *sense of smell*.
● 鼻が高い ▶ 彼は秀才の息子を持って鼻が高い He *is proud of* his brilliant son.
● 鼻高々 ● 鼻高々と (得意満面で) very proudly; (勝ち誇ったように) triumphantly. ▶ 彼は1等をとって鼻高々だった He *was glowing with pride* when he won first prize.
● 鼻であしらう ▶ 彼らは私の警告をふんと鼻であしらうだけだった (あざ笑う) They only *sneered at* my warning.
● 鼻にかける ▶ 彼女は自分の才能を鼻にかけている She *boasts of* [*is bragging about*, (話) *is stuck up with*] her talent. (**!** 逆に「少しも鼻にかけない」なら She's not a bit stuck up in spite of her talent. などという)
● 鼻につく ▶ 駄じゃれも乱発されると鼻につく Too many poor puns *make us sick*.
● 鼻の差 ● 鼻の差で勝つ win *by a nose*.

はな

- **鼻持ちならない** ▶彼は鼻持ちならない He *stinks* [*is disgusting*].
- **鼻を明かす** (出し抜く) outwit 《him》; 《話》 take the wind out of 《his》 sails.
- **鼻を(へし)折る** take [bring] 《him》 down a peg (or two) 《話》 cut 《him》 down to size.
- **鼻を鳴らす** (馬などが鼻息を荒立てる) snort; (犬がくんくんかぐ) sniff 《*at*》; (軽蔑・不満の意でふんと言う) snort, sniff; (甘え声を出す) say in a coaxing voice. ▶「ダイヤの指輪を買ってね」と彼女は彼に鼻を鳴らしてねだった "Please buy me a diamond ring," she asked him *in a coaxing voice*.

はな『鼻』 *The Nose*. (參考) 芥川龍之介の小説
はな 洟 〖鼻水〗 (nasal) mucus. (⇒鼻水)
-ばな -端 (⇒初め)
はなあかり 花明かり the gleam of cherry blossoms.
はなあらし 花嵐 a strong wind [a gale] during the cherry-blossom season.
はなあわせ 花合わせ Japanese card-playing. ● 花合わせをする play cards.
はないき 鼻息 ● **鼻息が荒い** (自信〖やる気〗闘志〗満々である) be full of confidence [drive; fighting spirit]. ▶彼は部下には鼻息が荒い (ごう慢だ) He is *arrogant* [*haughty*] to his subordinates.
- **鼻息をうかがう** (人を怒らせないように気を遣う) take care not to offend 《him》; 《人の顔色を見る》 be (obsequiously) sensitive to 《his》 mood.

はないけ 花生け a flower vase.
はないちもんめ 花一匁 *hanaichimonme*; (説明的に) a Japanese children's game of headhunting using *janken*.
はなうた 鼻歌 a hum. ▶彼は楽しそうに鼻歌まじりで車を走らせていた He *hummed* happily (*to himself*) as he was driving.
はなお 鼻緒 a (clog) thong. ▶私の下駄の鼻緒が切れた My *clog thong* has broken.
はながさ 花笠 a sedge hat adorned with (artificial) flowers.
はなかぜ 鼻風邪 ● 鼻風邪を引いている have a *head cold* [*a cold in the head*] (!) *head* の代わりに ×nose は不可; (鼻水が出る程度の) have the sniffles.
はながた 花形 a (shining) star. ● **花形産業** an industrial favorite. ● **花形選手** a star player.
はながつお 花鰹 shavings of dried bonito.
はながみ 鼻紙 a tissue. (⇒塵(ち)紙)
はなぐすり 鼻薬 ● 〖鼻の薬〗 medicine for the nose. ● 〖わいろ〗 a bribe; (機嫌取りのえさ) a sop 《*to*》. ▶鼻薬が効を奏したに違いない The *bribe* must have worked.
- **鼻薬をかがせる** give a bribe 《*to* an official》; grease 《his》 palm.

はなくそ 鼻糞 dried mucus; 《話》 (dried) snot. ● 鼻くそをほじる pick one's nose.
はなぐもり 花曇り cloudy weather during the cherry blossom season.
はなげ 鼻毛 hairs in the nostrils [nose]; nose hairs. ● 鼻毛を抜く pull out one's nose hairs; (鼻から毛を抜く) pull hairs out of one's nose.
はなごえ 鼻声 a nasal voice; 〖話〗 a twang. ● 鼻声でしゃべる talk *through* one's *nose* [*with a twang*].
はなござ 花茣蓙 a figured mat.
はなごよみ 花暦 a floral calendar.
はなざかり 花盛り (⇒満開) ● 花盛りの娘 a girl *at her best* [*in the flower of youth*]. ● ミニスカートが花盛り (=大流行) だったころ when miniskirts were *all the rage*.
はなさき 鼻先 the tip of one's nose. ● 鼻先に under one's nose; before one's eyes.
- **鼻先であしらう** sneer at 《him》.

はなさきじいさん『花咲爺さん』 *The Story of the Old Man Who Made Withered Trees to Flower*. (參考) 日本の昔話

:はなし 話 ● 〖話すこと〗 (a) talk; (会話) (a) conversation; 〖演説〗 a speech; (短いくだけた) a talk. ①〖~(の)話〗 ● 商売の話 a business *talk*. ● 世間話 (=雑談) をする make small *talk*. ● 内緒話をする have a private *talk*. (⇒内緒 ②) ▶ここだけの話だがこのダイヤにしてもらなんだ This diamond is, *between ourselves* [*you and me*, ×me *and you*], an imitation. ▶先生の話では健는病気だそうだ The teacher *says* that Ken is sick./According *to the teacher*, Ken is sick. (1) 前の方が普通. (2) ×According to the teacher's saying などとしないこと.
②〖話の[の]〗 ● 話の種 a topic for [of] *conversation*. ▶君は話が長い Your *talk* is too long. ▶あとで来て. 話があるの Come and see me later. I have somthing to *tell* you [〖話〗 I *want* (*to have*) *a word with* you]. (!) 前の方は「伝えたい事がある」の意, 後の方は聞き正しかり, 意見をする場合)
③〖話を〗 ● 話をする speak; talk (⇒話す ①); (話し合う) talk [speak] 《*to*, *about*》; have a talk [a conversation] 《*with*》; (演説する) speak, make [give] a speech, give 〖×make〗 a talk 《*to* the audience, *on* [*about*] the subject》 (!) on は専門的内容を暗示. ● 商売の話をする *talk* 《*about*》 business. (!) business, music, baseball, philosophy など, 話の内容を表す語が続く場合は, 時に about が省略される. ● 話を始める start [begin] to *talk*; start *a conversation*; (話の口火を切る) break the ice (!) 特に知識のない人同士の間で座をなごませるため). ▶何の話をしていたのかな Where were we (talking)? (!) 会話中に前の話を忘れたときの決まり文句) ▶パーティーではお互いに仕事の話をしないでおきましょう Let's not *talk* to each other *about* our work [〖話〗 Let's not *talk* shop] at the party.

会話 「その新企画はいつ始まるのですか, どういう方が参加なさるのですか」「今のところ, 詳しいお話はできません」"When are you going to start that new project? Who are going to be involved?" "At this point, I can't tell you anything specific about it."

❷〖話す内容〗 what 《one》 says; 〖報告としての話〗 an account, a story (!) 前の方は体験者・目撃者の詳細な報告. 後の方にはしばしば話し手の主観が含まれる); 〖知らせ〗 news; 〖物語〗 a story (!) 実話にも架空の話にも用いられる. ● 彼の話によると according to him [*what* he *says*, his *account*, his *story*, ×his talk]. (!) his story は話し手の疑念を暗示. 日常的には He told me [us] that …. の言い方が普通 ● 早い話が (=手短に述べると) to make [cut] a long *story* short. ● 話を合わせる (同意するふりをする) pretend to agree with 《him [what he says]》; (口裏を合わせる) (⇒口裏). ● 話のつじつまを合わせる adjust one's *story* to fit the fact. ▶彼はピカソの話をしてくれた He told us the *story* of Picasso./He told us about Picasso. (!) ×He told us Picasso. とはいわない (⇒話す ⑤))

会話 「ちょっといい話があるんだ」「ほんと? 何なの?」「課長に昇進したよ」「それはよかったね」 "I have some good *news*." "Really? What's it?" "I was just promoted to manager." "I'm very happy to hear that./(それはおめでとう) I'm very happy for

❸ [話題] a topic; a subject (⇨話題); [話の核心] the point. ●話をそらす（変える）change the *topic* [*subject*] 《*into*》. ●会合でその話を持ち出す bring up the *topic* [*subject*] at the meeting. ●話をもとに戻す get back to the *subject* one was talking about earlier. ▶話は違い[変わり]ますが，今日は家におられますか Not to change the *subject*, are you staying (at) home today? (❢ I don't mean to change .... の省略形)/(ところで[話はそれるが]) *By the way*, are you staying (at) home today? ▶話をそらさないでください Please don't try to change the *subject*./Will you stick to the *point*? ▶彼女は演説中によく話が飛んだ She often *jumped from one topic to another* in her speech. ▶旅行の話といえば，ロンドンに行ったことがありますか *Talking* [*Speaking*] *of* travel, have you ever been to London? (❢ 通例文頭で) ▶ワインの話となるとまあよくしゃべること *When it comes to* wine, he never stops talking.

❹ [相談] (a) consultation; [申し出] an offer; [交渉] (a) negotiation (❢ しばしば複数形で); [約束] a promise; [合意] (an) agreement; [協定] (an) arrangement; [了解] an understanding. ●うまい話（心が動く申し出）a tempting *offer*; (もうけ話) a lucrative *offer*. ●話をまとめる（取り決める）arrange ...（解決する）settle ...《*with*》. ▶その件でお話（＝相談）があるのですが I'd like to *talk to* you *about* the matter.

❺ [うわさ] a rumor. ▶彼はパリへたつという話だ *People say* [*They say*, 《書》 *It is said*] *that* he will leave for Paris. (❢ *People* [*They*] *say* .... では*that*は省略可)/I *hear* (*that*) he will leave for Paris./There is a *rumor* [(some) *talk*] that he will leave for Paris.

❻ [事柄，事情，わけ] ▶よくある話だ（これまでもそうだった）It's the (same) old *story*. ▶特に好ましくないことについて用いる)/(しょっちゅう起こる) That happens all the time./(仕方がない) It's just one of those things. ▶君は本気で我々の計画に乗る気はあるのか．それなら話は別だ（＝事情は違ってくる）Are you really interested in our project? That's another [a different] *story*./It's another [a different] *story* when you're really interested in our project.

●話が合う have something in common to talk about. ●話が合わない have nothing in common to talk about.
●話がうますぎる ▶その話はうますぎる That (*offer*) is too good to be true.
●話が落ちる ▶彼らは酔いが回ってきて話が落ちてきた When they got drunk, their talk *was getting indecent* [*dirty*].
●話が違う ▶それでは話が違う（話した内容）That's not *what* you *said*./(了解) That's not our *understanding*.
●話がつく（まとまる）come to an *agreement* [an *arrangement*, an *understanding*]《*with*》. ●話をつける（取り決める）arrange ...《*with*》; (解決する) settle ...《*with*》.
●話がはずむ have a lively [an animated] conversation 《*about*》.
●話が分かる ▶彼は話の分かる（＝話せる）人だ He's very *understanding*.
●話にならない ▶彼の提案は話にならない（話題にする[本気で考える]価値がない）His proposal is not worth *talking about* [*thinking about seriously*]. (❢ ... not worth *it*. とぼかして響きをやわらげることもある)/(問題にならない) His proposal is (quite) *out of the question*.
●話に乗る（提案などを受け入れる）accept a proposal 《*for*; *to do*》; accept an offer 《*of*; *to do*》; (話題などに興味を示す) show (an) interest 《*in*》. ▶うまく話に乗せられるとも be tempted to accept a proposal [an offer]. ▶彼女は野球の話（＝話題）に少しも乗ってこなかった She didn't *show* any *interest in the topic* of baseball.
●話に花が咲く ▶話に花が咲いた（活発な会話をした）We *had a lively conversation*./(会話が活発になった) Our *conversation became* more *lively*.
●話に実が入る ▶彼らは話に実が入って（＝熱中して）時のたつのを忘れた They *were engrossed in talk* [*conversation*] and lost all track of time.
●話の腰を折る ●彼女の話の腰を折る *interrupt* her talk; *interrupt* her during her talk.
●話半分 ▶彼の話は話半分に聞いておいた方がよい You should *discount half* of his story.
●話し言葉 (the) spoken language. ●話し上手 a good talker, a conversationalist; a good speaker (❢ 演説など改まった話が上手な人). ●話し手 a speaker. ●話し下手 a poor talker; a poor speaker.

-ぱなし -放し ❶ [...したまま] (⇨まま) ●電気をつけっぱなしにする leave [keep] the light on. (❢ 前の方は放置している状態を，後の方は意図的にする場合をいう) ▶ゆうべは窓を開けっぱなしにして眠った I slept *with* the window *open* last night.
❷ [...し続ける] (⇨続ける) ▶このところうちのチームは勝ちっぱなしだ Our team *has continued to* win [*winning*] the games lately./(連勝中である) Our team *is on a* winning *streak* these days.

はなしあい 話し合い 《have》a talk 《*with*》; 《have [hold, ×make]》a discussion (⇨❻相談); [会談，会議] 《hold [give, have]》a conference [a meeting]; 《conduct [hold]》talks (❢ 通例複数形で); [交渉] 《conduct》(a) negotiation 《*with*》. (❢ しばしば複数形で) ▶当面の難局を話し合いで解決することを双方に勧める urge them to solve the present difficulties by *negotiations*. ▶これ以上話し合いを重ねてもむだだ There's no point in further *talks*. ▶長い話し合いのあと彼らは合意に達した They reached an agreement after long *negotiations*. ▶その話し合いは行き詰まった[再開された] The *talks* [*negotiations*] broke down [resumed].

はなしあいて 話し相手 ●話し相手がほしい I want *someone to talk to* 《*with*》. (⇨相談 ❷)

*はなしあう 話し合う talk 《*to* [*with*] him 《*about* it》》 (⇨❻❼), have* a talk 《*with* him》; (徹底的に) talk 《*it*》over 《*with* him》; (議論する) discuss 《*it with* him》, have a discussion 《*about it with* him》 (❢ talk より堅い語だが，気軽な意見交換を意味し，日本語の「議論」「討論」とはずれがある (⇨議論)). ▶次に何をしようかと話し合った We *talked about* what we should do next. / We *discussed* [×*discussed about*] what to do next. ▶このことは父と十分に話し合った I *talked* this *over* [*discussed* this] *with* my father./I *had a good talk* [*a great deal of discussion*] *with* 《×*to*》 my father *about* this. ▶グリーンさん，その件について昼食を食べながら話し合いませんか Mr. Green, would you like to *discuss* the matter over lunch? (❢ 事情 ▶ 米英では日本のように夜に食事をしながら商談をする習慣はない)

はなしがい 放し飼い pasture; grazing. ●羊を放し飼いにする（放牧する）put the sheep out to pasture [《英》grass]. ●犬を放し飼いにする（つながずにおく）

leave a dog *at large*; (放す) *let* a dog *loose*.

はなしかける 話し掛ける speak* 「talk」 to .... ▶私は電車の中で知らない人に話しかけられた I *was spoken to* [×was talked to] *by* a stranger on the train. (**!** speak で他動詞扱い)

はなしごえ 話し声 a voice. (⇨声) ▶2階から数人の話し声が(=話しているのが)聞こえた I heard several people talking upstairs.

はなしこむ 話し込む (長い間話す) have* a long talk, talk for a long time; (話に夢中になる) be absorbed in talking. ▶夜遅くまで話し込む talk far into the night. ▶彼女は彼の仕事のことで彼と話し込んだ She *had a long talk with* him about his work.

はなしずき 話し好き ── **話し好きな** 形 talkative; (話) chatty.

はなしちゅう 話し中 (電話が)お話し中です The line is *busy* 《主に米》 [*engaged* 《英》]. ▶彼は今ほかの電話で話し中です He is *on* another line. ▶お話し中失礼いたしますが, ... I'm sorry to interrupt you, but ...

はなしぶり 話しぶり 《his》 way of talking [speaking]; the way 《he》 talks [speaks*] (⇨口ぶり); 『言葉つき』《his》 speech. ▶話しぶりで彼女が京都出身と分かった By *the way she spoke*, I could tell she came from Kyoto.

はなしょうぶ 花菖蒲 〖植物〗an iris.

はなじろむ 鼻白む (興ざめする) look embarrassed [hesitant, discouraged].

:**はなす 話す** speak*; talk; say*; tell*. (⇨言う 〖類語〗, しゃべる) ▶犬は(言葉を)話すことができない A dog can't *speak* [*talk*]. (**!** talk より speak の方が普通) ▶他の人が話している(=発言している)ときはおしゃべりをしないで聞きなさい Stop *talking* and listen while someone else is *speaking*. ▶話せば長くなりますが It's a long story. (**!** 詳しく話すのを避ける言い方) ▶話せば分かる *Talking* leads to understanding. ▶夫婦は一方から一方に話しかけることはあってもおしゃべりに発展することはなかった He and his wife [The couple, They] *spoke* sometimes, but seldom *talked*. (**!** 対照用例に注意 ⇨夫婦)

① 【 ... 〜を話す】 ●大声で話す *speak* [*talk*] loudly; *speak* [*talk*] up. ●英語で話す *speak* [《まれ》*talk*] *in* English. (**!** I speak English と言えるのは語学能力・習慣より, 特定の状況における伝達手段として英語を選ぶことをいう) ●ロンドンなまりで話す *speak with* a Cockney accent. ●電話で話す *speak* [*talk*] *on* [*over*] the telephone. ▶私は休暇のことであなたにいろいろ話すことがあります I have a variety of things to *tell* you about my vacation. ▶彼氏のことであなたにいろいろ(=多く)話したい I want to *tell* you a lot about my boyfriend. ▶彼女は私に彼の性格についてこっそり話してくれた She *told* me secretly [in secret] about his character. ▶何があったのか正直に話してください Please be honest and *tell* me what happened [*tell* me honestly]. ▶さあ, 何があったのかちゃんと(=正確に)話しなさい Now *tell* me exactly what happened.

② 【 ...に話す】 (話をする, 話しかける) speak [talk] to ...; (伝える) tell. (⇨⑤) ▶君に話したいことがある(伝える) I have something to *tell* [*say to*] you. (⇨④) ▶これがきのうあなたにお話しした本です This is the book I *told* you *about* [*mentioned*] to you] yesterday. (⇨⑤)

〖会話〗「どうして私に話してくれなかったの」「話したじゃないか」"Whý didn't you ↗*tell* me?" "I ↗*díd*." (**!** 反発を示す音調)

③ 【 ...（のこと）を話す】 (...のことを) speak 《about,

(やや書)of)》; talk 《about, of》 (**!** talk about＋人は「...のうわさをする, 〖書で言う〗の意にもなる》; (言葉・事実などを) speak; (物語・真実などを) tell; (少し触れる) mention, refer to ... (**!** mention より堅い語).
●物語を話す *tell* [×speak, ×talk, ×say] a story.
▶英語を話せますか Do you *speak* [〖まれ〗*talk*, ×say, ×tell] English? (**!** Can you ...? は能力を直接的に問うことになり失礼にあたることがある) ▶彼女は2か国語を話せる She *speaks* [*can speak*] two languages./She is bilingual. ▶彼は家族のことは何も話さなかった He never *spoke about* [*talked about*, *mentioned*, *referred to*] his family./He *said* [*mentioned*] nothing about his family. (**!** 前の文では his family を, 後の文では nothing を主語とする受身文が可) ▶何のことを話しているのですか What *are* you *talking about*? (**!** about は省略不可) ▶事情(=理由〖状況〗)を詳しく話してくれませんか Can you *tell* me the reasons [circumstances] in detail.

■● **DISCOURSE** ■●
実際, 世界には2つ以上の言語を話せる人は多い *Actually*, there are many people in the world who can *speak* two or more languages. (**!** actually (実際に)は主張を表すディスコースマーカー)

④ 【A(人)にBを話す】 tell A B, tell B to A (**!** B は物語・事実など); say B to A (**!** B は言葉など). ●彼に真相を話す(打ち明ける) *tell* him the truth; *tell* [*speak*, ×*say*] the truth *to* him. ▶彼女は私に二言三言話した She *said* [*spoke*] a few words *to* me.

⑤ 【A(人)にB(事・人)について〖のことを〗話す】 tell A about B; talk [speak] to A about [《やや書》of] B. ●その問題について聴衆に向かって話す (＝演説する) *speak* [*give a speech*] *to* an audience *on* the subject. (**!** この on は about と同じ意味だが, 専門的な内容を暗示する) ▶日本のことについてもっと私たちに話して(＝教えて)ください *Tell* us more *about* Japan. ▶そのことは後であなたにお話しします I'll *tell* you [*talk* (*to* you), *speak* (*to* you)] *about* it later. (**!** ×talk [speak] you about it ... は不可)/I'll *mention it to* you later.

⑥ 【 ...と話す】 talk to [with] ...; speak to [《主に米》with].... (**!** to は一方的に話しかける (⇨②), with は相手と(親しく)話し合うという含みがあるが, 区別しないことも多い. with は長時間親しく話をする場合に好まれる) ▶彼女はだれと話しているのですか Whó is it she's ↗*talking* [↗*speaking*] *tó*? (**!** (1) この文は Who is she *talking to*? の強調構文. (2) この文で「いったいだれと」を強調する場合は Who ís it ...? のように強勢が移動する) ▶ちょっとあなたと話したい(＝相談したい)ことがあるのですが I have something to *talk to you about*. (**!** about を忘れないこと)

:**はなす 離す** 〖引き離す〗 separate, 《書》 part (**!** 後の方は完全に分離すること); （引き離しておく） keep* ... separate [away, apart] (*from*) (**!** この separate は形容詞で /séprət/ と読む) (⇨引き離す); (取りのける) take* 《off》. ●机を窓から(もう少し)離す *put* [*move*] a desk (a little farther) *away* [*apart*] *from* the window. ▶母親を赤ん坊から引き離すのは残酷だ It's cruel to *separate* [*part*] a mother *from* her baby. ▶この子から目を離すな Don't *take* your eyes *off* the child. /(見張っていなさい) *Keep an eye on* the child. (後の方が自然) ▶種を5センチずつ離してまきなさい Plant the seeds five centimeters *apart* [*at intervals of* five centimeters]. ▶私が目を離したすきに彼は逃げた He ran away when I wasn't looking (at him). ▶私は彼

はなす 放す 〖つかんでいる物を放す〗let*... go, let go of ..., release (release の方が堅い語); 〖解き放す〗let... loose; 〖束縛などから解放する〗set*... free, release. ▶手を放して！ Let me go!/Take your hands *off* (me)! ▶彼はロープから手を放した He let go (*of*) the rope. (**!**〘話〙では of はしばしば省略される)/He let the rope *go*./He lost his grip *on* the rope. ▶犬を放すな Don't let the dog *loose*. ▶彼女はかごを開けてその鳥を放してやった She opened the cage door and set the bird *free* [*released* the bird].

はなずおう 花蘇芳 〖植物〗a redbud; a Juda's tree.

はなすじ 鼻筋 ▶鼻筋の通った美男子 a handsome young man with a *shapely* nose. (**!**「かっこうのいい鼻」の意)

はなずもう 花相撲 a special sumo tournament between regular ones.

はなせる 話せる ❶〖話すことができる〗 ▶英語の話せる秘書 an English-speaking secretary; a secretary who *speaks* English.
❷〖話の分かる〗understanding. (⇨話❻)

はなぞの 花園 a flower garden.

はなだいろ 縹色 (薄いあい色) pale deep blue.

はなだかだか 鼻高々 ── 鼻高々と〘副〙very proudly; triumphantly.

はなたけ 鼻茸 〖医学〗a nasal polyp.

はなたて 花立て a flower vase.

はなたば 花束 a bunch of flowers; (ブーケ) a bouquet /boukéi/. ▶彼女にバラの花束を贈る present *a bunch of* roses to her; present her (with) *a bunch of* roses. (⇨束)

はなだより 花便り (説明的に) a news about the cherry blossoms [how far the cherry trees are in bloom in various parts of Japan].

はなたれ 鼻たれ a snotty child (⦅children⦆); (若造) a fledg(e)ling (person).

はなぢ 鼻血 blood from one's nose, a nosebleed (**!**複数形はない). ▶昨夜ひどく鼻血が出た I *had* a bad *nosebleed* [a very *bloody nose*] last night./My *nose bled* badly last night. ▶あの女の子、鼻血が出ているよ That girl is *bleeding from* [*at*] *her nose*. (**!**at は「鼻の穴」からとは限らない)/That girl's *nose* is *bleeding*.

はなつ 放つ ❶〖光・熱・においなどを〗〘書〙emit (-tt-); (におい・熱などを) give*... off; (光・熱などを) send*... out. ▶このランプは強い光線を放つ This lamp *sends out* [*gives off*, 〘書〙*emits*] a powerful beam.
❷〖矢・弾丸などを〗shoot*; fire. ▶矢を放つ *shoot* an arrow. ▶礼砲を放つ *fire* a salute. ▶ヒット[二塁打; ホームラン]を放つ *hit* a single [a double; a home run].
❸〖動物などを〗let* (a police dog) loose; (解放する) set* (a bird) free. (⇨放す)

はなっぱし 鼻っぱし (⇨鼻っ柱)

はなっぱしら 鼻っ柱 ▶鼻っ柱が強い (小生意気な) impertinent; (我を張る) self-assertive.
▶鼻っ柱をへし折る make (him) humble; 〘話〙take (him) down a peg (or two).

はなつまみ 鼻つまみ (実にいやな奴) a jerk, 〘話〙a skunk; (厄介者) a nuisance.

はなづまり 鼻づまり ▶鼻づまりしている My *nose is stuffed* [*is stopped*] *up*. / I have a *stuffy* [*stuffed*] *nose*.

はなづら 鼻面 the tip of one's nose. (⦅回⦆鼻先)

はなでんしゃ 花電車 a decorated streetcar; a 'streetcar float'.

***バナナ** (1本の) a banana; (1房の) a bunch of bananas. ▶バナナの木[皮] a *banana* plant [skin]. ▶バナナの皮をむく peel (off the skin of) a *banana*.

はなのした 鼻の下 ▶鼻の下が長い ▶彼は鼻の下が長い (女性に甘い) He is *soft on women*.
▶鼻の下を伸ばす ▶あなた、鼻の下が伸びてるわよ You're starting to drool. (**!** drool は「よだれを流す」の意)

はなばさみ 花鋏 a pair of flower scissors.

はなはだ 甚だ 〖非常に〗very, very much; 〖大いに〗greatly; 〖過度に〗exceedingly; 〖極度に〗extremely. (⇨非常に) ▶君の発言ははなはだ迷惑だ What you said is *very* [*extremely*] annoying.

***はなはだしい** 甚だしい 〖重大な〗serious; 〖強烈な〗intense; 〖程度に大きな〗enormous; 〖極端な〗extreme; 〖誤りなどが目立つ〗glaring. ▶はなはだしい誤解 a *serious* [a *great*] misunderstanding. ▶はなはだしい相違 a *tremendous* [a *great*, a *marked*, a *striking*] difference. ▶はなはだしい損失 an *enormous* [a *heavy*] loss. ▶はなはだしい例をあげる cite an *extreme* case. ▶はなはだしい間違いをする make a *glaring* [〘書〙a *gross*, (重大な) a *serious*] mistake.

はなばなしい 華々しい 〖輝かしい〗glorious; 〖見事な〗splendid; 〖壮観な〗spectacular. ▶彼はその試合で華々しい活躍をした He played a *glorious* [a *splendid*] part in the game. ▶彼女は女優として華々しい生涯を送った She led a *glorious* career as an actress. ▶開会式は華々しく行われた The opening ceremony was *spectacular*.

はなび 花火 a firework; (爆竹) a (fire)cracker. ▶仕掛け花火 *set fireworks*. ▶花火大会に行く go to a *fireworks* (⦅米⦆) [a *firework* ⦅英⦆] display. ▶花火をする do *fireworks*. ▶花火を上げる set off [shoot off, display] *fireworks*. ▶最後の display は「花火大会をする」の意) ▶花火大会の晩はいい場所がとれた We had a good spot on the night of the *fireworks*.

はなびえ 花冷え chilly weather during the cherry blossom season.

はなびしそう 花菱草 〖植物〗a California puppy.

はなびら 花びら a petal /pétl/. ▶バラの花びら rose *petals*. ▶5弁の花びらのツバキ a five-*petaled* camellia.

はなふだ 花札 *hanafuda*; (説明的に) Japanese playing cards. ▶花札をする play cards [*hanafuda*].

はなふぶき 花吹雪 a shower of cherry blossoms falling in the wind.

はなぺちゃ 鼻ぺちゃ ▶あの人は鼻ぺちゃだ He has a *flat nose*.

***パナマ** 〖国名〗Panama /pǽnəmɑ̀ː/; (公式名) the Republic of Panama. (首都 Panama City) ▶パナマ人 a Panamanian /pæ̀nəmèiniən/. ▶パナマ(人)の Panamanian.
▶パナマ運河 the Panama Canal. ▶パナマ帽 a Panama hat.

はなまつり 花祭り 〖仏教〗the Buddha's birthday festival; the Flower Festival.

はなまる 花丸 (説明的に) an encircled flower seal (used by teachers to grade students' work and encourage them to study harder).

はなみ 花見 cherry-blossom viewing. ▶公園に花見に出かける go (out) to see [enjoy] the *cherry blossoms* at the park; go *cherry-viewing* in [*xto*] the park.
▶花見客 a cherry-blossom viewer.

はなみず 鼻水〖医学〗nasal mucus;《話》snot. ● 鼻水を垂らす snivel. ▶鼻水が出ているよ Your nose is running./（婉曲的）You've got a runny nose. (!) You have a running nose. とはあまりいわない)

はなみずき 花水木〖植物〗a dogwood.

はなみち 花道（劇場などの）an (elevated) aisle /áil/. ▶ほら, 横綱が花道をやって来る Here comes the *sumo* champion up the *aisle*.
● 花道を飾る ▶彼らは優勝して引退する監督の花道を飾った They won the tournament to glorify the retiring manager.

はなむけ 餞 a farewell gift [present]. ● 2 人にはなむけの言葉を述べる offer the two his *well-wishing* words.

はなむこ 花婿 a bridegroom. (⇨新郎)

はなむすび 花結び（バラ結び）a rose, a rosette;（蝶結び）a bow, a bowknot.

はなめがね 鼻眼鏡 鼻眼鏡をかけたシューベルトの肖像 the portrait of Schubert with *a pair of pince-nez* /pǽnsnèi/. ▶おばあちゃんは本を読むとき鼻眼鏡をかけている My grandma wears her glasses *on the tip of her nose* when she reads books.

はなもじ 花文字 an (ornate) initial;（古文書の大文字）a majuscule /mǽdʒəskjùːl/.

はなもち 花持ち ▶あじさいは花持ちが悪い Hydrangeas wither in a short time.

はなもちならない 鼻持ちならない （実にいやな）disgusting,《話》stinking;（吐き気をもよおさせる）nauseating.

***はなやか 華やか** 图 （豪華な美しさ）gorgeousness;（はで）showiness.
――**華やかな** 形 （豪華な）gorgeous;（はでな）《通例軽蔑的》showy. ● 華やかな衣装 a *gorgeous* dress. ▶会場は華やかな＝陽気で楽しい)雰囲気だった There was a *cheerful* atmosphere in the hall.
● 華やかに 副 （豪華に）gorgeously. ● 彼女は華やかに着飾っていた She was *gorgeously* dressed.

はなやぐ 華やぐ become* cheerful; be brightened. ▶その女優がステージに姿を現すと会場の雰囲気はぱっと華やいだ As soon as the actress appeared on the stage, the atmosphere of the theater (was) *brightened*.

はなよめ 花嫁 a bride. ● (やがて)花嫁になる人 a bride-to-be. ● 花嫁姿の娘 a girl in a *wedding* dress [in *bridal* costume].
● 花嫁衣裳 a wedding dress, bridal costume;（一式）a bride's outfit. ● 花嫁学校 a finishing schòol. ● 花嫁修業 domestic training.

はならび 歯並び a set of teeth. (⇨歯 ❶ ①)

はなれ 離れ（離れ家）a detached house;（離れ部屋）a detached room.
● 離れ島 an isolated [a solitary] island.

ばなれ 場慣れ 图 （経験）experience. ● よく場慣れした講演者 a well-*experienced* lecturer. ▶彼の仕事は多少場慣れが必要だ His job requires some *experience*.
――**場慣れする** 動 （舞台「演壇」に立つことに慣れる）get* used to the stage [platform];（あがらなくなる）get over one's stage fright.

―ばなれ ―離れ ● 金離れ (⇨金離れ) ● 映画離れの傾向 a trend not to go to the movies.

はなればなれ 離れ離れ ―― 離れ離れの 形 separated; （ちりぢりの）scattered.
――**離れ離れに** 副 separately;（独立して）independently. ▶彼の家族は離れ離れになった His family *separated* [*got separated*,（崩壊した）*split up*, *broke up*].

:はなれる 離れる 動 ❶［分離する, 去る］separate (*from*);〖去る〗leave*,（去って行く）go* away (*from*). ● そのグループから離れる *leave* [*separate from*] the group. ● 列から離れる（離脱する）*fall* [*drop*] *out of* the line. ▶故郷を離れて 5 年になる It is [has been] five years since I *left* home [my hometown]. ● 船は桟橋から離れていった The ship went（すべるようにゆっくりと）*drew*(d) *away from* the pier. ● 離れないでついてきなさい（くっついていなさい）*Keep close to* me./*Stick with* me. ▶彼の友人たちは 1 人ずつ（彼を見捨てて）離れていった His friends *fell away* one by one.

❷［位置・距離・年齢が］▶（危ないから）離れていろ（近寄るな）*Keep away* [*back*]*!* ●「離れろ」なら *keep* be *get* にする) ● その湖はここから遠く離れている The lake is *a long way* (*off*) [《やや書》*far away*, ×far] from here. (!) far は単独では通例類語例文・副文で用いる(⇨遠い)) ● 彼の家は駅から 8 キロ離れたところにある His house is five miles (*away* [*distant*, ×far]) *from* the station. (!) 距離を明示するときは *far* は不可)) ● その村と学校は約 3 キロ離れている The village and the school are about two miles *apart*./(村と学校間の距離は約 3 キロある) The distance between the village and the school is about two miles. ▶ベースから離れすぎるな Don't get too far *off* base. ● 郵便局はぼくの行く道筋からだいぶ離れたところにある The post office is rather *out of* my way. ● 彼らは年がかなり離れている（年齢に大きな差がある）There is *a great difference in* their ages.

会話「町は(ここから)どのくらい離れていますか」「5 キロほど離れています」"How *far away* [*off*] is the town?" "It's about three miles *away* [*off*]."

❸［精神的に］▶君のことが片時も心を離れない（気にかかっている）You've been *on my mind* all the time. ● 彼女の心はもう君から離れているよ She *no longer loves* [（興味を失っている）*has already lost interest in*] you. (!)「部下の心は君から離れている」では Your people *are no longer cooperative*. のようにいう)
――**離れて** 副 （あちらに）away;（隔たって）off;（分かれて）apart. ● 遠く離れて far *away* [*off*];（何マイルも離れて）miles *away* [*off*]. ● 16 キロ離れて *at a distance of* ten miles. ● 3 メートルずつ離れて（＝の間隔で）並ぶ line up *at intervals of* 10 feet. (!)**事情** 米英では日常語としては mile, foot の方が kilometer, meter より普通) ● 親元から遠く離れて暮らす live *far away* [*apart*] *from* one's parents;（別々に）live *separate* [*separately*] *from* one's parents. (!)この *separate* は形容詞で /sépərət/ と読む);（独立している）be independent of one's parents.

はなれわざ 離れ業（見事な）《やや書》a feat;（危険な）a stunt. ● 複雑な計算を一瞬のうちにするという離れ業を演じる perform the *feat* of doing the complicated calculations in a moment. ● 高いぶらんこの上で勇敢な離れ業を演じる do [perform] a brave *stunt* on a high trapeze /træpíːz/.

はなわ 花輪 （祝儀・葬儀用の）a wreath;（頭・首につける）a garland. (!) 勝利者に与えられる花輪の意では両方とも用いられる)

はなわ 鼻輪 a nose ring.

バニーガール a bunny (girl).

はにかみ bashfulness;（生来の内気）shyness.
● はにかみ屋 a bashful [a shy] person. (⇨内気) ● 彼女ははにかみ屋さんです She is *shy* [*bashful*]./She is a *shy* [*bashful*] girl.

はにかむ be shy; be bashful. (⇨照れる)

ばにく 馬肉 horseflesh; horse meat.

バニシングクリーム vanishing cream.

パニック (a) panic. ● パニックになって in (a) *panic*. ● パニックに襲われる *be panic-stricken*. ● その事件で町中がパニックに陥った The whole town got [was thrown] into a *panic* because of the incident./The incident caused a *panic* in the whole town.

はにゅうのやど　埴生の宿　(みすぼらしい家) a shabby house; a hovel.

バニラ　〘植物〙 a vanilla;〘エッセンス〙vanílla.

はにわ　埴輪　a clay image [figure]; (説明的に) a human figure or an animal made of clay during the prehistoric times in Japan.

バヌアツ　〘国名〙Vanuatu /vænuáːtuː/;（公式名）the Republic of Vanuatu.（首都 Port Vila）● バヌアツ人 a Vanuatuan. ● バヌアツ(人)の Vanuatuan.

***はね　羽, 羽根**　❶〘羽毛〙a feather; (特に大きく華やか) a plume (❗帽子などの羽飾りの意でも用いられる);《総称》plumage /plúːmidʒ/;（鳥の体をおおう feather や plume の集合体をさす）(鳥の綿毛, 柔毛) down. ● 赤い羽根(共同募金)運動 a 'Red *Feather*' community chest drive. ● 羽のついた帽子 a hat with *plumes*. ● その鳥はきれいな羽をしている The bird has beautiful *feathers* [*plumage*].
❷〘鳥や飛行機などの翼, 虫の羽〙a wing. (⇨翼) ● 羽を広げる[たたむ; はばたかせる] spread [fold; flap] (its) *wings*.
❸〘道具・器具の〙(バドミントン・羽根つきの) a shuttlecock; (プロペラ・扇風機などの) a blade.
● 羽が生えたように as if it had wings. ▶ 羽が生えたようにお金がなくなる Money disappears *as quickly as if it had wings*. ▶ iPod nano が羽が生えたように (=飛ぶように) 売れている iPod nano *is selling like hot cakes*. (❗通例通信社)
● 羽を伸ばす　▶ その夜は両親がいなかったので子供たちは羽を伸ばした (自由に楽しんだ) Their parents were not at home that night, so the children *enjoyed themselves freely* [〘話〙*went on the loose*].

はね　跳ね　(はねた泥) splashes of mud. ▶ ズボンの後ろにはねが上がっているよ There are *splashes of mud* on the back of your pants./The back of your pants *is splashed* [*is spattered*] *with* mud.

はね　撥ね　❶〘字の書き方〙hane; (説明的に) an upward stroke of the brush. ❷〘はねること〙ピンはね (a) kickback. (⇨ピンはね)

ばね　a (coil [spiral]) spring; (弾力) spring. ● ばねのきいた[きいていない]ベッド a springy [a springless] bed. ● 足腰のばねがなくなる lose *spring* in one's legs. ▶ このネズミ取りはばね仕掛けです This rattrap works [is worked] by a *spring*./This rattrap has a *spring* device.
● ばねばかり a spring balance.

はねあがり　跳ね上がり　❶〘物価・相場が〙a jump; a sudden rise. (⇨暴騰) ❷〘おてんば〙a tomboy; a filly.

はねあがる　跳ね上がる　(跳び上がる) spring* [jump] up; (急に上がる) shoot* up,〘話〙skyrocket. ▶ ガソリンの価格が最近はね上がった The price of gasoline *has shot up* [*skyrocketed*] lately.

はねおきる　跳ね起きる　(ぱっと立ち上がる) spring* [jump] to one's feet; (寝床から) spring [jump] out of bed.

はねかえす　跳ね返す　❶〘ボールなどを〙rebound. ❷〘拒絶する〙reject, refuse flatly. ❸〘不利な状況を〙overcome*.

はねかえり　跳ね返り　❶〘ボールなどの〙a rebound. ❷〘反動, 影響〙repercussions. ❸〘おてんば〙a tomboy; a filly.

はねかえる　跳ね返る　bounce back; rebound. (❗やや堅い語で, ボール・光だけでなく比喩的にも用いる) ▶ ボールが壁に当たってはね返った The ball *bounced* [*rebounded*] *from* [*off*] the wall. / The ball struck the wall and *bounced back*. ▶ 悪業は我が身にはね返る Our evil conduct will *rebound* [〘書〙*recoil*] on ourselves.

はねかかる　跳ね掛かる　(ばしゃんと) splash; (ぱっと) spatter; (べしゃっと) splatter. ▶ 泥水が車のフロントガラスにはねかかった Muddy water *splashed* (on [*against*]) the windshield of the car.

はねかける　跳ね掛ける　(ばしゃんと) splash; (ぱっと) spatter; (べしゃっと) splatter. ▶ バスが私の服に泥水をはねかけた The bus *splashed* [*spattered*] my clothes *with* mud./The bus *splashed* [*spattered*] mud *on* my clothes.

はねつき　羽根突き　Japanese battledore and shuttlecock. ● 羽根つきをする play *battledore and shuttlecock*.

はねつける　撥ね付ける　〘断固として激しく〙reject (❗refuse より強意だが);〘きっぱりと〙refuse; turn ... down. (⇨断る❶) ● 申し出を頭からはねつける flatly *reject* [*refuse, turn down*] an offer. ● その計画をはねつける *reject* [×*refuse*] the plan.

はねとばす　跳ね飛ばす　(水・泥などをばしゃんと) splash; (ぱっと) spatter; (べしゃっと) splatter. (⇨跳ねる❷)

はねのける　撥ね除ける　〘押しのける〙push (勢いよく) thrush]... aside [away];〘取り除く〙take*... out, remove. ● ふとんをはねのける push a quilt *aside*. ● 箱詰めする前に傷のある桃をはねのける *take out* bruised peaches before boxing them.

はねばし　跳ね橋　(城門側へ引き上げる) a drawbridge; (真ん中を引き上げる式の) a bascule bridge.

はねぶとん　羽布団　a down quilt,《米》a comforter,《英》a duvet /djuːvéi/.

はねぼうき　羽箒　a feather duster.

はねまわる　跳ね回る　jump around [《主に英》about] (⇨跳ぶ [類語], 跳ねる); (遊び騒ぐ) romp around [《主に英》about]. ▶ 子供たちは部屋中をはね回っている The children *are romping around* (in) the room.

ハネムーン　〘新婚旅行〙a hóneymòon. ● ハネムーン中のカップル a *honeymoon* couple; honeymooners.
● ハネムーンでハワイに行く go to Hawaii for [on] one's *honeymoon*. (×trip) ● (新婚旅行期間を過ごす) (spend one's) honeymoon in Hawaii.
● ハネムーンベビー a honeymoon baby; a baby on [during] the honeymoon.

パネラー　〘パネルディスカッションの一員〙a pánelist;《和製語》a paneler.

パネリスト　a pánelist.

***はねる　跳ねる**　❶〘跳び上がる〙jump; (水平方向に) leap*; (勢いよく) spring*; (ぴょんぴょん) hop (-pp-); (両足を交互に) skip (-pp-); (1回) bounce; (何度も) bound. (⇨跳ぶ❸, 弾む) ▶ トランポリンの上ではねる *jump* [*bounce*] (on *sth*) on a trampoline. ▶ 魚が水面ではねた A fish *jumped* out of the water [*broke* the water]. ▶ ウサギ[カエル]が小道をぴょんぴょんはって通った A rabbit [A frog] *hopped across* the path.
❷〘飛び散らす〙(ばしゃんと) splash; (ぱっと) spatter. ▶ 車が我々に泥をはねた The car *splashed* [*spattered*] mud *on* us [*us with* mud]. ▶ 壁に料理の油がはねた The cooking oil *spattered* on the wall. ▶ フライパンからぱんとはねた熱い油でやけどをした I was burned by the hot fat *popping* out of the frying pan.

はねる　撥ねる　❶〘採用を断わる〙reject, turn ...

パネル

down; (不適当なので削除する) get rid of ..., 《書》 eliminate. ●不良品をはねる reject [*get rid of*, *eliminate*] defective products. ▶彼は就職試験の面接ではねられた He *was rejected* [*was turned down*] in the job interview.
❷[その他の表現] ●上前をはねる skim some off the top. ▶王は首をはねられた The king had his head *cut off*. ▶彼は車にはねられた He *was* [*got*] *hit by a car*./He *was knocked down by a car*. (⚠ 前の方は「衝突する」、後の方は「ぶつかって倒れる」の意)

パネル a panel.
●パネルディスカッション 《hold》 a panel discussion. (⚠そこでの討論者はa panelist [✕a paneler] という)
●パネルヒーター an oil-filled electric radiator. (⚠ a panel heater とはいわない)

ハノイ 〖ベトナムの首都〗Hanoi /hænɔ́i/.

パノラマ a pànoráma. ●山頂からの見事なパノラマ a fine *panorama* [*panoramic* view] 《*of the city*》 from the top of the mountain.
●パノラマカメラ a panoramic camera; 《和製語》 a panorama camera. ●パノラマ写真 a panoramic photograph.

はは 母 ❶[女親] a mother; (母であること) motherhood. ●3人の子の母 a *mother* of three children. ●実の母 one's real *mother*; (血のつながった) one's birth [(生物学上の)] biological] *mother*; one's *mother* by blood. ●義理の母 a *mother*-in-law. ●まま母 a stepmother. ●未婚の母 an unmarried *mother*. (⚠ a single *mother* ということもあるが、この語は離婚や夫の死別で母子家族なっている場合にも用いる) ●母(親)のような女性 a *motherly* woman. ●母のない子 a *motherless* child. ●母なる人 Mother. ●(子を生んで)母になる become a *mother*. ▶彼女は優しい母になるだろう She will make a kind [a loving] *mother*. (⚠ become と異なり「そういう素質を持っている」の意)
❷[起源]《書》the mother. ●母なる大地 Mother Earth. ●必要は発明の母 (ことわざ) Necessity is *the mother of invention*.
●母の日 Mother's Day. (参考 《米》などは5月の第2日曜日、《英》は Lent (四旬節) の第4日曜日)

はは (笑い声) ha(-)ha!

*****はば 幅** ❶[横の長さ] (a) width, 《書》(a) breadth. (⚠ width は端から端までの距離に, breadth は表面上の広がりに重きを置く) ●幅10メートルの通り a street ten meters *wide* [*broad*, *in width*, *in breadth*]. ●幅の狭い[広い]川 a *narrow* [a *wide*, a *broad*] river. ●肩幅が広い have *broad* shoulders. ▶この船は長さ90メートル,幅20メートルだ This ship is 90 meters long and [by] 20 (meters) *wide*. (⚠ (1) ... is 90 meters by 20 (meters) のように long, wide を明示しないときは短い方が幅と解釈される. (2) 部屋や土地などの幅と奥行きを表す場合は大きい方の数値に long を,短い方に wide を用いる: 幅6メートル奥行き4メートルの部屋 a room six meters long and four wide. ただし奥行きに deep を用いると a room six meters wide and four deep となる)
会話「この道の幅はどのくらいですか」「11メートルです」 "How *wide* [How far *across*] is this road?" "It's 11 meters (*wide* [*across*])." / 《やや書》 "What is the *width* [*breadth*] of this road?" "It's 11 meters." /It has a *width* [a *breadth*] of 11 meters." (事情 米英ではヤード法を日常用いる. 11 meters は約 36 feet)
❷[ゆとり] ●彼は人間に幅が出てきた (心が広くなった) He's become *broad-minded*. ▶その言葉の解釈にはかなりの幅が持たせてある You are allowed much *latitude* in interpreting the word. ▶人生をもう

少し幅広く(=広い視野から)解釈すべきだ You should interpret your life *from a broader point of view*.
❸[開き] ●賃金の値上げ幅は大きくなかった The *range* of a raise was small. ▶彼は歩幅が大きい He walks with long *steps*.
●幅がきく ▶彼は政界ではなかなか幅がきく (影響を及ぼしている) He is very *influential* [is *a man of great influence*] in political circles./He *has* great *influence* in political circles.

ばば 馬場 riding grounds.

パパ 《話》 a dad, 《話》 a daddy. (⚠ papa は今はあまり用いられない) (⇨お父さん)

ばば(あ) 婆(あ) (老女) an old woman; (祖母) a granny.

パパイヤ 〖植物〗a papaya /pəpáiə/.

ははおや 母親 a mother. (⇨母)

ははかた 母方 one's mother's [(やや書) maternal] side. ●私の母方のいとこ a cousin on my *mother's side*; one of my *maternal* cousins. (⇨父方)

はばかり 憚り (遠慮) reserve (⇨遠慮); [(便所)] a bathroom (⇨便所).

はばかりながら 憚りながら (それはそうだろうが) I dare say ..., but (相手の意分を一応受け入れてやんわりと反論する言い方); (生意気なようですが) Excuse me for being a bit too forward, but.

はばかる 憚る (ためらう) (*to do*); (気おくれしている) be diffident 《*about doing*》, (遠慮する) 《書》 refrain 《*from doing*》. ●はばからずに意見を述べる (率直に) express one's opinion *frankly*. ▶彼はそれはおれのものだと言ってはばからない He *doesn't hesitate to* claim [(主張する) insists on claiming] it to be his possession. ▶パリでは恋人たちが人目をはばかることなく人前でキスしているのを見た I saw lovers kissing each other *openly* in public in Paris.

ははこぐさ 母子草 〖植物〗a cottonweed.

はばたき 羽ばたき (ゆっくりした) a flap; (小刻みで速い) a flutter. ●羽ばたく) ▶茂みの中で羽ばたきが聞こえた We heard a *flutter of wings* in the bush.

はばたく 羽ばたく (はばたと) flap (-pp-) [*beat**] (one's wings); (小刻みに早く) flutter (one's wings). ●世界にはばたく spread one's wings 《in the world》. ▶その鳥は必死にはばたいたが飛べなかった The bird *flapped* (its *wings*) hard but couldn't fly.

はばつ 派閥 a faction. ●党内派閥 intraparty *factions*. ●派閥を解消する disband [liquidate] *factions*. ●その党は三つの主要派閥に分かれている The party is split (up) into three main *factions*.
●派閥争い a factional strife [struggle, dispute]. ●派閥政治 factional politics

はばとび 幅跳び the lóng [《米》bróad] jump. ●立ち幅跳び the standing long *jump*. (⇨走り幅跳び)
●幅跳び選手 a long jumper.

ハバナ 〖キューバの首都〗Havana /həvǽnə/.

ばばぬき 婆抜き (トランプの) (play) old maid.

はばひろい 幅広い ●幅広い知識を持つ have a *wide* [a *broad*, an *extensive*] knowledge 《*of*》. ●幅広い論議 (広範囲な) a wide-ranging discussion. ▶そのアニメ作家は小さい子供から年配の人まで幅広いファンを持っている The animator has a *wide range of* fans from young children to elderly people.

バハマ 〖国名〗Bahamas /bəhá:məz/; (公式名) the Commonwealth of the Bahamas. (首都 Nassau) ●バハマ人 a Bahamian. ●バハマ(人)の Bahamian.

はばむ 阻む (妨げる) prevent [stop (-pp-)] 《him *from doing*》 (後の方が口語的); (妨害する) obstruct, block; (遅らせる) hinder, hamper. (⇨妨げる) ●経済成長を阻む *hinder* economic growth. ●軍隊の前進を阻む *check* the army's advance. ▶地元住民の強い反対で原子力船の寄港が阻まれた Strong opposition from the local people *prevented* the nuclear-powered vessel *from* calling at the port. ▶濃霧のため彼の視界を阻んだ A thick fog *obstructed* [*blocked*] the driver's view. ▶がけくずれに遭った被害者の救出作業が激しい雨に阻まれている Heavy rain *is hampering* the rescue operation of the landslide victims.

はばよせ 幅寄せ —— 幅寄せする 動 pull (a car) over; move a car (closer) to the side of the road.

パパラッチ [<イタリア語] [有名人を追い回すフリーのカメラマン] a paparazzo /pɑ̀:pərɑ́:tsou/ (複) paparazzi /-rɑ́:tsi/.

ババロア [<フランス語] Bavarian /bəvéəriən/ cream.

ハバロフスク [ロシアの都市] Khabarovsk /kəbɑ́:rəfsk/.

はびこる [雑草などが] (生い茂る) grow* thick [thickly] (!) thick の方は結果の状態に重点がある), grow rank; (おおい広がる) overrun*; (害虫・病気などが) (横行する) infest (!) しばしば受身で); (広く行き渡る) (書) prevail, (まん延する) go* rampant. ●ネズミのはびこっている家 a house *infested with* mice; a mouse-*infested* house. ▶雑草が庭一面にはびこっている Weeds *grow thick* [*grow rank*] in the garden./The garden *is overgrown* [*is rank, is overrun*] *with* weeds. ▶昔肺病が坑夫の間にはびこっていた Lung diseases used to *prevail* [*rage*, (書) *be prevalent, be rampant*] among miners.

パビリオン a pavilion.

パピルス [植物・紙] papyrus /pəpáiərəs/.

はふ 破風 [建築] a gable.

はぶ [動物] a *habu*, a poisonous snake found in Okinawa.

ハブ [車軸・中心] a hub. ●ハブ空港 a hub airport. ●ハブブレーキ (自転車の) a hub brake.

パフ (a powder) puff.

パブ 《英》a pub 《public house の略》. (⇨バー)

パプアニューギニア [国名] Papua /pǽpjuə/ Nèw Guinea /gíni/; (公式名) the Independent State of Papua New Guinea (首都 Port Moresby) ●パプアニューギニア人 a Papua New Guinean, a Papuan. ●パプアニューギニア(人)の Papua New Guinean, Papuan.

パフェ (a) parfait /pɑːrféi/.

***はぶく** 省く [除く] (削除する) delete; (除外する) exclude, (名簿・グループから) leave*... out; (省略する) omit (-tt-), leave ... out; (節約する) (労力・費用などを) save; (切り詰める) cut*... down, cut down on ...; (減らす) reduce. ●名簿から彼女の名前を省く *delete* [*omit, exclude*] her name *from* the list; *leave* her name *out of* the list. ●詳しい説明を省く *omit* [*leave out*] a detailed explanation. ▶私たちは経費を省かねばならない We must *reduce* [*cut down* (*on*)] our expenses. ▶機械のお陰で我々の手間と時間がうんと省ける Machines *save* us a lot of time and trouble.

はぶたえ 羽二重 *habutae*; (説明的に) smooth, glossy silk.

ハプニング [予期せぬ出来事] an unexpected [(びっくりさせるような) a surprising] event [incident]. (!) a happening は意外性を特に含まない「(偶発的な)出来事」の意)

はブラシ 歯ブラシ a toothbrush.

はぶり 羽振り ▶彼は会社で羽振りがよい (勢力がある) He is influential [has gained influence] in his company. ▶その時から彼は羽振りがよくなったようだ He seems to have *come up in the world* since then.

パプリカ (香辛料) paprika.

パブリシティ [広報活動] publicity.

パブリック [公の] public (↔private).
●パブリックインボルブメント [住民参加] public involvement. ●パブリックオピニオン [世論] public opinion. ●パブリックコース [ゴルフ] a public (golf) course. ●パブリックコメント [意見公募] public comment. ●パブリックスクール [全寮制の私立中学校] 《英》a public school. (!) 《米》では公立学校) ●パブリックリレーションズ [広報] public relations (略 PR).

バブル [あぶく] a bubble. ●日本のバブル経済[景気]の崩壊 the collapse [bursting] of Japan's *bubble* economy [*economic bubble*]. ▶バブルがはじけた The *bubble* economy has collapsed./The economic *bubble* has burst.

パブロフ [ロシアの生理学者] Pavlov /pǽvləv, -lɔ:f/ (Ivan Petrovich 〜). ●パブロフの条件反射 *Pavlovian* conditioned reflexes.

ばふん 馬糞 horse dung [droppings]; (肥料) horse manure.

はへい 派兵 —— 派兵する 動 ▶イラクに派兵する (軍隊を送る) *send* [《やや書》*dispatch*] *troops* to Iraq.

はべる 侍る ▶殿のおそばにはべる (=そばに仕える) *wait on* the lord *by* (his) *side*. ●芸者をはべらせる have *geisha* (girls) *wait on* (him).

バベルのとう バベルの塔 the Tower of Babel /béibl/.

はへん 破片 a fragment, a broken piece; (木・石などの一部) a chip; (ガラスなどのとがったかけら) a splinter. ●ガラスの破片 a *fragment* of broken glass; a *broken piece* of glass; a *splinter* of glass.

ぼぼたん 葉牡丹 [植物] an ornamental cabbage.

はほん 端本 (不完全な1組) an incomplete set of books; (1冊のみの) an odd volume.

はま 浜 a beach. (⇨浜辺)

はまかぜ 浜風 (浜に吹く風) the wind at the beach; (海岸から吹く風) the wind from the sea.

はまき 葉巻 (smoke) a cigar /sigɑ́:r/.

はまぐり 蛤 [魚介] a clam. (!) 二枚貝の総称としても用いられる) ●焼きハマグリ a baked *clam*. ●ハマグリの殻 a clamshell.

はましぎ 浜鷸 [鳥] a dunlin.

はまだらか 羽斑蚊 [昆虫] an anopheles; a malaria-carrying mosquito.

はまち [魚介] a young yellowtail. (!) 通例単・複同形, 肉は U)

はまちどり 浜千鳥 a plover (at the beach).

はまなす 浜茄子 [植物] a sweetbrier.

はまべ 浜辺 (海・湖・川の) a beach (!) 砂や小石などにおおわれた部分); (海辺) the seashore (!) 通例砂や岩がある); (砂浜) sand(s) (!) 通例複数形で). (⇨海岸) ▶彼は浜辺で寝転んで日光浴をしている He is lying *on the beach* [*the sand*(*s*)] in the sun.

はまや 破魔矢 a *hamaya*; (悪魔払いの) an exorcising /éksɔːrsàiziŋ/ arrow; (説明的に) an arrow with white feathers, which is believed to break the entry of evil spirits into the house.

はまゆう 浜木綿 a *hamayu*; (説明的に) a plant of crinum /kráinəm/ family that grows on the beaches with white fragrant showy flowers in the summer.

はまりやく 嵌まり役 ▶彼はその仕事にはまり役だ He is *the very* [*right*] *person* for the job. ▶淀君は彼女のはまり役だ She is *a natural* [*is naturally good*] for (the role of) Yodogimi.

はまる 嵌まる ❶ [ぴったり入る] fit (-tt-) 《in, into》. ▶窓が(窓枠に)うまくはまらない The window doesn't *fit in* [*into*] its frame. ▶この指輪は小さすぎて私の指にはまらない This ring is too small. It doesn't *fit on* my finger. ▶このコートはボタンがはまらない This coat doesn't *button up*.
❷ [落ち込む] *fall into* a pond. ▶車がぬかるみにはまって動けなくなった The car *got stuck* [*caught*] in the mud./The car (*got*) *bogged down* in the mud.
❸ [だまされる] ▶敵のしかけたわなにはまる *fall into* [*be caught in*] the trap set by the enemy; *fall into* the hands of the enemy.
❹ [のめり込む] 《話》get into...; (やみつきになる) 《話》get hooked 《on》. ▶彼女はフラメンコにすっかりはまっている She's heavily into dancing the flamenco. ▶インターネットってそんなにはまるものなんですか Is the Internet that much *captivating*?

はみがき 歯磨き [練り状の] toothpaste, dental cream; [粉の] tooth powder; [行為] toothbrushing. ●歯磨きをする brush one's teeth.

はみだす はみ出す ❶ [突き出る] ▶彼の足がふとんからはみ出していた His legs *were sticking out of* the *futon*. ▶彼のポケットから何かはみ出している (外に垂れている) There is something *hanging out of* his pocket.
❷ [押し出される] ▶我々はエレベーターからはみ出した We *were crowded* [*were pushed*] *out of* the elevator.
❸ [超える] ▶予算からはみ出す *go beyond* the budget.

バミューダ (⇨バーミューダ)

ハミング ― ハミングする 動 hum (a tune).

はむ 食む [食べる] eat; (動物が) feed; (家畜が) graze. ●高給を食む(=もらう) get [receive] a high salary.

ハム ❶ [肉] (a slice of) ham. ❷ [アマチュア無線家] a (radio) ham, a ham operator.
● ハムエッグは私の好きな食べ物です Ham and eggs is [ˣare] my favorite dish. ● ハムサラダ ham /an/ salad; (a) ham salad. ● ハムサンド a ham sandwich. ● ハムチーズロール a ham-cheese roll.

はむかう 刃向かう [反抗する] act in defiance of...; (敵対する) turn* [go*] against.... (⇨逆らう) ●権力に刃向かう *rise* [*revolt*] *against* those in power.

はむし 羽虫 [昆虫] a leaf beetle.

ハムスター [動物] a hamster.

ハムラビほうてん ハムラビ法典 the Code of Hammurabi /hæmurɑ́ːbi/.

『ハムレット』 *Hamlet*. (参考) シェイクスピア作の悲劇)

はめ 羽目 ▶困った羽目に陥って in an awkward plight [*predicament*]; 《話》in a pretty fix. ●辞職する羽目になる *be reduced to* resigning; (余儀なく) *be compelled to* resign; (結果として) *end up* resigning. ▶もうあんな羽目には二度と陥らないようにしようと思う I'm never going to get myself into that kind of (awkward) situation again.
会話 「おまえ、このごろずいぶん勉強がんばってるね。なんでそんなに変わったんだい」「やっぱりもう1年浪人するはめになりたくないからね」「その調子で!引き続きがんばれよ」 "Son, you're studying very hard these days. What's made you change so much?" "Well, I'd rather not *have to* wait another year before passing the college entrance exam." "That's the spirit, son. Keep the good work."
● 羽目を外す 羽目を外して(=思いきり楽しんで)よい時

と悪い時がある You ought to know when to *let yourself go* and when not to.
● 羽目板 (屋外の)《米》clapboard; 《英》weatherboard; (集合的) weatherboarding; (屋内の) wainscot; (集合的) wainscoting.

はめこむ はめ込む [ぴったり合わせて入れる] fit (-tt-); [ダイヤなどを] set*. ●ガラスを窓枠にはめ込む fit a pane *into* a window frame; set a pane *into* [*to*] a window frame. ▶指輪には小さなダイヤがたくさんはめ込まれていた The ring *was set with* a lot of small diamonds./There were a lot of small diamonds *set in* the ring.

はめころし 嵌め殺し [建築] (はめ込みの建具) fixed fittings.
● はめ殺し窓 a fixed (sash) window.

はめつ 破滅 ruin; destruction. ▶際限のない野望が彼の破滅を招いた His boundless ambition led to his *ruin* [(破滅させた) brought him to *ruin*].
── 破滅する 動 be ruined, ruin oneself; (破壊される) be destroyed. ▶人類はいつか環境破壊によって破滅するかもしれない The human race might *be ruined* [*be destroyed*] by environmental destruction someday.

*はめる 嵌める ❶ [ぴったり入れる] fit (-tt-) 《on, into》. ●びんにふたをはめる *fit* a cap *on* a bottle. ●上着のボタンをはめる *button up* [*do up*] one's jacket.
❷ [身につける] put*...on; (身につけている) wear*, have*...on. ●手袋をはめる *put* [(引っ張る) *pull*] *on* one's gloves. ●指輪をはめている *wear* a ring (*on* one's finger); *have* a ring *on* (one's finger).
❸ [計略にかける] (欺く) take*...in; (罪に陥れる) 《話》set*...up, frame*. ▶私は彼の話[計略]にはめられていた I *was taken in* by his stories [trick].

*ばめん 場面 [映画・劇などの] a scene; [光景] a sight. (⇨場) ●見逃せない一場面 a *scene* not to be missed. ▶昨夜のテレビの決闘の場面を見たかい Did you see the duel *scene* on TV last night?

はも 鱧 [魚介] a conger pike; a pike eel.

はもの 刃物 an edged tool; (集合的) cutlery.
● 刃物師 a cutler.

はもの 葉物 (葉を食べる野菜) green vegetables.

ハモる (曲・歌を) sing [play]... in harmony; harmonize 《on》.

はもん 波紋 ● a ripple. ●水面に波紋を描く form [make] *ripples* on the water surface. ▶水面に波紋が広がった *Ripples* spread across the water. ▶彼の報告は学生の間に大きな波紋(=騒ぎ)を引き起こした His report created a great *sensation* among the students.

はもん 破門 图 (弟子・会員の) (an) expulsion; (宗教上の) (an) excommunication.
── 破門する 動 expel; excommunicate. ●画壇から破門される *be expelled from* the painting circle.

ハモンドオルガン (商標) a Hàmmond órgan.

はや 早 (もはや, すでに) already; (今や) now; (早くも) so soon.

はや 鮠 [魚介] a Japanese dace.

はやあし 早足 ── 早足で 動 with quick steps; at a quick pace. ▶駅までは早足でも20分はかかります It takes at least twenty minutes to the station even if you *walk quickly* [*at a fast pace*].

*はやい 早い, 速い ❶ [時期] early; soon.
WORD CHOICE (時期的に)早い
early 時刻・時間帯が絶対的に早いこと。または通常よりも早いこと。▶朝早くに in the *early* morning.
soon 何らかの時点から、ほとんど間があいていないこと。▶できるだけ早くかけなおしますね I'll call you back as *soon* as I can.

はやい

頻度チャート
early
soon
20　40　60　80　100 (%)

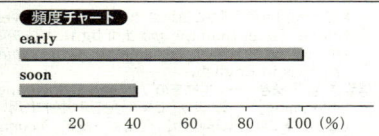

▶早い夕食を食べた I had [took] an *early* supper./I had [took] supper *early*. (❗「形容詞＋名詞」と「動詞＋副詞」の関係に注意 (⇨❷))
【...が[は]早い】 ▶電車は到着が 5 分早かった The train arrived five minutes *early*./The train was five minutes *early* (in arriving). ▶8 時では早すぎる Eight o'clock is too *early*. ▶老人はたいてい朝が早い Older people are usually *early* risers./Older people usually get up *early*. ▶早かったかしら，手が要るだろうと思ったものだから (I'm) sorry if I'm *early*, but I figured you'd need some help. ▶話すのはまだ早い It's too *soon* to tell. ▶終末は予想したより早かった The end came *sooner* than expected. ▶早ければ早いほどいい The *sooner*, the better. (❗これに対し The earlier, the better. は次のような場合に用いる:「明朝何時にまいりましょう」「早ければ早い方がいいよ」"What time shall I come tomorrow morning?" "The *earlier*, the better.")

❷ [速度] fast; rapid; quick (⇨[類語]); (動作がすばやいこと) speedy (❗quick より強意的); (動きが軽快で速いこと) swift; (遅れずすみやかに行う速さ) prompt.

WORD CHOICE 《速度が》速い

fast 人や物の動作・運動の速度が絶対的に速いこと.
● 脚の速い人 a *fast* runner.
[fast＋图] food/track/lane/bowler/pace

quick 主に動作が迅速・敏速・瞬間的で速いこと. ● 彼女の方をすばやくさっと見る have a *quick* look at her.
[quick ＋图] look / glance / fix / succession / word

rapid 主に物の成長・増加・反応などの速度が速いこと. ● その植物の短期間でのすばやい成長 the plant's *rapid* growth in a short time.
[rapid＋图] growth/succession/response/increase/rise

頻度チャート
fast
quick
rapid
20　40　60　80　100 (%)

● 速い馬 a *fast* horse. ● 速い列車 a *fast* [a *rapid*] train. (❗「急行列車」は an express,「朝早い列車」は an early train) ● 病気の早い回復 a *quick* [a *speedy*] recovery from sickness. ● 早い返答をする give a *quick* [a *prompt*] answer; give an answer *quickly* [*promptly*]; *be quick with* one's response. ● この時計は 3 分早い This watch is three minutes *fast* (⇔slow). ● あの投手はとても速球を投げる That pitcher throws a very *fast* ball. ● 彼女は呼吸も脈も速かった Her breathing was *fast* and her pulse was *quick*. (❗fast と quick の対照に注意) ● 月日の経つのは早い Time goes (by) *fast*. (⇨ 副❷)/(光陰矢のごとし)《ことわざ》Time flies (×like an arrow). (❗like an arrow をつけるのは和製英語)
会話「手紙全部書いちゃったよ」「全部だって！　早かったなあ！」"I've written all my letters." "All of them! You are *quick*!"
【...が早い[速い]】 ● 計算[決断]が早い *be quick at* figures [*in* making decisions]. ● 手が早い(すぐ暴力を振るう) *be quick to* use violence; (女性とすぐ関係を持つ) *be quick to* sleep with a woman. ● 車で行くより歩いて行く方が早いかもしれません It might be *quicker* (to go) on foot than by car. ● 彼は覚えが早い He is *quick to* learn./He is *quick at* [*in*] learning. (❗不定詞は特定の描写を，動名詞は一般的な性質を表すことが多い) / He is a *quick* learner. ● 彼女は歩く[話す]のが速い She walks [speaks] *fast*./She is a *fast* walker [speaker]. (❗後の文は一般的な性質を表し，次のような特定的な動作には用いられない: 彼は列車に間に合うように速く歩いた He walked *fast* [×He was a fast walker!] to catch the train.) ● 竹は生長が早い Bamboos grow *rapidly*. ● 川はこのあたりは流れが速い The river flows *rapidly* here.
会話「どちらの道を行くのが早いですか」「あまり変わりません」"Which way is *faster*?" "It's about the same."

❸ [その他の表現] ● ...するが早いか (⇨すぐ [...するとすぐに)])
● 早いこと[ところ] ▶雑事は早いこと片付けよう Let's finish the chores *as soon as possible*.
● 早い話が ▶早い話が，彼の言うことは信用できないということですね *In short* [*To be short*], you can't believe what he says.
● 早いもの勝ち 《ことわざ》First come, first served. (❗「先着順」「えこひいきはやめる」で日本語の語感とやや異なる (⇨先着))

── 早く，速く 副 ❶ [時期] early; soon; at once; right away [off]; immediately /ɪmíːdiətli/.

使い分け early, soon (⇨形 ❶ [類語])

at once 一定の時や出来事のあと時間をあけないで「すぐに」の意.
right away [off] at once の日常的な語で，《米》では at once よりくだけた語としてより好まれる.
immediately at once とほぼ同義だがやや堅い語. 日常会話ではしばしば強意的に用いられる.

▶早く来てください Come *early*. (❗朝早くまたは予定の時間より早くにという意) / (すぐに) Come *soon*. ▶早く帰ってきなさい Come back *early* [(すぐに) *soon*]./(ぐずぐずせずに) *Don't be long*. ▶彼は朝早く起きる He gets up *early* in the morning [*in the early morning*]./He is an *early* riser. ▶疲れていたので早く寝た I was so tired that I went to bed *earlier*. (❗*early* としてもこの意味を表せるが，*earlier* とする方が「いつもより早く (*earlier than usual*)」の意が明確になる) ▶彼は 1 時間早く来た He came an hour *early*. (❗この場合 *soon* は使えない) ▶仕事は思ったより早く終わった I finished the job *earlier* [*sooner*] than I (had) expected. (❗(1) *earlier* は予定の時刻より早く，*sooner* は予定の時間より短い時間で仕事が終わったことを表す. (2)《話》では *had* を省略することが多い) ▶早く行け Go *right away* [*at once, immediately*]. ▶できるだけ早く来なさい Come *as soon as you can* [《大至急》*as soon as possible*]. (❗ただし，次のような場合は *possible* に限る: 虫歯はできるだけ早く詰めてもらうのがよい It is advisable to have your tooth filled *as soon as possible*.)/《やや書》Come *at your earliest convenience*.
【早くても】 ▶建設には早くても 1 年はかかるだろう

The construction will take a year *at the soonest.*
会話 「いつ来られる」「早くてもあしたの午前中だな」 "When can you come?" "Tomorrow morning *at (the) earliest.*"
❷ [速度] fast; quick, quickly; rapidly; swiftly; promptly. (⇨形 ❷ [類語]) ▶早く食べなさい Eat *quick*. (❗(1) 命令文では quickly はあまり用いられない。(2) 次の soon との違いに注意: このリンゴは早く食べないと腐る This apple should be eaten *soon* or it will spoil.) ▶早くしなさい (Be) *quick*./(急いで) Hurry up./〔書〕 Make haste./(ぐずぐずするな) Don't be long (about it). ▶冬の日は早く暮れる The night falls *fast* in winter. ▶彼はあまり速く話すので言うことがよく分からなかった He spoke so *fast* that I couldn't follow him./He spoke too *fast* for me to follow (him). ▶時間が驚くほど早くたった It was surprising how *quickly* the time passed. ▶仕事が予定より早く進んでいる The work is going *ahead of* schedule.

はやうち 早撃ち ▶彼は早撃ちの名手だ He is *quick on the draw*./He is a *sharpshooter.*

はやうま 早馬 [速い馬] a fast horse; [昔, 急報のための使者が乗った馬] a post horse.

はやうまれ 早生まれ ▶早生まれの(＝1月1日から4月1日までに生まれた)子 a child born between January 1 and April 1. (⇨遅生まれ)

はやおき 早起き 图 [事] early rising; [人] an early riser.
● 早起きは三文の得 (ことわざ) The early bird catches the worm. (❗この英語は「早い者勝ちだ。のろのろしないで」の意にも用いられる)
── 早起きする get up early (in the morning).
● 早寝早起きする (⇨早寝)

はやおくり 早送り ── 早送りする fast-forward. ▶早送りボタンを押す push the *fast-forward* button.
── 早送りする 動 ▶ビデオを早送りする *fast-forward* a videotape; 〔話〕 *run* a video *up*.

はやがてん 早合点 ── 早合点する 動 jump to a conclusion [conclusions].

はやがね 早鐘 《ring [sound]》 a fire [an alarm] bell.
● 早鐘を打つ ▶胸が早鐘を打った My heart *palpitated* [*beat rapidly, pounded*].

はやがわり 早変わり ── 早変わりする 動 ▶(役者が) make* 《seven》 quick costume changes.

はやく 破約 a breach of promise. ● 破約する 動 break* [renege /ríŋg/ on] a promise.

はやく 端役 a small [a minor] part (↔a major [a leading] role). ▶端役の俳優 a bit actor. ▶端役を演じる play a *small* [a *bit*] *part.*

はやく 早く, 速く quick. (⇨早い [早く])

はやぐい 早食い ── 早食いする 動 bolt 《one's lunch》 (down); swallow 《food》 quickly; (がつがつ食べる) gobble 《one's food》 down [up] (in a hurry); eat* very quickly.

はやくち 早口 ▶早口で[に]話す speak fast [rapidly]. ▶早口の人 a fast-paced talker. (❗a fast talker は「話・かけして」「口のうまい人」の意)
● 早口言葉 a tongue twister.

はやくても 早くても quick. (⇨早い [早く])

はやくも 早くも ❶ [もうすでに] already. ▶早くも遺産相続の争いが起きている They are having trouble over inheritance *already*. (❗already は having の前に置くより文尾に置くよりあきれの含みがよりはっきり示される)
❷ [早くても] (⇨早い [早く])

はやさ 速さ quickness; rapidity; [速度] speed.

▶光の速さより速く進むことはできない We can't travel [move] faster than the *speed* of light. ▶彼の英語の上達の速さには驚いた I'm amazed at his *rapid* progress in English.

はやざき 早咲き ── 早咲きの 形 early(-flowering [-blooming]). (❗後の方は特に観賞用の植物に用いる) ▶このバラは早咲きだ This rose *blooms* [*flowers*] *early*./This is an *early* rose.

はやし 林 [森] a wood(s); [木立] a grove; [雑木林] a copse, (主に英) a coppice. (⇨森) ● 松林 a pine *wood* [*grove*].

はやし 囃子 a musical accompaniment; (祭礼の) festival music.
● 囃子方 a musician; an accompanist.

はやしたてる 囃し立てる (⇨囃す) ▶その政治家ははやし立てられて演壇を降りた(あざけられて) The politician *was booed* [*was jeered*] off the platform.

> **翻訳のこころ** 男子生徒たちは、口笛を吹いたり、拍手をしたりして、私と峰生をはやし立てた (山田詠美『ひよこの眼』) Whistling and clapping, the male students *teased* Mikio and me. はやし立てる」は tease (からかう)で表す。この語は「善意でも悪意でも相手に対して笑ったり、冗談を言ったりする行為」を表す。

はやじに 早死に ── 早死にする 動 die young; die early in life; 〔やや書〕 die an early death.

はやじまい 早仕舞い ── 早仕舞いする 動 (店を) close 《the store》 up earlier; (仕事を) knock off (work) earlier.

ハヤシライス (説明的に) rice with hashed meat [beef], hashed meat [beef] and rice.

はやす 生やす grow*. ▶あごひげを生やす[生やしている] *grow* [*have, wear*] a beard. ▶雑草を庭に生やしたままにする let the weeds *grow* in the garden.

はやす 囃す 〔〈やじる〉〕 jeer 《at》; 〔〈かっさいする〉〕 (声援する) cheer; (拍手する) applaud; (元気づける) encourage. (⇨囃し立てる)

はやせ 早瀬 rapids.

はやだし 早出し early shipment of 《vegetables [fruit]》.

はやだち 早立ち 图 an early start [departure].
── 早立ちする 動 start early.

はやて 疾風 a gale; a blast of wind.

はやで 早出 ▶明日は早出だ I must *go to work* [*the office*] *early.*

はやてまわし 早手回し ▶早手回しに(＝早目に)ホテルの予約をする make hotel reservations *early.*

はやとちり 早とちり ▶彼女はよく早とちり(＝早まった決定[判断])をする She often makes a *hasty decision* [*judgment*].

はやね 早寝 ── 早寝する 動 go to bed early. (⇨夜更かし) ▶早寝早起きする go to bed early and get up early. (❗keep early hours は今はまれ)

はやのみこみ 早呑み込み (⇨早合点)

はやば 早場 ● 早場米 early crop of rice.

はやばや 早々 ❶ [早く] early. (⇨早い [早く ❶]) ❷ [速く] quickly, promptly. (⇨早い [早く ❷])

はやばん 早番 (be on) the early [(三交替制の) morning] shift.

はやびけ 早引け ── 早引けする 動 (学校を) leave* school (an hour) early; (職場を) leave work [one's office] early [earlier than usual].

はやぶさ 隼 [鳥] a peregrine falcon.

はやべん 早弁 ── 早弁する 動 have* an early lunch; eat* one's (box) lunch earlier.

はやまる 早まる 〔〈軽率なことをする〉〕 be hasty; 〔〈繰り上がる〉〕 be brought forward; 〔〈やや書〉〕 be advanced.

はやみ (⇨早める❶) ● 早まったことをする do a rash thing. ● 早まって in a hurry; without (due) consideration. ▶家を買うときは早まってはいけない Don't *be hasty* in buying [purchasing] a house. ▶会の時間が早まった The Time of the meeting *was brought forward* [《やや書》*was advanced*].

はやみ 早見 a chart; a table. ●計算早見表 a (ready) reckoner.

はやみち 早道 a shortcut. (⇨近道)

はやみみ 早耳 ▶君は早耳だね You are *quick-eared*./You have a good nose for news.

はやめ 早目, 速目 ── **早目[速目]に** 📖 (定刻より早くて) early (⇨早く); (普段より早く) earlier (than usual); (余裕を持って) in good time; (定刻より速めに) ahead of time; (予定より速めに) ahead of schedule. ▶彼はいつもより早めに来た He came a little *earlier* than usual. ▶早めに予約しないと切符が手に入りません You can't get tickets unless you book them *early*.
〈会話〉「それは土曜日に持っていくよ」「もう少し早めに渡してもらえないかなぁ」"I'll bring them around on Saturday." "Can't you let me have them a bit *sooner*?"

はやめし 早飯 (早めの食事) an early lunch [supper]. ▶彼は早飯だ(食べるのが速い) He eats 〈lunch〉 *very fast*.

はやめる 早める, 速める ❶【時期】quicken, 《書》hasten /héisn/; (繰り上げる) bring* [put*]... forward, 《やや書》advance. ●死期を早める (不幸などが) quicken one's death; *hasten* one's end. ▶出発を土曜から金曜に [1 週間だけ] 早めた We *brought forward* our departure from Saturday to Friday [by one week].
❷【速度】quicken, speed*... (up). ●足を速める *quicken* one's steps [pace]. ●仕事を速める *speed up* one's work. ▶列車は速度を速めてきた The train began to *put on* [*gather*] *speed*./The train began to *accelerate*./(乗っている人を主語にして) We were *running* [*going*] *faster and faster*.

はやり 流行 图 (a) fashion; (傾向) a trend; (一時的の) a fad, 《やや書》(a) vogue.
── **はやりの** 圏 fashionable, trendy; (人気のある) popular. (⇨流行(%))
● はやり歌 a popular song. ●はやり風邪 (流行性感冒) 〈suffer from〉 influenza [《話》(the) flu]. ●はやり言葉 (流行語) a vogue word, a word in vogue; (専門語的になった) a buzzword. ●はやり目 (流行性結膜炎)【医学】〈suffer from [catch]〉 epidemic conjunctivitis; (一般的に) pinkeye.

はやりすたり 流行り廃り ▶名前はちょうど服同様にはやりすたりがある Names, just like clothes, *go in and out of fashion*.

はやりたつ 逸り立つ (しきりに...したがる) get [become, grow] impatient; (気負い立つ) get excited.

*__**はやる 流行る**__ ❶【流行する】come* into fashion [《やや書》vogue]; (人気がある) be popular. (⇨流行, 人気) ●はやっている歌 a *popular* song. ▶ロングスカートがまたはやってきた[はやっている] Long skirts *have come into fashion* [*are in fashion*] again. ▶このヘアスタイルは今ははやっていない This hairstyle *is out of fashion* [《やや書》*vogue*, *style*] at present./(もうはやらなくなった) This hairstyle *has now gone out* (of fashion [*vogue*]). ▶今はどんなえりがはやっていますか What kind of collar *is popular* now? ▶週末を田舎で過ごすのがはやっている It's *fashionable* [*fashion*] to spend the weekend in the country.
❷【繁盛する】(繁盛する) prosper, flourish, thrive* (⇨繁盛する); (商売がうまくいっている) do* good business. ●はやっている店 a *prospering* [a *flourishing*, a *thriving*, (うまくいっている) a *successful*] store. ▶この食料雑貨店ははやっている. This grocery store *is prospering* [*is doing good business*]./(得意客が多い) This grocery store *has* [*attracts*] *a lot of customers*. ▶近所にスーパーができてから, うちの店ははやらなくなった We have become less *prosperous* [(商売で落ち目になった) Our business has gone downhill, (客足が減ってきた) We have been losing customers] since a new supermarket opened in the neighborhood.
▶あの医者ははやっている The doctor *has a large practice*. (❗ practice は「業務」の意で, a large practice は内容的には「多くの患者 (many patients)」をさす)
❸【病気が広まる】spread*, go* around. ▶関東地方で流感がはやっている (The) flu *is spreading* [*is going around*, (猛威を振るっている) *is raging*] in the Kanto district./(話) Influenza *prevails* [*is prevalent*] in the Kanto district./Lots of people have got (the) flu in the Kanto district.

はやる 逸る (興奮する) be [get*, feel*] excited ⟨*at*⟩; (あせる) be impatient. ●はやる気持ちを抑える control one's *eagerness* [*impatience*]. ▶彼はパーティーのことを考えると心ははやった He *was excited* [*was thrilled*] when he thought of the party.

はやわかり 早分かり quick understanding, (早合点) (⇨早合点) ●早分かりする be quick to understand; 《話》be quick on the uptake. (❗ uptake は「吸収すること」) ●国文法早わかり a quick and easy handbook of Japanese grammer.

はやわざ 早業 quick work, a quick job; a lightning trick. ▶あまりの早業でトリックを見破れなかった I couldn't see through the trick because he had done it *so quickly*.

*__**はら 腹**__

▣ **WORD CHOICE** ▣ **腹**

stomach 胃部, または腹部全体のこと. 日常的文脈・専門的文脈を問わず, 幅広く用いられる. ●腹が痛い[腹をこわす] have *stomach* pains [troubles].

belly 胃部・腹部のこと. 通例くだけた文脈で用いる. ●太鼓腹 a big *belly*.

abdomen 腹部・腹腔部のこと. 主に専門的・医学的文脈で用いる. ●上[下]腹部 the upper [lower] *abdomen*.

▣ **頻度チャート** ▣

stomach ███████████████████
belly   ██████████
abdomen ██

0   20   40   60   80   100 (%)

❶【腹部】a stomach; 《話》a belly; an ábdomen (⇨類語); 《話・幼児語》(ぽんぽん) one's tummy. ①【~腹】 ●太鼓腹 a potbelly. ●ビール腹 a (big) beer *belly*.
②【腹が】 ▶腹が痛い I have a *stomach*ache./I have a pain in the *stomach*./My *stomach* aches. ▶腹が一杯だ I'm full. (⇨腹一杯) ▶彼は背が高くどっしりとし, 腹が出ていた He was tall and heavily built, with a big *stomach*. ▶腹が張る

は

My *stomach* feels bloated [(もたれる) heavy]. ▶腹がへったときこれを食べてください Please have this when you *get* [*become*] *hungry*. (❗日常会話では get の方が普通) ▶腹がへっているときに酒を飲んではいけない You'd better not drink alcohol when you *are hungry* [(すきっ腹の時に) *on an empty stomach*].

③**[腹に]** ▶この食物は腹にもたれた This food lay heavy on my *stomach*. ▶運動不足で腹にぜい肉がついてきた I'm getting flabby around the waist for lack of exercise.

④**[腹を]** ▶彼の腹をなぐる hit him in the *stomach*. ▶彼女は妊娠して大きな腹をしている She *is very pregnant*./(婉曲的) She *is expecting* (*a baby*). ▶子供は腹をすかして帰ってきた My child came home *hungry*. ▶スマートに見えるようにと彼は腹を引っ込めていた He kept [held] his *stomach* in, trying to look better.

❷**[物の中央]** (内部の空間) a belly. ● 船の腹 the *belly* of a ship.

❸**[考え, 心]** (理性的な心) (a) mind; (情緒的な心) (a) heart.

● **腹が黒い** ▶彼は執念深く冷血で腹が黒いやつだ He is a vengeful, cold-blooded, and *black-hearted* [(悪意のある) *evil-minded*] man.

● **腹が据(*)わる** ▶腹のすわった(=毅然(きぜん)とした)人 a *resolute* person; (度胸のある人) a *brave* [(度胸のある) *plucky*] man [woman]. ▶その知らせで動揺したが, すぐ腹がすわってきた(気を静めた) I was agitated by the news, but I *pulled* myself *together* [(度胸がすわった) *plucked up* my *courage*] at once.

● **腹が立つ** ▶彼のものの言い方に腹が立った I *got angry* [(主に米話) *mad*] at his way of speaking. ▶The way he spoke *made* me *angry* [(いらいらさせた) *annoyed* me, (むっとさせた) *offended* me, (米話) *burned* me *up*]. (⇨④)

● **腹がふくれる** (満腹になる) have a full stomach. ▶牛乳を飲むと腹がひどくふくれる(=張る) Milk makes my *stomach swell* badly.

● **腹が太い** ▶彼は腹が太い(=心が広い) He is *big-hearted* [(寛大だ) *generous*, *broadminded*]./(根性がある) He has a lot of *guts*.

● **腹に一物(いちもつ)** ▶彼は腹に一物ありそうな(=何かたくらんでいそうな)人だ(話)He seems to *be up to something*.

● **腹に据えかねる** ▶彼の傲慢(ごうまん)さは腹にすえかねる I *can't put up with* [*can't stomach*] his arrogance.

● **腹の皮がよじれる** ▶ポールホーガン主演の『クロコダイルダンディー』を見るたびにおかしくて腹の皮がよじれる Every time I watch *Crocodile Dundee* starring Paul Hogan, my *sides split* with laughter.

● **腹の中** ▶腹の中を見せない conceal one's true intentions; (本性を現さない) do not show one's true colors. ● 腹の中で笑う laugh *in* one's *sleeve*; grin *inside*. ▶彼は腹の中(=心)は親切な人だ He is a kind man *at heart*. ▶あの男の腹の中(=考え)は分からない I don't understand what he is thinking [(腹積もり) what he has in mind]. ▶彼の心を見すかすことができない(=分からない). で「彼の心を見すかすことができない」の意

● **腹の虫** ▶それでは彼の腹の虫がおさまらない(=気持ちを静められない)だろう It *won't soothe* his *feelings* [(怒りを静める)] calm down his anger].

● **腹を痛める** ▶彼女はとても貧しかったので自分の腹を痛めた子を捨てざるをえなかった She was forced to abandon *her own child* because she was very poor.

● **腹を抱える** ▶子供たちは腹(=横腹)を抱えて笑った The children laughed, *holding* their *sides*./(二つ折りになって) The children *doubled* (*themselves*) *with* laughter.

● **腹を決める** ▶彼を支持しようと腹を決める *decide* [*make up* one's *mind*] *to* back him up.

● **腹を切る**(切腹する) kill oneself by cutting open one's stomach with a dagger; commit harakiri suicide; (手術を受ける) have an operation on the stomach.

● **腹をくくる** ▶腹をくくっている(決意している) *be very determined* (*to* do); (覚悟をしている) be prepared (*to* do).

● **腹を壊す** ▶腹をこわしている I am having *stomach* trouble./(下痢をしている) I have loose bowels [diarrhea]. (⇨腹痛) /dàiərí:ə/ は医学用語]

● **腹を探る** ▶その問題について彼女の腹を探った I *sounded* her [her views] *out* on the problem.

● **腹を立てる** ▶be *get angry* [(主に米話) *mad*] 《*with* [*at*] + 人, *at* [*about*] + 物・事》 (心の平静さを失う) lose one's temper, get upset. ▶彼女がうそを言ったので腹を立てている I'*m angry with* [*mad at*] her for telling me a lie./(ひどく) I *resent* her telling a lie. (⇨怒る) ▶そんなに腹を立てるなよ. Don't *get upset*./(落ちつけ) Calm down. ▶彼は利口じゃないんだ. だからいちいち腹を立てちゃいけないよ(=我慢しなさい) He's not clever. So *be patient with* him.

● **腹を割る** ▶腹を割って話し合う talk *frankly* 《*with*》; have a *heart-to-heart* talk 《*with*》.

はら 原 (野原) a field; (平原) a plain.

***ばら 薔薇** (花) a rose; (木) a rosebush. ● バラのつぼみ a *rose* bud. ● バラのとげ a *rose* thorn. ● バラの花束 a bouquet of *roses*. ● バラのように赤い唇 *rose-red* lips; *rosy* lips. ● ばら色 (⇨薔薇色)

ばら ― ばらの 形 loose. ● ポケットのばら銭をじゃらつかせる jingle some coins [change] in one's pocket. (❗(1) 動詞が jingle なので, *loose* coins としない. (2) 特定の小銭は the change) ▶鉛筆をダースではなくばらで買いたい I want to buy pencils *loose*, not by the dozen.

はらあて 腹当て (よろい) a breast plate; a bib; an apron.

バラード [詩・音楽] a ballade /bəlάːd/; [ラブソング] a ballad /bǽləd/.

はらい 払い [支払い] (a) payment (⇨支払い); [請求書] a bill; [勘定(書)] an account. ● 現金払い *payment* in cash. ● 一括払い *payment* in a lump sum. ● ボーナス一括払い single *payment* at bonus season. ● 全額払い *payment* in full. ● 分割払い *payment* by installments [on account]. (❗後の方は「つけ[(内金としての)一部]払い」の意にもなる) ● 年払い[月々12回払い]をする pay in yearly [12 monthly] installments. ▶今月は酒屋の払いが多い We have a lot of *bills* (*to pay*) *for sake* this month.

はらいおとす 払い落とす ● オーバーの雪を払い落とす *shake* [*brush*] the snow *off* one's overcoat. ● たばこの灰を払い落とす *knock off* one's cigarette ash.

はらいこみ 払い込み (支払い) (a) payment; (入金) a deposit.
● 払い込み期日 the date of payment. ● 払い込み金額 the amount paid. ● 払い込み資本 paid-in [up] capital.

はらいこむ 払い込む [支払う] pay*; [金などを預ける] deposit. ● 年会費をA銀行で払い込む *pay* the annual fee *through* A bank. ▶私は彼の口座に100万円払い込んだ I *paid* [*deposited*] a million

はらいさげる　払い下げる (民間に売り渡す) sell*... off; (処分する) dispose of .... (❗「払い下げ」is a sell-off, (×a) disposal) ▶政府は大会社に国有林を一部払い下げた The Government sold off (a) part of the national forest to big companies.

はらいせ　腹いせ ▶腹いせをする take it out (on him); vent one's anger (on). (⇨八つ当たり)

はらいっぱい　腹一杯 ▶腹一杯だ I am full./(十分に食べた) I've eaten my fill./I've had enough.

はらいのける　払い除ける ▶食べ物にとまっているハエを払いのける brush [(手であおいで) fan] some flies away from the food. ▶手を払いのける (振り払う) shake [throw] off (his) hand; brush away (his) hand.

はらいもどし　払い戻し a refund /rɪ́fʌnd/; (税金などの) a rebate /rɪ́ːbeɪt/. (❗日本語の「リベート」のような悪い含みはない) ▶切符[チケット]の払い戻し (get) a refund on the ticket. ▶予約キャンセルの場合、料金の払い戻しは行われません If canceled, no refund will be made.

はらいもどす　払い戻す pay*... back, repay*; refúnd, make* a refúnd. (⇨返金) ▶運賃 [1,000円]を払い戻してもらう have one's fare [1,000 yen] refunded. ▶試合が雨で流れ、入場料は払い戻された Admissions were refunded when the game was rained out.

会話 「これを返品しますので払い戻していただけますか」「それはできかねますが」「ああそうですか」"May I return this and get a refund?" "I'm afraid not." "Oh, thanks anyway."

ばらいろ　薔薇色 图 rose (color).
— **薔薇色の** 圏 rosy, rose-colored. ▶彼の未来はばら色だ He has a bright [a rosy, (有望な) a promising] future. ▶人生はいつもばら色(＝楽しい、楽)と限らない Life is not all roses [not always a bed of roses].

‡**はらう　払う** ❶[支払う] pay*; (返済する) pay ... back, repay* (❗後の方が堅い語). ▶勘定[借金]を払う pay one's bill [debts]. (⇨支払う) ▶(彼に)借入金を払う pay (him) back the loan; pay the loan back (to him). ▶その本の代金を払う pay for the book. (❗×pay the book とはいわない) ▶つけて、後で払います Charge it, and I'll pay it later. ▶君へのお金をあすまでに払います I'll pay you the money [the money to you] by tomorrow. ▶あなたにいくら払いかえばいいですか (借りがありますか) How much do I owe you? ▶ここは私に払わせてください I'd like to [Let me] pay for this./(私が負担する)

会話 「それいくら？」「私たちが払えない額よ」"How much does it cost?" "More than we can afford."

会話 「そのテーブルにいくら払いましたか」「1万円払いました」"How much did you pay for the table?" "I paid ten thousand yen."

❷[取り除く] (手・ブラシなどでほこりなどを) brush ... off [away]; (ほこりを払う) dust ... (off); (枝を切り落とす) cut*... off. ▶いすのほこりを払う dust the chair. (⇨払い落とす, 払い除ける) ▶彼は起き上がってズボンについた泥を払った He got up and brushed [(ばんばん叩いて) slapped] some dirt off his pants. ▶私たちはその木の枝を払った We cut [(勢いよく切り落とした) lopped, (刈り込んだ) trimmed] some branches off the tree.

❸[注意・敬意を]pay*; (敬意を) show*. ▶だれも彼の助言に注意を払わなかった No one paid any attention to his advice. ▶その子供たちは先生に敬意を払った The children showed [paid] respect to their teacher./The children respected their teacher.

❹[売却する] sell*; (処分する) dispose of .... ▶古新聞を回収業者にはらう sell some old newspapers to a junk dealer; (リサイクルに持って行って) take old newspapers to a recycle center [shop] and get some money.

はらう　祓う (厄払いをする) exorcize; drive* (an evil spirit) out; (清める) purify. ▶お経をあげて家から悪霊をはらう exorcize (an evil spirit from) the house by chanting prayers.

ばらうり　ばら売り ── ばら売りする 動 sell* (them) separately. ▶この色鉛筆をばら売りしてもらえますか Can I get these colored pencils loose?

バラエティ　variety /vəráɪəti/. ▶バラエティに富む be full of [rich in] variety.
● バラエティショー a variety show; (米) vaudeville /vɔ́ːdəvɪl/.

パラオ [国名] Palau /pəláʊ/; (公式名) the Republic of Palau. (首都 Koror) ▶パラオ人 a Palauan. ▶パラオ語 Palauan. ▶パラオ(人[語])の Palauan.

はらおび　腹帯 (腹巻き) a stomach band; (妊婦の) a maternity belt; (馬の) a saddle girth.

はらかけ　腹掛け (職人の) a workman's apron; (腹当て) a bib; an apron. (⇨腹当て)

はらがまえ　腹構え ── 腹構えする 動 (心の準備をする) prepare oneself (for); get [be] ready (for, to do).

はらぐあい　腹具合 ▶腹具合が悪い I have something wrong with my stomach./I have an upset stomach [a stomach upset]. (❗stomach trouble は「胃腸の病気」の意味でここでは不適)

パラグアイ [国名] Paraguay /pǽrəɡwaɪ/; (公式名) the Republic of Paraguay. (首都 Asuncion) ▶パラグアイ人 a Paraguayan. ▶パラグアイ(人)の Paraguayan.

はらくだし　腹下し (下痢) diarrhea; (下剤) (a) laxative.

パラグライダー (器具) a paraglider; (スポーツ) paragliding.

パラグラフ　a paragraph.

はらぐろい　腹黒い [人が] sly, crafty, (二心のある) duplicitous; [計略をねる] scheming, designing, (悪意を持った) evil-minded; [考え・計画などが] dark. ▶腹黒い人 a scheming person; a schemer.

はらげい　腹芸 ▶腹芸を使う use visceral /vɪ́sərl/ communication [《話》 belly language] (❗belly language は body language (身体語) に合わせて作られた言葉); (説明的に) use a clever technique to make one's real intentions understood without verbal interaction.

ばける [列などが] be broken up; [髪が] be disheveled /dɪ́ʃévld/, be disarranged.

はらこ　腹子 (a) hard roe; (salted) fish eggs. ▶タラの腹子 (タラコ) cod roe.

はらごしらえ　腹ごしらえ ▶仕事を始める前にちょっと腹ごしらえをしておこう We'll have [eat] a light meal before we start to work.

はらごたえ　腹応え ▶今夜の食事は腹応えがなかった The dinner tonight stuck to my ribs [was not satisfactory to me].

はらごなし　腹ごなし ▶昼食のあと腹ごなしに散歩をした We took a walk for [to help] digestion after lunch.

パラサイト [他に寄りかかって生活する人] a parasite (↔ an independent).

- **パラサイトシングル** 'parasite single'; (説明的に) an unmarried young man or woman who continues living with his or her parent(s) like "parasite" even after he or she becomes economically independent and who enjoys a carefree and well-to-do life style as a single.

パラジウム 【化学】palladium /pəléidiəm/ 《元素記号 Pd》.

パラシュート 〚落下傘〛 a parachute /pǽrəʃùːt/.

はらす 晴らす ▶ 〚追い払う〛drive*... away, 《やや書》dispel (-ll-); 〚明らかにする〛clear. ● うさを晴らす *drive away [dispel]* one's gloom. ● 疑惑を晴らす *clear* oneself of the doubt. ● 積年の恨みを晴らす *settle* old scores 《*with* him》.

はらす 腫らす ▶ 彼女は目を赤く泣きはらしていた Her eyes *were swollen* from crying.

ばらす 《分解する》take*... apart [to pieces]; 《殺す》《話》do*... in, 《俗》bump (...) off; 《暴露する》reveal, disclose. ● 彼の秘密をばらす *reveal [disclose, lay bare]* his secret; give him away. ● このエンジンをばらして調べなさい *Take* this engine *apart [to pieces]* and check on it.

バラスト 〚道路・線路用の砂利〛ballast /bǽləst/.

パラソル a párasòl. (⇨傘)

パラダイス Paradise, paradise; 《比喩的》a paradise 《*of, for*》.

パラダイム 〚枠組〛a paradigm.
● パラダイムシフト 〚理論的枠組の変更〛a paradigm shift.

はらだたしい 腹立たしい 〚いら立たせる〛irritating, annoying (⇨苛〘い〙立つ); 〚しゃくにさわる〛offensive.
〔翻訳のこころ〕思い出そうとして, 思い出せないものを抱えるほど, 腹立たしいことはない (山田詠美『ひよこの眼』) Nothing's more *annoying [irritating]* than having in mind something that you want to recall but you can't. (❢ *annoying* は「気に障る」, *irritating* は「(ある程度の期間にわたって生じることについて)腹立たしく思う」の意)

はらだち 腹立ち anger; 《激怒》rage. ▶ 腹立ちまぎれに彼をどなりつけた I shouted at him in a fit of *anger [temper]*.

はらちがい 腹違い ● 腹違いの弟〚妹〛 a brother [a sister] born of a different mother. (❢ a half brother [sister], a stepbrother [a stepsister] は母だけでなく父の違う弟〚妹〛の意にもなる)

パラチフス 〚医学〛paratyphoid /pǽrətáifoid/.

ばらつき unevenness. ● 彼らの成績にはだいぶばらつきがある Their grades *vary* widely. (⇨ばらつく)

ばらつく 〚まちまちである〛vary《*in*》; 〚差が大きい〛《一定でない》be irregular; 〚一様でない〛be uneven; 〚髪などが乱れる〛be disarranged; 〚大粒の雨が〛spatter.

バラック a hut; 《掘っ建て小屋》a shack, a shanty; 《大きく醜い》《話》a barracks (❢ 単・複同形).

ばらつく 〚雨などが〛sprinkle. ● 小雨がぱらついている It's *sprinkling*.

はらつづみ 腹鼓 ● 腹鼓を打つ pat one's stomach after eating to one's satisfaction.

はらっぱ 原っぱ a [an open] field; a meadow (❢ 「牧草地, 放牧場」としても用いる. 野の花が咲く).

はらづもり 腹積もり ● 腹積もりはできている be ready《*for*; *to* do》. (⇨心積もり)

はらどけい 腹時計 ● one's stomach's time. ▶ ぼくの腹時計ではもう昼食時だ My stomach says it's lunch time.

パラドックス a paradox.

ばらにく 肋肉 ribs (of beef or pork).

パラノイア 〚妄想症〛〚医学〛paranoia /pǽrənɔ́iə/.

はらのむし 腹の虫 (⇨腹 〚成句〛)

はらばい 腹這い ● 腹ばいになる lie on one's stomach. ● 腹ばいになって前進する crawl forward *on one's stomach*.

はらはちぶ 腹八分 ● 腹八分にしておけ 《食べすぎるな》Don't eat too much.
● 腹八分目に医者いらず 'Being moderate in eating will keep you healthy.'/Feed by measure and defy the physician./Temperance is the best physician.

はらはら ── **はらはら(と)** 〚副〛 ❶ 〚散り落ちる様子〛 ▶ 桜の花びらがはらはらと落ちている The petals of cherry blossoms *are fluttering (down)* to the ground. ▶ 涙が彼女のほおをはらはらと流れ落ちた Tears *trickled* down her cheeks.

❷ 〚気をもむ様子〛 ▶ 母親は赤ん坊がよちよち歩くのをはらはらして見ていた The mother *nervously* watched her baby toddling along.

── **はらはらする** 〚動〛《不安である》feel* uneasy [nervous]. ● はらはらする試合 an *exciting [a thrilling]* game. ▶ その映画は私をはらはらさせた The film *thrilled* me.

ばらばら ❶ 〚砂や雨など小粒のものが続けて落ちる様子〛 ▶ あられ〚大粒の雨〛がばらばら降ってきた Hail stones [Large drops of rain] began to *patter down*. (❢ その音は the *patter* of hailstones [raindrops] (on the roof))

❷ 〚分散した状態〛 ▶ 子供たちがばらばら散っていった The children *scattered in all directions*./The children *dispersed*. ▶ 破産して家族はばらばらになった The bankruptcy caused the family to *split up [break up]*. ▶ 私は古新聞がばらばらにならないようひもでしっかり縛った I bound up the old newspapers tight with string so that they wouldn't be scattered around. ● 彼は自転車〚時計〛を直すため部品をばらばらにした He *took* the bicycle *apart* [the clock *to pieces*] to fix it. ▶ 彼女はその花びんを落としてばらばらに壊してしまった She dropped the vase and it *broke into pieces*. ▶ 夫婦の気持ちは間もなくばらばらになっていった The couple came to *feel apart* before long.

❸ 〚乱れた状態〛 in disorder. ▶ 子供がそろえて置いてあるカードをばらばらにした The child put the cards *out of* their correct order.

❹ 〚統一のない状態〛 ● ばらばらの記述 (一貫しない) an *inconsistent* account. ▶ 委員会はその件に関して意見がばらばらで結論を出すに至らなかった The committee had *widely varying* opinions on the matter and couldn't come to a conclusion. (❢ 次のようにもいえる: As opinions varied on the matter, the committee ....) ▶ 値段が店によってばらばらだ The prices *vary* from store to store.

● ばらばら殺人事件 a mutilation murder. ● ばらばら死体 a dismembered body. (❢ *dismember* は「手足などを切り取る」の意)

ぱらぱら ❶ 〚粒状のものが続けて落ちる様子〛 ● 料理に塩をぱらぱら振りかける *sprinkle* salt *on* one's food; *sprinkle* one's food *with* salt. ▶ 雨がぱらぱら降り始めたので私たちは急いで下山した As it began to *sprinkle*, we hurried down the mountain.

❷ 〚本などをめくる様子〛 ▶ 本のページが風でぱらぱらめくれた There was a *flutter of pages* (of a book) in the wind. ● 彼は本をぱらぱらめくった He *leafed [thumbed, flipped] through* a book.

❸ 〚まばらな様子〛 ▶ 会合の出席者はぱらぱらだった There was only a *scattering* of people at the meeting./(数が少なかった) There was *only a small* attendance at the meeting. ▶ 彼がおじぎをするとぱらぱら弱々しい拍手が起こった There was

はらびれ 腹鰭 〖魚介〗a pelvic fin.
パラフィン paraffin (wax).
●パラフィン紙〖主に米〗waxed [wax] paper. (**!**この意では通例 paraffin paper とはいわない); (特に料理に用いる)〖英〗greaseproof paper.
パラフレーズ 〖名〗a paraphrase 《of》.
—— **パラフレーズする** 〖動〗paraphrase.
はらぺこ 腹ぺこ ▶腹ぺこだ I'm *very hungry*./〖話〗(空腹で死にそうだ)〖米〗I'm starved./I'm starving. ▶戦争中は食うものがなく皆腹ぺこだった We all *went hungry* without having enough food during the war.
パラボラ a parabola /pərǽbələ/, a parabólic anténna /〖話〗a dish.
はらまき 腹巻き a bellyband; (説明的に) a wide stomach sash for keeping the abdomen warm.
ばらまく ばら撒く (四方に) scatter. (⇨撒(*)く ❶)
● 灰を凍った道路にばらまく *scatter* ashes *on* [(一面に) *over*] the icy road; *scatter* the icy road *with* ashes. ● うわさをばらまく(=広める) *spread* a rumor. ● 選挙で金をばらまく(=ばく大な金を遣う) *spend* a great deal of money [*throw* one's money *around*] in the election. ▶多量のちらしがばらまかれた(=配られた) Great quantities of leaflets *were distributed*.
はらむ 孕む 〖子を宿す〗become* pregnant; 〖風を受けてふくらむ〗swell* in the wind; 〖含む〗involve; (伴う) accompany. ▶この事業は失敗すれば全財産を失う危険性をはらんでいる This project *involves* the risk of losing all my fortune [money].
パラメーター 〖数学〗a parameter /pərǽmətər/.
パラメディック 〖上級救急救命士〗a paramedic.
はらもち 腹持ち ▶力仕事をする人は腹持ちのいいものを食べたがる Manual workers want to eat things that *wear well* [*keep them going longer*].
バラモン a Brahman, a Brahmin. (〖参考〗インドのカースト制度の4階級中, 最高位の僧)
● バラモン教 Brahmanism. ● バラモン教徒 a Brahmanist.
バラライカ [<ロシア語]〖楽器〗a balalaika. ● バラライカ奏者 a balalaika player. ● バラライカを弾く play the balalaika.
パラリンピック the Paralympics. (**!**複数扱い) ▶パラリンピックは「もう一つのオリンピック」と呼ばれる The *Paralympics* are sometimes called 'the other Olympic Games.'
パラレル 〖名〗〖スキー〗 ▶パラレルで滑る ski in a *parallel* position.
—— **パラレル** 〖形〗(並列の) parallel.
● パラレル伝送 〖コンピュータ〗parallel transmission. ● パラレルプリンター a parallel printer. ● パラレルポート a parallel port.
はらわた 腸 〖大・小腸〗the intestines; 〖腸の全体〗the bowels (⇨腸(ちょう)); 〖魚などの内臓〗the guts.
● 魚のはらわたを抜く gut a fish; take out *the guts* of a fish.
● はらわたが腐る ▶あの男ははらわたが腐っている (心が堕落している) He is *corrupted*./He has a *corrupt heart*.
● はらわたが煮え繰り返る ▶その話を聞いてはらわたが煮え繰り返った The story *made* my *blood boil*. ▶彼ははらわたが煮え返る思いで(吐きながら)つばを拭き取った He *was seething* as he wiped the spit off. (**!**通例進行形で用いる)

はらん 波乱 〖もめごと〗(a) trouble; 〖社会的な騒動〗(a) disturbance, 〖激震〗ups and downs. ● 政治的波乱を巻き起こす cause [raise] a political *disturbance*. ● 波乱に富んだ[波乱万丈の]一生を送る lead a life full of *ups and downs*; (出来事の多い一生を送る) lead an *eventful* [a *stormy*] life.
はらん 葉蘭 〖植物〗a cast-iron [shield-flower] plant, an aspidistra.
バランス balance. (⇨釣り合い, アンバランス) ● バランスのとれた[とれていない]食事 a (*well*-)*balanced* [an *unbalanced*] diet. ● 需要と供給のバランス a *balance* of supply and demand; a supply-demand *balance*. ● 片足でバランスをとる *balance* (*oneself*) on one leg. ● 仕事と遊びのバランスをとる *keep* [*preserve*] *a balance between* work and play. ● バランス感覚がすぐれている have a good sense of *proportion*. ● バランスを崩しながら一塁へ送球する throw to first off *balance*. ▶彼はでこぼこの斜面でバランスを崩して転倒した He lost [was thrown off] his *balance* on a bumpy slope and tumbled down. ▶(一国の)輸入と輸出はバランスがとれていなくてはならない A nation's imports and exports should *balance* [*be balanced*].
● バランスシート 〖貸借対照表〗a balance sheet.

*はり 針 ❶ 〖裁縫・注射・レコード用などの〗a needle; 〖計器の〗a pointer, a needle; 〖時計の〗a hand; 〖留め針〗a pin; 〖ホッチキスの〗a staple; 〖釣り針〗a hook; 〖虫の〗a sting; 〖植物のとげ〗a thorn; 〖縫合の一針〗a stitch.
①〖～針, 針の～〗● 編物[縫い]針 a knítting [a séwing /sóuiŋ/] nèedle. ● 注射針 (皮下注射針) a hypodermic needle. (**!**(1) 単に a needle ということもある. (2)「皮下注射器」は a hypodermic syringe) ● 糸を通した針 a *needle* and thread. (**!**単数扱い) ● 針の先 the point of a *needle*. ▶磁石の針は北を指す A compass *needle* points to the north. ▶彼は腕の傷口を5針縫った It took five *stitches* to close up the wound in his arm./The wound in his arm needed five *stitches*.
②〖針に〗● 針(の穴)に糸を通す thread a *needle*; pass [get] thread through the eye of a *needle*. ● 針にえさをつける bait a *hook*.
③〖針で〗● 針で刺す prick 《one's finger》 with a *needle* [a *pin*]; (虫が) sting 《him *on* the neck》. ● チョウをピンで(=ピンで)留める fasten a *butterfly* with a *pin*; pin a butterfly. ▶足に針で刺すような痛みを感じた I felt a *stinging* pain in my [the] leg.
❷〖(比喩的に)とげ〗● 針を含んだ言葉 sharp [*stinging*] words.
❸〖はり治療〗(⇨鍼(は))
● 針のむしろ ● 針のむしろに座る心地である feel as if (one were) lying on the bed of *thorns*.
● 針刺し a pincushion. ● 針仕事 needlework; sewing. ● 針箱 a séwing bòx [kìt]; a workbox.
はり 張り (⇨張り合い) ● 張りのある声 a *strong* [豊かな] a *rich*] voice; a voice full of life. ● 張りのある若い肌 one's *fresh* and youthful skin.
はり 梁 a beam.
はり 鍼 (針) a needle; (鍼術) acupuncture; 〖医学〗stylostixis. ● 針を施す acupuncture.
● 鍼医 an acupuncturist.
はり 玻璃 (水晶) crystal; (ガラス) glass.
ばり 罵詈 abuse. ● 罵詈雑言を浴びせる hurl [shout, scream] (a stream of, a torrent of) *abuse* at 《him》/*abuse* 《him》.
バリ 〖インドネシア南部の州〗Bali /báːli/. ● バリ(人)の Ba-

-ばり -張り ● 革張りのいす a chair *covered with leather*; a *leather-covered* chair. ● バルザック張りの小説 a novel written *in the style* [*manner*] *of Balzac*.

パリ [フランスの首都] Paris /pǽris/. ● パリ市民, パリっ子 a Parisian /pərízən/.
● パリ祭 the Fourteenth of July. [参考] フランス革命(1789年)の記念日

バリア [障壁] a barrier.
● バリアフリー (⇨バリアフリー)

はりあい 張り合い ● 張り合いのある(=やりがいのある)仕事 a *challenging* [*a rewarding*] job; a job *worth doing*. ● 張り合いのない人生を送る (退屈な) lead a *dull* life; (目的のない) lead an *aimless* [*a purposeless*] life. ● 生きる張り合いがない have nothing *worth* living for; have nothing to live for. ▶家のローンの返済があったのでかえって仕事の張り合いが出た I felt (all) the more inclined to work hard because I had a home loan to pay off.

はりあう 張り合う (競争する) compete [contend] 《*with*, *against*》, rival. ▶彼らはライバル会社と激しく張り合っている They *are* keenly *competing with* [*against*] their rival company. ▶2人は社長の地位につこうとお互いに張り合った The two *rivaled* [*competed with*] each other *for* the presidency.

はりあげる 張り上げる (声を) raise one's voice; (叫ぶ) shout 《*at*》; yell 《*at*》. ▶「あなた！」妻は大声を張り上げた "Mr. Bush!" My wife *shouted at the top of her voice*. (■夫をたしなめたりするときに、姓で呼んで改まった口調になることがある)

バリアフリー ● バリアフリーの公共施設 (障壁なしの) *barrier-free* public facilities. ● バリアフリー化(する) incorporate *barrier-free* design.

バリアント [異形] a variant 《*of*》.
パリーグ [野球] the Pacific League.
はりいた 張り板 a fulling board.
ハリウッド [米国の映画製作の中心地] Hollywood /hɑ́liwùd/.
バリウム [化学] barium 《元素記号 Ba》. ● バリウムを飲む take a *barium* sulphate 《米》[*meal* 《英》] (before an X-ray is taken of one's stomach).
はりえ 貼り絵 a collage /kəlɑ́ːʒ/. ▶彼女は色紙を使って貼り絵を作った She made a *collage* out of colored paper.
バリエーション (変化) (a) variation; (多様) (a) variety. ▶彼がチームに入って司令塔になれば攻撃にバリエーションが出てくるだろう When he joins us and directs the offense, our team will have more *variations* in the pattern of attack.
はりえんじゅ 針槐 [植物] a false acacia. 《同》ニセアカシア》
はりかえる 張り替える, 貼り替える (壁紙・障子・ふすまを) repaper; (いすなどを) re-cover.
はりがね 針金 wire. ▶「針金1本」は a (piece of) wire. ● 針金で縛る bind (them) with *wire(s)*; wire (them) together.
はりがみ 張り紙 [掲示用] (手書き・印刷による) a notice (■材質は紙に限らない); (印刷した小さい) a bill; (ポスター) a poster /póustər/; [表示用] (のり付き) a sticker; (ラベル) a label /léibl/; (付箋) a tag (■しばしば複合語で). ●「指名手配」の張り紙 a "wanted" *notice*. ● 音楽会の張り紙 a concert bill. ▶張り紙お断り [掲示] Do not stick any bills. ▶箱に「割れ物」の張り紙がついていた On the box was a *sticker* saying "Fragile."

バリカン 《a pair of》hair clippers. [参考] フランスのバリカン製造会社 Barriquand et Marre より

ばりき 馬力 ❶ [馬力] a horsepower (略 ~) (略 hp, HP). ▶もっと馬力のある車がほしい I want a car with more *power*.
[会話]「このエンジンは何馬力ですか」「20馬力です」"What is the *horsepower* of this engine?/How many *horsepower* does this engine have?" "It is [It has] 20 *horsepower*." (■「20馬力のエンジン」は a twenty-*horsepower* engine)
❷ [精力] energy. ●馬力がある be energetic. ● 馬力をかける(全精力を出す) apply [devote] all one's *energy* [*energies*] 《*to*》. ● 馬力をかけて仕事をする work hard.
❸ [荷馬車] a wagon; a cart.

はりきゅう 鍼灸 acupuncture /ǽkjupʌ̀ŋktʃər/ and moxa treatment. (⇨鍼灸(しんきゅう))
はりきる 張り切る [頑張る] work [try] hard 《*to do*》; [元気でいる] be vigorous, be energetic; [熱中している] be enthusiastic 《*about*》; [心がはっている] be eager 《*to do*》.
はりくよう 針供養 *harikuyo*; (説明的に) a memorial service for broken needles.
はりぐるみ 張りぐるみ ● 張りぐるみのいす an upholstered chair.
バリケード a barricade /bǽrikèid/; (道路の) 《put up》 a road block. ● 机で入り口にバリケードを築く *barricade* the entrance with desks. ● 彼らを入れないようにバリケードを築く build *barricades* to keep them out.
ハリケーン a hurricane /hə́ːrəkèin/.
はりこ 張り子 ● 張り子の虎 a paper tiger, 《米》a paper-mâché /pèipərməʃéi/ tiger.
はりこみ 張り込み a stakeout; (待ち伏せ) (an) ambush; (監視) (やや書) surveillance. ● メディアの張り込みに悩まされている人 the victim of a media *stakeout*. ● 張り込み中である be on a *stakeout*. (⇨張り込む)
はりこむ 張り込む ❶ [監視する] keep* a (close) watch 《*on*》; keep 《him [a place]》under watch《(やや書) surveillance》, 《話》stake 《a place》out. ❷ [奢発する] give* 《him an expensive coat》generously; (自分のことで) treat oneself 《*to* an expensive coat》.
はりさける 張り裂ける ▶悲しみのために彼の胸は張り裂けそうであった His heart nearly *broke* with sorrow.
パリジェンヌ [＜フランス語] a Parisienne /pəriːzién/.
はりしごと 針仕事 《do》needlework. (=裁縫)
パリジャン [＜フランス語] a Parisian /pərízən/.
はりせんぼん 針千本 [魚介] a porcupine fish; a balloonfish.
はりたおす 張り倒す (ぶちのめす) knock 《him》down [flat]; (平手で強く打つ) slap (-pp-) 《him》hard.
はりだし 張り出し (張り紙) a notice; a poster; a bill. ● 張り出し舞台 an apron stage. ● 張り出し窓 a bay window; (弓形の) a bow window. ● 張り出し横綱 an extra *yokozuna* [grand champion].
はりだす 張り出す, 貼り出す ❶ [掲示する] put* ... up. ❷ [出っ張る] (せり出す) stick* out (⇨突き出る); (頭上に) overhang*; (上方に横たわる) overlie*. ▶その家は大きなバルコニーが前庭に張り出していた The house had a large balcony *hanging over* [*overhanging*] the front garden. ▶高気圧が北海道上空に張り出してきている A high pressure system *is moving over* Hokkaido.
はりつく 張り付く stick [adhere; cling] 《*to*》. (同 くっつく)

はりつけ 磔 (十字架への) (a) crucifixion. (!the Crucify はキリストの磔にする) ▶はりつけにする crucify. ▶はりつけになる be crucified.

はりつける 張り付ける ●壁にポスターを張り付ける stick [(特にのりで) paste (up)] posters on the wall; paste [×stick] the wall with posters. ▶ロッククライマーが岩壁に身を張りつけて(=しがみついて)いた The climber was clinging to the cliff face.

ぱりっと ●ぱりっとしている (身なりが) look smart [handsome]《in one's coat》(!後の方は主に男性に用いる) be smartly [crisply] dressed; (紙・せんべいなどが) be crisp.

はりつめる 張り詰める ●【氷が】 freeze* [be frozen] all over. ▶湖に氷が張り詰めた The lake has (been) frozen all over.
●【緊張する】 be tense [strained]; strain one's mind [nerves]. ▶張り詰めた雰囲気 (厳粛な) a solemn [(緊張した) a tense] atmosphere. ▶式典の間中大変気の張り詰めていた I was (feeling) very tense throughout the ceremony. ▶降伏をラジオで聞いたとき、私は張り詰めていた気が抜けてぼんやり立ちつくした When I heard the news of our surrender on the radio, my strained [tight] nerves slackened and I stood there in a daze.

パリティ [コンピュータ] a parity. ●パリティチェック a parity check.

はりとばす 張り飛ばす slap (-pp-) (his) face hard; slap (him) hard (⇨張る 他 ④).

バリトン (声域) báritòne; (歌手) a baritone. ●バリトンで歌う sing (in) baritone. ▶彼はすばらしいバリトンの声をしている He has [speaks in, sings in] a fine baritone voice.

はりねずみ 針鼠 [動物] a hedgehog; a porcupine (!後の方が大きい).

ばりばり ●【かみ砕く音】 ▶ライオンがばりばり骨をかみ砕いた The lion crunched the bones. (!crunch は「音を立ててかみ砕く」の意)
●【強い力で引き裂く[はがす]様子】 ▶帆が強風でばりばり破れた The sails were ripped in a gale. ▶バイクがばりばりエンジンをふかす音がした I heard a bike revving up.
●【その他の表現】 ▶ばりばり働く work very hard; (猛烈に) work like blazes [(話) (馬車馬のように) like a horse]. ▶ばりばりの現役である be very active on the front line. ▶タオルがばりばりに凍っていた The face towel was frozen stiff [like a board].

ぱりぱり ●【新しく張りがある様子】 ▶ばりぱりのお札 a crisp [a crackling] bank note. ▶ぱりぱりの新しいシャツ a crisp new shirt; (糊(ʳ)がよくきいている) a well starched new shirt. ▶レタスの葉は新鮮でぱりぱりしていた The lettuce leaves were fresh and crisp.
●【裂けたり砕けたりする音】 ▶氷を踏むとぱりぱりと砕けた The ice cracked when I trod on it. ▶彼はビスケットをぱりぱり食べた He crunched the biscuits.

はりばん 張り番 (a) watch. (⇨見張り)

はりぼて 張りぼて (⇨張り子)

はりめぐらす 張り巡らす 【囲む】 surround; (ロープで) rope ... off; [(網などを)] set*... up. ▶刑務所の周りには高い壁が張り巡らされている The prison is surrounded by high walls. ▶彼らは世界中に情報網を張り巡らした They set up an information network all over the world. (!国家の戦略的情報は intelligence) ▶スタジオの天井にはライトの電線が縦横に張り巡らしてあった Strings of lights crisscrossed (on) the ceiling of the studio.

はりやま 針山 a pincushion.

バリュー [価値] value. ●ニュースバリュー (news) value. (⇨ニュース) ●ネームバリュー (⇨ネーム)

はる 春 ●【季節の】 spring, (the) springtime. ▶(1) 北半球では 3～5 月, 南半球では 9～11 月. (2) this, last, next などを伴う場合は前置詞をつけずにそのまま副詞としても用いる. ▶ある年の春に one spring. ▶毎年春になると every spring. ▶ここは春には大勢の人でにぎわう A lot of people visit here in 《主に米》 the spring [during the spring, for the spring]. (!前の二つは「…の期間中に」, for は「…を過ごすために」の意) ▶今年の春は例年になく寒かった It was [has been] unusually cold this spring. (!was はすでに春が過ぎ去っている場合に, has been は現在はまだ春の終わりである場合に用いる. this spring の代わりに in 《主に米》 the spring this year ともいえるが, in the spring of this year は避けた方がよい) ▶私の父は去年の春亡くなった My father passed away last spring [in 《主に米》 the spring last year]. (!last spring は今年の春がまだ来ていない場合に用いる) ▶来年の息子は今年の春大学に入る My son will get into [enter] college next spring. (!「今度の春」が目前の場合は this spring も可)《語法》米英では「春」に入学・入社のイメージはない) ▶もう春も終わりです Spring is going. ▶冬は過ぎ, 今は春です Winter is over [has gone]. It's spring now. ▶後半は Spring is here [now with us]./Spring has [《文》 is] come. ともいえる) ▶日本では 3 月, 4 月および 5 月が春(=春の月)です March, April, and May are the spring months in Japan. (!日本の春に特定する場合には左の必要)
●【人生の】 ▶我が世の春を謳歌(ᵒᵏ)する[している] enjoy [be at] the height of one's prosperity [(人気) popularity, (権勢) power].
—— 春の 形 spring; 《書・詩》 vernal. ▶ある春の日に one [on a] spring day; one day in 《主に米》 the spring. ▶今年の北海道は春の訪れが遅い Spring comes late [is late (in) coming] in Hokkaido this year. ▶春の足音が聞こえる(=すぐそこまで来ている) Spring is near at hand [just around the corner].
●**春一番** the first gale of the spring. ●**春がすみ** a spring haze. ●**春物** spring clothes [wear].

はる 張る 動 自 ●【伸び広がる】 (伸びる, 広がる) stretch out; (広がる) spread* (out). ▶その木の枝は四方に張っている The branches of the tree spread (out) in all directions./The tree spreads its branches in all directions. (⇨他 ②) ▶その草は根が張っている The grass is deeply rooted.
●【一面におおう】 ▶湖一面に氷が張った Ice has formed over the lake./The lake has (been) frozen [iced] over.
●【ふくらむ】 ▶お乳が張っている My breasts feel swollen with milk. ▶腹がガスで張っている My stomach is bloated with gas.
●【突き出る】 ▶彼はあご(骨)が張っている He has a strong square jaw.
●【その他の表現】 ▶気の張る(=堅苦しい)パーティー a formal party. ●気が張る (緊張する) be [feel] tense [nervous]. (⇨ストレス) ▶肩が凝る(=凝る) have stiff shoulders [(片方だけが) a stiff shoulder, (首どもの周辺をさして) a stiff neck]. ▶値の張る(=高価な)家具 expensive [《やや書》 costly] furniture. ▶値が張る be expensive; cost much.
—— 張る 他 ●【引っ張り渡す】 (綱などを心棒に張る) stretch; (ぴんと張る) strain; (ひも・電線などを張り渡す) string*. ▶綱をぴんと張る stretch a rope tight; strain [tighten] a rope. ▶針金を 2 本の柱の間に張る stretch [string] a wire between two posts.

● ギターに弦を張る *string* a guitár. ● 綱を張って囲う *rope off* (the place).
❷ [広げる] *spread*... (out); (十分に伸ばし広げる) *stretch*... (out). ● 幕を張る *spread* a curtain. ● (木が)枝を張る *spread* [*its*] branches. ● カンバスをわくにぴんと張る *stretch* a canvas *over* a frame. ● テントを張る *set up* [*pitch*] a tent. ● 帆を張る(=揚げる) *put up* [*hoist*] a sail [the sails]. ● テニスコートにネットを張る *put up* the net on the tennis court. ● 畑の周囲に[窓に]金網を張る *put up* wire netting *around* a field [*over* a window].
❸ [突き出す] ● ひじを張る *stick* [*push*] *out* one's elbows; (直角にする) *square* one's elbows. ● 胸を張る(自信・自尊で) *throw* [*swell*] *out* one's chest; (姿勢正しく) draw one's shoulders back.
❹ [平手で打つ] ● 彼の横っ面を張る *slap* him [*give* him *a slap*] *on* the face; *slap* his face. (❗後の方はなぐった部分に重点のある言い方) (⇒張り倒す, 張り飛ばす)
❺ [おおいをつける] ● 壁に新しい壁紙を張る *cover* a wall *with* new wallpaper. ● 床にタイルを張る *tile* a floor.
❻ [その他の表現] ● ふろに水を張る *fill* a bath *with* water. ● 宴を張る *hold* [*give*, [話] *throw*] a banquet. ● 勢力を張る *extend* influence (*over* a district). ● 論陣を張る *set out* an argument (*for*, *against*). ● 相場を張る *play* the market. ● 意地を張る be obstinate; be stubborn. ● 見えを張る show off; put on a good front.

はる 張る, 貼る 〖くっつける〗 put; 〖(ぴったりと) stick*; (のりで) paste〗; 〖こう薬を〗 plaster; 〖障子を〗 paper. ● 切手を封筒に張る *put* [*stick*] a stamp *on* an envelope. ● 壁にポスターを張る *put up* a poster /póustər/ *on* the wall; *paste* a poster *to* the wall. ▶その写真はアルバムに張りました I *pasted* [*put*] the picture in my album.

*はるか 遥か ❶ [距離] (遠くに) *far** (⇒遠い ❶ [類語]); (見える・聞こえる範囲で遠くに) in the (far) distance. ● はるかかなたに稲妻が光るのが見えた I saw a flash of lightning *far away* [*far off*, *a long way off*, *in the distance*]. ● 私の家ははるか山の上にある My house is *far up* the mountain. ● アインシュタインは時代のはるか先を行く人でした Einstein was *far ahead* [*in advance*] of his time.
❷ [時間] ● はるか紀元前 1000 年の昔は *as far back as* 1000 B.C. (❗西暦では×1,000 とコンマをつけない) ▶それははるか昔の出来事だった It was *a very old incident*./(ずっと前に起こった) The incident happened *a long time ago*.
❸ [程度] much; far. (❗いずれも通例比較級・最上級の前で用いる. by far, far and away はこの強意形. by far は後置可) ● 彼の車は私のよりはるかによい His car is *much* [*far*, *even*, 〖話〗 *a lot*, 〖話〗 *lots*] better than mine. ▶2 人のうちでは彼女の方がはるかに若い She is *by far* the younger of the two [the younger of the two *by far*]. ● 私はこの難民キャンプで, 成功することよりも人の役に立つことの方がはるかに重要であることを学んだ In this refugee camp, I have come to understand that being successful *can't hold a candle to* being of use. (❗A can't hold a candle to B は〖話〗「A は B よりはるかに劣る」の意)
会話「2 回目の方がよかったよね」「ええ, はるかによかったよ」"It was better the second time, wasn't it?" "*Very much* better."

はるかぜ 春風 a spring wind [breeze].
はるぎ 春着 〖春用の衣服〗 spring wear [clothes]; 〖正月用の晴れ着〗 a New Year's dress [suit].

バルキー ● バルキーセーター a bulky sweater.
バルク 〖積み荷〗 bulk. ● バルクカーゴ 〖ばら荷〗 a bulk cargo.
バルコニー a balcony. ● バルコニーへ出る walk out on [xin] the *balcony*. ▶バルコニーに洗濯物を干してはいけないことになっています We're not allowed to hang laundry on the *balcony*.
パルサー 〖電波天体〗〖天文〗 a pulsar.
はるさき 春先 ● 春先に in early spring; early in (〖主に米〗 the) spring.
バルサミコ 〖<イタリア語〗 ● バルサミコ酢 balsamico vinegar.
バルサム 〖芳香天然樹脂〗 balsam /bɔ́ːlsəm/.
はるさめ 春雨 〖春の雨〗(a) spring rain [shower]; rain in springtime.
はるさめ 春雨 〖食べ物〗 Chinese starch noodles.
パルス (電流) 〖電気〗 a pulse. ● パルス変調 pulse modulation. ● パルスレーダー pulse radar.
バルセロナ 〖スペインの都市〗 Barcelona /bɑ̀ːrsəlóunə/.
『**バルタイ**』 *Partei*. (参考) 倉橋由美子の小説
パルチザン 〖ゲリラ隊員〗 a partisan.
パルテノン 〖ギリシャの神殿〗 the Parthenon /pɑ́ːrθənɑ̀n/.
バルト ● バルト海 the Bàltic /bɔ́ːltik/ Séa. ● バルト三国 the Baltic States. (参考) エストニア・ラトビア・リトアニアの 3 共和国
はるとしゅら 『春と修羅』 *An Ashura in Spring*. (参考) 宮沢賢治の詩集
バルトリンせん バルトリン腺 〖解剖〗 the Bartholin's gland.
はるのさいてん 『春の祭典』 *Le Sacre du Printemps*; (英語名) *The Rite of Spring*. (参考) ストラビンスキー作曲のバレエ組曲
はるばしょ 春場所 〖相撲〗 the spring (grand) sumo tournament.
バルバドス 〖国名〗 Barbados /bɑːrbéidous/. (❗公式名も同じ). (首都 Bridgetown) ● バルバドス人 a Barbadian. ● バルバドス(人の) Barbadian.
はるばる 遥々 (長い道のりを) all the way; (遠くから) from far away [off], (書) from afar. ▶彼は北海道からはるばる上京した He came to Tokyo *all the way* from Hokkaido.
バルビタール 〖薬学〗 barbital. (参考) 鎮静・睡眠剤
ハルビン 〖中国の都市〗 Harbin.
バルブ 〖弁〗 a valve.
パルプ 〖製紙原料〗 wood pulp. ● パルプにする pulp.
パルプざい パルプ材 pulpwood.
はるまき 春巻き a spring [an egg] roll.
はるめく 春めく ▶だんだん春めいてきた It *is getting* more *like spring*./It has become springlike.
パルメザンチーズ Parmesan cheese.
はるやすみ 春休み (the) spring vacation [〖英〗 holidays]. (参考) 米英では Easter break [〖米〗 vacation, 〖英〗 holidays] がこれに当たる

はれ 晴れ 图 fair [快晴] clear] weather; (いい天気) nice [good, 〖主に英〗 fine] weather. (❗気象学上は clear (快晴), fair (晴)と区別するが, 天気予報では clear の中に fair も含めていうことが多い) (⇒天気) ▶あすは晴れでしょう It [The weather] will be *clear* [*fair*] tomorrow./(晴れ上がるでしょう) It will *clear up* tomorrow. (❗天気予報などでは, 該当地域の人々に話しかけるスタイルで We'll get (mostly) *clear* [*sunny*] *skies* tomorrow. などということも多い. mostly は「だいたい」の意) ● 今朝のテレビの天気予報で,「晴れ後曇り」だそうです This morning's TV weather forecast said, "*Fair*, later cloudy."

── 晴れの 形 〖格式ばった〗 formal, cèremónial; 〖

はれ 腫れ (a) swelling. ●その薬ではれが引いた The medicine made the *swelling* go down. ▶冷湿布をすると足首のはれが引くでしょう A cold compress will take away the *swelling* on your ankle.

はれあがる 晴れ上がる clear up. (⇨晴れる) ▶空はすっかり晴れ上がった The sky [It] *has cleared up*.

はれあがる 腫れ上がる swell* up. ▶彼の顔はひどく腫れ上がっていた His face *was* badly *swollen* [puffy and swollen].

ばれい 馬齢 ●馬齢を重ねる (むだに年をとる) grow older without any particular purpose.

バレエ [<フランス語] a ballet /bǽleɪ/. (❗「芸術の一部門としてのバレエ」は Ⓤ でしばしば the 〜) ●バレエのけいこをする practice *ballet*. ●バレエを見に行く go to (see) a [the] *ballet*. (❗は相手も知っているの意) ▶彼女はとてもバレエが上手だ She's a good *ballet* dancer./She dances *ballet* very well.

●バレエ曲 a ballet. ●バレエシューズ 《a pair of》 ballet shoes. ●バレエ団 a ballet company. (❗固有名詞は the ... Ballet のようにいう) ●バレエダンサー (男性・女性) a (professional) ballet dancer;(女性) a ballerina. (❗主演バレエダンサーは the lead dancer [(女性) the prima ballerina] 《with the Russian Ballet》という)

ハレーション [写真] (a) halation /heɪléɪʃən, hə-/.

パレード [行進] a parade. ●戦勝[優勝]パレード a victory [a victorious] *parade*. ▶サーカスの一団が町中をパレードした The circus *paraded* (through) [*had a parade through*] the town.

バレーボール [球技] vólleybàll. ●そのボールは Ⓒ ●バレーボールをする play *volleyball*. ●バレーボールの試合をする play [have] a *volleyball* game 《with, against》.

はれがましい 晴れがましい [公式の] formal, ceremonial; [すばらしい] grand. ●晴れがましい場所で話すspeak on a *formal* [a *ceremonial*, a *grand*] occasion.

はれぎ 晴れ着 ●晴れ着を着ている be (dressed) in one's (Sunday) best; be (dressed) in one's best clothes.

はれすがた 晴れ姿 ●晴れ姿(=晴れ着姿)の (dressed) in one's best. ●結婚式の時の娘の晴れ姿をカメラに収める take a photograph of one's daughter *in her wedding dress*. (❗成人式・卒業式などの場合はそれぞれの装いで訳語を工夫する必要がある) ●金メダルを授与される息子の晴れ姿を夢みる dream of seeing the *moment of* one's son's *triumph* when he is awarded a gold medal.

パレスチナ Palestine /pǽləstàɪn/. ●パレスチナ人 a Palestinian /pæləstíniən/. ●パレスチナ(人)の Palestinian.

***はれつ** 破裂 図 a burst; (血管などの) [書] (a) rupture; [爆弾などの] (an) explosion. ●タイヤの破裂 the *burst* of a tire; a tire *burst*. ●水道管の破裂した所 a *burst* in a water pipe. ●「破裂した水道管」は a *burst* water pipe. ●血管の破裂 the *bursting* [*rupture*] of a blood vessel.

── 破裂する[させる] 動 [中からの圧力で破裂する] burst*; [血管などの] (やや書) rupture; [爆発する] explode, blow*... up. (❗後の方が口語的。) ●破裂してこなごなになる *burst* into fragments. ●タイヤ[風船]を破裂させる *burst* a tire [a balloon]. ●かんしゃく玉を破裂させる *explode* a firecracker; (激怒する) *explode* [*burst*] *with* anger, [話] blow up. ▶こ

の冬凍結で水道管が破裂した The water pipes *burst* when we had the freeze this winter. ▶ボイラーは大きな音を立てて破裂した The boiler *burst* [*exploded*] with a loud noise. ▶爆弾が破裂した The bomb *exploded* [*blew up*].

●破裂音 an explosive sound; [音声] an explosive, a plosive.

パレット [<フランス語] a pálette. ●パレットナイフ a palette knife.

はれて 晴れて [正式に] officially; formally; (公然と) publicly; openly. ▶30年間の亡命生活の末に彼は晴れて故国の土を踏んだ He set foot in his homeland *publicly* after living in exile for thirty years.

はればれ 晴れ晴れ ── 晴れ晴れする 動 (気分が) feel cheerful [refreshed]. ●晴れ晴れした顔をしているhave a *bright* [a *cheerful*] look (on one's face). ●気分が晴れ晴れしない (憂うつだ) feel *gloomy* [*depressed*]. ●晴れ晴れとした気分で外出する go out *in high* [*good*] *spirits*.

はれぼったい 腫れぼったい swollen, (いくらか腫れた) puffy. ●腫れぼったい目 *puffy* eyes.

はれま 晴れ間 [雲の切れ間] a rift in the clouds; a patch of blue sky; [雨のこやみ] a lull in the rain. ▶午後には晴れ間も出るでしょう We'll get some sunshine in the afternoon.

ハレム a harem /héərəm/. (⇨ハーレム)

はれもの 腫れ物 [はれ] a swelling; [できもの] a boil; (腫瘍(ようよう)) a tumor. ▶彼は首にはれものができている He has a *swelling* on his neck. ▶顔にはれものができたA *boil* developed on my face.

●腫れ物に触るように ●はれものに触るように扱う treat [handle] (*him*) *with kid gloves*.

はれやか 晴れやか ── 晴れやかな 形 ●晴れやかな微笑をする give a *bright* [a *radiant*, (機嫌のよい) a *cheerful*] smile. ▶オーケストラの晴れやかな音楽が一段と大きくなるとドアが開いて新郎新婦が入ってきた As the orchestra swelled with *triumphant* music, the door opened and the bride and groom came in.

── 晴れやかに 副 ●晴れやかに(=華美に)装う be *gaily* dressed.

バレリーナ [<イタリア語] a ballerina. (⇨バレエ)

***はれる** 晴れる ❶ [天気が] (空が晴れ上がる) clear (up); become* clear; [霧が] clear (away); [上がる] lift; (消散する) disperse. ●よく晴れた青空 a *clear*, blue sky. ▶まもなく晴れそうだ It [The weather] will *clear up* soon. ▶空が晴れて星が出ている The sky is *clear* and the stars are out. ▶正午までには霧は晴れるだろう The fog will lift [*clear away*] by noon. ▶晴れた日にはここから富士山が見える We can see Mt. Fuji from here on a *clear* [*fine*] day.

> **古今ことばの系譜「ごんぎつね」**
> ある秋のことでした。二、三日雨がふりつづいていた間、ごんは、外へも出られなくて穴の中にしゃがんでいました。雨があがると、ごんは、ほっとして穴からはい出しました。空はからっと晴れていて、百舌鳥(もず)の声がきんきん、響いていました。It was autumn. The rain had been falling for a few days, and Gon had had to keep to his hole. So, when the rain finally stopped, he felt relieved and crept out. Outside he saw that the sky had already cleared up and the shrikes were noisily squawking. (❗(1)「からっと晴れた」は「晴れた」と言い換える。(2)モズの鳴き声の「きんきん」は擬音語にせず、squawk という動詞によって表す)(⇨『ごんぎつね』)

❷ [気分が] (一新する) be refreshed; (元気づく）

cheer up. ▶海外旅行でもすれば気が晴れるよ Traveling abroad will *cheer* you *up*.

翻訳のこころ 二人掛けの座席はいたるところで三人掛けになり、窮屈そうに身を寄せ合った乗客が、*擦れない顔付き*で扇子や団扇(うちわ)を使っている(竹西寛子『蘭』) On every bench for two, three people are seated. Squeezed next to each other, those passengers with *unhappy* [*depressed*] looks are using [waving] fans or *uchiwa*. (! 「濡れない顔付き」は look unhappy (楽しそうでない), depressed (意気消沈したように)と表す

❸ 《疑いが》 (消える) disappear, vanish; 《身のあかしが立つ》 (主語は人) be cleared (*of* the charge); (ぬぐい去られる) be dispelled. ▶その容疑者に対する私の疑いはやっと晴れた My doubts about the suspect *have been dispelled* at last.

はれる 腫れる (ふくれる) swell* (up); (炎症を起こす) be inflamed. ● 腫れた目 *swollen* eyes. ● (真っ赤に)腫れた傷口 an *inflamed* wound. ▶ねんざをした足首が腫れた My sprained ankle *has swelled* (*up*).

ばれる (明るみに出る) come* out, (やや書) come to light; (人の正体などが) be found out. (⇨発覚する) ▶今までのところその秘密はばれていない The secret *hasn't come out* so far. ▶彼が金を盗んだのがばれた It *came out* that he had stolen the money. ▶大きなうそほどばれにくい The greater the lie (is), the greater the chance (is that) it will be believed.

バレル 〖容量の単位〗 a barrel /bǽrəl/.

パレルモ 〖イタリアの都市〗 Palermo /pələ́ːrmou/.

ハレルヤ hallelujah, halleluiah /hæ̀ləlúːjə/. (! 「神をたたえよ」の意)

はれわたる 晴れ渡る clear up. ● 晴れ渡った青空 a *clear* [雲のない) a *cloudless*] blue sky.

ばれん 馬棟 a baren; (説明的に) a pad for printing woodcuts.

バレンタインデー 《*on*》 (Saint) Valentine's /vǽlən tàinz/ Day. (参考) 2月14日. その日に送るカードは a valentine (card))

はれんち 破廉恥 图 shamelessness; shamefulness. — 破廉恥な 圃 (人が) shameless; (行為が) shameful.

ハロ 波浪 waves.
● 波浪注意報 [警報] 〖issue〗 a high-sea warning [(米) advisory].

ハロウィーン Halloween /hæ̀louwíːn/. (参考) 10月31日の夜)

ハロー Hello /helóu, hə-/; Hallo /həlóu/.

ハローワーク (公共職業安定所) a public employment security office; (米) a career center, (英) an employment agency; (学生の為) a (job) placement center [bureau]; (和製語) a hello work.

ハロゲン 〖ハロゲン元素〗〖化学〗halogen /hǽlədʒən/.

バロック (様式・時代・音楽) the baroque /bəróuk/. (! 時に B-) ● バロック様式の建物 a *baroque* building.
● バロック音楽 baroque music. ● バロック建築 baroque architecture.

パロディー (a) parody (*of*, *on*).

バロメーター a barometer /bərámitər/. ▶体重は健康のバロメーターだと言われている The weight of one's body is called [said to be] a *barometer* of one's health.

バロン 〖男爵〗 a baron.

バロンドール 〖<フランス語〗 Ballon d'Or; European Footballer of the Year. (参考) フランス『フットボール』誌が主催して選出するヨーロッパ年間最優秀プレーヤー)

パワー power. (⇨力) ● 学生パワー student *power*.
● 老人〖ヤング〗パワー gray [youth] *power*.

● パワーアップ (⇨パワーアップ) ● パワーウィンドー 〖自動車の電動窓〗 a power window. ● パワーゲーム 〖権力闘争〗 a power game. ● パワーシャベル a power (-assisted) shovel. ● パワーステアリング power steering. ● パワーフレー 〖アイスホッケー〗 a power play. ● パワーリフティング 〖競技〗 powerlifting. (参考) 重量挙げの一種

パワーアップ ー パワーアップする[させる] 動 become* [make* 《it, him》] more powerful; strengthen. (! power up は「機械などが始動する」の意)

ハワイ 〖米国の州〗 Hawaii (略 Haw. 郵便略 HI); 〖ハワイ諸島〗 the Hawaiian Islands; 《愛称》 the Aloha State. ● ハワイ人 a Hawaiian. ● ハワイ(人)の Hawaiian.

ハワイアン Hawaiian; (音楽) Hawaiian music.
● ハワイアンギター a Hawaiian [a steel] guitar.

パワステ 〖「パワーステアリング」の略〗 (⇨パワー)

はわたり 刃渡り 〖刃物の刃の長さ〗 blade length; the length of a blade. ▶刃渡り15センチの短刀 a dagger with a *blade* fifteen centimeters *long* [with a fifteen-centimeters *blade*].

パワフル ー パワフルな 圃 (力強い) powerful; (強力な) high-powered. ● パワフルなエンジン a *powerful* [a *high-powered*] engine. ● パワフルなデータベースソフト a *powerful* database software.

***はん** 半 〖半分〗 half (覆 halves). (⇨半分) ● 8時 半に at *half* past 〖(米) after〗 eight; at 8:30 (「eight thirty」と読む). ● 半時間 *half* an hour; (! *half* hour. ● 1時間ごとに every *half* hour. ● 鉛筆を半ダース買う buy *half* a dozen pencils. ▶ 1か月半が過ぎた One month and a *half* has passed. (One *and a half* months has passed. (! 単・複扱いに注意. 前の方が普通の言い方)

***はん** 判 (印鑑) a signature [a personal] seal; (ゴム印) a stamp. ● 判を押す seal, put [set] a seal 《*to*》; stamp, put a stamp 《*on*》. ▶彼は保証人として書類に判を押した(署名捺印した) He signed the documents as a guarantor. (事情) 米英では通例サインですます)

● 判で押したように (いつもと同じように) invariably; exactly the same way.

はん 版 〖本の〗(改訂・増補を加えた) an edition; (増し刷り) an impression; (印刷すること, 発行部数) a printing (! 改訂などの有無は問わない). ● 初[再; 第3]版 the first [second; third] *edition*. ● 改訂[増補; 縮約]版 a revised [an enlarged, an abridged] *edition*. ● 重版 a second *impression*. ▶その本の第5版は数回版を重ねた The fifth *edition* of the book went through several *printings*.

はん 班 〖組〗a group; 〖分隊〗a squad. (! ともに単・複両扱い) (⇨班長)

はん 範 (手本) a model 《*of*》; (模範) an example 《*of*》. ● 日本の範にならう(=従う) follow the *model* of Japan. ● 範を垂れる(模範を示す) set an example 《*to*, *for*》. ▶教師は生徒の前に範を垂れないといけない Teachers must *set an example for* their students.

はん 藩 〖領主〗a (daimyo) domáin, a fief (覆 〜s); 〖一族〗a (feudal) clan (! 単・複両扱い). ● 彦根藩 Hikone Domain [Fief, xClan].

はん- 反- anti-; counter-. ● 反共産主義 *anti*communism. (⇨反共) ● 反主流派 the *anti*mainstream group. ● 反社会的行為 an *anti*social act. ● 反作用 *counter*action. (! ⇨反核, 反日)

はん- 汎- ● 汎アメリカ主義 Pan-Americanism. ● 汎アラブ主義(運動) Pan-Arabism.

ばん

ばん 晩 [日没から就寝時ごろまで] (an) evening; [就寝時ごろから, あるいは日没から日の出まで] (a) night. (⇨夜(⊕) 解説) ▶ 彼は東京を晩の7時に出発した He left Tokyo at seven *in the evening*. ▶ 晩方雪になった It began to snow toward *evening*. ● 金曜日の晩, 車で町に出かけよう Let's drive to town (on) Friday *evening* [*night*]. (❗ 前置詞 on. ただし〘話〙ではしばしば省略される. 「明日の晩」なら tomorrow evening [night] で前置詞はつけない (⇨朝 解説)) ▶ 私は彼女の所に3泊泊まった I stayed *three nights* at her place. ▶ 1晩中眠れなかった I couldn't sleep *throughout the night* [*all night* (long)].
● **晩ご飯** (a) dinner; (a) supper; an evening meal. (⇨夕食)

ばん 番 ❶ [順序, 順序] (順番) one's turn; (配列) order. (⇨順番) ▶ 私の番になった My *turn* has come./It has come to my *turn*. ▶ 今度は我々が行く番だ It's our *turn* to go. ▶ 彼は自分の番でないのに演説した He made a speech *out of turn* [*order*]. ▶ 彼は3番を打っている〘野球〙 He bats third. 会話 「次はだれの番だい」「私よ」"Whose *turn* is it (next)?" "Mine." / "Who's next?" "Me." 会話 「パパ, もう1回やってみていい?」「太郎の番がすんだらやってもいいよ」"May [Can] I have another go, Daddy?" "When Taro's had a *turn*, you can." 会話 「彼はクラスで何番ですか」「2番です」"Where does he stand [rank] in his class?" "He *stands* [*ranks*] *second* (in his class)."
【**〜番目**】 (⇨目❶) ▶ 彼は2番目に来た He was *the second* to come [that came]./He came *second*. (❗「彼は何番目に来たのか」は When [Where] did he come? という. それに対する答えは簡単に *Second*. でよい. また How many people came before he did? ともいう) ▶ 左から3番目が彼の息子さんです The *third* (boy) from the left is his son. ▶ 日本で5番目に大きな都市はどこですか What's the *fifth* largest city in Japan?
❷ [試合の回数] (野球・チェスなどの一勝負) a game; (ボクシングなどの) a match, a bout. ● 3番勝負 a three-*game* match; (トランプなどの) a rubber (of three games). ● 7番勝負のシリーズ a best-of-seven series. (参考 先に4勝した方が勝ち) ● 相撲で連続3番勝つ win three *bouts* in a row [get three straight wins] in the sumo tournament. ● チェスを1番やろう Let's play a *game* of chess.
❸ [見張り] watch; (監視, 警戒) guard; (見張り番) a guard; (守る人) a keeper. ● 工場の番をする *guard* the factory. ● 店番をする mind [〘米〙 tend] the store. 会話 「かばんの番をしててね」「いいよ」"*Watch* (over) [*Keep an eye on*] my bag." "Sure./Okay."
❹ [番号] a number. (❗ 通例序数詞アラビア数字の前で No., no. と略記する. 記号は #) ● 14番のバス a *number* [#] 14 bus. (❗ Take a bus *number* 14 as far as the station. (14番のバスに乗って駅まで行きなさい) のようにいうこともある) ● (電車などが) 3番ホームから出る leave from Platform [〘米〙 Track] *No.* 3. (❗❗❗ しばしば省略される) ● 図書目録が923局2540番にご請求ください Call us on 923-2540 to order the book catalog. ● 警察は110番でDial 110 for the police. (❗ one one oh あるいは double one oh と読む) ▶ 座席に1番から10番まで番号をつけてください Please *number* the seats from *No.* 1 to *No.* 10.

会話 「あなたの電話番号は何番ですか」「242-0175番です」"What is your (tele)phone *number*?" "(It's) two-four-two, oh-[zero-]one-seven-five."

ばん 万 ▶ 万(=万に一つも)遺漏(いろう)なきよう, お取り計らい願います *Do* make sure (that) everything is all right.
● **万やむを得ず** 万やむを得ない (=どうにもならない) 事情 《owing to》 absolutely unavoidable circumstances.

ばん 判 size. ● 大判のシャツ a large-*sized* undershirt. ● 菊判の本 a book in *kiku size*; a *kikusized* book. ● A4判の用紙 [スケッチブック] an A4 sheet [sketchpad].

ばん 盤 (板) a board; (ディスク) a disc. ● チェス盤 a chessboard. ● 碁盤 a go board (with four legs). ● 配電盤 a switchboard.

ばん 鷭 [鳥] a moorhen; a common gallinule.

バン (自動車の) a van; a wagon. ● ライトバン a delivery [〘米〙 light] *van*.

-ばん -版 an edition. (⇨版❶) ● 限定 [廉価, 普及; 豪華; 海賊] 版 a limited [a cheap; a popular; a deluxe; a pirated] *edition*. ● ポケット [ペーパーバック; ハードカバー; 卓上] 版 a pocket [a paper-back; a hardback; a desk] *edition*. ● 2005年版 the *edition* of 2005. ● (新聞の) 地方 [日曜] 版 the local [Sunday] *edition* (of a newspaper). (❗ 新聞のあるページに掲載される「地方版」は the local (news) page)

パン [<ポルトガル語] (パン一般) bread (❗ 狭義では食パンをさすので, 洋食などでパンを注文するときには注意が必要); (種々の形の小型パン) a (bread) roll; 〘米〙 (ハンバーガーなどの丸い小型のパン) a bun; (菓子パン) a sweet roll.

> 解説 (1) パンにはパン種 (yeast) を入れて作った leavened /lévnd/ bread とそうでない flat bread がある. 米英のパンは主に leavened wheat bread で, 白パン (white bread), ふすまのある小麦粉で作った黒パン (brown bread), ライ麦で作った黒パン (black bread, rye bread) などがある.
> (2) パン類の総称は bakery products, レストランのメニューでは breads and griddle cakes.

● 大型パン1本 [一かたまり] a loaf (of *bread*). ● フランスパン French *bread*. ● あんパン a *bun* stuffed with sweet bean paste. (参考 日本独特のパン) ● ロールパン a roll. ● パン2枚 [2切れ] two slices [two pieces] of *bread*. ● トーストにしたものは toast で ×bread とはいわない ● バター [ジャム] 付きパン *bread* and /ə/n/ bútter [jám]. (❗ 単数扱い) ● パンの皮 [耳] (a) crust. ● パンを焼く (作る) bake *bread*; (トーストにする) toast (a slice of) *bread*. ● パンをちぎる break *bread*. ● 古い [干からびた] パン stale *bread*. (❗ dry bread はバターなど塗ってないパン) 会話 「このパンはどんな味ですか」「甘口でしっとり [歯ごたえがあって, あっさりして] います」"What does this bread taste like?" "Well, it's a bit sweet and doughy [chewy and plain]."
● **パン粉** [くず] (bread) crumbs. ● **パン屋** (人) a baker; (店) a baker's (shop), a bakery. (❗ 販売のみの店は a bread shop)

はんい 範囲 (及び得る可能性のある) (a) range; (能力の) scope; (勢力・効力などの) a sphere; (活動・知力などの) a reach; (研究・知識などの) a field (⇨分野); (交際・興味などの) a circle; [限界] limits (❗ 通例複数形で); [程度] an extent. (⇨広範囲)
①【**〜範囲**】 ● 活動範囲 one's *scope* [*sphere*] of

はんい
activities. ● 勢力範囲 a *sphere* of influence. ● 守備範囲の広い内野手〖野球〗an infielder with wide *range*; a wide-ranging infielder. ▶その原理は適用範囲が広い The principle has [a wide *range* of] applications. ▶彼は交際範囲が広い He has a large (↔a small) *circle* of friends [acquaintances]. ▶数学の試験範囲は50ページから80ページまでです The exam in math *covers* pages 50 to 80. ▶ジャズは私の守備範囲(=専門領域)ではない Jazz is outside my *domain* [*field*; *sphere*] of knowledge.
② 〖範囲(内[外])で〗 ▶検査結果はすべて正常値の範囲内である The test results are all in the normal *range*. ▶この問題は科学の扱う範囲外である This problem is beyond [outside] the *scope* of science. ▶温度は10℃から20℃の範囲で上下した The temperature *ranged from* 10℃ *to* 20℃. ▶経費は予算の範囲内では収まらなかった(範囲を越えた) The expenses exceeded the *limits* of the budget. ▶自分のできる範囲で(=できる限り)やりましょう I'll do it *to the best of my ability*.
③〖範囲を〗 ● 調査の範囲を広げる[限定する] extend [limit] the *scope* of the inquiry. ▶その質問は生徒たちの知識の範囲を超えていた The question was outside the *range* [beyond the *limits*] of the students' knowledge.

はんい 犯意 〖法律〗malice; criminal intent. ● 計画的犯意を持って with malice aforethought.

はんいご 反意語〖言語〗an antonym /ǽntənɪm/; (反対語) an opposite. ▶ 'up' is the *antonym of* 'down'./'Up' and 'down' are *antonyms*. (❗複数形に注意)

はんいんよう 半陰陽 hermaphroditism; hermaphrodism.
— 半陰陽の 形 hermaphroditic; bisexual.
● 半陰陽者[動物] a hermaphrodite.

***はんえい** 反映 名 a reflection.
— 反映する 動 ▶この記事は世論を反映している This article *reflects* [*is a reflection of*, *is the mirror of*, *mirrors*] public opinion./(受身形で) Public opinion *is reflected* in this article. ▶サッカーは試合ぶりに国民性が反映しやすいスポーツと言われる Soccer is said to be a sport in which the national character is likely to *be reflected* in a team's playing style.

はんえい 繁栄 名 prosperity.
— 繁栄する 動 prosper; thrive; flourish. (⇨栄える, 繁盛)

はんえいきゅう 半永久 — 半永久的な 形 semi-permanent.

はんえり 半襟 a decorative, replaceable neckband (on an under-*kimono*).

はんえん 半円 名 a half circle; a semicircle.
— 半円の 形 semicircular.

はんおん 半音〖音楽〗a semitone, 《米》a half step. ● 半音上げる[下げる] sharp [flat] (a note); raise [lower] 《a note》 by a *semitone*.

はんか 反歌 (長歌の後に添える短歌) (説明的に) a *tanka* added to a *choka*.

はんか 販価 (「販売価格」の略) a selling price. ● 税込み[税抜き]販価 the tax-included [tax-excluded] *selling price*.

はんが 版画 a print, an engraving; 〖木版画〗a woodcut (❗版木は a woodblock); 〖石版画〗a lithograph /líθəɡræf/; 〖アクアチント版画〗an aquatint, an aquatinted picture; 〖メゾチント版画〗a mezzotint /métsoutɪnt/.

● 版画家 a block-print artist.

ばんか 挽歌 an elegy. ● 挽歌を捧げる offer an *elegy* 《to a dead person》.

ばんか 晩夏 late summer.

ハンガー a (coat) hanger. ● 上着をハンガーに掛ける put a coat on a *hanger*.
● ハンガーボード a pegboard; 《和製語》a hanger board.

バンカー 〖ゴルフ〗《米》a sand trap, a trap; 《英》a bunker. (❗《米》の bunker は sand trap 以外の障害物もさす) ● バンカーに入れる hit 《one's ball》 into a *bunker*; bunker 《one's first shot》.

ハンガーカーブ 〖野球〗a hanging curve; a hanger.

ハンガーストライキ (go on) a hunger strike.

はんかい 半開 — 半開の 形 half-opened. ● ドアを半開のままにしておく leave the door half open.

はんかい 半壊 — 半壊する 動 be partially destroyed.
● 半壊家屋 a partially destroyed house.

ばんかい 挽回 名 〖取り戻すこと〗recovery; 〖復活〗restoration. ● 名誉の挽回 *restoration* of one's honor; *recovery* of one's reputation. ● 退勢の挽回を図る try to *restore* [*retrieve*] one's declining fortunes.
— 挽回する 動 recover; regain. ● 勢力を挽回する *regain* one's power.

ばんがい 番外 an extra. ● 番外の余興 an *extra* [an *additional*] attraction.

はんがえし 半返し — 半返しする 動 (説明的に) send 《him》 as a return gift something equivalent to half of the money one received.

はんかがい 繁華街 (a) dówntòwn; busy streets.
● 繁華街へ(の) dówntòwn.

はんかく 反核 — 反核の 形 antinuclear.
● 反核運動 an antinuclear movement. ● 反核運動にたずさわっている人々 *antinuclear* activists.
● 反核集会 an antinuclear meeting.

はんがく 半額 (定価などの) half (the) price; (運賃などの) half (the) fare; (総額の) half the amount [sum] 《of》. ● 半額にする reduce the price *to half*; (5割引きにする) give [offer] a 50 percent discount. ● 半額で買う buy (it) *half-price* [*at half price*, *at a 50 percent discount*]. ▶12歳未満の子供たちの運賃は半額です Children under 12 travel *at half fare*.

はんかくめい 反革命 名 (an) antirevolution; (a) counterrevolution.
— 反革命の 形 antirevolutionary; counterrevolutionary.
● 反革命主義者 an antirevolutionary; a counterrevolutionary.

はんかこうひん 半加工品 semi-processed articles; half-finished goods.

ばんがさ 番傘 a *bangasa*; (説明的に) a coarse oilpaper umbrella.

***ハンカチ(ーフ)** a handkerchief (複) ~s, -chieves; 《話》a hankie, hanky. ● 胸ポケットにのぞかせるハンカチ a pocket-*handkerchief*, a display *handkerchief*. ● ハンカチを押し当てて泣く cry into one's *handkerchief*. ● ハンカチで手をふく dry [wipe] one's hands with [on] a *handkerchief*. ● ハンカチで鼻をかむ blow one's nose into [with, on] a *handkerchief*. ● ハンカチを振る wave one's *handkerchief* 《at him》.

はんかつう 半可通 a superficial knowledge 《of history》. ▶ぼくは英語に詳しいよと彼は言うが, 実は半可通だ He says he knows English very well, but actually he only acquires a *smattering* of

ハンガリー [国名] Hungary; (公式名) the Republic of Hungary. (首都 Budapest) ● ハンガリー人 a Hungarian; (総称) Hungarian people, (やや書) the Hungarians. ● ハンガリー語 Hungarian. ● ハンガリー(人[語])の Hungarian.

バンガロー [山小屋] a cabin; (ベランダ付きで軒が深い) a bungalow.

*__はんかん__ **反感** [悪感情] bad [ill] feeling; [嫌悪感] (やや書) (an) antipathy; [敵対心] (やや書) antagonism. ● 彼に反感を抱いている have *ill feeling toward* [*against*] him; feel (an) *antipathy to* [*toward*, *against*] him. ▶ 反感を買う ● 原住民の反感を買う cause [create] *ill feeling* among the natives; provoke the natives' *antipathy* [*antagonism*].

はんかん 繁閑 ▶ 繁閑にかかわらず, 午後 5 時まで勤務しなければならない You must work until 5 p.m. whether you are *busy or not*.

はんかん 繁簡 (繁雑と簡略) complexity and simplicity.

はんがん 半眼 ● 目を半眼に開いて with one's eyes half open [half-opened].

ばんかん 万感 ● 万感胸にせまる be filled [overwhelmed] with a rush of emotions. ▶ 彼女のまなざしには万感の思いがこめられていた Her eyes *spoke volumes*. (!speak volumes は「さまざまなことを雄弁に物語る」の意)

はんかんはんみん 半官半民 ▶ この法人は半官半民である (政府の財政的支援を受けている) This corporation is operated *with some government support*.

はんがんびいき 判官びいき sympathy for [support of] the weaker person. ● 判官びいきをする sympathize with [support] the weaker person.

はんき 反旗 ▶ 反旗を翻す ● 政府に反旗をひるがえす *revolt* [*rise* (*in revolt*)] *against* the government.

はんき 半期 a half term [(1 年) year]. ● 半期に一度の half-yearly; (やや書) semi-annual. ● 上[下]半期 the first [second] *half of the year*. ● 半期に一度の大バーゲン a *half-yearly* sale (*on* carpets).

はんき 半旗 a flag at half-mast. ● 国王の死を悼んで半旗を掲げる fly a *flag at half-mast*, mourning over the death of the king.

はんぎ 版木 a (printing) block; a woodblock.

ばんきしゃ 番記者 a reporter who watches every movement of some VIP.

はんぎゃく 反逆 [名] [反逆罪] treason; [反乱] (小規模な) (a) revolt; (大規模で組織的な) (a) rebellion. (⇨反乱)
— 反逆する [動] revolt (*against*); rebél (*against*). ● 反逆行為 an act of treason. ● 反逆者 a rébel; (裏切者) a traitor.

はんきゅう 半休 (米) a half-day, a half day, half of a day; (英) a half holiday. ▶ あすは半休だ Tomorrow is *a half day*.

はんきゅう 半球 a hemisphere. ● 東[西]半球 the Eastern [Western] *Hemisphere*.

ばんきょ 蟠居 — 蟠居する [動] (木がしっかり根を張る) take root firmly; (根拠地を設けて勢力をふるう) establish a base and wield power [hold sway] (*over* the areas).

*__はんきょう__ **反響** [名] [音の] an echo (複 ~es) (⇨響く ❷); [反応] (a) response; [大評判] (a) sensation. ● 大きな反響を呼ぶ create [cause] a great *sensation*; meet with a lot of *response*. ▶ 私たちの運動には何の反響もなかった There was no *response to* our movement.
— 反響する [動] echo. (⇨響く ❷)

はんきょう 反共 (主義) anticommunism. ● 反共主義者 an anticommunist. ● 反共政策 an anticommunist policy.

はんきょうらん 半狂乱 ● 半狂乱になって frantically.

ばんきん 板金 sheet metal. ● 板金加工 sheet metal processing. ● 板金工 a sheet metal worker.

バンク [銀行] a bank. ● メインバンク a main [a house, one's] *bank*. ● プライベートバンク a private *bank*.
● バンクカード a bank card.

パンク ❶ [タイヤの] (穴) a puncture; (破裂) a blowout; [パンクしたタイヤ] a flat tire, (主に米語) a flat.
● パンクを修理してもらう have a *flat tire* [*a puncture*] fixed. ▶ 途中でタイヤがパンクした Our car had a *flat tire* [*a puncture*, *a blowout*] on the way. (!our car の代わりに we も可)/The tire of our car *went flat* [*punctured*, *blew out*] on the way. ▶ 彼の自転車に乗ってたらパンクしてしまった I had a *flat tire* on his bike.
❷ [過食・殺到の結果として] ▶ 食べすぎておなかがパンクしそう (=はち切れそう) だ My stomach is about to *burst*. ▶ 首都高速連日パンク状態だ The metropolitan expressway *is overcrowed* from day to day. ▶ 電話回線はパンク寸前だ The phone lines are on the point of *being jammed*.

パンク [音楽の] (パンクロック) punk (rock). (!単に punk ということが多い)
● パンクバンド a punk band.

ハングアップ — ハングアップする [動] [コンピュータ] hang up. (働 フリーズ)

バンクーバー [カナダの都市] Vancouver /vænkúːvər/.

ハンググライダー [器具・人] a hang glider; (飛行) hang gliding. ● ハンググライダーで飛ぶ hang-glide; fly in a *hang glider*

パンクチュエーション [文法] [句読法] punctuation; [句読点] a punctuation (mark). (⇨働 句読点)

*__ばんぐみ__ **番組** (一般に) a program; (ショー) a show. (⇨放送). ● 子供向けのラジオ [テレビ] 番組 a radio [TV, a television] *program for* children. ● 2 時間番組 a two-hour *program* [*show*]. ● (電話での) 視聴者参加番組 a call-in (米) [a phone-in (英)] *program*. ● 新聞のテレビ番組欄 the TV *program* section of a newspaper. ● 夜の番組を見る [聞く] watch [listen in to] a late *program*. ▶ 今日のテレビ[ラジオ]番組はどんなのがありますか What *programs* are *on* TV [the radio] today?/What are today's TV [radio] *programs*?/What is *on* TV [the radio] today? ▶ これは彼が出ている番組だ This is the *program* [*show*] he is *on*. ▶ その晩はフランスのテレビ, ラジオはすべて定時番組をやめてベルリオーズのレクイエムを流した All French television and radio networks canceled their regularly scheduled *programs* and instead played the Berlioz's "Requiem" that night.

> **関連 番組の種類**: 映画番組 a móvie prógram/ドキュメンタリー a documentary/スポーツ番組 a spórts prógram/インタビューもの a tálk shów/クイズ番組 a quíz shów/歌謡番組 a músic shów/芸能ニュース show business news.

バングラデシュ [国名] Bangladesh /bàːŋɡlədéʃ/; (公式名) the People's Republic of Bangladesh. (首都 Dhaka) ● バングラデシュ人 a Bangladeshi. ● バングラデシュ(人)の Bangladeshi.

ハングリーせいしん ハングリー精神 a strong motivation, an aggressive ambition; 《和製語》 hungry spirit.

ハングル Hangul /hɑ̀ːŋgúːl/. (!個々の文字は a ～ (letter))

ばんくるわせ 番狂わせ an úpsèt; (意外な結果) an unexpected result; (思いがけないこと) a surprise. ▶彼が横綱を負かすという番狂わせがあった It was an *upset* [(大番狂わせ) a major *upset*] when he beat the grand champion./(予想に反して負かした) He *upset* /ʌpsét/ the grand champion.

はんぐん 反軍 (反乱軍) a rebel army.
- **反軍思想** (軍部に反対すること) antiwar ideas.

はんけい 半径 〖数学〗 a radius /réidiəs/ (圏 radii /-diài/, ～es). (⇨直径) ▶その建物から半径8マイル以内に[の] within an eight mile *radius* of [in a eight mile *radius* around] the building. ▶半径5センチの円をかく draw a circle with a *radius* of 5 centimeters.

はんけい 判型 (本の大きさ) the format of 《the magazine [the book]》.

パンケーキ ▶パンケーキを焼く make [ˣbake] a *pancake*.

はんげき 反撃 图 a counterattack. ▶3点入れて反撃に出る (野球で) rally with three runs; stage a three-run *rally*.
- **反撃する** 動 counterattack [make* a counterattack] 《on, against》; (戦い・争いで) fight* back 《against》.

はんけつ 判決 (一般に) (a) judgment; (裁判所の裁定) a ruling; (決定) (a) decision; (判事による刑罰の宣告) (a) sentence; (陪審員の評決) a verdict. ●判決をくつがえす reverse the *judgment* [*ruling*, *decision*]. ●彼に判決を言い渡す pass [pronounce] *sentence* on him. ▶法廷は彼に不利[有利]な判決を下した The court *decided* [*ruled*] *against* [*for*] him./The court *passed judgment against* [*for*] him. ▶彼は死刑の判決を受けた He *was given* [He *received*] *a sentence* of death./ He *was sentenced* to death. ▶そのスパイは有罪[無罪]の判決を受けた The spy *was found guilty* [*was found not guilty*].

はんげつ 半月 图 a half moon; (半月形) a semicircle. — **半月の** 形 semicircular.

はんげつばん 半月板 〖解剖〗(膝関節内の月状軟骨) a semilunar cartilage; (関節内の軟骨) a meniscus. ●半月板損傷 (suffer from) an injury to the *semilunar cartilage* [*meniscus*].

はんけん 半券 (a ticket) stub.

はんけん 版権 (a) copyright. ●版権を獲得[出願; 登録]する secure [apply for; register] a *copyright*. ▶だれが君の本の版権を持っているのですか Who has [holds] the *copyright on* [*for*] your book?
- **版権所有者** a copyright holder. ●**版権侵害** an infringement of copyright.

はんげん 半減 — **半減する** 動 (減らす) reduce by half, halve; (減る) be reduced by half, halve. ●出費を半減する *reduce* [*cut down*] the expenditure *by half*.
- **半減期** (放射能などの) a half-life.

ばんけん 番犬 a watchdog, a house dog.

はんこ 判子 (印鑑) a seal. (⇨印鑑)

はんご 反語 ❶ [表面とはうらはらの皮肉] irony /áiərəni/. ❷ [修辞疑問] a rhetorical /rit(ː)ríkəl/ question. (! Who knows? (= Nobody knows.) のように疑問文の形式で断定を強める文)
❸ [反意語] an antonym /ǽntənim/. (! up と

down, new と old のような関係) (⇨反意語)
- **反語的** 形 irónical.
- **反語的に** 副 irónically.

*****はんこう 反抗** 图 (抵抗) resistance 《to》; (反対) opposition 《to》; (権威などへの不従順) disobedience 《to》; (権威などへの反発) rebellion 《against》; (挑戦的態度) defiance. ▶親への反抗は成長の過程である *Resistance to* parents is in the process of growing up. ▶彼は反抗期だ He is at a *rebellious* age.
- **反抗的な** 形 (不順従な) disobedient; (反発する) rebellious (! 前の方は単に人のいうことを聞かないことを意味するが、後の方は口や態度で積極的に反発することを含意する); (挑戦的な) defiant. ▶彼は反抗的な子供だ He is a *disobedient* [a *rebellious*] child. ▶彼は上司に反抗的な態度を示した He took a *rebellious* [a *defiant*] attitude toward his boss.
- **反抗する** 動 (抵抗) resist; (反対する) oppose; (言うことを聞かない) disobey; (反発する) rebel (-ll-) 《against》; (公然と挑戦する) defy. ▶彼は母親に反抗した He *disobeyed* [*rebelled against*] his mother.
- **反抗心** a rebellious spirit.

はんこう 反攻 a counterattack 《on, against》. ●反攻に転じる make a *counterattack*. (⇨反撃)

はんこう 犯行 a crime; an offénse. (⇨犯罪) ●犯行を自供[否認]する confess [deny] (that one committed) the *crime*.
- **犯行現場** the scene of the crime.

はんごう 飯盒 〖携帯用食器セット〗 a mess kit.

ばんこう 蛮行 barbarism; a barbarous act.

*****ばんごう 番号** a number. ▶番号!《号令》《米》 Count off!/《英》 Number off!
① 【～の(番号)】 ●大きい[小さい]番号 a high [low] *number*. (! ˣa big [a small] number とはいわない) ●通し[一連の]番号 serial *numbers*. ●座席番号 a seat *number*. ●学籍番号 a student ID *number*. ●金庫の番号を忘れる forget the *combination* to a safe. ●*combination* は組み合わせの番号) ▶君の部屋の番号は何番ですか What is the *number* of your room [your room *number*]? (! 「105号室」なら Room No. 105 で, Room number one-o /óu/ - five と読む)
② 【番号〜】 ●カードを番号順に並べる arrange the cards in *numerical* order. ▶番号違いです (電話で) I'm afraid you have the wrong *number*.
③ 【番号が[を]】 ●座席に1から100の番号をつける *number* [*give numbers to*] the seats (from) 1 to 100. ▶すべての製品に番号がついている The products are all *numbered*.
- **番号札** a numbered [a number] ticket. (! 前の方が普通)

ばんこく 万国 图 all nations, all (the) countries on earth.
- **万国の** 形 international; universal; world.
- **万国旗** the flags of all nations. ●**万国博(覧会)** a world's fair; an international exposition.

ばんこく 万斛 ▶万斛の(=たくさんの)涙を流す shed *a flood of* tears.

バンコク 〖タイの首都〗 Bangkok.

はんこつ 反骨 (精神) an antiestablishment [a rebellious] spirit.

ばんこつ 万骨 ▶一将成りて万骨枯る (⇨一将[成句])

ばんごや 番小屋 a lodge; (見張り小屋) a watchhouse; (番兵などの) a watch box.

はんごろし 半殺し ▶彼は半殺しの目にあった He was beaten *nearly to death* [*within an inch of* his *life*, (こてんぱんに) 《話》 *to* (a) *pulp*].

はんこん 瘢痕 〘医学〙(傷跡) a cicatrix /síkətriks/.(⦿ cicatrices /síkətráisiːz/).

ばんこん 晩婚 (a) late marriage.(⇨結婚)▶彼は晩婚だ He *married late* (in life).

はんさ 煩瑣 → 煩雑な ⑩ troublesome.(⇨ 煩雑)

はんざい 犯罪 〘法律違反行為〙(a) crime (⚠個々の行為は Ⓒ);〘一般に違反行為〙an offénse (⚠通例軽い犯罪).(⇨平和)▶窃盗は犯罪だ Theft is a crime [χis criminal].(⚠形容詞の criminal は「犯罪の[に関する]」の意で限定的に用いられる)

①〖～犯罪〗• 軽(い)犯罪 minor [petty] *crime*; a minor [a petty] *offense*;〘法律〙a misdeméanor.• 重い犯罪 major [serious] *crime*; a major [a serious] *offense*;〘法律〙(a) felony.• 少年犯罪(非行) juvenile delinquency.(⚠「少年犯罪者」は a juvenile delinquent)• 凶悪犯罪(残忍な[極悪非道な]犯罪) an atrocious [a heinous] *crime*.• 性犯罪 sex [sexual] *crime*.• 組織犯罪 organized *crime*.• インターネット犯罪(Inter)net *crime*.(⚠(1) 通例 net crime.(2) 通例無冠詞)• 女性に対する犯罪 a *crime* against women.

②〖犯罪～〗• 戦争犯罪人 a war criminal.▶その男にはずいぶん犯罪歴(=前科)があった The man had a long *criminal* [*police*] record.

③〖犯罪が〗▶犯罪が増加しつつある *Crime* is on the increase [rise]./(犯罪率が) The *crime* rate is increasing.

④〖犯罪を〗▶犯罪を働く(犯す) commit (a) *crime*.• 犯罪を防止する(抑止する、撲滅する) prevent [deter; eradicate] crime.▶彼は犯罪を犯した He committed (a) *crime*.

• 犯罪現場(犯行現場)《at》 the scene of the crime [the crime scene].• 犯罪行為(犯行) a crime, a criminal offense;(犯罪の行為) a criminal act.• 犯罪者(犯人) a criminal;(法律違反者) an offender.• 犯罪心理学 criminal psychology.• 犯罪捜査 《conduct》 a crime [a criminal] investigation 《into》.• 犯罪対策 《take》 measures to prevent crime.• 犯罪防止 crime prevention.• 犯罪防止キャンペーン a campaign [a crusade] for *crime prevention* [*against crime*].

ばんざい 万歳 ❶ 〖祝福の叫び〗hurray /həréi/, hurrah /həráː/, banzai, viva /víːvɑː/.▶万歳三唱 three cheers《for》.(⚠ Hip, hip, hurray!を三度繰り返す)• 万歳を唱える hurrah《for》; cry [shout] *banzai*; give *cheers*《for》.▶万歳!合格したよ *Hurray!* I passed the test.▶女王陛下万歳 *Hurray* for [*Long live*] the Queen!(⚠〘英〙では後の方が好まれる)

❷〖降参〗▶もう万歳だ(万事休す) It's all over with me.(⇨お手上げ)

ばんさく 万策 ▶万策尽きた We tried everything and now we don't know what to do next./We have reached the end of our tether /téðər/[〘米〙rope].

はんざつ 煩雑 → 煩雑な 圏 (複雑な) complicated;(わずらわしい) troublesome.

ハンサム → ハンサムな 圏 handsome, good-looking.• ハンサムな青年 a *handsome* [a *good-looking*] young man.

はんさよう 反作用 (a) reaction.• 作用と反作用 action and reaction.• 反作用を起こす cause a *reaction*.

ばんさん 晩餐 dinner.• 晩餐[晩餐会]に招く invite《him》to *dinner* [a *dinner*].

• 晩餐会《give [hold]》a dinner (party); a banquet /bæŋkwət/.(⚠ banquet は祝宴などで形式ばったもので、通例スピーチを伴う)▶大統領の誕生日祝いで盛大な晩餐会が催された A magnificent *banquet* was given to celebrate [in honor of] the president's birthday.(⚠後の方が次に「人」がくるのが普通)

はんし 半死 → 半死半生 • 人を殴って半死半生にする(半殺しにする) beat《him》*nearly to death* [*an inch of*《his》*life*].

はんし 半紙 Japanese writing paper.

はんし 藩士 a clansman (⑰ clansmen); a retainer of a《daimyo》domain.

はんじ 判事 a judge, a justice.(⚠後の方は〘米〙では最高裁判事、〘英〙では最高法院判事をさす)• 首席[陪席]判事 a presiding /prizáidiŋ/ [an associate] *judge*.• 最高裁の判事 a Supreme Court *judge*.• 判事席 a judgment seat; the bench.• 判事補 an assistant judge.

ばんし 万死 • 万死に値する deserve *death*.
• 万死に一生を得る(⇨九死)

ばんじ 万事 everything; all.▶万事オーケーだ *Everything is all right* [O. K.]./*All is well*.▶万事休す *All is over* [*up*] (with me)./*It's all over* [*up*] *with me*.▶万事あとよく頼みます I will leave *everything* to you.▶万事うまくいった *Everything went well* [*right*].▶この世は万事金だ *Money is everything* in this world.

パンジー 〘三色スミレ〙〘植物〙a pansy.

バンジージャンプ (スポーツ) búngee júmping;(1回の降下) a bungee jump.• バンジージャンプをする人 a bungee jumper.

はんした 版下 (旧来の) a block copy, a copy for block printing;(現在の) a picture [〘図表〙a diagram,(文字中心の) a print] for a printing plate.

はんじもの 判じ物 a rebus;(なぞ) a riddle.

*はんしゃ 反射 图 (光、熱、音などの) reflection;(行動) a reflex /ríːfleks/;(能力) reflexes.• 乱反射 diffused *reflection*.• 光の反射 the *reflection* of light.• 条件反射 a conditioned [↔an unconditioned] *reflex* [*response*].

—— 反射的に 圖 • 反射的に頭をひょいと下げる duck one's head *by reflex action* [*in a reflex*,(本能的に) *instinctively*].

—— 反射する 働 reflect.▶地面に積もった雪に日光が反射した The snow on the ground *reflected* the sunlight.

• 反射運動 a réflex (mòvement).• 反射鏡 a réflex [a refléctìng] mirror.• 反射作用 a réflex (áction).• 反射神経 reflexes.• 反射神経がいい[遅い] have good [slow] *reflexes*.• 反射熱 reflected heat.• 反射望遠鏡 a refléctìng tèlescope; a reflector.• 反射炉 a reverberating furnace.

はんしゃかいてき 反社会的 —— 反社会的(な) 圏 anti-social.
• 反社会的行為 antisocial behavior.• 反社会的分子 antisocial elements.

ばんしゃく 晩酌 —— 晩酌(を)する 働 have a drink with one's dinner (at home).

ばんじゃく 盤石 (大きな岩) a huge rock.• 盤石の防御 an airtight defense.▶彼は盤石の態勢で(=周到な用意をして)選挙に臨んだ He ran for the election after *thorough* preparations.

はんしゅ 藩主 a *daimyo*; a feudal lord.

はんしゅう 半周 —— 半周する 働 go halfway around《the field》.

ばんしゅう 晩秋 • 晩秋に in late autumn [〘米〙fall]; late in (《主に米》the) fall (autumn).(

はんじゅく 半熟 —— 半熟の [形] 〔卵の〕soft-boiled; 〔食物の〕half-boiled. ▶卵は半熟にしてください〔レストランで〕I'd like my eggs *soft-boiled*. (⇨茹でる)

はんしゅつ 搬出 —— 搬出する [動] carry ... out 《*of*》.

ばんしゅん 晩春 ●晩春に in late spring; late in 《主に米》 spring.

はんしょ 板書 [名] ●板書を写す copy what *is written on the board*.
—— 板書する [動] write (...) on the blackboard.

はんしょう 反証 (a) disproof 《複 〜s》; (xa) contrary evidence. ●彼のアリバイについて反証をあげる *disprove* his alibi.

はんしょう 反照 〔照り返し〕reflection; 〔夕映え〕the evening glow.

はんしょう 半焼 —— 半焼する [動] be half destroyed by fire.

はんしょう 半鐘 a fire alarm; a fire bell. ▶半鐘が鳴っている There goes the fire bell./The fire bell is clanging.

***はんじょう 繁盛** [名] prosperity.
—— 繁盛する [動] prosper; flourish; thrive. (⇨栄える) ●繁盛している医者〔患者の多い〕a doctor with a large practice. ●彼の商売は繁盛している His business *is prospering* [*flourishing*, *thriving*]./He's doing good business./He has a very *successful* [a *thriving*] *business*./He *is successful in* his business.

はんじょう 半畳 ●半畳を入れる〔からかう〕tease; 〔やじる〕jeer 《*at*》; heckle (the candidate).

ばんしょう 万象 ⇨森羅万象

ばんしょう 万障 ●次回の会合には万障お繰り合わせの上御出席ください We would *really* like you to attend [We *do* hope that you will attend] the next meeting. (■「ぜひ」という気持ちを表すのに副詞 really や強調の助動詞 do を添える)

ばんしょう 晩鐘 a vesper (bell).

ばんしょう『晩鐘』 *The Angelus*. (参考) ミレー作の絵画. 原名は *L'Angélus*.

ばんじょう 万丈 ●万丈の気炎をあげる talk big. ●波乱万丈 (⇨波乱)

バンジョー 〖楽器〗a banjo 《複 〜(e)s》.

はんしょく 繁殖 [名] 〖動物が子を生むこと〗breeding; 〖動植物が増え広がること〗propagation; 〖書〗〖増殖を繰り返すこと〗multiplication. ●繁殖力の強い〔=多産な〕動物 a *fertile* [〖やや書〗a *prolific*] animal. ▶ネズミは繁殖が早い Mice *breed* [*propagate*, *multiply*] rapidly.
—— 繁殖する [動] breed*; 〖書〗propagate (oneself); multiply.
●繁殖期 the 《seals'》 bréeding sèason.

ばんしょく 伴食 ●伴食大臣〔名ばかりの〕a nominal Minister.

はんじる 判じる 〔判断する〕judge; 〔解釈する〕interpret 《dreams》.

はんしん 半身 〖上下の〗half (of) the body; 〖左右の〗one side of the body. ●上[下]半身 the upper [lower] *half of the body*. ●左[右]半身 the left [right] *side of the [one's] body*. ▶彼は半身不随だ He is paralyzed *on one side*.
●半身像〔胸像〕a bust. ●半身浴 〔説明的に〕soaking half of the body in warm water.

はんしんはんぎ 半信半疑 ●ニュースを半信半疑で聞く〔疑わしげに〕listen to the news *doubtfully* [*dubiously*, *suspiciously*]. 〔疑わしい〕▶その話に対して半信半疑だった I *was half in doubt about* the story./I *only half believed* the story./〔全面的には信じられなかった〕I couldn't *quite believe* the story.

はんしんろん 汎神論 pantheism /pǽnθiːɪzm/.
●汎神論者 a pantheist.

はんすう 反芻 —— 反芻する [動] 〔動物が〕ruminate; chew the cud. (■いずれも比喩的にも用いる) ●彼の忠告を反芻してみる *think deeply* [〖書〗*ruminate*] over his advice.
●反芻動物 a ruminant.

はんすう 半数 half 〖of〗. (■動詞は of の後の〔代〕名詞の数に一致する) ▶そのミカンの半数は腐っている *Half* (*of*) the oranges are rotten. (■of は しばしば省略される. ただし代名詞の場合は省略不可) ▶合格者は半数を越えた〔半数もいなかった〕More than [Less than, Fewer than] *half of* the applicants have been successful.

ハンスト 《go on》 a hunger strike. (⇨スト)

パンスト (xa) panty hose. (⇨パンティーストッキング)

はんズボン 半ズボン 《a pair of》 shorts.

***はんする 反する** 〔反対である〕〔相いれない〕be contrary 《*to*》; 〔正反対である〕be opposite 《*to*》; 〔背く〕run* counter 《*to*》; 〔規則などに違反している〕be against .... ▶彼の話は事実に反する What he has said *is contrary to* the fact. ▶その政策は我々の利益に反する The policy *runs counter to* [〔矛盾する〕*conflicts with*] our interests. ▶バイク通学は校則に反する Bike commuting *is against* the school rules. ▶自分の意志[良心]に反して行動するな Don't act *against* your will [conscience]. ▶私の期待に反して彼は今度の選挙に落選した He failed in the recent election *contrary to* [*against*] my expectation(s). ▶彼は私の警告に反して1人で山登りに行った (警告にもかかわらず) He went climbing alone *in spite of* [〖書〗*despite*, 〔無視して〕*in defiance of*] my warning. ▶私が忙しく働いているのに反して彼は何もしないで遊んでいる I'm busy at work, *while* he's idling about./*While* I'm busy at work, he's idling about.

***はんせい 反省** [名] 〖熟考〗reflection; 〖再検討〗review; 〔悔悟〕(a) regret. ●自分の行いについて彼に反省を求める ask him to *reflect on* his conduct. ▶これは反省の材料になる This will be material for my *reflection*. ▶彼には反省の色がまったくなかった He gave no sign of *regret* 《for it》.
—— 反省する [動] think*... over; reflect 《*on*; *that* 節》; 〖再検討する〗review; 〔悔しかったと悔やむ〕regret (-tt-); be sorry 《for》. (●後悔する) ●反省してみると on *reflection*. ▶自分のしたことを反省しています I'm *thinking over* what I did and *regret* it./I'm *sorry for* what I did.
●反省会 a review meeting.

はんせい 半生 〔現在までの人生〕one's 《past》 life; 〔一生の大半〕most [the best part] of one's life.
●半生を振り返る look back on [〖やや書〗reflect on] one's *life*.

ばんせい 万世 eternity.
●万世一系 an unbroken line 《of Emperors》.

ばんせい 晩生 ●晩生種の late 《rice》.

ばんせい 晩成 ●彼は晩成型だ He's a late bloomer. (⇨大器 [文例])

はんせいひん 半製品 (⇨ 半加工品)

はんせき 犯跡 ●犯跡をくらます destroy the evidence of a crime.

はんせき 版籍 〔領土と領民〕domains [land] and people.
●版籍奉還 〔説明的に〕the return of domains [land] and people to the Meiji Emperor in 1869.

ばんせつ 晩節 ●晩節を全うする remain an honora-

ble man throughout one's life.
はんせん 反戦 opposition to war.
● 反戦運動 an antiwar movement. ● 反戦集会 an antiwar rally. ● 反戦主義 pacifism. ● 反戦主義者 a pacifist. ● 反戦デモ an antiwar demonstration.
はんせん 帆船 〖米〗a sailboat; 〖英〗a sailing boat; 〖大型の〗a sáiling shíp 〖《書》vèssel〗.
はんぜん 判然 —— 判然とした 形 〖明らかな〗clear; 〖はっきりした〗distinct; 〖確定の〗certain. ● 判然とした相違 a *distinct* difference. ● この意味が判然としない This meaning is *not clear* 〖どちらともとれる〗is *ambiguous*〗. ▶ 彼がなぜ来なかったのかその理由が判然としない I cannot see *clearly* why he didn't come.
ばんせん 番線 〖鉄道の〗〖《米》a track; 〖英》a platform. ● 3 番線で on *track* [*platform*] 3. ● 3 番線から出る depart from [leave] *track* [*platform*] 3.
ばんぜん 万全 ● 万全を期すために (念には念を入れて) to make doubly sure. ● 万全の(=最も確実な)策を取る take the *surest* [(最も安全な) *safest*, (可能な限りすべての) *all possible*] measures.
ハンセンびょう ハンセン病 Hánsen's disèase; leprosy /léprəsi/. 〖《前の方が好まれる》〗 ● ハンセン病患者 a Hansen's (disease) patient.
はんそ 反訴 動 a cross-action; a counterclaim.
—— 反訴する 動 bring a cross-action《*against* him *for* it》.
● 反訴人 a counterclaimant.
はんそう 帆走 名 sailing.
—— 帆走する 動 ● ヨットで帆走する sail in a yacht.
はんそう 搬送 conveyance; transport(ation). (⇨運送)
ばんそう 伴走 —— 伴走する 動 accompany《a marathon runner》.
● 伴走車 an éscort vèhicle (càr, mòtorcycle).
ばんそう 伴奏 名 (an) accompaniment. ● ピアノの伴奏で歌う sing *to* a piano *accompaniment*; sing *with* (a) piano *accompaniment*.
—— 伴奏(を)する 動 accompany. ▶ 彼はピアノで彼女の伴奏をした He *accompanied* her *on* [*at*] the piano./He *played* a piano *accompaniment on* [*for*] her.
● 伴奏者 an accompanist.
ばんそう 晩霜 a late frost.
ばんそうこう 絆創膏 a stícking plàster, (バンドエイド)《商標》a Band-Aid, (包帯など固定用の) adhesive tape. ● 傷口に絆創膏を張る apply a (*sticking*) *plaster* on a cut. ● 包帯を絆創膏で止める hold a bandage on with *adhesive tape*.
はんそく 反則 名 〖規則違反〗(a) violation of the rules 〖個々の例は C〗, (特に競技の) foul play, a foul. ● 反則を記録する book a foul. ▶ これは反則だ It's *against the rules*.
—— 反則(を)する 動 violate [break] the rules (! 後の方が口語的); play foul, commit a foul.
はんそく 販促 〖販売促進〗sales promotion.
● 販促活動 sales promotion activity. ● 販促費 (sales) promotion costs [expenses]; the costs [expenses] for (sales) promotion.
はんぞく 反俗 resistance to convention.
● 反俗精神 an anticonventional spirit.
はんそで 半袖 ● 半袖のドレス a dress with *short sleeves*; a *short-sleeved* dress.
はんた 繁多 busyness. ● 繁多を極めている be very *busy*; have a lot to do; have pressure of work. (⇨多忙)

はんだ solder /sάdər/. ● はんだ付けする solder.
● はんだごて a soldering iron.
パンダ 〖動物〗a panda /pǽndə/. ● ジャイアント[レッサー]パンダ a giant [a lesser] *panda*.
ハンター 〖猟師〗a hunter.
‡**はんたい** 反対 名 ❶〖抵抗〗opposition《*to*》; 〖異議〗(an) objection《*to*》. ▶ そのダムは人々の強い反対にもかかわらず建設された The dam was built in spite of strong *opposition* from the people. ▶ 彼は我々の考えに反対の意を表した He raised [《やや書》voiced] an *objection to* our ideas./He spoke *against* [*in opposition to*] our ideas. ▶ 私の両親は私たちの結婚に大反対だった My parents were very much *against* our marriage.
❷〖逆〗the revérse; the opposite /άpəzit/; 《書》the cónverse; the cónverse. (⇨逆)

> 使い分け **reverse** 順序・上下・左右・表裏など逆の関係にあること。
> **opposite** 方向・位置などが正反対であること。比喩的に性質・傾向などについても用いられる。
> **contrary** 内容などが強い対立関係にあること。
> **converse** 論理学, 数学で命題が逆であること。

● それを反対側から見る look at it from the *other* side. ▶「右」は「左」の反対が 'Right' is the *opposite* 〖《反意語》the *antonym*, ×the *contrary*》of 'left'./'Right' and 'left' are *opposites* [*antonyms*]. ▶ 彼女はやせているが私はまったく反対だ She is thin and I'm quite the *opposite* [*reverse*]. ▶ 私が何を言っても彼女は反対を言う Whatever I say, she says the *contrary*. ▶ 名簿の順序が反対だ The names on the list are in *reverse* order.
—— 反対の 形 opposite《*to*》; contrary《*to*》; reverse《*to*》; (もう一方の) the other. ● 反対方向へ打つ go [hit] *the other* way; hit the ball to the *opposite* field. ● 車は反対の方向へ走って行った The car ran *the other* way./The car ran in [×to] the *opposite* direction. (⇨➡➡) ● 演奏会は彼の期待とは反対のものだった The concert was *contrary to* his expectation./The concert was the *reverse* [*opposite*] of what he (had) expected. (! *opposite* の方が強意的)
—— 反対に 副 ❶〖方向・位置などが〗(方向が) in the opposite direction, the other [wrong] way (around); (位置が) opposite, (裏表が) inside [wrong side] out; (上下が) upside down; (左右が) the right side left. ▶ 私の家はバス停の反対側(=向かい側)にある My house is *across* the road from [*opposite* (*to*), 《主に米》*across from*] the bus stop. (! *opposite* が具体的な位置を表す場合は to を省略して前置詞として用いる方が普通) ▶ シャツを裏表[前後]反対に着ているよ You're wearing your shirt *inside out* [*the other way*, (後ろ前に) *back to front*, (後ろ向きに) *backward*].
❷〖内容が〗(それどころか逆に) on the contrary (! 通例文頭・文中で用い, これから述べることがすでに示された[暗示された]ことと正反対であることを強調する); (そうする代わりに) instead (! 通例文頭・文尾で); (しかし一方では) on the óther hànd. ▶ 私は彼女は彼が好きだと思っていたら反対に嫌っていた I thought she liked him, but *on the contrary* she hated him. (! 前半と後半が逆の反対の意を表す) ▶ これで母さんが喜んでくれると思っていたら反対にこっぴどく叱られちゃった I expected Mom to be pleased with it, and got a good telling-off *instead*.
会話「山田はいつも遅れるんだよ」「反対に君はいつも早いね」 "Yamada's always late." "Yóu, *on the* ⌄*other hand*, are álways ⌄*early*."

— **反対する** 動 oppose; (異議を唱える) object 《to》; (意見に反対する) disagree 《with》; (...に反対している) be against ..., 《やや書》 be opposed to .... ▶彼は我々の計画に反対した He *opposed* [*objected to*] our plan. (❗)▶He objected our plan. とはいわない/(反対していた) He *was against* [*was opposed to*] our plan. ▶彼は私のアイディアは非現実的だと言って反対した He *objected that* my idea was impractical. ▶あなたの意見には反対です I *disagree* [*don't agree*] *with* you. ▶野党は与党の政策に真っ向から反対した The opposition parties *stood up to* the ruling party's policy.
• 反対給付〖法律〗counter performance; (返礼) a return. • 反対語 an antonym; an opposite. • 反対車線 the opposite lane. • 反対色 an antagonistic color; (補色) a complementary color. • 反対勢力 counterforce. • 反対尋問 a cross-examination.

はんだい 飯台 (⇨卓袱(しっぽく)台)
ばんだい 番台 (銭湯などの) the watch seat; the lookout seat.
はんたいせい 反体制 — 反体制(の) 形 antiestablishment.
• 反体制活動家[分子] a political dissident. • 反体制作家 an antiestablishment writer. • 反体制主義者 an antiestablishmentarian.
はんだくおん 半濁音 〖言語〗*p*-sound in Japanese.
はんだくてん 半濁点 the *p*-sound sign in Japanese. (「ぱ」「ぴ」の「゜」)
パンタグラフ a pántográph. (❗つづり字に注意)
バンダナ a bandan(n)a.
バンタムきゅう バンタム級 〖ボクシング〗(等級) the bantamweight class; (選手) a bantamweight.
パンタロン [<フランス語] 〖すその広がったズボン〗bell-bottoms. (❗ pantaloons は《主に米》で、男性用にも用いられるズボン一般を指す)

:はんだん 判断 图 (a) judgment (「判断力」の意では Ⓤ); 〖決定〗(a) decision; 〖結論〗(a) conclusion; 〖解釈〗(an) interpretation.
①【判断～】▶ 判断ミス an error of *judgment*. • すぐれた判断力がある have good (↔poor) *judgment*. • 判断力に欠ける lack *judgment*. • 判断力を発揮する use one's *judgment* (*in*).
②【判断が[は]】▶答えが正しいのかどうかは判断がつかない I can't *judge* [*tell*] whether the answer is right (or not). (⇨③) ▶彼の状況判断は正しい His *judgment* of the situation is right.
③【判断に】▶ ご判断に任せます I will leave it to your *judgment*. ▶その仕事を引き受けるべきかどうか判断に迷った(=心が揺れた) I wavered in my *judgment* whether I should accept the job (or not). ▶そのような結論が現実的かどうか判断に苦しんだ(=判断が難しかった) I found it difficult to *judge* whether such results were realistic (or not). ▶その計画を推進する決定は委員会の判断に基づいてなされた The decision to go ahead with the project was made on the basis of the *judgment* of the committee.
④【判断を】▶ 判断を下す make [form] a *judgment* (*on*). • 健全な判断を示す show [display, exercise] sound *judgment*. • 判断を誤る make an error in *judgment*; misjudge [him [the timing]]. • 判断を保留する reserve *judgment*. • 彼に判断を求める ask for *judgment*; ask for [seek] his *judgment*. • 彼の判断を十分尊重しています I fully respect your *judgment*.
⑤【判断で[は]】▶とっさの判断で on the instant [spur-of-the-moment] *decision*. ▶彼は自分の判断で(=自発的に)大学を変えた He transferred to another university on his own *initiative* [(責任で) by his own *responsibility*]. (❗)✕on his own judgment は不可) ▶私の判断(=意見)では彼は間違っている In [✕According to] my *judgment* [*opinion*, *view*], he is wrong./My *judgment* [*opinion*] is that he is wrong.

— **判断する** 動 judge; 〖決定する〗decide; 〖結論を下す〗conclude; 〖解釈する〗interpret.
①【動+判断する】▶ 自分で判断しなさい *Judge* for yourself.
②【...で[から]判断する】▶ 第一印象で[外見で]判断する *judge* 《him》*by* first impressions [*by* 《his》 appearance]. ▶手紙から判断すると母はだいぶ元気になっているようだ *Judging from* [*by*] her letters, Mother seems to be feeling a lot better. (⇨③)

■ **DISCOURSE**
人を外見で判断すべきとの意見には賛成しかねる、なぜなら人の外見には自分の意志で変えられないような側面がたくさんあるからだ I do not agree with the statement that a person should be *judged* by their appearance, **for** there are many aspects of one's appearance that can not be changed by one's own will. (❗ for ... (なぜなら...)は理由に用いるディスコースマーカー. 主節に続けて使うのが一般的)

③【...だと判断する】▶ 彼女は彼を 30 歳ぐらいだと判断した She *judged that* he was about thirty./《書》 She *judged* him (*to* be) about thirty. ▶彼の口ぶりから私の意見に賛成ではないと判断した I *judged from* what he said *that* he didn't agree with me. ▶私たちは彼にがんであることを知らせない方がよいだろうと判断した We *decided* (*that*) it would be better not to inform him of his cancer. ▶彼は彼女の言葉を脅迫だと判断した He *interpreted* [✕judged] her remark *as* a threat. /He *judged* her remark (*to* be) a threat. とすれば可)

ばんたん 万端 all; everything. ▶準備万端整った *Everthing's* [*All's*] ready.
ばんち 番地 (地番) a lot number; (各戸の家屋番号) a house number; (通りの番号) a street number [address]; (住所) one's address. ▶北町 1 丁目 5 番地 2 号に住んでいる live at 1-5-2 [5-2, 1-chome], Kita-machi. (❗後の方が正式)
パンチ ❶ 〖拳闘〗(ボクシング) a punch. • パンチを受ける get a *punch*. • パンチを応酬する exchange [trade] *punches*. (❗複数形に注意) • 彼のあごにパンチを食らわせる *punch* him (*out*) [*give* him a *punch*] *on* the chin; *punch* (*out*) his chin. (❗(1) out を添えるのは《米》. 「徹底的に」の意はほとんどない. (2)「あごに」は他に in [on] the jaw,「みぞおちに」は in (the pit of) stomach,「鼻に」は in [on] the nose)
❷ 〖ハサミ〗a punch. • 切符にパンチを入れる *punch* (a hole in) a ticket.
• パンチカード a punch(ed) card.
❸ 〖迫力〗▶ パンチのきいた歌《話》a *punchy* song. • パンチ力のある打者 a power hitter; a slugger. • パンチ力に欠けるチーム a punchless team.
パンチパーマ 〚have [get]〛a kinky perm. (⇨パーマ)
ばんちゃ 番茶 coarse green tea (made from tough tea leaves).
• 番茶も出花 'Even coarse tea tastes good when it is served for the first time.'/(ことわざ) Everything is good in its season.
パンチャー a puncher.
はんちゅう 範疇 a category. • ...の下位範疇に入る fall into [belong to] one of the subordinate

categories of ….
はんちょう 班長 a group [a squad] leader. ●2班の班長 the *leader* of *Group* two.
ばんちょう 番長 a leader of a group of juvenile delinquents.
パンチング 〖サッカー〗a punching. (⇨弾く)
パンツ 〖下着〗(男性用の) underpants;《英》pants;(短い) briefs,《米》shorts;(女性用の) panties,《英》pants;〖ズボン〗trousers,《米》pants;(半ズボン) shorts. ●海水パンツ swim(ming) *trunks*;(ビキニ水着の) bottoms. ●パンツルックの(=ズボンをはいている)少女 a girl *in pants*.
●パンツスーツ《米》a pantsuit;《英》a trouser-suit.
はんつき 半月き ▶半搗き米 half-polished rice.
はんつき 半月 half a month, half a month.(⦿事情 週単位で生活している米英人の場合 two weeks の方が自然な発想)▶半月ごとに twice a month; every two weeks; (やや雅) sèmimónthly.
ばんづけ 番付 〖順位表〗a list. ▶初場所の番付 the *rankings* [the (*ranking*) *list*] of wrestlers] for the New Year's Grand Sumo Tournament.
●長者番付に載る be put on the *list* of millionaires.
ハンデ a handicap. ●ハンデ3のゴルファー a golfer with a *handicap* of three; a 3-*handicap* player.
▶弱視は彼にとって大きなハンデだ Poor eyesight is a great *handicap* to him. / He is greatly *handicapped* by poor eyesight.
ばんて 番手 (糸の太さ) a (yarn) count. ●20番手の綿糸 No. 20 count cotton yarn. ●1番手の選手 a number one player.
はんてい 判定 图 〖判断〗a judgment; 〖決定〗a decision; 〖権限のある者の裁定〗a ruling; 〖審判の〗a call. ●審判の判定に従う obey the umpire's *call* [*decision*, *ruling*]. ●判定に抗議する argue [dispute] a call. ●判定勝ち[負け]する (ボクシングで) win [lose] (on) a *decision*; win [lose] by a *decision* (on points). ●「判定勝ち[負け]」は a win [a loss] on points, a points victory [defeat] (という). ●きわどい判定でセーフ[アウト]になる be safe [out] on a close call.
━判定する 働 judge; decide; rule; call.
ハンディー ━ **ハンディーな** 形 easily-handled, easy to use, handy (⦿英語の handy は「手近にあって便利な」の意が強い).
パンティー panties,《英》pants. (⦿ともに複数扱い)
パンティーストッキング (xa) panty hose /pǽnti hòuz/, pantihose (⦿複数扱い);《英》tights;《和製語》panty stocking.
ハンディキャップ a handicap. (⇨⦿ ハンデ)
ハンティング 〖狩猟〗hunting.
はんてん 反転 ━ **反転する** 働 〖ひっくり返る〗turn over; 〖元の方向へ戻る〗turn back, reverse one's course; 〖逆回転をする〗turn around [the other way].
はんてん 半纏 (羽織に似た上着) a *hanten* coat;(印半纏) a *happi* coat; a workman's livery.
はんてん 斑点 a spot; a speck (⦿ spot より小さい).
●布の上の斑点 a *spot* [a *speck*] on the cloth.
●茶色の斑点のある犬 a brown *spotted* dog; a dog with brown *spots*. (⇨まだら)
はんと 反徒 (謀反人) rebels. (⇨謀反)
はんと 版図 (a) territory. (⦿ 領土)
ハンド (手) a hand; 〖サッカーの〗handball.
●ハンドクリーム hánd cream. ●ハンドドリル a hánd drill. ●ハンドベル a handbell. ●ハンドマイク a hand-held microphone [〖話〗mike].

バント 〖野球〗a bunt. ●バントをする lay down [make] a *bunt*. ●バントを試みる attempt a bunt; make a bunt attempt. ●バントを失敗する fail to bunt. ●バントの構えをする take the *bunting* stance; square around to *bunt*. ●バントがうまいbe a good bunter. ●バントを決める bunt successfully. ●スリーバントしてファウルになる *bunt* foul for one's third strike. ▶彼は犠牲バントで走者を二塁に送った He sacrificed [bunted] the runner to second.(⦿走者を主語にすると The runner moved to second *on* his sacrifice *bunt*. となる)
⦅関連⦆いろいろなバント: 送りバント a sacrifice bunt/犠牲バント a sacrifice bunt/スクイズバント a squeeze bunt/スリーバント a two-strike [third-strike] bunt/セーフティーバント a individual offensive bunt/ドラッグバント a drag bunt/バスターバント a fake [a slash] bunt/プッシュバント a push bunt.

●バントエンドラン a bunt and run. ●バントヒット a hit on a bunt; a bunt single. ●バントヒットを打つ bunt safely; lay down a base-hit bunt.
バンド ❶〖ひも〗(輪状の) a band;(締め具付きの) a strap. ●ゴムバンド a rubber *band*. ●ヘアバンド a head*band*. ●腕時計のバンド《米》a watch*band*;《英》a watch*strap*(⦿皮・布製); a (watch) bracelet (⦿金属製).
❷〖洋服の〗a belt. (⦿a band とはいわないことに注意) (⇨ベルト)
バンド 〖楽団〗a band. ●ジャズ[ロック; ブラス]バンドを結成する form a jazz [a rock; a brass] *band*.
●バンドマスター 〖楽団の指揮者〗a bandmaster; a conductor. (⦿後の方は性差のない言い方) ●バンドマン a band player; (男の) a bandsman. (⦿つづり字に注意)
はんドア 半ドア ▶半ドアの half-opened. (⇨半開き)
ハンドアウト 〖資料用印刷物〗a handout.
はんとう 反騰 图 〖経済〗a sharp rise in《stock prices》after a fall; a rally. (⦿ 反落)
━反騰する 働 ▶円が反騰した The yen *rallied*.
はんとう 半島 a peninsula /pənínsələ/. ●能登半島 the Noto *Peninsula*.
はんどう 反動 (a) reaction. (⦿物理的な意にも政治的な意にも用いる) ●新しい思想に対する反動 a *reaction against* new ideas. ●反動的政策 a reactionary policy. ●バスの急な動きの反動で倒れる fall down *in reaction to* the sudden movement of the bus.
●反動勢力 the reactionary forces; the forces of reaction.
ばんとう 晩冬 late winter.
ばんとう 番頭 (商店・旅館などの) a head clerk. ●内閣の大番頭(=官房長官) the Chief Cabinet Secretary.
はんどうたい 半導体 〖物理〗a semiconductor.
はんとうまく 半透膜 a semipermeable membrane.
はんとうめい 半透明 ━ **半透明の** 形 translucent /trænslúːsnt/, semitransparent.
バンドエイド 〖絆創膏〗〖商標〗《米》(a) Band-Aid,《英》(an) Elastoplast.
はんどく 判読 ▶彼の筆跡は判読に苦しむ It's hard to read [make out, decipher] his handwriting./ His handwriting is hardly *readable* [*legible*].
ハンドクラフト 〖手工芸(品)〗《米》handcrafts;《英》handicrafts.
はんとし 半年 half a year, a half year; six months.
▶その雑誌は半年ごとに発行される The magazine is issued *every six months* [*semiannually*].
ハンドバッグ a handbag;《米》a purse (⦿《英》では

ハンドブック a handbook. (⇨便覧)
ハンドブレーキ 《米》a párking bràke, 《英》a handbrake.
ハンドボール 〖球技〗《play》handball.
パントマイム (a) pantomime, (a) mime. ●パントマイムをする perform a *pantomime* 《*of*》. ●パントマイムで道化を演じる *pantomime [mime]* a clown. ●パントマイム俳優 a pantomimist.
ハンドメード ●ハンドメードのマフラー a hand-made (↔ machine-made) scarf.
パンドラのはこ パンドラの箱 Pandora's /pǽndɔ́ːrəz/ box. ●パンドラの箱を開く open *Pandora's box*. (❗「思いがけない災いを招く」こと)
***ハンドル** 〖自動車の〗a steering wheel (❗×a handle とはいわない); 〖自転車・オートバイの〗a handlebar (しばしば複数形で); 〖ドアの〗a (door) knob. ●右ハンドルの車 a right(-hand)-drive car. (❗「ハンドルが右についている」は The steering wheel is on the right-hand side.) ●車のハンドルを握る (運転する) take the *wheel*, (運転中である) be at [behind] the *wheel*. ●車のハンドルを左に切る turn the *wheel* [あわてて, 急に] swerve] (to) the left. ●ぬかるみ道でハンドルをとられる lose control of one's car [bicycle] on a muddy road. (❗この場合には ×lose control of the wheel [handlebars]... とはいわない) ●ハンドルの前に座るsit behind the wheel. (❗日本語と英語の表現の違いに注意) ▶見事なハンドルさばきですね You're really a good driver.
●ハンドルネーム 〖パソコン通信用のニックネーム〗a handle; 〖和製語〗a handle name.
はんドン 半ドン (半日休みの日) 《米》《半休》
はんなき 半泣き ●半泣きで答える answer *half-crying*.
はんなま 半生 ― 半生の 形 (生煮えの) imperfectly boiled; (半焼けの) half-boiled; (生半可な) half-baked. ●半生のアスパラガス *imperfectly boiled* asparagus. ●半生知識 *half-baked* knowledge.
ばんなん 万難 ― 万難を排する overcome all the difficulties [obstacles]. ▶核戦争は万難を排して(=犠牲を払ってでも)回避しなければならない We must avoid nuclear war *at all costs [whatever the cost]*.
はんにえ 半煮え ― 半煮えの 形 half-boiled, not boiled [cooked] enough.
はんにち 反日 ― 反日(の) 形 anti-Japanese. ●反日感情 anti-Japanese sentiment [feeling].
はんにち 半日 half a day, a half day.
はんにゃ 般若 一般若の面 a mask of an ogress.
●般若湯 (酒) alcoholic drinks.
はんにゃしんぎょう 般若心経 *The Great Heart of Wisdom Sutra*. 〖参考〗大乗仏教の経典
はんにゅう 搬入 ― 搬入する 動 carry [bring; take]... in. ●bring ... in は中にいる人から見た場合, take ... in は外にいる人から見た場合) ●ピアノを部屋に搬入する *carry* the piano *into* the room. (❗搬入先を示す場合は into を用いる)
はんにん 犯人 〖犯罪人〗a criminal, a culprit (❗後の方は犯人と推定される人についていもう); 〖法律違反者〗an offender (❗criminal の婉曲的としても使う); 〖容疑者〗a suspect. ●犯人 〖窃盗; 誘拐〗犯 a murderer [a thief; a kidnapper]. (❗×a criminal in the murder case などとはしない) ●その犯人を逮捕する arrest the *suspect* [殺人犯] murderer]; (強盗) robber]. (❗厳密には裁判で有罪か確定する前は criminal, culprit, offender は不適) ●犯人を投獄する send the *criminal [offender]* to prison.

▶彼らは彼を犯人ではないかと疑っている They suspect [×are suspecting] him as the *criminal*. ▶だれが真犯人か Who is the real *culprit*? (❗おどけて「だれがやったのか」の意で「だれが犯人は」は Who did it?)
●犯人像 a profile [a description] of the murderer [robber, etc.].
ばんにん 万人 all (the) people, everybody. ●万人の認める真理 (a) *universal* truth. ●この小説は万人に理解される This novel is intelligible to *all people*. ▶この小説は万人向きだ (万人の好みを満足させる) This novel satisfies *all* tastes./(万人が気に入る) *Everybody* likes this novel.
ばんにん 番人 〖見張り番〗a guard /ɡɑ́ːrd/; a watch; (男の) a watchman (複 -men); 〖留守居〗a caretaker. ●入口に番人を置く place a *guard* [*watch*] at the door.
はんにんまえ 半人前 ― 半人前の 形 《話》green; (経験不足の) inexperienced; (未熟な) immature. ▶私は教師としてはまだ半人前です I'm *not yet well experienced in* teaching./(駆け出しで経験不足の) I'm still a *fledg(e)ling* teacher.
はんね 半値 half the price. (⇨半額)
ばんねん 晩年 ●晩年は in one's later years [life]; late in life.
はんのう 反応 名 (a) reaction (❗生物学的・化学的反応から事件や影響などに対する反応まで広く用いる); (a) response. (❗刺激に対する反応, または質問・提案・訴えなどに対する返答) (⇨反響) ●ツベルクリン〖化学; 連鎖〗反応 a tuberculin [a chemical; a chain] *reaction*. ●酸に対する鉄の反応 the *reaction* of iron to acid; the *reaction* of acid *on* iron. ●刺激に対する反応 the *reaction* [response] to a stimulus. ▶私たちの提案にはほとんど反応がなかった Our proposals met with little *response*. ▶彼らは私たちの訴えに何の反応も示さなかった They gave [made] no *response* to our appeal.
― 反応する 動 react 《*to*》; respond 《*to*》. ▶彼はその知らせ[君の招待]にどう反応しましたか How did he *react* to the news [*respond to* your invitation]?
●反応時間 a reáction time.
はんのう 半農 ―半農半漁の村 a farming and fishing village.
ばんのう 万能 ― 万能(の) 形 (多才な) 《米》all-around, 《英》all-round, versatile. ●万能選手 an all-around [a versatile] player [athlete] (❗《英》an all-rounder はスポーツに限らず「何でもよくできる人」の意.《米》an all-rounder は《まれ》)〖野球〗a utility player [man] (❗どのポジションもこなせる選手で, 補欠の含みがある). ●万能ナイフ (多目的) an all-purpose knife. ●万能薬 a cure-all,《やや書》(けなして) a panacea /pæ̀nəsíːə/.
はんのき 榛の木 〖植物〗an alder.
パンのき パンの木 〖植物〗a breadfruit (tree).
はんば 飯場 a bunkhouse (複 -houses /-ziz,《米》-siz/).
はんば 半端 名 〖半端物〗an odd item [piece]; (がらくた) odds and ends; 〖端数〗a fraction; 〖不完全〗incompleteness (⇨中途半端).
―半端な ●(残りの)半端な金 the *odd* money. ●半端仕事をする do *odd* jobs. ●半端な(=断片的な)知識 *fragmentary* knowledge. ▶その品は半端では売れません (セットを崩して売ることはできません) We can't break the set [pair].
バンパー (自動車の) 《主に米》a fender,《英》a bumper.
ハンバーガー a hamburger,《やや話》a burger.

ハンバーグ(ステーキ) a hamburg steak, a hamburger.

はんばい 販売 图 (a) sale; selling.
① 《～販売》▶現金販売 a cash *sale*; a *sale for* [×with] *cash*. ▶信用販売 a credit *sale*; a *sale on credit*. ▶訪問販売 call [door-to-door] *sales*. ●委託販売 consignment *sales*. ●カタログ販売 catalog *sales* [*selling*]. ●通信販売 mail order *sales* [*selling*]. ●大量販売 mass *sales* [*selling*]. ●値下げ販売 mark-down *sales*. ●自動販売機 a vénding machine.
② 《販売を》▶販売を促進する promote *sales*. ▶未成年者に対する酒類の販売を禁止する prohibit the *sale* of alcoholic drinks to minors.
③ 《販売は》▶販売は順調である[低迷している; 横ばいである] *Sales* are strong [weak; flat].
── **販売する** 動 sell*; [商5] deal* in .... (⇨売る) ▶この店は靴を販売している They *sell* [×are selling] shoes at this store. (▶一時的に売っているわけではないので進行形は用いない) / This store *deals in* [*carries*] shoes. ▶この品物はどこでも販売されている These goods *are on sale* everywhere.
●販売員[係] a salesperson; (働 salespeople); (男性) a salesman; (女性) a saleswoman. ●販売価格 a sélling príce. (☒ a sale price は「特売価格」) ●販売競争 sáles competítion. ●販売計画[戦略] a sáles ([広義で] a márketing) prógram [strátegy). ●販売政策 a sáles [×a sale] pòlicy. (☒ 形容詞的に用いる場合には複数形になる) ●販売促進 (⇨販促) ●販売代理店 a distributor; a sales [a sélling] àgent [ágency]; (特定メーカーの) an outlet. ●販売店 (販売会社) a dealer; (店) 《米》a store, (英) a shop 《中国》; 《新聞の》a delivery agent. ●販売部 a sales department. (⇨営業) ●販売網 a sales network. ●販売利益 a profit on sale. ●販売量[高] sales volume. ●販売力 sáles fòrce; sélling pòwer; márketing stréngth. ●販売ルート a sales channel.

バンパイア [吸血鬼] a vampire.

はんぱく 反駁 (an) argument; (a) refutation. (働 反論)

はんぱく 半白 (白髪の交じった髪) gray hair.

ばんぱく 万博 [「万国博覧会」の略] a world's fair, an international exposition.

パンパス [アルゼンチンの大草原] the pampas /pǽmpəs/ 〚単・複両扱い〛; 〚植物〛pampas grass.

はんぱつ 反発 图 (嫌悪, 反発作用) (a) repulsion; (反感) (an) antipathy; (抵抗) (a) resistance; (反対) (an) opposition; (反抗) (a) reaction; (権威などに対する) a rebellion. ▶彼に反発を感じる feel *repulsion* for him; feel *antipathy to* [*toward*] him. ▶彼の発言は組合の強い反発を買った His remarks met with great [strong] *opposition from* the union.
── **反発する** 動 repel (-ll-); resist; oppose; react; rebel (-ll-). ▶若者は年配の人たち[古い価値観]に反発した Young people *reacted* [*rebelled*] *against* their elders [the old values]. ▶磁石の同じ極は反発する The same poles of magnets *repel* (each other).

はんぶん 半分 ▶利益を半々に分ける divide [share] the profit(s) *fifty-fifty* [*equally*]. ▶水とミルクを半々に入れる put in water and milk *half-and-half*. ▶彼の生死の見込みは半々だ He has a *fifty-fifty* chance of being alive.

ばんぶん (⇨どんぶん)

ばんぶん 万分 [決して] never (⇨決して); [十分に]

fully (⇨十分に); [全く] quite (⇨全く❶).

ぱんぱん ▶ぱんぱんと柏手を打つ *clap* one's hands in prayer. ▶ふとんをぱんぱんたたく *slap* a futon. ▶腕がぱんぱんに張っている My arms *are really stiff*. ▶少年は風船をぱんぱんにふくらませた The boy *fully inflated* the balloon. (▶「ぱんぱんにふくらませた風船」は *a fully inflated* balloon) ▶花火がぱんぱんと鳴った The fireworks went off *with bangs*.

ばんばんざい 万万歳 the deepest [heartiest, warmest] congratulations 《on [upon]》 his success》.

はんびょうにん 半病人 a person in poor health; a semi-invalid.

はんびらき 半開き ── **半開きの** 形 half-open. ▶ドアが半開きだ The door is (left) *half-open* [*is not properly closed*]. ▶暴風雨の中を傘を半開きにして歩いた I walked in the storm with my umbrella *half-open*. / I walked under a *half-open* umbrella in the storm.

はんぴれい 反比例 〚数学〛inverse proportion. (㐧 正比例) (⇨比例)
── **反比例する** 動 ▶気温は高さに反比例する Temperature is *in inverse proportion* [*ratio*] *to* altitude.

はんぷ 頒布 图 (配布) distribution; (流通) circulation. ── **頒布する** 動 distribute.
●頒布会 (hold [have]) a special sale 《of》.

ばんぷう 蛮風 a barbarous [a barbaric] custom.

はんぷく 反復 图 repetition. ▶英語を学ぶには反復練習が大事だ *Repeated* practice [*Repetition*] is important in learning English. / It's important to practice *repeatedly* in learning English.
── **反復する** 動 repeat; do (it) (over) again. (☒ どちらも「1 回またはそれ以上繰り返す」の意); (何度も反復して) repeatedly; again and again; over and over (again).
●反復記号 〚音楽〛a repeat (sign).

はんぷく 反覆 [ひっくり返すこと] the overthrow 《of a government》; [反復] (⇨反復).

ばんぷく 万福 ▶貴家の万福を祈る I wish you *every happiness*.

パンプス 《a pair of》 pumps 《米》 [court shoes 《英》].

ばんぶつ 万物 everything, all things; (神が創造した世界) creation. ●万物の霊長 the lord of *creation*. ▶万物は流転する *All things* change. / *All things* are in flux, always changing. (☒ in a state of flux ともいう. 「流動的で」の意)

ハンブルク [ドイツの都市] Hamburg /hǽmbə:rg/.

パンフレット [表紙の付いた仮とじの小冊子] a pamphlet, a booklet; [写真・イラストなどをふんだんに使った商品などの説明パンフ] a brochure /brouʃúər/; [折りとたみ式の] a leaflet. ▶海外旅行のパンフレット an overseas travel *brochure*.

はんぶん 半分 图 [2 分の 1] (a) half (働 halves) 《*of*》. ▶ケーキの半分 *a half of* a cake. ▶8 の半分は 4 です *Half of* 8 is 4. ▶リンゴの半分は腐っている *Half* (*of*) the apples are rotten. (☒ 動詞の数は of の後の(代)名詞に一致する. また of はしばしば省略されるが, 代名詞の場合は省略できない: *Half of them* [*those*] are rotten. / *Half of* it [*that*] is rotten.) ▶この子供たちの半分は日本人で, 残りの半分は中国人だ One *half of* the children are Japanese and the other *half* are Chinese. ▶サンドイッチがあるんだけど半分食べてもいいよ I have some sandwiches. You can have *half* [×the half]. / (半分ずつしよう) 〚話〛 I'll *go halves* with you *on* my sandwiches. ▶そのリンゴを半分に切りなさい Cut the apple *in half*

[into halves, down the middle]. ▶彼は生徒数を半分(だけ)減らした He reduced the number of students *by half*. ▶そのパンは半分でも買えますか Can I buy the bread by the *half*-loaf?
— 半分の 形 half. ▶半分の分け前 a *half* share.
• 半分の紙 a *half* sheet of paper.
— 半分 副 half; [中途に] halfway; (まっ二つに) down the middle. ▶私の仕事は半分終わった My work is *half* done./I'm *halfway* through the work. ▶びんには水が半分入っている The bottle is *half-filled* with water. ▶私は彼の半分しか本[金]を持っていない I have only *half* as many books [much money] *as* he does. ▶(山を)だいたい半分くらい登ったね We are nearly *halfway* up the mountain.

> 翻訳のこころ 電車の中でうとうとしていたので、半分夢を見ているような感じだった(吉本ばなな『みどりのゆび』)I was dozing off on the train; so I felt as if I had been dreaming. (❗この「半分」は「あたかも、まるで」の意なので as if ... を表す)

はんぶんじょくれい 繁文縟礼 (形式的な規則や儀礼) red tape.
はんべい 反米 — 反米(の) 形 anti-American.
• 反米感情 anti-American sentiment [feeling].
ばんぺい 番兵 a sentry. (⇒歩哨(ほしょう)) • 番兵に立つ[に立っている] stand *sentry* [be on *sentry* duty].
• 番兵小屋 a sentry box.
はんべそ 半べそ — 半べそをかく be on the verge of tears.
はんべつ 判別 名 (a) distinction. (⇒区別)
— 判別する 動 ▶2語の意味の相違を判別する *distinguish [tell]* the difference in meaning *between* the two words.
はんぺら 半ぺら half a sheet.
はんぼいん 半母音 〖言語〗a semivowel; (渡り音) a glide.
はんぼう 繁忙 — 繁忙をきわめている be very busy 《doing; with》. (⇒忙しい)
ハンマー a hammer. ▶ハンマーでくぎを打つ *hammer* a wedge.
• ハンマー投げ the hammer throw. • ハンマー投げの選手 a hammer thrower.
はんみ 半身 ❶〖姿勢〗半身に構える (相手に対し体を斜めにした構え) take an oblique stance against one's opponent.
❷〖魚の切り身〗symmetrical half of a fish.
はんみょう 斑猫 〖昆虫〗a tiger beetle.
ばんみん 万民 all the people; all the citizens.
パンムンジョム 板門店 〖韓国と北朝鮮の国境沿い休戦ライン上の村〗Pànmùnjóm.
はんめい 判明 — 判明する 動 〖明らかになる〗become* clear; 〖知られる〗become known; 〖結局…であることがわかる〗prove, turn out 《to be》; 〖同一人[物]と確認される〗be identified. ▶その事故の原因が判明した The cause of the accident *has become clear* [*been identified*]. ▶その報道は誤報であることが判明した The news *proved* [*turned out*] (*to be*) false. (⇒分かる❸) ▶選挙結果はいつ判明しますか When will the results of the election *be known* [発表される] *be announced*]? ▶その死体の身元はまだ判明していない The body *is not yet identified*.
はんめし 晩飯 (a) supper, (a) dinner. (⇒夕食)
はんめん 半面 ▶彼女は口が悪い半面(=しかし)情のある人です She's sharp tongued, *but* she's a warm and loving heart. ▶この風刺小説はおもしろい反面(=しかし同時に)恐ろしくもある This satirical novel

is interesting *but at the same time* it is horrifying./(一方では) *While* this satirical novel is interesting, it is horrifying.
• 反面教師 a bad example; an example of how not to behave.
はんめん 半面 〖一方の面〗one side; (もう片方の面) the other side. (⇒一面)
ばんめん 盤面 ❶〖レコード・碁盤などの表面〗the surface of a 《go》 board. ❷〖局面〗盤面は彼に有利である The *game* is going in his favor.
はんも 繁茂 — 繁茂する 動 grow thick [rank]. (⇒茂る)
はんもく 反目 名 (反感) (an) antagonism; (敵対) (a) hostility.
— 反目する 動 ▶彼と反目している be *antagonistic to* [*toward*] him; be *hostile to* him; be *at odds with* him.
ハンモック a hammock. ▶ハンモックをつるす hang [sling] a *hammock*. ▶ハンモックに寝る sleep in a *hammock*. (❗彼が寝るハンモック」は the hammock he sleeps in)
はんもと 版元 (出版元) a publishing house [company].
はんもん 反問 — 反問する 動 ask [鋭く] shoot] (…) back.
はんもん 斑紋 (まだら模様) a mottled pattern.
はんもん 煩悶 名 〖悩み〗(a) worry, (やや書) distress; 〖苦悩〗(やや書) anguish, (an) agony; 〖苦しみ〗suffering.
— 煩悶する 動 worry 《about》; feel *distress* 《over》, be in *distress* [*anguish, agony*] 《over》; suffer 《for》.
はんもんてん 板門店 (⇒パンムンジョム)
ばんゆう 蛮勇 • 蛮勇を振るう ▶蛮勇をふるって(深く考えないで) recklessly; with reckless bravery. ▶行政改革の実を上げるには蛮勇をふるわなければ…という思い切った策を講じなければならないだろう They will have to *take drastic steps* in order to make the administrative reforms really successful.
ばんゆういんりょく 万有引力 • 万有引力の法則 the law of *universal gravitation*.
はんよう 汎用 • 汎用性のある general-purpose; (多目的の) multipurpose. • 汎用コンピュータ a *general-purpose* computer.
はんよう 繁用 busyness.
はんら 半裸 — 半裸の 形 half-naked.
ばんらい 万雷 • 万雷の拍手 (receive) tumultuous [thunderous] applause 《from the audience》. (❗他に a thunder [a storm] of applause なども用いられる)
はんらく 落落 〖経済〗a steep fall in 《stock prices》 after a rise. (⇔急騰)
はんらん 反乱 (大規模の) (a) rebellion (❗通例不成功に終わったものをさす. 成功すれば revolution になる); (小規模の) (a) revolt; (船内や軍隊内の) (a) mutiny. • 反乱を起こす rise in rebellion 《against》; revolt, rise in revolt 《against》; rise 《against》. • 政府に対する反乱を鎮める put down [suppress] a *rebellion* [a *revolt*] *against* the government. ▶反乱が起こった A *rebellion* [A *revolt*] broke out 《×happened》.
• 反乱軍 a rébel army; (やや書) insurgent forces [troops].
はんらん 氾濫 名 an overflow, a flood; 〖供給過剰〗(an) oversupply. • アメリカ映画の氾濫 the *flood* of American films.
— 氾濫する 動 overflow, flow [run*] over 《the banks》; be flooded. ▶台風の後その川は氾濫した

The river *overflowed* (its banks) [*was flooded*] after a typhoon. ▶書店に婦人雑誌が氾濫している The bookstores *are flooded with* women's magazines./There are *so many* women's magazines in the bookstores. (**!**「数」でなく「量」なら, たとえば「ラジオ・テレビ・映画などで英語が氾濫している」は There is *so much* English heard on the radio, TV, movies and so on. となる)

ばんりのちょうじょう 万里の長城 the Great Wall (of China).

はんりょ 伴侶 (⇨連れ) ● 人生の伴侶《書》a *companion* for life. (**!**「生涯の友」の意もある. 単に夫, 妻の意では a partner)

はんりょく 万緑 ● **万緑叢中**(%%)**紅一点** (⇨⑩ 紅一点)

はんれい 凡例 (辞書などの) explanatory notes (**!**図入りのものは an explanatory chart); a guide to using 《the dictionary》; (地図・図面などの略号・記号表) a key, 《やや古》a legend.

はんれい 判例 《やや書》 (a) (judicial) précedent. ● 判例に従う[従わない] follow the *precedents* [break with *precedent*]. ● 判例に基づいて《やや書》 in accordance with *precedent*.

はんれき 犯歴 (have) a criminal record.

はんろ 販路 (市場) a market; (販売店) an outlet. ● 販路を開拓する find [open] a new *market* 《for the products》. (⇨市場(%%))

はんろん 反論 图 [[反対意見]] (an) argument 《against》; [[論ばく]] (a) refutation.
── 反論する 動 argue 《against》; refute.

はんろん 汎論 an outline 《of》; an introduction 《to》.

ひ

ひ 日 ❶ [太陽] the sun (！「ひなた」「日光」の意でも用いる); (日光) sunshine, sunlight (！前の方がより強く「暖かいこと」を暗示); (太陽光線) sunbeams. ▶日は東から昇り西に沈む The *sun* rises in [×from] the east and sets in the west. ▶日がさんさんと輝いていた The *sun* was shining bright [brightly]. (！bright では輝いている状態に, brightly では輝いている様子に重点がある) ▶彼は日が沈んでからここを出発した He left here *after sunset* [(暗くなってから) *after dark*]. ▶私の部屋は日がよく当たる[当たらない] My room gets a lot of [doesn't get much] *sun* [*sunlight, sunshine*]./A lot of [No] *sun* [*sunlight, sunshine*] comes into my room. (⇨日当たり) ▶君は少し日に当たらないといけない You need (to get) some *sun*. ▶この箱は日の当たる[当たらない]所に置いておきなさい Keep the box *in the sun* [*out of the sun*, (日陰に) *in the shade*].

❷ [日中] (a) day (↔(a) night). ▶冬は日が短い The *days* are short in (《主に米》 the) winter. (！複数形で用いることに注意. 次例も同様) ▶夏が近づくにつれて日が長くなる The *days* grow [get] longer as summer approaches. ▶日差しの強い日はサングラスをかけます I wear sunglasses on sunny *days*. ▶もうすぐ日が暮れる It will get dark soon./Night [×Day] will fall soon. (！前の方が普通)

❸ [1日] a day; (期日) a date. ▶次の日(に) the next [following] *day*. ▶ある寒い[晴れた]日に on a cold [a clear] *day*. ▶結婚式の日を決める fix [set] the *date* for a wedding. (！for は予定を表す. the *date* of one's wedding は「結婚式のあった日」の意) ▶彼に初めて会った日は大変寒かった The *day* (that) [《書》 The *day* when] I first met him was very cold. (！《話》では通例 that を省略する) ▶日がたつにつれて彼は息子のことがだんだん心配になってきた As *time* [(the) *days*] went by, he became more and more anxious about his son. ▶郵便は日に 2 回配達される Mail is delivered twice *daily* [a *day*]. ▶彼は来る日も来る日もその仕事を続けた He went on with the work *day after day* [《やや書》 *day in, day out*]. ▶ある日おじの家へ遊びに行った I went to see my uncle *one day*. ▶締め切りの日が近づいている The closing *date* [The deadline] is approaching.

❹ [日数] ▶中間試験までもうあまり日がない We have only a few *days* left before the midterm exams.

❺ [時, 時代] (時) time; (時代) one's days. ▶若き日の楽しい思い出を話す talk about the delightful memories of one's younger days. (！日常会話では talk about how happy one was *when* one was young などという方が普通) ▶遊んで日を過ごす idle away one's *time*. ▶休日はいつも読書をして日を過ごす I spend my *time* reading on holidays. ▶世界から戦争がなくなる日が間もなくやって来るだろう 《書》 The *day* [*time*] will soon come when there will be no war in the world. (！The day と *time* ... が離れていうのが when は前の *day*, [*time*] when ... will soon come. の語順より普通)/There will be no war in the world someday.

❻ [その他の表現] ▶やっとの日を暮らす (その日暮らしをする) live (from) hand to mouth. (⇨その日暮らし)

● 日一日と day by day. (⇨[日に日に])

● 日が浅い ▶彼はこの会社に入社してからまだ日が浅い *It's not* [*It's not been*] *long* since he joined this company.

● 日が当たらない ▶日の当たらない人々 (不幸な人々) unfortunate people; 《やや書》 the unfortunate.

● 日暮れて道遠し The day is short and there is still a long way to go. / A man bas become old but has still a lot to do.

● 日に日に day by day. ▶日に日に寒くなってきた It's getting colder *day by day* [*from day to day*, (毎日) *every day*].

● 日を改めて ▶日を改めて(＝別の日に)お電話差し上げます I will call you *another day* (いつかある時) *some other time*].

● 日を追って day by day.

ひ 火 ❶ [火炎] fire; [炎] a flame; a blaze (！flame より大きくて激しい. 通例単数形で用いる); (たばこ・ライターなどの) a light. (⇨火遊び)

① 【火は[が]】 ▶火はまだ燃えている[もう消えた] The *fire* is still burning [has already gone out]. ▶紙は火がつきやすい Paper catches *fire* easily. (！×Paper is easy to catch *fire*. とはいわない) ▶火はたちまち家々に燃え移った The *fire* spread [ran] rapidly from house to house. ▶火が燃え尽きぬうちにそこを離れてはいけない Don't leave there before the *fire* has burned (itself) out. ▶これらのマッチは火がつかない These matches won't strike.

② 【火の】 ▶火のついたマッチを捨てる throw a *lighted* match. (！限定的に用いる場合は lit より lighted が普通) ● 火の車 (⇨火の車) ▶強風が吹いて火の回りが速かった A strong wind blew and the *fire* burned quickly.

③ 【火に】 ▶その建物は一面火に包まれた The building was enveloped *in flames* [*in a blaze*].

④ 【火を】 ▶家に火をつける set *fire* to a house; set a house *on fire*. (！set fire to は偶然・故意にかかわらず, 通例燃やしたくないと思っているものに火をつける場合に用いる) ▶火打ち石で火を打ち出す strike *fire* with a flint. ▶マッチでたばこに火をつける light a cigarette with a match. (！light は通例, ろうそく (candle) など本来火をつけて使うものに用いる) ▶たいていの動物は火を恐れる Most animals dread [are afraid of] *fire*. ▶ちょっと(たばこの)火を貸してください Give me a *light*, please. (！この場合 fire は使えない)

❷ [火事] (a) fire. (⇨火事) ▶火の用心をする look out for *fire*. ▶火の用心 (掲示) Beware of *fire*. ▶彼の家から火が出た A *fire* occurred [started] in his house./He had a *fire* started in his house. (！「から」は from ではない)

❸ [たき火・暖炉・炊事用などの] a fire. ● 火を消す put out [*extinguish*] a *fire*. ● 火をおこす make [build] a *fire*. ● 火にまきをくべる feed the *fire* with wood; feed wood to the *fire*. ▶部屋を暖かくするために火をたいた We made [lit, built] a *fire* to warm the room. ▶なべを火にかけなさい Put a pan on the *fire*. ▶こちらへ来て火にあたりなさい Come over here and warm yourself by [at]

the *fire*. ▶彼は炉に火を入れた He *fired* the furnace.
❹【火熱】a fire. ●火の気 (⇨火の気) ▶彼女はスープに火を通した She *heated* (*up*) some soup. ▶豚肉はよく火を通さないといけない Pork should be *well-cooked* [*be cooked well-done*].
❺【砲火】fire. ●火ぶたを切る (⇨火蓋) ▶銃が火を吹いた The gun *fired*.
❻【その他の表現】恥ずかしさで顔から火が出る思いだった I *flushed* [*blushed*] with shame./My *face was burning* with shame.
●火がつく ▶その子供は犬を見ると火がついたように泣き出した The child began to cry *frantically* [*wildly*] when he saw the dog.
●火に油を注ぐ 会話 「ジムと真紀は離婚を考えているんだ」「2 人ともどうしたのかしら。真紀の言い分をジムに話してみるわ」「そんなことをしたら火に油を注ぐことになるよ」"Jim and Maki are thinking about divorce." "What's the matter with them? I'll talk to Jim for Maki." "That'll [You'll] be just *adding fuel to the fire*."
●火の消えたよう ▶その町を訪れたとき火が消えたような寂しさだった When we visited the town, we found it *completely* [(*that*) *it was completely*] *deserted*.
●火のない所に煙は立たない《ことわざ》There's no smoke without fire./《ことわざ》Where there is smoke, there is fire.
●火の中水の底[中] ▶あなたの頼みとあれば、火の中水の底です If this is your request [what you want me to do], I'd *go through fire or water*. (❗(1) go through fire or water は慣用表現. (2) what you want me to do の you は強く読む)
●火を落とす extinguish [put out] a fire.
●火を見るよりも明らかだ ▶彼の成功は火を見るよりも明らかである His success is quite obvious [*as clear as day*(*light*)].

ひ 比 ❶【比率】(a) ratio /réiʃou/ (徼 ~s). (⇨比率)
●正比[反比] direct [inverse, reciprocal] *ratio*.
▶二つの容器の容積の比は 3 対 1 です There is a *ratio of 3 to* 1 between the volumes of the two containers. ▶3 対 5 の比は 3:5 または 3/5 と書かれる The *ratio of 3 to* 5 is written 3:5 or 3/5.
❷【比較】(a) comparison. (⇨比較) ▶私は英語では君の比ではない(君の方がずっと勝っている) You know English much [a lot] better than I./《やや書》I'm not your *equal* in English.
ひ 妃 a princess. (⇨妃殿下)
ひ 灯 a light. (⇨明かり❶) ▶谷の方に灯がともっているのが見えた I saw some *lights* burning in the valley. ▶何につけ伝統の灯をともし続けるには相当の努力が必要である It takes considerable efforts to *keep* traditions *alive*. (❗「絶える」場合は The tradition *died out*. など)
ひ 非 【過失】a fault (❗「過責任」を表すときは通例 one's ~);【誤り】an error (❗後の方が堅い語). ●自分の非を認める admit one's *mistake* [*error*]. ▶非は私にある It's mý *fault*./The *fault* is mine [lies with me]./I'm to blame.
●非の打ち所がない ▶君の英語は非の打ち所がない Your English *is perfect* [*leaves nothing to be desired*].
●非を鳴らす ▶政府の政策に非を鳴らす(=強く非難する) *denounce* the government's policy.
ひ 杼 (機織りの) a shuttle.
ひ 碑 (記念碑) a monument.
ひ 緋 scarlet. ●緋色のドレス a *scarlet* dress.
ひ- 非- un-; in-; non-. ●非科学的な *un*scientific.
●非人間的な *in*human. (❗*un*human はあまり使われない) ●非暴力(主義) *non*violence. (❗un-, in-, が非難の意を持つのに対し, non- には通例その含みはない)
ひ- 曾- (⇨曾(²)-)
-ひ -費【経費】expenses; (主に個人の) (an) expenditure;【支出】(a) cost. (⇨支出) ●国民医療費 national medical *expediture*.
*び 美【美しさ】beauty;【抽象的美】the beautiful.
●男性[女性]美 manly [womanly] *beauty*. ●自然の美 the *beauty* of nature; natural *beauty*.
●美的感覚 a sense of *beauty*; an esthetic sense. ▶美は見る人次第だ《ことわざ》*Beauty is in the eye* [×*eyes*] *of the beholder*.
び 微 (非常に細かなこと) minuteness /main(j)úːtnis/.
●微に入(ʼ)り細(ʂ)をうがつ (非常に詳細な説明をする) give a minutely detailed explanation.
ひあい 悲哀 (深い悲しみ) sorrow ●具体的にはしばしば複数形で;(悲しみ) sadness; (みじめさ) misery. ●人生の悲哀を感じる feel the *sorrows* of life.
ひあがる 干上がる dry up. ●あごが干上がる (⇨顎[成句]) ▶この川は夏になると干上がる This river *dries up* in (《主に米》the) summer.
ひあし 火脚 (火の回り) the spread of fire. ▶火脚が速かった The *fire* spread rapidly.
ピアス 《a pair of》pierced earrings. (❗単に earrings ということも多い) ●ピアスをつける put *earrings* into one's ears. ▶ピアスつけられないわ. だって耳に穴を開けてないんだもの I can't wear pierced *earrings* because my ears aren't pierced [I don't have pierced ears].
ひあそび 火遊び ── 火遊び(を)する 動 play with matches [fire]. (❗後の方は「愚かで危険なことをする」の意でも用いる) ●恋の火遊びをする play with love.
ひあたり 日当たり ●日当たりのよい[悪い(= 日の当たらない)]部屋 a *sunny* [*a sunless*] room. (⇨日❶)
ピアニスト a pianist /piˈænɪst, piːˈanɪst/.
*ピアノ【楽器】a piano (徼 ~s); (堅型の) an upright piano; (グランドピアノ) a grand piano; (ピアノ演奏) piano.
①【ピアノの~】●ピアノの先生 a *piáno* teacher.
②【ピアノが】▶彼女はピアノが上手だ She plays the *piano* very well./She is good at (playing) the *piano*./She is a good pianist.
③【ピアノに[で]】●ピアノに合わせて歌う sing *to the piano*. ●ピアノで伴奏する accompany《her song》*on the piano*. ▶彼女は映画音楽[ショパン]で弾いた She played screen music [Chopin] *on the piano*.
④【ピアノを】●ピアノを弾く play the *piano*. ●ピアノを弾きながら歌う sing *at the piano*. ●ピアノを練習する practice the *piano*. ●ピアノを教える[習う] (個人的に) give [take] *piano* lessons; (学校などで) teach [learn] *piano*.
●ピアノ演奏会 a piáno recital. ●ピアノ協奏曲 a piáno concèrto. ●ピアノ曲 a piáno pìece. ●ピアノ線 (a) piáno wire. ●ピアノソナタ a piáno sonàta.
ひあぶり 火炙り ▶彼女は見せしめのために火あぶりにされた She *was burned at the stake* as a warning to others.
ヒアリング【聴解】listening;【公聴会】a (public) hearing.
●ヒアリングテスト a lístening comprehènsion tèst. (❗a hearing test は「聴力検査」の意)
ひあんだ 被安打【野球】a hit allowed. ●7 回を投げて被安打 4 である allow four hits in seven innings.

ひいー 曽- ●ひいおじいさん one's *great*-grandfather. ●ひいおばあさん one's *great*-grandmother. ●ひい孫 a *great*-grandchild. (⇨曾(ソウ)孫)

ピーアール 名 [広報] public relations (略 PR, P.R.) (単数扱い); [宣伝] [広報的な] publicity; (実売目的な) advertisement. (⇨宣伝) ●ピーアール用パンフレット a *promotional* brochure. ●大いにピーアールになる get a lot of *publicity*.
— **ピーアールする** 動 publicize; advertise. (⇨宣伝する)
●ピーアール活動 a publicity campaign; (販売促進活動) (a) promotion.

ピーイーティー [ポリエチレンテレフタレート] PET. (⇨ペットボトル)

ピーエイチディー Ph.D. (*Doctor of Philosophy* の略) (⇨博士)

ビーエス [放送衛星] BS (*broadcasting satellite* の略).

ピーエス [手紙の追伸] PS, P.S. (*postscript* の略).

ビーエスイー [牛海綿状脳症, 狂牛病] BSE (*bovine spongiform encephalopathy* の略).

ピーエム [午後] p.m., P.M. [ラテン語 *post meridiem* (=afternoon) の略]. (用法は (⇨午前))

ピーエルオー [パレスチナ解放機構] PLO (*Palestine Liberation Organization* の略).

ピーエルほう PL法 [製造物責任法] the Product Liability Law.

ビーカー a beaker.

ひいき 晶屓 名 [愛顧] favor (「えこひいき」の意もあ る); [店などへの] patronage /pǽtrənɪdʒ/. ●ひいきの政治家 a *pro*-Japanese politician. ●彼は大のカラヤンびいきだった He was a big fan of (Herbert von) Karajan. ●その店をひいきにする *patronize* the store; (常連客である) *be a regular customer* [[書] *a patron*] *of* the store. ▶当店をごひいきにしていただきありがとうございます Thank you for your *patronage* of our store. ▶彼はこの旅館をひいきにしている (気に入った) This inn is his *favorite*./(常宿だ) This is his *regular* inn.
●**ひいき目に見る** ▶彼はいくらひいき目に見ても(=せいぜい)二流の物書きです He is *at (the) best* a second-rate writer. at (the) best は文頭・文尾でも用いられる.
●**ひいきの引き倒し** (ひいきをしすぎるとかえってその人を不利にする) If you give too much favor to 〈him〉, it will do 〈him〉 more harm than good.
— **ひいきの** 形 favorite. ▶ごひいきの歌舞伎役者はだれですか Who is your *favorite kabuki* actor?
— **ひいきする** 動 favor. (⇨えこひいき) ●弱い者をひいきする *favor* the underdog.

ひいく 肥育 名 fattening.
— **肥育する** 動 ●豚を肥育する *fatten* pigs 〈*up*〉.

ピーク [頂点, 最高の状態] a peak; the highest level [condition, point]. ●ピーク時 (最高時) a [the] *peak* hour [time, period]. ●ピークを越える pass a *peak*. ▶朝のラッシュアワーのとき混雑はピークに達する Congestion reaches a *peak* during the morning rush hours.

ビーグル [動物] a beagle. (参考) 小型の猟犬)

ピーケー a PK (*penalty kick* の略). ●PKを献上する gift [present] a *penalty*.
●ピーケー戦 (PK戦) a penalty shoot-out.

ピーケーエフ [国連平和維持軍] PKF (a (United Nations) *Peacekeeping Force* の略).

ピーケーオー [国連平和維持活動] PKO ((United Nations) *Peacekeeping Operations* の略).

ビーコン (信号灯) a beacon. ●ラジオビーコン (無線標識) a radio *beacon*.

ビーシー B.C., B.C. (*Before Christ* の略). (⇨エーディー)

ビージーエム background music; (和製語) BGM.

ビーシージー [医学] BCG (vaccine) (*Bacillus Calmette-Guérin* の略)

ピーシービー [ポリ塩化ビフェニール] PCB (*polychlorinated biphenyl* の略).

びいしき 美意識 a sense of beauty; an esthetic sense.

ヒース [植物] a heath(er) /hi:θ, héðər/; (ヒースの茂る野原) a heath.

ビーズ a bead. ●一連のビーズ a string of *beads*.
●ビーズのバッグ a *beaded* [×a bead] bag.
●ビーズ細工[飾り] beading; beadwork.

ピース [セットの中の1品] a piece. ●6ピース1セットのスプーン a set of spoons containing 6 *pieces*; a 6-spoon set.

ひいずるくに 日出ずる国 [日本の美称] the land of the Rising Sun.

ヒースロー ●ヒースロー空港 Heathrow Airport.

ヒーター a heater. (⇨ストーブ) ●オイルヒーター a kerosene (米) [a paraffin (英)] *heater*.

ビーだま ビー玉 a marble.

ビーチ ●ビーチパラソル a beach umbrella; (和製語) a beach parasol. ●ビーチバレー beach volleyball.
●ビーチボール a beach ball.

ひいちにちと 日一日と (⇨日 [成句])

ピーティーエー a PTA (a Parent-Teacher Association の略). ●PTAの会合 a *PTA* president [meeting]. ▶PTAはどんな活動をしていますか What activities is the *PTA* involved in?
●PTA会長 a PTA president.

ピーティーエスディー [心的外傷後ストレス障害] [医学] PTSD (*post-traumatic stress disorder* の略).

ひいては (同様に) as well. ▶核兵器廃絶はその国のためひいては世界平和のためになる The abolition of nuclear weapons does good to the country and the peace of the world *as well*.

ひいでる 秀でる [書] excel 〈*in, at*〉; be very good 〈*at*〉; [勝る] [書] surpáss. (⇨優れる) ●英語で他に秀でる *excel* [*surpass*] the others *in* English. ●一芸に秀でる be (a) *master* of an art.

ビート [拍子, 強拍音] a beat. ●強烈なビートのロックrock music with a strong [a powerful] *beat*.
●ビート族 (1人) a beatnik; (全体) the beat generation. ●ビート板 a kickboard; (米) a flutterboard; (英) a float.

ビート [甜菜] [植物] (a) beet.

ピート [泥炭] peat.
●ピートモス peat moss.

ヒートアイランド [大都市の高温域現象] a heat island (⇔cool island).

ヒートアップ ▶最近この分野での競争がヒートアップしている Competition *is heating up* in this field these days.

ヒートショック (a) heat shock. (参考) 急激な温度変化が体に及ぼす影響)

ヒートポンプ [熱ポンプ] a heat pump.

ビートルズ [英国のロックグループ] the Beatles.

ビーナス Venus. ●ミロのビーナス the *Venus* of Milo.

ビーナスのたんじょう 『ビーナスの誕生』(イタリア語名) *Nascita di Venere*; (英語名) *The Birth of Venus*. (参考) ボッティチェリ作の絵画)

ピーナ(ッ)ツ peanut. ●ピーナツの殻を割る crack open a *peanut*.
●ピーナツバター peanut butter.

ビーバー [動物] a beaver; (毛皮) beaver.

ひいひい ●(苦しくて)ひいひい言う shriek 〈in pain〉; (悲

鳴を上げる) scream [cry out] 《in terror [with pain]》(⇨悲鳴).

ぴいぴい ● ぴいぴい鳴らす whistle (! 口笛またはそれに似た音を出す); pipe (! 筒状の笛の音を出す). ▶ひな鳥が母鳥を求めてぴいぴい鳴いた The chicks *cheeped* after their mother. (! 鳥が普通さえずる声は chirp でよい) ● 彼のラジオがぴいぴい雑音を立てた His radio set *made a squeaking noise*. ● 彼は金がなくぴいぴいしている He is *very hard up*.

ピーピーエム 〖百万分率〗ppm; PPM 《*parts per million* の略》.

ビーフ 〖牛肉〗beef. ▶ビーフ2切れください Two *beefs*, please. (! 注文するときなど two pieces of beef より普通)
● ビーフシチュー beef stew. ● ビーフジャーキー (beef) jerky. ● ビーフステーキ a beefsteak. (! 料理名は U) ● ビーフストロガノフ beef stroganoff.

ビーフン 〖<中国語〗〖米粉〗rice vermicelli /vɜːrmɪtʃéli/; fine rice noodles.

ピーマン 〖<フランス語〗〖植物〗a green [a sweet] pepper, 《米》a bell pepper, a pimento [a pimiento] 《複 〜s》.

ビーム a beam.
● ビームアンテナ a beam antenna.

ひいらぎ 柊 〖植物〗a holly.

ヒール a heel. ▶ヒールの高い[低い]靴をはいている She wears [is wearing] high [low] *heels*.

＊ビール 〖<オランダ語〗beer /bíər/. (! 種類をいうときは C)

> 解説 ビールといえば通例 **lager** (beer) をいうが, これ以外にホップ味の強い **ale**, 黒ビールの **porter**, これよりさらに強い黒ビール **stout**, 苦みの強い **bitter** など多くの種類がある. ×dry (beer) は和製英語.

● 生ビール draft beer. ● びん[缶]入りのビール bottled [canned] beer. ● 冷やしたビール cold beer. ● 気の抜けたビール stale [flat] beer. ● 新種のビール a new (type of) beer, new beers) ● ビール1杯 a glass of beer; (ジョッキ1杯) a mug of beer. ● ビール作り beer making (書) brewing. ● 生ビールとラガーとどちらがいいですか Which *beer* do you prefer, draft or lager? ● ビールを2杯ください Two *beers*, please./Could I have two *beers*? (! 飲食店で注文する場合は two glasses [mugs] of beer とあまりいわない. また I'll have a Bud, please. (バドワイザー (Budweiser) をお願いします) のように銘柄を指定することもある) ● ビールはドイツの国民的飲料だ Beer is the national drink of Germany.
● ビール腹 (腹, 人)〖話〗a béer bélly (gùt); a potbelly. ● ビールびん a béer bòttle.

ヒールアウト ―― **ヒールアウトする** 動 〖ラグビー〗heel out.

ビールス a virus /váiərəs/. (⇨ウイルス)

ひいれ 火入れ 〖溶鉱炉などの〗initial kindling; (原子炉の) igniting, 〖加熱〗heating; 〖野焼き〗burning the weeds in the field.
● 火入れ式 a lighting [an igniting] cèremony.

ヒーロー 〖英雄〗a hero /híː(ː)rou/. (複 〜es).
● ヒーローインタビュー (スポーツ) a post-game interview; (和製語) a hero interview.

ビーンボール 〖野球〗a béan bàll. ● ビーンボール合戦 a *beanball* war. ● ビーンボール乱闘 a bean brawl. ● バッターにビーンボールを投げる throw a bean a batter. ● 身をかがめてビーンボールをよける duck a bean ball.

ひうちいし 火打ち石 《strike》(a) flint.

ひうん 非運, 否運 〖運の悪いこと〗bad luck, (a) misfortune. (⇨⇨不運)

ひうん 悲運 (悲しい運命) a sad [tragic] fate. ● 悲運の英雄 an ill-fated [(悲劇的な) a tragic] hero.

ひえ 稗 〖植物〗Japanese millet; barnyard grass.

ひえいせい 非衛生 insanitation. (⇨不衛生)

ひえいり 非営利 ―― **非営利の** 形 《米》nonprofit. 《英》nonprofit-making. (! それぞれ non-profit, non-profit-making ともつづる)
● 非営利企業 a nonprofit business. ● 非営利事業 a nonprofit undertaking. ● 非営利団体 《米》a nonprofit organization, 《英》a non-profit-making organization (略 NPO).

ひえき 裨益 (役に立つこと) help; usefulness; (利益) benefit; (寄与) (a) contribution.

ひえきる 冷え切る ❶ [体や食べ物が] be chilled to the bone. (⇨冷える) ▶スープは冷え切っていた My soup *has got completely cold*.
❷ [愛情が] ▶ 2 人の関係は冷え切って終わった Their relationship *has gone cold* and has ended.

ひえこむ 冷え込む ▶今夜はひどく冷え込みそうだ It's going to be *very cold* [It's going to *freeze*] tonight. ● あすは一段と冷え込むでしょう It will *get much colder* tomorrow.

ひえしょう 冷え性 ▶彼女は冷え性だ(=血液の巡りが悪い) She has (a) poor blood circulation.

ひえびえ 冷え冷え ▶今朝は冷え冷えする It's *chilly* this morning.

＊ひえる 冷える 〖冷たくなる〗get* [grow*, become*] cold; 〖冷やされる〗be chilled; be cooled; 〖冷たく[寒く]感じる〗feel* cold. ● よく冷えたビール *well-chilled* [*ice-cold*] beer. ▶今夜はよく冷える It's terribly *cold* [*chilly*] tonight. (⇨寒い) ● 体のしんまでひどり冷えてしまった I *was chilled* to the bone [marrow].

ピエロ 〖<フランス語〗〖道化師〗a clown. (! フランス語の pierrot /píːəróu/ より普通).

ヒエログリフ 〖象形文字〗a hieroglyph /háiərəglíf/.

びえん 鼻炎 (a) nasal inflammation, 〖医学〗rhinitis /raináitəs/.

ビエンチャン 〖ラオスの首都〗Vientiane /vjentjáːn/.

ビエンナーレ 〖<イタリア語〗a biennial /baiéniəl/ exhibition. (参考) 2 年に一度開催される美術展など.

ひおい 日覆い (⇨⇨ 日除け)

ひおうぎ 檜扇 〖植物〗a leopard flower.

ひおけ 火桶 (木製の小型火鉢) a small wooden (charcoal) brazier.

ビオトープ 〖特定の野生生物の生息区域〗a biotope /báiətoup/.

ひおどし 緋縅 ● 緋縅のよろい a *scarlet-threaded* suit of armor.

ビオラ 〖楽器〗a viola /vióulə/.

びおん 微温 ―― **微温の, 微温的な** 形 (生ぬるい) lukewarm; (手ぬるい) lax. ● 微温的な処置を取る take a *lukewarm* measure. ● 微温的な態度を取る take a *lax* attitude 《to, toward》.
● 微温湯 (ぬるゆ) lukewarm [tepid] water.

びおん 鼻音 〖言語〗a nasal (sound).
● 鼻音化母音 nasalized vowel.

ひか 皮下 ―― **皮下の** 形 〖医学〗subcutaneous /sʌ̀bkjuːtéiniəs/; hypodérmic.
● 皮下脂肪 subcutaneous fat. ● 皮下注射 a subcutaneous [a hypodermic] injection.

ひか 悲歌 an elegy.

ひが 彼我 (相手と自分) he and I; they and we. ▶彼我の戦力が伯仲している They are equal to *us* in

ぴか 美化 图 ●校内美化運動 a campus *clean-up* [*cleaning*] campaign.
—— **美化する** 動 (理想化する) idealize; (実際よりよく見せる) glorify; (掃除して) clean; (飾って) beautify. ●戦争を美化する *glorify* war.

***ひがい** 被害 [[物への害]] damage; [[人への精神的・肉体的な, 物への害]] harm; [[損失]] (a) loss. (⇨害, 損害)

① **[被害を]** ●被害を及ぼす do [cause] *damage* 《*to*》. ●被害を免れる escape *damage* 《*from*》; escape being damaged 《*by*》. ●その被害を最小限にとどめる minimize the *damage*. ●盗難にあって大きな被害を受ける suffer a great *loss from* a burglary. ●この地方は毎年台風が来るたびに大きな被害を受ける Every year when a typhoon comes, this district *suffers* a lot of [great, heavy] *damage*. (❗much damage ともいえるが ×many damages は不可. 後半は this district is badly damaged ともいえる) ●うちの家はその火事で被害を受けなかった Our house *wasn't damaged* [*harmed*] *by* the fire./The fire *did* no *damage* [*harm*] *to* our house.
会話 「衝突で車はどんな被害を受けましたか」「バンパーがひどく壊れました」 "What *damage* did the crash *do to* your car?" "The fender 《米》 [bumper 《英》] *was* badly *damaged*."

② **[被害が[は]]** ●被害が最もひどかった地域 the worst-*affected* [(人に対する被害) worst-*afflicted*] area. ●その地震による建物への被害は甚大だった The *damage* done to the buildings by the earthquake was extensive.
会話 「火事の被害(=損害額)はどのくらいでしたか」「2,000万円でした」 "How much did you lose in the fire?" "I lost 20 million yen."

●被害者 a victim; (死傷者) a casualty (❗通例複数形で). ●被害妄想 pàranóia; [[心理]] a persecution complex; (人) a paranoid. ●被害妄想になる get [become] páranòid.

ぴかいち ぴか— ——ぴか—の 形 far [by far, far and away] the best; top. (❗(by) far, far and away は最上級を強める) ●英語を話すことにかけては彼は学校でぴか—だ He is *by far the best* speaker of English in our school.

ひかえ 控え [[メモ]] a note (❗しばしば複数形で); [[写し]] a copy, a dúplicate. ●控えをとる (メモする) make a *note* 《*of*》; (写しを取る) make [take, (コピー機で) print, run off] a *copy* 《*of*》. ●控えの捕手 a backup catcher. ●控えの投手陣 a relief corps /kó:r/.
●控え室 a wáiting ròom. ●控え選手 a reserve player; a substitute. (⇨補欠) ●控え選手を出す put [insert] a *reserve* player in (a game).

ひかえめ 控え目 ——控え目な 形 [[度を越えない]] móderate; [[謙虚な]] modest. ●控えめな人 a *modest* [(感情を表に出さない) a reserved, (無駄なことは言わない) a discréet] person. ●控えめな要求をする make *moderate* [*modest*] demands. ●控えめの見積もりで at a *moderate* [a *conservative*] estimate. ●彼は態度がたいへん控えめだ He is very *modest* in his behavior.
—— **控えめに** 副 móderately; modestly. ●食べる eat *moderately*; (習慣として) be *moderate in* eating; (いつもより) eat less than usual. ●彼女は非常に控えめに自分のことを語った She spoke very *modestly* about herself. ●控えめに言っても君は無作法だったよ You were rude, *to say the least* [*to put it mildly*].

ひがえり 日帰り ●東京へ日帰り出張をする make *one day* business *trip* to Tokyo. ●日光は東京から日帰りできます From Tokyo you can *go to* Nikko *and come back in a day* [*on the same day*]. ●彼は息子と日帰りの予定で出かけています He's *away for the day* with his son.

***ひかえる** 控える ❶ **[抑制する]** (慎む) refrain 《*from*》; (判断などを差し控える) reserve; (体によくないものの量を減らす) cut* down 《*on*》; (度を越さない) be móderate 《*in*》. ●酒を控える *refrain from* (drinking) alcohol; *cut down on* drinking [alcohol]; *be moderate in* drinking; (飲み過ぎない) *do not drink too much*. ●判断を控える *reserve* [*stay*] judgment. ●コメントを控える *hold back* from giving one's comments. ●医者は当分外出を控えるように(=家にいるように)と言った The doctor advised me to *stay indoors* for the time being.
会話 「腕のいい建築家なのにどうして首にしたのですか」「そのことについて話すのは控えさせていただきたい」 "Why did you fire him? He's such a talented architect." "I'd *rather not talk about* it now."

❷ **[書き留める]** write* [put*]... down; (メモする) note... down. ●彼の住所を控えておく *write down* his address. ●その車のナンバーを控えておく *note down* [*make a note of*] the license number of the car.

❸ **[近くにある, 近くで待つ]** ●隣の部屋で控える(=待つ) *wait* in the next room. ●私たちはお正月を目前に控えてとても忙しい We are very busy *with* the New Year *close at hand* [*just before us*]. ●私の学校は北に海を控えている(=面している) My school *faces* the sea on the north. ●彼の背後にはある有力な政治家が控えている He *has* a certain influential politician *at his back* [*behind him*].
●彼はアメリカへの出発を2日後に控えている He *is leaving* for America in two days./(出発まであと2日ある) He has two days (left) until he starts for America. ●風邪を引かないようにね. 大事なコンサートを控えているのだから Be careful not to catch cold. You have a big concert *coming up*.

ひかがみ 膕 [[解剖]] (ひざの後ろのくぼんだところ) the hollow of the knee.

***ひかく** 比較 图 a compárison. ●彼の作品と彼女の作品では比較は(=比べ物)にならない There's no *comparison between* her work and his./His work *can't be compared with* [*can't be compared to*, (匹敵しない) *can't compare with*, *can't bear comparison with*] hers. (❗いずれも彼女の作品の方が断然優れていることを暗示)
—— **比較の** 副 comparatively; relatively. ●この店は比較的安い This store is *comparatively* [*relatively*] cheap.
—— **比較する** 動 compare 《A *with* [*to*] B》 (❗to は特に受身で好まれる); [[対比・対照する]] contrást 《A *with* [*and*] B》. (⇨比べる) ●その二つを比較する *compare* [*make a comparison between*, *contrast*] the two. ●都会生活と田舎の生活を比較する *compare* city life *with* [*to*] country life. ●私は何事にせよ彼と比較されるのは好きではない I don't like to *be compared to* [*with*] him *in* anything. ●トムと比較するとボブの方が客観的だ (*As*) *compared with* [*to*] Tom, Bob is more objective. (❗(1) as は通例省略される. (2) ×*Comparing with* [*to*] Tom, ... は不可) / *In* [*By*] *comparison with* Tom, Bob is more objective.
●比較級 [[文法]] the comparative (degree). ●比較研究 a comparative study. ●比較言語学

ひかれもの 引かれ者 (刑場に引かれていく罪人) a criminal dragged to prison [an execution ground].
- **引かれ者の小唄** (負け惜しみ) sour grapes; (強がり) a bluff.

ひかれる 引かれる 〖心引かれる〗be attracted 《by》(❗状態をいう場合は ... 《to》); 〖魅せられる〗be fascinated 《た eitid》/《by, with》, be charmed 《by, with》. (⇨魅了, 引く❹)

ひがわり 日替わり ● 日替わりのランチメニュー today's special lunch menu. ● 日替わり目玉商品 special bargain items today [of the day].
- **日替わり定食** a special set meal whose menu changes from day to day.

***ひかん 悲観** 图 péssimism; 〖失望〗disappointment.
　　―**悲観的な** 形 pessimístic; (希望の持てない) gloomy. ▶結果についてそんなに悲観的になるな Don't be so *pessimistic* [×feel so gloomy] *about* the results.
　　―**悲観する** 動 be pessimistic [feel gloomy] 《about》; take a pessimistic view 《of》; (がっかりする) be disappointed 《about, at》.
- **悲観論[主義]** péssimism. ● 悲観論[主義]者 a pessimist.

ひかん 避寒 ● 避寒のために in order to avoid the cold.
- **避寒地** a winter resórt. (❗「冬の行楽地」の意もある)

ひがん 彼岸 the equinoctial week. ● 彼岸の入り the beginning of the *equinoctial week*. ● 彼岸の中日 the equinox (day). (⇨春分, 秋分) ● 暑さ寒さも彼岸まで (⇨暑さ[成句])
- **彼岸桜** a cherry tree which blossoms around the spring equinoctial week.

ひがん 悲願 ● 悲願を達成する realize [fulfill] *one's long-cherished wish* [*desire*] (*to* do).

びかん 美観 a fine [a beautiful] sight. ● 美観を添える add to the *beauty* 《of》. ● 街の美観をそこなう spoil the *beauty* 〖(外観) *appearance*〗of the streets.

びがんじゅつ 美顔術 a facial; (a) beauty treatment. (❗後の方はパーマなども含む) ▶月に1回美顔術をしてもらっている I get a *facial* once a month.

ひがんすぎまで『彼岸過迄』 *To The Spring Equinox And Beyond*. (参考 夏目漱石の小説)

ひがんばな 彼岸花 〖植物〗a cluster-amaryllis.

ひき 引き 〖力添え〗(引き立て) favor; (縁故・コネ) connections, (話) a pull; 〖引っぱること〗(a) pull; (魚つりの) a bite, (強い引き) a tug. ● 社長の引きで課長になる be promoted chief of the section by the president's *favor* [through the president's *pull*]. ▶(釣りで)引きが強い There's a strong *pull* [a good *pull*] on the line./I can feel a (strong) *tug*.

ひき 悲喜 ● **悲喜こもごも** ▶私にとっては悲喜こもごもの一年だった I've experienced both *happy and sad* events this year./I've had both happy and sad experiences this year. ▶結果については悲喜こもごも(=悲しみと喜びが入りまざった気持ち)というところだ I have *mixed feelings of* happiness and sadness about the result.

-ひき 一匹 ● 5匹の猫 five cats. ● 数百匹の豚 several hundred pigs.

ひぎ 秘技 a special technique.

ひぎ 秘儀 (秘密の儀式) a secret ceremony.

-びき -引き ● 5パーセント引きで at a five percent *reduction* [*discount*]. (⇨割引)

ひきあい 引き合い ▶その製品に関して外国より引っ合い(=問い合わせ)があった We've received several *inquiries about* the product from abroad.
- **引き合いに出す** (言及する) mention; refer [make reference] to ...; (引用する) quote; cite. (⇨引用)
- キーツの1節を引き合いに出す *quote* a passage *from* Keats.

ひきあう 引き合う ❶〖引っ張り合う〗pull (a thing) against each other; (引きつける) attract each other. (⇨引く)
　　❷〖元が取れる〗pay*. ▶この取り引きは引き合わない This business doesn't *pay*. (❗「引き合う[合わない]取り引き」は paying [unprofitable] business) ▶値引きすると引き合わない It won't *pay* (us) to reduce the price.

ひきあげ 引き上げ, 引き揚げ 〖物価・賃金などの〗a rise (❗賃金の場合は《米》a raise, 《英》a rise); an increase, 《米話》a hike; 〖難破船の〗salvage.
- 石油価格の25パーセントの引き上げ a 25 percent *rise* in the price of oil. ▶彼は社長に5パーセントの賃金の引き上げを求めた He asked his boss for a 5 percent wage *raise* 《米》[*rise* 《英》]./He asked his boss to raise his salary by 5 percent.

ひきあげる 引き上げる, 引き揚げる
　　❶〖引っ張り上げる〗pull ... (up), draw* ... (up); 〖水準・賃金などを〗raise, 《米》hike; 〖沈没船を〗float, salvage (a sunken ship). ● おぼれている人を川から引き上げる *pull* [*draw*] (*up*) a drowning person *from* the river. ● (リールで)魚を引き上げる *reel in* a fish.
　　❷〖元の所へ戻る〗(立ち去る) leave*; (国・郷里へ帰る) return, go* back; (退却する) retreat 《from》; (撤退する) withdraw* 《from》; 〖本国へ送還される〗be repatriated 《from》▶彼は戦後中国から引き揚げてきた He returned [*was repatriated*] *from* China after the war.
　　❸〖取り戻す〗(投資した)資金を引き揚げる *pull out* the funding.

ひきあて 引き当て (抵当) (a) mortgage; (a) security.

ひきあてきん 引き当て金 an allowance; a reserve; a provision. ● 貸し倒れ引き当て金 an allowance [a reserve, a provision] for loan [credit] losses.

ひきあてる 引き当てる ❶〖くじを〗draw. ● くじで特賞を引き当てる *draw* (*获得する*) *win*] a special prize in a lottery.
　　❷〖当てはめる〗(⇨比べる) ▶我が身に引き当てて考えてくれよ Put yourself *in* my *position* [《話》*shoes*].

ひきあみ 引き網 a seine. ● 引き網漁をする *seine*; fish with a *seine*.

ひきあわせる 引き合わせる 〖紹介する〗introduce 《him to her》; (おぜん立てをする) arrange 《for them to meet》; (知り合わせる) bring* 《them》together; 〖照合する〗check 《A *with* [*against*] B》; (比べる) compare 《A *with* B》.

***ひきいる 率いる** 〖連れて行く〗take*; 〖指揮・統率する〗lead*; (楽団を) conduct, 《米》lead; (軍隊を) be in command of .... ● 青木大将に率いられた軍隊 an army *under the command of* [*commanded by, led by*] General Aoki.

ひきいれる 引き入れる ❶〖引いて中へ入れる〗pull 《into》; (ゆっくり, 滑らかに) draw 《into》. ● カートを電車に引き入れる *draw* a cart *into* a train. ▶彼は私を自分の家へ引き入れた He *pulled* me *into* his house.
　　❷〖誘い入れる〗win ... over 《to》. ▶彼は友人を味方に引き入れたがっている He wants to *win* his friend *over to* his side.

ひきうけ　引き受け　(仕事・責任などの) undertaking; (任務などの) (an) assumption; (地位・手形などの) acceptance; (株式・社債などの) underwriting.
● 引き受け業者 an accépting hòuse; an accéptor; an underwriter; an undertaker. ● 引き受け業務 únderwriting bùsiness. ● 引き受け銀行 an underwriting bànk. ● 引き受け契約 an underwriting còntract [agrèement]. ● 引き受け渡し documents against acceptance 《略 D/A》.

ひきうける　引き受ける ❶ 【受け入れる】(仕事・責任など を) take*, take ... on, 《書》undertake*; (任務など を) assume; (地位などを受諾する) accept. ● 重い責任を引き受ける take [assume, accept] heavy responsibility (for). ● その地位[注文]を引き受ける accept the position [order]. ▶これ以上仕事を引き受けられない I can't take on any more work [take any more work on (myself)]. ▶鳥にえさをやるのはぼくが引き受けよう I'll take it on myself to feed the birds./I'll feed the birds. ▶彼は議長役を引き受けた He took on [assumed] the role of chairman.
❷【世話をする】take* care of ...; (管理・管理を引き受ける) take charge of .... ● 彼の弁護を引き受ける (担当する) take charge of his defense. ▶おばが子供たちの世話を引き受けてくれることになった My aunt agreed to take care of [look after] my children.
❸【保証する】guarantée. ● 彼の借金の返済を引き受ける guarantee the payment of his debts; guarantee to pay his debts.

ひきうす　碾き臼　a hand mill; a quern.
ひきうつし　引き写し　【物】a copy, a trace; 【行為】copying, tracing. (⇒敷き写し)
ひきうつす　引き写す　copy ... (out [down]); (図面などを) trace. (⇒写す❶)
ひきうり　挽き売り　sales of ground merchandize.
***ひきおこす　引き起こす**　cause; (...に通じる) lead* to ...; (もたらす) bring*... about; (誘発する) induce. ▶その事故は欠陥ブレーキによって引き起こされた The accident was caused by faulty brakes.
ひきおとす　引き落とす ❶【送金する】charge 《100,000 yen》to one's 《bank》account. ● 引き落とされている be paid from [be charged to] one's 《bank》account.
❷【相撲で】pull (one's opponent) down.
ひきおろす　引き下ろす ❶【上から下へ】pull [(引きずって) drag (-gg-)] ... down; (降ろす) lower. (⇒下ろす❶❹) ❷【預金を】draw*... out. (⇒下ろす❹, 引き出す)
ひきかえ　引き換え　...と引き換えに in exchange for .... (⇒交換) ● 品物を代金引き換え渡しで注文する order goods C.O.D. (❕C.O.D. は cash [《米》collect] on delivery の略) ● 彼の愛と引き換えに何もかも捨てる give up everything else for his love. ▶彼らは人質と引き換えに大金を要求してきた They demanded a lot of money in exchange for hostages.
● 引き換え券 (手荷物などの) a cláim tàg [ticket]; (景品などの) a coupon.
***ひきかえす　引き返す**　(方向を変えて) turn back; 【帰って来る・行く】come* [go*] back; 【戻る】return; (船などが) put* back (to port). ● 途中から引き返す turn back halfway. ▶来た道を[出発点へ]引き返そう Let's go back the way we came [to where we started]. ▶もう引き返すこと(=後戻り)はできない There is no turning back. (❕慣用表現)
ひきかえ(て)　引き替え(て)　(...は反対に) on the contrary; (その代わりに) instead; (その一方で) on the other hand. (⇒反対に❷) ▶姉に引き替え(=と較べて)彼女はとても親切だ She is really kind compared with [to] her big sister. ▶彼女は背が高い。それに引き替え(=一方)息子は低い He is tall, while [but on the other hand,《書》whereas] his son is short. (⇒一方, 逆)

ひきかえる　引き換える, 引き替える　【交換する】exchange (for). ● 当たり券と賞品を引き換える exchange a prize for a winning ticket.
ひきがえる　蟇蛙　【動物】a toad.
ひきがたり　弾き語り　ピアノの弾き語りをする sing to one's own accompaniment on the piano [to one's own piano accompaniment].
ひきがね　引き金　a trigger. (❕比喩的には「過激かつ急激な行為の原因」の意) ● 引き金に指をかけている have one's finger on the trigger. ● 引き金を引く pull [squeeze] the trigger. ▶彼の暗殺が戦争の引き金となった His assassination triggered (off) the war.
ひきぎわ　引き際　男は引き際(=仕事を辞める時期)が大切だ A man must know when to quit [retire from] his job.
ひきげき　悲喜劇　a tragicomedy.
ひきこみせん　引き込み線　(鉄道の) a (railroad) siding, 《米》a sidetrack; (電気・電話などの) an incoming line; (アンテナなどの) a lead-in.
ひきこむ　引き込む　【中に引き入れる】draw* (導いて) lead*]... in (❕引き込んだ場所を示す時は into ...); 【魅力で引きつける】attráct; (魅了する) fascinate /fǽsənèit/; 【仲間に入れる】(⇒引きずり込む).
ひきこもり　引き籠もり　(事) hikikomori, withdrawing from society; (人) a hikikomori sufferer. ▶近年引きこもりの生徒が増えてきた More and more students are suffering from social withdrawal in recent years.
ひきこもる　引き籠もる　● 田舎に引きこもる retire to the country. ● 書斎に引きこもる shut oneself up in one's study. ▶彼は1日中家に引きこもっていた He kept indoors [stayed in, kept in] all day. ▶彼はクリスマス以来風邪で引きこんでいる (寝込んでいる) He has been laid up [(不本意ながら床から離れられない) been confined to bed] with a cold since Christmas.
ひきころす　轢き殺す　▶彼女は犬をひき殺してしまった She ran over [down] a dog and killed it.
ひきさがる　引き下がる　(退く) withdraw* (into one's room). ▶彼は強い反対にあい引き下がらざるをえなかった He had to back down [off] in the face of strong opposition. (❕しぶしぶ対案に賛成したことを暗示) ▶こんなに侮辱されておめおめと引き下がれない I can't [won't] take this insult lying down. (❕ take ... lying down は「甘んじて受ける」の意. 通例否定文で用いる)
ひきさく　引き裂く　(紙などを) tear*... (up), (ぐいと強く) rip (-pp-) ... (up); (人と人を) separate (⇒裂く); (統一集団を) tear ... apart. (❕通例受身で) ● 手紙をずたずたに引き裂く tear [rip] up a letter.
ひきさげ　引き下げ　価格引き下げ a price cut [reduction]; a cut [reduction] in price.
ひきさげる　引き下げる　【価格・率などを】bring*... down, lower (↔raise); 【賃金・価格などを削減する】cut*... (down), reduce. ● 品物の値段を引き下げる bring down [lower, reduce] the price of the goods. ● 彼の賃金を500円引き下げる cut (down) [reduce] his wages by 500 yen.
ひきざん　引き算　图 subtraction (↔addition).
── 引き算をする 動 subtráct. (⇒引く❽)
ひきしお　引き潮　the ebb (tide). (⇒潮) ● 引き潮に乗って沖へ運ばれる float away on the ebb. ● 引き潮

ひきしぼる 引き絞る 〔弓を〕draw a bow to the full; 〔強く絞る〕pull 《a rope》tight; 〔声を〕strain one's voice.

ひきしまる 引き締まる ●引き締まった体 a firm [a well-knit, (小さいながらも) a compact] body. ●引き締まった顔つき firm features. ●身の引き締まった肉 firm meat. ●口元の引き締まるような朝の空気 the bracing [crisp] morning air. ▶これから引き受ける責務の重さに身の引き締まる思いです I'm bracing myself for the great responsibilities I'm about to assume.

ひきしめ 引き締め tightening; restraint. ●金融引き締め政策を続行する maintain a tight money policy.

ひきしめる 引き締める 〔ロープ・予算などを〕tighten ... (up), 〔気を〕straighten oneself up; (えりを正す) shape up. ●手綱[金融]を引き締める tighten the reins [the money market] (■前の方は比喩的にも用いる). ●口元を引き締める tighten [compress] one's lips. ▶私は職員室に入る前に気を引き締めた I straightened myself up before entering the teachers' room.

ひしゃ 被疑者 (容疑者) a súspect.

ひきずりおろす 引きずり下ろす, 引きずり降ろす pull [drag] ... down. ●知事の座から引きずり降ろされる be forced to step down from the governorship. ▶彼の巨大な像は怒り狂った民衆によってロープを使って引きずり降ろされた His huge statue was pulled to the ground by angry citizens using rope.

ひきずりこむ 引きずり込む pull [(無理やり) drag (-gg-), (誘うように) draw*] ... in. (■引きずり込む場所を表すときは into ...) ●戦争に引きずり込まれる be drawn into [get involved in] the war.

ひきずりだす 引きずり出す pull [(無理やり) drag (-gg-), (誘うように) draw*] ... out. (■どこから引きずり出すのかを表すときは out of ...)

ひきずりまわす 引きずり回す pull [(無理やり) drag (-gg-)] ... around [about]. ●東京の名所めぐりに友人を引きずり回す take one's friend around [all over] Tokyo to see the sights.

ひきずる 引きずる 〔重い物を〕drag (-gg-); 〔軽い物・服のすそなどを〕trail; 〔服のすそなどが〕trail, drag 《on》. ●引きずる上げる pull [drag] ... up. ●長いスカートを引きずる trail one's long skirt. ▶彼は右足を引きずって歩いた He walked, dragging his right foot. ▶犬が皮ひもを引きずってあてもなく歩道をうろついていた A dog was wandering aimlessly on the sidewalk with its leash trailing behind it. ▶彼はやってしまった失敗をいつまでも引きずっている(=とりつかれている) He's always being haunted by his past failures.

ひきぞめ 弾き初め the New Year's first playing (of a musical instrument); (説明的に) the act of playing a musical instrument at the beginning of the New Year.

ひきたおす 引き倒す ●柱に綱をかけて引き倒す pull a rope down with a rope.

***ひきだし** 引き出し ❶〔机などの〕a drawer. ●引き出し一杯の書類 a drawerful of papers. ●引き出しの奥にいた the back of a drawer. ●引き出しを開ける open [pull open] a drawer. ●引き出しを閉める shut [close, push in] a drawer. ●引き出しをかき回す go [rummage] through a drawer.
❷〔預金などの〕(a) withdrawal. (⇒引き出す)

ひきだす 引き出す pull 《out of, from》, draw* 《out of, from》; (預金などを) withdraw* 《from》. ●銀行から金を引き出す draw [withdraw] one's money from the bank. ●これらの資料からその結論を引き出す draw 〚pull〛 the conclusion from these data. ▶コンピュータは一瞬のうちにその大学についての全情報を引き出す The computer pulls [takes] out all information about the university in a moment. ▶彼のいいところを引き出すようにしなさい Try to bring out the best in him.

ひきたつ 引き立つ ❶〔よりよく見える〕look better [finer, nicer]. ▶そのブローチをつけると彼女のドレスが引き立った Her dress looked better with the brooch. ▶その黒いドレスで彼女の白い肌は引き立った The black dress set off her fair skin. (■set ... off は「対照によってひき立てる」の意)
❷〔元気づく〕cheer up. ▶朗報で彼の気持ちは引き立った He cheered up at the good news./The good news cheered him up.

ひきたて 引き立て (引き立てる物・人) a foil 《for》; (愛顧) favor; (商店などのひいき) pátronage; (推薦) recommendation. ▶彼女は美しい姉の引き立て役だった She acted a good foil to her beautiful sister./She made her beautiful sister look even better. ▶一層の引き立てをお願いします I hope we may receive further favor. ▶毎度お引き立てありがとうございます (店主などが) Thank you for your patronage.

ひきたてる 引き立てる ❶〔よく見せる〕set* ... off. ▶額縁がその絵を引き立てている The frame sets off the picture./The frame makes the picture look better./The frame is a foil to the picture. (■a foil は「引き立てる物」の意)
❷〔鼓舞する〕(気を) cheer ... up. ▶その言葉は私の気を引き立てた The words cheered me up.
❸〔目をかける〕favor; (得意先となる) patronize (⇒引き立つ, ひいき); (支援する) back 《him》 up.

ひきちがい 引き違い ●引き違い戸 a double sliding door. ●引き違い窓 a double sliding window.

ひきちぎる 引きちぎる (物を) tear* ... off [out]. ●その雑誌の写真を引きちぎる tear a photo out of the magazine.

ひきちゃ 挽き茶 (抹茶) powdered green tea.

ひきつぎ 引き継ぎ (引き継ぐ) ●転勤の事に引き継ぎをした As I was going to be transferred, I explained to my successor all about the job.

ひきつぐ 引き継ぐ 〔人から〕take* 《his duties》 over 《from》; 〔人に〕hand 《one's duties》 over 《to》. ▶私は父からその仕事を引き継いだ I took the business over from my father./I carried on my father's business.

ひきつけ 引き付け ●引きつけを起こす have a convulsive fit; go into [have, suffer] convulsions.

ひきつける 引き付ける (磁力などが物を) attract; (人を魅了する) attract, charm; (人の心に訴える) appeal 《to》. ●人を引きつける人 (魅力的な人) an attractive [a charming] person. ●磁石は鉄を引きつける A magnet attracts [has attraction for] iron. ▶彼女の微笑に引きつけられた I was attracted [was charmed] by her smile. ▶この絵は私の心をとても引きつけた The painting appealed to me enormously.

ひきつづき 引き続き ●引き続き同じクラスを担任する continue to be in charge of the same class. ▶総会に引き続き分科会があった Section meetings followed the general meeting. ▶彼はちょっと一息つき、それから引き続き話を続けた He paused for a moment, and then went on to tell his story [continued to tell the story, went on with his story]. (⇒続ける)

ひきつづく 引き続く continue (⇨引き続き, 続く) ●引き続くインフレ a continuing [a long-drawn] inflation. ▶母が死に, 引き続くように父もこの世を去った My mother died, and *soon after that* my father followed her.
ひきづり 引き釣り (トローリング) trawling.
ひきつる 引きつる (筋肉が) get* (a) cramp (⇨痙攣(ﾘｬｸ)); (顔などが) twitch. ▶足の方にひきつった *get (a) cramp* in one's leg. ▶彼の顔は怒りで引きつった His face *twitched* [*worked fiercely*] with rage. ▶最後の方が急激で恐ろしい表情の変化を活写

ひきつれる 引き連れる ●子供を引き連れて遊園地へ行く *take* one's children *to* the amusement park.
ひきて 引き手 a handle; a pull; (ドアの) a knob; (戸などの) a catch.
ひきて 弾き手 a player; a performer. ●ピアノの弾き手 a piano *player*.
ひきでもの 引き出物 a present [a gift] (given to guests at a banquet).
ひきど 引き戸 a sliding door. ▶引き戸をぴしゃんと閉めた I slammed the *sliding door* shut.
ひきとめる 引き止める (-pp-); keep*; (行かせない) (やや書) detain. (⇨止(ﾄ)める ❹) ●あなたが本当に行きたいのならこれ以上引き止めません I won't *stop* [*keep*] you any longer if you really want to go. ▶どうか引き止めないでください Please don't *stop* me. /(行かせてください) Please let me go.
ひきとり 引き取り (⇨引き取る)
●引き取り手 (人の) a caretaker; (落とし物の) a claimant. ▶ぼくの古いカメラの引き取り手は現れなかった Nobody wanted (to have) my old camera.

ひきとる 引き取る ❶ [返してもらう] take... back. ●(店などが)不良品[欠陥商品]を引き取る *take back* defective [faulty] articles.
❷ [受け入れる] take*... in; [世話をする] take care of…. ▶彼女はその男の子を引き取って育てた She *took* the boy *in* and brought him up.
❸ [立ち去る] leave*; (出て行く) get* out (*of*).
❹ [息を] [書・婉曲的] breathe one's last; (死ぬ) die (〜d; dying), (婉曲的) pass away.
ビギナー [初心者] a beginner.
●ビギナーズラック [賭け事などで初心者が得る幸運] beginner's luck.
ひきなおす 引き直す (改めて引く) draw (a line) over again, redraw (a line); (風邪を) catch (a) cold again.
ビキニ [水着] a bikini. ●ビキニを着た女性 a woman in a *bikini*.
ビキニ [地名] ビキニ(環礁) Bikini /biki:ni/.
ひきにく 挽き肉 minced [(主に米) ground] meat.
ひきにげ 轢き逃げ a hit and run. ●ひき逃げした車[運転手] a hit-and-run car [driver]. ●ひき逃げされる be involved in [a victim of] a hit-and-run accident.
ひきぬき 引き抜き [物の] pulling out; [人材の] headhunting; poaching. (⇨引き抜く)
ひきぬく 引き抜く ❶ [物を] pull... out; (草・木などを) pull... up; (雑草・木などを根ごと) uproot, root... up. (⇨抜く) ●雑草を引き抜く *pull-up* weeds.
❷ [人材を] poach; (主に有能な人を) headhunt.
▶たった一人川て育てた社員をライバル会社に引き抜かれた We *had* our newly trained employee *poached* by a rival company.

ひきのばす 引き伸ばす, 引き延ばす ❶ [物を] (写真を) enlarge, blow... up; (ゴムなどを) stretch; (金属などを) draw*... out, (たたいて) beat*... out. (⇨伸ばす ●) ●写真を引き伸ばしてもらう have a photo *enlarged* [*blown up*]

❷ [時間・期間を] (長引かせる) draw... out; (期間を延長する) extend, prolong; (遅らせる) delay; (保留する) put*... off, postpone. (⇨延ばす ❷, 延期する) ●会議を引き延ばす draw [drag] out the meeting. ▶会社を相手に訴訟を起こせば相手は上告を繰り返して公判を10年にも渡って引き延ばしかねない If we filed a suit against the company, they could *extend* [*stretch*] it over ten years with appeal after appeal.
ひきはがす 引き剥がす (引っ張って) pull... off; (引き裂いて) tear... off. ●壁からポスターをひきはがす *pull* [*tear*] a poster *off* (a wall).
ひきはなす 引き離す ❶ [分離する] pull... apart, separate, (⇨後の方が堅い語) ●彼は取っ組み合いのけんかをしている少年たちを引き離した He *pulled* the fighting boys *apart*./He *separated* the fighting boys.
❷ [差を広げる] (競争でリードを広げる) stretch the lead (*over*); (競走で差をあける) outdistance. ●彼は2位の走者を大きく引き離してゴールインした He crossed the finish far *ahead of* the runner-up.
ひきはらう 引き払う (去る) leave*; (引っ越す) move (out) (*from*); (立ち退く) (書) vacate.
ひきふね 引き船, 曳き船 a tugboat.
ひきまく 引き幕 a (drawing) curtain; (舞台用の) a stage curtain.
ひきまど 引き窓 a skylight. (類) 天窓
ひきまわし 引き回し (連れ回すこと) taking ... around [about]; (指導) guidance; (昔の刑罰としての) public exposure. ●万事よろしくお引き回しください I would greatly appreciate your *advice*.
ひきまわす 引き回す [綱・幕などを] draw*... around; [あちこち連れて行く] take* (*him*) around [to many places]; [人を指図する] order (*him*) around [about].
ひきもきらず 引きも切らず (⇨ひっきりなし, 絶えず)
ひきもどす 引き戻す [引いて戻す] pull... back; [連れ戻す] bring*... back; [引き返す] go* back (⇨引き返す).
ひきもの 引き物 (⇨引き出物)
ひきゃく 飛脚 [歴史の] *hikyaku*; (説明的に) an express messenger (employed to convey urgent messages).
ひぎゃく 被虐・被虐性 masochism.
ひぎゃくたいじ 被虐待児 被虐待症候群 [医学] battered child syndrome.
ひきやぶる 引き破る tear*... (up), rip (-pp-) ... (up). (⇨引き裂く)
ひきゅう 飛球 [野球] a fly (ball). (⇨フライ) ●大飛球 a long *fly*.
ひきょ 美挙 (立派な行動や企て) a praiseworthy act [undertaking].
*ひきょう 卑怯 图 (臆病(ﾋｮｸﾋﾞｮｳ)) cowardice.
── 卑怯な 形 (不公正な) unfair; (臆病な) cowardly. ▶彼は卑怯なやり方でレースに勝った He won the race by (using) *unfair* means. ●相手の弱点につけこむとは卑怯だ It's *unfair* of you [You're *unfair*] to take advantage of an opponent's weakness.
● 卑怯者 (臆病者) a coward.
ひきょう 秘教 an esoteric religion.
ひきょう 秘境 unexplored [人があまり訪れない] rarely visited] regions. (⇨未踏) ●秘境にある温泉 (知られていない場所) a hot spring in an *unknown* place; (まったく人里離れた) a hot spring *totally secluded from the world*.
ひきょう 悲境 an unhappy situation; (逆境) one's adverse circumstances; (悲運) one's sad fate.
ひきよせる 引き寄せる draw* [pull]... (*near, up to*),

ひきより 飛距離 〖野球〗 distance of a batted ball; 〖ゴルフ〗 a carry 《of 300 yards》. ▶飛距離の長いフライ[ホームラン] a long fly [home run].

ひきわけ 引き分け a draw; (同点) a tie; (引き分け試合) a drawn 〖tied〗 game. ▶その試合は5対5の引き分けに終わった The game ended in a draw [a tie] 5-5. (! five-to-five または five all と読む. a 5-5 draw [tie] ともいう) ▶彼とは引き分けだった I drew with him./He and I were tied.

ひきわける 引き分ける 〖試合を〗 draw*; 〖相手と〗 draw 〖tie (～d; tying)〗 《with》. (⇨引き分け) ▶両チームは5対5で引き分けた The teams drew (the game) 《at 〖×by〗 5》. (! five-to-five と読む)

ひきわたし 引き渡し (物品の) (a) delivery; (権利などの) (a) transfer; (犯人などの) (an) extradition. ▶商品の引き渡し the delivery of goods.

ひきわたす 引き渡す 〖商品などを〗 deliver; 〖犯人などを〗 turn [hand]... over 《to》; (犯罪者を管轄国に)extradite... 《to》; (財産などを譲る) make*... over 《to》. ▶彼の身柄を日本に引き渡すよう公式に要請する make an official request for his extradition to Japan. ▶彼らは彼のおたずね者を警察へ引き渡した They turned [handed] over the wanted man [woman] to the police.

ひきわり 碾き割り ・ひき割り麦 ground barley.

ひきん 卑近 ── 卑近な 形 〖身近な〗 familiar; (日常的な) everyday; (ありふれた) common, ordinary; 〖分かりやすい〗 plain. ▶卑近な例をあげる give a familiar [a plain] example.

ひきんぞく 非金属 〖化学〗 nonmetal. ・非金属元素 a nonmetallic element.

ひきんぞく 卑金属 〖化学〗 (a) base metal.

ひく 引く　　　　　　　　　　　　　　INDEX

❶ 引っ張る	❷ 引っこめる
❸ 導く	❹ 注意・関心などを
❺ 辞書などを	❻ 電話・水道などを
❼ 線を	❽ 減じる
❾ 風邪を	❿ 下がる
⓫ 引用する	⓬ 受け継ぐ
⓭ 選び出す	⓮ 塗る
⓯ その他の表現	

WORD CHOICE　引く
draw いす・カーテン・弓・人など, 比較的軽い物を, 静かに引いたり, 引き寄せたりすること. ▶彼は椅子をベッドの方に引き寄せた He drew a chair to the bed.
pull ロープ・手・そり・ドア・引き金・人の袖などをぐいっと一気に強く引くこと. ●ロープを引っ張る pull the rope. ●母親は息子の身体を自分の方に引き寄せた The mother pulled her son toward her.

頻度チャート
draw
pull
　　　20　　40　　60　　80　　100 (%)

❶ 〖引っ張る〗 pull; draw*; (急にぐいと) jerk; (力を入れてやっとの思いで) haul; (ぐっと) tug (-gg-) 《at》; (船・車などを綱で) tow. (⇨引っ張る) ▶綱を引く pull (at [on]) a rope; give a pull at [on] a rope; give a rope a pull. ▶(注意を引くために)彼のそでを引く pull him by the sleeve; pull [tug] (at) his sleeve. (! 前の方は him に, 後の方は sleeve に重点がある) ●引き金を引く pull [squeeze, ×draw] the trigger. ●弓を引く draw [×pull] a bow. ●カーテンを引く (閉める) draw a curtain; (下ろす) lower a curtain. ●手綱をぐいと引く jerk reins. ●丸太を引く haul logs. ▶火事のときはこのレバーを引きなさい In case of fire pull this lever.

❷ 〖引っこめる〗 pull back; (引き上げる) draw* back, withdraw*. ●あごを引く draw in one's chin. ▶敵は国境から兵を引いた The enemy soldiers drew back [were taken away] from the border.

❸ 〖導く〗(手を取って) lead*. ●老人の手を引いて道路を横断する lead an old person (by the hand) across the road.

❹ 〖注意・関心などを〗 draw*; (引きつける) attract; (つかむ) catch*. ●人々の同情を引く draw the sympathy of other people. ▶彼は彼女の気を引こうとした He tried to attract [catch, draw] her attention. ▶なぜか彼に心が引かれる I feel somehow drawn [attracted] to him.

❺ 〖辞書などを〗 look 《a word》 up 《in a dictionary》; use [see*], 《やや書》 consult, 《やや書》 refer (-rr-) to 《a dictionary for a word》. ▶単語の意味が分からなければ辞書を引きなさい If you don't know the meaning of a word, look it up in a dictionary. (! ×... look up a dictionary は不可) ▶辞書の引き方が分からない I don't know how to use [consult] a dictionary.

❻ 〖電話・水道などを〗 install 《a telephone》; (敷設する) 《英》 lay* 《electricity [water]》 on. ▶彼は家に電話を引いた He had the telephone installed in his house. (! have+目的語+過去分詞(...してもらう)の構文) ●ガスはまだ引いていない We haven't received our gas supply yet./《主に英》 We haven't had gas connected yet.

❼ 〖線を〗 draw*; (定規などを使って直線を) rule. ●直線を引く draw a straight line. ●紙に罫(⁽⁾)を引く rule lines on paper [paper with lines].

❽ 〖減じる〗(数を) subtract, take* 《from》 (! 後の方が口語的); (税金などを) deduct 《from》; (値段などを) reduce, take... off. (! 後の方が口語的) ▶10から4を引けば6残る If you subtract [take] 4 from 10, you get 6./Ten minus four is six. ▶給料から税金と保険料が引かれる Taxes and insurance are taken out [are deducted] from your pay. ▶値段を1割引きしましょう I will reduce [lower] the price by 10 percent./I will take 10 percent off the price./I will give you a discount of 10 percent [(a) 10 percent discount]./I will discount 10 percent. (! 「引いてもらった」は I got (a) 10 percent discount (on the TV set).)

❾ 〖風邪を〗 catch*. ▶私は風邪を引きやすい I catch (a) cold [get a cold] easily./《やや書》 I am liable [subject] to colds. ▶私は風邪を引いている I have a cold.

❿ 〖下がる〗 (熱・はれなどが) go* down; (潮が) ebb (←flow); (洪水などが) go down, 《やや書》 subside. ▶熱が引いた My fever has come down [gone down]./(熱はもうない) My fever has [is] gone. (! be gone は文語的な表現で結果に重点がある) ▶潮が引いている The tide is on the ebb. ▶洪水がしだいに引いた The floods gradually went down [subsided].

⓫ 〖引用する〗 quote; cite. (⇨引用する) ●彼の本から1節を引く quote a passage from his book. ●過去の例を引く cite past examples.

⓬ [受け継ぐ](血筋を) be descended 《*from*》; be a descendant 《*of*》. ▶彼は貴族の血を引いている He *is descended from* [*a descendant of*] *a* noble family./《やや書》He *is of* noble birth [*descent*]. **⓭ [選び出す]** draw*. ▶おみくじを引く *draw* a sacred lot. ●カードを引く *draw* a card.
⓮ [塗る](床に油を) oil 《a floor》. (ワックスを) wax 《a floor》. (フライパンに) grease 《a pan》.
⓯ [その他の表現] ●手を引く (⇨手 [成句]) ●引く手あまた (⇨引っ張り凧[だこ]) ▶あの事故は彼の後の人生に尾を引いていた That accident *left its mark on* his life. ▶私は一歩も後へ引かなかった(=譲らなかった) I did not *yield* an inch./(主張を曲げなかった) I held [*stood*] *my ground*. ▶約束してしまったのだから今となっては引くに引けない Once I have made a promise, it's too late to *back out*.

***ひく 弾く** (楽器・曲を) play, perform 《＋曲, *on*＋楽器》. (🔲前の方が普通) ▶ギターを弾く *play* the guitar; (かき鳴らす) *pluck* [《米》*pick*] (the strings of) a guitar. ▶あなたはバイオリンが弾けますか Can you *play* [*perform on*] the violin? ▶彼はピアノでショパンの曲を弾いた He *played* [*performed*] Chopin *on* the piano. ▶何か楽しい曲を弾いてくれませんか Would you *play* me something happy [something happy for me]? ▶彼女はギターを弾きながら歌った She sang to her own accompaniment on the guitar.

ひく 退く draw* back. (⇨退[ひ]く, 引退する, 引く⓾, ⓯).

ひく 挽く, 碾く (のこぎりで) saw*; (うすで) grind*. ▶丸太を板にひく *saw* a log *into* boards. ●小麦をひいて小麦粉にする *grind* wheat *into* flour. ●ひきたてのコーヒー freshly *ground* coffee.

ひく 轢く (車が人などを) run*... over [*down*]. (🔲後の方は「はねる」の意) ▶彼は車にひかれた He *was run over* [*down*] by a car. (⇨轢[れき]殺す) ▶何か黒いものが突然前方に飛び出してきて私はもう少しでひきそうになった(かろうじて避けた) Just ahead of me something black suddenly jumped out, and I *narrowly missed* it.

びく 比丘 【仏教】a Buddhist priest.
びく 魚籠 a fish bàsket; a creel.

:ひくい 低い ❶ [高さが] low (↔high); (背が)(鼻が) flat (-tt-). ▶低い天井 a *low* ceiling. ▶日照りで川の水位が低い The river is *low* because of the drought /drάʊt/. ▶彼はクラスでいちばん背が低い He is the *shortest* (boy) in his class. ▶彼女は鼻が低い She has a *flat* [*a short, a small*] nose. (🔲(1) 日本語と異なり悪い意味はない. (2) a low nose とあまりいわない) ▶この場所は海面より低い This place is *below* (↔above) sea level. ▶野原に低く霧が立ちこめていた Fog hung *low* over the field./A *low* fog covered the field.
❷ [程度・地位・声など] (程度・声などが) low; (地位が) humble. ●低い声で話す speak in a *low* [(小さい) *a small*, (かすかな) *a faint*, (低くて太い) *a deep*] voice; speak *low* [(静かに) *quietly*]. ●声を低くする *lower* [*drop*] one's voice. ●低い生活水準 a *low* standard of living. ●低い収入で暮らす live on a *low* [*a small*] income. ●低くなる (⇨下がる ❶) ▶ここは夏でも気温が低い The temperature here is *low* even in (主に米) the summer. ▶この国は教育水準が低い Education *is of a low* level in this country. ▶彼は社会的地位が低い He is a man of *low* [*humble*] position. ▶封建時代には身分の低い小作人は軽視されることが多かった The *lowly* peasants were often thought lightly of in the feudal times. ▶彼は見知らぬ人にも腰が低い(＝礼儀正しい) He is *polite* [*courteous*] even *to* strangers.

びくう 鼻腔 (⇨鼻腔[びこう]))
びくしょう 微苦笑 — 微苦笑する 動 smile a faint, bitter smile.
ピクセル 【画素】【コンピュータ】a pixel.
ひくつ 卑屈 (奴隷根性) servility; (ぺこぺこすること) subservience. ●卑屈な態度をとるな Don't take a *servile* [*a subservient, a slavish*] attitude./Don't be *subservient*.
ひくつく (⇨びくびくする)
びくっと ●びくっとさせる startle, give a start [*a jump*]. ●びくっとする音を聞く; get jumpy (*at* the sound). ▶私はその叫び声を聞いてびくっとした I *was startled* to hear the cry./The cry *gave me a start*. ▶彼はびくっとして後ろに下がった He stepped back *with a start*.
ぴくっと ●ぴくっとする (無意識に) twitch, give a twitch (ぐいっと引く) [(ぐいっと押す) 引く] jerk, give a jerk. ▶釣りざおの先端がぴくっと動いた. 例のあたりの感じだった The tip of the fishing rod gave a slight jerk. It was the usual feeling of a fish pulling at the line.
ひくて 引く手 — 引く手あまた 引く手あまたである be in great demand; be much in demand. (🔲 be sought after はやや古風で堅い表現) ▶就職のときも彼は引く手あまただった He got a lot of job offers.
びくともしない ❶ [まったく動かない] will not [refuse to] budge (an inch). ▶5人がかりで押したが岩はびくともしなかった Five of us pushed the rock very hard but it wouldn't *budge* (*an inch*)./Five men's combined force *couldn't budge* the rock.
❷ [まったく平静である] remain completely calm, not turn a hair. ●敗北の知らせにびくともしないでいる hear the news of the defeat *without turning a hair*.

ビクトリア ●ビクトリア湖 Lake Victoria. ●ビクトリア女王 Queen Victoria.
ビクトリーラン a victory lap; 《和製語》a victory run. ▶レースが終わるとメダリストたちは競技場でビクトリーランをした After the race, the medalists ran [did] a victory lap in the stadium.
ピクニック a picnic. (🔲事情 《米》では自宅の庭などでの食事でもピクニックということもあり, 日本語のピクニックより意味範囲が広い) ●ピクニックに行く go on [*for*] *a picnic*, go picnicking (*in* the woods, *at* [*on*] the beach). ▶私たちは浜でピクニックをした We *picnicked* [*had a picnic*] at the beach.
ひくひく ▶私はほおの筋肉がひくひくするのを感じた I felt a muscle in my cheek *twitch*. ▶ウサギがその草をひくかいだ A rabbit *sniffed at* the grass.
びくびく — びくびく(して) 副(小心で) timidly; (気が落ち着かず) nervously; (心配で) uneasily. ▶彼女はびくびくしながらドアをノックした She *timidly* knocked on the door. ▶彼はびくびくして(=用心しながら)そのもろい橋を渡った He crossed the fragile bridge *cautiously*.
— **びくびくする 動** (恐れる) be afraid [scared] 《*of*》(🔲後の方が意味が強い); (不安・心配で落ち着かない) 《話》be jumpy. ▶ヘビにそんなにびくびくするな Don't be so *afraid of* snakes.
ぴくぴく ●ぴくぴく動く twitch. ●ぴくぴく引きつる目 *twitching* eyes. ●耳をぴくぴく動かす *twitch* one's ears. ▶何匹かの魚はまだぴくぴくしていた Some fish *were* still *twitching*.
ひぐま 羆 【動物】a brown bear.
ピグミー a Pigmy. (参考 アフリカ中部に住む背の低い民

族の総称》
ひくめ 低目《⇨高目》● 低目の球 a *low* ball. ● カーブを外角低めに投げる throw a curve *low* and outside. ▶ 今日は気温が少し低目だ The temperature is a little *lower* today.
ひくめる 低める ▶ お願いだから声を低めてください Please *lower* your voice.
ひぐらし 蜩 〖昆虫〗a clear-toned cicada /sikéidə/ [〖米〗locust].
ピクルス pickles /píklz/. ● キュウリのピクルス pickled cucumbers.
ひぐれ 日暮れ 〖日没〗(a) sunset; 〖たそがれ〗(evening) twilight, 《やや語》dusk (**!** twilight は薄明かり, dusk はそのうちより暗い時間帯); 〖夕方〗evening. ● 日暮れごろに toward *evening*. ▶ 私たちは日暮れ前に家路を急いだ We hurried home *at sunset* [*twilight, dusk*]. ▶ 彼らは日暮れ前に山小屋に着いた They arrived at the mountain cabin before *sunset* [*before it got dark*].
ひけ 引け 《⇨引け時》
● <u>引けを取る</u> be behind 《him》; (劣っている) be inferior to 《him》. ● 英語のクラスの他の者に引け目取っている be *behind* the rest of the class in English. ● 彼の作品は一流の作家のものと比べても引けを取らない (見劣りしない) His works compare favorably with those by first-class writers. ▶ 彼女はテニスではクラスのだれにも引けを取らない (断然まさっている) She is *second to none* in her class as a tennis player.
*****ひげ** 髭 ❶ 〖男性の〗(口ひげ) a mustache /mʌ́stæʃ/, 《英》a moustache /mustá:ʃ/ (**!** 非常に長い場合は複数形も用いられる. また, 時には顔全体のひげをさす; あごひげ) a beard /bíərd/; (ほおひげ) whiskers; (もみあげ) 《米》sideburns, 《英》sideboards.

mustache　beard　whiskers

①〖〜ひげ, ひげ〜〗● 濃い[薄い; 長い] ひげ a heavy [a light; a long] *mustache*. ● 無精ひげ (短い) stubble; (やや伸びた) three days' stubble, a three-day beard. ● 手入れの行き届いたちょびひげ a well-trimmed small *mustache*. ● 付けひげをしている wear a false *mustache* [*beard*]. ● 赤ひげの男 a red-*mustached* [-*bearded*] man; a man with a red *mustache* [*beard*].
②〖ひげを〗● ひげをそる shave (oneself) (**!** 習慣的行為には oneself は省略する), 《話》have a shave; (顔の) shave one's face; (床屋でそってもらう) have [get] a shave. ● ひげをきれいにそった a clean-*shaven* face. ● ひげをはやす[はやしている(=たくわえている)] grow [have] a *mustache* [a *beard*]. ▶ 彼は2日間ひげをそっていない He *hasn't shaved* for two days.
❷ 〖動物の〗(猫・ネズミなどの) a whisker; (魚の) a barbel.
● ひげの塵(ちり)を払う (権力のある者にこびへつらう) flatter [《話》butter up] a person in authority.
● ひげそり道具 sháving things [stʌ́f]; (**!** 前の方が普通);(揃いの一式) a sháving kit. ● ひげ面 (無精ひげの) an unshaven face; (ひげをたくわえた) a bearded [a whiskery] face.
ひげ 卑下 — 卑下して 副 humbly. — 卑下する 動 humble oneself.
ピケ 〖隊・隊員〗a picket. ● 工場にピケをはる *picket* a factory; (ピケ隊を) put [place] a *picket* in front of a factory. ● ピケを突破する break through a *picket* (*line*).
びけい 美形 (美貌) good looks; (美人) a beautiful [a good-looking] woman.
びけい 美景 beautiful scenery; a lovely [a fine] view.
ひげき 悲劇 名 (a) tragedy (↔(a) comedy). (**!** 演劇の一部門では無冠詞)
—**悲劇的な** 形 ● 悲劇的な事件 a *tragic* event (**!** a tragedy もこの意になる) ● 悲劇的な死を遂げる die a *tragic* death; die *tragically*.
● 悲劇俳優 a tragic actor [(女優) actress].
ひけぎわ 引け際 ❶ 〖身を引く間際〗▶ 引け際が肝心だ It's important to know *when to leave* [*quit*].
❷ 〖職場から退出する際〗▶ 電話が鳴ったのは会社の引け際だった The phone rang just as we were going to *leave* the office.
❸ 〖株取引で〗● 立ち会いの引け際に *at the close of* a trading session.
ひけし 火消し (消火) fire fighting [〖書〗extinguishing]; (消防士) a firefighter.
● 火消しつぼ a charcoal extinguisher. ● 火消し役 (騒動などの調停役) a trouble-shooter; (野球の救援投手) a fireman.
ひけつ 否決 名 (却下) (a) rejection.
— **否決する** 動 (提案などを) reject; (議案などを投票で) vote ... down. ▶ 6 対 5 で法案は否決された The bill *was voted down* [*was rejected*] by 6 (votes) to 5./They voted 6 to 5 to *reject* the bill. (to reject の 下に 〖結果〗を表す)
ひけつ 秘訣 the secret 《*of, to*》; the key 《*to*》; 〖こつ〗(やや話) a [the] knack 《*of, for*》. ● 私の成功の秘訣 the *secret of* [*key to*] my success. ● 《…する》秘訣を知っている have the *knack of* 《*doing*》. ▶ 健康を保つ秘訣は早起きすることです The *secret of* [*to*] staying healthy is to get up early.
ひけどき 引け時 (the) closing time [hour].
ひけめ 引け目 ● 引け目を感じる ● 数学で引け目を感じる *feel inferior to* him *in* mathematics. ● 彼女の前では引け目を感じる *feel small* in her presence.
ひげもじゃ 髭もじゃ ● 髭もじゃの顔 ... a face *with a stubbly* beard.
ひけらかす (得意げに) show*... off*; (これ見よがしに) 《話》parade; (知識をひけらかす) *show off* [*parade*] one's knowledge.
ひける 引ける (1日の業務を終える) get off (work); (終わる) be over; close. ● 学校が引けてから彼の家に寄ってみよう I will drop in at his house after school is over.
🗨 「仕事が引けた後でお誘いしていいですか」「まあ, それはありがとう」「仕事はいつ引けるのですか」"Could I invite you out *after* work?" "Oh, thank you so much." "What time do you *get off*?"
ひけん 比肩 名 equality.
— **比肩する** 動 (匹敵する) equal, be equal 《*to*》. ▶ 彼は数学では私と比肩する He *equals* [*is equal to*] me in mathematics. ▶ この発明に比肩するものはない Nothing *can be compared with* this invention.
ひげんぎょう 非現業 名 (事務職) clerical [desk] work. — **非現業の** 形 clerical.
ひげんじつてき 非現実的 非現実的な 形 unrealistic; (実用的でない) impractical.
ひけんしゃ 被験者 (試験の) an examinee; (実験・検査の) a subject. ● その実験の被験者 a *subject* for [the *subject* of] the experiment.
ひご 籤 *higo*; (説明的に) a thin strip whittled from a piece of bamboo.

ひご 庇護 图 protection. ●徳川幕府の庇護のもとで under the *protection* of the Tokugawa Shogunate.
── **庇護する** 動 protect.

ひご 卑語 〖卑猥(ひわい)な語〗(単語) a vulgar word; (単語・表現) a vulgarism. (⇨俗語)

ひごい 緋鯉 〖魚介〗a golden red carp.

ひこう 肥厚 〖医学〗hypertrophy /haɪpéːtrəfi/.
●肥厚性鼻炎 hypertrophic rhinitis.

ひこう 非行 (a) delinquency. ●(a) minor crime (の婉曲語) ●青少年非行 juvenile *delinquency*. ●非行に走る turn to *dilinquency* [*delinquent behavior*]. ●非行少年[少女] a juvenile delinquent; a delinquent boy [girl].

ひこう 飛行 图 〖1 回の〗a flight; 〖飛ぶこと〗flight, flying. ●夜間飛行 a night *flight*. ●試験飛行をする make a test *flight*.
── **飛行する** ●北[ニューヨーク]へ向けて飛行する *fly* north [*to* New York]. ▶イギリス海峡を最初に横断飛行した人はだれですか Who was the first person to *fly* (*across*) the English Channel? (⇨飛ぶ)
●飛行士 (パイロット) a pilot; (宇宙飛行士) an astronaut (⇨宇宙). ●飛行時間 flying hours; flíght tìme. ●飛行場 an airfield, 〘米〙an airdrome, 〘英〙an aerodrome. (⇨空港) ●飛行船 an airship. ●飛行艇 a flying boat.

ひごう 非業 ●非業の死を遂げる die a violent death; die violently.

びこう 尾行 图 ●彼に尾行をつける put a *shadow* [a *tail*] on him.
── **尾行する** ▶スパイの容疑者は探偵に尾行されていた The suspected spy *was being shadowed* [*was being tailed*] by detectives.
●尾行者 a shadow; 〘話〙a tail.

びこう 備考 图 (覚え書き) a note; (簡単な所見) a remark; (参照) a reference.
●備考欄 a remarks column.

びこう 微光 a faint light.

びこう 鼻孔 〖解剖〗(鼻の穴) a nostril.

びこう 鼻腔 〖解剖〗(鼻の内部) a nasal cavity.

ひこうかい 非公開 ── **非公開の** 形 (秘密の) secret; (部外者を閉め出した) closed, closed-door. ●非公開の計画 a *secret* plan. ▶その裁判は非公開で行われた The trial was held *behind closed doors* [*in camera*]. (⇨後の方は法廷用語)

***ひこうき 飛行機** a plane, 〘米〙an airplane, 〘英〙an aeroplane; 〖すべての航空機の総称〗an aircraft. (⇨航空機)

①**【〜飛行機】** ●軽飛行機 a light plane; a light *airplane*. (!両者とも特に自家用の) ●水上飛行機 a seaplane. ●模型[おもちゃの]飛行機を飛ばす fly a model [a toy] *airplane*.

②**【飛行機(の)〜】** ●飛行機の切符 an áirline [*pláne*] ticket. ▶ロビーで会ったばかりの男の人が飛行機の中で私の隣に座った The man I just met in the lobby sat next to me *on the plane*. (!この場合 in the plane としない方がよい) ▶彼は飛行機事故で死んだ He was killed in a *plane* accident [*crash*]. (!crash は墜落事故)

③**【飛行機が[は]】** ●飛行機が離陸[着陸; 墜落; 不時着]する The *plane* took off [landed; crashed; was forced to land]. ●彼の乗った飛行機は遅れた His *plane* [(便) *flight*] has been delayed. ▶飛行機がよく揺れた It was a bumpy flight.

④**【飛行機に[を, から]】** ●飛行機に乗る[から降りる] get on [off, ×from] a *plane* (*at*). ●飛行機を乗り継ぐ change planes. (⇨乗り継ぐ) ●飛行機に酔う get airsick. ●飛行機を操縦する pilot an *airplane*. ●太平洋航路に飛行機を就航させる operate an *airplane* [begin *air service*] on the Pacific route.

⑤**【飛行機で】** ●飛行機でハワイへ行く go to Hawaii *by plane* [*by air*] (!by は「手段」を表す); go to Hawaii *in* [*on*] *a plane* (!in, on は「乗って」の意); take a plane to Hawaii (!take は「利用する」の意); fly to Hawaii (!*fly* は「飛んで行く」の意で口語ではこの言い方が最も普通). ▶私は飛行機で旅行をしたことがない I have never traveled *by plane* [*by air, in a plane*]./I have never taken a *plane* [an *air*] trip.
会話 「彼らはどうやって行くのかな」「ニューヨークまではたぶん飛行機で行くつもりでいるよ」"How are they going?" "They think they might *fly* as far as New York."
●飛行機雲 a vapor trail; a contrail. ●飛行機代 (航空運賃) an áirline fàre.

ひこうしき 非公式 ── **非公式な** 形 (公でない) unofficial; (略式の) informal.
── **非公式に** 副 unofficially; informally. ●非公式に訪問する pay an *unofficial* [an *informal*, (私的な) a *private*] visit (*to*).

ひごうほう 非合法 illegality. ▶アメリカでの銃の所持は非合法化されるべきである Owning pistols [guns] ought to *be outlawed* in the United States.
●非合法活動 illegal [unlawful] activities.

ひごうり 非合理 图 irrationality.
── **非合理の** 形 irrational; unreasonable. ●非合理な制度 an *irrational* system.
●非合理主義 irrationalism.

ひこく 被告 a defendant (⇔a plaintiff); (刑事事件の) an accused person, 〘やや書〙the accused (!単・複両扱い).
●被告側弁護人[団] (the) counsel for the defense [accused]. (!「被告側弁護団」の意で用いる場合は複数扱い) ●被告席 the dock; the bar.

ひこくみん 非国民 (愛国心の薄い[ない]人) an unpatriotic /ʌnpèɪtriátɪk/ person; (売国奴) a traitor (to one's country).

ピコグラム 〖1 兆分の 1 グラム〗a picogram /píːkoʊɡræm/.

ひこつ 腓骨 〖解剖〗a fibula (複 〜s, -lae /fíbjəliː/).

びこつ 尾骨 〖解剖〗the coccyx /kάksɪks/ (複 〜es, coccyges /kɑksáɪdʒɪːz/). (⇨ 尾骶骨)

ひごと 日毎 ●日ごとに涼しくなってきた It's getting cooler *day by day* [*every day*, ×day after day]. (!(1) 完了形とともには用いない. (2) ×day after day と同じ状態が毎日[長い期間, 続く場合に用いる])

ひこばえ 蘖 〖切り株から出る新しい芽〗a sprout (from the stump of a tree); a shoot; a tiller.

ひこぼし 彦星 〖天文〗(牽牛(けんぎゅう)星) Altair.

ひこようしゃ 被雇用者 (従業員) an employee (⇔ employer).

ひごろ 日頃 ●日ごろ(=昔から)の恨みを晴らす settle [pay off] *old scores* 《*with* him》. ▶京都は日ごろ(=長い間)私が行きたいと思っていたところだ Kyoto is the place I've wanted *to visit for a long time*. ▶私は日ごろから(= 常に)健康には気をつけている I *always* take care of my health. ▶大事なのは日ごろの(=毎日の)勉強だ What counts is your *every-day* [〘日々の〙*daily*] study./It is important for you to study *every day* [×everyday]. (⇨普段)

ひこん 非婚 ── **非婚の** 形 non-marital (birth). (⇨ 未婚)

***ひざ 膝** 〖ひざがしら〗a knee /niː/; 〖座ったときの〗one's lap. (!単数形で用いる. ただし, their *laps*)

①【膝が】 ▶ひざがくがくした（震えた）My knees shook [knocked]. ▶彼のズボンはひざ(の部分)がぶかぶかれている His pants are baggy *at* the *knees*.

②【膝に】 ▶ひざ(の上)に両手を重ねてきちんと座る sit up with one's hands together in one's *lap*. ▶彼女はひざ(の上)に赤ん坊を乗せていた She held her baby on her *knee* [*lap*].

③【膝を】 ●片ひざをつく fall [go down, get down] on one's *knee*. ●ひざを曲げる[立てる; かかえ込む] bend [draw up; hug] one's *knees*. ●ひざを組む cross one's *legs* [×*knees*]. ●ひざついて祈る *kneel* in prayer; bend the *knee*(s). (⇨ひざまずく) ▶彼は転んでひざをすりむいた He fell and scraped his *knee*. ▶彼女はひざ立ちになって子供を着替えさせていた She was on her *knees*, helping her boy change his clothes. ●彼はひざをたたいて大笑いした He slapped his *knee* [(もも) *thigh*] /θái/ *and burst into laughter.* (事情) 相手の冗談などに「それはおもしろい」と同調するしぐさ（⇨［ひざを打つ］）

翻訳のこころ メロスは幾度となくめまいを感じ、これではならぬ、と気を取り直しては、よろよろニ、三歩歩いて、ついに、がくりとひざを折った（太宰治『走れメロス』）Melos felt dizzy many times. Pulling himself together, he took a couple of unstable steps and collapsed on [fell to] his knees at last. (❗(1) pull oneself together は「感情に流されそうな自分を勇気づけて冷静になるままように努力する」の意. (2)「よろよろ」という擬態語は英語にないので, take unstable steps (=不安定な足取りで歩く)と表す (3)「ひざを折る」は collapse on his knees (ひざをついて倒れこむ)と表す. 両膝をつくのを knees と複数形になることに注意)

④【膝まで[より]】 ●ひざまで水につかって立っている stand *up to the knees* [*knee-deep*] in (the) water. ●ひざまでのブーツをはいている wear *knee-high* boots. ▶ミニスカートは丈がひざよりも上だ Miniskirts are *above the knees*.

● ひざが抜ける ▶(ズボンの)ひざが抜けている be worn out at the knee. ●ひざががっくりしてひざが抜けた My knees gave way with disappointment.

● ひざが笑う ▶ひざが笑い始めた My knees began to *sag*.

● ひざ詰め談判 (⇨膝詰め)

● ひざを打つ snap one's fingers [×knees]. (事情) 人の注意を引いたり, うまくいった時のしぐさ)

● ひざを折る ▶彼はひざを折って祈り始めた He knelt (down) [*fell to* his *knees*] and started to pray.

● ひざを崩す ▶彼は私にひざをくずす(=もっと楽に座る)よう勧めた He told me to sit more comfortably.

● ひざを屈する ▶敵の前にひざを屈する yield to the enemy.

● ひざを正す sit up straight.

● ひざを乗り出す lean forward.

● ひざを交える ▶彼はひざを交えて(=親しく)話し合う have a *friendly* [(腹を割って)a *heart-to-heart*] talk with him.

●ひざ当て a kneecap, a kneepad ●ひざ掛け 《米》 a lap robe, 《英》 a rug.

ビザ a visa /víːzə/. ▶フランスへの入国ビザを必要とする need an entry *visa* for France. ●出国ビザの発給を拒否される be refused [denied] an exit *visa*. ●観光[就労]ビザで入国する enter the country on a tourist [a working] *visa*. ▶ビザが5月に切れるので更新の手続きをしなくてはならない My *visa* runs out 《書》 *expires*] in May, so I must apply for its renewal. ▶まだビザがおりません The *visa* has not yet been granted [been issued] to me.

ピサ ピサの斜塔 the Leaning Tower of Pisa /píːzə/.

ピザ [＜イタリア語] (a) pizza /píːtsə/ (pie). ●ピザ専門店 a pizzeria /piːtsəríːə/; a pizza house.

ひさい 非才 one's lack of ability; inability. ●浅学(ホシ)非才を顧みずin spite of my *lack of* knowledge and *ability*. (⇨浅学)

ひさい 被災 图 ●地震の被災地 the quake-hit area. ●水害の被災者 a flood *victim* [*sufferer*]. ●a victim of a flood, a sufferer [of] a flood も可だが, この形式は flood に修飾語をつけるときに好まれる

——被災する 動 suffer 《severe damage *from* a flood, flood damage》; fall victim 《of an earthquake》; be hit 《*by* a flood》.

ひさい 微細 —— 微細な 形 ●微細な変化 *minute* /main(j)úːt/ changes.

—— 微細に 副 ●微細に記述する describe 《it》 *minutely* [(詳細に) *in detail*]; give a *minute* [(詳細な) a *detailed*] description 《of》.

びざい 微罪 a petty [a minor] offense.

ひざかり 日盛り ●夏の暑い日盛り the *heat of summer*. ●日盛りに外を歩く walk in *the heat of the day*.

ひさく 秘策 ●秘策を練る work out a secret plan. ●秘策を授ける let 《him》 into [《話》 in on] the secret plan.

ひざこぞう 膝小僧 a knee; [膝のさら] a kneecap. ●ひざ小僧を出して show [expose] one's knees.

ひさし 庇 (家の) eaves, (帽子の) a peak, a visor. ●ひさしを貸して母屋を取られる (一部を貸したのが全部を奪われてしまう) One loses the whole by lending a part./A falling master makes a standing servant.

ひざし 日差し (陽光) sun, sunshine; (日光) sunlight. (⇨日光) ●暖かい春の日差し the warm spring *sunshine*. ▶日差しが強くなった *The sun* grew stronger. ▶私は暑い日差しの中を2キロ歩いた I walked two kilometers in the hot *sun*.

ひさしい 久しい ▶彼が亡くなって久しい It is [It has been] *a long time* since he passed away. ▶久しく(=長い間)彼とは会っていない I haven't seen him *for a long time*. ▶原子爆弾のために, 久しく人類を支えてきた高尚な感情が滅びされてしまった The atomic bomb [A-bomb] has ruined the noble sentiment that has *long* sustained human existence.

***ひさしぶり 久しぶり** for the first time in a long time [in many years, in ages]. (❗(1) after a long time ともいう. (2)《書》では「長い時の経過[留守; 音信不通; 別離]の後で」の意で after a long interval [(absence); silence; separation] などを用いることもある) ▶彼女から久しぶりに電話があった I had a call from her *for the first time in a long time* [*in many years*]./《書》I had a call from her *after a long silence*. ▶あんなに魅力のある人に会ったのは久しぶりだ It's [It's been] *a long time* since I met such a charming person. ▶久しぶりに最高のニュースを聞いたよ That's the best news I've heard *for a long time*. ▶久しぶりですね I haven't seen you *for a long time* [(*for*) *ages*, (*for*) *an age*]. (❗後の二つは口語的)/It's [It's been, ×This is] *a long time* [*ages, an age*] since I saw you last./Long time no see. (❗親しい間柄で用いる. これをもじって Long time no talk. ともいう)/(It's) good to see you again. (❗会う言い方は仕事上などの改まった場合に用いる.「お久しぶりに続く表現としては How have you been? (どうしてたの)や I could hardly recognize you. (だれだか分からなかった)などがある)

ひざづめ 膝詰め ▶刑事はひざづめで容疑者を問いただした The police detective sat *knee to knee with* the súspect and questioned him. (事情)文字どおりのざをつき合わせて相手を心理的に追い詰める動作)
・ひざ詰め談判 ・ひざ詰め談判をする[始める] have [enter into] direct negotiations 《with》.

ピザパイ（⇨® ピザ）

ひさびさ 久々（⇨久しぶり）

ひざまくら 膝枕 ▶彼女のひざ枕で眠った I went to sleep with my head *on* her *lap*.

ひざまずく [尊敬・祈りのために] kneel* /niːl/ (down); fall* [go* down, get* down] on one's knees. (事情)日本人の両手を合わせた動作に通じる心情を表す)▶ひざまずいて祈る kneel (down) to pray [in prayer]; pray *on one's knees*. ▶彼は彼女の足もとにひざまずいて許しを請うた He *knelt* at her feet [knelt to her] and asked for forgiveness.

ひさめ 氷雨 a (freezing) cold rain.

ひざもと 膝元 ▶ストーブをひざ元に引き寄せる draw a heater closer to oneself. ▶親のひざ元を離れる leave one's parents' home;(独立する)become *independent of* one's parents. ▶その事件は幕府のおひざ元で起こった The incident happened *very near* (the headquarters of) the Shogunate.

*****ひさん 悲惨**〖みじめさ〗misery;〖惨事〗(a) trage-dy;〖残酷〗cruelty. ・戦争の悲惨さ the *cruelty* [*misery*] of war.

—悲惨な 形 ・悲惨な生活 a *miserable* [a *wretch-ed*] life. ・悲惨な事故（恐ろしい）a *horrible* [a *ter-rible*] accident; (衝撃的な) a *tragic* accident. ・悲惨な最期を遂げる die a *tragic* [(無残な) a *cruel*] death.

ひさん 砒酸〖化学〗arsenic acid.
・砒酸塩 arsenate.

ひさん 飛散 名 scattering.
—飛散する 動 scatter. ▶粉塵(ﾁﾘ)があたり一面に飛散した Fine particles of stone *scattered* all around.

ビザンチン ・ビザンチン（様式）の Býzantine.

ひし 菱〖植物〗a water chestnut.

ひし 皮脂〖生理〗sebum.
・皮脂腺〖解剖〗a sebaceous /səbéiʃəs/ gland.

ひし 秘史 a secret history 《*of*》; unknown [hidden] historical facts [secrets].

ひじ 肘 an elbow. ・ひじの関節 an *elbow* joint. ・ひじを張る square [spread out] one's *elbows*. ▶彼をひじで横へ押しのける push him aside with one's *elbow*; elbow him aside. ▶テーブルにひじをつくな Don't rest your *elbows* on the table./Keep your *elbows* off the table. ▶彼の上着はひじがすり切れていた His coat was worn out at the *elbow*(s). (!単数形では片ひじのこと)
・ひじ当て elbow patches.

ひじかけ 肘掛け（いすの）an arm of a chair; an armrest.
・ひじ掛けいす 《sit in》an armchair. (⇨椅子)

ひしがた 菱形 a lozenge /lázindʒ/;〖数学〗a rhom-bus /rámbəs/.

ひじき 鹿尾菜〖植物〗brown algae /ǽldʒiː/.

ひしぐ 拉ぐ（押しつぶす）crush;（勢いなどをくじく）over-power.

ひししょくぶつ 被子植物 an angiosperm.

ビジター the visitors. ▶ジャイアンツはビジターのタイガースを本拠地に迎えた The Giants played host to the *visiting* Tigers.
・ビジターチーム a visiting team

ひしつ 皮質〖解剖〗the cortex; a cortical layer.

びしつ 美質 a good quality; a virtue; a grace. ・生来の美質 an inborn quality.

びしっと ▶松の枝がぴしっと折れた The branch of the pine tree *snapped off*. ▶彼は遅くまで家に帰らなかった息子をびしっと(=厳しく)しかった He scolded his son *sternly* for staying out late.

ぴしっと ・ぴしっと裂ける[割れる; 折れる] crack. ・ぴしっとむちを鳴らす *snap* [*crack*] a whip. ▶君のそのスーツ姿はぴしっと決まっている You look *perfectly* smart in that suit.

びしてき 微視的 microscopic (↔macroscopic).
・微視的経済学 microeconomics. ・微視的分析〖経済〗(a) microscopic analysis.

ひじてつ 肘鉄（冷たい拒絶）a snub,《やや話》a brush-off,《書》a rebuff. ・ひじ鉄を食う get a *snub* [*brush-off*]; meet with a *rebuff*. ・ひじ鉄を食わす give《him》the *cold shoulder* [a *brush-off*]; cold-shoulder《him》; brush《him》off.

ひじでっぽう 肘鉄砲（⇨肘鉄）

ひしと ・そうする必要性をひしと(=強く)感じる feel *keenly* the necessity of doing it. ▶姉妹はひしと(=しっかりと)抱き合った The sisters hugged each other *tightly*.

ビジネス business. (⇨仕事)
・ビジネス英語 búsiness Énglish. ・ビジネス街 a búsiness dìstrict [cènter]. ・ビジネスクラス a búsiness [an executive /igzékjətiv/] clàss. [参考] first class と tourist [economy] class の中間)・ビジネススーツ《米》a búsiness sùit,《英》a lóunge sùit. ・ビジネススクール a búsiness schòol [còllege]. ・búsiness school の《米》では「経営学大学院」) ・ビジネスチャンス《seize》a búsiness opportùnity《for》;《和製語》a búsiness chance. ・ビジネスホテル 'an economy hotel mainly catering for traveling office workers' (サービスなしの) a no-frills hotel (for business people);《和製語》búsiness hòtel. ・ビジネスマン（会社員）an óffice wòrker; a cómpany emplòyee; (実業家) a (business) executive; a búsiness pèrson. (! 特に性別を区別するときには a businessman, a businesswoman という)

ビジネスライク businesslike. (!日本語のような冷たい含みはない)▶彼はすべてにビジネスライクだ He's too *businesslike* in everything. (! too に注意)

ひしはい 被支配 ・被支配者《集合的》the ruled; ruled people.

ひしひし ・ひしひしとこたえる《事が主語》come home to《him》. ▶貧乏の辛(ﾂﾗ)さをひしひしと感じた I felt *keenly* the rigors of poverty. ▶先生の助言の重みがその後の人生で彼にはひしひしと感じられた The weight of his teacher's advice *came home* to him in his later life. ▶空港を一歩出るとこの北国の寒気がひしひしと(=体を突き刺すように)感じられた The moment I stepped out the airport, I felt the harsh air of this north country *pierce* my body [襲いかかる *close in on* me].

びしびし（厳しく）very hard, severely. ・びしびし取り締まる crack down on《motorcycle gangs》. ▶新人たちはその日のクラブでびしびし鍛えられた Newcom-ers got *severe* training in the club. ▶騎手が馬にびしびしむちを当てた The rider whipped his horse *very hard*.

ひじまくら 肘枕 —— 肘枕(を)する 動 rest one's head on one's elbow [arm].

ひしめく（push [shove] and) jostle. ▶店は買い物客でひしめき合っていた The store *was jammed to the rafters with* shoppers. (! to the rafters は「たる木に達するほど」の意で、屋内の密集・混雑ぶりを強調する)

ひしもち 菱餅 a *hishimochi*; (説明的に) lozenge-shaped rice cakes with three layers of red, white, and green (for the Girl's Festival).

ひしゃ 飛車 (将棋の) a *hisha*; (チェスの) a rook.

ひしゃく 柄杓 a ladle /léidl/. ●ひしゃくで水をくむ *ladle* water (*into* a bowl).

びじゃく 微弱 — 微弱な 形 slight, (very) weak. ●微弱な震動 a *slight* [a *weak*, a *faint*] shake.

ひしゃげる go* out of shape; (ひどく) be crushed (out of shape).

ひしゃたい 被写体 (対象) an object; (対象として選ばれた物 [人]) a subject.

びしゃもん(てん) 毘沙門(天) *Bishamonten*; (説明的に) the god of war, one of the seven gods of good luck.

ぴしゃりと ❶ [強く閉めたりする様子] (戸などを閉めるとき) with a slam, (平手打ちなどのとき) with a slap. (!) slam, slap は動詞としても用いられる） ●彼のほほをぴしゃりと打つ *slap* him on the cheek; *slap* his cheek. ●蚊 [ハエ] をぴしゃりとたたく *swat* a mosquito [a fly]. ▶彼は引き出しをぴしゃりと閉めた He shut the drawer *with a slam*./He *slammed* the drawer (shut).
❷ [断固として] (堅く) firmly, (明確に) definitely; (きっぱりと) flatly. (⇨ぴしゃんと) ▶彼女は彼の求婚をぴしゃりと断わった She *flatly* refused his marriage proposal.
❸ [正確に合致して] perfectly, exactly.

ぴしゃんと (!) 「ぴしゃりと」 より荒々しさなどが加わるので、hard, sharp など修飾語をつけて工夫する: with a *hard* [a *sharp*] slam) ▶彼らは私の鼻先で戸をぴしゃんと閉めた They *slammed* the door on me [in my face].

びしゅ 美酒 delicious *sake* [wine]. ●勝利の美酒に酔う enjoy a good drink to celebrate a victory.

ビジュアル — ビジュアルな 形 visual. ●ビジュアルアーツ the visual arts. ●ビジュアル効果 (a) visual effect. ●ビジュアルデザイン visual design.

ひじゅう 比重 specific gravity, relative density; [重要性] weight, importance. ▶金の比重はいくらですか What is the *density* of gold? (!) 比重が大きい [小さい] は have a high [a low] density) ▶学校生活でクラブ活動の占める比重は大きい Club activities *are given* great *weight* [*importance*] in school life.

びしゅう 美醜 beauty or ugliness; (器量) looks; appearance.

ひしゅうしょくご 被修飾語 [言語] a modified [a qualified] word.

ひじゅつ 秘術 the secret, a secret art [(技術) technique /teknı́ːk/]. ●秘術を伝授する hand down the *secrets* (*to* them). ●秘術を尽くして戦う fight to the best of one's ability; try every possible means to win.

***びじゅつ** 美術 art (!) 1部門をいうときは an 〜); the fine arts. (!) 以上いずれも絵画・彫刻・建築をさす. art は音楽・文学・劇・舞踊などを含めた「芸術」の意でも用いる) ●造形美術 plastic *arts*. ●近代美術 modern *art*. ●大学で東洋 [西洋] 美術を研究する study the Oriental [Western] *art* at college. ●美術専攻の学生 an *art* student; a student majoring in *art*. ●美術に興味がある be interested in *art* [*the fine arts*]. ●美術は選択科目です *Art* is an elective subject.
— 美術の 形 artistic.
— 美術的に 副 artistically.
●美術家 an artist. ●美術学校 an árt schòol.

●美術館 an árt gàllery [musèum]. ●近代美術館 a museum of modern art (近代美術館) のようにもいう) ●美術工芸 arts and crafts. ●美術書 an árt bòok. ●美術商 an árt dèaler. ●美術展 an art exhibìtion. ●(!) an exhibition of Western art (西洋美術展) のようにもいう) ●美術評論家 an árt crìtic. ●美術品 a work of art; (集合的) (fine) art. ●美術部 an árt clùb.

ひじゅん 批准 名 《書》ratification. ●包括的核実験禁止条約の批准が否決された *Ratification* of the Comprehensive Test Ban Treaty was rejected.
— 批准する 動 《書》ratify. ●条約を批准する *ratify* a treaty.
●批准書 an instrument of ratification.

ひしょ 秘書 a (private) secretary /sékrətèri/, 《to》) 米国の企業では an assistant (補佐役) の方が好まれる傾向にある); (集合的) the secretarial staff. ●医療秘書 a medical *secretary*. ●秘書の職を得る get a post [a position] as a *secretary*. ▶私はハリソンの秘書の山本と申します I am Yamamoto, (a) *secretary to* [*of] Mr. Harrison. ●彼女は社長秘書を務めた She was the president's *secretary* [(個人秘書) personal *assistant*]./She was [acted as] (a) *secretary to* [×*of*] the president. (!) 複数の社長秘書のうちの 1 人の意では a をつける. それ以外では通例無冠詞)
●秘書科 a secretarial course. ●秘書課 the secretarial section. ●秘書学校 a secretarial school. ●秘書官 a minister's secretary. ●秘書室 a secretariat(e) /sèkrətə́riət/.

ひしょ 避暑 ▶私たちは北海道に避暑に行くつもりです We are going to Hokkaido to *escape the summer heat*./We are going to *spend* [*pass*] the *summer* in Hokkaido.
●避暑客 a súmmer vìsitor. ●避暑地 a súmmer resòrt.

びじょ 美女 a beautiful woman [girl], 《やや古》 a beauty. (⇨美人) ●目のさめるような金髪の美女 (話) a striking blonde *bombshell*. (!) しばしば blonde とともに用いられる)

ひしょう 卑小 ●卑小な(=取るに足らない)考え a *petty* [a *trifling*] idea.

ひしょう 飛翔 名 [書] flight; (高所への) soaring.
— 飛翔する 動 fly; soar. ●大空を飛翔する *soar* high in the sky.

***ひじょう** 非常 [非常の場合] an emergency. ●非常事態 (⇨非常事態) ●国家の非常時 a national *emergency* [(危機) crisis]. ●非常の場合に備えるprepare for [provide against] *emergencies*; prepare for *the worst*. ▶非常の場合にはこの番号に電話をかけてください Call this telephone number *in an emergency*./In case of (an) *emergency* 《主に米》[*In the event of an emergency* 《書》] call this telephone number. ▶私たちは非常の場合に備えて貯金しておかなければならない We must save money *for an emergency* [*for a rainy day*].
●非常階段 an emergency staircase; (火災時の) a fire escape. ●非常口 (go out through) an emergency exit [door]. ●非常コック an emergency handle. ●非常手段 (take) emergency [(極端な) extreme, (例外的な) exceptional] measures. ●非常食 emergency rations. ●非常停止ボタン an emergency stop.

ひじょう 非情 [書] [無情, 冷酷) ●非情の人 a *heartless* [an *unfeeling*, (残酷な) a *cruel*] person.

びしょう 美称 (ほめていう呼び方) a eulogistic /jùːləd ʒístɪk/ name 《for》.

びしょう 微小 图 minuteness /maín(j)úːtnɪs/.
— **微小な** (非常に小さい) microscopic; minute.
- 微小な生物 a *microscopic* organism; a microorganism.
- 微小な音(=かすかな)音 a *faint* sound.
- 微小地震 a micro earthquake.

びしょう 微少 ● 微少な(=非常に少ない)量の鉛 a *very small* amount of lead.

びしょう 微笑 a smile. (!特に形容詞を加えなくてよい) ● 口元に微笑を浮かべて with [wearing] a *smile* on one's lips.

びしょう 尾錠 (ベルトなどの) a buckle. ● ベルトを尾錠でしめる *buckle* (up) a belt.

ひじょうきん 非常勤 — **非常勤(の)** 图 part-time.
- 英語の非常勤講師をしている be a *part-time* (→a full-time) teacher of English (*at*); teach English *part-time* (*at*). (!*at* の後はいずれの教育機関でもよい (⇒講師))

***ひじょうしき 非常識** — **非常識な** 图 absurd; (法外な) unreasonable; (思慮のない) thoughtless. ● 非常識である have no [lack, be lacking in] common sense. ● そんなことを言うなんて非常識だ It's *absurd of* you [You're *absurd*] *to* say such a thing. (!後の方が直接的で語調が強い)

ひじょうじたい 非常事態 — **非常事態(の場合)**an emergency; [状態]a state of emergency. ● 非常事態が起きたら if an *emergency* comes [《やや書》 occurs]. ● 非常事態にある be in a *state of emergency*. ● 非常事態を宣言する declare a *state of emergency*; declare an *emergency*.

ひじょうしゃ 非使用者 an employee.

びじょうじょ 美少女 a good-looking [a pretty, a beautiful] (young) girl.

ひじょうじょう 非上場 — **非上場の** 图 unlisted.
- 非上場株 an unlisted stock. ● 非上場企業 an unlisted company.

ひじょうせん 非常線 a cordon. ● その一帯に非常線を張る put a *cordon* around the area; cordon off the area. ● 警察の非常線を突破する break through the police *cordons*.

ひじょうな 非常な [程度が大きい] great; (極端な) extreme; [ものすごい] terrible; (強烈な) intense; (普通でない) unusual; (並外れた) extraordinary; (異常な) abnormal. ● 非常な驚き a *great* [a *complete*, a *total*] surprise. ● 非常な暑さ *terrible* [*intense, extreme*] heat. ● 非常な興味を示す show a *great* [an *intense*, a *strong*, an *abnormal*] interest (*in*).

***ひじょうに 非常に** very; much; very much; so; greatly; extremely; 《書》 most.

> **使い分け** **very** 最も一般的で, かつ口語的な語. 原級の形容詞・副詞または形容詞化した過去・現在分詞を修飾する. (逆に very がついているか, 次の much がついているかによって過去分詞の形容詞化の尺度となる.) 特に感情や心理状態を示す形容詞化した過去分詞 (pleased, tired などには very で修飾することが多い: I was *very* surprised *at* [to hear] the news. しかし, 動詞のもとの意味が強く働くと感じられる場合は **much**, **very much** を用いる: I was (*very*) *much* surprised *by* his sudden visit.
> **so** very の口語的な代用語. 特に女性が好んで使う.
> **greatly** 動詞・過去分詞を修飾することが多い.
> **extremely** 「大いに, 実に」という程度が高いことを表し very より強意的.
> **most** much の最上級の形だが, the をつけないで感情を含む形容詞・副詞を修飾する.

- 非常におもしろい本 a *very* [a *most*] interesting book. (! the móst interesting book は「いちばんおもしろい本」) ● 今日は非常に寒い It's *very* [*extremely*, (本当に) *really*] cold today. ▶ 私は彼が非常に好きだ I like him *very* [*so*] *much*. (!×I like him *much*. は不可)/I'm *very* [*so*] fond of him. (!《米》では主に女性が用いる) ● 彼はその知らせを聞いては非常に喜んだ He was *very* [*much*, *very much*] pleased at the news. (!(1) *very* が最も普通. (2) 通例 ×He was pleased at the news very much. とはしない) ▶ あの子は非常に親切なのでみんなに好かれている She is *so* kind [*such* a kind girl, 《書》 *so* kind a girl] (*that*) everybody likes her. (!(1) 《話》ではしばしば that を省略する. (2) 日常会話では Everybody likes her, she is *so* kind. などということも多い. (3) so+形容詞に続く名詞は必ず不定冠詞を伴う) ● その政治家は地元では非常に尊敬されていた The politician was *greatly* [*highly*] respected [People had *great* respect for the politician] in his [her] hometown.

びしょうねん 美少年 a good-looking [a handsome] boy.

びじょうり 非条理 (⇒不条理)

びしょく 美食 (うまい食べ物) delicious food; (栄養食) a nourishing diet.
- 美食家 (食通) a gourmet /ɡúərmeɪ/; an epicure.

びじょとやじゅう 『美女と野獣』 *Beauty and the Beast*. [参考] フランスの童話.

びしょぬれ びしょ濡れ ▶ 彼らは雨でびしょぬれになった They *got wet through* in the rain. (!次例より口語的)/They *got soaked to the* [×*their*] *skin* in the rain. (!*to the skin* は意味を強める. 省略可) ▶ 服を脱ぎなさい. びしょぬれじゃないの Take your clothes off! They *are soaking* (*wet*) [*are soaked through*]. (!後半は You're *all wet*. ともいえる) ▶ シャツは汗でびしょぬれだった My shirt *was wet through* [*dripping wet*] with sweat. (!主語は人も可)

びしょびしょ (したたるほど) dripping wet; (しみ通って) wet through; (浸るほど) soaked. (⇒びしょぬれ) ▶ 水があふれて床がびしょびしょになった The water overflowed and *flooded* the floor./The water overflowed and the floor *got very wet*. (!この場合 dripping [soaking] wet は不適

ビジョン [展望] (a) vision. ● ビジョンのある(=先見性のある, 想像力豊かな)リーダー a leader of *vision*.

ひじり 聖 (高僧) a high(-ranking) priest; (聖人) a saint; (達人) a master.

びしりと (閉めたり下ろしたりして音を立て) with a slam (⇒ぴしゃりと); (むちの音や物がはじける音がして) with a crack; (拒絶などはっきりと) flatly. ● ドアをぴしりと閉める slam the door. ▶ そのライオン使いはむちを何度もぴしりと鳴らした The lion-tamer *cracked* his whip many times.

びしれいく 美辞麗句 《軽蔑的》《use》 flowery [pretty] words. ● 美辞麗句の多い演説 a *flowery* speech.

びしん 微震 a slight earthquake [tremor].

びじん 美人 a beautiful [a good-looking] woman, 《やや古》 a beauty. ● 目を見張るような美人 a stunning *beauty*.
- 美人コンテスト a beauty contest.

ピジン [混成語] (a) pidgin.
- ピジンイングリッシュ pidgin English.

ビス [<フランス語] (ねじ) a screw /skruː/; (ねじくぎ) a bolt.

ひすい 翡翠 (宝石) jade.

ビスケット 《米》 a cookie, (主に英) a biscuit; (薄くてかりかりした) a cracker.

ビスコース 〖化学〗viscose.
ビスタ 〖細く長い眺め〗a vista.
● ビスタカー (列車の展望車) an observation car; (2階建ビスタ[電車]) a double-decker; 《和製語》a vista car.
ピスタチオ 〖＜イタリア語〗〖植物〗a pistachio /pistǽ-ʃiou/.
ヒスタミン 〖生化学〗histamine. ● 抗ヒスタミン剤 an antihistamine.
ヒステリー 〖＜ギリシャ語〗〖病気〗〖医学〗hysteria /histíəriə/; 〖発作〗〖医学〗hysterics /histériks/(〖!〗単・複両扱い.《話》では be in [have] *hysterics* の形で単に「感情的になっている[なる]」ことを表す). ● ヒステリーを起こす go into [have a fit of] *hysterics*; become *hysterical*. ● ヒステリーを起こしている be in a state of *hysteria*; be in *hysterics*.
ヒステリック —— **ヒステリックな** 形 hysterical. (⇒ヒステリー)
ピストル a pistol, 《主に米》a handgun; 〖回転弾倉の〗a revolver; 〖自動の〗an automatic (pistol); 〖銃器〗a gun. ● ピストルで撃つ shoot (it) with a *pistol*; (ねらって撃つ) fire a *gun* (*at*, *on*). ● ピストルを向ける point [aim] a *pistol* (*at*). ● 人質はピストルを突きつけられて手を挙げた The hostages held up their arms [hands] *at gunpoint*.
● ピストル強盗 (人) a robber armed with a gun [a pistol]; (事) an armed robbery.
ビストロ 〖＜フランス語〗〖小レストラン〗a bistro.
ピストン a piston. ● 駅とコンサート会場の間をバスがピストン輸送している Buses *shuttle* (*back and forth*) [There's a *shuttle* bus service] *between* the station and the concert hall.
ヒスパニック 〖米国のラテンアメリカ系住民〗a Hispanic.
ビスマルク 〖ドイツの政治家〗Bismarck /bízmɑːrk/ (Otto von ～).
ひずみ 歪み 〖板などの〗a warp (〖!〗複数形なし); 〖機械などの〗a strain; 〖音などの〗(a) distortion. ● 板のひずみ a warp in a board. ● ひずみのない音 a sound without *distortion*. ● 経済のひずみ (不均衡) economic *maladjustment*.
ひずむ 歪む warp, be [get] warped.
ひする 比する (⇒比べる)
びせい 美声 (*in*) a beautiful [a sweet] voice.
びせいぶつ 微生物 a microbe, a microorganism. ▶微生物で分解できる(＝生分解性の)プラスチックは環境にやさしい素材の一つである Biodegradable /bàioudiɡréidəbl/ plastic is one of the eco-friendly materials.
● 微生物学 microbiology.
ビゼー 〖フランスの作曲家〗Bizet /biːzéi/ (Georges /ʒɔːrʒ/ ～).
ひせき 秘跡, 秘蹟 〖キリスト教〗a sacrament; the sacrament. ● 秘跡を受ける receive *the sacrament*.
びせきぶん 微積分 〖数学〗differential and integral calculus.
ひぜに 日銭 a daily cash income. ▶商売をしていると日銭は入るが, まとまった金はなかなか用意できない Of course my business *brings in some cash daily*, but sometimes it isn't easy to have a sizable sum of money on hand.
ひぜめ 火攻め a fire attack. ▶敵城を火攻めにした They attacked by *setting fire to* the enemy's castle.
ひぜめ 火責め a torture by fire. ● 罪人を火責めにする *torture* the criminal *with fire*.
ひせん 卑賎 名 lowliness; humbleness.
—— **卑賎な** 形 lowly; humble. ▶彼は卑賎の素性を恥じなかった He was not ashamed of his *lowly* [*humble*] origins.
ひせんきょけん 被選挙権 eligibility for election. ● 被選挙権がある be eligible (*for*). ▶彼は市長の被選挙権がある He *is eligible for* the mayoral election [*to run for mayor*]. ▶知事の被選挙権は30歳からである A candidate for prefectural governor must be at least thirty./You have to be at least thirty in order to run for governor. (〖!〗be eligible は年齢以外の要素も含むので, 年齢だけを問題にする場合はこのようにする方がよい)
ひせんきょにん 被選挙人 a person eligible for election [elective office].
ひせんとういん 非戦闘員 a noncombatant.
ひせんろん 非戦論 pacifism. ● 非戦論を唱える cry against [be opposed to] (the) war.
● 非戦論者 a pacifist.
ひそ 砒素 〖化学〗ársenic 〖元素記号 As〗.
びそ 鼻祖 〖創始者〗the originator.
ひそう 皮相 —— **皮相(的)な** 形 superficial; 〖表面的な〗surface. ● 皮相的な見方 one's *superficial* view.
ひそう 悲壮 —— **悲壮な** 形 悲壮な決意で (断固とした) with *grim* determination; (哀れをさそう) with *pathetic* resolution. ● 悲壮な(＝悲劇的な)最期を遂げる die a *tragic* [英雄らしい a *heroic*] death.
ひぞう 秘蔵 —— **秘蔵の** 形 〖お気に入りの〗favorite; 〖大事な〗treasured. ● 秘蔵の品 a treasure. ● 秘蔵っ子 (⇒秘蔵(ひぞう)っ子)
—— **秘蔵する** 動 treasure 《a sword》.
ひぞう 脾臓 〖解剖〗a spleen.
びそう 美装 —— **美装する** 動 (美しく飾る) be beautifully dressed; (本を) be beautifully bound.
びぞう 微増 a slight increase (*in*).
—— **微増する** 動 increase slightly. ▶生産高は年々微増している The output *is increasing slightly* year by year.
ひそうぞくにん 被相続人 〖法律〗an áncestor.
ひそかに ひそかに (人に知られないように隠れて) secretly, in secret; (他人を入れないで内々に) privately; (人に気づかれないようそっと) stealthily; 〖心の中で〗in one's heart; inwardly. ● ひそかに出かける go out *secretly* [*in secret*]; slip out. ● 心中ひそかにほくそ笑む laugh *inwardly*; (やや話) laugh *up one's sleeve*. (〖!〗しばしば意地悪く) ▶心中ひそかに期するものがある I have a firm resolution *in my heart*.
ひぞく 卑俗 名 vulgarity. —— **卑俗な** 形 vulgar.
ひぞく 卑属 (子孫) a descendant. ● 直系卑属 a lineal *descendant*. ● 傍系卑属 a collateral *descendant*.
ひぞっこ 秘蔵っ子 (子供) one's favorite [darling] child; (弟子) one's favorite pupil.
ひそひそ (ささやくように) in a whisper; (低い声で) in a low voice. ▶彼らはよく隅でひそひそ話をしている They are often *whispering* [*speaking in whispers*] in the corner.
ひそみ 顰み (眉をしかめること) frowning; knitting one's brows.
● ひそみにならう (盲目的に人を真似る) imitate [(人に従う) follow] 《him》blindly.
ひそむ 潜む ❶〖潜在する〗lurk; (背後に) lie* behind (...). ▶うまい話には危険が潜んでいる Some dangers *lurk* in [*lie behind*] a tempting offer.
❷〖身を隠す〗hide* (oneself); (待ち伏せる) lurk. (⇒隠れる)
ひそめる 潜める (身を) hide* (oneself); (声を) lower

ひそめる [drop (-pp-)] 《one's voice》.

ひそめる 顰める （まゆを） frown 《on》; （寄せる）《書》 knit* 《one's brows》. [事情] 考えたり心配したりするときの表情

ひそやか 密やか （ひっそりとした） quiet; （さやかな） secret.

ひだ 襞 [折りひだ] a fold; （スカートなどの） a pleat; [ギャザー] gathers; [キノコの] a lamella. ● カーテン[シルクのドレス]のひだ the *folds* of the curtains [silk dress]. ● ひだのよった pleat; fold; gather.
● **ひだスカート** a pleated skirt; a skirt with pleats.

*__ひたい__ 額 a forehead /fɔ́ːrhed/ 《米》 fɔ́ːrhèd, 《英》 fɔ́rid/, [眉（まゆ）] a brow /bráu/. ● しわの寄った額 a *furrowed forehead* [*brow*]. ● 額の切り傷 a cut in [on] the *forehead* [*brow*]. ● 額の汗をふく wipe sweat from one's *brow* [*forehead*]. ● 額をこする rub one's *forehead*. [!] 思い出そうとするしぐさ ● 額にしわを寄せる wrinkle one's *forehead* [*brow*]; knit one's *brow(s)* [!] 複数形は「両の眉（まゆ）」の意. 不快や考え込むしぐさ); frown. ● 額（= 目）に手をかざしている He has a *high* [a broad (↔a narrow)] *forehead*. [!] broad は単に面積の広い額を, high は知性を備えた額を意味する
● **額に汗する** ● 額に汗して働く work [(金を稼ぐ) earn money] by the sweat of one's *brow* [!] 聖書に基づく慣用表現で文語的); work with one's own hands in sweat.
● **額を集める** ● 額を集めて相談する put one's *heads* [×*forehead*] *together*; 《話》go into a huddle.

ひだい 肥大 [名] (器官や組織の) [医学] hypertrophy.
—— **肥大した** [形] ● 肥大した心臓 an *enlarged* heart.

びたい 媚態 flirtation; 《書》 coquetry. [!] 媚（び）) ● 彼女は会社のどの男性にも媚態を示す She *flirts with* every man in the office.

びたいちもん びた一文 a penny (!! 《英》 1 ペニー, 《米》 1 セント), 《米》 a cent; (10 セント) 《米》 a dime.
● びた一文出さない won't give *a penny* (*for*).

ひたおし 直押し —— **直押しする** [動] push ahead 《with the plan》.

ひたかくし ひた隠し ● 彼はそのことをひた隠しにしていた He tried his best [hardest] to keep it hidden [(秘密に) secret, in the dark].

ひたき 鶲 [鳥] a flycatcher.

びだくおん 鼻濁音 [言語] a nasal sonant.

ピタゴラス [ギリシャの哲学者・数学者] Pythagoras /pəθǽgərəs/.

ひたしもの 浸し物 (⇒御浸し)

*__ひたす__ 浸す (ちょっと漬ける) dip (-pp-) 《in, into》; (漬けておく) soak 《in》; (体の部分を) bathe. ● 豆を水にひと晩浸す *soak* beans *in* water overnight.

ひたすら [ただ] only; [非常に] earnestly; [熱心に] very hard. (⇒一生懸命) ● 彼はひたすらがん細胞の研究に打ち込んだ He devoted himself *entirely* [*heart and soul*] to his research on cancer cells. [!] heart and soul は文尾に置いてもよい ● 母は息子の無事をひたすら祈った The mother *earnestly* prayed for her son's safety.

ひだち 肥立ち (産後の回復) recovery, convalescence 《after childbirth》. ● 彼女は産後の肥立ちがよい[悪い] She *is doing well* [*badly*] after childbirth.

ぴたっと ● ぴたっと（= 急に）雨がやんだ *Suddenly* it stopped raining.

ひたと ❶ [ぴったりと] ● ひたと彼の背後につく be *close behind* him.
❷ [突然] suddenly. ● 風がひたとやんだ The wind *has fallen*.
❸ [ひたすら] ● 顔をひたと見つめる stare 《him》 *straight* in the face.

ひだね 火種 [火火] a live charcoal to build a fire with; [原因] a cause. ● 両国の争いの火種 the *cause* of conflicts between the two countries.

ひたはしる 走る [ひたすら走る] run* and run; [急ぐ] run as fast as one can*; (必死に走る) run for one's life. ● 彼らは警察の手から逃れるためひた走った（必死に走った） They *ran for* their *lives* to escape from the police.

ひたひた ❶ [水などが静かに触れる] lap against…. ● 小波が岸辺にひたひた寄せていた Small waves *were lapping against* the shore.
❷ [ちょうど浸る量の] ● 魚をひたひたの水で煮る boil fish with water *that just covers it*.
❸ [着実に迫って] steadily; (威嚇するように) ménacingly. ● 大群衆がひたひた寄せてきた A large crowd closed in (on us). [!] close in は「(攻撃しようと)だんだん取り囲む」の意だが, gradually, steadily などを添えて意味を明確にできる

ひだまり 日だまり a (warm,) sunny spot [place].

ビタミン a vitamin /váitəmin/. [!] 通例複数形で) ● ビタミンの欠乏による病気 illness caused by *vitamin* deficiency. ● この野菜はビタミン K が豊富だ This vegetable is rich in *vitamin K*.
● **ビタミン剤** a vitamin pill; (丸薬) a vitamin tàblet. [!] 総合ビタミン剤は a multivitamin tablet [pill].

ひたむき —— **ひたむきな** [形] (熱心な) intent; (一つの目的を持った) single-minded. ● ひたむきな態度 an *intent* attitude. ● 仕事にひたむきである be *intent on* [*single-minded about*] one's work.
—— **ひたむきに** [副] intently; single-mindedly.

:**ひだり** 左 [解説・用例は (⇒左の)]
❶ [左(側)[手, 方]] left. [!] 通例 the [one's] ~)
①[左(の)~] left, left-hand. ● 左足 one's *left* leg. ● 左きき a *left-handed* person. ● 左ききの選手 a *left-hander*. ● 左投げの投手 a *left-handed* pitcher; a southpaw; a lefty. ● 左打ちのバッター a *left-handed* batter; a lefty. ● 彼は右投げ左打ちだ He bats left, throws right. [!] 日本語では語順が逆
②[左に[へ]] on the [one's] left(-hand [-side]); to the [one's] left. ● 左へ曲がる turn 《*to the*》 *left*. ● 左に見える see 《it》 *on* one's *left*.
❷ [左翼] (個人) a leftist [!] しばしば L-); (人々, 集団) the left (wing) [!] 集合的用い単・複両扱い. しばしば L- (W-)). ● 左(派)の left [!] しばしば L-); leftist [!] しばしば L-); left-wing.

ぴたり (正確に) right, just; (完全に) 《話》 dead. (⇒ぴったり) ● 彼はぴたりと当てた He guessed *right*. ● 車がぴたりと彼女の前に止まった A car stopped *dead* [*right*] in front of her. [!] dead では止まり方が完全であること, right では停止の位置が彼女の真ん前であることを意味する. ただし dead の前にポーズを置いた言い方 (right と同義になる) ● 矢がぴたりと的の中心を射た The arrow hit the bull's-eye. ● 発言や予想がぴたりと当たったときも比喩的に bull's-eye を用いる: それ[彼の言葉]はぴたりと当たった It [His words] hit the bull's-eye.)

ひだりうえ 左上 ● 左上の[に] at the upper left.

ひだりうちわ 左うちわ ● 彼は左うちわだ He's comfortably off though he doesn't work for money.

ひだりがわ 左側 the left (side), the left-hand side. (⇒右側) ● 左側通行 (掲示) Keep (to the) *left*. ● イギリスでは車は左側通行になっている They drive

ひだりきき 左利き 图 (人) a left-handed person; a left-hander. ● 左利きの 形 left-handed; lefty.

ひだりした 左下 ● 左下の[に] at the lower left.

ひだりづめ 左詰め ● 左詰めにする left-justify.

ひだりて 左手 the left hand; (左側) the left [left-hand] side. (⇨左側) ● 左手で持つ hold (it) in one's *left hand*.

ひだりまえ 左前 ● 左前である (金銭面で困っている) be hard up, be badly off; 《書・婉曲的》 be in straitened circumstances.

ひだりまわり 左回り ── 左回りの[に] 形 副 《米》 counterclockwise 《英》 anticlockwise. ● このロータリーでは車は左回りに進む All cars move *counterclockwise* [move to the *counterclockwise* direction] in this traffic circle.

***ひたる** 浸る [[浸水する]] be flooded (⇨漬かる); [[ふける]] (思索・空想などに) be lost [deep] 《*in*》, (酒・悲しみなどに) give* oneself over 《*to*》; (勉強・仕事などに 没頭する) be absorbed [engrossed] 《*in*》. ● 喜びに浸る bask *in* the pleasure 《*of*》; (我を忘れる) be beside oneself with joy. ● 絶望に浸る give oneself over to despair.

ひだるま 火達磨 (炎のかたまり) a mass of flames. ● そのヘリコプターは火達磨になって墜落した The helicopter *burst into flames* and went down.

ひたん 悲嘆 ● 悲嘆に暮れる grieve deeply 《*for* him; *over* it》. (⇨嘆く)

ひだん 被弾 ── 被弾する 動 ● 彼女は脚に被弾した A *bullet hit* her in the leg./She *was shot* in the leg.

びだん 美談 a beautiful [(道徳的に模範となる) a moral] story.

びだんし 美男子 a handsome [a good-looking] man 《複 men》.

びちく 備蓄 图 (大量の) a stockpile 《*of*》. ● 石油の備蓄基地 an oil *stockpile* base.
── 備蓄する 動 have ... in store; (大量に) stockpile, build a stockpile 《*of*》.

ぴちぴち ❶ [[元気のいい様子]] ● ぴちぴちした女の子 a *vibrant* [a *cheerful and lively* /láivli/] girl. ● 魚がぴちぴちはねる Fish are jumping *energetically*.
❷ [[勢いよく当たる様子]] ● 雨が窓にぴちぴちはね返っていた The rain *was pelting against* the window. ● フライパンの油がぴちぴちはねる The oil *spits* [*spatters*] in the frying pan.

ひちゃくしゅつ 非嫡出 illegitimacy.
● 非嫡出子 an illegitimate child; (私生児) a love child.

びちゃびちゃ ── びちゃびちゃの 形 [[ぬかるんで]] (雪解けで) slushy; (泥水で) muddy; [[ぬれて]] (water) soaking (wet). ● 雪解け道を歩いたらキャンバスシューズがびちゃびちゃになった The slushy road made my canvas shoes *very* [*soaking*] *wet*.

ぴちゃぴちゃ ❶ [[しぶきを上げる様子]] splash. ● 子供は水をぴちゃぴちゃするのが好きだ Children like to *splash* water.
❷ [[舌鼓を打つ様子]] smack. ● あの人はぴちゃぴちゃわせてものを食べる癖がある He has a habit of *smacking* his lips while eating his food.
❸ [[主に犬や猫などが舌を鳴らして飲む様子]] lap (-pp-) ... (up). ● 子猫たちがぴちゃぴちゃとミルクを飲み続けた The kittens kept *lapping* (*up*) milk. ● lap はさざ波の寄せる音などにも用いる)

ひちゅう 秘中 ● 秘中の秘 a top secret. (⇨極秘)

びちょうせい 微調整 图 fine-tuning; fine [minor] adjustment.
── 微調整する 動 ● 計画を微調整する *fine-tune* the plan.

ひちりき 篳篥 《楽器》 a *hichiriki*; (説明的に) an end-blown flute with seven finger holes in front and two holes in the rear, used in Japanese court music, similar to a recorder or flageolet.

ひつ 櫃 a chest. ● 米びつ a rice tub.

ひつあつ 筆圧 the pressure of the pen on the paper; the strength of one's brushstroke.

ひつう 悲痛 图 grief; sorrow.
── 悲痛 形 ● 助けを求める悲痛な叫び *heart-rending* cries for help. ● 悲痛な面持ち a look of sorrow; a *sorrowful* look.

ひっか 筆禍 ● その記事のために彼は筆禍を招いた His own article got him into trouble./His own article caused him a lot of problem.

ひっかかり 引っ掛かり ❶ [[引っ掛かるところ]] (ホックのような) a catch.
❷ [[関係]] ● 私はあの会社とは何の引っ掛かりもない I have no *connection* with the firm.

ひっかかる 引っ掛かる ❶ [[物が]] (かかって離れない) catch* 《*in, on*》; (捕えられる) be caught. ● クモの巣に引っ掛かる be [get] *caught in* a cobweb. ● たこが木に[枝の先に]引っ掛かった The kite *got caught in* the tree [*on* the tip of a branch]. ● 骨がのどに引っ掛かった (突き刺さった) I got a bone *stuck* [*caught*] *in* my throat. ● 留め金がうまく引っ掛からない The hook doesn't *catch*.
❷ [[だまされる]] ● 彼の策略に引っ掛かる be *cheated* [be *deceived*, 《やや話》 be *taken in*] by his tricks; *fall for* his tricks.
会話「や一い, 引っ掛かった(=私は君をひっかけた)」「じゃ, 今のは芝居だったの」「その通り. 君はまんまと引っ掛かったってわけさ」"Hey, *I had you*." "So you mean you were only acting?" "That's right. You totally *fell for* it."
❸ [[かかわり合う]] ● 悪い女に引っ掛かる get *involved* [《やや書》 *entangled*] *with* a bad woman.
❹ [[検査などに]] ● ドーピング検査に引っ掛かる *fail* a dope test.
❺ [[気になる]] ● ちょっと引っ掛かることがある I *have* something *on* [x*in*] *my mind*.

ひっかきまわす 引っ掻き回す [[場所をかき回して捜す]] rummage /rámidʒ/ 《about [around]》 《*in* [*through*]＋場所; *for*＋物》; [[混乱させる]] throw* ... into confusion; (かき乱す) upset*. ● 引き出しを引っかき回して鍵を捜す *rummage* (*about*) *in* the drawer *for* a key. ● クラスを引っかき回す *throw* the class *into confusion*; *upset* the class atmosphere.

ひっかく 引っ掻く scratch. ● 猫にひどく引っかかれた I was badly *scratched* by the cat. ● 彼はバラで手を引っかいた He *scratched* his hand *on* [x*with*] a rose (bush).

ひっかける 引っ掛ける ❶ [[くぎなどに]] catch*. ● 彼女はドレスをくぎに引っ掛けた She *caught* her dress *on* [x*with*] a nail./A nail *caught* her dress./Her dress *caught on* a nail.
❷ [[つるす]] hang*; [[急いで着る]] throw* [slip (-pp-)] (a coat) on. ● コートを掛けくぎに引っ掛ける *hang* one's coat *on* the peg.
❸ [[水などを浴びせる]] ● 猫につまずきそうになって持っていたコーヒーを引っ掛けてしまった I nearly tripped over a cat and *spilled* my coffee *on* myself.
❹ [[だます]] deceive; (まんまと) trick, cheat; 《やや話》 take* ... in; (誘惑する) seduce. ● 彼らは彼

うまく引っ掛けて大金を巻き上げた They *cheated* [*tricked*] him *out of* a large sum of money.

ひっかぶる 引っ被る ❶［被る］pull ... over one's head. (⇨被る❷) ❷［引き受ける］take; assume. (⇨被る❺)

ひつき 火付き ▶この木は火付きがいい This wood *kindles* [*catches fire*] easily.

ひっき 筆記 ── **筆記する** 動 ●講義を筆記する (書き留める) *write down* a lecture; (メモをとる) *take* [*make*] *notes of* a lecture.
  ●**筆記試験** a written examination. ●**筆記体** 《write in》script [cursive letters]. ●**筆記用具** writing materials.

ひつぎ 柩 a coffin, 《主に米》a casket (❗coffin の婉曲語). (⇨棺).

ひっきょう 畢竟 (つまり) in short (⇨つまり❷); (結局) after all; in the end (⇨結局).

ひっきりなし ●ひっきりなしの(=絶え間ない)騒音 (an) *incessant* noise. ▶ゆうべからひっきりなしに(=連続的に)雪が降っている It has been snowing *continuously* [*とぎれなく*) *without a break*] since last night. ▶今日はひっきりなしに(=次々と)来客があって I had visitors *one after another* [*one* visitor *after another*] today. (⇨絶えず) ▶その件に関する問い合わせの電話がひっきりなしにかかってきています Our phone has *been ringing off the hook* with inquiries about the matter. (❗《米》で「(電話が)かかりっぱなしである」の意)

ピッキング 图 lock picking. ●ピッキング対策 a measure against *lock picking*.
── **ピッキングする** 動 pick a lock.

ビッグ［大きい, 重大な］big.
  ●ビッグイベント a big event. ●ビッグニュース big news.

ピックアップ ❶［選択］▶読みたい本を5冊ピックアップした (選んだ) I *picked out* [*chose*, ×*picked up*] five books I wanted to read.
❷［小型トラック］a pick-up (truck).
❸［車で迎える］▶あした10時にピックアップしてくれますか *Pick* me *up* at 10 tomorrow, will you?

ビッグイヤー The Big Ear. (参考) UEFA チャンピオンズリーグ優勝トロフィーの愛称)

ビッグイニング［野球］a big inning. (参考) 3点以上が入るイニング)

ピックオフプレー (⇨牽制(球))

ひっくくる 引っ括る bind (old magazines); tie (a thief) (up). (⇨括る)

ビッグバン［宇宙爆発起源］［天文］the big bang.
  ●ビッグバン理論 the big bang theory.

ビッグベン［英国国会議事堂の時計塔］Big Ben.

***びっくり** 图 (a) surprise. (⇨驚き)
── **びっくりする** 動 be surprised [amazed, astonished, startled];［おびえる］be frightened;［不安になる］be alarmed;［衝撃を受ける］be shocked;［驚嘆する］《やや書》wonder,《書》marvel. (⇨驚く［類語］) ▶びっくりするじゃないか You *surprised* me./You did *startle* me. ▶彼は結婚すると言って私たちをびっくりさせた He *surprised* [*amazed*] us by saying that he was going to get married. ▶彼女の悲鳴にびっくりした I *was astonished at* her scream. ▶あの地震にはびっくりした I *was frightened* by the earthquake. ▶彼の腕前にはびっくりする We *are amazed* [*We wonder*] *at* his skill./We *are amazed* how skillful he is. ▶びっくりして目が覚めた I woke up *in surprise*. ▶君をびっくりさせることがある I have *a surprise* for you. ▶(贈り物・知らせなど)(息を止めていなさい) Hold your breath. (❗意外な知らせの前置き)

── **びっくりするような** 形 surprising, amazing, astonishing, startling;［おびえる］alarming;［驚嘆する］wonderful, marvelous. ●びっくりするような速度で with *amazing* speed.
  ●**びっくり箱** a jack-in-the-box. ●**びっくりマーク** (感嘆符) an exclamation point [《英》mark].

ひっくりかえす 引っ繰り返す ●［裏返す, 転がす］turn ... (over);［上下を逆にする］turn ... upside down;［傾けて倒す］tip (-pp-) ... over;［転覆させる］overturn, upset*. ●［引っくり返る］▶レコードを引っくり返す *turn* a record (*over*). ▶コップを(うっかり)引っくり返す *upset* a glass; (当たって) *knock* a glass *over*. ▶犬がいすを引っくり返した The dog *tipped* the chair *over*. (⇨倒す❶) ▶彼は部屋中を引っくり返したが財布は見つからなかった He *turned* the room *upside down* but couldn't find the wallet. (❗この turn ... upside down は「乱雑にする」の意)

ひっくりかえる 引っ繰り返る ●［裏返しになる, 転がる］turn over;［転覆する］overturn, upset*;［倒れる］fall* (down [over]); (勢いよく) tumble;［逆転される］be reversed. ▶石につまずいて引っくり返る *fall* [*tumble*] *over* a rock. ▶船があらしの中で引っくり返った The boat *turned over* [*overturned*, *upset*] in the storm./The storm *turned* the boat *over* [*overturned* the boat, *upset* the boat]. ▶いすにひどく背をもたれかけすぎたのでいすが引っくり返った I sat back too far in the chair and it *fell over*. ▶一審, 二審の有罪判決が最高裁で引っくり返った The guilty verdict in the first and second trial *was reversed* by the Supreme Court.

ピックルス pickles /píklz/. (⇨ピクルス)

ひっくるめる 引っ括るめる include. ▶この車は付属品を引っくるめて200万円だ This car costs two million yen, *including* extras [*inclusive of* extras, extras *included*].

ひつけ 火付け;(放火犯人) an arsonist. (⇨放火) ●**火付け役** (⇨火付け役)

ひづけ a date.
① ［～日付］▶正しい［正確な］日付 a correct [an exact] *date*. ▶5月3日の日付の手紙を受け取る receive 《his》letter *of* [*dated*] May 3(rd) [May (the) third, 《英》the third of May]. [❗of の方が口語的。3 は通例 (the) third と読む。(the) を省略するのは《米》)
② ［日付～］●(国際)日付変更線を越える cross the international *date* line.
③ ［日付は［が］］▶この手紙の日付は2005年5月1日となっている This letter *is dated* [《書》bears the *date of*] May 1, 2005. (❗《英》では 1 May, 2005 と書くことが多い。略記する場合は《米》5/1/05,《英》1/5/05) ▶この領収書には日付がない This receipt has no *date* on it [*is not dated*]./The *date* is not put on [*xin*] this receipt.
  ●**日付印** a datestamp.

ひっけい 必携 ●英語教師必携の本 a book *indispensable to* teachers of English. ●国文法必携(=便覧) a *handbook of* [*to*] Japanese grammar. ▶雨具必携のこと *Remember* [*Don't forget*] *to bring* an umbrella or a raincoat. (⇨雨具)

ひつけやく 火付け役 (扇動者) an agitator; (ごたごたを起こす人) a troublemaker, a firebrand. ▶例のごたごたの火付け役はだれか Who is the *leader* of the trouble?/Who caused the trouble?

ピッケル［<ドイツ語］an ice ax.

ひっけん 必見 ●必見のもの a must. (❗「どうしても...しなければならないもの」の意 (⇨必読)) ▶あの映画は必見だよ The film is a *must* [a *must-see*]./(見逃さない) You can't miss the film.

ひっこう 筆耕 copying; (人) a copyist.
ひっこし 引っ越し (⇨引っ越す) ●新居への引っ越し a *move into* a new house. ▶私は引っ越しで忙しかった I was busy with the *move*. ▶引っ越しは重労働だ *Moving*'s hard work./It's hard work to *move (out)*. ▶引っ越し先(=新しい住所)を教えてください Please let me know your *new address*.
● 引っ越し業者(会社) a móving còmpany; (業務) the móving bùsiness. ●引っ越しそば (説明的に) buckwheat noodles presented to one's new neighbors when one has just moved in.
● 引っ越しトラック a móving [a remóval] vàn.
● 引っ越しパーティー a housewarming (party).
● 引っ越し費用 (pay) the móving [remóval] expènses.

ひっこす 引っ越す move 《to, into》. ●東京から田舎へ引っ越す *move from* Tokyo *to* the countryside. ●アパートから新築の家へ引っ越す *move out of* an apartment *into* a new house. (🔔引っ越し先が場所の場合は to, 具体的な住居には into が多く用いられる) ▶私たちは次の日曜日に引っ越すことになっている We *are moving (out)* next Sunday. (🔔move out は「今住んでいる所を出て行く」の意) ▶娘が私の部屋もある大きな家を買ったのでそちらへ引っ越します My daughter bought a big house with a room for me. I'm *moving in* (there) with her. ▶「私たちのところに引っ越してくる」なら move in (here) with us. On there, here は大まかな場所をさし, 具体的な場所の直前に置く)

ひっこぬく 引っこ抜く pull ... up. (⇨引き抜く)
ひっこみ 引っ込み (引き下がること) (a) retreat; (a) withdrawal. ▶もう引っ込みがつかない It's too late now to *back out* (of it). (🔔back out (of it) は「(事業などから)手を引く」の意)/I have gone too far to *retreat*.

ひっこみじあん 引っ込み思案 (内気) shyness. ▶彼女はあまりにも引っ込み思案だ She is too *shy and withdrawn*.

ひっこむ 引っ込む ❶ (退く) (引退する) retire; (引き下がる) withdraw*. ●田舎に引っ込む *retire into* the country. ●奥の部屋へ引っ込む *withdraw into* the inner room. ●家に引っ込んでいる *stay [keep] indoors*. ▶お前は引っ込んでいろ You stay out of this!/Keep your nose out of this./(自分のことに気を配れ) Mind your own business. ▶やっと汗が引っ込んだ (出なくなった) I've stopped sweating.
❷ [くぼむ] sink*. ●引っ込んだ目 *deep-set* eyes.
❸ [後方にある] ▶教会は大通りから引っ込んだ所にある The church *stands back from* the main street.

*****ひっこめる 引っ込める** ❶ [引っ込ませる] draw*... in, [書] retract. ●腹を引っ込めておく *hold* one's stomach *in*. ●ちょっと触るとカメは首を引っ込めた The tortoise *drew in* its head [*pulled* its head *inside* the shell] at a touch.
❷ [撤回する] take*... back, 《やや書》withdraw*, [書] retract. ▶彼女について言ったことを引っ込める気はない I will not *take back* what I said about her.

ヒッコリー [植物] a hickory.
ピッコロ [<イタリア語] [楽器] a piccolo (複 ~s).
ひっさげる 引っ提げる ❶ [手に提げて持つ] carry 《a thing》 in one's hand.
❷ [率いる] lead; be in command of ....

ひっさつ 必殺 ●必殺の一撃 a *deadly* blow.
ひっさん 筆算 图 calculation with figures.
―― **筆算する** 動 do calculation [sums] on a piece of paper.

ひっし 必死 ―― **必死の** 形 desperate; (狂気のような) frantic. ●岸にたどりつこうと必死の努力をする make *desperate* [*frantic*] efforts to reach the shore.
―― **必死で[に]** 副 desperately; frantically; [命がけで, 力一杯] *for one's [《やや書》 for dear] life*. ●必死で助かを求める call *desperately* [*frantically*] for help. ▶彼らは最終バスに乗ろうとして必死で走った They ran *for their lives* [《話》 *like hell*] to catch the last bus. ▶世の中の変化が猛烈な勢いで進むので私たちはみんな追いつくのに必死です The world is changing so drastically that we are all running to catch up. (🔔「必死に」の訳語を用いなくても文脈的に意味することもできる)

ひっし 必至 ―― **必至の** 形 (避けられない) inevitable, unavoidable (🔔前の方が強意的); (確実な) absolutely sure. ▶石油不足は必至だ Oil shortage is *inevitable*./*Inevitably*, [It is *inevitable* that] we will suffer from oil shortage. ▶彼の勝利は必至だ His victory is *absolutely sure*.

ひっし 筆紙 ●筆紙に尽くしがたい (文章にはとても表現できない) be beyond description [expression].

ひつじ 未 the Ram.
● 未年 [十二支] the year of the Ram. (⇨干支(ᘓ)関連)

ひつじ 羊 [動物] a sheep (🔔単・複同形); (雄の) a ram, (雌の) a ewe /jú:/; (子羊) a lamb. ●羊の群れ a flock of *sheep*. ●羊の肉 mutton; (子羊の) lamb.
● 羊の皮を着た狼 a wolf in *sheep's* clothing.
● 羊飼い a shepherd /ʃépərd/; (女性の) a shepherdess. ● 羊雲 [気象] a floccus (複 -ci).

ひっしゃ 筆写 ―― **筆写する** 動 copy; transcribe.
ひっしゃ 筆者 (執筆者) a writer; (著者) an author; (書家) a calligrapher; (自分を称して), 《書》 we (🔔後の語は読者を含めた謙遜語). 文章に客観性を持たせようとする the present writer [author] などの使用は好ましくない)

ひっしゅう 必修 ―― **必修の** 形 required; (義務的な) compulsory.
● 必修科目 a compulsory [《米》 a required] (↔ an optional, 《米》 an elective) subject.

ひっしゅつ 必出 ●必出問題 all-important questions; questions which will surely be asked in the exam.

ひつじゅひん 必需品 a necessity; (やや話) a must (🔔通例単数形で). ●生活必需品 the necessities [necessaries] of life. (⇨生活)

ひつじゅん 筆順 the stroke order (of Chinese characters).

ひっしょう 必勝 ▶彼は今度のレースでの必勝を期している He is *determined to win* the race this time.

びっしょり ●びっしょり濡(º)れる be wet through; be drenched [be soaked] to the skin. (⇨びしょ濡れ) ▶彼女は暑い所で働いていたらびっしょり汗をかいた She *sweated a lot [heavily]* from working in the heat.

びっしり (密に) densely. ●ブナがびっしり生えている森 a forest *dense* with beech trees. ●かばんに本をびっしり詰め込む *stuff* books *into* a bag; *stuff* a bag *with* books. ▶その地域には小さな家がびっしり建てられている The area is built up with small houses. ▶劇場には人がびっしり入っていた The theater *was packed (full)* with people [*packed-out, jam-packed*] (🔔(1) with people はない方が普通. (2) packed full, packed-out, jam-packed の方が単なる packed より意味が強い)

ひっす 必須 ―― **必須の** 形 essential, indispensable. (⇨必要な)
● 必須アミノ酸 essential amino acids. ● 必須科目

ひっせい 畢生 — 畢生の 形 (死ぬまでの間) lifelong. ▶畢生の大事業 one's lifework.

ひっせい 筆勢 《with》a stroke of the pen;《with》(brush-)stroke.

ひっせき 筆跡 handwriting, writing. ▶斉藤氏の筆跡の手紙 a letter in Mr. Saito's *handwriting*. ●筆跡鑑定 hándwriting anàlysis. (❗「その筆跡を鑑定する」は analyze the *handwriting*.) ●筆跡鑑定家 hándwriting ànalyst.

ひつぜつ 筆舌 ●筆舌に尽くしがたい ▶その景色の美しさは筆舌に尽くしがたい The beauty of the scenery is *beyond 《all》 description* [*expression*]./The scenery is *too* beautiful *for words* [*description*].

*ひつぜん 必然 图 (避けられないこと) inèvitabílity; (必要性)(やや書) necéssity,《やや書》(a) need (❗複数形にしない). ▶彼がそこへ行かなければならない必然性(＝絶対的な必要性)がない There's no *absolute necessity* [*need*] for him to go there.
—— 必然の, 必然的な 形 inévitable; nécessary (❗叙述用法は《やや書》); (当然の) nátural. ▶彼らが離婚したのは必然の結果だった It was an *inevitable* [*necessary*] result that they got divorced./*It was inevitable* that they got divorced.
—— 必然的に 副 inévitably; nécessarily; (当然の結果として) as an inévitable [a nécessary] result [cónsequence] (❗ result より consequence の方が堅い言い方); (当然のこととして) as a matter of course. ▶彼は父親が死んだので必然的に就職しなければならなかった He *inevitably* [*necessarily*, 《絶対に》*absolutely*] had to get a job because his father died. (❗この absolutely は否定文では不可)

ひっそく 逼塞 — 逼塞する 動 (落ちぶれて身を隠す) live in obscurity.

ひっそり 副 quíetly; (孤独に) sólitarily; (平穏に) péacefully; (密かに) sécretly. ▶彼らは田舎でひっそり暮らしている They *live solitarily* [*live a solitary life*] in the country./They are enjoying a *peaceful life* in the solitude of the country.
—— ひっそりした 形 quíet, calm; (不活発な) inactive. ▶平日はひっそりしている The stores are *quiet* on weekdays. ▶9月の海辺はひっそりしていた (人気がなかった) The seaside *was deserted* in September.

ひったくり 引ったくり (行為) a snatch; (人) a snátcher. ▶ひったくりに注意《掲示》Beware of *snatchers*. ▶私はひったくりにあいました I've been *robbed* [×*snatched*] (*of my bag*). (❗具体的な物を主語にして My bag's been *snatched*. は可)

ひったくる 引ったくる snatch. ▶彼は有無を言わせず ⟨it⟩ *snatched*. ▶彼は彼女の手からバッグをひったくろうとした He tried to *snatch* [He *snatched at*, He made a snatch at] her hand.

ひったてる 引っ立てる march ⟨him⟩ off ⟨to⟩; (連行する) take ⟨him to⟩.

*ぴったり ❶ [急に] súddenly, all of a súdden. ▶列車が急にぴったり止まった The train stopped *suddenly* [*all of a sudden*]./The train came to a *sudden* stop. (⇨ぴたり)
❷ [密着して] (きつく) tíghtly; (密に) clósely. ●体にぴったり合うスカート a *close-*[*tight-*]*fitting* skirt. ▶このシャツはあまりぴったりしすぎている This shirt is *too tight*. ▶彼は先頭グループにぴったりついて走っている He's running *close* behind the first group.
❸ [正確に] exáctly, ríghtly. ▶彼はぴったり線にそって木を切った He cut the wood *exactly* along the line. ▶小包はぴったり5キロあった The parcel weighed *exactly* five kilos. ▶彼は彼女の歳をぴったり当てた He guessed her age *correctly* [*rightly*]. (❗《話》では correct, right も用いる) (⇨ぴたり)
❹ [申し分なく] pérfectly; (理想的に) idéally. ▶このクラスは初心者の要求にぴったり合っている This class complies *perfectly* with beginners' demands. ▶これは寒い冬の日などにはぴったりの料理だ This dish is *perfect* for a cold winter day. ▶その女性は彼の抱いている妻のイメージにぴったりの人だった The woman *satisfied* his *ideal* of a wife./The woman *satisfied* his image of an *ideal* wife.
会話「このイヤリングは私にはちょっと大きすぎるわ」「お嬢様にぴったりのものがございます」"These earrings are a bit too big for me." "I have *just* the thing for you, Miss."

ひつだん 筆談 — 筆談する 動 commúnicate by [in] wríting.

ひっち 筆致 (文字の) hándwriting; (文章や絵画の) a style, (a) tóuch. ●軽妙な筆致のエッセー an essay in a light *style* [*touch*].

ピッチ ❶ [速力] (a) speed; (歩み) a pace ●急ピッチで at a fast *pace*. ●ピッチを上げる・仕事のピッチを上げる[落とす] speed up [slow down] the *pace* of one's work; quicken [slacken] the *pace* of one's work. (❗後の方が堅い言い方)
❷ [音の高さ] (a) pitch.

ピッチ (サッカーなどの)《米》a field,《英》a pitch. (❗「フィールド」「グラウンド」と同義だが, 特にゴールライン・タッチラインに囲まれたプレーエリアをさす) ●サード・オブ・ザ・ピッチ『サッカー』thirds of the pitch. (参考 ピッチを3分割した各ゾーン. ディフェンディングサード・ミドルサード・アタッキングサードに分かれる)

ピッチアウト 图 [野球] a pítchout. ▶捕手は(投手に)ピッチアウトを要求した The catcher called for a *pitchout*.
—— ピッチアウトする 動 pitch out; make a pítchout.

ヒッチハイク 图 hítchhiking.
—— ヒッチハイクする 動 hítchhike 《to, into》; hitch a ride 《to, into》;《米話》thumb a ride,《英話》thumb a lift 〔参考〕親指を立てて (lift a thumb) 合図することから.

ピッチャー [野球の] a pítcher; a húrler. (⇨投手) ●ピッチャー返しの打球 a cómebacker. ●ピッチャー強襲のヒットを打つ single to the mound. ●ピッチャーゴロ a grounder to (a) pitcher;《和製語》pítcher's (grounder). ●ピッチャープレート the pitcher's plate [rubber]; the rúbber.

ピッチャー [水差し] a pítcher.

ひっちゃく 必着 ▶ひっちゃく届くこと Manuscripts *must reach* us *by* [*no later than*] February 15.

ひっちゅう 必中 ▶彼は一発必中の腕前だ He *always hits* [*never misses*] the target with his first shot.

ひっちゅう 筆誅 ●筆誅を加える denóunce ⟨him⟩ in wríting.

ひっちょう 必聴 ●ジャズファン必聴のレコード a *must* record for Jazz fans.

ぴっちり — ぴっちり(と)した 形 tight; well-fítting. ▶ぴっちりしたズボンをはくとお尻の線が丸見えになった The *tight* pants molded her hips and bottom completely.

ピッチング pítching. ●1安打ピッチング one-hit *pitching*. ▶タイガースはその新人の3安打ピッチング

助けられて3対1でジャイアンツを破った The Tigers beat the Giants 3-1 behind the rookie's three-hit *pitching*.
- ピッチングコーチ a pítching còach. • ピッチングマシン a pítching machine.

ひっつく 引っ付く stick 《to》. (⇨くっつく)

ひっつめ 引っ詰め a bun; (説明的に) a hairstyle in which a woman with long hair fastens it in a knot at the back of the head. ▶引っ詰髪にする [している] put [wear] one's hair in a *bun*.

ひってき 匹敵 图 〔対等〕 equality.
── **匹敵する** 動 〔対等である〕 equal; 〔互角である〕 match; 〔肩を並べる〕 compare 《with》 (❗通例否定文で); 〔同列にある〕 rank 《with》. ▶テニスでは彼に匹敵する者はいない No one can *equal* [*match*, *compare with*] him in tennis. ▶彼にテニスで匹敵[match]するものはいない(=だれにも引けを取らない) He is *second to none* in tennis. ▶この大学はアメリカの一流大学に匹敵する This university *ranks with* the best universities in the U.S.

ヒット 图 ❶〔野球で〕(安打) a hit, a safety; (単打) a base hit; a one-base hit; a single. • ヒットを打つ hit safely; have [get, make] a *hit*; single. • ヒット2本を許す allow [give up] two *hits*. • ヒット5本で3点をあげる score three runs on five *hits*. • ピッチャーからヒット3本を奪う get [collect] three *hits* off the pitcher. • レフトにヒットを放つ *single* to left. • 5打席でヒットが出ない go *hit*-*less* in five at-bats. • 相手チームをヒット3本に抑え hold the other team to three *hits*. ▶彼のヒットで2点入った His *hit* drove in two runs.
❷〔大当たり〕(的中) a hit; (成功) a success. ▶サザンオールスターズのヒットアルバムを持っていますか Do you have any Southern All Stars *hit* albums?
❸〔サイトの発見〕〔インターネット〕a hit.
── **ヒットする** 動 ❶〔大当たりする〕▶(映画などが)大ヒットする be a big [a great] *hit*; be a great [big] *success*. (❗特に映画などでは be a box-office *hit*)
❷〔サイトを発見する〕▶「城レストラン」を検索したらいくつかヒットした I got several *hits* in search for "castle restaurant."
• ヒットエンドラン (⇨ヒットエンドラン) • ヒットソング a hit song. • ヒットチャート a hit chart. • ヒットパレード(ヒット曲リスト) a hit parade.

ビット a bit. ▶ 64ビットプロセッサー a 64-*bit* processor. • キロビット a kilobit. • メガビット a megabit. • ギガビット a gigabit. • テラビット a terabit.

ピット 〔カーレースの給油・点検・修理場〕 a pit.
• ピットイン a pit stop.

ひっとう 筆頭 〔表の1番〕 the top [first] on the list; 〔長〕 the head. • 戸籍筆頭者 the *head* of a family. • 前頭(まえがしら)筆頭 the *top-ranking Mae-gashira* sumo wrestler.

ひっとう 筆答 ── **筆答する** 動 answer in writing.
• 筆答試験 a written exam.

ヒットエンドラン 〔野球〕 a hit and run; a hit-and-run play. • ヒットエンドランを行う make [execute] a *hit and run*. ▶ヒットエンドランのかかっている A *hit and run* is on. ▶そのバッターはヒットエンドランをうまくこなす The batter handles a *hit-and-run play*.

ひつどく 必読 ▶学生の必読書(読み物) required reading for students; (書籍) a book which every student *should* [*must*] *read* (❗ must は強制的に過ぎる場合もある). • 必読書 *must* books for students.

ヒットマン 〔殺し屋〕 a hit man; a hired killer.

ひっとらえる 引っ捕らえる catch. (⇨捕まえる)

ひっぱがす 引っ剥がす peel 《a wallpaper》 off. (⇨剥がす)

ひっぱく 逼迫 ── **逼迫した** 形 tight. ▶金融が逼迫している Money is *tight* [*scarce*]. ▶私たちの財政は逼迫している Our finances are *very tight*./(危機的である) Our financial situation is *critical*.

ひっぱたく (平手で) slap (-pp-) 《hard》. ▶彼の顔をひっぱたく slap him 《hard》; give him a 《hard》 slap in [across] the face. • 子供の尻をひっぱたく *spank* a child.

ひっぱりこむ 引っ張り込む draw* [pull, drag (-gg-)] ... into .... (❗後の方はど引っ張る力が強くなる) ▶彼はその新興宗教に引っ張り込まれた He *was dragged into* the new religion.

ひっぱりだこ 引っ張り凧 ▶彼女は若手女優として引っ張りだこだ(需要がある) She is *in great demand* [is *much in demand*] as a young actress. ▶(書) She is a very [a highly, a much] *sought-after* young actress.

ひっぱりだす 引っ張り出す ❶〔引っ張って外に出す〕 pull [draw] ... out. • たばこを1本箱から引っ張り出す *pull* [*draw*; (取り出す) *take*] *out* a cigarette *from* a pack; *pull* [*draw*; *take*] a cigarette *out of* a pack.
❷〔無理に表立った場所に出す〕▶彼らは彼を市長候補に引っ張り出した(=説得して立候補させた) They *persuaded* him to run for mayor.

ひっぱる 引っ張る ❶〔引く〕(手前に) pull (↔push); (軽くなめらかに) draw*; (強く) tug (-gg-); (急に) jerk; (重い物を引っ張る) drag (-gg-); (車・船などを綱で) tow (⇨引く); 〔引っ張って伸ばす〕 stretch. • ロープを引っ張る *pull* [*tug*] 《*at* [*on*]》 the rope (❗名詞形を用いて give a *pull* [a *tug*] at the rope, give the rope a *pull* [a *tug*] ともいえる); (ぴんと張る) *tighten* a rope, *stretch* a rope *tight*. • 彼のそでを引っ張る *pull* him *by* the sleeve; *pull* his sleeve. (❗前の方は人、後ろはそでを強調) ▶そりを引っ張って丘を上る *pull* 《ぐいと》 *tug*》 a sled *up* the hill. ▶彼をベッドから引っ張り出す *pull* [(無理やり) *drag*] him *out of* bed. • 網を引っ張る (たぐる) draw a net. ▶髪をそんなに強く引っ張らないで Don't *pull* my hair so hard. ▶ドアがかたくて引っ張っても開かない The door is stuck and I can't *pull* it *open*. ▶君の車は違法駐車でレッカー車に引っ張られていったよ Your car *was towed away* for illegal parking. ▶腰に巻いたロープが引っ張られる感じがした I felt a *pull* on the rope around my waist.
❷〔連行する〕(連れて行く) take*; (連れて来る) bring*. ▶その泥棒を警へ引っ張っていく *take* the thief *to* the police station. ▶彼をここへ引っ張ってきたまえ *Bring* him here with you.
❸〔その他の表現〕▶引っ張る打者 a pull hitter. ▶会社を引っ張っていくような社長が必要だ We need a president who has a strong leadership. ▶リストラで失業したとき、昔の友達が自分の会社に引っ張ってくれた When I lost my job under the company's downsizing plan, one of my old friends offered me a new job with his company. ▶4番打者は速球をレフト線へ引っ張った The cleanup *pulled* a fastball down the left field line.

ヒッピー a hippie, a hippy; 《やや古》 a Gypsy traveler.

ヒップ (腰回り) the hips, (ヒップのサイズ) one's hip measurement; (尻(しり)) the buttocks. • ヒップ丈のコート a *hip-length* coat. ▶彼女はヒップが大きい She is large around the *hips* [is *large-hipped*, is *wide-hipped*]./She has broad [big] *hips*.

ビップ 《やや話》a VIP. (⇨ブイアイピー)
ひっぽう 筆法 ❶【筆遣い】(文体) one's style of writing. ❷【方法】a way; a method.
ひっぽう 筆鋒 (筆の先) the point of a brush [pen].
● 鋭い筆鋒 (攻撃的な文章の勢い) a vigorous [a forceful] style.
ひづめ 蹄 a hoof (働 hooves, -fs).
ひつもんひっとう 筆問筆答 a written exam [test].
ひつよう 必要 图 (欲しいものが欠けている状態) need 《of, for》; (避けることができない状態) necessity 《of, for》. (❶いずれも「必要なもの・場合・理由」という具体的な意味では [C])

① 【必要を[に]】 ▶ 彼らの最低の必要を満たす supply [meet] their barest *needs*. ● 休養の必要(性)を感じる feel the *need of* [*for*] a rest; feel the *need to* take a rest. ● 運動の必要(性)をさとる realize the *necessity of* [*for*] taking exercise. (❶動名詞の場合は of が普通) ▶ この町には新しいバス路線が必要になってきた There is a growing *need for* a new bus route in this town. ▶ 必要に応じてその金を遣いなさい Use the money *as* (*it is*) *needed* [*you need it*].

② 【…する必要がある】 need to do; it is necessary (for 〈him〉) to do [that …]; (しなければならない) must do; have to do, 《話》have got to do.
▶ 彼はもっと勉強する必要がある He *needs to* [ˣ*need*] study harder. (⇨③)/He *has to* [*must*] study harder. (❶後の方が強意的 (⇨ねばならない)) / It's *necessary for* him to study [*that* he (*should*) study] harder. (❶この文節を用いるのは堅い表現. ˣHe is *necessary* to study harder. とはいわない)
▶ 君の時計は修理する必要がある 《物が主語》 Your watch *needs* [《主に英語》*wants*] repairing. (❶ need では Your watch *needs* [ˣ*wants*] *to* be repaired. の型も可. ˣYour watch needs to repair. は不可) / Your watch *is in need of* repair. / 《人が主語》 You *have to* have [get] your watch repaired. ▶ 彼にここにいてもらう必要がある I *need* him (to be) here. ▶ もし必要があれば(=必要なら)私が行きましょう I'll go, *if* (*it is*) *necessary*.

③ 【…する必要はない】 don't have to do, 《話》haven't got to do; don't need to do, 《主に英》needn't do (❶ need には助動詞と本動詞の二つの用法があるが, 今では助動詞としての用法が普通. 助動詞用法は通例否定文・疑問文で用い, 肯定文では通例用いない); It is not necessary to do. ▶ 君は急ぐ必要はないよ You *don't have to* [*need to*] hurry./It's not *necessary* [*unnecessary*] for you to hurry./There's no *need* [*necessity*] for you to hurry [ˣof your hurrying, ˣthat you should hurry]. (⇨②) ▶ 君は行く必要はなかった You *didn't háve to* go./You *didn't néed to* go. You needn't have gone. (❶いずれも実際に行った場合であるが, 初めの2文で have, need に強勢がない場合は「必要はなかったので行かなかった」の意となる)

● **必要に迫られる** ▶ 彼は必要に迫られて家を売った He sold his house *out of* [*from*] *necessity*./*Necessity* drove [compelled] him to sell his house. (⇨やむをえない)
● **必要は発明の母** (ことわざ) Necessity is the mother of invention.

── **必要な** 形 necessary 《*for, to*》; (条件として必要な) 《書》 requisite 《*for*》; [不可欠な] (本質的に) essential 《*for, to*》; (ある目的を達するために) indispensable 《*for, to*》. ▶ この仕事に必要な技能 the skills *necessary* [*in*] this job; the *necessary* skills *for* this job. ▶ 十分な睡眠とバランスのとれた食事は健康の維持には絶対に必要なものである(=必要だ) Good sleep and a well-balanced diet are *essential* [*indispensable*], absolutely *necessary*, an absolute *necessity*] *for* the preservation of health. ▶ 彼女はケーキを作るのに必要なものを買いに行った She went out [ˣ*shopping*] to buy what she *needed* to make the cake. (❶(1) go shopping では特別の目的がなく買い物に行く意であるからここでは不適切. (2) ˣ… buy the cake's necessities. とはいわない) ▶ 彼女は必要以上に子供の世話をする She takes care of her children more than (is) *necessary*.

── **必要とする** 動 need, be in need of …; 《やや書》require; (時間・労力などを) take* (❶主語は物・事) (⇨掛かる). (❶ともに通例進行形不可) ▶ 我々は君の援助を必要としている We *need* your help. (❶Your help is *necessary for* us. より普通)/We *are in need of* your help. ▶ この町が本当に必要としているのは図書館です What this town really *needs* is a library. ▶ この仕事は多少の技術を必要とする This job *needs* [*requires*] some skill./It *takes* some skill to do this job.

● **必要悪** a necessary evil. ● **必要経費** necessary expenses. ● **必要条件** a necessary [《書》a requisite] condition; a requirement.

ひつりょく 筆力 (⇨筆勢)
ビデ [<フランス語] a bidet /bidéi/.
ひてい 否定 图 (否認) (a) denial 《*of; that* 節》; (a) negation; (否定の返答語) a negative. ● 二重否定 a double negative.

── **否定の, 否定的な** 形 negative.

── **否定する** 動 deny; (いやと言う) say* no; (否定的に答える)《書》answer in the negative (↔affirmative). ▶ 彼は私の言うことを否定した He *denied* what I said. (❶通例 ˣHe denied *me*. とはいわない) ▶ 彼は彼女にコカインを手渡したということについては否定した He *denied* that he had passed any cocaine to her. (❶deny の後では, some と any の使用は否定文に準ずる)/He *denied* having passed [passing] any cocaine to her. ▶ 彼が偉大な科学者であるという事実は否定できない It cannot *be denied* that he is a great scientist./There is no *denying* (the fact) *that* he is a great scientist.

● **否定文** 【文法】a negative sentence.

びていこつ 尾骶骨 【解剖】the coccyx /káksiks/ (働 ~es, coccyges /kəksáidʒiːz/). (働 尾骨)
ビデオ (録画) (a) video (働 ~s); (録画装置) a video. (❶正式には a vídeocassètte [(カセット式の) a vídeocassette recòrder] ⇨ ビデオに録画する get [record] 《a TV program》 *on* (one's) *video* [*videotape*]; *videotape* [*tape*] 《a TV program》. ● 彼女の結婚式のビデオを見る watch a *video* of her wedding. ● ビデオを10時に(動くように)セットする set the *video* to go on at 10:00.

● **ビデオオンデマンド** video on demand. ● **ビデオカード** a video card; a graphics adapter. ● **ビデオ会議** a video conference. 《その装置は video conferencing》 ● **ビデオカメラ** a video camera. ● **ビデオクリップ** a video clip. ● **ビデオゲーム** a video game. ● **ビデオ撮影** a video shoot. ● **ビデオショップ**《米》a video store, 《英》a video shop; (レンタルの)《米》a video rental store, 《英》a video rental shop. ● **ビデオソフト** video software. ● **ビデオディスク** a videodisc (略 VD). ● **ビデオプロジェクター** a video projector.

ビデオカセット a vídeocassètte.
● **ビデオカセットレコーダー** a videocassette recorder (略 VCR). (❶ a video, a video recorder ともいう)
ビデオテープ (a) vídeotàpe, 《話》(a) video (働

ビデオデッキ ～s). (⇨ビデオ)
● **ビデオテープレコーダー** a videotape recorder (《略》VTR). ● **ビデオテープ録画** (a) videotape recording; (a) VTR.

ビデオデッキ a video deck, a VCR /víː siː áːr/ 《video cassette recorder の略》.

ピテカントロプス 《原人》a pithecanthrope.
● **ピテカントロプスエレクトゥス** 《直立原人》 *Pithecanthropus erectus*.

びてき 美的 —**美的な** 《圏》《やや書》aesthetic /esθétik/, 《米》esthetic. ● **美的センスがある[ない]** have an [no] *aesthetic* sense; have a [have no] sense of beauty.
● **美的価値** *aesthetic* value. ● **美的感覚** a sense of beauty; an esthetic sense.

ひでり 日照り dry weather; 《干ばつ》(a) drought /dráut/, a dry spell. ● **日照りに苦しんでいる地域** a *drought*-stricken area. ▶日照り続きで作物がだめになった The crops have failed because of a long spell of *dry weather* [a long *dry spell*]. ▶日照りが3か月続いた The *drought* lasted (for) three months./We had three months of *drought*.

ひでん 秘伝 the secret. (⇨秘術)

びてん 美点 〖長所〗a good point; 〖価値ある点〗a merit; 〖美徳〗a virtue. (⇨長所)

びでん 美田 a fertile farm(land); a fertile rich field. ▶児孫(じそん)のために美田を買わず I will not leave an *estate* to my descendants.

ひでんか 妃殿下 a princess; 〖敬称〗(日本の) Her (Imperial) Highness, (英国の) Her (Royal) Highness. (⇨殿下)

ひと 人 INDEX
❶ 一人の人間　❷ 他人
❸ 人柄　❹ 有能な人材
❺ 人類　❻ 客
❼ 大人

◀ WORD CHOICE ▶ 人，人々
people 通例無冠詞で用い，不特定の人の集合を総称的に表す．時に定冠詞を伴い，特定の国民や民族を表す．
▶人々は号泣していた *People* are crying.
person 通例 a person の形で不特定の個人を表す．時に，people のより改まった言い方として，複数形の persons を用いる．▶夜型の人 a night *person*.
one 単独で用い，不特定の個人を表す．時に修飾語を伴，前出の可算名詞を受けることもある．▶人は自分の言ったことを守るべきだ *One* should keep *one's* word.

❶ 〖一人の人間〗(男女ともに) a person; (男性) a man (《複》men), 《話》a guy; (女性) a woman (《複》women /wímɪn/); 〖不特定の〗someone, somebody; 〖一般に〗people; 《書》one. (⇨人間)
① 〖～(の)人〗▶目上の人 one's *superior*. ▶時の人 a *man* [a *woman*] of the news. ● **意志の強い[行動力のある；約束を守る]人** a *person* of will [action; 《his》word]. ● **普通の人** an ordinary [《平均的な》an average] *person*. ● **大勢の人** a crowd of *people*. ▶彼は実に変わった人だ He is really an odd *person* [*man*]./He is quite an *eccentric*. ▶どんな人でもこの法に従わねばならない Every *person* [*Everybody*] has to obey this law./*Nobody* is above the law. ▶彼は滋賀県の人です He is [comes] from Shiga Prefecture.
〖会話〗「あの男の人，だれだか知ってる?」「どの人?」「白いズボンをはいてる人」"Do you know who that *guy* [that *man*, he] is?" "Which *one*?" "The *one* in the white pants." (🚫 one は前出の名詞の代用として用いる．複数のときは ones を用いる (⇨[次例]))
〖会話〗「フランスの人たちには好感を持ったかい」「私が出会った人々はほとんどがすてきな方たちだったわ」"Did you like the *people* in France?" "Most of the *ones* I met were charming."
〖会話〗「その映画はそんなに人気があるのですか」「いつももうすごい人ですよ」"Is the movie as popular as all that?" "It's usually extremely *crowded*." (🚫 ...crowded *with people* の形は避けられる)
② 〖人の～〗● **人の一生** (one's) life, a *man's* life. (🚫 (1) この man は一般に「人間」の意であるが「男の一生」の意にもとれる. (2) *human* life は「人の(生)命」) ▶それが人の世の常だ That is the way of the (*human*) world. ▶突然背後の人の気配に気づいた I suddenly sensed *someone* behind me.
③ 〖人は[が]〗▶この人はだれですか Who is this *man* [*woman*]? (🚫 person を用いると「こいつはだれだ」の意. Who is this gentleman [lady]? の方が丁寧な言い方) ▶岸田さんという人がお見えです A (*man* named) Mr. Kishida is waiting to see you. (🚫 Mr. のような敬称のついた人名に a をつけると「...という人」の意) ▶人は自らの欠点に気がつかない *One* is blind to *one's* [《米》*his* or *her*] own faults. (🚫 日常的には one, one's の代わりに you, your が用いられる) ▶毎年どれくらいの人がここを訪れますか How many *people* [×persons] visit here every year? (🚫 persons は堅い語で人数が少ないときや数を明示するとき以外は用いない) ▶音楽を愛する人は幸福である *People* [*Those*] *who* love music are happy. ▶人は見かけによらない You shouldn't judge *people* by their appearances./Never judge from [by] appearances.
④ 〖人に[で]〗● **人によって異なる** be different *from person to person*. (🚫 対句的に用いた場合は無冠詞) ▶今夜人に会う約束がある I have to meet *someone* this evening./I have an appointment this evening. ▶ホールは人でいっぱいだった The hall was full of *people* [×men]. (🚫 men は「男たち」)
⑤ 〖人を〗▶あいつはいつだって人を待たせるんだから He always keeps *us* waiting.
〖会話〗「ここで何をしてるの?」「人を待ってるんです」"What are you doing here?" "I'm waiting for *somebody*." (🚫 口語では someone より普通)

❷ 〖他人〗other people, others. (🚫 後の方はやや堅い言い方. 自分以外のすべての人をさす．単数形は an(other) (person)) (⇨他人); 〖世間の人々〗people.
① 〖人の〗● **人の上に立つ** lead *other people*. ● **人の弱みにつけこむ** take advantage of *other people's* [*others'*] weak positions. ● **人の金に手をつける** pocket *someone else's* [*another person's*, ×another's] money.
② 〖人が〗▶人が何と言おうと私はそれをやる I'll do it whatever *other people* say about me.
③ 〖人に[も]〗● **人に頼る** depend on *others*. ▶このことは人には言うな Keep this secret (from *others*). ▶姉はスタイルがいいとよく人に言われる My sister *is* often *told* [×said] that she has a nice figure [×style]. (🚫 通例 by others はつけない)/*People* [×*They*] often say that my sister has a nice figure. (🚫 they を頻度や時を表す副詞とともに用いると特定の集団を表すことになり，この場合不可 (⇨❶))
④ 〖人を〗● **人をやって医者を呼ぶ** send *for* a doctor.

❸ 〖人柄〗(生まれつきの) nature; (他人から見た印象を総合した) personality; (道徳的性質としての) character. ▶彼は人を見る目がある[ない] He is a good [is no] judge of *character*.

ひとあし

❹ 〚有能な人材〛an able [a capable] person; 〚適任者〛the right person 《for》(⇨人材); 〚人手〛manpower; a hand. (⇨人手)
❺ 〚人類〛mànkind; man (❗(1) 無冠詞. (2)「男性」の意が強く感じられるので、次の語を用いることも多い); 〚動物と区別した人間〛the human race, a human being, a human. (⇨人類, 人間)
❻ 〚客〛a visitor. ▶ 今人(=来客)が来ている We have a visitor now.
❼ 〚大人〛an adult, 《話》a grown-up. (⇨大人)
● 人がいい 彼は人がいい He has a good personality./He is so good-natured./〚だまされやすい〛He is credulous. ▶ 彼は人のいい(=悪意のない)仕事一途な男です He's a well-meaning slave to his job. (❗「無礼・非常識な言動はあるが」といったことを含意する)
● 人が変わる 彼は人が変わった He has [《文》is] changed a lot./He is a new man.
● 人が悪い ill-natured, 《主に米話》mean.
● 人のうわさも七十五日 A rumor lasts only seventy-five days./《ことわざ》A wonder lasts but nine days.
● 人の口に戸は立てられない People will talk.
● 人の疝気(ｾﾝｷ)を頭痛に病む One has a headache about another person's colic./《ことわざ》The stone that lies not in your gate breaks not your toes.
● 人のふり見て我がふり直せ Correct your faults by observing other people's faults. / Learn wisdom by the follies of others.
● 人のふんどしで相撲を取る 'One wrestles by wearing another man's loincloth.'; (人の費用で利益を得る) gain profits at somebody else's expense; (人の手柄[お膳立て]を利用する) take advantage of somebody else's achievement [arrangements].
● 人もあろうに 人もあろうに彼がそう言ったのだ He, of all people, said so.
● 人を介する through another (person).
● 人をばかにする 人(=私)をばかにするにもほどがある You are [He is] making a complete fool of me! (❗主語は文脈による)
● 人を食う 人を食ったことを言う talk big.
● 人を呪わば穴二つ 《ことわざ》Curses come home to roost.
● 人を人とも思わない 人を人とも思わない(=高慢な)態度 an arrogant [a haughty] manner.
● 人を見て法を説け Adapt your speech to the audience./《ことわざ》All meat pleases not all mouths.

ひとあし 一足 ▶ 一足ごとに at every step.
● 一足違いで (わずかの差で) by a second. ● 一足…一歩前に出る take a step forward. ● 一足先に (少し早めに) a little early [earlier]. ● 病院まではほんの一足です It is only a few steps [a short walk] to the hospital./The hospital is only a few steps away. ● すみません、一足お先に失礼します Excuse me, I must be going now.

ひとあじ 一味 ▶ この味噌汁は一味足りない This miso soup needs a little more flavor.
● 一味違う (食べ物が) taste better [(特別の) special]; (芸能などが) have a taste of one's own; (際立たせる) set … off. ▶ 彼の芸は並の芸人からは一味違う His performance sets him off from other entertainers.

ひとあせ 一汗 ▶ ジョギングで一汗かいた I worked up a good sweat by jogging.

ひとあたり 人当たり ▶ 彼はだれにでも人当たりがよい He is friendly [affable] to everybody.

ひどい

ひとあめ 一雨 〚1回の雨降り〛a rainfall; 〚にわか雨〛a shower. ▶ 夜の間に一雨降った There was a brief rainfall during the night. (❗ overnight rain だと一晩中降ったのか、夜一時的に降ったのか分からない)
▶ 一雨こないかなあ We could do with a spot of rain. ▶ 一雨ごとに春らしくなる It becomes more springlike with each rainfall. ▶ 一雨きそうだ We're going to have a shower.

ひとあれ 一荒れ ▶ 一荒れ来そうだ It looks like we're going to have a storm. ▶ 今日の会議は一荒れしそうだ Today's meeting will be stormy, I'm afraid.

ひとあわ 一泡 ● 一泡吹かせる ▶ 彼らに一泡吹かせてやる I will give them a real scare. / I will scare [frighten] them to death.

ひとあんしん 一安心 (⇨安心) ▶ これで一安心だ This is a load [a weight] off my mind. (❗「気がかりがなくなった」の意)

ひどい ❶ 〚激しい〛(自然現象・行為が) violent; (天候・病気などが) severe; 〚強烈な〛(光・温度などが) intense; (風・光・色・香りなどが) strong; 〚はなはだしい〛bad; terrible; 《話》awful. ● ひどい暑さ violent [intense, terrible] heat. ● ひどい風 a violent [a strong] wind. ● ひどい雨 (大雨) a heavy rain. ● ひどい寒さの中で in the severe [intense, bitter] cold. ● ひどい頭痛がする have a bad [an awful, a terrible] headache; feel a violent [a severe] pain in the [one's] head. ● ひどい誤りを犯す make a terrible [〚重大な〛a serious, 〚大きな〛a great] mistake. ● ひどいせきが出る have a bad cough. ● ひどい傷を負う be badly [seriously] injured; hurt oneself badly [seriously]. ▶ ひどい暑さだ It's extremely [《話》terribly, 《話》awfully] hot./The heat is terrible. ▶ なんてひどい天気 What terrible [awful, 〚いやな〛nasty] weather! ▶ ひどい人込みだこと What a crowd!
❷ 〚むごい〛cruel; heartless; 〚つらい〛bitter; hard. ● ひどい仕打ち cruel treatment. ● ひどいことを言う say awful things 《about》. ● ひどい目にあう have a bitter [a terrible] experience; have a hard [a bad] time; (よけいなことをして) burn one's fingers. ● ひどい目にあわせる treat 《him》cruelly; 《話》work 《him》over. ▶ このためきっとひどい目にあうぞ You will pay 《dearly》for this. (❗「…の罰を受ける」の意) ▶ 自分の子供を虐待するなんてなんてひどい女なんだ She's so heartless [It's heartless of her, It's a shame for her] to treat her child cruelly. (❗ shame は「ひどいこと」の意)
❸ 〚悪い〛bad*; poor; (人[行為]が恥知らずの) disgraceful. ● ひどい道 a bad road; (でこぼこの) a rough road. ● 試験でひどい点を取る get a poor mark in the exam; do poorly in the exam. ● ひどい(=みじめな)生活をする lead a miserable life. ▶ こんなひどい映画は見たことがない This is the worst movie I've ever seen. ▶ その池(から)のにおいは本当にひどいよ The smell from the pond is really [×very] awful. ▶ 彼はほとんどの科目はまずまずの出来だが、数学はまったくひどいものだ《話》He does passably in most subjects, but his math is an absolute disaster.

会話 「なんだこれは. ひどいじゃないか, この鍋物は冷えきっているぜ」「本当? つっ返しなさいよ」"Oh no! This is disgusting [terrible], the casserole is stone cold." "Really? You should send it back."

会話 「ちょっと, あんたの今学期の成績, ひどいわよ」「母さん, 来学期は絶対がんばるよ」「期待してるわ」"Son, your grades for this term are very disappointing." "Mom, I promise I'll try harder next

term." "I hope you will."
❹ [〖過度の〗] excessive 《prices, demands》; [〖法外な〗] unreasonable 《prices, demands》; outrageous 《prices》; [〖不当な〗] unfair 《treatment, criticism》; unjust 《laws》.

ひといき 一息 ❶ [〖一呼吸〗] a breath. ●深く一息つく take a long [a deep] *breath*. ●ほっと一息つく (安心する) breathe a sigh of relief; feel relieved. (❗後の方が普通) ●一息に (⇨一気に)
❷ [〖少しの努力〗] もう一息で合格だ Just one more *effort*, and you will pass the exam.
●一息入れる (一休みする) take [have] a rest.

ひといきれ 人いきれ ●車内は人いきれでむっとしていた The train was jammed and *stuffy*.

ひといちばい 人一倍 ●彼は人一倍本を読む He reads *more books than other people do*. ●彼女は人一倍健康に注意する She takes *more care of herself* [《まれ》 her health] *than others* (do)./She is *extremely* careful about [of] her health. ●不登校の子は人一倍真剣にものごとを考えているのです Children who refuse to go to school are *much more serious thinkers than their peers*.

ひとう 秘湯 an unknown [〖ひなびた〗 a secluded] hot spring; (俗化から守られている) a hot spring best-kept secret.

ひどう 非道 图 inhumanity; (残忍) cruelty.
── **非道な** 形 ●非道な仕打ち *inhuman* [*cruel*] treatment.

びとう 尾灯 a táillight, 《英》 a rèar light.

びどう 微動 微動だにしない do not move [《やや書》 budge] an inch; stand firm like a rock.

ひどうめい 非同盟 ── **非同盟の** 形 nonaligned 《nations》.

ひとえ 単, 単衣 an unlined *kimono* (for summer wear).

ひとえ 一重 ●一重の 形 single. ●一重の赤バラ a *single* red rose. ●一重まぶた flat eyelids.

ひとえに 偏に [〖まったく〗] entirely, [〖書〗] solely; [〖ひたすら〗] earnestly. ●彼の成功はひとえに自らの努力による His success is *entirely* due to his efforts./He owes his success *entirely* to his efforts. (❗(1) このように owe は自分自身の行動の結果を示すのにも使える. (2) entirely の位置に注意) ●ひとえにおわび申し上げます I *earnestly* beg your pardon.

ひとおし 一押し 图 a push.
── **一押しする** 動 give ... a push. ●もう一押しでその仕事は完成だ Just *one more effort* and the work will be done.

ひとおじ 人怖じ ── **一人怖じする** 動 be shy. (⇨人見知りする)

ひとおもいに 一思いに (ためらわず) without hesitation; (きっぱりと) once and for all, résolùtely; (大胆に) boldly. (⇨思い切って) ●いっそ一思いに (= きれいさっぱりと) 死んでしまいたい I want to kill myself *once and for all*. (❗この場合 I'd like to ... とすると once and for all の強い願望det合わない)

ひとがき 人垣 a crowd (of people). ●沿道は女王のパレードを見ようとする人たちが人垣を作っていた *A crowd of people* lined the route of the Queen's motorcade.

ひとかげ 人影 (人の姿) a figure; (人の影) a silhouette /síluét/. ●遠くに黒い人影が見えた We saw a dark *figure* in the distance. ●人影が障子に映った A (man's [woman's]) *silhouette* fell on the paper screen. ●公園には人影がなかった The park *was* almost *deserted*.

ひとかたならぬ 一方ならぬ (⇨一方ならず) ●彼の知らせを聞いてひとかたならず喜んだ He was *very* [*not a little*] glad at the news./He was *extremely* pleased about the news.

ひとかたならぬ 一方ならぬ [〖多大の〗] great; [〖非常に〗] very; (少なからず) not a little. ●ひとかたならぬご親切ありがとうございました Thank you very much for all your kindness. ●あの人にはひとかたならぬお世話になりました I am *greatly* indebted to him.

ひとかど 一廉 ●彼はひとかどの人物だ He is *somebody* [《やや話》 *someone*] (in this field)./He is a person *of* (some) *importance*. ●彼はひとかどの学者だ He is quite a [《話》 *some*] *scholar*. ●《話》 He is *something of a scholar*. (❗いずれも単数可算名詞を修飾する場合に限る)

ひとがら 人柄 (a) personality; (性格) one's character. ●彼は人柄がいい He has a good *personality*. ●外観より人柄の方が大切です *Personality* is more important than looks. ●彼女はどんな人柄か (= 好きな人) ですか What kind of (×a) *person* is she?

ひとからげ 一絡げ ●一絡げにする lump ... together.
●十把一絡げ (⇨十把一絡げ)

ひとかわ 一皮 ●一皮むけば underneath (...). ([〖...の〗下に] の意) 紳士面をしているが, 一皮むけばあの男は詐欺師です He looks like a gentleman, but *underneath* he is an impostor./He is an impostor *behind the mask* of a gentleman.

ひときき 人聞き ●**人聞きが悪い** ●そんなふうに言わないで, 人聞きが悪いよ Don't talk like that. People would frown (on you) if they heard you. (❗後の文は People would not like it if .... ともいう) ●人聞きの悪い. 知らない人が聞いたら本気にしますよ That's *scandalous*! People will take it seriously.

ひときらい 人嫌い 图 misanthropy; (人) a misanthrope. ── **人嫌いの** 形 misanthropic.

ひときわ 一際 ●ひときわ (= 異常に) 大声で話す speak in an *exceptionally* loud voice. ●彼の仕事は他の人のよりひときわ目立つ (抜きん出ている) His work *stands out* from that of others./His work is really *outstanding*.

***ひどく** [〖非常に〗] very, 《主に女性語》 so (❗ともに形容詞・副詞を修飾); (ものすごく) terribly, 《話・主に女性語》 awfully; (極度に) extremely; badly* (❗動詞を修飾. want, need などとともに用いることが多い); [〖激しく〗] severely. ●ひどくしかられる be *severely* told off [*scolded*]. ●今日はひどく疲れた I'm *very* [《話》 *dead*] tired today./I'm quite [*completely*] exhausted today. (⇨全く) ●I'm tired *out* today. ●彼がいなくてひどく寂しい I miss him *very* [*so*] *much*. ●今日はひどく寒い It's *terribly* [*extremely, awfully, bitterly,* (凍えるほど) *freezing*] cold today. ●彼女はそれをひどく欲しがっている She *badly* wants it./She wants it *very much*. ●彼はその自動車事故でひどくけがをした He was *badly* [*severely, seriously*] injured in the car accident. ●彼の死を聞いてひどく悲しい I'm *extremely* sorry to hear of his death. ●雨がひどく降った It rained *heavily* [*hard*]./We had a *heavy* [×a hard] rain.

びとく 美徳 (a) virtue (⇔(a) vice). ●謙譲の美徳を発揮する show the *virtue* of modesty. ●親切は美徳だ Kindness is a *virtue*. (❗「いろいろな種類の美徳のうちの一つ」 の意では a)

ひとくい 人食い ●人食い人種 《集合的》 a cannibal tribe (❗単・複両扱い); (1 人) a cannibal.

ひとくぎり 一区切り ●やっと一区切りついた. 少し休もう We've come to the *end of a section* [《今はまれ》 *a stage*]. Let's have a break.

ひとくさり 一くさり (一段落) a passage. ●演説を一くさりぶつ make *a speech*.

ひとくせ 一癖 ▶あの人，一癖ありそう He gives me an impression that we have to be careful with him./《話》He seems to be an *awkward customer*./(変わり者だ)《話》He's a character (❗悪い意味はない).
● **一癖も二癖もある** ▶彼は一癖も二癖もある人だ He is *a very difficult person to deal with*.

ひとくち 一口 ❶ [食べ物，飲み物] (一口分の量) a mouthful; (食べ物の一口) a bite, (やや書) a morsel; (ぐいと一飲み) a gulp, a swallow; (一すすり) a sip. ● もう一口食べる have [take] *another mouthful of* food. ● ウイスキーをちびりと[ぐいっと]一口飲む take *a sip* [*a gulp*] of whiskey. ● それを一口で食べる eat it *at a bite*. ● ビールを一口で飲み干す drink the beer *at a gulp* [*in one gulp*]. ▶そのスープを何とか一口飲んだがそれ以上はだめだった I managed to get down *a mouthful of* the soup, but no more. ● 満腹です．もう一口も入りません I'm full [I've had enough]. I can't have another *bite*.
❷ [一言] a word. ▶一口に言えば彼の答えは「ノー」です His answer is no *in a word*./(要約して)*In short*, his answer is no. ▶一口に絵画といってもいろいろある (=あらゆる種類の絵がある) There are *all sorts of* paintings./There are [You can find] paintings and paintings.
❸ [割り当て・分け前・寄付などの一口] a share. ▶我々の計画に一口乗りませんか Won't you *take a share in* [(参加して) *join in*] our project?
● 一口カツ a pork nugget; a bite-sized pork cutlet. ● 一口話 a short comic [funny] story.

ひとくろう 一苦労 ▶彼の家を見つけるのに一苦労した I've had *some difficulty* (*in*) finding his house.

ひとけ 人気 ● 人気のない通り a *deserted* street. ● 人気(=人のいる気配)がする There is a sign of life. (⇨気配)

ひとけい 日時計 a sundial.

ひとけた 一桁 [数字のけた一つ] a digit. (❗0～9までの数字の意も由) (⇨桁) ● 一けた違う(=上[下]である) be one *digit* larger [smaller]. ● 平成一けた生まれの子供 children (who were) born in *the first nine years* of Heisei.

ヒトゲノム [生物] a human genom(e).

ひとこいしい 人恋しい ▶人恋しいと思う feel lonely (and want to have someone to talk to).

ひとこえ 一声 ● 一声叫ぶ give [utter] *a cry*. ● 総理大臣の一声 *one word* from the prime minister. ▶旅行で留守にされるときは一声かけてくださいね Let me know when you are away on a trip.

ひとこえ 人声 a voice. ▶隣りの部屋で人声がした *Voices* were heard in the next room.

ひとこきゅう 一呼吸 ▶一呼吸入れよう Let's *take a break* for a while.

ひとごこち 人心地 ● 人心地つく (ほっとする) catch one's breath, feel relieved; (さっぱりする) be refreshed.

ひとこと 一言 a (single) word. (❗single が入ると強意的) ● 一言で言えば in a word; (手短に) in short; (かいつまんで) to sum up. ▶彼女はフランス語は一言も話せない She *can't speak a* (*single*) *word* of French./She *can't speak* French *at all*. ▶私に一言いわせてください Let me say *a word* [*I* have my say]. (❗have one's say は「自分の意見を述べる」の意) ● 彼は驚いて一言も話せなかった He couldn't utter *a word* in surprise [was *speechless* with surprise]. ● 彼はいつも一言多い She has to say *one word* too many. ▶一言お祝いの言葉を申し上げます Let me say *a few words* of congratulations.

ひとごと 人事 other people's affairs. ● 人事とは思えない(=自分のことに思える) feel as if it were one's own affair. ▶これは人事ではない(=私にも関係する) This concerns me, too. ▶人事のように言うな Don't talk as if it were *none of your business* [*someone else's affairs*]. ▶よくもそんなに冷静でいられるね．話を聞いているとまるで人事みたいに聞こえるよ How can you be so detached? It sounds as if you're talking about *someone else*.

ひとこま 一駒 a [one] scene; (フィルムなどの) a frame. ● 日常生活のひとこま *one scene* [(映画の中の) *shot*] in our daily life.
● **ひとこま漫画** a cartoon.

ひとごみ 人込み [群衆] a crowd (of people). ● 人込みを避ける avoid *crowds* [*crowded places*]. ● 人込みに紛れて姿を消す disappear in the *crowd*. ▶彼らは人込みをかき分けて進んだ They fought their way through the *crowd*.

ひところ 一頃 (一時期) at one time; (以前) once. (⇨昔) ▶ひところよく川に魚釣りに行った *At one time* [*Formerly*] I used to go fishing in [×to] the river.

ひとごろし 人殺し 図 [行為] (故意の) a murder; (過失の) [法律] manslaughter; (故意・過失の) [法律] (人) a homicide. [人] a murderer; a homicide.
— 人殺し(を)する 動 murder; commit murder. (⇨殺人)

ひとさし 一差し [将棋]《play》a game of *shogi*; [舞] a dance.

ひとさしゆび 人差し指 the [one's] forefinger, the [one's] index finger. (⇨指)

ひとざと 人里 ● 人里離れた所 a *remote* [a *far-off*] country; a place *far from town* [《書》*from human habitations*].

ひとさま 人様 other poeple; others.

ひとさらい 人さらい (行為) kidnapping; (人) a kidnapper. (⇨誘拐)

ひとさわがせ 人騒がせ — 人騒がせな 形 (人の心をかき乱す) disturbing; (不安・恐怖心をかき立てる) alarming. ● 何とも人騒がせな話 a *disturbing* [an *alarming*] story. ● 人騒がせなことをする create a *disturbance*. ● (何でもないことに大騒ぎする) make [get into] a *fuss* over [about] nothing.

*****ひとしい 等しい** 形 [同一物でないが，数量・程度・大きさなどが等しい] equal (*to*); [同一物あるいは別の物の程度・大きさなどが内容的に同じ] the same; [価値・数量・意味などが同等の] equivalent (*to*); [...も同然で] as good as .... (⇨同じ) ▶二つの等しい部分 two *equal* parts. ▶その二つのボールは重さが等しい The two balls are *equal* [*the same*] in weight./The two balls are of *equal* [*the same*] weight. ▶この二つの文は意味が等しい These two sentences are *equivalent* in meaning. ▶1メートルは1ヤードに等しいとは言えない A meter is not quite *equal* [*equivalent*] to a yard. ▶無謀運転は自殺行為に等しい Reckless driving is *equivalent to* [*amounts to*] a suicidal act.
— 等しく 副 [平等に] equally; [同様に] alike; similarly; [...もまた] too, also. ● 万人を等しく遇する treat all people *equally* [*alike*]. ● 仕事量を等しくする *equalize* one's workload; *make* one's workload *equal*. ● その金は兄弟の間で等しく分けられた The money was divided *equally* [in *equal* parts] among the brothers. ● 彼も等しく(=また)望郷の念に駆られた He *also* [*too*] got homesick./He got homesick *as well* [*too*]. (❗

ひとしお 一入 (なおさら一層) all the more; (特に) especially. ▶見知らぬ町の喧騒(煎)に寂しさがひとしお身にしみた The bustle of an unfamiliar town made me feel *all the more* lonely.

ひとしお 一塩 アジの一塩物(=薄く塩を振ったもの) *lightly salted* horse mackerel.

ひとしきり 一頻り ▶午後ひとしきり雨が降ったあとはまた晴れた It rained *for a while* in the afternoon, but the skies cleared up again.

ひとしごと 一仕事 (一区切りの) a piece of work; (かなりの[きつい]仕事) hard [tough] work; (時間のかかる) time-consuming work. ▶教える準備をするだけでも一仕事だ It's *quite a job* making [to make] preparations for teaching.

ひとじち 人質 a hostage. ●彼を人質に取る take [hold] him (as a) *hostage*. ●人質を解放する release [free, set free] the *hostages*.

ひとしばい 一芝居 ▶あの子は病気じゃないよ. 同情を得るために一芝居打っているだけだよ She's not really ill; she's just *putting* it *on* to get sympathy.

ひとしれず 人知れず [秘かに] secretly, in secret; [心の中で] inwardly.

ひとしれぬ 人知れぬ unknown to other people [others]; [秘密の] secret; [隠れた] hidden; [内心の] inward.

ひとずき 人好き ●人好きのする女性 a *likeable* [(魅力的な) an *attractive*, (愛想のよい) an *amiable*] woman.

ひとすじ 一筋 (1本の線) a line. ●絵の中央の一筋の道 *a straight* road in the center of the picture. ●一筋の希望 *a ray* of hope. ▶彼女はバレエ一筋に生きてきた(=ひたすら打ち込んできた) She *has devoted herself entirely* to the ballet.

ひとすじなわ 一筋縄 ●一筋縄ではいかない ▶彼は一筋縄ではいかない(扱いにくい) He is *hard to deal with*./(手ごわい交渉相手だ) [話] He is a *tough negotiator*.

ひとずれ 人擦れ ●人擦れした sophisticated; worldly-wise. ●人擦れしていない unsophisticated; naive; innocent.

ひとそろい 一揃い (道具などの) a set; (服の上下) a suit. (⇨一式) ●百科事典一そろい a *set* of encyclopedia. ●上下一そろいの服 a *suit* of clothes.

ひとだかり 人だかり ▶店の前は黒山の人だかりだった There was a large [big, huge] *crowd* (of *people*) in front of the store.

ひとだすけ 人助け 人助け 名 a kind act, a help.
— 人助け(を)する 動 be kind to 《him》; help 《others》 (out).

ひとたび 一度 once; one time. (⇨一旦(穀))

ひとだま 人魂 the spirit of a dead person; (鬼火) a will-o'-the-wisp.

ひとたまり ●ひとたまりもなく (簡単に) very easily; (抵抗もなく) without any [the least] resistance; (どうしようもなく) helplessly. ▶チームはひとたまりもなく負かされた The team was *very easily* beaten.

ひとちがい 人違い — 人違いする 動 take [mistake] 《him》 for somebody else; (人を間違えて話しかける) speak to the wrong person.
会話「失礼ですが, 田中先生ではありませんか」「いいえ, 違います. 人違いですよ」 "Excuse me. Aren't you Mr. Tanaka?" "No, I'm not. You must have the *wrong person*."

:ひとつ 一つ 名 ❶ [1個] one. ▶リンゴは十のうち一つが腐っていた *One* out of ten apples was rotten [bad]. (!直前の apples に引かれて were が用いられることもあるが避けた方がよい) ▶ロンドンは世界最大の都市の一つです London is *one* of the largest cities in the world. ▶私は時計を 2 種類持っています. 一つは腕時計でもう一つは懐中時計です I have two watches. *One* is a wristwatch and *the other* is a pocket watch. (!2つあるもののうち最初に言及するものは one で, 残りの一つは the other で表す)
❷ [一体, ひとまとまり] ●一つに(=一体に)なって行動する act *united* [*in a body*]. ●持ち物を一つにまとめる put [(やや話) *lump*] one's things *together*; (荷造りする) *pack* one's things. ▶彼らは心を一つにしてその問題の解決にあたった They *became one* [(やや書) *were unified*] to solve the problem. (!日常会話では They worked together to solve.... などということが多い)

— 一つ(の) 形 ❶ [1 個の] one (!特に「一つ」の意を強調したり, 正確を要する場合以外は one より a, an が多く用いられる); [たった一つの] a single; (一つしかない) the (one and) only. ▶彼のたった一つの夢 his *one and only* dream. ▶テーブルの上にメロンが一つある There is a melon on the table. ▶リンゴが一つだけ残っている There's only *one* [×an] apple left. ▶よいニュースを君に教えてやろう I'll give you a good *piece of* news [×a good news]. (!news は Ⓤ. *a piece of* news より普通) ▶彼の作文には一つの間違いもない There is not a (*single*) mistake in his composition. (!*single* を省略する場合は a を /eɪ/ と読んで「一つ」を強調する)

> 解説 a/an と one はともに「ひとつ」のものを表すことができるが, いつでも交換可能というわけではない.
> (1) **数を強く意識する場合** ▶このステレオにはテープデッキが 1 台ついている This stereo has *one* [×a] tape deck. (!1 台ということを強調する言い方で, 2 本のテープは使えないことを暗示) ▶我々が注文したのはケーキ一つで, 二つではない It was *one* [×a] cake we ordered, not two. (!数を数えるときには two や three などに対応させて用いる)
> (2) **数の単位を表す語の前** ▶ hundred, thousand, million など数の単位を表す語の前では, one の代わりに a が可能なことがある. 他にも, 分数を表す quarter, third, half などの前, dollar, pound などお金の単位の前では one の代わりに a が用いられることがある. ▶その建物の中には 100 人の学生がいた There were a [one] hundred students in that building. (!(1) くだけた文脈では one の代わりに a が好まれる. ただし, a は数の表現の先頭にのみ用いられ, 途中には one を用いる: 2,152 two thousand *one* [×a] hundred (《主に英》and) fifty-two. (2) 正確さを意識するときは one を用いる: その建物の中にはちょうど 100 人の学生がいた There were exactly *one* hundred students in that building.) ▶そのゴルフ選手は賞金 150 万円を獲得した That golf player won a prize of *one* million five hundred thousand yen. (!数の表現が長くなる場合は *one* が普通)
> (3) **不特定などれか一つにふれるとき** ▶テープデッキじゃだめだ. その仕事をするには CD プレーヤーがいる *A* [×One] tape deck is no good. I need *a* [×one] CD player to do the job.
> (4) **他と比較して一つについて述べるとき** ▶1 人は日本から, 他の人はみな米国から来た *One* [×A] is from Japan and the others are from the United States. ▶その人たちのうちの 1 人は日本から来ています *One* [×A] of those people is from Japan. (!of 句を従えるのは one のみ)
> (5) **物語などで day, morning などの語とともに** ▶ある日のその男は町を出た *One* [×A] day the man went out of the town.

ひとつおき

❷【同じ】the same. ▶一つ屋根の下に住む live under *the same* roof [in *the same* house].

——一つ 副 ❶【1個, 1件】(一つにつき) each, 《やや書》apiece; (一つには) for one thing; (一つ一つ) one by one (一つずつ). ▶それは一つ 100 円です They are a hundred yen *each* [*apiece*]. ▶私はたばこをやめました. 一つにはたばこは体によくないのと, もう一つには妻がたばこの煙を嫌うからです I gave up smoking—*for one thing*, it's not good for the [my] health, and *for another* (*thing*) my wife hates cigarette smoke. (❗️... smoking, *partly because* it's ... and *partly because* my wife .... のようにもいえる)

❷【ちょっと】just; (1 回) once. ▶一つ彼に聞いてみてください Just ask him. ▶一つやってみよう I'll *just* try it./I'll have *a try* (↔a bad) mixer とう) ▶彼は会社をやめてからほとんど人付き合いをしなくなった He has *met* [*seen*] very few *people* since he retired from the company.

ひとっこ 人っ子 ● 人っ子一人 ▶人っ子ひとりいない There is not *a soul* to be seen [in sight]. (❗️否定文で)

ひとつずつ 一つずつ one by one; (各々) each. ▶彼はその問題を一つずつ処理した He dealt with the problems *one by one*. (⇨一つ一つ)

ひとづて 人づて ● 一人づてに 副 (受け売りの) secondhand; at second hand; (口伝えに) by word of mouth; (うわさで) by [from] hearsay. ▶彼女が結婚すると人づてに聞いています I know *secondhand* [*at second hand*] that she is going to get married.

ひとっとび 一っ飛び (⇨一(⁵⁄₂)飛び)

ひとつぱしり (⇨一(²⁄₂)走り)

ひとつひとつ 一つ一つ (一つずつ順番に) one by one; (各々) each. ▶卵を一つ一つ数える count the eggs *one by one*. ▶桃は一つ一つ紙で包んであった *Each* of the peaches have [The peaches were *each*] wrapped in paper. (⇨一つずつ)

ひとつぶ 一粒 (穀物・砂・塩などの) a grain; (液体の) a drop. (⇨粒(²⁄₂)) ▶1 粒の砂に世界を見る see a world in *a grain* of sand. ● 1 粒の雨 *a drop* of rain.
● 一粒種 one's only child.

ひとづま 人妻 another man's wife 《後》 other men's wives; (既婚女性) a married woman 《後》 -men).

ひとつまみ 一つまみ ——一つまみの 形 (指先でつまんだ量) a pinch (*of* salt); (ごく少数の) only a few; (一握りの) a handful (*of*). ● 一つまみの金持ち *a handful of* rich people.

ひとつめこぞう 一つ目小僧 a one-eyed goblin.

ひとつも 一つも 【一つも...ない】 not a (single); (何も...ない) (not) any; (not) anything. (⇨一つ) ▶彼らは事態の改善に一つも努力しなかった They did *not* make *any* effort to improve the situation. ▶彼に有利な証拠は一つもない There's *not a* (*single*) piece of evidence for him. ▶彼女は大きな輝く目以外にこれといった取り柄は一つもなかった She had *nothing* to recommend but a pair of big shining eyes.

ひとで 人手 ❶【動員可能な人員数】manpower; 【手助け, 人夫】a hand (「手助け」の意では常に単数形); 【援助】help. ● 人手を借りる ask for a *hand*. ▶人手が足りない We are *short-handed*./We are *short of hands* [*help*].

❷【他人の手】 ▶人手に渡る pass to [fall into] *other hands*. ▶人手にかかる (殺される) be murdered.

● 人手不足 a manpower [(肉体労働の) a labor] shortage; (一人の) shortage of manpower. ▶配管工は今人手不足だ (不足している) Plumbers /plʌ́mərz/ are *in short supply* right now.

ひとで 人出 【群衆】a crowd; 【人の数】the number of people. ▶通りは大変な人出だった There was a large [a big, a huge] *crowd* on 《米》[in 《英》] the street./The street *was* very *crowded*. ▶その祭りは人出が少なかった [多かった] There were [×was] a small [a large] *number of people* at the festival./There was a poor [a good, a high] *turnout* at the festival.

ひとで 海星 【動物】a starfish. (❗️単・複同形)

ひとでなし 人でなし ▶ a devil, a beast; 【冷酷な人】a cold-blooded [an inhuman, (無情な) a heartless] person; 【恩知らず】an ungrateful person. ▶この人でなし You jerk! (❗️《話》You beast. 大人が用いるとふざけていると受けとられることが多い)

ひととおり 一通り ——一通りの 形 【全体的のところ】(全般的な) general; (全部の) all. ▶日本語を一通り知っている have a *general* [a *basic*] knowledge of Japanese; (身につけている) have learned the *basics* of Japanese. ▶その本を一通り読む read *all* the books there. ● 教科書を一通り (=一そろい) 買う buy *a set of* textbooks. ● その事を一通り (=手短に) 彼に話す tell it to him *briefly*. ● その書類に一通り (=ざっと) 目を通す *look over* [*run through*] the papers; *glance over* [*through*] the papers.

❷【普通】一通りの心配ではない be *extremely* anxious about it. ▶辞書を編集する苦労は一通りではない It takes *extraordinary* trouble [It is *such an effort*] to compile a dictionary.

ひとどおり 人通り ● 人通りのない [多い; とだえた] 通り

ひととき 一時 ● 楽しい一時を過ごす have *a* good [*a* great] *time*. ● 今晩は楽しい一時を過ごせてとても幸せでございました I'm glad we had [could have] a lovely [a happy] evening with you.

ひととなり 人となり [人柄] one's personality; (性格) one's character; [生まれつきの性質] one's nature. ● 私が彼を尊敬するのはその人となりのためで財産のためではない I respect him not for what he has but for what he is.

ひととび 一飛び ● 大阪から香港まではほんの一飛びだ It's just *a short flight* from Osaka to Hong Kong. ● 夢の一飛びに(=いっぺんに)かなった My dream has come true *all at once* [*in an instant*].

ひとなか 人中 ● 人中で *in public*; *in company*. (⇨人中で)

ひとなかせ 人泣かせ ― 人泣かせな 形 troublesome 《problems》.

ひとなつ(っ)こい 人懐(っ)こい amiable; (友好的な) friendly; (話しかけやすい、親しみやすい) affable. ● 人懐っこい笑顔 an *amiable* [*a friendly*] smile. ● その犬は人懐っこい The dog *is friendly to* [*likes*] *people*.

ひとなみ 人並み ― 人並みの 形 (平均的な) average; (普通の) ordinary; (ありふれた) common; (まあまあの) 《やや書》 decent. ● 人並みの背の高さの人 a person of *average* [中位の *medium*] height. ● 人並みの生活をしている enjoy an *ordinary* [*a decent*] standard of living; (巨人) a giant.
● 人並み外れた ● 人並み外れた大男 an *extraordinarily* [*an uncommonly*] big man; (巨人) a giant.
― 人並みに 副 ● 人並みに風邪を引く catch (a cold *like other people*. ● 人並み以上に働く *work harder than others* (*do*). (❗ do を用いる方が口語的で普通) ● 彼には人並み以上に情にもろいところもある He has *as much of sentimental side as the next person*. (❗成句表現)

ひとなみ 人波 (押し寄せる群衆) a surging crowd. ● 人波にもまれる be shoved /ʃʌvd/ [jostled /dʒɑ́s(ə)ld/] *in the crowd*. (❗ be jostled and shoved ... と語を重ねると強調的になる)

ひとなめ 一なめ 名 a lick.
― 一なめする 動 ● アイスクリームを一なめする *lick* an ice cream; give an ice cream *a lick*. ● 火が山々を一なめした The fire *ate up* [*wiped out*,《やや書》 *licked up*] the mountains.

ひとなれ 人なれ ● 人なれしたサル a *tame* monkey.

ひとにぎり 一握り a handful 《*of*》. (⇨一掴(つか)み). ● 一握りの土地 a *tiny piece of* land. ● 一握りの革命分子 a *handful of* revolutionaries.

ひとねむり 一眠り 名 a (short) nap [sleep].
― 一眠りする 動 (仮眠する) take* [have*] *a* nap; (しばらく眠る) sleep* for a while; have some sleep.

ひとばしら 人柱 a human sacrifice.

ひとばしり 一走り 名 a (short) run, (ペンの) a stroke.
● 一っ走り使いに行く go on [run] an errand. ● ペンの一走りで書く write with a [at the] *stroke* of one's pen.
― 一走りする 動 make [take*] a short run. ● 公園を一走りする go for *a run* in the park.

ひとはた 一旗 ● 一旗あげる make [(あげようとする) seek] one's fortune.

ひとはだ 一肌 ● 一肌脱ぐ help; give 《him》 help; (困難な立場にある人を助ける) help 《him》 out.

ひとはだ 人肌 ● 牛乳を人肌に温める warm milk to *skin* [*body*] *temperature*.

ひとはな 一花 ● 一花咲かせる ● 彼も一花咲かせたことがあった He had *his day*.

ひとばらい 人払い ● 人払いをお願いしたいのですが I'd like to talk to you *in private*./I'd like to *have* this room *to ourselves*.

ひとばん 一晩 a night. ● 彼は友人の家で一晩泊まった He stayed *overnight* at his friend's house. ● 彼らは一晩中語り明かした They talked *all night (long)* [*throughout the night*]. ● 一晩待ってください。よく考えた上で決めたいと思います Please wait *until tomorrow* [《one night》]. I'll think it over and decide. (❗慣用表現で Let me sleep on it. ともいえる)
● 一晩泊まり an óvernight stay.

ひとびと 人々 people. (⇨人 ❶ ②) ● 多くの人々が負傷した A lot of *people* were injured.

ひとふで 一筆 ● 慶子は一筆で絵を描き上げた Keiko dashed the picture off *with* only *one stroke*.
● 一筆書き (説明的に) a picture or Chinese character drawn with a single stroke (of the brush).

ひとふろ 一風呂 ● 一風呂浴びる take [have] a bath.

ひとべらし 人減らし a personnel cut [reduction]; a cut [a reduction] in personnel.

ひとほね 一骨 ● 一骨折る make an effort.

ひとま 一間 a room. ● 一間のアパート a *one-room* apartment; a studio apartment.

ひとまえ 人前 名 [人の集まり] company. ● 人前に出ることを嫌う avoid *company*; (はにかみ屋である) be an íntrovèrt (↔an éxtrovèrt). (❗心理学用語で「内向性の人」)、(社交的でない) be not sociable.
● 人前(=体裁)をつくろう keep up appearances.
● 人前をはばからず泣く weep *openly*. ● 人前をはばかって (体裁上) for decency's sake.
― 人前で 副 (他人・公衆の面前で) in front of other people; in public; (他人、特にお客がいるところで) in company. ● 人前で話すのは難しい It's hard to speak *in front of other people* [*speak in public*]. ● 人前でそんな話をするな Don't tell a story like that *in front of other people* [*in company*]./Don't tell a story like that *in the presence of other people* [*when there are other people*]. (❗ when ... の方が口語的)

ひとにんせ 人任せ ● 彼はいつでも自分がすべきことを人任せにする He always *leaves someone to* do his job./He always *leaves* his job to someone else.

ひとまく 一幕 (劇) an act; (場面) a scene.
● 一幕見 seeing only one act of a play. ● 一幕物 a one-act play.

ひとまず (ともかく) anyway, anyhow; (差し当たり) for the time being, for the present. ● ともかく、一応、差し当たり ● ひとまず仕事を始めましょう We'll start working *anyway*. ● ひとまずこうしておきましょう。あとで変更することもあるでしょうが We'll leave things as they are *for the time being*, though we might make changes later.

ひとまちがお 人待ち顔 ● 人待ち顔である appear to be expecting [waiting for] someone.

ひとまとめ 一纏め 名 (ひと束) a bundle; (小さな包み) a package.
― ひとまとめにする 動 (一か所に集める) put ... together; (束ねる) bundle ... (up). ● これらの本はみなひとまとめにして彼の部屋に運んでください Please carry all these books to his room *in a bundle*.

ひとまね 人まね 图 mimicry. (⇨物まね)
— **一人まねする** 動 ●猿のように人まねをする *mimic people like a monkey.*

ひとまわり 一回り 图 [1周] a round; (競走路の) a lap; [大きさ] a size; [十二支の] twelve years. ●(人間的に)一回り成長する *grow (more) mentally mature.* ●これよりもう一回り大きな [小さな] 靴が欲しい *I'd like to have shoes one size larger [smaller].* ▶彼は奥さんより一回り年上だ *He is twelve years older than his wife.*
— **一回りする** 動 *go around* ⟨the pond⟩; (持ち場を) *do [make] one's rounds* ⟨of⟩.

ひとみ 瞳 【解剖】 a pupil. ●瞳を凝らす *look hard [intently]* ⟨*at*⟩; (目を凝らす) *strain one's eyes* ⟨*to do*⟩.

ひとみごくう 人身御供 a human sacrifice.

ひとみしり 人見知り — **人見知りする** 動 *be shy* (*with strangers*). ●人見知りしない人 (外向的な) an *outgoing* (社交的な) a *sociable* person; an éxtrovèrt (↔an íntrovèrt) (●心理学の用語で「外向性の人」). ●その赤ちゃんは人見知りしない *The baby takes to most strangers.* (❗️ *take to* は「好きになる」の意)

ひとむかし 一昔 (長い間) 〖話〗 an age (❗️通例複数形で); (10年) a decade. ●彼が大学を卒業したのは一昔前になる *It's (been) ages since he graduated from university.*

ひとめ 一目 [見ること] a look; (ちらり) a glance; 〖目撃〗 a sight. ●彼女をちらっと一目見る *have [take, cast] a glance at her*; *glance at her.* ●彼の喜びようが一目で分かった *I could tell at a glance how delighted he was.*/(容易に見てとれた) *His delight was plain to see.* ●ここから市が一目で見える (市全体を見ることができる) *Here we can see [get a view of, overlook] the whole city.*
● **一目惚れ** *love at first sight [glance].* ●彼女に一目ぼれする *fall in love with her at first sight [glance].*

ひとめ 人目 (other people's) attention [notice]. ●人目を避ける *avoid attention [notice]*; *avoid being seen.*
●**人目がうるさい** ▶人目がうるさいので(=あれこれうわさされるのが煩わしいので)多くの人とは会わない *I don't get together with many people for fear of gossip.*
●**人目に余る** ▶人目に余る行為のせいで, 人々は彼と距離を置いた *People stayed away from him because of his disgusting behaviors.*
●**人目に立つ** ▶彼は背が高いので人目に立つ(=人込みの中でも目立つ) *He's tall, so he stands out in the crowd.*
●**人目につく** *draw the attention* ⟨*of*⟩. ▶人目につくところで口げんかをするのはやめなさい *Stop quarrelling in a conspicuous place.* ▶人目につかないところ行こう *Let's go somewhere less public.*
●**人目を忍ぶ** ●人目を忍んで *secretly, in secret.* ●人目を忍ぶ恋人 *furtive lovers.*
●**人目を盗む** ▶そのいたずらっ子は人目を盗んで(=気づかれないように)となりの家の木からリンゴをもぎ取った *The naughty boy picked apples from the neighbor's tree, without being noticed.*
●**人目をはばかる** *try to avoid being seen.* ▶彼らは人目をはばからずにキスをした *They kissed each other without avoiding being seen* [人前で] *in public*]. ●彼らは人目をはばかって(=ひそかに)暮らした *They lived a secret life.*
●**人目を引く** *attract attention [notice].* ▶彼女のはでな服装は人目を引いた *Her showy dress was very eye-catching* [*a real eye-catcher*]. (❗️いずれ

もくだけた語で, よい意味で用いる)

ひとめぐり 一巡り 图 a round. (⇨一巡)
— **一巡りする** 動 *go around...* (⇨一回り); (旅行などで) *make a tour* (*around*); (循環する) *circulate.* ▶季節が一巡りしてまた春が来た *The seasons have gone around and it's now spring again.*

ひともじ 人文字 *letters formed by groups of people.* ●人文字でつづった 'HAKATA' 'HAKATA' *spelled in human letters.*

ひとやく 一役 a role.
●**一役買う [買って出る]** *play* [*offer to play*] *a role* ⟨*in*⟩.

ひとやすみ 一休み 图 (休息) a rest; (小休止) a break.
— **一休みする** 動 ▶ここで一休みしましょう *Let's take [have] a rest [a break] here.*

ひとやま 一山 ●一山500円のリンゴ *apples sold at 500 yen a pile [a lot].*
●**一山当てる** 〖話〗 *make a killing.* ●株で一山当てる (=もうける) *make a killing on the stock market.*

ひとやま 人山 ●バーゲンセールで人山ができた *A crowd of people [Crowds of people] gathered in a sale.*

ひとよせ 人寄せ an attraction.

ヒドラ [腔腸動物] a hydra.

ヒトラー 〖ドイツの独裁者〗 Hitler (Adolf ～).

*ひとり 一人, 独り** 图 代 [1人] one; [各人] each, every one. (❗️*each* の方が個別的を強調する) ●彼らを1人1人調べる (①各々人を調べる方を強調) *examine each* (*one*) [*every one*, ×*every*, ×*everyone*] *of them* (❗️×*examine them each* のように直接目的語の後において副詞としては用いない) ; (1人ずつ調べる) *examine them one by one* [(次々と) *one after another*, (一度に1人ずつ) *one at a time*]. ▶友人の1人がアメリカにたった *One of my friends [A friend of mine] has* [×*have*] *started for America.* (❗️後の方は「ある友人」の意) ▶男の子は彼1人で, 妹が2人いた *He was the only son. He had two sisters.* (⇨形)/*He had no brothers but two sisters.* ▶本校の学生の4人に1人が電子辞書を持っている *At our college, one student out of* [*in*] (*every*) *four has an electronic dictionary.* (❗️...*one out of* [*in*] (*every*) *four students* ... の語順も可. いずれも動詞は *one* に呼応する)

【**一人も…ない**】 ▶友人は1人も会いに来ない *None* [誰1人として] *Not one*, ×*No one*] *of my friends come to see me.* (❗️堅い〖書〗では *None* [*Not one*] に対応して *comes* も用いる) ▶通りには1人もいなかった *Nobody* ⟨〖書〗 *Not a soul*⟩ *was to be seen on the street.* (❗️*soul* は「人 (*person*)」の意) ▶この車にはもう1人も乗れません *There is no room for anybody else in this car./This car cannot hold anybody else.* (❗️前の方が普通)

— **一人 (の), 独り (の)** 形 [1人の] one (❗️特に「1人」を強調するときは1以外は不定冠詞 *a*, an で表す); [ただ1人の] the (*one and*) *only*; (1人ぼっちで寂しい) *lonely*; (1人だけで連れのいない) 〖やや書〗 *solitary* (❗️通例限定的に); (ただ1人の, 独身の) *single* ●1人旅をする *travel alone [by oneself]* (⇨形); *take a solitary journey.* ●独り居を楽しむ *enjoy solitude.* ●彼女はまだ独り身だ *She's still single* [*unmarried*]./*She's not married yet.*

— **一人 (で), 独り (で)** 副 [1人で] *each*; (単独で) *by oneself, alone*; (独力で) *by* [*for*] *oneself* (❗️*by* では「自分1人で」, *for* では「自分の利益のために」の含みを持つ). ▶私は彼らに1人2ドルずつやった *I gave each of them two dollars.* (❗️この *each* は

代名詞)/I gave them *each* two dollars. (❗ each の位置は、二つとる構文です ... them two dollars *each*. のように直接目的語の後も可) ▶パパ、ぼく1人で塗ったんだよ I painted it (by) *myself*, Daddy. ▶彼1人だけが試験に合格した He *alone* [*Only* he] passed the exam. (⇨-だけ❶) ▶お願い、1人にしてね Please leave me *alone*. (❗ この alone は形容詞) ▶私はたった1人でそこへ行った I went there *all alone* [*by myself*, *on my own*]. (❗(1) all は強意語. (2) all で修飾せず alone を文頭に出して意味を強めることもできる: *Alone*, he had crossed the Pacific Ocean in a tiny yacht. (たった1人で、彼は小さなヨットで太平洋を横断したのだった)) ▶乗っ取り犯は1人残らず射殺された The hijackers were shot dead *to the last* [(ややまれ) *to a*] *person*./The hijackers were (*one and*) *all* shot dead.

DISCOURSE
一人で旅をするのが好きな人もいる一方、友人と一緒に旅をするのが好きな人もいる Some people like to *travel alone*, **while** others prefer traveling with their friends. (❗ while (一方) は2つの要素を並べて対比を表すディスコースマーカー。前後で対照的な内容を述べる)

- 一人部屋 a single room.
- **ひどり** 日取り the date; (日程) the schedule. ● 会合の日取りを決める decide [fix, set] *the date for the meeting*. ● 旅行の日取りを決める set *the schedule for the trip*.
- **ひとりあたま** 一人頭 ▶その音楽会にひとり頭500円出した We paid 500 yen *a head* for the concert.
- **ひとりあたり** 一人当たり ● 1人当たりの国民所得 *per capita* national income. ▶ 1人当たり500円かかるだろう It will cost 500 yen *per head*.
- **ひとりあるき** 独り歩き, 一人歩き ── 独り[一人]歩きする **動** (1人で歩く) walk [外出する] go out] alone [by oneself]; (幼児が独立して歩けるようになる) become able to walk by oneself; (独立する) (⇨独り立ち). ▶その国の間違った印象だけが独り歩きしている Only a false impression of the country is becoming prevalent among people.
- **ひとりがち** 一人勝ち ── 一人勝ちする **動** ▶ゆうべのポーカーでは彼が一人勝ちした He was *the only winner* in the poker games last night.
- **ひとりがてん** 一人合点 ── 一人合点する **動** (性急に結論を出す) jump to conclusions [a conclusion]. (❗ that節を導く時は jump to *the* conclusion that ...); (勝手に思い込む) convince oneself 《*that* 節》.
- **ひとりぐらし** 一人暮らし ── 一人暮らし(を)する **動** (独居する) live alone [by oneself, in solitude]; lead a solitary life; (独身生活を送る) live single.
- **ひとりごと** 独り言 ● 独り言を言う talk *to oneself*. (❗ say to [tell] oneself は「心の中で考える」の意にもなる. monologue は劇の「独白(の場面)」); (ぶつぶつと) mutter [mumble] *to oneself*.
  会話 「何か言った？」「いや、独り言です」 "What did you say?" "Nothing, I was just *thinking aloud* [*out loud*]." (❗ think aloud は「考えごとを口に出す」の意. 通例進行形で用いる)
- **ひとりしばい** 一人芝居 (1人で演じる芝居) a one-person [a one-man, a one-woman] play [show].
- **ひとりじめ** 独り占め ── 独り占めする **動** get [(している) keep, have]... (*all*) *to oneself* (❗ all は「完全に」の意で強意語); 《話》hog; (人の時間・注目などを) monopolize.
- **ひとりずもう** 独り相撲 ● 独り相撲をとる《書》tilt at windmills (「いもしない敵にいどむ」の意); be blindly intent on 《do*ing*》.
- **ひとりだち** 独り立ち, 一人立ち ── 独り[一人]立ちする **動** become independent (*of*), 《話》stand on one's own feet. ▶彼は親から独り立ちしていい年頃だ He is old enough to *be independent of* his parents.
- **ひとりっこ** 一人っ子 an only child. (⇨一人息子)
- **ひとりでに** 独りでに (自然に) by [(まれ) *of*] *itself*, *on its own*; *of its own accord*; (自動的に) automatically. ▶戸がひとりでに開いた The door opened *by itself* (*automatically*). ▶彼女の風邪はひとりでに治った Her cold cleared up *on its own*. ▶彼女はひとりでに(＝思わず)口元がほころんだ She smiled *in spite of herself*.
- **ひとりね** 独り寝 ── 独り寝する **動** sleep alone.
- **ひとりぶたい** 一人舞台, 独り舞台 ❶[独演] a play [show] performed by one person, a monodrama.
  ❷[1人だけ特にすぐれていること] ▶試合は彼の一人舞台だった(＝だれも彼にかなわなかった) *Nobody was able to match* him in the game. ▶野球の話になると彼の一人舞台だ(＝話を1人で独占する) When it comes to baseball, he *completely monopolizes* the conversation.
- **ひとりぼっち** 独りぼっち ── 独りぼっちの **形** [ただ1人の] alone (❗ 必ずしも寂しさを意味しない); [仲間がなく1人の] 《やや書》solitary; [独りで寂しい] lonely. (⇨孤独) ▶独りぼっちの老人 a solitary [a lonely, ˣan alone] old man. ▶奥さんに死なれて彼は元の独りぼっちに戻った When he lost his wife, he was *alone* again.
- **ひとりむすこ** 一人息子 an [ˣthe] only son. (❗ the only son は「その一人息子」の意か、後に限定語句を伴うときに限り用いる. (⇨一人っ子)の場合も同様) ▶健は彼の一人息子である Ken is the *only son* (that) he has.
- **ひとりむすめ** 一人娘 an only daughter. (⇨一人息子)
- **ひとりも** 一人も not one. (⇨一人 [一人も...ない])
- **ひとりもの** 独り者 a single man [woman]. (⇨独身)
- **ひとりよがり** 独り善がり ── 独り善がりの **形** smug, complacent (❗ smug より強意的); (自己満足の) self-satisfied.
- **ひとわたり** 一渡り (⇨一通り)
- **ひな** 雛 a young [a baby] bird; (羽の生えたばかりの) a fledg(e)ling; (巣立つ前の) a nestling; [鶏などの] a chicken; (卵からかえったばかりの) a chick. ▶ひなが5羽かえった Five *chickens* (were) hatched.
- **ひなあられ** 雛霰 (説明的に) grilled bits of rice cake for the Girl's [Doll's] Festival.
- **ひなが** 日長 ▶日長になってきた The days are getting longer (and longer).
- **ひながた** 雛型 [見本・模型] a model; (小型模型) a miniature; [見本書式] a sample form.
- **ひなぎく** 雛菊 [植物の] a daisy.
- **ひなげし** 雛罌粟 [植物の] a corn [a field] poppy. [参考] よく麦畑に咲いているあざやかな赤い花がけしで、英国では戦死者を象徴する. ▶a Flanders poppy ともいう)
- ***ひなた** 日向 the sun (↔the shade). ● 日なたで乾かす dry (it) *in the sun*. ● 日なたで遊ぶ play in the *sunshine*. ▶彼は庭で日なたぼっこしていた He *was sunbathing* [*sunning* (*himself*)] in the garden.
- **ひなだん** 雛壇 (説明的に) a tiered /tɪərd/ stand for dolls (which are displayed for the Girl's [Doll's] Festival).

ひなどり 雛鳥 〘ひよこ〙a chick;《集合的》a brood;〘ニワトリのひな〙a chick; a chicken;《集合的》a brood (of chicks).

ひなにんぎょう 雛人形 a doll displayed at the Girl's [Doll's] Festival.

ひなびた 鄙びた ▶ひなびた温泉 a *rustic* hot spring; a hot spring in a *rural* setting. (❗*rustic* の方が俗化されていない素朴さを強調)

ひなまつり 雛祭り the Girl's [Doll's] Festival (celebrated on March 3). 〘事情〙 米英にはない

ひならず(して) 日ならず(して) soon. (⇨間もなく)

ひなわじゅう 火縄銃 a matchlock,《主に米》a harquebus.

***ひなん** 非難 图 〘批判〙(a) criticism;〘厳しい〙〘書〙censure;〘とがめること〙blame;〘穏やかな〙(a) reproach;〘公然の〙《やや書》a rebuke;〘名指しの不当な〙name-calling and finger-pointing;〘言葉や文章による攻撃〙an attack. ● 非難を免れる escape *criticism* [*reproach*]. ● 彼らの非難の的になる become the object of their *criticism* [*attack*]. ● 世間のごうごうたる非難にさらされる lay oneself open to furious public *criticism* [*censure*]. ▶そんなことをすると他人の非難を招くよ If you do such a thing, you will bring the *blame* of other people *upon* yourself. ▶首相はその政策で非難(=攻撃)を受けている[受けた] The Prime Minister is [came] *under fire* for the policy. (❗*fire* の代わりに attack も可) ▶そんな非難がましい顔しないでよ Don't look so *disapproving*.

── 非難する 動 〘人・行為を〙criticize;〘権威者が厳しく〙〘書〙censure;〘公然と〙denounce;〘人を〙〘責任があるとして〙blame;〘よくないことをしたと疑って〙accuse, point a [an accusing] finger 《at》;〘穏やかに〙reproach (❗怒りより失望の気持ちを表す);〘攻撃する〙attack;〘非とする〙disapprove 《of》. ▶彼女は夫のことをだらしないと言っていつも非難している She *is* always *criticizing* her husband *for* being sloppy [×that her husband is sloppy]. ▶君が悪いことをしたといって非難しているのではないのだ I'm not *blaming* you *that* you did (anything) wrong./I'm not *blaming* you *for* [*accusing* you *of*] your wrongdoing. ▶新聞は政府の政策を激しく非難した The press *criticized* [*censured, attacked*] the government's policy severely./The press strongly *denounced* the government's policy. ▶お互いに(どちらが悪いかなどと言って)非難し合うのはやめよう Let's not play the *blame* game. ▶「あなた美香に何をしたの」と彼女は非難するように言った。「その非難は自分に向けたらどうだ」と彼は応酬した "What did you do to Mika?" she said *accusingly.* "You can turn that *finger* around," he retorted.

***ひなん** 避難 图 〘風雨・危険などからの一時的避難〙《やや書》shelter;〘危険・災害などの回避〙evacuation,《やや書》réfuge. (❗この2語はしばしば交換可)

── 避難する 動 shelter, take [find, 《書》seek] shelter《from +危険な場所; at [in, under] +安全な場所》; evacuate. ● 通りから住民を避難させる *evacuate* the inhabitants from the street. ▶船はあらしを避けて入り江に避難した The boat *sheltered* [*took shelter, took refuge*] *from* the storm *in* a cove.
● 避難勧告 (issue) an evacuátion advísory 《for》. ● 避難民 a refugee;《危険地域からの》an evacuee. ● 避難所 a shelter [a refuge] 《from》.

びなん 美男 a handsome man.

ひなんくんれん 避難訓練 ● 火事・風水害の避難訓練 a fíre [an éarthquake] drill. ● 避難訓練をする practice *evacuation*.

ビニール 〘化学〙vinyl /váinil/. (❗英語では「ビニール製の」は通例 plastic という)●ビニールのレインコート a *plastic* raincoat. (⇨プラスチック)
● ビニールハウス a plastic greenhouse;《和製語》a vinyl house. ● ビニール袋 a plastic bag.

ひにく 皮肉 〘人を傷つける辛らつな〙sarcasm;〘笑いをさそうような〙irony. (❗「思いどおりにならぬ成り行き」の意では◎) ● 痛烈な皮肉 biting [keen] *sarcasm*; (a) biting [(a) bitter] *irony*. ● 運命の皮肉によって by the *irony* of fate. ● 皮肉な笑い (冷笑) a *cynical* smile; (心の中を隠す笑い) an *ironic*(*al*) smile; (相手の欠点をからかう笑い) a *satirical* laughter. ● 皮肉を言う make *sarcastic* [*ironic*(*al*)] remarks《about》; be *sarcastic*《about》. ●「何と思いやりのあること」と彼女は皮肉って言った "How unselfish you are!" she said *in sarcasm* [*irony*]. ▶皮肉にも消防署が全焼した *Ironically*, [It was *ironic*(al) that, The *irony* was that] the fire station (was) burned down.
● 皮肉屋 a sarcastic [an ironic(al)] person.

ひにくる 皮肉る (皮肉を言う) make sarcastic [ironic(al)] remarks《about》; be sarcastic《about》. (⇨皮肉)

ひにち 日日 a day. (⇨日 ❹)

ひにひに 日に日に (⇨日[成句])

ひにょうき 泌尿器 the urinary organs.
● 泌尿器科 urology.

ひにん 否認 图 denial /dináiəl/.
── 否認する 動 deny; make a denial of …. (⇨否定) ▶彼はその犯行を否認した He *denied* [*made a denial of*] the crime.

ひにん 避妊 contraception; (産児制限) birth control.
● 避妊薬 a contraceptive (pill). (⇨ピル) ● 避妊用具 a contraceptive (device). ● 避妊リング an IUD (intrauterine *device* の略).

ひにんじょう 非人情 ── 非人情な 形 heartless; inhuman; cold-hearted.

ひねくりまわす 捻くり回す (いじくる) ▶野の花は野にあるように生けなさい。ひねくり回してはいけません Wild flowers should be arranged the way they are in the field. Never *fiddle around with* them.

ひねくれもの ひねくれ者 a contrary person.

ひねくれる become crooked /krúkid/. (⇨ねじける ❷)

ひねしょうが ひね生姜 an old ginger /dʒíndʒər/ rhizome.

ひねた 〘穀物などが〙(more than one-year) old; (水分が少なくなった) shriveled;〘子供が〙(ませている) precocious (❗精神的な早熟またはそれからくる大人びた行動をいう). ● ひねた(=しおれた)野菜 withered vegetables. ● ひねた(=大人の顔)をした子供 a child *with an adult face*.

びねつ 微熱 a slight fever. ▶私は微熱がある I've got a *slight fever*./I'm *slightly* [《話》a bit] *feverish*.

ひねもす 終日 all day (long). (⇨終日(ﾋﾞ))

ひねり 捻り a twist; (回転) a turn. ● ボールにひねりを加えて投球する throw a ball by giving it special *spin*. ▶もう一ひねりすれば(=もう少し磨きをかければ)いいエッセーになると思う I think this will make a very tasteful essay if it is given a bit more polish.

ひねりだす 捻り出す ❶〘苦心して考え出す〙●案をひねり出す devise a plan. ● その問題の解決策をひねり出す *work out* [*hammer out*] a solution to the problem.
❷〘捻出する〙manage to raise《money》. ● 苦しい

ひねりつぶす 捻り潰す 〘指先でつぶす〙crush with one's fingers; 〘屈服させる〙crush 《one's enemy》. ▶その提案をひねりつぶす kill the proposal.

ひねりまわす 捻り回す ▶ピストルをひねり回す(=いじり回す) play 《toy》with a pistol.

＊ひねる 捻る ❶〘右か左へ回す〙twist,（激しくねじる）wrench;（スイッチなどを）turn, switch.●蛇口を左へひねる turn the faucet 〘英〙the tap〙to the left. ▶彼はサッカーをしていて足をひねった(=ねんざした) He twisted [wrenched, sprained] his leg while playing soccer. ▶彼はテレビの前に座ってスイッチをひねった He sat in front of the TV and *turned* [*switched*] it *on*.（❗×...turned its switch. とはいわない）
❷〘考えを巡らす〙●頭をひねる (⇨頭〘成句〙)●ひねった問題 a *tricky* [a *complex*] question.（❗tricky は「ひっかかりやすい」, complex は「複雑な」）▶(俳句を)一句ひねる *compose* 〘*work out*〙a *haiku*.
❸〘その他の表現〙▶なぜ彼女があんな男と結婚したのか皆首をひねった We *were* all *puzzled* why she married a man like that.

ひのあめ 火の雨 ▶火の雨が降った A *shower of sparks* flew. ▶彼らに火の雨が降りかかった *Sparks* rained down on them.

ひのいり 日の入り sunset,《米》sundown.（❗光景の描写では ⒞）

ひのうつわ 『悲の器』*Vessel of Sorrow*.（参考）高橋和巳の小説）

ひのうみ 火の海 a sea of flame.●火の海に包まれている be ablaze; be in flames.

ひのえうま 丙午 a *hinoeuma*;（説明的に）one of the signs of the Chinese zodiac; it is believed by some people that a woman born under that sign is firm and unyielding and brings bad luck to her husband.

ひのき 檜 『植物』a *hinoki*; a Japanese cypress.（❗檜材は ⒰）

ひのきぶたい 檜舞台 ●ひのき舞台を踏む（俳優が）appear on the boards of [perform on] a first-class stage;《比喩的》be in [get into] the limelight (of the political world).

ひのくるま 火の車 financial difficulties. ▶我が家の台所はいつも火の車だ Our family finances are always *in a tight corner*.

ひのけ 火の気（火）fire;（火の形跡）a sign of fire.（⇨火）●火の気のない部屋 an *unheated* room. ▶火の気のない山で火事が発生するときがある A fire sometimes breaks out in the mountain where there is no *sign of fire*.

ひのこ 火の粉 sparks. ▶燃えている建物が崩壊したとき火の粉がどっと飛び散った A shower of *sparks* flew into the air as the burning building collapsed.

ひのたま 火の玉 a fireball;（鬼火）a will-o'-the-wisp.

ピノッキオ Pinocchio /pinóukiou/.（参考）イタリアの児童文学者コッローディの童話『ピノッキオの冒険』の主人公）

ひので 火の手（火事）a fire;（炎）a flame.（❗しばしば複数形で）（⇨火事）▶火の手がその工場から上がった The *fire* started [broke out] in the factory.

ひので 日の出 (a) sunrise (↔(a) sunset). ●日の出を見る watch the *sunrise* [the rising sun]. ▶我々は日の出とともに出発した We started *at sunrise*.
●日の出の勢い ▶当時平家一門は日の出の勢い(=繁栄の絶頂へと驀進(ばくしん)中)であった The Heike clan was making a straight dash for the height of prosperity [勢力[人気]上昇中]〘書〙was very much *in the ascendant*] in those days.

ひのべ 日延べ ●日延べする 動（延期する）put off, postpone;（延長する）extend. ▶試合は雨のため2日間[金曜日まで]日延べされた The match *was put off for two days* [*until Friday*]. ▶会期を3日間日延べすることになりました We've decided to *extend* the session for three days.

ひのまる 日の丸 the Rising-Sun (Flag).
●日の丸弁当（説明的に）a box lunch with a pickled *ume* on top in the center of the rice.

ひのみ(やぐら) 火の見(櫓) a fire tower; a watchtower.

ひのめ 日の目 ●日の目を見る〘物・事が主語〙see the light of day;（実現する）be realized. ▶彼の映画は日の目を見ることがなかった His movie didn't *see the light of day*《公開されなかった》was not *shown to the public*].

ひのもと 火の元 （火）fire. ●火の元に気をつける be careful with *fire*.

ビバーチェ [＜イタリア語] 〘活発に〙〘音楽〙vivace /vivá:tʃei/.

ひばいひん 非売品 an article not for sale;《掲示》Not for sale. ▶この絵は非売品です This picture is *not for sale*.

ビハインド 〘相手チームに先行された〙behind.●3点のビハインドをはね返す（野球で）overcome a three-run deficit. ▶我がチームは3点のビハインドだ（野球で）We are three runs behind./We are trailng [down] by three runs.

ひばく 被爆 ●被爆する 動 be atom-bombed; be irradiated 《by a nuclear accident》.
●被爆者 an atomic bomb [an A-bomb] victim; a survivor of atom-bombing. ●被爆地区 an atom-bombed area [site].

ひばし 火箸 (a pair of) tongs.

ひばしら 火柱 ▶火柱が立った A *pillar of fire* shot up.

びはだ 美肌 (a) beautiful skin.

ひばち 火鉢 a *hibachi*;（説明的に）a small Japanese charcoal heating appliance somewhat resembling a brazier.（❗英語の hibachi は金属製の焼き肉を作る携帯用こんろのこと）

びはつ 美髪 beautiful hair.

ひばな 火花 sparks. ▶燃える薪(たきぎ)から火花が上がった The fire wood threw up *sparks*.
●火花を散らす（必死で戦う）fight desperately;（議論で）argue hotly. ▶二つのスーパーが商戦の火花を散らしている The two supermarkets are *very competitive with* each other./There is *a lot of competition between* the two supermarkets.

ひばらい 日払い ●日払いにする pay 《for a thing》in *daily installments*.
●日払い賃金 daily wages 《of 8,000 yen》.

ひばり 雲雀 『鳥』a (sky)lark.

ビバルディ 〘イタリアの作曲家〙Vivaldi (Antonio ～).

＊ひはん 批判 图 (a) criticism;（厳しい）〘書〙censure;（論評）(a) comment 《on, about》.（⇨批評, 非難）
●自己批判 self-criticism;（反省）self-examination.●批判の余地がある[ない] be open to [be beyond, be above] *criticism*. ●その作品に専門的な批判を2,3加える give a few expert *criticisms on* that work. ●建設的な批判を受け入れる accept constructive *criticism*. ▶私たちは日本に対する海外の批判をもっと謙虚に受けとめるべきだ We should take *criticism against* Japan from

ひばん

abroad more humbly. ▶批判に耳を傾けない個人や組織は必ず衰退していく、とぼくは思います I believe individuals and organizations that are not open to *criticisms* are bound to lose out.

── 批判的な 形 ● 彼に批判的な態度を取る take a *critical* attitude *toward* [*to*] him. ● 批判的な目で(=批判的に)あらゆる物事を見る look at everything critically [with a *critical eye*]. ● 政府に対して批判的である be *critical of* the government.

── 批判する 動 criticize; (論評する) comment 《*on, about*》. ▶彼はわいろを受け取ったと厳しく批判された He was severely *criticized for* taking bribes./His bribery *came in for* severe *criticism*.

● 批判票 a vote cast in criticism; a cénsure vòte.

ひばん 非番 ● 非番である[になる] be [go] *off* duty. ● 非番の日に on one's day *off*; on an *off*-day. ● 非番の警官 a policeman *off* duty; an *off*-duty policeman.

ひひ 〚動物〛a baboon /bæbúːn/.

ひび 罅 〚あかぎれ〛chaps. ● 壁のひび a crack *in* the wall.

● ひびが入る crack; be cracked. ● ひびの入った茶わん a *cracked* cup. ● その車のフロントガラスにはくもの巣のようなひびが入っていた The wind shield of the car was cracked in a spider web pattern. ● その出来事で彼らの友情にひびが入った(=関係が悪くなる) The happening caused a *crack* [〚書〛a *rift*] in their friendship.

ひび 日々 (毎日) every day; (来る日も来る日も) day after day; (日ごとに) day by day, daily. ● 日々努力する make *constant* efforts (*to* do). ● 忙しい日々(=生活)を送る lead a busy *life*. ● 日々の行動 *daily* activities.

ひびき 響き 〚馬が鳴く声〛a neigh /neɪ/. ● 馬が牧場でひひーんと鳴いていた Horses *were neighing* in the meadow. ▶馬が時折ひひーんと鳴いて駆けている Horses are running around with occasional *neighs*.

ひびき 響き ❶〚音響〛(a) sound. (⇒音〖響〗) ▶この鐘は響きがよい This bell has a good *sound*./This bell *sounds* [*rings*] well.

❷〚反響〛an echo (複 〜es) (⇒木霊〖こだま〛), 響く❷; 〚音響効果〛acoustics /əkúːstɪks/ (複数扱い). ▶このホールは響きがよい The *acoustics* of this hall are good.

❸〚振動〛(a) shock; (a) vibration. ● 地響き earth *tremors*.

❹〚音の感じ〛a tone; a ring. ▶彼の言葉には真実の響きがあった His speech had a truthful *tone* [a *ring* of truth about it]./His speech *sounded* (進行形不可)

ひびきわたる 響き渡る ▶教会の鐘が響き渡った The church bells *rang out*.

ひびく 響く ❶〚音が伝わる〛ring, sound. (⇒鳴り響く) ▶彼の怒声が家中に響いた His angry voice *rang* [*sounded*] *through* [*in*] the house. (❗through は「隅々にまで」の意)

❷〚反響する〛echo, resound. ▶轟音(ごうおん)がトンネル内に響いた A deafening roar *echoed* [*resounded*] *in* [*through*] the tunnel. / The tunnel *echoed* [*resounded*] with a deafening roar. (❗前者の方が普通)

❸〚悪影響を及ぼす〛affect, tell* on .... ▶連日の残業が体に響いてきた Working overtime every day is beginning to *affect* [*tell on*] me [my health].

❹〚広く知られる〛be well-known. ▶彼の名は日本中に響き渡った He *became well-known* [His name *resounded*] all over Japan.

びびたる 微々たる very few [little], only a few [little] (❗few は数, little は量に用いる); 〚程度が〛(わずかな) slight; (取るに足らない) insignificant. ● 微々たる変化 a *slight* change. ▶我々のもうけは微々たるものであった We made *very little* money./Our profit was *very small*. ▶野生動物が作物や家畜に相当な被害を与えるが、それは人が野生動物に与えてきた被害に比べれば微々たるものであろう Wild animals can do plenty of damage to our crops and cattle, but that will be *nothing* [*insignificant*] compared to what we have done to them.

***ひひょう 批評** 图 (a) criticism; (批評記事) a review; (論評) (a) comment 《*on, about*》.

> 〚使い分け〛**criticism** 文学・美術作品などの批評. 日常語としては欠点をあげて批判することを意味する.
> **review** 書物・映画・演劇などの批評.
> **comment** 観察し、熟慮した上での論評・意見.

● 新しい劇の批評を読む read the *criticism* of a new play. ● その本について批評を書く write a *review* about the book; *review* the book. ▶その映画は好意的な批評を受けた The movie got favorable *reviews*.

── 批評する 動 criticize; review; (論評する) comment [make* a comment] 《*on, about*》. (❗専門的な批評には or、くだけた内容の批評には about を用いる) ▶私の小説を読んで批評してくださいませんか Would you read and *criticize* [*comment on*] my novel? ▶私は批評されるのはいやだ I don't like being *criticized*.

● 批評家 a critic.

びびる (気後れする) get* nervous; (おびえる) be scared; (ちゅうちょする) hesitate 《*to* do》, 〚話〛chicken out 《*of* doing》.

ひびわれる 罅割れる crack; be cracked. (⇒罅〖ひび〛)

びひん 備品 (移動不可能な) a fixture; (移動可能な) fittings; 〚家具類〛(移動可能な) furniture; (移動不可能な) furnishings; 〚設備〛equipment 《*for*》. ● 台所の備品 a kitchen *fixture*. ● 事務備品 office *equipment*. ▶この本は学校の備品(= 所有物)です This book is the *property* of the school.

*ひふ 皮膚** skin. (❗the skin は総称としての皮膚をさす) ● 皮膚の色 a *skin* color; (顔色) a complexion. ● 皮膚炎を起こす get inflammation of the *skin*. ▶彼らは皮膚が白い[黒い] They have fair [dark] *skin*. (⇒色) ●「白人[黒人]だ」という場合には They are white [African-American]. とする. くわしくは(⇒黒人)) ● 彼女は皮膚がすべすべしている[強い; 弱い] She has (a) smooth [(a) strong; (a) delicate] *skin*. (⇒すべすべ) ▶彼女は皮膚が荒れている She has (a) rough [(あかぎれのした) (a) chapped] *skin*./Her *skin* is rough [chapped]. ●「皮膚が荒れる」は Her *skin* becomes rough [chapped].)

● 皮膚科医 a dermatologist; a skin specialist. (後の方が口語的) ● 皮膚科(学) dermatology. ● 皮膚がん skin cancer. ● 皮膚感覚 skin [cutaneous] sensation. ● 皮膚病 a skin disease.

ひぶ 日歩 daily interest; (率) a daily interest rate.

ビフィズスきん ビフィズス菌 bifidobacteria /baɪfɪdoʊbækˈtɪəriə/ (-rium).

ひふう 美風 a good custom [(伝統) tradition].

ひふう 微風 (a) breeze. (⇒そよ風)

ひふく 被服 clothes. (⇒衣服)

ひふく 被覆 covering; coating.

ひぶくれ 火ぶくれ a blister. ▶やけどして手を火ぶくれができた I *got blisters* on my hand from the burn./I burned my hand and it *blistered*.

ビブス a bib (@ bibs). (【参考】ピッチサイドのカメラマンや紅白戦トレーニング中のプレーヤーが身につける、オーバーオール状の胸当て)

ひぶそう 非武装 disarmament; (地域の) demilitarization.
・非武装地帯 a demilitarized zone 《略 DMZ》.
・非武装中立 unarmed neutrality.

ひぶた 火蓋 ・**火ぶたを切る** (戦闘の) open fire; (競技などの) start 《*doing*; *to do*》,《話》kick ... off. ▶2週間にわたるトーナメントの火ぶたが切って落とされた They *started* the first game of a two-week tournament.

ひぶつ 秘仏 (説明的に) an invaluable Buddhist statue not usually shown to the public.

ビフテキ (a) steak /stéik/, (a) béefsteak. (【前の方が普通→ステーキ》)

ひふようしゃ 被扶養者 a dependent.

ビブラート [<イタリア語]【音楽】(a) vibrato. ・ビブラートをかける use some *vibrato* (*for a note*).

ビブリオ a vibrio. (【参考】腸炎をおこす細菌)

ひふん 悲憤 indignation; resentment. ・悲憤慷慨(ﾞ)する be indignant 《*at*, *over*, *about*》; resent.

ひふん 碑文 an inscription; (墓碑銘) an épitàph.

びふん 微粉 fine powder.

びぶん 美文 elegant [flowery] language. ・美文調で《*write*》in an *elegant* [a *flowery*, an *ornate*] *style*.

びぶん 微分 名【数学】differéntial (↔integral); (微分学) (the) differential calculus.
ー**微分する** 動 differentiate.
・微分方程式 a differential equation.

ひへい 疲弊 ー**疲弊する** (人・国が) be exhausted; (国・土地が) (やや書) be impoverished.

ピペット 【化学】a pipet(te) /paipét/. (【参考】化学実験用のガラス管)

ひほう 秘宝 (a) (《書》cherished) treasure. (⇨宝)

ひほう 秘法 a secret method.

ひほう 悲報 ・悲報に接する receive the sad [mournful] news 《*of*; *that* 節》.

ひぼう 誹謗 名 (ののしり) abuse /əbjú:s/; (中傷) (a) slander, denigration.
ー**誹謗する** 動 abuse /əbjú:z/; slander, denigrate.

びほう 弥縫 ・弥縫策 (間に合わせの) a stopgap measure.

びぼう 美貌 (美しい顔立ち) good looks; (美しさ) beauty. ・美貌をあからさまに boast of one's *good looks*. ・彼女の美貌に魅かされる be captured by her *beauty*. ・美貌の婦人 a *beautiful* woman. ▶美貌は皮一重(ﾞ)(ことわざ) *Beauty* is only [but] skin-deep.

びぼうろく 備忘録 a memorandum; a datebook.

ひほけんしゃ 被保険者 an insured person,【法律】the insured (【1 人にも複数の場合にも用いる】).

ひほけんぶつ 被保険物 the article insured.

ヒポコンデリー【心気症】【医学】hypochondria /hàipəkándriə/; hypochondriasis.

ひぼし 日干し ・日干しにする dry 《fish》in the sun.

ひほん 秘本 (秘蔵本の) a treasured book; (春本) pornography.

ひぼん 非凡 ー**非凡な**【並外れた】extraordinary (↔ordinary);【めったにない】uncommon;【普通でない】unusual;【注目すべき】remarkable. ▶彼は音楽に非凡な才がある He has an *extraordinary* [an *unusual*, a *remarkable*] talent for music./He has a *genius* for music./He is a musical *genius*.

ː ひま 暇 ❶【時間】time (⇨時間); (自由な[あいた]時間) free [spare] time; (仕事から解放された) leisure (time). (⇨暇) ▶彼は暇さえあればテレビを見ている He spends all his *spare* [*free*] *time* (in) watching TV. (⇨暇な時はいつも) He watches TV whenever he is *free*. (⇨③) ▶忙しくて読書の暇がない I'm so busy that I have no *time* to read [for reading]./(時間をさくことができない) I'm so busy that I can't spare the *time* to read. ▶彼は暇がありすぎる He has too much *free* [*leisure*] *time*./(暇をもて余している) *Time* hangs heavily on his hands. ▶こういうことは暇がかかるものだ These things take *time*. ▶彼がテレビを見ている暇に(=間)私は宿題をすませた While he was watching TV, I finished my homework.
会話「今日は暇がないんだ」「じゃあ、いつ暇があるの」"I don't *have time* today." "When do you *have time*, then?"
❷【休暇】(仕事などを休んで)「時を表す名詞」+off; (公務員・軍人などの) leave (【「休暇期間」の意では《C》】. ・暇 [1 日暇] 1 週間暇; あす暇] をとる take some time [a day; a week; tomorrow] *off*.
▶私は 1 週間暇をもらって国へ帰った I was given a week's *leave* and went home.
・暇に飽かせて ▶彼は暇に飽かせて(=ゆっくり時間をかけて)散歩した He took [had] a *leisurely* walk.
・暇を出す (首にする) let 《him》go;《書》dismiss;《主に英話》sack;《話》fire. ▶その店員はよく遅刻したため暇を出された The clerk *was dismissed* [*was let go*] because he was often late.
・暇をつぶす kill time. (⇨暇つぶし)
・暇を盗む (時間を作る) make [find] time 《*to do*》.
ー**暇な** 形 **❶【時間】**(仕事がない) free; (忙しくない) not busy; (手があいている) not occupied. ・暇な時間を有効に使う [利用する] make good use of [take advantage of] one's *free time*. ▶暇なときにこの書類に目を通しておいてください Look into these papers when you are *free* [when you have *free time*, (暇ができたら) when you can find *time*]./Look into these papers in your *free* [*spare*] *time*.
❷【閑散】(不景気な) slow, slack; (不振な) dull. ▶盆休みの頃はたいていの商売が暇な時期です The *Bon* holidays are a *slow* [a *slack*, a *dull*] time for most businesses. ▶その店は午後 2 時から 4 時までが最も暇です The *slackest* hours at the store are between two and four in the afternoon.

ひまく 皮膜 (生物体の)【解剖】a membrane; (薄い膜) a film.

ひまく 被膜 a capsule; a film.

ひまご 曾孫 a great-grandchild (@ -children); (男の) a great-grandson; (女の) a great-granddaughter.

ひましに 日増しに (日ごとに) day by day; (毎日) every day. ▶日増しに寒くなってきた It's getting colder *day by day* [*every day*, *from day to day*].

ひましゆ 蓖麻子油 castor oil.

ひまじん 暇人 a person of leisure. ▶暇人の(=暇を持て余しているくせに)手紙の返事も寄こさない I know he *has a lot of time on his hands* [暇な時間がいっぱいある] he *has a lot of free time*], but he doesn't write back to me.

ひまつ 飛沫 spray; splash. (⇨飛沫(ﾞ))

ひまつぶし 暇つぶし ▶暇つぶしによく推理小説を読む I often read detective stories *to kill time*./I often *kill time* (by) reading detective stories.

ひまつり 火祭り a fire festival; (儀式) a fire ser-

ひまどる 暇取る take much time. (⇨回 手間取る)

ヒマラヤ〔山脈〕the Himalayas /himəléiəz/; the Himalaya Mountains.

ヒマラヤすぎ ヒマラヤ杉〔植物〕a Himalayan cedar.

『**ひまわり**』 The Sunflowers.(参考)ゴッホ作の絵画

ひまわり 向日葵〔植物〕a sunflower.

ひまん 肥満 fatness;(病的な)〖医学〗obesity. ●肥満(体)の fat (！婉曲的には stout,《書》corpulent を用いる);〖医学〗obese /oubí:s/;(太りすぎの)overweight. ●肥満になる get fat.(⇨太る) ●豊かさの象徴だった肥満は今や貧困の象徴となっている Being overweight was once the symbol of affluence, but it has now become the symbol [that] of poverty.
●肥満児 a fat [an obese, an overweight] child. ●肥満指数 an obesity index.

びまん 瀰漫 spread.(⇨蔓延(まんえん))

びみ 美味 — 美味な ⁅な⁆ delicious.(⇨おいしい)

:**ひみつ** 秘密 ⓐ（事柄）a secret,（状態）secrecy；⦅私的な秘密では⦆privacy,⦅な⦆a mystery.
①【〜(の)秘密】 ●企業秘密 an industrial secret. ●国家の［商売上の，軍事上の］秘密 a state [a trade; a military] secret. ●厳重に守られた秘密 a closely-guarded secret. ●公然の秘密 an open secret. ●成功の秘密 the secret of (one's) success. ●彼の出生の秘密 the mystery of his birth. ●君とぼくの間の秘密 a secret between you and me. ●信書の秘密を侵す violate the privacy of correspondence. ▶あなたの活力の秘密は何ですか What is the secret of your energy?
②【秘密は［が］】 ●秘密が漏れた The secret leaked [came, got] out. ▶私たちの間には何も秘密はない We have no secrets between us [from each other]. ▶この件に関しては秘密は厳重に守るべきだ Strict secrecy should be kept concerning this matter.
③【秘密を】 ●彼［新聞］に秘密を漏らす leak [let out] a secret to him [the press]. ●秘密を打ち明ける tell [confide,（暴露する）reveal] one's secret (to);（話）let (him) in on a secret. ●秘密を守る keep [guard] a secret. ●秘密を見破る discover [find out] the secret. ●秘密を探る trace a secret. ▶ぜひ私に秘密を教えてよ Do let me into the secret.

── 秘密(の) ⁅形⁆ secret;（私的な）private;（特に文書・話に関する）còonfidéntial;（隠された）hidden. ●秘密の情報 secret [classified] information. (！後の方は官公庁，特に軍に関する秘密)●秘密の話をする（打ち明け話をする）have a confidential talk;（秘密会談をする）have secret talks. ▶ここだけの秘密の話だが，彼は肺がんらしい I hear he's got lung cancer between ourselves [between you and me].

── 秘密に ⁅副⁆ secretly, in secret;（内々に）privately, in private.（⇨ひそかに，こっそり，内々）▶彼は妻にはそれを秘密にしていた He kept it secret [a secret] from his wife. (！前の方は形容詞，後の方は名詞)▶秘密にしておくと誓いなさい［約束しなさい］Swear [Promise] secrecy.

会話「このことは秘密にしておいてください．お願いします」「分かったね．秘密は守るよ」"Keep it under your hat. Please!" "I get it. My lips are sealed."
●秘密会議 a secret [a closed] meeting. ●秘密会談 secret talkings. ●秘密協定 a secret agreement. ●秘密警察 the security [secret] police. ●秘密結社 a secret society; an underground organization. ●秘密工作 a secret [an undercover] operation. ●秘密裁判 a secret trial. ●秘密主義 secretiveness. ▶彼は個人的な事柄に関しては秘密主義だ He is secretive [secret] about his personal matters. ●秘密選挙 a secret election. ●秘密諜報部員 a secret agent; a spy.（⇨スパイ）●秘密投票 a secret ballot. ●秘密文書 confidential documents. ●秘密兵器 a secret weapon.（「とっておきの有力な手段」の意でも用いられる）●秘密漏洩(ろうえい) leakage of a secret.

*:**ひみょう** 微妙 ─ 微妙な ⁅形⁆ 〖慎重さを要する〗delicate /délikət/;〖分からないほど微細な〗subtle /sʌ́tl/;（細密な）fine. ●微妙な立場にある be in a delicate position. ●これらの語の微妙な相違を見分ける see a subtle [a delicate, a fine] difference in meaning between these words.

ひむろ 氷室 an icehouse.

ひめ 姫 a princess. ●メリー姫 Princess [Lady] Mary. (！前の方は王の娘，後の方は伯爵以上の貴族の娘)

ひめい 悲鳴 a scream, a shriek. (！後の方がかん高い声)(⇨叫び声) ●悲鳴をあげて逃げる run away with a scream. ●恐ろしくて[痛くて]悲鳴をあげる scream [shriek, cry out] in terror [with pain].(⇨叫ぶ) ▶私は忙しくて悲鳴をあげたい気分だ（助けを求めたい）I'm so busy that I feel like crying [asking] for help.

ひめい 碑銘 an inscription; an epitaph.

びめい 美名 a good name. ▶平和のためという美名に隠れて多くの核実験が続けられてきている A number of nuclear tests have been carried on in the name [under the cloak] of keeping the peace.

ひめくり 日捲り a daily (pad) calendar.

ひめゆり 姫百合〔植物〕a red star lily; a morning-star lily.

ひめる 秘める〖隠す〗hide*;（人に話さないでおく）keep* ... to oneself;〖心に強く持つ〗have* ... in《him》. ●秘められた財宝 hidden treasure. ●その思いは胸に秘めておく keep the memory to oneself. ▶彼は強い意志を内に秘めている He has a strong will in [inside] him./He is strong-willed.

ひめん 罷免 ⓐ（a) dismíssal.

── 罷免する ⁅動⁆ dismiss [remove]《him》from office.（⇨免職）

*:**ひも** 紐 ❶〖物を縛る〗(a) string; (a) cord; a strap;（靴ひも）a (shoe) lace,《米》a shoestring;（犬・馬などの）《米》a leash,《英》a lead（⇨リード，綱(つな)）.

使い分け **string** 物をしばったりつるしたりするのに用いられるひも.
cord string よりも太いひも．ともに「1本のひも」は a (piece of) string [cord] という．ひも状のものを太い順に並べると rope（ロープ），cord, string, thread（糸）となる．
strap 物を固定するのに用いる帯状のひも．複合語で用いることも多い：カメラの(肩からかける)ひも a camera strap/ヘルメットなどのあごひも a chinstrap/（水着などの）肩ひも a shoulder strap.

●ひもを通したビーズ a string of beads. ●ひもを結ぶ［ほどく］tie [untie] a string. ●靴のひもを結ぶ［解く］tie [untie] one's laces, lace (up) [unlace] one's shoes. ▶彼はその箱をひもで縛った He tied the box up with string. (！文脈から複数の場合は with string (s は省略可)）▶私のくつひもがほどけた My shoestring [shoelace] came [got, ×went] loose.
❷〖条件〗strings. ●ひも付きの［でない］金 money with strings [no strings] attached.
❸〖売春婦の〗a pimp.

ひもく 費目 an item of expediture [expenses].

- 費目別に記載する itemize.
びもく 眉目 ●**眉目秀麗** 眉目秀麗(ˇˋ)の男性 a handsome [a good-looking] man.
ひもじい (be [feel]) very [really] hungry. ▶ひもじくて死にそうだ I'm starving to (death).
ひもち 日保ち ●日もちする牛乳 (英) long-life milk. ▶これはあまり日もちがしませんのでお早めに召し上がってください As this doesn't keep well [long], I hope you enjoy it as soon as possible. (⇨持つ❼)
ひもち 火保ち ▶この木炭は火もちがいい This charcoal burns [keeps burning] for a long time.
ひもつき 紐付き (⇨紐❷)
ひもと 火元 ●火事の原因 the origin of a fire. ▶火元は応接室だった The fire started [broke out] in the drawing room. ▶火元に注意せよ Look out for fire.
ひもとく 繙く ●歴史書をひもとく read a history book.
ひもの 干物 a dried fish [(貝) shellfish]. (! 若干しは half dried …などとする)
ひや 冷や (水) cold water; (酒) cold sake. ▶酒は冷やで飲みます I drink sake cold.
ひやあせ 冷や汗 (a cold) sweat. ▶彼女は多数の聴衆の前で上がって冷や汗をかいていた She was sweating with stage fright in front of a large audience. ▶まず手がふるえ, ついで冷や汗が体中に吹き出るのが分かった First my hands trembled and then sweat broke out all over my body. ▶ガスをつけたままなのに気づいたとき冷や汗が出た I came out in a cold sweat when I realized I left the gas on.
ビヤガーデン a béer gàrden.
ひやかし 冷やかし [からかい] teasing; [店で見るだけ] browsing. ▶冷やかし半分で teasingly, for fun.
●冷やかしの客 a browser.
ひやかす 冷やかす (軽くいじめて) tease; (からかう) make* fun of …; [店などを] browse (around)…. ▶彼は智子との婚約を友達に冷やかされた He was teased about his engagement to Tomoko by his friends. ▶ぼくはベッカム風の髪型を皆に冷やかされて切られちゃったんだ Everybody made fun of [(話) made a crack about] my Beckham's haircut and I snapped. ▶焼き物市で露店を冷やかして回るのはとても楽しいものですよ It'll be lots of fun to browse around one stall to another at a pottery market.
ひやく 飛躍 ❶ [急激な進歩] rapid progress. ▶近年科学は飛躍的に進歩した Science has made rapid [great] progress in recent years./Science has progressed [advanced] rapidly in recent years. (! 前の方が普通の言い方)
❷ [活躍] ▶政界に飛躍する play an active part [role] in political circles.
❸ [論理などの] a gap; [話などの] a jump. ●論理の飛躍 a leap in logic [argument]. ●話題の飛躍 a jump from one topic to another.
ひやく 秘薬 (秘密の薬) a secret medicine [remedy]; (妙薬) a specific medicine [remedy].
‡**ひやく 百** a [one] hundred (! 特に数を強調するときはone を用いる); [百番目の] the hundredth. ●1,100 one [a] thousand one [×a] hundred (! 英米の場合に限らず eleven hundred と読むことも多い) ●100 分の1 a [one-] hundredth. ●100 分の3 three-hundredths. ●百円ほどなく by hundreds; by the hundred(s). (! by the hundred は「百単位で」の意もある) ●百年 a century. ●百一番目の [the] one hundred and first. (! 101st と書く) ▶およそ 550 人の学生がそのデモに参加した About five hundred [×hundreds] (and) fifty students took part in the demonstration. (! and /n/と

弱く読む. and を省略するのは《主に米》) ▶何百人もの乗客がその事故で怪我をした Hundreds [×Hundred] of passengers were injured in the accident. (!「数百人の乗客」なら several [×some] hundred passengers で, some では「約百人」の意となる)
●**百も承知** ▶そのことは百も承知だ I know it perfectly [only too] well./I am well [quite] aware of it.
びやく 媚薬 (性欲増進剤) an aphrodisiac /ǽfrədíziæk/; (ほれ薬) (×a) lóve pòtion.
ひゃくがい 百害 ●**百害あって一利なし** It has only bad [harmful] effects 《on you》./It does 《you》all harm and no good.
ひゃくじゅう 百獣 ●百獣の王ライオン a lion, the king of beasts.
ひゃくじゅうきゅうばん 119番 ━━ **119 番する** 動 call [dial] 119; make an emergency call to the fire station. (⇨110 番 事情)
ひゃくしゅつ 百出 ▶その件について議論百出した Opinions varied widely on that point. ▶難問が百出した Difficult problems arose one after another.
ひゃくしょう 百姓 [大きな農場経営者] a farmer; [小作農] a tenant farmer, a peasant. (⇨農民, 農家)
●百姓をする engage in farming; be a farmer.
●**百姓家** a farmer's house; a peasant's cottage.
●**百姓仕事** fárm wòrk, farming.
ひゃくせん 百戦 ●**百戦百勝** 百戦百勝の invincible [victorious, unbeaten] 《teams》. ▶百戦百勝する win every battle; be victorious [unbeaten] in every battle.
●**百戦錬磨** ▶百戦錬磨の兵 a veteran.
ひゃくせん 百選 ●名曲 [名所] 百選 the selection of 100 famous pieces of music [places].
ひゃくたい 百態 ●美人百態 various postures of a famous beauty.
びゃくだん 白檀 [植物] a sandalwood. (! 材木の場合は U)
●**白檀香** 《burn》sandalwood incense.
ひゃくてん 百点 (得点) one [a] hundred points; (満点) a perfect score [mark], 《英》full marks (⇨満点). ▶試験で百点を取るのは難しいものだ It is hard to get a perfect score [full marks] in exams. ▶彼のやり方は百点満点だ (申し分ない) His way of doing things is perfect [leaves nothing to be desired]./I'll give him a perfect mark [《英》ten out of ten] for his way of doing things. ▶きみの彼女は百点満点で何点あげられる? How many points would you give your girlfriend out of a hundred?
ひゃくとおばん 110番 ━━ **110 番する** 動 call [dial] 110 /wán wán óu/; make an emergency call to the police. (事情) 警察・消防・救急車呼び出しの緊急電話番号 (emergency number) は《米》では 911,《英》では 999
ひゃくにち 百日 a [one] hundred days.
●**百日咳** 《catch》whooping cough; [医学] pertussis /pərtʌ́sis/.
ひゃくにちそう 百日草 [植物] a zínnia.
ひゃくにんいっしゅ 百人一首 (歌集) (説明的に) an anthology of one hundred tanka poems by one hundred famous poets; (カルタ) (説明的に) traditional Japanese cards based on one hundred famous tanka; (ゲーム) The One Hundred Poems Card Game.
ひゃくにんりき 百人力 图 great strength ▶君が加勢してくれれば百人力だ It'll be a great [big] help if you join us.

— 百人力 形 very powerful. ▶百人力の男 a herculean.

ひゃくねん 百年 a [one] hundred years. ▶ここで会ったが百年目 You're finished now that I've seen you here.

● 百年河清(かせい)を待つ (実現する見込みがない) There is no possibility that something will happen./《ことわざ》 When Gabriel blows his horn then this question will be decided.

● 百年祭 《米》 a centennial (anniversary), 《英》 a centenary (anniversary). (⇨一年祭) ● 百年の計 a far-sighted [a far-seeing] national policy.

ひゃくはちじゅうど 百八十度 (度数) one [a] hundred (and) eighty degrees. ● 180度の大転換をする do an *about-face*《主に米》 [an *about-turn*《主に英》] (*in* one's policy). (! (1) do の代わりに make も可. (2) 形容詞の complete をそえて強調することも可.)

ひゃくぶん 百聞 ● 百聞は一見にしかず《ことわざ》Seeing is believing. (! To see is to believe. より自然)

ひゃくぶんりつ 百分率 percéntage. (⇨パーセント)

ひゃくまん 百万 a [one] million. ● 250万 *two million(s)* and a half. (! 数詞がつくと millions とはしばなるが, 最近では《米》《英》とも複数形にしない傾向がある) ▶three million [xmillions] books (! 後に名詞がつく場合は常に単数形) ▶何百万人もの人々 millions [xmillion] *of* people.

● 百万長者 a millionaire. (● 億万長者) ▶だれが百万長者などになりたいのか Who wants to be a *millionaire*?

ひゃくめんそう 百面相 ●百面相をする pull [make] comic faces.

びゃくや 白夜 a night with [under] the midnight sun.

ひゃくやく 百薬 ●百薬の長 the best of *all medicines*. ● 酒は百薬の長 (⇨酒 [成句])

ひゃくようばこ 百葉箱 a box for outdoor meteorological instruments.

ひゃくらい 百雷 ●百雷のごとき拍手かっさい *thunderous* applause; a [the] *thunder* of applause.

ひやけ 日焼け 图 (ひりひりして痛い) (a) sunburn; (健康的な) a (sun)tan.

— 日焼ける 動 (赤く焦げる) get sunburned; (こんがりと) tan. ▶彼の日焼けした顔 his (*sun*)*tanned* face. ▶きれいな小麦色に日焼けする *tan* [*get tanned*] to a golden brown. ▶彼女はすぐ日焼けする She *tans* [*gets sunburned*] easily. ▶娘たちによっては見事に] 日焼けして帰ってきた My daughters came back with nice [wonderful] *tans*.

● 日焼け止めクリーム[オイル] (紫外線を遮断する) (a) sunscreen; (a) sunblock (! sunscreen より強力); (小麦色に焼く) suntan cream [oil].

ひやしちゅうか 冷やし中華 *hiyashichuka*; (説明的に) Chinese noodles served cold with shredded ham, cucumbers, eggs, etc. on top.

ヒヤシンス 【植物】 a hyacinth /háiəsinθ/.

*ひやす 冷やす ❶ [冷たくする] cool; (水で) ice. ▶冷蔵庫でビールを冷やした[冷やしておいた] I *cooled* the beer [*kept* the beer *cool*] in the refrigerator. (! 後の方の cool は形容詞) ▶お茶を氷で冷やしなさい *Cool* the tea with *ice*./*Ice* the tea. (! 「アイスティー」は iced tea) ▶ひざを冷やさないようにしなさい (=いつも温かい状態にしておきなさい) Keep your knees warm. (! 日本語の発想の違いに注意)

❷ [その他の表現] ▶頭を冷やす(=冷静になる) cool

[calm] down; 《命令文で》cool it. ▶私はその恐ろしい光景を見て肝を冷やした(=ぞっとした) I *was frightened* at the terrible sight.

ビヤだる ビヤ樽 a beer barrel.

ひゃっかじてん 百科事典 an encyclop(a)edia /ensáikləpí:diə/. (⇨事典, 辞典)

ひゃっかせいほう 百花斉放 ●《回》百家争鳴

ひゃっかぜんしょ 百科全書 an encyclop(a)edia.

ひゃっかそうめい 百家争鳴 free discussions among scholars of various schools.

ひゃっかてん 百貨店 a department store. (! 《英》でも通例 shop ではなく store を用いる (⇨デパート) ● 阪急[三越]百貨店 Hankyu [Mitsukoshi] *Department Store*. (! (1) 前後関係から明確なときは単に Hankyu [Mitsukoshi] ということもある. (2) 米英では Macy's (メーシーズ百貨店), Harrods (ハロッズ百貨店)など固有名詞のみからなることが多い)

ひゃっかにち 百箇日 the hundredth day after a person's death.

ひゃっかりょうらん 百花繚乱 ▶庭は百花繚乱だ The garden is overflowing with a profusion of flowers. ▶デジタルカメラ市場はまさに百花繚乱の状態だ The market is flooded with various kinds of digital cameras.

ひゃっきやこう 百鬼夜行 chaos; a state of complete disorder.

ひゃっけい 百計 (devise) various [hundreds of] plots.

びゃっこ 白狐 a white fox.

ひやっと ▶飛行機がひどく揺れたときはひやっとした I *shivered* [*felt a shiver*] when our plane shook hard. ▶その光景に背すじがひやっとした A chill ran down my back at the sight. ▶外はぽかぽか暖かかったが森に入るとひやっとした Outside it was comfortably warm but in the wood I *felt a chill in the air*.

ひゃっぱつひゃくちゅう 百発百中 ●百発百中する 動 hit the mark ten times out of ten; never miss the mark [target].

ひゃっぱん 百般 ●百般の 形 all kinds [sorts] of ....

ひゃっぽ 百歩 ●百歩譲っても even if I make a major concession to you.

ひゃっぽう 百方 ●百方手を尽くす try every [all] possible means (*to do*); leave no stone unturned (*in doing*).

ひやとい 日雇い (人) a day laborer. ▶彼は日雇いだ He is a *day laborer*./(日雇いで働く) He *works by the day*.

ひやひや 冷や冷や ——冷や冷やする 動 (怖がる) be afraid (*of*; *that*節); fear; (身震いして) shudder. ▶母親は自分の子供が自転車に乗って事故を起こすのではないかとひやひやしている The mother *is afraid* that her little boy may cause an accident on his bicycle. ▶綱渡りを見て観衆はひやひやした The spectators *shuddered* at the tightrope walk.

ビヤホール 《米》 a béer hàll, 《英》 a béer hòuse.

ひやみず 冷や水 cold water. ▶年寄りの冷や水 (⇨寄り [成句])

ひやむぎ 冷や麦 *hiyamugi*; (説明的に) Japanese (thin) noodles chilled in ice-cold water and served with thick soy-flavored dipping sauce.

ひやめし 冷や飯 cold cooked rice.

● 冷や飯を食う ▶彼は会社で冷や飯を食わされている He *is treated coldly* in his office./He *is given cold treatment* in his office.

ひややか 冷ややか ——冷ややかな 形 〖冷淡な〗 cold

(⇔warm); 〚冷静な〛 cool; 〚肌に冷たい〛 cold; chilly. ●冷ややかな態度をとる take a *cold* attitude 《toward》. ●人を冷ややかに迎える give 《him》 a *cool* reception [welcome].

ひややっこ 冷や奴　*hiyayakko*; (説明的に) chilled *tofu*, usually served with some toppings such as bonito flakes, chopped green onion and grated ginger.

ひやりと (⇨ひやっと)

ヒヤリング listening. (⇨ヒアリング)

*ひゆ 比喩 图 〚言葉のあや〛 a figure of speech (　直喩 (a simile /símɪli/)), 隠喩 (a metaphor) などを総称した言い方); 〚寓話(ぐうわ)〛 a fable, a parable.

—— 比喩的な 形 figurative; metaphorical. ▶その語は比喩的な意味で用いられている The word is used *figuratively* [in a *figurative* sense]. ▶英詩では「ばら」がよく「愛」の比喩的表現として使われる. The rose is often used as a *metaphor* of love in English poetry.

—— 比喩的に 副 figuratively; metaphorically.

ヒューズ a fuse /fjúːz/. ▶ヒューズが飛んだので取り換えなくてはならない The *fuse* has blown [(米) blown out], so I have to change it [replace it, put in a new one].

ヒューストン 〚米国の都市〛 Houston.

ビューティー 〚美しさ〛 beauty; 〚美人〛 a beauty. ●ビューティーコンテスト a béauty còntest. ●ビューティーサロン a béauty sàlon.

ひゅうひゅう (⇨ぴゅうぴゅう)

ぴゅうぴゅう ▶冬には北風がぴゅうぴゅう吹く The north wind *howls* /háʊlz/ in winter. ▶汽船が何度もぴゅうぴゅう汽笛を鳴らしながら港を出て行った The steamer *whistled* many times when she left port. (　she は汽船をさす) ▶戦場では弾丸がぴゅうぴゅう飛び交った Bullets *were whizzing* around in the battlefield.

ピューマ 〚動物〛 a puma.

ヒューマニスト 〚人道主義者〛 a humanitárian; 〚人間至上主義者〛 a húmanist.

ヒューマニズム 〚人道主義〛 humanitárianism; 〚人間至上主義〛 húmanism.

ヒューマン 〚人間〛 a human. ●ヒューマンアセスメント 〚人事評価〛 (an) employee evaluation. ●ヒューマンエラー human error. ●ヒューマンドキュメント the record of 《his》 life; a human document. ●ヒューマンリレーションズ 〚人間関係〛 human relations.

ピューリタン (清教徒) a Puritan; (道徳的に非常に厳格な人) 《軽蔑的》 a puritan.

ピューリッツァー ●ピューリッツァー賞 Pulitzer Prize.

ピューレ 〚<フランス語〛 purée. ▶トマトピューレ tomato purée.

ヒュッテ 〚<ドイツ語〛 〚山小屋〛 a mountain hut.

ビュッフェ 〚<フランス語〛 〚駅などの立食式の食堂〛 a buffet /bəféɪ/; 〚列車食堂〛 a buffét càr.

ぴゅんぴゅん ▶彼は高速道路をぴゅんぴゅん(=猛スピードで)飛ばすので私は生きた心地がしなかった I was scared to death when he drove along the expressway *at terrific* [(無条件茶な) *breakneck*] *speed*.

ひょいと ❶〚思いがけなく〛 unexpectedly; (突然に) suddenly. ▶私はひょいと外国に行きたくなった I felt like going abroad *suddenly* [*all of a sudden*]. ▶彼がひょいと訪ねてきた He paid me a visit *unexpectedly* [*out of the blue*]. /He *dropped in* on me. (　drop in は「ひょこり訪ねる」の意) ▶彼はひょいと会社を辞めたくなった He had *a sudden whim* to quit his company. (　whim は「理に合わぬ要求,

気まぐれ」の意)

❷〚急な動作を示して〛 ●かばんをひょいと網棚にほうり上げる *toss* a bag onto the rack. ●ホットケーキをひょいと裏返すこつを覚える get the hang of *flipping* (*over*) a pancake. ▶彼はひょいと頭を上げて私の方を見た He *popped* his head *up* to look at me. (　pop は急で軽快な動きを表す) ▶彼はひょいと子供を肩に乗せた He *snatched* the boy onto his shoulders. (　snatch は急に力ずくで取り去る動作を示す)

❸〚苦もなく〛easily; (軽々と) lightly. ▶彼はその石をひょいと持ち上げた He lifted the stone *so easily* [*lightly*]. ▶少年は自転車からひょいと降りた The boy stepped off his bike *with one easy movement*.

ひょいひょい ▶彼はひょいひょいと岩から岩へ跳んだ (身軽に) He jumped *lightly* from rock to rock. ▶彼女はひょいひょい外国へ出かける (何度となく) She goes abroad *as often as not* [*more often than not*].

*ひよう 費用 〚出費〛 (an) expense (　〚必要経費〛の意では通例複数形で); 〚支払うべき費用〛 (a) cost.

①〚~費用〛 ▶結婚式の費用 wédding expénses. ●訴訟費用 the *costs* of litigation.

②〚費用が[は]〛 ▶セントラルヒーティングを取り付けるのは大変費用がかかる It's quite an *expense* [It's a great *expense*, It's very *expensive*] to install central heating. (　この an expense は「費用がかかること」の意. quite a 〚《米話》は形容詞のつかない単数名詞を修飾して〛「たいへんな」「たいした」の意を表す慣用表現)/It *costs* too much [a great deal, a fortune] to install central heating. ▶思ったより費用がかかった My *expenses* were greater than I (had) expected. ▶家を新築する費用はどのくらいですか What is the *expense* [*cost*] of building a new house?/How much does it *cost* to build a new house?

③〚費用を[に]〛 ▶費用(=資金)を捻出する manage to raise the *fund*. ▶会社が旅行の費用を払ってくれる The firm pays [(負担する) bears] our traveling *expenses*. (　複数形に注意)/(会社の費用で旅行する) We travel *at* the firm's *expense*. (　「自分の費用で」なら at our own expense となる) ▶私たちは家の修理の費用を出し合った We shared our *expenses for* repairing the house.

DISCOURSE
費用の心配について言いたいのは，教育など費用に対する効果が高い投資は少ないということだ **As for** concerns about the cost, I have to say that few investments are more *cost-effective* than education. (　as for ... (...については)は関連を表すディスコースマーカー)

④〚費用で〛 ▶100ドルの費用で at an *expense* [a *cost*] of 100 dollars. ▶追加費用なしに at no extra *expense* [*cost*]. ▶それはわずかな費用で完成した It was completed at small (⇔great) *expense* [*cost*].

*ひょう 表 〚縦横の二つの軸による一覧表〛 a table; 〚項目を羅列した一覧表〛 a list. ▶上の表に示したように as *listed* above; as shown in the *table*. ▶表に載っている be on a *list*; be listed. ▶実験結果を表にする make the results of experiments into a *table*. ●学生の必読書を表にする *list* [*make a list of*] the books students should read. ●表計算ソフト a spreadsheet software.

ひょう 俵 a sack of 《potatoes [coal, flour]》.

ひょう 豹 〚動物〛 a leopard /lépərd/; 〚黒ヒョウ〛 a (black) panther /pǽnθər/. ●アメリカヒョウ a jaguar.

ひょう 票 a vote. ● 組織[保守; 同情]票《集合的》the organized [conservative; sympathy] *vote*. ● 浮動票 (⇒浮動票) ● 提案に対する賛成[反対]票 a *vote for* [*against*] the proposal. ● 票集めの方針 *vote*-catching [*vote*-getting] policies. ● 大量票を獲得する get [poll, secure] a heavy (↔a light) *vote*. ▶私は彼に1票を投じた I *voted for* him./I cast my *vote for* him. ▶法案は10票対8票で可決された The bill was passed by 10 *votes* to 8. (❗「1票差で」は by a single *vote*)
● 票が開(ひら)く 票が開き始めた The vote-counting began.
● 票を読む (票読みをする) project the vote count. (⇒票読み)

ひょう 評 〖批評〗criticism; (本・演劇などの) (a) review; 〖論評〗cómment 《*about, on*》. (⇒批判) 〖好意的な〗映画評を書く write a (favorable) *review of* a movie.

ひょう 雹 hail; (1粒の) a hailstone, a pellet of hail. (⇒あられ)

びよう 美容 (容姿を美しくすること・術) (a) beauty treatment. ● 美容と健康によい be good for one's health and *beauty*.
● 美容院 a béauty sàlon [pàrlor,《米》shòp]; (髪の) a hairdresser's. ● 美容学校 a beauticians' school. ● 美容師 a beautician; (髪専門の) a hairdresser. ● 美容整形 cosmetic surgery; (美顔整形) face lifting. ● 美容体操《do》cal(l)isthénics /kæləsθéniks/《単・複両扱い》.

*** びょう 秒** a sécond. ● 時も角度も表す (⇒分(ぶ))) ● 100メートルを11秒で走る run 100 meters in eleven *seconds*. ● 20秒目をつむる close one's eyes for twenty *seconds*. ● 10秒の遅れを出す make a ten-*second* [X-*seconds*] delay. ● 毎秒50メートル動く move 50 meters a [per] *second*. ● ものの数秒とたたないうちに in a matter of *seconds*. (❗ a matter of は時間・距離の短かさを強調する語句で, ここは「ほんの2-3秒ぐらいで」で「あっというまに」という感じを表す) ▶今1時4分23秒 [30秒] です It's four minutes twenty-three *seconds* [four and a half minutes] past one.

びょう 廟 (壮大な墓) a mausoleum /mɔ̀ːsəlíːəm/ 《複 ~s, -lea /líːə/》.

びょう 鋲 (金属板用の) a rivet; (紙・敷物などの) a tack; (靴底の) a hobnail. ● 鋲を打つ drive (in) a *tack*; (靴底に) put a hobnail on the sole [bottom]; hobnail (boots). ● 鋲で留める *tack*《a notice *to* a board》. (⇒画鋲(がびょう))

ひょうい 憑依 ── 憑依する 動 ● 悪霊が憑依する(=のりうつる) be possessed by an evil spirit.

ひょういつ 飄逸 ── 飄逸な 形 free and easy; happy-go-lucky.

ひょういもじ 表意文字 an ideogram, an ideograph.

*** びょういん 病院** a hospital. (⇒通院, 入院)

> 解説 (1) hospital は通例大きな総合病院をさす. 米国では通例入院が中心で, 最初に外来患者を診察するのは個人医院 (a doctor's [a physician's] office) や付属診療所 (a clinic).
> (2) hospital は通例《英》では「治療の場」(機能)を思い浮かべるが,《米》では「建物」を連想するため《米》用法では the を冠するのが普通.

① 〖~病院〗● 私立[国立; 総合; 救急]病院 a private [a national; a general; an emergency] *hospital*; (大学付属病院などの)《主に米》a medical center. ● 小児科[動物]病院 a children's [an animal] *hospital*. ● 慶応病院 the Keio *Hospi-tal*.

② 〖病院に〗▶けがをした人たちは病院に運ばれた The injured people were taken [(急送された) were rushed] to *the hospital*《米》[to *hospital*《英》]. ▶彼はまだ病院にいる(入院している)He's still in *the hospital*《米》[in *hospital*《英》]. ▶母の見舞いに病院に行った I went to *the hospital* to visit [see] my mother./I visited [went to see] my mother in (the) *hospital*. (⇒解説(2)) ▶すぐに病院に(=医者の診察を受けに)行った方がいいよ You'd better go and see your doctor [go to the doctor's (office)] right away. (❗(1) go to (the) hospital は通例入院が必要な病気を暗示するのでここでは不適. (2) the] doctor は「かかりつけの医者(family doctor)」の意) ▶彼は様子を見るために病院に入れられた He was put in a *hospital* for observation.

③ 〖病院で〗● 病院で看護師として働く work as a nurse at a *hospital*. ● 彼は病院で亡くなった He died in *the hospital*《米》[in *hospital*《英》].
● 病院長 the head of a hospital.

びょういん 病因 an etiology; the cause of a disease.

ひょうおんもじ 表音文字 〖言語〗a phonogram.

*** ひょうか 評価** 图 (証拠・能力などの) (an) evaluation; (格付け) a rating; (見積もり) an estimation; (税額の) (an) assessment; (意見) an opinion; (査定) (an) appraisal. ● 過大評価 overvaluation. ● 過小評価 undervaluation. ● 再評価 revaluation.
会話 「勤務評価の結果をもらったよ」「どうだった」「協調性は A の評価をもらったけど, 能率で C と評価されるなんて思ってもいなかった」"I just received the results of my performance *evaluation*." "How did you do?" "Well, I was given a *rating* of 'Excellent' for Cooperation, but I never expected to be *rated* 'Poor' for Efficiency."
── 評価する 動 evaluate; rate; estimate, value; assess. ● 学生の能力を評価する evaluate student's abilities. ● その家を4,000万円と評価する *estimate* [*value*] the house *at* 40 million yen; *rate* the house *at* [*as worth*] 40 million yen. ▶この作品をどのように評価していますか What's your *opinion* [What *opinion* do you *have*] of this work? ▶彼らは君を高く評価している They *think* highly of [*have a high opinion of*] you./They *regard* you *highly*. (❗いずれも進行形不可)
■ DISCOURSE
教師を評価すべきという考え方を支持する I support the view that teachers should be *evaluated*. (❗ I support the view that ... (... という意見を支持する) は賛成を表すディスコースマーカー)

● 評価益 valuátion [appráisal] gàin [pròfit]. ● 評価額 a value; a valuation; an assessment; an assessed [an appraised] value. ● 評価額10億円の土地 an estate with a *value* of a billion yen. ● 評価基準 a valuátion bàsis. ● 評価損 valuátion [appráisal] lòss.

ひょうか 氷菓 (アイスクリーム) (an) ice cream;《英》an ice; (シャーベット) a sherbet.

ひょうが 氷河 a glacier /ɡléiʃər/.
● 氷河時代 the ice age; the glacial epoch [period, era].

びょうが 病臥 ── 病臥する 動 be sick [ill] in bed; be laid up; (病気・老齢で寝たきりの) be bedridden.

ひょうかい 氷海 a frozen sea.

ひょうかい 氷塊 a block of ice; (浮氷) a floe; an ice floe.

ひょうかい 氷解 —— **氷解する** 動 be cleared up;《やや書》be dispelled. ▶彼の説明で彼女の誤解は氷解した His explanation *cleared up* [*removed*] her misunderstanding.

ひょうがい 病害 crop damage; damage from blight. ●病害虫 (⇒害虫)

ひょうき 表記 ❶[表記法] notation. ●音声表記(法) phonetic *notation*.
❷[表書き] ●表記の住所 the address *written* [*mentioned*] *on the cover*.

ひょうき 標記 [[表題] a heading; [目印・符号] a mark.

ひょうぎ 評議 名 (a) conference; (a) discussion.
—— **評議する** 動 (議論を戦わす) discuss; (会議を開く) hold a conference.
●評議員 a councilor; a member of a council.《米》a council person. ●評議(員)会 a council.

:**ひょうき 病気** ❶[不健康] (an) illness; (a) sickness; a disease /dizíːz/; an ailment; a disorder; trouble.

> 使い分け **illness, sickness** 「病気」の意を表す一般的な語. 多くの場合 illness が長期にわたる病気をいうのに対して, sickness は短期間の一時的な病気をいい, 吐き気を催すような気分の悪い状態もさす. ともに個々の病気を表すときは C. なお,《米》では sickness の方が好まれ, illness はやや堅い語.
> **disease** 特に病気の種類をいう.
> **ailment** 軽い慢性の病気.
> **disorder** 心身機能の不調による一時的な病気.
> **trouble** 局所の病気.

① [～病気] ●心の病気 mental *illness*. ●軽い[重い]病気 a slight [a serious, ×a heavy] *illness*. ●命取りの病気 a fatal [a deadly] *disease*. ●心臓の病気 (a) heart *disease*; heart *trouble*. ●腎臓の病気の人 a person with kidney *trouble*. ●ウイルス性の[恐ろしい; 子供がかかる]病気 a virus [a terrible; a childhood] *disease*.

② [病気が］ ●病気が治る get well; get over *illness*;《やや書》recover from *illness*; [書] be cured of one's *disease*. ▶彼の病気はよくなるどころか悪化した His condition got worse instead of improving./He got worse rather than better. (❗got iller はまれ)
会話「お子さんの病気はいかがですか」「おかげさまでだいぶよくなりました」「それはよかった. 引き続きお大事にね」"How is your (*sick*) child?" "He's a lot better now, thanks." "That's good. I hope he's well again soon."

③ [病気に] ●病気になる get [《やや書》become, (急に) [書] fall] ill [(主に米) *sick*]; [書] be taken ill (❗ill の叙述用法は《米》では堅い言い方. sick の叙述用法は《書》を除いて通例「むかついて吐き気がする」の意); (伝染性の病気に) catch a *disease*. ●病気に負ける give way to one's *disease*. ●重い病気にかかっている be seriously *sick* [*ill*]. (⇒重病) ▶彼は心配のあまり病気になった He was so worried that he got *sick*./He got *sick from* so much worry. ▶今までに大きな病気にかかったことがありますか Have you had any major *diseases*? ▶その葉っぱは病気にかかっている The leaves *are diseased*.

④ [病気を] ●病気を治す cure a *disease*. ●病気を治療する treat a *disease*. ●病気をうつされる(=もらう) catch a *disease* 《*from*》.

⑤ [病気で] ●肺の病気で死ぬ die *of* [×*from*] (a) lung *disease*. (❗死の直接的な原因を表す場合は from ではなくof (⇒死ぬ)) ●病気で寝ている be sick [*ill*] in bed (⇒④); 《やや話》be laid up *with sickness* [*illness*]. ●病気で学校を休む take a call in *sick*. ▶彼は病気で学校を休んだ He stayed away from school because he was *sick* [*ill*]./《やや書》He was absent from school because of *sickness* [*illness*].

⑥ [病気だ] ●彼は病気だ He is *sick* [*ill*]. (❗×He is a sickness [an illness]. とはいわない)/(具合がよくない) He's *not well*.
❷[悪癖] ●彼は例の病気が始まった He's got that *habit* again.
—— **病気(の)** 形 sick. (❗ill は通例限定的には用いない) ●病気休暇をとっている be on *sick* leave. ●病院へ友達の病気見舞いに行く go to the hospital to see one's *sick* friend; visit one's *sick* friend in hospital [《主に米》the hospital]. (❗×one's *ill* friend は不可. ただし副詞とともに用いて one's *very ill* friend のようにはいえる)

ひょうきん 剽軽 —— **剽軽(な)** 形 (こっけいな) funny, comical. ●ひょうきんなしぐさで with a *funny* [*comical*] gesture.
●ひょうきん者 a funny [a comical] fellow; a clown.

ひょうぐ 表具 mounting. ●源氏物語の絵巻物を表具してもらう *have* one's pictures of *The Tale of Genji mounted* on a scroll.
●表具師 a mounter; a scroll maker ●ふすま張り, 壁紙張りの paperhanging. それを業とする人は a paperhanger.

びょうく 病苦 ●病苦に堪える bear *the pain of illness*. ●病苦と闘う struggle with one's *illness*.

びょうく 病躯 a sick body. (⇒⑯ 病身) ●病躯を押して in spite of one's *poor health*.

ひょうけいさん 表計算 ●表計算ソフト a sprèadsheet sòftware.

ひょうけいほうもん 表敬訪問 《pay》a courtesy call 《*on*》《visit《*to*》.

ひょうけつ 氷結 —— **氷結した** 形 frozen.
—— **氷結する** 動 freeze.

ひょうけつ 表決 名 a decision.
—— **表決する** 動 make [take] a decision [a vote] 《*on*》. ●挙手によって表決する *vote* by a show of hands.

ひょうけつ 票決 名 a decision by vote. ●票決に付す put (the matter) to the vote. ▶票決の結果彼の案は不採用となった The vote went against his plan./His plan was voted down.
—— **票決する** 動 vote 《*on* a matter》, take a vote 《*on* a matter》. ▶法案は 15 対 3 で票決された (可決された) The bill was passed [(否決された) was defeated] by 15-3 vote [by 15 votes to 3]. (❗15-3 は 15 to 3 と読む)

びょうけつ 病欠 absence 《*from* school [work]》because of sickness [illness]. ●電話で病欠を届ける call in sick.
—— **病欠する** 動 be absent because of sickness; be off sick; (許可を得た上での) be on sick leave. ▶熱があるので病欠させてほしいのです I have a fever, so I'm thinking of *taking* a day *off sick* [a sick day]. ▶彼は学校を病欠した He *was absent* [*stayed away*] *from* school *because of sickness*. (❗後の方が口語的)

:**ひょうげん 表現** 名 [[表明] (an) expression; [[芸術作品などによる] (a) representation; [[言い回し] an expression. (⇒語句) ●思想の自由な表現 the free *expression* of thoughts. ●表現の自由 freedom of *expression*. (❗「言論の自由」は freedom of speech) ▶「亡くなる」は「死ぬ」の意の婉曲的な表現

ひょうげん "To pass away" is a euphemistic *expression* meaning "to die." ▶芸術は自己表現の一つの形式である Art is a form of self-*expression*.

— **表現する** 〖人・作品などが〗express; 〖言葉で〗put* (**!** 通例様態を表す副詞(句)を伴う。express より口語的); 〖絵などが〗represent; 〖感情などを〗give* expression to 〖one's feelings [anger]〗. ●自分の考えを英語で[上手に]表現する express oneself [*put* one's ideas] in English [cleverly, very well]. ▶その1節は彼の苦悩を表現している The passage *expresses* [gives *expression* to, *is expressive of*] his agony. ▶あの時のうれしさは言葉では表現できません I can't *express* (in words) [No words can *express*] how delighted I was at that time. (**!** that 節を用いて ×...*that* I was very delighted.... とはいえない)/I can't *put* my delight at that time in [into] words.(表現しがたい喜びを感じた) I felt *indescribable* [〖書〗 *inexpressible*] delight at that time.
● **表現力** (one's) power(s) of expression; (one's) expressive power(s).

ひょうげん 氷原 an ice field.
ひょうげん 評言 a (critical) cómment. (⇨批評)
ひょうげん 病原 the cause [origin] of a disease.
● **病原菌** a (disease) germ. ● **病原体** pathogen /pǽθədʒən/.

ひょうご 評語 〖評言〗(a) comment (⇨評言, 批評); 〖評点〗a grade (⇨評点, 点 ❷).

ひょうご 標語 〖うたい文句〗(スローガン) a slogan; (キャッチフレーズ) a catchword, a catch phrase; 〖座右銘〗a motto (復 ~es). ●「安全運転」という交通安全週間の標語 the *slogan* "Drive Safe(ly)" for the traffic safety week.

ひょうご 病後 ●病後療養中の人 a convalescent /kὰnvəlésnt/. ●病後の静養[回復]期 convalescence. ▶彼は病後に体が弱くなった He has become weak *after his sickness*.

ひょうこう 標高 an [the] altitude. (参考 海面からの高さ) ▶その山は標高 3,000 メートルある The mountain is 3,000 meters *above sea level* [*above the sea*]. ▶ここの標高はどれくらいですか What is the *altitude* here?

ひょうこん 病根 the cause of a disease. ●社会の病根を絶つ get rid of social *evils*.

ひょうさ 票差 ●わずかの[大きな]票差で勝つ win by a narrow [a large] *majority*; win by a narrow [a wide] *margin*. ●16 票差で勝つ win by a *majority* of 16 (votes).

ひょうさつ 表札 (戸口の番地札, 名札) a doorplate; (名札) a nameplate. (**!** 前の方は通例真鍮(しんちゅう)などの金属製, 後の方は金属・樹脂製) (事情 米英では表札に番地のみを書くことが多い)

ひょうざん 氷山 an iceberg.
● **氷山の一角** ▶今回の収賄事件は氷山の一角にすぎない The recent case of bribery is just [only] *the tip of the* 〖×an〗 *iceberg*.

ひょうし 拍子 ❶〖調子〗time. ●3 拍子の曲 a tune in triple [three-four] *time*. (**!** 2 拍子では duple /djúːpl/, two-four を, 4 分の 4 拍子では quadruple, four-four を用いる) ●手で拍子をとる beat [keep] *time* with one's hands.
❷〖はずみ〗(a) chance. ●何かの拍子に by some *chance*. ▶転んだ拍子に脚を折ってしまった I broke my leg when I fell down.

ひょうし 表紙 (本の) a cover, a binding. (**!** 日本語の「カバー」は英語では jacket または 〖英〗 wrapper) ●裏表紙 a back *cover*. ●背表紙 a spine. ●布表紙の本 a clothbound book; a book bound in cloth. ●本に表紙をつける (装丁する) bind a book.

ひょうじ 表示 — **表示する** 〖示す〗show; 〖指し示す〗indicate; (計器が) read; 〖言い表す〗express. (⇨示す) ▶価格はここに表示されている The price *is shown* [*is marked*] here. ●湿度計は 80 パーセントを表示している The hygrometer /haigrɑ́mətər/ *reads* [*indicates*] 80 percent./The hygrometer *reading* [*indication*] is 80 percent. (**!** a reading, an indication は「表示された数値」)

ひょうじ 標示 a sign; a mark. (⇨標識)
ひょうし 病死 图 death from a disease. (関連 サーズによる死亡 death *by* SARS)
— **病死する** die of a disease.

ひょうしき 標識 a sign /sáin/; 〖航空・航路の〗a beacon. ●交通(道路)標識 a traffic [a road] *sign*. ●「止まれ」の標識 a stop *sign*; a *sign* saying "Stop". ●標識に従って進む follow a *sign*.
● **標識灯** a béacon light.

ひょうしき 拍子木 wooden clappers.
ひょうしき 病識 one's consciousness of sickness [illness].
ひょうしつ 氷室 an icehouse.
ひょうしつ 病室 a sickroom; (大部屋) a (cancer) ward (**!**「病棟」をさす場合もある).
ひょうしぬけ 拍子抜け —**拍子抜けする** 動 (当てが外れる) be disappointed 《*to* do; *at*》.
ひょうしゃ 被用者 an employee.
ひょうしゃ 評者 a reviewer 《*of* a play》; a critic.
ひょうしゃ 病舎 (⇨匣 病棟)
ひょうしゃ 描写 a description; (絵・文章での) a portrayal. ●心理[自然]描写 psychological [naturalistic] *description*. ●性格描写 character *portrayal*.
— **描写する** 動 〖文章で〗describe, give* a description 《*of*》; 〖絵・文章で〗portray, 〖書〗depict. ●人物を描写する describe [*portray*] a character. ●その出来事を生き生きと[簡潔に; 詳細に]描写する give *a* vivid [*a* concise; *a* minute] *description of* the event.
● **描写力** the power of description.

ひょうしゃく 評釈 图 (an) annotation.
— **評釈する** 動 annotate 《a book [a text]》.
ひょうじゃく 病弱 — **病弱な** 形 ●病弱な (= 病気がちな)子供 a sickly child, a child (chronically) *in poor health*. ●病弱な体質である have a *sickly* [a *weak*] constitution.
ひょうしゅつ 表出 图 (an) expression.
— **表出する** 動 express 《one's feelings [emotions]》.

ひょうしゅつ 描出 (a) description; (a) portrayal. (⇨描写)

:**ひょうじゅん** 標準 图 a standard; 〖平均〗an average.
① 【標準~】 ●日本標準時 Japan *Standard* Time. ●世界標準時 Universal Time Coordinated. ●以前の Greenwich Mean Time に代わる正式名) ●標準サイズのスーツ a *standard*-size suit. ▶私の体重は標準以上[以下]だ My weight is above [below] *average*./(人が主語) I am above [below] *average* in weight.
② 【標準に[から]】 ●標準に達する[しない] come up to [fall short of] *standard*. ▶君の作品は標準に達していない[達している] Your work is below *standard* [up to *standard*]. ▶たいていのアメリカ人の標準からすると日本の校則は保守的だ Japanese school regulations are conservative *by* most American *standards*.

— **標準の, 標準的な** 形 standard, (普通の) normal;

ひょうしょう 【平均的な】 average; 【典型的な】 typical. ●標準的な問題 a standard question. ●私は標準的な日本人だ I'm an average Japanese. ●日本では働く女性が標準的に(=普通に)なりつつある Working women are becoming normal [the norm] in Japan.
— 標準化する 動 standardize.
●標準化 standardization. ●標準価格 a standard price. ●標準型 the standard type. ●標準語 the standard language; (日本の) standard Japanese. ●標準装備 standard equipment. ●標準偏差 『数学』 standard deviation.

*ひょうしょう 表彰 — 表彰する 動 《書》 commend 《for》; (栄誉を与える) honor 《for》; (賞を与える) award. ●彼はおぼれている少年を助けて表彰された He *was commended for* saving a drowning boy.
●表彰式 a commendation [an award] ceremony. ●表彰状 a commendation; 《米》 a citation 《for bravery》. ●表彰台 (mount) an honor platform.

ひょうしょう 氷晶 ice crystals; ice needles.
ひょうしょう 氷象 (a) representation; (象徴) a symbol; an emblem.
ひょうしょう 標章 (シンボルマーク) a mark; an emblem; a logo; (ステッカー) a sticker.

*ひょうじょう 表情 〔顔の〕 (an) expression, 《書》 a cóuntenance; 〔顔・顔の〕 a look 《通例単数形で. 感情を表す形容詞を伴うと「目つき」をさす〕; 〔顔〕 a face. ●顔の表情 an *expression* [*a look*] *on* one's face; one's facial *expressions*. ●表情の豊かな[乏しい]顔 an *expressive* [an expressionless, a wooden] face. ●心配そうな表情で彼を見る look at him with a worried *expression* [*look*]. ●表情を変える change (one's) *expression* [*countenance*]. ●その知らせを聞いて彼は表情が堅くなった His *face* hardened at the news. ●彼はうれしそうな表情をしている He looks happy./He has a happy *expression on* his face. ●彼女はほっとした表情を見せた She *showed that* she was relieved [*how relieved she was*].

ひょうじょう 氷上 ●氷上の輪舞 a round dance *on ice*. ●氷上ですべって転ぶ slip *on the ice*.
ひょうじょう 評定 a verdict. ●小田原評定 (⇨小田原評定)
びょうしょう 病床 a sickbed. (⇨病気) ●彼は病床にある先生を見舞った He visited his teacher in a *sickbed* [(病気の先生) his *sick teacher*]. ●彼は長年病床にある[ついている] He *has been sick in bed* [*He has been laid up*] for many years.
びょうじょう 病状 (健康状態) (a) condition. ●彼の病状は悪化した His *condition* turned [*got*] worse. ●病人の病状は変化がみられない There is no change in the *condition* of the patient.
ひょうしん 秒針 a second hand.
びょうしん 病身 ●(慢性的に)病身の妻 one's *invalid* [*ailing*] wife. ●母は病身だった My mother had a *weak constitution*./My mother was chronically *in poor health*.
ひょうする 表する express; offer; present. ●遺憾の意を表する express one's [*offer an expression of*] regret. ●祝意[謝意]を表する *offer* one's congratulations [gratitude]. ●弔意を表する *offer* [*present*] one's condolences. ●田中氏に敬意[謝意; 弔意; 祝意]を表して in honor [appreciation; congratulation; condolence] of Mr. Tanaka.
ひょうする 評する 〖批評する〗 críticize, (本・劇などを) review; 〖論評する〗 cómment 《about, on》; 〖評価する〗 (やや書) evaluate; 〖呼ぶ〗 call. ●彼を経営の神様と評する call him the god of management.
びょうせい 病勢 (a) condition (病状)
ひょうせつ 氷雪 ice and snow. ●氷雪に閉ざされる icebound and snowbound.
ひょうせつ 剽窃 plagiarism /pléidʒərìzm/.
— 剽窃する 形 plágiarize. (⇨盗用)
ひょうぜん 飄然 — 飄然と 副 ●彼は飄然と旅に出た He went on a trip *aimlessly* [*without purpose*].
ひょうそ(う) 瘭疽 〖医学〗 a whitlow. (!a felon は古い言い方)
ひょうそう 表装 图 (書籍の) binding; (書画の) mounting.
— 表装する 動 bind 《a book in leather [paper]》; mount 《a picture》.
ひょうそう 表層 the outer layer.
●表層構造 〖言語〗 surface structure.
びょうそう 病巣 the focus (of a disease) 《複 foci /fóusai/》. ●病巣を突き止める [切除する] detect [remove] the *focus*.
びょうそく 秒速 (⇨速度) ●秒速5メートルで at 《a speed of》 5 meters a [*per*] second.
ひょうだい 表題, 標題 (書名・劇名など) a title; (章や節などの) a title, a heading. ●その本には「星と祭り」という標題がつけられた The book *was entitled* [*was titled*] "Stars and Festivals." (!引用符とピリオドの位置関係については (⇨巻末 [句読法])
●表題音楽 program music.
ひょうたん 氷炭 ●氷炭相容れず (ことわざ) They agree like cats and dogs./They agree harp and harrow.
ひょうたん 瓢箪 a gourd /gɔːrd/.
●ひょうたんから駒 (冗談が本当になった) The joke has become a reality [has come true]./(思いがけない好結果を生んだ) It has unexpectedly brought about a happy result.
ひょうちゃく 漂着 — 漂着する 動 drift ashore. ●難民の乗った船がその島に漂着した A refugees' boat *drifted ashore on* the island.
●漂着物 a drift; (難破船の) flotsam.
ひょうちゅう 氷柱 (つらら) an icicle; (室内に立てる氷の柱) an ice pillar.
ひょうちゅう 標柱 (道標) a signpost; a guidepost; a leveling rod [staff].
びょうちゅうがい 病虫害 damage by blight. (!blight の中には insects (虫)による害も含まれる)
ひょうてい 評定 图 (ランク付け) a rating; (評価) an evaluation; (評点) a grade. ●勤務評定 an efficiency *rating*. ●5段階評定 the five rank system.
— 評定する 動 rate; evaluate.
ひょうてき 標的 ●標的となる be a *target* 《for》. (!射撃の標的は a target, 《書》 a mark. mark には比喩的用法はない) ●鉄道の駅や空港ビルがテロ攻撃の標的になる恐れがある Railroad stations and air terminals are potential *targets for* terrorist attacks [*for* terrorists].
びょうてき 病的 — 病的な 形 morbid. ●彼は火に対して病的な恐怖心を持っていた He had a *morbid* fear of fire.
ひょうてん 氷点 fréezing pòint (!無冠詞に注意; 〔話〕 freezing). ●氷点下の気温 a *below-zero* [*sub-zero*] temperature (!摂氏の場合); a temperature *below freezing point*. ●温度は氷点下(5度)に下がった The temperature dropped (to five degrees) *below freezing point* [*below zero*, 〔話〕 *below freezing*].
ひょうてん 評点 (評価点) a grade; (試験の点数) a

ひょうでん mark. (⇨点❷)

ひょうでん 票田 (有権者) voters, grass roots; (その支持) grass-roots support. ●大票田 a most populated section of a constituency where one can hope to get strong *grass-roots support*.

ひょうでん 評伝 a critical biography.

ひょうど 表土 topsoil.

びょうとう 病棟 a ward /wɔːrd/. ●隔離病棟 an isolation *ward*. ●産科[小児科]病棟 a maternity [a children's] *ward*. ●恵子は外科病棟で働いている Keiko works in the surgical *ward*.

*__びょうどう__ 平等 图 〖権利・機会などの均等〗equality; 〖公平無私〗impartiality. ●人種の平等を主張する claim racial *equality*. ●男女平等を要求する call for *equality* between [of] the sexes.
── 平等の 形 (同等の) equal /iːkwəl/; (特に数量などが同一の) even; (えこひいきのない) impartial. ●平等の権利 *equal* rights. ●平等の分け前をもらう get an *even* [an *equal*] share 《of》. ●人はみな生まれながら平等である All people [men] are created *equal*.
── 平等に 副 equally; evenly; impartially. ●機会を平等に与える give *equal* opportunities 《to》. ●彼らにその金を平等に分けてやる divide the money *equally* [*evenly*] among them. ●彼女は生徒を平等に扱った She treated her students *equally* [*impartially*], (公平に) *fairly*, (差別なく) *without discrimination*]./She was *impartial* [*fair*] *to* her students. ●仕事の量を平等にしよう Let's *equalize* our workload./Let's *make* our workload *equal*.
●平等主義 egalitarianism;《まれ》egalitárianism. ●平等主義者 an egalitarian.

びょうどく 病毒 a disease germ; (ウイルス) a virus. ●病毒におかされる be infected 《with》.

びょうにん 病人 a sick [⌐an ill] person (❗ill を用いると「悪人」の意); [患者] a patient; (介護を必要とする) an invalid. ●病人たちの看護をする take care of the *sick people*.

ひょうのう 氷嚢 an ice bàg [pàck].

ひょうはく 漂白 图 bleaching.
── 漂白する 動 ●ふきんを漂白する *bleach* a dish《米》[a tea《英》] towel.
●漂白剤 a bleach.

ひょうはく 漂泊 ❶ [さまよう] wander. (⇨さ迷う) ❷ [船が漂う] ●船が波間に漂泊していた A ship *was drifting* on the waves with its engine stopped [without its engine running].

:**ひょうばん** 評判 图 〖世間の評価〗(a) reputation, (定評) 〖どちらも複数形にしない〗; 〖名声〗fame; 〖人気〗popularity; 〖話題〗the talk 《of》; 〖うわさ〗a rumor. (⇨噂(ﾅｶﾜｻ), 定評, 名声)
① [=評判] ●その映画はすごい前評判だ (封切られる前に話題になっている) The movie *is* widely [much] *talked about* before it is released.
② [評判~] ●彼 [その劇] は評判倒れだった (評判ほどよくなかった) He [The play] was not so good as he [it] *was reputed to be*. (⇨⑥) ●あのホテルのサービスは評判どおりいい The service at the hotel is as good *as people say it is*./The service at the hotel *lives up to its reputation*.
③ [評判が[の]] ●評判の[の]悪い人 a person of bad [evil] *reputation*. ●評判の高い店 a store with an excellent *reputation*. ●彼は医者として評判がよい He has [enjoys] a good *reputation* as a doctor. (❗have a good [a bad] reputation の主語は通例人・会社・店などで、物・事は不可. 次の2例参照) ●その会社は仕事がお粗末なので評判が悪い The company has a bad *reputation* [*name*] *for* its poor work. ●その映画は若者の間では評判がよい The movie is *popular* (↔*unpopular*) *with* [*among*] young people. ●それ以来彼の評判が上がった[落ちた] His *reputation* has risen [fallen] since then. ●B さんは金のために彼女と結婚したという評判が立った The *rumor* got around that Mr. B had married her for money.
④ [評判に] ●彼はすぐれた指揮者として評判になった (=名をあげた) He has made a *name* for himself [his *name*] as an excellent conductor. ●彼女の突然の結婚は町中の評判(=うわさの種)になっている Her sudden marriage is the *talk* of the town. ●その随筆は学生たちの評判になった The essay won *popularity with* [*among*] students.
⑤ [評判を] ●彼はこの小説で評判を得た He won a *reputation for* this novel./This novel of his gave him a good *reputation* [brought him *fame*]. ●彼はその事件で評判を落とした He lost his *reputation* because of that affair./That affair ruined his *reputation*. ●その映画は大評判を呼んだ (=大当たりした) The movie *made a great hit*.
⑥ [評判だ] ●彼はずば抜けて頭がよいという評判だ He has *the reputation of* being an exceptionally bright boy./He has *a reputation* [*a name*] *for* exceptional brightness [*for* being exceptionally bright]. (❗前置詞, 冠詞に注意)/〖書〗He *is reputed* (*as* [*to be*]) an exceptionally bright boy. (❗He is said to be.... の方が口語的) ●その劇は今大評判だ (大変人気がある) The play is very *popular*./(大騒ぎになる) The play has caused a *sensation*.
── 評判の 形 〖よく知られた〗well-known; 〖人気がある〗popular; 〖悪名高い〗notorious /noutɔ́ːriəs/. (⇨人気, 悪名) ●彼女はこの町で評判の美人だ She is a *well-known* beauty in this town.

ひょうひ 表皮 图 a cúticle; 〖医学〗(an) epidermis /èpidə́ːrmis/.
── 表皮の cuticular, epidermic.

ひょうひょう 飄々 (気楽な) easygoing; (世俗を離れて) a little aloof from the world.

びょうぶ 屏風 a *byobu*; (説明的に) a folding screen (with two or more decorative panels), which serves as a room partition or a blind.

びょうへい 病弊 an evil (❗通例複数形で); a bad effect.

ひょうへき 氷壁 (岩壁状の氷) a cliff ice; (氷に覆われた岩壁) an icy cliff.

びょうへき 病癖 a bad habit.

ひょうへん 豹変 ●豹変する 動 change suddenly; (一変する) do a complete turnaround. ●君子は豹変する《ことわざ》(変化に対応して考えを改める) A wise man changes his mind, a fool never.

びょうへん 病変 a pathological change; a physical or mental change caused by a disease.

ひょうぼう 標榜 图 〖賛意を示して主張する〗(やや書) ádvocate the cause 《of》; 〖公言する〗《書》proféss.
── 標榜する 動 ●民主主義を標榜する *advocate the cause* of democracy. ●正義を標榜して *in the cause* of justice.

びょうほう 描法 a dráwing [a páinting] technique.

びょうぼつ 病没 ●病没する 動 die of disease. (◻病死)

ひょうほん 標本 a specimen /spésəmən/; (見本) a sample. (⇨見本) ●チョウの標本 butterfly *specimens*. ●月の岩石の標本 *specimens* of moon rocks. ● 昆虫を標本にする mount insects. ● 標本調査 a sample survey.

びょうま 病魔 ● 病魔を克服する overcome [get over] an illness. ● 病魔にとりつかれる be attacked by a disease.

ひょうめい 表明 —— **表明する** 動 〚述べる〛 express; (公式に) state. (⇨述べる) 〚宣言する〛 declare; 〚発表する〛 announce. ● 彼の提案に反対[賛成]を表明する declare (oneself) against [for] the proposal. ● 辞意を表明する announce one's intention to resign.

ひょうめい 病名 the name of a disease.

*****ひょうめん 表面** /sɔ́ːrfis/; (上面) the top (side). ❶〚外にあらわれた面〛a surface ● 月の表面 the surface of the moon. ● 池の表面 the surface [top] of a pond. ● 板の滑らかな[ざらざらした]表面 a smooth [a rough] surface of a board. ● (問題が)表面化する come to the surface; (明らかになる) come to light. ● 表面がきつね色になるまで肉をあぶる broil meat until the top side is brown.
❷〚うわべ〛the surface; (外見) (an) appearance; the outside; (見かけ) pretense. ● 表面だけのやさしさ surface [superficial] kindness. (⇨上辺(うわべ)) ▶彼のやさしさは表面だけだ His kindness is only on the surface [is all pretense, (やや話) is just a fake]. ▶彼は表面には[表面上は]社交的なように見えるが、内では孤独なのだ He seems outgoing on the surface, but inside he is lonely. ▶人を表面だけで判断するものではない You shouldn't judge people only by appearances.
● 表面張力〖物理〗sùrface ténsion.

ひょうめんせき 表面積 a surface area. (1 通例 a 〜)

ひょうよみ 票読み —— **票読みする** 動 (投票数を数える) count the votes; (得票数を見積る) estimate [(予測する) predict] the number of votes.

びょうよみ 秒読み a countdown. ● 秒読みを始める start a countdown. ● 秒読みの段階(=最終段階)に入る come to the final stage. ● 秒読みまで 20 分です It's twenty minutes to the countdown. (1 ロケット打ち上げの現場では「発射 60 秒前, 秒読み開始」T minus sixty seconds and counting. (T = time は発射予定時間)のようにいわれる)

ひょうり 表裏 (表と裏) the front and the back; (裏表) two sides. ● 裏表、陰日向(ひなた)
● 表裏一体をなす be inseparably related [combined].

びょうりがく 病理学 图 pathólogy.
—— **病理学上の** 形 pathológical.
● 病理学者 a pathologist.

ひょうりゅう 漂流 图 (a) drift. —— **漂流する** 動 drift. (⇨漂う)
● 漂流者 (難破者) a castaway. ● 漂流船 a drifting ship. ● 漂流物 a drift; (遭難船の) flotsam.

ひょうりょう 秤量 weighing. ● 秤量 10 キロのはかり a ten-kilogram balance [scale].

びょうれき 病歴 one's medical history, one's past illnesses. ● 彼の病歴を調べる check his medical history.

ひょうろうぜめ 兵糧攻め ● 兵糧攻めにする cut off the supply of food. ● 兵糧攻めで敵を降伏させる starve the enemy into surrender [out].

ひょうろん 評論 图 (a) criticism; (個々の) a critical essay; (新聞・雑誌の) (a) review. (⇨批評) ● 評論家 (⇨評論家)
—— **評論する** 動 criticize; review 《favorably》; comment, make comments 《on, about》.

ひょうろんか 評論家 a critic. ● 文芸評論家 a literary critic. ● 映画評論家 a movie critic [reviewer]. ● 野球評論家 (=解説者) a baseball commentator. ● 政治評論家 a political observer.

ひよく 比翼 ● 比翼の鳥 a pair of imaginary Chinese birds (which are believed to fly together all the time).
● 比翼塚 a lover's mound.

ひよく 肥沃 —— **肥沃な** 形 fertile /fɔ́ːrtl, -tail/; (豊かな) rich; (生産性の高い) productive. ● 肥沃な土地 fertile soil.

びよく 尾翼 (尾翼を含む尾部) a tail. ● 垂直尾翼 a vertical tail. ● 水平尾翼 a horizontal tail; tailplane.

びよく 鼻翼 the wings of a nose. (㉠ 小鼻)

ひよけ 日除け a sunshade; (窓の) a blind (1 一枚布のものをいう。よろい板のものは a Venetian /vɪníːʃən/ blind); (米) a (window) shade; (窓・入り口から突き出た) an awning /ɔ́ːnɪŋ/. ● 日除けを上げる draw up [raise], lift the blind(s). ● 日除けを降ろす pull down [lower, draw] the blind(s).

ひよけ 火除け prevention of fire; fire prevention; (予防策) a prevention against fire.

ひよこ a chick; a chicken. (1 後の方は成鶏も含む) ▶私は教職について 3 年ですがまだまだ教師としてはひよこです I have been teaching for three years but I'm quite a fledgling teacher yet. (1 fledgling は「羽が生えたもののまだ飛べないひな鳥」のことで比喩的に「経験不足の」の意)

ぴょこぴょこ ● ぴょこぴょこ飛ぶ hop (around). ● ぴょこぴょこ動く[動かす] bob (...) repeatedly. (⇨ぴょんぴょん)

ぴょこんと ▶少年はぴょこんと頭を下げた The boy bobbed his head briefly./The boy gave me a short bow. ▶水中からぴょこんと魚が現れた A fish suddenly popped up out of the water.

ひょっこ (⇨ひよこ)

ひょっこり (思いがけなく) unexpectedly; (急に) suddenly. ▶古い友達がひょっこり訪ねてきた An old friend of mine came to see me unexpectedly. ▶雲が切れて月がひょっこり顔を見せた The clouds broke suddenly to reveal the moon. ▶梅雨にひょっこり 1 日晴れの日がきた A sunny day interrupted the rainy season.

ひょっと ● ひょっとして[すると] (もしかして) by any chance; (もしかすると) possibly. (⇨もしかして、もしかして)

ひよどり 鵯 〖鳥〗a bulbul /búlbul/.

ぴよぴよ (擬音) cheep; peep, peep. ▶ひよこが巣の中でぴよぴよ鳴いている Chicks are cheeping in their nest. ▶どこか外でぴよぴよという鳴き声がする You can hear cheeps somewhere outside.

ひより 日和 〖天候〗weather; 〖晴天〗nice (《英》fine) weather; (⇨天気) ● 小春日和 (⇨小春日和) ▶ピクニックには絶好の日和です It's an ideal day [perfect weather] for a picnic.

ひよりみ 日和見 ● 日和見感染〖医学〗an opportunistic infection. ● 日和見主義 opportunism.
● 日和見主義者 an opportunist.

ひょろながい ひょろ長い ● ひょろ長い少年 a lanky [a gangling] boy. ● ひょろ長い路地 a long and narrow alley.

ひょろひょろ ❶〚不安定に〛unsteadily; (弱々しく) weakly; 〚不安定な〛unsteady; (弱い) weak; (ぐらつく) shaky. ▶倒れていた男がひょろひょろ立ち上がった The fallen man rose to his feet unsteadily./The fallen man staggered to his feet. ▶その患者はまだ足もとがひょろひょろしている The patient still walks weakly [unsteadily]. (1 形容詞で表せば、

He is still *weak* [*shaky*] just after his illness. (彼はまだ病み上がりでひょろひょろしている))
❷ [細くてもそろそう] thinly; [細く長い] lanky; (やせた) lean. ▶やせた土地に草がひょろひょろ生えている Grass grows *thinly* on the barren land. ▶彼女はひょろひょろして何かぎこちない She is a *lanky*, awkward girl. ▶早春になると若草がひょろひょろと顔を出した Lean shoots of grass sprang out in early spring.

ひょろり ●ひょろりとした(=やせて細い)青年 a *lanky young man*. (⇨ひょろひょろ)

ひよわ ひ弱 ― ひ弱な 形 weak; (生まれつき弱い) delicate.

ぴょんと ●ぴょんと跳ぶ (人が片足で、カエルなどが両足で) hop; (両足で体全部を用いて) jump;《書》leap. ▶ぴょんと跳んで with a hop [a *jump*]. ▶カエルがぴょんと水に跳び込んだ A frog *hopped* into the water. ▶彼女はぴょんと跳んで小川を渡った She *jumped* [*sprang*] *across the stream*. ▶彼はぴょんと跳びのいてその一撃を避けた He parried [evaded] the blow *with a jump*.

ひょんな ●きのう彼女とひょんな所で会った Yesterday, I met her at a place where I *least expected* to see her. ▶あの男とはひょんなことから知り合いになった I've come to know him *quite unexpectedly* [*まったくの偶然で*] *by sheer chance*].

ぴょんぴょん ●ぴょんぴょん跳ぶ jump; (小さく跳びはねる) hop. ▶カエルがぴょんぴょん跳んでいった A frog *hopped away*. ▶子ヤギはぴょんぴょんはねる習性がある Kids have a habit of *jumping* [*bouncing*] *up and down*.

ピョンヤン 〖北朝鮮の首都〗Pyongyang /pjáŋjɑ́ːŋ/.

ひら 平 ❶ [平ら] ●手の平 the *palm* of the [one's] hand.
❷ [並み] ●平の巡査 a *rank-and-file* cop. ●平の職員から係長に昇進する be promoted from *clerk* to section chief. (❗職名を表す場合は無冠詞) ●平社員)

―ひら ―片 ●ひとひらの紙切 a *piece* [a *sheet*, a *slip*] of paper. ●ふたひらの雪[雲] two *flakes* of snow [cloud].

ビラ (散らし) a handbill; (ポスター) a poster, a placard, a bill. (⇨ポスター) ●ビラをまく give out [distribute] *handbills*. ●ビラを張る put up a *poster*; stick [post] a *bill*.

ひらあやまり 平謝り ●平謝りする apologize profusely [(恐れ入って) humbly] 《to》; make profuse [humble] apologies 《to》.

ひらい 飛来 ―― 飛来する 動 fly*《to Japan》; (渡り鳥が) migrate《to》. ▶この鳥は冬になるとこの湖に飛来する These birds *fly* [*migrate*] *to* this lake each winter.

ひらいしん 避雷針 《米》 a lightning ròd, 《英》 a lightning condùctor.

ひらおよぎ 平泳ぎ (the) breaststroke. (❗競技種目としては通例 the をつける) ●平泳ぎの選手 a breast-stroker. ●平泳ぎをする do (the) *breast-stroke*.

ひらおり 平織り ●平織りの織物 a plain fabric; plain cloth.

ひらがな 平仮名 *hiragana*; (説明的に) the Japanese cursive syllabary.

ピラカンサ 〖植物〗a pyracantha.

ひらき 開き ❶ [開く(こと)] (an) opening. ●海開き the *opening* of a beach to swimmers.
❷ [差] (相違) (a) difference; (へだたり) a gap. ●年齢の開き the age *difference*. ●理論と実践の開きが大きい a *gap* between theory and practice. ▶彼らの

能力の開きは大きい There is a great *difference* [(書) *disparity*] *in* their abilities./Their abilities *differ* greatly.
❸ [魚の] ●あじの開き a horse mackerel *slit open and dried*.
●開き戸 a hinged door.

ひらきなおる 開き直る (話) take [assume] a somewhat attitude. ▶彼は急に開き直って「それがどうした」と言った He suddenly *turned defiant* [*shifted to a defiant attitude*] and said, "So (what) [What of it]?"

:ひらく 開く ❶ [開ける] open (❗「ひらく」「あく」を意味する最も一般的な語); (手紙などの封を) unseal; (包み・ドアなどを) undo*; (包み・荷物などを) unpack; (折りたたんだものを) unfold (⇔fold). ●口を大きく開く *open* one's mouth wide. ●手紙の封を開く *open* [*unseal*] a letter. ●包みを開く *undo* [*unpack*, *open*] a package. ●扇子を開く *unfold* [*open*] a fan. ●本を開く ●本の10ページを開いた They *opened* (the book) *to* [《英》*at*] page 10./(ページを繰って) They *turned to* page 10 (of the book). ▶ドアがさっと開いた The door *swung open* [ˣ*opened*]. (❗この open は形容詞)

❷ [咲く] (花などが) open, come* out; (つぼみなどが) unfold. ▶花が開き始めている The flowers *are opening* [*coming out, blooming*]. ▶桜の花が開いた The cherry blossoms *have come out*. (❗blossoms が主語のときは bloom は不可)/(花盛りだ) The cherry trees are in (full) bloom. ▶つぼみが開いた The buds *opened* [*unfolded*].

❸ [始める] (店などを) open; (開始する) start, begin*, 《書》commence (⇨始める); (創立する) set*... up, found, establish. ●銀座に店を開く *open* [*start*] a store on the Ginza. ●子供の学校を開く *set up* [*found, open*] a school for children. ●日蓮は日蓮宗を開いた Nichiren *founded* [*was the founder of*] the Nichiren-shu sect.

❹ [開催する] (パーティー・会などを) give*, hold* (❗前の方が口語的); (議会などを開会する) open. ●パーティーを開く *give* [*hold, have*, 《話》*throw*] a party. ●コンサートを開く *give* [*hold*] a concert. ●議会を開く *open* Congress 《米》[Parliament 《英》]. ●討論会は講堂で 10 時に開かれた The debate *opened* [*was held, took place*] in the auditorium at ten. ●国会が今開かれている The Diet *is now sitting* [*is now in session*].

❺ [開拓する] (道などを) open; (森などを) clear; (土地などを) open... up. (⇨切り開く) ●道を開く *open* [*build*] a road. ●(木を切り倒して)森を開く *clear* a wood. ●鉱山を開く *open up* [*develop*] a mine.

❻ [その他の表現] ●脚を開いて立つ stand *with legs apart*. ▶彼は駅の近くに食堂を開いている (経営している) He *keeps* [*runs*] a restaurant near the railroad station. ▶図書館は 5 時まで開いています The library *is open* [ˣ*opened*] until 5. ▶走者間の距離が開いた The distance between the runners *widened*. ▶彼は心を閉ざしているからそれを開いてくれる人が必要なのだ He's so defensive that he needs someone who can *get through to* him. (❗*get through to* は「気心が通じる」の意)

ひらぐも 平蜘蛛 〖動物〗a uroteid spider. ●平蜘蛛のようにあやまる (平身低頭する) apologize abjectly [on *one's* knees].

***ひらける 開ける** ❶ [開化・発展する] (文明化される) become* civilized; (近代化される) become modernized; (発展する) develop. ●開けた国 a *civilized* [a *developed*] country. ▶その町はだんだん開けて仙台で最大のベッドタウンの一つになった The town

has gradually *developed* [*grown*] *into* one of the largest bedroom towns in Sendai.
❷ [物事が分かる]（分別がある）be sensible. ●開けた人 a *sensible* person;（人づき合いのよい人）a *sociable* person;（世事に通じている人）a *man of the world*. ▶あの老人は開けた（=進歩的な）考えを持っている The old man [woman] has *progressive* ideas.
❸ [開通する] be opened. ▶二国間に新しい航空路が開けた A new airline *was opened* [《やや書》*was inaugurated*] between the two countries.
❹ [運がよくなる] ▶運が開けてきた Fortune has begun to *smile on* me./Luck is beginning to *turn in* my favor. (**!** in one's favor は「有利に」) / Luck *is coming* my *way*.
❺ [見晴らしが] （広がる）spread* out;（展開する）open. ▶すばらしい眺めが眼前に開けた A splendid view *opened* [*spread out*] before us.

ひらしゃいん 平社員 a mere employee, a rank-and-file employee.

ひらたい 平たい [平らな] flat (-tt-);（凹凸のない）even;（なめらかな）smooth（⇨平ら）; [平易な] plain, simple. ●平いなべ a *flat* pan. ●平たい表面 an *even* [a *smooth*, a *flat*] surface. ●平たい言葉で平たく言えば] in *plain* words; plainly.

ひらづみ 平積み ── 平積みする 動 stack《books》(up).

ひらて 平手 the palm of the [one's] hand. ▶ほおに強烈な平手打ちを食らわす give《him》a hard slap across the face; slap《him》hard across the face.

ひらなべ 平鍋 a pan.

ピラニア ［<ポルトガル語］〖魚介〗a piranha /pirάːnjə/《⑲ 〜, 〜s》.

ひらひら 副 ▶花びらがひらひらと散った Flower petals fell *fluttering* (to the ground). ▶チョウがひらひら飛んでいる A butterfly *is fluttering* [*flitting*] *about*.
── ひらひらする[させる] 動 flutter;（規則的に）wave. ▶旗が風にひらひらした A flag *waved* [*fluttered*] in the wind.
── ひらひら 名 ▶カーテンにひらひらがついている There are *frills* on the curtain.

ピラフ ［<フランス語］(a) pilaf(f) /piláːf, pilǽf/《⑲ 〜s》. (**!** 料理名では ⓤ) ●えびピラフ shrimp pilaf.

ひらべったい 平べったい flat. ●平べったい顔 a *flat* face.

ひらまく 平幕 〖相撲〗*hiramaku*,（説明的に）a *sumo* wrestler in the *makuuchi* division below *komusubi*.

ひらまさ 平政 〖魚介〗an amberjack.

ピラミッド a pýramid. ●ピラミッド型のウェディングケーキ a *pyramid-shaped* [a *pýramídical*] wedding cake. ▶ホテルからピラミッド群とスフィンクスが見えた We could see the *Pyramids* and Sphinx from the hotel. (**!** このように大文字で書かれることが多い)

ひらめ 平目 〖魚介〗a (left-eyed) flounder;（舌平目）a sole. (**!** いずれも単・複同形、肉は ⓤ) [事情] 米英ではカレイとの区別はあまりない)

ひらめき 閃き（考え・光などの）a flash,《話》an inspiration.（⇨光）●天才のひらめきを示す show *flashes* [*sparks*] of genius.

*ひらめく 閃く ❶ [ひるがえる] flutter. ▶旗が風にひらめいている A flag *is fluttering* [*waving*,（ばたばたとせわしげに）*flapping*] in the wind. ▶天才とは 1 パーセントのひらめきと 99 パーセントの努力だ Genius is one percent *inspiration* and ninety-nine percent perspiration. (**!** 押韻に注意)
❷ [ぱっと光る [浮かぶ]] flash. ▶遠くに稲妻がひらめいた Lightning *flashed* in the distance. ▶うまい考えがひらめいた A good idea *flashed into* my mind./A good idea *occurred* [*came*] to me *in a flash*./I hit upon [*came across*] a good idea.

ひらや 平家 a one-story [a one-storied, a single-story] house《⑲ houses /-ziz,《米》-siz/》.

ひらり （敏しょうに）nimbly;（早く）swiftly;（軽く）lightly. ▶殴られまいとひらりと身をかわす *dodge* a blow. ▶彼はひらりと小川を跳び越えた He jumped *nimbly* [*lightly*] across a stream. ▶彼女はひらりと馬から降りた She sprang *lightly* off her horse./She got off her horse *easily and skillfully*. ▶彼は剣をひらりと振った His sword *flashed* as he swang it.

びらん 糜爛 名 a sore;〖医学〗erosion. ●女性の糜爛（=腐乱した）死体 the decomposed body of a woman.
── 糜爛する 動 fester.

びり （成績などの）the bottom（↔the top）. ▶彼はクラスで成績はびりだ He is (*at*) *the bottom of* the class. ▶彼は競走でびり(=最後)だった He came in [*was*] *last* in the race.

ピリオド 《主に米》a period,《主に英》a full stop.（⇨巻末〖句読法〗）

ひりき 非力 ── 非力な 形 powerless.

ビリケン ［米国の福の神の像］a Billiken.

ひりつ 比率 (a) ratio /réiʃou/《⑲ 〜s》; [割合] (a) proportion.（⇨割合）●一国の女子に対する男子の比率 the *ratio* [*proportion*] of men *to* women in a country.

ぴりっと ●ノートを 1 枚ぴりっとはぎ取る *rip* a leaf from a notebook. ●ぴりっとした朝の冷気 *crisp* (*and refreshing*) morning air. (**!** *crisp* is cold, dry, fresh を合わせた感じの語) ●ソーダのあのぴりっとした味 the *piquant taste* [*piquancy*] of soda pop. ▶その料理はぴりっとした味がする The dish *tastes hot* [*pungent*]. / The dish *bites* [*stings*] the tongue. ▶このハムはブラックペッパーでぴりっとした味付けがしてある This ham *is spiced* with black pepper. ▶あの男にはぴりっとしたところがない（気迫に欠ける）He is lacking in *spirit*./（煮え切らない男だ）He's a *wishy-washy* fellow.

ひりひり ── ひりひりする 動 ❶ [痛みで]（ひりひりさせる）irritate;（うずいて、しみて痛む）smart;（ひどい痛みで痛む [痛みを与える]）sting*. ▶シャツの堅い襟で首がひりひりする The stiff collar of my shirt *irritates* [*hurts*] my neck. ▶煙が目にしみてひりひりする My eyes *are smarting from* the smoke./The smoke *stings* my eyes. ▶海岸で日光浴をしたので皮膚がひりひりした My skin *stung from* sunbathing on the beach. ▶風邪でのどがひりひりする I have a *sore* throat from a cold.
❷ [香辛料で]（辛い）be hot;（焼けるように辛い）burn. ▶このカレーはひりひりする（ほど辛い）This curry is [*tastes*] *too hot*./This curry *burns* my tongue [mouth].

びりびり ❶ [びりびり破る [破れる]] tear* /téər/ (up);（激しい力で）rip (-pp-). ▶彼は怒って手紙をびりびり破った He *tore up* the letter in anger. ▶彼は包みをびりびり引きちぎった He *ripped* the cover off. ▶彼女は手紙をびりびり破いて開けた She *tore* [*ripped*] the letter open.
❷ [小刻みに震える] shudder（⇨震える）;（反響して）resound. ▶地震の余波で家がびりびりと揺れた The house *shuddered* in the dying tremors of the earthquake. ▶彼は部屋がびりびりするほど音楽のボリュームを上げた He turned up the music so loudly that it *resounded through* the room.

ぴりぴり

❸ 〚電気刺激を受ける[与える]〛▶近づいてはいけません. 触れるとびりぴりっときますよ Stay away. You'll get an electric shock at a touch.

ぴりりと ──ぴりぴりする 動 ❶〚痛みで〛(刺すように) sting*; (肌などを赤くして) irritate. (⇨ぴりぴり❶)
❷〚香辛料で〛be hot [pungent]. (⇨ぴりっと, ひりひり)
❸〚緊張して〛tense. ▶レーサーたちはレースの直前ぴりぴりしている Racers are *very tense* just before their race. ▶彼女similarly何かあったのかしら. 最近すごくぴりぴりしていて声もかけられないわ〚話〛What's up with her? She's been all *edgy* [*on edge, uptight*] recently and I just can't speak to her.

ビリヤード billiards /bɪljərdz/. (〚単数扱い〛● ビリヤードをする play *billiards*. ● ビリヤードを 1 ゲームする have a game of *billiards*. ● ビリヤードの球[突き棒] a *billiard* ball [*cue*].

びりゅうし 微粒子 a (minute /main(j)úːt/) particle; 〚物理・化学〛a corpuscle /kɔ́ːrpəsl/.

ひりょう 肥料 (一般に) (a) fertilizer (〚化学肥料も含む〛; (動物の排泄(ᵉ)物などの) manure; (たい肥) compost. ● 天然肥料 natural *manure*. ● 化学肥料 chemical *fertilizer*. ● 畑に肥料をやる manure [fertilize] the fields; put *manure* [*fertilizer*] on [in] the fields.

びりょう 微量 a very small amount 《of》; a particle [a molecule] 《of》. ● 微量のダイオキシンを検出する find [detect] *a very small amount of* dioxin.

びりょく 微力 ▶微力ながらお役に立たせてください Let me *do my best* [*what I little*] to help you.

ピリンけい ピリン系 ●ピリン系の薬品 pyrazolone drugs. (〚参考〛アミノピリンやスルピリンなどの薬剤)

*:**ひる** 昼 ❶〚正午〛noon, midday. ● 昼休み a lúnch brèak [hòur]. (⇨昼休み) ▶彼は昼に戻るでしょう He'll be back at *noon* [*midday*]. (〚「昼に」が「正午きっかり」でなく時間的な幅を持つ場合は after [around] *noon*) ▶昼前に宿題をすませなさい Finish your homework before *noon*. ▶どこにお昼(=昼ご飯)を食べに行きましょうか Where shall we go for *lunch*?

❷〚昼間〛day, daytime (〚いずれも日の出から日没までの期間をさすが, day には「1 日」の意もあるので「昼」の意を明確にするときは daytime を用いる); (昼の明かり) daylight. ● 昼の学校 a *day* (↔a *night*) school. ▶昼のうちは雨が降ったりやんだりしました It rained off and on during the *day* [in the *daytime*]. ▶昼が短くなってきた The *days* are getting shorter. ▶彼は入学試験に通るため, 昼も夜も一生懸命勉強した He studied hard *day* and *night* [*night* and *day*] to pass the entrance exam.

●昼を欺く ▶通りは昼を欺く(=真昼のような明るさで) The streets are *as bright as daylight* [*day*].

ひる 蛭 〚動物〛a leech. ▶ヒルが脚に引っついていた I found a *leech* sticking [stuck] to my leg.

***ビル** a building (略 bldg.). ● オフィスビル an óffice building; (大規模の) an óffice blòck; a block of offices. ● 竹中ビル the Takenaka *Building*.
● ビル街 a street of large (office) buildings.

-びる ● 大人びる look grown-up. ● 古びる look outdated. ● ひなびる look countrified.

ピル 〚経口避妊薬〛the pill, the Pill. ● ピルを服用する take the *pill*. ● ピルを常用し始める [している] go [be] on the *pill*. ● ピルの常用をやめる come off the *pill*. ▶ピルはやめたわ I'm no longer on the *pill*.

ひるいない 比類ない (たぐいまれな) incómparable; (ずば抜けている) matchless; 〚書〛peerless; (並ぶものない) 〚書〛unparalleled. ● 原爆投下という人類史上比類ない犯罪 atom-bombing, the *unparalleled* crime in human history.

ひるがえす 翻す ❶〚決心などを〛(変える) change 《one's mind》; have* second thought 《米》 [thoughts 《英》] 《about》; (撤回する) take* 《one's words》 back. ● 初志を翻す *give up* one's original intention.
❷〚身を〛dodge; (向きを変える) turn. ● 身を翻して打撃を避ける *dodge* a blow. ● 身を翻して逃げる *turn around* 《about》 and run away.
❸〚旗などを〛flutter, fly*.

ひるがえって 翻って 〚さて〛now; 〚…に話を転じて〛turning to .... ● 翻って考えて(=再考して)みると on second thought 《米》 [thoughts 《英》]; on reflection.

ひるがえる 翻る 〚空中で揺れる〛fly*; 〚波のように揺れる〛wave; 〚はためく〛flutter; 〚ばたばたと〛flap (-pp-). ▶こいのぼりが風に翻っていた The carp streamers *were flying* [*waving*, *fluttering*, *flapping*] in the wind.

ひるがお 昼顔 〚植物〛a (field) bindweed.

ひるさがり 昼下がり early in the afternoon; in the early afternoon.

ビルディング a building. (⇨ビル)

ビルトイン 〚作りつけの〛built-in. (⇨内蔵)

ひるどき 昼時 (正午ごろ) 《at》 midday; around noon; (昼飯時) 《at》 lunchtime.

ひるね 昼寝 图 a nap, a daytime nap; (午睡) an afternoon nap.
── 昼寝する 動 take [have] a nap.

ひるひなか 昼日中 《in》broad daylight. (⇨真昼)

***ひるま** 昼間 day, daytime. (⇨昼❷) ▶彼女は昼間働いている She works *during the day*./She works *in* [*during*] *the daytime*. ▶フクロウは昼間寝て夜えさを捜す Owls sleep *by day* and hunt at night. (〚対照させて by day ... by night ということもあるが, やや古い) ▶彼女はまっ昼間から酒を飲み始める She begins to drink in the *broad daylight*. ▶彼は昼間(=午後)ずっと寝ていた He slept all (the) *afternoon*. (⇨昼)

ビルマ Burma. 〚参考〛ミャンマーの旧称〛

ひるむ 〚恐怖などで思わず身を引く〛flinch 《from》; (顔をひきつらせて) wince 《at》; (身を縮ませる) 《主に英》 shrink* 《from》. ● 大きな物音にひるむ *flinch* [*shrink*] at a loud sound. ● 獰犬にひるむ *shrink* (*back*) *from* a fierce dog. ● 一撃を食らってひるむ *flinch* [*wince*] with the force of the blow. ▶海に飛び込もうとしたがひるんでしまった I tried to dive into the sea, but I *flinched* [*shrank*] *from* doing it. (⇨ためらう)

ひるめし 昼飯 (have) lunch. (⇨昼食)

ひるやすみ 昼休み a lúnch brèak [hòur], a nóon brèak [《米》 rècess]. ● 1 時間の昼休みをとる take a one-hour *lunch break*; take an hour's *recess for lunch*. ● 昼休みにテニスをする play tennis during the [one's] *lunch* [*noon*] *break*.

ひれ 鰭 a fin. ● しり[背;尾]びれ an anal [a dorsal; a caudal] *fin*.

ヒレ (ヒレ肉) fillet, 《米》filet /filát, filéi/. ● ヒレ肉は高価だ *Fillet* is expensive. (〚ヒレ肉 3 枚 three fillets (of beef) では [C])
● ヒレステーキ a fillet stèak.

***ひれい** 比例 图 〚釣り合い〛(a) proportion; 〚比率〛 (a) ratio /réiʃou/. (⇨比率) ● 正[反]比例 direct [inverse] *proportion*.
── 比例する 動 ▶収穫高は 7 月の雨量の多寡(ᵏ)に比例する The amount of the crops is *in proportion to* the rainfall in July. ▶彼の出費は収入に比例して

ない His expenditure is *out of proportion* to his income. ▶売り上げが伸びたのに比例して利益が増えた Our profits increased *in proportion as* sales picked up./(応じて) *As* sales picked up [*With* a growth in sales], our profits increased.
● **比例代表制**〔選挙の〕proportional representation. ● **比例配分**〔数学〕proportional distribution.

ひれい 非礼 rudeness; impoliteness. (⇨無礼, 失礼)

びれい 美麗 ── **美麗な** 形 beautiful. (⇨美しい, 麗しい)

ひれき 披瀝 ── **披瀝する** 動 express one's opinion [views]; speak one's mind.

ひれつ 卑劣 ── **卑劣な** 形 (さもしい) mean; (軽蔑すべき) contemptible; (汚い) dirty; (意地の悪い) nasty.
● 卑劣な手を使って by (using) a *mean* [a *contemptible*, a *dirty*, a *nasty*] trick. ▶老人をだまして金を取るのは卑劣だ It's *mean* to cheat an old man [woman] (out) of his [her] money.
── **卑劣さ** 名 meanness.

ピレネー ● **ピレネー山脈** the Pyrenees /pírəniːz/. (！複数扱い)

ひれふす ひれ伏す ▶彼の前にひれ伏す *throw oneself* at his feet; (やや書) *prostrate oneself* before him.

ひれん 悲恋 tragic love 《*for* him》.
● **悲恋物語** a tragic love story.

ひろ 尋〔長さの単位〕a fathom. (！約 1.8m) ● 5 尋の深さを be five *fathoms* deep.

:ひろい 広い 形
［WORD CHOICE］ 広い, 幅広い
wide 物事の幅・領域などが広いこと。とくに両端間の距離を強調し、しばしば物事が多種多様であることを含意する。時に意味を強めるために wide-open などの複合語の形を取る。▶その単語は幅広い意味を持つ That word has a *wide* range of meanings.
broad 物事の範囲・範疇（はんちゅう）・意味・定義などが広いこと。特に面的な広がりを含意する。▶こうした幅広い範疇に入る歌 the types of songs in these *broad* categories.
large 面積が広いことを表す最も一般的な語。▶その部屋は 200 人を収容するだけの広さがある The room is *large* enough to accommodate 200 people.

頻度チャート
wide ▇▇▇▇▇▇▇▇▇▇
broad ▇▇▇
large ▇▇▇▇▇▇▇
20 40 60 80 100 (%)

❶〔幅, 面積, 空間〕wide; broad; large (⇨[類語]); big (-gg-) (！*large* より主観的でくだけた語); (極端に広く広大な) vast (！通例限定的に); (外へ広がるように広い) extensive; (部屋などの囲まれた空間が広い) spacious; (中に人や物が入った後でもゆとりがあるほど広い) roomy; (さえぎるものがなく広い) open (！通例限定的に). ▶広い川 a *wide* [a *broad*] river. ▶広い世界 the *wide* world. ▶広い船室 a *large* [a *spacious*, a *roomy*, ⊗a *wide*] cabin. ▶彼は肩幅が広い He has *broad* (→narrow) shoulders. (！この場合 wide はあまり用いない)/He is a *broad-shouldered* man. ▶この大学のキャンパスはとても広い The campus of this university is very *large* [*big*, *spacious*]. ▶こんな広い家に住むなんて気持ちいいでしょうね It must be

nice to live in a *big* place like this. ▶広い海が眼前に広がっていた A *wide* [A *broad*, A *vast*] ocean lay before us. (！sea の場合は a *wide* sea が普通)
❷〔抽象的範囲〕wide; broad; extensive. ▶広い意味では in a *broad* sense. ▶彼はその問題について広い知識を持っている He has *extensive* [*wide*, *broad*] knowledge of the subject. ▶私は趣味が広いが, 特に絵に興味がある I have *broad* interests, but mostly, I'm interested in painting. ▶彼は顔が広い(多数の知人がいる) He has a *wide* [a *large*] circle of acquaintances [friends]. ▶彼は心の広い人だ He is a *broad-minded* [a *big-hearted*, (寛大な) a *generous*] person.

── **広く** 副 ❶〔幅, 面積, 空間〕(幅広く) wide; (広範囲に) widely, extensively; (遠く広く) far and wide. ▶ドアを広く開けよ open the door *wide*. ▶これらの植物は広く分布している These plants are *widely* [*extensively*] distributed. ▶彼は世界を広く旅行した He has traveled *widely* [*extensively*, *far and wide*, 《話》*a lot*] in the world.
❷〔抽象的範囲〕(広範囲に) widely; (詳細に) extensively; (一般に) generally. ▶視野を広く持つ have *wide* views 《about》. ▶彼が偉大な物理学者であることは広く知られている It is *widely* [*generally*] known that he is a great physicist. ▶彼は中国文学に広く通じている He is *extensively* [*widely*] read in Chinese literature. ▶それは広く受け入れられている事実です It is a *universally* accepted fact.

── **広くする** 動 widen; broaden. ▶道路を広くする *widen* [*broaden*] the road. ▶視野を広くする *widen* [*broaden*] one's views. ▶ガレージを広くする *enlarge* a garage. ▶領土を広くする (拡張する) *extend* one's territory.

ひろいあげる 拾い上げる pick ... up (⇨拾う); (不遇の人を) pick 《him *for* the post》.

ひろいあつめる 拾い集める gather ... (together [up]); collect.

ヒロイズム heroism /hérouizm/.

ひろいだす 拾い出す pick ... out; select.

ひろいぬし 拾い主 the finder 《*of* a wallet》.

ひろいもの 拾い物 (掘り出し物) a find; (思わぬ幸運で得たもの) a windfall. ● 拾い物をする (物を拾う) pick up a thing; (幸運な見つけものをする) make a lucky [a rare] *find*.

ひろいよみ 拾い読み ── **拾い読みする** 動 (一部を読む) read from 《a book》; (飛ばし読みする) skip through 《a book》; (1 語 1 語読む) read 《sentences》word by word.

ヒロイン a heroine /hérouən/. (！英語では今は男女区別なく a hero を用いる) (⇨主人公, ヒーロー)

:ひろう 拾う〔拾い上げる〕pick ... up; 〔集める〕(拾い上げて) pick ... up; (移動しながら) 《主に書》gather; 〔選び出す〕pick ... out; 〔見つける〕find*. ▶たきぎを拾う *pick up* [*gather*] sticks for firewood. ● 活字を拾う *pick out* types. ● 勝ち点を拾う manage to *pick up* a point. ▶お前が落としたんだぞ 拾って拾え You dropped it, you *pick it up!* ▶ホテルの前で(車で)私を拾ってください Please *pick* me *up* in front of the hotel. ▶道で時計を拾った I *found* a watch on the road. ▶駅前でタクシーを拾おう Let's get [(手を上げて) *flag down*, *hail*, (乗る) *get in*] a taxi in front of the station. ▶その少年は果樹園でリンゴを拾い食いした The boy *picked* an apple *up* at the orchard and *ate* it.

*ひろう 疲労 fatigue /fətíːɡ/ (！過労・運動などからくる長期に及ぶ大きな疲れで休養を要する状態); weariness /wíərinəs/ (！体力・気力のなえた状態); exhaustion /iɡzɔ́ːstʃən/ (！ひどい疲労状態で一時的なも

ひろう

の)、▶(疲れ)
① 【疲労～】 ●疲労感 tired [fatigue] feeling. (**!** 後の方が語調が強い)
② 【疲労が】 ●だんだん疲労がたまってきた I'm getting more and more tired. ▶疲労が抜けた My fatigue disappeared [vanished].
③ 【疲労の】 ●疲労のピークにある be in a state of extreme fatigue. ▶彼は疲労の色を見せなかった He didn't show any signs of fatigue. ▶疲労のため彼は仕事を休んだ He stayed away from work because of fatigue [because he was tired].
④ 【疲労を】 ●疲労を回復する recover from one's fatigue. ●疲労を感じる feel tired [weary]; (極度に) feel tired [worn] out. (⇨①; 疲れる)
● 疲労困憊(こんぱい) ▶彼は疲労困憊の様子だ He looks completely [utterly, absolutely, ×very] exhausted./He looks tired out [worn out, 《話》 dead tired]./(顔に表れている) His exhaustion is visible in his face.
● 疲労骨折 【医学】 a fatigue [a stress] fracture.

ひろう 披露 图 【発表】 (an) announcement; 【紹介】 (an) introduction. ●ホテルで結婚披露宴を催す hold a wedding reception at a hotel.
── 披露する 動 ●婚約を披露する announce [make an announcement of] one's engagement. ●新製品を披露する introduce a new product 《to the market》.

びろう 尾籠 ▶尾籠な(=品のない)話ですが It is an indecent thing to mention, but ....

ビロード [<ポルトガル語] velvet. ●ビロード製品 velvet goods. ●ビロードのような velvety.

ひろがり (広さ) (an) extent; (空間・表面の) an expanse; (とぎれのない広がり) a stretch; (幅が広くなる) a spread. ●宇宙空間のぼう漠たる広がり the vast expanses of outer space. (**!** 複数形で広大さを強調する) ▶砂漠の広大な広がり以外何も見えなかった We could not see anything but a great stretch of desert.

:ひろがる 広がる spread* (out) (**!** 最も一般的な語); (長さ・範囲が伸びる) extend; (道・土地などが伸び広がる) stretch; (大きさ・数量・範囲などの点で) expand; (幅が広くなる) widen, broaden; (うわさが) go* [get*] around. ●がんが彼の体中に広がった The cancer spread throughout his body. ▶見渡すかぎりブドウ畑が広がっていた The vineyard stretched [extended] as far as the eye could see. ▶道路の向こう側には平な土地が広がっていた There was flat, open ground on the other side of the road. ▶その川は流れていくにつれて川幅が広がっている The river widens [gets wider] as it flows. ▶(恒常的な状態をいう場合は進行形にしない) ▶そのニュースはすぐに広がった The news went around [spread] quickly. ▶戦争に行かないことを支持する議論が若者の間に広がりつつある Arguments for not going to war are catching on with young people. ▶世の中に先行きの不透明感が広がっている(=漂っている) There is uncertainty about the future in the air. ▶小さな一口大のなすは皮が柔らかく、噛むと薄い塩味が広がった(=口一杯になった) A tiny, bite-size eggplant had a soft, tender skin. When I bit it, a slight salty taste filled my mouth.

ひろく 秘録 a confidential [a secret] document; (極秘録) a top-secret document.

ひろくち 広口 ❶ 【口の広いこと】 ●広口のつぼ a widemouthed jar. ❷ 【水盤】 a (flower) basin.

:ひろげる 広げる spread*... (out); (長さ・範囲・意味などを伸ばす) extend; (大きさ・数量・範囲などの点で)

ひろまる

expand; (折りたたんだ物を) unfold; (建物・事業などを) enlarge; (幅を広くする) widen, broaden; 〖開く〗 open. ●地図を広げる spread (out) a map; open [unfold] a map. ●事業を大規模に広げる expand [extend, enlarge] one's business on a large scale. ●道を広げる widen [broaden] a road. ●知識を広げる extend [expand, widen] one's knowledge. ●旅行をして視野を広げる widen [broaden] one's outlook by traveling. ●足を広げて立つ stand with one's feet (spread) apart. ●両腕を広げて彼を迎える welcome him with open arms [with arms open]. ▶その木は枝を四方に広げていた The tree spread [was spreading] its branches in all directions. ▶ワシは翼を広げて飛び立った The eagle spread (out) [expanded] its wings before flying away. ▶彼女はナプキンを広げてひざに置いた She unfolded the napkin and put it in her lap. ▶私はトマトを栽培するため菜園を広げた I enlarged [extended] the vegetable garden to grow tomatoes./I made the vegetable garden larger to grow tomatoes. ▶彼は桜の木の下で弁当を広げた He opened [(包みを開く) unpacked] his lunch (box) under the cherry tree.

ひろさ 広さ (面積) (an) area; (広がり) (an) extent; (幅) (a) width. ●彼の知識の広さ the extent [width, (膨大さ) vastness] of his knowledge. ▶この農場の広さはどれくらいありますか How large [big, ×wide] is this farm?/What is the area [extent] of this farm? (⇨面積) ▶あの家は広さ十分だ That house is large enough.

ピロシキ [<ロシア語] pirozhki. (**!** 複数扱い)

ひろそで 広袖 图 a wide sleeve. ── 広袖の 形 wide-sleeved.

ピロティー [<フランス語] pilotis /piːlɔːtiːz/. (**!** 複数扱い) ●ピロティー形式の市庁舎 a city hall built on pilotis.

ひろば 広場 (通りの集まってくる) a square (**!** 実際には四角形の広場とは限らない); (都市の) a plaza; 〖空き地〗 an open space [area]; (町なかの) a vacant lot.
● 広場恐怖症 【心理】 agoraphobia.

ひろはば 広幅 double-wide [double-width] cloth.

ひろびろ 広々 ── 広々とした 形 (⇨広い [類語])
●広々とした家 a spacious 〖《やや話》 a roomy〗 house. ●広々とした(=大きな)キャンパス a large [広大な] a vast] campus. ●広々とした(=開けた)眺め an open [a wide, (広大な) an extensive, (遮るものない) uninterrupted] view.

ヒロポン (覚醒剤の一種) 【薬学】 methamphetamin /meθæmféṭəmiːn/; 《話》 meth. (**!** 「ヒロポン」は日本の商標名)
● ヒロポン中毒者 《俗》 a meth addict.

ひろま 広間 a hall; (客船などの) a saloon.

***ひろまる 広まる** spread* (**!** 最も一般的な語); (うわさなどが) go* [get*] around; 〖流行する〗 come* into fashion [vogue], (力・影響などが行き渡る) 《書》 pervade. ▶市長が入院しているといううわさが市中に広まった The rumor spread [went around, (流布した) circulated] through the city that the mayor was in hospital [〖主に米〗 the hospital]. (**!** 次のようにもいえる) ▶There is a rumor (going around) that .... (**!** のようにもいえる) ▶彼の名声は日本中に広まっている His fame is spreading [増大している] is growing] throughout Japan. ▶平和を愛する心が世界に広まった The love of peace spread over [pervaded] the world. ▶ハイブーツが去年女性の間に広まった High boots came into fashion [became popular] among women last year.

(!)...caught on with women ... のようにもいえる (⇨広がる) ▶ その説は科学者の間で広まってきている(=支持を得てきている)ようである The theory seems to *be gaining ground* among scientists.

ひろめる 広める ● (うわさなどを流布させる) circulate; (知識などを普及させる)《書》diffuse; (思想などを宣伝する)《やや書》propagate; (大衆化する)《やや書》popularize. ● 悪いうわさを広める *spread* [*circulate*] a bad rumor. ● 知識を広める *spread* [*diffuse*] knowledge; (自分の知識を) *extend* [*expand*, *broaden*] one's knowledge. ● 共産主義[教義]を広める *propagate* communism [a doctrine]. ● ロック音楽を広める *popularize* rock; *make* rock *popular* 《among, with》.

ピロリきん ピロリ菌 (helicobacter) pylori.
ひろんりてき 非論理的 ● 非論理的な 形 illogical.
ひわ 鶸 〖鳥〗(マヒワ) a siskin; (カワラヒワ) an Oriental greenfinch.
ひわ 秘話 an unknown [秘められた] a secret story.
ひわ 悲話 a sad [a tragic] story.
ひわ 枇杷 〖植物〗a loquat /lóukwɑt/.
ひわ 琵琶 〖楽器〗a *biwa*, (説明的に) a 4-stringed or sometimes 5-stringed lute played with a large-sized plectrum, which was introduced from China to Japan in the Nara period. ● 琵琶を弾く play the *biwa*. ● 琵琶の伴奏で平家物語を語る recite the *Tale of the Heike* with *biwa* accompaniment.
ひわい 卑猥 ● 卑猥な 形 obscene. (⇨猥褻(ᵂᵃᵗˢ))
ひわだ 檜皮 (ヒノキの皮) *hinoki* bark.
● 檜皮葺き a *hinoki* bark thatch.
ひわたり 火渡り ▶ 修道僧が火渡りをしていた Monks *were walking barefoot over the fire*.
ひわり 日割り ● 日割りを定める (日程を立てる) make up a schedule. ▶ 利子[賃金]は日割りで計算されます The interest is [The wages are] calculated *daily* [*by the day*, 《主に米》*per diem* /pər díːem/].
ひわれ 干割れ dry up [parch] and crack. ▶ この板は干割れしないように日陰に置いておきなさい Place this board in the shade so that it won't *split*.
ひわれる 干割れる dry up [parch] and crack.
ひん 品 (細部にまで気を遣った上品さ) elegance,《話》class; (内から出る優美さ) grace; (洗練されていること) refinement; (おもむき) taste. ● 品のある elegant; graceful; refined. ● 品のある女性 an *elegant* [*graceful*] woman; a woman of *elegance* [*refinement*]. ● 品のない(=下品な)言葉遣いをする use *coarse* [*vulgar*] language. (!) 後の方が強意的) ▶ 彼女にはどこか品がある There's something *refined* about her./She has *class* (↔no class). ▶ 彼の冗談は品があった[なかった] His joke was in good [poor, bad] *taste*.
ひん 便 (列車・バスなどの運行) (a) service; (飛行機の) a flight; (郵便) mail. ● 空港までのバスの便がない There is no bus *service* to the airport. ● 帰りの便はミラノを17時30分に発ち、ダブリンに19時に到着いたします The return *flight* leaves Milan at 17:30 and arrives back in Dublin at 19:00. ▶ 彼はニューヨーク行きの3時の便に乗った He took the three o'clock *flight* to New York. (!「日本航空第76便で」は on JAL *Flight 76*) ▶ 夜の便があればそれに乗りましょう. その方が安いですから If there's a night *flight*, let's take that. It's cheaper.
会話 「イタリア行きの便についてお尋ねしたいのですが」「承知いたしました、少々お待ちください. 4便ございます」"I'd like to inquire [ask] about *flights* to Italy." "I see. One moment, sir. Yes, there are four *flights* out." (!) out は出発便を示す)

*びん 瓶 a bottle; a jar; a flagon; a decanter; a phial /fáiəl/,《書》a vial /váiəl/.

使い分け **bottle** 取っ手・注ぎ口がなく、口が細いもの.
jar 取っ手・注ぎ口がなく、口が広いもの.
flagon 主にワイン・リンゴ酒などの販売用に使われている取っ手付きで大型細口のもの.
decanter 栓の付いた細口の食卓用装飾瓶. 多くはワインなどのアルコール類を入れて注ぐために用いられる.
phial, **vial** 薬や香水などを入れる小瓶.

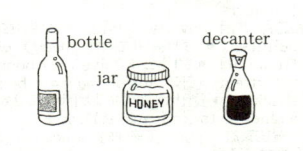

bottle / jar / decanter

● 空き瓶 an empty *bottle*. ● ビール瓶 a béer bòttle. ● ビール1瓶 a *bottle* of beer. ● ピーナツバター1瓶 a *jar* of peanut butter. ● 水を瓶に詰める[入れる] put water into a *bottle*; fill a *bottle* with water; *bottle* water. ● 1瓶いくらで売る sell (beer) *by the bottle*.

びん 敏 ▶ 彼は機を見るに敏である He is *quick* at seizing an opportunity./He is *quick* to grab an opportunity.
びん 鬢 the hair at the temples.

*ピン ● 〖留め針〗a pin; 〖ゴルフ・ボウリングの〗a pin. ● ヘアピン a hairpin. ● 安全ピン a safety *pin*. ● ピンで留める *pin (up)*《a notice *to* [*on*] a board》; fasten (a notice) with a *pin*. ● ピンを抜く *unpin*《a dress》; remove *pins* (from one's hair).
● ピンカール a pin curl. ● ピンセット (⇨ピンセット)
ピン ● ピンからキリまで ▶ 学者にもピンからキリまである There are all sorts of scholars./There are [You can find] scholars *and* scholars.
ひんい 品位 〖威厳〗dignity; 〖品性〗character; 〖優雅さ〗elegance. ● 品位のある dignified [(上品な) an *elegant*] lady. ● 品位を落とす[保つ] lose [maintain] one's *dignity*. ● 新聞の品位を高める elevate the *character* of a paper. ▶ うそをついて自分の品位を落とす[汚す] degrade [disgrace] oneself by telling a lie.
ひんかく 品格 (⇨品(²))
びんがた 紅型 〖染色法〗an Okinawan traditional dyeing; 〖染色した布地〗an Okinawan traditional dyed goods (characterized by bright colors).
びんかつ 敏活 ── 敏活な 形 quick; prompt.
*びんかん 敏感 ● 敏感な 形 sensitive (*to*); (低抗力が弱い) susceptible (*to*). ● 敏感な耳(=聴覚) a *sensitive* ear. ● 暑さに敏感である be *sensitive* [*susceptible*] to heat. ▶ 政治家はたいてい世論に敏感である Most politicians are *sensitive* to public opinion.
ひんきゃく 賓客 a guest (of honor).
ひんく 貧苦 poverty. ● 貧苦の底にある be poverty-stricken; be struggling with extreme poverty.
ピンク (淡紅色) pink. ● ピンクの pink; (ピンクがかった) pinkish. ▶ 彼女は色白でピンク色のほほをしている She has a fair skin and *pink* (赤い) rosy] cheeks.
● ピンク映画 a pornographic [a porn(o), a blue] movie [film].
ひんけつ 貧血 〖医学〗anemia /əníːmiə/. ● 貧血(症)

ビンゴ 〖ゲーム〗 bingo /bíngou/.

ひんこう 品行 〔道徳面から見た〕conduct; 〔ふるまい〕behavior 《⇒行い〔類語〕; 〔道徳観念〕morals.
① 〖品行が〗▶彼は学校での品行があまりよくない His *conduct* at school is not very good./He doesn't behave very well at school.
② 〖品行の〗▶品行のよい〔品行方正な〕人 a person of good *conduct* [high (↔loose) *morals*].
③ 〖品行を〗▶品行を慎む be careful in one's *conduct* [*behavior*]. ▶品行を改める improve one's *conduct* [*behavior*]; mend one's ways [*manners*].

ひんこん 貧困 poverty. (⇒貧乏) ●政治の貧困 poor politics. ●思想の貧困 *poverty* of ideas [thought]. ▶貧困にあえぐ live very poorly; live in extreme 〘書〙abject] *poverty*; be *poverty*-stricken. ▶貧困は犯罪の主な要因である *Poverty* is a chief factor in (causing) crime.
●貧困家庭 a poor 〘婉曲的〙a needy] family.

びんさつ びん札 a brand-new bill 〘英〙note]; a completely new bill 〘英〙note].

ひんし 品詞 〖文法〗a part of speech.

ひんし 瀕死 ——瀕死の 形 〔死にかけている〕dying; 〔死に近い〕near death. ▶瀕死の男 a *dying* man. ▶瀕死の重傷 a *critical* [a *fatal*] injury. (!瀕死の重傷を負う」は be critically [fatally] injured. fatal は強く死を含意する (⇒致命傷)) ▶彼は事故で瀕死の状態だった He *was dying* [*near death*] after the accident.

ひんしつ 品質 (a) quality. (⇒質) ●さまざまな品質の紙 paper of various *qualities*. ●品質がよい〔悪い〕be of high [low] *quality*; 〔優れている〕be superior [〔劣っている〕inferior] in *quality*. ●高品質の製品 a (high) *quality* product. ●品質を向上させる raise [改善する] improve] *quality*. ▶アルミの優秀さは軽さにある The excellence [superiority] *in quality* of aluminum is its lightness. ▶その時計は品質のよさで有名 The watch is famous for its (good) *quality*. (!quality には「良質」の意もある)
●品質管理 quálity contròl 《略 QC》. ●品質検査 a quálity inspèction. ●品質保証 〔表示〕Quality Guaranteed.

ひんじゃ 貧者 a poor person; 《総称的に》poor people, the poor.
●貧者の一灯 a widow's mite.

*__**ひんじゃく**__ 貧弱 名 poorness.
—— 貧弱な 形 〖乏しい〗poor; 〖不十分な〗meager. ▶貧弱な(=やせた)男 a *thin* man (本格が) a man of *poor* build; (服装が) a *poorly* dressed man. ▶彼の演説は内容が貧弱でした His speech was *poor* in content. ▶(中味が薄い) His speech *didn't* have *much* substance. ▶私の物理の知識は貧弱です I *don't* have *much* [I have a *poor*] knowledge of physics./My knowledge of physics is quite *limited*.

ひんしゅ 品種 〔動植物の種〕a breed; 〔動植物の変種〕a variety. ●豚の新品種 a new *breed* [*variety*] of pig. ●稲の品種を改良する improve the *breed* of rice [riceplants].
●品種改良 improvement of breed.

ひんしゅく 顰蹙 ——顰蹙を買う be frowned /fráund/ on. ▶コンサートで若いカップルがひそひそ話をしていてまわりの人たちのひんしゅくを買い，しっという声を浴びせられた At the concert, a young couple's whispers caused *black looks* and hushing noises from the people around them. (!a black look は

「非難[嫌悪]の視線」の意)

ひんしゅつ 頻出 ——頻出する 動 appear frequently. ●頻出する1,500語のリスト a list of 1,500 very frequent words. (!語順に注意)

びんしょう 敏捷 ——敏捷な 形 〔素早い〕quick; 〔軽やかな〕nimble, agile /ǽdʒl/. ●敏捷な動作 a *quick* [*nimble*] movement. ●動きが敏捷である be *quick* in one's movement; be *nimble* [*agile*].
—— 敏捷に 副 quickly; nimbly, agilely.

びんしょう 憫笑 ——憫笑する 動 smile with [in] pity.

びんじょう 便乗 ——便乗する 動 ●彼の車に便乗する (乗せてもらう) *get a ride* [*a lift*] in his car. ●時勢に便乗する (利用する) *take advantage of* the trend of the times.
●便乗値上げ an opportunistic price raise.

ヒンズーきょう ヒンズー教 Hínduism, the Hindu religion. ●ヒンズー教徒 a Hindu. ●ヒンズー教の Hindu.

ひんする 貧する become poor; fall [sink] into poverty.
●貧すれば鈍(ﾄﾞﾝ)する Poverty dulls one's mind./《ことわざ》He that loses his goods loses his sense.

ひんする 頻する ●絶滅[倒産]の危機に頻する *be on the verge* [*point*] of extinction [bankruptcy].

ひんせい 品性 character. ●品性を陶冶(ﾄｳﾔ)する cultivate [build (up)] one's *character*. ●あの人は品性がいやしい He's [She's] not of good *character*. (!low character はマイナスイメージが強すぎるので避けた方がよい) ▶そんなことを言うと品性が疑われるよ What you said just now [you're saying right now] will call your *character* in question. (!just now と right now の使い分けに注意)

ピンセット [<オランダ語] tweezers. (!複数扱い. 数える場合は a pair [two pairs] of ～)

ひんせん 貧賤 ——貧賤な 形 poor and humble.

びんせん 便箋 〔a sheet of〕notepaper [writing páper] (!後の方はレポート用紙, 原稿用紙の意でも用いる) (一つづりの) a notepad, a wríting pàd; (人・会社の名前・住所が入った) 〔a sheet of〕letterhead. ●便せんで手紙を書く write a letter *on a notepad*.

ひんそう 貧相 ——貧相な 形 〔貧相な〕poor; 〔みじめな〕miserable; 〔みすぼらしい〕shabby. ▶彼は貧相に見えた He looked *shabby*. ▶彼女はいつも貧相な身なりをしていた She was always *shabbily* [*poorly*] dressed.

びんそく 敏速 ——敏速な 形 〔すばやい〕quick; 〔きびきびした〕brisk; 〔求めに応じてすぐ〕prompt. ●敏速に行動する act *quickly*; be *quick in* action.

ひんそん 貧村 a poor village. (⇒⇔寒村)

ひんだ 貧打 〖野球〗poor batting [hitting].
●貧打線 a low-hit game.

ビンタ ▶ビンタを食らわす slap 《him》on the face; slap 《his》face. (⇒平手)

ピンチ ①a crisis 《略 crises /kráisi:z/》; 〔切迫した状態〕a pinch (!pinch は通例成句で用いる; 〔野球で特に投手にとっての〕a jam. ●ピンチに陥る *get into trouble* [*a jam*]. ●ノーアウト満塁のピンチを切り抜ける get out of a bases-loaded, no-out *jam*. ▶彼は私のピンチを救ってくれた He helped me *out of a crisis* [(切羽詰まったときに) *in* 〘米〙*at* 〘英〙*a pinch*, (板ばさみの窮地に立ったときに) 〔話〕*when I was in a fix*].
●ピンチヒッター 〖野球〗a pinch hitter; (一般に) a fill-in (*for*). ●ピンチランナー 〖野球〗a pinch runner.

びんづめ 瓶詰め ●瓶詰のジャム *bottled* jam. ●

ビンディング [<ドイツ語] 【スキー】 a binding /báindiŋ/.

ビンテージ vintage. ●ビンテージイヤー a vintage year. ●ビンテージモデル a vintage model. ●ビンテージワイン vintage wine.

ヒント a hint; (手がかり) a cue /kjúː/. (⇨暗示) ●彼にヒントを与える give [drop] him a hint 《as to, about》. ●ヒントを得る get a hint 《from》. ▶実際の事件からヒントを得た映画 a movie suggested by an actual incident.

ひんど 頻度 frequency. ●高い[低い]頻度 《with》 high [low] frequency. ●使用頻度順に in order of frequency in use. ●頻度が高く[低く]なってきている be increasing [decreasing] in frequency. ▶彼はかなりの頻度でここへやって来るHe comes here quite often [frequently]. (⚠前の方が口語的な (⇨度々)

ぴんと ❶ [物がきつく張られた様子を] (きつく) tightly. ●ぴんと張る tighten. ▶テニスコートにはネットがぴんと張られていた The net was hung tightly in the tennis court. ▶彼はロープをぴんと張った He tightened the rope./He stretched the rope tightly. ▶背筋をぴんと伸ばしていなさい Try to keep your back straight [upright]. ▶ウサギが耳をぴんと立てた The rabbit cocked (up) [pricked up] its ears.

❷ [物が勢いよくはね上がっている様子] (⚠適当な副詞がないので動詞で表す) ▶将軍のひげはぴんとはね上がって(=巻き上がって)いた The general's mustache curled up at the ends.

❸ [空気・気分などが緊張して] (形容詞で表して) tense, strained. ●ぴんと張り詰めた雰囲気 a tense atmosphere. ▶その部屋の空気はぴんと張り詰めていた The air in the room was tense.

❹ [直感的に物事を感じとる様子を] ●ぴんとくる ring a bell; (思い当たることが分かる) know intuitively [by intuition]; (心に思い浮かぶ) occur; (心に訴える) appeal. ▶彼女が彼の名前を言ったのでぴんときた Her mention of his name rang a bell. ▶彼がそれをやったのかもしれないとぴんときた It occurred to me that he might have done it. ▶校長先生の冗談は我々にはぴんとこなかった(要点が分からなかった) We couldn't get the point of our headmaster's jokes. ▶母さんはロックにぴんとこないと言う My mother says she doesn't find rock (music) appealing./My mother says rock music doesn't appeal to her. ▶私は彼に気がないということをそれとなく言ったが、彼はぴんとこないようだった I dropped a subtle hint that I was not interested in him, but he didn't seem to take it [pick it up]. (⚠ it は hint をさす)

ピント [<オランダ語] 【焦点】 a focus 《微》〜es; foci /fóusai/; 【要点】 the point. (⇨焦点) ●(写真などの) ピントが合っている[外れている] be in [out of] focus. ●カメラのピントを合わせる bring a camera into focus. ▶彼の議論はピントが外れている His argument is off (↔to) the point./His argument misses the point.

ピンナップ a pínup. ●ピンナップガール a pinup girl.

ひんにょう 頻尿 frequent urination, 【医学】 pollakiuria /pὰləkijúəriə/.

ひんのう 貧農 a poor farmer; (小作農) a peasant.

ひんぱつ 頻発 图 a frequent occurrence. ── 頻発する 動 ▶その交差点では事故が頻発する Accidents occur [happen] (very) frequently [very often] at the intersection. (⚠後の方が口語的)

ピンはね 图 〔話〕a kickback; (分け前) 〔話〕a cut. ── ピンはねする 動 pocket 《some of the money》. ▶手数料の10 パーセントをピンはねする pocket 10 percent of the commission; take 10 percent cut of the commission. ▶彼の賃金からピンはねする pocket a kickback from his wages.

ひんぱん 頻繁 ●人通りの頻繁な通り a busy street. ▶最近彼とは頻繁に(=何回も)会っている Recently I have met him many times [しばしば] very often, (やや書) very frequently]. (⇨度々)

ひんぴょうかい 品評会 a show; (農・畜産物などの) a fair; (美術品・製品などの展覧会) an exhibition /èksəbíʃən/. ●花[猫]の品評会 a flówer [a cát] shów. ●農産物品評会 an agricultural fair [show].

ぴんぴん 頻々 ── 頻々と ⚠ frequently; often.

ぴんぴん ── ぴんぴんしている 形 (生気がある) lively; (生きている) alive, live /láiv/; (活力のある) energetic. ▶あの魚屋ではぴんぴんしているロブスターを売っている 《米》 They sell live lobsters at the fish store./《英》They sell live lobsters at the fishmonger's. ▶彼は(元気で)ぴんぴんしているよ He's alive and kicking. (⚠成句表現) ▶あの老作家はぴんぴんして活躍してるよ The old writer is still very active. ▶うちのじいさんは80 だけどぴんぴんしていますよ My grandpa is hale and hearty at eighty. (⚠「老人が健康で元気な」の意の成句表現)

ひんぷ 貧富 wealth and poverty; 〘人〙(the) rich and (the) poor (⚠複数扱い. 日本語と英語では語順が逆になる). ●貧富の差 the gap [gulf] between (the) rich and (the) poor. (⚠ the を省略する時は両方ともする) ●貧富を問わず非difference be nakuてはならない Whether rich or poor, all have to work.

ピンポイント ●ピンポイント爆撃 pinpoint bombing.

*__びんぼう__ 貧乏 图 poverty. ●貧乏暮らしをする live in poverty. ●貧乏ゆすりをするな Don't jiggle [joggle] your leg(s)./Don't shake. ▶彼はいつも貧乏くじを引いている He is always the most unlucky of all./He always draws the short straw. (⚠ 慣用表現)

── 貧乏な 形 poor; (お金・生活必需品を欠いた) needy; (極貧の) poverty-stricken. (⇨貧しい) ●貧乏な人々 poor (↔rich) people; the poor (↔the rich); (婉曲的) the needy (⚠ 以上二つはいずれも複数扱い); (婉曲的) differently advantaged people. ●貧乏になる become poor; fall into poverty; be reduced to poverty. ●貧乏人の子供 poor people's children, the children of the poor. (⚠ the poor children は「かわいそうにその子供たち(は)」の意で、この場合は不可) ●貧乏神にとりつかれている be poverty-stricken. ▶彼は貧乏だったので大学に行けなかった He could not go to college because he was poor. ▶露骨な poor を避けて、He didn't have enough money to [He couldn't afford to] go to college. などということが多い) 《書》Poverty prevented him from going to college. ▶彼女は貧乏な家族に食べ物を与えた She gave some food to the poor [needy] family. ▶彼女は貧乏性 She worried a lot about little things and can never relax.

●貧乏暇なし (貧乏人は暇がない) The poor man has no (time for) leisure.

びんぼうものがたり 『貧乏物語』 A Story of Poverty. [参考] 河上肇の経済評論.

ぴんぽーん ❶ 【玄関のチャイムの音】 ▶ぴんぽーんと玄関のベルが鳴った "Ding-dong," went the doorbell.

❷ 【その通りだ!】 Bingo!; You've hit it!

ピンぼけ ▶この写真はピンぼけだ This photograph is out of focus [blurred, is not clear].

ピンポン ping-pong, table tennis. ●ピンポンをする

play *ping-pong*.
- ピンポン玉 a ping-pong ball.

ひんまげる ひん曲げる bend with a jerk. (⇨曲げる)

ひんみん 貧民 poor people, the poor, 《婉曲的》(恵まれない人々) the ùnderprívileged (❗いずれも複数扱い).
- 貧民街 the slums; a slum area. (⇨スラム)

ひんむく ひん剥く peel [pare] with a jerk. (⇨剥く)

ひんめい 品名 the name of an article.

ひんもく 品目 an item. ● 品目ごとに並べる arrange them *item* by *item*.

ひんやり ● ひんやりする feel nice and cool. ● ひんやりした cool; (冷たい) cold; (冷え冷えする) chilly. ▶ 夏は木陰に入るとひんやりする You *feel nice and cool* [It's *pleasantly cool*] under a tree in (《主に米》 the) summer. ▶ 石の床は足にひんやりした The stone floor *felt cold* on my feet.

びんらん 便覧 a manual (❗使用法・技術習得の原則や規則をまとめた本); (特定分野の手引書) a handbook. (❗両者交換可のこともあるが, 後の方が口語的で手軽さを含意) ● 学生便覧 a handbook *for* students; a student *handbook* [*manual*].

びんろうじゅ 檳榔樹 『植物』 a betel palm.

びんわん 敏腕 图 (有能) ability; (受け入れる能力) (a) capacity; (手ぎわ) (a) skill; (巧妙さ) cleverness.
- 敏腕をふるう show one's *ability* [*skill*] (《in; *in* doing》).
— 敏腕な 形 (有能な) able; capable. ▶ 彼女は敏腕弁護士だ She is an *able* [a *capable*, (てきぱきとした) an *efficient*] lawyer.

ふ

ふ **府** 【行政区】a prefecture (⇨県);【中心である場所】a center, 《書》a seat. ●大阪府 Osaka *Prefecture*. ●府庁 a *prefectural* office. ●学問の府 a *center* [a *seat*] of learning. ●立法の府《書》the legislature. (⇨国会)

ふ **歩** (将棋・チェスの) a pawn.

ふ **負** 負の数 a *minus* [a *negative*] number.

ふ **斑** ●黄色い斑入りの葉 a yellow *spotted* leaf; a leaf with yellow *spots*.

ふ **腑** 腑に落ちない ▶彼の説明はどうも腑に落ちない(=納得しがたい) I'm *not convinced of* his explanations./His explanations *are not very convincing*.

ふ **麩** fu; (説明的に) dried wheat gluten. ●生麩 fresh *fu*.

ふ **譜** 【楽譜】music; (総譜) a score;【囲碁・将棋の記録】a record;【系図】(a) genealogy;【図譜】a picture book.

ふ **分** 【パーセント】《米》a percent, 《英》a per cent. (! 単・複同形) (⇨パーセント) ●8分の利子で金を借りる borrow the money at [with] 8 *percent* interest.

> **翻訳のこころ** がたがたしながら、一人の紳士は後ろの戸を押そうとしましたが、どうです、戸はもう一分も動きませんでした (宮沢賢治『注文の多い料理店』) Shuddering, one gentleman tried to push open the door behind him. Did it open? No, it didn't budge even an inch. (! (1)「一分も」は even an inch (少しも)と表す. (2) budge は否定に用いられることが多く, don't budge は「まったく動かない」の意)

●分がある ▶彼の方に分がある (勝ち目がある) The odds *are in* his *favor*./(有利な立場にいる) He *is in an advantageous position*./He *has an advantage over* me [us].

ふ **歩** 【面積の単位】a *bu*. (参考 約 3.3m²);【歩合】(⇨歩合).

ふ **部** ❶【部門】a department; a division; a bureau /bjúərou/ (複 ~s, ~x /-z/).

> **使い分け department** 会社や官庁などの組織の中の部門を表す.
> **division** department と同義で用いられる. department が上位, division が下位の関係を作る傾向がある.
> **bureau** 米国官庁の大きく分かれた部門のほか, 支社や支局を表す.

●会社の営業部 the sales *department* [*division*] of a company. ▶阿部さん, どこの部にお られるのですか What *department* are you *in*, Mr. Abe? ❷【刊行物の単位】a copy. ●その小説を1万部印刷する print 10,000 *copies* of the novel. ❸【部分】a part, a portion. (⇨部分, 一部) ●『ハムレット』の第1部 the first *part* of *Hamlet*. ●(歌舞伎などの)昼の部 a daytime performance. ▶実際のパンフレットでは Performance: Daytime: 11:00- Night time: 19:00- などとする ▶その報告書は4部からなっている The report is in four *parts*. ❹【クラブ】a club. ●ラグビー部 a rúgby clùb. ●テニス部に入っている belong to [be a member of] the tennis *club*. ●部室 (⇨部室)

ファーザーコンプレックス 《suffer from》 an [the] Electra complex; (和製語) a father complex.

ファースト 【野球】(一塁) first (base), (! 無冠詞に注意); (一塁手) a first base player [(男の) baseman (複 -men)]. ●ファーストを守る play *first* (base). (⇨塁)
●ファーストコーチ a first base coach. ●ファーストゴロ a grounder to first. ●ファーストフライ a fly to first. ●ファーストミット a first baseman's glove [mitt]. ●ファーストランナー the runner on [at] first.

ファーストクラス first class. ●ファーストクラスのホテル a *first*class hotel. ●ファーストクラスで旅行する travel *first-class*.

ファーストネーム 《one's》 first name. ▶ファーストネームの美津子と呼んでちょうだい Just [You can] call me by my *first name*, Mitsuko.

ファーストフード fast (*slow*) food. ●ファーストフードの店 a *fast food* restaurant.

ファーストレグ (⇨ファーストレッグ)
ファーストレッグ a first leg. (参考 カップ戦で適用される2回戦制マッチの第一試合. 第二試合は second leg)

ファーストレディー 【大統領[州知事]夫人】 the first lady. (! しばしば the F- L-)

ファーブル 【フランスの昆虫学者】 Fabre /fáːbər/ (Jean Henri ~).

ファーポスト 【サッカー】a far post. ▶中村のキックはファーポストを抜けていった Nakamura's shot flew past the *far post*.

ファーマシー 【薬局】《米》 a drugstore, 《英》 a chemist's (shop), 《書》 a pharmacy.

ファーム(チーム) 【二軍】【野球】 a farm team [club].

ファール a foul. (⇨ファウル)

ぶあい 歩合 (率) a rate; a percentage; (手数料) a commission. ●公定歩合 the official discount [bank] *rate*. ●売り上げの10パーセントの歩合をもらう get a *commission* of ten percent [a ten percent *commission*] on sales.
●歩合給制 a commission-based pay system. ●歩合制 a commission(-based) system; a commission basis.

ファイア 【火, 炎】 fire. ●ファイアストーム (説明的に) singing and dancing around the bonfire (! a firestorm は「火事場のあらし」の意)

ファイアウォール 【コンピュータ】 a firewall.

ぶあいそう 無愛想 图【交際嫌い】unsociability.
—— 無愛想な unsociable; (人に) unfriendly; (ぶっきらぼうな) blunt; (冷たい) cold. ●無愛想な顔で私を見る give me a *cold* [an *unfriendly*] look. ●無愛想な返事をする make [give] a blunt answer; answer *bluntly*. ▶近所の人は私たちに無愛想だった Our neighbors were *unsociable* [*unfriendly*] to us.

ファイティングスピリット fighting spirit. (⇨ファイト)
ファイト 【闘志】(xa) fight; (闘う元気) fighting spirit. ●(闘志) ●ファイト満々である be full of *fight* [*fighting spirit*]. ▶彼のファイトがわいた His *fighting spirit* was aroused. ●(掛け声)ファイト, ファイト (がんばろう) Go, go, go!

ファイナリスト [決勝戦出場選手] a finalist. ●彼は競技会初出場でファイナリストになった(=決勝戦に残った) He *made the final* at his first competition.

ファイナル [決勝戦] the final(s). (⇨決勝)

ファイナンシャル financial.
●ファイナンシャルアドバイザー a financial adviser.
●ファイナンシャルプランナー a financial planner.

ファイバー (a) fiber. ●光ファイバー (an) optical *fiber*. ●ファイバーグラス fiberglass, glass fiber. ●ファイバーケーブル a fiber cable. ●ファイバースコープ a *fiber*scope. ●ファイバーボード [繊維板] fiberboard.

ファイリング [書類などの分類・整理] filing. ●電子ファイリングシステム an electronic *filing* system. ●ファイリングキャビネット a filing cabinet.

ファイル 图 a file. ●ファイル用カード a filing card. ●ファイル用ホルダー a *file* folder. ●ファイルをコピーする[削除する; つくる; 編集する] [コンピュータ] copy [delete, 《米》 erase; create; edit] a *file*. ●ファイルを開く[閉じる; 印刷する; 保存する] [コンピュータ] open [close; print; save] a *file*. ●隠しファイル [コンピュータ] a hidden *file*. ●テキストファイル (⇨テキスト)
── **ファイルする** 動 file 《papers》; keep* 《papers》 on file [in a file].
●ファイル管理 [コンピュータ] a file management. ●ファイルサーバ [コンピュータ] a file server. ●ファイル属性 [コンピュータ] a file attribute. ●ファイル名 [コンピュータ] a file name.

ファインセラミックス fine ceramics.

ファインダー [カメラ・望遠鏡の] a finder, a viewfinder.

ファインプレー (make) a brilliant [a superb] play; (捕球の) a beautiful [a spectacular] catch; a circus catch. (!「ファインプレー」は難しい飛球・ライナーの「好捕」の意で用いるのが普通だが, a fine play は広い意味で「すばらしいプレー」)

ファウル 图 [競技] a foul. ●ゴロのファウルを打つ ground [bounce] it *foul*. ●バックネットへファウルを打つ *foul* back to the screen. ●打球はファウルになった The ball went [fell] *foul*.

参考 サッカーでは, 以前はファウルの具体的な所作からそれぞれ pushing, tripping, holding などと細かく呼び慣わしていたが, 近年は「非スポーツ的行為 (unsporting behaviour)」に統一されている. 審判への[不当]抗議によるファウルを dissent.

── **ファウルする** 動 foul; commit a foul, [野球] foul (off) a pitch; foul away.
●ファウルグラウンド[ゾーン] [野球] the foul territory. (! foul ground とはいうが foul zone は和製英語) ●ファウルチップ [野球] a foul tip. ●ファウルフライ [野球] a foul fly, ●三塁へのファウルフライに倒れる *foul* out to third. ●ファウルポール a foul pole. ●ファウルボール [野球] a foul ball. ●ファウルライン a foul line. ●レフトのファウルライン沿いにフライを打ち上げる hit a fly ball down the left *field* (*foul*) *line*.

ファクシミリ [通信] facsimile, fax; [装置] a fax (machine); [複写されたもの] a facsimile, a fax. (⇨ファックス)

ファクス (a) fax. (⇨ファックス)

ファゴット [<イタリア語] [楽器] a bassoon /bəsúːn/. ●ファゴットを演奏する play the bassoon. ●ファゴット奏者 a bassoonist.

ファザコン [「ファーザーコンプレックス」の略] (⇨ファーザーコンプレックス)

ファジー ── **ファジーな** 形 [あいまいな] (像や思考が) fuzzy; (意味の) ambiguous.
●ファジーエンジニアリング fuzzy engineering. ●ファジー理論 fuzzy theory. ●ファジー論理 fuzzy logic.

ファシスト a fascist /fǽʃist/.

ファシズム [独裁的国家主義] fascism /fǽʃizm/. (! しばしば F-)

ファスナ(ー) 《主に米》 a zipper, 《主に英》 a zip (fastener). (! fastener は「ファスナー」より意味が広く,「締め具, 留め具」の総称 (⇨チャック)) ●ファスナー付きのコート a coat with a *zipper*. ●ファスナーを開ける open [undo, 《下げて》 pull down] a *zipper*; unzip 《one's skirt》. ●ファスナーを閉める close [do up, 《上げて》 pull up] a *zipper*; zip up 《one's skirt》. ▶かばんのファスナーが動かなくなった The *zipper* on my bag (got) stuck.

ぶあつい 分厚い, 部厚い thick. ●分厚い本 a thick book. ▶薄い絵本で分厚いメッセージが伝わるのはなぜなんでしょう Why is it that a thin picture book can deliver very heavy messages?

ファック 图 [性交] [卑] fuck. ── **ファックする** 動 fuck.

ファックス [通信] fax /fæks/; [装置] a fax (machine); [複写されたもの] a fax. (⇨ ファクシミリ) ●ファックスで送る send 《a letter》 *by fax* [*facsimile*]; *fax* 《a letter》. ▶返事はファックスでお送りします I'll *fax* you the reply [*fax* the reply *to* you]. ●ファックスナンバー a fáx nùmber.

ファッショ [<イタリア語] [独裁的国家主義] fáscism, Fascism.

ファッショナブル ── **ファッショナブルな** 形 [流行の] fashionable.

ファッション [流行] (a) fashion, (a) vogue. ●ミラノの最新ファッション the latest Milan *fashion*. ▶ロングスカートが今年のファッションだ Long skirts are *in* 《x a》 *fashion* this year. ●パリは世界のファッションの中心地です Paris is the *fashion* center of the world.
●ファッションショー a fáshion [a vógue] shòw. ●ファッションモデル a fáshion [a vógue] mòdel.

ファミコン [映像] a video (computer) machine; [商標] Nintendo Entertainment System (略 NES). ●ファミコン (*Family Computer*) は日本での商品名); (ゲーム) 《play》 a video game.

ファミリー [家族] a family.
●ファミリーカー a fámily càr. ●ファミリーネーム [姓] a fámily nàme; a surname. ●ファミリープラン [家族計画] fámily plànning; (携帯電話などの割引料金) 《主に英》 a mobile phone family plan. ●ファミリーレストラン a family restaurant.

ファラオ [古代エジプト王の称号] a pharaoh /féərou/.

ファラデー [英国の物理・化学者] Faraday (Michael ～).

ふあん 不安 图 [将来への] (an) anxiety 《about》; [思い悩み] (a) worry 《about》; [気持ちの落ち着かなさ] uneasiness; [悪い事が起こるのではないかという] (a) fear 《of》; [社会などの動揺] unrest. (⇨心配)
① [~不安] ●期待と不安 hopes and *fears*. ▶目下最大の不安は, 自分の会社がつぶれるのではないか. 先の不安は, 定年後の生活 The immediate *fear* is that my company could go bankrupt. The distant *fear* is my life after retirement. (!「つぶれるのではないか」は「つぶれるかもしれない」として, 仮定法の could で表す)
② [~不安を] ●不安を与える cause 《him》 *anxiety* [*uneasiness*]. ●不安を和らげる ease [relieve] *anxiety* [*uneasiness*]. ●社会不安を引き起こす cause social *unrest*. ●人々の心に不安をかき立てる stir up *anxiety* [*uneasiness*] in people's minds. ▶彼女は空爆で殺されるのではないかという不安

を覚えた She felt a *fear of* being killed in an airstrike. ▶彼女の将来に非常に不安をいだいていた He *was* very *anxious* [*worried, concerned*] *about* her future. ▶彼はその手術に少し不安を感じた He felt a little *uneasy about* the operation. ▶医師は彼の手術への不安を除こうとした The doctor tried to get rid of his *uneasiness about* the operation. ▶その悪夢は彼の心の奥に不安を残すことになった The nightmare left some *uneasiness* in the back of his mind.

③【不安で】▶私は不安で眠れなかった I couldn't sleep *with anxiety* [*worry*]. ▶彼女は一人取り残されてなんとなく不安であった She, left alone, had a vague feeling of *uneasiness*.

── **不安な** 形 (心配な) anxious; (落ち着かない) uneasy. ● 不安な状態 an *uneasy* condition. ● 顔に不安そうな様子を浮かべて with an *uneasy* look on one's face. ● 不安そうにたずねる ask *uneasily*. ▶彼は山中での不安な一夜を過ごした He spent an *uneasy* [*sleepless*] *a restless* night in the mountains.

● 不安神経症【医学】anxiety neurosis.

ファン [扇風機] a fan.
● ファンヒーター (通例電気の) a fan heater.

ファン [熱心な愛好者] a fan; (熱狂者) an enthusiast; (愛好者) a lover; (崇拝者) an admirer (❗高尚なものに用いる). ● 熱心な野球ファン an ardent baseball *fan* [*enthusiast*]; a baseball *devotee* [*freak*]. ● タイガースファン a Tigers *fan*. ● ビートルズの大ファン a great *fan* [a devoted *fan*, (崇拝者) a great *admirer*] of the Beatles; a Beatles devotee. ● 音楽ファン a *lover* of music; a music *lover*. ● スポーツファン an *enthusiast* for sports; a sports *enthusiast*. ▶彼のファン層は広い He has *fans* of a wide variety.

● ファン感謝デー a fan appreciation day. ● ファンクラブ a fán clùb. ● ファンレター a fán lètter. (⇒ファンレター)

ファンクションキー [コンピュータ] a function key.

ファンシーグッズ (キー・みやげ品などの小物) fancy goods.

ファンタジー [幻想, 空想] (a) fantasy.

ファンダメンタル [基本的な] fundamental.

*ふあんてい 不安定 ── 不安定な 形 ● 不安定な(=定まらない)天気 (×an) unsettled [*uncertain*, (変わりやすい) *changeable*] weather. ● 情緒的に不安定な(=変わりやすい)人 an emotionally *unstable* person. ● 不安定な(=永続性のない)地位 an *unstable* position. ● 不安定な(=固定しない)足場[仕事] an *unsteady* foothold [*job*]. ● 不安定な(=不安な)気持ち an uneasy feeling.

ファンデーション [化粧品] foundation cream; [婦人用下着] a foundation garment; (寝巻きを含む) lingerie /lɑ̀ːnʒəréi/.

ファンド [基金, 資金] funds.
● ファンドマネージャー [資金運用担当者] a fúnd mànager.

ふあんない 不案内 ▶京都はまったく不案内です I'm *a* complete [*a* total] *stranger in* Kyoto./I'm completely [totally, quite] *unfamiliar with* Kyoto.

ファンファーレ [<フランス語] a fanfare /fǽnfeər/.
▶ファンファーレで迎えられる be greeted with a *fanfare*.

ファンブル 名 [野球・アメフト] a fumble. (❗野球では通例ゴロについて用い、フライには drop を用いる)

── **ファンブルする** 動 fumble. ● ゴロをファンブルする *fumble* a ground ball.

ファンレター a fán lètter; 《集合的》 fán màil.

*ふい 不意 名 ● 不意を打つ take 《him》 by surprise; surprise 《him》. ▶その強盗は不意を打たれた The robber *was taken by surprise*./(油断しているところを捕らえられた) The robber *was caught off* (his) *guard*.

● **不意を突く** ▶我々は敵の不意を突いた We *took* the enemy *by surprise*./We *made a surprise attack on* the enemy./We *attacked* the enemy *without warning*.

── **不意の** 形 [突然の] sudden; [予期しない] unexpected. ● 不意の来客 (have) an *unexpected* visitor. ● 不意の訪問 (pay) a *surprise* visit.

── **不意に** 副 [突然] suddenly, all of a sudden; [思いがけなく] unexpectedly; [偶然に] by chance; [予告なしに] without warning [*notice*]. (⇒突然[類語]) ▶列車は不意に止まった Our train stopped *suddenly* [*all of a sudden*]./Our train came to a *sudden* [an *abrupt*] stop. ▶犬が不意に飛びかかってきた A dog *suddenly* jumped at me./A dog jumped at me *unexpectedly*. ▶不意に友達が訪ねてきた A friend of mine came to see me *without* (*previous*) *notice*.

● 不意打ち (⇒不意打ち)

ふい ▶せっかくのチャンスをふいにした I've lost [*missed*] a rare chance. ▶あんな努力したのにすべてがふいになった(=まったく駄目になった) All my hard work [my efforts] *came to nothing*.

ぶい 部位 a part, (人体の) a region. ● 身体各部位 the body *parts*; the *regions* of the body.

ブイ [浮標] a buoy /búːi, bɔ́i/; [救命具] a life buoy.

ブイアイピー (ややき) a VIP (a V.I.P.) (❻ VIPs, V.I.P.'s) (*very important person* の略).

フィアンセ [婚約者] (男性) a fiancé; (女性) a fiancée (❗発音はずれも /fìːɑːnséi/); (将来の夫[妻]) one's husband [wife] to be.

フィート a foot (略 ft.). ([参考] 約 30 センチ) ● 3 フィートの長さの棒 a three-*foot* [×*feet*] pole. ● 5 フィート 7 インチ five *feet* [(話) *foot*] seven (inches); 5 ft. 7 in. ; 5′ 7″. (❗ 後に数詞や tall などを伴わないときは feet が普通: five feet [×*foot*]; five feet [foot] tall. (2) 身長を表すときは feet, inches は略すことが多い) ▶1 フィートは 12 インチです There are twelve inches *to a foot*.

フィード ── **フィードする** 動 [サッカー] feed.

フィーバー ▶ゴルフフィーバー (×a) golf *fever*. ● フィーバーしている be crazy [*wild*] 《*about*》.

フィーフラ (⇒フィフラ)

フィーリング [感情] feeling(s); [雰囲気] an atmosphere, a feeling. ▶あの人とはフィーリングが合わない I don't like him for no reason at all. ▶彼女の新曲はフィーリングがいいね I like the *feeling of* her new song.

フィールズしょう フィールズ賞 a Fields prize. ([参考] 数学のノーベル賞といわれる)

フィールディング [野球] fielding.

フィールド [競技] a field.
● フィールドアスレチック a natural obstacle course; 《商標》 Field Athletic. ● フィールド競技 field sports; (種目) a field event. ● フィールドスロー [バスケ] a field throw. ● フィールドノート [実地踏査の記録] a field note. ● フィールドプレーヤー a field player. (❗ たとえばサッカーではゴールキーパーを除く 10 人のプレーヤーのこと) ● フィールドワーク [現地調査の] fieldwork.

ふいうち 不意打ち (make) a surprise attack. ● 不意打ち試験 (give) a *surprise* exam.

ブイエッチエフ [超短波] VHF (*very high frequency* の略).

フィガロのけっこん『フィガロの結婚』 *The Marriage of Figaro*. (参考) モーツァルト作曲のオペラ

フィギュア(スケート) figure skating. ●フィギュアスケートをする skate *figures*.

フィクション (小説) (集合的) fiction; (作り事) (a) fiction. ▶このラジオ番組は完全にフィクションです This radio program is entirely *fictitious*.

ふいご 鞴《《機械》》 bellows; the bellows.

ブイサイン a V sign /víːsàin/; a péace sign.

フィジー 〔国名〕 Fiji; (公式名) the Republic of the Fiji Islands. (首都 Suva) ●フィジー諸島 the Fiji Islands. ●フィジー諸島人 a Fijian. ●フィジー諸島(人)の Fijian.

フィズ 〔発泡性飲料〕 fizz.

ふいちょう 吹聴 ── 吹聴する 動 broadcast, tell* everybody (*about*; (*that*) 節) (⇨言いふらす); (自慢して) brag (-gg-) (*about*; (*that*) 節), boast (*of*, *about*; (*that*) 節).

ふいっち 不一致 (意見などの) (a) disagreement; (不和) (a) discord; (不調和) (a) disharmony. ●わずかな不一致を解決する resolve a slight *disagreement*. ●性格の不一致 (離婚理由としての) incompatibility; (個性のぶつかり合い) personality clash.

フィット ── フィットする fit (-tt-). (⇨合う❶)

フィットネス fitness. ●フィットネスクラブ a fitness club; (美容体操と美顔術の) a figure salon.

ブイティーアール (a) VTR (*v*ideotape *r*ecording [*r*ecording] の略).

ブイディーティー 〔(パソコンなどの)画像表示端末〕 VDT (*v*isual [*v*ideo] *d*isplay *t*erminal の略). ●VDT 症候群 〔医学〕 visual display terminal syndrome. (参考) パソコン作業などを長く続けた結果生じるさまざまな症状

ぷいと (突如) abruptly, suddenly; (思いがけなく) unexpectedly. ▶彼女はぷいと顔をそむけた She *abruptly* turned away her face. ▶彼は会社を辞めた He quit the firm *suddenly* [(予告・通知なしに) *without* (*giving*) *any notice*].

フィナーレ [<イタリア語] 〔終曲, 終幕〕 a finale /fináːli/.

フィナンシャル financial. (⇨ファイナンシャル)

フィニッシュ (競技・競走の) a finish.

フィファ 〔国際サッカー連盟〕 FIFA 《*F*ederation *I*nternationale de *F*ootball *A*ssociation の略》.

フィフティーン [ラグビーのチーム] a fifteen.

ブイヤベース [<フランス語] bouillabaisse /bùːləbéis/.

フィヨルド [<ノルウェー語] a fjord /fjɔːrd/, a fiord.

フィヨン [<フランス語] bouillon /búljan/.

フィラデルフィア 〔米国の都市〕 Philadelphia /filədélfiə/.

フィラメント (電球の) a filament.

フィラリア a filaria. ●フィラリア症 〔医学〕 filariasis.

ふいり 不入り ▶芝居は不入りだった The play *was poorly attended*./The play *drew only a small [limited] audience*.

フィリッピン (⇨フィリピン)

フィリピン 〔国名〕 the Philippines /fílipiːnz/; the Philippine Islands; (公式名) the Republic of the Philippines. (首都 Manila) ●フィリピン人 a Filipino; (女性) a Filipina. ●フィリピン(人)の Philippine.

フィル 〔「フィルハーモニー」の略〕 (⇨フィルハーモニー)

フィルタ(ー) (カメラ・濾過 (ろか) 器の) a filter; (たばこの) a filter tip. ●フィルター付きのたばこ a filter [a filter-tipped] cigarette; a filter tip.

フィルダースチョイス 〔野球〕 a fielder's choice. (参考) 日本語では通例狭い意味にしか用いないが, 本来は次の場合に記録される. (1) 先行走者をアウトにするために打者をアウトにしない. (2) 他の走者をアウトにするために別の走者の進塁を阻止しない. (3) 守備の警戒を解いて走者に進塁を許す ●フィルダースチョイスで出塁する be safe at first on a *fielder's choice*. ●フィルダースチョイスで 1 点取る score a run on a *fielder's choice*.

フィルタリング 〔〔情報〕選別〕 filtering.

フィルハーモニー a philharmonic orchestra. ●ウィーンフィルハーモニー the Vienna *Philharmonic* (Orchestra).

フィルム (a) film. ●高感度[カラー; 白黒]フィルム fast [color; black-and-white] *film*. ●フィルム 1 本 (カメラ用の) a roll of *film* (*with* 24 *exposures*) (!( ) 内は「24 枚撮りの」の意. また a 24 exposure *film* ともいう; (映画の) a spool の (米) [a reel (英)] of *film*. ●フィルムに収める film (it). ▶新しいフィルムをカメラに入れた I put [loaded] a new *film* into the camera. (!「カメラにフィルムを入れる」は load a camera [xa film].) ▶このフィルムはあと 5 枚残っている I have five exposures left on this (roll of) *film*. ●フィルムライブラリー [映画図書館] a film library.

フィレ (⇨ヒレ)

フィレンツェ 〔イタリアの都市〕 Florence.

フィン 〔足ひれ〕 (a pair of) flippers, (米) fins.

ぶいん 部員 (クラブの) a member (*of*) (⇨会員); 〔部局の〕 a staff member. (⇨職員)

フィンガー 〔手の指〕 a finger. ●フィンガーボール a finger bowl.

フィンランド 〔国名〕 Finland; (公式名) the Republic of Finland. (首都 Helsinki) ●フィンランド人 a Finn; (総称) the Finns, the Finnish. ●フィンランド語 Finnish. ●フィンランド(人[語])の Finnish.

ふう 封 ●手紙の封をする *seal* (*up*) a letter. ●手紙の封を切る *open* [*cut open*] a letter. ●遺言書の封を開く (開封する) *break the seal of* a will. ●(米英で公文書など重々しく封印されたものにも) break the seal and open ... などとして用いる.

ふう 風 ❶ 〔様式, 型〕(a) style (!行動・生活様式, その人[時代, 流派]独特の様式); (芸術などの様式) a manner; (流行の型) a fashion; (物[人]の型・種類) a type. ●洋風の家 a Western-*style* house; a house in the Western *style*. ●ロシア風に料理する cook ((in) the) Russian *style*. (!副詞句の場合 in, さらに the もしばしば省略される) ●ピカソ風の絵 a painting in the *manner* [*style*] of Picasso. ●当世風の結婚式 a wedding in the latest *fashion*. ●商売人風の男 a man of commercial *type*. ●現代風の考え方 a *modern* way of thinking. ●都会風の若者 an urbane /əːrbéin/ young person. ▶この建物は東洋風だ This building is (in) the Oriental *style*./This building has [shows] an Oriental *touch*.

❷ 〔やり方〕 a way; a manner; (a) fashion. (!way が多く口語的 (⇨方法)) ●こんな風にやりなさい Do it (in) this *way* [in this *manner*, in this *fashion*]./Do it like this. ▶どういう風にして英語を勉強したのですか How did you study English? ▶お母さんに向かってそんな風に口をきいてはいけない You shouldn't speak to your mother *like that* [*in that manner*].

会話 「私だったら彼の言ったことをそんな風に取らないわ」「じゃあどんな風に取るの」 "I wouldn't take his words *that way*." "Which *way* would you take

乱れている Public morals are loose these days. ▶このような慣習は風記上昇させるなど These customs are injurious to public morals.

ふうき 富貴 ・富貴な家に生まれる be born into a wealthy and aristocratic family.

ふうきり 封切り a premiere /primíər/. ・映画の封切りの release of a new movie. ・**封切り映画** a newly released film [movie]; a first-run film [movie].

ふうする 封する release /a movie).

ブーケ [花束] a bouquet /boukéi/.

***ふうけい 風景** [景色] scenery; a scene; a landscape; [眺望] a view; a sight. (⇨眺め)

> **使い分け scenery** 一地方全体の通例美しい自然の風景. 集合的に用い, 不可算扱い.
> **scene** 一目で見渡せる景色. 必ずしも自然の景色に限らない.
> **landscape** 一目で見渡せる陸地の自然の風景.

・アルプスの風景 the scenery of the Alps. ・街頭風景 a street scene. ・アルプスは風景の美しいことで有名だ The Alps are noted for their scenic beauty [beautiful scenery]. ・私の部屋から湖の風景が見える My room has [gives, (見渡す) [書] commands] a view of the lake. (⇨見晴らす)
・**風景画** a landscape. ・**風景画家** a landscape painter.

ブーケガルニ [香草の束] a bouquet garni.

ふうげつ 風月 ・風月をめでる enjoy the beauties of nature.
・風月を友とする ▶彼は退職後は風月を友とする日々を送っている After retirement, he is enjoying a poetic life in full contact with nature.

ブーゲンビリア [植物] a bougainvill(a)ea /bù:gən-víliə/.

ふうこう 風向 the wind direction. (⇨風向き)
・**風向計** an anemoscope.

ふうこうめいび 風光明媚 ▶ナポリは風光明媚の地として知られている Naples is famous for its beautiful scenery [beauty of scenery, scenic beauty].

ふうさ 封鎖 [名] [武力による] a blockáde; [資金などの凍結] a freezing (of funds). ・経済封鎖 an economic blockade. ・港の封鎖を解く lift [raise] the blockade of a port.
―― **封鎖する** [動] blockáde; [出入りを止める] block (... off); [凍結する] freeze*. ・港を封鎖する blockade a port. ・バリケードで通路を封鎖する block (up) a passage with a barricade. ▶パレードのため通りは一部 [全面的に] 封鎖された The street was partially [completely] blocked to traffic for the parade.

ふうさい 風采 [外見] (an) appearance; [押し出し] presence. (▶常に形容詞を伴う) ・立派な風采の男 a man of fine appearance [presence]; a handsome man.
・風采が上がらない ▶彼は風采が上がらない He is not attractive in appearance./He is an unimpressive-looking man./He doesn't look like much.

ふうさつ 封殺 [野球] a force-out. (⇨フォースアウト)

ふうし 風刺 [名] satire /sǽtaiər/. ・「風刺文・作品」の意では [] ▶その物語は風刺にあふれている The story is full of satire.
―― **風刺する** [動] sátirize. ▶その劇は政界を風刺したものだ The play is a political satire./The play is a satire on the political world.
―― **風刺的に** [副] satirically.
・**風刺(作)家** a sátirist. ・**風刺小説** a satiric(al)

---

them, then?" (▶which way は先行文の that way を受けて反駁する言い方で, 一般的には how を用いる)

[会話] 「この仕事にはさほど興味はないんだ」「そんな風に思ってるんだったら, どうして引き受けたりするの」 "I'm not very interested in this work." "If you feel like that [If that's how you feel, If that's the way you feel], whý táke it?" (▶×If that's the way how you feel, ... は不可.「why+原形動詞」の文は「その必要はないのに」を含意する言い方)

❸ [様子] (外観) a look; (an) appearance; an air. (▶後の2語は「見せかけ」の意にもなる) (⇨様子) ▶彼は一見学者風だ He has the look [appearance, air] of a scholar./He looks like a scholar. ▶なんでも知った風な口をきくな Don't speak as if you knew everything. ▶彼はそれにはまったく興味がないといった風だった He appeared [seemed] to have no interest in it./[米話] He looked like he had no interest in it. (⇨よう❷)

❹ [風習] (manners and) customs. ・都会の風に染まる be steeped in urbanity; be urbanized.
・土地の風に従う keep to the customs of the place.

ふうあい 風合い a [the] touch; a [the] feel. (⇨風合) ・絹の風合いをもつ布 a cloth which feels like silk.

ふうあつ 風圧 wind pressure. ・激しい風圧を受けて倒れる fall under strong wind pressure [(強風のために) because of a strong wind].
・**風圧計** a wind pressure gauge /géidʒ/.

ふういん 封印 a seal. ・封印を押す [破る] affix [break] a seal. ・封印のしてある箱 a sealed box; [書] a box under seal.

ブーイング [名] [野次] booing.
―― **ブーイングする** [動] boo. ▶彼らはアンパイアの判定にブーイングして抗議した They booed the umpire for his decision.

ふううう 風雨 wind and rain; [暴風雨] a storm. ▶そのベンチは風雨にさらされていた The bench was exposed to the wind and rain [the weather].

ふううん 風雲 ・**風雲急を告げる** ▶風雲急を告げる (=社会の大変動期にさしかかっている) We are heading for a time of great social upheaval./Great social upheaval is about to take place.
・**風雲児** (やや書) a hero (徴 ~es) in the turbulent days.

ふうか 風化 [名] (作用) weathering. ―― **風化する** [動] (岩などが) weather; [記憶などが] fade (away).

ふうが 風雅 [名] [優雅] elegance; [よい趣味が] taste; [上品] refinement. (⇨風流)
・**風雅な** [形] elegant; tasteful; refined.

フーガ [<イタリア語] [音楽] a fugue /fjú:g/.

ふうがい 風害 (suffer [receive]) damage from wind; wind damage.

ふうかく 風格 an air; [文芸上の] style. ・王者の風格 a kingly air. ・風格のある文章を書く write in a distinguished style of one's own. ▶彼は風格がある (威厳がある) He has an air of dignity./He is a dignified-looking man. (⇨個性)

ふうがわり 風変わり ―― **風変わりな** [形] (⇨変な) ・風変わりな男 an extraordinary [an odd, an unusual and strange] man. ・風変わりな家 a fantastic [a quaint] house. (▶前者は形が奇抜なこと, 後者は古風で趣のあること)

ふうかん 封緘 a seal. ―― **封緘する** [動] seal.

ふうき 風紀 public morals. (▶無冠詞複数扱い) ・風紀を乱す [よくする, 取り締まる] corrupt [improve, control] public morals. ▶このごろは社会の風紀が

/sətírik(əl)/ novel. ● 風刺漫画 a satiric(al) cartoon; a cáricatùre.

ふうしかでん 『風姿花伝』 *The Flowering Spirit: Classic Teaching on the Art of Noh*. (参考 世阿弥元清の能芸論書)

ふうじこめる 封じ込める (動きなどを) shut*... down; (国・思想などを) (やや書) contain; 〖閉じ込める〗 shut ... (up) 《in》, confine ... 《in》. (⇨閉じ込める)

ふうじて 封じ手 〖囲碁・将棋〗 (説明的に) the first move for the next day recorded in an sealed envelope; 〖相撲〗 a forbidden technique.

ふうしゃ 風車 a windmill. ● 赤い風車 〖映画名〗 *Moulin Rouge*.
● 風車小屋 a windmill (shed).

ふうしゅう 風習 (習慣) (a) custom; (しきたり) (a) convention; (風俗) manners. (⇨風俗, 習わし)

ふうしょ 封書 a (sealed) letter.

ふうしょく 風食 图 〖地学〗 wind erosion; (風化) weathering.
── **風食する** 動 ● 風食された岩 a *weathered* [a *wind-eroded*] rock.

ふうじる 封じる (黙らせる) silence, 《話》 shut*... up.
● 批判を封じる *suppress* [*silence*] criticism. ▶ 彼の口を封じるのは難しい It's hard to *stop* [*shut*] his mouth. (🚫口語的な表現)

ふうしん 風疹 〖医学〗 rubella /ruːbélə/; German measles (🚫単数扱い. 専門語ではない. 以前ほどは用いられない).

ふうじん 風塵 windblown sand.

ブース 〖仕切り部屋〗 a booth; (料金徴収所) a toll-booth.

ふうすいがい 風水害 storm and flood damage, damage from [(caused) by] a storm and flood(s). (⇨水害)

ブースター 〖増幅器〗 a booster.

ふうする 諷する (遠まわしにいう) say* obliquely; talk round《the problem》; (風刺する) satirize. (⇨風刺)

ふうせつ 風雪 wind and snow; 〖吹雪〗 a snowstorm; 〖大吹雪〗 a blizzard; 〖試練〗 hardships.
● 人生の幾多の風雪に耐える go through many *hardships of* [*in*] life.

ふうせつ 風説 a rumor. ▶ 風説が立つ *Rumor* has it that…/It *is rumored* that….

ふうせん 風船 a ballóon. ● ゴム[紙]風船 a rubber [a paper] *balloon*. ● 風船の束を上げる fly [send up] a bunch of *balloons*. ● 風船をふくらます blow up 《🏤書》 inflate 《↔deflate》 a *balloon*. ● はぐれた風船が木の先にひっかかってぱんと割れた A stray *balloon* got caught on a tree top and popped [burst (with a pop)].
● 風船ガム (a piece of) bubble gum. ● 風船玉 a toy balloon.

ふうぜんのともしび 風前の灯 ▶ 彼の命は風前の灯だ (1本の毛[糸]でぶらさがっている) His life *hangs by a hair* [*a thread*]. /(差し迫った危険にさらされている) His life *is in imminent* [《書》 *impending*] *danger*.

ふうそう 風葬 open-air burial.

ふうそく 風速 wind speed [velocity]. (🚫後の語は専門用語) ● 最大瞬間風速 the maximum instantaneous *wind speed*. ● 風速は15メートルです The wind is blowing at 15 meters [about 50 feet] per second. (事情 米英では a 34-mile-an-hour wind のように時速をマイルで用いて表す)
● 風速計 a wind gauge /géidʒ/.

*__ふうぞく__ 風俗 〖慣習〗 manners; (習慣) (a) custom (🚫しばしば複数形で); 〖風紀〗 public morals. ● 日本各地の風俗を調べる study the *manners* [*customs*] of all parts of Japan. ● 風俗を乱す corrupt *public morals*.
● 風俗営業 the entertainment and amusement trade. ● 風俗営業取締法 the Entertainment Establishments Control Law. ● 風俗画 a genre /ʃáːnrə/ painting. ● 風俗産業 the sex industry.
● 風俗習慣 manners and customs. ● 日米間にはとてもたくさんの風俗習慣の違いがある There are a lot of differences between Japanese and American *manners and customs*. ● 風俗小説 a genre novel. ● 風俗犯罪 an offence against public decency.

ふうたい 風袋 tare /téər/; packing. ▶ 風袋ごとで2キロだ This parcel weighs two kilograms *gross*. (🚫「風袋抜きで」は net)

ふうたろう 風太郎 (説明的に) a person who doesn't work and lives off his family and does what he wants to do.

ブータン 〖国名〗 Bhutan /buːtáːn/; (公式名) the Kingdom of Bhutan. (首都 Thimphu) ● ブータン人 a Bhùtanése. ● ブータン(人)の Bhutanese.

ふうち 風致 (自然界の美しさ) a scenic beauty.
● 風致地区 (自然保存地区) a nature preservation area; (都市周辺の緑地帯) a green belt.

ふうちょう 風潮 〖傾向〗 a trend, a tendency (⇨傾向); (ある時代・社会の) (the) climate; 〖時流〗 the current. ● 軍国主義の風潮 the *trend toward* militarism. ● 嘆かわしい社会風潮 a deplorable social *trend*. ● 時代の風潮に乗る〖逆らう〗 swim with [against] the *current* (*of the times*). ▶ 若者が物事を安易に考える風潮が強まっている There is a growing *tendency* for young people to take things easy. ▶ 働く女性に対する社会的風潮はかつてのように厳しいものではない The social *climate* is not so harsh toward working women as it used to be.

ブーツ (a pair of) boots. (⇨靴)

ふうてい 風体 an appearance; a look. ● あやしい風体の男 a suspicious-*looking* man.

ふうてん 瘋癲 ❶ 〖精神状態が不安定な人〗 a lunatic; a demented person. ❷ 〖定職のない人〗 a vagabond; a vagrant. ● フーテンの寅さん Torasan, the *vagabond*.

ふうど 風土 ① climate; (自然的特徴) natural features. ● 日本の精神的風土 the spiritual *climate* of Japan. ● 土地の風土に慣れる acclimatize [get *acclimatized*] *to* the land; get used to the *climate* of the land. (🚫後の方が口語的)
● 風土病 an endemic (disease).

フード 〖頭巾, 覆い〗 a hood /húd/; 〖食物〗 food /fúːd/. (⇨食べ物) ● フードつきのレインコート a raincoat with a *hood*; a *hooded* raincoat.

*__ふうとう__ 封筒 an énvelòpe. ● 和[西洋;薄茶色の事務用]封筒 an end-opening [a side-opening; a manila] *envelope*. ● 返信用封筒 a return *envelope*. ● 封筒にあて名を書く address an *envelope*; write an address on an *envelope*. ● 封筒に手紙を入れる put a letter into an *envelope*. ● 封筒に封をする seal [close] (up) an *envelope*. ● 封筒に切手を貼る put a stamp on an *envelope*.

ふうどう 風洞 ● 風洞実験を行う (do [conduct]) a wind tunnel test 《on, for》.

プードル 〖動物〗 (犬) a poodle.

ふうにゅう 封入 ── 封入する 動 enclose.

ふうは 風波 (⇨波風)

ふうばい 風媒 pollination by wind.
● 風媒花 an anemophilous flower.

ふうび 風靡 ── 風靡する 動 dominate; be dominant (*over*); be very influential [powerful]. ●一世(いっせい)を風靡する (⇨一世[成句])

ブービーしょう ブービー賞 〖最下位から二番目の賞〗a second-last prize. ▶ a booby prize は最下位の賞

ふうひょう 風評 (うわさ) a rumor; ((悪い)評価) a (bad) reputation. (⇨うわさ, 評判)

★**ふうふ 夫婦** a (married) couple, husband [《書》man] and wife.

> **解説** couple が一般的. couple より堅い結びつきを言うときは pair を用いることがある. いずれも単・複両扱い. 夫婦を構成する夫と妻に視点を置く場合は husband [man] and wife で通例無冠詞で用いる.

① 【〜夫婦】 ▶ 若夫婦 a young *couple*. ●老夫婦 an elderly [a senior] *couple*. (●後の方は「親夫婦」の意もある) ●新婚夫婦 a newly married [a newlywed] *couple*; (やや書) newlyweds. ●おしどり夫婦 a happy *pair*; a happy married *couple*. ●田中さん夫婦 Mr. and Mrs. Tanaka; Mr. Tanaka and his wife; the Tanakas. ▶ 彼らは似合いの夫婦だ They are a well-matched [a nice] *couple*. ▶ 私たち夫婦には子供がいません Our *couple* [*We, My husband and I*] have no children.

② 【夫婦(の)〜】 ▶ 夫婦げんかをする have a quarrel [a row /ráu/] with one's wife [husband]. ▶ 彼らは夫婦仲が悪い The *couple* don't get on well (with each other). ▶ 結婚記念日に夫婦水入らずで (=自分たちだけで)食事に出かけた The couple went out to dine *by themselves* on their wedding anniversary.

③ 【夫婦に】 ▶ 壮一は弥生と夫婦になった(=結婚した) Soichi *got married to* [×with] Yayoi. ▶ あの人たちはよい夫婦になりますよ I hope they'll make a nice *couple*.

④ 【夫婦で】 ▶ 我々は夫婦で共働きしている My wife and I are both working [both have jobs]. (●×I and my wife の語順は通例では不可) ▶ ご夫婦でおいでください Please come over with your wife [husband].

● 夫婦げんかは犬も食わない 'Even a dog will not eat a quarrel between husband and wife.' /(夫婦げんかの仲裁をするのはおろかである) It is foolish to intervene in a quarrel between husband and wife.

● 夫婦愛 married love; love between (a) husband and wife. ● 夫婦生活 (a) married life. ● 夫婦別姓 the use of different surnames by a married couple. (⇨別姓) ● 夫婦別れ (離婚) (a) divorce. (⇨離婚)

ふうふう ▶ 母親が子供のためにスープをふうふう吹いて冷ました The mother *blew on* the soup to cool it down for the baby. ▶ 彼は走った後で息切れして, ふうふういった He *was breathless* [*was out of breath, was breathing heavily*] after running. ▶ 英単語を毎週 100 覚えるのに彼はふうふういっている He *is really struggling* to memorize a hundred English words every week.

ぶうぶう ❶ (うるさい音を立てる) (豚などが) grunt. ● ほら貝をぶうぶう吹く blow on a conch-shell trumpet. ▶ 彼は車の警笛をぶうぶう鳴らした He *honked* the horn of the car.

❷ (しきりに不平を言う) complain, grumble. ▶ 私の母はいつも何かぶうぶう言っている My mother *is always complaining about* something. ▶ 生徒たちは宿題のことでぶうぶう言った The students *grumbled over* [*about*] their assignments.

ふうぶつ 風物 ● 自然の風物 natural *features*. ● 田園の風物 rural *scenes*. ● 日本の風物 Japanese things. (●things は常に複数形). Japanese things は「日本製品」の意) ▶ 風鈴は日本の夏の風物詩だ *Furin* brings us the real feeling of summer in Japan.

ふうぶん 風聞 (a) rumor. (⇨噂(うわさ))

ふうぼうガラス 風防ガラス 《米》a windshield; 《英》a windscreen.

ふうぼう 風貌 (顔立ち) features; (《書》) (a) appearance; 《書》(a) countenance. ● 温和な風貌である have a gentle *appearance*.

ふうみ 風味 (趣ある美味・香り) (a) flavor; (やや書) (a) savor. ● 風味を添える flavor. ● 風味が落ちる lose its *flavor* [*savor*]. ▶ そのコーヒーには何ともいえない風味がある The coffee has an exquisite *flavor*.

ブーム (にわか景気) a boom; (一時的大流行) a craze, 《話》(しばしば軽蔑的) a fad. ● 建築ブーム a building *boom* [*rush*]. ▶ 若い人の間で海外旅行がブームになっている Traveling abroad is the *craze* [the *fad, very popular*] among young people.

ブーメラン a boomerang.

ふうもん 風紋 ripple marks (*left on sand by the action of wind*). (●常に複数形で用いる)

ふうらいぼう 風来坊 a wanderer; (気まぐれな人)《やや書》a whimsical person.

フーリガン (サッカーの) a hooligan.

> **参考** 「フーリガン」とはあくまで便宜上の呼称で, 実際には特定の個人をさすのはまれ. 一般にサッカー場およびその周辺で暴力などの反社会的行為におよぶグループをさして用いられる.

ふうりゅう 風流 名 (優雅) elegance; (よい趣味) (refined) taste; (上品) refinement. ● 風流を解さない人 a person who doesn't understand *elegance*; 《やや書》a prosaic /prouzéiik/ person. ● 無風流 out of *taste*.

── **風流な** 形 elegant; tasteful; refined. ● 風流な人 a person of (refined) *taste*.

ふうりょく 風力 the force of wind, wind force [velocity]. (⇨風速)

● 風力発電 wind power generation.

ふうりん 風鈴 a *furin*; (説明的に) literally a wind bell [chime], a Japanese hanging bell made to tinkle in the wind and give people a feeling of relief from the heat of summer days.

ふうりんそう 風鈴草 〖植物〗a Canterbury bell; a campanula.

★**プール** 〖水泳用の〗a swimming pòol. ● 浅い[深い]プール a shallow [a deep] *pool*. ● 室内プール an indoor (*swimming*) *pool*. ● 温水プール a heated *pool*.

● プールサイド 《at》 the poolside. ● プール熱 (咽頭結膜熱) pharyngoconjunctival fever 《略 PCF》.

プール 名 〖蓄えること〗a pool.

── **プールする** 動 資金をプールする *pool* one's money [*fund, resources*].

ふうろう 封蝋 sealing wax.

ふうろう 風浪 wind and waves.

ふうん 不運 名 bad* luck; (ひどい) (a) misfortune. (⇨運, 災難) ▶ 最近は不運続きだ I'm having a run [a streak] of *bad luck* these days.

── **不運な** 形 不運な事故 an unlucky [an *unfortunate*] accident. ● 再々不運な目にあう have [suffer, 《やや書》meet with] frequent *misfortunes*. ▶ 彼は何て不運なんだろう What a stroke of *bad luck* [*misfortune*] he has! (●簡略して Whát lùck he has! とも). Whàt lúck... のように強勢を

ぶうん ― 置くと逆の意味になるので注意)
― 不運にも 圖 ▶不運にも彼は腕を折った Unluckily [Unfortunately, Unhappily], he broke his arm. (! It was《x a》bad luck 《unlucky, unfortunate,《x》unhappy》that he broke his arm. ともいえる)/He had the bad luck 《misfortune》to break his arm./He was unlucky enough to break his arm.

ぶうん 武運 the fortune(s) in war. ● 武運つたなく敗れる lose the battle. (! 特に武運の部分を訳出する必要はない) ● 武運の長久を祈ります I wish you good luck in war.

ブーン a boom (⇒ぶんぶん❶)

＊ふえ 笛 〘横笛〙a flute; 〘縦笛〙a recorder; 〘呼び子〙a whistle. ● 笛を吹く play the *flute* [*recorder*]; 〘呼び子を〙blow a *whistle*. ● 試合終了の笛を吹く blow the final *whistle*. ● 笛吹く少年 (⇒「笛吹く少年」) ▶警官は笛を吹いてその車に止まるよう合図した The police officer *whistled* the car to stop.
● 笛吹けども踊らず (働きかけてもだれも応じない) No one would follow his lead.

フェア 〘公正〙fair. ● フェアにやる play *fair* [×*fairly*]. ● 人をフェアに扱う treat him *fairly* [×*fair*]. ▶あなたにあらかじめ警告しておくほうがフェアだと思ったんです In the spirit of *fair play*, I thought you should be warned beforehand.
● フェアグラウンド〘ゾーン〙〘野球〙the fair territory. (!*fair ground* というのが *fair zone* は和製英語)
● フェアグラウンドへ打つ hit a ball *fair*. ● フェアボール 〘野球〙a *fair* (×*a foul*) ball.

フェア 〘博覧会,見本市〙a fair. ● 住宅フェア a house *fair* [*show*].

フェアウェー 〘ゴルフ〙a fairway.

フェアプレー 〘公明正大な試合〘行動〙〙fair play.
● フェアプレーをする play *fair* [×*fairly*].

フェアリー 〘妖精〙a fairy.
● フェアリーテール 〘おとぎ話〙a fairy tale. ● フェアリーランド 〘おとぎの国〙a fairyland.

ふえいせい 不衛生 图 insanitation.
― 不衛生な 形 unhygienic /ʌnhàidʒiénik/, 〘やや書〙insanitary; 〘健康に悪い〙unhealthy; 〘人が衛生に不注意な〙careless about hygiene [sanitation].
● 不衛生な環境 an *unhealthy* environment.

フェイドアウト 图 fade-out.
― フェイドアウトする[させる] 動 fade out [fade ... out].

フェイドイン 图 fade-in.
― フェイドインする[させる] 動 fade in [fade ... in].

ふえいよう 富栄養 **― 富栄養の** 形 eutróphic (↔ oligotrophic). ● 富栄養化 eutrophication.

フェイント a feint. (!英語では主にボクシング・フェンシングで用いる。サッカーなど他のスポーツで用いることはまれ)
● フェイントをかける feint [make a *feint*]《*to do*》.

フェース 〘顔〙a face; 〘岩面〙a face.
● フェースオフ 〘アイスホッケー〙(試合開始) a face-off. ● フェースタオル a fáce tòwel. ● フェースバリュー 〘額面価格〙fáce vàlue; 〘顔がきくこと〙《have》extensive contacts. ● フェースマーク 〘コンピュータ〙a smiley; an emoticon; 〘和製語〙a face mark.

フェーンげんしょう フェーン現象 〘＜ドイツ語〙〘気象〙a foehn (föhn) /féin/ phenomenon.

ふえき 不易 〘不変〙immutability; immutableness. ― 不易の 形 immutable, unchangeable.

フェザーきゅう フェザー級 the featherweight.

フェスティバル 〘祭り〙a festival.

ふえて 不得手 **― 不得手な** 形 〘へたな〙poor《*at, in*》, bad《*at*》(!後の方が口語的で意味が強い); 〘気が進まないものを表す〙weak《*in, at*》. (!通例 *in* は学科・分野, *at* は活動を表す) ▶彼は英語が不得手で He is *poor* [*bad, not good*] *at* English./He is *weak* [*poor*] *in* English./English is his *poor* [*weak*] subject.

フェニックス 〘不死鳥〙a phoenix /fíːniks/.

フェノール 〘化学〙phenol.

ブエノスアイレス 〘アルゼンチンの首都〙Buenos Aires /bwèinəs áiəriz/.

ふえふくしょうねん 『笛吹く少年』 *The Piper*. 〘参考〙マネの絵画. 原名 *Le Fifre*

フェミニスト 〘女性にやさしい男性〙a chivalrous [〘英書・米〙a gallant] man (複 men); 〘男女同権論者〙a feminist. (〘参考〙この語は男性による女性保護をも含意するという理由で,純粋に男女同権を主張し闘う人を a femaleist と呼ぶ人もいる。

フェミニズム 〘男女同権主義〙feminism.

フェライト 〘化学〙ferrite.

フェラチオ 〘＜フランス語〙an oral sex, (a) fellatio /fəléifiòu/. ● フェラチオをする fellate.

フェリー(ボート) 〘連絡船〙a ferry, a ferryboat.

＊ふえる 増える, 殖える

WORD CHOICE 増える
increase 税金・価格・割合・分量などが増加すること。増加内容を表す場合は in, 増加の幅を表す場合は from ... to などの前置詞が後続する。▶私立大学の数は 100 から 200 に増加した Private universities have *increased* in number from 100 to 200.
grow 物の数量・サイズ・程度などが増大すること。時に増加内容を表す in number [popularity, proportion, rate, size] などが後続する。▶彼の利益は着実に〘特筆すべき割合で〙増えている Their gain is *growing* at a constant [remarkable] rate.
multiply 物の数量・度合いなどが増加すること。時に昆虫や細菌などの増殖を含意する。▶トラブルの数が急に増えた The number of the troubles *multiplied* rapidly.

〘頻度チャート〙

increase ████████████████████████████████████

grow ███████████████████

multiply █

| | 20 | 40 | 60 | 80 | 100 (%) |

❶〘数・量が増す〙incréase; gain (!主語は人); multiply. (⇒類語; 増加する, 増す) ● 数[量]が増える *increase* in number [amount]. ● 経験が増える *gain* experience. ▶最近海外へ行く学生が増えている The number of students going overseas *has* (×have) *been increasing* lately./Students going overseas *have been increasing* in number lately. (!日常会話では More and more students are going overseas these days. などということも多い) ▶体重が 5 キロ増えた I've gained [*put on*] five kilograms. (!「体重が増える」は gain (in) weight, put on weight) ▶売り上げは 1 年で 2 [3] 倍増えた Sales *have doubled* [*tripled*] in a year. ▶妻の病気で彼の心配事が増えた His wife's illness *added* to his worries.
❷〘繁殖する〙(動物が) breed*; (動植物が)〘書〙própagàte. (⇒繁殖)

フェルト felt. ● フェルトペン a felt(-tip) pen. ● フェルト帽 a felt hat.

プエルトリコ 〘米国の自治領〙Puerto Rico /pwèərtərí:kou/.

フェルマータ 〘延音記号〙〘音楽〙a fermata.

フェレット 〖動物〗a ferret.
フェローシップ 〖研究奨学金〗a fellowship.
フェロモン 〖異性誘引ホルモン〗a pheromone /férə̀moun/.
ふえん 不縁 〖縁遠いこと〗one's poor prospect of marriage; 〖結婚の話が不成立であること〗failure of a marriage talk; 〖縁切り〗釣り合わぬは縁のもと An ill-matched couple will sometimes end in *divorce*.
ふえん 敷衍, 敷行 ▸敷延して述べる explain in detail, 《書》expound.
フェンシング fencing. ●フェンシングの選手 a fencer. ●フェンシングをする fence; do *fencing*.
フェンス a fence. ●フェンスを作る build [erect] a 《wire》*fence* 《around》. ●フェンス直撃の二塁打を打つ hit a double off the *fence* [wall]. ●ライナーでオーバーフェンスする hit a liner over the *fence*. ●フェンス際でフライを捕る catch a fly ball at [against] the wall.
フェンダー 《米》a fender, 《英》a wing; 《泥よけ》a mudguard.
ぶえんりょ 無遠慮 ― **無遠慮な** 形 〖遠慮のない〗unreserved (⇒遠慮); 〖ずけずけ言う〗outspoken; 〖失礼な〗impolite; 〖無作法な〗rude; 〖厚かましい〗impudent, cheeky. ●無遠慮なふるまい *unreserved* [*rude*] behavior. ●無遠慮なことを言う make *outspoken* [*impudent*] remarks. ●無遠慮な口のきき方をする(= 無遠慮に物を言う) speak *rudely* [*impudently*].
フォアグラ 〖<フランス語〗foie gras /fwà: grá:/; goose liver.
フォアハンド forehand.
●フォアハンドストローク a forehand (stroke).
フォアボール 〖野球〗a base on balls; a walk, a (free) pass; 《和製語》four balls. ●ストレートのフォアボールを walk on four pitches. ●フォアボールを出す give 《a batter》a walk; walk (a batter) (on balls). ●フォアボールを得る get [draw] a walk; take the ball four. ●フォアボールで一塁に出る walk to first (on balls); get [take] a base on balls. ●敬遠のフォアボールで歩かされる be intentionally walked. ●押し出しのフォアボールで1点取る score a run on a bases-loaded *walk*; walk [force] in a run.
フォーカス 〖焦点〗a focus 《複 ~es, foci /fóusai/》.
フォーク 〖民族, 民衆〗folk; 〖「フォークソング」の略〗(⇒ フォークソング).
フォーク 〖食卓用〗a fork.
フォーク 〖「フォークボール」の略〗〖野球〗a forkball.
フォークソング 〖民謡〗a fólk /fóuk/ sòng; fólk mùsic. ●フォークソング歌手 a fólk sìnger; a fólk musician.
フォークダンス 〖民族舞踊〗a folk dance. (❗現代風にアレンジしたものも含む)
フォークボール 〖野球〗a forkball.
フォークリフト a forklift (truck).
フォークロア 〖民間伝承, 民俗学〗folklore.
フォーシームファストボール 〖野球〗a four-seam fastball; a four-seamer. 《参考》ホップする速球. 人差し指と中指を縫い目に2回ずつ交差させて投げる; 《関連》ツーシームファストボール a two-seam fastball; a two-seamer).
フォースアウト 〖野球〗a force-out. ●フォースアウトにする make a *force-out*; force (a runner) out; put out (a runner) on a force play. ●ゴロを打ってフォースアウトになる ground into a *force-out*. ●二塁を踏んでフォースアウトにする step on second base for a *force-out*.

フォースプレー 〖野球〗a force (play). ●すべてのベースでフォースプレーができるように打者を歩かせる walk a batter to set up the force at all bases. ▸走者はフォース(プレー)でアウトになった The Runner was put out on a force play.
フォートラン 〖コンピュータ〗FORTRAN 《*formula translation* の略》.
フォーマット 名 〖書式〗〖コンピュータ〗a format.
― **フォーマットする** 動 〖初期化する〗format 《a disk》.
フォーマル ― **フォーマルな** 形 〖形式ばった, 正式の〗formal.
●フォーマルウエア a formal suit [dress]; 《集合的》formal wear.
フォーミュラ 〖公式規格〗a formula.
●フォーミュラカー 〖自動車競技用の規格車〗a fórmula càr. ●フォーミュラプラン 〖証券〗a fórmula plàn. ●フォーミュラワン Formula One (略 F1).
フォーム 《運動の》form. ●彼の走るフォームはすばらしい His running *form* [His *form* in running] is excellent./He has excellent running *form*.
フォームラバー 〖気泡ゴム〗foam rubber. ●フォームラバーの入っているクッション a cushion of *foam rubber*.
フォーラム 〖公開討論会〗a forum. ●(...を議題として) フォーラムを催す hold a *forum* (on ...).
フォールト 〖テニス・バレーボール〗a fault.
フォグライト 〖霧灯〗a fóg làmp, a fóg light.
フォックステリア 〖動物〗《犬》a fox terrier.
フォックストロット 《perform》a foxtrot. 《参考》社交ダンスの一つ)
フォッサマグナ 〖大地溝帯〗the Fossa Magna.
フォト 〖写真〗a photo 《複 ~s》; a photograph.
●フォトジャーナリズム phòtojóurnalism.
ぶおとこ 醜男 an ugly man 《複 men》.
フォルダ(ー) 〖コンピュータ〗a folder.
フォルテ 〖<イタリア語〗〖音楽〗《強く》forte (略 f).
フォロー ― **フォローする** 動 ❶ 〖追求する〗follow up.
●事件をフォローする *follow up* the case.
❷ 〖話を補う〗●彼の説明をフォローする *strengthen* his explanation.
❸ 〖補助する〗●彼の仕事をフォローする *help* him *with* his work.
フォローアップ 名 〖追跡調査〗(a) follow-up.
― **フォローアップする** 動 follow ... up.
フォロースルー follow-through.
フォワード 〖スポーツ〗a forward 《略 fwd》. (❗守備位置をさすときは Ⓤ) ●センターフォワード a centerforward. ●フォワードパス a forward pass.
ふおん 不穏 ― **不穏な** 形 〖不安にするような〗disturbing, 《書》disquieting; (恐ろしい兆候を示す) threatening, ugly. ●不穏な雲行き[情勢] a *threatening* situation. ●不穏な空気をはらむ(やや書) sense a feeling of *disquiet*; sense something *ugly* in the air. ▸軍部に不穏な動きがある Some *trouble* is developing [brewing] in the army.
●不穏分子 dissidents; trouble makers.
フォンデュ(ー) 〖<フランス語〗a fondu(e) /fand(j)ú:/.
フォント 〖同一書体の一揃い〗〖印刷〗a font.
ふおんとう 不穏当 ― **不穏当な** 形 《不適切な》improper. ●不穏当な発言をする make *improper* remarks.
ふか 鱶 〖魚介〗a shark.
ふか 不可 〖成績の〗《米》an F (❗*failure* の頭文字); 〖投票の〗a nay. ●不可とする(= 賛成しない) disapprove 《*of*》. ●数学で不可をとる fail [get an F in] mathematics. ▸(採決で)可とする者5名に対し不可が2名だった The ayes [yeas] were five against

two *nays* [*noes*]./Five were in favor of it, while two were *against* it.

ふか 付加 ── **付加する** add. (⇨付け加える)
- 付加価値 added value. ● 付加価値税〔英国〕 a value-added [×an added-value] tax〔略 VAT〕.(参考 それに類する米国の税は a sales tax)
- 付加疑問〖文法〗a tag question. ● 付加給付 a fringe benefit.(!しばしば複数形で)

ふか 府下 ── **府下に** 副 in the prefecture; (行政権内に) under the prefectural administration.

ふか 負荷〖化学〗a load.

ふか 孵化 图 hatch, incubation.(!前の方は日常的)
- 人工孵化 artificial *incubation*.
── **孵化する** 動 hatch; incubate.
- 孵化器 an incubator. ● 孵化場 a hatchery.

ふか 賦課 图 (税金を課すこと) imposition 〈on〉; (徴収すること) a levy 〈on〉. ● 賦課金をひとり 5,000 円取る *levy* 5,000 yen per person [head].
── **賦課する** 動 impose; levy.
- 賦課額 (査定で決められた税額) the amount assessed (in a tax).

ふか 部下 one's assistant; (見下して)《書》one's subordinate; (男の) one's man (複 men). ▶彼には多くの有能な部下がいる He has a lot of able *assistants* [*men* under him]. ▶彼女は私のおじの部下です She *works* for my uncle./My uncle is her boss. ▶彼は私の直属の部下である He *is under* my direct *supervision*.

ふ :**ふかい** 深い 形 ❶ 〔物が垂直・水平に〕 deep. ● 深い雪 *deep* snow. ● 奥深い森 *deep* woods. ● 深い守備をとる play *deep* [*back*]. ● 左中間の深いところへ打った fall into *deep* left center field. ▶湖はこのあたりがいちばん深い The lake is *deepest* around here.(!主語が他との比較の概念を含まない場合は最上級でも the がつかないことに注意. cf. The lake is *the deepest* in Japan.) ▶ここは泳げるほど深いですか Is this water *deep* enough to swim in?(!in に注意)

❷ 〔程度・状態・性質などが〕 deep; (深遠な)《書》profound. ● 深い傷[ため息] a *deep* wound [sigh]. ● 深い絶望 *deep* despair. ● 深い眠りに落ちる fall into a *deep* [(十分な) a *sound*] sleep. ● 学問の深い人 a person of *deep* [*profound*] learning. ● 深い憎悪を抱く have (×a) *deep-rooted* [(激しい) *fierce*] hatred 〈of, for〉. ▶彼の方が考が深い His thought is *deeper*. ▶その映画は私に深い感銘を与えた The movie made a *deep* [a *profound*] impression on me./I was *deeply* impressed by the movie. ▶彼は学識が深い He has a *profound* [a *deep*] knowledge./His knowledge is *profound*.

❸ 〔濃い〕(森・霧などが) dense, thick; (色が) deep.
● 深い霧 a *dense* [a *thick*, ×a *deep*] fog. ● 深い森 a *dense* [a *thick*, (繁茂した) a *luxuriant*] forest. ● 深い青色 *deep* blue.

❹ 〔親密な〕 close /klóus/. ● 彼女と深い関係にある have a *close* [(深刻な) a *serious*] relationship with her. ▶彼女に深く愛されている I am *deeply* loved by her.

*:**ふかい** 不快 图 (心地が悪いこと) discomfort; (腹立たしいこと) displeasure.
── **不快な** 形 (人を不愉快にさせるような) unpleasant; (人にとって気にくわない) disagreeable; (不快感を与える) offensive; (人をうんざりさせるような) disgusting. (⇨不愉快な) ● 不快なにおい an *unpleasant* [an *offensive*, a *disgusting*] smell. ● 人に不快なことを言うべきではない You should not say *unpleasant* things to [things to *displease*] other people. (!日本語につられて単に people だけでは不適当) ▶彼

は不快そうな顔をした He looked *displeased* [×unpleasant].
- 不快指数 the discomfort index《略 DI》; (温湿指数) the temperature-humidity index《略 THI》.(!英語ται今は後の方を用いる)

ふかい 部会〖部門〗a section;〖クラブの会合〗a club meeting. ● 産業部会 the industrial *section*.

ふかいかん 不快感 unpleasantness, an unpleasant feeling. ● 不快感を覚える (人が) feel *displeased* [(むかつくような) *disgusted*, (いらいらするような) *offended*, (心地が悪い) *uncomfortable*. ● 不快感を表明する express an *unpleasant feeling* [a *feeling of discomfort*]. ▶他人に不快感を与えるな Don't give other people [others] an *unpleasant feeling*. ▶若者たちはムカツクという言葉を異物(=なじみのないもの)に対する不快感を表すのに使っているようだ Young people seem to be using the word 'mukatsuku' to describe *a sense of disgust* toward anything unfamiliar.(!「ムカツク」は英語では stomach-turning (⇨むかつく)

ぶかいしゃ 部外者 (よそ者) an outsider; (かかわりのない人) a person not concerned. ● 部外者の意見を尊重する respect *outside* opinions. ● 部外者立入禁止 揭示 *Private*.

ふがいない 腑甲斐ない (根性のない)《話》gutless,《やや話》spineless; (失望させるような) disappointing; (屈辱的な) humiliating. ▶3 連敗するとはふがいない(=恥ずべき)連中だ They should *be ashamed of* themselves for having lost three consecutive games./It is *humiliating* to have lost three games in a row.

ふかいにゅう 不介入 (特に外国の内政に対しての) nonintervention〈in〉, (特に政治問題に対しての) noninterference〈in〉. ● 民事不介入 *no intervention* [*interference*] in civil affairs. ● 軍事不介入 *no intervention* [*interference*] in military affairs.
- 不介入政策 a policy of nonintervention.

ぶがいひ 部外秘 ── **部外秘の** 形 restricted. ● 部外秘の情報[書類] *restricted* information [documents].

ふかいり 深入り ── **深入りする** 動 go deep [far] into …. ● 事件に深入りする go *deep into* [get *deeply involved in*] an affair. ▶私たちはこんなに深入りしてはいけなかったのです We shouldn't *have gone* this *far*.

ふかおい 深追い ── **深追いする** 動 chase 〈him〉too far; pursue 〈the matter〉further [(しつこく) doggedly /dɔ́(ː)gidli/].

ふかかい 不可解 ── **不可解な** 形 mysterious; (なぞのような) enigmatic; (理解できない) incomprehensible. ● 不可解な事 a mystery; a *mysterious* affair. ● 不可解な行動 (×an) *enigmatic* behavior. ▶彼の突然の失踪は不可解だ His sudden disappearance is a *mystery*./It's *difficult to understand* why he suddenly disappeared.

ふかかち 付加価値 (⇨付加)

ふかぎゃく 不可逆 ── **不可逆的な** 形 irreversible.
── **不可逆的に** 副 irreversibly. ● 不可逆性 irreversibility.

ふかく 不覚 ● 不覚の(=思わず)涙を流す shed tears *in spite of* oneself. ● 前後不覚 (⇨前後 [成句])
- **不覚を取る** (不注意な失敗をする) make a careless mistake [a blunder]〈in〉; (油断していて負ける) lose〈a match〉when (I) do not fight hard.

ふかく 俯角 an angle of depression.

ふかく 深く deep; deeply. ● 深くする[なる] deepen.
● 深く切る[掘る] cut [dig] *deep*. ● 問題を深く掘り下げる go *deep* [*deeply*] into the subject. ● 深く

ふかく おじぎする bow /báu/ *deeply* [*low*]; *make a deep bow*. ●深く悲しむ feel sorrow *deeply*; feel *deep sorrow*. ●その映画に深く感動する be *deeply moved* [*impressed*] by the movie. ●浅い池を深くする *deepen* a shallow pool. ●ご親切に深く感謝いたします I am *deeply* grateful for [(心から) I *sincerely* appreciate] your kindness. ▶ジャングルはしだいに深くなっていった The jungle *was getting thicker*.

ふがく 富岳, 富嶽 Mt. Fuji.
●富嶽百景 (a selection of) one hundred pictures of Mt. Fuji.

ぶがく 舞楽 (説明的な) Japanese court music accompanied by ancient dances.
●舞楽面 a mask for court dances.

ふかくじつ 不確実 图 uncertainty. (⇨確実)
━ **不確実な** 形 uncertain; (信頼できない) unreliable; (不安定な) insecure. ●不確実な情報 *unreliable* information.

ふかくてい 不確定 ━ **不確定な** 形 indefinite; (はっきりしない) uncertain. ●不確定な要素 *indefinite* factors.

ふかけつ 不可欠 ━ **不可欠な** 形 indispensable, essential 《*to, for*》. (⇨必要な) ▶水は我々の生活に不可欠だ Water is *indispensable* [*essential*] *for* our life.

ふかこうりょく 不可抗力 图 (天災) an act of God.
━ **不可抗力の** 形 (避けられない) inevitable, unavoidable. ▶その事故は不可抗力だった The accident was *inevitable* [*unavoidable, beyond our control*].

ふかさ 深さ depth; (知的な) profundity. ●川の深さを測る measure [*sound*] the *depth* of a river. ●彼の知恵の深さ the *depth* [*profundity*] of his wisdom. ●10メートルの深さに[で] at a [×*the*] *depth* of ten meters. ●これくらいの深さの所 a place (which is) about this *deep* [《まれ》*depth*].
会話「プールの深さはどれくらいですか」「2メートルです」"How *deep* is the swimming pool?" "It's two meters *deep* [*in depth*]."

ふかざけ 深酒 ●深酒をする drink heavily [*hard, too much*].

ふかざら 深皿 a dish.

ふかし 不可視 invisibility.
●不可視光線 an invisible ray.

ふかしぎ 不可思議 ━ **不可思議な** 形 (神秘的な) mysterious; (奇妙な) strange.

ふかしんじょうやく 不可侵条約 a nonaggression pact [*treaty*]. (⇨条約)

ふかす 吹かす ●たばこを吹かす smoke (a cigarette). ●パイプを吹かす *smoke* a pipe; *puff* 《*away*》 *at* one's pipe. ●エンジンを吹かす run 《《話》*rev* 《*up*》》 the engine. ●バイクを吹かしている音 A the sound of a *revving* motorbike.

ふかす 蒸かす steam. (⇨蒸(む)す)

ふかち 不可知 ━ **不可知の** 形 『哲学』 (知ることができない) unknowable.
●不可知論 agnosticism. ●不可知論者 an agnostic.

ぶかつ 部活 club /kláb/ activities. (⇨クラブ)

ぶかっこう 不格好 ━ **不格好な** 形 (形の悪い) unshapely, ill-shaped; (無器用な) clumsy; (ぎさまな) awkward. ▶彼女のスカートは不格好だ. 座ると太ももがあらわに出します Her skirt *doesn't fit her well*. It rides up to her thighs when she sits down. ▶彼は不格好な手つきで箸(はし)を使う He uses chopsticks *awkwardly* [*clumsily*]./He is *awkward* [*clumsy*] at using chopsticks.

ふかっぱつ 不活発 ━ **不活発な** 形 《やや書》inactive; (沈滞した) dull. ●不活発な市場 an *inactive* [*a dull, a sluggish*] market.

ふかづめ 深爪 深爪をする cut a nail to the quick. (❗to the quick は「爪の下の生身まで」の意)

ふかで 深手 a serious [a severe] wound. ▶彼は市街戦で深手を負った He *got seriously* [*gravely*] *wounded* in the street fighting.

ふかなさけ 深情け deep love. ▶悪女の深情け (⇨悪女[成句])

*****ふかのう 不可能** 图 impossibility.
━ **不可能な** 形 impossible; (実行不可能な) impracticable. ●不可能な仕事 an *impossible* task. ●実行不可能な計画 an *impracticable* plan. ▶彼にとって不可能なことはない Nothing is *impossible* 《*to* [*for*]》 him. ▶それは不可能に近い It's almost 《《話》next to, ×*nearly*》 *impossible*. ▶彼がその試合に勝つのは不可能だ It's *impossible* for him to win the match./He *can't* [*is unable to*, ×*is impossible to*] win the match./The match *is impossible* [*not possible*] for him to win. (❗*not possible* は不定詞の目的語を主語にできる(⇨可能)) ▶この単語は翻訳不可能だ This word is *impossible* to translate. (❗It *is impossible to* [*We can't*] translate this word. ともいえる)/This word *can't* [×*is not able to*] be translated. (❗be (un)able to の後には通例受身は続かない)/《やや書》 This word *is not capable* [*incapable*] of translation [*being translated*].
会話「それを今日中に渡してください」「お言葉ですが, それはとうてい不可能(=問題外)です」"Let me have them by tonight." "I beg your ╲pardon. That's *out of the question*."

ふかひ 不可避 ━ **不可避な** 形 (避けて通れない) unavoidable; (必然的に起こる) inevitable.

ふかひれ (食材としての) shark fin.
●ふかひれスープ shark(-)fin soup.

ふかふか fluffy; (柔らかい) soft. ●ふかふかした毛のコート a *fluffy* woolen coat. ●できたてのふかふかしたパン freshly baked *soft* bread. ▶じゅうたんは歩くとふかふかしていた The carpet sank under my feet.

ぶかぶか 『物が大きすぎる様子』too big, too large; (だぶだぶの) baggy (❗ふくらんだ感じのものについて用いる). ●この帽子は私にはぶかぶか This hat is *too large* for me. ▶彼はぶかぶかのオーバーを着ていた He was in a *baggy* overcoat.

ぷかぷか ●(たばこなどを)ぷかぷかふかす puff 《*away*》《*at*》. ●(水などに浮かんで)ぷかぷかする (浮かぶ) float (lightly); (漂う) drift. ▶彼はよく本を読みながらぷかぷかパイプをふかします He often *puffs* 《*away*》 *at* his pipe as he reads. ▶魚がぷかぷか口を動かしている The fish *is puffing* its mouth. ▶木ぎれが水にぷかぷか浮いている A piece of wood *is floating* [×*floats*] on the water.

ふかぶかと 深々と ●deeply. ●深々と頭を下げる bow /báu/ *deeply* [*very low*] 《*to* him》; make a *deep bow* 《*to* him》. ●深々といすに座る *sit back* in a chair.

ふかぶん 不可分 ━ **不可分の** 形 (分割できない) indivisible; (切り離せない) inseparable 《*from*》. ▶その二つの問題は不可分の関係にある The two issues *are inseparable* [*can't be separated*] *from* each other).

ふかまる 深まる ▶夜が深まるにつれて寒くなった It got colder as the night *advanced* [*(進む) went on*]. ▶秋がだいぶ深まっていた We were well into fall 《米》 [autumn 《主に英》]. ▶両国の関係はいっそう深まった The relations between the two countries *have*

ふかみ 深み 深みのある研究 a *deep* [《やや書》a *profound*] study. ▶彼の詩には深みがない His poetry lacks [has no] *depth* [*profundity*].
● 深みにはまる（深い所に）fall into a *deep place* [the *depths*]《*of* a river》;（窮地に陥る）get oneself into a real *fix*.

ふかみどり 深緑 deep green;（暗い緑）dark green.

ふかめる 深める （深くする）deepen;（促進する）promote;（豊かにする）enrich;（育成する）cultivate. ●相互の理解を深める promote [deepen, develop] one's mutual understanding. ●友情を深める become very friendly 《with》, improve one's friendship 《with》.(!) *cultivate* a friendship は相手を利用する目的で付き合いを濃くするの意が強い）
● 経験を深める *enrich* one's experience.

ふかよみ 深読み ― 深読みする 動 ▶君は彼女の言ったことを深読みしている You are trying to read something more than she actually meant by her words. (!) ✕*read between the lines* は「表面に表れない相手の意図を的確に読み取る」の意でここでは不適）

ブカレスト〖ルーマニアの首都〗Bucharest /búːkərèst/.

ふかん 俯瞰 ―俯瞰する 動 look over... from above; have a bird's-eye view 《of the village》.
● 俯瞰図 a bird's-eye view.

ぶかん 武官 〖陸軍〗〖中国の都市〗a military [a naval] officer. (!) 英語では特に commissioned officer（士官）をいう）●大使館付き武官 a military [a naval] attaché.

ぶかん 武漢〖中国の都市〗Wuhan /wúːhɑ́ːn/.

ふかんしへい 不換紙幣 inconvertible paper money. (!)(1) 英語では米ドルと交換できない紙幣をも意味する。(2) nonconvertible は通用ใช้ない）

ふかんしょう 不干渉 （特に外国の国政に対しての）non-intervention 《in》;（特に政治問題に対しての）non-interference 《in》. ●他国の内政不干渉政策 a policy of *nonintervention in* the internal affairs of other countries.

ふかんしょう 不感症 图 （性的な）frigidity.
― **不感症の** 形 ▶彼はいわゆに不感症になっている（何とも思わない）He *thinks nothing of* [（何のやましさも感じない）*has no scruples about*] taking bribes.

***ふかんぜん 不完全** 图 〖欠けた部分のあること〗incompleteness; 〖完璧でないこと〗imperfection; 〖欠点〗a fault; 〖欠陥〗a defect.
― **不完全な** 形 incomplete; imperfect; faulty; defective. ●フランス語の不完全な知識 an *imperfect* [an *incomplete*] knowledge of French.
▶それは多くの点で不完全ではあるが価値の高い作品である It's *imperfect* in many respects, but a work of great value. ▶私のチョウの収集はまだ不完全だ My collection of butterflies is still *incomplete*.
● 不完全燃焼 incomplete combustion. ▶今日の試合は不完全燃焼のまま終わった（＝最善を尽くすことができなかった）ような気がする I feel as if 〖《話》like〗 I *couldn't do my best* in today's match.

ふき 蕗 〖植物〗a (Japanese) butterbur.
ふき 不帰 ●不帰の客となる〖書〗depart this life; make one's exit.
ふき 付記 an addendum (複 addenda);（注記）a (supplementary) note;（追伸）a postscript（略 P.S., p.s., PS).
ふぎ 不義 （不貞）adúltery. ●不義を犯す commit *adultery* 《with》. ▶天に代わって不義を討つ We strike the *unjust* on behalf of Heaven.
ふぎ 府議 〖「府議会議員」の略〗（⇨府議会）

***ぶき 武器** arms; a weapon /wépn/;《集合的》weaponry. (!) *arms* は兵器の総称で数詞 many などをつけない。この語は腕の延長としての武器のイメージが強い。一方、weapons は原爆を含むすべての武器を指す）●武器を携帯する carry a weapon. ●武器を供給する provide *weapons* 《for》. ●武器を取って敵に立ち向かう take up *arms* [rise in *arms*] against the enemy. ●捕虜から武器を取り上げる take the *weapons away* from the prisoners; disarm the prisoners. ●武器を捨てる lay down [《あきらめて》give up] one's *arms*. ●涙は女の武器 Women's tears are the best *weapon*.
● 武器弾薬 arms and ammunition.

ぶぎ 武技 martial arts.

ふきあげる 吹き上げる （風が）blow*... up,（液体などを勢いよく）shoot*... up, spout /spáut/. ▶風が落ち葉を吹き上げた The wind *blew up* the fallen leaves. ▶火山は溶岩を空高く吹き上げた The volcano *shot up* [*spouted*] lava high into the sky.

ふきあれる 吹き荒れる rage. ▶風が吹き荒れた The wind *raged* [*blew violently*].

ブギウギ 〖音楽〗bòogie-wóogie.

ふきおろす 吹き下ろす ●山から吹き下ろす風 a wind blowing down the mountain.

ふぎかい 府議会 a prefectural assembly.
● 府議会議員 a member of the prefectural assembly.

ふきかえ 吹き替え 〖映画などの代役〗a stand-in; 〖録音での〗dubbing.

ふきかえす 吹き返す （意識を取り戻す）come* around; come to oneself (!) この oneself は省略されることがある). ▶彼女は人工呼吸で息を吹き返した She *regained consciousness* [*came to 《herself》*] by artificial respiration.

ふきかえる 葺き替える reroof. (!) 「屋根の大々的修理をする」の意にも用いることができる）

ふきかける 吹き掛ける （息を）breathe 《on, upon》;（たばこの煙などを）puff;（スプレーで）spray. ●鏡に息を吹きかける *breathe* [*blow*] on the mirror. ▶彼は（たばこの）煙を私の顔に吹きかけた He blew [puffed] cigarette smoke in my face.

ふきけす 吹き消す blow*... out. ▶彼はろうそくを吹き消した He *blew out* the candle.

ふきげん 不機嫌 ― **不機嫌な** 形 bad-tempered; 〖怒ってむっつりした〗sullen /sʌ́ln/,《話》cross; 〖不快な〗displeased. ●不機嫌である be in a bad mood [temper]. ▶彼女は不機嫌な顔をしている She looks *sullen* [*displeased*]./She has a *sour* [a *long*] face.

ふきこぼれる 吹きこぼれる boil over. ▶台所で何か（なべ）が吹きこぼれている Something's [The pot *is*] *boiling over* in the kitchen.

ふきこむ 吹き込む ❶ 〖風・雪などが〗 ▶戸のすき間から（部屋に）雨が吹き込んだ Rain blew [was blown] *in* [*into*] the room] through a gap in the door.
❷ 〖息などを入れる〗 ▶風船に息を吹き込む（＝ふくらます）*blow up* a balloon.
❸ 〖感情・考えなどを〗 ▶生徒たちに学習熱を吹き込む *inspire* [*infuse*] students *with* eagerness to learn; *inspire* eagerness to learn *in* students; *infuse* eagerness to learn *into* students.
❹ 〖録音する〗 recórd. (!) アクセントに注意）●演説をテープに吹き込む *record* a speech *on* tape; *tape* a speech.

ふきこむ 拭き込む ●廊下をふき込む *polish* the floor *until it shines*; *polish* the floor *well*.

ふきさらし 吹きさらし ●吹きさらしのプラットホーム a (railroad) platform *exposed to the wind*;《更

ふきすさぶ 吹きすさぶ ●一晩中強風が吹きすさんだ The strong wind blew violently [(吹き荒れた) raged; (ひゅうひゅう吹いた) howled] all night.

ふきそ 不起訴〖法律〗(陪審制での) non-prosecution /-indáitmənt/. ●不起訴にする (人を) do not prosecute [indict /indáit/]; (提訴告発をとりやめる) drop charges 《against》. ▶彼は不起訴になった They decided not to prosecute him./He was spared charges./Charges were dropped against him.

ふきそうじ 拭き掃除 (ふくこと) wiping; (ごしごし磨くこと) scrubbing. ●床のふき掃除をする wipe the floor; (モップで) mop the floor.

ふきそく 不規則 ── 不規則な 形 irregular. (↔regular) ●不規則な生活をする live an irregular life; keep irregular hours. ●患者の呼吸は荒く不規則だった The patient's breathing was hard and irregular./The patient was breathing hard and irregularly [(and) at irregular intervals]. ●不規則動詞〖文法〗an irregular verb. ●不規則変化〖文法〗(an) irregular conjugation.

ふきたおす 吹き倒す blow*... down. ●多くの木を吹き倒す blow down a lot of trees.

ふきだす 吹き出す, 噴き出す ❶〖液体が〗spout /spáut/ [spurt] (out); (ほとばしる) gush (out); 〖煙・ガスなどが〗(勢いよく) jet (-tt-), jet out. ▶傷口から血が噴き出した Blood spouted [spurted, gushed] (out) from the cut. ▶煙が噴き出した Smoke jetted out.
❷〖笑い出す〗burst* out laughing [into laughter].
❸〖風が〗begin* [start] to blow.

ふきだまり 吹きだまり a drift. ●雪の吹きだまり (場所) the place where snow drifts; (たまった雪) a snowdrift. ▶雪が塀の向こう側に吹きだまりになっていた The snow lay drifted in at the other side of the wall.

ふきちらす 吹き散らす blow*... about, scatter. ▶強い風が書類を吹き散らした A strong wind blew about [scattered] the papers.

ふきつ 不吉 ── 不吉な 形 (悪い前兆になりそうな) óminous; (凶事を予感させる) sínister; (縁起の悪い) unlucky; (不安な) uneasy. ●不吉な夢[予言] an ominous dream [prediction]. ●不吉な兆し a sinister symptom; an evil omen. ●不吉な感じのする黒雲 sinister-looking [ominous-looking] black clouds. ●不吉な数 an unlucky number. 〖参考〗13 など) ▶失敗するんじゃないかという不吉な予感がした I had a premonition that I might fail. (❗️premonition は通例「不吉な, いやな」の意を含む) ▶西洋では黒猫が前を横切ると不吉だとされる In the West, a black cat is considered bad luck if it crosses your path.

ふきつける 吹きつける 〖風雨が〗blow* 《against》; 〖塗料を〗spray. ●ペンキを壁に吹きつける spray paint on the wall; spray the wall with paint. ▶風が窓に[顔に]強く吹きつけた The wind blew hard against the window [in my face].

ぶきっちょ ── ぶきっちょな 形 clumsy. (⇨不器用)

ふきつのる 吹きつのる (風などが) blow* harder.

ふきでもの 吹き出物 (発疹) a rash; (若者特有のいくつきても複数形にしない) 〖にきび〗a pimple, 〖英〗a spot (❗️通例複数形で); 〖はれもの〗a boil. ●吹き出物ができる have a rash [pimples] 《on one's face》. (⇨ぶつぶつ, にきび)

ふきとばす 吹き飛ばす 〖風などが〗blow*... off, (遠くへ) blow... away. (⇨飛ばす❶) ▶あらしで屋根がわらが数枚吹き飛ばされた Several tiles were blown off from the roof by [in] the storm./The storm blew several tiles off the roof. (❗️後の例の off は前置詞)

ふきとぶ 吹き飛ぶ ▶立て看板が強風で吹き飛んだ A billboard blew off in a gale [was blown off by a gale]./A gale blew off a billboard. ▶彼の一言で彼女の心配は吹き飛んだ Her anxiety vanished when he said that./His words dispelled her anxiety.

ふきとる 拭き取る wipe... off. ●窓の汚れを拭き取る wipe the dirt off [away from] a window.

ふきながし 吹き流し a streamer.

ふきぬけ 吹き抜け 〖建築〗a void; (階段の) a stairwell.

ふきぬける 吹き抜ける ▶寒風が松林の間をひゅうひゅうと吹き抜けている The cold wind is whistling through the pine trees.

ふきのとう 蕗の薹 a butterbur sprout.

ふきはらう 吹き払う ▶強風で雲が吹き払われた The strong wind blew away all the clouds in the sky./All the clouds in the sky were blown away by the strong wind.

ふきぶり 吹き降り rain with strong winds; (横なぐりの雨) a driving rain.

ふきまくる 吹き捲る ▶台風は一晩中吹きまくった The typhoon raged [blew very hard] all night.

ふきまわし 吹き回し (⇨風 〖成句〗)

ぶきみ 不気味 ── 不気味な 形 weird /wíərd/; uncanny; 《話》creepy (⇨気味 〖気味(の)悪い〗)

ふきや 吹き矢 (矢) a dart; (矢筒) a blowpipe, a blowgun. ●吹き矢を飛ばす blow [shoot] a dart 《with a blowgun》.

ふきやむ 吹き止む blow* over; (だんだん弱くなる) die (〜d; dying) down [away]. ▶風は夕方には吹き止んだ The wind blew over [blew itself out] by the evening.

* **ふきゅう 普及** 名 spread /spréd/ (❗️通例 the 〜); 〖大衆化〗popularization; 〖製品の浸透〗penetration; 〖拡散〗〖書〗diffusion. ●教育[インターネット]の普及 the spread of education [the Internet]. ●パソコンの普及率 the penetration rate [levels] of PC 《into the country》.

── **普及する** 動 〖広まる〗spread*, become* widespread; 〖広める〗spread, 〖知識などを〗《書》diffuse /difjúːz/, (思想などを宣伝して)〖書〗própagàte; 〖一般化になる〗become popular; 〖大衆化させる〗《書》popularize. ●知識を普及する spread [diffuse] knowledge. ▶今日では教育が非常に普及している Nowadays education is widely spread. ▶携帯電話は全国に普及している Cellular phones are widespread [広く使われている] (are in wide (spread) use, are widely used) all over the country. ▶DVD プレーヤーはますます普及している DVD players are becoming increasingly [more and more] popular.

■ **DISCOURSE**
イーメールが通信手段としてこれほど普及した今, 高校では英文ライティングに重点を置くべきである Now that e-mail has become such a popular means of communication, high schools should place a greater emphasis on English writing. (❗️now that ... (...した今) は因果関係を述べるときに用いるディスコースマーカー. now that 以下の節は通例現在完了形または現在形)

ふきゅう ●普及版 a popular edition.

ふきゅう 不休 不眠不休 (⇨不眠 (成句))

ふきゅう 不朽 ─ **不朽の** 形 (不滅の) immortal; (いつまでも続く) everlasting, enduring. ●不朽の名作 an *immortal* [an *enduring*] masterpiece. ●不朽の名声 *undying* fame.

ふきゅう 不急 ─ **不急の** 形 not urgent; not pressing.

ふきゅう 腐朽 名 decay; rot; (金属の腐食) corrosion. ●腐朽を防ぐ prevent 《it》 from *decay*; prevent *decay*.
─ **腐朽する** 動 decay; go* [fall*] into decay; rot (-tt-); corrode.

ふきょ 不許 ●不許複製 All rights reserved.

ふきょう 不況 名〖深刻で長期的な〗(a) depression;〖景気の一時的後退〗(a) recession;〖景気の不調〗slack business, a (business) slump;〖景気の沈滞〗stagnation;〖不況の時勢〗bad [hard] times. ●1930年代の世界的不況 the worldwide *depression* of the 1930s. ●長引く不況 a protracted *recession*. ●不況に陥る go into *depression*. ●不況のどん底にある be at the bottom [in the depths] of the *depression*. ●不況から抜け出す come [get, climb] out of the *depression*; (乗り切る) ride out of the *depression*. ●円高不況 *endaka* [yen appreciation] *recession*. ▶不況が深刻になった The *depression* [recession] has worsened [deepened]. ▶映画産業は厳しい不況に見舞われている The film industry is experiencing [is in the grip of] a severe *depression*. (❗(1) in the grip of ... 「...につかまえられて」の意. (2) 不況産業は a *depressed* industry)
●不況カルテル (form) a recession [a depression] cartel.

ふきょう 不興・不興を買う offend [give offense to]《him》; displease, 《やや書》incur《his》displeasure, 《話》get on《his》bad [wrong] side.

ふきょう 布教 propagation; (主にキリスト教の伝道) mission; (布教活動) missionary work.
─ **布教する** 動《書》propagate; (キリスト教) evangelize.
●布教者 a propagator; a missionary.

ふきょう 不器用 ─ **不器用な** 形 awkward, clumsy. (❗後の方が強意的で, 悪い結果を暗示する) ●手先が不器用だ be *awkward* [*clumsy*] *with* one's hands; 《話》be all thumbs. (❗(1)《英》で be all fingers and thumbs ともいう. (2)《話》で手先が一時的に思うように動かないときに用いることが多い) ●不器用な手つきで in an *awkward* way, awkwardly; with *clumsy* hands, clumsily.

ぶぎょう 奉行 〖歴史〗(江戸幕府の職制の一つ) a *bugyo* (働~s); a magistrate.
●奉行所 (特に町奉行の) a magistrate's office.

ふぎょうせき 不行跡 (不品行) misbehavior; (特に性的な) misconduct.

ふきょうわおん 不協和音 《書》(a) discord (↔concord), 《やや書》dissonance (↔consonance). ●彼らの間に不協和音が聞こえる There seems to be a note of *discord* among them./They don't seem to be in harmony.

ふきょく 部局 a department. (⇨部)

ふきょく 舞曲 dánce mùsic.

ぶきよさらば『武器よさらば』 *A Farewell to Arms*. (参考) ヘミングウェーの小説

ふきよせ 吹き寄せ ❶〖料理の〗a dish of nicely-assorted *tempura* or *nimono*; well-assorted dry Japanese sweets. ❷〖音楽の〗曲曲（ きょく）吹き寄せ a medley of tunes.

ふぎり 不義理 名〖社交上の〗neglect of social obligations; (忘恩) ingratitude (⇨義理);〖金銭上の〗an unpaid debt /dét/. ▶彼にそんなに不義理をすべきではない You shouldn't *be* so *ungrateful to* him.
─ **不義理な** 形 (恩知らずの) ungrateful.

ふきりつ 不規律 名 a lack of discipline; indiscipline; (不穏当) an impropriety.
─ **不規律な** 形 indisciplined; improper.

ぶきりょう 不器量 ─ **不器量な** 形 ●不器量な女 a plain〖《米》a *homely*〗woman. (⇨醜い)

ふきん 付近 名 a neighborhood;《書》vicinity. (❗後の方が範囲が広い)(⇨近所) ▶付近一帯は炎に包まれた The whole *neighborhood* was enveloped in flames.
【付近に［を, で］】 nearby (❗単独で副詞として用いる);〖...の近くに〗near ...;〖この辺りに〗around〖《主に英》round, 《主に米》about〗(...). ●その家の付近を捜索する search *around* [*about*] the house. ▶付近には家は一軒もなかった There was no house *nearby* [*around*]. ▶事故はどこかこの付近で起こった The accident happened somewhere *near* here [*around* here, *in* this *neighborhood*].
─ **付近の** 〖隣接した〗neighboring;〖すぐ近くの〗nearby;〖近隣の〗adjacent /ədʒéɪsnt/. (❗接している場合もある) ●付近の村々 the *neighboring* [*nearby*] villages; the villages *nearby*. ●現場付近の家 the houses *around* [*adjacent to*] the scene.

ふきん 布巾 (食器をふく)《米》a dísh tòwel,《英》a tea towel [cloth]; a kitchen towel.

ふきんこう 不均衡 (an) imbálance;〖不釣り合い〗disproportion;〖不平等〗(an) inequality. ●日米貿易の不均衡 the trade *imbalance* [xunbálance] *between* Japan and America; Japan's trade *imbalance* with the United States. ●富の不均衡 *inequalities* in wealth. ●輸入額と輸出額の不均衡を是正する correct〖《書》redress〗an *imbalance* between imports and exports.
─ **不均衡な** 形 unbalanced; disproportionate; unequal.

ふきんしん 不謹慎 ─ **不謹慎な** 形〖慎みに欠けること〗immodest; (不遠慮な) unreserved; (無分別な) indiscréet, thoughtless; (みだらな, 下品な) indecent /ɪndíːsnt/. ●不謹慎な冗談 an *indecent* joke. ▶彼女の言動は不謹慎のそしりをまぬがれないShe may well be criticized for her *lack of modesty* [*discretion*].

ふく 吹く ❶〖風が〗blow*. ▶風がひどく吹いている It [The wind] *is blowing* hard. (❗日常会話ではIt's very [really] *windy*. の方が普通) ▶風はどちらから吹いていますか Which direction *is* the wind *blowing* [*coming*] from?
❷〖人が〗blow*; (ぷっと吹く) puff /pʌf/. ●食べ物を吹いてさます *blow* (*on*) one's food to make it cool. ●ろうそくを吹き消す *blow* [*puff*] a candle *out*.
❸〖吹奏楽器を〗blow*; (演奏する) play. ●口笛を吹く whistle. ●笛[トランペット]を吹く *blow* a whistle [a trumpet]. (❗トランペットの場合は *play* the trumpet も可)

ふく 服 clothes /klóʊz, klóʊðz/;《集合的》clothing /klóʊðɪŋ/; (a) dress; (a) cóstume; wear; a suit; an outfit.

> **使い分け** **clothes** 「服」の意を表す最も一般的な語. 常に複数扱いで数詞は用いない. 「1[2]着」はa suit [two suits] of *clothes* という. 「多くの服」は many [much] *clothes*. (❗口語では many の方が普通)

clothing clothes より堅い語. clothes より意味が広く, 靴・帽子などを含むことがある.「1着, 1点」は an article (a piece) of *clothing*.「多くの服」は much (×many) *clothing*.
dress ある行事・目的にふさわしい服装または着飾るための衣服. 女性のワンピースの意では Ⓒ.
costume ある時代・地域・国民などに特有の衣服. 特に舞台で着られるようなもの.
wear 特定の目的のための服で, 複合語でよく用いられる. 特に商業用語. 集合的に用い単数扱い.
suit 一そろいの洋服で, 紳士用背広, 婦人用スーツをいう.
outfit 特定の場合に着る衣装一そろい.

① 【~(の)服】 夏服 súmmer clóthes [clóthing, wèar], ● 紳士〔婦人〕服 men's [women's] clothes; men's [ladies] wear. ● 和服 Japanese clothes; a kimono. ● 夜会服 évening drèss. ● 戦闘服 báttle drèss. 〖軍〗fatigues /fətí:gz/. ● 江戸時代の服 the *costume* of the Edo period. ● 宇宙服 a spáce sùit. ● スキー服 a ski *outfit* [*suit*].
② 【服を】服を着る [脱ぐ] put on [take off] one's *clothes*. ▶ 亜美は服をたくさん持っている Ami has a lot of *clothes*./Ami has a large *wardrobe*. (!) wardrobe は個人や劇団などが持っている全衣服の意) ● 彼はいい服を着ている He is wearing fine *clothes*. ● この進行形は「今"い"服を身につけている」という一時的な状態を表す)/(立派な身なりをしている) He *is* well *dressed*.
③ 【服は】 ▶ この服は彼女によく似合う This *dress* looks [These *clothes* look] very nice on her. (!) ×This clothes.... とはいわない)

*ふく **拭く** [表面を軽くぬぐう, (ふき取る) wipe ... away [off]; (乾かす) dry. ● 口をハンカチで*ふく* wipe one's mouth *with* [*on*] a handkerchief. (!) with は「…を用いて」, on は「…にこすりつけて」の意) ● 涙をふく wipe one's tears *away* [*off*]; *dry* one's tears. ● 体をタオルでふく *dry* oneself with a towel. ● テーブルをきれいにふく *wipe* a table clean; give a table *a good wipe*. ● 窓をふく (=きれいにする) *clean* the windows. ▶ 彼女は皿をふいて食器棚へしまった She wiped the plates (*dry*) and put them away in the cupboard.

ふく **副** [写し] a duplicate, a copy. (⇨ 口 ❸)
ふく **福** (good) luck; good fortune. ● 福の神 (⇨福の神) ▶ 笑う門には福来る (⇨笑う [成句])
● 福は内, 鬼は外 In with good luck, out with the evil spirit.

ふく **葺く** roof; (わら, かやなどで) thatch. ● かわらで屋根をふく *roof* a house with tiles. ● わらでふいた古い農家 an old farmhouse *thatched* with straws; a *thatched* old farmhouse.

ふく **噴く** [書] emit (-tt-); (煙を) smoke, jet (-tt-) out; (液体を) spout, spurt. ● 火を噴く burst into flames; (火山が) erupt. ▶ 三原山が煙を噴いている Mt. Mihara *is smoking*./Smoke is coming from Mt. Mihara. ▶ 近くで鯨が潮を噴くのを見た I watched a whale *blow* [*spout*] not far from me.

ふく- **副-** (代理[次位]の) vice-; (下位の) sub-; (共同の) co-; (補助の) assistant; (代理の) deputy; (補充の) supplementary; (追加の) additional. ● 副社長 [大統領] a *vice*-president. (⇨会社) ● 副議長 [会長] a *vice*-chairperson. ● 副操縦士 a copilot. ● 副大臣 (日本の) a senior vice-minister. 〖関連〗政務次官 a state secretary/政務官 a parliamentary secretary. ● 東京の副都心 a *subcenter* of Tokyo. ● 副支配人 an assistant manager. ● 副知事 a *deputy* governor;《米》(州の) a lieutenant governor. ● 副収入 *additional* income.

ふく **河豚** 〖魚介〗a *fugu*; a blowfish, a globefish, a swellfish, a puffer (fish).
● 河豚中毒 blowfish poisoning. ● 河豚料理 a blowfish dish.

ふく **武具** ● 武具一式 a suit of armor.
ふくあい **不具合** (欠陥) a defect, a fault (*in*); (不備) a flaw (*in*); (小さな技術上の問題) a glitch (*in*); (プログラムの誤り) a bug (*in*). ● 部品の不具合を直す correct a *defect in* [×of] a part.

ふくあつ **腹圧** 〖医学〗abdominal pressure.
ふくあん **腹案** (考え) an idea; (計画) a plan. ● 腹案を練る work out a *plan*.

ふくい **復位** 图 restoration; 〖書〗reinstatement.
— **復位する** 動 be restored (*to*); 〖書〗be reinstated (*in* one's former position, *as* a king).

ふくい **腹囲** (⇨ウエスト)
ふくいく **馥郁** ▶ バラの馥郁とした香りが応接間に漂っていた The *fragrance* of roses filled the drawing room.

ふくいん **幅員** the width of a road. ● 幅員 30 メートルの道路 a road 30 meters *across* [*wide*].

ふくいん **復員** 图 demobilization.
— **復員する** 動 be demobilized and sent home.
● 復員軍人 an ex-serviceman, an ex-soldier.

ふくいん **福音** 〖よい知らせ〗(a piece of) good news (*for*); 〖キリストの教え〗the gospel.
● 福音書 the Gospel. 〖参考〗新約聖書の *Matthew*, *Mark*, *Luke*, *John* の 4 書またはそのうちの 1 書)

ふぐう **不遇** (不運) one's ill fate. ● 不遇をかこつ complain about 〖書〗bemoan one's (*ill*) *fate*.
● 一生不遇である (世に認められない) *remain unknown* 〖obscure〗, (出世できない) *unsuccessful* all one's life.

ふくえき **服役** 图 (懲役) penal /pí:nl/ servitude. ● 服役中である be *in prison*.
— **服役する** 動 serve one's term [sentence]. ● 3 年間懲役する *serve* three years *in prison*.
● 服役者 a prisoner; (受刑者) a convict.

ふくえん **復縁** 图 a reconciliation with one's former husband [wife].
— **復縁する** 動 be reconciled with one's former husband [wife]. ● 彼女に復縁を迫る press her to come back to him; demand that she come back to him.

ふくおんせい **副音声** a SAP channel. (!) SAP は secondary *audio* program の略). ▶ この番組は副音声 (=他の言語) でも聴ける You can listen to this program in another language (spoken on the same channel).

ふくがく **復学** — **復学する** 動 return [come back] to school (after one's sickness). (!) 後の方が口語的)

ふくかん **副官** (⇨副官(ふっかん))
ふくがん **復顔** 图 (a) restoration of a dead person's facial features.
— **復顔する** 動 restore the facial features.
● 復顔像 a restored image of a dead person's face.

ふくがん **複眼** compound eyes.
ふくぎょう **副業** (have) a job on the side (!) ×a side job とはいわない); (アルバイト)《have》a part-time job.

ふくげん **復元** 图 ● 壁画の復元 the *restoration* of a wall painting.

ふくこう 復元する 動 ●古代ギリシャの遺跡の一部を復元する *restore* (a) part of the ancient Greek ruins. ●復元図 a *restoration*.

ふくこう 腹腔 〔解剖〕 the abdominal cavity.

ふくごう 複合 〔複合物〕 a compound; a composite; 〔複合体〕 a complex.
── 複合の 形 compound; composite; complex.
●複合汚染 compound pollution [contamination]. ●複合企業 a conglomerate /kəŋglάmərət/. ●複合競技 〔スキー〕 a combined race. ●アルペン〔ノルディック〕複合(競技) the Alpine [Nordic] combined (race). (参考) 前の方は滑降と回転の, 後の方は距離とジャンプの複合競技) ●複合語 a compound (word). ●複合ターミナル a combined transport terminal. ●複合肥料 (配合肥料) a compound fertilizer. ●複合輸送 combined transport.

ふくごうおせん 『複合汚染』 *Compound Solution*. (参考) 有吉佐和子の小説)

ふくこうかんしんけい 副交感神経 〔解剖〕 the parasympathetic nerve.

ふくさ 袱紗 a handkerchief-sized silk wrapper; (茶道用の) a small silk cloth for the tea ceremony.

ふくざい 服罪 ── 服罪する 動 (罪に服する) accept a 《jail [two-year]》 sentence; (刑期を務める) serve one's time.

ふくざつ 複雑 名 (a) complexity; (a) complication.
── 複雑な 形 complex (↔simple); cómplicàted; (やや書) íntricate; invólved; mixed.

> 使い分け **complex** たくさんの異なる部分からなっていて分かりにくいこと.
> **complicated** あまりに複雑なため分かりにくいこと.
> **intricate** 多くの細かい部分から成り立っていること.
> **involved** complicated とほぼ同意だが, 錯綜(さくそう)・混乱を強調する.
> **mixed** さまざまな種類のものがまざり合って複雑なこと.

●複雑な装置 a *complicated* [a *complex*, an *intricate*] device. ●長くて複雑な手順 a long and *complicated* [*involved, complex*] process. ▶それは事態をいっそう複雑にするだけだ It'll just further *complicate* the situation./It will only *make* the situation *more complicated*. ▶学生は数学を複雑で分かりにくいと思うかもしれない Students may think that mathematics is *too complex* [*complicated*] to understand. ▶そのことでは複雑な心境だ I have *mixed* feelings about it.

> ■ DISCOURSE
> コンピュータは実に生活を複雑にした Computers have **certainly** made life more *complex*. (!) certainly (実には主張を表すディスコースマーカー)

ふくさよう 副作用 a side effect. (! しばしば複数形で) ▶この薬は副作用があるかもしれない This medicine may have 《*harmful* [*adverse*]》 *side effects* 《on the patient》. ▶薬の副作用で気分が悪かった I suffered unpleasant *side effects* from the medicine.

ふくさんぶつ 副産物 a by-product; 〔事業・研究などの有益な〕 (a) spin-off.

***ふくし** 福祉 welfare, (やや書) well-being. (⇨幸福)
●社会福祉 social *welfare*. ●児童 [老人] 福祉 child [old people's] *welfare*. ●在宅福祉サービスを向上させる improve home *welfare* services. ●国民の福祉(=福利)に貢献 [を増進] する work for [promote] the *welfare* of the people. ●福祉国家 a *welfare* stàte. ●福祉事業 wélfare wòrk. ●福祉施設 wélfare facilities. ●福祉事務所 a wélfare òffice. ●福祉政策 a wélfare pòlicy.

ふくし 副使 a deputy [a vice] envoy. (⑳ 正使)

ふくし 副詞 〔文法〕 an adverb.
●副詞句 an adverb [an adverbial] phrase.
●副詞節 an adverb [an adverbial] clause.

ふくじ 服地 material for clothing.

ふくしき 複式 ── 複式の 形 〔複式記入の〕 double-entry; 〔複合の〕 composite; 〔組み合わせた〕 combined; 〔二重 [三重] の〕 two-[three-]fold. ●連勝複式 〔競馬〕 a quinella. (関連) 連勝単式 a perfecta)
●複式火山 a composite volcano. (!「二重 [三重] 式火山」(a two-[three-]fold volcano が含まれる)) ●複式学級 a combined class. ●複式簿記 double-entry bookkeeping.

ふくしきこきゅう 腹式呼吸 abdominal [《話》 belly] breathing. ●腹式呼吸をする do [perform] *abdominal respiration*.

ふくじてき 副次的 ── 副次的な 形 〔二次的な〕 secondary; 〔比較的重要でない〕 minor; 〔補助的な〕 《やや書》 subsidiary. ●副次的な問題 a *secondary* [*a subsidiary*] matter; a side issue.

ふくしゃ 複写 〔写し, 複写物〕 a copy; a duplicate /d(j)úːplɪkət/ (⇨写し); 〔正確な複写〕 a facsimile; 〔複製〕 a reproduction. ▶これがその本の複写版です This is a *facsimile* edition of the book. ▶その3枚の複写の用紙に書き込んでください Fill this out *in triplicate*.
── 複写する 動 ●その文書を複写する *copy* [*duplicate*] the document; *make* [*take*] *a copy of* the document. ●写真を複写する *reproduce* a photograph.
●複写機 a cópying [a dúplicating] machìne; a duplicator. ●複写紙 cópying [dúplicating] páper.

ふくしゃ 輻射 名 radiation. ── 輻射する 動 radiate 《from》.
●輻射熱 radiant heat.

ふくしゅ 副手 a subassistant 《to》.

ふくしゅう 復習 名 《米》 (a) review, 《英》 (a) revision.
── 復習する 動 ●今日の授業の復習をする *go over* 《米》 *do a review of, review*, 《英》 *revise* today's lesson.

ふくしゅう 復讐 名 〖私的なうらみによる〗 revenge; 〖不正に対する正義感による〗 《やや書》 vengeance. (! いずれか行為をさす場合には a をとるが, 複数形にはしない)
●復讐の鬼となるを obsessed with *revenge*. ●恐ろしい復讐を企てる seek a terrible *revenge* [*vengeance*] 《on him》.
── 復讐(を)する 動 〖被害者自身が〗 take* revenge, 《やや書》 revenge oneself 《on＋人, for＋事》; 〖被害者に代わって他の人が〗 avenge, revenge. (! 本来 revenge は被害者自身が, avenge は他人が被害者に代わって復讐することをいうが, 区別なく用いることも多い) ▶彼は裏切り者に復讐した He *took revenge on* [*revenged himself on*] his betrayer. ▶彼は彼らの家を燃やして父親が殺された復讐をした He *took revenge* [*vengeance*] *on* them *for* his father's death by burning their house. ▶日常会話では He *paid* them *back for* his father's death by burning their house. の方が普通)/He *avenged* [*revenged*] his father's death by burning their house. (! ×He *avenged* [*revenged*] them *for* his father's death .... のように復讐の相手を直接目的語にはしない)/He burned their house in

[out of] revenge for his father's death.
ふくじゅう 服従 〖言うことに従うこと〗obedience 《to》; 〖屈服〗submission 《to》.
——**服従する** 動 〖言うことに従う〗obey, be obedient 《to》; 〖屈服する〗submit 《to》. ●王に服従する *submit to* the king. ▶私は社長命令にただただ服従した I unquestioningly *obeyed* my boss's orders.
ふくしゅうにゅう 副収入 (an) additional income; (a) side income.
ふくじゅそう 福寿草 〖植物〗an adonis.
ふくしょ 副署 图 a countersign, a countersignature.
——**副署する** 動 ●文書に副署する *countersign* the papers.
ふくしょう 副将 a subcaptain.
ふくしょう 副賞 a supplementary prize. (⇔ 正賞)
ふくしょう 復唱 ——**復唱する** 動 repeat.
ふくしょう 複勝 ●(ある馬に)複勝で賭ける wager on a horse to *place* [*show*].
●複勝式馬券 a place [a show] ticket.
ふくじょうし 腹上死 ——腹上死する 動 die in the course of sexual intercourse.
ふくしょく 服飾 ●服飾雑誌 a fáshion màgazine. ●服飾デザイナー a fáshion [a drèss (and accessory)] designer. ●服飾品 (男性用)《米》(men's) furnishings; (女性用) women's clothes and accessories. (❗服とバッグなどまで含めたアクセサリー類)
ふくしょく 復職 ——復職する 動 return [go back, come back] to work 〖役職に〗one's position〗. (❗go back は外部の人からみた場合、come back は自分または内部の人からみた言い方。いずれも return より口語的)
ふくしょく(ぶつ) 副食(物) a side dish. (❗主料理に対する付随的な料理) (⇔おかず)
ふくしん 副審 an assistant referee; (線審) a linesman.
ふくしん 腹心 腹心の部下 one's right hand [(男の) right-hand man, (女の) right-hand woman]. (❗複数の部下をさすときに、one's right hand people ともいう)
ふくじん 副腎 〖解剖〗an adrenal /ədríːnl/ gland.
●副腎機能低下 hypoadrenalism. ●副腎髄質ホルモン adrenaline. ●副腎皮質ホルモン adrenal cortex hormone.
ふくじんづけ 福神漬け (説明的に)sliced vegetables pickled in soy sauce and *mirin* [sweet *sake*].
ふくすい 腹水 abdominal fluid; dropsy of the belly; 〖医学〗ascites. ●腹水がたまる have an accumulation of *fluid in the abdominal cavity*.
ふくすい 覆水 spilt water.
●覆水盆に返らず 'Spilt water can't be regained into the pot.'/〖ことわざ〗It is no use crying over spilt milk. (❗後の方のことわざは、There's no use [point] crying ....も可。意味は「いまさら元に戻せないことを悔むなんてばかげたことだ」なので、前の方が意味的に日本語のことわざに近い)
ふくすう 複数 the plural(略 pl(ur).). ●おそらくこれは複数の人間の仕業だ Probably, *more than one* person has done this. (❗more than one は「2人以上」の意だが one にひかれて単数扱い)
●複数形〖文法〗a plural form. ●複数名詞〖文法〗a plural noun.
ふくする 服する (命令などに) obey 《an order》; (刑に) serve 《a sentence》; (喪に) go* into [服している be in] mourning 《for one's mother》.

ふくする 復する return [be restored] 《to》. ●旧に復する return to the former state. ●健康が復する recover [regain] one's health.
ふくせい 複製 图 a reproduction; (精密な) a réplica; (原物どおりの複写) a facsimile /fæksíməli/; (まったく同じ物) a duplicate /d(j)úːplikət/.
——**複製する** 動 ●名画を複製する *reproduce* [*duplicate*] /d(j)úːplikèit/ a famous picture.
ふくせき 復籍 ——復籍する 動 restore one's family [school, college] register. (❗family register は戸籍)
ふくせん 伏線 (手掛り) a clue; (ヒント) a hint.
●伏線を張る ●物語の結末については第1章に伏線が張られている A *clue* to the ending of the story is provided in the first chapter./A *hint* about how the story ends is given in the first chapter.
ふくせん 複線 a double track; a two-track line.
●複線にする double-track.
●複線工事 double-tracking.
*****ふくそう 服装** dress; 〖正服〗clothes /klóuz, klóuðz/; 〖集合的〗clothing /klóuðiŋ/; 〖衣装〗(a) cóstume. (⇨服、衣装) ●服装を正す tidy up oneself [one's *dress*]. ●立派な[みすぼらしい]服装をしている be well [poorly, shabbily] *dressed*. ●仕事にふさわしい[ヒッピーのような; 年相応の]服装をしている *be dressed for* one's work [*like* a hippie; *for* one's age]. ▶私たちの学校では服装の自由が認められていない A free choice of *clothing* is not allowed at our school. ▶彼は服装をかまわない My He doesn't care about his *clothes* [(外見) his *appearance*]./〖話〗He is a careless dresser. ▶今日の会にはどんな服装で行くべきですか What should I wear to today's party? ▶服装は清潔でさっぱりしたものにしなさい *Dress* to look clean and neat. ▶運動しやすい服装でお越しください Please come in *clothes* suitable for exercise. ▶服装にはその人の個性が現れるものです Your character will be expressed *in the way you dress*. ▶服装ご随意 (招待状の後書き) Dress optional./(平服で) Informal dress.
●服装規定 a dress code.
ふくそう 福相 ——福相の 形 affluent-looking.
ふくそう 輻輳 congestion; crowding.
——**輻輳する** 動 congest; crowd. ●年末には事務が輻輳する We *are overcrowded with* business at the end of the year.
ふくぞう 腹蔵 ●腹蔵のない frank, candid. ●腹蔵のない意見 a *frank* [a *candid*] opinion. ●腹蔵なく話す speak *frankly* [*candidly*, 《話》 (*straight*) *from the shoulder*].
ふくそうひん 副葬品 〖考古学〗grave goods, tomb furnishings.
ふくそくるい 腹足類 〖生物〗gastropoda; (1匹) a gastropod. ——**腹足類の** 形 gastropodous.
ふくそすう 複素数 〖数学〗a complex number.
ふくたい 腹帯 a maternity belt.
ふくだい 副題 a subtitle.
ふくたいてん 不倶戴天 ●**不倶戴天の敵**(かたき)(死ぬまでの) a mortal; (やや書) 〖和解のない〗a sworn] enemy.
ふくちょう 副長 (軍艦の) a vice captain. ●支店の副長 (企業の) a deputy branch manager; an assistant regional manager.
ふくちょう 復調 图 ●復調のきざしが見える show signs of *recovery* [*improvement*].
——**復調する** 動 (運動選手や歌手などが) recover [regain] one's good form.
ふくつ 不屈 ——不屈の 形 (屈服しない) indomitable;

ふくつう　腹痛 (a) stomachache, 《やや話》(a) bellyache; 《幼児に多い痛みの激しい》colic; 《激しい運動などの後の筋肉の収縮による》stomach cramps; 《生理による》menstrual cramps. ▶腹痛がする I have a *stomachache*. / My stomach aches. / I am suffering from a *stomachache*. (❗I *suffer from a stomachache.* は「慢性の腹痛に悩んでいる」の意)/ I have a *pain in the stomach* [a *stomach pain*].

ふくとう　復党 ── 復党する 图 rejoin [return to] 《the Democratic Party》.

ふくどくじさつ　服毒自殺 ●服毒自殺をする commit suicide by taking poison; poison oneself.

ふくどくほん　副読本 a side [a supplementary] reader.

ふくとしん　副都心 a subcenter 《*of* Tokyo》.

ふくのかみ　福の神 the god of good fortune; the god of wealth.

ふくはい　腹背 ●腹背に敵を受ける(=前と後から) be attacked by the enemy both in the *front* and *the rear*.

ふくびき　福引き a lottery, a draw. ●福引きをする[引く] hold [draw] a *lottery*. ●福引きで賞品を当てる win a prize in a *lottery* [a *draw*].
●福引き券 a lottery ticket.

ふくびこう　副鼻腔 a paranasal sinus.
●副鼻腔炎 〖医学〗 sinusitis.

ふくぶ　腹部 〖解剖〗 the abdomen; the belly. (⇨腹) ▶腹部の激痛で病院に運ばれる be carried [brought] to a hospital for a severe pain *in the abdomen* [a severe *abdominal* pain].

ぶくぶく ●ぶくぶくと泡だつ液体 bubbly liquid. ▶なべの中に泡がぶくぶく出てきた Bubbles started to rise in the pot. ▶シチューがぶくぶく煮立ってきた The stew began to *bubble* [《ぐつぐつ煮える》*simmer*]. ▶彼はぶくぶく太っている He is *fat like a balloon*.

ふくぶくしい　福々しい ▶彼女は福々しい顔をしている She has a *rich-and-happy-looking round face*.

ふくふくせん　複々線 a four-track [a quadruple-track] line. (⇨複線) ●複々線の鉄道 a *four-tracked* railroad.

ふくぶくろ　福袋 《米》a grab bag, 《英》a lucky dip.

ふくぶん　複文 〖文法〗 a complex sentence.

ふくへい　伏兵 an ambush /æmbʊʃ/; 《予期せぬ障害》an unexpected impediment [obstacle, 《困難》difficulty]. ▶伏兵にあうて倒される be ambushed. ●伏兵にうたれて死ぬ be killed in the *ambush*.

ふくへき　腹壁 〖解剖〗 the abdominal wall.

ふくぼく　副木 a splint. ▶骨折した腕に副木をあてがらった I got my broken arm put in *splints*.

ふくほん　副本 a duplicate copy.

ふくまくえん　腹膜炎 〖医学〗 peritonitis /pèrətənáitəs/.

ふくませる　含ませる ●水分を含ませる soak [《書》saturate]... with water. ●赤ん坊に乳房を含ませる give the breast to a baby; suckle a baby.

ふくまでん　伏魔殿 the abode of all demons; 《罪悪の根源地》the hotbed of vice [crime, 《陰謀》intrigue].

ふくまめ　福豆 《説明的に》roasted beans which are scattered about on the *Setsubun* Day.

ふくみ　含み 〖言外の意味に〗(an) implication, 《特に単語の》a connotation 〖しばしば複数形で〗; 《発言などの》《やや書》an óvertòne (❗通例複数形で). (⇨含意)●含みのある返事 a reply with 《some》*implications*. ●性的な含みのある語 a word (loaded) with sexual *connotations*. ●皮肉な含みに富む論評 a

comment full of ironical *overtones*. ●含みを残しで later discussion. ▶彼は含みの多いものの言い方をする人なので真意が読みとりにくい He is difficult to understand because he always means more than he actually says.
●含み益 a latent [《隠れた》(a) hidden] profit.
●含み声 a muffled voice. ●含み資産 hidden assets. ●含み損 a latent loss. ●含み笑い a suppressed laugh [smile].

ふくみみ　福耳 plump ears; 《説明的に》ears with thick lobes which are believed to bring in luck and wealth.

◆ふくむ　含む ❶〖含有する〗《構成成分として》contain; 〖包含する〗《全体の一部として》include. ▶レモンは多くのビタミン C を含んでいる Lemons *contain* [×are containing] a lot of vitamin C./A lot of vitamin C *is found* [×is contained] in lemons. (❗ contain は進行形や受身は不可)▶価格には消費税が含まれている The price *includes* consumption [sales] tax. ▶英語は必修科目の中に含まれていない English *is excluded from* [*is not among*] the required subjects. ▶その飛行機には日本人 15 人を含む 120 人の乗客が乗っていた There were 120 passengers aboard the plane, *including* [×included] 15 Japanese.
❷〖口に〗▶口に食べ物を含んだまま話してはいけません Don't talk *with* your mouth *full* (*of* food).
❸〖心に留める〗keep* [bear*]... in mind. ▶このことをよく含んでおいてください I hope you'll *keep* this *in mind*.
❹〖暗に意味する〗imply. ▶彼のほほえみには重要な意味が含まれていた His smile *implied* something important.
●含むところがある　▶私は彼に含むところがある(=恨みを抱いている) I have [hold] a grudge against him./I owe him a grudge. ▶彼には含むところがある(=何か考えがあるらしい) It seems that he *has something in mind*.

ふくむ　服務 《公務》service; 《職務》(a) duty. (⇨勤務)
●服務規定 service [office] regulations.

ふくめい　復命 ── 復命する 動 report 《*to* him》on the mission one has carried out.

ふくめに　含め煮 (⇨含含める)

ふくめる　含める include. ●含めない do not include; exclude; leave [keep]... out. ▶送料を含めて 8,000 円になります It comes to [It will be] 8,000 yen, postage *included* [*including* postage, *inclusive of* postage].

ふくめん　覆面 a mask. ●覆面をした masked; veiled. ●覆面をかぶっている[かぶる] wear [put on] a *mask*.
●覆面パトカー an unmarked police car.

ふくも　服喪 mourning. ●服喪中である be in *mourning* 《*for* one's father》. ●服喪期間に入る go into *mourning* 《*for* one's father》.

ふくやく　服薬 ── 服薬する 動 take* medicine.

ふくよう　服用 ── 服用する 動 take* medicine. (❗水薬に限り drink も使える) ▶これらの錠剤を1日3回食後に服用してください *Take* these pills three times a day after meals.

ふくよう　複葉 ●複葉機 a biplane.

ふくよか ── ふくよかな 形 《丸々と太った》plump, chubby 《❗前の語は通例幼児女性と子供に用い、後の語は太り方をいう「は、fleshy の両面語。後の語は特に赤ん坊と子供によく用いられる》;《肉づきのよい》fleshy, buxom /bʌksəm/ 《❗後の語は通例女性の胸が豊かな状態や魅力的なものについていう》;《でっぷりした》stout.

(**!** fat の婉曲語) ● ふくよかなほほ *plump* [*fleshy*] cheeks. ▶彼女のことをふとると言うんじゃない. ふくよかと言いなさい Don't say she's fat; say she's *plump*.
ふくらしこ ふくらし粉 baking powder.
ふくらはぎ a calf (働 calves).
ふくらます 膨らます 〖膨張させる〗 swell*... (out); (空気・ガスなどで) blow*... up, 〖書〗 inflate; (まくら・クッション・チューブなどを) plump ... up, 〖原型になるよう揺さぶったり軽くたたくなどして〗; (息などで) puff ... up; 〖増やす〗 increase. (⇨膨れる) ● 予算をふくらます swell [*increase*] a budget. ● タイヤをふくらませる *blow up* [〖書〗*inflate*, ×*swell*] the tire. (**!**「ぱんぱんにふくらんだタイヤ」は a fully *inflated* tire) ▶イーストがパンをふくらませる The yeast *makes* the bread *rise*. ▶新入生は皆希望に胸をふくらませていた(=希望にあふれていた) All the freshmen *were full of* hopes.
ふくらみ 膨らみ (膨張してふくれ上がること) a swell; (内圧による) a bulge; (ふわっとしたふくらみ) a puff. (⇨膨らむ) ● 彼女の胸のふくらみは the *swell* of her breasts. ● ポケットのふくらみ a *bulge* in a pocket.
*****ふくらむ** 膨らむ swell*; expand (⇨膨張する); (中にものが詰まって) bulge /bʌldʒ/. ● 小銭でふくらんだポケット a pocket *bulging with* small coins. ● 風船がふくらんだ The balloon *has swelled* [*swollen*]. ▶つぼみふくらみ始めた The buds began to *swell* [*expand*].
ふくり 福利 welfare, 《やや書》well-being. (⇨福祉)
● 福利厚生 (従業員の) the welfare of employees [workers]. ● 福利厚生施設 (従業員のための) facilities for the welfare of employees [workers].
ふくり 複利 compound (↔simple) interest. ● 複利で計算する calculate at *compound interest*. ● 利子は複利です The interest is *compound*.
ふくりゅう 伏流 图 an underground stream [river].
— **伏流する** 動 flow underground.
● 伏流水 water flowing underground.
ふくれあがる 膨れ上がる ▶観衆は 7,000 人にふくれ上がった The audience *swelled* to 7,000 people. ▶彼の借金はひどくふくれ上がって返済不可能になった His debts *amounted to* so much 〖急速に〗*snowballed* so quickly] that he was unable to pay them back.
ふくれっつら 膨れっ面 ● ふくれっ面をした (子供のようにすねてむっつりした) sulky; (不機嫌で黙り込んだ) sullen.
● ふくれっ面をする go into a sulk; sulk.
*****ふくれる** 膨れる ❶〖膨張する〗(水分・空気が入って) swell*; (四方に) expand; (パンなどが) puff up, rise*. ▶水分を吸って木がふくれた The wood *has swelled* [*swollen*] (out) *with* moisture. ▶観衆が 1,000 人以上にふくれた The audience *has swelled* [*increased*] to over a thousand.
❷〖不満を示す〗(不機嫌に黙り込む) get* sullen; (すねる) get sulky, sulk; (口をとがらす) pout. ▶彼女はさっきのことでまだふくれている She's still *sulky* [*sulking*] *about* what happened earlier.
*****ふくろ** 袋 a bag; a sack; a pouch /paʊtʃ/.

> 使い分け **bag** 紙・ビニールの袋から布・プラスチック・皮製の袋まで一般的な語. キャンデー・ポテトチップスなどの袋詰めを《米》a *pack* of candy [potato chips], 《英》a *packet* of sweets [potato crisps] ともいう.
> **sack** 粗布・丈夫な紙・ビニール製の大型の袋で, 通例穀物・石炭・野菜などの保管・輸送に用いる.
> **pouch** ベルトに取り付けたり, ポケットに入れて携帯できるような小物入れ. 有袋類の袋も pouch.

● 買い物袋 (紙, ビニール)《米》a shopping *bag*,《英》a carrier (*bag*); (紙) a paper *bag*. ● ビニール袋 a plastic *bag*. ● 小麦粉〖ジャガイモ〗一袋 a *sack* of flour [*potatoes*]. ● お菓子を一袋食べてしまう eat a whole *bag* of sweets. ▶袋から持ち物を取り出した He took his things out of a *bag*.
● 袋のねずみ ● 袋のねずみである cannot escape; be trapped like a rat; be cornered. ▶彼は警官にビルに追い詰められて袋のねずみであった The police *trapped* him [*bottled him up*] in the building.
● 袋網 a bag net, a fyke (net). ● 袋帯 a double-woven *obi*. ● 袋織り (二重織り) double weaving.
● 袋とじ *fukurotoji* binding; bag-style binding.
● 袋縫い double sewing; (縫い目) a French seam. ● 袋耳 (すぐれた記憶力) a retentive memory; (織物の耳の袋織り) a double-sided woven edge.
ふくろ 復路 (帰路) one's way back. (⇨ 往路)
ふくろう 梟 〖鳥〗an owl /aʊl/. ▶ふくろうが鳴いている An *owl* is hooting.
ふくろくじゅ 福禄寿 *Fukurokuju*, (説明的に) the god of happiness, wealth and longevity. He is one of the seven gods of good fortune.
ふくろこうじ 袋小路 a blind alley; a dead end. ● 袋小路に追い詰められるを cornered in a *blind alley*.
● 袋小路に入る come to [reach] a *dead end* [a *deadlock*, an *impasse*].
ふくろだたき 袋叩き — 袋叩きにする 動 beat 〈him〉up, give 〈him〉a good beating. ▶彼は街の不良グループに袋だたきにされた He got *beaten up* by a street gang.
ふくろもの 袋物 (袋状入れの総称) bags.
● 袋物商 a dealer in bags.
ふくわじゅつ 腹話術 ventriloquism /ventrɪləkwɪzm/.
● 腹話術師 a ventriloquist.
ぶくん 武勲 a brilliant military feat. ● 武勲をたてる distinguish oneself in battle [battlefield].
ふけ dándruff. ● ふけが出る get *dandruff*. ● ふけだらけのえりの人 one's collar covered with *dandruff*.
● ひどいふけ性である have very bad *dandruff*.
● ふけ取りローション anti-dandruff hair lotion.
ぶけ 武家 〖家柄〗a *samurai* family; (階級) the *samurai* class; 〖人〗a *samurai* (働 ~).
● 武家の商法 (不慣れでへたな商法) an inexperienced and bungling way of doing business.
● 武家時代 〖歴史〗the age of *samurai* rule [ascendancy]. ● 武家政治 *samurai* government.
ふけい 不敬 disrespect; irreverence. ● 不敬な言動をする show disrespect (*for*); be disrespectful 《*to*》.
● 不敬罪 lese /liːz/ majesty.
ふけい 父兄 parents. (⇨父母)
ふけい 父系 图 the paternal line.
— **父系の** 形 one's paternal 《grandparents》; 《grandparents》 on one's father's side. (⇨ 父方)
ふけい 婦警 『「婦人警官」の略』a policewoman.
ぶげい 武芸 military [martial] arts. (**!** 常に複数形で用いる)
*****ふけいき** 不景気 图 (厳しい時世) hard [bad] times; (長期の不況) a depression; (一時的景気後退) a recession; (景気不振) a slump. ▶あの国はひどい不景気に苦しんでいます They are suffering from a serious *depression* in that country.
— **不景気な** 形 ❶ (商売などが) (活気のない) dull, inactive; (緩慢な) slack. ▶このごろは不景気です *Times are hard* [*bad*] 《×in》these days./These are the *hard times*./Business is dull [slack,

ふけいざい 不経済 ― **不経済な** 形 〖経済的でない〗 uneconomical; 〖むだな〗 wasteful. ● 不経済な生活の仕方 a *wasteful* [*uneconomical*] way of life. ▶彼女は不経済な女だ (節約がまったくできない) She's incapable of economies./(やたらと金を遣う) She spends money too freely. ▶安物を買うのはかえって不経済だ It can be *uneconomical* to buy cheap goods./Buying cheap things is a *false economy*.

ふけこむ 老け込む age (a lot). ▶奥さんに死なれて彼はずいぶん老け込んだ He *has aged a lot* since his wife died./His wife's death has *aged* him *a lot*.

ふけつ 不潔 ― **不潔な** 形 (汚れてきたない) dirty, filthy (❗後の方が激しい意); (きれいでない) unclean; (不衛生な) insanitary. (⇨汚い) ▶不潔な手でものを食べるな Don't eat with *dirty* [*unclean*] hands.

ふけやく 老け役 ● 老け役を演じる play the *part* [*role*] *of an old man* [*woman*]; do the *part* [*role*] *of an aged person*.

ふける 老ける grow* [become*, get*] old; age. ▶彼はずいぶんと老けた He's *become* much *older*./He's *aged* a lot. ▶彼は年よりは(=年の割に) [60 歳にしては] 老けて見える He *looks older* than he really is [than sixty]./He *looks* old for his age [for sixty].

ふける 更ける ▶夜も更けてきた (遅くなって) It's *getting late* (at night)./(夜が進行している)《書》The night *has far advanced*. ▶夜が更けるにつれて風が出てきた As *the night* went *on*, it got windy. ▶彼は毎日夜が更けるまで勉強した He studied *till late at night* [*far into the night*] every day. ▶秋も更けて(=けわとなって)めっきり涼しくなった We are now in the midst [height] of fall and it has become quite cool.

ふける 耽る ❶〖熱中する〗be absorbed 《in》, be intent 《on》; 〖専心する〗devote oneself 《to》; 〖我を忘れる〗be lost 《in》. ▶昨夜は読書にふけった I *was absorbed in* [*intent on*] reading last night. ▶彼は(すっかり)物思いにふけっている He *is* (deeply) *lost in* thought./He is (deep) in thought.
❷〖おぼれる〗give* oneself over 《to》; 〖思う存分…する〗indulge 《in》; 〖麻薬などに〗be addicted 《to》. ▶彼はばくちにふけった He *gave himself over to* gambling. ▶彼は飲酒にふけっている He *indulges* (*himself*) *in* drinking./He's *addicted to* drinking.

ふけん 父権 paternal rights.

ふげん 付言 ― **付言する** 動 make* some additional remarks; add 《*that* 節》.

ふけんこう 不健康 ●不健康そうな若者 an *unhealthy*-looking young man. ●不健康な食品 *unhealthy* [*unwholesome*] foods. ●不健康(=不健全)な遊び *unwholesome* amusements.

ふけんしき 不見識 ― **不見識な** 形 unwise; (無分別な) indiscreet. ▶公の席であのような発言をするとは君も不見識だ It's *unwise* [*indiscreet*] of you to make such remarks in public. (❗ indiscreet は人の秘密をばらすなど好ましくない行為を非難する形容詞)

ふげんじっこう 不言実行 Deeds are better than words./Actions speak louder than words. ●不言実行の人 a man of deeds, not of words.

ふけんぜん 不健全 名 unsoundness; unwholesomeness; unhealthiness.
― **不健全な** 形 (心身が健康でない)《やや書》unsound; (道徳的に有害な) unwholesome; (健康でない) unhealthy. ▶これらの雑誌は少年少女に対して不健全な影響を与える These magazines have an *unhealthy* [an *unwholesome*] influence on boys and girls.

ふこう 不幸 ❶〖恵まれない状態〗unhappiness; 〖大きな不幸〗(a) misery; 〖不運〗bad* luck, (ひどい) (a) misfortune, (不運) ▶いろいろな不幸にあう suffer various *misfortunes* [*miseries*]. ●不幸のどん底にある be in the depth of misery. ●自ら不幸を招く bring *misfortune* on oneself. ▶不幸は続くもの《ことわざ》*Misfortunes* [*Troubles*] never come singly. ▶他人の不幸につけこんで金もうけをするのはいかない It's wrong to profit from the *misery* of others.

❷〖近親者の死亡〗(死別) (a) bereavement /biríːvmənt/; (死亡) (a) death. ▶彼の家族に不幸があった There was a *death* in his family. ▶この度の〖ご子息の〗ご不幸をお聞きして大変お気の毒に存じます I'm very sorry to hear of your *bereavement* [*your son's death*].
● **不幸中の幸い** ▶彼女はハンドバッグを失くしたが財布が入っていなかったのは不幸中の幸いだった She lost her handbag [《米》purse], but it's a *good thing* money wasn't [she didn't have money] in it. (❗(1)《米》では handbag = purse で purse の方を多く使う. したがって「財布」の訳はこのように工夫する. (2)後半は but *luckily* none .... ともいえる.)
― **不幸な** 形 unhappy, (みじめな) miserable, 〖不運な〗unlucky, unfortunate. (⇨不運) ●不幸な人 [事故] an *unhappy* person [accident]. ●不幸な幼年時代を送る have an *unhappy* childhood. ●不幸な一生を送る lead an *unhappy* [a (*bitter* and) *miserable*] life.
― **不幸にも** 副 unluckily, unfortunately, 《やや書》unhappily. (⇨不運)

ふこう 不孝 undutifulness. (⇨親不孝)

ふごう 符号 〖印〗a mark; 〖記号〗a sign; 〖電信符号〗a code. (⇨印, 記号) ●モールス符号 the Morse code [*alphabet*].

ふごう 符合 ― **符合する** 動 (一致する) agree 《with》; (偶然に一致する) coincide /kòuinsáid/ 《with》. ▶彼の証言は犯人の自白とぴったり符合する His testimony *agrees* [*coincides*, *corresponds*] exactly *with* the criminal's confession. (❗ correspond to は類似・対応も表すので意味があいまいになる) (⇨一致)

ふごう 富豪 a very rich [wealthy] person. (⇨金持ち) ●大富豪 (百万長者) a millionaire; (億万長者) a billionaire.

ふこう 武功 (⇨武勲)

ふごうかく 不合格 〖失敗〗failure 《in》. ▶彼は入学試験に不合格だった He *failed* [(通らなかった) *didn't pass*] his entrance exam. ▶3 人がカンニングのため不合格になった (=はねられた) Three candidates *were rejected* because of cheating.
● **不合格者** an unsuccessful candidate. ● **不合格品** a reject.

ふこうせい 不公正 ― **不公正な** 形 unfair.

ふこうへい 不公平 名 〖公正でないこと〗unfairness; 〖えこひいきすること〗partiality; 〖不正・不当なこと〗injustice. (⇨公平) ▶だれに対しても不公平なふるまう behave without *partiality* [*injustice*] to anyone.
― **不公平な** 形 unfair; unjust; partial. ●不公平な

ふごうり 不合理 裁判 an *unfair* [an *unjust*] trial. ●不公平税制 an *unfair* tax system. ●不公平な判断を下す pass an *unfair* [a *partial*] judgment 《*on* it》. ▶彼に賞を与えないのは不公平だ You're *unfair* [It's *not fair* of you] not to give him the prize./It's *unfair* that he shouldn't be given the prize.
── 不公平に 副 unfairly; partially. ●生徒たちを不公平に扱う treat the students *unfairly*.

ふごうり 不合理 图 (論理的でないこと) illogicality; (理屈に合わないこと) unreasonableness; (無分別) irrationality.
── 不合理な 形 illogical; unreasonable; irrational. ●不合理な話 an *illogical* [an *unreasonable*] story. ▶彼の要求は不合理なようには思えなかった His demand didn't seem *unreasonable*.

ふこく 布告 图 (公然と発表すること) (a) declaration; (重大なことを広く公にすること) (a) proclamation.
── 布告する 動 ●宣戦を布告する make a *declaration* [a *proclamation*] of war 《*against*》; *declare* [《書》*proclaim*] war 《*against*》.

ぶこく 誣告 a false charge [accusation]; 『法律』a malicious prosecution; 『名誉毀損(ﾞ)』(口頭によるもの) a slander; (文書によるもの) a libel /láibl/.
── 誣告する 動 make a false charge 《*against*》; slander [libel] 《*against*》.

ふこくきょうへい 富国強兵 ●富国強兵策 a policy for making one's country wealthy and militarily strong.

ふこころえ 不心得 ── 不心得な 形 〘思慮のない〙 thoughtless; (軽率な)《やや書》imprudent; (分別を欠いた) indiscreet.
●不心得者 an imprudent [an indiscreet] person.

ぶこつ 無骨, 武骨 ── 無骨[武骨]な 形 〘頑丈だが洗練されていない〙 rugged /rágid/, and unrefined.

ふさ 房 〘果実の〙 a bunch, a cluster; 〘先を散らしたもの〙 (飾り房, トウモロコシの) a tassel; (羽毛の) a tuft; (緑飾り) a fringe. ●一房のブドウ a *bunch* [a *cluster*] of grapes. ●羽毛の房 a *tuft* of feathers.
●房のついたカーテン a *fringed* curtain.

ブザー a buzzer /bázər/. ●ブザーを押す[鳴らす] press [sound] a *buzzer*; buzz /báz/. ▶ブザーが鳴っている There goes [There's] the *buzzer*.

ふさい 夫妻 《⇨夫婦》●西垣(淳)氏夫妻 Mr. and Mrs. (Jun) Nishigaki (❗Jun を入れる方が正式); Mr. Nishigaki and his wife; the Nishigakis.

ふさい 負債 (a) debt /dét/; liabilities. 《⇨借金》●多額の負債を抱えている be heavily in *debt*. ▶その会社は5,400億円の負債を抱えて倒産した The company went into bankruptcy with *liabilities* [*debt*] of 540 billion yen.
●負債比率 a débt [a liabílity] ràtio; a debt-equity ratio.

ふざい 不在 图 (an) absence. (❗不在の期間・回数を表すときは 〖C〗)
── 不在である 動 (外出している) be out; (長く留守にしている) be away; (どこかへ行った) be gone; (家にいない) be not in, be not at home (『が主語が省略するのは《米》); (いるべきところにない) be absent 《*from*》. (⇨留守) ▶支配人は今不在です The manager is *out* [*not in* (the office)] now. ▶彼は出張で2週間不在です He *is away* on a business trip for two weeks.
●不在地主 an absentee landowner [landlord].
●不在者 an absentee /æbsntíː/. ●不在(者)投票 an absentee vote [ballot].

ぶざい 部材 materials for making components [parts].

ぶさいく 不細工 ── 不細工な 形 (ぎこちない) awkward; (無器用な) clumsy; (容貌など) plain, ugly. 《⇨不格好》▶なんてぶさいくな女なんだろう She's [She looks] *very plain*.

ふさかざり 房飾り (服・旗・カーテンなど) a fringe; a tassel.

*ふさがる 塞がる ❶〘通れない〙 be blocked, 《やや書》be obstructed. (⇨塞ぐ❶) ▶その道は雪でふさがっている The road *is blocked* by [with] snow.
❷〘空いていない〙 be occupied; (時間的に) be engaged; (手があいていない) be busy. ▶その部屋はふさがっている (現に) The room *is occupied*./(予約中で) The room *is reserved* [《主に英》*is booked*]. ▶私は金曜日の夜はふさがっている I'*m engaged* for [(別の約束がある)] I have another appointment on] Friday evening. ▶私は手がふさがっている My hands are full./I have my hands full. ▶彼女は料理で[来客で]手がふさがっている She *is busy cooking* [*engaged with* a visitor]. ▶その仕事で午前中がふさがってしまった The work *took up* [*occupied*, *engaged*] the whole morning. (❗後にくるほど堅い表現)/I *was occupied* [《話》*was tied up*] *with* the work all morning. ▶その席はふさがっている The seat *is taken*. ▶その電話(機)は今ふさがっている Someone is using the telephone./(話し中です) The line *is busy* [《主に米》*is engaged* 《英》]. ▶そのポスト(=職)はふさがった The position *was filled*. 会話 「ダブルの部屋をお願いします」「あいにく全部ふさがっています」"I'd like a double room, please." "I'm afraid we're fully *occupied*."
❸〘閉じる〙 (ひとりでに) close (up); (閉ざされる) be closed. ▶彼の目は今にもふさがりそうだ His eyes [eyelids] *are closing*. ▶傷口はふさがって順調に治っている The wound *has closed* (*up*) and is healing nicely. ▶私は開いた口がふさがらなかった I was speechless [dumbfounded]. (❗後の方が強意的的) (⇨唖然(ﾞ))

ふさぎこむ 塞ぎ込む (落胆する) get* depressed; (元気がない, 憂うつだ) feel* low 〖《話》blue〗. ▶ふさぎ込んでいる be in low spirits. ▶どうしてそんなにふさぎ込んでいるの Why *are* you *so depressed*? ▶失敗したからといってふさぎ込むな Don't *get depressed* [《話》*feel blue*] about your failure. ▶彼女が死んでから彼はふさぎ込んでいる He's *been feeling low* [*in low spirits, low-spirited*] since she died.

ふさぎのむし 塞ぎの虫 ▶彼はふさぎの虫に取りつかれている He is feeling low./《話》He is (down) in the dumps./He is depressed.

ふさく 不作 a bad* [a poor] crop [harvest]; a crop failure. 《⇨豊作》●不作の(=成果の少ない)年 a lean year. ▶今年は不作だった Crops were *poor* [*failed*] this year./We had *poor crops* this year. ▶今年の文学界は不作だった Few [No] good works appeared in the literary world this year.

ふさぐ 塞ぐ ❶〘穴などを〙 (覆って) cover; (詰めて) fill ... (in), stop (-pp-) ... (up); 〖通路などを〗block, (物が)《やや書》obstruct; 〖占有する〗take ... up, occupy. (❗前の方が口語的) ●板で穴をふさぐ *cover* a hole with a board. ●セメントで割れ目をふさぐ *fill* (*in*) [*stop* (*up*)] a crack with cement. ●手で耳をふさぐ *stop* [*cover*] one's ears with one's hands. (❗stop one's ears には「聞こうとしない」の意もある) ▶倒れた木が数時間道路をふさいでいた The fallen tree *blocked* [*obstructed*] the road for several hours. ▶ベッドが部屋の半分をふさいでいる The bed *takes up* [*occupies*] half the room.

ふさくい / ぶじ　1566

❷ [閉じる] close, shut*．(⇨閉じる) ▶目をふさぐ close [shut] one's eyes． ▶手をふさぐ cover one's eyes．(⇨❶) ▶傷口をふさぐ close the wound．

❸ [気持ちが] get* depressed．(⇨塞ぎ込む)

ふさくい 不作為 〖法律〗omission; forbearance．
● 不作為犯 a crime of omission．

***ふざける** ❶ [冗談で言う［する］] (冗談を言う) joke 《with＋人, about＋事》; [悪ふざけをする] play a trick [a joke] 《on＋人》． ▶ふざけて言っただけで彼女を怒らせるつもりはなかった I was only joking [I said it only as a joke, I said it just in fun]—I didn't mean to offend her． ▶ふざけたことを言うな Don't talk nonsense!/Stop your nonsense．

❷ [遊び騒ぐ] (子供が) romp 《about》． ▶波打ち際でふざけて水をかけあっている子供たち children splashing each other playfully at the water's edge． ▶子供たちは教室でふざけていて窓ガラスを割った The children broke the windowpane when they were romping 《about》 in the classroom． ▶車が動いているときは中でふざけるな (子供に) Don't play [《やや話》 act up] inside while the car's moving．

ぶさた 無沙汰 (long) silence．(⇨御無沙汰)

ふさふさ (髪などが豊かにある様子) thick; (あり余る) abundant． ●ふさふさとした尾 a bushy tail． ●ふさふさと垂れ下がっている藤の花 hanging clusters of wisteria flowers． ●彼女はふさふさした黒い髪をしている She has thick [abundant, a cluster of] black hair．

ぶさほう 無作法 〖名〗 [悪い行儀] bad manners; [無礼] rudeness．
—— 無作法な 〖形〗 (行儀の悪い) ill-mannered; (気配りがなく失礼な) impolite; (粗野で無礼な) rude． ●無作法なふるまいをする behave rudely． ▶彼は無作法だ He has bad manners．/He has [×knows] no manners． (❗この manners は good manners の意)/He is rude． ▶人を指すのは無作法だ It's rude [bad manners] to point at people．

ぶざま 無様, 不様 —— ぶざまな 〖形〗 (ぎこちない) awkward; (不器用な) clumsy; (不面目な) shameful, humiliating; (見苦しい) ugly; (だらしない) untidy． (⇨見苦しい) ●ぶざまな敗戦 a shameful defeat． ▶彼はぶざまな姿で(＝ふさわしくない服装で)パーティーに現れた He turned up at the party improperly [《だらしない服を着て》 untidily] dressed．

***ふさわしい** 相応しい (条件を満たした) suitable, 《やや書》 suited 《for, to》 (❗ suited は通例叙述的に); (好ましい) good* 《for; to do》; (資格・能力のある) fit (-tt-) 《for》; (その場によく調和した) 《やや書》 appropriate 《for, to》 (本来ふさわるべき) 《やや書》 proper 《for, to; to do》; (最適の) right 《for; to do》 (❗通例限定的に); (言動などが似合う) 《書》 becoming 《on＋事, to [for]＋人》; (値する) worthy 《of; of doing, 《まれ》 to do》． (❗ becoming, worthy は通例叙述的に, または意味の直後に置いて) (⇨適当 [類語], 適切) ●収入にふさわしい生活をする live within (↔beyond) one's income [means]． ▶彼はその仕事にふさわしい He is the right man for the job [to do the job]./He is a suitable [a fit, a proper] man for the job./He is a suitable [fit, proper] for the job (❗のように名詞の後に置くと一時的にふさわしいことを暗示) ▶このドレスは式によろしいでしょうか Is this dress suitable [good, appropriate, proper] for the ceremony? ▶その言葉は政治家にふさわしくない Those words aren't worthy of [becoming to] a statesman． ▶この靴はテニスにはふさわしくない(＝役に

立たない) These shoes won't do for playing tennis．

プサン 釜山 〖韓国の都市〗 Pusan /púːsɑːn/．

ふさんか 不参加 nonparticipation; (不出席) nonattendance． ●不参加である do not participate [decline participation] 《in a meeting》; do not attend 《a meeting》． ●会議への不参加を表明する express one's will not to attend [participate in] the meeting．

ふさんせい 不賛成 〖不承認〗 disapproval; [意見の不一致] disagreement． (⇨反対) ●不賛成だと首を横に振る shake one's head in disapproval． ▶その提案には不賛成だ I am against [don't agree to] the proposal./I'm opposed to the proposal． ▶君の意見には不賛成だ I can't agree with you [your opinion]．(⇨賛成する)

ふし 節 ❶ [関節] a joint; (特に指のつけ根の) a knuckle． ●体の節々が痛む I feel pain in every joint．
❷ [結節] (木・板の) a knot; (竹の) a bamboo joint, a node． (⇨節穴) ●この木材は節だらけだ This wood is full of knots./This is a knotty wood．
❸ [旋律] a tune, 《書》 a melody． (❗西洋の方は [音楽] では特に主旋律をさす) ●詩に美しい節をつけて吟じる recite a poem to a beautiful tune． ●節を口笛で吹く whistle the tune [melody]． ▶その歌の節は知っているが歌詞は知らない I know the tune to the song, but not the words．
❹ [箇所] a point． ●彼の言葉には疑わしい節がある There are some doubtful points [《話》 is something fishy] in what he says．

ふし 父子 father and child [son, daughter]．
● 父子家庭 a motherless family．

ふじ 藤 〖植物〗 a wisteria．
● 藤色 light purple． ●藤色の light purple; wisteria violet． ●藤棚 a wisteria trellis． ●藤づる a wisteria vine．

ふじ 不治 —— 不治の 〖形〗 (治らない) incurable． ●不治の病 an incurable disease． (❗「命取りの病」は a fatal [a killer] disease)

ふじ 不時 —— 不時の 〖形〗 unexpected 《visitors》; (不測の) unforeseen 《expenses》． ●不時の場合に (緊急時に) in an emergency; (まさかの時に) in time of need．

ふじ 富士 Mt. Fuji.
● 富士火山帯 the Fuji volcanic zone． ●富士五湖 the five lakes of Mt. Fuji． (❗of で富士山と湖の関係が深いことを暗示) ●富士額 a forehead whose hairline forms the inverted of Mt. Fuji．

ぶし 武士 a samurai; (戦士) a warrior; (家来) a military retainer of a daimyo．
● 武士に二言はない A samurai's word is as solid as a rock．
● 武士は食わねど高楊枝 'A samurai will use a toothpick even though he has not eaten.'/A noble-minded person will never lose his or her pride even in poor circumstances．
● 武士道 bushido; (説明的に) the ethical code of the samurai emphasizing absolute loyalty to his master．

***ぶじ** 無事 〖名〗 [安全] safety; [平穏] peace, quiet, quietness; [健康] good health． ●家族の無事を祈る pray for the safety of one's family．
—— 無事な 〖形〗 safe; [平穏な] peaceful, quiet; [健康で] well． ●太平無事の世の中に住む live in a peaceful world． ●あ, 無事でよかったと彼の母親はほっとため息をついて言った "Thank God [Heaven] (↘), you're safe!" his mother sighed with relief． (❗ Thank God [Heaven] は安堵(あんど)や

ふしあな 節穴 a knothole. ▶君の目は節穴か Where are your eyes?

ふしあわせ 不幸せ unhappiness. (⇨不幸)

ふしおがむ 伏し拝む prostrate oneself《before the image of Buddha》and pray.

***ふしぎ 不思議** 图 [[不思議な物・人・事]] (a) wonder; [[驚嘆すべきこと]] (a) marvel; [[不可解]] (a) mystery; [[奇跡]] a miracle. ●世界の七不思議 the Seven *Wonders* of the World. ●自然の不思議(な現象) a nature's *wonder*. ▶彼が彼女に腹を立てたのも不思議ではない It's *no wonder* (*that*) he got angry with her./*No wonder* he got angry with her. (❗この場合 that は通例省略される)/I don't *wonder* (*that*) he got angry with her. (❗自然だ) It's *natural that* he got [should have got] angry with her. (❗後の方が当然に思う気持ちが強い) (⇨当然)
── **不思議な** 形 [[奇妙な]] strange; [[驚くべき]] wonderful, marvelous (❗wonderful より強意的); [[不可解な]] mysterious; [[奇跡的な]] miraculous; [[理解できない]] incomprehensible. ●不思議な光景を見る see *strange* sights. ●不思議な出来事 a *mysterious* event. ▶彼が会合に出なかったとは不思議だ It's *strange* that he didn't [shouldn't have] come to the meeting. (❗should を用いる方が意外に思う気持ちが強い) ▶不思議な(=意外な)ことに彼は試験に失敗した *Surprisingly* [*To my surprise*], he failed the exam. ▶ジムとぼくは同じ学校に通っているが,不思議なことにめったに彼に会わない Jim and I go to the same school, but *strangely* [*oddly*] *enough* I rarely see him. (❗strange enough, strange to say とも言えるが, 前の方は《話》, 後の方は今はあまり用いられない) ▶この薬は風邪に不思議なほどよく効く This medicine has a *wonderful* [a *marvelous*] effect on a cold./This medicine works *like magic* [*magically*] to cure a cold. ▶This medicine does *wonders* for a cold. ▶彼の流感は完全に治ったのにせきがなかなか止まらないので医師も不思議がっている The doctor *finds it strange* that he is still coughing though he has full recovered from the flu.

ふしぎのくにのアリス 『不思議の国のアリス』 *Alice's Adventures in Wonderland*. (参考 キャロルの童話)

ふしくれだった 節くれ立った knotty, 《米》knobby, 《英》knobbly.

ふじさん 富士山 *Mt. Fuji*. (参考 草野心平の詩集)

ふしぜん 不自然 ▶彼のふるまいは不自然だった His behavior seemed *unnatural* [(ぎこちない) *awkward*]./He behaved in an *unnatural* manner.

ふしだら ── **ふしだらな** 形 [[だらしない]] loose; [[不道徳な]] immoral. (⇨だらしない) ●ふしだらな女 a *loose* [an *immoral*] woman.

ふじちゃく 不時着 ── **不時着する** 動 ●島に不時着する make a forced [[緊急の]] *an emergency*] *landing on* the island.

ふしちょう 不死鳥 a phoenix. (⇨回 フェニックス)

ふじつ 不実 ── **不実な** 形 [[誠実でない]] unfaithful; dishonest; insincere; [[事実でない]] false.

ぶしつ 部室 a clubroom; (校舎とは別棟の) a club house.

ぶしつけ 不躾 ── **不躾な** 形 [[無作法な]] impolite; (礼な) rude; [[無遠慮な]] blunt; [[無神経な]] insensitive. ●ぶしつけな質問 a *blunt* [an *insensitive*] question. ●大変ぶしつけなことを申し上げて恐縮に存じますが… I'm sorry to sound *crass* [*grossly insensitive*], but…. ▶ぶしつけですが,どちらへ行かれるのですか Where are you going, *if I may ask*? ▶人に収入のことをたずねるのはぶしつけです It's *rude* to ask people about their income.

ふして 伏して ▶この段伏して(=くれぐれも)お願い申し上げます Thank you in advance. (❗「前もってお礼を申し上げます」の意)

ふじばかま 藤袴 [[植物]] a thoroughwort.

ふしぶし 節々 ●体の節々が痛い I have pains in my *joints*./My *joints* give me a lot of pain.

ふしまつ 不始末 (誤った処置) mismanagement; (不祥事) misconduct; (不注意) carelessness. ▶火事はたばこの不始末が原因である The fire started because the cigarette *was not extinguished*. (❗extinguish は《書》「完全に火を消す」の意)

ふしまわし 節回し a tune; a melody.

ふじみ 不死身 ── **不死身の** 形 (不死の) immortal; (タフな) tough.

ふしめ 伏し目 ●伏し目になる drop [lower, cast down] one's eyes. ●伏し目がちにうなづく nod with *downcast eyes*.

ふしめ 節目 (転機) a túrning pòint; (大事な時) a (major [decisive]) juncture《*in* one's life》.

ふしゅ 浮腫 [[医学]] (an) edema. (⇨回 むくみ)

ぶしゅ 部首 (漢字の) a radical of a Chinese character.

***ふじゆう 不自由** 图 ❶ [[不便]] (an) inconvenience. ●テレビのない生活の不自由さ the *inconvenience* of life without TV. ●彼に不自由をさせる put him *to inconvenience*; *inconvenience* him. ▶住宅難でたいへん不自由している The housing shortage *causes* us a lot of *inconvenience*(s)./We *suffer* [*are put to*] great *inconvenience* because of the housing shortage.
❷ [[窮乏]] (貧乏) poverty. ●何不自由なく暮らす live *in comfort*; lead an *easy* life [a life of *ease*]. ▶彼はいつも金に不自由している(=不足している) He is always *short of* money. ▶あの人は金に不自由はない He has *plenty of* money./(金を自由に遣える) He *has* money *at his disposal*. ▶君に不自由はさせない You will *want for nothing*./You will have all you need. (❗ will の代わりに shall を用いるのは《書》)
── **不自由な** 形 ❶ [[不便な]] inconvenient. ▶田舎で生活するのは不自由だ It's *inconvenient* to live in the country.
❷ [[窮乏した]] ●不自由な暮らしをする live *in poverty*; lead a *hard* life; (暮らし向きが悪い) be badly [=well] off.
❸ [[身体の]] ●目が不自由だ (目が見えない) be *blind*; (婉曲的) (視力が弱い) have *weak* [*poor*] eyesight. ●足[手]が不自由だ have lost the use of one's legs [arms]. ▶彼は耳が不自由だ(=よく聞こえない) He doesn't hear *very well*./He is *hard of hearing*. ▶彼は体が不自由だ(=身体に障害がある)

ふしゅう 腐臭 ● 腐臭を放つ give out a *putrid smell*.
ぶしゅうぎ 不祝儀 (葬儀) a funeral.
● 不祝儀袋 an envelope for condolence money.

ふじゅうぶん 不十分 图 〖必要を満たすに足りないこと〗 insufficiency; 〖目的などに十分な条件を欠き不適当〗 inadequacy; 〖欠乏, 不足〗 lack, want; 〖不完全〗 imperfection. ● 証拠不十分で彼を釈放する release him on the grounds of *insufficient* evidence; set him free *for lack* [*want*] *of* (*sufficient*) evidence.
── 不十分な 形 (不足の, 十分でない) not enough, insufficient; (不適当な) inadequate; (能力が不十分な) incompetent; (不満足な) unsatisfactory; (不完全な) imperfect, incomplete. (⇨不完全) ▶ 彼の給料は二人の息子を大学に行かせるには不十分だ His salary is *not enough* [is *insufficient*, is *inadequate*] to send his two sons to college. ▶ 彼は英語教師として能力が不十分だ He is *incompetent* as an English teacher [*to teach* English, *for teaching* English]. ▶ 彼のレポートは不十分だ(不完全だ) His report is *imperfect*./(望むべき点が多い) His report *leaves much to be desired*./(不満足だ) His report is *unsatisfactory*.

ぶじゅつ 武術 martial [military] arts.
ふしゅび 不首尾 ● 不首尾に終わる end in failure; be unsuccessful.

ふじゅん 不純 impurity.
── 不純な 形 impure. ● 不純な(=不道徳な)動機から from *impure* [〖利己的な〗*selfish*, 〖私心のある〗*self-interested*] motives.
● 不純物 impurities.

ふじゅん 不順 ── 不順な 形 ● 不順な天候 (季節はずれの) *unseasonable* [〖定まらない〗*unsettled*, 〖変わりやすい〗*changeable*] weather.

ふじょ 扶助 〖援助〗 aid; 〖救済〗 relief. ● 相互扶助 mutual *help* [*aid*]. ● 政府[公共]の扶助を受ける receive government *aid* [public *relief*].

ふじょ 婦女 woman (働 women).
● 婦女暴行〖婉曲的〗(a) sexual assault; (a) rape. ● 婦女暴行を受ける be sexually assaulted; be raped.

ぶしょ 部署 one's post [station]. ● 部署につく[とどまる] take up [remain at] one's *post*.

*ふしょう** 負傷 图 (事故などによる) an injury, (まれ) a hurt; (弾丸・刃物などによる) a wound. (⇨怪我)
● 右肩の負傷 a *wound in* [an *injury to*, a *hurt on*] the right shoulder.
── 負傷する 動 (事故などで) be [get*] injured, be [get] hurt; (弾丸・刃物などで) be [get] wounded. (⇨怪我(を)する) ▶ その交通事故で多くの人が負傷した A lot of people *were injured* [×*was injured*] in the traffic accident. ▶ 彼はその戦いで足を負傷した He *was wounded* [×*was injured*] *in* the leg in the battle. (!「彼は事故で足を負傷した」は He *injured* his leg in the accident. で, wound とは異なり通例 ×He *was injured* in the leg .... とはいわない)
● 負傷者 an injured [a wounded] person; (総称) injured [wounded] people, 〖やや書〗 the injured [wounded]. (! the wounded はしばしば戦争による負傷兵をさす)

ふしょう 不詳 ── 不詳の 形 〖知られていない〗 unknown; (身元の) unidentified; (作者の) anonymous. ● 氏名不詳 The name is *unknown*. (⇨不明)

ふじょう 不浄 ── 不浄の 形 (汚れた) dirty, 〖やや書〗 unclean; (不純な) 〖やや書〗 impure. ● 不浄の(=不正な)金 *dirty* money.

ふじょう 浮上 ── 浮上する 動 (浮かび上がる) rise [come up] to the surface, surface; (順位などが上がる) go up [rise, advance] (*to* the top). ▶ 潜水艦がいきなり浮上してきた The sub(marine) *surfaced* suddenly.

*ぶしょう** 無精, 不精 ── 無精[不精]な 形 lazy. ● 筆無精(人) a *poor* [a *bad*] correspondent. ▶ 無精でまだ彼女に電話してないんだ I was too *lazy* to telephone her./I was *neglectful*. I haven't called her yet. (! *neglectful* は「(すべきだと承知の上で)(するのを)怠っておく」の意)
● 無精ひげ (短い) stubble, (やや伸びた) three days' stubble, a three-day beard. ● 無精者 a lazy fellow; (薄ぎたない怠け者) 〖話〗 a slob.

ぶしょう 武将 a commander of *samurai* army.
ふしょうか 不消化 indigestion; 〖医学〗 (消化不良) dyspepsia /dispépʃə/. ● ひどい不消化を起こす have [get] serious *indigestion*.
● 不消化物 indigestible food.

ふしょうじ 不祥事 (あってほしくない出来事) a deplorable event; (スキャンダル) a scandal.

ふしょうじき 不正直 图 dishonesty.
── 不正直な 形 dishonest.

ふしょうち 不承知 ● 不承知である (反対である) be against...; (賛成しない) disagree (*on, about*); (是認しない) disapprove (*of*). ▶ 彼はその件に[娘がその男と結婚することに]不承知である He *disagrees about* the matter [*disapproves of* his daughter marrying the man].

ふしょうぶしょう 不承不承 (very) reluctantly, (very) unwillingly. ● 嫌々(に)

ふしょうふずい 夫唱婦随 ▶ 夫唱婦随は昔の話だ The days of a dutiful and obedient wife is over.

ふじょうり 不条理 图 (an) absurdity.
── 不条理な 動 absurd; (不合理な) unreasonable. (⇨不合理)

ふしょく 腐食 corrosion; (特に, 酸による) erosion; (さびによる) rust.
── 腐食する[させる] 動 corrode; erode; (さびて) rust (...) away. (⇨腐る) ● 塩分で鉄柱が腐食した Salt *corroded* [*ate into*] the iron pillar.
● 腐食止め an ànticorrósive.

ふしょく 腐植 腐植土 humus (soil).

*ぶじょく** 侮辱 图 (an) insult (! 具体的な言動は Ⓒ); 〖法律〗 contempt /kəntémpt/. ● 法廷侮辱罪に問われるを charged with *contempt* (of court). ▶ そのような行為は女性に対するひどい侮辱だ Such conduct is a bad *insult* [is highly *insulting*] *to* women. ▶ 彼女は彼に侮辱的な言葉を浴びせた She hurled [flung] *insults* at him./She uttered *insulting* words to him.
── 侮辱する 動 insúlt. ▶ 彼は私を盗みをしたと言って侮辱した He *insulted* me by accusing me of stealing. ▶ 彼女は侮辱されて泣き出した She began to cry when she *was insulted*.

ふじょし 婦女子 women and children.
ふしょぶん 不処分 ● 不処分にする decide *not to punish* 《him》; decide *not to put* 《him》 *on probation*. (! put on probation は「保護観察処分にする」の意)

ふしん 不信 ❶ [不信用]discredit; (不信頼) (a) distrust. ● 不信を招く bring *discredit* 《*on*》. ▶ 彼は政治に不信の念を抱いている He has a *distrust* of politics./(あまり信用していない) He doesn't put much confidence in politics. ▶ 彼女の目には不信の色が表れていた Her eyes were filled with *distrust*.

ふしん

❷ [不実] faithlessness. ● 不信の行為 a *faithless deed*.

ふしん 不振 (不活発) dullness; (不景気) a [an economic] slump; (選手などの不調) a slump. (⇨不景気) ● 石油products不振 the oil industry *slump*. ● 食欲不振 a *poor* appetite. (減退) *loss of* appetite. ● 業績不振 a *poor* track record; a sales *slump*. ● チームの不振 a slumping [a lowly] team. ▶ 自動車業界はすでに不振期に入ってきている The car industry is already sinking into a *slump*. ▶ その店は売れ行き不振で店を閉めた The store shut down because of *poor* sales. ▶ その選手は打撃不振に陥っている The player is in a batting [hitting] slump.
— 不振の 形 (不活発な) inactive, slack. ▶ 商売が不振だ Business is *dull* [*slack, slow*].

ふしん 不審 图 [疑念] (a) doubt; [嫌疑] (a) suspicion.
— 不審な 形 ● 不審な行動を取る act *suspiciously* [奇妙に] *strangely*]. ● 不審な人物 a *doubtful* [(うさんくさい) a *dubious*, a *suspicious*] character. ▶ 不審な点があったら、私どもにお問い合わせください If you *have any doubt*(*s*), please refer to us. ▶ 不審な (= 奇妙な) ことがあればすぐ知らせてください If you come across *anything strange*, let me know at once.
— 不審(そう)に 副 ● 不審そうに彼を見る look at him *suspiciously* [*with suspicion*]. ▶ 警察は彼の行動を不審に思った The police *were* [×was] *suspicious of* his movements./The police thought his movements were *strange*.
● 不審船 a suspicious boat. ● 不審火 a fire suspected of arson. (**!** *arson* は「放火」の意).

ふしん 普請 图 building (of a house). ● 安普請の家 a *jerry-built* house.
— 普請する 動 build* (a house).

ふしん 腐心 — 腐心する 動 (骨折る) take* pains 《*to do*》; (非常に努力する) make* a great effort 《*to do*》; (苦労する) have* a lot of trouble 《*doing*》.

***ふじん** 夫人 a wife (圈 wives); (敬称) Mrs. /mísiz/. (**!** (1) [英] ではピリオドなし. (2) 正式には Mrs. +「夫の姓名」. Mrs. +「妻の旧姓名」で「未亡人」の意. 職業婦人や親しい者の手紙には一般の既婚婦人名もこれを使うことがある. (3) ×Mrs. Keiko (敬子夫人) のような言い方はしない. 加藤(安夫氏の)夫人 *Mrs*. (Yásuo) Káto.
● 社長夫人 the *wife* of a company president. ▶ 彼は夫人同伴でパーティーに出た He attended the party with his *wife*.

***ふじん** 婦人 a woman (圈 women); a lady. (**!** woman のより丁寧形で、当人を前にしたり商業宣伝文などで用いる) (⇨女) ● 老婦人 an elderly *lady*. ▶ ご婦人方はこちらへ This way, *ladies*! ▶ こちらのご婦人を席にご案内してあげて Show this *lady* to her seat.
● 婦人科 gynecology /gàinəkάləʤi/. ● 婦人科医 a wóman dòctor (**!** (1) 「女性の医師」は a fèmale [a wòman] dóctor. アクセントの違いに注意. (2) a lady doctor は侮辱的という人もいる) (⇨女 ④); a gynecologist. ● 婦人会 a women's association. ● 婦人記者 a woman reporter (圈 women reporters). ● 婦人警官 a policewoman (-women). ● 婦人参政権 female suffrage. ● 婦人雑誌 a women's [a ladies'] magazine. ● 婦人病 a woman's [a gynecological] disease. ● 婦人帽 a ladies' hat.

ふじん 布陣 图 (a) battle formation [[書] array]. ▶ 新内閣は最強の布陣で発足した The new government started with the best *lineup* of its ministers.
● 布陣する 動 go into battle formation; prepare for battle.

ぶじん 武人 a military figure; a soldier.

ふしんかん 不信感 (a) distrust; (疑念) (a) suspicion. ● ...に不信感を抱く have a *distrust* [be *distrustful*] 《*of*》.

ふしんしん 不信心 图 (やや書) impiety /impáiəti/.
— 不信心な 形 (やや書) impious /ímpiəs, impáiəs/.

ふしんせつ 不親切 ▶ 彼女は彼に不親切だった She was *not kind to* him. (**!** unkind は cruel, hard-hearted, unsympathetic など強いマイナスイメージを伴う語).

ふしんにん 不信任 nonconfidence.
● 不信任案 a nonconfidence vote [bill]. ▶ 内閣不信任案はわずかの差で否決された A vote [A bill] of *nonconfidence* in the Cabinet was defeated by a narrow margin. ● 不信任決議 a nonconfidence resolution. ● 不信任動議 a nonconfidence motion.

ふしんばん 不寝番 (行為) night watch; (人) a night guard. ● 不寝番をする keep *watch* during [throughout] the night.

ふす 付す (⇨付する)
ふす 伏す (⇨伏せる, 伏して)
ふず 付図 an attached map [図, 図形, 図表] diagram, [図, 図表] chart, [グラフ] graph, chart]. (**!** 海図, 水路図などは map でなく chart)

ぶす an ugly girl [woman (圈 -men)]; [米俗] a dog. (**!** 非常に無礼な言葉).

ふずい 不随 [麻痺, 略] parálysis. (⇨麻痺) ● 半身不随 *parálysis* on one side; [医学] hemiplegia /hèmiplíːdʒiə/. ● 全身不随 total [general] *paralysis*. ● 不随になる be paralyzed. ▶ 彼は全身[下半身]不随になった He *was* totally *paralyzed* [*was paralyzed* from the waist down].

ふずい 付随 — 付随する 動 (伴って生じる) accompany, be incidental 《*to*》; [書] attend. ● この件に付随する問題 problems *incidental to* [[書] *attendant on*] this matter. ▶ 税率の引き上げに付随して多くの問題が生じている A number of problems *have accompanied* the rise in taxes./The rise of tax rates has caused a lot of problems.

ぶすい 無粋, 不粋 — 無粋な, 不粋な 形 (気配りを欠いた) insensitive, (機転のきかない) tactless. ▶ 彼女の気持ちが分からないなんて信介も無粋な男だ It is *insensitive* of Shinsuke not to understand how she feels.

ふずいい 不随意 ● 不随意運動 involuntary motion. ● 不随意筋 [解剖] an involuntary muscle.

ふすう 負数 [数学] a negative number.

ぶすう 部数 the number of copies; (新聞・書籍などの発行部数) a circulation. ● 発行部数が多い have a large *circulation*. ▶ その雑誌は発行部数 20 万だ The magazine has a *circulation* of 200,000.

ぶすっと ❶ [押し黙ったさま] ● ぶすっとして sullenly.
● ぶすっとした顔 a *sullen* face [look]. ● ぶすっとする sulk. ▶ 彼女がまたぶすってしてる She *is sulking* again.
❷ [何かを強く突き差し込むさま] ▶ 彼はその男をナイフでぶすっと刺した He *stabbed* the man with a knife.

ぶすぶす ● ぶすぶす燃える smolder. ● ぶすぶす文句を言う grumble 《*about*》. ● (刃物などで) ぶすぶす突き刺す stab ... again and again. ● ボール箱にぶすぶす穴を開ける *poke* holes in the cardboard box with a nail.

ふすま 襖 a *fusuma*; (説明的に) a sliding door

ふすま covered with thick *fusuma* paper [cloth] on a wooden frame. (cf. 障子)

ふすま 麩 bran.

ぶすりと (⇨ぶすっと ❷)

ふする 付する 〖《付ける》〗(⇨付ける ❸); 〖(選択して)ゆだねる〗《やや書》submit (-tt-). ● 審議に付する《書》take (the matter) into deliberations. ● 公判に付する *bring* (the case) to trial. ● 火葬に付する cremate. ● 不問に付する (⇨不問)

ふせ 布施 ● お布施を包む make an *offering* (of money) (*to* a Buddhist priest).

***ふせい** 不正 图 (an) injustice; (a) wrong; (a) dishonesty; (an) illegality /ílìːgǽləti/. (❗いずれも具体的な行為を表す場合は 🄒)

> **《使い分け》 injustice** 正しさを欠いた不正.
> **wrong** 道徳に反する不正.
> **dishonesty** 人を欺いて行う不正
> **illegality** 法に反する不正 (= 違法).

①【不正~】● 公的資金の不正支出 *illegal* expenditure of public funds. ● 列車に不正乗車する (こっそり乗る) *steal a ride* on a train; (運賃をごまかす) *cheat on the train fare*. ▶ 彼は試験に不正行為 (= カンニング)をした He *cheated* on the exam.
②【不正を】● 不正を見逃す overlook an *injustice*. ▶ 彼は不正を認め, 自ら職を辞した He admitted the *injustice* and voluntarily stepped down from his job. ● 彼は不正を働いた He committed an illegal *act*./He did *wrong*. (❗wrong は名詞と堅い語) ▶ 不正を働いた銀行員は首になった The *dishonest* bank clerk was fired.
— **不正な** 圈 (ごまかしの) dishonest; (違法の) illégal; (不公平な) unfair. ▶ 彼は不正な手段で財を成した He made a fortune by *dishonest* [*illegal*, *unfair*] means. ▶ 公務員がわいろを受け取るのは不正なことだ It is *illegal* for public officials to take bribes.
● **不正疑惑** (an) illegal suspicion. ● **不正咬合**(ｺﾞｳ) 〖医学〗 malocclusion. ● **不正事件** (汚職事件) a corruption [a bribery, a graft] case. ● **不正(子宮)出血** dysfunctional uterine bleeding. ● **不正侵入** (コンピュータの) illegal computer access. ● **不正融資** illegal financing. ● **不正利得** dishonest gains. ● **不正利用** illegal [unfair] use.

ふせい 父性 paternity.
● **父性愛** paternal love.

ふぜい 風情 〖魅力〗(a) charm; 〖味わい〗(a) taste; 〖気品, 優雅さ〗élegance. ▶ 風情のある [ない] 庭 a *tasteful* [a *tasteless*] garden. ● ひなびた風情のある have a rustic *charm*. ● 風情を添える add a *charm*《*to*》. ▶ この町は以前の風情がなくなった This city has lost its *charm* [*elegance*].

ふせいかく 不正確 — **不正確な** 圈 (⇨正確な) ● 不正確な(= 間違った)答えをする give an *incorrect* answer. ● 計算が不正確だ be *inaccurate at* figures. ● 不正確な(= 厳密でない)推論 *inexact* reasoning.

ふせいこう 不成功 (失敗) failure. ● 具体的な事例をさすときは 🄒 (⇨失敗) ● 不成功に終わる be unsuccessful; end in failure; (失敗する) fail; (むだに終わる) come to nothing. ▶ 実験は不成功に終わった The experiment *ended in failure*. ▶ 最初の数編の小説はどれも不成功(= 失敗作)だった A couple of his first novels were *failures*.

ふせいじつ 不誠実 图 (誠意のなさ) insincerity; (不正直) dishonesty.
— **不誠実な** 圈 insincere; dishonest.

ふせいしゅつ 不世出 — **不世出の** 圈 (比類のない) incomparable, unparalleled.

ふせいせき 不成績 (悪い結果) poor [(不満足な) unsatisfactory, (期待に反する) 《やや書》 negative] results; (悪い成績) poor grades [(点数) marks]. ▶ 今年のレッドソックスは不成績に終わった The Red Sox had a *poor* [a disappointing] *season* this year.

ふせいみゃく 不整脈 an irregular pulse; irregular heartbeats; 〖医学〗 ar(r)hythmia.

ふせいりつ 不成立 (失敗) failure. (⇨成立) ▶ 交渉は不成立だった(= 失敗に終わった) The negotiations ended in *failure*. / The negotiations *fell through*. ▶ 議案は不成立だった(= 通らなかった) The bill *failed to pass*.

ふせき 布石 ● **布石を打つ** (必要な準備をする) make necessary arrangements 《*for*》.

:**ふせぐ** 防ぐ 〖予防する〗 prevent, keep* 《*from doing*》 (❗prevent の方が意味が強い); 〖寄せつけない〗keep ... off, (中に入れない) keep ... out; 〖用心する〗 guard 《*against*》; 〖保護する〗 protect 《*against*, *from*》. ● 事故を防ぐ *prevent* accidents. ● ポンドの下落を防ぐ *prevent* [*keep*] the pound *from* falling in value. ● 敵の攻撃を防ぐ *keep* the enemy's attack *off*. (= 食い止める) ● 間違いを防ぐ *guard against* mistakes [errors]. ▶ その医師団 [医薬] が病気が広がるのを防いだ The team of doctors [The medicine] *prevented* the disease 《*from*》 spreading. (❗from がない方は直接的な関与を, ある方は間接的な関与を表す) ▶ 手入れがよければ虫歯は防げる Tooth decay can be *prevented* by good care. ▶ 私は寒さを防ぐためにオーバーを着た I put on an overcoat to *keep out* [*protect* myself *against*] the cold. ▶ その柵(ｻｸ)が子供が道路に飛び出すのを防いでいる The fence *protects* the children *from* running into the road. (❗無生物主語の場合は通例 from の省略不可)

ふせじ 伏せ字 (理由があって印刷できない文字) unprintable words.

ふせつ 付説 an additional explanation.

ふせつ 符節 (割符) a tally (stick).
● **符節を合わせたように** ▶ 2人の話は符節を合わせたように一致した Their stories *tallied with* each other. / Their stories were exactly the same.

ふせつ 敷設 图 《やや書》 construction, building.
— **敷設する** 動 (ガス管などを敷く) lay; (建設する) build; construct. ● 光ファイバーのケーブルを敷設する *lay* a fiber-optic cable. ● 鉄道を敷設する *build* [*construct*] a railroad.

ふせっせい 不摂生 (健康に留意しないこと) neglect of one's health. ● 不摂生な(= 不健康な)生活をする lead an unhealthy way of life. ▶ 長年の不摂生がたたって胃かいようになった I got a stomach ulcer because I *neglected* my *health* for years.

***ふせる** 伏せる ❶ 〖下に向ける〗(身を伏せる) lie* down; (視線などを) cast* (one's eyes) down; (表を下にして) put* ... face down(ward); (上部を下にして) put ... upside down. ● 地面に身を伏せる *lie down* [*lie face down(ward)*] on the ground (❗前の方は単に身を横たえること, 後の方はうつ伏せになること); *throw oneself flat on the ground*. ● 本を机に伏せる *put* [*lay*] a book *face down(ward)* on the desk. ● たらいを伏せる *place* a tub *upside down* [*bottom up*]. ▶ 彼女はきまりが悪くなって顔を伏せた She got embarrassed and *looked down*.

❷ 〖秘密にする〗 make* ... a secret. ● この事は(彼には)伏せておいてくれ *Keep* this matter *a secret* 《*from* him》.

❸ 〖病気などで〗 ● 病気で伏せっている be sick [〖主

ふせん 〖英〗ill〗 *in bed*. (⇨寝る❸)

ふせん 不戦 ●**不戦勝** a win by default. ●**不戦勝**する win (a game) by default. ●**不戦条約** 〖conclude [violate]〗 an anti-war treaty [pact] 《with Japan》. ●**不戦敗** a loss by default. ●不戦敗になる lose (a game) by default.

ふせん 付箋 a tag, a label /léibl/, a slip of paper.
● 付箋を付ける tag; label; put a *tag* [a *label*] on.

ふぜん 不全 (不完全) imperfection; (必要を満たせないこと) insufficiency. ●**心不全** 〖医学〗 cardiac *insufficiency*; malfunction of the heart.

ふぜん 不善 ▶小人閑居して不善をなす (⇨小人(ɔょぅ)) [成句]

ぶぜん 憮然 ● 憮然として 〖茫然として〗 dumbfounded [stunned] 《by, at; to do》; (放心状態で) in a daze, in utter amazement; 〖落胆して〗 disappointed, in disappointments; 〖ため息をついて〗 with a sigh.

ふせんめい 不鮮明 ― **不鮮明な** 形 (明らかでない) indistinct; not clear. ▶この本の印刷は不鮮明だ The print in this book is *not distinct* [*not clear, indistinct*].

ふそ 父祖 ancestors. ●父祖伝来の ancestral. (⇨先祖)

ぶそう 武装 名 〖集合的〗 armament. (**!** 時に ～ s. 主に重兵器による武装)
● 武装化する militarize 《a nation》.
― **武装する** 動 arm oneself 《*with* a gun》; (状態) be armed 《*with* a gun》, be under arms. ●銃で武装させる *arm* 〈him〉 with a gun.
● **武装解除** disarmament; (国や地域などの) demilitarization; (建物や軍艦などの) dismantlement. ● **武装解除する** disarm; (国や地域などを) demilitarize; (建物や軍艦などを) dismantle. ● **武装警官** an armed police officer; a police officer under arms. ● **武装地帯** a militarized zone. (関連) 非武装地帯 a demilitarized zone) ● **武装中立** armed neutrality. (関連) 非武装中立 unarmed neutrality).

ふそうおう 不相応 ― **不相応な** 形 (ふさわしくない) unfit 《*for*》; unsuitable 《*for*》; (不釣り合いな) out of proportion 《*to*》; (似合いな) unbecoming 《*to*》. (⇨相応) ▶彼は身分不相応な高級車を乗り回している He drives around in a luxury car *beyond his means*. (**!** means は「収入」の意)

*ふそく 不足 名 ❶〖不十分〗(a) shortage;《書》(an) insufficiency 〖複数形なし〗; (a) scarcity; 〖欠乏〗(a) lack (**!** 複数形なし);《やや書》(a) want 〖複数形なし〗;《やや書》(a) deficiency; 〖不足額〗a déficit; 〖差額〗(a) difference.

┌─────────────────────────
│ 使い分け **shortage** 必要な分量より少ない状態.
│ **insufficiency** 必要なものが十分でないこと.
│ **scarcity** 需要に満たず, 手に入りにくいこと.
│ **lack** 必要なものがまったくないか十分でない状態のこと.
│ **want** 特に必要不可欠なものがまったくないか十分でない状態のこと.
│ **deficiency** 通常の機能のためには不可欠と思われるものがまったくないか十分でないこと.
└─────────────────────────

①〖～(の)不足〗●石油不足 a *shortage* 〖《書》a *dearth*〗 of oil; an oil *shortage* 〖《書》*dearth*〗; (供給不足) a *short* 〖an *insufficient*〗 *supply* of oil. ●準備不足 (a) *lack* of preparation; (不十分な準備) (an) inadequate preparation. ●準備不足の ill-prepared 《*for*》. ●説明不足 (a) lack of explanation; (十分な説明) (an) inadequate explanation. ●ビタミンCのひどい不足 a serious *lack* [*deficiency*] of vitamin C. ●歳入の不足(額) a *deficit* in revenue. ●今日の労働力の不足 the labor *shortages* of today. ▶最近の住宅不足は深刻だ The housing *shortage* is very acute these days./There is a very acute *shortage* of houses these days. ▶その地域では水不足がしばしば起こる Water *shortages* often occur in that area. ▶彼はまだ経験不足だ He's still *lacking in* experience. ▶最近は運動不足になりがちです I tend *not* to get *enough* exercise [I'm liable to *lack* exercise] these days. ▶ニューヨークタイムズの記事はあの事件について説明不足である The article in *The New York Times* is *short of* explanation of the event.

②〖不足を〗●不足を補う supply [meet] a *shortage*; make up (for) a *deficiency*. (⇨補う)
③〖不足で〗〖のために〗●睡眠不足のために *for* [*through*] *lack of* sleep; *for* [*from*] *want of* sleep; because one didn't sleep *well*. ●人手不足で困る suffer from a manpower *shortage* [a *shortage* of manpower]. ●情報不足でパニックになった A lack of information caused a panic.

❷〖不満足〗dissatisfaction, discontent; 〖不平〗(a) complaint. ●不足そうな顔をする look *dissatisfied* [*discontented*]. ●食べ物に不足を言う complain 〖ぶつぶつ言う〗 grumble] *about* the food. ▶彼なら相手にとって不足はない(=好敵手だ) He is a good match for me.

❸〖困窮〗want; need. ●何不足なく暮らす live in comfort 〖《書》plenty〗; (裕福である) be well off.
― **不足する** 動 run* *short* 〈*of*〉; 〖不足している〗be short 〈*of*〉. (⇨欠く, 足りない) ●食料が不足している We *are short of* food. (**!** 具体的な物についていう場合, We lack [are lacking in] food. のように lack を用いるのは非常に堅い言い方 (⇨図 ❶ ①))/We don't have enough food. (**!** There is a *shortage* [a *short supply*] of food./Food is scarce [in short supply]. なども可 (⇨図 ❶ ①)) ▶資金が不足してきた Our funds *are running short*./We *are running short* of funds.

ふそく 不測 ― **不測の** 形 (予知できない) unexpected, unforeseen (**!** 後の方がより口語的な) (偶然の) accidental. ●不測の災害に備える provide against an *unexpected* [an *unforeseen*] disaster.

ふそく 付則 (付け足した規則) an additional rule [regulation]; (補則) a supplementary provision.

ふぞく 付属 名 ●A大学付属高校 a senior high school *attached to* A University. ●車の付属品 *accessories* for a car; car *accessories*.
― **付属する** 動 be attached 《*to*》.

ぶぞく 部族 名 a tribe.
― **部族(間)の** 形 tribal. ●部族の一員 a tribal [*tribe*] member. ●男女に分けて, a tribesman, a tribeswoman ともいう) ●部族間の闘い *tribal* warfare.
● **部族意識** tribalism.

ふそくふり 不即不離 ● 不即不離の関係を維持する keep a relation neither too close nor too distant 《*with*》.

ふぞろい 不揃い ― **不揃いの** 形 (不均整の) irregular; (平らでない) uneven. ●これらのリンゴは大きさが不揃いだ These apples are *irregular* in size.

ふそん 不遜 ― **不遜な** 形 〖傲慢な〗insolent,《書》impudent (**!** 通例目上の人に対して); 〖横柄な〗árrogant (**!** 思い上がった) concéited; (人を見下した) contémptuous.

*ふた 蓋 〖箱・なべなどの〗a lid; 〖びんなどの〗a top (**!** lid より小さな容器の), a cap (**!** カメラのレンズや万年筆の

ふだ たなどにも用いる); 〘覆い〙 a cover. ▶ふた付きの lidded; covered. ▶ふたのない lidless; open. ▶ふたをする cover 《a box (with a lid)》; put the lid 《on a box》; cap 《a bottle》; (醜聞などに) hush up 《a scandal》; (ふたを) take the lid off 《a bottle》; (あける) open 《a bottle》; (覆いを) uncover 《a dish》. ▶ふたを(回して)しっかり閉めなさい Screw the cap tightly.

*__ふだ__ 札 a label /léibl/; a tag; a ticket.

〘使い分け〙 **label** 紙・プラスチック・布などでできており、物品に張り付けて中身・送り先・持ち主などを示す。
tag 紙・金属・プラスチック・皮などの細長い1片で、物に張り付けるものやひも付きのものがある。 labelと同じ目的の他に物の識別や分類に用いられる。
ticket 主に値段・品質などを示す。

● **名札** a nameplate; a náme tàg. (❗パーティーなどで胸につけたり、会議で机上に置くのは前の語) ● **番号札** a number tag. ● (手荷物の預かり札) a (baggage) claim tag [check]. ● **守り札** a charm, a talisman. ● **札付きのトランプの札** a (playing) card. (⇒カード)
● **札付きの悪党** (⇒札付き) ● **札を張る** (⇒レッテル)

*__ぶた__ 豚 〘動物〙 a pig, a hog; 〘去勢しない雄豚〙 a boar; 〘雌豚〙 a sow; 〘古〙 a swine (❗単・複同形); 〘豚肉〙 pork.

〘使い分け〙 **pig** 《英》では広く豚を意味する一般的な語だが,《米》では120ポンド以下の「子豚」の意で用いる。
hog 《米》で「成長した豚」の意だが,《英》では食肉用に去勢した雄豚をさすことが多い.

● **食肉用の豚** a pork pig. ● **焼き豚** roast pork; (丸焼きの) roast pig. ● **豚のように太った豚** be fat as a pig. ● **豚のようにがつがつ食べる** eat like a hog. ● **豚を飼う** breed 〘主に英〙 keep〙 pigs; raise hogs.
▶豚がぶうぶう鳴いている The hog [pig] is grunting.
● **豚に真珠** (ことわざ) cast [throw] pearls before swine. (⇒聖書から)
● **豚小屋** a pigsty; 《米》a pigpen, a hogpen.

ぶたい 付帯 ● **付帯決議** (補助的決議) (やや書) a supplementary resolution. ● **付帯工事** related work. (❗電気・ガス・水道など住宅建設に基本的に付随する工事をさす場合には, utilities work というとはっきりする) ● **付帯条件** (付随的な条件) an incidental [(書) a collateral] condition.

*__ぶたい__ 舞台 ● 〘芝居の〙 the stage.
① 〘~舞台〙 ● **回り舞台** a revolving stage. ● **初舞台** a debut /deibjú:, déibju:/. (⇒④; 初舞台)
② 〘舞台~〙 ● **舞台負けする** (=あがる) have stage fright. ▶彼は舞台度胸がいい He doesn't get stage fright.
③ 〘舞台に〙 ● **舞台に立つ** appear on the stage; make the stage appearance; (舞台に上がる) go on the stage. (❗最後の言い方は「俳優になる」の意にもなる) ▶彼女は5年ぶりに舞台にカムバックした She came back to the stage after five years' absence [a five-year interval, for the first time in five years].
④ 〘舞台を〙 ● **初めて舞台を踏む** make one's debut; make one's first appearance on the stage. ● **舞台を退く** (俳優が) retire from [quit] the stage. ▶ダンサーは活気あふれる舞台(=演技)を見せてくれた The dancers gave a vivid performance.
⑤ 〘舞台で〙 ● **舞台で演じる** perform [play] on the stage.
❷ 〘活動の場〙 the stage; (範囲) a sphere. ▶彼の活動の舞台は非常に広い He has a wide sphere of activity. ▶彼は政治の[国際]舞台で主導的な役割を果たしている He is playing a leading role on the political [international] stage. ▶彼女は活動の舞台を京都から東京に移した She transferred the sphere [scene] of her activity from Kyoto to Tokyo.
❸ 〘場面〙 a scene. ▶この小説の舞台は京都です The scene [(背景) setting] of this story is (laid) in Kyoto./This story is set in Kyoto. ▶舞台が変わった The scene (has) changed.
❹ 〘その他の表現〙 ● **独り舞台である** (=人気をひとり占めする) steal the show [scene].
● **舞台衣装** a stage costume [garment] (❗しばしば複数形で); (芝居の) a theatrical costume. ● **舞台裏** (⇒舞台裏) ● **舞台演出** stage direction [production]. ● **舞台演出家** a stage director 《主に米》[producer 《主に英》]. ● **舞台監督** (人) a stage manager; (事) stage management. ● **舞台稽古** (have) a stage [舞台衣装を着て行う) a dress] rehearsal. ● **舞台効果** stage effects. ● **舞台照明** stage lighting. ● **舞台装置** stage setting. ● **舞台中継** a stage relay; a drama relayed from the stage. ● **舞台俳優** a stage actor [actress, player].

ぶたい 部隊 (軍隊などの) a unit; (特別の任務の) a corps /kɔ́ːr/ (圏 ~ /kɔ́ːrz/). ● **医療部隊** a hospital unit; a medical corps. ● **部隊長** a commander.

ぶたいうら 舞台裏 (俳優の控え室) the greenroom.
● **舞台裏の工作** backstage [behind-the-scenes] maneuvering. ● **舞台裏で決定する** make a decision behind the scenes [stage].

ふたいてん 不退転 ● **不退転の決意で** with an indomitable resolve; resolutely.

ふたく 付託 ━━ **付託する** 動 ▶議案を委員会に付託する refer a bill to a committee.

ふたく 負託 ● **国民の負託にこたえる** live up to people's trust.

ぶたくさ 豚草 〘植物〙 (a) ragweed.

ふたけた 二桁 double digits.
● **二桁成長** double-digit growth. ● **二桁成長をする** grow at double-digit rates.

ふたご 双子 twins. (❗複数形に注意) ● **双子の姉[妹]** one's twin sister. ▶彼女は双子の女の子を産んだ She had [gave birth to] twin girls. (❗had は口語で用いるが、文脈によってはあいまい) ▶彼は双子です He is one of the twins. (❗He is a twin. はまれ。×He is one of twins. とはいわない.「彼らは双子です」は They are twins.)

ふたごころ 二心 ● **二心がある** be unfaithful [(やや書) disloyal] 《to》. ● **二心がない** be faithful [loyal] 《to》.

ふたござ 双子座 〘占星・天文〙 Gemini /dʒémənài/ (the はつけない); (双子宮) 〘占星〙 the Twins. (⇒乙女座) ● **双子座(生まれ)の人** a Gemini, a Geminian. (❗後者の方は形容詞にも用いる)

ふたことめ 二言目 ● **二言目には疲れたと言う (口をきくには必ず)** He never opens his mouth without saying, "I'm tired."/(いつも) He always says, "I'm tired."

ふたしか 不確か ━━ **不確かな** 形 〘不確実な〙 uncertain; (信頼できない) unreliable; (漠然とした) vague /véig/; (不明確な) indefinite /indéfənit/. ● **不確かな情報** unreliable information. ● **不確かな記憶** an uncertain [an unreliable, a vague] memory. ● **不確かな返事** an indefinite reply.

ふだしょ 札所 (説明的に) a numbered holy place (=temple) for pilgrims where they offer cards (and handcopied prayers) and get the temple's certificate of their visit. ●四国八十八か所札所 Pilgrims' Eighty-eight Holy Places in Shikoku.

ふたすじみち 二筋道 〖別れ道〗 a forked road; 〖相異なる2つの方向〗 two divergent ways.

***ふたたび** 再び 〖二度〗 again; twice; 〖もう一度〗 once more [again]; 〖二度目に〗 for the second time. ▶ ふたたび彼はオーケーと言った *Again* he said OK./He *again* said OK./He said OK *again*. ●またふたたびそのような誤りをするな Don't make that mistake *again* [*twice*]. (❗ twice は「二度」, again は「くり返し」に重点がある)/(くり返すな) Don't *repeat* such a mistake. ●彼はふたたび戻って来た He is back *again* [*once more*]. ●彼女はふたたびそれに挑戦した She tried it *again* [*a second time*]. ▶彼は1時間後ふたたび仕事を始めた He *resumed* his work after an hour. (❗ resume は「ふたたび始める」の意)

***ふたつ** 二つ two; 〖半分〗 a half (圏 halves); 〖両方〗 both. (⇨とも) ●リンゴを二つに切る cut an apple *in two* [*in half, into halves*]. ●紙を二つに折る fold the paper *in two* [*half*]; *double* the paper. ●一度に二つずつリンゴを取る take *two* apples at a time. ●このミカンを二つくだざい Give me *two* of these oranges. ▶彼女はケーキを二つとも食べた She ate *both* pieces of the cake. ▶それら二つとも欲しくない I don't want either [×both] of them. (❗ not both は部分否定で「二つは欲しくない」)/I want neither of them.
- 二つとない こんな絵は二つとない(=匹敵するものがない) This picture *has no equal* [*match*]./This picture is *unique* [*matchless*].
- 二つ返事 ●彼は二つ返事で(=すぐさま)その計画を承諾した He *promptly* [*readily*] consented to the plan.

ふたつき 札付き ●札付きの悪党 《やや書》 an *infamous* /ínfəməs/ [a *notorious*] villain /vílən/.

ふたて 二手 ●わたしたちは二手に(=二つのグループに)分かれて行方不明の少女を捜索した We divided into *two groups* and searched for the missing girl.

ふたとおり 二通り 〖二つ〗 two. ●二通りの解釈ができる 〖事が主語〗 admit of *two* interpretations. ▶それには二通りのやり方がある There are *two* ways of doing it./It can be done in *two* ways.

ふたどめ 札止め 〖入場券売り切れ〗 a sellout. ●サーカスは札止めの盛況だった All the tickets for the circus had sold out./The circus had completely sold out.

ぶたにく 豚肉 pork. (⇨豚)

ブタノール 〖化学〗 butanol /bjúːt(ə)nɔːl/.

ふたば 双葉, 二葉 a seed-leaf (圏 -leaves). (❗ 専門語で a cotyledon /kàtəlíːdn/) 〖栴檀(栴檀)〗 ●双葉(=芽)のうちに摘みとる nip ... in the bud.

ぶたばこ 豚箱 〖留置所〗 〖話〗 a lockup (⇨留置); 〖刑務所〗 〖話〗 a clink, 〖米話〗 a can. ●一晩豚箱に入る spend a night in a *lockup*.

ブダペスト 〖ハンガリーの首都〗 Budapest /b(j)úːdəpèst/.

ふたまた 二叉, 二股 圏 〖分岐したもの〗 a fork; 〖枝状のもの〗 a branch. ●二またに分かれる fork; branch off. ●二またをかける have it both ways. (❗ 両天びんにかける の意) ▶別荘へ行く道がここで二またに分かれる The road to the villa *branches off* here.
— 二叉(の), 二股(の) 圏 forked. ●二また道 a *forked* road. ●二またのソケット a *two-way* socket.
- 二また膏薬 〖どっちつかず〗 fence-sitting; 〖どっちつかずの人〗 a fence sitter; 〖節操のない人〗 a person

with no principles. (⇨日和(ひより)見)

ふため 二目 **二目と見られぬ** ●二目と見られぬ顔 a frightful [a hideous] face; a shockingly ugly face.

ふたもの 蓋物 an earthenware [a lacquerware] dish or bowl with a lid.

***ふたり** 二人 〖二人〗 two (people); 〖両方〗 both; 〖一組〗 a pair; 〖二人〗 double. ●二人ずつ組で *two by two*. ●二人一組になって *in pairs*. ●二人部屋 a *double* (↔ a single) room. ●二人目の息子 one's *second* son. ●自転車に二人乗りする ride a bicycle *double*. ●私たち二人はここに残ります The *two* of us stay here. (❗ us は同格の of. Two of us .... の of は部分の of で「私たちのうちの二人は」の意) ●二人のうちで年上はどちらですか Which is the older [×oldest] *of the two*? ●二人とも高校生です *Both* of them are [They are *both*, ×They both are] high school students./(高校へ行っている) They *both* go to high school. (❗ both の位置に注意(⇨とも)) ▶彼らは二人ともまだ来ない *Neither of* them has [〖話〗 have] come yet. ▶彼は母親と二人暮らしです He lives with his mother *alone*./He and his mother live (all) *by themselves* [*on their own*].

ふたん 負担 圏 〖過重な義務・責任〗 〖やや書〗 a burden; 〖責任・罪などの重圧〗 a load; 〖責任〗 responsibility. ●納税者の税負担 the *burden* of taxation *on* the taxpayer. ●負担をかける impose a *burden* (*on*). ●彼の負担を軽く[重く; 軽減]する lighten [increase; relieve] the *burden on* him. ▶来る日も来る日も病人の世話をするのは相当な負担です It's quite a *burden* to care for a sick person day in and day out. ▶彼は負担が大きすぎる He has too heavy a *burden*./That's *too much* for him. ▶その仕事をそんなに負担に感じなくてもいい You don't have to feel so much *responsibility for* the job.
— 負担する 動 〖支払う〗 pay*; 〖義務として引き受ける〗 bear*. ●だれが旅行費用を負担するのですか Who will *pay* your traveling expenses? ●会社がその事故の損害(賠償金)を負担した The company *bore* damages for the accident.

***ふだん** 普段 〖通常〗 usually; 〖普通〗 generally; 〖常に〗 always. (⇨いつも 解説) ●普段よくある間違い a *common* mistake. ●普段の出来事(=日常茶飯事) an *everyday* occurrence. ▶私は普段歩いて学校へ行く I *usually* walk to school. ▶私は普段から健康には気を付けている I *always* take care of my health. ▶彼は普段どおり9時に[普段より早く]家を出た He left home at nine *as usual* [*earlier than usual*]. ▶彼は普段と変わった様子もなかった There was nothing *unusual* [*strange*] about him.

ふだん 不断 ▶彼の成功は不断の(=変わらず続く)努力によるものだ His success is due to his *constant* [*unflagging*, *ceaseless*] efforts.

ブタン 〖化学〗 butane /bjúːtein/.

ぶだん 武断 ●武断主義 militarism. ●武断政治 military government.

ふだんぎ 普段着 〖平常の服装〗 everyday clothes [wear] (❗ いずれも集合的. clothes は複数扱い, wear は単数扱いで主に商用語); 〖正装に対して〗 an informal dress; 〖軽装〗 casual clothes [wear]. ▶彼は普段着のまま会社へ行った He went to the office *in everyday clothes*.

ふだんそう 不断草 〖植物〗 a (Swiss) chard.

***ふち** 縁 〖端〗 an edge, 〖やや書〗 a margin; 〖崖(がけ)などの〗 a brink (⇨端); 〖円形の物の〗 a rim, 〖容器の〗 a

brim (⚠ 水などを満たす場合); 〖平面・場所の境界部分〗a border, a verge. ● テーブルの縁 the *edge* of a table. ● 眼鏡の縁 the *rims* [*frames*] of the glasses. ● コップの縁 the *rim* of a glass. ● 湖の縁 on the *border* [*edge*] of a lake. ● 花で縁を取った歩道 a sidewalk with a *border* of flowers. ● 水をグラスの縁まで入れて fill the glass to the **brim** with water. ● 縁なしの眼鏡 *rimless* glasses. ● 縁なしの帽子 a *brimless* hat. ● 歩道の縁(石)《米》a curb; 《英》a kerb. ● 金縁《金縁》● このテーブルクロスは縁が青い This tablecloth has a blue *border*.

ふち 淵 〖川の〗a deep pool; (流れの中の) a deep place; 〖深い所〗the depths. ● 絶望の淵に沈んでいる be in the *depths* of despair. ● 破滅の淵(=瀬戸際)に立つ be on the *brink* of ruin.

ふち 不治 (⇨不治)

ふち 扶持 〖武士の給与〗a salary; a stipend /stéipend/; 〖書〗a emolument (⚠ 通例複数形で).

ぶち spots; (小さな斑点に)specks. (⇨斑点). ● ぶちのある spotted, mottled. ● 斑(ぶち)● ぶちの犬 a spotted [a mottled] dog. ● ぶちの猫 a tabby [a brindled] cat.

プチ 〖小さい〗petit /pətí/.
● プチ家出 a petit runaway; (説明的に) an adolescent running away from home for a short time. ● プチトマト (ミニトマト) a cherry tomato. (1) 小型のトマト a petit [a mini] tomato とはいわない. (2) a miniature tomato は可 ● プチナイフ 〖ペティナイフ〗(皮むき用の小型ナイフ) a páring knife (果物ナイフ) a frúit knife. (⚠(1) 前の方が普通. (2) 通例 a petit knife とはいわない ● プチパン (小型ロールパン) a petit pain (⑧ petits pains). ● プチフール (一口大のケーキ) a petit four (⑧ petit(s) fours). ● プチホテル a petit hotel.

ぶちあたる ぶち当たる hit (*against*); (勢いよく) run (*into*); (激しくぶつかる) crash (*against, into*); (どすんと) bump (*into, against*). ● 人にぶち当たる *hit againsst* a person. ● 電柱にぶち当たる *run* [*crush*] *into* a utility pole. ● 人生の壁にぶち当たる *run into* a brick wall in life. ● 多くの困難にぶち当たる *run into* 〖直面する〗*face*〛many difficulties.

ふちいし 縁石《米》a curb(stone);《英》a kerb (stone).

ふちかがり 縁かがり 图 a hemstitch.
— **縁かがり(を)する** 動 hemstitch; hem (-mm-).

ふちかざり 縁飾り edging; (フリルをつけた) a frill. ● フリルの縁飾りがしてあるブラウス a *frilled* blouse; a blouse *with frills*.

ぶちかます 打ち噛ます (ぶん殴る) bash《him *on* the head》; (体当たりする) hurl oneself《*at*》; (強い一撃を与える) give《him》a hard punch〖《話》a haywire〗《*in* the face, *on* the nose》.

ぶちこむ 打ち込む throw*《it *into* the river》; (刑務所へ) throw《him *into* jail [prison]》.

ぶちころす 打ち殺す kill; (残虐な手口で) butcher; kill cruelly [brutally].

ぶちこわし 打ち壊し ▶ 彼の不用意な発言のために懇親会はぶち壊しになった His careless remark *spoiled* [*ruined, upset, wrecked*] the convivial party.

ぶちこわす 打ち壊す (台なしにする) spoil*; (めちゃくちゃにする) wreck; ruin; upset*; (損なう)《書》mar (-rr-).

ふちどり 縁取り (衣服や紙の) a border; (房飾り) a fringe. ● レースの縁取りをしたハンカチ a *lace bordered*. ● 黒い縁取りの写真 a picture with a black *border*. ● 縁取りをする (⇨縁取る)

ふちどる 縁取る (花などで境界をつける) border, edge; (房飾り) fringe; (枠で) frame. ● レースで縁取ったハンカチ a *lace-edged* handkerchief. ● 彼女はドレスをレースで縁取っていた She *bordered* [*edged, trimmed*] the dress *with* lace. ● 花園はチューリップで縁取られていた The flower garden *was fringed* with tulips.

ぶちぬき 打ち抜き ● 6段ぶち抜きの大ニュース a big news item using six columns.

ぶちぬく 打ち抜く ❶〖貫通させる〗(弾丸などが) shoot*《him》through《the head》, pierce. ● 山にトンネルをぶち抜く dig a tunnel *through* a mountain. ● 壁をぶち抜いて大きな部屋を作る remove the wall to make one big room.
❷〖完遂する〗● 3日間のストをぶち抜く carry out a three-day strike.

ぶちのめす 打ちのめす (殴り倒す) knock ... down [flat to the ground]; (てんぱんにやっつける)《やや話》beat* ... to a pulp.

プチブル(ジョア) 〖＜フランス語〗〖小市民〗a petit bourgeois /pətì:-buərʒwá/ (⑧ petits bourgeois /-(z)/). ● プチブル根性 a *petit bourgeois* mentality.

ぶちまける (空にする) empty ... (out), dump; (怒りなどを) vent; (真実などを) tell*. ● 怒りを妻にぶちまける *vent* one's anger *on* one's wife《*by doing*》. ● ぶちまけたところ to tell (you) the truth; frankly (speaking); to be perfectly frank (with you). (⚠ 以上の句はいずれも通例文頭で)

ふちゃく 付着 — **付着する** 動 stick (*to*),《やや書》adhere (*to*). ● 血痕の付着したシャツ a bloodstained shirt.

ふちゃく 不着 nonarrival; (不配達) non-delivery.
● 不着郵便物 undelivered [lost,《やや古》misdirected] mail.

ふちゅう 不忠 图 disloyalty (*to*). — **不忠の** 形 disloyal.

*ふちゅうい **不注意** 图 carelessness; 〖怠慢〗negligence; 〖無思慮〗thoughtlessness. ▶ その事故は運転手の不注意によって起きた The accident happened through the driver's *carelessness* [*negligence*]./The accident was caused by the driver's *carelessness* [*negligence*]. ▶ 彼女は不注意からその花びんを割ってしまった She was *careless* and broke the vase.
— **不注意な** 形 careless (*of*); negligent (*of*); thoughtless (*of*); (無神経な) insensitive (*to*). ● 不注意な間違いをする make a *careless* mistake. ▶ 彼は不注意な運転で事故を起こした He drove *carelessly* and had an accident. ▶ 彼の不注意な発言が彼女の感情を害した His *careless* [*thoughtless, insensitive*] remarks hurt her feelings. ▶ 窓を開けっ放しにしていたとは彼は不注意だった It was *careless of* him [He *was careless*] *to* leave the window open./*Carelessly* he left the window open.(⚠ この意では He *carelessly* left ....の位置も可)

ふちょう 不調 (a) bad condition (⇨調子 ❶); 〖不成立〗failure. ● 不調である be *in bad* [*out of*] *condition*; (運動選手などが) be *off* [*out of*] *form*,《主に米》be *in a slump*. ▶ 今日はどうも体が不調だ I don't feel well today./I'm *not in good condition* today. ▶ あのチームは最近不調だ The team have been *off* [*out of*] *form* recently. ▶ 交渉は不調に終わった The negotiation ended in *failure*./(決裂した) The negotiation *broke down*.

ふちょう 府庁 a prefectural government office. (⇨県庁)

ふちょう 婦長 〖「(看護)師長」の以前の言い方〗a head nurse,《英》a senior nursing officer (⚠ 正式名).

ふちょう 符丁 〔符号〕a sign, a mark; 〔合い言葉〕a password; 〔暗号〕a cipher.

ぶちょう 部長 a (general) manager (⚠ ×Mr. General Manager のように呼び掛けには用いない); a department [a division] manager. ● 人事[営業; 購買]部長 a personnel [a sales; a purchasing] manager. ▶ミラーさん, こちらが輸出部長の阿部ですMr. Miller, this is Mr. Abe, manager of the Export Department.

● 部長代理 a deputy manager.

ぶちょうほう 不調法, 無調法 ❶〖不行き届き〗(あやまち) a blunder; (うかつなこと) carelessness; 〔下手なこと〕poorness. ▶不調法をする make a blunder; (礼を失する) be impolite. ▶口が不調法なるbe not a good [a smooth, (口達者な) a fluent] speaker.
❷〖酒が飲めないこと〗▶私, 不調法でしてNo, thank you. I don't drink.

ふちょうわ 不調和 图 lack of harmony, disharmony. (⇨調和) ▶不調和である do not harmonize 《with》, be out of harmony 《with》.
—— **不調和な** 形 disharmonious, 《書》inharmonious.

ふちん 不沈 ▶不沈戦艦といわれた大和もあえなく撃沈された The Yamato, a supposedly unsinkable battleship, was sunk too easily.

ふちん 浮沈 〔話〕ups and downs. (⇨浮き沈み) ▶我が国の浮沈にかかわる一大事 a grave matter vital to our country.

ぶつ 物 〖品物〗goods; an article; 〖お金〗money; 〔現金〕cash; 〔俗〕dough.

ぶつ 打つ ❶〖殴る〗hit*. (⇨殴る)
❷〖演説する〗give* a talk; give [make*] a speech. (⇨演説)

ふつう 普通 —— **普通の** 形 common (↔uncommon); ordinary (↔special, extraordinary); usual (↔unusual); general (↔specific); universal; normal (↔abnormal); average; medium.

使い分け	
common	様々な時代・場所に共通する一般性を持つこと.
ordinary	ありふれていて平凡で面白みのないこと.
usual	状況や展開などが通常通りであること.
general	およそ全体に当てはまる一般性を持つこと.
universal	例外なく全体に当てはまること.
normal	平均や基準から逸脱せず, 正常・普通であること.
average	ずば抜けた点がなく, 平均的で普通であること.
medium	サイズが大きすぎず小さすぎず, 中ぐらいで普通であること.

①〖普通の〜〗▶普通の状態に戻っている[戻る] be back [go back, 《やや書》return] to normal. ▶今では女性が結婚後も仕事を続けるのはごく普通のことだ It is now quite common for women to continue their work after marriage. ▶彼はごく普通のサラリーマンだ He's just an ordinary [《平均的な》an average] office worker. ▶指しゃぶりは幼児には普通の(=よくある)ことだ Thumb sucking is usual with [for] little children./It's usual [the usual thing, not unusual] for small children to suck their thumbs. ▶この本は普通の読者向きだ This book is suitable [《やや書》intended] for general readers.

【会話】「髪はどのようにカットいたしましょうか」「普通(の長さ)でお願いします」"How do you want your hair cut?" "Medium length, please."

【会話】「歯ブラシをください」「電動のですか」「いいえ, 普通のでいいです」"I'd like a toothbrush, please." "Electric?" "No, just an ordinary [a regular] one."

②〖…は[が]普通だ〗▶この方がそれより普通だ This is more common [normal] than that. ▶彼のふるまいはとても普通とはいえない His behavior is a long way [《やや書》far] from normal./His behavior is quite abnormal. ▶彼の身長は普通[普通以上; 普通以下]だ He's about [above; below] average in height.

—— **普通(に)** 副 〔通例〕usually, (一般に) generally; 〔普通程度に〕ordinarily; 〔正常に〕normally. ●普通にふるまう behave ordinarily [normally]. ▶彼は普通月曜日にここに来る He usually [generally] comes here on Mondays. ▶彼女は普通は朝食を取らない She doesn't usually [usually doesn't] have breakfast. ▶私は普通 11 時に寝る Generally [In general, As a rule], I go to bed at eleven.

● 普通科 a general course. ● 普通株〖証券〗《米》common stocks [shares]; 《英》ordinary shares [stocks]. 〖関連〗優先株《米》preferred stocks [shares]; 《英》preference shares [stocks]. ● 普通教育 general education. ● 普通銀行 an ordinary bank. ● 普通選挙 a universal [a popular] election. ● 普通名詞〖文法〗a common noun. ● 普通郵便 ordinary mail《主に米》[post《主に英》]. 〖関連〗速達 special [《英》express] delivery. ● 普通預金 an ordinary deposit. ● 普通預金口座 an ordinary deposit account. ● 普通料金 an ordinary rate; a normal fare. ● 普通列車 a local [a slow, 《米》an accommodation] train.

ふつう 不通 ▶不通になる (道路・交通などが閉鎖される) be blocked; (運行などが一時停止される) be suspended; (交通などが渋滞する) be tied up. ▶土砂崩れのため道路が不通になった The road was blocked by a landslide. ▶列車は不通だ The trains aren't running. ▶台風のため電話が不通となった The telephone service has been suspended [been cut off] because of the typhoon. ▶その事故のために交通が不通になっている Traffic is tied up because of the accident./The accident has tied up traffic [has caused a traffic tie-up].

ぶつえん 仏縁 〖仏教〗Buddha's guidance.

ふつか 二日 ● 2 日間滞在する stay for two days. ● 5 月 2 日に on May 2(nd). (⇨日付) ● 2 日目ごとに every other [second] day. ● 2 日おきに(3 日目ごとに) every three days; every third day. ● 二日酔い (⇨二日酔い)

ぶっか 物価 (commodity) prices. ● 物価を安定させる stabilize prices. ▶山口は比較的物価が安い Prices are lower [=higher] in Yamaguchi./Things are cheaper in Yamaguchi./Yamaguchi is a less expensive city. (⚠ 文脈があれば Yamaguchi is cheap. も可) ▶石油ショックの直後物価がはね上がった Prices jumped [rose rapidly, soared, 《話》skyrocketed] right after the oil shock [the energy crisis]. ▶この 3 年間で物価が安定していた Prices have been stable for the past three years.

● 物価指数 (消費者の) the consumer [(卸売りの) wholesale] price index 《略 CPI [WPI]》. ● 物価上昇 an increase [《米》a raise, 《英》a rise,《主に米話》a hike] in price. ● 物価水準 a price level. ● 物価政策 a price policy. ● 物価騰貴[下落] a rise [a fall] in price; a price rise [fall]. ● 物価動向 the trend [movement]

ぶっか 物価 price; price trend [movement]. ●物価変動 price fluctuations.

ぶっか 仏果 〖仏教〗 Nirvana /niərvάːnɑ/.

ぶつが 仏画 〖経典にのっとった絵〗 a picture that represents a fact in the Buddhist scriptures; a Buddhist picture; 〖仏の絵〗 a picture of Buddha 〖(僧の)〗 a Buddhist priest〗.

ぶつかき 打つ欠き 《氷》 cracked ice.

ぶっかく 仏閣 a (Buddhist) temple.

ふっかける 吹っ掛ける ● けんかを吹っ掛ける pick a quarrel 《with》. ● 議論を吹っ掛ける challenge 《him》 to a discussion. ● 難題を吹っ掛ける 《やや書》 impose a difficult problem 《on》. ● 途方もない値を吹っ掛ける ask 《him》 to pay a very high [《やや書》 an exorbitant] price; 《話》 try to rip 《him》 off.

ぶっかける 打っ掛ける ● 彼に水をぶっかける dash water on [over] him; dash him with water.

フッかすいそ フッ化水素 〖化学〗 hydrogen fluoride 《記号 HF》.

*__**ふっかつ** 復活__ 图 (a) revival; 《書》 (a) rebirth. ● 軍国主義の復活 the revival [rebirth] of militarism. ● キリストの復活 the Resurrection /rèzərékʃən/ (of Christ). ● 敗者復活戦 a consolation match [race]; a revival series.
— **復活する[させる]** 動 revive; 《流行・人気が戻る》 come* back. ● 旧制度が復活した The old system has (been) revived.
● **復活祭** Easter.

ふつかよい 二日酔い a hángòver. ▶今朝はひどい二日酔いで I have a terrible [a bad] hangover this morning.

*__**ぶつかる** ❶〖打ち当たる〗__ hit*, strike* 《against, up on》(❢ hit の方が口語的); 〖突き当たる〗《どんと》bump; 《ごつんと》knock; 《すさまじい音を立てて》crash; 《突っ込み》run* 《against, into》(❢ hit は当たったら跳ね返る, into ははめ込む感じ。したがって against には不動のものに当たる含みがある); 〖激しくぶつかり合う〗 collide 《with》 (⇨衝突する); 〖利害などが対立する〗 clash 《with》. ● いすにぶつかってひっくり返す knock over a chair; knock a chair over. ▶彼の車電柱にぶつかった His car hit [struck] (against) a telephone pole. (❢ 動いている物・人にぶつかる場合には against は常に省略される (⇨[第 2 文例]))/His car bumped into [knocked against] a telephone pole. (❢ knock には他動詞用法なし)/His car bumped [ran, knocked] into a telephone pole. (❢ 最後の文は電柱が倒れた様子などを含意する) ▶彼は車にぶつかった(偶然または故意に) He hit a car./(車にはねられた) He was hit by a car. ▶車がトラックに激しくぶつかった The car crashed into the truck./The car collided with the truck.
会話「ぶつかってごめんなさい」「前をよく見たらどうなの」"Sorry I bumped into you." "Why don't you look where you're going?"
❷〖事故・不幸などに出くわす〗meet* with …; 〖障害などに突き当たる〗《話》run* up against …; 〖立ち向かう〗 face. ● 困難にぶつかる[ぶつかっていく] meet with (face) a difficulty. (❢ meet with a difficulty は「困難に対処する」の意) ● 優勝候補と 1 回戦でぶつかる run up against the top favorite in the first match. ● 次の試合で彼らとぶつかる(= 対戦する) compete with [against] them in the next round.
❸〖行事・日時などがかち合う〗 clash 《with》; conflict 《with》; 〖ある日に当たる〗 fall* 《on》. ● 彼女の結婚式が私の試験とぶつかった Her wedding clashed [conflicted] with my examination./Her wedding fell on the same day as my exam. ▶二人の意見がぶつかった There was a clash of opinions between the two men. ▶今年の文化の日は日曜とぶつかる Culture Day falls on (a) Sunday this year.

ふっかん 副官 an adjutant; an aide-de-camp; an aide.

ふっかん 復刊 — **復刊する** 動 《雑誌などを》reissue; 《出版を再開する》《やや書》resume publication.

ふっき 復帰 图 (a) return; 〖もとの人気・地位への〗 a comeback; 〖財産の〗〖法律〗 reversion.
— **復帰する** 動 return; 〖戻って来る〖行く〗〗 come* [go*] back; 〖財産が〗〖法律〗 revert; 〖俳優・選手などが〗 make* a comeback. ● 職場に復帰する return [go back] to work. ▶沖縄は 1972 年日本に復帰した Okinawa was returned to Japan in 1972.

ぶつぎ 物議をかもす ● 大いに物議をかもす arouse /əráuz/ [cause, 《書》give rise to] much controversy; be openly [widely] criticized [discussed].

ふっきゅう 復旧 图 restoration /rèstəréiʃən/. ▶路線復旧のめどが立たない The prospect of reopening the line is still uncertain.
— **復旧する** 動 restore.
● **復旧工事** restóration [repáir] wòrks.

ぶっきょう 仏教 Buddhism.
● **仏教徒** a Buddhist. ● **仏教美術** Buddhist art.

ぶっきらぼう — **ぶっきらぼうな** 形 《無愛想な》 blunt, brusque; 《そっけない》 curt. ● ぶっきらぼうな返事をする give a blunt [a curt] answer; answer bluntly [curtly]. ▶彼は態度がぶっきらぼうだ He has a blunt [a brusque, a curt] manner.

ぶつぎり ぶつ切り chops 《of vegetables》; rough cuts. ● 肉[まぐろ]をぶつ切りにする cut meat [tuna] into chunks.

ふっきる 吹っ切る forget*; get* over; 《断ち切る》 break* off. ● 未練を吹っ切る foreget (the woman); get over one's romantic attachment 《to the woman》.

ふっきれる 吹っ切れる ▶彼の一言でわだかまりが吹っ切れた (= 彼の言ったことが彼に対する悪感情から私を自由にした) What he said freed me of my bad feeling toward him. ▶事件は公式には決着したが, 吹っ切れないものを感じている人が多い The case was settled officially, but many people still feel some niggling doubt(s). (❢ niggling は「何となく心にひっかかっている」の意)

ふっきん 腹筋 〖解剖〗 abdominal muscles. ● 腹筋を鍛える develop one's abdominal muscles. ● 腹筋運動を 10 回する do 10 situps.

ブッキング 〖予約〗 booking.

フック 〖ボクシング・ゴルフ〗 (a) hook. ● 左のフックを打つ hit 《him》 with a left hook.

ぶつぐ 仏具 Buddhist altar fittings.

ブックエンド 〖本立て〗 bookends.

ブックカバー a (book) jacket, a dust jacket [cover, wrapper]. (❢ a book cover は「本の表紙」の意)

ぶつくさ ● ぶつくさ言う grumble 《about》. (⇨ぶつぶつ)

ブックバンド a bookband.

ブックマーク 〖コンピュータ〗 a bookmark.

ブックメーカー 〖賭(か)けの胴元〗 a bookmaker; 《話》 a bookie.

ふっくら 《毛のようにふかふかした》fluffy; 《柔らかい》soft; 《ほおなどが丸々とした》 plump; 《丸い》 round. ▶彼女はふっくらした毛皮のコートを着ていた She wore a fluffy fur coat. ▶あの少女は赤いふっくらした頬をしている The girl has plump [round], rosy cheeks.

ブックレット 〖小冊子〗 a booklet.

ブックレビュー 〖書評〗a book review.

ぶつける 〖投げつける〗throw*, fling* 《at》(**!** fling の方が激しい動作を表す). 〖衝突させる〗run*, (どんと) bump, (がちゃんと) crash 《into, against》. 〖打ちつける〗hit*, strike*, (しばしば) knock 《against, on》. (⇨ぶつかる). ● 犬に石をぶつける throw [fling] a stone at a dog. ● 自動車を塀にぶつける run [bump, crash] one's car into a wall. ● 木の枝に頭をぶつける hit [strike, knock] one's head against the branch of a tree. ▶ ゆうぐれR街灯柱に車をぶつけた Someone hit the lamppost with their car last night. ▶ 彼の車はトラックにぶつけられた His car was hit by a truck.
[会話]「車はやられたのかい」「もうちょっとでぶつけられてばらばらになるところだったよ」 "Was the car damaged?" "Almost [Nearly] knocked to pieces."

ふっけん 復権 图 (a) restoration of (civil) rights; (a) rehabilitation. ● 浪漫主義の復権(=再生)a revival 〖書〗a resurgence] of romanticism.
—— **復権する** 動 restore (civil) rights; rehabilitate oneself; (以前の権力を再び握る) get back [return] to power.

ぶっけん 物件 〖対象物〗an object; (物品) an article, a thing; (売買対象としての不動産) a property. ● 課税対象物件 an object of taxation. ● 証拠物件として押収する hold 《it》in evidence.

ぶっけん 物権 〖法律〗a real right. ● 物権を設定する〖移転する〗create [transfer] a real right.

ふっけんしょう 福建省 〖中国の省〗Fujian /fjúːdʒjáːn/ Province.

ふっこ 復古 (復旧, 復元) restoration; (再活性化) revival. ● 復古調 a revival mood. ● 王制復古 the restoration of the monarchy. 〖参考〗英国史ではチャールズ二世 (Charles Ⅱ) の復位を the Restoration という.

ふつご 仏語 (フランス語) French.

ぶつご 物故 (a) death.
● 物故者〖法律〗the deceased. (**!** 単数または複数扱い (⇨死者))

ふっこう 復交 图 restoration.
—— **復交する** 動 restore (diplomatic) relations 《with》.

ふっこう 復興 图 〖復旧〗restoration; (回復) recovery; (再建) reconstruction; 〖古い習慣などの復活〗revival. ● 経済復興 economic recovery [reconstruction]. ● 文芸復興 (ヨーロッパ史上の) the Renaissance. ● 戦争で破壊された国の復興を支援する support the restoration of a war-torn country.
—— **復興する** 動 ● 復興させる reconstruct; revive. ▶ 町が復興した The town was reconstructed.

ふっこう 腹腔 (⇨腹腔(ふく))

ふつごう 不都合 图 (不便) (an) inconvenience. (⇨都合). ● 不都合を招く create inconvenience.
—— **不都合な** 形 inconvenient; (悪い) wrong; (不適当な) improper. ● 不都合なことをする do something wrong; misbehave.

ふっこく 復刻, 覆刻 —— **復刻〖覆刻〗する** 動 reprint 《a book》. ● 復刻版 a reprinted edition.

ぶっころす 打ち殺す (⇨打ち殺す)

ぶっこわす 打ち壊す (⇨打ち壊す)

ぶっさん 物産 (個々の工業製品・農産物) a product, (集合的) (農産物) produce. ● 滋賀県の物産展を display of the products (野菜・果物など) produce] of Shiga Prefecture.

ぶつし 仏師 a sculptor of Buddhist images.

ぶっし 物資 〖品物〗goods; 〖必需品〗commodities; 〖供給品〗supplies. ● 生活物資 daily necessities; essential commodities. ● 物資の不足 a shortage of goods [commodities, supplies]. ● 彼らに物資を補給する supply goods for [to] them; furnish supplies to them.

ぶつじ 仏事 a Buddhist memorial service.

ぶっしき 仏式 Buddhist rites. ● 仏式による葬儀 a Buddhist funeral.

***ぶっしつ** 物質 图 matter; (a) material; a substance.

[使い分け] **matter** 心・精神に対して, 視覚・触覚でとらえることのできる物質一般を表す.
material 物を作るための材料・資質となるもの.
substance やや堅い語で, 物を構成する特定の化学的・物理的特性を持つ物質.

● 化学物質 a chemical substance. ▶ 蒸気と水は同じ物質だ Vapor and water are of the same substance.
—— **物質の, 物質的(な)** 形 material; physical. (**!** 前の語は形・実体があることによば、後の語は心・精神に対して五感や科学的に認識できることをいう) ● 物質的な援助 material help [assistance]. ▶ その家庭は物質的に恵まれている The family is materially well-off.
● 物質界 the material [physical] world. ● 物質主義 materialism. ● 物質文明 material civilization. ● 物質名詞 〖文法〗a material noun. ● 物質欲 a desire for material possessions.

ぶっしゃり 仏舎利 〖仏教〗a bone of Buddha.

プッシュバント 〖野球〗a push bunt.

プッシュホン a push-button 〖米商標〗a Touch-Tone (tele)phone;《和製語》push phone. ● プッシュホンで911番に電話をかける punch [dial] 911.

ぶっしょう 物証 (物的証拠) (physical) evidence; (証拠物) real evidence. (**!** material evidence は「判断を左右するほどの重要な証拠」で, 物的証拠とは限らない) ● 物証が乏しい There is little evidence. ▶ 検察は物証を得られないまま起訴に踏み切った The prosecution brought a charge without evidence.

ぶつじょう 物情 ● **物情騒然** ▶ その国は物情騒然としている The whole country is in turmoil./There is prevailing unrest in the country.

ふっしょく 払拭 —— **払拭する** 動 dispel (-ll-) 《one's anxiety [fear, etc.]》; 〖書〗dissipate. ● 不信感を払拭できない cannot dispel one's distrust.

ぶっしょく 物色 —— **物色する** 動 look 《for》; search 《for》. (⇨捜す) ● 泥棒は宝石はないかと店を物色した (くまなく捜した) The thief searched [〖荒らし回った〗ransacked] the store for jewelry.

ぶっしん 仏心 Buddha's infinite mercy.

ぶっしん 物心 ● 物心両面において満たされている be satisfied materially and spiritually. ● 物心両面において援助する give 《him》material and moral support.

ぶっせき 仏跡 〖仏教〗〖仏教の聖地〗a sacred place of Buddhism; (釈迦の足跡) Buddha's footsteps.

ぶつぜん 仏前 ● 仏前に(=位牌(いはい)の前に)果物を供える offer fruit [✕fruits] before the tablet of the deceased.

ふっそ 弗素 fluorine /flúərɪn/ 〖元素記号 F〗.
● フッ素樹脂 fluororesin. ● フッ素樹脂コーティング fluororesin coating.

ぶっそう 物騒 —— **物騒な** 形 〖危険な〗dangerous; 〖不安定な〗unsettled; 〖騒然とした〗troubled. ▶ この辺は夜の一人歩きは物騒です It's dangerous for you to go out alone in this neighborhood after dark. ▶ 物騒な世の中になってきた Times are [The

ぶつぞう 仏像 an image of Buddha.
ぶつだ 仏陀 〘仏教〙(the) Buddha.
ぶったい 物体 (知覚されるもの) an object;〘物理〙a body. ● 未確認飛行物体 an unidentified flying object; a UFO (❗複数形は～s, ～'s).
ぶったおれる 打っ倒れる fall* down; fall to the ground;(くずおれる) collapse;(大きな音を立てて) crash;〘病気になる〙get [become] sick [ill]. ▶彼は仕事がきつくてぶっ倒れた He got sick because the job was too hard for him. (❗ fall down on the job は「その仕事をきちんとできない」の意の口語表現でここでは不適)
ぶつぎる 打つ切る chop (-pp-) down [(枝などを) off]; cut* down [off] with a decisive stroke.
ぶったくる 打ったくる rob (-bb-); take*... by force. ▶バーでぶったくられた I had to pay through the nose at the bar.
ぶったまげる 打つ魂消る 《話》be flabbergasted 《at, by》.
ぶつだん 仏壇 a household [a family] Buddhist altar.
プッチーニ 〘イタリアのオペラ作曲家〙Puccini /puːtʃíːni/ (Giacomo ～).
ぶっちぎり ▶タイガースはぶっちぎりの(=他のチームを大きく引き離す)8連勝をとげた The Tigers had an 8-game winning streak, building up a good lead over the other teams.
ぶっちょうづら 仏頂面 a sullen [a sour, a long] face. ● 仏頂面をする make [pull, put on] a sullen face.
ふつつか 不束 ▶ふつつか者ですが精一杯努めます Though I'm not well experienced, I'll try to do my very best.
ぶっつけほんばん ぶっつけ本番 ● ぶっつけ本番でスピーチをする make a speech impromptu; make an impromptu speech. ▶その時にはなればよっけ本番でやるよ When the time comes, I'll play it by ear. (❗「臨機応変にやる」の意の口語的成句表現)
ぶっつづけ ぶっ続け ● ぶっ続けで continuously. (⇨ぶっ通し)
ふっつり ❶ [前ぶれなく急に] abruptly;(突然)suddenly, all of a sudden. ▶彼はあの時以来ふっつり来なくなった He abruptly stopped coming just after that.
❷ [きっぱりと] completely;(この1回限りで) once and for all. ▶彼はふっつり酒をやめた He gave up drinking once and for all.
ぷっつり ❶ [一気に切れる] ▶ロープが重みでぷっつり切れた The rope snapped under the weight.
❷ [急に止まったりする] (⇨ふっつり❶) ▶話の最中に電話がぷっつり切れてしまった The telephone went dead in the middle of our conversation. (❗ dead に突然の意味が十分に含まれている)
ふってい 払底 图 shortage;(欠乏)scarcity /skéərsəti/.
—— **払底する** 動 run short; become [get, grow] scarce.
ぶってき 物的 [物質的] material;(有形の)physical; tangible. ● 物の証拠が不十分なため for insufficient physical [tangible] evidence. (❗ material evidence は「重要な証拠」の意 (⇨物証))
● 物的損害 material [physical] damage.
ふつわく 降って湧く ▶気の毒に彼は降って湧いたような災難にあった It is a pity that he met with an unforeseen disaster.

ぶってん 沸点 the bóiling pòint.
ぶってん 仏典 the sutras /súːtrəz/; the Buddhist scriptures.
ぶつでん 仏殿 the main temple building.
ふっと ❶ [息が吹き出る様子・音] ▶彼女はローソクの火を吹き消す blow out a candle. ▶彼女はふっと安堵(も)の息をついた She gave a sigh of relief./She sighed with relief.
❷ [急に] (⇨ふと) ▶彼はふっと海を見たくなった He was suddenly taken by the idea of seeing the sea. ▶ふっとそんな気がした It just occured to me./ It flashed across me.
ぶつど 仏土 〘仏教〙(浄土) the Pure Land.
ふっとう ▶ふっと吹き出す (⇨吹き出す❷)
*ふっとう 沸騰 图 boiling.
—— **沸騰する** 動 boil, come* to a boil. (⇨沸く, 沸かす) ▶水を沸騰させる boil water. ▶水が沸騰すると水蒸気になる When water boils, it changes into steam. ▶ふっとうしてなくなってしまった The water has boiled away [boiled dry]. ▶その問題をめぐって議論が沸騰した(=議論を戦わせた) We had a heated argument over the problem.
● 沸騰点 the bóiling pòint.
ぶつどう 仏堂 (寺) a temple;(仏殿) the main temple building.
ぶつどう 仏道 〘仏の教え〙the teachings of (the) Buddha, (the) Buddha's teachings;(仏教)Buddhism;(仏教僧の修行)Buddhist (ascetic) discipline;〘仏の悟り〙Buddhist enlightenment. ▶仏道に励む discipline oneself to attain Buddhist enlightenment.
ぶっとおし ぶっ通し ―― **ぶっ通しで** 副 (休まずに) without a break;(連続して)continuously. ▶昼夜ぶっ通しで練習する practice day and night without a break. ▶パーティーは3日間ぶっ通しで開かれた The party went on continuously for three days.
フットサル 〘5人制のミニサッカー〙futsal.
フットノート 〘脚注〙a footnote.
ぶっとばす 吹っ飛ばす (強打する) slug (-gg-);(なぐり飛ばす) knock (him) down [out]; belt;(投げ飛ばす) fling* (him) away;(車を猛スピードで走らせる) drive at a terrific speed, 《米話》barrel. ● ホームランをぶっ飛ばす slug a home run. ● 相手を土俵の外にぶっ飛ばす fling the opponent out of the ring. ▶あんな狭い道をぶっ飛ばすなんて無茶苦茶茶だ It's ridiculous to barrel down that narrow street. ▶ぶっ飛ばせば20分でいけると思う I think we can get there in twenty minutes if we speed up.
ぶっとぶ 吹っ飛ぶ [風で] be blown off [away];[なくなる] disappear;(払いのける) get* rid of..., dispel (-ll-). (⇨吹き飛ばす) ▶その事故で私の計画めちゃめちゃになってしまった(=台なしになった) The accident completely spoiled my plan.
フットボール 〘競技〙football;〘ボール〙a football. ● フットボールをする play (ˣa) football. ● フットボールの選手 a football player; a footballer. ● フットボール競技場 a football field [ground]. ● フットボールの試合 《米》a football game 〘英〙match.
フットライト 〘脚光〙footlights.
フットワーク 〘足さばき〙footwork. ● フットワークを乱す lose one's footwork. ▶彼はフットワークが軽い His footwork is light.
ぶつのう 物納 图 (税金の) tax payment in kind.
—— **物納する** 動 pay* (one's inheritance tax) in kind.
ぶっぱなす 打っ放す (ピストルを) shoot* 《at》; fire 《at, on》.
ぶっぴん 物品 goods; an article; a commodity.

- 物品税 a commódity tàx.
ぶつぶつ [発疹] a rash. ▶*a* rash で病気などが原因のいくつかの赤い小さいはれを(さす) ●ぶつぶつができる《人が主語》get a rash;《人・体の部分が主語》break [come] out in a rash; *A* rash breaks [comes] out 《*on* one's back》. ▶男の子の腕にはぶつぶつがちょっと出ていた The boy had *a* slight *rash* on his arm.
ぶつぶつ ❶ [意味不明のことや不平などを言う様子] 《動詞で表して》mutter; (つぶやく) mumble; (不平を言う) grumble 《*about*》. (!) grumble は不平を言うという意味を持つが, mumble は mumble a prayer (祈りをつぶやく) などといえるように不平の意味を含んでいない. mutter は文脈によってそのいずれにも用いられる ▶彼は何かわけの分からないことをぶつぶつ言っていた He *was* muttering [*mumbling*] something incoherent. ▶私の母はいつも父の浪費癖にぶつぶつ言っている My mother *is* always muttering [*grumbling*] *about* my father's extravagance.
❷ [音を立てて煮えたり, 沸き出たりする様子] 《動詞で表して》(ぐつぐつ煮える[煮る]) simmer (⇨ぐつぐつ); (ぶくぶく泡立つ) bubble. (⇨ぶくぶく)
ぶつぶつこうかん 物々交換 图 barter.
── 物々交換する 動 ●チョコレートとたばこを物々交換する barter tobacco *for* chocolate.
ぶつぶん 仏文 [フランス文学] French literature; (フランス文学科) the French literature course; (フランス語の文章) a French sentence; French writing;《an essay》written in French. ●仏文和訳 translation *from* French into Japanese.
ぶっぽう 仏法 the teachings of (the) Buddha, (the) Buddha's teachings; (仏教) Buddhism.
ぶっぽうそう 仏法僧 [鳥] a broad-billed roller.
ぶつま 仏間 a Buddhist family altar room.
ぶつめつ 仏滅 a *butsumetsu* day; an unlucky day; (説明的に) a day opposed to a *taian* day by *in-yo* divination. (⇨大安)
ぶつもん 仏門 ●仏門に入る become a Buddhist priest.
ぶつやく 仏訳 图 (a) French translation. (!) *a* をつけると「訳されたもの」の意
── 仏訳する 動 translate [put] into French 《from (the) Japanese》.
ぶつよく 物欲 ▶彼は物欲が強い He is very *materialistic* [a very materialistic person].
*ぶつり 物理 图 [物理学] physics (!) 単数扱い); physical science. ●応用[理論]物理学 applied [theoretical] *physics*.
── 物理的(な) 形 physical. ●物理的現象 a *physical* phenomenon (*a* phenomena). ●物理的変化 [法則] *physical* change [laws].
── 物理的に 副 physically. ▶そのような計画を実行に移すのは物理的に不可能である It is *physically* impossible to carry out such a plan.
●物理学者 a physicist. ●物理療法 (理学療法) physiothérapy; (米) physical therapy.
ぶつりあい 不釣り合い ── 不釣り合いの 形 (調和していない) ill-matched; (不均衡の) disproportionate.
▶不釣り合いな夫婦 an *ill-matched* couple. ▶彼の支出は収入と不釣り合いだ His expenditure is *disproportionate* [*out of proportion*] *to* his income. ▶このブラウスとスカートは不釣り合いだ The blouse *doesn't go* (well) *with* [*doesn't match*] the skirt.
ぶつりき 仏力 (the) Buddha's superpower.
ぶつりゅう 物流 (物的流通) physical distribution.
●物流管理 physical distribution management. ●物流業 the distributive trades [industry]. ●物流コスト distribútion còst. ●物流システム a physical distribution system.
ふづりょう 物量 the amount of materials; [(資源) resources]. ●物量に(= 物的優位に)物を言わせて taking advantage [on the strength] of one's *material superiority*.
ふつわ 仏和 ●仏和辞典 a French-Japanese dictionary.
ぶつん ▶ロープがぷつんと切れた The rope suddenly *snapped*. ▶電話がぷつんと切れた The telephone line *went dead*.
*ふで 筆 [毛筆] a (writing) brush; [絵筆] a (paint) brush; [ペン] a pen. ▶弘法にも筆の誤り 'Even an excellent calligrapher like Kobo-daishi sometimes makes mistakes with the brush'./(ことわざ) Even Homer (sometimes) nods. ▶弘法筆を選ばず (ことわざ) Bad workmen always blame their tools.
●筆が滑る make a slip of the pen.
●筆が立つ ▶彼は筆が立つ He writes well./He is a good writer. (!) 後の方は「いい作家である」の意にもなる
●筆を入れる (絵などに) touch up《a picture》, add a few touches 《*to* a picture》; (文章などに) make corrections 《*in* a manuscript》, correct 《a manuscript》.
●筆を置く (書くことをやめる) put down one's pen; stop writing.
●筆を折る [断つ] stop [give up] writing《novels》.
●筆を執る (執筆を始める) start to write; (ペンを執る) take up one's pen.
●筆を染める (やってみる) try one's hand at writing; (書き始める) start to write.
●筆を走らせる (書く) write; (描く) paint. ▶彼はさっそく友への手紙に筆を走らせた He soon *wrote* (a letter) to his friend.
●筆入れ (⇨筆箱) ●筆立て a pén [a péncil, a brúsh] stànd. ●筆箱 a pén [a péncil, a brúsh] càse.
ふてい 不定 ── 不定の 形 indefinite; (不確かな) uncertain; (不安定な) unsettled; (不規則な) irregular. ●不定の天候 *uncertain* [*unsettled*, 変わりやすい) *changeable*] weather. ●不定の収入 (an) *irregular* income.
●不定冠詞 [文法] an indefinite article. ●不定詞 [文法] an infinitive. ●不定愁訴 [医学] malaise /məléiz/. ●不定代名詞 [文法] an indefinite pronoun.
ふてい 不貞 ●不貞を働く commit adultery; be unfaithful《*to* one's wife》.
ふてい 不逞 ●不逞のやから (道義に従わない人たち) people without scruples [a sense of morality]; lawless people; (無礼な人たち) disrespectful [impertinent, rude] people.
ふていき 不定期 ── 不定期の 形 irregular (↔regular). ── 不定期に 副 irregularly.
●不定期便 an irregular [a non-scheduled] service.
ふていさい 不体裁 ── 不体裁な 形 (見苦しい)《やや書》unsightly; (ぶざまな) awkward. (⇨体裁)
ブティック [<フランス語] a boutique /bu:tí:k/.
プディング (⇨プリン)
ふてき 不適 ── 不適の (⇨不適当, 適不適)
ふてき 不敵 ── 不敵な 形 (大胆な) bold; (恐れを知らない) fearless; (大胆不敵な) daring. (⇨大胆な)
ふでき 不出来 ── 不出来な 形 (失敗した) unsuccessful; (不満足な) unsatisfactory; (へたな) poor.

● 不出来な成績 a *poor* [an *unsatisfactory*] grade.

ふてきかく 不適格 ― 不適格な 形 (不向きな) unfit, inadequate; (資格がない) unqualified. (⇨適任, 不適任) ● 不器用で外科医には不適格な a person who is clumsy and *unfit for* a surgeon.

ふてきせつ 不適切 ― 不適切な 形 (条件を満たしていない) unsuitable; (その場にふさわしくない) inappropriate. (⇨不適当) ● 不適切な例 an *unsuitable* [an *inappropriate*] example.

ふてきとう 不適当 ― 不適当な 形 (条件を満たしていない) unsuitable; (好ましくない) not good; (能力・資格に欠ける) unfit; (ふさわしくない) improper. [類語] ふさわしい) ● その仕事には不適当な人 an *unsuitable* [an *unfit*] person *for* the job. ● 不適当な発言をする make *improper* remarks. ● その本は高校生には不適当だ That book *isn't good for* high school students.

― 不適任 名 inaptitude; unsuitableness. (⇨適任)

― 不適任な 形 (不向きな) unfit; unsuitable; (不適格な) inadequate; (資格のない) unqualified. ● 彼女は秘書には不適任である She *is unfit* [*unsuitable*] *for* a secretary.

ふてぎわ 不手際 (⇨失敗 ❷) ● とんだ不手際 (=大失敗) をやらかす make a terrible *blunder*. ▶ 私どもの不手際でご迷惑をおかけしまして申し訳ございません We're sorry to have troubled you through our *error*.

ふてくされる ふて腐れる 〖すねる〗 sulk, get* *sulky*; 〖やけになる〗 get desperate. ● ふてくされている be *sulky*; 〖話〗 be in the sulks; be *desperate*.

ふでづかい 筆遣い 〖筆の運び方〗 (skillful) handling of one's brush [pen]; (画家・書家の) brushwork.

ふてっかく 不適格 (⇨不適格)

ふてってい 不徹底 ― 不徹底な 形 〖不十分な〗 not thorough, insufficient; 〖中途半端な〗 half, halfway; (一貫性のない) inconsistent. (⇨徹底) ● 不徹底な処置 *half* [*halfway*] measures.

― 不徹底に 副 ● 電話連絡はとかく不徹底に(=不正確に)なりやすい We tend to get information *inaccurately* when it is given by telephone.

ふてね ふて寝 ● 彼は昼までふて寝していた He *was sulking in bed* [*stayed in bed in the sulks*] until noon.

ふでぶしょう 筆無精 ● 彼は筆無精だ He is a poor correspondent./He is not a letter writer. (⇔筆まめ)

ふてぶてしい (ずぶとい) rude, 〖書〗 impudent.

ふでぶと 筆太 ● 筆太に書く write with a *bold stroke* [*bold strokes*] of one's brush [pen].

ふでまめ 筆まめ ● 筆まめな人 a good correspondent (❗ good に替えて grave, energetic などをその意に応じた形容詞と使える); a good letter writer (❗「手紙を書くのが上手な人」の意もある). (⇔筆無精)

*__**ふと** 〖突然に〗 suddenly; 〖偶然に〗 by chance, by accident; 〖何気ない〗 casually. ● ふとした. (⇨ふとした) ▶老人はふと立ち止まって振り返った The old man [woman] stopped *suddenly* and looked back. ▶ふと旅行をしたくなった I *suddenly* got a notion to travel./(急に衝動にかられた) I *had* [*got*, *felt*] *a sudden urge* [*itch*] to travel. ▶ふと街で彼に会った I met him on the street *by chance*./I happened [(言) *chanced*] to meet him on the street./I [*came across*, 〖話〗 *ran into*, 〖話〗 *bumped into*] him on the street. ▶ふとすばらしい考えが浮かんだ A bright idea *occurred to* me [*came across my mind*]./I *hit* on a bright idea. (⇨思い付く) ▶私は

この本を仕事から帰宅する途中ふと立ち寄った小さな本屋で見つけた I found this book in a small bookstore where I *casually* dropped on my way home from work. ▶ふと気がつくと(=知らぬ間に)列車はトンネルに入っていた The train had gone into a tunnel *before I knew it*.

*__**ふとい 太い** ❶ [幅・厚みのある] (回りが太い) thick; (大きくて太い) big (-gg-); (線・字などが) bold; (線・まゆなどが) heavy; (肥満した) fat (-tt-).

①【太い〜】 ● 太い首[柱] a *thick* neck [pillar]. ● 太い腕 *big* [*thick*] arms. ● 太い線 a *bold* [a *heavy*, a *thick*] line. ● 太いくぎ a *heavy* nail. ● 太い指 a *thick* [(ずんぐりした) a *stubby*] finger. ● 太い字で名前を書く write one's name with *bold* [*thick*] strokes. ● 太い足 *fat* [(太く短い) 〖話〗 *pudgy*] legs (❗いずれも肥満的に); (肉うきめいい) *heavy* legs. ● 黒い皮の太いベルト a *heavy* [(幅の広い) a *wide*, ×a *thick*] black leather belt. (❗語順にも注意)

②【…が[は]太い】 ▶アイススケートの選手は太くて丈夫なももをしている Ice skaters have very *thick* and strong thighs. ▶彼はまゆが太い He has *heavy* [(ふさふさした) *bushy*] eyebrows.

❷ [声が] ● 彼は太い声をしている He has a *deep* voice./His voice is *deep*.

❸ [図太い] (恥知らずの) shameless; (厚かましい) impudent; (大胆な) daring. ● 肝っ玉の太い男 a *daring* [a *bold*] man. ● 彼はそれをやるだけの太い神経を持っている He has *strong* nerves to be able to do that.

*__**ふとう 不当** 名 injustice; (不公平) unfairness. (⇨正当) ● その判決の不当性に抗議する protest against the *injustice* of the court's ruling [decision].

― 不当な 形 (不合理な) unreasonable; (公平でない) unfair; (不法な) illegal. ● 不当な差別 *unjust* discrimination. ● 不当な値段 an *unreasonable* price. ● 不当な(=無理な)要求をする make an *unreasonable* demand. ▶ぼくは彼から不当な扱いを受けた I received (×an) *unfair* treatment by him./I was *unfairly* treated by him.

― 不当に 副 unjustly; unfairly; unreasonably. ● 不当に非難する accuse (him) *unjustly*. ▶彼は不当に解雇された He was dismissed *unfairly*. ▶彼女は不当に逮捕された She was arrested *unlawfully* (正当な理由なしに) without due cause].

● 不当解雇 unfair dismissal. ● 不当行為 a wrongful deed. ● 不当判決 an unjust decision. ● 不当表示 (誤解を招きやすい) misleading representation. ● 不当利益 undue profit. ● 不当廉売 (ダンピング) dumping. ● 不当労働行為 unfair labor practices.

ふとう 埠頭 (突堤) a wharf /hwɔːrf/ (複) 〜s, wharves), a pier; (岸壁) a quay /kiː/.

ふどう 不動 ― 不動の 形 ● 不動の(=確固たる)信念 firm [(揺るぎない) *unshakable*] faith. ● 不動の(=不動の)決意 an *indomitable* [an *unshakable*] resolution. ● 政界に不動の(=確立した)地位を占める hold a *firmly established* position in political circles.

ふどう 浮動 ― 浮動する 動 float (*in* the air); (価格が) fluctuate.

● 浮動株 floating stocks. ● 浮動票 (⇨浮動票)

ぶとう 舞踏 a dance, dancing.

● 舞踏会 a dance (❗a dance party より普通. (正式で大規模な) a ball. ● 舞踏会を開く *give* [×open] *a dance* [a *ball*]. ● 舞踏病 〖医学〗 chorea; 〖話〗 the jumps.

*__**ぶどう 葡萄** 〖果実〗 a grape (❗一粒をさす. 通例は粒が

ぶどう

集まって房になっているので複数で表す); 〖木〗a (grape) vine. ▶ブドウ一房 a bunch [a cluster] of *grapes*.
• ブドウの収穫 a *vintage*. • ブドウの種 a grapestone. • ブドウのつる a grapevine. • 干しブドウ a raisin. • ブドウを作る植物 〖grow〗 *grapes*.
• ブドウ色 (a) wine color. • ブドウ園[畑] a vineyard; a vinery. (◉ vine は tree とは考えられないので orchard とはいわない) • ブドウ球菌〖医学〗a staphylococcus. • ブドウ栽培家 a grape grower. • ブドウ酒 (red [white, rosé /rouzéi/]) wine. • ブドウ棚 a grapevine trellis. • ブドウ糖 grape sugar; glucose /glúːkous/.

ぶどう 武道 the martial arts. (◉ 剣道・柔道・弓道などの武術の総称)

ふどうい 不同意 (一致しないこと) disagreement; (不可とすること) disapproval.

ふどういつ 不統一 〖まとまりのないこと〗lack of unity; 〖不調和〗disharmony; 〖一貫性のないこと〗inconsistency. (⇨統一) ▶その問題に関して政府では不統一が見られる(= 意見が分かれている) Government *is divided* on the issue.
——統一な 厖 (不調和な) inharmonious.

ふとうこう 不凍港 an ice-free port.

ふとうこう 不登校 (登校拒否) refusal to attend school; (学校嫌い) schóol phòbia. • 不登校の生徒 a student who refuses to go to school [suffers from *school phobia*]; a school-phobic student.

ふとうごう 不等号 a sign of inequality《記号 ≠; <, >》.

ふどうさん 不動産 real estate [property]; 〖法律〗immovables.
• 不動産開発 property development. • 不動産鑑定士《米》a real estate appraiser; 《主に英》a real estate surveyor. • 不動産業 real estate business. • 不動産業者《米》a real estate agent, a realtor /ríːəltər/;《英》an estate agent. • 不動産(取得)税 a real estate [property] (aquisition) tax. • 不動産仲介料 a real estate brokerage /bróukərid3/; a brokerage fee on real estate. • 不動産登記 real estate [property] registration. • 不動産取り引き a real estate transaction [deal].

ふとうしき 不等式 〖数学〗an (expression of) inequality.

ふどうそん 不動尊 「不動明王」の尊称 (⇨不動明王)

ふどうたい 不導体 a nonconductor.

ふどうとく 不道徳 immorality. —— 不道徳な 厖 immoral; (非倫理的な) unethical. (⇨道徳)

ふどうひょう 浮動票 《集合的》the floating vote,《主に米》the swing vote. ▶浮動票の獲得をねらう attempt to win *the swing vote*; (浮動期有権者に支持を訴える) woo swing《米》[floating《英》] voters.

ふとうふくつ 不撓不屈 —— 不撓不屈の 厖 unyielding,《やや書》indomitable. • 不撓不屈の精神 an *unyielding* [an *indomitable*] spirit.

ふとうへん 不等辺 • 不等辺三角形 a scalene /skeilíːn/ triangle. • 不等辺四辺形《米》a trapezium /trəpíːziəm/;《英》a trapezoid.

ふどうみょうおう 不動明王 *Fudo Myoo*, the god of fire;(説明的に) He is known by his flaming sword in his right hand and rope in his left hand, with which he slashes away material connections and binds up evil-doers.

ふとうめい 不透明 opacity /oupǽsəti/; (予測できないこと) (an) uncertainty.
—— 不透明な 厖 opaque /oupéik/ (↔transparent); ▶政策決定の仕方が不透明である It is *not clear* how

ふとした

the policy was decided. ▶景気の先行きは不透明である(不確実) The outlook of economy is *uncertain* [(複雑で分かりにくい) *murky*]. (◉「不透明な時代」は the age of murkiness)

ふどき『風土記』 *Records of Wind and Earth*; *A Topography*. 〖参考〗奈良時代の地誌

ふとく 不徳 lack of virtue.
• 不徳の致すところ ▶それは私の不徳の致すところです That's entirely my *fault*./(道義的に責任を感じる) I *feel morally responsible* for it.

ふとくい 不得意 图 a weak point. (◉ ×a poor point とはいわない) (⇨不得手)
—— 不得意な 厖 (へたな) bad,《やや書》poor; (弱い) weak. (◉ 能力・知力などが劣っていることを表す) ▶彼の不得意な科目はフランス語だ His *weak* subject is French./He *is weak* [*poor*] in French. ▶彼は友達付き合いが不得意です He *is not good at* mixing with his friends./(うまくやっていけない) He can't get along well with his friends.

ふとくさく 不得策 ▶(...するのは)不得策である It is (a) bad policy《*to* do》/It is not advisable《*to* do》.

ふとくてい 不特定 (決まっていない) indefinite. • 不特定多数の人 an *indefinite* number of people.

ふとくようりょう 不得要領 • 不得要領な (漠然とした) obscure, vague; (あいまいな) ambiguous. • 不得要領な返事をする give a *vague* [an *ambiguous*] answer.

ふところ 懐 ❶〖胸部〗(衣服の胸の部分)《書》a bosom (◉ 通例女性の衣服の胸の部分をさし、日本語の和服のふところとは意味が少しずれる);(内ポケット) an inside [an inner] pocket. ▶赤ん坊をふところに抱く hold a baby to one's *bosom* [*breast*]. ▶彼は財布を上着のふところから取り出した[に入れた] He took out the wallet from [put the wallet in] his *inside* jacket *pocket*.
❷〖金銭〗(金) money;(所持金) a pocket. (◉ 通例単数形で) • ふところと相談する consult one's *pocket* [*purse, pocketbook*].
❸〖包容〗▶私は大自然のふところに(いだかれて)育った I grew in the *bosom* of nature [(自然のままの田舎) the unspoiled countryside].
• 懐が暖かい ▶商売が繁盛し彼のふところは暖かくなった The business prospered and his *purse* grew *fat* (↔*lean*).
• 懐が痛む ▶結局ふところはそれほど痛まなかった. あまり支払う必要がなかったので It wasn't so *hard on* my *pocket* after all. I didn't have to pay for much.
• 懐が深い • 懐の深い男 a broad-minded man.
• 懐を肥やす ▶彼はふところを肥やした (私腹を肥やした) He *has lined* his (*own*) *pockets*. 〖慣用表現〗
• 懐刀 (懐剣) a dagger; (腹心の部下) one's right-hand man.

ふとさ 太さ (針金・ロープなどの) thickness; (直径) diameter; (声の) depth.
〖会話〗「その木の幹の太さはどのくらいですか」「50 センチほどです」"How *wide* is the tree trunk in *diameter*?/What is the *diameter* of the tree trunk?" "It's about fifty centimeters in *diameter*./It has a *diameter* of about fifty centimeters."

ふとざお 太棹 a *samisen* with a thick neck; a thick-necked *samisen*.

ふとじ 太字 • 太字で in bold type;(欧文) in Gothic type. • 太字で印刷する print in *boldface*《*to*》.

ふとした ▶ふとした(=偶然の)出会い an accidental [a *casual*] meeting. • ふとした(=ちょっとした)風邪 a *slight* cold; *a bit of* a cold. • ふとした(=何気ない)話の中で in a *casual* conversation. • ふとしたことから(=偶然に)彼と知り合いになる come to know him

ふとっちょ

by chance; *happen to* get acquainted with him. ● ふとした(=つまらない)ことからけんかする get into a fight over a *trivial* thing. ● ふとした出来心で(=衝動的に)金を盗む steal the money *on impulse*.

ふとっちょ 太っちょ 《話》a fatso (複 ～es), 《話》a fatty.

ふとっぱら 太っ腹 ── 太っ腹な 形 (気前のよい) very generous, big-hearted; (度量の広い) magnanimous.

ふとどき 不届き ── 不届きな 形 (けしからぬ) outrageous; (無礼な) rude.

ぶどまり 歩留まり a [the] yield (rate). ▶ここ十数年その会社では新入社員の歩留まりがいちじるしく低下している The rate of newly employed *workers who stay long* in the company has remarkably dropped in the last ten years or so.

ふとめ 太目 ── 太目の 形 rather thick. (⇨太い)
● 太めの女性 a *plus-sized* woman. ▶ 彼女性版のサイズより) ▶ 彼は少し太めだ He is a little *too heavy*. /《話》He is on the *plump* side.

ふともも 太腿 a thigh /θái/.

*** ふとる 太る** 動 get* [grow*] fat (-tt-) [stout] (❗ fat はしばしば軽蔑的に醜い太り方を意味するので避けた方がよい. stout はしばしば fat の婉曲語として用いられる); (丸々と) get plump (❗特に赤ん坊や女性に用いる); (体重が増える) gain [put* on] weight (⇔*lose*weight). ▶ 彼は年々太った He *got fatter* [*heavier*] every year. ▶ 彼女は少し太ったね She *is gaining* [*putting on*] a little *weight*. /She's *getting* [*growing*] a little *stout*. ▶ このように進行形で用いると婉曲的な言い方となる (⇨会話)) ▶ 彼は太りすぎているのでダイエット中です He's on a diet because he is a little *overweight* [a little too *heavy*, 《話》a bit *on the heavy side*, 《かっぷくがいい》rather *heavy-set*]. (❗ a little, a bit, rather などを添えて表現をやわらげることが多い) ▶ ウエストが太ってきた My waist *is expanding*. ▶ 君は太らなきゃあ, やせすぎだよ You need to *fill out*. You're too thin.

[会話]「一服どう」「いや, いらない. (たばこは)半年前にやめたんだ」「太った？」「5キロほどね. いったん減量したんだけど最近またその分太ってしまった」"Have a smoke?" "No, thanks. I quit six months ago." "(Did you) *gain weight?*" "About eleven pounds. I took it off for a time, but recently I've put it back on." (❗ put ... back on は「再び身につける」の意で言う方が日常的)

── 太った 形 fat (-tt-); (肉付きのよい頑丈な) stout; (丸々太った) plump (❗よい意味または婉曲的に); (特に赤ん坊・子供が) chubby. ▶ 太った中年の女性 a *stout* middle-aged woman. ● まるまる太った赤ちゃん a *plump* [a *chubby*] baby.

*** ふとん 布団, 蒲団** *futon* (❗ (説明的に) a set of Japanese mattresses and quilts; (敷き布団) a mattress; (掛け布団) a quilt /kwílt/; (寝具類) bedding; bedclothes.

[解説] 米英人にとって mattress はベッドに付属したスプリングの入ったもの. quilt はベッドの上にかける暖かい上掛けを意味するので, 日本の布団のことを明示するには上のように a Japanese mattress, a Japanese quilt または *futon* /fúːtɑn/ という. なお英語化した futon は布団に似たベッド用マットレスやソファーベッドをさす.

● 布団を敷く(畳に布団を広げる) spread [lay] (out) *futon* on the *tatami* (floor); make the [one's] bed. [事情] 米英では ベッドを整えること) ● 布団を上げる put away the *bedding*; (たたむ) fold up the

bedding. ● 布団を干す air the *bedding*; give the *bedding* a good airing. ● 布団を掛ける put on a *quilt*. ● 布団をかけて寝る sleep under a *quilt*. ● 布団蒸しにする confine 《him》 under several *futons* for fun.

ふとん『蒲団』 *The Quilt*. (〖参考〗田山花袋の小説)

ふな 鮒 〖魚介〗a crucian (carp). (❗ 通例単複同形. 肉は 1ウゴ)

ぶな 橅 〖植物〗a beech (tree).

ふなあし 船足, 船脚 ● 船足が早い[遅い] be fast [slow]; be a fast [a slow] boat.

ふなあそび 舟遊び, 船遊び boating. ● 舟遊びをする enjoy *boating*. (⇨ボート)

ぶない 部内 in [within] the department. ● 政府部内で in government circles. ▶ この情報は部内にとどめておいてもらいたい I hope you'll keep this information *in our department*.

ふないた 船板 (あげ板) a (ship) plank; (造船用の板) timber for building a ship; ship timber.

ふなうた 舟歌 a rower's [(男の) a boatman's, a sailor's] song; 〖ゴンドラこぎの〗a barcarol(l)e. ▶ ヴォルガの舟歌 *The Song of the Volga Boatmen*. (〖参考〗ロシア民謡) ▶ ショパンの『舟歌』*Chopin's Barcarolle*.

ふなか 不仲 (仲たがい)《書》discord. (⇨不和) ● 不仲である don't get along [on] well 《with》; be on bad terms 《with》.

ふながいしゃ 船会社 a shípping còmpany.

ふながかり 船繋かり 名 anchorage; mooring.
── 船繋かりする 動 come* to anchor; take* up moorings 《at Buoy No. 3》

ふなかた 船方 (⇨⑥ 船頭)

ふなじ 船路 〖針路〗a course; 〖いつもの航路〗a route; (定期船の) a line; 〖船旅〗a voyage.

ふなぞこ 船底 the bottom of a ship [a boat].
● 船底天井 (説明的に) a wooden ceiling shaped like the bottom of a boat.

ふなだいく 船大工 a shipwright.

ふなたび 船旅 (航海) a (sea) voyage; a sea trip; (観光の) a cruise. (⇨航海) ▶ 世界一周の船旅に出かける予定です We will go on an around-the-world *voyage*.

ふなだまり 船溜まり a fishing hàrbor.

ふなちん 船賃 (乗客の) a (boat) fare; (貨物の) a sea freight (charge). (⇨運賃)

ふなつきば 船着場 (港) a port; a harbor (❗ port は人工的, harbor は公共も利用した港); (波止場) a wharf /hwɔ́ːrf/ (複 ～s, wharves).

ふなづみ 船積み 名 shipment, shipping; lading.
── 船積みする 動 load (a ship *with* automobiles); ship (-pp-) 《goods 《a cargo of wool》》.
● 船積み港 a port of loading. ● 船積み書類 a shipping dòcuments. ● 船積み通知 a shípping advice; a notice of shipment.

ふなで 船出 名 (出航) sailing. (⇨出航)
── 船出する 動 sail (out) 《for》; set sail 《for》.
▶ その観光船は今朝ニューヨークへ向け船出した The sightseeing boat *sailed for* New York this morning.

ふなに 船荷 a shipment, a shipload; (a) cargo; sea freight.
● 船荷証券 a bill of lading (略 B/L).

ふなぬし 船主 a shipowner.

ふなのり 船乗り (❗主に水夫, 水兵)《詩》a mariner. ● 船乗りになる become a *sailor*; go to sea. (❗ go to *the sea* は「海に行く」の意)

ふなばた 船端, 舷 the side of a boat [a ship]. ● 船端から身を乗り出す lean over the *side of a boat*.

ふなびん 船便 sea mail [×sea post]; surface mail. (🔢陸上の便も含む) ●船便で送る send (it) by sea mail.

ふなべり 船縁 (⇨船端)

ふなむし 船虫 〖動物〗a sea slater.

ふなやど 船宿 〖釣り船の仕立てをする家〗a fishing boat agency; a fishing boat keeper's.

ふなよい 船酔い 名 seasickness. ▶それは船酔いの予防になります That helps to prevent seasickness.
— **船酔いする** 動 get seasick; be a bad sailor. (⇨酔う)

ふなれ 不慣れ — **不慣れな** 形 unaccustomed 《to》; (なじみの薄い) unfamiliar 《with, to》; (経験の浅い) inexperienced 《in, at》. ▶その間違いは彼の不慣れのためです The mistake is due to his inexperience./He made the mistake through inexperience. ▶彼は車の運転には不慣れだ He's an inexperienced driver./He's inexperienced in driving./He is unaccustomed to [not accustomed to] driving. ▶私はこの土地にはまだ不慣れです I'm still a stranger here./I'm still unfamiliar with this place./This place is still unfamiliar to me.

*ぶなん 無難 — **無難な** 形 (安全な) safe; (容認できる程度の) acceptable, 〖書〗 passable. ●無難な演技を選ぶ choose a safer [(より楽な) an easier] way. ●無難な(=まずまずの)演技 an acceptable [a passable] performance. ▶それは言わないでおいた方が無難でしょう It would be safer to leave it unsaid.

ふにあい 不似合い — **不似合いな** 形 〖書〗 unbecoming; (値しない) unworthy (🔢婉曲叙述的に); (適さない) unsuitable, unfit; (不釣り合いな) ill-matched. (⇨不向きな) ●紳士に不似合いなふるまい conduct unworthy of [〖書〗unbecoming to] a gentleman. ●不似合いな夫婦 an ill-matched couple [pair].

ふにおちない 腑に落ちない (⇨腑[成句])

ふにく 腐肉 (腐った) rotten meat; (腐って悪臭を放つ) putrid meat.

ふにゃふにゃ — **ふにゃふにゃの** 形 (張りのない) limp; (柔らかい) soft; (締まりのない) flabby; 〖頼りない〗 unreliable; (決断力のない) weak, 《話》 namby-pamby; (甘すぎる) too permissive. ●帽子がぬれて, ふにゃふにゃになった The hat got wet and went limp. ▶お前みたいにふにゃふにゃしたやつは男じゃない You aren't a man. You're too weak.

ふにょい 不如意 ●手元不如意である be hard up; be in financial difficulties; 〖書〗 in straitened circumstances. (🔢「以前と変わって経済的に苦しい状況にある」の意)

ふにん 不妊 sterility. ●不妊症の女性 a sterile /stérəl/ [〖書〗a barren] woman. ▶彼女は不妊症で二人には子供がなかった She was sterile and they had no children.
●**不妊手術** sterilization.

ふにん ●単身赴任者 a business bachelor. ▶彼は4月に東京へ単身赴任した In April, he left for his (new) post in Tokyo without taking his family.
●**赴任地** one's (new) post; the place of one's assignment.

ふにんき 不人気 — **不人気な** 形 unpopular 《with, among》. (⇨人気)

ふにんじょう 不人情 — **不人情な** 形 (思いやりのない) unkind; (冷たい心の) cold-hearted; (同情心のない) unsympathetic; (無情な) heartless.

ふぬけ ふ抜け 〖意志力のない人〗 a person of no will power; 〖いくじなし〗 a coward /káuərd/; a weakling; 《話》 a nàmby-pámby (person).

ふね 船, 舟 a ship; a boat;〖書〗a vessel; 〖汽船〗 a steamer. (⇨汽船)

■ WORD CHOICE　船

boat 各種の船を指す最も一般的な語. 小型から中型の船舶に用い, 通例大型船舶には用いない. ●漁船 a fishing boat.
〖形 名＋boat〗 fishing/new/flying/wooden/cruising/motor

ship 主に大型の客船・輸送船・軍用船のこと. ●客船 a cruise ship.
〖形 名＋ship〗 cruise/cargo/sailing

vessel 主に大型の船舶のこと. 通例, 改まった文脈で用いる. ●商船 a merchant vessel.

■ 頻度チャート

	20	40	60	80	100 (%)
boat					
ship					
vessel					

①〖〜船〗 ●釣り舟 a físhing bôat. ●東京行きの船 a ship (bound) for Tokyo.
②〖船は〗 ▶その船は処女航海に出た The ship sailed on her maiden voyage.
③〖船を[に, で]〗 ●船に乗る get on (↔off) a ship; go [get] on board (a ship). (🔢「船に乗る」は go [get] aboard a ship ともいう (⇨乗る, 乗船する)) ●船で北海道へ行く go to Hokkaido by ship [on a ship, 《話》 by boat]; take ship [〖《話》a boat〗] to Hokkaido. (⇨バス) ●船で旅行する travel by ship [sea]. ▶私は船に弱い(船酔いする) I'm a bad [not a good] sailor./I get seasick easily.
●**舟を漕ぐ** row a boat; (うとうとする) nod [doze] off to sleep.

ふねっしん 不熱心 名 〖怠惰〗 laziness; 〖無関心〗 indifference.
— **不熱心な** 形 lazy; indifferent; (興味のない) uninterested; (熱意がない) unenthusiastic.

ふねんせい 不燃性 名 incombustibility; nonflammability, noninflammability.
— **不燃性の** 形 incombustible; nonflammable, noninflammable; (耐火の) fireproof. ●不燃性のプラスチック nonínflammable plastics.

ふのう 不納 (支払いの不履行) nonpayment. ●税金の不納者(滞納者) a defaulting taxpayer.

ふのう 不能 ①不可能, 無能 ●性的不能 impotence. ▶彼は再起不能だ(健康の面で) He is past [beyond] hope of recovery./There is no hope of [《主に米》for] his recovery [that he will recover]./(第一線で) There is no hope of [《主に米》for] his comeback.

ふのう 富農 a rich [a prosperous] farmer.

ふのり 布海苔 〖海草〗 a glue plant.

プノンペン 〖カンボジアの首都〗 Phnom Penh /(pə)nàm pén/.

ふはい 不敗 — **不敗の** 形 ●不敗のチャンピオン the undefeated champion.

ふはい 腐敗 名 〖腐ること〗 rot; decay; 〖堕落〗 corruption. ●政治の腐敗 political corruption.
— **腐敗する** 動 ❶〖腐る〗 (細菌作用によって) rot 《-tt-》; (自然と徐々に) decay; (食物が悪くなる) go* bad; spoil. (⇨腐る)
❷〖堕落する〗 corrupt. ▶市政は汚職で腐敗している The city government has been corrupted through bribery.

ふばい 腐敗した 形 [腐った] rotten; spoiled; [堕落した] corrupt. ▶腐敗した政治家たち corrupt politicians.

ふばい 不買 a bóycott. (⇨ボイコット) ●不買(同盟)を解く lift a *boycott* 《*on* A's products》. ●不買運動をする stage a *boycott*. (❢「不買運動」は a boycott campaign ともいう)

ふはく 浮薄 ●浮薄である(浮いている) be frivolous;(ちゃんと取り合わない) be flippant;(浅薄な) shallow.

ふばこ 文箱 a box for letters and papers.

ふはつ 不発 a misfire. ●不発になる misfire;(ピストルが) snap.
●不発弾 a blind shell;《話》a dud (bomb).

ふばらい 不払い nonpayment.
●不払い手形 a dishonored bill [draft].

ふび 不備《欠陥》《やや書》a defect, defectiveness;(不足) lack,《やや書》deficiency;(不完全) imperfection. (⇨欠陥) ●不備のある defective;(不完全な) imperfect. ●構造上の不備 a *defect* in construction. ●不備を修正する correct a *defect*. ▶現在の教育制度には不備な点がいくつかある There are some *defects* [*imperfect points*] in the present education [educational] system.

ぶひ 部費 [部に納める金] a clúb fèe,《英》clúb dùes(複数扱い);[部に納められた金] club's money;(使途を分けた金) a clúb bùdget. ●ボールは部費で買う buy balls with *club's money*.

ふびじん 不美人 a plain [《米》a homely] woman [girl].

ふひつよう 不必要 ●不必要な 形 unnecessary, needless《無用》;[余計な] superfluous /s(j)ùːpə́ːrfluəs/《余計な》●不必要なもの *unnecessary* things. (⇨不用品) ●不必要な干渉 an *unwanted* interference. ●不必要に騒ぎ立てる make an *unnecessary* fuss《*about*》. (⇨必要 ① [文例])

ふひょう 不評 [不人気] unpopularity;[受けが悪いこと] an unfavorable reception;[悪評] a bad reputation [name]. ●不評である(=評判が悪い)《⇨評判 ③》.
●不評を買う ▶彼の演説は出席者の不評を買った(=好評を得られなかった) His speech *was not favorably* [*well*] *received* by those present. ▶彼はその長たらしい演説で不評を買った He got a *bad reputation for* his lengthy speech./His lengthy speech gave him a *bad reputation*.

ふひょう 付表 (添えられた表) an appended table.

ふひょう 付票 (荷物につける札) a tag.

ふひょう 浮氷 a floating ice;(一面の) an ice floe; a floe.

ふひょう 浮標 a buoy /búːi, bɔ́i/.

ふびょうどう 不平等 名 (an) inequality. ●男女間のさまざまな不平等 *inequalities* between men and women. ●不平等を是正する redréss [《書》rectify] *inequality*. ●不平等を助長する increase [増強する] reinforce] inequality.
— 不平等な 形 (等しくない) unequal;(不公平な) unfair. ●少数派の不平等な扱い the *unequal* treatment of minority groups.
●不平等条約 an unequal treaty.

ふびん 不憫 — 不憫な 形 (かわいそうな) poor;(哀れな) pitiful. ●ふびんな子 a *poor* [(不幸な) an *unhappy*] child. ▶その孤児をふびんに思った I pitied [*felt pity for*] the orphan. (⇨哀れむ)

***ぶひん** 部品 (機械などの) a part;(構成部分) a component (part)《*of, for*》. (❢にしばしば複数形で) ●自動車部品《米》automobile parts,《英》motorcar parts. ●予備部品 spare parts. ●部品を組み立てる put together [《やや書》assemble] the parts《*into* a car》. ●部品を調達する procure parts [components]《from》.
●部品メーカー a parts [a components] manufacturer; (parts) suppliers.

ふひんこう 不品行 (身持ちの悪さ) loose morals;(不道徳な行為) immoral conduct. ●不品行な男 a man of *loose morals*.

ぶふうりゅう 無風流 — 無風流な 形 (やぼな) unrefined; tasteless;(無粋な) prosaic; dull. (⇨無風流)●無風流で out of *taste*. ▶なんとも無風流な(=無粋でなんの面白味もない)男だ He is a complete bore.

ふぶき 吹雪 a snowstorm;(大吹雪) a blizzard. ●吹雪の中を[を押して] in [through] the *snowstorm*.

ふふく 不服 [異議](an) objection;[不満](a) discontent; (一時的な) (a) dissatisfaction;[不平](a) complaint. (⇨不満, 不平) ●不服を言う(反対する) object 《*to*》;(不平・不満を言う) complain《*about*》. ▶彼はその決定に不服を唱えた He raised [made] an *objection to* the decision. ▶彼はその案に不服そうだった He looked *dissatisfied* [*discontented*] *with* the plan.

ふふく 吹雪く ▶ふぶいている A snowstorm blows hard [rages].

ふふつせんそう 普仏戦争 〖歴史〗 the Franco-Prussian War.

ふふん humph /m̩m̩, m̩m̩m̩, hʌmf/. (❢ 疑い・軽蔑などを表して鼻で出す音) (⇨ふん) ●ふふんと笑う sneer (contemptuously [scornfully, disdainfully])《*at*》.
(❢ 副詞は添えなくてもよい)

***ぶぶん** 部分 名 a part; 《やや書》a portion; a division; a section; a piece.

> **使い分け** part 最も一般的な語で, 全体 (the whole) の一部をなす部分を示し, 以下の語の代わりに用いられる場合が多い.
> **portion** 割り当てられた部分.
> **division** 切ったり区分したりして得られる部分.
> **section** はっきりと分けられた部分をいい, division より小さいもの.
> **piece** 切断・分解された部分.

●その本の最初の部分 the first *part* [*portion*] of the book. ●冷蔵庫の冷凍庫部分 the freezer *section* of a refrigerator. ▶個々の部分ではなく全体を見るべきだ One has to look at the whole, and not just the individual *parts*. ▶彼の蔵書の一部分が火事で焼失した (A) *part of* [*Some of*] his books were burnt to ashes in the fire. (❢(1) 全体と一部とを対立させる場合を除いて part of は通例を省略する. (2) of の目的語が複数名詞の場合は後の言い方が普通) ▶彼はその土地の一部分を買った He bought a *piece* [a *portion*, (a small) *part*] of the land.
— 部分的な 形 ●部分的改訂 a *partial* (↔a total) revision (*of* a book).
— 部分的に 副 partly; partially. (❢ partly は全体に対して部分を強調. partially は状態・程度に力点を置く) ▶壁は部分的にツタでおおわれている The wall is *partly* covered with ivy [×ivies]. (❢ ivy は不可算名詞) ▶その仕事は部分的にしか終わっていないだけだ (未完成だ) The work is only *partially* finished.
●部分食 a partial eclipse of the sun [moon].

ふぶんりつ 不文律 an unwritten rule (法律) law].

***ふへい** 不平 [不満] (a) dissatisfaction《*with, at*》;(a) discontent《*with*》●前の語は一時的な不満, 後の語は根深い不満;[苦情](a) complaint《*about*》;[ぐち] a grumble. (⇨不満)

ふへい
① 【不平～】 • 不平不満 complaints and dissatisfaction [discontent]. • 不平たらたらである be full of complaints [grumbles].
② 【不平だ】 • 不平が多い have a lot of complaints. • それについて何か不平があるのですか Do you have any complaint(s) about it?
③ 【不平を】 • 不平を言わずに (不平ひとつ言わず) without (any) complaint. ▶彼はいつも何かにつけて我々に不平ばかり言っている He is always complaining to us about something. (**!** He is always making a complaint about something to us. のように名詞表現も可)/He is always grumbling at us about something. (「always＋進行形」は通例話し手の非難の気持ちを表す) ▶彼は部屋が暑すぎると(私に)不平を言った He complained [grumbled] (to me) that the room was too hot. (直接話法で "The room is too hot," he complained [grumbled] (to me). ともいえる)
• 不平分子 discontented elements. • 不平屋 a grumbler.

ぶべつ 侮蔑 名 (a) contempt.
—— 侮蔑的な 形 • 侮蔑的な態度をとる take a contemptuous attitude; be contemptuous 《of poor people》.
—— 侮蔑する 動 hold 《him》 in contempt 《for his foolish behavior》.

*****ふへん** 普遍 名 (普遍性) universality.
—— 普遍的な 形 universal; (一般的な) general. • 普遍的な妥当性がある have universal validity.
—— 普遍的に 副 universally. • 普遍的に認められる真理 a universally acknowledged truth.

ふへん 不変 —— 不変の 形 〖変わることのない〗unchangeable, (いつも同じの) invariable; 〖永遠の〗eternal; everlasting; 〖絶えず続く〗constant. • 不変の法則 an unchangeable [an invariable, (書) an immutable] law. • 不変の真理 eternal [everlasting] truths /trúːθs, -ðs/. • 不変の愛を誓う pledge everlasting [constant] love.

*****ふべん** 不便 名 (an) inconvenience. • 田舎生活の不便さ the inconvenience of country life. ▶新聞がなかったら日常生活にずいぶん不便を感じることだろう Without newspapers, we would feel a great deal of inconvenience [×feel very inconvenient] in our daily life. (⇒⤴)
—— 不便な 形 inconvenient. • 不便な場所[家] an inconvenient location [house]. • この家に応接間がないのは不便です It is [×We are] inconvenient not to have a reception room in this house. (**!** 人は主語にしない) ▶君の家は町に出るには大変不便だ Your house is very inconvenient for getting into town. ▶外国を旅行する者にとって最も不便なことの一つは言語の違いである One of the greatest inconveniences for foreign travelers is the differences of language.

ふべんきょう 不勉強 名 laziness. ▶これまでの不勉強がたたって落弟することになった I have to repeat the same year because I have not studied hard [have been lazy] in my studies] all this while. ▶不勉強で知りません I'm sorry. I don't know.
—— 不勉強な 形 lazy.

ふへんふとう 不偏不党 • 不偏不党の立場に立つ be nonpartisan; be neutral to any party; be on nonpartisan [neutral] ground.

*****ふぼ** 父母 one's mother and father; one's father and mother; (両親) one's parents. (⇒親❶) • 父母会に出る attend a P.T.A. meeting. (**!** 単にP.T.A. とはいわない)

ふほう 不法 名 (違法) illegality; 〖法律〗unlawfulness.
—— 不法な 形 違法な) illegal; 〖法律〗unlawful. • 不法な手段をとる take illegal measures [steps] 《to do》.
• 不法行為 an illegal [an unlawful] act; an illegality. • 不法就労者 an illegal worker. • 不法侵入 trespassing; a trespass. • 不法侵入者 a trespasser. • 不法占拠者 a squatter. • 不法駐車 illegal parking [trespass]. (⇒⤴) • 不法入国[滞在]者 an illegal alien.

ふほう 訃報 the news [report] of 《his》 death. (⇒悲報) ▶昨夜彼の訃報に接した I heard the news [was informed] of his death last night.
• 訃報欄 (新聞の) the obituary column.

ふほんい 不本意 unwillingness, reluctance. ▶不本意ながら計画を断念した We gave up the plan unwillingly [reluctantly, against our will]. (**!** いずれも文頭位も可) ▶試験は不本意(＝不満足)な出来だった The results of the examination were unsatisfactory [×unwilling].

ふまえる 踏まえる • 実験の結果を踏まえて(＝結果に基づいて)理論を展開する base a theory on the outcome of the experiment. • 実態を踏まえて(＝よく知った上で)問題を論じる discuss the problem with a full understanding of (the) actual conditions. • 自分の経験を踏まえて(＝経験から)話す talk from one's own experiences.

ふまじめ 不真面目 ▶彼はまじめなやつだ He is not a serious [an earnest] fellow.

*****ふまん** 不満 名 (a) dissatisfaction 《with, at》; (a) discontent 《with》. (**!** 前の方は一時的な不満、後の方は慢性的な不満); 〖不平〗 a complaint 《about》; 〖不賛成〗disapproval. (⇒不平) ▶賃金が低いため労働者の間に不満がつのった A lot of discontent grew among the workers because of their low wages. • その計画に不満を表明する express one's dissatisfaction at [one's disapproval of] the plan. • 食べ物に不満を言うな Don't complain [(ぶつぶつと) grumble] about food.
—— 不満な 形 dissatisfied, discontented; (うれしくない) unhappy, (結果などが期待のいかない) unsatisfactory. ▶だれもが不満な様子だった Everybody looked dissatisfied [discontented]. ▶私は今の仕事に大いに不満である I am very dissatisfied [discontented] with my present job. ▶その処置はだれにも不満であった The measure was unsatisfactory to everyone.

ふまんぞく 不満足 名 (a) dissatisfaction, (a) discontent.
—— 不満足な 形 dissatisfied; discontented; unsatisfactory. ▶私はその結果には不満足だ I'm dissatisfied [not satisfied] with the result.

ふみ 文 〖手紙〗a letter; 〖本〗a book.

ふみいし 踏み石 〖飛び石〗a stépping stòne (**!** 通例複数形で); 〖上がり口の〗a fumiishi, (説明的に) a massive flat stone at the (entrance) floor adjoining a Japanese-style room for taking off one's shoes before stepping onto it.

ふみいた 踏み板 (階段の) a step. (**!** a tread /tréd/ は step の足がふれる表面部分. a tread board ともいう)

ふみいれる 踏み入れる set* foot [×feet] 《in》; step (-pp-) 《into》.

ふみえ 踏み絵 (説明的に) an engraving of the Christ's crucifix used during the Edo Period to identify adherents of Christianity by having them step on it. • 踏み絵を強いる force 《him》 to take a loyalty test 《to》.

ふみかためる 踏み固める stamp [tread* /tréd/] 《the

ふみきり 踏み切り ❶〖鉄道の〗a (railroad) crossing;〖水平踏切〗a grade 《米》[a level《英》]crossing. ●無人踏切を渡る go over an unattended *crossing*. ●踏切で止まる stop at a (*railroad*) *crossing*.
❷〖跳躍〗a takeoff.
❸〖決断〗▶踏み切り(=踏み切り)がつかない I cannot make up my mind.
●踏切番 a gatekeeper, (男の) a gateman. ●踏み切り板 a springboard.

ふみきる 踏み切る ❶〖跳躍競技で〗take off. (*地面を強く踏んで飛び上がること*)
❷〖思い切ってする〗●結婚に踏み切る take the plunge and get married; (決意する) decide [make up] one's *mind* to get married. ●新しい事業に踏み切る *decide* to go ahead with a new business; (乗り出す) *launch* (*out*) *into* a new business; *start* a new business. ●ストライキに踏み切る (突入する) *plunge into* a strike. ●それを防ぐために強硬手段に踏み切る (取る) *take* strong measures to prevent it.

ふみこえる 踏み越える step (-pp-) *over*《a ditch》; (困難を乗り切る) *get* *over* [*overcome**]《difficulties》.

ふみこたえる 踏み堪える (土俵際で) *stand* firm [*hold** on]《*against* one's opponent's hard push》. ▶この不況の中で零細企業がふみこたえるのは容易ではない It is not easy for small firms to *keep going* [*hold on*] in this hard times.

ふみこみ 踏み込み ❶〖相撲などで〗《make》a dash 《*against* one's opponent》. ●踏み込みが足りない (相撲で) one's *dash* is not good enough; (問題へのかかわり方が) do not deal seriously [*face squarely*]《*with* the problem》.
❷〖警察の〗《make》a raid《*on*》.

ふみこむ 踏み込む (足を踏み入れる) step (-pp-) *into*…; (侵入する) *break* *into*…; (警察が急襲する) raid [*make* a *raid on*]《a house》. ●部屋に踏み込む *step into* a room. ●踏み込んだ議論をする discuss《*it*》*at greater length*; hold [have] an *in-depth* discussion《*on* the problem》.

ふみしめる 踏み締める step (-pp-) firmly《*on*》; (固める) stamp down hard《*on* the ground》. ●一歩一歩踏み締めて歩く walk *with* (slow but) *firm steps*.

ふみだい 踏み台 a (foot)stool, a stepladder;〖目的達成の手段〗a step, a stepping-stone. ●踏み台に乗る get on [《やや書》mount] *a stool*.
●踏み台にする ▶彼を踏み台にする(=出世のために利用する) use him as a *stepping-stone*《*to*; *to do*》.

ふみたおす 踏み倒す ●勘定を踏み倒す (払わずに行く) 《話》*jump* one's bill. ▶彼は借金を踏み倒した He *didn't pay* his debts./(計画的に支払わなかった) He dodged payment of his debts.

ふみだす 踏み出す (前に出る) step (-pp-) *forward*; (一歩進む) *take** a step*; (始める) *start*,《書》*enter on* [*upon*]…. ▶ドアの方に向かって一歩踏み出す *take a step* toward the door. ▶彼は実業界に第一歩を踏み出した He *took the first step into* the business world.

ふみだん 踏み段 (⇔踏み板)

ふみちがえる 踏み違える ❶〖人生の道を間違える〗take* a wrong step in life; go* away from the right path.
❷〖階段を〗●階段を踏み違える lose one's footing on the stairs; miss one's step on the stairs.
❸〖足の筋を違える〗sprain [*twist*] one's ankle. ▶階段から落ちたときひどく足を踏み違えた I *sprained* [*twisted*] *my ankle* badly when I fell downstairs.

ふみつくえ 文机 a réading dèsk.

ふみつける 踏み付ける 〖〖(強く) stamp《*on*》; (踏みつぶす[荒す]) trample … (down). (⇔踏む) ●その虫を踏みつける *stamp on* the insect.

ふみつぶす 踏み潰す trample《on …》; (足で強く踏む) stamp《*on*》. (⇔踏み付ける) ●その虫を踏みつぶす *stamp on* the worm. ▶村人の中には象に踏みつぶされて死821者もあった Some villagers *were trampled* to death by elephants.

ふみとどまる 踏み止まる (残る) stay, remain (*前の方が口語的*); (やめる) *give** … up*; (気持ちを抑える) *hold** oneself back*; *check oneself*. (⇔思いとどまる) ▶私はいったんは会社を辞めようと思ったが踏み止まった For a time I thought of leaving the company but I *thought better of it*. (*「思い直してそうすることをやめた」の意*)

ふみならす 踏み鳴らす stamp. ●床を踏み鳴らす *stamp* on the floor. ●いらいらして足を踏み鳴らす stamp (one's foot) impatiently.

ふみならす 踏み均す (足で平らにする) make* 《the ground》flat [level] by treading on it [with one's feet].

ふみにじる 踏みにじる (権利・感情などを) trample《*on*, *upon*》. ●花を踏みにじる *trample*《*on*》flowers; (踏み倒す) *trample down* flowers. ●他人の権利を踏みにじる *trample on* the rights of other people. ▶彼の好意を踏みにじる (無視する) *ignore* his favor.

ふみぬく 踏み抜く 〖踏んで穴をあける〗(床に) put* one's foot through the floor; (尖った物で足に) run《a nail》through one's foot; step (-pp-)《a nail》and get hurt badly.

ふみば 踏み場 ▶彼の部屋は足の踏み場もないほど散らかっていた His room was such an awful mess (that) I could hardly find a place to put my foot.

ふみばこ 文箱 (⇔文箱)

ふみはずす 踏み外す lose* [miss] one's footing. ▶彼は階段を踏み外して落ちた He *lost* his *footing* and fell down the stairs./He missed a step going downstairs (and fell down). ▶彼は人の道を踏み外した(=人の守るべき本分からそれた) He *strayed* [*deviated*] *from* the path of human decency [*morals*].

ふみまよう 踏み迷う (道に迷う) lose* one's way《*in* the forest》. ●悪の道に踏み迷う (踏み込む) fall into evil ways; (正道から外れる) go astray from the right path.

ふみもち 不身持ち (⇔身持ち)

ふみわける 踏み分ける ▶生い茂った草を踏み分けて河川敷を通り抜いた We went across the dry riverbed *pushing aside* tall grass that covered it.

ふみん 不眠・**不眠不休** ●不眠不休で働く (24時間ぶっ通しで働く) work around the clock; (昼夜働く) work night and day [*day and night*].

ふみんしょう 不眠症 insómnia. ●不眠症の人 an insomniac. ▶彼女は不眠症にかかっている She is suffering from *insomnia*.

‡**ふむ 踏む** ❶〖足で〗step (-pp-)《*on*》, tread* /tréd/《*on*》. ●アクセルを踏む *step on* an accelerator (pedal);《米話》*step on* the gas. ●一塁を踏む *step on* first base. ▶彼は私の足を(誤って)踏んだ He stepped [*trod*] *on* my foot. ▶その投手はジャイアンツに二塁を踏ませなかった The pitcher didn't allow

ふむき
the Giants to reach second base. ▶芝生を踏まないように Don't *tread on* the grass./《掲示》Keep off the grass.
会話「足をお踏みですよ」「すみません」"You're *ón* my ↘toe." "↗Sorry!" (❗ You're *stepping* [*treading*] *on* my toe. ともいう)
❷〖訪れる〗set* foot (*in*, *on*); visit. ●私は今までフランスの地を踏んだことがない I *have* never *set foot in* France [*on* French soil] before./I've never *visited* France.
❸〖見積もる〗éstimàte; (価格を) value. ●彼の年を40すぎと踏む *estimate* his age (*to be*) over 40 [(*that*) his age is over 40]. (❗後の方が口語的) ●その時計を1万円と踏む *value* [*put*] the clock *at* 10,000 yen.
❹〖手続きなどを〗~手続きを踏む go through [*complete*] the formalities. (❗前の方が口語的) ●課程を踏む *complete* a course.
❺〖その他の表現〗 ●怒って地団太を踏む stamp one's foot in anger. ●場数を踏む(=多くの〖幅広い〗経験を積む) have a lot of [*wide*] experience. ●ドジを踏む make [*commit*] a blunder.
●踏んだり蹴ったり (⇨踏んだり蹴ったり)

ふむき 不向き ── **不向きな** 形 (必要条件を満たしてない) unsuitable; (資格・能力に欠ける) unfit. (⇨ふさわしい) ▶そのドレスは彼女には不向きだ That dress *isn't suitable* [is *unsuitable*] *for* her. ▶彼は教師には不向きだ He is *unfit* [(やや話) *isn't cut out*] *for* teaching [*to be* a teacher]. (❗ be cut out for [to be] は通例否定文で用いる)

***ふめい 不明** 名 (無知) ignorance /íɡnərəns/. ●不明を恥じる be ashamed of one's ignorance.
── **不明の, 不明な** 形 (知られていない) unknown; (不明瞭(めいりょう)な) obscure; (身元未確認の) unidentified /ʌ́naidéntəfàid/. ●原因不明の病気 a disease of *unknown* origin. ●国籍不明の飛行機 an *unidentified* airplane. ▶彼女生死は不明です It is *unknown* [(確かでない) is *not certain*] whether he is alive or not. ▶作者の意図が不明だ(明らかでない) It is *not clear* what the writer wants to say. ▶彼がその女性を殺した動機は不明だ His motive for murdering the woman is *obscure*. ▶その男は身元不明です The man is *unidentified*. ▶息子がゆうべから行方不明です My son *has been missing* since last night.

ふめい 武名 ●武名をあげる win military fame; distinguish oneself by one's military bravery.

ふめいよ 不名誉 名 〖不面目〗(a) disgráce, (a) dishonor; 〖恥〗(a) shame; 〖信用失墜〗(a) discredit.
── **不名誉な** 形 ●不名誉な事件 a dishonorable [*shameful*] incident. ●それ[彼]は我が家にとって不名誉なことだ That [He] is a *disgrace* [a *shame*] *to* my family. ▶我がチームは不名誉な戦績を残した Our team left *dishonorable* results.

ふめいりょう 不明瞭 ── **不明瞭な** 形 not clear; (目・耳・心に) indistinct; (言葉・発音などが) (やや書) inarticulate. ●経理の不明瞭な点 points *unclear* in the accounting. ●あの老人は歯がぬけていて発音が不明瞭だ As the old man has lost all his teeth he [his pronunciation, his speech] *isn't articulate*.

ふめいろう 不明朗 ── **不明朗な** 形 (不公平な) unfair; (不正な, ごまかしの) dishonest, (問題のある) questionable. ●あのバーの不明朗な会計 *questionable* [*dishonest*] charges at the bar.

ふめつ 不滅 〖不死〗immortality. ●霊魂の不滅 the *immortality* of the soul. ▶バッハの音楽は不滅だ Bach's music is *immortal*. ▶彼は野球界の不滅の名選手だ He is one of the *immortals* [the *immortal* baseball players]. ▶我が巨人軍は永久に不滅です Our Giants are *immortal*./The Giants *forever*! (❗ forever は間投詞的で「…は永遠に」の意)

ふめん 譜面 a (musical) score; music.
●譜面台 a music stand.

ふめんぼく 不面目 (a) disgrace. (⇨不名誉)

ふもう 不毛 ── **不毛の** 形 (作物のとれない) barren, sterile /stérl/ (ともに比喩的にも用いる); (荒れた) waste. ●不毛の土地〖議論〗*barren* soil [*argument*].

ふもと 麓 (山の下のあたり) the foot (❗最も一般的な語); (低い部分) a bottom; (基の部分) a base. ▶彼の家は山のふもとにある His house is *at the foot* [*bottom*, *base*] of the mountain.

ふもん 不問 ── **不問に付す** leave [*pass*] (the case) unquestioned, let (the case) go unquestioned; (見逃す) overlook (the case).

ぶもん 武門 ●武門の出である come of a *samurai* [*military*] family.

ぶもん 部門 〖部類〗a class; 〖範疇(はんちゅう)〗a category; 〖企業などの組織上の〗a division; a department; a section. ●広報部門 the public relations *division* [*department*, *section*]. (❗順に範囲が狭くなる) ▶彼は年少部門で1等賞をとった He won (the) first prize in the junior *class* [*category*]. (❗ the は通例省略する)

ふやかす soak 〈lentiles /létlz/〉in water 〈until (they) become soft〉.

ふやける ❶〖ふくれる〗swell*; become* swollen [(パンなどが水分を含んで) soggy /sáɡi/]; (柔かくなる) become soft. ▶さっさと食べないとコーンフレークがふやけるよ Eat your cornflakes quickly. They're getting soggy. ▶プールから上がってしまい, 指先がふやけてしまっていた I found my fingertips all *wrinkled up* when I came out of the swimming pool. (❗ be wrinkled up は「しわだらけになる」の意)
❷〖精神的にだらしなくなる〗grow* lazy [(書) indolent]; slack off.

ふやじょう 不夜城 a brightly-illuminated all night place of entertainment.

***ふやす 増やす, 殖やす** 〖数・量を〗incréase; 〖物・事を増す〗add to…. ●人員〖人数〗を5人から10人へ増やす *increase* the personnel [the number of persons] from five to ten. ●貯金を増やす *add to* one's savings. ●知識を増やす *increase* [(向上させる) *improve, develop*] one's knowledge. ●借金を増やす *get* more deeply *in* debt. ●支持者を増やす (獲得する) *gain* supporters. ▶英語の語いを増やすことは重要だ It's important to *increase* [*enlarge, extend*] your English vocabulary. ▶もっと勉強時間を増やしなさい *Put* more hours *in* your study. ●給料を増やして(=上げて)もらった We had our salary *raised*. (❗「have+目的語+過去分詞」の構文)

***ふゆ 冬** 名 (the) winter. (参考 北半球では12〜2月, 南半球では6〜8月)(⇨春) ●冬に in 《(主に米) the》*winter*. ●冬を越す pass the *winter*. ▶ここ数日ほど冬めいてきた It *has* become winterlike for the past few days.
── **冬の** 形 winter; (冬特有の) wintry. ●冬の寒さ the cold(ness) of (the) *winter*. ▶(今年は)冬の間中風邪をひかなかった I haven't had a cold all this *winter*.
●冬鳥 a winter bird.

ふゆう 浮遊 ── **浮遊する** 動 (浮かぶ) float; (漂う) drift.
- 浮遊生物 plankton. • 浮遊物 a floating matter.

ふゆう 富裕 ── **富裕な** 形 rich, wealthy, 《話》well-to-do. ▶彼は富裕な家に生まれた He was born *rich* [*into a wealthy family*].
- 富裕層 the wealthy class.

ぶゆう 武勇 bravery; (戦闘での) 《主に書》valor /vǽlər/.
- 武勇伝 an episode of bravery [valor].

***ふゆかい 不愉快** 名 (不快さ) unpleasantness.
── **不愉快な** 形 (いやな) unpleasant; (気にくわない) disagreeable; (不快感を与える) offensive; (むかつくような) disgusting.
① 〖不愉快な～〗 ▶不愉快な思い出 an *unpleasant* memory. ▶彼は不愉快な男だ He is an *unpleasant* [a *disagreeable*, (気分が悪くなるほどいやな) a *disgusting*] man. ▶パーティーで不愉快な思いをした I had an *unpleasant* time at the party./I felt *displeased* [×unpleasant] at the party. ▶人に個人的な質問をするのは不愉快なものとされる(=まゆをしかめて嫌がられる) Asking personal questions *is frowned upon*.
② 〖…は不愉快だ〗 ▶彼の高圧的な態度は非常に不愉快だ His high-handed attitude is very *unpleasant* [*disagreeable*] (to me). ▶彼と話すのは不愉快だ It's *unpleasant* to talk to him./He is *unpleasant* to talk to. (❗最後の to を落とさないように言う)
── **不愉快に** 副 ▶彼は卑怯(ひきょう)者呼ばわりされて不愉快に思った (腹を立てた) He got *offended* [〖むかっとした〗 He *was disgusted*; (憤慨した) He *felt angry and resentful*] *at* being called a coward.

ふゆがた 冬型 ── **冬型の** 形 • 冬型の天候 *wintry* weather. • 冬型の気圧配置 a pressure pattern *characteristic of winter*.

ふゆがれ 冬枯れ • 冬枯れの景色 a *bleak and desolate*) winter landscape. • 冬枯れの木々 trees *denuded of their leaves in winter*; *nude* trees *of winter*.

ふゆきとどき 不行き届き 〖不注意〗carelessness; (うかつなこと) inattentiveness; 〖怠慢〗neglect; (a) negligence. (⇨怠慢) ▶この誤りは私の不行き届きのせいです This mistake is due to [is caused by] my *carelessness*./I made this mistake. I was *careless*. ▶彼は部下に対する監督不行き届きで非難された He was charged with *lack of supervision over his subordinates* 〖(男の) *men*〗.

ふゆげしょう 冬化粧 ▶北の山々の峰は早や冬化粧をしている Mountain peaks in the north *have already been covered with snow*.

ふゆごもり 冬籠もり • 冬ごもりをする stay indoors during the winter; spend the winter (months) indoors [(巣の中で) in the nest]; (冬眠する) hibernate.

ふゆじたく 冬支度 preparations for (the) winter. ▶北の国では夏が終わるとすぐに冬支度に入る People in the north countries begin to *prepare for the coming winter* just when the summer is over.

ふゆしょうぐん 冬将軍 'General Winter'; Jack Frost. ▶冬将軍がやって来そうだ It feels as though *Jack Frost is coming*.

ふゆぞら 冬空 the (gray [gloomy]) winter sky.

ふゆのたび 『冬の旅』 *Winter Journey*. (参考 シューベルトの歌曲集)

ふゆば 冬場 ── **冬場の** 形 winter (vegetables). • 冬場に in the winter months; during the winter.

ふゆび 〖冬の弱い日光〗 pale winter sunshine [sun]; 〖気象上の〗 a day with the minimum temperature below zero.

ふゆもの 冬物 (冬服) winter clothes [wear]; (冬物の商品) winter goods. ▶冬物最終処分 (掲示) Final Clearance Sale *on Winter Clothes* [*Goods*].

ふゆやすみ 冬休み the winter vacation. (事情 米英では the Christmas break [(米) vacation, 《英》holidays] がこれに当たる)

ふゆやま 冬山 〖冬枯れの山〗 bleak mountains in the winter; 〖冬山登山〗 mountain climbing in the winter, winter mountaineering. • 冬山登山する climb a mountain in the wintertime.

ふよ 付与 ── **付与する** 動 (権限・権力を) give, 《書》invest; (称号などを) confer (-rr-); 《書》bestow.
- 全権を付与する *invest* 〈him〉 *with* full authority [full authority *in* /him/].

ふよ 賦与 ── **賦与する** 動 (やや書) gift, 《書》endow /endáu/. (❗ともに通例受身で) ▶彼は生まれつき絵画の才能を賦与されている He *is endowed* [*is gifted*] *with* a talent for painting./He has a *natural* [an *innate*] talent for painting.

ぶよ 蚋 〖昆虫〗 a gnat /næt/; a midge. (❗《英》で gnat と midge を同じに扱うことがある)

***ふよう 不用, 不要** ── **不用**〖不要〗**の** 形 (さしあたり必要のない) unnecessary, (使われていない) out of use.
- 不用になる go *out of use*. • 不用の節は if you don't need it.
- 不用品 a discarded [an unwanted] article, an article for disposal. • 不用品即売会 (米) a garage [a yard] sale (参考 自宅の車車庫で行われる); (慈善市) a rummage /rʌ́mɪdʒ/ (米) [a jumble (英)] sale.

ふよう 扶養 名 support; maintenance. • 家族の扶養 the *maintenance* of one's family [one's wife and children]. ▶私には扶養家族が5人いる [多い] I have five *dependents* [a large *family to support*]. (⇨動)
── **扶養する** 動 (やや書) maintain. ▶私には両親を扶養する義務がある I have a duty to *support* [*maintain*] my parents.
- 扶養控除 deduction for dependents. • 扶養者 a support(er); (一家のかせぎ手) the breadwinner. • 扶養手当 a family allowance. (事情 《英》では「(政府が毎週支給する)児童手当」のこと)

ふよう 芙蓉 〖植物〗(米) a Confederate [a cotton] rose. (参考 本来は a Chinese mallow という。米国への渡りが南部だったので, このように呼ばれる)

ふよう 浮揚 ── **浮揚する** 動 (空中に) rise [float] in the air; (水上に) rise [come up] to the surface; (潜水艦などが) surface.
- 浮揚力 buoyancy /bɔ́ɪənsi/.

ぶよう 舞踊 a dance, dancing. • 日本舞踊 Japanese *dancing*. • 民族舞踊 a folk *dance*.
- 舞踊家 a dancer.

ふようい 不用意 ── **不用意な** 形 (準備ができていない) unprepared; (不注意な) careless; (無思慮な) thoughtless; (無分別な) indiscreet. • 不用意な発言を避ける (控える) avoid [refrain from] *careless* remarks. • 不用意に それを口に出す say it *thoughtlessly*.

ふようじょう 不養生 neglect of one's health; (不節制) intemperance. ▶医者の不養生 Doctors often *neglect* their own *health*./(ことわざ) Physician, heal thyself. (❗thyself は yourself の 《古》)

ぶようじん 不用心 ── **不用心な** 形 unsafe, inse-

ふようど 腐葉土 leaf mold, 《やや書》 humus.

ぶよぶよ ▶彼の体はぶよぶよしている His body is *flabby*. ▶畳が湿気でぶよぶよしている The *tatami* floor is *soggy* from the damp.

プラーク 〖歯科〗(dental) plaque /plǽk/.

フライ 〖野球〗a fly (ball). ●大[小]フライ a long [short] *fly*. ●内野[外野]フライ an infield [an outfield] *fly*. ●高いフライ a high [a towering] *fly*. ●犠牲フライ a sacrifice *fly*. ●センター[凡]フライを打つ hit a *fly* [a pop *fly*] to center; fly [pop up] to center. (1)「その結果アウトになると fly out [pop out] to center という. (2) 動詞の fly の過去形・過去分詞形は flied) ▶フライを捕る[落とす] catch [drop] a fly.

フライ 〖料理〗deep-fried food. ●エビフライ a *deep-fried* (*breaded*) *prawn*. ●フライにする deep-fry (*food*).

プライオリティー 〖優先順位〗priority.

ぶらいかん 無頼漢 (やくざ) a gangster; (ごろつき) a ruffian; (ならずもの) a rascal; (不良) a hooligan, a hoodlum.

フライきゅう フライ級 the flyweight. ●フライ級選手 a flyweight.

プライス 〖価格〗a price. ●プライスカード a príce càrd. ●プライスタグ a príce tàg. ●プライスリーダー制 price leadership.

ブライダル 〖婚礼(の)〗bridal. ●ブライダル産業 the bridal industry.

フライト 〖飛行機の便〗a flight. (⇨便(½)) ▶彼は午前10時発のフライトで大阪に行った He flew to Osaka on the 10 a.m. *flight*. ●フライトアテンダント〖客室乗務員〗a flíght attèndant. ●フライトコントロール〖航空管制〗(a) flíght contròl; 〖操縦装置〗a flight control system. ●フライトシミュレーター〖模擬飛行装置〗a flight sìmulator. ●フライトナンバー〖飛行便の番号〗a flíght nùmber. ●フライトバッグ〖機内持ち込みのショルダーバッグ〗a flíght bàg. ●フライトレコーダー〖飛行記録装置〗a flíght recòrder; a black box.

プライド 〖誇り〗pride;〖自尊心〗self-respect. 語感 日本語では「お高くとまっている」という含みがありマイナスイメージを持っているが, 英語では逆にプラスイメージが伴う. ●プライドを持っている be proud of [take *pride* in] 〈one's job〉. ●プライドを傷つける hurt 〈his〉 *pride*. ▶彼はプライドが高くて言い訳などしない He is too *proud* [has too much *self-respect*] to make an excuse. (!「プライドが高い」は ×His pride is high. とはいわない)

フライドチキン fried chicken.

フライドポテト 《主に米》French fries,《英》chips (!いずれも通例複数形で);《和製語》fried potato.

プライバシー privacy. ●プライバシーを侵害する invade 〈his〉 *privacy*. (!「プライバシーの侵害」は an invasion of *privacy*) ●プライバシーを守る protect [(尊重する) respect, (遵守する) guard] one's *privacy*. ●プライバシーに関わる事 one's *private* affairs. ●プライバシーの権利 right to [of] *privacy*. ●当方はあなたのプライバシーを絶対に守ります We absolutely guarantee your *privacy*. ●スターにはプライバシーはあまり許されない Stars don't get much *privacy*.

フライパン 《米》a frypan,《英》a frying-pan; (小さなフライパン)《主に米》a skillet.

プライベート — **プライベートな** 形 〖私的な〗private;〖個人的な〗personal. ●プライベートビーチ〖ホテルや個人専用浜辺〗a private beach. ●プライベートブランド a private brand. ●プライベートルーム〖私室〗a private room.

プライマリーケア 〖初期医療〗primary care; primary health care.

プライマリーバランス 〖基礎的財政収支〗primary balance.

プライムタイム 〖最も視聴率の高い時間帯〗《at》prime time.

プライムレート 〖最優遇金利〗the prime (lending) rate. ●短期[長期]プライムレート the short-term [long-term] *prime rate*; the *prime rate* on short-term [long term] loans. ●プライムレートを引き上げる[引き下げる] hike [cut] the *prime rate*.

プライヤー (ペンチ) a pair of) pliers.

フライング 图 〖競技〗a false start; a bréakawày. (!a flying start は「助走スタート」の意で, この意でも和製英語)

—— **フライングする** 動 make a false start; break away; jump the starter's gun.

ブラインド a blind. (!しばしば複数形で),《米》a (window) shade. ●ブラインドを上げる[降ろす] raise [lower, pull down] the *blind*(s) [*shade*(s)].

ブラインドタッチ touch-typing. (!blind touch より普通. ●ブラインドタッチで打てるようになる learn to *touch-type*.

ブラインドテスト 〖目隠しテスト〗《conduct》a blind test.

ブラウザ 〖閲覧ソフト〗a browser.

ブラウス a blouse;〖シャツブラウス〗a shirt blouse,《米》a shirtwaist. ●オーバーブラウス an overblouse. ●赤いシルクのブラウスを着た女性 a woman in a red silk *blouse*.

ブラウンかん ブラウン管 a cathode-ray /kǽθoud-/ tube, a (picture) tube. (!a Braun-tube はまれ)

ブラウンソース 〖料理〗brown sauce.

プラカード a plácard. ●プラカードをかかげる carry a *placard* 《that says "No More Wars"》.

ぶらく 部落 (小村落) a small village.

プラグ a plug /plʌ́ɡ/. 〖参考〗三叉ソケット(英国)に二叉プラグ(日本・米国)を差し込むのに使う補助具を a travel plug という) ●プラグをソケットに差し込む put a *plug* in the socket. ●プラグを差し込んで扇風機をつける *plug in* an electric fan. (!×plug an electric fan は不可)

プラグマティズム 〖実用主義〗pragmatism.

プラザ [<スペイン語] 〖広場〗a plaza.

ぶらさがる ぶら下がる (静止して) hang*; (だらりと, ぶらりと) dangle; (ゆらゆらと) swing*. ●つり革によら下がる *hang from* [*dangle from*, (つかまる) *hang on to*] a strap. ▶ぶどうが棚からぶら下がっていた The grapes *hung* (*down*) *from* the trellis. ▶鉄棒に 20 秒ぶら下がっていられますか Can you *hang from* a bar for 20 seconds?

ぶらさげる ぶら下げる hang*; suspend (!前の方が口語的); (ぶら下で); (手に下げて運ぶ) carry. ●洗濯物を物干し綱にぶら下げる *hang* the washing on the line.

***ブラシ** a brush /brʌ́ʃ/. ●靴[洋服]ブラシ a shoe [clothes] *brush*. ●ヘアブラシ a hairbrush. ●髪にブラシをかける *brush* one's hair; *give* one's hair a (*good*) *brush*. ●犬にブラシをかけてやる groom a dog with a *brush*. ●ブラシを使ってポニーテールにまとめる *brush into* a ponytail. ▶君の上着はブラシをかけないといけない Your coat needs [wants] *brushing*. (!〈話〉では need [〈まれ〉 want] to be brushed も可)

プラシーボ 〖偽薬〗a placebo. ●プラシーボ効果 the placebo effect.

ブラジャー [<フランス語] a bra /brɑ́ː/;《やや古》a

brassiere /brəzíər/. ●ブラジャーをつける put on [do up] a *bra*. ●ブラジャーをはずす take off [undo] one's *bra*. ▶彼女はブラジャーをつけない[つけていない] She doesn't wear a *bra*.

ブラジリア 〖ブラジルの首都〗Brasília. (■ -í- は本来のつづり字)

ブラジル 〖国名〗Brazil;《公式名》the Federative Republic of Brazil. (首都 Brasília) ●ブラジル人 a Brazilian;《総称》Brazilian people,《やや書》the Brazilians. ●ブラジル(人)の Brazilian.

ふらす 降らす ●弾丸の雨を降らす *shower* bullets 《*on*》. ▶その温暖前線が近畿地方に大雨を降らした The warm front *brought* heavy rain [rainfall] *to* the Kinki District.

＊プラス ❶〖加算・正数記号〗a plus (↔a minus). ▶2 プラス 4 は 6 Two *plus* four is [equals] six. (■ この plus は両言葉でその前の two という数値が主語となるため、単数動詞が呼応する。次例の方が口語的)/Two and four is [are, make(s)] six.
❷〖有利〗an advantage,《話》a plus. ▶これは会社に大変なプラスになる This is a great *advantage* [a big *plus*] to our company. ●彼の長所は常にプラス志向的(=物事を前向きに考える)という点です His strong point is that he always thinks *positive* [物事の明るい面を見る] looks on the bright side]. ●英語を知っていることは彼の仕事にプラスになっている Knowledge of English is a *plus* in his job.
❸〖電気などで〗●磁石にはプラスとマイナスがある A magnet has *positive* and negative *poles*.
●プラスイメージ a positive (↔negative) impression [image]. ●プラス記号 a plus (sign). ●プラス成長 (経済の) positive (↔negative) economic growth. ●プラスドライバー a Phillips head [a cross-head] screwdriver. ●プラスねじ a Phillips head [a cross-head] screw. (⇨プラスアルファ, プラスマイナス)

プラスアルファ ▶夏のボーナスは 2 か月分プラスアルファです The summer bonus is two months' salary *plus* something (extra) [*plus* a bit extra]. (■ ×plus α とはいわない

フラスコ 〖<ポルトガル語〗a flask /flǽsk, flɑ́ːsk/.

プラスチック plastic;(製品) plastics. (■日本語の「プラスチック」は主に塩ビ・合成樹脂に用いられるが、英語ではナイロン・ビニロン・セルロイドをさす(⇨ビニール))
●プラスチック産業 the plastics industry. ●プラスチック製品 plastic products [goods]; plastics; things made of plastic. ●プラスチック爆弾 a plastic bomb [explosive]. ●プラスチックマネー [「クレジットカード」の別称]《話》plastic (money). ●プラスチックモデル (プラモデル ともいう) ●プラスチックモデル (プラモデル の通称).

フラストレーション 〖欲求不満〗frustration. ●フラストレーションを感じる[がたまる] feel [get] *frustrated*.

ブラスバンド a brass band.

プラズマ plasma.
●プラズマディスプレーパネル a plasma display panel (略 PDP).

プラスマイナス plus or minus (記号 ±). ●プラスマイナスゼロになる come to [add up to] nothing. ▶当社は今年度はプラスマイナスゼロ(=純益ゼロ)になった We ended up with *no profit* this year./(ぎりぎり採算ベースに達した) We (finally) came up to the break-even [managed to break even] this year. ▶プラスマイナス 3 パーセントの誤差がある There is a margin of error of *plus or minus* 3 percent.

プラスミド 〖核外遺伝子〗a plasmid.

プラタナス 〖植物〗a plane (tree),《米》a sycamore. (■ 通例 ×a platanus とはいわない

フラダンス a húla, a hula-hula;《和製語》a hula dance. (■ その踊り手は a hula dancer) ●フラダンスを踊る dance the *hula*; hula.

ふらち 不埒 — **不埒な** 〖限度をこえてけしからぬ〗(無作法な) rude;(ふとどきな) outrageous;(許しの余地のない) inexcusable,(許せない) unpardonable. ▶なんとふらちな男だ What a *rude* fellow he is!

プラチナ platinum (元素記号 Pt).

ふらつく 〖めまいがする〗be [feel] dizzy [giddy];(よろよろする) stagger, be unsteady [《話》shaky] (on one's feet); [ぶらぶら歩く] wander around.
●態度がふらつく take an *uncertain* attitude 《*toward*, *to*》. ●彼は疲れ切ってふらついた He *was dizzy* because he was too tired. ●彼は通りをふらつきながら歩いていった He *staggered* down the street./He walked down the street *unsteadily*. ●酒を飲んだので頭がふらついた The *sake* made my head *swim*.

ぶらつく ❶〖人が〗(足の向くままに) stroll;(楽しい気分で) ramble;(あてもなく) wander. (⇨さまよう) ●町中をぶらつく *stroll around* the streets. ●森をぶらつく *ramble* [*stroll*] (*around*) in the woods. ●店の中をぶらつく *wander through* the store. ●公園をぶらつきましょう Let's *take a stroll* [(散歩する) *take a walk*] in the park. ▶ここは若者が大勢ぶらつくところだよ This is where a lot of young people *hang out*. (■ hang out は《話》で「ひんぱんに訪れる」の意) ❷〖物が〗swing*. (⇨ぶらぶら) ❶

ブラック ▶コーヒーはブラックが好きだ I like my coffee *black*.
●ブラックコーヒー black coffee. ●ブラックパワー [黒人の政治運動] Black Power. ●ブラックペッパー [黒コショウ] black pepper. ●ブラックホール 〖天文〗a black hole. ●ブラックボックス 〖航空〗a black box. (■ (1) a flight recorder と a voice recorder を収めた容器の通称. (2) 実際は黒色ではなく、目立つ明るい色) ●ブラックマーケット [闇市] a black market. ●ブラックマネー [不正資金] black money. ●ブラックユーモア black humor.

ブラックジャック 〖トランプ〗《主に米》blackjack, twenty-one;《主に英》pontoon.

ブラックバス 〖魚が〗a black bass.

ブラックリスト (make) a blacklist 《*of*》. ●ブラックリストに載っている人 a person on the *blacklist*. ●彼をブラックリストに載せる put [place] him on the *blacklist*; blacklist him.

フラッシュ (装置) a flash (■ 撮影方法・閃光(ツッ)をいうときは 〖〗), a flashlight (■ 閃光をいうときは 〖〗), a flashlamp;(使い捨て式電球) a flashbulb. ●フラッシュ付きカメラ a camera with a built-in *flash* unit. ●フラッシュをたく use a *flash*; set off [light] a *flashbulb*. ●フラッシュを浴びる be in a flood of *flashlights*;(急に有名になる) flash into fame. ▶彼が玄関口に出てくると、報道陣のフラッシュがたかれた Reporters' *flashbulbs* popped just when he appeared at the front door. ●フラッシュ撮影禁止 No flash photograph.
●フラッシュカード a flash card. ●フラッシュメモリ [コンピュータ] a flash memory. ●フラッシュライト [懐中電灯]《主に米》a flashlight.

ブラッシュアップ — **ブラッシュアップする** 動 brush ... up; brush up on .... ●英語をブラッシュアップする *brush up* (*on*) one's English.

フラッシュバック 图 a flashback. ●子供時代へのフラッシュバック a *flashback* to one's childhood.
— **フラッシュバックする** 動 flashback 《*to*》.

ふらっと (無意識に) unintentionally; (特に目的なく) aimlessly; (ふとした思いつきで) on a whim. ▶その少年はふらっと店のチューインガムに手を出した The boy grabbed a packet of chewing gums *unintentionally* at the store. ▶私は時々ふらっと旅に出たくなる Sometimes I feel like going on a journey *aimlessly*. ▶彼はふらっと海辺へ行く気になった He *had a whim to* go to the seaside. ▶ウイスキーを飲んで頭がふらっとした I *felt dizzy* after I drank whiskey./The whiskey made my head *swim*.

フラット 〖音楽〗a flat (記号 ♭);〖競技の記録〗flat.
• 10 秒フラットで in 10 seconds *flat*.

ぶらっと (⇨ふらっと) ▶旧友がぶらっとやって来た An old friend of mine *dropped in on* me [*at my house*].

プラットホーム a platform. (⇨ホーム)

フラップ 〖下げ翼〗a flap.

フラッペ [<フランス語] frappé.

プラトニックラブ 〖精神的恋愛〗platonic love.

プラトン 〖ギリシャの哲学者〗Plato /pléitou/.

プラネタリウム a planetarium (複 ~s, planetaria).

プラハ 〖チェコ共和国の首都〗Prague /prɑ́ːɡ/.

フラフープ a hula hoop. (❗もと商標) • フラフープをする hula-hoop.

ふらふら 副 ❶〖不安定に〗unsteadily, falteringly.
• ふらふらと立ち上がる *stagger* to one's feet. ▶彼は酔っ払ってふらふらと歩いた He got drunk and walked *unsteadily*. ▶彼はふらふらと酒場から出てきた He *wandered off* out of the bar.

❷〖当てなく〗aimlessly. ▶世界をふらふらさまよう *wander around* [*about*] the world. ▶彼はふらふらと仕事を替えていった He drifted *aimlessly* from job to job.

❸〖無意識に〗unconsciously. ▶彼はふらふらと発車寸前の列車に乗ってしまった *Unconsciously* he got on a train that was just leaving.

── **ふらふらする** 動 ▶シャンペンを一杯飲んだら頭がちょっとふらふらした With a glass of champagne, I felt kind of *light-headed*. (⇨ふらっと) ▶子供たちはぐるぐる回ってふらふらするのを楽しんでいる Children turn around and around and enjoy *feeling giddy* [*dizzy*]. (❗いずれも目が回って倒れそうになる感じを表す) ▶柳の長い枝がふらふらしていた The long branches of a willow tree *hung loose*.

── **ふらふらした** 形 ▶ふらふらした(=しっかりした方針のない)態度 an *uncertain* attitude. ▶彼はいつもふらふらして決断ができない He's too *indecisive* [(話) (優柔不断な) *wishy-washy*] to make a decision.

ぶらぶら ❶〖揺れ動く〗sway. ▶吹き流しが風にぶらぶら揺れていた A streamer *was swaying* in the wind. ▶彼は運動の前に手をぶらぶらさせた(=振り動かした) He *swung* his hands around before the exercise.

❷〖ゆったりとした気分で歩く〗(特に目的なく) wander /wɑ́ndər/; (楽しく) stroll, take* a stroll.
• 店内の商品をぶらぶら(=特に買う気もなく)見て歩く *casually* browse around in a store. ▶私たちはウィンドーショッピングをしながら銀座をぶらぶら歩いた We *strolled* along the Ginza window-shopping. ▶彼女は公園をぶらぶら歩いた She *strolled* [*took a stroll*] in the park.

❸〖仕事などしないで無為でいる〗be idle. ▶家でぶらぶらして過ごす *idle away* one's *time* at home. ▶彼は一日中ぶらぶらしている He is *idle* all day long. ▶彼はぶらぶらしている(仕事がない) He's *out of work* now./(目的のない生活をしている) He's leading an *aimless* life.

ブラボー [<イタリア語] Bravo! (❗演奏者に)/(お見事!) Well done!/(すてき!) Splendid!

フラボノイド 〖植物色素〗flavonoid /fléivənɔ̀id/.

フラミンゴ 〖鳥〗a flamingo /fləmíŋɡou/ (複 ~(e)s).

プラム 〖植物〗a plum.

フラメンコ [<スペイン語] flamenco /fləméŋkou/; (米) flamenco dancing; (曲, 歌) a flamenco (複 ~s) • フラメンコを踊る dance the *flamenco*.

プラモデル a plastic model. • プラモデルを作る build [make, (組み立てる) assemble] a *plastic model (car)*.

ぶらりと ❶〖たれ下がっているさま〗▶ヒョウタンがたくさん庭にぶらりと下がっていた Many gourds *were dangling* in the garden.

❷〖目的のないさま〗aimlessly; (怠けて) idly. ▶彼はよくぶらりと旅に出ることがある He often goes on a journey *without any particular aim*. ▶私は 1 日をぶらりと過ごした I spent the day *idly*.

ふられる 振られる be turned down; be refused.
▶ぼくは彼女に振られた(申し込みを断られた) I *was turned down* by her. (❗英語では能動形 She *turned me down*. の方が普通)/(捨てられた) She *left* [(突然に) jilted, (話) *dumped*] me./(絶交された) She *dropped* me. (❗後の 2 例は受身で用いることはない)

フラワー 〖花〗a flower.
• フラワーアレンジメント 〖生け花〗flower arrangement. • フラワーショー a flower show. • フラワーセンター a flower center.

ふらん 腐乱 图 decomposition;《書》putrefaction. ▶死体は腐乱の状態がひどく身元は確認できなかった The body *was* badly *putrefied* and we could not identify it.
── **腐乱させる** decompose,《書》putrefy.
── **腐乱死体** a decomposing [《書》putrefying] body.

フラン [<フランス語] 〖スイスの通貨単位〗a franc (略 F., Fr.).

プラン 〖計画〗a plan.

ふらんき 孵卵器 an incubator.

フランク 〖サッカー〗flank. (参考 ピッチ上の両タッチラインに近いスペース。サイド)

ブランク 〖空白, 空欄〗a blank; 〖途切れ〗a gap. ▶彼の運転歴には 5 年のブランクがある There is a *gap* of five years in his driving experience.

プランクトン 〖浮遊生物〗〖集合的〗plankton.

フランクフルト 〖ドイツの都市〗Frankfurt /frǽŋkfərt/.

フランクフルトソーセージ a frankfurter (和製語) a Frankfurt sausage.

フランクリン 〖米国の政治家・著述家・発明家〗Franklin (Benjamin ~).

フランケンシュタイン Frankenstein /frǽŋkənstàin/.

ぶらんこ a swing. • ぶらんこに乗る (1 回乗る) have a *swing*; (台座に乗る) ride on [get on, sit on] a *swing*; (遊ぶ) play on the *swing*. ▶うちの娘はぶらんこが好きだ My little girl likes to *swing*.

フランス 〖国名〗France; 〖公式名〗the French Republic. (首都 Paris) • フランス人 (男性) a Frenchman; (女性) a Frenchwoman; (総称) French people, (やや書) the French. (❗特に男女の区別をしない場合は通例 He [She] is French. のようにいう)
• フランス語 French. • フランス(人[語])の French.
• フランス革命 the French Revolution. • フランスパン (棒状の) French bread, a French loaf, a baguette /bæɡét/. • フランス料理 French food; (調理法) French cooking [cuisine]. • フランス料理店 a French restaurant.

ふらんすものがたり 『ふらんす物語』 *French Stories*. (参考 永井荷風の短編小説集)

プランター a planter.
フランダース 『「フランドル」の英語名』(⇨フランドル)
ブランチ 『昼食を兼ねた遅い朝食』brunch.
フランチャイズ 『フランチャイズ本拠地占有権』a franchise; 『地域内独占営業権』a franchise.
● フランチャイズ加盟 franchise participation. ● フランチャイズ契約 a franchise (agreement). ● フランチャイズチェーン a chain of franchise stores. ● フランチャイズ店 a franchise(d) store. ● フランチャイズ料 a franchise fee.
ブランデー brandy; (1杯の) a snifter of brandy.
● 紅茶にブランデーを少し入れる add a dash [a nip] of *brandy* to one's tea.
プランテーション 『大農園』a plantation.
ブランド 『銘柄』a brand. ● 有名ブランドの紅茶 name-*brand* [a famous *brand* of] tea. ● デザイナーブランドの服 *designer* clothes. ● ブランド志向が強い be brand-conscious; like *name products*. ● ノーブランド商品 generic *branded* goods; the generics.
● ブランドイメージ (improve [hurt]) one's brand image. ● ブランド商品 a brand name item; a name [a name-brand] product; a name brand. ● ブランド戦略 the brand strategy. ● ブランドマーク a brand mark.
プラント (a) plant.
● プラント輸出 plant export; the export of plant.
フランドル Flanders. (『参考』ベルギー西部・フランス北部・オランダ南西部を含む地域)
プランナー 『立案者』a planner /plǽnər/.
プランニング 『立案』planning.
フランネル 『毛織物』flannel /flǽnl/.
***ふり 振り** 图 ❶ 『様子』(外見) (an) appearance; an air; (見せかけ) (a) pretense; (a) show. ▶彼はなり振りかまわず働いた He worked hard without caring (about) *how he looked*./He worked hard, regardless of his *appearance*. ▶人の振り見て我が振り直せ 'Observe other people's *appearance* [*behavior*] and correct your own.'/《ことわざ》Learn wisdom by the follies of others.
❷ 『振動』(円状の) a swing, a sweep; (上下前後の) a shake; (尾や頭の) a wag. ▶腕をひと振りして水に飛び込む jump into the water with a *swing* of one's arms. ▶びんをひと振りする give a bottle a *shake*.
── **振りをする** 動 『実際そうであるかのように偽る』pretend, (巧みに) 『書』feign; make* believe (『!』pretend より口語的で, よく子供のまねごと遊びに用いられる (⇨ごっこ)); 『書』affect 『自分を他に印象づけようとする含意がある』; 『態度などを帯びる』assume (『!』必ずしも人を欺く意図を含まない); 『態度などを装う』『話』put*... on. ● 見て見ぬふりをする (⇨見て見ぬ振り)
▶彼はその話を知らないふりをした He *pretended* [*feigned*, *made believe*, *affected*] not to know the story./He *pretended* [*feigned*, *made believe*, *affected*] that he didn't know the story. (『!』to 不定詞の場合は主に身ぶりで, that節の場合は主に言葉で示す) /『書』He *pretended* [*feigned*, *affected*, *assumed*] ignorance of the story.

***ふり 不利** 图 (a) disadvantage; 『障害』a handicap. ▶この同盟は日本には非常に不利だ This alliance is very *disadvantageous* [a big *disadvantage*] to Japan.
── **不利な** 厖 disadvantageous (*to*) (『!』通例叙述的); 《好ましくない》unfavorable. ▶この点では外国人は不利な立場にある Foreigners are *at a disadvantage* [are *handicapped*] in this respect./Foreigners are in a *disadvantage* [an *unfavorable*] position in this respect. ▶彼女は私に不

利な証言をした She testified [gave testimony] *against* me. (『!』「不利な[に]」の意は前置詞 against (↔for) によっても表せる)

ふり 降り 『雨』rain, a rainfall; 『雪』snow, a snowfall. ▶この降りでは客は来ないだろう The customers will not come in this *rain*. ▶ひどい降りだ It's *raining* [*snowing*] hard.
ぶり 鰤 『魚介』a yellowtail. (『!』通例単・複同形. 肉は 🔵)

***ぶり -振り** ❶ 『…の後』after …; 『…以来』since …; 『…の期間で初めて』for the first time in 《ten years》. ▶私は8年ぶりに彼に会った I saw him *for the first time* in eight years./I saw him *after* (an [xthe] interval of) eight years [*after* an eight-year interval]. (『!』after eight years' interval とはあまりいわない)/《この前会ってから8年になる》It's [It's been] eight years *since* I saw him last. (『!』最初の表現がいちばん口語的) ▶登山者は5日ぶりに〔遭難後5日ぶりに〕救出された The climbers were rescued *after* five days [five days *after* the mountain accident]. ▶今年は20年ぶりの暖冬です This is the warmest winter in 《主に米》 [*for* 《主に英》] 20 years. / This is the warmest winter (that) we have had in 《主に米》 [*for* 《主に英》] the past [last] twenty years. ▶こんなくつろいだ気分になるのは何年ぶりかです I feel more relaxed than I've felt in 《主に米》 [*for* 《主に英》] … years. (『!』than 以下に否定が含意された言い方で, I haven't felt as relaxed in [for] … as this は通例問省略するのに相当する)
❷ 『様子, 仕方』a way. ▶仕事ぶりがよい (よく働く) work well (熱心に) hard, (積極的に) actively]. ● 生活ぶりがつましい (質素な生活をする) lead [live] a frugal life. ▶彼の話しぶりが気にくわない I don't like his *way* [*manner*] of speaking. (『!』次例の方が口語的) ▶ I don't like the *way* (that) he speaks.
▶彼らの暮らしぶりからすると相当裕福なようだ From the *way* they live, they seem to be quite well-off. ▶ [Judging from the way …, 《米》The way …. でもこの意は表せる)

ふりあう 振り合う ▶私たちは何度も手を振り合って別れを惜しんだ We were so reluctant to part that we *waved* good-by *to each other* over and over again.
ふりあおぐ 振り仰ぐ ● これから征服する山頂を振り仰ぐ *look up at* the (mountain) top we are going to conquer.
ふりあげる 振り上げる ● げんこつを振り上げる *raise* [*shake*] one's fist (in anger). ● 彼の竹刀を振り上げる *raise* 〔さっと〕 *throw up*, 〔猛然と〕 *fling up*〕 one's bamboo sword *over* his head.
ふりあてる 振り当てる (⇨割り当てる)
ふりあらい 振り洗い── 振り洗いする 動 wash 《a shirt》 by shaking (it) in soapy water.
フリー── フリーの 厖 『自由な』free; 『フリーランスの』free-lance. ● フリーのカメラマン a freelance [xa free] photographer. ● フリーで働く work *freelance*; do *freelance* work; *freelance*.
フリーウェア 『無料ソフト』a freeware.
フリーエージェント 『野球』a free agent. ● フリーエージェントの身分 free agency.
● フリーエージェント制 the free agent system; the FA system.
フリーキック 『サッカー・ラグビー』a free kick. ● 直接〔間接〕フリーキック a direct [an indirect] free kick.
フリークライミング 『登山』free climbing.
フリーザー a freezer.
フリーサイズ 《商品の表示》One size fits all. ▶このフ

フリージア

トッキングはフリーサイズです These stockings *stretch to fit* [×are free sizes].
フリージア 〖植物〗a freesia.
フリーズ ― **フリーズする** 動 〖コンピュータ〗freeze*.
フリースクール 〖自由学校〗a free school.
フリースタイル freestyle. ● フリースタイルの freestyle 《swimming [figure skating, gymnastics]》. ● フリースタイルで泳ぐ swim *freestyle*.
フリーズドライ 名 〖凍結乾燥〗freeze-drying. ― **フリーズドライの** 形 freeze-dried.
フリースロー 〖バスケット〗(sink) a free throw.
フリーセックス free love. (❗free sex とはあまりいわない)
フリーター a freelance worker; a job-hopping part-time worker [〘話〙part-timer]; 〘和製語〙a freeter. (参考「フリーター」は「フリー (free) 」と「アルバイター (Arbeiter) 」(ドイツ語)の合成語) ▶ フリーターは定職につかずアルバイトで暮らす若者のことをいう The word "freeter" refers to a young person who has no intention of taking a full-time job but flits from one part-time job to another (to make a living).
フリータイム 〖自由時間〗free time. ● フリータイム制 (英会話教室などの) a free time [a flexible time] system.
フリーダイヤル 《米》a toll-free call, 《英》freefone, freephone; 〘和製語〙free dial. (語法 米国では 1-800-…) ● フリーダイヤルで電話する 《米》make call 《them》 *toll-free*, make a *toll-free* call 《to them》; 《英》call 《their》 *freefone* [*freephone*] 《number》.
プリーツ a pleat. ● スカートのプリーツ pleats *on* the skirt. ● プリーツスカート a pleated skirt.
フリートーキング free conversation [〘討論〙discussion]; 〘和製語〙free talking.
フリーパス 〖無料入場[乗車]券〗a (free) pass; a free ticket.
フリーバッティング 〖野球〗batting practice; 〘和製語〙free batting. ● フリーバッティングをする take batting practice. ● フリーバッティングの投手をする pitch batting practice.
フリーハンド 〖器具を使わずに手で描いた〗fréehànd. ● フリーハンドで描く draw 《it》 *freehand*; do a *free-hand* drawing 《of it》.
ブリーフ (a pair of) briefs. (⇨パンツ)
ブリーフケース a briefcase.
フリーボール 〖アメフト〗a free ball.
フリーマーケット 〖蚤(⊘)の市〗a flea market.
フリーメール 〖コンピュータ〗(サービス) free email service; 〘和製語〙free mail.
フリーライター 〖自由契約の著述家〗a freelance writer; 〘和製語〙a free writer.
フリーランサー freelance; a freelancer. (❗自由契約の記者・写真家など)
フリーランス ― **フリーランスの** 形 freelance. (⇨フリー) ● フリーランスのジャーナリスト a *freelance* journalist.
プリインストール ● プリインストールする 〖コンピュータ〗pre-install.
ふりえき 不利益 〖損〗a loss; 〖不利〗(a) disadvantage. ● 不利益をこうむる suffer a *loss*.
ふりおくれ 振り遅れ 〖野球〗a late swing. ● 振り遅れのファウル a *late-swing* foul. ● 速球に振り遅れる swing late on a fastball.
ふりおとす 振り落とす throw*… off. ● 彼は馬から振り落とされた He *was thrown off* the horse.
ふりおろす 振り下ろす ● 刀を振り下ろす *swing* a sword *down*.

ふりかえ 振り替え (郵便の) postal transfer. ● 振り替えで送金する send money by *postal transfer*. ● 振り替え休日 a substitute holiday.
ぶりかえす ぶり返す ▶病気がぶり返さないように気をつけてください Take care not to have [suffer] a *relapse*. ▶寒さがぶり返した The cold *has returned* [*has come back again*]. (❗後の方が口語的)
*ふりかえる 振り返る ❶〖振り向く〗(体の向きを変える) turn around; (目・顔などの向きを変えて見る) look back 《at》; (見回す) look around. ● 振り返って私を見る *look back at* me; *turn* 《*around*》 *to look at* me. ▶彼は振り返って私と向かい合った He *turned around* and faced me.
❷〖回想・反省する〗(回顧する) look back 《on》; (思案・反省する) reflect 《on》. ▶過去を振り返らないで、未来に向けて生きなければ。あなたはまだ若いのだから Don't look back on the past. You should look forward to the future. You're still young. ▶彼女は過去の生活をじっくりと振り返ってみた She *reflected on* her past life.

DISCOURSE

決断は慎重に考えた後に下すべきだと言う人は多い。しかし振り返ると、私は即断が成功につながる経験を何度もした **Many people say that** decisions should be made after careful thinking. *Looking back,* however, I have had many experiences where quick decisions led to success. (❗Many people say that … (多くの人は…という)は譲歩を表すディスコースマーカー. however 以下に力点がある)

ふりかえる 振り替える change [transfer (-rr-)] 《A to B》.
ふりかかる 降り懸かる fall* 《on, over》; (起こる) happen 《to》. ▶火の粉が木に降りかかった Sparks *fell on* the tree. ▶不幸が彼女に降りかかった Misfortune *fell on* [*happened to*] her.
ふりかけ 振り掛け *furikake*, (説明的に) a mixture of sesame seeds, chopped seaweed, dried bonito shavings, salt, etc., which is sprinkled over rice.
ふりかける 振り掛ける ● 肉に塩とコショウを振り掛ける *sprinkle* [*dust*] salt and pepper *on* [*over*] the meat; *sprinkle* [*dust*] the meat *with* salt and pepper.
ふりかざす 振りかざす 〖振り上げる〗raise … 《over one's head》; 〖権力を行使する〗use [wield, (誇示する) show* off] 《one's authority》.
ふりかた 振り方 〖振る方法〗how to swing 《a bat》; 〖処し方〗a way to do. ● 身の振り方をよく考える think carefully how to *get along in the world*. (❗get along には「多少の困難はあるが(生活していく)」の含みがある)
ふりがな 振り仮名 (説明的に) *kana* written at the right side of [〖横書きの場合〗written above] *kanji* to show its pronunciation [how to pronounce it].
ふりかぶる 振りかぶる (刀などを) raise … high 《above one's head》; (ピッチャーがワインドアップする) wind* /wáind/ up. ● 振りかぶって投球する work out of the windup. ▶ピッチャー、振りかぶりました Here's the *windup*.
ブリキ [<オランダ語] tin, tinplated iron [steel]. ● ブリキ板 tin; tinplate. ● ブリキ缶 a (tin) can; 《英》a tin (can). ● ブリキ屋 a tinsmith.
ふりきる 振り切る 〖振り放つ〗tear* oneself away 《from》; (追っ手などを) shake*… off (⇨振り払う); 〖思いきり振る〗(バットやクラブを) take* a full swing.

ふりきれる
▶彼は泣く子供を振り切って家を出た He left home, *tearing himself away from* his crying child. ▶だれかにあとをつけられていたが、何とか振り切った Someone was following me, but I shook him *off* at last.

ふりきれる 振り切れる ▶体重計の針が振り切れた The pointer on the scales *went* [*jumped*] *off* scale. (❗ 後の scale は「目盛り」の意)

プリクラ a 'Print Club' photo-sticker machine. (❗ Print Club は商標)

フリゲートかん フリゲート艦 [小型駆逐艦] a frigate.

ふりこ 振り子 a pendulum /péndʒəlam/.
● 振り子時計 a pendulum clock.

ふりこう 不履行 nonfulfillment, a breach. ● 契約不履行で訴える sue 《him》 for *breach* of contract. ● 契約不履行である be in *breach* of contract; *have broken* [*violated*] the contract. ● 債務不履行になる go into *default*; *default* on the debt.

ふりこみ 振り込み ● (口座へ)自動振り込みになっている *be* electronically *deposited* into one's bank account.

ふりこむ 振り込む (口座に) pay* [*deposit*] 《money》 into 《his》 bank account. (❗ pay の方が口語的)

ふりこむ 降り込む (雨・雪が) come* into ...; (雨が) rain into .... ▶開けた窓から雨が降り込んだ It *rained into* the room through the open window.

ふりこめる 降り籠める ▶雨に降りこめられた I was unable to go out because it rained hard./The rains prevented me from going out. (❗ rains は「大雨」の意)

ブリザード [雪あらし] a blizzard.

ふりしきる 降り頻る (雨[雪]が絶え間なく降る) rain [snow] continuously; (雨[雪]が激しく降る) rain [snow] hard [heavily]. ▶降りしきる雨の中を出かける go out in the *heavy* [✕*hard*] rain. ▶朝から雨が降りしきっている It *has been raining continuously* [*hard*] since this morning.

ふりしぼる 振り絞る (声を) shout at the top of one's voice; (力を) put* forth [summon] all one's strength. ● 最後の力を振り絞って with the last of one's strength. ▶彼は石を動かそうとして力を振り絞った He *used* [*put forth*] *all* his *strength* to move the rock.

ふりすてる 振り捨てる (きっぱりと捨てる) desért, abandon. (⇨捨てる❷)

ブリストル [英国の都市] Bristol /brístl/.

フリスビー (遊具)(商標) a Frisbee /frízbi/. ● フリスビーを投げる toss a Frisbee. ● フリスビーをする play Frisbee.

ブリスベーン [オーストラリアの都市] Brisbane /brízbein, brízbən/.

プリズム a prism.

プリセプター [個人教師] a preceptor. (参考) 会社・病院などで新任の人に付き添って教える先輩)

ふりそそぐ 降り注ぐ [雨が] rain (hard) 《on》; [光が] shine*; (さんさんと) shed* the torrent of light 《on》. ▶雨が木の葉にしきりに降り注いでいる It's *raining hard* on the leaves. (❗「休みなく」の意なら steadily となる)

ふりそで 振袖 a long-sleeved *kimono* 《 〜s》.

ふりだし 振り出し ❶ [出発点] ▶野球の試合を振り出しに戻す make a game a new ball game. ▶もし計画が失敗したら振り出しに戻ってしまう If our plan falls through, we have to go back to *the starting point* [(話) go back to *square one*, (また最初から計画を練り直す) work on the plan *all over again*]. (❗ 二番目の言い方はチェスで最初の位置に戻ることから生まれた. start again from square one とも言う)
❷ [手形などの発行] issue; drawing.

ふりだす 振り出す ▶彼に10万円の小切手を振り出す *write* him *a check* for 100,000 yen.

ふりつ 府立 prefectural. (⇨県立)

ふりつけ 振り付け (やや専門) choreógraphy. ● 振り付けをする choreograph 《a ballet》.
● 振り付け師 a choreographer.

ぶりっこ ぶりっ子 ▶あの娘(こ)ってぶりっ子じゃない? That girl is always trying to be cute [a good girl], isn't she?

ブリッジ ❶ [橋, 船橋] a bridge; [渡線橋] an overpass. ❷ [歯・眼鏡の] a bridge. ❸ [レスリングの] a bridge. ❹ [トランプの] bridge. ● ブリッジを(ひと勝負)する play a game 《of》 *bridge*.
● ブリッジバンク (受け皿銀行) a bridge bank.

ふりつづく 降り続く continue to rain [snow], rain [snow] continuously. ▶もう3日も雪が降り続いている It *has been* [*has kept* 《on》] *snowing* for three 《consecutive》 days. ● on がある方が「3日も」という心だちの感が伝わる ▶こう雨が降り続くと気分が滅入ってしまう I feel depressed because it's been raining *for a long time*.

フリップ [テレビ放映用の大型図解カード] a flip chart.

ふりつもる 降り積もる ▶子供たちは降り積もった雪をふみしめて学校へ行った The children went to school walking slowly on the snow that *was* [*lay, piled*] *thick on the ground*.

ふりにげ 振り逃げ [野球] a dropped third strike.
● 振り逃げで出塁する reach first base on a *dropped third strike*.

ふりはなす 振り放す (⇨振り切る)

ふりはらう 振り払う shake* ... off. ● 傘に積もった雪を振り払う *shake* snow *off* one's umbrella. ▶彼女は肩に置いた彼の手を振り払って足早に立ち去った She *shook off* the hand he put on her shoulder and hurried away.

ぷりぷり ❶ [はちきれそうな, 張りがある] (肉うきぶんがよく) plump; (形や状態が満ちて) rich. ● ぷりぷりのおしり *plump* buttocks.
❷ [とても怒っている] ● ぷりぷりする get angry [(話) into a huff]. ● ぷりぷりしている be in anger [(話) a huff]. ▶「もう、うるさいわね」と彼女はぷりぷりして言った "Stop nagging," she said *snappishly*.

プリペイドカード [代金前払いのカード] a prepaid card.

ふりほどく 振りほどく break [shake* oneself] free 《of his hand(s)》. ▶「ちょっと, 離してよ」と言って彼女はその男の手を振りほどいた "Hey! Would you let go!" she said and *broke free of* the man's grip.

ふりまく 振り撒く ● 愛嬌を振りまく *turn on* one's charm. ● 微笑を振りまく give 《them》 a smile.

プリマス [英国・米国の都市] Plymouth /plíməθ/.

プリマドンナ [<イタリア語] [オペラの主役女性歌手] a prima donna /prí:mə dánə/.

ふりまわす 振り回す [振り動かす] shake*; swing*... 《around》; (威嚇のため刀などを) wave, (書) brandish; [乱用する] abuse 《one's authority》; [見せびらかす] show* 《one's knowledge》 off. ● 彼に向かってげんこつを振り回す *shake* one's fist at him. (事情) 威嚇(い)のしぐさ) ● おのを振り回す *swing* an ax(e). ▶彼に振り回された I was twisted [was turned] around his little finger. (● 慣用表現)

ふりみだす 振り乱す ▶髪を振り乱してwith one's hair *disheveled* /dɪʃévld/ [*tousled* /táuzld/].

ふりむく 振り向く (⇨振り返る) ▶名前を呼ぶと彼女はすぐに私の方を振り向いた When I called her name,

ふりむける she *turned around toward* me [*looked around at* me, *turned* her *face toward* me] right away. ▶振り向くとそこには１匹の子犬が座っていた I *turned around* [*looked back*] to find a puppy sitting there. ●近ごろの子供は甘いお菓子なぞ見向き(=見向き)もしない Children of today *don't care for* candy 《米》[*sweets*《英》]. (❗*care for* は「好む」の意で通例否定文・疑問文で用いる)

ふりむける 振り向ける turn《one's face》to [*to*-*ward*]《the right》. ●収入の多くを子どもの教育費に振り向ける *turn* [*apply*] much of one's income *to* one's children's educational expenses. ●都はその資金を大公園の建設に振り向ける(=充当する)ことを決定した The Metropolitan government decided to *appropriate* the funds for the construction of a large-scale park.

ふりやむ 降り止む stop (-pp-), (徐々に) let* up. ▶雨が降りやんだ The rain *has stopped* [*let up*]./It *has stopped* raining.

ブリュッセル [ベルギーの首都] Brussels /brǽslz/.

ふりょ 不慮 ── **不慮の** 形 [予期しない] unexpected, unforeseen; [偶然の] accidental. ●不慮の災難 an *unexpected* [*an unforeseen*] disaster. ●不慮の事故にあう meet with an accident. ●不慮の死を遂げる die an *accidental* death; be killed in an accident.

ふりょ 俘虜 (⇨捕虜(ほ))

ふりょう 不良 名 [非行者] [書] a delinquent /dilíŋkwənt/ (⇨非行); [乱暴者] a hooligan,《話》a hoodlum. (❗以上 3 語とも主に若者をさす) ●不良になる turn *delinquent*. ▶あの少女は不良だ That girl is a *delinquent*.

── **不良の** 形 [天候・成績などが] bad*; [素行が] delinquent; [発育・成長などが] poor; [製品が] defective (⇨欠陥). ●天候[成績]不良のために because of *bad* weather [one's *bad* grades, one's *poor* grades]. ●栄養[消化]不良をきたす suffer from *malnutrition* [*indigestion*]. ▶今年の稲は発育不良だ The riceplants are *underdeveloped* [show *poor development*] this year.

●不良グループ a group of hooligans [hoodlums]. ●不良債権 (⇨不良債権) ●不良少年 a delinquent boy; (乱暴な子供) a rough kid. ●不良導体 [電気] a nonconductor. ●不良品 [商業] an item of defective merchandise, 《話》a lemon (❗機械製品についてのみ); (不完全な製品) an imperfect product.

ふりょう 不猟 (have) a poor bag; (get) little game.

ふりょう 不漁 (have) a poor catch.

ぶりょう 無聊 [書] tedium; boredom; (倦怠感) ennui /ɑːnwíː/. ●無聊を慰める relieve (the) *boredom*.

ふりょうさいけん 不良債権 a bad debt; a non-performing loan. ●不良債権を処理する clear up [clean up, liquidate, dispose of] *bad debts* [*problem loans*]. ●金融機関の不良債権を公的資金で穴埋めする use taxpayer's money to offset financial institutions' *bad debts*.

ふりょき 『俘虜記』 *Taken Captive*. (参考 大岡昇平の小説)

ふりょく 浮力 buoyancy /bɔ́iənsi/, buoyant force. ●浮力が大である have great *buoyancy*.

ふりょく 富力 (富から生じる力) wealth and influence; means. ●加藤家は急速に富力を増した The house of Kato has rapidly grown in [increased] *wealth and influence*.

ぶりょく 武力 military force [power]; (武器) arms. ●武力に訴える appeal to *military force* [*arms*]. ●武力で紛争を解決する settle a dispute by (using *military*) *force*. ●武力介入 armed [military] intervention.

フリル a frill. ●フリルのついたエプロン a *frilled* [*frilly*] apron.

ふりわけ 振り分け 荷物を振り分けにしてかつぐ carry two bundles on one's shoulder, one hanging in front, and the other in the back.

ふりわける 振り分ける [[分配する]] divide ...《among》(⇨分ける ❶ ❷); (二つに) devide ... in two [half]; [[割り当てる]] assign, 《やや書》allot (-tt-). (⇨割り当てる)

ふりん 不倫 名 (行為) adultery. ●不倫の恋 *illicit love*. ●不倫の相手 (男から) a lady friend, (女から) a gentleman friend.

── **不倫(を)する** 動 commit adultery; have an (extramarital) affair《with》; 《話》cheat on《one's husband [wife]》.

会話 「花子と不倫(=浮気)をしてたんじゃないの」「とんでもない」 "Did you have an *affair* with Hanako?" "Of course I didn't."

プリン (a) custard pudding, (カラメル味の) (a) caramel custard.

プリンス [王子] a prince.

プリンセス [姫, 妃殿下] a princess.

プリンター a printer. ●レーザープリンター a laser *printer*. ●熱転写プリンター a thermal *printer*.

プリント 名 ❶ [配布物] a handout. (❗xa print とはいわない) (参考 日本語でも「ハンドアウト」と言うことが多くなってきた); [謄写版による印刷物] a mimeograph (❗mimeo と略すこともある), a mimeographed copy. ●プリントを配る give [pass] out the *handouts*《to》.

❷ [模様] ●花柄のプリント地 (a) *print* with a flower [a floral] design. ●プリントの服 a *print* dress.

❸ [写真] a print.

── **プリントする** 動 ●そのネガから写真をプリントする *print* a photograph from the negative. (❗写真屋にしてもらう場合は get a photograph printed from ... となる)

●プリント基板 [コンピュータ] a printed-circuit board《略 PC board》. ●プリント合板 printed plywood /plǽiwùd/. ●プリント配線 [コンピュータ] a printed wire.

プリントアウト 名 [コンピュータ] (a) printout.

── **プリントアウトする** 動 *print* ... out.

ふる 振る ❶ [振り動かす] shake*; wave; swing*; sway.

使い分け **shake** 具体的な動作から抽象的な動作まで幅広く用いられる語. 時に激しく振ることを表す.
wave 主に手あるいは手に持ったものを振ること. それによって応答・あいさつ・注意などさまざまな意図が伝えられる.
swing ある点を支点に振ること. 足や腕などをぶらぶらと振ること, または弧を描くように物を振ることをさす.
sway 風などが木をゆっくりと揺らすこと.

●薬びんを(よく)振る *shake* (*up*) a medicine bottle. ●首を横に振る *shake* one's head. (❗No の意で不承知・否定を表す. 否定疑問に対しては同意(はい)を示す. 英語では驚いたり, あきれたり, 信じられないといったしぐさを表すこともある) ●首を縦に振る *nod* (one's head). (❗Yes の意で承知!・肯定を表す. 否定疑問に対しては反対の主張(いいえ)を示す. また眠くてこっくりする様子にも nod を用いる) ●旗を振る *wave* a flag. ●彼女はハンカチを振る *wave* a handkerchief *to* [*at*] her. (❗

ふる wave her a handkerchief は不可) ●ボールをねらってバットを振る swing (the bat) [take a swing] at a ball. ●指揮棒を振る beat time with a baton /bɑtɔ́n/. ●彼は手を振って私にあちらへ行くよう[中に入るよう]合図した He waved me away [in]. 類語 後の方は日本式とは異なり, そろえた4指または立てた人差し指を自分の方に向けて前後に振る) ●彼女は私にさよならと手を振ったので私も手を振った She waved good-by to me [waved me good-by] and I waved back. ●彼は手を振ってタクシーに止まるよう合図した He waved a taxi to stop./(大声を出して止める) He hailed a taxi. ●彼は両手を[腰を左右に]振って歩いた He walked swinging his arms [swaying his hips from side to side]. ●犬が尾を振った The dog wagged its tail. ●薬はよく振ってから飲みなさい Shake the medicine well before taking [drinking] it. (🛈 水薬の場合は drink も可) ●彼は2–3回バットを振ってからバッターボックスに入った He took two or three practice swings and then stepped up into the batter's box.
❷ [振りかける] sprinkle. ●料理に塩を振る sprinkle salt on [over] the food ●over は料理全体に振りかけること; sprinkle the food with salt.
❸ [わきに書き添える] ●漢字にかなをふる attach kana to the Chinese characters.
❹ [捨てる] ●社長の地位を振る give up one's position as president of a company. ●彼を振った I turned him down. (⇨振られる)

*ふる **降る** fall*; [雨が] rain; [雪が] snow. ●午後にはひと雨降るかもしれない It may rain [We may have rain] in the afternoon. ●外は雨が激しく[しとしと]降っていた It was raining hard [was drizzling] outside. ●まもなく大粒の雨が降ってきた Very soon large drops of rain began to fall [ばらばらと patter down]. ●朝から雨が降ったりやんだりしている It has been raining off and on [on and off] since morning. ●7月初めから雨がほとんど降らない We have had [There has been] very little rain since the beginning of July. ●今日東京で初めて雪(=初雪)が降った Today we had the first snow of the year in Tokyo. ●一晩中雪が降り続いた The snow continued [kept falling] all night./(降りやまなかった) The snow never let up all night. ●気の毒に彼は降って湧いたような災難にあった (⇨降って湧く)
●降ればどしゃ降り 《ことわざ》 It never rains but it pours.;《米》 When it rains, it pours. (🛈「泣き面にハチ」の意だが, 時によいことにも用いる)

ふる 古 old. (⇨お古)
●古新聞 old newspapers.

フル ●時間をフルに活用する make full use of one's time;《やや書》 use one's time to the full. ●フル回転 (⇨フル回転) ●工場はフル操業している The factory is operating at full capacity [is going (at) full blast].

–ぶる –振る (装う) pretend; (...の振りをする) pose as .... (⇨振りをする) ●学者ぶる pretend to be [《やや書》 put on the airs of] a scholar. ●偉ぶる assume an air of importance.

ブルアウェイ [サッカー] pull away from the marker. (〔参考〕 マーカーの視野から消える動きをすること)

*ふるい **古い** ❶ [長い時間を経た］old; (非常に古い) ancient. (🛈 通例限定的に) ●古城 an old [an ancient] castle. ●私の古い(=昔の)友人 an old friend of mine; my old friend. ●古い(=古くから)の慣習 an old [a time-honored] custom. ●古いしきたりを破る break old conventions. ●日本は古い歴史のある国です Japan has an ancient [a long] history. ●この寺には400年の古い(=長い)歴史があるThis temple has a long [✕an old] history of 400 years.
❷ [新鮮でない] old; (古くなって味がない) stale. ●古い米 (古い) old rice. ●古くなったパン stale bread.
❸ [時代遅れの] out-of-date; (古めかしい) old-fashioned; (使い古した) worn-out; (文句などが陳腐な) hackneyed. ●古い考え方の outdated, old-fashioned] ideas. ●古い表現 a hackneyed [a trite] expression. ●古い上着 a worn-out coat. ●古い(=旧式の)ミシン an old style [type of] sewing machine; an out-of-date [an old-fashioned] sewing machine. ●そういう考え方は古い That kind of thinking is out-of-date [behind the times]. ●その服は今ではもう古い(流行遅れだ) That dress is now out-of-date [old-fashioned]. ●その手は古い. もうきかないよ It's the same old trick. It won't work.

ふるい 篩 a sieve /sív/; (主に料理用の) a sifter.
●ふるいにかける sift; sieve, put ... through a sieve; [選び出す] screen. ●小麦粉をふるいにかけてボールに入れる sift [sieve] the flour into a bowl.

ぶるい 部類 a group; (種類) a class; (範ちゅう) a category. (🛈 class より堅い語). ●同じ部類に属する belong to the same class. ●...の部類に入る come [fall] into the category of ....

ふるいおこす 奮い起こす ●勇気を奮い起こす pluck [summon, screw] up (one's) courage (to do).

ふるいおとす 篩い落とす (審査で) screen ... out; (雑草を取るように) weed ... out. ●30名の応募者がふるい落とされた Thirty applicants were screened out [were weeded out].

ふるいたつ 奮い立つ rouse /ráuz/; [(やや書) stir (-rr-)] oneself. ●奮い立たせてもう一度挑戦させる rouse him to challenge (it) again.

ふるいつく 震い付く embrace [hug (-gg-)] (out of excitement). ●震いつきたくなるような女だった She was so sexy I wanted to hug her./(抗しがたき) She was irresistibly sexy.

ふるいわける 篩い分ける (より分ける) sift; (選別する) screen. ●砂と小石をふるい分ける sift (out) pebbles from sand. ●応募者は履歴書をもとにふるい分けられた The applicants were screened based on their résumés.

*ふるう **振るう, 篩う** ❶ [振り動かす] shake*; (振る) wave; (大きく振り動かす) swing*. ●剣を振るう wield [(書) brandish] a sword (at).
❷ [行使する] use, (働かせる) exercise; (発揮する) show*. ●暴力をふるう use violence (on him). ●権力をふるう exercise [wield, show] (one's) authority (over). ●熱弁をふるう make [give] a passionate speech (about). ●彼は大工として腕をふるった He showed his skill as a carpenter.
❸ [元気・勢いがある] ●商売がふるわない Business is not active [is dull]. ●彼は成績がふるわない He is not doing well at school. (不振) ●あらしが夜通し猛威をふるった The storm raged all night.

ふるう 奮う pluck [summon] ... up. (⇨奮い起こす)

ブルー 色 ●ブルーカラー [労働者, 工員] a blue-collar worker. ●ブルージーンズ《米》 a blue jeans. ●ブルーチーズ [青カビチーズ] blue cheese.

ブルース (the) blues /blú:z/; (曲) blues. (🛈 単・複両扱い) ●ブルース歌手 a blues singer. ●ブルースを1曲ひく play a blues.

フルーツ [果物] (a) fruit. (🛈 通例 U として果物全体を表すが, 種類をいうときは C) ●市場でフルーツを少し買った I bought some fruit [✕fruits] at the

フルーティー

market.
- フルーツカクテル a fruit cocktail. • フルーツケーキ (a) fruitcake. • フルーツサラダ fruit salad. • フルーツジュース fruit juice. • フルーツパーラー a soda fountain; an ice-cream parlor;《和製語》a fruit parlor. • フルーツポンチ a fruit cup; a fruit cocktail;《和製語》a fruit punch.

フルーティー ── **フルーティーな** 形 〖果実の味のする〗fruity.

フルート 〖楽器〗a flute. • フルート奏者《米》a flutist;《英》a flautist /flíːtɪst/. • フルートを吹く play the *flute*.

ブルートゥース 〖コンピュータ〗Bluetooth.（参考 デジタル機器間の無線仕様）

ブルーベリー 〖植物〗a blueberry.

ブルーマウンテン Blue Mountain coffee.（参考 ジャマイカ産コーヒー豆）

プルーン 〖植物〗a prune.

ふるえ 震え a shake;（恐怖・嫌悪などによる）a shudder;（寒さなどによるかすかな）a shiver;（恐怖・興奮などによる急激な）a tremble. • 恐怖の震え a *tremble* of fear. ▶ 恐ろしくて震えが止まらなかった I couldn't stop *trembling* [*shuddering*] with fear.

ふるえあがる 震え上がる（激しく震える）tremble;（寒さなどで）shiver;（恐怖・嫌悪などで）shudder.（寒さで）寒さで震え上がる *shiver with* cold. ▶ 彼は死体を見て震え上がった He *shuddered* [*turned to jelly*] when he saw the (dead) body. ▶ 彼のこわい顔を見て彼女は震え上がった〔=背筋に寒気が走った〕《話》His hard look *sent shivers down her spine*.

***ふるえる** 震える shake*; tremble; shiver; shudder; quiver.

> 使い分け shake 身体や具体的な物が震えること. 声などが震える場合にも用いられる.
> tremble 主に恐怖や感動などの心的な要因によって身体（の一部）が震えること.
> shiver 寒さで身体が震えること. 恐怖などの心的な要因によって震える場合にも用いられる.
> shudder 心的な要因により身体が震えること. また, 乗物などが揺れる場合にも用いられる.
> quiver 唇やのど, あるいは声などが小刻みに震えていること.

• 震える手でそれをつかむ take it with *trembling* [*quivering*] fingers. ▶ 彼の声は怒りのあまり震えていた His voice *was shaking* [*trembling*] with anger. ▶ 彼女は興奮して震えていた She *was shaking* [*quivering*] with excitement. ▶ 彼女は寒さで震えた She *shivered with* cold. ▶ そのことを考えるだけで震えてしまう I *shudder to* think of it./Just to think of it [The very thought of it] makes me *shudder*.

プルオーバー a pullover.

フルかいてん フル回転 ▶ 機械をフル回転（=フル稼働）させても生産に間に合わない Our machines *are* now *in full operation*, but we can't keep up with demand. ▶ そのレストランはとても繁盛していてウェイトレスはフル回転で（休憩なしで）働いている The restaurant is crowded, and the waitresses are working without rest.

フルカウント 〖野球〗a full count; a three-two count.（参考 ボールの数を先にいう）• フルカウントで on [with] a *full count*. • フルカウントに持ち込む run the count *full*. • フルカウントからライトオーバーのホームランを打つ hit a *full-count* pitch over the right-field wall.

ふるがお 古顔 an old-timer.（⇨古株）

ふるかぶ 古株〖古い切り株〗an old (tree) stump;〖古参〗an old-timer（〖やや蔑称〗an old hand（=老練家）, an old [a long-time] member（古い会員）の意と《米話》で年寄り (an oldster) の意がある）

ブルガリア 〖国名〗Bulgaria /bʌlɡéəriə/；（公式名）the Republic of Blugaria.（首都 Sofia）• ブルガリア人 a Bulgarian. • ブルガリア語 Bulgarian. • ブルガリア（人[語]）の Bulgarian.

ふるき 古き （古い）old; （古い物）old things; （老いた人）old people. ▶ 古きよき時代《⇨良き》
• 古きを温（たず）ねて新しきを知る《⇨温故知新》

ふるぎ 古着 old clothes;〖着古しの〗used [secondhand] clothing.
• 古着屋（店）a secondhand clothes [clothing] store;（人）an old-clothes dealer.

ふるきず 古傷 （肉体的な）an old injury [wound];（精神的な）old wounds [sores]. • 古傷にさわる open (up) [reopen] *old wounds*. • 古傷をいやす lick one's *old wounds*. ▶ 古傷がまた痛む My *old injury* has begun to ache [hurt] again.

ブルキナファソ 〖国名〗Burkina Faso（〖公式名も同じ〗.（首都 Ouagadougou）• ブルキナファソ人 a Burkinabe. • ブルキナファソ（人）の Burkinabe.

ふるくさい 古臭い old;（時代遅れの）óut-of-dáte; old-fashioned;（新鮮味のなった）stale; hackneyed. • 古臭いしゃれ a *stale* joke. ▶「快刀乱麻を断つ」式の古臭い（=定形化して新鮮味のまったくない）表現 such a *hackneyed* expression as 'to cut the Gordian knot'. ▶ 彼の考えはもう古臭い His ideas are *out-of-date* [*old-fashioned*].

ふるくは 古くは many years ago, ages ago;（歴史をさかのぼれば）back in history.

フルコース 〖食事の〗a six-course dinner, a dinner of six courses（注 six は five のこともある. 通例 ×full course とはいわない時に a full course dinner ということがある）；〖ゴルフの〗a full course.

プルサーマルけいかく プルサーマル計画 the plutonium-thermal /pluːtóniəm-/ project.

ふるさと 古里 one's hometown, one's home.（⇨故郷（きょう））▶ 郷里の青空を見て, ここが自分のいる場所だと改めて（=もう一度）感じました Looking at the blue sky in my *hometown*, I realized once again that this is where I belong [that was where I belonged].（注 自分の故郷以外の場所でこの発言をしている場合は that was where I belonged となる）

ブルジョア 〖中産階級の人〗a bourgeois /buərʒwɑ́ː/（↔a proletarian）（注 日本語の「ブルジョア」が時にさす「金持ち」の意では用いない）；（その集合体としての中産階級）the bourgeoisie /bùərʒwɑːzíː/（↔proletariat）（注 単・複両扱い）；〖金持ち〗a rich [a wealthy] person.

ふるす 古巣 one's old home;（比喩的）the place [office, company, etc.] where one used to work. • 古巣のチームに戻る go back [return] to one's *old* [*former*] *team*.

フルスイング 名 a full swing [cut]. • フルスイングで打つ take a *full swing* at a pitch.
── **フルスイングする** 動 take a full swing《*at*》.

フルスピード • フルスピードで運転する drive《*at*》*full* [*top*] *speed*.（注《話》ではしばしば at は省略される）

ブルゾン 〖フランス語〗a blouson /blúːzɑn/.

ブルターニュ 〖フランスの半島〗Brittany.

フルタイム 《work》full-time（↔part-time）；〖サッカー〗full-time（参考 正規の 90 分間が終わった状態のこと）.

プルダウンメニュー 〖コンピュータ〗a pulldown menu.

ふるだぬき 古狸 an old fox, a foxy old man（⇨

men). (❗英語では fox (きつね)で表す)

プルタブ a (pull) tab.

ふるづけ 古漬け well-pickled vegetables.

ふるって 奮って 〚進んで〛(快く) willingly; (自発的に) voluntarily. ▶奮ってご参会ください Please *feel free to* attend the meeting./You *are cordially invited* to attend the meeting. (❗cordially は「真心をこめて」の意)

ふるっている 振るっている (意表をついた) extraordinary; (めったにない) uncommon; (ユニークな) special, 《話》unique; (例外的な) exceptional; (変わった) strange, unusual. ▶彼女のスピーチの出だしが実にふるっていたShe began her speech with *extraordinary* words.

ふるつわもの 古兵 an old soldier; (ベテラン) a veteran; an old hand; (経験豊かな人) an experienced person; (熟練した技の持ち主) a skilled person.

ふるて 古手 (⇨古株)

ふるどうぐ 古道具 (中古品) a secondhand [used] article; (古い家具) (an) old [(a) used] furniture. ●古道具を買いあさる hunt for *used articles*.
●古道具屋 (店) a secondhand store [shop]; (がらくた屋) a júnk shòp; (人) a dealer in secondhand articles; a junk dealer.

ブルドーザー a bulldozer, 《話》a dozer. ●ブルドーザーでならす〚掘る〛bulldoze (the ground).

ブルドッグ 〚動物〛(犬) a bulldog.

プルトップ pull top. ●プルトップ缶 a *pull top* can.
●プルトップ缶を空ける open a *pull top* can.

プルトニウム 〚化学〛plutonium /pluːtóuniəm/.
●プルトニウム爆弾 a plutonium bomb.

ブルネイ 〚国名〛Brunei /bruːnái/; (公式名) the Brunei Darussalam. (首都 Bandar Seri Begawan) ●ブルネイ人 a Bruneian. ●ブルネイ(人)の Bruneian.

フルネーム (正式の氏名) a [one's] full name; one's name in full. ▶フルネームで署名してください Sign your *name in full*, please.

フルバック 〚サッカー・ラグビー〛a fullback.

ふるびた 古びた ●古びた上着 an old [(すり切れた) a worn-out, (古風な) an old-fashioned] jacket.

ふるびる 古びる grow [become] old.

フルフェース a full face helmet.

フルブライト (奨学金) Fulbright (scholarship). ●フルブライト奨学生 a Fulbrighter; a Fulbright student [(研究者) scholar].

ぶるぶる ●ぶるぶる震える shake (❗最も一般的な語); (激しく) tremble; (かすかに) shiver. (⇨震える) ●ぶるぶる震えている手 shaking [trembling] hands. ●寒さでぶるぶる震える shiver with cold. ●犬は川から上がると体をぶるぶるっと振って水を落とした The dog *shook* itself *vigorously* when it came out of the river.

フルベース ●フルベースにする fill [load] the bases, 《話》load the sacks. ●フルベースで二塁打を打つ hit a double with *bases loaded*. ▶ツーアウトフルベースである The bases *are filled* [*are loaded*] with two outs./There are two outs *with the bases loaded*. ▶ワンアウトフルベースのピンチを脱する get out of a *bases-loaded* one-out jam.

ブルペン 〚野球〛a bullpen. ●ブルペンでウォーミングアップする warm up in the *bullpen*.
●ブルペンコーチ a bullpen coach. ●ブルペン捕手 a bullpen catcher.

ふるぼけた 古ぼけた (古くてうす汚い) old and grubby; (歳月を経て古くなった) 《やや書》time-worn; (旧式の) outdated.

ふるほん 古本 (中古本) a used [a secondhand] book. ●古本で買う buy 《(話)get》(a book) *secondhand*. (❗この secondhand は副詞)
●古本屋 (店) a secondhand bookstore; (人) a secondhand bookseller.

ブルマー 《a pair of》bloomers.

ふるまい 振る舞い ❶〚行い〛(人に対する) behavior; (道徳面から見た) conduct. (⇨行い) ●ふるまいをする behave [act] foolishly. ▶彼のふるまいは確かに異常だった His *behavior* was certainly out of the ordinary. ▶彼のふるまい方は気に入らない I don't like the way he *acts* [*behaves*] (toward me).
❷〚もてなし〛entertáinment; 〚おごり〛a treat. ●大盤ぶるまいする give 《him》a big feast.

*****ふるまう 振る舞う** ❶〚身を処する〛behave (❗behave (oneself) には「(子供などが)行儀よくする」の意もある), 《書》conduct oneself (⇨振る舞い); 〚行動する〛act. ●勇敢にふるまう behave [act] bravely. ●赤ん坊のようにふるまう behave [act] like a baby. ●思いどおりにふるまう have [get] one's (own) way. ▶彼はその老人に対して丁重にふるまった He *behaved* respectfully *to* [*toward*] the elderly person./He treated the elderly person with respect.
❷〚もてなす〛entertáin; 〚おごる〛treat. ●彼らに夕食をふるまう *treat* [*invite*] them *to* dinner.

フルムーン 〚満月〛a full moon.

ふるめかしい 古めかしい (古風な) old-fashioned. (⇨古い)

ふるもの 古物 a used article [item, thing].

ふるわせる 震わせる (上下・左右に動かす) shake* (❗最も一般的な語); (恐怖・怒りなどで激しく身震いする) tremble; (寒さでかすかに震える) shiver; (小刻みに震える) quiver. (⇨震える) ▶ガス爆発は町全体を震わせた The gas explosion *shook* the whole town. ▶彼は怒りにぴくぴく唇を震わせた His lips *quivered* with rage.

ふるわない 振わない (⇨振るう ❸)

ブルンジ 〚国名〛Burundi; (公式名) the Republic of Burundi. (首都 Bujumbura) ●ブルンジ人 a Burundian. ●ブルンジ(人)の Burundi.

ふれ 振れ (標準などからの離れ) (a) deviation 《from》.
●振れが著しい make a distinct *deviation* 《from the normal course》; deviate greatly 《from the set rule》.

ふれ 触れ (役所の告知) an official announcement [notice]. ●触れを出す make a public announcement 《that 節》; issue [put up, post] a *notice*.

ブレ (カメラの) a camera shake; (映像の) a blur. (⇨手ブレ)

ふれあい 触れ合い ●親子の触れ合い contact [touch] between parent and child; a parent-child contact [touch]. ●触れ合い動物園 a petting zoo. ▶彼は心の触れ合いを求めている He wants human contact.

ふれあう 触れ合う come* into contact 《with》. (⇨接触する)

フレアスカート a flared skirt.

ぶれい 無礼 图 rudeness; impoliteness. ●無礼を許す forgive 《his》*rudeness*. ●彼に無礼を働く behave [act] rudely to him; be rude to him.
── **無礼な** 形 (粗野で侮辱的な) rude; (礼儀に欠ける) impolite. (⇨失礼) ●無礼なふるまい *rude* behavior. ▶あんな無礼な人は初めてだ I've never met such a *rude* [an *impolite*] man like him./He is the *rudest* man I've ever met. ▶彼は無礼にも私の申し出を断わった He *rudely* [*impolitely*] rejected

ぶれいこう

my offer. (❗rudely, impolitely を文尾に置くと断わり方が無礼だったことになる)/He was *rude* [*impolite*] enough to reject my offer./He had the *rudeness* [*impoliteness*] to reject my offer.

ぶれいこう 無礼講する(=堅苦しい形式をはずす) drop formalities. ▶きのうのパーティーは無礼講で大いに盛り上がったよ We *let our hair down* and went a bit wild at the party last night. (❗*let one's hair down* は《話》で「(長い間の自制の後で)自由気ままにふるまう」の意)

プレー a play. ●見事な[へまな]プレー a fine [a bonehead] *play*. ●やさしいプレーを難しく見せる make easy *plays* appear difficult. ▶プレーボール (⇨プレーボール)

プレーイングマネージャー 〖野球〗a player [a playing] manager.

プレーオフ a playoff. (参考 プロ野球ではレギュラーシーズン後日本[ワールド]シリーズ前に行うシリーズ) ●プレーオフをする to play off, have a *playoff*. ●プレーオフに進出する make [get into] the playoffs. ●地区優勝決定プレーオフに全勝する sweep the Division Series *playoff*. ▶彼は18ホールのプレーオフライバルに勝った He won in an 18-hole *playoff* against his rival.

ブレーカー a (circuit) breaker.

プレーガイド a ticket agency [office], a play agency; (和製語) a play guide.

***ブレーキ** a brake. (❗しばしば複数形で) ●きいっというブレーキの音 a screech [a squeal] of *brakes*. ●ブレーキを踏む step on the *brake*(s). ●自転車のブレーキがきかなかった The *brakes* of the bike didn't work [failed].
●ブレーキをかける brake; put a brake [the brakes] on (❗比喩的にも用いる), apply the brakes. ●ブレーキをかけて車を止める *brake* a car to a stop. ●急ブレーキをかける *brake* suddenly [slam the *brakes* on] (*to* avoid a child). ●物価の上昇にブレーキをかける put a *brake* on rising prices. ▶彼らはその改革にブレーキをかけた They put *the brakes* on the reform.

フレーク a flake. ●ツナのフレーク tuna *flakes*.

ブレークスルー 〖突破〗a breakthrough.

ブレークダンス break-dancing.

ブレークポイント 〖テニス〗(win) a break point.

プレースキック 〖競技〗a placekick.
── **プレースキックする** 動 placekick; make a placekick.

プレート 〖野球〗the plate, (ホームプレート) the home plate, (ピッチャープレート) the pitcher's plate [rubber]; 〖地学〗a (crustal) plate. ●(投手が)軸足をプレートに付ける [から外す] toe [step off] the *rubber*.
●プレートアンパイア 〖野球〗a plate umpire. ●プレートテクトニクス 〖地学〗plate tectonics.

プレーバック a playback. (⇨再生)

プレーブック 〖作戦図をのせたノート〗〖アメフト〗a play book.

プレーボーイ (一般に遊び人) a playboy (↔a playgirl); (女好きの男) a ladies' man; (女性にもてる) 《話》a lady-killer.

プレーボール Play ball! (参考 試合開始の号令)

フレーム 〖枠〗a frame.

フレームワーク 〖枠組〗a framework.

プレーヤー ❶〖競技の〗a player ●一億円プレーヤー a million dollar (*player*). (❗*player* をつけずに用いることが多い) ❷〖CDなどの〗a player.

ブレーン 〖知的指導者〗《話》the brains (❗この形で一人にも複数にも用いる); 〖知能顧問団〗a brain(s) trust. (❗s を省略するのは《米》。単・複両扱い) ▶彼は大統領のブレーンだ He is *the brains* [✕*brain*] *behind* [an *adviser to*] the president.
●ブレーンストーミング brainstorming.

プレーン ●プレーンオムレツ a plain omelet. ●プレーンヨーグルト plain yog(h)urt.

プレオリンピック the Pre-Olympics, the Pre-Olympic Games.

ふれこみ 触れ込み (前宣伝) promotion; (an) advertisement; (an) announcement. ▶あの人は外科医という触れ込みだった He *gave himself out as* a surgeon.

ブレザー 〖ブレザーコート〗(替え上着) a sports jacket; (運動選手・学生の制服などの) a blazer. (❗✕a *blazer coat* とはいわない)

プレジャーボート (レジャー用小型船) a pleasure boat. (関連 a work boat 業務用小型船)

プレス 名 ❶〖プレス機械〗a press. ❷〖報道機関〗the press. ❸〖重量挙げ〗●プレスで100キロ持ち上げる lift 100 kilos in the *press*. ❹〖サッカーの〗pressing.
── **プレスする** 動 ●アイロンでワイシャツをプレスする press shirts with an iron; iron shirts.
●プレスキット 〖記者会見資料一式〗a press kit. ●プレスキャンペーン a press campaign. (参考 新聞が特定の問題を積極的に取り上げることで世論の関心を盛り上げる運動) ●プレスセンター a press center. ●プレスハム pressed ham. ●プレスリリース 〖報道陣に対する公式発表〗a press release. ●プレスルーム 〖記者会見室〗a press conference room; (報道記者室) a pressroom.

ブレスケア 〖口臭予防〗breath care.

フレスコ (壁画) a fresco. (❗画法をいうときは Ⓤ)

ブレスト 〖胸〗a breast; 〖平泳ぎ〗(the) breaststroke.

プレスリー 〖米国の歌手〗Presley /présli, préz-/ (Elvis ～).

ブレスレット 《wear》a bracelet.

プレゼンス 〖存在感〗presence.

プレゼンテーション 〖発表, 提示〗(a) presentation.
●プレゼンテーションをする give a *presentation*.

プレゼント 名 〖贈り物〗a present, a gift. ●クリスマスプレゼントをもらう get [be given] a Christmas *present* [*gift*]. ▶これはおばあちゃんへの[おばあちゃんから私たちへの]プレゼントです This is a *present for* Grandma [*to* us *from* Grandma].
── **プレゼントする** 動 ▶彼女誕生日に何をプレゼントしてくれましたか What did he *give* you for your birthday [as a birthday *present*]? (❗動詞の presént は公式に「贈呈する」場合に用い, この場合不自然)

ふれだいこ 触れ太鼓 ●両国界隈に触れ太鼓を回す make a parade of drums along the streets in Ryogoku announcing the opening of the *sumo* tournament.

プレタポルテ [＜フランス語] 〖デザイナーブランドの既製服〗a prêt-à-porter /prètɑːpɔːtéi/.

フレックスタイム ●フレックスタイム制度 〖自由勤務時間制〗《米》flextime, 《英》flexitime; the flexible working hours system. ▶君の会社ではフレックスタイムを導入していますか Do you work *flextime*?

プレッシャー pressure. ●プレッシャーが相当かかる feel [come under] a lot of pressure (*from*; *to do*).
●プレッシャーをかける put *pressure* (*on* him *to do*). ●プレッシャーに負ける〖打ち勝つ〗give in to [handle, (耐え抜く) withstand] *pressure*. (⇨圧力)

フレッシュ ── **フレッシュな** 形 fresh.
●フレッシュジュース fresh juice. ●フレッシュバター 〖無塩バター〗fresh butter.

フレッシュマン 〖大学の1年生〗a first-year student; 《米》a freshman (⑱ -men) (❗) (1) 女子学生にも用いる。(2) ×a fresh person とはいわない); 〖新入社員〗a new employee, a recruit.

プレッツェル a pretzel.

プレトリア 〖南アフリカの都市〗Pretoria /pritɔ́ːriə/.

プレハブ prefabrication.
● プレハブ住宅 a prefabricated house; 《話》a prefab /príːfæb/.

プレパラート 〖<ドイツ語〗 a prepared slide (for a microscope).

プレビュー 〖映画などの試写会〗a preview.

ふれまわる 触れ回る spread*... about; (言い触らす) tell* everybody 《about; that 節》(⇨言いふらす, 吹聴)

プレミア(ム) a premium /príːmiəm/. (❗ premia は premium の古い複数形) ●10 パーセントのプレミア付きで at a *premium* of 10 percent. ●プレミアを付ける put [place, set] a *premium* 《*on*》. ●プレミア付きで売られる be sold at a *premium*. ●映画のプレミア(ショー) a movie *premiere* /primíər/. ●プレミアム発行 a premium issue.

プレミアリーグ Premier League.

プレリュード 〖前奏曲〗a prelude 《*to*》.

‡**ふれる 触れる** ❶〖さわる〗(手や指などで軽くさわる, 物が接触する) touch; (手でさぐって知る) feel*. ▶手を触れるな Don't touch it [them]. (❗) with your hands は省略できる)/〖掲示〗Hands off. ▶彼は私の肩に手を触れた He *touched* my shoulder [me on the shoulder]. (❗)注意この焦点は彼の方が身体の部分, 後の方の文は人にある)/I felt his *touch* on my shoulder. ▶目の見えない人たちはしばしば物に触れてそれが何であるかわかる Blind people can often recognize things by *feeling* [*touching*] them. ▶警察の現場検証を考えて彼は現場に手を触れなかった He left the scene *untouched* for the police inspection. ▶ドアは軽く触れると開きます The door opens [will open] with [〖まれ〗at] a soft *touch*.

❷〖言及する〗refer (-rr-) to ...; (述べる) mention (❗の方が堅い語); (簡単に触れる) touch on [upon]... ▶要点に触れる come to the point. ▶その件に触れると彼は話題を変えた He changed the subject when I *referred to* [*mentioned*] the matter. ▶彼は数分間その話題に触れただけだった He only *touched on* the subject for a few minutes. ▶新聞にはその事故のことは何も触れられていない There is no *mention* of the accident in the paper. ▶彼の言葉は核心に触れている What he has said *is to* (⇔beside) *the point*.

❸〖そむく〗(法などを破る) break*, violate (❗後の方が堅い語); (...に反する) be against ... ▶交通法規に触れる *break* traffic regulations. ▶彼の今の行動は法律に触れている That conduct of his [×That his conduct] is *against* the law.

❹〖その他の表現〗▶彼の怒りに触れる (彼を怒らせる) *offend* him. ▶その薬は子供たちの目に触れないところに置いておきなさい Keep the medicine where the children *can't find* it [*out of sight of* the children]. ▶この金属は空気に触れるとすぐに腐食する This metal will corrode quickly in the open air.

ふれる 振れる ❶〖メーター・磁石の針が〗shake*; move; swing*; (前後左右に) sway*; (傾く) lean*; (方向がぶれる) be not in the right direction.
❷〖振り方がよい〗swing* well.

ぶれる ▶シャッターを押す時手がぶれてしまった I couldn't hold the camera *steady* [My hands *shook* a little] when I was pressing the shutter. ▶この写真はぶれている This picture *is out of focus* [*is blurred*].

ふれんぞくせん 不連続線 〖気象〗a line of discontinuity.

フレンチキス 〖ディープキス〗a French kiss (⇨ディープキス); 〖軽いキス〗a kiss (❗この意で a French kiss を用いるのは和製英語).

フレンチトースト French toast.

フレンチドレッシング French dressing.

フレンチホルン 〖楽器〗a French horn.

ブレンド a blend. ●おいしいブレンドコーヒー a good *blend* of coffee; good *blended* coffee.

フレンドリー ── フレンドリーな 形 〖友好的な〗friendly. ●フレンドリーな態度 a *friendly* attitude.

*ふろ 風呂 图 〖浴室〗《米》a bath-, 《米》a bath-room; 〖浴槽〗a bathtub, a tub, 《主に英》a bath.

> 解説 (1) 米英では風呂・トイレ・洗面所が一体となっている場合が多い。2階建ての家では通例寝室のある2階にある。(2) 米では bathroom は主に「トイレ」の意で用いる。(3) 米英では入浴の際、湯船につかって楽しむことは日本ほど多くない。シャワーで済ませることが多い。

● 風呂加減 (⇨湯 ⇨会話) ●露天風呂 an open-air [an outdoor] *bath*. ●ゆっくり風呂に入る take [〖英〗have] a long (⇔a quick) *bath*. ●赤ん坊を風呂に入れる give a baby a *bath*; bathe /béid/ 〖米〗[bath 〖英〗] a baby. ●風呂に水[湯]を張る fill the *bathtub* with water; run water into a *tub*, run the *tub* (for him). ●風呂を立てる get the *bath* ready; prepare a *bath*. ●風呂をわかす heat the *bath*. ●「風呂がわきましたよ」"Your *bath* is ready." ●彼は今風呂に入っています He's taking [〖英〗 having] a *bath* now./He's in the *bath* now. (❗ He's in the bathroom. は「トイレに入っている」の意)〖事柄〗米英では風呂の湯は一回ごとに流す) ▶夜遅く入る温かい風呂ほどよいものはない There's nothing like a hot *bath* late at night. ▶彼は風呂につかって歌を歌うのが好きです He enjoys singing in the *bathtub*.

● 風呂桶 〖米〗a bathtub, a tub; 《主に英》a bath.
● 風呂釜 a báth hèater. ●風呂代 a bathhouse charge. ●風呂場 a bathhouse; a public bath. (❗日本と異なり個室形式でなく, しばしば複数形で用いる)

プロ 图 a professional, 《話》a pro (⑱ ~s) (⇔an amateur). ●プロに転向する turn *professional*.
── **プロの** 形 professional. ●プロのサッカー選手 a *professional* [a *pro*] soccer player; a soccer *pro*.

フロアショー a floor show. (〖参考〗劇場ではなく、レストランやナイトクラブで行われるショー)

フロイト 〖オーストリアの精神医学者〗Freud /frɔ́id/ (Sigmund ~).

ブロイラー 〖肉をあぶり焼きする器具〗《米》a broiler; 〖食用若鶏〗a broiler (chicken).

ふろう 浮浪 ●浮浪(生活)をする 〖書〗lead a *vagrant* [a *vagabond*] life.
● 浮浪児 a street child. ●浮浪者 《米》a hobo, 《英》a tramp; (特に, 男の) 〖書〗a vagrant /véigrənt/, 《米話》a bum.

ふろうしょとく 不労所得 (an) unearned income.

ふろうふし 不老不死 图 ●不老不死を願う want to *live eternally*.
── **不老不死の** 形 (年老いない) ageless; (死なない) immortal. ●不老不死の薬 〖書〗the elixir /ilíksər/ of life.

ブロー 图 blow-dry.
——ブローする 動 ・髪をブローする *blow-dry* one's hair.
ブローカー [仲買人] a broker.
ブロークン **ブロークンな** 形 broken.
・ブロークンイングリッシュ (speak in) *broken* English.
ブローチ a brooch /bróutʃ, brú:tʃ/. ・ブローチをつけている[つける] wear [put on] a *brooch*.
フローチャート [流れ図] a flowchart.
フロート [飲料] a float; [山車(ﾀﾞﾉ)] (on) a float.
・コーヒーフロート a coffee *float*.
ブロードウェー [米国ニューヨーク市の大通り] Broadway.
ブロードバンド [広帯域高速大容量データ転送] broadband. ・ブロードバンドを利用する use *broadband*.
フローリング flooring.
***ふろく 付録** (書物・書籍・新聞・雑誌などの) a supplement (**!** 本文の内容を補うものでしばしば別冊の形をとる); (巻末の) an appendix (複 ~es, appendices); (余分なおまけ) something extra; (景品) a free gift.
・本の付録 a *supplement* [an *appendix*] to a book. ▶ 今月号には旅行特集の別冊付録がついている This month's issue has a travel *supplement*.
ブログ [日記形式のホームページ] a blog (《weblog の略》).
プログラマー a (computer) programmer.
プログラミング programming.
・プログラミング言語 prógramming lànguage.
プログラム [計画, 予定, 番組] a program /próugræm/; [コンピュータ] a program. ・プログラムの5番目の項目 the fifth (number [item]) *on the program*. ・そのコンサートのプログラムを買う get a *program for* the concert. ・プログラムに載っている be (put) on the *program*. ・コンピュータのプログラムを組む write a *program for* a computer.
・プログラム学習 programmed learning. ・プログラム言語 [コンピュータ] prógram [prógramming] lànguage.
プロジェクター a projector.
プロジェクト a próject. ・プロジェクトチームを組む set up [organize, form] a *project* team. ・国家[開発]プロジェクト a national [a development] *project*.
ふろしき 風呂敷 a clóth wràpper, a wràpping clòth. ・風呂敷包み a *parcel* [a *bundle*] wrapped in a *cloth*. ・風呂敷に包む wrap (it) in a *cloth*. ・大風呂敷を広げる (大げさに言う) talk big.
プロセス [過程, 進行] (a) process.
・プロセス制御 process control. ・プロセスチーズ process [processed] cheese.
プロセッサー [コンピュータ] a processor. ・フードプロセッサー a food processor. ・マイクロプロセッサー [コンピュータ] a microprocessor.
プロダクション [製作] production; [映画の製作所] a movie studio (複 ~s); [芸能プロダクション] a theatrical *agency*.
プロダクト a product.
ブロック 图 ❶ [政治·経済上の] a bloc; [街区] a block (**!** 四方を道で囲まれた一区画).
❷ [建築用の] a (concrete) block.
❸ [競技の] a block.
——ブロックする 動 [競技] block. ・(捕手などが)ホームをブロックする *block* the plate. ・スコールズのしなるようなシュートはかろうじてカラガーにブロックされた Scholes' whipping shot was narrowly *blocked* by Carragher.
・ブロック経済 bloc economy.

フロックコート a frock coat.
ブロックサイン [暗号化されたサイン] [野球] an encrypted signal [×sign]. (**!** この場合通例 a block sign とはいわない)
フロッグマン [潜水作業員] a frogman (複 -men); [潜水夫] a diver.
ブロッコリー broccoli /brákəli/.
プロッター [コンピュータ] (作図装置) a plotter.
フロッピー(ディスク) a floppy disk (**!** 単に a disk, a floppy ということも多い); a diskette. ・フロッピーにコピーする copy (a file) onto a *disk*. ・フロッピーをディスクドライブに入れる put [(やや書) set] a *disk* into the disk (《米》) drive. ・フロッピーをフォーマット[初期化]する format a *disk*.
・フロッピーディスクドライブ a floppy disk drive (《略 FDD》).
プロテイン [たんぱく質] protein /próuti:n/.
プロテクター a protector (**!** 特に「すね当て, レガーズ」は shin guards [pads] という; [野球の捕手·球審用の] a chest protector; [急所保護用のサポーター] an abdominal protector (**!** 通例単に a cup という).
プロテクト [保護] protection. ・プロテクトがかかっている be protected.
プロテスタント [教徒] a Protestant; [教義] Protestantism.
プロテスト [抗議] a protest.
・プロテストソング a prótest sòng. (参考) 社会批判を内容とする楽曲
プロデューサー a producer.
プロトタイプ [原型, 模範] a prototype.
・プロトタイプカー [試作車] a prótotype càr.
プロバイダー a provider.
プロパガンダ [思想·教養などの宣伝] 《make》 (×a) propaganda 《*for, against*》.
プロパン(ガス) propane gas; (液化石油ガス) liquefied petroleum gas 《略 LPG》.
プロピレン [化学] propylene /próupəli:n/.
プロフィール [横顔, 人物評] a profile /próufail/. (⇨ 横顔) ・首相のプロフィールを新聞で読む read a *profile* of the Prime Minister in the newspaper.
プロフェッショナル **——プロフェッショナルの** 形 professional. (⇨プロ)
プロペラ a propeller /prəpélər/.
・プロペラ機 a propeller-driven (air)plane.
プロポーション [均整] proportions. (**!** 通例複数形で) ・プロポーションのいい女性 a well-*proportioned* woman; a woman with a well-*proportioned* body.
プロポーズ 图 a proposal. ・彼のプロポーズを受け入れる accept his *proposal* (of marriage).
——プロポーズする 動 ・彼女にプロポーズする propose (marriage) *to* her; make a *proposal* (of marriage) *to* her. (⇨結婚)
プロポリス [蜂蝋] propolis.
ブロマイド [スターなどの写真] a star's picture [photo (複 ~s)]; [特定場所のスチール写真] a still. (**!** a bromide は「ブロマイド印画紙使用の写真」)
プロムナード [<フランス語] [散歩(道)] a promenade /pràmənéid/. 《米》では学年末のダンスパーティーをさすことが多い)
・プロムナードコンサート 《英》 a promenade concert, 《英話》 a prom. (参考) 通例, 聴衆は立ったまま演奏を聴く
プロモーション [販売の促進] (a) promotion.
・セールスプロモーション sales *promotion*.
・プロモーションビデオ a promótion vìdeo.
プロモーター [興行師] a promoter.
プロやきゅう プロ野球 pro(fessional) baseball.

フロリダ 〖米国の州〗Florida /flɔ́(:)ridə/《略 Fla. 郵便略 FL》.

プロレス(リング) professional 〖《話》pro〗 wrestling. ▶プロレスの選手 a professional wrestler.

プロレタリア 〖＜ドイツ語〗〖無産階級の人〗a proletarian /pròulətéəriən/ (↔a bourgeois); 〖集合体としての無産階級〗the proletariat(e) (↔bourgeoisie) (❢単・複両扱い).
- プロレタリア革命 a proletarian revolution.
- プロレタリア文学 proletarian literature.

プロローグ a prologue /próulɔ(:)g/ (↔an epilogue).

フロンガス chlorofluorocarbon /klɔ̀:rouflùərou-káːrbn/ 《略 CFC》. ▶フロンガスはオゾン層を破壊するといわれている It is implicated that *chlorofluorocarbon* [*CFC*] causes the breakdown of the ozone layer.

ブロンズ bronze.
- ブロンズ像 a bronze statue.

フロンティア 〖西部開拓時代の辺境・新分野〗the frontier /《米》frʌ́ntiər, 《英》frʌ́ntiə/.
- フロンティア精神 the frontier spirit.

フロント (ホテルの) the front 《米》[reception《英》] desk; the desk (❢単に front といえば、建物の「正面」をさす); 〖野球〗(球団経営首脳陣) the front office (❢(1) front office は本来は「運営事務本部」のこと. (2) サッカーでは同じ意味合いで board (理事会) がごく一般的に用いられる). ▶ホテルに帰ると彼女はフロントで鍵を(をもらった When she came back to the hotel, she collected her key from the *desk*.

ブロンド (金髪) blond hair; (金髪の女性) a blonde. (⇒金髪)

フロントエンジン 〖前置きエンジン〗a front engine.
フロントエンド 〖コンピュータ〗a front end.
- フロントエンドプロセッサー a front-end processor.

フロントガラス 《米》a windshield, 《英》a windscreen, 《和製語》a front glass.

フロントドライブ 图 〖前輪駆動〗front-wheel drive 《略 FWD》.
—— フロントドライブの 圏 front-drive.
- フロントドライブカー a front-(wheel) drive car.

プロンプター 〖役者を教える人〖装置〗〗a prompter.
プロンプト 〖コンピュータ〗(入力促進記号) a prompt.

ふわ 不和 〖ごたごた〗(a) trouble;〖仲たがい〗《書》discord;〖意見・利害の衝突〗(a) conflict;〖摩擦〗(a) friction. ▶家庭の不和を招く cause family *trouble* [*discord*]. ▶グループ内に不和を生じさせる cause *friction* in a group. ▶不和である を on bad terms 《*with*》. ▶絶え間ない夫婦間の不和が少年非行のもとになることがある Constant *discord* between husband and wife can cause juvenile delinquency. (❢(1) husband and wife の無冠詞に注意. (2) marital *discord* [*trouble*] は法律用語)

ふわたり 不渡り ▶不渡りを出す *dishonor* [*fail to pay*] a bill. ▶頂いた小切手は不渡りになります Your check *bounced*./You gave me a *bad check*.
- 不渡り手形 [小切手] a dishonored bill [《米》check], (米) 不渡り手形は NSF (= *N*ot *S*ufficient *F*und) 印とされる.

ふわふわ ❶ 〖軽く空中に浮かんでいる様子〗● ふわふわ浮いている float (lightly); (漂う) drift in the air. ▶羽根が数枚空中にふわふわ浮いていた A few feathers *were floating lightly* in the air.
❷ 〖柔らかく気持ちがよさそうな様子〗● ふわふわして fluffy; (柔らかい) soft. ▶ふわふわした毛のコート a *fluffy* woolen coat.
❸ 〖気持ちが浮ついている様子〗▶彼は若いころふわふわしていた He was *frivolous* when he was young.

ふわらいどう 付和雷同 —— **付和雷同する** 動 go with the crowd; (盲目的に他に同意する) agree with other people blindly.

ふわりと (柔らかに) softly; (ゆるやかに) gently; (軽く) lightly. ▶気球がふわりと着地した The balloon touched the ground *softly*. ▶クレーンは重い荷をふわりと持ち上げた The crane lifted the heavy load *lightly*.

*__ふん 分__ a minute /mínət/. (❢時刻・時間と角度のいずれにも用いる(⇒時(°))) ●1時間 [15度] 8分4秒 one hour [fifteen degrees], eight *minutes*, (and) four seconds. ▶時間は 1h 8′4″, 角度は 15°8′4″ としばしば略記する) ●10分間休憩をする take a rest for ten *minutes*; take a ten-*minute* rest. ●1分間に1キロメートルの速度で at (a speed of) 1 kilometer a [per] *minute*. ▶1時間は60分です There are sixty *minutes* in an hour./An hour has sixty *minutes*./Sixty *minutes* makes (❢sixty minutes という時間の長さの単位としてとらえる場合は単数扱い) ▶駅まで歩いて30分です It's (a) thirty *minutes*' [a thirty-*minute*, half an hour's] walk to the station. ▶彼は1分たがわず到着した He arrived *to the minute*. ▶今4時12分です It's 4:12 (《主に英》4.12). (❢日常的な略式の言い方. four-twelve と読む)/It's twelve *minutes* past [《米》after] four. (❢正式な言い方)

> **解説** 時刻の言い方:
> (*1*) 5分・10分・20分・25分の場合は minutes を省略可: 9時10分前です It's ten (*minutes*) to [《米》of] nine.
> (*2*) 15分は quarter, 30分は half で表す: 2時15分 [30分; 15分前]です It's (a) *quarter* past [*half* past; (a) *quarter* to] two. 《米》では a はしばしば省略する. なお, 《話》で「時＋分」の言うときは It's two fifteen [two thirty; one forty-five]. も可.
> (*3*) くだけた言い方では It's はしばしば省略される.

ふん 〖不審, 軽蔑〗huh /hʌ́/; humph /hm̩p, m̩m̩p, hʌ́mf/; 〖ためらい, 思案〗hum /hm:/. ▶彼は私の答えを聞いて(ばかにして)ふんと鼻をならした He *snorted* at my answer.

ふん 糞 excrement /ékskrəmənt/; (鳥やあまり大きくない獣の droppings; (牛馬などの) dung. ● ネズミ[羊]の糞 mouse [sheep] *droppings*.

*__ふん 分__ ❶ 〖分数・部分など〗(等分した一部分) a part. (⇒分数) 解説 ● 4分の1 a quarter; one [a] fourth. ● (後の方が堅い言い方) ● 4分の3 three quarters; three fourths. ● 5万分の1の地図 a map *on* [*with*] *the* [*a*] *scale of* 1:50,000 (❢one to fifty thousand と読む); a map drawn *to a scale of* 1:50,000 (❢drawn は「描かれた」); a one-to-fifty-thousand map. ▶ 1分は1時間の60分の1です A [One] minute is *a sixtieth part* [*one sixtieth*] of an [one] hour. ▶この市は東京の10分の1の大きさです This city is *one tenth* the size of [as large as] Tokyo. ▶彼はブラインドを4分の3ほど引いた He pulled down the shades *three quarters* of the way. (❢of the way は「ブラインドの走行程の」の意. 全体で副詞句となっている)
❷ 〖割り当て, 分け前〗a part, a portion; a share; (食べ物の 1杯分) a helping.

> **使い分け** part, portion ともに全体の一部分を意味するが, 後の方がある人・目的のために割り当てられた独立的な部分をさす. したがって「分け前」という意味にも用いる.
> share 受ける側からとらえられた「分け前」を表す.

- そのケーキを3(等)分する divide the cake into three (equal) *parts* [*portions*]. ● 大盛りのプディング一人分 a generous *helping* [*portion*] of pudding. ● 10月分の給料をもらう get one's pay *for* October. ▶ 自分の分をぺろりと食べた He ate his *portion* with good appetite. ● その利益の私の取り分は100万円だった My *share* [*portion*] of the profits was one million yen. ● これはあなたの分です This is your *share* [*yours*]. (❗*share* を用いると利益own分の分け前という意味になる。yours は漠然と「あなたの分」で,各人に割り当てられた量などを意味する)/This is *for* you. (❗相手に物を差し出すときの表現) ▶ 私は彼の分まで支払わされた I had to pay *for* him.
  【会話】「このケーキおいしい！」「私の分もとっておいて」 "What a delicious cake!" "Save some of it *for* me."

❸ 〖分量〗(割合, 比率) a percentage; (含有量) a cóntent; (ある金額などに相当する分量) worth 《*of*》. ● 1ドル分のバター a dollar's *worth of* butter. ● 2人分の仕事をする do the work of two people; do two people's work. ● このウイスキーはアルコール分が多い This whiskey has a high *percentage* of alcohol. ● 彼は3日[3人]分の食糧を買った He bought food *for* three days [people].

❹ 〖資力, 身分, 本分〗(資力) means; (立場) one's place; (運命) one's lot; (義務) one's duty. ● 分相応 [不相応] に暮らす live within [beyond] one's *means*. ● 分を知る know one's *place*. ● 分に安んじるを満足することを持つ be contented with one's *lot*. ● 己の分を尽くす do one's *duty* [*duties*]. ● 親しくても礼がを知られる(=なれなれしくないこと) Be friendly, but never familiar.

❺ 〖状態〗 condition(s); situation; things. ▶ この分では(=現状では)その事業は失敗に終わりそうだ *Judging from the present condition* [*As things are*, *As things stand*], the enterprise will end in failure. ▶ この分じゃ彼は成功しないよ *At this rate* [*If he goes on like this*], he will not succeed. ▶ この分ではあした雪になりそうだ It looks like snow tomorrow.

*ぶん 文 a sentence; 〖学校の作文〗a composition; 〖書き物〗writing; 〖文体〗(a) style. (⇨文章) ● 単[複; 重] 文 a simple [a complex; a compound] *sentence*. ● その文を受身の文に書き換える rewrite the *sentence* into a passive *sentence*. ▶ これはなかなかよい文だ This is a good piece of writing.
● 文は人なり (ことわざ) The style is the man.
● 文は武に勝る (ペンは剣より強い)《ことわざ》The pen is mightier than the sword /sɔ́ːrd/.

ぶんあん 文案 《make》a draft. ⇨下書き

ぶんい 文意 the meaning of a sentence. (⇨意味)
▶ これは文意不明だ I don't understand *the meaning of this sentence*.

*ふんいき 雰囲気 (an) atmosphere. (❗(1)単独で用いられると通例れる雰囲気を表す。(2) mood は「個人的な気分」の意なので注意) ● 暖かい[家庭的な; 友好的な; 張りつめた; 気まずい] 雰囲気の中で in a warm [a family; a friendly; a tense; an awkward] *atmosphere*. ● 雰囲気のよい喫茶店 a tearoom with (a nice) *atmosphere*. ▶ その部屋は重苦しい雰囲気に包まれていた There was a heavy *atmosphere* in the room./The *atmosphere* in the room was heavy.

ぶんいん 分院 a branch《hospital [temple]》.

ぶんえん 噴煙 smoke of a volcano; volcanic smoke. ▶ 霧島はもうもうと噴煙を上げていた Mt. Kirishima was belching [emitting] a thick column of *smoke*.

ふんか 噴火 名 (an) eruption. ● 火山の噴火 a volcanic *eruption*.
—— 噴火する 動 erupt. ● 噴火している be erupting; be in *eruption*.
● 噴火口 a crater. ● 噴火山 an active volcano.

:ぶんか 文化 名 (a) culture (❗具体的な個々の文化をいうとき以外は通例無冠詞); (文明) (a) civilization.

【使い分け】**culture** ある民族, 人間集団が産み出し, 習得し, 伝えていく生活様式・風俗・習慣・言語・思想・芸術などの総体をさす。
civilization 未開の状態が開化されたり, 科学・技術など社会が物質面で高度に発達している状態をさす。

① 〖～文化〗● 古代ギリシャ文化 ancient Greek *culture*. ● 異文化間の問題を研究する study cross-cultural [intercultural] problems [issues].
② 〖文化が〗● その国は文化が遅れている [進んでいる] That nation is behind [advanced] in *civilization*.
③ 〖文化を〗● 自分たち自身の文化を創造する create a *culture* of one's own. ▶ 古代ギリシャ人は高い文化を持っていた The ancient Greek had a high level of *culture* [(文明) *civilization*]. ▶ 私たちの新しい文化がこの地域でも栄え花開くでしょう Our new *culture* will flourish and bloom in this area. ▶ 民主的な文化がその国でも深く根付くことを望んでいます We hope (that) democratic *culture* will be deeply rooted in the country. ▶ 我が社の企業文化を育てるようあらゆる努力をするつもりです We intend to make every possible effort to develop our corporate *culture*. ▶ 文化を理解できる唯一の方法はその文化にどっぷりつかることだ The only way to understand a *culture* is to be immersed in it.
—— 文化(の) 形 (文化の[に関する], 文化的) cultural; (文化のある) cultured; (開けた) civilized. ● 文化的生活をする lead a *civilized* [ⓍA *cultural*] life; enjoy modern living. (❗後の方が口語的)
● 文化遺産 cultural heritage [assets]. ● 文化会館 a civic hall. ● 文化勲章 the Medal for [《英》the Order of] Culture. ● 文化圏 a culture [cultural] area. ● 同じ文化圏に属する belong to the same *culture* [*cultural*] area. ● 文化交流 cultural exchange. ● 文化功労者 a person of Cultural Merit. ● 文化国家 a cultured nation. ● 文化祭 (学校の) a school festival. ● 文化財 《⇨文化財》● 文化人 a person of culture; a cultured person. (❗いずれも「教養の高い人」の意) ● 文化人類学 cultural anthropology. ● 文化水準 cultural level; the level of culture. ● 文化センター a civic center. ● 文化庁 the Agency for Cultural Affairs. ● 文化の日 《×the》Culture Day.

ぶんか 分化 名 〖特殊化〗specialization (❗生物学の専門語としても用いる); 〖生物〗(形態的・機能的特殊化) differentiation. ▶ 医学は分化傾向をいっそう強めている Medicine is moving toward more *specialization*.
—— 分化する 動 specialize; differentiate.

ぶんか 文科 〖大学の文科系の学問〗the humanities, human studies.
● 文科系 《⇨文科系》

ぶんがい 憤慨 名 〖不正などに対する〗indignation; resentment. (❗不正を働いた者に対する恨みを暗示する) (⇨憤り)
—— 憤慨する 動 be [feel*] indignant; be [get*] very angry. (❗前の方は不正・卑劣行為など正当な理由で怒ること。後の方は主に個人的理由で怒ること) ● 人

ぶんかい 分解 图 [[要素への]] resolution; [[成分・元素への]] decomposition.
── **分解する** 動 [[構成要素に]] resolve 《into》; [[成分・元素に]] decompose; (分析する) analyze; (溶解する) dissolve; (小さな機械を解体する) take*... apart [to pieces]. ●水を酸素と水素に分解する resolve [decompose] water into oxygen and hydrogen. ●その時計を分解する take the watch apart [to pieces]. ●自動車を分解修理[=オーバーホール]する give a car an overhaul; overhaul a car. ●それは元素に分解する It resolves into its elements. ▶プリズムは光を分解する A prism decomposes light.

ぶんかい 分会 a branch (organization).
ぶんかいかい 分科会 a branch meeting.
***ぶんがく** 文学 图 literature. ●児童[純; 大衆; 近代]文学 children's [polite; popular; modern] literature. ●イギリス[アメリカ]文学 English [American] literature. ●国文学史 the [a] history of Japanese literature. ▶彼は文学愛好者です(文学趣味がある) He has a taste for literature [a literary taste]./(読書好きだ) He likes reading [is a lover of reading].
── **文学の, 文学的な** 形 literary. ●文学の才能がある have a literary talent.
●文学科 a literature department; a department of literature. ●文学界 the literary world. ●文学作品 a literary work; [[集合的]] literature, literary works. ●文学雑誌 a literary magazine. ●文学士 a Bachelor of Arts (略 B.A.). ●文学者 (作家) a writer; (文学研究者, 作家) a literary man [woman] (圈 はともに (-)men); (著述家) [書] a man [a woman] of letters.
●文学修士 a Master of Arts (略 M.A.). ●文学賞 a literary award. ●文学青年 a young literature lover. ●文学博士 a doctor of literature (略 Lit(t).D.). ●文学部 a college 《米》 [a faculty 《英》] of literature.
ぶんかけい 文科系 the humanities course. (⇨文系)
ぶんかざい 文化財 重要[無形]文化財 an important [an intangible] cultural asset.
ぶんかつ 分割 图 (a) division. ●株式分割 a (stock [share]) split [split-up].
── **分割する** 動 divide. (⇨分ける❶) ●財産を 4 人の子供に平等に分割する divide one's property equally among one's four children. ▶ドイツは第二次大戦後東西に分割された Germany was divided into East and West after World War Ⅱ. ▶クラスは 4～5 人一組の研究グループに分割された The class was sectioned into study groups of four or five.
●分割統治 divide-and-rule. ●分割払い (⇨分割払い)
ぶんかつばらい 分割払い payment by [in] installments /ɪnstɔ́ːlmənts/. ●車を分割払いで買う buy a car on the installment plan [《英》 on hire purchase]; 《米》 buy a car on time. ●分割払い方式 the installment [easy] payment plan [system].
ぶんかん 分館 an ánnex 《to a library》.
ぶんかん 文官 (軍人に対して) a civil servant.

ぶんき 噴気 ●火口からの噴気 hot gases [vapors] discharged from a crater.
●噴気孔 a fumarole.
ぶんき 奮起 ── **奮起する** 動 rouse /ráuz/ oneself.
●奮起させる stir ... (up). ▶彼の激励で私たちは奮起してもう一度挑戦した He stirred [inspired] us to try it again.
ぶんき 分岐 ── **分岐する** 動 (やや書) divérge 《from, into》, fork 《into》, branch (off) 《into》. ▶その道路は前方 2 キロの地点で幹線道路から分岐する The road diverges from the highway 2 kilometers ahead.
ぶんきてん 分岐点 (道や川の) a fork; (道や鉄道の) a junction (❗ (1) 語源からみて「合流点」の含みが強い. (2) 《米》では an intersection の方が一般的). ●人生の分岐点に(=岐路)に立つ 《⇨岐路》 ●この道をまっすぐ行って分岐点に来たら左へ進みなさい You go straight down this road until you get to the fork in the road. Go left.
ぶんきゅう 紛糾 图 [[複雑な事態]] (a) complication.
── **紛糾する** 動 become complicated; (混乱に陥る) fall [be thrown] into confusion. ●事態を紛糾させる make the situation complicated; complicate the situation. ●会議を紛糾させる throw a meeting into confusion.
ぶんきょう 文教 education. ●文教政策 an educational policy. ●文教地区 a school zone.
ぶんぎょう 分業 the division of labor. ●分業で仕事をする divide the work.
ぶんきょうじょう 分教場 ●山の分教場 a small branch school in the mountains [on the hillside, etc.].
ぶんきょく 分局 a branch office [bureau].
ぶんきょくか 分極化 图 polarization.
── **分極化する** 動 become polarized. ●分極化させる polarize. ●分極化している be polarized. ▶新空港建設の提案をめぐって周辺住民の意見は分極化した The proposed new airport polarized the opinions of local citizens./The opinions of local citizens became polarized on the new airport proposal.
ぶんぎり 踏ん切り ▶その計画を断念するかどうか踏ん切りがつかない I can't make up my mind whether to give up the plan or not.
ぶんきんたかしまだ 文金高島田 (説明的に) a sophisticated Japanese hairstyle arranged for a bride.
ぶんぐ 文具 (⇨文房具)
ぶんけ 分家 ── **一家分家する** 動 set up a branch family. (⇨本家)
ふんけい 刎頸 ●刎頸の友 an inseparable friend.
ふんけい 焚刑 (⇨火炙(あぶ)り)
ぶんけい 文系 the humanities course. (圏 理系) ▶彼は大学は文系に進むことにしている He is going to take the humanities course [study the humanities] in college.
ぶんけい 文型 a sentence pattern. ●基本文型 a basic sentence pattern.
ぶんげい 文芸 (文学) literature; (芸術と文学) art and literature. (⇨文学)
●文芸作品 a literary work. ●文芸雑誌 a literary magazine. ●文芸批評 literary criticism. ●文芸部 (クラブ活動) a literary club; (会社の) a literary section. ●文芸復興 the Renaissance. (❗ 一般的には a renaissance) ●文芸欄 (新聞などの) a literary column.
ふんげき 憤激 (a) rage; (a) fury. ●憤激している be in

ぶんけん a rage [one's fury]. ●憤激を招く enrage; infuriate. (⇨激怒)

ぶんけん 分県 ●分県地図 a map of prefectures [prefecture].

ぶんけん 分権 decentralization of authorities [power]. ●地方分権 decentralization.
— **分権化する** 動 decentralize.

ぶんけん 文献 (一連の学術的な) literature; (書物) a book; (記録資料) documents (🛈通例複数形で). ●参考文献 a bibliography; references. (🛈前の方が徹底さを含意) ▶彼はその問題に関して多くの文献を集めた He collected much [a large] *literature* on the subject.

ぶんげん 分限 one's status; one's position in society. (⇨分(ぶ)❹)

ぶんけんたい 分遣隊 a detachment.

ぶんこ 文庫 (図書館, 蔵書, 叢書(そう)) a library. ●岩波文庫 the Iwanami *Library*.
●**文庫本** ⇨文庫本

ぶんご 文語 literary language; (書き言葉) (the) written language. (⇨口語)
●**文語体** (*in*) a literary style.

ぶんごう 吻合 名 〖医学〗(an) anastomosis (複 -moses).
— **吻合する** 動 join; unite.

ぶんこう 分光 名 〖物理〗(分光すること) dispersion; (分光された光の帯) a spectrum.
— **分光する** 動 disperse.
●**分光器** a spéctroscòpe.

ぶんこう 分校 a branch school.

ぶんごう 文豪 a great writer; a literary master.

ぶんこつ 分骨 — **分骨する** 動 ▶私の骨は高野山に分骨してほしい I'd like you to *entomb part of* my *ashes* in Koyasan. ▶父の遺骨は郷里の墓地に分骨された *A part of* my father's *ashes was buried* in the family graveyard of his hometown.

ぶんこつさいしん 粉骨砕身 — **粉骨砕身する** 動 do one's very best; exert oneself to the utmost.

ぶんこぼん 文庫本 a paperback (edition), a pocket edition. ●文庫本に入っている[で出ている] be out in *paperback*. ●文庫本で読む read 《a novel》 *in paperback*.

ぶんさい 粉砕 — **粉砕する** 動 (押しつぶす) crush ... (to pieces); (破片を飛散させて壊す) shatter; (突然音を立てて打ち砕く) smash. ●敵を粉砕する *crush* the enemy.

ぶんざい 粉剤 〖農業〗powdered agricultural chemical.

ぶんさい 文才 ●文才がある have a *talent* [an *aptitude*] *for writing*.

ぶんざい 分際 ▶彼は学生の分際で高級な車を乗り回している He drives around in a luxury car *though* he is only a college student.

ぶんさつ 分冊 a separate volume. ●3分冊にして出版する publish 《the novel》 *in three volumes*.

ぶんさん 分散 名 〖雲・光・群衆などの〗dispersion; (離散, 崩壊) a breakup. ●光の分散 the *dispersion* of light.
— **分散する[させる]** 動 〖四方に散る・散らす〗scatter, 《やや書》disperse (⇨散らす); 〖解散する・させる〗break*(...) up; 〖中央集中の人口・産業などを〗decentralize. ●群衆を分散〔=解散〕させる *scatter* [*disperse, break up*] the crowd. ●国の産業を分散させる *decentralize* the nation's industry.

ぶんし 憤死 — **憤死する** 動 die of indignation; kill oneself in violent anger. ▶走者はバックホームされて本塁で憤死した The runner got thrown out at home.

***ぶんし** 分子 〖化学・物理〗a molecule /mάləkjùːl/; 〖数学〗a númeràtor (↔denominator); 〖一部の者〗an element. ●反動[不平]分子 reactionary [discontented] *elements*. ●党内の腐敗分子を一掃する clear the party of its corrupt *elements*.
●**分子構造** molecular structure. ●**分子式** a molecular formula (複 ~s, formulae). ●**分子生物学** molecular biology. ●**分子物理学** molecular physics. ●**分子量** molecular weight.

ぶんし 分詞 〖文法〗a (present [past]) párticiple.
●**分詞構文** a participial /pὰːrtɪsɪpɪəl/ construction.

ぶんし 文士 a literary man [artist]; (小説家) a novelist; (物書き) a writer. ●三文文士 a hack *writer*.

ぶんじ 文治 (⇨文治(ぶんち))

ぶんしつ 紛失 名 (a) loss. ●警察に宝石の紛失届を出す report the *loss* of one's jewelry to the police.
— **紛失する** 動 〖人が〗lose*; 〖物が〗(見当たらない) be missing; (消える) disappear. ●紛失した鍵(かぎ) a *lost* [a *missing*] key. ▶私は時計を紛失した I *lost* my watch./My watch has *disappeared* [*is missing*].

ぶんしつ 分室 a branch office.

ぶんしゃ 噴射 名 ●ガスの噴射 a *jet* of gas.
— **噴射する** 動 ●炎を噴射する *jet* (*out*) flames. ▶水が噴射した The water *jetted out*.

ぶんしゃ 分社 a branch shrine.
●**分社化** the split [split-up] of a company.
●**分社化する** split (up) a company.

ぶんじゃく 文弱 ●文弱に流れる have too much interest in literary [artistic, scholarly] pursuits and neglect one's 《military》duties.

ぶんしゅう 文集 (名詩名文選集) an anthology; (雑録) a miscellany. ●フォークナー文集 a *collection* of Faulkner's works.

ぶんしゅく 分宿 — **分宿する** 動 put up at different hotels.

ぶんしゅつ 噴出 名 a gush; a spout; eruption (🛈噴出物 Ⓒ). ●石油の噴出 a *gush* [a *spout*] of oil.
— **噴出する[させる]** 動 (液体が突然割れ目などから) gush(...) (*out*); (液体・炎などが[を]一直線に) spout(...) (*out*); (煙・煙などを激しく大量に) belch(...) (*out*); (溶岩などを) erupt.

ぶんしょ 焚書 book burning.

ぶんしょ 分署 a local tax office [police station].

ぶんしょ 文書 〖書類〗papers; (資料・証拠としての) a document (⇨書類); 〖通信文〗a letter, 《書》〖集合的〗correspondence; 〖記録〗a record; 〖書き物〗(a piece of) writing. ●公[私]文書 official [private] *documents*. ●外交文書 diplomatic *correspondence*. ●文書で回答する answer *in writing*. ▶その件で我々は合意したが, 文書の形では何もない We shook hands on it, but there's nothing *on paper*. ▶契約を文書にしてください I want to have a contract *on paper* [*in writing*].

***ぶんしょう** 文章 (書き物) writing; (一つの文) a sentence; (作文) a composition; (一節) a passage; (随筆, 小論) an essay; (文体) (a) style. ●文章を書く write 《a composition [an essay]》. ●文章にまとめる put 《one's ideas》 in *writing*. ▶彼は文章が上手[へた]だ He is a good [a poor] *writer*./He writes well [poorly]./He is good [poor] at *writing*.
●**文章家** a writer; (随筆家) an essayist.

ぶんしょう 分掌 名 division of duties.
— **分掌する** 動 ▶その業務を2つの課で分掌する

ぶんじょう 分乗 ── **分乗する** 動 ▶観光客の一行は2台のバスに分乗して出発した The party of tourists started in two buses. (❗特に「分ける」を強調する必要はない)

ぶんじょう 分譲 图 ●土地の分譲 sale of land in lots. (❗a lot は《主に米》で「土地の1区画」の意)
── **分譲する** 動 ●その土地を分譲する sell the land in lots; subdivide the land and sell it.
● **分譲住宅** a newly built house for sale.
● **分譲地** a (building) lot for sale;《米》a subdivision. ● **分譲マンション** a condominium /kàndəmíniəm/;《話》a cóndo (	複 〜s). (❗1戸または建物全体をさす)

ふんしょく 粉飾 图 (数字などの) window dressing; the manipulation of accounts.
── **粉飾する** 動 ●貸借対照表を粉飾する dress up the balance sheet.
● **粉飾決算** window dressing; the settlement of accounts based on window dressing [manipulation]. ● **粉飾決算する** windowdress the financial statements [accounts].

ふんしん 分針 a mínute hànd.

ふんじん 粉塵 (金属・岩石などの微細な粉) minute particles;《coal》dust.
● **粉塵公害** dust pollution.

ぶんしん 分身 (もうひとつの自分) one's [an] alter ego /íːgou/ (	複 egos), the other [another, the second] self (	複 selves). ▶他人を心の奥底から友とみなすことは彼[彼女]を自分の分身とみなすことである To regard another person truly as a friend is to regard him [her] as an alter ego. (参考 アリストテレスの言葉)

ぶんじん 文人 a literary man [woman] (	複 はともに (-)men).
● **文人墨客**(ぼっかく) literary men [women] and experts in calligraphy or ink drawing.
● **文人画** literati painting. (❗作品そのものをいう場合は C)

ふんすい 噴水 a fountain. ▶噴水が出ている The fountain is playing.

ぶんすいれい 分水嶺 a watershed,《米》a divide.

ぶんすう 分数 a fraction, a fractional number. (⇒一分の) ● **仮分数** a proper [an improper] fraction. ● **帯分数** a mixed number.

> 解説 **分数の読み方:**
> (1) 一般に $1/3$＝a [one] third, $3\,2/5$＝three and two fifths. 分子が2以上では分母に s をつける ただし $1/2$＝a [one] half [×second].
> (2) 複雑または大きな桁(けた)の数の分数の場合: $5/50+13$＝five over [by] fifty plus thirteen.
> (3) 単位の名詞を伴う場合: $3/4$ cup＝three quarters [fourths] of a cup, $1\,1/4$ cups of milk＝one-and-a-quarter cups of milk. (❗限定形容詞として名詞を修飾する場合はハイフンをつける. of はしばしば省略される)
> **用法:**「分数＋of＋图」が主語の場合, 動詞の数は名詞の数に呼応する: 作物[オレンジ]の3分の2が被害を受けた Two thirds of the crop was [of the oranges were] damaged.

● **分数式** a fractional expression. ● **分数方程式** a fractional equation.

ふんする 扮する ❶ [演じる] ▶弁慶に扮する play the role [part] of Benkei; act (as) Benkei. (❗as が省略された場合 act は他動詞).
❷ [変装する] (⇒変装する)

*****ぶんせき 分析** 图 (an) análysis (	複 analyses).

── **分析する** 動 analyze; carry out [make, do] an analysis (of). ▶その水を分析した結果, 化学汚染物質を含んでいることが分かった The analysis of the water showed that it contained chemical pollutants. ▶我々はなぜ失敗したのかを知るために綿密にその計画を分析した We analyzed the plan closely [made a close analysis of the plan] in order to see why it had failed.
── **分析的な** 形 analytical. ●物事を分析的に考える think analytically.
● **分析化学** analytical chemistry.

ぶんせき 文責 ▶この記事の文責は私にある I'm responsible for (the content of) this article.

ぶんせつ 分節 division into parts; (分けられた部分) a part;〖言語〗a segment.

ぶんせつ 文節〖文法〗(説明的に) the smallest unit of words that sounds natural in a spoken sentence.

ふんせん 噴泉 a (hot) spring that spurts water into the air;〖噴水〗a fountain.

ふんせん 奮戦 ── **奮戦する** 動 fight hard [bitterly, (負けを覚悟で必死に) desperately].

ふんぜん 憤然 ●憤然として in indignation; (激怒して) in a rage. ●憤然として立ち去る walk off in indignation [in a rage].

ぶんせん 文選 ── **文選する** 動 pick up [gather] type from cases for typesetting; (組版する) typeset, set type.

ふんそう 扮装 ❶ [役者の] (a) mákeùp. ●オセロの扮装をする make (oneself) up [do one's makeup] as Othéllo. ❷ [変装] (a) disguise. (⇒変装)

ふんそう 紛争 〖激しい論争〗(a) dispute; 〖もめごと〗(a) conflict, (a) trouble; 〖騒ぎ, 動乱〗(a) disturbance. ●大学紛争 disturbances at universities. ●国境紛争 a border dispute [conflict]. ●労使間の紛争の解決にあたる go about settling a dispute between employers and employees. (⇒争議) ●紛争中である be (involved) in conflict [a dispute]《with＋人, about [over]＋事》.

ぶんそうおう 分相応 (⇒分(ぶ)❹)

ふんそく 分速 ●分速15キロで at (a speed of) 15 kilometers a [per] minute.

ふんぞりかえる ふん反り返る ●いすにふんぞり返る(＝偉そうにいすに座る) sit back in a chair arrogantly; throw oneself back in a chair. ▶嫌な感じの男が何人か子分を従えてふんぞり返って私の方に近づいてきた An obnoxious man swaggered up to me accompanied by his henchmen.

ぶんたい 分隊 (陸軍の) a squad.
● **分隊長** a squád commànder.

ぶんたい 文体 (a) style. ●口語的な[洗練された]文体で書く write in a colloquial [a polished] style. ●漱石の文体をまねて書く write in the style of Soseki. ▶彼の文体は多少堅苦しいところがある His style (of writing) is somewhat stiff./He writes in a rather formal style.
● **文体論** stylistics. (❗単数扱い)

ふんだくる (力ずくで取る) snatch ... (off), grab (-bb-) ... (away) (❗後の方が乱暴); (法外な金額を要求する)《話》rip (-pp-)《him》off. ▶あのバーでビール1本で1万円もふんだくられた That bar ripped me off 10,000 yen for a bottle of beer.

ふんだりけったり 踏んだり蹴ったり ●踏んだりけったりの(＝ひどい)目に have a very hard time (of it); have a pretty bad time.
会話「サイクリングは楽しかった？」「帰りに自転車がパンクするし, それにわか雨に降られるし踏んだり蹴ったりだっ

ふんだん — **ふんだんに** 副 ● ふんだんに(=惜しげもなく)金を遣う spend (one's) money *freely*; 《やや書》 *lavish* (one's) money 《*on*》. ● ダイヤモンドをふんだんにあしらった王冠 a crown set with *plenty* of diamonds. ▶ふんだんに(=たっぷり)時間がある We have [There is] *plenty* of time./《書》We have time *in plenty*.

— **ふんだんな** 形 ● ふんだんな(=豊富な)資金 *abundant* funds.

*__ぶんたん__ 分担 名 [費用・仕事などの負担] a share; [計画的に割り当てた仕事] an assignment; [任意または偶発的な割り当て] 《古》(an) allotment. ● 分担が決まった仕事 an *assigned* [an *allotted*] task. ● 自分の分担の仕事をする do one's *share* of work; do one's *assignment*.

— **分担する** 動 [分け合う] share; [分割する] divide; [割り当てる] assign /əsáin/. ● 責任を分担する take [《やや書》 assume] one's share *of* the responsibility. ● 費用を分担する *share* [*split up*] the expenses 《*with* him, *between* the two》. ▶その仕事を我々 4 人で分担しよう Let's *divide* [*share*] the work *among* the four of us.

ぶんたん 文旦 〖『ザボン』の別名〗(⇨ザボン)
ぶんだん 分団 a branch (office) 《*of* a fire station》.
ぶんだん 分断 ● **分断する** 動 (分割する) divide ... 《*into*》; (遮断する) cut ... off 《*from*》. ▶ベルリンは戦後長い間東西に分断されていた Berlin had *been divided into* East and West Berlin for years after the war. ▶落石事故で南海線はあちこちで分断された The rockslide accidents *cut off* traffic in many places along the Nankai Line.
ぶんだん 文壇 the literary world, literary circles. ● 文壇で名をなす become famous [win fame] in the *literary world*; win *literary* fame.
ぶんち 文治 civilian control. ● 文治主義 the principle of civilian control [government].
ぶんちゅう 文中 ▶文中に文法上の間違いはない There are no grammatical errors *in the sentence*(*s*) [*composition*, *text*].
ぶんちょう 文鳥 〖鳥〗a Java sparrow. ● 手乗り文鳥 a tame Java sparrow.
ぶんちん 文鎮 a paperweight.
*__ぶんつう__ 文通 名 《やや書》 correspondence.
— **文通する** 動 《やや書》 correspond 《*with*》, exchange letters 《*with*》. ▶私は彼女と何年も文通している I *have been corresponding* [*exchanging letters*, *in correspondence*] *with* her for years.
ふんづける 踏ん付ける stamp 《*on*》; (踏みつぶす) trample ... (down); (踏み付ける; 上に乗る) step (-pp-) 《*on*》.
ふんど 憤怒 ⇨憤激.
ぷんと ▶彼女はぷんと顔をそむけた She *angrily* turned her face away. ▶その薬品はぷんと鼻をつく The medicine smells *pungent* [*bad*].
ふんとう 奮闘 名 (a) stréuous [(a) hard, (a) great] effort; [頑張り] hard work. (⇨努力, 健闘)
— **奮闘する** 動 make strenuous efforts 《*to do*》; work hard.
ふんどう 分銅 a weight.
ぶんとう 文頭 《*at*》 the beginning of a sentence.
ぶんどき 分度器 a protractor.
ふんどし 褌 a loincloth; *fundoshi*; (説明的に) an old Japanese men's underwear made of a long, narrow cloth which is rolled around the loin; 〚熱帯に住む男性の腰布〛a loincloth 《@-cloths /-klɔːðz, klɔːθs/》. ● 人のふんどしで相撲を取る (⇨人) [成句]
● ふんどしを締めてかかる straighten oneself up [roll up one's sleeves] and get to work.

ぶんどる 分捕る (奪い取る) seize /síːz/; (略奪する) loot; (力ずくで奪う) grab (-bb-); (ひったくる) snatch. ● アメリカのヘリコプターを分捕る *seize* an American helicopter.

ぶんなぐる 打ん殴る hit* [knock, punch] 《him》 hard, 《話》 wallop, 《米話》 slug (-gg-), give* 《him》 a hard blow [《話》 a real wallop]. (⇨なぐる)

ぶんなげる 打ん投げる throw* [fling*, (特に大きいものや重いものを) hurl] forcefully [violently].
ふんにゅう 粉乳 powdered [dry] milk.
ふんによう 糞尿 human waste, 《書》 excreta.
-ぶんの -分の over; (divided) by. ● 7分の20 twenty *over* seven (=$^{20}/_7$). ▶クラスの3分の1 [3分の2]は女生徒です One *third* [Two *thirds*] of the class is [《英》 are] girl students. (⇨分数)
ぶんのう 分納 — **分納する** 動 pay* 《the debt》 in 《three》 installments.
ぶんぱ 分派 (分離[分裂]集団) a splinter group; (政党などの) a faction; (宗派の) a sect. ● 分派活動 factional activities.
ぶんばい 分売 ● 分売はしない do not sell separately.
ぶんばい 分配 名 [配ること] (a) distribution; (配るために分けること) division. ● 富の分配 the *distribution* [*division*] of wealth.
— **分配する** 動 (配る) distribute 《*to*, *among*》; (均一に) divide 《*between*, *among*》; (分け合う) share 《*between*, *among*》. ● 子供たちに食物を分配する *distribute* [*hand out*] the food *to* the children. ▶彼の財産は3人の息子に均等に分配された His property *was distributed* [*was divided*, *was shared* (*out*)] equally *among* his three sons.
● 分配額 a share.
ふんぱつ 奮発 — **奮発する** 動 (思いきって...を買う) treat oneself 《*to*》. ▶彼女は奮発してシルクのドレスを買った She *treated herself to* a silk dress.
ふんばり 踏ん張り ● もうひと踏ん張りする make another effort 《*to do*》; renew one's effort 《*to do*》.
ふんばる 踏ん張る ● 足を踏ん張る stand firm; plant one's (both) feet firmly. ● 最後まで踏ん張る(=耐え抜く) hold out to the end. (⇨頑張る) ▶敵の執拗な攻撃にもかかわらず彼らは踏ん張った They held [stood] *firm* against the enemy's persistent attack.
ふんぱん 噴飯 ● 噴飯ものである be perfectly [utterly] absurd [ridiculous]; be perfect [utter, sheer] nonsense.
ぶんび 文尾 (⇨文末)
ぶんぴ 分泌 secretion. (⇨分泌(ひ))
ぶんぴつ 分泌 〖医学〗secretion /sikríːʃən/. ● 唾液(だ)の分泌 the *secretion* of saliva /səláivə/.
— **分泌する** 動 ● 胃液を分泌する 〖医学〗*secrete* gastric juice.
● 分泌作用 secretion. ● 分泌腺 a secretory /síkrətəri/ gland. ● 分泌物 a secretion.
ぶんぴつ 分筆 〖法律〗subdivision of a lot. ● 宅地を4つに分筆する *subdivide* the building lot *into* four parts.
ぶんぴつ 文筆 (文章を書くこと) writing; (著述活動) 《do》 literary work.
● 文筆家 (作家) a writer; (文人) a literary man [woman]. ● 文筆業 the literary profession.

ぶんびょう 分秒 a moment. ▶この事の処理は分秒を争う This must be dealt with *immediately* [*urgently*]./This is a matter of great [*extreme*] urgency. (⇨一刻)

ぶんぶ 文武 ▶文武両道に秀でている excel in both *literary and military arts*. (❗excel は進行形不可)

ぶんぷ 分布 图 (a) distribution.
── **分布する** 動 ▶その昆虫は日本に広く分布している The insects *are* widely *distributed* [*have a wide distribution*, *range* widely] in Japan. (ˣare ranging ... と進行形にはしない)
● **分布地図** a distribútion màp.

ぶんぶつ 文物 ▶日本の文物 *things* Japanese; Japanese *culture*.

ふんぷん 紛々 ▶彼女の過去に関しては諸説紛紛としている *Opinion is* [ˣOpinions are] *divided on* her past./There are *a lot of opinions* on her past.

ぶんぶん ❶【羽の音, うなる音】▶ぶんぶん羽音を立てる(蜂・蚊などの) buzz /bʌz/; (蜂など) hum. ● エンジンのぶんぶんうなる音 the *whine* of the engine. ▶夏になると食品の周りにはえがぶんぶん飛び回る Flies *buzz around* food in ((主に米)) the summer. ▶軽飛行機がぶんぶん飛んで行くのが聞こえる You can hear light airplanes *buzzing off*.
❷【棒などをうならすほど振り回す様子・音】▶杖をぶんぶん振り回す *twirl* a cane.

ぷんぷん ❶【臭】▶(においなど) strongly. ▶彼の息は酒のにおいがぷんぷんした His breath *smelled* [*reeked*] *of* alcohol. (❗reek は特に悪臭についていう) ▶海辺は腐った魚のにおいがぷんぷんしていた The beach *was filled with a strong smell of* rotten fish./Rotten fish *stank* on the beach. (❗stink は「悪臭を放つ」の意) ▶女性の一団がどやどや乗り込んできてエレベーターの中で香水のにおいをぷんぷんさせた A group of women piled into the elevator and *overwhelmed* me with perfume. (❗この overwhelm は「辟易させる」の意)
❷【非常に怒っている】angry, mad (-dd-). ▶彼は長く待たされてぷんぷん怒っていた He was *very* angry at being kept waiting so long. ▶彼女はぷんぷん怒っていた She *was* really *fuming*. (❗fume は自動詞で「非常に怒る」の意)

*__ふんべつ 分別__ [【慎重さ】 prudence, discretion /dɪskrέʃən/, 【判断力】 (good) sense, 【賢明さ】 wisdom; (才覚) wit(s). ▶分別ある人 a person of *prudence* [*discretion, sense*]; a *sensible* person (❗この方が普通). ▶侮辱されて分別を失う様 (one's *good*) *judgment* at the insult. ▶分別を働かせる use [exercise] *prudence* [*discretion*] (*in doing*). ▶分別を持ちなさい Be *sensible*./Why don't you be *reasonable*? (❗命令の意を持つ修辞疑問文) Why aren't you reasonable? と異なることに注意) ▶彼は分別のある行動をする He is *prudent* [*discreet*] *in* his behavior. ▶彼はそんなことをするほど無分別ではない He knows better [*has more sense*] than to do [ˣdoing] such a thing. ▶彼女には彼の申し入れを断わるだけの分別があった She had enough *sense* to decline his offer./She was *sensible* [*wise*] enough to decline his offer. ▶あのか, いくつになったら分別がつくようになるのだろう When will the poor fool learn *wit*?

ぶんべつ 分別 ▶ごみの分別収集 separate garbage collection. ▶分別収集する collect 《burnables and unburnables》 separately. ▶ごみは分別して出してください Please *separate* garbage *according to type* and put it outside.

ふんべん 糞便 (⇨大便)

ぶんべん 分娩 (⇨出産) ● 無痛分娩 painless *delivery*. ● 自然分娩 natural childbirth.
● **分娩室** a delívery ròom.

ふんぼ 墳墓 a tomb. (⇨墓)
● **墳墓の地** (先祖が埋葬されている場所) the place where one's ancestors are buried; (自分の一生を終えるつもりの地) a place to live for the rest of one's life.

ぶんぼ 分母 a denominator (↔a numerator). ● (最小)公分母 the (least) common *denominator*.

*__ぶんぽう 文法__ grammar. (❗つづり字に注意) ● 英文法 English *grammar*. ● 文法的な誤りをおかす make a *grammatical* mistake [a mistake in *grammar*]. ▶その文は文法的に正しい[正しくない] The sentence is *grammatical* [*ungrammatical*]./The sentence is *grammatically* correct [incorrect].
● **文法家** a grammarian. ● **文法書** a grammar (book).

ぶんぽう 分封 ── **分封する** 動 〖大名が〗 divide one's land and grant to one's subject(s); 〖ミツバチが〗 swarm; leave* the hive to establish a new one.

*__ぶんぽうぐ 文房具__ 《集合的》stationery (❗文房具の総称。つづり字に注意)〖関連〗stationary 立ったままの, 動かない); 〖筆記用具〗writing matèrials.
● **文房具屋** (店) a státionery stòre [shòp]; a stationer's; (人) a stationer.

ふんまつ 粉末 图 powder. ● 粉末にする powder. ● 粉末になる turn to *powder*.
── **粉末の** 形 powdered.
● **粉末コーヒー** powdered coffee.

ぶんまつ 文末 (at) the end of a sentence.

ふんまん 憤懣 (不正行為などに対する) indignation; (態度や言葉に表れる) resentment; (激しい) a rage. ● 憤懣やるかたない be filled with *indignation* [*resentment*]; be *indignant* [*resentful*] 《*at, about*》.

ぶんみゃく 文脈 context. ● この文脈では in this *context*. ● 文脈から単語の意味を知る learn the meaning of a word from its *context*. ● 文脈から切り離された彼の発言 his remarks taken [quoted] out of (ˣthe) *context*.

ぶんみん 文民 a civilian.
● **文民統制** civilian control.

ふんむき 噴霧器 〖スプレー〗a spray, a sprayer; (香水などの) an atomizer.

*__ぶんめい 文明__ (a) civilization. (⇨文化) ● 西洋[古代; 物質]文明 Western [ancient; material] *civilization*. ● エジプト文明はナイル川流域に起こったと言われている It is said that Egyptian *civilization* started in the valley of the Nile. ● 原始人は私たちが思っていたよりも *civilized* していた The primitive people *were* more *civilized* than we thought. ▶文明は世界を滅ぼす(＝世界を滅ぼす可能性がある)ほどまでに戦争を育ててしまった *Civilization* has nurtured war to the extent (that) it could destroy the world. (❗「世界を滅ぼす可能性がある」の意を表すのに could と仮定法を用いていることに注意)
● **文明開化** civilization and enlightenment. ● **文明国** a civilized country. ● **文明社会** a civilized society. ● **文明の利器** (現代の便利な物) a modern convenience. (❗modern conveniences では「近代[最新式]設備」の意) ● **文明病** diseases of civilization; (性病) a venereal disease.

ぶんめい 文名 《win [(確立する) build up, have]》a reputation as a good writer [a man of letters].

ぶんめん　文面（手紙の要旨）the content [《書》purport] of one's letter. ▶この手紙の文面から察すると, 彼はかなり困っているようだ Judging from (*the way he wrote*) this letter, he seems very troubled./(…のように読める) His letter reads that he is in trouble.

ぶんもん　噴門〖解剖〗the cardia.
● **噴門痙攣**(ケイレン)〖医学〗cardiospasm.

*****ぶんや　分野**（研究や活動の）a field,《やや書》a realm /rélm/. ●研究分野 a *field* of research. ●新分野を切り開く open (up) a new *field*. ▶あなたの専門分野は何ですか What is your special *field*?/What is your specialty? ▶彼は物理学の分野でよく知られている He is well known in the *field* [*realm*] of physics.

ぶんよ　分与 ── **分与する**〖動〗(財産を) settle 《an acre of land》on 《him》.〖!〗settle には生前または遺言による贈与の両方が含まれる; (配る, 分ける) distribute.

ぶんらく　文楽 *Bunraku*, a *Bunraku* puppet show;（説明的に）a classical Japanese puppet show where the puppets move to a story that is chanted to *samisen* music.

*****ぶんり　分離**〖名〗separation. ●政教分離 (⇨政教分離)
● 分離独立運動 a separatist movement.
── **分離する**〖動〗séparàte《A *from* B》. ●石を砂と分離する *separate* the stones *from* the sand. ▶クリームはミルクから分離した The cream *separated from* the milk.

ぶんりがくぶ　文理学部《米》the college [《英》the faculty] of literature and science.

ぶんりつ　分立〖名〗〖分離〗(a) separation;〖分割〗(a) division;〖独立〗independence. ●三権分立 *division* of power. (⇨三権分立)
── **分立する**〖動〗separate (*from*);〖独立する〗become* independent (*of*).

ぶんりゅう　噴流 a jet (stream).
ぶんりゅう　分流 a branch (of a river);（支流）a tributary;〖分かれた派〗a faction. (⇨分派)
ぶんりゅう　分留 fractional distillation.

*****ぶんりょう　分量** (a) quantity, (an) amount (⇨量);〖薬の服用量〗a dose /dóus/. ▶ここに十分な分量のミルクがあります We have a sufficient *quantity* [*amount*] of milk here.〖!〗《話》では We have *enough* milk here. の方が普通. ▶薬の分量を間違って飲まないように注意しなさい Be careful not to take a wrong *dose* of medicine.

*****ぶんるい　分類**〖名〗classification; sorting. ●植物の分類 the *classification* of plants.

── **分類する**〖動〗classify;（グループに分ける）group;（仕分けする）sort…(out). ●本を著者別[アルファベット順]に分類する *classify* the books *by* their authors [*in* 《×an》alphabetical order]; *sort* (*out*) the books *according to* their authors [*into* alphabetical order]. ▶それらは題目によって三つの種類に分類することができる They can *be classified* [*grouped, divided*] *into* three classes according to subjects. ▶その本は伝記として分類されていますかそれとも小説としてですか Is that book *classified as* biography or fiction? ▶この本はノンフィクションに分類される This book *comes* [*falls, is classified*] *under* "Nonfiction."
● 分類表 a classificátion tàble.

ぶんれい　奮励 ── **奮励(努力)する** exert oneself, try [do] one's best. (⇨頑張る)

ぶんれい　文例〖模範的な文, 文章〗model [exemplary] writing;〖用例〗an example;〖引用例〗a citation. ●手紙の文例集 a collection of exemplary letters.

*****ぶんれつ　分裂**〖名〗(a) division;（仲間割れ）a split.
● 細胞分裂 cell *division*. ●党の分裂 a *split in* the party.
── **分裂する**〖動〗〖意見などが分かれる〗divide; be divided（通例二つに分かれることを含意する. 明確にしたいときは into three などを後につける);〖政党などが分裂する〗split*, be split;〖関係が壊れる〗break* up. ▶その問題で我々の意見が分裂した We [Our opinions] *were divided on* the issue. (〖!〗この場合は We *divided on* the issue. とするのはまれ)/(意見が一致しなかった) We *didn't agree on* the issue./The issue *divided* us. ▶その政党は2派[右派と左派]に分裂した The party *split* (*up*) *into* two factions [the right and the left]. ▶消費税問題で党は大きく分裂している The party *is* deeply *split on* [*over*] the consumption tax issue.
● 分裂症〖医学〗(精神分裂症) schizophrenia. (〖参考〗日本では2002年に「統合失調症」に名称変更)

ぶんれつ　分列 ● (閲兵式の)分列行進する a march-past. ●分列行進をして通り過ぎる *march past*《the prime minister's stand》.

ふんわり〖副〗(柔らかく) softly;（軽やかに） lightly. ▶大きな雲がふんわり青空に浮かんでいる There is a large cloud floating *lightly* in the blue sky. ▶飛行船がふんわりと着陸した An airship landed *softly* on the ground.
── **ふんわりした**〖形〗● ふんわりしたセーター a *fluffy* [a *soft*] sweater. ● ふんわりしたカーペット a *deep-sinking* carpet.

へ

へ 屁 《卑》 a fart. ● 屁をひる 《卑》 fart. (⇨おなら)
● 屁とも思わない ▶ そんなことは屁とも思わない 《話》 I don't care [give] *a damn* about it.
● 屁にもならない ▶ そんなものは屁にもならない (＝取るに足らない)《話》 It's *not worth a fig*.

：へ 〔格助詞〕 ❶ [方向, 方角] (向かって) *for …*; (へ, まで) *to …*; (方へ) *toward …*. (⇨-に) ▶ 成田からローマへたつ leave Narita *for* Rome. (❕leave *from* Narita … や ×leave Narita *to* [*toward*] Rome は不可) ▶ ドアの方へ歩いて行く walk *to* [*toward*] the door (❕toward は方向を示すだけだが, to は到着点を含意し, ドアのところまで行ったことを暗示する) ▶ 一行はロンドンの方へ向かっていた The party was heading *for* London. ▶ 私たちは大阪へ向かう列車に乗り込んだ We took a train (bound) *for* Osaka. ▶ 3時までに家へ帰って来るんですよ You must come [get] (×to) *home* by three (o'clock). (❕home は副詞で「家へ」の意)

❷ [相手, 対象] *to …*; *for …*. (⇨-に) ▶ 月に1度故郷の両親へ手紙を書く I write *to* my parents at home once a month. ▶ これは彼への贈り物です This is a present [a gift] *for* him. (❕for は「…あての」)

❸ [中へ, 上へ] (中へ) *into …*; (上へ) *on …*. (⇨-に) ▶ 荷物はロッカーへしまいなさい Put your things (away) *into* the locker. ▶ 植木鉢はこの棚へのせておこう I'll put the flower pot *on* this shelf.

❹ [事態] (…しているときに) *just when* [*as*] …. ▶ 妹とけんかしているところへ友達がやって来た A friend of mine came *just when* [*as*] I was quarrelling with my sister. (❕just when はしばしば迷惑であることを暗示する)

ヘア [頭髪] hair; [陰毛] pubic hair. (❕英語の hair には pubic hair の意はない)
● ヘアオイル a hair òil. ● ヘアカット a haircut. ● ヘアスタイル a hairstyle; (男の) a haircut; (女の)《話》a háirdo (～s). ● ヘアスプレー a háir spráy. ● ヘアドライヤー a hair drýer [drier]. ● ヘアトニック a háir tònic. ● ヘアヌード a nude (photo) showing pubic hair. ● ヘアバンド a headband. ● ヘアピース 《婉曲的》 a háir pìece; (男性用) a háir toupèe /tuːpéɪ/. ● ヘアブラシ a hairbrush. ● ヘアピン (⇨ヘアピン) ● ヘアマニキュア háir còloring. ● ヘアリキッド háir líquid. ● ヘアローション háir lòtion.

ベア 《米》a (pay) raise; 《英》a (pay) rise. (⇨昇給)

ペア a pair. ● ペアで in *pairs*. ● ペア《そろいの服》を着ている若夫婦 a young couple in *matching* [(同じ)*the same*] clothes. (❕in pair look とはいわない) ▶ テニスで彼とペアを組むか I be paired [be *partnered* (*up*)] with him in tennis.
● ペアガラス (複層ガラス) double glazing; 《和製語》pair glass. ● ペアガラスの窓 a *double-glazed* window.

ヘアピン a hairpin; 《米》a bobby pin, 《英》a hairgrip. ● ヘアピンカーブ (道路の) a hairpin 《米》turn [《英》bend]. (⇨カーブ)

ベアリング [軸受け] a bearing.

***ヘい** 塀 《さく》a fence. (⇨壁) [注] ● れんが塀 a brick *wall*. ● 板塀 a board [a wooden] *fence*. ● 家に塀をめぐらす surround a house with a *wall* [a *fence*]; build a *wall* [a *fence*] around a house. ● 塀ごしに見る look over a *wall*. ● 塀に激突する crash into a *wall*. ● 塀際でフライを捕る catch a fly ball at [against] the wall; make a near-the-fence catch of a fly ball. ▶ 泥棒は塀をよじ登って庭に降りた The thief climbed over the *wall* (and got) into the garden.

へい 丙 [順序, 等級] (3番目) the third; (3級) (the) third (class); (成績の可) grade C, a "C" 《⑩ C's》. ● 物理で丙をとる get a *C* in physics.

へい 兵 [軍隊] an army; troops (❕「兵士」の集まりの意); (兵士) a soldier; men (❕将校に対して). ● 士官と兵 officers and *men*. ● 兵を挙げる raise an *army*. ● 兵を進める [引く] move [pull out] *troops*.

へい 弊 (悪い慣習) (an) evil practice; a bad custom; 《書》a malady. ● 多年の弊 (＝宿弊) を除く eliminate maladies of long standing. (⇨悪弊, 弊害)

ペイ [報酬] pay; (a) salary. (⇨給料) ▶ この値段ではペイしない (＝引き合わない) It doesn't *pay* at this price.

へいあん 平安 图 peacefulness; (平穏) peace; (平静) calmness. ● 心の平安 *peace* of mind.
—— 平安な 形 peaceful, calm /kάːm/.
—— 平安に 副 peacefully; in peace.
● 平安時代 [歴史] the Heian Period.

へいい 平易 —— 平易な 形 [平明な] plain; [簡単な] simple; [容易な] easy. ● 平易な英語で書かれた本 a book written in *plain* [*simple*, *easy*] English.
—— 平易に 副 ▶ 平易に言えば to put [putting] it *plainly* [*simply*]. ● 説明を平易にする *simplify* an explanation.

へいいん 兵員 (数) (the number of) soldiers. ● 兵員を増強 [削減] する increase [reduce] *the number of soldiers*; 《話》beef up [cut] *trooops*.

へいいん 閉院 —— 閉院する 動 [病院などが] (1日の業務を) close (down [up]); (廃院にする) close (down). (❕意味をはっきりさせるために for good など を添えることがある)

へいえい 兵営 barracks. (❕単・複両扱い)

へいえき 兵役 military service. ● 兵役に服する serve in the military [(陸軍) army, (海軍) navy]. ● 兵役を免除される be exempt from *military service*.

へいえん 閉園 图 closing (down) 《of a zoo [a kindergarten]》.
—— 閉園する 動 ▶ その植物園は午後6時に閉園する The botanical garden is *closed* at 6 p.m. ▶ 本日閉園 (掲示) *Closed* for Today.

ペイオフ a payout limit system; 《和製語》payoff.

へいおん 平穏 图 [平和] peace; [静けさ, 安らかさ] quiet, quietness; [平静, 落ち着き] calmness. ● 平穏無事に暮らす live *in peace and quiet*; live a *peaceful* [*quiet*] life.
—— 平穏な 形 peaceful; quiet; calm. ● 平穏な時代に in *peaceful* [*quiet*, *calm*] times. ● 平穏な土曜の晩 a *quiet* Saturday evening. ▶ その村は昔と同様だった The Village was as *calm and quiet* as it was.

へいか 兵火 [戦禍] war damage; the ravages of war; [戦火] war. ● 兵火の巷(ちまた) the scene of

へいか 平価 parity; par (value). ●購買力平価 purchasing power *parity*.
●平価切り上げ revaluation. ●平価切り下げ devaluation.

へいか 陛下 His [Her] Majesty; (両陛下) Their Majesties. (❗呼びかけや you の代わりに用いるときは Your Majesty. 両陛下に対しては Your Majesties. [His, Her, Your] Majesty は三人称単数扱い) ●天皇陛下 *His Majesty* the Emperor. ●皇后陛下 *Her Majesty* the Empress. ●女王陛下 *Her Majesty* the Queen. ●天皇皇后両陛下 *Their Majesties* the Emperor and Empress.

へいか 米価 the price of rice, the rice price. ●消費者[生産者]米価 the consumer [producer] *rice price*.
●米価審議会 the Rice Price Council.

へいか 米菓 rice crackers.

へいかい 閉会 ⓐ the closing of a meeting. ●閉会の辞を述べる give a *closing* address; make *closing* remarks. ▶閉会を宣言いたします. 皆様ありがとうございました I declare the *meeting closed*. Thank you Ladies and Gentlemen. ▶国会は閉会中です The Diet is not *in session*.
── 閉会する ⓥ close (a meeting).
●閉会式 the clósing (↔opening) cèremony.

*****へいがい 弊害** ⓐ a bad [an evil, a harmful] effect 《on》 (⇒害); [悪影響] a harmful [a bad] influence. ▶喫煙は健康にさまざまな弊害をもたらす Smoking brings about a lot of *bad effects on* [*causes a lot of harm to*] health.

へいかつ 平滑 ── 平滑な ⓐ smooth and flat.
●平滑筋 [解剖] a smooth muscle.

へいかん 閉館 ⓐ ●閉館時間を延長する extend the *opening* hours. (❗日本語と考え方が逆) ●本日閉館 (揭示) *Closed* today.
── 閉館する ⓥ ▶図書館は6時に閉館します This library closes at six.

へいがん 併願 ── 併願する ⓥ ▶二つの大学に併願する apply to two universities.

へいき 平気 ⓐ [平静な] calm /ká:m/; (冷静な) cool; [無関心な] indifferent 《to》, (心配しない) unconcerned 《about》. ▶彼は父の死の報に接しても平気なふりをした He pretended *calmness* to *be calm*, not to *turn a hair* at the news of his father's death. (❗最後は口語的な表現) ▶彼は危機にあっても平気な様子だった He looked *calm* [*cool*] in the crisis. ▶彼女は人が苦しんでいてもまったく平気だ(=無頓着(ちゃく)だ) She *is* quite *indifferent* [*shows* complete *indifference*] to other people's sufferings./She *is* quite *unconcerned about* other people's sufferings. ▶人が何と言おうと私は平気だ(=気にしない) I *don't care* [*couldn't care less*] 《about》 what people say. (❗通例 wh- 節の前では about は省略される) ▶暑さなんかまったく平気だ(=いやでない) I *don't mind* the heat at all. 会話(うっかりぶつかって)「おっと！ごめん！」「大丈夫. 平気だよ(=大したことない)」 "Oops /wúəps/! Sorry!" "That's OK. It *doesn't matter.*"
── 平気で[に] ⓥ calmly. ▶彼は平気で(=何事もなかったように)ふるまっていた He behaved *as* (*calmly as*) *if nothing had happened to* him. ▶彼は平気でうそをつく(何とも思わない) He *thinks nothing of* telling lies./(ためらわずに) He tells lies *without scruple*.

へいき 兵器 arms; a weapon /wépn/, (集合的に) weaponry. ●細菌[化学]兵器 a bacteriological [a chemical] *weapon*.

●兵器庫 an armory; an arsenal. ●兵器工場 an árms [a wéapons] fàctory.

へいき 併記 ── 併記する ⓥ ●両論を併記する write [put] down the opinions of both sides. (❗write... down は「...をしっかりと記録にとどめる」の意)

:**へいきん 平均** ❶ [均ずすこと] an average.
① 平均～ ▶このクラスの平均点は何点ですか What's [×How many is] the *average* grade in this class? ▶少年たちの平均身長は170センチです The *average* height of the boys is 170 centimeters [5.5 feet]./The boys *average* 170 centimeters [5.5 feet] in height. (❗この average は「平均して...になる」の意の自動詞) 事情 米英では単位は feet の方が普通) ▶東京の年間平均降雨量はサンフランシスコの約3倍である The *average* annual rainfall in Tokyo is about three times (as large as) that in San Francisco. ▶彼は成績は平均以上[以下]です His school work is *above* [*below*] *average*./He is *above* [*below*] *average* in school work.
② 平均は ●全国平均 the national *average*. ▶3と5と7の平均は5です The *average* of 3, 5, and 7 is 5.
③ 平均(して) ●期末試験で平均70点[良]をとる get an *average* grade of 70 [a B average] on the term exam. ▶彼は平均週5日働く He works five days a week *on* (*an* [*the*]) *average*./He *averages* five days' work a week. (❗この average は「平均して...する」の意の他動詞) ▶同国の経済は年平均約10パーセントの成長を続けてきた The country's economy has grown at an annual *average* rate of about 10 percent.

❷ [均衡] balance. ▶彼は体の平均を失って川に落ちた He lost his *balance* and fell into the river. ▶彼は片足で体の平均を保った He kept his *balance* [*He balanced himself*] on one foot.
── 平均の ⓐ average; (普通の) ordinary. ●平均的な学生 an *average* [an *ordinary*] student.
●平均株価 a stock (price) average; a market average. ●平均気温 the average temperature. ●平均給与 the average salary. ●平均寿命 the average life span [expectancy]. ●平均台 a balance beam. (❗競技種目をさす場合は (do) the ～) ●平均値 the mean (value). ●平均賃金 the average wage.

へいけい 閉経 ⓐ menopause, the change of life. ▶彼女は55歳のときに閉経をむかえた She reached the *menopause* at the age of fifty five.
── 閉経期の ⓐ menopausal.

へいげい 睥睨 ── 睥睨する ⓥ ▶天下を睥睨する(自分が乗り出す機会を虎視眈々とねらっている) carefully watch for a chance to come to the fore (as a politician); (にらみつけて周りを威圧する) domineer over people with a coercive look.

へいけものがたり『平家物語』 *The Tale of the Heike*. (参考 鎌倉時代の軍記物)

古今ことばの系譜『平家物語』
祇園(ぎおん)精舎(しょうじゃ)の鐘の声, 諸行無常の響きあり. 沙羅(しゃら)双樹(そうじゅ)の花の色, 盛者(じょうしゃ)必衰のことわりをあらわす. おごれる人も久しからず, ただ春の夜の夢のごとし. The bells of the Gion Temple tell us that all things are transient and not eternal. When we see the camellia flowers fall, we know that prosperity cannot continue forever. The life of the arrogant is never everlasting. All things are like dreams in a spring night.

(!)(1)「祇園精舎」は釈迦とその教団のために建てられた寺院。(2)「沙羅双樹」(sal trees)はフタバガキ科の常緑高木で、釈迦入滅の時に、その四方にこの木が一対ずつあったという。一説に、日本で見られるのはツバキ科蕃葉樹の「ナツツバキ」で、花は白く、朝咲いて夕方には散ることから『平家物語』でこのように述べられているという。sal という名はあまりよく知られていないので、ここではcamellia とした。

へいげん 平原 a plain. (⇨平野)

べいご 米語 American English;〖米国語法〗an Americanism (↔a Briticism).

***へいこう** 平行 图〖数学〗parallelism.
— 平行な 厖 parallel (to, with). ●線Aと平行な線を引きなさい Draw a line *parallel to* line A./Draw a *parallel to* line A.
— 平行する 動 ●鉄道は高速道路と平行して走っている The railroad line *runs parallel to* [*with*] the superhighway.
●平行線をたどる ▶彼らの話し合いは平行線をたどった(=議論がかみ合わなかった) Their discussions did *not get anywhere* [*got nowhere*]./(議論をし続けたが合意に至らなかった) They went on discussing but did*n't come to* [*reach*] *an agreement*.
●平行移動〖数学〗parallel translation. ●平行四辺形 a pàrállélogràm. ●平行線 parallel lines. ●平行棒〖体操〗(the) párallèl bárs. (!競技種目としてはつをつけるのが普通。「段違い平行棒」は (the) uneven (parallel) bars)

へいこう 平衡 〖釣り合い〗balance, equilibrium /ìːkwəlíbriəm/. (!前の方が一般的) ●釣り合い, バランス) ●体の平衡を保つ[失う] keep [lose] one's *balance*. ▶スケーターは体の平衡を失って転倒した The skater lost her *balance* [*equilibrium*] and fell.
●平衡感覚 the sense of balance [equilibrium].

へいこう 並行 — 並行して 副 go* abreast (of); (道などが並んで通る) run* side by side 《with》. ●彼と並行して走る run *abreast of* [*with*] him. ▶2人の容疑者の取り調べは並行して行われた The two suspects were interrogated *at the same time*.
●並行輸入 parallel importing.

へいこう 閉口 — 閉口する 動 〖悩まされる〗be annoyed (at, by, with) (=悩ます);〖当惑する〗be embarrassed. (⇨当惑する) ▶この暑さには閉口する(=我慢できない) I *can't stand* [*bear*] this heat. ▶彼の講演には全く閉口した(=うんざりした) His lecture was quite *boring*./〖話〗I *got sick and tired of* [*got fed up with*] his lecture.

へいこう 閉校 — 閉校する 動 close (down) the school (for good).

へいごう 併合 图 (BによるAの) the annexation 《of A by B》.
— 併合する 動 (国・領土を) (やや書) annex. (⇨合併, 吸収) ▶その小国はロシアに力ずくで併合された The small country *was forcibly annexed to* Russia.

***べいこく** 米国 〖国名〗the (United) States,《書》the United States of America 《略 the U.S.,《書》the U.S.A.》;《話》America. (首都 Washington, D.C.) (⇨アメリカ❶) ●米国人 an American ●米国(人)の American;(総称) American people,《やや書》the Americans.
●米国政府 the U.S. Government.

べいこく 米穀 rice.
●米穀商[店] a rice dealer [shop]. ●米穀年度 the rice year.

へいごま 貝独楽 (spin) a conch-shaped top.

へいこら — へいこらする 動 kowtow /káutáu/;(相手の言うなりとする) be submissive (to). (⇨ぺこぺこ)

***へいさ** 閉鎖 图 〖店・工場などの〗a close-down, a shut-down; (労働者の締め出し) (a) lockout.
— 閉鎖的な 厖 closed. ●閉鎖的な社会 a *closed* society.
— 閉鎖する 動 〖学校・道などを〗close (!使用を停止[中止]すること),〖店・工場などの業務を〗close down, (一時的に) shut*... down, (経営者側が) lock... out. ▶工場では閉鎖されるだろう The factory is going to *be closed down* [閉鎖になる) *close down*] soon. ▶空港は霧のため閉鎖された The airport *was closed* because of (the) fog. (⇨閉まる)

へいさく 平作 (平年作) an average crop [harvest].
べいさく 米作 〖栽培〗rice growing;〖米の収穫〗a rice crop [harvest].
●米作地帯 a rice-producing district.
へいさつ 併殺 a double play. (⇨ダブルプレー)
へいざん 閉山 — 閉山する 動 (登山を許可しない) close the mountain to climbers; (鉱山などを) close (down) the 《coal》 mine; shut* down the 《coal》 mine.
べいさん 米産 ●米産地 a rice-producing district. ●米産国 a rice-producing country.
へいし 兵士 〖陸軍の〗a soldier;〖海軍の〗a sailor. (⇨軍人, 兵隊)
へいし 閉止 (permanent) stopping.
へいじ 平時 — 平時の 厖 peacetime (↔wartime).
●平時に in *peacetime*. ●平時にも戦時にも in war and *peace*. (!語順に注意)
へいじつ 平日 (日曜日(と土曜日)以外の日) a weekday; (仕事の日) a workday; (日曜日(と土曜日)以外の1週間) a (wórking) wèek. ●平日どおり(いつものように) as usual. ▶あの店は平日は開いている That store is open *on weekdays*. (!《話》では on はしばしば省略する)
会話 「それでは朝食を食べる暇がないじゃないの」「そうだよ. 平日はね」 "So you don't have time to eat breakfast, do you?" "I don't, during the *week*."

へいしゃ 兵舎 bárracks. (!単・複両扱い)
へいしゃ 弊社 our company; we.
べいじゅ 米寿 one's 88th (calendar) year. (⇨還暦)
へいしゅう 弊習 ●弊習を打破する break an evil [a bad, a corrupt] custom.
べいしゅうきこう 米州機構 the Organization of American States (略 OAS).
へいじゅん 平準 ●国民の生活の平準化を推し進める go ahead with a plan to *equalize* the standard of living of the people.
へいしょ 兵書 a book on military science.
へいしょ 閉所 a small closed-in place.
●閉所恐怖症 claustrophobia /klɔ̀ːstrəfóubiə/. ●閉所恐怖症者 a claustrophobic.
へいじょ 平叙 ●平叙文 the statement of a fact.
●平叙文〖文法〗a declarative sentence.
へいじょう 平常 图〖標準となるもの〗normal;〖標準の状態〗normal conditions. ●平常心で行動する act *with* (one's) *presence of mind*. ▶水位は平常より15センチ高い[低い] The water level is 15 centimeters *above* [*below*] *normal*. ▶彼は平常どおり9時に[平常より15分遅れて]店を開けた He opened the store at nine o'clock *as usual* [15 minutes later *than usual*].
— 平常の 厖 (標準の) normal; (平素の) usual; (通常の) ordinary; (毎日の) everyday. ▶列車のダイヤは平常に戻った The railroad [train] service returned [was back,《書》was restored] to *normal*.
— 平常に 副 usually; normally; ordinarily. (⇨普

へいじょう 通, 普段, 通例, 通常)
● **平常点** (教室での) a grade 《米》[a mark 《英》] for 《his》 class participation.

へいじょう 閉場 ── **閉場する** 動 close (the meeting room for voting); 〖営業をやめる〗 close (down) [shut* down] 《the theater [market]》 (for good).

べいしょく 米食 ▶朝は米食だ We have a rice-based breakfast./We eat *rice* for breakfast. ▶日本人は米食だ The Japanese eat *rice* as a staple diet./The staple diet is *rice* here in Japan.（**!** a staple diet は「主食」の意）

へいしんていとう 平身低頭 ── **平身低頭する** 動 bow deeply; (ひざまずいて) go* [get*] down on one's knees. ● 平身低頭して(=謙虚に)謝る apologize (most) humbly; make a *humble* apology 《to》.

へいすい 平水 ❶〖平常の水のかさ〗the usual volume of water 《of the river》.
❷〖波立っていない水面〗the calm [undisturbed] surface of the river [lake].

へいせい 平成 Heisei. ▶私は平成元年卒業だ I graduated in 1989 [in *the* first *year of Heisei*].（**!** 特に日本の元号を明記する必要がある場合を除いて、西暦を用いる）

へいせい 平静 图 〖落ち着き〗calmness; 〖沈着〗《やや書》 composure, presence of mind; 〖穏〗peace; 〖静けさ、安らかさ〗quiet. ● 心の平静を保つ [失う] keep [lose] one's *composure* [*presence of mind*].
── **平静な** 形 calm; composed; peaceful; quiet.
● 平静な行動 *calm* [*composed*] behavior.
── **平静に** 副 ▶彼は怒りを抑えて平静に答えた He controlled his anger and answered *calmly*. ▶町はまもなく平静になった The town soon became *quiet* [*peaceful*].

へいぜい 平生 〖⇨日頃, 普段, 毎日, 平常〗

へいせき 兵籍 military status.

へいせつ 併設 ── **併設する** 動 (付属としてBにAを立する) set* up [establish] A as an ánnex to B; (付属しているの) be attáched 《to》. ▶その大学には幼稚園が併設されている A kindergarten *is attached to* the college.

へいぜん 平然 ── **平然とした** 形 (落ち着いた) calm; (冷静な) cool. 〖⇨平気〗
── **平然と** 副 calmly; coolly.

へいそ 平素 (⇨日頃(ご)) ▶平素のごぶさた(=長い間の音信不通)をおわび申し上げます I must apologize (to you) for my *long* silence.

へいそう 兵曹 (旧海軍の) a petty officer.
● **兵曹長** a chief petty officer.

へいそう 並走, 併走 ── **並走[併走]する** 動 run* abreast 《with》.

へいそく 閉塞 图 (a) blockage; 〖医学〗(管, 主に血管の) occlusion /əklúːʒən/. ● **腸閉塞**(=腸) ▶時代の閉塞感を打ち破る get rid of [do away with] the sense that the world is blocked up.
── **閉塞する** 動 block up; blocade.
● **閉塞前線** 〖気象〗an occluded front.

へいぞく 平俗 ── **平俗な** 形 mediocre; (俗な) vulgar; common; 〖文章などが〗(分かりやすい) easy; (単純明快な) plain; (文語に対し口語的な) colloquial.

へいそつ 兵卒 a private (soldier).

へいそん 併存, 並存 图 coexistence.
── **併存[並存]する** 動 coexist 《with》.

へいたい 兵隊 〖陸軍の〗a soldier; 〖軍隊の〗troops ● 軍人, 将校) 〖将校に対して〗(集合的) the rank and file (**!** 単・複両扱い). ● 兵隊ごっこをする play (at being) *soldiers*.

へいたん 平坦 ── **平坦な** 形 ● 平坦な小道 an *even* [a *flat*, a *smooth*] path. ● 道を平坦にする *level* a road. 〖⇨平ら, 平たい〗
● **平坦地** the flatlands.

へいたん 平淡 ── **平淡な** 形 (すっきりした) neat; (ごてごてしていない) not heavy; (気取り, 飾り気のない) unaffected; simple.

へいたん 兵站 ● **兵站部**(軍隊の) a supply base; (主に食糧の) a commissariat.

へいだん 兵団 a corps /kɔːr/ (**複** corps /kɔːrz/). (**!** 単・複両扱い)

へいち 平地 flat [level] land; flat [level] ground; (平らな地方) flat [level] country. (**!** 通例無冠詞)
● **平地に波乱を起こす** (わざともめごとを起こす) cause unnecessary trouble intentionally [on purpose].

へいちゃら (⇨へっちゃら)

へいちょう 兵長 (旧陸軍の) a lance corporal.

へいてい 平定 ── **平定する** 動 (鎮圧する) suppress, put*... down 《後の方が口語的な》; (制圧する) 《やや書》 súbjugate, 《書》 subject... to one's rule.
● 反乱を平定する *suppress* a rebellion [a revolt].
● 全国を平定する *bring* the whole country *under control*; *subject* the whole country *to* one's *rule*.

へいてい 閉廷 ── **閉廷する** 動 dismiss (a) court. ▶これより3月15日まで閉廷とする The court *is adjourned* until March 15.

へいてん 閉店 图 ▶本日閉店(=休業中) 〖掲示〗*Closed* today.
── **閉店する** 動 close 《a store》; (廃業する) close 《a store》 down. ▶午後7時に閉店します This store *closes* at seven./We *close* at seven. (**!** We= Our store. 次例も同様) ▶閉店しました We *are* [×were] *closed*.
● **閉店時間** the clósing tìme [hòur]. ▶閉店時間でございます (客に) I'm afraid it's time to *close*.

へいてん 弊店 our 《米》 store [《英》 shop]; we.

へいどく 併読 ── **併読する** 動 (新聞などを同時に) take* [subscribe to] two newspapers; (2つ(以上)の小説などを並行して読む) read* two novels at the same time.

へいどん 併呑 annexation. (⇨併合)

へいねつ 平熱 (a) normal (body) temperature. ▶薬で平熱になった My temperature *has become normal* with the medicine. 〖**事情**〗米英では37℃ (約99°F) を平熱としている ▶平熱より2度高かった My temperature was two degrees *above normal*.

へいねん 平年 〖例年〗a normal [an average] year (⇨例年); 〖うるう年でない年〗a common year. ▶今年の冬の降雪量は平年を上[下]回った Snowfall was *above* [*below*] *normal* this winter. ▶収穫高は平年並みでしょう The crops will be about the *average*.
● **平年作** a normal [an average] crop.

へいば 兵馬 〖兵士と馬〗soliders and horses; 〖軍備〗arms; armaments; 〖軍隊〗troops.
● **兵馬の権** ● 兵馬の権を握る(握っている) get [have] supreme command of the armed forces.

へいばい 併売 ── **併売する** 動 sell* 《workbooks》 together with 《textbooks》.

へいはつ 併発 图 〖余病〗a complication.
── **併発する** 動 ▶彼女は流感から肺炎を併発した Pneumonia followed her influenza as a *complication*./(流感が肺炎に進展した) influenza

へいはん 平版 (平版で刷ったもの) a planograph.
● 平版印刷 planography.

へいはん 平板 ― 平板な 形 〖文章・話などが〗(単調な) flat, monotonous; (退屈な) dull, boring. ● 平板に堕した描写 a *flat*, uninteresting description. ▶彼の講演は平板で(=退屈で)中座したい気持ちだった I felt like going out in the middle of his speech. It was so *boring*.

べいはん 米飯 boiled rice.

へいび 兵備 (⇨軍備)

へいふう 弊風 a bad [an evil] custom. ● 世の弊風に染まる be infected with the *evil ways* of the world.

へいふく 平伏 ― 平伏する 動 prostrate oneself (《*before*》 the king).

へいふく 平服 (普段着) everyday clothes [wear], an ordinary [an everyday] dress; (制服に対して私服) one's plain [civilian] clothes. ▶平服でご出席ください《招待状》No dress./《話》Dress casual.

へいへい (⇨へいこら)

―へいべい ―平米 ...square meters. ● 200 平米の土地 two hundred *square meters* of land.

べいべい (経験が乏しくだまされやすい人)《話》a greenhorn (! 通例男性); (新参者) a beginner, a novice /návɪs/.

へいへいたんたん 平々坦々 ● 平々坦々たる原野 the *very flat* wilds.

へいへいぼんぼん 平々凡々 ● 平々凡々たる(=変化がまったくない)凡庸な生活を送る lead a *humdrum* life.

へいほう 平方 a square. ● 100 平方メートルの土地 one hundred *square meters* of land. ● 3 フィート平方のテーブル a table 3 feet *square*. ● 5 の平方は 25 である The *square* of 5 is 25. ● 1 平方フィートは 144 平方インチである A *square* foot has 144 *square* inches.
● 平方根 a square root.

へいほう 兵法 (個々の戦いの) tactics; (戦争を大局的に見ての) strategy. (⇨戦術)

*__へいぼん 平凡__ ― 平凡な** 形 〖普通に見かける〗 common; 〖特別でなく普通の〗 ordinary; 〖ごく普通の〗(軽蔑的) mediocre /miːdióʊkər/; 〖特色のない〗(やや書) featureless; 〖事件のない〗 uneventful. ● 平凡な体験 a *common* experience. ● 平凡な人間 a mediocrity /miːdiákrəti/; (普通の平均的な人) an ordinary [an *average*] person. ● 平凡な顔 a *common* [a *featureless*] face. ● 平凡な日々 *uneventful* days. ▶彼は平凡な作家などではない He is no *ordinary* [*mediocre*] writer. (! この no は「決して...ない」の意の副詞)

へいまく 閉幕 the final curtain. ▶10 時閉幕 The *curtain falls* [*comes down*] at ten.

べいまつ 米松 〖植物〗a Douglas fir [pine, spruce]; an Oregon pine.

へいみゃく 平脈 〖解剖〗one's normal pulse.

へいみん 平民 (貴族に対して) the common [ordinary] people. (! 集合的に. 一人をさす場合は a commoner)

へいめい 平明 ― 平明な 形 ● 平明な文章 (平易な) *plain* [*simple*, (明快かつやさしい) *lucid*] writing.

へいめん 平面 图 ● 平面を a plane.
― 平面の 形 〖数学〗planar; (平らな) flat; (二次元の) two-dimensional.
● 平面鏡 a plane mirror. ● 平面図 〖建築〗 a (ground) plan. ● 家の平面図 a house *plan*; a

plan for a house. ● 平面図形 a plane figure.

へいもん 閉門 ― 閉門する 動 close the gate(s). (! 複数形 gates は 2 枚, 上の門扉のある門の場合). ▶閉門7時《掲示》*Closed* at 7 p.m.

へいや 平野 a plain. (! しばしば複数形で) ● 関東平野 the Kanto *Plain*(s).

へいゆ 平癒 a (complete) recovery.
― 平癒する 動 make* a recovery; recover (《*from*》). ▶1 日も早いご平癒をお祈りいたしております I'm praying for your quick [*speedy*] *recovery*.

へいよう 併用 ― 併用する 動 use ... together [along] (《*with*》); use both ... and ... (at the same time). ▶この薬は他のどの薬とも併用してはいけない Don't *take* this medicine *together with* any other medicine.

へいらん 兵乱 (⇨② 戦乱)

へいり 弊履 ● 弊履のごとく捨てる 'throw ... away like a pair of worn-out shoes'; (なんの役にも立たない) throw ... away as absolutely [completely, totally] useless; (気にもとがめることなく) throw ... away without a qualm /kwάːm/.

へいりつ 並立 ― 並立する 動 stand* side by side (《*with*》); (張り合う) rival (《*with*》); 〖両立する〗 (⇨両立).

へいりょく 兵力 (武力) military strength; force of arms. (⇨武力) ▶兵力に訴える resort [appeal] to *arms*. ● 兵力を増強する reinforce [build up] *military strength*.

ベイルート 〖レバノンの首都〗Beirut /beɪrúːt/.

へいれつ 並列 (電気の) parallel (↔series). ● 電池を並列につなぐ connect batteries *in parallel*.
● 並列回路 a parallel circuit.

:へいわ 平和 图 (a) peace. (! 形容詞的に用いることもある) ● 世界平和のために for world *peace*; for the *peace* of the world. ● 60 年間の平和 sixty years of *peace*; a *peace* of sixty years (! 「平和な一期間」の意のときは不定冠詞がつく). ● 永遠の平和 a lasting *peace*. ● 平和を維持する maintain [keep] *peace*. ● 平和を祈る pray for *peace*. ▶その会談が両国に平和をもたらした The talks brought *peace* to both [of the] countries. ▶日本人は平和を愛する国民である The Japanese are a *peace-loving people*./Japanese people love *peace*.
― 平和(的)な 形 peaceful. ● 平和な[世界] a *peaceful* nation [world]. ● 平和的手段によって by *peaceful* means. ● 原子力の平和的利用 *peaceful* uses of nuclear energy. ● 平和な生活をする lead [live] a *peaceful* life; live *peacefully* [*in peace*]. ▶その国は平和である It is *peaceful* in the country. ▶その 2 国は現在平和的な関係にある The two countries are *at peace* now.
― 平和(的)に 副 peacefully. ● その紛争を平和的に解決する settle the dispute *peacefully* (〖友好的に〗 *amicably*). ● 再び平和になった Peace has come again [《戻った》 has returned].
● 平和維持活動 a péacekeeping operàtion 《略 PKO》. ● 平和維持軍 a péacekeeping fòrce 《略 PKF》. ● その兵士は 1 人の平和維持軍の兵士 a peacekeeper). ● 平和外交 peaceful diplomacy. ● 平和教育 péace educàtion. ● 平和共存 peaceful coexistence. ● 平和憲法 Japan's "Peace" Constitution. ● 平和使節 a péace mìssion. ● 平和主義 pacifism. ● 平和主義者 a pacifist. ● 平和条約 a péace trèaty.

ペイン 〖苦痛〗pain.
● ペインクリニック 〖苦痛緩和専門病院〗a páin clìnic.
● ペインコントロール 〖苦痛の緩和〗páin contròl.

ペインティング painting.
● ペインティングナイフ 〖油絵用のへら〗a páinting

ペイント (ペンキ) paint. (⇨ペンキ)

へえ 〖驚き, 疑い〗(おお) Oh!; (おや, まあ) Well!; Oh dear!, (まさか) Indeed!; (ああ困った)(My) God! ▶へえ, そうですか *Oh*, is that so?/*Oh*, really? (⇨まあ 圖) ▶へえ, こいつは驚いた *Well*, what a surprise! ▶へえ, 信じられない I can't believe it./(まさか)〘話〙You ˇdon't say (so)! 〘皮肉っぽい感じを伴う〙▶へえ(本当なの？)(計報にに接するなどのときよう) ˇ*Oh*, ˇ*no*!

会話 「軍隊に入ろうと思ってるんだ」「へえ, なんと. 軍隊にね. それは一大決心だわね」"I'm going to join the army." "*Gee*!/*Boy*!/*ˇAre you*? Joining the army. That's a big decision." (❗(1) ˇ*Are you?* の音調では「あっそう」「本当？」くらいの意となる. (2) *Boy*! は男女共に用いるが, 黒人に対しては軽蔑的なので避ける)

ベーカリー 〖パン屋〗a bakery.
ベーキングパウダー báking pòwder.
ベークライト 〖合成樹脂〗〖商標〗Bakelite.
ベーコン bacon. ▶ベーコン一切れ a slice of *bacon*.
● ベーコンエッグ bacon and /ən/ eggs.

***ページ** ❶〖本などの〗a page (略 p., 圏 pp.); (本の1枚, 2ページ) a leaf (圏 leaves).
①〘ページの〜〙● 80 ページの雑誌 a magazine of eighty *pages*; a eighty-*page* magazine. ● ページの上[真ん]中, 下[の方]に at the top [middle, bottom] of a *page*. ● ページの端を折る turn down the corner of a *page*. (❗「端を折ったページ」は a dog-eared page という) ▶その語は 3 ページの 10 行目に出ている You will find the word at line 10 *on* [ˣin] *page* 3./You will find the word in the tenth line of the third *page* [of page 3].
②〘ページを〙● カタログのページをぱらぱらとめくる turn (over) the *pages* [*leaves*] of a catalog quickly; leaf through a catalog. ▶この辞書は 2,000 ページを越す This dictionary has more than two thousand *pages* [is over 2,000 *pages* long]. ▶今何ページをやっているの What *page* are we on? ▶本の 10 ページを開きなさい. 今日はここから始めますよ Open your book(s) *to* [〘主に英〙*at*] *page* 10. [Turn to *page* 10.] Here's what we're going to study today. (❗ˣthe page 10 とはいわない) ▶ 50 ページ以下を見よ See *p.* 50 ff. (❗ ff. is following pages の略)
③〘ページから[に, まで]〙● 10 ページから 15 ページまで読む read pages 10 to 15 [*pp.* 10–15]. ▶試験範囲は 25 ページから 50 ページまでです The exam covers *pages* 25 to 50. ▶ 30 ページに[から]続く Continued on [from] *page* 30.
❷〖その他の表現〗▶それは我が国の歴史に輝かしい 1 ページとして記憶されるでしょう It will be remembered as a glorious *page* in our history.
● ページビュー 〖コンピュータ〗page view 《略 PV》.

ページェント 〖歴史事件を演出した野外劇〗a pagent /pǽdʒənt/.
ベーシック 〖コンピュータ〗BASIC 《*Beginner's All-purpose Symbolic Instruction Code* の略》.
ページボーイ 〖ホテルなどの給仕〗a page boy.
ベージュ beige /béiʒ/. ● ベージュの beige.
ベース ❶〖塁〗a base, a bag. ● 一塁ベース (ˣthe) first *base*. ● ベースから離れている be off (ˣthe) *base*. ● ベースタッチする touch a *base*. ● ベースを踏む step on the *bag*. ● 一塁ベースを踏み損なう miss first *base*. ▶フルベースになっている The *bases* are loaded [full]. (❗ˣfull bases としない)
❷〖基礎〗a basis (圏 bases); a base. ▶その考え方が彼の議論のベースになっていた The idea was the *basis* [*base*] of his argument. (❗ *basis* の方が普通)
● ベースアップ (⇨ベースアップ) ● ベースキャンプ (set up) a base camp. ● ベースコーチ 〖野球〗a base coach. ● ベースライン 〖野球・テニス〗a baseline. ● ベースランニング 〖野球〗baserunning.

ベース 〖低音歌手, 低音楽器〗a bass /béis/; 〖低音(部)〗bass. (⇨バス) ● ベースを弾く play the bass.
● ベース奏者 a bassist.
● a pace. ● ベースを速める[ゆるめる] quicken [slow down] one's *pace*. ● ベースをつかむ[に乗る] find [get into] one's *rhythm*. ● 1 シーズン 50 本のホームランベースで 〖野球〗be on pace for a 50-homer season. ▶彼の仕事のベースは速い(＝速いベースで仕事をする) He works at a fast *pace*. ▶彼のペースについていけなかった I couldn't keep *pace* with him [keep up with his *pace*]. ▶マイペースでいきます(守る) I will keep (up) [(進む) go at] my own *pace* [ˣmy pace]./I'll *pace* myself. ▶午後は仕事のペースが落ちる The work *slacks off* in the afternoon./Everyone *slacks off* at his 〘話〙their] work in the afternoon.

ベースアップ 图 a (pay) raise 《米》[rise 《英》]; 〘話〙a pay [a wage] hike; 《和製語》base up. ▶去年は 5 パーセントのベースアップがあった We got a 5 percent *raise* [*rise*] last year./Our salary went up [rose] by 5 percent last year.
── **ベースアップする** 動 give*(him) a raise [a rise] (in salary); (賃金ベースを上げる) raise the wage base.

ペースト paste. ● ペースト状の pasty.
ベースボール 〖野球〗baseball. (⇨野球)
ペースメーカー ❶〖競走での〗a pacemaker, a pacesetter. ● ペースメーカーになる set the pace 《in a race》.
❷〖脈拍調整器〗a pacemaker. ● ペースメーカーをつけている be fitted with a *pacemaker*.

ペーソス 〖哀愁〗〖書〗pathos.
ベータ ● ベータカロテン 〖化学〗béta càrotene.
● ベータ線 〖物理〗beta rays. ● ベータ版 〖コンピュータ〗the beta version.
ベーダ 〖バラモン教の聖典〗the Veda(s).
ベーチェットびょう ベーチェット病 〖医学〗Behçet's disease.
ベートーベン 〖ドイツの作曲家〗Beethoven /béitouvn/ (Ludwig van ～).
ペーハー 〖水素イオン濃度指数〗pH /pìːéitʃ/《*potential of hydrogen* の略》. ● ペーハー 5.5 の酸性雨 acid rain with *pH* 5.5 [a *pH* of 5.5].
ペーパー 〖紙〗paper; 〖論文〗a paper; 〖紙やすり〗sandpaper.
● ペーパーカンパニー (名義だけの) a dummy (company), (にせの) a bogus company. (❗a páper còmpany は「製紙会社」の意) ● ペーパークラフト papercraft. ● ペーパータオル a paper towel. ● ペーパーテスト a written test [exam]. (❗a paper test は「紙質検査」の意) ● ペーパードライバー a driver in name [on paper] only, (説明的には) a person who has a driver's licence but never drives; 《和製語》a paper driver. ● ペーパーナイフ 《米》a letter opener, 《英》a paper knife. ● ペーパーバック a paperback (book). ● ペーパープラン a deskplan, a plan on paper.

ぺこぺこ (⇨ぺいぺい)
ベーリング ● ベーリング海峡 the Bering Strait.
ベール 〖顔をおおう布〗a veil. ● ベールをかぶる[上げる; 取る] wear [raise; lift] a *veil*. ● 霧のベール a *veil* of mist. ● その中のベールに包まれている be hidden in a

veil of mystery.

ベオグラード 〖セルビアの首都〗 Belgrade /bèlgréid/; 〖セルビア語〗 Beograd.

ペガサス 〖ギリシア神話〗 Pegasus.

べからず 〖してはいけない〗 do not, don't; 〖…禁止〗 (❗ 掲示などで「no＋名詞」で表す). ▸エチケットべからず集 the *don'ts* of etiquette. ▸花をとるべからず《掲示》 *Do not* [*Don't*] pick the flowers. ▸ごみ捨てるべからず《掲示》 *No* dumping./*No* litter. ▸芝生に入るべからず《掲示》 *Keep off* the grass.

べき 冪 a power. (❷ 累乗)

‐べき ❶〖義務〗 (…しなければならない) must 《do》, have* to 《do》 (❗ must は話し手の主観, have to は外部の客観的な事情による義務を表し, must の方が意味が強い). (…するべきです) should 《do》, ought to 《do》. (…するべきだ, ought to のように) should は主観的, ought to は客観的な意味合いを含む) ▸法律には従うべきだ You *must* [*have to*] obey the law. ▸君は言いたいことを言うべきだったのに You *should* [*ought to*] have said what you wanted to say. (❗ 実際は言わなかったことを含意) ▸こんな危険な場所へ行くべきではない You *mustn't* [*shouldn't, oughtn't to*] go to such a dangerous place again.
会話「彼はまだ学校に来ていません」「彼の家に連絡してみるべきだと思う?」 "He hasn't come to school yet." "Do you think we *should* try his home?" ❷〖…したらいいのか〗〖what などの疑問詞＋to 不定詞〗で表す. why は除く) ▸次に何をすべきか分からない I don't know *what* to do [*what I should* do] next. ▸いかに生きるべきかをもっと真剣に考えなさい Think more seriously about *how* to [*how you should*] live. ❸〖その他の表現〗 ▸今日すべきことは何もない I have nothing to do today. ▸他に何かやるべきことは? (Is there) anything else *to* be done? ▸出発すべき時間です It's time (for you) *to* start./It's time you started. (❗ (that) 節内の動詞は直説法過去)

DISCOURSE
選挙権を持つ年齢を引き下げるべきと考える I *am of the view that* the voting age *should* be lowered. (❗ I am of the view that ... (私は…という見方である)は二者択一を表すディスコースマーカー)

へきえき 辟易 ── 辟易する 動 ▸私は彼女の愚痴には辟易している(=うんざりしている) I *am fed up with* her complaints./*I'm sick and tired of* her complaints.

へきえん 僻遠 ●僻遠の地 a remote [a distant] place.

へきが 壁画 a mural; a wall painting. (❗ 主にフレスコ画(a fresco)をさす)

へきがん 碧眼 图 ⟨a pair of⟩ blue eyes.
── 碧眼の 厖 blue-eyed 《beautiful woman》.

へきぎょく 碧玉 a jaspar.

へきそん 僻村 a remote [an out-of-the-way] village.

へきち 僻地 a remote [an out-of-the-way] place, an isolated area.
● 僻地教育 education in a remote place [an isolated area].

へきとう 劈頭 the start [beginning]. (⇨冒頭) ● 劈頭第一に at the *very beginning*; first of all.

ペキニーズ 〖動物〗(犬) a Pekingese.

へきめん 壁面 (壁) a wall; (壁の表面) the surface of a wall.

へきれき 霹靂 a sudden peal of thunder. ●青天の霹靂 (⇨青天 [成句])

ペキン 北京 〖中国の首都〗 Beijing /bèidʒíŋ/.

‐べく(して) ──可く(して) ▸彼は大学に進むべく(=進むために)東京に来た He came up to Tokyo *in order to* [*so that he could*] go to college. ▸彼は勝つべくして勝った(=自然の成り行きで) It was *natural* that he should win./It was *natural* for him to win.

ヘクタール 〖面積の単位〗 a hectare 《略 ha.》. 〖参考〗 1 万平方メートル.

ペクチン 〖化学〗 pectin.

ヘクトパスカル 〖気圧の単位〗 hectopascal 《略 hPa》. ▸中心気圧は 950 ヘクトパスカルです The central barometric reading is 950 *hectopascals*.

ベクトル 〖＜ドイツ語〗 a vector /véktər/.

ベクレル 〖放射能の単位〗〖物理学〗 a becquerel.

ヘゲモニー 〖覇権〗 hegemony /hədʒéməni/.

へこおび 兵児帯 a *hekoobi*, 《略式的に》 men's or children's *obi* of thin soft wide cloth for an informal *kimono* such as a *yukata*.

へこたれる 〖落胆する〗 be discouraged, lose* heart; 〖意気消沈している〗 be depressed; 〖疲れ切る〗 get* tired [worn] out. ▸一度の失敗くらいでへこたれるな Don't *be discouraged* by one failure./Don't let one failure *discourage* you. ▸途中でへこたれずに(=粘り強く)最後までやれ Do it *persistently* to the end.

ベゴニア 〖植物〗 a begonia /bigóunjə/.

ぺこぺこ ❶〖ひどく空腹な〗 very hungry. ▸私はお腹がぺこぺこだ I'm *very hungry*./《死ぬほどに》 I'm *starving*./《主に米話》 Am I hungry! (❗ Am に強勢を置く)
❷〖卑屈に何度も頭を下げる〗●ぺこぺこする kowtow /káutáu/《to》(❗ 語源は中国語で,「頭を何度も下げる」の意); bow subserviently; 《迎合する》 flatter. ▸彼は人がぺこぺこするのを見るのが嫌いだ He doesn't like to see people *kowtowing*.

へこます 凹ます (くぼませる) dent, make* a dent in .... (⇨へこむ) ●洗面器をへこます *dent* [*make a dent in*] a washbowl. ●腹をへこます *flatten* one's stomach.

へこみ 凹み (物がぶつかってできた) a dent; (凹形の)《書》(a). concávity; (地面などの) a hollow; (急な; a depression. ▸車のへこみを直してもらえますか Can you fix a *dent* in the car?

へこむ 凹む ❶〖へこむ〗▸その事故で車のドアがへこんだ The door of my car *was dented* in the accident. ▸落石で屋根がへこんだ(=陥没した) The roof *caved in* by falling rocks.
❷〖気分が落ち込む〗▸私は成績が悪くてへこんだ The poor grades *made* me *feel depressed* /《話》 *got me down*].

ぺこりと ▸彼はぺこりと頭を下げて「おはよう」と言った He *bobbed* his head and said, "Good morning." ▸その歌手は聴衆に身をかがめぺこりと頭を下げた The singer *bobbed a curtsy* to the audience.

へさき 舳先 the bow(s) /báu(z)/ (↔stern). (❗ しばしば複数形で) ▸岸にへさきを向けた *head for* the shore.

‐べし (⇨‐べき) ▸若者はもっと注意深く運転すべし Young people *should* drive more carefully. ▸明朝 7 時駅に集合すべし You *are* (*requested*) *to* gather at the station at seven tomorrow morning.

へしおる へし折る break* 〖(ぽきんと) snap (-pp-)〗 ... off. ▸あの男の高慢の鼻をへし折ってやる He's too arrogant. I'll take him down a peg or two. (❗ 後半は口語的慣用句で,「やりこめる」の意)

ベジタリアン 〖菜食主義者〗 a vegetarian.

ペシミスト 〖悲観論者〗 a pessimist.

ペシミズム 〖悲観論〗 pessimism.

ぺしゃんこ (⇨ぺちゃんこ)

ペスタロッチ 〚スイスの教育学者〛 **Pestalózzi** (Johann Heinrich ～).

ベスト [**最良のもの**] the best. ● ベストコンディションである be in the *best* (possible) [in *top*] condition. ● ベストを尽くす do one's *best* 《*to* do》. ▶ 今まで読んだ本の中でおもしろさではこれがベストだ This book is the *most* [×*best*] interesting one I've ever read. ▶ 彼女の歌はベストテン入りしている Her song is in the *top* ten (of the chart) [one of the ten *best* songs]. (⚠ ×*best ten* の語順は不可) (事情) 米国ではこの種のランキングでいちばん定評のあるのは Billboard chart)/She is in the *top* ten singers [one of the ten *best* singers]. ▶ 私たちのチームはベスト8[4]に残った Our team got into the quarterfinals [semifinals].
● ベストセラー a bestseller, a best-seller. (⚠ 時に「本」以外にも用いる.「ベストセラー作家」 (a best-selling writer) の意でも用いる); (最もよく売れる本) the best-selling book. ● ベストドレッサー one of the best dressed men [women] (of the year). (⚠ 通例 ×a best dresser とはいわない) ● ベストメンバー the best members.

ベスト [チョッキ]《米》a vest,《英》a waistcoat. (⇨チョッキ)

ペスト [＜オランダ語]〚医学〛(the) plague /pléig/.
● ペスト菌 a plague bacillus. (֎ ～ bacilli)

ベスビオ ● ベスビオ山 Mount Vesuvius /vəsú:viəs/.

へそ 臍 a navel /néivl/,《話》a belly [tummy] button. ● へそ茶を沸かす (ばかばかしい) What a joke!/ (冗談はよせ) None of your jokes./(笑わせるなよ) Don't make me laugh!
● へそを曲げる (不機嫌になる) sulk; get cross [sulky] 《*at* it》.
● へその緒 a navel cord [string]; an umbilical cord. ● へそのごま naval fluff. ● へそ曲がり (変人) a perverse fellow;《米話》a crank.

べそ ● べそをかく (泣く) sob; (泣き出しそうだ) be on the verge of tears. (⇨泣く)

へそくり (秘密の貯金) secret savings; (隠された小遣銭 [小金]) extra money hidden away; (不時に備えた貯金)《話》a nest egg. ● へそくりをする save up secretly. ▶ 彼女は部屋のどこかにへそくりを隠している She hides her *secret savings* somewhere in her room.

:へた 下手 ━━ 下手な 形 poor; bad* 《*at*》; (熟練していない) unskilled 《*at*, *in*》, unskillful 《*at*, *in*, *with*》; (無器用な) awkward, clumsy 《*with*》.

> **使い分け** poor 最も一般的な語で, 主に技術や技量の低さを表す.
> bad 行動や作品などが標準のレベルに達しておらず, 未熟であることを表す. poor より強意的.
> unskilled 専門的な作業のための技術が, 特に積み重ねの訓練が足りないために十分習得されていないことを表す.
> unskillful 熟練していないことを表す.
> awkward ぎこちなさや不自然さによって行動が適切に行われていないことを表す.
> clumsy 主に人の不器用さ, また言葉や気の利かないことを表す. awkward と交換可能なことも多いが, より強意的で悪い結果を暗示する.

① [**下手な～**] ▶ 下手な職人 a *bad* [a *poor*, an *unskilled*] craftsworker [〚書〛artisan, (男の) craftsman, workman]. ▶ 下手な言い訳をするな Don't make a *poor* excuse [a *clumsy* apology]. ▶ 彼らの口論に下手に(=軽率に)口出ししたらかえって事がこじれるよ If you cut in on their argument *thoughtlessly*, it will make matters worse. ▶ いい場所を教えてくれたよ. 下手な(=場所[施設]が悪い)キャンプ場なんかよりずっといい Thanks for telling us about such a nice place (like that). It's much better than a camping site in a *poor location* [with *poor facilities*].

② [**…が下手だ**] ▶ 彼はドイツ語が下手だ He is a *poor* [a *bad*] speaker of German./He's not very good [(不得意だ) He's *weak*] *in* [*at*] German. (⚠ 通例 in は学科・分野, at は運用的技術を表す)/His German is poor [(ひどい) *terrible*]. (⚠ 反対にいい場合は He doesn't speak German (*very*) *well* [*good* German].) ▶ 彼は箸(の使い方が下手だ He is awkward [*clumsy*, *unskillful*] *with* chopsticks. (⚠ with は扱い方を表す)/He uses chopsticks *awkwardly* [*clumsily*]. ▶ テニスは好きよ. すごく下手だけど(=上手になる見込みがまったくない) I like tennis. I'm such a *hopeless* player, though. ▶ 彼は生きるのが下手で, 何でも一生懸命だった He *was poor at* coping with life's problems, taking everything too seriously.
● **下手な鉄砲も数撃ちゃ当たる** Even a poor shot will hit the mark sometimes.
● **下手の考え休むに似たり** Thinking it over is a waste of time if you are bad at thinking.
● **下手の長談義** 'A poor speaker makes a long speech.'/(ことわざ) Brevity is the soul of wit.
● **下手の横好き** One is very enthusiatic about it though one is not good at it.
● **下手をすると** ▶ 下手をすると(=注意しないと)この仕事は1週間で終わらないでしょう If we are *not careful* (enough) [(物事がうまくいかないと) If things *go wrong*], we won't get this work done [finished the work] in a week. (⚠ 前の方は「仕事をしてしまう」の意)

へた 蔕 (カキ・ナスなどの) a calyx /kéiliks/, (֎ ～es); a cup.

ベターハーフ《話・おどけて》one's better half. (⚠ 自分の配偶者をさすかなり古い言い方)

べたおくれ べた遅れ ▶ 山手線は目黒での事故でべた遅れになっている *All* the trains on the Yamanote Line *are delayed* by an accident at Meguro.

へたくそ 下手糞

へだたり 隔たり (距離・時間・身分などの) (a) distance; (相違) (a) difference; (大きな相違) a gap; (年齢・地位などの不釣り合い)〚書〛(a) disparity. ▶ 世代の隔たり the generation *gap*. ▶ 彼らの年齢の隔たり the *gap* [*disparity*] *in* their ages; their age *gap*. ▶ 彼らの考えは互いに大きな隔たりがある There is a great *difference* [*gap*] *between* their ideas. ▶ 北方領土問題をめぐって日露間にはまだ大きな隔たりがある On the Northern Territory issue, Japan and Russia *remain far apart from* each other.

***へだたる 隔たる** (距離的に) be … away 《*from*》, be … distant 《*from*》 (⇨距離); (意見などの) be apart 《*from*》; (年月が経つ) pass. ▶ その村はここから5キロ隔たっている The village is five kilometers *away* [*in distance*,《まれ》*distant*] *from* here. ▶ 彼らの意見はかなり大きく隔たっている Their opinions are very much *apart*.

べたつく ▶ 彼女の指はお菓子でべたついていた Her fingers *were sticky* with sweets. (⇨べたべた ❶ ❷)

へだて 隔て ● 隔てなく (⇨分け隔て)

***へだてる 隔てる** 動 (切り離す) separate; (仕切る) partition … off;〚疎遠にする〛estrange. ▶ 彼と彼女の

仲を隔てる *estrange* him *from* her. ● その部屋を食堂として使うためにカーテンで隔てる *partition off* the room with a curtain to use part of it as a dining room. ● 山田村から村ひとつ隔てた村 the next (village) but one from Yamada Village. ▶ 英国はイギリス海峡でフランスと隔てられている England *is separated from* France by the Channel.

── 隔てて 副 ● 3 メートル隔てて(=おきに) *at intervals* [*an interval*] *of* three meters; *every* three meters. ● 山を隔てて向こうにある村 a village *beyond* the mountain. ▶ あの人は川を隔てて真向かいに住んでいる He lives *across* [《主に米》*across from*] the river. ▶ 彼らはテーブルを隔てて座っていた They *were* sitting with a table *between* them [(テーブルをはさんで向かい合って) *across* the table *from* each other].

へばる [疲れ果てる] get* tired [worn] out; get exhausted. (⇒疲れる) ● 重労働でへばった The hard work *exhausted* me [*wore* me *out*].

へとへと (⇒くたくた)

べたべた ❶ [粘りつく] ● べたべたする (不快に粘りつく) sticky; (汗で) sweaty; (油で) greasy. ▶ 私の指はキャラメルでべたべたしていた My fingers were *sticky* with caramel. ▶ 少し歩いても体が汗でべたべたした I was *sweaty* after a short walk.

❷ [甘えてまといつく] ● べたべたする(=くっついて離れない) cling (on) 《to》, hang on 《to》. ▶ 少年は父親が家に戻るとべたべたして離れない The boy *never leaves* his father when he comes back home. ▶ 彼はいつも女の子とべたべたしている He *is* always *flirting with girls*.

❸ [塗りつけるさま] (厚く) thickly; (全体に) all over. ▶ 壁にビラがべたべた張ってある Bills *are pasted all over* the wall./The wall *is almost covered* with bills. ▶ 彼女はべたべたと化粧していた She was *very heavily* made up.

ぺたぺた ❶ [べたべた音を立てる] slap (-pp-). ● 彼女はぺたぺたスリッパの音を立てて廊下を歩いた She walked with her slippers *slapping* on the corridor. ▶ 彼はひげそったあとの顔にローションをぺたぺた付けた He *dabbed* after-shave *on* his face. (❗ dab は軽くたたく動作を表す. slap はこの場合強すぎる)

❷ [べたべたつける] (はる) stick*, plaster*, paste; (ペンキなどを) paint. ▶ 彼は雑誌から切り抜いた絵を壁一面にぺたぺた張った He *stuck* illustrations from magazines *all over* the wall.

べたぼめ べた褒め ── べた褒めする 動 praise ... to the skies; 《おじで》flatter (immensely); 《米話》lay* it on thick 《about》.

べたぼれ べた惚れ ▶ 彼は理恵にべたぼれだ He *is madly* [*head over heels*] *in love with* Rie.

べたやき べた焼き ● a contact print. ● べた焼きにする contact-print 《a negative》; make a *contact print* 《from a negative》.

べたゆき べた雪 wet snow.

へたりこむ sink* (down). ● 地面にへたりこむ *sink* to the ground. ● 疲れていすにへたりこむ *sink into* a chair from exhaustion.

べたりと (⇒べったり)

ペダル (ミシン・ピアノ・自転車・自動車などの) a pedal /pédl/. ● ペダルを踏む work a *pedal*; pedal 《a bicycle》.

ぺたんと ● ぺたんと床に座る *sink* to the floor; flop [plop] down on the floor. (❗ thump, thud のような荒々しく, 重い感じではないが,「ぺたん」ほど軽い感じはしていない)

ペチカ [<ロシア語] [[ロシア風の暖炉]] a Russian stove.

ペチコート a pétticoat.

へちま 糸瓜 [植物] a loofa(h), a sponge cucumber [gourd /gɔːrd/]. ● へちま水 loofa(h) juice.

ぺちゃくちゃ ● ぺちゃくちゃしゃべる 《けなして》chatter 《about》● chat は単に「おしゃべりをする」; (子供などが舌たらずに) prattle. ▶ まだ仕事が山ほどあるのに何をぺちゃくちゃ無駄口たたいているの? What's all this *chatter* [《話》 *jabber*] when there's lots of work to be done?

ぺちゃくちゃ (⇒ぺちゃくちゃ)

べちゃべちゃ ❶ [ぬれている様子] ● べちゃべちゃにぬれる be all wet. ● べちゃべちゃの髪を乾かす dry one's *soaking-wet* hair.

❷ [しゃべる様子] ● べちゃべちゃしゃべる chatter noisily.

ぺちゃぺちゃ ❶ [歩く音] ● ぺちゃぺちゃ音を立てて水たまりを歩く *squelch* across a pool of rain water.

❷ [しゃべる様子] ● ぺちゃぺちゃしゃべる chatter 《away》.

ぺちゃんこ [平らな] flat. (❗ 意味を強めると completely flat, (as) flat as a pancake のようになる) ● ぺちゃんこにする (押しつぶす) crush [press, 柔らかい物を] squash] 《it》 flat; (地震が家などを) flatten, level 《a house》 (to the ground). ▶ 大きな落石で車はぺちゃんこになった The car *got crushed flat* by a large falling rock.

ペチュニア [植物] a petunia.

べつ 別 图 ❶ [区別] (a) distinction; (差別) discrimination; (相違) (a) difference. (⇒別) ▶ 男女[年齢]の別だれでもコンテストに参加できます Anyone can take part in the contest *regardless* [*without distinction*] *of* sex [age].

❷ [除外] exclusion; (例外) an exception. ▶ 筋は別としてこの本はおもしろかった I found the book interesting *apart* [《主に米》*aside*] *from* the plot. ▶ 冗談は別として, あの男は教職には向いていないよ Joking *aside* [Joking *apart*, *Apart from* joking], he is not fit for the teaching profession. ▶ 彼の論文は少々の不備は別としてよくできている His thesis is good, *except for* a few minor flaws. (❗ except for ... は文修飾. except ... は語修飾語句を導く: Everyone *except* me went to the party. (私以外は全員パーティーへ行った) (⇒除く)) ▶ 普段昼食には酒を飲まないが日曜日は別だ I usually don't drink at lunch, but Sunday is an *exception*.

── 別の 形 (もう一つの) another; (ほかの) other; (異なる) different; (別々の) separate; (余分の) extra. ▶ この時計は気にいらない. 別のを見せてください I don't like this watch. Please show me *another* (one). ▶ 悪いけど今忙しいの. 別の時にしてくれない I'm sorry but I'm busy now. Can't you make it *another* [some *other*] time? ▶ 子供たちにはそれぞれ別の部屋がある The children have *separate* rooms. / (自分自身の部屋がある) The children have their *own* rooms [have rooms *of* their *own*]. ▶ 私たちはそれぞれ別々のルートを取って山頂に向かった We each headed for the top of the mountain, taking *a different* route from each other. ▶ 言うこととすることは別だ To say [Saying] is *one thing*, and to do [doing] is *another*. (❗ 不定詞を用いる方が明確で強意的なので, 話題の初めでは用いる) ▶ 電気代が別だとは知らなかった I didn't realize that electricity was *extra*. ▶ あら, すみません. 別の方だと思っていたものですから Oh, I beg your pardon. I thought you were *someone else*.

-べつ —別に 副 (余分に) extra; (加えて) in addition 《to》; (特に) especially, in particular (⇔特に). ▶私たちが別に食費を払うのは当然です It is natural that we should pay *extra* [make the *additional* payment] for food expenses. (**!**形容詞としては extra より additional の方が普通) ▶別にサービス料を申し受けます Attendance is charged *extra*. ▶定価とは別に消費税を支払わねばならない *In addition to* the price, we have to pay the consumption tax. ▶午後は別にすることがない I don't have anything *in particular* to do [I have nothing to do *in particular*] in the afternoon. ▶彼は別にこれという理由もなく学校を休んだ He was absent from school without any *special* reasons [for *no particular* reasons]. ▶負けたって別にいいじゃないか What does it matter if we lose [they win]?
会話「やあ智子, 変わりないかい」「いや別に」"Hi, Satoko. What's new?" "Oh, *nothing much* [*in particular*]."
会話「どうして行ったの」「いや, 別に」"Why'd you go?" "Oh, *no reason*."
会話「何か手伝えることはあるかい」「いや別になぁ。お気づかいありがとう」"Is there anything I can do to help?" "Nót ᵛ*particularly* [ᵛ*really*]. But thanks for concerns."
会話「彼はどんな話をしたの」「別に(=特別の話はしなかった)」"What did he say?" "*The usual things*."

-べつ -別 ●著者別図書目録 a catalog of books listed *by* author. ●年齢[年度]別人口 population *by* age [year]. ●その資料を題目別に分類する classify the data *by* [*according to*] subject (matter). ●受験者を都道府県別に分ける classify the applicants *by* prefecture. (⇨❶)

べつあつらえ 別誂え — 別誂えの 形 custom-made 《shoes》; 《shoes》 made to order.
べついん 別院 图 a branch temple.
べつうり 別売り ▶この車のカーナビは別売りです This car navigation system is *an extra-cost option*.
べっか 別科 a special course.
べっかく 別格 — 別格の 形 (特別な) special; (異なった) different; (例外的な) exceptional. ▶別格扱いを受ける be given special treatment; be *specially* treated. ▶彼の英語の運用力は別格だ He has an *exceptionally* good command of English./His English speaking ability is *quite different from* others. ▶あのホテルは別格だ The hotel *has no equal*./The hotel *is better than any others*./The hotel *is a class by itself*.
べっかん 別巻 a supplement 《to》.
べっかん 別館 an ánnex 《*to* a hotel》; (増設部分) an extension.
べつかんじょう 別勘定 a separate account; (割り増し勘定) an extra charge. ▶これは別勘定にしてください Please put this on a *separate account*.
べっき 別記 图 ●細則は別記とする Detailed regulations *are given elsewhere*.
— 別記する 動 state elsewhere.
べっきょ 別居 图 (a) separation.
— 別居する 動 ●(結婚生活が破たんをきたして) separate, live separately, be separated; (仕事などの都合で) live away [《書》 apart] 《from》. ▶彼女は夫と別居した She *got a separation* [*got separated, separated*] *from* her husband.
べつくち 別口 图 (別口座) a separate account.
— 別口の 形 (もう 1 つの) another; (異なった) different; (特別の) special. ●別口のパーティーにもちょっと顔を出す turn up at *another* party. ●別口の話情報 information from *a different source* [*somewhere else, another channel*].
べっけ 別家 图 〘分家〙 a branch family; 〘別宅〙 a second house.
— 別家する 動 set* up [start] a branch family.
べっけい 別掲 ●別掲の図表を参照のこと Refer to the diagram [(図形) the figure] *given separately*.
べっけん 瞥見 图 a glance; a glimpse.
— 瞥見する 動 take* a glance 《*at*》; catch* a glimpse 《*of*》.
べっけんたいほ 別件逮捕 图 (an) arrest on a different [a separate] charge.
— 別件逮捕する 動 arrest 《him》 [take* 《him》 in] on a different charge.
べっこ 別個 — 別個の 形 ●別個の問題 (それぞれ異なった) a *different* problem; (別の) another problem.
— 別個に 副 (別々に) separately; (一つずつ) individually.
べっこう 別項 (別の項目) another [a separate] heading [(細目) item]; (別の条項) another [a separate] article [clause, provision]. ▶この問題は別項で詳しく取り扱う予定である This problem will be dealt with in detail under *another heading*.
べっこう 鼈甲 tortoise-shell /tɔ́ːrtəsʃèl/. ●べっ甲のくし *tortoise-shell* comb.
● 鼈甲細工 tortoise-shell work.
べつこうどう 別行動 ●別行動をとる act separately [(個別の) respectively, individually, (異なった) differently]; take separate [respective, individual, different] action. ▶私たちはパリまで一緒に行ったがあとは別行動をとった(=そこで別れた) We went together as far as Paris, and *separated* there.
べっさつ 別冊 a separate volume; (雑誌の) an extra number. (⇨付録)
ペッサリー a pessary; a diaphragm /dáiəfræm/. (**!** 後の方が一般的)
ヘッジ 〘つなぎ売買, 保険つなぎ〙 〘経済〙 a hedge; hedging (transaction).
● ヘッジファンド a hédge fùnd.
べっし 別紙 (もう一枚別の紙) another paper [sheet]; (添付した紙) an attached paper [sheet]. ▶別紙参照 See [Cf.] *another sheet*.
べっし 蔑視 图 (⇨軽蔑) ●女性蔑視 séxism.
— 蔑視する 動 ●女性を蔑視する look down on women; have a sexist attitude.
べっしつ 別室 ●別室で in another room.
べっしゅ 別種 another [a different] kind. ▶それとは別種の植物 a *different kind* of plant *from* that one.
べっしょう 別称 another name 《of, for》. ▶浅草寺は浅草観音と別称されることもある Sensoji Temple *is sometimes called* Asakusa Kannon.
べっしょう 蔑称 a contemptuous [a disdainful, a derogatory] term. ●ジャップは日本人の蔑称で 'Jap' is (a term) *derogatory* [*contemptuous*] *of* a Japanese.
べつじょう 別条 (⇨❶ 異状) ▶彼は重傷を負っているが, 命に別条はない He is seriously injured, but his life is in no danger.
べつじん 別人 another [a different] person. ▶彼は結婚してから別人のようになった He has become *another man* since getting married./(大いに変わった) He has changed a lot since he got married. ▶彼は私たちが捜している人とは別人だ He is a *different person* from the one [He is *not the person*] we are looking for.

べつずり 別刷り ●別刷り15部 fifteen copies of the *off-print*. ▶ロンドンの劇場の別刷りが20ページ以上もこの本には入っている More than twenty pages of *separately printed pictures* of London theaters are inserted in this book.

べっせい 別姓 ●夫婦別姓を法律化する legalize the use of *different surnames* by a married couple. ▶今のところ夫婦別姓は法律上は認められない The law has not as yet allowed *married women to keep their maiden names* [*married couples to keep different surnames*] *after marriage*.

べっせかい 別世界 a different world; 〖宇宙〗 outer space. ▶クーラーのきいた部屋に入ったら涼しくてまるで別世界だった When I went into the air-conditioned room, it was so cool that I felt as if I were [〖話〗was] in a *different world*.

べっせき 別席 ▶このことは別席を設けて(≒別の機会に)話し合おう Let's talk about this matter another time.

べっそう 別荘 a cottage; a summer house (圈 houses /-ziz, 《米》-siz/); 〖庭付きで大きな〗a villa. ●貸別荘 a *villa* for rent 《米》[to let《英》]. ▶伊豆の別荘 one's *cottage* [*villa*] at Izu.

べっそう 別送 ●小包を別送する send a parcel *separately*.

べったく 別宅 a second house; (別邸) a villa.

へったくれ ▶相談もへったくれもあるものか。おれはそんなことには金は出さん I don't see any need to talk about it. I won't pay any money for that. ▶いやもへったくれもあるものか (いやとは絶対にいわせない) I won't take no for an answer./(文句なんかいっている場合ではない) Hang the complaints.

べつだて 別立て ─ 別立ての (特別に設けた) special; specially prepared; (別々の) different; (別の基準による) on a different basis. ▶新幹線と在来線の料金は別立てになっている The Shinkansen fares *are different from* the old-line (train) fares.

べったり ❶【粘りつく】●べったりくっつく[つける] stick. ▶ぬれたシャツが体にべったりついている My wet shirt *sticks* [*clings*] *to* the body.
❷【まとわりつく】▶子供たちは一日中母親にべったりくっついている The children *cling to* their mother all day long.
❸【厚く】thickly.
❹【一面に】all over. ▶紙一面に数字がべったり書いてある Numbers are written *all over* the paper.

ぺったり ●べったり床に座り込む sink to the floor; flop [plop] down on the floor. (⇨ぺたんと) ●窓ガラスにべったり顔をつける press one's face *against* the window. ▶雨に濡れた落ち葉がべったりアスファルトの道にくっついている Fallen leaves wet with rain *are stuck* on the asphalt road [pavement].

べつだん 別段 particularly. (⇨別に)

へっちゃら 会話 「先生に見つかったらしかられるよ」「へっちゃらさ」"If the teacher catches you, he will talk to you." "I *don't care at all* [*a bit*]./I *couldn't* [《米》*could*] *care less*."

へっつい 竈 (⇨竈(かまど))

べってい 別邸 a second residence (❗ second を省略した方がよいことがある); (別荘) a villa.

ヘッディング (⇨ヘディング)

ペッティング 图 petting. ── **ペッティングする** 動 pet.

べってんち 別天地 a different world. (⇨別世界)

ヘッド a head.

べっと 別途 ── 別途の 形 (追加の) extra. (⇨別に) ●別途料金を支払う pay an *extra* [an *additional*] charge (《for》it). ▶交通費は別途支給する We'll pay you the travel expenses *separately* [(後で) *later*].

***ベッド** (a) bed 〖家具としてのベッドは C, 「就寝」の意では U で通例無冠詞〗(⇨床(とこ)) ●シングル[ダブル]ベッド a single [a double] *bed*. ●補助ベッド an extra *bed*. ●(折りたためる)簡易ベッド《米》a cot,《英》a camp *bed*. ●ベビーベッド (四方を囲んだ)《米》a crib,《英》a cot; (携帯用の)《米・商標》a portacrib,《英》a cárrycot. ●寝心地のいい[堅い]ベッド a comfortable [a hard] *bed*. ●ベッドに入る get [(もぐり込む) climb] into (↔out of) *bed*. ●ベッドインする(性交する) go to bed (*with*); 〖和製語〗(*bed in*). ▶疲れたらベッドで横になりなさい Lie down on the *bed* if you're tired. (❗lie in bed はふとんの中に入っている状態)
会話「ベッドメーキングは自分でやるの?」「うん、毎日ね」"Do you ever make your *bed*?" "Yes, always." (❗整えられるように寝具を整えること.)
●ベッドカバー a bedspread. ●ベッドシーン a bedroom [❌a bed] scene. ●ベッドルーム a bedroom.

ペット a pet. (❗ 特に その中で犬, 猫などというときは a pet dog, a pet cat などという). ●家の中で飼うペット a house *pet*; 〖婉曲的〗an animal companion, a companion animal. ●ペットにリスを飼う have [《主に英》keep] a squirrel as a *pet*. ▶ペットは寂しさをいやしてくれるパートナーになることもよくある *Pets* often serve as companions to ease a feeling [sense] of loneliness.
●ペットショップ a pét shòp. ●ペット美容室 a pét groòming stòre (pàrlor, ❌barber). ●ペットフード pét fòod.

べつどうたい 別動隊, 別働隊 a detached [a separate] unit [corps /kɔ́ːr/ (圈 corps /kɔ́ːrz/)].

ヘッドギア〖競技〗headgear.

ヘッドコーチ a head coach.

ヘッドスライディング〖野球〗a headfirst [❌head] slide. ●二塁へヘッドスライディングする slide into second *headfirst*.

ベッドタウン《米》a bedroom town [community, suburb],《英》a dormitory town [suburb]; 〖和製語〗a bed town.

ペットネーム〖愛称〗a pet name.

ヘッドハンター a headhunter.

ヘッドハンティング headhunting.

ヘッドハント 图 headhunting.
── **ヘッドハントする** 動 head-hunt; go* headhunting. ▶彼女はライバル会社にヘッドハントされた She has *been headhunted* by a rival company.

ヘッドホーン (a pair of) headphones; (マイクつきの) a headset.

ペットボトル a plastic bottle; a PET bottle. (❗ PET は *p*olyethylene *t*erephthalate (ポリエチレンテレフタレートの略. 前の方が普通)

ヘッドライト a headlight;《英》a headlamp. (❗ともに複数形で) ●ヘッドライトを下げる dip the *headlights*. ▶霧が出ていたので、どの車もヘッドライトをつけていた It was foggy and all the cars had their *headlights* on.

ヘッドライン〖新聞などの見出し, ニュースなどの主な項目〗a headline. ●ヘッドラインニュース *headline* news.

べっとり (⇨べったり)

ヘッドロック (プロレスの) a headlock.

べつのう 別納 图 ●料金別納(郵便)〖表示〗postpaid.
── **別納する** 動 pay* separately.

べっぱ 別派 (別の宗派) a different sect; (党派) a different faction; (別流派) a different school.

べつばら 別腹 ▶たくさん食べたけれどケーキだけは別腹なのよね I've had enough, but there's always *room* for cakes. (❗room は「スペース」の意)

べっぴょう 別表 an attached list [table]. ▶詳しくは別表参照のこと Refer to the *attached list* for details.

へっぴりごし へっぴり腰 ●へっぴり腰で (腰がひけて) with one's bottom stuck out; (こわごわ) fearfully, nervously; (ぎこちなく) awkwardly; (自信なさげに) with bottom out, unsure of oneself.

べつびん 別便 ●小包を別便で送る send a parcel *under separate cover* [*by separate mail*, 《英》*by separate post*; (別に) separately].

べっぷう 別封 ●別封で under separate cover; in another packet.

べつべつ 別々 ── **別々の** 形 [[別個の]] separate; [[異なった]] different; [[めいめいの]] respective. ●別々の学校へ行く go to *different* schools. ▶子供たちは別々の部屋を持っている The children have *separate* [their *respective*, (個人用の) *individual*, (自分自身の) their *own*] rooms.
── **別々に** 副 [[離れて]] apart; [[個別に]] individually. ●犬と猫を別々にしておく keep the dog and the cat *apart* [*separate*]. ●贈り物を別々に包む wrap the gifts *individually*. ▶彼らは今は別々に住んでいる (=別居している) They are living *separately* [*apart*] now.

べっぽう 別報 different information [news].

へっぽこ (能なしの) dumb; incompetent; (役に立たない) useless; worthless.

べつむね 別棟 ▶兄弟はみな彼の屋敷内の別棟に住んでいた All his brothers lived in *detached houses* on his land.

べつめい 別名 (もう一つの名) another name 《*for*》; (特に犯罪者の) an alias /éiliəs/. ▶泥棒は本名ジョンソン, 別名をジョーンズという The thief's name is Johnson, *alias* Jones. (❗副詞用法).

べつもの 別物 ▶助け合いともたれ合いは別物 Mutual help and mutual dependence are two *different things* [(概念) *conceptions*].

べつもんだい 別問題 ●それは別問題として *apart* [《米》*aside*] *from it*. ▶それは別問題だ That's *another question* [*story*, *matter*]. / That's *a different story*.

へつらい (お世辞) flattery. (⇨へつらう, おべっか, お世辞)

へつらう flatter; (取り入ろうとする) play up 《*to*》; (機嫌をとる) curry favor 《*with*》; (おべっかを使う) 《軽蔑的》toady 《*to*》. ●上役にへつらう *flatter* [*play up to*, *toady to*] one's boss.

べつり 別離 ●別離(=別れ)の涙を流す shed tears at parting.

べつわく 別枠 ▶予算に別枠を設ける make a *separate item* [*heading*] in the budget.

へて (場所を) via /váiə/, by way of ...; (時間を)《two years》later. (⇨経る)

ペディキュア [[足の爪の手入れ]] (a) pedicure.

ヘディング 《サッカー》a header, heading. ●ヘディングシュートを決める score a goal with a *header*; head the ball into the goal. ▶前の方の goal は「得点」, 後の goal は「(相手チームの)ゴール」の意) ●テリーのヘディングは脅威だ Terry's *header* is dangerous.

ベテラン an expert /ékspə:rt/; (老練家) a veteran, (やや話) an old hand.
── **ベテランの** 形 (経験の豊かな) experienced; (熟達した) expert; (老練な) veteran. ●ベテラン弁護士 an *experienced* [a *veteran*] lawyer. ▶前の方はすぐれた知識や腕前を, 後の方は長年関与した結果としての巧みさを, 時に狡猾(ずる)さを含意する) ▶彼はベテランのドライバーだ He is an *expert* driver./He is *expert* [*an old hand*] *at* driving. ▶この道では彼はベテランだ He's an *expert* [a *veteran*] in this field./He is *an old hand at* these kind of things.

ヘテロセクシュアル 名 [[異性愛の人]] a heterosexual.
── **ヘテロセクシュアルの** 形 heterosexual. (⇨homosexual).

ぺてん (策略を用いること)《書》trickery (❗具体例は a trick); (金品をだまし取ること) swindling. (❗具体例は a swindle)《話》a con.
●ぺてんにかける play him a *trick*; play a *trick* on him; trick him 《*into*＋图, *doing*》. ●彼をぺてんにかけて金を取る *swindle* [《話》*con* (-nn-)] him *out of* his money; get the money from him by a *trick*. (⇨だます)
●ぺてん師 (詐欺師) a swindler; a fraud. (⇨詐欺)

へど 反吐 (吐いたもの) vomit. (=吐き気) ●へどが出る vomit, throw up (❗後の方が口語的の)《話》spew (up). ●へどが出そうな sickening; (不快にさせる) disgusting. ▶その光景を思い浮かべるだけでもへどが出そうだ The very thought of the sight is quite *disgusting*.

べとつく stick 《*to*》; be sticky. ▶やにはべとつく Tar *is sticky*.

ベトナム [[国名]] Vietnam /vi:etnáːm/; (公式には) the Socialist Republic of Vietnam. (首都 Hanoi)
●ベトナム人 a Vietnamese /viètnəmíːz/. ●ベトナム語 Vietnamese. ●ベトナム(人[語])の Vietnamese.
●ベトナム戦争 the Vietnam(ese) war.

へとへと ●へとへとに疲れる be (completely [absolutely]) exhausted; be tired out;《話》be dead tired (❗dead は「死ぬほど」の意). ●(仕事などが人を) へとへとにする very tiring; exhausting. ▶歩き回ってへとへとになった I walked and walked until I *was exhausted* [*was tired out*].

べとべと ●べとべとしている (べたつく) sticky; (ぬれている) wet (-tt-); (したたる larger) dripping wet; (汗で) sweaty. ▶私の手はジャムでべとべとしている My hands are *sticky with* jam. ▶雨で彼女の髪はべとべとにぬれた Her hair was *dripping wet in* the rain.

へどもど ▶彼女は問い詰められてへどもどした (=面食らってろくに返事もできなかった When she was pressed for an answer, she *was very confused* [*was bewildered*] *and couldn't give an intelligible answer*. (⇨どもどど)

へどろ (泥状の沈澱物) sludge; (水底の軟泥) ooze /úːz/; (ぬるぬるした土) slime /sláim/. ▶川底にはへどろがたまっていた The river bed was covered with thick *sludge* [*was thick with sludge*].

へなちょこ a worthless fellow [guy]; (くだらない人)《話》pipsqueak; (腰抜けの人) a milksop.

へなへな ❶ [[弱々しい様子]] ●へなへなと崩れる collapse *weakly* [(どうしようもなく) *helplessly*].
❷ [[態度などがしっかりしていない]] weak. ▶彼の部下に対する態度はへなへなだ His attitude toward his men is *weak*.

ペナルティー [[罰]] a penalty (参考) 日本語では競技用語から, 今は一般にも用いられるようになった); [[一般に, 罰金]] a fine, a penalty. (⇨罰金) ●ペナルティーを科する [科せられる, 支払う] impose [suffer; pay] a *penalty*.
●ペナルティーエリア《サッカー》a penalty box [area]. (❗box を用いることが多い) ▶シアラーがペナルティーエリア内で倒された Shearer was brought down in the *penalty box*. ●ペナルティーキック (⇨ペナルティーキック) ●ペナルティーゴール《サッカー》a penalty goal.

- **ペナルティーショット**〖アイスホッケー〗a penalty shot.
- **ペナルティーボックス**〖サッカー〗a penalty box.
- **ペナルティーライン**〖サッカー〗a penalty line.

ペナルティーキック〖サッカー・ラグビー〗a penalty (kick). ●ペナルティーキックをする take a *penalty kick*; kick a penalty. ●ペナルティーキックで点をとる〖ゴールで〗〖サッカー〗score a penalty goal [a point *on a penalty kick*].

ベナン〖国名〗Benin /bənín/; (公式名) the Republic of Benin. (首都 Porte Novo) ●ベナン人 a Beninese. ●ベナン(人)の Beninese.

ペナント〖野球などの優勝旗〗《米》a pennant. ●ペナントを争う〖獲得する〗compete for [win] the *pennant*.
- ペナントレース〖野球〗a pennant race.

べに 紅〖ほお紅〗rouge /rúːʒ/; 〖棒状の口紅〗(a) lipstick; 〖鮮紅色〗clear red. ●ほおに紅さす *rouge* one's cheeks; put *rouge* on one's cheeks.

べにざけ 紅鮭〖魚介〗a red (sockeye) salmon.

べにしょうが 紅生姜 red pickled ginger.

ペニシリン penicillin /pènəsílin/.
- ペニシリン注射 a penicillin shot [injection].
- ペニシリン軟膏 penicillin ointment.

ベニス〖イタリアの都市〗Venice. (⇨ベネチア)

ペニス a penis /píːnɪs/ (圈 〜es, penes /píːniːz/).

ベニスのしょうにん『ベニスの商人』*The Merchant of Venice*. (参考) シェイクスピアの喜劇)

べにばな 紅花 a safflower.

べにます 紅鱒 (⇨⑩ 紅鮭)

ベニヤいた ベニヤ板〖合板〗plywood. (! veneer はベニヤ板を構成する1枚1枚の薄い板)

ベニュー〖開催地〗a venue.

ベネズエラ〖国名〗Venezuela /vènəzwéilə, -wíːlə/; (公式名) the Bolivarian Republic of Venezuela. (首都 Caracas) ●ベネズエラ人 a Venezuelan. ●ベネズエラ(人)の Venezuelan.

ベネチア〖イタリアの都市〗Venice. ●ベネチアの Venetian /vəníːʃən/.

ベネルックス Benelux /bénəlʌks/. (参考) ベルギー(*Bel*gium)・オランダ (the *Ne*therlands)・ルクセンブルク (*Lux*embourg) の3か国)

へのかっぱ 屁の河童 ▶そんなことへのかっぱだ (朝飯前だ) Nothing could be easier. (⇨朝飯前)/(平気だ) I 〖ぞんざい〗could(n't) care less. (⇨へっちゃら)

への字 への字 ●口をへの字に結ぶ turn down the corners of one's mouth; (怒りを抑えて) be tight-lipped.

ペパーミント〖植物〗péppermint.

へばりつく へばり付く (べったりくっつく) cling* to ...; (ねばりつく) stick* to .... ▶泥が私にへばりついている The mud *has clung to* my shoes. ▶子供たちはその展示にへばりついて離れなかった The children were practically hanging all over the display, and staying put in front of it for a long time. (! (1) hang over は「身を乗り出している」の意. (2) stay put は「その場を離れない」のくだけた言い方)

へばる get* tired out, 《俗》be pooped. (⇨へたばる)

***へび** 蛇〖動物〗a snake, 〖書〗a serpent (! snake より大きな蛇や毒蛇). ●毒蛇 a poisonous (↔ non-poisonous) *snake*; a viper. ●蛇をとぐろ[枝に巻きついた] The *snake* coiled up [coiled (itself) around a branch].
- 蛇ににらまれた蛙 a frog that recoiled at the sight of a snake.
- 蛇の生殺し 《*in*》(a state of) limbo.
- 蛇使い a snake charmer.

ベビー〖赤ちゃん〗a baby. ●ベビーカー (折りたたみ式の) a stroller,《英》a push-chair. (! baby car は「小型自動車」) ●ベビーウェア〖服〗babywear; babies' wear. ●ベビーウォーカー《米》a go-cart;《英》a baby walker. ●ベビーオイル báby òil. ●ベビーサークル (赤ん坊の遊び場) pláypen;〖和製語〗a baby circle. ●ベビーシッター a baby-sitter. ●ベビーだんす a chest for babies' use. ●ベビーパウダー báby pòwder. ●ベビーフード báby fòod. ●ベビーブーム (⇨ベビーブーム) ●ベビーフェイス a baby face. ●ベビーベッド《米・英やや古》a crib,《英》a cot. ●ベビー用品 báby gòods.

ヘビーきゅう ヘビー級 the heavyweight. ●ヘビー級の選手 a heavyweight.

ヘビースモーカー a heavy smoker.

へびいちご 蛇苺〖植物〗an Indian strawberry.

ベビーブーム a baby boom.
- ベビーブーム世代 a baby boom generation. ●ベビーブーム世代に生まれた人 a baby boomer.

へびにピアス『蛇にピアス』*Snakes and Earrings*. (参考) 金原ひとみの小説)

ヘビメタ (「ヘビーメタル」の略)〖音楽〗heavy metal.

へびをふむ『蛇を踏む』*Treading on a Snake*. (参考) 川上弘美の小説)

ペプシン〖生化学〗pepsin.

ペプトン〖生化学〗peptone.

へべれけ ●へべれけに酔っ払う (話) get blind [dead, (酔っ払って騒ぐ) roaring] drunk. (⇨泥酔)

へぼ (へたな) poor, unskillful. ●へぼ将棋 a *poor* game of *shogi*. ●へぼ絵かき a *poor* painter.

ヘボン〖米国の宣教師・医師〗Hepburn /hépbɜːrn/ (James Curtis 〜). (参考) ヘボン式ローマ字を考案)
- ヘボン式 the Hepburn system of Romanization.

へま 〖事〗a blunder;〖人〗a blunderer. ●へまをやる make [commit] a *blunder*; blunder,《話》make a mess of it. ▶彼はへまな(= 不注意で失敗をする)男だが悪意はない He means well. He's only careless.

ヘミングウェー〖米国の小説家〗Hemingway (Ernest 〜).

ヘモグロビン〖<ドイツ語〗〖生化学〗hemoglobin /híːməɡlòʊbən/ (略 Hb).

:へや 部屋 a room;〖アパートの1世帯分の〗《米》an apartment,《英》a flat;〖相撲の〗a stable.

① 【〜部屋】 ●広い[狭い]部屋 a large [a small] *room*. ●xa wide [a narrow] *room* とはいわない ●空き部屋 a vacant [an unoccupied] *room*. ●小部屋 a small *room*; (納戸) a boxroom; (大部屋を仕切った) a cubicle. ●勉強部屋 a study. ●貸し部屋 a *room* for rent《米》[to let《英》]. ●井筒部屋 Izutsu *Stable*. ●私は彼と相部屋です I share a *room* with him. ▶私たちは3部屋のアパートに住んでいます We live in a three-*room*(*ed*) apartment.

② 【部屋〜】 ●部屋代 (a) *room* rent. ●部屋割りをする assign *rooms*.

[会話]「ここの部屋代はいくらですか」「月3万円です」 "What is the rent for this *room*?" "It's 30,000 yen a month."/"How much do you pay for this *room*?" "I pay 30,000 yen each month."

③ 【部屋が】 ●彼の家には部屋が5つあります His house has five *rooms*. ●部屋が空いた A *room* becomes vacant [available].

④ 【部屋に】 ●部屋に入る go [come] into a *room*; enter a *room*. (! 後の方が堅い言い方) ▶彼がやって来たらすぐに部屋に通してくれ When he arrives, *show* him *in* [*into* the room] immediately. ▶彼らはたった二部屋に8人で住んでいた The eight of them lived in only two *rooms*.

⑤ 【部屋を】 ●部屋を出る go [come] out of a

room; leave a *room*. ●部屋を借りる rent a *room*. ●部屋を探す look for [seek] a *room*. ●ホテルのツインの部屋を予約する reserve [book] a twin *room* at a hotel.
[会話]「いらっしゃいませ」「部屋をお願いします」「シングルですか、ダブルですか」「眺めのいい[道路に面していない]ダブルをお願いします」"Can I help you?" "Yes, I'd like a *room*, please." "Single or double?" "A double (*room*) with a good view [away from the road], please."
●部屋着〔寝巻きの上に着る〕《米》a bathrobe,《英》a dressing gown;〔女性用〕a negligee /nèɡləʒéi/(ネグリジェ).●部屋ばき(carpet) slippers.

へら a spatula /spǽtʃələ/.

べら 〖魚介〗a wrasse.

*****へらす** 減らす 〖数量・価格・速度・程度などを〗reduce;〖減量を徐々に〗decrease,〖消費量・費用などを切り詰める〗cut*... down.(⇨減る)●学生数を減らす *reduce* [*decrease*] the number of students.●一学級あたりの子どもの数を減らす *reduce* the number of pupils per [in a] class.●体重を3キロ減らす *reduce* [*lose*] one's weight by three kilograms.(!)いずれも意図的に体重を減らすこと.「(自然に)体重が減る」は lose (some) weight (one's はつけない)●税金を10パーセント減らす *reduce* [*lower*] taxes by 10 percent.●出費を減らす *cut down* (*on*) [*reduce*] one's expenses.▶前の方が口語的)●ウイスキーの量を減らす *cut down* (*on*) whiskey; drink *less* whiskey.

へらずぐち 減らず口 〔言わずもがなのことを言う〕say something nasty [spiteful] which is better left unsaid. ▶減らず口をたたく Hold your tongue! / Shut your mouth! / Shut up!

ベラスケス 〖スペインの画家〗Velázquez /vəlǽskəs, -láːs-/ (Diego Rodríguez de Silva y ~).

へらぶな 箆鮒 〖魚介〗a deepbodied crucian carp.

へらへら ●へらへら(=軽薄に[あいまいに; いやしそうに])笑う laugh frivolously [obscurely; obsequiously].▶彼の例のへらへら笑いが気にくわない I don't like the way he laughs *insincerely*. (!)現在形で習慣的な笑いであることが示される)●へらへら(=軽々しく)しゃべる talk carelessly [thoughtlessly, indiscreetly] like an idiot.

べらべら ●べらべらしゃべる chatter (away [on]), prattle. (!)べらべらよくしゃべる人は a chatterer, a prattler, 特に, 子供の場合は a chatterbox ということがある)●秘密をべらべらしゃべってしまう tell a secret *thoughtlessly*; give away a secret *foolishly*.▶彼はよくべらべらしゃべる(=おしゃべりだ)He is very talkative.

ぺらぺら ❶〔よくしゃべるさま〕〔止まることなく〕incessantly, continually;〔流ちょうに〕fluently.▶彼女はフランス語がぺらぺらだ She speaks French *fluently*. / She is a *fluent* speaker of French. / She speaks *fluent* French.▶彼女は2時間もぺらぺらしゃべっていた She has been chattering (*continuously*) for two hours. (!)この場合進行形を用いることで「ぺらぺら」が出るのは強調ではなくもよい)
❷〔本などを次々とめくる〕▶彼女は手帳をぺらぺらめくった She leafed [thumbed] through her notebook.
❸〔薄い〕(very) thin (-nn-);〔弱くすぐだめになる〕flimsy.●ぺらぺらの紙 *thin* paper.●ぺらぺらの服 a *flimsy* dress.

べらぼう ── **べらぼうな** 〖極度な〗extreme;〔不合理な〕unreasonable,〔法外な〕〖やや書〗exorbitant;〔ばかげた〕absurd.▶ひどい〕べらぼうな暑さ extreme

[耐えられない] *intolerable*] heat. ▶あのレストランはよくべらぼうな値段を請求する That restaurant often charges *unreasonable* [*exorbitant*] prices.
── **べらぼうに** 副 〔極度に〕extremely;〔ひどく〕《話》terribly,《話》awfully. ▶このドレスはべらぼうに値段が高い This dress is *terribly* [*awfully*] expensive.

ベラルーシ 〖国名〗Belarus /bèlərúːs/;〔公式名〕the Republic of Belarus.〔首都 Minsk〕●ベラルーシ人 a Belarusian. ●ベラルーシ語 Belarusian. ●ベラルーシ(人[語])の Belarusian.

ベランダ a veranda(h) /vərǽndə/,《米》a porch.

べらんめえ ●べらんめえ口調で in a dashingly spirited language of native Tokyoites. ▶べらんめえ, 何いってやんだ Don't talk nonsense, you dork!

へり 縁 〔角ばったものの〕an edge;〔円形のものの〕a rim;〔茶わんなどの〕a brim ●〔衣類の〕a hem;〔畳・じゅうたん・布などの〕a border. ●湖の縁を歩く walk along the *edge* of a lake.

ペリー 〖米国の提督〗Perry (Matthew Calbraith ~).

ベリーズ 〖国名〗Belize /bəlíːz/〔公式名も同じ〕. 〔首都 Belmopan〕●ベリーズ人 a Belizean. ●ベリーズ(人)の Belizean.

ベリーダンサー a belly dancer.

ベリーダンス a belly dance.

ベリーロール straddle, straddle roll. (〖参考〗走り高跳びの跳躍方法の一つ)

ヘリウム 〖化学〗helium /híːliəm/《元素記号 He》.

ヘリオトロープ 〖植物〗a heliotrope.

ペリカン 〖鳥〗a pelican /pélikən/.

へりくだる be modest;(《米》謙遜《けんそん》)

へりくつ 屁理屈 〔言い逃れ〕a quibble;〔あら探し〕a cavil. ●へりくつを言う〔細かいことを論じ, 肝心なことに話が行かないようにする〕quibble 《*about, over*; *with* +人》;〔けちをつける〕cavil 《*at, about*》;〔理屈をこねる〕chop logic.

ヘリコプター a helicopter;《米話》a copter,《話》a chopper.

ヘリポート a héliport;〔一機分の〕a hélipàd. ●海上ヘリポート an offshore (floating) *heliport*.

***へる** 減る ❶〖数量が減る〗decréase(↔increase), dwindle;〖減少する〗lessen,〔やや書〕〖数が少なくなる〗become* fewer;〖量が少なくなる〗become less.(⇨減少する)

> [使い分け] **decrease** 個数・人数・割合・規模などが減ること. 一度に大きく減るのではなく, 徐々に少なくすることを含意する.
> **dwindle** 数・規模・エネルギーなどが小さくなること. 特に, 減り方が大きく, 消えてなくなる場合などに用いられる.
> **lessen** 規模・程度などが減少すること. 減少の量は明確には示されない.
> **diminish** 量・規模・価値・力などが減ること. 時に減少した量よりも減少したこと自体に焦点が当てられる.

●数[量]が減る *decrease* in number [amount]. ●減ってなくなる *dwindle* (*away*) to nothing. ●体重が減る *lose* (↔gain) weight 《*from* 50 *to* 45 kilos; *by* 5 kilos》. (!)「体重が減る」は *a lose a lot of weight*) ▶近年志願者の数が急激に減ってきた The number of applicants *has* [×have] *decreased* [*fallen off*] sharply in recent years. ▶今月は売り上げが3パーセント減った Sales *have decreased* [*lessened*, 〔下落した〕*declined*, *fallen off*] by 3 percent this month./There is a *decrease* [*a decline*] in sales of 3 percent this month. (!)Sales *were down* 3 percent [We had 3 percent *smaller* sales] this month. の方

へる が口語的) ▶今年は昨年より事故が減った There were *fewer* [《話》*less*] accidents this year than last. (❗There weren't *as* [*so*] many accidents this year as last. の方が口語的) ▶犯罪は減る傾向にある(=減少している) Crime *is decréasing* [*on the décrease*]. ▶がんの死亡率は減って(=下がって)きている The death rate from cancer *is going down*. ▶そのスキャンダルのせいで彼の支持者が減った He *lost* some of his supporters because of the scandal. (《次例よりも口語的》) The scandal *diminished* his supporters [*caused the number of his supporters to diminish*]. ／(彼の支持者が減った) ▶川の水が減った(=水位が低くなった) The water in the river *has gotten low.*／The river *has sunk*. ▶食料が減った(=不足して)きた We *are running short of* food.／Our food *is running short*.

❷【その他の表現】▶腹が減る get [become] hungry. (❗前の方が口語的) ▶タイヤが減った The tire *has worn out*.

__へる 経る__ ❶【経過する】(時が過ぎる) pass; (過ぎて行く) go bý. (⇨経つ, 過ぎる) ▶月日を経るに従って as the days *go by*; as time *goes by*. ▶3年を経て彼は故郷に戻った He came home three years *later* [*after three years*, ×*in three years*]. ▶彼が家を出てから3年を経るIt is [has been] three years since he left home.／Three years *have passed* [*gone by*] since he left home.／He left home three years ago.

❷【通過する】(通り抜ける) go* [pass] through .... ●モスクワを経て(=経由して)パリへ飛ぶ fly to Paris *via* [*by way of*] Moscow. ●必要な手続きを経る go *through* the necessary formalities. ▶私たちは森を経て湖に来た We came *through* the forest to the lake.

❸【経験する】experience; go* through .... ●困難を経る *experience* [*go through*, 《やや堅め》 *undergo*] hardships. ▶出世の階段があっても, 販売員からレジ主任, 支配人補佐を経て支配人になれるってわけさ There's a clear corporate ladder. I mean you could go from clerk *to* cashier captain *to* assistant manager and then manager.

*__ベル__【呼び鈴】a bell; (玄関の) a doorbell. ●非常ベル an emergency *bell*; (火災の) a fíre alàrm; (防犯の) a búrglar alàrm.

①【ベルが】▶電話のベルが鳴った The telephone rang [went off]. (❗*go off* は「突然に鳴る」の意) ▶ベルが鳴っている There goes the *bell*.／The *bell* is ringing. (❗前の方が普通) ▶休み時間[授業の終わり]を知らせるベルが鳴った The *bell* rang for break [to end class].

__会話__「ベルが鳴っているから出てください」「はい」"Will you answer the *bell*?" "Yes, I will."

②【ベルを】▶ベルを鳴らす ring the *bell*. ●ベルを鳴らして召し使いを呼ぶ ring (the *bell*) for a servant.

__ベル__【米国の発明家】Bell (Alexander Graham /gréiəm/ ~).

__ペルー__【国名】Peru; (公式名) the Republic of Peru. (首都 Lima) ●ペルー人 a Peruvian. ●ペルー(人)の Peruvian.

__ベルギー__【国名】Belgium; (公式名) the Kingdom of Belgium. (首都 Brussels) ●ベルギー人 a Belgian. ●ベルギー(人)の Belgian.

__ベルサイユ__ ●ベルサイユ宮殿 the Palace of Versailles /veərsái/.

__ヘルシー__── __ヘルシーな__ 形 healthy. ●ヘルシーな食事 a *healthy* diet.

__ペルシャ__ Persia /pə́ːrʒə/. (【参考】1935年に Iran と改称)
●ペルシャ人 a Persian.
●ペルシャじゅうたん a Persian carpet [rug]. ●ペルシャ猫 a Persian cat. ●ペルシャ湾 the Persian Gulf. (❗(1)《話》で単に the Gulf ともいう. (2) アラブ諸国では the Arabian Gulf という)

__ヘルシンキ__【フィンランドの首都】Helsinki /hélsiŋki/.

__ヘルス__【健康】health.
●ヘルスクラブ a héalth clùb. (【参考】健康維持増進のための機器を備えた会員制のクラブ) ●ヘルスケア【健康管理】héalth càre. ●ヘルスセンター (娯楽施設)《米》a héalth spà;《英》a héalth fàrm. (【参考】運動・食餌で減量などの健康増進を目的とする施設); (保養地) a héalth resòrt. (❗*a health center* は《米》では「(学生または地域の)健康相談センター」,《英》では「保健所」) ●ヘルスメーター a báthroom scàle (❗《英》では ~s); (和製語) héalth mèter.

__ペルソナ__【<ラテン語】【(個人)】a persona /pərsóunə/.

__ヘルツ__【<ドイツ語】【振動数・周波数の単位】hertz /há:rts/ (略 Hz); 【単・複同形】●キロヘルツ kílohertz (略 kHz). ●メガヘルツ mégahertz (略 MHz). ●ギガヘルツ gígahertz (略 GHz).

__ベルディー__【イタリアの作曲家】Verdi /véərdi/ (Giuseppe ~).

__ベルト__ a belt; (座席の) a seat belt. ●ベルトつきのレインコート a *belted* raincoat. ●ベルトを締める fasten [buckle (up)] one's *belt*.
●ベルトコンベヤー a conveyor /kənvéiər/ belt, a conveyer. (❗(1) conveyor ともつづる. (2) a *belt conveyer* は普通ではない)

__ヘルニア__【医学】a rupture, (a) hernia /hə́:rniə/. ●ヘルニアになる rupture (oneself);《話》give oneself a *rupture*; (ヘルニアである) have a *rupture* [(a) *hernia*].

__ヘルパー__【助力者】a helper; 【家政婦】a (home) help.

__ヘルプ__【コンピュータ】help.
●ヘルプ画面 a hélp scrèen. (❗通例複数形で) ●ヘルプ機能 hélp fùnction.

__ベルファスト__【北アイルランドの首都】Bélfast.

__ヘルペス__【医学】herpes /hə́:rpi:z/.
●ヘルペス脳炎 herpes encephalitis.

__ベルベット__ vélvet. (⇨《同》ビロード)

__ベルボーイ__【ホテルなどのボーイ】a bellhop; a bellboy. (⇨ボーイ)

__ヘルメット__ a helmet; (オートバイ運転用などの) a crash helmet; (消防士の) a fireman's helmet; (建設現場用などの) a hardhat, a hárd hàt; (野球用の) a batting helmet (❗打撃用); a catcher's helmet (❗捕手用); (騎手の) a ríding càp.

__ベルモット__ (a) vermouth /vərmú:θ/. (【参考】食前酒の一種)

__ベルリン__【ドイツの首都】Berlin /bə:rlín/.
●ベルリンの壁 the Berlin Wall.

__ベルン__【スイスの首都】Bern(e) /bə́:rn/.

__ベレー__ (ぼう) ベレー(帽)【<フランス語】a beret /bəréi/.

__ペレストロイカ__【<ロシア語】【旧ソ連の民主化政策】perestroika.

__ヘレニズム__【ギリシャ的思想・文化】Hellenism.

__ヘレンケラー__【米国の社会福祉事業家】Helen Keller.

__ぺろ__ a tongue. (⇨《同》舌)

__ヘロイン__ heroin /hérouin/. ●ヘロイン常用者 a *heroin* addict.

__ぺろっと__ ●ぺろっと舌を出す stick out one's tongue (briefly [quickly]). ●ぺろっとなめる lick. (⇨ぺろぺろ) ●ぺろっと(=あっというまに)食べる eat(...) up [put (...) away] *in no time*. ●(皮などが)ぺろっとむける peel off.

へろへろ ●へろへろと倒れる collapse weakly; sink feebly to the ground. ●へろへろの紙 flimsy paper.

べろべろ ❶[なめるさま] ●べろべろなめる lick. ▶少年はアイスクリームの棒をべろべろとなめた The boy *licked* his fingers sticky with ice cream. (▮唇や舌で飲み食いをするときに出す音に slurp があるが、ぺろぺろ、ぴちゃぴちゃ、ぺちゃぺちゃなどが対応する: 猫が皿のミルクをぺろぺろなめていた The cat *was slurping* the milk in the dish.)
❷[酔っ払っているさま] べろべろに酔っている; 《話》 be dead [blind] drunk. ▶彼は昨夜べろべろに酔って帰ってきた He came home *dead [blind] drunk* last night.

ぺろぺろ ●ぺろぺろなめる lick. ▶犬が私の顔をぺろぺろなめた The dog *licked* my face.

ぺろりと (⇨ぺろっと)

べろんべろん (⇨べろべろ❷)

:へん 変 图 ❶[変化] a change; (移行) 《書》 (a) transition.
❷[変事, 非常事] (事故) an accident; (事件) an incident; (災害) a disaster; (非常の場合) an emergency. ●本能寺の変 the *incident* at the Honnoji Temple.
❸[通常と違った状態] strangeness.
❹[音楽] a flat 《記号 ♭》.
── **変な** 厖 strange; odd, 《話》 weird /wíərd/; 《やや古》 queer; peculiar; eccentric; funny; crazy; mad (-dd-); 《話》 out of one's mind (⇨おかしい❷, 妙); [怪しげな] suspicious, 《話》 fishy; [調子が悪い] wrong (▮通例叙述的に (⇨調子❸).

> **使い分け** strange 「変な」の意を表す最も一般的な語。以前に見聞きしたことがなく、明確な説明が難しいようなものであることを含意する。
> **odd** 普通の価値観や普段の状態などから考えると奇妙に思えることを表す。時に現実離れした奇妙さを示す。
> **queer** はっきりとは分からないが、どこか奇妙な点があることを表す。ただし、日常的な文脈で人に用いると「ゲイの」の意に解釈されることが多いので注意。
> **peculiar** 状況や物の性質などの奇妙さを表す。時に驚きを与えることを含意する。
> **curious** 物事の奇妙さを表す。人に対してはあまり用いない。否定的な意味はなく、興味を引くような面白みを含意する。
> **eccentric** 主に人の考えなどが風変わりであることを表す。必ずしも否定的な含意はなく、時に非凡さを表す。
> **funny** 物事の不可解さを表す。
> **crazy** 様子や行動などが奇妙で常識を外れていることを表す。
> **mad** 人が怒っている、または夢中になっている状態を表す。時に人・行動・様子などが普通ではないことも表す。
> **out of one's mind** 気が変であることを表す。

①[変な〜] ▶自動車のエンジンから変な音がした A *strange* [*An odd*] sound came from the car engine./The car engine made a *strange* [*an odd*] sound. ▶彼は変な(=不審な)目つきで私を見た He looked at me *suspiciously*./He gave me a *suspicious* glance. ▶網だなの上に変な物が置かれていた There was something *suspicious* on the rack.
②[...は[が]変だ] ▶彼女の態度はどこか変だ There is something *strange* [*odd, peculiar*] about her. ▶あんな女と結婚するなんて彼が変だ He is *crazy* [*mad*] to marry her. ▶今日の君は様子が変だ(=いつもの君らしくない) You *aren't yourself* today. ▶彼がそんなことをする[した]なんて変だ It's *strange* [*odd, funny*] that he should do [should have done] such a thing. (▮that 節内は … he does [has done, did] … の直説法も可能だが, should を用いると話し手の驚き・意外さを表す) ▶母親のデートのお膳立てをするなんて変だと思わないの Don't you think it's a little *weird* that you're trying to get your mother a date?
会話 「このヨーグルト何か変だな」「それはヨーグルトじゃなくてコテージチーズよ」 "There's something *wrong with* this yogurt." "It's not yogurt. It's cottage cheese."
── **変に** 副 ▶それは変に聞こえるかもしれないが事実だ It may sound *strange*, but it is true. ▶たぶん彼は暑さで頭が変になってしまったんだよ Perhaps he's *gone queer* (in the head) with the heat.

へん [軽蔑など] humph (▮h'm ともつづる), pooh, bah.

へん 辺 ❶[多角形の] a side. ●三角形の三つの辺 the three *sides* of a triangle. ▶この2辺は直角をなす These two *sides* form a right angle.
❷[近辺] a neighborhood. (⇨近辺, 辺り, 近所) ▶この辺はまったく初めてです(=地理が分からない) I'm quite a stranger *around* [*near*] here. (▮「この辺はよく知っています」は I know my way *around* [*near*] here.) ▶その辺のこと(=それに関すること)をもっと知りたい I want to know more *about* it.
❸[程度] ▶[話・授業などを] 今日はこの辺で終わろう That's all for today./[仕事などで] Let's call it a day./Let's end it here. ▶彼をどの辺まで信じてよいものやら I wonder *how much* I can trust him.

へん the left-hand (side) radical [component] of a Chinese character.

へん 編 ❶[作品の] ●1編の詩 a poem; a *piece of* [×a] poetry. ●前編 the first *part* [*volume, half*]; (見出しで) *Part* [*Volume*] 1. ●続編 a sequel 《*to*》; (続き) a continuation 《*of*》.
❷[編集] ▶博士編の辞書 the dictionary *edited* [《やや書》 *compiled*] by Dr.. (⇨編集)

── **へん** -遍, -返 (⇨回❶)

***べん 便** ❶[便利] convenience; [交通] service; [設備] a facility (▮通例複数形で). (⇨便利) ●水の便 the *convenience* of water. ●交通の便 transportation [communication] *facilities*; *facilities* for transportation [communication]. ▶この町はバスの便がよい[悪い] There is a good [poor] bus *service* in this town./The bus *service* is good [poor] in this town. ▶その病院は駅に近くて交通の便がよい The hospital *is convenient for* [*to*] the station. ▶家を買う前にその場所の交通の便をまず考慮すべきです Before you buy a house, you should first take into consideration the *convenience* of the location *for* transportation.
❷[糞] 《書》 feces /fíːsiːz/; 《書・婉曲的》 stool(s); [排泄(²⁾)作用] 《書》 excretion. ●堅い[軟らかい; 水のような]便をする have hard [soft, loose; watery] *stools*. ●血便が出る (⇨血便)

べん 弁 ❶[方言] (a) dialect; (なまり) an accent (⇨訛(ホミ)); [弁舌] speech; [演説] a speech. ●就任の弁 (give) an inaugural *speech* [*address*]. ●鹿児島弁で話す speak in Kagoshima *dialect* [with a Kagoshima *accent*].
❷[花弁] a petal. ❸[機械・臓器の] a valve.
● **弁が立つ** ▶彼はなかなか弁が立つ (話し方がうまい) He is quite a good [a fluent] speaker./(議論するのがうまい) He argues well.
● **弁を弄する** use casuistry [sophistry].

***ペン a pen. (▮万年筆・ボールペン・羽ペンなどを含む) ●ペンで書く write *with a pen* [*in pen*]. (⇨書く) ●ペン

へんあい

とインクで書く write *with* [*in*] *pen* and ink. (❗対句的に用いる場合は冠詞はつけない) ●ペン(=文筆業)で生計を立てる live [make a living] *by one's pen*. ▶このペンは書きやすい This *pen* is easy to write with. (❗with に注意)/This *pen* writes well.
- ペンを置く (書くことをやめる) put down one's pen; stop writing.
- ペンを折る stop [give up] writing [one's writing career].
- ペンを執る take up one's pen; (執筆を始める) start to write.
- ペンを走らせる (書く) write.
- ペン先 a nib, (米) a penpoint. ●ペン軸 a penholder. ●ペン習字 penmanship. ●ペンだこ a callus on one's middle finger (caused by writing).

へんあい 偏愛 图 (かたよった好み) (やや書) pàrtiálity (*to*); (えこひいき) (やや書) favoritism.
— 偏愛する 動 be partial (*to*); favor.

へんあつき 変圧器 a transformer.

へんい 変異 图 (地殻の) (a) (crustal) movement;〖生物〗(a) variation. ●突然変異〖生物〗(a) mutation.

へんい 変移 图 (a) change; (a) transition.
— 変移する 動 change (*into, to*).

べんい 便意 图 ●急に便意をもよおす urgently need to defecate; (英語) be taken short; (米語) suddenly feel *a call of nature*. (❗尿意の時にも用いる)

べんえき 便益 图〖便利〗convenience; facility;〖有益〗profit; advantage. ●便益を与える give [offer] *convenience* (*to*). ●…の便益を図る serve [administer to] (his) *convenience*.

へんおんどうぶつ 変温動物 〖生物〗a poikilotherm /pɔ̀ikiləθəːrm/; (一般に) a cold-blooded animal.

:**へんか 変化** 图 ❶〖変わること〗(全面的な変化) (a) change (*in, of*); (部分的な変化) (an) alteration; (変動) (a) variation (*in, of*); (変形) (a) transformation; (推移) (a) transition. ●天候の変化 a change *in* the weather. ●彼の態度の変化 his *change* of attitude. ●1日の気温の変化 a *variation in* temperature [a temperature *variation*] in a day. ●経済的変化を受ける undergo an economic *change* [*transformation*]. ●変化しやすい天気 changeable [*variable*] weather. ▶年よりはしばしば変化を恐れる Old people often fear *change*. ▶情勢に変化がない There is no *change* [*alteration*] *in* the situation./The situation remains unchanged.
❷〖変化に富むこと〗variety; diversity. (❗後の方が堅い語) ●変化に富んだ生活をする lead a life *full of change and variety*; lead a *varied* [(多事多難な) an *eventful*] life. ▶学校生活は変化に乏しいので我慢できないほど退屈だった The lack of *variety* made school life unbearably dull. ▶そこでの生活は単調で変化がない The life there is monotonous and doesn't *vary* (from day to day).
❸〖文法上の〗(動詞の) (a) conjugation; (格の) (a) declension. ▶動詞 come の変化が言えますか Can you *conjugate* the verb 'come'?
— 変化する 動 change; (部分的・断続的に) vary. (⇨変化❶) ▶状況は絶えず変化している Circumstances *are* always *changing*. ▶戦後東京はずいぶん変化した Tokyo *has changed* a lot [a great deal] since the war. ▶車窓の景色は時々刻々変化した The view from the train window *varied* every minute [from one minute to the next]. ▶彼のカーブは鋭く変化する[ほとんど変化しない] His curveball *breaks* sharply [has little break on

べんぎ

it].

へんか 返歌 a *tanka* sent in return.

*__べんかい 弁解__ 图〖言い訳〗(an) excuse /ikskjúːs/ (*for*);〖説明〗(an) explanation (*of, for*);〖正当化〗justification (*for*). ●そのようなミスに弁解の余地はない There is no *excuse* [*justification*] *for* such a mistake. ▶貧乏がお金を盗んだことの弁解にはならない Your poverty does not *justify* your stealing the money.
— 弁解(を)する 動 make* [offer] an excuse, excuse /ikskjúːz/ oneself (*for*); explain; justify. (⇨言い訳(を)する) ▶彼は遅れて来たことを弁解した He *made an excuse* [*excused himself*] *for* being late. ▶そのようなばかげたふるまいに対してどう弁解するつもりなのですか How are you going to *excuse yourself for* [*explain, justify*] such stupid behavior?/(弁解として言う) What are you going to say *in explanation* [*excuse, justification*] of such stupid behavior?

へんかきゅう 変化球 〖野球〗(throw) a breaking ball. (❗主にカーブ・スライダー・ナックルボールのように大きく曲がる球をいう。曲がりの小さな速球系のものは moving fastball という) ●変化球を打つのが上手な打者 a *breaking-ball* hitter.
● 変化球投手 a breaking-ball pitcher.

へんかく 変革 图〖変化〗(a) change;〖改革〗(a) reform;〖革命〗(a) revolution. ●思想の大変革 a *revolution* in thought. ▶労働者は社会変革を求めて世論に訴えた The workers agitated for social *reform*.
— 変革する 動 ▶我々の生活様式を変革する change [*reform*] our way of life.

へんがく 変額 variable.
● 変額年金 a variable annuity. ●変額保険 vari(rate) insurance.

べんがく 勉学 图〖勉強〗(a) study;〖学業〗(one's) studies. (⇨勉強) ●勉学に励む study hard; (研究を進める) pursue one's *studies*.

ベンガラ 〖赤色顔料〗red ocher;〖酸化鉄〗red (iron) oxide.

ベンガル ●ベンガル湾 the Bay of Bengal /beŋɡɔ́ːl/.

へんかん 返還 图 return, 〈書〉 restoration. ●北方領土の返還を要求する demand the *restoration* of the Northern Territories. ●沖縄返還(=復帰) the *reversion* of Okinawa.
— 返還する 動 ●優勝旗を返還する return [〈書〉 *restore*] the championship flag (*to*).

へんかん 変換 — 変換する 動 (変える) change; (切り換える) switch; (転換する) convért; (数式などを) transfórm. (⇨変える, 切り替える) ●ひらがなを漢字に変換する *convert* hiragana *to* kanji.

べんき 便器 〖便所用の〗a toilet (❗便座は a toilet seat); (小便用の) a urinal;〖室内用の〗(小便・大便用の) a chamber (pot); (病人のベッドに差し込む) a bedpan.

べんぎ 便宜 图〖都合のよいこと〗convenience (↔inconvenience);〖便宜を図る設備〗a facility (❗通例複数形で);〖利点〗(an) advantage. ●公衆の便宜を図る[尊重する] promote [respect] the public *convenience*. ●彼に研究の便宜(=設備)を与えてやる give [afford] him *facilities* for study. ●便宜上それをある所に置いておく leave it where it was *for convenience*(') *sake* [*for the sake of convenience*]. ▶東京では山を教育を受けられるという便宜がある Tokyo has the *advantage* of giving us a good education./(人が主語) In Tokyo we have the *advantage* of receiving [being able to receive] a good education. ▶この店では客の便宜を

図って買い物袋が用意されている At this store shopping bags are provided for the customers' *convenience*.
── **便宜的な** 形 expedient. (❗通例叙述的に) ● 便宜的手段を講じる use an expedient; (一時的な手段をとる) take *temporary* measures.
● **便宜主義** opportunism. ● **便宜主義者** an opportunist.

***ペンキ** [＜オランダ語] (house) paint. (❗paint のみでは絵の具の意にもなる) ● ペンキ用のはけ a *paint*brush. ▶ペンキがはげている The paint is coming [peeling] off. ▶ペンキ塗りたて《掲示》《米》Wet *paint*./《英》Fresh *paint*. ▶彼はドアにペンキを塗った He *painted* the door. (▶「ペンキで白く塗った」は He *painted* the door white.)
● **ペンキ屋** (店) a (house) páint stòre [shòp]; (人) a (house) painter. (❗看板をかく場合は house に代えて ad や signboard を用いる)

へんごう 変記号 a flat (記号 ♭).

へんきゃく 返却 名 (a) return; (金銭の) (a) repayment. ● 図書館への本の返却 the *return* of books *to* the library.
── **返却する** 動 return. (⇨返す)
● **返却ボタン** (自動販売機の) the change return button.

へんきゅう 返球 (外野からの) a throw-in; (捕手から投手へ、または初めの送球をした野手への) a return throw. ● ホームへ好［悪］返球する make a good [a bad] *throw*(-*in*) to home.

へんきょう 辺境 (遠隔地) a remote region; (国境地方) a border(land); (西部開拓時代の) the frontier.

へんきょう 偏狭 ── **偏狭な** 形 (了見の狭い) narrowminded (⇔broad-minded); (不寛容な) intolerant (❗以上は人について用いる); (狭い) narrow; (偏見のある) prejudiced. (❗最後の 2 語は心や見解についても用いる)

***べんきょう** 勉強 名 (勉学) (a) study; a lesson; work. (⇨[類語])
❶【～の (の) 勉強】● 学校の勉強 schoolwork. ● 受験勉強 studying for an (entrance) exam. ● 系統立った勉強 a systematic *study*. ● フランス語の勉強 the *study of* French; one's *lesson in* French.
❷【勉強が［の］】● 勉強がよくできる［できない］ do well [poorly] at school; make good [poor] grades. ▶彼は勉強が大変よくできる(=優秀な生徒) He's a very good student. ▶彼は勉強のしすぎで病気になった He got sick because he *studied* [*worked*] too hard.
❸【勉強を】● 勉強をする (⇨動) ● 勉強を怠る neglect one's *studies* [*lessons*]. ▶私たちは中学校で英語の勉強を始める We begin the *study* of [to *study*] English in junior high school. ▶父が勉強を見てくれた Father helped me with my *lessons*. (❗×Father helped my *lessons*. としない)
── **勉強する** 動 ❶【学ぶ】study, learn*, work.

┌─────────────────────────┐
│ 使い分け **study** 主に学校の勉強や専門の研究を行うことを表す。勉強することは自体に焦点が当てられる。比較的高度なレベルの勉強であることを含意する。
learn 主に楽器や語学などの知識や技術を習得することを表す。勉強だけでなく経験などによって学習する場合にも用いられる。
work 原義は「働く」であるが、文脈から「勉強する」の意が明らかな場合に用いられる。 │
└─────────────────────────┘

❶【(副＋) 勉強する】● もっと勉強する *study* [*work*] harder. ▶彼はよく勉強する He *studies* [*works*] *hard*. (❗×learn hard は不可)/He is a hard worker [a hardworking student]. ▶勉強し

ているときに話しかけないでください Please don't speak to me when I'm *studying* [*working*]. ▶彼は昨日は一日中勉強しないで本を読んでいた Yesterday I read books all day instead of *studying*.
会話「「どこで勉強しているのですか」「エール大学です」 "Where *are* you *studying*?" "At Yale University."
❷【...を勉強する】● 数学をよい本で勉強する learn math *out of* good books. ● 生物学を A 教授の下で勉強する *study* biology *under* professor A. (❗(1) ×learn は不可. (2)「先生から習う」は learn *from* a teacher)
❸【...のために勉強する】● 期末試験のために勉強する *study* [*prepare, work*] *for* the term exam. ▶我々は主に自分のために勉強するのだ We mostly *study for* ourselves. ▶彼は医者になるために勉強している He's *studying to* be a doctor.
❷【値引きする】(⇨負ける ❸)
会話「三つまとめて買うからちょっと勉強してちょうだい」「そうですね. 三つで 100 ドルならどうですか」「嬉しいわ. ありがとう」"Could you *knock down* [*drop*] the price a little if I buy three?" "Hmm. How about 100 dollars for three?" "That's great. Thanks."
● **勉強家** a hardworking [(やや書) a diligent] student; a hard worker. ● **勉強会** (会合) a stúdy mèeting; (仲間) a stúdy gròup [circle]. ● **勉強時間** one's study hours. ● **勉強机** a study desk. ● **勉強道具** a tool for study. ● **勉強部屋** a study (room).

へんきょく 編曲 名 (an) arrangement.
── **編曲する** 動 arrange. ▶この曲はピアノ用に編曲されている This music *is arranged* for the piano.
● **編曲者** an arranger.

へんきん 返金 名 a refund /rɪ:fʌnd/.
── **返金する** 動 give* a refund; pay back the money; (やや書) refund /rɪfʌnd/ 《him》《his》 money, refund 《his》 money 《to him》. ● 全額返金してもらう［を受ける］ have [get, receive] a full *refund*; have one's money refunded in full.
会話「この服大きすぎたの. 返金してもらえるかしら」「お客様、レシートをお持ちですか」「ええ、これです」「ありがとうございます. これが返金分でございます」"I'm afraid this dress is too big. I'd like to *have* my *money back*. [I'd like my *money back on* this dress./Can I *have* a *refund*?/(話) Can you take it back?]" "Have you got your receipt, ma'am?" "Yes, here it is." "Thank you, ma'am. Here's your *refund*."

ペンギン【動物】a penguin /péŋgwɪn/.

へんくつ 偏屈 ── **偏屈な** 形 (心のねじけた) warped /wɔ́:rpt/; (風変わりな) eccentric; (頑固な) obstinate; (心の狭い) narrow-minded. ● 偏屈者 a man [a woman] with a *warped* mind (❗通例 ×a *warped* man [woman] とはしない); (変人) an eccentric (person).

ペンクラブ (国際ペンクラブ) PEN 《International Association of *P*oets, Playwrights, *E*ditors, *E*ssayists and *N*ovelists の略》.

へんげ 変化 ❶【神仏の人への変身】(a) personification of a god. ▶神が少女の姿に変化する A god *changes* into the form of a young girl. ● A god *transforms* into a young girl.
❷【妖怪】a goblin; a monster.
❸【演劇】▶彼は七変化を見事に演じきった He performed superbly seven different roles in quick succession 《before the breathless spectators》.

へんけい

へんけい 変形 图 (ねじれ) a warp /wɔːrp/; (別の形への) (a) transformation; (本来の形をそこなうこと) (a) deformation. ● 背骨の変形 (a) *deformation* of the spine. ● 変形の土地 an irregularly-shaped plot.
― **変形させる** 動 warp; transform. (⇨変える) ▶熱で本の表紙が変形した Heat *warped* [×*transformed*] the book cover.
● **変形性関節炎**〖医学〗osteoarthritis. ● **変形文法** transformational grammar.

へんけい 変型 图 a variation.

べんけい 弁慶 ● 弁慶の泣き所 one's Achilles heel. (❗日本語では「むこうずね (shin)」のこと) ● 弁慶縞(じま) a two-color check pattern.

へんけいどうぶつ 扁形動物 a flatworm; a platyhelminth.

へんけん 偏見 (偏った考え) (a) prejudice; (先入観による好み) (a) bias /báiəs/. (❗よい意味にも用いる). ● 根深い人種的偏見 deep-rooted racial *prejudice*. ● 偏見のある態度 a *prejudiced* [a *biased*] attitude. ● 偏見のない意見 an *unprejudiced* [an *unbiased*, (公平な) an *impartial*] opinion. ● 偏見がない be free from *prejudice*. ● あらゆる偏見を捨てる put [cast] away all *prejudice*. ● 偏見なしに without *prejudice*. ▶彼は政治家に対して偏見を持っている He has a *prejudice* [a *bias*] *against* politicians./He *is prejudiced* [is *biased*] *against* politicians.

へんげん 片言 ● 片言隻語(せきご) (a) (piece of) word; a few words.

へんげん 変幻 変幻自在の changing-freely; (目まぐるしく変わる) ever-changing, fast-changing, kaleidoscopic.

*** べんご 弁護** 图 (一般にまたは法廷での) (a) defense (❗通例単数形で); (正当化) justification. ● 自己弁護 self-*justification*; self-*defense*. ▶彼の行為はまったく弁護の余地がない His action is quite *indefensible*./(正当化できない) Nothing can *justify* (him in) his action.
― **弁護する** 動 〖法廷で〗plead*; defend (❗defend は日常語では行為・意見についても用いる); 〖一般に〗(味方をして言う) speak* in defense of (him) [in (his) defense, for (him)]; (人・行為・意見などを正当化する) justify; 〖主義・政策などを主張する〗(書) advocate. ▶自分を弁護する *speak for* oneself. ▶私は自分の弁護をしてくれる有能な弁護士を頼んだ I got a good lawyer to *defend* me [*plead* my case, *plead for* me].
● **弁護依頼人** a client. ● **弁護団** (被告側) (defense) counsel, counsel for the defense; (原告側) counsel for the plaintiff. ● **単・複両扱い** ● **弁護人** (総称) (defense) counsel (⇨弁護団); a defense lawyer, an advocate. ● **弁護料** a lawyer's fee.

*** へんこう 変更** 图 (全面的な) (a) change; (部分的な) (an) alteration /ɔːltəréɪʃən/; (一部修正〗(a) modification. ▶住所の変更を市役所に届け出る have one's *change* of address registered at the city hall. ● 計画[時間]は予告なく変更になることがあります The plan [time] is subject to *change* [*alteration*] without notice. ▶この法律は多少変更の必要があります This law needs [wants] some *modification*(s)./This law needs to *be modified* to some extent (❗wants to be … も可能だが(まれ)). ▶このたび下記の住所に移転いたしましたが電話番号には変更はありません We have just moved to the following address. Our telephone number remains the same.
― **変更する** 動 change; (正式に) alter /ɔːltər/; (修正する) modify. ● 住所を変更する *change* [×*alter*] one's address. ● 予定を変更する *change* [*alter*] one's schedule.

へんこう 偏光 polarized light.
● **偏光顕微鏡** a polarizing microscope. ● **偏光板** a polarizing plate. ● **偏光フィルター** a polarizing filter. ● **偏光レンズ** a polarizing lens.

へんこう 偏向 图 (a) deviation 《from》. ● 右翼偏向 right-wing *deviation* [*deviationism*].
― **偏向する** 動 deviate 《from》.
● **偏向教育** politically biased education.

へんこうせい 変光星 〖天文〗a variable star.

べんごし 弁護士 图 ● 法律を専門とするすべての人に用いられる一般的な語》, 《米》an attorney; 〖法廷弁護士〗《米》a counselor, 《英》a barrister; 〖事務弁護士〗《英》a solicitor (主に訴訟依頼人のために法律事務を執行し、訴訟の準備をする). ● 刑事[民事]弁護士 a criminal [a civil] *lawyer*. ● 顧問弁護士 a legal advisor. ● 弁護士になる become a *lawyer*; enter the law; be admitted 〖《英》called〗to the bar. ● 弁護士を(開業)している practice law; be in law practice. ● 弁護士を頼む engage a *lawyer*.
● **弁護士会** a bar association; the bar. ● **弁護士事務所** a lawyer's office. ● **弁護士料金** a lawyer's [a retaining] fee.

べんざ 便座 a toilet seat.
● **便座カバー** a seat cover.

へんさい 返済 图 return; 〖金銭の〗(a) repayment (❗1回1回の返済や返済金 (money repaid) の意では ©). ● 家のローンの返済が滞る get behind in the loan *repayments* on the house. ● 借金の返済を迫る press 〈him〉 for *repayment* of the money; press 〈him〉 to pay the debt. ● 返済可能なクレジットを組む establish a *good line of credit*. ● 分割返済 *repayment* in installments [in easy *payment*s]; (債務・公社債などの) an amortization.
― **返済する** 動 return; (金銭を) repay*, pay* 《money》back. ● 利子をつけて借金を返済する *repay* [*pay back*] a loan with interest. ● 借金をきれいに返済する *pay* [*clear*] *off* one's debt. ● 働いて返済する work one's debt off; work out one's debt.
● **返済期限** the term of repayment; the repáyment tèrm. ● **返済期日** the repáyment dàte; (債務の) final maturity. ● **返済能力** ability to repay debt [loan]. ● **返済不能** default; repayment default.

へんざい 偏在 maldistribution. ● **富の偏在** the *maldistribution* of wealth.

へんざい 遍在 图 《書》omnipresence.
― **遍在する** 動 be present everywhere;《書》be omnipresent.

べんさい 弁済 图 repayment, payment. ● 債務の弁済を履行しない default on the loan.
― **弁済する** 動 repay* a loan.

べんざいてん 弁財天 *Benzaiten*; (説明的に) one of the seven deities of good fortune, and the only goddess of beauty and talent in the group.

へんさち 偏差値 〖統計〗deviation value; (テストの) a T-score. ● **偏差値の高い学生** a student with a high *T-score*.

へんしゅう 編集 图 (⇨🈩 編集)
― **編集する** 動 compile [edit] 《a dictionary》.

へんし 変死 ● 工事現場で発見された変死体 a *body* found at the construction site.

へんじ

— **変死する** 動 die 〈～d; dying〉 an accidental [(暴力・事故などによる) a violent, (異常な) an unnatural] death.

ːへんじ 返事 名 an answer 〈to〉; a reply 〈to〉; a response 〈to〉.

> 使い分け **answer** 質問や手紙などに対する返事を意味する最も一般的な語.
> **reply** 主に手紙・電話・呼びかけなどに対する返事. 時に返事の内容より返事の有無に焦点が当てられた.
> **response** answer より堅い語. 時に即座の返事であることを含意する.

① 〖～返事〗 ▶あいまいな返事 an ambiguous *answer* [*reply*]. ▶色よい返事をする give a favorable *answer* [*reply*] 〈to him〉; give 〈him〉 a favorable *answer*. ▶彼は私たちの提案に二つ返事で同意した He *readily* said yes [agreed] to [×with] our proposal.

② 〖返事が〗 ▶きのう彼から返事が来た I got [received] a *reply* from him yesterday. ▶1か月前に彼女に手紙を出したがまだ返事がない I wrote (to) her a month ago, but I've had no *answer* yet. (! to を省略するのは《主に米》) ▶ドアのベルを鳴らしたが返事がなかった I rang the doorbell but there was no *answer* [nobody answered]. ▶お返事が非常に遅れて申し訳ございません I apologize for taking so long to reply to your letter.

③ 〖返事に〗 ▶私は返事に困った I didn't know what I should *answer* [what to *answer*].

④ 〖返事を〗 ▶すぐに手紙の返事をください Please send [×write] an *answer* [a reply] *to* my letter soon./Please *answer* my letter soon. (! (1) write an answer は「(質問に対して)答えを書く」の意なのでここでは不可. (2) 単に「すぐに返事をください」なら Please write (me) back soon. も可) ▶彼は彼女が3月10日に日本を立ったと返事をしてきた He *wrote back* (saying [to say]) that she had left Japan on March 10th. ▶ご返事を(楽しみに)お待ちしています I am looking forward to your *reply* [(手紙) *letter*]. ▶彼は母親に返事をしなかった He didn't *answer* [*reply to*] his mother./He gave no *answer* [made no *reply*] to his mother. ▶今すぐ返事をしなくてもよい. 考えておいてくれ You don't have to *give me an answer* right away, think about it.

— **返事する** 動 answer; reply 〈to〉; respond 〈to〉. (! answer が最も一般的) (⇨ 図 ④) ▶どうもお返事申しあげにくいお話だとは存じますが... I don't know what to say. I appreciate the offer, but....

へんじ 変事 〖予期しない悪い出来事〗 a disaster; an accident; (突発的な出来事) an emergency.

べんし 弁士 〖演説者〗 a speaker, 《やや書》 an orator; 〖無声映画の〗 a narrator.

へんしつ 変質 名 〖質的変化〗 a change in quality, (a) transformation.

— **変質する** 動 change; be transformed 〈into〉. ▶熱はワインを変質させる Heat *turns* wine.
• 変質者 a pervert.

へんしつ 偏執 • 偏執狂 monomania /mɑ̀nəméiniə/; (人) a monomaniac. (! 一つのことに固執すること 〖人〗) • 偏執症 〖医学〗 (統合失調症の一つ) paranoia; (偏執病患者) a paranoid.

へんしゃ 編者 an editor; a compiler. (⇨ 編集する)

へんしゅ 変種 〖生物〗 a variety; (突然変異による) a mutation.

ːへんしゅう 編集 名 editing; compilation.
— 編集の 形 editorial.

へんしょく

— **編集する** 動 〖書物・新聞・放送番組・映画などを〗 edit (! 人の書いたものや作ったものを削る・直すなどに); 〖辞書・選集・資料集などを〗 compile (! 他の本などから資料を集めて). • テープを編集する *edit* a tape. • 手引書を編集する *compile* a guide book. ▶この本は上手に編集されている This book *is* well (↔badly) *edited*.
• 編集会議 an editorial [an editors'] meeting.
• 編集局長 a managing editor. • 編集室 an editorial office. • 編集者 an editor; a compiler.
• 編集長 the editor-in-chief; the chief editor.
• 編集部 an editorial department. • 編集部員 an editorial staff member. (! 集合的にいうときは an editorial staff で単・複数扱い) • 編集方針 one's editorial policy.

へんしゅう 偏執 (⇨ 偏執)

へんしょ 返書 a reply. (⇨ 返事)

ːべんじょ 便所 〖家庭の〗《米》a bathroom; a toilet; 《英》a lavatory, (英语では) a WC; 〖公共の場の〗《米》a rest room, a washroom; (男性用)《米》 the men's room, 《英語》the gents (! しばしば the G-. 単数扱い. 《掲示》Gentlemen); (女性用)《米》the ladies' [powder] room, 《英語》the ladies (! 単数扱い. 《英》《掲示》Ladies); 〖便器〗a toilet, a lavatory.

> 解説 (1) 《米》では **bathroom** が最も一般的な語で, 主に家庭の便所を表すが, レストランなどの公共施設のものをさすこともある. 《英》では **toilet** が最も一般的な語で, やや堅い語は **lavatory** 《話》では **loo** /lúː/ ともいう. WC は water closet の略で家の見取図や戸の表示用以外は 《やや古》.
> (2) 上にあげた語句は, toilet, lavatory を除き, いずれも婉曲語. 特に powder room は高級さ・上品さを暗示する.

• 公衆便所《米》a cómfort stàtion [ròom]; 《主に英》a (public) convenience. (! 以上はいずれも public toilets [lavatories] の婉曲語) • 水洗便所 a flush *toilet* [*lavatory*]. • 和式便所 (=便器) a *toilet* of squatting type. • 便所に入っている[行く] 《米》 be in [go to, use] the *bathroom*; 《英》be in [go to, use] the *toilet*. ▶便所はどこですか (家庭で) Will you show me where the *bathroom* is, please? (! 婉曲的に) May I use your *bathroom*?/Where can I wash my hands? ということも多い)/(公共の場で) Where [Which way] is the *rest* [*men's, ladies'*] *room*? (! which way の方が婉曲的)

へんじょう 返上 名 ▶休日返上で働く *give up* one's holiday to do the work; (週末も働く) work on [《英》at] the weekend as well.

— **返上する** 動 return; (あきらめる) give*... up. • 運転免許証を返上する *return* [give back] one's driver's license. • 汚名を返上する clear one's name.

ːべんしょう 弁償 名 (his) compensation, 《書》reparation. (⇨ 賠償)

— **弁償する** 動 compensate 《him》for (his) loss; pay* [make* up] for a loss. ▶君がそれを壊したんだから弁償しなければならない You broke it and you'll have to *pay for* it.
• 弁償金 (a) compensation 〈for〉. (! 複数形なし)

べんしょうほう 弁証法 dialectic.

へんしょく 変色 名 (a) change of color; discoloration.

— **変色する** 動 change color; (色が悪くなる) discolor; (色があせる) fade. • 変色した discolored; faded. ▶酸で青い布地が変色した The acid *dis-*

colored the blue cloth.
へんしょく 偏食 (a) correct an *unbalanced diet*. ▶太郎は偏食がひどい Taro has too many kinds of food he doesn't like to eat.
── **偏食する** 動 have* an unbalanced diet. ▶偏食する子どもは多い Many children *eat only what they like*.
ペンション [<フランス語] a small (inexpensive) hotel. (!)英国を除くヨーロッパ圏のものを a pension と呼ぶことがある
べんじる 弁じる (意見を述べる) make* a speech 《*about, on*》; argue 《*about; against*》.
ペンシルバニア [米国の州] Pennsylvania /pènsəlvéinjə/ (略 Pa., Penn(a). 郵便略 PA].
へんしん 返信 a reply; an answer. ●返信を書く reply to 〔*answer*〕 a letter. ●返信用はがき a replý càrd. ●返信用封筒 a stamped addressed envelope (略 S.A.E.). ●返信料 retúrn pòstage.
へんしん 変心 名 (心変わり) a change of heart [mind]; (裏切り) betrayal.
── **変心する** 動 have* a change of heart; change one's mind; (裏切る) betray.
へんしん 変身 名 (a) metamorphosis (複 -phoses); (通例よい方への) transformation.
── **変身する** 動 ▶彼女は魔女に変身した She *turned into* a witch.
へんじん 変人 an eccentric [an odd] person, an eccentric; (話) a freak.
ベンジン [化学] benzin(e) /bénzi:n/.
ペンス pence (略 p). (!)単数は a penny. 略記号にはピリオドをつけない
へんすう 変数 [数学] a variable.
へんずつう 偏頭痛, 片頭痛 [医学] 《(get [suffer from]》 (a) migraine /máigrèin/.
へんする 偏する be partial (*to*); be biased 《*against, toward*; in favor of》; be one-sided. ▶審判は一方に偏しないように心がけなくてはならない Judges should not be *partial to* [*toward*] one side.
へんせい 変成 ●**変成岩** a metamorphic rock. ●**変成作用** [地学] metamorphism.
へんせい 変声 (⇒声変わり)
●**変声期** the period when a boy's voice changes.
へんせい 変性 ●**変性アルコール** methylated [denatured] spirits [alcohol].
へんせい 編成 名 [組織すること] organization; [組織形成すること] formation. ▶次の列車は 8 両編成です (=8 両で構成されている) The next train *is made up of* eight cars [(英) carriages]./The next train *has* eight cars.
── **編成する** 動 organize; form. ●野球チームを編成する *organize* [*form*] a baseball team. ●予算を編成する *compile* [*draw up*] a budget. ●番組を編成する *arrange* [*draw up*] programs.
へんせい 編制 名 [組織すること] organization; [外形を整えること] formation. ●軍隊を戦時編制に替える *reorganize* the army for war.
── **編制する** 動 organize; form. ●兵士を3連隊に編制する *organize* soldiers *into* three regiments.
へんせいふう 偏西風 the westerlies; the prevailing westerly winds.
へんせつ 変節 名 (裏切り) (a) betrayal.
── **変節する** 動 betray.
●**変節者** a betrayer; 《書》a rénegàde.
べんぜつ 弁舌 (話すこと) speech. ●弁舌の巧みな人 an eloquent speaker.

●**弁舌さわやか** ▶彼は弁舌さわやかだった His *speech was eloquent,*/He spoke eloquently.
へんせん 変遷 [変化] (a) change; [推移] (a) transition ((!)change より堅い語); [浮き沈み] ups and downs. ●時代の変遷 the *changes* of the times. ●封建社会から近代社会への変遷 the *transition from* a feudal *to* a modern society.
へんそう 返送 ── **返送する** 動 send*… back; return.
へんそう 変装 名 (a) disguise /disgáiz/. ●変装用につけひげをつける put on a false beard as a *disguise*; *disguise* oneself *with* [*by* wearing] a false beard. ●夜のホームレスの変装を見抜く see through his homeless disguise.
── **変装する** 動 (仮装する) put* on a disguise (*to do*); disguise oneself (*as* a sailor). ●変装している wear a disguise; be disguised. ●変装した人 a person *in disguise*.
へんぞう 変造 名 [改変] alteration; [偽造] forgery.
── **変造する** 動 alter (documents); forge (a 10,000 yen bank note).
へんそうきょく 変奏曲 a variation.
へんそく 変則 ──**変則的な** 形 (正規の方法に従わない) irregular; (正常でない) anómalous; (例外的な) exceptional.
●**変則ダブルヘッダー** [野球] an unorthodox doubleheader. ●**変則投手** [野球] a junkballer.
へんそく 変速 ●5段変速の自動車 a car with five *gears.*
●**変速機** [装置] a gearbox; a transmission. ●**変速レバー** (米) a gearshift, (英) a gear lever [stick].
へんたい 変態 ❶ [動物の] (書) metamórphosis (複 -phoses /-siːz/). ❷ [性欲の] a sexual perversion; (人) a sexual pérvert.
へんたい 編隊 formation. ●編隊飛行 formation flying. ●編隊飛行をする fly in *formation*; do *formation flying*.
へんたいがな 変体仮名 (説明的に) cursive *kana* letters (that are of older origin than the ordinary *kana* letters used at present).
ペンタゴン [米国国防総省] the Pentagon. (参考) 建物が五角形であることから
べんたつ 鞭撻 名 (an) encouragement.
── **鞭撻する** 動 encourage (him *to do*). (⇒励ます)
ペンダント a pendant.
へんち 辺地 a remote place. (⇒僻地)
ベンチ a bench. (⇒椅子(゛)) ●公園のベンチ a park *bench*. ●ベンチに腰をかける sit on a *bench*. ●レギュラー選手をベンチに格下げする *bench* a regular player. ●ベンチ入りする make the team (club).
●**ベンチウォーマー** [控え選手] a benchwarmer. (!)「ベンチを暖める」は warm the bench) ●**ベンチシート** a bench seat. ●**ベンチプレス** bench press. ●**ベンチプレスをする** bench-press. ●**ベンチマーク** [コンピュータ]
ペンチ (a pair of) pliers.
へんちくりん 変ちくりん ──**変ちくりんな** 形 (妙な) strange; queer; (風変りな) odd; peculiar.
ベンチャー [冒険的事業] a venture. ●ジョイントベンチャー [共同企業体] a joint *venture*.
●**ベンチャー企業** a venture company. ●**ベンチャーキャピタル** (米) venture (英) risk) capital. ●**ベンチャー精神** a venturesome spirit. ●**ベンチャービジネス** [新興ビジネス] a venture business.
へんちょ 編著 ●山田太郎編著 Edited [*Compiled*] *by* Taro Yamada. (!)文字通りに written and edited… とはしない

へんちょう 変調 ❶【音楽】(⇨転調)
❷[調子が狂うこと] ▶最近体に変調をきたしている(=一体の具合がよくない) I'm *not feeling well* these days./I've been *feeling out of sorts* recently. (⇨体調, 気分)

へんちょう 偏重 图 undue emphasis《on》. ●学歴偏重 diplomaism.
── **偏重する** 動 ●学歴を偏重する place *undue* [*too much*] *emphasis on* educational background.

へんちょうし 変調子 (⇨変調)

べんつう 便通 a bówel mòvement [mótion], 《話》 a BM; 《米》《書》 a movement. ●便通をよくする help《him》have regular *bowel movements* [*motions*]. ▶日に何回ぐらい便通がありますか How often do your *bowels move* once a day? (!your *bowels* が主語) ▶便通はきちんとあります My *bowels moves* regularly [are regular]. ▶3日間便通がありません I haven't had a *bowel movement* [*motion*] [(便秘している) *have been constipated*, *have had constipation*] for three days.

ペンティアム 【コンピュータ】《商標》Pentium.

ペンディング ●ペンディングの not decided [settled], 《書》 pending. ▶その問題はまだペンディング(=未決定)になっている The problem *is* still *waiting to be settled*.

へんてこ 変梃 ── 変てこな 形 odd; strange. ●変てこな帽子《*in*》an *odd* hat.

へんてつ 変哲 ●何の変哲もない陶器 a very *ordinary* piece of pottery.

ヘンデル 【ドイツ生まれの英国の作曲家】Handel /hǽndl/ (George Friderick ~).

へんてん 変転 图 (変化) a (great) change; (展開) a development. ●変転きわまりない ever-changing. ▶人生は変転きわまりないものだ Life is full of *ups and downs*.
── **変転する** 動 change; develop.

べんてん 弁天 (⇨弁財天)

へんでんしょ 変電所 a (transformer) substation.

へんとう 返答 an answer, a reply. (⇨返事)

へんどう 変動 图 [変化] (a) change;【物価・相場などの】(a) fluctuation《*of*, *in*》;【社会などの激変】(an) upheaval. ●株価の絶えざる変動 a constant *fluctuation* in stock prices. ●政策の大変動を引き起こす bring about a great *change* in policy. ●為替レートの変動 a foreign exchange *fluctuation*.
── **変動的** 形 fluctuating; floating; variable; transitory; flexible.
── **変動する** 動 change; fluctuate. ▶物価は最近変動している Prices *are fluctuating* these days.
●変動為替相場制 the floating exchange rate system. ●ドルを変動為替相場制にする *float* the dollars. ●変動金利 the floating interest rate; the variable-rate interest. ●変動所得 transitory income. ●変動幅 a fluctuation band.

*****べんとう 弁当**【解説】lunch は弁当の一般的な語. 昼食という意もあるので区別するために a packed *lunch* ともいう. 野外で食べる弁当は a picnic *lunch*, 旅行や折り詰め弁当は a box *lunch* という. 「子供が学校へ持っていく弁当」は the children's [kids'] school *lunch* などという.

●弁当を詰める[作る] fill [fix] a *lunch* box; pack a *lunch*. ●弁当を食べる eat [have] (one's) *lunch*. ▶私は毎日工場に弁当を持って行く I take my *lunch* to the factory every day.
●弁当代 lúnch mòney. ●弁当箱 a lúnch bòx.

へんとうせん 扁桃腺 【解剖】the [one's] tonsils. (!その一つは a tonsil)
●扁桃腺炎 tonsillitis /tɑ̀nsəláitəs/. ●扁桃腺切除 (a) tonsillotomy; (摘出) (a) tonsillectomy. ●扁桃腺肥大 enlarged tonsils.

へんな 変な strange. (⇨変)

へんにゅう 編入 图【入学許可】admission; (転学) a transfer;【合併】incorporation.
── **編入する** 動 ●(小学)2年生に編入される be admitted to the 2nd grade; be accepted as a 2nd grader. ●村を隣接する市に編入する *incorporate* a village *into* a neighboring city.
●編入試験 a transfer admission test. ▶彼女は短大から4年制大学に入る編入試験を受けた She took an exam to *transfer from* the junior college *to* a 4-year college.

ペンネーム a pen name, a pseudonym /sjúːdənɪm/《*of*》. ●ペンネームを使う adopt [use] a *pen name* [a *pseudonym*]. ●キングというペンネームで小説を書く write novels under the *pseudonym* of King.

ベンネビス ●ベンネビス山【スコットランドの山】 Ben Nevis.

へんねん 編年 ●編年体の in chronological order. ●編年史 a chronicle.

へんのう 返納 ── **返納する** 動 (物・金を) return; (金を) pay* back; repay*; refúnd.
●返納金 a repayment; (a) réfund.

へんぱ 偏頗 图 partiality.
── **偏頗な** 形 partial《*to*》. (⇨片寄り)

へんぱい 返杯 ── **返杯する** 動 offer a cup of *sake* in return.

ペンパル a pén pàl.

へんぴ 辺鄙 ── **辺鄙な** 形 ●辺ぴな村 an *out-of-the-way*【人里離れた】a *remote* village.

べんぴ 便秘 constipation,《米》irregularity (!婉曲的な言い方).
── **便秘する** 動 ●便秘している be suffering from *constipation*; be *constipated* [《米》*irregular*]. ▶私は旅行するといつも便秘します I always *get constipated* when I travel.

へんぴん 返品 returned goods. 【事情】(1) 米国ではたいていの百貨店には返品用カウンター (Return Counter) がある. (2) Satisfaction guaranteed の表示があるものは返品がきくが, No returns の表示のものは返品できない) ▶この服はバーゲンで買ったから返品できない I bought this dress on sale and I can't *return* it [*take it back*]. ●「返品=払い戻し)のきかない品物」は a non-refundable item)
── **返品する** 動 return [(送り返す) send* back] goods.

ペンフレンド a pen pal,《英》a pen friend.

へんぺい 扁平 ── **扁平な** 形 flat.

へんぺいそく 扁平足 ●扁平足である have *flatfeet*; be flatfooted. ▶私はひどい扁平足だ I'm seriously splayfooted.

べんべつ 弁別 图 (a) distinction.
── **弁別する** 動 distinguish. ●善悪を弁別する draw a *distinction between* good and evil; *distinguish* good *from* evil. (⇨区別)

へんぺん 片々 ── **片々たる** 形 ❶[薄っぺらな] insignificant; unimportant; (価値のない) worthless.
❷[切れ切れの] ●片々たる(=断片的な)知識 *fragmentary* knowledge《*of* English grammar》.
❸[翻る] ●桜花が片々として舞い散っている The petals of cherry blossoms *are fluttering down* to the ground.

べんべん 便々 ●都会の片隅で便々と日を送る *idle* one's time *away* in the obscure corner of

town; lead an *idle* and obscure *life* in town.
● 便々たる太鼓腹 a *protuberant* belly; a potbelly.

ぺんぺんぐさ ぺんぺん草 〔植物〕(a) shepherd's purse. ● ぺんぺん草の生えた家(=人の住まないさびれた家) a deserted house.

へんぼう 変貌 图 (変化) (a) change; (変形) (a) transformation; (a) transfiguration. (⇨変化)
── **変貌する** 動 change 《into》; (変形する) transform [transfigure] 《into》. ● 近代的な町に変貌する a *change into* a modern town.

へんぽう 返報 图 (⇨報復, 仕返し)

べんぽう 便法 ● 便法を講じる resort to *expedient* means.

へんぽん 返本 ── **返本する** 動 return a book 《to the publisher》.

へんぽん 翻翻 ▶ 旗は風に翻翻と翻っていた The flag *was fluttering* [*flapping*] in the (strong) wind.

べんまく 弁膜 〔解剖〕a valve. ● 心臓弁膜症 valvular disease of the heart.

べんむかん 弁務官 a commissioner. ● 高等弁務官 a high commissioner.

へんむけいやく 片務契約 a unilateral contract [agreement].

へんめい 変名 图 (名前を変えること) a change of one's name; (変えた名前) another name; (偽名) a false [an assumed] name; an alias /éilias/.
── **変名する** 動 (改名する) change one's name; (偽名を使う) assume a false name. ● 変名を使って under a *false* [*an assumed*] *name*.

べんめい 弁明 图 〘言い訳〙(an) excuse 《for》; 〘説明〙(an) explanation 《of, for》. (⇨弁解) ● 彼に弁明を求める demand [call for] an *explanation* from him.
── **弁明する** 動 make* an excuse [excuse oneself] 《for》.

べんもう 鞭毛 a flagellum (圏 -lla, ～s). ● 鞭毛運動 flagellar movement. ● 鞭毛虫 a flagellate.

へんよう 変容 图 a (complete) change in appearance; 〘書〙transfiguration. ● キリストの変容〘キリスト教〙the Transfiguration.
── **変容する** 動 change 《completely》; 〘書〙transfigure. ▶ 50年ぶりの日本はすっかり変容していた After fifty year's absence, Japan looked completely different.

ペンライト a pénlight.

へんらん 変乱 (世の中の乱れ) social disturbances [confusions].

べんらん 便覧 (⇨便覧(ﾋﾞﾝﾗﾝ))

:**べんり 便利** 图 (便利さ) convenience; handiness.
── **便利な** 形 〘都合のよい〙convenient; 〘役に立つ〙useful; 〘手ごろな, 手近にある〙handy.

① 【便利な～】● 便利な道具 a *convenient* [a *handy*, a *useful*] tool. ● 会合を開くのに便利な場所 a *convenient* place for (holding) [*to* hold] a meeting; a place *convenient for* (holding) a meeting. ● 持ち歩きに便利な辞書 a *handy* dictionary *to* carry. ● 生活に便利ないろいろの物 various *conveniences* of life.

② 【…が[は, に]便利だ】▶ ピクニックのときは紙の皿が便利だ Paper plates are *convenient* [*handy*] on a picnic. ● 私にとってはバスで行くのがとても便利だ It is very *convenient* [a great *convenience*] for me to go by bus. (⚠ to me の代わりに不定詞(明示されていない場合も含む)の意味上の主語として for me も可. その場合には …*convenient* that I go by bus. ともいえる. ×I am very *convenient*…. とはいわない) ▶ 私の家は駅に近くて便利だ My house is *convenient to* 〘米〙[*for* 〘英〙] the station. / 〘書〙My house is *conveniently* [*handily*] located near the station. ▶ このカメラは持ち運びに便利だ This camera is *convenient for carrying*.

会話 「どこで落ち合おうか」「そうだな. ぼくの家がいちばん便利だな」"Where shall we meet?" "Well, my house is the most *convenient*."

● 便利屋 (人) a utility man, a handyman; (職業) handyman business.

べんりし 弁理士 a patent attorney [lawyer].

へんりん 片鱗 (一部) a part, a bit; (ちらりと見えること) a (brief) glimpse. ● 彼の天才の片鱗を垣間見る get a *glimpse* of his genius. ● 彼は子供のときから大器の片鱗をうかがわせた He gave us a *glimpse* [a *hint*] of great talent as a boy.

へんれい 返礼 a return. (⇨礼) ● 返礼として in return 《for》.

べんれい 勉励 图 hard working.
── **勉励する** 動 work laboriously [strenuously, very hard].

へんれき 遍歴 图 wanderings. ● 女性遍歴で有名な俳優 an actor famous [well-known] for his involvement [relations] with a number of women.
── **遍歴する** 動 wander around [about].

へんろ 遍路 〘巡礼〙a pilgrimage 《to》; 〘巡礼者〙a pilgrim. ● 四国八十八か所遍路の旅に出る go on [make] a *pilgrimage to* the eighty eight temples in Shikoku.

べんろん 弁論 (演説) public speaking; (証拠提示・論理的説明などによる論争) (an) argument; (議会・集会・討論会などでの賛否討論) (a) debate; (法廷での) pleading. (⇨申し立て, 陳述) ● (法廷での)口頭弁論 oral *proceedings*. ● 最終弁論 final [concluding] *arguments*.
● 弁論大会 a speech [an oratorical] contest. (⚠ 後の方が堅い表現) ● 弁論部 a debáting club; a debáte club.

ほ

ほ 歩 a step. (⇨一歩) ●3歩前へ出る[後ろにさがる] take three *steps* forward [backward]. ●歩を速める quicken 《↔slow》 one's *steps* [*pace*].
 ●歩を一(いつ)にする (歩調をそろえる) keep step 《with》.

ほ 帆 a sail. (**!**集合的に ⓤ で用いることもある) ●帆を揚げる put up 《hoist》 [*furl*, drop] a *sail* [the *sails*]. ●帆を下ろす haul down [lower, drop] a *sail* [the *sails*]. ●帆を張る[たたむ] unfurl [furl] a *sail*. ●帆を全部張っている be in 《やや書》 under] full sail.

ほ 補 ●警部補 《米》 a lieutenant; 《英》 an inspector. ●判事補 an *assistant* judge. ●外交官補 a *probationary* diplomat.

ほ 穂 [[穀物の]] an ear, a spike. ●稲の穂 an *ear* of rice. ●穂が出る[出ている] come into *ear* [be in (the) *ear*].

ボア [[動物]] a boa. [[参考]] 南米産の大蛇); [[襟巻き]] a boa.

ほあん 保安 ●保安係《集合的》the security staff; 《個人》a security staff member. ●保安官 a sheriff. ●保安要員 (警備員) a security guard 《警備》; (建物・設備などの補修員) a máintenance mechànic [男性] màn》. ●保安林 a forest reserve [preserve].

ほい 補遺 a supplement 《to》; an addendum 《addenda》.

-ぽい 子供っぽい 《軽蔑的》 childish. ●忘れっぽい forgetful. ●水っぽい 《軽蔑的》 watery. ●怒りっぽい be *easily* offended; get angry *easily*.

ホイール [[車輪]] a wheel. ●前のホイールキャップが外れている車 a car with the front *hubcap* missing.
 ●ホイールベース [前後の車輪軸間の距離] a wheelbase. (通例単数形)

ぼいき 墓域 the area of a burial ground [a cemetery].

ほいく 保育 ── 保育する 動 bring* 《a child》 up, raise; 《書》 nurture (**!**通例受身で).
 ●保育園 a (day) nursery, a day-care center; (2-5 歳児の教育機関) a nursery school. ([[事情]]《米》では通例 2-3 時間預かる) ●子供を保育園に預ける leave one's child in [at] a nursery; put one's child in a *nursery*. ●保育器 an incubator. ●保育士 a child carer; a nursery school teacher.

ボイコット 图 《集団での排斥》 boycott; (不買同盟) a boycott; a buyers' strike.
── **ボイコットする** 動 boycott 《Japanese products, the manager》.

ボイス ●ボイスメール voice mail. ●ボイスレコーダー (航空機の) a voice recorder.

ぼいすて ぼい捨て ── ぼい捨てする 動 toss ... away; throw*... away. (⇨ぼいと) ●彼はたばこを道路にぼい捨てした He threw a cigarette butt *out* on the street. ▶ぼい捨て禁止 《掲示》 No Littering.
 ●ぼい捨て禁止条例 a no littering ordinance; an ordinance against littering.

ほいつ 捕逸 (⇨パスボール)

ホイッスル 《referee's》 whistle /hwɪsl/. ●警笛
 ●ホイッスルを吹く whistle; blow (on) a *whistle*.

ホイップ 图 (泡立てること) whipping. ●ホイップ用の生クリーム whípping crèam; heavy cream.
── **ホイップする** 動 whip ... (up).
 ●ホイップクリーム whipped cream.

ほいっぽ 歩一歩 (一歩一歩) step by step; slowly but steadily. ●歩一歩と成功に近づく come *nearer and nearer* toward success; approach success *step by step*. (⇨一歩 ❶ [第 2 文例])

ぽいと ●ぽいと toss ... away; throw ... away. (**!**後の方は単に「捨てる」の意) ▶車の窓から空きびんをぽいと捨てた He tossed [《話》 chucked] an empty bottle out of the car window.

ぽいぽい (快く) readily; (何のためらいもなく) without a moment's hesitation. ▶彼は私が頼んだ仕事をほいほいと引き受けてくれた He *readily* took the job I asked him. ▶あんないいかげんな男の申し出にほいほい (= よく考えないで) 乗ったらたいへん目に合うよ If you accept such an irresponsible man's offer *without thinking it over*, you'll have a terrible experience.

ボイラー a boiler. ●ボイラーをたく stoke (up) a *boiler*.
 ●ボイラー係 a boiler attendant. ●ボイラー室 a boiler room.

ホイル foil /fɔɪl/. (**!**数えるときは a piece [a sheet] of 〜 (1 枚), a roll of 〜 (1 巻) などを用いる) ●アルミホイル aluminum *foil*; tinfoil. ●魚をホイル焼きにする wrap a fish in *foil* and broil 《米》 [grill 《英》] it.

ぼいん ●彼女はすごいぼいんだ (= 胸が大きい) 《話》 She's got big *boobs* [*knockers*].

ぼいん 母音 a vowel (↔a consonant). ●二重母音 a diphthong. ●半母音 a semivowel. ●長[短]母音 a long [a short] *vowel*.

ぼいん 拇印 a thumbprint. ●書類に拇印を押す put a *thumbprint* [make a *thumb imprint*] on the papers. ([[事情]] 米英でも人物証明に使うことがある)

ポインセチア [[植物]] a poinsettia /pɔɪnsétiə/.

ポインター (猟犬) a pointer.

ポイント ❶ [点, 地点] a point; (小数点) a (decimal) point (⇨点 ❶ ❸) ●タイ釣りのポイントに到着する get to a (good) *point* for fishing sea bream.
 ❷ [要点, 要所] the point ●チェックポイント a checkpoint. ●ポイントを述べる [外さない] come [keep] to the *point*. ▶そこがポイントだ That's the *point*.
 ❸ [得点] a point ●マッチポイント a match *point*. ([[参考]] テニスなどで試合の勝敗を決める最後の得点) ●ポイントをあげる win [gain, score] a *point*.
 ❹ [活字の大きさ] a point ●10 ポイント活字の本 a book printed in 10-*point* type.
 ❺ [鉄道の] 《米》 (the) switches, 《英》 (the) points.
 ●ポイントを稼ぐ (処世上有利になることをして点数を稼ぐ) 《話》 earn [get, win, score] Brownie points.
 ●ポインゲッター (高得点をとる選手) a high scorer.

ほう 方 ❶ [方向] (方角, 方面) a direction, a way; [...の方向に向かって] toward .... (⇨方向, 方角) ●両方を見る look both *ways*. ▶そっちの方へ行くと駅に出ますよ You will get to the station if you go that *way* [*in that direction*]. (**!**way は this, that などを伴って前置詞なしで副詞的に用いる) ▶彼は図書館の方へ歩いて行った He walked *toward* [*in the direction of*] the library. ▶熱海は横浜の

西の方にあります Atami lies *to* [*xin*] *the west of* Yokohama. (🔸*in* だと熱海は横浜の中にあるという意になる. *to* の方は しばしば省略する) ▶右の方に大きな建物があります There is a large building *to the right* [右側に] *on the right side*. ▶彼は本郷の方に(=あたりに)住んでいる He lives *somewhere* (*up*) Hongo *way*. (🔸*way* は「付近」の意で, 地名の後に置いて副詞的に用いる)

❷ [**方面, 部類**] (分野) a field; [側(がわ)] a side, one's part. ▶あの科学者はその方では秀でている That scientist is outstanding [《やや書》eminent] *in that field*. ▶私の方は(=私としては)その計画に異存はありません *For my part*, [(私個人としては) *Personally*, (私に関する限りは) *As far as I am concerned*, (私はどういえば) *As for me*], I have no objection to the plan. (🔸to はすでに記憶している事柄に関連して新しい情報を導入する) ▶彼はいつも負けている方を応援する He always supports the losing *side*. ▶間違いをしたのは秘書の方だ *It was* the secretary *who* [*that*] made the mistake. (🔸強調構文)/(間違いは秘書の側にある) The mistake is *on the secretary's side*./It is a mistake *on the secretary's part*. ▶君の方から彼に謝る必要はないよ *You* don't have to apologize to him.

❸ [**比較, 対比**] ▶こっちの方があの本よりずっとおもしろい *This* book is a lot more interesting than that one. (🔸is の [*話*] で比較級を強める) ▶二つのうちではこちらの方が安い *This* is the cheaper of the two. (🔸二つの比較には通例最上級でなく the＋比較級を用いる) ▶今日は家にいた方がいい *You should* stay at home today. (🔸*should* の代わりに *had better* を用いる方が命令的な言い方になる) (⇔いい⓯) ▶少し待った方がいいとは思わないか Don't you think it would *be better* to wait a bit? ▶どちらかというと物事を楽観する方だ He is *rather* optimistic. ▶彼は背はまあ高い方かしら He's *kind* [*sort*] *of* tall. (🔸*kind* [*sort*] *of* ... 《話》で「いくぶん, ある程度」の意) ▶あんな医者には行くくらいならじっと寝ている方がましだ(=寝ている方がよい) *I would rather* stay in bed *than* [寝ていても同じだ] I might as well stay in bed *as*] go to see such a doctor. ▶あの男とは付き合わない方がいいでしょう You *would* [*will*] *do well* to avoid him.

[会話] 「紅茶とコーヒーとどちらがよろしいですか」「紅茶の方がいいな」"Which would you like, tea or coffee?" "I'd *prefer* tea."

❹ [**側**] ▶彼はいつも君の方を支持している He always takes *your side*./He is always *on your side*.

*ほう 法 ❶ [**法律**] (the) law (🔸「国の法」の意では通例 the ～); (個々の) a law. (⇔法律) ▶国際法 international *law*. ▶特定の法は無冠詞 ▶法を守る [破る] (⇔法律) ▶法を曲げる bend [拡大解釈する] 《話》stretch] the *law*. ▶法の網をくぐる evade the *law*; escape from the clutches of the *law*. ▶法の名において in the name of the *law*. ▶法の下ではだれもが平等である All people have equal rights under [before, in the eyes of] the *law*. ▶君のやったことは法に反する What you did is against [is contrary to] the *law*.

❷ [**方法**] (組織的な) a method; (やり方) a way. (🔸日本語では「...法」はどちらかというと堅い表現なので, 日常的な *way* より *method* の方が適切なことが多い) ●英語教授法 the *method of* teaching [*xto* teach] English.

❸ [**道理**] reason. ▶そんな法はない That's against *reason*./That's unreasonable. ▶君がそれをやらな法はない There is no *reason why* you should not do it./There is no *reason* for your not doing it [*for you not to do it*]. (🔸後の to 不定詞の方が口語的)/(やるべきだ) You should do it.

ほう oh; well; why. (⇔へえ) ▶ほう, そうですか *Oh*, is that so? ▶ほう, これで *Well*, then? ▶ほう, うらやましいなあ *My*! How I envy you!

ほう 苞 [包葉] a bract.

ほう 砲 a gun.

ほう 報 a report; 《a piece of》 news [information]. ▶彼の死去の報に接した I received the *news* of his death./I received *information* that he died.

ほう- 訪- ▶訪日中の英首相 British Prime Minister *on a visit to* Japan [now *staying* in Japan]. ▶訪中する visit China.

*ほう 棒 [棒切れ] a stick; [丸棒] a pole; (さお) a rod; [こん棒] a club; [横木] a bar; [線] a line; (一本の) a stroke. ▶カーテンのつり棒 a curtain *rod*. ▶棒を集めて火をおこした We gathered some *sticks* to make a fire.

● 棒に振る ● 丸一日を棒に振る waste a whole day. ● チャンスを棒に振る *throw away* an opportunity. ▶その汚職事件で彼は一生を棒に振った The scandal *ruined* his career [life].

ぼう 坊 ❶ [僧] ●お坊さん a priest; a Buddhist priest [monk]. ❷ [**男の子**] a boy; (呼びかけ語) sonny. (⇔坊や, 坊ちゃん) ▶川島さん家(ち)の次男坊 Mr. Kawashima's second *son*.

ぼう 房 (刑務所などの) a cell.

ぼう 某 [知っていても明言せずに] certain; [ある] one. ●某氏 a *certain* person; Mr. So-and-so. ●某所 a *certain* place. ▶昨年の 5 月某日に *one* day [*on a certain date*] in May last year.

ぼう 暴 ●暴をもって暴に報いる 'return violence with violence'.

ぼう- 亡- ●亡夫 one's dead husband. (⇔亡夫)

ぼうあつ 暴圧 suppression. ▶反乱者に対する軍隊の暴圧 the army's *brutal suppression of* the rioters.

ほうあん 法案 a bill. ●法案を提出する introduce [propose] *a bill*. ●法案を可決する [否決する; 棚上げにする] pass [reject; shelve] *a bill*.

ぼうあんき 棒暗記 图 ●歴史的事実の棒暗記 the *rote-learning* of historical facts. (🔸[書] rote /róut/ は「機械的な繰り返し」の意で, 通例 by rote の形で用いる) (⇔動)

── 棒暗記する 動 learn ... by rote.

ほうい 方位 (方位計による方向・位置) a bearing; (方角) (a) direction. ●方位を定める [確かめる] find [get, take] one's *bearings*. ▶我々の船の方位は淡路島の西 50 度のところであった Our boat's *bearing* was 50° west of Awaji Island. (🔸50°は fifty degrees と読む)

ほうい 包囲 图 (敵軍の占領目的の) (a) siege. ●敵の包囲網を破る break through the enemy *siege* [*encirclement*]. ●城の包囲を解く raise [lift] the *siege* of the castle.

── 包囲する 動 ▶敵軍は城を包囲した Enemy troops *surrounded* [*besieged, laid siege to*] the castle.

ほうい 法衣 a priest's [(キリスト教で) clerical, canonical] robe. ●法衣をまとっている in a priest's robe [garb].

ぼうい 暴威 ●暴威をふるう rage; storm; (攻撃的に) tyrannize (over).

ほういがく 法医学 forensic /fərénsik/ medicine; [書] medical jurisprudence.

ほういつ 放逸 图 ●放逸に流れる be given to *dissolution*.

── 放逸な 形 dissolute; loose; licentious.

ぼういんぼうしょく 暴飲暴食 图 excessive [immoderate] eating and drinking. (🔲語順に注意)
── **暴飲暴食する** 動 eat* and drink* excessively [too much].

ぼうう 暴雨 a rainstorm; (大雨) a heavy rain.

ほうえ 法会 a Buddhist memorial service.

ほうえ 法衣 ⇨法衣(ほうい).

ほうえい 放映 图 televising.
── **放映する** 動 televise; broadcast*... on television. ▶オリンピックは全世界に放映されるだろう The Olympic Games will *be televised* [*be shown on TV*] all over the world.
● **放映権** televising [broadcasting] rights.

*ぼうえい 防衛** defense. (⇨国防) ▶正当防衛で彼を射殺する shoot him down in [×by] self-*defense*. ▶彼はタイトルの防衛に成功した He succeeded in *defending* his title.
── **防衛する** 動 defend. (⇨守る) ▶我々はその島を防衛するために2個連隊を派遣した We sent two regiments to *defend* [in *defense of*] the island.
● **防衛軍** defense forces [corps]. ● **防衛策** a defensive measure (*against*; *to do*). (🔲しばしば複数形で) ▶テロに対して防衛策を講じる take *defensive measures against* terrorism. ● **防衛省** the Ministry of Defense. ● **防衛大学校** the National Defense Academy. ● **防衛大臣** the Minister of Defense. ● **防衛費** the (national) defense expense [cost]; (防衛支出) defense spending; (防衛予算) the defense budget. ● **防衛力** defense capacity; defensive strength. (🔲 defense force とはいわない) ▶国境の防衛力を強化する build up [strengthen] *defenses* on the border.

:**ぼうえき 貿易** trade; (交易) commerce.
① 【~貿易】 ▶外国[自由; 保護]貿易 foreign [free; protective] *trade*. ▶片[2国間; 三角]貿易 one-way [bilateral; triangular] *trade*. ▶対外[国際]貿易 external [international] *trade*. ▶日中貿易は近年著しく拡大した Sino-Japanese *trade* [*Trade* between Japan and China] has expanded remarkably in recent years.
② 【貿易~】 ▶日米貿易摩擦 the U.S.–Japan *trade* dispute [friction]; Japan's *trade* dispute [friction] with the U.S. ▶日本貿易振興会 the Japan External *Trade* Organization (略 JETRO). ▶日本の対中国貿易赤字は200億ドルに達した Japan's *trade* deficit (↔surplus) with China amounted to 20 billion dollars./Japan ran up a surplus of 20 billion dollars in its *trade* with China.
③ 【貿易が】 ▶日本はアメリカとの貿易が盛んです Japan *does* a lot of *trade* with the U.S./Japan *trades* a lot *with* the U.S.
④ 【貿易を】 ▶日本は貿易を自由化するよう求められた Japan was asked to liberalize *trade*. ▶アジア諸国との貿易を促進する promote *trade* with Asian countries.
● **貿易相手国** a tráding pàrtner. ● **貿易会社** a tráding [an impórt-éxport] còmpany. ● **貿易外収支** the invisible balance of trade; invisible trade balance. ● **貿易協定** (sign) a tráde agrèement (*between* Japan and America). ● **貿易自由化** tráde liberalizàtion. ● **貿易収支** the balance of trade; tráde bàlance. ● **貿易商** a (foreign) trader. (🔲語 輸出業者 an exporter/輸入業者 an importer) ● **貿易障壁** (clear away [remove]) tráde bàrriers. ● **貿易風** a tráde wind. (🔲通例複数形で) ● **貿易不均衡** (correct [redress]) the tráde imbálance. (🔲この場合通例 unbalance は用いない)

ぼうえき 防疫 prevention of epidemics. ▶防疫対策を講じる take preventive [[医学]] prophylactic] measures against epidemics. (🔲「コレラの防疫対策」なら an epidemic of cholera または a cholera epidemic とする)

ほうえつ 法悦 (宗教上の) (a) religious ecstasy; religious exaltation; (一般的に) (an) ecstasy. (⇨陶酔) ● **法悦にひたる** go [get] into *ecstasies* (*over* the beauty of ...).

ほうえん 方円 ▶水は方円の器に従う (⇨水[成句])

ほうえん 砲煙 gun smoke; artillery smoke; battle smoke. ● **砲煙弾雨** (=激しい砲弾の撃ち合い)の中をくぐる make progress under *a rain* [*a shower*] *of shells*; come through *the thick of a battle*.

ほうえん 豊艶 ── **豊艶な** 形 voluptuous; buxom; 《話》 curvaceous.

ほうえん 防炎 fire protection. ▶防炎加工のしてある fire-proofed (curtains).

ほうえん 防煙 smoke protection. ▶火災が発生するとこのシャッターは自動的に下り防煙する When a fire breaks out, this shutter comes down automatically to *protect* the other parts of the building *from being filled with smoke*.

ぼうえんきょう 望遠鏡 a telescope. ▶天体[屈折; 反射; 電波]望遠鏡 an àstronómical [a refracting; a reflecting; a radio] *telescope*. ▶望遠鏡で見える星 stars that can be seen *with a telescope*. ▶私は望遠鏡で星を観測した I observed the stars *through a telescope*.

ぼうえんレンズ 望遠レンズ a télephoto léns.

ほうおう 法王 (ローマ法王) the Pope.
● **法王庁** the Vatican.

ほうおう 法皇 an abdicated emperor who has joined a Buddhist order.

ほうおう 訪欧 图 (go on) a visit to Europe.
── **訪欧する** 動 visit Europe.

ほうおう 鳳凰 (想像上の鳥) a Chinese phoenix.

ほうおん 報恩 ▶報恩の気持ちを表して in return for (his) kindness; to show [express] one's gratitude for (his) kindness.

ぼうおん 忘恩 ingratitude, ungratefulness.
● **忘恩の徒** an ungrateful person. (🔲 ungrateful は日本語の「忘恩」より意味が広く, Don't be *ungrateful*. (お礼を言うのを忘れないでね) のようにも用いる)

ぼうおん 防音 ── **防音の** 形 soundproof. ● **防音のしてある部屋** a *soundproof* room.
● **防音装置** soundproof equipment. ● **防音装置を施す** soundproof (a room).

ほうか 邦貨 (in) Japanese currency. ▶邦貨に替える change (US dollars) for the yen.

ほうか 放火 图 (やや書) arson. ▶彼は放火の容疑で逮捕された He was arrested for [on a charge of] *arson*.
── **放火する** 動 ▶家に放火する set fire to a house; set a house on fire.
● **放火犯(人)** an arsonist. ● **放火癖** pyromania.
● **放火魔** a pyromaniac /pàirəméiniæk/; 《話》 a fírebùg.

ほうか 放歌 ▶放歌高吟(こうぎん)する sing lustily.

ほうか 法科 the law department; the department of jurisprudence. ▶法科の学生 a law student.
● **法科大学院** a law school.

ほうか 法貨 [『法定貨幣』の略] legal tender.

ほうか 砲火 (artillery) fire. ▶集中砲火 concentrated (*artillery*) *fire*. ● **砲火を浴びせる** pour (*shell*)

ほうが *fire* 《on》. ●砲火を交える exchange *fire* 《with》. ▶我々は敵の砲火にさらされた We were exposed to [浴びた] were under] enemy's *fire*.

ほうが 邦画 a Japanese film [《主に米》movie].

ほうが 奉賀 ━ **奉賀する** 動 congratulate.

ほうが 萌芽 (発芽状態) budding; a sign 《of》(❗ しばしば複数形でいろいろの兆候を示す). ●悪の萌芽を(=芽のうちに)摘み取る nip an evil in the bud. ▶彼は幼少にして数学の天才の萌芽が見られた He showed *signs* of a mathematical genius in his early childhood.

ぼうか 防火 fire prevention, the prevention of fire.
●防火訓練《conduct》a fire drill. ●防火建築 a fireproof building. ●防火装置 fire prevention equipment. ●防火(地)帯《参考》延焼を防ぐための空間帯) a firebreak. ●防火壁 a fire wall; (シャッター) a fireproof shutter. ●防火用水 fire-fighting water.

ぼうが 忘我 《be in》complete forgetfulness of oneself. ●忘我の境に入る forget [lose] oneself 《in one's work》.

ほうかい 崩壊 图 (a) collapse; (破滅) ruin; (没落) a fall. ●家庭の崩壊 (一家の没落) the *ruin* [*fall*] of one's family; (離婚などによる) (a) family *breakdown*; the *break-up* of one's home (❗その結果生じる「崩壊家庭」は a *broken* home).
━ **崩壊する** 動 (つぶれる, つぶす) collapse; (ばらばらになる[する]) break* (...) down [up]; (破滅する[させる]) ruin. ▶その建物は崩壊しかかっていた The building *was collapsing* [*falling down*]./(崩壊寸前だった) The building was on the verge of collapse. ▶彼が死んだら家庭は崩壊するであろう His family will *be ruined* [*break up*, ×collapse, ×break down] if he dies./His death will *ruin* his family.

ほうがい 法外 ━ **法外な** 形 unreasonable; 『過度の』excessive. ●法外な要求をする make an *unreasonable* [an *excessive*] demand. ●法外な値段を支払う pay an *exorbitant* price.
━ **法外に** 副 unreasonably; excessively.

*ぼうがい 妨害 图『行為』(邪魔) obstruction; (干渉) interference; (中断) interruption; [物, 人] an interruption; (乱すもの[人]) a disturbance. (⇨邪魔) ●妨害行為 《an》*obstructive* behavior. ●(走者の)守備妨害 runner's interference. ●(捕手の)打撃妨害 catcher's interference. ●走塁妨害 obstruction. ●公務執行妨害(罪)で逮捕される be arrested on the [a] charge of *obstructing* government officials in carrying out their duties. ▶私はその計画を実行し始めるとすぐに妨害にあった As soon as I started the project, I met with *interference*. ▶車の騒音は私たちの生活の妨害になる The noise of cars *disturbs* [is a *disturbance* to] our life.
━ **妨害(を)する** 動 [『進行を止める』(完全に) block, 《やや書》obstruct; [『かき乱す』disturb; [『干渉する』] interfere 《with》; [『中断させる』] interrupt. (⇨口出しする) ●計画を妨害する *block* [*obstruct*, *interfere with*] a plan. ●議事の進行を妨害する *obstruct* proceedings; (長々と演説をして)《主に米》*filibuster*. ●捕手に守備妨害をする interfere with a catcher. ●走者に走塁妨害をする obstruct a runner. ▶数人の学生が大声で話をして講義を妨害した Several students *interrupted* the lecture by talking loudly. ▶安眠を妨害するな Don't *disturb* my sleep [me while I am sleeping].

ぼうがい 望外 ━ **望外の** 形 unexpected; (身に余る) undeserved. ●望外の喜び an *unexpected* pleasure. ▶実験を重ねていくうちに我々は望外の成果を得た After a lot of experiments, we got a far better result than we had expected.

ーほうがいい ー方がいい (⇨いい❼⓭)

*ほうがく 方角 [『方向』] a direction; (進む) a way. (⇨方向, 方(がた)) ●大阪の方角に in the *direction* [×way] of Osaka. ●方角違いの方へ行く go in [×to] the wrong *direction*. ▶彼はあちらの方角へ行った He went off in that *direction*. ▶郵便局はここからどっちの方角ですか Which *direction* [*way*] is the post office from here? ▶駅は反対の方角にあります The railroad station is the other *way*. ▶ごいっしょの方角なら車にお乗せしましょう If you are going my *way*, I'll give you a ride 《主に米》[a lift 《主に英》]. (❗ a ride to you としない).

ほうがく 邦楽 Japanese (classical) music.

ほうがく 法学 (the) law, 《書》jurisprudence. ●法学を学ぶ study *law* [*jurisprudence*].
●法学士 (学位) Bachelor of Laws 《略 LL.B.》; (人) a bachelor of Laws. ●法学者 a jurist.
●法学博士 (学位) Doctor of Laws 《略 LL.D.》; (人) a doctor of Laws. ●法学部 the law school.

ほうかご 放課後 after school. ▶放課後野球をしよう Let's play baseball *after school*.

> **翻訳のこころ** それは, 秋の学園祭についての話し合いが持たれた放課後のことだった (山田詠美 『ひよこの眼』) It was one afternoon after school when we had a talk about [over] the fall school festival. (❗ (1) 授業は通例午後に終わるので, ここでは one afternoon after school としたが, 午前中に授業が終わる場合は one morning となる. (2) 「秋の学園祭」は fall school festival. 秋に行われる学校行事には autumn でなく fall をつけるのが普通)

ほうがちょう 奉加帳 (社寺への奉納金[品]の台帳) a list of donations (to the shrine [temple]). ●奉加帳を回す(=寄付をつのる) collect donations.

ほうかつ 包括 ━ **包括的(な)** 形 (総合的な)(やや書) còmprehénsive, (一切を包んだ) (all-) inclusive, òveráll (❗ 限定的に). ●中東の包括的平和 *comprehensive* peace in the Middle East.
━ **包括的に** 副 comprehensively; inclusively.
━ **包括する** 動 《書》comprehend; include.

ほうかび 防黴 mold [(革製品などにつく白ゆ) mildew] prevention. ●防かび塗料 *anti-mold* paint; *mold-preventive* paint.

ほうかん 宝冠 a crown; (帯状の) a diadem.
●宝冠章 Orders of the Precious Crown.

ほうかん 法官 (⇨⓵ 裁判官)

ほうかん 砲艦 a gunboat.

ほうかん 幇間 (太鼓持ち) a professional male entertainer.

ほうかん 包含 ━ **包含する** 動 include, contain; (意味に) imply. ▶多くのことわざには 2 つの意味が包含されている Many proverbs *contain* [*imply*] two meanings.

ほうがん 砲丸 a shot. (⇨砲丸投げ)

ほうかん 防汗 ━ **防汗の** 形 (汗による害を防ぐ) sweatproof; preventive of sweat damage. ●防汗の腕時計 a *sweatproof* wristwatch.

ぼうかん 防寒 ●防寒用として as a protection *against* the cold. ●防寒具 an outfit for cold weather. ●防寒下着 thermal underwear; 《話》 thermals. ●防寒服 clothes for cold weather.

ぼうかん 傍観 ━ **傍観する** 動 ▶彼は彼らのけんかをただ

ぼうかん 傍観しているだけだった He just *looked on* as they were fighting./He just *stood by and watched* their fight./He just remained an *onlooker* [a *bystander*] while they were fighting.
● 傍観者を an ónlòoker; a býstànder.

ぼうかん 暴漢 a thug, a hoodlum. ● 暴漢に襲われる be attacked by a *thug*.

ほうがんし 方眼紙 graph [《英》section] paper. ● 3ミリ方眼紙 a *graph paper* ruled into 3-millimeter squares.

ほうがんなげ 砲丸投げ the shot put. ● 砲丸投げの選手 a shot-putter. ● 砲丸投げをする put [《えいと力を込めて》heave] the *shot*. (**!**) (1) throw も可能だが、軽々しい投げ方を連想させるのが普通ではない。 (2)「円盤投げをする」は throw 《×put》 the discus)

ほうがんびいき 判官びいき ⇨判官(はんがん)びいき

***ほうき** 放棄 图 [《権利・地位・計画などの》 abandonment; 《権利などの正式の》 (a) renunciation. ● 戦争放棄を宣言する declare the *renunciation* of war. ● 戦争放棄条項が日本、アジア(= 日本とその他のアジア)の平和と安定に役立った The war-*renouncing* clause (of our Constituiton) has served to maintain peace and stability in Japan and the rest of Asia.

── 放棄する 動 [《あきらめる》give *... up (**!** 最も日常的な語); 《完全に》 abandon; 《正式に》《やや書》 renounce; 《ついに》 relinquish; 《書》 《権利・自由などをやむをえず譲り渡す》 surrender. (⇨捨てる❷) ● 計画を放棄する *give up* [*abandon, relinquish*] one's plan. ● 燃えている船を放棄する *abandon* a burning ship. ● 職場を放棄する go on (a) strike. (⇨スト) ▶ 彼女はその土地の所有権を放棄した She *renounced* the ownership of the land. ▶ 我々は決して自由を放棄しないだろう We shall [will] never *surrender* our liberty. (**!** shall の方が決意の度合いが強い)

ほうき 箒 a broom. ● 竹ぼうき a bamboo besom /bíːzəm/. ● ほうきの柄 a broomstick. ● ほうきで掃く sweep 《a room》 with a *broom*.
● 箒星 a comet.

ほうき 法規 (法律と規則) laws and regulations. ● 交通法規 traffic *regulàtions*.

ほうき 蜂起 图 an uprising.

── 蜂起する 動 (反乱として立ち上がる)《やや書》 rise (up) in revolt 《against》; (反乱を起こす) revolt [rebel] 《against》; (武装して立ち上がる)《やや書》 rise (up) in arms 《against》; take* up arms 《against》.

ぼうぎ 謀議 图 (a) conspiracy, a plot. ● 共同謀議する joint *conspiracy*. ▶ 謀議をめぐらす (⇨謀略)

── 謀議する 動 《やや書》 conspire (together) 《to kill him》; plot 《to kill him; his murder》.

ほうきぼく 箒木 《植物》a broom [a summer] cypress; a burning bush; a kochia.

ほうきぐさ 箒草 〖『ホウキギ』の別名〗(⇨箒木)

ぼうきゃく 忘却 图 《やや書》 oblivion. ● 忘却のかなたに沈む fall [sink] into *oblivion*.

ぼうぎゃく 暴虐 (行為) atrócities (⇨残虐); (暴君による) tyrannies /tírəniz/. ● 暴虐の限りを尽くす commit all sorts of *atrocities*.

ほうきゅう 俸給 pay, (a) salary. (⇨給料)
● 俸給生活者 a salaried worker [employee]; a white collar worker.

ほうぎょ 崩御 图〖天皇・皇后・皇太后・太皇太后が死去すること〗 one's death [《婉曲的》 demise].
── 崩御する 動 pass away; 《書》 decease.

ぼうきょ 暴挙 (暴力) violence, force; (不法行為) an outrage. ● 暴挙に出る 《やや書》 resort to *violence*;

commit an act of *violence*. ● 民主主義に対する暴挙 an *outrage* against democracy.

ぼうぎょ 防御 图 defense. ● 国の防御 national *defense*. ● 防御態勢をとる be [stand] on the *defense*.
── 防御する 動 defend. (⇨守る) ● 爆弾から身を防御する *defend* oneself *from* [*against*] bombing.
● 防御戦 defensive warfare. ● 防御率 (⇨防御率)

ほうきょう 豊凶 ● 今年の豊凶を占う divine the (rice) harvest of the year.

ほうきょう 豊胸 large [well-developed] breasts. ▶ 彼女は豊胸手術を受けた She had an operation to make her breasts fuller./She had breast implants (to increase the size of her bust).

ぼうきょう 望郷 ● 望郷の念 homesickness. ● 望郷の念に駆られる feel [get, 《やや書》become] homesick 《for》 (**!**) feel が最も普通); have a feeling of *homesickness*. (**!** ×have a homesick は不可) ▶ 彼の望郷の念は交響曲となって表れた His *longing for home* found expression in his symphony.

ぼうぎょりつ 防御率〖野球〗an earned run average 《略 ERA》. (**!**) earned run は「自責点」● 先発 31試合で防御率 2.07 の 23勝 4敗である go 23-4 with a 2.07 *ERA* in 31 starts. ● 防御率が 4点以下である have an *earned run average* below four. ● チーム防御率が 5.10 である have a 5.10 team *ERA*. ▶ 彼の防御率は 4.20 に上がった His *earned run average* rose to 4.20.

ぼうぎれ 棒切れ a stick. (⇨棒)

ほうぎん 邦銀 a Japanese bank overseas.

ほうぎん 放吟 ── 放吟する 動 sing loudly.

ぼうぐ 防具 a protector; 《集合的》protective gear.

ぼうぐい 棒杭 a stake.

ぼうくう 防空 air defense.
● 防空壕 an air-raid shelter. ● 防空施設 air defense facilities.

ぼうぐみ 棒組み〖印刷〗galley setting. ● 棒組みにする set type in a galley.

ぼうグラフ 棒グラフ a bar chart [graph].

ぼうくん 亡君 亡君 (= 死んだ君主) の恨みをはらす avenge one's *deceased* [*late*] lord 《on》.

ぼうくん 暴君 a tyrant /táiərənt/, a despot.

ほうけい 方形 a square. ● 方形の土地 a *square* plot of land.

ほうけい 包茎 a phimosis. ● 包茎手術を行う operate on a *phimotic* penis.

ほうげい 奉迎 图 a welcome 《to the Prince》.
── 奉迎する 動 welcome 《the Emperor》.

ぼうけい 亡兄 one's dead [《婉曲的》 dear departed, deceased, (最近死んだ) late] brother.

ぼうけい 傍系 ── 傍系の 形《やや書》subsídiàry; (重要でない) minor.

ほうげき 砲撃 图 (a) bombardment, fire. ● 砲撃を開始する [やめる] open [cease] fire 《on》.
── 砲撃する 動 bombard; fire 《at, on》; shell 《the enemy's trenches》.

ぼうげつ 某月 a certain month.

ほうける 呆ける ── 遊びほうける (子供が遊びに夢中だ) be absorbed [deep] in play; (快楽にふける) be given to the pursuit of pleasure. (⇨遊び呆ける)

ほうけん 奉献 ── 奉献する 動 《やや書》dedicate. (⇨奉納)

ほうけん 宝剣 a treasured sword.

ほうけん 封建 ── 封建的な 形 ▶彼はとても封建的だ He is very *feudal* [《権威的だ》*authoritative*].
● 封建時代 the feudal times. ● 封建社会 a feudal society. ● 封建主義 feudalism. ● 封建制度 the feudal system; feudalism.

ほうげん 方言 (a) dialect; (単語) a dialect word. (⇨ 訛(なま)り) ▶東北方言で話す speak *in* Tohoku *dialect*.

ほうげん 放言 ━ 放言する 動 (無責任な発言をする) make* an irresponsible [(不適切な) an improper, (遠慮のない)《書》an unreserved] remark. (⇨ 失言)

*__ほうけん__ 冒険 图 (an) adventure (❗多少危険を伴うわくわくするような経験. 具体例は Ⓒ); a venture (❗ 生命・金銭的危険を伴う試み); [危険な諸(も)け] a risk, a gamble. ●数多くの冒険をする[経験する] have [experience] a lot of *adventures*. ●命がけの冒険をする risk one's life. ●冒険談を聞かせる tell 〈him〉about one's adventures. ▶彼はアマゾンの秘境への冒険に出かけた He *ventured* to the unknown Amazon. ▶見もしない土地を買うのは冒険(=危険)だ Buying the land you've never seen is a *risk* [a *gamble*].
━ 冒険する 動 (危険を覚悟で) run* [take*] a risk [risks]; (運にまかせて) take a chance [chances]. ●冒険家 an adventurer; (冒険好きな人) an adventurous person. ●冒険心 (have) an adventurous spirit. ●冒険的事業 (ベンチャービジネス) a (business) venture (⇨ベンチャー); (一かバかの) a risky business. ●冒険物語 an adventure story; a story of adventure.

ぼうけん 望見 ━ 望見する 動 look at 《Mt. Fuji》 from a distant place; see* 〈him〉 from afar [a long distance].

ぼうげん 暴言 暴言(=乱暴な言葉)をはく use *violent* [(無礼な) *rude*, (口汚くののしる) *abusive*] *language*.

ほうげんものがたり『保元物語』 *Hogen Monogatari*: *Tale of the Disorder in Hogen*. 《参考》鎌倉時代に成立した軍記物語

ほうこ 宝庫 (宝を入れる倉) a treasure house (複 houses /-ziz,《米》-siz/), a treasury. ●知識の宝庫 a storehouse 《源泉》 a source》 of knowledge; (豊富な知識) a wealth of knowledge.

ほうご 法語 (⇨法話)

ほうご 防護 图 protection 《from》.
━ 防護する 動 protect 《from》.
●防護服 a protective suit. ●防護壁 a protective wall.

*__ほうこう__ 方向 [方角, 方面] (a) direction; (道筋) a way; [進路, 方針] a course. (⇨方角, 方(ほう))
①【方向~】 ●方向転換をする (向きを変える) make a change of *direction* [*course*]; (主義・政策・態度などの) do an about-face 《米》[an about-turn 《英》] (in). ●方向感覚を失う lose one's sense of direction; get [be] disoriented (❗形容詞として a disoriented whale などのようにも用いられる) ●明確な方向性を打ち出す hammer out a definite course of *direction*. ●人生のはっきりした方向性がない have no clear *direction* in one's life. ▶彼は方向音痴だ He has no [a terrible] *sense of direction*.

> **📘 DISCOURSE**
> 1990年代の政策の方向転換によって, 貧富の差は大きくなっている On account of the *change* in policy in the 1990s, the gap between the rich and the poor has been growing. (❗ on account of ... (...が原因で)は理由に用いるディスコースマーカー)

②【方向が】 ▶方向が分からなくなってしまった. ここはどこだ I've lost my sense of *direction* [my *bearings*]. Where am I?
③【方向を】 ●方向を誤る (道などの) go the wrong way [in the wrong *direction*] (❗ way では通例 in を省略し副詞的に用いる); take the wrong road [×way]; (職業の) choose the wrong kind of job [the wrong career]. ●音のする方向を見る look *in* [×at] *the direction* [×way] *of* the sound. ●人生の方向を決定する determine the *course* of one's life; decide one's future. ▶船は北の方向を進んだ The ship sailed *toward* [*in the direction of*] the north.

④【方向へ[から, に]】 ●反対の方向へ行く go *in* [×to] the opposite [other] *direction*; go the other *way*. ▶彼はどっちの方向へ行きましたか Which *direction* [*way*] did he go?/What *direction* did he go in? (❗ *In* what direction ...? は今はあまり用いない) ▶彼は駅の方向へ走って行った He ran *toward* [*in the direction of*] the station. ▶海の方向から風が吹いて来る The wind is blowing *from the direction of* the ocean. ▶その湖はこの地点から南の方向にある The lake lies (*to* the) south of this point.
●方向指示器 (自動車の)《米》a turn signal;《英》an indicator. ●方向舵 (飛行機の) a rudder. ●方向探知機 a diréction finder; (電波探知機) a radar.

ほうこう 彷徨 图 wandering /wɑ́ndəriŋ/; roaming.
━ 彷徨する 動 ●ロンドンの町を彷徨する *wander* (*around*) the streets of London. ●荒野を彷徨する *roam* the wilds.

ほうこう 芳香 (a) fragrance /fréigrəns/,《やや書》(a) pérfume; (いいにおい) a good [a pleasant, a sweet] smell. ●芳香を放つ give off [release] a *fragrance*; smell good [pleasantly, sweetly]. ▶部屋には何ともいえぬ芳香が漂っていた The room was filled with an inexpressibly *good smell*. (❗ 場所を言わない場合の主語は The air ... となる)
●芳香剤 an aromatic.

ほうこう 咆哮 图 (猛獣がほえること) a roar. ●ライオンの咆哮が聞こえる hear the *roar* of lions.
━ 咆哮する 動 roar.

ほうこう 奉公 图 service; (徒弟の年季奉公) (an) apprenticeship. ●息子を店に奉公に出す *apprentice* one's son to a storekeeper. ●年季奉公をする serve one's *apprenticeship*.

> **古今ことばの系譜『坊っちゃん』**
> この下女なもと由緒のあるものだそうだが, 瓦解(がかい)のときに零落して, つい奉公までするようになったのだと聞いている. だから婆さんである. この婆さんがどういう因縁(いんねん)か, おれを非常に可愛がってくれた. Kiyo, I had heard, came from a good family, but had lost everything at the time of the Restoration, and was finally reduced to working as a servant. By this time she was well on in years. This old woman, for what reason I do not know, was always extremely good to me. (Burton Watson) (❗(1)「瓦解」は明治維新. 維新に伴い, 武家階級の多くは零落した. (2)「だから婆さんである」は「維新からかなりの月日がたっているから, 今では年寄りである」という意味. これに対する を well on in years のその意味だから適切な訳になっている) (⇨『坊っちゃん』)

━ 奉公する 動 serve 《the family》.
●奉公人 (召し使い) a servant; (従業員) an employee; (徒弟) an apprentice.

ほうこう 放校 expulsion from school. ▶彼は放校になった He was expelled from school/《話》He got thrown out of school.

ほうごう 法号 (戒名のうち「院」「居士」の部分) ranking words in a posthumous Buddhist name.

ほうごう 縫合 图 a suture /súːtʃər/.
— **縫合する** 動 ●傷を縫合する *put stitches in* a wound; *stitch* [*sew*] *up* a wound.
● 縫合糸 a suture.

ぼうこう 膀胱 【解剖】the bladder.
● 膀胱炎【医学】cystitis /sistáitis/. ● 膀胱結石【医学】a cystolith; a vesical calculus.

ぼうこう 暴行 【暴力行為】violence; (an) outrage (❗ 後の方が意味が強い); 【法律】(暴行殴打) assault and battery; 〚婦女暴行〛(a) rape; 【法律】assault. ●暴行を加える use *violence on* him; 《話》rough him up; 《書》commit an *outrage on* him.
— **暴行する** 動 ●婦女を暴行する *rape* [〚婉曲的に〛 *attack*, *assault*] a woman.
●暴行罪 a crime of violence. ●暴行犯(人) a rapist. ●暴行未遂 an attempted assault.

ほうこうづける 方向付ける ●会社の将来を方向付ける会議を開く hold a meeting to *shape* the future *direction* [*course*] of the firm.

***ほうこく 報告** 图 a report /ripɔ́ːrt/ (*of*, *on*). (❗ on は詳しい報告に用いる) ●中間 [年次; 最終] 報告 an interim [an annual; the final] *report*. ● 委員会の報告(書)を提出 [受理]する present [receive] a *report of* the committee meeting.（❗ 委員会が作成した報告(書)の場合は the committee's *report*）
● 口頭 [文書] で報告をする make an oral [a written] *report*. ● その事故の詳細な報告書を作成する draw up a detailed *report on* the accident.
— **報告する** 動 report (*on*), make* [give*] a *report* (*of*, *on*). ●その証人は彼をそこで目撃したと報告した The witness *reported* having seen him there [*that* he had seen him there]. ▶ 彼はその自動車事故のことを警察に報告した He *reported* the car accident *to* the police.
●報告者 a reporter.

ほうこく 報国 services rendered to one's country.

ぼうこく 亡国 ❶〚亡びた国〛a ruined country. ●亡国の民 people whose country was ruined.
❷〚国を亡ぼすこと〛●亡国的な思想を持つ have [harbor] thoughts *ruinous to* one's *country*.

ぼうさ 防砂 prevention of soil erosion; erosion control.

ぼうさい 亡妻 one's dead [〚婉曲的〛dear departed, deceased, (最近死んだ) late] wife.

ぼうさい 防災 disaster prevention; prevention of [×from] disasters.
● 防災訓練 a disaster drill. ●防災設備 disaster prevention facilities. ● 防災対策 disaster prevention measures. ●防災都市 a disaster-proof town. ●防災の日 Disaster Prevention Day.

ぼうさい 防塞 a fort; (大規模なもの) a fortress; (バリケード) a barricade.

ほうさく 方策 (対策) measures; (一連の処置のうちの一つ) a step. (⇨方法) ●犯罪を防止する方策を講じる take *measures* [*steps*] to prevent crimes; take *measures* against crimes.

ほうさく 豊作 〚特定の作物の〛a good [a large, a bumper] crop (*of* rice [wheat, corn, grain]); 〚全作物の〛a good [a large, a rich] harvest. (❗ (1) a good rice harvest のように特定の穀物をさすこともできる. (2) 果物や野菜の場合は crop を用いることが多い) ●リンゴの大豊作 a bumper *crop* of apples; a bumper apple *crop*. ●豊作続きを記録する a succession of good (⇔poor) *crops* [*harvests*]. ▶今年は米が豊作だった There was [We had] a *good crop* of rice this year./The rice crop was *good* [*fine*] (⇔

poor, small) this year.
● 豊作貧乏 豊作貧乏だ We've had a rich crop but poor prices.

ぼうさつ 忙殺 — **忙殺される** 動 (大変忙しい) be very busy (*with*; *doing*). ●今は仕事に忙殺されている be very busy (大量の仕事に圧倒される) be swamped] *with* work at the moment.

ぼうさつ 謀殺 图 a (premeditated) murder.
— **謀殺する** 動 murder.

ほうさん 放散 動 diffusion.
— **放散する** 動 diffuse 《light [heat, liquids, gas(s)es]》.

ほうさん 硼酸 【化学】boric acid.
●硼酸水 a boric acid solution.

ぼうさん 坊さん a priest; a Buddhist priest [monk].

***ほうし 奉仕** 图 (a) service. ●無料奉仕 free *service*; *service* without reward. ●社会奉仕 volunteer social *service*.
— **奉仕する** 動 ●国家に奉仕する *serve* [*render services for*] one's country. ▶ 本日は卵を特別奉仕 (=値引き)しています《話》Eggs are *on special* today. (❗ special は「特別奉仕の(品)」の意. 例：The supermarket is having a *special* on strawberry. (あのスーパーでは今イチゴの特売をしている))
●奉仕価格 a bárgain príce. ●奉仕活動 volunteer work. ●奉仕品 a bargain.

ほうし 芳志 ▶ ご芳志を賜り誠にありがたく厚く御礼申し上げます I would like to express my sincere thanks for *your kindness* [(贈り物) *present*].

ほうし 放恣 ●放恣な生活を送る lead a *loose*, *self-indulgent* life. (⇨放縦)

ほうし 法師 a Buddhist priest [monk]. ●一寸法師 (⇨一寸)

ほうし 胞子 【生物】a spore.

ほうじ 邦字 (日本の字) Japanese characters; (漢字とかな) *kanji* and *kana*.
● 邦字新聞 a newspaper in Japanese; a Japanese-language newspaper (❗ 単に a Japanese newspaper ということもある).

ほうじ 法事 a Buddhist [a memorial] service 《for》. ●きのう亡母の法事を営んだ We held a *memorial service for* our (dead) mother yesterday. (❗ a memorial service で母は亡くなったことは明らかなので dead はなくてもよい)

‡**ぼうし 帽子** 〚縁のない〛a cap (❗ 野球帽 (a baseball cap) のようなひさし (a visor, a peak) のついたものを含む); 〚縁のついた〛a hat; 〚あごの下でひもを結ぶ〛a bonnet 〔参考〕乳児用. 以前は女性が着用した.
①【~帽子, 帽子の~】●狩猟用帽子 a húnting cáp. (❗ 日本語のハンチング (a sports cap) とは異なる) ●中折れ帽(子) a felt hat. ●山高帽(子) 《米》a derby, 《英》a bowler. ●帽子の縁 the brim of a hat.
②【帽子】●帽子をかぶる [かぶっている] put on one's *hat* [wear one's *hat*, have (got) one's *hat* on]. (❗ put one's *hat* on, have (got) on one's *hat* の語順も可. have (got) on... on は通例進行形不可) ●帽子を(気取って)ななめにかぶる cock one's *hat*.
●帽子を深くかぶる pull one's *hat* over one's eyes. ●帽子を脱ぐ take off one's *hat*; take one's *hat* off. ▶ 彼女は帽子をかぶって [かぶらずに] 出て行った She went out with her *hat* on [without a *hat*, bare headed].
③【帽子に】●彼は帽子に手を当てて[を上げて]私にあいさつした He tipped [raised] his *hat* to me. (❗ 前の方は帽子をちょっと持ち上げること. 後の方が丁寧

あいさつ).
- **帽子掛け** a hatrack, a hatstand; (木の枝状の) a hat tree. **帽子屋** (人) a hatter, (婦人帽の) a milliner; (店) a hát shòp, a millinery.

ぼうし 防止 ⓢ prevention. (⇨予防) ▶青少年犯罪の防止 the *prevention* of juvenile crime.
—— **防止する** 動 ▶犯罪の拡大を防止する *prevent* the spread of crime; *prevent* crime *from* spreading. (⇨防ぐ)

ぼうし 亡姉 one's dead [〖婉曲的に〗 dear departed, deceased, 〖最近死んだ〗 late] sister.

ぼうし 某氏 a certain person [〖男〗 gentleman]; Mr. So-and-so.

ぼうじ 房事 a marriage act; the conjugal bed. ●房事にふける indulge in *sexual pleasures*.

ほうしき 方式 〖体系的方法〗 a system; 〖方法〗 a method; 〖形式〗 a formula (複 ~s, formulae); 〖手続き〗 (a) procedure. ●デジタル方式 a digital *system*. ●所定の方式に従う follow the standard *system* [*formula, method, procedure*].

ほうじちゃ 焙じ茶 (xa) roasted [toasted] tea.

ぼうしつ 防湿 —— **防湿の** 形 (水蒸気を通さない) moistureproof; dampproof.
●**防湿剤** (乾燥剤) a drying agent; a desiccant. ●**防湿層** 〖建築〗 a damp(proof) course.

ぼうじま 棒縞 thick, vertical stripes.

ほうしゃ 放射 ⓢ (光・熱などの) radiation; (光・熱・音・臭気などの) 〖書〗 (an) emission.
—— **放射する** 動 《やや書》 radiate, 《書》 emit (-tt-). ▶太陽は光と熱を放射する The sun *emits* [*radiates, sends out*] light and heat.
●**放射熱** radiant heat. ●**放射冷却現象** the radiation-cooling phenomenon.

ほうしゃ 硼砂 〖化学〗 borax.

ぼうじゃくぶじん 傍若無人 —— **傍若無人な** 形 (尊大な) árrogant; (目上の人に対して横柄な) ínsolent. ●傍若無人なるまい *arrogant* [*insolent*] behavior. ●傍若無人に振る舞う behave *arrogantly* [*insolently*].

ほうしゃじょう 放射状 —— **放射状の** 形 radial.
—— **放射状に** 副 radially. ▶スポークは中心から放射状に伸びている The spokes *radiate* (*out*) from the center.
●**放射(状)道路** radial roads.

ほうしゃせい 放射性 —— **放射性の** 形 radioactive.
●**放射性元素** a radioactive element. ●**放射性降下物** radioactive fallout. ●**放射性廃棄物** radioactive waste. ●**放射性物質** a radioactive substance.

ほうしゃせん 放射線 radioactive rays; radiation.
●放射線をかけ過ぎる expose 《a cancer patient》 to overdoses of *radiation*.
●**放射線技師** a radiologist. ●**放射線病** [障害] radioactive sickness. ●**放射線療法** radiotherapy. ●**放射線療法士** a radiotherapist.

ほうしゃのう 放射能 radioactivity, radiation. ●放射能漏れ a leak of *radiation* [*radioactivity*]; a *radiation* [*radioactivity*] leak. ●放射能の影響 *radiation* effects. ●高レベルの[許容数値内の]放射能を検出する detect a high [the acceptable] level of *radiation* [*radioactivity*]. ●放射能に汚染される be contaminated by *radioactivity*].
●**放射能汚染** radioactive contamination [pollution].

ほうしゅ 法主 the head of a Buddhist sect.
ほうしゅ 砲手 a gunner.
ぼうじゅ 傍受 —— **傍受する** 動 monitor; intercept; pick ... up.

ほうしゅう 報酬 ❶〖給料〗 pay; (医師など専門職への謝礼) a fee. ●その仕事に対する報酬 the *pay* for the job. ▶弁護士の報酬は大変高い The lawyer's *fee* is very high. ▶彼は無報酬で働いた He worked *without pay* [*for nothing*].
❷〖報い〗(奉仕や善行に対する) (a) reward. ●報酬を要求する[受け取る] claim [receive] a *reward*. ▶彼は功労に対する報酬としてお金をもらった He was given money in *reward* [as a *reward*] *for* his services./He *was rewarded with* money *for* his services.

ほうじゅう 放縦 —— **放縦な** 形 (だらしない) loose; (ままな) self-indulgent; (ふしだらな)《やや書》 dissolute. ●放縦な生活を送る lead a *loose* [a *dissolute*] life.

ぼうしゅう 防臭 deodorization.
●**防臭剤** a deodorant; a deodorizer.

ほうしゅく 奉祝 ⓢ a celebration. —— **奉祝する** 動 celebrate.

ほうしゅく 防縮 ●防縮加工する preshrink. ●防縮加工済みのワイシャツ a *preshrunk* shirt.

ほうしゅつ 放出 —— **放出する** 動 〖熱や光を〗 send ... out, give* ... off, 《書》 emit (-tt-); (放射する)《やや書》 radiate; 〖物資・放射能などを〗 release.
●**放出物資** released goods.

ほうじゅん 芳醇 —— **芳醇な** 形 (まろやかな)《やや書》 mellow; (こくのある) full-bodied. ●芳醇なワイン *mellow* wine.

ほうじゅん 豊潤 —— **豊潤な** 形 rich; (完全に熟した) ripe; mature. ●豊潤な含み a *rich* sound. ●豊潤な果物 a *rich* fruit. ●豊潤な肉体 mature, *voluptuous* body.

ほうしょ 奉書 (a sheet of) *hosho* paper; (説明的に) thick and soft traditional Japanese paper of high quality.

ほうじょ 幇助 —— **幇助する** 動 assist; support; (犯罪を) aid and abet (-tt-).
●**幇助者** a supporter; (犯罪の) abettor.

ぼうしょ 防暑 protection from the heat.
●**防暑服** summer clothes.

ぼうしょ 某所 a certain place. ●都内某所で *somewhere* in Tokyo.

ぼうじょ 防除 prevention 《of》. ●虫害防除 *prevention* of insect [vermin] damage.
—— **防除する** 動 prevent.

ほうしょう 法相 〖法務大臣〗 the Minister of Justice.

ほうしょう 報償 ⓢ compensation. (❗報償金は ⓒ)
●遺族に一律 2,000 万円の報償を提示する offer the bereaved twenty million yen each *for* [*in compensation for*] the loss of their [his, her] family member.
—— **報償する** 動 compensate 《for》.

ほうしょう 褒章 an award; a medal of merit [honor]. ●褒章を与える[受ける] give [receive, get] an award; be awarded a prize.

〖関連〗**日本の褒章**: 紅綬褒章 the Medal with Red Ribbon/緑綬褒章 the Medal with Green Ribbon / 黄綬褒章 the Medal with Yellow Ribbon / 紫綬褒章 the Medal with Purple Ribbon / 藍綬褒章 the Medal with Blue Ribbon/紺綬褒章 the Medal with Dark Blue Ribbon.

ほうじょう 芳情 (⇨圝 芳志)
ほうじょう 法城 〖仏教の本山〗 the head temple of a Buddhist sect; 〖拠り所としての仏教〗 Buddhist teachings that support one's life; Buddhism;

ほうじょう [聖域] a sanctuary; holy precincts.
ほうじょう 豊穣 a good crop [harvest] (of the year). ●五穀豊穣を祈る pray for a rich [bumper] harvest of the grains.
ほうじょう 豊饒 fertility.
── 豊饒な 形 fertile. ●豊饒な土地 fertile land.
ほうしょう 傍証 (状況証拠)【法律】(a piece of) circumstantial evidence.
ほうしょう 帽章 a badge on a cap.
ほうじょうき『方丈記』 *Record of the Ten-Foot-Square Hut*; *Hojoki: Visions of a Torn World*. [参考] 鴨長明の随筆

> **古今ことばの系譜** 『方丈記』
> 行く川のながれは絶えずして、しかも本の水にあらず. よどみに浮かぶうたかたは、かつ消えかつ結びて久しくとどまりたるためしなし. 世の中にある人とすみかと、またかくの如し. The river never stops flowing. The water is always new and never the same. Bubbles in a pool form and vanish, and do not stay for long. People in this world and their abodes change in the same way. (❗ (1) pool は「川で水が流れずにとどまっているところ」の意. (2) abode は「住まい」の意の文語で、庵のような小さい粗末なものも含みうる)

ほうじょうきたい 胞状奇胎 【医学】a vesicular mole.
ほうしょうきん 報奨金 a (¥100,000) reward. ●報奨金を出す offer [give] a *reward*.
ほうしょく 奉職 ── 奉職する 動 work. (⇨勤める)
ほうしょく 宝飾 jewels and ornaments; (集合的) jewelry. (❗その中の1点は a piece of jewelry.
ほうしょく 飽食 图 (書) satiation /sèiʃiéiʃən/.
── 飽食する 動 (書) be satiated (with food and drink).
ぼうしょく 防食 图 prevention of corrosion [(さび) rust].
── 防食の 形 corrosion-proof[-resistant]. ●防食工事をする do work to prevent corrosion [rust]; protect (a bridge) from corrosion [rust].
●防食剤 an anticorrosive (agent).
ぼうしょく 望蜀 ●望蜀の言(げ)であるが... It would be asking too much (for the moon), but ....
ぼうしょく 暴食 overeating. (⇨暴飲暴食)
ほうじる 奉じる ❶[奉納する] present. ●神前に舞を奉じる *present* a dance *to* the god; *present* the god *with* a dance.
❷[心から従う] (命令に) obey; (宗教的教えに) believe in (Buddhism). ●勅命を奉じて by Imperial order.
❸[捧げ持つ] hold (a flag) upright in front of one's body.
ほうじる 報じる (報道する) report. (⇨報道) ●すべての新聞がその列車事故を報じている The train accident *was reported* in all the newspapers./It *was reported* in all the newspapers that there was a train accident./All the newspapers have *reports of* [*on*] the train accident.
ほうじる 焙じる roast; toast (tea leaves).
***ほうしん** 方針 (政府・会社などの政策) a policy; (生活・行動上の信条) a principle; (行動の方向・やり方) a course; (計画) a plan. ●方針を変える change one's *policy* [*course*, *plan*, *tack*]. ●外交 [教育, 営業; 施政] 方針を立てる decide on one's foreign [educational; business; administrative] *policy*. ●一定(いってい)の (党の) 方針に従う follow a definite *policy* [the party *line*]. ▶私は人には本を貸さない方針です I make it my *principle* not to lend a

book to other people [others]. (⇨主義) ▶お手数ですが宿泊者名簿にご記入ください. ホテルの方針ですので May I trouble you to sign the register? It's our hotel *policy*.
ほうしん 放心 absent-mindedness; (書) abstraction. ●放心している be *absent-minded* [(書) *abstracted*]. ●放心して absent-mindedly. ▶彼女は放心したような顔つきをしていた She looked *absent-minded*./She had an *abstracted* look on one's face.
ほうしん 砲身 a barrel of a gun; a gun barrel.
ほうじん 邦人 (外国にいる日本人) a Japanese national; (日本人) Japanese people. ●在留邦人 *Japanese nationals* (living) abroad. ●邦人誘拐事件 an abduction of *Japanese nationals* [*people*].
ほうじん 法人 a corporation, 【法律】a juridical [a legal] person; (法人団体) a corporate body; an incorporation. ●会社を法人組織にする *incorporate* a company.

> **関連** いろいろな法人: 医療法人 a medical corporation/営利[非営利]法人 a profit-making [a non-profit] corporation/学校法人 an educational foundation/現地法人 a locally incorporated company; a company incorporated abroad/財団法人 a foundational juridical person/宗教法人 a religious corporation.

●法人株主 a corporate stockholder. ●法人所得税 corporate income tax. ●法人税 corporátion táx. ●法人組織 a corporate organization.
ぼうしん 防振 ── 防振の 形 vibration-proof [-resistant].
●防振装置 a vibration-proof device.
ぼうじん 防塵 图 protection against [from] dust.
── 防塵の 形 dust-proof.
●防塵カバー a dúst còver. ●防塵めがね (a pair of) dust-proof glasses.
ぼうず 坊主 a bonze /bánz/, a Buddhist monk.
●坊主憎けりゃ袈裟まで憎い 《ことわざ》 (私を愛するなら私の犬も愛して) Love me, love my dog.
●坊主丸儲け A Buddhist monk's income is clear profit.
●坊主頭 a close-cropped [a short-cropped] head; (毛をそった頭) a shaven head.
ほうすい 放水 图 drainage.
── 放水する 動 ●ダムから放水する *discharge water* from a dam. ●燃えさかる家に放水する *spray* [*squirt*] *water on* a furiously burning house.
●放水車 water truck. ●放水路 a drain (canal).
ほうすい 豊水 ●豊水期 a high-water season.
ぼうすい 防水 ── 防水の 形 (水がしみ込まない) waterproof; (水が入らない) watertight. ●防水加工したコート a *waterproof* coat. ●防水(加工)する waterproof (a jacket); make (a box) watertight. ▶このコートは防水性だ This coat is *water-proof* [*proof against damage of water*]. (❗ ×proof against water とは言わない)
●防水シート (a) tarpaulin. ●防水時計 a waterproof watch. ●防水扉 a watertight door.
ぼうすい 紡錘 a spindle.
●紡錘形 a spindle shape.
ほうすん 方寸 〘非常に狭い土地〙a very small piece of land; 〘心の中〙one's mind. ●思いを方寸に納める keep an idea [a thought] in one's *mind*.
ほうせい 法制 legislation. ●内閣法制局 the Cabinet Legislation Bureau. ●内閣法制局長官 the

Director-General of the Cabinet Legislation Bureau. ●**法制史** a history of law. ●**法制審議会** the Legislative Council.

ほうせい 砲声 **the roar of a heavy gun.** ▶敵の砲声がどーんどーんと遠くに聞こえた We heard the distant *rumbles of* enemy *artillery*. (❗artillery は集合的に「大砲」)

ほうせい 縫製 machine sewing. ▶この服は縫製がいい This suit is carefully sewn./This suit is well-made.

ほうせい 暴政 (a) tyranny /tírəni/. ●暴政をしくimpose tyranny 《on》.

ほうせき 宝石 a jewel (❗装身具の意では複数形で), 《集合的》jewelry; (原石を加工研磨したもの) a gem; (原石) a precious stone. ●傷のない宝石 a clean stone. ●宝石をちりばめた冠 a *jeweled* crown; a crown set [studded] with *jewels*. ●指輪に宝石をちりばめる set *gems* in a ring; set a ring with *gems*. ▶彼女は高価な宝石を身につけていた She wore rich *jewels*. ▶彼女の宝石はみな泥棒に盗まれた All her *jewelry* was stolen by a thief.
●**宝石商** a jeweler, a gem dealer. ●**宝石店** a jeweler's (shop). ●**宝石泥棒** a jewelry thief. ●**宝石箱** a jéwel [a jéwelry] bòx.

ぼうせき 紡績 spinning.
●**紡績会社** a spínning còmpany. ●**紡績機** a spinning machine. ●**紡績業** the spinning industry. ●**紡績工場** a spínning mill.

ほうせつ 包摂 〖哲学〗subsumption.
——**包摂する** 動 subsume. ▶A は B に包摂される A is subsumed under B.

ぼうせつ 防雪 protection from [against] snow.
●**防雪林** a snowbreak (forest).

ほうせん 奉遷 ▶ご神体を奉遷する move the object of worship (in a shrine).

ぼうせん 防戦 图 (a) defénse; (防御戦)《やや書》defensive warfare. ▶挑戦者はあごに強烈な一発をくらって防戦一方だった The challenger had to *defend himself all the time* after he received a heavy blow on the chin.
——**防戦する** 動 defend oneself 《against》.

ぼうせん 傍線 a sideline. ●傍線を引く draw a *sideline*.
●**傍線部** a sidelined part.

ぼうぜん 茫然 ——**茫然とする** 動 〖物も言えないほど驚く〗be dumbfounded; 〖びっくり仰天する〗be stunned, 《書》be stupefied, 《話》be flabbergasted. ●彼の大胆さに茫然とする *be dumbfounded* [*stunned*] by his boldness. ▶彼は彼女の死の知らせに茫然とした[茫然自失した] He *was stunned by [at, to* hear] the news of her death.
——**茫然と(して)** 副 ●茫然として(=放心状態で)そこに立ちつくす stand there *in a daze*. ●茫然と(=あっけにとられて)彼を見つめる stare at him *in utter amazement*; (口をぽかんと開けて) gape at him.

ほうせんか 鳳仙花 〖植物〗a touch-me-not. (❗触れると実がはじけて種子が飛び散るのでこの名がある。正式には a garden balsam /bɔ́ːlsəm/)

ほうそ 硼素 〖化学〗bóron (元素記号 B).

ほうそう 放送 图 broadcasting; 〖放送番組〗a broadcast, a program; 〖アナウンス〗an announcement.

①【～放送】●ラジオ放送 a radio *broadcast*. ●テレビ放送 a TV *broadcast*; a telecast. ●生放送 a live /láiv/ *broadcast*. ●再放送 a rebroadcast; a rerun. ●全国放送 a nationwide *broadcast*. ●深夜放送 a late night *program*. ●国際放送 international *broadcasting*. ●衛星放送 satellite broadcasting; (その番組の一つは a satellite broadcast); *broadcasting* via satellite. ●AM [FM] 放送 an AM [an FM] *broadcast*. ●生(中継)放送 a live (relay) *broadcast* (*from*). ●車内放送 (make) an *announcement* over [on] the train's public address [PA] system. ●音声多重方式による野球の(日英) 2 か国語放送 the bilingual (Japanese and English) *broadcast* of a baseball game by multiplex; the bilingual (Japanese and English) multiplex *broadcast* of a baseball game.

②【放送～】●民間[公営; 地方; ラジオ; テレビ]放送局 a commercial [a public; a local; a radio; a television] (*broadcasting*) station. ●放送中《掲示》On the air. ▶この番組の放送時間は午前 10 時から 11 時までです The air time of this program is from 10 to 11 a.m. (❗air time は放送局の 1 日の放送時間ということもある)

③【放送を】●NHK の[短波; FM] 放送を聞く listen to *broadcasts on* NHK radio [*on* short wave; *by* FM].

——**放送する** 動 broadcast* 《news》; (ラジオで) radiobroadcast*; (テレビで) televise. ▶彼の演説はきのうラジオで放送された His speech *was broadcast* (*ed*) *by radio* [*on the radio*] yesterday. (❗by では手段を強調する) ▶その野球の試合はテレビの 2 チャンネルで午後 6 時から生放送されます The baseball game *is televised* live on Channel 2 from 6 p.m. ▶今 3 チャンネルでは何が放送されていますか What's *on* on Channel 3 now?
●**放送衛星** a bróadcasting sàtellite. ●**放送記者** a nétwork [a rádio, a TV] repòrter. ●**放送劇** a broadcast play. ●**放送権** broadcasting rights 《*to*; *for*》. ▶ワールドカップの独占放送権を得る acquire exclusive *broadcasting rights to* [*for*] the World Cup. ●**放送作家** a bróadcasitng writer; (テレビ[ラジオ]の) a television [a radio] writer. ●**放送事業** the broadcasting business [industry]. ●**放送室** (学校の) a school broadcasting room; (放送局の) a studio. ●**放送大学** the University of the Air; 《英》the Open University. ●**放送網** a (radio [television]) network.

ほうそう 包装 图 (包むこと) wrapping; (荷作りすること) packing. (⇒包み)
——**包装する** 動 wrap (-pp-); pack; (進物用に) gift-wrap (-pp-). ▶これを進物用に包装してください Would you *wrap* this as a gift? 《事情》米英では a Gift-wrapping counter へ持って行き包装してもらう。通例有料。
●**包装紙** wrápping pàper; a wrapper.

ほうそう 疱瘡 〖医学〗(天然痘) smallpox; (種痘) a vaccination against smallpox.

ぼうそう 暴走 图 〖自動車などの〗reckless driving; (盗んだ車での) a jóyride; 〖動物の群れの〗a stampede; 〖野球の〗a reckless baserunning.
——**暴走する** 動 ▶彼は車を暴走させた He *drove* his car *recklessly*.
●**暴走族** a motorcycle gang.

ほうそうかい 法曹界 legal [《やや書》judicial] circles.

ほうそく 法則 (学問・自然科学上の) a law; a principle. ●自然の法則《集合的》the *law* of nature; natural *law*. (❗その一つをさす場合は a ~ となる) ●重力の法則 the *law* [*principle*] of gravity. ●需要と供給の法則 the *law* of supply and demand. (❗語順に注意)

ぼうだ 滂沱 ▶涙が滂沱として下る Tears stream [(滝のように) cascade] down one's cheeks.

ほうたい 包帯 (a) bandage /bǽndidʒ/. ●1巻きの包帯 a roll of *bandage*. ●足に包帯を巻く bandage one's foot; put a *bandage* on [around] one's foot. ●傷の包帯を取る take a *bandage* off the wound. ●けがをした指に包帯をしている have a *bandage* on one's injured finger. ▶彼は1週間はど包帯をしていた He *was in bandages* for a week or so.

ほうだい 邦題 a Japanese title.

ほうだい 砲台 a battery.

-ほうだい -放題 ●食べ放題 (⇨食べ放題) ●言いたい放題のことを言う say *what one feels* (like saying); (遠慮なく言う) speak *without reserve*. ▶彼は何でも我がままの放題[=思いどおりにする] He *has* [*gets*] his *own way* in everything./He *does whatever* he *likes* [*wants*].

ぼうだい 膨大 ― 膨大な 形 (数量・額が) (巨大な) huge; (広大な) vast; (並外れて大きい) enormous; (驚くほど大きい) tremendous; (計り知れない) immense. ●膨大な金額 a *huge* [a *vast*, an *enormous*] amount of money.

ぼうたおし 棒倒し a "pushing-down-the-pole" game.

ぼうたかとび 棒高跳び the pole vault. ●棒高跳びをする選手 a pole-vaulter.

ぼうだち 棒立ち ●棒立ちになる stand upright [erect]. ●恐怖で棒立ちになる *stand petrified* with fear. ●(ボクシングで)ロープに追い詰められて棒立ちになる be on the ropes and unable to defend oneself.

ぼうだま 棒球 [野球] a nothing ball [pitch]. ▶彼は棒球しか投げられない He's got nothing on the ball.

ほうたん 放胆 ― 放胆な 形 bold; fearless; (大胆不敵な) intrepid. ●放胆な作戦 *intrepid* tactics. (❗単・複両扱い)

ほうだん 放談 a free [(形式ばらない) an informal] talk. ●時事放談 a *free talk* on current topics.
― 放談する 動 talk freely (*about*, *on*, *of*).

ほうだん 法談 (⇨法話)

ほうだん 砲弾 a shell.

ぼうだん 防弾 ― 防弾の 形 bulletproof.
●防弾ガラス bulletproof glass. ●防弾チョッキ a bulletproof jacket.

ほうち 放置 ―― 放置する 動 leave*. ●駅前に自転車を放置する *leave* one's bicycle in front of the station. ●病人を路上に放置しておく *leave* a sick person (*unattended*) on the street. ●事態を放置する(=そのままにしておく) leave the situation *as it is*. ▶その農場は放置されていた (荒れるに任されていた) The farm *was left* (*to run*) *wild*. (❗( )内を省くと放置した結果だけを、( )内を含むとそこに至る過程をも暗示する)/(手入れされていなかった) The farm *was* (*left*) *uncared for*.

ほうち 報知 图 information; (報告) a report; (告知) (a) notice. ●火災報知機 a fire alarm.
― 報知する 動 inform [notify] 《*A of B*》.

ほうちく 放逐 expulsion; (国外へ) banishment.
― 放逐する 動 expel (-ll-) 《*from*》; banish 《*from*》; 《書》 oust 《*from*》. ▶彼は国外へ放逐された(=追い出された) He *was expelled from* his [the] country.

ほうちこく 法治国 a law-governed state.

ほうちゃく 逢着 ―― 逢着する 動 face; 《書》 encounter. ●困難に逢着する be faced with difficulties.

ぼうちゅう 忙中 忙中閑あり 'You can always find leisure time even when you are very busy.'/ (だれが見ても忙しそうな人があえて上手にひまを作るものだ)《ことわざ》 The busiest men can [have] find the most leisure.

ぼうちゅうざい 防虫剤 (虫よけ) an insect repellent; (衣類の) mothballs.

ほうちょう 包丁 a kitchen knife (圈 knives).
●包丁研ぎ knife-sharpening; (人) a knife-sharpener.

ほうちょう 放鳥 ― 放鳥する 動 set* a bird free.

*ぼうちょう 膨張 图 expansion. ●金属[通貨]の膨張 the *expansion* of metals [currency]. (❗「通貨の膨張」 is inflation (of currency) ともいう)
― 膨張する[させる] 動 expand (❗物質の体積が全体に膨張すること (⇨拡大する)); swell* (❗空気や水が入ってふくれ上がること (⇨膨らむ)). ●急速に膨張する人口 a rapidly *expanding* [(増加する) *increasing*] population. ▶鉄は熱で膨張する Iron *expands with* heat [when (it is) heated]./Heat *expands* iron. ▶ガスが膨張して気球が破裂した The gas in the balloon *expanded* [*was expanded*, ×swelled] *and exploded*. (❗*swell* は体積のいものには用いない。The balloon *swelled*. は可)
●膨張率 the rate of expansion; the expansion rate.

ぼうちょう 防潮 protection from [against] the encroachment of the sea.
●防潮堤 (堤防) a seawall.

ぼうちょう 防諜 protection from espionage.

ぼうちょう 傍聴 图 hearing; [出席] attendance. ▶(裁判で)一般の傍聴が許された The public were admitted to the court. ▶公判は傍聴禁止で行われた The trial was conducted in camera [with closed doors]. (❗*in camera* は「非公開で」の意)
― 傍聴する 動 listen to ...; hear*; attend. ●公判を傍聴する *attend* a trial. ●国会を傍聴する *visit* the Diet in session.
●傍聴券 an admission ticket. ●傍聴席 seats for the public; (法廷・議場などの) the public [visitors'] gallery. ●傍聴人 a hearer; a visitor in the gallery; 《集合的》 the gallery; an audience.

ほうっておく 放っておく (構わずにおく) leave* [let*]... alone; (わきへおく) lay*... aside. (⇨放置) ▶彼は今不機嫌だから放っておきなさい He's sulking now. *Leave* [*Let*] him *alone*.
会話 「また彼は約束を破ったのよ」「彼がそんなことをしたのを放っておくつもり?」 "Yet again he's broken his promise." "*Are you letting* him *get away with it*?" (❗*get away with ...* は「(よくない事)をまんまとやり通す」の意)

ぼうっと ❶ [はっきりしないで] dimly; (かすかに) faintly; (定かでなく) indistinctly. (⇨ぼんやり❶) ▶暗やみに何かぼうっと人影かのようなものを見た I saw something figure-like *dimly* in the dark./I saw a *vague* figure in the dark.
❷ [放心して] in a daze; (うっかりと) absent-mindedly; (うつろに) vacantly. (⇨ぼんやり❷) ●ぼうっと空を眺める look *vacantly* at the sky. ▶私はぼうっとして自分の駅で降りるのを忘れた I *absent-mindedly* missed my station. ▶彼女は彼に死なれたショックでぼうっとなっているようだった She seemed *dazed* [*numb*] *from* the shock of his death. (❗*from* の代わりに *with* も可)
❸ [火などが] ●ぼうっと火がつく catch fire. ▶枯れた草に火がぼうっとついた The dry grass *caught* fire. (❗「ぼうっと」に当たる言葉はないが、早い動きを示す *catch* でその様子を伝える)
❹ [汽笛の音] (⇨ぼうっと❶)

ぼうっと ❶ [汽笛の音] ▶船が港を出るとき汽笛をぼうっと鳴らした The steamer *blared* its *horn* as it sailed

out of the harbor. ▶遠くで汽車のぼうという音が聞こえた I heard the train *whistle* in the distance.
❷【顔などが】●ぽうっと赤くなる blush, flush, turn red. ▶彼女は当惑して顔がぽうっと赤くなった She *blushed* with embarrassment.
❸【放心して】▶彼は彼女の美しさにぽうっとなった He *was stunned* [*was carried away*] by her beauty.

ほうてい 法廷 （裁判所）a court (!「裁判」の意では Ⓤ. 正式には a court of law, a law court などという); (裁判が行われる部屋) a courtroom.
①【～法廷】●小法廷 a petty *court* [*bench*]. ●大法廷 the full *court* [*bench*].
②【法廷は】●法廷は3日後に開かれる The *court* will be held [《やや書》be in session] three days from now.
③【法廷に[で]】● 法廷に出頭する appear in *court*. ▶その件は法廷に持ち出さないことにした We decided *not to bring* the case *to court* for trial./ (示談で解決することにした) We decided to settle the case *out of court*. ▶法廷では真実を言わないといけない You have to tell the truth in [×at] *court*. ▶彼らは国を相手に損害賠償を求めて法廷で争った They brought a suit for the damages *against* the Government.
●法廷通訳 courtroom interpreting; （人）a courtroom interpreter. ●法廷闘争 a court battle; (訴訟) a suit. ●法廷闘争に持ち込む appeal to a *court* (*of law*). ●法廷侮辱罪 contempt of court. ●法廷弁護士《英》a barrister.

ほうてい 奉呈 信任状を奉呈する *present* one's credentials *to* the president [Emperor, Queen].

ほうてい 法定 ── 法定の 🄵 (法律上正当な); (法律で決められた) legal /líːɡl/; 《書》 statutory.
●法定貨幣 legal tender; lawful money [currency]. ●法定金利 the legal interest rate. ●法定最低賃金 (the) legal minimum wage. ●法定準備金 [statutory] reserves. ●法定相続人 a legal heir /éər/. ●法定代理人 a legal representative. ●法定伝染病 a legal communicable disease. ●法定労働時間 (the) statutory working hours [workweek].

ぼうてい 亡弟 one's dead [《婉曲的》dear departed, deceased, 《最近死んだ》late] brother.

ほうていしき 方程式 【数学】an equation. ●1次 [2次; 3次; n次] 方程式 a linear [a quadratic; a cubic; *n*th-degree] *equation*. ●連立方程式 simultaneous *equations*. (!複数扱い) ●方程式を立てる[解く] set up [solve] an *equation*.

ほうてき 放擲 ── 放擲する 🄳 abandon 《one's duty》.

ほうてき 法的 ── 法的な 🄵 (法律にかなった) legal. ●法的措置を取る take a *legal* action. ▶それは法的には正しいかもしれないが道徳的には間違っていると思う That may be *legally* right, but I think it's morally wrong.

ほうてん 宝典 『大切な本』a precious book; 『日常生活に便利な本』a handbook; a manual. ●育児宝典 a handbook of childcare; a childcare handbook.

ほうてん 法典 a code. ●ハムラビ法典 the *Code* of Hammurabi. ●民法典 a civil *code*.

ほうでん 宝殿 『宝物殿』a museum; 『神殿』a shrine; (神聖な場所) a sanctuary.

ほうでん 放電 🄰 《書》 (electric) discharge.
── 放電する 🄳 《書》 discharge (electricity).
●放電管 【電気工学】a discharge tube.

ほうてん 傍点 (side)dots. ●傍点を打つ put *dots* alongside the words in order to show emphasis.

ほうと 方途 （何をなすべきか）what to do; (手段・方法) a way, a means; (対応策) a measure 《*to* do》.

ぼうと 暴徒 (破壊的群衆)a mob, rioters. ●暴徒を扇動する[追い払う] stir up [disperse] a *mob*. ▶暴徒は鎮圧された The *mob* was [were] put under control.

ほうとう 宝刀 a treasured [a valuable] sword. ▶この刀は先祖伝来の宝刀だ This sword is a valuable family heirloom.

ほうとう 放蕩 （快楽にふけり金銭・精力を乱費すること）《書》dissipation; (金銭の浪費) prodigality; (色狂い) dissoluteness. ●放蕩にふける indulge in *sensual pleasures*. (!sensual pleasures は「美食, 性行為など肉体的歓び」の意)
●放蕩者 a dissipated《書》[a prodigal, a dissolute] man.

ほうとう 砲塔 (旋回式の) a (gun) turret.

ほうどう 報道 🄰 a report 《*of, on*》 (!on は通例詳細なものに用いる); 『ニュース』 news; (放送) a newscast; 『取材』coverage. ●その事故の報道 a *report of* the accident. ●その殺人事件について断片的な報道をする make a fragmentary *report of* the murder case. ●新聞報道によると according to a newspaper *report*. ●報道の自由を脅かす threaten freedom of the press.
── 報道する 🄳 report; (取材して) cover. ●すでに報道したとおり as previously *reported*. ▶その事故は新聞ではどのように報道されていますか How is the accident *reported* [*handled*] by (the) press [in the newspapers]? ▶大統領は重体だと報道されている It *has been reported* that the president is seriously ill. ▶すべての新聞がハイジャック事件を詳しく報道した Every paper *covered* the hijack in detail./Every paper *gave* detailed *coverage to* the hijack.
●報道員 [記者] a (news) reporter 《*on, for, from, with*》. ●報道カメラマン a néws photògrapher. (!a news cameraman はニュース映画のカメラマンをさすことがある) ●報道官 (米政府の) the Press Secretary (to the President). ●報道関係者 (people connected with) the press. (!the press では単・複両扱い) ●報道関係者からの問い合わせ an inquiry from *the press*. ●報道管制 a blackout on news; a news blackout; news censorship (!前の二つは「報道させない」場合, 後の方は「検閲をパスしたもののみ報道させる」場合); (婉曲的) news management. ●報道機関 néws mèdia. (!単・複両扱い (⇨マスコミ)) ●報道写真 a néws phòtograph. ●報道写真家 a news photographer; (写真に重点を置いた) a photojournalist. ●報道陣 the press (!単・複両扱い); the newspeople, (男の) the newsmen; 《英》the néwspaper repòrters, (男の) the pressmen.
●報道番組 a repórting prògram; (解説を主にした) a news commentary program.

ぼうとう 冒頭 [初め] the beginning, the start; (話などの) the opening; (文などの) the head. ●冒頭から from the *beginning* [*start*]. ●演説の冒頭に at the *opening* [*beginning*] of one's speech. ●手紙の冒頭で at the *head* of the letter. ▶その小説は冒頭に挿し絵がある The novel *opens with* an illustration.
●冒頭陳述 an opening statement.

ぼうとう 暴投 🄰 【野球】(打者への) a wild pitch; (野手への) a wild throw, an overthrow; 『クリケット』a wide ball. ▶藤井投手の暴投で三塁へ進む get to

third *on* Fujii's *wild pitch*. ● 二塁手へ(高い)暴投を投げる *overthrow* the second baseman.
— 暴投する 動 throw* [pitch] wild; throw a wild ball.

ぼうとう 暴騰 名 a sharp [a sudden] rise, a jump.
— 暴騰する 動 rise* sharply [suddenly]; go* up sharply [suddenly]; jump; (打ち上げ花火のように)《話》skyrocket. ▶ 昨年は物価が暴騰した Prices *rose sharply* [*jumped, skyrocketed*] *last year.*/There was a *sharp rise* [a *jump*] *in* prices last year.

ぼうどう 暴動 a riot; (騒動) a disturbance; (反乱) an uprising. ● 人種暴動 a ráce *riot*. ▶ 暴動を起こす start a riot; raise [start] a *riot*; create a *disturbance*. ▶ 暴動を鎮圧する put down [suppress] a *riot* (▮前の方が口語的だ); 《書》quell a *disturbance*. ▶ 学生の暴動が起こった A student *riot* broke out [×*happened*].

ぼうとく 冒瀆 名 (神聖なものへの) (a) blasphemy /blǽsfəmi/; (不敬) (a) profánity. (▮前の方がより過激. ともに具体的言動の場合は C)
— 冒瀆的な 形 blásphemous; profáne.
— 冒瀆する 動 blasphéme.

ぼうどくマスク 防毒マスク a gás màsk.

ほうなん 法難 《仏教》(suffer) religious persecution.

ほうにち 訪日 a visit to Japan. — 訪日する 動 visit Japan. (⇨訪問)

ほうにょう 放尿 名 urination; micturition.
— 放尿する 動 urinate; discharge urine; relieve oneself.

ほうにん 放任 名 (無干渉) noninterference. ● 放任主義の子供を育てる bring up one's children *on a let-alone* [*a hands-off*] *principle*.
— 放任する 動 【干渉しない】do* not interfere *(with)*; 【そのままほうっておく】let* [leave*] ... alone. ▶ 彼は子供を放任している He doesn't *interfere* [(寛大すぎる) *is too permissive*] *with* his children./He lets his children do as they want to.

ほうねつ 放熱 — 放熱する 動 (熱を作り出す) radiate [(放出する) give* out, (放散する) disperse] heat. ● 放熱器 a radiator.

ほうねつ 防熱 — 防熱の 形 heat-resistant.

ほうねん 放念 ▶ そのことはどうぞご放念ください Please forget it.

ほうねん 豊年 a good [《米》a banner] year for crops; a fruitful [an abundant] year. (▮後の方は農作物以外についても用いる) (⇨豊作)
● 豊年満作 (豊作) a bumper harvest [crop].

ほうねん 防燃 — 防燃の 形 fire-resistant. ● 防燃加工をする make 《the cloth》 *fire-resistant*.

ぼうねんかい 忘年会 a year-end party (held to help people forget the troubles of the past year).

ほうのう 奉納 — 奉納する 動 《やや書》dedicate. ● 神社に灯籠を奉納する *dedicate* [*offer*] a lantern *to a shrine*.
● 奉納試合 a kendo exhibition held at a shrine.
● 奉納相撲 a ritual sumo bout held at a shrine.

ほうはい 澎湃 ▶ 自由を求める声が澎湃として起こった(=勢いをもって起こった) The demand for freedom *rose strongly* among people./People's demand for freedom *surged up*.

ぼうはく 傍白 《演劇》 an aside.

ぼうばく 茫漠 ▶ 茫漠たる原野 a vast stretch of the wilds. ▶ あの先生の講義は茫漠としていて(=とりとめがなく, 首尾一貫していないので)つかみ所がなかった His lecture was so *rambling and incoherent* that I couldn't get his point.

ぼうはつ 暴発 — 暴発する 動 (銃が) go* off accidentally [by accident].

ぼうはてい 防波堤 a breakwater; (海岸浸食防止の) a seawall.

ほうばん 邦盤 a record [a disc, a CD] of Japanese music [songs].

ぼうはん 防犯 crime prevèntion.
● 防犯課 the department of crime prevention. ● 防犯カメラ 《on》a secúrity càmera. ● 防犯訓練 a crime prevention drill. ● 防犯週間 Crime Prevention Week. ● 防犯ビデオ 《on》a secúrity video. ● 防犯ベル (盗難報知器) a búrglar alàrm; (ポケット用の) a pager (⇨ポケットベル).

ほうひ 包皮 《解剖》the foreskin; the sheath.

ほうひ 放屁 — 放屁する 動 break* wind; pass gas. (⇨おなら)

*****ほうび** 褒美 (a) reward 《*of* + 金額, *for* + 行為》; 《賞》a prize. ▶ 彼に 1 万円を彼に与える *reward* him *with* 10,000 yen 《*for* his help》; give him a *reward* of 10,000 yen 《*for*》; give him 10,000 yen *in* [*as a*] *reward* 《*for*》. ▶ 彼は努力を認められてたっぷりほうびをもらった He *was* amply [highly] *rewarded for* his efforts.

ぼうび 防備 defense. ▶ 防備を固める strengthen the *defense* 《*against*》. ● 無防備の defenseless. (⇨無防備)

ぼうびき 棒引き ▶ 彼の借金を棒引きにする *write off* [*cancel*] his debts.

ぼうびろく 忘備録 (⇨備忘録)

*****ほうふ** 豊富 名 richness, 《やや書》abundance, 《書》plenty.
— 豊富な 形 rich, 《やや書》affluent; (あり余るほどの) abundant, plentiful; (十分な) ample. ● 鉄分の豊富な野菜 vegetables *rich in* iron. ● 豊富な運動量 a *large quantity of* motion [練習 *exercise*]. ▶ この地域は米が作れるほど豊富な雨量がある This area has *ample* rainfall for growing rice. ▶ この土地は鉱物が豊富だ This land is *rich* [*abundant, affluent*] *in* minerals./《書》This land abounds *in* [*with*] minerals. ▶ 彼は語彙(ぃ)が豊富だ He has a *large* [a *rich*, a *wide*, an *extensive*, ×*many*] *vocabulary*. ▶ 彼は教職の経験が豊富だ He has *a lot of* [*plenty of*] experience in teaching. ▶ そのメニューは選択肢が豊富だ(=豊富な選択肢がある) There are *abundant* choices in the menu./(幅広い選択肢がある) There is a *wide* range of choices in the menu.
— 豊富に 副 ▶ 知識を豊富にする *make* one's knowledge *richer*; 《やや書》*enrich* one's knowledge. ● 語彙(ぃ)を豊富にする *enrich* [*increase, build, develop, enlarge*] one's vocabulary. ● 食物は豊富にある We have *an abundant* [a *plentiful*] supply of food./We have *plenty of* [a *great deal of*] food./We have food *in abundance* [*in plenty*]. ▶ その店はブランド品を豊富にそろえている(= 豊富な種類を持っている) The store has an *abundant* variety of brand-name goods.

ほうふ 抱負 (大志) (an) ambition; (熱望) (an) aspiration (▮2 語ともしばしば複数形で); (計画) a plan. ▶ 抱負を語る talk about one's *ambitions*; tell 《*us*》one's *plan* 《*for* the future》.

ぼうふ 亡夫 one's dead [《婉曲的》dear departed, deceased, (最近死んだ) late] husband.

ぼうふ 亡父 one's dead [《婉曲的》dear departed,

ぼうふう deceased, (最近死んだ) late' father.

ぼうふう 暴風 a windstorm (! 雨を伴わない); (強風) a gale (! a storm より弱いが船のマストが折れることもある); a storm (! 雨やしばしば雷も伴う). (⇨暴風雨).
- 暴風警報 a stórm [a gále] wàrning. ● 暴風圏 a stórm zòne.

ぼうふうう 暴風雨 a storm, a rainstorm. (⇨暴風)
- 雷を伴う暴風雨 a *thunderstorm*. ▶暴風雨が一日中荒れ狂った The *storm* raged all day. ▶航海中私たちの船は何度も暴風雨にあった Our ship met with [was caught in] a *storm* many times during our voyage.

ぼうふうりん 防風林 a windbreak.

ほうふく 法服 〖裁判官の〗a judge's gown [robe]; 〖僧侶の〗a priest's robe (⇨法衣).

ほうふく 報復 图 (個人的な復讐(ふくしゅう)) revenge; (仕返し) retaliation; (主に国家間の) reprisal /rɪpráɪzəl/. (⇨復讐) ● 報復措置をとる take *retaliatory* measures (*against*).
― 報復する 動 retaliate; (復讐する) revenge oneself [take* revenge] (*on*).

ほうふくぜっとう 抱腹絶倒 ▶彼はその冗談に抱腹絶倒した He shook [*His sides shook*] *with laughter* at the joke. ▶×He shook his sides... は不可(!) (笑い転げた)《話》He *laughed his head off* at the joke.

ぼうふざい 防腐剤 (an) antiseptic; 〖(食品の)保存料〗(a) preservative.

ほうふつ 彷彿 ▶あの子は彼の死んだ父親をほうふつとさせる (=思い浮かばせる) The boy *reminds* me *of* his dead father./(よく似ている) The boy *closely resembles* his dead father.

ほうぶつせん 放物線 图 a parabola /pərǽbələ/. ● 放物線を描く draw 〖書〗describe] a *parabola*.
― 放物線(状)の 形 pàrabólic.

ぼうふら 〖動物〗a mosquito larva (圏 〜s, larvae); (くねくねする動きから) a wriggler.

ほうぶん 邦文

ほうぶん 法文 〖法令の文章〗the text of the law; legal sentences; 〖法律と文学〗law and literature. ● 法文化する make ... into a law. ▶法文に規定されているように as provided for in the *law*.
● 法文学部〈米〉the college of law and literature;〈英〉the faculty of law and literature.

ほうへい 砲兵 an artillerist, (男の) an artilleryman (圏 -men).
● 砲兵隊 the artillery. (! 単・複両扱い)

ぼうへき 防壁 a protective wall.

ほうべん 方便 (急場しのぎの方策)《書》an expedient (! 道徳上不正だと思われる手段も含めて); (手段) a means (! 単・複同形). ▶彼を納得させる方便を考えなければならない I must think out an *expedient* [a *means*] to convince him. ▶うそも方便 (⇨嘘 [成句])

ぼうぼ 亡母 one's dead 〖婉曲的〗dear departed, deceased, (最近死んだ) late] mother.

ほうほう 方法 〖やり方〗a way, a manner (! way より堅い語); (組織的な) a method, (体系立った) a system; 〖扱い方〗an approach; 〖手続き〗(a) procedure (⇨手続き); 〖手段〗a means (! 単・複同形); 〖対策〗measures; 〖様式〗a style.

① 〖〜の(方法)〗▶ 英語を教える最善の方法 the best *way* [*method*] of teaching English. ▶彼女独特の表現方法 her *manner* of expression peculiar to her. ▶そのコンサートのチケットの入手方法 a *means* of getting [obtaining] a ticket for the concert. ▶従来の方法に従う follow the usual [(伝統的な) traditional] *method*.

② 〖方法が[は]〗▶人それぞれ違った練習方法がある There are different *methods* of exercise for different people. ▶海外を旅行する最も安上がりな方法は何ですか What is the cheapest *way* of traveling [*to* travel] abroad?/What is [are] the most inexpensive *means of* traveling [×to travel] abroad? ▶それしか方法はない It's the only *way* to go.

③ 〖方法を〗▶ この箱を開ける方法を知っていますか Do you know *how to* open this box? ▶彼はその問題に対して分析的な方法をとった He took an analytic *approach to* the problem. ▶彼らは新しい経営方法を導入した They introduced a new management *system*. ▶彼はその実験の方法を学生に説明した He explained to the students the *procedure for* [*to be* followed in] the experiment. ▶その病気を予防するためにあらゆる方法を講じなければならない We have to take every possible *measure to* prevent [all the preventive *measures against*] the disease.

▶ DISCOURSE
以下の方法を提案したい **I would like to** suggest the following *measures*. (! I would like to ...(...したい)は主張を表すディスコースマーカー。I want to ...よりもフォーマルで,論文に適している)

④ 〖方法で〗▶ 私と同じ方法でもう一度やってごらん Try it again in the same *way* [*manner*, *method*] as I did. (! 他の 2 語と異なり,way では前のinと後のas の省略されることが多い) ▶ 君がいちばんいいと思う方法でそれをやりなさい Handle it *how* [*the way*] you think best.

● 方法論 (a) methodology. ● 最も有効な方法論 the most effective *methodology* of foreign language teaching.

ほうぼう 〖魚介〗a sea robin; a gurnard.

ほうぼう 方々 〖いろいろな場所で〗in various places; 〖至る所〗everywhere; 〖あちこち〗here and there.
● 世界のほうぼうから日本に来る come to Japan from *various* [*all*] *parts* of the world. ▶ほうぼうへ移動する a move *from place to place*. ▶いなくなった犬をほうぼう探した I looked *everywhere* [*all over*] for my lost dog. ▶ その植物はほうぼうにある The plant is *here and there*.

ぼうぼう ❶ 〖果てしない〗vast. ▶ぼうぼうたる砂漠がずっと延びていた A *vast* desert extended far out before my eyes.
❷ 〖草などが茂りすぎて〗▶ 空き家の庭は草ぼうぼうだった The garden of the empty house *was overgrown with* weeds./Weeds were *rank in* the garden of the empty house. ▶ 彼の頭髪は手入れもされずにぼうぼうに伸びていた His hair was left to grow *thick and wild*.
❸ 〖勢いよく〗hard; (激しく) fiercely; (炎に包まれて) in flames. ▶ 乾いた木がぼうぼう燃えていた Dry wood was burning *fiercely* [*vigorously*]. ▶ 家がぼうぼう燃えていた [燃え上がった] The house was *in flames* [burst *into flames*].

ほうほうのてい ほうほうの体 ▶ ほうほうの体で逃げる (大あわてで) run away *in a great hurry*; (命からがら) run *for one's life*.

ほうぼく 放牧 图 grazing.
― 放牧する 動 ▶ 牛を放牧する put cattle out to (×a) pasture (! 成句なので冠詞をつけない); graze [*pasture*] cattle.
● 放牧地 a pasture. (! a meadow は「特に干し草を作るための牧草地」)

ぼうまい 亡妹 one's dead 〖婉曲的〗dear depart-

ほうまつ 泡沫 ●**泡沫候補** an unlikely [a minor] candidate.

ほうまん 豊満 ― 豊満な 形 plump; (セクシーな) voluptuous. ●大柄で豊満な胸の女性 a large, full-breasted woman.

ぼうまん 膨満 (膨張) distention; (鼓腸) flatulence. ●腹部膨満 abdominal distention [flatulence]. ●膨満感を覚える have a sensation of distention [flatulence].

ほうまんけいえい 放漫経営 loose [(慎重を欠いた) careless, (無責任な) irresponsible] management.

ほうみょう 法名 [戒名] a posthumous /pástʃəməs/ Buddhist name; [僧としての名前] a Buddhist name.

ぼうみん 暴民 rioters; riotous people; a mob.

ほうむ 法務 ●**法務局** the Regional Legal Affairs Bureau. ●**法務省** the Ministry of Justice. ●**法務大臣** the Minister of Justice.

ほうむる 葬る ❶ [埋葬する] bury /béri/ ▶彼は共同墓地に葬られた He was buried [was laid to rest] in the cemetery.
❷ [もみ消す] cover [hush]... up; [忘れ去る] bury; [望みや機会をくじく] kill. ●その疑惑はやみに葬る cover [hush] up the corruption scandal. ▶その出来事がやがて過去のこととして葬り去られるだろう The event will soon be buried in the past. ▶不幸な事件で彼の野望は葬り去られた An unfortunate accident killed his ambition.

ほうめい 芳名 [[「相手の名前」の意の尊敬語]] your (honored) name. ●**芳名録** a visitors' book [register].

ぼうめい 亡命 名 [政治的亡命] [国際法] political asylum; [敵側へ] defection; [国から追放されて] exile.
―― **亡命する** 動 seek [take*] political asylum 《in》; defect 《to》; (避難する) seek refuge 《in》. ●亡命して異国で暮らす live in exile. ●**亡命者** a political refugee; (敵側への) a defector; (追放人) an exile. ●**亡命政府** a government in exile.

* **ほうめん 方面** ❶ [方向, 地域] (方向) a direction; (地域) an area (! 広大な地域にも町の1地区のような狭い場所にも用いる); (地方) a district. ▶東京方面に行く電車はすべて通勤客で超満員だった All trains going in the direction of Tokyo [All trains (bound) for Tokyo] were overcrowded with commuters. ▶九州方面は豪雨に見舞われた A torrential rain hit the Kyushu district.
  会話 「火事はどこだ」「渋谷方面だ」"Where is the fire?" "It's in the Shibuya area./It's somewhere in [around] Shibuya./(話) It's out Shibuya way."
  ❷ [分野] a field; (物・事態などの様相・面) an aspect. ●物理学の方面で活躍している be active in the field of physics. ●あらゆる方面の(=職業、地位の)人 people from every walk [all walks] of life. ●お仕事はどういう方面ですか What field [What kind of business] are you in? ●あらゆる方面からその問題を話し合いましょう Let's discuss the problem in all its aspects [(あらゆる角度から) from all angles]. ▶その話は確かな方面(=情報源)から聞いた I got the news from a reliable [当やや書) source (《やや書》 quarter]. (! 「情報源は確かでないが」は from an unidentified source)

ほうめん 放免 ―― **放免する** 動 release [《書》 discharge] 《him》 from prison. ●仕事から放免される be freed from work. ▶彼は無罪放免となった He was acquitted of the charge./He was found innocent and was released [was set free].

ほうもう 法網 ●**法網をくぐる** evade the law; (法の支配から) escape the clutches of the law; (犯罪すれすれの行為をする) sail close to the wind.

ほうもう 紡毛 spun wool.

ほうもつ 宝物 a treasure; (家伝の) an heirloom. (⇒宝) ▶その寺の宝物は今公開されている The temple's treasures are on view now.
●**宝物殿** a building for storing treasures; a treasure house.

* **ほうもん 訪問** 名 a visit 《from, to》; (短期で正式の) a call 《on, at》. (! 《米》では訪問の長短や種類を問わず visit が一般的。《英》では call が一般的で, visit は長期の訪問や仕事・公式の訪問に限られる) (⇒動)
  ●彼の訪問を受ける get a visit [receive a call] from him. ▶首相は中国を訪問中です The Prime Minister is on a visit to [is visiting] China.
  ―― **訪問する** 動 visit; (特定の目的で) pay* a visit 《to》; (職務・儀礼で) call 《on+人, at+場所》. (⇒訪ねる) ●生徒の家庭を次々に訪問する visit [call at] one's students' homes one after another; pay a round of visits to one's students' homes. ▶京都は毎年多くの観光客が訪問する Kyoto is visited by a lot of tourists every year./A lot of tourists visit Kyoto every year. (! 場所を主語にした visit の受身は, by 以下が不特定多数であるときや, Our school has been visited by the Prime Minister. (我が校は総理大臣の訪問を受けたことがある)のように知名度の高い人であるときを除いて通例不可)
  ●**訪問介護員** (⇒ホームヘルパー) ●**訪問看護** home-visiting nursing; (在宅ケア) domiciliary care (! 病院看護 (hospital care) に対比して用いられる). ●**訪問着** a (women's) semi-formal kimono. ●**訪問客[者]** a visitor; (職務・儀礼で短時間の) a caller. ●**訪問販売** door-to-door [call] sales.

ほうもん 砲門 ●**砲門を開く** (砲撃を始める) open fire 《on the closing enemy》.

ぼうや 坊や ❶ [男の子] a boy; (息子) a son; (子供) a child (愛 children); [呼びかけ] (my) boy; son, sonny; 《話》 kid. (⇒坊ちゃん) ▶あれがあなたの坊や? Is that your son [little boy]?
❷ [世間知らずの青年] ●坊や坊やした青年 a young man looking like a mere boy. (! a stripling は《やや古》)

ほうやく 邦訳 (a) Japanese translation. (! 「邦訳書[版]」の意では C) ▶この小説は邦訳が出ている A Japanese translation of this novel is available.

ほうゆう 朋友 a friend; (仲良し) a good [a great] friend.

ぼうゆう 亡友 one's dead [late] friend.

ほうよう 抱擁 名 an embrace; a hug. (! 後の方が口語的)
―― **抱擁する** 動 embrace; hug (-gg-). (⇒抱く)

ほうよう 法要 a Buddhist service. (⇒法事)

ぼうよう 茫洋 ―― **茫洋たる[とした]** 形 vast; (際限ない) limitless; (底知れない) unfathomable. ●茫洋たる大海原 a vast (expanse of the) sea.

ほうようりょく 包容力 ●**包容力のある人** a broad-minded person.

ぼうよみ 棒読み ―― **棒読みする** 動 (一本調子で読む) read*... monotonously [《やや書》 in a monotone]. ▶彼のスピーチは用意したものを棒読みしているだけでつまらなかった His speech was dull because he only read what he had prepared.

ボウラー (ボウリングをする人[選手]) a bowler.

ほうらく 法楽 ●**口の法楽をする** 《食べ物が主語》 tickle

ほうらく 崩落 图 (a) collapse; (陥没) a cave-in; (岩盤などの) a fall; (相場などの) a crash; a break. (⇨暴落)
── **崩落する** 動 collapse; cave in. ▶トンネル崩落事故の12人の犠牲者 twelve victims of the tunnel cave-in.

ほうらく 暴落 图 a sudden [a sharp] fall [turn-down《やや書》decline]; (株式の) a slump 《→a boom》, a collapse, a (nose) dive, a tumble, (突然の) a crash. ●株式市場の暴落 a *collapse* [a *crash*] of the stock market; a break.
── **暴落する** 動 ▶株価が暴落した Stock prices *fell sharply* [*went down sharply, slumped, plummeted*, (大暴落した) *crashed*]. There was a *sharp fall* [a *slump*, a *crash*] *in* stock prices.

ほうらつ 放埓 ── **放埓な** 形 (だらしない) loose; (気ままな) self-indulgent; (ふしだらな)《やや書》dissolute. (⇨放縦)

ほうり 法理 the principle of law.

ほうり 暴利 unfairly large profits. ●暴利をむさぼる make *unfairly large profits*;《軽蔑的》profitéer 《*from*》. (⚠「暴利をむさぼる人」は *a profiteer*)

ほうりあげる 放り上げる (ひょいと放る) toss ... up; (投げ上げる) throw*... up.

ほうりき 法力 (仏法の) the great power of the teachings of Buddhism.

ほうりこむ 放り込む throw*... in [into《a room》]. ▶開けてある窓から手紙を放り込む (場所を特定せずに) *throw* a letter *in* at [through] the open window. (⚠「彼女の部屋に」と場所を特定すると *throw* a letter *into* her room through the open window となる) ▶チョコレートを口に放り込む *throw* [*pop*] a piece of chocolate *into* one's mouth.

ほうりだす 放り出す 動 ❶【外へ投げ出す】throw*... out. ▶引き出しの中の物を放り出す *throw* things *out of* the drawer. ▶酔っ払いの男を通りに放り出す *throw* [《話》*kick*] *out* the drunken man *into* the street.
❷【放棄する】give*... up, abandon.《前の方が口語的》▶仕事を放り出す *give up* one's work. ▶妻子を放り出す(＝見捨てる) *desert* [《話》*walk out on*] one's wife and children.
❸【解雇する】dismiss,《話》fire. (⇨解雇) ▶彼は会社から放り出された He *was dismissed* [*was fired*, 《くだけた英語》*was sacked*] *from* the company.

‡**ほうりつ** 法律 (法律全般) (the) law [「国法」の意では通例 the ~,「法の力」の意では無冠詞]; (個々の法律) a law; (法学) law. (⇨法, 規則)
① **【法律～】** ●法律違反 a violation [a breach] of the *law*. ▶彼は法律上不利な立場にある He is in a *legally* unfavorable position.
② **【法律が[は]】** ▶バスの中での飲酒を禁止する法律がある[ない] There is a *law* [no *law*] against drinking in buses. ▶法律は未成年者の喫煙を禁じている The *law* forbids minors to smoke [prohibits minors from smoking]. (⚠後の方が堅い表現) ▶週末ごとに家に帰ってはいけないという法律はないでしょう There's no *law* that says I can't go home every weekend, is there [×can I]?
③ **【法律が】** ●法律の条文 the letter of the *law*. ●法律の網をくぐる evade the *law*; escape from the clutches of the *law*. ▶残念だが君の法律の解釈は間違っている I'm sorry to say that your interpretation of the *law* is wrong.
④ **【法律に[で]】** ●法律に照らして処理[処分]する deal with《a case, him》according to the *law*.

▶彼は法律に明るい He is learned /lə́ːrnid/ [an expert] in the *law*./He is a good *lawyer*. ▶ここで集会を開くと法律に触れる(＝法律違反だ) It is *against the law* [It is *illegal*, It is *unlawful*] to hold a meeting here. ▶あなたの国ではギャンブルは法律で認められていますか Is gambling *legal* in your country?

解説 **illegal** は「法律に違反した, 違法の」状態を表す. 反対語の **legal** は「法律に合致した, 合法の」状態を表すとともに,「法律関係の, 法律上の」という日本語に当たることも多い. (⇨①) **unlawful** (非合法的な)および反対語の **lawful** (合法的な)は illegal, legal より総括的で, 道徳・宗教なども含めた広い意味での合法, あるいはそむいていない状態をいうが, 今日ではやや古風な語.「違法の」の意では illegal が,「道徳的に禁じられた」の意では illicit が用いられることが多い.

⑤ **【法律を】** ●法律を守る keep [《やや書》observe, (従う) obey, (厳密に)《やや書》abide by] the *law*(s). ●法律を破る(＝犯す) break [go against, violate] the *law*(s). ●法律を学ぶ study [《英》read] *law*. ●法律を改正する amend [revise] a *law*. ▶職場での差別を禁止する法律を制定した They enacted a *law* [《書》legislated] against discrimination in the workplace.
●法律家 a lawyer. (⚠特に弁護士のこと) ●法律学 jurisprudence. ●法律事務所 a láw òffice [fìrm]. ●法律相談 《hold》(a) legal consultation. ●法律用語 a legal term. (⇨④ **解説**)

ほうりなげる 放り投げる throw*. (⇨投げる, 放る)

ほうりゃく 方略 a plan; (目的達成のための戦術) (a) strategy; (悪巧み, わな) a scheme; a ruse.

ほうりゃく 謀略 a plot; a conspiracy (⚠人と組んでの陰謀). (⇨計画, 陰謀)

ほうりゅう 放流 图 (水の) a discharge. ●ダムからの水の放流を調整する adjust a *discharge* of water from a dam.
── **放流する** 動 (水を) discharge; (魚を) stock. ●川に魚を放流する *stock* a river *with* fish.

ほうりゅう 傍流 a branch; (川の) a tributary.

ほうりょう 豊漁 a good [a big, a large] catch (of fish). ⇨大漁

***ほうりょく** 暴力 violence; (力ずくで) force. ●家庭内暴力 family [domestic] *violence*; *violence* in the family. ●校内暴力 school *violence*. ●暴力に訴える appeal [《やや書》resort] to *violence*. ●暴力を振るう use *violence* 《on him》. ●暴力で金を奪う take money 《*from* him》 *with violence* [*by force*]. ▶暴力は弱さの一つの形である *Violence* is a [one] form of weakness.
●暴力行為 (an act of) violence. ●暴力団 a gang (⚠単・複同扱い. 一人一人の団員は a gangster); a crime [a criminal] syndicate.

ボウリング (ゲームの) bowling. ●ボウリングをする bowl; enjoy [×play] bowling. ▶放課後ボウリングをしに行こう Let's go *bowling* after school.
●ボウリング場 a bówling àlley.

ほうる 放る 動 ❶【投げる】throw*. (⇨投げる) ●窓から空き缶を放る *throw* (荒々しく) *fling*, (低いと) *toss*, 《話》*chuck*] an empty can *out of* the window.
❷【構わないでおく】neglect《one's family》. ●庭を(手入れせずに)放っておく *neglect* a garden. ●家を放って(＝見捨てて)出て行く *desert* [《話》*walk out on*] one's family. ●しばらく彼を放っておく(＝一人にしておく) *leave* [*let*] him *alone* for a while.
❸【せずにおく】leave*... undone; [《中途でやめる》

ボウル (容器) a bowl. ●サラダボウル a salad *bowl*.
●ボウル1杯のイチゴ a *bowl* of strawberries.

ほうるい 堡塁 a fort; (大規模で半永久的な) a fortress.

ほうるい 防塁 (⇨堡塁)

ほうれい 法令 laws and ordinances. (!*ordinance* は政令や市町村の条例) (⇨法律)

ほうれい 亡霊 the soul of the dead; [幽霊] a ghost. ▶ハムレットは父の亡霊を見た Hamlet saw the *ghost* of his father.

ほうれつ 芳烈 ─ 芳烈な 形 fragrant; aromatic.

ほうれつ 放列 ❶ [軍隊で] ▶一斉射撃のために放列をしく place guns in position to fire a volley.
❷ [カメラなどの] ▶彼はカメラの放列をしいた(=ずらりと並べた) He set up *a battery* [*an array, a row*] *of cameras*.

ほうれつ 砲列 (⇨放列❶)

ほうれんそう [植物] spinach /spínɪtʃ, spínɪdʒ/.

ぼうろ 防霧 ─ 防霧の 形 (結露防止の) dew-condensation preventive (windowpanes).

ほうろう 放浪 ─ 放浪する 動 [さまよう] wander (around [about]); (自由に楽しく) roam (about); [さすらう] drift. ▶何か月もヨーロッパを放浪する *wander* [(話) *bum*] *around* Europe for months.
●放浪者 a wanderer; a roamer; a drifter.
●放浪生活 (lead) the life of a wanderer. ●放浪癖 (have) wanderlust.

ほうろう 報労 ●報労金 (pay) a reward for one's labor.

ほうろう 琺瑯 (集合的) enamel. ●ほうろう引きの鍋 a enameled pan.
●ほうろう質 (歯の) enamel. ほうろう容器 enamelware.

ほうろう 望楼 (遠くを見るためのやぐら) a watchtower.

ほうろうき 『放浪記』 *A Journal of Wandering*. (参考) 林芙美子の小説

ほうろく 焙烙 (素焼きの土なべ) an earthenware pan (for roasting beans)

ぼうろん 暴論 (不合理な発言) an absurd remark [statement]; (極端な意見) an extreme opinion.
●暴論を吐く make an *absurd remark*; give an *extreme opinion*.

ほうわ 法話 a talk [a lecture] on Buddha's teaching. ●法話をする preach [deliver] a *sermon*.

ほうわ 飽和 saturation. ●飽和状態になる reach *saturation* point; become *saturated*.
●飽和点 (a) saturation point. (!比喩的にも用いられる)

ほえごえ 吠え声 (犬などの) a bark; (野獣の) a roar.

ほえづら 吠え面 a tearful face.
●吠え面をかく 《米》 laugh out of the other side of one's mouth; 《英》 laugh on the other side of one's face. (!「今はうまくいっているが、将来はそういはいかない」の意) ●あとでほえ面をかくYYou'll pay (dearly) for this!

ポエム [(1編の詩) a poem.

*****ほえる** 吠える [犬が] (わんわん) bark (*at*); (きゃんきゃん) yelp; [猟犬が] bay (*at*) (!*bark* より継続的に); [猛獣が] roar; [人が] howl (*at*). ▶その犬は私にほえついた The dog *barked at* [*to*] me. (!受身は *I was barked at* by the dog. *at* を落とさないこと)
▶ほえる犬はかまない (ことわざ) *Barking* dogs don't [seldom] bite.

ほお 頬 a cheek. (!左右をさすときは複数形) ●リンゴのような[ふっくらした]ほおの少女 a rosy-*cheeked* [a plump-*cheeked*] girl; a girl with rosy [plump] *cheeks*. ●ほおをつねる pinch [tweak] one's *cheek*. ●ほおを染める redden one's *cheeks*; (赤面する) blush. ●彼女のほおにキスをする kiss her on the *cheek*. ▶興奮で彼のほおは赤くなった His *cheeks* flushed [burned] with excitement.
▶病後で彼のほおはこけていた His *cheeks* were hollow [sunken] after the illness. ▶彼女はしかられてほおをぷっとふくらませた She puffed her *cheeks* out when she was told off.

ポー [米国の詩人・作家] Poe /póu/ (Edgar Allan ~).

ボーイ [少年] a boy (⇨少年); [ホテルなどの] 《主に米》 a bellboy, 《米》 a bellhop, 《主に英》 a porter; [レストランの] a server; = a waitperson; [客船の] a steward; [寝台車の] 《米》 a porter.

ボーイスカウト the Boy Scouts; (団員) a boy scout.

ボーイソプラノ [音楽] (声) a boy soprano voice; (人) a boy soprano.

ボーイッシュ ─ ボーイッシュな 形 [男性[少年]風の] boyish. ●彼女のボーイッシュな髪型 her *boyish* haircut.

ボーイハント 《have》a hunt for a boyfriend. (!この意では a boy hunt とはいわない)

ボーイフレンド a bóyfriend. (!女性から見た男性の恋人で通例一人だけ。単なる男友達の意では a (male) friend)

ポーカー [トランプ] poker. ●ポーカーをする play *poker*.

ポーカーフェース [何食わぬ顔] 《話》 a poker face.
●ポーカーフェースを決め込む keep a *poker face*.

ほおかぶり 頬被り ●ほおかぶりする cover one's head and cheeks with a towel and tie it under one's chin. ●もめ事にほおかぶりを決めこむ(=知らないふりをする) *pretend not to know* the trouble.

ボーカリスト a vocalist.

ボーカル a 《Jazz》 vocal. (!しばしば複数形で) ●ロックバンドでボーカルをやっている be a *vocalist* in a rock band; sing with a rock band.

ボーキサイト [地学] bauxite.

ボーク [野球] a balk. ●ボークをする[犯す] commit [make] a *balk*; balk. ●ボークで生還する score on a *balk*. ▶ピッチャーはボークをとられた The pitcher was called for a *balk*/The pitcher was charged with a *balk*.

ポーク [豚肉] pork. ●ポークカツ breaded deep-fried pork cutlet. (参考) 和製洋食 ●ポークソテー (a) sautéed [(a) sauté] pork. ●ポークチョップ pork chops.

ほおげた 頬桁 prominent [projected] cheekbones; [解剖] the zygoma (複 ~ta).

ボージョレ [フランスの地方] Beaujolais. (参考) ワインの名産地)
●ボージョレヌーボー Beaujolais nouveau.

ほおじろ [鳥] a (Japanese) bunting.

ホース a hose /hóuz/. ●消火用ホース a fíre hòse.
●ホースで水をかける water 《the garden》 with a *hose*; hose 《the lawn》. ●車をホースで水洗いする *hose down* [*off*] a car (with water).

ポーズ ❶ [姿勢] a pose /póuz/. (⇨姿勢) ●単なるポーズ(=見せかけ) a mere pose; (take) *a pose*. ●ガッツポーズをする (⇨ガッツ) ▶彼女は写真をとってもらうためにポーズをとった She *posed for* her photo. ●モデルは休憩後元のポーズを再とた The model resumed her *pose* after a break.
❷ [小休止] a pause /pɔ́ːz/. ●ポーズを置く pause (briefly); take a 《brief》 *pause*.

ほおずき 〖植物〗 a ground cherry; a Chinese lantern (plant).

ほおずり 類擦り ▶赤ちゃんにほおずりをする press one's cheek on a baby's.

ボーダーライン a borderline. ▶彼は合否のボーダーライン上にあった He was on the *borderline* between passing and failing./He was a *borderline* case in the exam.

ポータブル 〖持ち運びできる機器〗 a portable.
● ポータブルコンピュータ a portable computer. ● ポータブルビデオカメラ a cámcòrder.

ボーダレス 〖無境界〗 borderless. ● ボーダレス化 becoming *borderless*. ● 情報[金融]のボーダレス時代に生きる live in a *borderless* age of information [the money market].

ポーチ 〖玄関口〗《on》a porch; (階段のついた) a stoop; 〖小物入れ〗a pouch /paʊtʃ/. ● ウエストポーチ a waist pouch.

ポーチドエッグ a poached egg.

ホーチミンし ホーチミン市 〖ベトナムの都市〗 Hồ Chi Minh City.

ほおづえ 類杖 ▶ほおづえをつく rest one's chin on one's hand(s) [cupped hands].

ぼーっと dimly. (⇨ぼうっと)

ぼーっと (⇨ぼうっと)

ポーツマス 〖英国・米国の都市〗 Portsmouth /ˈpɔːrtsməθ/.
● ポーツマス条約 〖歴史〗 the Treaty of Portsmouth.

*****ボート** a boat /boʊt/ (**!** 小型の船の総称);〖手こぎの〗《米》a rowboat,《英》a rowing boat (**!** 日本語のボートは厳密にはこの意); 〖モーターで動く〗a motorboat; (大型の) a powerboat. ▶川にボートをこぎに行く go to the river to row a *boat*; go boating [for a row] *on* 〈xto, xin〉the river. ▶ボートを2時間借りる rent a *rowboat* for two hours.
● ボートピープル 〖漂流難民〗 boat people. ● ボートレース a regatta /rɪˈɡɛtə/《**!** 複数のレースが行われる競技会);(主に英) a boat race.

ボード 〖板〗(a) board. ▶ハードボード 〖硬質繊維板〗 hardboard. ● マザーボード 〖回路基板〗〖コンピュータ〗 a mother *board*.
● ボードゲーム 〖盤上ゲーム〗 a board game.

ボードセーリング boardsailing. ▶windsurfing の正式名。そのボードは a sailboard という)

ボードビル 〖寄席〗〖演芸〗《米》vaudeville /ˈvɔːdəvɪl/,《英》variety, a variety show.

ポートフォリオ 〖資産構成, 作品集〗a portfolio. ● 分散型[最適]ポートフォリオ 〖経済〗 a diversified [an optional] *portfolio*.

ポートレート 〖肖像画〗a portrait. (⇨肖像)

ポートワイン port (wine). (**!** wine をつけない方が普通)

ボーナス a bonus. 事情 米英では会社が大きくもうかったときにだけ支給される)● 多額のボーナス a large *bonus*. ● ボーナスを支給する pay *bonus*. ● 月給3.8か月分のボーナス (get [receive]) a *bonus* equivalent to 3.8 months' salary. ▶冬の(=年末の)ボーナスは手取りで50万だった I got a year-end *bonus* of 500,000 yen after tax.
● ボーナス支給率 a bonus payment rate. ● ボーナストラック 〖音楽〗 a bonus track.

ホーバークラフト a hovercraft (複 ~(s)).

ほおばる 類張る ▶食べ物を口一杯にほおばる fill [cram] one's *mouth* with food; cram food *into* one's mouth; have a big mouthful of food. ● 食べ物をほおばったまましゃべる speak *with* one's *mouth full*. ▶彼は食べ物をほおばっていたので私に返事ができなかった He *had so much* food *in* his *mouth* that [He had his *mouth full* and] he couldn't answer me.

ほおひげ 類髭 whiskers. (⇨ひげ)

ホープ a hope. ▶日本音楽界のホープの一人 a *hope* of Japanese musical world.

ほおべに 類紅 blusher,《米》blush(-on);〖古〗rouge /ruːʒ/. ● 頰紅を付ける put on some *blusher*, rouge one's cheeks.

ぽーぽー

ほおぼね 類骨 cheekbones. ▶ほお骨が出ている have high *cheekbones*.

ホーマー a homer. (⇨ホームラン)

ホーム ❶〖プラットホーム〗《米》a track,《英》a platform. ● 発車[到着]ホームへ a departure [an arrival] *platform*. ▶有楽町寄りの端で待つ wait on the Yurakucho end of the *platform*. ● 6番線ホームから出る leave from *track*《米》[*platform*《英》] 6. ● 〘Track [Platform] ×(... the 6th としない)▶2番ホームの列車は20時8分発の東京行きです The train at *track*《米》[*platform*《英》] 2 leaves for Tokyo at 20:08.
❷〖ホームベース〗the home plate, home. ● ホームベースを踏む step on [cross] the *plate*. ● ホーム(ベース)をブロックする block the *plate*. ● ホームベース上のクロスプレー a close play at the plate. ● 浅い外野フライでホームへ突入する race to home on a shallow outfield fly.
❸〖本拠地〗(⇨ホームグラウンド, ホームゲーム, ホームチーム)

ホームアンドアウェー 〖サッカー〗 home-and-away. ▶すべての試合はホームアンドアウェー方式で行われる All matches are played on [over] a *home-and-away* system.

ホームイン ── **ホームインする** 動 reach [come*, get*] home; (本塁を踏む) cross the [home] plate. 〖和製語〗home-in. ● 走者をホームインさせる drive in [home] a runner. ● 彼のヒットでホームインする come across on his single. ● 長駆ホームインする sprint home all the way from first base.

ホームグラウンド 〖本拠地〗《on, at》one's home ground; (本拠地球場)〖野球〗the home field [grounds]. ● ホーム(グラウンド)で試合をする play a game at *home*. ▶我々はホームグラウンドで戦うので有利だ We are at [have] a *home-field* advantage over them.

ホームゲーム (野球などの) a home game (↔a road [an away] game).

ホームコメディー a situation comedy;《話》a sitcom;〖和製語〗a home comedy. (⇨ホームドラマ)

ホームシック homesickness. ▶彼は大変なホームシックにかかった He became [got] very [terribly] *homesick*.

ホームショッピング home shopping.

ホームスチール 〖野球〗 a steal of home.
── **ホームスチールする** 動 steal home.

ホームステイ a homestay. ▶学生時代にアメリカ人家庭に1か月ホームステイしたことがある I *stayed with* an American family [*in* America *on* a *homestay* program] for a month when I was a student. (**!** do a homestay は元来和製英語であるが英語圏で用いられつつある) ▶彼は今カナダでホームステイしている He is now on a *homestay* visit in Canada.

ホームストレッチ ● ホームストレッチにかかる come into the homestretch [《英》the home straight].

ホームスパン 〖手織りのラシャ〗homespun,(毛織物) homespun fabric.

ホームセンター a home center (❗《米》では通例建材を扱っている);《英》a DIY store (❗DIY は do-it-yourself の略).

ホームタウン 〖故郷〗one's hometown.

ホームチーム 〖地元チーム〗the [one's] home team.

ホームドクター a family doctor;《和製語》a home doctor.

ホームドラマ a drama of family life,《和製語》a home drama;〖連続メロドラマ〗a soap opera;〖連続コメディー〗(family) situation comedy, a sitcom (参考) 同じ登場人物の毎回違った愉快な番組).

ホームバー a home bar.

ホームバンキング home banking.

ホームビデオ a home video.

ホームプレート home plate [base], the plate.

ホームページ a website; a homepage. (❗後の方は通例 a website の最初のページのみをさす) ●人気歌手の公式[非公式]ホームページ an official [an unofficial] website for a popular singer. ●ホームページを作る create a website. ●ホームページを見る view [訪れる] visit, (アクセスする) access) a website. (⇨アクセス❷) ●ホームページで求人を始める start offering jobs on a homepage. ▶三省堂のホームページの URL を教えてください Please tell me a URL of the website for Sanseido. ▶詳しくは弊社ホームページをご覧ください For more details, please visit our company's website. ▶あなたのお気に入りのホームページはどこですか What is your favorite website? ▶ハッカーがホームページに侵入した A cracker attacked [broke] the website./The website was illegally accessed.

ホームベース (⇨ホームプレート)

ホームヘルパー 〖訪問介護員〗《米》a home care [a home health] aide, a personal care worker;《英》a home help;《和製語》home helper.

ホームメード ── **ホームメードの** 形 〖自家製の〗homemade. ●ホームメードのアイスクリーム homemade ice cream.

ホームラン a home run,《話》a homer. ●ソロホームラン a solo [a bases-empty] home run. ●ツーラン[スリーラン]ホームラン (hit) a two-run [a three-run] home run. ●満塁ホームラン (⇨満塁). ●大ホームラン a long home run. (❗a big home run は「重大な(局面での)ホームラン」の意) ●二者連続ホームラン back-to-back home runs. ●アベックホームラン home runs hit in tandem in a game. ●ホームランダービーのトップに立つ lead the home run derby. ●ホームランを打つ hit [belt, strike, deliver] a home run;《話》homer. ●ホームラン狙いのスイングをする take a home run swing; swing for the fences. ▶彼は今季 50 本のホームランを打った He hit [slammed] fifty home runs this season.

●ホームラン王 a home run king. ●ホームラン王のタイトルを獲得する win the home run king title. ●ホームラン競争 (オールスター戦前などの) a home run derby. (❗「ホームラン王争い」の意にもなる) ●ホームランバッター a home run hitter [slugger, ×batter]. ●ホームランボール a home run ball. (❗「ホームランを打たれる投球」と「ホームランになったボール」の両方の意がある)

ホームルーム 〖教室,生徒全体〗a homeroom;〖時間,授業〗homeroom, a homeroom period. ●朝[帰]りのホームルーム a short homeroom (period) at the beginning [end] of the (school) day. (❗(1) 前の方は《米》では a homeroom in the morning も可. (2) 単に a short homeroom (period) ということが多い) ●ホームルーム活動 a homeroom activity. ●ホームルーム中 during homeroom [the homeroom] period].

ホームレス a homeless [a street] person;《集合的》homeless [street] people,《やや書》the homeless.

ポーランド 〖国名〗Poland; (公式名) the Republic of Poland. (首都 Warsaw) ●ポーランド人 a Pole. ●ポーランド語 Polish. ●ポーランド(人間)の Polish.

ボーリング 名 〖穴を掘ること〗boring.
── **ボーリングする** 動 bore.

ボーリング 〖ゲームの〗(⇨ボウリング)

ホール 〖会館,大広間〗a hall. ●ダンス[コンサート]ホール a dance [a concert] hall. ●カーネギーホール Carnegie Hall.

ホール 〖ゴルフの〗a hole. ●ホールアウトする complete the round. ▶hole out は「ホールに球を入れる」の意 (⇨[第 2 文例])) ▶最終ホールはパースリーだ The last hole is par three. ▶山田は 5 メートルのパットをホールに入れた Yamada holed (out) from 5 meters. ▶彼は 7 番ホールでバーディーを取った He got a birdie on the seventh.

●ホールインワン (get) a hole in one.

*****ボール** ❶ 〖球〗a ball. ●テニスボール a tennis ball. ●ボール投げをする play catch. ●ボールを投げる throw [pitch] a ball. (❗pitch は主に「投げが打者に対して投げる」の意. throw にはそれ以外に「送球する」の意もある) ●ボールを受ける(打つ; 受けそこなう) catch [hit; miss] a ball. ●ボールが高めに浮く get the ball up. ●ボールを持つ[キープする]〖サッカー〗hold the ball.

❷ 〖野球のボール球〗a ball. (↔a strike). ●〖審判が〗ボールを宣言する call (a pitch) a ball. ●ボールに手を出す swing at a ball; chase a bad pitch. ●ボール球を見送る take a ball. ●外角遠く外れたボール a ball way outside. ●フォークボールを投げてボールになる throw a forkball for a ball. ●ボールカウントがスリー(ストライク)スリー(ボール)だった The count was three (balls) and two (strikes) [×two strikes and three balls]. (❗語順に注意)

●ボールガール a ball girl. (⇨[ボールボーイ]) ●ボールベアリング 〖球軸受け〗〖機械〗a ball bearing. ●ボールボーイ a ball boy. (❗男女を区別しない場合は a ball person) ●ボールポゼッション〖支配〗〖サッカー〗(ball) possession.

ボール 〖容器〗a bowl. (⇨ボウル)

ボールがみ ボール紙 (厚紙) cardboard; (合板紙) pasteboard.

ホールケーキ (eat) a whole cake.

ホールド 〖レスリング〗〖押さえ込み〗a hold;〖登山〗〖登る際の手がかり〗a hold;〖野球〗a hold (参考) リリーフ投手がリードを保ったまま別の投手へ引き継いだ場合に与えられる成績).

ホールドアップ 〖強盗〗a holdup,《話》a stickup. ▶ホールドアップ! (手を上げろ) Hold'em [《話》Stick'em] up! (❗'em は them (=your hands) のこと)

ホールトマト a whole tomato.

ボールばこ ボール箱 a carton (⇨カートン); a cardboard box.

ボールペン a ballpoint (pen). (❗《英》では《商標》Biro から a biro /báiərou/ (複 ~s) ともいう.

ポールポジション the pole position.

ポーロ [<ポルトガル語] a small round cookie [biscuit].

ほおん 保温 ── **保温する** 動 keep* (it) warm.

ぼーん (鐘などが鳴る) ring*; toll. (❗toll は鐘がゆっくり鳴る音だが,通例 1 回ではなく続けて鳴るのをさす) ▶お寺の鐘がぼーんと鳴った A long, muffled dong sounded from a temple. (❗日本の鐘は音の質が違

ボーンヘッド 〖間抜けなプレー〗〖野球〗a bonehead play (❗ bonehead は「ボーンヘッドをする選手」); 〘話〙a boner. ● ボーンヘッドをしでかす make a *bonehead play*; pull a boner.

ほか 外, 他 图 ❶〖他の物・人〗another; other(s); the other; the others; something [someone] else; 〖残りの物・人〗the rest.

> **解説** (1) another は「もう一つの物，もう一人の人」の意で，形容詞として使う場合は通例単数名詞を修飾し，その前に冠詞，this, that, my などはつかない。
> (2) 代名詞としての other は単数形でも複数形でも用いるが，単数形のときは any, some, no などを伴う。形容詞としては，普通は複数名詞を修飾するが単数名詞を修飾する場合は any, some, no などを伴う。the other は二つ[二人]の中でもう一方を，the others は他の物[人]が二つ[二人]以上ある場合に用いる。
> (3) else は不定代名詞，疑問詞, no-, any-, some- のつく副詞の後にくる。

▶ ほかに質問はありませんか Do you have any *other* question(s)? (❗ s がある場合は話し手が複数の質問を予想していることを暗示) ▶ ほかにだれがパーティーに来ますか Who *else* is coming to the party? ▶ ほかにお茶のほしい方はいらっしゃいませんか Who *else* would like some tea? ▶ ほかにデザートを召し上がりたい方はいませんか Would anybody *else* like dessert? (❗ 前の方が口語的) ▶ ほかにすることがなかったので午後はずっとテレビを見て過ごした I had nothing *else* to do, so I spent the whole afternoon watching television. ▶ こんなに安く買えるところはほかにありません You can't buy it cheaper anywhere *else* [at any *other* store].

会話 「印象派がすごく気に入ったわ」「ほかにはどれが気に入った？」"I liked the Impressionists a lot." "Which *others* [ˣWhich *else*] did you like?" (❗ *else* は which とともには用いない)

会話 「ほかに何かございますか」「これだけにしておきます」(店での) "Anything *else*, sir [ma'am]?" "That's all for now."

❷ 〖…を除いて〗except …, but …; except for …, apart 〖(米) aside〗from …; other than …, besides …. (⇨以外)

> **解説** except, but は全体に対する一部の例外を表す。except の方が強意的. いずれも主に every, any, no, およびその合成語や all などを修飾し，必ずその後に置く. except for, apart 〖(米) aside〗from は「…の点は別として」の意で文全体を修飾し，通例文頭・文尾に置く. other than, besides は主に否定文で except とほぼ同じ意で用いる。

▶ あの店は日曜のほかは毎日営業している That store is open every day *except* on Sunday(s). ▶ 私は 2, 3 のすり傷のほかにけがはありません *Except for* [*Apart from*] a few scratches, I'm not hurt. ▶ 彼のほかにだれもそんなことはしないだろう Nobody *except* [*but*] him would do such a thing. (❗ 反語的に) Who *but* [ˣ*except*] him would do such a thing? (ともいえる)/Nobody would do such a thing *except* [*but*] him./*Except for* [ˣ*Except*, ˣ*But*] him, nobody would do such a thing. ▶ 私は家に帰るしかなかった I had no choice [nothing to do] *but* to come home./There was nothing for it *but* (to) [nothing to do *but*] come home./(私にできることはただ家に帰ることだった) All I could do was (to) come home. (❗ 〘話〙では通例 to を省略する) ▶ 彼女は彼を助けるしかほかに手がないことを知っていた She knew that there was no other way *but* to help him. ▶ 私には彼のほかに親しい友人はいません I have no close friends *except* [*besides*] him./I don't have any *other* close friends [any close friends *other*] than him./(私の唯一の親しい友人です) He is my only close friend.

❸ 〖…に加えて〗besides …; in addition to …; apart 〖(米) aside〗from …. ▶ 山田さんほか 3 名 Mr. Yamada and three *others*; three (people) *besides* Mr. Yamada. ▶ この店はパンのほかにケーキも売っている This shop sells cakes *besides* [*in addition to*] bread. ▶ 週末にはジョギングのほかにいつも何をしますか What do you usually do on weekends *besides* to go jogging? (❗ do が前にくるときは besides is to または to を省略不可)

● ほかでもない ▶ そのような発言をしたのはほかでもない社長だった Such remarks were made by *none other than* the president. ▶ 君に話というのはほかでもないが神戸への出張の件よ *All* I want to talk to you about is your business trip to Kobe.

── ほかの 形 other; another; (異なった) different.
● ほかの人たち *other* people; *others*. (❗ other people が普通) ▶ 何かほかの本 some *other* book(s). ● 彼のほかの二人の友達 his two *other* friends. ● だれかほかの人のペン somebody *else*'s [some *other* person's] pen. (❗ 後の方が口語的) ▶ この帽子は気にいらない，ほかのを見せてください (他の一つ) I don't like this hat. Please show me *another* (one)./(他のいくつか) Please show me some *others* [*other* ones]./(違うもの) Please show me a *different* one. ▶ ほかの子供たちは家に帰った The *other* children went home. ▶ ほかの日に来れませんか Can't you come any [some] *other* day? (❗ some は話し手が肯定的な答えを期待していることを示す) ▶ 彼女はクラスのほかのだれよりも頭がいい She is smarter than any *other* student [ˣstudents] in her class. (❗ She is smarter than the *other* students in her class. より強意的. 同様の内容は She is the smartest student in her class., またさらに強意的な She is the smartest of all the students in her class. でも表せるが，日常会話では最初の訳文のように「比較級＋than any other …」の方が普通) ▶ ほかのことを話しましょう Let's talk about something *else* [some *other* thing]. ▶ 私の学校には 5 人の外国人の先生がいる. 3 人はアメリカ人でほかの 2 人はカナダ人だ There are five foreign teachers in my school. Three are Americans and the *other* two [ˣthe two *other*] are Canadians. (❗ 語順に注意. the *other* two の代わりに the rest ともいえる)

ほか 簿価 〖『帳簿価額』の略〗(a) book value (関連 市場価値 a market value).

ほか a stupid [a careless] mistake, a blunder. (❗ a serious [a major] blunder ははったりして「大ぽか」だが，単に a blunder でも文脈によっては「大ぽか」の意にもなる) ● ぽかをやる make [commit] a *blunder*.

ぼがい 簿外 ── 簿外債務 off-balance sheet liabilities. ● **簿外資産** off-balance sheet assets. ● **簿外取引き** an off-balance (sheet) transaction; off-balanced [off-balance] trading.

ほかく 捕獲 ── 捕獲する 動 capture, catch. ● 敵の軍艦を捕獲する *capture* an enemy ship. ● 猿を捕獲する *catch* a monkey (alive).

ほかげ 火影 〖火の光〗firelight; 〖ともし火に映し出された姿〗a figure in the firelight.

ほかげ 帆影 (a) sail [sails] seen in the distance. (❗ 無冠詞の sail は 1 隻の船の帆 1 枚または全部の帆

ほかけぶね 帆掛け舟 《米》a sailboat; 《英》a sáiling bòat; (大型帆船) a sáiling ship.
ぼかし (色の) gradation; shading.
***ぼかす** (輪郭などを) blur (-rr-); (色を) gradate; (態度を) take* an uncertain attitude; (答えを) 《やや書》make* a noncommittal answer. ▶彼は自分の仕事については話をぼかした He was intentionally *vague* about his job.

ほかならない 外ならない ▶その人はきのう通りで出会った人にほかならなかった He was *none other than* the man [*the very* person] I saw on the street yesterday. ▶その成功は君の絶えざる努力の結果にほかならない(=まったく君の努力による) The success is *entirely* due to your constant efforts.

ほかならぬ 外ならぬ ▶ほかならぬ君のことだから[君の頼みだから]その秘密を教えてあげよう Since it is you and none other [it's you who are asking], I'll tell you the secret. ▶後ろから声をかけられた。振り返ってみるとそれはほかならぬ内田だった Someone called me from behind. I turned and found it to be *none other than* Uchida [be Uchida, *no less*]. (❗後の言い方は単независ前の語の重要性を強調して「なんとまあほかならぬ…」の感じになる)

ほかほか (暖かい) warm; (熱い) hot (-tt-). ▶羽ぶとんはほかほかしてよく眠れた The down quilt was (*comfortably*) *warm* and gave me a good sleep. ▶ごはんは湯気が立ってほかほかです The boiled rice *is steaming hot*.

ぼかぼか ぼかぼか殴られる be hit hard repeatedly. (⇨ぽかぽか❷).

ぽかぽか ❶ [暖かさ] ▶日が差してぽかぽか暖かい It is *pleasantly warm and sunny*. /The sun is *pleasantly warm*. ▶この半島ではほとんど一年を通じてぽかぽかした陽気です It is warm and sunny almost throughout the year in this peninsula.
❷ [続けて打つ様子] ▶調子がよかったので打撃練習で彼はぽかぽかと長打を打った He was in his best condition and hit a long ball in practice *over and over again* [*again and again*].

***ほがらか 朗らか** ── 朗らかな 形 [快活な, 陽気な] cheerful, sunny; [楽しげな, 愉快な] merry. ●朗らかな女の子 a *cheerful* [a *sunny*, a *merry*] girl. ●朗らかな性格である have a *cheerful* [a *sunny*] disposition.
── 朗らかに 副 ●朗らかに笑う laugh *cheerfully* [*merrily*].

ぽかりと ❶ [打つ様子] ▶ぽかりと打つ whack 《him》, give 《him》 a whack. ▶だれかが後ろから私の頭をぽかりとたたいた Someone *whacked* me on the head from behind.
❷ [急に割れたり開いたりする様子] ▶目の前に洞窟(ど)の入り口がぽかりと開いていた The entrance of a cave stood *wide open* in front of us. ▶道路にぽかりと一つ穴が開いた A hole *gaped* in the road. ▶大きな球がぽかりと割れた The big ball *split* [*came apart*] *with a pop*.
❸ [空中に浮かぶさま] (⇨ぽっかり❷)

ほかん 保管 图 [行為, 状態] safekeeping; [状態] (主に警察による) custody; (個人による) keeping; (倉庫での) storage. ●彼に宝石の保管をまかせる leave the jewelry with him for *safekeeping*.
── 保管する 動 (を預かる, 預かる) keep*. ●金庫に[子供の手の届かない所に]保管しておく keep 《it》 in a safe [out of the reach of children]. ●倉庫に家具を保管する put the furniture *in storage*. ▶その書類は顧問弁護士が保管しています Those documents are *in* *safekeeping* *with* my lawyer. /Those documents *are in* the custody [keeping] of my lawyer.
●保管銀行 (証券の) a custódian bànk. ●保管所[庫] a safe(-)deposit. ●保管人 [機関] a custodian. ●保管料 storage (charge).

ほかん 補完 ── 補完する 動 supplement; complement.

ほかん 補巻 a supplement 《to》.

ほかん 母艦 a mother ship.

ぽかんと ❶ [大きく口を開けて] ▶少年は口をぽかんと開けて行列を見ていた The boy was looking at the procession *with his mouth wide open*. /A boy *was gaping at* the procession. (❗gape at … は「ぽかんと口を開けて見とれる」の意)
❷ [ぼんやりと] absent-mindedly; (うつろに) vacantly. ●彼はそこにぽかんと立っていた He stood there *absent-mindedly*. ▶彼女は(わけが分からなくて)ぽかんとした顔をしていた She looked *blank* [had a *blank* look on her face]. ▶彼は非番のときは ぼかんとして(=何もしないで) 1 日を過ごす He spends the day *idly* when he is off duty.

ほき 簿記 bookkeeping. ●商業簿記 commercial *bookkeeping*. ●単式[複式]簿記 single-entry [double-entry] *bookkeeping*. ●簿記をつける keep *the books* [*the accounts*].
●簿記係 a bookkeeper.

ボギー [ゴルフ] a bogey /bóugi/. ●ダブルボギー a double *bogey*. ●ボギーをたたく make a *bogey* 《on the 14th》; bogey 《the 14th [twice in the first three holes]》.

ぽきぽき ▶枝をぽきぽき折る snap [×crack] twigs. ▶彼は指の関節をぽきぽき鳴らした He cracked [×snapped] his knuckles.

ボキャブラリー [語彙(い)] vocabulary. (⇨語彙) ●ボキャブラリーが豊富である have a large [a rich, ×much, ×many] *vocabulary*. ▶私はボキャブラリーが貧困だから(=限られているから)いい言葉がなかなか出てこない Because of my limited *vocabulary*, I have trouble making nice-sounding [good-sounding] remarks [phrases].

***ほきゅう 補給** 图 supply. ●燃料補給 the supply of fuel; (給油) refueling.
── 補給する 動 ●船に燃料を補給する supply the ship *with* fuel; *refuel* the ship.
●補給路 a supplý ròute.

ほきゅう 捕球 图 [野球] a catch. ❶通例ノーバウンドの捕球については (⇨キャッチ) ●後ろ向き捕球 an over-the-shoulder catch. ●片手捕球 a one-hand(ed) catch.
── 捕球する 動 ●ライナーを捕球する catch a liner; *make a catch* of a liner.

***ほきょう 補強** reinforcement. (⇨強化)
── 補強する 動 reinforce; (強化する) strengthen. ▶その堤防を補強しないといけない We have to *reinforce* the dike. /The dike needs some *reinforcement*.
●補強工事 reinforcement work.

ほきん 保菌 ▶保菌者 a (HIV) carrier.

ぼきん 募金 (1 人 1 人からの) a collection; (資金調達) fund raising. ●共同募金 《米》commúnity chèst. ●街頭募金 a street *collection* of contributions. ●彼のために 100 万円の募金を集める *collect* [*make a collection of*] a million yen for him.
●募金運動 a fund-raising campaign [drive] 《for》; a campaign [a drive] to raise funds 《for》.

ぼきんと ●ぼきんと音を立てる snap, crack. (⇨ぽきぽき)
●ぼきんと音を立てて with a snap [a crack]. ▶庭師が小枝をぼきんと折った A gardener *snapped (off)* a twig. ▶彼女が倒れたとき, 腕の骨がぼきんといった When she fell, a bone in her arm *cracked*. ▶彼はぼきんと棒を折った He broke a stick *with a snap*.

ぼく 僕 I

ほくい 北緯 the north latitude. ▶この市は北緯42度41分にある This city is (situated) in [at] latitude forty-two *degrees* forty-one minutes north. (🛈通例 lat. 42°41′N と略記する)/The latitude of this city is 42°41′N.

ほくおう 北欧 Scandinavia /skændinéivia/; [[北ヨーロッパ]] Northern Europe. ●北欧人 a Scandinavian.

ぼくが 墨画 (⇨墨絵)

ほくがん 北岸 the northern coast.

ぼくぎゅう 牧牛 cattle on the pasture; cattle put to grass.

ほくげん 北限 the northern limit ((of)); the northernmost point.

ボクサー [[拳闘家]] a boxer; [[犬]] a boxer.

ぼくさつ 撲殺 ── 撲殺する 動 beat* [club (-bb-)] ((him)) to death.

*****ぼくし** 牧師 a minister; a clergyman (圏 -men); a pastor; a parson; a rector;《集合的》the ministry [clergy] (🛈複数扱い);《呼びかけ》Reverend.

┌─────────────────────────────────┐
│ 解説 (1)《米》では minister が一般的. clergy-│
│ man も「牧師」の意で用いるが, 本来は広く各宗教・│
│ 宗派の聖職者をさす.《英》では英国国教会派の牧師│
│ を clergyman, そうでない牧師を minister という.│
│ 教会・教区を預かる牧師は pastor だが英国国教会│
│ 派では parson, 米国聖公会では rector という.│
│ (2)「…牧師」という場合は the Reverend [the│
│ Rev.] (Taro [T.] Abe, Mr. Abe, *Abe) で, い│
│ ずれも書き言葉としては正式な表現であるが, 話し言葉│
│ としては the Rev. を用いるのがくだけた表現.│
└─────────────────────────────────┘

●牧師になる become a *minister*; (牧師の一員になる) enter the ministry; (聖職につく) take (holy) orders; enter the Church. ▶彼はその地域の教会の牧師です He is the *minister* at the local church. ▶牧師様, こんにちは How are you, *Reverend*?
●牧師館 a parsonage; a rectory.

ぼくしゃ 牧舎 a stable; (羊小屋) a sheepfold; (牛舎) a cowhouse, a cowshed.

ぼくしゅ 墨守 adherence ((to)). ●旧習を墨守する adhere [stick] to old customs.

ぼくじゅう 墨汁 India [China] ink. ●墨汁で書く write *with* [*in*] *India ink*.

ぼくしょ 墨書 ── 墨書する 動 write* in India [China] ink.

ほくじょう 北上 ── 北上する 動 go* [move, head] north(ward); go (×move, ×head) up.

*****ぼくじょう** 牧場 a stock farm (🛈 a livestock farm も可);《米国などの広大な》a ranch; [[放牧地]] a pasture. ●牧場を経営する run a *ranch* [a *stock farm*]. ▶牧場で(雇われて)働く work *on a ranch* [a *stock farm*]. ▶牛の群れと牧場で草を食べているCows are grazing peacefully in [on] the pasture.
●牧場主 a stock farmer;《米》a rancher.

ほくしん 北進 ── 北進する 動 move north(ward).

ぼくしん 牧神 [[ギリシャ神話]] Pan; [[ローマ神話]] Faunus, a faun.

ボクシング boxing. ●ボクシングの試合 a *bóxing* màtch (×*game*); a fight. ●ボクシング選手権保持者 a champion boxer. ●ボクシングをする box《*with* him, *against* him, a 12-round match》; do [×play] boxing.

ほぐす (糸などのもつれを) disentangle; (緊張などを) relieve, ease; (ばらばらにする) loosen. (⇨ほぐれる) ●緊張をほぐす *relieve* [*ease*] the tension. ●固まった地面をほぐす *loosen* the solid ground. ●サケの身をほぐす *flake* salmon.

ぼくする トする ❶[占う] tell* [read*, predict] ((one's future)).
❷[占って決める] decide ((to buy land)) by following the fortune-teller's predictions.

ほくせい 北西 the northwest (略 NW). (⇨東) ●北西の west-northwest. ●北西の風 a north-west [(ほぼ北西の)] a northwesterly wind.

ぼくせき 木石 ▶あの男は木石漢だ(=人を思いやる優しさなどみじんもない人だ) He has no milk of human kindness in him. (🛈慣用表現. シェークスピア作 *Macbeth* より)

ぼくそう 牧草 grass; pasture.
●牧草地 (干し草・放牧用の) grassland(s), meadow(s); (放牧用の) (×a) pasture. (🛈 a pasture は1区画の牧場)

ほくそえむ ほくそ笑む chuckle to oneself; (喜ぶ) gloat ((*over*)) (🛈 自分の成功や人の失敗に満足を示す). ▶彼はライバルの失敗にほくそ笑んだ He *gloated over* his rival's failure.

ぼくたく 木鐸 (舌が木製の鈴) an old-time Chinese bell with a wooden tongue; (社会の指導者を) a leader. ▶新聞は社会の木鐸(=世論を導くもの)である Newspapers stir up [lead] public opinion.

ほくたん 北端 [[最も北の所]] the northernmost part; the northern end [(先端) tip]. ▶この岬は日本の北端にある This promontory is at *the northern end* of Japan.

ぼくちく 牧畜 (家畜全般の) stock [livestock] farming; (主に牛の) cattle breeding.
●牧畜業者 a stock [a livestock] farmer [raiser]; a cattle breeder.

ぼくてき 牧笛 a shepherd's pipe.

ほくとう 北東 the northeast (略 NE). (⇨東, 北西)

ぼくとう 木刀 a wooden sword.

ぼくどう 牧童 a boy herder; (特に羊の) a shepherd /ʃépərd/ boy; (牛の)《米》a cowboy.

ほくと(しちせい) 北斗(七星) [[天文]]《米》the Big Dipper, 《英》Charles's Wain;《米》the Plow, 《英》the Plough (🛈発音はともに /pláu/).

ぼくとつ 朴訥 ── 朴訥な 形 rustic (🛈 いい意味で「田舎の人らしい特質をそなえた」の意); 素朴な simple; (実直な) honest. ●ぼくとつな青年 a *rustic* young man.

ぼくねんじん 朴念仁 ▶あの人は朴念仁(=口数も少なく人付き合いも苦手な人)だ He is not sociably disposed [sociable].

ぼくはべんきょうができない『ぼくは勉強ができない』 *I Cannot Study Well*. (参考 山田詠美の小説)

ほくぶ 北部 the north; (北の地方) the northern part;《米国の》the North. (⇨南部)

ぼくふ 牧夫 a herdsman (圏 -men).

ほくべい 北米 North America. ●北米の North American. ●北米大陸 the North American Continent.

ほくへん 北辺 the northern place [land]; (北の果て) the northern end [(先端) tip] (⇨北端).

ほくほく ●ほくほくする (自然と笑みがれる) beam [smile] happily; (ふかしたいもなどがふんわりした) soft and fluffy. ▶彼女はその知らせを聞いてほくほくした She was *all smiles* to hear the news./She *smiled happily* to hear the news.

ほくほくせい 北北西 the north-northwest.
ほくほくせいにしんろをとれ 『北北西に進路を取れ』 *North by Northwest*. (参考) ヒッチコック監督の映画)
ほくほくとう 北北東 the north-northeast 《略 NNE》.
ぼくめつ 撲滅 图 (根絶) eradication; (全滅) extermination.
── **撲滅する** 動 eradicate, root out; exterminate, get* rid of. ●性犯罪を撲滅する *eradicate* [*root out*, (力ずくで) *stamp out*, (一掃する) *wipe out*] sex crime. ●伝染病を撲滅する *eradicate* [*stamp out*] infectious diseases. ●害虫を撲滅する *exterminate* [*get rid of*] harmful insects.
ほくめん 北面 the north face. ●アイガーの北面を登る climb the *north face* of the Eiger.
ほくよう 北洋 the north sea [ocean]. ●北洋漁業 north-sea fisheries.
ぼくよう 牧羊 sheep farming. ●牧羊犬 a sheepdog. ●牧羊者 a sheep farmer [breeder]; a shepherd. ●牧羊地 a pasture; (イギリスの) a sheep walk; (オーストラリアの) a sheep run.
ほぐれる (ほどける) get* untied; (もつれなどが) loosen, get [come*] loose; (緊張などが) relax. (⇨ほぐす) ●筋肉がほぐれた My muscles *relaxed*. ●彼のジョークで室内の緊張がほぐれた His joke helped (to) *ease the tension in the room*. (2 to は《話》では通例省略される)
ほくろ a mole. ●付けぼくろ a beauty spot [mark]. ●私は顔にほくろがある I have a *mole* on my face.
ぼけ 呆け senility /sənílətɪ/. ●老人ぼけ (遠回しに) second childhood; (痴呆症)〖医学〗senile dementia. (⇨ぼける)
ぼけ 木瓜〖植物〗a Japanese quince; a flowering quince.
ほげい 捕鯨 whaling, whale fishing [fishery]. ●捕鯨を禁止する ban *whaling*. ●捕鯨業 whalery. ●捕鯨船 a whaler (2「捕鯨船員」の意もある); a whaling ship; a whale catcher [chaser]. ●捕鯨船団 a whaling fleet.
ぼけい 母系 ── 母系の 形 (やや書) maternal, on the maternal side. ●母系社会 a matrilineal /mèɪtrəlíniəl, mæt-/ society.
ぼけい 母型〖印刷〗a matrix /méɪtrɪks/ (複 〜es).
ほけきょう 法華経〖仏教〗the Lotus Sutra.
ほげた 帆桁 a sail yard; a (sail) boom.
ほけつ 補欠 (代わりの人) a súbstitute 《*for*》. ●生徒の補欠募集をする recruit students to fill vacancies. ●補欠選挙《米》a special election; 《主に英》a by-election. ●補欠選手 a substitute player; (控えの) a reserve, 《米》a bench warmer (2「補欠選手である」は be on [warm] the *bench*); a sub; an extra. ●補欠名簿 a waiting list.
ぼけつ 墓穴 a grave. ●墓穴を掘る《話》dig one's own grave (2 破滅でいかない大損害などの場合にも用いる); bring about one's own ruin.
ほけっと absent-mindedly; (何をする事もなく) idly; (うっかり) carelessly. (⇨ぼんやり) ●彼はほけっと玄関の前に立っていた He stood *absent-mindedly* in front of the door. ●私は日曜日はほけっとして過ごします I spend my time *idly* on Sundays./I *idle away* my time on Sundays.
***ポケット** a pocket.
① 〖〜ポケット〗●ズボン[上着]の(片側の)ポケット a trouser [a jacket] *pocket*. ●(上着の)胸[内/わき]ポケット a breast [an inside; a side] *pocket*.
② 〖ポケットの〗●ポケットのないズボン *pocketless pants*《米》[*trousers*《英》]. ●ポケットの中を探る feel in one's *pocket*《*for* the key》. ●私はいつも時計をズボンのポケットに入れている I always carry my watch in my trouser *pocket*.
③ 〖ポケットに[から]〗●ポケットに入れる put (it) in [into] a *pocket*; pocket (it). ●ポケットから取り出す take (it) out of one's *pocket*. ●彼はポケットに両手を突っ込んで歩いていた He was walking with his hands in his *pockets*. (2「ポケットに両手を突っ込む」は put one's hands in [into] one's *pockets*) ●彼はポケットに手を入れてサングラスを取り出してかけた He reached into his *pocket* and slipped sunglasses on.
●ポケットキャッチ〖野球〗(make) a basket catch. (2 x a pocket catch は不可だが a vest-pocket catch は可) ●ポケットチーフ a pocket handkerchief. ●ポケット版 (本の) a pocket(-size(d)) edition. ●ポケットブック a pocketbook, a pocket book. (2「札入れ」の意もある) ●ポケットベル a (pocket) pager, 《米》a beeper, 《英》a bleep, a bleeper;《和製語》pocketbell. ●ポケットマネー pocket money.
ぼけなす 惚け茄子《話》a dimwit;《話》a bonehead;《話》a blockhead.
ポケベル 〖「ポケットベル」の略〗a pager. (⇨ポケット)
ぼける 呆ける ❶ 〖頭が〗get* [go*] senile /síːnaɪl/. ●母はそのうちぼけるのではないかと心配している My mother worries about *going senile*. ●祖父は年をとってぼけてきた My grandfather is getting old and *senile*. (2「ぼけ老人」は a *senile* old man [woman]) ●彼はぼけてしまって子供のようだった He was quite childish in his *senility* /sənílətɪ/. ●彼は休み明けでぼけている His head is still on vacation 《主に米》[holiday《英》]./He *is out of it* after the vacation. (2 out of it は「ぼけっとして」の意の口語的慣用表現)
❷ 〖輪郭が〗●ピントがぼけた写真 a *blurred* picture; a picture *out of focus*.

***ほけん** 保険 insurance; 〖保険契約〗an insurance (policy).
① 〖〜保険, 保険〜〗●健康保険に入っていますか《米》Have you got *health insurance*? (事情) アメリカでは公的な健康保険がないので、各自が保険会社と契約する)

関連 いろいろな保険: 医療保険 medical insurance/介護保険 nursing care insurance/海上保険 marine insurance/火災保険 fire insurance / がん保険 cancer insurance / 簡易保険 postal life insurance/強制保険 obligatory insurance/健康保険 health insurance/災害保険 casualty insurance/失業保険 unemployment insurance/自動車保険 car insurance/社会保険 social insurance/終身保険 whole life insurance/傷害保険 accident insurance/生命保険 life insurance /《英》assurance/相互保険 mutual insurance/団体保険 group insurance/任意保険 voluntary insurance/年金保険 annuity insurance/養老保険 endowment insurance.

会話 「保険証を忘れたのですが…. これは保険がきかないんでしょうか」「残念ですが…. 今日は全額を現金でお支払いいただくことになりますが、次回保険証をお持ちくださったときに還付いたします」"I forgot to bring my health *insurance* card. This can't be covered by *insurance*?" "I'm sorry you'll have to pay

the full amount in cash, but you'll get a reimbursement the next time you come with it."
② [保険が] ▶私の家には5,000万円の火災保険がかけてある My house *is insured against* fire for fifty million yen./The fire *insurance* on my house is fifty million yen.
③ [保険に] ▶生命保険に加入する take out [buy] *insurance on* one's life; take out [buy] a life *insurance policy*. ▶彼は日本生命保険に入っている He *is insured* [*holds a policy*] *with* the Nippon Life Insurance. ▶宝石商は常に十分な保険に入っている Jewellers *are* always very well *insured*.
④ [保険を] ▶保険を申し込む[解約する; 更新する] apply for [cancel; renew] an *insurance (policy)*. ●財産に火災[損害; 盗難]保険をかける *insure* one's property *against* fire [damage; theft]. ▶彼は1,000万円の生命保険をかけた He *insured himself* [*his life*] *for* ten million yen./(かけていた) He *had* [*carried*] ten-million-yen *insurance* on his life.
⑤ [保険で] ▶その損害は保険で償われる The damage is covered by *insurance* (*money*).
● 保険医 a doctor who accepts health insurance patients. ● 保険会社 an insurance company; an insurer. ● 保険勧誘員 an insurance salesman [saleswoman]. ● 保険業 the insurance business [industry]. ● 保険業者 an insurer, an underwriter. ● 保険金 (receive [collect]) the insurance (money). ● 保険金受取人 a beneficiary. ● 保険契約者 a policyholder; (被保険者) the insured (person) (『単・複両扱』). ● 保険証券 an insurance policy. ● 保険診療 health insurance treatment. ● 保険代理業[店] an insurance agency. ● 保険料 insurance; (掛け金) a premium; an insurance premium. ● 自動車の保険料を払う pay the *insurance on* one's car.

ほけん 保健 preservation of one's health. ● 世界保健機関 World *Health* Organization (略 WHO). ● 保健衛生 sanitation. ● 保健師 a (public) health nurse. ● 保健室 (米) an infirmary;(英) a sick [a first-aid] room. ▶田中先生、ちょっと気分が悪いのですが、保健室へ行っていいですか I'm not feeling very well, Mr. Tanaka. May I go to the *infirmary*? ● 保健所 a (public) health center. ● 保健体育 health and physical education.

ほけん 母権 maternal rights.

ほ こ 矛 a pike; 『武器』arms.
● 矛を収める stop fighting; break off a battle.
● 矛を交える fight; go into battle.
● 矛を向ける turn one's attack 《on, against》; attack 《him》.

*ほ ご 保護 图 (a) protection (!保護する物・人の意では ⓒ); 『保存』preservation; (国土・資源の) conservation; 『未成年者に対する』custody. ● 文化財の保護 the *preservation* of cultural assets. ● 自然[環境]保護 (the) *conservation* of nature [the environment]. ● 両親の保護のもとで under the *protection* of one's parents. ● 警察の保護を求める ask for police *protection*; (警察に身辺保護を求める) ask the police for *safekeeping*. ● 生活保護 (⇨生活保護) ● 保護観察処分を受ける do [be put on] probation. (!前の方は《話》)
—— 保護する 動 protect; 『風雨から』shelter (⇨守る); 『破壊・腐朽から』preserve. ● 国内産業を保

護する *protect* [*safe-guard*] home industries. ● 野生生物を保護する *conserve* [*preserve*] wildlife. ● 森林を保護する *conserve* [*preserve*] forests. ▶サングラスは太陽の光から目を保護する Sunglasses *protect* [*shield*] the eyes *from* [*against*] the sunlight./Sunglasses are a *protection for* the eyes *against* the sunlight. ▶生け垣が風から花を保護している The hedge *shelters* the flowers *from* the wind. ▶その家出少女は警察に保護された[されている] The runaway girl was taken into [is in] police *custody*.
● 保護観察官 a probation officer. ● 保護関税 a protective tariff. ● 保護区域 a 《wildlife》 reserve; a 《game》 preserve; a 《bird》 sanctuary. ● 保護国 a protectorate /prətéktərət/. ● 保護司 (無報酬の) a voluntary probation officer. ● 保護者 a protector, a guardian; (両親) parents; 『法律』(後見人) a guardian. ● 保護色 protective coloring; (一つの) a protective color. ● 保護団体 a protection organization. ● 保護鳥 a protected bird. ● 保護鳥獣 (禁猟鳥獣) forbidden game. ● 保護貿易 protective (↔free) trade; (主義) protectionism. ● 保護領 a protectorate. ● 保護林 a forest preserve.

ほ ご 反故 (紙屑(¾)) wastepaper.
● ほごにする ▶約束をほごにする(=破る) *break* one's promise.

ほ ご 補語 『文法』a complement. ● 主格[目的格]補語 a subject [an object] *complement*.

ほ ご 母語 one's native language, 《主に英》one's mother tongue. (『参考』幼児期に最初に習得した言語)

ほ こう 歩行 图 walking. ● 歩行困難である have difficulty (in) *walking*.
—— 歩行する 動 walk. (⇨歩く)
● 歩行器 (米) a walker, (英) a walking frame. ● 歩行器にすがって少しずつ[よちよち]歩く inch [toddle] along on a *walker* (主に米) [a *zimmer frame* (英商標)]. (! walkerはリハビリ用、小児用のいずれもさすが、(英)の小児用は a baby walker という) ● 歩行訓練 walking exercises. ● 歩行者 (⇨歩行者)

ほ こう 補講 (やや書) a supplementary lecture [(学課) lesson]. (⇨補習)

ぼ こう 母校 one's old school, 《書》one's alma mater /ǽlmə mɑ́ːtər/. (! ラテン語で「自分を育ててくれた母」の意)。 ▶ハーバード大は私の母校だ Harvard (University) is my *alma mater*./I went to Harvard (University). ▶私は2年ぶりに母校を訪問した I visited my *old school* for the first time in two years.

ぼ こう 母港 a home port.

ほこうしゃ 歩行者 a pedestrian. ● (道路を)歩行者専用化する pedestrianize. ▶歩行者優先 Pedestrians have the right of way./(歩行者に道を譲れ)(掲示) Yield to pedestrians. ▶歩行者通行禁止 (掲示) No pedestrians.
● 歩行者専用区域 a pedestrian mall 《米》[precinct 《英》]. ▶その橋は歩行者専用だ The bridge is for *perdestrians* only. ● 歩行者天国 a 'pedestrian paradise'; 《英》a pedestrian precinct; (車のない散歩道) a car-free [a vehicle-free] promenade.

ぼ こく 母国 one's home country.
● 母国語 (⇨母語)

ほこさき 矛先 (槍の) a spearhead. ● 議論の矛先を鈍らせる blunt the *edge* of one's argument. ▶彼らは攻撃の矛先を敵の司令部に向けた They directed

the *attacks* against the enemy's headquarters.
ボゴタ [コロンビアの首都] **Bogotá** /bòugətá:/. (参考) 旧称 Santa Fé de Bogotá)
ぼこぼこ ●ぼこぼこの (でこぼこのある様子) bumpy, full of bumps. ●ぼこぼこ音のする bubbly. ●蚊にたくさんくわれて腕中がぼこぼこになっている My arms are *very bumpy* with a lot of mosquito bites. ●水道管の割れ目からぼこぼこ水が出ている Water is welling up *in bubbles* from the broken pipe.
ほこら 祠 a small shrine.
ほこらしい 誇らしい proud. ●誇らしげに proudly; (勝ち誇ったように) triumphantly. ●母校を誇らしく思う be proud of [take pride in] one's old school. ●息子を誇らしく眺める look on one's son *with pride*. ●look on … は「…をある感情をもって見る」の意を表すときに用いる)
***ほこり** 誇り pride (!軽蔑的に「うぬぼれ」の意でも用いる);【自尊心】self-respect;【名誉となる人[物]】an honor, a credit (⇨名誉). ●誇り高い男 a *proud* man; a *self-respecting* man. (!後の方は通例否定文で用いる) ●彼の誇りを傷つける hurt [wound] his *pride*. ●…ということを誇りに思う I'm proud [(光栄に思う) I'm honored] that …. ●私は日本人であることを誇りに思っている I am proud of [take pride in, pride myself on] being a Japanese. ▶彼らは我が校の誇りだ(=名誉だ) They are an *honor* [a *credit*] *to* our school./They are the *pride* of our school. (!主語が複数であっても honors, credits, the prides とはしない) ●どんな人にも誇りはある Everybody has their *pride*. ●質問するなんて彼の誇りが許さない His *pride* will not allow him to ask questions./(彼は誇りが高すぎて質問できない) He is too *proud* to ask questions. (!「彼の誇りが高い」は ×His pride is high. とはいわないことに注意)
***ほこり** 埃 dust. (!「立ち上るほこり」の意ではしばしば a ~) ▶テーブルの上にほこりがたまっていた *Dust* lay on the table./The table was covered in *dust*. (!後の方は埃が相当にたまっていることを含意する) ●彼女は家具のほこりを払った She *dusted* the furniture./She swept [×cleaned] the *dust* away from the furniture. ▶車がもうもうとほこりを巻き上げながら通り過ぎて行った The car raised a cloud of *dust* as it passed by. ▶なんてほこりっぽい道なんだ What a *dusty* road it is!/How *dusty* the road is!
***ほこる** 誇る be proud 《*of* (doing); *that* 節》, take* pride 《*in*》, pride oneself 《*on*》(⇨誇り), 組織・場所が誇りとして持っている》boast. ●君たには人に誇れるものがあるか Do you have anything you *are* [can be] *proud of*? ●彼は仕事早速いのを誇っている He *is proud of* his quick work [*that* he can do his work quickly]. ●その大学は立派な図書館を誇っている The college *boasts* a fine library.
ほころばす 綻ばす ●【衣服を】tear* [rip (-pp-)]… open; split*; 【口元を】wear* [(急に) break*into] a smile.
ほころび 綻び a split [an open] seam. ●ほころびを直す sew up a *split seam*. ▶ほころびができた The seam has split.
ほころびる 綻びる ●【縫い目が】come* apart [undone], split*; 【口元が】【人が主語】break* into a smile, grin (-nn-); 【花が開く】open. ▶ズボンの縫い目がほころびた The pants 《米》[trousers 《英》] *split* along the seam. ●桜の花がほころび始めた The cherry blossoms began to *open* [*bloom, come out*]. ●「安全な日本社会」の神話はほころびて(=崩れ)きている The myth of 'a safe Japanese society' is being shattered [falling apart]. (!

being shatterd は外的要因に, falling apart は内的要因による)
ほこぶ 綻ぶ (⇨綻びる)
ほさ 補佐 图 《事》assistance; (補佐する人) an assistant. ●部長補佐 an *assistant* general manager. ●大統領補佐官《米国》a Presidential aide.
—**補佐する** 動 assist; help; 《書》aid. ●議長を補佐する *assist* the chairperson.
ほさき 穂先 the tip of an ear; (刃の切っ先) the point of a sword.
ほざく ▶何をほざいているんだ, だまれ None of your damned nonsense! You just shut up!
ほさつ 捕殺する 動 (動物を捕まえて殺すこと) catch* and kill.
ほさつ 補殺 【野球】an assist. ●補殺なしのダブルプレー an unassisted double play. (参考) 1 人の野手が送球することなく 2 つのアウトを取る) ▶二塁手に補殺が記録された The second baseman got credited for an *assist*. (参考) 二塁ゴロを一塁に送球した場合など)
ぼさつ 菩薩 【仏教】a Bodhisattva /bòudisǽtvə/.
ぼさっと absent-mindedly. (⇨ぼんやり, ぼけっと)
ボサノバ [<ポルトガル語]【音楽】bossa nova.
ぼさぼさ ▶彼はいつもぼさぼさの髪をしている He always has *unkempt* [*disheveled*] hair./He always wears his hair *unkempt* [*disheveled*]. ▶ぼさぼさしていると飛行機に乗り遅れるぞ 《話》If you *dilly-dally* [*dawdle*], you'll miss the plane.
ほされる 干される be left out in the cold; be ignored.
ぼさん 墓参 ●墓参をする visit 《his》grave [tomb /túːm/].
‡**ほし** 星 ❶【天体】a star. ●星の【天文】stellar. ●星の多い starry. ●星の出ている夜 (=星月夜) a starry [《書》a starlit] night. ●星の出ていない夜 a starless night. ●星の降るような夜空 a *star*-filled [a *starry*] night sky. ●望遠鏡で星を観測する observe the *stars* through a telescope. ●星を眺め look up at the *stars*. ▶空に星が輝いている *Stars* are [There are *stars*] twinkling in the sky./(星が多い) The sky is *starry*. ▶星が出た The *stars* came out. ▶星が流れた A *star* [(流星) A meteor] shot across the sky.
❷【運勢】one's star [fortune]. ●星占い (個々の占い) a horoscope; (占星術) astrology. (⇨占い) ▶私は幸運[不運]な星の下に生まれた I was born under a lucky [an unlucky] *star*.
❸【星印】a star, an asterisk (*). ●星形の starlike. ●星(印)をつける mark 《it》with a *star* [an *asterisk*]; star; asterisk.
❹【斑点】 a spot; (牛馬の顔の) a blaze; (目の星) a white speck. ●目に星が出る have a white *speck* in one's eye.
❺【的の中心】the bull's eye.
❻【花形】a star. ●文学界の星 a *star* of the literary world; a literary *star*.
❼【勝利】a win. ●(白)星をあげる have [make] a *win*. ●黒星を喫する be beaten [defeated]; suffer a defeat.
❽【犯人】a culprit; (容疑者) a suspect. ●星を挙げる arrest [catch] the *culprit*. ▶「星の目星はついているのか」と彼は言った "Do you have a *suspect*?" he said.
●星の数ほど ●そんな本なら星の数はどあるよ There are a *countless number* of books of that kind.
●星空 a starry sky. ●星祭り (⇨圏 七夕 (ᵗᵃⁿᵃᵇᵃᵗᵃ))
ほし- 干し- dried.
ほじ 保持 图 ●世界記録保持者 a world-record *holder*.

— **保持する** 動 keep*, hold*, maintain, preserve. (⇨保つ) ▶秘密を保持する keep a secret. ▶タイトルを保持する hold the title.

ぼし 母子 mother and child. (1)通例無冠詞に用いる.《米》では冠詞をつけていうこともある) ▶母子ともに元気 Mother and child are both doing well.
▶**母子家庭** a fatherless family; a single-parent [a one-parent] family. (1)後の方は父子家庭の場合もあり, 文脈がないとはっきりしない) ▶**母子手帳** a maternity health-record book. [参考] 米英にはない)

ぼし 拇指 (手の第一指) the thumb.
ぼし 拇趾 (足の第一指) the big toe. (⇨外反母趾)
ぼし 墓誌 (追悼的に) a record of life and death of a deceased person in the slab of the tomb.

ほしあかり 星明かり starlight. ▶星明かりで in (the) [by] starlight.

ほしあげる 干し上げる ❶ [よく乾かす] dry completely. ❷ [水をなくす] ●池の水を干し上げる drain the water from the pond. ❸ [食べ物をまったく与えない] starve; do not give (him) any food for a long time.

ほしい 欲しい want; would like; wish; hope.

> 使い分け **want**「欲しい」の意を表す最も一般的な語. やや無作法に響き, 目上の人物に対して用いることはまれ.
> **would like** 控え目に「欲しい」ことを表す. 依頼や質問を丁寧に行うときに用いられる.
> **wish**「…であることを願う」「…したい」の意を表す. 時に得られる可能性が低いものを欲する場合に用いる.
> **hope**「…であることを望む」「…したい」の意を表す. 時に抽象的なものを欲する場合に用いる. 具体的なものに用いることはまれ.

▶欲しい物を(何でも)あげよう I will give you anything you want. ▶欲しいだけ取りなさい Take as many [much] as you want. (1)many は数を, much は量を問題にする場合)
①[〜が欲しい] ▶新車が欲しい I want [I'd like] a new car./I wish (that) I had [×have] a new car. (1)that は通例省略され, that 節中は仮定法過去形. 現在車がないことに残念だという気持ちを表す (⇨②)) ▶(プレゼントなどをもらって) まあ, これ前から欲しかったのよ My, this is just what I've long wanted.
会話「何が欲しいですか」「コーヒーが欲しいです」"What would you like [《やや書》care for]?" "I'd like some coffee." (1)(1) care for は通例否定文・疑問文で用いる. (2)「コーヒーはいりません」は I don't want any coffee, thanks. で I wouldn't like any coffee. とはいわない)
②[〜して欲しい] ▶もっと勉強して欲しい I want [I'd like] you to study harder. (1)継続状態を表す場合には want A doing を用い, 主に否定文で用いる: 私がここにいる間は歌を歌わないで欲しい I don't want you singing while I am here.) / 《書》 I wish you would study harder. / I wish you studied harder. (1)勉強する可能性がないことを暗示. ×I want [I'd like] (that) you study harder. とはいわない (⇨①)) ▶きみもあしたまでに準備[修理]して欲しい I want it (to be) ready [repaired] by tomorrow. (1)to be がない方が直接的) ▶彼は女店員に指輪を見せて欲しいと言った He said to a saleswoman, "I'd like to see some rings." (1)Please show me some rings. より丁寧な表現)/He asked a saleswoman to show him some rings. ▶彼は早く(病気が)よくなって欲しい I hope (that) he will get [he gets] well soon. (1)×I wish he would …. はよくならないであろうということを前提とするので不可) 会話「彼も来るの?」「来て[来ないで]欲しいな」"Is he coming, too?" "I hope so [not]."

ほしいまま 欲しいまま ▶欲しいままにふるまう have one's own way. ▶権力を欲しいままにする exercise one's power [authority] to the full (over); (乱用する) abuse one's power [authority]. ▶現代随一の画家として名声を欲しいままにする enjoy the reputation of being the best painter of the day.

ほしうらない 星占い (占星術) astrólogy; (個々の占い) a hóroscope. ▶星占いの結果 a cast [read] one's hóroscope. ▶星占いでは今週はいいことずくめだ My horoscope for this week is full of good news.

ポシェット [<フランス語] a pouch /páutʃ/, a pochette /poʊʃét/. ▶ウエストポシェット a waist pouch.

ほしがき 干し柿 a dried persimmon.

ほしかげ 星影 starlight. ▶星影さやかな夜 a clear starlit night; a bright starry night.

ほしがる 欲しがる ▶(〜欲しい) ▶そのおもちゃを欲しがって泣く cry for the toy. ▶その子はキャンデーを欲しがった The child wanted (to have) some candy. ▶これは君が欲しがっていた参考書だ This is the study aid you have wanted [(しきりに) have been wishing for].

ほしくさ 干し草 hay. ▶干し草を作る make hay.

ほしくず 星屑 stardust; a multitude of stars in the night sky.

ほしくる (⇨ほじる)

ポジション [[位置, 地位]] a position. ▶スコアリングポジションに進む move into scoring position. ▶(野球で)彼は3つのポジションを守る He plays three positions.

ほしつ 保湿 ▶保湿クリーム móisturing crèam. ▶**保湿剤** a moisture-preservative.

ポジティブ (積極的な) positive. ▶ポジティブシンキング[前向きな考え方] positive thinking.

ほしとりひょう 星取り表 a scóre shèet.

ほしのり 干し海苔 a dried sheet of sea laver /léivər/.

ほしぶどう 干しぶどう a raisin /réizn/, (種なし) a currant. (1)通例複数形で)

ほしまわり 星回り ▶one's star. ▶星回りがいい be born under a lucky star. ▶星回りが悪い be born under an unlucky star; be ill-starred.

ほしもの 干し物 (洗濯物) the washing,《米》the wash. (1)集合的に. 単数扱い) ▶干し物を取りこむ take [get] the washing in. (⇨洗濯)

ほしゃく 保釈 图 [法律] bail. (⇨釈放) ▶保釈を認める grant bail. ▶保釈金を1万ドルとする set bail [《主に米》bond] at ten thousand dollars. ▶保釈願いan application for bail. ▶保釈中である be out on bail; be under bail. ▶保釈保証人になる put up bail (for him).
— **保釈する** 動 bail [《主に米》bond]… out; release … on bail.

ぼしゃる go* to pieces; (計画などが) fall* through. ▶その計画は資金不足でぼしゃってしまった The plan fell through [went to pieces] for lack of funds.

ほしゅ 保守 图 [習慣・考え方の維持] conservatism; [よい状態の維持] maintenance. ▶エレベーターの定期保守点検をする carry out routine maintenance of the elevator 《米》[lift 《英》].
— **保守的な** 形 conservative. ▶保守的な意見 a conservative opinion. ▶英国民は保守的な国民だ The British are a conservative people. ▶彼女の結婚に対する考えはひどく保守的である Her attitude toward marriage is very conservative./She is very conservative in her attitude toward mar-

ほしゅ 捕手 〖野球〗a catcher. (⇨キャッチャー) ● 正[控えの]捕手 a regular [a backup] catcher. ● 捕手用マスク a catcher's mask. ● 捕手をする play catcher. ● 山田投手[ジャイアンツ]の捕手をする catch Yamada [for the Giants].

ほしゅう 捕囚 (捕らわれの身) a prisoner; a captive.

ほしゅう 補修 图 repair. ● 補修中である be under *repair*.
— **補修する** 動 repair. (⇨直す, 修理する)
● 補修工事 repair works.

ほしゅう 補習 〖進学など〗an extra lesson; 〖補講〗a supplementary lesson [lecture]. ● (英語の)補習(授業)を受ける take *extra* [*supplementary*] *lessons* (in English).

ほじゅう 補充 — **補充する** 動 〖空所を満たす〗fill (up); 〖再び満たす〗refill, 《書》replenish; 〖不足を補う〗supply. ● 欠員を補充する *fill* (*up*) a vacancy. ● タンクに水を補充する *refill* [*replenish*] the tank *with* water. ● 必要部品[不足分]を補充する *supply* necessary equipment [deficiency]. ● 軍隊に新兵を補充する *recruit* an army.
● 補充兵 a recruit.

***ぼしゅう** 募集 图 ❶〖人の〗recruitment. ● 募集に応じる apply 《for》(⇨応募する); (広告を見て) answer an *advertisement* 《for clerks》. ● 事務員募集《広告》Clerks wanted./Wanted clerks. (❗ Clerks are wanted から) ● 伊藤君は花嫁募集中だ Ito is *on the lookout for* a future Mrs. Ito.
❷〖寄付などの〗(a) collection. ● 募集額 the amount (of money) *to be raised*. ● 基金募集を始める start a fund (⇨)
— **募集する** 動 ❶〖社員などを〗(求める) look for ..., 《書》seek*; (新入者を) recruit; (広告で) advertise for ...; 〖志願・投稿などを促す〗invite. ● 学生(新会員)を募集する *recruit* students [new members]. ● 新聞で教員を募集する *advertise for* teachers in the newspaper. ● 論文を一般から募集する(= 公募する) *invite* public contributions of papers. ● この工場は従業員を募集している The factory *is looking for* [*seeking, accepting applications for*] workers. (❗ 最後は「応募受付中」の意)
❷〖寄付金などを〗collect; (大規模に) raise. ● 慈善事業への寄付金を募集する *collect* contributions [money] for charities; *make* [*take up*] *a collection* for charities. ● 新しい学校の建設資金を募集する *raise* a fund [money] *for* a new school. (❗ money は無冠詞) ● 公債を募集する *raise* a loan.
● 募集人員 the number to be admitted 《*to* a club》. ● 募集要項 guidelines for applicants; (冊子) an application booklet.

ぼしゅうだん 母集団 〖統計〗a population; a universe. (❗ 前の方が普通)

***ほじょ** 補助 图 help, 《やや書》assistance, 《書》aid; support. (❗ help が一般的な語. assistance は help より堅い上品な語. aid は主に公的な援助. support は財政的・精神的支援) ● 財政的補助 financial *aid* [*assistance, support*]. ● 補助的な手段 auxiliary [subsidiary /sʌbsídièri/] measures. ▶彼女は国の補助を受けて生活している She lives *on* (the) national relief *funds*.
— **補助(を)する** 動 help, 《書》assist, 《書》aid; support; (補助金を出す) subsidize /sʌ́bsədàiz/. (

助ける, 援助する) ● 学費[生活費]を補助する *help* 《him》*with* 《his》school [living] expenses. ▶彼女は父親の仕事の補助をした She *helped* [*assisted*] her father *with* the work. (❗ ×She *helped* [*assisted*] her father's work. とはいわない)
● 補助員 an assistant. ● 補助金 a subsidy /sʌ́bsədi/. ● 補助席 a spare [an extra] chair; (米などの) a jump seat.

ぼしょ 墓所 a burial ground; a graveyard.

***ほしょう** 保証 图 〖品質・借金などの〗a guarantee; 〖商品の品質保証〗a warranty /wɔ́ːrənti/; 〖借金などの担保〗(a) security; 〖確言, 確約〗(an) assurance. ● 返品保証つきの商品 goods with a money back *guarantee* [*warranty*]. ● 連帯保証 a joint *guarantee*. ● サービス[商品取り替え]保証 a *guarantee for* service [replacement]. ● 製品保証 a pródúct *guarantee* 《wàrranty》. ● 信用保証 a crédit *guarantèe*. ▶彼が成功するという保証はない There is no *guarantee that* he will succeed. ▶このテレビは1年間の保証がついている This TV set comes with a one-year *guarantee* [*warranty*]./This TV set *is guaranteed* [*is warranted*] for one year.
— **保証する** 動 〖商品・事などを〗guarantee, 《書》warrant; 〖確言する〗assure; 〖確実にする〗ensure, 《米》insure; 〖真実性・人格などを〗vouch 《for》. ● この機械の品質を保証する *guarantee* [*warrant*] the quality of this machine. ● 商品の破損に対して保証する *guarantee* goods *against* breakage. ▶彼にその地位を保証する *guarantee* him the post [the post to him]; *ensure* him the post [the post *for* him]. ▶努力してみますがうまく行くかどうかは保証できません I'll try, but I can't *guarantee* success. ▶食料の供給を保証します We *guarantee* (you) the supply of food./We *guarantee to* [*that* we will] supply you with food. ▶彼はそれは純金だと保証した He *guaranteed* that it was pure gold./He *guaranteed* it (to be) pure gold. (❗ that 節を用いた前の方が普通) ▶彼の誠実さは保証します I (can) *assure* you *of* his sincerity./I (can) *assure* you (that) he is sincere./I *vouch for* [(責任を負う) *answer for*] his sincerity.
● 保証期間 the period of guarantee; the warranty period. (❗ 「(商品が)保証期間内である」は be under guarantee [warranty]) ▶保証期間は3年です The *warranty* period is three years./The *guarantee* is good [valid] for three years. ● 保証金 security [guaranty] money. ● 保証書 a guarantee [a warranty] 《*on* a camera》. ● 保証人 (⇨保証人)

***ほしょう** 補償 图 compensation, 《書》reparation. (⇨賠償, 償い) ● 1万ドルの補償を請求する claim 10,000 dollars *damages*. ● 補償として100万円受け取る receive one million yen *in compensation* [*as a compensation*] 《for one's injury》.
— **補償する** 動 compensate 《him *for* it》. ▶会社は彼がけがに対して補償をした The company *compensated* him *for* his injury.
● 補償金 (a) compensation; 〖法律〗damages.

ほしょう 歩哨 a sentry, 《古》a sentinel. ● 歩哨に立つ[に立っている] be on *sentry* duty. ● 歩哨を置く post a *sentry*. (⇨番兵)

ほしょう 保障 图 〖安全保障〗security. ● 社会保障 social *security*. ● 安全保障理事会 (国連の) the Security Council. ● 日米安全保障条約 the U.S.-Japan *Security* Treaty.
— **保障する** 動 guarantee; (権利する) secure. ● 平和を保障する *secure* peace. ● 権利を保障する *secure*

ほしょう 堡礁 a barrier reef (⇨ ～s).
ほしょう 慕情 (a) love 《*for*》; (得がたいものに対する強いあこがれ) (a) yearning 《*after*》.
ほしょうにん 保証人 a guarantee /ɡærəntíː/; (契約・協定などの) a guarantor /ɡǽrəntɔːr, -tər/; (借金・人(の行為)などの) (a) surety /ʃúərəti/; (署名に加わる連帯保証人) 《米》a cosigner, (身元照会先) a reference, 《英》a referee. ● おじにローンの保証人になってくれるよう頼んだ I asked my uncle to *act as guarantee* 《やや書》to *act as surety*, to *stand surety*] *for* my loan. (❗ as の後の不定冠詞は通例省略される)/I asked my uncle to *guarantee* my loan [to be my *guarantor for* the loan]./《米》I asked my uncle to *cosign* 《*for*》my loan [to be my *cosigner for* the loan].

ほしょく 補色 complementary colors.
ほしょく 捕食 图 predation.
── **捕食の** 形 predatory.
── **捕食する** 動 prey 《*on* insects [mice]》.
● 捕食動物 a predator; a predatory animal.

ほじる 鼻[歯]をほじる pick one's nose [teeth].
● 耳をほじる *remove* earwax; *clean* one's ears.
● 彼のプライベートな問題をほじる (せんさくする) *pry into* his private affairs; (干渉する)《話》*poke* [*stick*] one's *nose into* his personal affairs.

ほしん 保身 self-protection. ● 保身の術にたけている be good at keeping one's interests; be clever at defending [protecting] one's position.

ほす 干す ❶ [乾かす] dry; [つるす] hang; [空気にさらす] air. ● 洗濯物を外に[ロープに]干す *hang* the washing out (to *dry*) [the washing on a line].
● セーターを干す(＝空気にさらしてよく乾かす[においを抜く])*air* one's sweater (*out*). (❗《米》で out を添えることもある) / 魚を日なたに干した I *dried* fish in the sun. (❗干し魚は dry [dried] fish)
❷ [空にする] empty; (飲み干す) drink*... down [*off*].

ボス a boss. (❗ 「上司」の意の boss には悪い響きはない。やたらといばっていて, 何でも自分勝手に取り仕切る人を非難していう場合にも用いる) ▶ 彼はその町の政治ボスだ He's the political *boss* of the city.

ポス [販売時点情報管理の略]〖商業〗POS 《point of sale の略》.
● ポスシステム a POS system.

ほすう 歩数 the number of steps. ● 歩数を数える count one's steps.
● 歩数計 a pedometer.

ほすすき 穂薄 (説明的に) *susuki*, Japanese pampas grass, in feathery, silvery plumes.

ポスター a poster /póustər/; (公示・広告など) a placard; (ビラなども含む広告類一般の) a bill. ● 選挙[指名手配]のポスター an election [a wanted] *poster*.
● ロックコンサート[スター]のポスター a *poster* for a rock concert [*of* a rock star]. ● ポスターを張る[引きはがす] put up [tear off] a *poster*.
● ポスターカラー poster paints [colors].

ポスティングシステム [入札制度][野球] a pósting sỳstem.

> フリーエージェント権を獲得していない日本人選手が所属球団の許可を得て，メジャーリーグ入りを希望した場合，30 球団が入札を行い，最高額(選手が所属する日本球団に支払う)を提示した球団が独占交渉権を得る。

ホステス [パーティーなどの女主人] a hostess; [バーの女性接客係] a bar hostess; [話] girl; 《米》a barmaid (❗《米》では「女性のバーテン」の意).

ホスト [パーティーなどの主人役] a host; [放送番組などの司会役] a host. ● ホスト役を務める act as *host* 《*at a party*》.
● ホストクラブ a 'host club'; (説明的に) an entertainment club which provides male companions for women.

*ポスト ❶ [地位, 任務] a post /póust/, a position. ● 教授のポストにつく take [get] a *post* as a professor. ● ポストのあくのを待つ wait for the vacant *post*. 《⇨地位》▶ ポストが人を変える People change when they are given a *position* of responsibility./Given a *position* of responsibility, a person changes. (❗前の方は人に, 後の方は地位に焦点がある)
❷ [郵便の] 《米》a mailbox, 《英》a postbox; (円筒状の) a pillar box.
❸ [サッカーの] a post. ▶ ルーニーのシュートがポストを叩いた Rooney hit the *post*. (❗「…のシュート」を省略した表現)

ポスト [それ以降の, その次の] post. ● ポスト小泉政権 post Koizumi government. ● ポスト構造主義 [歴史] post-structuralism.

ポストカード [郵便はがき] a postcard.
ホストコンピュータ(ー) a host computer.
ポストハーベスト [収穫後の農作物の処理] post-harvest treatment.
ホストファミリー a host family. ● ホストファミリーをする[＝引き受ける] accept an overseas student in one's home and take care of him or her as a member of one's family.
ポストプレー [サッカーで] post-play.
ポストモダニズム [脱近代主義] postmodernism.
ポストモダン [脱近代主義の] pòstmódern.
ボストン [米国の都市] Boston.
ボストンバッグ (旅行用) a tráveling bàg, 《主に米》a (hand) grip (❗a Boston bag は《古》).
ボスニア・ヘルツェゴビナ [国名] Bosnia-Herzegovina /bázniə-hə̀rtsəgouvíːnə/ (❗公式名も同じ). (首都 Sarajevo) ● ボスニア人 a Bosnian. ● ボスニア語 Bosnian. ● ボスニア(人の語)の Bosnian.
ホスピス a hospice. (⇨ 緩和ケア)

ほする 保する ▶ 彼の安全は保しがたい I cannot *assure* you *of* his safety./I cannot *assure that* he is safe.

ほする 補する (担当を命じる) appoint 《him *as* [*to be*] principal of Tokyo high school》.

ほせい 補正 图 ● 補正予算を組む make [draw up] a *supplementary* [a *revised*] budget.
── **補正する** 動 (修正する) revise; (補足する) supplement.

ほぜい 保税 ● 保税上屋 a bonded shed. ● 保税貨物[品] bonded cargo [goods]; cargo [goods] in bond. ● 保税制度 the bond [bonded] system.
● 保税倉庫 a bonded warehouse. ● 保税倉庫に入れる bond 《goods》. ● 保税倉庫から出す take 《goods》out of bond.

ぼせい 母性 maternity, motherhood. ● 彼女は彼に母性愛のような感情を持った She felt something like *maternal* love for him. ▶ 彼女の母性愛がかき立てられた Her *maternal* love [*The mother in her*] was stirred.
● 母性本能 maternal [mothering, motherly] instinct(s).

ぼせき 墓石 a gravestone; a tombstone.
ほせつ 補説 图 a supplementary explanation.
── **補説する** 動 supplement 《the text》with addi-

ほせん 保線 maintenance of tracks.
- 保線区 a railroad section. ●保線工事 track (maintenance) work. ●保線作業員 a linesman; 《米》tracklayer;《英》a platelayer.

ほぜん 保全 图 (保存) preservation; (機械などの) maintenance; (自然の) conservation. ●森林保全 the forestry *preservation* [*conservation*] ; the *preservation* [*conservation*] of forests. ●環境保全 the environmental *protection* [*conservation*].

── **保全する** 動 preserve; maintain; conserve.
- 領土を保全する *preserve* the territorial integrity.
- 保全管理人【法律】a receiver.

ほせん 母船 a mother ship.

ぼぜん 墓前 ●墓前に花を捧げる put flowers *before 《his》 grave* [*tomb*].

ほせんこく 母川国 a state of origin.

ほぞ (木材の)《fix》a tenon (*into* a mortise). ●柱にほぞ穴をあける cut a mortise in [mortise]《a pillar》.

ほぞ 臍 (へそ) the navel.
- ほぞを固める make up one's mind; resolve; determine.
- ほぞをかむ deeply regret; feel very sorry.

***ほそい 細い** ❶ [物・声などが] thin (-nn-) (↔thick); fine; slender; small; narrow.

> **使い分け thin** 物の細さを示す最も一般的な語. 特に人の体(の一部)の細さを表すことが多い.
> **fine** 糸や髪の毛などが非常に細いことを表す.
> **slender** 主に人の体の細さを表す. thin に比べて細いことによって魅力的という肯定的な含意がある.
> **small** 土地などが細いことを表す.
> **narrow** 主に道路などの横幅が長さの割合と比較して細いことを表す.

- 細い糸 a *thin* [a *fine*] thread. ●細い声で話す speak in a *small* [a *weak*] voice. ●先の細いペン a *fine* (point of a) pen; a pen with a *fine* point. ●細い指をしている have *slender* [*thin*] fingers.
▶ 我々は山道を登って行った We climbed a *narrow* mountain path. ▶ その棒は先が細くなってがっている The stick *tapers (off)* to a point. ▶ 彼女の腰のくびれはかなり細くなっていた Her waist had grown decidedly *thinner*.(!比較級に注意)
会話「その上着はいかがですか」「ウエストのところが少し細すぎるようだ」"How about the jacket?" "It seems a bit too *small* in the waist."

❷ [その他の表現] ●彼女は食が細い(=あまり食べない) She doesn't eat much./She is a *light* [a *small*, a *poor*] eater.

ほそう 舗装 图 pavement.
── **舗装する** 動 ●道をコンクリート[アスファルト]で舗装する *pave* a road *with* concrete [asphalt].
- 舗装道路 a paved road. ●舗装 a pavement.

ほそうで 細腕 ●女の細腕で(=他の助けを借りないで)レストランを経営している She runs a restaurant *by herself* [*on her own*].

ほそおもて 細面 a pleasant oval face.

ほそく 歩測 ── **歩測する** 動 pace out [off]《the distance》.

ほそく 捕捉 图 (捕まえること) capture.
── **捕捉する** 動 catch; take [catch, lay] hold of.
- 彼の発言の真意は捕捉しがたい(=理解するのは難しい) It's not easy to find out what he really means.

ほそく 補則 supplementary rules.

ほそく 補足 图 ●補足説明をする give a *supplementary* explanation. (⇨補う)

── **補足する** 動 (不足を補って完全にする) complement; (付加的に) add; (十分にするために) supplement. ●互いに補足しあう *complement* each other. ●それにもう一例補足する *add* another example *to* it; *supplement* it *with* another example.

ほそじま 細縞 ── **細縞の** 形 ●細縞のスーツ a *pin-striped* suit.

ほそづくり 細作り ●細作りの縄 a thin [a fine] rope.
- 細作りの(=細身の)娘 (⇨細身) ●細作りで上品な顔の婦人 a woman with *fine* features.

ぼそっと ●ぼそっと言う(聞き取りにくい低い声で言う) say in a low voice; (ささやく) whisper. ●ぼそっと(=ぼんやりと)立っている be standing《there》*absentmindedly*. ▶ 彼は好きだと言った He *whispered* (that) he liked her.

ほそながい 細長い ●[周囲の細い] slender《vases》; [縦長の]; long《windows》; [幅の狭い] narrow《tables》; [細い切れ, 区画] a strip《*of* paper [land]》.

ほそぼそ 細々 ●細々と(=かろうじて)暮らす make a poor [a scanty] living《as; (by) do*ing*》; scrape by [along]《*on* 70,000 yen a month》. ▶ 兄は田舎で細々と雑貨屋をやっている My brother in the country runs a small drugstore, which *brings him* [*brings in*] only a meager income.

ぼそぼそ (⇨ぼそっと)

ほそみ 細身 ●細身の刀 a *narrow-*(bladed) sword. ●細身のズボン(a pair of) *narrow* trousers《主に米》pants. ●細身の娘 a *slender* girl; a girl of *slender* build.

ほそめ 細目 ❶ [開け方] ●細目のズボン slightly tight pants《米》[trousers《英》]. ●ドアを細目に開けておく leave the door *ajar* [*slightly open*, *a little open*]. ●細目に(=細い)切る cut ... *fine*. ▶ 彼は細目だ He is *rather thin*./He is *lean*. (! thin は「不健康に細い」, lean は「健康的だが細い」の意)
❷ [細い目] ●細目を開く open one's eyes a little.

ほそめる 細める ●目を細める (まぶしさ・近視などで) squint one's eyes. ●目を細めて見る squint《*at*》(⇨目 ❶ ④).

ほそる 細る (やせる) become* thin (-nn-); (端のところで次第に細くなる) taper (off). ●最近食が細っている I *have lost* my appetite lately.

***ほぞん 保存** 图 [腐敗・破壊などから守ること] preservation; [変化・損傷を受けないようにすること] preservation; conservation. ●史跡の保存 *preservation* [*conservation*] of historic spots. ●この絵は保存状態がよい[悪い] This painting is in a good [a poor] state of *preservation*.

■ DISCOURSE ■

古い建築の保存は難しい. ひとつには安全面の問題がある. …もうひとつには費用の問題がある *Preserving* old architecture is difficult. **For one thing**, there is the problem of safety. … **For another (thing)**, there is the problem of cost. (! for one thing ... for another thing 〜 (ひとつには…もうひとつには〜)は列挙に用いるディスコースマーカー)

── **保存する** 動 [害・破壊などから価値あるものを] preserve; [現在の状態のまま] conserve; [取っておく] keep* (!意味の広い語). (⇨保つ) ●重要文書を保存する *preserve* important documents. ●天然資源を保存する *conserve* natural resources. ▶ この牛乳は長期間保存できる(=保存がきく) This milk can *be kept* [*be preserved*] for a long time.
- 保存血液 stored blood. ●保存食 (保存のきく食

ほだ 物) nonperishables. ● 保存料 a preservative. ● 保存療法 〔医学〕 a conservative treatment.
ほだ 榾 〔薪〕 firewood.
ポタージュ 〔＜フランス語〕 potage /poʊ(ː)tάːʒ/; thick soup.
ぼたい 母体 the mother's body; 〔基礎〕 the basis. ● 母体保護のために for the health of the *mother*. ● 抵抗運動の母体 the *basis* of the resistance. ● 母体保護法 the Maternity Protection Law.
ぼたい 母胎 (in) one's mother's womb.
ぼだい 菩提 ● 菩提を弔(とむら)う pray for ((the repose of)) the dead. ● 菩提寺 one's family temple.
ぼだいじゅ 菩提樹 〔植物〕 a lime (tree); 〔米〕 a linden. (❗ linden には詩的な響きがある)
ほだぎ 榾木 firewood.
ほだされる ● 彼の熱意にほだされる be touched [moved] by his eagerness. ▶彼は情にほだされやすい He is *very sympathetic*./He is a *very sympathetic person*.
ほだし 絆し 〔自由を束縛するもの〕 ties; bonds (❗ 主に複数形で. 単数形でも可).
ほたてがい 帆立貝 〔魚介〕 a scallop, a scollop.
ぼたぼた (⇨ぽたぽた)
ぽたぽた ●ぽたぽた落ちる drip, fall in drops; 〔しずくが小さい流れになって〕 trickle down. (⇨たらたら) ▶汗が彼の額からぽたぽた落ちていた Sweat *was dripping* (*down*) from his forehead./Sweat *was trickling* from his forehead. (❗ drip は名詞にも用いられる: 水がぽたぽた落ちているのが聞こえる I hear the *steady drips* of water.)
ぼたもち ぼた餅 a *botamochi*; (説明的に) a soft rice cake covered with sweetened bean paste. (⇨お萩(はぎ)) ▶棚からぼた餅 (⇨棚) 〔成句〕
ぼたやま ぼた山 〔主に英〕 a slag heap.
ぽたり 〔水滴の落ちる音〕 a drop. ▶雨のぽたり(ぽたり)と落ちる音がする I hear the *drip*(-*drip*) of the rain (*from* the roof). ▶水道の蛇口からぽたりぽたりと水がもれている Water *is dripping* from the faucet./The faucet *is dripping* water./The faucet [tap] has a *drip*.
ぽたりぽたり (⇨ぽたり)
ほたる 蛍 a firefly, 〔米〕 a lightning bug. ● 蛍石 〔鉱物〕 fluorite, fluorspar. ● 蛍狩り firefly catching. ● 蛍を見に行く go out to catch fireflies. ● 蛍火 the glow [light] of a firefly. ● 蛍袋 a bellflower.
ほたるいか 蛍烏賊 〔魚介〕 a firefly squid.
ほたるがわ 『蛍川』 *River of Fireflies*. 〔参考〕宮本輝の小説
ほたるのはか 『火垂るの墓』 *Grave of the Fireflies*. 〔参考〕野坂昭如の小説
＊ボタン 〔＜ポルトガル語〕 ❶ 〔服の〕 a button /bʌ́tn/. ● 三つボタンの服 a three-*button* suit. ● ボタンダウンのシャツ a *button*-down shirt. ● ボタンを(きちんと)かける fasten (up) *buttons*; button (up) 〔a coat〕. ● ボタンをはずす undo *buttons*; unbutton 〔a coat〕. ● 上着にボタンを縫いつける[つけてもらう] sew a *button* [have a *button* sewn] on a coat. ● シャツの上のボタンが二つ取れた[取れている; 取れかかっている] The top two *buttons* of my shirt came off [are missing; are loose].
❷ 〔機械などの〕 a (push) button. ● 押しボタン a push button. ● 〔機械・ベルなどの〕ボタンを押す push [press] the *button*.
● ボタンを掛け違える ▶私たちはボタンを掛け違えたまま議論していたことに気付いた We realized that we *started off on a wrong foot* with our argument.

ボタンホール a buttonhole.
ぼたん 牡丹 〔植物〕 a (Japanese tree) peony.
ぼたんざくら 牡丹桜 (八重桜) a double-flowered cherry tree.
ぼたんゆき 牡丹雪 large snowflakes.
ぼち 墓地 a graveyard; (教会付属の) a churchyard; (共同の) a cemetery (❗ 公営のものは a public ～, 私営のものは a private ～). ● a burial place [ground] は通例古代・先史時代などの古い墓地である). ● 青山墓地 Aoyama *Cemetery*. ● 公園墓地 a memorial park.
-ぽち (⇨-ぽっち)
ホチキス a stapler. 〔参考〕日本語の「ホチキス」は発明者 Hotchkiss の名から) ● ホチキスの針 a staple. ● ホチキスでとじる staple 〔sheets〕 together. ▶そのカタログの表紙に名刺がホチキスでとめてある The catalogue has a business card *stapled to* the front cover.
ぽちぶくろ ぽち袋 (小さなのし袋) a small *noshi* envelope.
ぼちぼち ❶ 〔よくも悪くもない様子〕 会話 「お仕事の方はいかがですか」「ぼちぼちですね」 "How's your business?" "*Just* só-sò./Só-sò!" (❗ 前の方は「さほどよくはない」の意. 後の方は満足していることを控えめにいう表現で, 率直な方では It's not perfect but it's Okay, I guess. などとなる)
❷ 〔ゆっくりとした様子〕 (⇨ぽつぽつ)
ぽちゃぽちゃ ●ぽちゃぽちゃしている (丸くかわいく) plump; (筋肉がたるんだ) flabby; (でぶ) fat. ▶赤ん坊はぽちゃぽちゃした体をしている The baby has a *plump* body. ▶彼女はぽちゃぽちゃした手をしている She has *plump* hands.
ぽちゃん 〔音〕 a splash. ▶リンゴが川にぽちゃんと落ちた An apple fell into the river *with a splash*. ▶魚が頭をあげて水中から飛び跳ねた A fish jumped out of the water *making a splash*.
ほちゅう 補注 ● a supplementary note.
ほちゅうあみ 捕虫網 a butterfly [an insect] net.
ほちょう 歩調 〔歩く速度〕 (a) pace; 〔歩き方〕 (a) step. (❗ いずれも歩くとき以外にも用いられる) ● 速い[ゆっくりした]歩調で at a fast [a slow] *pace*. ● 彼女に合わせて歩調を早める[ゆるめる] quicken [slacken] one's *pace* to match hers.
● 歩調を合わせる ● 歩調を合わせて歩く walk in step ((with)). ▶彼は他のみんなとは歩調が合わない He is *out of* [is *not in*] *step with* the rest. (❗ (1) 意見・考えなどが一致しないこともいう. (2) the rest は the other people, the others ともいい,「自分以外の他の人たち」の意. (3) 日本語に引かれて everyone else とするのは不可) ▶私は彼らに歩調を合わせていけなかった(＝仕事などでついていけなかった) I was unable to *keep pace* [*step*] *with* them.
ほちょうき 補聴器 ● 補聴器を使う[つけている] use [wear] a *hearing aid*.
ぼつ 没 ● 紀元前 56 年没 Died in 56 B.C. (❗ d. 56 B.C. と略記する)
● 没になる ▶私の随筆は紙面の都合で没になった(＝活字にならなかった) My essay *was not published* because there was not enough space. (❗ 内容が基準に達しなくて「没になった」は My essay *was rejected* [*was turned down*].)
ぼっか 牧歌 图 ● a pastoral /pǽstərəl/ song [(詩) poem]; 〔まれ〕 a pastoral.
● 牧歌的な 形 〔田園ふうの〕 pastoral, idyllic /aidílik/. ● 牧歌的な風景 a *pastoral* landscape.
ぼつう 没頭 ● 没我の境に入っている be absorbed in ((reading [one's work])).
ほっかい 北海 a northern sea; (英国東の) the North Sea. ● 北海油田 the North Sea oil fields. (❗ 「北海油田産の石油」は the North Sea oil)

ぼっかく 墨客 (説明的に) an artist who paints and/or writes with a Chinese brush.

ほっかぶり 頬被り ⇨頬(ǔ)被り

ぽっかり ❶ [幅広く] wide open; (口を開けた) agape /əgéip/. ▶ぽっかりと口を開けている穴 a *gaping* hole. ● 口をぽっかり開けて with one's mouth *agape* [*wide open*]. ▶傷口がぽっかり開いていた The cut was *wide open*.
❷ [軽く] lightly. (! 副詞を添えなくても動詞でその意が出ている場合が多い) ▶雲がぽっかり空に浮かんでいる A cloud is floating (*lightly*) in the sky.
❸ [急に] suddenly. ▶弟がその時だし抜けにぽっかり姿を現した Just then my brother *turned* [×*showed*] *up suddenly* (*out of nowhere*). (! show up は「予定した人が現れる」の意)

ほっき 発起 图 proposal. (⇨提案) ● 市長の発起で at the *proposal* of the mayor.
── **発起する** 動 propose; (事業などを) promote.
● **発起人** (提起者) a proposer; (会社設立者) a promoter.

ぼっき 勃起 图 an erection.
── **勃起する** 動 get* [have*] an erection. ● 勃起したペニス an *erect* penis. ● 勃起不能 impotence. ● 勃起不能の impotent.

ぼっきゃく 却 ● 自己を没却する do not care about oneself; think nothing of oneself.

ほっきょく 北極 the North [Arctic] Pole. (⇨南極) ● 北極回り(の空路)でパリに行く fly to Paris by the route across the *North Pole*.
── **北極の** 形 arctic. ● 北極海 the Arctic Ocean. ● 北極圏 the Arctic Circle. ● 北極光 the northern lights; the auróra boreális. ● 北極星 the polestar (! しばしば the P-, the Pole Star); the North Star, Poláris. ● 北極探検(隊) an arctic expedition. ● 北極地方 the Arctic (region); the north polar region. ● 北極点 the geographical north pole.

ほっきょくぐま 北極熊 [動物] a polar bear.

ぽっきり ❶ [折れる様子の] (⇨ぽきんと) ❷ [それだけ] ● 2,000円ぽっきり only [just] 2,000 yen.

ほっく 発句 [連歌の] the first seventeen syllable line of a *tanga*; a *haiku*. (⇨俳句)

ホック a hook /húk/; (一対) a hook and eye (複) ~s and ~s). (⇨スナップ) ● ホックを留める (unhook) (! a dress). ▶スカートはスナップよりホックの方がしっかりとまると思う I think *hooks and eyes* would hold the skirt better than snaps.

ボックス a box (⇨箱); (劇場の) a box; (レストランなどの) a booth. ● 電話ボックス (主に米) a phóne [téléphone] bòoth; (主に英) a phóne [téléphone] bòx; (英) a cáll bòx.
● ボックスシート a box seat.

ぽっくり [下駄] (a pair of) lacquered wooden *geta* with high soles.

ぽっくり [急に] suddenly, all of a sudden; (思いがけなく) unexpectedly. ▶ぽっくり死ぬ a *sudden* [an *unexpected*] death. ▶その青年は外国でぽっくり死んだ The young man died *suddenly* abroad.

ほっけ [魚介] an Atka mackerel.

ほっけ 法華 ❶ [お経] (⇨法華(ǔ)経) ❷ [宗派] (日蓮宗) the Nichiren sect; (天台宗) the Tendai sect.
● **法華の太鼓** ● だんだんよく鳴る法華の太鼓 The more you know about it, the more it grows upon you [you come to like it].

ホッケー [スポーツ] hockey /háki/. ● (米) ではアイスホッケー (ice hockey), (英) では陸上ホッケー (field hockey) をさすのが普通 ● ホッケーをする play *hockey*.

ぼっけん 木剣 a wooden sword.

ぼつご 没後 after one's death. ● 没後100年を記念するコンサート a concert to mark the *centennial* (米) [*centenary* (主に英)] of *one's death*.

ぼっこう 勃興 图 a rise. ── **勃興する** 動 rise*.

ぼっこうしょう 没交渉 ● 世間と没交渉の生活を送る live *isolated* from the world. ▶彼とはここ 2, 3 年間没交渉になっている I *have lost touch* [*have been out of touch*] with him for the past few years. (! いずれも touch の代わりに contact も可)

ほっこく 北国 a northern country. (⇨北国(ǔ))

『**ボッコちゃん**』 *Bokko-chan*. (参考 星新一の小説)

ぼっこん 墨痕 ● 墨痕鮮やかにしたためられた書状 a letter written with fine [skillful] strokes of the (writing) brush.

ほっさ 発作 an attack; (軽い) a fit. (! 後の方は「感情の激発」の意でも用いる) ● 心臓 [ぜんそく] の発作に襲われる have a heart [an asthmatic] *attack*. ▶彼は絶望のあまり発作的に屋上から飛び降りた He jumped from the rooftop *in a fit* of despair.

ぼっしゅう 没収 图 confiscation; (罰として没収) forfeiture /fɔ́:rfətʃər/. ● 財産の没収 the *confiscation* of (his) property.
── **没収する** 動 confiscate; (罰として没収される) forfeit /fɔ́:rfət/. ▶彼は免許証を没収された His license *was confiscated* (by the police)./He *forfeited* his license (by killing a person in an accident). (⇨取り上げる)
● 没収試合 a forfeited game. ● 没収物 a confiscated item; a confiscation.

ぼつしゅみ 没趣味 ● 没趣味な 形 ● 没趣味な文章(おもしろくない) a *dull* [a *tasteless*] prose. ● 没趣味な(=単調な)日常生活 a *monotonous* [a *drab*] everyday life. ● 没趣味な (退屈な) a *dull* [a *boring*] person; a bore; (趣味をもたない) a person *who has no hobby* [*pastime*].

ぼっしょ 没書 (不採用な) a rejected manuscript [letter to the editor]. ● 没書にする reject [turn down] a manuscript [a contribution].

ほっしん 発心 ── **発心する** 動 [[信仰心をもつ]] become* religious; get* religion; (信仰に心が動かされる) be religiously awakened; [[決心する]] make* a resolution; make up one's mind《to do》.

ほっしん 発疹 ● 発疹 (on the back). ▶私はストレスが原因の発疹が時々できる I sometimes break [come] out in a *rash* when I'm stressed.

ほっす 払子 a *hossu*; (説明的に) a duster-like article a Buddhist priest has in his hand when he gives a religious talk in a dignified manner.

ほっす 法主 (⇨法主(ǔ))

ほっする 欲する want, 《書》desire; (…を欲しがる) wish for …. (⇨望む, 欲しい) ▶彼はおのれの欲するままに行動する He acts as he *wishes* [*pleases*].

ぼっする 没する ❶ [[沈む]] (太陽などが) go* down, set*, sink* (in the west, below the horizon). ● (船などが) 水中に沈む *go down under* [*sink into*, *sink under the surface of*] the water. ▶雪はひざを没するほどの深さだった The snow was [lay] knee-deep. ❷ [[死ぬ]] die (~d; dying).

ぼつぜん 没前 before one's death; before one dies.

ほっそく 発足 图 (an) inauguration.
── **発足する** 動 (設立する) set*… up; (始める) start. ▶特別委員会が発足した The special committee *has been set up* [*been established*].

ほっそり ● ほっそりした slim (-mm-); (やや書) slender (! 前の語より優美さが強調される). ▶黒を着るとほっそり見える Black is a slimming color./Black

ほったてごや 掘っ建て小屋 a hut;《しばしば軽蔑的》a shanty, a shack.

ポツダム 《ドイツの都市》Pótsdam. ●ポツダム宣言 the Potsdam Declaration.

ほったらかす 《世話をしない》neglect;《…しないでおく》leave*; undone. ●ほったらかしの子供 a *neglected* [an *uncared-for*] child. ●家族をほったらかす *neglect* one's family. ●仕事をほったらかす *leave* one's job *undone*; *neglect* one's task. ●道路はほったらかしにされてひどい状態だった The road was in bad condition from *neglect*.

ほったん 発端 《起こり》an origin;《始まり》a beginning. ●事の発端の *origin* of an affair. ●事の発端から from the (very) *beginning* [*start*].

ぼっち 没地 the place of one's death.

-ぼっち ▶100円ぼっちしかない I have *only* one hundred yen. (🚫) では I *only* have óne hundred yen. というのが普通 ●彼の言うことにはこれっぽっちの真実もない There isn't *a grain* [*an ounce*] of truth in what he says.

ホッチキス a stapler. (⇨ホチキス)

ぼっちゃり ●ぼっちゃりしたほっぺ *chubby* [*plump*] cheeks. ●ぼっちゃりした少女 a *chubby* [a *plump*] girl.

ぼっちゃん 坊ちゃん 《敬称》your [his, her] son;《呼びかけ》boy;《年少者や男の子》son. ●彼は坊ちゃん育ちで《=過保護に育ったので》世間知らずだ He's had a *sheltered upbringing* and doesn't know (anything about) the world. (🚫) 主語は she とすれば「お嬢さん育ち」となる
●坊ちゃん刈り a boy's haircut;《説明的に》a style of a boy's hair in which it is cut evenly in the front and short around the neck.

ぼっちゃん『坊っちゃん』 *Botchan*. 〔参考〕夏目漱石の小説

古今ことばの系譜 『坊っちゃん』
卒業してから八日目に校長が呼びに来たから、何か用だろうと思って、出掛けて行ったら、四国辺のある中学校で数学の教師がいる。月給は四十円だが、行ってはどうだという相談である。（略）この相談を受けた時、行きましょうと即座に返事をした。Eight days after the graduation the director of the school asked to see me. I went to his office wondering what he wanted. A middle school in Shikoku needed a mathematics teacher. The salary was forty yen a month. ... when I heard the details I answered immediately that I would go. (Burton Watson)(🚫)(1)「呼びに来た」といっても校長自ら来たのではない、用務員などに呼びに来させたのであろうから、訳のようになる。(2) A middle school ... は He said なしで話した内容を示しているが、これによって原文のスピーディな語りの調子が出る) (⇨奉公)

ほっつきあるく ほっつき歩く wander [《やや書》roam] about;《遊び歩く》《話》gad (-dd-) about. ▶こんな時間までどこをほっつき歩いてたのだ Where have you been all this while?

ボッティチェリ 〔イタリアの画家〕Botticelli /bàtitʃéli/ (Sandro 〜).

ぼってり ●ぼってりした唇 thick [*fleshy*] lips. ●ぼってりした中年女性 a *stout* [a *fat-looking*] middle-aged woman. ●ぼってり着込んだ彼の姿《主に書》his *heavily*-clad figure.

ぽってり (⇨ぼってり)

ほっと ●ほっと息をつく give [breathe, utter,《書》heave] a sigh《*of*》; sigh. (🚫)《悲哀・疲労・安堵》・賞賛・あきらめなどから》音でわかるくらい深く息を

つく ●ほっとしたことには to one's relief. ▶聴衆はその演技にほっと賛嘆の溜(ﾀﾒ)め息をもらした The audience *gave a sigh of* admiration at the performance. ▶母は息子が無事だと聞いてほっとした The mother *gave a sigh of relief* [*felt relieved*] when she heard her son was safe./The mother *felt relieved* (to hear) that her son was safe. 〔会話〕「あなたの血液検査の結果は陰性です」「あー、ほっとしましたよ」"The results of your blood test are negative." "What a *relief*!/That's a *load off my mind*!"

ホット ── **ホットな** 〔形〕〔新しい; 熱い〕hot (-tt-);《最新の》the latest;《人気のある》popular. ●ホットな観光スポット a *popular* tourist spot.
●ホットカーペット an electric carpet;《和製語》a hot carpet. ●ホットカーラー《温熱で髪を巻く器具》a hot roller. (🚫)(1) しばしば複数形で. (2) この意では a hot curler はまれ. (3) an electric hair curler は1本のこてのような形のもので髪を巻く器具》●ホットケーキ《米》a hót càke, a pancake. ●ホットコーナー〔野球〕the hot corner. 〔参考〕三塁手の守備位置 ●ホットコーヒー (hot) coffee. (🚫) hot はつけないのが普通. 単に hot とはいわない (⇨コーヒー) ●ホットドッグ a hot dog. ●ホットニュース hot news; the latest news. ●ホットプレート a (portable) hotplate. ●ホットマネー〔国際短期資金〕hot money. ●ホットライン a hot line《*to*》. ●ホットリスト〔コンピュータ〕a hotlist.

ぽっと ●ぽっと顔を赤らめる blush;《紅潮させる》flush. ▶スイッチをひねるとガスはぽっと《=勢いよく》点火した I turned on the gas and it lit *vigorously*.

ポット 《紅茶の》a teapot;《コーヒーの》a coffeepot;《魔法瓶》a thermos (bottle《英》).

ほっとう 没頭 ── **没頭する** 〔動〕〔夢中になる〕be absorbed《*in*》;〔努力・注意を集中する〕concentrate《*on*》;〔捧げる〕《やや書》devote oneself [one's time]《*to*》;〔一心に従事する〕occupy oneself, be occupied《*with*, *in*》. (⇨専念) ●読書に没頭する be *buried* [*be engrossed*] *in* one's book. ●彼はウイルスの生態研究に没頭した He *devoted himself to* the research of the virus's behavior.

ほっとうにん 発頭人 《張本人》the author of the plot; a conspirator;《首謀者》the ringleader.

ほっとく 放っとく (⇨放っておく)

ぼっとで ぽっと出 ●ぽっと出の《a girl [a boy]》fresh from the country.

ぼつにゅう 没入 ── **没入する** 〔動〕●仕事に没入している《=夢中になっている》be absorbed in one's work. (⇨没頭)

ぼつねん 没年 the year of one's death;《享年(ｷｮｳﾈﾝ)》one's age at death.

ぽつねんと all alone; by oneself. ▶老人が一人庭の奥を見つめぽつねんと座っていた There I found an old man sitting *by himself* looking into the far end of the garden.

ぼっぱつ 勃発 图 an outbreak, a sudden occurrence.
── **勃発する** 〔動〕break* out, occur (-rr-) suddenly. ▶第一次世界大戦は1914年に勃発した World War I *broke out* in 1914.

ほっぴょうよう 北氷洋 《北極海》the Arctic Ocean.

ホップ ❶〔植物〕a hop;《苦み料》hops.
❷〔跳び方〕a hop. ●ホップ・ステップ・ジャンプ《三段跳び》《話》*hop*, step, and jump. (🚫) the triple jump が普通
❸〔投球の〕a hop. ●ホップする速球 a fastball with a *hop*; a hopping fastball.

ポップ 《話》pop. (!*popular* (*song*) から) (⇨ポピュラー))
- ポップシンガー a pop singer. ●ポップスター a pop star. ●ポップフライ (⇨ポップフライ)

ポップアート pop art.
ポップアップ 〔飛び出す絵本〕a pop-up.
- ポップアップメニュー 〔コンピュータ〕a pop-up menu.

ポップコーン popcorn, (電子レンジで作る) microwave popcorn.
ポップス pop music, 《話》pop;(その歌)a pop (song). (!pop は popular の略)
- ポップコンサート a pop concert.

ポップフライ 〔野球〕a pop (fly); a pop-up. ●ポップフライを打ち上げる pop-up. ●一塁へのポップフライでアウトになる pop out to first.

ほっぺた 頬っぺた a cheek. (⇨頬(ﾊ))
- ほっぺたが落ちそう ほっぺたが落ちそうなほどおいしい be [taste] absolutely delicious.

ほっぽ ぼっぽ(=ふところ)が暖かい have a fat purse.
ほっぽう 北方 图 the north. (⑱ 南方) ▶スウェーデンはデンマークの北方にある Sweden is [lies] (*to the*) *north of* Denmark. (!to の ばしばは省略する) ▶スウェーデンはヨーロッパの北方(= 北部)にある Sweden is *in the northern part of* [*in the north of*] Europe. (!上例と比較. スウェーデンはヨーロッパ大陸に位置しているので to the north of とはならないことに注意. Sweden is *in northern* Europe. ともいう (⇨南部)) ▶その村は町の北方 10 マイルの所にある The village is ten miles *north of* the town.
— 北方の 厖 north; northern. (!後の語は方位のやや不明確なときに用いる傾向がある)
— 北方へ 副 northward; toward the north; north.
- 北方領土 the Northern Territories.

ほつほつ 图 (発疹(ﾊｯｼﾝ)) a rash; (斑点(ﾊﾝﾃﾝ)) spots; (草かぶれ) a nettle. ▶熱が出てぼつぼつできた I had a *rash* when I ran a high fever.

ぼつぼつ 副 ❶ 〔ゆっくり〕slowly, at a slow pace; (着実に) steadily, (のんびりと) leisurely, (徐々に) gradually, (少しずつ) little by little. (⇨ぽちぽち) ▶ガイドが我々にぼつぼつ登るように助言した The guide advised us to climb *slowly* [*at a slow pace*]. ▶その店では午前中はぼつぼつ仕事をする At the shop they work *leisurely* in the morning. ▶ぼつぼつ桜の花が咲き始めた The cherry blossoms have begun to bloom *little by little*.
❷ 〔間もなく〕soon, (程なく) before long. ▶ぼつぼつ来るんじゃないかな He will come *soon*. ▶ぼつぼつ出かけようか Let's get going *soon*.

ぼつぼつ 图 a rash; spots. (⇨ほつほつ 图)
ぼつぼつ 副 (⇨ぼつぼつ 副, ぼちぼち 副 ❶) ▶ぼつぼつ水が落ちている Water is falling *in drops*. ▶雨がぽつぽつ降り始めた It began to rain (*lightly*)./Rain began to fall *in light drops*. ▶青い海に小さい島がぽつぽつ(= 点々と)ある The blue sea *is dotted with* small islands. ▶避暑に来ていた人たちもぽつぽつ帰り始めた People who had stayed here to avoid the heat of the summer began to *trickle home* [to go home *by twos and threes*].

翻訳のこころ 大通りにはクリスマスソングが流れ, 薄青い夕暮れに, ネオンがぽつぽつきはじめていた (江國香織『デューク』) Christmas songs were heard in [on] the main (×big) street and neon lamps began to light here and there in the pale blue dusk. (!(1) 「大通り」は街中の主な通りの意なので a main street とする. (2) 「ぽつぽつ」は here and there (あちらこちらに) と表す. (3) 「夕暮れ」は dusk)

ぽっぽと ▶列車がぽっぽと走っていった The train went *puffing away*. ▶ふろから上がると体中がぽっぽとほてった I was *steaming hot* after the bath.

ぽっぽや 『鉄道員』 *Railroad Man*. [参考] 浅田次郎の小説
ほっぽらかす (⇨ほったらかす)
ぼつらく 没落 图 ▶帝国の没落(= 滅亡) the *downfall* [*fall*] of an empire.
— 没落する 動 ▶どうして彼の家族は没落(=滅亡)したのか What brought about the ruin 〔転落〕*downfall*〕 of his family? (⇨落ちぶれる)

ぽつり ▶雨がぽつりと落ちてきた A *drop* of rain came down. ▶彼はぽつりと(=不意に)自分がやったと言った He *unexpectedly* said (that) he had done it. ▶彼女はぽつりと(=ひとこと)いいですと言った She let out *a single word of* "yes."/She simply said "Yes."

ボツリヌスきん ボツリヌス菌 a botulinus; a botulinum.
- ボツリヌス菌中毒 botulism.

ぽつりぽつり (⇨ぽつぽつ) ▶老人は昔のことをぽつりぽつり話した *Little by little* the old man [woman] talked about his [her] old days.

ほつれ ▶髪のほつれをかき上げる comb back one's *loose* [*loosely hanging*] *hair* with one's fingers. ●布の切り口のほつれ *frayed threads* at the cut edge of cloth.

ほつれる (髪・ひもなど) get*[come*] loose; (衣服・ロープなどが) become* frayed.
ボツワナ 〔国名〕Botswana /bɑtswɑ́ːnɑ/; (公式名) the Republic of Botswana. (首都 Gaborone) ●ボツワナ人 a Botswanan; (総称) Botswana. ●ボツワナ(人)の Botswanan.

ぽつんと ▶廊下を歩いていると窓辺に彼が一人ぽつんと立っているのが見えた I saw him standing *all alone* [*on his own*] by a window in the corridor. ▶木が 1 本ぽつんと野原に立っている A *solitary* tree stands in a field. ▶天井からしずくがぽつんと落ちてきた A *drop* of water fell from the ceiling.

ほてい 布袋 *Hotei*; (説明的に) one of the seven gods of good luck. He is the god of contentment and happiness with a big belly and happy, smiling face. He carries a large cloth bag full of daily necessities on his back.
- 布袋腹 a big belly; (太鼓腹) a potbelly.

ほてい 補訂 — 補訂する 動 rivise and enlarge 《a dictionary》.
- 補訂版 a revised and enlarged edition.

ほてい 補綴 (⇨補綴(ﾎﾃｲ))
ボディー 〔体〕a body. ▶このドレスはほっそりしたボディーラインがくっきり出るようなデザインになっています This dress is designed to outline your slender *body*. (!「ボディーラインを強調する服」は tight clothes, a slinky dress などという)
- ボディーウェア bodywear. ●ボディーシャンプー liquid soap;《和製語》body shampoo. ●ボディースーツ a bodysuit. ●ボディーブロー 〔ボクシング〕a body blow. ●ボディーボード (板) a body board; (行為) body boarding. ●ボディーランゲージ 〔身体言語〕body language.

ボディーガード a bodyguard. ▶大統領のボディーガードが角に立っていた The President's *bodyguard* was [were] standing at the corner. (!一人にも集合体にも用いる)

ボディーチェック ❶ 〔空港などでの〕a body search; a security check. (!この意での ×body check は和製英語 (⇨❷)) ●ボディーチェックを受ける be body searched, 《話》be frisked; undergo a *body*

ボディービル

search.
❷【アイスホッケー】a body check. (参考) 相手選手の動きを体当たりで妨害すること)

ボディービル body-building. ●ボディービルをする人 a body-builder. ●ボディービルをする work out with weights.

ボディコン 〚曲線美を強調する服〛tight-fitting [skin-tight] (women's) clothes. 注 body conscious などは用いない

ほてつ 補綴 〚医学〛a prosthesis.

ポテト a potato /pətéitou/ (複 ～es). ●ベークドポテト a baked *potato*. ●マッシュポテト mashed *potato(es)*;《英》mash.
●ポテトチップス《米》(potato) chips,《英》(potato) crisps. ●ポテトフライ《米》French fried potatoes, French fries,《英》(potato) chips.

ほてり 火照り (顔面の) a glow; a flush; (赤面) a blush.

***ホテル** a hotel /houtél/; (自動車旅行者用の) a motel /moutél/; (古風な) an inn. ●神戸ホテルに泊まる stay at the Kobe *Hotel* [(the) *Hotel* Kobe]. 注 この言い方は《米》では無冠詞のことが多い ●三つ星のホテル a three-star *hotel*. ●ホテルに部屋を予約する reserve [make a reservation for] a room at a *hotel*; reserve a *hotel* room. ●ホテルに着く arrive at a *hotel*; (記帳をすませる) check in at a *hotel*. ●ホテルを出る leave a *hotel*; (手続き後) check out of a *hotel*. ▶どこのホテルに泊まるつもりですか Which [What, Where] *hotel* are you going to stay at [in]?
●ホテルマン a hotel employee. 注 a hotel man は「経営者」の意)

ほてる 火照る (紅潮させる) flush; (燃えるように熱く感じる) burn*; (熱く感じる) feel* hot. ▶彼女はほてった顔をしていた She *was flushed* with the heat. ▶私は恥ずかしくて顔が火のようにほてるのを感じた I *felt burning hot* in the face with shame. ▶日焼けをして顔がほてる I *feel hot* in the face from sunburn. ▶彼は熱で体がほてっていた He *was burning up* with fever. 注 進行形のみ ▶少し走ると体がほてってきた When I ran awhile, the *heat rose* through my body.

ほてん 補填 ── **補填する 動** ●損失を補填する *make up* the loss. ●赤字を補填する *make good* the loss.

ポテンシャル 〚潜在能力, 可能性〛(a) potential.

ポテンヒット (⇒⑨ テキサスヒット)

***ほど 程** ❶【比較】①【A ほど B ではない】not as [so] B as A. 注 (1) so を用いるのは《米》では文語的. (2) B は形容詞・副詞または「形容詞+a(an)+名詞」) ▶私は彼ほど料理はうまくない I can't cook as [so] well *as* he can. 注 so を用いる場合, so に強勢を置くと私も彼も料理がうまいことを前提とするが, not に強勢を置くと as と同様にそのような含意はない)/I can't cook *better than* he can./I'm *not such a* good cook [(書) *as* good a cook, ×as a good cook] *as* he is. ▶それは思ったほど高くなかった It was *not so* expensive *as* I (had) [×I've] expected./It wasn't *more* (《やや書》was *less*) expensive *than* I (had) [×I've] expected. 注 いずれもくだけた言い方では had を省略する ▶私は兄ほどたくさんのお金 [本] を持っていない I don't have *as much* money [*many* books] *as* my brother. 注 (1) much は不可算名詞と, many は可算名詞複数形とともに用いる. (2) ×… have money as much [books as many] as…, は不可)
会話 「簡単？」「君が考えているほど簡単ではないよ」"Is it easy?" "*Not so* easy *as* you might think."
②【A ほど B なものはない】nothing be as B as [more B than] A. 注 B は形容詞 ▶そのチームで真紀子ほど背が高い者はいない Makiko is taller *than any other* member [*the other* members, ×any other members] in the team. 注 any other … の方が強意的)/Makiko is the tallest in the team./《やや書》Nobody [No one] in the team is *as* [*so*] tall *as* Makiko. 注 「真紀子と同じ背の高さまでくる人はいない」の意. *Nobody* [*No one*] in the team is taller *than* Makiko./Makiko is *as* tall *as any* member in the team. は「真紀子と同じ背の高さの人はいるかもしれないがそれ以上の人はいない」の意) ▶彼の音楽ほどすばらしいものはない There's *nothing as* wonderful *as* [*more* wonderful *than, like*] his music./《やや書》*Nothing* is *as* wonderful *as* [*more* wonderful *than*] his music./(他のどの音楽よりも)《やや書》*No other* music is *as* wonderful *as* [*more* wonderful *than*] his. ▶父が死んだときほど悲しいことはなかった I was *never* [I'd *never* been, ×I've never been] sad*der than* when my father died.

❷【程度】①【…ほど～だ】(…なほど A だ) so A ((that) 節); 《口話》では that を省略することが多い; too A to (do); (…するほど十分に A だ) A enough to (do). 注 (1) 以上いずれも A は形容詞・副詞 ▶部屋は字が読めないほど暗かった The room was *so* dark (*that*) I couldn't read./《口話》I couldn't read, the room was *so* dark./The room was *too* dark (*for* me) *to* read. ▶それは言葉で表せないほどすばらしい It's *too* wonderful *for* words./It's *beyond description*. ▶彼が私にとってどれほど大切かは言葉ではちょっと言い表せないか I just can't tell you *how much* he means to me. ▶私にはすることが山ほど(=たくさん)ある I have *a lot of* things [*a pile of* work] to do.

②【…ほど…ではない】▶彼はそれを信じるほどのばかではない He is not foolish *enough* [He knows better *than*] *to* believe it. 注 He is not *so* foolish *as to*…. ともいえるが一般的ではない ▶その子はそれほど(=あまり)わんぱくではない The boy is not *very* [《口話》*(all) that*, 《書》*so*, ×as] naughty. 注 so は The boy is *not* so naughty *as* he was [I thought]. (以前[思った]ほどわんぱくではない)の省略表現 (⇒❶) ▶彼はこれという(=とりたてていう)ほどの詩は書いていない He wrote *no* poems *to speak of*. 注 *to speak of* は通例否定文で用いる)

❸【およそ】about, around; some (注 複数の数詞の前で用いる); (…かそのくらい) or so. (⇒約) ●50 分ほど歩く walk for *about* [*some*] fifty minutes; walk for fifty minutes *or so*. ●1 週間ほど前 *about* [×*some*] a week ago; a week *or so* ago. ▶あの人には 2 回ほどしか会っていない I've only met him (*about*) twice. 注 日本語でぼかし語として用いられる場合は訳す必要はない: それを三つほどいただくわ I'll take (×about) three of them.)

❹【すればするほど】the (+比較級), the (+比較級). 注 前の the は 「…するほど」, 後の the は 「それだけいっそう」の意 ▶多ければ多いほどよい *The more, the better*. ▶宝石は大きければ大きいほど高い *The bigger* a jewel is, *the* more expensive it is [×*the* more it is expensive]. ▶上へ登るほど空気は新鮮になるだろう *The* higher you climb, *the* fresher the air will become./*As* you climb higher, (*so*) the air will become fresher. 注 前の言い方より口語的. 未来のことでも前半の節は現在時制

●**程がある** ▶我慢にもほどがある(我慢の限度にきた) I've reached the *limit(s)* of my patience./(堪忍袋の緒が切れた) This is the last straw. 注 慣用表現

ほどあい (もう彼[それ]には我慢できない) I can't be patient with him [of it] any longer. ▶冗談にもほどがある (冗談が過ぎる) You are carrying your joke too far./(ほどほどにしろ) Don't carry your joke too far. ▶のうずましいにもほどがある(=何というあつかましさだ)《話》What a nerve!

ほどあい 程合い ── **程合いの** 形 suitable; right. ▶湯は程合いの熱さまで冷えた The hot water cooled down [off] to *just the right* temperature.

ほどう 歩道 (車道に対する)《主に米》a sidewalk,《英》a pavement (*!*《米》では「車道」の意); (散歩道) a walk; (遊歩道) a promenade (*!*《英》では特に海辺のものをさす),《英話》a prom. ▶横断歩道 ⇨ 横断歩道 ● 動く歩道に乗っている stand on a moving *sidewalk*.
● **歩道橋** a pedestrian bridge [《主に米》overpass,《英》flyover]; (二つの建物を結ぶ) a walkway.

ほどう 補導 名 guidance. ▶青少年の補導 the *protection and guidance* of youth.
── **補導する** 動 guide. ▶警察に補導される(=捕まって注意される) be caught and admonished by the police.

ほどう 舗道 a paved road.

ほどく 解く (結び目などを) undo*, untie (〜d; -tying). (⇨解く❶) ● 靴のひもをほどく *undo* [*untie*] one's shoelaces; *unlace* one's shoes. ▶縫い目をほどく *undo* [*unpick*] the seams. ▶編み物をほどく *undo* [*unravel*] one's knitting.

ほとけ 仏 (the) Buddha /búːdə/, a Buddha (*!* つづり字に注意. h を抜かす誤りが多い); [故人]《書》the deceased (*!* 単・複両扱い); [死人] a dead person.
● 無縁仏 (⇨無縁) ▶彼女は仏の慈悲にすがった She threw herself on the mercy of (the) *Buddha*.
▶知らぬが仏 ⇨知らぬ [成句]
● **仏作って魂入れず** One makes a Buddha image, but fails to put a soul in it./(最後の仕上げをしていない) You do not put the finishing touches to your work.
● **仏の顔も三度まで** Even a Buddha gets angry if he is stroked on the face three times./(どんな人の忍耐にも限度がある) There is a limit to anyone's patience.
● **仏心** (慈悲深い心) a merciful heart.

ほとけのざ 仏の座 [植物]〚キク科の〛a nipplewort [参考] 春の七草の一つ); 〚シソ科の〛a henbit; a perfoliate-archangel.

ほどける 解ける (ひもが) come* loose [undone]; (もつれた糸・編み物などが) unravel /ʌnrǽvəl/, get* unraveled. ▶靴ひもがほどけた My shoelaces *came undone*.

ほどこし 施し (行為) almsgiving /ɑ́ːmzgìvɪŋ/; charity; (物) alms (*!* 単・複同形); a handout. (*!* a cash handout, a handout of money のように用いる.「乞食に与える物」という意識がつきまとう語) ▶私は人の施しは受けない、これからは自力で生活しますI won't take *charity*. I live on my own from now on. ▶我々は政府の施しを求めているのではない. ただ欲しいのは仕事なのだ We're not asking for government *handouts*. We're just asking for our jobs.

*ほどこす **施す** ❶[与える] give*. ▶金をいくらか施す *give*〖him〗a little money; *give* a little money 〖*to* him〗. ▶彼に傷の応急手当を施しておいた I *have given* him first-aid treatment for the injury.
❷[行う] do*. ▶人に多くの親切を施す *do* other people [others] many kindnesses. ▶こうなってはもう手の施しようがない(=できることは何もない) Under the circumstances, nothing can be done

[there's nothing we can *do*].
❸[その他の表現] That work *did* her credit [credit *to* her]. ▶ハンカチには花の刺しゅうが施されてあった The handkerchief *was embroidered with* flowers.

ほどちかい 程近い near; a short way from.... ● ハイドパークに程近い高級ホテル a high class hotel *near* [*not far from*] Hyde Park.

ほどとおい 程遠い far from.... (⇨遠い❸)

ほととぎす [鳥] a little cuckoo /kúːkuː/(㊹〜s);〚植物〛a toad lily.

ほどなく 程なく (間もなく) soon,《やや書》before long; (じきに) shortly. (⇨ 間もなく)

ほとばしる (力強く噴き出す) spurt; (大量に噴き出る) gush. ▶血が傷口からほとばしり出た Blood *spurted* [*gushed*] from the wound.

ほどへて 程経て after a while. (*!* 数年から数十分まで不定の時間の長さを表す)

ほとほと まったく 形 quite, utterly;〚本当に〛really. ▶私はほとほと自分がいやになった I am *utterly* [*completely*] disgusted with myself. ▶こういう生活がほとほといやになった I am *quite* tired of [am sick and tired of] this life./《話》I'm *fed up with* this life. ▶彼のことではほとほと手を焼いている I'm *quite* at a loss what to do with him.

ほどほど 程々 名 moderation.
── **ほどほどの** 形 moderate.
 会話 「戦争はもう始まってしまったのだからあとは早く終わるよう願うか」「同感だ. ほどほどのうちにね」"Now the war has started, I hope it'll end soon." "So do I. Within a *reasonable* period of time."
── **ほどほどに** 副 moderately. ● ほどほどに酒を飲む(適度に) drink *in moderation* ▶ほどほどに酒を飲む人 be a *moderate* drinker という); (飲み過ぎない) don't drink too much [《書》to excess]. ▶何事もほどほどに Be *moderate* in all things. ▶酒はほどほどにしておけ《話》*Go easy on the sake!* (*!* 命令文〔的〕に用いることが多い)

ぽとぽと ● ぽとぽとしずくが落ちる drip. ▶レインコートから廊下にぽとぽと水が落ちているよ Your raincoat *is dripping* with water onto the hall floor./Water *is dripping* (*down*) from your raincoat onto the hall floor.

ほとぼり ● ほとぼりが冷める ▶事件のほとぼりが冷めるまで(=世間の人々が興味を失うまで)彼は身を隠していた He hid himself until *the public lost interest* in the affair [興奮が冷める] *the excitement* about the affair *cooled down*, (うわさが静まるまで) *the rumors* about the affair *died down*].

ポトマック ・ ポトマック川 the Potomac /pətóumək/.

ボトム 〚底〛the bottom;〚下半身用の衣服〛bottoms (↔tops) (*!* (1) 通例複数形で. (2) パジャマなどのズボンをさす).

ボトムアウト ── **ボトムアウトする** 動 〚相場などが底入れする〛bottom out.

ボトムアップ ● ボトムアップ式の〚下から上への〛bottom-up (↔top-down).

ほどよい 程よい (度を越していない) reasonable; (最適の) right; (適度の) moderate. ● ほどよい運動量 a *moderate* amount of exercise. ● ほどよく(=心地よく)疲れる be *pleasantly* tired. ▶学校は駅からほどよい距離のところにある Our school is a *reasonable* [㾱 a good] *distance* away from the station. (*!* good を用いると「かなりの」の意) ▶彼はほどよい時間に現れた He appeared at the *right* [*appropriate*] time. ▶この部屋はほどよい(=快適な)暖かさだ This room is *comfortably* warm.

ほとり (⇨河畔、湖畔) ● その川のほとりに near [by, on]

ぽとりと the river (!後の語ほど川に近い); on the bank of the river. ▶湖のほとりを歩く walk along the edge of the lake.

ぽとりと ぽとりと落ちる drop; fall; 《水滴が》drip.

ボトルキープ the keeping of one's own bottle of liquor in one's favorite bar;《和製語》bottle keep.

ボトルネック〚支障〛a bottleneck.

ほとんど 殆ど ❶〘肯定的に〙almost (!形容詞・過去分詞の前で), nearly; (およそ) about (⇨約); (ほとんど…も同然) as good as, practically, virtually; (大部分が) mostly.

> 解説 **almost** は「あとわずかなところで到達していない」ことを, **nearly** は「接近していてあともうすぐで到達しそう」なことを強調する. したがって almost の方が nearly より強意的で, almost＝very nearly と考えてよい. (i) nearly は very, pretty, not などの修飾を受けるが, almost は受けない. (ii) almost is no, never などの否定語や any (どんな…にも), the same, the only, the first などの語を修飾できるが, nearly はできない. (⇨❷)(iii) almost は感情・思考を示す形容詞・動詞を修飾できるが, nearly は時間・位置・具体的な状態を示す語しか修飾できない.

● ほとんど満員の電車 a train almost [about] full; a near-full [an almost full] train. ● ほとんど 1 年中家にいる stay (at) home most of the year. ▶ほとんど(すべて)の学生が英語を勉強している Almost all (of) the students are [Almost every student is] studying English. (!almost の代わりに nearly も可. almost や nearly は名詞を直接修飾することはできないので ×Almost [×Nearly] the students…. は不可)/(大部分の)学生が英語を勉強している Most students [Most of the students] are studying English. (!前の方は学生一般を, 後の方は特定の学生集団をさす. ×Most of students…. や ×The most students…. は不可) ● 昼間はほとんど(いつも)家にいます I nearly [almost] always stay [I'm usually] (at) home during the day. (!×I nearly [almost] stay…. は不可) ▶夏休み中はほとんどずっと北海道にいた I was in Hokkaido almost all the summer vacation. (!×I was almost in Hokkaido during the summer vacation. は不可) ▶我々はそこほとんど 1 時間(ぐらい)待った We waited there for almost [nearly, about] one hour. (!almost は通例, nearly は常に 1 時間を下回るが, about では 1 時間前後をさす) ▶それはほとんど夢のようだった It was almost [×nearly] like a dream. ▶図書館はほとんど完成しました The library is almost [nearly] completed. ▶それはほとんど不可能だ It's almost [nearly, next to, practically, virtually] impossible. ▶このことをほとんど忘れていた I almost [×nearly] forgot about it. ▶私はあなたと体重はほとんど同じです I weigh about [almost] the same as you. (!これは量についてであるが, 質については The town is much [almost] the same now as it used to be. (その町は今も昔ほとんど変わりがない)のようにいう)/I weigh about [almost, nearly] as much as you. ▶彼らはほとんどが学生だった They were mostly [〘主に〙] mainly] students./Most of them were students. ▶彼はほとんど死んだも同然だ He is practically [as good as, all but] dead.

会話「もう終わったの?」「ほとんどね」"Are you through (with it)?" "Almost [Just about]."

会話「そこでは何をしたの?」「ほとんど観光だよ」"What did you do there?" "Sightseeing, mostly."

❷〘否定的に〙(ほとんど…ない) hardly; scarcely; few; little*.

解説 **hardly** と **scarcely** は動詞を修飾するときは, 通例 be 動詞・助動詞の直後, 一般動詞の前に置き, 頻度を表す場合は通例 ever, at all を, 程度を表す場合はしばしば at all を伴う. 名詞を修飾するときは通例 any を伴い数量がほとんどないことを表す. scarcely の方が客観的でやや堅い訳. **few** は複数可算名詞の前で, **little** は不可算名詞の前で数量がほとんどないことを表す. いずれも, 不定冠詞を伴った a few や a little (⇨少し) と聞き分けが難しいため, 書き言葉以外では very, so, too などの修飾語を伴うのが普通. なお, little は副詞として動詞を修飾することがある.

▶彼はお金を持っていない He has hardly [scarcely] any money. (!(1) hardly, scarcely は既に否定の意を含んでいるので ×He doesn't have hardly [scarcely] any…. とはしない. (2) He hardly [scarcely] has any money. の語順も可)/He has very little money. (!His money is little. のような叙述用法は文語的)/He has almost no money. ▶彼にはほとんど会わない I hardly ever [almost never, 〘やや書〙very seldom] see him./〘話〙I see very little of him. (!(1) little は名詞. (2)「よく会う」は I see a lot of him.) ▶その事件についてほとんどだれも知らない Hardly anyone knows [Almost no one knows, Very few people know] the incident./The incident is almost unknown. ▶彼は昨夜ほとんど眠れなかった He could hardly [scarcely] sleep last night. (!この用法の hardly, scarcely は助動詞 could を修飾している)/He hardly [scarcely] slept (at all) last night./He could sleep [slept] very little last night. (!この用法の little は通例 very を伴い, 動詞より後に置く) ▶彼はひと言もしゃべらなかった He spoke hardly [scarcely] a word./He hardly [scarcely] spoke a word.

会話「彼にはフランス語の知識がありますか」「ほとんどありません」"Does he have any knowledge of French?" "Hardly [Scarcely] (at all)./Very little."

会話「ここにはよく来るの?」「ほとんど来ません」"Do you come here often?" "Hardly ever."

ほなみ 穂波 (説明的に) (a field of) rice [wheat, etc.] plants in ear waving in the wind.

ポニーテール《a girl with》a ponytail. ● 髪をポニーテールにしている have a ponytail; wear one's hair in a ponytail.

ほにゅう 哺乳 feeding. ● 哺乳ビン《米》a nursing bottle,《英》a feeding bottle. ● 哺乳類〘動物〙a mammal.

ぼにゅう 母乳 mother's milk, breast milk. ● 赤ん坊を母乳で育てる feed a baby on mother's milk; breast-feed (↔bottle-feed) a baby.

ほぬの 帆布 sailcloth.

ほね 骨 ❶〘人間などの〙(a) bone (!集合的には Ⓤ); (骨格) a skeleton. ● 魚の骨 a fish bone. ● 骨つきの肉 meat on bone. ● 魚を骨ごと食べる eat the fish bone(s) and all. ● 折れた骨を接ぐ set a broken bone. (!「骨を接いでもらう」は have a broken bone set) ● 魚の骨を取る bone a fish; take the bones out of a fish. ▶くしの中には骨で作られているものもある Some combs are made of bone. ▶この魚は骨が多い This fish has a lot of bones in it./This is a bony (↔a boneless) fish. ▶右腕の骨を折った I broke (a bone in) my right arm./I had my right arm broken. ▶あのおばあちゃんもとうとう骨になってしまった(＝死んでしまった) The old woman is dead [is gone, has passed away] after all. (!後の二つは婉曲的)

❷ 【気骨】 backbone (🅘 通例否定文で), spine; (気概) spirit. ▶骨のある人 a person *of spirit* [(不屈の精神) *fortitude*]; a person *with* spine. ▶あの男は骨がない He has no *backbone* [*spirit*].
・**骨が折れる** ▶骨の折れる仕事 laborious [*painstaking*, *backbreaking*] work; a *hard* [a *heavy*] job. ▶━は楽な仕事 an *easy* job. ▶ロシア語を覚えるのは骨が折れる Russian *is a hard* [*a difficult*] language *to learn*./*It is hard to* learn Russian. ▶その計画を実行するのに骨が折れた I *found it hard to* carry out the plan./I *had difficulty (in)* carrying out the plan. (🅘 *in* は通例省略する)
・**骨と皮になる** ▶彼女は長患いで骨と皮ばかりになっていた She was *very thin* [*skinny*] after a long illness./(話) She had become *all* [*only*, *just*] *skin and bone(s)* from a long illness. (🅘 ×*bone(s) and skin* とはいわない)
・**骨にしみる** (骨身にしみる)(⇨骨身 [成句])
・**骨の髄まで** ▶今日は骨の髄まで寒さがしみる Today I feel chilled *to the bone* [*marrow*]./ The cold bites me *through and through* today. ▶彼は骨の髄まで(＝徹頭徹尾)悪人だった He was a villain *through and through*./He was a *complete* villain.
・**骨までしゃぶる** ▶金貸しはその老人の骨(の髄)までしゃぶった (話) The money lender *bled* the old man [woman] *dry* [*white*].
・**骨を折る** ▶彼は君のためにいろいろ骨を折った He took a lot of *trouble* for you.
・**骨を埋める** ▶その医師は骨を埋める(＝残りの人生を過ごす)覚悟で離島に行った The doctor went to that isolated island with the intention of *staying there for the rest of* his *life* [(そこを最後の住む場所にする) *making it* his *final home*].
・**骨を拾う** (遺骨を)gather one's ashes.

ほねおしみ 骨惜しみ ━ ・骨惜しみをする (労を惜しむ)spare oneself. ・骨惜しみせずに(...する)《do》 without *sparing oneself*; *spare no effort* [*pains*] 《*to do*》; (骨を折る) take (great) pains [the trouble] 《*to do*》.

ほねおり 骨折り (苦労) trouble, pains (🅘 前の方が口語的); (つらい労働) labor; (労力) (an) effort; (尽力) a service, 《書》 good offices. ・無駄な骨折りに unrewarded *pains*. ▶その仕事はきつかったが骨折りがいがあった The work was really hard but it was worth the *trouble*. ▶彼は私たちのためにその切符を手に入れようと大変な骨折りをしてくれた He *took* [*had*] *a lot of trouble* [(話) *broke his neck*] *getting* the tickets for us./He *took great pains to* get the tickets for us. ▶大変な骨折りで彼らは車をぬかるみから引き出した With great *effort*, they pulled the car out of the mud.
・**骨折り損のくたびれもうけ** (ことわざ) Much pains, no gains./(骨折って獲た獲物はろうそく代にもならないくらい)《やや話》 The game is not [won't] worth the candle.

ほねおる 骨折る (⇨骨折り, 骨 [骨を折る])
ほねぐみ 骨組み (人・動物の骨格) a frame; (特に男性の体格) (a) physique, (人体の形と大きさ) (a) build (🅘 男女について用いられるが, 女性は通例 a figure を用いる); (枠組み) a framework, (構造体) a structure; (概要) an outline. ▶家の骨組みが the *frame* of a house. ▶がんじょうな骨組みの男性 a man of strong *build*; (体格のよい) a *well-built* man. ▶その計画の骨組みができ上がった I have completed the *outline* [*framework*] for the plan.

ほねつぎ 骨接ぎ bonesetting; (接骨医) a bonesetter. (⇨接骨) ▶骨接ぎをする set a bone [bones].

ほねぶし 骨節 ❶ 【関節】 a joint. (⇨骨太)
❷ 【気骨】 backbone (🅘 通例否定文で), spine; (気概) spirit. (⇨骨 ❷)
・**骨っ節の太い** large-boned.

ほねっぽい 骨っぽい 〖小骨の多い〗 bony; 〖気骨のある〗 (a man) with spirit. (⇨気骨, 骨 ❷)

ほねなし 骨なし ▶あいつは骨なしだ(気骨のない) He has no backbone./He is spineless.

ほねぬき 骨抜き ━ ・骨抜きの (骨を取った) boned; (肝心な箇所を抜かれた)《書》 eviscerated; (薄められた) watered-down. ▶法案を骨抜きにする *eviscerate* [*water down*] a bill. ▶民営化法案は族議員の手で骨抜きにされた The privatization bill *was watered down* by the interested group of Diet members.

ほねばった 骨ばった bony /bóuni/. ▶彼は骨ばった顔をしている He has a *bony* [an *angular*] face.

ほねばなれ 骨離れ ▶この魚は骨離れがいい We can *bone* this fish easily./We can easily *take out bones* from this fish.

ほねぶと 骨太 ━ 骨太の 圏 large-[big-]boned; (がっしりした) sturdily built. ・骨太の男 a *sturdily built* man. ・骨太の政策 a *large-boned* policy. ・骨太の(＝力強い)作品 a *dynamic* work.

ほねぼそ 骨細 ━ 骨細の 圏 fine-boned. ▶彼女は骨細で少年のようにすらっとしている She is fine-boned [exquisitely boned] and boyishly slender.

ほねみ 骨身 ・**骨身にこたえる** 彼の言葉が骨身にこたえた His words *cut me to the bone*.
・**骨身にしみる** ・骨身にしみる寒さ bone-chilling cold. ▶寒さが骨身にしみた I *was chilled* [*frozen*] *to the bone*.
・**骨身を惜しまない** ▶彼女は家族を養うため骨身を惜しまず働いた She worked *as hard as she could* [*without sparing herself*] to support her family.
・**骨身を削る** (懸命に事に当たる) work very hard 《*at*; *to do*》; (骨折る) break one's neck 《*to do*》. ・彼女の骨身を削るような(＝骨の折れる)努力 her *painstaking* efforts. ▶彼はローンを返済するために骨身を削って働いた He *toiled* (*away*) to pay back the loan.

ほねやすめ 骨休め (くつろぎ) relaxation; (休息) a rest. ▶骨休めにテレビで野球を見る watch a baseball game on TV *for relaxation*.
━ 骨休めする 動 ▶ゆっくり骨休めするために有馬温泉に行く go to the Arima hot springs *for* [*to take*, *to get*] *a good rest*.

****ほのお** 炎 a flame; (一瞬激しくゆらめく) (a) flare; (激しく燃え上がる) a blaze. ・燃えるろうそくの炎 the *flame* of the burning candle. ・マッチの炎 the *flare* of a match. ▶その建物は炎となって燃え落ちた The building fell *in flames*. ▶風が出てきて炎はますます大きくなってきた The *flames* are getting higher and higher as the wind is rising. ▶「助けて」と叫ぶ声が炎の中からした "Help!" cried a voice in the *blaze*./A cry for help came from the *blaze*.

ほのか ━ ほのかな 圏 (かすかな) faint; (薄暗くぼんやりした) dim (-mm-). ▶ほのかな明かり a *dim* [a *faint*] light. ▶ほのかにバラの香りがする There's a *faint* [a subtle /sʌ́tl/, a delicate /délikət/] fragrance of roses.

ほのぐらい ほの暗い dim (-mm-). ▶薄暗い ・ほの暗いランプの明かりの下で in the *dim* lamplight. ▶もう夜は明けていたが, あたりはまだほの暗かった It was after dawn, but still *a little dark*.

ほのじ ほの字 ▶彼はあの娘(ニ)にほの字だろう He cares for that girl, doesn't he?/He has a crush on that girl, right?

ほのじろい 仄白い ▶夕闇にほの白くうかぶ夕顔の花 whitish moon-flowers in the gathering dusk; moon-flowers looking whitish in the fading light.

ほのぼのと ❶〖薄暗くぼんやりと〗dimly. ❷〖心暖まる〗
● ほのぼのとした話 a *heartwarming* story.

ほのめかす 仄めかす ❶ hint; (言葉・態度などで) imply, suggest. ▶彼は自殺をほのめかした He *hinted* [*dropped a hint*] *that* he might kill himself./He *hinted* (*at*) the possibility of suicide. (〖後の方は堅い言い方〗) ▶その記事は真犯人はA氏であるとほのめかしていた The article *hinted* [*implied*, *suggested*] *that* Mr. A was the real culprit.

ホノルル 〖米国の都市〗Honolulu /hɑnəlúːluː/.

ホバークラフト a hovercraft.
● ホバークラフト港 a hoverport.

ほばく 捕縛 ── 捕縛する 動 capture; arrest.

ほばしら 帆柱 a mast.

ほはば 歩幅 a step; (大きな) a (long) stride. ● 大きな[小さな]歩幅で歩く walk with long [short] steps.

ホバリング ── ホバリングする 動 〖ヘリコプターが空中に停止する〗hover.

ほぼし 母斑 〖医学〗a nevus /níːvəs/ (覆 nevi /níːvaɪ/).

ぼひ 墓碑 a gravestone, a tombstone /túːmstòun/.
● 墓碑銘 an epitaph. (〖氏名と生没年だけのものから墓碑文を添えたものまでをいう〗)

ポピー 〖植物〗a poppy.

ほひつ 補筆 ── 補筆する 動 add ... to improve (the manuscript).

ポピュラー popular. (⇨ポップ)
● ポピュラー音楽 popular music. ● ポピュラーソング a popular song.

ポピュリスト 〖人民主義者〗a populist.

ぼひょう 墓標 a (wooden) grave post.

ボビン 〖糸巻き〗a bobbin.

ほふく 匍匐 ● 匍匐前進する crawl [creep] foward on the ground.

ボブスレー 〖そり〗a bobsleigh, a bobsled; 〖競技〗bobsledding. ● ボブスレーに乗る bobsleigh, bobsled.

ポプラ 〖植物〗a poplar. ● ポプラ並木 a row of *poplars* [*poplar* trees].

ポプリ 〖<フランス語〗(花香) (a) potpourri /pòupuríː/.

ほふる 屠る (動物・対戦相手を) slaughter.

ほへい 歩兵 a foot soldier, (男の) an infantryman (覆 -men); 〖集合的に〗the infantry (覆 単・複両扱い).

ほへい 募兵 ── 募兵する 動 invite《young people》to enter the army; recruit.

ボヘミア 〖チェコの地方〗Bohemia /bouhíːmiə/. ● ボヘミア人 a Bohemian. ● ボヘミア(人)の Bohemian.

ボヘミアン a bohemian /bouhíːmiən/. (〖!〗時に a Bohemian)
● ボヘミアングラス Bohemian glass.

ほほ 頬 a cheek. (⇨頬)

ほぼ 略 〖約〗about, around; (大ざっぱに) roughly /ráfli/; 〖ほとんど〗almost, nearly; 〖事実上〗practically; 〖大部分〗mostly, for the most part. (⇨約)
● ほぼ1割 *almost* [*roughly*] 10 percent. ▶仕事はほぼ終わった My work is *almost* [*nearly*, *practically*] finished. ▶彼が試合に勝つと言ってはほぼ間違いはない It is *probable* to say that he will win the game./He will *probably* win the game.

ほぼ 保母 (保育所の) a nursery school teacher.

ほほえましい 微笑ましい 〖心暖まる〗heartwarming; 〖楽しくさせる〗pleasant. ● ほほえましい光景[話] a *heartwarming* scene [story]. ▶子供が父親と遊んでいるのは見ていてほほえましかった It was *heartwarming* [*pleasant*] to see a child playing 《play》 with his father. (〖!〗文型上は play も可能だが、日本語で「遊んでいるのを」を「遊ぶのを」とした場合と同じく play では不自然)

ほほえみ 微笑み a smile. (⇨微笑, 笑み, 笑い) ● 幸せうなほほえみを浮かべる smile happily; give 《him》 a happy *smile*.

ほほえむ 微笑む smile 《at》. (⇨笑う❶) ● 彼にほほえみ返す *smile* back at him; return his [×my, ×her] *smile*. ● 彼にやさしくほほえみかける give him a kind *smile*; *smile* kindly *at* him.

ほまれ 誉れ 〖名誉〗honor, credit. ● 家門の誉れ an *honor* [a *credit*] *to* one's family. (⇨名誉) ● 彼は秀才の誉れ(=評判)が高い He has *a reputation for* [*the reputation of*] being a brilliant student. (〖!〗後の方は being を省略可)

ほむぎ 穂麦 wheat [barley, oats, corn] in ear.

ほむら 炎 (⇨炎)

ほめい 墓銘 (墓碑銘) an epitaph.

ほめごろし 褒め殺し ● 褒め殺しにする try to harm 《him》 by giving undue praise to 《him》.

ほめそやす 褒めそやす (⇨褒め称える)

ほめたたえる 褒め称える 〖大いにほめる〗praise ... highly [to the skies]; 〖書〗acclaim. ▶彼の新作映画は本年度最高作としてほめたたえられた His new movie *was acclaimed* as the best of the year.

ほめちぎる 褒めちぎる (⇨褒める) ● 彼の勇気ある行動をほめちぎる *praise* his courageous act *very highly* [*to the skies*].

ポメラニアン 〖動物〗(犬) a Pomeranian.

__ほめる__ 褒める ❶〖高く評価して〗praise, 〖書〗commend; 〖感心して〗admire; 〖よく言う〗say good things《about》, speak* highly [favorably, 〖やや書〗well] of ... (⇨感心する, 賞賛する) ▶先生は彼を勤勉だと言ってほめた The teacher *praised* his diligence [*him for* his diligence]. (〖!〗that 節は用いない。praise は日常語としてはやや堅い語で、yet The teacher said he was very diligent. などで表されることが多い) ▶その作品はすべての批評家に大そうほめられた The work was highly *praised* [*very highly spoken of*] by all the critics./The work *won high* [*great*] *praise* from all the critics. ▶彼の行為はいくらほめてもほめきれない His deed is *beyond* (*all*) *praise*. / We can*not praise* his deed *enough*. (〖!〗enough の代わりに too much を用いると「ほめすぎることはできない」の意にもなりあいまい) ▶それはあまりほめられたことではない(=賞賛に値しない) It does not deserve any *praise*./(名誉とならない) It does not do him any *credit*.

❷〖お世辞で〗compliment. (⇨お世辞) ● 彼女の服をほめる *compliment* her [*pay* her *compliments*] *on* her dress. (〖!〗×*compliment* her dress は不可) 会話「料理がお上手ですね」「ほめてくださるなんてうれしいわ」"You're a good cook." "Thank you for your [the] *compliment*./I'm flattered (to *be complimented*)." (〖!〗()内は会話体では通例省略される)

ホモ 图 〖同性愛〗homosexuálity; (同性愛者) a homoséxual, 〖話・軽蔑的〗a homo (覆 ~s) 〖以上の語は女性同士の場合も含まれる〗; (主に男性の) 〖話・軽蔑的〗a queer, 〖話〗a gay (〖!〗女性同士の場合は a lesbian /lézbiən/ を用いる。いずれも侮蔑(ぶべつ)的な語ではない)。

── ホモの 形 homosexual, 〖話〗gay.

ホモサピエンス
- ホモ牛乳 [均質牛乳] homogenized milk.

ホモサピエンス (ヒト) Homo sapiens /hòumə séipienz/.《書》現生人類の学名)

ホモセクシャル《⇨ホモ》

ほや 火屋 [ランプの] (筒状の) a chimney;(球形の) a globe.

ほや 海鞘 [魚介] a sea squirt.

ぼや a small fire. ▶ぼやで済んだ The fire was put out before it got serious.

ぼやかす (意味・真意を) make*... vague [ambiguous,《書》equivocal]. ●わざとぼやかした返事をする give an *equivocal* [(言質を与えない) a *noncommittal*] reply.

ぼやく complain《about》; grumble《about》;(いつもぶつぶつ言う)《話》gripe《about》.

ぼやける (薄暗さ・遠方のために) dim (-mm-), become* dim;(不明確な輪郭・高速のために) blur (-rr-), become blurred ● 以上は記憶・思考などにも用いる;(画像・音声が) become fuzzy. ●ぼやけた記憶 *dim* memories. ▶涙で視界がぼやけた Tears *dimmed* [*blurred*] my eyes./My eyes *were dim* [*were*] *dimmed*,《were》*blurred*] with tears. ▶この写真は少しぼやけている This picture is a bit *fuzzy* [*blurred*,(焦点が合っていない) *out of focus*].

ぼやっと《⇨ぼんやり》

ほやほや (新鮮な) fresh;(できたてで熱い) hot (-tt-). ▶このクッキーはできたてのほやほやです These cookies are *fresh from the oven* /ˌʌvn/. ▶彼はほやほやの新人です He is a *fresh* newcomer./(大学出たての) He is *fresh from* [*out of*] college. ▶彼らは新婚ほやほやです They have *just* married./They are *newlyweds*.

ぼやぼや ●ぼやぼやしている (注意がたりない) careless;(うっかりしている) absent-minded;(怠けている) idle;(てきぱきしない) slow. ▶ニューヨークでぼやぼやしてると裸にされるよ In New York you'll be ripped off if you're *careless*. ▶ぼやぼやしている生徒はそのクラスではおいてきぼりにされた The *idle* students [(理解が遅い者) *slow* learners] were left behind in the class. ▶その忙しい料理店ではぼやぼやしていると,注文したいものが何もとれないよ If you're *slow* in ordering at that busy restaurant, you won't (manage to) get anything you want. ▶ぼやぼやするな《気を付けろ》Watch out./Look out.

ほゆう 保有 ── 保有する 動 hold*,《書》possess.《⇨持つ 3》[類語] ●核兵器を保有する *hold* nuclear weapons. [関連]▶ 核保有国 a nuclear power/核を保有しない国 a nuclear-free nation)

ほよう 保養 图 [休養] (a) rest;(健康維持・病後の) preservation of one's health;(病後の) recuperation《養生・静養・療養などを広く含む》;[気晴らし]《る》recreation;(骨休め) a relaxation.《養生・休養などを含む》●保養に行く go to《Hakone》to *get some rest* [《書》*recuperate*, *recreate*《oneself》, *relax*]; go to《Hakone》for one's *health* [《書》*recuperation*, *recreation*, *relaxation*]. ● for one's *health* は養生・静養・療養などを広く含む》●目の保養となる (事または主語が) *delight* one's eyes;(人が主語が) *feast* one's eyes《on》.
── 保養する 動 take* [have*] a rest;《書》recuperate; recreate [refresh]《oneself》;(oneself), relax.
- 保養所 (病後の人の) a convalescent /ˌkɒnvəˈlɛsnt/ home [hospital];(会社などが所有する) a company-owned recreation facility. ● 保養地 a héalth resòrt.

ほら look; here, there. ▶ほらごらん,向こうに船が見えるよ Oh, *look*, you see a boat over there. ▶ほら,

太郎が来たよ ↘*Here* comes [ˣhas come, ˣcame] ↙Taro. ● [!](1) 眼前の動作を感嘆的にいう表現.(2) 代名詞が主語なら Hére he ↘comes. の語順となる.少し距離があれば here の代わりに there を用いる) ▶ほらあなたの捜していた本よ *Here's* the book(s) you've been looking for. [!] 主語が複数でも《話》では Here's が可》▶ほら,鐘が鳴っているよ ↘*There goes* [ˣis going] the ↙bell! ▶ほらね,言ったとおりでしょう ↘*There* [↙*There nów*, *Thére you* ↙*are*]! I ↘told you só.《⇨それ》▶ほらまた始まった *Thére* [*Hére*] you ↙go agáin!

ほら 法螺 (信じがたい話) a tall story [tale];(自慢) brag,《話》big talk. ● ほらを吹く brag《about》,《話》talk big《about》.
- ほら吹き a braggart.

ぼら 鯔 [魚介] a gray mullet.

ホラー horror.
- ホラー映画《主に米》a hórror mòvie;《主に英》a hórror film.

ほらあな 洞穴 a cave;(大きくて深い) a cavern;(野獣の住む) a den.

ほらがい 法螺貝 [魚介] a trumpet shell;(大きな) a conch (shell). ● ほら貝を吹く blow a *conch horn*.

ポラロイドカメラ [商標] a Polaroid《camera》.

ボランチ [<ポルトガル語] [サッカー] a defensive midfielder; a holding player [midfielder] [!] a holding player [midfielder] は 21 世紀に入ってから英国で一般的に使われ始めた用語).

ボランティア (人) a volunteer /vàləntíər/《for; to do》. ● ボランティア活動をする work as a *volunteer*. ▶彼女は週末はボランティアとして病院で働いた She worked as a *volunteer* [*volunteered*] at the hospital over the weekend. ▶阪神・淡路大震災の前までは多くの日本人はボランティア活動に関心がなかった Not many Japanese took interest in *volunteer* activities [*work*] before the Great Hanshin-Awaji Earthquake.

ほり 彫り (平面・立体的の) carving;(石・木・金属などに線で書いた) engraving. ▶彼女は彫りの深い=凹凸のはっきりした)顔をしている She has *clear-cut* [(のみで彫ったような) *chiseled* /tʃízld/,(岩のように際立った) *craggy*] features.

ほり 堀 a moat.《⇨外堀》● 堀を巡らした城 a castle surrounded by a *moat*. ● 堀を掘る dig a *moat*.

ポリ ❶ [「ポリス」(警官)の略] 《話》《俗》a cop; a police officer;(集合的) police [!] 複数扱い).
❷ [「ポリエチレン(製の)」の略] plastic [polyethylene] (bag). ● [!] 前の方が普通 ● ポリ袋 a plastic bag.《⇨ポリ袋》

ほりあてる 掘り当てる ● 石油を掘り当てる *strike* [*hit*] oil.

ポリープ [医学] a polyp /pɑ́lɪp/. ● ポリープを取ってもらう have *polyps* removed (from the intestines).

ポリウレタン [化学] polyurethane /pùːljuːə(ː)rəθeɪn/.

ポリエステル [<ドイツ語] [化学] polyester.
- ポリエステル樹脂 polyester resin. ● ポリエステル繊維 polyester fiber.

ポリエチレン [<ドイツ語] [化学] polyethylene /pɑ̀liéθəlìːn/,《英》polythene.

ポリオ《話》polio; [医学] poliomyelitis. ● ポリオの予防注射をしてもらう be vaccinated against *polio*.
- ポリオ患者 a *polio* victim.

ほりおこす 掘り起こす dig*... up [out]. ●凍ていた地面[木の根]を掘り起こす *dig up* frozen land [the tree by its roots]. [!] ジャガイモなど容易に掘り出せるものは *dig potatoes* などとなる) ▶野に埋れた人材を掘り起こす *find* [*discover*] hidden talents.

ほりかえす 掘り返す dig*... up.

ポリグラフ 〖うそ発見器〗a polygraph, 《話》a lie detector.

ほりごたつ 掘り炬燵 a *horigotatsu*; (説明的に) a *kotatsu* around which you can sit at the table because the heat source is sunken below the floor. (⇨炬燵)

ほりさげる 掘り下げる 〖下へ掘る〗dig*... down; 〖探究する〗dig (やや書) delve into .... ▶その事件を掘り下げて調べる dig into the case.

ポリシー 〖方針, 主義〗a policy.

ポリス 〖警察〗the police; (警官) a police officer. (⇨警察, 警官)
● ポリスボックス 〖交番〗a police bòx. (事情 米英には日本の交番に当たるものはない)

ポリス 〖古代ギリシャの都市国家〗〖歴史〗a polis.

ほりだし（もの） 掘り出し(物) (価値のある見つけ物) a find; (得な買い物) a (good) bargain 《話》buy. ▶彼の新しい車はまさに掘り出し物 His new car is a real *find* [*bargain*].

ほりだす 掘り出す ● 落花生を掘り出す dig (*up*) peanuts. ● がれきの中から死体を掘り出す dig out the body *from* the debris /dɪbríː/; dig the body *out of* the debris.

ホリデー 〖休日〗a holiday. (⇨休日)

ほりぬきいど 掘り抜き井戸 an artesian well.

ポリネシア 〖南太平洋の島群〗Polynesia /pὰlənífːɜ/.
● ポリネシアの Polynesian.

ポリバケツ a plastic bucket 〖(主に米)〗pail〗.

ほりばた 堀端 a bank [a side] of a moat; a moatside. ● 堀端にある柳 willow trees *on* [*along*] *the moat*; *moat-side* willow trees.

ボリビア 〖国名〗Bolivia; (公式名) the Republic of Bolivia. (首都 La Paz) ● ボリビア人 a Bolivian.
● ボリビア(人)の Bolivian.

ポリフェノール 〖化学〗polyphenol.

ポリぶくろ ポリ袋 a plastic bag; (密封保存用の) 〖もと商標〗a ziploc(k). ▶紙袋にしますかポリ袋にしますか (スーパーなどで) Paper or *plastic*?

ポリプロピレン 〖化学〗polypropylene.

ぼりぼり ❶ 〖強〖かく様子〗〗● ぼりぼりかく scratch. ▶そんなにぼりぼりかくな Don't *scratch* yourself so hard.
❷ 〖堅いものをかむ音〗● ぼりぼり食べる crunch (on). (! munch (on) は「もぐもぐ食べる」の意) ▶彼はぼりぼりビスケットをかじった He *crunched* (*on*) biscuits.

ポリマー 〖重合体〗〖化学〗polymer.

ほりもの 彫り物 〖彫刻作品〗(平面・立体的) a carving; (立体彫像) a sculpture; 〖木[金属・石]版画〗an engraving; 〖入れ墨〗a tatóo (働 ~s).

***ほりゅう** 保留 图 (延期) (a) deferment; (一時的停止) (a) suspension; (留保) (a) reservation.
—— 保留する 動 defer (-rr-); postpone; put*... off (! 以上三つは「延期する」の意。後になるほど口語的に); suspend; reserve. ● しばらく再判断を保留する *defer* [*suspend, reserve*] judgment for the time being.

ボリューム ❶ 〖音量〗volume. ● ステレオ[ラジオ]のボリュームを上げる[下げる] turn up [turn down] (the *volume* on) the stereo [radio]. ● ボリュームをいっぱいにしてステレオをかける play a stereo at full [maximum] *volume*.
❷ 〖分量〗● ボリュームのある食事 a *substantial* [a *heavy*] meal. (! 後の方は「量が多い上に消化にも悪い」の意) ● ボリュームのある(= 厚い) 本 a *thick* book. ● ボリュームラベル 〖コンピュータ〗a volume label.

ほりょ 捕虜 a prisoner of war 《略 POW》(! 文脈によっては prisoner だけでこの意を表す); a captive. ▶兵士たちは捕虜になった The soldiers were taken [held] *prisoner* [*captive*]. (! 主語が複数でも prisoner, captive は単数形・無冠詞)
● 捕虜収容所 a detention camp; a prisoner-of-war [a POW] camp.

ポリようき ポリ容器 a plastic container.

ほりわり 掘り割り (水路) a canal; a ditch. (! 後の方は道路脇や畑の区画・灌漑(かんがい)用)

***ほる** 掘る dig*, 《書》excavate; (溝を) trench; (鉱石を) mine; (油田を) drill. ● ジャガイモを掘る(= 掘り出す) dig (*up* [*out*]) potatoes. ● 石炭[金]を掘る *mine* coal [gold]. ● 地面に穴を掘る dig *a hole in* the ground. ● 山にトンネルを掘る dig [bore, cut] a tunnel *through* a mountain. ▶彼は砂浜を掘って貝を捜した He *dug* the beach for seashells.

***ほる** 彫る (彫って刻む) carve, (のみで) chisel; (表面に名前などを) inscribe, engrave. ● 木を彫って仏を作る *carve* [*cut*] wood *into* a Buddha; *carve* [*cut*] a Buddha *out of* wood. ● 机に名前を彫る *carve* [*inscribe, engrave, cut*] one's name *on* a desk; *inscribe* [*engrave*, ×*carve*, ×*cut*] a desk *with* one's name.

ぼる (法外な値を要求する) overcharge; (高値を吹っかける) 《話》rip (-pp-) ... off. ▶あのレストランでぼられた I *was overcharged* [*was ripped off*] at that restaurant.

ポルカ a polka /póulkə/. ● ポルカを踊る polka; dance the *polka*.

ボルシェビキ <ロシア語> a Bolshevik /bóulʃəvɪk/ (働 ~s, Bolsheviki /bóulʃəvíːkɪ/).

ボルシチ <ロシア語> bors(h)cht /bɔːrʃt/, borsch /bɔːrʃ/.

ホルスター 〖ピストル用革ケース〗a holster.

ホルスタイン 〖乳牛〗《米》a Holstein; 《英》a Frisian.

ホルダー 〖紙ばさみ〗a folder.

ポルターガイスト 〖駆霊〗a poltergeist /póultərgaɪst/.

ボルチモア 〖米国の都市〗Baltimore /bɔ́ːltəmɔ̀ːr/.

ボルテージ 〖電圧〗voltage /vóultɪdʒ/ (⇨電圧); 〖熱気〗(感情の激しさ) voltage; (熱意) enthusiasm. ● ボルテージが高い演説をする give a high-*voltage* [気迫あふれる] a high-*spirited*] speech. ● ボルテージが上がる get more enthusiastic 《*about*》.

ボルト 〖ねじ〗a bolt. ● ボルトを締める fasten a *bolt*.
● ボルトで止める fasten 《*wheels*》with a *bolt*; bolt 《*wheels*》.

ボルト 〖電気〗a volt /vóult/ (略 V, v); (ボルト数) voltage. (⇨電圧) ● 100 ボルトの電流 a 100-*volt* current.

ボルドー 〖フランスの都市〗Bordeaux /bɔːrdóu/.
● ボルドー液 Bordeaux mixture. (参考 農薬の一つ)

ポルトガル 〖国名〗Pórtugal; (公式名) the Portuguese /pɔːtʃəgíːz/ Republic. (首都 Lisbon) ● ポルトガル人 a Portuguese (! 単・複同形); (総称) Portuguese people, 《やや書》the Portuguese (! 複数扱い), ● ポルトガル語 Portuguese. ● ポルトガル(人[語])の Portuguese.

ボルネオ 〖マレー諸島最大の島〗Borneo /bɔ́ːrniòu/.

ポルノ 图 pornography /pɔːrnágrəfi/, 《話》porn(o) /pɔ́ːrn(oʊ)/. (! いずれも本や映画や写真などを集合的に表す)
—— ポルノの 形 pornographic; 《話》porn(o).
● ポルノ映画 a porn(o) film 〖(主に米)〗movie〗.
● ポルノ俳優 a porn(o) star [figure]. (! ポルノ女優は特に a porn(o) queen という)

ホルマリン formalin /fɔ́ːrmælɪn/.

ホルムアルデヒド 〖化学〗formaldehyde /fɔːrmǽldəhàɪd/. (参考 防腐・消毒剤)

ホルムズ ● ホルムズ海峡 the Strait of Hormuz /hɔ́ːrməz, hɔːrmúːz/.

ホルモン a hormone /hɔ́ːrmoun/; 〖医学〗(内分泌腺) an endocrine [a ductless] gland. ● 男[女]性ホルモン a male [female] (sex) hormone. ● 環境ホルモン (⇨環境) ● ホルモンの障害に苦しむ suffer from a hormonal disturbance.
▶ ホルモン剤 a hórmone drùg. ● ホルモン焼き (臓物焼き) barbecued entrails.

ホルン 〖楽器〗a horn /hɔ́ːrn/. ● ホルンを吹く (演奏する) play the horn; (鳴らす) blow [sound] a horn.

ほれいしゃ 保冷車 (トラック) a refrigerated truck [van]; (貨車) a refrigerated car.

ボレー 〖スポーツ〗a volley. ● ボレーの応酬をする volley.

ほれこむ 惚れ込む 〖話〗(⇨惚れる); (感служ) admire. ● あんな男にほれこむなんてあなたはばかだ What a fool you are to fall for a man like him. ▶ 彼は彼女にほれこんでいる He is crazy [mad] about her. ● 社長は彼の才能にほれこんでいる The president admires [×is admiring] his talents.

ほれぼれ 惚れ惚れ —— 惚れ惚れする 動 (魅惑的な) fascinating /fǽsəneitiŋ/; (魅了される) be fascinated 〈by〉; (見とれる) admire. (⇨魅了)

ほれる 惚れる 〖愛している〗love, be in love 〈with〉; 〖恋に落ちる〗fall* in love 〈with〉, 〖話〗fall for …; 〖魅了される〗be charmed [attracted] 〈by〉. ● 一目で彼女にほれる fall in love with [好きになる] come to love] her at first sight. ● 彼女にぞっこんほれている be madly [be head over heels] in love with her. ● 彼の人柄にほれる be attracted by his personality.

ボレロ 〖＜スペイン語〗❶〖服〗a bolero /bəlérou/ (jacket). ❷〖音楽〗a bolero. ● ラベルの『ボレロ』 Ravel's Bolero.

ほろ 幌 a top, a hood /húd/. ● オープンカーのほろ the top of a convertible. ● ほろをたたむ[掛ける] put down [pull up] the top [hood]. ● ほろを掛けたうば車 a baby carriage with the hood up.

ぼろ 〖使い古した布きれ〗(a) rag, old cloth; 〖ぼろ着〗rags, ragged 〖衣類〗clothes. ● ぼろをまとった男 a ragged man; a man dressed in rags. ● ぼろ [切れ] ないかな. 窓をふくのにいるんだ Do you have any rags? I need some to wash the windows.
● **ぼろを出す** expose one's faults [defects, (弱点) weakness]. ● ぼろを出さぬように(=体裁を保とうと) a try to keep up [save] appearances. ● それは巧妙な作り話だったが結局はぼろが出た It was a clever invention, but ultimately it did not hold water. (❗hold water は「筋が通る」の意で通例否定文で用いる)

—— **ぼろの** 形 (使い古した) worn-out; (衣服などが) ragged. (⇨ぼろぼろ❶) ● ぼろ(=荒れはてた)アパート a run-down [安っぽくて汚らしい] 〖話〗a crappy] apartment.
● **ぼろ屋** a rag collector, (男の) a ragman; 《米》a junk dealer [男の junkman].

ぼろい ● ぼろい(=やたらもうかる)仕事 an easy-money [〖俗〗a big-money] job. (⇨ぼろ儲け)

ぼろきれ ぼろ切れ (⇨ぼろ)

ぼろくそ ぼろ糞 (けなす) 〖話〗run 〈him, it〉 down; (悪口を言う) call 〈him〉 (a thousand) names; speak badly [ill] of; abuse.

ホログラフィー holography.

ホロコースト 〖ユダヤ人大虐殺〗the Holocaust.

ポロシャツ a polo shirt.

ホロスコープ 〖星占い〗a horoscope.

ぼろっちい (みすぼらしい) shabby; seedy. (⇨ぼろ)

ほろっと (⇨ほろりと)

ほろにがい ほろ苦い 〖少し苦い〗slightly bitter; 〖甘く苦い〗bittersweet. ● ほろ苦い思い出 one's bittersweet memory.

ポロネーズ 〖＜フランス語〗〖音楽〗a polonaise /pɑ̀ləneiz/.

ほろばしゃ 幌馬車 a covered wagon. (参考) 米国の開拓時代に大陸横断に使われた大型の幌馬車は a Conestoga (wagon), a prairie schooner ともいう

*****ほろびる** 滅びる 〖国家・政府などが倒れる〗fall*; 〖絶滅する〗(生物などが) become* extinct; (種族・習慣などが) die out 〈～d; dying〉; 〖滅びされる〗be destroyed. ● 滅びてゆく文明 a dying civilization. (❗dying を人や生物に用いると「死にかけている」の意となるので注意) ● その政権はいつ滅びましたか When did the government fall? / (いつ倒されたのか) When was the government overthrown? ● その部族は滅びつつある The tribe is dying out [絶滅寸前だ] is on the verge of extinction, is on the way out]. ● 古くからの習慣はなかなか滅びない Old customs die hard [don't die so easily]. ● 核戦争で人類は滅びるだろう The human race will be destroyed by nuclear war. ● その文明は突然滅びた (=崩壊した) The civilization suddenly collapsed [(消滅した) died, 〈書〉perished].

*****ほろぼす** 滅ぼす 〖破壊する〗destroy; 〖破滅・没落させる〗ruin; 〖政府などを倒す〗overthrow*. ● その都市は敵に滅ぼされた The city was destroyed by the enemy./ (陥落した) The city fell to the enemy. ▶ 彼は酒で身を滅ぼした He ruined himself [his life] by drinking./Drink was his ruin.

ほろほろ ● 涙がほろほろとこぼれた Silent tears welled up and ran down my cheeks. ● 山ばとがほろほろと鳴いている I hear a pigeon cooing./I hear the cooing of a pigeon.

ぼろぼろ —— **ぼろぼろの** 形 ❶〖衣類などが〗(破れた) ragged /rǽgid/; (使い古した) worn-out; (布・衣類などがすり切れた) threadbare; (ちぎれた) tattered. ● ぼろぼろの靴 worn-out shoes. ● ぼろぼろの服を着た見知らぬ人がやって来た A stranger in ragged clothes [in rags] came along. ▶ 私のコートは何年も着てぼろぼろになった My coat became threadbare through years of use.
❷〖乾燥してばらばらで〗coarse; dry. ● このごはんはぼろぼろ This boiled rice is coarse. ▶ この古い木はさわるとぼろぼろ崩れる This old wood crumbles at the touch. ▶ パンのくずがぼろぼろテーブルに落ちた Bread crumbs fell onto the table.

ぼろぽろ ● 彼女の指の間から豆がぼろぼろ床に落ちた Beans fell through her fingers onto the floor. ▶ 大粒の涙がぽろぽろ彼女のほおを伝って流れた Big tears trickled down her cheeks.

ほろほろちょう ほろほろ鳥 〖鳥〗a guinea fowl [(雌) hen].

ぼろもうけ ぼろ儲け easy money [gain]. ● 土地を売ってぼろ儲けする sell land and make easy money. ● 株でぼろ儲けする 〖話〗make a killing on the stock market. ● 〖慣用表現〗

ほろよい ほろ酔い ● ほろ酔い気分である be slightly drunk [〖書〗intoxicated]; 〖話〗be tipsy.

ほろりと ● ほろりとさせる(=感動的な) a moving [touching] story. ● ほろりと酔う get slightly drunk. ● 涙を一滴ほろりと流す drop [〖書〗shed] a tear. ▶ その話に私はほろりとした (=感動して涙を流した) I was moved to tears by the story./The story moved me to tears.

ぽろりと ● ぽろりと秘密を漏らす let out [slip] a secret

ぼろん let a secret out も可);《話》let the cat out of the bag. ▶彼女の手から指輪がぼろりと落ちた *fell*［すべって］*slipped*] off her hand. ▶彼女の目からぼろりと涙が落ちた A tear *dropped* from her eyes. ▶リンゴを噛んだとたん彼の歯がぼろりと欠けた When he tried to bite into an apple, his tooth *chipped*.

ぼろん ●ギターをぼろんと鳴らす *twang* [*pluck*] a guitar.

ホワイト〚白〛white.
● ホワイトカラー〚事務[頭脳]労働者〛a white-collar (↔a blue-collar) worker. ● ホワイトクリスマス a white Christmas. ● ホワイトゴールド white gold. (参考) 白金 (platinum) の代用として用いられる合金)
● ホワイトソース white sauce. ● ホワイトボード a whiteboard. ● ホワイトリカー〚焼酎〛Japanese distilled liquor. (❗white liquor は「パルプ溶液」の意 (⇨焼酎)

ホワイトデー (説明的に) March 14, when some Japanese men give gifts back to women from whom they received Valentine's Day gifts; 《和製語》White Day. (⇨バレンタインデー)

ホワイトハウス〚米国大統領官邸〛the White Hòuse.

:**ほん** 本〚書物〛(単行本) a book;《書》a volume (❗特に大型の本).
①【～の】●絵本 a picture *book*. ●科学[歴史]の本 a scientific [a history] *book*; a *book* on science [history]. ●料理の本 a cookbook;《主に英》a cookery *book*. ●ハードカバーの本 a hardcover *book*. ●クロース装丁[革表紙]の本 a clothbound [a leather-bound] *book*. ●3冊で一組の本 a set of three *books*. ●5巻ものの本 a *book* in [×of] five volumes; a five-volume *book*.
②【本(に)は】●この本はよく売れる This *book* sells [×is sold] well. ▶その本は5万部売れた Fifty thousand copies of the *book* were sold. (❗a copy は同じ本の1冊をいう) ▶その本は300ページ以上ある The *book* has more than 300 pages. ▶この本は初心者向きだ This *book* is (intended) for beginners. ▶その本にはどんなことが書いてありますか What does the *book* say?
③【本の】●本の表紙 a (*book*) cover. (❗「本のカバー」は a (*book*) jacket という) ▶彼はいわば本の虫だ He is, so to speak, a *bookworm*.
④【本を】●本を開く[閉じる] open [close] a *book*. ●本を書く[出版する] write [publish] a *book*《about, on》. ❗about は一般的な内容を, on は専門的な内容を暗示する) ●ロンドンへ本を注文する order a *book* from [×to] London. ▶その本を数日貸してくれませんか Would you lend me the *book* for a few days? ▶彼は図書館から数冊本を借りた He borrowed a few *books* from [out of] the library. ▶彼はよく本を読む He reads a lot of *books*./He reads a lot./He's a great reader. ▶彼は子供たちに毎晩本を読んでやる He *reads* to his children every evening. ▶S社から本を出す予定です I'm planning to have a *book* published by S publishing company.

ホン〚音の強さの単位〛a phon /fάn/. ▶交通の騒音が70 ホンだった The traffic noise registered [was] 70 *phons*.

ほん- 本-〚主な〛main, head;〚本当の〛real;〚本物の〛genuine /dʒénjuin/;〚正式の〛regular;〚この〛this;〚現在の〛present. ●本社 the *head* [*main*] office;《当社》this [*our*] company. ●本名 one's *real* name. ●本真珠 a *genuine* [a *real*] pearl.

-ほん -本 ●チョーク数本 several *pieces* of chalk. (❗×several chalks は不可); ひも2本 two *strings*; two *pieces* of string. ●ビール5本 five *bottles* of beer. (⇨一本)

ぼん 盆〚器〛a tray.

ぼん 盆麻〚「盂蘭盆(ご)」の略〛the *Bon* Festival, the *Obon* holiday; (説明的に) a Buddhist festival for honoring the spirits of ancestors, which are supposed to be visiting with the living on August 15 (=July 15 by the lunar calendar). It is held from August [July] 13 to 16.
● 盆と正月が一度に来たよう It's like the Bon Festival and the New Year all rolled into one. (❗米英では It's like Christmas and Easter all rolled into one. という. また単に It's like Christmas and Easter. ということも多い)
● 盆踊り the *Bon* Festival dance.

ボン〚ドイツの都市〛Bonn.

ぽん ❶〚ぽんと音がする〛pop (-pp-); (ぴしゃりと打つ) clap (-pp-); (はじけて) crack; (肩などを軽くたたいて) pat (-tt-). ▶ウエーターがびんのコルクを抜くと, ぽんと音がした When the waiter uncorked the bottle, it *popped*. ▶クリが火の中でぽんとはじけた A chestnut *cracked* in the fire. (❗トウモロコシがはねるのは pop) ▶彼が私の肩をぽんとたたいた He *patted* [*clapped*, *tapped*] me on the shoulder.
❷〚ぽんと投げたり気前よく出すさま〛●週刊誌を私にぽんと投げて寄こす *toss* me the weekly; *toss* the weekly *to* me. ▶彼はぽんと全額払った He *generously* paid the whole amount.

ほんあさ 本麻〚形〛(衣料品など) (natural) linen. ●本麻のジャケット a *linen* jacket.

ほんあん 翻案〚名〛adaptation. (❗「翻案された物」の意では〚C〛)
── 翻案する〚動〛●小説を舞台用に翻案する *adapt* a novel *for* a play; *adapt* a play *from* a novel.

ほんい 本位 ●自己本位の人 a *self-centered* [a *selfish*, a *self-love*] person. ●若者本位のテレビ番組 *youth-oriented* TV programs. ●人物本位で採用する employ people *on the basis of* personality. ●金本位制度 the gold *standard* (system). ●興味本位 (⇨興味) ▶私たちは品質本位で電気製品を買う We buy electrical appliances *on the basis of* quality./Quality comes *first* when we buy electrical appliances.
●本位貨幣 standard money. ●本位記号〚音楽〛a natural.

ほんい 本意 one's real intention. (⇨本心) ▶妥協するのは本意ではなかった I *was reluctant to* compromise. (❗be reluctant の代わりに be unwilling を用いると妥協しなかった場合も含むので注意) ▶彼をだますのは本意ではなかった(=だまそうとしなかった) I *didn't really mean to* deceive him.

ほんい 翻意 ●翻意を促す urge《him》to change his decision《to do》; (再考を促す) urge《him》to reconsider.

ほんいん 本院〚分院に対して〛headquarters (❗単・複両扱い); the head [main] hospital;〚この院〛(議会) this House; (病院) our hospital.

ほんいんぼう 本因坊 a *Honinbo*; the grand master of go. ●本因坊位を獲得する win the title of *Honinbo*.

ほんえい 本営 headquarters. (❗単・複両扱い)
ほんおどり 盆踊り (⇨盆)
ほんか 本科 a regular course.
●本科生 a regular student.
ほんかい 本懐 ●本懐を遂げる realize one's *long-cherished desire* [*dream, ambition*].
ほんかいぎ 本会議 ●衆議院本会議《書》a plenary

ほんかく 本格 ── **本格的な** 形 (本物の) real; (食べ物が伝統製法の) authentic; (全面的な) full-scale.
● 本格的な登山家 a *real* mountaineer; (専門家) an *expert* climber, an *expert* in mountaineering. ● 本格的な冬の訪れ the coming of *real* winter. ● 本格的な調査 a *full-scale* investigation. ▶ 彼らは少し殴り合いをしたが本格的なけんかにはならなかった(=避けられた) They exchanged a few blows, but a *real* fight was averted. ▶ あのレストランでは本格的なフランス料理を出す They serve *authentic* French dishes at that restaurant.
── **本格的に** 副 本格的にピアノの勉強をする take piano lessons *in earnest*. ▶ 雨は本格的(=本降り)になってきた The rain was coming down *in earnest*. (⚠️ ×be in full swing は組織されたものの活動が最高潮に達していることを示す表現なので, 自然現象に用いるのは不可)

ほんがく 本学 our school [college].

ほんぐうぼうにっき『本覚坊遺文』 *Memories of the Priest Honkaku*. (参考) 井上靖の小説

ほんどり 本歌取り (an) adaptation of an old poem [song].

ほんがわ 本革 (real) leather. ● 本革のジャンパー a *leather* windbreaker.

ほんかん 本官 〖正式の官職〗 the regular government office [employment]; 〖本務の職〗 one's principal office [position]. ● 本官に任命される be appointed to the position of a regular government employee.

ほんかん 本管 a main (pipe). ● 水道[ガス]の本管 a water [gas] *main*. ● ガスの本管を止める turn off the gas at the *main*.

ほんかん 本館 the main building.

ほんがん 本願 (仏の) Buddha's wish to relieve people of their sins; (宿願) a long-cherished desire [dream]. ● 本願成就を祈願する pray for the realization of one's *dream*.

ほんき 本気 名 earnestness; seriousness.
── **本気の** 形 (まじめな) earnest; (真剣な) serious. ● 冗談ではない, 本気なのだ I'm not joking. I'm *serious* [I mean what I say].
── **本気で** 副 earnestly, in earnest; seriously. ● 本気で勉強する study *earnestly* [*in earnest*]. ● 本気で努力する make an *earnest* effort (*to do*). ● 彼の冗談を本気にする take his joke *seriously*. ● 本気で行政改革に取り組まなければならない We must start working on administrative reforms *in all seriousness*.
会話 「ボブは本気でメアリーと結婚する気なの?」「そんなこと私には分からないわ. 本人に聞いてみてよ」 "Is Bob (really) *serious about* marrying Mary?/Is Bob *in* (deadly) *earnest to* marry Mary?" "Don't ask me. Ask him."
会話 「それ, あなたにあげるわ」「本気でそう言ってるの?」「そうよ」 "I'll give it to you." "Do you *mean* that?" "I mean it."

ほんぎ 本義 (文字・言葉の本来の意味) the central meaning (*of* 'take'); (原義) the original meaning; (根本の意義) the basic [fundamental] principle (*of* education).

ほんぎまり 本決まり ▶ 彼の昇進が本決まりになった It has definitely [最終的に] finally] been decided that he (《主に英》should) be promoted. (⚠️ formally (正式に)を用いるなら decided の次に置くのがよい)

ほんきゅう 本給 (基本給) one's basic pay.

ほんきょ 本拠 〖根拠地〗 the base; 〖本部〗 the headquarters; 〖活動・主義などの拠点〗 the stronghold; 〖スポーツチームのホーム〗 the home (ground).

ほんぎょう 本業 one's main [regular] occupation [(仕事) job]. ● 本業に専念する devote oneself to one's *main occupation*.

ほんきょく 本局 one's main office; (地区内の) a central office. ▶ 郵便物は本局が配達する The *central post office* delivers letters and other postal matter.

ほんきょち 本拠地 (⇨本拠)

ほんぐもり 本曇り 本曇りになってきた It's getting *heavily overcast*./The sky is *clouding over*.

ぼんくら 图 (人) a blockhead; a halfwit. ▶ このぼんくら! You *blockhead*!
── **ぼんくらな** 形 blockheaded; half-witted; stupid.

ほんけ 本家 〖分家に対して〗 the head [main] family (違い) 米英には本家・分家の概念はない); 〖元祖〗 an originator; 〖製造元〗 an original maker [manufacturer].

ぼんけい 盆景 a miniature landscape garden arranged on a tray; a tray landscape.

ほんけん 本件 this case [matter].

ほんけん 本絹 《a *kimono* (made) of》 pure silk.

ほんげん 本源 〖根源〗 a source; an origin; 〖根本〗 the principal [first] cause. ● テムズ川の本源をたずねる go [trace] back to the *source* of the Thames.

ぼんご 梵語 名 〖サンスクリット〗 Sanskrit.
── **梵語の** 形 Sanskrit.

ボンゴ 〖楽器〗 a bongo (drum). (⚠️ 通例一対で用いられるので複数形で)

ほんこう 本校 (分校に対して) the main school; (当校) this [our] school.

ほんこく 翻刻 名 (復刻) reprinting. ── **翻刻する** 動 reprint.
● 翻刻本 a reprint.

ほんごく 本国 one's own [native, home] country, 《書》 one's homeland, 《書》 one's native land; 〖移住者から見て〗 《やや書》 one's mother country [motherland]; (特にドイツ人に対して) 《やや書》 one's fatherland; (米国・オーストラリアの白人移民の) the old country. ● 本国に帰る go [return] *home*. (⚠️ この home は副詞) ● 本国に送還される be sent back to one's own [*home*] country; (亡命者・捕虜などの) 《やや書》 be repatriated.
● 本国政府 the home government.

ほんごし 本腰 ● **本腰を入れる** 本腰を入れて(=本気で)仕事に取りかかる set to work *in earnest*; get down to work. ● その問題に本腰を入れて取り組む *be serious about* tackling the problem.

ぽんこつ 《話》 a piece of junk.
● ぽんこつ車 (廃車) a wreck; (おんぼろ車) an old wreck; 《英話》 an old banger; 《話・やや古》 a jalopy /dʒəlάpi/.

ホンコン 香港 〖中国の特別行政区〗 Hong Kong.

ほんさい 本妻 one's legally wed [legal, lawful] wife.

ぼんさい 凡才 (並の才能) average [ordinary] ability; (並の才能の人) a person of average [ordinary] ability.

ぼんさい 盆栽 a *bonsai* (⚠️ 単・複同形), a *bonsai* tree; (説明的に) a potted dwarf tree (pruned and pinched to produce a desired shape or effect).

ぼんさく 凡作 a mediocre work.

ほんざん 本山 (寺院の) the head temple of a Buddhist sect; 〖元締め〗 the center. (⇨総本山)

ほんし 本旨 (本来の趣旨) the original purport; (真の目的) the true aim [objective]. ●本旨を失う lose the *true aim* 《*of* education》. ●本旨に反する go against the *principle* 《*of* education》.

ほんし 本紙 have [this] newspaper; [『付録に対して』] the main section. ●本紙記者 our correspondent [reporter]. ●本紙読者 our readers. ●本紙に既報の通り as already reported in *our columns*.

ほんし 本誌 our [this] magazine [journal].

ほんじ 本字 [『漢字』] a Chinese character; [『略字・俗字に対して』] an original character.

ほんじ 梵字 Devanagari; Sanskrit characters.

ほんしき 本式 (⇨正式, 本格的な) ●本式の晩さん会 a *formal* [a *regular*, a *full-course*] dinner. ●英語を本式に習う take *regular* lessons in English; (系統だてて) study English *systematically* [in a *systematic* way]. ▶さて、本式に寝るとしようか Well, I'll go to bed.

ほんしけん 本試験 the final exam.

*ほんしつ 本質 图 [『真髄』] essence; [『特質』] nature. (⇨深奥, 核心) ●民主主義の本質 the *essence* of democracy. ●愛の本質 the *nature* of love.
—— **本質的 形** essential. ●本質的な相違 an *essential* difference 《*between*》.
—— **本質的に 副** essentially. ▶その2案は本質的に同じです The two ideas are *essentially* the same.

ほんじつ 本日 today. (⇨今日(³)) ▶本日休業〖掲示〗 Closed (for) *today*.

ほんしつ 凡失 a silly [a foolish, a stupid] error. (⇨凡ミス)

ほんしゃ 本社 (本店) the head [『米』home] office; a headquarters [『単・複数扱い』] ; (当社) our company [firm]. ●東京に本社のある会社 a Tokyo-*based* company; a company which *is*) *based* in Tokyo. ●同社は本社を日本から香港へ移転させた The company shifted their *headquarters* from Japan to Hong Kong.

ほんしゅう 本州 Honshu; the Main Island of Japan.

ほんしゅつ 奔出 图 a gush. (❷ 複数形なし) ●情熱の奔出にまかせる give oneself to a *gush of passion*.
—— **奔出する 動** gush out.

ホンジュラス 〖国名〗Honduras; (公式名) the Republic of Honduras. (首都 Tegucigalpa) ●ホンジュラス人 a Honduran. ●ホンジュラス(人)の Honduran.

ほんしょ 本書 this book.

ほんしょ 本署 [『支署などに対して』] headquarters (❹ 単・複数扱い); the principal office, (警察の) police headquarters; [『この署』] this office, (警察の) this station.

ほんしょう 本性 (⇨正体) ●本性を現す reveal one's *true nature* [colors]; betray oneself; give oneself away 《*by* do*ing*》. ▶生(³)酔い本性を違(³)わず (⇨生酔い [成句])

ほんしょう 本省 (中央官庁) the ministry proper.

ほんしょう 梵鐘 a Buddhist temple bell.

ほんしょく 本職 ❶ [『本業』] one's (regular) job [work, 『書』occupation, (知的職業) profession, (手仕事) trade]. (⇨職業) ●彼の本職は大学の教授[大工]です He is a university professor *by profession* [a carpenter *by trade*]. ❷ [『専門家』] a professional; an expert; a specialist. ●本職の画家 a *professional* painter. ●本職からダンスを教えてもらった I took dance lessons from a *professional*.

ほんしん 本心 [『真の意図』] one's *real* [*true*] intention(s). ●本心を打ち明ける confide one's *real intention* 《*to*》. ●彼の本心が分からない I don't know his *real intention*./I don't know if he means what he says.

ほんじん 本陣 a *honjin*; (説明的に) an officially appointed hotel with accommodations for a *daimyo* and his train.

ぼんじん 凡人 『普通の人』an ordinary [a common] person; 『凡才』a mediocrity. ▶それは凡人の力には及ばない It's beyond (the ability of) an *ordinary person*.

ポンず ポン酢 [<オランダ語] *ponzu*; (説明的に) juice pressed from a bitter orange.

ほんすじ 本筋 the main subject [(話題) topic, (目的) purpose]. ●本筋から外れる stray [〖書〗digress] from the *main subject* [*topic*, (要点) *point*] 《*of* his talk》. ●本筋を見失う lose track of the *main purpose*. ▶まず上司に相談するのが本筋(=あるべき順序)だと思う I think it's *proper* to consult your boss first.

ほんせい 本性 (⇨本性(³))

ほんせき 本籍 one's permanent [legal] residence; (登録上の住所) [『書』] one's domicile /dáməsàil/. ▶彼は本籍を東京から広島に移した He transferred his *legal residence* from Tokyo to Hiroshima. ▶彼女の本籍は名古屋にある She *is legally domiciled* in Nagoya.
●**本籍地** the place where one is legally domiciled; one's permanent domicile.

ほんせん 本船 a mother ship.
●**本船渡し** [『商業』] free on board (略 F.O.B., f.o.b.).

ほんせん 本線 a main; [『米』a trunk] (⇨branch) line; (この線) this line. ●山陽本線 the Sanyo (Main) *Line*.

ほんせん 本選 (予選に対し) the final test [(競技) competition]. ●本選に残る be qualified for *the final competition*.

ほんぜん 本然 —— **本然の 形** 眠ければ眠る. それは人間本然の欲求だ When you feel sleepy, you sleep. That's *nature* for humans to do so. (⇨本来)

ほんぜん 翻然 —— **翻然と 副** suddenly; all of a sudden. ▶青年は翻然と非を悟った The young man *suddenly* realized that he was in the wrong.

ほんそ 本訴 〖法律〗(反訴に対し) a main action.

ほんそう 本葬 (hold) a formal funeral. (❷密葬)

ほんそう 奔走 图 (走り回ること) running around 《『主に英』about》; (努力) (an) effort; (世話) 〖書〗good offices. ●恩師の奔走のお陰で彼は留学することができた He was able to study abroad with the *help* [through the *good offices*] of his former teacher.
—— **奔走する 動** (努力する) make* an [every] effort 《*to* do》; (忙しく動き回る) be busy 《do*ing*; *with*》. ●金策に奔走する make *every effort* to raise money; be *busy* raising money.

ほんぞう 本草 ●**本草学** a study of plants, minerals, and animals used in Chinese medicine.

ほんそく 本則 [『法令の本文』] the main body of laws; [『原則』] principles.

ぼんぞく 凡俗 —— **凡俗な 形** (ごく普通の) ordinary; (よくも悪くもない) mediocre; (一般大衆の) 〖書〗vulgar.

ほんぞん 本尊 the principal deity /díːəti/ (of the temple). ▶この寺のご本尊は観世音菩薩(³)である This temple *is dedicated to* Kannon.

ぼんだ 凡打 凡打する[に終わる] hit *a routine fly* [〖ゴ

ほんたい 本体 (機械などの) the (main) body.
ほんたい 本隊 the main body [force]. ●別動隊が本隊と合流した The separate unit joined the *main force*.
ほんたい 本態 ●本態性高血圧〖医学〗essential hypertension.
ほんだい 本題 the main subject. ●本題に戻る[からそれる] return to [stray from] the *main subject*.
ぼんたい 凡退 ―三者凡退に退ける retire the three batters [the side] in order. ●8回(の1イニング)を三者凡退に抑える pitch a one-two-three eighth inning. ―三者凡退となった〖野球〗 They went down one-two-three [in order].
ほんたく 本宅 one's (family) home [residence].
ほんたて 本立て a bookend (❢通例複数形で).
ほんだな 本棚 a bookshelf (⊛ -shelves). (⇨棚)
ほんだわら 馬尾藻〖植物〗a gulfweed.
ぼんち 盆地 a basin; (谷間) a valley. ●ナイル盆地 the Nile *basin*; the *basin* of the Nile.
ポンチ (a bowl of) punch /pʌ́ntʃ/. ●フルーツポンチ (⇨フルーツ)
ポンチョ [＜スペイン語] a poncho.
ほんちょう 本庁 〖中央官庁〗the central government office.
ほんちょうし 本調子 　(正常の状態) the normal [good] condition. ●本調子を取り戻す regain one's *normal condition*. ―きょうは本調子ではない(＝体調が悪い) I'm not in *good condition* [《話》*shape*] today./(いつもの調子ではない) I'm not up to my *usual form* today./(最高の調子ではない) I'm not at my *best* today.
ほんて 本手〖囲碁・将棋〗the orthodox move.
ほんてん 本店 (銀行その他の会社の本社) headquarters (❢単・複両扱い); the head [main] office.
ほんでん 本殿 the main shrine.
ぼんてん 梵天〖宇宙創造の神〗Brahma.
ほんと truly; self. (⇨本当)
ほんど 本土　the mainland. ●日本本土　Japan proper. (❢(1) proper は名詞の後につけて「厳密な意味での」の意。(2) the Mainland of Japan は日本の「本州」のこと)
ぼんど (⇨ぼんど)
ポンド ❶〖重さの単位〗a pound /páund/ 《記号 lb》. 〖参考〗1 ポンド＝454 グラム. ●20 ポンド 20 *pounds* [*lbs*]. ●ポンド価 the pound.
❷〖貨幣単位〗a pound /páund/ 《記号 £》. 〖参考〗(1) 1 ポンド＝100 ペンス. (2) 英貨ポンド正式には a pound sterling という) ●それは5 ポンド10 ペンスした It was [cost] £5.10 [*five pounds* (and) ten (pence)]. (❢and と pence を省略するのは《話》)
ほんとう 本当 图 ❶〖真実〗reality; 〖真実〗truth; 〖事実〗a fact. (⇨型〖類語〗) ●あなたの夢が本当になればよいと思います I hope your dream will become a *reality* [come *true*]. ●それが本当なら彼らは驚くでしょう If that's *true*, they will be surprised. ●すぐに成功してみせるさ, 本当だよ(＝約束するよ) I'll make it soon, *I promise*. (❢make it は succeed の意の口語的慣用表現) ●来週行くよ, 本当よ(＝うそじゃないよ) I'll come next week, *honest* I will.
〖会話〗「駅で彼女に会ったんだ」「えっ, 本当？」 "I met her at the station." "Oh, *really*?" (❢*really* はこの例のような驚きのほか, 興味・疑い・不満なども表す)
〖会話〗「大学をやめようかと思ってるのよ」「本当ですか(＝本気でそういっているの)」 "I think I'll drop out of college." "Do you *mean* that?"

〖会話〗「明日飛行機で行くのよ. 心配でたまらないわ」「大丈夫だよ. ぼくは長年飛行機で飛んでるけど, ぼくびっくすることなんか何もないよ. 本当だよ」"I'm going to fly in an airplane tomorrow, so I'm nervous." "Don't worry! I've been flying for years. And believe me, there's nothing to be nervous about." (❢このように挿入的に用いる)

〖会話〗「あなた, 学生さんですか」「はい, 神戸大学の学生です」「本当ですか(＝まさか), 私もそうなんです」 "Are you a student?" "Yes, I'm a student at [*of*] Kobe University." "*No ⤴kidding!* [You don't ⤵say!] So am I." (❢いずれも「うそっ」といった気持ちのこもった驚きを伝える)

【本当は】 (本当のことを言えば) to tell (you) the truth; (見かけ・予想に反して) in fact, actually; (実際は, 本来なら) really. (⇨型(5)) ●本当は彼女に会いたくないんだ To tell (you) the truth [〖書〗In (all) truth], I don't want to see her./*The truth [fact] (of the matter) is (that)* I don't want to see her. ●彼は彼女に会ったが, 本当は会いたくなかった He saw her, but *in fact* [*actually*, *really*] he didn't want to. ●本当はそんなことを言うべきではない You *really* shouldn't say that.

❷〖その他の表現〗●その事についてはお父さんと相談するのが本当だと思う I think you *should* talk to your father about it. (❢次例より口語的)/I think it is *proper* [*right*] to talk to your father about it. (⇨正しい, 適切な)

― 本当の 形 real; true; actual; genuine.

〖使い分け〗 **real** 作り出されたものではなく本物であることを表す.
true 現実に起きた出来事であることを表す. また, 物事はこうあるべきだという基準と一致していることを表す.
actual 想像や仮定に対して, 本番・現実・実際であることを表す.
genuine でっちあげられた物でないことを表す. また, その場のものであることを表す.

●本当の金(ﾈ) *genuine* [*real*, *true*, ×*actual*] gold. (⇨純金) ●本当の友達 a *true* [a *real*, a *genuine*] friend. (⇨親友) ●本当の自分 one's *real* self. ●それは本当の話です That's a *true* story./That's *true*. ●だれも彼女の本当の歳を知らない No one knows her *true* [*real*, *actual*] age./No one knows how old she *really* is. ●彼が今ハワイにいるのは本当だ It is true [a fact] that he is in Hawaii now. (❢×It is true [a fact] for him to be in Hawaii now. は不可)/*Truly*, he is in Hawaii now.

― 本当に 副 ❶〖実に, まったく〗

〖解説〗強調を表すには主に次の三つの方法がある.
(1) 強調の副詞を用いる. いずれも本義から意味が拡大して very の強意語として用いられる: (非常に) very much, so; (実に) really; (偽りなく) 《やや書》truly; (確かに) certainly, surely; (絶対に) absolutely; (極度に) extremely; (まったく) quite, 《話》just; (ひどく) 《話》awfully, 《話》terribly.
(2) 動詞に do をつける. 彼にあいつは大嫌いだ I *dó* hàte him. (❢do に強勢を置く. be 動詞の場合は be に強勢を置く: 私は本当に元気なんです I *ám* [xdó be] fine. cf. Dó be quiet.)
(3) 感嘆文を用いる. 本当に気持ちのいい日だ What a beautiful day!

●本当に幸せです I'm *very* happy (*indeed*). (❢*indeed* をつけるとより強意的)/*How* happy I am! ●彼は本当に親切です He is *really* [*truly*, 《主に米話》*real*, 《主に米話》*sure*] kind. ●パーティーは本当に楽しかった I enjoyed the party *very much*./I *really* [*very much*] enjoyed the party./I had a *very* [*a really*] good time at the party. ▶本当にごめんなさい I'm *so* [*extremely*, *terribly*, *awfully*] sorry. (❗いずれも主に女性語) ▶本当にそうですかAre you *quite* sure? ▶彼のコンサートは本当にすばらしかった His concert was *just* splendid.

❷ [*実際に*] really; actually; in fact. (⇨実際) ▶本当にそれが要るんだよ *I tell you* I need it./I need it, *I tell you*.

会話 「ごめんなさい, ママ」「本当にすまないと思っているの?」"I'm sorry, Mummy." "Are you *really* sorry?"

会話 「彼, 本当に婚約したんだよ」「とても信じられないよ」"He's *actually* engaged." "Would you believe it!"

❸ [*相づちの強調*] 会話 「ほら雨がやんだよ」「まあ, 本当に(そうだわ)ね」"Look. It's stopped raining." "Oh yes. Só it ＼has."

会話 「いいお天気ですね」「本当に(そう)ですね」"Nice day, isn't it?" "It cértainly [《主に米語》súre] ＼is."

会話 ▶「この犬は大きくなったね」「本当に(そう)だわ」"Hásn't this dog ＼grown!" "He hás ＼indeed." (❗前半は感嘆文の一種)

会話 ▶「きれいな夕焼けだね」「本当にね」"What a beautiful sunset!" "*I know.*"

ほんとう 本島 the main island.

ほんとう 奔騰 ― **奔騰する 動** soar; jump; skyrocket. ▶金の相場が奔騰した The price of gold *has suddenly jumped*.

ほんどう 本堂 the main [inner] temple, the main building (of a temple).

ほんどう 本道 【本街道】a main road; a highway (⇔a bypath, a side road); 【正しい道】the right way. ● 人生の本道を踏み外す wander away from the *right path* in life. ● 教育の本道 the *right* [*best*] *way* to educate people.

ほんどおり 本通り a main 《米》[a high 《英》] street. ● ケンジントン本通り *High Street* Kensington.

ほんにん 本人 (⇨当人, 自分, 自ら) ▶彼は君本人に話をしたいと言っている He wants to talk to you *personally* [*in person*]. ●本人がそういうのなら本当だろう It'll be true if he [she, (当該の人) the person concerned] says so.

ほんぬい 本縫い the final sewing.

ほんね 本音 (真の意図) one's real [true] intention. ● 本音を吐く say *what one really thinks*; reveal [disclose] *one's real intention(s)*. ● 建前と本音を使い分ける use one's words or *actual intentions* depending on the occasion. ▶今の言葉は本音ですか Do you *really mean* what you've said?

ボンネット 【車の】《米》a hood /húd/, 《英》a bonnet /bάnit/; 【帽子の一種】a bonnet.

ほんねん 本年 the current year; (今年) this year. ● 本年度の経済成長率 the economic growth rate of the *current* (*fiscal*) *year*. ▶本年もよろしくお願い申し上げます I hope (that) our good relationships will continue this year. (❗事情 米英には日本で年賀状に書くような特別な決まり文句はない)

*****ほんの** 【単なる】mere; 【ささやかな】small; 【わずかな】slight; 【ただ…だけ】only, just 【just の方が口語的】; 【単に】《やや堅》merely; 【わずかに】slightly. ● ほんのちょっと仕間 *just a moment* [*a minute*]. ▶彼の父が死んだとき彼はほんの子供だった He was a *mere* child when his father died./He was *only* [*just*, *merely*, 《主に書》*but*] a child when his father died. (❗an only child は「一人っ子」の

意)/He was *no* [*nothing*] *more than* a child when his father died. ▶ほんのお礼のしるしにこの本を差し上げます I'd like to give you this book as a *small* [*a slight*] token of my gratitude. ▶図書館はほんの名ばかりであった It was a library in name *only* [*only* in name]. ● 私はほんの数ドル[少しのお金]しか持っていない I have *only* a few dollars [*a little money*]. ▶この食物はほんの少し辛い This food is *just a little* [*slightly*, 《話》*a little bit*] hot.

*****ほんのう 本能** 名 (an) instinct. ● 自己防衛の本能 the *instinct* of self-protection; an *instinct* to protect oneself.

―― **本能的な 形** instinctive.

―― **本能的に 副** ▶彼は本能的に身の危険を感じた He felt *instinctively* [*by instinct*] that he was in danger./*Instinct* told him that he was in danger./His *instincts* sensed danger. ▶動物は本能的に火を恐れる Animals have an *instinctive* fear [*dread*] of fire.

ほんのう 煩悩 (説明的に) all human desires and passions that disturb your mind. (参考 キリスト教でいう seven deadly sins―pride, covetousness, lust, anger, gluttony, envy, and sloth もこれに類する。● 煩悩を断つ cut off [get rid of] *all human desires and passions*. ▶煩悩 (= 世俗的な欲望) に勝つのは難しい It is difficult to overcome *earthly desires*.

ほんのくぼ 盆の窪 the hollow of the nape.

ほんのり (わずかに) slightly; (かすかに) faintly. ● ほんのりとした匂い a *slight* [*a faint*] smell. ▶彼は酒を飲むとほんのり桜色になる He flushes *slightly* [*a little*] pinkish when he drinks alcohol. ▶そのお菓子はほんのりレモンの香りがする The cake smells *slightly* [*faintly*] of lemon. ▶東の空がほんのりと明けてきた There is a *faint* [ˣa *slight*] light in the eastern sky.

ほんば 本場 (原産地, 発祥地) the home; (生産の中心地) the center of production; (発祥地) the birthplace. ● 立憲政治の本場 the *birthplace* [*home*] of constitutional government. ● 本場のスコッチ genuine [*real*, *authentic*] Scotch. ▶この市は繊維産業の本場です This city is the *home* of the textile industry. ▶彼のフランス語は本場仕込みだ He has learned his French at a prestigious place [*in France*, *in Paris*]. (❗(1) prestigious は「権威のある」の意。(2) 場所を明示する方が自然)

ほんば 奔馬 a runaway horse; a horse running wildly.

● 奔馬性肺結核 〚医学〛galloping consumption.

ほんばこ 本箱 a bookcase. ● ガラス戸入りの本箱 a glass-fronted *bookcase*.

ほんばしょ 本場所 〚相撲〛a regular [a seasonal] *sumo* tournament.

ほんばん 本番 acting before the audience; 〚映画〛acting before the camera; (1回に映す場面) a take; 〚ラジオ・テレビ〛going on (the) air. ▶今のは試しだ。今度が本番だ That was just a trial run, now comes *the real thing* [now, we're *on*].

ほんびき ぼん引き (売春の客引き) a pimp, 《英話》a ponce. ● ぽん引きをする pimp.

ほんぶ 本部 (中心となる事務所) the head office (⇔a branch office); (軍隊・警察などの司令部) headquarters (単・複両用); (活動の中心地) a center; (大学などの事務局) an administration building. ▶FBI 本部はワシントン D.C.にある FBI *headquarters* is [are] in Washington, D.C./FBI *has its headquarters* [*is headquartered*] in

Washington, D.C.
ぼんぷ 凡夫 （普通の人）an ordinary person (⑳ people).
ポンプ a pump. ●蒸気ポンプ a stéam pùmp. ●手押しポンプ a hand pump. ●ポンプで井戸から水を汲み上げる pump water up from a well. ●船底の水をポンプで排出する pump the water out of a ship; pump out a ship.
●ポンプ室 a pump room. ●ポンプ車 (消防用の) a pumper.
ほんぷく 本復 ──本復する 動 〖全快する〗recover from one's illness; be restored to health.
ほんぶたい 本舞台 ❶〖本番の舞台〗▶彼はすでに5歳のときに本舞台を踏んだ He made his debut on the stage at an early age of five.
❷〖活動の晴れの場〗a public place. (⇨檜(⑴)舞台)●政界の本舞台を踏む appear on the political stage; make a debut as a politician.
ほんぶり 本降り a heavy rain; (ひっきりなしに降る雨) a steady rain. ▶まもなく雨が本降りになってきた It soon began to rain very hard〖本格的に〗in earnest〗.
ほんぶん 本分 one's duty. ❶〖義務〗●本分を尽くす〖怠る〗do〖fail in, neglect〗one's duty. ▶勉強するのが学生の本分だ A student's duty is〖It's a student's duty〗to study.

▣ **DISCOURSE**
もちろん学生の本分は勉強だ。しかし、他の活動にもかかわるべきだ Of course, students must study. However, they should engage in other activities as well. (❗Of course (もちろん) は譲歩を表すディスコースマーカー。However 以下に力点がある)

ほんぶん 本文 (挿し絵・注などに対して) text; (主要部分) the (main) body. ▶この本は本文の部分はそんなに多くない There's not so much text in this book. ▶この情報は注ではなく本文で扱うべきだ You should treat this information in the main body of the text, not in the notes.
ボンベ ＜ドイツ語＞ (円筒形の容器) a cylinder, (小型の) a canister. ●(プロパン)ガスボンベ a (propane) gas cylinder. (❗a gas bomb は「(毒)ガス弾」) ●酸素ボンベ an oxygen cylinder. ●調理用ガスボンベ a cooking-gas canister.
ボンベイ 〖インドの都市〗Bòmbáy. (参考)ムンバイ (Mumbai) の旧称)
ポンペイ 〖イタリアの都市〗Pompeii /pɑmpéii(ː)/.
ほんぽ 本舗 (⇨⑲ 本店)
ほんぽう 本邦 (我が国) this〖our〗country. ●本邦初演の戯曲 a play which was staged for the first time in Japan.
ほんぽう 本俸 (基本給) one's basic pay.
ほんぽう 奔放 ──奔放な 形 (形式にとらわれない) free; (抑制されず気ままな) unrestrained, uninhibited; (芸術家などが因襲にとらわれない) bohemian. ▶時に彼女の自由奔放な態度は無礼に思えることがある Sometimes her unrestrained manner seems rude.
ぼんぼり 雪洞 （あんどん）a paper-covered stand lamp; (手にもつ) a paper-covered hand lamp.
ぼんぼん 〖良家の息子〗a son of a respectable family. (⇨ぼっちゃん, 若旦那)
ぼんぼん 〖花火や時計などの音〗●薪をぼんぼんくべる feed the fire with wood at a furious pace. ●花火をぼんぼん (＝立て続けに) 打ち上げる set off fireworks in quick succession [one after another]. ●その古い時計がぼんぼんと鳴った The old clock went ding-dong.
ボンボン ＜フランス語＞〖洋菓子〗a bonbon.
ぼんぼん ❶〖破裂音, 爆発音〗●ぼんぼんと音を立てて with pops (ばんばんと). ●ぼんぼんと鳴るpop. (❗日本語のぼんぼんは複数音を示すが、英語のpop は複数音ではなく「ぼんと音がする」の意なので工夫がいる) ●花火がぼんぼんと上がった The fireworks were set off with bangs. ●クリスマスイブに、シャンパンがぼんぼん鳴った On Christmas Eve, champagne bottles kept on popping.
❷〖無造作に行う様子〗▶彼はいつもぼんぼんものを言う He is outspoken in his remarks./He always speaks frankly and directly〖話〗straight from the shoulder]./He doesn't mince (his) words.
●ぼんぼん蒸気 a steam passenger launch.
ポンポン 〖帽子などの玉房, 応援用飾り〗a pompon /pámpɑn/.
ポンポンダリア 〖植物〗a pompon (dahlia).
ほんま (本当) truth. (⇨本当) ▶ほんまかいな Is that true?/Really? ▶ほんまに彼女のこと好きやで I love her truly.
ほんまつてんとう 本末転倒 ▶それでは本末転倒だ You're giving priority to a less important thing.
ほんまる 本丸 (城の内部のとりで) the inner citadel /sítədl/ (of a castle).
ほんミス 凡ミス a careless [a silly, a stupid] mistake; 〖野球などで〗a careless [a silly, a stupid] play, 《話》a bonehead play.
ほんみょう 本名 one's real name (↔false name).
▶会員登録は本名でお願いします Please register as a member in your real name.
ほんむ 本務 ❶〖本来の努め〗●本務をおろそかにする neglect one's duty. ❷〖兼務に対し〗one's main [principal] work [job].
●本務校 the school [college] where one is (employed as) a regular (teacher).
ほんめい 本命 (競馬・競技・選挙などの) the favorite, a prospective winner; 《米話》a shóo-in.
ほんもう 本望 ●本望を遂げる realize one's long-cherished desire [dream]. ▶彼女はさぞかし本望だろう She must be very [quite, completely, perfectly] satisfied.
ほんもと 本元 (⇨本家)
ほんもの 本物 名 ▶この真珠は本物そっくりだ These pearls look real [genuine].
──**本物の** 形 (外見と内容が同じの) real; (正真正銘の) genuine; (基準にそう) true; (人工的でない) natural. ●本物の紳士 a true [a real] gentleman. ●本物の証明書 a genuine [an authentic] certificate. ●本物の(＝天然の)石を使った暖炉 a native stone fireplace. ▶彼のピアノ演奏は本物だ (専門家のように演奏する) He plays the piano expertly./His performance on the piano is the real thing. (❗the real thing は「人」についてほめて用いられる: He is the real thing.)
ほんもん 本文 (⇨本文(ﾊﾞﾝ))
ほんや 本屋 〖小売店〗《米》a bookstore, 《英》a bookshop; (人) a bookseller; 〖出版社〗a publisher. (⇨書店)
*****ほんやく 翻訳** 名 (a) translation. ●自動翻訳 automatic translation. ●翻訳業を work as a translator. ●ヘブライ語から英語への聖書の翻訳 the translation of the Bible from Hebrew into English. ●バルザック[フランスの小説]を翻訳で読む read Balzac [a French novel] in translation. ●この詩は英語からの翻訳だ This poem is a translation from the English (original). (❗the をつけてその詩の英語版をさすので the は省略できない) ▶彼は翻訳がうまい He is a good translator./He is clever at translation. (⇨訳(ﾔｸ))

ぼんやすみ ── **翻訳する** 動 translate. ●その詩を英語に翻訳する translate [《やや話》put] the poem *into* English. /《やや話》do an English *translation* of the poem. ●フランス語へ逐語的に翻訳する make [do] (it) a word-for-word *translation into* French. ●その劇はギリシャ語から英語に忠実に翻訳された The play *was* closely *translated from* Greek *into* English. ▶彼の詩は日本語に翻訳できない His poetry does not *translate* [cannot *be translated*] *into* Japanese. (⇨訳す)
●**翻訳家** a translator. ●**翻訳権** the right to translate [of translation]. ●**翻訳書** a translation.

ぼんやすみ 盆休み the *Bon* holidays.

***ぼんやり ❶**[定かでなく]dimly; (かすかに) faintly; (区別がつかず) indistinctly. ▶ぼんやりと見える山影 the *dim* [*vague*] outline of a mountain. ▶遠くに山がぼんやり見える You can see mountains *dimly* [*faintly*] in the distance. ▶ずっと遠くにぼんやり人影が現れた There appeared in the far distance an *indistinct* human figure.
❷[うっかりと] absent-mindedly; (うつろに) vacantly. ▶彼女はよくぼんやりして傘を電車の中に置き忘れてくる She often leaves her umbrella in the train *absent-mindedly*. ▶彼は海をぼんやり見るのが好きだ He likes gazing *vacantly* at the sea. ▶ほかのことを考えてぼんやりしていた I was *absent-minded* thinking about something else./My mind was wandering.
❸[態度や様子があいまい] (漠然と) vaguely /véigli/; (あいまいに) obscurely; (どちらともとれる) ambiguously. ▶私はそのことをぼんやりとしか思い出せない I can only remember it *vaguely*. ▶彼女は何かぼんやりした分からない事を言って人をとまどわせるのが好きです She enjoys puzzling other people [others] by expressing herself *obscurely* [*unclearly*]. ▶彼の政治的立場はぼんやりとしか報じられていなかった His political position was *ambiguously* reported.
❹[なす事もなく]idly; (目的もなく) aimlessly. ▶私はふつう日曜は一日ぼんやり過ごします I usually spend the whole day *idly* on Sundays. ▶私はぼんやりと旅をして回るのが好きです I like traveling around *aimlessly* [*for no specific purpose*].
❺[よく気を配らずに] carelessly; (無頓着に) negligently. ▶ぼんやり運転していたら曲がる所を見逃すよ If you drive *without looking ahead carefully*, you will miss your turn.

ぼんよう 凡庸 ── **凡庸な** 形 (平凡な) commonplace; (良くも悪くもない) mediocre /miːdióukər/; (並の) ordinary.

ぼんよみ 本読み ❶[読書家]a great reader; (熱烈な) an avid reader; (本の虫) a bookworm.
❷[演劇などで](脚本を) script reading. ●本読みをする read the script with other actors.

***ほんらい 本来** ── **本来の** 形 original; essential; natural. ●人間本来の性質 human *nature*. ●その語の本来の意味 the *original* meaning of the word.
── **本来** 副 ❶[元来]originally; [本質的に]essentially; [生来]naturally, by nature. ▶この詩は本来フランス語で書かれていた This poem was *originally* written in French. ▶お金は本来(=それ自体)悪いものではない Money is not bad *in itself*.
❷[あるべき規準によれば] ▶本来ならば母がお伺いすべきですが.... My mother ought to visit you, but ....
▶本来ならば(=厳密に言うと)これは私の仕事ではない *Strictly speaking*, this is not my job.

ほんりゅう 本流 the mainstream, the main current. ●政界の本流から外れている be outside [out of] the political *mainstream*.

ほんりゅう 奔流 [激しい流れ]a rushing stream, a torrent. ●奔流をなして流れる flow [rush] in *torrents*.

ほんりょ 凡慮 ordinary mind; ideas that come from ordinary people. ●凡慮の及ぶところではない It's something beyond our thoughts.

ほんりょう 本領 (特性) one's characteristic; (実力) one's (real) ability; (専門) one's specialty. ●本領を発揮する show oneself at one's best; show one's *real ability*; (得意の分野にいる) be in one's element.

ほんるい 本塁 [野球]the home plate, home. ●(捕手などが)本塁をブロックする block the *plate*. ●本塁を死守する protect the *plate*.

ほんるいだ 本塁打 a home run, a homer. ●特大本塁打 a tape-measure home run [shot]. ●本塁打を打つ hit a home run [a homer].
●**本塁打王** a home-run king.

ほんろう 翻弄 ── **翻弄する** 動 (波が) toss ... about; (人が) trifle (*with*); make* fun [a fool] of ....
●**翻弄される** (波に) be tossed (back and forth); (...のなすがままである) be at the mercy of .... ●松坂は相手チームの強打者を翻弄した Matsuzaka *made fools of* the opposing team's sluggers.

ほんろん 本論 [主題]the main subject; (主な問題点) the main issue.

ほんわか ▶この裏通りにはほんわかとした(=暖かくてくつろいだ)雰囲気がただよっている A *warm and relaxed* [*comfortable*] atmosphere prevails in this alley.

ほんわり 本割り [相撲]*honwari*; (説明的に) the schedule of *sumo* bouts carried out according to the *torikumi* program.

ま

ま 間 ❶ [時間] time; (暇) leisure; (合間) an interval; (休止) a pause.
① [間が] ▶忙しくてくつろぐ間がない I'm so busy (that) I have no *time* to relax. ▶出発までにまだじゅうぶん間がある There is plenty of *time* before we (×will) start. ▶彼は日本に来てまだ間がない He has *not* been *long* in Japan./*It's not been* [*isn't*] *long* since he came to Japan.
② [間の[に, も]] (⇨間(ﾏ)) ▶あっという間に in an instant; in no time (at all). ▶演説は間の取り方が難しい It's hard to *pause* [*make a pause*] properly when you give a speech. ▶私が止める間もないうちに彼はそれを買ってしまった He bought it *before* I could stop him. ▶知らない間に夜が暗くなっていた He was [had] gone *before* I knew it.
③ [間を] ▶少し間をおいてから話す speak after a short *interval* [*pause*]. ▶2時間の間をおいて(2時間間隔で) at *intervals* of two hours, at two-hour *intervals*; (2時間後に) two hours later, after (an interval of) two hours. (⇨後)
❷ [空間] (a) space; (間隔) an interval. ▶間をあける leave (a) space 《between》. ▶一定の間をおいて柱を立てる put up posts at regular *intervals*.
❸ [部屋] a room. ▶日本間 a Japanese-style *room*. ▶ふた間の家 a two-*room*(ed) house. ▶6畳の間 a six-tatami [a six-mat] *room*.
• 間がいい (タイミングがいい) be timely (⇨タイミング); (運がいい) be lucky [fortunate].
• 間が抜ける ▶そんなことをするとは彼は間が抜けている It's *stupid* of him to do that./He's *stupid* to do that.
• 間が持てない ▶電車の中ではすることがないので間が持てない I *cannot fill (in) the time* as I have nothing to do on the train.
• 間が悪い (きまりが悪い) feel awkward [embarrassed]; (運が悪い) be unlucky.
• 間を持たせる ▶雑談をして間を持たせる *fill (in) the time* by chatting.

ま 真 ▶真新しい車 a *brand*-new car. ▶橋の真下に *right* under the bridge. ▶その町はここから真北の方 The town lies *due* north of here.
• 真に受ける (⇨真に受ける)

ま 魔 (悪魔) a devil /dévl/, an evil /íːvl/ spirit; (害悪, 不運) evil. ▶魔よけ a charm against evils. (⇨魔除け) ▶魔の金曜日 an *unlucky* Friday. ▶魔の踏み切り a *fatal* railroad crossing.
• 魔がさす ▶彼女が時計を万引したなんて魔がさしたに違いない *Something* must have *got into* her to make her shoplift a watch./(書) She must have been possessed by an *evil spirit* to have shoplifted a watch.

***まあ 副** ❶ [ちょっと] just. (**!** 通例命令文の前に置き, 命令・提案・助言をやわらげる) ▶まあ考えてごらん *Just imagine!* ▶まあおかけください *Just sit down, please*.
❷ [やや] rather; fairly (⇨かなり [類語]); [およそ] about; [言ってみれば, 例えば] let us say, (let's) say; [いわば] as it were, 《話》so to speak; [おそらく] maybe. ▶その芝居はまあ失敗だった The play was *rather* a failure. (**!** rather は「a+程度を表す名詞」の前に置く. ひどい失敗を暗示する婉曲表現)
▶彼女はまあ好きなほうだ I *rather* [《話》*kind of, sort of*] like her. (**!** (1) kind [sort] of はしばしば /kàində/, /sɔ́ːrtə/ と発音される. (2) 会話では次のようにも用いる:「彼女が好きなんでしょ」「まあね」"You like her, don't you?" "I *rather do./Kind* [*Sort*] *of*.")
▶まあそんなところだ(いくつか例をあげた後で) It's something *like* that./(話を切り上げるときに) That's (just) *about it* [*all*]./(相手に同意して) That's *about the size of it*./(概数に対して) That's *about right*. ▶彼は来ますよ, まあ10分もすれば He'll be here in, (*let's*) *say*, ten minutes. ▶彼はまあ生き字引といったところだ He is, *as it were* [*so to speak*], a walking dictionary. ▶今夜はまあ雨だろう *Maybe* it will rain tonight. ▶彼はまあ紳士といえる人だ He *might* be called a gentleman./《話》He is *a kind* [*a sort*] *of* (×a) gentleman. (**!** A kind [a sort] of の後は通例無冠詞の単数名詞) ▶彼女は60を越えているでしょう I *would* [*should*] *say* she is over sixty. (**!** would, should は断定を避けた控えめな気持ちを表す. would の方が好まれる)
❸ [催促, なだめ] ▶まあ(=お願い), そんなに怒らないで *Please don't be so angry!* (⇨どうか) ▶まあお座りなさい *Do sit down*. (**!** (1)(相手が座るのをためらっているような状況で用いる. (2) ...↘*down*. と下降調にすると「座れといったら座れ」の意)

―まあ 間 ❶ [驚きなど] oh /óu/; well; (oh) dear; (Good) Heavens [《やや古》gracious]; my; 《米話》say, 《古》I say; 《英やや古・米》why /wái/.

使い分け	
oh	驚き・喜び・不快・感動などさまざまな感情を表す最も一般的な語.
well	予想外の出来事などが起きた際の驚きや愉快さを示す.
dear	好ましくないことに対する驚き・後悔・いら立ち・同情などの感情を表す. 通例 "oh dear" の形で用いられる.
(Good) Heavens [gracious]!/(My) goodness!/Goodness (gracious) me!	驚き・困惑・怒りなどを示す. Oh (my) God! などの下品な言い方に対する婉曲表現.
my	主に驚き・当惑・感動などの感情を表す. "My" あるいは "oh my" の形で用いられる.
say	驚き・喜び・賞賛を表す.
why	意外さによる軽い驚き・ためらいなどを表す.

▶まあ, きれいな花ことだ *Oh* [*My* (*my*)], what a beautiful flower! (**!** 感嘆文だけでもこの意を表せる) ▶まあ, どうしたの *Well*, what's the matter? ▶まあ大変, どこへ鍵(￣)を置いたのかしら *Oh dear* [*My goodness*]! Where have I put my keys? ▶まあよかった, 彼は無事だった Thank God [*goodness, heaven*(*s*)]! He's safe. ▶あらまあ, 箱がからっぽだ *Why*(, *why*)! The box is empty. ▶まあ, こんな所でお会いするなんて(世間なんと狭いものですね) *What a small world!*/(考えてもごらんなさい)《話》*Fancy meeting you here!* (**!** 命令文による一種の感嘆表現) ▶よくもまあ私にそんな口がきけますね *How dare you say such a thing to me!*
❷ [応答, 反応] ▶まあ, それで? *Well, then?* ▶まあ仕方がないさ *Oh well, we can't help it* [*it can't be helped*]. ▶まあまあ, それはお気の毒に *Dear, dear! I'm sorry to hear that*. ▶まあ, それはよい考えだわ

Say, that's a good idea.
●会話「彩子が結婚するんですって」「まあ,本当なの?」 "I hear Ayako's getting married." "Oh, really?" (≒単に Oh?, Really? とも)
●会話「君がその花びんを割ったの?」「ええ,まあそういうことです」"Did you break the vase?" "Well [Why], yes."

まあい 間合い (ちょうどよい間隔) a suitable distance [interval]; (頃合い) the right time (⇒頃合い); (潮) high time. (⇒潮時)

マーカー a marker (pen).

マーガリン margarine /má:rdʒərən/, 《英話》marge /má:rdʒ/.

マーガレット 〖植物〗a marguerite /mà:rgəri:t/.

マーキュロクロム [赤チン] 〖商標〗Mercurochrome /mərkjúərəkròum/. (▮現在は製造中止)

マーク 图 〖目印〗a mark (⇒印); [ある内容を表す記号など] a sign; 〖銘柄〗a brand; 〖商標〗a trademark; [敵の選手の] marking. ●クマのマークのスポーツシャツクマ a Bear *brand* sports shirt. ●その会社の(トレード)マーク the company's *trademark*. ●平和の(シンボル)マーク a peace *symbol* [*emblem*]. (▮(1) 前の方は抽象的,後の方は具象的な図案など。(2) ×…*symbol mark* とはいわない) ●その船には赤十字のマークがついていた The ship *was marked with* a red cross.
―― **マークする** 働 [敵の選手を] cover, 〖サッカーなど〗《英》mark; 〖要注意人物を〗keep watch on (⇒ブラックリスト).

マークアップ [利幅] a markup.

マークシート a mark-sense, a mark-sensing card. ●マークシート方式のテスト a computer-graded [a computer-scored] test. (▮a mark-sheet test は《英》ではコンピュータ時代以前に使われた,正解の番号に穴を開けたシートを作って答案の上に重ねて採点した旧式のもの)

マーケット 〖市場〗a market. ●家の近くのマーケットで肉を買う buy some meat at the *market* near one's house. ●新型車のマーケット(≒市場)の開拓をする develop [find] a *market for* new models. ●フリーマーケット a flea *market*.
●マーケットシェア a *market* share. (⇒シェア) ●マーケットリサーチ 〖市場調査〗márket resèarch.

マーケティング 〖市場戦略〗marketing. ●国際[グローバル]マーケティング international [global] *marketing*.
●マーケティング計画 a márketing plàn. ●マーケティング戦略 a márketing stràtegy. ●マーケティングリサーチ 〖市場調査〗márketing resèarch.

まあじ 真鯵 〖魚介〗a saurel.

マーシャルしょとう マーシャル諸島 〖国名〗the Marshall Islands; (公式名) the Republic of the Marshall Islands. (首都 Majuro) ●マーシャル(諸島)人 a Marshall Islander. ●マーシャル(諸島)語 Marshallese. ●マーシャル(諸島)(人[語])の Marshallese.

マーシャルプラン 〖第二次大戦後の欧州復興計画〗the Marshall Plan.

マージャン 〈中国語〉 mah-jong /mà:dʒɔŋ/. ●マージャンのパイ (*mah-jong*) tile. ●マージャンをする play (a game of) *mah-jong*.
●マージャン屋 a mah-jong parlor.

マージン ❶ [利ざや] a (profit) margin. ●化粧品の商売はマージンが多い[少ない] The (*profit*) *margin* is large [small] in the cosmetics business./The cosmetics business has a wide [a narrow] *margin* (of profit).
❷ [余白] a margin. (⇒余白)

まあたらしい 真新しい brand(-)new. ●真新しい帽子 a *brand*(*-*)*new* hat.

マーチ 〖行進曲〗a march.

マーフィーのほうそく マーフィーの法則 Murphy's Law.

マーブル (大理石に似た模様) marbling; (ビー玉) a marble.

マーボーどうふ 麻婆豆腐 〖料理〗*mabo dofu*; (説明的に) fried *tofu* with ground meat in a spicy sauce seasoned with chili pepper.

まあまあ ❶ [そこそこの程度] ●まあまあの給料 a decent [a moderate] salary. (▮前の方は「かなりいい」こと,後の方は「平均以下」であることを表す婉曲表現) ●英語の試験はまあまあできたと思う I think I did *fairly well* [*well enough*, 《話》okay] on the English exam. ●値段はまあまあだ(=あまり高くない) The price is *reasonably* (high). /It's *reasonably* priced. ●彼はそのアルバムでまあまあの成功を収めた He had a *nice little* success with the album.
●会話「芝居はどうだった?」「まあまあだった」"How was the play?" "*Not too* [*so*] *bad*." (▮なかなかよかった「大の控えめな表現)/(たいしてよくなかった) 《話》(*Only*) *só-só*./(可もなく不可もない) *Neither good nor bad*." (▮中立的な表現)
●会話「やあ,ニック元気かい」「まあまあだ」"Hi, how's it going, Nick?" "*Could be better*." (▮I を省略したくだけた慣用表現.「最高にいいよ」なら Couldn't be better.)
❷ [なだめて] ●まあまあ次郎,泣かないで ↘*Come on* [*Come, Now, There*], ↗*Jiro. Stop crying*.

マーマレード marmalade /má:rməlèid/.

マーモット 〖動物〗a marmot. (▮日本語の「モルモット」とは別の動物)

マーラー 〖オーストリアの作曲家〗Mahler (Gustav ~).

まい 舞 a dance; dancing. ●日本古来の舞 a traditional Japanese *dance*. ●舞を舞う perform a *dance* (*to*).

***まい―** 毎― ❶ [...ごとに] (すべての...も) every ...; (各 ...) each .... (▮前の方は全体的かつ個別的,後の方は個別的。いずれも単数名詞を従える) ●毎日そこへ行く go there *every* [*each*] day. (▮(1) ×on every [each] day は不可. (2) each は「全体」を暗示する語とはいっしょに使えない: ほぼ毎日 almost [nearly, practically] *every* [×*each*] day/例外なく毎日 *every* [×*each*] day (without exception) ●その雑誌なら毎号読んでいます I read *each* issue of that magazine./I never miss an issue of that magazine.
❷ [...につき] a, per. (⇒-に付き) ●毎秒 60 メートルで走る run (at) 60 meters *a* [*per*] second.

***まい** -枚 〖紙・ガラスなどの〗a sheet of ...; (四角の形が整っている紙など); a piece of ...; 〖形・大きさが整っていない紙など〗; 〖パンなどの〗a slice of .... (⇒一枚) ●数枚の紙 several *pieces* [*sheets*] of paper. ●1 枚の紙切れ a *scrap* of paper. ●食パン 2 枚 two *slices* of bread. ●写真 3 枚 *three* pictures. ●80 円切手を 5 枚ください Please give me *five* eighty-yen stamps. ●フィルムはあと何枚残っていますか How many exposures have you got left?

-まい ●あしたは雨は降るまい I don't think it will rain tomorrow. ●彼はとうてい試験には受かるまい He *can't* possibly pass the exam. (▮possibly は can't を強める) ●彼は決してそこへは行くまい He *will never* go there. ●いったいどうしてそんな危険を冒したの,警告されていなかったわけじゃあるまいし Whatever made you take such a risk? It wasn't *as if* you hadn't been warned.

-まい -米 rice. ●白米 polished *rice*. ●国[外国]産米 domestic [foreign, imported] *rice*. ●カリフォ

まいあがる ルニア米 rice from California; Californian [Californian] rice.

まいあがる 舞い上がる 〚鳥などが〛soar, fly* up; 〚風で〛be blown up 《◆吹き上げる》;《渦を巻いて》be whirled up; 《揺り動かされて》be stirred up. ▶ワシが空高く舞い上がった The eagle *soared* high into the sky. ▶風が吹くたびにほこりが舞い上がった Every gust of wind *whirled* [*stirred*] *up* the dust. ▶彼は志望大学に合格して舞い上がった He *felt elated* to have been admitted to the university of his choice.

まいあさ 毎朝 every morning. ●毎朝早く起きる get up early *every morning* [毎日朝早く] early *in the morning every day*]. (⇨每-)

マイアミ 〚米国の都市〛Miami /maiǽmi/.

まいおき 舞扇 a dáncing [a dánce] fán; a fan for dancing.

まいおさめる 舞い納める finish dancing.

まいおりる 舞い降りる (さっと降りる) swoop down; (飛んできて降りる) flutter down. ●ふわりと舞い降りる *flutter lightly down*.

マイカー（個人用）one's own car; a private car; (家族用) a family car. ●マイカーで通勤する go to work [commute] in [×on, ×by] one's *own car*. ●マイカー族 an owner driver.

まいかい 毎回 ▶彼は会合には毎回出席する He *never fails to* attend the meeting. ▶私は試験を毎回(=必ず)ミスをする I make some mistakes in (each and) *every* exam. (！( )内を加えると「毎回毎回こりもせず」という感じを伴う) (⇨每-)

まいき 毎期 every [each] term.

まいきょ 枚挙 ●枚挙にいとまがない be too numerous to mention 《数え上げる》enumerate, count].

マイク a mícrophòne,《話》a mike. ●ハンド[つり下げ]マイク a hand-held [a suspended] *microphone*. ●ワイヤレスマイク a wireless *microphone*. ●隠しマイク a concealed [a hidden] *microphone*,《俗》a bug. ●感度のよいマイク a sensitive *microphone*. ●マイクに向かって[を通して]話す speak into [through, over] a *microphone*. ▶彼に向けてマイクを突き出す hold a *microphone to* him; (先を向ける) point a *microphone at* him. ▶入っていますか、マイクは入っていますか Are we on? Is the *mike* working?

マイクロ 〚極小, 微小〛micro-. ●マイクロウェーブ (⇨同 マイクロ波) ●マイクロキュリー〚放射能の強さの単位〛〚物理〛a microcurie. ●マイクロコンピュータ a microcomputer. ●マイクロ波〚物理〛a microwave. ●マイクロバス a minibus.《米》a microbus. (！前の方が普通) ●マイクロフィルム (a) microfilm. ●新聞をマイクロフィルムに収める *microfilm* the newspapers. ●マイクロマシン a micromachine. ●マイクロメーター〚計測器具〛a micrometer. ●マイクロリーダー a microreader.

マイクロソフト Microsoft Corporation.《参考》米国のコンピューターソフトウエアメーカー》●マイクロソフトを使ってプログラムを組む use *Microsoft('s)* software to write a program.

マイクロホン a mícrophòne. (⇨同 マイク)

まいげつ 毎月 every month. (⇨毎月(まいつき))

まいこ 舞子 a *maiko* (複 〜s); (説明的に) a young apprentice geisha girl.

まいご 迷子 a lost [a stray] child (複 children). ▶その子は森の中で迷子になった The child *got lost* [*lost his way*] in the woods. ▶迷子のご案内を申し上げます。赤い帽子をかぶった2歳ぐらいのお子様をお預りしています。お心当たりの方は近くの店員にご連絡ください We have a *lost child* looking for her parent. Would the guardian of a two-year-old girl wearing a red hat please contact one of the storeclerks in your vicinity.

まいごう 毎号 (⇨毎-)

まいこつ 埋骨 — 埋骨する 動 彼は妻の隣りに埋骨されている His ashes *are buried* next to those of his wife./He *is buried* with his wife.

まいこむ 舞い込む (花びらなどが) come* fluttering 《into a room》; (手紙などが) receive [get*] 《a letter》unexpectedly.

マイコン a mícrocompùter,《話》a micro (複 〜s). (⇨コンピュータ)

まいじ 毎時 every hour. ▶その列車は毎時240キロ(の速さ)で走る That train runs at (a speed of) 240 kilometers *an* [*per*] hour. (！(1)《話》ではしばしばatも省略される. (2)しばしば 240 kph [KPH]と略記する) ▶列車は毎時0分[毎時30分]に発車する Trains leave *every hour* on the hour [on the half hour].

まいしゅう 毎週 every week. ●毎週一度の会合 a *weekly* meeting. ▶毎週日曜日にそこへ行く go there *every* Sunday (日曜日にはいつも) on Sundays,《話》Sundays]. ▶彼は毎週電話をくれた He gave me a (phone) call *every week* (週に一度) once a week, weekly]. (⇨每-, 週) ▶毎週火曜日の9時に来られますか Can you come at nine *every* Tuesday?

まいしょく 毎食 every [each] meal.

まいしん 邁進 — 邁進する 動 ●仕事[研究]に邁進する *push ahead* [*forward, on*] *with* one's work [study].

まいすう 枚数 the number of sheets. (⇨一枚) ▶試験が終わったら回収した解答用紙の枚数を確認してください When the exam is over, please check *how many* answer sheets you've collected.

まいすがた 舞姿 one's dáncing [dánce] stànce.

まいせつ 埋設 — 埋設する 動 ●ガス本管を埋設する *lay* a gas main *underground*.

まいそう 埋葬 名 burial /bériəl/. ▶彼の埋葬式を営む hold his *burial* service.
— 埋葬する 動 bury /béri/; 《婉曲的》lay 《him》to rest [sleep].

まいぞう 埋蔵 — 埋蔵する 動 ●莫大な量の石油が埋蔵されている海域 a sea area with vast oil *deposits*. ●埋蔵金 the buried /bérid/ gold. ●埋蔵物 (鉱石などの) deposits; (持ち主不明の発掘物)《法律》(a) treasure trove. ●埋蔵量 (oil) reserves [deposits].

まいちもんじ 真一文字 ●(矢などが) 真一文字に飛ぶ fly in a *straight line*. (！「一直線に飛ぶ」の意) ●真一文字に突進する dash *straight ahead*. ●真一文字に口(=唇)を結んでいる keep one's lips *tightly* closed.

まいつき 毎月 every month. ●毎月一度の会合 a *monthly* meeting. ▶毎月そこへ行く go there *every month* (月に一度) once a month, monthly]. (⇨每-)

まいど 毎度 every [each] time. ▶彼は毎度(=毎回)失敗している He fails *every* [*each*] *time*. ▶毎度(=度々)お手数をおかけして申し訳ありません I'm sorry to trouble you *so often*. ▶彼が遅れて来るのは毎度(=いつも)のことだ He *always* comes late. ▶毎度ありThanks (a lot). ▶毎度ありがとうございます。またお越しください Thank you very much (for your patronage). Please come again.

まいとし 毎年 every year. (⇨毎年(まいねん))

マイナー ●マイナーな(=重要でない)詩人 a *minor* [an

マイナーリーガー a minor leaguer.

マイナーリーグ 〖野球〗a minor league; the minor leagues 〖参考〗米国の2大リーグの下位のリーグの総称.　▶選手をマイナーリーグへ落とす send a player down to the *minors*.　▶マイナーリーグから昇格する be promoted from the *minors*.

*__マイナス__　❶【引き算・負記号】a minus (↔a plus).　▶6マイナス10はマイナス4 Six *minus* ten is *minus* [〖数学〗*negative*] four.　▶温度はマイナス20度だ The temperature is *minus* 20 (degrees) [20 (degrees) *below zero*].　▶年間の最低気温は摂氏マイナス5度で最高気温は35度だ The annual range of temperature is from −5℃ to 35℃. (⇨温度)　❷【不利】a disadvantage.　▶核家族のマイナス面 the *disadvantage*(s) of a nuclear family.　▶彼のまじめさがかえってマイナスになった His diligence turned out (to be) a *disadvantage* after all.　❸【電気など】　▶磁石にはプラスとマイナスがある A magnet has positive and *negative* poles.
● マイナスイオン negative ion /áiən/ ● マイナスイメージ a negative (↔positive) image.　● マイナス記号 a minus (sign).　● マイナス成長（経済の）negative (economic) growth.　● マイナスドライバー a slotted-head [a flat-tip] screwdriver; 〖和製語〗a minus driver.　● マイナスねじ a slotted screw.

*__まいにち　毎日__　every day.　● 毎日の(=1日1日の)生活 one's *daily* (〖日常の〗*everyday*) life. (✕one's every day life は不可)　▶彼は毎日そこへ行く He goes there *every day* [(1日単位で) *daily*, (日に一度) *once a day*].　▶彼は毎日のように電話をしてきた He called me up almost *every day* [almost *daily*]. (⇨毎一)　▶私は毎日毎日(=来る日も来る日も)その仕事をした I worked on it *day after day* [*eight days a week*].　▶day by day は「日ごとに」の意. 後の方は誇張表現で日本語の「1週間に10日来い」に通じる言い方

*__まいねん　毎年__ every [each] year; annually.　● 毎年の行事 an *annual* [a *yearly*] event.　▶私は毎年[毎年夏休みには；毎年1回は]帰省する I go home *every year* [*every summer vacation*; at least *once a year*].　▶毎年今ごろは雨が多い We have lots of rain about this time *every year* [about this time of (the) year]. (⇨毎一, 年)

マイノリティー （=1国内の少数民族）the minority (group); （その一員）a minority.

まいばん　毎晩 every evening [night].　● 毎晩のテレビ番組 *nightly* TV programs.　▶毎晩外出する go out *every evening* [*every night, nightly*]. (⇨毎一, 晩, 夜)

まいひめ　『舞姫』 *The Dancing Girl*; *The Dancer*.　〖参考〗森鷗外の小説

『マイフェアレディー』 *My Fair Lady*. 〖参考〗バーナード・ショーの戯曲『ピグマリオン』を原作としたミュージカル・映画

マイペース　❶【速度】(run *at*, do one's work *at*) one's own pace.　❷【方法】(do one's work *in*) one's own way.　(❗ 単に「マイペースでやる」なら go one's (own) way も可)

マイホーム 〖我が家〗one's (own) home [house].　▶彼は東京の郊外にマイホームを持っている He has a *house of his own* [*owns a house*] in the suburbs of Tokyo.
● マイホーム主義 a family-oriented [a home-oriented] way of life.　● マイホーム主義の男 a family man, a family-minded man.

まいぼつ　埋没　——埋没する 動 be buried /bérid/ (*under* snow).　▶仕事に埋没する be buried [bury oneself] in one's work.

まいもどる　舞い戻る　▶犯人は凶行現場に舞い戻るだろう The criminal will come back [return] to the scene of the crime. (❗ 前の方が口語的)

まいゆう　毎夕 every evening. (⇨毎晩)

まいよ　毎夜 every evening [night]. (⇨毎晩)

まいる　参る　❶【行く】go*; （相手のところへ行く）come*.　（=行く）ただ今参ります I'm *coming*./(店員が) I'll be right *with you*. (❗ right は「すぐに」の意)

❷【来る】come*; 〖到着する〗arrive.　▶すぐ戻ってまいります I'll be [*come*] back in a moment./I'll be right back. (❗ 本来の文脈では be は come と同義)　▶間もなくお車が参ります Your car will *arrive* [*be here*] soon, sir.

❸【参拝する】　▶寺[神社]に参る visit a temple [a shrine]; worship [go worshipping] at a temple [a shrine]. ❗ 前の方は観光の意も表すが, 後の方では参拝の意が明確になる)

❹【負ける】〖耐えられない〗can't stand [bear]; (あきらめる) give up.　▶参ったと言う admit [acknowledge] one's *defeat*.　▶この寒さ[暑さ]には参った(=耐えられない) I *can't stand* [*bear*] this cold [heat]./This cold [heat] *is* quite *unbearable*.　会話 「どうだ, 参ったか」「参った」"Now, do you *give up*?" "I give up./You beat me. (❗ 以上現在形に注意)/You've got me."

❺【困る】（困惑する）be embarrassed （*by, at*）; (閉口する) be beaten; (窮地に立っている) 〖話〗be in a fix; 〖疲れはてる〗be tired out, be exhausted; 〖苦しむ〗suffer (*from*); 〖体調を崩す〗collapse.　▶精神的に参る *be* emotionally *exhausted*.　▶彼のマナーの悪さには参ったよ I *was embarrassed by* [*at*] his bad manners.　▶これには完全に参った This *beats me* altogether.　▶彼は徒歩旅行の後すっかり参っていた(=疲れきっていた) He *was tired out* [*was exhausted*] after the walking trip.　▶彼は風邪で参っている He *is suffering from* a cold.　▶休暇を取らないと体が参ってしまいますよ If you don't take a vacation, you'll *collapse* (燃えつきる) *burn yourself out*].

❻【ほれこむ】be [fall*] in love (*with*).　▶彼はあの娘にすっかり参っている He *is madly in love with* [〖話〗*is crazy about*] that girl.　▶彼女は男の子がみんな参ってしまう(=夢中になる)ほどの美人だった She was such a beauty that she *drove* all the boys *wild* [〖話〗*crazy*].

マイル a mile.　〖参考〗約1.6キロ）　● 5マイル半 five *miles* and a half; five and a half *miles*.　● 時速50マイルで走る run at 50 *miles* an [per] hour.
● マイルを貯める[使う] accumulate [use] mileage points.　● マイルストーン 〖里程標〗a milestone.

マイレージ　● マイレージ（=マイルを貯める[使う]）(⇨マイル)　● マイレージサービス a frequent-flier service; a mileage accumulation service.

まいわし　真鰯 〖魚介〗a pilchard.

マインド 〖精神〗mind.　● 消費者マインド the consumer *mind*.

マインドコントロール 名 mind control; （洗脳）brainwashing.

——**マインドコントロールする** 動 brainwash 《him *into doing*》.

__まう　舞う__ 〖舞いを〗dance (⇨踊る); 〖チョウ・木の葉などが〗flutter (about); (回転しながら) whirl; 〖鳥が〗fly; (旋回して) circle; (空高く舞い上がる) soar.　▶四

の葉が風に舞っている The leaves *are fluttering* [*whirling*] in the wind.

まう 眩う (⇨眩(ﾏ)ﾙ)

マウイ ●マウイ島 Maui.

まうえ 真上 ─ 真上に 〓 (…の真上に) right [just] above (…); (…の真上に) right over (…); 〔まっすぐ頭上に〕 right overhead. (⇨真下) ▶月を見に来て！ 真上に出ているよ Come (and) look at the moon, it's *right over* (our heads). (❗️) (1) right overhead ともいう。(2) くだけた言い方では and はしばしば脱落する.

まうしろ 真後ろ ─ 真後ろに 〓 (すぐ真後ろに) just [right, directly] behind …; just at the back of …. (⇨うしろ) ▶小犬が彼女の真後ろにいた A puppy was *just behind* her.

マウス [ハツカネズミ]【動物】a mouse (複 mice).

マウス [コンピュータの] a mouse (複 mice). ▶マウスで操作する operate with a *mouse*. ▶開きたいファイルのアイコンをマウスでダブルクリックしてください Double-click on the icon for the file you want to open using your *mouse*.
● マウスパッド a mouse pad. ● マウスポインター a mouse pointer. ● マウスボタン a mouse button.

マウス [口] a mouth.
● マウスピース (楽器・ボクサーの) a móuthpìece.

マウンテンバイク a móuntain bìke.

マウンド 〔野球〕 the mound. ●マウンドに立つ take [立っている] be on] the *mound*; (投球する) *pitch*.
● マウンドを降りる leave the *mound*.

マウントクック [ニュージーランドの山] Mt. Cook.

★まえ 前 【❶場所】 (前部, 前面, 前面) the front /frʌ́nt/ (⟷ the back); (乗り物などの前部) the fore (part).
❶【前の】 (正面の, 最前の) front; (前方の) fore; (順序中の) previous. ▶前の席に座る take a front seat; sit *in the front*. (⇨❸) ▶列車の一番前の車両に座席を見つける find a seat in *the foremost car* [in the car *at the front*] of a train. ▶前のページに on *the previous* page. ▶前の席に座っていいかな。後ろだと酔うんだ Do you mind if I sit *in the front*? I get carsick if I sit in the back.
❷【~(の)前の[に, で, を]】 (…の前に) in [at] the front of … (特定の空間内で前の部分をいう。またその位置を強調する場合); (…の前方に) in front of … (⟷ behind), before … (❗️ before の「場所」を表す用法は, 順序の場合、「(身分の高い人の)前に[で]」の場合, right before one's eyes, before one's very eyes などの表現を除いて《書》); (…の進行方向の前方に) ahead of …; (…の面前で) in the presence of …. ● 教室の前の方に座る sit *at* [*in*] *the front of* the classroom. (❗️ stand *in front of* the class は,「(先生などが)生徒の前に立つ」の意) ▶ハンドルの前に (＝運転席に) 座る sit *behind* [*at*, ×*in front of*] the wheel. ●聴衆の前で話す speak *in front of* the audience; (話しかける) address the audience. ●建物の前を通過する pass *the front of* [*in front of*] the building. ▶バスの前の方はすいていた The *front* of the bus was not crowded. ▶彼の前に突然猫が現れた Suddenly a cat appeared *in front of* him. ▶駅前の本屋はとても大きい The bookstore *across* (*the street*) *from* the station is very large. (❗️ 通りを隔てて駅前にある場合)/The bookstore *in front of* the station is very large. (❗️ 駅のすぐ前にある場合) ▶ 私は人の前で侮辱された I was insulted *in front of* other people [(公然と) *in public*]. ▶母[母]の前でそのことは話さないでください Don't talk about it in his *presence* [*in the presence*] of my mother]. (❗️ Don't talk about it when he [my mother] is there. の方が口語的)
▶彼は危険を前にしても冷静だった He remained calm even *in the presence of* [*in the face of*] danger. ▶彼は私の10メートル前を走っていた He was running ten meters *ahead of* me.
❸【前に[を, へ, から]】 (前方へ) forward (⟷ backward), 《書》 forth; (前方の位置に) ahead; (前方に, 最前に) in front (⟷ behind). (❗️ ahead と異なり静止状態を表す. この意で用いられるのは今は《まれ》の❷). ●前に進む go [step] *forward*; 《やや書》 proceed. ●1歩前に出る take a step *forward*. ●前に進み出て握手する come *forward* [*forth*] and shake hands. ●前にならえ！ 〔号令〕 Stand at arm's length! ▶この単語は5ページほど前に(＝戻った所に)初めて出てくる This word first appears about five pages *back* [*ago*]. ▶彼をもっとよく見ようと何列か前に出た I moved *up* several rows to see him better. (❗️ up は問題となる位置への接近を表す) ▶前を見ろ Look *forward* [*ahead*]./Look *to the front*./Look *in front of* you./Look where you're going. ▶前に進め！ 〔号令〕 Forward march! ▶我々は前から2列目[彼より3列前]に座ったWe sat in the second row from *the front* [three rows *ahead of* him].
会話「ごめんなさい」「どうして前を見て歩かないんだ」"Oh, sorry." "Why don't you look *where you are going*?"

❷【時】 (以前) before; (以前に一度) once; (昔は) formerly, in former days; (昔は…だった) used to 《do》 (⇨以前); (この前) last, last time (⇨この前❷). ▶その町には前に行ったことがある I (have) visited that town *before*./I once [*formerly*] visited that town. ▶彼は以前ほど勉強しない He doesn't study as hard as he *used to* [as (he *did*) *before*, as he *did* (*once*), 《書》 as once he *did*]. ▶彼女は前より元気そうだった She looked better than *last time*.

①【前の】 (時間・順序が) previous, 《やや書》 prior, (時間的にすぐ前の) last; (昔の) former; (古い) old. ●前からの約束(＝先約) a *previous* [a *prior*] engagement. (❗️ *prior* の方が優先性を強調する) ●米国の前の大統領 the *former* President [the *ex-*President] of the United States. ●小泉氏の前の総理大臣 the prime minister *before* [《書》 *prior to*] Mr. Koizumi. ●2日前の新聞 a two-day-*old* newspaper; a newspaper from two days *ago*. ▶今度の秘書の方が前の秘書よりタイプを打つのが速い The new secretary types faster than the *old* one. ▶彼女はその前の晩に彼に会ったと言った She said that she had seen him the night *before* [the *previous* night]. (❗️ the night before の方が口語的)/(直接話法で) She said, "I saw him *last night*."

②【~前に[から, まで]】 before …, earlier than …; (今より…前に) … ago (は過去時制で); (時刻で, …分前に) to …, 《米話》 of …, 《米話》 till; (事前に) in advance, 《主に米》 ahead of time. (⇨前もって) ●7時15分前に at a quarter *to* [*of*] seven. (❗️ at six forty-five ともいう) ●5時[出かける]ちょっと前にお電話ください Call me a little *before* five [*before* you go out, ×*before* you *will* go out]. (❗️ 時を表す副詞節では未来のことでも will は用いない) ▶私は発車の10分前に駅に着いた I arrived at the station ten minutes *before* the train started. (❗️ before によって時間的な順序関係が明示されるので, had arrived としないことが多い) ▶「夫は3年前に死んだ」と彼女は言った She said, "My husband died three years *ago*." (❗️ 間接話法では例えば She said that her husband had died three years *before* [×*ago*]. のように言い換え可) ▶京都には何年前に来ら

まえあき 前開き ● 前開きのブラウス a blouse that opens [buttons] *in front*.

まえあし 前足 [脚部] a foreleg (↔a hind leg); [足先] a forefoot (⑱ -feet); (犬・猫などの) a forepaw; (馬・牛などの) a forehoof (⑱ 通例 ~s).

まえいわい 前祝い 图 ● 前祝いに in anticipation of 《one's birthday, a success, a victory》.
── 前祝い(を)する 動 celebrate ... *in advance [ahead of time]*.

まえうけきん 前受け金 advance received [receipt]; an advance payment.

まえうしろ 前後ろ ● 帽子を前後ろにかぶっている wear one's cap 《*with the*》*front side back* [(後ろ向きに) *backward*, (後ろ前に) *back to front*].

まえうり 前売り 图 《切符》an *advance sale*, a sale *in advance*.
── 前売りする 動 sell 《it》*in advance*.
● 前売券 an advance [a reserved] ticket.

まえおき 前置き (予備的な) a prelíminàry remárk; (導入的な) an introductory remark. ● 少し前置きをする make a few *preliminary remarks*. ● 部長の話はいつも前置きが長い The General Manager always makes long *introductory remarks*.

まえかがみ 前かがみ ● 前かがみになる bend forward; stoop. ● 前かがみで歩く walk with a *stoop*. (歩くとき身をかがめる) *lean forward* when one walks.

まえがき 前書き a preface /préfəs/; a fórewòrd. (⇨ 序文)

まえかけ 前掛け an apron /éiprən/. (⇨エプロン)

まえがし 前貸し 图 an advance; advance payment.
── 前貸する 動 ● 彼に5万円を前貸しする *advance him 50,000 yen* [50,000 yen *to him*];《話》*pay him 50,000 yen up front*.

まえがしら 前頭 a *maegashira*; (説明的に) a sumo wrestler of the *makuuchi* division ranking below *komusubi*.

まえがみ 前髪 (おかっぱにした)《主に米》bangs,《英》a fringe; (人・馬などの) a forelock. ● 前髪を下ろしている wear one's *hair* down *in front*.

まえがり 前借り ── 前借する 動 ● 給料から2万円を前借りする get an advance of 20,000 yen [have 20,000 yen advanced] on one's salary.

まえきん 前金 advance payment. (⇨前払い)

まえげいき 前景気 a prospect; an outlook. ● 前景気は良い The *prospects* are bright [promising]. ● 前景気は悪い The *outlook* is gloomy [bleak].

まえこうじょう 前口上 (芝居などの) a prologue 《*to*》; (本題に入る前の) an introductory remark. (⇨前置き)

マエストロ[<イタリア語]【芸術の大家】 a maestro /máistrou/《⑱ ~s, -tri》.

まえせつ 前説 an introductory remark.

まえせんでん 前宣伝 advance advertising; advance publicity.

まえだおし 前倒し 图《米》front-loading. (❗繰り延べ執行]は back-loading) ● 公共事業の前倒し the *front-loading* [《やや書》*front-loaded execution*] of public works projects.
── 前倒しする 動 front-load.

まえだれ 前垂れ (⇨前掛け, エプロン)

まえづけ 前付け (書物の) front matter; preliminaries.

まえのめり 前のめり ● 前のめりになる lurch forward; nearly fall forward.

まえば 前歯 a front tooth (⑱ teeth).

まえばらい 前払い 图 advance payment; prepayment. ● 給料の前払い(金) an *advance* on one's salary. ● 退職金前払い制度 a system of a retirement allowance paid in advance. ● 支払いは全額前払いとなります Payment is required *in advance* for full amount. ● お支払いは郵便振替による前払いでお願いいたします For payment, please *pay in advance* by postal money order.
── 前払いする 動 ● 税金を前払いする *pay* the tax *in advance*. ● 会社は君の給料の一部を前払いしてくれるだろう They will *advance* you part of your salary.

まえぶれ 前触れ [[前兆]]a sign; (吉凶などの) an omen /óumən/; (好ましくないことの) a warning; [[予告]] (previous) notice. ● 春の前触れ a *sign* of spring. ● 台風の前触れ a *sign* [*a warning*] of a typhoon. ● 前触れもなく訪ねる call on 《him》without 《*previous*》*notice*. ● 何の前触れもなく雨が降り出した It started to rain without any *warning* at all.

まえまえ 前々 ● 前々から (長い間) for a very long time; (以前からずっと) all the time, àll alóng. ● そのことは前々から知っていた I've known it *for a very long time*. / I've known [knew] it *all along*.

まえみごろ 前身頃 (衣服の) the main front piece [part].

まえみつ 前褌 【相撲】《grab》 the front of a *mawashi*; the front of a (belted) loincloth.

まえむき 前向き ●前向きの(=建設的な)批判[意見] constructive criticism [opinions]. ●前向きの(=積極的な)姿勢を取る take a *positive* [a *forward-looking*] attitude. ●その問題に前向きに対処する deal with the problem *constructively* [*productively*]. ▶私が求めたいのは前向きの考えです All I want is thinking *positive*.

まえもって 前もって beforehand, in advance (!後の方が堅い語), 《主に米》ahead of time; (もっと早く) earlier. ●8月分の仕事を前もってする do work *ahead* for August. ●前もって温めておいたオーブンに入れる put ⦅it⦆ into the *preheated* oven. ▶いらっしゃるのなら前もって知らせておいてくださればよかったのに I wish you would have given me a notice that you were going to come./I wish you would have let me know *beforehand* [*in advance*, *earlier*] that you were going to come. ▶遅れるようでしたら前もって電話で連絡してください Call *ahead* if you're delayed. ▶なぜ前もってそう言わなかったんですか Why didn't you say so *before*? ▶前もって決めておいた時間にはだれも来なかった Nobody came at the *appointed* time.

まえやく 前厄 the year before an unlucky age.

まえわたし 前渡し (金銭の) advance payment, payment in advance (⇨前払い); (物品の) delivery ⦅*of* the goods⦆ in advance.

まおう 魔王 the Devil, Satan /séitn/ (!キリスト教での悪魔の王).

まおとこ 間男 (行為) ⦅commit⦆ adultery; ⦅have⦆ extramarital affairs; (人) a paramour; an illicit lover.

まがいもの まがい物 [模造品] an imitation; [いんちき品] a fake; [偽物] a counterfeit. ●まがい物のダイヤ an *imitation* [a *fake*] diamond.

まがう 紛う ▶まがう方(も)なく unmistakenly; without doubt; certainly; definitely.

マカオ [中国の特別行政区] Macao /məkáu/.

まがお 真顔 ●真顔で(真剣な顔で) with a *serious* look; (笑いのない顔で) with a *straight face*. ●真顔になる become *serious*.

まがき 籬 a hedge.

まがし 間貸し ── 間貸しする 動 rent [⦅英⦆ let] (out) a room (to a student); (下宿人を置く) take in a lodger [⦅英⦆ boarder].

まかじき 真舵木 [魚介] a (blue) marlin.

マガジン [雑誌] a magazine. ●マガジンラック a magázine ràck.

まかす 負かす [相手・敵などを打ち破る] (スポーツ・碁などで) beat*; (戦いなどで) defeat; (議論などで勝つ) ⦅話⦆ get* the better of.... ▶彼らは我がチームを3点差で負かした They *beat* our team by three points. ▶彼はその試合でこてんこてんに負かされてしまった He *was beaten* completely / ⦅話⦆ He was beaten hollow] in the game. (⇨負ける) ▶彼女は議論で私を負かした She *beat* [*got the better of*] me in the argument.

まかず 間数 the number of rooms. ▶彼女の家は間数が多い Her house has many [a lot of] *rooms*.

__まかせる 任せる__ ❶ [ゆだねる] leave ⦅*A to B*⦆; (信用して大事なものを委ねる) entrust [trust] ⦅*A with B*⦆. (!entrust の方が普通). ●財産管理を彼に任せる *leave* one's property in his charge; put one's property under his charge. ●一切を運に任せる *leave* everything to chance. ▶その問題の解決は弁護士に任せた I *have left* the lawyer *to* settle the problem [the settlement of the problem *to* the lawyer]. ▶子供たちの世話を彼女に任せられるだろうか Can we *leave* our children *to* her to look after?/⦅信用して⦆ Can we *entrust* her *with* the care of our children [our children *to* her care]?/Can we *trust* her *to* look after our children? ▶承知した．一切任せておいてくれ OK, I *leave* everything *to* me./You can *count on* me. I'll take care of everything.

会話 「パーティーにはだれを呼ぼうか」「一切君に任せるよ」"Who shall we invite to our party?" "I *leave* it all ⦅*up*⦆ *to* you."

❷ [放任する] [(...にまで)] let*... do; (放っておく) leave*. ●自然の成り行きに任せる let ⦅the matter⦆ take its (own) course. ●激情に身を任せる(=身をゆだねる) *give oneself up to* one's passions. ▶家のことは妻に任せている I *let* my wife keep house. ▶彼は畑を荒らすに任せた He *let* the fields run to waste./He *left* the fields running to waste.

❸ [存分に使う] ●力に任せて(=全力で)彼を殴る hit him *with all* one's *strength*. ●暇に任せて読書する read *at* one's *leisure*. ●金に任せて(=費用に構いなしに)家を建てた He had his house built *regardless of* its cost.

まがたま 勾玉 a comma-shaped bead (for ornament).

まかない 賄い ●賄いつきの下宿 a *boarding*house. (⇨下宿) ▶ぼくは賄いつきで月5万円払う I pay 50,000 yen a month for room and *board* [*board* and *lodging*].

__まかなう 賄う__ [食事を] serve ⦅him⦆ a meal; provide ⦅him⦆ (with) a meal (!with を省略するのは⦅米⦆); [費用などを] pay, cover, meet*. ▶彼の収入は家計を賄うに十分だ His income is large enough to *pay* [*cover*, *meet*] the household expenses.

まかふしぎ 摩訶不思議 ●摩訶不思議なこと a complete mystery. ●摩訶不思議な事件 a *very mysterious* case.

まがまがしい 禍々しい ●まがまがしい静けさ an ominous silence. (⇨不吉)

まがも 真鴨 [鳥] a mallard.

まがり 間借り 名 ●間借り生活をする live in lodgings; live in a rented room.

── 間借りする 動 rent a room ⦅*from*⦆.

●間借り人 a lodger, ⦅米⦆ a roomer; (アパートや貸しビルなどの借り手) a tenant. ●間借り料 room rent; the rent for a room.

まがりかど 曲がり角 [街角] a (street) corner (⇨角⦅₁⦆); [道路の屈曲部] a bend, a turn (⇨カーブ); [転換期] ⦅at⦆ a túrning pòint. ▶学校制度もついに曲がり角にきた The school system has reached a *turning point* [(危機) a *crisis*] at last.

まがりくねる 曲がりくねる (川・道などが) wind* /wáind/; twist and turn. (⇨曲がる) ●曲がりくねった道 a *winding* road. ▶小道は山腹を曲がりくねって上っている The path *winds* [*twists and turns*] *up* the side of the mountain. ▶小川は谷間の中を曲がりくねって流れている The stream *winds* [*twists*] *through* the valley.

まかりでる 罷り出る (人の前に出る) present oneself; appear; (退出する) leave; withdraw.

まかりとおる 罷り通る ●なぜこんな不法行為がまかり通るのか理解できない We can't understand why such an illegal act *goes unpunished* [*unchecked*].

まかりならぬ 罷りならぬ ▶ここで喫煙[撮影]することはまかりならぬ No Smoking [No Photographs]/Smoking [Taking photographs] *is* strictly *prohibited* here.

まがりなりにも 曲がりなりにも (どうにかこうにか) somehow; (不満足ながら) though not satisfactorily;

まかりまちがう 罷り間違う （最悪の場合には） if (the) worst comes to (the) worst 《《米》ではしばしば the を省略する》; （事態がうまく行かなければ） if things go wrong. ▶まかり間違えば命を落とすことになるだろう If the worst comes to the worst, you will lose your life.

まかる 負かる （⇨割引，値引き）▶少し負からないかね Please give me a *discount*?/Could you *make* it a little *cheaper*?

*****まがる** 曲がる ❶ [まっすぐでなくなる] (直線の物が力を受けて) bend*; （弧を描いて）curve; （向きを変える）turn; （曲がりくねる）wind* /wáind/; （ねじれる）twist; [まっすぐでない] crooked /krúkid/; （よじれている）awry /ərái/. （⇨曲げる）● 曲がった道 a *curving* [a *curved*, a *turning*, a *winding*, a *twisted*, a *crooked*] road. ● 曲がった針金 a *twisted* [a *bent*, a *curved*, a *crooked*, xa *curving*, xa *winding*] wire. ● 道の曲がった所 a *turn* [a *curve*, a *bend*] in the road. ● 鉛は容易に曲がる Lead *bends* easily. ▶その道路はそこで左へ曲がっている The road *turns* [*curves*, *bends*] (to the) left there. ▶その川はくねくね曲がって流れている The river *winds* its way. /The river follows a *winding* course. ▶ネクタイが曲がっているよ．直しなさい Your tie is *awry*. Straighten it.
❷ [かがむ] be bent (*with*). ▶彼は老齢で腰が曲がっている He *is bent* [bowed /báud/] *with* (old) age. (❗単に「腰が曲がっている」の場合には His back is *bent* [*bowed*], xHe is bent [bowed]. はよくない)/He *stoops with* [*from*] age. ▶背中が曲がっているよ．まっすぐに座りなさい Don't *slouch*. Sit up straight. (❗slouch /sláutʃ/ は「だらけた姿勢で前かがみになる」)
❸ [心がねじける] be twisted. ▶彼は根性が曲がっている His mind *is all twisted* [(やや書) *distorted*]./(物事を素直に見ない) He can't see things straight.
❹ [進行方向を変える] turn. ● その角(º)を曲がったところにある銀行 the bank *around* the corner. ▶車は角を右へ曲がった The car *turned* the corner to the right./The car *turned* (to the) right [*made a right* (*turn*), *took a right* (*turn*)] at the corner. ▶角を曲がろうとして自転車から落ちた I fell off the bicycle *going around a corner*. ▶彼のカーブは鋭く曲がる His curveball breaks sharply.
❺ [その他の表現] ▶曲がった（＝不正な）ことのきらいな人 a person who hates anything *unfair*. ▶曲がりなりにも （⇨曲がりなりにも）

マカロニ [＜イタリア語] macaroni /mǽkəróuni/. ● マカロニウエスタン [イタリア製西部劇映画] a spaghetti western; 《和製語》a macaroni western. ● マカロニグラタン macaroni au gratin.

まき 巻 （書物区分） a volume, a book. ● 巻 1 the first *volume*; *Volume* [*Book*] Ⅰ [One].

まき 槇 [植物] a podocarpus.

まき 薪 《a piece of》(fire) wood. ● 暖炉用に薪を割る chop *wood* for a fireplace. ● 薪をくべる put *wood* on a fire.

まきあげる 巻き上げる ❶ [巻いて上げる] （カーテンなどを） roll ... up; （風が落ち葉などを） whirl ... up, whirl ... into the air ▶突風が街路の落ち葉を巻き上げた A gust of wind *whirled up* the fallen leaves from the street.
❷ [だまし取る] cheat (him out) *of* his money); swindle 《money *out of* him》; （暴力・脅迫によって） rob (-bb-) （him *of* his money》. ▶青年はその女性から 500 万円をまんまと巻き上げた The young man succeeded *in cheating* [was skillful enough *to cheat*] the woman (out) of 5 million yen.

まきあみ 巻き網 a purse seine /séin/; a round haul net. ● 巻き網漁船 a purse seiner.

まきえ 撒き餌 （魚の）《scatter》chum; ground bait; (鳥の)《sprinkle, scatter》food.

まきえ 蒔絵 gold [silver] lacquer work.

まきおこす 巻き起こす [引き起こす] cause; [生み出す] create. ▶この手紙は政府内にひと騒動巻き起こすだろう This letter will *cause* a tumult in the government.

まきがい 巻貝 [魚介] a conch (榎 ～es, ～s); (貝殻) a spiral shell.

まきかえし 巻き返し （返り咲き） a comeback （❗通例単数形で); （回復）(a) recovery. ● 巻き返しを図る try to come back, try to make [stage] a comeback; try to make [stage] a (dramatic) recovery. ● 巻き返しに転じる(＝勢力を盛り返す) regain one's power [strength].

まきかえす 巻き返す [巻き戻す] rewind* /riwáind/ (⇨巻き戻す); [もとの状態に戻る] come* back; (戦ってもとに戻る) fight* back. (⇨巻き返し)

まきがみ 巻紙 （手紙用の） rolled letter paper; （トイレの） a roll of toilet paper [toilet tissue, bathroom tissue].

まきげ 巻き毛 curly hair, (a) curl; （巻きひげ状の細長い）a ringlet. （⇨カール, 髪）

まきこまれる 巻き込まれる （⇨巻き込む）

まきこむ 巻き込む ❶ [回転物などに] catch*. ● 指をローラーに巻き込む *catch* one's fingers [*get* one's fingers *caught*] *in* a roller. ● ダンプカーに巻き込まれる be [*get*] *caught under* a dump truck. ● 渦に巻き込まれる be *caught in* [《書》*be engulfed*] *in* a whirlpool.
❷ [関係に引き入れる] involve 《*in*》. ● 犯罪に巻き込まれる *get involved* [*get caught up*] *in* a crime. ▶ジョー, ごたごたに巻き込まれるなよ Stay out of trouble, Joe.

■ **DISCOURSE** ■
私の意見は，昨今幼児が巻き込まれるひどい犯罪があまりに多いという事実に拠っている My opinion is supported by the fact that there have been so many terrible crimes *involving* children. (❗My view [opinion] is supported by the fact that ...（私の見方は…という事実に拠っている）は理由に用いるディスコースマーカー)

マキシ [くるぶし丈のスカートなど] 《話》a maxi.

マキシシングル a maxisingle. (｜参考｜ 12cm 盤 CD で発売されるシングル)

まきじた 巻き舌 ● 巻き舌で（＝r 音をふるわせて）話す speak with a *trill*; roll [trill] one's r's.

まきじゃく 巻き尺 a tape measure, a méasuring tàpe. (⇨物差し)

まきずし 巻き鮨 *nori*-roll *sushi*; （説明的に） vinegared rice rolled in dried laver with some ingredients.

まきぞえ 巻き添え ● 巻き添えを食う get involved [mixed up] (*in* a quarrel). ▶彼の家のそばで走行中の車からの発砲事件があり，彼は巻き添えを食って(＝偶然弾に当たって)死んだ There was a drive-by shooting by his house, and he *got shot by accident* and died.

まきた 真北 ● 真北に due north, exactly to the north. (❗due (正確に) は東西南北の四方位に用いる

まきちらす 副詞)▶駅はここから真北10キロの地点にあります The station is ten kilometers *due north of* here.

まきちらす 撒き散らす [ばらまく] scatter ... around [［主に英］about]; (投げ散らかす) throw*... around [［主に英］about]; (水・粉などを振りかける) sprinkle (⇨撒く❶); [うわさなどを広める] spread*. ▶床に水をまき散らす sprinkle [(飛び散らす) splash] water *on* the floor. ●金をまき散らす (浪費する) scatter [(やや話) throw] one's money *around*; (ばかげたむだ遣いをする) squander one's money (*on*).

まきつく 巻き付く wind* /wáind/; [蛇などが] coil; [つるなどが] twine (*around*). ▶ツタが木に巻きついていた The ivy *wound* [*twined*] *around* the tree. (❗ wound は /wáund/ と読む)

まきつける 巻き付ける wind* /wáind/ [twist] ... around. (⇨巻く❷) ●棒にロープを巻きつける *wind* a rope *around* [*to*] a stick. ●髪の毛をカーラーに巻きつける put one's hair in curlers.

まきとる 巻き取る wind*; (じゅうたんなどを筒状に) roll. ▶フィルムを巻き取る *wind* /wáind/ [×roll] the film onto another reel.

まきば 牧場 [［放牧地］] a pasture, grazing land; a meadow. (⇨牧場(ぼくじょう))

まきひげ 巻き髭 [［植物のつる］] a tendril; a cirrus (複 cirri). ●巻きひげのある cirrose; cirrate. ●巻きひげ状の cirrose.

まきもどし 巻き戻し rewind. (⇨巻き戻す)

まきもどす 巻き戻す rewind* /riwáund/. (❗ 過去・過去分詞は通例 rewound /riwáund/) ●テープを巻き戻す *rewind* a tape.

まきもの 巻き物 a horizontal scroll containing either calligraphy or picture. ●巻物を広げる[巻く] unfold [roll up] a *scroll*.

まきゅう 魔球 an unhittable breaking ball [pitch].

まきょう 魔境 an ominous threatening place.

まぎらす 紛らす (人を) divert, distract; (時間を楽しく)(やや書) beguile; (悲しみなどを) hide*, drown. ▶話をして気を紛らす *divert* oneself *by talking; distract* oneself *with* talk. ●本を読んで退屈な時間を紛らす *beguile* the tedious hours *with* a book [*by* reading a book]. ●悲しみを笑いに紛らす *hide* [*conceal*] one's grief with a smile. ●悲しみを酒で紛らす *drown* one's sorrows (in drink). (❗ 成句的表現)

まぎらわしい 紛らわしい [［混乱させる］] confusing; [［惑わせる］] misleading; [［あいまい］] ambiguous. ▶この二つの単語は大変紛らわしい These two words are very *confusing*.

まぎれこむ 紛れ込む ●人込みの中に紛れ込む *mingle with* the crowd, (消える) *disappear in* the crowd. ▶ひょっとして私の本が君の本の中に紛れ込んでいませんか Isn't my book *among* yours by any chance?

-まぎれに -紛れに ▶悔しまぎれに(=悔しさに駆り立てられて) driven [spurred on] by chagrin /ʃəɡrín/. ▶彼女は腹立ちまぎれに(=かっとなって)夫をののしった She swore at her husband *in a fit of anger* [(腹いせに) *out of spite*]. ▶彼は苦しまぎれに(=窮地に追い込まれて)うそをついた *Driven into a corner*, he told a lie.

まぎれもない 紛れもない 形 (間違いのない) unmistakable; (見てすぐ分かる) obvious. ●紛れもない事実 an *unmistakable* [an *obvious*] fact (明白) (絶対的真実) the [×an] absolute truth; (議論の余地のない事実)(やや書) an indisputable fact.

── **紛れもなく** 副 ▶そのダイヤは紛れもなく(=疑いもなく)本物だ The diamond is *undoubtedly* genuine.

*****まぎれる 紛れる** (人の気持ちが) be diverted; (時間が)(やや書) be beguiled (⇨紛らす); [［混ざり合う］] mingle with ...; [［見えなくなる］] be lost (*in*). ●音楽で気が紛れる *be diverted* by the music. ●人込みに紛れて逃げる *mingle with* the crowd and escape. ●闇に紛れる *be lost* in the dark; (闇に乗じる) take advantage of the dark(ness). ●どさくさに紛れて車を盗む steal a car *in* [*during*] the confusion. (⇨どさくさ ［成句］) ▶彼の話で彼女の悲しみは紛れた His talk *distracted* her (mind) *from* grief. ▶忙しさに紛れてごぶさたしておりました I was too busy to write (to) you. (❗ to を省略するのは［米・英話］)

まぎわ 間際 ●閉店間際に *just before* the closing time. ▶私は出発間際にその手紙を受け取った I *was* (*just*) *about to* start [*was on the point of* start-ing] when I got the letter. ▶彼は死ぬ間際まで意識がはっきりしていた His mind was clear *up until* his last moments. (❗ up は until を強める)

まきわり 薪割り wood chopping. ●薪割りをする chop firewood.

*****まく 幕** ❶ [［カーテン］] a curtain; (舞台の) the curtain. ●幕を上げる[降ろす] raise [lower] a *curtain*; (劇場で) ring up [down] *the curtain* (❗ ベルを合図に上げ下げすること). ●幕を引く draw [close] *the curtains*. ●紅白の幕を張る stretch a red and white *curtain*. ●盛んな拍手のうちに幕が降りた There was loud applause as the *curtain* came down [fell, dropped] (↔went up, rose). (語法 欧米では通例劇場の幕は左右に引かず,上下に動かす)

❷ [［劇の一幕］] an act. ●序幕 the first [opening] *act*; *Act* I. ●3幕ものの劇 a three-*act* play; a play in three *acts*. ●ハムレットの第2幕第3場 (*in*) *Act* II, Scene iii *of Hamlet*. (❗ *act* two, scene three と読む. また引用の出典の場合は *Hamlet* II, iii のように略記する) ▶この劇は3幕ものです This is a three-*act* play./This play has three *acts*. ▶この劇の一番の見どころは3幕目です The best part of the play comes in the third *act*.

❸ [［終わり］] ▶ついにその不思議な物語も幕となった And here the mysterious story *has come to an end* [*been played out*]. ▶その芝居はハッピーエンドで幕となった The curtain *came down* on the play with a happy ending. (❗ ×a happy end とはいわない)/The play *ended* happily.

❹ [［場合］] ▶ここは君の出る幕ではない(君の知ったことではない) It's none of your business./(余計なお世話だ) Mind your own business./(君と関係がない) That has nothing to do with you. ▶さあ君の出る幕(=番)だ Now it's your *turn*.

●幕を開ける open [draw] the curtains; (始まる) open (↔close), start, begin. (⇨始まる)

*****まく 巻く** ❶ [［包む］] (巻きつける) wrap (-pp-); (包帯を) bandage. ●マフラーを首に巻く *wrap* a muffler *around* one's neck; *wrap* one's neck *with* a muffler. (❗ 前の方が普通) ●指に包帯を巻く put a bandage *on* [*around*] one's finger; *bandage* (*up*) one's finger.

❷ [［物を巻く］] wind* /wáind/ ... (up); (丸める) roll ... (up); (糸を) reel; (ぐるぐる巻く) coil ... (up). ●時計のねじを巻く *wind* (*up*) a clock. ●フィルムを巻く *wind* [*advance*, ×roll, ×coil] the film. (❗ wind は全部で, advance は1こまずつ巻くこと) ●地図を巻く *roll* (*up*) a map. ●釣り糸を巻く(=たぐり寄せる) *reel in* [*up*] the line. ●ロープをぐるぐる巻く *coil* (*up*) a rope.

*****まく 蒔く** plant; sow*. (❗ sow は特に大量にばらまく場合に用いられる) ▶庭にヒマワリの種をまく *plant* sun-flower seeds *in* the garden. ●畑に種をまく *sow*

まく seed *in* the field; *sow* the field *with* seed (⚠単に *sow* the field ともいう. seed は農作物などで大量に扱うときは集合的で Ⓤ); *seed* the field. ● 疑いの種をまく〔比喩的〕*sow* the seeds of suspicion.
- **まいた種は刈らねばならぬ**（自業自得）〔ことわざ〕As you sow, so you reap.
- **まかぬ種は生えぬ**〔ことわざ〕You can't make an omelet without breaking eggs. (⚠英語の方には「犠牲」の意味合いもある)

*__まく__ 撒く ❶ [まき散らす] (四方にばらまく) scatter; (液体・粉末などを振りかける) sprinkle. ● 道路に砂利をまく *scatter* gravel *on* [*over*] the road (⚠ over は道路一面に無造作にまくことを暗示); *scatter* the road *with* gravel (⚠ 道路一面に敷きつめることを暗示). ● 街路に水をまく *sprinkle* water *on* the street; *sprinkle* the street *with* water (⚠ sprinkle は通例意図的に狭い面積にまくことを暗示); *water* the street. ● ビラをまく(=配る) *distribute* handbills. ▶節分に豆をまいた We *scattered* [*threw*] *around* parched beans on *Setsubun*—on the evening of February 3. (⇒撒*()き散らす)
❷ [尾行などをはぐらかす] ● 警官をまく (追跡の手がかりを失わせる) *throw* the police *off* (*the scent* [*track, trail*]); (かいくぐり逃れる) *lose* the police; (まんまと逃れる)〔話〕*give* the police *the slip*.

まく 膜 [薄い膜] a film; (温めたミルクなどにできる膜) (a) skin; [粘膜] (a) mémbrane. ● よどんだ水面に張っている膜 a *film* on the stagnant water.

まくあい 幕間 《米》an intermíssion; 《英》an interval. ● 幕あいに軽食を取る take a snack in the *intermission*. ● 10分の幕あいに during a ten-minute *intermission*.

まくあけ 幕開け (幕を開けること) opening the curtains. ● 芝居の幕開け the opening of a play. ● マルチメディア時代の幕開け (やや書) the *dawn* of the multimedia age.

まくうち 幕内 (階級) the *makuuchi* or senior grade division; (力士) a *makuuchi sumo* wrestler. ● 幕内に上がる enter the *makuuchi* division.

マグカップ a (coffee [beer]) mug. (⚠ a mug cup とはいわない) ● コーヒーマグカップ a cóffee *múg*.

まくぎれ 幕切れ (結末) an end. ▶その事件の幕切れはあっけなかった(=突然の幕切れだった) The incident came to a sudden [an abrupt] *end*.

まぐさ fodder; (干し草) hay. (⚠ fodder は草とは限らず根菜なども含む)

まくしあげる 捲し上げる (⇒捲る)

まくした 幕下 [相撲] (階級) the *makushita* or junior grade division; (力士) a *makushita sumo* wrestler. ▶彼はまだ幕下だ He is still in the *makushita division*.

まくしたてる 捲し立てる ● 戦争反対論をまくし立てる *argue furiously* against war. ▶彼は男女共同参画社会の理念をとうとうとまくし立てるが, 家庭では亭主関白の生活を送っている He *spouts* the ideals of a gender equality society, and yet he leads the life of a male chauvinist at home.

まぐそ 馬糞 horse dung; (肥料) manure.

まぐち 間口 [正面] a frontage /fráɪntɪdʒ/; [横幅] (a) width. (⇒幅) ● 間口が20メートルの建物 a building with a *frontage* [a *width*] of 20 meters. ● 商売の間口を広げる expand one's *scope* of business.

マクドナルド McDonald's /məkdánldz/.

マグナカルタ [大憲章] the Magna C(h)arta /mǽgnə kɑ́ːrtə/; the Great Charter.

マグナム [大型連発拳銃] a magnum (handgun).

マグニチュード a magnitude. ▶マグニチュード5.6の地震があった There was an earthquake of *magnitude* [an earthquake registering a *magnitude* of] 5.6 (on the Richter scale). ▶阪神大震災はマグニチュード7.2を記録した The Great Hanshin Earthquake registered a *magnitude* of [*measured*] 7.2.

マグネシウム [化学] magnesium /mæɡníːziəm, -ʒəm/ (元素記号 Mg).

マグネット a magnet.

まくのうち 幕の内 (⇒幕の内(弁当))
● 幕の内(弁当) an entr'acte /ɑ́ːntrækt/ box lunch; (説明的に) a traditional Japanese box lunch including rice balls and assorted side dishes.

まくひき 幕引き ● 戦争の幕引きをする(=終わらせる) *put an end to* the war.

マグマ [地学] magma.

*__まくら__ 枕 a pillow. (⇒枕元) ● 枕をして眠る sleep with one's head on a *pillow*. ● 本を枕にする *pillow* one's head *on* a book. ● ひじを枕にして横になる lie down with one's head (*pillowed*) on one's arm.
- **枕を交わす** sleep (*with*).
- **枕を高くして眠る** sleep in peace [without fear, without worries].
- **枕を並べる** 枕を並べて寝る sleep *side by side*.
- **枕絵** an erotic picture. ● **枕カバー** a pillowcase; a píllow slip. ● **枕木** 《米》a (cross) tie; 《英》a sleeper. ● **枕経**(*きょう*) (説明的に) sutra recitation at the bedside of a dead person before the body is placed in a coffin. ● **枕詞**(*ことば*) (説明的に) a conventional epithet mostly used in *waka*.

まくらのそうし 『枕草子』 *The Pillow Book of Seishonagon*. [参考] 清少納言の随筆

> **古今ことばの系譜** 『枕草子』
> 春は曙、やうやうしろくなり行く山ぎは、すこしあかりて、紫だちたる雲のほそくたなびきたる In spring it is the dawn that is most beautiful. As the light creeps over the hills, their outlines are dyed a faint red and wisps of purplish cloud trail over them. (Ivan Morris) (⚠(1)「しろくなり行く」に対し (light) creep,「たなびく」に対し trail という動詞の選択に工夫がある. (2)「紫だちたる」は「紫がかった」の意なので purplish. (3) wisps of purplish cloud は「幾筋かの紫色の雲」の意. 「ほそくたなびきたる」雲は一筋ではないだろうから, この意に訳されている) ● 眞虫(*まむし*)

まくらもと 枕元 ● 枕元に (ベッドのかたわらに) at [by] one's bedside; (ベッドの頭に) at the head of one's bed. ● 枕元に呼ぶ call (*him*) *to* one's bedside. ▶彼の枕元に本が数冊置いてあった There were some books *at* his *bedside*.

まくりあげる 捲り上げる (⇒捲る)

まくる 捲る ❶ [服などを] (端から丸めて) roll ... up; (たくし上げる) tuck ... up; (すそを持ち上げて) hold*... up. ● ワイシャツをひじの上までまくる *roll* [*tuck*] one's shirt sleeves *up* above one's elbows. ● ズボンのすそをまくり上げる *tuck up* one's pants 《米》[*trousers* 《英》].
❷ [しきりに[盛んに]...する] ● しゃべりまくる talk and talk; talk on and on. (⚠ on は継続の意を表す副詞)

まぐれ(あたり) まぐれ(当たり) 〔話〕a fluke /fluːk/; 以下のすべてのほか全く・野球などで広く使われ; [予測の] a lucky guess; [テニス・ゴルフ・玉突きなどの] a lucky [a chance] stroke; [射撃の] a lucky [a chance] shot. ● まぐれ(当たり)で勝つ[試験に合格する] win [pass an exam] *by a fluke*. ▶あれはまった

まくれる くのまぐれだった It was a sheer *fluke*./(幸運だった) It was just *luck*.

まくれる get* rolled [curled] up.

マクロ [巨視的] macro.
● マクロ経済学 màcroeconómics. ● マクロ経済政策 macroeconomic policy.

まぐろ 鮪 [魚介] a tuna. (❗通例単・複同形. 肉は Ⓤ)
● マグロの刺身 slices of raw *tuna* (fish).

まぐわ 馬鍬 a harrow.

まくわうり 真桑瓜 [植物] an Oriental melon.

まけ 負け (敗北) (a) defeat (↔ (a) victory); (試合などの) a loss (↔ a win). ● 負け投手 a *losing* (↔ a *winning*) pitcher; a loser (↔ a winner). ● 負けがこむ(=勝ちより負けの回数が多くなる) suffer more *losses* than wins. ● 貫禄(ﾛｸ)負けする lose in dignity [(存在感) presence]; (威圧される) be overawed by 《his》 dignified presence. ● かみそり負けをする get a razor *rash*. ▶どうやら君の負けだね I'm afraid you have *lost*. ▶私の負けだ You win!! (❗日本語の発想と時制の違いに注意)

● 負け犬 (敗北者) a loser. (❗*underdog* は主に「試合などで負けそうな人」のこと)

まげ 髷 (男性の) a topknot; (女性の) a chignon /ʃíːnjɑn/. ● まげを結う have one's hair dressed into a *topknot* [a *chignon*].

まけいくさ 負け戦 (戦いに負けること) a defeat; (負けた戦い) a losing battle. (㊙ 勝ち戦)

まけおしみ 負け惜しみ sour grapes. (❗『イソップ物語』の話から) ● 負け惜しみを言う人 a bad (↔ a good) loser; a poor (↔ a good) sport. ▶彼女は負け惜しみが強い(=負けを認めない) She refuses to admit her *defeat*./She is a bad [poor] loser. ▶それは負け惜しみだよ I think it's just sour grapes. ▶負け惜しみを言うな Don't cry [×say] sour grapes.

まけこし 負け越し [相撲] a [one's] *makekoshi* eighth loss, a *makekoshi* 7-8 record, a losing record.

まけこす 負け越す (負けた回数が勝った回数より多くなる) suffer more losses than wins; (相撲で) have* a losing record. ▶我がチームは 4 シーズン連続で負け越している We have four consecutive losing seasons.

まけじだましい 負けじ魂 (競争心) a competitive spirit; (闘争心) fighting spirit; (不屈の心) an indomitable [an invincible] spirit.

まけずおとらず 負けず劣らず (同様に) as ... as; (…に劣らず) no less ... than ...; (等しく) equally. ▶彼女は夫に負けず劣らず頑固だ She is as stubborn as her husband./She is no less stubborn than her husband. (⇨勝る [勝るとも劣らない]) ▶彼らは2人とも負けず劣らずよく勉強した They both studied equally hard.

まけずぎらい 負けず嫌い — 負けず嫌いな 形 (競争心の強い) competitive; (屈しない) indomitable.

まけっぷり 負けっぷり ● 負けっぷりが良い[悪い] be a good [a bad] loser.

マケドニア [国名] Macedonia /mæsədóuniə/; (公式名) the Former Yugoslav Republic of Macedonia. (首都 Skopje) ● マケドニア人 a Macedonian. ● マケドニア語 Macedonian. ● マケドニア(人[語])の Macedonian.

まげもの 曲げ物 a round chip box [container].

まげもの 髷物 (時代物) a novel [a film, a play] set in the days of the *samurai*.

⁑まける 負ける ❶ [敗北する] (試合・賭けに) lose* (↔ win); (負かされる) be beaten, be defeated (*in*, *at*). (❗後の方が堅い言い方. 前の方は主に競技に, 後の方は主に戦いに用いられる) ▶試合に負ける lose [be *beaten in*] a game. (❗後の方は完全にやっつけられることを指す) ▶テニスで負ける *lose at* tennis (×*lose* tennis としない); *be beaten* [*be defeated*] *at* tennis. ▶負けたよ You beat me./I give up. (❗現在形に注意) ▶巨人は 2 対 1 で [1 点差で] 負けた The Giants *lost* (the game) *to* the Tigers (by a score of) 2-1 [by one run]. (❗(1) ×*lost* the Tigers としない. (2) 2-1 is two-to-one と読む) ▶私は弟とトランプをしていつも負ける I always *lose at* cards *to* my brother./I'm always *beaten* [*defeated*] *at* cards *by* my brother. ▶総選挙で我が党は反対勢力に負けた Our party *was defeated by* our opponents *in* the general election. ▶相手チームに 3 点差で負けている We *are* three points [(サッカーなどで) goals, (野球などで) runs] *behind* the other team. ▶パチンコで 5,000 円負けた(=失った) I *lost* 5,000 yen at pachinko.

❷ [屈する] (参る) give* in, 《やや書》 way 《to》; 《書》 yield 《to》; (悲しみなどに打ち負ける) 《やや書》 be overcome 《by, with》. (⇨負けん気) ▶彼は酒の誘惑に負けた He gave in [gave way, yielded] to the temptation of *sake*. ▶彼女にしつこく金をせがまれてとうとう負けてしまった He pressed me so hard for money that I finally *gave in* to him. ▶彼女は悲しみ [暑さ] に負けてしまった She *was overcome with* grief [by the heat]. ▶病気に負けないよう(=耐えるために)体力をつけなさい You should build up your strength to resist disease. ▶私はうるしに負けた(=かぶれた) I've got a rash from lacquer.

❸ [値引きする] (値段を切り下げる) cut*, lower, 《やや書》 reduce; (割引する) give* a discount, discount. ▶彼らは 1,000 円 [1,000 円に] 負けてくれた They cut [lowered, reduced] the price by [to] 1,000 yen. (❗(1) ×cut [lowered, reduced] 1,000 yen としない. (2) 「彼らに 1,000 円 [1,000円に] 負けさせた」は I cut [(話) beat] them down by [to] 1,000 yen. とする) ▶現金なら 2 割負けましょう We give you a discount of 20 percent [(a) 20 percent discount] for cash. ▶これ少し負けられませんか Could you come down a little (on the price)?/Could you give me a discount on this?/Will you take a little off [(主に米話) a bit less]?/(婉曲的) Can you give me a special price?

❹ [劣る] ▶彼は英語ではだれにも負けない(=劣らない) He is *second to none* in English. ▶彼は走ることではだれにも負けたくなかった(=越されたくなかった) He wanted to be a faster runner than anyone else./《やや書》He did not want to *be outdone* by anyone in running.

● 負けるが勝ち (ことわざ) Sometimes the best gain is to lose./(負けば勝つ) She stoops to conquer. ●「屈辱を忍んで勝つ」の意》

⁂**まげる 曲げる** ❶ [物・体の部分を] (まっすぐな物を力を加えて) bend*; (弧を描くように) curve; (ねじる) twist (↔ straighten). ● 針金を曲げる bend a wire. ▶彼はペンを拾い上げようと腰を曲げた He bent down to pick up the pen. ▶彼は口をへの字に曲げて不満を示した He turned down his mouth [lips] at the corners showing a complaint. 事情▶ 欧米では「腹立ち, 落胆」を示すときのしぐさ. 「不満」は push one's lower lip out (特に男性が) 下唇を突き出す), pout (子供が口をとがらす という)

❷ [真実・信念・主義などを] (ゆがめる) 《やや書》 distort; (主義などからそれる) 《やや書》 depart, deviate 《from》. ● アリバイを作るために事実を曲げる *distort* [*twist*] the fact to make an alibi. ▶彼は最後まで自分の信条を曲げなかった(=堅持した) He stuck

まけんき 負けん気　●負けん気の（競争心の強い）competitive；（屈しない）indomitable．●負けん気を起こす try hard *not to be beaten* ［《書》*not to yield*］．▶ちびのくせに負けん気だけは人一倍強い Though he is only a small boy, he has a very *competitive mind* ［*attitude*］.

まご 孫　a grandchild（《複》-children）；（孫息子）a grandson；（孫娘）a granddaughter．●初孫 one's first *grandchild*．▶お孫さんがおありですか Do you have any *grandchildren*?/Are you a grandfather［a grandmother］?

まご 馬子　a packhorse driver．
— 馬子にも衣装 Clothes make the man./《ことわざ》Fine feathers make fine birds./《ことわざ》The tailor makes the man.

まごい 真鯉　《魚介》a black carp．

まごがいしゃ 孫会社　a company affiliated with a subsidiary (*of* Toyota)．

まごこ 孫子　**孫子の代まで**　▶その話は孫子の代（＝後世）まで伝えられるだろう The story will be handed down to future generations［《書》to posterity］.

まごころ 真心　（誠心誠意）；（やや書）cordiality；（温かい）heartiness；（誠意）sincerity．●真心のこもった贈り物 a *hearty* ［*heartily*］心尽くしの*a thoughtful* present．●真心をこめて来客をもてなす entertain one's guest *with all* one's *heart* ［*heartily*］.

まごつく 動　《当惑する》be confused, bewildered；《途方に暮れる》be at a loss．●慌てる《類語》▶英国に行ったとき習慣の違いにたいへんまごついた I *was very confused* by the difference in customs when I went to England．▶外国人に話しかけられてまごついた I *was bewildered* when a foreigner spoke to me．▶彼は返答にまごついた He *was at a loss* (what) to answer [for an answer]./He *didn't know* what to answer．（後の文の方が口語的）
— まごつかせる 動　confuse, bewilder．▶彼は多くの質問をして私をまごつかせた He *confused* me with [by asking] a lot of questions.

まごでし 孫弟子　a pupil of one's pupil．

まこと 誠, 真　❶《真実》truth．（⇨本当, 誠実）●まことのことを言う tell the *truth*．▶それはうそかまことか Is it *true* or false [false or *true*]?
❷《誠意》（うそを言わない）sincerity；（道徳的に誠実な）integrity；（裏切らない）(good) faith．●まことを尽くす do *in good faith*, do *sincerely*．

まことしやか 真しやか　●まことしやかなうそをつく tell *plausible* ［いかにも]*feasible*] lies．（⇨もっともらしい）▶彼女の話はまことしやかだからたいがいの人はそれを信じるだろう She is so *plausible* that most people will believe her story.

まことに 誠に　《本当に》really, truly；《非常に》very, very much; greatly；《心から》heartily; sincerely；《書》truly; from (the bottom of) one's heart．（⇨本当 ③）▶彼はまことに有能な男だ He is *really* [*truly*] an able man．▶ご面倒をおかけしてまことに申し訳ありません I'm *very* [*really*, 《話》*terribly*, 《話》*awfully*] sorry to have troubled you．▶ご親切まことにありがとう存じます I'd like to thank you *very much* [*heartily*] for your kindness./I'm *truly* grateful to you for your kindness.

まごのて 孫の手　a back scratcher．《語源》米英にはない）

まごびき 孫引き　名 a secondhand quotation．
— 孫引きする 動　quote 《a passage》 secondhand．

まごまご — まごまごする 動　（⇨まごつく）▶まごまごしていると急がないとバスに乗りそこなうよ *Hurry up* or you'll miss the bus./*Hurry up!* The bus is going to leave．

まこも 真菰　《植物》wild [water] rice．

マザー 《母親》a mother；《女子修道院長》a mother．

マザーグース Móther Góose．《参考》英国の童謡集の作者とされる伝説上の人物）●マザーグースの唄 a *Mother Goose* rhyme．

マザーコンプレックス (suffer from) an [the] Oedipus /édəpəs/ complex；《和製語》a mother complex．（⇨マザコン）

マザーテレサ 《マケドニア出身の修道女》Mother Theresa．《参考》1979年にノーベル平和賞受賞）

マザーボード 《コンピュータ》a mother board．

まさか 副　《驚き・疑惑・否定の応答》Not　really! (!下降上昇調でいうと「いえ別に、それほどではない」といった控えめな否定表現になる）; You don't say (so)! (!so は通例省略される）; No!; Never!; That's impossible!；《冗談でしょ》You múst be joking 《話》kidding．；《嘘でしょ》《主に米》No way．(!これを切り返す場合 Yes, way. (そのまさかなんだ)のようにもいえる）▶まさかここで君に会うとはね I *never* expected to meet you here./《話》*Fancy* meeting you here!　▶彼はまさかそんなことをしたはずがない He *can't* have done such a thing.
会話「彼は 90 を越えてると思うよ」「まさか」"He's over ninety, I guess." "*Not really!*/*Well, I never* (*did*)!" ●He isn't!, He can't be! などでもまさかの意を表すことができる）
会話「彼はきのう交通事故で亡くなったよ」「まさか（＝冗談でしょ）」「本当なんだ」"He was killed in a traffic accident yesterday." "*You're kidding* [*joking*]!/*No* kidding!" (!下降上昇調でいうと「いや冗談なんかじゃない」の意となる）/（本気で言っているのじゃないでしょうね) You don't mean that, do you? (信じられない) I don't believe it!" "I'm serious."
【まさか…ではないでしょうね】surely … not; Don't tell me．(!話し手の驚き・疑惑・念を押す気持ちなどを表す）▶まさかあんな男の言うことを信じてるんじゃないだろうね *Surely* you *don't* believe such a fellow! (!You don't believe such a fellow, *surely*. のように文尾の位置も可）▶だれのせいですって？まさかジョンじゃないでしょ Who did you say was to blame? *Surely not* John? ▶それはまさか本当の話じゃないでしょう *Don't tell me* it's a true story．
— まさか 名　《緊急》an emergency；《必要》need．（⇨万一）▶まさかのときに in an [in case of] *emergency*; in time [case] of *need*．●まさかの場合に備えるprepare for the *worst*．
●まさかのときの友こそ真の友《ことわざ》A friend in need is a friend indeed．

まさかり 鉞　an ax(e), a broadax(e); a battle-ax(e)．

まさき 正木　《植物》a spindle tree．

まさぐる （手でいじる）finger；（もてあそぶ）play [toy] 《with》；（手で触れる）touch．

まさご 真砂　sand．（⇨《倒》砂）

マザコン 《〖「マザーコンプレックス」の略〗》（⇨マザーコンプレックス）▶マザコンの男(の子) a mama's《米語》 a mummy's《英語》 boy．▶彼はマザコンだ（＝母親から精神的にぜんぜん独立していない） Spiritually, he is not at all independent of his mother．●spiritually は文末に置いてもよい）/《話》He's still tied to his mother's apron strings./《話》He still hasn't cut the apron strings.

まさしく　正しく [[確かに]] certainly; surely; [[疑いもなく]] undoubtedly; [[まぎれもなく]] definitely; [[本当に]] really; [[正確に]] just, exactly. (⇨正に) ▶これはまさしく今までに見た最高の映画だ This is *certainly* [*surely*] the best movie I've ever seen. ▶その犯人はまさしく女性だ The criminal is *undoubtedly* a woman. ▶彼はまさしくこの家に住んでいた He lived in this *very* house. (⇨正に) ❶
会話 「第一子というのは後から生まれた子よりも親に従順なのでしょうか」「まさしくそうですね」 "Are first-born children more obedient to their parents than later children?" "It's *definitely* true."

マサチューセッツ [[米国の州]] Massachusetts /mǽsətʃúːsɪts/ (略 Mass. 郵便略 MA).

*ま**さつ　摩擦** 图 [[物理]] (a) friction (❗比喩的に「意見の衝突, あつれき」の意にも用いられる. 具体例は ⓒ); [[もめごと]] (a) trouble; [[こすること]] rubbing. ●両国間の貿易摩擦を除く[避ける;　引き起こす;　緩和する] remove [avoid; cause; reduce] trade *friction* [*conflict*] between the two countries.
── 摩擦(を)する 動 rub (-bb-). ●冷水[乾布]摩擦をして皮膚を鍛える *rub* one's skin with a cold wet [a dry] towel to make it strong. ●木片を摩擦して火をおこす make fire by *rubbing* two pieces of wood together.
●摩擦音 [[音声]] a fricative (sound). ●摩擦熱 frictional heat.

まさに　正に ❶[[正確に]] just; exactly; [[本当に]] really; [[まったく]] quite. ▶それはまさに私が欲しいと思っていたものだ That is *just* [*exactly*] what I wanted./(ほかならぬ) That is the *very* thing I wanted. (❗very は形容詞で強調的に用い, this, that, one's などを, 後に修飾句[節]を伴う) ▶彼はまさにこの仕事に打ってつけの人だ He is *júst* [*exáctly*] the right man for the job. ▶彼はまさに紳士だ He is *really* [*really* is] a gentleman. (❗後の方が強意的)/He is a *real* gentleman. ▶まさにそのとおりだ That's *quite* [*precisely*] right. / *Exactly*. / ˇThat's ít. ▶彼はまさに(=文字どおり)絶望のどん底にあった He was *literally* in the depths of despair./(正真正銘的) He was in the *very* depths of despair. (❗この意での very は通例唯一無二のものを修飾し, 語の持つ重大さや深刻さを強調する)
会話 「休みはどうでした」「まさに申し分なしだったよ」 "What sort of holiday did you have?" "*Quite* perfect."

❷[[今にも…しようとしている]] be just going to 《do》; be about to 《do》 (❗be going to より差し迫った未来を表し, 通例未来を表す副詞[句]を伴わない); be on the point of 《doing》 (❗前の二つより強意的). ▶電話が鳴ったときぼくはまさに出かけようとしていた I *was just going to* leave [*about to* leave, *on the point of* leaving] when the telephone rang. ▶その銀行はまさに破産の危機にひんしている The bank is *on the verge* [*brink*] *of* bankruptcy.

まざまざ ── まざまざと 副 (鮮やかに) vividly; (はっきりと) clearly; (明確に) distinctly. ▶その光景をまざまざと思い出す recall the scene *vividly* [*clearly*].

まさめ　正目 图 straight grain. ── 正目の 形 straight-grained.

まさゆめ　正夢 [[予言的な夢]] a prophetic dream. ▶きのう見た夢が正夢になった(=夢が本当になった) The dream (that) I had yesterday came true [proved *prophetic*].

*ま**さる　勝る**　be better 《than》, be supérior 《to》; 《書》surpáss. ▶この製品は質の点であれよりずっと勝っている This product is much *better than* [much *superior to*] that in quality. ▶知識の点で彼に勝る者はいない No one *is ahead of* [*surpasses*] him in knowledge./No one can beat him for knowledge. ▶健康は富に勝る Health *is above* [*better than*] wealth. ▶1日の仕事を終えたあとのよく冷えたビールに勝るものはない There's nothing like a good cold beer at the end of a day's work. ▶彼の妹は聞きしに勝る美人だった His sister was much *more* beautiful *than* I had heard.
●勝るとも劣らない　▶太郎は兄に勝るとも劣らず利口だ Taro is *not* [*no*] *less* clever *than* his brother. (❗ not less ... than は「同等またはそれ以上」, no less ... than は「まったく同等」を表すのが原則であるが, 日常会話では区別なく用いることが多い)

まざる　混ざる, 交ざる mix. (⇨混じる, 混ざる)

まし　増し　❶[[増すこと]] (an) increase. ▶賃金の3割増し a 30 percent *increase* 《米》 raise, 《英》 rise 》 in wages; a wage *increase* 《主に米話》 hike 》 of 30 percent. ▶休日料金は2割増しだ They charge 20 percent *extra* on [ˇin] holidays. (❗ extra は「割増[追加]料金」の意) ▶日増しに暖かくなっている It's getting warmer and warmer *day by day*.

❷[[勝ること]] ((...より)よい) be better 《than》; (...する方がまし) might as well 《do》; (...するよりむしろ...したい) would rather ... 《than》. ▶もっとましなことが言えないのか Can't you say anything *better than* that? ▶つまらぬことを言うくらいなら黙っている方がましだ It is *better* to keep silent *than* to talk nonsense. ▶親友を裏切るくらいならむしろ死んだ方がましだ I'd *rather* [*sooner*] die *than* betray my best friend./I'd *prefer* to die *rather than* 《to》 betray [*instead of* betraying] my best friend. (≒むしろ) ▶彼に金を貸すくらいなら捨てた方がましだ(=彼に金を貸すのは捨てたも同然だ) You *might as well* throw your money away *as* lend it to him. ▶遅くてもしないよりはまし(ことわざ) *Better late than never*.
会話 「あのナイフ全然切れないんだ」「これなら少しはましかしら」 "That knife won't cut at all." "Is this one any *better*?"

まじ　▶それまじかよ Are you serious [kidding, sure]?/No fooling [kidding]!/Really?/Do you mean it? ▶この契約がとれなかったらうちは倒産だ, まじで(=それが事実だ) If we don't get the contract this time, we'll go broke. That's a *fact*.

マシアス・ギリのしっきゃく 『マシアス・ギリの失脚』 *The Failure of Mathias Giri*. ([参考] 池澤夏樹の小説)

*ま**じえる　交える**　●私情を交える *bring in* personal feelings 《into》. ●私情を交えずに 《talk》 *impartially*. ●敵と砲火を交える *exchange* fire with the enemy. ●息子ととさつを交えて(=率直に)話し合う have a *heart-to-heart* [a *frank*] *talk* with one's son.

ましかく　真四角 图 a square. ── 真四角の 形 square. (⇨四角)

まじきり　間仕切り 图 a partition. ── 間仕切り(を)する　●広間を三つに間仕切りする *partition* [*divide*] a hall *into* three parts. ●間仕切りをして居間と食堂を分ける *partition off* the living room from the dining room. ●居間兼食堂の部屋を間仕切りする build a *partition* between a living room part and a dining room part of the room.

マジシャン [[手品師]] a magician, a conjurer.

ました　真下 ── 真下に 形 right [just] under [below]. (❗ under は「真下に」, below は「より下

マジック

方に」の意)●橋の真下に *right under* [×*below*] the bridge. ●*below* では「橋より下流に」の意。●線の真下に署名する sign *just below* [*under*] the line.

マジック 〘手品, 魔術, 魔法〙magic; 〘マジックペン〙(先の細い) a felt-tip (pen); (先の太い) a marker (pen), 《米》a (magic) marker; 〘商標〙(a) Magic Marker; 〘和製語〙a magic pen.
●マジックインキ a (magic) marker, a marker [a felt-tip] pen. (❗ Magic Inkは日本の商標) ●マジックテープ〘商標〙Velcro, a Velcro closure. (❗ 柔らかい loop tape と堅い hook tape からなる) ●マジックナンバー the magic number 《*for*》. ●マジックハンド (伸縮自在ばさみ) a (manipulator arm; 〘和製語〙a magic hand. ●マジックミラー a one-way mirror.

***まして** 〘ましてい…ない〙let alone; much less (❗ 前の方が口語的。いずれも否定的文脈の後で); 〘言うまでもなく〙not to mention, not to speak of…, to say nothing of… (❗ 以上三つは通例名詞(句)の前で)
▶私はドイツ語を読むことさえできない。まして書いたりできない I can't even read German, *let alone* [*much less*] write it. ▶その町には美術館がある。まして図書館は当然ある There's a museum in the city, *not to mention* [*not to speak of, to say nothing of*] a library. ▶彼は人に優しい。まして子供には当然です He's kind to other people [others], *and even more* to children. (❗ He's kind to other people, *much* [*still*] *more* to children. は《まれ》)
❷ [...よりも] than …. (❗ 形容詞・副詞の比較級の後で) ▶彼女は以前にもまして美しくなった She's become more beautiful *than* ever [*before*]. (❗ *ever* では「以前のどの時よりも」の意, *before* では単に「以前よりも」の意)

まじない 呪い (呪文) a spell; (魔除けの言葉・動作・物) a charm. ●まじないを唱える recite a *spell* [a *charm*].

まじなう 呪う cast [put] a spell 《*on*》.

まじまじ ●まじまじと見つめる gaze intently 《*at him*》; gaze intently into 《his》face; stare 《him》in the face.

***まじめ** 真面目 ━━ **真面目な** 形 serious; earnest; (やや書) sober; honest /ɑ́nəst/.

> 〘使い分け〙 **serious** 主に人の様子や物事の内容などが冗談や遊び半分ではなく真剣であることを表す。
> **earnest** 人が何かに対して熱心で真剣であることを表す。時に軽蔑的に「くそまじめな」(too *serious*) の意でも用いられる。
> **sober** 人の性格や態度などが正直で落ち着いていることを表す。
> **honest** 「正直な」の意で、人のまじめさを表す。

●まじめな学生 a *hard-working* [an *earnest*] student (❗ a diligent student より普通。an earnest student は「くそまじめな学生」の意にもなり); (勉強家) a *hard* worker. ●まじめな顔でこっけいな話をする tell a funny story with a *straight* face. ●彼女はいつもまじめな顔をしている She always wears a *serious* [a *sober*] face. / She always looks *serious* [*sober*]. (❗ look serious は深刻に考え込んでいる様子も表す) ▶まじめな話だが私のところで働く気はあるか *Seriously* (speaking) [*Speaking seriously*], do you have any intention of working for me?

━━ **真面目に** 副 (本気で) seriously; (熱心に) earnestly; (熱心に) hard [×*hardly* にとない)。 ▶私の質問にまじめに答えなさい Answer my question *seriously* [*in all seriousness*]. (❗ 後の方が強意的)
▶私は冗談のつもりで言ったが彼はまじめに受けとった I said it as a joke, but he took me *seriously*.

まじわる

▶彼は大変まじめに英語を勉強した He studied English very *hard* [*diligently*]. ▶まじめにしろ Be *serious*!/(遊んでないで) Stop [〘話〙Quit] playing around. (❗ 子供に対して)

━━ **真面目さ** 名 (本気) seriousness; (真剣) earnest (❗ この場合通例 in earnest (まじめに) の熟語で用いられる。

まじめくさる 真面目くさる pretend to be serious. (⇒真面目) ▶山田先生は時々まじめくさった顔で冗談を言う Mr. [Ms.] Yamada sometimes cracks a joke with a *straight* face.

ましゃく 間尺 ●**間尺に合わない** ▶税務署員をごまかそうとするのは間尺に合わない(＝割に合わない) It *does not pay* (you) to be dishonest with the tax collector.

ましゅ 魔手 ●魔手にかかる fall into the *clutches* 《*of*》; be [fall] prey 《*to*》; fall victim 《*to*》. ●魔手にかかっている be in a person's *clutches*. ●魔手から逃れる escape the *clutches* 《*of*》.

ましゅつ 魔術 (魔法, 手品) mágic. (⇒魔法, 手品)
●魔術師 (魔法使い, 手品師) a magician. (❗ 比喩的にも用いる: 言葉の魔術師 a *magician with words*)

マシュマロ a marshmallow /mɑ́ːrʃmèlou/.

まじょ 魔女 a witch (↔a wizard).
●魔女狩り a witch hunt. ●魔女裁判 a witch trial.

ましょう 魔性 ━━ **魔性の** 形 (魅惑的な) seductive; (悪魔のように人を引きつける) devilish. ●魔性の女(魅惑的な女) an enchantress; (男を破滅させる美女) a siren.

ましょうめん 真正面 ●**真正面に**[の] (…の向かい側に) just opposite [〘主に米話〙across from]…; (…の前に) right in front of …. ▶私の家は郵便局の真正面にある My house is *just opposite* [*across from*] the post office. ▶猫がバスの真正面に飛び出して来た A cat ran out *right in front of* the bus.

マジョラム 〘植物〙a (sweet) marjoram.

まじりけ 混じり気 ●混じり気のない(＝純粋な)クローバーのはちみつ *pure* clover honey. ●混じり気のない(＝心からの)賞賛 (a) *genuine* praise.

まじりもの 混じり物 (不純物) a impurity. (❗ 通例複数形で)

***まじる** 混じる, 交じる 〘混じり合う〙mix 《*with*》; mingle 《*with*》; blend 《*with*》. (⇒混ざる) ▶人込みに混じる *mingle with* the crowd. ●悪意が混じった(＝を帯びた)言葉 compliments *tinged with* malice. ▶油は水と混じらない Oil doesn't *mix* [*blend*] *with* water./Oil and water don't *mix* [*blend*]. ▶彼女の黒髪に白髪が交じっていた She had black hair *mixed with* gray./Her black hair *was streaked with* gray. (❗ be streaked with …は「…でしまがついている」の意) ▶彼女にはアメリカ人の血が混じっている(＝混血だ) She is *half*-American./She has American blood in her. ▶雑草が花に交じっていた(＝花の中に)生えていた Weeds were *among* the flowers. (❗ among の後は複数名詞)

まじわり 交わり 《やや書》(an) association. (⇒交際)

***まじわる** 交わる ❶〘物が物と交差する〙cross, 《やや書》intersect. ▶二つの通りはここで[この点で]交わっている The two streets *cross* each other [*intersect*] here [at this point; in front of this department store]. ▶直線 xy と点 m で交わるように直線 ab を引け Draw line ab so that it *cuts* line xy at point m.

❷〘交際する〙(⇒付き合う)●よい[悪い]友達と交わる *keep* good [bad] *company*.

ましん 真芯 (野球のバットなど) a sweet spot; good wood. ●スライダーを真芯でとらえる hit a slider squarely [on the nose]; meet a slider on the nose; get *good wood* on a slider. ▶彼女はテニスラケットの真芯でボールを打った She hit a ball with the *meat* of the tennis racket.

まじん 魔神 a devil; (イスラム神話) a genie, a jinn(i).
マシンガン a machine gun.
マシンご マシン語 〖コンピュータ〗machine language.

ます ❶〖数・量などが〖を〗〗incréase; 〖力・重さなどが〖を〗〗gain; 〖水かさが〗rise*; 〖物・事を〗add to.... (⇨増える, 増やす) ●数[量]が増す *increase* in number [amount]. ●速度を増す *gain* [*gather, pick up*] speed. ●重要性を増す take on an *added* significance (❗ take on は「帯びる」の意); become *more* important. ▶需要が3割増した The demand *has increased* by 30 percent. ▶その女優は人気が増してきた The actress *is gaining* in popularity./The actress *is getting more* popular. (❗ 後の方が口語的) ▶川の水かさが増した The river *has risen*. ▶その本を読んで興味が増した The book *added* to my interest. ▶前にも増して彼が必要だ We need him *more than* before.

ます 升, 枡 〖計量器〗a measure; (説明的に) a square wooden measuring cup. ●1 升枡 a one-*sho measure*. ●升売りする sell *by the measure*.
●升酒 *sake* served in a square wooden measure cup. ●升席 a box (seat).

ます 鱒 〖魚介〗a trout. (通例単・複同形. 肉は Ⓤ)

＊まず ❶〖第一に〗(何よりも先に) first, first of all (❗ ともに通例文頭・文尾で. 後の方が強意的); (列挙して) first(ly), in the first place, to begin [start] with, for a start. (⇨まずもって)

> **解説** first(ly), in the first place, to begin [start] with は事柄を列挙する場合, 最初の要素の前で用いる. 2番目の要素の前では second(ly), in the second [next] place, then, next などを, 3番目の要素の前では third(ly)を用いる. 3番目以降の要素が最後の要素の場合は finally, last(ly), last of all などがいろいろな組み合わせで用いられる.

▶まずこの仕事を片づけなければならない I have to finish this job *first (of all)./The first thing* I have to do is (to) finish this job. (❗ to を省略する方が口語的) ▶まず最初に彼女が到着した She arrived *first./*She was *the first* to arrive. ▶彼をその地位につけるのに反対する理由は二つある. まず彼はあまり経験がないし, それに支持する人も少ないです There are two reasons against giving the position to him. *First*(*ly*) [*In the first place, To begin with*], he doesn't have much experience. *Second*(*ly*) [*In the second place, Then*], (その上) *Besides*, few people support him. ▶まずこの仕事から〖議長を選ぶことから〗始めよう Let's *begin with* this job [*by electing* a chairperson].
〖会話〗「夏休みにはどこに行ったの?」「まず箱根に行って, それから下田に行ったよ」"Where did you go for your summer vacation?" "*First* to Hakone and then to Shimoda."

❷〖ともかく〗anyway, anyhow. (⇨とにかく)

❸〖およそ〗about; (ほとんど) almost, nearly; (十中八九) probably. ▶まずみなところで That's *about* it. ▶(数字について) That's *about* right. ▶彼が生きていることはまず間違いない I'm *almost* sure that he is alive. ▶彼のことだからまず成功するでしょう *Probably* he will succeed./He is *most likely to* succeed. ▶地図と磁石を持っていけば, 道に迷うことはまずないでしょう(=迷うはずがない) If you take a map and a compass with you, you *can't* get lost. ▶彼を納得させることはまず間違いない You *can't* go wrong, if you convince him. ▶それをやることはまずないだろうな I don't think I'll *ever* do it.

ますい 麻酔 〖状態〗anesthesia /ˌænɪsθíːʒə/; 〖薬〗 (an) anesthetic. ●全身〖局部〗麻酔 general [local] *anesthesia*. ●麻酔をかける anesthetize /əˈnɛsθɪtaɪz/. ●全身麻酔をかけられている be under general *anesthesia* [a general *anesthetic*]. (❗「(医者が)麻酔をかける」なら put (him) under ... となる) ▶麻酔が切れてきた The effect of an *anesthetic* is wearing off. ▶彼は麻酔からさめた He came out of the *anesthesia*./The *anesthetic* wore off.
●麻酔医 〈米〉an anesthesiologist /ˌænɪsθiːziˈɑlədʒɪst/; 〈英〉an anesthetist /əˈnɛsθətɪst/.
●麻酔銃 a tranquilizer gun.

まずい ❶〖味が悪い〗bad*; (ひどい) terrible, 《話》awful. ●まずいビール (気の抜けた) *flat* beer. ●まずそうな料理 an *unappetizing* [an *uninviting*] dish. ▶この肉はまずい This meat is [tastes] *bad*./This meat doesn't *taste good*.
❷〖下手な〗poor, bad* (❗ 後の方が口語的で意味が強い (⇨下手)); (ぎこちない) clumsy. ●まずい弁解をする make a *clumsy* [a *poor*] apology. ▶彼女は料理がまずい She is a *poor* cook [✗cooker]./She is *poor* [*bad*] at cooking.
❸〖都合が悪い〗(不適当な, 思わしくない) wrong; (立場・時間などが具合の悪い) awkward /ˈɔːkwərd/; (好ましくない) unfavorable; (分別のない) unwise. ●まずい印象を彼に与える make an *unfavorable* impression on him. ▶どうもまずい時に来ましたね You've come at the *wrong* [an *awkward*] time. (❗「まずい場所に」なら to the wrong place となる) ▶まずいことになってしまった Things *have become awkward* [*gone wrong*]./We are now in an *awkward* situation. ▶そんなことをしてはまずいよ It would be *unwise* of you to do that. (❗ It's unwise....ではすでになされた行為に対する言い方になる)/(しない方がよい) You *shouldn't* [You *would be wiser not to*] do that. (❗ 後の方はそんなことをすれば取り返しがつかなくなることを暗示) ▶まずいことに(=運悪く), 私が訪ねたときには彼は留守だった *Unluckily* he was not at home when I came over. ▶彼女はまずいことになったと思った. 彼女の気を悪くさせたくなかったので He felt *bad*. He didn't want her to be upset.
❹〖醜い〗ugly. ▶彼女の犬はまずい顔をしているが, とても人なつこい Her dog looks *ugly*, but he's very friendly. (⇨醜い)

ますかがみ 増鏡 *Masukagami*. (〖参考〗室町時代の歴史物語)
マスカット 〖植物〗a muscat /ˈmʌskət/.
マスカラ ●マスカラをつけている[つける] wear [apply, put on] mascára.
マスキングテープ 〖塗装のはみ出し防止テープ〗a másking tàpe.
マスク ❶〖面, 覆面〗〖ガーゼ・野球の捕手などの〗a (face) mask; 〖フェンシング選手などの〗a face guard ●ガスマスク 〖防毒面〗a gás màsk. ●デスマスク 〖死面〗a déath màsk. ●ライフマスク a life màsk. ●酸素マスク an óxygen màsk. ●流感予防のマスクをかけている wear a flu [a gauze] *mask*.
❷〖容貌〗looks, features. ▶彼はマスクがいい He has good *looks*./He is good-looking [handsome].
マスクメロン 〖植物〗a múskmèlon.

マスゲーム group [mass] gymnastic exercises; gymnastic exercises by a group of people.

マスコット a mascot /mǽskɒt/. (!)幸運をもたらすとされる動物・人・人形など》
・マスコットガール a mascot;《和製語》a mascot girl.

マスコミ(ユニケーション) 〖大衆伝達機関〗the (mass) media (!)単・複両扱い〗;〖大衆伝達〗mass communications. ・マスコミの時代 the age of *the mass media*. ▶[その事件]はマスコミを大いににぎわした He [The incident] got a lot of attention from *the media*.

:まずしい 貧しい ❶〖貧乏な〗poor (!)最も一般的な語〗;(必需品に困窮した)(やや書〗needy; (極度に貧しい) poverty-stricken; (暮らし向きがよくない) badly-off (worse-off; worst-off);(叙述的に). (⇨貧困)
・貧しい人 a *poor* person; (総称) *poor* people, (やや書) the *poor* (!)(婉曲的)needy](!)複数扱い).
▶その老人は貧しい暮らしをしている The older person is *poor* [*badly-off*]./The older person *lives in poverty*. (!)書〗The older person is *in want*. (!)in want は「必需品を欠いた」) ▶彼は貧しい家に生まれた He was born *poor*./He was born of a *poor* family./He comes from a *poor* family [*background*]. (!)この場合 came は不可) ▶彼らは貧しくて子供に靴を買ってやれない They are too *poor* [(十分な金がない)They didn't have enough money, (余裕がない)They can't afford] to buy shoes for their children. (!)露骨な poor を避けて後の二つのようにいうことが多い)
❷〖貧弱な〗(やや書)poor; (乏しい)scanty; (十分でない)(やや書)insufficient. ▶ぼくの英語の単語力は貧しい My vocabulary in English is quite *poor*. ▶私の貧しい才能ではとてもそんなことはできない I can't do it with my *poor* ability.

マスター ❶〖経営者〗a mánager;(バーの)《米》a barkeeper,《英》the landlord (*of a pub*); (店の)《米》a storekeeper,《英》a shopkeeper;〖所有者〗an owner. ・店の主人の意では通例 master は用いない.呼びかけるときは名前か Excuse me, sir. (男性に), Excuse me, ma'am. (女性に)という
❷〖修士〗a master, a master's degree. (⇨修士)
❸〖熟達〗・フランス語をマスターする *master* [*learn*] French. ・master は「熟達の域に達する」, learn は「学んで習得する」の意. 日本語の「マスターする」は learn に相当することも多い
・マスターキー a master key, a passkey. ・マスターコピー a master copy. ・マスターファイル 〖コンピュータ〗a master file. ・マスタープラン 〖基本計画〗a master plan.

マスターズ 〖ゴルフ〗the Masters (Tournament). (参考)世界4大ゴルフトーナメントの一つ)

マスタード mustard /mʌ́stərd/.
・マスタードガス 〖化学〗mustard gas.

マスターベーション ❷ masturbation.
— **マスターベーションする** ⦿動 masturbate.

マスチフ 〖動物〗a mastiff. (参考)闘犬・番犬用の犬)

マスト a mast /mǽst, mɑ́ːst/. ・3本マストの船 a three-*masted* ship.

マスプロ(ダクション) 〖大量生産〗mass production.
・マスプロ教育 education conducted on a mass-production basis. ・マスプロ大学 《米話》a diploma [a degree] mill. (!)卒業証書[学位]を簡単に出す大学のこと)

***ますます 益々** 〖だんだん多く〗more and more; 〖だんだん少なく〗less and less; 〖増加して〗increasingly; 〖それだけますます〗(all) the more (*for*; *because* 節); 〖all の続く方が普通の, 〗すればするほど…だ〗the +比較級..., the + 比較級...; 〖ずっと,絶えず〗all the time. ▶まわりの多くの人があの町にやって来た *More and more* people came to the town. ▶このごろ大学に入るのはますます難しくなってきている It's getting *more and more* [*increasingly*] difficult to get into college these days. ▶ますますその絵が好きになっていった I liked the picture *more and more* [*less and less*]. ▶事態はますます悪化した Things went *worse and worse* [*from bad to worse*, *worse than ever*]. ▶彼らを見ると彼はますます怒った The sight of them made him *angrier*. ▶彼は素直な人のでますます彼が好きになった I've come to like him *all the better* [*more*] *for* his frankness [*because* he is frank with me]. ▶彼は飲めば飲むほどますますしゃべらなくなる *The more* he drinks, *the less* talkative he gets. ▶物価はますます上がっていく Prices are going up [*rising*] *all the time*. ▶ます(=さらに)困ったことには雪が激しく降り出した *To make* (xthe) *matters worse* [*What was worse*], it began to snow heavily.
(会話) 「あの人は来ないよ」「それならますます結構だわ」 "He's not coming." "So *much the better*."

まずまず (話)só-sò.▶彼の成績はまずまずだ His grades are *not bad* [(話) *so-so*]. ▶英語の試験はまずまずだった I did *fairly well* on the English exam.
(会話) 「調子はどうだい」「まずまずだ」 "How's everything?" "*So-so!/Can't complain!*"

ますめ 升目 ❶〖升で計った量〗measure.
❷〖チェス盤などの〗・原稿用紙の升目 the *squares* on the manuscript paper.

マスメディア the (mass) media. (⇨マスコミ)

まずもって (まず何よりも先に)first of all; (何よりも)more than anything else, before anything else. (⇨何より①)

ますらお 益荒男 (雄々しい男子) a storng, brave man; a manly man. ・ますらおぶり manliness.

マズルカ 〖＜ポーランド語〗a maz(o)urka /məzɔ́ːrkə/.
・マズルカを踊る dance the *mazurka*.

まぜあわせる 混ぜ合わせる, 交ぜ合わせる mix ... up, mix ... with [and].... (⇨混ぜる)

ませいせっき 磨製石器 〖考古〗a ground stone tool.

まぜかえす 混ぜ返す (⇨混ぜ返す)

まぜごぜ 混ぜごぜ a jumble (*of*). ・まぜごぜにする jumble... (up [together]). ▶使用済み切手と未使用切手が箱の中にまぜごぜに入っていた Used stamps and new ones *were jumbled up* [*together*] in the box.

まぜごはん 混ぜご飯 cooked rice with various ingredients.

まぜっかえす 混ぜっ返す (人の話にちゃちゃを入れる) confuse ... by joking; (小ばかにする) make* fun of ..., ridicule.

まぜもの 混ぜ物 (混合物) a mixture; (食品添加物) an additive. ・混ぜ物のある[ない]ミルク *impure* [*pure*] milk. ・混ぜ物をする (不純にする) make ... less pure; adulterate.

マゼラン ・マゼラン海峡 the Strait of Magellan /mədʒélən/.

ませる — **ませた** 形 (早熟な) precocious /prikóuʃəs/.
・ませた(=大人のような)口をきく talk *like a grown-up* [*in a grown-up manner*]. ▶彼女は7歳の女の子にしてはませている She is *precocious* for a seven-year-old girl. ▶その子は年よりませた顔をしている The child *looks old for* his age [*older than* his years].

***まぜる 混ぜる, 交ぜる** 〖混合する〗mix (!)最も一般的な語); blend; mingle; (薬品などを) compound

/kəmpáund/; (水などで薄める)(やや書) dilute; (不純に)(やや書) adulterate; [かき回す] stir (-rr-).

使い分け mix 二種類以上の思想・感情・飲食物・性質・化学薬品などを均質に混ぜ合わせることを表す. 時に区別のできないものを混同してしまうことを意味する.
blend 二種類以上の様式・色・歌声・飲食物などを混ぜ合わせることを表す. しばしば混ざり合って調和することを含意する.
mingle 匂い・感情・人間関係などが混ざり合うことを示す. 混ざってももとの要素は消えないことを含意する.

● セメントと砂を3対1の割合で混ぜる *blend* [*mix*] cement *and* sand in the ratio of 3 to 1. ● 卵に牛乳をよく混ぜる *mix* some milk *up* well *into* the eggs; (卵と牛乳を) add eggs to milk and mix [beat] well. (参考) 料理の本にはたいてい Add eggs to milk, one at a time, beating well after each. (卵を牛乳に加える. 1 個ずつよくかきまぜること) のような表現で書かれている) ● 絵の具を混ぜる *mix* [*blend*] the paints. ▶ パンを作るため小麦粉に水を混ぜる We *mix* [*blend*] flour *with* water to make bread. ▶ レモンとオレンジの汁を混ぜてはいけません Don't *mingle* lemons *with* oranges. ▶ 牛乳に水を混ぜることは法で禁じられている It is against law to *dilute* [*adulterate*] milk *with* water. ▶ シチューは泡が出てくるまで混ぜていないとだめですよ Don't stop *stirring* the stew until bubbles start to appear. (⇨ かき回す, 掻き混ぜる)

マゾ (マゾヒスト) a masochist; (マゾヒズム) masochism.
マゾヒスティック ― **マゾヒスティックな** 形 masochistic.
マゾヒスト [被虐性愛者] a masochist.
マゾヒズム [被虐性愛] masochism /mǽsəkɪzm/.
まそん 磨損 名 abrasion; wear and tear; attrition.
― **摩損する** 動 wear down.

＊また 又 副 ❶ [同様に] (…も) also, too, as well; (…もそうである) so ＋助 ＋主語. (―も, 同様)

解説 (1) also, too, as well はいずれも肯定文で用いる. (⇨(3)) also はやや堅い語. 通例, 一般動詞の前, be 動詞の後, 最初の助動詞の後に置く (⇨ [第1文例]). too は also よりくだけた語で, さらに強意・対照の度合いが強く感情がこもる. too よりさらにくだけた言い方が as well. too, as well は強調する部分が句や節で文の前に置かれることがある(その場合は下降上昇調で as ↘well, ↘too と読む)が, 通例, 文尾または強調する語の直後に置く.
(2) 「so＋助動詞＋主語」も肯定文で上の三つの語句とほぼ同じ意で用いられるがもっぱら主語を強調する: 彼は泳ぎができるが, 彼女もまたできる He can swim, and *so* can ↘*she* [and shé can ↘*too*, and shé can ↘*also* (swim)]. 前文が助動詞を含まない場合は do, does, did などを用いる: 彼も泳ぎだし, 彼女もまた泳いだ He swam, and *so* did ↘*she*.
(3) 否定文では, also, too, as well の代わりに **not … either** を, 「so＋助動詞＋主語」の代わりに 「**neither** [**nor**] ＋助動詞＋主語」を用いる: 彼は泳がなかったし, 彼女もまた泳がなかった He didn't swim, and shé didn't ↘*either* [(やや書)(and) néither did ↘*shé*, (書)(英) nór did ↘*shé*].

▶ 智史は今日もまた知子とデートした Satoshi *also* had a date with Tomoko ↘today. (話)では Satoshi, が修飾する語句が強く読まれるが, (書)では Satoshi, had a date, with Tomoko のどれが修飾されるのかあいまいなので, Satoshi had a date with Tomoko *also* today [today *also*]. のように修飾する語句の直前または直後に置く. 後に置く方が強調的)/Satoshi had a date with Tomoko ↘*today* ↘*too* [*as* ↘*well*]. ▶ 私もまた彼に会ったことがある I have séen him ↘*too* [*as* ↘*well*]./I, ↘*too*, have seen him. (**!** (1) 堅い言い方だが, 書くときは前の文より明確. (2) as well は主語の後では避けた方がよい. (3) コンマは主語が代名詞以外のときに多い)/I ↘*also* have [I, ↘*also*, have] seen him. (**!** also が主語を強調することを明確にするには直後に置く. 《書》ではコンマを使った後の言い方の方が明確だが, いずれも too や as well の方が普通.

❷ [繰り返して] (再び) again; (もう一度) once more [again]; (いつの日か) someday, (いつか) sometime; (いつかそのうち) some other time; (別の時に) another time; (後で) later. (⇨ 再び, いつか) ▶ 彼はまた宝くじに当たった He won a prize in the public lottery *again* [*once more*]. (**!** × … once more again は不可)/(もう一つ当たった) He won *another* prize in the public lottery. ▶ 彼はまた帰ってきた He has come back *once again* [*once more, a second time*]. (**!** 単に again ですますこともある. また 1 回目に戻ってきた場合でも again をつけることもある) ▶ いずれまた遊びに行きます I'll come (and) see you *someday* [*sometime, some other time*]. (**!** (話) では and はしばしば省略される) ▶ その話はまた(の機会に)しよう Let's talk about [discuss] it (*at*) *another time*. ▶ またお電話します I'll call you *later* [*some other time*]. ▶ あしたもまた暑くなりそうだ It's going to be *another* hot day (tomorrow). ▶ ほらまた始まったよ (またかよ) There you [Here we] go *again*. (**!** 後の方は困った状況に自分も巻き込まれているという含みを伴う)/He is at it *again*. (**!** いずれも不愉快な話や行為の繰り返しに対して発する慣用的口語表現)

❸ [その上] (A そして B も) A and (also) B, A and B too [as well] (⇨ ―も ❷); (さらに) besides [what is more, (書)] moreover]; (さらによい [悪い] ことに) (and) what is better [worse]. (⇨ その上) ▶ 彼は医者でもあり, また作家でもある He is a doctor *and* /ænd/ a writer. (**!** a doctor *and* /ənd/ writer は 「医者でかつ作家」くらいの意で上例ほど強意的でない)/He is a doctor *and also* a writer [*and* a writer *too*]. (**!** 後の方が口語的. 他に writer の方を明確に強調するには a writer *as well as* a doctor やさらに強調して *not only* a doctor *but* (*also*) a writer を, 両方を強調するには *both* a doctor *and* a writer を用いる) / (医者である上に作家だが) *Besides* being a doctor, he is (*also*) a writer. ▶ 彼は帰りが遅かった, また(＝おまけに)酔っ払っていた He came home late, *and besides* [*what's more*, (さらに悪いことに) *what is* [*was*] *worse, to make matters worse*], he was drunk./He came home late. /*Also*, he was drunk. (文頭位で接続詞的に用いるのはくだけた言い方) ▶ 彼は字が読めないしまた書くこともできない He *can't* read *or* [×*and*] write. (**!** 両方とも否定する場合は and は不可)/He can *neither* read *nor* write. (⇨ または) ▶ 私はパーティーに行けなかった. また行きたくもなかった I couldn't go to the party, *and* I didn't want to *either* [(書) *nor* did I want to]. (⇨ ❶ 解説 (3))

❹ [その他の表現] ▶ じゃあまた(後で[あす; 来週]) See you (later [tomorrow, next week])! [(話) 親しい人の間で用いる. See you は /sɪːjə/ と読む] ▶ 木の葉が 1 枚また 1 枚と地面に落ちる Leaf *after* leaf [One leaf *after* another] fell to the ground. ▶ 食べ物をむだにする人もいれば, また(＝だが一方で)十分にない人もいる Some people waste food, *while* [*but*] others don't have enough to eat. (**!** 日常会話では but の方が普通) ▶ 失敗はしたが, また(＝他方に)いい経験になっ

た I failed, but *on the other hand* it was a very good experience for [to] me. (⇨一方) ▶君はまた(=いったい)なんでそんなことをしたんだ Why *on earth* [*in the world*] did you do that? (❗ また は疑問詞を強める) ▶彼はまた=まあそれにしても)なんて間抜けなんだ *But* how silly he is! (❗ but は感嘆文の前に添えて感情を強める)

── またの 形 ●またの日(に)(別の日) *another* day; (いつかそのうち) *some other* day; (翌日) the *next* day. (⇨2) ●またの(=別の)名を「のっぽ」という *An-other* name of his is "Lofty." (❗ another の前に通例限定語句は来ない)/(…とも呼ばれている) He is *also* called "Lofty."

また 股, 叉 〖人体・木などの〗a crotch; (また状のもの) a fork; 〖もも〗a thigh. ●内股で歩く walk pigeon-toed; 〖米〗toe in (↔out). ●股(=脚)を広げていすに座る sit on a chair with one's *legs* [(ひざ) *knees*] apart. ●彼の股の所をけさ kick him in the *crotch*. ●木の股に座る sit in the *crotch* of a tree. ●二また道 a *forked* road. ●三つまたの枝 a three-*forked* [a three-*pronged*] twig. ●歩くときは外股にならないようにしなさい Don't *turn* your toes *out* when you walk. ▶道はそこで二またに分かれている The road *forks* there.
●股にかける ▶世界を股にかける travel all over the world.

まだ ❶〖いまだに〗still; yet.

> 使い分け **still** 特定の状態が現在・過去・未来のある時まで継続しており、それが予期した以上に長く続いていることを表す.
> **yet** 通例否定文で用い, 現在・過去のある時までに期待していた事がまだ起こっておらず, 驚き・不満に思っていることを表す. それがのちに起こるであろうという話し手の気持ちを暗示する.
> still は通例一般動詞の前, be 動詞・助動詞の後に置く. yet は通例文尾に置く.

①〖まだ…である〗still. (❗ 進行形や継続を表す動詞とともに用いる. 通例この意で yet を用いるのは堅く古めかしい言い方) ▶太郎はまだ眠ったままだ Taro is *still* asleep./Taro remains sleeping. ▶いやあだ, まだ雨が降っている Oh, dear, it's *still* raining. ▶田中さんはまだ入院している Mr. Tanaka is *still* in (the) hospital./Mr. Tanaka *still* is in (the) hospital. (❗ is を強く読み, 前の言い方より強意的. いずれも を用るのは《米》) ▶彼女はまだ京都に住んでいる She *still* lives in Kyoto. (❗ She lives in Kyoto yet. はこれから先も京都に住み続けることに疑問を感じている表現) ▶外はまだ 1 時間は明るいだろう It will be light outside for an hour *yet*. (❗ ある状態が将来どれほど長く続くかを強調する場合は, 肯定文でも yet が普通に用いられる) ▶彼はまだ(=いつかわからない)心変わりするかもしれない He may *still* [《書》*yet*] change his mind./He may change his mind *yet*. (❗ (1) この用法では活動を表す動詞とともに用いることも多い. (2) yet は通例文尾に置く. 助動詞の後ろに置くのは《書》)
会話「ところでまだ間違っているよ」「まあ! 今度はちゃんとうまくやったと思ったのに」"And *still* you've got it wrong." "Oh dear! And I thought I'd been so clever this time."

②〖まだ…ない〗not(…) yet; still(…) not; (一度も…ない) have never (*done*). ▶まだ彼は帰宅していない He hasn't come home *yet*. (❗ (1) yet は否定文では He hasn't *yet* come home. のように本動詞の前にも置くのが堅い言い方. (2) yet を強く発音すれば still を用いた場合と同じような含みがある. (⇨〖次の訳 注記(2)〗). (3) yet は通例現在完了形, また《米》ではしばしば過去形にも用いる. 過去完了形にも用いることもできるが, He hadn't come home *by that time*. のように by 句を用いる方が好まれる)/By that time. /He *still* hadn't [has *still* not] come home. (❗ (1) still は常に否定語より前に置く. ある状態が予想以上に長く続くことを表し, 話し手のいらだちを暗示する. (3)《話》ではさらに強調されて He *still* hasn't come home *yet*. となることがある) ▶真実はまだ分からない The truth has *not* been found *yet*. ▶彼らはまだ本当の空腹を知らない They have *not* known real hunger *yet*. ▶私はまだ海外へ行ったことがない I have *never* been abroad. (❗ この意で never の代わりに not ever を用いるのはまれ)/I *never* have been abroad. (❗ have を強く読む. 前の言い方より強意的)/*Never* have I been abroad. (❗ さらに強調的でかつ文語的・詠嘆的な表現. 倒置形になることに注意) ▶私はまだその話は聞いていない I have *still* [《書》*yet*] *to* hear that story. (❗ 聞いていないのが不思議[不本意]であることを暗示する)

会話「コンサートはもう終わりましたか」「いいえ, まだです(=まだ終わっていない)」"Has the cóncert / fínished yet?" "(No,) *not* ˋyet." (❗ yet はしばしば短い否定の答えで not の直後で使われる. 下降調も可)

> 解説 「まだ」が「今までのところ」といった意のときは so 〖《書》thus〗far や as yet でも表せる. 前の方は通例現在完了形, 時に現在形とともに用いる: まだ彼から何の返事も受け取っていない I haven't received any answer from him *so far* [(*as*) *yet*]. (❗ as yet は通例否定文・疑問文で用い,「先のことは分からないが」という含みがある. as yet を文頭に置いた場合 as は省略不可) 現在以外の特定のある時を基準にするときは as yet のみ可: そのころまだ彼は有名になっていなかった As yet [×So far], he had not become famous.

③〖まだ…か〗still. ▶年をとってもまだ愛していてくれますか Will you *still* love me when I'm old? ▶まだここにいるのですか. とっくに帰ったと思っていました Are you *still* here? I thought you'd gone home ages ago. (❗ still を強く読み驚きやいらだちを暗示する)

❷〖わずかに, やっと〗

> 解説 **only** は書き言葉では通例修飾する語句・節の直前か, 時に直後に置かれる. 話し言葉では一般動詞の直前 [be 動詞・助動詞の後に置かれる傾向があるが, only に修飾される語が強く発音されるため, あいまいさはない.

▶彼はまだ子供だ He is *only* a child. (❗ He is *still* a child. は「依然として子供だ」の意. an *only* child は「一人っ子」の意) ▶まだ 9 時だ. 寝るには早すぎる It's *only* nine; it's too early to go to bed. (❗ ×It's still nine. とはいわないことに注意) ▶ここへ来てまだ 1 か月にしかならない It is [It's been] *only* a month since I came here./*Only* a month has passed since I came here.

❸〖さらに〗(もっと) more (❗ この意では more に限らず比較級を用いることによって表せる);〖比較級を強めて〗still, even,《書》yet (❗ still, yet は another なども強める) ▶この子はまだ背が伸びるだろう This boy will grow taller. ▶することがまだたくさんある I still have a lot *more* to do. ▶まだもう一つ[いくつか]尋ねたいことがある I have *still* [*yet*] *another* question [*more* questions] to ask you.
会話「たばこはまだ(=残っている)?」「2,3 本ね」"Have you any cigarettes *left*?" "A few."

❹〖どちらかと言えば〗(⇨むしろ) ▶これでもまだましな方だ Even this is a little *better than* [*not as bad as*] the others. ▶彼に頼るくらいなら自分 1 人でやった

マタイ がまだました I'd *rather* do it by myself *than* count on him.

マタイ Matthew. (参考) 十二使徒の1人

まだい 真鯛 [魚介] a red sea bream.

まだい 間代 (部屋代) (a) room rent. (⇨部屋 ❷)

マタイじゅなんきょく 『マタイ受難曲』 *St. Matthew Passion*. (参考) バッハ作曲の音楽作品

またいとこ a second cousin /kʌ́zn/.

またがし 又貸し 名 [土地・建物などの] a sublease.
— **又貸しする** 動 ● 部屋を又貸しする *sublet* [*sublease*] a room. ● 本を又貸しする lend a borrowed book to another.

マダガスカル [国名] Madagascar /mǽdəgǽskər/; (公式名) the Republic of Madagascar. (首都 Antananarivo) ● マダガスカル人 a Malagasy; a Madagascan. ● マダガスカル語 Malagasy; Madagascan. ● マダガスカル(人[語])の Malagasy; Madagascan.

またがみ 股上 (ズボンの股からウエストまでの寸法) a rise. ● 股上 27 センチのズボン pants with a *rise* of 27 centimeters.

またがり 又借り — **又借りする** 動 borrow ... secondhand.

*****またがる** ❶ [人が] ● 馬にまたがる get on [(やや書) mount] a horse (!乗る動作をいう); (両足を広げて座る) sit astride ((主に米) of) a horse; (乗って行く) ride on horseback.
❷ [領土・期間などが] extend, stretch, spread*. (⇨亘(ﾜﾀ)る) ● 2か国 [10年] にまたがる *extend over* two countries [ten years]. ● 4年にまたがる計画 a four-year program. ● 村は川の両岸にまたがっている The village *extends* across [lies on both sides of] the river.

またぎき 又聞き 名 secondhand information, hearsay.
— **又聞きする** 動 hear 《the news》 secondhand; learn by hearsay.

またぐ ● 溝をまたいで渡る *stride over* [*across*] the ditch. ● 敷居をまたぐ *cross* the threshold.

またぐら 股座 a crotch; a thigh. (⇨股)

またした 股下 an inseam. (!股の付け根からくるぶしまで, ズボンの下の長さにもいう) ● 股下を計る take *inseam* measurements. ● 彼女は股下75センチのジーンズをはいている She wears jeans with an *inseam* of 75 centimeters./Her jeans measure 75 centimeters *from the crotch to the bottom*.

またしても ● 2,3日前に買ったばかりの傘をなくしてしまったのでまたしても買わなくてはならない I've lost my umbrella I bought only a few days ago. I must buy one [×it] *yet again*. ● 同じようなミスをまたしてもやるなんて, 彼はこりない人ね He made *yet another* mistake of the same kind. He never learns a lesson.

まだしも ● 咳だけならまだしも熱もある I have *not only* a cough *but also* a fever. ● 命をとられるよりは金をとられるほうがまだましだ I am *luckier* to be robbed of money *than* to be killed. (!「比較級 + than」を用いて表現する)

またぎれ 股擦れ ● その赤ちゃんはまたずれになっている The baby has a *sore* crotch.

またせる 待たせる [いやおうなしに] make*... wait; [待たせておく] (命令や依頼して) have*... waiting; [待たせ続ける] keep*... waiting. ● 長らくお待たせしました 《日本人的発想》 I'm sorry to *have kept* you *waiting* so long./ I'm sorry I *have kept* you *waiting* so long./(話) (ごめん, お待たせしたかしら) Sorry, I hope you haven't been waiting long [haven't had a long wait]. ● さらにくだけて, Sorry you had to wait long, huh? のようにもいう)/(米英人的発想) Thank you very much for waiting so long. ● はい, お待たせしました (商品などを手渡すときに) Here you are! ● 外に車を待たせてある I *have* a car *waiting* outside. ● 人を待たせてはいけません You should not *keep* people *waiting*./(時間は厳守すべきだ) You should be punctual. ● 待たされている間テレビでトーク番組を見ていた While I *was made to wait*, I was watching a talk show on TV.

またたき 瞬き (目の) a blink; (星の) a twinkle.

またたく 瞬く [光・星が明滅する] 《やや書》wink, 《やや書》blink; (きらきら光る) twinkle. ● またたく間に (一瞬に) in an instant [a second]; (すぐに) in no time. ● 遠くで明かりがまたたいていた A light *was winking* [*blinking*] in the distance. ● 星が空にまたたいている Stars *are twinkling* in the sky. ● そのスポーツカーはまたたく間に走り去った The sportscar speeded away *in an instant*.

またたび 木天蓼 [植物] a silver vine.

またたびもの 股旅物 a drama depicting the adventure of a wandering gambler.

またとない 又ない ● またとない (= 二度とない) 機会 a *golden* [*a once-in-a-million*] opportunity. ● またとない (= 比類のない) 品 a *unique* [*a matchless*] article. ● こんなにいい賭けの材料はまたとない It's *as good a thing to bet on as any*. (!最上級表現の一つで「どれにも劣らない」の意)

マタニティードレス a matérnity drèss [clòthes].

マタニティーブルー [出産後の情緒不安定症] (suffer) post-natal depression; (軽いうつ状態) (experience) the maternity blues [×blue].

まだの 又の another. (⇨又 [また] の)

または (A または B) A or B; either A or B. (!後の方が選択の意を強く表す)

> **解説** (1) いずれも A, B は文法的に対等の関係にある語・句・節. (2) いずれも後に動詞が続く場合, 動詞の数は B に呼応するのが原則だが, either A or B では複数扱いのこともある.

● 黒または青のインクで書く write in black *or* blue ink. ● あすは雨または雪でしょう It's going to rain *or* snow tomorrow. ● 山田か田中, または小川がその本を持っている Yamada *or* Tanaka [Yamada, Tanaka,] *or* Ogawa has the book. ● またはその和子がそこに着けば電話をしてくるだろう If *either* Hiroshi *or* Kazuko arrive there, they will call us./《書》If *either* Hiroshi *or* Kazuko arrives there, he or she will call us. ● 父または私が行きます *Either* my father *or* I am going. (!(1) 呼応のわずらわしさを避けて *Either* my father *or I will* be going./*Either* my father is going *or I am*. ともいえる. (2) 通例一人称を後に置く. *Either* I *or* my father .... の形は避ける)

またまた 又々 again. (⇨又 ❷)

まだまだ ❶ [依然として] still; (なおいっそう) 《比較級を強めて》much, far, still, even, a lot, 《話》lots (!much が最も一般的); (まだ...ない) not(...) yet, still (...) not. (⇨まだ ❶) ● 当地は3月でもまだまだ寒い It's *still* cold here even in March. ● 君はまだまだ勉強しなければならない You must work *much* [*still*, *even*] *harder*. ● 人間はまだまだ多くの困難を乗り越えねばならないだろう People [We] will have to get over *far* [*a lot*] *more* difficulties. ● 彼女はまだまだ若い She is quite a young woman yet.

❷ [その他の表現] ● 確かに彼は腕を上げたが, 作品の出来栄えはまだまだだ Indeed, he has improved in his skills, but his works *leave much to be desired*. ▶(ほめられた人が謙遜そんして)私なんかまだまだです I'm *not any good* at it. (❗決まり文句)

マダム ●有閑マダム a leisured *lady*. ▶*madam* は女性への呼びかけ語. しばしば ma'am と短縮される)(⇨奥様). ●バーのマダム《米》a (woman) *saloon keeper*,《英》a (woman) *publican*. (❗ママ)
●マダムキラー a *lady killer*;《和製語》a *madam killer*.

またも(や) 又も(や) (⇨またしても)

まだら 斑 〖不規則な〗a *mottle*; 〖斑点はんてん〗a *spot*; (細かい) *speckles* (⇨斑点). 〖光線・毛皮の〗a *dapple*. ●まだらのある *mottled*; *spotted*; *speckled* (⇨ぶち); (馬などが) *dappled*. ●白黒まだらの犬 a *white and black* dog (❗a *white* and a *black* dog は「白い犬、黒い犬 1 匹ずつ」の意); a white dog *spotted with* black [with black *spots*].
●まだら模様 a mottled pattern [design]. ●まだら模様の卵 a *speckled* egg; an egg with 《brownish》 *speckles* on it.

まだるっこい (のろい) slow; (回りくどい) roundabout. ▶年を取るとすることがまだるっこくなる People do things *slowly* [People become *slow* of doing things] when they get old. ▶彼女のしゃべり方は腹が立つほどまだるっこい She speaks in an annoyingly *roundabout* way.

※まち 町

WORD CHOICE 町

city 社会基盤が整った一定規模の町や市のこと. New York City (ニューヨーク市)のように, 狭義では行政上の「市」をさす. ●町の中心部 *inner city*.
〖形+city〗 large/central/central/big

town village と city の中間程度の規模を持つ集落. city に対して, 小ささ・身近さ・温かさ・懐かしさなどを含意する. ●彼は今, 町にいるよ He's in *town* now.
〖形+town〗 small/little/new/home/old

頻度チャート
city ━━━━━━━━
town ━━━━━━
   20   40   60   80   100 (%)

a town; a city. ●活気のある町 a lively [(刺激のある↔boring)] *town*. ●町外れに on the outskirts of the *town*. ●(⇨町中, 町並み) ▶彼は山あいの小さな町に住んでいる He lives in a small *town* in the mountains. ▶私は用事のために町に来ています I'm now in *town* (↔out of town) on business. ▶このように近くの町という場合は通例無冠詞) ▶そのうわさは町中に広まった The rumor got about through the whole *town* [throughout the *town*]. ▶町中の人が私たちを歓迎してくれた The whole *town* welcomed us. (❗*town* は「町の住民」の意で集合的に単・複両扱いだが, the whole で修飾される と単数扱い) ▶母は町に買い物に行った My mother went to (the) *town* [〖繁華街に〗《主に米》went *downtown*] to do some shopping. (❗この downtown は副詞)/My mother went shopping in *downtown*. (❗この downtown は名詞)
●町工場 a small-scale factory in a town.
●町役場 a town [a city] office; (建物) a town [a city] hall.

※まち 街 (街路) a street. ●(⇨街角, 街着) ●街へ行く go *downtown* [×to downtown]. (❗downtown は「繁華街へ」の意の副詞) ●街で友達に会った I saw a friend *on*《米》[*in*《英》] the *street*. ▶彼は本の代金を払ってピカディリーの街の喧騒けんそうへ出た He paid for the book and walked out into the busy *streets* of Piccadilly.

翻訳のこころ 十二月の街は, 慌ただしく人が行き交し, からっ風が吹いていた〈江國香織『デューク』〉In the streets [town] during December, people were hurriedly coming and going, and a strong dry wind was blowing. (❗(1)「人(が)行き来する」のは街の場合なので, town より streets の方が適切. (2) come and go は日本語とは順序が逆になることに注意)

●街明かり city lights. ●街角 (⇨街角) ●街着 townwear.

まち 襠 (衣服・手袋などの) a gusset /ɡʌ́sɪt/; (スカートに付ける) a gore. ●まちを入れる insert a *gusset* in 《a garment [a glove]》; insert a *gore* in 《a skirt》. ▶このバッグはまちが広い[大きい]ので荷物がたくさん入ります This bag has wide [large] (side [(底の)bottom]) *gussets* and it can hold many things. (❗「横[底]のまち」をはっきりと表す場合に side [bottom] を入れる)

-まち -待ち (a) wait. ●10 分待ち《There is》 a ten-minute *wait* [a wait of ten minutes].

まちあいしつ 待合室 〖駅・病院などの〗a wáiting ròom; 〖ホテルなどの〗a lounge /láʊndʒ/.

まちあいせいじ 待合政治 (説明的に) behind-the-scenes negotiations in decision making among politicians.

まちあかす 待ち明かす sit up all night expecting for a person to come; wait the whole night 《for》.

まちあぐむ 待ち倦む (⇨待ち兼ねる)

まちあわせる 待ち合わせる (⇨会う, 約束) ▶私は彼女と 6 時に駅で待ち合わせています I *have arranged to meet* [*have made an appointment to meet*] her at the station at six (o'clock).

まちい(しゃ) 町医(者) 《英》a general practitioner (略 GP). (🎯 開業医)

まちうける 待ち受ける ●吉報をいまや遅しと待ち受ける *wait for* good news eagerly [(いらいらして) impatiently]; (楽しみにして待つ) *be looking forward to* receiving good news (❗be looking と進行形にすると待つ気持ちが強く示される); (予期して待つ) expect good news.

まぢか 間近 (⇨近い) ▶2 人の結婚は間近に迫っている The date for their marriage *is getting near.*/《結婚式は》《話》 Their wedding *is just around the corner*.

※まちがい 間違い ❶〖誤り〗a mistake; an error; (無知・不注意によるばかげた) a blunder (❗後の方ほど非難の意が強くなる); (不注意による軽い) a slip,《話》a slip-up; (落ち度, 過失) a fault (❗one's fault は過失責任を暗示).

使い分け mistake 知識・技術の不足や誤解などによる誤りや, 広く判断の誤りをさす.
error 計算や文字の誤りなど, うっかりまたはやむを得ず基準・規則・正しい行動などから外れることを表すことが多い. mistake と交換可のこともあるがやや堅い語で, 道徳的な意では mistake でなく error を用いる: 自分の間違いを悔い改める repent one's *errors* [wrongdoings, ×mistakes]. (❗この場合 error はやや古風)

●テスト[計算]でつまらない間違いをする make a *slip* on a test [a small *error* in one's calculations]. ▶それは何かの間違いでしょう It must be a *mistake*. ▶彼の答案にはつづりの間違いがたくさんあった His

まぢかい

paper had a lot of [was full of] spelling *mistakes* [spelling *errors*, *errors* in spelling, *misspellings*]./There were a lot of spelling *mistakes* in his paper. ▶また同じ[ひどい]間違いをしたんだね You think I'm going to work with you, you *are mistaken* [《話》you've (got) *another think coming*]. ▶電話番号をお間違いだと思いますよ I'm afraid you have the *wrong* number. ▶だれにだって間違いはあるものです Anyone can make [sometimes makes] a *mistake*./Everybody makes *mistakes*.

❷〖失敗〗 a mistake; an error; a blunder. (⇨❶)〖類語〗 ▶彼を信用したのが間違いの元だった(=彼を信用するという誤りを犯した) I made a mistake in [*made the mistake of*] trusting him. (❗I made a mistake [was mistaken] that I trusted him. は不可)/*It was a [my] mistake that* I (should have) trusted him. (❗should have を用いる方が後悔などの感情が強い)/*It was a blunder* [*a mistake*, *an error*] *for* me to trust him. ▶あの戦争は完全に間違いだった The war was a complete *mistake*.

❸〖事故〗 an accident; (何かの出来事)something. ▶彼に途中で何か間違いが起こったのでなければよいが I hope he hasn't had an *accident* [I hope nothing has happened to him] on the way.

❹〖男女間の〗 ▶間違いを起こす commit an *indiscretion* (*with* him). (❗婉曲表現)

❺〖その他の表現〗 ▶彼はまだ生きているって, 何かの間違いだろう(=生きているはずがない) He's still alive? He *can't* be. ▶彼なら間違いない(=信用できる) He *can be trusted* [*is trustworthy*].

会話「彼はいつ辞めたんだい」「ぼくの記憶に間違いがなければ(=正確に覚えていれば)去年の春だったと思うよ」"When did he quit?" "Sometime last spring, *if I remember rightly* [*right*, *correctly*]."

まぢかい 間近い be (near [close]) at hand;《話》be just around the corner; 〖近づく〗draw [get*] near (❗draw より get の方が口語的). ▶クリスマスも間近い Christmas is coming soon [*getting near*, (*just*) *around the corner*,《やや書》(*near* [*close*]) *at hand*].

まぢがいない 間違いない 形 ▶彼の当選は間違いない It *is certain* [×*sure*] *that* he will win the election./He will *surely* [*is sure* to] win the election. (⇨必) ▶彼が世界タイトルを獲得するのはほぼ間違いない I'm almost *certain* [*sure*] (*that*) he will win the world title.

会話「彼は君の案に同意するだろうか」「彼がぼくの案に同意するかだって？ そりゃもう間違いないさ」"Will he agree to your plan?" "Will he agree to my plan? *No doubt about* it [You'd *better believe* it]."

DISCOURSE

大型ショッピングセンターが近所に建設されれば, 交通渋滞や公害, そしてポイ捨てにつながることは間違いない. 端的に言うと, 静かな環境が損なわれるだろう If a big shopping center [mall] were built in our neighborhood, it would *surely* cause traffic jams, pollution, and litter. *In short*, the quiet atmosphere would be ruined. (❗in short [brief],; in a word, (端的に言うとは言い換えに用いるディスコースマーカー. 直前の内容を短くまとめた内容を述べるときに用いる)

── 間違いなく 副 ▶後で間違いなく来てください *Be sure*

まちがえる

to come later./Don't [×Never] *fail to* come later. (❗Never では習慣的行為を意味する)/Come later *without fail*. (⇨必) ▶天気は週末には間違いなくよくなるでしょう The weather this weekend *will certainly* improve.

会話「どれが私の？」「どれだって？ 間違いなくあの青いのだよ」"Which one's mine?" "Which one? That blue one, *surely*."

まちがう 間違う 動 ❶〖正しくない結果を出す〗make a mistake [an error, (大失敗) a blunder, (軽い) a slip] 〈*in*〉. (⇨間違える ❶) ▶間違っている; be mistaken; be wrong; be in the wrong; be not correct.

┏━━━━━━━━━━━━━━━━━━━━━━━━┓
┃ 使い分け **be mistaken** 人の記憶・信念・判断など
┃ が正確ではなく誤解や思い違いをしていることを表す.
┃ **be wrong** 人や物事が法的・道徳的に正しくないこと,
┃ 人が意見・判断・答えなどを誤っていること, 物事が事
┃ 実や正答と異なっていることを表す.
┃ **be in the wrong** 人が争い・過失などにおいて法的・
┃ 道徳的に責任があることを表す.
┃ **be not correct** 人・物事が事実や一定の基準に合っ
┃ ていないことを表す.
┗━━━━━━━━━━━━━━━━━━━━━━━━┛

▶その答えは間違っている The answer *is wrong* [*is not right*]. ▶そんなことをするなんて君は間違っている (道徳的に間違っている) You *are wrong* [*It is wrong of you*] *to* do such a thing./(判断・方法などにおいて間違っている) *It is wrong for* you *to do* [*that you should* do] such a thing. (❗この場合は It is wrong で若干の区切りのをつけて訳す) ▶彼が有罪である と考えるなんて君は間違っている You *are wrong* [*mistaken*] *in* thinking he is guilty. (❗mistaken の方が意味が弱い) ▶この手紙は住所が間違っている This letter is *wrongly* addressed [is addressed *wrong*(*ly*)]. (❗wrong は口語的で, 動詞の前には用いない)/The address on this letter *is wrong* [*is not correct*].

会話「君はそのことに関してまったく間違っていたよ」「そう？」"You *were* quite *wrong* about it." "Was I?"

会話「あらごめんなさい」「また何を[何か]間違ったの？」"Oh I'm sorry." "Now what have you done *wrong*?" (❗この wrong は副詞)

❷〖取り違える〗(⇨❶) ▶彼は間違って私のかばんを持って行った He took my bag *by mistake*.

❸〖失敗する〗 ▶一歩間違えは大事故につながる A single *mistake* [A *false* step] would lead to a serious accident. (⇨形)

❹〖その他の表現〗 ▶間違っても(=どんな状況下でも)そんなことをするな You should *never* do such a thing *under any circumstances*. ▶間違って(=うっかり)機械を作動させてしまった I started the machine *accidentally*.

── 間違った 〖正確・適切さに欠ける〗wrong (↔right); incorrect (↔correct); 〖事実に反する〗false; 〖判断を誤った〗mistaken; 〖論理性に欠ける〗《書》erroneous. ▶間違った答えをする give the *wrong* [the *incorrect*] answer. ▶間違った評価をする have a *mistaken* opinion 〈*of*〉. ▶宗教について間違った観念を持つ have a *false* idea about religion.

まちがえる 間違える ❶〖正しくない結果を出す〗make a mistake [an error, (大失敗) a blunder, (軽い) a slip] 〈*in*〉. (⇨間違える ❶); 〖思い違いをする〗 mistake* (❗通例受身不可). ▶計算をいくつか間違える make a few *mistakes* [*errors*, *slips*] *in* calculation. ▶方向[道]を間違える *mistake* the direction [road]; take the *wrong* direction

[road]. (!後の方が口語的) ●来る日を間違える come on the wrong day. ▶私は住所を書き間違えた I made a slip when I was writing the address./(間違った住所を書いた) I wrote the wrong address. ▶彼女は日にちを間違えていた [間違えた] I was mistaken about [mistook, made a mistake about] the date. ▶彼女は間違えて鏡に1,000円の値札をつけてしまった She labeled a mirror wrongly at one thousand yen. ▶たぶん君は彼が言ったことを間違えてとった(=誤解した)んだよ Perhaps you misunderstood him.
会話「君, せりふを間違えているよ. 最初からやり直して」「いいや. 今度は間違えないようにするわ」"You have the line wrong. Please start back at the beginning." "All right. I'll try not to get it wrong this time."
❷【取り違える】(AをBと) mistake*《A for B》; (AをBと混同する) confuse《A with [and] B》. ▶彼は私を押し込み強盗と間違えた He mistook [took] me for a housebreaker [a burglar]. ▶あなたの傘と私のとを間違えたようです I think I've confused your umbrella with mine.
会話「失礼ですがどこかでお目にかかりませんでしたか」「いえ, そんなことはないと思いますが. きっとどなたか他の人と間違えておられるんです」「いや, これはどうも. 私の思い違いでしょう」"Excuse me, but don't I know you from somewhere?" "No, I don't think so. You must have me confused [mixed up] with someone else." "Oh, I'm sorry. I guess I made a mistake."
❸【失敗する】(⇨間違う❸)

まちかど 街角 ●街角で at [on, ×in] a street corner. ●街角(=通り)で彼に会う meet him on《米》[in《英》] the street.

まちかねる 待ち兼ねる (待ち切れない) can* hardly wait《for》;(熱心に[いらいらして]待つ) wait eagerly [impatiently]《for》;(楽しみにする) look forward to …(!…は名詞または動名詞)(我慢できないほど) be impatient《for; to do》. ▶彼女は夏休みを待ちかねている She can hardly wait for the summer vacation./She is looking forward to the summer vacation. ▶彼がお待ちかねよ He's (getting) impatient to see you. ▶彼は待ちかねて家に帰ってしまった He could no longer wait and so went home.

まちかまえる 待ち構える (待つ) wait《for》;(注意して待つ) watch《for》. ●彼を攻撃するチャンスを待ち構える watch for a chance to attack him. ▶報道陣は首相が到着するのを今か今かと待ち構えていた The reporters were impatiently waiting for the prime minister to arrive.

まちくたびれる 待ちくたびれる get* [grow*] tired of waiting《for》. ▶私はタクシーを待ちくたびれて歩いて帰った I got [grew] tired of waiting for a taxi and walked home.

まちこがれる 待ち焦がれる (⇨焦がれる)

まちじかん 待ち時間 a《long》wait. ▶自分の順番がくるまでの待ち時間が2時間あった I had a two-hour wait [I waited two hours] before my turn came around.

まちすじ 町筋 a street.

まちどおしい 待ち遠しい 〖楽しみに待つ〗look forward to …;〖待ち切れない〗just can't wait《for》;〖いらいらして待つ〗wait impatiently《for》. ▶あなたからの便りが待ち遠しい I'm very much looking forward to hearing《×to hear》from you. (!特に待ち遠しい気持ちを表す場合, 進行形で用いることが多い) ▶クリスマスが待ち遠しい I just can't wait [I can hardly

wait] for Christmas to come. ▶彼がやって来るのが待ち遠しい I am impatiently waiting for him to come. ●お待ち遠さま I'm sorry to have kept you waiting./Thank you for waiting. (⇨お待ち遠さま)

まちなか 町中 dówntòwn. ●町中に住む[へ行く] live [go] downtown. ▶町でばったり彼女に会った I came across her on《米》[in《英》] the street.

まちなみ 町並み (家の並び) a row of houses along the street. ●美しい町並みを保存する preserve beautiful rows of houses in the town.

まちにまった 待ちに待った long-awaited. ●待ちに待った明石海峡大橋の開通 the long-awaited opening of Akashi Kaikyo Bridge.

マチネー [<フランス語] 〖昼興行〗a matinee /mætənéɪ, mátɪnèɪ/, a matinée.

まちのぞむ 待ち望む 〖待つ〗wait eagerly《for》;〖楽しみに待つ〗look forward to …. ▶息子はクリスマスを待ち望んでいる My son is looking forward to Christmas.

まちはずれ 町外れ ●町外れにある be on [in] the outskirts of a town [a city]. ▶日暮れごろ山崎の町外れに着いた We reached the outskirts of Yamazaki toward evening [at dusk].

まちばり 待ち針 a marking pin.

まちびと 待ち人 ●待ち人来たらず The person you are waiting for will not turn up.

まちぶぎょう 町奉行 〖歴史〗a city [a town] bugyo [magistrate].

まちぶせ 待ち伏せ ── 待ち伏せする 動 (襲うために) ambush [lie* in wait]《for him》;(隠れて待つ) hide*《oneself》and wait《for him》.

まちぼ(う)け 待ちぼ(う)け ●きのうは彼女に待ちぼうけを食わされた I waited for her yesterday but to my disappointment she did not show up.

まちまち ── まちまちの 形 〖さまざまな〗《書》various;〖異なった〗different. ●まちまちの服装をしている be in different clothes.
── まちまちに 副 〖さまざまに〗《書》variously;〖異なって〗differently. ●まちまちに評価される be variously [differently] estimated.
── まちまちである 動 (多様である) vary;(異なる) be different. ●箱の大きさは小さいのから大きいのまでまちまちだ The boxes vary in size from small to large. ▶その件について彼らの意見はまちまちだ Their views vary (widely) [They have (widely) varying views] on the subject./Their views are (widely) different from each other./(意見は分かれている) Their views are divided on the subject.
会話「彼は何時に仕事に出かけますか」「日によってまちまちです」"What time does he go to work?" "It varies from day to day."

まちもうける 待ち設ける (待ち受ける) wait for … (⇨待ち受ける);(期待する) expect. (⇨期待する)

まちわびる 待ちわびる be eagerly [impatiently] waiting《for》. ▶彼女は恋人のアメリカからの帰りを待ちわびている She is impatiently waiting for her boyfriend's return from America.

まつ 待つ

WORD CHOICE 待つ

wait 人・物・出来事などを待ち構えること. または, 特定の場所で, あるいは, 特定の時間まで待つこと. ●電話が鳴るのを wait for the phone to ring. ●待機時間[者リスト] waiting time [lists].
look forward to 特定の時期・出来事などを心から楽しみにして待つこと. ●君と会うのを楽しみに待つ look forward to meeting you.

まつ

頻度チャート
wait
look forward to
20　40　60　80　100 (%)

❶ [待ち受ける] wait 《for》,《書》await; [楽しみに待つ] look forward to ...; [予期する] expect.

解説 wait は他動詞の await に対して自動詞用法が一般的で,「…を待つ」の意で目的語をとるときは wait for とする. ただし,「機会・順番」を取る好機を待つ wait for [wait] the chance to come into power./私は自分の順番を待った I waited [waited for] my turn.
(2) 抽象的なものが主語になるときは wait for より await の方が適切: 幸福が彼を待っていた Happiness awaited him. ただし目的語を明示しない文脈では await は不可: 彼がオフィスに戻ると山のような仕事が待っていた There was a pile of work waiting [×awaiting] when he returned to the office.

▶私は彼を 1 時間待った I waited for him for an hour./I waited an hour for him.(❗前の方は「1 時間」,後の方は「彼」に重点がある) ▶私は彼女到着を待っています I'm waiting for his arrival./I'm waiting for him to arrive (×that he will arrive). ▶だれを待っているんですか Who [《書》Whom] are you waiting for? ▶ちょっと待ってください Wait a minute [a moment], please./One [Just a] moment, please.(❗後の方が堅い言い方. 《話》では Just a second. ともいう)/《電話で》(切らずにそのまま) Hold the line [Hold on], please. (❗《電話で》お待ちになりますか は Do you want to hold?/Would you like to hold?) ▶あなたのお便りを待っています I'm looking forward to hearing 《×to hear》 from you./I'm looking forward to 《×expecting》 a letter from you./(待ち切れずにうずうずしている) I can't wait 《×await》 to hear from you. (❗await is to 不定詞とともには用いない) ▶あす 6 時にお待ちしております I'll see [I'm expecting, ×I'll wait for] you at six tomorrow. (❗(1) I'm expecting... の方が改まった言い方. (2) wait は継続を表す動詞なので時点を示す時刻とは用いない) ▶その打者はカーブを待っている The batter sits on [waits for] a curve.

会話「やっと来たね」「ずいぶん待った?」"At last you've arrived." "Have I kept you waiting long?/(Have you) been here long?" (❗《話》の方では you しばしば省略される)

会話(受付で)「ABC 会社の金子ですが, 営業の野村様と 10 時にお約束しています」「お待ちしておりました. ただ今お呼びしますのであちらでおかけください」"I am Kaneko from ABC Company. I have made an appointment to see Mr. Nomura of the Sales Department at 10 o'clock." "He's expecting [×waiting for] you. Would you like to take a seat over there? I'll call him right away." (❗wait を用いると時間に遅れている人を待っているようになるので不適)

❷ [頼る] depend on ....(⇨次第) ▶問題の解決は今後の研究に待つ We depend on our further research for the solution of the problem [for the solution of the problem on our further research]. (❗この例のように on 句が長い場合や句を強調する場合には, 後の方の語順をとる)/The solution of the problem depends on our research in the future.
●待てど暮らせど　▶待てど暮らせど彼は現れなかった I waited and waited, but he never showed up.

*まつ 松 〖植物〗(木) a pine (tree); (材) pine. ●赤[黒; 五葉]松 a Japanese red [black; white] pine.
●松かさ a pine cone. ●松葉 a pine needle.
●松林 a pine grove. ●松原 a pinery; a pine grove. ●松やに (pine) resin /rézin/; (松やにの残留樹脂) rosin. ●(バイオリンの弦に松やにを塗る rosin one's bowstring.

まっ 真っ―　▶真っただ中 in the middle of ....(⇨真ん中, 真っ最中) ▶真っ裸の stark-naked.(⇨丸裸)

まつえい 末裔 a descendant. ▶有名な武将である加藤清正の末裔だと言う人がたくさんいる There are a lot of people who profess that they are descendants of [that they are descended from] the famous general Kato Kiyomasa.

まっか 真っ赤 ── 真っ赤な 形 (鮮明な赤の) bright red; (濃い赤の) deep red; (深紅の) crimson; (緋色《ぅ》の) scarlet. ●真っ赤な服 a scarlet [a crimson] dress. ●真っ赤な(=まったくの)うそをつく tell a downright [an outright] lie; 《話》lie through one's teeth.

── 真っ赤に 副 ▶真っ赤に燃えているストーブ a red-hot stove. ▶(当惑して)耳の付け根まで真っ赤になる blush [flush] (up) to the ears. ●怒って真っ赤になる turn red [crimson, scarlet, purple] with rage; flush with rage.(⇨赤くなる) ▶彼はワインを 2 杯飲むと顔が真っ赤になった He turned crimson in the face after a second glass of wine. ▶彼の目は真っ赤で血走っていた His eyes were all red and bloodshot.

マッカーサー [米国の軍人] MacArthur /məkáːrθər/ (Douglas ~).
まつかざり 松飾り (⇨⑥) 門松
まっき 末期　the end (of); (明確な時期区分の) the last period; (病気の) the terminal stage. ●明治末期 toward [at, ×in] the end of the Meiji period. ●末期の(がん)患者 a terminal (cancer) patient.
●末期医療 terminal care. ●末期がん terminal cancer.
マッキントッシュ 〖コンピュータ〗《商標》Macintosh.
マッキンレー マッキンレー山 Mt. McKinley.
まつくいむし 松食い虫 〖昆虫〗a pine sawyer.
まっくら 真っ暗 図 complete [total] darkness.
●真っ暗(がり)の中に一人座る sit alone in complete darkness.

── 真っ暗な 形 completely dark; pitch-dark. ▶その部屋は真っ暗だった It was completely dark [pitch-dark] in the room./The room was in complete darkness [in pitch darkness]. ▶停電で部屋が真っ暗になった The room went black when the power failed. ▶就職できなかったらお先真っ暗 My future is very bleak if I can't find a job./(どうしてよいか分からない) I don't know what I'm going to do if I can't find a job.
まっくらやみ 真っ暗闇 complete [total] darkness.
まっくろ 真っ黒 ── 真っ黒な 形 deep-black, coal-black, pitch-black. ▶彼の髪は真っ黒だ His hair is deep-black./He has deep-black hair. ▶手を見てごらん. 真っ黒に汚れてるじゃないの Look at your hands. They're (as) black as coal. ▶彼は真っ黒に日焼けした He got thoroughly tanned. ▶パンは真っ黒に焦げた The bread burned [was burned]

まつげ 睫 an eyelash, a lash.（❗通例複数形でまつげ全体を集合的に表す）●付けまつげをしている wear false *eyelashes*.

まっこう 真っ向 ― 真っ向から 副 〖正面から〗head on; 〖きっぱりと〗flatly. ●労使の真っ向からの対決 a *head-on* confrontation between labor and management. ●彼女の申し出を真っ向から拒絶する refuse [reject] her proposal *flatly*. ●真っ向から風を受けて走る run *against* [《やや書》（風をものともせずに）*in the teeth of*] the wind. ●自動車は真っ向から塀に突っ込んだ The car crashed into the wall *head on*.

まっこう 抹香 incense (powder). ●抹香臭い（香の）smell of *incense*;（仏教じみている）sound [look] pious. ●抹香臭い話 a pious talk.

まっこうくじら 抹香鯨 〘動物〙a sperm whale.

まつごのみず 末期の水 ●父の末期の水をとる be present at one's father's deathbed;〘話〙be with one's father when he dies.

マッサージ 名 (a) massage /məsɑ́ːʒ, mǽsɑːʒ/.
── **マッサージ（を）する** 動 massage; give (him) a massage. ●マッサージをしてもらう have a *massage*. ●背中をマッサージしてもらう have one's back *massaged*.
●マッサージ師 a massagist, a massager. ●マッサージ療法 massotherapy.

まっさいちゅう 真っ最中 (right) in the middle of ...; at the height of ....（⇨最中）●今選挙運動の真っ最中です The election campaign is now *in full swing*.

まっさお 真っ青 ― 真っ青な 形 ●真っ青な空 in a *deep blue* [in an *azure*] sky. ●真っ青な海 the *deep blue* sea. ●その現場を見て真っ青になる *turn deathly pale* [*go white, lose color*] at the scene.（⇨青くなる）▶どこか具合か悪いの？ 真っ青だよ Is there something wrong? You look *deathly pale*. ▶彼は怒りで真っ青だった He was *white* with rage.

まっさかさま 真っ逆様 ●真っ逆様に川に落ちる fall *headlong* [*headfirst*,（もんどり打って）*head over heels*] into the river.

まっさかり 真っ盛り ●夏の真っ盛りに *in the height of* (the) summer.（⇨最中, 満開）

まっさき 真っ先 ― 真っ先に 副 （何よりも先に）first of all, first (and foremost). ●真っ先に彼に電話をした I called him (up) *first of all*. ●彼は現場に真っ先に駆けつけて来た He was *the first* (person) *to* rush to the scene. ●会議で真っ先に出たのがこの問題でした This was the *first and foremost* question raised at the meeting.

まっさつ 抹殺 ── 抹殺する 動 ❶〖殺害する〗kill;（計画的に）murder. ●彼らは反対派を抹殺した They *murdered* [《処分した》*got rid of*] those who opposed.
❷〖否認する〗deny;〖無視する〗ignore. ▶彼の意見は抹殺された His opinion *was* completely *ignored*.
❸〖消去する〗rub (-bb-) ... out [off],《書》erase.（⇨消す❷）

まっさら 真っ更, 真っ新 ●真っさらの背広 a *brand-new* suit.

まっし 末子 the [one's] youngest child（⇨末(ばっ)子）

まつじ 末寺 a branch temple.

まっしぐらに（全速力で）at full [top, high] speed.（❗《米話》ではしばしば at を省略する）●ゴール [特価品売り場] に向かってまっしぐらに突進する make a dash *for* the goal [the bargain counter].

まつじつ 末日 the last day（*of* May）.

まっしゃ 末社 a subordinate shrine.

マッシュポテト mashed potatoes [potato],《英話》マッシュ.

マッシュルーム 〘植物〙a mushroom.（❗食べ物としては Ⓤ）

まっしょう 末梢 ── 末梢的な 形（ささいな）trivial;（周辺的な）peripheral;（本質的でない）nònesséntial.
●末梢神経 〘解剖〙peripheral nerves.

まっしょう 抹消 ── 抹消する 動 〖線を引いて〗（名前などをリストから）cross ... off,（単語などを）cross ... out;〖削除する〗delete ...《from》. ●（リストから）彼の名前を抹消した cross his name *off* (the list).

まっしょうじき 真っ正直 ── 真っ正直な 形 perfectly [absolutely] honest; quite [perfectly] straightforward.

まっしょうめん 真っ正面 right in front.（⇨真正面）

まっしろ 真っ白 ── 真っ白な 形 ●真っ白い(な)ドレス a *pure white* dress. ●真っ白な歯 *pearly white* teeth. ▶彼の髪は真っ白だ His hair is *snow-white* [《as white as snow》]. ▶そのニュースに私は頭の中が真っ白になった My mind went *blank* when I heard the news.

まっしん 真っ芯 （⇨真芯）

まっすぐ 真っ直ぐ ── 真っ直ぐな 形 ❶〖物が〗（一直線の）straight;（直立の）upright, erect. ●2点を結ぶまっすぐな線を引きなさい Draw a *straight* line between the two points.
❷〖人・性格が〗（正直な）honest /ɑ́nɪst/,《やや書》upright. ●彼はまっすぐな性格だ He is an *honest* [an *upright*] man./He is honest [*upright*]. ▶彼はまっすぐな人生を送った He led [lived] an *honest* life.

── **真っ直ぐ（に）** 副 （曲がらずに）straight;（直立して）upright, erectly;（他へ寄らずに）direct(ly);（正直に）honestly. ●まっすぐ立つ stand *straight* [*upright*]. ●くぎをまっすぐに打つ hammer a nail in *straight*. ▶この道をまっすぐ100メートル行きなさい Go *straight* a hundred meters along this street. ▶放課後まっすぐ家に帰りなさい Go *straight* [*right*] home after school. ▶体をまっすぐにしなさい Hold yourself upright [*erect*]./Straighten《*yourself*》*up*. ▶彼はくいをまっすぐに固定した He set the post *upright*. ▶彼はまっすぐ医者の所へ行った He went *direct* [*straight*] to the doctor.（❗*directly* には「すぐに」の意もあるので *direct* を用いる方がよい）

まっせ 末世 a degenerate [a corrupt] world.（❗world の代わりに society（社会）, age（時代）を用いることもできる）

まっせき 末席・末席を汚(けが)す ●委員の末席を汚す（＝委員である名誉を得ている）*have the honor* of being a committee member.

まっせつ 末節 a trivial matter; trifles; a minor detail. ●枝葉末節にこだわる （⇨枝葉〖成句〗）

まっそん 末孫 a distant descendant;〘集合的〙distant posterity.

まった 待った （⇨待つ❶）●待ったをする（囲碁・将棋などで）retreat [withdraw] a move;（相撲で）call "Not ready" ●〘直接話法で〙, give a not ready signal. ▶ちょっと待った Just a moment./*Wait a moment*. ▶社長は時々我々の企画に待ったをかける（＝一時的に停止を命ずる）The president sometimes *calls* [*orders*] *a temporary halt* to our plan. ▶（時間的に）待ったなしだ（＝今を外して時がない）It is now or never.

マッターホルン 〘スイスとイタリアの国境にまたがる山〙the Matterhorn /mǽtərhɔ̀ːrn/.

まつだい 末代 ●末代まで (何代も何代も先まで) for generations to come; (いついつまでも) forever, eternally. ●恥を末代にさらす One's shame will live [will be remembered] *forever*. ▶人は一代名は末代 《ことわざ》 Worthy men shall be remembered [never be forgotten].

まったく 全く ❶ 【完全に】 quite; absolutely; completely; totally; utterly; entirely.

> **使い分け** **quite** 「まったく」の意の最も一般的な語. 通例この用法の quite は、極限またはそれに近い比較の余地のない形容詞や副詞 (amazing, awful, certain, complete, empty, enough, exhausted, extraordinary, finished, full, perfect, ready, (all) right, sure, unique, wrong など), 極限・完結を暗示する動詞 (agree, believe, cover, finish, forget, refuse, reject, ruin, understand など), 相違・反対を表す語 (another, contrary, different, opposite など)を修飾する.
> **absolutely** 話し手の主観的で強い確信を表す. 通例 all, every, no, always, never などの全体を暗示する語のほか, 極限に近い状態を表す語や強い感情を表す語とともに用いられる.
> **completely** すべての部分がそろい欠けるところがなく完全である状態を表す. 完結・達成などを暗示する.
> **totally** 「あらゆる点で」「全面的に」の意で, 人や物事の状態・性質の程度を強調する.
> **utterly** 話し手の感情を強く表す. 否定的で好ましくない意の語と用いることが多い. 好ましい意の語の場合は, 通例極限状態を表す語と用いる.
> **entirely** 全体に渡って当てはまることを表す. 例外が一切無いことを含意する.

▶まったく同感です I *quite* [*completely*, *totally*, *utterly*, *entirely*] agree (with you). (❗ *completely* と *entirely* については I agree with you *completely* [*entirely*]. の語順も普通に用い, より強調的)/(まったく君の言うとおりだ) You are *quite* [《話》 *dead*] right. (❗ You said it!/You can say that again. などのようにもいえる)/(まったく同意見だ) I have the *very* same opinion as you./(これ以上は賛成しようがないほどだ) I couldn't agree more. ▶彼はまったく疲れきっていた He was *quite* [*absolutely*, *completely*, *utterly*] exhausted. (❗ ...*quite* tired のように quite を比較の余地のある形容詞と用いると「とても」「まあまあ」疲れた」の意となる)/(話) He was *júst* tired ╲out. ▶それはまったくそうでない It is *not quite* [*ábsolùtely*, *completely*, *totally*, *entirely*, *áltogèther*] false. (❗ 部分否定) ▶彼はまったくについてはまったく違った意見を持っている He has *quite* a different opinion about that. [❗ ...a *quite* different opinion の語順が普通)/He has *quite* a *completely* [a *totally*, an *entirely*] different opinion about that. ▶それはまったく偶然の出来事だったんだよ It was *quite* an accident. ▶まったくばかげてる That's *absolute* [*complete*, *total*, *utter*, 《話》 *downright*] nonsense!/What a *perfectly* ridiculous thing! (❗ *perfectly* は通例好ましくない意の形容詞と用いしばしば皮肉を含意) ▶あなたの誕生日のことをまったく忘れていた I forgot *all* about your birthday./I *completely* [*clean*] forgot about your birthday.

❷ 【少しも...ない】 not (...) at all; not (...) in the least [slightest]. (❗ *not ... at all* より強調的) ▶その子はまったく人見知りしない The child is *not at all* [*in the least*, 《話》 *a bit*] shy with strangers. (❗ ...*not a little* shy は 《書》 で「少なからず人見知りする」の意となるので注意) ▶彼はまったくその状況を知らなかった He didn't know the situation *at all* [*in*

the least, *in the slightest*, 《話》 *one (little) bit*]./He *really* [《話》 *júst*] didn't know the situation. (❗ He didn't *really* know.... では「あまり知らなかった」, He didn't *just* know.... では「単に知っていただけではない」の意)/He was *completely* [*entirely*] unaware of the situation. (⇨❶)

会話 「疲れましたか」「いいえ, まったく」 "Are you tired?" "No, *not in the least* [*not in the slightest*]./*Not at all.*"

❸ 【本当に】 really; (実に) indeed (❗ 通例 very を伴う形容詞・副詞の後で); (非常に) very. (⇨本当 ③) ▶まったく暑いですね It's *really* [(ものすごく) *terribly*, 《話》 *awfully*] hot./It's *very* hot, indeed./What a hot day (it is)! ▶まったく(=実の[正直な]ところ)そのニュースには驚いた *Truly* [*Really*], I was surprised at the news.

会話 「本当に気持ちのいい日だこと!」「ね! まったく夏みたい」 "What a beautiful day!" "Isn't it! *Júst* like summer."

会話 「彼女は優しい母親になるでしょうね」「まったくだね」 "She will make a kind mother." "*I knów*./*You can say that again*./《主に英》 *Quite* (*so*)./《話》 *I'll say*."

会話 「彼のどこがいいの?」「何てこと言うの, まったく」 "What's good about him?" "*Honestly*!" (❗ 憤慨・不信・当惑を表す)

まつたけ 松茸 【植物】 *matsutake*, a *matsutake* mushroom; (説明的に) a fragrant mushroom which grows chiefly in a red-pine forest in the fall.
●松茸ごはん (説明的に) rice cooked with thinly sliced *matsutake* and seasoned with soy sauce.

まっただなか 真っ只中 ●混乱のまっただ中で *in the middle* [《書》 *midst*] *of* confusion.

まったり ●まったりとした (柔らかくてこくがある) smooth and rich; (なめらかで柔らかい) creamy. ●まったりとした味 a *smooth and rich* taste. ▶今週はずっと忙しかったのでこの週末はまったりと[(=のんびりと)過ごしたい I just want to spend this weekend *relaxing* [(何もしないで) *doing nothing*] because I have been very busy this week.

まったん 末端 【終わり】 the end; (先端) the tip. ●行政機構の末端 the *smallest unit* of the administrative organization; a *terminal* administrative organization.
●末端価格 (小売価格) the retail price; (麻薬などの) the street price [value]. ●末端消費者価格 an end-user[-consumer] price. ●末端冷え性 《suffer from》 (medical) poor circulation in the extremities [hands and feet]. ●末端肥大症 【医学】 acromegaly.

マッチ 【マッチ棒】 a match. ●(はぎ取り式の)紙マッチ a matchbook. ●マッチ1箱 a box of *matches*. (小箱に入った) ●マッチの先 a *match* head. ●マッチの軸 a matchstick. (❗ 特に燃えさし) ●マッチをする strike [light] a *match*. ●マッチで火をつける light 《a lamp》 with a *match*. ●マッチ遊びをする play with *matches*. ●すみませんがマッチを貸してもらえませんか Excuse me. Do you (happen to) have a *match*?
●マッチ箱 a matchbox.

マッチ 【試合】 a match. ●タイトル[リターン]マッチ a title [a return] *match*.
●マッチプレー match play. ●マッチポイント a match point. ●マッチポイントをつかむ[切り抜ける] have [save, survive] a *match point*.

マッチ 【釣り合い】 (⇨調和, 釣り合い) ●マッチさせる

まっちゃ 抹茶 powdered green tea. ●抹茶をたてる make *powdered tea*.

まってい 末弟 the [one's] youngest brother.

マット a mat. (❢しばしば複合語で) ●ドアマット a dóor màt. ●バスマット a báth màt. ●床にマットを敷く spread a *mat* on the floor. ●マットで靴をぬぐう wipe one's shoes on the (door) *mat*. ●マット運動 mat exercises.

まっとう 真っ当 =真っ当な形 straight. (⇒まともな)

まっとうする 全うする ●責務[責任; 任務]をまっとうする fulfill [perform, 《書》discharge] one's duty [responsibility; mission]. ●天寿をまっとうする die of old age; die a natural death.

マットレス a mattress.

まつのうち 松の内 the first seven days of the New Year.

マッハ 〖飛行物体の速度の単位〗Mach /máːk/ (number), mach (略 M). ●マッハ2.5で飛ぶ fly at *Mach 2.5*.

まつばがに 松葉蟹 〖動物〗(ズワイガニ) a snow crab.

まつばぎく 松葉菊 〖植物〗an ice plant.

まつばだか 真っ裸 名 stark-nakedness. (⇒裸)
── 真っ裸の 形 stark-naked. ●真っ裸で泳ぐ swim *stark-naked* [*in the nude*].

まつばづえ 松葉杖 a crutch. ●ひと組の松葉杖 a pair of *crutches*. ●松葉杖をついて歩く walk on *crutches*.

まつばぼたん 松葉牡丹 〖植物〗a rose moss.

まつび 末尾 the end. ●手紙の末尾に at *the end of* a letter. ●末尾の数字 the last number.

まつぴつ 末筆 ●末筆ながら 〖参考〗このように書く習慣は米英にない。特別の前置きなく, Please give my best wishes [regards] to all your family. (ご家族の皆様によろしくお伝えください) などと書く)

まっぴら 真っ平 ●そこへ行くのはまっぴらだ I will never go there./(どんな手段を使っても行かない)《主に書》I will *not* go there *by any (manner of) means*. ●戦争はもうまっぴらだ(=もうたくさんだ) We've had *enough* of wars./No more wars! ●彼らに金を貸すなんてまっぴらだ Don't Lend them money? *Never!* 〖会話〗「それを私にくれない」「まっぴらごめんだ」"Will you give it to me?" "*No way* [*Definitely no*]." (❢ no way は《話》で「どんなことがあってもいやだ」の意)

まっぴるま 真っ昼間 ●真っ昼間に in broad daylight. (⇒真昼, 白昼)

まっぷたつ 真っ二つ ●スイカを真っ二つに割る cut a watermelon right [*just, exactly*] *in half* [*two*].

まつぶん 末文 (手紙文の終わりの結びの文) the closing sentence of a letter; (文章の終わり) the end of a sentence.

まつぼう 末法 〖仏教〗the degenerate times. ●末法思想 (説明的に) the thought based on the prediction that Buddhism becomes weak in the degenerate times.

まつまい 末妹 the [one's] youngest sister.

まつむし 松虫 〖昆虫〗a *matsumushi*; (説明的に) a species of cricket. (⇒鳴く) 関連

まつよいぐさ 待宵草 〖植物〗an evening primrose.

まつよう 末葉 ❶〖時代の終わりごろ〗toward the end (of the 20th century). ❷〖末孫〗a distant descendant.

＊まつり 祭り (宗教上の, または定期的な行事の祭りの) a festival; (宗教上の祝祭, または祝祭日) a feast. (⇒お祭り) ●京都の時代祭り Jidai *Festival* in Kyoto. ●祭りを催す [祝う] hold [celebrate] a *festival*. ●その祭りの呼び物 the chief attraction of the *festival*. ●秋祭りが行われている [近づいている] The autumn *festival* is going on [drawing near]. ●クリスマスは西洋では大切な祭りだ Christmas is an important *festival* [*feast*] in the West. ●いつまでもお祭り気分でいてはいけない You shouldn't be in (a) *festive* mood forever. ●もう後の祭りだ (⇒後の祭り)

まつりあげる 祭り上げる (名目上だけの地位に) 《話》kick 《him》upstairs 《to》; (…に仕立て上げる) set* 《him》up as .... ●彼はその会社の会長に祭り上げられた He *was kicked upstairs* to chair of the company.

まつりゅう 末流 (子孫) a descendant (⇒子孫); (末派) a minor branch.

＊まつる 祭る 〖神社を建てて〗《やや書》dédicate,《書》enshrine (❢主語は神社); 〖神として〗《やや書》deify /díːəfài/; 〖崇拝して〗wórship. ●東照宮は徳川家康を祭ってある The Toshogu Shrine *is dedicated to* [*enshrines*] Tokugawa Ieyasu. ●彼は神として祭られている He *is deified* [*worshiped* as a god].

まつる (裁縫) whip; sew with overcast stitches); hem; hemstitch.

まつろ 末路 (最後の日々) one's last days; (死)《書・婉曲的》one's [the] end (❢通例単数形で, 幸福な死にも用いる). ●悲劇的な末路を迎える meet [come to] a tragic *end*. ●英雄の末路は時として哀れだ Heroes sometimes have miserable *fates*./The *last days* of heroes are sometimes miserable. (⇒最期)

まつわりつく 纏わり付く 〖付きまとう〗follow 《him》about; 〖ぴったりくっつく〗cling* to .... ●大勢のファンがその歌手にまつわりついていた I saw a lot of fans *hanging around* the singer.

まつわる 纏わる ❶〖関連する〗be associated 《with》. ●この湖にまつわる悲しい物語がある There is a sad story *about* this lake.
❷〖付きまとう〗●彼女は母親にまつわって離れなかった She *was hanging around* her mother.

＊-まで (副助詞) ❶〖時〗until ..., till ..., to ..., up to ..., into ..., through ....

使い分け **until, till** 肯定文では通例継続を表す動詞と用い,「…までずっと」という状態の終了時を表す。否定文では通例瞬間を表す動詞を用いて動作の開始点を表す。He didn't come *until* [*till*] six o'clock. では彼がちょうど6時に来たことが含意される。six o'clock のような時点でなく, 日, 週, 月, 年などのように期間を表す場合には注意が必要。例えば He didn't come *until Monday*. では英語では Monday を含まないのに対し, 日本語の「月曜まで」は月曜を含むので,「彼は日曜まで来なかった」「月曜になって来た」となる。till と until には意味的な違いはないが, 文頭では until の方が好まれる。

to 期間の終わりを表し,「A から B まで」を表すには from A *to* [*till, until*] B を用いるが, この場合終わりに B が含まれるかどうかは不明。(cf. through)

up to 「…まで」の意で限度を示し, 文頭に用いる場合が多い。

into 「(深く)…まで」の意で時間の推移を表す: 夜ふけまで far *into* the night.

through 「(…の始めから終わりまで通して) ずっと」の意。《米》では「A から B まで」を表すには (from) A *through* [《話》*thru*] B を用いることがあるが, この場合 B は常に終わりに含まれる。(cf. to)

● 今まで (⇨今 ❶ ⑤)　▶3時まで彼女を待ったが彼女は来なかった I waited for her *till* [*until*, ×by, ×to] three o'clock, but she didn't appear.　▶夏休みはあと3週間ある We have another three weeks *to* [*till*] the summer vacation./We have three weeks to go *before* the summer vacation.　▶彼らは6月から9月までヨーロッパを旅行した They traveled in Europe *from* June *to* [*till*] September./They took a European tour (*from*) June *through* September.　▶バスが止まるまで降りてはいけない Don't get off the bus *till* [*until*] it stops.　▶仕事が済むまでそこを離れられません *Until* we've finished our work we can't leave there.　▶先週までのところ彼からの返事は受け取っていなかった *Up to* last week, I hadn't received a reply from him.　▶月曜日に試験が二つあるのできのうは夜遅くまで勉強した Since I'm going to have two exams on Monday, I studied (*till*) late at night yesterday.　▶面会時間は公式には8時までです(=に終わる) Visiting time stops officially *at* eight.　▶彼女は死ぬまで結婚しなかった She remained single *all her life*.　(!) 日本語につられて ×She didn't get married until she died. としない

会話 「そのショーは何時までですか」「10時ごろまでです」 "*Until* what time [How late, How long] will the show go on?" "*Until* around ten o'clock."　(!) (1) How late は遅くまで続くことを前提とした言い方。(2) How long が最もよく用いられるが、時間の長さを問う言い方なので "For two hours." のような応答も可/(何時に終わりますか) "What time will the show end?" "Around ten o'clock."

【…までに(は)】 by …, by the time (that)… (!) 節を従える場合は前置詞 by の代わりに接続詞的に用い、that は通例省略する); (…前に) before …

解説 until, till, by はいずれも時間の終点を表すが、until, till が「…までずっと」と終点までの継続状態に重点があるのに対して、by は「…までに終わる」と行為・状態の終了する最終限度に重点がある。

▶明日9時までにここへ来ていただきたいのです I'd like you to come here *by* [*before*, ×till, ×until] 9 o'clock tomorrow.　(!) (1) by は厳密には「9時までに」、before が漠然と「9時より前に」の意。(2)「遅くとも9時までには」の意では… no later than 9 o'clock tomorrow. などという。　▶いつまでにそれをしてしまわねばならないのですか When do you have to finish it *by*?　▶彼がここへ着くまでには仕事を終えているだろう I will finish my job *before* [*by the time*, ×*by*] he gets here.　(!) (1) 時を表す従属節内は未来の内容を表していても現在形を用いる。(2) I will finish my job… の部分は「…仕事を終えよう」のように意志の意にもなる。(3) 節に完了形を用いた I will have finished my job… は、特定の未来時点までに仕事を終了していることを明示する言い方となるが、日常英語では上例のように未来形ですますことが多い)

❷ [場所] to …, up to …, as far as …. (⇨へ)

使い分け to 「…へ」「…まで」の意で方向と到着点を表す。
up to 「…に至るまで」という気持ちを強調する。
as far as 「(ある場所)まで」と限度を示す。
so far as 主に否定文とともに用いられる。

▶家(駅)まで送ってやるよ (歩いて) I'll walk you home [*to* the station]./(車で) I'll drive you home [*to* the station].　▶彼は飛行機でパリまで行った He flew *to* [*as far as*] Paris.　(!) to ではパリが最終地点であることを、as far as では飛行機以外の交通機関でさらに別の目的地へ向かったことを含意)　▶(乗り物など)渋谷まで料金はいくらですか What's the fare *to* Shibuya?

会話 「ここからロンドンまでのくらい距離がありますか」「約50マイルです」 "How far is it from here *to* London?" "It's about fifty miles."

会話 「どこまでドライブしようか」「丘の頂上まで行きましょう」 "How far will we be going for a drive?" "Let's drive up *to* [*to*, ×till] the top of the hill."　(!) 前置詞の till, until は時間にのみ用い、場所には用いない。ただし接続詞では until [till] we reach the top of the hill. は可で、until の方が好まれる)

❸ [程度、範囲] (…に至るまで) to …, up to …; (…する程度まで) as [《やや書》so] far as …; (…さえ) even.　●最後まで戦う fight *to* the last; fight it out.　(!「論じて決着をつける」の意もある)　▶水は私たちの首のところまで来た The water came *to* [*up to*] our necks.　▶気温は40度まで上がった The temperature went *up to* 40 degrees.　▶そのバスは80人まで乗れる The bus can hold *up to* [×until] 80 people.　▶彼らは歩けるところまで行った They went *as far as* they could walk.　▶彼女は(とりあえず)熱海までの切符を買った She bought a ticket for *as far as* Atami.　▶彼ははかとまでは言わないがよくつまらない質問をする I won't *go so* [*as*] *far as to* say that he is a fool, but he often asks silly questions.　(!) go as [so] far as to do で「…しさえする」の意)　▶1番の生徒までもその難問には答えられなかった *Even* the top student couldn't answer the difficult question.　▶ずうずうしくもそんなことまで期待しているの? Dare you *even* hope for ˇsuch a thing?　(!) hope に強勢を置くと「…を期待しているの」の意)

❹ […だけ] (単に) only, just, simply, 《やや書》 merely.　▶念のため彼に尋ねようとしたまでだ To make sure, I *only* [*just*, *simply*, *merely*] tried asking him.　▶(授業などで)今日はこれまで *That's all* [*So much*] for today.　▶彼らがその計画に反対するのなら強引にそれを推し進めるまでだ If they object to the plan, we can *only* [《やや書》 *do nothing but*] push on with it forcibly.

❺ [必要がない] ▶そんな大雨の中を出かけるまでもない You *don't have to* [*don't need to*, 《主に英》*needn't*] go out in the heavy rain. (⇨必要 图 ③)

マティーニ (カクテル) martini (cocktail).
まてがい 馬刀貝 〖魚介〗 a razor clam [shell]; a jackknife clam; a pen shell.
まてき『魔笛』 The Magic Flute. (参考 モーツァルト作曲の歌劇)
-までに(は) until. (⇨-まで ❶)
まてんろう 摩天楼 a skyscraper (!) 60階前後以上); a high-rise building (!) 10–60階程度).

*まと 的 ❶ [弓道・射撃などの標的] a target; a mark.　●(銃で)的をねらう aim (one 's gun) at the *target* [*mark*].　▶鉄砲の弾が的に当たった [的を外れた] The bullet hit [missed] the *target* [*mark*].

❷ [対象] an object, a target, a focus, a center.

使い分け object 感情や思考を伴う行為、または(性的な)興味などの対象となるものを表す。
target 爆撃などの物理的な攻撃、また嫉妬などの精神的な攻撃の的であることを表す。
focus 興味や注目の対象となる人や状況などを表す。時に複数存在する候補の中から選び出されたものであることを含意する。
center 人の関心などの中心的な存在であることを表す。

まど 窓 ●疑惑[関心; 賞賛]の的 an *object* of suspicion [interest; admiration]．●注目の的 the *focus* [*center*] of attention．▶彼はみんなの尊敬[羨望(ﾎ)]の的である Everyone respects [is jealous of] him．▶次例より一般的)/He is the *object* of everyone's respect [jealousy]．▶そのような政策は非難の的になりやすい Such a policy becomes an easy *target* for [the easy *target* of] criticism．❸【急所】▶君の質問は的外れだ Your question is *beside the point*．/（論じている問題とは関係がない）Your question isn't connected with [*is irrelevant to*] the subject we are discussing．▶議論の的を一点に絞った方がよい It would be better to *narrow* your argument *down* to one point．●的を射る ▶彼の提案は的を射ている His suggestion *is* (*right*) *to the point* [*is quite appropriate*]．

*:**まど 窓** a window;（船・飛行機の）a port, a porthole.

> 解説 **window** は壁にあいている空所，その空所を閉じる戸そのもののどちらにも用いる。　米英の窓は通例上下に動かす上げ下げ窓（a sash window, 《米》a vertical (sash)）か，外[内]側に押し[引き]出して開く 開き窓（a casement (window)）のどちらかで，日本式の引き違い窓は a sliding window という。

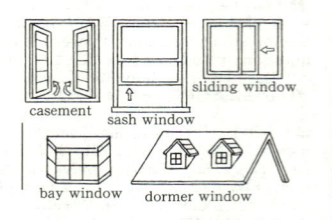

①【〜窓】●出窓（台形）a bay（弓形）a bow *window*．●天窓 a skylight．▶目は心の窓と言われる They say the eyes are the *windows* of the soul．
②【窓〜】●窓側の席 a seat by the *window*; a *window* seat．●窓ふきをする clean a *window*．▶外でスポーツに興じる子供たちの声が（締め切った）窓越しに聞こえた The sounds of children playing sports outdoors filtered in *through* the windows．(⇨⑤)
❸【窓に】●窓に鉢植えの花を並べる arrange potted flowers in the *window*．●窓にカーテンをつける fit curtains on the *window*．▶彼女は窓に映った自分の姿をじっと見つめた She stared at her own image reflected in the *window*．
④【窓を】●窓を開けっ放しておく keep [leave] the *window* open．(❗ keep は暑さなどのために意図的に開けておくのに対し，leave は開いたまま放っておくの意。open は形容詞)　▶窓を開けて[閉めて]くださいますか Could you please open [close] the *window*?

> 解説 「窓を開ける」は上の例文にもあるように一般に open the *window* で表せるが，窓の種類によってさらに適切な表現が可能なこともある: *slide* the *window open*（横に引いて開ける）/*push* the *window open*（押して開ける）/*pull* the *window open*（手前に引いて開ける）/*raise*（↔down）the *window*（上げて開ける）/（自動車の）*lower* the *window*, *roll down* the *window*（❗ roll down は特にハンドル式の場合）．

⑤【窓から】▶彼は窓から外を見ていた He was looking out of [《米》out] the *window*．▶ホテルの窓から富士山が見えた We saw Mt. Fuji through [from] the hotel *window*．▶列車の窓から顔を出してはいけません Don't put your head [×face] out of [《米》out] of the train *window*．▶窓からそれを渡してください Pass it to me through the *window*．
●窓ガラス a windowpane．(❗ a window pane と 2 語にもつづる)　●窓枠 a window frame;（上げ下げ窓の）a window sash．

まどあかり 窓明かり ●窓明かりで by the light (coming) through a window．
まとい 纏い a fireman's standard．
まといつく 纏い付く (⇨絡み付く)　▶つたが木にまといついていた（＝巻きついていた） Ivy *twisted* (*itself*) [*coiled* (*itself*),《やや書》*twined* /twáind/] *around* the tree．
まとう be clothed [《古・文》clad] (*in a coat*)．(⇨着る)
まどう 魔道 ●魔道におちる go astray [wrong]; fall into evil courses．
まどう 惑う be puzzled; be perplexed. (⇨迷う❷)
まどお 間遠 ― 間遠に 形（時間）at long intervals;（距離）in the distance．
まどぎわ 窓際 ●窓際に near [beside, by, at] the window．(❗ near が最も遠く，at が最も近い)　●（乗り物の）窓際の席 a *window* seat（↔aisle seat）．
●窓際族 'window gazers'; sidetracked employees．
まどぐち 窓口 a window; [受け付け先] a desk; [仲介者] a contact．●切符を売る窓口 a tícket *window*,《米》a wicket．●出納窓口 a cashier's *window*,（窓口係）a clerk;（銀行の）a teller．
まどべ 窓辺 ●窓辺に near the window．(⇨窓際)
まとまった 纏まった ❶【多くの】（比較的多い）fairly large;（かなりの額・量の）《話》tidy．▶彼はまとまった金を預金からおろした He withdrew a *fairly large* [*a tidy*] sum of money from his bank account．
❷【決定的な】definite /défənit/．▶その件に関して私はまとまった意見を持っていない I have no *definite* opinion on the matter．
❸【結びつきのよい】close-knit;（よく組織だった）well-organized．●よくまとまった家庭 a *close-knit* family; a very *united* family．
まとまり 纏まり（一貫性）coherence;（統一）unity;（秩序）order;（解決）(a) settlement．●まとまりのあるクラス a *close-knit* class．●まとまりがつく（＝成果がある） get somewhere（↔nowhere）．●まとまりのない（＝一貫していない）議論 an *incoherent* argument; an argument which *lacks coherence*．●まとまりのない（＝構成のまずい）文章 *poorly-arranged* [*poorly-organized*] writing．▶彼らはまとまりがない There is no *unity* among them．▶5 時間も討議したのにまとまりがつかなかった We *got nowhere* even after five hours of discussion．
*:**まとまる 纏まる** ❶【決着がつく】（意見が一致する）agree 《*on*》;（意見の一致を見る）come* to [arrive at, reach] an agreement 《*with*》;（問題・紛争などが解決する） be settled;（結論が下される）be concluded;（完成する）be completed．(⇨纏まった❷)　▶詳細はまだまとまっていない The details *haven't been agreed on* yet．▶彼の提案を採択することで話がまとまった We *agreed to* adopt [*that* we 《主に英》 *should*) adopt] his proposal．▶その件で彼らと話がまとまった We *came to an agreement with* them about the matter．▶その取り引きはまとまらなかった（＝失敗に終わった） The deal *fell through* [*ended in failure*]．

まとめ ❷ [集まる, 統一される] (寄せ集める) be collected; (いっしょにする) be brought [be put] together; (団結する) unite, be united. (⇨纏める❶❸) ● 4人がつまたまって外出する go out *in groups of* four. ▶彼の随筆は1冊の本にまとまった His essays *were collected* [*were put together*] *into* one volume. ▶彼らは一つにまとまってその問題を解決した They *united* [*were united*] *to* find a solution to the problem. ▶彼らはよくまとまっている(=仲がよい) They *are in* perfect union.
❸ [整う] (よく整理されている) be well-arranged; (考えなどが系統立てられている) be well-organized; (考えなどが具体化される) take* shape; (取り決められる) be arranged. ▶彼の論文はよくまとまっている His thesis *is well-arranged* [*well-organized*]. ▶私たちの計画はまとまってきた Our plans are beginning to *take shape*. ▶三本君と藤井さんの間に縁談がまとまった A marriage *has been arranged* between Mr. Mimoto and Miss Fujii./《人が主語》Mr. Mimoto and Miss Fujii are getting married.

まとめ 纏め (要約) a summary; (結論) a conclusion. ● 簡単なまとめをする give [make] a brief *summary*.

まとめやく (主催者) an organizer; (争いの仲裁者) a mediator, an arbitrator; (特に会社の紛争の) a troubleshooter; (特に戦争などの) a peacemaker; (意見の調整役) a coordinator; (議長) a chairman, a chairwoman (⑱-men). ▶彼はまとめ役には向かない He is not fit for the job of a coordinator.

***まとめる 纏める** ❶ [集める] (散在している物・人を1か所に集める) gather; (目的を持って選択して集める) collect; (いっしょにする) put* [get*, bring*]... together (❗ gather, collect より口語的); (グループに[分類して]集める) group. ● 資料を1冊の本にまとめる *gather* [*collect*, (編集する) *compile*] data *into* a book. (❗ collect は組織的にまとめることをいうが, gather にはこの意味はない) ● 荷物をまとめる *get* one's things *together*, (寄せ集める) *gather* one's things *up* [*together*]. ● テーブルの上にまとめて置いてある郵便物 a pile of mail *collecting* on a table. ▶その落ち葉をまとめて焼いてください Please *gather* [*collect*] the fallen leaves and burn them. ▶本は主題別にまとめてある The books *are* filed [*according to*] subjects. ▶そんな大勢の人を一度に案内するのは無理だから 11 人か 12 人ずつのグループにまとめよう We can't show around that many all at once, so we need to *get* them *together* in groups of eleven or twelve.

❷ [整える] (整とんする, 手はずを整える) arrange; (考え・計画などを具体的なものにする) put* [get*]... into shape; (系統立てる) organize; (編集する) 《やや書》compile; (要約する) sum (-mm-) ... up, summarize (❗ 前の方が口語的); (意見の違いなどを調整する) adjust; (統一する) unify; (合体させる) unite. ● 縁談をまとめる *arrange* a marriage. ● 考えをまとめる *put* [*get*] one's thoughts *into* shape; *put* [*get*, *gather*] one's ideas *together*; *collect* [*compose*] one's thoughts. ▶みんなの意見をまとめる (意見の相違などを調整する) *adjust* differences of opinion; (みんなを同意させる) *get* everyone *to agree*; (要約する) *summarize* everyone's opinions. ▶顧客リストをまとめる *compile* a list of one's customers. ● 持ち物をまとめる (=荷造りをする) *pack* one's things. ▶人をまとめるのがうまい He's a good *leader* [*organizer*]. (⇨纏(㊗)め役) ▶そのチームをまとめるのは難しい It's difficult to *get* the team *together*. ▶調査結果は私がまとめます I'll *sum up* the investigation's findings.

❸ [決着をつける] (紛争などを解決する) settle; (結末をつける) conclude; (商談などを取り決める) arrange, (最終的に) close; (調停する) 《やや書》mediate; (完成する) complete, finish. ● 紛争をまとめる *settle* [*mediate*] a dispute. ● 交渉をまとめる *conclude* negotiations; *bring* negotiations *to a conclusion*. ● 商談をまとめる *close* [*arrange*, *strike*] a bargain. ● 卒業論文をまとめる *complete* a graduation thesis. ▶この契約を今日中にまとめるようにしよう 《話》Let's try to get this deal sewed up today.

—— **まとめて** 副 (みんないっしょに) all together; (支払いなどを一度に) in a [one] lump (sum); (同時に) all at once. ● 1年分の給料をまとめてもらう *get* a year's pay *in a lump* [*all at once*]. ▶全部まとめていくらですか How much is it *all together*?

***まとも** —— **まともな** 形 (正直) honest /ánɪst/; (きょうな) straight; (本気の) serious; (分別のある) sensible; (世間並みの) decent; (適切の) proper. ● まともな仕事 a *proper* job. ● まともな意見を述べる express a *sensible* opinion. ● まともな暮らしをする lead [live] a *decent* life; live *decently*. ▶彼はまともなやり方で金を得た He got money by *honest* means. ▶彼はまともな人間だ He is an *honest* [(社会的にちゃんとした) a *respectable*] man. ▶そんなことをするとは君はまともじゃないね(=頭がおかしいね) It's *crazy* of you [You're *crazy*] to do such a thing. (❗ 前の方が普通) ▶まともな生活をするというのが大事なことだ I think the most important thing is to lead a *decent* life.

—— **まともに** 副 [[正面から]] (直接に) right; (まっすぐに) straight; [[まじめに]] (正直に) honestly (⇨形); (本気で) seriously. ▶ボールがまともに私の顔に当たった The ball hit me *right* [*straight*, 《話》*flush*] in the face./(当たった部分に焦点を置いて) The ball hit my face *straight*. ▶彼女は母の顔をまともに見られない She can't look her mother *straight* [*right*] in the face. ▶こんな朝早くては頭がまともに働かない I can't think *straight* this early in the morning. ▶釈放のとき彼はまともに暮らすことを誓った He vowed to go *straight* when he was released. (❗ 成句的表現) ▶彼の冗談をそんなにまともに取るな Don't take his joke so *seriously*.

マドモアゼル [<フランス語] (...嬢) Mademoiselle /mædəmwzél/ (略 Mlle.) (⑱ mesdemoiselles /mèidəmwzél/). (❗ (1) 英語の Miss に相当. (2)「お嬢さん」と呼びかけにも用いられる)

マドラー a muddler.

マドラス [[インドの都市]] Madrás. (参考) チェンナイの旧称

まどり 間取り ● 家の間取り the *plan* of a house; the *arrangement of rooms* in a house. ▶彼は間取りのいい家に住んでいる He lives in a house with a good (⇔a bad) *floor plan*./He lives in a well-*planned* (⇔a badly-planned) house.

マドリード [[スペインの首都]] Madrid /mədríd/.

マドリガル [[無伴奏多声楽曲]] [[音楽]] a madrigal.

マドレーヌ [<フランス語] a madeleine.

マドロスパイプ a seaman's (tobacco) pipe.

まどろっこしい (⇨まだるっこい)

まどろむ doze (off), take* [have*] a doze; (特に昼間に) take [have] a nap. ▶気持ちよくまどろむ have *a comfortable doze*.

まどわす 惑わす [[心を混乱させる]] confuse; [[当惑させる]] perplex, puzzle; [[誘惑する]] tempt, seduce; [[だます]] deceive.

まとわりつく 纏わり付く (付きまとう) follow 《him》 around [about]; (しがみつく) cling 《to him》. ● まと

マトン [羊肉] mutton /mʌ́tn/.
マドンナ [＜ラテン語] [聖母] the Madonna /mədánə/. ●マドンナ像(の絵) a Madonna.
マナー [行儀，礼儀] manners. (❗この意では ×manner とはいわない) ●テーブルマナー table *manners*. ●マナー違反(行為) a breach of *manners*. ●携帯電話をマナーモードに切り換える change one's cell phone into the silent mode. ●彼はマナーが悪い He has no *manners*./His *manners* are bad./He is bad-*mannered* (↔good-mannered).

まないた 俎 a cútting [a chópping] bòard.
●まないたに乗せる ●私は不公平な税の問題をまないたに乗せ，彼らと話し合うつもりである I will *take up* the matter of unequal taxation and discuss it with them.
●まないた(の上)の鯉 ●彼は今やまないたの上の鯉だ(＝どうしようもない状況に直面している) He *is* now *confronted with a hopeless situation*.

まなかつお 真魚鰹 [魚介] a harvest fish; a butterfish.
まなざし 眼差し a look; (一べつ) a glance. ●やさしいまなざしで彼を見る give him [look at him with] a tender *look*; *look on* [*at*] him tenderly. (❗*look on* は特にある感情をもって見る)
まなじり 眦 ●まなじりを決して(＝非常な決意をして)事に当たる do one's job *with great determination*.
まなつ 真夏 ●真夏に in the middle [height] of summer; in midsummer. (❗夏至の頃をさすこともある)
●真夏日 (説明的に) a day on which the temperature is 30 degrees Centigrade [30℃] or over.
まなつのよのゆめ 『真夏の夜の夢』 *A Midsummer Night's Dream*. (参考 シェイクスピアの戯曲)
まなづる 『真鶴』 *Manazuru*. (参考 志賀直哉の小説)
まなづる 真名鶴 [鳥] a white-naped crane.
まなでし 愛弟子 one's favorite [《やや書》 beloved /bilʌ́v(i)d/] pupil [disciple /disáipl/].
まなび 学び ●学びの園 [窓] a school.
まなびや 学び舎 a school.
まなぶ 学ぶ ❶ [身につける] (教わって) learn*; (個人教授で) take* lessons (*in*); (習得する) acquire. (⇨習う) ●教訓を学ぶ *learn* a lesson (*from*). ●スペイン語を学ぶ *learn* [*acquire*] Spanish. ●彼は外国旅行から多くを学んだ He *has learned* a lot *from* [*out of*] his travels abroad.

DISCOURSE
英語は早く学び始めるほど良いという考え方には賛同できない。ひとつ例を挙げよう。以前同級生に，英語圏の国に住んだことがないのに英語がとてもよく話せる人がいた I do not agree with the idea that the earlier we start *learning* English, the better chance we will have to *master* it. **Let me give you an example.** I once had a classmate who spoke English very well even though she had never lived in an English-speaking country. (❗Let me give you an example. (一例を挙げよう)は具体例に用いるディスコースマーカー。数文にわたる長い例に用いるとよい)

❷ [学科として勉強する] study; [科目を専攻する] specialize in ...; (学部生が)《米》major in ... (❗major in は大学学部レベルの大まかな分類に，specialize in は大学院レベル以下にさらに細かい専門的分類に用いる (⇨専攻)); [課程を履修する] take* a course in ...; [大学などで教育を受ける] be educated 《*at*》. (⇨勉強) ●彼は中学校から学び始める We begin to *study* English in [×from] junior high school in Japan. ●彼女は大学で心理学を学んだ She *studied* [*majored in, took a course in*] psychology at college. ●相田教授から法律を学んでいます I'm *studying* [《英》*reading*] the law from [《英》under] Prof. Aida. ●彼はハーバードで学んだそうだ I hear he *was educated* [*was a student*] at Harvard./I'm told he *went to college* at Harvard.

❸ [その他の表現] ●よく学びよく遊べ 'Work hard, play hard.'/(ことわざ) All work and no play makes Jack a dull boy.

まなむすめ 愛娘 one's beloved /bilʌ́v(i)d/ [dear] daughter.
マニア a maniac /méiniæk/. (❗(1) mania /méiniə/ は「熱狂」の意で，人はささない。(2) 病的なまでの執着心を含意)，an enthúsiàst. ●彼は切手マニアだ He is a stamp-collecting *maniac* [*enthusiast*]./He has a *mania* [*a craze*] *for* stamp collecting. (❗日常会話では He *is crazy about* (collecting) stamps./He *is* really *into* stamps. などという方が普通)

*****まにあう** 間に合う ❶ [時間の上で] (一般に) be in time (*for*; *to do*) (↔be late); (乗り物に) catch* (↔miss), get*, make*. ●彼はかろうじてその列車に間に合った He *was* just *in time for* [*to catch*] that train./He just *caught* [*got*, 《話》*made it to*] that train. ●彼は夕食に間に合うように帰宅した He came home *in time for* dinner. ●今からではもう間に合わない (＝遅すぎる) だろう It'll *be too late* now.

会話「9時で間に合う(＝十分に早めに着く)よね」「ゆうゆう間に合うようにそれより早く出た方がいいよ」"Nine o'clock *will be soon enough*, won't it?" "You'd better leave before that, so you'll *be in* good [plenty of] time."

会話「手紙じゃ間に合わないよ」「それなら彼に電話してみたら」"A letter wouldn't *be quick enough*." "Why don't you call him, in that case?"

❷ [役に立つ] (用が足りる) do* (❗通例 will を伴う); (目的にかなう) serve 《his》 purpose, answer 《his》 purpose; (分量的に十分である) be enough. ●ペンは持っていないが，鉛筆で間に合うだろう I don't have a pen, but a pencil *will do* [*will serve* (my purpose), will *answer my purpose*]. ●これだけあれば当座は間に合うだろう This *will do* [*will be enough* to manage] for the time being. (❗be enough の主語は代名詞のみで ×This money is enough .... のような言い方は不可)

❸ [なくて済む] do* [manage] without ..., 《やや書》 dispense with .... (❗通例 can, must, have to などを伴う) ●君に手伝ってもらわなくても間に合う I *can do* [*manage*] *without* your help.

❹ [その他の表現] ●これは今度の月曜日には間に合わない (＝月曜日までに準備できていない) だろう This won't *be ready* by next Monday.

会話「今日は何かご用はありませんか」「ええ間に合ってるわ，ごくろうさん」"Do you have any orders today, ma'am?" "No, we don't have any. Thanks anyway."

まにあわせ 間に合わせ (物) a makeshift; [一時しのぎ] (人，物) a stopgap. ●間に合わせの処置を取る take *makeshift* [*stopgap*, (一時的な) *temporary*] measures. ●箱をテーブルの間に合わせにする use a box *as a makeshift for* a table.

まにあわせる 間に合わせる (用意する) get* ... ready;

まにうける　(なんとかする) manage 《with》; (…で済ます) make* do with …. ● 締め切りに間に合わせる meet the deadline 《for》. ▶これをあすまでに間に合わせて (=用意して) ください Get this *ready* by tomorrow. ▶当分このカメラで間に合わせよう (=済ませよう) I'll *manage with* this camera [*make do with* this camera] for the time being.

まにうける　真に受ける　(言葉どおりに取る) take* 《him》at 《his》word; (本気にする) take ... seriously. ▶彼女の約束を真に受けてはいけない You should not *take* her promise *seriously*.

マニキュア　(a) manicure /mǽnikjùər/. ● つめの手入れやマニキュアを塗ること、足の場合は pedicure); (液) nail polish, 《米》nail enamel, 《英》nail varnish. ● つめにマニキュアをする *manicure* [塗る) polish, do] one's nails. ● 赤いマニキュアをしている wear red *nail polish*. ● マニキュアをしてもらう have a *manicure*.
● マニキュア師 a manicurist. ● マニキュア除光液 nail polish remover.

まにし　真西　be due west. (⇨真北)

まにまに　間に間に　波[風]の間に間に漂う drift *at the mercy of* the waves [the wind].

マニュアル　[[指導書, 手引書]] a mánual. ● マニュアル通りにする do 《it》out of the *manual*. ● トレーニング[セールス]マニュアル a tráining [a sáles] mànual.
● マニュアル車 a manual transmission car; a car with manual transmission. (❗(1) 単に a manual ということもある. (2) ×a manual car とはいわない)

マニラ　[[フィリピンの首都]] Manila /mənílə/.
● マニラ麻 Manila hemp.

まにんげん　真人間　an honest man. ● 真人間になる turn over a new leaf.

*まぬがれる　免れる**　❶[[逃れる]] (災難などから未然に) escape; (救われる) be saved from …. (⇨逃れる) ● 地震を免れた建物 the building that *escaped* the earthquake. ● 間一髪のところで死を免れた I narrowly *escaped* [×escaped from] death. (❗*escape* from は「現実に束縛されていてそこから逃げる」の意で, ここでは I *had* a narrow *escape from* death. ▶彼はあやうく殺されるところを免れた He narrowly *escaped* being [×from being, ×to be] killed. ▶破損船は沈没を免れた The damaged ship *was saved* [*was rescued*] from sinking.
❷[[避ける]] (意識的に) avoid; (策を用いて巧みに)《やや書》evade; (ずるけたりして) shirk. ▶彼は私の質問に答えずに責任を免れようとしている He's trying to *avoid* [*evade*] (taking) his responsibilities without answering my questions. ▶彼の解雇は免れない His dismissal *cannot be avoided* [*is unavoidable, is inevitable*].
❸[[免除される]] be freed 《from》. ▶彼は兵役を免れた He *was freed* [《やや書》*was exempted*] *from* military service.

マヌカン　[<フランス語] a mannequin. ([[参考]] 商品の衣服などを身につけ宣伝・販売する女性店員)

まぬけ　間抜け　❷[[ばかもの]] a fool, a stupid fellow, 《話》a blockhead, 《話》an idiot. ▶この間抜けやYou *silly* boy!/You *idiot*!/What an *idiot* [a *fool*] (you are)!
── **間抜けな**　圏 foolish, silly, stupid (⇨愚か); (頭の鈍い) dull-witted.

*まね　真似**　❶[[模倣]] (an) imitation, [[ものまね]] mimicry /mímikri/. ● 通例ふざけたり, からかったりすることを意含する) ● まねをする (⇨まねる) ● 声まね vocal *mimicry*. ● まねをして発音の仕方を習う learn how to pronounce *by imitation*. ▶彼はゴリラのまねが上手だった He was a good *mimic* of gorillas./He *mimicked* [*imitated*] gorillas very well. ▶彼のまねをして (=見習って) 早寝[早起き]をしようと思う I'll *follow* his *example in* keeping early hours. (❗keep early hours は元は「早寝早起きする」であったが, 今は「早寝する」「早起きする」のいずれか一方をさすのが普通) ▶彼は若者たちに髪形, 衣装をまねる国民的英雄である He is a national hero whose model of hair-style or fashion young people *follow* [*imitate*].
❷[[ふり]] (a) pretense. ● 死んだまねをする *pretend to* be dead; *make a pretense of* being dead; *fake* [《話》*feign* [書]] death. ● カウボーイのまねをして遊ぶ play cowboy.
❸[[ふるまい]] ● ばかなまねをする do a foolish thing; (物笑いになる) make a fool of oneself (❗主語が複数の場合は fools になる); (わざと) play [act] the fool. ▶ばかなまねはよし Stop *making* such a *fool of yourself*. ▶ばかなまねをするな Don't be foolish [a *fool*].
❹[[その他の表現]] ▶その操作は彼の仕方を見よう見まねで覚えた I learned how to operate it *by watching* his *example*. ● (⇨真似事)

マネ　[[フランスの画家]] Manet /mænéi/ (Édouard 〜).

マネー　[[お金]] money.
● マネーゲーム [[投機的な投資・資金運用]]《play》the money game. ● マネーサプライ [[通貨供給(量)]] the money supply. ● マネービル [[利殖]] moneymaking; [[和製語]] money building. ● マネーフロー money flow. ● マネーロンダリング [[資金洗浄]] money laundering.

マネージャー　[[店・芸能人・《米》学校の運動部などの]] a manager; [[プロボクサーの]] a manager; [[スポーツチームの]] the team's caretaker (❗この場合 manager は「監督」). ● ケアマネージャー [[介護支援専門員]] a nursing care manager.

まねき　招き　(an) invitation. (⇨招待)

まねきねこ　招き猫　a beckoning cat; (説明的に) a figure of a lucky cat, usually made of clay, porcelain or wood, which sits with its paw raised and bent as if beckoning customers to enter.

マネキン　[[人形]] a mannequin, a manikin (❗今は a dummy が普通); [[ファッションモデル]] a model.

*まねく　招く**　❶[[手招きする]] beckon. ▶彼は中に入るよう手で招いた He *beckoned* (to) me *to* come in [*beckoned* me *in*]. ([[事情]] 米英人の手招きする行為は, 手のひらを自分に向けて人指し指を前後に動かす)
❷[[招待する]] invite [《話》have] 《him》《to+場所など》; ask 《him》《to+場所など》. (⇨招待する) ● 家の中へ招き入れる ask [歓迎して] welcome 《him》in; (先導して) lead 《him》inside. ▶お招きいただきありがとうございました It was (so) kind of you to *invite me*./《話》Thank you for *having me*.
[[会話]] 「彼を今晩食事に招いたらどう?」「それはいいですね」"Why don't we *invite* [*ask*] him *to* dinner tonight?" "That's a good idea."
❸[[来てもらう]] (専門的指示を得るため) call … in; (雇う) employ, 《主に英書》engage. (❗employ は給与支給, engage は雇用契約を暗示し, 敬意は伴わない) ▶我々は彼を顧問として招いた We *called* him *in* [*employed* him, *engaged* him] *as* an adviser.
❹[[引き起こす]] cause, bring* … about (❗前の方がより直接的な原因を表す); (結果として至る) lead* to …, result in … (❗後の方が堅い言い方); (よくない事をもたらす)《やや書》give* rise to …. (⇨引き起こす, もたらす) ▶賃金の値上げは物価高を招く Higher

まねごと 真似事 ▸裁判[民主主義]のまねごと a *mockery* of justice [*democracy*]. ▸料理のまねごとをしているだけだ(=ちょっとかじる程度だ) I just *dabble* at cooking. ▸私のピアノはほんのまねごとです(=未熟だ) I'm just a *novice* pianist.

マネジメント [経営管理] management. ●アセットマネジメント [資産運用] asset *management*. ●ケアマネジメント [在宅介護支援] care *management*. ●リスクマネジメント [危機管理] risk *management*. ●トップ[ミドル]マネジメント [企業の最高[中間]管理組織部門] top [middle] *management*.
●マネジメントシステム [管理システム] a management system.

＊まねる imitate; (そっくりに) copy; (おどけて) mimic (-icked; -icking); (サルまねする)《軽蔑的》ape; [手本にする] model (*on*, *after*); follow (*his*) *example*. (⇨まね) ▸子供は親のやり方をまねるものだ Children *imitate* [*copy*] the (way) their parents do. ▸その男の子は彼女の声をまねて私たちを笑わせた The boy made us laugh by *mimicking* her voice. ▸この絵はゴッホのまねだ This painting is an *imitation* [(複製だ) a *reproduction*, (偽作だ) a *counterfeit* /káuntərfɪt/] of a Gogh /góu/. ▸彼女はその写真の髪型をまねて自分の髪を整えた She *modeled* her hair *on* the picture.

まのあたり 目のあたり ●目のあたりにする(目の前で見る) see (*it*) *just* [*right*] *in front of* one's *eyes*; (it) *before* one's *very eyes*; (自分の目で[直接に; 現場で]見る) see (*it*) *with* one's *own eyes* [*firsthand*; *on the scene*].

まのび 間延び ●間のびした(=退屈な)話 a *dull* talk. ●間のびした顔 a *stupid-looking* face.

マノン 〘サッカー〙 Man on! ((参考)「敵のプレーヤーが(死角から)来てるぞ、注意しろ」の意の掛け声)

まばたき 瞬き 图 [無意識的] a blink; [合図などするための意識的な] a wink. ●まばたきもせず私をじっと見つめる stare at me without *blinking* [a *blink*].
— 瞬きする 動 ▸太陽がまぶしくてまばたきする *blink* in the sun(light).

まばたく 瞬く blink [wink] (one's *eyes*). (⇨瞬き)

まばゆい 眩い (⇨眩(まぶ)しい) ▸まばゆいばかりの海原 the *glaring* [*dazzling*] sea.

まばら — **まばらな** 形 sparse; thin (-nn-); (ちりぢりに) scattered; (薄くなった)まばらな髪 *thin* hair. ●まばらな拍手 a smattering of applause (*for him*). ▸その会合の出席者はまばらだった The meeting was *sparsely* [*thinly*] attended./The attendance at the meeting was *sparse* [*thin*].
— まばらに 副 sparsely; thinly; (あちこち) here and there. ▸まばらに生えている数本の木々 a few *sparse* trees. ▸その村には人家がまばらにしかなかった The houses *were scattered* in the village./There was a *scattering* of houses in the village.

＊まひ 麻痺 图 [医学] paralysis; (無感覚) numbness. ●小児麻痺 infantile *paralysis*; (話) polio. ●心臓麻痺で亡くなる die of heart *failure*.
— 麻痺する 動 get* paralyzed; (無感覚になる) get numb (*with*). ▸彼の左腕は麻痺していた His left arm *was paralyzed*. ▸病気を主因にして The disease *has paralyzed* him from the waist down. (その病気で彼は腰から下が麻痺したということもいえる) ▸唇が寒さで麻痺していた My lips *were numb from* [*with*] cold. (《米》では from の方が好まれる) ▸列車の運行停止で商品の流通が麻痺した Railroad stoppages *have paralyzed* the flow of goods.

まひがし 真東 ▸真東に due east. (⇨真北)

まびきうんてん 間引き運転 ●間引き運転をする (走行間隔を開ける) thin out train [bus] runs; (本数を減らす) reduce the number of train [bus] runs.

まびく 間引く (間隔を開ける) thin (-nn-) ... out; (数を減らす) reduce. ●タマネギの苗を間引く *thin out* onion plants.

まびさし 目庇 (かぶとの) a visor; (帽子の)《米》a visor, 《英》a peak.

まひる 真昼 [正午間] broad daylight; [正午] (high) noon, midday; [日中] daytime, day. ●真昼に at *noon* [*midday*]; in the *daytime*; (白昼公然と) in broad *daylight*.

マフィア [<イタリア語] the Mafia /máːfiə/. (❗単・両扱い)

マフィン a muffin.

まぶか 目深 ●帽子を目深にかぶる pull one's hat *down over* one's *eyes* [*all the way down to* one's *brows*]. ●帽子を目深にかぶっては wear one's hat *down over* one's *eyes*.

まぶしい 眩しい [目がくらむほど強い] dazzling; [ぎらぎらするようにひかり強く激しい] glaring. ●まぶしいほど美しい女 a woman of *dazzling* beauty. ●まぶしい日光 the *glaring* sunshine. ▸車のライトがまぶしくて目がくらんだ The lights of the car *dazzled* me [*blinded* my eyes]./The light of the car *came into* my *eyes* and I couldn't see anything. ▸熱帯の太陽がまぶしく照りつけた The tropical sun *glared down* (*on* us). ▸鏡の光の反射がまぶしかった The reflection of light in the mirror was *very bright*.

まぶす (振りかける) dust (*with*), sprinkle (*with*); (表面をおおう) coat (*with*, *in*) ●ドーナツに砂糖をまぶす *dust* a doughnut *with* sugar [*sugar on* a doughnut]. ●餅にきな粉をまぶす *coat* a rice cake *with* [*in*] soybean flour.

まぶた 瞼 图 (単に a lid ともいう) ●上[下]まぶた an upper [a lower] *eyelid*. ▸彼は一重[二重]まぶただ He has flat [double] *eyelids*. ▸まぶたが重い(=眠い) I *feel sleepy*. ▸まぶたを閉じると両親の面影が浮かんだ When I closed [shut] my *eyes*, I saw the images of my parents.
●まぶたの母(記憶の中の母) a mother who lives in one's memory.

まふゆ 真冬 ●真冬に in the middle [depths] of winter; in midwinter. (❗冬至の頃をさすこともある)
●真冬日 (説明的に) a day on which the temperature is below zero degrees Centigrade [0℃].

マフラー [襟巻き] a scarf (複 ~s, scarves), 《古》a muffler; [消音器] 《米》a muffler, 《英》a silencer. ●マフラーを首に巻く[巻いている] put on [wear] a *scarf* around one's neck.

まほう 魔法 mágic; (呪文(じゅもん)による) a spell; (悪事のための) witchcraft; (悪霊を使った) sorcery.

① 【魔法の~】 魔法のつえ[じゅうたん; 鏡] a *magic* wand [carpet; mirror]. ▸魔法の円の中にいればあなたの身に害は及びません If you stay inside a *magic* circle, no harm will come to you.

② 【魔法に[を]】 魔法にかかる[かかっている] fall [be] under a *spell*. ●魔法をかける cast a *spell* [work *magic*] (*on* him); put [lay] (him) under a *spell*. ●魔法をとく break [remove] a *spell*. ▸魔女は魔法を使い王子をカエルに変えた The witch used [practiced] *magic* to turn the prince into a frog./The witch turned the prince into a frog by *magic*.
●魔法使い a magician; (魔女) a witch, (男の) a wizard. ●魔法びん (商標) a Thermos, 《米》

まほうじん Thermos [a vacuum] bottle, 《英》a Thermos [a vacuum] flask. (!) jar, pot などとはいわない)

まほうじん 魔方陣 a magic square.

マホガニー 〖植物〗(a) mahogany. (!) 木材は Ⓤ)
● マホガニーのテーブル a *mahogany* table.

マホメット 〖イスラム教の創始者〗Mahomet. (⇨ムハンマド)
● マホメット教 Islam. (⇨イスラム教) ● マホメット教徒 a Muslim.

まぼろし 幻 (幻影) a vision; (実態のないもの)《やや書》a phantom, (錯覚) (an) illusion. ● 幻の(＝珍種の)魚 a fancy fish. ▶彼女は死んだ我が子の幻を見た She saw her dead baby in a *vision*.

＊まま 儘 ❶ […動作・状態の継続〗keep*; remain; leave*. (⇨のまま)

> 使い分け **keep** 人の感情や状態, 物の状態を維持する. 意図的にそうしていることを含む.
> **remain** 人や物の状態がそのまま維持されることを表す.「未だに」の意を含意する.
> **leave** ある物事をそのままにしておくことを表す. 本来は処理すべきことを放置していることを含意する.

● 窓を開けたままにしておく *keep* [*leave*] the window open. (!) open は形容詞. keep は「意図的に開けたままにしておく」, leave は「単に放っておく」の意) ▶先生が出ていったあと生徒たちはしばらく黙ったままでいた The students *kept* [*remained*] silent for some time after the teacher (had) left. ▶医者が来るまで彼女を寝かしたままにしておきなさい *Keep* her in bed till the doctor comes. ▶彼は物事をやりかけのままにしておくのを好まない He doesn't like to *leave* things unfinished. ▶ただ疲れただけです. しばらくこうさせてください I'm only tired. Just let me *be* for a while.

❷ 〖様態〗(a) 〖…のとおりに〗as 《＋節》. (⇨ありのまま) ●物事をあるままに見る see things *as* they are. ▶君の思うままにしてよろしい You can do *as* you like [please, 《書》wish]./You can have it (in) your own way. ▶君の髪型は今のままでいい I like your hair *as* [*the way*] it is. ▶彼の財力なら何でも思いのままだ His fortune enables him to do *whatever* he wants to.
(b) 〖付帯状況〗 ● with …を用いて表す場合が多い) ▶口に食べ物をいっぱい入れたままでしゃべるな Don't speak *with* your mouth *full*. ▶彼は帽子をかぶったままで入ってきた He came in *with* his hat *on*. ▶彼女はやかんを沸騰させたまま台所から出て行った She left the kitchen *with* the kettle *boiling*. ▶彼は腕を組んだままそこに座っていた He was sitting *with* his arms *folded*. (!) 後の2例で, 現在分詞・過去分詞のいずれを用いるかは主述関係による. cf. *The kettle was boiling*. (やかんが沸騰していた)/*His arms were folded*. (彼は腕を組んでいた)

❸ 〖…に従って〗according to …. ▶父は医師のすすめるままに田舎へ転地した My father moved to the country for a change (of air) *according to* the doctor's advice.

❹ 〖その他の表現〗▶彼は出かけたまま帰っていません He left home, and hasn't come back yet.

まま 間々 〖「時々」と「しょっちゅう」の中間の頻度を表す〗(よく) fairly often, (たまに) more often than not; (時々) sometimes; (時に) now and again [then], from time to time. ▶ままあることだ (頻度が下がる) ▶今ではバスで駅まで行くことがままある I take a bus to the train station *more often than not*.

ママ 〖母〗《口》a mom, a mommy, mama; 《英》a mum, mummy (お母さん); 〖バーの〗《米》a (woman) saloon keeper, 《英》a (woman) publican. (!) (1) 米英では通例男性. (2) 複数形では woman を women と変化させる).

ままおや 継親 a stepparent.

ままこ 継子 a stepchild (働 -children); (男性の) a stepson; (女性の) a stepdaughter. ● ままこ扱いをする be hard on one's *stepchild*. ● まま子扱いをする treat (him) as 〖話〗like] an outsider.

ままこ 継粉 an undissolved lump of flour.

ままごと 飯事 ● ままごとをする play house.

ままちち 継父 a stepfather.

ままならない ▶人生はままならない (望むようにはいかない) Life *doesn't go just as* we wish./Life *doesn't go the way* we want it to.

ままはは 継母 a stepmother.

ままよ 儘よ ▶人が何と言おうとままよだ I *don't care* what people say.

まみず 真水 fresh water.

まみなみ 真南 真南に due south. (⇨真北)

-まみれ -塗れ (⇨塗れる) ●血まみれの衣服 blood-stained clothes. ▶ほこりまみれになった I *got dusty all over*. ▶彼の顔は泥まみれだ His face *is covered* [*is heavily smeared*] *with mud*./His face is muddy all over.

まみれる 塗れる (覆われている) be covered 《with》; (汚れる) be smeared [(しみがつく) stained] 《with》. ●一敗地にまみれる suffer a crushing [an overwhelming] defeat. ▶彼の新しい靴は泥にまみれた His new shoes *were covered* [*smeared*] *with mud*.

まむかい 真向かい (⇨向かい) ● 駅の真向かいの店 a store *just* [*right*] *opposite* 《主に米話》*across from* the station; (真ん前の) a store *just* [*right*] *in front of* the station.

まむし 蝮 〖動物〗a (pit) viper.

＊まめ 豆 (一般的に) a bean; (大豆) a soy bean; (エンドウ) a pea. ● 煮豆 boiled [cooked] *beans*. ● 豆をまく (畑に) sow *beans* 《in the field》; (節分で) scatter parched *beans* (to drive out evil spirits on February 3).
● 豆科 the pulse family; the pulses. ● 豆かす bean cake. ● 豆がら beanstalks or pods left after the beans have been taken out. ● 豆まき (節分の) a bean-scattering ceremony. (⇨節分)

まめ — **まめに** 副 (勤勉に) hard, diligently; (陰日向(ひなた)のない) faithfully. ●まめに働く work *hard* [*diligently*]; beaver away 《at》. ●まめにノートをとる *take notes diligently* (入念にノートをとる) take careful notes 《on the lecture》. ●まめに働く人 an eager beaver. ●筆まめ

まめ 肉刺 (水ぶくれ) a blister; (うおのめ) a corn. ▶足の親指にまめができている A *corn* has formed on my big toe./I have a *corn* on [xin] my big toe.

まめ- 豆- (小さい) miniature; (小型の) baby; (超小型の) midget. ● 豆電球 a *miniature* bulb. ● 豆本 a *miniature* book. ● 豆台風 a *small* typhoon. ● 豆自動車 a *midget* car. ● 豆鉄砲 a peashooter. (⇨鳩 〖成句〗) ● 豆絞り a spotted pattern. ● 豆単 (小形の単語集) a *pocket-size*(*d*) wordbook. ● 豆炭 an oval [an egg-shaped] briquette. ● 豆粒のように小さく見える look as small as a *pea*; (遠くで人が) look like an ant (!) 主語が複数のときは look like ants.

まめつ 磨滅 图 wear.
— **磨滅する** 動 wear down. ● 磨滅したタイヤ a *worn-down* tire. ▶タイヤが磨滅した The tire *has* (*been*) *worn down*.

まめまめしく ●まめまめしく (＝勤勉に) 働く work *hard*

まもう 磨耗
── **磨耗する** 動 be worn down [away]; wear down [away]. (‼away はすり減ってなくなることを含意する《磨滅》)

***まもなく 間もなく** soon, presently (‼後の方が堅い語); (ほどなく) before long (‼soon とほぼ同意だが, やや文語的); (じきに) shortly (‼以上の語より短い時間を表す); (ほとんど) nearly; (しばらくしたら) in a little [a short] while. ▶彼は間もなく帰って来るでしょう He will come back *soon* [*before long*, *shortly*, *in a little while*, *in a short while*]. (⇨すぐ❷) ▶その本は間もなく(＝近いうちに)出版されます That book is fòrthcóming [coming out soon]. ▶間もなく彼はその事件を知った He *soon* [*Soon* he] knew the incident. (‼soon は過去形では通例文尾では用いられない)/He knew the incident *before long* [×*shortly*]. (‼shortly は通例単独では過去形では用いられない)/(主に書) *It was not long before* he knew the incident. ▶彼らは大学を卒業後間もなく結婚した They got married *soon* [*shortly*] after they (had) graduated from college. ▶間もなく夏休みになる The summer vacation is coming *soon* [(話) is *just around the corner*]. ▶彼女が死んで間もなく(＝もうすぐ)10年になる It's been *almost* [*nearly*] ten years since she died./She has been dead for *almost* [*nearly*] ten years.

まもの 魔物 a demon /díːmən/; a devil /dévl/; an evil /íːvl/ spirit. (⇨悪魔) ▶金は魔物 The love of money is the root of all *evil*.

まもり 守り defense. (⇨守備) ▶固い守り strong *defense*. ▶空の守りを固める strengthen the *defense* [×*guard*] of the air. ▶守りにつく《野球》take the field. ●守り専門の選手 a *defensive* replacement. ▶守りの上手な外野手 a good outfielder.
●**守り刀** a dagger for self-defense. ●**守り神** a guardian deity. ●**守り札** a paper charm.

‡**まもる 守る** ❶ [遵守する] (法・規則を) 《やや書》observe, obey (↔break*); (命令などを) obey, follow (↔disobey); (慣習・教えなどを) follow,《やや書》observe. (‼observe は「自発的意志によってきちんとやるに」, obey は「権威に服して従順に」, follow は「内容のとおりに」の意) ●交通規則をきちんと守る *observe* the traffic rules strictly. ●速度制限を守る *obey* the speed limit. ●仏教の教えを忠実に守る *follow* [*observe*, (実行する) *practice*] the Buddhist teachings. ●医師の注意を守る *follow* [×*obey*, (聞く) *take*] *the doctor's advice*. ●親の言いつけを守りなさい You should *obey* [*follow*] the orders of your parents./You should *obey* [*be obedient to*] your parents.

❷ [履行する] (約束・秘密などを) keep*; (主義・決心などを頑固に) stick* [《書》adhere] to…. ●固く守られた秘密 a well-*kept* secret. ●主義を固く守る *stick* to one's principles. ●約束を守る *keep* one's promise [*word*]. (⇨約束) ▶予約時間を守ってください (医院などで) Please *keep* your appointment.

❸ [防御する] (攻撃・脅威から) defend; (危険から) protect, keep*; (盾(☆)のように)《やや書》shield; [[危害から見張る]] guard. ●彼女を危険から守る *defend* [*protect*, *guard*, *keep*] her *from* [*against*] danger. (‼from は防御の姿勢から, against は積極的な攻撃を暗示) ●敵国から守る *defend* [*protect*] one's country *against* the enemy. ●彼の留守宅を守る(＝管理する) take charge of [(世話する) look *after*] the house while he is away. ▶こんな薄いコートでは寒さから身を守れないだろう Such a thin coat won't *protect* you *from* [*give a protection against*] the cold./You can't *protect* yourself *from* the cold *with* such a thin coat./Such a thin coat won't be a protection against the cold. ▶その建物が風から彼を守ってくれた The building *shielded* him *from* [*against*] the wind. ▶国民は自分で自分を守るしかない。だから貯金するのだ The (Japanese) people have to *protect* themselves. That is why they save money.

❹ [維持する] keep*,《やや書》maintain. ●平和[沈黙]を守る *keep* peace [silence, (黙っている) silent]; *maintain* peace [silence].

❺ [その他の表現] ●セカンド[ショート]を守る play second (base) [shortstop]. ▶どのポジションを守っていますか What position do you play? ▶時間を守ることは大切なことだ It's important to *be punctual*./Punctuality is an important matter. ▶今のところ彼は1敗を守っている So far he *has played quite well* with only one defeat.

まやかし a fake; a counterfeit. (⇨偽物(にせ)) ▶政治家のまやかしにはうんざりだ I am sick and tired of the *deceit* by politicians.

まやく 麻薬 a drug, (話) dope; (鎮痛などの麻酔薬) a narcotic. (‼drug はヘロイン (heroin), モルヒネ (morphine), アヘン (opium) などの麻薬, さらに LSD などの幻覚剤を含めもう。それ以外にマリフアナ (marijuana), コカイン (cocaine) なども含む) ●麻薬の乱用 *drug* abuse; abuse of *drugs*. ●麻薬の取り引き *drug* traffic [*trafficking*]; traffic in *drugs*.
●**麻薬常習者** a drug addict; a habitual drug user; a narcotic. ●**麻薬中毒** narcotic [*drug*] addiction; narcotism. ●**麻薬取締法** the Narcotic Control Act. ●**麻薬密売人** a drug [a dope] dealer. ●**麻薬密輸組織** a drug-[a dope-] smuggling ring.

まゆ 眉 /áibràu/, a brow. (‼通例複数形) 眉をかく pencil one's *eyebrows*. ●眉を上げる raise one's *eyebrows* [an *eyebrow*] 《at the news》. (‼複数形は驚き・ショックを, 単数形は驚き・軽蔑・非難・疑いなどを表す) ▶彼のおじさんは濃い眉をしている His uncle has thick [bushy] *eyebrows*.
●**眉につばをつける** ▶彼の言うことは何でも眉につばをつけて聞くべきだ We have to *take* everything that he says *with a grain of salt*.
●**眉に火がつく** ▶彼は眉に火がつくのを(＝差し迫った危険を)感じ, 走り始めた Sensing *imminent danger*, he started to run.
●**眉一つ動かさない** ▶彼は彼女の死の知らせを眉一つ動かさずに(＝表情を変えずに)聞いた He heard the news of her death *without changing his expression*.
●**眉を吊り上げる** get angry.
●**眉をひそめる** ▶彼はその知らせを聞いて眉をひそめた He frowned /《書》knitted his (eye)brows 《at the news》. (‼不快・心配・思索などを表す)
●**眉を寄せる** (困惑・不機嫌などの表情で) bring one's eyebrows closer (together); knit one's (eye) brows.
●**眉形** the shape of an eyebrow. ●**眉毛** (⇨眉毛) ●**眉墨** an eyebrow pencil.

まゆ 繭 a cocoon. ▶繭から糸を取る reel silk off *cocoons*.
●**繭玉** a New Year's decoration of a willow branch hung lots of cocoon-shaped rice cakes and dumpling.

まゆげ 眉毛 an eyebrow. ●眉毛を抜く pluck ones

eyebrows.

まゆつばもの 眉唾物 (うさん臭い話)《話》a fishy story;(疑わしい事) a dubious matter. ▶それは眉唾物だ(=信じられない)/You can't readily believe it./(話を割り引いて受け取らなくはならない)《やや話》It must be taken with a grain [a pinch] of salt.

まゆね 眉根 ●眉根にしわを寄せる frown; knit one's brows.

まよい 迷い (ためらい) hesitation; (自己不信) self-doubt; (錯覚) (an) illusion. ●迷いが生じる(ためらう) hesitate《about》;(揺れ動く) waver. (⇨迷う ❸)
●迷いがさめる be disillusioned; awake from an *illusion*; (正気・理性を取り戻す) come to one's senses.

‡**まよう 迷う** ❶ [道に迷う] get* [be] lost, lose* one's [the] way; (はぐれる)《やや書》stray. ▶彼らは森の中で道に迷った They *got lost* [*were lost*, *lost their way*] in the wood(s). ▶子犬が私たちの家に迷い込んできた A puppy *strayed into* our house. 会話「道に迷ったようですが, どうなさいましたか」「ええ, どのバスに乗ったらいいのかちょっと分からなくなってしまって」"You look *lost*. Can I help you?" "Yes, please. I've had a little mix-up (in) finding the right bus." (❗have a mix-up は「頭が混乱している」の意の口語的慣用表現)

❷ [当惑する] (途方に暮れる)《やや書》be at a loss; (困惑する) be puzzled; be perplexed. ▶どうしたらよいか迷った I *was at a loss* [*was puzzled*]《*about* [*as to*]》what to do. (❗wh- 節[句]の前では前置詞はしばしば省略される. 次例の方が日常的か)/I *didn't know* what to do.

❸ [ためらう] hesitate; (思案する) wonder《wh- 節[句]》; (気持ちが揺れる) waver (⇨ためらう); (決心がつかない) be undecided. ▶さんざん迷った末 after so much *hesitation*. ▶彼はどっちの道を取ろうかまだ迷っている He *is* still *hesitating* [*is* still *undecided*, *is* still *not sure*, *is* still *of two minds*,《主に英》*is* still *in two minds*]《*about*》which way to take. ▶彼はどのセーターを買うか迷った He *wondered* [couldn't decide] which sweater to buy. ▶彼は決断に迷った He *wavered* in his resolution./His resolution *wavered*.

❹ [心を奪われる] ●恋に迷う (夢中になる) be lost in love; (盲目的になる) be blind with love. ●女に迷う(=魅せられる) be charmed [《やや書》captivated] by a woman.

まよえる 迷える stray《sheep》.

まよけ 魔除け (魔力のあるもの) a talisman (複 ~s); (お守り) an amulet, a charm《*against* evils》. ●魔除けに as a *talisman*.

まよこ 真横 ●真横から (right) from the side. ●人の真横に stand right at《his》side. ▶車は真横からの突風で対向車線へ押しやられた My car was pushed (×off) into the opposite lane by the gale blowing *from the side*. (❗off があると「道から外に吹き飛ばされた」の意になる)

まよなか 真夜中 ●(*in*) the middle of the night. (❗midnight は「夜の 12 時」の意. ただし形容詞的用法では「真夜中の」の意にも: 真夜中の訪問 a *midnight* visit) ●真夜中過ぎまで勉強する study till after [past] *the middle of the night*. (❗till after midnight は「夜の 12 時過ぎまで」の意) ▶彼は時々真夜中に電話をかけてくる He sometimes calls me up *in the middle of the night* [《夜遅く》*late at night*].

マヨネーズ [<フランス語] mayonnaise /méiənèiz/.
●マヨネーズをかける put *mayonnaise*《*on*》; dress《a green salad》with *mayonnaise*.

まよわす 迷わす (当惑させる) puzzle,《書》perplex; (判断を誤らせる) mislead*; (誘惑する) tempt, seduce. ▶大衆はデマに迷わされやすい The public can *be* easily *misled* by rumors.

マラウイ [国名] Malawi; (公式名) the Republic of Malawi. (首都 Lilongwe) ●マラウイ人 a Malawian. ●マラウイ(人)の Malawian.

マラカス [楽器] (a pair of) maracas. (❗通例一つずつ両手に持つので複数形だが. 一つは a maraca) ●マラカスを振る shake the *maracas*.

マラソン a marathon /mǽrəθàn/. ●マラソン走者[選手] a *marathon* runner; a marathoner. ●マラソンをする run [do] a *marathon*. ●フルマラソンを完走する complete a full *marathon*. ●ハーフマラソン a half *marathon*. ●いつかボストンマラソンに出たい I hope to be [take part] in the Boston *marathon* someday. (❗go on the Boston *marathon* ともいう)
●マラソンコース a márathon còurse.

マラリア malaria /məléəriə/. ●マラリア患者 a *malarial* patient. ●マラリアにかかる come down with *malaria*. ●マラリアにかかっている be suffering from *malaria*.

まり 毬 a ball. ●まりをつく bounce a *ball*.

マリ [国名] Mali; (公式名) the Republic of Mali. (首都 Bamako) ●マリ人 a Malian. ●マリ(人)の Malian.

マリア ●聖母マリア the Blessed /blésid/ Virgin (*Mary*), the Virgin *Mary*.

マリアナ ●マリアナ諸島 the Mariána Islands.

マリーゴールド [植物] a marigold.

マリッジ [結婚] a marriage.
●マリッジブルー the marriage blue. (参考 結婚直前の人に見られる情緒不安定な状態) ●マリッジリング [結婚指輪] (wear) a wédding rìng.

マリネ (a) marinade. (❗種類をいうときは [C]) ●サケのマリネ *marinated* salmon.

マリファナ (smoke) marijuana /mǽrəwá:nə/,《巻きたばこの》《話》a joint.

まりも 毬藻 [植物] a marimo (複 ~s); (説明的に) a ball-shaped green alga that grows in a freshwater lake or pond.

まりょく 魔力 (不思議な力) mágic, magical power; (魅力) (a) charm.

マリン [海の] marine.
●マリンスノー marine snow. (参考 海水中を沈降する白色の粒子) ●マリンスポーツ water [ocean] sports. (❗marine sports はあまり用いない) ●マリンブルー (濃い青色) marine blue.

マリンバ [楽器] a marimba. ●マリンバを演奏する play the *marimba*. ●マリンバ奏者 a marimbist.

*‡**まる 丸** [円] a circle. ●二重丸 a double *circle*. ●丸を描く draw a *circle*. ●正しい答えに丸 (= 丸印) をつける mark a correct answer with a *circle*. (事情 米英ではチェック印(✓) ((米) check, (英) tick) を用いる方が普通) ▶正しいと思う文の番号を丸で囲みなさい Draw a *circle* around [Enclose with a *circle*, Circle] the number of the sentence you think right.

まるー 丸- [十分の] full; [完全の] whole; [たっぷりの] good. ●丸坊主の頭 (⇨丸坊主) ●丸 3 日間 for three *full* [*a full* three, *fully* three] days (❗for *full* three days は (古・詩)); for three *whole* days (the *whole* three days); for a *good* three days; 《話》for three *solid* days [three days *solid*]. ▶その仕事を完成するには丸 1 年かかる It will take a *full* [a *whole*, a *good*,《話》a *solid*] year

まるあらい to complete the work.

まるあらい 丸洗い ― 丸洗いする 動 ●着物を丸洗いする wash a kimono without taking it apart. ●丸洗い可能な掛け布団 a Japanese quilt which can be washed whole.

まるあんき 丸暗記 ― 丸暗記する 動 ●その課を丸暗記する learn the (whole) lesson by heart [(機械的) by rote].

まるい 丸い, 円い 形 〖円形の〗 round; 〖環状の〗 circular; 〖球状の〗 round, 〖やや書〗 spherical. ●円いテーブル a round table. ●背中の丸い round-shouldered. ●角の丸いテーブル a table with rounded (⇨sharp) corners. ▶地球は平たくなく丸い The earth is not flat, but round.

● 丸く丸まる〖収める〗 (円満に収まる/収める) work out [work (it) out] peacefully.

― 丸くなる 動 ●〖物が〗 round; 〖動物・人が寝て〗 curl [huddle] (oneself) up, lie* curled [huddled] up; 〖人柄が〗 grow, mellow, mellow. ●背中を丸くする (人が) hunch one's shoulders; (猫が) arch its back. ●驚いて目を丸くする round one's eyes [open one's eyes wide] in surprise. ●鉛筆の芯(_しん_)が丸くなった The point of a pencil got dull [blunt]. ▶彼女は年とともに少し丸くなってきた He has mellowed a little with age.

まるうつし 丸写し 名 an exact [a carbon] copy (of).

― 丸写しする 動 ●彼女の詩の一節を丸写しする copy a stanza from her poem. (**!** copy は「ただ単にそのまま写す」の意と「盗み写す (plagiarize)」の意の両方を含む)

まるおび 丸帯 a one-piece sash.

まるがお 丸顔 a round face. ●丸顔の少女 a girl with a round face; a round-faced girl.

まるがかえ 丸抱え ▶宴会は会社の丸抱えだった We had a banquet (entirely) at the company's expenses./The banquet was (entirely) financed by the company./The company paid all the expenses of the party.

まるかじり 丸齧り ●リンゴを丸かじりする eat an apple, skin and all. (⇨丸ごと).

まるがっこ 丸括弧 a parenthesis (複 parentheses). (⇨括弧)

まるがり 丸刈り ●丸刈りにしてもらう get a close crop; have one's hair closely cropped [cut]. ●丸刈りの少年 a boy with close-cropped hair. ▶彼は丸刈りにしている He has a close crop [a close haircut].

まるき 丸木 a log.
●丸木橋 a log bridge. ●丸木船 a dugout (canoe /kænúː/).

マルキシズム 〖マルクス主義〗 Márxism.

マルク 〖ドイツの旧通貨単位〗 a mark; a deutsche mark 《略 DM》.

マルクス 〖ドイツの経済学者〗 Marx /máːrks/ (Karl ~).
●マルクス経済学 Marxian economics. ●マルクス主義 Márxism. ●マルクス主義者 a Marxist. ●マルクスレーニン主義 Marxism-Leninism.

まるくび 丸首 ●丸首のセーター a round-neck sweater /swétər/; a crew neck; (とっくり襟(_えり_)の) 〖主に米〗 a turtleneck; 〖主に英〗 a poloneck. ●丸首のシャツ a T-shirt.

まるごし 丸腰で unarmed; without a sword [a gun]; without carrying any weapon.

まるごと 丸ごと ●豚を 1 匹まるごと焼く broil 〖英〗 grill] a pig whole; broil a whole pig. ●魚を丸ごと(=骨ごと)食べる eat a fish, bones and all. ●リンゴを丸ごと(=皮ごと)かじる eat an apple, peel and all; (皮をむかずに) eat an apple without peeling it.

〖翻訳のこころ〗 彼の下役との関係はまるごとの人間関係でなく, 仕事という側面についての上下関係だけであるはずです (丸山眞男 『「である」ことと「する」こと』) His (of the section chief) relationship with his underlings are not based on overall personal relationship; superior-inferior relationship is supposed to be based solely on their work relationship. (**!**「まるごと」は over-all (全体の, あらゆる面での)の意と表す)

マルコポーロ 〖イタリアの旅行家〗 Marco Polo /máːrkou póulou/.

まるさ 丸さ roundness. (⇨丸味)

マルセイユ 〖フランスの都市〗 Marseilles /maːrséi/.

まるぞめ 丸染め ●丸染めにする dye 《a kimono》 without taking it apart.

まるぞん 丸損 ●丸損する suffer a total [a complete, a dead] loss.

まるた 丸太 a log.
●丸太小屋 a log cabin.

マルタ 〖国名〗 Malta /mɔ́ːltə/; (公式名) the Republic of Malta. (首都 Valletta) ●マルタ人 a Malta. ●マルタ語 Malta. ●マルタ(人[語])の Malta.

まるだし 丸出し exposed. ●太ももを丸出しにして歩く walk with one's thighs exposed. ●方言丸出しで話す speak with a broad dialect.

マルチ multi-. ●マルチタスク(の) 〖コンピュータ〗 multitasking. ●マルチユーザー(の) 〖コンピュータ〗 multiuser.
●マルチ商法 multilevel merchandising [sales]; pyramid selling. ●マルチ人間 a multitalented person. ●マルチヒットゲーム 〖野球〗 a multi-hit game. (〖参〗 1 選手が 2 本以上のヒットを打った試合) ●マルチホームランゲーム 〖野球〗 a multi-homer game. ●マルチメディア (⇨マルチメディア)

マルチメディア 〖複合媒体〗 multimedia. (**!** 単数扱い) ●双方向型マルチメディア interactive multimedia.
●マルチメディアパソコン 〖コンピュータ〗 a multimedia PC.

まるっきり (少しも…でない) not … at all [in the least]; (完全に) completely. (⇨全く) ●まるっきり分かりません I don't understand it at all. ▶彼にはそれをする意志などまるっきりない He has no intention whatever of doing it. (**!** whatever は形容詞的用法で no または any を伴った名詞の後でそれらを強調するために用いる) ▶そのことに関しては正義はまるっきり素人だ(=ほとんど経験がない) Masayoshi has very little experience in it. ▶ふるさとはまるっきり変わってしまった My hometown has [〖文〗 is] changed completely.

まるっこい 丸っこい roundish. ●丸っこい字を書く write roundish characters.

まるつぶれ 丸潰れ ▶計画が丸つぶれになった The plan completely miscarried./The plan was wrecked.

***まるで** **❶** 〖あたかも〗 as if, as though 《+節》; (…のような[に]) (just) like ….

〖解説〗(1) as if [though] 節中は通例仮定法を用いるが, 主節が現在形の場合, as if [though] 節には直説法現在形を用いることがある. この場合, 現在の事実または未来の実現性が強調されていることに注意: 彼はまるで私を疑っているかのような物の言い方をする (=どうも疑っているらしい) He talks as if he is suspicious of me./彼はまるで今にも泣きそうだ(=今に泣きだすだろう) He looks as if he is going to cry.

まるてんじょう 丸天井 【建築】(アーチ形の) vault; (半円形の) a dome.

まるどり 丸取り ━ 丸取りする 動 take all 《the profits》 for oneself.

まるなげ 丸投げ ━ 丸投げする 動 (仕事を全部下請けに回す) farm out the whole of 《its》 work to a subcontractor.

まるのみ 丸飲み ━ 丸飲み(に)する 動 swallow ... 《whole》. ● 食べ物を丸飲みにする swallow food. ● 話を丸飲みする swallow a story whole.

まるはだか 丸裸 ━ 丸裸の 形 《話》 stark-naked /-kídid/. ● 丸裸になる strip oneself stark-naked. ● 丸裸にする strip 《him》 stark-naked [naked to the skin]; strip 《him》 of all 《his》 clothes. ▶子供たちは川岸で丸裸で遊んでいた The children were playing on the riverside stark-naked [《何も身につけないで》 with nothing on, in the nude]. ▶株の暴落で丸裸になった(＝全財産を失った) I have lost all my property in the stock market crash.

まるばつ ○× ● ○×式のテスト a true-false test 《事情》; 米英では正解にチェック印(✓)の《米》 check, 《英》 tick を用いるのが普通; (多肢選択式の) a multiple-choice test.

まるひ 丸秘 ━ 丸秘の 形 《情報・文書が》 confidential; (政府・軍の) classified (⚠通例限定的に). ▶そのデータは丸秘扱いになっている The data is treated as 《highly [strictly]》 confidential. ● 丸秘情報 confidential information. ● 丸秘書類 confidential papers.

まるぼうず 丸坊主 ● 丸坊主の頭 (できるだけ短く刈った) a close-cropped [《剃った》 a close-shaven] head. (⚠ close は /klóus/; ● 木を丸坊主にする cut off all the twigs and some of the branches. (⇒

丸刈り)

まるぼし 丸干し 名 (a) 《fish》 dried whole; (イワシの) a dried sardine. ━ 丸干し(に)する 動 dry 《fish》 whole.

まるぽちゃ ちゃぽちゃ ━ 丸ぽちゃの 形 plump 《face》.

まるまげ 丸髷 ● 丸髷に結う do one's hair in an oval chignon.

まるまど 丸窓 a round [a circular] window; (飛行機の) a porthole.

まるまる 丸々 ❶ 【丸く太っている】 (人・顔などが丸々と) round; (子供などが丸ぽちゃの) chubby; (人・体の部分が肉うきのよい) plump (⚠ fat のように悪い意味はない); (豊満な) full. ● 彼の丸々とした顔 his round [plump] face. ● 丸々と太った赤ちゃん a plump [a chubby] baby.

❷ 【完全, 全部】 (全体の) whole; (完全な) complete; (すべての) all. (⇒全部) ● まるまる 1 万円をなくす lose a whole [正味の》 a clear] ten thousand yen. ● 商売でまるまる損をする suffer a complete [a dead] loss in 《one's》 business. ● 石油を外国にまるまる依存する completely [entirely] depend on other countries for oil. ● 金をまるまる引ったくられた I had all the [×the whole] money snatched. (⚠冠詞の位置に注意)

まるまる 丸まる (丸くなる) curl (up). (⇒丸い)

まるみ 丸味 roundness. ● 丸味のある roundish; rounded. ● 丸味をつける round; make 《it》 round; (角などを削って) round 《a corner》 off.

まるみえ 丸見え ▶君の部屋は外から丸見えだ We can see everything in your room from the outside.

まるめこむ 丸め込む (口車に乗せる) wheedle; (おだてる) 《話》 sweet-talk; (信用させてだます) 《話》 con (-nn-); (説得する) persuade; (説きふせて味方に) win*... over. ● 彼女は父親を丸め込んで小遣いをもらった She wheedled [sweet-talked, persuaded] her father into giving her pocket money. ▶彼は彼女を丸め込んで味方にした He won her over to his side.

まるめる 丸める (丸くする) round; (背中を) stoop; (体を) curl [huddle] 《oneself》 up; (巻く) roll; (紙などをもみくちゃにする) crumple; (紙などをボール状にする) make* a ball (of); (ball ... up). ● とがった机の角を丸める round off the sharp-pointed edge of the desk. (⚠round ... off は「角を落とす」) ● 丸めた雑誌で彼をたたく hit him with a rolled magazine. ● 丸めてあるマットレスを広げる unroll a rolled-up mattress. ▶その母音を発音するときは唇をこのように丸めなさい When you pronounce that vowel, round your lips like this. ▶彼は背中を丸めて入り口を通り抜けた He stooped to go through the gateway. ▶毛布がソファーの上に丸めて置いてあった A blanket lay crumpled on the sofa.

マルメロ [＜ポルトガル語] 【セイヨウカリン】【植物】 a quince.

まるもうけ 丸儲け ━ 丸儲けする 動 (利益をあげる) make a clear profit (of 100,000 yen); (ぼろもうけする) 《話》 clean up (at a gamble).

まるもじ 丸文字 smooth, rounded, flowing script. ▶彼女は漢字を丸文字で書く The lines of her kanji are rather rounded.

まるやき 丸焼き ● 豚を丸焼きにする bárbecue a pig; roast a pig whole. ● 豚の丸焼き a roasted pig.

まるやけ 丸焼け (⇒㊥ 全焼)

***まれ 希** ━ 希な 形 【珍しい】 rare (変化形は (-rer; -rest) もあるが実際に使われることは少なく, very [extremely] rare などのように程度の副詞を添えることが多い); (めったにない) uncommon; [普通でない] unusual, 《話》 unique. (⇒㊥) ● まれな美人 a woman of *rare* [*uncommon*] beauty. ●まれな出来事 an *uncommon* occurrence. ●彼が怒るのはまれな事だ *It's unusual* [*very rare*] *for* him *to* get angry./(めったに怒らない) He *rarely* [*hardly ever*,《書》*seldom*] gets angry. (**!** 強調構文で *It is rarely* [《書》*seldom*] *that* he gets angry. ともいえる (⇒ ▣))

── **まれに** ▣ *rarely*,《書》*seldom*; *hardly ever*. (⇒めったに) ▶こんなに楽しい人はまれにしかいない I've *rarely* [*hardly ever*] met such a delightful person./I've *hardly* met *anybody* who is *so* delightful./Such a delightful person is *rare* [《書》is *seldom* to be seen). ●彼女はごくまれにしか図書館に行かない She visits the library only on *rare* occasions./She *rarely* [*seldom*], *if ever*, visits the library. ▶「*rarely* [*seldom*], *if ever* は「仮にあったとしてもごくまれに」という慣用的表現)
● **まれに見る** ▶彼はまれに見る(＝例外的な)才能の持ち主だ He has *exceptional* ability.

マレーシア【国名】Malaysia /məléiʒə, -ʃə/《公式名も同じ》. (首都 Kuala Lumpur) ●マレーシア人 a Malaysian. ●マレーシア語 Malaysian. ●マレーシア(人[語])の Malaysian.

マロニエ【＜フランス語】【セイヨウトチノキ】【植物】a horse chestnut.

まろやか ── **まろやかな** 形 (練れて口当たりのよい) smooth, mild, mellow. ▶この 17 年ものウイスキーは実に味がまろやかだ This 17-year-old whiskey is very *mellow*.

マロン【＜フランス語】【栗】【植物】a marron.
● マロングラッセ a marron glacé.

まわし 回し【相撲】*mawashi*; a sumo wrestler's loincloth or belt. (**!** 単に belt ということが多い) ●化粧回し a *sumo* wrestler's belt with an embroidered hanging cloth. ●回しをとる get a hold of 《his》*belt*. ●左手で回しをとって with a left-handed *belt* hold.

まわしのみ 回し飲み ▶グラスのワインを回し飲みする pass a glass of wine *around* and *drink from* it *in turn*.

まわしもの 回し者 a spy.

まわしよみ 回し読み ▶私たちはその漫画を回し読みした We *passed* the comic (book) *around* and *read* it *in turn*.

*****まわす 回す** ❶【回転させる】turn;（周りを）revolve;（自体を中心に）rotate;（高速に）spin*.（⇒回る[類語]）●エンジンでプロペラを回す *turn* [*revolve*, *rotate*] a propeller for an engine. ●車のハンドルを右へ回す *turn* the (steering) wheel to the right. (**!** *turn* the handle は「取っ手を回す」の意) ●棒の先で皿を回す *spin* a plate on the end of a stick. ●洗濯機を回す(＝つける) *turn* [*switch*] *on* a washing machine;（洗濯をする）do the washing. ▶もう一度 [3 回]つまみを回しなさい *Turn* the knob again [three times]./*Give* the knob another *turn* [three *turns*].
❷【順に送る】pass [hand]... around [on]《*to*》(**!** pass は順に回すこと, hand は手渡すことに重点がある;（転送する）forward, send*... on《*to*》. (⇒回送する) ●杯を回す *pass around* a sake cup. ●回覧を次の人に回す *pass* [*hand*] a notice *on to* the next person. ●その手紙は営業所内に[営業所を次々に]回された The letter *was passed around* the office [*was passed from* office *to* office). (**!** *from* A *to* A の型では A は無冠詞であることに注意) ●塩を回してください *Pass* [x*Turn*] (me) the salt, please.
❸【移す】▶車を玄関に回してくれますか Will you *bring* [*send*] the car 《*around*》*to* the front door? (**!** *bring* は運転者に, *send* は運転手以外の人にいう場合) ●彼は本店から地方支店に回された He *was transferred from* the head office *to* a local branch. ●この電話を内線 10 番へ回していただけますか Could you *transfer* this call *to* extension 10, please?/Could you give me extension 10, please?

まわた 真綿 *floss* (silk). ●真綿のような flossy.
● **真綿で首を絞める** ▶それは真綿で首を締めるようなものだ (それは苦しめるようだ) It seems (that)《he》is being tortured by slow degrees./(やわらかなひふめのようだ)《比喩的》That is a case of the velvet paw of the cat.

*****まわり 回り, 周り** ❶【円周】(a) circúmference;【周囲の状況】surróundings (⇒周囲);【環境】(an) envíronment (⇒環境);【近所】a neighborhood (⇒近所, 付近).
①【周りが[は]】▶こんなに周りがやかましくては考えるのも大変だ It's hard to think with all this noise (*all*) *around*. ●私の家の周りは住宅地です My *neighborhood* is a residential area.
②【周りの】▶周りの建物 the *surrounding* buildings. (⇒周囲 ②) ●周りの雰囲気に呑まれる be overwhelmed by the atmosphere *around* one.
③【(...の)周りに[は]】*around*(...),《主に英》*round*(...);《主に英書》*about*(...). ●家の周りに広い芝生がある There is a big lawn *around* the house. ●周りに立っていた人々はみな疲れた様子だった All the people standing *around* looked tired. (**!** この *around* は副詞)
④【周りを】▶周りを見渡す look *around*. ●高いフェンスに周りを囲まれた家 a house *surrounded* by a high fence. ●地球は太陽の周りを回っている The earth goes [moves, turns] *around* the sun. (**!**《英》では円周運動を表す場合 round を用いることが多い)
❷【巡回】a round. ●あいさつ回りをする pay [make] a *round* of visits. ●得意先回りをする make [do, go] the *round*(s) among one's clients.
❸【経由】▶...回りで《やや書》by way of ...《話》のときには by を省略する); via /váiə/.... ●北極回りで by way of [*via*,（飛行機が）*over*] the North Pole.
❹【行き渡ること】▶風が強くて火の回りが早かった The fire *spread* fast [quickly] because of the strong wind. ●この酒は回りが早い This alcohol *works* [*takes effect*] quickly.

まわりあわせ 回り合わせ (人生の有為転変) the wheel of Fortune. (●巡り合わせ)

まわりくどい 回りくどい roundabout;《書》circuitous /sərkjúːətəs/. ▶回りくどいことを言うな Don't talk in a *roundabout* way./(要点に触れよ) Come [Get] to the *point*.《常套句》Don't beat around《英》about) the bush. (⇒遠回し)

まわりこむ 回り込む go *around* to the front 《*of*》. ●スライディングしてホームへ回り込む slide clear around the catcher. ●打球に(対して) circle a ball; move in front of a ball.

まわりどうろう 回り灯籠 a revolving lantern.

まわりぶたい 回り舞台 a revolving stage.

まわりまわって 回り回って ▶回り回って(＝多くの回り道をして)ようやく駅に行く道を見つけた *After many detours*, I finally found my way to the railroad station. ●そのダイヤは回り回って(＝何度も持ち主が変わって)彼女のものとなった The diamond *changed hands a lot of times*, and finally it came into her possession. (**!** finally に替えて at last とすると

彼女がそのダイヤを待ち望んでいたことになり、ここでは不

まわりみち　回り道　●回り道をする take [go by] a roundabout route [way]; (迂回(うかい)する) make a detour (➪). ▶私は回り道をして学校に行った I took a roundabout route to school./I went to school by a roundabout route. ▶ずいぶんと回り道をした(=曲折を経た)がやっと目的を達成できた I had a lot of twists and turns [ups and downs], but I could finally achieve [finally achieved] my goal.

会話「ほかに何か用はない?」「郵便局に寄ってくれる? でもちょっと回り道になってしまうかしら」"Anything else I can do for you?" "Can you drop in [《主に英》call] at the post office or is that a bit out of your way?"（❗be out of one's way は「道筋から外れる」こと）

まわりもち　回り持ち　●回り持ちで (順ぐりに) in rotation; (交替で) by turns, in turn.

＊**まわる　回る**

WORD CHOICE　回る, 回転する

spin　物体が特定の場所で軽やかに高速で回転すること. ▶コインが回っている The coin is spinning.
revolve　物体が特定の点や軸を中心として重々しくゆっくりと回転すること. ▶回転ドア a revolving door.
rotate　機械部品などが回転すること. または, 人が仕事を輪番で行うこと. ▶ヘリコプターの回転プロペラ rotating helicopter blades.

頻度チャート

spin ▇▇▇▇▇▇▇▇▇▇
revolve ▇▇
rotate ▇

20　40　60　80　100 (%)

❶[回転する] turn ((a)round); revolve; rotate; spin*. ▶風車(かざぐるま)は風に吹かれて勢いよく[くるくる]回った The pinwheel turned rapidly [around and around] in the wind. ▶船は岬を回った The ship turned [rounded] the cape. ▶地球は地軸を中心に回り(=自転し)ながら太陽の周りを回って(=公転して)いる The earth revolves [turns, moves] around the sun, while rotating [turning] on its axis. (⇨自転, 公転) ▶部屋がぐるぐる回っているような気がした I felt as if the room were [《話》 was] spinning (around). ▶換気扇は電気で回る The ventilating fan is run [is operated, (まれ) is turned] by [on] electricity. (❗by では「電気が回転させている」, on では「電気で人が回転させている」の意となる) ▶父の形見の時計は私の細い手首にはめるとぶかぶか回っている The watch was given as a keepsake of my father swims on my thin wrist. ▶あの美少女の前に出ると口がよく回らなくなった(=うまくしゃべれなかった) In front of that beautiful girl, I had a dry mouth. (❗have a dry mouth は「しゃべれない, 口が回らない」の遠回しな言い方)

❷[巡回する] (見て回る) look around (in), have* [take*] a look (a)round (in), go* around …; (仕事などで) do* [make*, go] the round(s) (of); (旅行者・見学者・芸人など) make a tour (of), tour. ▶本屋を見て回る(何軒も) go around bookstores; (1軒の中を) look around (in) a bookstore. ▶得意先[親戚(しんせき)]を回る make [do, go] the rounds of one's customers [relatives]. ▶(ヒットを打って)一塁を大きく回る take a big turn at first. ▶先生は今往診に回っています The doctor is doing his rounds [is out on his rounds] now. (❗do [be out on] one's rounds は習慣的行為を示し, 文脈によってご用聞き・配達・警備などしごとの内容が明らかになる. 通例, 主語に注意) ▶彼は今北海道を回っている He is making a tour [touring (in), traveling around] Hokkaido. ▶ランナーは三塁を回って本塁に向かった The runner rounded third base.

❸[迂回(うかい)する] (回り道をする) take* [go* by] a roundabout route (⇨遠回り); (…経由で行く) go via /váɪə/ …; (寄り道する) go [come*] (a)round to …. ▶香港を回ってオーストラリアに行く go to Australia via [《やや書》 by way of] Hong Kong; (旅の途中で立ち寄る) go to Australia after stopping over at [in] Hong Kong. ▶途中で郵便局へ回る go around to the post office on the way. ▶橋が壊れていたので別の道を回って行った We went by another route because the bridge was broken. ▶勝手に回ってください Come around to the kitchen, please.

❹[あちこち動く] (町中を歩き回る) walk around [about] (in) the town. ▶そこらじゅうを捜し回ったが鍵(かぎ)は見つからなかった I looked all over [looked and looked], but I couldn't find the key.

❺[行き渡る] (酒はみんなに行き(だけわたる)かな Is there enough (sake) to go around? ▶酒[毒]が回った(=効いた) Alcohol [Poison] took effect (on him). ▶忙しくて手が回らない I am so busy that I can't attend [get around] to it. (❗前の方は「注意が向かない」, 後の方は「暇がない」の意)

❻[過ぎる] ▶5時を回った(=過ぎた)ところだ It has just turned five./It's just past [《米》after] five.

まわれみぎ　回れ右　●回れ右をする do an about-face 《米》 [an about-turn 《英》]. ▶回れ右! 《米》About-face!/《英》About-turn! ▶彼女はぼくの姿を見るとさっと回れ右をして逃げて行った The moment she caught sight of me, she turned around and ran away.

＊**まん　万**　ten thousand. (❗英語では「万」という単位はない. 1万は 10×1,000＝ten thousand, 10万は 100×1,000＝a [one] hundred thousand とする. なお 100万は a [one] million) ●2万5,000 twenty-five thousand. ●35万冊の本 three hundred (and) fifty thousand books. (❗and は 《米》ではしばしば省略する) ●何万[何十万]冊かの本 tens [hundreds] of thousands of books. (❗複数形に注意) ●1万分の3 three-ten thousandths. ●5万分の1の地図 (⇨万分の一) ▶彼が成功する可能性は万に一つもない There is not the slightest possibility of his success.

まん　満　●満5年 five full years; a full five years; fully five years. (❗full five years は 《古・詩》) (⇨丸一) ▶満18歳になる be 18 years old. (事情 米英では満年齢のみを用いる)

●満を持す wait until the time is ripe; (やる気満々で) be raring (to do).

−マン　●銀行マン (行員) a bank clerk; (窓口係) a teller; (事業家) a banker.

＊**まんいち　万一**　●(緊急の場合) (an) emergency; (最悪の場合) the worst; (まさかの時) a rainy day. ●万一(=非常)の場合には in an emergency; in case of emergency. ▶万一の場合に備えておかなければならない We must provide for [《古》against] a rainy day [an emergency]./We must prepare for the worst. ▶万一の事が私に起これば, 私のすべてのお金はあなたのものです If the worst [anything] were to happen to me, all my money would be yours.

——**万一**　副　if … were to …, if (by any chance)…

まんいん

should …. (🛈 were to と should の違いについては (⇨もし❹)) ▶万一君が先にここへ着いたら外で待っていなさい If (by any chance) you should get there ahead of us, wait outside. (🛈 were to も可)

*まんいん 満員 ── 満員の 形 (込み合った) crowded; (いっぱいの) full. ●満員の(=収容能力いっぱいの)聴衆 a capacity audience. ●超満員である be overcrowded; be crowded beyond capacity. ▶バスは学生で満員だった The bus was crowded with [xby] students. (🛈 crowded は受身というより形容詞的性格が強いので with を伴う。また much でなく very で修飾する)/(すしづめだった) The bus was packed [《話》jam-packed] with students. (🛈 後の方が強意的) ▶ホテルは満員(=満室)だった There were no vacancies at the hotel./(予約済みだった) The hotel was (fully) booked up. ▶球場は(野球ファンで)超満員だった The stadium was filled to capacity (with baseball fans). ▶満員《掲示》(劇場など)《主に米》Full house, 《英》House full/(ホテルなど) No vacancy /(立ち見席以外満員 Standing room only 《略 SRO》/(満員札止め) Sold out.
●満員電車 a crowded [a packed, a jammed, a full] train. (🛈 packed, jammed は crowded より込み方がひどい。a jam-packed train ともいう)

まんえつ 満悦 ─満悦の体(てい)である appear greatly [heartily, thoroughly] satisfied 《with》; look very pleased 《with, at, about; that》.

まんえん 蔓延 图 spread. ●病気の蔓延を防ぐ check [prevent] the spread of a disease.
── 蔓延する 動 spread.

まんえんがんねんのフットボール『万延元年のフットボール』 The Silent Cry. 《参考》大江健三郎の小説

マンオン (⇨ 图 マノン)

*まんが 漫画 『漫画本』a cómic, 《米》a comic book, a manga; 『時事風刺』a cartoon /kɑːrtúːn/《通例１こま》; 『人物風刺』a caricature /kǽrikətʃùər/《通例１こま》; 『こま続き』a comic strip, 《英》a strip cartoon. ●政治漫画 a political cartoon. ●漫画的(=こっけいな)comic-like, comical; funny. ●漫画チックな (=漫画風の) manga-style. ●漫画をかく draw a cartoon. ●新聞の漫画を読む read a comic strip in the newspaper. ●テレビの漫画を見る watch a cartoon on TV [a TV cartoon]. ▶『テレビ漫画『ドラえもん』』は the TV cartoon "Doraemon". ▶少年漫画本はすごくよく売れる Boys' comic books [Comic books for boys] really sell well. ▶新聞にブレア首相の風刺漫画が出ている There is a cartoon of Prime Minister Blair in the newspaper.
●漫画映画 a cartoon (movie《主に米》[film《主に英》]); an animation; 《書》an animated cartoon. ●漫画家 a cartoonist; (人物風刺の) a caricaturist; (アニメの) an animator. ●漫画喫茶 a manga cafe; (説明的に) a coffee shop with a lot of comic books, where customers can buy drinks and read comic books.

●まんかい 満開 (木・植物など) full bloom [blossom] (🛈 通例南の方は観賞用の花、後の方は果樹や草木の花についていう); 『盛り』one's best. ●桜が満開だ The cherry trees are in full bloom [blossom]./The cherry blossoms are fully out [at their best].

まんがいち 万が一 (⇨万一) ▶万一あしたの雨の場合は行きません If it should rain tomorrow, I won't go.

まんがく 満額 the full amount 《of》. ●満額回答する (満額与える) offer the full amount of the union's demand; (満額要求に応じる) accept [meet] the union's demand for the full amount. ●退職金を満額支払う pay the full amount of a retirement allowance; pay a retirement allowance in full.

まんがん 万巻 ●万巻の書 a large number of books; tens of thousands of books.

まんがん 満願 fulfillment of a vow. ▶満願の日がきた The term of my vow ended.

マンガン 『化学』manganese 《記号 Mn》.

まんかんしょく 満艦飾 ●軍艦に満艦飾を施す deck the whole warship with flags (and lights). ●満艦飾の(=着飾っている)女性 a woman dressed up to the nines.

まんき 満期 『保険などの』maturity; 『契約などの期限』expiry; expiration. ▶私の生命保険は今年の５月に満期になります My insurance policy will mature in May this year.
●満期手形 a matured note; a due bill. ●満期日 the maturity [due] date; the date of maturity.

まんきつ 満喫 ── 満喫する 形 ●田舎の生活を満喫する enjoy country life to the full.

マングース 『動物』a common mongoose.

マングローブ 『植物』a mangrove (tree).

まんげきょう 万華鏡 a kaleidoscope /kəláidəskòup/.

まんげつ 満月 a full moon. ●満月の夜 a full-moon night; a night when the moon is full. ●今夜は満月だ[に近い] The moon is full [nearly full] tonight.

まんげん 万言 ▶万言を費やす give a wordy [a lengthy] explanation.

まんこう 満腔 ── 満腔の 形 heartfelt; sincere. ●満腔の敬意を表する express one's heartfelt [《最大限の》utmost] respect 《for》.

マンゴー 『植物』a mango /mǽŋgou/《復》~s, ~es》.

マンゴスチン 『植物』a mangosteen.

まんざ 満座 all those present; everyone there. ●満座の中で before the whole group.

まんさい 満載 (いっぱいの積み荷) a full load [《船・飛行機などの》cargo]. ●石炭満載のダンプカー a dump truck carrying [with] a full load of coal.
── 満載する 動 (荷物などを) carry a full load [cargo] 《of》; (記事などを) be full of …. ▶船はコーヒー豆を満載していた(=十分積んでいた) The ship was fully loaded [《限度まで積んでいた》loaded to capacity] with coffee. ▶『ニューズウィーク』の最新号は日本の記事を満載している(=いっぱいある) The latest issue of Newsweek is full of articles on Japan.

まんざい 漫才 (こっけいなやりとり) a comic dialogue by two comedians; (早口での掛け合い)《英》a cross talk.
●漫才師 a pair of comedians, a comic duo (🛈 ともに２人組);《英》a cross-talk comedian.

まんさく 万作 『植物』a witch hazel.

まんさつ 万札 a ten-thousand-yen bill [note]; a 10,000-yen bill.

まんざら (まったく…というわけではない) not(…) altogether [completely, entirely]. (🛈 部分否定) ▶それはまんざら捨てたものでもない It is not altogether bad.
●まんざらでもない ▶彼は私の提案にまんざらでもない(=かなり興味がある)という顔をした He looked pretty interested in my proposal.

まんざん 満山 the whole mountain; the whole hill.

まんじ 卍 a swastika. 《参考》ナチスの紋章は卐

まんしつ 満室 no vacancies [vacancy]. ▶当ホテ

まんしゃ 満車 〘掲示〙Full./No Vacancy.

まんしゅう 満州 〘現在の中国東北地方〙Manchuria /mæntʃúəriə/.
● 満州国 Manchukuo.

まんじゅう 饅頭 (a) *manju*; (説明的に) a kind of Japanese-style bun usually stuffed with sweetened bean paste.

まんじゅしゃげ 曼珠沙華 〘植物〙a cluster-amaryllis.

まんじょう 満場 (会場全体) the whole house [(参加者) assembly; (聴衆) audience]. ● 満場一致で ⇨満場一致 ● 満場をどっとわかせる (話) bring the (*whole*) *house* down. ▶彼の演技は満場をうならせた (=深い感動を与えた) His performance made a deep impression on [deeply impressed] the *whole audience*.

まんじょういっち 満場一致 ùnánimity. ● 満場一致の unanimous /juː(ː)nǽniməs/. ▶その提案は満場一致で可決された The proposal was adopted *unanimously* [by a *unanimous* decision].

マンション 〘分譲マンション〙《米》a condominium /kὰndəmíniəm/, (米話) a condo (⑱ ~s), 《英》a flat; 〘賃貸マンション〙(建物全体)《米》an apartment building [house, complex], 《英》a block of flats; (1戸分)《米》an apartment, 《英》a flat. (!) mansion は「大邸宅」の意で, 共同住宅の1戸分をさして mansion とはいわないが,《英》では大きな建物全体の名称として Victoria Mansions のように複数形で使われることがある) ● ワンルームマンション《米》a one-room apartment, a studio (apartment); 《英》a studio (flat), a bed-sitter, 《英話》a bedsit.

まんじり ● **まんじりともしない** ▶昨夜はまんじりともしなかった (一睡もしなかった) I *didn't sleep a wink* last night./(まったく眠れなかった) I couldn't get a wink *of sleep* last night.

まんしん 満身 ● 満身の力を込めて with all one's strength [〘主に書〙might];《やや古》by [with] might and main.
● 満身創痍 ▶彼は満身創痍だった He was wounded /wúːndid/ [was injured] *all over*./He had injuries *all over*.

まんしん 慢心 图 (うぬぼれた) pride; (思い上がり) self-conceit.
── 慢心する 動 be proud; be conceited. ▶彼は金持ちの子供だというだけでひどく慢心している He *is puffed up with pride* only because he is a son of a rich man.

まんすい 満水 ▶湖は満水だ The lake *is full* [*is filled to capacity*]. ▶ダムは満水になった The dam's water level *has peaked*.

まんせい 慢性 ── 慢性の 形 chronic (⇔acute). ▶頭痛が慢性化してしまった I have developed a *chronic* headache.
● 慢性病 a chronic disease [illness]. ● 慢性疾患者 a chronic patient [invalid].

まんせき 満席 〘掲示〙《主に米》Full house./《主に英》House full./(立ち見席のみ) standing room only 《略 SRO》. ▶ホールは満席だった (満員) The hall *was full* (*up*)./(座席はみな占められていた) All (*of*) *the seats were occupied* in the hall.

まんぜん 漫然 ● 漫然とした (=散漫な)講演 a *rambling* lecture. ● 漫然と (=目標もなく) 暮らす live aimlessly [*without an aim*]; (何もせずにゆったり過ごす) *idle* one's time *away*; (座ってだらだらと時間をつぶす)《やや話》(just) sit around (*doing*). (⇨ぼんやり ❹)

*****まんぞく** 満足 图 (a) sàtisfáction (⇔(a) dissatisfaction); (!)「満足させるもの」という具体的な意味以外は通例無冠詞); conténtment (⇔discontent). (!)前の方は欲求・欠乏などが十分満たされたときの満足の状態をいうのに対し, 後の方は現状に満足していてそれ以上望まない心の状態をいう) ● 満足を感じる[得る, 与える] (⇨動) ▶彼はとても満足げにうなずいた He nodded *with great satisfaction* [ˣvery satisfactorily]./(満足した表情で) He nodded with a very *satisfied* [*contented*, ˣcontent] look. (!) content は限定的には用いない) ▶彼はその報告に満足の意を表した He expressed *his satisfaction with* [*at*] the report. ▶彼女は私の満足のゆくようにピアノを弾いた She played the piano *to my satisfaction*. (!) 堅い言い方で, She played the piano as [(the) way] I wanted her to. の方が普通) ▶幸福は満足にある Happiness consists in *contentment*. (!) この語は限定的には用いない)
── 満足な 形 satisfactory《to+人, for+事・物》; 〘完全な〙perfect; 〘必要十分な〙enough. ● 顔に満足な表情を浮かべて with a look of *satisfaction*. ● 五体満足な(=肉体的に異常のない)赤ちゃん *a physically normal* baby; a baby in a physically *normal* state. ● 満足な(=十分な)食べ物 *enough* [〘やや書〙*sufficient*] food. ▶彼の仕事は私には満足なものではなかった His work wasn't *satisfactory to* [ˣfor] me. ▶彼は満足な(=正規の)教育を受けていない He has had no *regular* education.

── 満足に 副 (満足のように) satisfactorily; (正しく) properly; (完全に) perfectly. ▶彼女は満足に本も読めない She can't even read a book *properly*.

── 満足する 動 (満足する[している]) be satisfied 《with》(!)受身の意を強調する場合は by も用いる); be conténted [content] 《with》(!) contented の方が一般的. content は内心で満足している状態を強く表す); (満足を感じる) feel* satisfaction [contentment]; 〘うれしい〙be happy《about, with》(!)口語的で意味の広い語); 〘喜んでいる〙be pleased《with》. ● 満足させる satisfy; please. ▶そんな薄給では彼は満足しないだろう He will not *be satisfied* [*happy*] *with* such a small salary. (!) 否定文では happy の方が強い不満を表す)/(事が主語) Such a small salary will not *satisfy* him. ▶優勝できたので大いに満足した I *was greatly satisfied* [*very happy*, *very pleased*] *to* win the championship./(満足を感じた) I *felt great satisfaction at* winning the championship./(満足を得た) I *got* [*received*] *great satisfaction from* winning the championship. (!) 事が主語にして Winning the championship *gave me great satisfaction* [*was a great satisfaction* to me]. ともいえる. 後の言い方では不定冠詞を用いることに注意) ▶私は今の生活に満足している(=甘んじている) I *am content*(*ed*) [*feel contentment*] *with* my present life. (!) この場合 satisfied は内心の方が強い意 (⇨图)) ▶ご満足していただけたでしょうか(=来てくれてありがとうございます) (レストランなどで) Thank you for coming. (!) Are you satisfied? などとは言わない) ▶彼女を満足させるのは難しい She's hard to *please*./It's hard to *please* her.

● 満足感 a feeling of satisfaction [contentment].

マンタ 〘魚介〙a manta (ray).
まんだら 曼荼羅 a mandala.
マンダリン 〘植物〙a mandarin (orange).
まんタン 満タン ● タンクを満タンにする *fill up* a tank. ▶満タンにしてください *Fill it up*, please. (!)男性はit

まんだん 漫談 (お笑い独演)stand-up (comedy); (こっけいなおしゃべり) a comic chat. ▶漫談をする do *stand-up*; (演芸で) give a comic chat.
・漫談家 a stand-up comic [comedian].

マンチェスター 〖英国の都市〗 Manchester /ˈmæntʃɛstər/.

まんちゃく 瞞着 ── 瞞着する ■ deceive. (⇨騙(認)す, ごまかす)

まんちょう 満潮 (a) high [full] tide 〖満ち(てくる)潮 (a flood tide); 〖川・湖の〗 high water. (⇨高潮, 上げ潮) ・満潮時に at *high tide*; when the *tide* is *high* [*full, in*]. ▶干潮は満潮と満潮の中間に起こる Low tide occurs halfway between *high tides*.

マンツーマン ・マンツーマンの訓練 one-to-one [one-on-one] training. ・マンツーマンで教える teach (him) on a *one-to-one* basis; (個人教授する) give (him) a private lesson.
・マンツーマンディフェンス a man-to-man [a person-to-person] defense. (❗性差を意識する人は後の方を好む)

マンデラ 〖南アフリカの政治家〗 Mandéla (Nelson Rolihlahla 〜).

まんてん 満天 ・満天の星 a star-filled [-spangled] sky.

まんてん 満点 ❶〖最高点〗a perfect score; 〖英〗full marks. (⇨点) ▶満点を取る get a *perfect score* [*full marks*] (*in an English exam*). ・200 点満点で 150 点とる get a score of 150 *out of 200*.
❷〖申し分ない〗 (⇨申し分(の)ない) ・その食べ物は栄養満点だ The food is *very* nutritious. ▶君の仕事は満点だ Your work *is perfect* [〖書〗 *leaves nothing to be desired*]./I can't ask for anything *more* about your work.

まんてんか 満天下 ・満天下の人 (全世界の人) people *all over the world*; the whole world.

マント [<フランス語] a cloak; a mantle; 〖ケープ〗 a cape.

マントひひ マント狒狒 〖動物〗 a hamadryas baboon.

マンドリン 〖楽器〗a mandolin /ˈmændəlɪn/. ・マンドリンを弾く play the mandolin. ・マンドリン奏者 a mandolinist.

マントル 〖地学〗the (Earth's) mantle.

マントルピース a mantelpiece.

*__まんなか__ 真ん中 the middle; the center (❗ middle は通例, 平面・線・面・時間の近中間部分を, center は円や球などの中心点をさし, 細長いものには用いない); 〖中心部〗 the heart. ・真ん中の息子 one's *middle* son. ・髪を真ん中で分ける part one's hair *in the middle*. ・道の真ん中に立つ stand *in the middle of the road*. ・ちょうど部屋の真ん中に座る sit right *in the center* [*middle*] *of the room*. ・真ん中へ速球を投げる throw a fastball down the middle. ▶(写真などを説明して) 3 人の女の子の真ん中にいるのが私よ I'm the *middle* one of the three girls. ▶その硬貨は真ん中に穴があいている The coin has a hole *in the center*. ▶彼はパリの真ん中に住んでいる He lives *in the heart* [*center*] *of* Paris. ▶これら二つの町の真ん中 (= 中間) に小さな村がある There is a small village just *midway* [*halfway*] *between* these two towns.

まんにん 万人 all (the) people. (⇨万人(認))

マンネリ(ズム) (型にはまった考え) a stereotype; (文体・画法などの) mannerism. ▶我々の生活がマンネリ化してきている Our life is becoming *routine* [*stereotyped*, ×*mannerism*]./We're getting into a *rut*.

まんねん 万年 ten thousand years; eternity.
・万年候補 An ever unsuccessful candidate.
・万年青年 a Peter Pan. ❗Never-never Land という想像の国に住みいつまでも成長しない少年から)
・万年雪 perpetual [eternal] snow. ・万年暦 a perpetual calendar. (⇨万年床, 万年筆)

まんねんどこ 万年床 ▶彼は万年床だ His *futon* has been laid down for a long time.

まんねんひつ 万年筆 a fountain pen. (⇨ペン) ▶この万年筆はインクがなくなっている This *fountain pen* is dry [*out of ink*].

まんねんれい 満年齢 (⇨満)

まんばい 満杯 ── 満杯である ■ be full (*of*); be filled up (*with*).

マンハッタン 〖米国ニューヨーク市の特別区〗 Manhattan.

マンパワー 〖人的資源〗manpower.

まんぱん 満帆 ・順風満帆 (⇨順風 [成句])

まんびき 万引き (行為)shoplifting, 〖話〗lifting; (人) a shoplifter. ▶万引きの常習犯 a habitual *shoplifter*. ・本の万引きで捕まる be caught (in the act of) *shoplifting* a book.

まんぴつ 漫筆 random notes; (新聞・雑誌の) a causerie /kòuzəríː/.

まんびょう 万病 all sorts [kinds] of diseases. ・万病に効く薬 a cure-all. ▶風邪は万病の元 A cold may lead to [can be the cause of] *all sorts of diseases*.

まんぴょう 満票 (すべての票数)the whole number of votes; (全員一致) a [×an] unanimous vote. ・満票で選ばれる be elected *by a unanimous vote* [*unanimously*].

まんぴょう 漫評 (気楽にする批評) a rambling criticism.

まんぷく 満幅 ・大統領に満幅の信頼を置く put [place] *complete trust* in the President.

まんぷく 満腹 a full stomach. ▶もう満腹です. あと一口も入りません I'm full (up) [(十二分に食べた) I've had enough, I've had eaten my fill]. I couldn't eat another bite. ▶満腹で走ってはいけません You shouldn't run *on* [*with*] a *full stomach*. (❗ on は「…のときに」の意)

まんぶん 漫文 random notes.

まんぶんのいち 万分の一 a ten-thousandth. ・5万分の1の地図 a map on a scale of *1:50,000* (*one to fifty thousand* とよむ); a map on the scale of *one-fifty-thousandth*.

まんべんなく 満遍なく ・さくにまんべんなく(=全体に)ペンキを塗る paint the fence *all over* [(むらなく) *evenly*]. ・全教科をまんべんなく(=均等に)勉強する study every subject *equally* well.

マンボ (音楽)mambo; (踊り) a mambo (🅿 〜s). ・マンボを踊る dance the *mambo*; mambo.

まんぽ 漫歩 a stroll. ・公園を漫歩する *stroll around* (*in*) *the park*.

まんぼう 翻車魚 〖魚介〗 a head-fish; an ocean sunfish.

マンホール a manhole, a utility hole. (❗性差を意識する人は後の方を好む) ・マンホールのふた a *manhole* [*utility*] cover.

まんぽけい 万歩計 (歩数計) a pedómeter.

マンマーク 〖サッカー〗 man-marking.

まんまえ 真ん前 ▶私の家の真ん前にバス停がある There is a bus stop *just* [*right*] *in front of* my house./(通りを隔てた先に) There is a bus stop

まんまく 慢幕 〖式場などの周りに張りめぐらす幕〗 a curtain.

まんまと (すっかり) completely; (首尾よく) successfully. ● まんまと一杯食わされる be *completely* [*nicely*] taken in.
> 翻訳のこころ 私の疑惑が，まんまと的中していたのだ (太宰治『猿が島』) My suspicion has turned out [proved (just)] right. (1)「的中する」は turn out [prove] right. right は「まんまと」に当たる. (2) just turn out [prove] right にその意味が含まれているので，通例不要)

まんまるい 真ん丸い (⇨丸い) ● まんまるい月(=満月) a *full* moon.

まんまん 満々 ▶彼は自信[やる気]満々だ He *is full of* confidence [*drive*]. ▶この長雨で川は満々と水をたたえている The river *is very full* due to this long rain.

まんまん 漫漫 ● 漫漫たる大海 *vast* [*wide*] *expanses* of sea.

まんまんなか 真ん真ん中 right in the middle 《*of*》. (⇨ど真ん中, 真ん中)

まんめん 満面 ● 満面に笑みを浮かべて彼女を見る look at her *smiling all over*. ▶彼は満面に笑みをたたえていた He was *all smiles*.

マンモグラフィー 〖乳房X線撮影〗〖医学〗mammography.

マンモス 〖氷河時代の巨象〗 a mammoth /mǽməθ/.
● マンモス企業 a *mammoth* enterprise. ● マンモス大学 a *mammoth* university. ● マンモスタンカー a *mammoth* tanker.

まんゆう 漫遊 (周遊) 《make》 a tour; 《make [take]》 a pleasure trip. (⇨旅, 旅行)

まんようしゅう 『万葉集』 The Ten Thousand Leaves. (〖参考〗奈良時代の歌集)

まんりき 万力 《米》a vise /váis/, 《英》vice.

まんりょう 万両 〖植物〗Ardisia crenata.

まんりょう 満了 圏 the end, 《やや書》expiration /èkspəréiʃən/. ● 任期満了 the *expiration* [*end*] of one's term of office.
── 満了する 動 《やや書》expire; (終わる) come to an end. ▶彼の任期は 2008 年 4 月 30 日に満了する His term of office is due to *expire* on April 30, 2008.

まんるい 満塁 ● 満塁ホームランを打つ hit a *bases-loaded* home run; hit a *grand slam*. ● 2 本のシングルとフォアボールで満塁にする *load the bases* on two singles and a walk. ● 打者を歩かせて満塁策をとる walk the batter intentionally to *load the bases*. ▶ツーアウト満塁だ Two down and *the bases are loaded* [*are filled*]./The *bases are loaded* with two outs./There are two outs with the *bases loaded*.

み

み 身 ❶ [体] (肉体) a body; (自分の体) oneself (■再帰代名詞として). ・身を乗り出す (前方へ) lean forward; (窓などから) lean out of 《a window》. ・高価な服を身につけている wear expensive clothes; have expensive clothes on. ・彼は身も心もその仕事に打ち込んでいる He devotes *himself* [his *body* and soul] to the work./He is devoted to the work *body* and soul. (■後の body and soul は副詞的) ▶彼らは岩の後ろに身を隠した They hid (*themselves*) behind the rock. ▶彼女は身を投げるようにしてベッドに横たわった She threw *herself* down on the bed. (■ ... threw her body ... はしない方がよい) ▶電話が鳴ったとき彼は何も [下着しか] 身につけていなかった He *had* nothing [nothing but his underwear] *on* when the phone rang. ▶警官は勤務中は拳銃を身につけて(=携帯して)いなければならない A police officer [(男の) A policeman] on duty must *carry* a revolver 《with him》.

❷ [自分自身] oneself. ・危険から身を守る protect *oneself* from [against] the danger. ・彼はばくちで身を滅ぼした He ruined *himself* by gambling./Gambling brought him to ruin [ruined him]. ▶彼に近づかないほうが身のためだ You stay away from him if you know what's good for *you*. (■強迫的命令文. 普通は It'd be better for you to stay away from him. などという)

❸ [立場, 身分] (立場) a place; (社会的地位) a position. ・身の程を知っている know one's *place*. (⇨身の程) ・身に合う(=分相応の)暮らしをする live within one's *means*. ・私の身にもなってください Put yourself in my *place* [*position*, 《話》 *shoes*]. ▶私たちは患者の身になって考える(=共感する)必要がある We must *sympathize with* our patients./《話》《慣用的に》We must put ourselves into our patients' shoes.

❹ [肉] meat. (■通例食用の獣肉をいい, 魚肉には用いない. ただし「カニの身」は例外的に crabmeat) ・赤[脂]身 lean [fat] *meat*. ・この取りたてのタイの身はとてもおいしい The *flesh* of this fresh-caught sea bream is delicious.

❺ [その他の表現] ・身の引きしまるような冷たい風 a *bracing* cold wind. ・身の回り (⇨身の回り)

・**身が入る** ▶勉強に身が入らない(集中できない) I *can't concentrate on* my studies./(あまり興味を持てない) I can't take much interest in my studies.
・**身が持たない** ▶睡眠不足で身が持たない I'm afraid my *health* will *break down* from lack of sleep.
・**身から出たさび** ▶それは身から出たさびだ You've *asked* for it./You had it *coming*. (■have it coming は「当然の報いを受ける」の意の口語的慣用表現. it は漠然と問題になっている事柄をさす)
・**身に余る** ▶身に余る(=自分にはもったいない)光栄です It's an *undeserved* honor./I don't *deserve* such a great honor.
・**身に覚えがない** ▶身に覚えのないことだ(何も知らない) I *don't know anything* about it./(無実だ) I'm *innocent* (of the crime).
・**身にしみる** ▶親の意見が身にしみた(=痛切に感じた) My parents' advice *came home to* [*hit home with*] me. ▶彼の親切が身にしみた(=深く感謝した) I *was deeply grateful for* [*was deeply touched by*] his kindness.
・**身につく** ▶教養を身につける *acquire* culture. ・芸を身につける *master* an art. ▶外国語はそう簡単には身につくものではない A foreign language is not so easy to *learn* [《書》 *master*]./You can't *learn* a foreign language so easily. (■後の方が日常的な言い方)
・**身につまされる** ▶友人の死を聞いて身につまされた(痛切に感じた) The news of my friend's death *came home to* me./(ひどく気の毒に思った) I *felt deeply sorry* [*felt deep sympathy*] *for* my friend's death.
・**身の置き所がない** ▶恥ずかしくて身の置き所がなかった(=どうしてよいか分からなかった) I was so ashamed that I *didn't know what to do with myself*.
・**身の振り方** ・身の振り方を決める determine *the course of one's life*; determine one's *future*. ▶卒業後の身の振り方(=何をするつもりか)を決めましたか Have you decided *what* you're going to do after graduation? ▶今後の身の振り方(=将来)について先生と相談した I talked with my teacher about my *future*.
・**身もふたもない** ▶身もふたもないことを言うね You're *too outspoken*.
・**身も世もない** ・身も世もなく泣く cry one's *eyes* [*heart*] *out*.
・**身を入れる** ・身を入れて仕事をしなさい *Put yourself* [*your heart*] *into* your work./(積極的に興味を持って) *Take an active interest in* your work./(没頭して) *Devote yourself to* your work. (⇨❶ [第1文例])
・**身を置く** ・雑踏の中に身を置く be among [in] the crowd.
・**身を起こす** (出世する) rise 《*to*》. ・貧困から身を起こす *rise from* poverty.
・**身を固める** ▶いつ身を固める(=家庭を持つ)つもりなの When are you going to *settle down* and have a family?
・**身を切る** ・身を切るような寒さ a *piercing* cold. ・身を切るような北風 a *cutting* [a *biting*] north wind.
・**身を焦がす** ・身を焦がすような恋 a *burning* love.
・**身を粉(こ)にして** ・身を粉にして働く work *oneself* [one's *fingers*] *to the bone*.
・**身を沈める** (身投げをする) throw oneself 《*in*》; (落ちぶれる) lower oneself 《*to*》.
・**身を捨ててこそ浮かぶ瀬もあれ** 《ことわざ》No pain, no gain.
・**身を立てる** ・文章で身(=暮らし)を立てる *live on* one's writing; *live* [*make a living*] *by* one's pen. ▶私は作家として身を立てたい(=地位を確立したい) I'd like to *establish myself* as a writer.
・**身を投じる** throw oneself 《*in*, *into*》. ▶彼は政界に身を投じた He *threw himself into* the political world.
・**身を挺(てい)する** ▶彼はおぼれかけた子供を身を挺して救った He saved the drowning child *without regard to* his own safety.
・**身を引く** ・学長の地位から身を引く(=学長を辞任する) *resign* (one's *position* [*post*]) as president. ・第一線から身を引く(=引退する) *retire from* the

front line.
- **身を潜(ひそ)める** ▶ 彼は木の中に身をひそめた(= 隠れた) He *hid* in [among] the bushes.
- **身を任せる**

  翻訳のこころ 列車の振動に身をまかせて、ひさしもやがてゆっくりと目を閉じた(竹西寛子『蘭』) *Allowing himself to move with the train, Hisashi, before long, also closed his eyes gently*. (⚠(1)「身(をまかせる)」は his body が himself が適切. (2)「やがて」は before long (間もなく)と表す. (3)「ゆっくりと」は gently (緩やかに, 静かに)と表す)
- **身をもって** ▶ 私は地震の恐ろしさを身をもって(= 自分自身で)体験した I experienced the terror of an earthquake *personally*.
- **身をやつす** ▶ 大道芸人に身をやつす disguise *oneself* as a street performer.
- **身を寄せる** ▶ 私はしばらくおじの所に身を寄せた I *stayed with* my uncle for a while.

***み 実** ❶[果実] fruit (⚠通例単数形で集合的に用いる. 種類をいうときは [C] (⇨果物)); (堅果) a nut; (イチゴなどの柔らかい) a berry. ▶実が熟す grow ripe; ripen.
- **実のなっている木** a tree *in fruit*. ● 木の実を割る[拾い集める] crack [gather] *nuts*. ▶この木は実がならない This tree does not bear [produce] much *fruit*./This tree is a poor [a good] bearer.

❷[実質] substance; (中身) contents; (汁物などの具) an ingredient (⚠だし昆布なども含む必要な材料をさす). ● 実のない[ある]演説 a *thin* [a *substantial*, 《話》 a *meaty*] speech.
- **実を結ぶ** ▶ 彼の努力は実を結んだ His efforts *bore fruit* [《報われた》 *paid off*]. (⚠前の方はやや堅い言い方)

み 巳 the Snake.
- **巳年** [十二支] the year of the Snake. (⇨干支) 関連項

み 箕 a winnow. ▶ 箕でふるう winnow 《grain》.
みー 未ー un-; in-; (まだ…ない) not(…) yet (⇨まだ).
- **人跡未踏の** *un*trodden; virgin; (探検されていない) *un*explored. ● 未経験の *in*experienced. ▶ それは未解決のままだ We haven't solved it *yet*./It remains *un*solved.

-み -味 ▶ 苦味がある have a bitter *taste*. ● 赤[青]味がかった reddish [bluish]. ▶ 赤味を帯びた空 a sky with a *tinge* of red. ▶ 彼の話にはこっけい味がある His story *has a touch* [*a tinge*] of humor./His story *is tinged* with humor.

みあい 見合い [見合いをすること] marriage arrangement; [両家を交えての] (説明的に) a party [a dinner] where prospective marriage partners are introduced to the family members of each other; [当人同士の] (説明的に) the first date through the go-between's arrangement. 【事情】 日本式の見合いは米英にはない. ● 見合い結婚 (⇨見合い結婚) ▶ 私はあすおじの紹介で見合いをする I'll have the first date with [meet] a *prospective marriage partner* through my aunt's arrangement tomorrow. (⚠日常会話では文脈から明らかな場合, 上例の a prospective marriage partner (結婚相手になるかもしれない人)の代わりに a man [a woman] や 単に 名前を用いてもよい)

みあいけっこん 見合い結婚 an arranged marriage (↔ a love marriage); (説明的に) a marriage arranged by a go-between. ▶ 姉は見合い結婚です My sister had an *arranged marriage*.

***みあう 見合う** [つり合う]《書》 be proportionate 《to》; [適合する] suit. ● 生活費の上昇に見合った給料 pay *proportionate to* increased living costs.
- **年齢に見合った服装をする** wear clothes *suitable for* one's age. ● 収入に見合った生活をする live *within* (↔ beyond) one's *income* [《やや書》 *means*].

みあきる 見飽きる (⇨飽きる) ▶ 海はもう見飽きた. 家へ帰ろう I've *seen enough* of the sea. Let's go home. ▶ 小さい子供は同じ絵本を何度見ても見飽きないものだ Young children never *tire* [*get tired*] *of* looking at the same picture book.

みあげる 見上げる ❶[上を見る] look up 《at》; (視線を上げる) raise one's eyes 《toward》. ● 見上げるばかりの大男 a *towering* man. ▶ 彼は空を見上げた He *looked up at* the sky.

❷[感心する] (賞賛する) admire; (尊敬する) respect; (尊敬して仰ぎ見る) look up to…. ▶ 君の勇敢な行為はなかなか見上げたものだ I *admire* (you *for*) your brave deed./Your brave deed *is admirable*.

みあたらない 見当たらない (見つけられない) can't be found; (なくなっている) be missing. (⇨見つかる) ▶眼鏡が見当たらない I can't find my glasses./My glasses *are missing*. (⚠どこだろうか) Where are my glasses? ▶ タクシーは1台も見当たらなかった Not a single taxi *could be seen* [*was in sight*].

みあやまる 見誤る (人を) mistake* [take*] 《him》 for 《his brother》. (⇨間違える) ● 信号を見誤る *misread* a signal.

みあわせる 見合わせる ❶[互いに見る] ▶ 顔を見合わせる look at each other.
❷[差し控える] ▶ 試合開始を10時まで見合わせる(= 延期する) *put off* [*postpone*] starting the game *to* [*until*] 10 o'clock. (⇨延期) ▶ 雨で遠足を見合わせる(= 中止する) *cancel* [*call off*] the picnic because of rain. (⇨中止) ● その案を見合わせる(= 断念する) *give up* the idea. (⇨断念)

みいだす 見出す find*. (⇨見付ける)
ミーティング [会, 集会] a meeting.
ミート [食用の肉] meat.
- **ミートソース** meat sauce. ● **ミートボール** a meatball. ● **ミートローフ** a meatloaf.

ミート [野球の] ▶ ミートのうまい打者 a contact hitter.
- **ミートする** meet a ball; lay the bat on the ball.
ミーハー (教養の低い人) a lowbrow (↔ a highbrow).
ミイラ 《ポルトガル語》 a mummy. ● ミイラ化した遺体 a *mummified* body.
- **ミイラ取りがミイラになる** go out for wool and come home shorn.

みいられる 魅入られる (とりつかれる)《やや書》be possessed 《by》; (魅了される) be fascinated 《by》.
みいり 実入り one's income. ▶ 実入りのいい商売 a *profitable* business. ▶ 嫌な仕事だが実入りは多い(= 実収入は多い) I don't like the job, but *the net income is large* [《大いにもうかる》 I can *make a lot of money* out of it]. (⇨収入)

みいる 見入る gaze 《at》. (⇨見詰める, 見とれる)
みうけ 身請け ─── **身請けする** 動 ransom 《a geisha》; set* 《a geisha》 free by paying a ransom.
- **身請け金** a ransom.
みうける 見受ける ❶[見る] see*. (⇨見る)
❷[…のようだ] (見える) look; (思われる) seem, appear. (⇨よう) ❸ ● 見受けたところ apparently; (どう見ても) to [by] all appearances. ▶ お見受けしたところ何か困りのようですね You *seem* to be having trouble.

みうごき 身動き ▶ 借金で身動きができない《話》be *up to* one's *ears* in debt. ▶ どうしてあわてて家なんか買うの

みうしなう

ローンで身動きがとれなくなるよ What makes you rush to buy a house? You'll *lock* your*self into* a mortgage. ▶彼らが行き過ぎるまで彼は茂みに隠れて身動き一つしなかった He hid [lurked] in the bushes, not *moving a muscle*, while they passed. ▶満員電車の中で身動き一つできなかった I couldn't *move an inch* in the crowded train./(向きを変えるだけの余地がなかった) I didn't have enough space to *turn around* in the crowded train. ▶居間は家具で身動きができないほどだった(=一杯だった) The living-room was *over-crowded with* furniture. ▶彼女はそこで身動きもせずに立っていた She stood there *motionless*.

みうしなう 見失う lose* sight of ..., lose;〖足どりを〗lose track of .... ● 人込みで彼を見失う *lose* (*sight of*) him in the crowd. (**!**) lose him は文脈によっては「彼をまく」の意にもなるので注意

みうち 身内 〖家族〗a family;〖親類〗a relative (⇨親類);〖子分〗a follower. ● 身内の争い a *family* [a *domestic*] discord. ● うちの身内には医者が多い We have a lot of doctors *in our family*. ▶身内の者だけで結婚式をすませた Only the *close relatives* were present at the wedding.

みうり 身売り ━ **身売りする 動** sell* oneself ((*into* bondage)). ● 工場を身売りする *sell out* [〖英〗*up*] one's factory.

みえ 見え 〖見せびらかし〗show;〖虚栄心〗vanity. ● 見え坊 (見えを張る人)〖話〗a showoff;〖かっこつける男〗(軽蔑的) a fop. ● 見えで〖見えを張って〗out of *vanity*; for *show*; just to show off. ▶彼は見えでそう言っただけだ。本心はそうではない He said that just *for show*. He doesn't really mean it.

● **見えも外聞もない** 〖もう見えも外聞もない〗(=人が私をどう思おうとかまわない) Now I don't care what other people [others] (will) think of me.

● **見えを切る** (自信のある態度を装う) put on an air of confidence.

● **見えを張る** show off; (体面を繕う) keep up appearances.

みえかくれ 見え隠れ ▶月が雲間に見え隠れした The moon *was seen off and on* [I *caught brief glimpses of* the moon] among the clouds. (**!**) off and on は on and off ともいう

みえすく 見え透く ● 見え透いたうそ 《やや書》a *transparent* lie;〖明らかなうそ〗an *obvious* [〖やや書〗a *blatant*] lie. (**!**) blatant には「恥知らずなほど露骨な」の意) ▶彼の本心は見え透いている His real intention is *obvious* [〖やや書〗*transparent*]./I *can see* his real intention.

みえっぱり 見えっ張り 〖話〗a showoff. (⇨見え)

みえみえ 見え見え ▶見え見えだ be too obvious; (見えていている)《やや書》be transparent.

:みえる 見える ❶〖目に映る〗see* (**!**) 人が主語。しばしば can を伴い継続的意味または知覚努力を表す); (現れる) appear (**!**) 物が主語). ▶物がダブって〖曲がって〗見える be *seeing* things double [warped]. (**!**) 通例進行形で) ▶空を見たが何も見えなかった I looked at the sky, but *saw* nothing. ▶その建物からは港全体がよく見える We can *see* the whole harbor from the building. (⇨見渡す) ▶彼女は彼が見えなくなるまで手を振った She *waved* to him until she could no longer *see* him. ▶海が見えてきた The sea *came into sight* [*view*]./We *came in sight* of the sea. (**!**)「見えなくなった」は The sea *was out of sight* [*view*].) ▶水平線に太陽が見えてきた The sun *appeared* on the horizon. ▶下着が見えています Your underwear *is showing*. (**!**) 常に進行形で) ▶大部分の星は肉眼では見えない Most stars *are* not *visible* [are invisible] to the naked eye.

会話 (心理テストで)「この絵には何が見えますか」「コウモリが見えます」"What do you *see* in this picture?" "I *see* [(...のように見える) It looks like] a bat." (**!**) 後の方は ❹ の意)

❷ 〖伺われる〗 ▶彼の作文には進歩の跡が見えない I *can't see* any (signs of) improvement in his composition.

❸ 〖視力がある〗 ▶事故で目が見えなくなる *lose* one's *sight* in an accident. ▶目の手術をして見えるようになる *regain* one's *sight* after an eye operation. ▶猫は暗がりでも目が見える Cats *can see* in the dark. ▶このごろ目がよく見えて衰えている よ I can't *see* things well these days./My eyesight is failing these days. ▶祖母は白内障でほとんど目が見えない My grandmother *is* almost *blind with* cataract. ▶彼は左目が見えない He's *blind* [*of*] his left eye.

❹ 〖思われる〗 (視覚的印象によって) look; (視覚による判断によって) appear; (五感による判断によって) seem. ▶思う) ▶彼女は年の割に若く見える She *looks young* [×*younger*] for her age./She *looks younger* than she really is./She doesn't *look* her age. ▶彼は正直者のように見える He *looks like* an honest man./He *appears* [*seems*] (*to* be) an honest man./He *looks* [*appears*, *seems*] *as if* he *was* [《やや書》*were*,〖話〗*is*] an honest man. ▶彼女は心配しているようには見えないえ She doesn't *seem to* be worried. (**!**) It doesn't *seem* (to me) *that* she is worried. より口語的) ▶彼は酔っ払っていると言ったがそうは見えなかった He said that he was drunk, but he didn't *look* it [×*so*].

❺ 〖来る〗 come*; (到着する) arrive. ▶客が見える前に居間の掃除をする clean the living room before the guests *come* [*arrive*]. ▶今晩お客さんが見えます We're having [expecting] guests this evening.

会話「ご面会の方がお見えです」「どなた？」 "There's someone *to see you*." "Who is it?" (**!**) it で受けることに注意

みお 澪 a channel.

みおくり 見送り ❶ 〖送別〗〖話〗a send-off. ● 盛大な[心温まる] 見送りを受ける be given a good [a heartwarming] *send-off*. ● 兄を見送りに駅へ行く go to the station to *see* my brother *off* [×*see off my brother*]. (⇨見送る ❶)

❷ 〖延期, 見通し〗(⇨見送る ❸) ● 見送りの三振をする strike out looking.

***みおくる 見送る** ❶ 〖送別する〗see* ... off. ● 子供が学校に行くのを見送る *see* the children *off* [×*see off the children*] *to* school. ● 客を玄関まで見送る *see* a visitor *out* [*to* the door]. ▶多くの友達が私と駅まで行ってくれた A lot of my friends *saw* me *off* at the station. (**!**) ... came to the station to *see* me *off*. ともいえる)

❷ 〖じっと見る〗watch. ▶私は彼の後ろ姿を(=彼が去って行くのを)見送った I *watched* him *going away*.

❸ 〖延期する〗postpone, put*... off (**!**) 後の方が口語的); (棚上げにする) shelve;〖機会などを逃がす, 申し出を断る〗〖話〗pass ... up. ● 決定を見送る *postpone* [*put off*] (making) a decision. ● 海外旅行の機会を見送る *pass up* a chance to travel abroad. ● 電車を見送る(=次の電車を待つ) *wait for* the next train. ▶その会社は今年は新規採用を見送るそうだ They say (that) the company will *not employ* new workers this year. ▶私はまた昇進を

みおさめ 見納め for the last time; (…の最後を見る) see the last of …; (最後に一目見る) take a last look at …; (見る最後の機会である) be the last chance to see. ▶この世の見納めに before one dies. ▶それが彼の見納めになった That was *the last* I ever *saw of* him.

みおつくし 澪標 a wooden post for marking a channel. ▶澪標が澪の位置を示す *Wooden posts* mark a navigable channel.

みおとし 見落とし (an) oversight; (うっかりした手抜かり) an inadvertent omission. ▶多少の見落としは仕方がない A few *oversights* are inevitable. ▶その誤植は校正者の見落としが原因だった The misprint was due to a proofreader's *oversight*.

みおとす 見落とす overlook; (うっかり逃す) miss. ● 要点を見落とす(＝つかみそこなう) *miss the point*. ▶私は誤りを見落としてしまった I *overlooked* [*failed* to *notice*] the error.

みおとり 見劣り ▶これはあれより見劣りする This *does not look* [*is not*] *as* good [*nice*] *as* that.

みおぼえ 見覚え (⇨覚える❶) ▶そのサインに見覚えがありますか Do you *recognize* [✕Are you recognizing] the signature? (❗ *recognize* は以前に見たことがあるのでだれ[何]であるか分かること) ▶彼の顔には見覚えがあるのだが名前を思い出せない I *know* him *by sight* [(以前会ったことがある)]I *have seen* him *before*, (よく見かける顔である) He *looks familiar*, but I can't remember his name.

みおも 身重 ━ 身重の 形 (妊娠中の) pregnant.

みおろす 見下ろす [人・建物・場所が] look down 《at, on, over》; [建物・場所が] (見渡す) overlook. ● 2 階の窓から(彼を)見下ろす *look down* 《at him》*from* the upstairs window. ▶私たちの学校は海を見下ろす丘の上にある Our school stands on a hill, *looking down on* [*overlooking*] the sea.

みかい 未開 ━ 未開の 形 (原始的な) primitive; (文明化されていない) uncivilized; (未開発の) undeveloped. ● 未開の土地 *undeveloped* land; (荒地) wild land.
● 未開社会 a primitive [an uncivilized] society. ● 未開人 (特に野蛮な)《しばしばけなして》a barbarian; 《古・けなして》a savage. (❗ a primitive man は「原始人」⇨野蛮〔野蛮人〕)

みかいけつ 未解決 ━ 未解決の 形 unsolved; unsettled; [未決定の] pending. (⇨解決) ▶その領土問題は依然として未解決のままである The territorial issue is still [still remains] *unsettled*.

みかいたく 未開拓 ━ 未開拓の(＝研究されていない)分野 an *unexplored* field; the frontier(s) 《*of*》.
● 未開拓地 (未耕作) uncultivated [virgin, (未開発) undeveloped] land.

みかいはつ 未開発 ━ 未開発の 形 (開発されていない) undeveloped; (活用されていない) untapped. ● 未開発の土地 *undeveloped* land.

みかえし 見返し (本の) an endpaper.

みかえす 見返す 〖見直す〗go* over [look over, check] 《one's exam paper》again; 〖振り向いて見る〗look 《じっと》stare》back 《*at*》; 〖見た人を見る〗return 《his》look [stare]; 〖仕返しをする〗get* revenge 《on *him*》 get back 《*at*》; (最後に打ち負かす) 《やや話》have* [get] the last laugh 《*on*》.

みかえり 見返り (報酬(ほうしゅう)) (a) reward. ● 見返りの (担保を取っての) 〖金融〗collateral /kəlǽtərəl/ (fund). ● 見返りに in return 《*for*》, as a *reward* 《*for*》. ● (人に)親切にしてあげてその見返りを求める do 《him》a favor and ask 《him》a favor *in return*. ▶彼に何か頼むと必ず見返りを要求してくる He always wants [demands] some *reward* for his help.

みがき 磨き (洗練) refinement.
● 磨きをかける ● 腕に磨きをかける *improve* one's skill. ● 演技に磨きをかける *refine* [*polish*] one's performance. (❗「磨きのかかった演技」は one's *refined* [*polished*] performance) ▶私は留学する前に英語に磨きをかけなければならない I must *improve* [(忘れかけているので) *brush up* 《on》] my English before I study abroad.

みがきあげる 磨き上げる polish … (up) (❗ up は「完全に」の意); (きれいにする) clean … (up). ● 靴をぴかぴかに磨き上げる *polish* [*shine*] one's shoes. ● ドアの取っ手をぴかぴかに磨き上げる *polish* the brass knob till it shines brightly. ● 窓ガラスを磨き上げる *give* the windows *a* thorough [*a* good] *clean-up*; *clean up* the windows spotlessly (❗「よごれた点がないように」の意). (⇨磨く)

みがきこ 磨き粉 polishing powder.

みがきにしん 身欠き鰊 dried fillets of herring.

みかぎる 見限る (見放す) give* … up; (見切りをつける) give up on … (❗ give up より強意的); (背を向ける) turn one's back on …. (⇨見限す)

みかく 味覚 (a sense of) taste; a palate /pǽlət/. ● 味覚(＝好みに合う suit one's *palate*; be to one's *taste*. ● 味覚(＝食欲)をそそる stimulate [tempt, whet] one's appetite. ▶彼は風邪で味覚がにぶくなった His cold impaired his *sense of* taste.

みがく 磨く ❶ 〖物を〗(つやが出るように) polish … (up) (❗ up は強意語); (ごしごしこすって) scrub (-bb-), rub (-bb-); (表面の不用物をはがす) scrape; 〖金属を〗burnish; 〖ガラス・レンズなどを〗grind /gráind/; 〖靴を〗shine (❗ 過去・過去分詞は 〜 d); 〖歯を〗clean, brush. ● 靴を磨く *polish* [*shine*] one's shoes; *give* one's shoes *a polish* [*a shine*]. ● (汚れを落とす) *clean* [*brush*] one's shoes. ● 床をきれいに磨く *polish* [*rub*] up the floor; *polish* [*scrub*, *scrape*] the floor *clean*. ● なべを磨く *scrub* [*scrape*] a pan *out* [*clean*]. ● 磨けば光る逸材 (米) a diamond in the rough; (英) a rough diamond.
❷ 〖技能を〗improve; 〖忘れかけた語学を〗brush up 《on》…; 〖文章などを〗refine, polish … (up). ● 腕を磨く *improve* [*develop*] one's skill. ● 文体を磨く *refine* one's writing style.

みかくにん 未確認 ━ 未確認情報 unconfirmed news [information]. ● 未確認飛行物体 a UFO; an unidentified flying object.

みかけ 見掛け 〖全体の外観の印象〗(an) appearance, a look; 〖見せかけ〗(a) show. (⇨外見) ● 見かけは in *appearance*. ▶彼は見かけは利口そうだが実はそうではない He *looks* [*appears*, is *apparently*] clever, but in fact he isn't. (❗ ✕*Apparently*, he is …. のように文頭位も可 (⇨見える)) ▶見かけどおり彼女は行動力がある She is *as* active *as* she *looks*. ▶彼は見かけほど若くない He is not as young as [is older than] he *looks*./(実際より若く見える) He *looks* younger than he (really) is.
● 見かけ倒し ▶それはただの見かけ倒しだった It was *not as* good *as* it *looked*./It *seemed* good but was *not really*.
● 見かけによらず ▶人は見かけによらない A person cannot be judged by his *appearance* [*looks*]./《ことわざ》*Appearances* are deceptive. ▶彼女は見かけによらず行動力がある Contrary to *appearances*

[(そうは見えないが) She doesn't *look like* it but] she is active.

みかげいし 御影石 granite /grǽnit/.

みかける 見掛ける 〔目にする〕see*; (ちらっと) catch* sight of ...; 〔見つける〕find*. ▶近ごろはあまりホタルを見かけなくなった We *see* [*find*] hardly any fireflies these days. ▶彼が家に入っていくのを見かけた I *saw* him entering the house. ▶あの人だれ? よく見かける顔なんだけど Who's that? *I've seen* her *around* 〔(見覚えのある) She looks *familiar*〕.
【会話】「きのう駅であなたを見かけたわ。あなたは私に気づかなかったけど」「ほんと？ 何時ごろ?」「8 時半ごろ」「それは私じゃないわ。だってきのうの 8 時半には家に帰っていたもの」"I *saw* [*caught sight of*] you at the station yesterday, but you didn't see me." (**！** *see* では文脈によっては 2 人が話をしたと考えられる場合もある) "Really? When?" "At about 8:30." "That wasn't me. Yesterday at 8:30 I was back home."

*****みかた 味方** 图 a friend (↔enemy); (対立する一方の側) (one's) side; (ペアでする試合の) a partner.
①【～の味方】• 貧乏人の味方 a *friend of* [*to*] poor people 〔(やや書) the poor〕. (**！**(1) 冠詞は常に a. (2)〖米〗では of が普通) ▶この問題ではいつも君の味方だ I'm always *on* your *side* in this matter. ▶彼らはかつては我々の味方だったが、今は敵だ They were once our *friends*, but now they are our enemies. ▶いったいだれがどっちの味方だ (試合などで) Who's playing *on* whose *side* [*team*]?
②【味方に】• 彼女を味方に引き入れる win [gain] her *to* one's *side*. (**！** 主に説得によって)
③【味方を】
〖翻訳のこころ〗私は、なんだか味方を得たような気分になり、気持ちがらくになるのを感じた (山田詠美『ひよこの眼』) Feeling somehow (that) I had someone on my side, I felt relieved. (**！**(1)「味方」は someone on my side (自分の側にいる人) と表す. (2)「気持ちがらくになる」は feel relieved と表す)
—— 味方(を)する 動 take* sides (*with*), take (his) side, take the side (*of* him); 〔支持する〕support, stand* by ...; (支援・援助する) back (him) up. ▶彼は味方をしないでくれ Don't take sides with him (*against* us). ▶彼は常に我々の味方をしてくれる He always *supports* us [*backs* us *up*].

みかた a view (*of* ..., の観点); (観点) a point of view, a viewpoint; (見地) a standpoint; (角度) an angle. ▶その事について悲観的な見方をする take a pessimistic *view* of it. ▶経済的な見方をすれば from an economic *point of view* [*viewpoint*, *standpoint*]. ● 別な見方でそれを論じる discuss it from another *angle*. ● 地図の見方 (表題) a *guide to* the map. ▶彼と私ではものの見方がまったく違う He and I have very different *points of view* [*viewpoints*]. ▶この問題は幾通りもの見方ができる There are several *ways to look at* this problem.

みかづき 三日月 a crescent (moon); 〖新月〗a new moon. ● 三日月形の crescent.

みがって 身勝手 (自分本位) selfishness; (利己主義) egoism. (⇨我が儘)

みかねる 見兼ねる (平気で見ていられない) cannot bear [stand] to see. ▶彼が悲嘆にくれるのを見るに見かねて助ける決心をした I *couldn't stand to see* him suffer distress so I decided to help him.

みがまえる 身構える (...の姿勢をとる) take* a posture (*of*); (...する準備をする) get* ready (*to* do); (気を引きつめる) be on one's toes. ▶彼と話をするときいつも身構えてしまう I *am always on my toes* [

feel nervous] when I talk with him.

みがら 身柄 〖「身柄」に当たる英語はなく、「犯人の身柄」=「犯人」と考える〗• 彼の身柄を拘束する take *him* into custody. ▶彼の身柄を引き取る take custody of *him*.

みがる 身軽 —— 身軽な 形 〔軽快な〕light; 〔敏捷(びんしょう)な〕agile /ǽdʒəl/, nimble. ● 身軽な服装をしている be *lightly* [*casually*] dressed.
—— 身軽に 副 • 身軽にさくを乗り越える get over the fence *lightly* [*nimbly*]. ● 身軽に(=あまり荷物を持たずに)旅をする travel *light*. (**！** 慣用的な言い方)

みかわす 見交わす (互いに見る) look at each other; (目くばせをする) exchange glances.

みがわり 身代わり 〖人〗a substitute (*for*) (⇨代わり); (他人の罪・責任を) a scapegoat; 〖行為〗substitution. ▶殺人犯の身代わりにさせられる be made the *scapegoat* for the murder someone else committed. ▶彼は息子の身代わりになって死んだ He died *for* [*in place of*] his son./He sacrificed his life *for* [*to save*] his son.

*****みかん 蜜柑** a satsuma; a mandarin (orange); a tangerine. ● ミカンの実(肉の)一袋 a segment [a section] of a *mandarin*. ● ミカンの皮をむく peel an *orange*. ● ミカン畑 a tangerine grove.

みかん 未刊 —— 未刊の 形 unpublished.

みかん 未完 图 incompletion. (⇨未完成)
—— 未完の 形 • 未完の大作 an *unfinished* [an *incomplete*] masterpiece. ▶未完 (書き物の終わりに) To be continued.
● 未完の大器 ▶彼は未完の大器(=末頼もしい青年)だ He is a young man full of promise.

みかんせい 未完成 图 incompletion.
—— 未完成の 形 (不完全な) incomplete; (出来ていない) unfinished. ▶その詩は未完成だ The poem is *unfinished* [*undone*]./The poem *is not completed* yet.

みかんせいこうきょうきょく『未完成交響曲』the Unfinished Symphony. 〖参考〗シューベルト作曲の交響曲

みき 幹 a trunk, a tree-trunk.

*****みぎ 右** ①【右(側[手、方])】right. (**！** 通例 the [one's] ～) ▶かしら右〖号令〗Eyes *right*! ● 右向け[回れ]右 (⇨回れ右)
①(右の〜) right; 〖右手[側、方]の〗right-hand. (⇨右側, 右利き, 右手) ● 右ハンドルの車 a car with a *right-hand* steering wheel. ▶彼は右投げ左打ちだ He bats left, throws *right*. (**！**(1) 英語と日本語の順序の違いに注意. (2)「右ききの投手」は a *right-handed* pitcher, a *right*-hander) ▶右足が痛む My *right* leg hurts.
【会話】「写真の右上の男の人はだれ?」「私の右うしろの人のこと?」"Who's the man at the upper *right* of the picture?" "The one behind me [backward] to my *right*, you mean?"
②〖右に[へ]〗on the right (side); to the right (side).

〖解説〗次の 2 文の違いに注意: 彼の右(隣)に座る sit *on* his *right* [*on* the *right side* of him]./彼の右(手)に座る sit *to* his *right* [*to* the *right side* of him]. (**！** 2 者の間に何人かの人が座っていることを暗示する)

● 最初の曲がり角を右に曲がる take the first turning *on* [*to*] the *right*. ● 取っ手を右に(=時計回りに)回す turn a handle *clockwise*. ● 右ヘゴロを打つ hit a grounder to the *right* side of the infield. ▶その角を右に曲がると銀行があります Turn (*to* the) *right*

みぎあがり 右上がり ● 右上がりの成長をする（=着実に成長する）grow *steadily*. ▶彼は右肩上がりに書く He has a tendency to write *slanting upward from left to right*./His handwriting tends to *slant upward from left to right*.

みぎがわ 右側 the right (side). (⇨右) ● 右側の引き出し the *right-hand* drawer. ● 道の右側を歩く walk on the *right side* of the street. ● 右側通行 *right-hand* traffic. ● 右側通行しなさい Keep (to the) *right*. ▶君の右側に座っていたあの女性はだれですか Who was that woman sitting on your *right* (side) [*right-hand side*]?

みきき 見聞き ▶見聞きしたことを全部ノートに書きとめた I wrote down in my notebook everything I *saw and heard*.

みぎきき 右利き 图 (人) a right-handed person; a right-hander. ── 右利きの 形 right-handed.

ミキサー (台所用品) a blender,《英》a liquidizer;(コンクリートミキサー) a concrete [a cement] mixer;(音量調整装置[係]) a mixer.

みぎした 右下 ● 右下の[に] at the lower right.
みぎづめ 右詰め ● 右詰めにする right-justify.
みぎて 右手 [手] the [one's] right hand (⇨手);[方向, 位置] the right. (⇨右) ● 公園の右手に *to the right* [*on the right side*] of the park. ● 前の方は「右の方向に」, 後の方は「右側の位置に」の意)

みぎひだり 右左 right and left. (⇨左右)
みぎまえ 右前 ● 着物を右前に着ている A *kimono* is worn *with the right side over the left*.
みぎまき 右巻き ── 右巻きの[に] 形 副 clockwise (↔ anticlockwise, counterclockwise); (巻き貝が) dextral (↔sinistral). ● (つるなどが) 右巻きに巻きつく twine *clockwise*.

みぎまわり 右回り ── 右回りの[に] 形 副 clockwise. (⇨左回り)

みきり 見切り ● 見切り発車する start a train before all passengers are on board; [比喩的に] (早くやり過ぎる) 《話》jump the gun.
● 見切りをつける (断念する) give... up;(手を引く) wash one's hands《of》. ▶我々はその計画に見切りをつけた We *gave up* (on) [(捨てた) *abandoned*] the plan. (! のある方が強意的)
● 見切り品 (処分商品) cléarance gòods; (割引品) a bargain.

みぎり 砌 ● 上京のみぎり *when* you come up to Tokyo. (⇨折❶) ● 幼少のみぎり *when* one is young. (⇨頃)

みきる 見切る (全部見る) read* through [over]《a manuscript》;(見限る) give*... up;(安売りする) sell*... off.

みきれい 身奇麗 ── 身奇麗な 形 neat and tidy. (⇨小奇麗)

みぎわ 汀 (水際) the waterside;(渚) a beach.
みきわめる 見極める [最後まで見る] watch《it》to the end;[確かめる] make* sure《of; that 節》;[真相を究明する] get* to the bottom of...; investigate.

みくだす 見下す despise;《話》look down on [upon].... (⇨軽蔑)

みくだりはん 三下り半 (説明的に) a note of divorce (given by a husband to his wife unilaterally during the Edo period). ▶今は下手をすると夫の方が三下り半を突きつけられる A husband will *be divorced one-sidedly* today if he is not good enough. ● 女性からの離婚状は dear John letter という

みくびる 見縊る underestimate, sell*《him》short. ▶君は彼の実力を見くびっては (=過小評価してはいけない You should not *underestimate* [(判断を誤る) *misjudge*] his ability.

みくらべる 見比べる 《A を B と》compare《A *with* B》. (⇨比べる)

みぐるしい 見苦しい [醜い] ugly, unsightly; [下品な] indecent; [服装などがみすぼらしい] shabby; [恥ずべき] shameful; (不名誉な) disgraceful. (⇨醜い)
● 見苦しい混乱 *ugly* [*unsightly*] disorder. ● 見苦しい服装をしている be *shabbily* dressed. ▶彼女の態度は実に見苦しかった (=不愉快だった) I found her manner extremely *unpleasant*.

みぐるみ 身ぐるみ ● 身ぐるみ (=持っているものすべてを) はぎ取られる be robbed [stripped] of *all* (*that*) *one has*.

ミクロ ── ミクロの 形 micro /máikrou/. ● ミクロの世界 the *micro*world.
● ミクロ経済学 microeconomics.

ミクロネシア [国名] Micronesia /màikrəníːʒə/; (公式名) the Federated States of Micronesia. (首都 Palikir) ● ミクロネシア人 a Micronesian. ● ミクロネシア(人)の Micronesian.

ミクロン [<ギリシャ語] a micron /máikrɑn/.
みけいけん 未経験 ── 未経験の 形 inexperienced;(未熟な)《話》green. ▶彼はその仕事はまだ未経験だ He is *inexperienced* at [*new to*] the job.
● 未経験者 an inexperienced person.

みけた 三桁 (数) three figures. ● 三桁の数字 a *three-digit* number. ▶117 は三桁(の数字)である The number 117 contains *three digits*./117 is a *three-digit* number.

みけつ 未決 ── 未決の 形 (未解決の) pending; (未

みけねこ 三毛猫 a tortoiseshell /tɔːrtəsʃèl/ (cat). 〔(略式)〕 ぶち猫 a tabby cat.

ミケランジェロ 〖イタリアの画家・彫刻家・建築家〗Michelangelo /màɪkəlǽndʒəlou/ (~ Buonarroti).

みけん 未見 彫 unread. ▶ 未見の書物 a book one *has not read*.

みけん 眉間 the middle of the eyebrows /áɪbràuz/; 〖解剖〗the glabella. ▶ 眉間にしわを寄せる(=違和感を催せる) knit [draw together] one's *brows*; frown. (⇒額) ▶ 彼女が投げつけた雪球が彼の眉間に命中した The snowball she threw hit him right *between the eyebrows* [*eyes*].

みこ 巫女 a *Shinto* maiden; (説明的に) a maiden in the service of a *Shinto* shrine.

みこうにん 未公認 ▶ 彼女は未公認ではあるが 100 メートル競走で 10 秒台を何度か出している She *has unofficially recorded* ten seconds something in the 100m dash a few times.
- 未公認記録 an unofficial record.

みこし 神輿 a portable shrine. ▶ みこしをかつぐ carry a *portable shrine*; (比喩的に) flatter 《him *into* doing》.
- みこしを上げる (立ち上がる) rise; (仕事などに取りかかる) start work; get started.

みこす 見越す expect; allow 《*for*》. (⇒見込む, 見込む) ▶ 渋滞を見越して早朝に出発した *In expectation* [*anticipation*] *of* heavy traffic I started early in the morning.

みごたえ 見応え ▶ NHK のそのテレビドラマは見ごたえがある The TV drama by NHK is really *worth seeing* [*watching*].

***みごと** 見事 图 ▶ お見事! (よくやった) *Well-done!*/(演奏[演技者]に対して) *Bravo!*/(すばらしい) *Excellent* [*Admirable*, *Fantastic*, *Wonderful*, *Beautiful*]*!*

── 見事な 形 〖すばらしい〗wonderful; 〖並以上に立派な〗fine; 〖壮麗な〗splendid, magnificent; 〖美しい〗beautiful; 〖優秀な〗excellent; 〖驚くべき〗marvelous; 〖あっぱれな〗admirable; 〖とびきりすぐれた〗superb. (❗wonderful, splendid, magnificent, excellent, marvelous, admirable, superb など を強めるときは通例 very でなく absolutely など を用いる) ▶ 見事な作品 a *wonderful* [a *fine*, a *nice*] piece of work. ▶ 見事な一鉢の菊 a pot of *beautiful* chrysanthemums. ▶ 見事なロングシュートでゴールを決める score a goal on a *beautiful* long shot. ▶ 彼の昨夜の演奏は実に見事だった The performance he gave last night was absolutely *superb* [*とても上手だった*] *very skillful*]. ▶ 彼のふるまいはお見事だった His conduct was *admirable*.

── 見事に 副 (上手に) very well; (完全に) completely; (美しく) beautifully. (⇒立派に) ▶ 見事に踊る dance *beautifully*. ▶ 彼は試験に見事に(=首尾よく)通った He *successfully* passed the exam. ▶ その試みは見事に成功した The attempt was *completely* [*highly*] successful. ▶ その計画をめちゃめちゃにしてくれたね What a *fine* mess you've made of the plan! (❗皮肉として).

みことのり 詔 an Imperial edict [rescript].

みごなし 身ごなし a bearing. ▶ 彼女の身ごなしは上品だった She *carried herself* gracefully.

***みこみ** 見込み ❶ 〖望み〗(a) hope; 〖可能性〗(a) likelihood, (a) possibility 〖前の方が実現可能性が高い〗; 〖成功の〗(a) chance; 〖成功・利益などの〗prospects. ▶ 回復の見込みのない患者[症状] a *hopeless*

case. ▶ 見込みのある青年 a *promising* young person; a young person with bright *prospects*. ▶ (勧誘の対象となるような)見込み客 a *prospective* client; a prospect. ▶ 彼の回復の見込みはほとんどない There is very little *hope* [*chance*] *of* his recovery. (❗hope は彼の回復に対する話し手の希望が示されるが, chance にはその含みはない)/He has very little *hope* [*chance*] *of recovery*. (❗前の文は客観的, 後の文は主観的表現) ▶ ハイキングは取り止めになる見込みだ There is a *likelihood* [*possibility*] *that* the hiking will be canceled./The hiking is *likely* [×*possible*] *to* be canceled. ▶ それは不可能ではないが, 見込みは薄い It isn't impossible, but just *unlikely*. ▶ 彼が勝つ見込みは十分ある He has a good *chance* of winning [×*to* win]./There is a good *chance* [〘話〙The odds are] *that* he will win.

❷ 〖予想〗expectation(s). (⇒予想) ▶ それは見込み違いだった (期待外れだった) It didn't come [live] up to my *expectations*./(誤算だった) It was my miscalculation. ▶ 彼女は今年自動車の免許を取る見込みです She *is expected to* get a driver's license this year.

みこむ 見込む 〖予想する〗expect; anticipate; 〖当てにする〗rely [count] on ...; 〖信用する〗trust; 〖考慮する〗take* (it) into account; 〖時間・費用などを見越しておく〗allow; 〔...のために余裕を見る〕 allow for ...; 〖見積もる〗estimate. ▶ 昇給を見込んで *in expectation* [*anticipation*] *of* a wage increase. ▶ 昼食に 1 時間見込んでおく *allow* an hour *to* have lunch [*for* lunch]. ▶ 私の見込んだ(=心にかなった)女性 a woman *after* my (*own*) *heart*. ▶ 君を友人と見込んで頼みがある *Trusting* you as a friend, I'd like you to do something for me. ▶ 交通渋滞を見込んで私たちは朝早く出発した *Allowing for* the traffic jam, we started early in the morning. (❗... in the morning, *allowing for* the traffic jam. の語順も可) ▶ 彼は社長に見込まれて(=社長の信任を得て)課長に昇進した He won the president's confidence [*favor*] and was promoted to head of the section.

みごもる 身ごもる ▶ ...の子を身ごもる *get pregnant* by .... (⇒妊娠する) ▶ きわめて深刻なのは雌クジラの多くが子を身ごもったまま殺されていることです What's most serious is that many of the female whales are killed while still *bearing unborn calves*.

みごろ 身頃 the body of a *kimono*.

みごろ 見頃 ▶ 見頃だ be at [×in] one's best. ▶ 桜の花は 4 月が見頃だ The cherry blossoms are *at* their *best* [(満開だ) *in* (*full*) *bloom*, 〘話〙*fully out*] in April.

みごろし 見殺し ▶ 見殺しにする leave 《him》to his fate [in the lurch] (❗成句表現); desert [leave]《him》without help (in a difficult situation).

みこん 未婚 (結婚していない) unmarried; (独身の) single. ▶ 未婚の女性 an *unmarried* [a *single*] woman. ▶ 未婚の母 an *unmarried* [a *single*, (婉曲的な) a *lone*] mother. (⇒非婚, 片親)

みこん 未墾 ── 未墾の 形 uncultivated 《land》; unreclaimed 《marshland》.

ミサ (a) Mass /mæs/, (a) mass. ▶ ベートーベンの「荘厳ミサ」 Beethoven's *Missa Solemnis*. ▶ ミサに出る attend [go to] *mass*. ▶ ミサを捧げる read [say, offer] *mass*. ▶ ミサを行う hold *mass*.
- ミサ曲 a mass.

ミサイル a missile /mísl/. ▶ 巡航ミサイル a cruise *missile*. ▶ 地対空ミサイル a surface-to-air *missile*

みさお 操 [貞操] chastity. (⚠chastity は「性的関係になること、性行為を行わないこと」の意。米英ではエイズの蔓延(まんえん)を防ぐために、学校教育で chastity program が組まれている) ●操を守る be faithful to one's husband [wife].

みさかい 見境 (識別) discrimination; (理性) reason. ●見境がなくなる lose one's *reason*. ●見境なくほめる give *indiscriminate* praise 《*to*》. ▶(前後の)見境もなく(=最初によく考えないで)服を買うな Don't buy clothes *without first thinking carefully*.

みさき 岬 (大きな) a cape; (絶壁の) a headland, a promontory /prάmǝntɔːri/; a point 《通例地名とともに用いる》. ●ホーン岬 *Cape Horn*; the Horn. ●足摺岬 Ashizuri *Headland*.

みさげる 見下げる despise;《話》look down on ....(⇨蔑).▶彼はなんと見下げ果てた人間だ What a *mean* fellow you are!

みさご 鶚 [鳥] an osprey.

みささぎ 陵 an Imperial mausoleum《複 ~s, -lea》. (⇔) 御陵)

みさだめ 見定め ●善悪の見定めがつかない can*not* tell right *from* wrong; can*not* distinguish right *from* wrong [*between* right *and* wrong].

みさだめる 見定める (確かめる) make* sure 《*of*; *that* 節》; 《書》ascertain. ●状況を見定める *make* sure how things are going 《やや書》stand]; take stock of the situation.

みざるきかざるいわざる 見猿聞か猿言わ猿 see no evil, hear no evil, speak no evil.

:みじかい 短い 形 [長さ・時間的] short (↔long);[つめ・芝生など短く切った] close;[短時間の、簡潔な] brief. ●短い休暇[旅行] a *short* holiday [trip]. ●短い一生を送る lead a *short* life. ●つめを短く切る cut [trim] one's nails *close*. ●短い報告をする make a *brief* [a *short*] report. ▶この上着はそでが私には短すぎる This coat is (too) *short* in the sleeves for me.

── **短くする** 動 shorten《a skirt》; make*《a skirt》shorter. ●髪を短くしてもらう *have* one's hair cut *short*《*close*, xshortly》.▶「短い髪」= *short* hair) ●夏になると夜が短くなる The nights *get shorter* in 《主に米》 the summer. ▶彼は不要な語を削って記事を短くした He *shortened* the article by deleting unnecessary words.

みじかめ 短め ●短目の[で] rather short; (短すぎる) a little too short. ●shortish は「長くも短くもない」と「かなり短い」の両方の意で用いられるので注意) ▶近ごろはスカート丈は短めになっています The length of skirts is becoming *rather short* these days. ▶(髪は)後ろを短めにしてください I'd like my hair cut *a little short* at the back.

ミシガン [米国の州] Michigan 《略 Mich. 郵便略 MI》.

ミシシッピ [米国の州] Mississippi /mìsǝsípi/《略 Miss. 郵便略 MS》. ●ミシシッピ川 the Mississippi.

みじたく 身支度 (⇨支度 ❷) ▶彼女は急いで身支度を整えた She *dressed* [*got dressed*] in a hurry. (⚠《話》では後の方が普通)

みしみし ▶この床はみしみし音がする(=きいきい鳴る) This floor *creaks*.

***みじめ 惨め ── 惨めな** 形 miserable, 《書》wretched; [後の方がより悲惨な様子が外に表れているとい] [不幸な] unhappy. ●みじめな生活をする lead a *miserable* [a *wretched*, an *unhappy*] life; live in *misery*. ●空腹でみじめな思いをする feel *miserable from* hunger. ▶太郎は彼女のことでみじめな気持ちでいた Taro felt *unhappy* about her.

みしゅう 未収 ── 未収の 形 uncollected; (受領できる) receivable. ●未収金 uncollected balance; bills [商店など] accounts] receivable. ●未収配当金 a dividend receivable.

みしゅうがく 未就学 ── 未就学の 形 preschool 《education》. ●未就学児童 a preschool child; a child *of preschool* age; a preschooler.

***みじゅく 未熟** 名 (熟さ) immaturity.
── **未熟な** 形 [成熟していない] immature; [経験がない] inexperienced 《*in, at*》,(話)green; [熟練していない] unskilled 《*in, at*》; [へたな] poor 《*at*》. ●未熟な労働者 an *unskilled* worker. ▶彼の運転技術は未熟だ He is *poor* [*inexperienced*] *at* driving./He is a *poor* [an *inexperienced*] driver.
●未熟児 a premature baby. ●未熟者 an inexperienced [《話》a green] person;《話》a greenhorn.

みしょう 未詳 ── 未詳の 形 [知られていない] unknown; [特定できていない] unidentified.

みしょう 実生 a seedling.

みしらぬ 見知らぬ [見たことのない] strange; [よく知らない] unfamiliar; [未知の] unknown. ●見知らぬ町 a *strange* [an *unfamiliar*] town. ●見知らぬ人 a stranger.

みしりおく 見知り置く ▶お見知りおきを願います I'm pleased to *make your acquaintance*./I'm glad to meet you.

みしる 見知る be acquainted《*with*》; know* (personally).

みじろぎ 身じろぎ ●身じろぎ一つしない(=少しも動かない) do not move a muscle 《*to do*》; remain completely still. ●身動き

ミシン a séwing /sóuiŋ/ machine. ([参考] 日本語のミシンは machine がなまったもの) ●ミシンでドレスを縫う make a dress on a *sewing machine*.
●ミシン針 a sewing-machine needle.

みじん 微塵 [断片] a fragment; (小片) a piece. ●みじんに砕ける be broken to *pieces* [into *fragments*]. ●みじん切りにする chop《it》up; (細かく切る) cut《it》into small *pieces*. (⚠「みじん切りの玉ねぎ」は finely chopped onions) ▶彼には彼女をだまそうなんて気はみじんも(=少しも)なかった He didn't have the *slightest* intention of deceiving her.

みじんこ 微塵子 [昆虫] a water flea.

ミス [未婚女性の姓・姓名につける敬称] Miss (⇨さん); [未婚女性] an unmarried woman. ●2008年のミス日本 Miss Japan (for) 2008.

ミス ❶[間違い] a mistake (⚠xa miss とはいわない); (スポーツ・校正・計算などの) an error. ●スペルのミス spelling *mistakes* [*errors*]. ●医療ミス (医療過誤) a medical *error* [xmistake]. ●ミスをする make [xdo] a *mistake*; make [commit] an *error*. ▶ちょっとした計算のミスをした I made a small *error in* my calculations.
❷[落ち度] a fault. ▶それは君のミスだ It's your *fault*.

:みず 水 water.

解説 (1) 日本語の「水」は冷水に限られるが、water は温度に関係なく用い、湯も含む。(⇨湯)
(2) 液体として見た場合は無冠詞、場所空間として見た場合は the がつく：油は水に浮く Oil floats on *water*./丸太が水に浮いていた There was a log floating on *the water*. (⇨❹)

ミズ　1732　みずかけろん

①【～水】● 水道の[井戸]水 tap [well] water. ● 海の水 sea water. ● 井戸[川]の水がかれた The well [river] has dried up. (❗×The water in the well [river] has dried up. とはいわない)
②【水～】● 水不足 (a) water shortage; (a) shortage of water. ● レタスを水洗いする rinse the lettuce; wash the lettuce in water. ▶これまでの努力がすべて水の泡になった (⇨水の泡)
③【水が[は]】● 今朝(蛇口を開けたが)水が出なかった This morning I turned on the tap but water didn't come out. ● (水道の)水が出しっ放しになっていた The water was left running. (❗水のだくことに注意) ● この水は飲める This water is good to drink. ● 夏には水が不足する We have a short supply of water in 《主に米》 summer./We are short of water in 《主に米》 the) summer.
④【水に】● ひざまで水につかって歩く walk [wade] in water up to one's knees. ● 水に映った自分の姿を見る see oneself in the water. (⇨解説(2))
⑤【水を】● (水道の)水を出す[止める] turn on [off] the water (supply). (❗supply を省略する方が口語的) ● 水を1杯[少し]ください Let me have a glass of [some] water. ▶彼女は花に水をやった She poured water on [watered] the flowers. ▶涼を求めて庭に水を打った I watered the garden to enjoy a cool breeze. ▶トイレの水を2度流した I flushed the toilet twice. (❗「トイレの水が流れなかった」 The toilet wouldn't flush.) ● 水濡れ注意 《表示》 Keep dry.

● 水が合わない ▶新しい職場の水が合わない I can't adapt (myself) to my new workplace./I don't feel comfortable in my new workplace.
● 水清ければ魚棲まず If water is clear, no fish will live in it./《ことわざ》(ものごとの度が過ぎるのはよくない) Too much of one thing is not good.
● 水と油 ▶2人の関係は水と油だ 'The two are like oil and water.' (❗日本語との語順の違いに注意) / The two are as different as night and day 《米》 [chalk and cheese 《英》]. (❗後の方の頭韻に注意)
● 水に流す ▶水に流そう。もう済んだことだから Forget it [Let's forgive and forget, 《ことわざ》 Let bygones be bygones]. It's ancient history. (❗口論などの後で)
● 水は方円の器(うつわ)に従う 'Water takes the shape of its container.'
● 水も滴る ▶水も滴る若だんな a strikingly good-looking young master.
● 水も漏らさぬ ▶水も漏らさぬ(=すきのない)警戒をする keep an airtight watch 《on》.
● 水をあける ▶彼は他の選手に大きく水をあけた He had [got] a big lead over the other swimmers.
● 水を打ったように ▶法廷は水を打ったように(=ピンが落ちたら聞こえるほど)静かだった The court was so quiet (that) you could have heard a pin drop.
● 水を得た魚のように ▶彼女は舞台に出ている時はまさに水を得た魚のようだ(=本領を発揮している) She's in her element (when she's) on the stage.
● 水をさす (関係などを壊す) ruin [destroy, wreck] a relationship 《with, between》; (計画などのじゃまをする) interfere with 《his plan》, throw [pour] cold water on 《his plan》.
● 水を向ける (誘いをかける) induce 《him to do》.

ミズ Ms. /míz/ (❷ Ms(e).s.) (⇨-さん) (❗既婚・未婚を区別したくない時 Miss., Mrs. の代わりに用いる敬称)

みずあか 水垢 《米》 scale, 《英》 fur. ●やかんの内側に水垢がついた Scale formed on the inside of the kettle.

みずあげ 水揚げ ❶【陸上げ】 unloading. ●船荷の水揚げをする(=船の荷を降ろす) unload a ship.
❷【漁獲量など】 a (fishing) catch. ●イワシの水揚量が多い have a large catch [haul] of sardines.
●タクシーのその日の水揚げ(=売上高) the day's takings of a taxi.
❸【切り花の】 ●この花は水揚げがよい These flowers are doing well.

みずあさぎ 水浅葱 (薄い青) light [pale] blue. ●水浅葱の light [pale] blue.

みずあそび 水遊び ●水遊びをする play with water [川など水のある場所で] (in the water); (手足をばたばたさせて) dabble 《in the water》.

みずあたり 水あたり ●外国へ行ったら水あたりに気をつけなさい You should take good care [should be careful] when you drink water abroad. It sometimes disagrees with you.

みずあび 水浴び bathing /béiðiŋ/, 《英》 a bathe; (主泳) a swim, swimming. ●水浴びをする swim, (主英) bathe, 《英》 have [take] a bathe 《in a river》. ●水浴びに行く go swimming [for a swim, for a bathe]. (⇨海水浴)

みずあめ 水あめ starch syrup.
みずあらい 水洗い (⇨水 ②)

みすい 未遂 ●未遂の attempted. ●自殺未遂 (an) attempted suicide. ●強盗[殺人]未遂 attempted burglary [murder]. ●クーデター未遂 an abortive coup /kuː/. ●テロリストたちは彼の暗殺を企てたが未遂に終わった The terrorists attempted his assassination but failed.

みずいらず 水入らず ●きのうの家族水入らずで(=家族だけで)外食した My family ate out alone [all by ourselves] yesterday./(外食を楽しんだ) My family enjoyed eating out together yesterday.

みずいり 水入り 《相撲》 mizuiri; (説明的に) a temporary halt by sumo referee because of a long bout.

みずいろ 水色 light [pale] blue.

*みずうみ 湖 a lake. ●琵琶湖は Lake Biwa または時に the Lake of Biwa のようにいう (⇨-湖(ᶜ)) ●湖で泳ぐ swim in a lake. ●湖でひとこぎする have a row on a lake. ●湖のほとりに一軒の別荘があった There was a villa on the lake.

ミズーリ 〖米国の州〗 Missouri /mɪzúəri/ 《略 Mo. 郵便略 MO》.

みすえる 見据える (じっと見つめる) gaze [stare] fixedly /fíksɪdli/ 《at》; (見定める) make* sure. ●状況を見据える make sure how things stand.

みずおと 水音 ●水音たてて with a splash. ●風呂場からぽたぽたと水音が聞こえてきた I could hear water dripping in the bathroom.

みずかがみ 水鏡 ●水鏡に映して見る look at one's reflection in the water.

みずかき 水かき (鳥などの) a web; (アザラシなどの) a flipper; (水掻き足) a webbed foot. ●水掻きのある webbed. ●水掻き足のある web-footed.

みずかけろん 水掛け論 《have》 an endless [(不毛の) a fruitless] argument [dispute] 《with》.
会話「ちょっとお客様、かばんの中を見せていただけませんか」「何で？」「そこの本をかばんに入れられましたね」「そんなことしてませんわ。失礼ね」「分かりました。それでは水掛け論になりますから警察を呼びましょう」"Excuse me, madam. Do you mind if I take a look in your bag?" "What for?" "I saw you put that book in your bag." "I never did. Excuse ˇme." "Right. Well, then that is getting us nowhere [we have something of an impàsse]. I'll call the police." (❗前の方は「こんな押し問答(=that)をして

みずかげん 水加減 the quantity of water 《*for* boiling rice》.

みずかさ 水嵩 the volume of water. ▶川の水かさが増した The river has risen [swelled]. (⇨増水)

みずかす 見透す see* through .... (⇨見抜く)

みずがめ 水瓶 a watar jar [(取っ手つき) jug].

みずがめざ 水瓶座 〔占星・天文〕 Aquarius /əkwέəriəs/ (**!** the はつけない); (宝瓶(ﾎｳﾋｮｳ)宮) 〔占星〕 the Water Bearer [Carrier]. (⇨乙女座) ●水瓶座(生まれ)の人 an Aquarius, an Aquarian. ▶後の方は形容詞としても用いる)

みずから 自ら 〔自分自身で〕 oneself; 〔直接に〕 personally, in person. (⇨自身, 自分) ●自らたたき上げた男 a *self*-made man.

みずがれ 水涸れ (かんばつ) (a) drought /dráut/; (水不足) (a) shortage [a lack] of water, (a) water shortage.

みすぎ 身過ぎ (生活) a living. (⇨生活, 生計)

みずき 水木 〔植物〕 a dogwood. (**!** 花水木 a flowering dogwood もさす)

みずぎ 水着 《主に米》 a báthing sùit, 《英》 a báthing còstume; (特にワンピース型の) a swimsuit; 〔ビキニ〕 a bikini (bathing suit); 〔男性用の水泳パンツ〕 《a pair of》 swimming trùnks. ●セパレーツ型の水着 a two-piece *bathing suit*. ▶彼女は水着姿です She looks good in a *bathing suit* [*wear*]. /《今はやや古》 She is a *bathing* beauty.

みずききん 水飢饉 (水不足) (a) water shortage; (干ばつ) (a) drought.

ミスキャスト miscasting. (**!** miscast は動詞)

みずきり 水切り (遊び) duck(s) and drake(s). ●水切り遊びをする skip [skim] stones 《on the pond》. ●花の水切りをする cut the stem of a flower in the water.
●水切り台 (食器の) 《米》 a dráinbòard; 《英》 a dráining bòard. ●水切りボール a colander.

みずぎわ 水際 the waterside, the water's edge; (岸) the shore.

みずぎわだつ 水際立つ ●水際立つ(=すばらしい)演技 a superb [a *magnificent*, a *splendid*] performance.

みずくさ 水草 a waterweed; 〔水生植物〕 a water plant; 〔イネ科の〕 a water grass.

みずくさい 水臭い ▶私に水臭い(=よそよそしい)のね You're *unfriendly* [《冷たい》 *cold*] to [toward] me. /《堅苦しい》 You're *formal* to [with] me. ▶水臭いじゃないか, はっきり言ってくれよ What an *unfriendly* thing to say! You should be more frank with me. ▶時には寄ってくれよ, そう水臭いこと言わずに Stop over once in a while. Don't *be such a stranger*.

みずぐすり 水薬 (an) liquid medicine. ●水薬を飲む take [drink] a *liquid* medicine.
●水薬瓶 a phial; 《書》 a vial.

みずけ 水気 (湿り気) moisture; (汁) juice. ●水気の多い 《xa》 *juicy* fruit. ●野菜を洗って水気を完全に切る wash vegetables and *drain* them thoroughly.

みずげい 水芸 《do [perform]》 a water trick.

みずけむり 水煙 ●水煙を立てる send up a *cloud of spray*; raise *spray*.

みずご 水子 (流産した胎児) a miscarried fetus; (堕胎した胎児) an aborted fetus. ▶流産した子供のために水子供養をしてもらった We attended Mass for our miscarried child's soul.

みずごえ 水肥 liquid fertilizer.

みずごけ 水苔 〔植物〕 (a) sphagnum (**!** sphagna); bog moss; peat moss.

みずごころ 水心 ▶魚心あれば水心 (⇨魚(ｻｶﾅ)) 〔成句〕

みずごす 見過ごす overlook. (⇨見落とす, 見逃す)

みずごり 水垢離 ●水ごりをとる purify oneself by pouring water over one's body; perform one's cold-water ablutions.

みずさいばい 水栽培 hydroponics (**!** 単数扱い); tank farming. ●水栽培をする use *hydroponics* to grow ....

みずさかずき 水杯 ●水杯を交わす exchange cups of water to drink as a farewell [a sign of the final farewell].

みずさきあんない 水先案内 pilotage. ●水先案内をして安全に入港させる *pilot* a ship safely into the harbor.
●水先案内船 a pilot boat. ●水先案内人 a pilot.

みずさし 水差し (water) jug, 《米》 a pitcher.

みずしげん 水資源 water resources.

みずしごと 水仕事 household work that uses (a lot of) water. ●水仕事をする do kitchen work; (洗濯をする) do the washing.

みずしぶき 水しぶき (はねた水) a splash; (水煙) spray. (⇨しぶき) ●水しぶきをあげてプールに飛び込む dive into the pool with a *splash*; splash into the pool.

ミスジャッジ ▶審判がミスジャッジした The umpire made a *bad call*. /The umpire made the *wrong decision*.

みずしょうばい 水商売 the bar [night club, restaurant] business; a chancy [a risky] business. ▶彼女は水商売の女です She is a *bar* girl. / She works in a *bar*.

みずしらず 見ず知らず ●見ず知らずの人(=まったく知らない人) a complete [a total, a perfect, an utter] stranger.

みずすまし 水澄まし 〔昆虫〕 a whirligig beetle.

みずぜめ 水攻め ●城を水攻めにする (水浸しにする) *flood* a castle; (給水路を断つ) *cut off the water supply to* a castle.

みずぜめ 水責め (大量の水を飲ませる拷問) water torture. ●水責めにする *torture* a person *by water*.

ミスター 〔男性の姓・姓名につける敬称〕 Mr. (⇨~さん)

みずたき 水炊き *mizutaki*, (説明的に) boiled chicken and vegetables that are eaten after being dipped in a special sauce.

みずだし 水出し ●お茶 [コーヒー] を水出しする make tea [coffee] by using cold water; use only cold water when making tea [coffee].

みずたまもよう 水玉模様 polka dots. ●水玉模様のスカート [ネクタイ] a *polka-dot(ted)* skirt [tie].

みずたまり 水たまり a puddle; (大きな) a pool (of water); (雨降りでできた水たまり) a *puddle* of rain.
●道路の水たまりにはまる slip [fall, take a false step] into a *puddle* in the road.

みずっぱな 水っ洟 ●水っぱなが出る have a runny [a running] nose. ▶水っぱなが出ているよ Your nose is *running*. ●水っぱなをする snivel.

みずっぽい 水っぽい watery; (こくがない) thin (-nn-).
●水っぽいスープ *watery* [*thin*] soup.

みずでっぽう 水鉄砲 water [a squirt] gun.

ミステリアス — ミステリアスな 〔形〕 〔不可解な, 神秘的な〕 mysterious. ●ミステリアスな殺人事件 a *mysterious* murder case.

ミステリー 〔神秘〕 mystery (**!** 「謎(ﾅｿﾞ)」の意では [C]); 〔推理小説〕 a mystery (novel).

みすてる 見捨てる 〔不当なまたはむごいやり方で〕 desert

みずどけい 〚完全に捨て去る〛abandon; 〚親密な人・物との関係を絶つ〛《書》forsake*. ●祖国を見捨てる abandon [forsake] one's country. ▶彼は有名になると家族を見捨てた He deserted [abandoned,《話》walked out on] his family when he became famous. ▶このスリラー映画もなかなか〔そう〕見捨てたものではない (＝かなりよい) This thriller is fairly good [(そう悪くない) not so bad].

> 翻訳のこころ 僕はあの広い屋敷の中で、ひとりぼっちで、世界中から見捨てられたように感じた（村上春樹『レキシントンの幽霊』） Alone in that big [huge] house, I felt as if I had been deserted [abandoned] by the whole world. (❶ be deserted は「捨てられる」の意を表す一般的な表現。be abandoned は「(保護したり責任をもってくれるはずの人に)捨てられる」の意を含む)

みずどけい 水時計 a water clock.
みずとり 水鳥 a water [an aquatic] bird;《集合的》waterfowl.(▶特にアヒル・カモ・ガンなど)
みずな 水菜 〖植物〗mizuna; a potherb mustard.
みずに 水煮 ●水煮にする boil in water; cook plain. ●サケの水煮, boiled salmon /sǽmən/. ●パック入りの[缶詰の]たけのこ水煮 a water-packed [canned] bamboo shoot (boiled plain).
みずぬき 水抜き ●浴槽の水抜きをする drain a bathtub. ●水抜き穴 a drain hole.
みずのあわ 水の泡 ❶〚水が作る泡〛(⇨泡) ❷〚むだなこと〛 ▶これまでの努力がすべて水の泡になった All my efforts came to nothing [were wasted, were in vain,《話》went down the drain].
みずのみびゃくしょう 水飲み百姓 (貧しい農民) a poor peasant.
みずば 水場 a place for drinking water; (野生動物の) a water(ing) hole.
みずはけ 水はけ drainage /dréinidʒ/. ▶この土地は水はけがいい[悪い] This soil has good [bad] drainage.
みずばしょう 水芭蕉 〖植物〗a giant skunk cabbage.
みずばしら 水柱 ●水柱を立てる send up a column of water.
みずばら 水腹 ❶〚水などを飲みすぎた時の腹具合》 ●お茶を飲みすぎて水腹になった My stomach is distended from drinking too much tea. ❷〚水を飲んで空腹をしのぐこと〛 ▶若い頃は1日水腹で過ごすこともあった Sometimes I had to live only on water for a whole day when I was young.
みずひき 水引 ●水引をかける tie a gift with red and white [black and white] paper strings.
みずびたし 水浸し ― 水浸しになる 動 be flooded 《with, by》; be submerged 《by》. ●完全に水中に没することで、冠水などに用いる) ●水道管が破裂して地下室が水浸しになった The water pipe burst [《米》bursted] and the basement was flooded (with water).
みずぶき 水拭き ― 水拭きする 動 wipe 《the floor》with a damp cloth.
みずぶくれ 水膨れ a blister. ●水ぶくれができた[つぶれた] A blister formed [burst,《米》bursted].
みずぶとり 水太り ― 形 flabby 《thighs, bottoms》. ― 水太りする 動 get* fat and flabby.
みずぶね 水船 (難破して浸水した船) a waterlogged wreck; (飲料水を運ぶ船) a water boat; (水槽の) a water tank.
ミスプリント a misprint; a printing [a typographical, a printer's] error; a typo. ▶この本にはミスプリントが多い This book is full of misprints.
みずべ 水辺 the waterside, the water's edge. ●水辺を散歩する take a walk along the waterside.
みずほ 瑞穂 fresh ears of rice.
瑞穂の国 〖「日本」の美称〗Japan.
みずぼうそう 水疱瘡 〖医学〗chicken pox. ▶水ぼうそうは子供がよくかかる病気の一つだ Chicken pox is a kind of disease common among children.
＊みすぼらしい (着古した、ぼろを着た) shabby; (粗末な)《やや書》miserable. ●みすぼらしい服 shabby clothes. ●みすぼらしいかっこうをした老人 a shabby [shabbily] dressed] old person. ●みすぼらしい小さな家 a shabby little house.

> 翻訳のこころ なぜだかそのころ私はみすぼらしくて美しいものに強くひきつけられたのを覚えている（梶井基次郎『檸檬』）I remember that in those days I would [used to] be strongly attracted by something beautiful but [×and] modest [humble]. (❶ (1)「みすぼらしくて美しい」は意味的には相反する語なので, but でつなぐ. (2) miserable, shabby, rugged (みすぼらしい)は,「美しさ」の意を全く含まない語なので, ここでは不適切)

みずまき 水撒き watering. ●水まきをする water; sprinkle water 《on》.
みずまくら 水枕 a water pillow.
みずまし 水増し 名 (帳簿の) padding. ●水増し入学させる admit more students than the previously stated number.
― 水増しする 動 (経費などを) pad.
みすます 見澄ます observe; watch carefully.
ミスマッチ 〚不釣り合い〛 a mismatch 《between》. ▶ダークスーツにスニーカーではどう見てもミスマッチだ A dark suit and sneakers are a total mismatch./ A dark suit does not at all go with sneakers.
みずまわり 水回り (説明的に) a living area where a great deal of water is consumed in a house or building, such as a kitchen, a bathroom, etc.
みすみす 〚すぐ目の前で〛before one's very eyes; 〚不必要に〛needlessly; 〚どうしようもなく〛helplessly. ▶みすみす泥棒に逃げられた The thief escaped before my very eyes.
みずみずしい 〚新鮮な〛fresh; 〚生き生きして若々しい〛fresh and youthful. ●みずみずしい肌 fresh and youthful skin.
みずむし 水虫 〖医学〗《get》athlete's foot. (❶ 無冠詞)
みずもの 水物 ▶勝負は水物だ (賭けみたいなものだ) Every game is a gamble./ (偶然に支配される) Every game is ruled by chance.
みずもれ 水漏れ a leak [《やや書》(a) leakage] of water. ●このタンクでは水漏れがあるようだ It seems (that) water is leaking out of this tank.
みずや 水屋 ●(神社・寺院の)(説明的に) a washstand for visitors at a shrine or temple; (茶室の) a small kitchen in a tea-ceremony room. ❷〚食器入れの戸棚〛a cupboard /kʌ́bərd/.
みずようかん 水羊羹 soft sweet bean jelly.
みする 魅する fascinate; charm. (⇨魅惑)
みずわり 水割り (a glass of) whiskey and /ən/ water. ●水割りにする dilute [mix]《brandy》with water.

:みせ 店

WORD CHOICE 店
store 身近な商品などを売る小規模な小売店舗。およそ2:1の割合で《主に米》。●小さな雑貨店 a small grocery store.
〚形 名＋store〛department/grocery/general/furniture

みせいねん

shop 身近な商品などを売る小規模な小売店舗. およそ2:1の割合で《主に英》. ただし, 商品の種類を明示して... shop と言う場合は《米》でも用いる. ● 地元のコーヒー店 a local coffee *shop*.
〖形 图+shop〗 coffee/antique/copy/dress/retail

▸頻度チャート◂
store
shop
20 40 60 80 100(%)

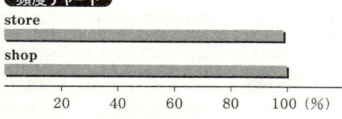

《主に米》a store,《主に英》a shop.
① 【店〜】 ● 店先で in front of a *store*.
② 【店は〔が〕】 ▶あの店はとても安い[高い] That *store* is very cheap [expensive, ×high]. ▶あの店は新鮮な野菜を売っています They sell fresh vegetables at that *store*./That *store* sells fresh vegetables. (❗前の方が普通) ▶あの店は日曜日は休みですか[開いていますか] Is that *store* closed [open] on Sundays? ▶この店は何時に開きますか[閉まりますか] What time is this *store* opened [closed]?
会話「この辺には野菜や果物を買ういいお店はあるかしら」「もちろんあるよ. すぐ近くにぼくがいつも行くいい店があるんだ」"I wonder if you have good *stores* for fruit and vegetables." "Sure we do. There's a nice *place* I always go to just around the corner." (❗place は口語で「店」「レストラン」のいずれにも用いられる)
③ 【店を】 ● 店を始める start a business;《話》set up shop. ● 店をのぞく(=立ち寄る) drop into a *store*. ● 店を手伝う help out in a *store*. ▶彼女は銀座に店を出している She has [《経営している》runs, keeps] a *store* on Ginza. ▶彼は午前 9 時に店を開ける He opens (⇔closes) his *store* at 9 in the morning. (❗at 9 a.m. とするより普通)
④ 【店に[で]】 ● 店に入る go into [enter] a *store*. ● 店に来る come to a *store*. ▶彼はその店でかばんを買った He bought a bag at that *store*. ▶あの店で靴下を売っているかしら I wonder if they sell socks at that *store*. (❗they を主語に用いていることに注意)

|翻訳のこころ| 小十郎が山のように毛皮をしょってその家の敷居を一足またぐと, 店では また 来たかというようす笑っているのだった (宮沢賢治『なめとこ山の熊』) Whenever Kojuro stepped into the store with a big [a huge] bundle of bear skins on his back, the store people [employees] would put on a sneering smile, as if to say, "He's back again." (❗(1) a sneering smile は「嘲(*あざけ*)るような笑い」の意. (2)「また来たか」は be back again (また戻ってきたか)と表す)

● 店を畳む close (down) a store; close up《米》[shut up《英》] shop.

みせいねん 未成年 ▬▬ 未成年の 形 a minor (▶ 18 歳[《米》の一部の州では 21 歳] 未満の者);《未成年期》《法律》one's minority. ● 未成年の minor, underage. ▶彼はまだ未成年です He is still a *minor* [in his *minority*]./(成年に達していない) He is still *underage*./He is not yet *of age*. ▶ 未成年者の飲酒は禁じられている *Minors* are forbidden to drink alcohol. ▶ 未成年者お断り《掲示》No minors./Adults only.

みせいり 未整理 ▬▬ 未整理の 形 unarranged; unclassified; unfiled; unsorted. ▶ここの本は未整理だ I *have not arranged* [*classified*, *sorted*] these books yet. ▶手紙を未整理のまま引き出しに入れてお

みせびらかす

いた I kept my letters *unfiled* in a drawer.

みせかけ 見せ掛け (a) pretense;《装い》(a) show;《偽り》a sham. ▶彼の愛情はただの見せかけだった His love was just a *pretense* [a *show*, a *sham*,《米話》a *put-on*]. ▶誰が 1 位になるかがはじめから分かっていたのならあの審査は見せかけ(=茶番劇)だったのだ If it was a foregone conclusion who would win the prize, the judging part was just a *charade* /ʃəréid/.
▬▬ 見せ掛けの 形 《装った》pretended;《偽りの》sham;《米話》put-on. ▶彼の見せかけの友情にだまされてはいけない Don't be taken in by his *pretended* [*sham*] friendliness.

みせかける 見せ掛ける 〖《偽って》ふりをする〗 pretend《*to do*; *that* 節》;《巧みに装う》《書》feign;《これ見よがしに》make* a show [a pretense] 《*of*》. (⇨振り, 装う) ● 勉強しているように見せかける *pretend to* be studying; *pretend that* one is studying; *make a pretense* [*a show*] *of* studying. ● 実業家のように見せかける *pose as* a business executive 〖《男の》a businessman〗. ● 指輪を本物のダイヤのように見せかけて《偽り》売りつける *pass off* a ring《on him》as real diamond. ▶彼は金持ちではない. そう見せかけているだけ He's not a rich man; he's just *pretending* [*feigning*, *putting it on*,《話》*putting on an act*]. (❗put on は「装う」, put on an act は「お芝居をする」)

みせがね 見せ金 show money.
みせがまえ 店構え the appearance of a store.
みせじまい 店仕舞い ▬▬ 店仕舞いする 動 《閉店する》close, shut*;《一時的に営業を停止する》close up one's store;《廃業する》close [shut] one's store down, go* out of business.
● 店仕舞いセール a clearance [《米》a closing-out] sale.

みせしめ 見せしめ 《警告》a warning,《戒め》an example. ● 彼を見せしめにする make an *example* of him. ● 見せしめのために彼を罰する punish him as a *warning* to other people.

ミセス 〖既婚婦人の姓・姓名につける敬称〗 Mrs. /mísiz/ (⇨〜さん);〖既婚女性〗 a married woman (⓮ women). ● ヤングミセス a young *married woman*. (❗×a young Mrs. とはいわない)

みせつける 見せつける make* a demonstration [display,《やや軽・軽蔑的》parade]《*of*》;《やや軽・軽蔑的》show*... off, parade. ● 仲のよいところを見せつける *make a demonstration of* love. ▶テニスのプロの力量はまざまざと見せつけられた(=いやというほど思い知った) I *fully realized* that professional tennis players are too great to be equaled.

みせどころ 見せ所 (⇨見せ場) ▶ここは君の腕の見せ所だ This is where you can show your skill./Now is the time to show your skill./This is a good chance for you to show your skill.

みぜに 身銭 ● 身銭を切る ▶ 身銭(=自腹)を切って入場券を買う get [buy] an admission ticket *out of one's own pocket*.

みせば 見せ場 《ショーなどの》a highlight;《物語の通例最後の》a climax;《最もよかったところ》a high point [《話》spot]. ▶この劇の見せ場は the *highlight* [*high point*] of this play. ● 見せ場を作る create a *high point*; set up a *climax*.

みせばん 店番 《店員》《米》a salesclerk,《英》a shop assistant. ● 店番をする watch [《米・英古》tend, 《古》mind] a store.

みせびらかす 見せびらかす show*... off. ▶ 友達に車を見せびらかす《得意になって》*show off* one's car *to* one's friend;《しばしば軽蔑的・やや話》*parade*

みせびらき 店開き ―― 店開きする 動 (新しく開店する) open a new store. ▶駅の近くに新しい百貨店が店開きした A new department store *opened* near the station.

みせもの 見世物 a show. ▶私は見世物にされた I *was* shamefully *exposed to* public view.
● 見世物小屋 a shów tènt.

みせや 店屋 (主に米) a store, (主に英) a shop. (⇨店)

みせられる 魅せられる ▶私は美しい聖堂に魅せられた I *was charmed* [*fascinated*] *by* the beautiful cathedral. (⇨魅惑)

:みせる 見せる ❶ [人に見えるようにする] show*. ● 他の者にいい手本を見せる *set* the other people [others] *a good example*; *set* a good example *to* the other people. ▶それをご両親に見せましたか Did you *show* it *to* your parents? (!×*show* your parents it の語順は不可) ▶あなたに見せたいものがあります Let me [I want to] *show* you something. ▶指導員がどうすべるか実際にやって見せてくれた The instructor *showed* us [*demonstrated*] how to ski. ▶工場をお見せ(=ご案内)しましょう Let me *show* you *around* our factory. ▶インフルエンザは依然衰える気配を見せていない The flu is still *showing* no signs of abating.
会話 (店)「あの指輪を見せてください」「はいどうぞ」 "Could you *show* me [Could I see] that ring?" "Here you are." (!くだけた言い方では Let me *have a look at* that ring, please. なども)
会話 「新車を買ったんだよ」「すごい！ 見せてよ」 "I've bought a new car." "Great! Let me *see* it."
会話 「検問にひっかかったんだ」「で、どうなったの？」「運転免許証を見せるように言われたんだ」 "I was stopped by the police at a checkpoint." "What did they do?" "They *asked for* my driver's license." (! ask me to show より ask for の方が普通)
❷ [姿を現す] appear, 《話》; show* up. (!《話》) turn up しばしば「思いがけず姿を見せる」の意) ● 会合に姿を見せる *appear* [*show* up] *at* a meeting.
❸ [見せかける] pretend (*to* do; that 節). ● こわくないふりをして見せる *pretend* not *to* be afraid; *pretend that* one is not afraid. ▶若く見せるためにはでな服を着る wear showy clothes to *make* oneself *look* young. (⇨見せ掛ける)
❹ [自信・決意の表示] ▶やつを必ず打ちのめしてみせる I *shall* beat him up. (!この shall は強い決意を表し, /ʃæl/ と強く読む) ▶必ず1週間で終えてみせます I'll definitely finish it in a week's time, *I promise (you)*.

みせる 診せる (⇨診る) ● 彼を医者に診せる(=連れて行く) *take* him *to* the doctor. ▶君は足を医者に診せた方がいいかもしれません Maybe you should *see* the doctor *about* your leg.

みぜん 未然 ● 未然に防ぐ ▶彼のたくらみを未然に防ぐ *nip* his plot *in the bud* (!慣用表現); (最初に挫折(_ざ)させる) *thwart* his plot *at the very beginning*. ▶彼の機敏な行動が事故を未然に防げた His quick action *prevented* an accident.

みそ 味噌 ❶ [調味料] *miso*, soybean paste. ● 味噌漬けにした大根 a radish preserved in *miso*. ● 減塩味噌 reduced-salt *miso*. ● 味噌汁 (⇨味噌汁)
❷ [特色] ▶そこが味噌だ (長所) That's the *good thing about* it./(コツ) That's the *trick about* it./(重要な点, 問題点) That's the *point* (*I want to make*).

● 味噌もくそもいっしょにする mix up good things with bad ones.
● 味噌をつける (へまをやる)《話》 make a mess of it, 《俗》 blow it; (面目を失う) lose face.

みぞ 溝 ❶ [排水路] a ditch, (深い) a trench; (排水溝) a drain, (道路沿いの) a gutter. ● 溝を掘る dig a *ditch*; ditch 《the ground》.
❷ [溝やレコード盤などの] a groove.
❸ [気持ちの] a gap; (大きな) a gulf (働 ~s). ▶彼らの間には溝がある There is a *gap* of feeling between them. ▶彼との溝がだんだん広がってゆくのを感じていた I was sensing a real *gap* [*distance*] growing between him and me. ▶外交と世論との溝はいつの時代にもある *Gaps* between diplomacy and public opinion have existed in all ages [generations]. (!in all ages は「昔からずっと」, in all generations は「あらゆる世代に」の意)

みぞう 未曾有 ―― 未曾有の 形 unprecedented; unheard-of; (これまでの記録を破る) record-breaking.

みぞおち 鳩尾 the pit of the stomach; 《話》 the solar plexus.

みそか 晦日 the last day of the [×a] month; (大晦日) 《on》 New Year's Eve. (⇨大晦日)

みそぎ 禊 ● みそぎをする 《書》 perform one's ablutions (!*ablutions* は「宗教的儀式で水で身を清めること」); purify oneself with water.

みそくそ 味噌糞 (⇨糞味噌)

みそこなう 見損なう ▶私はその映画を見損なった I *missed* (*seeing*) [*failed to see*] that film. ▶あの男を見損なったよ I *misjudged* him. (!「判断を誤る」の意で, 文脈しだいで「見直す」の意にもなるので注意)/(失望した) I *am disappointed in* him.

みそさざい [鳥] a wren.

みそじ 三十路 (30歳) the age of thirty; (30代) 《in》 one's thirties.

みそしき 未組織 ―― 未組織の 形 unorganized.

みそしる 味噌汁 《a bowl of》 *miso* soup. ● あさり[豆腐とわかめ]の味噌汁 *miso* soup with asari clams [tofu and seaweed] in it.

みそっかす 味噌っ滓 (味噌をこした後のかす) *miso* lees; (仲間はずれにされた子) a child who is excluded.

みそっぱ 味噌っ歯 a decayed (milk [baby]) tooth (働 teeth).

みそはぎ 禊萩 [植物] a purple loosestrife.

みそめる 見初める (一目ぼれする) fall* in love 《with a girl》 at first sight. ▶彼がパーティーで見初めた女の子 the girl *he fell in love with* at a party.

みそら 身空 ▶彼女は若い身空で未亡人になって大変苦労した She lost her husband when *she was young* and had a very hard time.

みぞれ 霙 sleet. ● みぞれの sleety. ▶外はみぞれが降っている It's *sleeting* outside. ▶雨がみぞれに変わった The rain turned to *sleet*.

みそれる 見それる (⇨御見知)

-みたいだ (見える) look; (思える) seem; (外見から…思える) appear; (聞いたところから…思える) sound. (!~らしい) ▶あの岩は人の顔みたいだ That rock *looks like* a human face. ▶彼は病気みたいだ He *looks* sick./He *seems* [*appears*] (*to be*) sick./*It seems* [*appears*, ×*looks*] *that* he is sick. ▶君はまるで酔っ払ったみたいだ You *look as if* you were [《話》 are] drunk. (⇨まるで) ▶まるで彼の話はうそみたいだ *It sounds as if* his story is not true.

-みたいな (⇨-よう❸)

みたけ 身丈 (身長) height (⇨身長); (着物の寸法) the length of a *kimono*.

みだし 見出し [新聞などの] a headline; (全段抜きの大

みだしなみ 身嗜み 〖外見〗(an) appearance. ▶彼女はいつも身だしなみがきちんとしている She is always careful about her (*personal*) *appearance* [about *the way she dresses*]. ▶後の方は口語的)/She always *keeps* herself *neat* [*tidy*]./She *is* always *neatly* [*tidily*] *dressed*.

***みたす** 満たす ❶〖満足させる〗satisfy; (要求・必要などに応える) meet*; (不足を補う) supply. ▶リンゴで空腹を満たす *satisfy* one's hunger *with* an apple. ▶この本は我々の好奇心を満たした The book *satisfied* our curiosity. ▶彼の報告は私の出した条件を満たしていない His report doesn't *meet* my requirements. (❗meetは否定文・疑問文・条件文で用いることが多い)

> **翻訳のこころ** しかしどうしたことだろう, 私の心を満たしていた幸福な感情はだんだん逃げていった (梶井基次郎『檸檬』) I wonder what has happened, because the happy feeling that filled my heart has gradually faded [gone] away [×escaped]. (❗(1)「(心を)満たす」は fill one's heart と表す. (2)「(感情が)逃げていく」は fade [go] away (消え去っていく)と表す. ここでは escape (逃げる)は不適切)

DISCOURSE
以下の条件を満たす限り賛成だ I agree, **provided** that the following conditions are *met*. (❗ provided ... (ただし...)は条件付き賛成を表すディスコースマーカー)

❷〖いっぱいにする〗fill 《a glass *with* water》.

***みだす** 乱す 〖静かな状態を〗disturb; 〖整とんされたものを〗《書》disarrange; 〖混乱させる〗throw*... into confusion [*disorder*]; 〖交通・通信などを〗disrupt; 〖髪などを〗dishevel; 〖心を〗(混乱させる) confuse; (ろうばいさせる) upset*. ▶(乱れる) • 世界の平和を乱す *disturb* world peace. ▶髪を乱して走る run *with* one's hair *disheveled*. ▶風紀を乱す(= 堕落させる) *corrupt* public morals. ▶その攻撃は敵の秩序を乱した The attack *threw* [*put*] the enemy *into disorder* [*confusion*]. ▶列を乱すな(=列から出るな) Don't *get* [*fall*] *out of* line.

みたて 見立て ❶〖診断〗(a) diagnosis /dàiəɡnóusis/; (❀ diagnoses). ▶見立ての確かな医師 a physician skilled in *diagnosis*. ▶見立て違いを(=誤診する) make a wrong *diagnosis*. ▶その医師の見立てでは肝臓障害だ The doctor's *diagnosis* is [The doctor *diagnosed*] liver trouble.

❷〖選択〗(a) choice; (a) selection. ▶見立てがうまい make a good *choice* [*selection*] 《*of*》. ▶このネクタイはどなたのお見立てですか Who *chose* this tie for you?

みたてる 見立てる 〖選ぶ〗choose* [select] 《a tie》 《*for* him》; 〖診断する〗diagnose /dàiəɡnóus/ 《his illness》《*as* flu, *as* serious》.

みたない 満たない ▶当時のことを信じていた人は半数に満たなかった Fewer than half of them believed it at that time.

みたま 御霊 the spirit of a dead person. (⇨霊)

みため 見た目 ▶彼は見た目ほど悪い子ではない He is not such a bad child [〖書〗so bad a child] *as* he *looks*. ▶その車は見た目は大したことないが, 私には十分役立っている The car is not much *to look at*, but it is useful to me. ▶この服は見た目はよくないが機能的である This dress isn't very nice-*looking* [*good-looking*], but it's functional. (❗「見た目によい服」は a nice-*looking* dress)

みだら 淫ら ── 淫らな 形 lewd; (下品な) indecent; (わいせつな) obscene; (性的にふしだらな) promiscuous. ▶みだらな夢を見る have a *lewd* dream. ▶みだらな生活をする lead a *promiscuous* life. ▶その男は少女にみだらな行為をしたとして逮捕された The man got arrested for committing an *obscene* act on the girl.

みたらしだんご 御手洗団子 a *mitarashidango*; (説明的に) small rice-flour dumplings on a bamboo stick, which are dipped in soy-and-sugar syrup.

みだりに 濫りに 〖理由なしに〗for no reason, without (good) reason; 〖許可なしに〗without permission [〖(許)〗leave]; 〖軽々しく〗in vain. ▶みだりに動物の生命を奪うな Don't take the life of any animal *without reason*. ▶みだりに学校の構内に入るな Don't enter the school grounds *without permission*. ▶みだりに神の名を口にするな Don't take the Lord's name *in vain*.

みだれ 乱れ (混乱) (a) confusion; (秩序などの) disorder. ▶心の乱れを隠す hide one's *confusion*. ▶社会の乱れ social *disorder* [(不安) *unrest*]. ▶列車ダイヤの乱れ *irregularities* in the train timetable.

みだれかご 乱れ籠 a clóthes bàsket; 《米》 a hamper.

みだれがみ 乱れ髪 untidy [disheveled /diʃévld/] hair; 〖書〗hair in disarray.

みだれがみ 『みだれ髪』 *Tangled Hair*. (参考 与謝野晶子の歌集)

みだれとぶ 乱れ飛ぶ ▶栃木の優勝が決まった瞬間座布団が乱れ飛んだ(=無数の座布団が土俵めがけて投げ込まれた) The moment Tochiazuma beat his opponent and won the championship, a countless number of seat cushions *were hurled at* the ring from everywhere. ▶首相が辞任を決定したといううわさが乱れ飛んでいる There are rumors *flying about* [*around*] that the Prime Minister has decided to resign.

***みだれる** 乱れる ❶〖場所・物などが〗(順序・秩序などが混乱している) be in disorder; (混乱する) fall* [be thrown] into disorder; (混沌(泟)としている) be in chaos; (整とんされたものが乱れる) 《書》 be disarranged; (交通・通信などが) be disrupted. ▶乱れた生活をする lead a *disorderly* [堕落した] *corrupt*] life. ▶部屋の中は乱れていた(=散らかっていた) The room *was in disorder* [*in a mess*]. (❗後の方が口語的) ▶その事故で交通が乱れた The accident *disrupted* traffic. ▶彼の服装はいつも乱れている(=だらしがない) He is always *untidily* [*sloppily*] dressed. ▶彼女の髪は乱れていた Her hair was *untidy* [*disheveled* /diʃévld/].

❷〖心・風紀などが〗(気が動転する) be upset; (道徳などが腐敗する) be corrupted. ▶彼はその悲報を聞いて心が乱れた The news *upset* him [心を引き裂いた] has *torn* his heart]. ▶このごろ日本語が少し乱れている The Japanese language today *is* somewhat *corrupted*./We are rather careless in speaking Japanese these days. ▶彼はお酒が強くて, いくら飲んでも乱れた様子を見せたことがない He holds his liquor well. He never *loses* his *composure*, no matter how much he drinks. (❗hold one's liquor well (酒に強い)はくだけた言い方)

DISCOURSE
上記の理由から，日本語は乱れているのではなく単に変化していると私は思う **For these reasons**, I believe the Japanese language is not *being corrupted*, but merely changing. (❗for this reason [these reasons]、(上記の理由から)は結論に用いるディスコースマーカー)

みち 道

WORD CHOICE 道, 道路
street 主に舗装・整備された都心の道路. Baker Street のように地名の一部として用いられることも多い. ●道を渡る cross the *street*.
road 主に舗装・整備された道路. 時に比喩的に用いて，目標までの到達過程を含意する. ●交通量の多い道 busy *road*.
path 人や動物が通る小道. ●道に沿って歩く walk along the *path*.

頻度チャート
street				
road				
path				
20	40	60	80	100 (%)

❶ [道路] a road; (幹線道路)《主に米》a highway (❗《英》では堅い語); (街路) a street, an avenue, a boulevard, a thoroughfare; (道筋) the way, a route; (小道) a lane, a path, a pass; (路地) an alley; (通路) a passage.
①[道は] ●神戸-大阪間の道は混んでいた The *road* [*highway*] from Kobe to Osaka was crowded. ▶町の中の道は舗装が行き届いている The *streets* of the town are well paved. ▶道は牧草地を抜けて丘の頂上まで続いていた The *path* ran [led] through the meadow up to the hilltop. (❗× ... was running [leading].... は不可) ▶夜もこの時間になればあの道はすいているだろう There won't be much traffic *on* [×in] that *road* at this time of night. (❗(1) traffic は「交通量」の意. (2) このように路上での移動が問題になっている文脈では in は用いない) ▶すべての道はローマに通ず〈ことわざ〉All *roads* lead to Rome. (❗「一つのことをするにもいろいろな方法がある」の意)
②[道に[で]] ●道に迷う lose one's *way*; get lost. ▶道で立ち話をするな Don't stand chattering together *on*《米》[*in*《主に英》] the *street*.
③[道を] ●道を間違えている [間違える] be on [take] the wrong *way*. ●来た道を戻る go back the *way* one came. ●森に道をつける make [(切り開く) cut out] a *road* through a forest. ▶私たちは最も近い道を通って駅へ行った We took the shortest *way* to the station. ▶この道を行けば元町通りに出られますか Does this *road* [*street*] lead (us) to Motomachi?/Does this *road* [*street*] take us to Motomachi?/Is this the right *way* to Motomachi? ▶私たちは景色の美しい海岸沿いの道を進んだ We took the scenic coastal *route*. ▶ニューヨークを見物していたときには人に道をたずねられて困った When I went sightseeing in New York, I was often (rather) surprised by being asked for *directions*. (⇨道順)
〖会話〗「すみませんが，郵便局への道を教えていただけませんか」「あいにくよく知らないのです」「いやどうも」"Excuse me. Could you tell [×teach] me the *way* to the post office, please?(❗以下のたずね方より丁寧で適切)/Which *way* is the post office, please?/How do I get to the post office?" "Sorry, I'm not really sure." "Well, thanks anyway."
❷[途中] ●私たちは学校へ行く[から帰る]道で彼に出会った We met him on our *way* to [(back) *from*] school. (⇨途中) ▶彼らは破滅への道をたどっていた They were *on* the *way* [*road*] to ruin.
❸[行く手, 通り道] the [one's] way. ●道をあけるstep [move] aside; make way 《for him》; (障害物を除いて) clear the *way*. ●後進に道を譲る make *way* for a younger generation. ●パトカーに道を譲る make *way* for the police car; give *way* [《米》*yield*] *to* the police car. ▶道をふさぐな Don't stand [be] in my *way*./(どいてくれ) Get out of my *way*./(通してくれ) Let me through.
❹[距離] (a) distance. ●50 キロの道を行く cover [go, walk] (a *distance* of) 50 kilometers [31 miles]. 〖事柄〗 米英ではマイルの方が適切 ●道を急ぐ(=足を速める) quicken one's stride [pace]. ▶秋田まで[この先]まだ道は遠い It's still a long *way* to Akita [*to* go, ahead (of me)]. (❗ a long *way* の代わりに ×far は不可 (⇨遠い))
❺[方法, 手段, 進路] (方法) a way; (手段) a means(❗単・複同形); (進路) a course. ●生活の道 a *means* of living. ●我が道を行く go [take] one's (own) *way*. ●道を誤る (職業選択を) make the wrong choice of one's job; (判断を) make the wrong decision. ●栄光への道を歩む follow the *path* to glory. ▶取るべき道は他になかった I had [There was] no other *way* [*choice*] (about it). ▶それが取るべき正しい道だ That's the proper *course* to take.
❻[研究・活動などの] (分野) a field; (事柄) a subject. (⇨専門, 方面, 領域) ●彼はその道の達人だ He is an expert [an authority] on that *subject* [in that *field*]. ●彼は医師の道を選んだ He has chosen his career as a doctor./(医学で身を立てていくと決めた) He has decided to make his career in medicine.
❼[道徳] a moral principle, morals. ●人の道を説く teach 《him》 *the moral principles*. ●人の道を踏みはずす stray [go astray] from *the moral principles*.
──**が開ける** find a way.

みち 未知 ●未知の(=見知らぬ)土地 a *strange* land. ●未知の世界に踏み込む venture into the *unknown* world.

みちあんない 道案内 图 〖事〗 guidance; (車の同乗者などによる) navigation; 〖人〗 a guide; a navigator.
──**道案内する** 動 ▶駅まで道案内する show 《him》 *the way* to the station.

みちいと 道糸 a fishing line; a fishline.

みぢか 身近 ──**身近な** 形 (近い) close; (なじみの) familiar; (一般的な) common. ●彼の身近な人々 people *close* to him. ▶テレビのお陰でイギリスも身近なものになった Television has pulled England *closer* to us. ▶月は別格として火星は地球の住人には最も身近な星である Except for the moon [Putting the moon aside], Mars is the most *familiar* planet for inhabitants of Earth [a planet most *familiar* to the inhabitants of the earth].
──**身近に** 副 ●...を身近に置く keep... *close at hand* [at one's elbow]. ●...を身近に感じる feel... *close* [*familiar*] to one.

みちがえる 見違える (⇨間違える❷) ▶彼女は見違えるほど変わった She has changed so much (that) I *can hardly recognize* her.

みちかけ 満ち欠け ── **満ち欠けする** 動 (月が) wax and wane.

みちくさ 道草 ●道草を食う hang around [《やや書》 loiter] on the way. ▶道草しないで学校からまっすぐ家に帰りなさい Come straight home from school (and don't *hang around*).

みちしお 満ち潮 (a) flood tide. (❗「満(ち)ている潮」は (a) high tide) (⇨満ち潮, 上げ潮)

みちじゅん 道順 the way, a route; (道順の説明) directions. (⇨道❶) ●道順をたずねる ask ⟨him⟩ for *directions*.
会話 「はい, これが私の住所です」「1 丁目の 1 の 14 ね, 分かった」「道順はいらない？」「いや, いいえ. 分かると思うよ」"Here's my address." "OK, it's 1-14, 1-chome. (I) got it." "Do you need *direction*?" "No, thanks. I think I can find it."

みちしるべ 道しるべ [道標] a signpost, 《古》 a guidepost.

みちすう 未知数 〖数学〗 an unknown quantity. (❗比喩的にも用いられる) ▶彼は教師としてはまだ未知数だ He is still an *unknown quantity* as a teacher./ His ability as a teacher is still *unknown*. (❗まったく (completely), どちらかと言うと (relatively) などで unknown を修飾することができる)

みちすがら 道すがら on the [one's] way 《to》; (途中ずっと) all the way; (行きながら) as one goes [walks].

みちすじ 道筋 (ある所から別の所までの道) a route; (経路) a course. ●町に行くいつもの道筋 the usual *route* to the town.

みちたりる 満ち足りる (満足する) be satisfied 《with》. ●満ち足りた生活 a *satisfied* life. ●満ち足りた気持ち a *contented* feeling.

みちづれ 道連れ a fellow traveler, 《書》 a traveling companion. ●道連れになる happen to meet and *travel together*.

みちならぬ 道ならぬ immoral; illicit. ●道ならぬ恋 an *illicit* love affair.

みちのり 道のり (距離) a distance; (旅程) a journey; (車での) a ride; (歩いての) a walk. (⇨道❹) ●5 マイルの道のりは長かった It took a long time to put it to practical use. ▶実用化に至る道のりは長かった It took a long time to put it to practical use.
会話 「ここから京都までの道のりはどれくらいですか」「車で[歩いて] 20 分(の道のり)です」"*How far* is it from here to Kyoto [to Kyoto from here]?/What is the *distance* from here to Kyoto [between here and Kyoto]?" "It's 20 minutes' [a 20-minute] *ride* [*walk*]."

みちばた 道端 the roadside. ●道端に by [at, on] the *roadside*. ●道端の花 *roadside* flowers; flowers at the *side of the road*.

みちはば 道幅 the width of a road [a street]. ●道幅を広げる widen the road. ▶車が 2 台すれ違うには道幅が広くない The road is not *wide* enough [is too narrow] for two cars to pass each other.

みちひ 満ち干 the ebb and flow. (⇨潮)

みちびき 導き guidance. (⇨指導) ●導きのもとで under the *guidance* 《of》.

***みちびく 導く** ❶ [案内する] (同行する) guide; (先に立って) lead*; (道順を示す) show*, 《やや書》 conduct. ●彼らを広間へ導く show [*guide*, *lead*] them into the hall.
❷ [指導する] guide; (教える) teach*. ●生徒たちを導く *teach* the students. ●若者を正しい道に導く *guide* [*lead*] the young people to the right path. ●一国を導いて困難を切り抜けさせる *guide* a country through its difficulties.
❸ [ある結果に到らせる] lead*. ●そのチームを優勝へと導く *lead* the team *to* victory. ▶とばくが彼を破滅へ導いた Gambling *led* [*brought*] him *to* ruin.
❹ [その他の表現] 義務感に導かれる be *guided* by one's sense of duty.

みちみち 道々 (⇨道中)

みちゃく 未着 ●小包は未着だ The parcel *has not (yet) arrived*. ▶その請求書は未着です The bill *has not (yet) been delivered*.

みちゆき 道行き (歌舞伎などで) the scene of lovers' trip; (衣服) a kind of women's coat for a *kimono*.

***みちる 満ちる** ❶ [いっぱいになる] fill 《with》, become* full 《of》; (いっぱいである) be full 《of》, be filled 《with》. ●半数に満たない (⇨満たない) ●水が水槽に満ちた Water *filled* the tub. (❗×Water *filled in* the tub. としない)/The tub *filled with* water. ▶彼の心は喜びに満ちた His heart *filled* [*flowed*] *with* joy./(満たされた) He *was filled with* joy./Joy *filled* his heart. (❗二つ目の言い方が最も普通) ▶彼は自信に満ちている He *is full of* [*is filled with*] confidence. (⇨溢(あふ)れる)
❷ [月が] (しだいに満ちる) wax; (満月である) be (at the) full; [潮が] (しだいに満ちる) flow; (満潮である) be in [high]. ▶潮が満ちて来た The tide *is flowing* [*coming in*].

みつ 密 ●親子の関係を密に(=密接に)する develop *close* relations between parent and child. (❗無記載に注意) ●密に詰める pack 《things》 *close*. ▶この市は人口が密だ This city *is densely* [*thickly*] *populated*.

みつ 蜜 (蜂(はち)蜜) honey; (花蜜) nectar; (糖蜜) 《米》 molasses (❗単数扱い), 《英》 treacle. (⇨蜜蜂) ▶ハチが蜜を吸っている Bees are sucking *nectar*.

みつあみ 三つ編み ●髪を三つ編みにする braid (❗主に米) [plait (❗主に英)] one's hair. ●髪を三つ編みにしている少女 a girl with [wearing] her hair *in braids* [*plaits*].

みつうん 密雲 (厚く重なった雲) dense [heavy, thick] clouds.

みつおり 三つ折り ── 三つ折りの 形 threefold. ●手紙を三つ折りにする *fold* a letter *in three*.

みっか 三日 ●3 日間 for *three days*. ●3 月 3 日に on March 3(rd), (⇨日付) ●3 日ごとに (⇨二日 [2 日おきに]) ▶彼は三日坊主(=何事にもがんばり続けることのできない人)だ He can't stick to anything (for very long).
●三日にあげず ▶彼は三日にあげず(=ほとんど毎日)やってくる He comes over *almost every day* [×everyday].
●三日天下 (短命の支配) a short-lived reign.
●三日ばしか three-day measles. (⇨風疹(ふうしん))

みつが 密画 a minutely executed drawing.

みっかい 密会 名 a secret meeting.
── **密会する** 動 ●彼らと密会する *meet* them *secretly*.

みつがさね 三つ重ね ●三つ重ねのサンドイッチ a triple-decker sandwich.

***みつかる 見付かる** find*. (⇨見付ける) ▶私の財布はまだ見つからない (まだ見つけていない) I *haven't found* [×found out] my wallet yet./(見つけられていない) My wallet *hasn't been found* [(出てこない) *hasn't turned up*]./(所在不明だ) My wallet *is still missing*. ▶気に入ったカーペットを見つからない I can't *find* [×find out] a carpet I ＼like. ▶彼は金を盗んでいるところを見つかった(=現場を押さえられた) He *was caught* (*in the act of*) stealing the money. ▶仕

みつぎ 事が見つかった I've found [got] a job. ▶そんなものおよそ見つかるわけがない = 千し草の山の中の針を探すようなものである It's like looking for a needle in a haystack.

みつぎ 密議 a secret [a private] conference. ●密議をこらす have [hold] a secret conference 《with》.

みつぎもの 貢ぎ物 《pay》 (a) tribute 《to a ruler》.
みっきょう 密教 esoteric Buddhism.
みつぐ 貢ぐ ●金を貢ぐ give money 《to one's lover》.
ミックス 图 ●ケーキミックス (a) cake mix.
── ミックスする 動 mix 《colors》. ●卵と酢をミックスしたもの a mixture of eggs and vinegar.
●ミックスサンド 《主に米》 club [×mix] sandwich.
●ミックスジュース mixed [×mix] (fruit) juice.
●ミックスダブルス 《テニスなど》 mixed doubles.

みつくち 三つ口 〖『口唇裂』の俗称〗 a cleft lip. (❗ harelip は「うさぎのくちびる」の意でひどい差別語)

みつぐみ 三つ組み ●三つ組みの 形 ●三つ組みの杯 a set of three 《sake cups》.

みつくろい 身繕い (⇒身支度, 支度 ❷)
みつくろう 見繕う 〖自分の裁量で...を選ぶ〗 choose* ... at one's discretion. ▶ワインを適当に見つくろっておいてほしい I'd like you to choose (me) wine at your discretion./I'll leave the choice of wine to you [your discretion].

みつげつ 蜜月 a honeymoon. (⇒ハネムーン) ▶彼らの蜜月の期間はもはや終わった Their honeymoon is already over.

:**みつける** 見付ける
<u>**WORD CHOICE**</u> 見つける
find 偶然によって，あるいは意図して人・物などを見つけること．時に find out の形で用い，真相・実態などの解明を含意する．▶行方不明中の子供は未だ見つかってない The missing child has not been found yet.
discover 重要性の高い未知の事実・場所・事柄などを新たに発見すること．▶アメリカはコロンブスによって見つけられたのですか Was America discovered by Columbus?
detect 組織的・体系的調査によって，秘匿された物や見つけにくい物を発見すること．▶その池で毒物が見つかった The poison was detected in the pond.

頻度チャート
find ████████████
discover ███
detect █

20　40　60　80　100 (%)

find*;《多数の中から》 spot (-tt-); find ... out; discover; detect. ●職を見つける〔得る〕 find [get] a job; 〔探す〕 look [hunt] for a job. ●未知の惑星を見つける discover an unknown planet. ●新しい方法を見つける〔見つけ出す〕 find (out) [discover] a new method. ●見つけしだい撃ち殺す shoot 《him》 on [at] sight. ●引き出しを整理しているとき偶然古い写真を数枚見つけた When I was straightening up the drawers, I found [came across,《やや話》 ran across, ×found out] some old pictures. ▶トムの帽子を見つけてあげてください Please find Tom his cap./Please find Tom's cap for him. ●彼が死んでいるところを見つけられた(=彼が死んでいるのが見つかった) He was found dead. (❗ dying なら「死にそうな状態のところを」の意) ●私は友達がやぶの中に隠れているのを見つけた I found [detected] my friends

hiding in the bush. ▶彼はとても背が高いので人込みの中でも見つけることができる He is such a tall man that you can easily spot〔(目にとまる) catch sight of〕 him in the crowd. ▶私は店で少年が電卓を万引きしているところを見つけた(=現場を押さえた) I caught a boy (in the act of) stealing a pocket calculator in the store.

みつご 三つ子 triplets (❗ そのうちの 1 人は a triplet); (3歳児) a three-year-old child.
●三つ子の魂百まで〔ことわざ〕 The child is father of the man. (❗ W. Wordsworth の詩 The Rainbow から．この father は「源，原点」の意)／The fox may grow grey but never good.

みっこう 密行 ── 密行する 動 travel [fly*] incognito 《to》; go* secretly 《to》.
みっこう 密航 ── 密航する 動 (船・飛行機に隠れて) stow away. ▶彼は貨物船で神戸に密航した He stowed away on a cargo ship to Kobe.
●密航者 a stowaway.

みっこく 密告 图 information;〔内報〕《話》 a tip-off.
── 密告する 動 ●警察に密告する inform 《against [on, upon] him》 to the police;《話》 tip off the police 《about him》.
●密告者 an informer;〔裏切り者〕 a betrayer.

みっさつ 密殺 ── 密殺する 動 butcher 《a cow》 illegally [unlawfully].
みっし 密使 〔書〕 an emissary.
みつじ 密事 a secret. (⇒秘密)
みっしつ 密室 〔出入り不可能の部屋〕 a locked room;〔秘密の部屋〕 a secret room. ●密室での behind closed doors. ▶大事なことが密室で決められた A crucial matter was [Crucial matters were] decided behind closed doors.
●密室政治 closed-door politics.

みっしゅう 密集 图 ●建物密集地帯 a built-up area. ●人口密集地域 a densely populated district. ▶彼はその市の住宅密集地域に住んでいる He lives in a built-up part of the city.
── 密集する 動 ●その地域はアパートが密集している(=接近して建っている) The apartments stand close together in that area.

みっしゅっこく 密出国 图 (不法出国) a smuggling.
── 密出国する 動 smuggle oneself out of a country. ▶彼を密出国させる smuggle him out of a country.

みっしょ 密書 a secret [a confidential] letter [message].
ミッション 〔使節団, 使命〕 a mission. ●訪中ミッション a mission to China.
ミッション 〔自動車の変速機, 伝動装置〕 a transmission
ミッションスクール a Christian school. (参考) a mission school は後進地域の布教のための学校)

みっせい 密生 ── 密生する 動 《植物が主語》 grow* thick [thickly, rank];《場所が主語》 be thick 《with》. (⇒茂る)
みっせつ 密接 ── 密接な 形 close. ▶彼はその事件と密接な関係がある He has a close connection [is closely connected] with the event.
みっそう 密送 ── 密送する 動 send* 《a thing》 secretly.
みっそう 密葬 ●密葬を行う hold a funeral within the family circle.
みつぞう 密造 ── 密造する 動 make [produce] ... illegally; (酒を) bootleg (-gg-).
●密造酒 bootleg (liquor);《米話》 moonshine.
みつぞろい 三つ揃い a three-piece (suit).
みつだん 密談 ── 密談する 動 talk secretly 《with》.

みっちゃく have* a private talk 《*with*》; talk behind closed doors. ▸この件は密談したことがある We talked about it *behind closed doors*.

みっちゃく 密着 图 (付着) adhesion.
── **密着する** 動 adhere 《*to*》; stick 《*to*》. ●密着させる stick ... firmly 《*to*》. ●日常生活に密着した(=基礎を置く)思想 thought *based on* daily life.
●**密着取材** close reporting.

みっちり (徹底的に) thoroughly, completely. ▸彼女はイギリスでシェイクスピアをみっちり研究した She studied Shakespeare *thoroughly* in England.

みっつ 三つ three. ●三つのリンゴ *three* apples. ●三つの子供 a child of *three* (years); a *three*-year-old child; (話) a *three*-year old. ●三つに分ける divide 《it》 into [×in] *three*. ●手紙を三つに折る fold a letter in [into] *three*. ●三つ目の問題 the *third* question.

みっつう 密通 ── **密通する** 動 commit (-tt-) adultery; have* extramarital affairs; have illicit intercourse 《*with*》.

みってい 密偵 a spy. ⇨スパイ, 探偵

ミット (野球の) a mitt. ●キャッチャーミット a catcher's mitt. ●ファーストミット a first baseman's glove [mitt].

***みつど 密度** density. ●人口密度 the *density* of population; population *density*. ●この物質は密度が高い This substance is *of* high *density*.

ミッドナイト 《*at*》 midnight.

ミッドフィールダー 《サッカー》 a midfielder.

みつどもえ 三つ巴 ●三つ巴の戦 (=三者間での)戦 a *three-way* [a *three-sided*] fight 《between A, B and C》.

***みっともない** [恥ずべき] shameful; (不名誉な) disgraceful, dishonorable; [上品でない] indecent; [その場にふさわしくない] improper; [みすぼらしい] shabby; [似合わない] [書] unbecoming; (醜い) ugly, unsightly. ●みっともないふるまい *disgraceful* [*shameful*] behavior; *improper* behavior 《for an occasion》. ●みっともない身なりをしている be *shabbily* dressed. ▸そんなこと言ってみっともない(=恥ずかしい)と思いませんか Aren't you *ashamed of* saying that? ▸食事中に音を立てるのはみっともない(=無作法だ)It is *bad manners* to make (a) noise while you are eating. ●みっともない(=恥を知れ)! Shame on you! 《*! What a shame*! は「それは残念だ」の意》

みつにゅうこく 密入国 图 (不法入国) a smuggling; illegal entry into a country.
── **密入国する** 動 smuggle oneself into a country; enter a country illegally. ●多くのメキシコ人をアメリカに密入国させる *smuggle* a lot of Mexicans *into* America.
●**密入国者** a smuggler; an illegal immigrant; (密航者) a stowaway.

みつば 三つ葉 [植物] a honewort.

みつばい 密売 ── **密売する** 動 sell* ... illegally; traffic 《*in* drugs》.
●**密売人** an illicit seller [dealer]; a 《drug》 trafficker; (麻薬の) a pusher. ●**密売品** illicit goods.

みつばち 蜜蜂 a bee, a honeybee. ●ミツバチの巣 (蜜房) a honeycomb; (巣箱) a beehive.

みっぷう 密封 密封する 動 seal ... (up). ●密封した手紙 a *sealed* letter.

みっぺい 密閉 ── **密閉する** 動 (おおう) cover 《a box》 tightly 《with a lid》; (栓をする) cork 《a bottle》; (密封する) seal 《a parcel》 up; (空気が入らないようにする) make* 《a container》 airtight. ●密閉した容器 an *airtight* container.

みつぼうえき 密貿易 图 (密輸) smuggling.
── **密貿易(を)する** 動 ●ヘロインを密貿易する *smuggle in* [*out*] heroin. (! in は「持ち込む」, out は「持ち出す」の意)

みつぼし 三つ星 [天文] Orion's Belt. ●三つ星レストラン a *three-star* restaurant.

みつまた 三つ又 ●三つ又のやす [道具] a trident. ●三つ又のフォーク a *three-pronged* fork.

みつまた 三椏 [植物] a *mitsumata*; a paper bush.

みつまめ 蜜豆 (デザート) a *mitsumame*; (説明的に) a mixture of agar cubes, chopped fruit and boiled red beans, topped with molasses or syrup.

みつめ 三つ目 ── 三つ目の 形 three-eyed 《monsters》.

***みつめる 見詰める** gaze [stare] 《*at*》 (! stare は好奇心などでじろじろ見る); look hard [intently] 《*at*》; (話) eye; (動きを目で追う) watch (intently). (⇨見る ❶) ●彼女の目[顔]を見つめる (じっと) *gaze into* her eyes [face]; (まじまじと) *look intently into* her eyes [face]; (じろじろ探るように) stare *her in the eye* [the face]. ●自分の内面を見つめる *look inward*. ▸さあ説明してとばかりに彼をじっと見つめる *eye* him, waiting for an explanation.

みつもり 見積もり (仕事・価値などの) an estimate /éstəmət/; (商品・証券などの時価の) (a) quotation; (品質・寸法・重量などの) (an) appraisal, (an) appraisement; (経費などの) a projection. ●概算見積もりを取る[提出する] get [submit] a rough [an approximate] *estimate* 《for the project》. (⇨見積もる) ▸この見積もりは5月末日まで有効となります The *quotations* will be supported until the end of May.
●**見積もり価格** an estimated [a quoted] price.
●**見積書** a written estimate.

みつもる 見積もる (仕事・価値などを) estimate /éstəmèit/, make* an estimate /éstəmət/ 《*of*》; (商品・証券などの時価の) quote; (品質・寸法・重量などを) appraise; (経費などを) project. ●屋根の修理の費用を200万円と見積もる *estimate* the cost of repairing the roof *at* [*to be*] 2 million yen; *estimate* 《that》 the repair to the roof will cost 2 million yen; *make* [*give*] *an estimate of* 2 million yen *for* the repair to the roof. ●家の建築を見積もる(=見積書を作る) *estimate for* building the house. ●損失を過大[過小]に見積もる *overestimate* [*underestimate*] the losses. ●少なく[内輪に; ざっと見積もって] at a low [a moderate; a rough] *estimate*.

みつやく 密約 (秘密の約束)a secret promise [(了解事項) understanding]. ●密約を結ぶ make a *secret promise* [*agreement*] 《with》.

みつゆ 密輸 图 smuggling. ●麻薬の密輸 drug-*smuggling*.
── **密輸する** 動 ●ヘロインをイギリスへ[から]密輸する *smuggle* [《話》 *run*] heroin *into* [*from, out of*] England. ●税関の目をごまかして拳銃を密輸する *smuggle* pistols *through* [*past*] the Customs.
●**密輸人**[業者, 船] a 《drug》 smuggler. ●**密輸品** smuggled goods.

みつゆにゅう 密輸入 ── **密輸入する** 動 smuggle 《into》. ●珍しい動物を密輸入する *smuggle* rare animals *into* a country.

みつゆび 三つ指 ●三つ指をつく bow politely with three fingers of both hands on the *tatami* [floor].

みつりょう 密猟 ── **密猟する** 動 poach. ●ウサギを密

みつりょう 猟する *poach* rabbits; *hunt* rabbits *illegally*.
● 密猟者 a poacher.

みつりょう 密漁 ━ 密漁する 動 poach.
● 密漁者 a poacher. ● 密漁船 a póaching bòat.

みつりん 密林 a thick [a dense] forest; (熱帯の) the jungle.

みつろう 蜜蝋 (木材のつや出し材料) beewax.

**みてい 未定 ━ 未定の 形 (未決定の) undecided; (定まっていない) unfixed; (不確実な) uncertain. ▶ 会合の日取りはまだ未定です The date of the meeting *is* not yet *decided* [*fixed*].
● 未定稿 an unfinished manuscript.

ミディ MIDI (Musical Instrument Digital Interface の略). ● ミディポート a *MIDI* port.

ミディアム medium. ● ミディアムレア *medium* rare. ▶ ステーキはミディアムにしてください I'd like my steak *medium*, please.

みてくれ 見てくれ (外観) (an) appearance. (⇨体裁) ▶ このケーキは見てくれはよくないが味はいい This cake doesn't *look* so good, but it is delicious.

みてとる 見て取る ● 一目で状況を見て取る(=理解する) grasp [*realize, take in*] the whole situation at one glance. ● 彼の笑いの底[奥]にあるものを見て取る *see through* his laughter. ▶ その瞬間に彼は自分が歓迎されない客であると見て取った(=気づいた) At that very moment, he *knew* [*realized, understood*] that he was not a welcome guest.

みてまわる 見て回る look around. (⇨回る❷)

みてみぬふり 見て見ぬ振り ● 見て見ぬ振りをする (⇨見[成句])

みてもらう 診てもらう see* [(書) consult] a doctor. (⇨診る)

みとう 未到, 未踏 ━ 未到[未踏]の 形 (探究[踏査]されていない) unexplored; (足を踏み入れていない) untrodden; (未開墾の) virgin. ● 前人未到の領域を研究する study an *unexplored* field. ● 人跡未踏の森 *untrodden* [*virgin*] woods.

みどう 御堂 a temple.

**みとおし 見通し ● ❶ [遠景] a perspective; [視界] visibility. (⇨視界) ▶ この部屋からはずっと向こうの湖まで見通しがきく(=見える) From this room I *can see* a lake far ahead. ▶ 霧の中では見通しがきかない In a fog the *visibility* is very poor [it is difficult to *see*].

❷ [成功・利益などの見込み] prospects 《for》; [展望] an outlook 《for》; [予測]《書》(a) prediction; a forecast. ▶ 将来の見通しは明るい The *prospects for* the future are [The *outlook for* the future is] good (↔poor). (❗前の方には感情的要素が入る) ▶ 景気回復の見込みは立たない(=望みはない) There's no *hope* [*prospect*] *of* economic recovery.

❸ [先見の明] foresight; [洞察力] (an) insight. ● 先の見通しがきく have (good) *foresight*; be able to see far into the future.

みとおす 見通す ● [見抜く] see* through …; [予測]《書》predict; foresee*. ● 将来を見通す *see into* the future.

みとがめる 見咎める question.

みどく 未読 ━ 未読の 形 unread /ʌnréd/ (newspapers).

みどく 味読 ━ 味読する 動 read* 《a book》with appreciation; enjoy 《a book》.

みどころ 見所 ● [注目点] a highlight; [将来性] promise; [よい点] a good point. ● その試合の見所は the *highlight* of the game. ▶ 彼は俳優としてなかなか見どころがある He shows great [a lot of] *promise* as an actor./He's a very *promising* actor [an actor full of *promise*].

ミトコンドリア 《生物》a mitochondrion (履 -dria).

みとどける 見届ける [確かめる] make* sure 《of; that 節》; (自分の目で見る) see* … with one's own eye; [最後まで見る] watch (it) to the end. ▶ 彼がバスに乗るのを見届けた I *made sure that* he took the bus. ▶ 彼は長生きして二人の孫が成長し結婚するのを見届けた He lived to *see* both his grandchildren grown and married.

みとめ(いん) 認め(印) a private seal; a signet. ● 認め(印)を押す stamp [affix] one's *private seal* 《on a document》.

**みとめる 認める ● ❶ [判断する] (事実[正当]と認める) recognize; (是認する) approve of …; (同意する) agree 《to》; (容認する) accept; [真偽を認める] (しぶしぶ) admit (-tt-), acknowledge; (自発的に) confess (to …). (❗しばしば自責の念を伴う) ▶ 彼らは敗北を認めた They *recognized* [*admitted, acknowledged*] their defeat. ▶ 彼女が偉大なランナーであることはだれでも認めている Everybody *recognizes* [*is recognizing*] *that* she is a great runner./Everybody *recognizes* her as [*to be*] a great runner. (❗裁判所などの公の機関が「法律上正当と認める」の意では xto be も用いる(⇨認定)) ▶ 父は私が彼と結婚することを認めてくれないでしょう Father will never *approve of* [*agree to*] my marrying him./(許可しない) Father will never *allow* [*permit*] me to marry him. (⇨❷) ▶ 彼の理論は妥当なものとして広く認められている His theory *is* widely *accepted as* valid. ▶ 彼は自分の罪を認めた He *admitted* [*acknowledged, confessed* (to)] his guilt./He *admitted* [*acknowledged, confessed*] *that* he was guilty./He *admitted* [*acknowledged, confessed*] himself (*to be*) guilty. ▶ 彼は金を盗んだことを認めている He *admits* [*acknowledges*] *that* he stole the money./He *admits* [*acknowledges*] having stolen [xto have stolen] the money. (❗ admit の場合, 完了形の代わりに *admits* stealing the money. も可) ▶ 彼は子供をひいたことを認めた He *confessed* (*that*) he had run over the child./He *confessed to* having run [*running*] over the child.
会話 (裁判で)「異議あり」「異議を認めます」"Objection." "(Your objection is) sustained."

❷ [許可する] (積極的に禁止しない) allow, 《話》let*; (積極的かつ正式に)《やや書》permit (-tt-). ▶ この部屋では喫煙が認められていない Smoking *is* not *allowed* [*permitted*] in this room. ▶ いつもより早く帰ることをお認めください Please *allow* [*permit*] me *to* go home earlier than usual. (❗ permit は許可を与える人の権威を含意)/Please *let* me go home earlier than usual. ▶ 新車を買うなんて絶対に認めませんよ(=聞き入れないよ) I won't *hear of* your buy*ing* a new car. (❗通例 will [would, could] not とともに用いる)

❸ [気にする] see*; (気づく) notice; (発見する) find*. ▶ そこには人影は認められなかった There was not a person to *be seen* there./Nobody could *be seen* there. ▶ エンジンに異状は認められません I can't *find* anything [I *find* nothing] wrong with the engine./The engine is all right.

❹ [評価する] recognize; (重んじる) think* highly [well, much] of … (❗ much は通例否定文で). ▶ 我々はみな彼の能力を認めている All of us *recognize* his ability.

**みどり 緑 [緑, 緑色] (a) green (❗種類をいうときは ©); [緑の草木] greenery (❗主に装飾用のもの); [葉

みどりご

緑(の草木)〖〖書・詩〗verdure; 〖食用の緑の葉の野菜〗greens. ●いろいろな緑 a variety of *greens*. ●ドアを緑に塗る paint the door *green*. ●緑がかった黄色 *greenish* yellow.

―緑の 形 green. ●緑の野原 *green* fields. ▶緑(の木々)の中に宮殿のような建物が見えた I could see palace-like buildings among the *greenery*. ▶緑の中にいれば落ちつき安らぐのはなぜでしょう Why is it that *greenery* has a soothing effect on our nerves [makes us feel calm and at ease]?/Why do we feel calm and at ease when we're surrounded by *greenery*?
●緑のおばさん 《英》a lollipop lady. ●緑の黒髪 (つやのある黒髪) glossy black hair. ●緑の日 (植樹日) Arbor Day (参考 英・カナダでは植樹祭の日); (日本の) Greenery Day. ●みどりの窓口 a JR ticket counter.

みどりご 嬰児 a baby; an infant.
みとりざん 見取り算 ●見取り算をする work out a *written-down problem* on an abacus.
みとりず 見取り図 a plan; (略図) a sketch.
みどりむし 緑虫 〖動物〗an euglena.
みとる 看取る 〖見守る〗be at 《his》 bedside; 〖看病する〗nurse 《him》, take* care of 《him》; attend 《him》. ●父の死を看取る be *at* one's father's *bedside* through his last days. ●母の最期を看取る *attend* one's mother on her deathbed.
ミドルエージ 〖中年〗middle age. (参考 40 歳から 60 歳ぐらいをさす)
ミドルきゅう ミドル級 the middleweight [×middle]. ●ミドル級の選手 a middleweight.
ミドルクラス 〖中産階級〗the middle class.
ミドルネーム one's middle name. (事情 洗礼名や旧姓で, 頭文字だけで略記されることが多い)
ミドルホール 〖ゴルフ〗a par-four hole.
みとれる 見とれる 〖魅了されて[感心して]見る〗look in fascination [admiration] 《at》; 〖魅了される〗be fascinated 《by, at, with》. ●人形に見とれる gaze [look] *at* a doll *in admiration*; gaze [look] *admiringly* at a doll. ▶彼はしばしその景色の美しさに見とれて立っていた He stood *admiring* [*fascinated by*] the beauty of the scene for a while.
ミトン a mitten, a mitt. (❗通例複数形で, 一対は a pair of *mittens* [*mitts*]) (⇨手袋) ●オーブン用ミトン oven *mitts* 《米》[*gloves* 《英》].

‡みな 皆 〖だれも〗everyone, everybody (❗後の方が口語的) (⇨だれでも); 〖どれも〗everything; 〖どの…も〗every 《+単数名詞》; 〖すべての(物)〗all. ▶皆疲れていた *Everyone* was [×were] tired. (❗今は通例 ×*All* were tired. のように *all* を「すべての人」の意で用いない) ▶彼らは皆イギリス出身です They are *all* [×They *all* are, ×*All* they are] from Britain./They *all* [*All of* them, ×*All* they] come from Britain. (❗(1) *all* の後に代名詞が続くときは間に of が必要. (2) *all of* … を否定するときは none of … を用いる: *None of* them [×*All* of them *don't*] come from Britain. (彼らは皆イギリス出身ではない) *Not all* of them come from Britain. (彼らが皆イギリス出身というわけではない)の意で, 部分否定 (⇨全部 ①)) ▶私には皆の言うことがひと言も理解できなかった I couldn't understand a word *anyone* said. ▶子供たちは皆寝た *All* 《*of*》 the children went to bed. (❗特定の子供をさす場合. 次例と比較) ▶子供は皆いたずらをするものだ *All* 《*of*》 children can be naughty sometimes. (❗世間の子供一般をさす場合) ▶彼は私たち皆を招待した He invited *all of* us [*us all*, ×*all us*]. (❗「*all of*+代名詞」が動詞・前置詞の目的語のときは「代名詞+*all*」の語順も可) ▶私は皆で(=全部で) 6 冊の本を買った I bought six books *altogether* [*in all*].
会話「彼女が言ったことは皆本当ですか」「そうです」"Is [×Are] *everything* she said true?" "Yes, it is [×they are]." (❗*everybody* や *everyone* と異なり, 動詞も代名詞も通例単数形で応)

みなおし 見直し (再検討) (a) review. ●年金制度の全面的な[包括的な]見直し an overall [a comprehensive] *review* of the pension plan.
みなおす 見直す 〖再び目を通す〗look … over [through] again; (再点検する) go over; 〖再検討する〗review, run a review 《of》; 〖より高く評価する〗think* better of 《him》, 〖書〗have* a higher regard for 《him》; (より信頼する) give* 《him》 more credit. ●その書類を発送する前に見直す *look over* the document *again* [*go over* the document] before sending it out. ●日本家屋のよさを見直す(=再認識する) *recognize* the merits of Japanese houses *again*. ▶今教育制度が見直されています The educational system *is* now *under review* [*being reviewed*]. ▶あれ以来彼を見直した I *thought better of* him after that.
みなぎる 〖満ちている〗be full 《of》; (あふれるばかりである) be bursting 《with》; 〖におい・感情などが全体に広がる〗〖書〗pervade. ▶今朝は力がみなぎっている感じがする I feel *full of* vitality this morning. ▶何もかも生気があふれていた Everything *was bursting with* life. ▶町全体に異様な空気がみなぎっていた A strange atmosphere *prevailed over* [*pervaded*] the whole town.
みなげ 身投げ ――**身投げする** 自 throw* oneself 《into a river》; drown oneself 《in a river》; kill oneself by jumping 《into a river》.
みなごろし 皆殺し the killing of all people; (民族の) genocide. ▶彼の家族は皆殺しにされた *All* the members of his family *were killed* [*were murdered*].
みなさん 皆さん 《呼びかけ》everybody, everyone; 《話》folks; (男性に) gentlemen /dʒéntlmən/ (❗×/-men/ と発音しない); (女性に) ladies; (小・中学生に) boys and girls; (演説などの始めに) ladies and gentlemen. ▶皆さんお静かに願います *Everybody!* Be quiet, please! ▶待ってください, 今帰り支度をしておられる皆さん, 聞いてください, お願いします Just a minute, please. *Those of you* about to leave, listen, please.
みなし 見做し ●みなし課税 deemed taxation. ●みなし法人課税 taxation on deemed corporations. ●みなし労働(時間) deemed working hours.
みなしご 孤児 (⇨孤児(ː))

‡みなす 見做す regard 《A *as* B》, look on [upon] 《A *as* B》; 〖数に入れる〗count 《A 《*as*》 B》; 〖考える〗consider 《A 《*to be*》 B》, think* of 《A *as* B》; 〖(誤って)解する〗take* 《A *for* [*to be*] B》. (⇨考える, 思う ❹) (❗以上いずれも通例進行形不可) ●彼を英雄とみなす *regard* [*look upon*] him *as* a hero; *consider* him 《*to be*》 a hero. (❗*consider* 《*that*》 he is a hero の方が口語的) ▶彼はその仕事に適任だとみなされている He *is regarded* [*is looked upon*] *as* 《being》 fit for the job./He *is considered* [《やや書》*reckoned*] 《*to be*》 fit for the job. (❗受身では *to be* は通例省略する) ▶だまっている人は計画に賛成しているものとみなしていいですか May I *suppose* [*take*

みなづき 水無月 [6月] June; (陰暦の) the sixth month of the lunar calendar.

＊みなと a harbor (❗自然の地形を利用した避難港); a port (❗港湾設備や背後の都市を含む商港). ●港に立ち寄る call at a port. ●船が港に入った The ship came into [made, (港に着いた) reached] (a) port. (❗通例 a は省略される.「港を出る」は leave [clear] (a) port) ●船は山々な港に停泊していた The boats were all in port [in (the) harbor].
港町 a port (town). ●港横浜(=横浜港) the port of Yokohama, Yokohama Port [×Port Yokohama] ●長崎は港町だ Nagasaki is a port [a seaport].

みなまたびょう 水俣病 Minamata disease; a disease caused by mercury poisoning.

:みなみ 南 図 south, South. (❗通例 the 〜) (⇨東)

> 解説 《米》では特に「南」の方角は地図の下方にあたるので, down で表すことがある.「北」には up を用いる: ニューヨークから南のフロリダまで行く go from New York down to Florida./北の方に住む live up north.

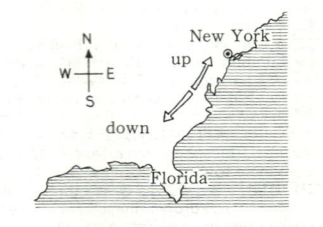

N / W-E / S / New York / up / down / Florida

—— **南の** 形 south; southern; southerly. ●駅の南口(出口) the south exit of a station; (入り口) the south entrance to a station. ●南向きの部屋 a room facing south.
—— **南に** 副 (南方に) (to the) south; (南部に) in the south; (南側に接して) on the south (side).; [南へ(向かって)] to [toward] the south; southward. ●南に針路をとる take a southerly course. ●南へ旅する travel (down) south.
●**南アメリカ** South America. ●**南回帰線** the Tropic of Capricorn. ●**南風** a south wind. (⇨東風) ●**南シナ海** the South China Sea. ●**南十字星** the Southern Cross. ●**南太平洋** the South Pacific. ●**南半球** the Southern Hemisphere. ●**南ヨーロッパ** the Southern Europe.

みなみアフリカ 南アフリカ [国名] South Africa (❗地域をもさす); (公式名) the Republic of South Africa. (首都 Pretoria) ●南アフリカ人 a South African. ●南アフリカ(人)の South African.

みなみな 皆々 (だれもかれも) everybody; (どれもこれも) everything. (⇨皆) ●皆々様 everyone. (⇨皆さん) ●当ホテルにご滞在中の皆々様へ To each and every guest (staying) at this hotel.

みなもと 源 [出所, 水源] a source; [起源] (an) origin; [根源] the root; (初め) a beginning. ●うわさの源をつきとめる trace the source of the rumor. ●利根川は大水上山に源を発している The Tone River rises [has its source] in Mt. Ominakami. ●現代文学の源を探ってみたい I hope to look for the origin(s) of modern literature.

みならい 見習い [実習] (practical) training; [徒弟] しての修業] apprenticeship; [仮採用] probation; [実習生] a trainee; [徒弟] an apprentice. ●見習いの店員[教員] a trainee salesclerk [teacher]. ●見習いのパン職人として働く work as an apprentice to a baker [a baker's apprentice]. ●彼は1か月間見習いだ He's on probation for a month. ●彼は大工の見習いをしている He's learning to become a carpenter.

みならう 見習う (模範にする) follow 《his》 example; (まねる) imitate. ●友人を見習ってまじめに勉強しなさい You should follow the example of your friend and study hard./You should study hard after the example of your friend [(友人がやるように) as your friend does].

みなり 身なり [外見] (an) appearance; [服装] dress.
①【身なりが[の]】 ●身なりのよい[悪い]人 a well-dressed [a poorly-dressed] person. ●身なりがよいも be well dressed. ●身なりが悪いも be poorly [badly, shabbily] dressed. (❗shabbily は特にみすぼらしい感じ)
②【身なりを】 ●きちんと身なりを整える dress neatly; tidy oneself up. ●人前に出てもおかしくないように身なりを整えなさい Make yourself look presentable.
③【身なりに[で]】 ●身なりに構わない be careless about one's dress [appearance]. ●身なりで人を判断するな Don't judge people by their appearances.

ミナレット [イスラム教寺院の尖塔] a minarét.

みなれる 見慣れる ●見慣れない顔 an unfamiliar face; (見知らぬ人) a stranger. ●こういう光景は子供のときから見慣れている I have been used [been accustomed] to seeing such sights since I was a child. (❗後の場合, ...to see も可)

ミニ mini.
●ミニカー (小型自動車) a minicar; (おもちゃ) a miniature car. ●ミニコミ communication by small publications. ●ミニコミ誌 a magazine with a very small circulation. ●ミニコンポ a miniature audio system. ●ミニスカート a miniskirt, (やや話) a mini. ●ミニディスク a Mini Disk, a MD. ●ミニバイク 《米》 a minibike; (原動機付け自転車) a moped /móupéd/; (スクーター) a (motor) scooter.

＊みにくい 醜い [容貌(ちう)などが醜い] ugly; (器量のよくない) plain, 《米》 homely (❗ugly は嫌悪を起こさせる意味の強い語で人には通例 plain, homely を用いる); [恥ずべき] shameful; (不名誉な) disgraceful, 《米》 dishonorable; [目ざわりな] 《やや書》 unsightly. ●醜い犬 an ugly dog. ●醜い行動 shameful [disgraceful] conduct. ●醜い建物 an ugly [an unsightly, (粗悪な) a shoddy] building. ●彼は醜いあざが顔にある He has an ugly [an unsightly] birthmark on his face.

みにくい 見にくい hard [difficult] to see; (字が読みにくい) difficult to read; (不鮮明な) indistinct. ●この眼鏡では見にくい(=よく見えない) I cannot see well through [with, ×by] these glasses.

ミニチュア a miniature 《of a car》. ●ミニチュアカー a miniature car.

ミニマム [最小[最低(限)]の] a minimum.
●ミニマムアクセス [最低輸入枠] minimum access.

みぬく 見抜く [見通す] see* through ...; [正体などを見破る] find* ... out; [気づく] notice; [感知する] perceive. ●彼のうそを見抜く see through his lies [him]. ●彼の胸の内を見抜く see into his mind. ●正体を見抜く find 《him》 out. ●一見してそれが偽物

みぬふり 見ぬ振り ▶見ぬ振りをする (⇨見る [成句])

みね 峰 (とがった山頂) a (mountain) peak; (山頂) the top of a mountain, the mountaintop, the summit (❗ 前の二つより堅い語); (尾根) a ridge; 〖刀の〗 the back 《of a sword》.

みねうち 峰打ち ●峰打ちにする strike 《him》 with the back of one's sword.

ミネソタ 〖米国の州〗 Minnesota /mìnəsóutə/ 《略 Minn. 郵便略 MN》.

ミネラル a mineral.
  ● ミネラルウォーター 《a glass of》 mineral water.

ミネルバ 〖ローマ神話〗 Minerva. (⇨参考) 知恵と武勇の女神)

みの 蓑 a straw raincoat.

みのう 未納 ▶彼は授業料が未納だ He *has not yet paid* his tuition fees./He *is in arrears* /ərìərz/ *with* his tuition fees.
  ● 未納金 arrears.

***みのうえ 身の上** ❶〖境遇〗 (一身上の問題) one's personal affairs [matters]; (経済的な生活状態) circumstances. ●身の上相談欄 〖新聞などの〗 the *personal-advice* column. ▶何人かの人が私のところへ身の上相談に来た Some people came to ask for my advice [to talk with me,《書》to consult (with) me] about their *personal affairs*. (❗ consult me のように with を用いないのは me を専門家の場合) ▶彼は恵まれない身の上だった He was in poor *circumstances* [素性が] *from a disadvantaged background*].

❷〖経歴〗 (生涯) life; (過去) one's past; (履歴) one's personal history. ▶彼女は身の上話 [自分に起こった一連の不幸な出来事]をぽつりぽつりと語り始めた She started to tell the *story of her life* [自分のことについてすべてを] *tell all about herself*] little by little.

みのがし 見逃し ●見逃しの三振をする 〖野球〗 look at strike three; strike out [be struck out] looking.

***みのがす 見逃す** 〖うっかり逃す〗 miss; 〖見落とす〗 overlook; 〖大目に見る〗 overlook; let* 《it》 pass [go].
 ●好機を見逃す *miss* a chance. ●見逃せない芝居 a play (that) we can't *miss*; a play that is a *must*. (❗ must は〖ぜひ見るべき(もの)〗の意の名詞. a *must* play ともいえる) ●投球を見逃す look at [take] a pitch. ●サインを見逃す *miss* a sign. ▶私たちはそのテレビの番組の冒頭の部分を見逃してしまった We *missed* 《*seeing*》 [*missed out on*] the start of the TV program. ▶予習してこなかったのは今回が最初なので見逃してあげよう I will *overlook* the fact that you didn't prepare today's lessons because it's the first time.

会話 「二度とカンニングはしません。お願いです, 今回は見逃してください」「それは職員会議で決めることです」"You'll never catch me cheating on an exam again. Just *let me off the hook* this time. Please!" "I'll never cheat .... より説得力のある言い方. let ... off the hook は「…を窮地から救う」の意の口語表現) "That's up to the faculty meeting to decide."

みのかわ 身の皮 《衣服》 one's clothes.
 ●身の皮を剥ぐ 《生活のために自分の衣服を売る》 sell one's clothes for a living.

みのけ 身の毛 ●身の毛がよだつ ●身の毛のよだつ話 a *hair-raising* [《血も凍るほどの》a *bloodcurdling*, 《背筋が寒くなるような》*bone-chilling*] story. ▶それを見て[考えただけで]身の毛がよだった(=身震いした) I

shuddered [*was horrified*] at the sight [the mere thought] of it./The thought [The mere thought] of it made *my hair stand on end*.

みのしろきん 身代金 a ransom. ●(...に対して) 5,000万円の身代金を要求する demand a *ransom* of fifty million yen (for ...).

みのたけ 身の丈 height. (⇨背❸, 身長) ▶元就は, 戦国乱世には珍しく, 天下を取ることなど望まず, 身の丈=自分のあるべき身分)に合った生き方をしていた Unlike his contemporaries who lived in the turbulent states of warring states, Motonari never aspired to gain the control of the country, and lived a life *knowing his* (×own) *place*. (❗ his own place とすると自分の国や地域などの地理的な意味になるので, ここでは不適切)

みのほど 身の程 《地位》 one's place; 《限界》 one's limitations. ●身の程をわきまえる know one's *place* [*limitations*]. ▶彼は身の程知らずだ He doesn't know his *place* [*limitations*].

みのまわり 身の回り ●彼の身の回りの世話をする take care of [look after] him. (❗「自分の身の回り」を oneself を用いる)
 ●身の回り品 one's things [belongings] (❗ 前の方が口語的); 〖書〗 one's personal effects.

みのむし 蓑虫 a bagworm.

古今ことばの系譜 『枕草子』

蓑虫, いとあはれなり. 鬼のうみたりければ, 親に似たればにて, 恐しき心あらむとて, 親のあやしき衣(ぎぬ)ひき着せて「今, 秋風吹かむをりぞ来むとする. 待てよ」と言ひ置きて逃げて去(い)にしも知らず, 風の音を聞き知りて, 八月ばかりになれば「ちちよ, ちちよ」とはかなげに鳴く, いみじうあはれなり. I feel very sorry for the basket worm. He was begotten by a demon, and his mother, fearing that he would grow up with his father's nature, abandoned the unsuspecting child, having first wrapped him in a dirty piece of clothing. "Wait for me," she said as she left. "I shall return to you as soon as the autumn winds blow." So, when autumn comes, the wretched child hears it and desperately cries, "Milk! Milk!" (Ivan Morris). (❗ ここでは「父が鬼, 母が人間」としているが, 「母が鬼, 父が人間」という解釈もある. 〖⇨『枕草子』

みのり 実り 《収穫》 (a) harvest; 《収穫高》 a crop.
 ●実りの多い(=有益な)議論 a *fruitful* (↔a *fruitless*) discussion. ▶実りの秋(=収穫期)がやって来た The *harvest season* has come. ▶今年は米の実りがよかった[悪かった] We had a good [a poor] *crop* of rice this year.

***みのる 実る** (実を結ぶ) bear* fruit [×fruits]. (❗ 比喩的にも用いる) ▶たいていの果樹は秋に実る Most fruit trees *bear* [*produce*] *fruit* in autumn. ▶彼の努力は実った[実らなかった] His efforts *bore fruit* [*bore no fruit*]. ▶今年は稲がよく実った(=豊作だった) We *have had a good crop of rice* [*a good rice crop*] this year.

みば 見場 ●見場がいい look good [nice, attractive]; be good [nice] to look at. ●見場が悪い look ugly [bad, awkward]. (⇨体裁, 見栄え)

みばえ 見栄え ●見栄えがする (すてきに見える) be *nice-looking*; 《人をひきつける》 attractive. ●見栄えのしない *poor-looking*; *unattractive*. ▶その赤いスカーフをすると彼女は見栄えがするよ She *looks attractive* [*nice*] in the red scarf.

みはからう 見計らう ●贈り物の品を見計らう *choose* a *suitable* gift. ▶ころ合いを見計らって彼を訪問した I *chose* the *right* [*proper*] *time to visit him*./

みはったつ (ちょうどよいときに) I visited him *at the right* [*proper*] *time*.

みはったつ 未発達 ― 未発達の 形 undeveloped; (発達不十分の) underdeveloped. ▶彼は心身ともに未発達だ He is *not well developed* either in mind or body./His body and mind are *not well developed*.

みはっぴょう 未発表 unpublished. ●未発表の論文 an *unpublished* paper.

みはてぬ 見果てぬ ●見果てぬ夢 an unfulfilled dream [(望み) hope, (大望) ambition].

みはなす 見放す [あきらめる] give* up on ...;[見捨てる] abandon. (➾見捨てる) ▶医師は祖父を見放した The doctor *gave up on* my grandfather.

みはば 身幅 the width of a kimono.

みはらい 未払い ― 未払いの 形 (まだ払われていない) unpaid, outstanding; not yet paid; (支払うべき) payable. ▶未払いの給料 *unpaid* wages [salary, pay]. ▶本の代金がまだ未払いになっている I *haven't paid for* the books *yet*. ▶その封筒には「未払い請求書」のスタンプが押してあった The envelope had "*Over Due*" stamped on it. ⚠封筒の中身が支払い期限の過ぎた請求書 (an overdue account) であるという標示。

●未払い金 (主な営業取り引き以外の取り引きから生ずる債務) accounts payable; (遅延金) arrearages.
●未払い利息 unpaid [未収の) accrued] interest; interest payable.

みはらし 見晴らし a view (*of*). (➾眺め) ▶海の見晴らしがよい部屋 a room with a fine *view of* the sea.
●見晴らし台 a lookout; a gazebo /gəzéibou/; an observation platform.

みはらす 見晴らす ▶この窓から港が見晴らせる(=眺められる) (人が主語) We can *get* [*have*] *a view of* [(見える) *see*] the harbor from this window./(場所が主語) This window *has* [*gives*] *a view of* the harbor./(見渡す) This window *looks* (*out*) *over* [*overlooks*, (書) *commands a view of*] the harbor.

みはり 見張り [監視] (a) watch; (警護, 警備) guard; (警戒) a watch; [見張り人] (男の) a watchman (複 -men); a guard; a lookout; (海水浴場などの) a lifeguard. ●見張りに立つ stand *guard*. ▶すべての門に見張りを置く place a *watch* [a *guard*, *lookouts*] *at* every gate. ⚠この watch と a guard は「一団の見張り人」の意で, watches, guards と交換可. ▶その容疑者に見張りをつける put a *watch* [a *lookout*] *on* the suspect.
●見張り所 a lookout; (番小屋) a watchhouse.

みはる 見張る ❶ [人・場所・活動などを] watch; keep* a watch 《on》. ▶囚人を厳重に見張る *watch* [*guard*] a prisoner carefully; *keep a careful watch on* a prisoner. ▶万引きを見張る(=警戒する) *be on the lookout* [*the watch, the alert*] *for* a shoplifter; *watch out* [*look out, keep a lookout*] *for* a shoplifter.
❷ [目を] open one's eyes (wide). ●驚きのあまり目を見張ってそれを見る look at it *with* one's *eyes wide open* in astonishment [wonder].

みはるかす 見晴るかす (➾見晴らす)

みびいき 身びいき 名 (えこひいき) (《やや書》favoritism; (縁故者登用) 《やや書》 nepotism.
── 身びいきする 動 practice nepotism; be partial to one's relatives; show* favoritism.

みひつ 未必 ●未必の故意 [法律] willful negligence; *conscious* negligence.

みひとつ 身一つ ― 身一つで 副 alone; by oneself. (➾単身)

みひらき 見開き a spread. ●見開き2ページ a two-page *spread*; two facing pages.

みひらく 見開く open 《one's eyes》 wide. ●目を見開いて with one's eyes (wide) open.

みふたつ 身二つ ― 身二つになる (出産する) give birth to a baby.

*__**みぶり 身振り**__ (しぐさ) (a) gesture; (動作) a motion. ▶怒った身振りをする make an angry *gesture*; make a *gesture* of anger. ▶彼は部屋に入るよう [座るよう] 身振りで合図した He *motioned* (*to*) me *to come into the room* [*to sit down*]. ⚠He *gestured to* me *to come into the room* [*to sit down*]. も可/He *motioned* me *into* the *room* [*to a chair*]. ⚠「motion＋人」の後には方向を表す語句が続く) ▶彼女は大げさな身振りで[身振り手振りで]そのときの状況を説明した She explained how it happened *with* exaggerated [a lot of] *gestures*. ⚠言葉をいっさい使わない(使えない)場合は, たとえば ...*in* dramatic *pantomime*. のようにもいえる
●身振り言語 body language.

みぶるい 身震い 名 (全身の激しい) a shudder; (小刻みな) a tremble; (寒さなどによる一時的な) a shiver.
── 身震いする 動 shudder; tremble; shiver. (➾震える) ▶目の前の光景に彼は身震いした He *shuddered at* the sight before him.

*__**みぶん 身分**__ ❶ [地位] a position, standing, (a) status; (社会的階級) a social class [level], (a) rank; (身元) one's identity.

> **使い分け** position 特定の組織の中での地位を表す一般的な語.
> **standing** position より漠然と身分の上下に言及する語.
> **status** 法律・社会・職業上の地位で, 特に他の人から見たもの.

●あらゆる身分の人々 people of all *ranks* [*social classes*]; people from all *walks* [*every walk*] *of life*.
① [身分が] (社会的に) 身分が高い人 a person of high (↔low) (social) *position* [*standing*]. ⚠単に a person of *position* [*standing*] ともいう) ▶彼は私とは身分が違う(=私より身分が高い)と思っている He thinks he is in a higher [a different] *social class* than I am./He thinks he belongs to a different *social class* from me. ▶公務員は身分が安定している The *position* of government employees is guaranteed.
② [身分を] ●身分を隠す hide [conceal] one's *identity*. ▶もし私が試合に出て収入を得ればアマチュアとしての身分を失うことになる I'll lose my amateur *status* if I get paid for playing.
❷ [その他の表現] ▶結構なご身分ですね(=うらやましい暮らしをしていますね) You lead an enviable life./You are in a well-off *position*. ▶身分相応な(=収入に合った)生活を送るようにしなさい You should live *within* (↔beyond) your *income* [《やや書》 *means*].
●身分証明書 an idéntity [an identificátion] càrd; an ID (card).

みぼうじん 未亡人 a widow. (➾やもめ) ●戦争未亡人 a war *widow*. ●岸氏の未亡人 Mr. Kishi's *widow*; the wife of the late Mr. Kishi. ●未亡人になる become a *widow*. ●戦争[交通事故]で未亡人になる *be widowed* by the war [in a traffic accident].

*__**みほん 見本**__ a sample, a specimen (⚠ほぼ同意だが, sample は全体の質を示す見本, 特に商業見本に

specimen は同類のものの見本・標本・適例をさす; (書物・雑誌の見本) a sample copy; [手本] a model, an example. ● この本の現物見本 a *sample copy of* this book. ● 薬草の見本 *specimens* of wild herbs. ● 見本として come [be] up to the *sample(s)*. ● 見本をいただけますか May I have a *sample*? ▶これは室内楽のよい見本だ This is a fine *specimen* of chamber music. / This is a good *example* of chamber music. ▶彼女は正直の見本のような人だ She is a *model* of honesty.
● 見本市 a tráde fàir. ● 見本刷り a specimen page. ● 見本帳 a sámple [a páttern] bòok.

*みまい 見舞い 〔訪問〕 a visit; 〔容体を問うこと〕〔やや書〕 an inquiry (*about* his health); 〔見舞いの言葉〕 an expression of one's sympathy (*for* [*with*] him). ● 火事見舞いに行く visit (him) to express one's sympathy after a fire. ▶私は入院中のおじを見舞いに行った I *visited* [*went to see*] my uncle in (《主に米》 the) hospital. / I went to (《主に米》 the) hospital to *visit* [*see*] my uncle. (❗(1) いずれも 《英》 では通例 the は省略する。(2) 文脈で明らかな場合は in [to] the hospital となる)
● 見舞客 a visitor. ● 見舞金 a present [a gift] of money. ● 見舞状 (容体を問う) a letter of inquiry; (回復を祈る) a get-well letter [card]; (被災者への) a letter of sympathy. ● 見舞い品 (贈り物) a present [a gift] (*to*); (被災者への救援物資) relief (goods). (⇨商品)

みまう 見舞う ❶ 〔見舞いに行く〕visit [go to see] (him) in 《主に米》 the) hospital (⇨見舞い); 〔容体を問う〕 ask about (his health); inquire about (his health); (第三者を通じて) ask [inquire] after (him [his health]). (❗いずれも inquire より ask を用いる方が口語的)
❷ 〔襲う〕 ● 不幸に見舞われる(=遭遇する) meet with misfortune. ▶この地域は昨夜暴風雨に見舞われた This area *was* (*hard*) *hit* [*was struck*] *by* a storm last night. (❗hit はしばしば hard を伴う) ▶2年に3年に1回, 首都圏は相当な雪に見舞われる The capital and its surrounding areas [×the capital area] *get* a heavy snowfall every two to three years.

みまもる 見守る 〔見て番をする〕 watch (over ...); (目を離さずに) keep* an [one's] eye (*on*); 〔成り行きなどを〕 watch (and see). ● 何が起こるか見守る *watch and see* what happens. ● 家族に見守られ息を引きとる pass away *with* all one's family *at* one's bedside.

みまわす 見回す look around [《主に英》 about].... ▶彼は用心深くあたりを見回した He *looked around* him [×himself] cautiously. ▶私は空席がないかと教室を見回した I *looked around* the classroom *for* an empty seat.

みまわり 見回り 〔〔巡回〕〕 a round; (警官などの) patrol. (⇨巡回) ● 見回りの人 a patrol officer, (男の) a patrolman; a watch, (男の) a watchman.

みまわる 見回る (巡回する) patrol (-ll-); (視察する) inspect.

みまん 未満 under ...; (...より少ない) less than....
● 5歳未満の子供 children *under* [*less than*] five (years of age). (❗「5歳以下の子供」は children of five *and under* という)

‡みみ 耳 ❶ 〔器官〕(人・動物の) an ear.
① 〔耳の〜〕 ● 耳の穴 (話) an earhole. ● 耳の掃除をする clean one's *ear(s)*. ● 耳のうしろに手をあてる put [cup] one's hand behind one's *ear*. 〔事情〕よく聞くためのしぐさ ● 耳の付け根まで赤くなる blush to the roots of one's *ears* [*hair*].

② 〔耳が〕 ▶耳が痛い I have a pain *in* my *ear*. / I have (an) earache.
③ 〔耳に〕 ● 耳に栓をする stop (up) one's *ears*; (耳栓をする) put earplugs in one's *ears*. ● 耳に鉛筆をはさむ have a pencil *behind* [×on] one's *ear*.
④ 〔耳を〕 ▶彼の耳を引っ張る pull him *by* the [×his] *ear*. (〔事情〕しかるときなどの行為) ▶すさまじい音がしたので思わず耳をふさいだ I covered my *ears* unconsciously when I heard a loud crash.
❷ 〔聞く力〕(聴覚) an ear (❗「聞き分ける力」の意では通例単数形で); (聴力) hearing. ▶耳が鋭い have a keen [a sharp] *ear*. ▶彼は耳がよいので言葉を覚えるのが早かった He had a good *ear* and (so) picked up languages quickly. ▶彼は耳が聞こえなくなった He lost his *hearing*. / He went deaf. ▶彼女は音楽を聞く耳を持ちあわせている [ない] She has a good [has no] *ear for* music.
❸ 〔端〕 an edge; (食パン・チーズなどの切れ端) a heel; (パンの皮) a crust. ● 耳折れ本 a *dog-eared* book. ● ページの耳を折る turn down the *edge of* the page; dog-ear the page. ● サンドイッチ用にパンの耳を切り落とす cut the *crust* off the bread for the sandwiches.
❹ 〔その他の表現〕 ▶ちょっとお耳を拝借 (Can I have) a word *in* your *ear*? / (書) Please lend me your *ears* for a minute.

● 耳が痛い ▶それは耳の痛い話だ (=痛い所にふれる) The story *touches* me *on the raw*. (❗「耳の痛いことを言う人」は a pebble in (his) shoe などという)
● 耳が遠い be hard of hearing; be a little deaf.
● 耳が早い ▶彼は耳が早い He has *sharp ears*.
● 耳に入れる ▶それを彼の耳に入れておこう (=知らせよう) I'll *let* him *know* [I'll *tell* him] *about* it. ▶君の耳に入れたいことがある I have some news for you.
● 耳にする ▶変な音を耳にした A strange sound *came to* [*reached*] my *ears*. / (書前の方が口語的) I *heard* [(ふと耳にした) *overheard*] a strange sound. ▶彼が離婚すると耳にした (=うわさを聞いた) I *hear*(*d*) [(たまたま耳にした) *happened to hear*] that he is going to get divorced.
● 耳にたこができる ▶その話は耳にたこができるほど聞いた I'*m sick and tired of* (hearing) the story. / I have heard *enough of* the story.
● 耳につく ▶波の音が耳について眠れない I can't sleep, because the sound of the waves *is ringing in* my *ears*.
● 耳に残る ▶父の最後の言葉が今も耳に残っている My father's last words still linger *in* my *ears* [*mind*].
● 耳を疑う ▶彼が亡くなった奥様のあとを追って自殺したと聞いて私は耳を疑った I couldn't believe my *ears* when I heard he committed suicide to follow his deceased wife.
● 耳を貸す ▶だれが何と言おうと, 彼は耳を貸さなかった [聞く耳を持たなかった] No matter who opposed him, he wouldn't *listen*. (❗would は「どうしても...する」という固執の意を表す)
● 耳を傾ける ▶彼らは一心に耳を傾けて(音楽を)聴いた (話) They were *all ears* (listening to music). / They listened (to music) *intently* [*with all* their *ears*].
● 耳を澄(す)ます ▶耳をすましたが何も聞こえなかった I listened *attentively* [*strained* my *ears*], but heard [could hear] nothing. (❗could をつければ努力を強調する)
● 耳をそばだてる prick up one's ears; keep one's ears open.
● 耳をそろえる ▶借金は月末までに耳をそろえてお返しし

す I'll *pay off* all the debts by the end of the month.
- 耳をつんざく 耳をつんざくジェット機の爆音 the *ear-splitting* noise of the jet.
- 耳をかして get out [*that* she has come].

みみあか 耳垢 earwax. ▶耳あかを取る remove *earwax*; clean one's ears.

みみあたらしい 耳新しい new; (新奇な) novel. ●私に耳新しい話 a story I have never heard before; a story *new* to me.

みみうち 耳打ち ▶耳打ちする 動 ●彼に何か耳打ちする(=ささやく) *whisper* something *in* [*into*] his *ear*. ●彼に外へ出るように[彼女が来たと]耳打ちする *whisper* to him to get out [*that* she has come].

みみかき 耳掻き an earpick. 事情 米英では綿棒(a Q-tip)を用いるのが一般的)

みみがくもん 耳学問 second hand information [knowledge]. ▶耳学問で覚える learn about (it) [acquire knowledge] by *listening to other people*; listen and learn.

みみかざり 耳飾り an earring; an eardrop. (⇨イヤリング)

みみくそ 耳糞 earwax. (⇨耳垢(忠))

みみざとい 耳聡い be quick of hearing; have* sharp ears.

みみざわり 耳触り ▶耳触り(=聞いたときの感じ)のいいことをいう say something nice (to the ear).

みみざわり 耳障り ●耳ざわりな音(大きくて不快な) a *harsh* sound; (不快にさせる) an *offensive* sound, a sound *offensive to* [*that offends*] *the ear*; (ぎいぎいいう) a *grating* sound. !以上の sound の代わりにしばしば noise(不快な雑音・騒音にも用いる) ▶彼の声は耳ざわりだ His voice has a *harsh* voice./His voice *grates on* me [my ears]. ▶自動車の警笛は耳ざわりだ The sound of an auto horn is *offensive to the ear*.

みみず an earthworm. ●みみず腫れ a welt; a weal.

みみずく 〚鳥〛 a horned [an eared] owl /áʊl/.

みみせん 耳栓 (insert) an earplug.

みみたぶ 耳たぶ an earlobe.

みみだれ 耳垂れ discharge from the ear(s); 〚医学〛 otorrhea. ●耳垂れがしている have *running ears*.

みみっちい (けちな) stingy; (狭量な) mean. (⇨けち)

みみどおい 耳遠い (よく聞こえない) be hard of hearing; (聞き慣れない) be unfamiliar (*to*).

みみなり 耳鳴り ▶耳鳴りがする I have [There is] a ringing in my ears. / My ears are ringing [singing].

みみなれない 耳慣れない unfamiliar; strange. ●耳慣れない医学用語 an *unfamiliar* medical term.

みみなれる 耳慣れる get* used to hearing. (⇨ 聞き慣れる)

みみもと 耳元 ●耳元で near [close to] one's ears. ●耳元でささやく[どなる] whisper [shout] *in* (his) *ear*. (⇨耳打ち)

みみより 耳寄り ▶君に耳寄りな話(=歓迎すべき知らせ)がある I have (×a) *welcome news* for you. ▶それは耳寄りな(=元気づける)話だ That's an *encouraging* story.

みみわ 耳輪 an earring. (働 耳飾り, イヤリング)

みむき 見向き ▶彼らは彼の絵には見向きもしなかった(=何の興味も示さなかった) They *showed* no *interest in* [(注意を払わなかった) *paid* no *attention to*, *took* no *notice of*] his painting.

みめ 見目 looks. ●(容貌(镇), 器量) ●見目うるわしい beautiful; pretty; good looking; attractive.

みめい 未明 ●6日の未明に *before dawn* [〚やや書〛 *daybreak*] on the morning of the 6th.

ミモザ 〚植物〛(オジギソウ) a mimosa. !その花は 〚U〛
●ミモザサラダ a mimosa salad.

みもしらぬ 見も知らぬ ●見も知らぬ人 a perfect [a complete, a total, an utter] stranger.

みもだえ 身悶え ●身もだえして苦しむ *writhe* /ráɪð/ in agony.

みもち 身持ち (品行) morals. ▶あの男は身持ちが悪い He leads a loose life./He has loose *morals*./He is a man of loose *morals*.

★**みもと 身元** (本人であること) one's *identity*; (素性) one's *background*. ▶その被害者の歯型鑑定による身元確認 the dental *identification* of the victim. ●身元不明の死体 an *unidentified* body. ●興信所に彼の身元調査を依頼する ask a private detective agency to look into his *background*. ▶被害者の身元は分からない The *identity* of the victim is unknown./The victim *has not been identified*. ▶私は身元を証明するものは何も持っていなかった I had nothing to prove my *identity* [to *identify myself*].
- 身元保証人 〚法律〛 a guarantor /ɡǽrəntɔːr/; (照会先) a reference; (親代わりの人) 〚法律〛 a guardian.

みもの 見物 ●〚見るに値するもの〛 something well worth seeing; (悪い意味で) a sight. ▶今度の選挙は見ものだ. どの党が勝つのかね I think the coming election is *something to watch*. Which party do you think is going to win?/(好奇心でいっぱいだ) I'm *very curious to see* which party will win in the coming election.

みもの 実物 〚実の部分を食べる野菜〛 fruit vegetables.

みや 宮 〚皇居〛 the Imperial Palace; 〚皇族〛(男性) a prince; (女性) a princess; 〚神社〛 a Shinto shrine. ●三笠宮 *Prince* Mikasa.

★**みゃく 脈** 〚脈拍〛 a pulse. (! 通例単数形で) ●弱い脈 a weak [a feeble] *pulse*. ●整[不整]脈 (have) a regular [an irregular] *pulse*. ●脈を数える[とる] count [take, feel] one's *pulse*. ▶私の脈は速い[遅い] My *pulse* is quick [slow]. ▶脈が速く打つ The *pulse* beats quickly.
- 脈ある ●まだ脈がある(=いくらか希望が残されている) There is still *some* [*a ray of*] *hope*.
- 脈圧 pulse pressure. ●脈圧計 a sphygmometer; a sphygmomanometer. ●脈管 a vessel.

みゃくうつ 脈打つ beat*; pulsate. ▶心臓が激しく脈打つ My heart *beat* fast.

みゃくどう 脈動 图 (a) pulsation. ── **脈動する** 動 beat*; pulsate.

みゃくはく 脈拍 a pulse; 〚脈拍数〛 a pulse rate. ▶私の平常の脈拍は 70 です My normal *pulse rate* is (at) seventy.

みゃくみゃく 脈々 ── **脈々と** 副 〚途切れることなく〛 continuously, ceaselessly. ●脈々と(=何世代も)続いてきた伝統 a tradition which has been maintained *for generations* [has been handed down *from generation to generation*].

みゃくらく 脈絡 〚論理的一貫性〛 consistency; coherence /kouhíərəns/; (つながり) connection. ●脈絡のない議論 an *incoherent* argument. (⇨まとまり) ▶彼女はよく脈絡のない(=今まで話していたこととまったく関係のない)話をし始める She often says something which *has nothing to do with* what she was talking about just before./She often *jumps from topic to topic* (in her talk).

みやけ 宮家 (皇族の家) the house [family] of an Imperial prince.

みやげ 土産 (主に自分のための旅の記念品) a souvenir /sùːvəníər/; (他人への) a present, a gift (🔘 後の方が堅い語), (記念祭などに出る小さな) a memento. ● ハワイの土産 a *souvenir* [帰国土産] a *homecoming present* [for] of Hawaii. ● 京都(見物)の土産に人形を買う buy a doll as a *souvenir* of (one's sightseeing in) Kyoto. ▶ 君に土産を買って来てやるよ I'll buy a *present* [a *souvenir*] for you. (🔘 漠然と I'll buy *something* for you. とも) ▶ これはいい土産になるだろう This will make a good *souvenir*. ● さあ、土産だよ Here's *something* [a *present*] for you. (🔘 親しい間柄では近所の方が普通)
● **土産話** (tell) a story [(give) an account] of one's trip. **土産物店** a souvenír [a *gift*] shòp.

みやこ 都 (首都, 中心地) a capital. ● 音楽の都ウィーン Vienna, the music *capital*. ● 都落ちする (都を去る) leave the *capital*; (都会を離れて地方へ転動・転居する) 《話》 get sent to the boondocks [boonies]. ▶ 奈良は 710 年から 794 年まで日本の都だった Nara was the [×a] *capital* of Japan from 710 to 794. ▶ 住めば都 (⇒住む [成句])

みやこごう 宮号 an official name of an Imperial prince.

みやこどり 都鳥 『鳥』 an oyster catcher.

みやこわすれ 都忘れ 『植物』 a China aster.

みやさま 宮様 a prince; a princess.

みやすい 見やすい easy to see; [活字・筆跡などが] clear, easy to read, legible. (⇒易い)

みやだいく 宮大工 (説明的に) a carpenter who specializes in building shrines, temples, and palaces.

みやびやか 雅びやか — 雅びやかな 形 (上品な) elegant, refined; (優美な) graceful.

みやぶる 見破る [正体などを] find*... out; [見透かす] see* through.... (⇒見抜く) ● 彼のたくらみを見破る *see through* his ruse /rúːz/.

みやま 深山 deep mountains.
● 深山おろし strong [violent] wind blowing down from deep mountains.

みやまいり 宮参り (説明的に) a newborn baby's first visit to a Shinto shrine, when it is a month old. ● 宮参りに連れて行く take one's baby to a Shinto shrine for blessing.

みやる 見遣る (遠くの方を見る) look at (a tree) in the distance; (ちらりと見る) glance (*at*). (⇒ちらっと)

ミャンマー 〖国名〗 Myanmar; (公式名) the Union of Myanmar. (首都 Yangon) (〖参考〗 旧称はビルマ (Burma)) ● ミャンマー人 a Myanmarese; a Burmese /bə̀ːrmíːz/. (🔘 後の方が一般的) ● ミャンマー語 Myanmarese; Burmese. ● ミャンマー(人[語])の Myanmarese; Burmese.

ミュージアム [博物館, 美術館] a museum.
● ミュージアムショップ a museum shop.

ミュージカル a musical (comedy).

ミュージシャン [音楽家] a musician.

ミュージック [音楽] music.
● ミュージックシーン a music scene. ● ミュージックホール a music hall. ● ミュージックボックス a music box.

ミューズ [ギリシャ神話] Muse. (〖参考〗 主神 Zeus の娘で芸術と学問の九つの各分野をつかさどる女神 The (nine) Muses の 1 人)

ミュータント [突然変異体] a mutant.

ミュール (靴) mules. (🔘 通例複数形で)

ミュンヘン [ドイツの都市] Munich /mjúːnik/.

みよ 御代 a reign. ● 明治天皇の御代に in [under] the *reign* of Emperor Meiji.

みよう 見様 the way of looking at things. ▶ あの猪の絵は見ようによってはバクにも豚にも見える That picture of a wild boar looks like a tapir /téipər/ or a pig by the *way* you see it.
● **見よう見まね** ▶ 見よう見まねで魚がおろせるようになった I've learned [技術を身につけた] I've got the skill] how to clean fish by *following the other people's example* [by *watching other people*].

*みょう 妙 图 ❶ [奇妙] strangeness.
❷ [玄妙] (神秘) a mystery; (奇跡) a miracle.
● 自然の妙 the *mystery* of nature.
❸ [巧妙] (うまさ) cleverness; (妙技) a knack.
● 人の操縦にかけた妙を得ている have a *knack* of managing people; be *clever* [*skillful*] at managing people.

— **妙な** 形 (奇妙な) strange, (変わった) odd, 《話》 weird; (好奇心をそそる) curious; (独特に奇妙な) peculiar; (わけの分からない) funny. (⇒変な) ● 妙な経験をする have a *strange* [a *funny*] experience. ● 妙な人 (変人) an *odd* [a *curious*] person; (不審人物) a *suspicious* person. ● 妙な顔をする make a *strange* face. ● 妙な癖がある have *peculiar* habits. ● 妙なことに彼は結局試験に合格した *Strange to say* [*Strangely* (*enough*), *Oddly enough*], he passed his exam after all. ▶ 彼がまだ来ないのは妙だ It's *strange* (that) he hasn't come yet.

— **妙に** 副 strangely; oddly; (極度に) extremely; (異常に) unusually. ● 妙にふるまう behave *oddly*.
● 妙にそのことが気にかかる be *unusually* [*extremely*] anxious [concerned] about it; feel *very* uneasy about it. ▶ その山は今日は妙に美しかった The mountain was *strangely* [*unusually*] beautiful today.

みょう- 明- ● 明二十日に *tomorrow*, (on) the twentieth. ● 明 2009 年に *next year*, in 2009.

みょうあん 妙案 a good idea. (⇒名案)

みょうおう 明王 (不動明王) *Fudo Myoo*, the god of fire. (⇒不動明王)

みょうおん 妙音 very sweet sounds [voices, music].

みょうが 茗荷 [植物] a *myoga*, (説明的に) a plant whose stem resembles that of a Japanese ginger, but only buds sprouting from the root itself are eaten.

みょうが 冥加 (神の恩恵) (a) blessing; God's [divine] protection; (恩恵に対するお礼) an offering.
● **冥加に余る[尽きる]** This is more than I deserve.

みょうぎ 妙技 (離れ技) a feat; (すばらしい演技) a wonderful performance. ● 妙技を披露する perform a *feat*; give a *wonderful performance*.

みょうけい 妙計 (⇒名案)

みょうごにち 明後日 (the) day after tomorrow. (⇒明後日)

みょうごねん 明後年 the year after next.

みょうじ 名字, 苗字 one's family name, one's surname. ● 結婚前の名字 one's maiden name. ▶ 私の名字は上原です My *family name* [*surname*] is Uehara. / (名字に重点を置いて) Uehara is my *family name*. (🔘 日本人の名字は名前の最初に来るので last name を用いるのは不適切) (⇒姓)

みょうしゅ 妙手 (よい手筋) a clever [(しびれるような) a spectacular, a fantastic] move. ● move を idea に替えると「妙案」 ● 妙手を打つ make a *clever move*.

みょうしゅ 妙趣 a subtle charm; an indescribable charm.

みょうしゅん 明春 next spring; this coming spring.

みょうじょう 明星 ❶ [金星] Venus. (⇒明けの明星,

みょうじん 明神 a gracious god.
みょうせき 名跡 the family name. ▶彼は父の名跡を継ぎ幸四郎を名乗った He *renamed himself Koshiro* after his father.
みょうだい 名代 (代理) a deputy; a proxy. ●…の名代を務める act as a person's *proxy*; act as *deputy* for a person. ●名代で by *proxy*.
みょうちょう 明朝 tomorrow morning. ●明朝に (×on) tomorrow morning.
みょうにち 明日 tomorrow. (⇨明日(ᵗ))
みょうねん 明年 next year. (⇨来年)
みょうばん 明晩 tomorrow evening [night]. ●明晩に (×on) tomorrow evening [night].
みょうばん 明礬 alum.
みょうみ 妙味 a subtle charm; a nice point.
みょうやく 妙薬 a wonder [a miracle] drug 《*for*》; a specific medicine 《*for*》. (⇨特効薬)
みょうり 名利 (⇨名利(ᵐ))
みょうり 冥利 〖神仏の守り〗 a divine protection; 〖至福〗 bliss; perfect happiness.
● **冥利に尽きる** ▶この難局に我が国のかじ取りの大任を与えられたことは男冥利に尽きると申さねばなりません I *feel perfectly happy* [quite honored] to burden myself with the heavy responsibilities to get our country out of these difficulties.
みより 身寄り (⇨親類) ▶身寄りのない子 a child without *relatives* (to depend on).
ミラー a mirror. ●ミラーボール a mirror ball.
†**みらい** 未来 图 the future; (人・国などの前途) a future. (⇨将来) ●未来を予測[予言]する foretell [predict] *the future*. ▶遠い未来に何が起こるかだれにも分からない No one can tell what will happen *in the* distant (↔near) *future* 〖書〗 What *the* distant *future* holds for us.》 ▶彼には画家としての洋々たる未来がある He has a great [a bright] *future* (ahead of him) as a painter./(前途有望だ) He is a (very) *promising* painter.
── **未来の** 圈 future; (予想される) prospective. ●未来の総理大臣 a *future* prime minister. ●未来の出来事 *future* events. ●未来の妻 one's *future* [*prospective*] wife. ●未来永劫(ᵉᵍᵒ) for all of eternity; forever and ever.
●**未来学者** a futurist. ●**未来完了** 〖文法〗 the future perfect. ●**未来時制** 〖文法〗 the future tense. ●**未来派** futurism.
ミラクル 〖奇跡〗 a miracle.
ミラノ 〖イタリアの都市〗 Milan /mɪlǽn/. ミラノ(人)の Milanese /mɪ̀lənízː/.
ミリ milli-. (〖「…の 1,000 分の 1」の意〗)
●ミリグラム a milligram 《略 mg》. ●ミリバール (気圧の単位) a millibar 《略 mb》. (注) 現在はヘクトパスカルを用いる》 ●ミリメートル a millimeter 《略 mm》. ●ミリリットル a milliliter 《略 ml》.
ミリオンセラー a million seller.
ミリタリズム 〖軍国主義〗 militalism (↔pacifism).
みりょう 未了 ── 未了の 圈 (未完成の) unfinished; (未解決の) pending. ▶審議未了の議案 a *pending* bill. ●その仕事を未了のままにしておく leave the work *unfinished*.
みりょう 魅了 ── 魅了する 動 fascinate; charm. (⇨魅惑) ▶その劇は観客を魅了した The play *fascinated* the audience.
*‡**みりょく** 魅力 图 (魅了する力) (a) charm, (a) fascination; (訴えかける力) appeal; (引きつける力) (an) attraction. ●性的魅力 sex *appeal*. ▶彼女の魅力のとりこになっている be captivated by [be a captive of, be bewitched by] her *charms*. ●魅力のある申し出 an *attractive* [an *inviting*] offer. ●魅力を感じる be [feel] *attracted to* her. ▶今日日本の古典文学は若者にとってあまり魅力がない Today classics of Japanese literature have almost no *appeal to* [*attraction for*] young people./(若者の心に訴えない) Today classics of Japanese literature hardly *appeal to* the young. ▶その分譲マンションの最大の魅力は交通の便がよいことです One of the biggest *attractions* of the condominium is [lies in] its convenience [easy access] to public transportation. ▶彼女は人間的魅力のない[にあふれている]人です She has no [lots of] *personality*.
── **魅力的な** 圈 (外見で人を引きつける) attractive; (うっとりさせる) charming, fascinating (以上の順で意味が強くなる); (かわいらしい) pretty (〖注〗通例成人男性には用いない). ●魅力的な青年 an *attractive* [a *charming*, a *fascinating*] young man. (〖注〗 *charming* は日本語の「チャーミング」と異なり, 親切さや愛想のよさなども含む内面的魅力をいい, 老若男女に対しても用いる. 上の者から下の者に用いるのが普通) ▶青い服を着たあなたはとても魅力的です You look very *attractive* in blue.
みりん 味醂 *mirin*; sweet *sake* 《for seasoning》.
●みりん干し (a) dried fish seasoned with *mirin*.

## ‡みる 見る	INDEX
❶ 目で	❷ 見物する
❸ 読む	❹ 確かめる, 調べる
❺ 世話をする	❻ 判断する
❼ 試みる	

WORD CHOICE 見る
see 意識せず自然と目に入ること. 時に見るつもりのないものを偶然見てしまうことをも含意する. ▶彼が金を盗んでいるのを見た I *saw* him stealing money.
look 静止した対象を意識して見ること. ▶彼は立ち止まって時計を見た He stopped to *look at* his watch.
watch 通例動きのある対象を意識して見ること. ●テレビを見る *watch* TV.

頻度チャート
see
look
watch
20 40 60 80 100 (%)

❶【目で】 see* (〖注〗進行形では用いない); look 《*at*》; watch (⇨【類語】); (じっと見る) gaze 《*at*》; (じろじろ見る) stare 《*at*》; (ちらっと見る) glance 《*at*》; (ちらっと目に入る) catch* a glimpse 《*of*》. ▶パジャマ姿でうろうろしかって. 近所の人に見られたらどうするの You can't walk around in pajamas. Imagine what the neighbors say when they *see* you. ▶見たことのない車が家の前に止まっているのに気づいた I noticed a *strange* car standing in front of my house.
①【…を見る】 ●テレビ[野球の試合]を見る watch television [a baseball game]. ●野球の試合を見に行く go to *see* a baseball game. (〖注〗重点が「行く」ことに移るため *see* を用いる) ●映画[劇]を見る (劇場・映画などで) see a movie [a play]; (テレビでじっと) *watch* a movie [a play] 《*on* TV》. ●変な夢を見る have [×see] a strange dream; 《やや古》 dream a strange dream. ●賛美歌集を見ながら歌

みる

う sing *from* one's hymn /hím/ book. ▶彼は空を見ていた He *was looking* (*up*) *at* [×watching, ×seeing] the sky. ▶何を見ているのですか What *are* you *looking at*? (❗*at* を落とさないこと) ▶みんな，こちらを見なさい *Look* [×Look *at*] this way, everybody. ▶彼は警官を見て逃げた He ran away *at the sight of* [*when he saw*] a police officer. (❗後の方が普通の言い方) ▶私は蛇は(=を)見るのも嫌だ I hate [can't stand] the very [*mere*] *sight of* snakes./Just the *sight of* snakes disgusts me. 会話「ご注文は何になさいますか」「メニューを見たいのですが」"May I take your order, please?" "I'd like to *see* the menu, please."

②【〜を見る】鏡で自分の姿をよく見てみなさい *Take a good* [*a close*] *look at* yourself in the mirror./*See* [*Look at*] yourself carefully in the mirror. ▶じろじろ人を見てはいけません Don't *stare at* people. (❗*stare* は人に関して使うとき，好奇心・猜疑(ぎ)心または非友好的感情でじろじろ見ることを含意する) ▶彼女はじっと優しく彼を見た She *gazed* lovingly *at* [(やや書) *on*] him. ▶彼はまっすぐ彼女を見て「愛しています」と言った He *looked* her [×at her] (straight) in the eye(s) and said, "I love you." ▶私はちらっと時計を見た I *glanced* [*gave a* quick *glance*] *at* my watch. (⇨[次の例]) ▶私はパレードが通ったとき，ちらっと王子を見た I *caught a glimpse of* the Prince as the parade went by. (❗glance, ちょっと前から見ないときにちらっと見るのは catch a glimpse) ▶ちょっと見て彼は重病と分かりました I could tell *at a glance* that he was seriously ill. (❗understand の意で tell は，肯定文で一回限りの過去の行為でも could を用いることができる)

会話 (店で)「何にいたしましょうか」「いいんです，今はちょっと見てるだけですから」「どうぞ(=いいですよ)」"Can I help you?" "Not right now, thanks. I'm just *looking*." "Fine."

③【〜が...するのを見る】▶私は彼が通りを横断[横断している]のを見た I *saw* him cross [*crossing*] the street. (❗(1) cross は私が見たときには仕事横断していたことを，crossing は横断している途中にあったことを含意する。(2) ×I saw that he crossed [was crossing] the street. とはいわない。(3) 受身では He *was seen* to cross [*was seen crossing*] the street. となるが，前の方は「だれかに見られた」，後の方は「話し手が目撃した」の意) ▶私は彼がいじめられるのを何回も見た I've often *seen* him bullied. (❗see は only と受身の関係 (He was bullied) にある) ▶私は太陽が水平線の下に沈むのを見ていた I *watched* the sun set [*setting*] below the horizon. (❗受身の ×The sun was watched to set [setting].... は不可)

❷【見物する】(花・名所などを) see*; 【見に訪れる】visit; 【見て回る】(店内などを) take* [have*] a look (*around*); (案内に従って) tour. ●公園に桜を見に行く go to *see* the cherry blossoms in the park. ▶京都には見る所がたくさんある There are a lot of sights [places to *see*, places to *visit*] in Kyoto. ▶この博物館を見るのはこれが初めてです This is my first *visit to* this museum./This is the first time I've *visited* this museum./I've never *visited* this museum.

❸【読む】read*; (ちょっと読む) glance at ...; (さっと目を通す) look ... through. ▶今日の新聞を見ましたか Have you *read* [*seen*] today's paper? (❗Have you seen ...? では「軽く見出しを見た」の意味，または新聞などを尋ねる言い方にもなる) ▶私はその雑誌を医院の待合室でちょっと見ただけでした I only *glanced at* [*looked through*] the magazine in the doctor's waiting room.

❹【確かめ，調べる】(事を) see*; (安全性などを) check; (単語などを) look ... up; 【吟味する】look ... over [*through*]; (誤りを正す目的で) take* [have*] a look (*at*). ●ブレーキを見る *check* the brakes. ▶ドアをノックする音がした。だれなのか見て来て There's a knock on the door. Go and *see* [(米話) Go *see*] who it is. (❗it で受けることに注意) ▶辞書での単語を見なさい *Look up* the word *in* your dictionary. ▶彼が小切手に書かれたサインをよく見た(=確かめた) He *took a good look at* the signature on the check.

❺【世話をする】look after ..., take* care of ...; (番をする) watch, keep* an [*one's*] eye on ...; 【手助けする】help. ●彼の宿題を見てやる *help* him *with* his homework/×help his homework は不可); *help* him (*to*) do his homework (❗*to* を省略する方は直接的援助，to のある方は間接援助を表す) ▶しばらくの間赤ちゃんを見ていてください Please *look after* [*take care of*, *watch*, *keep an eye on*] my baby for a while.

❻【判断する】judge; 【A を B とみなす】look on [*regard*] (《A *as* B》); 【見こす】allow; 【見つもる】estimate. ●空模様から見て (*judging*) *from* [*by*] the look of the sky. ▶彼の行動を疑いの目で見る *look on* [*regard*] his actions *with* suspicion. ▶乗り換えに 30 分見る *allow* 30 minutes to change trains. ▶私は彼のことを友達とは見ていない I don't *look on* [*regard*] him *as* a friend. ▶私の見るところ(=意見では)その本はまったく駄作だ *In my opinion* [*view*], that book is just trash. (⇨意見) ▶見たところ(=見かけは)彼らは仲のよい友人のようだ *Seemingly* [*Apparently*] they are close friends. (❗*Apparently* は文脈によって「明らかに」の意にもなるので注意)/They *seem* [*appear*] *to be* close friends. ▶どう見ても(=あらゆる点から見て)彼女は 40 を越えている She's over 40 (years of age) *in every respect* [*way*]. ▶彼の言うことはどう見ても(=明らかに)間違っている *Obviously*, he is wrong./He is *obviously* wrong./It is *obvious* (that) he is wrong. ▶まだ来ていないところを見ると，彼はバスに乗り遅れたにちがいない *Seeing* (*that*) he isn't here yet, he must have missed the bus.

❼【試みる】try, have* a try 【話】a go 《*at*》, give* (*it*) a try (⇨試みる); 【...してみて気づく】《*do*》and [*to*] find*. ▶もう一度やってみます I'll *try* again./I'll *have* another *try*. (⇨やってみる) ▶このケーキを召し上がってみてください Please *try* [×try eating] this cake. ▶我々が火事の現場に急行してみると家全体に火が回っていた We rushed to the scene of the fire *and found* the whole house in flames.

● 見て見ぬ振りをする pretend not to see [(気づかないふり) notice, (知らないふり) know]; turn a blind eye 《*to*》; shut [*close*] one's eyes 《*to*》; look the other way; 【話】wink at 《him [his bad thing]》. ▶人がいじめられているのを見て見ぬふりをすることはできない I cannot *turn a blind eye* when someone is being bullied.

● 見ぬ振りをする pretend not to see; (不正などを) close one's eyes to ...; (やや書) connive /kənáiv/ *at* .... ▶彼はそのけんかを見ぬ振りをした He *closed* [*shut*] his *eyes to* the fight. ▶彼女が見ぬ振りをしていて私に気づかれないようにちらちらと私を見ているのに気づいた I noticed that she *was stealing glances* [*secretly glancing*] at me.

● 見る影もない ● 見る影もなくやせ細った人 a *misera*-

- **見るに耐えない[忍びない]** ▶彼女があんなに悲しんでいるのは見るに耐えない I *can't bear to* see her so sad./(見るのはつらい) It is painful to see her so sad.
- **見るに見かねて** ▶見るに見かねて彼を助けた I *couldn't stand by* and helped him./(気の毒に思って助けた) I felt so sorry for him that I helped him.
- **見るべき** ▶見るべき名所 the sights *worth seeing*.
- **見るも** ▶見るも哀れな miserable *to the eye*.

みる 診る (診察する) see, 《書》 consult. ●医者に診てもらう see [《書》 consult] a [one's] doctor. ● one's doctor は「かかりつけの医者」/ ●医者に胃を診てもらう have one's stomach *examined* by a doctor; have a doctor *examine* one's stomach. ●脈を診る take [feel] (his) pulse. ▶医者に風邪を診てもらいましたか *Have* you *been* to [*Have* you *seen*] the doctor about your cold? ▶息子が熱を出しているのですが, 先生, 診ていただけますか My son has a fever. Will you *have* [*take*] *a look at* him, Doctor?
会話 「あんまり気分がよくないんだ」「医者に行って診てもらいなさいよ」"I don't feel very well." "Go and *see* [《米話》 Go *see*] a doctor."

みるがい 海松貝 【魚介】a trough shell.
みるからに ▶彼は見るからに(=一見して)神経質そうだ I can tell *at a glance* he is highly strung. ▶彼は見るからに(=あらゆる点で)英国紳士だ He is *every inch* an English gentleman./(明らかに) *Obviously* [*Evidently*], he is an English gentleman. (⇨見る❻)

*****ミルク** milk. ●粉ミルク dried [powdered] *milk*; *milk* powder. ●コンデンスミルク condensed *milk*. ●ミルクで子供を育てる bring up a child on the *bottle*; bottle-feed a child. ●コーヒーはどのようになさいますか. ブラックですか, それともミルクを入れますか How would you like your coffee? With or without cream [Black or white]? (**!** (1) 最近では前の方が普通. (2) 《話》 ではミルクを入れたコーヒーを white coffee という. コーヒーに入れるものは cream)
●ミルクスタンド a milk bar. ●ミルクセーキ a milk shake. ●ミルクチョコレート (a) milk chocolate. ●ミルクティー tea with milk. (**!** 《英》 では単に tea というのが普通)

みるみる 見る見る (一瞬のうちに) in a moment [an instant, a minute]; (非常に早く) very fast [rapidly, quickly]. ▶船は船員もろともみるみる沈んでしまった The ship sank with all her crew *in a moment* [*an instant*]. ▶彼はみるみるうちに英語が上達した He has made (×a) *rapid* progress in English./His English has *rapidly* improved.

みるめ 見る目 ●人を見る目がある be a good (↔poor) judge of people. ●陶器を見る目がある have *an eye for* pottery; be a *good judge of* pottery; be a connoisseur /kὰnəsə:r/ of pottery. (**!** この connoisseur は「鑑定家」の意) ▶君はものを見る目があるね You have a good one when you *see* it.

ミレー 〖フランスの画家〗 Millet /mi:jéi/ (Jean François ～).
ミレニアム 〖千年(間[紀])〗 a millennium /miléniəm/. (圏) millennia, ～s)
みれん 未練 〖愛着〗a lingering attachment [preference]; 〖残念な気持ち〗 (a) regret. ●彼女にまだ未練がある I still have a *lingering attachment* [*some feelings*] *for* her./(忘れられない) I still can't put her out of my mind./I'm not yet *over* her. ▶彼は未練を残して故郷を去った He left his hometown *with regret*. ▶彼は未練がましくもな く家を売り渡した He sold the house off *without regret*.

ミロ 〖スペインの画家〗 Miró /miróu/ (Joan ～).
みろくぼさつ 弥勒菩薩 Miroku(-bodhisattva).
ミロのビーナス the Venus of Milo /máilou, mí:-/.
みわく 魅惑 图 (a) fascination; (魅力) (a) charm.
—— **魅惑的な** 圏 ▶彼女は魅惑的なほほえみを浮かべて彼を見た She looked at him with a *fascinating* [a *charming*] smile.
—— **魅惑する** 動 fascinate; charm. (**!** 前の方が強意的) ▶聴衆は彼のすばらしい奇術に魅惑された The audience *was fascinated by* [*with*] his wonderful magic./(とりこになった) The audience *fell under the spell of* his wonderful magic.

みわけ 見分け (区別) (a) distinction. ●見分けがつく(違いが分かる) can tell the difference; (見分けできる) can tell, can distinguish. (**!** tell は通例 can を伴う) ●見分けがつかない(=見ても分からないほど変わる) change beyond [out of] (all) recognition. ▶ラバと馬の見分けがつきますか Can you *tell the difference* [Can you *distinguish*] between a mule and a horse? ▶その双子はそっくりなのでさっぱり見分けがつかない Those twins are so alike (that) I *can never tell* [I *can never distinguish*, I never *know*] *one* from the other. (**!** I *can't tell* them *apart* [*distinguish* them]. ともいえる)

みわける 見分ける (区別する) tell*, distinguish 《A *from* B》 (**!** tell は通例 can を伴う); (違いが分かる) know* 《A *from* B》. (**!** 通例否定文・疑問文で) (見分け, 区別する) ▶群衆の中で彼を見分ける(=見つける) *pick* him *out* [×up] in the crowd. ▶闇の中で人影[だれなのか]を(やっと)見分けることができた I could *make* a figure *out* [*make out* who it was] in the dark. (**!** 「見分ける」「分かる」の意の make out は肯定文で過去の一回限りの行為でも could を用いることができる)

みわすれる 見忘れる forget; fail to [do not] recognise. (⇨忘れる)
みわたす 見渡す (一望する) look out 《on, over》, overlook; (見下ろす) look down 《on, over》. (⇨見下ろす) ●聴衆を見渡す look over [(全体を) (やや書) survey] the audience. ▶ホテルの部屋から町全体が見渡せた Our hotel room *looked out over* [*overlooked*, 《書》 *commanded a view of*] the whole city./We *could see* the whole city from our hotel room./There was [We had] a full *view of* the city from our hotel room./(大げさな言い方で) We *got a bird's eye view of* the city from our hotel room. ▶見渡す限り麦畑が広がっていた The wheat field stretched *as far as the* [×one's] *eye could see*. (**!** as far as the eye could *reach* より普通. as far as I [we] could see も可能だが「(視界がはっきりしないが)そこで見た限りでは」の意になることもある)

みをもって 身を以って (みずから) personally; (かろうじて) barely, narrowly (escape death).
みんい 民意 (国民の意思) the will of the people; (世論) public opinion. ●民意を反映する reflect *the will of the people* [*public opinion*].
みんえい 民営 private management [operation].
みんえいか 民営化 privatization. ●郵政民営化 the *privatization* of the postal service. ●民営化に賛成[反対]である be in favor of [against] *privatization*.
—— **民営化する** 動 privatize; sell* [transfer] to private ownership [hand]. ▶国鉄は分割・民営化された The JNR *was devided and transferred to private ownership* [*privatized*].

みんか 民家 a (private) house.

みんかん 民間 图 ●民間(=人々の間)に広まっているうわさ a rumor widespread *among the people*.
―― 民間の 形 (公的でない) private; (軍人・官吏に対して一般人の) civil, civilian; (商業的の) commercial; (民衆の) folk.
●民間外交 nongovernment(al) diplomacy. ●民間活力 the vitality of the private sector. ●民間機 a civil [a civilian] airplane. ●民間企業 a private enterprise. ●民間人 (軍人・官吏に対しての) a civilian. ●民間信仰 folk belief. ●民間設備投資 private capital expenditure. ●民間団体 a private organization; (非政府の) a non-governmental organization (略 an NGO). ●民間伝承 folklore. ●民間部門 a private sector. ●民間放送 commercial broadcasting. ●民間融資 commercial loan; commercial lending. ●民間療法 folk remedies [医療] medicine].

みんぎょう 民業 private enterprise.
ミンク a mink; (毛皮) mink. ●ミンクのコート a *mink coat*. (💡[話]では単に a mink ともいう)
みんぐ 民具 articles for everyday use.
ミンクくじら ミンク鯨 a minke whale.
みんげいひん 民芸品 (a) folkcraft.
みんけん 民権 [the people's] rights. ●民権を主張する assert the *people's rights*.
●民権運動 a civil rights movement.
みんじ 民事 civil affairs. ―― 民事の 形 civil.
●民事再生法 the Civil Rehabilitation Law. ●民事裁判 a civil trial. ●民事事件 a civil case. ●民事訴訟 a civil action [suit]. ●民事訴訟法 the Code of Civil Procedure.

みんしゅ 民主 ―― 民主的な 形 democratic (↔undemocratic). ▶ 我々は民主的にその会議を運営していた We chaired the meeting *democratically* [in a *democratic* way].
―― 民主化する 動 democratize ⟪a country [a system]⟫.
●民主化 democratization. ●民主国家 a democracy. ⟨⇒民主国⟩ ▶ 民主国家ではすべての国民は平等の権利を持っている In a *democracy* all citizens have equal rights. ●民主社会 (a) democratic society. ●民主主義 (⇒民主主義) ●民主制 a democratic system. ●民主政治 a democratic (form of) government. ●民主党 (日本の) the Democratic Party of Japan; (米国の) the Democratic Party.

みんじゅ 民需 (民間需要) the private demand. (⟨⇔官需⟩) ●民需を拡大する expand the *private demand*.
●民需産業 civilian industry.
みんしゅう 民衆 the people; (やや書) the (general) public. ⟨⇒大衆⟩
みんしゅく 民宿 a tourist home; (英) a guesthouse, a hostel.
みんしゅこく 民主国 a democratic state [country, nation] ⟨⇒国⟩; a democracy. ●西欧民主諸国 Western *democracies*.
みんしゅしゅぎ 民主主義 democracy. ▶ 民主主義は古代ギリシャに始まった *Democracy* originated in Ancient Greece. ●民主主義者 a democrat.
みんじょう 民情 the actual living conditions of the people. ●民情を視察する observe *how the people live*.
みんしん 民心 popular [public] sentiment [feeling]; feelings of the people. ●民心の安定を図る work to put the *public feeling* at rest.
ミンスク 〖ベラルーシの首都〗 Minsk.

みんせい 民生 public welfare.
●民生委員 a local welfare commissioner; a social worker. ●民生局 the Public Welfare Bureau.
みんせい 民政 (a) civil administration [government].
みんせん 民選 ●民選議員 a popularly-elected representative; a representative elected by the people.

みんぞく 民族 图 〖人種〗 a race; 〖国民〗 a people; (歴史・言語などを共有する) a nation; an ethnic group (💡 特有の文化・宗教・言語などを共有する集団。特にある地域の原住民や国・都市などの少数民族について用いる). ●異民族 an alien *race*. ●少数民族 (個々の) a minority *race* [*people*]; (少数民族集団) *ethnic* minorities. ●農耕[狩猟]民族 an agricultural [a hunting] *people*. ●日本民族 the Japanese *people*. ●多民族国家 a multi*racial* nation. ●単一民族国家 a *racially* homogeneous nation.
―― 民族の, 民族的な 形 racial; national; ethnic.
●民族の偏見 *racial* prejudice. ●民族意識 racial [national] consciousness. ●民族衣装 native [national] costume; ethnic clothes. ●民族移動 a racial migration. ●民族運動 a racial movement. ●民族音楽 ethnic music. ●民族学 ethnology. ●民族自決 racial [national] self-determination. ●民族宗教 the folk religion. ●民族主義 racism, racialism; nationalism. ●民族主義者 a nationalist. ●民族浄化 ethnic cleansing /klénziŋ/ [〖古〗 purification]. ●民族性 racial [national] characteristics. ●民族舞踊 ethnic dance. ●民族紛争 (an) ethnic conflict. ●民族料理 ethnic food.

みんぞくがく 民俗学 folklore.
●民俗学者 a folklorist.
ミンチ minced [〖米〗 ground] meat; (牛肉の) minced beef, 〖米〗 ground beef, 〖英〗 mince.
●ミンチパイ (a) mince pie.
みんちょう 明朝 〖歴史〗 (中国の) Ming; the Ming dynasty; 〖活字〗 Ming-cho type.
みんていけんぽう 民定憲法 a democratic constitution.
ミント 〖ハッカ〗 (a) mint.
みんど 民度 (人民の文化水準) the cultural [(道徳的) moral] standard of the people; (生活水準) the standard of living of the people; a living standard. ▶ あの国は民度が低い The people in that country have a low *standard of living*.

みんな everybody; all. ⟨⇒皆⟩ ▶ みんな死ぬほど心配しているんだよ 〖話〗 *People* have been worried sick. (💡 この表現は関係する人の多くを漠然とする)
みんぺい 民兵 〖集合的〗 (the) militia /məlíʃə/ (💡 単・複両扱い); (男性の) a militiaman (🅂 -men), (男女共用) a militia member.
みんぼう 民望 popularity. ⟨⇒衆望⟩
みんぽう 民放 commercial broadcasting.
みんぽう 民法 (法律) the civil law; (法典) the civil code.
みんゆう 民有 ―― 民有の 形 private; privately-owned. ●民有地 private land.
みんよう 民謡 a fólk sòng (💡 現代的なフォークソングは modern folk といって区別することがある); (伝承的で物語性のある) a ballad /bǽləd/. ●日本の民謡 a Japanese *folk song*.
みんりょく 民力 a nation's financial [economic] power.
みんわ 民話 a fólk tàle [stòry]; (伝説) a legend (💡 集合的には Ⓤ); (民間伝承) 〖集合的〗 folklore.

む

む 無 nothing; [ゼロ] zero. ●(努力などが)無になる come to *nothing* [[書] *naught*]; be brought to *nothing*. ▶無から有は(=何も)生じない《ことわざ》Nothing comes of [from] *nothing*.
●無にする ▶彼の親切を無にしてしまった I let everything he did for me *come to nothing*.

むい 無位 ●無位無官の人 a commoner; a person with no social rank.

むい 無為 图 idle.
── 無為に 副 idly, in idleness. ●無為に暮らす live *in idleness*; lead an *idle* life; idle 《one's time》away.

むいか 六日 ●6日間病気で寝る be sick in bed for *six days*. ●6月6日に on June 6(*th*). (⇒日付)

むいぎ 無意義 ── 無意義な 形 insignificant; meaningless. (⇒無意味)

*__むいしき__ 無意識 ── 無意識の 形 [思わず知らずの]involuntary; [意識不明の, 何気ない] unconscious. ▶彼は3日間無意識状態だ He has been *unconscious* for three days (running).
── 無意識に 副 ●無意識にそれをした I did it *involuntarily* [*unconsciously*], (考えずに) *without thinking*]. ▶彼女はその男を見て無意識に叫び声を上げた She gave an *involuntary* cry at the sight of the man.

むいそん 無医村 a doctorless village; a village without a doctor.

むいちぶつ 無一物 ●無一物である(=お金や財産などを何一つ持っていない) be penniless. ●無一物になる lose everything.

むいちもん 無一文 ── 無一文の 形 penniless. (⇒文無し) ▶今彼の身にもしものことがあれば彼の家族は無一文のまま残されることになるだろう If something happens to him now, his family will be left *penniless* [(何も受け取るものがない) *empty-handed*].

むいみ 無意味 ── 無意味な 形 ●無意味な(=意味のない)議論 a *meaningless* [a *senseless*] argument. ●無意味な抵抗 (a) *useless* resistance. ●無意味なこと(=わけの分からないこと)を言う talk *nonsense*.

むいん 無韻 ── 無韻の 形 unrhymed; blank.
●無韻詩 an unrhymed poem; (弱強五歩格の無脚韻詩) blank verse.

ムース [<フランス語] [整髪料, 菓子] (a) mousse /múːs/.
●チョコレートムース chocolate mousse.

ムース [動物] (ヘラジカ) a moose.

*__ムード__ (an) atmosphere. (❗mood は主に個人または集団の [気分や, 気分]の意; 広まる楽観ムード a *mood* of growing optimism)(⇒雰囲気) ●ムードのある人 a person with a certain [a lot of] *atmosphere*. ▶その部屋はいいムードがあった The room had a nice *atmosphere* [was full of *atmosphere*].
●ムード音楽 mood music. ●ムードメーカー a creator of a cheerful atmosphere; [(和製語)] a mood maker.

ムートン [<フランス語] sheepskin.
ムールがい ムール貝 [<フランス語] [魚介] a blue mussel.
ムーンストーン (a) moonstone. ([参考] 6月の誕生石)
ムーンライト [月光] moonlight.

むえき 無益 图 uselessness.
── 無益な 形 useless; futile /fjúːtl, -tail/. (⇒無駄) ●無益な本 a *useless* book. ●無益な試みをする make a *futile* [a *useless*] attempt.

むえん 無塩 ●無塩食 salt-free diet. ●無塩バター salt-free [unsalted] butter.

むえん 無煙 ── 無煙の 形 smokeless.
●無煙炭 anthracite; hard coal. ●無煙ロースター a smokeless grill.

むえん 無縁 ●無縁である (関係がない) have no relation 《to》; be irrelevant 《to》; (縁者がない) have no relatives. ●無縁の墓 an unknown [an unidentified] person's grave; (弔う縁者のない) a neglected grave.
●無縁仏 (説明的に) a person who died leaving no one to attend to his grave.

むが 無我 图 (無私) selflessness.
── 無我の 書 selfless. ●無我の境地に達する[にいる] attain [be in] a state of (perfect) *selflessness* [(没我) *self-effacement*].

むかい 向かい ●向かいの 書 opposite. ●向かいの家 the house *opposite* (mine); (通りの向こう側の) the house *across the street*. ●川の向かい側に住む live *on the opposite* [*other*] *side of* the river; live *across* the river. ▶学校は教会の向かいにある Our school is *opposite* (to) [《主に米話》*across from*] the church. (❗ to なしで opposite を前置詞として用いる方が普通. in front of the church では単に「教会の前の場所に」という漠然とした言い方になる. *Across from* the church is our school. のように倒置構文を用いると church からの視点が強調される)

むがい 無害 ── 無害な 形 harmless 《to》; (薬などが) [書] innocuous. ●人畜無害 *Harmless* [*No harm*] *to* animals and humans. (❗殺虫剤などの表示) ▶私はもう年だから人畜無害だよ I'm a *harmless* old man. ●この薬は無害だ This medicine is *harmless* [*innocuous*]./This medicine will do you *no harm*.

むがい 無蓋 ── 無蓋の 形 (屋根のない) open.
●無蓋貨車 《米》a flatcar, 《米》a freight car, 《米》a gondola (car); 《英》a wagon.

むかいあう 向かい合う [互いに向き合う] face 《with》each other. ▶その二人は向かい合ってテーブルについた The two sat at the table *facing each other*./The two sat *across* the table *from each other*./The two sat *face to face with each other across* the table. ●愛と舞はテーブルに向かい合って座っていた Ai and Mai were sitting *across from each other* at the table. ▶彼の家は私の家と向かい合っている His house is *opposite* (to) [《主に米話》*across from*] mine. (❗ to は省略する方が普通) / His house *faces* mine.

むかいあわせ 向かい合わせ ●向かい合わせの2枚の鏡 two *facing* mirrors; two mirrors *facing in opposite directions*. ●向かい合わせに座る(=向かい合って座る) (⇒向かい合う)

むかいかぜ 向かい風 a head [an adverse, an unfavorable, a contrary] wind. ●向かい風に逆らって進む go *against the wind*.

*__むかう__ 向かう ❶ [面する] face. ●鏡に向かう(=鏡をのぞく) look in a mirror. ▶フェンスに向かって立つ

むかえ

stand *opposite* the fence. ▶彼は大群衆に向かって演説を始めた He *faced* the large crowd and began to make a speech. ▶彼はいつも夜遅くまで机に向かっている He always *sits at* his desk till late at night. ▶写真の向かって右から3人目が私のおばです The third person from the right in the picture is my aunt. ▶よくも面と向かってそんなことが言えるな How dare you say such a thing to my *face* (↔*behind my back*)? (❗単に …*to* me? ともいえる)

❷ 【対する, 刃向かう】 ●風に向かって(=逆らって)走る run *against* the wind. ●犬に向かって石を投げる throw a stone *to* [(めがけて)*at*] the dog. (❗at では石が実際に犬に当たったかどうか不明だが to では当たったことを含意する) ●彼に向かって手を振る wave *at* him. (❗at は目標を示す) ▶敵が向かってきた The enemy advanced *on* [(四方から) closed in *on*] us. (❗on は攻撃を含意する) ▶彼女はナイフを持って私に向かってきた She *came at* me with a knife.

❸ 【目指す】 (出発する) start 《*from*》; leave* 《*for*》 (⇨出発する); (向かって進む) head 《*for*》. ▶東京へ向かう leave *for* Tokyo. ▶彼はあす成田を発ってパリに向かう He leaves [*starts from*] Narita *for* Paris tomorrow. (❗He *is leaving*…. と進行形にすると, そのことがあくまで予定であることを意味する。それに対し現在形ではそのことが動かない事実として語られている) ▶私たちは南[ロンドン]に向かって進んでいる We *are heading* south [*for* London, *toward* London]. (❗for は目的地, toward は方面, 方向を表す) ▶彼は急いで学校に向かった He *made for* school. (❗make for … は「へすばやく進む」の意) ▶彼女はバイクに乗って町に向かった She got on her bike and rode off toward town. (❗車の場合は drove off とよる)【会話】「田中はどこ?」「今ごろはもう(名古屋を出て)大阪に向かっているはずだよ」"Where's Tanaka?" "By now he should *be* (heading out of Nagoya) *on* his *way to* Osaka."

❹ 【方向に傾く】 ▶彼は日ごと快方に向かっている He *is getting better* [*is taking a turn for the better*] day by day. ▶冬に向かうと(=冬が近づくにつれて)風邪をひく人が多くなる With the approach *of* winter more and more people catch (a) [get a] cold.

むかえ 迎え ●迎えに寄る(誘いに立ち寄る) call for …; (車で迎えに行く) pick … up. ●ホテルに迎えの車を差し向ける send a car around to *pick* (him) *up* at [ˣ*to*] a hotel. ●彼を駅に迎えに行く[来る] go [come] to the station to *meet* him; go [come] to *meet* him at the station. ▶彼女は学校へ娘を迎えに行った She went to school to *take* her daughter *home* [(車で) *pick up* her daughter]. ▶空港に迎えに来てください Please come and *meet* me at the airport.

むかえいれる 迎え入れる receive; (歓迎する) welcome. ▶彼の二塁打で2人の走者を迎え入れた His double brought in [home] two runners.

むかえうつ 迎え撃つ meet*; (ミサイルを) intercept.

むかえざけ 迎え酒 ●二日酔いを治すために迎え酒をする have *a hair of the dog* to cure one's hangover. (❗a [the] hair of the dog that bit (him) は「(彼に)かみついた犬の毛の少の傷が治せる」との迷信に由来する慣用表現)

むかえび 迎え火 *mukaebi*; (説明的に) the bonfire lit to welcome the spirits of one's ancestors. (⇨送り火)

むかえぼん 迎え盆 *mukaebon*; (説明的に) the first day of the Bon Festival. (⇨送り盆)

*★**むかえる 迎える** ❶ 【出迎える】(会う) meet*; (車で迎えに行く) pick … up (⇨出迎え); 【歓迎する】 welcome,

---

むかし

greet (❗後の方は言葉・動作などを伴う); (しばしば正式に) receive. ●彼は玄関で客を迎えた He welcomed [*greeted, received*] his guest at the (front) door. ▶その店は客を迎える準備ができている The store is ready to *receive* customers. ▶彼を暖かく迎えてやってほしい。ずっと昔からの友だちだからね You must make him *welcome*. He is a very old friend of mine. (❗この welcome は形容詞で「歓迎される」の意)

❷ 【来てもらう】(招待する) invite; (呼ぶ) call. ●専門家を迎える *invite* [*call*] a specialist. ▶当日彼らは彼を講師に迎えた They *invited* him *to* give them a lecture on that day.

❸ 【ある時期・状態になる】 (入る) enter; (達する) reach; (巡って来る) come* around. ●新時代[新たな局面]を迎える *enter* a new era [a new phase]. ●老い[大場]を迎える *reach* old age [(its) climax]. ●新年を迎える greet [*welcome*, (祝う) celebrate] the New Year. ▶彼は20歳の誕生日を迎えた His twentieth birthday *came around*.

むかく 無学 图 (無知) ignorance; (文盲) illiteracy.
—**無学な** 形 (無教育の) uneducated; (文盲の) illiterate /ɪlɪtərət/. ▶無学だからといって卑屈になることはない You need not feel small because you are ˇ*uneducated*.

むかくめん 無額面 ●無額面株式 《株式》 a no-par (value) stock.

むかご 零余子 《植物》 a propagule.

▪**むかし 昔** (ずっと前に) a long time ago, long ago; (かって) once (❗通例 be 動詞, 助動詞の後, 一般動詞の前に置く。これは強勢を受けないのが普通。(現在または過去のある時より前に) before (⇨以前), (以前に) formerly, in former times [days]; (過去に) in the past, 《話》 in the old days; (大昔に) in old [ancient] times. (❗(1) in the old world と言ってるその意を表すこともある。(2) before, in the past は通例過去・現在[過去]完了時制とともに用い、その他は通例過去時制とともに用いる)

> **解説** (1) used to と would: 上記の副詞(句)以外に,「昔」の意味は /júːstə/, would によっても表せる。**used to** は (a) 過去の状態や習慣的行為を現在と対比して表したり, (b) 過去の習慣的動作を表す。**would** はもっぱら (b) の用法で, 主に書き言葉で用いられ, used to より回顧の気持ちが強い。また, いずれも漠然とした過去を表し, sometimes, every Sunday, for years, in one's childhood などの漠然と頻度や時を表す副詞(句)を伴うことができるが, ten times, for ten years, in 1990 など明確な頻度や時の副詞(句)とともには通例用いない。
>
> (2) used to の否定文・疑問文・付加疑問文
> 否定文: He never used to…./He didn't use [used] to…./《英書やや古》 He used not to…./《英やや古》 He use(d)n't to….
> 疑問文: Did he use [used] to…?/《書やや古》 Used he to…?
> 付加疑問文: He used to…, didn't he?
> 実際には否定文の never used to を除いて普通の過去形を用いる方が一般的。

❶ 【昔(は)】 ▶昔, 京都は日本の首都でした Kyoto was the capital of Japan *a long time ago* [*long ago*]. ▶昔は婦人に選挙権が与えられていなかった *Formerly* [*In former times*, 《話》*In the old days*], the right to vote was not given to women. ▶私は昔京都に住んでいた I (*once*) lived in Kyoto. (❗once なくても「昔」の意は表せる)/I *used to* [ˣ*would*] live in Kyoto. ▶昔はよく妹と散歩したものだ I often *used to* [*would* often] take a walk with my sister. (!used often to の語順は堅い言い方) 会話「テニスをおやりですか」「昔は時々やりましたが最近はやりません」"Do you play tennis?" "I *used to* sometimes, but not recently."

②【昔に[を]】●昔をしのぶ look back on one's *past*; recall one's *younger days*. ▶彼らは1500年の昔にそこに住みついた They settled down there *as early* [*as far back*] *as* 1500.

③【昔から】●昔からの(=昔の)友人 an *old* friend of mine. (⇨友達) ●昔からの習慣 an old [(伝統的な) a *traditional*] custom. ●彼は昔から(=ずっと)大阪に住んでいる He has *always* lived in Osaka. (!この用法は普通は通例完了形と用いる)/(子供のころから) He has lived in Osaka *since* he *was a child* [(やや書) *since* his *childhood*]. ▶(ずっと)昔から君を知っているような気がする I feel I've *always* known you.

── 昔(の) 形 old; (大昔の) ancient; (過去の) past. ●昔なじみの顔 old familiar faces. ●昔々 long, long ago; once upon a time. (!おとぎ話などで最初に用いる句) ●昔の友人 (⇨図 ③) ●昔の面影 one's *former* self [appearance]. ●昔かたぎの大工 a carpenter who sticks to *old-time* ideas. ●昔ながらのふるさと one's home town *exactly the same as before*. ▶それは何年も昔のことだ It was *ages* [*a very long time*] *ago*. ▶私たちはいっしょに遊んだ昔の日々を思い出した We remembered the *old days* when we had played together. ▶その町は昔のままだった The town was exactly the same *as before*./(書) The town was as it *had been*. ▶彼は今では昔のように暇ではない He isn't as free as he *used to* be [he (once) *was*, (once) he *was*]. (!*once* は省略данных などで be 動詞(や助動詞)が強勢を受ける場合はその前に置くのが普通)
会話「夕べはどこにいたの」「そんな昔のこと, 覚えてないね」"Where were you last night?" "That's *a long ago*, I don't remember." (!映画『カサブランカ』(*Casablanca*) の中の名セリフの一つ)

●昔取った杵柄(誠) (*with*) skills acquired in the past.

むかしつ 無過失 ●無過失責任【法律】liability without fault.

むかしばなし 昔話 (おとぎ話) an old tale; (伝説) a legend; (思い出話) stories of one's past.

むかち 無価値 ── 無価値な 形 valueless; worthless.

むかつく ❶【吐き気がする】feel* [be] sick (!(米)では文脈上明らかな場合以外は to one's stomach をつける); [吐き気・嫌悪を催す] be [feel] disgusted; be stomach-turning [(非常にむかつく) is stomach-churning]. ●空腹になると胃がむかつく I *feel sick* to my stomach when I get hungry./My stomach *turns* [(激しく) *churns*] when I get hungry./Hunger *makes* me *sick* to my stomach [*turns* my stomach].
❷【腹が立つ】●彼の態度にむかついた His attitude *disgusted* me [*made* me *sick*, 《米話》*burned* me *up*]./I was disgusted at [by] his attitude./His attitude *was disgusting* [*stomach-turning*] *to* me. (!「超むかつく」は stomach-churning が当たる)
会話「何で私にどなるのよ」「むかついているからだよ」"What are you yelling at me for?" "Because I'm pissed off."

むかっぱら むかっ腹 ●むかっ腹を立てる (わけもなく腹を立てる) get angry for no reason; (突然) fly into a temper [a rage, a passion] for no reason.

むかで 百足 【動物】a centipede.

むかむか ── むかむかする 動 [吐き気がする] feel* sick; [嫌悪がさす] be disgusted. (⇨むかつく) ●むかむかして in disgust.

むがむちゅう 無我夢中 ●無我夢中で(=命からがら)逃げる run away *for dear life*. ●新作に無我夢中(=忘我の状態)である[になる] *be in* [*go into*] *ecstasy* over the new work. (⇨夢中)

むがわせ 無為替 ●無為替輸出 no-draft export. ●無為替輸入 no-draft import.

むかん 無官 (⇨無位)

むかん 無冠 ▶ジャーナリストを無冠の帝王と呼ぶことがある Journalists are sometimes called *uncrowned kings*.

むかんがえ 無考え ── 無考えな 形 thoughtless; reckless; rash.

むかんかく 無感覚 ── 無感覚の 形【光・刺激などに】insensitive, 《書》insensible (!sensible の反対の意ではないことに注意); [まひした] numb; [植物の] insensitive. (⇨無神経) ●痛みに無感覚である be *insensitive* [*insensible*] *to* pain. ●(指などが)寒さで無感覚になる become *numb* [*dead*] *from* [《まれ》*with*] the cold.

むかんけい 無関係 ── 無関係の 形 unrelated 《*to*》, unconnected 《*with*》; (見当違いの) irrelevant 《*to*》. (⇨∼関係) ●無関係である have nothing to do 《*with*》; have no connection 《*with*》; be not connected 《*with*》. ▶私はそのことと無関係だ I *have nothing to do with* the matter. ▶その二つの事件は全く無関係だ The two events are completely *unrelated* [*unconnected*].

むかんじしん 無感地震 an unfelt earthquake. (⇔有感地震)

むかんしん 無関心 indifference 《*to, toward*》; unconcern 《*for, about*》. (⇨関心) ▶彼は政治に無関心だ He *is indifferent to* [*unconcerned about*] politics./He *has no interest in* politics.

むかんどう 無感動 ── 無感動な 形 unmoved (!通例叙述的に); impassive, apathetic. ●無感動な表情 an *impassive* [an *emotionless*] expression.

*むき 向き ❶【方向, 方角】a direction, a way. (⇨方向) ●アンテナの向きを変える change the *direction* of the antenna. ●ソファーの向きをくるりと変える turn the sofa around. ▶風の向きが北に変わった The wind *changed* [*shifted*] *to* the north. (!日本語の「向き」に引かれて The wind *direction* [The *direction* of the wind] changed to the north. というのはやや冗漫) ▶この家は向きが悪い This house faces the wrong *way* [*in* the wrong *direction*]. (!このままだと米英人には分からないので, According to the traditional belief in Japan, this house ... とするがよい) ▶私の家は東向きだ My house *faces* [*looks*] east./My house faces *toward* [*to*] the east.

❷【適合】(適している) be suitable 《*for*》; (主に仕事・役割などに) be suited 《*to, for*》. (⇨向く) ●子供向きの本 a book (*suitable* [(企画された) *designed*]) *for* children; a children's book. ●向き不向き (⇨)

❸【傾向】a tendency. ▶彼には他人の問題を軽視する向きがある He tends to [has a *tendency* to] make light of other people's problems.

❹【人】▶ご希望の向きにはこの本をお送りします We send this book to *those* who ask for it.

むき ●むきになる (本気になる) get serious; (怒る) get upset; (興奮する) get excited. ▶彼はむきになって(=猛烈に)そのうわさを否定した He *fiercely* denied the rumor. ▶そうむきになるな Don't be so seri-

むき ous./(かりかりするな) Don't get upset [《話》get up tight]./(力まないで) Take it easy.

むき 無期 —— **無期の** 形 indefinite. ● 無期停学になる be suspended *indefinitely* [*for an indefinite period*] from school. ● 無期懲役に処せられる be sentenced to *life* imprisonment; be imprisoned *for life*; get [be given] life.
—— **無期に** 副 indefinitely.

むき 無機 inorganic (↔organic).
● 無機化学 inorganic chemistry. ● 無機化合物 an inorganic compound. ● 無機肥料 inorganic fertilizer. ● 無機物 inorganic matter, an inorganic substance; (鉱物質) a mineral.

むぎ 麦 (小麦) wheat,《英》corn; (大麦) barley; (ライ麦) rye; (カラス麦) oats. ● 麦を作る grow [raise] wheat. ● 麦打ちをする flail [thresh] wheat [barley]. ● 麦踏みをする tread barley [wheat] (plants).
● 麦秋 early summer. (⇨麦秋(ばくしゅう)) ● 麦粉 wheat [rye] flour /fláuər/. ● 麦作 (栽培) wheat cultivation; (作柄) a wheat crop. ● 麦茶 barley tea. ● 麦とろ boiled rice and barley topped with grated yam. ● 麦笛 an oaten pipe;《古》an oat. ● 麦飯 cooked rice and barley.

むきあう 向き合う face each other. (⇨向かい合う) ▶ やはり旅はたった一人で自分と向き合いながら (= 自分の内面を見つめながら) 歩くのでなければ、無意味ということか To me traveling is meaningless, unless I go [×walk] alone *looking into my inner self*.

むきかわる 向き変わる turn (a)round.

むきげん 無期限 —— **無期限の** 形 indefinite. ● 無期限ストに入る go on an *indefinite* [a *no-time-limit*] strike; go on strike *for an indefinite period*.
—— **無期限に** 副 indefinitely; for an indefinite period [time].

むきず 無傷 —— **無傷の** 形 (傷のない) flawless; (完全な) perfect; (けがのない) unhurt, unwounded; (無事な) unharmed. ● 無傷の宝石 a *flawless* gem. ▶ 彼は燃えている家から無傷で脱出した He got out of a burning house *unhurt* [*unharmed*].

むきだし 剥き出し ● むき出しの (= 裸の) 肩 *bare* [*naked*] shoulders. (⇨裸) ● 腕をむき出しにする *bare* one's arms. (⚠「腕をむき出しにして」は with one's arms *bared*) ● 敵意をむき出しにする (= 露骨に表す) *show* one's hostility *openly*.

むきだす 剥き出す (⇨剥き出し) ● 歯をむき出す show one's teeth. ▶ その子は歯をむき出してにっこと笑った The child *grinned*. ▶ 犬は怒って歯をむき出した The dog *showed* [*bared*] its teeth angrily.

むきどう 無軌道 —— **無軌道な** 形 (無節操な) unprincipled. ● 無軌道な (= ふしだらな) 生活をする lead a *loose* life.

むぎとへいたい 麦と兵隊』 *Wheat and Soldiers*. (参考) 日野葦平の小説

むきなおる 向き直る turn around [round, about].
● 向き直って私を見る *turn around* and look at me.

むきふむき 向き不向き ▶ 人にはそれぞれ向き不向きがある Everyone is talented in his [her] way.
会話 「テレビのクイズ番組に出る気はないかい」「うーん、クイズ番組に出るなんていうのは人によって向き不向きがあるからね」"Won't you like to go on a TV quiz show?" "Well, being a quiz show contestant is not for everyone."

むきみ 剥き身 —— **剥き身の** 形 shelled 《peas [prawns]》; shucked 《peas [oysters, clams]》; peeled 《prawns》. ● あさりのむき身 shelled short-neck clams.

むきむき 向き向き ▶ 人には向き向き (= それぞれの好みや適性) がある Everybody has their own *taste* or *aptitude*.

むきめい 無記名 —— **無記名の** 形 (署名のない) unsigned; (氏名等が記入されていない) unregistered; (白地のままの) in blank. ● アンケートに無記名で答える answer a questionnaire *unsigned*. ● 無記名投票で決める decide by [in a] *secret* (↔open) ballot.
● 無記名株『株式』a bearer stock; a stock to bearer; an unregistered stock.

むきゅう 無休 ● 無休で働く work *without a holiday*. ▶ 年中無休《掲示》Open throughout the year./ Open 7 days a week.

むきゅう 無給 —— **無給の** 形 unpaid《work》. ● 無給の幹事 an *unpaid* [《名誉職の》an honorary] secretary. ● 無給で働く work *without pay*.

むきゅう 無窮 infinity; eternity. (⇨無限, 永遠)

むきょういく 無教育 —— **無教育の** 形 (教育のない) uneducated; (教養のない) uncultured; (無学の) illiterate /ilítərət/. (⇨無学)

むきょうそう 無競争 ● 無競争で当選する be elected *unopposed*.
● 無競争選挙 an uncontested election.

むきょうよう 無教養 —— **無教養な** 形 uncultured.

むきょか 無許可 —— **無許可で** 副 [無断で] without permission;『認可を受けずに』without a license.
● 無許可で露店を出している keep a stall *without a license*.

むきりょく 無気力 名 languor.
—— **無気力な** 形 (不活発な) inactive, lethargic; (ものうげな) languid; (元気のない) spiritless.

むぎわら 麦藁 straw.
● 麦わら細工 straw work. ● 麦わら帽子 a straw hat.

むきん 無菌 名 (状態) asepsis. —— **無菌の** 形 aseptic; (殺菌した) sterilized.
● 無菌飼育 (実験用動物など) aseptic feeding. ● 無菌室 an aseptic [a sterilized, a germfree] room. ● 無菌培養 aseptic culture.

****むく 向く** ❶ [向きを変える] (体の) turn; (目・顔などの) look. ● 右を向く turn (to the) right. ● 後ろを向いて彼を見る *look back at* him. (⇨振り向く) ● 彼は怒って私の方を向いた He *turned to* [*toward*] me in anger.
❷ [面する] face; (建物・窓などが見晴らす) look out on…. ● 南を向いた部屋 a room *facing* south (⚠ a south-facing room とはしない方がよい). ▶ そのホテルは海に向いている The hotel *faces* [*looks out on*] the sea. ▶ その窓は庭に向いている The window *opens onto* [*on*] the garden.
❸ [適する] suit, be suitable 《for》; (ふさわしい) be fit 《for; to do》 (⚠ suitable より意味が広い語). ● 女性に向いた仕事 a job *suitable* [*fit*] *for* a woman; a *suitable* [a *fit*] job *for* a woman. ▶ その土地は野菜の栽培に向いていますか Does the soil *suit* [*Is the soil suitable for*] vegetables? ▶ この土地は石が多くて農業には向かない These fields are too rocky for farming. ▶ 彼女は教師に向いていない She *isn't suited to be* a teacher [*for teaching*]. (⚠ be suited は主に仕事・役割などに向いていることをいう. suited の代わりに good enough を用いるほうが口語的)/《話》She *isn't cut out to be* a teacher [*for a teacher, for teaching*]. (⚠ be cut out は通例否定文で用いる) / (教えるのが本当にへただ) She *isn't any good at* teaching. ▶ あなたは本当にセールスの仕事に向いた性格のように思えますよ You dó sèem to have the personality *for* sales.

❹ [気持ちなどが傾く] (…したい気がする) feel* like (doing). ▶このところあまり仕事に気が向かない I don't *feel like* working [*am not inclined to* work] these days. ▶気の向くようにしなさい Do *as you like.*
❺ [その他の表現] ▶ついに彼にも運が向いてきた Fortune *smiled on* [*upon*] him at last.

*む**く 剝く** (果物・野菜などを) peel, pare. (【厳密には peel は手で, pare はナイフでむくことだが, pare の代わりに peel を用いることも多い) ▶リンゴの皮をむく *peel* [*pare*] an apple. ▶彼女はバナナの皮をむいてくれた She *peeled* me a banana [a banana *for* me].

むく 無垢 ▶無垢な(=純真な)少女 an *innocent* girl. ▶白無垢の(=純白の)ドレス a dress of *pure* white.

むくい 報い (罰) (a) punishment (⇔罰); (天罰)〔書〕 (a) retribution (*for*); (善行の) (a) reward (*for*). ▶悪事の報いを受ける receive *punishment for* one's wrongdoing. ▶それは当然の報いだ That's *what you deserve*. (【よい意味にも悪い意味にも用いる)/(いい気味だ) That [It] *serves you right*. (【くだけた会話では *Serve(s) you right*. ともいう) ▶彼は警告を無視して後で報いを受けた He disregarded the caution and *paid for* it later.

むくいぬ 尨犬 [動物] a shaggy dog.

*む**くいる 報いる** [報酬で] reward; [行為で] repay*, return. (【悪に対しても用いる) (⇔礼) ▶彼の働きに賞を与えて報いる *reward* him with a prize *for* his work. ▶彼の親切に報いる *return* [*repay*] his kindness. ▶彼の功労に対してどのように報いたらよいだろう How can I *reward* [*repay*] (him *for*) his services?

むくげ 木槿 [植物] a rose of Sharon /ʃéərən/; an althea.

むくち 無口 ▶彼は無口だ (あまりしゃべらない) He doesn't *talk much*./(口数が少ない) He's a man of *few words*./He's a *reticent* man. ▶(おとなしいタイプだ) He's the *quiet* [*silent*] type.

むくどり 椋鳥 [鳥] a starling.

むくみ 浮腫み (はれ) swelling. ▶脚にむくみが出ている I have a *swelling* on my leg./(むくんでいる) My leg *is swollen*.

むくむ 浮腫む (はれる) swell*. ▶彼は糖尿病で脚がむくんでいる His legs *are swollen* with diabetes.

むくむく ▶夏の青空に雲がむくむくと出ていた There were *towering masses of clouds* in the blue summer sky. ▶燃えているビルから煙がむくむくと出た Smoke *billowed up* from the burning building.

むぐら 葎 [植物] a creeper.

むくれる (むっとする) get* sullen; (怒る) get angry. ▶真由美はむくれた顔をしている Mayumi looks *sullen* [*angry*]. ▶彼は何でもないことですぐむくれる He easily *gets sullen* [*angry*] at nothing.

むくわれる 報われる be rewarded. (⇔報いる) ▶彼女の努力は十分報われた Her efforts *were well rewarded*./Her efforts paid off well enough. ▶正直は必ず報われる It *pays* to be honest./It *pays* you if you are honest./Honesty *pays* you (well).

-むけ -向け ▶輸出[南米]向けの品物 goods *for* export [South America]. ▶この雑誌は少年向けです This magazine is (*designed*) *for* boys. ▶その番組は中国向けに放送されている The programs are beamed *to* [*at*] China.

むげ 無碍 图 (障害がない) freedom from obstacles. — **無碍の** 形 obstacle-free.

むけい 無形 ▶有形無形の援助 *moral* and *material* support.

●無形固定資産 intangible fixed assets. ●無形文化財 an intangible cultural asset [treasure].

むげい 無芸 ▶無芸の人 a man [a woman] of *no accomplishments*. ●無芸大食の人 a glutton. ●多芸は無芸 (⇔多芸) [成句]

むけいかく 無計画 — **無計画な** 形 unplanned; (無謀な) (むこうみずな) haphazard. ▶無計画な住宅政策 an *unplanned* [*haphazard*] housing policy.

むけいけん 無経験 ▶無経験である have no experience (*in*); be inexperienced (*at, in*). (⇔経験)

むけいこく 無警告 — **無警告の** 形 surprise (attacks). — **無警告で** 副 without warning; (通告なしに) without notice.

むけつ 無欠 — **無欠の** 形 flawless; perfect; impeccable. ▶完全無欠の absolutely *perfect*.

むけつかくめい 無血革命 〔やや書〕 a bloodless revolution.

むけっきん 無欠勤 ▶彼は昨年無欠勤だった He *didn't stay away from work* last year.

むけっせき 無欠席 perfect attendance (at school). ▶彼は昨年学校を無欠席で通した (=1度も休まなかった) He *didn't stay away from school* last year./He *never missed school* last year.

むげに [きっぱりと] flatly; [そっけなく] bluntly; [即座に] 〔やや書〕out of hand. ▶むげに断わる refuse (it) *flatly* (out *of hand*); give (him) a *flat* refusal. ▶「むげに断わるわけにはいかないからね」と彼は言った "I can't *say no* to you," he said.

:**むける 向ける** ❶ [向かせる] (顔・視線・背などを) turn; (注意などを) direct; (銃などを) aim, point. ▶彼に背中を向け *turn* one's back *on* him. ▶銃を彼に向け *aim* [*point*] one's gun *at* him. ▶背を壁に向けて立つ stand with one's back *to* [*against*] the wall. ▶こっちに顔を向けなさい *Turn* your face this way [(私の方に) *toward* me]. ▶将太は私の忠告に注意を向けようとしなかった Shota wouldn't *pay* [*turn, direct*] his attention *to* my advice. ▶彼らの怒りは私に向けられていた Their anger *was against me*.

❷ [差し向ける] send*. ▶警官を事故現場に向ける *send* a policeman *to* the scene of the accident. ▶お迎えの車を差し向けましょう I'll *send* a car *around* to pick you up.

❸ [当てる] ▶全精力をその仕事に向ける *put* all one's energies *into* the job; *devote* [*apply*] all one's energies *to* the job. ▶研究に心を向けなさい *Put* [*Set, Apply*] your mind *to* your studies.

むける 剝ける (皮が) peel (off). ▶背中の皮がむけ始めた The skin on my back has begun to *peel* (*off*). ▶バナナはすぐ皮がむける Bananas *peel* easily.

むげん 無限 图 infinity; 〔永遠〕 (an) eternity. — **無限の** 形 (計り知れない) infinite (↔finite); (限度のない) limitless, boundless; (永遠の) 〔やや書〕 eternal; (無尽蔵の) inexhaustible. ▶無限の可能性 *infinite* [*limitless*] possibilities. ▶無限の活力 *boundless* energy. ▶我々の時間は無限ではない Our time is not *unlimited*. ▶愛は無限です. 人に与えれば与えるほど豊かになってゆくのだから Love is *inexhaustible*; the more you give (to others), the more you have.
— **無限に** 副 infinitely; limitlessly; boundlessly.
●無限軌道 a caterpillar, a caterpillar track.
●無限責任 unlimited liability.

むげん 無間 incessancy.

むげん 夢幻 图 an illusion; a phantasm. — **夢幻の** 形 phantasmal.

むげんだい 無限大 [名]【数学】infinity. ── 無限大の [形] infinite.
むこ 婿 [娘の夫] a son-in-law (徽 sons-,《英語》~s); [花婿] a (bride)groom. ●婿を取る(親の立場から) adopt a son-in-law into one's family; (子の立場から) take a husband. ●婿(養子)になる[行く] marry an heiress; marry into the family of one's bride. ●婿入り (⇨婿入り)
むごい [残酷な] cruel; [冷忍な] brutal; [無慈悲な] merciless; [恐ろしい] terrible, horrible. ●むごい主人 a cruel [a merciless] master. ●むごい死に方をする die a terrible [(悲惨な) a tragic] death. ●彼らにむごいことをする Don't be cruel to them./Don't treat them cruelly.
むこいり 婿入り ▶彼は金持ちの家へ婿入りした He married into a wealthy family.
*__むこう__ 向こう ❶ [反対側] the opposite side; (もう一方の側) the other side. ▶川の向こうに病院があります There is a hospital on the opposite side [across, over] the river. (▮ across は「平面的なものを横切ったところに」、over は「…の上を越えたところに」の意) ▶彼の車は道路の向こうに止まっている His car is standing at the other side of the road [across the road from here, over the road]. ▶丘の向こうに小さな村がある There is a small village beyond [(背後に) behind] the hill. (▮ beyond は「越えた向こう側に」の意で次に高さのあるものが来ることが多い) ▶彼は運動場の向こうの方へ歩いて行った He walked (down) to the far side of the playground. ▶彼はテーブルの向こうから話しかけてきた He spoke to me from across the table. ▶風は向こう(=反対方向)から吹いている The wind is blowing from the opposite direction. ▶センターは向こう向きで大飛球を捕った The center fielder caught the long fly over the shoulder [made an over-the-shoulder catch of the long fly].

❷ [あちら] (あそこに[の]) over there. ▶はるか向こうに in [×at] the far distance; far away; a long way off. ●2マイル向こうのガソリンスタンド a gas station two miles away [at a distance of two miles]. (▮ 前の方が口語的) ●向こうを向く(向きを変える) turn around; (顔をそむける) turn away. ▶向こうのあの白い建物が見えますか. 郵便局はその向こう(=通り過ぎたところ)です Do you see that white building over there? The post office is just past [after] it. ▶我々は庭の向こうの端にクルミの木を植えます We're going to plant walnut trees at the far end of the garden. ▶彼がはるか向こうからやって来るのが見える I can see him coming from a long way off. ▶飛行機は山の向こうへ飛んで行った The airplane flew away over the mountain. ▶向こうへ着いたらすぐ手紙を出します I'll write to you as soon as I get there. ▶向こうへ行け Go away!/(出て行け) Get out!

❸ [今後, 未来] ▶向こう1週間の仕事のスケジュールを立てる plan one's work schedule for the next [following] week. ▶4月1日から向こう1週間休暇をとります I'll take a week's vacation starting from April 1./I'll be on a week's vacation from April 1.

❹ [相手] (相手側) the other side. ▶費用は向こう持ちです It's 《his [her, their]》 expense. ▶向こうの言い分もよく聞きなさい Listen well to what the other side [party] has to say. ▶最初に手を出したのは向こう(=彼, 彼女, 彼ら)だ It was he [she, they] who attacked me first.

● 向こう三軒両隣 (場所的に) one's next-door neighbors and the three across; (親しくしている隣人) one's close neighbors.

●向こうに回す ▶チャンピオンを向こうに回して(=対抗して)善戦する put a good fight against a champion. ●世論を向こうに回して(=反対して)立ち上がる rise in opposition to public opinion.

● 向こうを張る ▶その両社は市場を支配しようと向こうを張っている(=張り合っている) The two companies are competing (with each other) to get control of the market.

●向こう正面 (相撲の) the south side of the sumo ring; (劇場の) a seat in front of the stage.

むこう 無効 [名] invalidity; [無効にすること] invalidation. ── 無効の [形] invalid; (契約などの)【法律】 void. ●無効の切符 an invalid [an unavailable] ticket. ●無効にする make (it) invalid [void]; invalidate. ●無効になる become invalid [void]; do not hold good. ▶その契約は無効です The contract is invalid (null and void). ▶このためにその協定は無効になった This made the agreement invalid [void].

●無効投票 a spoilt [an invalid] vote.

むこういき 向こう意気 ●向こう意気が強い (強気の) aggressive; (闘志満々の)《話》scrappy; (威勢のいい)《話》gutsy; (競争心の強い) competitive.

むこうがい 無公害 ── 無公害の [形] pollution-free. ●無公害エンジン a pollution-free engine. ●無公害車 a pollution-free automobile.

むこうぎし 向こう岸 the other side of a river. ●向こう岸の灯火 lights on the opposite bank. ●向こう岸へフェリーで渡る cross the river by ferry; take a ferry to the other side of the river.

むこうきず 向こう傷 a cut on one's [the] forehead; a slash across one's face.

むこうずね 向こう脛 a shin. ●向こうずねをいすにぶつける bang one's shin against the chair.

むこうっつら 向こうっ面 ●彼の向こうっ面を張りとばす punch him across the face.

むこうはちまき 向こう鉢巻き (説明的に) a towel tied around the head with its knot in front.

むこうみず 向こう見ず ── 向こう見ずな [形] reckless; (大胆な) daring; (軽率な) rash. (⇨無謀)

むこくせき 無国籍 ── 無国籍の [形] stateless. ●無国籍者 a stateless person. ●無国籍船 a stateless ship.

むごたらしい (残酷な) cruel. (⇨むごい)

むことり 婿取り ●婿取りする (親の立場から) adopt a son-in-law into one's family; (子の立場から) take a husband.

むこん 無根 ●事実無根のうわさ a groundless [an unfounded] rumor.

むごん 無言 ── 無言の [形] (黙っている) silent; (口をきこうとない) mute (▮「口をきけない」の意もある). ●無言の抗議 a silent [a mute] protest. ●無言の(=暗黙の)了解 a tacit understanding. ●無言電話がかかってくる get a silent telephone call. ●無言で in silence, silently; mutely; (一言も言わないで) without (saying) a word; without speaking. ▶彼女はしばらく無言のままだった She remained silent for some time. ▶近ごろ無言電話がかかってきて気持ちが悪い For the last few weeks I've had telephone calls which are silent when I pick up the receiver. It's really weird.

●無言劇 (a) pantomime.

むさい messy; untidy. (⇨むさ苦しい)
むざい 無罪 [名] innocence. ●無罪を主張する assert one's innocence [that one is innocent]; plead not guilty. ▶彼は無罪放免となった He was ac-

むさく quitted of the charge./He was found *innocent* and was released [was set free].
── 無罪の 形 innocent; not guilty (⚠裁判などで用いる言葉). ●無罪の判決 a decision of '*not guilty*'. ▶トムは放火罪で起訴されたが無罪になった Tom was charged with arson but *found innocent* [*not guilty*]. (⚠found は過去分詞)

むさく 無策 ●政府は地価の下落対策に無為無策だ The government takes *no* (*effective*) *measures against* the fall in land prices.

むさくい 無作為 ── 無作為の 形 unintentional; (統計などで) random.
── 無作為に 副 unintentionally; at random. ●無作為抽出法 random sampling. ●無作為標本 a random sample.

むさくるしい むさ苦しい (汚い) messy; (乱雑な) untidy. ●むさ苦しい部屋 a *messy* room. ▶むさ苦しい所ですが，どうぞお上がりください Please come in and make yourself at home. (⚠Our house is messy, but.... などの直訳は避けた方がよい)

むささび 〖動物〗a flying squirrel.

むさつ 無札 ●無札乗車する get a free ride; ride 《a train》 without a ticket.

むさべつ 無差別 名 indiscrimination.
── 無差別の 形 indiscriminate /ìndiskrímənət/. ●無差別に人を殺す kill people *indiscriminately*. ●無差別〖柔道〗the open division. ●無差別爆撃 indiscriminate [random] bombing.

むさぼりくう むさぼり食う devour; eat*... greedily. ▶犬は残飯をむさぼり食った The dog *devoured* the left-overs.

むさぼりよむ むさぼり読む devour 《a book》; 〖熱心に読む〗read* 《a book》 avidly. ▶私はその新聞記事をむさぼり読んだ I *devoured* the newspaper article./(熱心に) I *eagerly* read the newspaper article.

むさぼる 〖がつがつ食べる〗eat*... greedily; devour. (⚠比喩的にも用いる) ▶その子はクッキーを全部むさぼるように食べた The child *devoured* all the cookies. ▶その会社は暴利をむさぼっている The company *is making undue profits* [*is profiteering*].

むざむざと (たやすく) easily; (惜しげなく) without regret; (抵抗せずに) without any resistance. ▶彼はむざむざと殺された He was *easily killed* [*was killed without any resistance*]. ▶むざむざと仕事を辞めようとはしない I'm not going to quit my job *without regret*.

むさん 霧散 ── 霧散する 動 disperse.

むざん 無残 ── 無残な 形〖恐ろしい〗horrible; 〖残酷な〗cruel, merciless; 〖悲惨な〗tragic. ●無残な光景 a *horrible* [a *cruel*, (ぞっとするような) an *appalling*] sight. ●無残な最期を遂げる meet with a *tragic* end [*death*].
── 無残に(も) 副 cruelly; without pity [mercy].

むさんかいきゅう 無産階級 the proletariat /pròulətéəriət/. ●無産階級の人 a proletarian /pròulətéəriən/. ●無産階級による革命 a *proletarian* revolution.

:むし

WORD CHOICE 虫

insect 広く昆虫一般のこと. ●6本足の虫 six-legged *insects*.
bug 小さな虫の総称. 時に比喩的に用いて，コンピュータプログラムなどの欠陥[バグ]をさす. ●このいらだたしい虫を払い落とす shake off this irritating *bug*.
worm ミミズや毛虫など, 地面を這う細長い形状の虫の総称. ●あたりではい回る虫たち *worms* wriggling about.

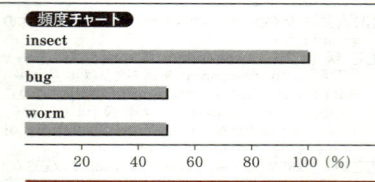

頻度チャート	
insect	██████████
bug	███
worm	██
	20 40 60 80 100 (%)

❶〖昆虫〗an insect; a bug; 〖ミミズ・ウジ虫など〗a worm /wə́ːrm/; 〖毛虫・イモ虫など〗a caterpillar; 〖ガなど〗a moth /mɔ́(ː)θ/; 〖鳴く虫〗a cricket; 〖害虫〗vermin 〖集合的に用い通例複数扱い〗; (寄生虫) a parasite, a parasitic worm.
①《虫が》●(草地などに)虫がつく be infested with *insects* [*vermin*]. ▶野原で多くの虫が鳴いている A lot of *insects* are chirping [singing] in the field. (※米英人は虫の鳴き声を the noise of *insects* と表現することもある) ▶梅雨の間この溝には虫がわいた *Worms* bred in this drain [This drain was infested with *worms*] during the rainy season. ▶このクリには虫が入っている These chestnuts are *wormy*.
②《虫に》●虫に刺された I've been bitten [been stung] by an *insect*. (⚠「虫の刺し傷」は an *insect* bite (⇒虫刺され)) ●このセーターはすっかり虫に食われている This sweater is all *moth* eaten. (⚠「虫食いのセーター」は a *moth*-eaten sweater)

❷〖気持ち, 感じ〗●これくらいでは腹の虫がおさまらない This won't soothe my anger.

❸〖熱中する人〗●彼は本の虫だ He's a bookworm. (⚠時に軽蔑的.「本にくう虫」の意にも用いる)(仕事の虫になっている) He's *addicted to* books. ●彼は仕事の虫だ(=仕事だけが生きがいだ) *All* he *lives for* is his career./(仕事中毒だ)《話》He's a workaholic.

❹〖その他の表現〗▶一寸の虫にも五分の魂 (⇒一寸〖成句〗) ▶たで食う虫も好きずき (⇒蓼〖成句〗)
●虫がいい ●虫のいい男 a *selfish* man. ▶それは虫がよすぎる That's [You're] asking too much. (⚠前の方は話の内容に, 後の方は人に関心がある)
●虫が知らせる ▶彼が事故にあうだろうと虫が知らせた I had a premonition [a hunch] that he would have an accident. (⇒虫の知らせ)
●虫が好かない ●虫の好かない人 a *disagreeable* person. ▶彼は虫が好かない I just can't take to him. (⚠take to ... は「...を好きになる」の意)/He's *not my favorite* sort of person.
●虫が付く ▶娘に悪い虫がつくのではと心配している I am worried that my daughter may have an undesirable boyfriend.
●虫の居所が悪い (機嫌が悪い) be in a bad mood.
●虫も殺さぬ ●虫も殺さない顔をしている be innocent-looking.
●虫を殺す (かんしゃくをこらえる) keep [control] one's temper.

むし 無視 ── 無視する 動 〖認めるのを拒絶する〗ignore,《話》brush ... aside [off]; 〖熟慮の上で取り上げない〗disregard; 〖注意を怠る〗pay no attention to ...; 〖おろそかにする〗neglect; 〖気にとめない〗take* no notice of ...; (公然と) defy. ●少数意見を無視する *ignore* [*disregard*] a minority opinion. ●法律を無視する *defy* the law. ▶彼らが君のことを何と言おうと無視しなさい *Ignore* [*Pay no attention to*, *Don't take any notice of*, ˣ*Disregard*] whatever they say about you.
▶彼女にあいさつしたが完全に無視された I greeted her, but she *ignored* me completely [《話》cut

むし me *dead*]. ▶運転手は赤信号を無視した The driver *went through* [*ignored*,《話》*jumped*] the red light. (‼後の二つは故意に，最初のはうっかりかは故意に) ▶彼は危険を無視して燃えている家の中へ飛び込んで行った *In spite of* [《書》*Regardless of*] the danger, he rushed into the burning house. ▶2人のうち片方の人だけを招待したらもう1人は無視された(=の者にされた)と思うでしょう If only one of the two people is invited, the other will feel *left out*. ▶あの人は芸能界では無視できない(=考慮に入れるべき)人だ He is a man to be *reckoned with* in the world of show business.

むし 無死 — 無死満塁です〖野球〗The bases are full [*loaded*] with no outs.

むし 無私 — 無私の 形 *unselfish*;《書》*selfless*; (公平無私の) *disinterested*. ▶無私の精神 *unselfish* [*selfless*] *spirit*. (⇨公平①)

むじ 無地 — 無地の 形 (模様のない) *plain*. ▶赤い無地の布 *plain* red cloth.

むしあつい 蒸し暑い *sultry*; (じめじめする)《話》*muggy*; (べとべとする) *sticky*. ▶今日はとても蒸し暑い It's so *sultry* [*muggy*] today./It's so *hot and humid* today.

◾ DISCOURSE
日本の夏は非常に蒸し暑い．その一方で冬にはかなり寒くなり，多くの地域では大雪が降る Summer in Japan is very *hot and humid*, *however*, it gets quite cold in winter and snows heavily in many regions. (‼; however，(一方では)は対比を表すディスコースマーカー．however の前後では対照的な内容を述べる)

むしかえす 蒸し返す ❶〖議論などを〗(軽蔑的) *rehash*; (不愉快な話題などを)《話》*drag ... up* (-gg-). ▶彼らはその議論を何度も蒸し返した They *rehashed* the arguments again and again. ▶そのことは蒸し返さないでくれ Don't *start* that (*all*) *over again*. **❷**〖料理を〗*steam ... over again*

むしかく 無資格 無資格の医師 an *unqualified* [(免許を持たない) an *unlicensed*] *doctor*.

むじかく 無自覚 — 無自覚な 形 *unconscious* 《*of*》.

むしかご 虫籠 an *insect càge*.

むしがし 蒸し菓子 (蒸しようかん・ういろうなど) *steamed cake*.

むしき 蒸し器 a *steamer*.

むしくい 虫食い ▶虫食いだらけの桃 a *worm-eaten peach*. ▶虫食いの背広 a *moth-eaten* suit.
● 虫食い算 *arithmetical restoration*.

むしくだし 虫下し a *vermifuge*.

むしけら 虫けら a *worm*; an *insect*. (⇨虫) ▶虫けら同然の人 a *good-for-nothing*; a *worthless* person.

むしけん 無試験 ▶無試験でこの学校に入学した I got into this school *without taking an exam*.

むじこ 無事故 ▶私は20年間無事故で I have had *no accidents* in [*for*] *the past twenty years*.

むしさされ 虫刺され an *insect bite*; a *sting*.

むしず 虫酸 ▶虫ずが走る・むしずの走るような(=いやな)奴 a *disgusting* [《やや話》a *sickening*] *fellow*; (おっかかい)《俗》a *creep*. ▶あいつのことを考えるだけでむしずが走る The mere thought of him *disgusts* me [*makes me sick*,《話》*gives me the creeps*].

むしタオル 蒸しタオル a *steamed towel*.

むじつ 無実 图 *innocence*. ▶彼の無実が証明された His *innocence* was proved./He was found *innocent* [*not guilty*]. (‼後の文の方が普通の言い方)/(無罪を宣告された) He was *acquitted*.
— 無実の 形 (人が) *innocent*; (事が他の) *false*.
● 無実の罪で on a *false* charge; under a *false* accusation.

むじな 狢, 貉〖動物〗(アナグマ) a *badger*; (タヌキ) a *raccoon dog*. ▶彼らは一つ穴のむじなだ They are both of a hair (‼通例悪い意味に用いる)/They are in the same boat.

むしなべ 蒸し鍋 a *steamer*.

むしのいき 虫の息 ▶彼は虫の息だ(=死の寸前の状態だ) He is breathing faintly./He is dying. ▶その少年はその翌朝虫の息の状態で発見された The boy was found *dying* [*barely alive*] the next morning.

むしのしらせ 虫の知らせ ▶虫の知らせで彼が事故にあうような気がした I had a *premonition* [a *hunch*] that he would have an accident. (‼前の方は「悪い予感」,後の方は「直感」のこと)

むしば 虫歯 *tooth decay*; (悪くなった歯) a *bad* [a *decayed*] *tooth* (‼後の方が堅い語. tooth の変化形は《俚》*teeth*)); (虫歯の穴) a *cavity*. ▶虫歯を防ぐ *prevent tooth decay*. ▶虫歯を詰めてもらう have one's *cavity* [*bad tooth*] *filled*. ▶虫歯が3本ある[ない] have three [no] *cavities*. ▶虫歯を抜いてもらう have one's *bad tooth* pulled out.

むしばむ 蝕む (病気などが冒す) *affect*, *erode*; (しだいに損なう) *undermine*; (酸が金属をおかすように) *corrode*; (弱める) *weaken*. ▶がんにむしばまれた肉体 a body *eroded* by *cancer*. ▶深夜の仕事で彼の健康がむしばまれ始めた Late night work began to *affect* [*undermine*] his health.

◾ 翻訳のこころ 生活がまだ蝕まれていなかった以前私の好きであった所は，例えば丸善であった(梶井基次郎『檸檬』) Maruzen was one of my favorite spots in those days when my life had not yet been eroded [affected]. (‼(1)「蝕まれる」は be eroded (徐々に冒される), be affected ((病で)[のために])冒される)と表す．(2)「例えば丸善であった」は，for example とせずに Maruzen was one of ... (...の一つが丸善だった)とする方が分かりやすい)

むしパン 蒸しパン a *steamed bun*.

むじひ 無慈悲 — 無慈悲な 形 *merciless*; (無情な) *heartless*; (残酷な) *cruel*.

むしふうじ 虫封じ (説明的に) an *incantation* or a *charm* for curing children's tantrums.

むしぶろ 蒸し風呂 a *steam bath*; a *sauna*; (トルコ風の) a *Turkish bath*. ▶まるで蒸しぶろの中にいるようだ(=ひどく蒸し暑い) It's terribly hot and humid.

むしぼし 虫干し 图 (空気・日光に当てること) *airing*.
— 虫干しする 動 ▶衣類を虫干しする *air* one's clothes; hang one's clothes up to *air*.

むしほん 無資本 ▶無資本で without funds [*capital*].

むしむし ▶むしむしする (⇨蒸し暑い)

むしめがね 虫眼鏡 a *mágnifying glàss*, a *magnifier*. ▶虫眼鏡で昆虫を見る look at an insect through a *magnifying glass*.

むしもの 蒸し物 (料理) *steamed food*; a *steamed dish*; (蒸し菓子) a *steamed cake*.

むしゃ 武者 a *warrior*; a *soldier*; a *samurai*.
● 武者人形 a *warrior doll*.

むしやき 蒸し焼き ▶蒸し焼きにする *bake* [(肉を) *roast*] ... in a (*covered*) *casserole*.

むじゃき 無邪気 图 *innocence*.
— 無邪気な 形 *innocent*; (子供のように) *childlike* (‼ *childish* は悪い意味で「子供っぽい」の意); (うぶな) *naive*; (あどけない) *artless*. ▶彼女は赤ん坊のように無邪気だ She is as *innocent* as a baby.

むしゃくしゃ — むしゃくしゃする 動 (いらいらする) *get**

むしゃしゅぎょう

[be] irritated (**!** be は状態を表す); (気にさわる) get [be] upset; (機嫌が悪い) be in a bad mood [temper]. ▶彼女しゃくしゃくしているみたい。きっと奥さんとけんかでもしたんだよ He looks *irritated and upset*. He must have had a quarrel with his wife.

むしゃしゅぎょう 武者修行 ● 武者修行に出かける set out on a journey around the country to *improve one's skill in martial arts*.

むしゃぶりつく cling* to [throw* one's arms around, take* tight hold of]《one's mother》and not let go.

むしゃぶるい 武者震い ● 武者震いする 動 tremble [quiver] with excitement.

むしゃむしゃ ▶ライオンがえさをむしゃむしゃ(=がつがつ)食べた A lion *devoured* its food. ▶彼はサラダをむしゃむしゃ(=口をもぐもぐさせて)食べた He *munched* his salad.

むしゅう 無臭 ― 無臭の 形 odorless.

むしゅうきょう 無宗教 ▶彼は無宗教だ He *doesn't believe in any* particular *religion*./《書》He is completely *irreligious*.

むしゅうにゅう 無収入 ● 無収入で[の] without any income.

むじゅうりょく 無重力 zero gravity; (無重量の状態) the condition of weightlessness. ● 無重力状態になる become *weightless*.
● 無重力飛行 a zero-gravity [a weightless] flight.

むしゅく 無宿 名 homelessness. ― 無宿の 形 homeless.
● 無宿者 a homeless person; 《総称的に》the homeless.

むしゅみ 無趣味 ● 無趣味である(=これといった趣味がない) have *no* particular *hobbies*.

***むじゅん** 矛盾 名 (相反すること) (a) contradiction; (首尾一貫しないこと) (an) inconsistency. ▶この世には多くの矛盾が存在する There are a lot of *contradictions* in this world. ▶彼の理論は矛盾だらけだ His theory is full of *inconsistencies*.
― 矛盾した[する] 形 contradictory《to》; inconsistent 《with》. ▶彼はよく矛盾したことを言う He often makes a *contradictory* statement./He often *contradicts himself*. ▶2人の証人は互いに矛盾する証言をした The two witnesses gave *contradictory* testimony.
― 矛盾する 動 contradict. ▶彼の話はその証拠と矛盾している His account *contradicts* [*is inconsistent with*] the evidence.

むしょ 務所 [『刑務所』の俗語的表現] a prison;《俗》the slammer;《米話》a pen (**!** *pen*itentiary の略).

むしょう 無償 ― 無償の 形 free.
― 無償で 副 (無報酬で) for nothing;《書》gratis; (無料で) free of charge. ● 無償で働く work *for nothing*.
● 無償交付 〖株式〗 free issue [distribution]; bonus issue. ● 無償サンプル a sample of no (commercial) value; a free sample. ● 無償資金協力 grant assistance.

むじょう 無上 ― 無上の 形 highest; greatest. ● 無上の光栄である feel *highly* honored; consider it *the highest* [*greatest*] honor《to do》.

むじょう 無常 ― 無常の 形 (変わりやすい)《書》mutable; (つかの間の)《書》transient;《書》evanescent; (一定しない) uncertain. ▶人生は無常だ Nothing is certain [Everything is *uncertain*] in this world./'Life is but an empty dream.'
● 無常観 a sense of transience [(むなしき)《書》vanity] of life.

むじょう 無情 ― 無情の 形 heartless; (冷たい心の) cold-hearted; (冷淡な) cold; (冷酷な) cruel; (無慈悲な) merciless. ● 無情な言葉 *heartless* [*cold*] remarks.
― 無情にも 副 heartlessly; cruelly.

むじょうけん 無条件 ― 無条件の 形 unconditional.
― 無条件で 副 unconditionally. ● 政治犯を無条件で釈放する release the political prisoner *unconditionally*.
● 無条件降伏 (an) unconditional surrender.

むじょうということ『無常といふ事』*On Transience*.〖参考〗小林秀雄の評論集

むしょうに 無性に [非常に] very; [極度に] extremely; [圧倒的なほど] overwhelmingly. ● 無性に腹が立つ get *very* [*extremely*] angry. ● 無性にうれしい[悲しい] be *overwhelmingly* glad [grieved]. ▶無性にあの人に会いたい(=会いたくてたまらない)《話》I'm *dying to* see him.

むしょく 無色 ● 無色透明のガラス *colorless*, transparent glass.

むしょく 無職 ― 無職の 形 without an occupation; [失職した] jobless, unemployed. ▶彼は無職だ (定職がない) He *has no* (regular [steady]) *job* [*occupation*]./(失業している) He *is out of work* [*a job*,《やや書》*employment*]. ▶母は無職です(=働いていない) My mother *doesn't work* [(働きに行っていない) *go to work*].

むしよけ 虫除け(薬) an *insect rep*è*llent*. (⇨防虫剤)

むしょぞく 無所属 ― 無所属の 形 independent, unattached. ● 無所属で立候補する run《主に米》[stand《英》] in an election *independently of* any party [as an *independent*].
● 無所属議員[候補者] an independent. (**!** 時に I-)

むしる 毟る 鶏の毛をむしる pull [pluck] (the) feathers from [off] a chicken; pluck a chicken. ▶庭の草をむしる weed the garden.

むしるし 無印 ― 無印の 形 (ブランド名のない) unbranded;《米》generic; (印のない) unmarked.
● 無印商品 generic products. ▶あのスーパーには無印商品がたくさんそろえてある They carry a wide range of *generic products* [(小売店の自社ブランド)《米》*store brands*;《英》*own brands*] at that supermarket.

***むしろ ❶** [Aよりむしろ B] B rather than A; not so much A as B; [(Aするより)むしろ Bしたい] would [had] rather B (than A) (**!** A, B は動詞の原形. had rather より would rather の方が普通. いずれも通例 'd rather と省略される); [むしろ…であればと望む] I would rather 《(*that*)節》. (**!** that 節内の動詞は通例仮定法). ▶私にはこの戦いの相手は悪というよりはむしろ無知であることがわかってきた I have come to understand that the battle here is against ignorance *rather than* against evil [*isn't so much against* evil *as* ignorance]. ▶パーティーに行くよりもむしろ家にいたい I'd *rather* stay home *than* go to the party. (ともいえる)/I'd *prefer* to stay home *rather than* to go [go, ×*going*] to the party. (**!** I prefer と異なり, 仮定法を用いた I would prefer の後では動名詞は不可) ▶むしろそれをすぐにやってしまいたい I'd *rather* you *did* it at once. (**!** did は仮定法過去形. I wish you did it at once. という方が普通)〖会話〗「しばらくソファーで横になったらどう?」「ありがとう, でもむしろこの方がいいよ」"Why don't you lie down on the sofa for a while?" "Thank you,

but I'd rather not." (❗ not は that I didn't lie … という否定の that 節の代用形。ただし that 節内が肯定の場合には ×I'd rather so. とはしない)
❷ [いやむしろ] (or) rather. ▶彼は同意した, というよりはむしろ(=もっと正確に言えば)反対はしなかったのだ He agreed, *or rather* he didn't object.
❸ [どちらかといえば] if anything. ▶彼はむしろ以前より幸せそうだ *If anything*, he seems happier than before.

むしろ 筵　a straw mat. ●むしろを編む make [weave, 《主に米》braid, 《主に英》plait] a straw mat.

むしん 無心　❶ [無邪気] innocence. ●無心に遊んでいる be playing *innocently*.
❷ [ねだること] a request. ●彼に金の無心をする ask [beg] him *for* some money.

むじん 無人　(人の住んでいない) uninhabited; (人の乗り組んでいない) unmanned; (捨てられた) deserted.
●無人の家 a *vacant* house.
●無人宇宙ステーション an *unmanned* space station. ●無人スタンド a self-service gas station. ●無人島 an *uninhabited* [a *desert*] island /áiləndʒ/. ●無人踏切 an *unattended* crossing.

むじん 無尽　a mutual loan association.

むしんけい 無神経 ── 無神経な 形 (他人の気持ちなどに) insensitive; (非難などに) thick-skinned. ▶彼女が夫の死を無視しているときに奥さんのことをのろしるなんて君は無神経だ It's very *insensitive* of you to talk fondly about your wife when she is saddened by [very sad about] her husband's death. (❗ 前の方が強調の傾向)

むじんぞう 無尽蔵　▶我々は天然資源を無尽蔵でないことを忘れがちだ We tend to forget natural resources are not *inexhaustible* [*infinite*].

むしんろん 無神論　atheism /éiθiizm/.
●無神論者 an atheist.

***む**す 蒸す　steam. ●サツマイモを蒸す *steam* sweet potatoes.

むす 生す　(生まれる) be born; (コケ・草が生える) grow*.

むすい 無水 ── 無水の 形 anhydrous.
●無水アルコール pure [absolute] alcohol. ●無水物 an anhydride.

むすう 無数 ── 無数の 形 countless, 《やや書》innumerable, 《主に書》numberless. ●無数の星 *countless* stars; 《書》stars *beyond* [*without*] *number*. ●無数の困難に直面する face *innumerable* difficulties.

***むずかしい** 難しい 形　❶ [困難な] difficult; hard; tough; troublesome; complicated; serious; delicate.

| 使い分け | difficult 実行や理解などが困難であることを表す。時に hard に比べて問題や行動自体が複雑であることを含意する。 |

tough 状況・問題の解決や対処が困難であることを表す。不可能ではないが精神的・身体的に非常に骨が折れることを含意する。

hard 実行や解決が困難であることを表す。difficult と交換可能な場合も多いが, 時に問題や行動自体の複雑性よりも状況的な難しさを含意する。

troublesome さまざまな問題や面倒を引き起こしうる状況やものなどを表す。

complicated 構造・状況・手続きなどが非常に複雑で込み入っているために対応が困難であることを表す。

serious 「重大な」の意が中心だが, 時に状況や症状が深刻で対処が困難であることを表す。

delicate 深刻な状況や問題を引き起こす可能性があるため, 扱いに慎重さが必要となることを表す。

① 【難しい～】 ●難しい立場 a *difficult* [(微妙な) a *delicate*] situation. ●難しい手続き complicated procedures. ●難しい病気 a *serious* illness. ●(慎重を要する)難しい手術 a *delicate* operation.
②【…は難しい】▶テストはとても難しかった The test was really *difficult* [*hard*, *tough*]. ▶彼女にはその問題を解くのは難しい It is *difficult* for her to solve the problem. (❗ ×It is difficult that she solves the problem. は不可)/The problem is *difficult* for her to solve (×it). (❗ The problem is 文の主語であり solve の目的語であるから it は不要)/She has *difficulty* (*in*) solving the problem. (❗(1) in は通例省略をる。(2) ×She is *difficult* to solve .... は不可 (⇨易しい)) ▶ジョンを納得させるのは難しい It is *hard* to convince John./John is *hard* to convince (×to be convinced).
❷ [できない] ▶(婉曲的に)それは難しいよ I'm afraid I *can't* do it./I *don't* think it's *possible*.
❸ [気難しい] *difficult*; (怒りっぽい) *touchy*; (好みが) *particular* (*about*) (⇨うるさい); (顔つきが) sullen, sour /sáuər/. ●難しいお客 a *difficult* [a *tough*] customer. ●難しい顔をしている look *sullen*; wear a *sullen* look [a *sour* face]. (❗「難しい顔をする」は make [pull] a sour face)

── 難しく 副 ●物事を難しく考えるは take things (*too*) *seriously*. ●難しく(=専門的に)言えば in technical language [terms].

むずかしさ 難しさ　difficulty.

| DISCOURSE | 団体競技に参加することで, 協力することの難しさを知った. …その一方で, 団体競技によって私は協力することの喜びを知った By participating in team sports, I have learned the *difficulty* of collaboration. … **On the other hand**, I experienced the joy of collaboration. (❗ on the other hand (一方)は対比を表すディスコースマーカー。前後で対照的な内容を述べる) |

むずがゆい むず痒い　(人・体の部分が) itch, feel* itchy. (⇨痒い)

むずかる (赤ん坊が) fret (-tt-), be fretful. ▶子供は疲れるとぐずるものだ When children are tired, they *get fretful*.

***むすこ** 息子　a son; 《話》a boy. (❗ 成人した息子にも用いる) (一人息子). ▶私には息子が2人と娘が1人いる I have two *sons* and one daughter. ▶おまえなんか息子じゃない You're no *son* of mine! (❗ You're not my son. より意味が強い)

むすっと ●むすっとしている look sullen; remain silent in a bad temper [mood]. ▶彼女はむすっと黙り込んで座っていた She sat *in sullen silence*.

むずと ●むずと(=突然荒々しく)つかむ grab [seize]《a thing [him]》. ▶彼は私の手首をむずとつかんだ He *grabbed* [*seized*] me by the wrist.

むすばれる 結ばれる　(結婚する) get* married 《to》; be united in marriage.

むすび 結び　[結末] an end; [結論] a conclusion. ●結びの一番 [相撲] the *final* [*last*] bout. ●結びの言葉 the *closing* remarks.

むすびつき 結び付き　(関係) (a) connection; (つながり) ties (❗ 通例複数形で). ▶私とその家族との結びつきはとても強い My *connection with* the family is very tight. ▶我が国は他国との結びつきを強めないといけない We must strengthen *ties to* [*with*] other nations.

むすびつく 結び付く　(密接な関係を持つ) have* a close connection, be closely connected 《with》. ▶今日の科学技術は軍事戦略に結びついている

Technology of today *has a close connection with* [×*to*] military strategy. ▶彼の実直さとそのような凶悪な犯罪とは結びつかない(=似つかわしくない) His honesty doesn't *fit in with* such a heinous crime.

翻訳のこころ 僕は父を愛していた. 尊敬もしていたけれどそれ以上に, 精神的にも感情的にも深く父に結びついていた (村上春樹『レキシントンの幽霊』) I loved and respected my father. Above all, I was deeply [closely] connected [attached] to him spiritually and emotionally. (❗ connect は「結びつく」の一般的な語. attach は幼い子どもが母親に対して愛着を感じるような結びつきを表す)

むすびつける 結び付ける ❶[**結わえつける**] tie ... (up) (〜*d*; *tying*); (しっかりと固定する) fasten. (⇨繋(ツナ)ぐ❷) ●旗をさおに結びつける *fasten* a flag *to* [*on*] a pole.
❷[**関係づける**] (⇨関係) ● A と B を結びつけ(て考え)る *connect* [*link*] A *with* B. ●運命が彼らを結びつけた Fate *brought* them *together*. ●うそつきというと政治家と結びつける人がある People [Some people] *associate* lying *with* politicians.

むすびめ 結び目 ●結び目を解く *untie* (↔*tie*) *a knot*.

:むすぶ 結ぶ

WORD CHOICE 結ぶ, 結びつける
tie ひもなどを結ぶこと. または, ひもなどを使って物を結びつけること. 比喩的に, 人や国を関係付けることも含意する. ●青いリボンで結ばれた贈り物 a present *tied* with blue ribbon.
knot 結び目を作って, ひもなどをきつく結ぶこと. ●(もつれて)結び目ができたロープ the *knotted* rope.

頻度チャート

tie ████████████████████
knot ██████████████████
20 40 60 80 100 (%)

❶[**ひもなどをつなぎ合わせる**] tie ... (up) (〜*d*; *tying*); (結び目を作る) knot /nɑ́t/ (-tt-); (縛る) bind*. ●靴のひもを結ぶ(*up*) *tie* one's shoelaces. ●包みをひもで結ぶ *tie* [*bind*] a package *with* a string. ●切れたひもを結び合わせる *knot* a broken string. ●結び合わせたシーツを使ってバルコニーから脱出する escape from the balcony using bed sheets *tied* [*knotted*] *together*. ▶その女の子は髪にリボンを結んでいた The girl had a ribbon *tied* in her hair. ▶彼女は背中で帯を結んだ She *knotted* the sash in the back.
会話「どのくらいきつく結んだらいい?」「できるだけきつくして」"How tight do you want the *knot*?" "Make it as tight as you can."
❷[**2点をつなぐ**] (連結物でつなぐ) connect; (密接に連結する) link; (直接結合する) join. (⇨繋(ツナ)ぐ❷) ● 2 点間を線で結ぶ *draw* a line *between* two points; draw a line *connecting* two points. ●東京と名古屋を結ぶ高速道路 the expressway that *connects* [*links*] Tokyo *with* [*and*] Nagoya. ▶その二つの島は橋で結ばれている The two islands *are connected* [*are linked*, *are joined*] *by* a bridge. ▶私たちはみんな友情で結ばれている We *are* all *linked* in friendship.
❸[**関係を結ぶ**] form [enter into] a relationship *(with)*; (条約などを締結する) conclude. ●彼と交友関係を結ぶ *form* a friendship *with* him; (仲良くなる) make friends with him (❗複数形に注意). ●平和条約を結ぶ *conclude* [(調印する) *sign*] a peace treaty *(with)*. ▶日本は戦争中ドイツと同盟を結んでいた Japan *was allied with* [*to*] Germany during the war. ▶アメリカ軍はイギリス軍とともにドイツとの戦争を戦った The American armed forces [services] *joined hands with* the British in the war against Germany. ▶健と美紀はいずれ結ばれる(=結婚する)運命だったんだ Ken and Miki were destined to *get married* eventually.
❹[**締めくくる**] (終わらせる) end, 《やや書》 conclude 《*with*, *by* doing》. ●好きな言葉で演説を結ぶ *end* [*conclude*] one's speech *with* one's favorite words. (⇨締めくくる)
❺[**固く閉じる**] ▶彼は口を固く結んだ He *closed* [*shut*] his lips *tight*./He *tightened* his lips.
❻[**実を結ぶ**] bear* fruit. ▶彼の研究はついに実を結んだ His studies *bore fruit* at last.

むずむずする ❶[**かゆくて**] (人が) have* [feel*] an itch /ítʃ/; (人・体の部分が) itch. ▶私は背中がむずむずする I *have an itch* on my back./My back *itches* [*is itching*, *is itchy*]. ●鼻が少しむずむずする(=くすぐったい) I *have* a slight *tickle* in my nose./My nose *tickles* [*is tickling*] a little.
❷[**早くしたくて, 欲しくて**] (話) itch 《*to* do》, have* an *itch* 《*for*》. (❗動詞の itch は通例進行形で用いる (⇨うずうず)》 ▶彼女は外国へ行きたくてむずむずしている She's *itching* [*has an itch*] *to* go abroad./She's *very eager to* go abroad. ▶彼は冷たいビールを飲みたくてむずむずしていた He *had an itch for* (a) cold beer.

*****むすめ 娘** a daughter, a girl; [若い未婚の女性] a girl; (成人した) a young woman (⑱ women) [lady]. (❗young lady は呼びかけや丁寧な言い方で用いる). ●娘時代の友達 a *girlhood* friend. ●娘盛りである be in the prime [bloom] of *girlhood*. ●娘心に気を配る be sensitive to *girlish sentiments* [*feelings*]. ▶彼女は娘時代をパリで過ごした She spent her *girlhood* in Paris.
●**娘一人に婿八人** ▶この品物は娘一人に婿八人だ(=欲しがっている人が多い) This article *is wanted by very many people*./This article *is much in demand*.
娘婿 one's son-in-law. (⑱ sons-).

むせい 無声 ●無声映画 a silent movie [film].
●無声音 [音声] a voiceless sound; an unvoiced sound.

むせい 無性 — **無性の** 形 asexual; sexless.
●無性生殖 asexual reproduction.

むせい 夢精 [生理] (a) nocturnal emission; 《have》a wet dream. (❗「性夢」の意もある)

むぜい 無税 — **無税の** 形 tax-free; (税金のかからない) free of tax; (関税のかからない) duty-free. ●無税で商品を買う buy goods *tax-free* [*duty-free*].

むせいげん 無制限 — **無制限の** 形 unlimited; (条件をつけない) unrestricted. ●無制限の自由 *unlimited* freedom. ●無制限に入場を許す admit people *without any restriction* [*freely*]. (⇨制限)

むせいふ 無政府 ●無政府状態(に陥る) (become) anarchy. ●無政府状態にある be in a state of *anarchy*.
●無政府主義 anarchism. ●無政府主義者 an anarchist.

むせいぶつ 無生物 an inanimate object; a lifeless thing.
●無生物主語 [文法] an inanimate subject.

むせいらん 無精卵 [生物] (未受精卵) an unfertilized egg; a wind egg.

むせかえる 噎せ返る ❶[**ひどくむせる**] be badly choked 《*with* smoke》. ▶部屋のたばこの煙で私はむせ返った The tobacco fumes almost *choked* me

in the room.
❷【大いにむせび泣く】sob (-bb-) bitterly.

むせき 無籍 ●無籍者 a person without a registered domicile.

むせきつい 無脊椎 ―― 無脊椎の 形 invertebrate /ɪnvə́ːrtəbrət/.
● 無脊椎動物 an invertebrate animal.

＊むせきにん 無責任 名 irresponsibility; lack of responsibility.
―― 無責任な 形 ● 無責任な親 *irresponsible* parents. ▶赤ん坊を1人車に残すなんて君は無責任だ It's *irresponsible* of you [You're *irresponsible*] to leave your baby alone in the car.

むせっそう 無節操(移り気)inconstancy. ● 無節操な奴《書》an *inconstant*［道義心のない］an *unprincipled*］fellow.

むせびなき 嗚咽泣き《give》a sob.

むせびなく 嗚咽泣く sob (-bb-); give* a sob.

むせぶ 噎ぶ ● 涙にむせぶ be choked *with* tears; (すすり泣く) sob.

むせる 噎せる(息が詰まる)choke《on》; be choked《with, by》. ● 彼女はたばこの煙にむせた She *choked on* the cigarette smoke./She *was choked with* [*by*] the cigarette smoke.

むせん 無銭 ● 無銭飲食する get out of a restaurant *without paying the bill*. ● 無銭旅行する travel *without money*.

むせん 無線(放送)radio, 《英古》wireless; (受信機)a radio (複 ～s). ● 無線で交信する communicate *by radio*. ● 無線で通信を送る send(↔get, receive)a message *by radio*; radio a message. ● 送受信両用無線機 two-way *radios*.
● 無線技師 a radio operator; a radioman.
● 無線局 a rádio stàtion. ● 無線操縦(⇨無線操縦)
● 無線タクシー a radio dispatched taxi. ● 無線電信 radiotelegraph(y). ● 無線電話機 a radiotelephone, a radiophone; (携帯用の)a walkie-talkie. ● 無線ラン『コンピュータ』a wireless LAN.

むせんそうじゅう 無線操縦 名 radio [《英古》wireless]control.
―― 無線操縦する 動 control《it》by radio; radio-control.

むせんまい 無洗米 pre-washed rice.

むそう 無双 ―― 無双の 形 unique; matchless.
● 無双窓 a hit-and-miss window.

むそう 夢想 名 ［夢］a dream; ［空想］(a) fancy; ［白昼夢］a daydream. (⇨夢, 空想)
―― 夢想する 動 dream《of》; daydream《about》.
▶私はパイロットになることを夢想した I *dreamed* of becoming a pilot. ▶再び君に会おうとは夢想しなかった I never *dreamed* of seeing you again.
● 夢想家 a dreamer; a daydreamer.

むぞうさ 無造作 ―― 無造作な 形 ［さりげなく］casually; ［たやすく］easily; ［すぐに］readily; ［ぞんざいに］carelessly. ● 無造作に問題を解く solve the problem *easily* [*without difficulty*]. ● 無造作に了承する consent *readily*; give one's *ready* consent. ▶彼は札束を無造作につかんかばんに入れた He clutched wads of money *casually* [*carelessly*] and put them into his bag.
● 無造作ヘア casual hairstyle.

ムソルグスキー［ロシアの作曲家］Mussorgsky /məsɔ́ːrgski/ (Modest ～). (❗Mousorgsky ともつづる)

＊むだ 無駄 名 (浪費) (a) waste; (無益) no good [use, point]. ● むだを省く save [(減らす) reduce, (切り詰める) cut down on, (避ける) avoid] *waste*.
▶そのような授業はすべて時間のむだだと彼は思った He felt that all such classes were a *waste* of time.
―― 無駄な 形 (浪費的な) wasteful; (結果的に不成功の) useless; (結果的に不成功の) vain (❗通例限定的に用い, 叙述用法を 副 としては in vain を用いる); (努力などが実りのない)《やや書》fruitless; (特定の目的のない) idle (❗通例限定的に); (不用な) unwanted. ● 資源のむだな使い方 a *wasteful* use [a *waste*] of resources. ▶そんなことを議論してもむだだ *It is useless* [*fruitless*] (*for* us) *to discuss it./It is useless* [*no good, no use*] *discussing it./There is no use* [*no good, no point*] (*in*) *discussing it.*
《話》では通例 in は省略される. ほぼ同様の内容が I don't see the point [any point] in discussing it. (私にはそれを議論する価値が分からない) などでも表せる ▶彼を説得しようとしたがむだだった I tried to persuade him, but *I couldn't* [it was *useless*]./I tried to persuade him(, but) *in vain* [*to no purpose*]./I tried *in vain* [*vainly*] to persuade him. (❗in vain, vainly は強調のため文頭に置かれることもある) ▶うそをついたってむだだよ Lying *won't get* you *anywhere* [*will get* you *nowhere*].
会話「NHKのど自慢大会に出ないかい」「出てもむだだよ. 『鐘三つ』なんて無理なんだから」"Won't you like to enter a singing contest of NHK?" "What's the point? I won't be able to pick up the three gongs."
会話「試合を延ばしたらどうだい」「そんなことしたってむだだよ」"How about postponing the game?" "That's *no good*."
―― 無駄になる 動 (無に帰す) come* to nothing. ● すべての努力がむだになった All my efforts *came to nothing* [*were wasted*]. ▶彼に対する忠告はむだになった My advice *was wasted* on him. (⇨無駄にする)
―― 無駄にする 動 (浪費する) waste, squander《on》; (捨てる)《話》throw*... away; (無にする) let*... come to nothing; (台なしにする) spoil*, ruin. (⇨駄目) ▶そんなばかげたことに時間をむだにしてはいけない You shouldn't *waste* [*squander*] your time *on* such silly things. ▶昇進のチャンスをむだにしてはいけない You shouldn't *throw away* [*waste*] your chance of promotion. ▶この週末をむだに過ごしたくはない I don't want to *idle away* this weekend.
▶一刻もむだにすることはできない There's no time to *lose* [*to be lost*]. (❗前の言い方が普通)

むだあし 無駄足 ▶パン屋さんが休みでむだ足になった I went to the bakery (only) to find it closed. (❗to は結果の意を表す不定詞)
● 無駄足を踏む go [(踏ませる) send《him》] on a fool's errand.

むたい 無体 ―― 無体な 形 unreasonable. (⇨無理 ❶, 無理な)

むだい 無代 ―― 無代の 形 free. (⇨無料)

むだい 無題(芸術作品名の題)No title.

むだがね 無駄金 ● むだ金を使う waste money《on clothes》.

むだぐち 無駄口 idle talk. ● むだ口をたたく Stop your *idle* talk./Quit talking *nonsense*./《話》Quit yapping.

むだげ 無駄毛 ● むだ毛をそる shave off one's *unwanted* hair. ● むだ毛を処理する remove [shave] *unwanted* hair.

むだじに 無駄死に 名 ▶彼の死はむだ死にだった His death was *meaningless*.
―― 無駄死にする 動 die in vain.

むだづかい 無駄遣い 名 (a) waste. (⇨無駄) ● エネルギー[資源]のむだ遣い a *waste* of energy [resources].
▶タクシーに乗るのはお金のむだ遣いだよ It's a *waste* of money to take a taxi. ▶彼女は息子にお金をむだ遣

むだばなし いしないように言った She told her son not to *waste* [(貯金する) to *save*] his money./(注意するように言った) She told her son to *be careful with* his money. (⇨無駄にする)

むだばなし 無駄話 ③ idle talk;《話》chit-chat.
── 無駄話をする ⓓ talk idly; make small talk;(ぺちゃくちゃしゃべる) chatter.

むだぼね 無駄骨 ●努力が水の泡に終わった Our efforts have failed [gone to waste].
● 無駄骨を折る waste one's time and labor; make vain [fruitless] efforts.

むだめし 無駄飯 ● 無駄飯を食う (仕事もせずに暮らす) lead an idle [a useless] life.

****むだん** 無断 ── 無断で ⓐ 〚予告なしに〛 without notice; 〚許可なしに〛 without permission 〚《書》leave〛. ● 無断で学校を休む stay away from school *without notice*; 《話》(サボる) skip school;(ずる休みする) play truant 〚《米話》hook(e)y〛. ● 無断で会社を欠勤する stay home from work *without permission* [*leave*, (病欠の電話をすること) *calling in* (*sick*)]; 《話》go AWOL /éiwɔːl/ (**!** AWOL は *A*bsence *W*ithout (*O*fficial) *L*eave の略). ▶今朝お車を無断でお借りしました I *took the liberty of* borrowing your car this morning. (**!** 改まった言い方で通例 I, We が主語)

むだんしゃくよう 無断借用 ● 無断借用する use … without asking permission; borrow … without authorization. (⇨無断)

むたんぽ 無担保 ── 無担保の ⓕ unsecured; uncovered. ● 無担保で融資する give a loan *without security*; give an *unsecured* loan.
● 無担保社債 an unsecured [an uncovered] bond; an unsecured [a naked] (corporate) debenture.

むち 鞭 a whip〚(柄に革ひもの (lash) のついたもの); (棒の) a rod; 〚とう・竹などの〛 a cane. ● むちで打つ (鞭打つ) 〚ことわざ〛むちを惜しむと子供がだめになる Spare the *rod* and spoil the child. (**!**「かわいい子には旅をさせよ」に相当する) ● 厳しいしつけは愛のむち Strict discipline is a special kind of love.

むち 無知 ignorance /íɡnərəns/ 《*of, about*》. ● 無知のために out of [from, through] *ignorance*. ● 自分の無知を恥じる be ashamed of one's *ignorance* [(知識の欠如) *lack of knowledge* 《*of, about*》].
── 無知な ⓕ 無知な人 *an ignorant* person. ● 法律に関しては無知だ I *am ignorant of* [*about*] law./I don't know anything about law./I have *no knowledge of* law.

むちうちしょう 鞭打ち症 (ˣa) whiplash, a whiplash injury. ▶私は車の衝突事故でむち打ち症になった I suffered from (a) *whiplash injury* in a car crash./The car crash gave me *whiplash*.

むちうつ 鞭打つ ⓓ (むちで) whip (-pp-); lash;(特に体罰として) flog (-gg-);(罰として) give* [him] the rod [the cane, (ten) lashes]. ● 公然とむち打つ *whip* (him) publicly. ● 馬をむち打って走らせる *whip* a horse on [along]. ● 老体にむち打って(=老齢にもかかわらず)働く *work in spite of* one's old age.

翻訳のこころ メロスは、わが身にむち打ち、ついに出発を決意した (太宰治『走れメロス』) Beating himself up [reprimanding himself], Melos finally decided to depart. (**!** beating himself up, reprimanding himself は「精神的に自分自身を奮い立たせる」の意)

むちこく 無遅刻 ● 無遅刻無欠席 perfect attendance and punctuality. ▶彼は3年間無遅刻だった He *has never been late for* school [the office]

for three years./He *didn't come late* to school [his office] for three years.

むちつじょ 無秩序 ③ disorder;(大混乱) (a) chaos /kéias/. (⇨混乱) ●軍隊は無秩序状態にある The troops are in (a state of) *chaos*.
── 無秩序な ⓕ disordered; chaotic.

****むちゃ** 無茶 ── 無茶な ⓕ 〚道理にかなわない、値段・要求などが法外な〛 unreasonable;〚理屈・常識に合わない〛 absurd;〚はしゃげた〛 ridiculous;〚過度の〛 excessive;〚軽率な〛 rash;〚考えのない〛 thoughtless;〚向こう見ずの〛 reckless. ● むちゃな値段 an *unreasonable* price. ● むちゃな運動 *excessive* [*immoderate*] exercise. ● むちゃな要求 an *excessive* [(法外な)《書》an *exorbitant*] demand. ● むちゃな計画 a *rash* scheme. ● むちゃな運転 *reckless* driving. ● むちゃ(に)と言うな Don't be *unreasonable* [*absurd, ridiculous*]!/(たわごとを言うな) Don't *talk nonsense*. ▶こんな寒い日に川へ泳ぎに行くなんてむちゃだ It's *ridiculous* [*absurd*] to go swimming in the river on a cold day like this. ● むちゃなことをしちゃだめだ Don't do anything *rash* [*reckless*]./(自分の限界を心得ているべきだ) You should know your limitations.

むちゃくちゃ 無茶苦茶 (無茶、めちゃめちゃ) ● むちゃくちゃな(=はしゃげた意) an *absurd* [a *ridiculous*] opinion. ▶今日はむちゃくちゃ(=ひどく)寒い It's *extremely* [*terribly, bitterly*] cold today.

むちゃくりく 無着陸 ● 無着陸飛行 a nonstop flight 《*from* London *to* Tokyo》. ●パリへの無着陸飛行に成功する succeed in *flying nonstop* to Paris.

****むちゅう** 夢中 ── 夢中な ● (我を忘れる) be beside oneself 《*with*》; (熱中する) be intent 《*on*》; (仕事などにふける) be absorbed [be engrossed] 《*in*》, (異性・趣味・スポーツなどに無我夢中である)《話》be crazy [mad, wild] 《*about*》;(恋する) be [fall] deeply in love 《*with*》. ● 喜びで夢中である be beside oneself with joy. ● 仕事に夢中である be intent on one's work; *be absorbed in* one's work. ▶彼女は音楽に夢中 She's *crazy* [*mad, wild,* (熱心だ) *enthusiastic*] *about* music. ▶彼は読書に夢中だ He *is absorbed* [*is engrossed*] *in* reading. ▶彼は金もうけに夢中 He's *mad for* money./(金もうけをしようと決心している)《やや書》He *is bent on* making money [moneymaking]. ▶彼はあまりに彼女に夢中なので彼女の欠点が見えない He's so much *in love with* her [so *crazy about* her] that he can't see her faults.
── 夢中で ⓐ 〚狂ったように〛 frantically, 《話》like crazy, 《話》like mad;〚命がけで〛 for dear life, for one's life;(必死に) desperately; 〚有頂天になって〛 with ecstasy. ● 夢中で逃げる run *for dear* [*one's*] *life*. ● 夢中で戦う fight *desperately*. ▶彼は入学試験のため夢中で勉強した He studied *desperately* [*eagerly, like crazy*] for the entrance exam. ▶ desperately では試験に失敗しないかと不安な気持ちで、eagerly は合格したいと積極的な気持ちで、like crazy は気が狂ったように猛烈に、の意) ▶遊び資金稼ぎのアルバイトに夢中でほとんど授業に現れない学生もいる Some students hardly show up for classes, because they are *preoccupied with* working part-time to make money [xto finance] for their leisure activities. (**!** show up for classes は「授業にでる」の意の慣用表現)

むちゅう 霧中 ● 霧中信号 a fog signal.

むちん 無賃 ● 無賃で free (of charge). (⇨無賃乗車)

むちんじょうしゃ 無賃乗車 ③ (ただ乗り) a free ride.
── 無賃乗車する ⓓ ride* free; have* [get*] a free ride; (こっそり乗る) steal* a ride 《*on* a train》.

- 無賃乗車者 a free passenger.

むつ 〖魚介〗a Japanese bluefish.

むつう 無痛 ── 無痛の 形 painless.
- 無痛分娩 painless childbirth [delivery]; (半麻酔状態での) delivery in twilight sleep.

むつき 睦月 〖1月〗January; (陰暦の) the first month of the lunar calendar.

むっく(り) ▶彼は寝床からむっくり(=突然)起き上がってきた He *suddenly* got out of his bed. ▶むっくりした体つきの男がやって来た There came a man of *bulky* [*stout*] build.

むつごと 睦言 «whisper» sweet [soft] nothings; «have» pillow talk.

むつごろう 〖魚介〗a mudskipper.

ムッシュ(ー) [＜フランス語] (...さま) Monsieur /məsjóːr/〘略 M.〙. (❗(1) 英語の Mr. に相当. (2) 呼びかけにも用いる)

むっちり ●むっちりした (堅太りの) plump; (赤ん坊などが) chubby; (肉感的な) 〖やや俗〗voluptuous. ●彼女のむっちりした乳房 her *firm* breasts.

むっつ 六つ six. ●六つ目の the sixth. (⇨三つ)

むっつり ●むっつりした (不機嫌な) sullen; (言葉数が少ない) taciturn. ▶彼は一日中むっつりしていた He was *sullen* all day. ▶「知らんね」と彼はむっつりして答えた "I don't know," he answered *sullenly*.
- むっつりすけべ a lecher behind one's austere face. ●むっつり屋 a sullen person; (無口な) a person of few words, a taciturn person.

むっとする ❶〖腹を立てて〗become* sullen; (感情を害する) get* offended. ▶ジョンソンはそのきつい言葉にむっとした Johnson became *sullen at* the harsh words.
❷〖熱気などで〗●むっとする(=胸を突くような)においがする *a foul* [*a nasty*] smell. ●部屋は熱気でむっとしていた It *was* very hot and *stuffy* in the room./The room *was* chokingly filled with heat.

むつまじい 睦まじい 〖和合した〗harmonious; (仲がいい) be on good terms «with». ●(仲)睦まじい夫婦 *a harmonious* [*a happy*] couple. ●(仲)睦まじく暮らす live *harmoniously* [*in harmony, happily*].

むつみあう 睦み合う like each other and become* friendly; make* friends «with»; 〖話〗hit* it off «with».

むて 無手 ── 無手で 副 (武器なしで) unarmed; (手ぶらで) empty-handed; (資本なしで) without capital.

むていけい 無定型 ●無定型詩 formless verse; (無脚韻の) blank verse. ●無定型短歌 a formless *tanka*.

むていけん 無定見 (信条のないこと) lack of principles. ▶あいつは無定見だ He has *no principles* (of his own).

むていこう 無抵抗 名 nonresistance.
── 無抵抗の 形 nonresistant. ●無抵抗の住民を殺す kill *nonresistant* inhabitants.
- 無抵抗主義 the principle of nonresistance. ▶インドはマハトマ・ガンジーの無抵抗主義による諸政策に導かれてついに英国の支配から独立した India led by Mahatma Gandhi's policies of *passive resistance*, finally gained (its [〖古〗her]) independence from the British rule.

むてかつりゅう 無手勝流 (戦わずに勝つこと・方法) (a way of) winning without fighting; (自己流) one's own way 〖fashion〗.

むてき 無敵 ── 無敵の 形 〖書〗invincible; 〖無比の〗unequaled; unrivaled; matchless.
- 無敵艦隊 (スペインの) the Invincible Armada /àːrmáːdə/.

むてき 霧笛 a foghorn. ●霧笛を鳴らす sound a *foghorn*.

むてっぽう 無鉄砲 ── 無鉄砲な 形 reckless; rash. (⇨向こう見ず)

むでん 無電 radio;《英古》wireless. (⇨無線)

むてんか 無添加 ── 無添加の 形 additive-free.
- 無添加化粧品 cosmetics containing no chemicals specified for indication. ●無添加食品 additive-free food(s).

むてんぽはんばい 無店舗販売 non-store retailing.

むとう 無糖 ── 無糖の 形 sugarless; sugar-free; unsweetened. ●無糖タイプの缶コーヒー *sugarless* canned coffee.
- 無糖ヨーグルト unsweetened yog(h)urt; plain yog(h)urt.

むどう 無道 ── 無道な 形 (道理に外れる) unreasonable; (非道な) unjust.

むとう(か) 無灯(火) ●無灯火で運転する drive «a car» *without lights*.

むとうせい 無統制 ── 無統制の 形 uncontrolled.

むとうはそう 無党派層 independents, independent voters.

むとうひょう 無投票 ●無投票で市長に3選される be chosen mayor for a third term of office *without voting*.

むどく 無毒 ── 無毒の 形 nonpoisonous; nontoxic.

むとくてん 無得点 ── 無得点の 形 scoreless. ▶試合は無得点引き分けに終わった The game ended in a *scoreless* tie. ▶その投手は相手チームを無得点に抑えた(=シャットアウトした) The pitcher *shut out* the other team.

むとどけ 無届け ●無届けで(=予告なしに)欠席する be absent *without notice*. ●無届け(=当局への事前通知なしの)デモ a demonstration held *without previous* [*advance, prior*] *notice to the authorities*.

むとんちゃく 無頓着 ── 無頓着な 形 (気にしない) careless; (無関心な) indifferent, unconcerned. ●身なりに無頓着だ be *careless about* [be *indifferent to*] one's dress. ▶マルコは何が起ころうと無頓着だ Malcolm doesn't *care* «*about*» what happens.

むないた 胸板 ▶太郎は次郎よりもずっと胸板が厚い Taro has thicker *chest* than Jiro. (❗特に厚い胸板の人を「たるのように丸い胸の人」の意で,He is barrel-chested. ということがある)

むなぎ 棟木 a ridgepole.

むなくそ 胸糞 ●胸糞が悪い «人が主語» be disgusted «at, with, by»; «事が主語» be disgusting [《話》nauseating /nɔ́ːzièitiŋ/]. ▶前の彼女が新しい彼氏と連れ立っているのを見て胸くそが悪くなった It was *nauseating* to see my former girlfriend walking with a new boyfriend.

むなぐら 胸倉 ●胸倉をつかんでにらみつける grab «him» by the collar [lapels] and glare angrily. (❗ lapels は背広などの前えり)

むなぐるしい 胸苦しい 〖圧迫を感じる〗feel* tight in the chest; 〖痛みを感じる〗feel chest pains.

むなげ 胸毛 chest hair. ●胸毛のある男 a man with a *hairy* chest; a *hairy*-chested man.

むなさき 胸先 a chest. (⇨胸元)

むなさわぎ 胸騒ぎ 〖不安〗uneasiness. ●胸騒ぎがする feel uneasy «about»; (悪い予感がする)《書》have a presentiment «that him».

むなざんよう 胸算用 ── 胸算用する 動 (当てにする) rely on ...,《話》count on .... ▶父のお金がすべて手に入るものと胸算用する *count on* [*rely on*,《主に文》]

むなしい 空しい, 虚しい 形 〖空虚な〗empty; 〖効果のない〗vain, fruitless; 〖役に立たない〗useless, futile.
● むなしい夢 an *empty* dream. ● むなしい望み a *vain* hope. ▶彼女の努力はすべてむなしかった All her efforts were *useless* [*fruitless, futile*]./(報われなかった) Her efforts *were not rewarded* [無駄に終わった] *came to nothing*, (実を結ばなかった) *didn't bear fruit*].

― 空しく, 虚しく 副 〖いたずらに〗in vain, uselessly, to no purpose; 〖ぼんやりと〗idly, in idleness. ▶我々は彼の気持ちを変えようとしたがむなしく終わった We tried *in vain* to make him change his mind. (❗*in vain* の位置は文尾でも可)/We *vainly* [*Vainly* we] tried to make him change his mind. ▶むなしく時を過ごしてはいけない Don't pass your time *idly*./Don't idle your time away.

むなしさ 空しさ, 虚しさ emptiness; (無価値) 〖書〗vanity. ● 人生のむなしさ the *emptiness* of life. ● 人の欲望のむなしさ the *vanity* of human wishes.

むなだか 胸高 ● 帯を胸高にしめる wear an *obi* high *(a)round* one's *waist*.

むなつきはっちょう 胸突き八丁 a very steep ascent near a mountaintop. ▶交渉は胸突き八丁にさしかかった The negotiations *have entered the final stage*.

むなびれ 胸鰭 a pectoral (fin).

むなもと 胸元 (胸部) a chest; a breast. ● 打者の胸元を攻める pitch a batter high and tight [in and on the hands]. ▶彼はナイフを私の胸元につきつけた He pointed his knife at my *chest*.

むに 無二 ● 無二の親友 one's best friend. ● 当代無二の詩人 the *greatest* [〖書〗*peerless*, 〖書〗*unrivaled*] poet of the day.

ムニエル [<フランス語] ● シタビラメのムニエル sole *meunière* /məːnjéər/.

むにゃむにゃ ● むにゃむにゃ言う (=分かりにくくつぶやく) mumble. ▶浩一は1人のときよく何かむにゃむにゃ言っている Koichi often *mumbles* when he is left alone.

むにんか 無認可 ● 無認可の保育所 an *unauthorized* day-care center.

むにんしょう 無任相 (⇨無任所大臣)

むにんしょだいじん 無任所大臣 a minister without portfolio.

:**むね** 胸 ❶ 〖胸部〗a chest; a breast; 《主に書》a bosom /búˈ(ː)zəm/; (女性の胸) a bust.

> **使い分け** chest 肋骨に囲まれた部分で心臓などを含んだ胸部全体をさす。胸部のけがや病気を示す際にも用いる。
> breast 盛り上がった胸の上部をさす。主に女性の(一方の)乳房を意味する。
> bosom 胸部・特に女性の胸をさす。
> bust 主に女性の胸の大きさや胸自体をさす。

① 【~胸】 ● 大きい(=幅の広い)胸 a broad (↔a narrow) *chest*; (乳房が大きい) large (↔small) *breasts*. ● 厚い[薄い]胸 a deep [a flat] *chest*.
② 【胸が[は]】 ▶胸が痛い[苦しい] I have a pain [a tightness] in my *chest*. ▶彼女は胸が豊かだ She is full-breasted [full-bosomed] (↔flat-chested)./She has large *breasts* [a full *bust*]. ▶彼女の胸はふくらみ出した Her *breasts* are developing.
③ 【胸に】 ▶彼女の胸に飛び込み rush into his arms. ▶赤ん坊は彼女の胸に抱かれて眠っていた The baby was sleeping in her *breast* [*bosom*]. ▶彼女は赤ん坊を胸に抱きしめた She held her baby against her *breast* [*bosom*].
④ 【胸を】 会話 「ちゃんと『気をつけ』の姿勢になってますか」「うん、ちょっと違うなあ。胸を張って腹を引っ込めなくちゃ」"Am I standing 'at attention' correctly?" "No, not exactly. You're supposed to keep your *chest* out and your stomach in."
⑤ 【胸で】 ▶胸でテープを切る *breast* the tape. (❗この場合 breast は上品な語でないので *cross* the finish をすすめる人も多い)

❷ 〖心臓・肺・胃など〗(心臓) a heart; (肺) a lung; (胃) a stomach. ● 胸を病む have *lung* [*chest*] trouble; (結核を) suffer from *tuberculosis*. ● 胸焼け (⇨胸焼け) ▶少し走ったら胸がどきどきした I felt my *heart* pound [beat fast] after running a little. ▶あいつを見るだけで胸が悪くなる The mere [very] sight of him makes me sick. (⇨むかつく)

❸ 〖心, 思い〗(情緒的な) a heart; (理性的な) a mind.

① 【胸の~】 ● 彼に胸のうち(=胸中)をあかす unburden one's *heart* to him. (⇨胸中)
② 【胸が[は]】 ▶胸が張り裂けるような声で in a *heart*-breaking [a *heart*-rending] voice. ▶あの孤児のことを思うと胸が痛む My *heart* aches for the orphan./I feel sorry for the orphan. ▶期待感で胸が高鳴った My *heart* beat [〖書〗*throbbed*] with expectation. ▶彼は胸がいっぱいになって言葉が出なかった He was too moved to speak./Words stuck in his *heart* with emotion. (❗この stick (in) は「(車などが)…にはまって動かなくなる」の意の比喩的用法) ▶その手紙を読むうちに彼は胸がいっぱいになった(=胸がつまった) He got all *choked up* [*had a lump in his throat*] as he read the letter.

> 翻訳のこころ 今после心は未来の画策のために詰まっている (横光利一『蝿』) Now his mind is filled with the future plans [plans for the future]. (❗(1)「胸」は mind (理性的なはたらきをする心)と表す。(2)「詰まっている」be filled with (満たされている, 一杯である)と表す)

③ 【胸に】 ▶彼の忠告が私の胸にこたえた His advice *came home to me*./心をえぐった) His advice *cut me to the heart* [*the quick*]. ▶彼女はその秘密を胸に秘めていた She *kept* the secret *to herself* [*in her bosom*]. ▶君の胸に聞きなさい Ask yourself.

● 胸が騒ぐ feel uneasy 《about》. ▶何か胸が騒ぐ I have a feeling that something bad is going to happen.
● 胸がつぶれる ▶突然の悲報に胸がつぶれた My *heart was broken* by the sudden sad news.
● 胸がふさがる ▶その痛ましいニュースに胸がふさがった My *heart was choked* with the distressing news.
● 胸が焼ける have heartburn. (⇨胸焼け)
● 胸に一物(いちもつ) ▶彼は胸に一物ありそうな様子だ He seems to have *a plot in mind*./He seems to *be hiding* his intentions.
● 胸に迫る touch one's heart. ▶万感胸に迫って言葉が出なかった I was so *full of emotion* that I couldn't speak.
● 胸にたたむ ▶それはだれにも言わずに胸にたたんでおいてください Don't tell anybody and *keep* it *to yourself*.
● 胸に手を当てる[置く] ▶そのことを胸に手を当てて考えてごらん Consider it *carefully*./Think carefully about it.
● 胸のすくような brilliant; exhilarating. ● 胸のすくような快挙 a *brilliant* achievement.
● 胸のつかえが下りる ▶それで胸のつかえが下りた It was *a weight off my mind*.
● 胸を痛める ▶彼の健康のことで胸を痛める(=心配する)

worry about [over] his health.
- **胸を打つ** ●胸を打つ場面 a *touching* scene. ▶私はその光景に胸を打たれた I *was touched* [*was moved*] by the scene./(胸のつまる思いがした) I *felt a lump in my* [*the*] *throat* when I saw it.
- **胸を貸す** (相撲で) allow a junior *sumo* wrestler to practice on one. (**!** on は「...を相手にして」の意)
- **胸を借りる** ▶私は先輩の胸を借りて練習した I *was allowed to* practice on my senior.
- **胸を焦がす** ●恋に胸を焦がす be deeply in love 《*with her*》.
- **胸をたたく** (自信を示して) strike one's chest with a fist.
- **胸を突かれる** (突然のことに驚く) be startled. ▶私は娘の言葉にはっと胸を突かれた I *was startled by* what my daughter said.
- **胸をなで下ろす** ▶彼が無事に着いたので胸をなで下ろした(=心から重荷を取り除いた) His safe arrival *took a load off* my *mind*./I *felt relieved* [*sighed with relief*, gave *a sigh of relief*] to hear that he had arrived safely.
- **胸を張る** (得意げに) thrust [throw] out one's chest; expand one's chest. ▶しゃんと胸を張って!(体をまっすぐにせよ) Straighten yourself up!/(元気を出せ) Keep your chin up! /[参考] 米英では chin は意志・決断の象徴
- **胸をふくらませる** ▶彼は希望に胸をふくらませて上京した He went to Tokyo (with his *heart*) *full of hope*./He went to Tokyo *with so much hope*.

むね 旨 ❶[内容] ●小包が着いた旨の手紙 a letter *saying that* [(趣旨) 《書》 *to the effect that*] the parcel has arrived. ●その旨彼に伝える tell him *so* [《書》 *to that effect*].
❷[主義] ▶我が社は「安全第一」を旨としています Our *motto* is "Safety First."

むね 棟 〔屋根の〕 the ridge; 〔建物〕 a house (🏠 houses /-ziz, 《米》 -siz/). ▶その火事で2棟が全焼した That fire burned down two *houses*.
- **棟上げ式** the ceremony of the completion of the framework of a house.

むねあて 胸当て (よろいの) a breastplate; (野球の) a chest protector; (エプロンなどの) a bib.
むねかざり 胸飾り a breastpin; a brooch; (飾り花の) a buttonhole.
むねさんずん 胸三寸 (a) thought. (⇨考え)
むねつ 無熱 ── 無熱の 形 nonfebrile; unfeverish.
むねやけ 胸焼け heartburn. ▶食べ過ぎてひどく胸焼けがする I ate too much and now I have bad [slight] *heartburn*.
むねわりながや 棟割り長屋 (全体) 《米》 row houses, 《英》 terraced houses; (一戸) 《米》 a row house, 《英》 a terraced house.
むねん 無念 〔残念〕 regret; 〔悔しさ〕 mortification; 〔無想〕 freedom from all thoughts. ●無念を晴らす(=復讐(ふくしゅう)する) revenge oneself 《*on*》.
むのう 無能 〔無能力〕 incompetence; 〔非能率〕 inefficiency. ●無能のため解雇される be dismissed for *incompetence* [*lack of ability*].
── 無能な 形 ●無能な役人 an *incompetent* [an *inefficient*] official. ▶彼は医者として無能だ He is *no good* as a doctor.
むのうやく 無農薬 ●無農薬野菜 *organic vegetables*. ▶無農薬野菜はひどく割高なので買う気になれない I'm discouraged from buying *organic vegetables* because they are very expensive. ●**無農薬農家** an organic farmer. ●**無農薬農法** an organic farming method. ●**無農薬フルーツ** organic fruit.

むのうりょく 無能力 名 incompetence. (⇨無能)
── 無能力な 形 incompetent.
- **無能力者** 〔法律〕 a person without capacity [legal competence].

むはい 無配 ▶M株は無配になった(=無配株になった) M stock became a *non-dividend payer*. ▶K社は今期も無配を余儀なくされた K had to *suspend payments of dividends* this term again.
- **無配株** a non-dividend payer.

むはい 無敗 ── 無敗の 形 undefeated. ▶今シーズンは6勝無敗だった We've had six wins and *no defeats* this season.
むはいとう 無配当 (⇨無配)
むばんそう 無伴奏 ── 無伴奏の 形 unaccompanied. ●無伴奏バイオリンソナタ a sonata for *unaccompanied* violin. ●無伴奏で歌う sing a cappella.
むはんのう 無反応 ▶私たちの訴えに彼らは無反応だった They showed *no reaction* to our appeal./They gave *no response* to our appeal.
ムハンマド 〔イスラム教の創始者〕 Muhammad /məhǽ-məd/. (**!** Mahomet ともいう)
むひ 無比 ── 無比の 形 (唯一の) unique; (対抗するものがない) 《書》 unrivaled, matchless; (並ぶものがない) 《書》 unparalleled; (匹敵するものがない) 《書》 unequaled.
むひはん 無批判 ── 無批判の 形 uncritical, unquestioning.
── 無批判に 副 uncritically.
むびゅう 無謬 名 infallibility.
── 無謬の 形 infallible.
むひょう 霧氷 (hoar)frost, 《書》 rime.
むびょう 無病 ●無病息災である be in good health; (年配者が) be hale and hearty.
むひょうじょう 無表情 ── 無表情の 形 impassive; (ぼんやりとした) blank, vacant. ●無表情な顔をしている have an impassive [a *poker*] face. (**!** 後の方は無表情を装った顔) ▶彼は死刑の宣告を受けた時石のように無表情のままであった His face remained as *impassive* as stone when he was sentenced to death.
むふう 無風 ── 無風の 形 windless; calm /káːm/. (⇨風(🌬)) ▶政局は現在無風状態だ The political situation *is settled down* [*is stable*] at present.
むふんべつ 無分別 名 indiscretion; (思慮のないこと) thoughtlessness.
── 無分別な 形 ●無分別なことをする do something *indiscreet* [(軽率な) *rash*]. ▶彼は無分別にもそのわいろを受け取った He *had the indiscretion* [*was so indiscreet as*] to take the bribe. / It *was thoughtless* of him [He *was thoughtless*] to take the bribe.
むべなるかな 宜なる哉 ▶光陰矢のごとしということわざがあるが、むべなるかな(=まったくその通りだ) A proverb says that time flies. Indeed, that is *quite right*.
むへん 無辺 ── 無辺の 形 infinite; limitless; boundless. ●広大無辺の vast and boundless; immeasurable.
むほう 無法 ── 無法の 形 lawless.
- **無法地帯** a lawless zone. ● **無法者** a lawless man; an outlaw; (ならず者) a rascal.

むぼう 無謀 名 recklessness.
── 無謀な 形 reckless; (軽率な) rash; (思慮のない) thoughtless. ●無謀な運転 *reckless* driving. ▶この悪天候に飛行機で飛ぶなんて無謀だ It's *reckless*

むほうしゅう 無報酬 ●無報酬の仕事 an *unpaid* task;（自発的にする）a *voluntary* task. ●無報酬で働く work *for nothing* [*without pay*].

むぼうび 無防備 ── 無防備の 形 defenseless;（都市などが）unfortified;（非武装の）unarmed. ●我々は敵の攻撃に対してまったく無防備であった We were utterly *defenseless* against the enemy attack. ●無防備都市 an open city.

むほん 謀反 〔反逆〕treason;〔反乱〕(大規模で組織的な) (a) rebellion; (小規模な) (a) revolt, (an) insurrection; (上官に対して) (a) mutiny. (⇨反乱) ●謀反を起こす revolt [rebél] (*against*). ●謀反人 a rébel.

むま 夢魔 (have) a nightmare.

むみ 無味 ●無味無臭の液体 a *tasteless*, odorless liquid.

むみかんそう 無味乾燥 ── 無味乾燥な 形 (退屈な) dull, boring, dry. ●無味乾燥な話 a *dull* [an *uninteresting*] story. ●彼の講義は無味乾燥だった I found his lecture *boring* [*dry*].

むめい 無名 ── 無名の 形 (知られていない) unknown; obscure; (名前の知れない) nameless. ●無名の作家 an *unknown* [an *obscure*] author. ●無名の墓 a *nameless* grave. ▶彼は 30 歳代後半まで芸術家としては無名であった He did not become *known* [was *not famous*] as an artist until he was in his late thirties. ●無名戦士 an unknown soldier. ●無名戦士の墓《米》the Tomb of the *Unknowns*;《英》the Grave of the *Unknown Warrior*.

むめい 無銘 ── 無銘の 形 unsigned; without the maker's name.

むめんきょ 無免許 ── 無免許の 形 (もぐりの) unlicensed; (免許なしで) without a license. ●無免許運転する drive *without a driver's license* [《英》*a driving licence*].

むもう 無毛 ── 無毛の 形 hairless;〔生物〕glabrous. ●無毛症〔医学〕atrichia; atrichosis.

むもくてき 無目的 ── 無目的な 形 aimless; purposeless.

── 無目的に 副 without any specific aim [purpose]; aimlessly.

むやみに 無闇に 〔向こう見ずに〕recklessly, rashly; 〔過度に〕excessively (⇨むやみやたら); 〔不当に〕unreasonably; 〔無差別に〕indiscriminately. (⇨やたらに) ●むやみにスピードを出す speed *recklessly*. ●むやみに酒を飲む drink *excessively* [*too much*]. ●他人をむやみに非難する blame other people [others] *unreasonably* [*indiscriminately*].

むやみやたらに (過度に) excessively. (⇨無闇に) ▶むやみやたらに酒を飲むと体に悪いよ *Excessive* drinking is bad for your health. ▶彼の演説はむやみやたらに長かった His speech was *much too long*. (*!* much は too を強調する)

むゆうびょう 夢遊病 sleepwalking;《書》somnambulism /sámnæmbjəlìzm/.

●夢遊病者 a sleepwalker;《書》a somnambulist.

むよう 無用 ── 無用の 形 ❶〔役に立たない〕useless, of no use.

❷〔不必要な〕unnecessary; needless. (*!* 主に限定的に) ●無用の混乱を招く give rise to *unnecessary* confusion. ▶心配はご無用(です) *Don't* worry (about it)!/*You don't have to* [*need not*] worry

(about it). (*!* 前の方が口語的)/*There is no need for* you to worry./You *have no need* to worry.
❸〔用事のない〕●無用の者立入禁止《掲示》No admittance except on business./No trespassing.
❹〔してはならぬ〕forbidden;《書》prohibited. ▶他言は無用 You *must not* tell it to anybody. ▶開放無用《掲示》*Close* the door after you. ▶*after* you は後にいる人にドアを閉めるの意で、状況が異なることに注意/Not to be left open.
●無用の長物 a thing that is worse than useless; (品物) a white elephant; (人) a good-for-nothing.
●無用の用 a thing apparently useless but in fact very useful.

むよく 無欲 名 (無私) unselfishness.
── 無欲の[な] 形 unselfish; generous.

むら 村 ❶〔行政区画〕a village (*!*《米》では通例 a small town, a town を用いる); (小村) a hamlet. ●隣[小さな]村 a neighboring [a small,《話》a tiny] *village*. ●村外れに on [×in] the outskirts of a *village*.
❷〔同業者の〕a colony. (*!* 単・複両扱い) ●芸術家村 an artists' *colony*; a *colony* of artists.
●村役場 a village office.

むら 斑 ── むらのある〔色や音が〕uneven;〔行動や感情が〕erratic. ●色にむらがある[ない]ポスター an unevenly [an evenly] painted poster. ●大きさにむらがある vary [*be irregular*] in size. ▶彼は気分に[彼の仕事には]むらがある He [His work] is *erratic*.

むらおこし 村興し ●村興しをする make a village prosperous; revive the *village* economy.

むらがる 群がる 〔寄り集まる〕gather;〔大勢の人が集まって混み合う〕crowd;〔押し合いながら移動する〕throng;〔動物・人が群れをなして集まる〕flock;〔昆虫・人などがうようよする〕swarm. (⇨集まる) ▶アリは虫の死がいに群がっている Ants *are gathering* [*swarming*] *around* the dead worm. ▶記者たちは質問しようと大臣の周りに群がった The reporters *gathered* [*crowded*] around the minister to ask questions. ▶観光客が群がってやって来た Sightseers came *in flocks* [*swarms*].

むらぎ 斑気 (気まぐれ)《やや書》(a) caprice /kəprí:s/; a whim. (⇨気まぐれ) ●むら気の娘《やや書》a *capricious* [a *whimsical*] girl; (気むずかしい) a *moody* girl.

むらさき 紫 〔赤みがかった〕purple;〔青みがかった〕violet;〔植物〕a gromwell. ●紫の purple; violet. ▶彼の唇は寒さで紫色だ His lips are *purple* from the cold.

むらさきキャベツ 紫キャベツ 〔植物〕(a) red cabbage. ●料理した葉 [Ⓤ]

むらさきしきぶ 紫式部 〔植物〕a Japanese beautyberry.

むらさきしきぶにっき『紫式部日記』 *The Diary of Lady Murasaki*. 〔参考〕紫式部の日記

むらさきずいしょう 紫水晶 amethyst.

むらさきつゆくさ 紫露草 〔植物〕a spiderwort.

むらざと 村里 a village; (小集落) a hamlet.

むらしゃかい 村社会 a village community.

むらす 蒸らす keep* the lid on [×keep《cooked rice》steamed] for a while after turning off the heat. (*!* steam は「(火にかけて蒸し器などで)蒸す」ことで、「蒸らす」は火からおろして熱い湯気を使うことで意味が異なり、ここでは不可)

むらすずめ 群雀 a flock of sparrows.

むらはちぶ 村八分 ostracism. ●村八分にする *stop*

accepting [《やや書》 *ostracize*] 《him》 as a member of the group. ● 近所の人から村八分にされる *become an outcast* among [《やや書》 *be ostracized* by] one's neighbors.

むらびと 村人　a villager. ▶ 村人たちはみんなその計画に反対していた The *villagers* were all against the plan./The whole *village* was against the plan. (！この village は集合的に「村民」の意)

むらむら ▶ 怒りがむらむらと私のなかに沸き上がった Anger surged (*up*) [*boiled up*] within me. ▶ 彼はそのむらむらとする衝動を抑えることができなかった He couldn't suppress the *rising* impulse.

***むり** 無理 图　❶ [道理に合わないこと] unreasonableness. ● 無理のない（道理に合った）reasonable;（自然な，当然の）natural. ● 無理のない姿勢 a *natural* posture. ▶ 無理を言うな，仕事中は会えないんだ You must be *reasonable* [Be *reasonable*]. I can't meet you while I am at work.

❷ [不可能] impossibility. ▶ 無理を承知で仕事を頼んだ I asked for the job *though I knew it was extremely difficult*.

❸ [強制] compulsion. ▶ 彼は無理を押して働き続けた He *forced* himself *to* work continuously.

会話「よろしければ私と踊っていただけますか」「喜んで．でも無理(を)しなくていいわよ」「無理なんかしてません」"If you don't mind, could you dance with me?" "With pleasure. But don't *feel obliged*." "It's not that."

❹ [過度] (an) excess; [過労] overwork.

● 無理が通れば道理が引っ込む When unreason prevails, reason gives way./When falsehood speaks, truth keeps silent.

● 無理もない ▶ 彼がそれを信じるのも無理はない（= 十分な理由がある）He *has every* [*good*] *reason to* believe it./He *may well* believe it. (！may well をこのように三人称主語と用いると「彼はおそらくそれを信じるだろう」の意にもとられるため，You *may well* believe it. のように二人称主語に限る方が無難)（信じて当然だ）It is natural (*that*) he *should* believe [*believes*] it. (！後の方が強意的，この場合 should は省略不可．It is *natural for* him *to* believe it. ともいえる)（不思議ではない）*It is no wonder* (*that*) [《話》*No wonder*] he believes it. (！信じてもとがめるわけにゆかない) I can hardly blame him *for* believing it./(理解できる) *It is understandable that* [*Understandably*,] he believes it.

— 無理な 形　❶ [道理に反した] unreasonable;（不当な）unjustifiable;（不自然な）unnatural. ● 無理な注文 (= 要求) をする make an *unreasonable* [（不可能な）an *impossible*,（過度の）an *excessive*,（不当な）an *unfair*] demand 《*on* him》;（要求[期待]しすぎる）ask [expect] too much 《*of* him》. (⇨❷, ❹)▶ それは無理(な注文)だ Your demands are *unreasonable*./You're asking [expecting] too much. (！That's too much to ask [expect]. のようにも言える)《話》That's a *tall* order. ▶ 夏に雪を期待するなんて無理だ It's *unreasonable* to expect snow in 《主に米》the summer./(期待できない) We can't expect snow in 《主に米》the summer.

❷ [不可能な] impossible. ▶ その仕事を全部するなんて無理だ I can't [It is *impossible* for me to,《やや書》I am unable to] do all the work. (！×I am *impossible* to do.... とはいわない．「...無理だと思う」という場合は I don't think I can.... となり，I think I *can't*.... は主張が強い場合を除いて《まれ》)▶ 彼は下半身が麻痺しています．おそらく歩行は無理でしょう He is paralyzed from the waist down. I'm afraid he

won't walk. (！won't be able to... に比べて気遣いのある表現)

会話「これを 6 時までに修理できますか」「それは [6 時は] 無理です」"Can you fix this by six o'clock?" "That's [Six is] ˇ*impossible*, I'm afráid."

❸ [強制的な] forced;（強制的な，義務的な）《書》compulsory;（力づくの）《書》forcible. ▶ 無理やり彼に運動をさせる get *excessive* exercise. ▶ 子供にそんな行動を期待するのは無理だ It's *too much* to expect children to act like that.

— 無理に 副　by force,《やや書》forcibly;（意に反して）against one's will. (⇨無理やり) ● 子供に薬を無理に飲ませる *make* the child take the pill; *force* the child *to* take the pill. (！force, make は「いやがるものを…させる」という強い強制力を示す) ● 無理に笑う (= 作り笑いをする) *force* a smile; give a *forced* smile. (⇨形 ❸) ● 無理に (= 力づくで) ドアを開ける *force* a door open; *force* open a door (！以上いずれも open は形容詞); open a door *by force*. ▶ 私は行きたくなかったが彼に無理に行かされた I didn't want to go, but he *forced* me (*to*) [*made* me (*go*)].

— 無理(を)する 動　（働きすぎる）work too much,《やや書》overwork;（筋肉などを極度に使う）strain oneself. ▶ 彼は無理をして（=長時間がたって）病気になった He got sick from *overwork* [because he *worked too much*]. (！from は原因を表す) / He *overworked* and became sick. ▶ 無理するな Don't *work too hard*./(のんきにやりなさい) Take it easy. (！《米話》では別れのあいさつとしても用いる)

むりおうじょう 無理往生　● 無理往生させる force 《him》to 《do》.

むりおし 無理押し　— 無理押しする 動　● 要求[提案]を無理押しする *push* one's claim [proposal]. ● 法案を無理押しする *force* a bill *through* Parliament.

むりかい 無理解　— 無理解な 形　unsympathetic; inconsiderate.

むりからぬ 無理からぬ （もっとも な）reasonable;（当然の）natural. (⇨無理[無理もない]) ▶ 彼が怒ったのも無理からぬことだ *No wonder* (*that*) [*It's no wonder* (*that*), *It is natural that*] he got angry. (！最初の言い方は《話》で, natural の場合 that は省略される)

むりさんだん 無理算段　▶ フランクは無理算段 (= 無理してお金を用意して) レストランを開店した Frank *scraped the money up* [*together*] to start a restaurant.

むりし 無利子 图　non-interest; no interest.

— 無利子の 形　interest-free. ▶ ただ今 6 か月の無利子貸し付けをご提供中です We are now offering six months' *interest-free* credit to our customers.

● 無利子債券　a non-interest-bearing bond.
● 無利子預金　a non-interest-bearing deposit.

むりじい 無理強い 图　compulsion;《書》coercion.
● 無理強いされて under *compulsion* [*coercion*].

— 無理強いする 動　force [compel] 《him *to do*》. (⇨無理に)

むりすう 無理数　 [数学] a surd; an irrational number.

— 無理数の 形　surd; irrational.

むりそく 無利息　(⇨無利子)

むりなんだい 無理難題　● 無理難題を吹っかける make an *unreasonable* demand 《*on* him》; ask *too much* 《*of* him》.

むりむたい 無理無体　— 無理無体な 形　extremely unreasonable.

— 無理無体に 副　forcibly.

むりやり 無理やり （力ずくで）by force. ● 無理やり彼から金を奪う take the money from him *by force*.

- 無理やり彼女を働かす make her work (❗強い強制を表す. make her work *against* her *will* とすれば「本人の意に反し」の意が加わる); *force* [*compel*] her *to* work (❗force は make と同様強い強制を表す. compel は force より意味は弱く,「不本意ながらもさせる」の意). (⇨無理に)

むりょ 無慮 (およそ) as many as …; no less than …; no fewer than …. ▶無慮1万人が亡くなった No fewer than 10,000 people were killed.

＊むりょう 無料 ── 無料の 形 free. ●無料配達 *free* delivery. ▶今夜のコンサートの無料の切符が2枚あります I have two *free* tickets for tonight's concert. ▶このパンフレットは無料です These brochures [pamphlets] are *free* (*of charge*). ▶このサービスは無料です There is *no charge* [*No charge is made*] for this service./We give this service *for nothing*.

── 無料で 副 free (of charge), for nothing, 《話》for free. ▶君には無料で1部あげよう I'll give you a *free* copy. ▶6歳未満の子供は無料で入れます(＝入場無料です) Children under six are admitted *free* (*of charge*). (❗「入場無料」〖掲示〗は Admission free)

むりょう 無量 ── 無量の 形 immeasurable; infinite. ▶感慨無量だ My heart is filled with deep emotion.

むりょく 無力 名 powerlessness; (病人・幼児などの) helplessness; 〖無能〗impotence; (技量の) incompetence.

── 無力な 形 powerless; helpless; impotent; incompetent. ▶群衆を静めるには彼は無力だった He was *powerless* to stop the mob. ●無力感 an impotent feeling.

むりん 無燐 ●無燐洗剤 (a) phosphorus-free detergent.

むるい 無類 ── 無類の 形 《書》matchless; 《書》unequaled. (⇨無比)

＊むれ 群 〖集団〗a group (❗一定のつながりを持った人や動物の集団); 〖人の〗a crowd; 〖獣の〗a herd; 〖羊・鳥の〗a flock; 〖魚の〗a school; 〖虫の〗a swarm; 〖猟犬・オオカミの〗a pack; 〖ライオンの〗a pride. (❗以上の語は原則として,全体をひとまとまりとして見るときは単数扱い, 個々の人や動物に重点を置くときは《英》では複数扱い, 《米》では単数動詞, 複数代名詞で呼応さすのが普通。●移民の群れ a *group* of immigrants. ●人の群れ a *crowd* of people. (❗以上と2例とも複数扱い) ●牛〖象〗の群れ a *herd* of cattle [elephants]. ●魚の群れ a *school* [《同一種の》a *shoal*] of fish. ●ハトの群れ a *flock* [《飛行中の》a *flight*] of pigeons. ●群れをなす(＝群れる) group [herd, flock] together. (❗すべて人にも使える) ●群れをなして生息する live *in herds* [*flocks*]. ▶羊の群れがやって来た。道をあけよう A *flock* of sheep is coming. Let's make way for them.

むれたつ 群れ立つ (群れを作って立つ) stand* in flocks; (群れを作って飛び立つ) fly* away in flocks.

むれとぶ 群れ飛ぶ fly* in flocks; fly in great numbers.

むれる 蒸れる ❶〖熱が通る〗●よく蒸れている be well *steamed*.

❷〖蒸し暑い〗be sultry; 〖(体の部分が)汗をかく〗get* [feel*] sweaty /swéti/. ▶この建物は蒸れて暑い It is hot and *stuffy* in this building. ▶この靴下は足が蒸れる(＝汗てにおう) My feet *get sweaty* in these socks.

むろ 室 (地下貯蔵庫) a cellar.

むろあじ 室鯵 〖魚介〗a brownstriped mackerel scad.

むろざき 室咲き ●室咲きの花 a hothouse [a greenhouse] flower.

むろまち 室町 ●室町時代 〖歴史〗the *Muromachi* period.

むろん of course; naturally. (⇨もちろん)

ムンク 〖ノルウェーの画家〗Munch /múŋk/ (Edvard ～).

むんずと (⇨むずと)

ムンバイ [＜ヒンズー語] 〖インドの都市〗Mumbai /mùmbáɪ/. 〖参考〗旧称ボンベイ

むんむん ●むんむんする (湿度が高くて) steamy; (通風が悪くて) be stuffy. ▶その部屋は窓をみんな閉めたのでむんむんしていた The room *was stuffy* with all the windows closed. ▶会場は若い女性の熱気でむんむんしていた(＝が充満していた) The hall *was filled with* the young women's enthusiasm.

め

め 目
INDEX

❶ 器官　　　　　　　❷ 視力, 視覚
❸ 視線　　　　　　　❹ 目つき
❺ 鑑識眼　　　　　　❻ 見方
❼ 経験　　　　　　　❽ 台風などの
❾ ざる・織物・木などの

❶ [**器官**] an eye (🛈 通例複数形で); (眼球) an eyeball.
① 【〜(の)目】 ● はれぼったい [かわいい] 目 puffy [lovely] *eyes*. ● つり[たれ]目 slanted [droopy] *eyes*. ● 黒い目の娘 a girl with dark [black] *eyes*. (🛈 通例 a black eye は目の周りの打撲によるあざをさす) ▶ 彼女は大きく青いきれいな目をしている She has beautiful big [×big beautiful] blue *eyes*.
② 【目が[は]】 ▶ 彼は目が赤い(=充血している) His *eyes* are bloodshot. ▶ 彼は目がひどくくぼんでいた His *eyes* were deeply sunken [deep-set]. (🛈 通例前の方は病気や老齢でやられた様子を, 後の方は彫りの深い顔をいう)/He had deep sunken [deep-set] *eyes*. ● 目がひりひり[ごろごろ]します My *eyes* feel irritated [sandy]. ▶ どこに目がついているんだ(=よく見ろ) Where are your *eyes*?
③ 【目の】 optic. ● 目の神経 an *optic* nerve. ● 目のごみ a foreign body [object] *in the eye*. ● 目の玉 (⇨目玉) ● 目の前で交通事故があった There was a car accident right in front of [before, under] my *eyes*. (⇨目の前 ❶)
会話「それはどこにあるの」「君の目の前(=鼻先)だよ」"Where is it?" "Right under [before] your *nose*."
④ 【目を】 ● 目を泣きはらす cry one's *eyes* out. ● 目を細める (まぶしくて, よく見えなくて) screw up one's *eyes* (近視などで) squint one's *eyes*, (愛着・笑みなどで) crease one's *eyes*. (🛈 narrow one's eyes は通例疑いや敵意のためにまゆをひそめる表情) ● 目を閉じる close [shut] one's *eyes*. ▶ その小さい男の子は目を大きく見開いて巨大な象を見た The little boy gazed at the huge elephant, (with his) *eyes* wide open. (🛈 この open は形容詞/目を丸くして) The little boy looked round-*eyed* at the huge elephant./(目を皿のようにして) 《話》 The little boy was *all eyes* as he looked at the huge elephant. ▶ ブラインドを開けると彼女は目をぎゅっとつむった When she drew up the blind, she squeezed her eyes tight shut. ▶ 彼は戦争で片目を失った He lost an *eye* in the war. ▶ 彼は驚いて目をぱちくり[白黒]させた He blinked [goggled] (his *eyes*) in amazement. ▶ 彼は封筒を取り上げ郵便局の消印を目を細めて見た He picked up the envelope and *squinted* at the postmark. ▶ 会話をするときには相手の目を見なさい, でないと相手の話に興味がないとか聞いていないと受けとられます Look into the other person's *eyes* [Make *eye* contact with the other person] during a conversation; otherwise, he thinks you are not interested in or listening to what he is saying.
⑤ 【目で】 ▶ 彼が歩いているのをこの目で見たのです I saw him walking *with* my own [×these] *eyes*.

❷ [**視力, 視覚**] an eye (🛈 しばしば複数形で); (視力) eyesight, sight; 《やや書》 vision. ● 目の錯覚 an *optical* illusion. ● 目に見えない細菌 an *invisible* germ. ● 目の届く限り一面に(=見渡す限り)麦畑が広がっていた The wheat field stretched as far as the [×one's] *eye* could see. (⇨見渡す) ● 目がよい have good (*eye*)*sight*; have sharp [good] *eyes*. ▶ 彼は片目が見えない He is blind *in one eye*. ▶ 彼女は目が見えなくなった She has lost her (*eye*)*sight*./She has become *blind*. ▶ 目がかすみます Things look blurred./I have blurred *vision*. ▶ 彼の目は昨年以来めっきり衰えた His (*eye*)*sight* has failed badly since last year. ▶ 暗闇でも目がきく動物もいる Some animals *can see* in the dark. ▶ 我々日本人は食物を味わうだけでなく目でも(=見て)楽しむのです You know Japanese people [《やや書》 the Japanese] enjoy *looking at* food as much as we enjoy tasting it. (🛈「我々」はことさらに訳さない方がよい)

❸ [**視線**] an eye (🛈 通例複数形で); (見ること) a look. ● 伏し目になる drop [lower] one's *eyes*. ● 目と目を見かわす exchange *looks* 《with》. ● 目をそらす look away 《from》. ▶ 彼女と目が合うと私は手を振った When our eyes met [I caught her *eye*], I waved to her. ▶ 目のやり場がない I don't know where to rest my *eyes* [which way to *look*]. ▶ 窓の方へ目を向けたが何も見えなかった I looked at the window, but didn't [couldn't] see anything.

❹ [**目つき**] (目の表情) an eye (🛈 しばしば複数形で); (様子) a look. (🛈 感情を示す形容詞を伴う) ● 落ち着いた[しっとの]目で私の方を振り向く turn to me with a tranquil [a jealous] *eye* [*look*]. ● 不信[尊敬]の目で人を見る *eye* [*look at*] 《him》 with disbelief [respectfully, admiringly]. ▶ 彼女はけげんな目をしていた She *had* a puzzled *look* in her eye(s)./She *looked* puzzled. ▶ 父は私をきびしい目で見た Father *gave me* a severe *look*./Father *looked at* me severely. ▶ 真理は私に話すなと目で合図した Mari *winked at* me [signaled to me with her eyes, signaled to me with a wink] not to speak.

❺ [**鑑識眼**] an eye (🛈 通例単数形で); (判断力) judgment. ▶ 彼は絵を見る目がある He has an *eye* [a *good eye*] *for* art. ▶ この詩を鑑賞するには詩人の目がいる It needs a poet's *eye* [(洞察力) *insight*] to appreciate this poem.

❻ [**見方**] (観点) an eye (🛈 しばしば複数形で); (見地, 見解) a point of view, a viewpoint. ● 法の目から見れば *in the eyes of* the law. ● 別の[公平な]目で情勢を見る look at the situation *with* another [an impartial] *eye*. ▶ 私たちは彼の目から見れば赤ん坊だ We are babies in his *eyes*. ▶ 作家の目から見ると, これらの文学作品は批評に値しない *From* a writer's *point of view*, these literary works are beneath criticism [review]. ▶ これがアメリカ人の目から見た日本観です This is Japan *as* Americans *see* it [*as seen by* Americans]. ▶ 長い目で見ればその家は今買っておいた方がいいでしょう *In the long run* it would be better for you to buy the house now [《話》 the house would be a good

buy (for you)].
❼ 【経験】(an) experience. ▶アメリカ旅行中何度も恐ろしい目にあった I had a lot of frightening *experiences* during my trip in America. ▶大雨が降った後ひどい目にあった We had a terrible *time* after it had rained heavily.
❽ 【台風などの】●台風の目 the center [*eye*] of a typhoon;《比喩的》the stórm cènter. ●針の目(=穴) the *eye* of a needle; a needle's *eye*.
❾ 【ざる・織物・木などの】(網・ざるの目) a mesh; (織り方) texture; (木目, 石目) grain; (チェス盤などます目) a square; [[のこぎり・やすりなどの]] a tooth (⑧ teeth). ▶2インチの目の網 a net of two-inch *meshes*. ▶目の細かい[荒い]ざる a fine-*meshed* [a coarse-*meshed*] strainer. ▶目のゆるい[荒い; つんだ]布地 cloth of loose [coarse; close] *texture*; loose [coarse; close] cloth. ▶目の細かい木材[石材] wood [stone] of fine *grain*; fine-*grained* wood [stone]. ▶碁盤の目 *squares* on a go board. ▶のこぎり[やすり]の目 the *teeth* of a saw [a file].

● 目がくらむ ▶目がくらむようなダイヤモンド a *dazzling* diamond. ▶彼は金に目がくらんだ He *was* blinded [*was dazzled*] *by* money.
● 目が肥えた ▶目の肥えた聴衆 an *appreciative* audience.
● 目が覚める wake (up); (正気を取り戻す) come to one's senses. ▶目が覚めるような(=鮮やかな)赤いドレス a *brilliant* red dress. ▶目が覚めるような(=息をのむほどの)ホームラン a *stunning* homerun. ▶今朝ののどが痛くて目が覚めた I *woke up* [(目を覚まされる) *was awakened*] *with* a sore throat.
● 目が据わる ▶彼は飲むにつれて目が据わってきた As he drank more, his eyes *grew fixed* [*took on a fixed look*].
● 目が[の]高い ●目の高い(=鑑賞力のある)観客 an *appreciative* audience. ▶彼はさすがに目が高い(=違いの分かる目を持っている) He *has* a truly *discerning eye*.
● 目が届く ▶親の目の届かない所で(=いない所で)悪い事をする do bad things *behind* one's parents' *backs*. ▶目の届かない所に行っては絶対だめよ I told you to stay close. Don't ever leave my *sight*.
● 目がない ▶彼女は甘いものに目がない She *loves* [*is very fond of*,《話》*is crazy about*] sweets./She *has* a *weakness for* sweet things./She *has* a *sweet tooth*.
● 目が回る ▶運動をやりすぎて目が回った(=めまいがした) I *felt giddy* [*dizzy*] from too much exercise. ▶今日は目が回るほど(=大変)忙しい I'm *very* busy [《話》(*as*) *busy as a bee*] today.
● 目から鱗(⅔)が落ちる ▶突然目から鱗が落ちた Suddenly *the scales have fallen from* my *eyes*./I *was* suddenly *awakened to the truth*.
● 目から火が出る ▶鴨居に頭をぶつけて目から火が出た I saw stars when I hit my head against the lintel.
● 目じゃない ▶彼は私の目じゃない(=相手にならない) He is *no match* for me. ▶他の女は目じゃない(=意味を持たない) Other girls *mean nothing* to me.
● 目と鼻の先 ▶駅は家から目と鼻の先です (非常に近い) The station is *very close to* my house./(石を投げると届く距離にある) The station is just *a stone's throw* from my house.
● 目に余る ▶目に余る(=堪えがたい)行為 the conduct one can't stand [*bear*, (認める) *approve*].
● 目に入れても痛くない ▶孫娘は目に入れても痛くない My granddaughter is the apple of my *eye*.
● 目に浮かぶ ▶あの美しいシーンが目に(=心に)浮かぶ The beautiful scene *comes to mind* [*into* my *mind*]./(...を心に描く) I *can* (just) *picture* the beautiful scene.
● 目に映る ▶目に映るすべてのものが私には珍しかった Everything that *met* my *eyes* [I *saw*] was new to me.
● 目に角(㋖)を立てる (ひどく怒ってにらみつける) look at 《him》very angrily.
● 目に染みる ▶煙が目に染みた The smoke *stung* my *eyes*. ▶5月は新緑が目に染みる(=鮮やかである) The fresh green is *vivid* in May.
● 目にする ▶これは街でよく目にする光景である This is the scene we often *see* on the street.
● 目に立つ ▶目に立つ(=目立つ)色 a *striking* color.
● 目に留める ▶彼女の赤いドレスが私の目に留まった(=注意を引いた) Her red dress *caught* my *eye* [*drew* my *attention*, *attracted* my *attention*]./ Her red dress *caught* my *eye* [*drew* my *attention*, *attracted* my *attention*].
● 目に入る ▶彼は立ち止まって彼女をにらんでいたが彼女は彼のことは目にも入らないかのように通り過ぎた He stopped to glare at her, but she passed as if she didn't even *see* him.
● 目には目を歯には歯を an eye for an eye (and a tooth for a tooth).
● 目に触れる ▶赤ちゃんは目に触れるものは何でも口に入れようとする Babies try to put everything they *see* into their mouths.
● 目に見える ▶目に見えて(=著しく)進歩する make (xa) *remarkable* [*marked*] progress《*in*》. ▶彼は目に見えて(=急速に)快方に向かっている He is getting better (*very*) *quickly*. ▶その結果はすでに目に見えている(=明らかだ) The outcome is already *too obvious*.
● 目にも留まらぬ ●目にも留まらぬ(=稲妻のような)速さで *as* quick as lightning.
● 目に物言わせる ▶目で物言わすことができる(=目で何でも意思伝達できる) You can *communicate* anything *with* your *eyes*.
● 目に物見せる ▶目に物見せてやるぞ(=こらしめてやるぞ) I'll *teach* you *a lesson*.
● 目の色を変える ▶彼は目の色を変えて(=狂ったように)勉強している He is studying *like mad* [*crazy*]. ▶ゴルフのこととなると彼の目の色が変わる(=目がきらきら[きらり]と輝く) His *eyes sparkle* [*flash*] when it comes to golf.
● 目の上のこぶ (いつもじゃまになるもの) a constant hindrance《*to*》. (⇨ 目の敵(㋕), 目の前)
● 目の付け所 ▶目の付け所がいい You *aim at the right thing*./Your *aim is right*. ▶そこが目の付け所だ That's *the point*.
● 目の保養 ▶展示中の数々の美術品は目の保養になった A (good) number of works of art on show were a feast for my [*the*] *eyes*.
● 目は口ほどに物を言う The eyes are as eloquent as the tongue.
● 目も当てられない ▶その光景は目も当てられないひどいものだった The sight was *too* terrible [*horrible*] *to look at*./That was an *unbearable* sight *to see*.
● 目を疑う ▶一瞬自分の目を疑った I couldn't believe my *eyes* for a moment.
● 目もくれない ▶私の忠告に目もくれない(=無関心だ) *be indifferent to* [(耳を貸さない) *turn a deaf ear to*, (無視する) *ignore*] my advice.
● 目を覆う (目をそむける) avert one's eyes《*from*》.
● 目を覆う(=正視できない)惨状 a terrible scene

one can *hardly look at*.
- **目をかける** ▶先生は目をかけている(=ひいきする) The teacher *favors* him.
- **目をかすめる** ▶目をかすめて(=こっそりと)酒を飲む drink *on the sly*. ▶彼は両親の目をかすめて(=両親の陰で)たばこを吸った He smoked *behind* his parents' *backs*.
- **目を配る** (注意して監視する) keep an eye out 《*for*》; (目を離さず見る) keep an eye 《*on*》. ▶親は常に子供たちに目を配る必要がある Parents should always *keep an eye on* their children.
- **目をくらます** (うまく人をまいて逃げる) 《話》 give 《him》 the slip. ▶容疑者は警察の目をくらませて逃げた The suspect *gave* the police *the slip*.
- **目を凝らす** ▶真二はその消えかかった字を読もうと目をこらした Shinji strained his *eyes* to read the faded letters./Shinji looked hard at the faded letters.
- **目を皿のようにする** ▶目を皿のようにして(=非常に注意深く徹底的に)探す look for 《it》 *very carefully and thoroughly*. ▶彼は目を皿のようにしたが霧の中では何も見えなかった He *strained* his *eyes*, but could see nothing in the fog.
- **目を三角にする** (目に怒りの表情を浮かべる) put on an angry look in one's eyes; (まゆをつり上げる) lower one's eyebrows (❗日本語に引かれて raise … とすると非難や疑念, 失望の表情になる).
- **目をつける** (獲得しようと) have an [one's] eye 《*on* it [him]》.
- **目をつぶる** ▶社長は彼の過失に目をつぶった (大目に見た) The boss *overlooked* [*winked at*] his fault./(見て見ぬふりをした) The boss *closed* [*shut*] his *eyes* to his fault. (❗*turned a blind eye to* his fault ともいう)
- **目を通す** ▶書類に目を通す look over [through] the papers; (ざっと) run 《one's eye(s)》 over [skim 《through》] the papers.
- **目を盗む** ▶親の目を盗んで(=内緒で)賭けトランプをする play cards for money *without the knowledge of* one's parents.
- **目を離す** ▶本から目を離す look *up* from the book. ▶あの子から目を離せない I can't take my *eyes* off that child. (❗このように通例否定文で)/(監視している) I have to *keep an eye* on that child.
- **目を光らせる** (油断なく見る) keep a watchful eye 《*on*》. ▶警察は麻薬の密輸に目を光らせている The police *keep a watchful eye on* drug trafficking.
- **目を引く** (⇨目に留める)
- **目を伏せる** ▶私たちはお互いに目を伏せて通り過ぎた We passed each other *with* lowered *eyes*. ▶彼は恥じて目を伏せた He looked [cast his *eyes*] down in shame. (❗この意の「伏し目」は downcast eyes)
- **目を丸くする** ▶その小さい男の子は目を丸くして(=大きく見開いて)巨大な象を見た The little boy looked *round-eyed* at the huge elephant. (⇨❶④)
- **目を回す** (気絶する) faint; (ひどく忙しい) be extremely busy 《*doing*; *with*》. ▶議会の準備で目を回す be extremely busy preparing for the conference.
- **目を見張る** 会話 「ショーはいかがでしたか」「あんまりすばらしくて目を見張った」 "What [×How] did you think of the show?" "I *was amazed* how good it was."
- **目をむく** (怒ってにらみつける) glare 《*at* him》; give 《him》 an angry glare. ▶彼は目をむいて私をどなった He shouted at me *with an angry glare*.

*め **芽** (種から出たばかりの) a seedling; (茎・枝になるべき) a sprout, a shoot; (葉・花になるべき) a bud. ▶芽キャベツ (⇨芽キャベツ) ▶レタスの芽 lettuce *seedlings*. ▶木の芽が出始めた New *buds* are beginning to sprout from the trees [appear on the trees]./The trees are budding [coming into *bud*]. (⇨芽ぶく) ▶間もなく豆の芽が出て来た *Sprouts* of beans were (coming) up in a short time. ▶ジャガイモは芽が出る前に食べた方がよい You should eat potatoes before they start *sprouting*.
- **芽が出る** ▶彼もやっと芽が出て来た At last he is on the way to success.
- **芽を摘む** ▶悪の芽を摘む nip crime *in the bud*.

-**め** -目 ❶ [順序] (❗通例序数詞で表す) ▶彼女の3番目の子供 her *third* child. ▶二つ目の角を右に曲りなさい Turn right at the *second* corner. ▶郵便局は角から5軒目です The post office is the *fifth* building from the corner. ▶母が死んで10年目になる It's been 《米》 [《英》] *ten* years since my mother died. ▶2人が結婚して5年目に子供が生まれた They had been married *for five years* when a baby was born. ▶父は私が生まれてから7年目に死んだ My father died *seven* years after [×since, ×from] I was born.
会話 「青山氏は何代目の社長ですか」「父親の跡を受けた2代目です」 "*How many* presidents *were there* [*have there been*] before Mr. Aoyama?" "He is the *second* president after his father." (❗How many ... are there ...? は時間的順序を問題にする場合の最も普通の聞き方)/"What *number* president is Mr. Aoyama?" "He is the *second* president in succession to his father." (❗現役の社長でない場合は is の代わりに was を用いる)
会話 「新神戸駅はここからいくつ目のバス停でしょうか」「四つ目です」 "*How many* stops away is Shin-Kobe Station?" "(It's) four stops away."

❷ [程度, 傾向] (いくぶん) rather; (少し) a little, 《話》 a (little) bit; (多少...の) on the ... side. ▶彼女はいつもより早めに出かけた She left *a little* [*a (little) bit*] earlier than usual. (❗「できるだけ早目」だと as early as possible) ▶彼女はきつめのスカートをはいている She wears a *rather* tight skirt [a skirt *on the tight side*]. ▶窓を少し細めに開けてください Please open the window *a little* [*a (little) bit*]. ▶聴衆は少なめにみても300人は来ている There is an audience of three hundred *at least*.

めあかし 目明し a private investigator in the Edo period. (⇨岡っ引き)

めあたらしい 目新しい new; (新奇な) novel; (独創的な) original. (⇨新しい)

めあて 目当て ❶ [目的] an aim; (意図) an intention. (⇨目的) ▶君の目当ては何だ What is your *aim*? ▶彼女は金目当てにその老人と結婚した She married the old man *for* the money./She was *after* his money when she married the old man.
❷ [目印] (道しるべ) a guide; (陸標) a landmark. ▶あの高い建物を目当てにして歩いて行きなさい Go on with that tall building as your *guide*.

めい 命 (命令) an order (⇨命令); (運命) (a) fate (⇨運命)

めい 姪 a niece.

めい 銘 [刻み込まれた文句] an inscription; (メダルなどの) a legend; [作者名] a signature. ●刀に銘が入っている刀 a sword with the *signature* of the smith (chiseled) on the tang. ●座右の銘 (⇨座右の銘)

めい- 名- (すぐれた) excellent; (すぐれて立派な) fine;

-めい (偉大な) great; (著名な) famous.《やや書》noted.
-めい -名 ●数名の人 several people. ●10名の生徒 ten students. (!) 英語では「名」に当たるものがない. 数をずばりいうだけでよい)
めいあん 名案 a good idea [plan]. ▶それは名案だ That's a *good idea*. (!) 単に Thát's an idéa. ともいう) ▶名案が浮かんだ A *good idea* occurred to [came over] me./I hit upon a *good idea*. ▶どうしても名案が浮かばないよ(=考えあぐねている)《話》I'm at my wits' [×wit's] *end*.
めいあん 明暗 light and shade. ●人生の明暗 the *bright and dark sides* of life.
●明暗を分ける (運命を決する) decide one's fate; (結果を決める) decide the outcome 《*of*》.
めいあん『明暗』*Light and Darkness*. [参考] 夏目漱石の小説)
めいい 名医 a skilled doctor, a doctor of doctors.
めいうつ 銘打つ give (exaggerated) names 《*to*》; name. ●健康食品と銘打ってある商品 an article *labeled* (as) health food.
めいうん 命運 (重大な運命) one's [the] destiny; one's [the] fate. (!) 後の方は本人にとって不本意な結末に至ることを暗示する) ●国家の命運をかけた戦争 a war that decides the *destiny* of a nation.
めいえん 名園 a noted [a famous, a well-known] garden.
めいえん 名演 a wonderful [an excellent, a great] performance.
めいおうせい 冥王星 [天文] Pluto.
めいか 名花 (美しい花) a beautiful flower; (美人) a beauty.
めいか 名家 a good [(すぐれた) a distinguished] family. (⇨名門) ▶彼女は近郷一の名家の出だ She comes from the most *distinguished family* in that district.
めいか 名菓, 銘菓 (すぐれた) a confection of high quality; (有名な) a confection from a famous [prestigious] shop.
めいが 名画 『絵の』(すぐれた) a great picture, a masterpiece; (有名な) a famous picture; 『映画の』an excellent film.
めいかい 明快 — 明快な 形 ●明快な(=はっきりした)答えをする give a *clear* answer. ●明快な指示を出す give《him》clear [(具体的ではっきりした) *specific*] instructions.
めいかい 明解 图 (a) clear [lucid] explanation.
— 明解な 形 clear; lucid.
めいかく 明確 (明瞭(めいりょう)さ) clarity.
— 明確な 形 ●明確な説明 a *clear* explanation.
●明確な(=確定的な)答え a *definite* answer.
— 明確に 副 ●その二つを明確に区別する make a *clear* [a *sharp*] distinction between the two; distinguish the two *clearly* [*sharply*]. ●その事について自分の態度を明確にする make one's attitude *clear* about the matter.
めいがら 銘柄 (商標) a brand; (株式の) a name, an issue. ●人気銘柄 a *brand* leader. ●優良銘柄 a (good) quality *name*. ●指標銘柄 a benchmark. ▶ビールであればこの銘柄でもよい Any *brand* will do as long as it's beer.
●銘柄売買 a sale by trademark [brand].
●銘柄品 a brand name, a brand-name product.
めいかん 名鑑 ●商工人名鑑 a business directory.
めいき 名器 a famous [(すぐれた) an excellent] utensil [(楽器) instrument]. (!) utensil は家庭内, 特に食器関係の器にみを指す語) ●名器ストラディバリウス a *famous* [a *celebrated*] Stradivarius /strǽdivéəriəs/. ▶彼の作になる茶器は有名だが, 真に名器と言えるものは数少ない He had made many famous tea-things, but really *good* ones are rare.
めいき 明記 — 明記する 動 (はっきり書く) write ... clearly; (具体的に書く) specify. ●契約書に日付が明記されている The date *is specified* in the contract.
めいき 銘記 — 銘記する 動 ●彼の言葉を心に銘記する *keep* [*bear*] his words *in mind*. (⇨覚える ❶)
めいぎ 名義 one's name. ▶この土地は妻の名義になっている This land is (registered) *in* my *wife's name* [*in the name of* my wife]. ▶大部分の土地を妻の名義に変更した (=妻に譲った) I *transferred* a large part of the land to my wife.
●名義書き換え (株券などの) a transfer.
めいきゅう 迷宮 a maze, a labyrinth /lǽbəriɵ/. (!) 後の方が堅い語)
めいきゅういり 迷宮入り 图 ▶その事件は迷宮入りの(=秘密に包まれた)ままだ The case *is still shrouded in mystery*./ (未解決だ) The case *is still unsolved*.
— 迷宮入りする 動 go unsolved.
めいきょうしすい 明鏡止水 ▶明鏡止水の心境です My mind is as serene as a *polished mirror* and still water.
めいきょく 名曲 (よい曲) good music; (すぐれた) an excellent piece of music; (有名な) a famous song; (傑作) a (musical) masterpiece.
めいきょく 名局 『囲碁・将棋』(有名な対局) a famous [(すばらしい) a well-played] game 《*of*》.
めいぎん 名吟 an excellent *tanka* [*haiku*, poem].
めいく 名句 (すぐれた句) an excellent phrase [*haiku*]; (有名な句) a famous phrase [*haiku*].
めいくん 名君, 明君 a wise [an enlightened] monarch [ruler, king].
めいげつ 名月, 明月 a bright moon; 『満月』 a full moon. ●中秋の名月 the harvest moon. ●名月の夜 a bright moonlight night.
めいけん 名犬 a fine [a smart] dog.
めいけん 名剣 (すぐれた剣) an excellent sword; (有名な剣) a famous sword.
めいげん 名言 『言い習わし』a (wise) saying; 『格言』 a maxim; (機知に富んだ言葉) a witty remark. ▶それは名言だ That's well said.
めいげん 明言 图 (はっきり言うこと) a definite /défənit/ statement; (言) (a) declaration.
— 明言する 動 say [state] definitely; (宣言する) declare.
めいこう 名工 (すぐれた職人) a master [a (highly) skilled] craftsperson; (有名な職人) a famous craftsperson.
めいさい 明細 『詳細』 details, particulars; 『内訳』 a breakdown. ●電話の明細を記入した請求書を求めるask for an *itemized* phone bill.
— 明細な 形 detailed; (書) minute /main(j)úːt/.
●明細書 (勘定などの) a (detailed) statement; (設計の) specifications; (有価証券の) a portfolio.
めいさい 迷彩 ●迷彩をほどこす camouflage /kǽməflɑ̀ːʒ/《a tank》.
●迷彩服 (wear) camouflage.
めいさく 名作 (すぐれた作品) a great work (!) 具体的に a great novel, a famous story などとしてもよい); (傑作) a masterpiece.
めいさつ 名刹 a famous temple.
めいさつ 名察 clear [great] insight. ▶ご名察 You guessed right!
めいさん 名産 a well-known [a special] product, a (local) specialty. ▶北海道の名産は何ですか What's the *specialty* of Hokkaido?

めいざん 名山 a noted [a well-known] mountain.

めいし 名刺 (総称的に) a card; (訪問用の)《米》a cálling càrd,《主に英》a vísiting càrd; (業務用の) a búsiness càrd. (!) a name card は「名札」。名刺を差し出す give [《手渡す》hand]《him》one's *card*. ▶日本の業界では初対面では名刺の交換がよく行われます In the Japanese business world, people often exchange their *cards* at their first meeting. (事情) 名刺は主に商用に使うが、本来米英では一般人が初対面のときに用いる習慣はない。また、商談の最初でなく最後に連絡用に渡すのが一般的)
- 名刺入れ a cárd càse. • 名刺判 (写真の) a 6.0× 8.3cm photograph size. (!) (1) 前の方が横、後の方がたての長さ。(2) ×は by と読む

めいし 名士〖著名人〗a famous figure, a celebrity;〖有力者〗a personage,〖重要人物〗a notable (通例複数形で). (⇨大物) • 土地の名士たち local *celebrities* [*notables*]. • 当代一流の名士 a leading *celebrity* of the day. • 町の名士の 1 人 one of the *celebrities* [*personages*] of the town.

めいし 名詞〖文法〗a noun.

めいし 明視 clear vision.
- 明視距離 the range [the field] of clear vision.

めいじ 名辞 (概念を言葉で表したもの) a term.

めいじ 明示 ── 明示する 動 (はっきりと示す・言う) show [indicate, express]... clearly. • 会員証を明示する(=見せる) *show* one's membership card.
- 理由を明示する(=十分に説明する) *explain* the reason *fully*.

めいじ 明治 Meiji. (⇨平成)
- 明治維新〖歴史〗the Meiji Restoration.

めいじつ 名実 • 名実相伴う (a person) worthy of the name.
- 名実ともに ▶彼は名実ともに偉大な科学者だ He is a great scientist *both in name and in reality*.

めいしゃ 名車 (すぐれた車) a car of high quality; (有名な車) a noted car.

めいしゃ 目医者 an éye dòctor (眼科医) an oculist.

めいしゅ 名手 an expert 《at, in》. • 弓の名手 an *expert in* archery; an *expert* archer. ▶彼は犠牲バントの名手である He is a *master* at rolling sacrifice bunts.

めいしゅ 名主, 明主 a wise monarch.

めいしゅ 名酒 *sake* of high quality.

めいしゅ 盟主 the leader《of an alliance》.

めいしゅ 銘酒 a famous brand of *sake*; *sake* of a superior brand.

めいしょ 名所 a place of interest; a noted place;〖観光地〗the sights. • 桜の名所 a *place famous* [*noted*] *for* its cherry blossoms. • 奈良の名所を見物する see the *sights* of Nara. (!)《話》*do* Nara は単に「奈良を見物する」意. *do* the sights of ... は《英古》
- 名所旧跡 places of scenic beauty and historical interest.

めいしょう 名匠 (すぐれた学者・芸術家) a great scholar [artist]; (有名な学者・芸術家) a well-known [a famous, an eminent] scholar [artist]; (巨匠) a great master; (名工) (⇨名工).

めいしょう 名相 (すぐれた《総理》大臣) a great (prime) minister; (有名な《総理》大臣) a prominent (prime) minister.

めいしょう 名将 a great [a famous] commander [general; (野球の) manager].

めいしょう 名称 a name. • この会に名称をつける name [give a name to] this society.

めいしょう 名勝 (景色の美しい土地) a beauty spot; a scenic spot; a place of scenic beauty.

めいしょう 明証 图 (決定的な証拠) conclusive evidence [proof]; (動かぬ証拠) irrefutable evidence [proof]; (明確な証拠) positive evidence [proof].

── 明証する 動 prove conclusively [irrefutably].

めいじょう 名状 • 名状しがたい be beyond description; indescribable.

めいじょう 名城 (すばらしい城) a grand [a splendid, a magnificent] castle; (有名な城) a famous castle.

めいしょく 明色 a bright (¬a dark) color.

めいじる 命じる ❶〖命令する〗order; command; direct; instruct; tell*. (⇨命令する)
❷〖任命する〗appoint. (⇨任命する)

めいじる 銘じる 肝に銘じる (⇨肝 [成句])

めいしん 迷信 (a) superstition. ▶4は不吉な数ということは迷信だ [という迷信がある] It's [There's] a *superstition* that four is an unlucky number. ▶私はそんな迷信は信じない I don't believe in such a *superstition*. ▶彼は大変迷信深い He is very *superstitious* [a very *superstitious*] man].

めいじん 名人〖大家〗a master;〖専門家〗an expert《at, in, on, with》; a wizard《at》. • 彫刻の名人 a *master* [an *expert*, a *wizard*] *at* carving. • 射撃の名人 a *master* shot; an *expert with* a gun (!) with は「...を扱う」の意). • 変装の名人 an *expert in* disguise. • チェスの名人 a chess *expert* [*wizard*]; an *expert* chess player.
- 名人気質(かたぎ)《a man with》the spirit of a master artist. • 名人芸《give》a masterly [a masterful] performance.

めいすい 名水 (きれいな水) clean [clear] water

めいすい 銘水 (有名な水) famed natural water.

めいする 瞑する (安らかに死ぬ[眠る]) die [rest] in peace. (⇨死ぬ) • もって瞑すべし (⇨以て [成句])

めいせい 名声〖有名であること〗fame (!) 一般的な語で、時に好ましくないことを含意する); (偉業に基づく高名さ)《書》renown;〖よい評判〗(a) reputation. (⇨評判) • 名声の高い人 a man of great [high] *fame*. • 名声を得る win [gain] *fame*. • 富と名声を追い求める seek *fame* and fortune. ▶彼は多くの発明で世界的名声を博した He won [achieved, (確立した) established] world-wide *fame for* his inventions. ▶彼女の名声が上がった Her *reputation* has grown. ▶そのうわさは彼の名声に傷をつけた The rumor injured his *reputation* [*good name*]. ▶浜氏は画家として名声が高い Mr. Hama is *famous* [*well-known*,《書》*renowned*] *as* a painter. (⇨有名)

めいせき 名跡 (有名な遺跡) famous historic remains.

めいせき 明晰 ── 明晰な 形 (頭脳・思考などが) clear. ▶彼は頭脳明晰だ He has a *clear* head./He is *clear-headed*./(頭が高い) He is intelligent.

めいせん 名川 a famous river.

めいせん 銘仙 *meisen* silk fabrics [cloth].

めいそう 名僧 an eminent priest.

めいそう 迷走 ── 迷走する 動 (はぐれる)《やや書》stray; (さまよう) wander.
- 迷走神経〖解剖〗a vagus /véigəs/ nerve, a vagus(復) vagi /-dʒai/).

めいそう 瞑想 图 瞑想にふける be lost in *meditation* [*contemplation*]. (⇨思索)

── 瞑想する 動 • 過去のことを瞑想する *meditate on* [*contemplate*] the past.

めいだい 命題〖論理〗a proposition.

めいだん 明断 ●明断を下す pass a clear judgment.
めいちゃ 銘茶 a famous [a well-known] brand of tea.
めいちゅう 命中 ── 命中する 動 (矢・弾丸などが) hit (↔miss); 《the mark》. ▶矢はほんの真ん中に命中した The arrow *hit* the target right in the center [《話》*hit* the bull's eye]. (❗後の方は比喩的にも用いる)
めいちょ 名著 (すぐれた[有名な]本) a great [a famous] book; (傑作) a masterpiece.
めいちょう 明澄 ── 明澄な 形 clear (sound).
めいちょう 迷鳥 a stray bird of passage; a stray migrant.
めいっぱい 目一杯 ▶目一杯勉強させていただいてこのお値段です This is *the best* [*lowest*] price we can offer. ●子育ては親を目一杯利用してという若い人が多い There are many young couples who want to *make the best use of* their parents in raising their children. ●目一杯借金をしてこの狭いマンションしか買えなかった I could only afford (to buy) this small apartment, though I borrowed money *as much as I could*.
めいてい 酩酊 intoxication.
── 酩酊する 動 be intoxicated. (⇨酔っ払う)
めいてつ 明哲 sagacity; great wisdom; (人) a sage /séidʒ/; a very wise person.
めいてんがい 名店街 (説明的に) a street lined with famous stores.
めいど 明度 brightness.
めいど 冥土 (あの世) the other world, 《書》the netherworld. ●冥土の旅 a journey to *the netherworld*.
●**冥土の土産** ▶それは本当にいい冥土の土産（=いい思い出）になるだろう It will be a really *good memory* (to take with me to the netherworld). (📖 米英には「冥土の土産」といった発想はない)
メイド a maid. (⇨メード)
めいとう 名刀 (すぐれた刀) an excellent sword; (有名な刀) a famous sword.
めいとう 名湯 a hotspring renowned for its medicinal properties.
めいとう 名答 [『正しい答え』] a right answer; [『うまい答え』] a clever answer. ▶ご名答 You're right!/《話》You've got it!
めいとう 明答 名 (はっきりした答え) a definite answer.
── 明答する 動 answer definitely; give a definite answer. (⇨確答)
めいとう 銘刀 a fine sword inscribed with a swordsmith's name.
めいどう 鳴動 名 rumbling. ▶大山(戀)鳴動してねずみ一匹 《大山》[成句]
── 鳴動する 動 rumble.
めいにち 命日 the anniversary of 《his》death.
めいば 名馬 (すぐれた馬) a fine horse; (有名な馬) a famous horse.
＊**めいはく 明白** ── 明白な 形 (はっきりした) clear; (単純明快な) plain; (疑問の余地のない) obvious; (証拠から明らかな) evident; (推論によって) apparent; (言葉などが暗示的でなく明瞭(ﾘｮｳ)な) explicit (⇨明らか). ●君が間違っていることはだれの目にも明白だ It is *obvious* [*evident*] to everyone that you're wrong.
── 明白に 副 ●明白に述べる state 《it》 *clearly* [*explicitly*]. (❗that 節, wh- 節を目的語に取ることもできる. その場合は clearly [explicitly] の後に)
めいばん 名盤 (すぐれたレコード [CD]) a good record [CD]; (有名なレコード [CD]) a famous record [CD].

めいび 明媚 ── 明媚な 形 picturesque; beautiful. ●風光明媚 (⇨風光明媚)
めいひつ 名筆 (作品) a splendid drawing [painting, calligraphy]; (画家・書家) a master hand [painter, artist calligrapher].
めいひん 名品 a masterpiece; (逸品) a gem.
めいびん 明敏 ── 明敏な 形 sagacious; quick-witted; bright; intelligent.
めいふく 冥福 ●冥福を祈る pray for *the repose of* 《his》*soul*. ▶ご冥福を祈ります May 《his》*soul rest in peace!*
めいぶつ 名物 ❶ [名産] a special [a noted] product; a (local) specialty. (⇨名産) ●カキは広島の名物だ Oysters are a *special product* [a *specialty*] of Hiroshima.
❷ [呼び物] an attraction; (特色) a feature.
●名物男 (人気の人物) a popular figure.
めいぶん 名分 ●大義名分 (⇨大義) [成句]）
めいぶん 名文 a fine piece of writing; (1節) a beautiful passage.
●名文家 a fine [great] writer; a stylist.
めいぶん 名聞 (a) reputation. (⇨評判)
めいぶん 明文 [法律] (規定, 条項) a provision. ▶言論の自由は憲法に明文化されている 《書》Freedom of speech *is provided for* in the constitution./《書》The constitution *provides that* we have freedom of speech.
めいぶん 銘文 (碑文・刻銘) an inscription; (墓碑銘) an epitaph.
めいぼ 名簿 (名前の一覧表) a list (of names); (公式の登録簿) a register; (通例住所も記した) a directory; (会社・学級・団体などの) a roll. (❗roll と directory は事物形式の名簿もさす) ●乗客名簿 a pássenger [xa passenger's] *list*; (飛行機の) a bóarding *list*. ●会員名簿 a *list* of members; a mémbership *list* [*dìrectory*]. ●学生名簿 a stúdent *dìrectory*; a *register* of students. ●同窓会名簿 an alúmni *dìrectory*. ●名簿を作る make a *list* (*of*). ●名簿に載っている be (put) on the *list* [*roll*]. ●彼を名簿から削除する strike him off the *list* [*roll*].

めいほう 名宝 famous treasures.
めいほう 盟邦 an ally; allied nations [countries].
めいぼう 名望 (名声) fame; renown; good reputation; (人気) popularity.
●名望家 a person of renown; a person of repute.
めいぼう 明眸 bright and beautiful eyes.
●明眸皓歯(ｺｳｼ) *beautiful eyes* and pearly teeth; (人) a beautiful woman; a beauty.
めいぼく 名木 (有名な木) a famous tree; (形のよい木) a graceful tree.
めいぼく 銘木 high-grade [high-quality] wood.
めいみゃく 命脈 life. ●命脈を保つ keep alive; survive.
＊**めいめい 銘々** 名 each. (⇨それぞれ, 各自)

> **解説** **each** の用法: (1) 形容詞, 代名詞, 複数形の主語と同格になる副詞として用いる.
> (2) 単数扱いで形容詞の場合は単数可算名詞を修飾する.
> (3) 否定文中で主語に用いることはできない.
> (4) 代名詞は he, his で呼応するのが原則だが《話》では they, their で呼応することが多い. 特に性差別の立場から《話》だけでなく普通の《書》でも their が好まれる傾向がある. 女性だと分かっている場合は she, her で呼応する. he or she, his or her で呼応することもあるが, 堅い《書》以外では通例用いない.

メーデー

メートル 〘計器〙 a meter. ●ガス[水道; 電気]のメーター a gás [a wáter; an eléctric] méter. ●パーキング[駐車]メーター a párking méter. ●メーターを調べる read the meter.

メーデー May Day. ●メーデーのパレード[集会] a May Day parade [rally]. (!〘英〙では5月第1月曜日のthe May Day bank holiday, 〘米・カナダ〙では9月第1月曜日の Labor Day がこれに当たる)

メード a maid, 〘古〙a maidservant; (家事をする) a housemaid; (ホテルの) a chambermaid.

メードインジャパン ⟨a camera⟩ made in Japan; ⟨a camera⟩ of Japanese make.

***メートル** 〘長さの単位〙a meter /míːṭər/ (略 m). ▶それは長さ3メートル, 幅1メートルある It is three *meters* long and one *meter* wide.
●メートルを上げる (酒を飲んでメートルを上げる(=大きいことを言う) talk big under the influence of alcohol.
●メートル法 the metric system ▶日本はメートル法を使っている We use the *metric system* in Japan.

メーリングリスト 〘コンピュータ〙a máiling list.

メール (電子メール) email, e-mail (⇨イーメール), (郵便) mail, 〘英〙post. ●エアメール airmail. ●ダイレクトメール direct mail (略 DM); (軽蔑的) júnk màil. ●メールを送る[受け取る] send [receive] an email. ▶私はたいてい日に何度かメールをチェックする I usually check my *email* several times a day. ▶詳細はメールでお知らせします Further information will be sent to you by *email*. ▶今は電車に乗るとみんな携帯電話でメールを打っている When you ride a train these days, you see everybody busily tapping out *email messages* on their cell phones. ●メールアカウント an email account. ●メールアドレス an email address. ●メールオーダー (⇨メールオーダー) ●メールサーバー a mail server. ●メールソフト email software. ●メール友達 an email friend. (⇨メル友) ●メールボックス a mailbox. ●メールマガジン an email magazine [newsletter].

メールオーダー ⟨by⟩ mail order. ●メールオーダーのカタログ a *mail-order* catalog.

メーン (主な・重要な) main.
●メーンアンプ a main amplifier. ●メーンイベント the main event. ●メーンコース the main course. ●メーンスタンド the grandstand; 〘和製語〙a main stand. ●メーンストリート the main 〘英〙high street. ●メーンディッシュ (食事の主料理) the main course. ●メーンテーブル the main table. ●メーンテーマ the (main) theme. ●メーンバンク 〘主要取り引き銀行〙the main bank. ●メーンフレーム 〘コンピュータ〙a mainframe. ●メーンポスト the main flagpole; 〘和製語〙the main pole. ●メーンマスト the mainmast.

めおと 夫婦 (⇨夫婦(ふ̅う̅ふ̅)) ●夫婦茶碗 a pair of teacups [rice bowls] for husband and wife.

メカ ▶ぼくはメカ(=機械類)にはまったく弱いんだ。君は強そうだね I don't know anything about *machines* [I can't repair or handle any *machines*] well]. It seems that you are a good mechánic.

メガー 〘巨大な〙mega.
●メガキャリア 〘巨大航空会社, 巨大通信企業〙a mega carrier; a mega airline. ●メガバンク a mega bank.

めがお 目顔 a look. ▶スカーレットが彼を愛していることは目顔で分かった I realized by the *look* on her face that Scarlet loved him.

めかくし 目隠し 图 (目を被う布) a blindfold; (窓の) a (window) shade, 〘英〙a blind.
—— 目隠し(を)する 動 put a blindfold [blind-fold.

めかけ 妾 a mistress; a concubine. ●妾を囲う keep a *mistress*.

めがける 目掛ける (...を向ける) aim ⟨at⟩. ▶彼はその猫をめがけて石を投げた He threw a stone at [to] a cat. (!at では実際に当たったかどうかは不明だが, to では実際に当たったことを含意する) ▶彼は出口をめがけて突っ走った He dashed *for* [*toward, to*] the exit. (! for は「目標物に向かって」, toward は単に「...の方向に」, to は到達を意味するが, for は「...の方に」の意)

めかじき 女舵木 〘魚介〙a swordfish; a broadbill.

めかしこむ めかし込む dress up ⟨in⟩.

めがしら 目頭 ●目頭が熱くなる ●目頭の熱くなるような光景 a *moving* [a *touching*] sight. ▶感動して目頭が熱くなった It was so *moving* (that) I *almost wept*./I was *moved to tears*.
●目頭を押さえる ▶ハンカチで目頭を押さえる dab one's *eye*(*s*) [(涙をぬぐう) wipe one's tears] with a handkerchief.

めかす (盛装する) dress up ⟨in⟩. ▶すっかりめかしこんだ女性(話) a woman *dressed to the nines*.

めかた 目方 weight. (⇨重量, 体重) ●目方で売る sell ⟨it⟩ *by weight*. (!×by the weight は不可)

めかど 目角 (⇨目尻)
●目角を立てる look daggers at ⟨him⟩.

メカトロニクス 〘機械電子工学〙mechatronics.

メガトン 〘核爆発力の単位〙a megaton (略 MT).

メカニズム a mechanism. ●ライフル[脳]のメカニズム the *mechanism* of the rifle [brain].

***めがね** 眼鏡 ❶ 〘眼鏡〙glasses; 〘米古・英〙spectacles, 〘話〙specs; 〘英古・米〙eyeglasses. (!数えるときは a pair [two pairs] of glasses という. 眼鏡の片方をさすときは a lens)
① 〘~眼鏡〙 ●近視用眼鏡 *glasses* for a near-sighted (主に米) [a shortsighted (主に英)] (↔a farsighted (主に米), a longsighted (主に英)) person. ●度の弱い[強い]眼鏡 weak [strong, thick] *glasses*. ●遠近両用眼鏡 bifocals. ●金縁[細いメタルフレーム]の眼鏡 gold-rimmed [wire-rimmed] *glasses*. ●縁なし眼鏡 rimless glasses. ●水中眼鏡 (水泳用) swímming gòggles; (潜水用) a fáce màsk. ●彼の眼鏡ではないようだ. たしか次郎のだよ. そんなのを持っているからね Those *glasses* don't look like his. They must be Jiro's. He has a *pair* like that.
② 〘眼鏡~〙 ●眼鏡のフレーム [縁; つる] the frame [rim; temples] of a pair of *glasses*. (! 眼鏡は眼鏡のレンズ以外の枠組全体) ●眼鏡越しに見る look ⟨at him⟩ over (the rim of) one's *glasses*.
③ 〘眼鏡が[を]〙 ●眼鏡をかけて見る look at [see, watch] ⟨it⟩ through *glasses*. ●眼鏡をかけた若い男 a young man in *glasses* [with *glasses* (on)]. ●眼鏡をかける[はずす] put on [take off] one's *glasses*. ▶彼は眼鏡をかけている He wears *glasses*. ▶ゆげで眼鏡が曇った My *glasses* were misted over [were fogged] with steam.
❷ 〘眼識〙judgment. ▶彼は私の眼鏡違いだった I misjudged him. / 文脈によって「見直した」「見損なった」のどちらにもとれる)/(期待外れだった) He didn't meet [come up to, live up to] my expectations. /He fell short of my expectations.
●眼鏡にかなう ▶彼の眼鏡にかなう(=気に入られる) find favor with him; win his favor.
●眼鏡ケース a glásses càse. ●眼鏡橋 a two-arched bridge. ●眼鏡屋 (店) an optical shop; (人) an optician; 〘掲示〙Optician.

めがねざる 眼鏡猿 〘動物〙a tarsier; a specter lemur.

メガバイト 〖情報量の単位〗a megabyte (略 MB).
メガヘルツ 〖電波周波数の単位〗a megahertz /méɡəhə̀ːrts/ (複 ～, ～es)(略 MHz).
メガホン a megaphone. ▶私は手をメガホンのようにして彼を呼んだ I called him through cupped hands.
めがみ 女神 a goddess (→a god).
メガロポリス 〖超巨大都市圏〗a megalopolis /mèɡəlάpəlis/.
めきき 目利き (鑑定) judgment, connoisseurship /kάnəsəːrʃip/; (人) a judge; a connoisseur. ▶彼女は浮世絵にかけては大した目利きだ She is a good *judge* of the *ukiyoe* prints./She has a sharp *eye* for the *ukiyoe* prints.
── **目利き(を)する 動** judge.
メキシコ Mexico /méksikòu/; (公式名) the United Mexican States. (首都 Mexico City) ●メキシコ人 a Mexican. ●メキシコ(人)の Mexican.
めきめき ❶〖上達などが著しいさま〗(著しく) remarkably; (際立って) markedly; (速く) rapidly. ▶その若いピアニストは国外でめきめき腕を上げた The young pianist grew *remarkably* skilled [made *remarkable* progress] abroad.
❷〖物が音を立てて壊れるさま〗 ▶大工が木の板をめきめきはいでいった The carpenter tore [pulled] off the wooden boards *with a loud noise*.
めキャベツ 芽キャベツ (Brussels) sprouts.
-めく 〖…のように〗like. ▶だいぶ春めいてきた It has become more spring*like*.
めくぎ 目釘 a rivet (of a sword hilt).
めくじら 目くじら ●**目くじらを立てる** 〖つまらない事に目くじらを立てるな(=欠点をはにくり出すな) Don't *find fault with* trivial [*trifling*] matters.
めぐすり 目薬 (洗眼液) eyewash, eye lotion; (点眼液) eyedrops. ●**目薬をさす** apply *eye lotion*; put *drops* in one's eyes.
めくそ 目糞 (⇨目脂(2))
●**目くそ鼻くそを笑う** (ことわざ) The pot calls the kettle black.
めくばせ 目配せ winking. ▶彼に(意味ありげな)目配せをする give him a (suggestive) *wink*; *wink* (suggestively) *at* him. ▶(2 人が)目配せを し合う exchange [〖話〗trade] *glances*. ▶すぐに出発するように彼に目配せをした I *signaled* him *with a wink* [*gave him a sign with the eye*] to start at once.
めくばり 目配り ── **目配りする 動** take good care of …; be very careful about …; pay close attention to ….
***めぐまれる 恵まれる** be blessed 《with》; 〖才能などに〗be gifted [〖書〗be endowed] 《with》; 〖資源などに〗be rich 《in》; 〖天候・事情などに〗be favored 《by》. ●音楽的才能に恵まれている *be blessed* [*be gifted*] *with* musical talent; *have a gift* [*a talent*] *for* music. ●美しい自然に恵まれている *be rich in* [*be blessed with*] natural beauty; *have beautiful scenery*. ●地理的に恵まれている *be favored* geographically. ●恵まれた家庭環境の *happy* home environment. ●(経済的に)恵まれない人々 the underprivileged. (❗複数扱い) ▶彼女は 4 人の子宝に恵まれた(=を持っている) She has four children./〖おどけて〗She *is blessed with* four children. ▶私はこれまでずっと健康に恵まれてきた I've enjoyed good health all my life.
めぐみ 恵み (恩恵) a blessing; (施し) charity. ●恵み深い人 a *benevolent* [a *merciful*] person. ●恵みの(=ありがたい)雨 a *welcome* rain. ●神の恵みにより by the grace of God. ●健康は私たちにとって大きな恵みだ Good health is a great *blessing* to us.
めぐむ 芽ぐむ bud (-dd-), come* into bud. ▶このあたりでは木々が芽ぐみ始めた[芽ぐみ始めた] The trees are *in bud* [are beginning to *bud*] around here.
めぐむ 恵む 〖哀れんで施す〗give* 《him money》 out of pity [charity]. ▶どうか次の食事のために少しお金を恵んでください Please *spare* some money for my next meal.
めぐらす 巡らす ❶〖囲む〗surround, 《やや書》enclose. ▶庭に垣を巡らす *surround* [*enclose*] a garden *with* a fence. ▶彼の家には生け垣が巡らしてある His house *is surrounded* [*is enclosed*] *by* [〖まれ〗*with*] a hedge./A hedge *surrounds* [*runs around*] his house. (❗いずれも ×is running [surrounding] とはいわない) (⇨囲む)
❷〖十分考える〗think about 《the plan》carefully; (思いを巡らす) turn 《the events of the day》 over in one's mind; (たくらむ) plot (-tt-) 《his murder》. ▶人は しばしば過去のことに思いを巡らす(=回顧する) People often *look back on* old times.
めぐり 巡り 〖遍歴〗a tour; 〖循環〗circulation; 〖一周〗(⇨一周). ●名所巡りをする *make a tour of* [*tour*] famous places. ●血の巡りが悪い have (a) poor [(a) bad] (blood) *circulation*; (頭が鈍い) *be not intelligent*, 〖話〗be slow on the uptake.
めぐりあう 巡り合う 〖思いがけず出会う〗meet* … by chance, 〖話〗come* across … (⇨会う❷); 〖親子などが再会する〗be reunited 《with》. ▶彼は 40 歳まで幸せに巡り合わなかった He didn't *find* [*acquire*] happiness until he was forty.
めくりあげる 捲り上げる ●ワイシャツのそでをめくり上げる *roll* one's shirt sleeves *up*. ●ズボンのすそをめくり上げる *tuck up* one's pants. (⇨捲(ま)る)
めぐりあわせ 巡り合わせ (運などの思わぬ訪れ) a stroke (❗主に幸運に用いる); (運命) one's fate. ●不思議な運命の巡り合わせで *by a stroke of luck*.
***めくる 捲る** (ページなどを) turn … 《over》. ●本をめくる *turn* 《*over*》the pages of a book; (ぱらぱらと) *leaf through* a book. ●新聞の(ページ)をめくる *turn* the newspaper page. ●トランプを 1 枚めくる *turn* a card *up*; (1 枚取る) pick a card. ●テーブルのクロスをめくる *pull* the cloth *off* the table. ▶起きなさい、でないとふとんをめくるからね Wake up, or I'll *strip* the bed.
***めぐる 巡る** ●池を巡る *go around* a pond. ●諸国を巡る *travel around* the countries. ●金の分配を巡る争い a dispute *over* the distribution of money. (⇨ついて) ▶季節が巡る The seasons *come around* [*rotate*]. ▶またう 3 年が巡ってきた The leap year *has come around*.

■ **DISCOURSE**
本稿では「ゆとり教育」を巡る現在の問題を論じる **This paper discusses** the current problems *regarding* the "yutori" education. (❗This paper discusses … (この論文は …を論じる) は論文の目的を紹介する表現. 序論でよく用いられる)

めくるめく 目眩めく (目がくらむ) be dazzled. ●目くるめくような日光 *dazzling* sunlight.
めくれる 捲れる be turned up. ▶彼女のめくれた厚い唇 her thick *turned-up* lip. ▶強風で傘がめくれてしまった My umbrella *was blown inside out* by the strong wind.
めげる (がっかりする) be disappointed; (勇気がそがれる) be discouraged; (落ち込んでいる) feel* really down. ●夏の暑さにもめげない 《やや書》 *undaunted* by the summer's heat. ▶彼は直面した幾多の困難にもめげなかった 《書》 He *was not discouraged* by a great number of difficulties he had encountered.

めこぼし 目こぼし 名 (見逃すこと)《やや書》connivance /kənívəns/.

━━目こぼし(を)する 動 (見逃す) overlook; (大目に見る)《やや書》connive 《at》; (目をつぶる) shut one's eyes 《to》.

メコン ▶メコン川 the Mekong /méikɔ́(ː)n/.

めさき 目先 ❶【目の前】目先の利益にとらわれる seek 《one's》 *immediate* interests.
❷【現在】目先のことばかり考える think only of [about] *the present*. ▶あいつは目先のことしか見えない男だ He cannot see beyond [further than] *the end of the nose*. (❗日本語との違いに注意)
❸【先見】目先がきく be farsighted; have *foresight*. ▶目先がきかない be shortsighted [be nearsighted]; have no *foresight*.
❹【様子, 趣向】●目先の変わった提案 a *new* [a *novel*] suggestion.
● 目先を変える try [do] something new.

めざし 目刺し dried sardines (put onto [on] a skewer [a straw]).

*めざす 目指す【目標を】aim 《at, for; to do》; 【方向・場所を】head 《for》. (❗その他前置詞(句) toward (…に向かって), for (…を求めて), after (…を求めて)などによっても表せる) ●ゴールを目指して走る run *toward* the goal. ●独立を目指して戦う fight *for* independence. ▶彼は医者を目指している He *aims to* become [*at becoming*] a doctor./His aim is to become a doctor. ▶この飛行機はパリを目指して北上中です Our plane is *heading* north *for* Paris.

めざとい 目敏い【目が速い】sharp-eyed. ●高行はほんのちょっとした間違いにも目ざとい Takayuki is *sharp-eyed* enough to find [*have sharp eyes*] for] a slightest mistake. ●部屋に入ると彼女は目ざとく(=すぐに)机の上に書き置きを見つけた She entered the room and found *at once* [*quickly* noticed] a note on the desk./*The moment* she entered the room, she found a note on the desk.
❷【目がさめやすい】《やや書》be easily awakened.

めざまし 目覚まし 目覚まし(目覚まし時計) an alarm (clock). (❗旅行用のものは a traveling alarm clock) ●目覚ましを8時にセットする set the *alarm* (*clock*) for [×at] eight o'clock. ▶彼は目覚ましが鳴らなかったので寝過ごした He overslept because his *alarm* didn't go off [ring].

めざましい 目覚ましい (著しい) remarkable; (驚くべき) amazing; (すばらしい) wonderful, splendid; (輝かしい) brilliant; (画期的な)《やや書》epoch-making.
●めざましい業績 a *remarkable* [a *wonderful*, a *brilliant*, a *great*, an *outstanding*] achievement. ●めざましい発達をとげる achieve a *remarkable* [an *amazing*, a *brilliant*] development.
●めざましい発見をする make an *epoch-making* discovery. ●英語がめざましく上達する make (×a) *remarkable* progress in English.

めざましどけい 目覚まし時計 (⇨目覚し)

めざめる 目覚める wake* (up), awake* (❗wake より堅い語. 特に比喩的に用いることが多い). ●(すっかり)目覚めている be (wide) *awake*. (❗この awake は形容詞で叙述用法のみ) ●長い眠りに目覚める *wake* (*up*) from a long sleep [a dreadful dream]. ●責任感に目覚める awake *to* [*become aware of, realize*] one's responsibility. ▶彼は7時に目覚めた He *woke* (*up*) at seven. ▶目覚めると時計が7時を打っていた I *awoke* to hear the clock striking seven.

める 目ざる (目の荒い) an openwork (bamboo) colander.

めされる 召される ●神[天国]に召される go to heaven; pass away. (❗いずれも「死ぬ」の婉曲的表現)

めざわり 目障り ❶《話》an eyesore (❗見ると不快になる物); a distraction (❗気を散らす物・人). ▶あの木は目障りだ That tree is an *eyesore* [an *offense to the eye*]. /(視界を遮る)《やや書》That tree spoils [《やや書》obstructs] the view.

*めし 飯 ❶【ご飯】 boiled [cooked] rice. (⇨ご飯)

> **解説** 普通 rice だけで十分. 欧米人は米を野菜として食べるので cooked rice は日本風のご飯でなく「スープの具にしたりバターでいためて料理した米」という意も含む.

❷【食事】a meal; (食物) food; (朝食) breakfast; (昼食) lunch; (夕食) dinner, supper. ●飯を食べる have a meal. ▶彼は三度の飯より芝居が好きだ He likes (seeing) plays better than anything else.
❸【生計】a [one's] living; a [one's] livelihood.
● 飯の食い上げ ▶そんなことをして見ろ, 飯の食い上げだぞ Do such a thing, and you'll lose your job.
● 飯の種 ●会社は気に入らないが飯の種だから仕方ない《話》I don't like the company, but it's where I get my *bread and butter* [I must bring home *the bacon*]. (❗bring home the groceries ともいい「生活費を稼ぐ」の意の慣用表現)
● 飯を食う ▶作家では飯は食えない I can't earn my *living* [my *daily bread*] as a writer.

めじ 目地 (継ぎ目) a joint.

メシア【<ヘブライ語】the Messiah /məsáiə/. (⇨救世主, キリスト)

めしあがる 召し上がる【「食べる, 飲む」の尊敬語】eat*; have*. (⇨食べる, 飲む) ●昼食は何を召し上がりますか What would you like (*to have*) for lunch? ●一つ召し上がれ Have one. ▶ごく親しい間柄などでない限り Eat one. とはいわない

会話「ここで召し上がりますか」「いや, 持って帰ります」 "Will this be to *eat* here?/Will you *be eating* here?" "No, to go, please." (❗店では (Is this) for here or to go? などが慣用的表現)

めしあげる 召し上げる (没収する) confiscate. ●召し上げられる be confiscated; forfeit.

めしかかえる 召し抱える employ [hire]《him》 as a retainer [a servant].

めした 目下 (年下の人) one's junior (❗地位についても用いるので, 年齢の場合は younger people [people who are younger] than one の方が明確); (部下) one's assistant [junior];《しばしば軽蔑的》one's inferior.

めしつかい 召し使い a servant; [お手伝いさん] a maid;《やや古》a housemaid. ●召し使いを置く[雇う] keep [employ] a *servant*.

めしつかう 召し使う employ [hire]《him》 as a servant; take [hire] into one's service.

めしどき 飯時 mealtime.

めしとる 召し捕る arrest [catch, capture]《an escaped convict, a criminal》.

めしべ 雌蕊 【植物】a pistil (↔stamen).

めじまぐろ めじ鮪 【魚介】a young tuna.

メジャー ❶【巻き尺】a tape measure. (⇨物差し)
❷【大きい方の, 主要な】major /méidʒər/.
❸【国際石油資本】the majors, the Seven Sisters.
● メジャーカップ【計量カップ】a méasuring cùp;《和製語》a measure cup. ● メジャー投手【野球】a major-league pitcher.

メジャーリーガー【野球】a major leaguer.

メジャーリーグ (米国プロ野球の) the major /méidʒər/ leagues, the majors, the big leagues. (❗(1) 使

めじり 目尻 ●目じりの上がった女性 a *slant-eyed* woman. ●目じりのしわ crow's feet; the wrinkles [lines] *at the ends of the [one's] eyes*.
●**目じりを下げる**（うれしそうな顔をする）look happy;（色目を使う）make eyes《*at* her》;[話] give《her》the eye].

めじるし 目印 [○や×などの] a mark; [標識] a sign; [目印になる建物など] a landmark.（⇒印）●読んでいる箇所の目印として, 本に紙切れをはさむ put a piece of paper in the book to *mark* one's place. ●時計台がその大学の目印です The clock tower is a *landmark* [*a guide*] to the college.

めじろ 目白 [鳥] a (Japanese) white-eye.

めじろおし 目白押し ●劇場前に人々は目白押しに並んだ The front of the theater was thick with people standing in line. ●新しい企画が目白押しだ There's *a flood of* new plans.

＊めす 雌 a fémale (↔male),《話》a she;（鳥）a hen;（象など大型動物の）a cow;（ウサギなど小形動物の）a doe.
●雌猫 a female cat; a she-cat; a tabby.

めす 召す [[「呼び寄せる」「何かを身に受け入れる」の意の尊敬語]] ●お年を召したご婦人 an *elderly* lady.（!) an old lady と同じ丁寧）●お風邪を召しませんよう Please take [Take] care not to *catch* (a) [*get* a] cold.（!) 公式の場以外では, please は自分より社会[身体]的弱者に対して用いる）●コートをお召しください *Please put* your coat *on*.
会話「京都はお気に召しましたか」「ええ, とっても」 "How do you *like* Kyoto?" "I like it so much."

メス [<オランダ語]（手術用の）a scalpel, a (surgical) knife.
●**メスを入れる**（手術をする）operate《*on* a patient》.
●無駄な歳出にメスを入れる cut wasteful expenditures. ●その汚職事件にメスを入れるべき(=徹底的に調べる)時だ It's high time we *probed*《✕probe》*into* the payoff scandal.（!) that 節内の動詞は通例直説法過去形）

‡めずらしい 珍しい ❶[まれな] rare（!) 通例「貴重」の意を含む. 変化形については（⇒まれ)];（珍奇な）curious;（めったにない）uncommon;[普通でない] unusual;[独特で他にない] unique. ●珍しい本 a *rare* book. ●珍しい光景 a *rare* [*a curious*] sight. ●珍しい名前 an *uncommon* name. ●珍しい経験 an *unusual* [*a unique*] experience. ●こんな大きなリンゴはこの果樹園では珍しい Such a big apple is *rare* in this orchard. ●彼が机に向かっているとは珍しい It's *rare* [*unusual*] for him to sit at his desk./ We rarely [*hardly ever*,《書》*seldom*] find him at his desk. ●こんなところで会いかかるとは珍しい It's quite *unusual* to see you here. ●今朝は珍しく暖かい It's *unusually* [*exceptionally*] warm this morning.
❷[目新しい] new;（新奇な）novel. ●珍しい経験 a *novel* experience. ●見るもの聞くものすべてが珍しい Everything I saw and heard was *new* [*interesting*] *to* me.
❸[その他の表現] 珍しい(=予期しない)客 an *unexpected* visitor《✕guest》.（!) guest は「招待客」）

●100 歳以上まで生きる人は珍しい(=ほとんどない) *Very few* people live to be over one hundred years old. ●近年では珍しい大雪[大地震]だった It was the heaviest snowfall [the severest earthquake] (that) we had had in recent years.

めせん 目線 one's eyes.（⇒視線）

メソジスト（教徒）a Méthodist.
●メソジスト教会 the Methodist Church.

メゾソプラノ [<イタリア語]【音楽】mezzo-soprano,（歌手）a mezzo-soprano《複 ～s》.

メゾネット【建築】《英》a maisonette.（!)《米》では a duplex apartment がこれに近い）

メゾピアノ [<イタリア語]【音楽】mezzo piano《略 mp》.

メゾフォルテ [<イタリア語]【音楽】mezzo forte《略 mf》.

メソポタミア Mesopotamia /mèsəpətéimiə/.（参考）イラクのチグリス・ユーフラテス両河川の地域一帯
●メソポタミア文明 the Mesopotamian civilization, the civilization of Mesopotamia.

めそめそ 副（涙を出して）tearfully. ●めそめそした声で in *a weepy* [*a tearful*] voice. ●子供がめそめそ母親にしがみついた The child hung onto his mother *tearfully* [*in tears*].
── **めそめそする** 動（すすり泣く）sob. ●めそめそするな! Stop *crying*!

めだか 目高 [魚介] a (Japanese) killifish《複 ～》.

メタげんご メタ言語 [言語] (a) metalanguage.

めだしぼう 目出し帽 (⇒目出帽)

メタセコイヤ [植物] a metasequoia.

めだち 芽立ち sprouting; budding.

‡めだつ 目立つ 動 ❶[人目を引く] be conspicuous; be noticeable; be remarkable; be prominent; be striking; be outstanding; stand* out.

> **使い分け** **be conspicuous** 存在感の大きさによって目立つことを表す. 時に否定的な意味も含む.
> **be noticeable** 変化や差異, または見た目の特徴などが容易に認識されるほど顕著であることを表す.
> **be remarkable** 物事の奇妙さや卓越性が際立っていることを表す.
> **be prominent** 容易に観察が可能な場所に位置しているため目立つことを表す.
> **be striking** 容易に認知できるほど目立つことを表す. 特に類似性や相異の程度に関して用いることが多い.
> **be outstanding** 同様のカテゴリーに属した人や物の中で特に目立っていることを表す. しばしば優れて目立つことを含意する.
> **stand out** 人が傑出して目立っていることを表す.

●目立つ相違 a *remarkable* [*a striking*] difference. ●目立つ服 a *striking* dress;（はでな）a *showy* [*a flashy*, *a gaudy*, *a loud*] dress（↔a sober, a conservative）dress. ●目立たないように(=品よく控え目に)"T.S." とイニシャルの入ったハンカチ a handkerchief *discreetly* initialed "T.S." ●彼はいつも目立とうとする He always tries to make himself *conspicuous* [（他人の注意を引きつけようと）to *attract* other people's *attention*] by telling jokes. ●彼女は高校時代普通で目立たない生徒でした She was an ordinary, *inconspicuous* student in her high school years. ●彼女の服のしみは目立たない The spots on her dress *are* not *noticeable*. ●その家は変わった色をしているので目立つ The house *stands out* [*is prominent*, *is striking*,《やや書》*is noticeable*] because of its unusual color. ●彼は画家としてひときわ目立つ存在だ He *is outstanding* [*is prominent*] *as* a painter./He

めたて

stands out from the other painters.
❷【その他の表現】▶このカーペットの色ははこりが目立たない(=汚れを示さない) The color of this carpet *doesn't* show the dirt. ▶このごろでは海外で休日を過ごす人が目立ってきている(=ますます多くの人が海外で休暇を過ごす) *More and more* people spend their vacation abroad nowadays. ▶彼女は目立ちたがり屋だ(=注目の的になりたがる) She's such a *show-off*. /(話) She's such a *show-off*. /《話》 She's such a *show-off*./《話》She's such a *show-off*./《話》She's such a *show-off*. ▶注目の中心/(話) She's such a *show-off*./《話》She's such a *show-off*. /《話》 She's such a *show-off*./《話》She's such a *show-off*. center of attention./《話》She's such a *show-off*.

── 目立って 副 conspicuously; noticeably; remarkably; prominently; strikingly; outstandingly. ●フランス語が目立って上達する make 〈a〉 *remarkable* progress in French. ▶最近交通事故が目立って増えてきた The number of car accidents has *noticeably* increased recently.

めたて 目立て ▶目立てをする set 〈a saw〉; sharpen [hone] the teeth of 〈a saw〉.

メタノール [<ドイツ語] 〖化学〗 [⇔メチルアルコール]

メタファー [[隠喩, 暗喩]] 〖修辞〗 〈a〉 metaphor.

メタボリズム [[新陳代謝]] metabolism.

メタボリックしょうこうぐん メタボリック症候群 〖代謝症候群〗〖医学〗a metabolic syndrome.

めだま 目玉 an eyeball. (⇔目) ▶目玉をぎょろつかせる roll [goggle] one's *eyes*.
● 目玉が飛び出る 目玉が飛び出るような値段 an *eye-popping* [〖法外な〗(書) an *exorbitant*] *price*.
● 目玉商品 a loss leader; 《話》 an eye-catcher.

めだまやき 目玉焼き a fried egg; 《米話》(片面を焼いた) an egg sunny-side up. ▶卵はどうしましょうか. スクランブルですか, 目玉焼きですか How do you want [like] your eggs, scrambled or *sunny-side up*?

メダリスト a medalist. ●ゴールドメダリスト a gold *medalist*.

メタリック ── メタリックの 形 〖金属性の〗 metallic.

メダル a medal /médl/; (主に装飾用の) a medallion.
● 金メダル 〈win〉 a gold *medal*.

メタルテープ [[録音テープ]] a metal tape.

メタンガス 〖化学〗methane /méθein/ (gas).

めちゃ 目茶 ▶めちゃな話 an *unreasonable* story. ●めちゃ[めっちゃ]かわいい赤ちゃん an *absolutely* lovely baby. ▶めちゃ[めっちゃ]くやしい How disappointing!

めちゃくちゃ (⇔めちゃめちゃ)

めちゃめちゃ ❶【壊れたり乱雑なさま】▶野良犬が花壇をめちゃめちゃにした Stray dogs *messed up* the flower garden. ▶花びんが石の床に落ちてめちゃめちゃに(=粉々に)なった The flower vase fell on the stone floor and *smashed into pieces*.
会話「面接はどうだった?」「いやー, めちゃめちゃだった」"How was the interview?" "Oh, it was *terrible* [〖大失敗〗 *a disaster*]."
❷【道理に合わないさま】▶彼の言っていることはめちゃめちゃだ What he's saying doesn't *make any sense at all*./What he's saying is *quite unreasonable*.

メチルアルコール 〖化学〗methyl alcohol /méθl ǽlkəhɔ(:)l/, wood alcohol, méthanòl.

メッカ [[イスラム教の聖地]] Mecca; [[あこがれの土地]] a mecca; [[活動・産業の中心地]] the center, the capital. ▶裕福な人たちのバカンスのメッカ a vacation *mecca* for wealthy people. ▶ブロードウェーはミュージカルのメッカだ Broadway is a [the] mecca of musicals. (❢ *the* を用いると, ミュージカルといえばブロードウェーしかないことを強調) ▶メンフィスはロックンロールのメッカだ Memphis is *the rock'n'roll center* [*capital*] *of* the world.

めつき 目つき a look (in one's eye). ●目つきの悪い[鋭い]男 a man with a sinister [a sharp] *look*. ▶彼はずる賢そうな目つきをしていた He had *a crafty look* (in his eye). ▶彼女は疑わしそうな目つきで私を見た She gave me a suspicious *look*.

めっき 图 plating/; [[特に金の]] gilding. ▶めっきがはがれた The *gild* has come off.
── めっきする 動 plate; gild. ● 皿を金めっきする *plate* a dish *with* gold; *gild* a dish. ▶この時計は銀めっきがしてある This watch *is plated with* silver./This is a silver-plated watch.
● めっきがはげる ▶彼のめっきはすぐにはげた(=本性が現れた) His real nature was soon revealed.

めっきゃく 滅却 ── 滅却する 動 [[消滅させる]] (雑念などを) shake off [free oneself of] 《worldly thoughts》; 《敵を》 destroy.

めっきり (非常に) very much, 《話》 a lot; (かなり) considerably; (著しく) remarkably; (際立って) noticeably. ▶彼はめっきり老けこんできました He has grown *much* [《話》*a lot*] older. (❢ いずれも比較級を強める) ▶ここのところめっきり寒くなった It has turned *considerably* colder recently.

めっきん 滅菌 sterilization. (⇔殺菌)

めっけもの めっけ物 (掘り出し物) a 〈lucky〉 find. (⇔掘り出し物) ▶最終戦の入場券を手に入れられただけでもめっけもの(=幸運)だ You were *lucky* even (in) getting a ticket for the final game.

めつけやく 目付け役 a superintendent officer (in the feudal age); (監督者) an overseer.

めっしつ 滅失 ── 滅失する 動 (価値のあるものが) be destroyed.

メッシュ (a) mesh. ●メッシュの(下着の)シャツ a mesh undershirt 《米》[vest 《英》]. ▶この靴は甲の部分がメッシュになっている The upper sides of these shoes are made of *mesh*.

めっする 滅する [[消滅する]] (死ぬ) die; (消えてなくなる) disappear; [[消滅させる]] 《敵を》 destroy; 《私心・我欲などを》 overcome, rise above 《selfishness [self-interest]》.

メッセージ (声明) a statement; (あいさつの言葉) a speech; (伝言) a message /mésidʒ/.

メッセンジャー a méssenger.
● メッセンジャーボーイ a messenger boy.

めっそう 滅相 ●滅相もない Nonsense!/How absurd [ridiculous]!/It's out of the question. (⇔とんでもない)

めったうち めった打ち ▶めった打ちにする 《話》 beat 〈him〉 up; beat 〈him〉 mercilessly [brutally]; 《投手を》 bunch hits 《off the pitcher》; tag [touch] 《the pitcher》.

*めったに rarely, 《書》 seldom; hardly [scarcely] ever. (❢ *hardly* [*scarcely*] *ever* は前の2語より情緒的だが, 意味・用法上3者は交換して用いられる) ▶あのような美しい景色を見たことはめったにない I have *rarely* [*hardly ever, seldom*] seen such a beautiful sight./《書》Rarely [*Hardly ever, Seldom*] have I seen such a beautiful sight. (❢ 文頭では語順倒置が起こることに注意) ▶私はめったに病気はしません I'm *almost never* sick. ▶そんなチャンスはめったにない Chances like that are *few and fár betwéen*. (❢ 「きわめてまれな」の意の慣用表現)
会話「彼女はめったに学校に遅刻しないね」「ええ, そうですね」 "She is *rarely* late for school, is she?" "No [Yes], she *rarely* is." (❢ *rarely* などの準否定語では付加疑問は肯定文になる)

めったやたらに 滅多やたらに (⇔やたらに)

めっちゃ (⇔目茶 ●)

めつぶし 目潰し ▶目つぶしを食わす throw 《ashes [sand]》into 《his》eyes to blind 《him》.

めつぼう 滅亡 图 [[没落]] a fall, a downfall; [[破滅]] ruin. ●国家[マヤ族]の滅亡 the *fall of* a nation

めっぽう [the Maya]. ▶核兵器は人類を滅亡に導きかねない Nuclear weapons may lead to the extinction of the human race.
—— **滅亡する** 動 (⇨滅びる)

めっぽう 滅法 ● めっぽう強い be *extremely* strong. ● めっぽう高い(=法外な)値段 an *unreasonable* price. ▶めっぽう暑い It's *terribly* [*extremely*, (耐えがたいほど) *unbearably*] hot.

めづまり 目詰まり ● 目詰まりをおこす be *clogged* [*choked*] (*up*) 《*with*》. ▶フィルターが目詰まりしてクーラーがきかない The air-conditioner does not work properly because the filter *is clogged up*.

メディア a medium (複 media /míːdiə/). ● マスメディア the (mass) *media*. ▶テレビは世論形成に最も影響力のあるメディアです Television is the most influential *medium* for forming [molding] public opinion. ● メディアリテラシー [メディア情報の利用・分析能力] media literacy.

メディカルチェック メディカルチェック [健康診断] a (medical) checkup (×check); a medical exam.

*__めでたい__ 形 [喜ばしい] happy, 《書》 joyful; [さい先のよい] auspicious. ● めでたい出来事 a *happy* [a *joyful*] event. ● このめでたい日に on this *happy* [*joyful, auspicious*] occasion. ▶彼が優勝したって, それはめでたい He won the championship. I'm really *happy* to hear that. (❗ほかに That's great., That's good [happy] news. (よい[めでたい]知らせだ)なども可)
—— **めでたく** 副 happily; auspiciously; [首尾よく] successfully. ▶彼らはめでたく(=めでたいことに)ゴールインした ˇHappily, they got ˇmarried. ▶その話はめでたく終わる The story ends *happily* [has a happy ending].

めぼう 目出帽 a ski màsk; a Balaclava.

めでる 愛でる [かわいがる] love; [ほめる] admire; [満喫する] appreciate, enjoy.

めど 目処 (見通し) (a) prospect 《*of*》; (可能性) (a) possibility. ● 7月末頃をめどに(=までに) *by* around the end of July.
● 目処がつく ▶やっと完成のめどがついた(=見えるところまできた) The completion is at last *in sight*. ▶それはいつ終わるのかめどがつかない There is *no prospect of* [(分からない) There is *no telling*] when it will be finished. (❗when 以下は名詞節なので will が必要)

めどおし 目通し looking through 《a book》.

めどおり 目通り ● 目通りを許される be granted an *audience* 《with the king》.

めとる 娶る get married 《*to* her》.

メドレー [混合曲] a medley /médli/; [陸上競技・水泳の] a medley relay [race]. ● 3曲メドレーで歌う sing a *medley* of three songs. ● 400メートル個人メドレー the individual 400-meter *medley* (*race*). ● メドレーリレー a medley relay.

メトロ [<フランス語] [パリなどの地下鉄] the metro (複 ~s). (❗しばしば the Metro) ● メトロで by *metro*.

メトロノーム [<ドイツ語] [音楽] a métronome.

メトロポリス a metrópolis. (⇨都市①)

めなだ 赤目魚 [魚介] a redlip mullet.

メニエルびょう メニエル病 [医学] Meniere's /meinjéərz/ disease [syndrome].

メニュー ❶ [献立] a menu. (⇨献立) ● コース用のメニュー a table d'hôte *menu*. ● メニューにある be (listed) on the *menu*. ▶今日のメニューは何ですか What is today's *menu*?/What is on the *menu* (*for*) today? ▶メニューを見せていただけますか Could you give me the *menu*, please? ▶メニューは驚くほど多かった The *menu* was surprisingly large.
❷ [コンピュータ] [コンピュータ] (参考 利用できる作業の選択肢一覧) ● メニュー選択式の [コンピュータ] menu-driven. ● メニューバー [コンピュータ] a menu bar.

メヌエット [<ドイツ語] [音楽] a minuet /mìnjuét/.

めぬきどおり 目抜き通り (都市の大通り) 《*on*》 the main street; 《英》 (*in*) the high street. ● 目抜き通りにある銀行 a bank on the *main street*.

めぬり 目塗り
—— **目塗りする** 動 plaster (a wall [a ceiling]).

めのう 瑪瑙 [鉱物] an agate /ǽɡət/.

めのかたき 目の敵 ● 目の敵にする always treat 《him》 like an enemy.

めのこ(ざん) 目の子(算) counting with one's eyes; (概算) (make) a rough estimate. (⇨概算)

めのたま 目の玉 an eyeball. (⇨目玉)

めのまえ 目の前 ❶ [面前] (…の面前で) in the presence of …; (すぐ前で) before 《his》 (very) eyes, right in front of 《him》; [話] under 《his》 (very) nose; [面と向かって] to 《his》 face. ● 彼を目の前でほめる [非難する] praise [blame] him *in his face*. ▶彼は目の前で私の妻を侮辱した He insulted my wife *in my presence*. (❗…in my presence より … when I was there の方が口語的) ▶私たちのすぐ目の前で事件は起こった The incident occurred *before our very eyes* [*right under our noses*]. ▶バスのドアは私の目の前でぴしゃりと閉まった The bus door closed sharply *in my face*.
❷ [直前] 試験は目の前に迫っている The exam *is close at hand* [[話] *just around the corner*].
● 目の前が暗くなる ▶突然目の前が暗くなり意識を失った Suddenly it *got dark before my eyes* and I lost consciousness. ▶末期の胃がんと聞いて目の前が暗くなった(=絶望した) *I was thrown into despair* when I was told that I have had terminal stomach cancer.

めばえ 芽生え ❶ [芽が現れること] sprouting.
❷ [事の始まり] ● 彼らの間の恋の芽生え the *beginning* of love between them.

めばえる 芽生える [芽ぶく] bud (-dd-); sprout (⇨芽); [成長し始める] begin* to grow. ● 2人の間に愛が芽生えた Love *has begun to grow* between them.

めはし 目端 ● 目端がきく (機転がきく) be quick-witted; be tactful.

めばち [魚介] a big-eyed tuna.

めはな 目鼻 [目と鼻] the eyes and the nose; [顔の造作] features. (⇨目鼻立ち)
● 目鼻がつく ▶我々の計画は目鼻がついてきた(=具体化する) Our plan is beginning to *take shape*.

めばな 雌花 a female [植物] a pistillate] flower.

めはなだち 目鼻立ち (見かけ) looks; (顔立ち) features. ● 目鼻立ちのいい顔 a well-*featured* face. (⇨容貌(½¾)) ● 目鼻立ちの整った男性 a *handsome* [(顔だちのよい) a *good-looking*] man; a man of regular *features*.

めばり 目張り a wéather strip. ● 窓を目張りする seal up the windows; weatherstrip the windows.

めばる 眼張 [魚介] a darkbanded rockfish.

めびな 女雛 a doll representing the Empress. (⇨男雛)

めぶく 芽ぶく bud (-dd-), come* into bud; sprout. (❗ bud は葉だけでなく花芽(=つぼみ)にもいう)

めぶんりょう 目分量 ● 目分量で計る measure 《salt》 *by* (*the*) *eye*; (大ざっぱにやる) go by rule of thumb.

めべり 目減り (減少) a decrease; (損失) a loss. ▶イ

めぼし ▶ンフレで預金が目減りした The *value* of my deposit *has decreased* because of inflation.

めぼし 目星 ▶犯人がだれなのか目星はつくよ We can *make a (pretty) good guess* as to the identity of 〖(誰)can *spot*〗 the criminal.

めぼしい 〖主要な〗chief; important (⇨主な); 〖値打ちのある〗valuable. ●その作家のめぼしい作品 the *chief* [*notable*] works by the writer. ●めぼしい(=貴重な)物は全部盗まれた All the *valuables* were stolen.

めまい 图 (ふらふらする) dizziness, giddiness; 〖医学〗vértigò. ▶めまいの発作に見舞われたときは、両ひざの間に顔をうずめなさい Put your head between your knees when you have a *dizzy* spell.

━━めまいがする 動 feel dizzy [giddy]. ●めまいがするような高さ *a dizzy* [*a giddy*] height.

めまぐるしい 目まぐるしい (速い) quick; (目を回すような) dizzying. ●世の中のめまぐるしい変化 the *quick* [*dizzying*] change(s) in 〖xof〗 the world. ▶テニスボールはネットをはさんでめまぐるしく飛び交った The tennis ball flew *quickly* back and forth across the net.

めめしい 女々しい (男らしくない) unmanly; (女のような) womanish; (意気地のない) sissy (❗次の例のように名詞としても用いられる). ▶そんな女々しいことをするな〖言うな〗Don't be such a *sissy*.

***メモ** 图 (簡潔な記録) a note (❗内容的に豊富なものをさすときは通例複数形で); (備忘・伝達用の) a memorandum (複 ～s, memoranda), 〖話〗a memo (複 ～s); (婉曲的) a reminder. ●メモを見ながら〖なしで〗しゃべる speak from [*without*] *notes*. ▶ちょっとメモでも入れておいてください Give him a gentle *reminder*.

━━メモする 動 ●彼の講義をメモする take [make] *notes* [*a note*] *of* 〖(米)*on*〗his lecture. ▶私は彼の名前をすばやくノートにメモした I *jotted* his name *down* on the notebook. (❗ jot … down は「(すばやく)書き留める」の意)

●メモ用紙 mémo [nóte] pàper; (走り書き用) (米) scrátch pàper; (英) scráp pàper; (はぎ取り式の) a memo pad.

めもと 目元 ●目元の涼しい〖愛らしい〗少女 a girl with *clear* [*lovely*] *eyes*. ●目元がぱっちりしている have *bright eyes*. ▶彼は目元が母親にそっくりだ He really takes after his mother *around his eyes*.

めもり 目盛り a scale; (やや書) a graduation. ●定規の目盛り the *scale* [*graduations*] on a ruler. (❗on の代わりに of も可) ●摂氏の目盛りのついた温度計 a thermometer with a Celsius *scale* [Celsius *graduations*].

メモリアル 〖記念碑〗a memorial.
●メモリアルホール 〖記念館〗a memorial hall; 〖葬儀場〗a funeral hall.

メモリー 〖記憶,記憶装置〗(a) memory. ▶このコンピュータはメモリー容量が大きい This computer has a large *memory*.

めもる 目盛る graduate. ●この定規はインチとセンチで目盛ってある This ruler *is graduated* in both inches and centimeters.

メモワール 〖＜フランス語〗〖回想録〗memoires /mémwa:rz/.

めやす 目安 〖基準〗a (rough) standard; 〖見当〗a rough idea; 〖目標〗the goal, the aim. ▶だれが勝つかだいたいの目安はつくよ I have a *rough* (話)a *pretty good*〗*idea* as to who will win. ▶月曜日を一応の目安(=仮の締切日)にこれを仕上げます The tentative deadline for finishing this work is Monday.

めやすばこ 目安箱 a *meyasubako*; (説明的に) a box placed in front of the supreme court by shogun Tokugawa Yoshimune to receive complaints, suggestions or appeals.

めやに 目脂 gum; 〖話〗sleep. ●目をこすって目やにを取る rub the *sleep* out of one's eyes.

メラニン 〖生物〗〖黒色素〗melanin.
メラネシア 〖太平洋の島々〗Melanesia /mèlənǐ:ʒə/.
メラノーマ 〖悪性黒色腫〗〖医学〗a melanoma.
メラミンじゅし メラミン樹脂 〖化学〗melamine resin.

めらめら ▶古い木造の家がめらめら燃えた The old wooden house was *in flames* [*on fire, blazing*]./〖火が主語〗The flames *licked* the old wooden house. (❗lick は火がついていくさまによく用いられる) ▶彼は怒りがめらめらと燃え上がった Anger *flamed* (*up*) within him.

メランコリー 〖憂鬱(ゆうつ)〗melancholy.
メリーゴーラ(ウ)ンド (ride (on)) a merry-go-round; (米) a carousel; (英) a roundabout.
メリーランド 〖米国の州〗Maryland /mérələnd/ (略 Md. 郵便略 MD).
メリケン 〖アメリカ〗American.
●メリケン粉 (小麦粉) flour.

めりこむ めり込む (沈む) sink* in …; (はまり込む) stick* in …. ▶車が泥の中にめり込んだ The car *sank* [*stuck, got*] *bogged down*] *in* the mud.

メリット 〖利点,長所〗an advantage; (a) merit. ▶本当の事を話してもメリットはほとんどない There are few *advantages* [There's little *merit*] in telling the truth. (❗前の方が普通)

▎▎▎▎ DISCOURSE ▎▎▎▎
早期外国語学習には明らかにメリットがある Studying a foreign language at an early age **clearly** has some *benefits*. (❗clearly (明らかに)は主張を表すディスコースマーカー)

めりはり 〖音声の高低・強弱〗modulation, range; 〖変化・相違〗(変化) a change; (相違) (a) distinction. ▶彼女の歌声はめりはりに欠ける She lacks *modulation* [*range*] in her singing voice. ▶日本の四季にはめりはり(=はっきりとした相違)がある There are *distinct differences* between the seasons in Japan. ▶彼は演説にめりはりをきかせる(=演説の大切な点に(声を大きく)ジェスチャーを豊富にまじえて)力を入れる) He *puts emphasis on* the important points (with raised voice and a lot of gestures) in his speech.

めりめり ▶めりめりっと天井にひびが走った Cracks ran on the ceiling with *ripping noises*. ▶その木造の家はめりめりと音を立てて倒れた The wooden house collapsed with *a groaning* sound.

メリヤス [＜スペイン語] 〖編んだ〖knit〗goods, knitwear. ●メリヤス生地 *knitted* fabrics. ●メリヤスのシャツ a *knit*(*ted*) undershirt.
●メリヤス編み stockinet (stitch).

メルカトルずほう メルカトル図法 Mercator('s) /mərkéitər(z)/ projection.
メルシー [＜フランス語] 〖ありがとう〗merci; thank you.
メルトダウン 〖炉心溶融〗meltdown.
メルとも メル友 an email friend [pal], an e-friend, an e-pal.
メルヘン [＜ドイツ語] a fairy tale. (⇨童話)
メルボルン 〖オーストラリアの都市〗Melbourne /mélbərn/.
メルルーサ [＜スペイン語] 〖魚介〗(ギンダラ) a common hake.

メロディー 〖旋律〗a melody; a tune. (⇨旋律)

メロドラマ (a) melodrama;〔テレビ・ラジオの連続版〕a soap opera,《話》a soap.

めろめろ ▶妻は孫のことになるとめろめろだ My wife *is too fond of* our grandchildren./《話》My wife *has a soft spot for* [*is nuts about*] our grandchildren. ▶彼は飲むとめろめろになる He *gets deadly drunk* whenever he drinks.

メロン 〖植物〗a melon.

めん 面 ❶〖顔〗a face.
❷〖お面〗a mask;〔剣道の防具〕a fáce guàrd. ●面をかぶる〔つける〕put on a *mask* [a *face guard*].
❸〖表面〗a surface /sə́ːrfɪs/;〔平面〕a plane;〔結晶体の小面〕a facet. (⇨表面, 平面) ▶その山の北面を登る climb the north *face* of the mountain. ▶立方体には6面がある A cube has six *surfaces* [*faces*]. ▶ヨットが湖面を走っている Yachts are sailing on (the *surface* of) the lake.
❹〖方面〗(局面) an aspect, a phase; (点) a respect, a point; (側面) a side; (分野) a field; (ページ) a page. ●あらゆる面で in every *respect*.
●この面＝点では in this *respect*. ●別の面＝角度から見る view《a subject》from a different *angle* [別の観点から》a different *point of view*]. ●その問題のあらゆる面を考慮する consider every *aspect* [all *sides*] of the matter. ●新聞の経済面 on the financial *page* [*column*] of the newspaper. ●その計画の経済的な面をよく考えなさい Consider the economic *aspects* of the plan. ●その面では(=に関しては)君に言うことは何もない I have nothing to say to you *about* [〖書〗*in respect of*] academic grades. ●我が家は健康面では不運続きだ《話》Health-*wise*, we've had a bad run of luck. ▶彼には人並みにやさしい面もある He has as much of a kind *side* as other people.
●面が割れる ▶容疑者は監視カメラで面が割れた(=だれであるかわかった) The suspect *was identified* by the security camera.
●面と向かう ●面と向かって言う say *to*《his》*face*(↔ behind《his》back). ●面と向かって座る sit *face-to-face*《with》. ●困難に面と向かう *face* difficulties; *face up to* difficulties.

めん 綿 cotton. ●綿100パーセントのシャツ a 100 percent *cotton* [a pure-*cotton*, an all-*cotton*] shirt.
●綿織物 cotton fabrics; (綿製品) cotton goods. ●綿花 (raw) cotton.

めん 麺 noodles. ●麺棒 a rólling pìn.

***めんえき** 免疫 图 〖医学〗immunity.
──**免疫の** 形 immune《*to, from*》. ▶はしかに免疫ができる become *immune to* measles. ▶予防注射をすれば百日ぜきには免疫ができる Vaccination *immunizes* /ímjənàiziz/ people *against* whooping cough /kɔ́(ː)f/. ▶彼女は母親の小言には免疫ができているShe *is immune* [〖平気だ〗《やや書》*impervious*] *to* her mother's complaints [*naggings*].
●免疫学 immunology. ●免疫グロブリン immunoglobulin. ●免疫体 an antibody. ●免疫不全症 an immunity deficiency disease. ●免疫療法 immunotherapy.

***めんかい** 面会 图 ●面会を申し込む ask for [request] an *interview*《with him》(!*request* はやや堅い語で, 丁寧さを暗示); ask for《him》. ▶面会謝絶〔掲示〕No visitors. ▶その患者は面会謝絶だ The patient doesn't *see any company* today. (!*company* は集合名詞で来客 (visitors) の意) ▶田中さんという方が面会に見えています。お通ししましょうか There's a Mr. Tanaka to *see* you, sir. Shall I show him in?
会話「面会の方が見えています」「どなた？」"Here is someone (who wants) to *see* you." "Who is it?" (!A *gentleman* [*lady*] wants to see you. の型も見かけるが, 上のように There's …, Here's … を用いる方が唐突感がないので好まれる)
──**面会する** 動 (会って話す) see*; (約束して会う) meet*,《米》meet with …; (見舞う) visit; (取材・公式会見をする) have* an interview《*with*》. ▶今日の午後社長と面会することになっている We *are meeting*《米》*meeting with*》the president this afternoon.
●面会時間 vísiting hòurs. ●病院の面会時間 a hospital's *visiting hours*. ●面会人 a visitor.

めんかん 免官 图 (a) dismissal.
──**免官する** 動 dismiss《him》from a government post.

めんきょ 免許 《米》(a) license,《英》(a) licence.
●免許を取る get [《やや書》obtain, ×take] a *license*. ●彼に免許を与える *license* him《*to do*》; give him a *license*《*to do*》. ●免許を停止[取り消し]される have one's *license* suspended [canceled]. ●無免許で運転する drive without a *license*. ▶彼は開業医の免許を持っている He *has a license* [*is licensed*] to practice as a doctor.
●免許証 (認可証) a license; (職業・身分などの証明書) a certificate. ●運転免許証《米》a driver's *license*;《英》a driving *licence*. (!アクセントに注意) ●免許状《免状》教員免許状 a teacher's [a teaching] *certificate*. ●免許料 a license fèe.

めんくい 面食い ▶彼女は面食いだ She likes [is easily attracted by, can't resist,《やや話》goes for] good-looking men.

めんくらう 面食らう (まごつく) be embarrassed《*by, about*》; (ろうばいする) be confused; be bewildered [〖書・やや古〗confounded, upset]. (⇨慌てる❶, まごつく) ▶あの個人的な質問には面食らってしまった I *was embarrassed by* the personal questions.

めんこ 面子 *menko*; a Japanese children's game using stiff pieces of paper with pictures on them.

めんこい (かわいい) pretty; cute.

めんざい 免罪 图 (an) acquittal; (宗教上の) remission of a sin. ●免罪となる be *acquitted of* a crime.
──**免罪する** 動 acquit《him *of* a crime》.
●免罪符 an indulgence.

めんし 綿糸 〖織物用糸〗cotton yarn; 〖縫い糸〗cotton thread.

めんしき 面識 acquaintance. ▶彼とは面識がない I don't *know* him *personally*./《書》I'm *not acquainted with* him./《書》I have *no acquaintance with* him./(まったく知らない人だ) He is a total [a perfect] stranger to me.

めんじゅうふくはい 面従腹背 a Judas kiss;《ことわざ》Many kiss the hand they wish to cut off.

***めんじょ** 免除 图 〖義務などの〗(an) exemption;〖罰・負債などの〗《書》(a) remission.
──**免除する** 動 ▶彼の試験を免除する *excuse* [《書》*exempt*] him *from*《taking》the examination. ▶彼らは税金を免除されている They *are exempt from*《paying》taxes./They *are free of* taxes.

めんじょう 免状 (証明書) a certificate; (許可証) a license; (卒業証書) a diploma. ●免状料 a license fèe.

めんしょく 免職 (a) dismissal. ●懲戒免職《get》disciplinary *dismissal*. ▶彼は職務怠慢で免職になった He *was dismissed* [*was discharged*] from

めんじる 免じる (⇨免除) ●若さに免じて(=を考慮して)許される be pardoned *in consideration of* one's youth. ▶君のお父さんに免じて(=のために)過失を大目に見ておこう I'll overlook your fault *for* your father's *sake*.

めんしん 免震 ━━ **免震の** 形 earthquake-proof.
●免震構造 seismically isolated structure.
●免震工法 seismic /sáizmik/ isolation.

メンス [<ドイツ語] menstruation; the menses; 《婉曲的》one's period [hormones]. (参考) 今は「生理」が普通》(⇨生理❷) ●メンスになっている menstruate; have one's *period* [*hormones*].

めんする 面する [向き合う] face; [大胆に立ち向かう] confront. (⇨直面する) ▶庭に面した窓 a window *on* the garden. ▶その建物は海に面している The building *faces* [*looks out on*] the sea.

めんぜい 免税 图 tax exemption; exemption from (paying) tax.
━━ **免税の[で]** 形 (関税が) duty-free; (税金が) tax-free. ●免税品のウイスキー *duty-free* whiskey. ▶空港では免税で時計が買える You can buy a watch *duty-free* at the airport.
●免税店 a duty-free shop. ●免税点 the tax exemption limit. ●免税品 a duty-free article. (!《話》では a duty-free ともいう)

めんせき 免責 (責任の除外) (an) exemption from responsibility [obligation].
●免責条項《法律》an escape [an exemption] clause.

めんせき 面責 ━━ **面責する** 動 reprove [reproach] 《him》to 《his》face.

めんせき 面積 (an) area; (床面積) (a) floor space (⇨建て坪). ▶この図形の面積はいくらですか What is the *area* of this figure? (!「…を求めよ」なら Find the area…. という) ▶この庭の面積は 300 平方メートルです The *area* of this garden is 300 square meters./This garden is [covers] 300 square meters in *area*./This garden has an *area* of 300 square meters. (⇨広さ)

めんせつ 面接 图 [面接試験] (一般に) an interview; [口頭試問] an oral examination.
━━ **面接する** 動 ●彼に面接する have an *interview with* him; interview him. ●就職の面接ではいつもあがってしまう I always get nervous *at* a job *interview*./(面接を受けるときに) I always get nervous when I have an *interview* [I am interviewed] *for* a job.

めんぜん 面前 ●他人の面前(=前)で *in front of* other people; (いる前で) *in the presence of* other people. ●公衆の面前で *in public*. (⇨人前)

めんそ 免租 tax exemption. (⇨免税)
●免租地 a tax haven.

めんそ 免訴 (an) dismissal. ●免訴にする dismiss 《a case *against* him》.

めんそう 面相 (⇨容貌, 人相) ●どうもうな面相の犬 a fierce-*looking* dog. ▶彼はひどい面相だ He is such a fright./He is a perfect fright.

メンター [指導者, 助言者] a mentor.

めんたいこ 明太子 *mentaiko*; (説明的に) salted cod's roe spiced with hot red pepper.

メンタルテスト [知能検査] a mental test; an intelligence test. (!現在では後の方が普通)

メンタルトレーニング [頭脳訓練] mental training.

メンタルヘルス [心の健康] mental health.
●メンタルヘルスケア [心の健康づくり] mental health care.

めんだん 面談 图 a face-to-face talk; (面接) an interview. ▶委細面談《広告》Particulars will be arranged *personally*.
━━ **面談する** 動 (相談する) talk … over 《*with*》; (面接する) have an interview 《*with*》.

メンチ (ひき肉) minced meat. (⇨ミンチ)
●メンチカツ a fried cake of minced meat. ●メンチボール a meatball.

めんちょう 面疔 [医学] a facial furuncle /fjúərʌŋkl/; a boil.

メンツ [<中国語] [面目] face; [名誉] honor. (⇨威信, 体面) ●メンツを失う[保つ] lose [save] *face*. (!もと one's をつけたのが今は《まれ》) ●メンツにかけても約束を守らないといけない *be on* one's *honor* to keep one's promise; be (in) *honor bound to* keep one's promise. ●メンツにこだわる be overly concerned about one's personal *honor*.

メンテ [「メンテナンス」の略] (⇨メンテナンス)

めんてい 免停 [「免許停止」の略] suspension of a license. ●免停を食う have one's license suspended 《*for* drunken driving》.

メンテナンス maintenance /méintənəns/. ●メンテナンスフリーの[で] *maintenance*-free.

メンデル [オーストリアの修道士・植物学者] Mendel /méndl/ (Gregor Johann /jóuhɑ:n/).
●メンデルの法則 Mendel's law.

メンデルスゾーン [ドイツの作曲家] Mendelssohn (Felix 〜).

***めんどう 面倒** 图 ❶ [手数] trouble (⇨迷惑); [難しさ] difficulty. ▶それを説明するのは少しも面倒ではありません[たいへん面倒だ] It's no *trouble* [great *trouble*] to explain it. ▶その仕事は少々面倒だった I had some *difficulty* [*trouble*] *with* the work./I had some *difficulty* [*trouble*] (*in*) doing the work. (!通例 in は省略する) ▶それでは事はますます面倒になるだけだ That only *complicates matters* more and more.
❷ [いざこざ, もめごと] trouble. (!通例, よくないことをして警察・教師などの権威者にやっかいになることを暗示。「政治的・社会的紛争」の意でははしばしば 〜) ●面倒に巻き込む get 《him》into *trouble*. ▶あの子はいつも面倒を起こしている That boy is always causing *trouble*./《軽蔑的》That boy is a troublemaker. ▶彼の身に何か面倒なことがあったに違いない He must have run into *trouble*. (!run into は「…に遭遇する」の意)
❸ [世話] care. (⇨面倒見) ▶自分で面倒をよく見るならその犬を飼ってもよい You may have [《主に英》keep] the dog if you *take good care of* it [*look after* it well] yourself.
●面倒をかける ●彼に面倒をかける give [cause] him trouble; trouble [bother] him; put him to trouble. ▶面倒をおかけしてすみませんでした I'm sorry to *have troubled* [*bothered*] you. (面倒をかけた後の言葉。かける前は次例を参照) ▶ご面倒をおかけしますがこの箇所を説明していただけませんか I'm sorry to *trouble* [*bother*] you, but could you explain this passage?/May I *trouble* [*bother*] you to explain this passage?
━━ **面倒な, 面倒くさい** 形 (やっかいな) troublesome, 《やや書》bothersome; (あきあきする) tiresome. ●面倒な仕事 a *troublesome* [a *bothersome*] task. ▶彼女のぐちを聞くのが面倒くさくなってしまった I've just felt it *troublesome* [*tiresome*] to hear her complaints./(うんざりして) I've gotten [become] (*sick and*) *tired of* (hearing) her complaints. ▶小口の注文のときは面倒くさってなかなか応じてくれない When you give them a small order, they can't *be bothered* to accept it.

めんどうみ　面倒見　▶あいつは面倒見のよい男だ(部下の世話をよくする) He *takes good care of* his subordinates./(親切で助けになる) He is very *kind and helpful* (*to* his students).

めんとおし　面通し　《米》a (police) lineup;《英》an identification parade.

メントール　menthol.

めんとり　面取り　(角材を45度に) chamfer, cut [make] a chamfer on《a beam, wood》;(角に丸味をつける) round off《the corners, the edges》.

めんどり　雌鳥　『雌の鳥』a hen (bird);『鶏の』a hen.

めんば　面罵　— **面罵する 動** abuse《him》to《his》face.

***メンバー**　『構成員』a member;『選手』a player;『出場選手の顔ぶれ』a lineup (⚠ 通例単数形で).　●先発メンバーを発表する announce the starting *line-up*.　●(野球チームの)登録メンバー(表) a team roster.　●(野球チームの)登録メンバーに入っている be on the roster.　▶あの人はその委員会(チーム)のメンバーだ He is a *member* of the committee [team]./He is *on* [✕*in*] the committee [team]. (⚠前の方より普通の言い方. on は所属を表す.「テニスクラブのメンバーだ」なら He is *in* [*belongs to*] a tennis club. となる)　▶彼らはチームのベストメンバーで試合をした They had a game with the best *players* of their team.

会話「もう(チームの)メンバーはそろったかい」「今のところ2人足りないんだ」"Have you got a full team?" "So far, we're two people short [short of two people]."

めんぴ　面皮　(⇨面(㋥)の皮)
●**面皮を失う** humiliate oneself; lose face.
●**面皮を剥(は)ぐ** put《him》to shame; humiliate.

めんぷ　綿布　cotton fabrics [cloth].

めんぼう　綿棒　《米商標》a Q-tip, a Q-Tip, a q-tip,《英》a cotton bud [swab].　●綿棒で耳あかを取る clean one's ears with a Q-tip.

めんぼく　面目　『メンツ』face;『名誉』honor;『名声』(a) reputation;『威信』prestige;『信用』credit. (⇨メンツ)　▶こんな間違いをしてまことに面目ない I've *disgraced myself with* this mistake./I'm very *ashamed of* this mistake./(弁解のしようがない) I *have no excuse for* this mistake.　▶そんなことをすれば彼の面目にかかわる(= 名声を損なう) That would cost him his *reputation*.　▶面目にかけても彼女にうんと言わせてみせる *On* my *honor*, I'll get her to say yes.
●**面目丸(まる)つぶれ**　▶私は面目丸つぶれだった I *lost face* completely./I suffered total *loss of face*.
●**面目を施す**　▶彼は試合に勝って面目をほどこした[保った] He won the game and *saved face*./His victory did him *credit*.

メンマ　[<中国語] (説明的に) Chinese bamboo shoots, boiled, fermented and seasoned for use in cooking.

めんみつ　綿密　— **綿密な 形**　『細密な』《書》minute /máin(j)úːt/;『精密な』close;『詳細な』detailed;『注意深い』careful;『人・物事が念入りな』scrupulous;(徹底した) thorough.　●綿密な観察 (a) *minute* [*close*] observation.　●綿密な(= 詳細な)報告 a *detailed* [a *minute*] report.　▶彼は仕事が綿密だ He is *scrupulous in* his work./He works with *scrupulous* care [very *carefully*].
— **綿密に 副** minutely; closely; (詳細に) in detail.　●殺人事件を綿密に調査する make a *close* [a *careful*, a *thorough*] investigation of the murder; investigate the murder *closely* [*carefully*, *thoroughly*].　●綿密に計画を練る *work out* a plan.

めんめん　面々　(1人1人) each [every] one.　●出席していた面々 *every* [*each*] *one* of those present. (⇨だれ(に)も 代 ❶)

めんめん　綿々　●綿々と語る talk *endlessly*; continue talking (for hours).　●綿々たる(= あふれる)情緒 a *flood* of emotion.

めんもく　面目　❶ 『名誉』honor. (⇨面目(めんぼく))
❷ 『様子』(an) appearance.　▶体育館は建て直され面目を一新した The gym was rebuilt and *looked completely different*.
●**面目躍如**　▶彼は面目躍如たる[となる]講演をした He gave a lecture that won him *honor* [did him *credit*].　▶我々にそんなことを言うとは彼の面目躍如たるものがある(= いかにも彼らしい) It's *just like* him to tell us about it.

めんよう　綿羊　『動物』a sheep (複 ～).

めんるい　麺類　noodles.

も

も 藻 〖植物〗 alga (複 algae /ǽldʒiː/); (水草) waterweed; (海藻) seaweed.

も 喪 mourning. ●喪に服する[喪が明ける] go into [out of] *mourning*. ▶彼女は父が死んだので喪に服していた She *was in mourning* for her (dead) father. ▶in mourning で父が亡くなっていることは明らかなので dead はつけないのが普通

‡も 〘副助詞〙 ❶ 〖…もまた〗 too, also, as well; (…もまた(…でない)) (not) … either. (⇨又 ❶〘解説〙)

〘解説〙(1) also は too, as well より堅い語. **too と as well** では as well の方がくだけた語.
(2) too, as well は通例文末に置く. too はまた文中で用いられる場合もあるが, その場合コンマで区切られることもある. also は通例動詞の前, be 動詞・助動詞の後に置く.
(3) too, as well では強勢の位置によって意味が変わる. たとえば I went to Paris last year ＼*too* [*as well*]. において, 強勢を I に置けば「他の人も行ったが私も」, Páris に置けば「他へも行ったがパリにも」, lást year に置けば「一昨年も行ったが昨年も」の意になる.

▶彼もひどい風邪を引いている He *also* has a bad cold./He has a bad cold *too* [*as well*]. ▶私もコーヒーはほしくない I d*on't* want any coffee *either*. (!否定文では ×too, ×also, ×as well は不可)
〘会話〙「彼はこの本がうまく読めない」「私もだ」 "He can't read this book well." "I c*an't* read it, *either*./*Neither* [*Nor*] can I./*Nor* me./Me *neither*." (!(1) 最後の二つの応答はくだけた言い方. (2) Me neither は通例間にコンマを入れない. cf. Me(,) too)
〘会話〙「今日は疲れた」「私もだ」 "I'm tired today." "*So* am I./I am *too* [*as well*, ×also]./Me(,) *too*./Same here." (!短い返答には also は用いない. 最後の二つはくだけた言い方)
〘会話〙「楽しい休暇を過ごしてね」「あなたもね!」 "Have a good holiday!" "*And* you (*too*)!/Yes, *same to you*!"

❷ 〖A も B も〗 A *and* B; (A も B も両方とも) both A and B; (A のみならず B も) not only A but also B; B as well as A (!二つとも B に意味の重点がある); (A も B も(…でない)) neither A nor B. (!以上の A, B は文法的に対等の語・句・節) (⇨又 ❸)▶昼も夜も night *and* day; day *and* night. ▶何マイルも何マイルも歩く walk miles *and* miles. ▶何年も何年も for years *and* years. ▶彼は和食も洋食も好きだ He likes *both* Japanese food *and* Western food. ▶彼女は主婦のみならずピアニストでもある She is *not only* a housewife *but* (*also*) a pianist./She is a pianist *as well as* a housewife. ▶学校へ行くときはバスも自転車も使わない. 歩いて行きます I go to school *neither* by bus *nor* by bicycle. I walk.

❸ 〖中には…も〗 ▶だれもが犬好きなわけではない. 好きな人もいればそうでない人もいる Not everybody likes dogs; *some* (people) ╱*do*, *some* [*others*] ╲*don't*.
〘会話〙「このリンゴすっぱくないの？」「おいしいのもあるわよ」 "Aren't these apples sour /sáuɚ/?" "*Some* of them are all right."

❹ 〖程度〗 (数[量, 時間, 距離, 回数]が…もの多くの) as many [much; long; far; often] as …; (数・量が…ほども多くの) no less [fewer] than …. (!いずれも…は数詞. 一般に no less than の方が as 型より強意的) ▶彼の書斎には 3,000 冊もの本がある There are *as many as* [*no less than*, *no fewer than*] three thousand books in his study./There are three thousand books, *no less*, in his study. ▶雨の中を 5 時間も歩かねばならなかった I had to walk *as long as* five hours in the rain. ▶彼は仕事で今年ニューヨークへ 10 回も行った He went to New York on business *as often as* ten times this year. ▶彼の年収は 1,000 万円にもなる His annual income comes to *no less than* [*as much as*, ×no fewer than] ten million yen. (!不可算名詞の場合 ×no fewer than は不可) ▶出発までに 10 分もない We have [It's] *less than* ten minutes before we start. (!less than は「…より少ない」の意)

❺ 〖どちらか, どちらでも〗 (A でも B でも) A or B; (A か B かどちらか) either A or B; (A であろうとなかろうと) whether A or not; (A も B も…ない) not A or B, neither A nor B. ▶君は行っても残ってもいい You can [may] (*either*) go *or* stay. (!either のある方が選択の気持ちが強い) ▶今日でもあすでも出かける用意はできています I'm ready to leave *either* today *or* tomorrow. ▶君は好きでもきらいでもその本を読まねばならない You must read the book, *whether* you like it *or not*. ▶彼はラジオも聞かないしテレビも見ない He doesn't listen to the radio *or* [×and] watch TV. (!次例より口語的)/He *neither* listens to the radio *nor* watches TV.

❻ 〖…すら〗 (…でさえ) even (!; (…さえしない) not so much as. (⇨でも, -さえ) ▶彼女はお茶の 1 杯も出そうとしなかった She did*n't* *even* [*so much as*] offer me a cup of tea.

〘翻訳のこころ〙何年か前までは, 家族で避暑地に滞在する生活もあった (竹西寛子『蘭』) Until a few years ago, our family *even* enjoyed the luxury of staying in a summer resort. (!「-も」にあたる even は二つのものを比較して, 一つを強調するときに用いる. したがって, ここでは今の余裕のない生活に比べて豊かであった以前の生活を強調している)

❼ 〖…でも〗 even if [though]…; (…だけれども) though …, although …; (…にもかかわらず) in spite of …. ▶雨がやまなくても出発しなければならないだろう I will have to start, *even if* [*though*] it doesn't stop raining. ▶雪が降っていても外は寒くはなかった *Though* [*Although*] it was snowing, it wasn't cold outside.

モアイ a moai. (参考 南太平洋のイースター島などにある巨石顔画像)

‡もう ▣ ❶ 〖すでに〗 alréady; yet; (今ごろは) by now, by this time.

〘解説〙**already** は通例肯定文で用い, 一般動詞の前, be 動詞・助動詞の後, 文尾, 時に文頭に置く. **yet** は通例疑問文で用い, 文尾に置く. 両方とも現在の時点での状態について用いるため, 通例現在完了形, 時に現在時制で用いる. また未来の特定の時点についている場合はそれぞれ過去時制・未来形でも用いる.

▶もう暗くなった It's *already* dark. ▶もう宿題は終

った I have *already* finished [《米》I *already* finished] my homework. (❗《米》では本来現在完了形を用いる場合でもしばしば過去形が用いられる)/I have finished my homework *already*! (❗前の方より強意的) ▶彼らはそのことをもう知ってるの？ Do they know about it *yet*? ▶駅に着いたときにはもう電車は出ていた The train had (*already*) left [The train *already* left] when I arrived at the station. (❗過去完了形を用いる場合はそれだけで時間関係が明らかなため already は省略可) ▶彼はもう青森に着いてるだろう He will have reached Aomori *already* [(今ごろまでには) *by now*, *by this time*]. ▶あいにくもう遅すぎるんだよ It's too late (*now*), I'm afraid.

会話 「先に宿題をしなさい」「もうしました」"You must do your homework first of all." "I *already* háve." (❗強意的に短く答える場合は already を助動詞の前に置く)

会話 「あなたはもう今日の新聞を読みましたか」「はい読みました[いいえまだです]」"Have you read today's newspaper *yet*?" "Yes, I have [No, not yet/ No, I haven't]." (❗(1) 疑問文で Have you read today's newspaper *already*? のように already を文尾に用いると「そんなに早く読んだのですか」という話し手の驚き・意外さを表す. (2) Have you *already* read today's newspaper? のように already を文中に置くと, 話し手は相手が新聞を読んでいることは知っているが, それを確認する文となる)

❷ 【間もなく】soon, presently (❗後の方が堅い語); (ほどなく) before long; (じきに) shortly; (今は) now. ▶彼はもうすぐここに来るでしょう He will *soon* come here./He will come [be] here *soon* [*before long*, *shortly*]./*It will not be long before* he comes here. (❗(1) 時間の短さを強調する. (2) ... before he *will* come here. はまれ) ▶もう冬です It's winter *now*./Winter *has come*./Winter *is here* [*is now with us*]. ▶もう10時だよ It's *getting on* toward 《主に米》[*for* 《主に英》] ten o'clock. (❗be getting on toward ... は「...に近づきつつある」の意の口語的慣用表現) ▶もうそろそろおいとまいたします I must be leaving [going] *now*. (❗進行形にすることによって唐突感を柔らげる)/*Now* I really must go./I must say good-by *now*./*It is about time* (for me) *to go*. ▶もう大人なんだから大人らしくしなさい You're a man [a woman] *now*, act like one. ▶もう休暇は終わったのだから一生懸命勉強しなければならない *Now that* the vacation is over [Since the vacation is over *now*], you should study hard.

会話 「おいとましなくちゃなりません」「もうですか」"I must be off." "*So soon?*"

❸ 【さらに】(もっと) more; (程度・距離がそれ以上に[の])further; (もう一つの) another.

① 【もう～】 ▶もう何も言うことはない I have nothing *more* [*further*] to say. (❗後の方が堅い言い方) ▶二つのうちの一方は白でもう一方は黒だ Of the two, one is white and *the other* is black. (❗二者のうちの残りの一方は the other)

会話 「もう１杯お茶をいかがですか」「もう結構です」"Would you like *another* cup of tea?" "No *more*, thank you."

会話 「申し訳ありません, 締め切りを少し遅らせていただけませんか」「今でもう1週間遅れているのですよ. もうあとどのくらいで仕上るのですか」「後3日いただけたら満足のいくものにしてみせます」"I'm sorry to say, but could I ask you to extend the deadline for a little while?" "You're *already* one week behind. How much longer will it take you to finish the work?" "If you give me *another* three [three *more*, an *extra* three] days, I promise you a satisfactory job." (❗(1) three days more は《まれ》だが three days extra は可. (2) already は ❶ の意)

② 【もう一度】 ónce móre [agáin]; (再び) again. ▶もう一度彼女に会いたい I'd like to see her (*once*) *again* [*once more*]. ▶もう一度おっしゃってください Would you please say it *again*?/《米話》Can you run it [that] by me *again*?/I Bég your ⤴pardon? (❗(1) 後の方は相手の言葉が聞き取れなかったときの決まり文句. くだけた言い方では略して Bég your ⤴pardon?/Párdon (me)? ともいう.《主に米》では Excuse me?,《英》では Sorry? も用いる. (2) その他親しい間柄では What did you say?/How's that?/What? なども用いられる. (3) *Again.*/*Once more.* は例えば教師が発音の練習をしている学生に対していう言い方) / Could you *repeat* that, please? ▶さあもう一度泳ごう Come on, let's have *another* swim.

③ 【もう少し】 some [a few, a little] more.

解説 (1) some は可算名詞の複数形・不可算名詞, a few は可算名詞の複数形, a little は不可算名詞の前で用いる.
(2) 否定文・疑問文では some は通例 any となる.

▶もう少しで列車に乗り遅れるところだった I *nearly* [*almost*] missed the train. (❗nearly は「乗り遅れそうだった」こと, almost は「乗り遅れなかった」ことに意味の重点がある) ▶(かろうじて間に合った) I *barely* caught the train. ▶お湯がもう(少しで)沸騰するよ The water's *nearly* boiling. ▶(励まして)ほらもう少しだ We're almost there. (❗慣用表現)

会話 「もう少しスープを召し上がりますか」「ありがとう, もう十分いただきました」"Would you like *some* [*a little*,《まれ》any] *more* soup?" "I've had enough, thank you." (❗相手にものを勧める場合肯定の答えを期待するので通例 any ではなく some を用いる)

会話 「さておいとましなくちゃ」「まあもう少しいいでしょう」"I really must go now." "Oh please stay *a little* [*a bit*] *longer*."

会話 「ねえ, どうしてもそこがうまく弾けないの」「そうね, もう少しじゃない」"See, I just can't get that right." "Well, you *almost* got it."

④ 【もう...しない】 not ... any longer [《話》more], no longer;《書》no more.

解説 (1) **not ... any longer [more], no longer** は「以前はそうであったが, 今では(そしてこれからも)もう...しない」のように過去を顧みる場合と「これからもう二度と...しない」のように将来について述べる場合に用いる.
(2) **no more** を過去を顧みる場合に用いるのは古い用法.

▶彼はもうここには住んでいない He does*n*'*t* live here *any more* [*longer*]. (❗any more [longer] は通例文尾に)/He *no longer* lives here./He lives here *no longer*. (❗no longer は後の例のように通例動詞の前, または be 動詞・助動詞の後で用い, 文尾に置く言い方でまれ) ▶もう我慢ならん (非難, 苦痛などに対して)《話》I can't take it *any more*./(やめてくれ)《話》That dóes it! ▶彼女はもう二杯上歩けない She *can't* walk *any farther*《主に米》[*any further*《主に英》,《まれ》*any more*]. (❗距離を表す場合は farther, further を用いる方が普通)/She can walk *no farther*《主に米》[*no further*《主に英》]. (❗前の方より堅い表現) ▶もうこんなは

もう かげたことは真っ平だ I won't have *any more* [×*any longer*] of this nonsense.
会話「もう持ってられないよ」「じゃあ手を放せよ」"I can't hold this *much longer*." "Let go of it, then."
❹〖その他の表現〗▶もううるさいわね What a nuisance! ▶もうたくさんだ Oh, that's enough. (やめにしよう) Enough is enough. ▶(かくれんぼうで)もういいよ All hide.
会話「本当にすみません」「もういいんだよ」"I'm terribly sorry." "(Just) forget it." (❗感謝と聞き返しに対しても用いられる. just は強意語)
会話「雨になるだろうと思うよ」「もう, そんなこと言わないでよ」"I think it's going to rain." "*Oh*, don't say that."

もう 吽 ▶もうと鳴く (牛が) moo,《やや古》low;(雄牛が低い深い声で) bellow. ▶雄牛がもう鳴いている A bull *is bellowing*.

もう 毛 (割合・長さ・通貨などの単位) a *mo* (毫 ~);one-tenth of a *rin*. ▶日歩5厘4毛の利息で at 0.54 percent interest per day. ▶彼の打率は3割7分2厘5毛だった He hit [*batted*] .3725. (❗ point three seven two five と読む)

もう 蒙 (無知) ignorance.
—— 蒙を啓(ひら)く (啓蒙する) enlighten.

-もう -網 ▶鉄道網 a *network* of railroads; a railroad *system*. ▶通信網 a communications *network*. ▶ラジオ[テレビ]放送網 a radio [a TV] *network*. ▶情報網 an intelligence *network*.

もうあい 盲愛 图 blind love.
—— 盲愛する 動 love ... blindly; (猫かわいがりする) dote on [upon]《one's grandchildren》.

もうい 猛威 (大氾) rage, (激しさ) violence; (はびこり) rampancy. ▶あらしが夜通し猛威を振るった The storm *raged* [*was violent*] all night. ▶昨年インフルエンザが猛威を振るった Influenza *raged* [*was rampant*] last year.

もうう 猛雨 a torrential rain; a heavy rain.

もうか 猛火 raging fire [flames]. ▶猛火に包まれ[れている] be in *raging flames*; be in a *big fire*.

もうがっこう 盲学校 a school for the blind; a school for the visually impaired [handicapped]. (❗ a blind school ともいうが避けたほうがよい)

*****もうかる 儲かる** 《物が主語》(利益があがる) yield profits, be profitable;(採算が取れる) pay*;《人が主語》(利益を得る) make* a profit; (金をもうける) gain; (金をもうける) make money. ▶もうかる商売 a *profitable* [a *paying*] business. ▶その取り引きでかなりもうかった The deal *yielded* large [*big*] *profits*./The deal was very *profitable*. ▶この商売はもうからない This business *yields no profit*./This business *doesn't pay*./There is no *gain* in this business. ▶それで1万円もうかった I got ten thousand yen *for* it./I *made a profit of* [*gained*] ten thousand yen *on* it.▶(節約できた) It *saved* me 10,000 yen.

もうかん 毛管 a capillary (tube).
●毛管現象 a capillary phenomenon. ●毛管作用 a capillary action.

もうぎゅう 猛牛 a fierce [a savage] bull.

もうきん 猛禽 a bird of prey; a raptor.

もうけ 儲け 〖利益〗 (a) profit; gain(s) (❗しばしば複数形で); money; 〖利息〗 returns; 〖利ざや〗 a (profit) margin. (⇨利益 ❶) ▶丸もうけする make a clear *profit*《of》. ▶一もうけする(=一財産作る) make a *fortune*. ▶ぼろもうけ (⇨ぼろ儲け) ●金もうけ (⇨金儲け) ▶彼はその土地を売って大もうけした He made a large [a *huge*] *profit on* the land./He made a large *profit from* [*on*] the sale of the land./He made a large *profit from* selling the land. ▶品物を100ドルで買って110ドルで売れば10ドルのもうけになる If you buy an article for 100 dollars and sell it for 110 dollars, you make a *profit* of 10 dollars. ▶小さなホテルを経営するだけではもうけにならない There's no *profit* [*gain*] *in* running a small hotel only. ▶彼らのもうけは薄利多売によるものだった Their *profit* was based on low margin and high volume. ▶投資した金のもうけは非常に少なかった The *returns on* the money I invested were very low.
●儲け口 (金もうけになる仕事) a moneymaking job.
●儲け物 (⇨儲け物)

もうげき 猛撃 — 猛撃する 動 ▶猛撃を加える make [launch] an *assault* [a *violent attack*]《on the enemy》.

もうけもの 儲け物 〖思いがけない授かり物〗 a windfall; 〖天のたまもの〗 a godsend; 〖買い得品〗 a good buy [bargain].

*****もうける 設ける** ❶〖設立する〗(設置する) set*... up, establish (❗前の方が口語的に); (組織する) organize;(規則などを定める) lay*... down. ▶仙台に支店を設ける *set up* [*open*] a branch office in Sendai. ▶(大学が)歴史の講座を設ける *establish* [*create*] a history course. ▶委員会を設ける *organize* [*set up*] a committee. ▶厳しい規則を設ける lay down rigid rules. ▶基準を設ける *set* a standard.
❷〖用意する〗 prepare;(あらかじめ備える) provide. ▶子供用の席を設ける *prepare* [*provide*] seats for children. ▶酒席を設ける(=宴会を催す) give a feast.

*****もうける 儲ける** 〖利益をあげる〗 make* a profit《on, from》; profit《from》; 〖利益を得る〗 gain; 〖金もうけする〗 make money; 〖働いてかせぐ〗 earn (⇨利益❶). ▶家を売ってもうける make a *profit on* one's house [*from* selling one's house]. ▶戦争でもうける *benefit from* war. ▶彼は株で100万円もうけた He *made a profit of* a million yen on the stock market. ▶その会社はもうけている The company *is making money*. ▶飛行機で出張したら1日もうけた I *saved* a day when I went on a business trip by air.

もうけん 猛犬 a fierce [a ferocious] dog. ▶猛犬注意《掲示》 Beware of the *dog*!/(説明的に) This home is protected by an *attack dog*.

もうげん 妄言 violent [abusive] language.
●妄言多謝 Please forgive my unreasonable statement. (⇨暴言)

もうこ 猛虎 a fierce [a savage] tiger.

もうこ 蒙古 (⇨モンゴル)
●蒙古斑 a Mongolian spot.

もうこう 猛攻 — 猛攻する 動 make a violent attack《on》; attack《him》fiercely [violently].

もうこん 毛根 the root of a hair; a hair root.

もうさいかん 毛細管 (⇨❷ 毛管)

もうさいけっかん 毛細血管 a capillary (vessel).

もうし 孟子 〖古代中国の思想家〗 Mencius /ménʃiəs/.

もうしあげる 申し上げる 〖「言う」の謙譲語〗 say*, tell*, mention, state. ▶as I *mentioned* [*stated*] before. ▶下記の所へ転居いたしましたのでご通知申し上げます Allow me to inform you that we have moved to the following address.

もうしあわせ 申し合わせ (取り決め) (an) arrangement; (合意) (an) agreement; (承諾) consent.
●申し合わせにより by *arrangement*; by (mutual)

もうしあわせる *agreement* [*consent*]. ▶そのことについて彼と申し合わせができている[できた] We are in [came to an] *agreement* with him about it.
● 申し合わせ事項 an agreed(-upon) item.

もうしあわせる 申し合わせる arrange, make* an arrangement ((*with*)); agree ((*on*)). ● 申し合わせた(=定められた)時間に at the *appointed* time [*hour*]. ● まるで前もって申し合わせたように as if *arranged* [*agreed*] beforehand. ▶彼と利益の分配について[利益は等分しようと]申し合わせた I *arranged with* him *about* the division of profits [*to divide* profits equally, *for* an equal division of profits].

もうしいで 申し出で an offer. (⇨申し出)

もうしいれ 申し入れ 〖正式な訴え〗《書》representations (*to*+人, *about*+事); 〖提案〗a proposal (*for*; *to do*); 〖申し出〗an offer (*of*; *to do*); 〖要求〗a demand (*for*; *that* 節); (要請) a request (*for*; *that* 節). ▶私たちは新しい橋を建設してほしいと市長に強力な申し入れをした We made strong *representations* to the mayor to build a new bridge.

もうしいれる 申し入れる 〖要請する〗(当局に正式に)《書》make* representations (*to* the council *about* it); (要請する) request (him *to do*; *that* 節); 〖苦情・抗議をする〗complain (*to*+人, *about*+事). (⇨申し入れ)

もうしうける 申し受ける 〖「受ける」などの謙譲語〗receive (⇨受け取る❶); (請求する) charge. ▶送料は別途申し受けます We'll *ask* you *to pay* a delivery charge for it separately.

もうしおくり 申し送り — **申し送りする 動** (先方に言ってやる) send word ((*to*)); (命令・業務などを後任に伝える) hand (one's duties) *over* ((*to*))

もうしおくる 申し送る ▶その事件を彼に申し送る(=引き継ぐ) *hand* the case *over to* him.

もうしおくれる 申し遅れる ▶申し遅れましたが(=もっと早く言うべきでしたが) I should [ought to] have said earlier. ▶申し遅れましたが,宮田均と申します. カメラマンをやっております I *should have introduced myself first*. My name is Hitoshi Miyata. I'm a photographer.

もうしかねる 申し兼ねる 〖「言い兼ねる」の謙譲語〗▶誠に申しかねますがそれをしていただけないでしょうか Might I ask you *to do* it?/*Would it be too much to ask* you to do it? ▶彼の字がうまいとはとても申し兼ねる I *can't possibly say* that his handwriting is good. (**!** possibly は can't を強調する)

もうしきかせる 申し聞かせる 〖「言い聞かせる」の謙譲語〗▶息子に二度とそんなことをしないように申し聞かせておきます I'll *give* my son *a good talking-to* not to do that again.

もうしご 申し子 ▶神の申し子 a heavenly-sent *child*. ▶コンピュータ時代の申し子 a *child* of the computer age. ▶日本サッカーの申し子 a *product* of Japanese soccer. (**!** この場合通例 a child of … とはいわない)

もうしこし 申し越し (伝言) sénding wòrd; (手紙で) writing ((*to*)).

もうしこみ 申し込み ❶〖申し出〗an offer (*of*); (提案) a proposal (*for*); (要求) a request (*for*). ● 結婚の申し込みを受ける[受け入れる: 断わる] receive [accept; refuse] a *proposal* (of marriage) ((*from* him)). (⇨申し込む❶)

❷〖応募〗(an) application (*to*+人・団体, *for*+事). ● 会員の申し込み an *application for* membership; a membership *application*. ● 申し込みを受けつける[締め切る] accept [close] *applications*. ● 早めに[早速]申し込みをする make early [*immediate*] *application*. ▶その職に30人の申し込みがあった We have had [received] thirty *applications for* [×*to*] the post. ▶彼は空手部に入部の申し込みをした He made an *application to* the *karate* club for membership. (⇨申し込む❶) ▶見本はお申し込みあり次第お送りいたします The sample will be sent *on request* [*application*].

❸〖挑戦〗a challenge ((*to*)); 〖参加〗an entry ((*for*)). ● 試合の申し込みを受け入れる accept (*his*) *challenge* to a game. ▶マラソンレースの参加申し込みが200人あった There were two hundred *entries for* the marathon.

❹〖予約〗a reservation. ▶ホテルの予約申し込みをする make a hotel *reservation*; make a *reservation* at a hotel.

● 申込者 an applicant ((*for*)). ● 申込書 (fill out 《米》[in 《英》]) an application (form).

もうしこむ 申し込む ❶〖申し出る〗propose; (頼む) (やや堅) request, (やや følg) ask for … . ▶彼に借金を申し込む request a loan *from* [*of*, ×*to*] him. (×*request* him a loan は不可) ▶彼に結婚を申し込まれた He *proposed* (marriage) [*made a proposal*] *to* me. (**!** marriage は省くことが多い)/He *asked* me to marry him.

❷〖応募する〗apply (*to*+団体, *for*+事). (**!** 正式に申し込むこと) ▶あの会社に就職を申し込む apply for a job *with* that company; apply [*make an application*] *to* that company *for* a job. ▶就職希望者は人事課に申し込むこと Job seekers should *apply* at the personnel office.

❸〖挑戦する〗challenge; 〖試合に登録する〗enter ((*for*)). ▶私たちは彼らにバスケットボールの試合を申し込みました We *challenged* them *to* a basketball game [*to have a game of basketball*]. ▶100名の選手がマラソンレースに参加を申し込んでいます One hundred competitors *have entered for* the marathon.

❹〖予約する〗reserve, 《英》book. ▶ホテルに部屋の予約を申し込む *reserve* [*make reservations for, book*] a room at a hotel.

もうしそえる 申し添える 〖「言い添える」の謙譲語〗give a supplementary explanation; add. ▶以上ご参考までに申し添えておきます This, I've *added* for your information.

もうしたて 申し立て (陳述) a statement; (被告人の抗弁)〖法律〗a plea; (裁判所への)〖法律〗(file) a petition. ▶破産申し立て the *filing* of the bankruptcy petition.

もうしたてる 申し立てる (述べる) state; (抗弁する)〖法律〗plead*; (上告する)〖法律〗appeal. ▶証人は以前その男を見たと申し立てた The witness *stated* that she had seen the man before. ▶その判決に不服を申し立てるつもりだ I'll *appeal against* the sentence. ▶彼女はその決定に異議を申し立てた She *made* [*raised, voiced, lodged*] *an objection to* the decision.

会話 「被告人の申し立ては?」「私はここに無罪を申し立てます」"How do you *plead*?" "I am authorized to *plead* [*enter a plea of*] not guilty." (**!** 罪状を読み上げた後のやり取り)

もうしつける 申し付ける order. (⇨命令する) ▶私でお役に立つことがありましたら何なりとお申し付けください *Tell* me whatever I could do for you.

もうしつたえる 申し伝える tell. (⇨伝える)

もうしで 申し出 an offer (*of*; *to do*); 〖要求〗a request (*for*; *that* 節); 〖提案〗a proposal (*for*); 〖申し込み〗(an) application (*for*). ● 申し出をする make an *offer*. ▶援助の申し出を受け入れる[断わる]

accept [decline] an *offer of* help. ▶数カ国から援助の申し出があった We had *offers* of help from several countries.

もうしでる 申し出る offer; 〔提案する〕propose; 〔応募する〕apply (*to*＋団体, *for*＋事); 〔届け出る〕report《*to*》; 〔権利を主張する〕claim. ▶彼への援助を申し出る *offer to* help him. ▶計画を申し出る *propose* [*suggest*] a plan. ▶奨学金を申し出る *apply for* a scholarship. ▶警察に申し出る *report*《*it*》*to* the police. ▶だれもそれが自分のだと申し出なかった Nobody *claimed* it.

もうしのべる 申し述べる 〔「述べる」の謙譲語〕express. (⇒述べる)

もうしひらき 申し開き 图 〔説明〕(an) explanation; 〔自己弁護〕self-defense; 〔自己の正当化〕self-justification.
── **申し開きする** 動 explain; defend [justify] oneself. (⇒説明, 弁解)

もうしぶん 申し分 ●**申し分(の)ない** 〔よい, 適した〕good; 〔完璧な〕perfect; 〔理想的な〕ideal; 〔満足な〕satisfactory. ▶ピクニックには申し分ない日だ It's a *good* [a *perfect*, an *ideal*] day for a picnic./The weather is *all right for* a picnic. ▶彼はその地位に申し分ない人だ He is the most *suitable* man *for* the position. ▶彼女の演技はまったく申し分がない Her performance *is quite satisfactory* [《堅い》*leaves nothing to be desired*, 《完全な》*is perfect*, 《まったくすばらしい》《話》*is just splendid*]. ▶扱いは申し分なかった They treated us *remarkably well*.

もうします 申します speak*. (⇒申す, 言う)

もうじゃ 亡者 ❶〔死者〕a dead person; the dead ▶仏教では死者全員を指して用いる.
❷〔…に執念を燃やしている人〕●がりがり亡者 a very greedy 〔《主に米》grabby〕person. ●金の亡者 a money-grubbing freak, a money-grubber. ●権力の亡者 a person with an unquenchable thirst [an insatiable appetite] for power. (**!** 前の方は「抑えられない熱望」, 後の方は「いくら与えても満たすことのできない欲望」の意)

もうしゅう 妄執 ▶妄執にとらわれている be obsessed with [by] the *delusion*《*that* 節》.

もうしゅう 猛襲 ── **猛襲する** 動 make a fierce attack《on the enemy》.

もうじゅう 盲従 blind obedience.
── **盲従する** 動 ▶上役に盲従する *obey* one's boss *blindly* [《理屈抜きで》*without question*]. (⇒従う)

もうじゅう 猛獣 a fierce animal; a beast of prey; a predatory animal; 〔野獣〕a wild animal; 〔狩猟用の物〕big game 《**!** 象・ライオンなどを集合的にいう》. ▶猛獣狩りをする shoot *big game*.
●猛獣使い a trainer [a tamer] of wild animals.

もうしょ 猛暑 〔焼けつくような暑さ〕scorching [great, intense, fierce] heat. ▶猛暑続きを spell of *scorching weather*. ▶今日は猛暑だ It's *scorching hot* today. (**!** ここは scorching は誤同用法)

もうしょう 猛将 a valiant general [admiral]. (**!** general は陸軍大将, admiral は海軍大将を表す)

***もうしわけ 申し訳** 〔弁解〕an excuse《*for*》; 〔謝罪〕an apology; 〔正当化〕justification. ▶この大失災については申し訳が立たない I have no *excuse for* this blunder I made. (⇒言い訳) ▶これで申し訳が立つ Now I can *justify myself*.
●申し訳程度の 〔名ばかりの〕(全額が) nominal; 〔行為・事柄が〕token; 〔ごく小さい〕very small; 〔ほんの少しの〕only a little. ●申し訳程度の料金 a *nominal* fee. ●申し訳の昇給 a *token* [《わずかの》a *slight*] increase in salary. ▶それは図書館といって

も申し訳程度のものです《話》It's a *poor excuse for a library*. ▶息子は父の申し訳程度に私の手伝いをした My son helped me *only a little* [〔ほんの短時間〕*only for a short time*, 〔いいかげんに〕《only》*half-heartedly*].
●**申し訳ない** ▶遅くなって申し訳ありません *I'm sorry (that)* I'm late [*to be late, for being late*]. (**!** 《話》では that は通例省略する)《すみません》. ▶申し訳ございません, 鍵をなくしてしまいました *I'm sorry* I lost the key./I *apologize*《*to* you》*for* losing the key. ▶実に申し訳ないこと(＝間違い)をしてしまいました I have made an *inexcusable mistake*. ▶ご不便をかけ申し訳ございませんでした 《車内放送で》We *regret* [×*regretted*] any inconvenience caused. (**!** sorry または apologize といっていないことに注意)

もうしわたす 申し渡す 〔宣告する〕sentence; 〔命じる〕order; 〔告げる〕tell. (⇒言い渡す) ▶裁判官は彼に懲役5年を申し渡した The judge *sentenced* him to five years in prison.

もうしん 盲信 图 a blind belief《稀～s》.
── **盲信する** 動 believe ... blindly.

もうじん 盲人 a visually impaired [an unsighted] person ▶blind は個人を修飾する限定用法は避けられる; 《総称》the blind; 〔視覚障害者〕visually impaired [handicapped] people; people with visual impairment.
●盲人用信号機 a traffic signal for visually impaired people《やや書》the blind.

もうす 申す speak*. (⇒言う)

もうすこし 申少し some more. (⇒もう❸③)

もうせい 猛省 serious [grave] reflection [reconsideration]. ▶犯した過ちについて君の猛省を促したい 《やや書》I must urge you to *reflect on* your mistakes *seriously*.

もうせん 毛氈 a carpet; a rug.

もうぜん 猛然 ── **猛然と** 動 〔猛烈に〕fiercely; 〔激しく〕violently; 〔断固として〕resolutely /rézəlùːtli/; 〔勇敢に〕bravely; 〔必死で〕desperately. ▶犬が猛然と泥棒に襲いかかった The dog *fiercely* attacked the robber. ▶彼は猛然とその計画に反対した He *violently* [《強く》*strongly*] objected to the plan. ▶彼らは猛然と敵に立ち向かった They *bravely* stood up to the enemy.

もうせんごけ 毛氈苔 〔植物〕a sundew.

もうそう 妄想 〔間違った信念〕a delusion; 〔とんでもない空想〕a wild fancy. ●誇大妄想 *delusions* of grandeur [persecution]. (⇒誇大, 被害) ▶彼は自分が英雄だという妄想を抱いている He is *under the delusion that* he is a hero.
●妄想症 〔医学〕delusional insanity; paranoia.

もうだ 猛打 hard hitting. (⇒強打)
── **猛打する** 動 get a lot of hits. ●猛打賞試合 a three-hit game. ●K投手に猛打を浴びせる light up [pound] K with for a lot of hits.

もうたくとう 毛沢東 〔中国の政治家・思想家〕Mao Zedong /máu dzədúŋ/. (**!** Mao Tsetung /tsətúŋ/ ともつづる)

もうちょう 盲腸 〔解剖〕〔虫垂〕the (vermiform) appendix; the cecum,《英》caecum. ▶盲腸を取ってもらう have one's *appendix* removed [out]. ▶彼は盲腸の手術を受けた He was operated on for *appendicitis*. ▶あなたは盲腸かもしれません You might have *appendicitis*.
●盲腸炎 〔医学〕appendicitis /əpèndəsáitis/.

もうつい 猛追 ── **猛追する** 動 run [rush, dash] in hot pursuit《*of*》; chase《him》energetically.

もうでる 詣でる (⇒参拝する, 参る❸)

もうてん 盲点 〔気づかない弱点〕a blind spot. (**!** 「目

もうとう の網膜の盲点」の意もある）
- **盲点をつく** 税法の盲点をつく（＝つけ込む）take advantage of a *blind spot* [(抜け穴) *a loophole*] in the tax laws.

もうとう 毛頭 [少しも…でない] not (...) at all; not the léast...; no 《＋图》whatever. ▶そのことについては疑う気は少しもありません I *don't* doubt it *at all*./There is *no* doubt *whatever* about it./There's *not the least* doubt about it. (❗ not は is にはかからないので ×There isn't .... とは通例いわない) ▶あなたの生き方にとやかく言うつもりは毛頭ありません *Nothing is farther from* my *intention than* to meddle in your life.

もうどう 妄動 a rash behavior [conduct].
もうどうけん 盲導犬 《米》a seeing eye dog, 《英》a gúide dòg.
もうどく 猛毒 图 (a) very strong [(死に至らす) a deadly] poison.
― **猛毒の** 形 highly [violently] poisonous.
もうねん 妄念 (⇨妄執)
もうばく 猛爆 heavy bombardment. ▶その都市は猛爆を加えられた The city *was heavily bombarded*.
もうはんたい 猛反対 fierce [violent] opposition.
もうひつ 毛筆 a (writing) brush.
もうひとつ もう一つ 形 (さらに一つ) another, one more. (❗後の方は数を強調する) ▶リンゴをもう一つ食べる eat *another one more* apple.
[会話]「ケーキをもう一ついかが？」「もうけっこう」"(How about) *another* piece of cake?" "No more, thanks."
― **もう一つ** 副 ❶ [さらに一層] ▶父は母よりもう一つ厳しかった My father was *still* [*even*] stricter (with me) than my mother. (❗いずれも比較級を強める)
❷ [もう少しというところで] ▶彼の言葉にはもう一つ（＝ほんの少し）説得力がない His words are *a little bit* lacking in persuasive power./(十分に) His words are not persuasive *enough* [(あまり) not *very* persuasive].
[会話]「体の調子はいかがですか」「もう一つ（よくない）です」"How are you feeling?" "Not *very* [*too*] well./(万全とは言えない) Not my very best."

もうふ 毛布 a blanket. ▶電気毛布 an electric *blanket*. ▶毛布にくるまる be wrapped [wrap oneself up] in *a blanket*. ▶彼女は彼に毛布をかけてやった She put the *blanket* over him.

もうべんきょう 猛勉強 ― 猛勉強する 動 ●英語を猛勉強する *study* English *very hard*. (⇨がり勉, 勉強)
- 試験のために猛勉強する（＝詰め込み勉強をする）*cram* for the exam.

もうぼ 孟母 Mencius' mother.
- **孟母三遷の教え** 'Mencius' Mother changed houses three times for her son's education.'/(ことわざ) Change of pasture makes fat calves.

もうまい 蒙昧 图 ignorance.
― **蒙昧な** 形 ignorant; unenlightened.
もうまく 網膜 [解剖] a retina /rétənə/ (圈 ～s, retinae /-niː/)
- **網膜剥離** [医学] detachment of the retina.
- **網膜炎** [医学] retinitis.

もうもう ▶車がもうもうと砂埃をあげて走り去った The car passed by, raising *clouds of* dust. ▶その家からもうもうと煙が出ているのが見えた I could see *a lot of* [(柱状の) *a column of*] smoke rising from the house. ▶浴室は湯気がもうもうと満ちていた The bathroom *was densely filled with* steam. ▶その部屋はたばこの煙でもうもうとしていた The room *was thick with* [*was full of*] cigarette smoke.

もうもく 盲目 图 (目が見えないこと) blindness. ▶盲目になる go [become] *blind*. ▶彼は片目 [左の眼] が盲目だ He is *blind in* [《書》*of*] one eye [*in* the left eye, ×*of* the left eye]. (❗後の言い方のように具体的な場所をさすときは in のみ可) ▶恋は盲目《ことわざ》Love is *blind*.
― **盲目の, 盲目的な** 形 blind. ●盲目的な愛情 *blind love*.
― **盲目的に** 副 ▶盲目的にその教えを信じてはいけない Don't believe the doctrine *blindly* [*uncritically*].

もうら 網羅 ― 網羅的な 形 (包括的な) comprehensive; (余すところのない) exhaustive.
― **網羅する** 動 [含む] (中身の全体として) contain; (全体の一部として) include; [範囲が...にわたる] cover. ▶そのリストはその本の単語を全部網羅している The list *contains* [*covers*] all the words in that book. ▶彼の研究は英文学の全分野を網羅している His studies *cover* the whole field of English literature.

もうれつ 猛烈 ― 猛烈な 形 (激しい) violent; (激しい) fierce; [強烈な] intense; (強い) strong. ●猛烈なあらし a *violent* [a *fierce*] storm. ●猛烈な暑さ *violent* [*fierce*, *intense*] heat. ●猛烈な競争 *fierce* [*keen, severe*] competition. ●猛烈な反対 *fierce* [*strong*] opposition. ●猛烈な速度で at a *terrific* speed.
― **猛烈に** 副 violently; fiercely; intensely; [ひどく] terribly. ●猛烈に攻撃する make a *violent* [a *fierce*] attack [attack *on*]; attack (an enemy) *violently* [*fiercely*]. ●猛烈に働く work *very hard* (狂ったように);《話》*like mad*.
- **猛烈社員** a fiercely working employee; (仕事中毒者)《しばしば軽蔑的》a workaholic.

もうれんしゅう 猛練習 hard [(集中的な) intense, (厳しい) strict] training [practice, exercise].
もうろう ― **もうろうとした** (ぼんやりした) dim (-mm-)-; (不明瞭な) indistinct; (漠然とした) vague; (気が遠くなって) faint; (めまいがして) dizzy; (疲労・病気・打撃などで)《話》groggy; (病気のためにうわごとを言って) delirious. ●記憶がもうろうとしている have a *dim* [a *vague*] memory (*of*). ●暑さで意識がもうろうとする feel *faint* [*dizzy*] from the heat. ▶まだ頭がもうろうとしている（＝はっきりしない）My head is *not clear* yet./I'm feeling *groggy*. ▶彼は高熱で意識がもうろうとしている He is *delirious* with a high fever.

もうろく 图 ▶もうろくした老人 a *senile* old man; a *dotard*.
― **もうろくする[している]** 動 get [be] senile; fall into [be in] one's dotage. ▶彼はもうろくしてきた He's getting [going] *senile*.

もえあがる 燃え上がる burn* [flare] up;（急に）burst* into flames. ▶一陣の風に火は燃え上がった A gust of wind made the fire *burn* [*flare*] *up*.
もえうつる 燃え移る (火が) spread* (*to*) ▶「延焼」はthe spread of fire); (火がつく) catch* fire. ▶火はすぐに隣接する建物に燃え移った The fire soon *spread to* the adjoining buildings.
もえかす 燃え滓 cinders.
もえがら 燃え殻 (石炭や木の) a cinder (❗通例複数形で); (灰) ashes.
もえぎ 萌黄 (色) yellowish [light] green. ●萌黄のyellowish [light] green.
もえさかる 燃え盛る blaze; burn brightly and fiercely.
もえさし 燃えさし (木・石炭などの) (やや書) embers; (木の燃えさし)《書》brands. ●燃えさしの薪 a *half-burned* log.

もえたつ 燃え立つ (盛んに燃える) blaze; burn strongly and brightly; (感情あふれ立つ) blaze [burn furiously] 《*with* fighting spirit; *for* [*to* win] the championship》.

もえつきしょうこうぐん 燃え尽き症候群 〖医学〗 burn-out syndrome.

もえつきる 燃え尽きる (火などが) burn* (itself) out; (精力を使い果たす) use up all one's energies, (やや話) burn oneself out.

もえつく 燃え付く ▶この木はなかなか燃えつかない This wood won't *catch fire* [*kindle*] easily.

もえでる 萌え出る burst into leaf. ▶5月には木々の若葉が萌え出る In May all the trees *burst into leaf*.

もえひろがる 燃え広がる (火が) spread*. ▶火事は急速に燃え広がった The fire *spread* rapidly.

もえる 燃える ❶ [燃焼する] burn* (⇨焼く ❶); (明るく炎を上げて) blaze; (炎・煙を出さずに) glow. ●燃えやすい (=可燃性の)材料 inflammable [《米》 flammable] (↔nonflammable) material. (❗ inflammable is nonflammable と混同しやすいことから工業用語では通例 flammable が用いられる) ●燃えるような夕焼け a *fiery* [a *flaming*] sunset. ▶その家は燃えていた The house *was burning* [*on fire*, *in flames*]. ▶暖炉で火[石炭]が燃えている A fire *is burning* [The coal *is glowing*] in the fireplace. ▶木造家屋は燃えやすい Wooden houses *burn* [*catch fire*] easily. (❗ ×Wooden houses are easy to burn. とはいわない) ▶木が燃えると炎が出る When wood *burns*, it makes a flame [a blaze]. ▶私たちはキャンプファイヤーが燃えているのを見た We saw a campfire *blazing*. ▶山腹は真っ赤なモミジで燃えるようだ The hillside *glows* [*flames*] with red maples.
❷ [感情が高ぶる] ▶彼女は音楽に対して燃えるような情熱を持っていた She had a *burning* passion for music. ▶彼は怒り[野心]に燃えていた He *is burning with* anger [ambition]. (❗ 通例進行形で用いる) ▶彼は名声に燃えていた He *was burning for* fame [*to* win fame].

もえる 萌える bud; sprout. ●若草萌える春 in spring when young buds begin to *grow*.

モーグル (スキー競技) moguls, mogul skiing.

モーゲージ 〖抵当〗 a mortgage /mɔ́ːrɡidʒ/. ●モーゲージ証券 mortgage-backed securities 《略 MBS》. ●モーゲージローン a mortgage loan.

モーション (動作) a motion. ▶ピッチャー第1球のモーション振りかぶりました The pitcher winds up for the first pitch. (❗ スポーツの実況中継などでは一つ一つの動作を伝えるときは現在形で用いる)
●モーションをかける (働きかける) get to work on …; (女性にいい寄る) make a pass at 《her》.

モーセ 〖古代イスラエルの預言者・律法者〗 Moses /móuziz/.
●モーセの十戒 the Ten Commandments.

モーター a motor, (エンジン) an engine.
●モーターショウ 《米》 an auto show; 《英》 a motor show. ●モータードライブ 〖フィルムの高速巻き上げ装置〗 a motor drive. ●モーターバイク a motorcycle, 《話》 a motorbike. ●モータープール (駐車場) 《米》 a parking lot; 《英》 a car park. (❗ motor pool は軍隊・官庁の「配車用自動車の集まり」の意) ●モーターボート a motorboat, (高速モーターボート) a speedboat.

モータリゼーション 〖車社会化〗 motorization /mòutaraizéiʃən/.

モーツァルト 〖オーストリアの作曲家〗 Mozart /móutsɑːrt/ 《Wolfgang Amadeus ~》.

モーテル 〖自動車旅行者用の簡易ホテル〗 a motel /moutél/.

モード 〖流行の型〗 a mode.

モーニング ❶ [朝] (a) morning.
❷ [服] a morning dress. (❗ morning coat (上着) としものズボンとシルクハットの一式 (⇨モーニングコート))
●モーニングカップ a cóffee mùg; 《和製語》 a morning cup. ●モーニングコール (⇨モーニングコール) ●モーニングセット breakfast special; 《和製語》 a morning set. (⇨モーニングサービス)

モーニングコート (燕尾服) a mórning còat (❗ a mourning coat は「喪服」), tails (❗ 複数形で), a tailcoat, a cutaway; (男性の礼装) a mórning drèss.

モーニングコール 《make [give]》 a wake-up [《英》 an early morning] call; 《和製語》 a morning call. ▶モーニングコールをご希望でしょうか Do you want a *call* in the morning? ▶6時にモーニングコールをお願いします Will you give me a *wake-up call* at six?/Could you *wake me up* at six?

モーニングサービス breakfast special. (❗ morning service は「朝の礼拝」の意) ●モーニングサービスを食べる have the *breakfast special*.

モービルハウス 〖トレーラー型の移動住宅〗 a mobile house.

モービルホーム 〖トレーラー型の移動住宅〗 a mobile home.

モーリシャス Mauritius; (公式名) the Republic of Mauritius. (首都 Port Louis) ●モーリシャス人 a Mauritian. ●モーリシャス(人)の Mauritian.

モーリタニア Mauritania; (公式名) the Islamic Republic of Mauritania. (首都 Nouakchott) ●モーリタニア人 a Mauritanian. ●モーリタニア(人)の Mauritanian.

モール 〖ショッピングセンター, 散歩道〗 a mall. ●ショッピングモール a shópping màll.

モールス ●モールス符号 Morse (code). ●モールス符号による通信 a message *in Morse (code)*.

もがく struggle; (苦痛のために) writhe /ráið/. ●もがき struggle to one's feet. ●自由になろうともがく struggle to get free. ▶絶望の谷間でもがき苦しむことは終わりにしようではありませんか Let us not *wallow* in the valley of despair.

もがりぶえ 虎落笛 the whistle of a cold north wind.

もぎ 模擬 ●模擬裁判 a mock trial; 〖法律〗 (法学生の) a moot court. ●模擬試験 (⇨模試) ●模擬店 (パーティーなどの) a buffet; (大学祭などの) a stall; (屋台) a booth; (売店) a stand. ▶ホットドッグの模擬店 a hot dog *stand*.

もぎとる もぎ取る 〖折り取る〗 break* … off; 〖引きちぎる〗 tear*; 〖ねじり取る〗 wrench; 〖果物を〗 pick. ●彼の手からナイフをもぎ取る *wrench* the knife *from* [*out of*] his hand.

もぎり a ticket colléctor [tàker].

もく 目 〖囲碁〗 (石) a piece, a stone; (盤の目) a point. ●3目勝つ[負ける] win [lose] by *three points*.

もぐ pick; (むしり取る) pluck. ▶ブドウを1房もぐ *pick* a bunch of grapes. ▶もぎたてのリンゴ an apple (*picked*) right *off* the tree; a freshly *picked* apple.

もくあみ 木阿弥 元の木阿弥 (⇨元 [成句])

もくぎょ 木魚 《strike》 a wooden drum (in a Buddhist temple).

もくげき 目撃 ── 目撃する 動 ●事故を目撃する (見る)

see an accident (*with* one's *own eyes*); (まのあたりに見る) (やや書) *witness* an accident. ▶私は男が窓をこじ開けようとしているのを目撃した I *saw* a man *trying to force the window open*.
- **目撃者** a *witness* (*to*). ● **目撃者の話** an *eyewitness account* (*of*).

もぐさ moxa /ˈmɒksə/.

もくざい 木材 wood; (建築用の) (主に米) *lumber*; (英) *timber*. (⇨木材)

もくさつ 黙殺 ── 黙殺する 動 ● 彼の提案を黙殺する (=無視する) *ignore* [*take no notice of*] his proposal.

もくさん 目算 (おおよその見積もり) a *rough estimate*; (見込み) an *expectation*. (!しばしば複数形で) ▶目算を立てる *make a rough estimate* (*of*). ▶それについては私の目算が狂った It didn't come up to my *expectations*./I (*badly*) *miscalculated* it.

もくし 黙視 ── 黙視する 動 (見て見ぬふりをする) *shut* [*close*] *one's eyes* (*to*); (傍観する) *look on* (*at*).

もくじ 目次 a *table of contents*. (!本の目次見出しとしては Contents が普通)

もくしつ 木質 ── 木質の 形 *woody*;〖植物〗*ligneous*. ── **木質化する 動** *lignify*.
- **木質繊維** *wood fiber*. ● **木質部** *xylem* /ˈzaɪləm/.

もくじゅう 黙従 名 *blind obedience*; *acquiescence*.
── **黙従する 動** *obey blindly*; (書) *acquiesce* /ˌækwiˈɛs/ (*in*).

もくしろく 黙示録 〖聖書〗the *Revelations*; the *Apocalypse*.

もくず 藻屑 (海藻) (a) *seaweed*. ● 海の藻屑と消える *be drowned at sea*; *be killed in a naval battle*.

もくする 目する (みなす) *regard*; (認める) *recognize*.

もくせい 木星 〖天文〗*Jupiter*. ● **木星の** *Jovian*.

もくせい 木犀 〖植物〗a *sweet-scented olive*; *devilwood*. ● **キンモクセイ** a *sweet-scented orange-colored olive*. ● **ギンモクセイ** a *sweet-scented white olive*.

もくせい 木製 ● 木製のテーブル a *wooden table*; a *table made of wood*. (⇨木造)

もくぜん 目前 ❶ 【場所】▶事故は我々の目前で起こった The accident happened *right before our eyes*.
❷ 【時間】▶目前の(差し迫った)*imminent* (!通例不快なことに用いる); (やや書) *impending*. (!通例限定的に用いる) ▶目前の危機 *imminent* [*impending*] *danger*. ● 目前の(=当面の)利益 *immediate advantage*. ▶試験は目前に控えて(=間近にして)必死に勉強する *study earnestly* [*very hard*, *desperately*] *with the exam close at hand*. (!desperately には「だめだと思いながらも」のマイナスイメージがある) ▶選挙が目前に迫っている The election will be held *very soon* [(やや書) is (*close*) *at hand*]. ▶彼女は結婚を目前に控えている She *is about to be married*.

もくぜん 黙然 ● 黙然と *silently*; *in silence*.

もくそう 黙想 *meditation*. (⇨瞑想) ● 黙想にふける *be lost in meditation* [*contemplation*].

もくぞう 木造 (木製の) *wooden*. ● **木造の家** a *wooden house*; (特に板張りの) (米) a *frame house*. ▶私の家は木造です My house *is made* [*is built*] *of wood*. (! wooden は補語に用いないので ×My house is wooden. としない)

もくぞう 木像 (立像) a *wooden statue* [(彫像) *image*, (偶像) *idol*].

もくそく 目測 名 *measure by* (the) *eye*. ▶とぶ川の幅の目測を誤る *misjudge the width of a ditch*. ▶フライの目測を誤る *misjudge a fly ball*.
── **目測する 動** ▶その距離を目測する *measure the distance by* (*the*) *eye*.

もくだく 黙諾 ── 黙諾する 動 *give* (*one's*) *tacit consent* (*to*).

もくたん 木炭 *charcoal*.
- **木炭画** a *charcoal* (*drawing*).

もくちょう 木彫 *woodcarving*; *wooden sculpture*.
- **木彫像** a *wooden sculpture*.

もくてき 目的 (a) *purpose* /ˈpɜːrpəs/ (*of*, *in*); an *aim*; an *end*; an *object* (*of*); an *objective*; a *goal*.

> 使い分け **purpose** 「目的」の意を表す最も一般的な語。目的が達成されるまでの過程が重要視される。
> **aim** 広く「目的」を表す。purpose と交換可能な場合も多いが、より具体的で明確な目的であることを含意する。
> **end** 最終的な目的を表す堅い語。目的に至る過程より目的が達成されるか否かに焦点が当てられることを含意する。
> **object** 主に行為や計画などの直接的な目的を表す。時に個人的な目的であることを含意する。
> **objective** 堅い語で、政治やビジネスなどに関連した目的を表す。時に遠からず達成が可能であることを含意する。
> **goal** 最終的、また長期的な目的を表す。達成に苦労を要するが達成後はそれが大きく報われること含意する。

①【〜目的、目的〜】▶最終目的 the final *purpose*. ▶研究目的 the *aim of* study. ▶究極[本来]の目的 the *ultimate* [*primary*] *purpose* [*aim*, *object*]. ▶目的意識がない *have no sense of purpose*.

②【目的は】▶彼の目的は湯川博士のような偉大な物理学者になることだった His *purpose* [*aim*, *objective*, *goal*] *was to be a great physicist like Dr. Yukawa*. ▶人生の目的は何か? What is the *purpose of life*? (!What is life for? より普通)

③【目的の】▶目的のない人生 *life without aim* [*purpose*] (!無冠詞); *life with no object*; an *aimless* [(書) a *purposeless*] *life*. ▶彼は目的のためには手段を選ばない He *would use any means* [*何でもやる*] *do anything*] *to achieve his end*.

④【目的に[を]】▶目的にかなう *answer* [(書) *serve*] *one's purpose*. ▶目的を果たす[達する] *achieve one's purpose* [*aim*, *object*, *objective*]. (!achieve の代わりに (書) *attain* も可) ▶彼は人生に確固たる目的を持っていた He *had a definite purpose* [*aim*, *object*, *goal*] *in life*.

⑤【目的で】▶彼はそれを買う目的で(=買うために)そこへ行った He *went there* (*in order*) *to buy it*. (!(1) 次例より口語的。(2) 書き言葉以外では通例省略される)/He *went there for the purpose of* [*with the aim of*, (意図) *with the intention of*, (書) *with a view to*] *buying it*. ▶彼は商売の目的でアメリカへ立った He *left for America for business purposes*./*Business took him to America*.

- **目的格**〖文法〗the *objective case*. ● **目的語**〖文法〗an *object* (*word*). ● **目的税** an *object tax*. ● **目的物** the *object*. ● **目的論**〖哲学〗*teleology*.

もくてきち 目的地 *one's destination*. ● 目的地に着く *reach* [*arrive at*] *one's destination*.

もくとう 黙祷 a *silent prayer*. ▶1分間の黙祷を捧げる *offer a one-minute silent prayer* (*for*); *offer a minute of* (×a) *silent prayer* (*for*). ▶1分間黙祷を捧げよう Let us observe a minute's *silence* for the victims.
── **黙祷する 動** *pray in silence* [*silently*].

もくどく 黙読 图 silent reading.
　― **黙読する** 動 read (it) silently [to oneself].

***もくにん 黙認** 图 tacit admission [permission].
　― **黙認する** 動 admit [(許す) permit] 《it》 tacitly; (罪・誤りなどを大目に見る) overlook; pass ... over 《!》 いずれも時に無意図的》; (寛大に扱う) tolerate.

もくねじ 木ねじ a wood screw.

もくぜん 黙然《もくねん》 (⇨黙然(もくねん))

もくば 木馬 a wooden horse; (小児用の) a rócking hòrse.
　● 回転木馬 a merry-go-round;《米》a carousel;《英》a roundabout.

もくはん 木版 (版木) a wooden block; (術) woodblock printing.
　● 木版画 a woodcut; a wood engraving; a wood-block print.

もくひ 黙秘 图 ● 黙秘権を行使する exercise the right to *silence*; 《米話》take the Fifth (Amendment). 《! 後の方の句は『米国憲法修正第5条により自分に不利な証言を拒否し黙秘権を行使する』の意》
　― **黙秘する** 動 ● その件について黙秘する keep [remain] *silent* about it;《法律》stand mute about it.

*:**もくひょう 目標** a goal; (目的) an object; (達成可能で大きな) an objective; (ねらい) an aim (⇨目的); (達成目標,標的) a target; (訪問者の目印) a landmark.
① 〖〜(の)目標〗 ● 人生の目標 one's *aim* [*object, purpose*] in life. ● 長期[中期;当面]の目標 a long-term [a medium-term; a near-term] *target*. ● 生産[販売]目標 a production [a sáles] tàrget. ● 数値目標 a numerical *target*. ● 最終目標 an end *goal*; an ultimate *target*.
② 〖〖目標を〗〗 ● 目標を設定する set [establish] a goal [a target]. ● 目標を高く[低く]設定する set one's *goal* [*target*] high [low]. ● 目標を達成する achieve one's *goal* [*objective, aim*]. 《! achieve の代わりに《書》attain も可》● 目標を越える exceed [surpass] one's *goal* [*target*]. ● 私たちの部署は5年連続で売り上げ目標を達成した Our division reached its sales *target* for the fifth straight year.
③ 〖目標〖は〗に〗 ▶ 敵の目標は我が国の軍事基地だった The enemy's *target* was our military bases. ▶ 1か月1万円貯金することを目標にした I've set a *goal* to save [a *target* of *saving*] 10,000 yen a month. ▶ 寄付金は200万円の目標(額)に達しなかった Contributions did not reach the *target* of [come up to the *targeted*] two million yen. ▶ 近くに何か目標になるものがありますか Is there any *landmark* near there?
　● 目標管理 management by objective(s)《略 MBO》. ● 目標圏 a target range. ● 目標設定 goal setting.

もくぶ 木部 (木質部) xylem.

もくへん 木片 (大きな) a block (of wood); (小さな) a chip [a piece] of wood; a wood chip; (極小の) a (wood) splinter.

もくめ 木目 the grain. 《!「板目,柾目(まさめ)」は the cross [straight] grain.》● 木目が細かい[粗い] have fine [coarse] *grain*. ● 木目にそって in the direction of *the grain*.

もくもく ● もくもくと立ちのぼる夏の雲 *massively* rising summer clouds. ● もくもくと立つ砂あらし rising *columns* of *sandstorm*. ● 工場の煙突から煙がもくもくと出ていた *Volumes* of *smoke* were pouring from the factory chimneys./The factory chimneys *were belching* (*out*) smoke.

もくもく 黙々 (黙って) silently, in silence. ● もくもくと山を登る climb a mountain *silently*. ● もくもく(=話もせずに)食べる eat *without conversation*. ▶ 彼はもくもくと働いている(=仕事に熱中している) He *is absorbed in* his work.

もぐもぐ ● もぐもぐ食べる munch. ● もぐもぐ(不明瞭に) 何か言う mumble. ▶ 馬がもぐもぐ草を食べているのを見た I saw a horse *munching* grass. ● もぐもぐ言わず にはっきり言いたい事を言いなさい Don't *mumble* and speak up what's on [in] your mind 《! on では「気になっていること」,in では「考えていること」の意》.

もくやく 黙約 a tacit agreement [understanding]; an implicit promise 《*with, between*》.

*:**もくよう(び) 木曜(日)** Thursday (略 Th., Thur(s).). (⇨日曜(日))

もくよく 沐浴 图 purification of oneself.
　― **沐浴する** 動 wash oneself; perform one's ablutions; (斎戒(さいかい)沐浴する) purify oneself.

もぐら 〖動物〗 a mole.
　● モグラ叩き《play》whack the mole. 《! 比喩的な意味でも用いられる》● モグラ塚 a molehill.

もぐり 潜り 图 diving.
　― **もぐりの** 圈 (無資格の) unqualified; (無免許の) unlicensed. ● もぐりの医者 an *unqualified* [*unlicensed*] doctor. ● もぐりで(=無許可で) without a license.

もぐりこむ 潜り込む ● ベッドに潜り込む get [climb] *into* bed. ● 「ふとんに潜り込む」は get 《×climb》*into* one's *futon*. ● 敵陣に潜り込む(=潜入する) *infiltrate* (*into*) [*slip into, sneak into*] an enemy camp. ● infiltrate は主に軍事・政治用語》.

*:**もぐる 潜る** ❶ 〖水中に〗 dive*, make* a dive 《*in, into*》. ● 潜りに行く go (skin-)diving. ● アワビを採るため海に約6メートルの深さまで潜る *dive for* abalones *to* a depth of some 20 feet [6 meters]. ▶ 彼は水中に潜った He *dived into* [*in*] the water./He *went down under* the water. ● He *disappeared under* the water. (水中に姿を消した)とすると文脈によっては「おぼれた」とも受け取られる》● 彼は3分間水に潜っていた He *was* [*stayed, remained*] *under* the water for three minutes.

❷ 〖中や下に入り込む〗 get* 《*into*》; (はって) creep* [crawl*] 《*into, under*》; (穴を掘って[掘るように]) burrow (oneself) 《*into, under*》. ● ベッドに潜る *get into* bed. ● 床下に潜る *crawl under* the floor. ● 地中深く潜る *burrow* deeply *into* [*through*] the ground.

❸ 〖当局などから逃れて潜伏する〗 ● 地下に潜る go underground.

もくれい 目礼 a nod. ● 彼に目礼をする *nod to* him; greet him with a nod [with one's eyes]. ● 彼女と目礼を交わす exchange *nods* with her.

もくれい 黙礼 ― **黙礼する** 動 bow 《*to*》 (in silence). 《! 特に無言を強調するときに in silence を添える》.

もくれん 木蓮 〖植物〗 a magnolia.

もくろう 木蝋 vegetable wax; Japan wax.

もくろく 目録 (一覧表) a list; (体系的な) a catalog 《! list より完全でないが検索機能を伴う》. 《英》では catalogue ともつづる》. (⇨リスト) ● 図書[蔵書]目録 a library *catalog*. ● 著者目録 an author *catalog*. ● 目録に載っている be (put) on [in] a *list* [*catalog*]. ● 目録を作る make a *list* [a *catalog*] 《*of*》.

もくろみ (計画) a plan; (たくらみ) a scheme /skiːm/, a design; (陰謀) a plot (⇨計画), an intention. (⇨意図) ▶ 研究はもくろみどおり(=計画どおり)に進んでいる The study is going (on) *as planned*. (⇨計画 ❷ 〖第3文例〗) ● もくろみが外れた My plan

もくろむ (計画する) plan (-nn-); (陰謀を) plot (-tt-); (空想的な計画, 悪だくみ) scheme /skíːm/, design; (いたずらなどを)《話》be up to …; (意図する) intend;〚ひそかに心に抱く〛have*… in mind. 脱税をもくろむ scheme [plan] to evade taxes; scheme [plan] tax evasion. ▶彼らが何をもくろんでいるのか知らない I don't know what they are up to.

*__もけい 模型__ a model; (小型模型) a miniature /mínətʃər/. 縮尺模型 a scale model. 実物大模型 a full-[a life-]size model; a mock-up. ●船の模型を作る make a model of a ship.
●模型地図 a relief map. ●模型飛行機 a model (air)plane.

もげる (取れる) come* off.

もこ 模糊 曖昧模糊とした dim; vague. (⇒曖昧[成句])

もこく 模刻 模刻した作品 an imitation; a reproduction.

もこもこ ▶もこもこした子犬 a fluffy little dog.

もごもご (もごもご言う) mumble; (もごもご食べる) munch; (うごめく) squirm. (⇒もぐもぐ)

もさ 猛者 (腕っぷしの強い男) a tough guy (選手player).

モザイク〚技法〛mosaic /mouzéiik/;〚絵, 模様〛a mosaic.
●モザイク細工 mosaic work. ●モザイク病〚植物〛mosaic disease.

もさく 模作 an imitation 《of》.

もさく 模索 模索する 動 grope 《for an answer》. (⇒暗中模索)

もさっと ▶もさっとしている〚風采の上がらない〛unimpressive; unattractive;〚気のきかない〛lumpish; clumsy.

もさもさ ❶〚動作が鈍いさま〛▶もさもさするな Don't dawdle./Be quick about it.
❷〚茂って見苦しいさま〛(⇒ぼうぼう❷)

モザンビーク〚国名〛Mozambique; (公式名) the Republic of Mozambique. (首都 Maputo) ●モザンビーク人 a Mozambican. ーモザンビーク(人)の Mozambican.

:**もし if.** ❶〚現在・未来について不確実なことを表す〛▶もしあす雨なら行かない If it rains [×will rain] tomorrow, I'll not go out. (❗単に条件を述べるだけなので仮定法は用いない(⇒解説 Ⅱ))▶もし3時までにその手紙を書き終えたら私が出してあげましょう If you have [×will have] finished writing the letter by three o'clock, I'll mail it. ▶もし自由時間があればそこへ行くつもりです If I have any [some] free time, I'm going to go there. (❗some は自由時間があると予想していることを暗示)▶もしストがなければあす帰ります I'll be back tomorrow unless there's [if there's not] a strike. (❗unless は「…でない限り」という除外の意を含み if ... not より強意的)▶あなたは会議に出るんですか, もしそうなら[もしそうでないなら]私は出ません Are you going to go to the meeting? If so [not], I won't.

> **解説** Ⅰ (1) if 節は未来を表す場合でも未来時制は用いないが, 主語の意志を表す場合 will, would を用いる: もしそうしてくだされば大変ありがたいのですが If you will [would] do so, I would be much obliged. (❗would の方が丁寧な感じを伴う)
> (2) if 節が主節の行為の結果についていうときは will が可: もしきみが喜ぶならここにいることにするよ If it will make you happier (as a result), I'll stay here.

❷〚現在の事実に反する仮定を表す〛(❗if 節は過去形, 主節は通例助動詞の過去形＋動詞の原形)▶もし十分な金があればその車を買えるのだが If I had enough money, I could buy the car. ▶もし彼がここにいれば援助してやれるのに If he was [《やや書》If he were,《書》Were he, ×Was he] here, I would help him. (❗仮定法では be 動詞は通例 were を用いるが主語が単数の場合は日常会話では was の方が普通. ただし次例のような慣用的な言い方では were を用いる) ▶もし私があなたならそんなことはしないだろう If I were [《話》was] you, I wouldn't do that. ▶もし忠告の表現で直接 Don't do that. というより丁寧でなければいっしょのですが If I was not [×Unless I was] busy, I'd come [×go] with you. (❗unless は仮定や想像上のことには通例不可) ▶もし空気がなければ我々は生きてゆくことができないだろう If it were not for [Without,《書・古》But for,《書》Were it not for, If there were no, ×Weren't it for] air, we could not live.

> **解説** Ⅱ 直説法現在と仮定法過去: 直説法現在と仮定法過去はともに現在または未来のことについて用いるが, その内容に関する話し手の確信度に差がある: If it is [was, were] true, I should know it. (もしそれが本当だとしたら知っておくべきだが)の後の方ほど「本当だ」という話し手の確信度は低くなる.

❸〚過去の事実に反する仮定を表す〛(❗if 節は過去完了形, 主節は通例助動詞の過去形＋動詞の原形) ▶もし君がもっと一生懸命勉強していたら試験に合格したであろう If you had studied [《書》Had you studied] harder, you would have passed the exam. ▶もし君の助けがなかったら成功できなかっただろう If it had not been for [Without,《書・古》But for,《書》Had it not been for, ×Hadn't it been for] your help, I could not have succeeded. ▶もしその電車に間に合っていたら今ごろはそこで待っているところでしょう If I had caught the train, I would [should] now be waiting there. (❗主節は現在時に言及しているので「助動詞の過去形＋動詞の原形」となっていることに注意) ▶もしあなたが来ると知っていたら家にいたのに If I had known [《話》I'd have known] you came over [were coming], I'd have stayed (at) home. (❗この述語動詞は仮定法でも, 中に組み込まれた節では直説法を用いることに注意)

❹〚未来について実現性の乏しい仮定を表す〛(❗if 節には should, または were to を用いる. should は実現可能なことを, were to は実現可能なことから不可能なことまでを表す) ▶もしトムに出会ったら電話するように伝えてください If you should [《書》Should you] run into Tom, tell him to call me up. (❗堅い言い方で特に可能性の低さを強調するとき以外は単に If you run into Tom, ... と❶の形式を用いる方が普通) ▶もし私が死ねば家族はどうなるだろう If I were to [《書》Were I to] die, what would become of my family? (❗if 節に were to を用いた場合は主節には過去形の助動詞を用いる)

> **解説** Ⅲ 「もし…ならば」の意味は if 以外に suppose [supposing] (that), provided [providing] (that), on condition that, in case by よっても表現できる. ただし微妙な意味の違いがある. **suppose, supposing** は「もし…だとしたらどうしますか」という what if? の意を含んでいるため主節はしばしば省略される: もし彼が来ないとしたらどうしよう Suppose [Supposing] he doesn't come (, what shall I do)?/もしライオンがおりから逃げたらどうなるだろう Suppose [Supposing] a lion should [were to] break out of the cage (, what would happen)?

provided, providing, on condition that は強い限定的な条件を表す. provided の方が一般的に: もし面倒なことさえなければここにいてもよろしい You can stay here *provided* [*providing, on condition that*, (...さえすれば) *as long as*] you cause no trouble.
in case は《米》では if と同様に用いることもあるが, 通例主節の後で「...の場合に備えて」という意で用いられる: もし雨が降るといけないから傘を持って行きなさい Take an umbrella with you, (just) *in case* it rains [*should rain*]. (⇨場合)

もし 模試 〖「模擬試験」の略〗a mock [a practice] exam 〖〖書〗 examination. (⇨試験)

****もじ** 文字 〖〖アルファベットの〗〗a letter; 〖〖漢字などの〗〗a character. (⇨字) ▶ギリシャ文字 Greek *letters*. ●小文字で書く write in a small (↔a capital) *letter*. ●small letter は「小文字」の意(「小さな文字」の意にもなる) ●女文字(=女の筆跡)の手紙 a letter (written) in a (delicate) female hand. ●金文字入りの本 a book *lettered* in gold. ●(時計などの)文字盤 a dial. ▶その子は英語のアルファベットの 26 文字が全部書ける The child can write all the 26 *letters* of the English alphabet. ▶この絵は文字がないころに描かれた This picture was drawn when there were no *letters*. ▶私は彼の言葉を文字どおりに受け取った I took what he said *literally* [in a *literal* sense]. ▶文字は人なり Your *handwriting* shows your character [personality]. ●文字言語 written language. ●文字多重放送 a teletext. ●文字化け 〖〖コンピュータ〗〗garbling; (文字) garbled [〖書〗(おかしな)funny] characters.

もしか(したら) perhaps, maybe. (⇨多分)
もしかして ▶もしかしてあなたは山田さんですか Are you Mr. Yamada, *by any chance*? (❗by any chance を文中のどこに置くかは補語の長さによる: Are you *by any chance* a member of the city redevelopment committee?)/Well, *if* it isn't Mr. Yamada!

もしかすると (ひょっとすると) possibly (❗perhaps, maybe は可能性は低い); (おそらく) perhaps, maybe. (⇨~かもしれない) ▶もしかすると彼はそれを知っているかもしれない *Possibly* he knows it./He *may possibly* know it. (❗may とともに用いると確率はさらに低くなる)/He *might* know it.

もしき 模式 ●模式図 a relief map.
もしくは or; either ... or .... (⇨または)
もじづら 文字面 the appearance of written words. (⇨字面(じづら))
もしも if. (⇨もし)

****もしもし** ❶〖〖電話で〗〗hello. (❗上昇調で発音)
[会話]「もしもし」「はい, 田中さんのお宅でしょうか」「はい, そうですが, どちら様でしょうか」「阿部でございます」"*Hello*." "*Hello*. Is this 〖〖英〗〗that〗 the Tanaka's (house)?" "Yes, it is. Who's speaking, please?" "This is Mrs. Abe."
❷〖〖呼びかけ〗〗 excuse me; 《米》say, 《英》I say. ▶もしもし, 何か落としましたよ *Excuse me* [*Say*], ma'am. You've dropped something.

もじもじ ── もじもじと 副 hesitantly; (恥ずかしそうに) shyly; (落ち着かなさそうに) uneasily.
── もじもじする 動 (ためらう) hesitate. ▶その男の子は入るかどうか決めかねてもじもじしていた The boy *hesitated* as he couldn't decide whether to come in or not. ▶彼女は彼と初めて出会ったとき, もじもじしてしゃべれなかった When she first met him, she was too *shy* to speak.

もしや if. (⇨もし, もしかすると)
もしゃ 模写 (写し取ること) copying; (模倣) mimicry; (写し) a copy; (複製) a reproduction. ●絵の模写 a *copy* of a picture. ●声帯模写 vocal *mimicry*.
── 模写する 動 ●北斎の絵を模写する *copy* a picture by Hokusai.

もじゃもじゃ ▶彼のまゆ毛はもじゃもじゃしている He has *bushy* [*shaggy*] eyebrows. ▶彼女はもじゃもじゃの毛深い男が嫌いです She hates *thickly-haired* men. ▶何かびんの中でもじゃもじゃ動いている There is something *swarming* in the bottle.

もしゅ 喪主 the chief mourner. ●chief mourners とすると主だった会葬者, つまり最も近い身内の人たちをさす)

モジュール 〖〖建築・コンピュータ〗〗 a module. ●モジュール化 modularization. ●モジュール式家屋 a *modular house*.

モジュラージャック (電話線の) a modular jack.
もしょう 喪章 (胸章) a mourning ribbon; (腕章) a mourning band.
もじり (パロディ) a parody (*of, on*).
モジリアーニ 〖〖イタリアの画家〗〗 Modigliani /mòudi:ljá:ni/ (Amedeo ~).
もじる parody. ▶ミルトンの詩をもじる *parody* [*make a parody of*] Milton's poems. (❗make の代わりに write, compose も可)

もす 燃す burn. (⇨燃やす)
もず 百舌 〖鳥〗 a shrike /ʃráik/.
モスキート 〖蚊〗 a mosquito.
●モスキート級 the Mosquito. (〖参考〗アマチュアボクシングの最軽量級)

モスク 〖イスラム教徒の礼拝所〗 a mosque.
もずく 〖植物〗 *mozuku*; alga-like seaweed.
●もずく酢 *mozuku* served in vinegary sauce.
モスグリーン (コケ色) moss green. ●モスグリーン(色)の moss green.
モスクワ 〖〖ロシアの首都〗〗 Moscow.
もすそ 裳裾 a train. (⇨裾❶)
モスリン 〖織物〗 muslin /mʌ́zlin/.
もする 模する imitate. (⇨まねる)
もぞう 模造 名 imitation. (⇨偽)
── 模造する 動 imitate; (偽造する) counterfeit /káuntərfit/; fake.
●模造紙 Japanese vellum paper. (❗通例 imitation paper とはいわない) ●模造真珠 an imitation pearl. ●模造品 an imitation; (にせ物) a counterfeit; a fake.

もぞもぞ ●もぞもぞ(=落ち着きなく)動き回る move around *restlessly*. ▶虫が背中をもぞもぞしているような気がした I felt as though [if] some insects were *crawling* [*creeping*] about over my back.

もだえる 〖〖のたうち回る〗〗〖書〗writhe /ráið/; (ひどく苦しむ) be in agony. ▶痛くてもだえる *writhe* in [with] pain.

もたげる 頭をもたげる raise [rear] one's head. ▶国家[民族]主義が頭をもたげ始めた Nationalism began to *rear* its (ugly) *head*./(力を持ち始めた) Nationalism began to *gain power*.

もたせかける もたせ掛ける lean* (*against*); (安定するように置く) rest (*against*). ▶はしごを壁にもたせかけなさい *Lean* [*Rest, Put*] the ladder *against* the wall.

もたせる 持たせる ❶〖〖持つように仕向ける〗〗 ▶たくさんの荷物を夫に持たせる have her husband *carry* a lot of parcels. ▶宝くじは彼に一時の夢を持たせた The public lottery *gave* him *a short-lived dream*. ▶例のご本は午後にでも秘書に持たせます(=届けさせます)

I'll *send* my secretary (*along*) *with* your book in the afternoon.
❷〖現状を保たせる〗keep*; (やや書) preserve. ●氷で魚をもたせる *keep* fish fresh with ice. ●切りバラをもたせるよい方法 a good way to *preserve* cut roses in good condition [to *prolong* the life of cut roses]. ▶手持ちの金でもう2週間もたせなくてはならない(=食いつながねばならない) I have to *live on* the money I have for two more weeks. ▶せめてもう1年はこの自転車をもたせたい I'd like to *use* [to go *on using*] this bike for at least one more year.
❸〖取らせる〗(負担させる) have* [make*]《him》pay; (あげる) give*. ●彼に費用の全額をもたせる *make* him *pay* all the expenses. ●タクシー代はぼくにもたせてください *Let* me *pay* the driver. ●妹が来たのでリンゴをもたせた(=持ち帰らせた) I *gave* my sister some apples *to take home* when she came over [came to see me].
❹〖持つように図る〗●論文に一貫性をもたせる *give* one's essay *consistency*; *make* one's essay *consistent*. ●仕事にゆとりをもたせる *give*《him》more time to do the work; (計画する) plan out a *leisurely* work schedule.

もたつく (時間がかかる) take* *time* (*to do*); (手間どる) be slow (*in*). ●切符を買うのにずいぶんもたついた It *took* me [I *took*] *a lot of time* to buy the ticket. (⇨かかる)●工事がもたついている(=ほとんど進んでいない) The construction is *making hardly any* [*very*] *little*] *progress*.

モダニスト 〖現代主義者, 近代主義者〗a *modernist*.
モダニズム 〖現代主義, 近代主義〗*modernism*.

もたもた ── **もたもたする** 動 be slow; dawdle. ●もたもたするな Be quick (about it)./《話》Don't *dilly-dally*./Make it *snappy*./《英》Look sharp.

もたらす 〖持って来る〗bring*; 〖引き起こす〗bring ... about, cause (前の方は因果関係が明確である場合、後の方は直接的な場合に); 〖生み出す〗produce, (利益を) yield; 〖伝える〗introduce. ●彼に吉報をもたらす *bring* good news to him; *bring* him good news. ●戦争は彼らの生活に大きな変化をもたらした The war *brought about* great changes in their lives. ●洪水は町の方に大きな被害をもたらした The flood *caused* [*did*] a lot of damage *to* the district. ▶その実験はよい結果をもたらした The experiment *produced* fine [good] results. ●鉄砲はポルトガル人によって日本へもたらされた Guns *were introduced into* Japan by Pòrtuguése. ▶世界に自由をもたらすために戦おう Let us fight to free the world.

もたれかかる　もたれ掛かる ●つえにもたれ掛かる *lean on* one's stick. (⇨もたれる)
もたれる ❶〖寄りかかる〗lean* (*on*, *against*, *over*). ●壁にもたれる *lean against* the wall. ●いすにもたれて座る *sit back in* [×on] a chair. ●手すりにもたれるな Don't *lean on* [*over*] the rail. (！on は「ひじをついて」, over は「身を乗り出して」の意)
❷〖食物が〗●胃にもたれる [lie*, sit*] heavy *on* one's stomach; (消化しにくい) be hard to digest; be not easily digested. ●胃にもたれる食物 *heavy* food.

モダン ── **モダンな** 形 〖現代的, 近代的〗modern.
●モダンジャズ modern jazz. ●モダンダンス modern dance. ●モダンバレエ modern ballet.

もち 餅 ❶〖耐久性〗●持ちがよい be durable; (衣服・素材などが) wear well; (品質・性能が) last* (for) a long time; (食べ物が) keep well [(for) a long time]. ●持ちのよい衣類 *durable* clothing; clothing that *wears well*. ●火持ちのいい炭 *long-*

burning charcoal. ●この靴は持ちが悪い These shoes *wear badly* [*don't last long*]. ●夏の野菜は持ちが悪い The vegetables *don't keep well* [*long*] in (《主に米》the) summer.
❷〖負担〗●費用はすべて会社持ちだ All the expenses *are paid by* the company. ▶夕食は私持ちだ The dinner *is on* me. (⇨奢(おご)る❶)

もち 餅 (a) rice cake (made from glutinous rice). ●もちを焼く toast [grill] (a) *rice cake*. ●もちをつく (全過程) make *rice cake*; (べったんべったんと) pound steamed rice into *cake*.
●もちはもち屋〖ことわざ〗Every man to his trade./Every man as his business lies.
●もち菓子 (a) sweet rice cake. ●もち花 a New Year's decoration of a willow branch with lots of round *mochi* [rice cake]. ●もち屋 (店) a rice-cake shop [store]; (人) a rice-cake dealer.
もちあい 持ち合い ❶〖力がつり合っていること〗両者の力は持ち合いだ The two *are well matched*.
❷〖相場に変動がないこと〗●相場は持ち合いだ The market *is steady*.

*<u>**もちあがる**</u> 持ち上がる ❶〖上へ上がる〗▶この箱は重くてぼくでは持ち上がらない This box is too heavy for me to *lift*.
❷〖事が起こる〗happen, come* up. ▶何が持ち上がったんだ What *happened*?/What's *up*? ●新しい問題が持ち上がった New problems *came up* [(不意に)《話》*cropped up*].
❸〖その他の表現〗●私たちのクラスは山田先生が持ち上がった Mr. Yamada continues to be in charge of our class.

もちあげる 持ち上げる ❶〖上に上げる〗lift ... (up); (重い物を) heave*. (⇨持つ❶) ●その重い荷物を持ち上げてトラックに載せる *lift* (*up*) [*heave*] the heavy box *onto* the truck.
❷〖おだてる〗●彼を持ち上げて歌を歌わせる *flatter* him *into* singing.

もちあじ 持ち味 〖人の〗(特別な才能) a special ability (！しばしば複数形で); (魅力的個性) an attractive personality; (人が持っているもの) what one has; 〖物の〗(特性) a special quality. ●絹の持ち味を十分に生かす use the *special qualities* of silk to full advantage. ▶君の持ち味を生かしなさい Make the most of your *special abilities* [*what you have*].

もちあるく 持ち歩く ●彼はいつもノートパソコンを持ち歩いている He always *carries* his notebook PC *around* [*about*] (*with* him).

もちあわせ 持ち合わせ ●今まったく持ち合わせがありません I have no *money on* [*with*] me now. (！金などの小物には on の方が普通)
もちあわせる 持ち合わせる 〖偶然持っている〗happen to have; 〖身につけている〗have* ... with [on,《主に英》about] one. (⇨持ち合わせ)
もちいえ 持ち家 one's own house [home]; a house of one's own.

モチーフ 〈フランス語〉〖文芸・音楽の〗a motif /moutíːf/(複 〜s); a motive; (テーマ) a theme /θiːm/. (⇨主題)

*<u>**もちいる**</u> 用いる 〖道具・材料・言葉などを〗use (⇨使う, 利用); 〖方法・考えなどを〗adopt. (⇨採用) ●火を用いる *use* fire. ●旧式なやり方を用いる *adopt* [*employ*] an old method. ●与えられた語を用いて空所を埋めなさい Fill in the blanks *with* [(by) *using*] the words given. ▶この素材は広く用いられている[用いられるようになった] This material *is in* [*has come into*] wide *use*. (！use の名詞の発音は /juːs/) ●この会社は日本式の経営方式を用いている This company *adopts* the Japanese management style.

もちうた 持ち歌 one's repertoire /rəpərtwɑ:r/ of songs. (⇨レパートリー)

もちかえり 持ち帰り ●持ち帰り用の料理《米》a takeout, a carryout;《英》a takeaway. (⇨持ち帰る)

もちかえる 持ち替える ●その重い荷物を持ち替える shift the heavy baggage *from one hand to the other*.

もちかえる 持ち帰る ●［持って帰ってくる］bring*... back [(自宅へ) home];［持って帰って行く］take*... back [home]. ▶持ち帰るためのピザを二つください Could I have two pizzas *to go* [*take out*], please?/Two *takeout* [《英》*takeaway*] pizzas, please.
会話 「こちらで召しあがりますか。お持ち帰りですか」「持ち帰ります」"Is that *for here* or *to go*?" "*To go*."

もちかける 持ち掛ける ●彼に話(＝ある提案)を持ちかける approach him *with* a proposal; (持ち出す) *bring up* a proposal *to* him. ●彼女に結婚話を持ちかける (＝結婚を申し込む) propose *to* her.

もちかぶ 持ち株 ●持ち株会社 a hólding còmpany. ●持ち株会社所有の会社 a holding. ●持ち株制度 stock ownership. ●従業員持ち株制度 an employee(s) stock ownership plan [scheme]; an employee stock [share] purchase plan.

もちきり 持ち切り ●町じゅうが彼の話でもちきりだ He is *the talk of* the whole town. (■ talk は U で「うわさの種」の意) ●新聞はその事件のこともちきりだ The newspapers *are full of* the news of the incident.

もちきれない 持ち切れない ▶荷物を全部は持ちきれなかった I *was unable to* [*could not*] *carry* all of my belongings.

もちくさ 餅草［植物］a mugwort.

もちくされ 持ち腐れ ●宝の持ち腐れ (⇨宝［成句］)

もちくずす 持ち崩す ●身を持ち崩す ruin oneself 《by gambling》;《やや話》go to the dogs. ●身を持ち崩した人 a degenerate.

もちげい 持ち芸 one's specialty. (⇨十八番)

もちこす 持ち越す ●結論を持ち越す[＝延期する] put *off* [*postpone*] a decision. ●その議題は来週まで持ち越された(＝途中で延期された) The topic *was carried* [*was held*] *over* till next week.

もちこたえる 持ち堪える［最後までがんばる］hold* out 《against》;［重みに耐える］hold, bear*;［困難を乗り越えさせる］《やや話》tide ... over; [もつ] last (out); ［病気・困難などを切り抜ける］《やや話》pull through(...). ●攻撃を持ちこたえる hold out against an attack. ▶床は families重さを持ちこたえられなかった The floor couldn't *hold* [*bear*] the weight of the furniture. ▶この金で今月は持ちこたえられるだろう This money will *tide* me *over* [*last* (me)] this month. ▶患者は冬を持ちこたえた The patient *lasted* (*out*) [*pulled through*] the winter.

もちごま 持ち駒 ●［将棋の］a captured piece;［いつでも使える人・手段］a person [a means] available for a particular task.

もちこみ 持ち込み ●申し訳ございませんがそのかばんは機内へのお持ち込みはできません I'm sorry, but it isn't possible to *take* that bag on the plane. (■ 不可能 を使った断り方に注意) ●試験場に辞書の持ち込みは自由です You can [are allowed to] *take* your dictionaries *into* the examination room. ●持ち込み原稿 (依頼されてない原稿) unsolicited manuscripts. ●持ち込み手荷物 (機内への) a carryon; 《a piece of》carry-on baggage [luggage]. ●持ち込み料 (ホテルへのワインなどの) corkage.

もちこむ 持ち込む ❶［持って入る］(⇨持ち込み) ●図書館に食物を[機内に爆発物を]持ち込む bring food *into* a library [explosives *aboard* a plane]. ●麻薬を国内に持ち込む(＝密輸入する) *smuggle* drugs *into* a country.
会話 「ごめんなさい。靴をはき替えるの忘れちゃった」「あなたが持ち込んできたこの泥をちょっと見てごらんなさい」"Sorry I forgot to change my shoes." "Just look at the mud you've *brought in* here."
❷［解決を要するものを］●その事件を裁判に持ち込む *bring* the case *into* court. ●賃金紛争を調停に持ち込む *submit* [*refer*] a pay dispute *to* arbitration.
❸［未解決のまま次の状態に］●試合を引き分け[同点]に持ち込む *bring* a game *to* a draw [a tie]. (■「同点に持ち込む」場合は tie the score [the game] も可) ●試合を延長戦に持ち込む *send* [*put*] a game *into* extra innings.

もちごめ 糯米 glutinous rice.

もちさる 持ち去る ●主人の金を持ち去る(＝持ち逃げする) *make off* [*away*] *with* the master's money; *run away* [*off*] *with* the master's money.

もちじかん 持ち時間 one's allotted time 《for》. ▶持ち時間が切れました Sorry, *your time's up*. ▶スピーチの持ち時間は10分です You *have* ten minutes *for* your speech./Ten minutes *are allotted to* [*for*] your speech.

もちだし 持ち出し ●この辞書は図書館の外に持ち出しはできない You are not allowed to *take* this dictionary *out of the library*. ▶その費用の一部は会社がもってくれますが、残りは持ち出しになります Our company takes care of part of the expenses, but we have to *pay* the rest *out of our own pockets*.

もちだす 持ち出す ❶［持って出る］take* [carry] ... out; (こっそり) smuggle ... out. ●重要書類を金庫から持ち出す *take* [*carry*] *out* important papers *from* the safe; *take* [*carry*] *out* important papers *out of* the safe.
❷［話題などを］raise, bring*... up; (提案する) propose, suggest. ●その問題を今日の会議に持ち出す *raise* [*bring up*] the subject *at* today's meeting.

もちつき 餅搗き rice-cake making. (⇨餅)

もちつき 望月 (中秋の名月) the moon on August 15th by the lunar calendar; (満月) a full moon.

もちつもたれつ 持ちつ持たれつ ●持ちつ持たれつの関係 a *give-and-take* relationship. ●持ちつ持たれつ(＝互恵性)がどんな関係にも大切だ *Reciprocity* is the key to every relationship.

もちてん 持ち点 points allotted beforehand to each contestant [athlete, player].

もちなおす 持ち直す ❶［もとのよい状態に戻る］rally;《話》pick up. ▶病人[株式市場]が持ち直した The patient [The stock market] *has rallied* [*picked up*].
❷［持ち換える］▶私は荷物を持ち直した I *shifted* the baggage *from one hand to the other*.

もちにげ 持ち逃げ ── **持ち逃げする** 動 make off [away] with ...; run away [off] with ...●会社の収益金を持ち逃げする *make off* [*run away*] *with* the company('s) profits.

もちぬし 持ち主 (法的所有者) an owner; (財産・性質などの)《書》a possessor; (会社・ホテルなどの) a proprietor. (⇨持つ) ●持ち主不明の品物 an *unidentified* article. ▶この土地の持ち主はだれですか Who *owns* [*is the owner of*] this land? ▶この家は持

もちネタ 持ちネタ 主が3回変わった This house *has changed hands* three times. ▶彼は豊かな才能の持ち主だ He *has [possesses]* great talent. ▶この(落とし物の)時計の持ち主はだれですか Will anyone *lay claim to* this watch? (❗ *lay claim to* は「…に対する所有権を主張する」の意)

もちネタ 持ちネタ (手品などの仕掛け) one's tricks [gimmicks].

もちのき 糯の木 〖植物〗 a ilex.

もちば 持ち場 〖受け持ちの場所〗 (部署) one's post; (巡回区) one's beat, one's round(s). ●持ち場を離れる〖捨てる〗 leave [desert] one's *post*. ●持ち場を回る walk [patrol] one's *beat*; make one's *rounds*.

もちはこび 持ち運び ●持ち運びができる〖便利な〗 portable. ▶このパソコンは持ち運びに便利だ This PC processor is easy to *carry*.

もちはこぶ 持ち運ぶ carry. (⇨運ぶ❶)

もちはだ 餅肌 (a) soft, smooth [velvet] skin.

もちぶん 持ち分 (費用・仕事・財産などの) one's share; (株・所有地の) one's holdings.

モチベーション 〖動機づけ〗 (a) motivation.

もちまえ 持ち前 (⇨特徴) ●持ち前(=生まれつき)の音楽的才能 a *natural* [an *inborn*] ability in music.

もちまわり 持ち回り ▶議長は委員の持ち回りで務めます The post of the chairperson *rotates among* all the committee members./The committee members take the chair *in rotation*. ▶持ち回りで各自の家を会場にした We *took turns* offering our house as a meeting place.
●持ち回り閣議決定 a round-robin Cabinet decision.

もちもの 持ち物 (所持品) one's things, one's belongings (❗後の方が堅い語, いずれも複数扱い); (財産) one's property, one's possessions (❗複数扱い); (旅行時の手荷物) 〈主に米〉 baggage, 〈主に英〉 luggage (❗ともに数えるときは a piece [two pieces] of ~). ▶これはあなたの持ち物ですか Is this *yours*?

もちゅう 喪中 ●喪中である be in mourning 《*for*》. (⇨喪) ▶喪中につき今年年末年始のごあいさつは遠慮させていただきます We would refrain from sending our New Year greetings since we are *in mourning*. 解説 米英にはこのような文面を書いて喪中はがきを出す習慣はない
●喪中はがき (説明的に) a postcard which notifies one's friends and acquaintances that one is in mourning and will not send New Year greetings.

もちよる 持ち寄る (持って来る) bring*. ▶彼らは食べ物を持ち寄ってパーティーを開いた They *brought* some food and gave a party./They had a party, each *bringing* some food. (❗これを a potluck party という)

*__もちろん__ of course /əfkɔːrs/; 〖当然〗 naturally; 〖言うまでもなく〗 needless to say (⇨言うまでもなく); 〖確かに〗 certainly, surely, 〈話〉 sure, (やや書) to be sure. ▶君が困っているならもちろん手伝うよ If you're in trouble, I'll *certainly* help you. ▶もちろん彼はその提案を断るだろう *Naturally*(,) he will refuse the proposal. (❗この意では文修飾語として用いられ, 文頭の位置が普通) ▶新鮮な空気はもちろん健康によい *Needless to say,* [*It goes without saying that*] fresh air is good for the health. (❗後の方は文語的)

会話 「あなたの車を借してくれませんか」「もちろんいいですよ」 "Will you lend me your car?" "*Of course* [*Certainly, Surely,* 〈話〉 *Sure*] I will. ❗ I will は省略してもよい)/〈話〉 I *sure* will./〈米話〉 *Sure thing*./〈話〉 *OK*./〈話〉 *Why not?*/*By all means*." (❗〈米〉 では Sure., 〈英〉 では Certainly., Of course. が一般的. By all means. は丁寧な返答)

会話 「それ本当にあなたのなの」「もちろん」 "Is that really yours?" "*Why, yes!*" (❗ 単なる質問に対して日本語に引かれて of course を用いると「分かりきってるじゃないか」という意となり無礼な感じを伴うこともある)

会話 「私の誕生パーティーにあなたもいかが」「もちろん喜んで(=是非ともうかがうわ)」 "Why don't you join us at my birthday party?" "You bet (your life)." (❗勧誘に対する返事に of course を用いると「当たり前のこととして」という奇妙な感じになるので不適切)

会話 「怒ってないだろうね」「もちろんだよ」 "You're not angry?" "*Of* ╲*course* [╲*Certainly*] not." (❗日本語に引かれて not を落とさないこと)

【…はもちろんのこと】 〖…は言うまでもなく〗 not to mention …, to say nothing of …, not to speak of … (❗最初の言い方が最も口語的); 〖A だけでなく B も〗 B as well as A; not only A but (also) B. ▶彼はイギリスへはもちろんのことアフリカへも行ったことがある He has been to Africa, *not to mention* [*to say nothing of, not to speak of,* ×*let alone*] England. ▶彼女は英語はもちろんのことフランス語も話せる She can speak French *as well as* English./She can speak *not only* English *but (also)* French. ▶彼が私たちを助けてくれるのはもちろんのことだと思っています I *take* (it) *for granted* that he will help us. ▶彼は英語も話せない, ドイツ語はもちろんのことだ He cannot speak English, *let alone* [*much less*] German. (❗いずれも否定文の後で用いる)

もつ 持つ INDEX

❶ 手で	❷ 携帯する
❸ 所有する	❹ 担当する
❺ 負担する	❻ 開催する
❼ 持ちこたえる	❽ その他の表現

WORD CHOICE 持つ

have 具体的な事物や, 抽象的な能力・権利・地位などを持つこと. ▶彼女は優れた記憶力を持っている She *has* a good memory.

hold 具体的な事物を手で握って持つこと. または, 比喩的に, 財産・権力・意見などを保持すること. ●飲み物のグラスを手に持って *holding* a glass in my hand.

possess 財産・不動産などの法的な所有権を持つこと. または能力・権利・特性などを持つこと. ▶我々は持っていたものすべてを失った We lost everything we *possessed*.

(❗ ❶–❸ の have の用法は (⇨表, 解説))

❶ 〖手で〗 (一般に) have* (got) (❗状態を表す)(⇨解説); (落とさないように) hold* (❗動作または状態を表し, しばしば持ち方に言及する); (自分の手でつかむ) take*. ●箸を正しく持って *hold* one's chopsticks properly. ●手に本を持った男の子 a boy who *has* a book in his hand; a boy *with* a book in his hand. ●このロープの端を持っていなさい *Hold* the end of this rope. ▶彼は私の手を持った He *took* my hand./He took me by the [×his] hand. (⇨つかむ) ●かばんを一つお持ちしましょう Let me *take* one of your bags./Let me *help* you *with* one of your bags.

❷ 〖携帯する〗 (身につけて持っている) have* (got) (⇨ ❸ 解説); (持って移動する) carry. ▶彼はいつもたくさんお金を持っている He always *has* [*carries*] a lot of money on [with] him. (❗文脈から明らかな場合,

on [*with*]+代名詞は省略可. お金のような小さな物については 通例 on を用いる方が普通.(《主に英》about も用いられる)▶その通りは同じようなスーツを着てブリーフケースを持ったサラリーマンであふれていた The street was crowded with similary-suited and briefcase-carrying [《話》-*toting*] office workers.

会話「スーツケースをお持ちしましょうか」「ご親切にありがとうございます」"May I *carry* your suitcase?/Can I *help* you *with* your suitcase?" "That's very kind of you."

❸ [所有する] have* (got); possess /pəzés/; own; keep*; hold*.

使い分け have (got) 何かを「持つ」ことを表す最も一般的な語. 単に手に持っていることから, 権利・能力として所有していることにまで幅広く用いられる.
possess 法的な所有権を有することを表す堅い語. 性質や能力などの所有も意味する
own 法的な所有権を有していることを表す. 通例安価なものに対しては用いない.
keep 手放しもせずに持ち続けることを表す.
hold 物を手で持つことを表す. 時に強く握ることを含意する. そこから財産・権力・意見などを保持することも表す.

解説 have (got) が ❶~❸ までの「持っている」という状態を表す語義で用いられる場合, 《米》《英》および現在時制または過去時制によって以下のような用法上の違いが見られる.
(i) 従来《英》では否定文と疑問文において, do を用いない場合は Have you (*got*) much money?(《今》君はお金をたくさん持っていますか)のようにその時の特定事項に言及し, do を用いる場合は *Do* you *have* much money?(一般論で君はたくさんお金を持っていますか)のように習慣や一般性に言及するとされてきたが, 今日ではあまりこの区別は守られていない.
(ii) have got について: (a) 形には完了形であるが, 意味は現在のことを表す. また, この用法では ×have gotten とはしない. (b) 通例進行形・命令形・受身は不可. また, 一般に (to) 不定詞・分詞形では用いない. (c) have だけの場合と異なり have got は got に強勢が置かれ, しばしば 've got, 's got のように短縮され, くだけた会話では 've ['s] は脱落し, 単に got となることがある: そこに何を持ってるの What you *got* there? (d) 質問に対する短い答えや付加疑問では通例用いない: 「ライターをお持ちですね」「はい持っています」"You've got a lighter, *haven't* you [×haven't you got]?" "Yes, I *have* [×have got]."

▶彼女は3人の子供を持っている She *has* [×is having] three children. (!この用法の have は通例進行形・受身は不可)▶私は車を持っていません I don't *have* a [×any] car. (!any は通例単数可算名詞の前には用いられない)/I *have* no car. ▶この机を10年間持っています I *have had* [《使っている》 *have used*] this desk for ten years. ▶私が持っている本をあなたに見せてあげよう I'll show you the book I *have* [*I've got*]. (!単に I'll show you *my* book. ともいえる)▶彼は私に悪い感情を持って(=抱いて)いた He *had* [*held*] ill feeling toward me. ▶彼は莫大な財産を持っている He *has* [*possesses*] great wealth. (!通例進行形・命令形・受身は不可)▶あなたは持って生まれたすぐれた才能がある You have a great talent you were born *with*. ▶彼は軽井沢にホテルを持っている He *has* a hotel in Karuizawa./He *owns* [*holds*, 《経営している》*keeps*, *runs*] a hotel in Karuizawa. (!own は通例進行形・命令形不可. hold は通例進行形不可)▶休みの間その本持っていていいですよ You can *keep* the book during the holidays. ▶彼は幅跳びの記録を持っている He *holds* the broad-jump record.

❹ [担当する] ●4年生を教えている *have* [《教える》*teach*] fourth graders; (担任する) *take* [*be in*] *charge of* a fourth-year class.

❺ [負担する] ●費用を持つ *pay* [*bear*] the expense; *pay* [《話》*foot*] the bill (*for it*). ▶これはぼくが持つよ(代金はぼくが支払うよ) I'll *pay for* this./(ぼくのおごりだ)《話》This is *on* me.

❻ [開催する] ●会合を持つ *have* [*hold*] a meeting. (!*have* は受身不可)(⇒開く❹)

❼ [持ちこたえる] *last* (out), hold* (out) (!いずれも out は「困難に屈せず」の含みを持つ(⇒持ちこたえる)); (形・色・においなど使用に耐えて) *wear**; (悪くならずに) *be good*, *stay* (good); (人が生き延びる) *live*; (危機・災害などを越えて) *survive*; (分量的に十分ある) *be good*. ▶この天気はどのくらい持つだろう How long

		(米)	(英)
平叙文	現在	I **have** (話) I'**ve got**	I **have** (話) I'**ve got**
	過去	I **had**	I **had** [×**had got**]
否定文	現在	I **don't have** (any+名) (話) I **haven't got** (+名) (I **have no** (+名))	I **haven't**　　　　　　(any+名) I **don't have** (話) I **haven't got** (+名) (I **have no** (+名))
	過去	I **didn't have** (any+名) (I **had no** (+名))	I **hadn't**　　　　　　(any+名) I **didn't have** (I **had no** (+名))
疑問文	現在	**Do** you **have** ...? (話) **Have** you **got** ...?	**Have** you ...? (No, I **haven't**.) (話) **Have** you **got** ...? (No, I **haven't**.) **Do** you **have** ...? (No, I **don't**.)
	過去	**Did** you **have** ...?	**Did** you **have** ...? [×**Had** you ...?]

もつ will this nice weather *last* [*hold*]?/How long is it going to *stay* fair? ▶これだけあれば1週間は持つ This supply will *last* (us) (for) a week. (❗通例受身・進行形不可)/This supply *is good* for a week. ▶この靴は長く持つだろう These shoes will *last* long [*wear* well, *be good* (for) a long time]. (❗(1) ×*last well*, ×*wear long* とはいわないが, These are *long-lasting* [*-wearing*] shoes. は可. (2)「電池」のような消耗の程度が外見から判断できないものは次のような表現が可: This battery will *have a life* of two years at least.) ▶彼はあすまで持たないだろう He will not *live* until tomorrow./(その夜を持ちこたえないだろう) He will not *live out* [*live through*, *last out*] the night. ▶この家はもう一度大地震がくれば持たないだろう This house won't *survive* another big earthquake. ▶この魚はあまり持たない This fish does not *keep* well [*long*]. (❗long は肯定文では通例 (for) a long time となる)/(すぐ腐敗する) This fish *spoils* [*goes bad*] easily.
❽【その他の表現】 ▶この会社は彼でもっている(=彼が主な支えとなっている) He *is* the chief *support* of this firm. ▶十分に休養を取らないと体が持たないよ(=健康を失う) Take a good rest, or you will *lose* your *health*.

もつ [内臓] entrails, 《話》guts (❗いずれも主に「腸」をさす); (レバー) a liver; (鳥の) giblets.
 ●もつ鍋 *motsunabe*, (説明的に) a kind of a pot dish in which several kinds of entrails are used. ●もつ焼 roast giblets.

もっか 目下 *present*; (今は) now. (⇨今❶) ▶目下経済危機にみまわれています We are in an economic crisis *at present*. ▶彼女は目下留学中だ She is *now* studying abroad.
—— 目下の 形 (現在の) *present*; (現時点の) *current*
 ▶目下の問題 the *present* problem. ▶目下の関心事 one's *current* interest. ▶目下の急務 the first thing one has to do *right now*. ▶彼の給料は目下のところ(=当分は)月いちやっている His pay will do *for the present* [*for the time being*, 《話》*for now*].
 ▶目下の状況ではストライキの早期解決の望みはほとんどない There is little hope of an early settlement of the strike under the *present* circumstances.

もっか 黙過 ── 黙過する 動 connive (*at*).

もっかん 木簡 (歴史的に) a narrow strip of wood on which messages were written in ancient China and Japan.

もっかんがっき 木管楽器 a woodwind instrument; (オーケストラの木管楽部) (the) woodwinds.

もっきょ 黙許 tacit permission. (⇨黙認)

もっきん 木琴 [楽器] a xylophone /záiləfòun/. ●木琴を演奏する play the xylophone. ●木琴奏者 a xylophonist.

モックアップ [実物大の模型] a mock(-)up.

もっけのさいわい ▶彼にそこで会えたのはもっけのさいわい(=思いがけない幸い)だった It was quite a *stroke of luck* that I ran into him there./By an amazing *stroke of luck*, I met him there.

もっこ 畚 a large basket for carrying earth.

もっこう 木工 (技術) woodworking; carpentry; (技術, 木工品) 《主に英》 woodwork. ●木工をする do *woodwork*.
 ●木工所 a wóodworking plànt. ●木工職人 a woodworker.

もっこう 黙考 meditation. (⇨沈思(ちんし)黙考)

もっさり (⇨もっさと)

もったい ●もったいをつけて話す speak with an *air of* (great) *importance*. (⇨もったいぶる)

もったいない ❶[むだである] be wasteful, be a waste.
 会話「あの靴は捨てたよ」「なんてもったいない!」"I threw those shoes away." "What a *waste*!"
 会話「1時間ほど休憩しない?」「だめよ, 時間がもったいない」"Why don't we take a rest for around an hour?" "No, it's a *shame* to waste time."
❷[よすぎる] be too good (*for*). ▶この車は私にはもったいない This car *is too good* for me. ▶これはもったいなくて捨てられない This *is too good* to throw away. ▶そんなほめの言葉は私にはもったいない(=値しない) I don't *deserve* such praise. ▶あなたはウエートレスにしておくにはもったいない人だ You've got something *better than* being a waitress.

もったいぶる [気取る] put* on airs, give* oneself airs. ●もったいぶって (ご大そうに) 《軽蔑的》pompously; (いかにも大事そうに) with an air of great importance.

もって 以て ❶[【道具・身体の一部などを】使って] with ...; [【手段・方法】によって] by ..., by means of .... (⇨で) ▶書面をもって(=手紙で)答える reply (to 〈him〉) by letter [[書いたもので]] *in* writing. ▶言葉をもって意志疎通する communicate *by means of* words. ▶彼の頭脳をもってすればその計画はきっと成功すべきだ./(彼の頭脳ならその計画を成功させるはずだ) His brains should make the plan successful. (❗前より堅い言い方) ▶私はそれがいかに重要であるかを身をもって(=体験に基づいて)知った I learned *by* [*from* (my own)] experience how important it was.
❷[【...の】原因・理由で] because of ..., on account of ...; for .... (❗for で特定の言い回しや否定的文脈でのみ用いる). (⇨ため) ▶老齢(のうれい)をもって引退する retire *because of* old age. ▶雅代は美人をもって聞こえていた (美人で有名だった) Masayo was famous [well-known] *for* her beauty./(美人として知られていた) Masayo was famous [well-known] *as* a beauty.
❸[区切りに] ▶彼は4月1日をもって(=4月1日に)我が社の社長になる He will become president of our company *on* [(4月1日より) *as of*, *as from*] April 1. (❗as of [from] は堅い言い方. 《米》 では as of の方が好まれる) ▶これをもって質疑応答は打ち切ります So much for questions and answers.
 ●もって瞑(めい)すべし ▶それだけ多くのことを成し遂げたのだから, もって瞑すべしだ(=それで満足すべきだ) Since you have accomplished so much, you *ought to be contented*.

もってくる 持って行く *take**; (持って歩く) *carry*; (相手のいる所へ持って行く) *bring**. ▶皿をあっち[台所]へ持って行く *take* the dishes *away* [*to* the kitchen]. ▶雨が降るといけないから傘を持って行きなさい *Take* an umbrella (with you) [*Carry* an umbrella] in case it rains. (❗take は「携帯する」の意では with one を伴うことが多い. carry もしばしば with 句を伴う)
 会話「ぼくがそのバッグを持って行きますよ」「気をつけて. かなり重いわよ」"Let me *take* [*carry*] the bag for you." "(Be) careful. It's rather heavy."
 会話「パーティーに何を持って行きましょうか」「花を持って来てくださる?」"What shall I *bring* [×*take*] to your party?" "Could you *bring* some flowers?"

もってうまれた 持って生まれた [天性の] *natural*; [生得の] *inborn*; [生来の] *innate*. ●持って生まれた才能 a *natural* [an *inborn*] *ability*.

もってくる 持って来る *bring** (↔*take**); [取って来る] *get**; [行って取って来る] *fetch*, 《話》*go** (and) *get*. ▶私に水を持って来てくれ *Bring* me some

もってこい

water./*Bring* some water *to* [*for*] me. (❗*to* は方向, *for* は利益を表す. 最初の文はその両方の意を持つ)/*Get* me some water./*Get* some water *for* [×*to*] me. ▶私は傘を持って来るのを忘れた I forgot to *bring* my umbrella (*with* me). ▶私の帽子を持って来てください Please *fetch* [*go* (*and*) *get*] me my hat./Please *fetch* [*go* (*and*) *get*] my hat *for* me. (❗Please *go and fetch* me my hat. ということもあるが避ける方がよい)

もってこい 持って来い ── 持って来いの 形 (最適の) right; (理想的な) ideal; (最も必要を満たした) most suitable. (⇨誂(*²)え向き) ▶疲れている時は1杯の熱いココアがもってこいだ (話) A cup of hot chocolate always *hits the spot* when you are tired. (❗飲食物に関しては普通)

もってのほか 以ての外 ●もってのほかの(=ふらちな)ふるまい *outrageous* behavior. ▶君がそんな要求をするとはもってのほかだ(=問題外だ) It's *out of the question* for you to make such demands. ▶無免許運転などもってのほかだ(=問題外だ) Driving without a license is completely *out of the question*. ▶私に向かってそんな口答えするなんてもってのほかだ(=よくも言えたものだ) How dare you [(絶対にしてはいけない) *Don't you dare*] talk back to me like that!

もってまわった 持って回った ●持って回った言い方をする talk in a *roundabout* way. (⇨回りくどい)

*もっと (❗日本語の「もっと」は英語の形容詞・副詞の比較級で通例表す) ▶問題をもっと(=さらに深く)調査する go *further* into the matter. ●もっと(たくさん)睡眠をとる sleep *more*.

[解説] (1) 形容詞・副詞の比較変化: 一般的な原則の概略は次のとおり(便宜上, 例は比較級のみ):
(a) [形容詞] (ⅰ) 単音節語はすべて -er, -est をつける: bigger, cleaner, harder.
(ⅱ) 2音節語は -er, -est などの語尾変化形と more, most を添える変化形の両方が可能なものが多いが, 後の方が一般的になる傾向がある: cleverer/ more clever, narrower / more narrow, gentler/more gentle. 特に, -er, -ow, -le, -some で終わる形容詞は最近 more, most を添えて変化させる傾向が強い. 今日2音節語の中で -er, -est の語尾変化のみが可なものは -y で終わる語: easier, prettier, happier. ただし, 形容詞語尾 -ly で終わる語は more, most を添える変化の方が一般的: more friendly [likely, lively].
(ⅲ) 3音節以上の語は通例 more, most を添える: more beautiful [comfortable, dangerous]. ただし, 否定接頭辞が付加されることによって3音節語になったものは通例 -er, -est をつける: uneasier, unhappier, unkinder.
(b) [副詞] 副詞の比較変化に関しても形容詞の場合とほぼ同様の規則が当てはまる. 単音節副詞 (hard, fast, soon, late, near) および early は -er, -est の語尾をつけ, それ以外の副詞は more, most を添えて変化させる. ただし, often と seldom については両方の変化が可であるが, often は more, most を添える方が一般的.
(c) [不規則変化] good/well (better, best), bad (worse, worst), far (farther/further, farthest/furthest), much/many (more, most), little (less, least)
なお, 両方の変化形が可な場合は, -er, -est の語尾変化の方がくだけた言い方. どちらの変化形かはっきりしない場合は more~, most~ にしておく方が無難.
(2) 最上級と定冠詞: 限定用法の形容詞が比較級で用いられる場合は必ず定冠詞が必要だが, 叙述用法の形容詞の場合は定冠詞は省略可. 副詞の最上級の場合, 定冠詞はあることもないこともあるが, 'of＋名詞句' などの限定表現を伴う場合は定冠詞をとりやすくなる. 一般に -est の語尾変化による形の方が most を添える形より, また(米)の方が(英)より定冠詞をとる傾向が強い.

▶今日はもっとすることがある I have something *more* to do today. ▶外へ出て他の子ともっと遊びなさい You should get out and play with other children *more*. ▶もっと(もっと)本[お金]が欲しい I want (*many*) *more* books [(*much*) *more* money]. (⇨ずっと❶) ▶彼らはもっと遠くへ旅を続けた They traveled *further* (米話・英) [*farther*(米書)] on. ▶もっと(長く)ここにいてくださいませんか Could you stay here (*much*) *longer*? (❗*much* は比較級を強める)/(仮定法を使って) I wish you stayed here *more* of the time. (❗「いてくれればいいのになあ」という意で強い願望を表す) ▶もっと(しっかり)英語を勉強しなさい Study English (*much*) *harder*. ▶もっとましなものがないのですか Don't you have [Isn't there] anything *better*?
[会話]「もっといるだろうな」「もっとって, どれ[いくつ]くらい？」"I shall want *more than* that." "How much [many] *more*?"
[会話]「遅くとも6時までにはそこに行くよ」「よかった！もっと遅くなるかと思ってたわ」"I'll be there by six at the latest." "Fine! I thought you'd be *later than* that."

モットー a motto /mάtoʊ/ (優 ~(e)s). ▶「努力」が私のモットーで "Work hard" is my *motto* [(処生訓) *maxim*]./I have "Work hard" as my *motto*.

:**もっとも 最も** (❗日本語の「最も」は, 英語では通例形容詞・副詞の最上級で表す (⇨一番❸). 比較変化については(⇨もっと [解説])) ●最もよい本 *the best* book. ●最も重要な事 *the most* (↔*the least*) important thing. ●最も一生懸命働く work *hardest*. ●最も勇敢に戦う fight *most* bravely. ▶彼は今までで最も偉大な詩人だ He is *the greatest* poet that (has) ever lived.

もっとも 尤も 接 (しかし) however; but; (とは言っても...だが) though (...), although .... (⇨しかし) ▶彼は試験に合格したと言った. もっとも後になってそれはうそだと分かったが He said he passed the exam. Later, *however*, it proved (to be) false. (❗however は通例コンマで区切る. 文頭・文中・文尾で用いられる) ▶彼は利口だ. もっとも彼の兄ほどではないが He is ╲clever, *though* [*although*] (he is) nót as clever as his ╲brother. (❗この場合 though 節は常に主節の後にコンマやダッシュ, 読むときはその前にポーズを置く)/(話) He is clever. He isn't as clever as his ╲brother, *though* [×*although*]. (❗この though は副詞で通例文尾に用い, 文頭では用いない. although はこの用法はない) ▶もっとも(＝もちろん)皆がその提案に賛成したわけではないが *Of course*, not everyone agreed to that proposal.

── **もっともな** 形 [理にかなった] reasonable; [当然な] natural; [正当な] just; [納得させる] convincing. ●もっともな要求 a *reasonable* [a *just*] claim. ●もっともな議論 a *convincing* argument. ●もっともなことを言う talk sense. ▶君が自分の息子の自慢をするのももっともだ You *may well* be proud of your son. ▶彼がそう言うのももっとも(なこと)だ *No wonder* [*It's no wonder* (*that*)] he says so./It is *natural* that he should say so./*It is natural for* him *to* say so. (❗後の方がより堅い言い方になる)

もっともらしい (本当のように思われる) plausible. ●もっともらしい弁解をする make a *plausible* [(理にかなった) a *reasonable*] excuse. ●もっともらしいうそをつく

もっぱら 専ら [他を排して] exclusively; [全面的に] entirely; [ひとえに] (やや書) solely. ▶この週刊誌はもっぱら女性向けだ This weekly (magazine) is *exclusively* for women [for women *exclusively*]. ▶余暇をもっぱらスポーツに向けた I devoted my spare time *entirely* [*solely*] to sports.

モップ a mop. ●モップで床掃除をする *mop* the floors.

もつやく 没薬 myrrh.

もつれ [糸・髪などの] a tangle; [事柄の] (a) complication; (a) confusion. ●ブラシ[くし]で髪のもつれを取る brush [comb] the *tangles* out of one's hair. ▶釣り糸がもつれた The fishing lines *have become* [*got*] *tangled* (*up*).

もつれこむ もつれ込む ▶試合は延長戦にもつれ込んだ(=入った) The game *went* [*ran*] *into* extra innings.

もつれる [糸・髪などが] tangle, get tangled [entangled]; [事柄などが] (混乱する) get confused; (複雑になる) get complicated. ●もつれた髪 *tangled* [*entangled*] hair. ▶ロープがもつれた The ropes *tangled*. ▶足がもつれた(=よろけた) I *tripped*.

もてあそぶ 玩ぶ play [toy] (*with*); (人・感情などを) trifle (*with*). ●ライターをもてあそぶな Don't *play* [*toy*, (話) *fool around*] *with* the lighter. ▶彼は私の愛情をもてあそんだ He *trifled* [*played*, *toyed*] *with* my affection.

もてあます 持て余す ▶彼はこの仕事をもて余していた(どう処理したらいいか分からなかった) He *didn't know what to do with* this task./(余りにも負担だった) This task *was too much for* him. ▶私は退屈で時間をもて余していた Time *hung heavy on my hands*. (!) (1) 退屈 時間がなかなか過ぎないこと. (2) 次のようにいうこともできる: 彼女が時間をもて余しているようだったので 2, 3 個人的な質問をしてみようと思い立った Since she seemed to have *plenty of time*, I decided to ask her a few personal questions. ▶両親でさえあの子をもて余していた(=監督できない) Even the parents *can't control* [*have no control over*] that child.

もてなし [厚遇] hospitality (!) 食事などを出して手厚くもてなすこと); [待遇] treatment; [受け入れ] a reception; [歓迎] a welcome. (⇨接待) ●心からのもてなしを受ける receive hearty *hospitality* [*treatment*] (!) 次の言い方の方が普通); receive a hearty *welcome* [*reception*]. ●おもてなしにおおずかりありがとうございました Thank you for your kind *hospitality*. (!) 訪問先を辞する際の言葉で非常に丁寧な言い方. Thank you for the wonderful evening. などという方が普通

*もてなす [歓待する] entertain; [待遇する] treat (!) well など常に様態の副詞(句)を伴う). ●夕食に客を招いてもてなす *entertain* a guest *to* [*at*] dinner; *host* a dinner party. ▶彼らは私たちを温かくもてなしてくれた They *treated* us very *warmly*./(歓迎してくれた) They *gave* us *a* warm *welcome* [*reception*].

もてはやす [ほめたてる] praise (⇨称賛); [ちやほやする] make* much of .... ●若者にもてはやされている(=人気がある) be popular among [with] young people.

モデム [コンピュータ] a modem. (!) modulator＋demodulator の短縮語) ●内蔵モデム an internal *modem*. ●モデムカード a modem card. ●モデムボード a modem board.

もてもて 持て持て ▶彼は女の子にもてもてだ He *is very popular with* girls.

モデラート [＜イタリア語] [音楽] moderato /màdərá:tou/.

もてる 持てる [人気がある] be popular (*with, among*); [好かれる] be liked (*by*). ●彼は若い女性に大変もてる He is very *popular with* [*among*] young women.

*モデル a model. ●ファッションモデル a fashion *model*. ●写真のモデル a photographic *model*. ●その小説の主人公のモデル the *model* for the hero of that novel. ▶その小説はある昔話をモデルにして作られた The novel was *modeled on* an old tale. ▶彼女は画家のモデルをしている She works as an artist's *model* [*sitter*]./She *models* [*sits*] *for* an artist. ●モデルガン a model gun. ●モデルケース [代表例] a typical case (*of*). (!) 通例 model case とはしない) ●モデルスクール a model school. ●モデルチェンジ a model changeover; change to a new model. (!)「モデルチェンジする」は change the *model*) ●モデル賃金 model wages. ●モデルハウス (米) a model home; (英) a show house [home]. ●モデルルーム a model apartment. (!) 通例 ×a model room とはしない)

モデレーター a moderator. (!) chairperson の婉曲語として用いられる)

:もと 元, 本, 基 [器] ❶ [起こり] (起源) (an) origin; (根源) the root; (源) a source; (始め) the beginning. (⇨発端, 始め) ▶彼の冗談が口論のもとだった His joke was the *origin* of the argument. ▶風邪は万病のもとだ A cold is the *root* [*source*, *beginning*] of all diseases. ▶その時計はもとから(=初めから)壊れていた That watch was out of order from the *beginning*. ▶ガス漏れのもとは彼の部屋だった The gas leak *originated* in his room. ▶その詩ははじめフランス語で書かれていた The poem was *originally* written in French.

❷ [原因] (a) cause. (⇨原因) ▶彼の心配のもとが何であったかだれも知らない Nobody knows what the *cause* of his trouble was. ▶大雨がもとで大変な洪水が起こった The heavy rain *caused* serious floods./We had serious floods *because of* the heavy rain. ▶彼は過労がもとで死んだ He died *from* overwork. (!) from は原因を表す (⇨死ぬ))

❸ [土台] a foundation; [基礎] a basis (複 bases). ▶農業は国の基だ Agriculture is the *foundation* [*basis*] of a nation. ▶この記事は事実をもとにしている This article *is based on* facts. (⇨基づく ❶)

❹ [資本] (資本金) capital; (原価) (a) cost; (出資金) (an) investment. ▶この商売を始めるにはずいぶん元がかかる We need a large amount of *capital* to start this business.

❺ [材料] (a) material; (料理などの) an ingredient. ▶この薬は何をもとにして作っているのですか What (*material*) is this medicine made from?

●元が取れる ▶この商売では元が取れない I can't recover the *cost* [*get a return on my investment*] in this business. /(割に合わない) This business doesn't pay.

●元も子もない ▶それでは元も子もない(=すべてを失うだろう) You will *lose everything*.

●元をただせば ▶小切手といっても元をただせば(=実際は)ただの紙切れだ A check is *really* no more than [*nothing but*] a piece of paper.

── 元(の) 形 (以前の) former, ex-. (!) 後の方が堅い語) ▶彼は元首相だ He is a *former* prime minister [an *ex-premier*]./(かつて首相だった) He was once [*formerly*] a prime minister. (!) once の方が口語的) ▶元そこには本屋がありました There *used to* [×would] be a bookstore there. (!) 現在と対比

した過去の状態を表す. There *was*... でも表せる)▶その本は元の所に戻しておいてください Please put the book back *where it was*./(あるべき場所に) Please put the book back in its *(proper) place*. ●彼女はもう元の彼女ではない She is no longer *what she was* [*used to be*]. (! 通例悪い意味に用いる. 日常会話では She has changed a lot. の方が普通) ●彼は元どおりの健康体にはならないでしょう He will never be as healthy *as he was* [*as he used to be, as before*]. ●雨が降ってきたので我々はもと来た道を引き返した We went back the way we came because it began to rain.

● **元のさやに収まる** ▶彼らは離婚寸前までいったが結局は元のさやに収まった(=再びいっしょになった) They were on the point of divorce, but they *got back together again* after all.

● **元の木阿弥**(もくあみ) ▶今や元のもくあみだった(=出発点に戻った) Now, we're back *where we started from* [*to square one*].

もと 下 ●先生の指導[監督]の下に *under* the direction [supervision] of a teacher. ●浅野博士の下で物理学の研究をする study physics *under* Dr. Asano. ●夫の下を去る leave one's husband. ●一撃の下に彼を倒すと knock him down *with* [*at*] *one* [*a single*] *blow*.

もとい 基 (基礎) a foundation; a base.

もとうけ 元請け (業者) the original contractor.

もどかしい (もどかしがる) be [feel*] impatient 《*for*》, (いらいらする) be irritated; (いらいらさせる) be irritating. (⇨いらいら, いらいら) ▶英語が通じないのでもどかしかった I couldn't make myself understood in English and it was *frustrating* [I *was frustrated*]. (!「目的が達せられないでいらいらする」は irritating では不適) ▶もどかしい思いで私は父の帰りを待った I was *impatiently* waiting for my father's return.

> **翻訳のこころ** まるで, 解けない問題を一つ抱えているような気分でいた. 私は, 自分自身をもどかしく思った(山田詠美『ひよこの眼』) I felt as if I had one unresolved problem [unanswered question] within me, and *was frustrated* with myself. (!(1)「もどかしい」は be frustrated (《何かが達成されなくて》欲求不満を抱く)と表す. (2) unresolved problem は「一般的で重大, 長期的な問題」, unanswered question は「短期間に解決が得られるような特定の問題」の意)

ーもどき ー擬き pseudo- /s(j)úːdou-/. ●科学もどきの *pseudo*scientific. ●芝居もどきのせりふ play*like* lines.

もときん 元金 (a) principal (⇨元金(がんきん)); (資本金) capital. (⇨元手)

モトクロス (a) motocross /móutoukrɔ(ː)s/.

もとごえ 元肥 base manure. ●元肥を施す apply manure before sowing [planting].

もとじめ 元締め (全体をまとめる人) a manager; (勘定の締めくくりをする人) a chief treasurer; (親分) a boss.

*****もどす 戻す** ❶[元の場所・状態へ戻す] return, put*... back (! 後の方が口語的); (復帰させる) restore. ●本を書棚に戻す *put* the book *back* on the shelf; *return* the book *to* the shelf. ●それを元に(入っていた)所に戻す *put* it *back* in its (proper) place [where it was, where it belongs]. ●彼を元の仕事に戻す(=復職させる) *restore* him [*put* him *back*] to his old job. ●時計を10分戻す *put* [*turn*] *back* one's watch (by) ten minutes. ●この電話交換台に戻していただけないでしょうか Could you please *return* me to the switchboard? ●彼女はテーブルから立ち上がりいすを元に戻した She rose from the table and *pushed* her chair *in*.

❷[吐く] vomit, 《話》throw*... up. ●戻しそうになる(米) feel sick to one's stomach; 《英》 feel *sick*. ▶彼は食べたものを戻した He *has thrown up* what he ate.

もたせん 元栓 a main cock [valve]. ●ガスの元栓を閉める turn off the gas *main* [the gas at the *main*].

もとちょう 元帳 a ledger. ●売掛金[買掛金]元帳 an account receivable [payable] *ledger*. ●仕入れ先元帳 a purchase [a creditor] *ledger*. ●得意先元帳 a sales [a debtor, a customers] *ledger*.

*****もとづく 基づく** ❶[根拠とする] be based 《*on, upon*》. ●彼の忠告に基づいて行動する act *on* his advice. 《従って》 ▶この小説は事実に基づいている This novel *is based on* facts. ▶日本のビジネスは相互信頼に支えられている Japanese business relationships *are built on* mutual trust.

❷[起因する] (...による) be due to ...; (由来する) come* 《*from*》; [起因する]《書》originate 《*in, from*》. ●彼の成功は努力に基づく His success *is due* [*attributable*] *to* his efforts.

もて 元手 [資本金] capital; [資金] a fund.

もとどおり 元通り (以前と同じように) (*as* ...) *as before*; (元あった所に) *where* 《it》 *was*. ●壊れた城を元通りにする(=修復する) restore a ruined castle. ●元通り健康になる recover [regain] one's health. ●おもちゃを元通りにしまう put back the toys *where they were*.

もとなり 本成り — 本成りの [形] 《a fruit》 grown near the root of the vine.

もとね 元値 (仕入れ値) the cost, the cost price. [関連] 小売り値 the retail price) ●元値で売る sell at the *cost price* [至近価].

もとばらい 元払い ●運賃元払い(=支払済) freight *paid*.

もとめ 求め [依頼] (a) request; [要求] a demand 《*for*》; [購入] purchase. ●求めにより *by request*; *at one's request*. ▶お求めの本は在庫がありません The book you *ask* [*xasked*] *for* is not in stock. ▶どんな色のセーターをお求めですか (店員が客に) What color sweater would you like [do you want]? (前の方が丁寧な言い方).

もとめて 求めて (いやがらずに) willingly; (喜んで) readily; (自発的に) voluntarily. (⇨進んで)

*****もとめる 求める**

WORD CHOICE 求める

require 事物・権利・支払いなどを当然のこととして相手に要求すること. ●我々は1万ドルの支払いを求められている We are *required* to pay 10,000 dollars.

claim 当然付帯すべき事柄や, 自らの当然の権利などを声高に要求・請求すること. ●損失に対して賠償金を求める *claim* money for loss.

demand 特定の行為・行動などを, ごく当然のこととして, 高圧的に相手に要求・主張すること. ●支配者はすべてをあきらめるよう我々求めた The ruler *demanded* that we give up everything.

頻度チャート

require ████████████████████

claim ██████████

demand ███████

20 40 60 80 100 (%)

もともと

❶【要請する】(...を) ask (for...), (人に...を) ask 〈him〉 for...;(正式に, 丁寧に)《やや書》request; 〖要求する〗(強く) demand; (当然の権利として) claim;〖欲する〗want.

①【…を求める】● 許可を求める ask [request] permission 《to do》. ▶政府は経済援助を求めた The government demanded [called for] economic aid. ▶彼女は心のふれ合いを求めている She wants human contact. ▶求む受付係〖広告〗Wanted a receptionist. ▶A receptionist is wanted. より) ▶彼女は大声で助けを求めた She called [cried] for help. ▶昨今は英語力が大いに求められている The ability to use [to communicate in] English is in (×a) great demand these days./There is much [a great] demand for the ability to use English these days. ▶公共の場所での禁煙を求める声が高まっている There is a great cry for a ban on smoking in public places. ▶彼は握手を求めて手を差し出した He extended his hand for a handshake.

②【(人)に…を求める】● 彼に着席を求める request him to sit down; request (of him) that he (《主に英》should) sit down. ● 彼に謝罪を求める demand an apology for [from] him. (⚠目的語が具体的な物の場合は from の方が好まれる); demand that he (《主に英》should) apologize. (⚠ ×demand him to apologize は不可) ▶私は彼に助言を求めた I asked him for advice [to advise me]./I asked [requested] his advice./I asked [requested] advice from him. (⚠(1) 最後の例は前の 2 例よりやや堅い言い方. (2) ×I asked him (his) advice. とはいわない. (3) I asked that he (should) advise me. とすると, 彼に直接求めるのではなく彼以外の人に頼んで求めるの意) ▶彼に多くを求めすぎてはいけない Don't ask too much of him.

DISCOURSE

多くの場合, 日本のポップス歌手が米国市場で成功するのは難しい. 主な理由として, 両国の聴き手の求めるものが非常に異なることがある It is often difficult for Japanese pop singers to succeed in the U.S. market, **mainly because** audience expectations are very different. (⚠mainly [partly] because ...(主に[部分的に]...のため)は理由に用いるディスコースマーカー)

❷【捜す】look for...;《書》seek* (for...) (⚠for がある方は強意的); (綿密に) search for...;〖追い求める〗pursue. ● 名声[問題の解決]を求める seek (for) fame [a solution to the problem]. ● 快楽を求める seek [pursue] pleasure. ● 金(な)を捜しだすって in search of gold. ● 幸福を追い求めて in pursuit of happiness. ▶多くの人が職を求めている Lots of people are looking for jobs [are after jobs, 《書》are seeking (for) employment] now. ▶大学は真理を求める所だ A university is the place where you search for truth.

❸【購入する】buy*, 《書》purchase /pə́ːrtʃəs/; (入手する) get*. (⇨買う)

*もともと 元々 **❶**【初めから】from the beginning [start]; (元来) originally; (生来) by nature, naturally. ▶彼女は元々彼なんか好きではなかった From the beginning [start] she didn't like him. ▶人間は元々社会的動物だ A human being is originally a social animal./We [People] are basically social animals.

会話 「彼は今ニューヨークに住んでいるよ」「元々どこの出身なの?」 "He's living in New York." "Originally where does he come from?"

❷【損も得もない】(やってみて)うまくいかなくても元々 You'd be none the worse for trying. (⚠none the worse for doing は「...したからといってちっとも悪くはない, 元々だ」の意) / Even if you couldn't make it, you wouldn't be worse off than you are now. (⚠wouldn't 以下は「今の状態より悪くはの意)

もとゆい 元結 (もとどり) the topknot; (もとどり用の糸・ひも) (a) paper string for tying the hair.

もとより 〖始めから〗from the first; (元来) originally; 〖もちろん〗of course. ▶もとよりそれは覚悟の上でした I was prepared for that from the first. ▶彼女は英語はもとよりドイツ語も話せる (言うまでもなく) She can speak German, not to mention [to say nothing of, not to speak of, ×let alone] English./(英語だけでなく) She can speak not only English but (also) German [German as well as English]. (⇨のみならず**❶**)

もどり 戻り〖帰り〗(a) return (⇨帰り); 〖釣り針のかかり〗a barb; 〖相場の回復〗〖経済〗a rally of shares; economic recovery. ▶私は毎年戻り年賀を出している Every year I write New Year's cards after I get them.

● 戻り売り selling on a rally. ● 戻り梅雨 the rainy season that has come back.

もとる ● 人道にもとる(=道理に背く)罪 a crime against humanity. ▶このようなことをもらうは私の良心にもとる It is [goes] against my conscience to accept such money.

*もどる 戻る **❶**【元の位置・状態に戻る】return, get* back (⚠後の方が口語的); 〖戻って行く・来る〗go* [come*] back. (⚠go と come の区別は ⇨行く) ● 急いで戻る go back quickly; hurry back. ● 出張から戻る return [get back] from one's business trip. ● 仕事に戻る get back to work. ▶彼は元来た道を戻っていった He has gone back the way he came. ▶今すぐそれを取りに戻りましょうか Shall I go back for it? ▶第 6 課に戻ろう Let's get back [return] to Lesson Six. ▶いつ東京に戻られますか When will you go back to Tokyo? (⚠東京以外で聞く場合)/When will you come back to Tokyo? (⚠東京にいる人がいない人[これから出かける人]に聞く場合) ▶自分の席に戻りなさい Go back to your seat. ▶なくしたさいふが戻ってきた(=私のところに戻された) The lost wallet was returned to me. (取り返した)I got my lost wallet back. ▶すぐに戻ります I'll be back in a minute./I'll be right back. (⚠be は come と同義で)(長くかからない)I won't be [take] long.

会話 「戻ってきてどのくらいになるの」「そんなにたってないよ」 "How long have you been back?" "Not long."

❷【引き返す】turn back; (船などが) put* back. ● 途中で戻る turn back halfway. (⇨引き返す) ▶船は港に戻った The ship put back to port.

❸【意識・健康などを取り戻す】recover; regain; (回復される) be restored. ▶彼女の意識がすっかり戻った She recovered [regained] her full consciousness./She completely came to her senses. ▶私は医師からもう元へは(=元には戻れない)と言われた My doctor told me my body won't recover its former condition. ▶秩序がすぐに戻った Order was quickly restored.

もなか 最中 a wafer cake filled with sweetened bean jam.

モナコ Monaco; (公式名) the Principality of Monaco. (首都 Monaco) ● モナコ人 a Monegasque; a Monacan. ● モナコ(人)の Monegasque;

『モナリザ』Monacan.
『モナリザ』 **the Mona Lisa** /móunə li:sə/. (参考) ダビンチ作の絵画. イタリア名は *La Gioconda* /lɑː dʒouˈkɑːndɑ/)
モニター 图 ❶ [監視装置] a monitor. ●高解像モニター a high-resolution *monitor*. ●マルチスキャンモニター [コンピュータ] a multi-scanning *monitor*.
❷ [意見提供者] (テレビの) a test viewer; (ラジオの) a test listener; (商品の) a (consumer) tester.
── モニターする 動 monitor 《a TV program》.
●モニターテレビ a monitor (screen).
モニタ(ー)リング [継続監視] monitoring.
●モニタリングポスト [放射線観測装置] a monitoring post.
モニュメント [記念碑] a monument.
もぬけのから もぬけの殻 ●警察が彼の家に踏み込んだときには、もぬけの殻だった(=空だった) When the police raided his house, they found it *empty* [*deserted*]. (! 後半は …, they found (that) *it was empty* [*deserted*]. ともいえる)
モネ [フランスの画家] Monet /mouneí/ (Claude ～).

もの 物

WORD CHOICE もの
thing 具体的, あるいは, 抽象的な事物全般のこと. しばしば, 関係代名詞節などが後続し, その内容が具体的に説明される. ●次に私が聞いたもの the next *thing* that I heard.
object 触知可能な具体的な事物・物体のこと. しばしば物体の正体が不明確であることを含意する. ●未確認飛行物体 unidentified flying *object*. ●何か脚が足をかすめた Some *object* brushed against my legs.
stuff 実相が不明確である具体的, あるいは抽象的事物のこと. しばしば口語で用いる. ●甘いもの sweet *stuff*.

頻度チャート
thing ████████████████████
object ████
stuff ██
  20 40 60 80 100 (%)

❶ [物体, 物品] a thing; stuff; an object (⇒ [類語]); (物品) an article; (物質) substance (! 物を構成する物質で特に化学成分を持った物質); (材料) (a) material; (何かあるもの) something (! 否定文・疑問文では通例 anything); (すべてのもの) everything; (どれでも) anything; (何も…ない) nothing. ●ねばねばする sticky *stuff*; a sticky *substance*. ●書く物 sómething to write with (! with に注意); (筆記用具) writing *matèrials*. ●物に執着する be attached to *things*. ●家の中の物は残らず燃えた All the *things* in the house were burned. ●その店ではいろいろな物を売っている They sell various (kinds of) *things* at that store. ●私は甘いものが嫌いだ I don't like sweet *things* [*stuff*]. ●私は眼鏡なしでは遠くの物が見えない I can't see distant *objects* without glasses. ●この粉状の物は何ですか What is this powdery *substance*? ●何か冷たい飲み物をいただけますか Could I have *something* cold to drink? (! 肯定の返事を期待する言い方では疑問文でも something を用いる) ●それは蛇のようなものでした It was *something* like a snake. ●どれでも好きな物を取りなさい Take *anything* [*whatever*] you like. ●このセーターは気に入りません. もっと安いもの[あの棚にあるもの]を見せてください I don't like this sweater. Show me a cheaper *one* [the *one* on the shelf]. (! *one* は形容詞・限定詞を伴って前出の可算名詞の代わりとして用いられる) ●その橋は板を 2-3 枚並べただけの粗末なものでした The bridge was a crude *one* with two or three planks laid side by side. ●それは私の欲しい物ではない That is not *what* [*the one*] I want. (! *what* は先行詞を含んだ関係代名詞)

❷ [所有物] (私のもの) mine; (あなたのもの) yours; (彼のもの) his; (彼女のもの) hers; (彼らのもの) theirs; (所有物) one's possessions; (身の回り品) one's belongings, (話) one's things. ●この本は私のものです This book is *mine*. /(私に属する) This book *belongs to* me. ●この公園は公共のものでだれでも利用できる This park is public *property* and anyone can use it.
[会話] 「これはだれのものですか」「田中さんのものです」 "*Whose* is this?" "It's Mr. Tanaka's."
❸ [品質] ●物がいい[悪い] be of good [bad, poor] *quality*. ●物のいい品 *quality* goods.
❹ [物事] ●ものの見方 the way you see *the world*. (! この world は「個人の経験する世界・世の中」の意) ●ものには順序がある There is a proper order in doing *anything*. ●ものは考えようだ It (all) depends on *how you look at it*. ●欲しいだけ服を持っている娘なんてものはいない There's no such thing as a young woman who has all the clothes she needs.

DISCOURSE
上記より文学はものの見方を形作る上で重要な役割を持つと我々は結論する **Based on the above, we can conclude that** literature plays a significant role in influencing one's *thinking*. (! Based on the above, we can conclude that … (上記より我々は…と結論する) は結論に用いるディスコースマーカー)

❺ [言葉] ●一言もものを言わないで without saying a *word*. ●彼はものの言い方を知らない He doesn't know the proper way of *speaking*.
[会話] 「結婚した相手が悪かったのかもね」「気をつけてものを言えよ」 "Maybe you married the wrong woman." "Watch *your mouth*."
❻ [道理, 知識] ●ものの分かった人 a *sensible* person. ●ものの分かった[分からない]ことを言う talk *sense* [*nonsense*].
❼ [その他の表現] ●[…ものだ] ●事故は起こるものだ [傾向] Accidents *will* happen. ●人はだれでもいつか間違いをするものだ [真理] We all make mistakes sometime. ●彼女に会いたいものだ [希望] I'd like to see her. ●放っておいてもらいたいものだ [願望] I *wish* you wouldn't keep hustling me. ●親の言うことは聞くものだ [義務] You *should* [*ought to*] obey your parents. ●この川でよく泳いだものだ [習慣] I *used to* [(主に書) *would*] often] swim in this river. (⇒昔)

●**物にする** (習い覚える) learn; (熟達する) master; (入手する) get. ●英語をものにする *learn* [*master*] English. (! 今は learn の方が普通) ●車の運転をものにする *learn* (how) *to* drive a car. ●アジア選手権で日本は韓国を下してオリンピック出場権をものにした (=勝ち取った) In the Asian championships, Japan defeated South Korea to win a ticket to the Olympics.
●**物になる** ●将来ものになりそうな男 (将来性のある) a *promising* man; (大きな可能性のある) a man of great *possibilities*. ●大工としてものになるまで (=一人前の大工になるには) 10 年かかる It takes you ten years to become a full-fledged carpenter.
●**物は言いよう** ●ものは言いようだ It depends on *how*

[the way] you *say* it.
● 物は相談 ●物は相談だが Let's *talk* the *matter over* (and try to come to an agreement).
● 物は試し ●ものは試しだ、やってみよう Let's *have a try* [*give it a try*] and see what will happen.
● 物を言う ●金にものをいわせて by the power of money. ●ものをいう世の中だ Money *talks*. (注 を奏すると) Money *does work*. (注 *does* は強意の助動詞) ●結局実力がものをいう Real ability will *win* in the end.

もの 者 a person. (⇒人) ●君は何者だ(名前は) *Who* are you?/(職業は) *What* are you? (注 ぶしつけな聞き方)

ものいい 物言い ❶[言い方] ●彼女の物言い the way she speaks; her way of talking.
❷[異議] ●審判の判定に物言いをつける protest against [raise an objection to] the referee's decision.

ものいう 物言う ❶[話す] speak; say. (⇒話す) ●彼は私に何か物言いたげであった He looked as if he wanted to *say* something to me.
❷[効を奏する] work; (役に立つ) help. ●地道な練習の積み上げが本番のレースで物を言う Constant efforts in practice will *work* at a real race [*help* you to *win* a race]. (注 この will は通例強勢を受け「…するものだ」の意)

ものいみ 物忌み ―― 物忌みする (説明的に) purify oneself by abstaining from going out or eating certain foods for a certain period of time.

ものいり 物入り (出費) expenses. (⇒出費)

ものいれ 物入れ [容器] a container; [押し入れなど] a closet; (車の小物入れ) a compartment; [ポケット] a pocket.

ものうい 物憂い (人がけだるい) listless, 《やや書》 languid /lǽŋgwid/; (時なだるい) lazy. ●春の日の物憂い気分 the *languor* of a warm spring day. ●物憂い夏の午後 a *lazy* summer's afternoon. ●物憂い天候 *depressing* weather. ●物憂い気持ち a *languid* feeling.

ものうり 物売り (人) a person selling things; a peddler.

ものおき 物置 (貯蔵室) a storeroom; (納屋) a barn; (小屋) a shed; (押し入れ) 《米》a closet.

ものおじ 物怖じ ―― 物怖じする 動 (内気な性格の) shy; (おどおどした) timid. ●ものおじしない子 a *fearless* child. ●彼は人前でもものおじしない(=怖がらない) He doesn't *get scared* in public.

ものおしみ 物惜しみ ―― 物惜しみする 動 ●彼は物惜しみする(=けちだ) He is a *miser*. ●彼は物惜しみしない(=気前がよい) He is *generous*.

ものおと 物音 a noise. (⇒音(1))

ものおぼえ 物覚え (記憶力) a memory. ●彼は物覚えがいい [悪い] He has a good [a poor] *memory*./(学ぶのが早い[遅い]) He is quick [slow] to *learn*. (⇒覚え) ●近ごろ物覚えが悪い(記憶力が衰えてきている) My *memory* is failing these days./(忘れっぽい) I am *forgetful* these days.

ものおもい 物思い ●物思いにふける be lost [deep] in *thought* [*meditation*].

ものかき 物書き a writer.

ものかげ 物陰 (暗がり) the shadow(s). (⇒陰) ●物陰にひそむ lurk in the *shadow*(*s*) [*dark*]. (隠れる) hide oneself; (通例悪事をするために) lurk.

ものかげ 物影 (物の姿) a shape, a form. ●暗がりの中で物影(=人影)の動くのが見える see [認める] make out] a figure moving in the dark.

ものがたい 物堅い (慎み深い) modest; reserved; (律儀な) conscientious; dutiful.

*****ものがたり 物語** 物語 a story; [冒険・魔法などが出てくる架空の話] a tale (注 story より堅い話); (教訓的なたとえ話) a fable; (超現実的空想小説) a romance. ●ウサギとカメの物語 [書名] *The Tales of the hare and the tortoise*. ●伊勢物語 [書名] *The Tales of Ise*. ●イソップ物語 [書名] *Aesop's Fables*. ●彼は子供に悲しい [冒険] 物語を話してやった She told her child a sad *story* [a *story* of adventure].

ものがたる 物語る [語る, 書] tell* (*of*); [示す] show*, [書] indicate; [証明する] prove*. ●砲弾の傷だらけのビルが激しい戦闘を物語っていた The shell marked buildings *told of* the fierce battle. ●その事件は彼の正直さを物語るものだった That incident *showed* [*indicated*] his honesty. ●それは彼の無実を物語っている It *proves* his innocence.

ものがなしい 物悲しい sad; (心細く悲しい) plaintive. (⇒物寂しい)

ものぐさ 物臭 [状態] laziness; [人] a lazy person, [話] a lazybones (注 単・複同形).

モノグラフ [小研究論文] a monograph.

モノグラム [組み合わせ文字] a monogram.

ものぐるおしい 物狂おしい 形 frantic; distracted.
―― 物狂おしげに frantically; distractedly.

モノクロ (白黒の) black-and-white; (単色の) monochrome.

ものごい 物乞い 名 [事] begging; [人] a beggar; 《米話》a panhandler.
―― 物乞いする 動 ●通りすがりの人に物乞いする *beg* (for) money (注 alms /ɑːmz/ from passersby (注 alms は衣類・食料も含む); *beg* passersby for money; 《米話》*panhandle* passersby.

ものごころ 物心 ●物心がつく (物事を理解し始める) begin to understand things. ●物心ついて以来 since I *was old enough to understand things*; (ever) since I *can remember*.

ものごし 物腰 (態度) (a) manner; 《書》(a) demeanor. ●丁寧な [気取った] 物腰で in a polite [a grand] *manner*. ●彼女は物腰が柔らかい She has a gentle *manner*./Her *manner* is gentle. (穏やかな話し方する) She is soft-spoken.

*****ものごと 物事** things. ●彼は物事をまじめに [安易に] 考えすぎる He takes *things* too seriously [easy]. (注 ×serious, ×easily は不可) ●物事はあるがままに見よ See *things* as they are. ●彼はいつも物事を思いどおりにやりたがる He always wants to do *things* his way. ●物事を中途はんぱにするな Don't do *things* by halves./Don't leave *things* half-done. ●物事にはすべて裏表があるものだ There are two sides to *everything*.

*****ものさし 物差し** (定規) a ruler, a rule; (測定器) a measure (注 日本語のメジャーより意味が広く容量や重さなどの測定にも用いる); (判断の尺度) a yardstick. ●30センチの物差し a 30-centimeter *ruler* [*rule*]. (注 ×30-centimeters…とはない) ●物差しでテーブルの長さを測る measure the table *with* a *ruler* [a *rule*]. ●自分の物差しで人の能力を測る measure 〈his〉 ability by one's own *yardstick*.

ものさびしい 物寂しい (なんとなく寂しい) lonely. (⇒寂しい) ●今日は物寂しい *Somehow* I am feeling *lonely* today./*I don't know why*, but I feel *lonely* today.

ものさわがしい 物騒がしい (うるさい) noisy; (世の中が物騒な) troubled; unsettled.

ものしずか 物静か ●物静かな 形 [口数の少ない] quiet; [平静な] calm; [穏やかな] gentle. ●物静かな女性 a *quiet* lady. ●彼は私に物静かに話しかけた He spoke to me *gently*.

ものしり 物知り 〚知識豊かな人〛a knowledgeable person; 〚特定のことに詳しい人〛a well-informed person; 〚学識のある人〛a learned /lɚːrnid/ person. ▶彼は鳥については物知りだ He is *knowledgeable about* birds./He *has a good* [*a wide*] *knowledge of* birds.
● 物知り顔 with a knowing look.

ものす 物す 一句物す *compose a haiku*.

ものずき 物好き (好奇心) curiosity; (人) a curious person. ▶物好きで君を手伝っているのではない I'm not helping you *just out of curiosity* [(全く楽しみのためだけに) *just for the fun of it*]. (! 後の方は for fun を強めた言い方) ▶そんな古い本を買うなんて君も物好きだ What a *curious* [(気まぐれな) *a whimsical*] *person* you are to buy such an old book!

ものすごい 物凄い 〚形〛〚恐ろしい〛terrible, horrible, 〚程度が〛great, (話) awful; (途方もない) tremendous. (⇨すごい) ▶ものすごい音を立てる make a *terrible* [a *terrific*, (すさまじい) a *tremendous*] noise. ● ものすごい暑さ extreme [*intense*] heat. ● ものすごい(=恐ろしい)形相で見る give (*him*) a *fierce* look.
—**物凄く** 〚副〛extremely; (話) terribly; (話) awfully. ▶ものすごくでかい男 a *great* big man. ▶外はものすごく寒い It's *extremely* [*terribly*, *awfully*] cold outside. ▶彼はものすごく食べた He ate an *awful* lot.

ものする 物する (⇨物す)

モノセックス —**モノセックスの** 〚形〛〚パーティー・学校などが〛男〚女〛性だけの〛monosexual. (⇨ユニセックス)

モノタイプ 〚自動鋳造植字機〛(a) Monotype.

ものだね 物種 (⇨命) 〚成句〛

ものたりない 物足りない 《人が主語》be not quite satisfied [*happy*] 《*with*》; 《事が主語》be not satisfactory. ▶彼の説明ではもの足りない I'm *not quite satisfied with* his explanation./His explanation *is not satisfactory* to me [*not satisfying*]. ▶この絵はどこかもの足りない I feel that *something is missing* from this picture./This picture seems to *be lacking in something* (*appealing*).

モノトーン 〚名〛〚単調, 単一色〛monotone.
—**モノトーンの** 〚形〛monotonous.

ものともしない ● 苦難をものともせず *in* (*the*) *face of* great hardship, (かまわず) *in spite of* great hardship. ▶彼女は苦労をものともしない(=何とも思わない) She *makes nothing of* her trouble.

ものとり 物取り (泥棒) a theif. (⇨泥棒) ▶これは物取りの仕業だ This must be the work of a *theif*.

-ものなら 《接続助詞》❶〚仮定〛▶行けるものなら行ってみたい *If I could*, *I'd like to go*. ▶私をぶてるものならぶってみろ Beat me *if you can*./*I dare you to beat me*.
❷〚想定〛▶ひとたびその歌を聞こうものなら(=聞いたら最後)決して忘れないだろう *Once* you have heard the song, you will never forget it.

ものなれた 物慣れた experienced 《nurses [pilots]》; practiced 《hunters [skills]》; skilled 《craftspeople》.

ものの 《副助詞》(ほんの) only; (…以内[以下]で) less than…. ▶ものの 20 分もたたないうちに [20 分で] 彼はすべての問題に答えた He answered all the questions in *less than* [*only*] twenty minutes. ▶ものの 3 人もいれば十分だ *Only* three people are enough.

-ものの 《接続助詞》(…けれども) though…, although…. ▶その申し出を引き受けたもののどうしたらいいのか分からなかった *Though* [*Although*] I accepted the offer, I didn't know what to do. (! (al) though 節の後置も可. また I accepted the offer, *but…*. も可)

もののあわれ 物の哀れ pathos /péiθəs/ 《*in*》.

もののかず 物の数 ▶お前はものの数に入っていない. 黙っていろ Man, you don't *count*, shut up! (! 呼びかけの man は《米》では女にも用いるが,《英》では男のみ)
● 物の数ではない ▶私の苦労なんて君のに比べたらものの数ではない(=何でもない) My efforts are *nothing compared to yours*.

ものnoけ 物の怪 an evil spirit; (死霊) the spirit of a dead person; (生霊) a wraith. ▶彼は物の怪にとりつかれているようだ He seems to be possessed by an *evil spirit*.

もののほん 物の本 ● 物の本によると *according to a book* on [*about*] *the subject* …; It says in some *book that* ….

もののみごとに 物の見事に ▶彼はものの見事にハムレットを演じた He played Hamlet *marvelously* [*splendidly*].

ものび 物日 (祝・祭りの日) a festival; (国民の祝日) a national holiday; (a) red-letter day.

ものほし 物干し ● 洗濯物を物干しロープにかける hang clothes on a *clothesline*. (! 竿につるす場合は hang clothes from a pole) 〚事情〛米英ではロープにかけて干す)

ものほしげ 物欲しげ —**物欲しげな** 〚形〛wistful. ● 物欲しげな目つきをして with *wistful* eyes. ● 物欲しげに見る look *wistfully* 《*at*》.

ものほしそう 物欲しそう (⇨物欲しげ)

モノポリー 〚独占〛a monopoly; 〚卓上ゲームの〛《商標》Monopoly.

モノマー 〚単量体〛〚化学〛a monomer.

ものまね 物まね 〚名〛(おどけた) an impression; 〚まね〛an imitation. (⇨まね) ▶彼はものまねがうまい He is a good mimic./He is good at *mimicking*.
—**物まね(を)する** 〚動〛(おどけて) mimic; (模倣する) imitate; (そっくり) copy; do [give] impressions 《*of a star player*》; (声による) do voices. (⇨まねる)

ものみ 物見 ❶〚見物〛sightseeing. ● 物見遊山に行く go on a pleasure trip. ❷〚見張り〛a watch; a guard; (斥候(せっこう)) a scout. ❸〚望楼〛a watchtower.

ものみだかい 物見高い (好奇心が強い) curious.

ものめずらしい 物珍しい curious. ▶物珍しそうに curiously; with a curious look. ▶物珍しさから out of [*from*] curiosity. (⇨好奇心) ▶だれもが物珍しそうに私を見た Everyone looked at me *curiously*.

ものもうす 物申す (ものを言う) speak (⇨言う); (抗議する) protest (⇨抗議する).

ものもち 物持ち (財産家) a rich person; a rich man [*woman*]. ▶彼女は物持ちがいい She uses her things carefully and keeps them for a long time. ▶(がらくたを)一杯持っている人を皮肉ってきみは大した物持ちだね You own a great deal of property.

ものものしい 物々しい 〚厳重な〛strict; 〚もったいぶった〛pompous; 〚堂々とした〛stately; 〚威圧感のある〛intimidating. ● 物々しい態度で in a *pompous* [a *stately*] manner. ● 物々しい正面玄関 the *intimidating* [*pompous*] front door. ● 物々しい警戒をする keep 《a》*strict* [《a》*close*] watch 《*on*》; guard 《the place, him》*heavily* [*strictly*].

ものもらい 物貰い ❶〚乞食〛a beggar.
❷〚麦粒腫(ばくりゅうしゅ)〛a sty, a stye. (! 発音はいずれも /stái/)

ものやわらか 物柔らか 〚名〛(穏やか) gentleness.
—**物柔らかな** 〚形〛gentle. ● 物柔らかな態度で in a

モノラル ― モノラルの 形 〖立体音響でない〗monaural.

モノレール 〖単軌鉄道〗a mónorail; 〖車両〗a monorail car; 〖列車〗a monorail train. ●モノレールで行く by [on a] *monorail*.

モノローグ 〖独白〗a mónologue. (!)〖米〗ではまた monolog も用いる.

ものわかり 物分かり ― 物分かりのよい〖理解のある〗understanding; 〖分別のある〗sensible; 〖寛大な〗lenient. ●物分かりのよい人 a *sensible* [an *understanding*] person. ●その生徒は物分かりのよい返事をした The student made [ˣgave] an *understanding* reply.

ものわかれ 物別れ ▶話し合いは物別れに終わった They failed to reach [come to] (an) *agreement*./(決裂した) Their talks broke down.

ものわすれ 物忘れ forgetfulness. ●年のせいで物忘れがひどい be very *forgetful* with age.

ものわらい 物笑い a laughingstock. (⇨笑い物) ●物笑いにされるぐらいならここにいたくない I won't stay here to be *laughed at*.

-ものを (⇨-のに)

モバイル ― モバイルの 形 〖可動性の, 移動式の〗mobile /móubəl/.
●モバイル広告 mobile advertising. ●モバイルコマース mobile commerce. ●モバイルコンテンツ mobile contents. ●モバイルコンピュータ a mobile computer. ●モバイルコンピューティング mobile computing. ●モバイル通信 mobile communications. ●モバイルバンキング mobile banking. ●モバイルプリンター a mobile printer. ●モバイルプロセッサー a mobile processor. ●モバイル放送 mobile broadcasting. ●モバイルマーケティング mobile marketing.

もはや 最早 (もはや…ない) no [not … any] longer, 《話》not … any more; (今は) now; (今ごろは) by now, by this time; (すでに) already. (⇨もう❶, ❸, ❹) ▶父はもはやこの世にはいない My father is gone now [is *no longer* alive]. (!)My father is *no more* (in this world). は古風なまたは文学的な言い方) ▶あの強盗ももはやこれまでだ *It's all over* [《話》*all up*] *with* the robber.

*もはん 模範 〖手本〗a model; a pattern; 〖例〗an example.
①【模範に】▶彼は父親を模範にした He followed the *example* of his father./He *modeled* [*patterned*] *himself on* his father. ▶その庭は日本庭園を模範にして(=模して)作られた The garden *was modeled after* the Japanese garden. ▶その少年に必要なのは模範になるような父親である What the boy needs is a father who is a *role model*.
②【模範を】▶彼は皆によい模範を示した He set a good *example* to [for] everyone [set everyone a good *example*].
③【模範で】▶彼の運転は立派な運転の模範である His driving is a *model* [a *pattern*] of what driving should be.
― 模範的な 形 model; (よい例になる) exemplary.
●模範演技 a model [an exemplary] performance. ●模範解答 a model answer. ●模範生 a model [an exemplary] student.

モビール 〖動く彫刻〗a mobile /móubəl/.
モビールハウス (⇨モービルハウス)
モビールホーム (⇨モービルホーム)
モビリティー 〖移動性〗mobility.
もふく 喪服 mourning. ●喪服を着ている wear *mourning*; be in *mourning* [*black*].

モヘア 〖アンゴラヤギの毛〗mohair /móuheər/.

もほう 模倣 名 imitation; 〖模写〗a copy. ●模倣によって英語の発音を学ぶ learn English pronunciation *by imitation*.
― 模倣する 動 imitate; (そっくり) copy. (⇨まねる) ▶その建物はベルサイユ宮殿を模倣して作られた The building was built *in immitation of* the Versailles Palace.

もまれる 揉まれる 〖手などで〗be rubbed; 〖群衆に〗be jostled 《*in a crowd*》; 〖困難やあらしに〗be tossed [《やや話》be knocked] about. ▶世間の荒波にもまれて(=もろもろの苦難の末)彼は人間が一回りも二回りも大きくなった He has become more mature (than before) as a result of (going through) various hardships.

もみ 籾 〖殻のついた米〗rice in the husk; 〖籾殻〗chaff.

もみ 紅 red silk.

もみ 樅 〖植物〗a fir (tree).

もみあう 揉み合う 〖押し合う〗push and shove /ʃʌ́v/; jostle; 〖争う〗struggle 《*with*》.

もみあげ 揉み上げ sideburns; 〖英〗sideboards. ●もみあげを伸ばす grow [wear] one's *sideburns* (long).

もみくちゃ 揉みくちゃ ― 揉みくちゃにする 動 (しわくちゃにする) crumple … (up). ●紙をもみくちゃにして丸める *crumple* a piece of paper (*up*) into a ball. ▶満員電車でもみくちゃにされた(=押しまくられた) I *was pushed and shoved* in the jam-packed train.

もみけす 揉み消す ❶〖物を〗(押しつけて) stub … out (-bb-); 〖火をおおって〗smother. ●たばこを灰皿にもみ消す *stub* [*crush*] *out* a cigarette in an ashtray.
❷〖悪事などを〗cover [口止めして] hush] … up. ●事件全体をもみ消す *cover* [*hush*] the whole affair *up*.

もみじ 紅葉 〖カエデ〗a (Japanese) maple; 〖紅葉(もみじ)〗red leaves. ▶きのう日光へ紅葉狩りに行った I went to Nikko to see the *scarlet maple* [《米》*fall*, 《英》*autumn*] *leaves* yesterday.
●もみじを散らす (顔などを) blush.
●紅葉下ろし momijioroshi, (説明的に) grated radish with red pepper. ●紅葉マーク (高齢者運転標識) an "elderly driver" sticker.

もみすり 籾摺り removing the husks from rice.
●籾摺り機 a husker.

もみで 揉み手 ― 揉み手をする (手を温めるために) rub [(恐怖や苦痛などのために) wring] one's hands. (事情) 米英では頼んだりわびるときなどの動作ではない. したがって訳では工夫することが必要) ▶彼はもみ手をして(=へり下って)少し金を貸してもらえまいかと言った He said *humbly* that he would be very grateful if I could lend him some money.

もみりょうじ 揉み療治 (a) massage. (⇨マッサージ)

*もむ 揉む ❶〖人・人の体を〗massage /məsάːʒ, mǽsɑːʒ/; (筋肉などを) knead /níːd/; (こする) rub … (down) (-bb-). ●もんで彼の首の筋違いを治す *massage away* the crick in his neck. ▶彼女は私の肩をもんでくれた She *massaged* [*gave a massage to*, *rubbed*] my shoulders.
❷〖心配する〗worry. ▶その件で気をもむなよ Don't *worry about* it.

*もめごと 揉め事 (争い事) (a) strife; (困難な事) (a) trouble. (⇨トラブル) ▶あの家族ではもめ事が絶えない There is constant (family) *strife* in their family./They always have *troubles* within the family.

もめる 揉める 〖ごたごたする〗have* trouble 《*with+*

もめん 人, about＋事); 〖論争する〗have a dispute 《with ＋人, about〖on〗＋事); 〖気にかかる〗be worried 《about》. ▶そのことできのうの会議はひどくもめた We had a heated *dispute* [*argument*] in yesterday's meeting *about* that matter./Yesterday's meeting was *noisy* over that matter.

もめん 木綿 cotton; 〖綿布〗cotton cloth. ●木綿のシャツ a *cotton* shirt.
● 木綿糸 cotton (thread); (紡績の) cotton yarn.
● 木綿糸を通した針 a needle *and cotton*. ●木綿製品 cotton goods.

もも 〖植物〗〖木〗a peach (tree);〖果実〗a peach (!食べ物としては [U]). ●桃の花 a *peach* blossom.
● 桃の節句 the Girl's [Doll's] Festival.

もも 股, 腿 a thigh /θái/.

ももいろ 桃色 pink. (!英語の pink にはわいせつな意味はない. cf. blue) ●桃色の花 a *pink* [a *rose-colored*] flower. ●桃色がかったドレス a *pinkish* dress.

ももだち 股立ち *momodachi*; (説明的に) open parts of both sides of the waist [of the mid-thigh] of the *hakama*.

ももたろう『桃太郎』 *Momotaro, or the Story of the Son of a Peach.* 〖参考〗日本の昔話

ももちどり 百千鳥 many birds; various kinds of birds.

ももひき 股引き (下着用) long underpants, 《話》long johns; (作業用) close-fitting trousers [pants].

ももわれ 桃割れ the *momoware* hairstyle; (説明的に) a kind of Japanese girls' former hairstyle.

もんんが『動物』 a small Eurasian flying squirrel.

もや 靄 (a) mist; (a) haze. (⇨霧❶) ●もやに隠れる be hidden in *mist*. ▶その川はよくもやが立ちこめる *Mists* often hang over the river.

もやい 舫い 〖海事〗moorings; a painter. ●もやいを解く untie a *painter*.
● 舫い船 a moored boat.

もやう (船を係留する) moor.

もやし (大豆の) bean sprouts. ●もやしっ子 (説明的に) a tall pallid child with little muscular strength.

__もやす 燃やす__ burn. ●情熱を燃やす *burn* with enthusiasm 《*for*》. (⇨熱中する❷) ●この紙くずをみんな燃やしてしまおう Let's *burn* (*up*) all this waste paper. ▶たき火をもっと燃やそう Let's *make* the fire *burn* more.

もやもや ▶この森の空気は何かもやもやしている The air in this wood is somewhat *hazy*. ▶頭がもやもやする I feel *blurred* in the head. ▶2人の間にはもやもやした気持ちがあった There was something *odd* [*awkward*] hanging over their relationship.

もやる 靄る (もやがかかる) become covered in a haze.

*__もよう 模様__ ❶〖図案〗a pattern /pǽtərn/ (!線や形を繰り返した装飾的な); a design (!意匠を凝らした芸術的な);〖虫や鳥の羽根の〗(a) marking (!通例複数形で). ●幾何学的な模様 geometric *patterns*.
● 壁紙の模様 wallpaper *patterns*; a *design* on wallpaper. ●花模様のあるドレス a dress with flower *patterns* [*designs*]; a flower-*patterned* dress. ●水玉模様 polka dots; a polka-dot *pattern*. ▶このカーペットにはかわいい模様がついている This carpet has a pretty pattern.

❷〖様子〗a look, an appearance;〖兆候, 気配〗a sign, an indication;〖状況〗the state of affairs [things]. (⇨様子) ●この空模様では from the look of the sky. ●荒れ模様の天気 *stormy* weather.
●事故の模様を報道する report *how* the accident *happened*. ●部屋の模様替え（＝家具の配置換え)をする *rearrange*; (改装する) *redo* a room. ▶雨模様です It *looks like* rain./It *looks as if* 〖《話》*like*〗it's going to rain. ▶物価は上がる模様です There is a *sign* of a price rise./Prices *seem* to go up. ▶この模様では, その法案は否決されそうだ In the present *state of things* [As *matters stand* now], the bill will be rejected. ▶今, 試合の模様はどうですか How's the game *going* now? ▶投資家はほぼ模様眺めに回った Many of the investors have taken a *wait-and-see* outlook [*have sat tight*].

*__もよおし 催し__ (集会) a meeting; (行事) an [a social] event; (式典) a ceremony; (宴会) a party; (デパートの) a sale. ●催しをする hold [have] a *meeting*; (余興をする) give [provide] *entertainment*; (特売をする) have [hold] a *sale*. ●その展覧会はある出版社の催しで（＝主催で）開かれた The exhibition was held under the *auspices* /ɔ́:spɪsɪz/ [*sponsorship*] *of* a publishing company. ▶この雑誌は町の催しに（＝町で何が行われているのかを知るのに）便利です This magazine is useful to see *what's going on* [*happening*] in town.

__もよおす 催す__ ❶〖会などを開く〗 hold, give* (!hold より口語的); 〖行う〗have*. ●コンサートを催す *hold* [*give*] a concert. ●彼のために送別会を催した We *held* [*gave, had*] a farewell party for [in honor of] him./We *gave* [ˣheld, ˣhad] him a farewell party. (!(1) 受身は A farewell party *was held* [*given, ˣhad*] for him./He *was given* [ˣheld, ˣhad] a farewell party. (2) くだけた言い方では throw も用いられる: ささやかなパーティーを催す *throw* a little party)

❷〖気分などを起こす〗●眠気〖寒気〗を催す feel sleepy [*chilly*]. ▶彼女はその写真を見て吐き気を催した She *felt* sick when she saw the picture./The picture *made* her *sick*.

もより 最寄り ●最寄りの（＝いちばん近い）駅 the *nearest* railroad station. ●最寄りの（＝近所の）スーパーマーケットに買い物に行く go shopping at the supermarket *in the neighborhood*; go shopping at the supermarket *nearby* [at the *nearby* supermarket].

モラール 〖やる気, 士気〗morale.

もらい 貰い (心付け)《書》a gratuity, a tip; (施し物) alms.

もらいうける 貰い受ける (もらう) get. (⇨貰う) ●隣から子犬をもらい受ける *get* a puppy from one's next-door neighbor.

もらいご 貰い子 〖養子〗an adopted child;〖里子〗a foster child.

もらいさげ 貰い下げ ▶先生は警察署に非行生徒をもらい下げに行った The teacher went to the police station to *get custody* of the delinquent student.

もらいさげる 貰い下げる ▶その土地は政府からもらい下げてもらった The land *was granted* from the government.

もらいじこ 貰い事故 (説明的に) a traffic accident for which one is not responsible. ●もらい事故にあう（＝交通事故に巻き込まれる）get involved in a traffic accident.

もらいちち 貰い乳 ▶彼女は乳腺炎にかかっていたので赤ん坊はもらい乳で育てた As she caught mastitis, she fed her baby on *another woman's milk*.

もらいて 貰い手 ▶子犬のもらい手がいない I cannot

もらいなき 貰い泣き ― 貰い泣きする 動 cry [weep] in sympathy.

もらいび 貰い火 ▶私の家は隣からのもらい火で全焼した My house was burned down by the fire which started in the next house.

もらいみず 貰い水 ●隣家でもらい水をする get water from one's next-door; go next door for water.

もらいもの 貰い物 a present (from).

もらいゆ 貰い湯 ●隣家でもらい湯する go next door for a bath.

もらう 貰う ❶ [受ける] (得る) get*; (差し出されて受け取る) receive (get より堅い語); (与えられる) be given; (持つ) have*; (代金として) take*; (賞などを) be awarded. ●許可をもらう get [have, 《やや書》 obtain] permission. ▶誕生日のプレゼントに時計をもらった I got [received, was given] a watch as my birthday present. ▶いくらもらったの How much did they give you? ▶水を1杯もらえませんか Can [Could] I have a glass of water? ▶部屋代として月3万円もらいます I'll take [(徴収する) collect] 30,000 yen a month for the room rent. ▶彼はノーベル平和賞をもらった He received [was awarded] a Nobel Peace Prize. ▶この前の仕事では月に1,500ドルもらって(=かせいで)いました In my last job I was making 1,500 dollars a month. ▶私は数学で優をもらった I got an A in math. ▶法廷の書記の仕事がもらえそうなんだ It looks like I'm in line for a clerkship (of the court). (!) be in line for は「…の見込みがある」の意
[会話] 「いくらだい」「525円です」「よし、それをもらおう」 "How much is it?" "It's 525 yen." "All right. I'll take it." (! この take は「選び取る」の意)
❷ [家に迎える] (養子に) adopt; (妻に) marry. ▶彼はおばの養子にもらわれた He was adopted into his aunt's family. ▶どうして嫁をもらわないのか Why don't you get married? (! 場合によりプライバシーの侵害になる質問)
❸ […してもらう] gét* [háve*] (it) dòne (! get の方が口語的); (頼んで) ask (him) to do; […してほしい] want [would like] (him) to do (! would like の方が間接的で丁寧な言い方). ▶(かかりつけの)医者に見てもらう see the [one's] doctor; go to the doctor('s). ▶私は彼にエンジンの調子を調べてもらった I got [had] the engine checked by him./(頼んだ) I asked him to check [I had him check] the engine./He checked the engine of my car. ▶私は先生に私の書いたものをチェックしてもらった I got [asked] my teacher to check my essay. (! have は目上の人または料金を払って「させる」の意. 「もらう」場合に用いるので ×I had my teacher check my essay. は不可) ▶この領収証にサインしてもらいたい I want [I'd like] you to sign this receipt. ▶いつ始めてもらえますか When can you start? ▶給料を上げてもらった I got [They gave me] a raise. (! 《英》 では salary の代わりに rise を用いる. ×I had my salary raised. とは通例いわない)

もらす 漏らす ❶ [知らせる] (秘密などをこっそり) leak ... (out); (意図的に) reveal; (通例何気なく) let* ... out; [告げる] tell*. ▶彼は敵に秘密の計画を漏らした He leaked (out) [revealed, gave away, told, (暴露した) betrayed] the secret plans to the enemy. ▶彼はうっかり意中の候補者の名を記者団に漏らしてしまった He accidentally let out [let slip] the name of a possible candidate [a candidate of his choice] to the press corps.

❷ [しそこなう] fail (to do); (捕らえそこなう) miss. ●最後の単語を聞き漏らす fail to catch the last word; miss the last word.

❸ [小便などを] ●小便を漏らす wet one's pants [(女子の) panties].

❹ [その他の表現] ▶彼は仕事のことで不満を漏らしていた(=言っていた) He was complaining [making complaints] about his job. ▶彼は後悔のため息を漏らした(=ついた) He sighed [heaved a sigh] with regret.

モラトリアム [(債務支払い)猶予] a moratorium.
●モラトリアム人間(精神的に未熟な若者) a mentally immature young man [woman].

モラリスト <フランス語> [道徳家] a moralist.

モラル [道徳] morals; [徳性] morality. ●(道徳) モラルの問題である a moral question. ●モラルに欠ける have no [be lacking in] morals.
●モラルハザード [倫理ική的] a moral hazard.

*もり 森 a wood; (a) forest; a grove. (⇨森林)

> 使い分け wood forest より小さく grove より大きく、人の往来があるような森. 複数形で用いることが多いが、その場合《米》では a をつけて woods を単数扱いにすることがある: 家の近くに森がある There is a woods 《米》 [There is a wood 《英》, There are woods 《英》] near the house.
> forest 天然の(大)森林で小動物や野獣の住む所.
> grove 手入れした小さな森 [木立, 林].

●森の鳥 wood [woodland] birds; birds of the woodland(s). ●森へ散歩に行く go for a walk in [xat, xto] the woods. ●木を見て森を見ず (⇨木(成句))
●森番 a forest watch.

もり 守り ●赤ん坊の守りをする (世話する) take care of [look after] a baby; (親の留守中に雇われて) baby-sit (for+雇い主) (! 過去形は baby-sat より did baby-sitting の方が普通).

もり 盛り ▶あのそば屋は盛りがよい [少ない] That soba shop serves us (with) a generous [a small] helping of soba.

もり 銛 a harpoon (! 主に捕鯨用); a fish(ing) spear. ●もりを打ち込む harpoon (a whale).

もりあがり 盛り上がり (a) swell; a rise; [絶頂] a climax.

もりあがる 盛り上がる 動 [ふくれる] swell*; [起こる] arise*; [催しなどが] (活気づく) come* to life, 《話》 warm up; (最高潮に達する) reach the climax; [感情的に] become* excited. ▶会場に着いたときパーティーは盛り上がり始めていた [最高に盛り上がっていた] The party had just started to warm up nicely [was in full swing] when we got there.

── 盛り上げる [積み上げる] heap [pile] up; [活気づける] bring* ... to life, 《話》 warm ... up. ▶彼らは歌や踊りでパーティーを盛り上げた Their songs and dances brought the party to life./They warmed up the party with songs and dances [by singing and dancing].

もりあわせ 盛り合わせ (すしなどの) the assorted selection. ●さしみの盛り合わせ assorted sashimi.

もりかえす 盛り返す [勢いを] regain one's power [strength]; [選手・俳優などが]《話》come* back; [株が] rally.

もりがし 盛り菓子 (説明的に) a heap of dry Japanese sweets or sweetened bean-jam buns on a tray, to the spirit of a dead person.

もりきり 盛り切り ●盛り切り一膳のご飯 a single helping of rice in a rice bowl.

もりこむ 盛り込む 〚取り入れて同化する〛《やや書》incorporate; 〚含む〛include. ● みんなの考えをその計画に盛り込む *incorporate* everyone's ideas *in* [*into*] the plan.

もりじお 盛り塩 *morijio*; (説明的に) a heap of salt set at the entrance of a (high-class) Japanese restaurant for luck.

もりそば 盛り蕎麦 *morisoba*; (説明的に) Japanese buckwheat noodles served on a bamboo platter.

もりだくさん 盛りだくさん ● 盛りだくさんな(=多彩な)行事 *colorful* events. ● 盛りだくさんの(=ぎっしり詰まった)プログラム a *full* program.

もりたてる 守り立てる (支持する) support; (支援する) back ... up.

もりつけ 盛り付け ▶ この盛りつけはすてきですね I love this *arrangement*.

もりつける 盛り付ける 〚皿に盛る〛dish ... up; (きれいに) arrange; 〚皿に分ける〛dish ... out.

もりつち 盛り土 (造成用の) a fill; (墓の) a mound.

モリブデン 〖化学〗molybdenum 〘記号 Mo〙.

もりもり ▶ その若い男はもりもり仕事をした The young man worked *vigorously*. ▶ 彼は元気もりもりだ He's *full of energy* [*vitality*]. ▶ そのレスラーの筋肉はもりもりしている The wrestler has *bulging* [*well-developed*] muscles./The wrestler is *very muscular*. ▶ 腹をすかせた少年はもりもりごはんを食べた The hungry boy *devoured* his bowl of rice.

もりわける 盛り分ける dish (sandwiches) out.

もる 盛る ● 土を盛る(=積む) *heap* [*pile*] up earth. ● 茶わんにご飯を盛る (食物を出す) *serve* rice *in* a bowl; (いっぱい入れる) *fill* a bowl *with* rice. ● 肉料理は大皿に盛って出された The meat was served *on* a big plate.

もる 漏る leak. (⇨漏れる) ▶ このバケツは水が漏る This bucket *leaks* [*is leaky*].

モルジブ Maldives /mɔ́:ldi:vz, mǽldaivz/; (公式名) the Republic of Maldives. (首都 Male) ● モルジブ人 a Maldivian. ● モルジブ(人)の Maldivian.

モルタル mortar /mɔ́:rtər/, (❗レンガなどの接合用); stucco (❗壁の仕上げ塗り用). ● モルタルを塗る mortar 《a house》. ● モルタル塗りの家 a *mortared* [a *stucco(ed)*] house.

モルト malt /mɔ́:lt/.
● モルトウイスキー malt whiskey.

モルドバ Moldova, (公式名) the Republic of Moldova. (首都 Kishinev) ● モルドバ人 a Moldovan. ● モルドバ(人)の Moldovan.

モルヒネ 〚<オランダ語〛〚薬剤〛morphine /mɔ́:rfi:n/.
● モルヒネ(の注射)を打つ give (him) a shot of *morphine*.
● モルヒネ中毒 morphine poisoning, morphinism. ● モルヒネ中毒患者 a morphine addict, morphinomaniac.

モルモット 〚<オランダ語〛a guinea /gíni/ pig. (❗(1)日本語と同様、比喩的にも用いられる。(2) a marmot とは異なる動物) ● 彼は自分の患者を新薬のモルモットとして利用した He used his patients as *guinea pigs* for a new medicine.

もれ 漏れ 〚穴などの〛a leak, (やや書) (a) leakage; 〚抜け落ち〛(やや書) (an) omission. ● ガス漏れ a gas leak. ● 情報の漏れ a *leak* [(a) *leakage*] of information. ● 名前の漏れ the *omission* of names 《*from*》.

もれきく 漏れ聞く (うわさに聞く) hear (secondhand); 〚ふと耳にする〛overhear* 《their conversation》. ● 漏れ聞くところによると I hear that ...; From what I've heard.

もれなく 漏れ無く ● 空所を漏れなく(=すべての空所を)埋める fill in [《米》out] all the blanks. ● 漏れなく(=徹底的に)調査する make a *thorough* [an *exhaustive*] investigation 《*into* it》. ● 漏れなく(it) *thoroughly* [*exhaustively*]. ● 応募者全員にも漏れなく化粧品のサンプルをお贈りします All applicants, *without* any exception, will receive free cosmetics samples as a present.

*もれる 漏れる ❶ 〚水・ガスなどが〛leak (out), escape. ● 水の漏れるバケツ a *leaky* bucket. ● 壊れたパイプからガスが漏れていた The gas *was leaking* [*escaping*] from the broken pipe. ▶ 光がカーテンのすき間から漏れていた Lights *were shining through* a chink in the curtains. ▶ 窓からは明かりが漏れていなかった No lights *came from* the windows. ▶ 彼の口から思わずくすっと笑いが漏れた An involuntary chuckle *escaped* his lips. ▶ おしっこが漏れそう I want to *leak* badly. (❗leak は「小便する」の意) ▶ 咳(ਢき)をしたときにお小水が漏れることはないでしょうか When you cough, does your water *come away from* you?
❷ 〚秘密などが〛leak (out); get* out. ● 秘密が漏れた The secret *has leaked* (out) [*got out*].
❸ 〚抜け落ちる〛(意図的または時にうっかりして) be omitted 《*from*》; (削除される) be left (*off* [*out of*] a list); (欠けている) be missing. ● 彼の名前は名簿から漏れていた His name *was omitted from* the list./His name *was off* [*out of*] the list./His name *was not on the list*. ▶ 〚単に「載っていない」の意〛▶ 彼は選考に漏れた(=選ばれなかった) He *was not chosen* [*selected*].

*もろい 脆い (壊れやすい) fragile; (弱い) weak. ● もろい花びん a *fragile* vase. ● もろい関係 a *fragile* relationship. ● 情にもろい have a *tender* heart.

もろきゅう *morokyu*; (説明的に) slices of cucumber served with unrefined *miso*.

もろくも 脆くも (容易に) easily; (難なく) without difficulty. ● もろくも敵に敗れる be beaten [be defeated] *easily* by the enemy.

もろこ 諸子 〚魚介〛a minnow.

もろこし 〚植物〛sorghum.

もろざし 諸差し 〚相撲〛*morozashi*; a both-hands-inside grip. ● 諸差しになる get a *both-hands-inside grip*.

モロッコ Morocco /mərákou/; (公式名) the Kingdom of Morocco. (首都 Rabat) ● モロッコ人 a Moroccan. ● モロッコ(人)の Moroccan.

もろて 諸手 ● 諸手を挙げて ● 諸手を挙げて賛成する (心から) agree 《*to* it [*with* him》》 *whole-heartedly*; (全面的に) agree *completely*.

もろともに 諸共に together 《*with*》.

もろに 〚完全に〛completely; 〚まともに〛right; (真っすぐに) straight. ● もろに負ける be *completely* defeated. ● もろにドアにぶつかる bump *right* into the door.

もろは 諸刃 ●諸刃の剣 a double-edged sword. ▶ その契約は我々にとって有利にも不利にも働く The contract will *cut both* [*two*] *ways* for us.

もろはだ 諸肌 ●諸肌を脱ぐ (上半身の肌を出す) strip to the waist; (全力で)do one's best; do all one can.

もろびと 諸人 many people; everyone; all the people.

もろみ 醪味 (酒) unrefined *sake*; (しょうゆ) unrefined soy sauce.

もろもろの 諸々の all; various; all kinds [sorts] of.

*もん 門 a gate. (❗通用門・城門・改札口など出入り口

を総称する語.門扉が両開きの場合はしばしば gates とする)●表[裏]の門 the front [back] *gate*. ●門から入る[出る] enter at [go out of] the *gate*. (🛈 日本語の「から」に引かれて from を用いないこと)●門をくぐり抜ける go [pass] through the *gate*. ●学校の正門は昼間は開いている The main *gate to* [*of*] the school is (kept) open during the day.
●門を叩く knock at the gate; (弟子入りをお願いする) ask to become a pupil.

もん 文 ●昔の貨幣の単位 a *mon*(貫 〜); a thousandth of a *kan*;〖足袋・靴の大きさの単位〗a *mon* (参考 約 2.4cm).●10 文の足袋 size 10 *tabi*.

もん 紋 (家紋) a family crest; (紋章) a coat of arms (⇨紋章).

もんえい 門衛 a doorkeeper. (⇨門番)

もんか 門下 ●門下生 a pupil; a student. (⇨弟子)

もんがいかん 門外漢 〖専門外の人〗a layman; (部外者) an outsider.

もんがいふしゅつ 門外不出 ●門外不出の名画 a great painting which has never been loaned [lent] out; a jealously guarded painting of great value. (🛈 jealously は「用心に用心を重ねて」の意)▶この絵は当館めの門外不出です This picture *is never allowed to take out of* the museum.

もんかしょう 文科省 〖「文部科学省」の略〗(⇨文部科学)

もんがまえ 門構え ●立派な門構えの家 a house with an imposing *gate*.

モンキー 〖猿〗〖動物〗a monkey.
●モンキースパナ[レンチ] a (monkey) wrench. (🛈 monkey を省略するのは (主に英))

もんきりがた 紋切り型 ●紋切り型の(＝型にはまった) あいさつ *stereotyped* [*conventional*] greetings.

****もんく** 文句 图 ❶〖語句〗words; (表現) an expression; (言葉遣い) wording. ●名文句(＝有名な引用句)a famous *quotation* 〈*from*〉.●それを表現するいい(＝ぴったりの)文句を思いつく find the right *word*(*s*) [*expression*] to describe it. (🛈 1 語の文句では word を用いる)

❷〖不平〗a complaint; (ぶつぶつ言う不満) a grumble;〖異議〗(an) objection. ●母は私の通知表の文句たらたらだった Mother was full of *complaints about* my report card. ▶彼の提案に文句はない I have no *objection* to his proposal. ▶文句なしに(＝疑いもなく)彼がチームで一番の選手です He is *without doubt* [*undoubtedly*] the best player on 〖×of〗 the team. ▶彼女の演奏は文句のつけようがなかった(＝完璧(なん)だった) Her performance was *perfect*. ▶彼はいつもぼくの作品に文句をつける(＝あら捜しする) He is always *complaining about* [*criticizing*, 〈やや書〉*finding fault with*〗my works. (🛈 always とともに進行形で用いると通例非難を暗示する)▶何か文句でもあるの？ Do you have something to say?

── 文句を言う 動 (不満を言う) complain 〈*about*＋事, *to*＋人; *that* 節〉; make* a complaint 〈*about*〉; (ぶつぶつ言う) grumble 〈*about*＋事, *at*＋人〉; (反対する) object 〈*to*〉.●給料が安いといって雇い主に文句を言う *complain to* the employer *about* one's small pay (🛈 語順を変えて *complain about* one's small pay *to* the employer も可); *complain to* the employer *that* one is poorly paid. ▶私には何も文句を言うことはない I have nothing to *complain* [*grumble*] *about*./(まったく満足している) I'm completely satisfied.

もんげん 門限 〖寮の〗(a) curfew; (家庭の) returning home time. ●門限に遅れる be late for the *curfew*. ●門限を守る observe the *curfew*.

▶門限は何時ですか What time do you have to get [return] home?/What time is the door closed [locked] at night? ▶門限は午後 10 時ですが,門限後に帰ると寮から締め出されるはめになりますよ We have a 10 p.m. *curfew*. You'll have to be locked out of the dorm, if you get back *after* 〈×the〉 *curfew*.

もんこ 門戸 ●諸外国に門戸を開く open (↔close) one's *doors* to foreign countries.

モンゴル Mongolia /mɑŋɡóʊljə/. (🛈 公式名も同じ)(首都) Ulan Bator. ●モンゴル人 a Mongolian; a Mongol. ●モンゴル語 Mongolian. ●モンゴル(人[語])の Mongolian.
●モンゴル帝国 the Mongol Empire. ●モンゴル相撲 the Mongolian sumo wrestling.

もんごん 文言 (語句) words; a phrase; (表現) an expression.

もんさつ 門札 a doorplate; a nameplate.

もんし 門歯 〖解剖〗an incisor /ɪnsáɪzər/.

もんし 悶死 ── 悶死する 動 die in great agony.

もんじゃやき もんじゃ焼き *monjayaki*; (説明的に) a thin soft cake made by baking shredded cabbage, shrimp, cuttlefish, etc. on a hot plate and then by pouring a mixture of flour and water on them, and finally by mixing all of them, which is usually eaten hot.

もんじゅのちえ 文殊の知恵 ●三人寄れば文殊の知恵 (⇨三人 [成句])

もんしょう 紋章 (貴族個人の) a coat of arms (参 coats of arms); (家・組織の) a crest.
●紋章学 heraldry.

もんしろちょう 紋白蝶 〖昆虫〗a cabbage butterfly.

もんしん 問診 oral questions by a doctor. ▶医師はその患者の病歴について問診をした The doctor asked the patient some questions about his medical history.

モンスーン the monsoon.

モンスター a monster.

もんせき 問責 ── 問責する 動 censure [officially criticize] 〈*him for* it〉. ▶その問題を早急に処理しなかったので彼は問責された He *was censured for* failing to deal with the problem quickly.

もんぜつ 悶絶 ── 悶絶する 動 faint in great agony.

もんぜん 門前 ●門前に in front of a gate.
●門前市を成す (絶え間なく客が来る) have a constant stream of customers.
●門前の小僧習わぬ経を読む (ことわざ) The sparrows near a school sing the primer. (🛈 primer はここでは「ラテン語初級読本」の意)
●門前払い ●門前払いをする (面前で戸を閉める) shut [slam] the door in 〈his〉 face; (面会を拒否する) refuse to see 〈him〉. ●門前払いを食う(＝追い返される) be turned away.
●門前町 a temple [a cathedral] town.

モンタージュ 〖＜フランス語〗〖技法〗montáge;〖写真〗a montage (picture [photograph]);〖米〗a composite (photograph),〖英〗an identikit picture.

****もんだい** 問題 ❶〖設問〗a question; (数学などの) problem; (プリントなど全体としての) a paper. ●問題に答える answer a *question*. ●数学の問題を解く solve a *problem* in math(ematics); solve a math(ematical) *problem*. (🛈 通例 ×answer a *problem* とか ×solve a *question* とはいわない)●練習問題をする do an *exercise* 〈*in* math〉. ▶先生は常に難しい問題を出した The teacher gave [set] us difficult *questions* [*problems*] for homework. ▶テストで問題を解くのに約 2 時間かかった It took me

about two hours to answer the *questions* [to solve the *problems*] in the test. この種の問題はよく試験に出る *Questions* of this kind are often asked in the exam. ▶ご質問の問題文は決して誤りではありません The sentence of *concern* in your question is not wrong at all.

❷ 〖解決を要する事柄〗a question; (困難な) a problem; (政治・経済上の) an issue; (研究課題, 話題) a subject; (警察など専門機関の調査を要する) a case.
● 未解決の問題 an open *question*; an unsolved *problem*. ● 社会問題に取り組む tackle a social *problem* [*question*, *issue*]. (!)英語では a major political *issue* (大きな政治問題), a serious pollution *problem* (深刻な公害問題)などのように具体的にいうことが多い ● 領土問題を解決する settle a territorial *issue* [論争] *dispute*]. ● 興味をそそる問題を論ずる discuss an interesting subject. ● 食糧問題を解決する solve [settle] the food *problem*. ▶いかにして労力を省くかという問題が提起された The *problem* of how to save labor was raised. ▶問題はだれがそれを取り扱うかだ The *question* is who will deal with it./(要は) The *point* [*thing*] *is*, who will deal with it? (! 前の文より口語的な表現) ▶次の問題(=議題)は校内暴力の問題です The next *subject* is the *problem* of the school violence.

❸ 〖疑問〗question. ▶その実験結果が問題になった The result of the experiment *was called in(to) question*. ▶彼の指導力に少し問題がある[まったく問題はない] There is some [no] *question about* his leadership.

❹ 〖不都合〗trouble; (やっかいな人・事) a problem.
● 問題を起こす cause (some) *trouble*. ▶いちばん問題なのは資金が不足していることだ The main *trouble* [The biggest *problem*] is lack of funds. (! ... is that we don't have enough funds. とも言える) ▶もしその秘密が漏れたら問題だぞ(=やっかいなことになる) You'll get into *trouble* if the secret leaks out. ▶次郎は問題だよ, だって身勝手だからね Jiro is a *problem*, because he is selfish. ▶彼は優秀な生徒で, 大きな問題を起こしたことはない He's an excellent student and has never been in any serious *trouble*. ▶彼の教え方に問題がある There is something *wrong* [*Something* is *wrong*] *with* his way of teaching. ▶問題はその男が信用できるかどうかだ The *question* is whether [〖英語〗if] the man can be trusted./〖話〗The question is, can the man be trusted?

〖会話〗「終電車に間に合いそうもないわ」「それなら問題ない. 車で送ってあげるよ」"I'm afraid I won't be in time for the last train." "That's no *problem* [No *problem*]. I'll see you home in my car."
〖会話〗「この洗剤はウールに使えますか」「ウールは大丈夫です. 全然問題ありません」"Can this detergent be used with wool?" "Wool's fine. No *trouble* at all."

❺ 〖関係する事柄〗a matter; a question. ● 金銭問題 money *matters*. ● 人道問題 a humanitarian *question*. ▶それは私の個人的問題だ That's my private *matter* [personal *problem*]. ▶良し悪しの問題ではなく好みの問題だ It's not a *question* of right or wrong, but it's a *matter* of taste. (! *matter* を否定文で用いて ✕it is not a matter of .... とは通例いわない) ▶君のうそがばれるのは時間の問題だ It's just a *matter* of time before your lie is discovered. ▶彼がここへ来るかどうかは(私には)あまり問題ではない It doesn't *matter* much (*to* me) whether he comes [✕he will come] here. (! *matter* は「重要である」の意の自動詞で, 通例主語 it

とともに wh- 節[句]や that 節を従え, 主に否定文・疑問文で用いる) ▶大学は中退しました. それが何か問題ですか I dropped out of college. What does that have to do with anything? (! That has nothing to do with anything. (=そんなことは何の関係もない)の反語表現)

■ DISCOURSE
この問題に関しては異なる見解がある There are different views **concerning** this *matter*. (! *concerning* ... (...に関して)は関連を表すディスコースマーカー)

❻ 〖その他の表現〗● 問題の(=話題になっている)人物 the person *in question*. ● (不良債権を抱えて)問題のある会社[銀行] a *problem* company [bank]. ● 問題意識がある (批判力がある) have a critical mind; (事情に通じている) be aware 《*of*; *that* 節》. ● 問題にしない (大目に見る) overlook (*it*); (無視する) neglect (*it*, him). ▶君の提案は問題にならない(=問題外だ) Your proposal is *out of the question*. (! the に注意)/〖話〗Your suggestion is *out*. ▶彼の発言は問題だと思う I think his remarks are *controversial* ones. ▶金の面に関しては問題ない(=満足)かい Are you *happy about* the financial side of it?

● 問題児 a problem child. ● 問題集 a collection of questions [problems]. ● 問題用紙 a question sheet, 〖米〗an exam.

モンタナ 〖米国の州〗Montana 《略 Mont. 郵便略 MT》.

もんち 門地 (生まれ) birth; (家系) lineage. (⇨家柄)

もんちゃく 悶着 〖もめごと〗(a) trouble; 〖口論〗a quarrel. ● 悶着を起こす (人が) get into trouble 《*with*》; (人・事が) cause *trouble*.

もんちゅう 門柱 a gatepost.

もんつき 紋付 a crested *kimono*; a *kimono* with one's family crest(s). ● 紋付の crested.
● 紋付袴(ᵇᵃᵏᵃᵐᵃ) (説明的に) formal Japanese clothes for men consisting of a *hakama* and a *haori* imprinted with one's crest(s). (⇨袴, 羽織(ᵉᵗᶜ))

モンテカルロ 〖モナコの都市〗Monte Carlo.

モンテスキュー 〖フランスの思想家〗Montesquieu /mɑ̀ntəskjúː, mɑ́ntəskjùː/ (Baron de la Brède et de 〜).

モンテネグロ 〖国名〗Montenegro; (公式名) the Republic of Montenegro. (首都 Podgorica) ● モンテネグロ人 a Montenegrin. ● モンテネグロ(人)の Montenegrin.

モンテビデオ 〖ウルグアイの首都〗Montevideo /mɑ̀ntəvədéiou/.

もんと 門徒 (門弟) a disciple /disáipl/; (信奉者) an adherent 《*of* the Shingon denomination》; (信者) a believer 《*in*》.

もんとう 門灯 a gate lamp.

もんどう 問答 questions and answers; 〖対話〗a dialog(ue). ● 押し問答をする argue back and forth. ▶問答無用 No argument./It's no use talking./〖話〗Don't waste your breath.

もんどころ 紋所 one's family crest.

もんどりうつ 翻筋斗打つ (宙返りをする) turn [do] a somersault. ▶彼は足を踏みはずしてもんどり打って(=まっ逆さまに)谷に落ちていった Missing his step, he fell into the gorge, *turning completely over* as he went. (⇨真っ逆様)

モントリオール 〖カナダの都市〗Montreal /mɑ̀ntriɔ́ːl/.

もんなし 文無し ━ 文無しの 彫 penniless. ● 文無しで without a penny [〖米〗a cent]. ▶彼はまったくの文無しだ He is absolutely *penniless*./He

もんばつ doesn't have a single penny./He has no money at all./《話》He is flat broke. ▶彼は文無しになった He has become penniless./He has spent the [his] last penny./《話》He has gone broke.

もんばつ 門閥 〖血筋〗(家系) lineage; (生まれ) birth (⇨家柄); 〖名門〗a distinguished family; good birth.

もんばん 門番 a doorkeeper, a gatekeeper; (ホテルなどの)《米》a doorman,《英》a porter. ●門番をする keep [guard] the gate. ●門番小屋 a gatehouse.

もんぴょう 門標 (⇨㊙ 門札)

もんぶかがく 文部科学 ●文部科学省 the Ministry of Education(, Culture, Sports, Science and Technology). (🔲 正式の場合以外は(　)内は省略される) ●文部科学大臣 the Minister of Education (, Culture, Sports, Science and Technology).

モンブラン 〖アルプス山脈中の最高峰〗Mont Blanc /mɔ́ːn blɑ́ːŋ/.

もんぺ women's loose work-pants.

もんめ 匁 a momme (㊤ 〜); (昔の通貨単位) a [one] sixtieth of a ryo; (重さの単位) a [one] thousandth of a kan (〖参考〗3.75g).

もんもう 文盲 図 illiteracy /ilítərəsi/. ── 文盲の 形 illiterate.

もんもん 悶々 ●悶々として worriedly. ●悶々とする (=思い悩む) worry oneself 《about》; brood 《about》.

もんよう 紋様 a pattern.

モンローしゅぎ モンロー主義 the Monroe Doctrine; Monroeism.

や

や 矢 ❶ [武器の] an arrow; [投げ矢] a dart. ●矢のように速い be (as) swift as an *arrow*. ●矢を射る [放つ] shoot an *arrow* 《at》. ●矢を弓につがえる put [fix] an *arrow* to the bow. ▶彼は矢を的に命中させた He shot the *arrow* straight into the target. ❷ [その他の表現] ●質問の矢を放つ fire [shoot] questions 《at him》. ●彼は矢のように部屋から出て行った He shot out of the room. ●その任務には彼に白羽の矢が立った He *was chosen* [*was selected, was singled out*] for the task. ▶矢は放たれた(=さいは投げられた) The die is cast.
● 矢でも鉄砲でも持ってこい (何でも来い) Let'em all come! (❗相手方の挑戦を受けて)
● 矢の催促 ●彼は私に金を返せと矢の催促をした He pressed me hard to return the money.
● 矢も盾もたまらず ●矢も盾もたまらない (話) be dying 《for, to do》.

や 野 ❶ [野原] a field. (⇒野⁰) ❷ [民間] (⇒民間)
● 野に下る (役人をやめる) leave public [government] service; (権力の座から離れる) go out of power.

や 輻 (スポーク) a spoke.

—や (そして) and; (または) or. なにやかや (⇒何や彼⁽か⁾や) ▶父は午前中ずっと新聞や雑誌を読んでいた My father was reading newspapers *and* magazines all morning.

—や —屋 ❶ [家] a house. (⇒空き家, あばら屋)
❷ [その職業を営む人・店] ●技術屋 a practitioner. ●事務屋 (官僚) a bureaucrat; (事務員) an office worker. ●何でも屋 (便利屋) a handyman; (どれも一流でない) a jack-of-all-trades. ●がらくた屋 (人) a júnk dèaler; (店) a júnk shòp.
❸ [そのような性質の人] ●気取り屋 an affected person. ●目立ちたがり屋 a show-off, a showboat.

やあ 《呼びかけ》Hello (there)./Hi (there). (❗there を添える方が親しみの度が強い) ▶やあ, 宇佐美君! *Hi*, Usami!

やあい 《呼びかけ》Hey. ▶やあい, 意気地なし Hey, coward!

ヤード a yard (略 yd.). [参考] 1 ヤード＝3 フィート(約 91.4 センチ)
●ヤードポンド法 the yard-pound system.

やい 《呼びかけ》Hey. (⇒おい)

やいた 矢板 a sheet pile.

—やいなや —や否や as soon as .... (⇒—否や)

やいのやいの ●やいのやいのと…しつこく迫る press hard for ...; make an urgent demand for ...; be urgent for ...; urge 《him》 to 《do》. ▶借金取りにやいのやいの言われてまいっている I'm really *hard pressed* for payment of the debt.

やいば 刃 (⇒刃物)
● 刃にかかる ●敵の刃にかかる be killed by the sword of 《an [one's]》 enemy.

やいやい 《呼びかけ》Hey, dummy [jerk]!

やいん 夜陰 ●夜陰に乗じて under 《×the》 cover of night [darkness].

やえ 八重 ●八重咲きの花 a double (↔a single) flower [blossom]. ●八重歯 a double tooth.

やえい 野営 图 camping.
——野営する 動 ●川のそばで野営する camp [pitch camp, make camp] for the night by a river. ●野営(=キャンプ)している兵士たち the soldiers in the camp. ●野営地 camp, 《主に米》a campground, 《主に英》a campsite.

やえざくら 八重桜 [植物] (花) double cherry blossoms; (木) a double-flowered cherry tree.

やえむぐら 八重葎 [植物] cleavers; (昔の床склад用) a bedstraw.

やえん 野猿 a wild monkey.

やおちょう 八百長 a fix, 《米》a sétup; (作り事) a pút-up jòb. ●競馬で八百長を仕組む fix [rig] a horse race. ▶あの野球の試合は八百長だ That ball game is a *fix* [*is fixed, is rigged*].

やおもて 矢面 ●矢面に立つ bear the brunt of 《the attack [the criticism, the questioning]》. (❗brunt は「(攻撃などの)ほこ先」の意。通例この形で成句として用いる)

やおや 八百屋 [店] (青物専門の) a fruit and vegetable store, 《英》a greengrocer's (shop); (食料雑貨の) a grocery (store) (❗《米》ではここで野菜・果物も扱っている), 《英》a grocer's (shop); [人] 《英》a greengrocer.

やおよろず 八百万 ●八百万の神 (無数の) a myriad of gods; (あらゆる種類の) all kinds of gods.

やおら ●やおら(=ゆっくり)立ち上がる rise [get] *slowly* [(物静かに) *gently, quietly*] to one's feet.

やかい 夜会 ●夜会を催す give an *evening party* [舞踏会》a *ball*].
● 夜会服 an évening drèss. (❗男の服にも用いる)

やがい 野外 in the open air. ▶子供は野外で遊ぶのが好きである Children like to play *in the open* (*air*) [*outdoors, outside, out of doors*].
● 野外演奏会 an open-air concert. ●野外活動 《do》 outdoor activities. ●野外劇 an open-air play; (主に歴史的・宗教的な事件などを扱う) a pageant /pǽdʒənt/, an open-air theater. ●野外研究 《do》fieldwork. (❗「実地調査, フィールドワーク」の意) ●野外料理パーティー 《主に米話》a cookout.

やがく 夜学 (a) níght [(an) évening] schòol. (⇒定時制 [定時制高校]) ●夜学で英語を学ぶ learn English at *night school*. ●夜学の高校に通う go to *night* (senior) *high school*.

やかた 館 (大邸宅) a mansion, a palace /pǽləs/; (城) a castle.

やかたぶね 屋形船 a roofed pleasure boat.

やがて ❶ [間もなく] soon, presently (❗soon より強い語); (ほどなく) before long; (すぐに) shortly; (しばらくしたら) in a little [a short] while; (そのうちに) in time; (十分時がたてば) in (the) course of time (❗the は省略されることもある); (いつか) someday; (遅かれ早かれ) sooner or later. (⇒間もなく, すぐ❷) ▶やがて君は後悔するでしょう You will be sorry for it *soon* [*before long, shortly, in a* (*short*) *while, in time, in* (*the*) *course of time, someday*]. ▶やがてみんな家路についた Everyone started for home *after a while*. ▶やがて私たちは道を間違えたのに気づいた *It was not long before* we realized we were on the wrong way. (❗主に《書》)

やかましい ❶ 喧しい 形 ❶[音が] noisy; loud.

	教室 (class-room)	ハエ (fly)	音 (noise)
やかましい		×	loud
うるさい	noisy	annoying	loud annoying

使い分け **noisy** 雑音 (noise) があって不快なこと。**loud** 音や声が大きくてうるさいこと。
「やかましい」、「うるさい」について修飾するものを英語で表すと下表のようになる。

(annoying の用例は (⇨うるさい))

● やかましい車 [テレビの宣伝] a *noisy* car [TV commercial]. ● やかましい音楽 *loud* music. (**!** 無冠詞) ● 2階のやかましい話し声 *loud* (talking) voices from upstairs. ▶「やかましい」と先生がどなった "*Don't be noisy* [静かに] *Be quiet*, (黙れ) *Shut up*," shouted the teacher. (**!** 2番目の言い方が最も普通、最後はかなり乱暴な言い方。But with ×Noisy! とはしない) ▶この店はやかましい It's *noisy* in this store. (**!** it で漠然と状況を表し、副詞(句)で場所を表す) / This store is full of *noise*. ▶こうやかましくては勉強できない I can't study with all this *noise*.

❷[厳しい] (人・物が) strict, severe; (人が厳格な) stern. (⇨厳しい) ● やかましいおやじ a *strict* [a *stern*] father. ● やかましい規則 a *strict* [a *severe*] rule. ● 生徒にやかましい先生 a teacher who is *strict* [*stern*, *severe*] *with* his [her] students. ▶母は行儀作法にやかましい My mother is *strict about* [*on*] manners [etiquette]. ▶「がみがみやかましい母親」は a *nagging* mother)

❸[好みなどが] particular, 《話》 fussy 《*about*》. ▶彼は食べ物にやかましい He's *particular* [*fussy*] *about* his food. (**!** ×He's a *particular* man about his food. は不可)

── やかましく 副 ❶[音が] noisily; loudly. (⇨形 ❶ [類語]) ▶エンジンはやかましく回転した The engine ran *noisily*. ▶彼はやかましくギターをかき鳴らした He strummed [played] his guitar *loudly*. (**!** 《話》では *loud* も使う)

❷[厳しく] strictly. ▶医者は安静にしているようにとやかましく言った The doctor *strictly* told [ordered] me to lie quietly. / (何度も) The doctor told me *again and again* [*over and over again*] to have a complete rest.

❸[しつこく] persistently. ▶彼は金を貸せとやかましく言った He *kept* (*on*) asking me to lend him money. (**!** on を用いるとしつこさ、いらだちの気持ちを強調する) / He *persistently* asked me to lend him money. ▶彼はやかましく質問をする He *annoys* [*bothers*, *troubles*] me *with* questions.

やかましや 喧し屋 (下らないことをつべこべ言う人) a nitpicker; (口うるさい人) a nagging person.

やから 族, 輩 [一族] a clan; [連中] 《話》 a bunch, 《話》 a lot 《単・複両扱い》. ▶あんな不逞(てい)の輩には近づくな Stay away from those lawless people [that *bunch*]. (**!** that には軽蔑の意が含まれている)

やかん 夜間 night. ● 夜間に (夜に) at *night*; (夜のうちに) in [during] the *night*. (⇨夜中) ▶夜間に外出してはいけない Don't go out *at night* [*during the night*]. ▶市内全域に夜間外出禁止令が施行されている A *night-time* curfew is in force throughout the city. / The whole city is (placed) under curfew.
● 夜間学校 (夜学) (a) night [(an) évening] schòol. ● 夜間勤務 night wòrk; night dùty. (⇨夜勤) ● 夜間試合 (ナイター) a night gàme. ● 夜間部 (大学の) the night schòol.

やかん 薬缶 a kettle; a teakettle (**!** 特に茶を沸かすための). ● やかんをかける put a *kettle* (*on* the stove, *over* the fire). (**!** I'll put the kettle on. はお茶を入れるときによく用いられる言い方) ● やかんで湯を沸かす boil water in a *kettle*; boil a *kettle*.

やき 焼き ❶[焼くこと] ▶イワシだって焼き方一つでおいしく食べられる Sardines are tasty if they *are broiled* properly. ❷[焼き物] ▶益子焼きの陶器 Mashiko *ware*. (⇨焼き物)
● 焼きが回る (年をとってぼける) become weak in one's mind [judgment] because of old age; become senile. ● 焼きを入れる (強くこらしめる) teach (*him*) a lesson; (殴ってこらしめる) punish 《*him*》 by beating.

やき 夜気 night air. ▶冷たく湿った夜気は病人によくない The cold and moist *night air* is bad [harmful] for a patient [a sick person].

やぎ 山羊 《動物》 a goat; (雄) a he-goat, 《話》 a billy-goat; (雌) a she-goat, 《話》 a nanny-goat; (子) a kid. ▶ヤギがめえと鳴いた A *goat* bleated [said "baa"].
● 山羊皮 goatskin. ● 山羊髭 a goatee.

やきあがる 焼き上がる (⇨焼く) ▶ケーキはふっくらと焼きあがった The cake *was baked* soft. (⇨焼ける) ▶お写真はすぐ焼きあがります Your picture will *be printed* [*ready*] in a second.

やきあみ 焼き網 a grill; a gridiron /grídàɪərn/; a grid.

やきいも 焼き芋 a baked [a roasted] sweet potato (複 ~es).

やきいれ 焼き入れ tempering. ● 焼き入れされた刀 a *tempered* sword; (急冷硬化された) a sword hardened by *quenching*.

やきいろ 焼き色 ▶肉に軽く焼き色をつける *brown* the meat slightly. ● 焼き色のいい nicely browned.

やきいん 焼き印 a brand. ● 自分の飼い牛に M の焼き印を入れる *brand* one's cattle *with* an M; *put* an M *brand on* one's cattle.

やきうち 焼き打ち, 焼き討ち ● 焼き討ちにする set fire 《*to*》; set ... on fire.

やきえ 焼き絵 a pyrography (複 -phies). (**!** 「焼き絵技法」の意では Ⓤ)

やきがね 焼き金 (行為) branding; (印) a brand. (⇨焼き印)

やききる 焼き切る cut ... off by burning 《with a blowtorch》; burn ... off.

やきされる 焼き切れる be burned out, burn out. ▶ヒーターのコイルが焼き切れた The heater coil *is* [*has*] *burned out*.

やきぐし 焼き串 a skewer. ● 焼き串に刺す skewer 《pieces of meat, vegetables》.

やきぐり 焼き栗 a roasted chestnut.

やきごて 焼き鏝 an [a heated] iron; (焼き印を入れる) a brándìng iron.

やぎざ 山羊座 《占星・天文》 Capricorn (**!** the はつけない); (磨羯(まかつ)宮) 《占星》 the Goat. (⇨乙女座)

やきざかな 焼き魚 a grilled [a broiled] fish.
やきしお 焼き塩 baked salt.
やきすてる 焼き捨てる ●古い書類を焼き捨てる *burn (up)* old papers; *throw* old papers *into the fire*.
やきそば 焼きそば fried noodles; chow mein /tʃáu méin/.
やきたて 焼きたて ●焼きたてのパン *freshly baked* bread; bread *hot [fresh] from the oven* /ʌvn/.
やきだまきかん 焼き玉機関 a hot-bulb [a semi-diesel] engine. (参考) 内燃機関の一種
やきつく 焼き付く (焼きつけられる) be branded 《*on, in*》. ▶その悲惨な光景が心に焼きついて離れない The tragic scene *is branded on* [*is burned into*; (深く刻まれる) *is imprinted on*] my memory.
やきつくす 焼き尽くす (建・建物などを) 《書》consume, burn*... down; (やや書) reduce ... to ashes. ▶火事は市の中心部を焼き尽くした The fire *reduced* the central part of the city *to ashes*.
やきつけ 焼き付け 图 (写真の) printing.
── 焼き付ける 動 (写真を) print (off) 《a photograph》; (陶器に絵などを) bake.
やきどうふ 焼き豆腐 grilled *tofu*; broiled [(焦げ目をつけた) browned] *tofu*.
やきとり 焼き鳥 *yakitori*; (説明的に) grilled chicken skewered on a bamboo stick.
やきなおし 焼き直し (作品・話などの) 《話》a réhash.
やきなおす 焼き直す (話) réhash.
やきにく 焼き肉 broiled [grilled] meat; (説明的に) thinly sliced beef dipped in soy sauce and broiled on a grill.
●焼き肉屋 a chophouse.
やぎのうた『山羊の歌』*Goat Songs*. (参考) 中原中也の詩集
やきのり 焼き海苔 grilled laver.
やきば 焼き場 (火葬場) a crematorium (複 ~s, -toria); 《主に米》a crematory.
やきばた 焼き畑 ●焼き畑農法 slash-and-burn agriculture [farming]. (!)後の方が口語的)
やきはまぐり 焼き蛤 a baked clam.
やきはらう 焼き払う burn*... down [off]. ▶川東の街は空襲で焼き払われてしまった The part of the town east of the river *was completely burned down* [(完全に破壊された) *was completely destroyed*] by the air raid.
やきふ 焼き麩 a *yakifu*; puffed wheat gluten.
やきぶた 焼き豚 roast pork.
やきまし 焼き増し ●写真を焼き増しする *print [make] a copy of* the photograph.
やきめし 焼き飯 (stir-)fried rice.
やきもき ── やきもきして 副 anxiously, with (great) anxiety. ▶母は息子の(帰り)をやきもきして待った The mother waited for her son *with great anxiety*.
── やきもきする 動 (心配する) worry, be anxious 《*about*》; (いら立つ) fret (-tt-) 《*about, over*》. ▶君はやきもきしすぎる You *worry* too much.
やきもち 焼き餅 (嫉妬(ど)) (a) jealousy. ●焼きもち焼き a *jealous* person. ●焼きもちを焼いている be *jealous* 《*of*》.
やきもの 焼き物 ❶[陶器] (a piece of) pottery; (磁器) china(ware), porcelain; (土器) earthenware. (⇒陶器)
❷[料理] (a) broiled [(a) grilled] fish [meat]; (焼き菓子) baked sweets. ●タイの焼き物 a *broiled* sea bream.
●焼き物師 a potter.
*やきゅう 野球 baseball. ●野球をする play *baseball*. (!) ×*play the* baseball としない) ●野球のボール a *baseball*. ●高校野球 (senior-)high-school *baseball*. ●軟式[硬式]野球 rubber-ball [hard-ball] *baseball*. ●プロ[ノンプロ]野球 professional [non-professional] *baseball*. ●少年野球チームのメンバー a member of a boys' *baseball* team. ●阪神と巨人の野球の試合をテレビで見た We watched a *baseball* [a *ball*] game between the Tigers and the Giants on TV.
●野球界 baseball circles; the game. ●野球解説者 a baseball commentator. ●野球記者 a baseball reporter [writer]. ●野球狂(人) a baseball nut; a baseball freak. ●野球場 a baseball ground [field]; (観客席のある) a (baseball) stadium, 《米》a ball park. (!)メジャーリーグの球場名は通例 ...Park, ...Stadium, ...Field) ●野球選手 a baseball [a ball] player. ●野球殿堂 the Baseball Hall of Fame. ●野球熱 a baseball fever. ●野球部 a baseball club. ●野球帽 a baseball cap.
やぎゅう 野牛 a wild ox; a bison /báisn/; (複 ~, ~s); (米国産) an American bison (!)俗に buffalo という); (欧州産) a wisent. ●野牛の群れ a herd of *bison*.
やぎょう 夜業 níght wòrk. (⇒夜なべ, 夜勤)
やきん 冶金 metallurgy /métəlɜ̀ːdʒi/.
●冶金技師 a metallurgical engineer.
やきん 夜勤 图 níght dùty; [夜業] night-work; [交替制の] the nightshift (!)通例夜10時から朝8時まで); 《米》the graveyard shift (!)通例夜12時から朝8時まで). ●夜勤の労働者 a worker on the *nightshift*; a *night* worker. ▶彼は今夜は夜勤だ He is *on duty tonight.*/He is *on night duty [on the nightshift]* today.
── 夜勤(を)する 動 work (on the) nightshift.
●夜勤手当 a night-work [a nightshift] allowance.
*やく 役 图 ❶[役割] (分担された) a part; (社会的に果たすべき) 《やや書》a role; [義務] duty; [仕事] a job; [機能, 職務] a function. (⇒役割, 役目) ●自分の役を果たす do one's *part* (with); do (carry out, 《やや書》perform) one's *duty*. ●母親の役を果たす (母親代わりに) play [(書) fulfill] the *role* of mother; (母親として) play [(書) fulfill] one's *role* as a mother. ●調停役を引き受ける take on 《やや書》 assume the mediation *role*; act *as* mediator. ▶部屋の掃除は君の役だ It is your *duty* [*job*] to clean the room./Your *duty* [*job*] is to clean the room. ▶彼はその計画で重要な役を果たした He played an important *part* [*role*] in the project.
❷[芝居の役柄] a role, a part; (配役) a character. ●主役 the léading ròle [pàrt]. (⇒主役) ●脇役 a suppórting ròle. ●王様の役を演じる play the *role* [*part*] of the king. ●リア王の役を演じる play (the *role* [*part*]) of King Lear. ●一人二役を演じる play two *roles* [a double *role*]. ●男優たちに役を割り当てる assign *roles* to the actors. ●刑事の役でデビューする make one's debut in the *role* of a detective. ●うまく自分の役をこなす act one's *part* well. ●自分の役になりきっている[いない] stay in [come out of] one's *character*. ▶彼はその劇でどんな役を演じますか What *role* [*part*] will he play in the drama? ▶弁慶は彼の当たり役だ He is perfect for the *role* of Benkei. ▶彼は殺人犯の役を与えられた He was cast *as* [*for the part of*] a murderer.
❸[地位] (任命された責任のある地位) 《書》a post; (相対的な社会的地位) 《書》a position; [官職] 《書》

書) office. ● 支配人の役を与えられる be given a *post* as manager. ● 彼はその会社で責任のある役を受け持っている He holds a responsible *post* [*position*] in the company. ● 政府内で彼はどんな役にありますか What *office* does he hold in the government?

── **役に立つ** 形 useful 《*to*＋人, *for* [*in*]＋事》, of use 《*to*＋人, *in*＋事》; helpful 《*to*＋人》, of help 《*to*＋人》.

> [使い分け] **useful** 考え・制度・機械・道具・情報などが有用であることを表す.
> **helpful** 主に人や情報が状況の改善などの助けになることを表す.
> **of use, of help** of の後に名詞を伴って、それぞれ useful, helpful の意を表す.
> 動詞 help も物や事を主語にして「一助となる」の意を表す.

● 役に立つ道具 a [×an] *useful* tool. ● 役に立つ人物 a *helpful* person. ● 役に立たない機械 a *useless* machine; a machine of *no use*. ● この本は君の[旅行の; 英語を勉強するのに]役に立つだろう This book will be *useful to* you [*for* traveling; *in* learning English]. ● そのコンピュータは大変役に立った The computer was very *useful*. ● そのコンピュータは肯定文では用いない: The computer was*n't* [was *not of*] *much use*. (2) use が no, any, much, what, how much などを伴うときは of は省略されるが、そうでないときや little, some, great などを伴う場合は、通例 of は省略不可) ● 何かお役に立つことがありますか Can I help you?/Can I be of any *help* [*service*] *to* you? (*!* service を用いる方が丁寧. 決まった言い方で of は通例省略しない)/(何か役に立ちたいのだが) Can't I do something for you? ● その経験が難局を乗り切るのに役に立った The experience *helped* me *to* overcome the difficulty. (*!* このように物事が主語のときは to を省略しない方が普通 (⇒助ける)) ● そのことを考えても何の役にも立たない It's (*of*) *no use* [It's *no good*] thinking about it. (*!* (1) 後の方が口語的. (2) 前の方の of は《話》では通例省略される. (3) *It's no use* [*good*] (*for* us) *to* think about it. も可/*There is no use* (*in*) [*no good*] thinking about it. (*!* 前の方の in は《話》では通例省略される)/(反語的) *What's the use* [*good*] *of* thinking about it? (*!*「そんなことを考えて何の役に立つんだ」の意. *What good would it do to* think about it? ともいえる.) ● このデータはどれもこれもさっぱり[あまり]役に立たない None of these data *help* [*helps*] at all [*very much*]. ● この飾りは実用にも役に立っている The ornament also *serves* some practical purpose. ● (質問の返事や助言などをした後で)お役に立てれば幸いです I hope that [this] *helps*. (*!* that [this] は今言ったこと. 親しい間柄では I は省略される)

> [会話]「本当にどうもありがとう」「どういたしまして、お役に立ててうれしいです」"Thank you very much indeed." "You're welcome. I'm glád to have been *of help*./I'm glád I could *help* you."

:**やく 焼く** ❶ [物を燃やす] burn*. (*!* burn の過去・過去分詞は《米》では burned が普通. ただし、過去分詞の形容詞用法では burnt も可.《英》では burned は自動詞用法のみで、その他の場合は burnt が普通) ● 秘密書類を焼く burn secret papers. ● きのうの火事で彼は家を焼いた(＝焼かれた) He *had* his house *burned* [《英》*burnt*] (*down*) in the fire yesterday.

❷ [食べ物に火を通す] roast; grill; broil; toast; bake; fry; barbecue.

> [使い分け] **roast** 主に肉・野菜を直火で焼くこと.
> **grill** 主に肉や魚を網で焼くこと. ただし《主に英》では直火で焼くときにも用い、その場合、《米》では通例 **broil** を用いる.
> **toast** 食パン・チーズ・ベーコンなどをこんがり焼くこと.
> **bake** パン・ケーキ・魚などを直火に当てずにオーブンで焼くこと.
> **fry** フライパンなどに油やバターをひいて肉などを焼くこと. deep とともに用いることで日本のフライのようにたっぷりの油で揚げることをさす.
> **barbecue** 肉・野菜などを野外で焼き網・串・かまどなどの器具を使って焼くこと. 特に牛・豚などを丸焼きにすることをさすこともある.

● 肉をキツネ色に焼く *roast* the meat brown. ● 焼きたてのパン freshly *baked* bread. (⇒焼きたて) ● 炭火で焼いたステーキ a charcoal-*broiled* [a charcoal-*grilled*] steak. ● オーブンは肉を焼くのに用いられます An oven is used to *roast* meat. ● 今では魚を炭で焼く人はほとんどいない Very few [Hardly any] people today *broil* fish over charcoal. ● 彼女はケーキを堅く焼いた She *baked* the cake hard. ● トーストを焼きすぎて焦がした I *burned* the toast.

❸ [皮膚を日光に焼く] tan (-nn-). (⇒日焼け) ● 海岸で女性が背中を焼いているのをよく見かける We often see some girls *tanning* their backs on the beach.

❹ [焼いて作る] ● 炭を焼く *burn* charcoal. ● 陶器を焼く *fire* [*bake*] (clay to make) pottery. ● れんがを焼く *bake* [*burn*, *make*] bricks.

❺ [写真を] print. ● このネガを3枚焼いてください *Print* [*Make*] three copies from this negative for me.

❻ [その他の表現] ● 彼のいたずらにはほとほと手を焼いている I'm quite *at a loss what to do with* his mischief. ● 私の個人的なことによけいな世話を焼かないで(＝干渉しないでください) Don't *meddle* [*interfere*] *in* my private affairs.

*やく **約** about, 《話》around, 《書》approximately; 《話》... or so; some (*!* 数詞の前に限る); (ほとんど) nearly, almost. ● 約20分待つ wait (for) *about* [*some*, *nearly*] twenty minutes. (*!* about は「20分前後」, some は「はっきりしないが20分ほど」, nearly は「20分近く」の意.「約1年」 about [*nearly*] *a* year などでは some は不可); wait (for) twenty minutes *or so*. ● 約50〜60人の人々 *some* [×about] fifty or sixty people. ● 彼は約7時に到着した He arrived (at) *about* [*around*, ×*some*] seven o'clock. (*!* at は通例省略する)

やく 厄 [[災い]] (a) misfortune; (不運) bad luck; [[厄年]] (⇒厄年).

やく 訳 [[翻訳]] (a) translation; [[訳文]] a translation; a version. ● 逐語訳 (直訳) a literal [a word-for-word] translation. (⇒直訳) ● 正確な [大ざっぱな] 訳 an exact [a rough] *translation*. ● 聖書の日本語訳 a Japanese *translation* [*version*] of the Bible. ● 日本語訳で読む read (it) in a Japanese *translation*. ● 訳をつける(＝訳す) (⇒訳す) ● この訳はうまい[へただ] This *translation* is well [poorly] done./This *is* skillfully [poorly] *translated*.

やく 葯 (花の) an anther.

やく 妬く (嫉妬(ᴸᶻ)する) be jealous 《*of*》; (うらやむ) be envious 《*of*》, envy. (⇒焼き餅)

ヤク [[動物]] a yak.

やぐ 夜具 bedding. (⇒寝具)

やくいん 役印 (職印) an official seal.

やくいん 役員 (会などの) an officer, an official; (会社

やくえき などの取締役) an executive (officer), a director. (!「最高経営責任者」は the chief executive officer, the CEO) ●役員の選挙を行う hold an election of *officers*.
● 役員会 (取締役会) a board of directors; (会議) a meeting of officers. ●役員会の決定 a board decision.

やくえき 薬液 (水薬) liquid medicine; (飲み薬) oral medicine.

やくおとし 厄落とし (⇨厄払い)

やくがい 薬害 drug [chemical] poisoning; damage caused by medicine [chemicals]; (農薬による害) damage from agricultural chemicals.

やくがく 薬学 图 [薬剤学] pharmacy; [薬理学] pharmacology.
— 薬学の 形 pharmaceutical.
● 薬学者 a pharmacologist. ● 薬学博士 a doctor of pharmacy 《略 Pharm.D》. ● 薬学部[科] the pharmacy department; the department of pharmacy.

やくがら 役柄 ❶ [任務の性質] the nature of one's duty. ▶役柄上，部下の何人かに解雇通告をせざるをえなかった Because of my *duty*, I had to give some of my staff a dismissal notice.
❷ [劇などの役] a role; a part. ▶彼はテレビドラマで恍惚の人の役柄を見事に演じた He played the *role* of a senile man very well in a TV drama.

やくぎょう 訳業 (翻訳の仕事) the transláting bùsiness; (翻訳) (a) translation.

やくげん 約言 ── 約言する 動 (要約する) make a summary (*of*); summarize; sum up.

やくご 訳語 (相当語句) an equivalent; an equivalent word in translation. ▶日本語の「義理」に相当する正確な英語の訳語はありますか Is there a precise English *word* [*equivalent*] for the Japanese "giri"?

やくざ (1人) a (member of) *yakuza* (!単・複同形. 総称的には the *yakuza*, the Japanese mafia (単数扱い, the Japanese criminal underworld は単数扱い); a gangster; [暴力団] a gang; [ごろつき] 《話》a tough; (若者の) 《話》a hoodlum. ●やくざ稼業から足を洗う go straight; make a clean break with the *gang* [*mob*].
●やくざ映画 a gangster movie.

やくざい 薬剤 (医薬) (a) medicine, a drug; (化学薬品) chemicals. ●薬剤を散布する spray *chemicals*.
● 薬剤師 a pharmacist;《米》a druggist,《英》a chemist.

やくさつ 扼殺 strangulation. (⇨絞殺)

やくさつ 薬殺 ── 薬殺する 動 kill ... by using poison [poisoned food].

やくし 訳詞 (a) translation of words of a song.
● 訳詞岩谷時子 words translated by Tokiko Iwatani.

やくし 訳詩 (a) translation of a poem; a translated poem.

やくし 薬師 (仏, 如来) *Yakushi*; the healing Buddha; (お堂) a temple dedicated to *Yakushi*.

やくじ 薬事 ●中央薬事審議会 the Central *Pharmaceutical Affairs* Council.
● 薬事法 [法律] the Pharmaceutical Affairs Law. ▶その男は薬事法違反で逮捕された The man was arrested for violating the *Pharmaceutical Affairs Law*.

やくじ 薬餌 medicine and diet.
● 薬餌に親しむ take medicine regularly.
● 薬餌療法 treatment by medicine and diet.

やくしゃ 役者 (男, 女) an actor, (女性) an actress; a player.

> 使い分け actor, actress 舞台・映画・ラジオ・テレビなどの劇の俳優で，これを職業とする人をいう. actor は女優も含めて俳優をさすことが多く，最近では女優自身も actress より actor と呼ばれることを好む傾向がある.
> player プロ・アマを問わず，芝居をする人の意. ただしプロの役者の意では actor より大げさな語.

● 舞台役者 a stage *actor* [*actress*, *player*]. ● 花形役者 a star *actor* [*actress*]. ● 大根役者 a bad [a poor, 《話》a lousy] *actor* [*actress*]; 《話》a ham (*actor*). ● 役者稼業 the *stage* career. ● 役者になる become an *actor* [an *actress*]; (舞台に立つ) go on [take to] the *stage*. ● 役者を辞める retire from [leave] the *stage*.
● 役者が一枚上 ▶彼は多くの面で私より役者が一枚上だ He is *a cut above* me in many ways.
● 役者がそろう ▶役者がそろった All the leading actors gathered together. (!一般的な意味では actors を persons などと替えるとよい)

やくしゃ 訳者 a translator.

やくしゅ 薬酒 medicinal liquor.

やくしゅ 薬種 ingredients for (making) Chinese medicine.
● 薬種商《米》a druggist;《英》a chemist.

やくしゅつ 訳出 图 (a) translation. (⇨翻訳)
— 訳出する 動 translate.

***やくしょ** 役所 a public [a government] office.
● 区役所 a ward office. ● 市役所 a city hall; a municipal office. ● 役所に勤める work for the (*local*) *government*. ▶もう少し具体的に work for *the government* [*prefecture*, *city*, *ward*, *town*] office ともいえる. work for *a public office* も可).
● お役所仕事 (⇨お役所仕事)

やくしょ 訳書 a translation. (⇨訳本)

やくじょ 躍如 ── 躍如たる (生々しい) vivid; (写実的な) realistic. ▶対戦相手をすべて一本で下すとは彼女の面目躍如たるものである It is *characteristic of* her to defeat all her opponents *by ippon*. ▶ピカソの『ゲルニカ』はスペイン動乱の様子を躍如たらしめている *Guernica* by Picasso *vividly* depicts the Spanish civil war.

やくじょう 約定 a contract. (⇨契約)
● 約定利率 the contracted (interest) rate; the contractual (interest) rate.

やくしょく 役職 (管理職) a managerial [an administrative] post [position]. ●役職につく take [hold] a *managerial post*.

やくしん 薬疹 [医学] a drug eruption.

やくしん 躍進 图 ▶日本経済の躍進 the *rapid* [*remarkable*] *progress* of the Japanese economy.
● 人類にとっての大躍進をとげる take a giant *leap* for mankind.
— 躍進する 動 advance rapidly [remarkably]; make rapid [remarkable] progress.

***やくす** 訳す translate. ●訳しにくい語句 a phrase difficult [hard] to *translate*. ●英語の小説を日本語に訳す *translate* 《やや話》*put*] an English novel *into* Japanese. ●詩をイタリア語から訳す *translate* a poem *from* Italian. ▶エゴは日本語では自我と訳される Ego *is translated as jiga* in Japanese.

やくす 扼す [動かないように押さえ込む] hold ... down (⇨押さえ付ける); [要所を押さえるように位置する] (占領する) occupy; (支配する) command.

やくする 約する ❶ [約束する] promise; make a

やくせき

promise. (⇨約束)

❷【短縮する】shorten; abbreviate; (簡略化する) simplify. ● 手続きを約する *simplify* the procedure. ● 「生活協同組合」は約して「生協」と言う 'Co-operative society' *is abbreviated* [*shortened*] *to* 'co-op'.

❸【約分する】(⇨約分)

やくせき 薬石 ● 薬石効なく彼は亡くなった He passed away in spite of all the medical treatment he had received [had been given].

やくぜん 薬膳 medicinal cooking [dishes].

やくそう 薬草 a (medicinal) herb.
● 薬草園 a hérb gàrden.

:やくそく 約束 图 a promise; one's word; an appointment; an engagement; a date.

> **使い分け** promise 私的な口約束から公約にまで幅広く使用される語。日本語の「約束」は相手との取り決めの意が強いが promise は「こうする」という自分の誓い・宣言を意味する。
> **word** 主に「口約束」の意で用い、言葉に対して責任を持つことを含意する。
> **appointment** 日時や場所を明確に指定した面会などの約束を表す。また、医師の診察や職務上の面接の予約の意でも用いる。promise はこの意では不可.
> **engagement** 主に「婚約」の意で用いるが、時にフォーマルな会合や面会などの約束を表す。
> **date** 日時を設定した人に会う約束という意で用いる。男女間のデートを示すことが多い。

①【~の(約束)】● 堅い約束 a solemn *promise*. ● 口約束 a verbal *promise*; (口先だけの約束) a mere *promise*. (⇨口約束) ● 援助の約束 a *promise* of help.

②【約束が[は]】▶他に[すでに]約束がある I have another [a previous] *appointment*. (**!** 後の方は I already have an *appointment*. の方が口語的) ▶歯医者に10時に診てもらう約束があります I have an *appointment* [xa promise] *with* the dentist at ten./I have a ten-o'clock *appointment with* the dentist. ▶人と6時に会う約束がある I have an *appointment to* meet somebody at six. ▶親しい人との私的な約束の場合は I'm meeting [I'm going to meet, I've made plans to meet] 《Taro》 at six. などが普通) ▶昼食の約束は40分後ですよ Your lunch *appointment* is in forty minutes. ▶約束は5時だ The *appointment* is *for* [*at*] five o'clock. (**!** *for* はすでに約束してある時刻に言及する場合に, *at* はこれから会う時刻を決める場合に用いる) ▶約束が違う That is not *what you promised* [*said*]. ▶約束は約束だ A *promise* is a *promise*. ▶今晩彼と食事の約束がある I have a dinner *engagement with* him *for* tonight./《話》I have a dinner *date with* him *for* tonight.

③【約束の】▶彼らは約束の時間に約束の場所にやって来た They came to the *appointed* place [their appointments] *at* the *appointed* time. ▶約束の自転車はいつ買ってくれるの When are you going to buy me the bicycle you *promised*?

④【約束を】● 約束を守る keep a [one's] *promise* ● 約束を果たす carry out [《やや書》fulfill] one's *promise*. ● 約束を破る break [go back on] one's *promise*. (**!** 特定の約束ではなく総称的にいう場合 promise は (one's) *promises*, a *promise* となる) ● 約束を取り消す withdraw one's *promise*; (婚約) break (off) one's *engagement*; (予約) cancel one's *appointment* (*with* a dentist). ▶我々は彼女から再会の約束を取りつけた We secured a *promise* to meet us again from her. ▶約束をすることと

やくたたず

それを守ることとは別問題だ Making *promises* and keeping them are two different things. (⇨動)

会話「彼は約束を守るだろうか」「これまではいつだってそうだったけどね」"Will he keep his *word*?" "He always has." (**!** この has は has always kept his word の省略形で, has に強勢を置く)

⑤【~で】▶次の日に払うという約束でそのお金を借りた I borrowed the money *on the promise that* I would pay [(条件で) *on condition that* I paid] it back the next day. (**!** 後の場合も I would pay となることがある)

── **約束する** 動 promise, make* a promise; give* one's word; (日時などを指定する) appoint. (⇨決める) ▶彼は約束したとおり8時に駅にやって来た He came to the station at eight as (he) *promised*./(約束を守ってやって来た) He *kept* his *promise* [his *word*] and came to the station at eight. (**!** 前の文より口語的)

会話(受付で)「こんにちは, 営業部のビル・ハリスさんにお会いしたいのですが」「お約束しておりますでしょうか」"Hello. Can I see Mr. Bill Harris of the Sales Department?" "*Is* he *expecting* you?" (**!** Do you have an appointment with him? より感じのよい尋ね方)

会話「あしたそっちへ行くよ」「約束する?」「ああ, 約束するよ」"I'll come over tomorrow." "*Promise?*" "Yes, I *promise*." (**!** (1) I promise you. は通例警告・脅迫を表し不可. (2) 改まった関係の場合は次のようなやり取りも可:「そのことを約束してくださいますか」「はい約束します」"May I have your word on [for] that?" "Yes, you have my word.")

①【~を約束する】▶彼は経済的援助を約束した He *has promised* his financial support.

②【~する(と)約束する】▶母は私に新しいドレスを買ってあげると約束したの My mother *promised* me a new dress. (**!**「(他の者にでなく)私に」の意で253の相手である me に重点を置くと My mother *promised* a new dress *to* me. となる) ▶彼はそこへは行かないと約束した He *promised* [xpromised with me] not *to* go there. (**!**(1) He *promised* me not to go there. の型は to 不定詞の意味上の主語が He か me かあいまいになるので避ける. (2) He did*n't promise to* go [xnot going] there./He *made* no *promises* about going there. は「そこへ行くとは約束しなかった」の意. (3) 不定詞の代わりに動名詞は不可)/He *promised* (me) [*gave* me his *word*] *that* he wouldn't [xdidn't] go there. (**!** that は省略可. that 節内の動詞は通例 will, would を伴う) ▶私たちは3年後にきっとまた会いましょうと約束した We *said* we would definitely get together again in three years. (**!** このような破っても信義を問われないような内容に対して promise を用いるのは不自然) ▶彼女と1時喫茶店で会おうと約束した I *made* an *appointment* [*an arrangement*] to meet her in a coffee shop at one o'clock. ▶彼の将来は約束されている(= 有望である) He has a very *promising* future.

● 約束手形 a promissory note.

やくたい 益体 ● 益体もない (価値のない) worthless; (つまらない) trivial; (ばかげた) silly. ● そんな益体もないことにかかわり合うな Don't get involved in such *trivial* matters [*silly* things].

やくだく 約諾 ── **約諾する** 動 declare [confirm] an agreement; agree to a contract.

やくたたず 役立たず ── **役立たずの** 形 (物事が) useless; (人が) worthless, 《話》gòod-for-nóthing (**!** 限定的に. a góod-for-nòthing はそのような人をいう). ● 役立たずのがらくた *useless* junk. ● 役立たずの

やくだつ 役立つ useful. (⇨役)
やくだてる 役立てる ((うまく[十分に; できるだけ])利用する) make* (good [enough; the best]) use of ...; (...に利用する) put* ... to (good) use 《in》. ● 原子力を平和目的に役立てる use atomic energy for peaceful purposes. ● 経験をその仕事にうまく役立てる put one's experience to good use in the work.
やくちゅう 訳注 (翻訳と注釈) translation and notes, attentions; (訳者の付けた注) a translator's notes. ● 安達氏訳注の本 a book translated and annotated by Mr. Adachi.
やくつき 役付き ・役付きになる(=管理職につく) take a managerial position; be promoted to management.
やくづくり 役作り studying a role; learning to play a part.
やくて 約手 〖『約束手形』の略〗(⇨約束)
やくとう 薬湯 a herbal [a medicinal] bath.
やくどう 躍動 ── 躍動する 形 (活発な) lively /láivli/; (精力的な) energetic. ● 体育館で躍動する少女たち lively girls moving about [girls moving about energetically] in the gym. ● 青春の血を躍動させる (=かき立てる) stir the hot blood of youth.
やくとく 役得 《書》 a perquisite /pə́ːrkwizit/, 《話》 a perk. (❗通例複数形で) ● 役得のある仕事につく get a job with (some) perks.
やくどく 訳読 verbal [oral] translation. ● 文法訳読式教授法 the grammar translation method.
やくどく 薬毒 a poisonous substance in medicine.
やくどころ 役所 (適所) one's niche; (天職) one's vocation, 《書》 one's calling. (❗calling は主に聖職者・医師の仕事などに用いる (⇨適役, はまり役)
やくどし 厄年 an unlucky year [(年齢) age]; (人生で危機が訪れる年齢) a climacteric /klaimǽktərik/ (age) 〖参考〗 日本では数え年で (男) 25,42,61 歳, (女) 19,33 歳だが, 西洋では暦年で7年ごとにそうした時期が訪れるとされる. cf. the seven year itch (結婚7年目ごろに騒ぎ出すといわれる浮気の虫); (特に男の) a mid-life crisis.
やくにん 役人 a government [a public] official, a public [a civil] servant; (官僚) a bureaucrat /bjúːəkrӕt/. (❗前の方の言い方に比べ, この語はマイナスイメージを持っている). 《公務員》● 役人になる(=become a public [a civil] servant. ● 役人を辞める (=公職を去る) leave [resign from] public office. ▶彼は文部科学省の役人だ He is an official [has a post] in the Ministry of Education.
● **役人根性** officialism.
やくば 役場 ● 村役場 a village office. ● 町役場 a town hall.
やくばらい 厄払い 名 exorcism /éksɔːsizm/.
── **厄払い(を)する** 動 drive out [exorcise] evil spirits. (⇨祓(は_ら)う)
やくび 厄日 (縁起の悪い日) an ill-omened day; a jinxed day; (災難が実際に起こる日) a bad [an unlucky] day.
やくびょう 疫病 a plague /pléig/.
● **疫病神** a deity of plagues. ● 疫病神のように嫌う avoid 《him》 like the plague; hate 《him》 like poison.
やくひん 薬品 〖医薬〗 (a) medicine, a drug; 〖化学薬品〗 chemicals. (⇨薬)
● **薬品会社** a drúg còmpany.

やくぶそく 役不足 〖会話〗「校正の仕事はあんき気に入ると思うよ」「君には役不足じゃないか」"I think I'd probably like proofreading." "You're a little overqualified (for it), aren't you?"
やくぶつ 薬物 a medicine; a drug. (⇨薬(く_すり))
● **薬物アレルギー** a drug allergy. ● **薬物依存症** 〖医学〗 drug dependence. ● **薬物検査** (スポーツ選手への) a dope [a drug] test. (⇨ドーピング). ● **薬物治療** 〖医学〗 medication; drug treatment. ● **薬物乱用** substance [drug] abuse.
やくぶん 約分 名 〖数学〗 reduction (of a fraction).
── **約分する** 動 reduce 《to》. ▶ 4/8 を約分すると 1/2 になる If you reduce 4/8 to its lowest terms, you get 1/2. (❗four eighths, one half と読む)/ 4/8 can be reduced to 1/2.
やくぶん 訳文 a translation.
やくほん 訳本 a translation. ● 『エデンの東』を日本語の訳本で読む read East of Eden in a Japanese translation.
やくまわり 役回り (割り当てられた仕事) one's assignment. ● いやな役回りを彼にさせる assign a disagreeable role [part] to him.
やくみ 薬味 (a) spice. ● 薬味を加える add spice 《to》.
● 薬味のきいた食べ物 spicy food.
やくめ 役目 (a) role; duty; (a) responsibility; a function. (⇨役, 役割) 例 通訳の役目を引き受ける take on [《やや書》 assume] the role of interpreter. ● 子供のしつけは親の役目だ It is parents' duty [responsibility] to discipline their own children.

*__やくめ__ 役目 〖仕事〗 a job; 〖任務〗 (a) a role, a part; 〖責任〗 (a) responsibility; 〖機能〗 a function. (⇨役, 役割) ● 通訳の役目を引き受ける take on [《やや書》 assume] the role of interpreter. ● 子供のしつけは親の役目だ It is parents' duty [responsibility] to discipline their own children.
やくめい 役名 (役職名) an official position [title]; (芝居における役の名前) the name of one's role.
やくよう 薬用 ● それは今ではもっぱら薬用です It's now used only for medicinal purposes.
● **薬用植物** a medicinal plant [herb]. ● **薬用石けん** medicinal soap.
やくよけ 厄除け (お守り) a talisman; a charm.
やぐら 櫓 (城などの) a turret /tə́ːrət/; (塔) a tower /táuər/. ● 火の見やぐら a fire tower.
● **櫓ごたつ** (説明的に) a kotatsu with a latticed square wooden frame and a coverlet over it.
● **櫓太鼓** (説明的に) a drum that is played on a yagura (tower) to announce the performance of sumo.
やくり 薬理 ● **薬理学** pharmacology. ● **薬理作用** medicinal action.
やくりきし 役力士 〖相撲〗 (三役の力士) an upper-rank sumo wrestler.
やくりょう 訳了 completion of the translation 《of the original》. ▶ その小説の訳了にどのくらいかかりますか How long will it take you to complete [finish] the translation of the novel?
やぐるま 矢車 a wheel with spokes in the shape of an arrow.
やぐるまぎく 矢車菊 〖植物〗 a cornflower.
やぐるまそう 矢車草 (ユキシタ科) a Rodger's bronze leaf; 〖『矢車菊』の別名〗 (⇨矢車菊).
やくろう 薬籠 (薬箱) a médicine chèst; (救急箱) a first-aid kit.
● **薬籠中(ちゅう)の物** ▶ 数百の兵卒を自家薬籠中の物とする(=自分の思いどおりにする) have several hundreds of private soldiers at one's disposal.

*__やくわり__ 役割 〖仕事の一部〗 a part; 〖役目〗 a role; 〖仕事〗 a job; 〖機能〗 a function. (⇨役, 役目) ▶ 当委員会の役割は新社屋を設計することだ The function of this committee is to lay out our new office. ▶このソファはベッドの役割もする(=としても役に立つ) This sofa can *serve* [用いられる] can *be used*] *as* a bed. ▶大気は温室のような役割をする(=働きをする) The atmosphere *acts like* a greenhouse. ▶ライオンは群れで狩りをし、役割分担をした(=連携した)攻撃方法をとる Lions are pack hunters. They use *coordinated* attack patterns.

やけ 自棄 (すてばち) desperation; (絶望) despair. ●やけになって desperately; in despair. ●失敗してやけになる *get* [*become*] *desperate* at the failure. ▶試験に失敗して彼はやけになった(=失敗を彼を絶望に追い込んだ) Failure in the examination drove him to *despair*.
 ●やけのやんぱち ●やけのやんぱちで(捨てばちになって) in desperation.
 ●やけ食い comfort-eating.

やけあと 焼け跡 the ruins of a fire; (火事の後の残骸(ぎい)) *debris*/dɑbríː/; *after* a fire. ●焼け跡に死体を見つける find a corpse among the *debris*.

やけい 夜景 a night view [scene].

やけい 夜警 (行為) night watch; (人) a (night) watchman (働-men), a night guard. ●夜警をする keep (the) *night watch*; keep *watch at night*. ●ビルの夜警をする *guard* a building *at night*.

やけいし 焼け石・焼け石に水 ▶1万円では焼け石に水だ Ten thousand yen is only *a drop in the ocean* [*bucket*]. (❗(only) a drop ... は「取るに足らない」の意の慣用句)

やけおちる 焼け落ちる (全焼する) be burned down; be burned to the ground.

やけくそ desperation. (⇨やけ)

やけこげ 焼け焦げ a burn. ●カーペットの焼け焦げが *burn* in [(表面) on] the carpet. ▶君のたばこの火でワイシャツに焼け焦げができた(=焼いて穴ができた) You *burned a hole* in my shirt with your cigarette./Your cigarette *burned a hole* in my shirt.

やけざけ やけ酒 ●やけ酒を飲む (やけになって酒を飲む) drink in desperation; (酒に悲しみを紛らす) drown one's sorrows in drink.

やけしぬ 焼け死ぬ be burned to death (*in* the fire).

やけだされる 焼け出される be burned [(英) be burnt] out of one's home; be made homeless by the fire. ●焼け出された人々 burned-out people; ((広い意味で)火事による犠牲者) *fire* victims.

やけただれる 焼けただれる (やけどで化膿する) get burned to the point of suppuration; (やけどで水ぐれになる) get burned and blistered. ●焼けただれたタンカー a *burnt* tanker.

やけつく 焼け付く ▶焼けつくような暑さだ It's *burning* [(やや話) *scorching*] hot.

やけど 火傷 図 (火・酸などによる) a burn; (熱湯・油などによる) a scald /skɔ́ːld/. ●軽い[ひどい]やけど a slight [a serious, a deep] *burn*. ●やけどの跡 a *burn* (scar). ●やけどで死ぬ be scalded to death. (❗ burned to death は「焼死する」) ●右足に2か所やけどの跡がある have two *burns* on the right leg.
 ――火傷(を)する 動 get* [be] burned; get [be] scalded; burn* [scald] oneself; have* a burn [a scald]. ●酸[ストーブ、ライター]で手にやけどする *burn* one's hand *by* the acid [*on* the stove; *with* a lighter]. ●熱い紅茶で舌にやけどする *burn* one's tongue *on* [*by*] the hot tea. ●ギャンブルで大やけどする(=大損する) *suffer* a heavy *loss* [(話) *get* badly *burned*] *at* gambling. ●皮膚にドライアイスでやけどすることがある Dry ice can burn the skin.
 会話 「どうしたの？ やけどしたの？」「うん、このとおりさ」"What's the matter? *Have* you *burned yourself*?" "This is it."

やけに [ひどく] terribly, 《話》 awfully. ▶今日はやけに寒い It's *terribly* [*awfully*] cold today.

やけの 焼け野 ●焼け野(が)原 war-scorched earth; a stretch of land left in burnt ruin by war.

やけのこる 焼け残る escape [survive] 《×from》 the fire. ●焼け残った家 a house *survived* [*saved from*] *the fire*. (⇨焼ける ❶)

やけぶとり 焼け太り profit from a fire; be better off than before a fire broke out. ▶その火事で彼の商売は焼け太りした His store was burned down in the fire, which, however, made him do bussiness on a larger scale than before.

やけぼっくい 焼けぼっくい ●焼けぼっくいに火がつく ▶焼けぼっくいに火がついた The *embers* of old love flared up again between them.

やけやま 焼け山 a scorched mountainside.

__やける__ 焼ける (⇨焼く) ❶ [燃えて灰になる] burn; be burned, 《英》 be burnt. ▶彼の原稿は火事でみな焼けてしまった His manuscripts *were* all *burned* (*up*) in the fire. ▶その大火で多くの家が焼けた A lot of houses (*were*) *burned down* [(*were*) *burned to ashes*] in the big fire. ▶幸いにもその建物は焼け残った Fortunately the building remained *unburned* [*survived the fire*].
 ❷ [食物が] (オーブン・直火で) be roasted; (直火で)(米)be broiled, 《主に英》 be grilled; (焼き網・鉄板などで) be grilled; (オーブンの中で直火を当てず) be baked. (⇨焼く ❷ [類語]) ▶ジャガイモは1時間で焼ける The potatoes *bake* for [×in] an hour. ▶肉が焼けた The meat *has been roasted* [*been grilled*].
 ❸ [日に] (sun)burn*; tan (-nn-), get* a (sun)tan. (⇨日焼け) ▶彼女の皮膚はすぐ日に焼ける Her skin *sunburns* [*tans*] easily. ▶暑い日差しで背中が焼けた The hot sun *burned* my back./My back (*was*) *burned* in the hot sun. ▶彼は仕事で働くのでよく日に焼けている Since he works in the sun, he *has a good* (*sun*)*tan* [*is* really *tanned*].
 ❹ [変色する] (色が悪くなる) discolor; (色があせる) fade. ●強い日光に当てても焼けないという保証付きの生地 cloth guaranteed not to *discolor* in strong sunlight. ▶カーテンは日光に当たって色が焼けた The curtains *faded* in the sunlight./Sunlight *faded* the color in the curtains.
 ❺ [空が] glow, 《書》 be aglow 《*with*》; be red. ▶空が夕日で真っ赤に焼けていた The sky *glowed* [*was aglow*] *with* the setting sun.
 ❻ [世話が] give* trouble. ▶4人の小さな子供は本当に世話が焼ける Four little children *give* us *a lot of trouble*.

やける 妬ける (うらやむ) be jealous [envious] 《*of*》. ▶(前の方がねたみの感情が強い) ▶やけるねえ I'm [I feel] *envious* of you./I envy you.

やけん 野犬 a stray [an ownerless] dog. ●野犬狩り a dog hunt. ●野犬狩りをする hunt [catch] *stray dogs*. ●野犬捕獲人 a dogcatcher.

やげん 薬研 a druggist's mortar; a mortar used for grinding drug ingredients.

やご [昆虫] a larva of a dragonfly.

やこう 夜光 light in the dark;【気象】(夜間に見える大気光) nightglow. ●夜光時計 a watch with a luminous dial. ●夜光塗料 luminous paint.

やこう 夜行 ●夜行(列車)で行く go by [on a] *night*

やごう train. (⇨列車③)
● **夜行性動物** an animal active at night, 《書》a nocturnal animal.

やごう 屋号 [[商店の]] the name of a store; [[歌舞伎俳優の]] another professional name for a *kabuki* actor to assume.

やこうちゅう 夜光虫 [[動物]] a noctiluca /nàktəlúːkə/.

*****やさい** 野菜 vegetables (**!**「野菜の」の意では vegetable); (葉菜類) greens, green vegetables. ● 野菜を作る grow [raise] *vegetables*. ▶ もっと野菜を食べなさい You should eat more *vegetables* [*greens*]. ▶ トマトは野菜か果物か Are tomatoes *vegetables* or fruit? ▶ 取りたての野菜は煮すぎてはいけない Fresh *vegetables* should not be overcooked.
● **野菜サラダ** green salad. (**!** vegetable salad より普通) ● **野菜ジュース** vegetable juice. ● **野菜食** a vegetable diet. ● **野菜スープ** vegetable soup. ● **野菜畑** (家庭の) a vegetable [a kitchen] garden; (市場向けの)《米》a truck farm [garden],《英》a market garden. ● **野菜料理** a vegetable dish.

やさがし 家捜し ━━ **家捜しする** 動 search the house thoroughly [everywhere in the house]《for it》.

やさがた 優形 a slender figure. ● **優形の男** a slim man; a man with a *slender build*.

やさき 矢先 [やじり] an arrowhead. ● **攻撃の矢先に立つ** bear the brunt of an attack. ▶ 出かけようとした矢先に彼女が来た I *was just about to* go out [*was on the point of* going out], *when* she came.

*****やさしい** 易しい 形 [[容易な]] easy; [[単純な]] simple; [[平易な]] plain.

┌─ **使い分け** ─────────────────────┐
│ **easy** 解決・操作・習得・実行などを行うのが苦 │
│ 労や努力を必要とせずに容易に行えることを表す. 人に │
│ とって容易である点を強調する. │
│ **simple** 考え・問題・構造・規則・作業などが複雑な点 │
│ を有しておらず, 理解や実行が容易であることを表す. 対 │
│ 象自体の構造の単純さを強調する. │
│ **plain** 人の言葉に難解な語や構造がなく易しいこと │
│ を表す. │
└─────────────────────────┘

● **やさしい問題** an *easy* [a *simple*] question 《to answer》. ▶ この本はやさしい英語で書かれている This book is written in *easy* [*simple*, *plain*] English. ▶ この問題を解くのは(君には)やさしい It's *easy* 《for you》 to solve this problem. (**!** ×It is *easy that* you solve this problem. は不可)/This problem is *easy* 《for you》 to solve (×it). (**!** ×*You are easy* to solve this problem. は不可 (⇨難しい))
━━ **易しく** 副 (簡単に) simply; (平易に) plainly. ● やさしく説明する explain《it》*simply* [*plainly*].

*****やさしい** 優しい 形 [[親切な]] kind;《書》(限定的に) kindly; [[温和な]] gentle, mild; [[思いやりのある]] tender; (情け深い) tenderhearted; (性格などが) sweet.

┌─ **使い分け** ─────────────────────┐
│ **kind** 人や行動の親切さを示す一般的な │
│ 語. sweet と異なり, 目上の人に対しても用いられる. │
│ **kindly** 行動の様子や態度が, 外見から読み取れる │
│ 優しさを表す. 通例自分より年下や弱い者に優しい場 │
│ 合に用いる. │
│ **gentle** 人や行動などに含まれる温和さを表す. 男女 │
│ ともに用いられる. │
│ **mild** 性格が優しく, めったに怒らず落ち着いている │
└─────────────────────────┘

ことを表す.
tender 主に行動などが愛情を伴って優しいことを表す.
tenderhearted 「情にもろい」という意を含んだ優しさを表す.
sweet 親しい人物の思いやりのある優しさを表す. 異性に対して用いることが比較的多く, いとしくなるような優しさを含意する.

▶ 彼は私にとても優しい He's very *kind* [*good*] *to* me. (**!** (1) good では病人・老人などに必要なものを与えて親切なことを暗示する. (2) kind の代わりに kindly は不可) ▶ 彼女は大変優しいご婦人だ She is a very *kind* [*kindly*, *gentle*, *tender*] old lady. (**!**《米》では男性に対して He is very *gentle*. という(女性的な男性を暗示することがある)) ▶ 美紀子は気立ての優しい人だ Mikiko is a *kindhearted* [a *tender-hearted*] woman. ▶ これは環境に優しい製品だ This is an environmentally-friendly product. ▶ これは地球に優しい肥料です This is an earth-friendly fertilizer. ▶ 我が党は人に優しい政治をめざしている Our party aims at people-friendly politics.
会話 「これおじさんからなんだ」「こんなにすばらしいプレゼントをあなたにくださるなんて何て優しいんでしょうね」"This is from my uncle." "How *kind* [*sweet*] (it is) of him to give you such a nice present!" (**!** 女性表現. 特に sweet は女性に好まれる)
━━ **優しく** 副 kindly; gently; tenderly. ● **優しく言う** say *kindly* [*gently*]. ▶ 彼女は私たちを優しく見つめた She looked *kindly* at us. ▶ 彼女は赤ちゃんを優しく抱き上げた She took the baby into her arms *gently*. ▶ 彼に優しくしてあげてね. まだこの仕事に慣れていないのだから Go easy on him—he's new to the job. (**!** 「お手柔らかにやる」の意. 通例命令文で)

やさしさ 優しさ kindness; gentleness; tenderness.

やし 椰子 [[植物]] [ヤシ科の木の総称] a palm (tree); [ココヤシ] (木) a coconut (palm), a coco《俗》〜s); (実) a coconut; [ナツメヤシ] (木) a date palm; (実) a date.
● **ヤシ油** coconut oil.

やし 香具師 a faker《at a fair》.(⇨的屋《てきや》)

やじ 野次 [行為] (演説での) heckling; (不満・嫌悪の) booing, hooting; [声] a heckling voice; (ぶうぶう) boos; (ほうほう) hoots; (嘲笑《ちょうしょう》の声・言葉) jeers; (口笛, どなり声) catcalls. ● **うるさい野次** loud boos [hoots]. ● **聴衆の野次を無視する** ignore the boos of the audience. ● **(野球の)ベンチの野次将軍** a bench jockey. ● **野次を飛ばす** heckle. (⇨野次る)

やじうま 野次馬 (見物人) an onlooker,《米話》a rubberneck. ▶ 事故が起きるとたいてい野次馬が多数集まる Accidents usually attract a crowd of *onlookers*.

やしき 屋敷 [大邸宅] a mansion,《書》a residence; [家屋敷] the premises; [敷地] a home [a residential] site. (⇨邸宅) ● **家屋敷を売り払う** sell 《his》*house and estate*. ● **屋敷内に** on *the premises*.

やじきた 弥次喜多 (気の合う者同士) birds of a feather; inseparable friends; (好一対のこっけい者) a good pair of comedians.

*****やしなう** 養う ❶ [扶養する] support,《やや書》maintain. ▶ 彼は妻子を養うために一生懸命に働いた He worked hard to *support* [*maintain*, *provide for*] his family. ▶ 彼の給料は 6 人家族を養うには不十分だった His salary was not adequate to *support* [*for the support of*] a family of six.

❷ 〖養育する〗(子供を) bring*... up; (人・家畜などを) raise. ▶彼はおじに養われた He *was brought up* [*was raised*] by his uncle.
❸ 〖養成する〗(みがく) cultivate; (形成する) form; (徐々に育てる) develop; (増進させる) build* ... up; (向上させる) improve. ● 物事に対する批判眼を養う *develop* [*cultivate*] a critical eye for things. ● 英会話力を養う *develop* [*improve*] one's English-speaking ability [one's skill in speaking English]. ▶早起きの習慣を養うようにしなさい You should *form* [*develop, cultivate*] the habit of getting up early. ▶最後の語が一番堅い ▶病後は体力を養う必要がある You must *build up* [*develop*] your (physical) strength after your sickness.

やしゃ 夜叉 a *yaksha*; a man-eating demon.
やしゃご 玄孫 a great-great-grandchild; a great-great-grandson; a great-great-granddaughter.
やしゅ 野手 a fielder ▶内野手 an infielder と外野手 an outfielder に分かれる; (投手以外の) a position player.
● 野手選択〖野球〗a fielder's choice.
やしゅ 野趣 ● 野趣に富んだ[あふれる](田舎らしい) rustic; pastoral (❗やや詩的な語); (自然な) natural; (素朴な) simple, unsophisticated. ▶彼女の家の庭は彼女の素朴な人柄を映して野趣あふれるものになっている Her garden has *natural* beauty of its own which is a perfect reflection of her down-to-earth [*simple*] personality. (❗前の方はほめ言葉だが, 後の方は「お人よしの」「愚かな」の意に取られやすいので避けた方がよい)
やしゅう 夜襲 a night attack [raid]. ● 敵に夜襲をかける make a *night attack* [*raid*] *on* the enemy; (夜陰に乗じて) attack [raid] the enemy under cover of darkness.
やじゅう 野獣 a wild animal [beast]. (⇨けだもの)
● 野獣派〖美術〗Fauvism; (画家) the Fauvists.
やしょく 夜食 a late-night light meal [snack], (子供がこっそり食べる) a midnight feast; (1日の4回目の食事) a supper.
やじり 矢尻, 鏃 an arrowhead.
やじる 野次る ● (特に選挙候補者を)からかったり質問攻めにして〗heckle; 〖不満・嫌悪などで〗(ぶうぶう) boo; (ほうをふく) hoot (at ...); 〖あざける〗jeer (at ...).
● 候補者をやじる *heckle* the candidate. ● 選手をやじる jockey [ride] a player. ● やじり倒す *shout* [*hoot*] (him) *down*. ● やじって演壇から退場させる *boo* [*jeer*] (him) *off* the platform. (⇨野次)
やじるし 矢印 an arrow. ● その場所に矢印をつける mark the place with an *arrow*. ● 矢印にそって進む follow an *arrow*.
やしろ 社 a (*Shinto*) shrine.
やじろべえ 弥次郎兵衛 a (children's) balancing toy.
やしん 野心 〖成功・権力などを得ようとする大望〗(an) ambition (*for*); 〖よい意味でも悪い意味でも使う〗; 〖偉大なものへの強い願望〗(an) aspiration (❗しばしば複数形で); 〖下心〗plot; designs. ● 野心を実現する realize [achieve, fulfill] one's *ambition*. ▶彼の野心は億万長者になることだ His *ambition* is to be a billionaire./He has an *ambition* [He has *aspirations*] *to be* a billionaire./He is *ambitious to* be a billionaire.
● 野心家 a ambitious person; a person of ambition; (野心満々の人) a person (who is) full of [filled with] ambition. ● 野心作 an ambitious work.
やじん 野人 (いなか者) a redneck; a country bump-

kin; an uncouth barbarian.
やす (魚を刺して捕る道具) a fish spear.
やすー 安ー ● 安月給 a *low* monthly salary.
ーやす ー安 ● (株式で) 5円安 fall five yen.
やすあがり 安上がり ● 安上がりな生活をする live *cheap*. (⇨安い [安く]) ▶その国を旅行する最も安上がりな方法を教えてください Please tell me the *cheapest* [*most economical*] way of traveling in the country.

:**やすい 安い** 〖物が〗cheap (↔dear); 〖expensive (↔expensive) と異なり, 通例比較変化しない〗; low-priced (↔high-priced); 〖値段が〗low (↔high).

使い分け cheap 旅費・経費・商品の価格が安いこと. 時に安っぽく質が悪いことを含意.
inexpensive 品質や効果の割りには金額が低額であること. cheap の婉曲語としても用いる.
low-priced 値段の安さを客観的に述べる語.
low 商品や給料などの金額が通常より安いことを示す語.

解説 cheap, inexpensive, low-priced はその中に「価格」の意が込められているので, 通例 price (価格), salary (給料), cost (費用), wage (賃金), fee (料金)など, すでに「価格」の意を含む語とは用いない: 安い費用 low [×cheap, ×inexpensive, ×low-priced] cost. なお, くだけた言い方では a *cheap* price/The price (of ...) is *cheap*. などということもあるが, 避けた方が無難.
---

①〖安い〜〗▶あの店で安い時計を買った I bought a *cheap* [an *inexpensive*] watch at that store. ▶その家具を安値で買った I bought the furniture at a *low* [(格安の) a *bargain*] price./(安く買った) I bought the furniture *cheap* [*inexpensively*]. (❗cheap は副詞 (⇨圖)) ▶(その家具は格安品だった) The furniture was a (good) *bargain* [〖話〗a good *buy*]. ▶こんな安い給料で生活するのは大変だ It's hard to live on a *low* [a *small*, ×a *cheap*] salary like this.
②〖...が[は]安い〗● 今はリンゴが安い Apples are *cheap* [*low in price*] now./The price of apples is *low* now./Apples are selling *cheap* now. ▶神戸は東京に比べると物が安い Things are *cheaper* [(物価が) Prices are *lower*] in Kobe than in Tokyo. (❗文脈があれば Kobe is cheaper than Tokyo. もよい) ▶あの店は安い That store is *cheap*./They sell *cheap* at that store. (何でも安く手に入る) You can get anything *for very little* [*great prices on anything*] at that store. (❗for very little money の省略形で for は「交換」の意. great は「You (=客) にとってすばらしい」ことから「安い」の意となる) ▶この辞書がいちばん安い This one is the *cheapest* [*least expensive*] of those dictionaries. ▶その値段なら手袋は安い At that price the gloves are *cheap*.
会話「もう少し安いのはありますか」「ございます. こちらへどうぞ」"Do you have something *less expensive*?" "Sure. Over this way."
● 安かろう悪かろう cheap and inferior in quality; 〖主に英〗cheap and nasty.
―**く** 圖 cheap, cheaply; inexpensively; 〖安い値段で〗at a low price. (⇨圖) ● 車を安く売った I sold the car *cheap* [*cheaply*, 〖話〗*on the cheap*]. (❗sell, buy, get とともに用いる場合は cheaply より cheap の方が普通) ▶少し安くなりませんか(=値引いてくれませんか) Can't you *cut* [*reduce*] *the price* a little?/Can't you make it a little

cheaper?/Will you give me a little discount?/Will you take a little *off*? ▶そではこんなに安くしていませんよ(=安く買えない) You can't get it *cheaper* [もっと払わなくてはならない] You have to pay much more] anywhere else. ▶砂糖の値段が安くなった(=下がった) The price of sugar *has gone down* [*fallen*].

*やすい 易い 〖容易な〗easy; 〖簡単な〗simple. (⇨易しい) ▶言うはやすく行うは難し 《ことわざ》(That's) *easier* said than done. (❗には *easier* は副詞)

―やすい ―易い (...する傾向がある)(本来的・習慣的に) be apt 《*to* do》; (好ましくないことを身に招く) be liable 《*to; to* do》; (...することがありやすい) be easy 《*to* do》; (簡単に...する) 動詞+(目的語+) easily.
● 信じやすい(=すぐに信じる) *be* (too) *ready to* believe; (やや軽) credulous. ● 解きやすい問題 an *easy* [*a simple*] problem *to* solve; a problem *easy* [*simple*] *to* solve. ● 使いやすい辞書 a user-*friendly* dictionary. ● 日本人の英語学習者が犯しやすい間違い an error *common among* Japanese learners of English. ● 彼は風邪を引きやすい He catches (a) cold *easily*. /×He is easy to catch cold. とはいわない/He is *apt* [*liable*] *to* catch (a) cold. ●「風邪を引きやすい人」は a person *apt* [*liable*] *to* catch (a) cold で, ×an apt [a liable] person *to* catch (a) cold とはいわない ▶彼の字は読みやすい His writing is *easy to* read./(はっきりと字を書く) He writes clearly [×in clear letters]. ▶ガラスは割れやすい Glass breaks *easily* [*easily breaks*]./Glass is *easily* broken. ▶この皿で ×Glass is *easy* to break. とはいわない. これは「ガラスを割ることはやすい」の意/Glass is fragile. ▶このペンはあのペンより書きやすい This pen writes *better* than that one.

やすうけあい 安請け合い 图 a hurried promise; an rash agreement.
—安請け合いをする 動 (性急に約束する) make rash promises; (すぐさま約束する) promise too readily; (軽々しく引き受ける) take on (it) lightly.

やすうり 安売り 图 a (bargain) sale. (❗通例単に a sale という)
—安売りする 動 have a sale 《*on* goods》; sell [offer]《goods》cheap [割引価格で] at reduced [low] prices, (見切って) at a sacrifice].
● 安売り店 a díscount stòre [shòp, hòuse]; a cut-rate store.

やすき 易き ● 易きに就く (安易な方法を選ぶ) take the easy way out; follow the beaten path.

やすっぽい 安っぽい cheap, tawdry. ● 安っぽい洋服 [人間] a *cheap* dress [person]. ● 自分を安っぽくするまねはするな Don't *cheapen* yourself [*make* yourself *cheap*].

やすで 安手 安手の 形 rather cheap.

やすね 安値 a low; a low price. (⇨安い) ● 最安値 (new (record)) *low*; the lowest price. ● 安値引け (register) a *low* close. ● 安値引ける close *low* 《*at*》. ● 安値をつける hit [touch, dip to] the *lows*. ● 史上最安値を記録する register an all-time *low*. ● (他店より)安値で売る undersell. ● 安値で買う buy cheap.

やすぶしん 安普請 ● 安普請の家 a jerry-built [a cheaply-built, a poorly-built] house (❨複❩ houses /-ziz, 《米》-siz/).

やすまる 休まる 〖体が〗 be [feel*] rested;〖心が〗be [feel] relieved; feel at ease [at rest, at peace]. ● 心[体]の休まる暇がない I have no moment of *ease* [*rest*]. ▶心の悩みを話してくだされば気が休まるでしょう You will *feel relieved* [*better*,

×*rested*] if you tell me your worries.

*やすむ 休む ❶〖休息, 睡眠〗(a) rest. ▶さあ, 一休みしよう Let's *take* [*have*] *a rest* now./Let's rest now. ▶お父さまはまだお休みですか Is your father still *in bed*? ▶ゆうべはよくお休みになりましたか Did you *sleep* well [*have a good sleep*] last night?
❷〖休憩時間〗a break; (授業間の)《米》(a) recess /ríses, ri:ses/. (⇨休憩, 昼休み). ● 10 分間の休み a ten-minute *break* [*recess*].
❸〖休止〗a break, a pause;〖中断〗interruption. ● 休みなく働く work without a *break* [*a rest*, *interruption*]; work continuously. ▶休みなく雨が降った There was no *break* in the rain./It rained continuously [incessantly].
❹〖休日〗a holiday; 〖休暇〗《主に米》a vacation, 《主に英》a holiday; 〖都合でとる休暇〗「期間」+off. (⇨休暇《類語》). ● 1 日 [2 週間] 会社から休みをとる take a day [two weeks] *off* from the office. (❗1 日休みをとるときは通例 take a *vacation* といわないが, 2 週間なら take a *vacation* of two weeks のようにいえる) ▶休みにはどこへお出かけですか Where are you going for [during] your *vacation* 《米》 [*holiday*(*s*) 《英》]? (❗for は「休みを過ごすために」, during は「その期間」の意) ▶あすは休みだ Tomorrow is a *holiday* [my day *off*]. (❗前の方は祝祭日などの公休日, 後の方は個人的にとる休みのこと) ▶毎週金曜は休みです We are *off* on Friday(s)./We have Friday(s) *off*.
❺〖欠席, 欠勤〗absence. ▶彼は今日は休みだ He is *absent* 《*from* school [work]》 today. (❗日常会話では He hasn't come [isn't here] today. などの方が普通. He is *off* today. または He *has* a day *off* today. とすれば「休暇をとっている」の意 (⇨❷))
❻〖休校, 休業〗▶あしたは学校が休みです We *have no school* [*classes*, *lessons*] tomorrow. ▶流感のため学校は 2 日間休みになった Our school (*was*) *closed* for two days because of the flu. ▶その店は月曜が休みだ The store *is closed* [*is shut*] on Monday(s).

やすみやすみ 休み休み ▶我々は休み休み山を登った We went up the mountain *taking a rest* now and then. ▶ばかも休み休み言え None of [《話》Cut out] your nonsense!/Don't say silly things./That's silly!

やすむ 休む ❶〖休息する〗rest, take [have*] *a rest*. (⇨休憩) ● 休む暇がない have no time to *rest*. ● 木陰で横になって休む lie and *rest* in the shade of a tree. ● 仕事をやめて休む *rest* [*take a rest*] from (one's) work. ▶彼は 1 時間休んで再び仕事を始めた He *had* an hour's *rest* [He *rested* for an hour] and started work again.
❷〖休暇をとる〗take* [have*]《a day》off. (⇨休暇, 休み❹) ▶次の月曜は休みます I'll *take* next Monday *off*./I'll *take* a day off next Monday. ▶仕事を二日ばかり休ませてもらってもよろしいでしょうか Is it all right if I *take* two days *off* work?
❸〖欠席・欠勤する〗be absent 《*from*》, stay away 《*from*》. (❗前の方は堅い言い方) ▶彼はきのう仕事を休んだ He *was absent* [*stayed away*] *from* work yesterday. (❗次例の方が口語的)/He *didn't go to* [He *missed*] work yesterday. ▶彼は 1 週間学校を休んでいる He *has been absent from* school for a week. (❗日常会話では He *hasn't been at* [*hasn't come to*] school for a week. などという方が普通) ▶来週先生の授業を休ませていただきたいのですが I'd like to *be excused from* [*I can't come to*, I *won't be in*] your class next week. (❗最初の表現が丁寧で穏やかな言い方. because 節などで理由を

やすめ　えるのが普通）▶今朝病気で休むと電話で(会社に)連絡した I called in sick this morning.
❹ [さぼる] 《学校などを休みする》 play truant [《米話》hook(e)y], 《話》 skip (-pp-) school; 《授業を欠席する》《話》 cut* 《a class》. ▶あの先生の授業は一度も休んだことがない I *have* never *cut* [*missed*] his class.
❺ [眠る] sleep*; [就寝する] go* to bed. ▶早く休む *go to bed* early. ▶彼はよく休んでぐっすり眠っていた He was fast [sound] *asleep*./I found him fast *asleep*. (《後の方は「行ってみたら…と分かった」という場合》▶父はまだ休んでいる（=寝ている）Father is still *in bed* [×*in a bed*]. ▶お休みなさい. (⇨お休み)
❻ [中止・中断する] suspend 《business》; [遊休している] lie* [stand*] idle. ▶彼はもう10時間も休まずに（=休憩せずに）働いている He has been working for ten hours *without a break* [*a rest*, 《ペースをゆるめないで》*without letting down*, 《ぶっ続けで》*on end*]. ▶その農地[機械]は休んでいる The farmland [machinery] *is lying* [*standing*] *idle*.

やすめ 休め　《号令》(Stand) at ease!; Stand easy! 《後の方が楽な姿勢》

やすめる 休める　[体などを] rest, give*... a rest; [心を] set* [put*] 《his mind》 at ease [at rest]. ▶頭[目]を休める *rest* one's brains [eyes]. ▶仕事の手を休める *rest* from 《one's》 work. ▶機械を休める *stop* a machine.

やすもの 安物　《安い品物》a cheap thing [article]; 《集合的》cheap goods. (!この場合は cheap に代えて inexpensive とることが多い) ▶一目見ればその時計が安物かどうかが分かる I can tell at a glance whether the watch is *cheap* or not. ▶それはそこらの安物のバッグとは違うよ. ちゃんとしたブランドものだよ It's not some *cheap* bag [That bag is not *a dime a dozen*《米話》 [*two a penny*《英》]]. It's a good brand.
● 安物買いの銭失い Buying cheap things is a waste of money [《不経済》a false economy]./《代金だけのものしか得られない》You get what you pay for./《ことわざ》一文惜しみの百知らず Penny-wise and pound-foolish. (!P- p- の頭語に注意)

やすやす ―やすやすと 形　very easily, with great ease; 《難なく》without difficulty [trouble]; 《すぐに》readily. ▶やすやすと勝つ win *very easily* [《話》*hands down*]. ▶《大差で》win *by a large margin*.

やすやど 安宿　a cheap hotel [inn].

やすらか 安らか　―安らかな 形　《穏やかな》peaceful; 《心配のない落ち着いた》quiet; 《安心して》at ease. ▶家庭で安らかな夜を過ごす spend a *quiet* [*peaceful*] evening at home. ▶あの人のそばにいると気持ちが安らかになる I *feel at ease* [*feel at peace with the world*] when I'm around him.
―安らかに 副　peacefully, in peace. ▶安らかに死ぬ die *peacefully* [*in peace*]; die a *peaceful* death. ▶赤ちゃんは母親に抱かれて安らかに眠っていた The baby was sleeping *peacefully* in its mother's arms.

やすらぎ 安らぎ　《心の平静》peace of mind. ▶心の安らぎを覚える have *peace of mind*; 《心が楽になる》feel *at ease*. ▶そこは心の安らぎが得られるところだ It's a place where you can find *peace*.

やすらく 安らぐ　●心が安らぐ（=心の安らぎを覚える）have peace of mind. (⇨安らぎ)

やすり 鑢　a file. ●紙やすり sandpaper. ●つめを切ってやすりをかける clip and file one's fingernails. ●《紙》やすりをかけて塗料を落とす *sand out* the rust.

やすんじる 安んじる　[満足する] content oneself 《with》, be content(ed) 《with》. ▶彼は現状に安ん

じている He *is content*(*ed*) *with* things as they are.

やせ 痩せ　《やせた人》a lean person; 《病的な状態》emaciation.
● やせの大食い ▶彼は大の大食いだ He never gains weight in spite of eating much.
● やせ薬 a redūcing rèmedy.

やせい 野生　―野生の 形　●野生での繁殖が難しい can hardly breed *in the wild*.
―野生する 動　▶この花は野生している This flower *grows wild*.
● 野生植物 a wild plant. ● 野生生物 《集合的》wildlife. ● 野生動物 a wild animal.

やせい 野性　名　wild nature.
―野性的な 形　wild; 《粗暴な》rough. (!ともに人に用いると「乱暴な」という悪い意味になる)

やせうで 痩せ腕　《細い腕》a thin arm. (⇨細腕)

やせおとろえる 痩せ衰える　●やせ衰えて骨と皮ばかりになる be reduced to skin and bones. ▶彼は長患いでやせ衰えている He looks *thin and weak* after being sick for so long [his long illness].

やせがた 痩せ型　a slim figure. ●やせ型の若い男 *slim* [a *slender*, 《筋肉質で》a *lean*] young man.

やせがまん 痩せ我慢　▶彼ははほんとうは欲しいのにやせ我慢しているんだ《自尊心が許さない》He really wants it, but he *is too proud* (*to say so* [*to admit it*])./《そうでないふりをしている》Though he really wants it, he's *pretending* he doesn't.

やせぎす 痩せぎす　―痩せぎすな 形　《やせて骨ばった》bony; [痩せた] skinny; scrawny. (!いずれも好ましくない状態をさす); [健康で細い] lean. ▶彼女はやせぎすだ She is *too thin*.

やせこける 痩せこける 動　become* very thin.
―痩せこけた 形　《話》skinny; 《書》emaciated.

やせち 痩せ地　poor [《不毛の》sterile, 《やや書》barren] land.

やせつち 痩せ土　poor [《不毛の》sterile, 《やや書》barren] soil.

やせっぽち 痩せっぽち　《話》a skinny person. ▶アンはやせっぽちだ Anne is *skinny* [*skin and bone*(*s*), a *skeleton*].

やせほそる 痩せ細る　get thin(ner). ●悩みでやせ細る *lose a lot of weight* from one's worries. (⇨痩せる)

*やせる **痩せる 動**　❶ [人が]（体重がへる）lose* weight; 《細くなる》get* [become*] thin (-nn-); 《減食などをして》slim (-mm-). ●10キロやせる *lose* ten kilos. ▶彼女は病気以来ずいぶんやせた She *has lost* a lot of *weight* since her sickness./She *got* a lot *thinner* after her sickness. ▶私は甘いものは食べません. やせようと（=減量しようと）思っていますから I don't eat sweets—I'm trying to *slim* [*reduce my weight*]. ▶彼女はとてもやせている She's too *thin*./《話》《しばしば軽蔑的》She's *skinny*.
❷ [土地が] become* poor. ▶その土地はやせている The land is *poor* [*barren*].
―痩せた 形　❶ [人が] thin (-nn-); 《病気などでやつれたときにも用いる》; 《ほっそりと美しい》slim (-mm-), slender; 《贅い肉の》lean; 《標準体重に足りない》underweight (↔overweight). ●やせた馬 a *thin* [a *lean*] horse.
❷ [土地が] poor; 《不毛の》barren, sterile. ●やせた土地 poor [*barren*] land.

やせん 夜戦　a night battle; night operations.

やせん 野戦　a (land) battle.
● 野戦病院 a field hospital.

やそう 野草　(a) wild grass. (!種類は Ⓒ)

やそうきょく 夜想曲　《音楽》a nocturne.

やだ (⇨嫌(%)) ▶やだわ，家に財布を忘れてきちゃった *Oh no*, I left my purse at home.

やたい 屋台 a booth; a stand ; 〚(主に英)〛 a stall (with a roof carried by cart). ●街角にホットドッグの屋台を出す set up a hot dog *stand* [*a stand selling hot dogs*] on [at] the corner of a street.

やたいぼね 屋台骨 〚土台〛 a foundation; 〚財産〛 one's fortune; (富) wealth. ▶バブル経済の崩壊が会社の屋台骨を揺るがせた The collapse of the "bubble economy" shook the company to its *foundations*.

やたて 矢立 a portable ink-and-brush case.

やだま 矢弾, 矢玉 arrows and bullets. ●矢弾の中を進む move forward in a *shower of bullets* [*arrows*].

やたら ― やたらに 副 〚過度に〛 too much, excessively; 〚無差別に〛 indiscriminately; 〚手当たり次第に〛 at random; 〚惜しげなく〛 freely; 〚ひどく〛 terribly; 〚向こう見ずに〛 recklessly. ●やたらに本を読む read books *at random*. ●金をやたらに遣う spend (one's) money *lavishly* [*recklessly*, (湯水のように) *like water*]; *be lavish with* one's money. ●やたらに(=次々と)ドレスを新調する have new dresses made *one after another*. ●やたらに働く 〚話〛 work *like crazy* [*like hell*]. ●やたらに(=盲目的に)信用する trust (him) *blindly*. ●今日はやたらに眠い I am *much too* [*terribly*] sleepy today. ▶その悪者はやたらに発砲した The gangster fired his gun *at random*. ▶やたらにブレーキを踏むな 〚話〛 *Go easy on* the brakes! (❗「ほどほどにする」の意で，通例命令文で)

● **やたらめったら ― やたらめったら(=ひどく)忙しい** be *extremely* busy.

やちゅう 夜中 (late) at night; (前の日の) (late) last night.

やちょう 夜鳥 a nocturnal bird.

やちょう 野鳥 a wild bird; 〚集合的〛 wild fowl /fául/. ●野鳥観察 bird-watching, birding. ●野鳥観察家 a bird-watcher, birder.

やちん 家賃 (a) (house) rent. ●1か月分の家賃を前納する pay one month's *rent* in advance. ●家賃を値上げする raise the *rent*. ▶このアパートの家賃は月12万です The *rent for* [×of] this apartment is 120,000 yen a month. ▶家賃はいくら払っているのですか How much *rent* do you pay? ▶毎月高い家賃を払っている I pay a high (↔a low) *rent* every month. ▶彼は家賃を3か月滞納している (払っていない) He hasn't paid the *rent* for the past three months./(遅れている) He's three months behind with his *rent*. ▶家賃が上がった The *rent* has gone up.

やつ 奴 〚男〛〚話〛 a fellow, 〚話〛 a guy; 〚主に米話〛 a boy (《成人男性にも用いる》); 〚主に英話〛 a chap. ●いい奴 a nice *fellow* [*guy, boy, chap*]. ▶かわいそうな奴 Poor *fellow*! ▶なんて奴だ What a *fellow* [*a guy*]! ▶きっと手伝ってくれる奴がいるに違いないさ There must be *someone* [*some guy*] who'll help.

翻訳のこころ それにしても心というやつは何という不可思議なやつだろう (梶井基次郎『檸檬』) Come to think of it, what a mysterious thing that *stuff* [*thing*] named 'the mind [heart]' is. (❗(1) stuff は特定の呼び名がないようなものをさす語。guy は主に人のことなので，ここでは不適切。(2) mind は理性的な働きをする「心」, heart は感情的・情緒的・精神的な働きをする「心」)

やつあたり 八つ当たり ▶彼女は子供たちに八つ当たりした She *took it out on* her children.

やっか 薬価 the price of medicine. ●薬価基準 the official prices of medicines.

やっか 薬科 ●薬科大学 a college of pharmacy.

やっか 薬禍 a physical trouble caused by medicine. (⇨⓮ 薬害)

****やっかい 厄介** 名 ❶〚面倒〛 (a) trouble; 〚小さな〛 bother; 〚心配〛 (a) worry. ●彼にやっかいをかける *trouble* him (*with, about*); give him [put him to, get him into] *trouble*. ●警察のやっかいになる (なっている) get into [be in] *trouble with* the police. ▶やっかいをかけてすみません I'm sorry to *have troubled* [(that) I *have troubled*] you. (❗ 面倒をかける前に言うなら I'm sorry to *trouble* you.)/I'm sorry for the *trouble* I caused./I'm sorry (that) I caused you so much *trouble*. ❷〚世話〛 care. ●やっかいになる (依存する) depend (*on*); (世話になって暮らす) live (*on, off*); (滞在する) stay (*with*+人, *at*+場所). ▶まだ親のやっかいになっているのですか Are you still *dependent* [×*depending*] *on* your parents?/*Are* you still *living* [〚話〛 *sponging*] *on* [*off*] your parents? ▶後の方は軽蔑的な言い方) ▶一晩おじの家にやっかいになった I *stayed* overnight *with* my uncle.

●やっかい払い ●彼をやっかい払いする get rid of him. ▶彼がよそへ引っ越した，いいやっかい払いだ 〚話〛 He's moved out, and *good riddance* (*to* him [×me])! (❗ to 以下である方が強意的)

― **やっかいな** 形 〚面倒な〛〚書〛 troublesome; 〚負担になる〛 burdensome; 〚困難な〛 difficult. ●やっかいな仕事 a *troublesome* [*a burdensome, difficult*] task. ●やっかいな子供 a *troublesome* child. ●やっかいなことを避ける avoid *trouble*. ▶やっかいなことに機械が動かない The *trouble* is (that) [〚話〛 *Trouble* is,] the machine doesn't work. ▶定刻に着かなかったらやっかいなことになりかねない If we don't arrive on time, we may get into *trouble*. ▶そんなことをすればやっかいなことになるよ It'd be asking for *trouble*. ▶子供は時にやっかいなことがある Children can be a *nuisance*.

●やっかいもの (人, 物) a nuisance (*to*); (負担に) 〚書〛 a burden (*to*); (人) a troublemaker.

やつがしら 八つ頭 〚植物〛 a yam.

やっかみ 〚羨望(浮)〛 envy; 〚しっと〛 jealousy. (⇨妬(浮)み)

やっかむ 〚羨望(浮)する〛 envy; 〚しっとする〛 be jealous (*of*). (⇨妬(浮)む)

やっかん 約款 an article; a clause; (契約条項) a stipulation; (法律の条項) a provision. ●約款の規定により支払う make payment as stipulated in the *contract*. ●条約の約款に違反する violate an *article* of the treaty.

やっき 躍起 ●躍起になって(=半狂乱になって)助けを求め cry for help *frantically* [(必死に) *desperately*]. ●試験にパスしようと躍起になる(=必死に努力する) make desperate efforts [try very hard, (総力をあげる)〚話〛 *go all out*] to pass the exam. ●彼はその賞を得ようと躍起になっている 〚話〛 He's *out for* [*out to* win] the prize. (⇨*out winning*... も可)

やっぎや 矢継ぎ早 ●矢継ぎ早に質問を浴びせる ask (him) a lot of questions *in rapid succession*; *shower* questions (*on* him); *shoot* [*fire*] questions (*at* him).

やっきょう 薬きょう a cartridge (case); (米) a shell.

やっきょく 薬局 a pharmacy, 《主に米》 a drugstore (❗ 薬のほかに日用雑貨も扱う), 《英》 a chemist's (shop); (病院内の) a (hospital) dispensary, a hospital pharmacy.

やっこ 奴 (しもべ) a manservant, a footman. ◆奴さん he; that guy;《英話》that bloke;《米俗》that dude. ● 冷や奴 (⇨冷や奴)
 ● 奴凧 (説明的に) a kite in the shape of a feudal footman with his sleeves outspread.
 ● 奴豆腐 tofu cut into cubes.
やっこう 薬効 the (good) effect of a medicine.
 ● リューマチに薬効のある温泉 a hot spring which *is good for* [*effective against*] rheumatism. ● 薬効のある草 a *medicinal* herb. ● 漢方薬はすぐには薬効が現れない Chinese medicine does not *take quick effect*.
やっざき 八つ裂き 八つ裂きにする tear ... to bits [pieces]; tear [pull]... apart.
やっさもっさ ❶ [ごった返して] ▶in confusion; in a muddle [jumble]. ▶急病人が出て, 教室はやっさもっさした With a sudden illness, our class *was thrown into confusion*.
❷ [もつれて] ▶交渉はまとまらずやっさもっさの状態になっている We failed to reach agreement and the negotiations *are in a tangle* [*are tangled up*].
やっす (変装する) disguise oneself 《*as a beggar*》.
やった (でかしたぞ！) Well done!; (お見事！) Excellent!; (うまいぞ！) Bravo! ▶やった, ホームランだ He did it! It's a homer.
 会話 「彼, チャンピオンになったぞ」「やったね！」 "He won the championship." "*Fantastic!*"
 会話 「みち子, 動物園に連れて行くよ」「やったあ！」 "I'll take you to the zoo, Michiko." "*That's great!/Yippee!*"
やっつ 八つ eight. ● 八つ目の the eighth /eitθ/.
やっつけしごと やっつけ仕事 ▶[間に合わせの仕事] a (quick) patch-up job; [[急いでした]雑な仕事] a slipshod job (done in a hurry), 《話》sloppy work.
やっつける (負かす) beat*, defeat (⇨負かす); (仕返しする) get; (こらしめる) let* (him) have it. ● 敵をやっつける *defeat* an enemy.
 会話 「どうしてそんなに必死で彼をやっつけようとするの？」「どうしてそうしてはいけないの. 私を裏切った当然の報いじゃないの」"Why are you totally out to *get him*?" "Why shouldn't I be? That's what he gets for cheating on me."
やっで 八つ手 [植物] a Japanese fatsia.
やっていく やって行く [[暮らしていく]] get* along [on]; [[人と仲よくやっていく]] get along [on] 《*with*》; [[事を何とか処理する]] manage (to do); (...なしで済ます) do* without .... ▶今月は5万円でやっていかなければならない I must *get along* [*manage* (*to live*), (収支を合わせる) *make* (*both*) *ends meet*] *on* 50,000 yen this month. ▶君がいなくても何とかやっていくよ I'll *manage* [do] without you. ▶彼は奥さんとうまくやっていくだろう He will *get along* [*on*] (well) *with* his wife. ▶彼は5時間の睡眠時間でやっていける(=5時間しか睡眠時間は要らない) He only needs five hours of sleep.
やってくる やって来る come* (*to*); [[近寄って来る]] come up (*to*), approach; (回って来る) come around; [[季節などが巡って来る]] come around; [[会いに来る]] come and [to] see; [[現れる]] appear, turn [[《話》show*]] up; [[訪問する]] visit, call 《*on* ＋人, *at*＋場所》. (⇨来る)
やってのける やって退ける do*; get*... done. ● その難事業を見事にやってのける(=成し遂げる)《やや書》accomplish [[《話》*pull off*]] the difficult enterprise. ● たくさんの宿題を1時間かそこらでやってのける(=やってしまう) *get* a lot of homework *done* in an hour or so.
やってみる (試みる) try; (一か八か) take* a chance. ▶それはやってみる価値がある It's worth *trying* [*a try*].
 会話 「私にはうまくできそうにないわ」「でもやってみないと分からないでしょう」"I don't think I'd be good enough." "You don't know until you *try* [*give it a try*], do you?"
 会話 「このロボットはどんなふうに動くのかしら」「やってみましょうか」"I wonder how this robot works?" "Let me *give you a demo*." (! *give a demo* は《話》「やって見せる, 実演する」の意)
やってらんない ▶あんな人ともうやってられないよ(=いっしょに仕事を続けていけない. 言うことがころころ変わるんだから) I *can't go on working* [(付き合いきれない) *can't get along*] *with* him any longer. He says something different every minute.
やっと ❶ [ついに] at last, 《書》at length; (いろいろあって最後に) finally. (⇨送語 [類語]) ▶やっと彼女から手紙が届いた *At last* [*Finally*] I got a letter from her. (! She's here, *at last*! (やれやれやっと彼女が来た)のように感情のこもった表現の場合 finally は不可) /《やや書》*It was a long time before* I received a letter from her. ▶ハリス博士, やっとじかにお目にかかれて大変うれしいです I'm delighted to meet you *finally* in person, Dr. Harris.
 会話 「試験が終わったよ」「じゃあやっとのんびりできるのね」"I've finished my exams." "So you can relax [you feel relaxed] *at last*."
❷ [かろうじて] barely, (only) just (! 後の方が口語的); (苦労して) with (great) difficulty; (危ういところで) narrowly. ● やっと終電車に間に合う be *just in time* for the last train. ▶やっと5時までに仕事を終えることができた I *barely* finished [(*only*) *just* finished, (なんとか終わった) *managed to* finish] the job by 5 o'clock. ▶家のガレージは車1台がやっとだ Our garage has *barely* [*just*] enough space for one car./《やや書》Our garage houses *only just* one car. ▶彼はやっとのことで怒りを抑えた He withheld his anger *with the greatest difficulty*. ▶食べてゆくのがやっとだ I have *barely* [(*only*) *just*] *enough* money to live on./*All* [*The best*] *I can do* is (to) support myself. (! 前に do が来る場合に限り, to の省略可)
やっとこ (工具) 《a pair of》pincers [nippers, (針金切り) pliers].
やっとこさ (⇨やっと)
やっぱり (⇨やはり)
ヤッホー yo-ho, yoo-hoo. ▶彼はヤッホーと叫んだ He shouted "*Yo-ho!*"/He *yo-hoed*.
やつめうなぎ 八つ目鰻 [魚介] a lamprey (eel).
やつら 奴等 ▶奴らの仕業に違いない I'm sure *they've* done it./That's *their* mischief, I'm sure.
やつれた ❶ [やせ衰えて] (睡眠不足・心配などで) haggard; (病気などで) gaunt, 《やや書》emaciated. ● やつれた顔 [人] a *haggard* face [person].
❷ [見苦しい] ▶やつれた身なりをしている wear *shabby* clothes; be *shabbily* [*poorly*] dressed.
やつれる become* haggard 《*from*》(a lack of sleep); become gaunt [《やや書》emaciated] 《*from* illness》. (⇨やせる)
やど 宿 (泊まる所) a lodging; (ホテル) a hotel /houtél/; (古風な) an inn. ● スキー宿 a ski *hotel*. ● 一夜の宿を求める ask for a night's *lodging*. ▶ 宿はすでに決まった We decided on our *lodging* right away. ▶彼はその夜ホテルに宿をとった(=泊まった) He *stayed* [《主に英》*put up*] *at* a *hotel* [*an inn*] for the night. (! *for* は「...を過ごすために」の意)

やとい ●宿帳 (宿泊人名簿) a hotel register. ●宿帳に記入する register at a hotel. ●宿賃 hotel charges.
やとい 雇い (雇用) employment; (使用人) an employee. ●臨時雇い temporary *employment*; (人) a temporary *employee*, (話) a temp. ●雇い人 (使用人) an employee. 雇い主 an employer.
やといいれる 雇い入れる employ, 《米》hire; (一時的に) 《英》hire. (⇨雇う [類語])
*****やとう 雇う** employ; hire; (新規に採用する) recruit.

> 使い分け **employ** 職員として正式に長期に人を雇うこと.
> **hire** 《米》では employ とほぼ同意.《英》では通例特別な目的のために一時的に雇う場合に用いる.

▶タクシーを1台雇う *hire* a taxi. ▶召使いを雇う *hire* a servant. ▶そのホテルは5人の料理人を雇っている The hotel *employs* five cooks. ▶彼女はオペレーターとして雇われている She is *employed* 《英・豪》*is engaged*] as an operator. ▶その男はうちで雇っていない. どこで働いているのかも分からない He's not on our *payroll*. I don't know who he works for. (**!** payroll は「従業員名簿」の意)
やとう 夜盗 (人) a burglar; (行為) (a) burglary.
やとう 野党 an opposition party; the opposition (**!** しばしば the O-), 《英》the Opposition (**!** 集合的で単・複両扱い). ●野党の労働党 the *opposition* Labour Party. ●野党第一党 the No. 1 *opposition party*. ●野党である[になる] be in [go into] *opposition*.
やどかり 宿借り 〖動物〗a hermit crab.
やどす 宿す ❶ [妊娠する] become pregnant 《by him》. ●彼の子を宿している be pregnant with his child; be carrying his child.
❷ [表面に持つ] ▶月影を宿している (=映している) 鴨川の流れ the water of the Kamogawa River that *reflects* the moon.
やどなし 宿無し 〖定住する家のない人〗a homeless person; (総称) the homeless; 〖浮浪者〗a tramp.
やどぬし 宿主 〖宿の主人〗the proprietor of an inn; 〖寄生生物の〗the host.
*****やどや 宿屋** an inn; (日本式旅館) a Japanese-style hotel [inn]. ●宿屋の主人[女将(ホル)] the landlord [landlady] of an *inn*. (⇨旅館)
やどりぎ 宿り木 〖植物〗mistletoe /mísltòu/, 《書》parasite.
やどる 宿る ❶ [風雨を避ける] 〖take* shelter; 〖精神的に住む〗dwell*. ●健全な精神が彼の身体に宿っている A strong mind *dwells in* his body./A sound mind *in* a sound body. (**!** 慣用的表現で「健全な肉体に健全な精神が宿るように」の意で教育の理想を述べた言葉) ▶神は万物に宿る Gods *exist in* all things.
やどろく 宿六 ▶うちの宿六 (=亭主) my (old) man; my hubby.
やどわり 宿割り ●宿割りをする assign *lodgings*.
やとわれ 雇われ ●雇われ店長 a *hired*《bar》manager.
やな 梁 /wíər/ a fish tràp. ●やなを仕掛ける set a *weir* [*a fish trap*].
やながわなべ 柳川鍋 a *yanagawanabe*; (説明的に) a pot of open-cut loaches and slivers of burdocks cooked with beaten egg.
やなぎ 柳 〖植物〗a willow (tree) (**!** 通例「しだれ柳 (a weeping willow)」をさす); (コリヤナギ) an osier. ●柳に風 (と受け流す) ▶彼は非難を柳と受け流した He took the criticism *in stride*. ●柳に雪折れなし (ことわざ) Better bend than

break. ●柳の下のどじょう ▶柳の下にいつもどじょうはいない 'Good luck doesn't always repeat itself.'/(ことわざ) There are no birds of this year in last year's nests./《米》You can't make a soufflé /suːfléi/ rise twice. (**!** スフレを焼くときは二度ふくらませることはできない」の意) ▶柳の下にどじょうが2匹いないとも限らないでしょう (雷が2度は落ちないなどとだれも言っていない) Who's saying lightning can't strike twice?
●柳行李 a wicker trunk. ●柳腰 a willowy waist. ●柳細工 osier goods. ●柳刃 a long, slender kitchen knife for *sashimi*.
やなみ 家並み a row of houses /háuziz, 《米》-siz/.
やなり 家鳴り ▶新築の家は家鳴りがすることがある Newly built houses will sometimes let out cracking sounds (until the wooden structures are settled).
やに 脂 〖木の〗resin; 〖たばこ〗tar. ●目やに gum; 《話》sleep. (⇨目脂)
やにさがる 脂下がる ▶彼女からデートに誘われたので彼はやに下がっている He has a complacent smile on his face because she asked him out.
やにっこい 脂っこい (やにが多い) resinous; (人がしつこい) persistent.
やにょうしょう 夜尿症 〖医学〗nocturnal enuresis /ènjuəríːsis/.
やにわに suddenly; abruptly. (⇨突然 [類語]) ●彼をやにわに襲う attack him *suddenly*; make a *sudden* attack on him.
やぬし 家主 (男性の) a landlord; (女性の) a landlady; 〖家の所有者〗the owner of a house.
*****やね 屋根** a roof (複 ~s). ●屋根は /rúːvz/ とも /rúːfs/ とも読む》 ●(競技場の) 屋根付き観覧席 the *covered* [*roofed*] stands. (**!** 単数扱い) ●赤い屋根の家 a house with a red *roof*. ●屋根伝いに from *roof* to *roof*. ●屋根にアンテナを取りつける put [install] an antenna on the *roof*. ▶私の家の屋根はかわら[わら]ぶきです My house has a tile [a thatched] *roof*./My house is *roofed* with tiles [thatch]. ▶彼らは3年間同じ屋根の下で暮らした They lived under the same *roof* [shared the same *roof*] for three years.
●屋根板 a (roof) shingle. ●屋根裏部屋 an attic,《書》a garret. (**!** garret は小さくて居心地が悪い感じを伴う)
会話「(オープンカーの) 屋根を上げようか. 寒くなるかもしれないよ」「いいの, 開けておいて. 風に当たっていたいの」"Should I put the *top* up? It might get cold." "No, keep it down. I want to feel the air."
やねのうえのバイオリンひき『屋根の上のバイオリン弾き』*Fiddler on the Roof*. (参考) 米国のミュージカル
やば 矢場 (屋外の) an archery ground; (屋内の) an archery gallery.
やばい (危険性の高い) 《話》chancy, risky; 《主に英》dicey.
やはず 矢筈 ❶ [矢の] the end notch of an arrow. ❷ [掛け軸をかける道具] a gadget for hooking a scroll to the hanger.
やばね 矢羽根 the feathers (of an arrow).
*****やはり** ❶ [同様に] also, too,《やや話》as well;《否定文を受けて》either; neither, nor. (⇨又 [類語]) ●彼もやはりそこにいたのです He was *also* there./He was there too [*as well*].
❷ [たとえそうでも] even so; (それでもなお) still (**!** 接続詞的に);(それにもかかわらず) all [just] the same,《やや書》nonetheless,《書》nevertheless. ▶この本にはいくつか間違いがあるが, やはり一読の価値はある

This book has some mistakes; *even so* [*still*], it's worth reading. ▶彼はかなり傲慢(訟)だが、やはり私は彼が好きです He is rather haughty, but I like him *all the same* [*nonetheless*].

❸【依然として】*still*. ▶やはり君は間違っていると思う I *still* think (that) you are wrong. ▶彼は今でもやはり勉強家です He works *as hard as before*.

❹【思ったとおり】*as one* (had) *expected*. ▶やはり彼は来なかった He didn't come *as I* (had) *expected* [心配していたとおり *feared*]. ▶やはり(=確かに)新米がいちばんおいしい *Sure enough*, this year's rice (crop) [✕new rice] is the best. (❗ new rice は「新種の米」の意で不可)

会話「あの人たち別れたんだって」「やはりね(=そうなるんじゃないかと思った)」"They broke up." "I thought that would happen./(思っていたとおりだ) That's just what I've thought."

❺【結局】(意図・計画などに反して) *áfter àll*. (❗ この意では通例英文尾に置く) (⇨結局) ▶他に約束があったが、やはりパーティーに行くことに決めた I had another appointment, but I decided to go to the party *after all* [考え直して] *on second thought*].

やはん 夜半 (夜中) night; (真夜中) the middle of the night. ▶彼は夜半過ぎまで勉強していた He studied until after [*past*] *the middle of the night*. (⇨夜中)

やばん 野蛮 ━━ **野蛮な** 圏 savage, barbarous (いずれも通例非難の意で「残虐な」ことをいう.前の方が強意的); (野蛮人の) barbarian; (野蛮人のように粗野な) barbaric. ● 野蛮な行為 a *savage* [a *barbarous*] act.
● 野蛮人 a *barbarian*; a *savage*.

やひ 野卑 ━━ 圏 (下品な) vulgar, crude; (粗野な) coarse, rude; (いやしい) mean, (主に書) base.

やぶ 藪 [低木の茂み] a bush; (密集した) a thicket; [草むら] a (grass) tussock. ● 竹やぶ a bambóo thicket [*grove*]. (⇨竹)
● **やぶから棒** ● やぶから棒に (出し抜けに) abruptly; (突然) suddenly, (話) *all of a sudden*; (予告なしに) without any notice; (思いがけなく) unexpectedly. ▶彼はやぶから棒に現れたので驚いた I was surprised at his *sudden* appearance.
● **やぶをつついて蛇を出す** ▶彼はやぶをつついて蛇を出すようなやつではない He is not the sort of person to wake a sleeping dog. (⇨藪蛇)

やぶいしゃ 藪医者 a quack (doctor).

やぶいり 藪入り (説明的に) a very short homecoming holiday (which was formerly given to a servant and an apprentice twice a year).

やぶか 藪蚊 [昆虫] a striped mosquito.

やぶく 破く *tear**. (⇨破る, 裂く)

やぶける 破ける *break**. (⇨破れる, 裂ける)

やぶこうじ 藪柑子 [植物] a spearflower.

やぶさかでない (進んで...する) be willing 《*to do*》. ▶あやまちを改めるのにやぶさかでない I'm *willing* [(ためらわない) *don't hesitate*] *to* correct my errors.

やぶさめ 流鏑馬 archery on horseback.

やぶにらみ 藪にらみ a squint.

やぶへび 藪蛇 ▶ういつはやぶへびだ It's just like waking a sleeping dog./(ことわざ) Let sleeping dogs lie.

*****やぶる 破る** ❶【紙・布などを裂く】tear* /téər/; (乱暴に) rip (-pp-); [ばらばらに壊す] break**. ● ドアを破って開ける *break* the door *open*. ● その手紙の封を破って開ける *tear* [*rip*, ✕*break*] *the letter open*. ▶彼はくぎにひっかかって破った He *tore* [*ripped*] his coat on a nail./(裂いて穴をあけた) He caught his coat on a nail and *tore* a hole in it. (❗ The nail *tore* a hole in his coat. ともいえる) ▶彼は怒って手紙をずたずたに破った He got angry and *tore up* the letter [*tore the letter* (*in*)*to pieces*]. ▶その小説は最後のページが破り取られていた The last page had *been torn* [*been ripped*] *out of* the novel. (❗ 能動文で Someone had *torn* [*ripped*] *out* the last page *from* the novel. ともいえる)

❷【平静状態を乱す】 (断つ) break*; (かき乱す) disturb; (だめにする) spoil*. ● 重苦しい沈黙を破る *break* the heavy [*oppressive*] silence. ● 調和を破る *spoil* [*disturb*] the harmony.

❸【限界を越える】 break*. ● これまでの世界記録を破る *break* [*beat*] the existing world record (*in*). ● 牢[自分の殻]を破る *break out of* prison [*one's shell*]. ▶彼は警察の警戒網を破って逃げた He *broke through* a police cordon.

❹【決められた事柄にそむく】 break*; (違反する) violate; (無視する) ignore. ● 規則を破る *break**; (従わない) *disobey* [*violate*] the rule. (❗ 後の方が堅い語) ● 約束を破る *break* (↔*keep*) [*go back on*] one's promise. (❗ 後の方が口語的) ● 伝統を破る *ignore* [*break with*] tradition. (❗ break with ... は「...との関係を断つ」の意)

やぶる 破る、敗る [勝負で人を負かす] beat*, defeat. (⇨負かす) ▶阪神は巨人を 10 対 0 で破った The Tigers *beat* [*defeated*, 《米》*shut out*, ✕*broke*] the Giants (by a score of) 10-0. (❗ 10-0 は ten to zero [*nothing*] と読む)

やぶれ 破れ [裂け目, ほころび] a tear, a rip. ● 服の破れをつくろう *mend* [*fix*] *a tear* in a dress.

やぶれかぶれ 破れかぶれ ▶もう破れかぶれだ I'm desperate.

*****やぶれる 破れる** ❶【破った状態になる】 (壊れる) break*, be broken; (裂ける) tear*, be [*get**] torn; (すり切れる) wear* out, be worn out. ● 破れた服 a *torn* dress. ● 破れた靴 *worn-out* shoes. ▶冬には水道管がよく破れる The water pipes often *break* [(破裂する) *burst*] in (《主に米》the) winter. ▶彼の上着はくぎにひっかかって破れた His coat *tore* [✕was torn] on a nail. ▶彼女のジーンズは破れている She has a *tear* in her jeans. (❗ この tear は「裂け目」の意)

❷【成功の見込みがなくなる】● 恋に破れる be *disappointed* in love. ▶彼の社長になるという夢は破れた(= 砕かれた) His hope of becoming president *was shattered* [*destroyed*].

やぶれる 敗れる (試合などで) (⇨負ける) be beaten, lose*; (戦いなどで) be defeated. (⇨負かす) ▶巨人は阪神に 10 対 0 で敗れた The Giants *lost* (the game) *to* [*were beaten by*] the Tigers (by a score of) 10-0. (⇨敗る [文例]) ▶彼女は準々決勝でウィリアムズに 1-6, 3-6 で敗れた She *fell to defeat* in the quarter finals to Williams 1-6, 3-6.

やぶん 夜分 night(time). ▶夜分こんな[遅い]時間にお電話してすみません I'm sorry for calling you at this time [at this late hour] of (the) *night*.

やぼ 野暮 ━━ **野暮な** 圏 (単純で事情にうとい) unsophisticated; (凡でつまらない)(話) corny; (人の気持ちに鈍感な) insensitive; (作法のあかぬけしない) unrefined. ▶私はそんなことを言うほどやぼじゃない I wouldn't be *so inelegant* as to say such a thing. ▶彼は彼女の申し出を断わるなんてやぼな(=ばかな)奴だな It was *stupid* of you to refuse her offer.
● 野暮用 (private) business; (雑用) a small job. ▶ちょっとやぼ用があってね There was *some stuff* I had to do. (❗ something のくだけた言い方)

やぼう 野望 (an) ambition. (⇨野心) ▶信長には天下

をとるという野望があった Nobunaga had an *ambition* to conquer the whole country.

やぼったい 野暮ったい (⇨野暮) ●やぼったい男 an *unsophisticated* [《無作法な》a *rude*] man. ●やぼったい女 a *dowdy* woman. ●やぼったい(=粗野な)デザイン a *crude* design.

やま 山

WORD CHOICE 山

mountain 通例高く険しい山脈や連山のこと。ただし、高い山の少ない英国では、比較的低いものも mountain と呼ばれる。●標高 4,000 メートルの山に登る climb a 4000-meter *mountain*.

hill mountain より低くなだらかな丘や小山のこと。Capitol Hill (米国の国会議事堂のある丘), Beverly Hills (ハリウッド近くの高級住宅街)など、固有名詞の一部にもなる。●町を見下ろす小山 the *hill* overlooking the city.

頻度チャート

mountain	
hill	
20 40 60 80 100 (%)	

❶ [山岳] a mountain; (小山) a hill; (鉱山) a mine. (⇨鉱山)

①【〜以】● 伊吹山 *Mt.* [*Mount*, ×Mountain] *Ibuki*. (！山の名前の前では Mountain は用いない。山脈の場合は the Rocky *Mountains* (ロッキー山脈)のようにいう) ●樹木[モミ]でおおわれた山 a forested [a fir-covered] *mountain*. ●はげ山 a bare [a deforested, a bald] *mountain*. ●雪をいただいた山 a snow-covered [a snow-capped, 《書》a snow-clad] *mountain*. ▶富士山は日本でいちばん高い山です *Mt.* Fuji is the highest *mountain* in Japan.

② 【山に[を, で]】● 山に登る go up [climb (up), 《書》ascend] a *mountain*. (！climb up は「よじ登る」感じ) ●山を下りる go down [《書》descend] a *mountain*. ●山に行く go to the *mountains*. (！複数形に注意) ●山を越えて隣の町へ行く go over a *mountain* to the next town. ●山で夏を過ごす spend the summer in the *mountains*. ●山で命を落とす lose one's life on the *mountain*.

③ 【山が】● 海より山が好きだ I prefer the *mountains* to the seashore. ▶日本は山が多い Japan has a lot of *mountains*./Japan is a *mountainous* country. ▶大雨で家の裏の山が崩れた(=山崩れを引き起こした) The heavy rain caused a landslide on the *hill* behind my house. ▶そこに山(エベレスト)があるからだ Because it is there. (！英国の登山家 Mallory の有名な言葉)

❷ [積み上げた物の山] (整然とした) a pile, a stack (！pile は通例同種類の物の山、stack は形も大きさも同じ物がたくさんきれいに積み重ねられたものをいう); (雑然とした) a heap (！同種でなくてもよい); (商品とか組) a lot. ●ひと山 500 円のリンゴ apples sold at 500 yen a *pile* [a *lot*]. ●ごみの山 a *heap* [a *mountain*] of garbage; a dump *heap*. ●山のような大波 *mountainous* waves; a *mountain* of waves. ▶彼の机には書類が山のように(=山積みにして)置いてある There's a *mountain* of papers on his desk. (⇨山積み) ▶山ほど仕事が待っていた (⇨山程)

❸ [物の高くなった部分] ●タイヤの山(=接地面) the *tread* of a tire. ●ねじの山 the *thread* of a screw.

❹ [投機, 推測] (a) speculation; (推測) a guess 《〜es》. (⇨投機, 推測) ●株で一山当てる make a *fortune* [《話》a *pile*] on the stock market.

❺ [山場] (事件・物語などの) the climax; (変動する量・割合などの) the peak; (危機) the crisis 《crises》(⇨峠); [終局] the end. ▶ここがこの物語の山だ This is *the climax* of the story. ▶今が景気の山 Now it's *the peak* of business.

●山が見える ▶事件の山はもうすぐ見えてくるだろう *The end* of the case will be in sight soon.

●山を当てる ●試験でうまく山を当てる *have a good shot at* the questions on an exam. ▶山が当たった I guessed right (↔wrong)./I succeeded (↔failed) in my guess [*speculation*]. ▶「試験で山が当たった」は I guessed *right* (↔wrong) about what would be on the exam.〕

●山をかける[張る] ●山をかけて[張って]株を買う buy stocks *on speculation*. ●山を張る打者 a guess hitter. ●カーブなどに山を張る look for a curveball.

●山を越す ▶その患者は山を越した The patient *has passed the crisis*.

●山を踏む (犯罪を犯す) commit a crime.

やまあい 山間 a mountain valley; (狭い) a glen; (切り立つ山にはさまれた) a ravine [rəˈviːn]. ●山間の集落 a village in [among] the *mountains*.

やまあらし 山荒し a 《動物》porcupine, 《米》a hedgehog.

やまあるき 山歩き ▶山歩きが好きだ I love walking in the *hills*./I love *hill*-walking.

やまい 病 (a) sickness, (an) illness; (病名のはっきりしている) (a) disease. (⇨病気) ●不治の病 an incurable *disease*. ●病を患う suffer from *sickness* [*illness*].

●病膏肓(ぶ)に入る (治療できないほどに病気が重くなる) be incurably ill; be too seriously ill to be cured; (ひどく物事に熱中する) be devoted 《to》; 《書》be absorbed 《in, by》; 《話》be crazy 《about, over, for》.

●病は気から (ことわざ) (心配のあまり《不死身と言われる》猫でも死んだ) Care killed a cat.

やまいぬ 山犬 (オオカミの類) a *yamainu*; (説明的に) a wild dog closely related to a Japanese wolf; a wild dog.

やまいも 山芋 《植物》a yam.

やまうば 山姥 a legendary monstrous woman who lived in the mountains.

やまおく 山奥 the heart of the mountains. (⇨奥) ▶彼らは山奥に住んでいる They live *in the heart of the mountains* [*deep in the mountains*].

やまおとこ 山男 【登山家】a mountain climber; (本格的な) a mountaineer; an alpinist; 【山の住人】a woodman (⑱ -men).

やまおり 山折り (折り紙で) 《make》a mountain fold. (⇨谷折り)

やまおろし 山颪 a (cold) wind blowing down a mountain.

やまが 山家 a house in a mountain village. ●山家育ちである be brought up [《米》be raised] in a mountain village; (いなか育ちである) be country-bred.

やまかがし 《動物》a grass snake; a Japanese water snake.

やまかけ 山掛け a *yamakake*; (説明的に) a dish of sliced [cubed] raw tuna topped with raw grated yam.

やまかげ 山陰 a shady [a north] side of a mountain.

やまかじ 山火事 a forest [×a mountain] fire.

やまかぜ 山風 a mountain wind; a wind that blows through the mountain; (夜間, 山頂より吹き下ろす冷えた風) a cold night wind that blows

やまがたな 山刀 a woodcutter's hatchet.
やまがっこ 山括弧 (かぎがっこ) pointed [broken] brackets.
やまがら 山雀 〘鳥〙a varied tit.
やまがり 山狩り ── 山狩りする 動 (山で狩りをする) hunt [shoot] in the mountains; (山に逃げ込んだ犯人などを捜す) search [しらみつぶしに捜す) comb] the mountain [hill] for a criminal [(脱獄囚) an escaped prisoner].
やまかん 山勘 (推量) a guess; (当て推量) guesswork; (直感)〘話〙a hunch. ▶山勘で by *guess* [*guesswork*]; at a *guess*; on a *hunch*. ▶山勘が当たった[外れた] My *guess* was right [wrong]./I guessed right [wrong]./I made a right [a wrong] *guess*.
やまぎわ 山際 ● 山際(=山のすぐそば)の家 a house *close by a hill* [*a mountain*].
やまくずれ 山崩れ a landslide,〘英〙a landslip;〘土石流〙a debris flow. ▶山崩れでたくさんの家が埋まった A lot of houses were buried by [in] the *landslide*.
やまぐに 山国 (国) a mountainous country; (地方) (a) mountainous country (❗country が「地方」の意の場合は単数形で通例無冠詞), a mountainous region.
やまけ 山気 (投機心)(やや書) a speculative bent [disposition]. ▶山気のある男 a man with a *speculative bent*. ● 株に山気を出す(やや書) *speculate in* stocks [on the stock market].
やまげら 山啄木鳥 〘鳥〙a grey-headed [a grey-faced] woodpecker.
やまごえ 山越え ── 山越えする 動 go over [across] a mountain.
やまごもり 山籠り ── 山籠りする 動 stay in the mountains for a long time; (修行者が) practice religious austerities at a mountain temple.
やまごや 山小屋 a (mountain) hut; (スキー・狩猟用などの) a lodge.
やまざくら 山桜 〘植物〙(木) a wild cherry tree; (花) wild cherry blossoms.
やまざと 山里 (山中の村) a mountain village; (山に近い村) a village near the mountain.
やまざる 山猿 a wild monkey; (いなかの人をあざけって)〘話〙a country bumpkin; a boor.
やまし 山師 〘投機師〙a speculator;〘詐欺師〙a swindler.
やましい feel* guilty (*about*), have* a guilty conscience. ▶私にやましいところはない I have nothing to *feel guilty about*./I have a clear conscience.
やましごと 山仕事 a job people do in the mountains.
やますそ 山裾 the foot of a mountain.
やませ 山背 a cold, damp north-east wind that blows in the summer (*in* the Tohoku region).
やまたかぼう(し) 山高帽(子) 〘米〙a derby;〘英〙a bowler (hat).
やまだし 山出し 山出しの青年 a young man *fresh from the country*; a rustic young man.
やまつなみ 山津波 ●山津波に襲われる be hit by a landslide,〘主に英〙a landslip.
やまづみ 山積み ●山積みの本 a pile [a heap] of books. (❗pile は整った一積み、heap は整っていない一積み) ▶机の上に書籍が山積みになっている Papers *are piled (up)* on the desk./The desk *is piled (high)* with papers.
やまて 山手 the residential area. (⇨山の手)
やまでら 山寺 a temple on [in] the mountain; a mountain temple.
やまと 大和 *Yamato* (, ancient Japan).
● 大和芋 a Japanese yam shaped like a ginkgo leaf. ● 大和絵 (a) *Yamato-e*; (説明的に) a traditional style of Japanese painting inspired by Zen Buddhism and developed by the Tosa and Kano schools of painting. ● 大和言葉 a native Japanese word. ● 大和魂 the Japanese spirit. ● 大和朝廷〘歴史〙the *Yamato* (Imperial) Court. ● 大和撫子(なでしこ)(日本女性) a Japanese woman. ● 大和民族 the *Yamato* [the Japanese] race.
やまとものがたり『大和物語』 *Tales of Yamato*. (参考) 平安時代の歌物語
やまどり 山鳥 a copper pheasant.
やまない やまない ▶お2人の末長いお幸せを祈ってやみません I hope (both of) you will be very happy forever.
やまなり 山鳴り the rumbling of a mountain. ▶山鳴りが続いている The *rumbling of the mountain* still continues./The mountain still continues *to rumble*.
やまなり 山形 (野球で)山なりのボールを投げる throw [投手が] pitch] a lob pitch; pitch a blooper (ball).
やまねこ 山猫 〘動物〙a wild cat; (オオヤマネコ) a lynx. ● 山猫スト a wildcat strike.
やまのおと『山の音』 *The Sound of the Mountain*. (参考) 川端康成の小説
やまのかみ 山の神 [山の守り神] a mountain god; 〘女房〙〘話〙my (old) woman;〘話〙my missus; 〘俗〙my ball and chain.
やまのて 山の手 〘山に近い地区〙the hilly section; 〘住宅地区〙the residential area [district],〘米〙the uptown (❗日本語の「山の手」の持つ上品さはない). ▶東京の山の手に住む live in *uptown* Tokyo; live *uptown* in Tokyo; live *in the residential area* of Tokyo.
● 山手線 the Yamanote (Loop) Line.
やまのは 山の端 the ridge of a mountain. ▶夕日が山の端(=山の稜線の向こう)に沈む The sun goes down *behind the mountain*.
やまのぼり 山登り mountain-climbing; mountaineering. (⇨登山)
やまば 山場 〘絶頂〙a climax;〘危機〙the crisis, the critical moment;〘転換点〙a túrning pòint. (⇨山❺) ▶委員会の審議は数日のうちに山場を迎える(=最終段階に達する) であろう The committee's deliberations will come [grow, draw] to *a head* in the next several days.
やまはだ 山肌 the surface of a mountain; mountain surface. ▶その山肌はむき出しになっている The *surface of the mountain* is bare.
やまばと 山鳩 〘鳥〙(キジバト) a turtledove; (特に北米の) a mourning dove.
やまばん 山番 a forest keeper [ranger]; the keeper of a forest.
やまびこ 山彦 an echo (複 ~es). (⇨木霊)
やまひだ 山襞 the folds of a mountain.
やまびらき 山開き the beginning of the mountaineering season. ▶富士山の山開きは7月1日です Mt. Fuji will be opened [open] to climbers on July 1.
やまぶき 山吹 〘植物〙a Japanese rose. ● 山吹色 bright yellow.
やまぶし 山伏 (説明的に) a Buddhist monk practicing asceticism in the mountains.
やまぶどう 山葡萄 〘植物〙(木) a wild grapevine;

やまふところ 山懐 ・山懐の温泉地 a spa nestling in the *heart* [《書》*bosom* /búzəm/] *of the mountains*.

やまぼこ 山鉾 a *yamaboko*; (説明的に) a festive float, on which there is a structure symbolizing a mountain topped with a halberd or a pike.

やまほど 山程 ▶私には山ほど仕事が待っていた (山のような) *Piles* [*Heaps, Mountains*] *of* work *was* [×*were*] waiting for me. (**!** 「多量」の意ではいずれもしばしば 〜s で用いる. 動詞の数は of に続く名詞に一致)/(たくさんの) *A lot* [*Lots*, 《話》*Tons*] *of* work was waiting for me.

やまみち 山道, 山路 a móuntain páth [tràck, (車が通れる) ròad]. ▶山路を登りながら, こう考えた (⇒『草枕』)

やまめ 山女 [《魚介》] a brook char [trout].

やまもと 山元 ❶[山の持ち主] an owner of a mountain [a mine]. ❷[鉱山・炭鉱の現場] a mine; a colliery.

やまもり 山盛り ・山盛りのミカン a *heap* of oranges. ●大さじに山盛り1杯の砂糖 a *heaped* [《米》a *heaping*] tablespoonful of sugar. ●彼の皿に食べ物を山盛りにする *heap* his plate *with* food; *heap* food *on* his plate.

やまやき 山焼き ── 山焼きする 動 burn the dead grass of a hill.

やまやま 山々 ❶[大いに] very much. ▶あなたと食事に行きたいのは山々なのですが, 今晩は約束があります I'd *very much* like to eat out with you, but [*Much as* I wish to eat out with you,] I have an appointment for tonight. (**!** 後の方は as much as の最初の as が省かれたもので, 省略形が普通. 譲歩節を導く) ❷[多くの山] ・伊豆の山々 the *mountains* of the Izu Peninsula.

やまゆり 山百合 [《植物》] a goldband [a golden-banded] lily.

やまよい 山酔い ── 山酔いする 動 suffer from mountain sickness.

やまわけ 山分け ── 山分けする 動 (…を等分に分ける) split* [divide]... equally [evenly, fifty-fifty]. ▶盗んだ金を仲間3人で山分けする *split* the stolen money *equally* between the three of us. ▶賞金を山分けする *divide* the prize money *fifty-fifty* [on a *fifty-fifty* basis].

やまんば 山姥 (⇒山姥(やまうば))

*やみ 闇 darkness; (暗い所) the dark; (夜の暗闇) night. ●闇に紛れて部屋に忍び込む sneak into a room *under cover of darkness*. ▶明かりがすべて消え, 私は闇の中に残された All the lights went out and I was left *in the dark*. ▶彼は夜の闇の中へ出て行った He went out into the *night* [the *darkness* of the night]. ▶前途は闇だ We have a dark future before us. ▶一寸先は闇 (⇒一寸 [成句])

● 闇から闇へ葬る ▶汚職事件は闇から闇へ葬られた(=もみ消された) The scandal *was hushed up* [*was covered up*].
● 闇市 (⇒闇市) ● 闇行為 black-market activities. ● 闇相場 [値] a black-market price. ● 闇取引 (⇒闇取引) ● 闇商人 a black marketeer.

やみあがり 病み上がり ・just recovered from sickness; (回復期にある) cònvalescent. ▶彼は病み上がりでまだ体が弱っている He is still weak *after* his *recent sickness* [*illness*]. (⇒上がり)

やみいち 闇市 a black market. (**!** 単数形で) ▶その時計は闇市で買った I bought the watch *on the black market*.

やみうち 闇討ち 《make》a sudden attack under cover of darkness. ●闇討ちを食うを be suddenly attacked in the dark; (不意打ちを食う) be caught off guard; be taken by surprise.

やみくもに 闇雲に [《でたらめに》] at random; haphazardly /hæpházərdli/; [[突然]] suddenly; (出し抜けに) abruptly.

やみじ 闇路 ・闇路を照らす light that illuminates the *dark path* [*road*]. ●恋の闇路に踏み迷う lose control of oneself in love; be blinded in love.

やみしょうぐん 闇将軍 a political wirepuller of absolute power.

やみじる 闇汁 (説明的に) mixed stew whose materials are brought together by each member of the eating party and cooked in the dark for secrecy and eaten there just for fun.

やみつき 病み付き (an) addiction 《*to*》. ▶彼はテレビゲームに病みつきになって毎日している He's *addicted to* video games and plays every day.

やみとりひき 闇取引 black-marketing; (不正な取り引き) illegal [《話》under-the-counter] trade; (裏取引) backdoor dealings.

やみなべ 闇鍋 (⇒闇(やみ)汁)

やみよ 闇夜 ・闇夜に on a dark [a moonless] night.
● 闇夜のからす It's like searching for a crow on a dark night./(ことわざ) It is ill to drive black hogs in the dark.
● 闇夜に[の]ちょうちん A lantern on a dark night is a great relief to me in need./《ことわざ》 Long looked for comes at last.
● 闇夜の鉄砲 It's like firing a gun at random in the dark of night.

やむ 止む [[雨などが]] stop (-pp-), 《話》let up; [[風などが]] (しだいにおさまる) die down 《〜d; dying》. (**!** 音などの場合は通例 die away) ▶雨が止んだ The rain *has stopped* [*let up*]./It has stopped raining [×*to* rain]. ▶今朝から雨が降ったり止んだりしている It has been raining *off and* on [*on and off*] since this morning. ▶朝にはあらしは止んでいた *There was no* storm in the morning. ▶赤ん坊は泣き止んだ The baby stopped crying.

やむ 病む (病気になる) get* sick. (⇒病気 ❶)

やむなく (⇒やむをえない [やむをえず])

やむにやまれず (⇒やむをえない [やむをえず])

やむにやまれぬ (⇒やむをえない)

やむをえない 形 [[避けられない]] unavoidable; (必然的な) inevitable; [[必要な]] necessary. ●やむをえない事情のために owing to [through] *unavoidable circumstances*. ▶それはやむをえないことだ It cannot be helped.

── **やむをえず 副** unavoidably; (必然的に) inevitably. ▶彼はやむをえず(家を売った (=売る以外に他の手段はなかった) He *had no* (*other*) *choice but to* sell his house./(必要に迫られて) He was driven by necessity to sell his house. ▶私はやむをえず(=余儀なく)退職した I *was obliged* [*was compelled, was forced*] *to* quit my job. (**!** 後の方ほど意味が強くなる)

やめ 止め a stop. ・止めにする stop 《*doing*》. (⇒止め)

*やめる 止める 動 ❶[中止する] stop (-pp-) 《*doing*》, 《話》quit*; (一時的に) suspend; (予定された事を) cancel, 《話》call ... off; [[終わらせる]] end. ・バスの運行を(一時)止める *suspend* a bus service. ▶おしゃべりは止めてくれませんか Will you please *stop* talk-

やめる

ing [✗*to talk*]? ▶太郎, やめなさい. いらいらさせないから *Stop it* [(もうたくさん) *That's enough*], Taro. It's getting on my nerves. (❗他に相手の発言や行動を制止するのにも Oh, còme ón! や Please を (❗pli:z) と長く発音する言い方もよく用いられる) ▶両国は戦争を止めることに同意した The two countries agreed to *stop* [*end*] the war. ▶NHK は今朝の対談番組を止めた NHK *canceled* a regular morning talk show. ▶組合はストライキを止めるよう指示された The labor union was ordered to *call off* [*end*] the strike.

❷ [断念する] give*... up; (誓って) swear* off ...; [縁を切る] be through (*with*). ▶彼は酒を止めた He *gave up* [*stopped*, (話) *quit, swore off*] drink*ing*. ▶そんなものは止めたほうがいい. 体に毒だ You should *cut* that stuff *out*. It's terrible for you. ▶家を買うのを止めた I *gave up* the idea of buying a house. (❗まだ買うという行動はとっていないので ✗I gave up buying a house. は不可) (買わないことに決めた) I *decided not to* buy a house. ▶先生のクラスの受講を止めたいのです. 思ったよりはるかに難しいものですから I'd like to *drop* your course. It's much harder than I expected. ▶行こうかな, それとも止めようかな Will I go or won't I?

会話「それ, 彼に送るわ」「止めろよ」"I'll send it to him." "*Don't.*"

❸ [廃止する] abolish, do* away with .... (❗後の方が口語的に); [取り除く] get* rid of .... ▶死刑を止める *abolish* the death penalty. ▶悪い習慣を止める *get rid of* a bad habit. ▶私たちの学校は制服を止めた Our school *did away with* uniforms.

── 止めさせる 動 ▶彼がそこへ行くのを止めさせる *stop* him (*from*) *going* there (❗(話) では from はしばしば省略される); *make* him *stop going* there. ▶彼に夜ふかしの習慣を止めさせる *get* him *out of* the habit of keeping late hours. ▶医者は彼を説得して酒を止めさせた The doctor *persuaded* him *to give up* drinking./The doctor *persuaded* him *not to* drink./(書) The doctor *dissuaded* him *from* drinking. ▶どうして彼らを説得してそれを止めさせなかったの Why didn't you *talk* them *out of* it?

やめる 辞める 動 [去る] leave, (話) quit*; [退職する] (定年などで) retire 《*from*》; [役職などを辞職する] resign 《*from, as*》. ▶彼は学校 [会社, その仕事] を辞めた He *left* [*quit*] school [the company; the job]. (❗(1) left school は《英》では「卒業した」の意もある. (2) leave の場合は辞める理由が不明であることが多いのに対し, quit の場合は通例自己の意志で辞めることを含む) ▶彼は 60 歳で会社を辞めた He *retired* [✗*resigned*] *from* the company *at* (the age of) sixty. ▶彼は委員 [議長] を辞めた He *resigned from* the committee [*as* chairman, the chairmanship].

── 辞めさせる 動 ▶社長は彼を辞めさせた(＝首にした) The president *dismissed* him [(話) *fired*, 《英話》 *sacked*] him (*from* the company). ▶彼は窃盗をして学校を辞めさせられた(＝退学させられた) He *was expelled from* school for stealing.

やもうしょう 夜盲症 【医学】 nyctalopia, (鳥目) night blindness.

やめる ▶ 《女性》 a widow (⇒未亡人); 《男性》 a widower. ▶やもめになる become a *widow* [*widower*]; lose one's husband [wife]; be widowed. ▶彼女のやもめ暮らしも 3 年ほどになる She has been a *widow* for some three years now.

やもり 【動物】 a gecko /gékou/ 複 ～(e)s.

*やや [少し] a little, (話) a (little) bit; (少しばかり) slightly; (いくぶん) rather (❗控えめにいってかえって意味を強める), 《やや書》 somewhat (❗rather より客観的な語); (ある程度まで) to some extent. ▶やや疲れた I'm *a little* [*a* (*little*) *bit, slightly, rather*] tired. ▶彼の英語はやや上達した His English has improved *a little* [*somewhat, to some extent*]. ▶君はやや今の政治家と似ている You look *rather* like that statesman.

ややこしい [複雑な] complicated, complex, intricate (⇒複雑); [やっかいな] troublesome. ▶話(＝事態)をややこしくするな Don't make the situations *complicated*.

ややもすれば [しがちである] (本来的・習慣的に) be apt (*to* do); (おそれがある) be liable (*to* do; *to*); (性質的に) be prone (*to* do; *to*). (⇒勝ち) ▶若い人はややもすれば誘惑に負けやすい Young people *are apt* [*liable, prone*] *to* give way to temptation. ▶人はややもすれば迷信に陥りやすい People *are liable* [*prone*] *to* superstition.

やゆ 揶揄 [ひやかし] 《やや書》 ridicule. ▶その政治家を揶揄する 《やや書》 *ridicule* [(笑い物にする) *make fun of*, (あざける) 《書》 *deride*, (からかう) *tease*] the politician.

やよい 弥生 ▶弥生式土器 *Yayoi* ware. ▶弥生時代【歴史】 the *Yayoi* period; (説明的に) an archaeological period in Japan after [following] the *Jomon* period (lasting from the third century B.C. to the third century A.D.).

─やら [副助詞] ❶ [不確かさを示す] ▶彼が何やら言っているがよく聞こえない Though he's saying some*thing*, I can't hear him well. ▶今日亀山さんという人があなたに会いに来ました *A* Mr. Kameyama came to see you today. ▶彼は来るのやら来ないのやらはっきりしない It's uncertain *whether* he will come *or not*.

❷ [並べていう] (または) or; (...や...やらで) what with [by]... and what with [by]. (❗ what with ... は「原因・理由を, what by ... は「手段・方法を示す」) ▶第二外国語としてフランス語やらドイツ語をとらないといけません You have to take [study] French *or* German as a second language. ▶貧困やら病気やらで彼女は人生に絶望した The *What with* poverty *and* (*what with*) sickness [Partly because she was poor and partly because she was sick], she gave up her life. (❗後の what with は省略されることが多い)

── ─やら [終助詞] [...かしら] I wonder 《*wh*- 節》. ▶この橋はいつ完成するのやら *I wonder when* this bridge will be completed.

やらい 矢来 a (split-rail) bamboo [log] fence of rough construction.

やらい 夜来 ▶夜来の雨 the rain that has been falling since last [the previous] night.

やらかす (する) do*; (失敗などを) make*. ▶彼は次に何をやらかすか分からない There is no knowing what he will do next. ▶彼はまたとんでもない失敗をやらかした He *made* a real blunder again.

会話「白状することがあるんだ」「まあ何をやらかしたの」"I've got a confession to make." "Now what *have you been up to?*" (❗be up to は (話) で「(よくないこと)をしている」の意)

やらす 遣らす ▶

やらずのあめ 遣らずの雨 a rain which begins to fall just as a guest is about to leave.

やらずぶったくり 遣らずぶったくり [与えずに取り上げるだけの] all take and no give. ▶彼はやらずぶったくりの男だ He is all take and no give.

やらずもがな 遣らずもがな ▶最終回にやらずもがなの 2 点を取られた They scored two runs in the last

やらせ inning, but they couldn't get any if we played better [properly].

やらせ 遣らせ ▶このドキュメンタリー映画はやらせだ(=でっち上げられたものだ) This documentary film *has been faked* [*has been fixed*; *has been staged*].

やらせる 遣らせる (無理に) make*... do; (好きなように) let*... do. ●彼女は意に反してそうやらされた She *was made to* [They *made* her] do so against her will. (!受身の場合 to が必要) ●子供たちの好きなようにやらせるつもりだ I'm going to *let* my children do as they like. ▶ちょっとやらせてみて *Let* me *have a try* 《話》 *a go*》 *at* it.

やられる (被る) suffer; (負かされる) be defeated [beaten]. ●こてんぱんにやられる *suffer* a terrible *defeat*. ▶彼はインフルエンザにやられた(=で寝込んでしまった) He *has come down with* (the) flu.

やり 槍 a spear; (騎兵の) a lance; 〖槍投げの〗 a javelin. ●槍を構える hold a *spear* for an attack. ●槍で突く spear; thrust a *spear* 《*into*》; lance.

やりあう 遣り合う (議論する) argue 《*with*》; (言い争う) quarrel, have* a quarrel 《*with*》; (戦う) fight* 《*with*, *against*》; (かかわる) tangle 《*with*》. ▶宗教のことであなたとやり合うつもりはない I'm not going to *argue with* you about your religion.

やりいか 槍烏賊 〖動物〗a spear squid.

やりがい 遣り甲斐 ●やりがいのある (やる価値のある) worth doing; (報いられる) rewarding. ●やりがいのある仕事 a job *worth doing*; a *rewarding* job; a challenge.

やりかえす 遣り返す (言い返す) retort, answer back; (仕返しをする) get* back 《*at*》. ▶「よけいなお世話よ」と彼女はやり返した "Mind your own business," she *retorted*.

やりかけ 遣り掛け ── **遣り掛けの** 形 (終えていない) unfinished; (半分しかしていない) half-finished, half-done. ▶やりかけの仕事がたくさんある I have a lot of *unfinished* work to do.

やりかける 遣り掛ける ▶仕事をやりかけたままにしてはいけない Don't leave the work *half-finished* [*half-done*].

*__やりかた__ **遣り方** 图 a way; (...の仕方) how to 《do》; (手段) a means. (⇨方法, 仕方) ●ちゃんとしたやり方で in the right *way*. ▶そのやり方で可能だと思いますか Do you think it's possible (*in*) that *way*? (!《話》ではしばしば in を省略する) ●本当にそのやり方分かってるの? Do you really know the *way* to do it [*how to do* it]? ▶彼は自分なりのやり方でそうした He did it (*in*) his *own way*. ▶それはやり方次第だ It (all) depends on *the way* [(on) *how*] you do it. ▶やり方さえ間違えなければ我々は彼らとの合意に達することができるかもしれない If we *play* our *cards right*, we may be able to come to an agreement with them. (!慣用表現)

やりきる 遣り切る (⇨遣り遂げる)

やりきれない 遣り切れない (⇨堪(た)らない) ▶ああ, こう寒くてはやりきれない(=耐えられない) Oh, I *can't stand* [*bear*] this cold. ▶新聞では毎日のように親による子供の虐待や子殺しのような悲惨な事件が報道され, 本当にやりきれない The newspapers report tragic incidents such as parents' cruelty to their child and infanticide almost every day, which *makes* me really *disgusted*. (!which は先行文全体をさす)

やりくち 遣り口 (やり方) a way. ▶あの男のやり口にはかむかする I'm disgusted with his *way of doing things* [*the way* he *does things*].

やりくり 遣り繰り ── **遣り繰りする** 動 (何とかやっていく) manage; (暮らしていく) get along. ●金[時間]をうまくやりくりする *manage* money [time] well. ●何とかやりくりして収入の範囲でやっていく *manage to* make (both) ends meet; *juggle* household expenses to make (both) ends meet. ●月10万円でやりくりする *manage* [*get along*] on 100,000 yen a month. ▶彼女は家計をやりくりするのが上手だ She *manages* the household [the family budget] well./She is a good (household) manager.

●**遣り繰り算段** ●やりくり算段して資金を調達する *manage to* raise fund 《*for*》. (⇨算段)

やりこなす 遣りこなす (⇨やってのける)

やりこめる 遣り込める (言い負かす) talk 〖《主に米》argue〗... down. ▶彼はやりこめられた He *was talked down*.

やりすぎ 遣り過ぎ ▶それはやり過ぎだ(= 行き過ぎだ) That's *going too far*.

やりすぎる 遣り過ぎる ●やり過ぎるな (勉強・運動・仕事などを) Don't *overdo it* [*things*].

やりすごす 遣り過ごす (通り過ごさせる) let*... go past. ●追っ手をやり過ごす *let* a pursuer *go past*.

やりそこなう 遣り損なう (失敗する) fail. ▶今度やりそこなったらおしまいだ If I *fail* this time, it's all up with me. (! be all up with は《話》で「万事休す」の意)

やりだま 槍玉 ●**槍玉に挙げる** ▶我々は彼を槍玉にあげた(= 槍玉にする) We *made a victim of* him.

やりっぱなし 遣りっ放し ●やり放しにする leave 《the work》 half-done [*unfinished*].

やりて 遣り手 (敏腕家) a capable person, 《話》a hotshot; 〖新進気鋭の人〗 an up-and-coming person; 〖積極的な事業家〗《話》a wheeler-dealer (しばしば悪い意味で抜け目なく商売をする人をいう); 〖精力的に働く人〗 a go-getter. ●警察署随一のやり手刑事 the most *capable* detective [the number one *hotshot* (detective)] in the police station.

やりとおす 遣り通す ▶これをやるからには最後までやり通しなさい If you do this, *do it all the way*. (⇨遣り遂げる)

やりとげる 遣り遂げる carry... out 〖やや書 through〗 (! through の方が最後までやり通す意が強い); 〖努力の末成就する〗 accomplish, 〖完了する〗 finish. ●使命をやり遂げる *accomplish* [*perform*, *carry out*] a mission. (! 後の方は口語的) ●やり始めたことは最後までやり遂げなさい You must *carry through* to the end what(ever) you set out doing. (! 目的語が長い場合, 特に関係節の場合の語順に注意)

やりとり 遣り取り 图 (交換) an exchange. ●情報[意見]のやりとり an *exchange* of information [opinions].

── **やり取りする** 動 ▶その件について彼と電話でやり取りする *toss* the matter *back and forth with* him on the phone. ▶彼とは長いこと手紙のやりとりをしている I *have exchanged* letters [《文通する》 *corresponded*] *with* him for a long time.

やりなおし 遣り直し (やり直すこと) redoing. ▶済んだことはやり直しがきかない What is done cannot be undone. (⇨遣り直す)

やりなおす 遣り直す (再びする[始める]) do* [start, begin*] (all) over again; (再出発する) make* a fresh start; (外国語などを磨き直す) brush... up, brush up on...; (繰り返す) repeat. ●*start again* from the beginning [《話》from *scratch*]. ●同じ学年をもう一度やり直す *repeat* the grade. (! *repeat the same grade* は冗語的なので避ける) ▶私は英語をやり直したい I want to *brush up* (on) my English. ▶間違えたらもう一度やり直さなければなりません If you make a mistake, you'll have to *do* it *over*. (❗*do ... over* は《米》で「〔課題など を〕やり直す」の意) ●彼女は人生をやり直す決心をした She decided to *make a fresh* [*a new*] *start* in life./She made up her mind to *have* her life *over again*.

やりなげ 槍投げ 〖競技〗 the javelin, javelin throw. ● 槍投げの選手 a *javelin* thrower. ● 槍投げをする throw a *javelin*.

やりにくい 遣り難い ▶(私には)この仕事はやりにくい(=難しい) This work *is difficult* [*hard*] (for me) *to do*. ▶彼とは仕事がやりにくい It's *hard* for me [I find it *hard*] *to* work with him. (⇨難しい)

やりぬく 遣り抜く carry ... out 〖《やや書》through〗; get* through with .... (⇨遣り遂げる)

やりのこす 遣り残す ▶多くの計画をやり残している We *have left* many projects *unfinished*.

やりば 遣り場 ▶目のやり場に困った I didn't know *which way to look*. ▶彼はやり場のない怒りを感じた(=どう怒りを表していいか分からなかった) He *didn't know how to give vent to* his anger.

やりみず 遣り水 (庭の) an artificial stream guided into a garden from a river.

やる 遣る ❶ [行かせる, 送る] send*. ● 子供を学校へやる *send* one's child *to* school. (❗「行かせる」の意のほかに学費を出したりする含みがある) ● パンを買いに使いをやる *send for* some bread. (❗使いに行く者を明示する場合は *send* him *for* [*to buy*] some bread とする)

❷ [他の場所へ移す] ● 窓の方に目をやる (=顔を向ける) *turn* one's face *toward* the window; (見る) *look at* the window. ● 私の眼鏡をどこへやった(=置いた) Where did you *put* my glasses?

❸ [与える] give*. ● 犬にえさをやる *give* food to a dog; *feed* a dog. (❗*feed* は子供・病人・動物などに食物を与えること) ● 花に水をやる *water* flowers.

❹ [する] do*. ● 大学で経済学をやる(=勉強する) *study* [専攻する《米》*major in*] economics at college; (経済学専攻の学生だ)《米》be an economic *major*. ● それを立派に [さっさと] やってのける *make* an excellent [a quick] *job* of it. ▶あの映画館では何をやっていますか(=上映していますか) What is *showing* [is *on*] at that movie theater? ▶1杯やりませんか(=飲みませんか) Won't you *have a drink*?/How [What] about (having) *a drink*? ● このようにやることなすことすべてうまくいかない Whatever I try ends in failure these days./I never get a break now. ● もうやるしかない 〖話〗 Here goes nothing. (❗「うまくいく公算が少ないか」という含みのあるひっ迫した状況での言い方) ● さあやろう. やればできるさ Let's *get going* 《主に米話》[*get cracking*《主に英話》]. We can *work it out*. (❗後の文は励ます言葉)

[会話]「試験で1番になったよ」「よくやったね」"I've come first in my exam." "Haven't you *done well* [*Well done*, Good (for you)]!"
[会話] (勝者・成功者などに)「やりましたね」「ええやりましたよ」"You *made it*." "Yes, I *made it*." (❗*make it* の意「うまくいく」の意)

❺ [してあげる] ▶私は息子に自転車を買ってやった I bought my son a bicycle./I bought my son a bicycle for [×to] my son. (前の方が「物」, 後の方が「人」に重点を置いた言い方 (⇨買う②)) ▶宿題を手伝ってやろう I'll *help* you *with* [help you (to) *do*] your homework.

❻ [...するぞ] (❗強い意志を表す) ▶必ず君を助けてやる I *will* help you. (❗*will* に強勢を置く) ❺ の I'll .... と比較)

やるかたない 遣る方ない ▶憤懣(ま)やる方ない I don't know how to vent [give vent to] my anger.

やるき 遣る気 (気力) drive; (動機づけ) (a) motivation. ● やる気満々である be full of *drive* 《for》; have a lot of *drive* 《for》; be highly motivated 《*to do*》. ● やる気を起こさせる(=動機づける) motivate《him *to do*》; (勇気づけ) inspire《him *to do*》. ● やる気のない lack *drive*. ▶彼がなぜ仕事に対してやる気をなくしたのか分からない I don't understand why he has lost his *motivation to* work. ▶その先生は生徒にやる気を(さらに)起こさせるために毎年学年当初にある宿題を出した The teacher gave out some assignment at the beginning of every year to *inspire* [*motivate*] his students (to try harder). ▶練習なんかやる気にならない I don't *feel like* practicing.

やるせない 遣る瀬ない 〖みじめな〗 miserable, 〖書〗 wretched; 〖どうすることもできない〗 helpless; 〖意のままにならない〗 frustrated. ● やるせない思いをする feel *miserable* [*helpless*].

ヤルタ 〖ウクライナの都市〗 Yalta /jɔ́ːltə/. ● ヤルタ会談 〖歴史〗 the Yalta Conference.

やれ ❶ [間投詞として] ▶やれ, 恐ろしや *Oh*, *no*! How dreadful! ▶やれ, 命は助かった *Thank God*, I escaped death. ▶やれ, 疲れた *Oh*, I'm tired to death.

❷ [二つのことを並列して] ▶彼はやれ寒いだの, やれ腹が減っただのと文句を並べる He complains that it is cold *and that* he is hungry./He complains of cold weather *and* his hunger.

やれやれ 〖安心〗 well; 〖失望, 困惑〗 oh, (oh) dear; 〖励まし〗 go on. ▶やれやれと思う give a sigh of relief; feel relieved. ▶やれやれ, やっと借金を返した *Well*(, *well*)*!* I've got out of debt at last. ▶やれやれ(=ひゃあ)やっと試験が終わった *Whew*, I'm glad the exams are over. ▶やれやれ, また遅刻したわ *Oh dear*, I'm late again. ▶やれやれ, 助かった *Thank God* [*goodness, Heaven*(*s*)]*!*

やろう 野郎 [男] a man, a fellow, 《米》a guy, 《英》a chap; (あの男) he. ▶この野郎！ You *rascal*! ▶この馬鹿野郎が！ You *idiot* [*fool*]*!* ▶これは野郎の仕事だ This is a *man's* job.

やわ 柔 ━ 柔な 形 (しっかりしていない) not strong [firm] (enough); soft; weak. ● やわな体 a *weak* body. ▶そんなやわな神経ではつとまらない You are *too nervous* [*sensitive*]. That won't do./You can't get it over with such *weak* nerves.

やわ 夜話 a relaxing evening story.
やわはだ 柔肌 soft [tender] skin.
やわら 柔 *yawara*, an old word for *judo*.

やわらかい 柔らかい, 軟らかい soft (↔hard); tender (↔tough); gentle (-ler; -lest); mild.

使い分け	**soft** 触ると簡単に変形するほど柔らかいことを表す. **tender** 主に食べ物が柔らかく噛みやすいことを表す. 時に柔らかいことが意外であることを含意する. **gentle** 雨・風・匂い・音などが穏やかで柔らかいことを表す. **mild** 味や口当たりなどの柔らかさを表す.

● 柔らかいまくら a *soft* pillow. ● 柔らかい肉 *tender* [×*soft*] meat. ● 赤ん坊の柔らかい肌 a baby's *tender* [*soft*] skin. ● 柔らかい声で話す talk in a *soft* [a *gentle*] voice. ● 絹は感触が柔らかい Silk is [feels] *soft* to the touch. ▶彼の口調は柔らかだったが言葉にはとげがあった His tone was *gentle*, but his words contained a sting.

やわらぐ 和らぐ 〖心・態度・怒りなどが〗 soften; 〖痛み・緊張・心配などが〗 ease; 〖風・あらしなどが〗 die (〜d; dying) down. ▶彼に対する心が和らいだ My heart *softened* toward him. ▶薬を飲むとすぐ頭痛は和らいだ My headache *eased* soon after I took the medicine./The medicine soon *eased* [(鈍らせた) *dulled*] my headache. ▶暑さ[寒さ]が和らいだ The heat [cold] *has got less*./It has got less hot [cold].

やわらげる 和らげる 〖態度などを〗 soften; 〖調子などを〗 tone ... down; 〖衝撃などを吸収して〗 absorb; 〖痛みなどを〗 ease; 〖人の気持ちなどを〗 calm. ●態度を和らげる *soften* one's attitude. ●批判の調子を和らげる *tone down* 《one's》 criticism. ●爆発の衝撃を和らげる *absorb* the shock of the explosion. ●痛みを和らげる *ease* the pain.

ヤンキー 〖「米国人」の俗称〗《話》a Yankee; 〖不良, 不良っぽい人〗 a (juvenile) delinquent.

ヤング (若者たち) young people;《やや書》the young (*!* 集合的に用い複数扱い);(若者1人)《話》a youngster.
● ヤングアダルト (10代後半または20代前半の若者) a young person in one's late teens or early twenties; a young adult. ● ヤングエグゼクティブ (若い経営者) a young executive. ● ヤングコーン (トウモロコシの若い穂) a young corn. ● ヤングパワー youth power;《和製語》young power. (関連 老人パワー gray power)

やんごとない noble(-blooded); royal; highborn. ●やんごとないお方 a *noble-blooded* person; a person *of noble blood*.

ヤンゴン 〖ミャンマーの都市〗 Yangon. (参考 旧称ラングーン (Rangoon))

やんちゃ (わんぱく) naughtiness, mischief. ●やんちゃな男の子 a *naughty* [a *mischievous*] boy.

やんばるくいな 〖鳥〗an Okinawa rail.

やんま 〖昆虫〗a large dragonfly.

ヤンママ a young mother; (元不良の) a young mother who was once a delinquent.

やんや ▶観客はやんややんやの大かっさいを送った The audience gave 《him》 an enthusiastic [a tumultuous, a wild] applause.

やんわり (やさしく) gently; (穏やかに) mildly. ●泣いている子にやんわり話しかける speak *gently* to the crying child.

ゆ

ゆ 湯 ❶ [温められた水] (hot) water.

> 解説 日本語では「湯」と「水」を区別するが、英語では特に cold water と区別して hot water という以外は単に water を用いる。

● ぬるま湯 (⇨湯垢) ぬるま湯 lukewarm *water*. ▶沸騰した湯を注ぎなさい Pour in *boiling* (*hot*) *water*. (!) boiling hot water は「煮えたぎる湯」という感じ) ▶沸かした湯を飲みなさい You'd better drink *boiled water*. ●お湯とお茶の葉をどちらを先に入れるのですか Which do you put in first, the tea leaves or the *water*? ▶湯を少し出してくれますか Run some *warm water*, will you?
❷ [ふろ] a (hot) bath. (⇨風呂) ●湯冷めする catch [get] a (slight) chill after a *bath*. (⇨湯冷め) ▶彼はゆったり湯につかった He took [《英》had] a leisurely (*hot*) *bath*.
● 湯船 a bathtub; a tub; a bath.
- **ゆあか 湯垢** 《米》scale;《英》fur. ●湯あかがつく be covered with the *scale*. ●湯あかをとる remove the *scale*.
- **ゆあがり 湯上がり** ●湯上がりの (just) after taking a bath. ●湯上がりのほてった身体 one's body still hot *after taking* [《英》*having*] *a bath*.
- **ゆあたり 湯中り** ── 湯中りする 動 be affected by staying in the bath too long [taking a bath too many times].
- **ゆあつ 油圧** oil [hydraulic /haidrɔ́:lik/] pressure. ●油圧計 an oil pressure gauge /géidʒ/. ●油圧ブレーキ oil [hydraulic] brakes.
- **ゆあみ 湯浴み** (⇨⑲ 入浴)
- **ゆいあげる 結い上げる** ●髪を結い上げる (上へあげる) put up one's hair; (結い終える) finish doing [dressing] one's hair.
- **ゆいいつ 唯一** ─ 唯一の 形 the [one's] only; [唯一無二の] one and only (!) only の強調形); [たった一つの] sole (!) やや書) Only より強意的); [一つしかなく独特の] unique. ▶その莫大(ばく)な財産の唯一の相続人 the *only* [*sole*] heir /éər/ to the large fortune. ▶私の唯一の希望 my *one and only* hope; all I want 〈is ...〉. ▶彼はそれができる唯一の人だ He is the *only* [*sole*] person that can do it.
- **ゆいがどくそん 唯我独尊** (⇨自負, 自惚れ) ●天上天下唯我独尊 (⇨天上 [成句])
- **ゆいごん 遺言** 图 a [one's] will,【法律】one's last will and testament; (口頭の) one's last words. ●遺言状を作成する make [draw up] a *will*. ▶父の遺言に従って会社を相続した I inherited the company in accordance with my father's *will*.
── **遺言する 動** ▶彼は全財産を次男に与えると遺言した He *willed* all his property *to* his second son. / He *willed* his second son all his property. / He left all his property to his second son *in his will*.
● 遺言執行者 an executor.
- **ゆいしょ 由緒** ●由緒ある(=歴史上重要な)寺 a *historic* (俗に) a historical] temple. (「歴史に関する」の意) ●由緒ある(=立派な家系の)一族 a family of *good lineage* /líniidʒ/. ▶彼は由緒ある生まれだ He is *of noble* [*good*] *birth*. / He is *wellborn*. (!) 前の方が普通)

ゆいしんろん 唯心論 spiritualism; idealism.
● 唯心論者 a spiritualist; an idealist.
- **ゆいのう 結納** (説明的に) a ceremonial exchange of engagement gifts. ●結納を交わす exchange engagement gifts [presents].
● 結納金 engagement [《書》betróthal /bitróuðl/] mòney. ● 結納品 engagement gìfts; engagement prèsents.
- **ゆいび 唯美** ─ 唯美的(な) 形 esthetic /esθétik/.
● 唯美主義 estheticism. ● 唯美主義者 an esthete /esθí:t/. ● 唯美派 the art-for-art's sake school.
- **ゆいぶつ 唯物** ● 唯物史観 historical materialism.
● 唯物弁証法 materialistic dialectics. (!) 単数扱い) ● 唯物論 materialism. ● 唯物論者 a materialist.
- **ゆう 夕** (an) evening. ●朝に夕に morning and *evening*. (⇨朝晩)
● 夕景色 an evening scene.
- **ゆう 有** (存在) existence; (所有) possession. ●有が無かを有を生じさせる make something out of nothing. (⇨無)
- **ゆう 勇** courage; [勇敢] bravery; [武勇]《書》valor.
● 勇を鼓す summon up one's courage 《to do》.
- **ゆう 雄** (すぐれている人・物) ●私学の雄 one of the *best* private universities.
- **ゆう 優** an A; Excellent, Very good. (!!!) 米英では A, B, C, D, F の 5 段階に成績を分けるのが普通. F は failure (落第) の頭文字) ●英語で優をとる get an *A* in English. ●全科目優で卒業する graduate with straight *A's*. ▶そのレポートには優をつけた I marked [rated] the paper "*A*."
- **ゆう 言う** say*; tell*; speak*. (⇨言(い)う)
- **ゆう 結う** [結髪] tie (〜d; tying); [髪を]do* (up) [arrange, dress]《one's hair》. ▶彼女は日本髪に結ってもらった She *had* her hair *done* [*arranged*, *dressed*] in Japanese style. ▶彼女は髪を束髪(たばね)に結い上げた She *put up* [(うしろで束ねた) *tied back*] her hair in a bun.
- **ユーアールエル** [コンピュータ] the URL (*for*, *of*)《uniform [universal] resource locator の略》. (参考) インターネット上のアドレス
- **ゆうあい 友愛** friendship; companionship; (男子間の) fraternity; (同じ目的で結ばれた者同士の) fellowship.
- **ゆうあかり 夕明かり** ●薄れゆく夕明かりの中で in the fading (evening) twilight; at dusk.
- **ゆうい 有為** ── 有為の 形 (有望な) promising 《young people》; (有能な) able; (才能豊かな) talented.
- **ゆうい 有意** ── 有意の 形 (意味のある) significant.
● 有意差【数学】a significant difference.
- **ゆうい 優位** ● 優位になる [立つ] have [gain (⇔lose)] the *superiority* 《*over*》; have [win, gain] an *advantage* 《*over*》; (地位が) have a *better position* 《*than*》. ▶インドはパキスタンより軍事力で優位に立った India achieved military *supremacy over* Pakistan. ▶当社は競合他社より明らかに[わずかに]優位に立っている We *have a* distinct [*a* slight] *advantage over* our rivals.
── 優位な 形 superior 《*to*》.
- **ゆういぎ 有意義** ── 有意義な 形 (意味のある) mean-

ゆいん … ingful; (意義深い、重要な)《やや書》significant; (役に立つ) useful. ● 有意義な議論 a *meaningful* discussion.
　会話「なんだか時間をむだに使わせてしまったみたいね」「とんでもない、有意義だったよ」"I feel like you wasted so much time." "Oh, no. It was time *well spent*."
　── 有意義に 副 ● 休日を有意義に過ごす spend a holiday *meaningfully* [*usefully*]; (うまく利用する) *make good use of* a holiday.

ゆういん 誘引 (⇨勧誘) ● 誘引物質〖化学〗an attractant.

ゆういん 誘因〖原因〗a cause; (直接原因) an immediate cause; (刺激)《やや書》(an) incentive 《to》. ▶よい成績をとることが時に一生懸命勉強する誘因となる Getting good grades is sometimes an *incentive to* do 〖動機〗a *motive for* doing〗hard work.

＊ゆううつ 憂鬱 名〖落胆〗depression (❕「意気消沈」から単なる「気落ち」まで意味が広い); 〖陰気な暗い気持ち〗gloom; (書) melancholy (❕気質として悲しい気分になったり物思いにふけったりすること).
　── 憂鬱な 形 depressing; gloomy; (書) melancholy; (みじめな) miserable; (悲しい) sad. ● 憂鬱な天候 *depressing* [*gloomy*, *miserable*] weather. ● 憂うつな音楽 *melancholy* [*sad*] music. ● 憂うつである be [feel] depressed; (元気がない) be in low spirits, (話) be in the blues. ● 憂うつな表情をしている have a *gloomy* expression. ▶雨の日は憂うつな気分になる〖憂うつになる〗I *feel depressed* [*melancholy*, (話) *blue*] on rainy days./Rainy days give me a feeling of *depression* [*melancholy*]./Rainy days are *depressing* to me [*depress* me, (話) *give* me *the blues*]. (⇨②)
　── 憂鬱に 副 ● 憂うつにさせる depress《him》; make《him》feel depressed; (話) give《him》the blues. ▶将来のことを考えると憂うつになった I *felt gloomy* thinking about the future./My heart sank when I thought about the future.
● 憂鬱症〖医学〗melancholia. ● 憂鬱症患者 a melancholiac.

ゆうえい 遊泳 名 swimming. ● 遊泳禁止〖掲示〗No Swimming Here. ▶彼は政界での遊泳術にたけている(＝身を処する方法をよく心得ている) He knows very well how to get along in the political world.
　── 遊泳する 動 swim.

＊ゆうえき 有益 名 ● 有益な 形〖役に立つ〗useful; 〖ためになる〗instructive; 〖有利な〗profitable. ● 有益な情報 *useful* information. ▶君の忠告は彼にとって問題の解決に〗とても有益だった Your advice was very *useful* to him [*for solving the problem*]. ▶この本はおもしろくもあり有益でもある This book is both interesting and *useful* [*instructive*, (情報の点で得るところの多い) *informative*]. ▶海外旅行は有益な経験です Traveling abroad is an *instructive* [a *profitable*] experience. ▶良書を読むことは有益です It is *instructive* [*profitable*] to read good books.

　DISCOURSE
　一見すると, 協同学習は個別学習よりも生徒にとって有益である. しかし私の経験では, 個別学習のほうが効果的だ **Apparently**, cooperative learning is more *beneficial* for students than independent learning. However, in my experience independent learning is more effective. (❕*apparently* (一見すると)は譲歩を表すディスコースマーカー)

　── 有益に 副 usefully; (有利に) to advantage. ▶私たちはその待ち時間を有益に使った We spent the waiting time *usefully*./We used the waiting time *to advantage*.

ユーエスエー the U.S.A. (⇨米国)
ユーエスビー〖コンピュータ〗USB《*universal serial bus* の略》. (参考) インターフェース規格の一つ)

ゆうえつ 優越 名 superiority. ● 優越的な態度をとる assume an air of *superiority*.
　── 優越する 動 be superior《to》. (⇨勝る, 優れる)

ゆうえつかん 優越感 a sense of superiority; (a) superiority complex. (❕精神分析の用語としても用いられる) ● 優越感に浸る indulge oneself in a sense of *superiority*. ● 彼に優越感を抱く have a *sense of superiority to* [*over*] him; feel *superior to* him.

ユーエッチエフ〖極超短波〗UHF, U.H.F., uhf, u.h.f. 《*ultrahigh frequency* の略》.

ゆうえん 幽遠 ● 幽遠の境地 the *other-worldly* state of mind.

ゆうえん 悠遠 ── 悠遠の 形 (原始の) primeval /praɪmí:v(ə)l/. ● 悠遠の昔 the *primeval* times.

ゆうえん 優艶 ● 優艶な 形 graceful; elegant.

ゆうえんち 遊園地 an amúsement pàrk; (運動設備のある) a recreátion gròund.

ゆうおう 勇往 ● 勇往邁進する push on *with unyielding*〖《書》*indomitable*〗*spirits*.

ゆうが 優雅 (優美) grace; (上品) elegance.
　── 優雅な 形 graceful; elegant; (安楽な) easy. ● 優雅な生活を送る lead a *high*〖(のんびりした) an *easy*, (ゆったりとした) a *leisurely*〗life. ▶恭子は身のこなしが優雅だ Kyoko has a *graceful* carriage.
　── 優雅に 副 ● 優雅に踊る dance *gracefully*.

ゆうかい 幽界 the world of the dead; the other world.

ゆうかい 誘拐 名〖特に身代金目当ての〗(a) kidnapping; (an) abduction. (❕後の方はやや堅い語)
　── 誘拐する 動 kidnap; abduct. ▶テロリストはその政治家を誘拐して巨額の身代金を要求した The terrorists *kidnapped* [*abducted*] the politician and demanded an enormous ransom.
● 誘拐罪 kidnapping. ● 誘拐事件 a kidnapping.
● 誘拐者 a kidnapper; an abductor.

ゆうかい 融解 ── 融解する 動 melt; fuse; liquefy.
● 融解点〖物理〗the mélting pòint.

ゆうがい 有害 ── 有害な 形 harmful; (危険な) hazardous; (悪い) bad*. ● 有害な化学物質 *harmful*〖(毒性の)《書》*noxious*〗chemicals. ● 喫煙は健康に有害である Smoking is *bad for* [*harmful to*, *hazardous to*] our〖the〗health./(害を与える) Smoking *damages* our health.

ゆうがい 有蓋 ── 有蓋の 形 covered, roofed.
● 有蓋貨車 (米) a boxcar; (英) a goods wagon.

ゆうがいむえき 有害無益 ● それは有害無益だ It does no good, only harm.

ゆうがお 夕顔〖植物〗a bottle gourd; (ヨルガオ) a moonflower, angel's tears.

ゆうかく 遊郭 a licensed red-light district.

ゆうがく 有額 ● 賃上げの要求に有額の回答をする offer a certain sum of money in reply to the demand for higher wages.

ゆうがく 遊学 ● 故郷を出て東京に遊学する leave one's hometown to study in Tokyo. ▶2人はイギリスに遊学(＝留学)中に知り合った They got to know while (they were) studying in Britain.

ゆうかしょうけん 有価証券 securities. ● 有価証券偽造罪の罪を規定する prescribe punishment for [of] counterfeiting *securities*.
● 有価証券報告書 a financial statement.

ゆうかぜ 夕風 an evening breeze.

ゆうがた 夕方 (an) evening.

解説 日本語の「夕方」は日没ごろから暗くなるまでの間をいうが、英語の **evening** は日没前から就寝時ごろまでの幅広い時間をいい、日本語の「夜」に当たることも多い。

● 夕方6時に at six (o'clock) *in the evening* [*at night*]. (**!** at night は単に「昼」でないことを示す) ▶彼が訪ねてきたのは寒い冬の夕方だった It was on a cold winter *evening* that he came to see me. ▶夕方私は料理をするのに忙しい I'm busy cooking *in the evening*. ▶5月6日の夕方ガス爆発があった There was a gas explosion on [×in] the *evening* of May 6. (**!** 特定の日の夕方の場合, 前置詞は in ではなく on. ただし時刻を伴う場合は in も可 (⇨午前)) ▶私は彼に昨日の夕方会った I met him yesterday [last] *evening*. (**!** last evening はあまり用いない. 誤りとする文法家もいる)

ゆうがとう 誘蛾灯 a light trap (for exterminating insects).

ユーカリ 〖植物〗 a [×an] eucalyptus /jùːkəlíptəs/ (圏 eucalypti /-tai/, 〜es), a eucalyptus tree.

＊ゆうかん 勇敢 图 bravery; courage.

━ **勇敢な** brave; courageous. (**!** 後の方は堅い語で精神面を強調する (⇨勇ましい)) ▶勇敢な兵士 a *brave* [*courageous*] soldier.

━ **勇敢に(も)** 圖 bravely; courageously; (大胆に) boldly. ▶勇敢に戦って死ぬ die *bravely*. ▶彼はその子を救うために勇敢にも燃え盛る家に飛び込んだ He *bravely* rushed [It was *brave of* him to rush, He was *brave* (enough) to rush] into the burning house to rescue the boy.

ゆうかん 夕刊 an evening (news)paper. (**!** 朝刊と区別するときは an evening edition ともいう)

ゆうかん 有閑 ━ **有閑階級** the leisure class; the leisured class(es). ●有閑マダム a leisured lady; a lady of leisure.

ゆうかんじしん 有感地震 a felt earthquake. (翻 無感地震)

＊ゆうき 勇気 图 cóurage; bravery (⇨勇敢); boldness; 〖度胸〗nerve; 〖気力〗heart.

使い分け courage 恐怖・不安・危険などに屈さず、信念や責務に従って行動する勇気を表す.
bravery 危険や困難に大胆に立ち向かう行動の勇敢さを表す. courage より危機度が高い状況であることを含意する.
boldness 勇敢さよりも大胆さ・無謀さ・強引さを含意する. 時に批判的に用いられる.

①〖勇気が〗▶彼には提案を断わる勇気がなかった He didn't have the *courage* [〖話〗the *guts*] to decline the offer. ▶異議を唱えるには勇気がいる It takes *courage* [*nerve*] to oppose other people [others]. ▶私はその知らせに勇気がわいた I *was encouraged at* [*by*] the news./I took *courage* [*heart*] *from* the news./(それを聞いて) I *was encouraged to* hear the news. ▶彼女に金をあげると言いたいのは山々だが、あえて口に出す勇気がない I'd very much like to ask her for some money, but I don't *dare* (*to*) [I'm *afraid to*]. (**!** (1) *dare to* の *to* はしばしば省略される. (2) 後の言い方の方が口語的) ▶彼の加入で我がチームは勇気百倍だ His joining our team gave us a lot of *courage*.

②〖勇気を〗● 勇気を失う lose *courage* [*heart*]; (落胆する) be discouraged; (おじけづく) lose one's *nerve*. ● 勇気を出す gather [〖奮い起こす〗pluck up, summon] one's *courage* 《*to do*》. ● 勇気を出して(= 思い切って)意見を述べる *venture* (*to express*) an opinion. ▶彼の演説は我々に勇気を与えた(= 勇気づけた) His speech *encouraged* us./We *were* [*felt*] *encouraged* by his speech. ▶時には(= 必要な時にはいやと言う勇気を持て Be *brave* enough to say no when you need (to). (**!** (1) 後の方の to はある方が口語的. (2) この to を代不定詞 (pro-infinitive) といい、前の to say no を受ける) ▶一瞬恐怖が心をよぎったが彼は勇気をふりしぼって(= 心を強固にして)水中に飛び込んだ A fear flashed across his mind, but he *steeled himself to* dive into the water.

━ **勇気の)ある** 圏 courágeous; (勇敢な) brave. ●勇気ある発言 a *courageous* statement. ●勇気のある男 a man *of courage*; a *courageous* man (**!** 前の方が強意的); (度胸のある人) a man *of nerve* [〖話〗*with plenty of guts*]. ▶この消防士たちの勇気ある行動が多くの人の命を救った These fire fighters' acts of *bravery* [*brave acts*] saved a lot of lives.

ゆうき 有期 ━ **有期の** 圏 (期限付きの) for a definite period; (終了させられる) terminable. ●有期刑に処せられる be sentenced to *imprisonment for a definite term* [*period*].

●有期公債 a fixed term loan [bond].

ゆうき 有機 ━ **有機の, 有機的な** 圏 organic (⇔ inorganic). ━ **有機的に** 圖 organically.

●有機化学 organic chemistry. ●有機化合物 an organic compound. ●有機栽培 organic growing [cultivation]. ●有機栽培されている be organically grown [cultivated]. ●有機酸 〖化学〗an organic acid. ●有機水銀 〖化学〗organic mercury. ●有機水銀中毒 organic mercury poisoning. ●有機体 an organic body; an organism. ●有機農業 organic farming. ●有機物 organic matter; an organic substance. ●有機肥料 organic fertilizer. ●有機野菜 organic vegetables.

ゆうぎ 友誼 friendship.
●友誼団体 a friendly organization.

ゆうぎ 遊技 ━ 遊技をする play a game.
●遊技場 an amusement center.

ゆうぎ 遊戯 图 (遊び) play; (ルールのある遊び) a game. ━ **遊戯をする** 働 (幼稚園児などが) play and dance.
●遊戯室 (部屋) a playroom; (戸外) a playground. (⇨遊び〖遊び場〗) ●遊戯療法 play therapy.

ゆうきづける 勇気づける encourage; 〖元気づける〗cheer ... up. (⇨勇気②)

ゆうきゅう 悠久 图 eternity.
━ **悠久の** 圏 eternal; everlasting. ●悠久の(= 変わらずに続く)大地 *unchanging* earth. ●悠久の(= 記憶にない)昔から from time *immemorial*.

ゆうきゅう 遊休 ━ **遊休の** 圏 idle, unused.
●遊休地 idle land; unused land. ●遊休資産〖資本〗idle (unemployed, dormant] assets [capital]. ●遊休施設 idle facility. ●遊休設備 idle equipment.

ゆうきゅうきゅうか 有給休暇 a paid vacation《米》[holiday《英》]. ●5日間の有給休暇を取る take five days off *with pay*. ▶今有給休暇中だ I'm *on a paid vacation*.

ゆうきょう 幽境 a secluded place; a place in total seclusion.

ゆうきょう 遊侠 ●遊侠の徒 a *chivalrous* person.

ゆうきょう 遊興 〖快楽〗pleasure; 〖娯楽〗amusement. ●遊興にふける indulge in [〖追求する〗《やや書》pursue] *pleasure*.

ゆうぎょう 遊興税 (an) amusement [entertainment] tax.

ゆうぎょう 有業 ●**有業者** working people. ●**有業人口** the working population.

ゆうぎり 夕霧 (an) evening mist. ▶あたり一面に夕霧が立ちこめている An *evening mist* hangs all around.

ゆうぐ 遊具 《a piece of》playground equipment; a children's plaything.

ゆうぐう 優遇 [名] 《よい[親切な]待遇》good [kind] treatment.
— **優遇する** [動] ●彼を優遇する give him *good treatment*; *treat* him 《very》*well*. ▶この社会では老人は優遇されていない In this society elderly people don't *receive kind treatment* [*are* not *treated kindly*]. ▶この会社では経験者を優遇する《=十分に給料を出す》This company *pays a good salary to* experienced employees [workers]./The experienced employees of this company *are well-paid*.
●**優遇税制** a preferential tax system 《for doctors》.

ユークリッド 〖ギリシャの数学者〗Euclid /júːklɪd/.
●**ユークリッド幾何学** Euclidean /juːklídiən/ geometry.

ゆうぐれ 夕暮れ ●夕暮れに in the twilight [evening]; at twilight 《↔at dawn》〚やや書〛at dusk. (⇨日暮れ)

ゆうぐん 友軍 a friendly 《同盟の》[an allied] army.
●**友軍機** a plane of an allied air force.

ゆうぐん 遊軍 reserve forces [corps].

ゆうけい 有形 — **有形の** [形] 〚見て《金銭》評価できる〛tangible; 〚目に見える〛visible. ●有形無形の援助を受ける (⇨有形無形)
●**有形資産** 〖法律〗tangible assets; tangibles.
●**有形文化財** 〖法律〗tangible cultural assets [properties].

ゆうげい 遊芸 ●遊芸のたしなみがある have (some) artistic accomplishments. (🔍 個々の芸事をいう方が普通)

ゆうけいむけい 有形無形 ●有形無形の援助を受ける receive both *spiritual and material* [*material and moral*] support 《from》.

ゆうげき 遊撃 ●**遊撃手** 〖野球〗a shortstop. (⇨ショート) ●**遊撃戦** 《ゲリラ戦》guerrilla warfare. ●**遊撃隊** a flying squad.

ゆうげん 幽玄 suggested deepness of feelings; unfathomable profundity. ●幽玄な尺八の調べ a *shakuhachi* tune that evokes our deep feelings; a profound *shakuhachi* tune.

ゆうげん 有言 ●**有言実行** ▶彼女は有言実行の人である She does what she says she will do./She is a woman of her word 〚話〛a doer〛. (🔍 米英で基本的な考え方)

ゆうげん 有限 — **有限の** [形] limited.
●**有限会社** 《米》a corporation; 《米》an incorporated company 《略 Co.》Inc.》; 《英》a limited company 《略 Co. Ltd.》. ●**有限会社田中商会** Tanaka & Co. *Inc.* [*Ltd.*]. ●**有限数** a finite 《↔an infinite》number. ●**有限責任** limited liability.

ゆうけんしゃ 有権者 〚投票者〛a voter; 〚選挙人〛an elector; 《選挙民》《集合的》the electorate (🔍 単複両扱い)

*****ゆうこう** 有効 [名] ❶ 〚効力・効果がある〛effectiveness; 《法的な》validity. ❷ 〚柔道〛a yuko. ●有効で破る defeat 《him》by *yuko*.
— **有効な** [形] 《効果のある》effective; 《法的な》valid.

▶10年間有効なパスポート a passport *valid* for 10 years. ●有効な方法 an *effective* measure. ●4月1日から有効な《=発効する》規則 a rule *effective* from April 1. ●**有効数字** 3桁 〖数学〗three significant figures. ▶図書貸出カードは1年間有効で更新もできる The library card *is valid* [*good*] for a year and renewable. ▶この契約は2009年まで有効である The contract will *be in effect* [*runs*] until 2009.

■ **DISCOURSE**
しかし私の見方では、この主張は今でも有効である In my point of view, however, this argument is still *valid*. (🔍 in my point of view, ... 《私の見方では》は主張を表すディスコースマーカー)

— **有効に** [副] ●有効に使う make good use of 《it》; 《効果的に》use 《it》*effectively*. ▶その法律は先月有効になった《=発効した》The law *became effective* [*came into effect*, *took effect*] last month.
●**有効求人数** effective job offers. ●**有効求人倍率** the job-offers-to-applicants ratio. ●**有効性** efficiency. ●**有効成分** an effective ingredient. ●**有効投票** a valid ballot.

ゆうこう 友好 [名] 《a》friendship. ●両国間の友好を促進する promote *friendship* between the two countries. ●アメリカとの友好関係を維持する[断つ] maintain [break off] *friendly relations* with America. ●会は友好裡に終わった The meeting ended on [xin] a *friendly* note.
— **友好的な** [形] friendly 《to, toward》. ●彼に友好的な態度をとる take a *friendly* attitude toward [to] him. ●その問題を友好的に解決する settle the matter in a *friendly* way.
●**友好協定** a friendship agreement; 《書》a concord. ●**友好国** a friendly nation. ●**友好条約** a treaty of friendship; a treaty of amity.

ゆうごう 融合 [名] 《a》fusion; 〚融和〛《a》harmony. ●核融合 〖物理〗(nuclear) *fusion*. ●形式と内容の完全な融合 a total *fusion* [*harmony*] of form and content.
— **融合する[させる]** [動] fuse. ▶彼のデザインには快適さと美しさが融合されている His design is the *fusion* of comfort and aesthetic.

ゆうこうきげん 有効期限 the term of validity. ●その法律の有効期限 the term of *validity* of the law. ●そのクレジットカードの有効期限 the *expiration date* of the credit card. ●**有効期限の切れた切符** an *expired* ticket. ▶これは有効期限が満了した《切れた》This has expired. (🔍 満了日は the expiration [expiry] date 《of a passport》という)/《これはもう有効でない》This is *not valid* any more.

ゆうこく 夕刻 ●夕刻に in the evening. (⇨夕方)

ゆうこく 幽谷 an unexplored valley [《深くけわしい谷》ravine]. ●深山幽谷 (⇨深山幽谷)

ゆうこく 憂国 patriotic concern for the future of one's country.
●**憂国の士** a patriot. (🔍 patriotism は正に「愛国」であり、憂国もそれから出たものには違いないが、少し異なる)

ユーゴスラビア Yugoslavia /juːgoʊsláːvɪə/. (📖 バルカン半島の旧連邦共和国)

ゆうこん 雄渾 — **雄渾な** [形] powerful [forceful] 《writing》.

ユーコン ●**ユーコン川** 〚北米大陸の大河〛the Yukon.

ユーザー a user 《↔a maker》. ●ユーザーを獲得する hook users. ●ユーザーが定義できる user-definable. ●**ユーザーフレンドリーなパソコン** a *user*-friendly 《↔user-hostile》PC. ●**エンドユーザー** an end(-)user; an ultimate user. ●**大口ユーザー** a major user.

ゆうざい

- ユーザーアカウント 〖ユーザーの識別情報〗《コンピュータ》 a user account. ● ユーザーインターフェイス 《コンピュータ》 a user interface. ● ユーザー辞書 《コンピュータ》 a user dictionary. ● ユーザー車検 (説明的に) an automobile inspection procedure done by a car owner. ● ユーザーズマニュアル a user's manual. ● ユーザー設定 the user's setting. ● ユーザー登録 user registration. ● ユーザー登録をする register oneself as a user. ● ユーザー名 a username.

ゆうざい 有罪 图 guilt. (⇨無罪)
── **有罪の** 形 guilty. ● (被告が法廷で)有罪を認める[認めない] plead *guilty* [not *guilty*]. ▶ 彼は殺人の有罪判決を受けた He *was found guilty* [*was convicted*] of murder. (⇨後の方は堅い言い方)

ゆうさんかいきゅう 有産階級 the propertied classes; the bourgeoisie /bùərʒwɑːzíː/ (● 単・複両形い). ● 有産階級の人 a bourgeois (● 単・複同形. しばしば軽蔑的)(資産家) a man of property.

ユーザンス 〖手形期限〗 an usance.

ゆうし 有史 (歴史) (recorded) history.
● 有史以前 (先史) prehistory. ● 有史以来 (歴史上) in history; (歴史が始まってから) since the beginning of history. ● 有史時代 historic (⇔prehistoric) times.

ゆうし 有志 〖自発的に参加する人〗 a volunteer; 〖関心のある人〗 an interested person; (人たち) those interested. (⇨同好) ● 有志による寄贈 vóluntary contributions. ● その運動に参加する有志を募る ask for *volunteers for* the campaign.

ゆうし 勇士 〖勇敢な戦士〗 a brave soldier; 〖勇者〗 a brave man (圏 men); 〖英雄〗 a hero (〜es). (⇨英雄)

ゆうし 勇姿 a brave [a heroic; 《書》a valiant] figure.

ゆうし 雄姿 (堂々とした姿) a magnificent [《書》a gallant, (壮厳な) a majestic] figure. ● 富士山の雄姿 a *magnificent* [a *majestic*] view of Mt. Fuji.

ゆうし 融資 图 〖資金の供給〗 financing; 〖貸付金〗 a loan. ● つなぎ融資 bridge *financing*; a bridge *loan*. ● 企業向け融資 a business [a corporate] *loan*. ● 有[無]担保融資 a secured [an unsecured] *loan*. ● 財政投融資 fiscal investment and *loan* program. ● その会社への融資を打ち切る cut off one's *financing* to the company. ● 銀行に100万円の融資を申し込む ask the bank for a *loan* of one million yen. ● 銀行から融資を受ける get a *loan* from the bank [a bank *loan*]; 《やや書》be *financed* by [*x*from] the bank. ● 不正融資を受ける obtain a fraudulent *loan*. ● 融資の返済 repayment of the *loan*. ● 融資を返済[完済]する repay [pay off] a *loan*.
── **融資する** 動 finance; make 《him》 a loan. ● 企業に融資する 《やや書》 *finance* an enterprise. ▶ 銀行はその会社に5,000万円融資した(= 供給した) The bank *provided* fifty million yen *for* the company./《書》The bank *furnished* the company *with* fifty million yen.
● 融資金額 the amount financed; the amount of a loan. ● 融資限度 the credit limit [line, ceiling]. ● 融資残高 the balance of (outstanding) loans; the outstanding balance of loans. ● 融資条件 the terms of a loan.

ゆうじ 有事 ● 有事(= 緊急事態発生)の際に in an *emergency*; 《主に米》in case of (an) *emergency*. (⇨緊急)
● 有事関連法 emergency-related bills. ● 有事立法 legislation to deal with emergencies.

ゆうしかい 有視界 a visual area.

ゆうしょう

● 有視界飛行 visual flight [flying].

ゆうしかく 有資格 形 (適格品) qualified; (免許のある) licensed; (法的に資格のある) eligible; (...の権利で与えられている) entitled. ● 有資格の学生相談員 a *qualified* counselor.
● 有資格者 a qualified person. ● 開業有資格者 a licentiate /láisénʃiət/. (● 医師・弁護士など) ▶ 老齢年金受給の有資格者はふつう65歳からです You won't be *eligible for* [be *entitled to*] an old-age pension until you're 65.

ゆうしき 有識者 a well-informed [〖学識のある〗 a learned /lə́ːrnid/] person; 〖学識者〗 an intellectual; (専門家) an expert.

ゆうしてっせん 有刺鉄線 barbed wire; 《米》barbwire. ● 有刺鉄線の柵(*) a *barbed-wire* fence.

ゆうしゃ 勇者 a brave man (圏 men) 〖戦士〗〖書〗warrior).

*ゆうしゅう **優秀** 图 excellence; 〖優越〗 superiority.
── **優秀な** 形 excellent; 〖他よりすぐれた〗 superior; 〖傑出した〗 outstanding. (⇨立派な) ● 優秀な学生 an *excellent* [a *superior*, an *outstanding*] student. ● 最優秀選手 〖野球〗 the most *valuable* player (略 MVP). (参考 ワールドシリーズやオールスター戦の、最優秀選手を含む優秀選手は top guns) ● 試験で優秀な成績をとる get *excellent* [*brilliant*] results on 〖主に英〗 in] the exam; get *high* marks on [〖主に英〗 in] the exam. ● 数学で優秀賞をもらう receive an award [a prize] for *excellence* in mathematics. ● 彼は化学が優秀です He is *excellent* [*doing very well*, ×*superior*] in [*at*] chemistry. ● 他者との比較では superior を用いる: 耕一は私より化学が優秀です Koichi is *superior to* [×than] me in chemistry.

ゆうしゅう 有終 ● 有終の美を飾る ▶ 我々の仕事に有終の美を飾ろう(= 立派に仕上げをしよう) Let's do our work *to perfection*. ▶ 彼は晩年オスカー賞を得て俳優としての生涯に有終の美を飾った He *rounded off* his career as an actor by winning an Oscar in his later years.

ゆうしゅう 幽囚 ● 幽囚の身となる be captured; (幽閉される) be confined 《in》; be in confinement.

ゆうしゅう 憂愁 ● 憂愁を帯びた表情 one's *melancholy* look.

ゆうじゅうふだん 優柔不断 图 indecision.
── **優柔不断な** 形 indecisive, 《話》 wishy-washy; (決断力のない) irresolute; (弱腰の) 《話》 weak-kneed. ▶ あの男はすぐれたリーダーになるには優柔不断に過ぎる He is too *indecisive* to make a good leader.

ゆうしゅつ 湧出 ● 石油の湧出量 *output* of oil.
── **湧出する** 動 gush [well] 《*out, forth*》.

ゆうしゅん 駿駿 a fine horse.

ゆうじょ 遊女 (中世の) a *geisha*; (江戸時代の) a prostitute.

*ゆうしょう **優勝** 图 〖勝利〗 (a) victory; 〖選手権〗 a championship. ● 団体[個人]総合優勝 a team [an overall individual] championship. ● メジャーリーグのリーグ優勝シリーズ the League Championship Series. ● 優勝決定戦をする play a playoff (game); play off a tie.
── **優勝する** 動 〖選手権争奪戦に勝つ〗 win* the championship [tournament, title]; 〖優勝旗を獲得する〗 《米》 win the pennant. ● 弁論大会に優勝する *win* a speech contest; (1等賞[1位]を取る) *win* [*take*] *first prize* in a speech contest. ● 日本シリーズに優勝する *win* the Japan Series. ▶ 私たちの学校は野球の県大会で初優勝した Our school *won* its first *championship* in the prefectural

baseball tournament. ▶タイガースがリーグ優勝した The Tigers captured [won] the *pennant*. ●優勝旗 a championship flag; 《米》(プロ野球などの) a pennant. ●優勝経験《have》the experience of having won a championship [having become a champion]. ●優勝経験者 a former champion. ●優勝行進 a victory parade; a victorious parade. ●優勝候補 a favorite. ●優勝者 a champion; (勝者) a winner. ●優勝戦(選手権大会) a championship (⚠しばしば複数形で); (勝ち抜き試合の) a championship tournament; (決勝戦) a final (⚠しばしば複数形で). ●優勝チーム the champion(ship) team; the winning team. ●優勝杯 a championship cup; (賜杯) a trophy cup. ●優勝劣敗 (適者生存) the survival of the fittest.

ゆうしょう 有償 —— 有償の 形 (金銭を支払っての) for a consideration. ●有償である have to pay 《for》; be charged 《for》.
●有償契約 a contract for a consideration;〖法律〗an onerous contract.

ゆうしょう 勇将 a brave general.
●勇将のもとに弱卒なし 'There is no cowardly soldiers under a brave general.'/(ことわざ) Such as the captain is, such is the soldier./Like master, like man./Like mistress, like maid. (⚠後の2例は皮肉として用いられるので注意)

***ゆうじょう** 友情 (a) friendship. ●真の[親しい; 暖かい]友情 a true [an intimate; a warm] *friendship*. ●友情のきずなを維持する keep up the bonds of *friendship*. ●友情をはぐくむ[断つ] cultivate [break up] a *friendship*《with》. ●変わらぬ友情を誓い合う pledge to maintain a permanent [〖書〗an everlasting, (生涯続く) a life-long] *friendship*. ●友情から out of *friendship*. ●友情に厚い人 a *friendly* [(親切な) a *kind*] person. ▶彼と私の友情は長く続いた The *friendship* between him and me [My *friendship* with him] lasted for a long time.

DISCOURSE
数年前, 私はお金を貸したことで, 友人を失った. ...よって私は, 友人にお金を貸すと友情が壊れる可能性があると考える Several years ago, I lost a friend by lending them money. ... Therefore, I am of the opinion that lending money to a friend can break up the *friendship*. (⚠therefore (よって)は結論に用いるディスコースマーカー. 前の部分と直接的なつながりが必要)

ゆうじょう 『友情』 *Friendship*. (⚠参考) 武者小路実篤の小説)

***ゆうしょく** 夕食 (a) supper, (a) dinner.

|使い分け| **supper** 夕方から夜10時ごろまでにかけて1日の最後にとる食事で, 朝食 (breakfast), 昼食 (lunch) とともに軽い食事のこと.
dinner 1日のうちで最も主要な食事. 通例夕食がこれに当たるが, 日曜・祭日は昼食が dinner となる場合もある. 区別するために昼食を an early dinner, 夕食を a late dinner と言うこともあるが, an early dinner は普通は早目に食べる夕食のことである.

●ロースト ビーフの夕食 a *dinner* of roast beef; a roast beef *dinner*. ●夕食に出かける go out for *dinner*. ●簡単な夕食をとる have a small *supper* [×*dinner*]. (⚠dinner はごちそうを含意するのでこの場合は不可だが「ささやかな夕食会 (a dinner party) にする」の意でも可) ▶うちの夕食は6時です We have [eat] *dinner* at six o'clock./Our *dinner* hour is

six o'clock. (⚠前の言い方が普通) 夕食ですよ(= 夕食ができました) *Dinner*'s ready. ▶今晩は私の夕食は用意しなくていいよ You don't have to get my *supper* [*dinner*] ready tonight.
会話「今日の夕食は何ですか」「てんぷらです」"What's [What are we having] for *supper* today?" "(There's [We're having]) tempura." (⚠答えとして単に Tempura. だけでもよいが, ×Tempura is. は不可)

ゆうしょく 有色 ●有色人種 a colored race; people of color. (⚠無礼な言い方) ●有色野菜 colored vegetables.

ゆうしょく 有職 —— 有職の 形 working; 《a person》 with a job [having a regular job]; (定職を持つ人) a jobholder.

ゆうしょく 憂色 a worried [an anxious] look. ●憂色に包まれる be filled with anxiety; be very much worried. ▶夫人の顔に憂色が漂っている She looks worried./Her face tells how she is worried.

ゆうじん 友人 a friend. (⇨友達)

ゆうじん 有人 —— 有人の 形 manned.
●有人宇宙計画 a manned space program. ●有人宇宙船 a manned spaceship. ●有人宇宙飛行 a manned spaceship flight. ●有人飛行 a manned flight.

ゆうしんろん 有神論 《やや書》theism /θí:izm/ (↔atheism). ●有神論者 a theist.

ゆうすい 湧水 spring water.

ゆうずい 雄蕊 (おしべ) a stamen.

ゆうすう 有数 —— 有数の 形 〖著名な〗《やや書》eminent; prominent; 〖指導的な〗leading; 〖名高い〗distinguished. ▶日本有数の科学者の1人 one of the most eminent [leading, distinguished] scientists in Japan. ▶日本は世界有数の輸出国だ Japan is a *leading* export country in the world.

ゆうずう 融通 名 accommodation. ●資金の融通 financial *accommodation*.
●融通無碍 ▶彼は融通無碍に対処する He *adapts* so *easily* [*readily*] that he can deal successfully with anything.
── 融通する 動 〖貸す〗lend; 〖便宜をはかって供給する〗《書》accommodate. ▶彼に5万円融通する *lend* him 50,000 yen. ▶私は銀行から500万円融通してもらった The bank *accommodated* [*supplied*] me *with* a loan of 5,000,000 yen./(借りた) I *borrowed* 5,000,000 yen *from* the bank.
── 融通が[の]きく 形 〖柔軟な〗flexible (↔inflexible); (物事が) elastic; 〖応用性のある〗《文》▶adaptable. ●融通がきく人 a *flexible* [an *adaptable*] person. ●融通がきく規則 *flexible* [*elastic*] (↔inflexible) rules. ●融通をきかせろ Be more *flexible*. ▶私のおじは大金の融通がきく(=自由にできる大金を持っている) My uncle has a large sum of money *at his disposal*.
●融通手形 an accomodation bill [《米》paper]; a finance bill.

ゆうすずみ 夕涼み ▶土手で夕涼みをした I *enjoyed* the (*cool*) *evening breeze* on [at] the bank./I *cooled myself* on [at] the bank *in the evening*.

ユースホステル a youth hostel /hástl/.

ゆうする 有する have; own; possess. (⇨持つ)

ゆうせい 有声 —— 有声の 形 〖言語〗voiced.
●有声音 a voiced sound. ●有声化 voicing; vacalization.

ゆうせい 有性 —— 有性の 形 〖生物〗sexual; sexed.
●有性生殖 sexual reproduction.

ゆうせい 郵政 postal service [administration]. ● 日本郵政公社 Japan Post.

ゆうせい 遊星 (惑星)【天文】a planet.

ゆうせい 優生 ― **優生学** eugenics. (**!** 単数扱い) ● 優生保護法 the Eugenic Protection Act.

ゆうせい 優性 图【生物】dominance.
― **優性の** 形 dominant (↔recessive). ● 優性の法則 a law of *dominance*.
● 優性遺伝 dominant heredity. ● 優性形質 a dominant (character).

ゆうせい 優勢 图 (力・数などでの優位) predominance; (優越) superiority; (勝ち越し) the lead.
― **優勢な** 形 predominant; superior. ▶ 国会ではA党の勢力が優勢だ The A Party *predominates* [*is predominant*] in the Diet. ▶ 敵は我が軍より数において優勢だ The enemy is *superior* in number to our troops./The enemy *outnumbers* our troops. ▶ 現在我々のチームが優勢だ Our team *is now leading* [*in the lead*]. ● 優勢勝ち a decision. ● 優勢勝ちする win a decision 《over》.

ゆうぜい 有税 ― **有税の** 形 taxable.
● 有税品 taxable [(関税) dutiable] goods; (課税対象となる) goods subject to taxation [duty].

ゆうぜい 郵税 [『郵便料金』の旧称] (⇨郵便)

ゆうぜい 遊説 图 canvassing (**!** 投票を求めて選挙区をくまなく回ったり人を訪問すること); 《米》stumping, 《米》barnstorming (**!** 《米》政治演説をしながら各地を回ること).
― **遊説する** 動 canvass; 《米》stump, 《米》barnstorm. ● 投票の依頼のために選挙区を遊説する *canvass* one's district *for* votes. ● 全国を遊説して回る *canvass* [*stump*] the whole country.

ゆうせつ 融雪 a thaw; thawing; [融けた雪] melted snow.
● 融雪期 the tháwing tìme [pèriod]. ● 融雪洪水 a flood caused by melted snow.

***ゆうせん 優先** (順序・時間などの) priority (**!**「優先すべきこと」の意では ⓒ); (順序・重要性などの) precedence; (選択などの) preference. ● 最優先事項 a first [a top, a highest] *priority*. ▶ この契約では君より私の方に優先権がある I have *priority over* you in this contract. ▶ それは最優先の議題である That is *highest on* [*at the top of*] the agenda. ▶ 会員は優先的に切符が手に入る Members *are given priority* in getting tickets. ▶ 幹線道路を走っているからこちらに(走行の)優先権がある We have the *right of way*, because we're on a main road.
― **優先する** 動 ▶ 憲法は他の一切の法律に優先する The Constitution *takes priority* [*precedence*] *over* all other laws. ▶ 日本は産業の発展を優先させてきた Japan *has given* (x a) *priority* [*precedence*] *to* industrial progress. ▶ 彼は何よりも仕事を優先させた He *placed* [*set*] his work *above* everything.
● 優先順位 the order of priority. ● 優先席 (老人などの) a priority seat.

ゆうせん 有線 cable; closed-circuit.
● 有線テレビ cable television; (共同アンテナの) community antenna television (略 CATV); (ローカル向けの) closed-circuit television. ● 有線放送 cable broadcasting.

ゆうせん 郵船 a mail steamer.

ゆうぜん 悠然 图 (平静) calmness; (沈着) 《やや書》 composure.
― **悠然とした** 形 calm; composed.
― **悠然と** calmly; composedly; leisurely.

ゆうぜん(ぞめ) 友禅(染め) *yuzen* dyeing; (説明的に) one of the (silk) *kimono* dyeing processes, the characteristic pattern of it being the clearly printed flowers and birds, plants and trees, or mountains and rivers.

ゆうそう 勇壮 ― **勇壮な** 形 (雄々しい) heroic /həróuik/; (勇敢な) brave; (鼓舞する) stirring. ● 勇壮な行進曲 a *stirring* march.

ゆうそう 郵送 图 (⇨郵便)
― **郵送する** 動 《主に米》mail, send 《it》 by mail; 《主に英》post, send 《it》 by post. ▶ 彼に本を郵送する *mail* a book *to* him; *mail* him a book. ▶ その本が郵送されてきた (=郵便で届いた) The book came *by mail* [*in the mail*]. ▶ 印刷物は安く郵送できる Printed matter can *be mailed* cheaply.
● 郵送料 postage.

ゆうそうじん 遊走腎【医学】a floating kidney.

ゆうそくこじつ 有職故実 the knowledge about the usages and practices at ancient imperial court and in *samurai* society.

ゆうだ 遊惰 ● 遊惰な生活を送る lead an *idle* life [spend *idle* days] without having a regular job.

ユーターン 《do [make]》 a U-turn. ● 車をユーターンさせる turn a car in a *U-turn*. ● ユーターン就職する return to one's hometown to get a job after studying or working for a certain period in a big city. ▶ ユーターン禁止 (掲示) No *U-turn(s)* (allowed).

ゆうたい 勇退 图 (自発的退職) voluntary retirement; (定年前の退職) early retirement.
― **勇退する** 動 retire early [voluntarily]; take early [voluntary] retirement.

ゆうたい 郵袋 a mailbag.

ゆうたい 優待 ― **優待する** 動 (手厚く扱う) treat ... hospitably; (特別有利に) treat ... preferentially.
● 高齢者を優待する *treat* elderly people *hospitably* [*preferentially*].

ゆうだい 雄大 图 ● ナイアガラ瀑布の雄大さ the *grandeur* [(壮大) *magnificence*] of Niagara Falls.
― **雄大な** 形 ● アルプスの雄大な眺め a *grand* [a *magnificent*, a *majestic*] view of the Alps.

ゆうたいけん 優待券 [『音楽会などへの招待券』] a complimentary ticket 《to, for》; [『銀行・ホテル・クラブなどの優待カード』] a courtesy card; [『割引券』] a discount coupon.

ゆうたいるい 有袋類 ― **有袋類の** 形【動物】marsupial. ● 有袋類の動物 a marsupial.

ゆうだち 夕立 a shower ● (1) ばらばらと降るにわか雨で「夕立」の激しさはない. (2) 英国では April shower といい4月に多く, 開花を呼ぶ慈雨の感を持つ; (スコール) squall; (説明的に) a sudden brief downpour.
● 夕立にあう be caught in [x by] a *shower*. ▶ 夕立がありそうだ We're going to have a *shower*.

ゆうだん 勇断 勇断を下す make a *resolute* [a *drastic*] decision 《about, on; to do》.

ゆうだんしゃ 有段者 a rank holder.

ゆうち 誘致 图 (勧誘) invitation.
― **誘致する** 動 (招く) invite; (引きつける) attract. ● 観光客をこの町に誘致する *attract* tourists to this town. ▶ 我が町にハイテク産業を誘致したいものだ We'd like to *invite* high-technology industries *to* our town.

ゆうちょう 悠長 ― **悠長な** 形 leisurely (⇨のんびり); (人が) easygoing (⇨呑気(°ん)); ● 悠長に構える take things easy. ▶ そんな悠長にしていられない I can't take [spare] my time for that now. ▶ なんと悠長な話だろう What a *slow* process (it is)!

ゆうづき 夕月 an evening moon; a moon in the

evening.
● 夕月夜 a moonlight evening; a moonlit evening.

ゆうづる『夕鶴』Twilight Crane.(参考 木下順二の戯曲)

ユーティリティー a utility room. (註 台所に隣接し, 洗濯機・乾燥機・アイロンなどを備えた家事室)

ゆうていもく 有蹄目〖動物〗(総称) the ungulates.
● 有蹄類の動物 an ungulate.

ゆうてん 融点〖物理〗the mélting pòint; the point of fusion.

ゆうと 雄図 (雄大な計画) a grand [(書) a grandiose] plan; an ambitious enterprise.

ゆうと 雄途 雄途につく launch [(書) embark] on an ambitious enterprise [a long journey].

***ゆうとう** 優等 honors /ánərz/. ● 優等で大学を卒業する graduate from college with honors. ● 彼は高校で優等生だった He was an honor student in high school.
● 優等賞 an honor (prize).

ゆうとう 友党 an allied political party.

ゆうとう 遊蕩 dissipation. (⇨放蕩)

ゆうどう 誘導 图 〖案内〗guidance; 〖指図〗instructions; 〖電気〗induction.
── **誘導する** 動 guide; (先導する) lead. (⇨導く) ● 管制官は飛行機を誘導した The air controller gave instructions to the plane. ● 船長は巧みに船を港へ誘導した The captain skillfully led [guided, piloted] the ship to the port.
● 誘導尋問 (ask) a leading question. ● 誘導装置 (ミサイルなどの) a guidance system. ● 誘導体 〖化学〗a derivative. ● 誘導ミサイル〖軍事〗a guided missile.

ゆうどうえんぼく 遊動円木 ● 遊動円木を渡る walk on (渡り切る) walk across] a swinging log [bar].

ゆうとく 有徳 ── 有徳の 形 virtuous. ● 有徳の人 a man [a woman] of virtue.

ゆうどく 有毒 ── 有毒な 形 poisonous, 《やや書》toxic.
● 有毒ガス poisonous gas. ● 有毒廃棄物 toxic waste.

ユートピア 图 〖理想郷〗(a) utopia. (註 しばしば Utopia) ── **ユートピアの** 形 utopian.

ゆうなぎ 夕凪 an evening calm.

ゆうに 優に (十分に) well; (たっぷり) good 《a ~ の形で数詞の前に置くのが普通》; (楽に) easily. ● 彼の財産は優に 100 億円以上あった His assets amounted to [were] well over ten billion yen. ● そこへ行くのに優に 2 時間かかった It took a good [(まるまる) a full, (書) fully] two hours to get there. ● 彼は彼女より優に頭一つ背が高かった He was a good head taller than her. ● この部屋は優に 100 人収容できる This room can easily seat [《やや書》accommodate] 100 people.

ゆうのう 有能 ● 有能な人 a person of ability; an able [a capable, a competent] person. (⇨能力) ● 有能な秘書 an able [(てきぱきと仕事をする) an efficient] secretary.

ゆうばえ 夕映え (夕映える) the evening [sunset] glow. ● 夕映えの空 the sunset sky.

ゆうばく 誘爆 ── 誘爆する 動 cause an explosion; explode by an external cause.

ゆうはつ 誘発 ── 誘発する 動 (誘引する) induce; (引き起こす) cause; (触発する) touch [trigger] ... off. ● ショートした火花があの大爆発を誘発した Sparks from a short-circuited electricity caused [were the cause of] the loud explosion. ● 何が戦争を誘発したのか What triggered off [touched off] the war?

ゆうばれ 夕晴れ a clear sky in the evening.

ゆうはん 夕飯 (1日の主要な食事) (a) dinner; (a) supper 《後に dinner をとった場合》. (⇨夕食) ● 夕飯に何を食べましたか What did you have for dinner [supper]?

ゆうひ 夕日 the setting [evening] sun. ▶夕日が西に沈みかけている The sun is setting in [xto] the west. ▶彼は背に夕日を浴びて歩いていた He was walking with his back shone by the setting sun. ▶西の空が夕日で燃えている The western sky is glowing with the setting sun.

ゆうひ 雄飛 ── 雄飛する 動 ● 海外に雄飛する go overseas full of ambition; (大活躍している) be very active in a foreign country.

ゆうび 優美 grace; (上品) elegance.
── **優美な** 形 graceful; elegant. ▶富士山は優美な姿をしている Mt. Fuji is graceful in shape.

ゆうびょう 有病 ● 有病率〖医学〗a morbidity rate.

ゆうびるい 有尾類〖動物〗the tailed amphibians.

ゆうびん 郵便 《主に米》mail, 《主に英》post.

> 解説 mail, post ともに不可算名詞で,「郵便(制度)」,「(集合的) 郵便物」の意を表す. いずれも後の意のときは単数扱いで, 数えるときは a piece of mail のようにいう.

①【~郵便】● 小包郵便で by parcel post [×mail]. ● 外国国内;普通郵便 foreign [domestic; ordinary] mail [post]. ● 航空郵便 airmail. (⇨航空便) ● 電子郵便 electronic mail《略 email, e-mail》. ● 書留郵便 registered mail《米》[post《英》]. (⇨書留) ▶この手紙の速達郵便でお願いします I'd like to send this letter by special delivery [《英》by express], please. (⇨速達)

②【郵便(は)】● 今日は郵便がたくさん来て I had a lot of mail [post] today./A lot of mail [post] came [arrived] today. ▶私あての郵便がありますか Is there any mail [post] for me? ▶郵便はもう来ましたか Has the mail [post] come yet?

③【郵便に[を]】● 郵便にあて名を書く address the mail. ● 郵便を仕分けは sort the mail. ● 郵便を配る[運ぶ; 転送する] deliver [carry; forward] the mail. ● 郵便を受け取る receive the mail. ● 午前中の郵便に間に合う [遅れる] catch [miss] the morning mail.

④【郵便で】● by mail [post]. ● 郵便で送る《主に米》mail;《主に英》post. (⇨郵送, 出す) ● 彼に郵便で小包を送る send him a parcel by mail [post]; mail [post] him a parcel; mail [post] a parcel to him.

── **郵便の** 形 postal.
● 郵便受け[ポスト]《英》a postal order. ● 郵便為替 a money order;《英》a postal order. ● 郵便為替で1万円を送る send 10,000 yen by money order [《英》postal order]. (註 a mail order は「郵便による注文」の意) ● 郵便切手 a postage stamp. (註 堅い言い方で日常的には stamp のみでよい) (⇨切手) ● 郵便業務 postal service. ● 郵便小包 a postal package. ● 郵便私書箱 a post-office box (略 POB, PO Box). ● 郵便書簡 a lettercard. ● 郵便制度 a postal system. ● 郵便配達人《主に米》a mail carrier, 《主に米》(男の) a mailman, 《主に英》a postal carrier, 《主に英》(男の) a postman. ● 郵便振替 postal transfer. ● 郵便保険 (簡易保険) postal life insurance. ● 郵便料金 (全体の) postal charges; (1回の) postage. ▶イタリアへの手紙の航空郵便料金はいくらですか What [How

ゆうびんきょく much] is the airmail *postage for* [*on*] a letter to Italy, please? ▶ **郵便列車** a mail [xa post] train.

ゆうびんきょく 郵便局 a post [xa mail] office 《略 p.o., P.O.》. ● **郵便局員** a postal [《主に米》a mail] clerk;（集配人）《主に米》a mail carrier,（男の）a mailman;《主に英》a postal carrier,（男の）a postman. ● **郵便局長** a postmaster [xa mailmaster].

ゆうびんちょきん 郵便貯金 postal savings. ▶ 10万円の郵便貯金がある I have *postal savings* of 100,000 yen./I have a *deposit* of 100,000 yen *in the post office*.
— **郵便貯金(を)する** 動 deposit one's savings in the post office.

ゆうびんはがき 郵便葉書 a postcard（!米国では私製と官製があるが, 英国では私製の絵葉書に限られる）;《米》a postal card（!主に官製の）. ● **郵便葉書で通知を受ける** receive《a》notice *by postcard*.

ゆうびんばこ 郵便箱《各家庭の郵便受け》《米》a mailbox,《英》a létter bòx;《ポスト》《米》a (roadside) mailbox,《英》a postbox.（⇨ポスト）

ゆうびんばんごう 郵便番号《米》a zip code（!5けたの数字）;《英》a postcode, a postal code.（!数字とアルファベット）▶ 日本の郵便番号は7けたです Japanese *zip code* [*postcode*] is a seven-digit number.

ゆうびんぶつ 郵便物（集合的に個人に届く郵便物全部）《主に米》mail,《主に英》post;（時に）postal matter.（⇨郵便）● **第3種郵便物** the third-class matter; the third class. ● **多くの郵便物を取り扱う** handle a lot of *mail* [*post*]. ● **郵便物を発送する** send out (the) *mail*.

ユーフォー 〔未確認飛行物体〕a UFO, a U.F.O. /júːèfoʊ, júːfou/（複 ～'s, ～s）《an *unidentified flying object* の略》.

ゆうふく 裕福 — **裕福な** 形 （財産・地位のある）wealthy;（金持ちの）rich, well-off,《話》well-to-do. ▶ 彼女は裕福な家庭の出です She comes from a *rich* [*a wealthy*, *a well-to-do*] family. ▶ 彼らの暮らしぶりからすると相当裕福らしい From the way they live, they seem to be quite *well-off* [*well-to-do*].

ユーフラテス — **ユーフラテス川** the Euphrates /juːfréɪtiːz/.

ゆうべ 夕べ ❶【昨夜】（⇨昨夜）
❷【夕べ】an evening;（夜会）an evening. ▶ 昨日音楽の夕べが公会堂で催された A musical *evening* was held at the public hall yesterday.

ゆうへい 幽閉 名（監禁）（やや書）confinement.
— **幽閉する** 動 ▶ 彼をロンドン塔に幽閉する *confine* him in the Tower of London.

ゆうべん 雄弁 名（やや書）eloquence. ● **雄弁を振るう** speak eloquently [with great *eloquence*]《about it》.
— **雄弁な** 形 《書》eloquent. ▶ それは事実を雄弁に語っている That *says a lot about* the fact./《書》That *is eloquent of* the fact. ▶ 目は口より雄弁だ Eyes are more *eloquent* than lips.
● **雄弁家** an eloquent [a skillful] speaker,《書》an orator.

ゆうほう 友邦 a friendly nation;（同盟国）an ally, an allied nation.

ゆうほう 雄峰 a majestic peak [mountain].

*ゆうぼう 有望 — 有望な** 形（将来性のある）promising;（見込みのある）hopeful（!通例叙述的に用いる）. ▶ 彼は前途有望な若者だ He is a *promising* young man./He is a young man of *promise*./He shows（xa）great *promise*./（大きな可能性を秘めている）He is a young man *of great possibilities*./He is a young *hopeful*.（!この hopeful は名詞）

ユーボート 〔ドイツの潜水艦〕a U-boat.

ゆうぼく 遊牧 — **遊牧の** 形 nomadic. ● **遊牧生活をする** lead a *nomadic* life.
● **遊牧民**（人々）nomads, nomadic people;（人種）a nomadic tribe.

ゆうほどう 遊歩道（海岸に沿った）a promenade /prɑ̀mənéɪd/,《英語》a prom.

ゆうみん 遊民 idle people. ● **高等遊民**《be among the [be one of those]》jobless college graduates.

*ゆうめい 有名** 名 〔名声〕fame;（悪名）notoriety /nòʊtəráɪəti/.（⇨形）▶ 彼は歌手として一躍有名になった He suddenly became *famous* [*very well known*,（人気が出る）*popular*] as a singer. ▶（名声を得た）He suddenly won *fame* as a singer. ▶ その小説は彼女を有名にした The novel *made* her *famous*./（名声をもたらした）The novel *brought fame to* her.
— **有名な** 形 （一般によい意味で）famous; famed;（話）big-name;（書）celebrated;（よく知られた）well-known;（名高い）noted;（卓越した）prominent, distinguished;（悪名高い）notorious.

【使い分け】**famous** 人や物事が広く有名であることを示す最も一般的な語. 通例, 肯定的な意味合いで用いられる.
famed「名高い」「名声を得た」の意を表す.
big-name 人や企業などにおいて能力・人気・実績などが一流であるために有名であることを表す.
celebrated 人や物が高い功績などによって有名であることを表す. 多くの人々の話題となるような有名さを含意する.
well-known 人や物事がよく知られていることを客観的に表す. 肯定的な文脈にも否定的な文脈にも用いる.
noted 人や物事の有名さを表す. 時に famous よりも限定的な分野での有名さを含意する.
prominent 特にその分野における技能や技術が一流であることを表す.
distinguished 人が優秀で際立っていることを表す. 主に専門的な仕事などに従事している人物の有名さを含意する.
notorious 人や物事の悪名高さを表す. 肯定的な文脈では用いない.

① 【有名な～】● 有名なオーケストラ a *famous* [a *well-known*,《話》a *big-name*] orchestra. ● 有名な芸術作品 a *famous* work of art. ● 有名なくざ a *notorious* gangster. ▶ 彼は有名な作家だ He is a *famous* [a *well-known*, a *noted*, a *prominent*, a *distinguished*] novelist.

② 【有名だ】▶ 有馬は温泉で有名だ Arima is *famous* [*well known*] *for* its hot springs.（!*for* に続く語句は所有代名詞を伴うことが多い）/（温泉地として）Arima is *famous* [*well known*] as a hot spring resort. ▶ 日本はすぐれた車を作ることで有名である It is *well known* [x*famous*] that Japan produces excellent cars.（! well-known は限定的に用いる場合はハイフンを用いてつづり, 叙述的にはこのように well known と分離するのが普通）▶ この地域は犯罪があるで有名である This part of the city is *notorious* [x*famous*] *for* its crimes [（高い犯罪率で）its high crime rate].

● **有名人**（知名人）a famous [a well-known] person,（名士）a celebrity,（大物）《話》a big [a famous] name. ● **有名税** a price for one's fame. ▶ プライバシーが狭められるのも有名税の一つだ

ゆうめい Well-known people have to stand lots of inconveniences, and encroached privacy in one of them. ● 有名大学 a famous [一流の《やや書》a prestigious] university. ● 有名ブランド（商品）《米》a name [《xa famous》] brand, brand name goods;（英）goods from famous companies;（会社）a famous [a well-known,《米》a name] company;（人気銘柄）a popular brand. ● 有名無実（⇨有名無実）

ゆうめい 勇名 ― 勇名を馳(は)せる distinguish oneself《in》; be famous《as an arctic explorer; for his conquest of K2》.

ゆうめい 幽明 ― 幽明境(さかい)を異(こと)にする（死であの世に行く）depart this life; go west.

ゆうめい 幽冥 ― 幽冥界 the abode of the dead;『ギリシャ神話』the Hades /héidiːz/.

ゆうめいむじつ 有名無実 ― 有名無実の社長（名目上の）the *nominal* president;（名ばかりの）the president *in name only*.

ゆうめし 夕飯（⇨夕飯(ゆうはん)）

*****ユーモア** 〖おかしさ〗humor /hjúːmər/;〖冗談〗a joke (*!* 日本語の「ユーモア」はこの語が適する場合もある). ▶ ユーモアのある話 a story of *humor*; a *humorous* story. ▶ ユーモアのある人 a humorist. ▶ 彼はユーモアが分かる[分からない] He has a good sense [has no sense] of *humor*./He sees [can't see] the point of *jokes*.

ゆうもう 勇猛 ― 勇猛な 形〖勇敢な〗brave;〖恐れを知らない〗《やや書》fearless;（大胆な）daring.

ゆうもや 夕靄 ―（an) evening haze [mist]. ▶ 川面(かわも)には夕もやが立ちこめていた An *evening mist* hung over the river.（⇨霧）

ユーモラス ― ユーモラスな 形（ユーモアのある）humorous /hjúːmərəs/（⇨ユーモア）,（人を楽しませる）amusing;（おかしい）funny.

ユーモレスク 〖音楽〗a humoresque /hjùːmərésk/.

ゆうもん 幽門 〖解剖〗the pylorus /pailɔ́ːrəs/《働 pylori /-rai/》.
● 幽門狭窄(きょうさく)〖医学〗pyloric stenosis. ● 幽門痙攣(けいれん)〖医学〗pylorospasm.

ゆうもん 憂悶 ― 憂悶する 動 be worried《over a private matter》.

ゆうやく 勇躍 ▶ 彼は勇躍（＝元気いっぱいに）出発した He set off [out] *in high spirits*.

ゆうやく 釉薬〖陶磁器の〗(a) glaze.

ゆうやけ 夕焼け an evening glow; a sunset (glow [color]); an after-glow. ▶ 夕焼け空 the sky *at sunset*.

ゆうやみ 夕闇 dusk;（日没後の薄明かり）twilight.（*!* 前の方が文語的でより暗い）▶ 夕闇が迫るころに at *dusk*; as *dusk* falls [gathers].

ゆうゆう 悠々 ― 悠々とした 形（落ち着いた）calm, composed;（急がない）leisurely;（安楽な）comfortable. ▶ 悠々とした（＝俗世間にわずらわされることなく）余生を送る spend the rest of one's life *free from worldly cares*.

― 悠々(と) 副（容易に）easily;（十分な）enough. ▶ あなたならゆうゆうと競走に勝つだろう You can win the race *easily* [*without difficulty*]. ▶ 電車にゆうゆう(と)間に合った（＝十分時間があった）I was *in plenty of time* [*well in time*] for the train. ▶ その男はゆうゆうとビールを飲んでいた The man was drinking a glass of beer *in a leisurely manner* [*xleisurely*].（*!* ... a *leisurely* glass of beer. も可）

〖会話〗「列車に間に合ったの？」「ゆうゆうさ．あり余るぐらいたっぷり時間があったよ」"Did you catch your train?" "*Easily*. Lots of time to spare."

翻訳のこころ 眼の大きな蝿は，今や完全に休まったその羽根を広げると，悠々と青空の中を飛んでいった（横光利一『蝿』）Gathering [Putting] the strength in those well rested wings, that big-eyed fly *easily* flew away all by itself into the blue sky.（*!*「ただひとり」で「飛んでいった」を修飾するので fly away の近くに置く）

● 悠々自適 ▶ 彼は退職後悠々自適の生活をしている（＝安楽に暮らしている）He has been living *comfortably* [*in comfort*] since he retired.

ゆうよ 猶予 名〖延期〗(a) postponement;〖期間の延長〗(an) extension;〖遅延〗(a) delay;〖支払いなどの〗grace. ●〖刑の執行猶予〗〖法律〗probation; (a) stay (of execution);（執行延期の判決）a suspended sentence;（特に死刑の）a reprieve. ▶ 彼の手術は一刻の猶予も許されない He must have an operation *without delay*. ▶ 一刻の猶予もなかった There was not a *moment* to lose. ▶ 彼は5年間の執行猶予を与えられた He was put on five years' *probation* [*probation* for five years]./He was given five years' *probation*. ▶ 彼は懲役5年執行猶予1年の判決を受けた He was sentenced to five years in prison with a *stay* of one year.（*!* stay は「刑の執行の延期[停止]」をいう）

― 猶予する 動 ▶ その代金の支払いを5日間猶予してあげよう I'll give you five days' *grace* to pay me the money.（*!* 日常会話では five more days でよい）▶ 彼は刑の執行を猶予された He was given [《書》was granted] a *reprieve*.（*!* reprieve は「死刑執行の延期」をいう）

-ゆうよ -有余 ● 3年有余 *a little more than* three years. ● 50年有余 fifty-*odd* years.（⇨②❶）

ゆうよう 有用 ― 有用な 形 useful;（助けになる）helpful. ▶ 彼は当社にとって有用な人材です He is a *useful man* to our company.

ゆうよう 悠揚 ● 悠揚迫らず・悠揚迫らぬ態度で with composure; with an air of perfect coolness; calmly; with perfect aplomb.

ゆうよく 有翼 ― 有翼の 形 winged.

ゆうよく 遊弋 ― 遊弋する 動 cruise; patrol (-ll-).

ゆうらく 遊楽 ― 遊楽する 動 abandon oneself to pleasure; indulge (oneself) in pleasure.

ユーラシア 〖ヨーロッパとアジアの総称〗Eurasia /juəréiʒə/.
● ユーラシア大陸 the Eurasian Continent.

ゆうらん 遊覧 ― 遊覧船 a pléasure bòat. ● 遊覧バス a síghtseeing bùs. ● 遊覧飛行 a síghtseeing flìght.

*****ゆうり** 有利 ― 有利な 形〖好都合な〗favorable;〖有益な〗advantágeous;〖利益になる〗profitable. ● 有利な立場 a *favorable* [an *advantageous*] position. ● 有利な商売 a *profitable* business. ▶ その状況は彼にとって有利になるだろう The situation will be *advantageous to him*./The situation will be [work] *to his advantage*. ▶ 早くから訓練を積んできたという点で彼は私より有利であった He *had the advantage* over me because of his early training. ▶ その証言は彼女に有利である The evidence [witness] is *in her favor*.

ゆうり 遊里（⇨遊郭）

ゆうり 遊離 separation;（孤立）isolation. ▶ 君たちの議論は現実から遊離している（＝まったく現実的でない）Your argument is *far from realistic* [*completely unrealistic*].

ゆうりすう 有理数〖数学〗a rational number.

ゆうりょ 憂慮 名〖将来への不安〗(an) anxiety;〖悩み〗(a) worry;〖懸念〗concern;〖動揺〗disturb-

ance. (⇨心配)
── 憂慮する 動 worry 《about》. ●憂慮すべき(=重大な)事態 a serious [a grave, a disturbing] situation. ▶彼は事態を非常に憂慮していた He was very concerned [disturbed, worried, anxious] about the situation.

ゆうりょう 有料 (料金) (a) charge. ▶配達は有料です There is a charge for delivery./Delivery is charged.
●有料コンテンツ fee-charging contents. ●有料サイト a fee-charging site. ●有料駐車場 a toll parking lot. ●有料トイレ a pay toilet. ●有料道路 a toll road. ●有料老人ホーム a fee-charging nursing home [《英》old people's home].

ゆうりょう 優良 ── 優良な 形 (品質などが) superior; (成績などが) excellent; (一流の) gilt-edged; 《話》blue-chip. ●健康優良児 a child in excellent health.
●優良株 a blue chip. ●優良企業 a blue-chip company. ●アジアを代表する優良企業 the best of Asian companies.

*ゆうりょく 有力 ── 有力な 形 [強力な] strong; [指導的な] leading (!限定的に); [影響力のある] influential; [勢力のある] powerful. ●日本の有力な五つの新聞(=有力5紙) five leading Japanese papers. (!語順に注意) ●有力な意見 an influential [(支配的な) a dominant] opinion. ●有力な派閥 a powerful faction. ●有力な証拠を握っている have strong [《説得力のある》convincing] evidence. ▶彼はその賞の最も有力な候補者です/He is the strongest candidate for the prize./He is the most likely candidate to win the prize. ▶彼は政界の有力者だ He is an influential man [《話》a big man, (指導者) a leader] in politics.

ゆうれい 幽霊 a ghost, 《話》(おばけ) a spook; (まぼろし) 《やや書》a phantom. ●幽霊の話 a ghost story. ▶彼は幽霊を見たかのように真っ青だった He looked (as) pale as if he had seen a ghost. ▶その山小屋は幽霊が出ると言われている They say the mountain hut is haunted.
●幽霊会社 a bogus company. ●幽霊船 a phantom ship. ●幽霊屋敷 a haunted house. (!haunt は「(幽霊などが)...に出没する」の意)

ゆうれい 優麗 ── 優麗な 形 elegant and beautiful.

ゆうれき 遊歴 ── 遊歴する 動 ●ヨーロッパを遊歴する (旅する) travel around Europe; (めぐり歩く) wander [《話》knock] around (in) Europe. (⇨歩き回る)

ゆうれつ 優劣 (差) (a) difference. ●優劣を競う struggle [《書》strive] for superiority; (競争する) compete 《with him》 (for superiority). ▶我々はその車の優劣(=長所と短所)を論じた We discussed the mérits and démerits of the car. (!対照姿勢に注意) ▶両者は優劣つけがたい It is hard to decide which one is better than the other./(はとんど差がない) There is hardly any difference [There is nothing to choose] between the two.

ユーロ (欧州通貨単位) a euro /júɜrou/ (複 ~s); (欧州(連合の)) Euro-.
●ユーロ円 Euroyen. ●ユーロ債 a Eurobond. ●ユーロ市場 the Euromarket. ●ユーロダラー Eurodollar. ●ユーロ通貨 Euromoney; Eurocurrency. ●ユーロトンネル (海峡トンネル) the Channel Tunnel. (!Eurotunnel は運営企業)

ゆうわ 宥和 (なだめること) appeasement.
── 宥和する 動 ●怒れる人々を宥和する 《やや書》appease [《書》conciliate] angry people.
●宥和策 an appeasement policy.

ゆうわ 融和 (親睦(しん)) (a) friendship; (友好関係) a harmonious relationship. ●両国間の融和をはかる attempt to establish the harmonious relationship [the friendly relations] between the two countries.

*ゆうわく 誘惑 名 (a) temptation; 《やや書》(a) lure; (an) enticement; seduction. ●誘惑に勝つ[と戦う] overcome [fight] temptation. ●酒を飲みたいという誘惑に負ける give way [《書》yield] to the temptation to drink. ▶東京は誘惑が多い Tokyo is full of temptations [enticements].
── 誘惑する 動 tempt; lure; entice; seduce.

> 使い分け tempt 話し手自身の欲求や他者が話し手に何らかの行動を取らせようとすること。通例，行うべきでない行動を取らせることを含意する。
> lure 主に好奇心や興味をかきたてて誘い込んだり引き付けたりすること。
> entice その気がない人を言葉や金品などで巧みに誘惑して行動させること。
> seduce 誘惑して堕落・陶酔させること。主に性的な誘惑を表す。

●女の子を誘惑する seduce a girl. ▶彼らはその少年を誘惑して金を盗ませた They tempted [(そそのかして) enticed, ×lured] the boy to steal the money. (!lure は to 不定詞をとらない)/They tempted [enticed, lured] the boy into stealing the money. ●誘惑者 a tempter; a seducer.

ゆえ 故 (理由) a reason; (原因) a cause. ●故あって for a certain [some] reason. (!前の方は話し手に理由が分かっているとき、後の方は分かっていないときに用いる) ●故なく for no reason; without reason. ▶故あってその計画は棚上げになった For some reason the project was shelved.

-ゆえ 《接続助詞》 (...のため) because .... (⇨ため❷) ▶疲れたため早めに就寝した Because [Since, As] I was tired, I went to bed early. (!後の方ほど意味は弱くなる)

ゆえき 輸液 名 an infusion; (点滴注入) a drip; (その液) drip.
── 輸液する 動 infuse drip 《into the veins》; put 《a patient》on a drip.

ゆえつ 愉悦 exuberance; joy.
── 愉悦する 動 enjoy; take delight [great pleasure] 《in》.

ゆえに [したがって]《やや書》therefore; [...なので] because .... (⇨だから) ▶我思うゆえに我あり I think, therefore I exist [am].

ゆえん 所以 (理由) (a) reason; (根拠) (a) ground. (⇨理由, 訳(2)) ▶私が君に大いに期待するゆえんはここにあります This is (the reason) why I expect a lot of you.

ゆえん 油煙 (すす) soot /sút/; lampblack. ▶石油ストーブから油煙が出ている The kerosene heater is smoking.

ゆか 床 a floor; 《集合的》flooring. ●床をはがす tear up [break open] the floor. ●床に倒れる fall to [on] the floor. ●床を掃く[ふく] sweep [wipe, (モップで) mop] the floor. ●部屋の床を板で張る floor the room with boards. ▶床が抜けた The floor gave way [collapsed]. ▶床に手をついて腕立て伏せを50回するんだ Drop to the floor and try to do 50 push-ups.
●床運動 a floor exercise. ●床暖房 floor heating. ●床面積 the amount of) floor space. (⇨建て坪)

*ゆかい 愉快 名 [楽しさ] (an) enjoyment; [喜び] (a) pleasure; [おもしろさ] fun. ●愉快愉快 How enjoy-

able [*pleasant*]!/What *fun* [×a fun]!
— **愉快な** 形 〖人を満足させる〗pleasant; 〖人を楽しませる〗enjoyable; 〖人をおもしろがらせる〗amusing; (人が陽気な) cheerful, jolly. (⇨面白い) ● 愉快な話 an *amusing* story. ▶彼といっしょに飲んでとても愉快だった I had a very *enjoyable* [*pleasant, good*] time drinking with him./(楽しんだ) I very much *enjoyed* drinking with him. (!very much は文尾も可)/I had a lot of *fun* drinking with him. ▶今夜は愉快にやろう(= 楽しもう) Let's *enjoy ourselves* [*have fun*] tonight. (!×Let's enjoy tonight. は不可) ▶彼はとても愉快な人だ He is a very *cheerful* [*jolly*] person./He is good [*great*] *fun*. (!×a good [*a great*] fun は不可)
● **愉快犯** (行為) a crime for pleasure; (人) a criminal for pleasure.

ゆかいた 床板 floorboards; flooring. ● 廊下にひのきの床板を張る floor the corridor [《米》hallway] with *hinoki* boards. ● 床板をはがす tear up the *floorboards*.

ゆかうえ 床上 ● 床上浸水 inundation above floor level [above the floor]. ▶床上浸水家屋は500戸を超えた More than five hundred houses were flooded *above floor level* [*above the floor*].

ゆがく 湯がく ● ホウレンソウをゆがく *blanch* spinach /spɪntʃ/. ● ジャガイモをゆがく *parboil* potatoes.

ゆかげん 湯加減 ▶(風呂は)自由に湯加減を調節できます You can control [adjust] the temperature of bath water as you like.
会話「湯加減はいかがですか」「ちょっと熱すぎます」"How do you find the bath?" "It's a bit too hot."/(簡潔に How's the bath? ともいえる. 応答で「ちょうどいい加減だ」なら "It's warm enough." などという)

ゆかしい 床しい ❶ 〖人柄が〗(気品のある) graceful; elegant; (心がひきつけられる) charming; attractive. (⇨奥ゆかしい)
❷ 〖昔しのばれる〗(an event) redolent of the past. ▶式は昔ゆかしく執り行われた The ceremony was held [performed] according to the *time-honored* ritual.

ゆかした 床下 ● 床下浸水する be flooded *below the floor*.

ゆかた 浴衣 a *yukata*; (説明的に) an informal light cotton *kimono* worn in (the) summer.

ゆがみ 歪み 〖板などが反る〗a warp /wɔːrp/; 〖よじれる〗a twist; (ひずみ)《やや書》(a) distortion. ● 床の歪みが *warp* in the floor.

＊ゆがむ 歪む 〖板などが反る〗warp /wɔːrp/, be warped; 〖よじれる〗twist, be twisted; (ひずむ) be distorted. (!以上はすべて比喩的にも用いられる) ● ゆがんだ画像 a *distorted* image. ▶この板の木製の枠は日に出しておくとゆがむよ This board will *get warped* [This wooden frame will *get twisted*] if you leave it out in the sun. ▶彼の顔は苦痛でゆがんだ His face (*was*) *twisted* [*was distorted*] with pain./He *twisted* [*distorted*] his face with pain./He grimáced in pain. ▶彼は何でもがゆがんだ物の見方をする He has a *distorted* [a *twisted*, a *warped*] view of everything.

ゆがめる 歪める (顔・事実などを) twist, distort (⇨歪む [第2文例]); (心・判断などを) warp. ● 真実をゆがめる *twist* [*distort*] the truth.

ゆかり 縁 〖つながり〗(a) connection; 〖関係〗(a) relation. ● 深いゆかりがある *be closely connected* 《*with*》. ● シェイクスピアゆかりの地 a place remembered in connection with Shakespeare. ▶私は彼とは縁もゆかりもない I have no *connection* [*relation*] whatever 《何の関係もない》/have nothing to do》with him./(まったく知らない人だ) He is a perfect [a total] *stranger* to me.

ゆかん 湯灌 ― 湯灌(を)する 動 (仏葬で) wash the dead body clean before burial.

:ゆき 雪 snow; 〖降雪〗a snowfall; 〖1片の雪〗a snowflake.

> 解説 **(1)** snow は「雪」そのものを全般的にとらえる場合には無冠詞, 1回の降雪として見た場合には a がつく: 去年の冬に大雪があった We had a heavy *snow* last winter. (1回性)/去年の冬は大雪だった We had heavy *snow* last winter. (全般的)
> **(2)** snows と複数形になると「積雪(量)」「積雪地帯」を意味する: エベレスト山の積雪地帯 the *snows* of Mt. Everest.

① 【〜雪】● 深い雪 deep *snow*. ● ぼたん雪 *snow in large flakes*. ● 万年雪 eternal [perpetual, everlasting] *snow*. ● 新しく降り積もった雪 newfallen *snow*; (新雪) fresh *snow*. ● 降りしきる雪 (*in*) a heavy snowstorm.
② 【雪が[は]】▶雪が降り出した It began to *snow*./The snow began to fall. ▶朝降り積もった雪は夕方には解けてしまった The snow which piled up in the morning melted away by the evening. ▶ここは冬でも雪は少しも[ほとんど]降らない We have no [very little, hardly any] *snow* here even in winter./It never [hardly ever] *snows* here even in winter. ▶雪が3メートル積もっている The snow is [lies] three meters deep.
③ 【雪の】snowy. ● 雪の降る日には on a *snowy* day. ● 雪の多い冬[地方] a *snowy* winter [district]. ● 雪のように白い (as) white as *snow*. ▶1メートルほど積もった雪の中を歩いて学校へ行った I walked to school through the *snow* lying about one meter deep. ▶子供たちは雪の中で遊ぶのが好きだ Children like playing in the *snow*.
④ 【雪に[を]】▶雪に埋もれる be buried under the *snow*. ● 雪におおわれた屋根 the roofs (which are) covered with *snow*; *snow-covered* roofs. ● 雪をいただいた山々 *snow-capped* mountains. ▶雨は雪に変わった The rain changed to [into] *snow*. ▶その村は1週間前から雪に閉じ込められている The village *has been snowed in* [*up*] for a week.
⑤ 【雪で】▶車は雪で動けなくなった The car got stuck in the *snow*. ▶大雪で山に登ることができなかった Because *it snowed* heavily [Because of the heavy *snow*], we couldn't climb the mountain./《物が主語》《書》 The heavy *snow* prevented us from climbing the mountain.

● **雪男** an abominable snowman; a yeti (!チベット語より). ● **雪女** a snow fairy; a snow nymph.
● **雪風** a wind with snow. ● **雪靴** (かんじき)《a pair of》snowshoes; (わらの長靴) straw boots.
● **雪雲** a snow cloud. ● **雪景色** a snow scene; a snowscape. ● **雪煙** a cloud of snow; (そりの走行などで)《send up》a spray of snow. ● **雪つぶて** a snowball. ● **雪野原** a snowfield; (果てしない) an expense of snow. ● **雪庇(せっぴ)** snow sticking out from the eaves (尾根) the ridge (of a mountain). ● **雪祭り** a snow festival. ● **雪道** a snowy road. ● **雪娘** (⇨[雪女]) ● **雪山** a snow-covered [a snowy] mountain.

ゆき 行き (⇨行(い)き)

ゆき 裄 (説明的に) the length of the sleeve measured from the center of the neck. ● 裄を縮める

ゆきあう shorten [take in] the *sleeves*. ▶この着物は裄が短すぎる The *sleeves* of this kimono is too short for me. (⚠ *The kimono ... has too short sleeves* for me は不可)

ゆきあう 行き会う 行き会う
ゆきあかり 雪明かり snowblink; snowlight. ●雪明かりで by snow light; in the light reflected off the snow.
ゆきあそび 雪遊び ●雪遊びをする play with snow.
ゆきあたりばったり 行き当たりばったり (⇨行(ゆ)き当たりばったり)
ゆきあたる 行き当たる (⇨行(ゆ)き当たる)
ゆきあらし 雪嵐 a blizzard. ▶雪嵐が何日も吹き荒れた A *blizzard* has raged for days.
ゆきうさぎ 雪兎 ❶[雪で作ったウサギ] a snow rabbit with *yuzuriha* ears and red nandin eyes. ❷[動物] a snowshoe hare.
ゆきおれ 雪折れ ── 雪折れする 動 break under the weight of snow. ▶柳に雪折れなし 'Willow branches do not break under the weight of snow.'/(ことわざ) Oaks may fall when reeds stand the storm.
ゆきおろし 雪下ろし ●雪下ろしをする remove [(掃いて) sweep, (シャベルでかいて) shovel] snow off the roof.
ゆきかう 行き交う (⇨行(ゆ)き交う)
ゆきかえり 行き帰り (⇨行(ゆ)き帰り)
ゆきかかり 行き掛かり (⇨行(ゆ)き掛かり)
ゆきかき 雪掻き (行為) snow shoveling; (道具) a snow shovel. ●雪かきをする (除雪する) clear [remove] snow 《*from* the road》; clear 《the road》 of *snow*; (シャベルでかいて) shovel snow away 《*from* the road》.
ゆきがけ 行き掛け (⇨行(ゆ)き掛け)
ゆきがこい 雪囲い a protection from snow; a protective board [covering, shed] from snow. ●植木に雪囲いをする cover a tree [a plant] from snow.
ゆきかた 行き方 (⇨行(ゆ)き方)
ゆきがっせん 雪合戦 ●雪合戦をする have a *snowball fight*.
ゆきき 行き来 (⇨行(ゆ)き来)
ゆきぐに 雪国 (国) a snowy country; (地方) snowy country. (⇨山国) (⚠ それぞれ説明的に a country [an area] where it snows a lot ともいえる)
ゆきぐに 『雪国』 *Snow Country*. (参考) 川端康成の小説)
ゆきくれる 行き暮れる ▶見知らぬ土地で行き暮れて不安が募った I was a stranger there and felt uneasier when it got dark.
ゆきげしょう 雪化粧 ▶山々は雪化粧をしていた The mountains *were covered* [(山頂付近に) *were crowned*] *with snow*.
ゆきさき 行き先 (⇨行(ゆ)き先)
ゆきしつ 雪質 the quality of snow. ●雪質によってワックスを替える change [use different] wax by the *quality of snow*. ▶ここの雪質はスキーには向かない The *snow* here is not good for skiing.
ゆきしろ 雪代 (雪解け水) snow water.
ゆきすぎ 行き過ぎ (⇨行(ゆ)き過ぎ)
ゆきすぎる 行き過ぎる (⇨行(ゆ)き過ぎる)
ゆきずり 行きずり (通りすがりの人) a passerby (複 passersby); (赤の他人) a total [a complete] stranger. ●行きずりの恋 [縁] a *casual romance* [relationship].
ゆきぞら 雪空 a snowy sky.
ゆきだおれ 行き倒れ (⇨行(ゆ)き倒れ)
ゆきたけ 裄丈 the length of a sleeve.

ゆきだるま 雪達磨 a snowman (複 -men). (⚠ この語は女性を含まないので a snow figure が好まれる) ●雪だるまを作る make [build] a *snow figure* [a *snowman*].
●雪だるま式に ▶彼の借金は雪だるま式に増えた His debt *has snowballed*.
ゆきちがい 行き違い (⇨行(ゆ)き違い)
ゆきつく 行き着く (⇨行(ゆ)き着く)
ゆきつけ 行きつけ (⇨行(ゆ)きつけ)
ゆきづまり 行き詰まり (⇨行(ゆ)き詰まり)
ゆきづまる 行き詰まる (⇨行(ゆ)き詰まる)
ゆきつもどりつ 行きつ戻りつ ●行きつ戻りつする go back and forth 《hesitating to enter the jeweler's shop》; walk up and down 《the room》.
ゆきづり 雪吊り *yukizuri* (説明的に) fixing the branches of a tree by suspended ropes to protect them from breaking off under the weight of the snow.
ゆきどけ 雪解け 名 a thaw /θɔ́ː/. (⚠ (1) 通例単数形で. (2) 比喩的にも用いる) ●外交関係の雪解け a *thaw* in diplomatic relations.
── 雪解けする 動 thaw. ▶3月に雪解けした The snow [It] *thawed* in March./We had a *thaw* in March.
●雪解け水 snow water. ●雪解け道 a slushy road.
ゆきとどく 行き届く (⇨行(ゆ)き届く)
ゆきどまり 行き止まり (⇨行(ゆ)き止まり)
ゆきなやむ 行き悩む ❶[進むのに苦労する] be hampered to proceed; 《物事が主語》make* it hard to move forward. ▶倒木にはばまれて我々は行き悩んだ Fallen trees blocked our way and *make* our *going* very *difficult*.
❷[思うようにいかず苦労する] be bothered [troubled] 《*with*》; be worried 《*about*》.
ゆきのした 雪の下 [植物] (a) saxifrage /sǽksəfridʒ/.
ゆきば(しょ) 行き場(所) (⇨行(ゆ)き場(所))
ゆきはだ 雪肌 [積もった雪の表面] the surface of the snow; [白い肌] (a) fair skin; (白くてなめらかな) (a) marble skin. (⚠ snow-white, snowy white, as white as snow は頭髪・ひげなどに用いるのが普通) ▶彼女の露出した肩は雪肌で魅力的であった Her exposed shoulders were *as white as marble* and very attractive.
ゆきひら(なべ) 行平(鍋) a *yukihira* pan; (説明的に) originally a glazed earthenware pan with a handle, a very short spout and a lid for making porridge, now also said of a pan made of metal.
ゆきふり 雪降り a snowfall; (雪の降る日) a snowy day. ▶雪降りの日はなるべく家にいる I stay at home [won't go out] on a *snowy day*, if possible.
ゆきみ 雪見 snow [snowscape] viewing; [雪見の宴] a sake-drinking party for enjoying a snowscape.
●雪見障子 (説明的に) a *shoji* whose lower half can be pushed up to reveal a glassed window. ●雪見灯籠(どうろう) a three-legged low stone lantern 《installed in the garden》.
ゆきみず 雪水 [雪解け水] snow water; [雪を解かした水] water made from snow.
ゆきめ 雪目 名 snow blindness. ── 雪目の 形 snow-blind.
ゆきもよう 雪模様 ▶今日は雪模様だ It looks like snow./It threatens to snow.
ゆきやけ 雪焼け ── 雪焼けする be tanned by

ゆきやなぎ 雪柳〖植物〗a spirea /spaɪrɪːə/.
ゆきよけ 雪除け (⇨雪掻(ㅤ)き)
ゆきわたる 行き渡る (⇨行(ㅤ)き渡る)
ゆきわりそう 雪割り草〖植物〗a hepatica.
ゆく 行く go*. (⇨行(ㅤ)く)
ゆく 逝く pass away. (⇨死ぬ)
ゆくえ 行方 ❶〖所在〗one's whereabouts. (!単・複両扱い) ▸行方不明 (⇨行方不明) ▸彼の行方は分からない His *whereabouts* is [are] unknown./We don't know *where he is* [*has gone*]. ▸我々は彼女の行方を見つけることはできなかった We couldn't find out her *whereabouts*./(書) We couldn't locate her. ▸警察は殺人犯の行方を追っている The police *are looking* [*searching*, *hunting*] *for* the murderer./The police *are after* the murderer. ▸納税者は払った金の行方を知る権利がある Each taxpayer has the right to know *where* his money *goes*. ▸彼は家賃を払わずに行方をくらました(=姿を消した) He disappeared (*from*) his home) without paying the house rent.
❷〖進む(べき)方向〗the direction; (試合などの) the outcome. ▸飛んでいくボールの行方を見る (ゴルフなどで) look in the *direction* of one's ball. ▸7回裏の彼のツーランホームランで試合の行方は決まった The two-run homer he hit in the bottom of the seventh inning decided the *outcome* of the game.
ゆくえふめい 行方不明 ▸行方不明の犬[手紙] a *missing* dog [letter]. ▸彼は行方不明です He is *missing*. ● 行方不明者〖集合的〗the missing.
ゆくさき 行き先 one's destination. (⇨行(ㅤ)き先)
ゆくさきざき 行く先々 ▸彼らは行く先々で(=どこへ行っても)歓待を受けた They were welcomed *wherever they went*.
ゆくすえ 行く末 ▸行く末頼もしい(=前途有望な)学生 a *promising* student. ▸子供の行く末(=将来)を案じる worry about [be anxious about] one's child's future.
ゆくぐち 湯口 (湯の出口) a hot-water hole [突き出た形の器口], (温泉の噴出口) a hot-spring hole. (!単に a hot spring ともいう)
ゆくて 行く手 ▸行く手に(=前方に)灯が見えてきた We saw a light *ahead of* us. ▸行く手は(=将来は)多難だ We have a lot of difficulties *in the future* [前途には] *ahead of* us, *before* us]. ▸(前途) トラックが行く手をふさいだ(=じゃました) A truck stood [got] *in* our *way*. ▸彼が行く手をさえぎったので家に入れなかった He barred my *way*, so I couldn't enter the house.
ゆくとし 行く年 ▸行く年来る年 *the old year* and the new year; (擬人化して) *the outgoing year* and the incoming year.
ゆくゆく 行く行く (いつか) sometime, someday; (将来) in the future. ▸ゆくゆくはパリに旅行するつもりです I will take a trip to Paris *sometime* [*someday*].
ゆくりなく(も) quite unexpectedly.
*****ゆげ** 湯気 steam. ▸湯気が立っているごはん (a bowl of) *steaming* rice. ▸スープ皿から湯気が立っていた *Steam* rose from the plate of soup. ▸湯気は(より普通) ▸やかんがストーブの上で湯気を立てている The kettle *is giving off steam* [*is steaming* (*away*)] on the stove. ▸ふろ場の鏡が湯気で曇った *Steam* formed on the bathroom mirror./The bathroom mirror (got) *steamed up* [(曇っていた) was clouded with *steam*].
ゆけつ 輸血 ⓝ a (blood) transfusion. ▸輸血を受ける get [be given] a (*blood*) *transfusion*.
—— 輸血する 動 transfuse. ▸その患者に大量の輸血をする *transfuse* a lot of blood *into* the patient. ● 輸血供給者 a blood donor. ● 輸血後肝炎〖医学〗post-transfusion hepatitis. ● 輸血性肝炎〖医学〗transfusion hepatitis. ● 輸血反応 a blood transfusion reaction.
ゆけども 行けども ▸行けども行けども目的地に着かなかった We *went* [*walked*, (自転車で) *cycled*, (自動車で) *drove*] *on and on*, *but* we did not arrive at our destination.
ゆけむり 湯煙 (thick) steam rising from hot water.
ゆさい 油彩 (画法) oil painting. ● 油彩画 an oil painting; a painting in oils.
ゆざい 油剤 (説明的に) chemical products that contain oil or fat except for soaps, paints, glycerin, etc.
ゆさぶり 揺さぶり〖揺すること〗a shake; (ぐらぐらさせること) a jolt. ▸揺さぶりをかける shake; jolt; give a jolt; (事の成り行きに水をさす)〖話〗rock the boat.
ゆさぶる 揺さぶる (荒々しく) shake*; (急激に) jolt. (⇨揺する) ▸投手を揺さぶる *shake* [bother] a pitcher. ▸その汚職事件は政界を根底から揺さぶった The scandal *shook* (*up*) [*jolted*] the political world to its foundation.
ゆざまし 湯冷まし cooled boiled water.
ゆざめ 湯冷め —— 湯冷めする 動 catch [get] a (slight) chill after a bath. ▸パジャマを着ないと湯冷めするよ If you don't put on [wear] your pajamas, you'll *get cold*.
ゆさゆさ ▸ゆさゆさ揺れる move up and down. ▸枝をゆさゆさしたら栗がばらばら落ちた I *shook* the branches (*hard*) until many chestnuts fell to the ground.
ゆさん 遊山 (go on) an excursion; a jaunt; (ピクニック) a picnic. (⇨物見)
ゆし 油紙〖医学〗oil(ed) paper.
ゆし 油脂 oils and fats. ● 油脂化学 fatty chemistry.
ゆし 諭旨 ▸彼は諭旨免職となった He *was* (*officially*) *advised* to tender his resignation.
*****ゆしゅつ** 輸出 图 export (⇔import).
①〖～輸出、輸出～〗▸再輸出 re-export. ● 輸出主導型の経済 an *export*-led [*export*-driven] economy. ▸輸出貿易は日本にとって不可欠である The *export* trade is essential to Japan. ▸このおもちゃは外国への輸出用に作られる These toys are manufactured for *export* to foreign countries.
②〖輸出が[は]〗▸昨年の輸出(額)は輸入(額)を上回った Last year's *exports* exceeded [were greater than] imports (in value). ▸対米輸出(額)は17.3パーセント増加した *Exports* to the US [The US-destined *exports*]) increased by 17.3 percent. ▸ドル高で米国の輸出は打撃を受けた The strong dollar hurt US *export*. ▸世界的な景気後退で日本の輸出が伸び悩んだ The worldwide recession slowed Japan's *export*.

🟥 **DISCOURSE**
量の面では輸出は減少したが、総額の面では増加した In terms of the amount, *exports* have dropped, but in terms of the total value, they have risen. (!in terms of ... (...の面では)は関連を表すディスコースマーカー)

③〖輸出を〗● 輸出を抑える[減らす] restrain [constrain, reduce] *exports*. ▸政府は金の海外に

ゆしゅつにゅう

の輸出を禁じた The government has banned the *export* of gold *to* foreign countries.
── **輸出する** 動 export (↔impórt). ▶日本はカメラを世界各国に輸出している Japan *exports* cameras *to* many different countries in the world.
- 輸出依存度 export dependency; the degree of dependence on [upon] exports. ● 輸出価格 export prices. ● 輸出額 the volume of export; exports (❗通例複数形で). ● 輸出課徴金 an export surcharge. ● 輸出関連株 export-related stocks. ● 輸出規制 export control; control of export. ● 輸出業 export business [trade]. ● 輸出業者《会社；国》 an (oil) exporter; an export agent [an exporting firm; an exporting country]. ● 輸出許可書 an export permit (略 E/P). ● 輸出禁止 an export ban; a ban on exports; an embargo on export. ● 武器輸出禁止 an arms embargo. ● 輸出禁制品《集合的》 contraband of goods. ● 輸出自主規制 self-restrictions on exports. ● 輸出奨励金 an export subsidy. ● 輸出申告(書) (an) export declaration (略 ED). ● 輸出(数)量 export volume. ● 輸出税 an export tax; export duties (❗単数扱い). ● 輸出高 exports. (❗通例複数形で) ● 輸出超過 a favorable balance of trade. ● 輸出手続き export formalities. ● 輸出品 an export (❗しばしば複数形で);《集合的》exported goods. ▶車は日本の主要な輸出品である Automobiles are the chief *export* of Japan [Japan's major *export* item].

ゆしゅつにゅう 輸出入 import and export (❗(1)しばしば形容詞的に用いる。(2)語順は交換可); importation and exportation. ▶たばこ製品の輸出入を禁止する ban the *import and export* of tobacco products.
- 輸出入業 import and export business [trade]. ● 輸出入業者 an importer and exporter. ● 輸出入品〔額〕imports and exports.

ゆしょう 油床《石油鉱床》an oil deposit.

ゆず 柚子【植物】yuzu, a kind of citrus fruit.
- ゆず湯 a hot bath scented with *yuzu*, traditionally taken on the winter solstice day).

ゆすぎ 濯ぎ ● ゆすぎをしっかりする give (the shirt) a thorough *rinse*; rinse (the shirt) thoroughly.

ゆすぐ 濯ぐ rinse ... (out). (⇨すすぐ)

ゆすぶる 揺すぶる (⇨揺さぶる, 揺する)

ゆすらうめ【植物】a Nanking cherry.

ゆすり【行為】(強要) extortion; (恐喝) blackmail;【人】an extortioner; a blackmailer. (⇨ゆする)

-ゆずり −譲り (...から得る) inherit [get*] (*from*). ● 親譲り (⇨親譲り) ▶彼の頑固さは父親ゆずりだ He *inherits* his stubbornness *from* his father./His stubbornness *comes from* his father.

ゆずりあい 譲り合い【妥協】(a) compromise;【互いに譲ること】(make) mutual concessions. ● 譲り合いの精神 a spirit of give-and-take.

ゆずりあう 譲り合う (⇨譲る❷❸❹) ▶譲り合って(=互いに譲歩して)問題を解決する settle the matter *by making mutual concessions*. ● 道を譲り合う make way for [give way to] each other. ● 席を譲り合う offer a seat to each other.

ゆずりうける 譲り受ける (財産などを) inherit (*from*); (買い取る) buy* (*from*); (事業などを) take* (a business) over (*from*). ▶父親から財産を譲り受ける *inherit* a fortune *from* one's father. ▶ノートパソコンを彼から安く譲り受けた I *bought* a notebook (computer) cheap *from* him.

ゆずりは 譲葉【植物】yuzuriha, (学名) Daphniphyllum macropodum.

ゆずりわたす 譲り渡す (財産などを)【法律】transfer (-rr-), make*... over 《*to*》; (権力などを) hand... over 《*to*》. (⇨譲る)

ゆする【強要する】extort;【恐喝する】blackmail. ▶彼から金をゆすり取る *extort* money *from* him; *blackmail* him *for* money; obtain money *by extortion* from him.

ゆする 揺する shake*; (ゆっくりと) rock; (ぶらんこなどを) swing*; (左右に大きく) sway. (左右に揺れる【類語】)
- 体を揺すって笑う *shake* with laughter. ● 木を揺すって果実を落とす *shake* fruit (*down*) *from* a tree. ● 赤ちゃんを揺すって寝かす[抱いて揺する] *rock* a baby to sleep [in one's arms]. ● 音楽に合わせて体を揺する *sway* (one's body) to [in time with] the music. ▶彼は息子の肩を(つかんで)揺すった He *shook* his son by the shoulder./He *shook* his son's shoulder.

:ゆずる 譲る ❶【譲渡する】pass ... on 《*to*》; (財産などを)【法律】transfer (-rr-), make*... over 《*to*》; (権力・責任などを) hand ... over 《*to*》; (会社などを) turn ... over 《*to*》;(王位を)【書】abdicate. ▶野党に政権を譲る *hand over* power *to* the opposition party. ▶これは父からもらったカメラです This is the camera my father *passed on to* me. ▶彼は一人息子に全財産を譲った He *transferred* [*made over*] all his property *to* his only son. (❗×He transferred [made over] his only son all his property. は不可) ▶彼は自分の店を息子に譲った He *transferred* his store *to* his son.

❷【与える】give*; (売る) sell*. ▶彼はバスで妊婦に席を譲った He *gave up* [*offered*] his seat *to* a pregnant woman on the bus. ▶彼に車を安く譲った I *sold* him my car cheap. (❗×I *sold* my car *to* him cheap. は不可)

❸【あける】(道をあける) make* way 《*for*》(❗比喩的にも用いる); (道を譲って先に行かせる) give* way 《*to*》,《米》yield 《*to*》. ● 後進に道を譲る *make way for* younger people. ▶(走行中の車はすべて救急車には道を譲らないといけない All traffic must *make way for* [*give way to*, *yield to*] ambulances.

❹【譲歩する】concede; make* a concession 《*to*》(❗しばしば複数形で). ▶その点は譲ります I'll *concede* [*give in on*] that point. ▶彼は脅迫者に一歩も譲らなかったHe never *made concessions* [(屈服する) *gave in*] *to* the blackmailer./He *held* his ground against the blackmailer.

❺【先へ延ばす】put*... off, postpone. (❗前の方が口語的) ▶その件の議論は後日に譲ることにしよう Let's *put off* [*postpone*] discussing the matter until some other day.

ゆせい 油井 an oil well.

ゆせい 油性 ── 油性の 圏 (油だらけの) oily.
- 油性塗料 oil (↔water) paint. ● 油性廃水 oily wastewater.

ゆせいかん 輸精管【解剖】a spermaduct.

ゆせん 湯煎 ── 湯煎する 動 ▶味噌を湯せんする put *miso* in a pan [a bowl] and heat it up over hot water.

＊ゆそう 輸送 名 《米》transportation,《英》tránsport. ● 海上[陸上; 鉄道; 航空]輸送 sea [land; rail; air] *transportation*; *transportation* by sea [land; rail; air]. ● 長距離輸送 long-distance *transportation*. ▶列車は必要不可欠な輸送機関だ The train is the essential means of *transportation* [《英》*transport*].
── **輸送する** 動 (長距離を大がかりに) transport (❗人の輸送にも用いる); (車で) haul; (船で) ship (-pp-) (

ゆそう 油送 ●油送管 an oil pipeline. ●油送船 an oil tanker.

ゆそう 油層 an oil stratum. ●油層を発見する strike oil.

ゆそうせん 油槽船 a tanker, an oil tanker.

ユタ 〖米国の州〗Utah /júːtɔː, -tɑː/〖略 Ut. 郵便略 UT〗

***ゆたか** 豊か —— 豊かな 形 ❶〖裕福な〗(金持ちの) rich; (富裕な) wealthy (⚠ rich より堅い語); (社会・環境などが)《やや書》affluent; (暮らし向きがよい) well-off (↔badly-off). ●豊かな社会 an *affluent* society. ▶彼は豊かな暮らしをしている He is *well-off*. ▶音楽は我々の生活を豊かにする Music makes our life *rich* [《やや書》*enriches* our life].
❷〖豊富な〗(たくさんある) rich; (あり余るほど豊かな) abundant; (たっぷりの) plentiful; (十二分な) ample. (⇨豊富) ●豊かな黒髪 *rich* [*abundant*] black hair. ●豊かな収穫 a *rich* [a *plentiful*, an *abundant*] harvest. ●豊かな(=肥沃(な)な)土地 *rich* [*fertile*] land. ▶その国は天然資源が豊かである The country is *rich* [*abundant*] *in* natural resources. ▶その会社は資本が豊かである The company has *a lot of* capital.
❸〖その他の表現〗●想像力豊かな人 an *imaginative* person; a person of *remarkable* [*fertile*] *imagination*. ●経験豊かな教師 an *experienced* teacher; a teacher of *rich experience*. ▶彼は才能豊かな作家だ He is a *gifted* writer./He has the *gift of* writing well.

ゆだき 湯炊き —— 湯炊きする 動 cook rice in boiling water from the start.

ゆだく 油濁 ▶タンカーから流れ出た原油で沿岸が10キロにわたり油濁した The *oil* from the tanker *polluted* the sea along coast for as long as ten kilometers.

ゆだねる 委ねる leave*. (⇨任せる❶❷)

ゆだま 湯玉 bubbles rising to the surface of boiling water.

ユダヤ Judea /dʒuːdíːə/. ●ユダヤ人 a Jewish person. (⚠ a Jew は時に侮蔑的なのでさける) ●ユダヤ(人)の Jewish. ▶彼はユダヤ人だ He is *Jewish* [a Jew]. ●ユダヤ教 the Jewish religion; Judaism. ●ユダヤ教徒 a Judaist.

ゆだる 茹だる be boiled. ▶スパゲッティはよくゆだったらざるに取ります The spaghetti *is boiled* very well and drained in a colander.

ゆたん 油単 a cover for a chest of drawers; (説明的に) cloth or oiled paper to protect a chest of drawers from dirt or moisture.

***ゆだん** 油断 图〖不注意〗carelessness;〖怠慢〗negligence;〖うかつ〗inattention. ●人の油断につけこむ catch《him》off (his) guard. ▶ちょっとした油断が事故につながる A little *carelessness* [*negligence*] causes accidents. ▶油断は禁物だ(=油断するな) Don't be caught *off* (your) *guard*.
●油断大敵 Security is the greatest enemy.
●油断もすきも(ならない) ▶近ごろ泥棒が多くて油断もすきもならない So many cases of theft have [*has* been] reported recently, so we cannot be too careful.
—— 油断する 動 (警戒を怠る) be off (one's) guard; (不注意である) be careless [negligent, inattentive]. ●人を油断させる throw [put]《him》off (his) *guard*. ▶すりに油断するな Don't *be off* [*Be on*] (your) *guard* against pickpockets./(心身しろ) Look [Watch] out for pickpockets./*Beware of* pickpockets. ▶いつの世でも、権力というものは油断ならない In any age [generation], we must be on our guard against power and authority.

ゆたんぽ 湯湯婆 a hòt-wáter bòttle (for foot warming); a foot warmer.

ゆちゃ 湯茶 ●湯茶の接待を受ける be served with tea [coffee].

ゆちゃく 癒着〖医学〗adhesion. ●政財界の癒着(=腐敗した関係) the *corrupt relationship* between political and business circles.

ユッカ〖植物〗a yucca /jʌ́kə/.

ゆづかれ 湯疲れ —— 湯疲れする 動 feel weak after a long hot bath.

***ゆっくり** ❶〖遅く〗slowly; (徐々に) gradually; (ゆったりと) leisurely; (急がずに) unhurriedly; (着実に) steadily. ▶ゆっくり食事をする have a *leisurely* meal; (時間をかけて) take one's time (in) eating. ▶ゆっくり行け Go *slowly* [*slow*]. (⚠ 命令文では後の方が普通)/(速度を落とせ) Slow down. ▶体力が弱っていたので彼の病気の回復はゆっくりだった He was physically so weak that he *was slow to* get better [*improve*]. ▶日曜日には人々が公園をゆっくり歩いているのを見かける On Sundays people are seen walking *leisurely* [strolling] in the park.
❷〖十分に〗▶彼らはゆっくり飛行機に間に合った They were *well* in time for their airplane. ▶いつもの忙しい時が過ぎて、彼らはゆっくり休むことができた They had a *good* rest after the usual busy hours. (⚠ この場合の good は「十分に、よく」の意で多くの名詞にかかる) ▶最終的に決める前に彼はゆっくりその計画を考えた Before reaching his final decision, he *thought over* the plan. (⚠ think ... over は「…を熟考する」の意)
❸〖その他の表現〗●彼はゆっくり(=時間をかけて)風呂に入る He takes a *long time* over his bath. ▶もう少しゆっくりしていってくださればよろしいのに You should've *stayed* a little *longer*.
会話「これがお部屋の鍵です。どうぞごゆっくり(=くつろいでください)」「ありがとう」 "This is the key to [xof] your room. Please *make yourself at home* [〖楽しいご滞在を〗 Have a pleasant stay]." "Thanks."
会話「ちょっと失礼します。すぐ戻ります」「どうぞごゆっくり。私は急ぎませんから」 "Excuse me a moment. I'll be back soon [It won't take time]." "Please *take your time*. I'm in no hurry."

ゆったり 副 (ゆとりがある) (空間的に) spaciously; (心理的に) relaxedly /rilǽkstli/. ▶ゆったりと時を過ごす have a *relaxing* time. ▶その家はゆったり間取りがしてある The house is *spaciously* laid out.
—— ゆったりした 形 (広々とした) spacious; (くつろいだ) relaxed; (寛大な) generous; (衣服が) loose. ●ゆったりした部屋 a *spacious* room. ●ゆったりした服 *loose* clothes. ▶私は心のゆったりした人が好きだ I like a *generous* person.
—— ゆったりする 動 (くつろぐ) feel* relaxed, relax; (気楽にする) take* it easy. ●この場合の it はその時の状況を広くさす) ▶休みのときにはゆったりしなさい *Take it easy* when you're on holiday.

ゆでだこ 茹で蛸 a boiled octopus. ▶彼は酒が回るとゆでだこのようにまっ赤になる When he gets drunk, his face always turns as red as a *lobster*.

ゆでたまご 茹で卵 a boiled egg. (関連 固ゆで卵 a hard-boiled egg/半熟卵 a soft-boiled egg)

ゆでる 茹でる boil. ▶パスタを腰がなくならない程度にやわらかくゆでる *boil* pasta until (it gets) tender but

ゆでん 油田 an oil field, an oilfield. ●北海油田 the North Sea *oilfields*. ●海底油田 a submarine *oil field*.

ゆどうふ 湯豆腐 *tofu* simmered in stock.

ゆどおし 湯通し ── 湯通しする (織物を) dip 《new cloth》into warm water; (食材などを) dip 《vegetables [plates]》 into boiling water for a moment.

＊**ゆとり** ●ゆとりのある教育 education *free of pressure*. ▶我々には子供を大学に通わせるゆとりはありません We can't *afford* to send our children to college. (⇒余裕)

ユニーク ── ユニークな 形 [独特で他にない] unique. ●ユニークな作家 a *unique*, [独創的な] an *original*, [匹敵する者がない]《書》an *unequaled*, 《書》an *unrivaled* writer. ●彼はユニークな (=他の人と違った) 考え方をする He has a *different* way of thinking [thinks *differently*] *from* others. ▶君の発想はとてもユニークだ Your idea is absolutely [《話》so, 《話》very] *unique*.

ユニオンジャック [英国国旗] the Union Jack.

ユニオンショップ a union shop. (参考) 被雇用者の労働組合への加入を義務づけ, 組合の除名と同時に職場も解雇される制度.

ユニコーン [一角獣] a unicorn.

ユニセックス ── ユニセックスの 形 unisex 《clothing [shops]》.
●ユニセックスサロン (理容院と美容院が一緒になった) a unisex hairdresser's salon.

ユニセフ [国連児童基金] UNICEF /júːnisef/. (参考) the *U*nited *N*ations *I*nternational *C*hildren's *E*mergency *F*und (国連国際児童緊急基金) の略. ただし 1953 年に United Nations Children's Fund (国連児童基金) と改称, 略称は同じ.

ユニット [構成単位] a unit. (⇒単位)
●ユニットキッチン a unit kitchen. ●ユニットケア unit nursing care. ●ユニット工法 (prefabricated) box unit construction. ●ユニット住宅 [プレハブ住宅] a prefabricated [《話》a prefab] house. (! 通例 a unit house とはいわない) ●ユニットバス a modular bathroom; 《和製語》a unit bath.
●ユニットプライス [単位価格表示] unit pricing; [単位価格] a unit price.

ユニバーサルサービス [全国均質サービス] universal service.

ユニバーサルデザイン [万人向け設計] universal design.

ユニバーシアード the Universiade. (! the World University Games (国際学生競技大会) の通称)

ユニホーム a uniform. (⇒制服) ●野球のユニホーム a baseball *uniform*. (参考) 上着は a jersey, ズボンは baseball pants. ●ユニホームを着た選手 a player in *uniform*. (! 複数のときは players in *uniform*(s))
●(野球選手が)ユニホームを脱ぐ (=引退する) hang up one's spikes.

＊**ゆにゅう** 輸入 名 import (⇔export).
① [~輸入] ●直[平行; 緊急] 輸入 direct [parallel; emergency] *import*. ●逆輸入 reverse import; reimport.
② [輸入(の)~] ●米 [農作物] の輸入自由化 liberalization of rice [agricultural product] *imports*; *import* liberalization of rice [agricultural products]. ●輸入住宅を建てる build a house with *imported* materials. ●高い輸入障壁 a severe [a heavy] *import* barrier. ▶原油の輸入価格が上がった *Import* prices of crude oil have risen [gone up]. ▶フランスからの輸入ワインを買った I bought some *imported* wines from France.
③ [~輸入が] ●輸入(額)が輸出(額)を上回っている *Imports* exceed [are greater than] exports (in value). ▶近年アジアからの輸入が急増している [伸び悩んでいる] In recent years, *imports* from Asia have rapidly increased [have made little increase].
④ [~輸入を] ●日本は外国からの車の輸入を奨励[規制]してきた Japan has promoted [restricted] the *import* of cars *from* abroad.
── 輸入する 動 impórt (↔expórt). ▶日本は中東から多くの原油を輸入している Japan *imports* a lot of crude oil *from* the Middle East.
●輸入依存度 import dependency; the degree of dependence on [upon] imports. ●輸出額 the volume of import; imports (! 通例複数形で). ●輸入課徴金 an import surcharge. ●輸入規制 import restrictions. (! 通例複数形で) ●輸入業 import business [trade]. ●輸入業者 (会社; 国) an 《orange》 importer. ●輸入許可書 an import permit. ●輸入禁制品 contraband of import; import prohibited goods. ●輸入証明書 a certificate of importation; an import certificate. ●輸入申告(書) (an) import declaration. ●輸入(数)量 import volume. ●輸入税 an import tax; import duties (! 単数扱い). ●輸入代理店 an import agent. ●輸入高 imports. (! 通例複数形で) ●輸入超過 (貿易赤字) a trade deficit. ●輸入手続き import procedures. ●輸入品 an import (! しばしば複数形で); an imported item; 《集合的》 imported goods. ●東南アジアの安い輸入品 cheap *imports* from Southeast Asia.
●輸入木材 imported timber. ●輸入割当 an import quota.

ゆにょうかん 輸尿管 [解剖] the ureter.

ユネスコ [国連教育科学文化機関] UNESCO, Unesco /juːnéskou/ 《the *U*nited *N*ations *E*ducational, *S*cientific and *C*ultural *O*rganization の略》.

ゆのし 湯熨し 名 steaming of cloth; (毛織物の仕上げ工程で行われる作業) crabbing.
── 湯のしする 動 steam [crab] 《cloth》.

ゆのはな 湯の花 hot-spring mineral deposits, [地学] sinter.

ゆのみちゃわん 湯飲み茶碗 a (tea)cup. (⇒茶碗)

ゆば 湯葉 (flat sheets, rolls or strips of) dried soybean milk skin.

ゆはず 弓筈 (説明的に) the part where the string of a bow is attached to the curved bamboo [wood, etc].

＊**ゆび** 指 ❶ [手足の] [手の] a finger (! 通例親指 (thumb) を含まない (⇒①)); [足の] a toe.

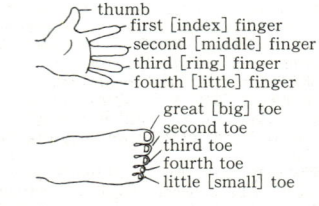

- thumb
- first [index] finger
- second [middle] finger
- third [ring] finger
- fourth [little] finger

- great [big] toe
- second toe
- third toe
- fourth toe
- little [small] toe

ゆびおり

①【〜(の)指】● 薬指 the third *finger*, (特に左手の) the ring *finger*. (❗結婚式のときには四本目の finger という) ● 太い指 a thick (↔a slender) *finger*. ● 人は手に10本, 足に10本の指がある Human beings have ten *fingers* and ten *toes*. (❗このような場合 fingers は thumb を含む)

②【指の[に]】● 指輪を指にはめる[はめている] put on [wear] a ring on one's *finger*. ● 鉛筆を指にはさむ hold a pencil between one's *fingers*. ▶彼の手袋は親指に穴があいている There is a hole in the *thumb* of his glove.

③【指を】● 指を組み合わせる interlace one's *fingers*; lace one's *fingers* together. ● 指をとじる close one's *fingers*. ● 指をくわえて with a *finger* in one's mouth. ● 指をしゃぶる suck one's *finger(s)*. ● (親指と) 指を鳴らす[はじく] snap one's *fingers*. (❗注意を引いたり, 「しめた」というしぐさ) ● 指を立てる lift one's *finger*. (❗ウェーターなどを呼ぶ動作) ▶2人は小指をからませて約束した They linked their *fingers* as a sign of promise.

④【指で】● 指で10まで数える count ten on one's *fingers*. (⇒数える) ● 豆を指でつまんで食べる eat beans with one's *fingers*. ▶彼は虫を親指で押さえた He put the worm under his *thumb*. ▶彼は硬貨をぽんと指ではじき上げた He flipped a coin. (⇒じゃんけん) ▶彼は人差し指と親指でオーケーの合図をした His *forefinger* and *thumb* signaled okay.

❷【その他の表現】▶彼は現代のオペラ界で3本の指に入る名テノール歌手である He is among the three greatest tenors in the contemporary world of opera.

- 指一本 ▶彼には指1本触れさせない I will never let you lay a *finger* on [let you *touch*] him. (❗I *shall* never.... とすれば決意の度合いが強まる)
- 指をくわえる ▶彼女はその指のダイヤの指輪を指をくわえて (=うらやましそうに) 見ていた She was looking *enviously* [(物欲しそうに) *wistfully*] at the diamond ring.
- 指先 a fingertip, the tip of a finger. ● 指先が器用だ be clever [skillful] with one's fingers.
- 指サック a fingerstall; (親指の) a thumbstall.
- 指人形 a finger puppet; (手人形) a hand 《米》 [a glove 《英》] puppet.

ゆびおり 指折り ● 日本で指折りの作曲家 one of the best [(指導的な) *leading*, (著名な) 《やや書》 *eminent*] composers in Japan.

- 指折り数える (指を折りながら数える) count on one's fingers. ▶その子はクリスマスの来るのを指折り数えて (=熱心に [しきりに]) 待っていた The child was *eagerly* [*impatiently*] waiting for [(楽しみに) was *very much looking forward to*] Christmas.

ユビキタス [<ラテン語] 【いつでもどこにでもある】 ubiquitous /juː(ː)ˈbɪkwɪtəs/.
- ユビキタスコンピューティング ubiquitous computing. ● ユビキタス社会 a ubiquitous society.

ゆびきり 指切り (説明的に) make a promise by locking [linking] each other's little fingers. ▶指切りげんまん, 嘘ついたら針千本飲ます Cross my heart and hope to die. (Jesus told me not to lie.) (❗「胸で十字を切って約束する. 破ったら殺されてもいい」の意. 通例省略される)

ゆびさき 指先 (⇒指)

ゆびさす 指差す point 《*at, to*》. (❗at は対象物そのものを, to は対象物の位置している方向をさす) ▶メニューの中から自分の欲しいものを指差して注文する *point out* what one wants from a menu. ▶彼は写真の男を指差して, 「これがぼくだ」と言った He *pointed at* a

man in [×of] the picture and said, "This is me." ▶人を指差すのは失礼だ It's not polite to *point at* people. ▶彼はその建物の方を指差した He *pointed to* the building.

ゆびずもう 指相撲 《fight* [do*, ×play]》 *yubizumo* wrestling; (説明的に) mock wrestling done between erect thumbs of two people while their fingers are tightly clasped together.

ゆびづかい 指使い fingering; how to work one's fingers. ▶ギターのコードを弾く指使いは初めは難しい The *fingering* to play chords on the guitar is difficult at first.

ゆびぬき 指貫き (裁縫用の) a thimble. ● 指貫きをはめる put a *thimble* on one's finger. ● 指貫きをはめて縫い物をする wear a *thimble* when one sews.

ゆびぶえ 指笛 指笛を吹く whistle through one's fingers.

*ゆびわ 指輪 a ring. ● 婚約[結婚]指輪 an engágement [a wédding] *ring*. ● ダイヤの指輪 a diamond *ring*. ● 指輪をはめる put a *ring* on (one's finger). ● 指輪を抜く take [slip] a *ring* off (one's finger). ● 結婚式で指輪を交換する exchange *rings* during a marriage ceremony. ▶恭子は左の中指に金の指輪をはめている Kyoko has [wears] a gold *ring* on her left middle finger.

ゆぶね 湯船 a bathtub, a tub. ● 湯舟につかる soak [be] in the *bathtub*.

ゆまく 油膜 an oil film; (事故などで水面に流出した) an oil slick. ▶単に a stick というう

ゆみ 弓 a bow /bóu/; 【弓術】 archery. ● 弓の名人 an expert archer. ● 弓で矢を射る shoot an arrow by a *bow*. ● 弓に矢をつがえる put [fix] an arrow to the *bow*.

- 弓折れ矢尽きる (力尽きる) one's strength gives out; (万策尽きる) exhaust every possible means.
- 弓を引く draw [bend] a bow; (反抗する) rebel [revolt] 《*against*》.

ゆみがた 弓形 ── 弓形の 形 bow-shaped. ▶その鉄の橋は弓形になって川にかかっていた The iron bridge *arched* over the river.

ゆみず 湯水 (水) water.
- 湯水のように使う ● 金を湯水のように使う spend money *like* water [*very extravagantly*].

ゆみなり 弓形 ▶横綱は土俵際で押し出されまいと弓なりになって必死にこらえた The Grand Champion defended, *arching* his *body backward* in a desperate effort not to be pushed out of the ring.

ゆみはり 弓張り ● 弓張りをする string* a bow; put* a string on a bow.
- 弓張り月 a crescent moon.

ゆみや 弓矢 (a) bow and arrow (徽 bow and arrows). ▶彼は弓矢でシカを仕留めた He shot the deer with a *bow and arrow*.

‡**ゆめ 夢** ❶【睡眠中の】a dream; (悪夢) a nightmare. (⇒悪夢)

①【〜夢】● 正[逆]夢 a prophetic [an opposite] *dream*. ● (悪) 恐ろしい[変な; 楽しい; 不吉な] 夢 a terrible [a strange; a pleasant; an ominous] *dream*. ● こわい夢を見る have a *nightmare*. ▶私の見た失恋の夢が逆夢でありますように I hope my *dream* about lost love will go by contraries [(現実のものにならない) won't come true].

②【夢〜】● 夢判断をする interpret [read] one's *dream*. ● 夢うつつでベルの鳴るのを聞く listen *half asleep* to the bell ringing.

ゆめ

③【夢の】● 夢のような計画 a dreamlike scheme. ● 夢のように(はかなく)消える vanish like a dream. ● 夢の中で英語を話す speak English in one's dream [while one is dreaming]. ▶加藤先生と再び会えるような夢だ It's like a dream to meet Mr. Kato again.

④【夢を[に]】● 夢を見る dream 《of, about; that 節》 (▲過去・過去分詞形は dreamed /drí:md (米), drémt (英) / が普通); have [書] dream, ×see, ×watch] a dream. (! dream a dream の場合は通例名詞の前に形容詞が入る) ▶私、あなたを夢をよく見るのよ I often dream about you./I see a lot of you in a dream. ▶試験に合格した夢を見た I dreamed [had a dream] that I passed the exam. ▶まるで夢を見ているような気分だった I felt as if I were dreaming [in a dream]. ▶夢でも見ているんだろう You must be dreaming! (!「ばかなことを言うな」の意) ▶亡き母が私の夢に現れた My dead mother appeared in my dream.

⑤【夢から[で]】● 夢からさめる wake from a dream. ● 夢でうなされる be frightened [troubled] by a nightmare.

❷【心に描く】a dream; (大望) (an) ambition; (幻想) a vision; (取りとめのない空想) (a) fancy.

①【～夢】● 途方もない[漠然とした]夢 a wild [a vague] dream. ● 大きな夢 a high ambition. ● 将来の夢を語る talk about one's dream for the future. ▶海外旅行は私の長年抱き続けている夢です Traveling abroad is my long-cherished dream ▶ともいえる. it is Never [Little] did I dream .... (▲否定を強調して Never in my wildest dreams had I thought I would ... ともいえる. ただし Never [Little] did I dream .... は文語的)/(思ってもみないことであった) Studying abroad was the last thing I was expecting. ▶それは夢にも思わないほどの(=夢のような)大金であった That was more money than I had ever dreamed of./That's a lot of money beyond my wildest dreams.

②【夢(の)～】● 夢の国 (a) dreamland. ● 夢多き少女 a fanciful girl. ● これは料理をする人にとってはまさに夢のキッチンだ This kitchen is a dream come true for any cook. (!《夢(③》)の意) ▶人は夢の中でよりよい自分を探している In dreams you search for a better self.

③【夢が[は]】● 私の夢が実現した My dream has come true [《やや書》has been realized]./《やや書》My dream has become a reality. ▶私の夢は外交官になることです My dream is [It is my dream] to become a diplomat. ▶私の夢は広まった My dream has spread. ▶その戦争で母国へ帰るという彼女の夢ははかなく破れた The war shattered [dashed] her dream of going back home. (!後の方は新聞用語)

④【夢に】● 夢に破れた人々 burned-out dream chasers. ▶直子は宇宙飛行士になることを夢に描いている Naoko is dreaming of becoming an astronaut. (!「夢に描く」の意の前置詞は of が普通) (夢を持っている) Naoko has a dream of becoming an astronaut. ▶あの若者は夢にあふれている That young man has a lot of dreams [is filled with ambitions].

⑤【夢を】● 夢を抱く have [cherish] a dream. (⇒夢見る) ● 夢を追う chase a dream. ● 彼の夢を実現させる realize [fulfill] his dream; turn his dream into reality. ▶あなたはどんな夢を持っていますか What dreams do you have for the future?

古今ことばの系譜 夢
陸上をやめようと思ったこともありました. でも, 一度夢をあきらめかけた私が結果を出すことで, 今, 暗闇にいる人や苦しんでいる人に,「夢を持てば, また必ず光が見えるんだ」ということを伝えたい, そのメッセージにもなるんだと, 走りながら自分に言い聞かせていました. (東京国際マラソンで見事に復活優勝した高橋尚子選手の優勝インタビュー)

There were times when I thought about ending my career as an athlete. Although I almost gave up my dream at one time, I realized that if I could get a good result I would be able to show people who have lost hope or are facing hardships that if they hold on to their dream, one day they will be able to see light. I ran, telling myself that I am carrying that message to them. (ヘラルド朝日 2005 年 11 月 23 日) (!見出しには "Takahashi teaches us to hold on to our dreams" とある. 本文の their dream は単数形は「配分単数」といい, 複数形ではないことに注意: We have a nose.)

⑥【夢にも...ない】▶勉強を怠けようとは夢にも思っていない I wouldn't dream of neglecting my studies. (!現在のことを述べるときは would [should, could] を伴う) ▶留学するなんて夢にも思っていなかった I never [《書》little] dreamed that I would study abroad. (!否定を強調して Never in my wildest dreams had I thought I would ... ともいえる. ただし Never [Little] did I dream .... は文語的)/(思ってもみないことであった) Studying abroad was the last thing I was expecting. ▶それは夢にも思わないほどの(=夢のような)大金であった That was more money than I had ever dreamed of./That's a lot of money beyond my wildest dreams.

⑦【夢だ】▶人生は現実であって夢ではない Life is a reality [is real] and not a dream.

● 夢を結ぶ (夢を見る) have a dream; (眠りにつく) go to sleep.
● 夢物語 a pipe dream. (!麻薬による幻のような夢想)

ゆめ 努 ● ゆめ...なかれ never 《do》. (⇒努々(ゅめ))

ゆめうつつ 夢現 ▶私の一生は夢うつつ(=夢と現実)の境をさまようがごときものに思える I feel I have been moving between dreams and reality all through my life. ▶ウインブルドンに移って以来夢うつで(=半分夢の中で)小鳥の声を聞くことがある Since I moved to Wimbledon, I hear, half in a dream [half dreaming, half sleeping, half asleep], the singing of birds in the morning.

ゆめうらない 夢占い ● 夢占い(=夢判断)をする interpret [read] one's dream.

ゆめがたり 夢語り ●【見た夢の話】a talk about a dream (one has had); 【夢物語】a pipe dream (⇒夢).

ゆめごこち 夢心地 ● 夢心地で (half) in a dream; (まるで夢のように) as if in a dream.

ゆめじ 夢路 ● 夢路をたどる have a dream; (気持ちよく眠る) sleep well, have a good sleep.

ゆめまくら 夢枕 ▶母が夢枕に立った(=夢に現れた) My mother appeared in my dream.

ゆめまぼろし 夢幻 dreams and illusions. ● 夢幻のような話 a dream-like story; an illusory story. ▶夢幻の世の中だ Everything in this world is ephemeral.

ゆめみ 夢見 ▶夢見がよかった[悪かった] I had a good [a bad] dream. ▶夢見心地だった (夢を見ているようだった) I felt as if I were in a dream.

ゆめみる 夢見る dream 《of, about》. (⇒夢 ❷) ● 夢見るような表情 a dreamy look. ● 栄光[外国で働くこと]を夢見る(=夢に描く) dream of [×dream] glory [working abroad]. ▶彼女は夢見るような目をしていた She had a dreamy [faraway] look in her eyes.

ゆめゆめ 努々 ▶ゆめゆめ自分の息子を疑うことなかれ

ゆもと　湯元　the source of a hot spring.

ゆや　湯屋（銭湯）a public bath.

ゆゆしい　由々しい ●由々しい(=重大な)事態 a *grave* [a *serious*] situation.

ゆらい　由来 图（起源）(an) origin. ●その寺の名の由来をたどる trace the *origin* of the name of the temple.

——由来する 動　外国語に由来する日本の言葉 Japanese words of foreign *origin*. ▶その建築様式はギリシャに由来する That style of architecture *originates* [has its *origin*] *in* Greece. (❗(1) 後の方が口語的. (2) 前の方は originated と過去形でもよい)

ゆらぐ　揺らぐ　[[揺れる]]（人が迷う）waver*（信念などが）be shaken. (⇨ぐらつく) ▶私の信念が揺らいだ My belief *was shaken*.

ゆらす　揺らす　shake*; swing*; sway; rock; jiggle. ▶ジェラードのロングシュートがゴールネットを揺らした Gerrard *rattled* the net from the distance.

ゆらめく　揺らめく　[[炎などが]]（ゆらぎの）waver;（ちらちらと）flicker.

ゆらゆら ●ゆらゆら揺れる［揺らす］（大きく左右に）sway;（つるしたものなどが繰り返し）swing;（ゆっくりと）rock;（軽く小刻みに）jiggle. (⇨揺れる) ●ゆらゆらと腰をふるフラダンサー a *jiggly* hula dancer. ▶波の上で小舟がゆらゆら揺れた A small boat *swayed* on the waves. ▶母親が大きなかごに入っている赤子をゆらゆらさせた The mother *rocked* the baby in a large basket. ▶かげろうがゆらゆら立っていた I saw the heat haze *shimmering*.

ゆらり ●ゆらりと揺れる（不安定に）waver;（大きく左右に）sway. ●弾丸が当たり, 彼はゆらりとして倒れた A bullet hit him and he *wavered* and fell down. ▶ヒョウタンが強風にゆらりゆらり揺れていた Gourds *were swaying* in the strong wind.

ゆられる　揺られる（⇨揺れる）▶私たちはバスに揺られながら山道を上がって行った We went up the mountain path on a *jolting* bus./Our bus *jolted* along up the mountain path. ▶釣り船にひどく揺られて吐気がした The fishing boat *tossed* badly, and I felt like vomiting.

ゆらんかん　輸卵管〔解剖〕an oviduct.

ゆり　百合〔植物〕a lily. ●白［黒］ユリ a white [a black] *lily*. ●姫ユリ a morning-star *lily*. ●山ユリ a golden-banded *lily*. ●鬼ユリ a tiger *lily*. ●鉄砲ユリ a trumpet *lily*. ●ユリのように白い肌 *lily-*white skin.
●百合根 a lily bulb.

ゆりいす　揺り椅子　a rócking chàir,《米》a rocker.

ゆりうごかす　揺り動かす　[[揺する]] shake*;（大きく左右に）sway;（揺りかごなど）rock;（感情を与える）sway. (❗しばしば受身で)▶彼の言葉に揺り動かされた He *was swayed* by the words.

ゆりおこす　揺り起こす　shake* (him) awake [from sleep, out of sleep]. ▶彼女は子供を揺り起こした She *shook* her child *awake*.

ゆりかえし　揺り返し（⇨ 揺り戻し）

ゆりかご　揺り籠　a cradle. ●赤ん坊を揺りかごに入れて揺る rock a baby in a *cradle*.
●揺りかごから墓場まで from the cradle to the grave.

ゆりかもめ　百合鴎〔鳥〕a black-headed gull.

ゆりもどし　揺り戻し（余震）an aftershock.

ゆりょう　湯量　the volume of hot water. ▶箱根の温泉は湯量が豊富だ Hot springs in Hakone have rich *volumes of water*.

***ゆるい　緩い** 形　[[結び目などが]] loose;[[スピードが]] slow;[[斜面が]] gentle;[[地盤が]] not firm, soft;[[規則などが]] lax. ●緩いスピードで at a *slow* speed. ●緩い坂 a *gentle* [a *gradual*] slope. ●（投手が投げる）緩いボール an off-speed pitch. ●（弱い打球）a soft [a weak] grounder; a slow roller. ▶この結び目は緩い This knot is *loose*. ▶この学校の校則は緩い The regulations of this school are *lax* [*not strict*].

——緩く 副　loosely. ▶2本のロープは緩く結びつけられている The two ropes are *loosely* tied together. ▶大雨で地盤が緩くなっている The heavy rain made the ground *soft*.

ゆるがす　揺るがす　shake*;（しだいにそこなう）《やや書》undermine. ●天地を揺るがすほどの大爆発 an explosion large enough to *shake* heaven and earth. ●世界を揺るがすようなニュース world*-shaking* [earth*-shaking*] news. ▶長年にわたる赤字が会社の基盤を揺るがすようになった The losses over the years began to *undermine* the foundation of our company.

ゆるがせ　忽せ ●ゆるがせにする neglect《one's work, *to do*》; be negligent《*of, in doing*》. ▶法律の文章は一字一句ゆるがせにできない Legal sentences have to be *precise* in the use of words./Legal sentences demand exact use of words.

ゆるぎない　揺るぎない（堅い）firm;（堅固な）solid;（しっかりした）secure;（安定した）steady. ●揺るぎない信念 an *unshakable* [a *firm*] belief.

ゆるし　許し（権威のある人による究極的な）permission,《書》leave;［罪などの重大な過失に対する］forgiveness;［失敗などを放免すること］pardon. (⇨許可) ●それをする許しを彼から得る get [obtain] *permission* from him to do it; get his *permission* to do it. ●彼の許しを得て［得ないで］外出する go out with [without] his *permission*. ●その罪に対し神の許しを請う ask [beg] His [God's] *forgiveness* for the sin; ask [beg] Him [God] to *forgive* the sin. (❗ His, Him の大文字に注意) ▶だれの許しを得てこの部屋に入ったのか By whose *permission* [(権限) *authority*] did you enter this room?/Who gave you *permission* to enter this room?/Who *permitted* [*allowed*] you to enter this room?

***ゆるす　許す** 動　❶［許可する］allow《A *to do*》; let*《A *do*》;《やや書》permit (-tt-)《A *to do*》;（入ることを認める）《やや書》admit (-tt-);（是認する）approve《*of*》;（承諾する）《やや書》consént《*to*》.

> 使い分け　permit 行動が人・制度・組織・環境によって公的に許可されること.
> allow「してもよい」の意を表す語で, 公的な許可と私的な許可の両方に用いる. 時に許可した後の判断は当事者に委ねられ, 許可してもそれが行われない可能性を含意する.
> let 人の意志どおりに行動させること.

●天候が許せば if the weather *permits*;《書》weather *permitting*《略 WP》. (❗通例文尾に置く. 日常的には if we have nice weather の方が普通) ▶旅行に行くのを父は許してくれたが母は許してくれた(=行かせてくれた) My mother *allowed* me *to* [*let* me, ×*let* me *to*] go on a journey though my father didn't *permit* it. (❗「父は許可しなかったが, 母は行くのを止めなかった」ぐらいの意 (⇨［類語］)) ▶ここでは狩猟は許されていない Hunting is not

ゆるみ 緩み

permitted [ˣallowed, ˣlet] here./You *are* not *permitted* [ˣallowed] *to* hunt here. (ˣallowed については (⇨[類語])) ▶門番は門を通り抜けるのを許してくれた The gatekeeper *permitted* [*allowed, let*] me through the gate. (❗️me の後に *to* pass (let では pass)が省略されていると考えられる) ▶時間が許す限り手伝ってあげよう I'll help you as [so] long as time *permits*. ▶おじに金銭上の世話になることは彼のプライドが許さなかった His pride would not *allow* him *to* [He was too proud to] take financial support from his uncle. ▶彼はその大学に入学を許された He *was admitted to* [ˣwas *permitted to, was allowed to*] get into, *was accepted* by] the college. ▶事態は一刻の猶予も許さない The situation *allows* [《書》*permits*] (*of*) no delay. (❗️「(物・事が)…の余地がある」の意で、通例否定文で用いられる。of はしばしば省略される) ▶父は私が彼女と結婚することを許さなかった My father didn't *approve of* [*consent to*] my marriage to [ˣwith] her.

❷【容赦する】forgive*; pardon; excuse; (大目に見る) overlook; (寛容さを示す) tolerate; (罪を罰せずに) condone /kəndóun/.

> 使い分け **forgive** 明らかな過ちや罪に対して怒りを静めて許すこと．
> **pardon** 人の罪などを権威者が容赦すること．《話》で用いるとちょっとした失礼に対して許すことを表す．
> **excuse** ちょっとした過失や失礼などを許すこと．目上の人物から容赦してもらうことを含意する．

▶今度だけは君の失敗を許してやろう I'll *forgive* [*excuse, overlook*] your mistake just this once. ▶こんなことを言うのをお許しください Pardon [*Forgive*] me for saying so./Pardon [*Forgive*] my saying so. (❗️so は次にいうことをさす. so の代わりに this も可) ▶本当にごめんなさい．どうかお許し(=謝罪の気持ちを受け取って)ください I'm terribly sorry. Please *accept* my *apologies*. (❗️Please forgive me. より丁寧な言い方) ▶先生は私の遅刻を許してくれた The teacher *excused* me *for* being late./The teacher *excused* my coming late. (❗️ˣThe teacher *excused* that I was late. とはいわない) ▶どんな理由にせよ彼の行為は許されるものではない No matter what reasons he has, his act *is inexcusable*. ▶息子がぶらぶらしているのを黙っておくわけはいかない I can't *tolerate* [*have*] my son idling about. (❗️この have は通例否定文で) ▶彼は人の失敗を許さない(=不寛容だ) He *is intolerant of* other people's [others'] faults. ▶彼の暴力行為は許せないいまでも理解はできます His act of violence could be understood, if not *condoned*.

❸【心などを許す】(信用する) trust; (信用して秘密などを打ち明ける) confide in …; (油断している) be off (one's) guard. ▶あの男に心を許してはいけない You should not *trust* [*confide in*] that man. ▶私には心を許せる(=信頼できる)友人が何人かいる I have several *trustworthy* [*reliable*] friends. ▶気を許しているすきに金を盗まれた I had my money stolen while I was off my *guard*.

❹【その他の表現】●スペースの許す範囲内に記事を縮める compress the article to fit the space *available*. ▶彼は古代ともに許す(=一般に認められている)古代史の大家だ He *is acknowledged as* [*It is generally accepted that* he is] an authority on ancient history. ▶大統領は普通の人のめんどうを見る生活を望んだが, それは許されようもなかった(=そうする権利はなかった) The president longed for the relaxed life of an ordinary man but he *had no right to* it. ▶先

発投手はシングルヒットを3本許しただけだった The starter allowed (gave up) only three singles.

ゆるみ 緩み (ロープなどの) slack. ●ロープのゆるみ the *slack* in a rope. ▶彼の気のゆるみから火事が出た The fire broke out because he was *careless* about fire.

***ゆるむ 緩む** 〘結び目などが〙loosen; 〘緊張などが〙relax. ●結び目が緩む a *loose* [a *slack*] knot. ▶彼のロープを握る手が緩んだ His grip on the rope *loosened*. ▶このねじはよく緩む This screw often *comes* [*works*] *loose*. ▶気が緩んだ(=油断しているすきに財布をすられた I *was relaxing* my *guard* [*was off* (my) *guard*] when I had my wallet picked. ▶近ごろは規律も緩みがちだ Discipline tends to *relax* [*be relaxed, be lax*] these days. ▶寒さが緩んできた The cold *is letting up*./It's *getting less cold*.

ゆるめ 緩め ●帯を緩めに(=強くなく)締める wear one's *obi not too tight* [ほんの少し緩く) *a bit loosely*]. ●小麦粉をいつもより緩めに溶く(=少し水の量を多くして混ぜる) mix flour with *a little more* water than usual. ●お通じが緩めである have *a little* [*a rather*] *soft* stool.

***ゆるめる 緩める** ❶【張力を弱める】(結び目などを) loosen (↔tighten); (力などを) relax, (特に綱などを) slacken. ●ベルト[ネクタイ]を緩める *loosen* one's belt [tie]. ●ねじを緩める *loosen* a screw. ●綱[弦]を緩める *slacken* the rope [string]. ●ロープを握る手を緩める *loosen* [*relax, slacken*] one's grip on the rope.

❷【和らげる】(緊張などを) relax, ease; (特に規則などを) loosen; (減じる) lessen. ●警戒を緩める *relax* one's guard (*against*). ●規則を緩める *relax* a rule. ●取り締まりを緩める *relax* [*loosen*] control (*over*). ●両国間の緊張を緩める *relax* [*lessen, ease*] the tension between the two countries. ▶テストが終わっていないのだから気を緩めて(=努力を怠って)はだめだ Don't *relax* your *efforts* because the tests aren't over.

❸【速度を落とす】slow down [*up*]; (減じる) lessen, slacken. ●自動車の速度を緩める *slow down* one's car; *lessen* [*slacken*] the speed of one's car. ●歩調を緩める *slacken* one's pace. ▶バスの運転手は速度を緩めた The bus (driver) *slowed down* [*up*]./The bus (driver) *slackened* speed.

ゆるやか 緩やか ──**緩やかな** 形 gentle; (のろい) slow. ●緩やかな坂 a *gentle* [a *gradual*] slope. ●緩やかな流れ a *gentle* [a *slow-flowing*] stream. (⇨緩める)

ゆれ 揺れ a shake; (a) swing; sway; (a) rock; a jolt. (⇨揺れる) ●船の揺れ the *rock* [(横揺れ)the *roll*, (縦揺れ) the *pitch*] of a ship. ●車の揺れ the *jolts* of a car. ●(小さな)地震の揺れ an earth *tremor*.

ゆれうごく 揺れ動く waver; flicker; sway. (⇨揺れる) ●炎が揺れ動いていた The flames *were wavering* [*flickering*]. ▶2人の意見の間に立って心が揺れ動いた I *wavered* [*swayed*] between the two opinions. (⇨揺れる [最後から2番目の文例])

ゆれもどし 揺れ戻し an aftershock. (⇨揺り戻し)

***ゆれる 揺れる** shake*; quiver, tremble, swing*; sway; rock; jolt; flicker.

> 使い分け **shake** 地面などが地震で大きく揺れること. また, 身体や精神状態が揺れる際にも用いる.
> **quiver** 小さいものが小刻みに揺れること. 木などの大きなものには用いられない.

tremble ものが小さく揺れること.
swing ものが上側を支点として繰り返し揺れること. 体の一部やものが振り子のように揺れることを示す.
sway 人や比較的大きなものがゆっくりと大きく揺れること.
rock ものが下側[地面との接地点]を支点として前後・左右にゆっくりと揺れること.
jolt 強い衝撃などによって激しく一度揺れること.
flicker 主に光や炎などが揺れること.

▶地震で家が揺れた I felt the house *shake* [*rock*] in the earthquake. (❗「揺れを感じたこと」に重点を置いた表現)/The house *shook* [*rocked*] in the earthquake. (❗(1)「家」に重点を置いた表現. (2) in の代わりに from も可)/The earthquake *shook* [*rocked*] the house. (❗「地震」に重点を置いた表現) ▶木の葉が風で揺れている The leaves *are shaking* [*quivering, trembling*] in the wind. ▶木々が強風で揺れていた The trees *were swaying* in the strong wind. ▶バスが通ると家が揺れた The house *trembled* [(震動した)*vibrated*] when a bus went by. ▶振り子が左右に揺れた The pendulum *swung* to and fro. ▶船は波に揺れた The ship *rocked* [*pitched* and *rolled*] on [in] the waves./The ship *was rocked* [*was pitched* and *rolled*] by the waves. (❗rock は方向を問わずに揺れた[揺らす], pitch は縦に, roll は横[左右]に揺れた[揺らす]) ▶道が悪くてバスががたがた揺れた The bus *jolted* [*bumped*] (*along*) over the rough road. (❗along は「揺れながら進む」の意を明確にする) ▶(空港でぼくのバッグがベルトコンベアの上を小刻みに揺れながら出てきた My bag came *jiggling* on the conveyor belt. ▶その申し出を受け入れようか受け入れまいかと彼女の心は揺れた(=迷った) She *wavered* [*swayed*] between accepting and refusing the offer. ▶スウェーデンの社会福祉制度は経済危機に見舞われ揺れている(=土台を揺るがされている) Sweden's social welfare system is severely *undermined* by the country's economic crisis.

ゆわえる 結わえる tie (〜d; tying); knot (-tt-); make* a knot; fasten; bind*. (⇨くくる, 縛る ❶, 結ぶ ❶)

ゆわかし 湯沸かし a (tea)kettle. (⇨やかん) ●ガス[瞬間]湯沸かし器 a gas [an instantaneous] water heater; 《英話》a geyser /ɡíːzər/. (❗特に家庭用)

ユングフラウ [<ドイツ語] the Jungfrau /júnfrau/. ([参考] アルプス山脈中の高峰の一つ)

よ

よ 世 ❶ [世間, 世の中] the world; [人生] life; [社会] society. (⇨世の中)
①《世の》● 世の荒波 the rough dealings of the *world*; (人生のさまざまな困難) the hardships of *life*. ● 世のためになる benefit the *world* [the *society*]. ▶それが世の常というものだ That's the way of the *world*./それが世の中だ That [Such] is *life*. ▶世の(=世間一般の)親たちは何と言うだろう What would parents *in general* say?
②《世に》● この世に生を受ける(=生まれる) come into the [this] *world*; be born. (⚠後の方が普通の言い方) ● 世に名高い万里の長城 the Great Wall which is well known *to* [×by] the *world*. ▶これが世に言う(=いわゆる)受験地獄だ This is the so-*called* [*what is called*] "examination hell."
③《世を》▶彼は世をはかなんで自殺した He lost all his hopes (in the *world*) and killed himself./(絶望して) He killed himself in despair.
❷[時世, 時代] (the) time(s). (⇨時代 ❷) ● 世の移り変わり the change of *times*. ● 世に遅れないでついてゆく keep up with *the times*. ● 世の流れに従う [逆らう] swim with [against] the tide.
● 世が世なら ▶世が世なら彼は有名な作曲家になっていたかもしれない *If times had been better* [If he *had lived in better times*], he might have been a famous composer.
● 世に出る (有名になる) become famous; (出世する) get on [rise] in the world; (出版される) be published; (市場に出る) be put on the market. ▶彼は歌手として世に出た He *became famous* as a singer. ▶彼の全集がいよいよ世に出ることになった His complete writings will be *on sale* at last.
● 世に問う ▶2004年に彼は研究成果を世に問うた(=出版した) He *published* the results of his research in 2004.
● 世も末 (この世の終わり) the end of the world. ▶殺人や誘拐が横行している. これじゃ世も末だ Murder and kidnapping are rampant. This is *the end of the world*!
● 世を去る ▶彼は昨年この世を去った He *passed away* last year. (⚠die の婉曲表現)
● 世を忍ぶ (世間から隠れて暮らす) live in seclusion. ● 世を忍ぶ仮の姿 an assumed self to *live in seclusion*.
● 世を捨てる give up [《やや書》 renounce] the world.
● 世を渡る (暮らしてゆく) live; (生計を立てる) make a [one's] living. ▶彼は世を渡る術(ｽ)を知らない He doesn't know how to *make a living*.

よ 夜 (a) night. (⇨夜(ﾖﾙ)) ▶夜が明けた *Morning* [*Day*, *Dawn*, ×*Night*] broke. (⚠主に書き言葉. 日常会話では It's morning./Morning has come [is here]. の方が普通)/《やや書》 It [(The) *morning*, (The) *day*] dawned.
● 夜の目も寝ない ▶彼女は夜の目も寝ないで(=徹夜して)レポートを書いた She *stayed up all night* to write a paper.
● 夜も日も明けない ▶ケータイなしでは夜も日も明けない(=1日も生活できない) I *cannot live even a day without* the cellphone.
● 夜を明かす ▶彼は森で夜を明かした He spent the *whole night* in the woods.
● 夜を徹する ▶彼女は夜を徹して(=夜通し)夫の看病をした She looked after her husband *all through the night* [*throughout the night*].
● 夜を日に継ぐ ▶何十人もの医師や看護士が何日も夜を日に継いで(=昼夜の別なく)働いた Dozens of doctors and nurses have worked *night and day* for days.
● 夜釣り night fishing.

よ 余 ● 60余年 60-odd years. (⇨余り ❷ [文例])

よあかし 夜明かし 名 (⇨⇔徹夜)
— **夜明かしする** 動 ● 夜明かしをしてセーターを編み上げる *sit* [*stay*] *up all night* to finish knitting a sweater; finish knitting a sweater without sleeping all night.

よあけ 夜明け (a) dawn,《やや書》daybreak (⚠dawn より少し時刻が遅い). ● 夜明けから日暮れまで from *dawn* till dusk [*dark*]. ▶7月3日の夜明けに山頂に到着した We reached the summit *at* (the break of) *dawn* on July 3. ▶彼は夜明け前にその町を出た He left the town before *dawn* [*daybreak*].

よあけまえ『夜明け前』 *Before the Dawn*. (参考 島崎藤村の小説)

古今ことばの系譜『夜明け前』
木曾路はすべて山の中である. あるところは岨(ｿﾜ)づたいに行く崖の道であり, あるところは数十間の深さに臨める木曾川の岸であり, あるところは山の尾をめぐる谷の入り口である. 一筋の街道はこの深い森林地帯を貫いていた. The Kiso Road lies entirely in the mountains. In some places it cuts across the face of a precipice. In others it follows the banks of the Kiso river, far above the stream. Elsewhere it winds around a ridge and into another valley. All of it runs through decent forest. (William Naff) (⚠ lies in..., cuts across..., follows..., far above..., winds around... and into..., runs through... など, 動詞と前置詞を多様に利用して, 訳文が単調散漫にならないように工夫しているところに注意)

よあそび 夜遊び — **夜遊びする** 動 enjoy nightlife; go out a lot at night. ▶この町には夜遊びするところも大してない There isn't much *nightlife* in this town.

よあつ 与圧 ● 与圧室 a pressure cabin. ● 与圧装置 a pressurization apparatus; pressurization equipment. ● 与圧服 a pressure suit.

よあるき 夜歩き — **夜歩きする** 動 ▶病身の人が夜歩きするのはよくない It's not good for a weak person to *go out at night*.

よい 良い, 好い, 善い

WORD CHOICE よい

good 人や物の外面・内面・質・程度が申し分なく良好であること. ▶それは我々にとってよい知らせだ That news is *good* for us.
fine 主に物が高級で上質であること. 特に自然の美しさや, 芸術・食品などの上等さを含意する. ● 海を望むよい景色 a *fine* view over the sea.
nice 人や物の気質・雰囲気が申し分なく良好であること. ● よい人 a *nice* guy.

よい

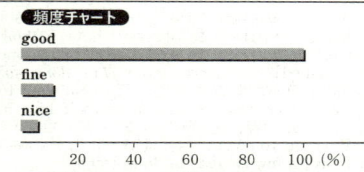

頻度チャート
- good
- fine
- nice

20　40　60　80　100 (%)

❶ [好ましい] **good***. (⇨いい ❶) ▶お金を持ってきてよかった It's good [(It's a) good thing] (that) I have brought some money on me. (⚠ 会話では ( ) 内を省略して Good thing I've brought…. のようにいう)/(運がよかった) It's fortunate that [Fortunately] I have brought some money on [with] me. (⚠ money のような小物では on が普通) ▶うそをつくのはよくないことだ It is wrong [bad, not right, not good] to tell lies. (⚠ not good は通例「(一般論として・道徳的に)よくない」ではなくて「(特定の状況で)適切でない」の意) ▶あそこの店でスーツをクリーニングしてもらったけどなかなかよかったわよ I had a suit cleaned there. They did a good job.

会話「そのコンサートはどうだった」「なかなかよかったよ」 "How was the concert?" "Fantastic [Splendid]."/"How did you like the concert?" "I really enjoyed it."

会話「その映画はよかったですか」「ぜんぜんよくなかった(=だめだった)よ」 "Was the film any good?" "(It was) no good at all." (⚠ (1) この good は名詞で通例 any, no などを伴う. (2)「まあまあよかった」なら It was good but not great. などという)

DISCOURSE
結論として私は，情報技術は世界をよりよくしたと考える **To conclude**, I am of the opinion that information technology has made the world a better place. (⚠ to conclude, (結論として)は結論に用いるディスコースマーカー)

❷ [うれしい] **be glad, be pleased**; (安心する) **feel* relieved**. ▶みんな無事でよかった I'm glad [I feel relieved] that we're all safe./(みんな無事なことに) Thank God [goodness, heavens] we're all safe. ▶ロンドンに来てよかった I'm pleased (that) we came to London. ▶ああよかった(=ほっとした) What a relief!

会話「昇進したよ」「まあ，よかったね. そうなると思ってたよ」 "I've been promoted." "Oh good for you [Oh, that's great, How nice, I'm so glad [very happy] for you]! I knew you would be."

会話「遅くても6時にはそこに行くよ」「よかった！ もっと遅くなるかと思ってたわ」 "I'll be there by six at the latest." "Fine! I thought you'd be later than that."

❸ [望ましい] (…であればいいのだが) **wish**. (⇨いい ❷) ▶彼女にその秘密をしゃべらなければよかった(のにしゃべってしまった) I wish you had not told her the secret. (⚠ 過去の事実に反する願望を表す)/I am sorry (that) you told her the secret. ▶よかれと思って言ってくださっていることは分かっています I know you mean well.

会話「ご忠告ありがとう. そうしてみるわ」「あとでそうしてよかったと思うよ」 "Thanks for the advice. I think I'll try it." "You won't regret it [be sorry]."

【よかったら】 ▶よかったら(=ご希望なら)ケーキを召し上がってください Help yourself to the cake if you ˇlike. ▶よかったら(=ご迷惑でなければ)それは私がやりましょう I'll do it, if you don't ˇmind. (⚠ 反対がない

と思われるような提案・要望などに添えたり, 他人の申し出などを断わる際に用いる. 「よかったら少しお金を貸していただけませんか」のように相手の意向が不明の場合は Could [Would] you lend me some money? などとする) ▶よかったらその靴どこで買ったのか教えてくださらない? Would you mind telling me where you got [bought] your shoes?

❹ [許可] **can*, may***. (⇨いい ⓮) ▶私が子供のころはこの川で泳いでもよかった I could swim in this river when I was a child. (⚠ このように過去の一般的な許可を表す場合は could を用いる. 次例と比較) ▶私は1時間だけでも外出してよかった I was allowed to [had permission to, ×could] go out only for an hour. (⚠ 過去に1回限りが許されたことには could は用いない)

❺ [助言] (…すべきだ) **should do, ought to do**. (⇨いい ⓯) ▶もっと分別があってもよさそうなものだ You should [ought to] know better. ▶私といっしょに来たらよかったのに You should have come with me. ▶手紙くらい書いてくれてもよかったのに You might have written a letter to me. (⚠ might に強勢を置いて不満・非難を表す)

❻ [十分である]

翻訳のこころ セリヌンティウスは無言でうなずき, メロスをひしと抱き締めた. 友と友の間は, それでよかった (太宰治『走れメロス』) Celenuntius nodded in silence and strongly [earnestly, lovingly] embraced Melos. That was enough [all that was needed [necessary]] between the friends. (⚠ (1)「ひしと」は strongly (強く), earnestly (誠実さをもって), lovingly (愛情をこめて) などで表す. (2)「(それで)よかった」は enough (充分である), all that was needed [necessary] (必要なのはそれだけだった)と表す)

よい 酔い ❶ [酒による酔い] **drunkenness**, 《書》 **intoxication**. ● 酔いが回っている [回る] to be [get] drunk. ▶2～3時間休んだら酔いが覚めた A few hours' rest sobered me (up)./I sobered up [became sober] after a few hours of rest. ❷ [乗り物酔い] **motion sickness**, 《婉曲的》**motion discomfort**; (車) **carsickness**; (飛行機) **airsickness**; (船) **seasickness**. (⇨酔う) ● 酔い止め薬 motion sickness drug [pills].

よい 宵 **early evening**. ▶宵に in the early evening. ▶まだ宵の口だ (⇨宵の口) ● 宵の明星 (⇨宵の明星) ● **宵闇** the evening twilight.

よいこ 好い子 (⇨好(ˇ)い子)

よいごこち 酔い心地 ▶いい酔い心地だ How I feel glorious on wine [beer, sake]!/Sake makes me feel glorious.

よいごし 宵越し ● **宵越しの金は持たない** ▶あの男は宵越しの金は持たない 'He spends the day's earnings by the end of the day.'/(気前よく金を使う) He is very generous with his money.

よいざまし 酔い覚まし ▶冷たい水に手をつけると酔い覚ましになる If you put your hands in cold water for a while, it will help sober you up.

よいざめ 酔い覚め ▶酔い覚めの水 water to quench one's thirst with after sobering up. ▶酔い覚めの水を1杯飲んだ After I sobered up, I drank a glass of water to quench my thirst.

よいしょ 圖 【よいしょ】《主に英話》**oops-a-daisy** /ˈwʊpsədèizi/ (⚠ 人がよじ登るのを手伝う際の掛け声) 【えんやら】 **yo-ho** /jòuhóu/ (⚠ 力仕事をするときの掛け声, 「よいと巻けはろ」 **yó-hèave-hó** (⚠ 錨(ˇˇ)などを巻き上げるときの掛け声). ● よいしょと (=体を重そうにいすから立ち上がる lift himself heavily out of a chair;

(さあいくぞと言って) stand out of a chair, saying, "*Well, here goes.*" ▶私たちはよいしょよいしょと言って彼が木に登るのを後押ししてやった We helped him climb the tree, repeating *oops-a-daisy*. (! このように直接的な言い方をする場合は helped him to climb とはしない) ▶彼はよいしょよいしょと言って岩を動かしていた He *was yo-hoing* again and again while (he was) moving the rock.
会話「スーツケースを網棚に上げていただけませんか」「いいですよ、よいしょ」"Would you mind putting my suitcase up on the rack?" "Not at all [《やや書》By all means]. *There you go.*"

── **よいしょする** 動 ●上司をよいしょする(=おだて上げる) *flatter* one's boss.

よいしれる 酔いしれる ●成功に酔いしれる(=陶酔する)《書》*be intoxicated with* [*by*] one's success; *be greatly excited by* one's success.

よいっぱり 宵っ張り〖夜遅くまで起きていること〗sitting [staying] up late at night;〖人〗a night person,《話》a night owl. ▶彼は宵っ張りの朝寝坊だ He keeps late hours. は「夜ふかしをする」の意で,「朝寝坊」は含まない)

よいつぶれる 酔い潰れる get* [be] dead drunk, get [be] blind drunk;《話》get [be] plastered (! be では状態も表す). ●酔いつぶれて意識を失う *drink oneself* unconscious [(人事不省に) into a stupor].

よいどめ 酔い止め (薬) motion sickness drug [pills].

よいどれ 酔いどれ a drunken person; (いつも酔っぱらっている人) a drunkard;《古》a sot.

よいね 宵寝 ─ **宵寝する** 動 go to sleep [(一時的に) take a nap] early in the evening.

よいのくち 宵の口 ▶まだ宵の口だ It's still *early evening*./The evening is still young.

よいのみょうじょう 宵の明星 the evening star.

よいまちぐさ 宵待ち草〖植物〗(月見草) an evening primrose.

よいまつり 宵祭り the eve (of a festival).

よいん 余韻 〖残る音〗a lingering sound; (残響) rev*è*rber*à*tions; 〖残る感覚〗a lingering sensation. ●寺の鐘の余韻 the *reverberations* of a temple bell. ●『第九』演奏終了後の余韻にひたる[を楽しむ] enjoy the *pleasant sensation that lingers on* after Beethoven's No. 9 Symphony

***よう 用** ❶〖用事〗something to do; business; work; an errand; an engagement.

> **使い分け** **something to do** 漠然と「何かをすること」を表す。
> **business** 処理すべき課題や用件を広く表す。私用・公用の両方に用いる。時に用事があってどこかに来る「行く」ことを含意する。
> **work** 主に仕事上の用事を表す。労力を要する義務的な用事であることを含意する。
> **errand** 人などにどこかへ用事を済ませに行くこと,またはその目的を表す。
> **engagement** 主に人と会う約束によってできた用事を表す。

●用を言いつける (仕事を与える) give *work* to 《him》; (あれこれ命じる) order 《him》about [around]. ●これといった用もない街をぶらつく stroll around the streets with *nothing* special *to do*. ●あしたは1日中用がある I *have something* [*some work*] *to do* all day tomorrow./(忙しい) I'm *busy* [《やや書》*engaged*] all day tomorrow. ▶いずれも決まったことなので現在時制を用いる. will を使うと,単なる予想を表す) ▶今日はもう用がない I have *nothing more to do* today./(もう仕事を済ませた) I've done [finished] my *work* today./*I'm done for* today. ▶彼は用があって名古屋に行った He went to Nagoya *on business*./*Business* took him to Nagoya. (! 後の方が堅い言い方) ▶何の用かね? What do you want? (⇒用もない) ▶町に二, 三用がある I have a few *errands* to do in town.

❷〖働き, 使用〗use /júːs/. ●紳士[婦人]用上着 a men's [ladies'] jacket. ●家庭[業務]用コピー機 a copier *for* family [business] *use*. ▶私はもうこの本には用がない I have no (further) *use for* this book. (! 次の方が口語的)/I don't want this book any more [any longer]. (! ×I want this book no more.=不可(やや書》)

❸〖その他の表現〗●用があったら電話をください Call me (up) if you *want* [*need*] anything. ▶彼に用があるのですが(=彼と話したい) I'*d like* [I *want*] *to talk to* him. (! 前の方が丁寧) ▶君にもう用はない(二度とかかわりを持たない) I'll never have anything *to do with* you again./((やや書》*I have nothing to do with you from now on.*) ▶君に用はない(さっさと消えろ) Go about your own business. (! 本来は「自分の仕事に取りかかれ」の意)
会話「ちょっと君に用があるんだ」「何でしょう」"I *want* you a minute." "Yes?" (⇒用例 ❶)

●用が足りる ▶それなら電話で用が足りる(=処理できる)《話》That can *be taken care of* with a phone call.

●用を足す〖仕事をする[済ませる]〗do [finish] one's business [work]; (使いをする) go on [run] errands《*for him*》;〖大小便をする〗《婉曲的》go to the bathroom; (訳) 《婉曲的》relieve oneself. ▶フランス語で用が足せますか Can you make yourself understood in French? (! 「フランス語で相手に言いたいことを伝えることができるか」の意)

●用をなす ▶この車は用をなさない(=役に立たない) This car is *useless* [*of no use*].

***よう 酔う** ❶〖酒に〗get* [be] drunk,《書》get [be] intoxicated. (! be drunk [intoxicated] は「酔っている」という状態を表すことが多い) ●ワインで少し酔う *get a little drunk* [(ほろ酔いになる)《話》*get tipsy*] *on* wine. ●酔った勢いで on a *drunken* [《米》*a drunk*] impulse. ●酔って帰宅する come home *drunk*. ●酔って眠る *drink oneself* to sleep. (! sleep は名詞) ●酔ってけんかになる get into a *drunken* brawl 《*with*》. ●酔って千鳥足で歩く stagger *drunkenly*. ▶彼は酔って車を運転した He drove while (he *was*) *drunk* [*intoxicated*]./(《やや書》(戯言的) He drove *under the influence* (*of alcohol*).

❷〖乗り物に〗●船[車; 飛行機]に酔う get seasick [carsick; airsick]. ▶彼は船に酔わない He never *gets seasick*./He is *a good* (↔a bad) sailor. ▶彼女はひどく車に酔う She *suffers* terribly *from carsickness.*

❸〖うっとりする〗●喜び[成功]に酔っている *be intoxicated with* joy [success]. ▶彼女の華麗なスケーティングが観衆を酔わせた Her fantastic skating *entranced* all the spectators.

よう〖呼びかけ〗hey;〖あいさつ〗hello,《米話》hi /hái/ (⇒こんにちは);〖だれかに〗well done, good; (演者に向かって)《やや古》bravo.

よう 洋 ●洋の東西を問わず whether in the East or the West; everywhere in the world; all over [throughout] the world.

よう 要 ▶要は不断の努力だ The *point* is that [《話》The *point* is,] you should make constant

efforts. (!(1) 後の方が口語的. (2) point の代わりに thing を用いて The *thing* is, you should make constant efforts. のようにもいえる)
● 要を得る ● 要(=要点)を得ている be *to the point*. (⇨要ము)
よう 陽 ● 陰に陽に (⇨陰(%))
よう 癰 『医学』(吹き出物) a carbuncle.

:-よう -様

INDEX

❶ 方法, 仕方　　　　❷ 様子, 有り様
❸ 類似, 例示　　　　❹ 目的
❺ 願望　　　　　　　❻ 指示・依頼の趣旨
❼ その他の表現

❶ 〖方法, 仕方〗 a way, a manner (⇨仕様); how to (do); 〖…のとおりに〗 as 《+節》, 《話》the way 《+節》. ▶物は考え様だよ Everything depends on your *way* of thinking. ▶三者三様の考え方がある Different people have different ways [*manners*] of thinking. ▶この機械はどのように操作するかご存じですか Do you know *how* to operate this machine? ▶このようにしなさい Do *like* this./Do (*in*) this *way*. (!《話》では in はしばしば省略される) ▶教えられたように描きなさい Paint *as* [*the way*] you are taught [told]. ▶ごめんなさいって言ったのよ. それ以外言い様がないじゃないの I've said I'm sorry. What else can I say? 会話 「行こうかな, それともやめようかな」「お好きなように. 決めるのは君なんだから」"Should I go or shouldn't I?" "*As* you like. It's for you to decide." 会話 「彼は辞めるぞって脅したんだよ」「知るもんか. 彼は彼のやりたいように(=やりたいことを)すればいいさ」 "He's threatened to resign." "I couldn't [《米話》could] care less. He can do what he likes." 会話 「その仕事に君を推薦しましょう」「お礼の申し上げようもありません」"I'll recommend you for the job." "Can I ever thank you enough!"

❷ 〖様子, 有り様〗 (思われる) seem, sound, appear; (見たところ) look; 〖まるで…のように〗 as if 《+節》.

使い分け seem 話し手の主観的な判断によって「…のように思える」の意を表す. 主に見た目が判断基準となるが, それに限定されない.
look 見た目からその状態や特徴を判断し,「…のように見える」の意を表す.
appear seem とほぼ同じ意味だが, やや堅い語. しばしばその判断が誤りであることを含意する.

解説 seem, appear の後の to 不定詞には be のほか, know, think などの状態動詞がくる. 動作動詞の場合は完了形にする (⇨第 2 文例). seem の場合は進行形も可: 彼は来月上京するようだ He *seems* to *be going* to Tokyo next month.

▶彼は病気のようだ It *seems* [*appears*] that he is sick. (!《話》では that がしばしば省略される. さらにくだけた言い方では *Seems* he is sick. のように it も省略される)/He *seems* [*appears*] (*to be*) sick. (!It seems [appears] that … より口語的) ▶彼女はその事を知らなかったようだ She doesn't *seem* to have known it./It doesn't *seem* (*that*) she knew it. (!She *seems* not to have known it. や It *seems that* she did*n't* know it. より普通) ▶あの人はあほうだ He *looks* foolish./He *looks* (*like*) a fool. (!(1) 前の方が一般的. (2) like を省略するのは《主に英》) ▶それはよい考えのようだ That *sounds like*《米》[That *sounds*《英》] a good idea. ▶あなたはよく分かっていないようね I don't *think* you quite understand. ▶彼は何でも知っているように話した [話す] He spoke [speaks] *as if* he knew everything. (!as if 節内の内容が主節の動詞が示す時と同じ時のことを表す場合は仮定法過去または《話》直説法過去, それ以前のことを表す場合は仮定法過去完了を用いる: 彼はまるで彼を見たかのように話した [話す] He spoke [speaks] *as if* he *had seen* it.) ▶今夜は雪のようだ It *looks like* snow tonight./It is *likely* to snow tonight./It *looks as if* it were [《やや話》was, 《話》is] going to snow tonight. (!(1) looks の代わりに seems も可. (2)《米話》では It *looks* [It *seems*, *Seems*] *like* it's going to snow tonight. のようにいうことも多い) ▶あれはジムの声のようだ That *sounds like* Jim's voice [Jim]. (!Jim だけでも sound, hear などと連語すると Jim's voice の意になりうる. cf. Can you hear *me*? (私の声 [言うこと] が聞こえますか)) ▶間違えたようです I'm afraid I've made a mistake. (!言いにくいことなどを相手に言わなければならないときの話し手の申し訳ない気持ちを表す) 会話 「彼は渡米するんですか」「そうではないようです」"Is he going to America?" "It *seems* [*appears*] not." (!「そのようです」なら It *seems* [*appears*] so./So it *seems* [*appears*]. ×It seems [appears] so. とはいわない)

❸ 〖類似, 例示〗(種類) a kind, a sort (⇨種類); (…のような) like …; (たとえば…のような) such as …; (…のように) as 《+節》.

① 〖…(の)ような〗 ● バナナやパパイヤのような熱帯果実 tropical fruits *such as* [*like*] bananas and papayas; *such* tropical fruits *as* bananas and papayas. (!like … より such (…) as の方が大げさな表現) ●このような本 (1 種類) books *of this kind* [*sórt*] (this kind を強調した言い方); thèse kind of books; *this kind of* book [books] (!堅い表現); (2 種類以上) thèse kinds of books. ▶どのような動物でしたか What *kind* [*sort*] *of* animal was it? (!通例 *an* animal とはしない) ▶彼は我々を裏切るような男ではない He is not *the kind* [*sort*] *of* (×a) man to betray us./He is the last (man) *to* betray us. (!the last man は「最も…しそうにない男」の意) ▶その料理はカレーのようなものです. ただそれほど辛くない The dish is *a kind of* curry, except (that) it is not particularly hot. (!except (that) は「…ということを除いて」の意. ややくだけた言い方に用いられる) ▶ぼくは彼のような強いボクサーになりたい I want to be a strong boxer *like* him. (!次例より口語的)/I want to be *such* a [×a *such*] strong boxer *as* he [《話》him]. ▶彼は近いうちに東京へ行くようなことを言っていた He said something *like* going (up) to Tokyo soon. ▶落ち着いて手紙が書けるような喫茶店はないでしょうか Is there a tearoom where you can settle down to write a letter? (!一般の人を表す you を用いた修飾節によって「…のような」の意を含ませる言い方) ▶この本は子供でも読めるようなやさしい英語で書かれている This book is written in *such* easy English *as* even children can read it. (!この as は関係代名詞) ▶それは金をどぶに捨てるようなものだ That is *like* [*a case of*] throwing money down the drain. 会話「私の新しいレインコートいいと思う?」「ええ, 私もそんなようなのを持ってるよ」"Do you like my new raincoat?" "Yes, I've got one *like* that."

② 〖…(の)ように〗 ● いつものように *as usual*. ● ご存じのように *as* you know. ● 湯水のように金を遣う spend money *like* water. ▶ちょうどミツバチがみつを好むようにフランス人はフランスワインを好む French people love their wine (*just*) *as* [《話》*like*] bees love honey./《書》(*Just*) *as* bees love honey, so French people love their wine. ▶彼が言ったようにこのことはまだ定説になっていない *As* 《話》*Just like*] he said, this view is not accepted yet. (**!** as 節を主節の後へ置くと「彼は定説になっていると言ったが，そうはなっていない」の意ともとれないないなるので注意) ▶彼らはアリのように働いている They are working *like* (so many) ants. ▶彼はウサギのように臆病に(らく)な He was (as) timid *as* a rabbit. ▶彼はもう昔のように強くない He is no longer *as* strong *as* he was./He isn't *as* [*so*] strong *as* he used to be.

❹［目的］to 〈*do*〉; in order to 〈*do*〉; so as to 〈*do*〉《口語》; so that 《+節》. (⇨ため❶) ● 後の二つは「…のために」を強調する言い方。（⇨ため❶）▶言う事を理解してもらえるよう彼はゆっくり話した He spoke slowly (*in order* [*so as*]) to make himself understood./He spoke slowly *so that* [《話》*so*, 《書》*in order that*] he *could* make himself understood. (**!** could の代わりに would, 《書》might も可) ▶彼に会わないように遠回りをした I took a roundabout way *so as* [*in order*] *not to* see him. ▶この場合は以来 as [in order] の省略は不可)/I took a roundabout way (*so as* [*in order*]) to avoid seeing him./I took a roundabout way *so* (*that*) I *would* [《英》*should*, 《書》*might*, ×*could*) not see him.

《話》「見て，ママ，一番てっぺんよ」「落ちないように(気をつけて)ね」"Look, Mommy. I'm right at the top." "Be careful *not to* fall. (**!** ×in order [×so as] not to fall cannot 用いない)/*Mind* (*that*) you don't fall." (**!** 後の方は通例命令文で用いられる)

《話》「どうしてごみを玄関に置いておくの」「ごみを出し忘れないようによ」"Why is the garbage left at the front door?" "*So* (*that*) I remember to take it out." (**!** That's so... の省略文で，( )内の that は《話》ではしばしば省略される)

❺［願望］▶長生きされますように *May* you live a long life! ▶彼が無事そこへ到着するよう神に祈った I prayed to God that he *might* arrive there safe(ly).

❻［指示・依頼の趣旨］▶彼に連絡しておくように《軽い命令》*Be sure to* contact him. ▶母は早寝早起きをするよう言った My mother told me to keep regular [《今はまれ》early] hours.

❼［その他の表現］▶泳げるようになる(= 習得する) *learn to* swim. (**!** learn how to swim は「泳ぎ方を学ぶ」の意なようになるかどうか分からない) ▶それが分かるようになる *come to* [×become to] understand it. ▶どうして彼を知るようになったの How did you *get to* know him?

＊—よう ❶［意志］will; (…しようとする) try 〈*to do*〉. ▶今度来るときはフランス人形を持って来てあげよう I *will* bring you a French doll next time I come here. ▶彼に君の手伝いをさせよう I *will* have him [get him to] help you. (⇨させる) ▶彼はその不快な思い出を忘れようとした He *tried to* forget the uncomfortable memory.

❷［勧誘］Let's .... / How [What] about ...? / Why not 〈*do*〉? / What do you say to 〈*doing*〉? (**!** いずれも口語的な表現) ▶放課後テニスをしよう *Let's* play tennis after school./*How* [*What*] about playing tennis after school? ▶この辺で昼食でもしようか *Let's* have lunch near here, *shall we* [《話》*right*, 《話》*OK*]?

ようありがお 用あり顔 ▶彼は何か用あり顔である He seems to have something he wants to talk with me [he wants me to do for him].

‡ようい 用意 图 ［準備］preparation(s) 《*for*》(**!** 個々

の準備は ～s); arrangements 《*for*》. (⇨準備) ● 5人分の夕食の用意 the *preparation* of dinner *for* five people. ▶朝食［お風呂］の用意ができました Breakfast [Your bath] *is ready*. ▶あと 30 分で(出かける)用意ができます I can *be ready* (*to go*) in half an [《米》a half] hour. ▶(あなたに)車の用意(=手配)がしてあります I *have arranged* a car (*for* you). (⇨手配) ▶《a car を主語に受身で》我々はいつでもその質問に答える(心の)用意がある We *are* always *prepared* to answer the question [*for* the question]. ▶(競走で)位置について！用意！どん！On your mark(s), *get set, go*!/《英》*Ready, steady, go*!

《会話》「では，第 1 問を出しますが用意はいいですか」「え，用意は万全よ」"Well, *are* you *ready for* your first question?" "As *ready* as I'll ever be./I'm all *set*."

● 用意周到 用意周到な(= 非常に注意深い)計画を立てる make a very *careful* plan.

—— 用意(を)する 動 prepare (for ...), get (...) ready 《*for*》(**!** 後の方が口語的); (手配する) arrange. ● 昼食の用意をする *prepare* lunch; *get* lunch *ready*. ▶月曜までにその金を用意しなければならない I have to *get* the money *ready* [*find* the money] by Monday. ▶傘を用意して(= 持って)行った[来た]方がいいですよ It would be better for you to *take* [*bring*] an umbrella (with you). (**!** with you がある方が「携帯する」の意が強い)

＊ようい 容易 —— 容易な 形 easy (-sier; -siest); ［簡単な］simple (-ler; -lest). ● 容易な仕事 an *easy* task. ● 容易ならぬ(= 重大な)事柄 a *serious* [a *grave*] matter. ▶そのテストは容易だった The test was *easy* [*simple*]. ▶中国語に熟達するのは容易なことではない It's not *easy* [no *easy* matter] to master Chinese. ▶戦争を始めるのは容易だが，終わらせるのは難しい War is easy to start, but difficult to end.

—— 容易に 副 easily, with ease; (難なく) without difficulty [trouble]; (すぐに) readily. ▶君だって容易にその問題に答えられる You can *easily* [*readily*] answer the question. ▶それで事が容易になった It made the matter *easy* [*easier*]./《書》It *facilitated* the matter. ▶この窓は容易に(= どうしても)開かない This window will not open. (**!** will は習性を表す) / (拒む) This window *refuses to* open.

ようイオン 陽イオン 〔物理〕 a positive ion /áiən/.

ようい く 養育 ❷ —— upbringing.

—— 養育する 動 bring ... up; 《主に米》 raise. ▶私はおばに養育された I *was brought up* [*was raised*] by my aunt.

● 養育費 the expense of bringing up a child.

よういん 要因 a factor; (原因) (a) cause. ● 失敗の主要因 a major [a chief] *factor in* the failure; the main [principal] *cause of* the failure.

よういん 要員 personnel. (**!** 複数扱い) ● 保安要員 security *personnel*. ● 編集要員(= 部員)募集《広告》Editorial staffers invited. ▶彼は今シーズンは代打要員に回された He was put to playing as a pinch-hitter this season.

よううん 妖雲 an ominous cloud.

ようえい 揺曳 ▶朝霧が揺曳する中で in the morning mist that *is hanging around*. ▶水平線を揺曳する船の煙 the *trailing* smoke of a ship over the horizon.

ようえき 用益 (使用と収益) use and profit.

● 用益権 〔法律〕usufruct. ● 用益権者 〔法律〕usufructuary. ● 用益物権 〔法律〕usufructuary rights.

ようえき 葉腋 〖植物〗 an axil.
ようえき 溶液 a solution.
ようえん 妖艶 ── 妖艶な 形 bewitching; glamorous.
ようおん 拗音 〖言語〗 a contracted sound (in Japanese).
ようか 八日 ●8日間 for *eight* days. ●5月8日に on May 8(*th*). (❗*th* の発音は /éiθ/) (⇨日付)
ようか 沃化 〖化学〗 iodation /àiədéiʃən/.
● 沃化亜鉛 zinc iodide /àiədàid/. ● 沃化銀 silver iodide. ● 沃化物 (an) iodide.
ようか 養家 (養子縁組を正式にした) an adoptive family; (法的手続きを経ていない) a foster family. ● 養家の父(=養父) an adoptive [a foster] father.
ようが 洋画 〖西洋画〗 a Western [a European] painting; (油絵) an oil painting. 〖外国映画〗 a foreign movie [film]. ● 洋画家 an artist of Western painting; an oil painter.
ようが 陽画 a positive (↔a negative) (picture).
ようかい 妖怪 〖幽霊〗 a ghost; 〖鬼〗 a goblin; 〖怪物〗 a monster.
ようかい 容喙 ── 容喙する 動 meddle 《*in* one's son's business》. (⇨口出し)
ようかい 溶解 名 〖物理・化学〗 dissolution; melting.
── 溶解する 動 (液体の中へ) dissolve; (熱で) melt. (⇨溶ける, 溶かす) ● 塩は水に溶解する Salt *dissolves* in water.
ようがい 要害 〖要塞(さい)〗 a fort; (大きい) a fortress; [とりで] a stronghold. ● 要害堅固な(=強固に要塞化した)城 (やぐ書) a *strongly fortified* (難攻不落の) an *impregnable*] castle.
ようかいご 要介護 ● 要介護者 a person requiring long-term care. ● 要介護認定 long-term care requirement certification. ● 要介護認定を受ける be certified as requiring long-term care.
ようがく 洋学 Western [European] learning (that was introduced in the Edo period).
ようがく 洋楽 Western [European] music.
ようがさ 洋傘 an umbrella.
ようがし 洋菓子 a (Western-style) cake (❗切り分けた一片は a piece of cake); (総称) Western-style confectionery. (⇨菓子)
ようかん 羊羹 *yokan*, sweetened bean jelly.
ようかん 洋館 a Western-style house.
ようがん 溶岩 lava. ● 溶岩が火山から流出した *Lava* flowed forth from the volcano./The volcano spouted [spewed forth] *lava*.
● 溶岩ドーム a lava dome. ● 溶岩流 a lava flow; a stream of lava.
ようき 妖気 ● 妖気のただよう (薄気味悪い) weird /wíərd/; uncanny; (この世のものとは思えない) unearthly (*beauty*).
ようき 容器 a container. (⇨器, 入れ物)
ようき 陽気 名 〖天気〗 weather; 〖時候〗 a season. ● 春らしい陽気になった The *weather* has become springlike. ● 陽気のせいでついこっくりが居眠りしてしまった Because of *warm weather* I nodded off in spite of myself.
── 陽気な 形 cheerful; (活気があって) lively; (笑い興じて) merry. ● 陽気な人 a *cheerful* person. ● 陽気な酒つき (have) *cheerful* looks. ● 陽気なおしゃべり *lively* chatter. ● 激しい労働にもかかわらず人々はとても陽気な People are very *cheerful* in spite of the heavy labor. ● その楽団は陽気な音楽を演奏した The band played *lively* music.
── 陽気に 副 cheerfully; merrily; lively. ● 陽気に笑う laugh *merrily*; have a *merry* laugh. ● 人々

はパーティーで陽気に歌っていた People were singing *cheerfully* [*merrily*] at the party.
ようぎ 容疑 (a) suspicion; (罪名) a charge. ● 窃盗の容疑で彼を逮捕する arrest him *on suspicion of* [*on a charge of, for*] theft. ● 彼に殺人の容疑をかける *suspect* him *of* murder. ● 彼は盗みの容疑がかかっている He *is suspected* [*under suspicion*] *of* stealing. ● 彼の証言で私の容疑は晴れた His testimony cleared me *of* [*from*] *suspicion*.
● 容疑者 a suspect, a suspected person. ● 殺人容疑者 a murder *suspect*; a *suspected* murderer; the alleged *murderer*.
ようきひ 楊貴妃 〖唐の玄宗の妃〗 Yang Kuei-fei /jáːŋ gwéifeɪ/, Yang Guifei /-gwíːfeɪ/.
*****ようきゅう** 要求 名 a demand 《*for*; *that* 節》; a claim; (要請) a request. ● 賃上げ要求 (make) a *demand for* higher wages. (⇨動) ● 彼の要求を満たす[しりぞける] meet [reject] his *demand* [*request*]. ● 彼に無理な要求をする *ask* too much *of* him.
── 要求する 動 demand 《*to* do; *that* 節》; claim; require; ask.

| 使い分け | **demand** 謝罪や説明, また何らかの行為を強く要求することを表す. **claim** 主に金銭の支払いを当然の権利として要求することを表す. **require** 規則や作業の上で必要となるものを要求することを表す. **ask** 丁寧に要求することを表す.「お願いする」という含意があり, 時に「あてにする」ことを表す. |

● (彼に)説明を要求する *demand* an explanation 《*from* [*of*, ˣ*to*] him》. ● 昇給を要求する *demand* a pay raise; *make* [*put in*] *a claim for* a pay raise; *ask for* a pay raise. ● お金の返済を彼に要求した I *demanded that he* (*should*) *pay* the money back. (❗ (1) ˣI *demanded* him *to* pay the money back. とはいえない. (2) 受身形は It *was demanded that he* (*should*) *pay* the money back. で, ˣHe *was demanded to* pay ... は不可) ● 彼女は会社に5,000 ドルの損害賠償を要求した She *claimed* 5,000 dollars (in) damages [damages of 5,000 dollars] against the company. ● 学校は学生に制服着用を要求した The school *required* the students *to* wear uniforms./The school *required that* the students (《主に英》 should) wear uniforms. ● 我々の肉体は常に水分を要求する(= 必要とする) Our body always *needs* water.
● 要求払い 〖経済〗 payment on demand.
ようきゅう 洋弓 (⇨アーチェリー)
ようぎょ 幼魚 (⇨稚魚)
ようぎょ 養魚 fish breeding; pisciculture.
● 養魚池 a bréeding pònd; a cúlture pònd. ● 養魚場 a físh fàrm. ● 養魚槽 a fish-breeding tank.
ようきょう 容共 acceptance of communism.
● 容共派 a pro-communist group [faction].
ようぎょう 窯業 the ceramics industry.
ようきょく 陽極 〖物理〗 the anode /ǽnoud/ (↔cathode); the positive (↔negative) pole.
ようきょく 謡曲 a *No*(*h*) chant [song].
ようぎん 洋銀 German silver, nickel silver.
ようぐ 用具 (道具) a tool, an implement (❗通例 tool より大きい); (装備) 〖集合的〗 equipment; (装備一式) an outfit. ● 園芸用具 gárden tòols. ● 農業用具 fárm *implements*. (❗plow (すき)など) ● スキー用具 skíing *equipment*; a skíing *òutfit*. ● 筆

記用具 writing *matèrials*.
ようくん 幼君 a young lord.
ようけい 養鶏 poultry farming [raising, breeding].
● 養鶏家 a póultry [a chícken] fàrmer [ràiser, brèeder]. ● 養鶏場 a póultry [a chícken] fàrm.
ようげき 要撃 ━ 要撃する 動 lie in ambush /ǽmbuʃ/ for the enemy; ambush. ▶我が軍は敵を背後から要撃した We *ambushed* the enemy from behind.
ようけつ 要訣 the crucial point.
ようけつ 溶血 图 『医学』hemolysis.
━ 溶血性の 形 hemolytic.
● 溶血性貧血 hemolytic anemia.
ようけん 用件 business. (⇨用❶)▶用件に入りましょう Let's get down to *business*. ▶留守中に電話が鳴ったら用件(=伝言)を聞いておいてください If the phone rings while I'm gone, take (↔leave) a *message*. (⇨会話))▶兄は留守です.ご用件を承っておきましょうか My brother is not in. Would you like to leave (↔take) a message (with him)? ▶ご用件は? (店員が客などに) What can I do for you?/Can [May] I help you?/(戸口に来た人に) What do you want?/What's your business here?/(電話を取り次ぐときに) May I ask what it is about?/What are you calling about?
会話「お隣の奥さんがお見えです」「そう,用件を聞いておいてくれ」"It's Mrs. Abe from next door." "Well, find out *what she wants*." **❶**(1)「奥さん」と言わずに親密の度合いにより姓をいったり名をいったりする. (2) find out … は「(何の用なのか)聞き出してくれ」で第2例の take a message とばば同意)
ようけん 洋犬 a European breed of dog.
ようけん 要件 『必要条件』a necessary [an essential] condition;(資格などの) a requirement (しばしば複数形で);『大事な用事』important business. ● 要件を満たす satisfy [meet] the *necessary conditions* [*requirements*] (*for*).
ようげん 用言 『文法』(説明的に) a technical term to denote verbs, adjectives, and adjectival verbs collectively in Japanese grammar.
ようげん 揚言 ━ 揚言する 動 speak boastfully (*of*); boast (*of, that* 節);(公言する) declare 《*that* 節》.
ようこ『*杳子*』*Yoko*. (參)古井由吉の小説)
ようご 用語 『専門語』a term;《集合的》『書』(a) terminology. (**❶** 一つ一つは [C];『言葉遣い』language. (⇨言葉) ● 法律用語 legal *terms* [*terminology*]; the *terms* [*terminology*] of law. ● 専門用語 technical *terms*. ● 近松の用語 Chikamatsu's *language*. ● 難しい用語を使う use difficult *terms* [*words*]. ▶これを医学用語で何と言いますか What is the medical *term for* this?
ようご 養護 (看護) nursing;(世話) care.
● 養護学級 a class for disabled [handicapped] children. ● 養護学校 a school for disabled [handicapped] children. ● 養護教諭 a school nurse. ● 養護施設 a nursing institution. ● 養護老人ホーム a nursing home (for the aged).
ようご 擁護 图『擁護』defense;『支持』support;『保護』protection.
━ 擁護する 動 ▶彼の意見を擁護する発言をする speak *in defense* [*support*] *of* his opinion. ▶憲法を擁護する *defend* the constitution. ▶人権を擁護する *defend* [*protect*] human rights.
ようこう 洋行 ━ 洋行する 動 go overseas [abroad]; travel overseas [abroad]. ▶洋行帰り a person who has (just) returned from abroad; a returnee from abroad.
ようこう 要項 『必要な事項』important [essential] points;『指針』guidelines.
ようこう 要綱 『重要事項の大要』an outline [要点] the gist] of essential points;『趣意書』a prospéctus. ▶講演の要綱 an *outline* [the *main points*] of one's speech.
ようこう 陽光 sun, sunshine. ▶真夏の陽光 summer's *sun*; hot [glaring] *sunshine* in the height of summer.
ようこうろ 溶鉱炉 a blast furnace.
ようこそ ▶ようこそと手を振る give 《him》a *welcoming* wave. ▶ようこそ日本へ *Welcome* to Japan. ▶ようこそ皆さん *Welcome*, friends! ▶ようこそいらっしゃいました It's *really* [*so*] *nice* of you to come [to have come]. (**❶** to come の方が普通/We're delighted to have you here. (**❶**単に (It's) nice [good] to meet [see] you. や, Thank you so much for coming./Thank you for joining us./I'm glad you could come [make it]. などの方が日常的な言い方)
ようさい 洋菜 Western vegetables introduced to Japan.
ようさい 洋裁 dressmaking. ▶洋裁(=服の縫い方)を教えてくれますか Can you teach me 《*how*》 *to sew a dress*?
● 洋裁学校 a dréssmaking schòol. ● 洋裁師(婦人服の仕立屋) a dressmaker;(男物の) a tailor. ● 洋裁店 a dressmaker's (shop).
ようさい 要塞 a fort;(大規模な) a fortress.
ようざい 用材 『材木』《米》lumber,《英》timber;『材料』materials. ● 建築用材 bùilding *matèrials*.
ようざい 溶剤 (a) sólvent.
ようさいるい 葉菜類 leafy [green] vegetables.
ようさん 葉酸 『生化学』folic acid.
ようさん 養蚕 sericulture. ● 養蚕をする《主に米》raise [《英》keep, rear] silkworms.
● 養蚕家 a sericulturist. ● 養蚕業 the sericultural industry.
ようし 用紙 (a) paper;(書式が印刷された) a form,《主に米》a blank. ● 申し込み用紙 an applicátion fòrm [blànk]. ● 印刷用紙 printing *paper*. ● 新聞(印刷)用紙 newsprint. ● 解答用紙 an ánswer shèet. ● 試験用紙 (問題が印刷されたもの) a *paper*, an exam(ination) *paper*. ● 投票用紙 a ballot.
ようし 用紙 (和紙と対比して) Western paper.
ようし 要旨 『要点』the (main) point;『骨子』the gist /dʒist/;『要約』a summary;『概要』an outline. ▶彼の話の要旨を述べる give the *main points* [the *gist*] of what he said.
ようし 容姿 『容姿』one's looks;『姿』a figure. ● 容姿端麗な女性 a *good-looking* woman; a woman with a *nice* [*a good, a lovely*] *figure*. (⇨スタイル)
ようし 陽子 『物理』a proton.
ようし 養子 an adopted child [son] (《復》children); 『婿養子』a son-in-law (《復》 sons-, 《英語》 ~s). ● その男の子を養子にする *adopt* the boy. ▶その家の養子になる(子供が) *be adopted* into the family;(引き渡される) be handed over to the adopting parents;(婿になる) marry an heiress. (⇨婿)
● 養子縁組み (an) adoption.
:**ようじ** 用事 『するべき事』things to do;『仕事』business;『人に頼まれた』an errand (⇨使い ❶);『会合の約束』an engagement. (⇨用 ❶) ▶今日は用事がたくさんある have a lot of *things to do* today. ▶二, 三用事[自分の用事]を済ませてくるよ I'll go and take

ようじ care of a few *things* [my *business*]. ▶あなたは京都へ用事で行ったのですか，それとも遊びに行ったのか Did you go to Kyoto *on business* or for pleasure?

ようじ 幼児 an infant, a little [a small] child (複 children); [よちよち歩きの] a toddler.
●**幼児期** childhood. ●**幼児教育** preschool education. ●**幼児語** (赤ちゃん言葉) baby talk. ●**幼児自閉症** 〖医学〗 infantile autism. ●**幼児性** infantile. ●**幼児服** children's clothes.

ようじ 幼時 (one's) infancy, (early) childhood. (⇨幼年)

ようじ 用字 (説明的に) an individual's characteristic use of Chinese characters and *Kana* in writing ▶一部の学者は最近の用字用語の混乱を嘆いている Some scholars regret the confused state of [the lack of integrity in] today's Japanese writing.

ようじ 楊枝 (つまようじ) a toothpick. ●ようじを使う pick one's teeth; use a *toothpick*.

ようしき 洋式 (a) Western style. ●洋式の便所 a *Western-style* toilet.

ようしき 様式 图 ●生活様式(=の仕方) one's *way* [(流儀) *mode*, (習慣) *manner*] of life; one's lifestyle. ●古典的な建築様式 classic *styles* of architecture.
── **様式化する** 動 (やや書) stylize.

ようしつ 洋室 a Western-style room.

ようしゃ 容赦 图 ❶〖許し〗forgiveness; pardon. (⇨許し) ▶その事はもはや容赦できない(=我慢できない) I can't *put up with* [*tolerate*] it any longer. (❗前の方が口語的) ▶バーゲン商品のお取り替えはご容赦願います Goods bought on sale [(英) *on offer*] cannot be exchanged.
❷〖手加減〗●容赦なく(=慈悲をかけることなく)彼を罰する punish him *without mercy* [*mercilessly*]. ●情け容赦のない人 a *merciless* [(冷酷な) a *relentless*] person.
── **容赦する** 動 (許す) forgive, pardon; (寛容を示す) tolerate; (大目に見る) overlook. (⇨許す❷) ▶彼は敵に容赦しない He shows no *mercy* [(寛大さ)《書》 *leniency*] to his enemies.

ようじゃく 幼弱 ●幼弱な子 an infant [a child] with a weak constitution.

ようしゅ 洋酒 Western [foreign] liquors.

ようしゅ 洋種 a foreign species 《*of* azalea》.

ようしゅつ 溶出 图 〖化学〗 elution. ── **溶出する** 動 elute.

ようじゅつ 妖術 magic; sorcery; (魔女の) witchcraft. ●妖術をかける practice [work, use] *magic* 《*on* him》.
●**妖術師** a magician; (男) a sorcerer, (女) a sorceress; (男) a wizard, (女) a witch.

ようしゅん 陽春 spring; (陽気のいい) a balmy spring.

ようしょ 洋書 (外国の本) a foreign book; (西洋の本) a Western book.

ようしょ 要所 〖重要な場所〗a key position; (軍事上の) a strategic point; 〖重要な点〗 a key point. ●要所要所に at *key points*. ●要所を固める fortify *strategic points*.

ようじょ 幼女 a little girl.

ようじょ 養女 an adopted daughter, a foster-daughter. (⇨養子)

ようしょう 幼少 (幼年時代) infancy. ●幼少の頃は one's *infancy* [early childhood]; when one is very young (❗前の方が口語的)

ようしょう 要衝 (重要地点) an important point; (軍事上の) a point [a place] of strategic impor-

tance.

ようじょう 洋上 ●洋上を漂う小舟 a boat drifting *on the ocean* [*sea*].

ようじょう 養生 ●養生のために for one's health; (病後の保養のために) for (one's) *recuperation*, to recuperate. (⇨保養)
── **養生する** (体を大事にする) take care of oneself [one's health]; (病気から回復する) 《書》 recuperate /rik(j)úːpəréit/.

ようしょく 洋食 Western food [dishes]. ●洋食の食べ方 Western table manners.
●**洋食店** a Western food [Western-style] restaurant.

ようしょく 要職 an important post [position]. ●その会社の要職にある hold an *important post* [*position*] in the company.

ようしょく 容色 (美貌) good looks; beauty. ●容色が衰える lose one's *good looks* [*beauty*].

ようしょく 養殖 (魚・貝などの) culture; farming. ●カキの養殖 the *culture* of oysters; oyster *farming* [*culture*]. ●真珠の養殖場 a pearl *fàrm*.
── **養殖する** 動 (育てる) raise; cultivate; farm; (繁殖させる) breed.
●**養殖魚** farm-raised fish. ●**養殖真珠** a cultured pearl.

ようしょっき 洋食器 《集合的》 (Western-style) tableware.

ようしん 痒疹 〖医学〗 prurigo /pruərάigou/ (複 -s).

＊**ようじん 用心** 图 〖注意〗care, caution (⇨注意); 〖警戒〗 (a) precaution. ●用心深い人に医者に診てもらいなさい See a doctor *as a precaution* [(念のため) *just in case*]. ●我が家では用心のために犬を飼っています We have [(主に英) keep] a dog for *protection* [(泥棒よけとして) as a *protection* against thieves].
── **用心(を)する** 動 take＊ care 《*of*; *to* do; *that* 節》, be careful 《*of*, *about*; *to* do; *that* 節》; be cautious 《*of*; *to* do; 〖警戒する〗 take precautions 《*against*》. ●火の用心をする *take precautions against* fire. ▶用心して通りを渡りなさい Cross the street *with care* [*caution*]. /*Be careful* when you cross the street. ▶道路が凍っているので転ばないように用心しなさい Since the roads are icy, *take care* [*be careful*] not to slip. /Since the roads are icy, *take care* (*that*) you don't slip. (❗ that 節中に未来を表す助動詞を用いない) ▶用心しろ (*Be*) *careful*!/*Take care*!/(古) *Have a care*! ▶満員バスの中ではすりに用心しなさい *Look* [*Watch*] *out for* pickpockets in crowded buses. (❗ 掲示などではしばしば *Beware of* pickpockets .... とする)

ようじん 要人 a very important person; a VIP /víːaipíː/ 《複 VIPs》.

ようじんぶかい 用心深い 形 careful, cautious. (⇨注意深い) ▶彼女はとても用心深いので寝る前に必ずドアを確かめる She is very *careful* [*cautious*] and never fails to check the door before she goes to bed.
── **用心深く** 副 carefully, cautiously. ▶私は用心深くその動物に近づいた I approached the animal *cautiously*.

ようじんぼう 用心棒 a bodyguard; a security guard; (ナイトクラブなどの) a bouncer 《*at* a bar》.

＊**ようす 様子**
WORD CHOICE 様子
look 人や物の外観・外見・風貌のこと．特に人の場合は特定の表情や目つきを含意する．▶君の様子から見ると，昨夜は飲みに行ったようだね From the *look* of you, I'd say that you were out drinking last night.

ようず

appearance 人や物の外観・外見のこと. しばしば内面と異なる見せ掛けとしての外面を含意する. ●この様子から判断すると judging by the *appearances*.
air 人や物の外見・雰囲気・態度のこと. 通例改まった文脈で用いる. ●ほっとした様子で with an *air* of relief.

❶ [外見, 模様] a look (**!** しばしば複数形で); (an) appearance; an air. ●がっかりした様子で with a *look* [an *air*] of disappointment; with a disappointed *look* [*air*]. ●その建物の様子から見て by [from] the *appearance* [*look*(s)] of the building. ●みすぼらしい様子の男 a poor-*looking* man. (⇨ような, 風采(ﾌｳｻｲ)) ●彼は健康がすぐれない様子だ He *looks* in poor health./He *seems* [*appears*] (to be) in poor health. (**!** look, seem, appear の違いは ⇨ よう❷)) ●彼は非常に興奮した様子で戻って来た He returned, *looking* very excited.
会話「トムはどんな様子だった?」「相変わらずだったよ」"How [×What] *was* Tom *looking*?" "Just the same as he always does." **!** look は通例進行形は不可だが, 一時的な様子についいう場合は可)

❷ [状態, 情勢] a state; a situation; (a) condition (⇨状態); [一般事情] things. ●様子を探る inquire into the state of *things*; see how *things* go. (**!** 後の方が口語的) ●この様子(=情勢)では当分問題は解決しそうにない Under the present *situation* [*conditions*] the problem is unlikely to be solved for the time being. ●町の様子はどうだ? How do *things* go in the town?/What's it *like* in the town? ●赤ん坊の様子がおかしい(=具合が悪い) There's *something* wrong [*Something* is wrong] with the baby. ●君の様子を見に来たよ I've come to see *how you are getting along* [*on*]. ▶しばらく様子を見よう(=静観しよう) Let's *wait and see* [×wait to see] for some time.

❸ [態度] a manner; (ふるまい) behavior. ●親しげな様子で in a friendly *manner*. ▶このごろ彼は様子が変だ These days his *behavior* is strange [unusual]./These days he is strange [unusual] in his *behavior*.

❹ [兆候, 気配] a sign; 《やや書》(an) indication. ●少しも恐れる様子はなく without any *signs* of fear. (**!**「少しも恐れる様子はない」は show no *sign*(s) of fear) ●その家には人の住んでいる様子はない There is no *sign* [are no *signs*] of people living in [(人の)life at] the house. ▶彼は疲れていたがそんな様子は見せなかった Though he was tired, he gave no *indication*.

ようず 要図 〔地図〕a rough map; 〔図面〕a (rough) sketch.
ようすい 用水 〔飲料用〕city water; 〔灌漑(ｶﾝｶﾞｲ)用〕water for irrigation, irrigation water; 〔消火用〕water for fire fighting, fire-fighting water. ●用水池 a reservoir /rézərvwùːr/. ●用水路 an irrigation channel [canal, ditch].
ようすい 羊水 [解剖] amniotic fluid; one's waters. ●羊水過多症 [医学] polyhydramnios.
ようすい 揚水 ── 揚水する 動 pump up water. ●揚水ポンプ a wáter pùmp; 〔発電所の〕a stórage pùmp.
ようすこう 揚子江 [中国の川] the Yangtze /jǽŋtsi/ River. [参考] 正式名は長江 (⇨長江))
ようずみ 用済み ●ご使用済みの本はお返しください Please return the books when you *have finished* [*have done*, 《話》 *are through*] *with* them. ▶あの男はもう用済みだ(=必要じゃない) We *don't need* him *any more*./He is *no longer useful* to us.
*ようする 要する ❶ [必要とする] need, 《主に英》

ようせき

want, 《やや書》 require; (努力などを) 《やや書》 demand. ●生産に要する労力 the labor *required for* [*involved in*] the production. ▶その資料は再検討を要する We *need to* [×*need*, しなければならない *have to*] check the data again./《事が主語》される必要がある) The data *need* [*want*, *require*] checking again./The data *need to be* checked again. ▶彼は健康上少し休養を要する He *needs* (to take) [*requires*] a little rest for his health./His health *requires* [×*needs*] *that* he 《主に英》 should) take a little rest. (**!** He *should* take a little rest for his health. (休養を取るべきだの)のようにいうことも多い)

❷ [時間を] take*; [金を] cost*. (⇨掛(ｶ)かる❾, 要(ｲ)る❷) ▶病気が回復するにはしばらく時間を要するでしょう It will *take* time to recover from the sickness.
ようする 擁する ❶ [抱きかかえる] embrace; hug (-gg-); hold* in one's arms.
❷ [勢力下に持つ] (統率する) lead*; command; (雇用する) employ. ●社員4万人を擁する大企業 a large company *with* 40,000 employees; a large company which *employs* 40,000 people.
❸ [持つ] have; (所有する)〈書〉 possess. ●巨富を擁する have 〈書〉 *possess*] a colossal fortune; *be in possession of* enormous fortune.
❹ [支える] ●幼君を擁する *back up* [*support*] a young lord.
ようするに 要するに [短く言えば] in short; to make 《米》 [cut 〈英〉] a long story short; [〈書〉] to sum up. ▶要するに彼はすぐれた経営者なのです *In short* [*In a word*, *In brief*, *To sum up*], he is an excellent manager. ▶要するに(=てっとり早く言えば)彼はじゃまされたくなかったのだ〔話〕 *The long and short of it is*, he didn't want to be disturbed.
ようせい 幼生 (幼虫・オタマジャクシなど) a larva.
ようせい 妖精 a fairy; 〔小妖精〕an elf (ꝏelves).
ようせい 要請 图 (a) request 《*for*; *that*節》. ▶彼女〔社長〕の要請でそこへ行った I went there *at her request* [*at the request of the president*]. ▶市民は市長の寄付要請に応じた〔を拒んだ〕 The citizens agreed to [rejected] the mayor's *request for* contribution.
── 要請する 動 make* a request 《*for*》, 《やや書》 request, 《やや書》 call on 《*for*, *to do*》; (頼む) ask. ●救助を繰り返し要請する *make* repeated *requests for* help. ▶彼に市長への立候補を要請した We *requested* [*called on*, *asked*] him to run for mayor. ▶イラン政府は日本に経済援助を要請した The Iranian Government *made a request to* [*called on*] the Japanese Government *for* economic aid. ▶〔Government は今は単独では *the* をつけないのが普通だが, このような「…政府」という場合は必ず *the* をつける)
ようせい 陽性 ── 陽性の 形 (性格が) cheerful; (反応が) positive (↔negative). ▶彼のツベルクリン反応は陽性だった His tuberculin reaction proved *positive*. ●陽性反応 a positive reaction. ●禁止薬物使用の検査で陽性反応が出る test *positive for* doping.
ようせい 養成 图 training 《*of*》.
── 養成する 動 (技術者などを) train; (才能・品性などを) cultivate, develop. (⇨養う)) ●看護師を養成する *train* nurses. ●専門的知識を養成する *cultivate* [*develop*] a technical knowledge. ●養成学校 a tráining schòol 《*for*》.
ようせき 容積 (容量) (a) capacity; (体積) a volume. ▶この缶は4リットルの容積がある This can

ようせつ 夭折 ― **夭折する** 動 die prematurely [young]; die a premature [an untimely] death. (⇨若死に、早死に)

ようせつ 溶接 welding. ● 折れたパイプを溶接する weld a broken pipe.
● 溶接機 a wélding machìne. ● 溶接工 a wélder.

ようせん 用船, 傭船 (船) a chartered ship [boat, vessel]; (雇うこと) chartering.
● 用船契約 a charter. ● 用船契約をする charter a ship [a boat]. ● 用船主 a charterer. ● 用船料 chárter hire.

ようせん 用箋 (便せん) létter pàper; (メモ用の紙) mémo [nóte] pàper (⇨メモ); (原稿用紙) mánuscript pàper; (書くための紙) wríting pàper.

ようせん 溶銑, 熔銑 molten iron.

***ようそ 要素** 〖構成要素〗 an element; 〖要因〗 a factor. ● 人間の生命の不可欠な要素 the essential *elements* of human life. ● 彼の成功に不可欠の要素 a *factor* essential to [for] his success.

ようそ 沃素 〖化学〗 iodine /áiədàin/ 〖元素記号 I〗.

ようそう 洋装 ― **洋装する** 動 be dressed in Western-style clothes.
● 洋装店 (婦人用) a dress-shop.

ようそう 様相 〖物事の側面〗 an aspect; 〖進展の段階〗 a phase. ▶事態はただならぬ様相を帯びている Things are taking on [《やや書》 assuming] a serious *aspect*. ▶戦争は違った様相を呈し出した The war entered a different *phase*./We entered a different *phase* in the war.

-ようだ (⇨-様(よう)❷)

ようたい 様態 (状態) a state; a condition.

ようだい 容体 the condition (*of* a patient). ▶彼の容体は思わしくない [今のところ落ちついている] He is not in favorable [now in stable] *condition*. ▶彼女の容体は急変した Her *condition* took a sudden turn (for the worse).

ようたし 用足し 〖用事〗 business; (人に頼まれた) an errand; 〖排泄〗 (⇨便所). ● 用足しに出かける go out on *business*; go on an *errand*.

ようたし 用達 (納入業者) a purveyor. (⇨御用 ❸)

ようたつ 用達 (⇨用足し)

ようだてる 用立てる ● 彼女に10万円用立てる (貸す) *lend* her one hundred thousand yen; (便宜をはかる) *accommodate* her *with* a loan of one hundred thousand yen.

ようだん 用談 (a) business talk. ▶ランチをしながら用談しましょう Let's *talk business* over lunch.

ようだん 要談 (have) a talk on [about] important matters.

ようだん 溶断 ― **溶断する** 動 fuse. ●酸素溶断機 an oxygen fusing machine.

ようだんす 用箪笥 a chest of drawers; 《米》 a bureau.

ようち 夜討ち 夜討ちをかける (敵に) make a night attack 《on the enemy》, attack 《the enemy》 by night; (新聞記者などが) make a surprise visit late at night. ▶きのうX社の記者に夜討ちをかけられた A reporter for X *came to my house late at night* unexpectedly.
● 夜討ち朝駆け ●…に夜討ち朝駆けをかける come to … late at night and early in the morning.

ようち 幼稚 ― **幼稚な** 形 (子供っぽい) childish, infantile /ínfəntàil/; (未熟な) immature /ìmət(j)úər/; (原始的な) primitive; (粗末な) crude. ● 幼稚なふるまい *childish* behavior.
● 幼稚化 (⇨幼児化) 〖医学〗 infantilism.

ようち 用地 a site; (土地) land. ● 新空港の用地 a *site for* a new airport. ● 建築用地 a búilding *site* (《米》 *lòt*). ● 農業用地 farmland; *land* for agricultural use.

ようち 要地 an important place; (軍事上の) a strategic point.

ようちえん 幼稚園 (a) kindergarten. ▶長男は幼稚園へ通っています My oldest son goes to [is in, 《やや書》 attends] *kindergarten*. (❗この場合は無冠詞) (⇨学校 [解説])
● 幼稚園教諭 a kindergarten teacher; a kindergart(e)ner. ● 幼稚園児 a kindergarten pupil; a kindergart(e)ner.

ようちゅう 幼虫 (一般的に) a larva (複 larvae /lάːviː/); (カブトムシなどの) a grub, (ハエなどの) a maggot; (チョウなどの) a caterpillar.

ようちゅうい 要注意 ▶医者から肝臓が要注意だと言われた My doctor told me that I *need special medical attention* for my liver.
● 要注意人物 a marked person (❗「有望な人」の意もある); a person on the blacklist; (危険人物) a security risk. ● 要注意人物名簿 a blacklist.

ようちょう 幼鳥 an unfledged bird; a fledg(e)ling; a young bird.

ようちょう 羊腸 (羊の腸) (a) sheep's gut. ● 羊腸たる (=曲がりくねった)山道 a winding [a zigzag] path (up the mountain).

ようつい 腰椎 〖解剖〗 a lumbar.
● 腰椎骨 the lumbar vertebrae /vάːrtəbriː/. (❗複数形で. 単数形は vertebra). ● 腰椎麻酔 lumbar anesthesia.

ようつう 腰痛 〖医学〗 lumbago /lʌmbéigou/; (背中を含めて) 《やや話》 (a) backache. ● 腰痛に悩む suffer from *lumbago* [*backache*]. ▶加藤先生は腰痛できのう学校を休んだ Mr. Kato didn't come to school yesterday because he had a *backache* [an *ache in his back*].

ようてい 要諦 crucial importance; 《書》 the quintessence. ▶商売の要諦は上手に広告することである Clever advertising is *the quintessence* of marketing.

***ようてん 要点** the point; 〖要旨〗 the gist /dʒíst/.
● 要点をついている [外れている] be to [off] *the point*.
● 要点をつかむ grasp [get, (分かる) see] *the point* (*of*). ▶彼の話の要点を聞かせてください Give me the *gist* [the (main) *point*] of what he said. ▶要点を外さないでくれないか Will you stick [keep] to *the point*?

ようでんき 陽電気 〖電気〗 positive (↔negative) electricity.

ようでんし 陽電子 〖物理〗 a positron.

ようと 用途 a use /júːs/. ● 用途が広い have a variety of *uses*; be used /júːzd/ in many ways. ● 用途が限られている have only limited *uses*.

ようど 用土 special soil for gardening.

ようど 用度 (事務用品の供給) the supply of stationery and other office equipment.
● 用度係 a clerk in charge of office supplies.

ようとうくにく 羊頭狗肉 'to hang a sheep's head and sell dog's meat'; (偽りの見せかけ) a false facade /fəsάːd/; 〖ことわざ〗 He cries wine and sells vinegar.

ようどうさくせん 陽動作戦 ● 陽動作戦に出る make a feint (operation); feint.

ようとして 杳として ● 男の行方は杳として知れない The man's whereabouts are [is] *in mystery*./No

ようとん 養豚 pig [hog] raising. (❗ hog は120ポンド以上の特に食用に去勢された豚)
- **養豚家** a píg fàrmer. • **養豚場** a píg fàrm.《英》a piggery.

-ような (⇒-様(ょぅ) ❸)

ようなし 洋梨 〖植物〗a pear.

-ように (⇒-様(ょぅ) ❸❹❺❻)

ようにく 羊肉 mutton; (子羊の) lamb.

-ようになる (⇒-様(ょぅ) ❼)

ようにん 容認 ── **容認する** 動 〖認める〗admit; 〖受け入れる〗accept; 〖許す〗allow. (⇒認める, 許す)

ようねん 幼年 • 幸せな幼年時代を過ごす have a happy *childhood*. (⇒幼少)
- **幼年期** (子供時代) childhood; (赤ん坊の頃) infancy. • **幼年期に** in (one's) *childhood* [*infancy, early childhood*].

ようは 要は in short, in a word. (⇒要, 要するに)

ようはい 遥拝 ── **遥拝する** 動 bow to 〈the Imperial palace〉from a distant place.

ようばい 溶媒 〖化学〗a solvent.

ようはつ 洋髪 a Western-style hairdo.

ようばん 洋盤 a European or American record.

*__ようび__ 曜日 会話 「今日は何曜日ですか」「日曜日です」"What *day* (*of the week*) is it today?" "(It's) Sunday." (❗ of the week がないと「何日ですか」の意にもなるが、「何曜日ですか」の意で用いることが多い)

ようひし 羊皮紙 parchment.

ようひん 用品 (台所などの) a utensil; (品物) goods (❗ 複数形で); (備品) equipment (❗ 集合的); (道具) things; (装備一式) an outfit. • 台所用品 kitchen *utènsils* [*things*]. • スポーツ用品 spórting gòods. • 事務用品 óffice *equipment*. • スキー用品一式 a skíing òutfit [*an outfit for* skiing]; skíing *equipment*.

ようひん 洋品 《米》haberdashery. (❗ 男子用服飾品)
- **洋品商** a haberdasher. • **洋品店** (男子用服飾品店) a haberdashery; (衣料品店) a clothing store; (ブティック) a boutique /buːˈtiːk/.

ようふ 妖婦 a seductive woman (圏 ~ women); (魔性の女) a femme fetale /fèm fətǽl/ (圏 femmes fatales /~, -z/) (❗ フランス語).

ようふ 養父 a foster father,《書》an adoptive father. (❗ 後の方は法的に養子にした場合) • **養父母** foster parents,《書》adoptive parents.

ようふ 洋舞 a Western-style dance.

ようふう 洋風 图 (a) Western style.
── **洋風の** 形 Western-style. • ジャガイモを使った洋風の煮物 Western-style stew using potatoes.
- **洋風建築** Western-style architecture.

*__ようふく__ 洋服 〖衣服〗clothes /klóuz, -ðz/ (❗ 複数扱いで数えられることもしばしばあるが、many, much のいずれをつけることもできるが、《話》では many の方が普通),《主に書》clothing; 〖和服に対して〗Western clothes; 〖ドレス〗a dress; 〖スーツ〗a suit; 〖着るもの〗something to wear. (⇒服)

> **使い分け** **clothes** 上着・下着など, 個々の衣類の集まりを表す一般的な語.
> **clothing** 集合的に用い, 帽子などを含め身につけるもののすべてをいう. 数えるときは a piece [an article] of clothing のようにする.
> **dress** 通例婦人や女の子の服を表すが, 特定の目的のための男女の服装の意も含み, この場合は不可算名詞扱い: in full *dress* (正装して, 礼服で) (⇒服)

- **洋服を着る**[**脱ぐ**] put on [take off] one's *clothes*. (❗「洋服を着ている(状態)」なら wear one's *clothes*, have one's *clothes* on) ▶ 私は洋服を2着作った (=作ってもらった) I had two *suits* (*of clothes*) [two *dresses*] made. (❗ ×two clothes のように数詞とは用いない)
- **洋服掛け** a cóat hànger. • **洋服だんす** a wardrobe. (⇒たんす) • **洋服屋** (店) a tailor's (shop), a tailor, (婦人服の) a dressmaker's (shop); (人) a dressmaker.

ようぶん 養分 nourishment; nutrient. (⇒栄養)

ようへい 用兵 (戦略) (a) strategy; (個々の戦術) tactics (❗ 単・複両扱い).

ようへい 葉柄 〖植物〗a leafstalk.

ようべん 用便 用便を足す go to the bathroom. (⇒用 ❸, 便所)

ようぼ 養母 a foster mother,《書》an adoptive mother. (❗ 後の方は法的に養子にした場合)

ようほう 用法 (使用法) directions; (語の使い方) usage; (用途) a use. • その薬の用法 the *directions* for the use of the medicine. • その語の正しい用法 the correct *usage* of the word. (⇒使い方) ▶ 決められた用法・用量を守って服用してください Follow the *directions* for the dosage of a *drug*.

ようほう 養蜂 beekeeping; apiculture /éipikʌltʃər/.
- **養蜂家** a beekeeper; an apiarist. • **養蜂場** an apiary.

ようぼう 要望 (a) request; 〖願望〗a wish; 〖要求〗a demand. • **要望にこたえる** meet《書》grant〈his〉request(s) [wish(es)] [*for*]. • 彼の要望に[にこたえて]会議を開く have a meeting *at* [*in answer to*] his *request*. ▶ 諸般の事情からご要望には添いかねます The circumstances would not allow me to comply with your *request*. ▶ ご要望に添えるようにいたします We'll attend to your *request*.

ようぼう 容貌 (見かけ) looks; (顔だち) features. (❗ 目, 鼻, 口など顔の造りの一つをいう場合は単数形で) ▶ 彼女は美しい容貌をしている She has good *looks* [fine *features*]./She is *good-looking*.

ようぼく 幼木 a young tree.

ようま 洋間 a Western-style room.

ようまく 羊膜 〖解剖〗the amnion.

ようみゃく 葉脈 the veins /véinz/ (of a leaf).

ようむ 要務 an important job [duty].

ようむいん 用務員 《米》a janitor,《英》a caretaker;《婉曲的》a custodian.

ようむき 用向き business. (⇒用 ❶)

ようめい 幼名 one's childhood name.

ようめい 用命 an order. ▶ 何なりとご用命下さい We are ready to receive your *orders*./We are always at your service. ▶ お気軽に当店へご用命ください We are entirely at your service.

ようもう 羊毛 图 wool; (a) fleece (❗ ❶ 1 頭ひと刈り分の場合は ℂ). • 羊毛のような woolly. • 羊毛を刈る shear [fleece] sheep. ▶ 羊毛は熱湯で洗うと縮む *Wool* shrinks when (it is) washed in hot water.
── **羊毛(製)の** 形 woolen.
- **羊毛製品** wool [woolen] goods. (❗ 後の方が普通)

ようもうざい 養毛剤 a háir tònic.

ようもく 要目 important items.

*__ようやく__ 〖ついに〗at last, at long last (❗ (1) 文頭または文尾に用いる. (2) 前の方が日常的。); (いろいろあって最後に) finally (⇒ついに); 〖かろうじて〗barely, (only) just (❗ やっとで); 〖困難を伴って〗with difficulty; 〖次第に〗gradually. (⇒やっと) ▶ 彼はようやく試験に合格した He passed his exams *at last*./He *finally* passed his exams. ▶ 彼はようやく列車に

ようやく に合った He *barely* caught the train./He was *just* in time for the train. ▶ようやくあたりが明るくなり始めた It's *gradually* getting light. ▶彼らは(のびのびになった後)ようやく交渉のテーブルについた They *came around to* sitting at the negotiating table. ▶電話で10分は話してからようやく(相手が)彼だと分かった I talked on the phone for ten minutes or so before I recognized him.

ようやく 要約 图 a summary (*of*); [文学作品などの] a digest. ●その報告の要約 a *summary of* the report.
── 要約する 動 ●その記事を100語で要約する *summarize* [*give a summary of*] the article in 100 words; (話) *boil* the article *down to* 100 words. ●その問題を簡潔に要約する *sum up* the matter briefly.

ようゆう 溶融, 熔融 (炉心の) (a) meltdown.

ようよう 洋々 ●洋々たる(=広々とした)海 a *broad* [a *vast*, (限りない) a *boundless*] expanse of ocean. ●前途洋々たる学生 (将来が明るい) a student with a *bright* future; (前途有望な) a *promising* student.

ようよう 要用 an important matter. ▶まずご要用のみにて失礼いたします Anyway, please forgive me for mentioning only *important matters*.

ようらく 瓔珞 (仏像の) a necklace; stringed ornaments.

ようらん 洋蘭 [植物] an orchid, a tropical orchid.

ようらん 要覧 (調査概説) a survey; (概略) an outline. (⇨便覧(ﾍﾞﾝﾗﾝ)). 学内要覧 (大学の) a bulletin; 《米》a college catalog; 《英》a university calendar.

ようらん 揺籃 揺籃期にある be in the cradle; in its infancy. ●揺籃の地 (発祥地) a birthplace.

ようりく 揚陸 [上陸] (a) landing; [陸揚げ] unloading.
●揚陸艦 [軍事] a lánding ship.

ようりつ 擁立 ●市長候補に擁立する *back*《him》*up*[*support*《him》] as (a) candidate for mayor.

ようりゃく 要略 the gist.

*****ようりょう** 要領 ❶[要点] the point. ▶彼女の説明は簡潔で要領を得ていた Her explanation was brief and *to the point*. ▶彼の返答は要領を得ていない(=見当違いだ) His answer is off *the point*.
❷[こつ] (話) a [the] knack (*of*, *for*), (話) the hang (*of*). (⇨こつ). ▶すぐにその機械の操作の要領は分かるよ You'll get the *knack*[*hang*] *of* operating the machine soon.
❸[手際] ●彼は要領よくその仕事をした He did the job *efficiently*./He was *efficient in* doing the job. ▶彼女は何事にも要領が悪い(=不器用だ) She is *clumsy* in everything. ▶彼は要領のいい[悪い]やつだ He's a *smooth* [a *clumsy*] fellow.

ようりょう 用量 (薬の) the amount (*of medicine to be taken* [*used*]).

ようりょう 容量 (a) capacity. (⇨容積). ●その水槽の容量は100リットルです The *capacity* of the water tank is 100 liters./The water tank has a *capacity* of 100 liters.

ようりょく 揚力 lift.

ようりょくそ 葉緑素 chlorophyll /klɔ́ː(ː)rəfɪl/.

ようりょくたい 葉緑体 chloroplast.

ようれい 用例 (典型的な例) an example; (例文) an example sentence; (説明のための) an illustration. ▶この辞書は用例が多い This dictionary gives [has, shows, cites, (含む) contains] a lot of *examples*.

ようれき 陽暦 (太陽暦) the solar calendar.

ようろ 要路 ❶[主要な交通路] an arterial road; (幹線道路)《米》a highway, 《英》a trunk road.
❷[重要なポスト] an important post. ●政府の要路を占める hold an *important post* in the government.

ようろ 溶炉, 熔炉 a smélting fùrnace.

ようろう 養老 ●養老院 a nursing home; an old people's home. ●養老年金 an old-age [a retirement] pension. (⚠《英》では後の方が一般的). ●養老保険 endowment insurance; old-age insurance. ●養老保険に入る take out *old-age insurance*.

ヨークシャテリア [動物] (犬) a Yorkshire terrier.

ヨーグルト [<トルコ語] yog(h)urt /jóugərt/. ●プレーンヨーグルト plain *yoghurt*.

ヨーチン [「ヨードチンキ」の略] (⇨ヨード)

ヨーデル a yodel. ●ヨーデルを歌う do [make] a *yodel*; yodel.

ヨード [化学] iodine /áiədàin/ 《記号 I》.
●ヨードチンキ tincture of iodine; (話) iodine. ●ヨードホルム [化学] iodoform. ●ヨード卵 an iodine-enriched egg.

ヨーヨー (おもちゃの) a yo-yo /jóujòu/.

*****ヨーロッパ** Europe. ●ヨーロッパの European. ●ヨーロッパ人 a European.
●ヨーロッパ大陸 the European Continent. (⚠英国人は単に the Continent という). ●ヨーロッパ連合 the European Union 《略 EU》.

よか 余暇 leisure, leisure time (⚠仕事や義務から解放された自由時間の意で、日本語の「レジャー」の持つ余暇を楽しむ意味はない); (あいた時間) spare time; (自由時間) free time. ●余暇にする仕事 a spare-time job. ●余暇のある生活をする lead a life of *leisure*. ●余暇を上手に活用する make good use of one's *leisure time*. ▶彼女は余暇に花を生ける She arranges flowers in her *spare* [*free*] *time*./(余暇を過ごす) She spends her *spare* [*free*] *time* (in) arranging flowers.

よか 予価 an expected price; a probable price. ▶予価5,000円《表示》*Probably* ¥5,000.

よか 予科 a preparatory course.

ヨガ yoga /jóugə/. ●ヨガをする practice [do] *yoga*. ●ヨガ行者 a yogi; (女性) a yogini. ●ヨガマット a yoga mat.

よかく 予覚 ●危険を予覚する sense danger.

よかく 余角 [数学] a complementary angle.

よかぜ 夜風 a night breeze [wind]. ▶夜風が身にしみた The *night wind* was terribly [biting] cold.

よかつ 余割 [数学] a cosecant /kousi:kænt/.

よかった (⇨良い ❸)

よからぬ 良からぬ ●彼のことでよからぬうわさが立っている A *bad* rumor about him is spreading. ▶そのことがよからぬ結果をもたらした That brought about a *bad* result. ●彼らは何かよからぬことをたくらんでいる They are up to something *bad*.

よかれ 善かれ ●よかれと思ってしたことがあだになった What I had done *hoping for the best* [*with the best of intentions*] turned out to be a bad thing.

よかれあしかれ 善かれ悪しかれ for better or worse; for good or ill; right or wrong. ●善かれ悪しかれテレビは子供に大きな影響を与えている *For better or worse* [(いずれにしても) *Anyway*], TV has a great influence on children.

よかん 予感 a hunch; (通例悪い)《やや書》a premonition; 《書》a presentiment. ●不吉な予感 an ominous *premonition* [*presentiment*]. ●災害が起こる予感がする have a *premonition* [*presentiment*]

of disaster. ▶彼が勝つような予感がする I have a *hunch* [My *hunch* is] that he will win.
よかん 余寒 the lingering cold. ●余寒厳しい折から as it is still very cold though it is spring according to the calendar; in this *lingering cold* of winter.
よき 予期 名 [『予想』] expectation(s); anticipation. (⇨予想) ・予期に反して against [contrary to] (all) *expectation*(*s*).
── **する** 動 expect; anticipate. ▶予期していたとおりその法案は否決された The bill was rejected as we (*had*) *expected*./At (*had been*) *expected*, the bill was rejected. ▶予期せぬ事がそこで起こった Unexpected things happened there.
よき 良き (よい) good. ●古きよき時代 the *good* old [×old good] days. ●今日のよき(=めでたい)日に on a *happy* day like this.
よぎ 余技 (趣味) a hobby. ●余技としての料理 cooking as a *hobby* (気晴らし), a *pastime*].
よぎしゃ 夜汽車 a night train.
よぎない 余儀ない unavoidable. (⇨やむをえない)
よきにつけあしきにつけ 良きにつけ悪しきにつけ ▶よきにつけ悪しきにつけ人の運命は決まっている Each of us has a desfiny, *for good or* (*for*) *evil*. (⇨善われ悪しかれ)
よきょう 余興 (an) entertainment. ▶彼は余興に歌を歌った He sang a song for [by way of] *entertainment*.
よぎり 夜霧 a night fog. (⇨霧)
よぎる ▶いろいろな不安が心をよぎった(=心に浮かんだ) Anxieties *flashed* [*flitted*] *through* my mind.
* **よきん 預金** (a) deposit (が貯金); (銀行口座) an account. ・30,000 円の預金をする *deposit* [make a *deposit of*] 30,000 yen (*in a bank*). ●預金を引き出す withdraw one's *deposit* (*from a bank*); (口座から現金で) withdraw (10,000 *yen from* one's *account*). ●銀行に預金口座を開く open an *account* at a bank. ●預金口座に 8,000 ドル預ける deposit 8,000 dollars in one's *account*. ・定期預金を[解約する] buy [cancel] a time *deposit*. ●預金獲得競争 a *deposit* battle; a battle for *deposits*. ▶彼女の預金口座に 50,000 円振り込んだ I paid 50,000 yen into her *bank account*. ▶彼はその銀行に預金がたくさんある He keeps [has] a large *deposit* in the bank. ▶預金残高を教えてくださいませんか Could you tell me my *bank balance*?

> **関連 いろいろな預金**: 外貨預金 a foreign currency deposit/積立預金 an installment deposit/定期預金 a time [a fixed] deposit/当座預金 a checking 〈米〉[a current 〈英〉] account/普通預金 an ordinary deposit/無利息預金 a non-interest-bearing deposit/利付き預金 an interest-bearing deposit.

●預金(支払い)準備率 the reserve (requirements) ratio; the bank reserve ratio. ●預金者 a depositor. ●預金証書 a deposit certificate; a deposit note; a deposit receipt. ●預金通帳 a bankbook; a deposit book. ●預金利息 interest on deposits.

* **よく 良く** ❶ [十分に, うまく] (上手に, 満足に, 十分に) well* (**!** 通例動詞より後に置く); (まったく) quite (**!** 通例動詞・形容詞の前に置く); (完全に) completely, fully, perfectly (⇨完全に); (綿密に) thoroughly /θʌ́ːrouli, θʌ́rəli/を; (正確に) exactly; (綿密に) closely; (注意して) carefully; (容易に) easily; (一生懸命に) hard; (見事に) nicely; (巧みに) skillfully. ●よく訓練された看護師 a *well*-trained nurse. ●地図をよく見る look at the map *closely* [*carefully*]; have a *good* [a *close*] look at the map. ●講師の話をよく(=注意深く)聞く listen *carefully* [*attentively*] to the lecturer. ●飲み込む前によくかみなさい Chew it *well* [Chew it *up*] before you swallow it. (**!** 日本語の「よく」は上にあげた訳語の他に, 「完全に, 最後まで」の意の副詞 up や out を伴った句動詞で表されることも多い: 部屋をよく掃除する *clean up* [*out*] (*a room*) ●ゆうべはあまりよく眠れなかった I could*n't* [did*n't*] sleep *very well* last night. (**!** not (…) very well は「あまりよく…ない」の意)/I did*n't* have a *very good* sleep last night. (**!** good は well に対応する形容詞) ▶この話はよくできている This story is *well* written. ▶おっしゃる意味がよく分かりません I don*'t* quite [*completely, fully, thoroughly*] understand what you mean./I don't understand *exactly* what [what *exactly*] you mean. (**!** (1) いずれの副詞も否定文で用いると部分否定で「よくは…ない」の意. また通例 very などの修飾は受けない. (2) この用法の exactly は通例疑問詞とともに用いる) ●うちの赤ん坊はよく食べる Our baby is a *good* eater./Our baby eats *a lot*. ●彼は クラスで一番よく勉強する He is the *hardest* worker [(一番よくできる) is the *best* student, is doing *best*] in his class. (**!** best はそれぞれ good, well の最上級)/He works [studies] (*the*) *hardest* in his class. (**!** 副詞の最上級の前に the をつけることもある (⇨最も)) ▶よくやりましたね You have done it *well* [*nicely, skillfully*]./《話》 You've done a *good job*. / *Good for* you! (**!** 他人の成功をたたえたり, 他人の行動に賛意を示す決まり文句)/*Well done*! (**!** 成功した人にいう決まり文句. しばしば教師が生徒の答案などに書く) ▶もう一度よく考えた方がいい You should *think it over* again [*give it a second thought*].

会話 「彼の経歴を知っていますか」「いいえ, よくは知りません」"Do you know his background?" "I don't know it *well* [*for certain,* 《話》 *for sure*]." (**!** not … for certain [sure] は部分否定で「はっきりは …ない」の意. 通例 know, tell などの動詞と用いる)

❷ [しばしば] often, frequently (**!** often の方が口語的 (⇨度々 **解説**); (習慣的に) habitually; (普通) usually; (大ぎう) a lot (**!** 後に名詞を伴うときは a lot of … の形で「多くの」の意 (⇨多く)). ▶彼はよく土曜の夜は外食します He *often* [*usually*] eats out on Saturday nights. ▶この地方よく地震がある This area is *often* [*frequently*] hit by earthquakes./Earthquakes are *frequent* [×often] in this area./《やや書》 This area is subject to *frequent* earthquakes./There are *a lot of* earthquakes in this area. ▶あなたのことは田中さんからよく聞いています I've heard *a lot* about you from Mr. Tanaka. ▶彼にはよくあることだが, 今日も学校を休んでいる *As is often the case* [*As is usual*] *with* him, he hasn't come to school today. (**!** as は関係代名詞で he 以下を受ける) ▶日曜の朝私たちはよくテニスをしたものだ We *often used to* [*would often*] play tennis on Sunday mornings. (⇨昔 **解説**) ▶よくある間違いです It's a *common* mistake (we make)./It's a mistake we *tend to* make. (**!** tend to do は「…する傾向がある」の意) ▶よくあることですよ It's *just one of those things* (that happen to everybody)./That's an *everyday* [*a common*] occurrence. (**!** 形容詞の everyday は 1 語続けて書く) / These things happen. ▶こんなことはよくあることだ(=あなただけのことではない) You're *not alone* in the trouble of this sort. ▶よくある(切ない)話だ (That's the) *same old*

story.
会話「彼はよく学校に遅刻するの?」「ええしょっちゅうよ」"How *often* is he late for school?" "He's late all the time."

❸ [良好, 好意] (健康な) well*; (親切な) kind, good*. ▶早くよくなってね I hope you get *well* [feel *better*, (回復する) *recover*] soon. ▶彼はよくなってきています(=快方に向かっています) He is getting [becoming] *better*./He is taking a turn for the *better*./His health *is improving*. ▶彼は私に大変よくしてくれる He is very *kind* [*good*] *to* [×*for*] me. ▶天気がよくなったらピクニックに行きましょう If the weather *improves* [(晴れたら) *clears up*], let's go on a picnic. ▶クラスのみんなが彼のことをよく言わない(=けなす) Everyone in his class *criticizes* him. (■言わないのは(↔well) of は今はあまり用いない) ▶ストに参加するのはよくて(=せいぜい) 10人くらいです *At most* [*At best*] ten of us will join the strike. ▶太郎はよく生きて10歳ぐらいまでだろうと医師は言った Doctors said we'd be lucky if Taro lived to be 10.

❹ [驚き, 感嘆] ▶あんな狭い部屋でよく3人も生活していますね(=不思議だ) *I wonder how* the three people can [(驚きだ) *It is amazing that* the three people can] live in such a small room. ▶よくご無事で(=無事なのがとてもうれしい) *I'm* ＼*so glád* (*that*) you are ／*safe* [*to* find you ／*safe*]. ▶よく来てくださいました(⇨ようこそ) ▶よくも口答えができたもんだ *How dáre* you ánswer [tálk] ＼back? (■強い非難を表す. 単に驚きを表す場合は次の2例のように いう) ▶よくそんなことを頼めるね *How can* you ásk ＼*such a thing?* ▶あいつはなんてよくしゃべるんだ *How* he *dóes* ＼*talk!*
会話「君の欠点は怠け者だってことだな」「よく言うよ」"The trouble with you is you're lazy." "You *can* ＼*talk.*"

*よく 欲 (a) desire 《*for, to* do》; (a) lust 《*for*》; greed 《*for*》; 《書》 avarice; (an) ambition 《*to* do》.

使い分け desire 実現が決して不可能ではないことに対する欲求や欲望を表す. 性的な欲望(sexual desire)の意で用いられることも多い.
lust 破廉恥や暴力など好ましくないことへの欲望, または強い性欲を示す.
greed 「強欲さ」「貪欲さ」を表す. 特に食欲・金銭欲・権利欲に対して用いる. また, 非常に自分本位の欲求であることを含意する.
avarice 金銭や権力に対する強欲さを表す.
ambition 大成への野望や名誉欲などを表す. 時に長期に抱いていることを含意する. 必ずしも否定的に用いられるわけではない.

① [～欲] ●強い権力欲 a *lust* [a strong *desire*] *for* power. ▶彼は名誉欲がない(あまりない; 強い) He has no [doesn't have much; has a strong] *desire for* fame. ▶彼女は知識欲が旺盛(おうせい)だ She has a great *desire for* knowledge [*to* learn]. (■日常会話では She really wants [is trying hard] to learn. などということが多い)

② [欲が] ●欲が出る get *greedy*. ▶彼は欲が深い(=欲張りだ) He is *greedy*. ▶彼は欲がない He has no *ambition*./(金もうけに関心がない) He isn't interested in *making money*./(私利がない) He is an *unselfish* [a *disinterested*, ×an uninterested] man.

③ [欲の[に]] ▶彼は欲のかたまりだ He is *greediness* itself./He is full of *greed*. ▶私は欲に目がくらんだ I was *blinded* by *greed* [*avarice*]./*Greed* blinded me.

④ [欲を] ●欲を言えばきりがない The more one has, the more one wants./(やや書) Our *desire* knows no bounds. ▶あなたは学校の成績はよいが, 欲を言えばもう少し深く(物事を)考えられればよいのだが Your (school) grades are good, but *I wish* you could think more deeply.

● 欲の皮が突っ張る ▶欲の皮が突っ張った老人 an *avaricious* [a *greedy*] old man [woman]. (■前の方が意味が強い)

● 欲も得もない ▶欲も得もなく働く work with no thought of gain or greed.

● 欲をかく (欲を出す) get greedy. ▶彼は欲をかいたあまりすべてを失った He *got greedier* and ended up losing everything.

よく 翼 (鳥・飛行機などの) a wing. ●水平[垂直]尾翼 a horizontal [a vertical] tail.

よく- 翌- (次の) next; (次に続く) following. ●翌3月10日に (on) *the next* [*following*] day, March 10(th). (⇨翌日)

よくあさ 翌朝 the next [following] morning.

よくあつ 抑圧 图 suppression; (政治的な) oppression; (感情などの) repression.
—抑圧する 動 ●言論の自由を抑圧する *suppress* freedom of speech. ●抑圧された欲望 *suppressed* [*repressed*] desires.

よくいえば よく言えば ▶彼女はよく言えば倹約家, 悪く言えばけちだ *If we speak well of* her, she's thrifty, but if not, stingy./She is thrifty *at best* and stingy at worst.

よくか 翼下 (勢力下) under one's power [influence]. (⇨傘下)

よくき 欲気 (意欲) eagerness; (入手欲) acquisitiveness; (欲深) greediness. ●欲気を出す be eager 《*for, to* do》; be acquisitive 《*of*》; be greedy 《*for, to* do》.

よくげつ 翌月 the next [following] month.

よくご 浴後 after one's [a] bath.

よくさん 翼賛 图 assistance; support; (協同) cooperation.
—翼賛する 動 help; support; cooperate.

よくし 抑止 (抑止するもの) a deterrence. ●犯罪の抑止力 (やや書) (act [serve] as) a *deterrent* to crime. ●核の抑止力 (やや書) (maintain) a nuclear *deterrent*; nuclear *deterrence*.

よくしたもので ▶世間はよくしたもので決して悪は栄えない *You don't have to worry.* God never permits evil to thrive [flourish].

よくしつ 浴室 《米》a bath, 《英》a bathroom. (⇨風呂(ふろ))

よくじつ 翌日 ●翌日に (on) the next [following] day. (■前置詞は省略する方が普通) ▶彼女はその翌日もう一度やって来た She came again *the next day*. ▶大学を卒業した翌日彼は故郷を後にした He left home *the day after* he graduated from college.
● 翌日配達 overnight delivery.

よくしゅう 翌週 the next [following] week.

よくじょう 浴場 a bath(room); [ふろ屋] a bathhouse; a public bath. (⇨風呂(ふろ))

よくじょう 欲情 sexual desire; (色情) passion; (激しい欲情) (a) lust. ●欲情をあおる物語 (やや書) a story that inflames one's *sexual desire*.

よくしん 欲心 (願望) (a) desire 《*for* fame》. (⇨欲)

よくする 浴する ●恩恵に浴する(=利益を受ける) benefit; get benefit 《*from*》. ●光栄に浴する(=光栄にも...する) have the honor 《*of doing; to* do》.

よくせい 抑制 图 (a) control; [感情・活動などの] (a)

restraint; 〔制止〕(a) check. ▶物価高は抑制がきかない The rising prices are *out of control* [*hand*].
──**抑制する** 動 control; 〈やや書〉restrain; 〔欲望などを〕repress. ●感情を抑制する *control* [*restrain*, *repress*] one's emotions; (自制する) *control* oneself. ●インフレを抑制する *control* [*check*] inflation. ●彼女の活動を抑制する *restrain* [*put a restraint on*] her activity.

よくぞ ▶よくぞ(＝ようこそ)はるばるおいでくださいました I'm very glad (that) you've come [It's very kind of you to have come] all the way to see us. ▶よくぞ言った《話》Well said!/《話》(認めたくなくが) You said it!

よくそう 浴槽 a bathtub, a tub.

よくち 沃地 (⇨動 沃土)

よくちょう 翌朝 (⇨翌朝(ょくあさ))

よくど 沃土 〔土〕rich 〔fertile〕soil; 〔土地〕fertile [rich] land.

よくとくずく 欲得ずく ── **欲得ずくの** 形 〔利己的な〕selfish, self-interested; 〔金目的な〕mércenary. ●欲得ずくで out of *selfish* [*mercenary*] motives.

よくねん 翌年 the next [following] year. (**!** in は省略する方が普通 (⇨翌日)) ▶彼女は帰国した翌年結婚した She got married *the year after* she returned home.

よくばり 欲張り 〔人〕a greedy [a grasping] person; (けち, 守銭奴) a miser; 〔行為〕greediness. (⇨欲)

よくばる 欲張る be greedy. ▶そんなに欲張るな Don't *be so greedy*. ●その子は欲張ってケーキを全部食べた The child ate all the cake *greedily*.

よくぶかい 欲深い greedy; (けちな) stingy. (⇨欲)

*** よくぼう** 欲望 desire (*for, to do*); (a) lust (*for*) (**!** 通例悪い意味で用いる。) 〔野望〕(an) ambition (*to do*). (⇨欲, 欲求) ●激しい欲望 an intense [a keen] *desire*. ●富と権力に対する欲望 a *desire* [a *lust*] *for* wealth and power. ●欲望を満たす〔抑える〕satisfy [suppress, curb] one's *desire*. ●世界征服の欲望を抱く have an *ambition to* conquer the world.

よくめ 欲目 (偏見) (a) prejudice. ●欲目で見る(＝偏見を抱いている) be prejudiced, be biased. ●親の欲目 the *partial eyes* of one's parents.

よくも ▶よくも私にそんなことが言えるね How can 〔(図々しくも) *dare*〕you say such a thing to me? ▶よくもだましたな You *did* deceive me! (**!** did を強く発音する)

よくや 沃野 a fertile [a rich] plain.

よくよう 抑揚 (an) intonation. ●抑揚をつけて話す speak with an *intonation*. ●抑揚のない(＝単調な)声で話す speak in a *monotonous* voice [(一本調子で) in a *monotone*]. ●抑揚をつけて詩を読む *intone* a poem.

よくよう 浴用 ──**浴用石けん**(*x*a) báth [tóilet] sòap. ●浴用タオル a bath towel.

よくよく 副 〔非常に〕very, very much; 〔注意深く〕very carefully 〔closely〕; 〔慎重に〕carefully. ▶よくよく金に困っている be *very* hard up for money. ●その問題をよくよく考える consider the matter *carefully* [〔十分に〕*fully*]; *think* the matter *óver*. (**!** think over the matter とはあまり言わない) ▶交差点を渡るときは車によくよく気をつけないといけませんよ You *do really* have to watch out for cars when you cross an intersection. (**!** 強意の助動詞 do と副詞 really 〔本当に〕による二重強調。do の方を強く読む)
──**よくよくの** 形 very; (やむをえない) unavoidable. (**!** 連related語によって種々の形容詞をとる) ●よくよくの頑固者 a *very* obstinate person. ●よくよく(＝まったく)のばか an utter [a *downright*] fool. ●よくよくの事情で under *unavoidable* circumstances. ●よくよく考えた上で after *careful* [*mature*] consideration. ▶あの人が金を貸してくれと言うのはよくよくのことだ(＝他にはどうしようもなかったに違いない) He must have *had no choice but to* ask us for money.

よくよく── 翌々── ▶私が到着した翌々日に彼が会いに来た He came to see me *two days after* my arrival [I arrived].

よくりゅう 抑留 (an) internment; 〔拘留〕detention. ▶彼はその国で3年間抑留生活を送った(＝抑留されていた) He was *interned* [*was detained*] in the country for three years.

*** よけい** 余計 ── **余計な** 形 〔余分の〕extra; (お金・時間などが) spare; 〔不必要な〕unnecessary, needless; 〔過多の〕too many [much]; 〔要求されない〕uncalled-for. ●よけいな費用 *extra* expenses. ●よけいなひと言 an *unnecessary* 〔書〕a *superfluous*〕remark; one word *too many*. ●よけいな物 *unnecessary* things; things we don't need. ▶よけいなお金は一文もない I don't have any money *to spare* [*spare* money]. ▶これは一つよけいだ This is one *too many*. ▶よけいな心配はするな Don't worry *too much* (about it). /(あまり深刻に考えるな) Don't take it *too seriously*. ▶(話のついでに)よけいなことを言ってしまった I said more than I meant to. ▶よけいなことをしてくれたものだ(＝そんなことはしてくれなくてもよかったのに) You needn't have done it. ▶よけいなお世話だ Mind your own business./It's none of your business. (⇨世話)

〔会話〕「あまりにも根を詰めすぎてあなたは疲れ切っているんだと思うわ, よけいなことを言うようだけど(＝求められて言うわけではないが)」「大丈夫だよ, 眠れなかっただけさ」「よけいなお世話かもしれないけど, ちょっと聞いてもらえるかしら」「えー, 何？」「その眠れないことで医者に診てもらうほうがいいと思うわ」"You're exhausted from pushing yourself too hard, that's what I think. Not that you asked me." "I just didn't sleep well. I'm fine." "I was wondering if I might possibly offer you some advice." "Oh, what?" "I think you should see the doctor about your insomnia."

── **余計** 副 extra; too much. ●50円よけいに払う(追加する) pay fifty yen *extra*, pay an *extra* fifty yen (**!** an *extra* fifty dollars のような場合も, fifty dollars をまとまった 1 単位と考える。したがって an を落とさないこと); (払い過ぎる) pay fifty yen *too much*. ▶注文より 3 箱よけいに送ってきた They sent three boxes *more than* we ordered. (**!** ... three *more* boxes *than* ... より普通/〈やや書〉They sent three boxes *in excess of* what we ordered. ▶彼は私よりよけいに勉強する He studies *harder than* I do [〔話〕than me, 〔書・古〕than I]. ▶ディスコへは行くなと言われてよけいに行きたくなった When I was told not to go to the disco, I was *all the more* tempted to (go there). ▶欠点があるからこそよけいに彼が好きなのです I love him (*all*) *the more for* his faults [*because* he has faults]. (**!** all はつける方が普通)

よけつ 預血 ── **預血する** 動 (説明的に) donate blood on condition that one get blood donation when one need it.

*** よける** 避ける 〔すばやく身をかわす〕(横に動く, 身をかがめるなど) dodge; (身をかがめて) duck; (打撃を) parry; 〔意識的に避ける〕avoid. ●カーブを身を引いて避ける bail out [duck away] on a curveball.

▶彼はすばやくボールを避けた He *dodged* the ball quickly. ▶彼は犬をよけようとしてハンドルを右に切った He turned the wheel right to *avoid* the dog.

よけん 与件 〖哲学〗 given conditions; data.

よけん 予見 图 foresight.
— **予見する** 動 (予知する) foresee; (予言する)《やや書》predict.

よげん 予言 (科学的推論による) (a) prediction; (予言者の) (a) prophecy /práfəsi/. ▶彼の予言は当たった[外れた] His *prophecy* came true [failed].
— **予言する** 動 (一般に)《やや書》foretell*, predict, prophesy /práfəsài/. ●未来を予言する *foretell* [*predict, prophesy*] the future. ▶占い師は女王の死を予言した The fortuneteller *foretold* [*prophesied*] the death of the queen 《*that* the queen would die》. ▶一部の学者は世界的な食糧危機が起こると予言している Some scholars *predict* [*prophesy*]《*that* there will be》a worldwide food crisis.
●予言者 a prophet; (女の) a prophetess.

よげん 余弦 〖数学〗 a cosine《略 cos》.
●余弦定理 the theorem of cosines.

よげん 預言 图 (a) prophecy.
— **預言の** 形 prophetic《*of*》.
— **預言する** 動 prophesy /práfəsài/.
●預言者 a prophet; a prophetess. ●預言書 the Prophets.

:**よこ** 横 ❶ [左右の長さ・幅] (短い幅) width, 《書》breadth; (長い幅) length.

解説 日本語では、縦は上下の長さ、横は左右の長さを表すが、英語では、長さの大小を考え、長い方を length、短い方を width で表すので、これらの語は必ずしも日本語の縦横と一致しない。例えば横 5cm, 縦 3cm の長方形は、図のように考える。

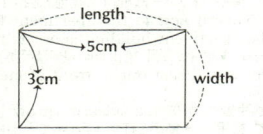

英訳すれば a rectangle 5cm *in length* [*long*] and 3(cm) *in width* [*wide*] となる。なお、はっきり縦よこということを示す height または high を用いる場合、長さの大小に関係なく、縦は height、横は width となるので、a rectangle 5cm *in width* [*wide*] and 3(cm) *in height* [*high*] となる。いずれも long, wide, high を用いる方が口語的。

▶この絵は横 80cm 縦 50cm ある This picture is eighty centimeters *long* [*in length*] and fifty centimeters *wide* [*in width*]./This picture is eighty *by* fifty centimeters.《!この by は寸法を表す。英語では「横×縦」のように横の数字が先に来ることが多い。例えば a 5-by-8 inch card は、横 5 インチ縦 8 インチのカード》

① 【横の】(水平の) horizontal《⇔vertical》; (クロスワードパズルの)横の 5, 5 across.《横の5』は 5 down》●横の線を引く draw a *horizontal* line; draw a line *horizontally*.

② 【横に[で]】(横切って) across; (横向きに) sideways; (斜めに) askew; (水平に) horizontally. ●テーブルを横にして運ぶ carry a table *sideways*. ●帽子を横にかぶっている wear a hat *askew* [*to the side*]. ●横に伸びる extend *transversely*; (生地が) stretch *sideways*. ●首を横に振る shake one's head《*at it*》.《!不賛成・不承知などを示す》●髪を横で分ける part one's hair *on the left side*. ▶鏡は横にひび割れていた The mirror was cracked *across* [*from one side to the other*, (*from*) *side to side*]. ▶私はその入り口から横になって通らなければならなかった I had to go through the door *sideways*. ▶彼は夕食後しばらく横になった He *lay down* for a while after supper.

❷ [そば, わき] (側面) a side.《⇒側（_{がわ}）②》●横から見た view《*it*》*from the side*. ●横にそれる deviate *sideways* [*laterally*] ●家の横にあるガレージ a garage *at* [*by*] *the side of* [(隣に) *next to*] a house. ▶あなたの横に座ってもよいですか May I sit *by* [*at*] *your side* [(かたわらに) *beside* you, (隣に) *next to* you]? ▶彼は横の入り口から入った He entered *by* [*at*, *through*] *the side* door. ▶彼は入り口の横に立っていた He was standing *beside* [*by*] the entrance.《!by は漠然と「…の近くに」を表す》▶彼は自転車に乗っている妻の横に並んでジョギングする He jogs *alongside of* his wife on her bike. ▶バスは横倒しになっていた The bus lay *on its side*. ▶横を向かないで正面を向きなさい Don't look [*turn*] *away* but look straight ahead.《!look [*turn*] *away* は「顔をそむける」とも》▶彼女がベンチに座れるよう彼は横に寄った He *moved over* to make room for her on the bench. ▶彼らは横に=わき)へ寄って私を通してくれた They stepped *aside* to let me pass. ▶横から口を出す《=干渉しないでくれ Don't *interfere in* [*meddle in*, (鼻を突っ込む)《話》*poke your nose into*] my affairs./(自分のことをしっかりやれ) Mind your own business.

●横の物を縦にもしない ▶彼は横の物を縦にもしない(=怠惰で何もしない) He is too lazy to do anything.

よこあい 横合い ●横合いから殴りかかる hit at《him》from the side. ●横合いから(=横)から口を出す《⇒横❷》

よこあな 横穴 a cave.
●横穴式石室 〖歴史〗 an ancient stone chamber in a tunnel tomb.

よこあるき 横歩き ●横歩きする move [walk] sideways.

よこいっせん 横一線 ●横一線に並んでいる be running neck and neck《*with*》.《!比喩的にも用いる》

よこいと 横糸 the weft; the woof《織 ~s》《⇔warp》.

よこう 余光 〖日没後の光〗 an afterglow; 〖先人の余徳〗 the remaining influence;《one's grandfather's》good reputation.

よこう 余香 (a) lingering scent. ●仏間にただよう余香 the *scent* of burnt incense *still lingering* in the family-altar room.

よこうえんしゅう 予行演習 a rehearsal; (軍事の) preliminary exercises. ●予行演習をする rehearse《a play》; have [hold] a *rehearsal*《for a play》.

よこおよぎ 横泳ぎ ●横泳ぎする do [swim] the sidestroke.

よこがお 横顔 a profile /próufail/. ●彼の横顔を描く draw his *profile*; draw him *in profile*. ▶彼女が横を向いたので横顔が見えた She turned sideways so I saw her *profile*.

よこがき 横書き horizontal writing. ●横書きにする write《it》horizontally [from left to right].

よこかぜ 横風 a side wind.

よこがみやぶり 横紙破り ●横紙破りをする(道理に反して自分の思いどおりにする) have one's own way against all reason.

よこぎ 横木 a crossbar, a bar.

よこぎる　横切る　cross, go* across .... (⇨渡る, 横断する) ●通りを走って[歩いて]横切る　run [walk] across a street. ●芝生を横切ってガレージの方へ行く go [近道のために] cut] across the lawn (and) toward the garage. ●車の流れを横切る cross the street through the traffic. ▶犬が目の前を横切った A dog crossed right in front of me [(私の通る道) my path].

よこく　予告　图　(公の) a preliminary announcement; (通知) a notice; (警告) a warning. ●3か月前の予告で[予告なしに]解雇される be dismissed at three months' notice [without (previous) notice].

── **予告する 動** announce (beforehand), make* a preliminary announcement 《of》; give* notice. ●本の近刊を予告する announce a book as in preparation. ●1か月前に解雇[退職]を予告する give 《him》a month's notice; give a month's notice to 《him》. ●彼に立ち退きを予告する give him (xa, xthe) notice to leave [that he should leave].

●**予告編** (映画などの) a trailer, 《米》a preview.

よこぐみ　横組み　(印刷) horizontal typesetting. ●横組みにする typeset [set type] horizontally.

よこぐるま　横車　── **横車を押す** (道理に反して自分の思いどおりにする) have one's own way against all reason.

よここう　an adit.

よこざま　横様　●横さまに倒れる fall on one's side.

よこじく　横軸　(グラフの) the horizontal axis; the x axis; (機械の) a horizontal shaft.

よこしま　邪ま　●よこしまな(=悪い)行い bad [邪悪な] wicked /wikid/, (不正な) wrong] behavior; (悪行) a wrongdoing.

よこじま　横縞　horizontal stripes.

よこしゃかい　横社会　a solidarity society.

よこす　寄越す　[[送る]] send*; [[こちらに手渡す]] hand ... over; [[与える]] give*. ●手紙をよこす send me a letter; (書く) write (to) me. ▶15分したら車をよこしてください Send the car in fifteen minutes. ▶君の財布をよこせ Give [Hand over] your wallet (to me). ▶彼は遅れるという伝言をよこした He sent me a message that he would be late.

***よごす　汚す**　[汚くする] make*... dirty [filthy] (!! filthy の方がひどい汚れ), dirty (!! 前の方が口語的); [[染みをつける]] stain; (点々と) spot (-tt-); [[特に排泄(#)物で)表面だけ[少し]]] 《書》soil; [汚染する] pollute, contaminate. (⇨汚染) ●指をインクで汚す stain [spot] one's fingers with ink. ▶新しい服を汚してはいけない Don't make [get] your new dress dirty./Don't dirty [soil] your new dress.

よごずき　横好き　●下手の横好きで油絵をもう10年ほど描いています I have been doing oil painting for pleasure about ten years, though I'm a poor painter.

よこすべり　横滑り　图　(車の) a skid. ●横滑りした路上のタイヤの跡 skid marks on the road.

── **横滑りする 動** (車の) skid; go into a skid. (⇨スリップ) ▶法相が閣内で横滑りするだろう The Minister of Justice will be given another portfolio [will be shifted to another position]. ▶portfolio は「特定官庁の大臣の地位」, shift は「ずらして動かす」の意.

よこずわり　横座り　── **横座りする 動** (説明的に) sit on the floor with one's lower legs to one's side.

***よこたえる　横たえる**　lay*. (⇨横たわる) ●まくらに頭を横たえる lay [xlie] one's head on a pillow. ●彼は疲れ切ってベッドにどっかと身を横たえた He laid [threw] himself down on the bed exhausted. (!! threw では身を投げ出すニュアンス)

よこだおし　横倒し　●車を横倒しにする push a car over sideways [sidelong]. ▶バイクが横倒しになった The motorcycle fell sideways [横にひっくり返った) was turned over sideways].

よこだき　横抱き　●子供を横抱きにする carry [hold] a child under one's arm.

***よこたわる　横たわる**　lie* (down), lay* oneself (down). (!! (1) 動作を表す場合は通例 down を伴う. (2) 両語の意味と語形変化に注意: lie 《自 横になる》: lay; lain; lying /láiiŋ/. lay 《他 横にする》: laid; laid; laying.) ●彼はベッドに大の字になって横たわっていた He was lying at full length on the bed. (!! lie in bed は「寝ている」の意)/He was stretching 《himself》out on the bed. ▶彼はソファーに横たわって新聞を読んだ He lay [laid down] down on the sofa and read a newspaper.

よこちょう　横町　(路地の) an alley; (本通りと平行して走る横道の) a side street.

よこづけ　横付け　── **横付け(に)する 形** park a car [船を) moor a boat] alongside.

よこっちょ　横っちょ　(⇨横, 側面) ●子供が横っちょから飛び出して来たのでぼくは夢中でハンドルを切った A child ran out suddenly into the street, and I turned the wheel instinctively.

よこっつら　横っ面　(ほお) a cheek. ●彼の横っ面を張る slap his face; slap him on the face; give him a slap on the cheek.

よこっとび　横っ飛び　(⇨横跳び)

よこづな　横綱　a grand champion 《sumo wrestler》, a yokozuna. ●横綱になる win the rank of grand champion in sumo.

●**横綱審議会** the Yokozuna Deliberation Council.

よこて　横手　▶アパートの横手に墓地がある There is a graveyard next to the apartment building./The apartment building is beside the graveyard. ▶横手から目の前ににゅっと手が突き出された An arm was thrust out in front of me from the side.

●**横手投げ** (野球の) a sidearm throw [pitch].

よこて　横手　●横手を打つ (感心して両手を打ち鳴らす) clap one's hands in admiration.

よごと　夜ごと　every night. ⇨毎晩

よことび　横跳び　●この種の猿は通常は木の上で暮らしているが地上を移動するときは横跳びをする This species of monkey usually lives in trees but moves on the ground jumping [skipping] sideways. ▶彼は横跳びになってボールをとった He flew sideways and caught the ball.

よこどり　横取り　── **横取りする 動** (盗む) steal; (途中で奪う) intercept; (ひったくる) snatch. ●(人が乗ろうとしている)タクシーを横取りする steal 《his》cab.

よこなが　横長　●横長の 形 long (sideways); (長方形の) oblong. (!!「縦長の」の意にもなる)

よこながし　横流し　●**横流し(に)する 動** (闇市場で売る) sell 《goods》on the black market; (違法に売る) sell 《goods》illegally [through illegal channels].

よこなぐり　横殴り　(吹き降りの) driving; (斜めからの) slanting. ●横殴りの雨 a driving rain. ▶横殴りの雨が降っている It's raining slantingly./The rain is pouring down in slanting sheets.

よこなみ　横波　a side wave. ●横波を受けて転覆する be hit by side waves and tip over.

よこならび　横並び　(横に1列に並ぶこと) standing side by side. ●横並びの意識 (have) a sense that

よこばい 横這い (カニの) a sideways movement. ●横ばいで移動する move [(歩く) walk] *sideways*. ▶売り上げは横ばいである Sales *remain at the same level* [have leveled off]./Sales are flat [unchanged].

よこはば 横幅 会話「その板の横幅はどのくらいありますか」「3メートルです」"How *wide* is [What is the *width* of] the board?" "It's three meters *wide* [*in width*]."

よこばら 横腹 ● one's [the] side. ●船の横腹 the side of a ship. ▶走りすぎて横腹が痛い My side aches from running too fast./I have a pain in *my side* because I ran too fast.

よこぶえ 横笛 a flute.

よこぶり 横降り ●横降りの雨 a slanting [(横なぐりの) a driving] rain. ▶雨は今度は横降りになった Now the rain has come down *slantwise*.

よこみち 横道 ●[わき道] a side road; [[間違った方向]] a wrong way. (⇨脇道)
● 横道にそれる (正しい方向から) deviate from the right way; (話の脱線する) wander from the subject, 《書》digress /dáigrés/ (from the subject).

よこむき 横向き ●横向きに小道を歩く walk *sideways* through the path. ●横向きに(=横腹を下にして)寝る lie (down) *on* one's *side*.

よこめ 横目 ● sideways [a sidelong] glance. ●彼を横目で見る look *sideways* [*sidelong*] at him; cast a *sideways* [a *sidelong*] glance at him.

よこめし 横飯 (西洋料理) Western food [dishes].

よこもじ 横文字 (西洋の言語) a European [a Western] language; (ローマ字) the Roman alphabet.

よこやり 横やり (an) interruption.
● 横やりを入れる (じゃまをする) interrupt 《him》; (口をさしはさむ)《話》cut [break, butt] in 《*on* a conversation》; (干渉する) poke [stick] one's nose 《*into*》.

よこゆれ 横揺れ 图 (船などの) a [the] roll (↔a [the] pitch); (地震の) (a) lateral vibration. ●船の横揺れ the *roll* of a ship.
── 横揺れする 動 sway; (船などが) roll; (地震が) vibrate laterally. (⇨揺れる)

よごれ 汚れ ●[ほこり・ごみなどの] dirt; [染み] a stain; (点々とした) a spot; [こすってできる] a smudge. ●しつこい汚れ a stubborn [a tough] *stain*. ●インクの汚れ ink *stains* [*spots*]. ●汚れのない(=ごみのない清潔な)台所 a *clean* [a *spotless*] kitchen. ●シャツの汚れを取る take off *stains* from one's shirt; (きれいにする) clean one's shirt. ●ほおにすす[インク]の汚れがついている have a *smudge* of soot [ink] on one's cheek. ●彼は車の汚れを洗い落とした He washed the *dirt* off the car. ●このカーペットは汚れが目立たない This carpet doesn't show *dirt*.
● 汚れ物 soiled [dirty] things (❗具体的にはclothes, towels, sheets などと置き換えればよい); (洗濯物)《集合的》washing [《米》wash], laundry.

よごれやく 汚れ役 the part of an outcast from society.

よごれる 汚れる (❗*filthy* の方がひどい汚れを含意); [染みがつく] be stained; [液体・油などで] be smeared; [表面が、わずかに] 《書》be soiled; [汚染される] be polluted. (⇨汚す) ●汚れた手で with *dirty* [*unclean*] hands. ●血で汚れたシャツ a shirt *stained* [*smeared*] with blood; a *blood-stained* shirt. ▶私のズボンは汚れてきたから洗濯しなければならない My trousers [《米》pants] *are getting dirty* and need washing. ▶白い布はすぐ汚れる White cloth *is easily stained* [*soiled*]./White cloth *stains* [*soils*] easily. ▶大気はスモッグでひどく汚れている The air has *been polluted by* [*with*] smog.

よこれんぼ 横恋慕 ── 横恋慕する 動 love someone's wife [husband, boyfriend, girlfriend]; love someone who belongs to another.

よこわり 横割り ●横割り行政 《have》a contact between related departments; departmental corporation.

よさ 良さ, 善さ (よい点) a good point; (長所) a merit; (美点) (a) virtue; (質のよさ) (a) good quality, quality. ▶私には彼のよさが分からない I can't see his *good points* [*merits*, *virtues*]. ▶使ってみてその辞書のよさが分かった I found the dictionary *good* after I used it.

よさい 余財 ●余財がある have money to spare. ▶これといった余財もない I don't have any *surplus funds* to speak of.

よざい 余罪 other crimes. ●余罪がいくつかあると思われる be suspected of some *other crimes*. ●その男の余罪を追及する question the man about *other crimes*.

よざくら 夜桜 ●夜桜を見に行く go to see *cherry blossoms* at night [(ライトアップされた桜) the *cherry blossoms* lit up at night].

よさむ 夜寒 the night cold 《you experience at the end of autumn》.

***よさん 予算** a budget (❗国家に限らず個人の予算にも用いる); [見積もり] an estimate; [予算案] a budget (bill).
① 【〜予算】 ●補正[追加; 総]予算 a revised [a supplementary; the total] *budget*. ●家庭[国家; 市]の予算 a family [a national; a municipal] *budget*. ●本予算 a main *budget*; principal *estimates*; (当初予算) an initial *budget*. ●暫定[特別]予算 a provisional [a special] *budget*. ●来年度の予算案を提出する present [submit] the *budget* for the forthcoming year. ●屋根の修理費の予算 an *estimate* of the cost of repairing the roof.
② 【予算(案)は】 ▶予算案は否決された[通過した] The *budget* was rejected [(was) passed, (承認された) was approved]. ▶ご予算はどのくらいでしょうか (店の人が客に) About how much would you like to spend [pay]?/(価格の範囲は) What (sort of) *price range* were you thinking of? (❗後の言い方は過去進行形によって現在の態度をぼかし、断定を和らげる言い方。答えは必ずしも between A and B (AとBの間)という必要はなく、About 20,000 yen. などという)
③ 【予算の】 budgetary. ●予算の均衡 *budgetary* balance. ●予算の作成[編成] formulation [compilation] of the *budget*. ●予算の範囲内で within (the limits of) the *budget*. ●予算の繰り越し carry over (of *budget*). ●予算の都合で for *budgetary* reasons.
④ 【予算(案)を[に]】 ●予算を立てる budget 《1,000,000 yen *for* new books》. ●予算を作成する make [write, compile] a *budget*. ●予算を切り詰める cut (down) [reduce] a *budget*. ●予算を超過する exceed the *budget* [*estimate*]. ●予算案を審議する discuss the *budget* bill. ●交際費を予算に組む include social (接待費) entertaining expenses in a *budget*; *budget* social expenses. ●予算を配分する allot the *budget*《*to*》. ●予算を決定する set the *budget*.
⑤ 【予算で[が]】 ●50億円の予算でダムを建設する construct a dam *on a budget* [*at an estimated*

よし all right. (⇨よろしい, よしよし)

よし 止し ▸止しにする それはよしにしよう (しないことにしよう) Let's not do it./(中止にしよう) Let's stop doing it.

よし 由 (手段) a way; a means. ● 彼がどこにいるのか知る由もない There is no *way* [*means*] of knowing where he is. ▸お元気の由(＝と聞いて)何よりです I'm very happy *to hear* you are very well.

よし 葦〘植物〙a reed.
● 葦の髄から天井覗く (狭い視野で勝手な判断をする) make a judgment with narrow-minded views; 《ことわざ》To look at heaven through a keyhole.

よし 良し ▸この魚は煮てよし, 焼いてよしです This fish is *good* either for boiling or broiling. ▸もう帰ってよし You *may* go home now.
● 良しとする ● 彼の案でよしとする (案を承認する) *accept* his plan; (満足する) *be satisfied* with his plan.

よじ 余事 ● 余事(＝当面の仕事とは関係のない事柄)に関心を向ける direct one's attention to *what does not concern his present job*. ● 本業の合間にちょこちょこ余事をする do some business on the side [beside one's fulltime occupation].

よしあし 善し悪し (善悪) good or bad; (正誤) right or wrong. (❗いずれも文脈によって or の代わりに and も用いる) ● 事の善し悪しの区別がつく know [can tell, distinguish] *right* from *wrong*; know the difference between *right and wrong*. ● 善し悪しにかかわらずそれをしなければならない Whether it is *good or bad* [*right or wrong*], we must do it. ▸天気の善し悪しにかかわらず出かけよう Let's start, (come) *rain or shine* [*whether it rains or not*]. (❗前の方は成句表現) ▸素直なら善し悪しだ(＝よいとは限らない) Obedience is *not always good*./(利点と欠点がある) Obedience has *both mérits and démerits* (⇨対照強勢に注意)

よしきり 葦切り〘鳥〙(オオヨシキリ) a great reed warbler; (コヨシキリ) a black-browed reed warbler.

よじげん 四次元 ▸四次元の空間 (хa) space of *four dimensions*; *four-dimensional* space.

よしごい 葦五位〘鳥〙a Chinese little bittern.

よしず 葦簀 a reed screen. ● よしず張りの夏祭りの小屋 a temporary hut made of *reed screens* for a summer festival.

よじつ 余日〘残された日〙remaining days; 〘またの日〙some (other) day.

よしない 由無い ❶〘理由がない〙without reason [cause]. ● よしない反対《make》an objection *without reason*.
❷〘方法がない〙● よしなく退却する have *no way* but to retreat [pull back]. ● やいやい言われてよしなく (＝やむを得ず) 従う yield to 《his》persistent demand.

よしなに ▸どうぞよしなにお取り計らいください I'll leave the matter to you. /「あなたにお任せします」の意.

よじのぼる よじ登る ▸崖によじ登る climb (up) [(すばやく) scramble up] a cliff. (⇨登る)

よしみ ▸友達のよしみ(＝友情から)彼に金を貸す lend him some money *out of friendship* [*for friendship's sake*]. ● 会議のあと山田君と昔のよしみで(＝旧交を暖めるために)一杯やった After the conference, I had a drink with Mr. Yamada *to renew* our *friendship*.

よしゅう 予習 图 preparation(s).
——予習(を)する 動 ● 授業の予習をする prepare one's lessons.

よじょう 余剰 (a) surplus. (⇨剰余) ● 余剰人員を削減[カット]する《話》cut the *deadwood* out. (❗ deadwood は「不要な人員」「売れ残り」の意の口語的表現)
● 余剰金〔額〕a surplus. ● 余剰在庫 surplus stock. ● 余剰農産物 farm surpluses; surplus agricultural [farm] products. ● 余剰米 surplus rice.

よじょう 余情 (⇨余韻) ● 余情のある俳句 a *haiku* poem that suggests something deep; a *haiku* poem full of suggested meanings.

よじょうはん 四畳半 ▸四畳半の部屋 a four and a half *tatami* size room.

よしよし 〘ほめて〙(いいぞ, その調子) Great! Keep it up./(いい子) Good boy [girl]! // 〘慰めて〙There, there [now]. ▸よしよし, すぐよくなるよ There, now, you'll soon get better. ▸よしよし, 分かった See right. I agree with you. ▸よしよし, もう泣くんじゃない Come, come, stop crying.

よじる 振る ▸行列を見るために身をよじる(＝ねじる) twist (around) to see the procession. ● 苦痛で身をよじる *writhe* /ráið/ [*twist*] with pain. ● やつをくすぐってやったら, 体をよじって声を立てて笑った I tickled him and he laughed all the more, *squirming*.

よじれる 捩れる be twisted. ▸バッグのストラップがよじれています The strap of your bag is *twisted*. ▸ケンのジョークでぼくたちは腹の皮がよじれるほど笑った We laughed *convulsively* at Ken's joke./Ken's joke had [left] us in stitches. (❗前の方は体をよじらせて笑うこと, 後の方は「止められないほど大笑いする」の意の口語表現)

よしわるし 善し悪し good or bad. (⇨善し悪(ᵃ)し)

よしん 与信 ● 与信管理 credit control [management]; control of making credits. ● 与信業務 credit business [activities]; operation of making [granting] credits.

よしん 予診 a preliminary medical examination.

よしん 予審 a preliminary hearing [examination].
● 予審判事 a magistrate.

よしん 余震 an aftershock. ▸余震が続いている There has been a series of *aftershocks*. ▸数回余震が感じられた We felt several *aftershocks* [*aftershocks* several times].

よじん 余人 ▸彼は余人をもって替えがたい No one can replace him.

よじん 余燼 (残り火) embers (❗炎は出ていない); (くすぶり) a smolder (❗通例単数形で. ❗いずれも比喩的にも用いられる) ▸少年は大火の余燼がくすぶる中を母親を捜しまわった The boy walked around the ruins of the big fire, *embers* still smoldering red hot, looking for his missing mother.

よしんば 縦しんば ▸よしんば(＝たとえ)地震があってもこの建物は大丈夫だ This building will be safe *if* an earthquake hit here. ▸よしんば君の言うことが正しくても, あんな言い方はないだろう *Even if* what you said was right, I don't think it was a good manner to put it like that.

***よす** 止す 〘中止する〙stop (-pp-); 〘取り止める〙cancel, call ... off; 〘断念する〙give*... up. (⇨止(°)める) ● おしゃべりよす Stop [《話》Quit] chattering [talking]. (❗×Stop [Quit] to chatter. は不可) / Don't chatter./No chattering! ● 外出のはよします I've decided not to go out./I think I'd better *not* go out./I'll *give up* the idea of going out. (⚠×I'll give up [stop] going out. は不可)

よすが ▶この写真集は先生をしのぶよすがとなる(=想い出させてくれる) This photographic album *helps us remember* [*reminds us of*] our teacher. ▶彼は身を寄せるよすが(=頼れる人)もない He has no one to ask for help [turn to].

よすてびと 世捨て人 a hermit; a recluse.

よすみ 四隅 ▶部屋の四隅 four corners of a room.

よせ 寄せ 〚囲碁・将棋〛the last [concluding] moves; the ending stages of a game.

よせ 寄席 (説明的に) a theater for *rakugo* or comic storytelling; (演芸場) a variety [《米》a vaudeville] theater.
● 寄席演芸 variety; a variety show; 《米》vaudeville. ● 音楽堂 《英》19 世紀から 20 世紀初めの寄席 ⒸまたはU寄席演芸 ⓊS(をさす)● 寄席芸人 a variety entertainer; 《米》a vaudevillian.

よせあう 寄せ合う ▶トムとメリーは体を寄せ合って座っていた Tom and Mary sat very *close together*. ▶ぼくたちは体を寄せ合って寝たのですぐに暖かくなった We *cuddled up close together* in bed and got warm soon.

よせあつめ 寄せ集め (ごた混ぜ) a jumble [a medley] 《of》. ▶寄せ集めの軍隊 a *medley* army. ●寄せ集めの(=にわか作りの)チーム a *scratch* [a *pickup*] team. ● 寄せ集めの材木で犬小屋を作る make a kennel with [using] a *jumble* of odd pieces of pillars and boards.

よせあつめる 寄せ集める (集める) gather ... (together [up]); (収集する) collect (⚠切手・模型など研究や趣味などで集めること). (⇨集める) ▶落ち葉を寄せ集める *gather* (熊手(のようなもの)でかき集める) *rake* (*up*) fallen leaves (*together*). ▶彼女は床に散らかっている服を寄せ集めた She *gathered up* the clothes on the floor. ▶この博物館は世界中からいろいろと珍しい自動車の模型を寄せ集めている They *have collected* [ˣ*gathered*] a lot of rare model cars from all over the world at this museum.

よせい 余生 ● 余生(=残りの人生)を社会奉仕にささげる devote *the rest of* one's *life* to social service. ● 余生(の年月)を安楽に送る spend *the rest of* one's *years* [one's *remaining years*] in comfort.

よせい 余勢 ● 余勢を駆る ▶初戦で大勝した余勢を駆ってそのチームは決勝戦に進出した *Encouraged* by the overwhelming victory in the first game [*match*], the team reached the final.

よせがき 寄せ書き a card or paper with one's words of good wishes or names. ▶私たちは彼のために寄せ書きをした We *wrote our words of good wishes and names* on *a card* for him.

よせざいく 寄せ木細工 wooden mosaic work; (床なら) parquetry /pάːrkɪtri/. ● 寄木細工の床 parquet.

よせづくり 寄せ木造り joined woodblock construction. ● 寄せ木造りの仏教彫刻 a Buddhist sculpture made by joining blocks of wood.

よせぎれ 寄せ切れ ▶寄せ切れでクッションを作る make a *patchwork* cushion.

よせつける 寄せ付ける ● 寄せつけない do not allow 《him》 to come near; keep 《him》 at a distance [arm's length]; (敵軍を) keep 《the enemy》 at bay. ▶彼女には男を寄せつけぬ何かがある She has something (in her) that *forbids* men *to approach* her. ▶彼女は食欲旺盛で風邪なぞ寄せつけない She has good appetite and *fights off* colds. ▶彼は数学ではクラスのだれも寄せつけない He is *by far*

the best math student in his class./He's *far ahead of* the other classmates *in* math.

よせて 寄せ手 an attacking force.

よせなべ 寄せ鍋 (説明的に) Japanese-style stew of fish, vegetables, etc. cooked at the table.

よせむね 寄せ棟 ● 寄せ棟造り 〚建築〛a house with a hip [a hippled] roof.

*****よせる** 寄せる ❶〔近づける〕(移動させる) move 《to》; (引き寄せる) pull [draw]*... (up) 《to》(⚠draw は pull よりもゆっくりなめらかな動作を表す); (近くへ持ってくる) bring*... close [near] 《to》; (物をわきへ置く) put*... aside. ● いすをテーブルの近くに寄せる *pull* [*draw*] *up* a chair to the table. ▶テーブルを少し右に寄せなさい *Move* [*Pull*] the table a little *to* the right. ▶自転車をわきへ寄せなさい Put the bicycle *aside*.(⚠車などでは Pull the car over (to the side). という)/(じゃまにならない所に移しなさい) *Move* the bicycle *out of the way.* ▶あの哲学者はいかめしい風貌で人を寄せつけない感じがする The philosopher looks grim and *unapproachable*.

❷〔手紙などを送る〕send*; (寄稿する) contribute 《to》. ● その雑誌に詩を寄せる *contribute* poems *to* the magazine. ▶祝電が全国各地から寄せられた Congratulatory telegrams *were sent in* from all parts of the country.

❸〔身・心などを寄せる〕● 貧しい人々に同情を寄せる(=同情する) feel sympathy [*compassion*] *for* [*sympathize with*] poor people [《やや書》the poor]. ● 信頼を寄せる *put* one's *trust* 《*in him*》; *trust* (him). ▶彼は身を寄せる所がない He has no place to *go* (to). (⚠*place* ではこの to は省略可. cf. He has no house to go to.) ▶彼女はしばらくの間姉のところに身を寄せている(=家に泊まっている) She *is staying with* her sister for a while. ▶彼女は新任の先生にひそかに思いを寄せている 《話》 She *has a crush on* her new teacher. ▶近いうちに寄せていただきます I'll *visit* [*call on*, *drop in on*] you one of these days. (⇒寄る)

よせん 予選 〚レースなどの〛 a (trial [preliminary]) heat; 〚競技などの〛 a preliminary; 〚サッカーなどの〛 a qualifying round, a qualifier. ● ワールドカップ予選 a World Cup *qualifier*. ● 100 メートル競走の 2 次予選を通過する get through the 2nd *heat* in the 100-meter dash. ● 「1 次予選」の 「1st *heat* という」● 予選落ち[通過] 〚ゴルフ〛miss [make] the cut. (⚠*cut* は本選出場のための基準点)
● 予選落ちする one's [a] missed out. ● 予選通過者 a qualifier.

*****よそ** 余所 (どこか他の場所) some other place; (別の場所) another place. ● どこかよそで遊ぼう Let's play *somewhere else* [*at some other place*]. ● よその家ではおとなしくしていなさい Be good at *someone else's* house. ● よその人(=見知らぬ人)から物をもらってはいけません Don't accept presents from *strange* people [*strangers*]. ▶彼は勉強をよそに(=しないで)遊んでばかりいる He is always playing *instead of* studying. (⚠この進行形＋*always* は話し手のいらだちを含意)

よそいき 余所行き (⇨余所行(ⓟ)き)

*****よそう** 予想 図 〔予期〕expectation(s); anticipation; 〔予測〕a forecast 《*for, of*》; 〚競馬〛(a) prospect; 〔推測〕a guess; 〚書〛(a) supposition; 〔見積もり〕an estimate, estimation.
① 〜(の)予想〕● (桜の)開花予想 the cherry blossom *forecast*. ● 今年のリンゴの収穫の予想は明るい The *prospects for* [*of*] this year's apple harvest are bright (↔*gloomy*). (⚠通例複数形で)

よそう

②【予想～】 ● 予想外の unexpected. ● 予想外に〔予想以上に〕beyond (one's) expectation(s), more than expected; (予想に反して) against [contrary to] (all) expectation(s). ▶その試験は予想以上に難しかった The exam was more difficult *than* (*I had*) *expected* [《話》*than I expected*]. (**!**) expect は比較を表す文脈では, 主節が現在形であってもしばしば過去完了形となる; She is prettier *than* (*I had*) *expected* [x*than I have expected*]. (彼女は予想以上にかわいい)) ▶予想どおりそのチームが優勝した The team won the championship *as* (*we had*) *expected* [《話》*as we expected*]./*Predictably*, the team won the title. (**!**) Predictably は文修飾語. 未来時制の文には用いない) ▶結果は予想以上〔どおり; 外れ〕だった The result exceeded [came up to; fell short of] my *expectations*.

③【予想が】 ▶彼女の予想が当たった〔外れた〕She guessed right [wrong]./Her *guess* was right [wrong]. ▶何が起こるかまったく予想がつかない *It's impossible* [*isn't possible*] *to* tell what will happen./《話》*You can't tell* [*There's no telling*] what will happen.

④【予想に】 ● 予想に反して against [contrary to] (all) expectation(s).

⑤【予想を上回る】 ● 予想を上回る exceed [《書》surpass] 《his》expectations. ● 予想を裏切る disappoint one's *expectations*. ▶売り上げは予想をはるかに下回った Sales fell [came] a long way short of our *expectations*. (**!**)「…下回っている」は … are (a long) way below (our) *expectations*) ▶選挙結果の最高と最低の予想をしてください Give us the best and the worst *scenario* of the election outcome. (⇒図)

⑥【予想では】 ▶私の予想では彼らは来月結婚するだろう My *guess* is *that* they will get married next month./(思う)《主に米語》I *guess* (*that*) they will get married next month. (**!**) that は通例省略する)

—**予想する 動** 〖予期する〗expect; anticipate (**!**)前の方は当然起こると確信していることを示す. 後の方は前もって察知すること, または何かに備えることをいう); 〖推測する〗guess; suppose; 〖見積もる〗estimate.

●戦争になると予想していた in expectation [*anticipation*] *of* war. ●今年の夏は非常に暑くなると予想される *It is expected* (*that*) we will have a very hot summer this year./The weather *is supposed to get* very hot this summer. ▶彼は来週来ると予想している I *expect* him *to* come next week./I *expect* (*that*) he will come next week. (**!**)後の方は客観的な言い方で, 単なる予想を表すだけだが, 前の方は来てほしいという話し手の期待を表す)

● 予想額 an estimated amount. ● 予想屋 (競馬などの) a tipster.

よそう 装う ❶ 〖食器に盛る〗● スープを(お玉で)皿によそう *ladle* /léidl/ soup into a plate. ▶ご飯をよそうのを手伝ってくれませんか Could you help me (to) *serve* [*dish up*] rice?.

❷〖よそおう〗(⇒装(そ²)う)

よそおい 装い ● 夏の装いをした女性 a lady *in* [*wearing*] summer *dress*. ● 最新流行の装いをしている *be dressed in the latest fashion*. ▶その店は装いも新たになった(=改装された) The store *has been remodeled* completely.

よそおう 装う ❶ 〖着飾る〗〘動作〙dress (oneself) (*in*), 《書》attire oneself (*in*) (**!**)通例「公の席に出席するために盛装する」の意); 〘状態〙wear*, be (dressed) in ..., 《書》be attired (*in*). ● はでに装っている *be gaily dressed*. ● 王衣を身に装っている *be* attired *in* royal robes.

❷〖振りをする〗pretend 《*to do*; *that* 節》(**!**)最も一般的な語); (悪意なく)〈やや書〉assume; (巧みに見せかける)《書》feign; (…ぶる)《書》affect. ● 平気を装う *affect* [*assume*] an unconcerned air. (**!**)前の方は「強がりで」, 後の方は「相手を心配させないように」ということを含意) ▶彼は病気を装った He *pretended* [*affected*] *to* be sick./He *pretended that* he was sick./He *pretended* [*feigned*, *affected*] sickness.

*よそく 予測 名 (科学的根拠に基づく)(a) prediction; (予報) a forecast (⇒予言); (見積もり) an estimate. ● 統計的予測 statistical *prediction*. ● 景気予測 a business *forecast*. ● 予測を下回る 1.3 パーセントの伸び a smaller-than-*expected* 1.3 percent increase. ● 会社の年間売り上げ予測が当たった〔はずれた〕 The company's annual sales *forecast* was right [wrong].

—**予測する 動** predict; forecast. ● 未来を予測する *predict* [*forecast*] the future. ▶彼は近い将来大きな地震が起こるだろうと予測した He *predicted* [*forecast*(*ed*)] *that* a strong earthquake would occur in the near future.

会話 「大統領選挙はどちらが勝つでしょうか」「現時点では非常に接戦で予測はできません」"Who's going to win the presidential election?" "It's too close to *predict* [《米話》*call*] at this point."

よそごと 余所事 (かかわりのない事) none of one's business; (関心のない事) a matter of no concern. ▶彼らの離婚は私にはよそ事とは思えない(=大いに関心がある) Their divorce is *of great concern to* me.

よそじ 四十路 forty years old.

よそながら 余所ながら ▶よそながら(=ひそかに)あなたのことを案じておりました I was *inwardly* worried about you.

よそみ よそ見 ▶よそ見しないで歩きなさい Look where you're going./Don't look the other way. (⇒脇見(ペ゜き)) ▶彼はよそ見していて電柱にぶつかった He *was looking the wrong way* and ran into a telephone pole. ▶事故はドライバーのよそ見(=不注意)が原因だった The accident was caused by the driver's *carelessness* [*inattention*].

よそめ 余所目 (⇒傍目(ばた゜))

よそもの 余所者 a stranger; (部外者) an outsider. ● よそ者扱いされる be treated as an *outsider*. ▶そこでは私はよそ者のような気分だった I didn't feel (that) I belonged there.

よそゆき 余所行き (晴れ着) one's best clothes; 《話・おどけて》one's Sunday best; (正装) formal dress. ● よそ行きの服をまとう in one's *best clothes*. ● よそ行きの(=改まった)言葉を遣う use *formal* language.

よそよそしい 余所余所しい 〖冷淡な〗cold; 〖友好的でない〗unfriendly, 《話》standoffish; 〖態度などが隔たりのある〗distant; 〖形式ばった〗formal. ● よそよそしい出迎えを受ける a (*formal*) welcome. ● よそよそしい態度で in an *unfriendly* [a *distant*] manner. ▶彼はいつも私によそよそしい He is always *cold and distant* to me./He is always *unfriendly* [*formal*] to me. ▶彼女にはどこかよそよそしいところがあった There was a certain *coldness* in [to] her. (**!**) to ではだれが何してもそれとなく気がつく, in では内包されていて必ずしもそうではないという含みがある) ▶彼の事業が失敗したとたん, 友人たちはよそよそしい態度を取り始めた As soon as his business failed, his friends started *giving* him *the cold shoulder*. ● *give ... the cold shoulder* は《話》で「冷たくあしらう」の意)

よぞら 夜空 a [the] night sky. (⇨空) ● 夜空に輝く星 stars shining in the *night sky*. ▶ 甲子園の夜空に花火が上がっていた Fireworks exploded in the *evening sky* over Koshien.

よた 与太 ● よたを飛ばす talk nonsense; talk irresponsibly.

よたか 夜鷹 [鳥] a jungle nightjar.

よだかのほし 『よだかの星』 *The Nighthawk Star*. (参考) 宮沢賢治の童話

よたく 預託 ── 預託する 動 deposit.
 ● 預託金 a deposit.

よたもの 与太者 a thug;《英古・米》a tough;(ちんぴら) a hooligan.

よたよた ● よたよた歩く（赤ん坊が）toddle;（あぶなげに）totter;（重い物を持って、酔っ払って倒れそうに）stagger. ▶ 赤ん坊が母の方へよたよた歩いて行った A baby *toddled* [*tottered*] toward its mother. ▶ 酔っ払いがよたよた歩いて行った A drunkard *staggered* along. ▶ 負傷兵がよたよた立ち上がった A wounded soldier *staggered* to his feet.

よたる 与太る ❶ [よたを飛ばす] (⇨与太)
 ❷ [不良のように行動する] play the gangster.
 ❸ [よたよたする] (⇨よたよた)

よだれ（唾液）saliva /səláivə/;（垂れた）drool. ● よだれをたらす slobber /slábər/;《書》salivate. ▶ 赤ん坊はよだれを流していた The baby *was slobbering* [*drooling*]. ▶ 私はそのケーキを見るとよだれが出た The cake made my *mouth water*./My *mouth watered* at the sight of the cake. (❗このようなケーキは a mouth-watering cake) ▶ この美しい絵がよだれが出るほど欲しい I would very much like to get this beautiful painting. (❗This beautiful picture *makes* my *mouth water* [*makes* me *drool*]. のような表現は、文字どおり絵に食べ物のおいしそうな様子が描かれていない限り使えない) ▶ 彼女は男たちが自分を見てよだれをたらすのには慣れていた She was used to men *drooling over* her.
 ● よだれ掛け a bib.

よたろう 与太郎 a blockhead;《米俗》a jerk;《英俗》a charlie.

よだん 予断 prediction.
 ● 予断を許さない ▶ 実際何が起こるかは予断は許さない We *can't predict* [*tell*] what will actually happen./There is *no telling* [*knowing*] what will actually happen.

よだん 余談 a digression. ● 余談になりますが（ちょっと話をそらせていただきますと）if you'll allow a slight *digression*, …;（ところで）by the way, incidentally. ▶ 彼の話は余談が多かった There were a lot of *digressions* in his speech. ● 余談はこれくらいにしておきましょう So much for the *digressions*.

よち 予知 图 (知識・経験などに基づく) (a) prediction, a forecast (❗後の方が口語的で確度合いが高い); (先見(の明)) foresight. ● 予知能力のある人 a person *of foresight*; a person who can *foresee* the future.
 ── 予知する 動 ▶ 地震を予知する make a forecast [a prediction] of earthquakes; forecast [predict, foretell] earthquakes.

よち 余地 [[余っている空間]] room, space, [[可能性]] room《for》; [[活動などの]] scope.
 ❶ [余地がある] ▶ もう 1 人入る余地がある There is *room* [*space*] *for* one more person. ▶ 会場は満員で立錐(すい)の[足を踏み入れる]余地もなかった The hall was so full that there was no standing *room* [no *room* for me to step in]. ▶ その辞書は大いに改善の余地がある There is plenty of *room for* improvement in the dictionary. ▶ この問題

はまだ議論の余地がある This question leaves *room for* [*is still open to*] discussion. ▶ その仕事には想像力を働かせる余地がない[十分にある] The job gives no [full] *scope for* the imagination. ▶ 君のしたことは弁解の余地がない What you did *allows* [《書》*admits*] *of* no excuse. (❗通例否定文で用いる。受身は不可)/Your conduct leaves no *room for* defense. ▶ 彼の無実は疑う余地もない There is *no doubt* about his innocence.
 ❷ [《余地を》] ▶ さらなる交渉の余地を残す leave *room* for further negotiation. ▶ 父は大学進学に関して私自身に選択の余地を与えてくれなかった My father didn't leave [give] me any *choice* about going on to college.

よちょう 予兆 an omen. ▶ 大地震の予兆があった There was an *omen* of a severe earthquake.

よちよち ● よちよち歩く toddle;（老人などがすり足で）shuffle. ▶ その赤ん坊はよちよち歩きを始めた [よちよち歩いて部屋に入って来た] The baby started *toddling* (*about*) [*toddled into* the room].

よつ 四つ ● 四つに組む (真剣に取り組む) come* [get*] to grips 《with》; get down to 《it; doing》; [[力士が]] grip each other's belts.

よつあし 四つ足 four legs; (けだもの) a quadruped /kwɑ́drəped/; an animal with four legs [feet]; a four-legged animal.

よっか 四日 ● 4 日間 for *four days*. ● 4 月 4 日に on April 4(*th*). (⇨日付)

よっか 翼下 (⇨翼下)

よっかかる 寄っ掛かる lean*. (⇨寄り掛かる)

よつかど 四つ角 [[十字路]] a crossroads (❗単数扱い); a crossing; [[街角]] a, (street) corner. ● 四つ角での交通事故 traffic accidents at a *crossroads*. ● その四つ角を左に曲がる turn (to the) left at the *crossroads* [*crossing, corner*].

よつぎ 世継ぎ [[後継者]] a successor《to》; [[相続人]] (男) an heir /eər/ 《to》, (女) an heiress 《to》.

よっきゅう 欲求 (a) desire《for; to do》; an appetite《for》; [[意志]] (a) will. (⇨欲, 欲望) ● 性的欲求 (a) sexual *desire*. (⇨性欲) ● 知的欲求を満たす satisfy one's *desire* to learn. ● 人々の真相を知りたいという欲求を喚起する whet people's *appetite for* the truth. ● 生への欲求 one's *will* to live. ▶ 彼はいつも欲求不満のはけ口を私に求める He always vents his *frustration* on me.

よつぎり 四つ切り (写真) a quarter, a photo of quarto size. ● 四つ切りにする print a photo [have a photo printed] in *a quarter size* [in *quarto size*].

よつご 四つ子 (1 人) a quadruplet /kwɑdrúːplet/;（全員）quadruplets.

よっつ 四つ four; (4 歳) four years old. ● 四つ目の the fourth. (⇨三つ)

よつつじ 四つ辻 (⇨四つ角)

よって 因って ❶ [そこで] so; therefore. (⇨だから)
 ❷ [それに基づいて] based on; consequent. ● よって起こった外交関係の悪化 the deterioration of diplomatic relations brought about *by* that action. ● 敗北のよって来たるところを考える think about the *cause of* [*reason for*] the defeat. ● この薬の効果は人によって異なる The effect of this medicine differs *from* person *to* person.

よつであみ 四つ手網 a four-armed fishing net.

よってたかって 寄ってたかって (⇨寄る ❷)

ヨット a yacht (❗小型の主に競走用帆船に、帆のない動力つきの豪華船の意にも用いる);《米》a sailboat,《英》a sailing boat (❗主に小型の帆船で、通例日本語のヨットに相当する). ● ヨット乗りに行く《主に米》go sail-

よっぱらい 酔っぱらい a drunken person;《話》a drunk. ●酔っ払い運転でつかまる be caught for *drunken* [《米》*drunk*] *driving*.

よっぱらう 酔っ払う get* [be] drunk. (⇨酔う)

よっぽど 余っ程 (⇨余程)

よづめ 夜爪 ●夜爪を切る cut one's nails at night.

よつめがき 四つ目垣 a *yotsumegaki*;(説明的に) a latticed bamboo fence.

よつゆ 夜露 night dew. (⇨露) ●夜露に当たるな Don't expose yourself to the *night dew*.

よづり 夜釣り night fishing. ●夜釣りに行く go fishing at night.

よつんばい 四つん這い ●四つんばいになって *on all fours*. ●四つんばいになって転げ回る[急な坂をよじ登る] crawl about [go up the steep hill] *on all fours* [*on one's hands and knees*].

***よてい** 予定 图 (一般的に計画) a plan (❗しばしば複数形で);(時間ごとに区切られた計画) a schedule;(活動計画) a program.

①【～(の)予定】●出版予定 a publishing *schedule*. ●当初の予定 the original *schedule*.

②【予定～】●出産予定日 the [one's] *due date*. ●出発[到着]予定時刻 the estimated time of departure [arrival]《略 ETD [ETA]》. ●工事は予定どおりに進んでいる The construction is going *according to* (the) *schedule* [*plan*]./The construction is going *as scheduled* [*planned*]. ●飛行機は予定どおり3時45分に出発でした The flight [plane] will depart *on schedule* [*as scheduled*] at 3:45. ●予定外に(=予定より)多くの学生がコンサートに集まった More students attended the concert than we (had) *planned on* [(予期していたより)than we (had) *expected*].

③【予定が[は]】●今日は予定がぎっしりつまっている I have a tight [a heavy, a full, ×a hard] *schedule for* today./I'm quite *booked up* today. ●それで予定がすっかり狂った That upset my entire *schedule*. ●予定が変更された The *schedule* has been changed. ●週末の予定がまだ立っていない I haven't set the *schedule* for the weekend yet. 会話「飛行機は予定どおりに到着しますか」「20分ほど遅れます」"Is the flight *on schedule*?" "It is about twenty minutes later." 会話「このあとの予定はどうなっていますか」「特に予定はありません(=特別何もすることがない)」"What's your *schedule* [What are your *plans*] *for* later?" "I have *nothing* particular *to do*."/"What *are* you *going to* do after this?" "I have no particular *plans* for later." (⇨動)

④【予定に】●予定によれば according to one's *schedule*. ●予定に変更がある There's a change in the *schedule* [*plan*]. ●駅で彼女に会うのは予定に入れていない(=計画していない) I don't *plan* to meet her at the station.

⑤【予定を】●週末の予定を立てましたか Have you made any *plans* for the weekend?

⑥【予定より】●列車は予定より2時間遅れで到着した The train arrived two hours behind (⇔ *ahead of*) *schedule* [*time*]. (❗(1) time を用いる方が堅い言い方)(2) The train arrived two hours *late*. ともいえる. この方が口語的)

⑦【予定だ】(⇨動) ●新校舎は来月完成の予定です The new school building *will* be completed next month. ●彼女と10時に会う予定で I'*m going to* meet [I'*m meeting*] her at ten. (❗前の方はあらかじめ決めた主語の意図、後の方は通例時の副詞を伴って取り決められた近い未来の予定を表す; I'm *supposed to* meet her at ten./《書》I *am to* meet her at ten. ●列車はあと30分で大阪に到着の予定でございます The train *will* arrive [*is due to* arrive, *is expected to* arrive, *is scheduled to* arrive, *is to* arrive] in Osaka in 30 minutes. (❗三つ目以降は堅い言い方) ●出産は12月の予定です I'*m expecting* a baby in December. (❗a baby は省略可)/I'*m going to* [×I'll] have a baby in December./My baby *is due* in December.

―― 予定の 圈 scheduled;(約束された) appointed;(計画された) planned. ●彼らは駅に予定の時間に着いた They arrived at the station at the *scheduled* [*appointed*, (決まった) *fixed*, ×*promised*] *time*. ●それは私の予定の行動でした That was my *planned* action.

―― 予定する 動 schedule《*to* do; *for*+日・時》(❗通例受身で);(計画する) plan (-nn-)《*to* do; *on* doing》(❗しばしば進行形で); be to do (❗堅い言い方. 通例正式な予定を表す);(到着予定である) be due 《*at, in; to do*》;(…するつもりである, 現況から判断して近く…しそうだ) be going to do;(…することになっている) be supposed to /səpóusftə/ do. (⇨图⑦) ●誕生日に友人を招くことを予定している I'*m planning to* invite [*on inviting*] my friends on my birthday. (❗後の方が口語的) ●会合はあす午後3時に予定されている The meeting *is scheduled for* [×at] 3 p.m. tomorrow. (❗×The meeting is scheduled *to be held* at 3 p.m..... のように受身の不定詞を伴うことは不可)

●予定地 a proposed site. ●新工場建設予定地 a *proposed* construction *site* of [for] a new factory. ●予定調和 preestablished harmony. ●予定納税 estimated tax prepayment. ●予定日 the expected date《*of* confinement》. ●予定表 a schedule.

よてき 余滴 (残ったしずく) drippings;《比喩的》(残りを拾い集めたもの) gleanings. ●編集余滴(=こぼれ話) *gleanings* from editor's notebooks.

よど 淀 backwater;―, a stagnant pool.

よとう 与党 the ruling [government] party; a party in power. ●与党の民主党 the *ruling* Democratic Party. ●与党である[になる] be in [come into] *power*.

よとうむし 夜盗虫〖昆虫〗an armyworm; a cutworm.

よどおし 夜通し (一晩中) all night (long);(夜の間ずっと) throughout the night. ●私は腹痛のため夜通し眠れなかった I couldn't sleep *all night* (*long*) [*throughout the night, all through the night*] because I had a stomachache.

よとぎ 夜伽 ―― 夜伽する 動〖寝ずの番をする〗(看病) keep vigil [sit up all night] beside the bed of a sick person; (警護・通夜で) keep vigil [an all-night watch]《*over* him》;〖女が男と〗serve as a bedmate.

よとく 余得 an extra profit (❗件数をいうときは C);(仕事または地位がらみの利得) a perk,《書》a perquisite.

よとく 余徳 influence [good reputation]《*of* one's late father》.

よどみ 淀み a stagnant [a standing] pool;(停滞) stagnation.

よどみ 澱み a sediment (❗複数形なし); (a) deposit.

よどみなく　淀みなく 〚流暢(ﾘｭｳﾁｮｳ)に〛 fluently; 〚口ごもらずに〛 without hesitation [faltering].

よどむ　淀む ● よどんだ空気 stale air. ● よどんだ水 stagnant [still] water. (⚠ 《 》には「沈澱している, 悪臭がある」の含みはない) ● この川の水はよどんでいる The water in this river is stagnant.

よどむ　澱む deposit; settle.

よなおし　世直し (a) social reform. ● 世直しをする carry out social reforms; make a better society.

***よなか　夜中** 〚漠然と夜中〛 night; 〚真夜中〛 the middle of the night (⇒真夜中); 〚夜中の1-3時ごろ〛 (in) the small hours. ● 夜中に in the middle of the night; (夜に) at night; (夜の間に) during [in] the night. ● 夜中じゅう雨が降った It rained all night [long] [all through the night, throughout the night]. ● 夜中に地震があった There was an earthquake during the night.

よなが　夜長 ● 秋の夜長を読書で過ごす spend long autumn evenings [nights] reading books.

よなき　夜泣き ● 赤ん坊がよく夜泣きをするのでこちらも眠れない Our baby often cries at night and we cannot get a good night's sleep.

よなき　夜鳴き ● 夜鳴きそば (そば) cooked noodles sold (late) at night by a hawker; (売る人) a hawker of cooked noodles. ● 夜鳴き鳥 a bird that sings at night.

よなべ　夜なべ 图 night-work. —— 夜なべ(を)する 動 work at night.

よなよな　夜な夜な every night; night after night.

よなれた　世慣れた (世才のある) worldly-wise (⚠ 通例叙述的に); (世間なれした) sophisticated. ● 世慣れた人 a sophisticated person; a man [a woman] of the world. ● 彼は年の割になかなか世慣れている He is rather worldly-wise [He has seen a lot of life] for his age.

よにいう　世に言う (いわゆる) what is [was] called; what they call. ● これが世にいう生麦事件である This is what is called the Namamugi Incident.

よにげ　夜逃げ —— 夜逃げする 動 run away under cover of darkness; 《英語》 do a moonlight flit.

よにも　世にも ● 世にも不思議な事件 (極度に) an extremely strange incident; (今まで聞いた中で最も) the strangest incident (that) I have ever heard of. ● 彼女は世にもまれな美人だ She is a rare beauty.

よねつ　予熱 preheating.
● 予熱炉 a prehéating fùrnace.

よねつ　余熱 (残っている熱) remaining [residual] heat; (廃熱) waste heat. ● フライパンの余熱で目玉焼きを作る make a sunny-side up by using the remaining heat of the frypan. ● ごみ processing 焼却の余熱を利用した温水プール a swimming pool heated by using the waste heat from incinerated garbage.

よねん　余念 ● 余念がない ● 読書に余念がない (=夢中だ) be absorbed [engrossed] in reading. ● 研究に余念がない devote oneself to one's studies. ● 仕事に余念がない (=忙しい) be busy with one's work.

よねんせい　四年生 (小学校の) a fourth-year pupil; 《米》 a fourth grader; 《英》 a fourth-former. (⇒一年生, 学年)

よのつね　世の常 ● 浮き沈みは世の常だ We all experience ups and downs./Life is full of ups and downs. ● 正直者が損をするのは世の常(=世の習い)だ It's everyday experience that honest people tend to lose out. ● 孟母は世の常の母親ではなかった The mother of Mencius was no ordinary mother.

***よのなか　世の中** 〚世間〛 the world; (社会) society; 〚人生〛 life; 〚時勢〛 times; 〚時代〛 an age; 〚漠然とした事態〛 things. (⇒世間) ● 世の中そんなに甘くはない The world [society] is not so permissive as you expect it to be. ● 彼は世の中をよく知っている He knows a lot about the world./He has seen a lot of the world. ● 近ごろは世の中が(=何もかも)どんどん変わっている These days everything is changing rapidly.

よのならい　世の習い (⇒世の常) ● 秀才が出世するとは限らないのが世の習いだ Bright students do not always get on in the world. That's life. ● 栄枯盛衰は世の習いだ (=人生には浮き沈みがある) Every life has its ups and downs 〚書〛 vicissitudes〛.

よは　余波 (災害・戦争などの) an aftermath; (なごり) an aftereffect (⚠ しばしば複数形で). ● 戦争の余波 the aftermath of the war. ● 石油ショックの余波 the aftereffects of the oil shock.

よばい　夜這い —— 夜這い(を)する 動 steal into a woman's bedroom at night.

よはく　余白 (a) (blank) space, a blank; 〚欄外に〛 a margin. ● 余白を残す〚埋める〛 leave [fill in] (a) space. ● ページの余白に書き込みをする write notes (down) in the margin of a page.

ヨハネスブルグ 〚南アフリカ共和国の都市〛 Johannesburg [/dʒouhǽnəsbɜ̀ːrɡ/].

よばれる　呼ばれる ❶ 〚声をかけられる〛 be called (out). (⚠ out を伴うと「大声で」の意) ● 名前を呼ばれたら手をあげなさい Raise your hand when your name is called (out).
❷ 〚称される〛 be called. ● 私は友人に「さち」と呼ばれています I am called 'Sachi' by my friends.
❸ 〚来させられる〛 be called; be sent for. ● 彼は職員室に呼ばれた(=呼び出された) He was called to the teachers' room. ● 彼女は重病だったので息子が呼ばれた(=呼び寄せられた) She was very sick, and her son was sent for (呼び戻された) was called home〛.
❹ 〚招待される〛 be invited, be asked. (⚠ 前の方が普通) ● 彼の結婚披露宴に呼ばれた I was invited to his wedding reception. ● 僕はそのパーティーには呼ばれていません I haven't been invited [been asked] to the party.

—よばわり　—呼ばわり ● 泥棒呼ばわりされて迷惑この上ない It really annoys me that they call me a thief. (⚠ call を強めて, brand (烙印(ﾗｸｲﾝ)を押す), label (レッテルをはる), denounce (公然と非難する: denounce me as a thief) のようにもいえる)

よばん　夜番 (行為) night watch; (人) a night watchman (國 watchmen) [guard]. ● 夜番をする guard (a bank) at night; keep a night watch.

よばんだしゃ　四番打者 〚野球〛 a cleanup (hitter); a number-four hitter. ● 四番打者を敬遠する walk a cleanup intentionally.

***よび　予備** 图 〚余分〛 (蓄え) a reserve; (非常用品) a spare; (補充用) (a) báckùp. (⇒スペア) ● 予備に金をいくらかとってある〚とっておく〛 have [keep] some money in reserve 〔for〕. (⚠ keep の場合は命令形・受身形可)
—— 予備(の) 形 〚余分の〛 spare; 〚準備の〛 preparatory; (予行の) preliminary; 〚非常用にとっておいた〛 reserve. ● 予備のタイヤ a spare (tire). ● 予備のワイン a backup wine bottle.
● 予備軍 the reserve(s). ● 生活習慣病予備軍 a reserve body of sufferers from lifestyle-related

よびあげる

illnesses. ● 予備校 《⇨予備校》● 予備交渉《enter into》preliminary negotiations. ● 予備知識《have》a preliminary [a background] knowledge《of》. ● 予備調査《make》a preliminary survey. ● 予備費《have》a reserve fund [a fund in reserve]. ● 予備品 a back-up (supply).
● 予備部品 spare parts.

よびあげる 呼び上げる　[大きな声で呼ぶ] call (out) 《his name》(❗call 自体である程度大きな声を含意. call out は shout, cry と似た意味になる); [呼び寄せる] call 《him》to《a party》.

よびあつめる 呼び集める　call ... together; (集合させる) assemble.

よびいれる 呼び入れる　call 《him》into《the house》.

よびおこす 呼び起こす　❶[目を覚まさせる] wake* 《him》up; 《やや書》awake*. ❷[思い出を] recall ... (to one's mind). ●事故の記憶を呼び起こす recall the accident; bring back the memory of the accident.

よびかけ 呼び掛け　(訴え)(an) appeal; (要請)(a) request; (呼称)(a form of) address. ●教会の募金の呼び掛けに応じる agree to the church's appeal [request] for charity.

よびかける 呼び掛ける　❶[声をかける] ▶2階から彼に呼びかけた I called to him from upstairs. ❷[訴える] ▶市民に節水を呼びかける appeal to the citizens to save water.

よびかわす 呼び交わす　▶登山者たちはお互いの名を呼び交わして居場所を確認し合った Climbers called each other's name to locate their positions.

よびこ 呼び子　(blow) a whistle.

よびこう 予備校　a preparatory school for university entrance examinations (❗単に preparatory school といえば,《米》では大学進学のための寮制の私立学校,《英》では public school 進学のための私立小学校); (日本の予備校・進学塾) a cram school 《受験用の詰め込み勉強をさせる》. ▶彼は浪人して予備校に通っている He is a high school graduate who failed to enter a college and goes to a cram school to study for the next chance.
● 予備校生 a cram school student.

よびごえ 呼び声　a call; (叫び声) a cry. ●荒野の呼び声 the call of the wild.
● 呼び声が高い ▶彼は次期社長として呼び声が高い(=評判である) He is very much talked about as the next president.

よびこみ 呼び込み　(人やサーカスなどの) a barker.

よびこむ 呼び込む　▶私を家に呼び込む(=呼び入れる) call me into one's house. ●客を呼び込む call in shoppers by barking.

よびさます 呼び覚ます　《⇨呼び起こす》

よびすて 呼び捨て　▶私を呼び捨てにしないで (姓だけで) Don't call me by my last name only. / (敬称なしで) Don't call me without "Miss." ["Mr.", "Mrs."]

よびだし 呼び出し　❶[召喚] ●警察からスピード違反で呼び出しを受ける receive a summons for speeding from the police. (❗「…に呼び出しを受ける」は be called [《書》summoned] to ... でよい) ▶青山様にお呼び出し申し上げます. フロントまでお越しください Paging Mr. Aoyama. Please be at the front desk. (❗Paging .... は We're paging .... の略で,「(マイクなどで)捜しています」の決まり文句)
❷[相撲] 呼び出し係) an [a ring] announcer.
● 呼び出し状 (召喚状) a summons.

よびだす 呼び出す　[呼び寄せる] call 《him》《to＋場所・人》; [来いと命令する] tell* 《him》to come《to one's room》; [書] summon 《him》《to》

(court); [呼び出し放送で] page. 《⇨呼び出し》●彼をその喫茶店に呼び出す call him [tell him to come] to the coffee shop. ●彼を電話口に呼び出す get him on the phone. ▶デパートで母を呼び出してもらった I had my mother paged at the department store.

よびたてる 呼び立てる　▶こんなに遅くお呼び立てして申し訳ありません I'm very sorry to have asked you to come this late at night.

よびつける 呼び付ける　[呼び出す] call 《him》to 《before》…; (召喚する) summon. ▶彼は上級生に呼びつけられた He was called to [before] his senior.

よびとめる 呼び止める　call to《him》to stop; [タクシーを] hail, 《大きく手を振って》flag (-gg-) ... down. ▶彼はタクシーを呼び止めた He hailed [flagged (down)] a taxi.

よびな 呼び名　❶[通称] a popular name. ▶彼はトンちゃんの呼び名をちょうだいしていた He was popularly called Ton-chan. ❷[名前] a name; (専門用語) a term.

よびならわす 呼び習わす　(習慣として呼ぶ) call ... customarily. ▶このためその像は「ビリケン」と呼び習わされている For this reason the statue is customarily called "Billiken."

よびみず 呼び水　(ポンプの) pump priming.
● 呼び水となる start; (刺激となる) be a stimulant 《to》, stimulate 《to; …into》. ▶リーダーの逮捕が呼び水となって暴動が起きた The leader's arrest stimulated them to get up a riot [引き金になる) triggered off the riot].

よびもどす 呼び戻す　call ... back; (命令によって) recall. ●父の病気で家に呼び戻される be called home because one's father is sick. ●旅行先から呼び戻される be called back from one's trip. ▶大使はロンドンから呼び戻された(=召還された) The ambassador was called back from London.

よびもの 呼び物　[特に人を引きつける物] the main [a special, a chief] attraction; [中心となる出し物] the feature. 《⇨ハイライト》▶綱渡りがサーカスの呼び物です The highwire act is the main attraction at [the feature of] the circus.

よびや 呼び屋　a promotor《of》.

よびょう 余病　(合併症) a complication. ▶余病に肺炎を併発した Pneumonia followed as a complication.

よびよせる 呼び寄せる　[[呼ぶ] call《him》《to＋人・場所》; [来てもらう] have*《him》come《to＋人・場所》. 《⇨呼び出す》

よびりん 呼び鈴　a bell; (玄関の) a door-bell; (ブザー) a buzzer. ▶ほら, 呼び鈴が鳴っているよ There's [There goes] the bell. (❗これはその場にいる人の注意を引くための発言で, 単に「呼び鈴が鳴っている」は The bell is ringing.)

よぶ 呼ぶ　❶[声をかける] call, (大声で) call ... out; (注意を引くため大声で呼ぶ) hail. ●大声で彼の名前を呼ぶ call out his name. ●助けを呼ぶ(=求める) call for help. ▶あっ, ママが呼んでるわ. じゃあね! Oh, there's my mom calling me. Bye! ●通りで見知らぬ人が突然私の名前を呼んだ A stranger suddenly called my name [me by name] on the street. ▶彼は通りでタクシーを呼んだ He hailed a taxi on the street.
❷[称する] call; (敬称で) address. ▶私の名前は幸子ですが友人はさちと呼びます My name is Sachiko but my friends call me Sachi. ●あなたのネコを何と呼んでいるの What [×How] do you call your cat? ▶学生たちは彼を教授と呼んでいる The students address him as "Professor." (❗×Call

him as "Professor" とはいわない)
❸ 【来させる】(通電話などで) call; (呼びに行く, 呼びで来る) get*; (他の人に呼びに行かせて) send* for ...; (召喚する)《書》summon. ▶救急車[警察]を呼ぶ Call an ambulance [the police]. ▶彼は医者を呼んだ (来るように頼んだ) He *called* in a doctor./(呼びにやった) He *called* [*sent*] *for* a doctor. (▲*call in* the doctor とすれば「かかりつけの医者」の意) ▶部長を呼んで来てあげましょう I'll *get* [go and *get*,《話》go *get*] the manager *for* you./I'll *get* [go and *get*,《話》go *get*] you the manager. (⚠*go* (and) *get* の形は原形でのみ用いる) ▶タクシーを呼んでください Will you *call* me a taxi [a taxi *for* me]? ▶(亀田)社長, お呼びですか Did you want (to see) me, Mr. Kameda?/Did you want me, sir [(くだけて) boss]?（⚠過去形を用いると丁寧さが増す）▶田中さんがお呼びです Mr. Tanaka *wants* [*is calling*] you.
❹ 【招待する】invite, ask. ▶今夜友達を夕食に呼んでいる I've *invited* [*asked*] some friends *to* dinner this evening.
❺ 【引き起こす】cause. ▶彼の小説は大きな反響を呼んだ (= 大評判になった) His novel *caused* [*made*] a great sensation. ▶この映画は大変な人気を呼んだ (= 勝ち得た) This movie *has won* great popularity.

よふかし 夜ふかし ── 夜ふかし(を)する 動 stay [sit] up late at night;《米・英礼》keep late hours. ▶早寝・読書をして夜ふかしをする stay [sit] up late reading. (⇨徹夜)

よふけ 夜ふけ ▶夜ふけに late at night; (真夜中に) at midnight. ▶深夜, 真夜中)

*よぶん **余分** 名 an extra; 〔過多〕(an) excess; 〔余剰〕(a) surplus.
── 余分の 形 extra; spare; too much; surplus. (⇨余計な) ●余分の切符が1枚ある have one *extra* ticket. ●余分の時間はない have no time *to spare* [no *spare* time].
── 余分に 副 (⇨余計(に)) ●余分に働く do *extra* work; work *overtime* [*extra*].

よぶん 余聞（こぼれ話）a tidbit. ●政界余聞 a piece of political *gossip*; a *tidbit* of information in the political world.

よへい 余弊〔いまだに残っている弊害〕long-lasting evil effects;〔...にともなって生じる弊害〕resulting evils. ●共産主義国家の余弊を絶やせないならない cannot do away with the *evils* of the communist country.

*よほう **予報** a forecast;〔予測〕(a) prediction. ●天気予報 a wéather fòrecast [repòrt]. ●長期[短期]予報 a long-[short-]range *forecast*. ●天気予報[係] a weather forecaster; (男の人) a weatherman. ●地震の予報 an earthquake *prediction* [*forecast*]. ●テレビ[ラジオ]の天気予報を聞く listen to the weather *report* on TV [the radio]. ●最近の(天気)予報はよく外れる[当たる] The recent *forecasts* often prove wrong [right]. ▶予報ではあしたは雨だ The (weather) *forecast* [The weather forecaster] says that it's going to rain tomorrow./《やや書》According to the (weather) *forecast* [the weather forecaster], it will rain tomorrow./The weatherman *forecasts* [×says] rain for tomorrow./Tomorrow's weather *forecast* is for rain.

*よほう **予防** 名 (防止) (a) prevention; (用心) (a) precaution. (⚠似た「予防策」の意では [C])
① 【〜の予防】 ●火災[病気]の予防 the *prevention* of fire [disease]. (⚠前の方は fire prevention ともいう) ●彼は盗難の予防(策)として鍵(穴)をつけた He installed a lock as a *prevention* against theft.
② 【予防〜】 ●火災予防週間 Fire *Prevention* Week. ●この種の事故に対して予防策を講じる take *preventive* measures [take *precautions*] against accidents of this kind. ●予防線を張る (⇨予防線)
── 予防する 動 (防ぐ) prevent《A from B》. (⇨防ぐ) ●インフルエンザが広がるのを予防する *prevent* the flu *from* spreading; *prevent* the spread of the flu. ●虫歯を予防する *prevent* tooth decay; (保護する) *protect* one's teeth *from* decay.
●予防医学 preventive medicine. ●予防注射 a preventive injection [《話》shot]《against》. (⇨予防接種)

よぼうせっしゅ 予防接種 名 (病原菌などの) (an) inoculation; (ワクチンの) (a) vaccination. (⚠両者とも「予防注射」の意にも用いる)
── 予防接種(を)する 動 ●彼にその病気の予防接種をする *vaccinate* him *against* the disease. ●コレラの予防接種を2回受ける be inoculated [vaccinated] *against* cholera twice; get two inoculations [vaccinations] *against* cholera;《米話》get two *shots* of cholera.

よぼうせん 予防線 ●予防線を張る ▶私は後で非難されないように予防線を張った I took every *precaution* so as not to be criticized later.

*よほど **余程** ❶ 【ずいぶん】(非常に) very, (very) much (⚠very は原級, much は比較級を修飾 (⇨大分解説)); (大いに) a great deal, 《やや書》greatly, 《話》a lot; (相当に) considerably (⚠通例最新級・比較級を修飾) (⇨大分) ▶今日はよほど気分がよい I feel *much* [*a lot*, *a great deal*] better today. ▶彼はその話がよほどおもしろかったようだ It seems that he was *very much* [*greatly*, 《話》*very*] amused by the story. (⚠very では amused は完全に形容詞化しており, ... the story was *very* amusing to him. ともいえる) ▶この仕事はよほど(= 十分)注意しないと危険だ If you aren't careful *enough* with this task, it can be dangerous.
❷ 【思い切って】 ▶よほど彼に言ってやろうかと思った(= 言ってやりたい気が大いにあった) I had a good mind to tell him.

よぼよぼ ── よぼよぼの 形 (体が弱い) frail, feeble; (老齢で震えたり, 足が乱れたり) shaky, 《話》doddering; (もうろくした) senile /síːnail/. ●よぼよぼの老婦人 a *frail* [a *doddering*] old lady.

よまいごと 世迷い言 a useless complaint; a grumble. (⇨愚痴)

よませる 読ませる ▶彼女の自伝はなかなか読ませるね Her autobiography *is very absorbing*.

よまつり 夜祭り a night festival.

よまわり 夜回り 名 a night patrol; (記者の) a night visit. ●夜回りの記者 a reporter on his [her] nightly rounds.
── 夜回り(を)する 動 patrol《the residential quarters》; (記者が) make [do] the rounds of people at night to collect information.

よみ 読み ▶相手の次の出方(= 手)は私の読みどおりだった His next move was just as I *had expected*.
●読みが深い ▶彼は読みが深い(= 洞察力がある) He has a [is a man of] deep (↔shallow) *insight*./《話》He has a lot of *insight*.

よみ 黄泉 the land of the dead; 〔ギリシャ神話〕Hades; 〔ギリシャ神話・ローマ神話〕the Underworld.

よみあげざん 読み上げ算 (説明的に) computation of the figures, read by another person, on an abacus.

よみあげる　読み上げる　(名前などを順番に) call ... off; (声をあげて読む) read*... out. ●1節をよく通した声で読み上げる read out the passage in a clear voice. ▶彼は合格者の名前を読み上げた He *called off* the names of successful applicants.

よみあさる　読み漁る　(広く[むさぼるように]読む) read 《a book》 widely 《voraciously》.

よみあやまる　読み誤る　●read* wrong; (読み間違える) misread*; (間違った発音で読む) mispronounce; (解釈を間違える) misinterpret; (判断を誤る) misjudge.

よみあわせ　読み合わせ　●読み合わせをする〘間違いがないか読み合う〙(⇨読み合わせる), 〘俳優が脚本を読み合う〙read through 《their》 parts together.

よみあわせる　読み合わせる　collate the copy with the original by reading aloud.

よみおとす　読み落とす　miss ... in reading. ▶彼はその論文の大切な箇所を読み落とした He *failed to [didn't] read* the important points [passages] of the thesis.

よみおわる　読み終わる　(始めから終わりまで読む) read*... over [through]. ▶やっと『風と共に去りぬ』を読み終わった I finally *read over [through] Gone with the Wind./I finally finished reading* [×to read] *Gone with the Wind*.
〔会話〕「あの本もう読み終わったの?」「読み始めたばっかりよ」"*Have* you *finished* [*Are* you *through* (*with*)] that book?" "I've only just begun it."

よみかえす　読み返す　read* again; reread (**！**変化形は read に同じ). ▶良書を読み返す *read* a good book *again*; *reread* a good book. ▶彼女は恋人からの手紙を何度も読み返した She *read* a letter from her lover *over and over again* [(繰り返し) *repeatedly*].

よみがえる　蘇る　〘生き返る〙revive; (息を吹き返す) come* [bring] (back) to life; (元気にする) restore (*to* health); revitalize. ●廃棄物を資源としてよみがえらせる *recover* waste materials as resources. ▶その音楽を聞いたとたん失った記憶がよみがえった The moment I listened to the music, my lost memory *revived./The music suddenly brought back my lost memory.* ▶その情景を見た私の心に20年前の頃がよみがえった The scene *reminded me of* the days of twenty years ago. (**！** remind は「思い出させる」の意)

よみかき　読み書き　●読み書きができない can't *read* or [×nor, ×and] *write*; can neither *read* nor *write*; be illiterate. ●読み書きそろばんを習う learn *reading*, *writing* and arithmetic [the three R's].

よみかた　読み方　●読み方を練習する practice *reading*. ●その漢字[行]の二通りの読み方 two *readings* of [to, for] the Chinese character [the line].

よみがな　読み仮名　(⇨ルビ)

よみきり　読み切り　●読み切り小説 a novel complete in one issue of a magazine; a complete(-in-one-issue) story. 〔関連〕連載物 a serial)

よみきかせる　読み聞かせる　●子供たちに絵本を読み聞かせる read a picture book to children.

よみきる　読み切る　finish reading. (⇨読み終わる)

よみくだす　読み下す　●条文を読み下す go *through* the text (*of* a treaty) (*quickly*). ●読み下す(=日本語の語順にあえて) read classical Chinese writings by arranging them in the Japanese word order.

よみごたえ　読みごたえ　●読みごたえのある本 (内容豊かな本) a book of much substance; (読んでためになる本) a rewarding book; (読む価値のある本) a book worth reading.

よみこなす　読みこなす　(よく読める) read* well; (読んで会得する) read and digest 〘(掘り下げる) delve 《*into*》〙; (理解する) understand*. ▶『源氏物語』を読みこなすのは骨が折れる It's hard to *read The Tale of Genji well./It's hard to read for the deeper meaning of The Tale of Genji*.

よみこみ　読み込み　●読み込み中〘コンピュータ〙loading.

よみこむ　読み込む　❶〘深く読む〙read* thoroughly. ❷〘コンピュータ〙read in.

よみさし　読みさし　●読みさしの本 the book one *is reading*; a half-read [-/red/] book. ▶彼は本を読みさしにして, あたふたと部屋から出て行った He hurried out of the room without finishing the book./He hurried out of the room, leaving the book *half-read*.

よみじ　黄泉路　the road to the Underworld. (⇨黄泉) ●黄泉路の旅 one's journey to the Underworld.

よみすごす　読み過ごす　miss reading; (飛ばす) skip. ▶どうやらその記事[最後の章]を読み過ごしてしまったらしい I seem to have *missed reading* the article [*have skipped* the last chapter].

よみすすむ　読み進む　go* on reading.

よみすて　読み捨て　throw 《a magazine》 away after reading it (for a few hours' pleasure).

よみせ　夜店　a night stand [〘(主に英)〙stall]. ●夜店を出す open [set up] a *night stand*.

よみだし　読み出し　(a) readout. ●読み出し専用記憶装置 read-only memory (略 ROM).

よみだす　読み出す　❶〘読み始める〙begin* to read. ▶きのうからあのベストセラー小説を読み出した I *began to read [began reading]* the best-selling novel yesterday.
❷〘データなどを〙〘コンピュータ〙read* out; make a readout 《*of*》.

よみち　夜道　●夜道を1人で歩くのは危ない It's dangerous (for you) to *walk* alone *at night*.

よみちがえる　読み違える　(誤読する・誤解する) misread*; (判断を誤る) misjudge; miscalculate. ▶彼の反応を読み違えた I *miscalculated* his reaction.

よみつぐ　読み継ぐ　(中断していた本を) resume reading [×to read]. ▶『吾輩は猫である』は世代から世代へと読み継がれている(=受け継がれて読まれている) "I am a cat" *has been read* from one generation to the next.

よみて　読み手　〘読む人〙a reader (⑳ 書き手); 〘読み上げる人〙a reciter; 〘短歌などの〙a writer; a composer.

よみで　読みで　▶あの本は読みでがある It will take a long time to read that book through. (⇨読みごたえ)

よみとおす　読み通す　read*... over [through]; read ... from beginning to end. ▶その本を読み通すのに10日間かかった It took me ten days to *read over* the book [*read* the book *from cover to cover*].

よみとく　読み解く　(暗号などを) decode; decipher; (難解な文章を) decipher.

よみどころ　読みどころ　a passage [a chapter] worth reading; (最高にいい部分) the highlight(s).

よみとばす　読み飛ばす　skim through [over] 《a book》.

よみとりき　読み取り機　〘コンピュータ〙a reader. ●読み取り機にカードを入れてドアの鍵を開ける swipe one's card to unlock the door. (〔関連〕このような磁気カー

よみとる 読み取る（意味・人の考え・感情などを）read*; （読んで理解する）read and understand*. (⇨読む❸) ▶彼の顔つき[言葉]からいらだっていることが読み取れた I *read* irritation on his face [in what he said]. ▶行間の意味を読み取ることが大切です It's important to *read* between the lines.

よみとれる 読み取れる (⇨読み取る)

よみなおす 読み直す ●答案を読み直す *read* one's exam paper *over again*.

よみながす 読み流す read* without a pause; run* [skim (-mm-)] through 《a book of jokes》. ●700年前の写本を読み流す=すらすら読めることを be able to *read* a 700-year-old manuscript *smoothly* [*easily*].

よみにくい 読みにくい hard [difficult] to read; (書いた文字が) illegible, unreadable; (内容が複雑・論理的でないなどで) unreadable. ▶このサインは読みにくい (=読み取りにくい、読めない) This signature is *illegible*.

よみのくに 黄泉の国 (⇨黄泉)

よみびと 詠み人 a writer; a composer; an author. ▶詠み人知らず Author unknown./Anonymous 《略 Anon.》.

よみふける 読み耽る（没頭する）be absorbed in (reading)《a book》. ▶彼は本を読みふけっていて母親が呼んだのも聞こえなかった He *was absorbed in* [*was poring over*; *was engrossed in*] a book and didn't hear his mother call.

よみふだ 読み札 a card to be read in a game of *karuta*.

よみもの 読み物 (新聞・雑誌の)《集合的》 reading (matter). (⇨読む❶)[最後の文例]▶軽い読み物 light *reading*. ●子供向き読み物 *reading*[本] a *book*] for children; (児童文学) juvenile *literature*.

よみや 夜宮, 宵宮 (⇨宵(よい)祭り)

よみやすい 読み易い easy to read; (書いた文字が) legible, readable; (内容が) readable.

:**よむ 読む, 詠む ❶**[読んで理解する] read*. ●カント[楽譜; 時計]を読む *read* Kant [music; the clock]. ●グラフを読む *read* a graph. (▶文字以外のものを注意深く見て理解する場合) ▶本を読んでいると電話が鳴った。「やあ、おばあちゃん、おれや」と電話の向こう側で男の声がした I *was reading* when the telephone rang. "Hi, Granny. It's me," said a male voice at the other end of the line. (▶The telephone rang while I was reading. の組み立て方より話の流れが自然になる) ▶その新聞は広く読まれている The paper *is* widely *read* paper. (❗The paper has a wide [a large] circulation. ともいえる) ▶彼が自殺したことを新聞で読んだ I *read* in the paper *that* he committed suicide./I *read about* [*of*] his suicide in the paper. (❗that 節、of 句では「を読んで知っている」の意で know にほぼ相当する. about 句では「について詳しく読む」ことを暗示し、可の場合可) ▶彼は日本の詩をよく読んでいる He's *well-read* in Japanese poetry. ▶この本は寝る時に読むのにちょうどよい This book makes perfect bedtime *reading*. (❗この reading は「読み物」の意で名詞)

❷[声を出して読む] read* (aloud [out, 《話》 out loud]). (❗朗読) ●判決文を読む *read out* the sentence. (❗read out は比較的短い内容や聞き手に関心のあるものに用いる) ●子供に本を読んでやって寝かせた I *read* the child *to* sleep. (❗(1) この sleep は名詞. (2) ×read the child sleeping とはいわない. (3) 自分が「本を読んで寝てしまう」場合は *read* oneself *to* sleep) ▶母は私に聖書を読んでくれた Mother *read* me the Bible./Mother *read* the Bible *to* [*for*] me. ▶寝る前に本を読むのもものだ I used to *be read to* [×*for*] before my bedtime. (❗read to A (A に読んで聞かせる)の受身で to は省略不可)

❸[推察する] read*. ●その手紙から彼の手[心]のうちを読み取る *read* his intentions [his mind, his heart, his thoughts] through [from] the letter. ●彼の表情から不満の気持ちを読み取る *read* discontent *in* [*on, from*] his face; read in [*on, from*] his face that he is discontented.

❹[詩歌を]compose; write*; make*. ●俳句を1句詠む *compose* a haiku.

よめ 嫁 [息子の妻] one's daughter-in-law (複 daughters-, 《英語》 〜s); [妻] one's wife (複 wives); (話・おどけて) one's missis; [花嫁] a bride.
①【嫁の[と]】▶彼女には嫁のもらい手がない She has no one who will *marry* her. ▶あの家は嫁と姑の仲がよくない The *wife* and her mother-in-law in that family don't get along [on] well.
②【嫁に】▶息子の嫁にもらう have (her) as a *wife* for one's son. ●娘を金持ちの嫁にやる *marry* one's daughter (*off*) to a rich man [into a rich family].
③【嫁を】▶彼はついに嫁をもらった(=結婚した) He *got married* at last.
●嫁に行く ▶彼女はまだ嫁に行く年ではない She isn't old enough [is too young] to *marry*./《書》She still hasn't reached a *marriageable* age.

よめ 夜目 ●教会は夜目にもそれとすぐ分かった I found the church easily enough *in the dark*.
●夜目遠目笠(かさ)のうち Any woman looks more beautiful when seen in the dark, at a distance, or under a sedge hat.

よめい 余命 one's remaining days. ●平均余命 life expectancy. ▶彼は寿命いくばくもない He has only *a few days to live*./《話》His *days* are numbered.

よめいびり 嫁いびり ●嫁いびりをする pick on one's daughter-in-law.

よめいり 嫁入り [結婚] (a) marriage; [結婚式] a wedding. ●嫁入り支度をする make preparations for *marriage*. ●嫁入り前の(=婚期に達している)娘が2人いる have two daughters of *marriageable age*.
●嫁入り衣装 a wédding drèss. ●嫁入り道具 a bride's [a bridal] outfit; 《やや書》a trousseau /truːˈsoʊ/ (複 〜s; trousseaux /-z/).

よめとり 嫁取り ●嫁取りする (親の立場から) adopt a daughter-in-law into one's family; (子の立場から) take a wife.

よめな 嫁菜 [植物] a starwort.

:**よめる 読める ❶**[読む能力がある] can* [be able to] read. ●前の方が口語的)●字の読めない人 an illiterate /ɪˈlɪtərət/. ●ドイツ語読める *can* [*be able to*] *read* German. ●彼は人の心が読める He *can read* minds./He is a mínd rèader.

❷[読まれる] read*. ●この法律の本は簡単に読める This book about law *reads* easily. (❗本などが主語になるこの用法は様態の副詞が必ず必要で、通例現在形で用いるが、This book about law *read* easily in those days. (その当時では簡単に読まれた)のように時間的制限がある場合は過去形も可)/This book about law is easy to *read* [×read it]. ●第3条はふた通りに読める(=解釈できる) Article 3 *reads* [*can be read*] (in) two ways./Two *readings* of Article 3 *are possible*.

❸[判読できる] be legible [readable]. (⇨判読)

よもぎ ❹[その他の表現] ●行間を読む(=言外の意味を読み取る) *read* between the lines. ●読んで字のごとく(に) *literally*; as its name indicates. ●1 行飛ばしで読む *skip* (*over*) a line.

よもぎ 蓬[植物] a mugwort.

よもすがら 夜もすがら (⇨夜通し)

よもや (Not) really! (⇨まさか 鬭)

よもやまばなし 四方山話 a small talk. (⇨世間 ①)

****よやく 予約** 图 ❶ [ホテル・座席などの] a reservation, 《主に英》(a) booking. ●予約をとっておく hold a *reservation*. ●予約を確認する (ホテルに対して) confirm one's *reservations*; confirm 《one's room》*reservation*; (航空会社に対して現地で) reconfirm one's *reservation*. ▶(航空券の)予約の確認をお願いします Reconfirmation, please. ▶全席予約済みです All seats (*are*) *reserved* [(*are*) *booked*]. (**!** *are* を省略するのは掲示文) ▶A ホテルの[その便の]予約がとれない I can't get a *reservation at* A Hotel [*on* the flight]. (**!**いずれも前置詞のは不可) ▶レストランに電話して夕食の予約をしよう I'll call up the restaurant and make a *reservation* for dinner. ▶3 か月先まで[来月まで(=今月中は)]予約でいっぱいです We're fully *reserved* [*booked* (*up*)] for the next three months [until next month].

会話「テーブルの予約は承っておりますか」「はい、田中の名前で3名、午後7時の予約ですが」"Do you have a table *reservation*?" "Yes, I do. The name is Tanaka, three people for [at] 7 p.m."

会話「キャンセルした場合の払い戻しに関しての予約条件はどうなっているの」「出発の 30 日前なら全額払い戻しになります」"What do the *booking* conditons say about the refund for cancellation?" "If it's 30 days before the departure, you get 100 percent back." (**!**このような旅行業界用語としては《米》でも booking が普通)

❷ [医院・会合などの] an appointment. (⇨約束[類語]) ●あすの予約を取り消す[変更する] cancel [change] one's *appointment for* tomorrow. ▶5 時に歯医者の予約をしている I have an *appointment with* [×*of*] the dentist at five./I have a dental *appointment* at five. ●あの歯医者は予約制だ That dentist sees you by *appointment* only [only by *appointment*].

❸ [新聞・雑誌の] a subscription. ▶ニューズウィーク誌の1年間の購読予約をした I *subscribed* [made a *subscription*] to *Newsweek* for a year.

― 予約する 動 ❶ [ホテル・座席などを] reserve, make* [get*] a reservation, 《主に英》book. ●インターネットで切符を予約する *reserve* a ticket on the internet. ▶彼は 5月10日午後のパリ行きの便の席を二つ予約した He *has reserved* [*booked*] two seats on an afternoon flight for Paris on May 10. ▶A ホテルに予約している I've *reserved* [*made a reservation for*, *booked*] a room at [in] A Hotel. (**!**(1)《米》では1室の予約でもしばしば made *reservations* となる. (2) 日本語的に ×…reserved A Hotel は不可. 訳例のほかに reserve *a hotel room* ともいう)/I have a room *reserved* at [in] A Hotel. ▶2晩予約してあるはずですが (ホテルのフロントで) I think you have a room *reserved* (for me) for two nights./I think I have a *reservation for* two nights. ▶切符を予約しましょうか Shall I *reserve* [book] a ticket *for you*?/Shall I *book* [×reserve] you a ticket? ▶今すぐ[早目に]予約しなさい. でないとコンサートの切符が手に入りませんよ *Book* now [early], or you won't get a ticket for the concert. (**!** reserve は他動詞なので不可) ▶今晩 8 時に 5 人予約したいのですが (レストランに電話で) I'd like to *reserve* a table for five at eight this evening. (**!**(1)…a table for eight this evening for five. のようにもいえる. (2)「美濃吉を 8 時に予約する」は reserve a table at Minokichi for [at] eight o'clock)

❷ [医院・会合などで] make an appointment.

会話「もしもし、今日の午後3時に[田中先生の診察を]予約したいのですが」「はい、お名前をどうぞ」"Hello. I'd like to *make an appointment for* three o'clock this afternoon [*to see* Dr. Tanaka]?" "Yes. May I have your name please?"

会話「その小説、次に読ませてもらえますか」「悪いけどだめよ. 息子がもう予約しているの」"Can I read that novel after you?" "Can't be done, I'm afraid. My son *has* already *spoken for* it." (**!**しばしば受身で物にも人にも用いられる:その本は(他の人が)予約済みです The book *is* already *spoken for*.)

❸ [新聞・雑誌などを] (予約購読する) subscribe 《*to*, *for*》.

❹ [その他の表現] ●テレビドラマをビデオで録画予約する *preset* a video recorder to record a television play.

●予約金 a deposit. ●予約席 a reserved seat. [参考] その座席は reserved と表示される. ●予約販売 sales [selling] by subscription.

****よゆう 余裕** ❶ [余地] room, space; [時間・金銭・体力の] time 《*money*, *energy*》to spare 《*for*》; [余剰] (a) surplus.

①[余裕が[は]] ▶その船にはまだ 5 人乗れる余裕がある The boat has enough *room for* five more persons. ▶時間[金]の余裕がない I have no *time* [*money*] *to spare*./I *am pressed for* time [money]. ▶旅行する余裕はない I can't *afford* (*to* take) a trip./I can't *afford* the *money* [*time*] for a trip. (**!** afford は can, could, be able to を伴って通例否定文・疑問文で用いる. ×I can't afford to have money [time] to take a trip. とはいわない)/I *don't have enough* [I *have no*] *money* [*time*] to take a trip. ▶バスにはまだ 30 分の余裕がある(=30分残っている) We have thirty minutes left before the bus leaves. ▶私には生活の余裕がほとんどない I have very little to live on.

②[余裕の] ●余裕のある生活をする live in comfort [a comfortable life]; be well [comfortably] off. ●余裕のない生活をする make a bare living (その日暮らしをする) live from hand to mouth.

③[余裕を] ●昼食に1時間の余裕を見る allow oneself an hour to have lunch; allow (a margin of) one hour for lunch [to have lunch]. ●旅費[交通渋滞]のための余裕を見ておく *make allowance*《*s*》*for* travel expenses [a traffic jam]. ●時間の余裕[考える余裕]をください Give me *time* [*time* to think]. ●約束の場所には(十分)余裕をもって着くようにしなさい Try to arrive at the appointed place with (plenty of) *time to spare*.

❷ [気持ちの] calmness; 《書》composure. ●余裕を失う lose one's *composure* [(沈着) *presence of mind*]. ●余裕を見せる show [(表す) display; (示す) exhibit] *composure*. ▶彼は余裕しゃくしゃくとしている He is *calm and composed*./His manners are *easy and relaxed*. ●あの人は先輩に助言を求めるだけの心の余裕がない(=心が狭い) That man is not broad-minded enough to ask his seniors for advice.

翻訳のこころ 花を買う余裕はお金ではなくて心の余裕だというのが祖母は言っていた（吉本ばなな『みどりのゆび』）My grandmother used to say that you buy flowers not with money to spare but with heart to spare. (❗ この spare は動詞で、「努力して何らかの結果を出したり、それを他人に与えたりする」の意)

よよと ●よよと泣く cry bitterly [(身を震わせて) convulsively]. ●よよと泣き伏す (=泣き崩れる) collapse in tears; collapse crying hard.

より (糸のねじれ) a twist. ●よりをかける give (it) a twist. ●彼女はお客様のために腕によりをかけて (=最善を尽くして) ごちそうを作った She *did* her *very best* to cook a good dinner [cook dinner] for her guests.
● よりを戻す ●あの2人はよりを戻した (=仲直りした) They *made it up* [和解した]《やや書》 *got reconciled* with each other. ●太郎とは別れたんだけど、彼はよりを戻して (=再び迎え入れて) ほしいと言っているのよ Taro and I broke up but he wants me to *take him back*.

:-より 《格助詞》❶ 『起点』(場所) from ...; out of ...; (時間) at ...; since .... (⇨から) ●彼らはローマに向けロンドンより出発した They started *from* [*left*] London for Rome. ●10 時より開会します We are going to open the meeting *at* [x*from*] ten (o'clock).
❷ 『比較の基準』(...よりも) than ... (❗ 形容詞・副詞の比較級の後に用いる) (⇨解説); (A よりむしろ B) not so much A as B; more [rather] B than A (❗ A, B は文法上同等のもの); (...より上位に) above ....

┌─────────────────────────────────┐
│ **解説** than の後には I, we, you, he, she, they など主格の人称代名詞が続く場合、主語の後に助動詞や動詞句を従えるのが最も普通の言い方。助動詞や動詞句を省略した上で than が接続詞であることを意識した than I のような言い方をするのは《書・古》で日常語としては大げさに響く。than が前置詞として用いられる場合、《話》では本来主格の人称代名詞が続くべきところ than me のように目的格を従えることもあるが、文にあいまいさが出てくることが多いので注意: 彼はあなたに対して私がするよりもひどい扱いをする He *treats you worse than me*. (❗ これは ...*than* I *do*. の意だが、*than* I *treats* me. (彼は私よりもあなたに対してひどい扱いをする) の意にもとれる) また、than の後では、前後関係から明らかな部分が省略されることも少なくない。 │
└─────────────────────────────────┘

● 愛より金を大事にする value money *above* love.
●彼は私より 3 センチ背が高い He is three centimeters taller *than* I am [《話》 me, 《書・古》 I]./He is taller *than* I am [《話》 me] by three centimeters. (❗ この by は「...だけ」という差額を表す) (⇨解説) ●靖より美紀子の方がずっと早く来た Mikiko came much earlier *than* Yasushi (did). ●彼は他のだれ [どの生徒] よりも足が速い He runs faster *than* anyone else [any other student, xany other students]. (❗ Nobody (else) [No (other) student] runs faster than he does. は堅い言い方) ●これはあれよりも質においてまさって [劣って] いる This is superior [inferior] *to* that in quality. ●私はコーヒーより紅茶の方が好きだ I prefer tea *to* [xthan] coffee./I like tea better *than* coffee. (❗ (1) この言い方が口語的。(2) 動詞が like の場合は通例 more より better が好まれる) ●彼女は以前よりきれいになった She's prettier *than* [she used to be]. ●テニスよりも英語の勉強がしたい I'd rather study English *than* play tennis. ●彼は俳優というよりむしろテレビタレントだ He is *not so much* an actor *as* a TV star./He is *more* [*rather*] a TV star *than* an actor./He is a TV star *rather than* an actor.

▶ **DISCOURSE**
以上より、子供は勉強よりも遊ぶべきと結論する **In this way, I conclude that** children should spend *more* time playing rather *than* studying. (❗ In this way, I conclude that ...(以上より、私は...と結論する) は結論に用いるディスコースマーカー)

❸ 『限定』(...よりほかは) except ...; but .... (⇨ほか)
●三郎よりほかにだれも部屋にいなかった There was nobody in the room *except* [*but*] Saburo. ●そうするより仕方がない I have *no* (*other*) choice *but* to do so./There is no other way *but* to do so./(そうするよりほかはしようがあるまい) I can't *help* doing so.

-より 寄り ●北 [西] 寄りの風 a *northerly* [a *westerly*] wind. ●あの政治家は少し [ずいぶん] 右寄りだ That politician is a little [far] *to the right*. ●プラットホームの上野寄りのところで待っているよ I'll be waiting (for you) *on* the Ueno *end of* the platform.

よりあい 寄り合い a meeting; (集まり)《やや書》a gathering.
● 寄り合い所帯 寄り合い所帯のチーム a *scratch* [a *pickup*] team. ●新しい連立政権は数党の寄り合い所帯だ The new coalition government is a *mixed group* of several parties [(構成されている) *is made up of* several parties].

よりあつまる 寄り集まる get together; gather.
よりいっそう より一層 ●より一層の努力を望む ask for *more* effort. ●より一層勉強する study *much* [*still, even*] *harder*. (❗ いずれも比較級を強める (⇨一層, 益々))

よりいと 縒り糸 twisted thread [yarn].

よりかかる 寄り掛かる lean*《on, against, over*》. (⇨もたれる) ●杖(?)に寄りかかる *lean on* one's stick.
● 親に寄りかかる (=頼る) *lean* [*depend*, *rely*] *on* [*upon*] one's parents.

よりき 与力 a *yoriki*; (説明的に) a supervisor of detectives in the Edo-period police system.

よりきり 寄り切り 『相撲』 *yorikiri*; (説明的に) frontal force out.

よりきる 寄り切る 『相撲』 force《him》 out (of the ring).

よりけり 因りけり depend on .... ●それを買うかどうかは値段によりけりだ Whether we buy it or not *depends on* the price. ●冗談も時によりけりだ You must choose the right time when you crack jokes.

よりごのみ 選り好み (⇨選(?)り好み)

よりすがる 寄りすがる (すがりつく) cling*《to》; (頼る) depend《on》. (⇨すがる)

よりすぐり 選りすぐり (⇨選りすぐる)

よりすぐる 選りすぐる choose carefully; make a careful selection《of》. (❗ pick and choose は「選り好みをする」の意でここでは不適) ●選りすぐった商品 a selection; a choice; ● the best [choice, choicest] article.

よりそう 寄り添う ●彼女に寄り添う (=ぴったりくっつく) *stick close to* her. ●彼に寄り添うように (=近くに) 座[立つ, 歩く] sit [stand, walk] *close to* him.

よりつき 寄り付き ❶ 『控えの間』an anteroom《of a Japanese-style restaurant》.
❷ 『庭園内の腰掛け』a bench.
❸ 『道路から玄関へのアプローチ』an approach;《車用の》a driveway.
❹ 『取り引きで午前・午後の最初の立ち会い』an open-

よりつく 寄り付く (⇒近付") ❶) ▶ほら穴に寄り付くな(=離れていろ) Keep away from [Keep off] the cave.

よりどころ 拠り所 (根拠) (a) foundation; (典拠) (an) authority; (支え) support. ▶新聞を拠り所にして彼はそう言った He said it *on the authority* [*foundation*] *of* the newspaper. ▶キリスト教は彼の心の唯一の拠り所である Christianity is his only *support* [*anchor*]. ▶彼は信仰を拠り所とした生活をしている His life *is founded on* faith.

よりどり 選り取り ── **選り取りする** 動 choose; make one's choice 《*of*》; (自由に選ぶ) take one's pick [choice].
● **選り取り見取り** ▶選り取り見取りで500円 *Take* your *pick* for 500 yen./*Choose* anything you like for 500 yen.

よりによって (すべての...の中で) of all 《places [people, things]》. ▶よりによってこんな所で君に会うとは *Of all* places to meet you here!/Fancy meeting here *of all* places! ▶よりによってこの忙しい時に(=忙しい時に限って)そんなことを頼まないでくれ Don't ask me to do that *just when* I'm busiest.

よりぬき 選り抜き ── **選り抜きの** 形 [精選した] select; (主に飲食物に関して) choice; [最上の]the very best. (⇒選(*り*)抜き) ▶選り抜きのチーム a *select* [*the very best*, ×*selected*] team; an all-star team. ▶選り抜きの物[人]《話》the best [pick] of the bunch.

よりみち 寄り道 ── **寄り道する** 動 (不意に立ち寄る) drop in 《*on* him, *at* a place》; (道草を食う) hang around on the way. ▶帰りに彼の家に寄り道した I *dropped in at* his home 《*on* him》 on my way home. ▶寄り道せずにまっすぐ帰った I went straight home (without *hanging around* [*stopping*] *on the way*).

よりめ 寄り目 ── **寄り目の** 形 cross-eyed. ▶彼女は寄り目だ She is *cross-eyed*.

よりも better .... (⇒上 ❷)

よりよい より良い better 《*than*》, superior 《*to*》. (❗前の方が口語的) (⇒い ❶)

よりよく 余力 (余った力)[金] energy [money] to spare. ▶余力がある[ない] have the *energy* [no *energy*] *to spare*.

よりわける 選り分ける [[分類する](選り出す)] sort ... out; (仕分ける) assort; (分類する) classify; [別々にする] separate 《A *from* B》. ▶書類を選り分ける *sort out* [*assort*, *classify*] the papers. ▶よいリンゴと悪いリンゴを選り分ける *separate* the good apples *from* the bad.

＊よる 夜 (a) night; (an) evening.

> 解説 「夜」に相当する英語として、日没から日の出までの暗い間を night, 日没就寝時の10時ごろまでの人々が起きて活動している時間を evening という。ただしこの区分は絶対的なものではなく、話し手の主観による。

① **[〜(の)夜]** ▶あの夜は蒸し暑かった That *night* was sultry./It was sultry (on) that *night*. (❗通例 on は省略される) ▶私はその夜ホテルに泊まった I stayed at a hotel for the *night*. (❗for は「...を過ごすために」の意) ▶私たちはあすの夜パーティーを開きます We're having a party tomorrow *evening*. ▶土曜の夜映画に行くつもりです We're going to go to the movies (on) Saturday *night*. (❗《話》ではば on を省略する)

② **[夜(の)〜]** ▶夜の学生 a *night* student. ▶夜の仕事(do) a *night* job. ▶夜の神戸港 Kobe Port *by night*. ▶夜遅くまで till late at *night*; far into the *night*. ▶夜じゅうあらしが吹き荒れた The storm raged all *night* [all through the *night*, throughout the *night*]. (❗後の二つは all night を強めた言い方) ▶父はいつも夜遅く家に帰って来る My father usually comes home late at *night*. ▶朝型の人もいれば夜型の人もいる Some people are morning people and some are night people. (❗単数形は a *night* person)

③ **[夜が[は]]** ▶夜が早い go to bed early. ▶天気のいい夜はテントで寝る sleep out in the tent *on fine nights*. (❗特定の日の夜には前置詞 on を用いる。ただし最初を伴う場合は in も可 (⇒午前)) ▶夜が明けた Morning [Day, Dawn, ×Night] broke. (⇒夜(*け*)) ▶夜は読書に最適です *Night* is the best time for reading. (❗night は総称的に用いられ無冠詞) ▶夜はいつも何をなさっていますか What do you usually do *in the evening*(s) [*at night*(s)]? (❗複数形が習慣的行為を強調。後の方は昼間との対比を含んだ言い方) ▶朝の来ない夜はない There's no *night* which isn't followed by dawn.

④ **[夜に]** ▶彼は6月2日[元旦]の夜に自動車事故にあった He had a car accident on the *night* of June 2 [New Year's *night*]. (⇒③) ▶夜にならないうちに家に帰ろう Let's go home before (it gets) dark [before *night* comes]. (❗× ... before it doesn't get dark [night doesn't come] や × ... before it *will* get dark [night *will* come] は不可) ▶彼は昼寝て夜小説を書いている He sleeps during the day [by day] and writes novels *during the night* [*by night*]. (❗by night は通例 by day または during the day と対句で用いられるが文語的)

＊よる 因る，拠る ❶ [次第である] depend 《*on*》. ▶彼の成功は努力いかんによる His success *depends on* his efforts 《*on*》 whether he can keep up his efforts). (❗《話》では on はしばしば省略される) ▶彼は相手によって言うことを変えるので困る He changes what he says *depending on* who he's speaking to. That's the trouble with him. ▶それは事情による That (all) [It all] *depends*.

❷ [起因する] be due to ...; be caused 《*by*》. ▶その事故は彼の不注意な運転によるものであった The accident *was due to* [*was caused by*] his careless driving./The accident happened *because of* his careless driving.

❸ [基づく] be based 《*on*》; be founded 《*on*》. ▶彼女の研究は正確なデータによる Her research *is based on* accurate data.

❹ [行使する] appeal 《*to*》; 《書》have* recourse 《*to*》. ▶武力による *appeal* [*resort*] *to* arms; use force.

❺ [その他の表現] ▶ご依頼によって *at* your request. ▶彼の援助によって *by* his help. ▶医師の勧めによって *on* the doctor's advice. ▶憲法第9条によって *under* Article 9 of the Constitution. ▶人を見かけによって判断してはいけない Don't judge a person *by* appearances [his (or her) looks]. ▶警察の話[発表]によれば[今日の新聞の報道]によれば彼は自殺したそうだ *According to* the police [today's paper], he committed suicide. (❗( )内の意も according to に含まれる。The police say [Today's paper says] (that).... の方が口語的な話 ① [第2文例])

＊よる 寄る ❶ [近寄る] (近くに来る) come* close

[near]《to》;[近付く］approach (⇨近付く❶);［位置を移動する］move《to》. ▶もっとそばへ寄りたまえ Come closer [nearer] to me. ▶もう少し左へ寄ってください Move a little more to the left, please. ▶わきに寄って彼らを通してやりなさい Step aside [Pull over] and let them pass. (!前の方は歩行者に、後の方は車の運転者に対する言い方) ▶私の学校から少し南に寄ったところに本屋があります There is a bookstore a little (to the) south of my school. ▶ライトは右中間に寄った The right fielder shaded to right center.

❷ [集まる] (会う) meet*; (集合する) gather, get* together. ▶後の方が口語的的(⇨集まる)

❸ [立ち寄る] (ひょっと訪れる) drop (-pp-) in [(ついでに寄る)《米・英話》stop (-pp-) in, 《英》call (in)] 《on＋人, at＋場所》, drop [《米・英話》stop, 《英》call] by (場所); (旅行などの途中で立ち寄る) stop off 《in [at]＋場所》; (飛行機で旅行の途中立ち寄る) stop over, make a stopover 《in》. ▶今度近くへ index いでの節はうちへお寄りください Drop in on us [at our house,《話》and see us] the next time you come around here. (!drop in and see … の言い方は drop が drops, dropped, dropping となる場合は and の代わりに目的を表す to を用いて to see … のようにいう) ▶東京へ行く途中会議に出るために名古屋に寄った On my way to Tokyo I stopped off in Nagoya to attend the meeting. ▶シカゴへ行く途中2日間ハワイに寄った I stopped over in Hawaii for two days on my way to Chicago. ▶あす事務所に寄っていいか？ 話があるんだ Can I come by your office tomorrow? We need to talk.
会話「由美が会社の帰りにちょっと話をしに寄るって言ってたの」「そう、よろしく言っといて」"Yumi said she'd stop by for a chat on her way from work." "Well, tell her I said hello."
会話「ご注文の本が入りました」「分かりました。そのうち取りに寄ります」"Your book's come in, sir." "Right. I'll drop by and pick it up sometime."
● 寄ってたかって ▶年上の少年たちはその年下の少年を寄ってたかっていじめた The older boys joined together [ganged up] to bully the younger one.
● 寄らば大樹の陰 A big tree is a good shelter.
● 寄ると触ると ▶彼らは寄ると触ると近所の人のうわさ話をする Whenever they meet [get together], they gossip about their neighbors./《書》They never meet [get together] without gossiping about their neighbors.

よる 縒る ● 何本かの糸をよってひもを作る twist [《やや書》twine] /twáin/ some threads into a string; make a string by twisting [twining] some threads together.

ヨルダン [国名] Jordan /dʒɔ́rdn/; (公式名) the Hashemite Kingdom of Jordan. (首都 Amman) ● ヨルダン人 a Jordanian. ● ヨルダン(人)の Jordanian.

よるのおんな 夜の女 《古》a streetwalker; 《米話》a hooker /húːkər/.

よるひる 夜昼 ● 夜昼ぶっ通しで復旧作業をする work night and day to restore 《telephone service》.

よるべ 寄る辺 ● 寄る辺(＝頼れる人)のない老人 an old man [woman] who has no one to depend upon [turn to].

よるなか 夜中 ● 夜夜中に late at night.

よるをかけて 『夜を賭けて』 Through the Night. (参考) 梁石日の小説

よれい 予冷 名 pre-cooling.
── 予冷する 動 pre-cool; cool in advance.

よれい 予鈴 the first bell; the warning bell. ▶予鈴 が鳴ったので生徒はぞろぞろと教室に入った The first bell rang [sounded] and students filed into the classroom./Students filed into the classroom at the warning bell.

よれよれ ── よれよれの 形 (使いくたびれた) worn-out; (見すぼらしい) (けなして) shabby; (すり切れている) frayed. ● (服などが)よれよれになる [＝しわくちゃになる] become wrinkled. ▶よれよれのレーンコートを着た男は刑事だった The man in the worn-out [shabby, frayed] raincoat turned out to be a detective.

よれる 縒れる be twisted. (⇨捩(を)れる)

よろい 鎧 (a suit of) armor. ● よろいをつける put on armor. ● よろいかぶとに身を固めた武士 an armored warrior; a warrior (clad) in armor.

よろいど 鎧戸 (日よけ・通風用の) a louver (door [window]); (シャッター) a shutter. ● よろい戸を閉める put up the shutter.

よろく 余禄 (余分の利益) an additional profit; a windfall profit.

よろける (つまずく) stumble; (今にも倒れそうによろよろ動く) stagger. (⇨よろめく) ● 石につまずいてよろける stumble over [on] a stone.

よろこばしい 喜ばしい (うれしい) glad (-dd-); (幸せな) happy. (⇨嬉(を)しい) ▶それは喜ばしい知らせだ That's welcome [good, great] news.

*よろこばせる 喜ばせる (うれしがらせる) please; (満足させる) satisfy; (大喜びさせる) delight. ▶彼女を喜ばせるのは難しい It's difficult to please [satisfy] her./She's difficult to please [satisfy]. ▶彼の贈り物が両親を大いに喜ばせた His present delighted his parents [made his parents very happy, gave great pleasure to his parents].

*よろこび 喜び (a) pleasure; (a) delight; (a) joy; (an) enjoyment. (!冠詞がつくとそれぞれ具体的な意味を表す)

使い分け pleasure 満足感や幸福感を含意した喜びを表す.
delight pleasure より大きな喜びを表す. プレゼントをもらった時などに用いられる. 喜びが身体にあふれて外面に現れていることを含意する.
joy 気分を高揚させ、興奮させるような喜びを表す. 結婚のような意義の大きいことへの深い喜びを含意する.
enjoyment 主に「娯楽」を楽しむことから得られる喜びを表す.

● 読書の喜び the pleasure of reading. ▶彼は喜びを体で(＝いろいろな身ぶりで)表した He expressed his pleasure [joy] with various gestures. ▶彼女は喜びで顔を輝かせていた She beamed with pleasure [delight, joy]. ▶彼は大喜びでそのプレゼントを受け取った He accepted the present with real delight. ▶彼らは喜びのあまり跳び上がった They jumped for joy. ▶長い間会わなかった親友に会うのは大きな喜びである It's (a) great pleasure to see a close friend after a long time.
会話「お宅の息子さんがエッセーコンテストで1位だったと新聞に出ていました. さぞお喜びのことでしょう」「ありがとうございます. 本当にうれしく思っています」"I read in the paper that your son was awarded the first prize in the essay contest. You must be very proud of him." "Well, thank you very much. We're really happy for him." 事情 身内がほめられた場合、日本人は He was very lucky, indeed. (本当に運がよい子です)とか We're all surprised. (みんなびっくりしています)などという謙遜した言い方をしがちであるが、米英では上記のように率直に喜びを表明するのが普通.
● 喜び事 a happy event.

*よろこぶ 喜ぶ (うれしく思う) be glad《at, about, of; to

do; *that* 節); (幸運で喜ぶ) *be happy* 《*about, over, at; to do; that* 節》; (満足する) *be pleased* 《*at, about, with; to do; that* 節》; (大いに喜ぶ) *be delighted* 《*at, by, with; to do; that* 節》(! *pleased* する意味が強い); (大いにうれしがる) (書) *rejoice* 《*at, over; to do; that* 節》; (喜んでする) *be willing* [*ready*] 《*to do*》. ▶彼はその結果を聞いて大変喜んだ He *was very glad* [*pleased, delighted*] *at* [*to know*] the results. (! (1) *pleased* は形容詞化しているため much ではなく very で修飾するのが普通. (2) *very delighted* は (話) で用いられ, 普通は (very) much で強める)/The results *pleased* [*delighted*] him greatly./He *rejoiced at* [*to know*] the results. ▶あなたが新しい仕事を得たことを大変喜んでいます I'*m very glad* [*happy, pleased*] *about* your new job./I'*m very glad* [*happy, pleased*] *that* you have got a new job. ▶彼女はこんな贈り物は喜ばないだろう She won't *be pleased* [*happy, delighted*] with [×at] this present. ▶喜んでお伴します I'll *be glad* [I'd *be happy*, I'd *be pleased*, I'm (*very*) *willing*, I'm *ready*] *to* go with you. ▶これは喜ぶべきことだ This is a matter for *joy*. ▶彼女からラブレターの返事が来たので彼は跳び上がって喜んだ He jumped *for joy* with her answer to his love letter. ▶彼は妻がはでな服を着るのを喜ばない (= 好きでない) He doesn't *like* his wife to wear a showy dress.
会話 「パーティーにいらっしゃいませんか」「喜んでうかがいます」"Will you come to the party?" "Yes, I'll *be glad* [*pleased, delighted*] *to*./(Yes [Thank you],) *with pleasure*."
会話 「手伝ってくれる?」「喜んで」"Will you help me?" "*Certainly*./*Surely* [(話) *Sure*]./*With pleasure*./(もちろん) *Of course, I will*." (! 親しい間柄では (I'm) *happy* [*glad*] *to*./(I'd) *love to*. なども用いる)

よろしい 宜しい 形 ❶ [許可] may; can*.

解説 (1) You may …. は上位の者が下位の者に許可を与えるときの言い方. 尊大な感じがあるのでそれを避けて You *can* …. を用いることが多い.
(2) 質問では *Can* [*Could, May,* (英) *Might*] *I* …? があり, 後の方ほど丁寧な言い方となるが, *Might I* …? はあまり用いられない. これらの質問に対する応答は *Might* [*Could*] *I* …? の場合を含めて *can, may* が用いられ, 例えば肯定では *Yes, you can* [*may*]./*Of course you can* [*may*]./*Yes, of course*./*Certainly*./《話》 *Sure*. などが, 否定では *No, you can't*./*No, I'm afraid you can't*. などが用いられる. *Yes, you may. や No, you may not.* は尊大にひびくこともある. 強い否定では *No, you must not*. が用いられる. ×*Yes, you could* [*might*]. という言い方はないので注意. また, この意味で直接話法を間接話法に言い換える場合については (⇒[第1文例]).
(3) Do you *mind* (*if* 節; *doing*) …? は「…をいやに思いますか」と丁寧に相手の意向を尋ねる言い方. *Would you mind* …? ではさらに丁寧になる. ×*Don't* [×*Will*] *you mind* …? とはいわない. くだけた会話では *Do* [*Would*] *you mind* が省略されて *Mind* …? ということもある. また, I *wonder if* …? を使う場合については (⇒会話 [第3例]). 快諾の応答は, *No, I don't mind at all.* / *Not at all.* / *Of course* [*Certainly, Surely*] *not.* と否定で答えるのが普通だが, 《話》では *Yes, certainly*./*Sure*./*All right*. などと肯定で答える場合もある. 断わる場合, *Yes, I do mind*. (だめです) では強い断わりになるので, 代わりに何らかの理由を述べて断わることが多い.

▶父は私に行ってもよろしいと言った My father said to me, "You *may go*."/(間接話法) My father told me that I could [×*might*] *go*. (!「かもしれない」の意では *may→might* が可だがこの場合は不可 (⇒解説 (2))) ▶この鉛筆を使ってもよろしいですか *Can* [*May*] I use this pencil?/《話》*Is it all right* [*OK*] *if* I use [(*for me*) *to use*] this pencil? ▶あなたは行かなくてもよろしい (= 行く必要がない) You *don't have to go*. / You *can* [*may*] *nót go*. と *not* に強勢を置いていうこともできる. You *cán't* [*máy not*] *go*. は「行ってはいけない」の意)
会話 「お電話をお借りしてよろしいですか」「ええどうぞ」"Can [Could, May] I use your phone?" "Yes, you *can* [*may,* ×*could*]./Yes, *certainly*./*Of course*./*Sure*(*ly*)."
会話 「もう一つどうぞ」「よろしいの?」"Have another one." "*May* I?" (! 相手に利益になる場合は, 例えば *Would you like to* have another one? などとことさら丁寧な表現を使わなくてもよい場合も多い)
会話 「ラジオの音を小さくしてもよろしいですか」「ええどうぞ」"*May* I turn down the radio?/(*Would you*) *mind if* I *turned* [*my turning*] down the radio?/I *wonder* [(より丁寧に) I *was wondering*] *if* I *could* turn down the radio?" (! 後の文は May I …? と同じ言い方の文尾は上昇調. したがってこのように疑問符をつけることがよくある) "No, I don't *mind at all*./No, *please do*./《話》 *Sure*." (⇒解説 (3))
❷ [適する, 都合がよい] *all right* 《*for, to*》; 《話》OK, O.K.; [役立つ, 間に合う] *will* *do. ▶それでよろしいか Is that *all right* [*OK*]?/*Will* that *do*? ▶何時がよろしいですか What time would *be good* [*convenient*] *for* you?
会話 「このいすで間に合いますよね?」「さしあたってそれでよろしいでしょう」"This chair *would do*, wouldn't it?" "It *would do* for the time being."
会話 「紅茶とコーヒーとどちらがよろしいですか」「紅茶の方がいいわ」"Which *would* you *like,* tea or coffee?" "I'd *prefer tea*." (! *Which do you like, …?* より丁寧)
[よろしければ, よろしかったら] ▶よろしければ今夜お会いしたいのですが I'd like to meet you tonight, if it's *all right for you* [いやでなければ] if you *don't mind*, (都合がよければ) if it's *convenient* (*for you*)]. ▶よろしければ (= ご希望なら) その本をお貸しします You can borrow the book if you *like* [*want to*]. ▶よろしかったら私たちのクラブにお入りになりませんか *Would you like* [*care*] *to* join our club? ▶よろしかったら私の最近の論文をお読みいただきたく存じます I *thought* you *might like to* read my recent paper. (! 前の例文よりさらに控えめな言い方)
── よろしい 副 *all right;* (話) OK. ▶よろしい. 私が代わりに行きましょう *All right* [*OK*], I'll go for you.
会話 「絶対に行くと決めているんだ」「よろしい. ぼくが君に忠告しなかったなんて言わないでくれよ」"I'm quite determined to go." "*Well*, don't say I didn't warn you."

よろしき 宜しき ▶彼の指導よろしきを得て私は泳げるようになった It's thanks to his *good coaching* that I've got the knack of swimming.

*よろしく 宜しく

解説 日本語で「あいさつ」や「依頼」の後につける「よろしく(お願いします)」は英語では言わないことが多い. また, 内容をくみ取って別の表現が必要な場合もある.

❶ [あいさつ] ▶はじめまして, 藤本です. よろしく How do you do? [Hello.] I'm Fujimoto. (! 前の言い方は改まった表現. 「よろしく」は表現しない. (I'm)

pleased [(It's) nice] to meet you. (お会いできてうれしい)をつけることが多い)
❷ [依頼] ● 会議の後, 部屋の片付けをよろしく(=片付けてください) *Please put the room in order after the meeting*. ▶ この件についてお力添え[至急お返事]いただきますようよろしくお願い申し上げます *Thank you for your help with [your prompt attention on] this matter*. (❗依頼の手紙の結句として) ▶ そちらの方よろしくお願いします(=これをあなたに任せます) *I'll leave it to you*.
会話 「私がそれを買ってきてあげます」「そうですか. よろしくお願いします」 *"I'll go and get [buy] it for you." "Thank you./Thanks."*
❸ [伝言] *give* one's (*best*) *regards* [*wishes*] 《*to*》 (1) *regards* は面識のある人に, *wishes* は面識のない人に用いる. (2) *best* をつける方が丁寧; 《話》 *say hello* 《*to*》. ▶ ご家族の皆様によろしく *Please give* [*send*] *my* (*best*) *regards to your family*./*Please say hello to your family* (*for me*)./《米普まね・英話》 *Please remember me to your family*. (❗これらに対して *I'll be sure to do that*. などと応答する) ▶ 父からもよろしくとのことです *My father gives you his regards* [*his regards to you*]./*My father told me to say hello*. ▶ 秀雄によろしく *Give my love* [《米》 *best*] *to Hideo*./*Say hi to Hideo for me*. (❗いずれもくだけた表現) ▶ 今年もよろしくお願いいたします *Please treat me this year as well as you did last year*. 事情 米英では新年のあいさつとしてこのように言うことはまれで *A Happy New Year*. だけで十分)

よろず 万 ❶ [多いこと] ● よろずの神々 *a myriad* [*myriads*] *of gods*. ❷ [万事] ▶ よろずご相談を承ります *Don't hesitate to ask me anything*.
● よろず屋 (雑貨店) *a general store*; 《広くを知っている人》 *a Jack-of-all-trades* (働 *Jacks-*).

よろめく 〚ふらふらする〛 *stagger*, 《つまずいて》*stumble*; 《今にもころびそうに》*totter*; 《酔っ払いのように》*reel*.
● 重い荷を背負ってよろめく *stagger under a heavy load*. ▶ よろめきながら階段をおりる *totter down the stairs*. ▶ その一撃で彼はよろめいた *The blow sent him staggering* [*reeling*]. ▶ その酔っ払いはよろめきながらドアの方へ行った *The drunken man staggered* [*reeled, stumbled and lurched*] (*along*) *toward the door*.

翻訳のこころ 私は心の中で大きくよろめくものを覚えたのである (太宰治『猿ヶ島』) *I felt* (*that*) *my mind wavered* [*vacillated*] *greatly*. (❗(1) 「よろめく」は *waver, vacillate* (《決心・決断などについて》心が揺らいだりちゅうちょする). *stagger, totter* は身体的な動きについてなのでここでは不適. (2) 通例 *waver, vacillate* の主語となるのは「人, 心, 気持ち」. したがって「心の中で大きくよろめいた」とする方が分かりやすい)

よろよろ (⇒よたよた).
よろん 世論 *public opinion*. (⇒世論(ぜん)).
よわ 余話 *the remnants of information; a tidbit*.
よわ 夜半 *midnight*. (⇒夜半(ぜん)).
よわい 弱い 形 〚力・精神力・能力が〛 *weak; feeble*; 〚虚弱な〛 *delicate* /délikit/, 〚病弱な〛《やや書》*weakly*, 〚酒などが〛 *weak; light; mild*; 〚音・光などが〛 *weak; faint; pale*. (⇒弱る)

使い分け **weak** 体・力・精神力・競争力・説得力・光・音・アルコールなどの弱さを幅広く示す最も一般的な語.
feeble 体・知能・安定性などが非常に貧弱であることを表す. 時に哀れみや軽蔑を含意する.
delicate 体の病弱さや皮膚の繊細さを表す.

weakly 人の行動に力が無く弱々しいことを表す.
light お酒の弱さなどを表す.
mild 薬の効き目・副作用が弱いこと, 石けんなどの刺激が少ないことを表す.
faint 音・光・匂い・動作・記憶などが弱く消え入りそうなことを表す.
pale 色合いの薄さ, 特に光の弱さなどを表す.

① 【弱い~】 ● 弱い人 *a weak person*; 《総称》 *weak people*, 《やや書》 *the weak*. ● 弱いチーム *a weak team*. ● 弱い立場 *a weak position*. ● 弱いビール *light* [*weak*] *beer*. ● 弱いたばこ *a mild* [ㄒa *weak*] *cigarette*. ● 弱い声で *in a weak* [*a feeble*, (かすかな) *a faint*] *voice*. ● 秋の午後の弱い日差し *the pale sun of a fall* [《主に英》 *an autumn*] *afternoon*.
② 【...が[の]弱い】 ● 心臓が弱い *have a weak heart*; (気が弱い) *be shy* [*timid*]. ● 視力が弱い *have poor* [*weak*] *eyesight*. ● 頭が弱い *be weak-minded* [*feeble-minded*]. (❗前の方には「気の弱い」という意もある) ● 意志が弱い *have a weak* (↔*strong*) *will*. ● 性格の弱い人 *a person of weak character*. ▶ 彼は体が弱い (健康上) *He is delicate* [*poor*] *in health*./*He is in delicate* [*poor*] *health*./(体質上) *He has a weak* [*a delicate*] *constitution*.
③ 【...に弱い】 ● 熱に弱い *be weak against heat*. ● 船[車]に弱い *get seasick* [*carsick*] *easily*. ● 風邪に弱い *catch* (*a*) *cold easily*; (抵抗力がない) *have little resistance to colds*. ▶ 彼は物理に弱い (=物理が不得意だ) *He is weak in* [*at*] *physics*. (❗主に *in* は学科, *at* は活動を表す) ▶ 彼は酒に弱い *He gets drunk easily*./*He is a poor drinker*. ▶ それらの植物は寒さに弱い(=耐えられない) *Those plants can't stand cold* (↔*are hardy*). ▶ 私の目は光に弱いのでサングラスをかけています *I wear sunglasses because my eyes are sensitive to the light*. ▶ 彼はかわいい子に弱い *He has a weakness for a pretty girl*.
—— 弱くする 動 *make** 《*it* [*him*]》 *weak*(*er*), *weaken* (❗前の方が口語的) (⇒弱める); 〚つまみなどをひねって〛 *turn ... down*. ● 暖房を弱くする *turn down the heat*.
—— 弱くなる 動 *grow** [*become**] *weak*(*er*), *weaken*; 〚音・風など〛*die* (~*d; dying*) *down*. (⇒弱る, 弱し) ▶ 彼の脈はだんだん弱くなった *His pulse became fainter*.

よわい 齢 (⇒⑧ 年齢).
● 齢を重ねる (歳をとる) *get old*.

よわいものいじめ 弱い者いじめ *bullying*. ● 弱い者いじめをする人[子] *a bully*. ● 弱い者いじめをする *bully the weaker people* [*the weak*]; *play* [*act*] *the bully*. ▶ 弱い者いじめをするなんて君たちは最低だ *You are the lowest of the low to pick on people weaker than you are*.

よわき 弱き (弱い者たち) *the weak* (❗複数形扱い). ● 強きをくじき弱きを助ける *crush the strong and help the weak*.

よわき 弱気 图 (弱さ) (a) *weakness*; 〚株式〛 *bearishness*.
—— 弱気な 形 *weak*; (弱腰の) 《話》 *weak-kneed*; *bear*; *bearish*. ● 弱気な人 *a person of weak character*. ▶ 弱気を出すな *Don't be so weak-kneed*.
● 弱気相場 〚経済〛 *a bear* [*a bearish*] *market*.
よわごし 弱腰 ● 弱腰である *be weak* [*決断力がない*] *weak-kneed*《*to*》.
よわさ 弱さ (体力・精神力・知力などの) (a) *weak-*

ness. ● 彼の失敗は性格[心]の弱さが原因だ His *weakness* of character [mind] caused his failure.

よわたり 世渡り 图 ● 世渡りがうまい(=出世の方法を知っている) know how to *succeed* [*get ahead*, 《話》*make it*] *in the world*.
—— **世渡りする** 動 (何とか無難に暮らして行く) get along in the world [in life].

よわね 弱音 ● **弱音を吐く** (泣き言を言う) whine; (不平を言う) complain. ● 弱音を吐くな Stop *whining!*/(運動などで人を励まして) Never *say die*! ▶「その仕事はできない」と彼は弱音を吐いた "I can't do the job," he *whined* [*complained*].

よわび 弱火 (弱い炎) a low flame; (弱い熱) low heat. (!) 炎が出ない電気こんろなどには後の方を用いる) ● 弱火にする set 《the heat [×gas]》 low (↔high); lower [decrease (↔increase)] the heat 《under the pan》. ● ...を弱火でいためる pan-fry ... over a *low flame*. ▶弱火にして, ふたをして, 10 分ほどとろ火で煮てください Lower (the) heat; cover; simmer 10 minutes. (!) 料理の解説書などでしばしば the が省略される)

よわふくみ 弱含み [[相場が値下がりする気配であること]] a weak tone.

よわまる get* [grow*] weak; (体力などが) weaken; [[風・音・火などが]] (急に) fall*; (しだいに) die (〜d; dying) down [away]; [[衰える]] 《やや書》decline. ▶彼の声の調子が弱まった His voice *fell* [*lowered*]. ▶風は弱まってきた The wind *is dying down* [*going down*, 《書》*abating*].

よわみ 弱味 (a) weakness (⇒弱点, 欠点); [[弱い立場]] a weak position; [[弱腰]] a weak attitude. ● 彼の弱味につけ込む take advantage of his *weakness(es)* [*weak position*]. ● 彼女の弱味(=彼女にとって不利なこと)を握っている [握る] have [get] *something* on her. (!) on は「不利益」を表す)

よわむし 弱虫 [[臆病(おくびょう)者]] a coward; [[非力な人]] a weakling; [[女々しい男]] 《話》a sissy; [[腰抜け男]] 《軽蔑的》a milksop; [[泣き虫]] 《話》a crybaby.

よわめる 弱める [[勢いを]] weaken; [[ガス・音量などを]] turn ... down; [[速度を]] slow ... down. ● 抵抗力[結束]を弱める *weaken* one's resistance [unity]. ● ガスを弱める *turn* the gas *down*.

よわよわしい 弱々しい 形 weak(-looking); delicate; feeble. ● 弱々しい声で in a *weak* [a *feeble*, 《かすか

な》a *faint*] voice.
—— **弱々しく** 副 weakly; feebly.

よわりめ 弱り目 ● **弱り目にたたり目** ▶その一家にとっては弱り目にたたり目だった Things went from bad to worse for the family. (!) ことわざの「弱り目にたたり目」は Misfortunes never come singly. (不幸は単独で来ない)という)

よわる 弱る ❶ [[弱くなる]] get [become*, grow*] weak, weaken; [[衰える]] 《やや書》decline; (やや話》fail. ▶彼の体は日ごとに弱っている He *is getting weaker* every day./His strength *is weakening* day by day./His health *is declining* [*failing*] day by day./He *is declining* [*failing*] *in* health day by day. ▶彼女は空腹で[手術のあとで]弱っている She *is weak with* hunger [*after* the operation]. ▶病気のために彼女の心臓は弱ってしまった Her heart *became weak from* [×*by*] the sickness./The sickness *weakened* her heart.
❷ [[困る]] be troubled (*with*); (途方に暮れる) be at a loss. (⇒困る) ▶どう答えてよいか弱った I *was at a loss for* an answer [*what to say*]./I *didn't know* what to say. ▶彼にお世辞を言われて弱った(=困惑した) I *was embarrassed by* his flattery.

*よん 四 four; [[4 番目の]] the fourth. (⇒三; 四番)

よんく 四駆 (四輪駆動の車) a four-wheel-drive [a 4WD] car; a car with four-wheel drive.

よんこままんが 四こま漫画 a four-frame comic strip [《英》strip cartoon]. (!) 「1 こま漫画」は a (single-frame) cartoon)

*よんじゅう 四十 forty; [[40 番目の]] the fortieth. (⇒二十, 五十)

よんだい 四大 [[「四年制大学」の略]] a university; a four-year college.

よんダブリューディー 4WD (四輪駆動の車) a four-wheel-drive [a 4WD] car; a car with four-wheel drive.

よんどころない unavoidable. (⇒やむをえない)

よんばん 四番 ● 四番打者 (⇒四番(ばん))打者)

よんびょうし 四拍子 ● 4 拍子の曲『音楽』a tune in *quadruple* /kwɑdrúːpl/ *time*.

よんもじことば 四文字言葉 a four-letter word.

*よんりん 四輪 ● 四輪駆動の車 a *four-wheel-drive* [a *4WD*] *car*; a car with *four-wheel* drive.
—— **四輪車** a four-wheeled vehicle.

ら

-ら -等 (⇨-達)

ラージヒル 〖スキー〗 the large hill. ● K 点 120 メートルのラージヒル the K-120 *large hill*.

ラード 〖豚脂〗 lard.

ラーメン [<中国語] ramen, Chinese noodles in soup. ● しょうゆ[みそ, 塩]ラーメン *ramen* in soy sauce [miso; salt] soup.

ラーゆ 辣油 [<中国語]〖とうがらし入りのごま油〗 spicy sesame oil.

らい 来‐ (次の) next; (来たるべき) coming. ● (⇨来年, 来月, 来週) ▶ 彼は来春卒業だ He will graduate *next* [in the *coming*] spring. (❗×in next spring は不可)

-らい -来 (以来) since …; (…の間) for …; (…の間に初めての) in …. (通例否定文・疑問文, 最上級のあとなどで用いる)(⇨以来, -振り) ▶ 中学卒業後彼に会っていない I haven't met [seen] him *since* we left junior high school. (❗「昨年来」なら since last year) ▶ 彼とはここ数か月連絡をとっていない I haven't been in touch with him *for* the last few months. ▶ こんな台風が東京を襲ったのは20年来のことだ This is the severest typhoon that Tokyo has experienced *in* twenty years.

らい 来意 ▶ 彼に来意を尋ねる (訪問の目的) ask him the *purpose of* [(理由) the *reason for*] his *visit*; (何の用かを) ask him what he wants with me [us].

らいう 雷雨 a thunderstorm, a thundershower. ▶ 昨夜はひどい雷雨だった Last night there was [we had] a heavy *thunderstorm*.

らいうん 雷雲 a thundercloud.

らいえん 来援 ― 来援する 動 come to [and] help. (❗and は口語的)

らいえん 来園 图 ▶ 皆様のご来園をお待ちしております We look forward to your visiting [visit with] us.
― **来園する** 動 come to 《the kindergarten [the zoo]》.

らいえん 来演 ― 来演する 動 come to give a 《piano》 performance. ▶ 7月4日ロンドンフィル来演 The London Philharmonic Orchestra comes [come] here to *give* its [their] *performance* on July 4.

ライオン 〖動物〗 a lion; (雌) a lioness; (子) a cub.

ライオンズクラブ 〖国際的社会奉仕団体〗 Lions Clubs International; (正式名) the International Association of Lions Clubs.

らいが 来駕 ● 来駕を請う ask for 《his》 visit; ask for the pleasure of 《his》 presence [attendance]; request 《his》 presence [attendance].

らいかい 来会 ● ご来会の皆様 people who are present; (呼びかけで) ladies and gentlemen. ▶ 総会への来会者は年々減っている Fewer people come to [attend] the general meeting year after year. (❗「来会者」全体は the attendance という) ▶ 多数[少数]の来会者 (There was) a large [a small] *attendance* (at the meeting).

らいかん 来館 ● 来館者 a visitor. ● 来館者数 the number of visitors (*to* the library [museum]).

らいかん 来観 ▶ 私たちの絵の展覧会にお誘いの上ひご来観ください We are looking forward to your coming with your friends to the exhibition of our paintings.

らいかん 雷管 a detonator. (⇨信管)

らいき 来季 (来シーズン) the next season.

らいき 来期 (来年) the next year; (学期) the next term; (決算上の) the next term. (⇨来年度) ● 来期の配当予想 the estimated *next* dividend payment.

らいきゃく 来客 (訪問者) a visitor, a caller; (招待客) a guest; 《集合的》 company (❗1人の場合もある). 会話 「阿部さんにお会いしたいのですが」「阿部はただ今来客中です」 "I'd like to meet Mr. Abe." "I'm sorry but he has a *visitor* right now."
● 来客名簿 a visitors' book.

らいぎょ 雷魚 〖魚介〗 a snake-head mullet.

らいげき 雷撃 图 ❶ 〖雷にうたれること〗 ▶ 雷撃死する be struck dead by lightning.
❷ 〖魚雷攻撃〗 a torpedo /tɔːpíːdou/ attack.
― **雷撃する** 動 ▶ 敵艦を雷撃する fire [launch] a *torpedo at* an enemy ship.

らいげつ 来月 next month (❗×in next month は不可); the coming month. ● 来月の5日に on the fifth of *next month*. ▶ 彼女は来月結婚する She is getting married *next month*. ▶ 来月から始めよう Let's start (×from) *next month*.

らいこう 来光 the sunrise (seen from the top of a high mountain).

らいこう 来校 ― 来校する 動 come to school. ▶ 文化祭には3日間で2,000人が来校した We had two thousand visitors to our Culture Festival over the three-day period.
● 来校者 a visitor.

らいこう 来航 ― 来航する 動 ▶ ペリーの艦隊は1853年に浦賀に来航した Perry's fleet came to [visited] Uraga in 1853.

らいこう 来港 ― 来港する 動 come to 《Japan》; visit.

らいさん 礼賛 图 (賞賛) praise; (崇拝) worship. ● 神を礼賛して *in praise of* God.
― **礼賛する** 動 praise; worship.

らいしゃ 来社 ▶ 午後2時にご来社ください Please *come to* our *company* [(事務所) *office*] at two (o'clock) in the afternoon.

らいしゃ 来車 a visit by car. (⇨来訪)

らいしゅう 来秋 next autumn (《米》 fall) (❗×in next autumn [fall] は不可); the coming autumn [《米》 fall].

らいしゅう 来週 next week; the coming week.
● 来週の今日 (⇨今日(きょう) 解説) ▶ 来週の土曜日に *next* Saturday (❗×on next Saturday は不可. 同じ週の土曜日にいえば「今週の土曜日」の意にもなる); on Saturday *next week*. ● 来週中に within [in] the *next week*. ▶ ウィンブルドンのテニス大会は来週ですか Is the Wimbledon tennis tournament held *next week*?

らいしゅう 来襲 (an) attack 《on》. (⇨襲来)

らいしゅん 来春 next spring (❗×in next spring は不可); the coming spring.

らいじょう 来場 ▶ 本日はご来場まことにありがとうございます Thank you very much for coming 《to the

らいしん 来信 a letter received.
らいしん 来診 ▶田中先生に来診をお願いしましょう Let's send for Dr. Tanaka. (⇨往診)
らいじん 雷神 the god of thunder.
らいしんし 頼信紙 a telegram form [blank].
ライス 〖米〗(cooked) rice.
ライスカレー curry and [with] rice. (❗単数扱い)(参考) curried rice は「ドライカレー」の意 (⇨カレー)
ライスペーパー rice paper.
らいせ 来世 (次の世) the next life [world]; (死後の世) the life [world] after death, the afterlife. ●来世を信じる believe in *the life after death*.
ライセンス 〖免許〗(a) license. (⇨免許) ●クロスライセンス a cross license.
●ライセンス契約 《make》 a license contract [agreement] 《with》; 《make》 license arrangements. ●ライセンス生産 license production. ●ライセンス料 a license fèe; a lìcensing fèe.
ライター 〖たばこの〗a (cigarette) lighter. ●ガスライター a gas *lighter*. ●ライターの石 a (*lighter*) flint. (❗✗*lighter stone* とはいわない) ●ライターをつける light [strike, (ぱちん と) flick] a *lighter*. ●ライターでたばこに火をつける light a cigarette from a *lighter*; use a *lighter* to light a cigarette.
ライター 〖作家〗a writer. (⇨作家) ●フリーのライター a free-lance *writer*.
ライダー 〖乗り手〗a rider.
らいたく 来宅 ▶ご来宅をお待ちしております I am waiting for you [your] coming *to our home* ▶せっかくご来宅いただきましたのに留守にしており失礼いたしました I am sorry I was out when you *visited* [*called on*] me.
ライチー 〖植物〗litchi /líːtʃi/.
らいちょう 来聴 图 ●スピーチコンテスト来聴歓迎 *Welcome* to the Speech Contest.
—**来聴する** 動 attend (a lecture).
らいちょう 雷鳥 〖鳥〗(a snow) grouse /gráʊs/ (複 ~, ~s); a ptarmigan /táːrmɪɡən/ (複 ~, ~s).
ライティングデスク a wríting dèsk.
ライティングビューロー a wríting dèsk;《英》a (writing) bureau (複 ~s, ~x /-z/) (❗bureau は《米》では「整理だんす」)
らいてん 来店 ▶またのご来店をお待ちしております《米英人的発想》Please come again (to our store [shop]).《日本人的発想》We are expecting you again.
らいでん 来電 a telegram. (⇨電報)
ライト 〖明かり〗the light; (光) light; (灯火) a light. (⇨明かり, 光) ●車のライト the headlights [headlamps] of a car. ●サーチライト a searchlight. ●ライトをあてる light; throw [《やや普》cast,《主に書》shed] *light* (*on*). ●ライトをつけている[つけたままの]自動車 a car with its *lights* on. ●すべての車はライトをつけていた All the cars had their *lights* on. ●展示品はきわめて効果的にライトが当てられていた The display *was lit* (*up*) very effectively. ▶警官が振るライトの誘導で車はそろそろと事故現場の脇を通り抜けていった Police *flares* guided the cars as they crawled by the accident.
●ライトペン a light pen.
ライト 〖野球の右翼〗right field; 〖野球の右翼手〗a right fielder; 〖思想上の右派〗the right wing. (⇨右翼) ●ライトを守る play *right field*. ●ライトにヒットを放つ make a hit to *right* (*field*). ●ライト打ちの打者 a *right-field* hitter. ●ライトオーバーの二塁打を打つ hit a double over the *right fielder*. ●ライト線へライナーを打つ hit a line drive to the *right-field* corner.
●ライトスタンド the right field stands;《和製語》the right stand.
ライト —ライトな 形 〖軽い〗light. ●ライトビール a *light* beer.
ライト 〖米国の飛行機製作者〗Wright (Wilbur〔Orville〕).
ライトアップ 图 (投光照明) (a) flóodlight; (電飾) (an) illumination. (❗いずれもしばしば複数形で)
—**ライトアップする** 動 floodlight (過去・過去分詞形は light* に同じ); illuminate. ▶みどりの日に東京タワーは緑色にライトアップされた On Greenery Day (the) Tokyo Tower *was floodlit* green [*was lit* green *by floodlights*].
らいとう 来島 動 come to [visit] this island. ●冬には何種類かの渡り鳥が来島する Some kinds of migratory birds *fly to this island* in winter.
らいどう 雷同 ●付和雷同 (⇨付和雷同)
ライトきゅう ライト級 the lightweight. ●ライト級の選手 a lightweight (boxer).
ライトバン a mínivàn; (荷物運搬用) a delívery trùck《米》[vàn《英》];〖ワゴン車〗《米》a station wagon,《英》an estate car. (❗a light van は「軽量のバン」の意で, 車の型式としては用いない)
ライトブルー light blue.
ライトプロテクト 〖コンピュータ〗write protection. ●ライトプロテクトをかける (書き込み禁止にする) write-protect.
ライナー ❶〖野球の〗a liner, a line drive. ●ハーフライナー a soft liner;《和製語》a half liner. ●弾丸ライナー a hot liner; a bullet; (俗) a frozen rope.
●ライナーのヒット a line single. ●ライナーを打つ line; hit a *liner*. ●ライナーを捕る catch [grab] a *liner*. ●ライナーを打ってアウトになる *line* out.
❷〖外洋定期船〗a liner.
ライナーノート a liner note,《英》a sleeve note. (❗通例複数形で)
らいにち 来日 图 ▶ビョークの来日コンサート Björk's Japan concert [concert in Japan].
—**来日する** 動 〖日本に来る〗come to [visit,《着く》arrive in] Japan. ●来日中である be *in Japan*. ●来日中の親善使節団 a goodwill mission *on a visit to Japan* [*now staying in Japan*].
らいにん 来任 (⇨赴任)
らいねん 来年 next year; the coming year. ●来年の5月に[next] May (❗in next May は不可. その年の1-3月ごろにいうと「今年の5月」の意にもなる); in May *next year*;《英まれ》in May *next*. ●来年の今ごろ about this time *next year*. ●来年の計画を立てる make plans for *next year*. ▶彼は来年65歳で退職する He retires at 65 *next year*.
●来年のことを言うと鬼が笑う (来年のことなど分からない) There is no telling [knowing] what will happen next year./(ことわざ) Nothing is certain but the unforeseen.
らいねんど 来年度 ●来年度の計画 plans for *the next fiscal* [*financial*] year.
らいはい 礼拝 worship. (⇨礼拝(ホシ))
らいはる 来春 next spring. (⇨来春(ショッポ))
ライバル a rival (*in*); a competitor. ▶その選挙で彼の最大のライバル(候補)はだれですか Who is his greatest *rival* (candidate) *in* the election? ▶私たちはクラスの首席を目指すよきライバルでした We were good *competitors* for the top of our class. (❗*rival* は敵対関係や対抗心を含むのでここでは不適当)

らいひ ―**ライバルの** 形 rival. ● ライバル意識をあおる encourage *rivalry* 《with him, *between* them》.

らいひ 来否 ▶ご来否早めにお知らせください Please let us know *whether you come or not* at the earliest opportunity.

らいびょう 癩病 (⇨ハンセン病)

らいひん 来賓 a guest; a visitor. (⇨客❶)
● 来賓席 the guests' seats;《掲示》For guests.

ライフ [［命, 生活, 人生］] life (❗一つの命, 具体的な生活や人生は [C];［一生］ a life 《lives》.
● ライフサイエンス［生命科学］ life sciences. (❗複数形に注意) ● ライフスタイル a lifestyle. ● ライフステージ stages of life. ● ライフセービング［人命救助(法)］ life saving.

ライブ ▶この CD は 2004 年のウィーンフィルのニューイヤーコンサートのライブ録音です This CD was recorded *live* at the 2004 New Year concert by the Vienna Philharmonic Orchestra. (❗ライブ録音は *live* recording)
● ライブコンサート a live concert. ● ライブショー a live show. ● ライブハウス a place with live (rock) music.

ライフサイクル ［生涯［循環］過程］ a life cycle.
● ライフサイクルアセスメント［製品の循環過程における環境影響評価］ the assessment of (its) life cycle. ● ライフサイクルコスト［製品の生涯費用］ the cost of (its) life cycle.

ライフジャケット ［救命胴衣］ a life jàcket.
ライプツィヒ ［ドイツの都市］ Leipzig /láipsig, -sik/.
ライフボート ［救命艇］ a lifeboat.
ライフライン ［生活線］ a lifeline. ▶ニューヨークの地下鉄は何百万人の人々のライフラインである New York subway system is a *lifeline for* millions of people.

ライブラリー ［図書館］ a library. ● 視聴覚ライブラリー an audio-visual *library*.

ライフル a rifle.
ライフワーク one's lifework.
らいほう 来訪 a visit. ▶ご来訪をお待ちしております I am expecting you.
● 来訪者 (訪問者) a visitor. (⇨訪問)

ライム a lime.
ライむぎ ライ麦［植物］rye.
ライむぎばたけでつかまえて『ライ麦畑でつかまえて』 *The Catcher in the Rye*. (参考 サリンジャーの小説)

ライムライト (舞台照明用の) a limelight; [脚光] the limelight. (⇨脚光)

らいめい 雷名 one's fame; one's good name. ● 雷名をとどろかす be world-famous; enjoy a worldwide reputation.

らいめい 雷鳴 (a clap [a peal, a crash, a roll] of) thunder. ▶突然雷鳴がした Suddenly it *thundered* [the *thunder* came].

らいゆう 来遊 ― 来遊する 動 come (to Kobe) for pleasure;《米》spend a vacation 《in Kobe》;《英》spend a holiday 《in Kobe》.

らいらく 磊落 ― 磊落な 形 openhearted.
ライラック ［植物］ a lilac /láilək/.
らいりん 来臨 ▶式典には皇太子殿下のご来臨を得て執り行われた The Crown Prince *honored* us *with his presence* at the ceremony.

らいれき 来歴 a history. ● 故事来歴 (⇨故事)
ライン ［線, 直線］ a line. (⇨線, 直線) ● 合格ライン (=水準)に達していない be below [be low] the passing mark. ● サイド［タッチ］ライン a side [touch] *line*. ● (ディフェンスの)最終ライン［サッカー］ the last *line* of defense. ● ラインを上げる［下げる］［サッカー］ push forward [pull back] the *line*.

● ラインアウト［ラグビー］ a line-out. ● ライン組織 a line organization. ● ラインダンス line dancing. ● ラインドライブ［野球］ a line drive. ● ラインプリンター［コンピュータ］ a line printer.

ライン ● ライン川 the Rhine /ráin/.
ラインアップ ［野球］ a lineup. ● ラインアップを発表する announce the *lineup*. ● スターティングラインアップ (=先発メンバー)から外れている be out of the starting *lineup*. ● ラインアップに復帰する get back in the *lineup*. ● ラインアップカード (メンバー表) a lineup card.

ラインズマン ［線審］ a linesman (複 -men);《男女共用》a line umpire.

ラインナップ (⇨ラインアップ)
ラウドスピーカー ［拡声器］ a loudspeaker.
ラウンジ ［休憩室, 社交室］ a lounge.
ラウンド ❶［ボクシングやレスリングの回］● 10 ラウンドに in the tenth *round*. ● 第 1 ラウンドでリードする take the first-*round* lead.

❷［ゴルフのひと試合］● ゴルフをワンラウンドやる play a *round* of golf.

❸［一斉協議］● ドーハラウンド the Doha *round*.

ラオス ［国名］ Laos /láːous/;《公式名》the Lao People's Democratic Republic. (首都 ビエンティアン) ● ラオス人 a Laotian /leióuʃən/. ● ラオス語 Laotian. ● ラオス(人［語］)の Laotian.

ラオチュー 老酒 [<中国語] Chinese (rice) wine.
ラガー ［ラグビー］ rugby,《英語》 rugger. (⇨ラグビー)
● ラガーメン *rugger* players.
ラガー ［ラガービール］ lager /láːgər/ (beer).
らかん 羅漢 a *rakan*;《説明的に》a Buddhist who has attained spiritual release from Karma through severe religious practices.

らがん 裸眼 the naked eye. ▶右目の視力は裸眼で 1.0 だ Vision *in* my right *naked eye* is twenty-twenty. (⇨視力)

:**らく** 楽 名 ❶［安楽］ comfort;［気楽］ ease;［心配・苦痛などからの解放］ relief. ▶どうぞお楽にしてください Please make yourself *at home* [*comfortable*]./Please *relax*. ▶私達両親に楽をさせてやりたい I wish to make my parents live *in comfort* [*comfortably*]. ▶その薬を飲めば少しは楽になるでしょう The medicine will give [bring] you some *relief*. ▶以前より暮らしは楽になった (=よりよい状態になっている) We *are better off* than before. ▶罪を告白したら気持ちが楽になるよ You'll *feel better* if you confess your guilt.

❷［容易］ easiness. ▶昨今は先生をするのも楽ではないよね It isn't *easy* being a teacher these days, you know. ▶雑誌の編集は楽じゃない (=楽な仕事でない) Editing a magazine is no *easy* job.

● 楽あれば苦あり After pleasure comes pain./No pleasure without pain.

― **楽な** 形 [安楽な, 快適な] comfortable;［気楽な, 容易な］easy. ● 楽な生活を送る lead a *comfortable* [an *easy*] life. ● 楽に (=寝心地のよい)ベッド a *comfortable* [×an *easy*] bed. ▶もっと楽な姿勢で座りなさい You'd better sit in a more *comfortable* position. (❗×easy position は不自然) ● 楽な気持ちでやりなさい (かたっくせずに) Take it *easy*./(緊張せずに) Just *relax*. ▶ゆったりした服の方が楽だ Loose-fitting clothes are more *comfortable*./We feel more *comfortable* in loose-fitting clothes. ▶ぼくには飛行機で行く方が楽だ It is *easier for* me to go by plane.

― **楽に** 副 (容易に) easily; (安楽に) comfortably; (難なく) without (any) difficulty. ▶この問題は楽に解ける I can solve this problem *easily* [*with*

らくいん *ease, without (any) difficulty*]./(解くのが容易だ) This problem *is easy* (for me) to solve. ▶法案は楽に議会を通過した The bill passed *comfortably*./「かなりの余裕をもって」の意）台所の電化でいぶん楽になった(=手間が省ける) Electrical appliances in the kitchen *have saved* a lot of *trouble*. ▶この車は楽に5人乗れる(=十分なスペースがある) This car *has enough room* [*is large enough*] for five people./This car seats [*sits*] five passengers *comfortably*.

らくいん 烙印 a brand.
● 烙印を押される be branded (as) (a traitor).

らくいん 落胤 an illegitimate child (@ children) (of a nobleman).

らくいんきょ 楽隠居 ● 楽隠居の身である live happily [comfortably, relaxed] in retirement; enjoy happy [confortable, relaxed] retirement.

ラグーン 〖潟〗a lagoon.

らくえん 楽園 a paradise. (⇨天国) ● 地上の楽園 an earthly *paradise*. ● 野鳥の楽園 a *paradise for* wild birds.

らくがき 落書き 图 〖壁・公衆便所などの〗graffiti /grəˈfiːtiː/ 〖単・複両扱い〗;〖なぐり書き〗a scribble; a scrawl.
── 落書きする 動 ● 壁に落書きする scrawl [scribble, write] *graffiti* on the wall; *scribble* [*scrawl*] on the wall. ▶落書きするな〖掲示〗No *Graffiti*./No *Scribbling*.

らくがん 落雁 *rakugan*; 〖説明的に〗dry Japanese sweets made of soybean flour and sugar.

らくご 落伍 ── 落伍する 動 ●10人の走者のうち4人が落伍した Four of the ten runners *dropped out*. (⇨脱落)
● 落伍者(脱落者) a dropout; (失敗者) a failure.

らくご 落語 comic storytelling (usually in a classical style). ● 個々の話は a comic story)

DISCOURSE
落語を英訳することは困難だ．落語には「だじゃれ」と呼ばれる同音語があるが，これらを英語でも同音語に訳すことは不可能に近い…さらに，背景の違いがある It is difficult to translate *Rakugo* into English. In Rakugo, they use "dajare" (play on words which have the same sound but different meanings). It is next to impossible to translate them into corresponding English homonyms. ... **Then again**, Rakugo world is foreign to the English-speaking world. (■ Then (again), (さらに)は追加に用いるディスコースマーカー.)

● 落語家 a professional comic storyteller.

らくさ 落差 〖落下距離〗a drop; 〖ギャップ〗a gap; (相違) a difference. ● 落差15メートルの滝 a fifteen-meter waterfall. ● 現実と理想との落差(=ギャップ)を埋める fill [bridge] the *gap* [*difference*] between realities and ideals. ▶その滝の落差は15メートルだ The waterfall has a *drop* of 15 meters [*is* 15 meters high].

らくさつ 落札 图 a successful bid.
── 落札する 動 make a successful bid (*for*). ● 我が社はそのビル建設請負契約を落札した Our company *has made a successful bid for* a contract for the construction of the building./Our company has won a contract for the construction of the building. ▶(骨董〖とう〗の)つぼは日本人の大金持ちに落札された(=競り落とされた) The antique pot *was knocked down to* a Japanese millionaire.
● 落札者 a successful bidder. ● 落札値 (契約値) a contract price; (最高入札値) the highest bid.

らくじつ 落日 the setting sun.

らくしゅ 落首 (説明的に) a short anonymous satirical poem (put up in the street in the Edo period).

らくしょう 楽勝 an easy victory [win], 《話》a walkover, 《話》a walkaway. ▶その試合は楽勝だった The game was an *easy victory* [*win*]./(私たちは楽勝した) We *won* the game *easily* [*hands down*]./We had an *easy win* [won an *easy victory*] at the game. ▶テストは楽勝だった 《話》The test was *a cinch* [*a piece of cake, a breeze*].

らくしょうか 楽勝科目《米話》a gut course.

らくじょう 落城 图 the fall of a castle.
── 落城する 動 fall (to the enemy).

らくせい 落成 图 completion.
── 落成する 動 ▶新校舎は3月に落成した The new school building *was completed* in March.
● 落成式 (hold) an inauguration [a completion] ceremony.

らくせき 落石 falling rocks [stones]. ▶落石で道がふさがった *Fallen rocks* blocked the road. ▶落石注意〖掲示〗Watch for falling rocks.

らくせき 落籍 (⇨身請け)

らくせつ 落雪 a fall of masses of snow; (落ちた雪) masses of snow that fell. ▶落雪があった *Masses of snow fell down* the mountain.

らくせん 落選 ── 落選する 動 ▶彼は次の選挙で落選するだろう He will *lose* the next *election*./He will *not be elected* [*be defeated*] in the next election.

らくだ 駱駝 〖動物〗a camel. ● ラクダのこぶ a hump.

らくたい 落体 a falling body.

らくだい 落第 图 ❶〖留年，再履修〗▶彼は数学で落第点をとった He got a *failing grade* [mark] in math. (■ 通例成績の「不可」は F で表す) ❷〖失格〗▶彼はセールスマンとしては落第だ He's a *failure* as a salesman.
── 落第する 動 ❶〖留年・再履修する〗▶彼は落第した(進級できなかった) He *failed to pass on to the next grade*./(再履修しなければならなかった) He had to *take the same course again* [*repeat the same course*].
❷〖試験に落ちる〗fail, 《米話》flunk; (落とされる) 《米話》be flunked (*in*). ▶君は数学を落第したと思うよ I'm afraid you've *failed* [《米話》*flunked*] math.
● 落第生 《米》a repeater.

らくたん 落胆 ── 落胆する 動 be discouraged [disappointed] (*by, at*), lose heart; (意気消沈している) be depressed (*by, at*). ▶その失敗で[その結果に]彼は落胆してしまった The failure [The result] *discouraged* him./He *was discouraged by* the failure [*at the result*].

らくちゃく 落着 ● 一件落着 The problem [trouble] *has been settled* (satisfactorily).

らくちょう 落丁 a missing page. ▶落丁しているPages are *missing*.

らくちょう 落潮 〖引き潮〗the ebb; (引いていく潮) an ebb tide (⇨引き潮); 〖落ち目〗loss of popularity (⇨落ち目).

らくちん 楽ちん 〖『楽』の児童語〗(⇨楽) ● 楽ちんないすa *conforbable* chair.

らくてん 楽天 ── 楽天的な optimístic. (⇨楽観) ● 楽天家 an optimist. ● 楽天主義 óptimism.

らくど 楽土 a paradise.

らくに 楽に (⇨楽 [楽に])

らくね 楽寝 ── 楽寝する 動 have a restful sleep [

らくのう 酪農 /déəri/ (farming).
- 酪農家 a dairy farmer; (男) a dairyman.
- 酪農場 a dairy (farm). ● 酪農製品 dairy products (goods).

らくば 落馬 图 a fall from a horse;《話》a spill.
── 落馬する 動 fall from [off] a horse. ● 落馬して死ぬ die in a spill.

らくはく 落魄 ── 落魄する 動《書・やや古》live in reduced circumstances; come down in the world; be laid low. (⇨零落)

らくばく 落莫 ● 落莫たる廃坑 a dreary mine now abandoned. ● 秋風落莫 a bleak wind-swept scene in late autumn.

らくばん 落盤 a cave-in (of a mine).

らくび 楽日 the last [closing] day of a performance.

ラグビー 〖スポーツ〗rugby;（正式には）rugby football;《英話》rugger. ● ラグビーをする play rugby. ● ラグビーの選手 a rugby player. ● ラグビーの試合 a rugby match.
- ラグビーボール a rugby ball.

ラグマット a rag mat.

らくめい 落命 ── 落命する 動 ● 戦場で落命する be killed in action [in the battlefield]. (⇨死ぬ)

らくやき 楽焼き rakuyaki ware; (説明的に)《a piece of》 hand-made pottery glazed and baked in low temperature;（素人が作った）《a piece of》pottery painted by amateurs (as a souvenir).

らくよう 洛陽 〖中国の古都〗Luoyang /lwɔːjáːŋ/.
- 洛陽の紙価を高からしめる 'raise the price of printing paper in the capital'; become a bestseller; The book is selling like hot cakes.

らくよう 落葉 图 the fall of leaves;（落ち葉）fallen leaves.
── 落葉する 動 （木が）shed [lose, drop]《its》leaves;（葉が）fall.
- 落葉樹 a deciduous tree.

らくらい 落雷 a thunderbolt. (⇨雷) ● 落雷による被害 lightning damage. ▶船のマストに落雷があった The mast of a boat was struck by a bolt of lightning [a thunderbolt].

らくらく 楽々 (⇨楽[楽に]) ● 楽々英作文（書名などで）English Writing Without Tears.

ラグランそで ラグラン袖 raglan /rǽglən/ sleeves.

らくるい 落涙 ── 落涙する 動 shed tears.

ラクロス 〖スポーツ〗lacrosse /ləkrɔ́ːs/. ● ラクロスをする play lacrosse. ● ラクロスの選手 a lacrosse player.

ラケット （テニス・卓球などの）a racket (❗ 卓球では《米》a paddle,《英》a bat ともいう) ● テニスのラケット a tennis racket.

ラゴス 〖ナイジェリアの旧首都〗Lagos /léigɑs/.

ラザーニャ ［＜イタリア語］〖パスタ料理の一つ〗lasagna /ləzάːnjə/.

ラジアルタイヤ a radial tire.

＊らしい ❶【思われる】seem; appear; (見える) look. (⇨ーよう ❷ ［類語］) ▶今日彼はひどく怒っているらしい He seems [appears, looks]《to be》very angry today. (❗ look では to be は通例省略される) / It seems [appears, ×looks]《that》he is very angry today. (❗ この文では that がしばしば省略される) ▶あすは雨らしい It looks [seems] like rain tomorrow. (❗ like は《米》では《第6文例》) ▶私は警官らしい背の高い男性に話しかけた I spoke to a tall man who seemed [appeared] to be a policeman. (❗ 程度を表すことができない名詞(や形容詞)の前では通例 to be は省略される) ▶ビル内をくまなく探したが，爆破装置あるいはそれらしいもの（＝それに似たもの）はなかった We searched the building from bottom to top, but there was no trace of an explosive device or anything resembling one. ▶彼は帰る途中どこかで時計を落としたらしい It seems that he lost [He seems to have lost] his watch somewhere on the way home. ▶彼はその事実を知らないらしい He didn't seem [He seemed not] to know the fact. (❗ to 不定詞には通例 know, hear, think などの状態動詞, 完了形, 進行形がくる(⇨[第2文例]))/It didn't seem that he knew [It seemed that he didn't know] the fact. (❗ seem の前の言い方の方が口語的) ▶どうやら雨らしい It looks like rain./It is likely to rain./It looks as if [《話》like] it's going to rain.

会話 「美智子はどうかしたの」「彼女やめたのよ. そうらしいわ」"What's happened to Michiko?" "She's resigned, só it ╱ seems." (❗ it seems so ともいえる)

❷【言われている】▶彼は近く政界を引退するらしい People say《that》[They say《that》,《書》It is said that] he will retire from the political world soon./I hear (that) he will retire from the political world soon. (❗ ..., I hear. のように最後に置くこともある)

❸【ふさわしい】(ぴったりである) be fit《for; to do》; (特徴を示している) be like ...; (値する) be worthy of ....
- レディーらしくないふるまい conduct unfit for a lady; (レディーに似合わない)《書》conduct unbecoming [not becoming] to a lady. ● いかにも芸術家らしい（＝その名にふさわしい）芸術家 an artist worthy of the name. ▶あんな侮辱的な言葉を遣うなんて君らしくないよ It's not fit for [It's not like,《書》It does not become] you to use insulting words like that! ▶子供じみた行動はいかにもあの男らしいよ Childish behavior is just like him. / It is characteristic [typical] of him to behave childishly.

ラジウム radium /réidiəm/〖元素記号 Ra〗.
- ラジウム温泉 a radium hotspring. ● ラジウム療法 radium therapy.

ラジエーター 〖放熱器, 冷却器〗a radiator /réidièitər/.

＊ラジオ 〖放送〗(the) radio /réidiou/; 〖受信機〗a radio (機～を) (set) (set)《話》この set は通例省略する). ▶その部屋ではラジオがかかっていた The radio was playing [on] in the room.

①【～ラジオ】● AM [FM; 短波]ラジオ an AM [an FM; a shortwave] radio. ● ポータブルラジオ a portable radio. ● トランジスタラジオ a transistor [a solid-state] radio. ● 目覚し付きラジオ a radio alarm.

②【ラジオ～】● ラジオ英語講座 a radio English course [program]. ● 特にラジオ用に書かれた脚本 a script written specially for radio. ● ラジオ関係で働く work in radio.

③【ラジオの[に]】● ラジオのダイヤルを回す dial the radio. ● ラジオの音を大きくする[しぼる] turn up [down] the radio. ● ラジオに出る go [be] on the radio (❗ be では状態を表す); go on the air. (❗ 後の言い方はテレビの場合が多い)

④【ラジオを】● 運転中はラジオを聞く listen to (the) radio while at the wheel. (❗ テレビと対照的に用いる場合は the が省略されることが多い(⇨⑤)) ● ラジオをつける[消す] turn on [off] the radio. (❗ turn のほかに put, switch も可) ● ラジオをつけっ放しにしておく leave the radio on. ● ラジオを NHK に合わせる tune the radio to NHK. ▶彼はラジオをかけたまま

ラジカセ 眠ってしまった He fell asleep with the *radio* on. (⚠ *with* は付帯状況を示す)
⑤【ラジオで】● ラジオで音楽を聞く listen to music *on* [*over*] *the radio*. (⚠ *on* の方が普通) ● ラジオで宣伝を流す put an ad [*advertise*] *on radio and TV*. ● 鉄道スト があることをラジオで聞いた I heard *on the radio* that there's going to be a train strike. ● 彼の演説はきのうのラジオで放送された His speech was broadcast *on the radio* [*by radio*] yesterday. ● 手紙を表す句の後では *radio* は無冠詞/His speech *was radioed* yesterday.
● ラジオアイソトープ 【化学・物理】 a radioisotope. ● ラジオコメディー a radio comedy. ● ラジオコンパス a radio compass. ● ラジオゾンデ 【気象】 a radiosonde. ● ラジオ体操 radio (gymnastic) exercises. ● ラジオ聴取者 a radio listener; 〔集合的〕 a radio audience. ● ラジオドラマ a radio play. ● ラジオニュース radio news; the news on the radio. ● ラジオ番組 a radio program. ● ラジオビーコン 【無線標識】 a radio beacon. ● ラジオ放送 radio broadcasting. (⚠ 具体的な放送は ⓒ) ● ラジオ放送局 a radio station.

ラジカセ a radio-cassette player, a radio and tape player; (大型) a boom box.
ラジコン radio control. ● ラジコン操作のモデルカー a radio-controlled model car.
らししょくぶつ 裸子植物 a gymnosperm.
ラシャ [<ポルトガル語] 【厚地の毛織物】 wool(en) cloth.
らしょうもん 『羅生門』 *Rashomon*. (参考 芥川龍之介の小説)
らしん 裸身 a naked /néikid/ body; (裸の状態)《hide one's》nakedness. ● 裸身をさらす expose one's *naked body*.
らしんばん 羅針盤 a (mariner's) compass.
ラス 【建築】 a lath. ● ワイヤーラス a wire *lath*.
ラスク (パンや卵から作る菓子) rusk.
ラスト 【最後, 最終】 the last; final.
● ラストシーン the last scene. ● ラストナンバー the last number. ● ラストボール 【野球】 (フルカウントからの) a payoff pitch; a 3–2 pitch; (和製語) a last ball.
ラストオーダー last orders, 《米》 a last call. ● 〔店で〕 ラストオーダーです *Last orders*, please!
ラストスパート ● ラストスパートをかける (競技で) make [put on] the *final* [*last*] *burst* [*spurt*] (of speed); (仕事などで) make the *final push*.
ラスベガス 【米国の都市】 Las Vegas /lɑːs véigəs/, (話) Vegas.
ラズベリー 【植物】 a raspberry.
らせん 螺旋 —— 螺旋形の 〔形〕 spiral; screw-shaped.
● らせん階段 a *spiral* [a *winding*] staircase. ● らせん状 in a *spiral*.
らぞう 裸像 (絵・写真の) a nude figure [picture]; (彫刻の) a nude statue.
らたい 裸体 a naked body; a nude body. (⇨裸)
● 画家のため裸体でポーズを取る pose nude [*in the nude*] for an artist.
● 裸体画 a nude (picture).
らち 埒 ● 埒が明かない ● 我々はそれについて何度も話し合いをしたが埒が明かない We have talked about it again and again but we *are getting nowhere*.
● 埒もない らちもないことを言う say silly things; talk nonsense.
らち 拉致 abduction.
—— 拉致する 〔動〕 abduct; (連れ去る) take ... away.
● 拉致被害者 an abductee.
らちがい 埒外 ● らち外にある be beyond the pale

(まったく受け入れがたい) be completely unacceptable. ● 彼女の行動はまったく常識の埒外 Her behavior is completely *beyond the pale* [*bounds*] of common sense.
らっか 落下 a fall, a drop. (⇨落ちる)
らっか 落花 —— 落花狼藉(ろうぜき) ● 落花狼藉たり be in utter [great] confusion; be chaotic /keiɑ́tik/.
ラッカー 【塗料】 lacquer /lǽkər/. ● ラッカーを塗る lacquer 《a desk》.
らっかさん 落下傘 a parachute /pǽrəʃùːt/. ● 落下傘で降りる make a descent by *parachute*; make a *parachute* descent; parachute.
● 落下傘部隊 a parachute troop, a paratroop.
● 落下傘兵 a paratrooper.
らっかせい 落花生 【植物】 a peanut, 《主に英》 a groundnut.
***らっかん** 楽観 〔名〕 ● 彼の病状は楽観を許さない His sickness doesn't allow for any *optimism*./We can't be *optimistic* [*hopeful*] about his sickness.
—— 楽観的な 〔形〕 optimistic. (希望に満ちた) hopeful.
—— 楽観する be optimistic 《*about*》; take an optimistic view 《*of*》; (物事の明るい面を見る) look on the bright side of things.
● 楽観論[主義] óptimism. ● 楽観論[主義]者 an óptimist.
らっかん 落款 (署名) a signature; (印) a seal (which calligraphers and artists use to sign their works).
ラッキー lucky. (⇨運, 幸運)
会話 「寝る前にもう 1 杯どう? おれのおごりで」「わあ, ラッキー!」 "How about another drink before bedtime? I'm buying." "Hey, that's a *break*!" (⚠ *break* は 〔話〕 で 『幸運』 の意)
● ラッキーセブン 【野球】 the seventh inning.
● ラッキーゾーン a lucky zone. ● ラッキーヒット 【野球】 a cheap hit.
らっきゅう 落球 —— 落球する 〔動〕 (flub [muff] and) drop [miss] the ball.
らっきょう 【植物】 a shallot (bulb); (漬物) a pickled shallot.
ラック 【棚】 a rack.
らっけい 落慶 the completion of a temple [a shrine] building. ● 本堂の落慶式を行う hold a ceremony to celebrate the completion of the main hall of a temple.
ラッコ 【動物】 a sea otter.
ラッシュ ● ゴールドラッシュ a gold *rush*. ● ラッシュアワー (⇨ラッシュアワー)
ラッシュアワー ● 朝のラッシュアワーに during [in] the morning *rush*(*-hour*). ● ラッシュアワーの混雑 〔交通量〕 *rush-hour* congestion [traffic].
ラッセル [<ドイツ語] 【医学】 (気管支の) a rhonchus /rɑ́nkəs/《 rhonchi /-kai/》; (肺の) a rale /rǽl/.
ラッセルしゃ ラッセル車 a snowplow /-plàu/. (参考 日本語は考案者の Russel から)
らっぱ 喇叭 〔軍隊の〕 a bugle /bjúːɡl/; 〔音楽隊の〕 a trumpet. ● らっぱを吹く blow a [sound a, play the] *bugle* [*trumpet*]; (自画自賛する) blow one's own *trumpet* [*horn*]. ● らっぱ飲みする drink 《beer》 (straight) from a bottle.
● らっぱズボン bell-bottoms.
らっぱずいせん 喇叭水仙 【植物】 a daffodil.
ラッピング wrapping. ● 〔店で〕 プレゼント用にラッピングしてください Please *gift-wrap* this [it].
ラップ 【包装用の】 〈a piece of〉 wrápping film, plastic film [wrap], 《主に英》 clingfilm. ● 文脈があれば単に wrap も可。Saran Wrap 《商標》 ● ラップで

ラップ 包む[を掛ける] wrap ⟨it⟩ up in *wrapping film*.
ラップ 〚音楽〛rap (music).
・ラップミュージシャン a rapper.
ラップタイム a lap time.
ラップトップ a laptop (computer). ・ラップトップに打ち込む type at a *laptop*.
らつわん 辣腕 ── 辣腕の 形 sharp; (抜け目のない, 鋭い) shrewd.
・辣腕家 a sharp [a shrewd] person. (⚠)(1) 通例 person の代わりに具体的に politician (政治家), businessman (事業家)などを入れて用いる. (2) 辣腕事業家を《話》で a go-getter とか a wheeler-dealer という)
ラディッシュ 〚植物〛a radish.
ラテン Latin. ・ラテン語(の) Latin.
・ラテンアメリカ Latin America. ・ラテン音楽 Latin music. ・ラテン民族 the Latin peoples [races].
らでん 螺鈿 ── 螺鈿細工 mother-of-pearl work.
ラトビア 〚国名〛Latvia; (公式名) the Republic of Latvia. (首都 Riga) ・ラトビア人 a Latvian. ・ラトビア語 Latvian. ・ラトビア人(語) Latvian.
ラドン 〚化学〛radon /réidɑn/; 〚元素記号 Rn〛.
ラニーニャ [<スペイン語] La Niña. (⇨ エルニーニョ)
・ラニーニャ現象 La Niña phenomenon.
らば 騾馬 〚動物〛a mule.
ラバー 〚ゴム〛rubber.
・ラバーソール (ゴム底の靴) rubber-soled shoes.
ラパス [ボリビアの首都] La Paz /lɑ pɑ́ːz/. (参考) 法律上の首都は Scre (スクレ)
ラビオリ [<イタリア語] 〚パスタ料理の一種〛ravioli.
らふ 裸婦 a nude (woman) (複 -men), a woman in the nude.
・裸婦画 a nude.
ラフ 〚ゴルフ〛the rough. ・ラフな(=略式の)服装で in casual [informal, ×rough] wear.
・ラフプレイ rough play.
ラブ ❶〚愛情〛love. **❷**〚無得点〛〚テニス〛love.
・ラブゲーム 〚テニス〛a love game. ・ラブコール (⇨ラブコール) ・ラブシーン a love scene. ・ラブストーリー a love story. ・ラブセット 〚テニス〛a love set. ・ラブソング a love song. ・ラブホテル a motel, a hotel; (和製語) a love hotel. ・ラブレター a love letter. ・ラブロマンス a romance.
ラブコール a phone call to one's sweetheart; (和製語) love call. ▶監督はその大物女優に映画出演のラブコールを送った The director *eagerly asked* the great actress to appear [play a role] in his movie.
ラプソディー 〚狂詩曲〛〚音楽〛a rhapsody.
ラブラドルレトリバー 〚動物〛a Labrador (retriever).
ラブラブ 付き合ってまだ3か月のあの2人はラブラブだ They met only three months ago and *are deeply in love* (with each other).
ラベル a label /léibl/. (⇨レッテル)
ラベル [フランスの作曲家] Ravel /rəvél/ (Maurice ∼).
ラベンダー 〚植物〛lavender /lǽvəndər/. ・ラベンダー香水 lávender wàter.
ラボ 《話》a lab (laboratory の略).
ラマ 〚動物〛a llama /lɑ́ːmə/.
ラマーズほう ラマーズ法 the Lamaze /ləmɑ́ːz/ method. ・ラマーズ法講習を受ける take Lamaze classes.
ラマきょう ラマ教 [<チベット語] Lamaism /lɑ́ːməizm/. ・ラマ教徒 a Lamaist.
ラマダン [<アラビア語] 〚断食月〛Ramadan /rǽmədɑn/. (参考) イスラム暦第9の月で断食が行われる)
ラム 〚子羊〛a lamb; (子羊の肉) lamb. ▶ラム2切れください Two *lambs*, please. (⚠注文するときは可算名詞扱い)
ラム [コンピュータ] RAM 《random-access memory の略》.
ラムしゅ ラム酒 rum.
ラムネ 《米》lemon soda, 《英》lemonade.
ラリー ❶〚テニス・卓球などの〛a rally. ▶2人は強烈なラリーを数回繰り広げた They powerfully hit the ball back and forth several times./Powerful *rallies* went on several times between them. **❷**〚自動車の長距離競走〛a (car) rally. ・パリ・ダカールラリー the Paris-Dakar *Rally*.
らりる (舌がもつれる) be thick in one's speech; cannot speak clearly; (ふらふらする) feel* dizzy.
られつ 羅列 名 (an) enumeration.
── 羅列する 動〚書〛enumerate; list mechanically. ▶次に彼女は来なかった理由を羅列し始めた And then, she began to *enumerate* the reasons [*give one* reason *after another*] for not coming.
-られる (⇨-れる)
ラワン 〚植物〛(材) lauan /ləwɑ́ːn/; (木) lauan.
らん 乱 (騒乱) (a) disturbance; (反乱) a riot; (a) revolt; (戦乱) a war. ・乱を起こす rise in revolt; raise a *riot*. ・乱を治める suppress [put down] a *riot* [a *revolt*]; (平和を回復する) restore the peace.
らん 蘭 〚植物〛an orchid.
らん 欄 〚囲ったところ〛space; [コラム] a column. ・氏名を記入する欄 the *space* to write one's name in.
・新聞のスポーツ欄 the sports *column* [*section*] of a newspaper. (⚠「新聞の広告欄」は the classified *section* [《英》the advertising *columns*] *of* a newspaper)
ラン [コンピュータ] LAN (local area network の略).
らんうん 乱雲 a nimbus (複 ∼es).
ランエンドヒット 〚野球〛a run and hit; a run-and-hit play.
らんおう 卵黄 (a) yolk /jóuk/, the yolk of an egg.
・卵黄2個 two *egg yolks*.
らんがい 欄外 a margin. ・37ページの欄外の注 a note *on the margin* [a *marginal* note] of page 37. ・欄外に書き込む write ... down *in the margin*.
らんかいはつ 乱開発 名 (やや書)indiscriminate exploitation; overexploitation.
── 乱開発する 動 森を乱開発する *exploit* the forests *indiscriminately*; overexploit the forests.
らんかく 乱獲, 濫獲 indiscriminate hunting [fishing]; overhunting; overfishing. ▶パンダは乱獲のため絶滅の危機にひんしている Pandas are on the brink of extinction because of *indiscriminate hunting* [because they have *been heavily hunted*].
── 乱獲[濫獲]する 動 hunt [fish] indiscriminately; overhunt; overfish.
らんかく 卵殻 an eggshell.
らんがく 蘭学 Dutch studies.
・蘭学者 a Dutch scholar.
らんかん 卵管 〚解剖〛an oviduct, a fallopian tube. (⚠(1) 通例複数形で. (2) 後の方が普通)
・卵管結紮(ケツ) 〚医学〛fallopian ligation. ・卵管破裂 tubal rupture.
らんかん 欄干 a railing; [橋・バルコニーなどの] a parapet.
らんぎょう 乱行 (やや書)debáuchery. ・乱行いちじるしい若者 (やや書) a debauched young man; a young debauchee /dèbɔːtʃíː/.

らんぎり 乱切り ●にんじんの乱切り carrots chopped into chunks; carrots cut into warped wedges. ●乱切りにする cut into warped wedges.

らんきりゅう 乱気流 (air) turbulence. ▶飛行中乱気流に巻き込まれた We experienced some *turbulence* during the flight.

ランキング a ranking. ●世界ランキング3位を第三位 be third in the world *rankings*. ●大学の偏差値ランキング university [college] *rankings* based on the T-scores of applicants. ●ランキング上位のテニス選手 a high-*ranking* tennis player. ●ランキング1位になる rank [be ranked] first.

ランク (a) rank. ▶東京は物価の点で世界第1位にランクされている Tokyo *ranks* first in prices in the world.
●ランクアップ a rise in one's ranking. ●ランクアップする rise 《*from* 7th *to* 5th *in* the world rankings》.

らんくいば 乱杭歯 (不揃いな歯) a snaggletooth (愈-teeth); (悪い歯並び) irregular teeth. ●乱杭歯だったので歯列矯正用の金具をはめていた As the alignment of my teeth was crooked, I used to wear braces.

らんくつ 濫掘, 乱掘 图 indiscriminate digging.
——**濫掘[乱掘]する** 動 dig ... up indiscriminately.

ランゲージ 〖言語〗 (a) language.
●ランゲージラボラトリー a language laboratory.

らんげき 乱撃 (⇨乱射)

らんこう 乱交 (グループでする性交) group sex; (不特定多数の人との性交) promiscuous sex.
●乱交パーティー a sexual orgy.

らんこうげ 乱高下 图 (株価などの) wild fluctuations (in stock prices); volatility.
——**乱高下する** 動 ●株価は乱高下した Stock prices *fluctuated wildly*.

らんごく 乱国 a disturbed [a troubled] country.

らんさく 濫作, 乱作 图 overproduction.
——**濫作[乱作]する** 動 ●小説を乱作する write too many novels;《書》churn out novels.

*****らんざつ 乱雑** 图 〖順序・配列が乱れている状態〗disorder;〖ごちゃごちゃに混ざり合った状態〗(a) clutter, (a) confusion;〖取り散らかした状態〗(a) mess.
——**乱雑な** 形 ●乱雑な部屋 an *untidy* [《やや書》a *messy*,《やや書》a *disorderly*] room; a room *in a clutter*. ●乱雑な字で書き込まれたページ a *scribbled* page
——**乱雑に** 副 ●床の上に乱雑に散らばった書類 papers thrown *in disorder* [*confusion*] on the floor.

らんし 乱視 图 〖医学〗astigmatism.
——**乱視の** 形 astigmatic.

らんし 卵子 〖生物〗an ovum /óuvəm/, (愈 ova); an egg.

ランジェリー 〖<フランス語〗〖婦人肌着類〗lingerie /làːnʒəréi, -riː/.

らんししょく 藍紫色 indigo purple.

らんしゃ 乱射 图 random [wild] shots, random fire.
——**乱射する** 動 ●ライフルを乱射する *fire* one's rifle *wildly* [*blindly*, *at random*,（無差別に）*indiscriminately*].

らんじゅく 爛熟 ▶その時イギリスの文学は爛熟期に達した At that time English literature reached its [came into] *full maturity*.
——**爛熟した** 形 overripe;〖文化などが〗matured.

らんじゅほうしょう 藍綬褒章 the Medal with Blue Ribbon.（⇨褒章 関連）

らんしん 乱心 madness; derangement.
●乱心者 a madman; a deranged person.

らんしんらんりょう 乱診乱療 ●乱診乱療する give《a patient》*unnecessary treatment*.

らんすう 乱数 random numbers.
●乱数表 a table of random numbers.

らんせ(い) 乱世 〖社会が乱れた時期〗turbulent [troubled] times;〖激動変革の時期〗the period [time] of social upheaval [violent changes]. ●乱世を生き抜く live out *the days of violent changes*.

らんせい 卵生 图 〖生物〗ovipartity /òuvəpǽrəti/.
——**卵生の** 形 oviparous《animals》.

らんせん 乱戦 〖混乱した戦い〗a confused fight;〖乱闘〗《やや書》a melee /méilei/; a dogfight. ▶その野球の試合は大乱戦になって勝負の行方は分からなくなった The final result of the baseball game became unclear (with) both teams scoring a lot of runs [乱打戦で] in a slugfest].

らんそう 卵巣 〖解剖〗an ovary /óuvəri/. (⚠ しばしば複数形で)
●卵巣摘出手術 an ovariectomy. ●卵巣ホルモン ovarian /ouvéəriən/ hormones.

らんぞう 濫造, 乱造 图 overproduction; excessive production.
——**濫造[乱造]する** 動 overproduce; produce [manufacture, make] in excess [carelessly; recklessly].

らんそううん 乱層雲（気象）nimbostratus.

らんたいせい 卵胎生 〖生物〗ovoviviparity.
——**卵胎生の** 形 ovoviviparous.

ランダウンプレー（⇨挟殺）

ランダム random. ●ア(ッ)トランダムに選ぶ pick《them》*at random*.
●ランダムアクセスメモリー 〖コンピュータ〗random-access memory (略 RAM). ●ランダムサンプリング random sampling.

ランタン a lantern.

ランチ 〖船〗a launch /lɔːntʃ, lɑːntʃ/.（⚠ 動力つきで川・湖・港内での観光・運搬用大型ボート)

ランチ 〖昼食〗lunch;（昼の定食）a set lunch. ●お子様ランチ a special dish for children; a kiddie special lunch. ●ランチタイムに at [during] lunchtime. ●ランチを食べる have *lunch*.

らんちきさわぎ 乱痴気騒ぎ ●乱痴気騒ぎをやる have a wild party;《やや話》go on a *drinking spree*.

らんちゅう 蘭鋳（説明的に）a globular goldfish with lumps on the head and no dorsal fin.

らんちょう 乱丁 incorrect [imperfect] collating.

らんちょう(し) 乱調(子) ❶〖株価の〗fluctuation《s》(in stock prices). ▶このところ株価の乱調が続いている Stock prices *have been fluctuating* for sometime. ❷〖演奏中の〗(a) confusion; (a) loss of control.

ランチョン (a) luncheon.
●ランチョンマット a place mat;（和製語）a luncheon mat.

ランデブー 〖<フランス語〗《やや書》a rendezvous (愈 ～ /-vùːz/).（⇨デート）●（宇宙船が）ランデブーする（=宇宙空間で出会う） rendezvous [have a *rendezvous*]《*with*》.

らんとう 乱闘 a confused [a free] fight;（取っ組み合いの）a scuffle. ●ビーンボールを巡っての乱闘 a bean brawl. ●ベンチ総出の乱闘 a bench-clearing brawl. ▶彼らは警官隊と乱闘になった They *scuffled with* the police.

らんどく 乱読 ——**乱読する** 動 read indiscriminately; read everything one can get one's hands on.（⚠ read at random は「量とは無関係に行き当たりばったり読む」の意)

ランドスケープ 〖景観〗a landscape.

ランドセル [<オランダ語] a satchel /sǽtʃəl/.（事情 米英では日本のようなランドセルはない。 各自好みのバッグを用いるのが普通)

ランドマーク 〚その土地の目印・象徴的な建物〛a landmark.

ランドリー a laundry /lɔ́ːndri/.（⇨コインランドリー）

ランナー 〚走者〛a runner /rʌ́nər/.
● ランナーズハイ 〚スポーツ〛a runner's high.

らんない 欄内 ● 欄内に記入する fill in [《米》fill out, 《英》fill up] the blanks. ▶申込書は指定の欄内に記入の上, 郵送してください Fill in [*out*] the application form as designated and send it by mail.

らんにゅう 乱入 图 （侵入）《やや書》(an) intrusion.
—**乱入する** 動 ▶デモ隊が大学構内に乱入した The demonstrators *broke into* the university campus.
● 乱入者 an intruder.

ランニング running /rʌ́niŋ/. ● ランニングをする go *running*. ● 公園へランニング(をし)に行く go *running* in [×to] the park. (*!* to では「公園へ[まで]走って行く」の意)
● ランニングキャッチ 〚野球〛《make》a running catch. ● ランニングコスト rúnning còsts [expènses].（*!* いずれも複数形で）● ランニングシャツ (下着)《米》a sleeveless undershirt,《英》a vest;（スポーツ用）《和製語》a running shirt. ● ランニングシューズ rúnning shòes. ● ランニングホーマー 〚野球〛《hit》an inside-the-park homer,《和製語》A running homer.

らんのう 卵嚢 an egg case;（カマキリ・ゴキブリなどの）an ootheca /ouəθíːkə/（֍ -cae /-kiː/);（サメ・エイの）a sea purse.

らんばい 乱売 图 ▶暖冬なので冬物の乱売が至るところで行われている Winter clothes *are being sold dirt cheep* everywhere because of the mild winter.
—**乱売する** 動 （めちゃくちゃ安く売る）《話》sell (it) dirt cheep; (他店より安く売る) undersell;（原価を切って売る）sell at a loss.

らんぱく 卵白 albumen /ælbjúːmən/; (an) egg white.

らんばつ 乱伐 图 （無謀な森林伐採）deforestation.
—**乱伐する** 動 deforest. ● 山の木を乱伐する fell [*cut down*] trees in the mountain *recklessly* [*indiscriminately*].

らんぱつ 乱発 图 （紙幣などを）overissue.
—**乱発する** 動 overissue《bank notes》.

らんはんしゃ 乱反射 图 diffusion.
—**乱反射する** 動 duffuse.

らんぴ 乱費 图 waste; squandering.
—**乱費する** 動 waste; squander.

らんぴつ 乱筆 图 （走り書き）(a) scribble; hasty writing. ▶乱筆乱文をお許しください Please excuse my *hasty writing* [*poor handwriting*]. （事情 米英ではこのような謙遜表現は慣用的でないない)

らんぶ 乱舞 —**乱舞する** 動 （気が狂ったように踊る）dance wildly [*madly*];（歓喜して踊る) dance for joy.

ランプ 〚光源としての〛a lamp. ● 石油[アルコール]ランプ an oil [a spirit, an alcohol] *lamp*. ● ランプのしん [ほや] a *lamp* wick [chimney]. ● ランプのかさ a *lamp*shade. ● ランプをつける[消す] light [put out] a *lamp*.

ランプ 〚高速道路の〛a ramp.

ランプ 〚牛の尻肉〛rump.
● ランプステーキ a rump steak.

らんぶん 乱文 (⇨乱筆)

らんぽう 卵胞 〚解剖〛an ovarian follicle. (*!* 単に a follicle ともいう)
● 卵胞ホルモン estrogen.

*****らんぼう** 乱暴 图 violence. ● 数々の乱暴狼藉(ろうぜき)を働く commit acts of vandalism.
—**乱暴な** 形 〚暴力的な〛violent; 〚荒々しい〛rough; 〚無謀な〛reckless; 〚不注意な〛careless; 〚無礼な〛rude; 〚不合理な〛unreasonable. ● 乱暴な態度 *violent* [*rude*, 《けしからぬ》*outrageous*] behavior.
● 乱暴な(=ずさんな)翻訳 a *loose* translation. ● 乱暴な運転手 a *reckless* [a *careless*] driver. ● 乱暴な筆跡 *careless* handwriting. ● 乱暴な要求 an *unreasonable* demand. ● 乱暴な言葉遣いをする use *violent* [*rough*] language; have a *rough* tongue; (口論をする)《話》talk *rough*. ● 乱暴な手段を用いる take *violent* measures. ▶乱暴なことはしなくてもその問題は解決できる You can solve the problem in non-*violent* ways [*without violence*].
—**乱暴に** violently; roughly; rudely; carelessly. ● 乱暴に彼を押しのける push him away *violently* [*roughly*]. ● 機械を乱暴に扱う treat a machine *roughly*.
—**乱暴を(する)** 動 彼に乱暴(を)する use *violence* on him; do *violence* to him.（⇨暴力, 暴行）
● 女性に乱暴する(=女性を犯す) sexually assault a woman; rape a woman.
● 乱暴者 a wild fellow, a rough,《話》a rowdy.

らんま 乱麻 快刀乱麻を断つ（⇨快刀 [成句]）

らんま 欄間 *ranma*;（説明的に）a wooden panel used as a decorative transom above paper-covered sliding doors. (*!* a transom は「ドア上部の明かり取りの窓」の意)

らんまん 爛漫 ● 桜花爛漫である Cherry blossoms are *at their best* [*prime, in full bloom*].

らんみゃく 乱脈 （ずさんな）careless. ● 乱脈な経理 *careless* accounting. ● 市の経理は乱脈を極めていた(=めちゃくちゃだった) The city's accounting was *in a terrible* [*an awful*] *mess*.

らんよう 乱用 图 ● 職権の乱用 the *abuse* /əbjúːs/ of one's official authority.
—**乱用する** 動 特権を乱用する *abuse* /əbjúːz/ one's privileges.

らんらん 爛々 ● 爛々とした(=きらきら輝く)目《with》bright [《ぎらぎら輝く》glaring] eyes.

らんりつ 乱立 ▶この地域にはスーパーが乱立している There are *too many* supermarkets in this district.

らんりゅう 乱流 turbulence. (⇨乱気流)
● 乱流抑制 turbulence suppression.

り

- **り 利** 〖有利〗(an) advantage;〖利益〗(a) profit, (a) gain;〖利子〗interest. ● 地の利を得る get the *advantage* of a good location. ● 利にさとい have a quick eye for a *profit* [for *gain*]. ▶利が利を生む *Interest* bears *interest*.
- **り 里** 〖長さの単位〗a ri. (❶単・複同形)（参考）約3.9 km)
- **り 理** 〖道理〗reason (⇨道理);〖真理〗truth. (⇨一理)
  ● 理に落ちる (話が理屈っぽくなる) become argumentative.
  ● 理の当然 (⇨当然)
- **-り -裏，-裡** ● 暗々裏に in secret, secretly;《approach》by stealth /stélθ/, stealthily. ● 成功裏に終わる《事が主語》come to a successful end; be a《great》success.
- **リアクション** a reaction.
- **りあげ 利上げ** 图 a rise in the interest rate.
  ―― **利上げする** 動 raise the interest rate.
- **リアス** 〖<スペイン語〗ria.
  ● リアス式海岸 a saw-toothed [ria] coastline.
- **リアリスト** 〖現実主義者〗a realist.
- **リアリズム** 〖現実主義〗realism.
- **リアリティー** 〖現実性〗reality.
- **リアル ―― リアルな** 形 (真に迫った) real; (写実的な) realistic. ● リアルな描写をする give a *realistic* description《*of*》.
- **リアルタイム** 〖即時・同時進行〗real time. ● リアルタイム為替レート a *real time* foreign exchange rate. ● その試合をリアルタイムで実況する broadcast the game in *real time*.
- **リーガー** メジャー[マイナー]リーガー a major [a minor] *leaguer*.
- **リーグ** a league. ● セントラル[パシフィック]リーグ the Central [Pacific] *League*. ● メジャーリーグの野球選手 a major-*league* ball player; a major *leaguer*.
  ● リーグ戦 (個々の試合) a league game [match] (⇨試合); (リーグ内の全試合) the league series; (一般に総当たり戦)《米》a round robin. ● 六大学野球リーグ戦 the Big-Six-University Baseball *League* Tournament.
- **リース** 〖花輪〗a wreath /ri:θ/.
- **リース** 〖賃貸借契約〗a lease. (⇨賃貸) ● 5年間リースでその機械を使う use the machine *on* a 5-year *lease*.
  ● リース業 a léase sèrvice. ● リース業者 a léasing còmpany.
- **リーズナブル** (手頃な) reasonable. ● リーズナブルな値段 (*at*) a *reasonable* price.
- **リーダー** 〖指導者〗a leader. ● リーダーシップをとる take on [assume, play] the *leadership* (role)《*of*》. ▶彼は組合のリーダーだ He is the *leader* of the union.
- **リーダー** 〖読本〗a reader. ● 英語のリーダー an English *reader*.
- **リーチ** 〖手の長さ〗a reach. ● リーチが長い have a long *reach*.
- **リーチ** 〖マージャンの〗a standing hand. ● リーチをかける declare a *standing hand*.
- **リーディング** 〖読むこと〗reading.
- **リーディングヒッター** 〖野球〗(シーズン途中の, またはチーム内の) a leading hitter;（シーズン成績としての) batting king [champion]. ▶彼は目下リーグのリーディングヒッターだ Now he leads the Pacific League in batting.
- **リード** 〖先頭〗the lead. (❶リードしている距離・時間などをいうときは a lead) ● リードを奪う 〖奪われる; 広げる〗 gain [lose; stretch] the *lead*. ● 相手チームを2点リードする have *a lead* of two points [a two-point *lead*] over the opposing team; *lead* the opposing team *by* two points. ▶ジャイアンツはタイガースに3点リードされている The Giants are trailing the Tigers by three runs. ▶ジャイアンツは5点リードされていたのをはね返した The Giants overcame the five-run deficit. ▶ランナーは一塁ベースから少しリードした The runner took a little *lead off* first base.
  ● リードオフマン 〖先頭打者〗〖野球〗a lead-off man [hitter]. ● リードギター (人) a lead guitarist; (パート) lead guitar. ● リードタイム 〖経済〗(事前所要時間) lead time. ● リードボーカル (人) a lead vocalist; (パート) lead vocal.
- **リード** 〖音楽の〗a reed.
  ● リードオルガン a reed organ.
- **リード** 〖犬・馬などの綱ひも〗《米》a leash,《英》a lead. ● リードをゆるめる loose a *leash*. (⇨ひも, 綱(⅔))
- **リーフ** 〖葉〗a leaf.
  ● リーフパイ a leaf pie.
- **リーフ** 〖暗礁〗a reef.
- **リーフレット** 〖ちらし〗a leaflet.
- **リール** (釣りざおの) a (fishing) reel; (テープなどの巻き枠) a reel. ● リール付き釣りざお a fishing rod and (a) *reel*. (❶単数扱い) ● リールで巻き上げる reel《a fish》in. ● オープンリールのテープレコーダー a reel-to-reel taperecorder.
- **りんりん** (⇨りんりん)
- ***りえき 利益** ❶ 〖もうけ〗(a) profit, gain(s) (❶しばしば複数形で);〖収益〗returns. (⇨儲(¾)け)
  ① 【〜利益】 ● 相当な [法外な] 利益 a handsome [an exorbitant] *profit*. ● 不正な利益 ill-gotten *gains*. ● 純[総]利益500万をあげる make a net [a gross] *profit* of five million yen.
  ② 【利益が[は]】 ● 利益が出る yield a *profit*. ▶この商売は利益が大きい[小さい] The *profit* from this business is large [small]. /(利益を生む) This business yields large [small] *profits*. ▶1日の利益はどのぐらいですか How much [What] *profit* do you make a day?
  ③ 【利益の】 ● 利益のあがる商売 a *profitable* (↔an unprofitable) business. ● 利益の増加 a rise [a surge] in *profits*. ● 利益の減少 a fall [a drop, a decline] in *profits*. ▶彼は利益のためなら何でもするだろう He would do anything for *gain*.
  ④ 【利益を】 ● 利益を出す (事が) yield a *profit*; (人が) make a *profit*. ▶彼は家を売って1,000万円の利益を得た He made [gained] a *profit* of ten million yen on [from] the sale of his house.
  ❷ 〖得〗 interest(s) (❶しばしば複数形で); (恩恵) benefit; (有利) advantage,《書》profit; (有益) use, good (❶ use より口語的). (⇨得, 益)
  ① 【〜利益】 ● 目先の利益だけを考える consider one's immediate *interests* only. ● 公共の利益を

リエゾン

はかる promote the public *benefit* [*good*, *interests*].
②【利益が】▶数学を勉強して何の利益があるのか (反語的) What's the *use* [*good*] of studying mathematics? (⇨得①)
③【利益に】▶それは君の利益に反するだろう It will be against your *interests*. ▶寝る時刻を過ぎてまで勉強しても何の利益にもならない There is no *advantage* [*profit*, (効果) *point*] *in* studying past your bedtime. ▶新しい道路は山間の住民の利益になるだろう The new road will *benefit* the people living in the mountains.
④【利益を】▶私はこの本から大いに利益を得た I *have benefited* greatly *from* [*by*] (*reading*) *the book*./I *have gained* great *benefit* from the book.
• 利益供与 an illegal payoff. • 利益計画 profit planning. • 利益社会 【社会学】(the) Gesellschaft. (関連) 共同社会 Gemeinschaft). • 利益団体 an interest group. • 利益配当 (株式の配当金) a dividend; (利益の分配) profit sharing. • 利益分配[配分] profit sharing. • 利益剰余金 (留保利益) an earned surplus. • 利益率 a profit ratio.

リエゾン [<フランス語] 〖連声〗〖言語〗 a liaison /liéizn/.

りえん 梨園 the world of *kabuki* actors. • 梨園の名門 a distinguished family in the *kabuki* actor's world.

りえん 離縁 (a) divorce. (⇨離婚)
• 離縁状 a letter of divorce (from a husband to his wife).

リオデジャネイロ 〖ブラジルの都市〗 Rio de Janeiro /ríːou dei ʒanéərou/.

りか 李下 ▶李下に冠を正さず 'Do not touch your headgear under a plum tree, because people will suspect that you have stolen some plums.'/Caesar's wife must [should] be above suspicion. (❢ 慣用表現)

りか 理科 ❶【教科】science; 【学問の総称】natural science(s) (❢ 通例複数形. 個々をさすときは a natural science).
❷【大学の理科系部門の総称】the science course. • 理科系に進む take the *science course* (in college).
• 理科室 a science room [(実験室) laboratory].
• 理科大学 a college of science.

リカー 〖蒸留酒〗 liquor.

‡りかい 理解 图 understanding, (書) comprehension; 〖把握〗grasp; 〖値打ちの理解〗 appreciation.
• 理解ある(=物分かりのよい)人 an *understanding* person. (❢ 「理解力に優れている人」 (a person of understanding) の意もある) ▶理解を越えている(=理解できない) be above [beyond] (his) *understanding* [*grasp*, *comprehension*]; be above [beyond] 《him》; be over 《his》head. • 理解力をテストする試験 an examination (designed) to test *understanding*. • 国家間の相互理解を深める develop [promote] mutual *understanding* between the nations.

── 理解する 動 understand*, (話) make*... out (❢ 通例疑問文・否定文に用いる. 受身は不可), (書) comprehend; 〖把握〗 grasp; 〖正しく認識する〗 appreciate. (⇨分かる❶) • 西洋文化を正しく理解する *appreciate* Western culture. ▶彼の言っていることが理解できなかった I couldn't *understand* [*make out*, (米やや話) *figure out*, *grasp*] what he said. (❢ 日常会話では「彼の言っていること[考え]を理解する」は *understand* [×*grasp*] him, *make* [*figure*] him *out* とすることも多い) ▶彼がなぜ学校をサボったのかどうも理解できない I just can't *understand* why he cut school./I just can't *understand* his [(話) him] cutting school. (❢ (1) 否定語の前の just は否定の強調. (2) 「理解できない」は I *don't understand....* で表すことも多い) ▶彼にはこの問題をはっきり理解している He *understands* [×*is understanding*] this matter clearly. (❢ 「だんだんと理解してきた」は He's beginning to *understand....* とする)/He *has* a clear *understanding of* this matter. ▶彼の講義は私にはさっぱり理解できない I can't *understand* his lecture at all./His lecture is quite *over my head*./I can't *make head or tail of* his lecture. ▶彼の作品は当時はあまり理解されなかった His works *were* not fully *appreciated* at that time. ▶少年は幼くて母親の死が理解(=実感)できなかった The boy was too young to *realize* the death of his mother.

りがい 利害 [利害関係] an interest. ▶私はあの会社に利害関係がある I have an *interest* in that firm. ▶この件では彼らの利害が一致している They have [share] common *interests* in this matter. ▶この件では彼らの利害は相反[衝突]している Their *interests* conflict [clash] in this matter.
• 利害関係者 the interested parties [persons]; the parties concerned. • 利害得失 the advantages and disadvantages 《*of*》.

りかがく 理化学 physics and chemistry.

りがく 理学 (physical) science.
• 理学士 Bachelor of Science《略 B.Sc.》. • 理学博士[修士] Doctor [Master] of Science《略 D.Sc. [M.Sc.]》. • 理学部 the college [department] of science. • 理学療法 physiotherapy; (米) physical therapy. • 理学療法士 a physiotherapist; (米) a physical therapist.

りかけい 理科系 the science course. (⇨理系)

リカバリー 〖回収, 回復〗(a) recovery.
• リカバリーショット 〖ゴルフ〗(hit) a recovery shot.

りきえい 力泳 ── 力泳する 動 swim with strong strokes, swim hard [as hard as possible].

りきがく 力学 dynamics. (❢ 単数扱い)
• 力学的エネルギー mechanical energy.

りきさく 力作 a tour de force; (傑作) a masterpiece. ▶展覧会に出展された絵はいずれも力作ぞろいだ All the paintings at the exhibition are *masterpieces*.

りきし 力士 a sumo wrestler. • 大型力士 a heavyweight *sumo wrestler*. • 力士の最高位に昇る obtain the highest *sumo* rank.

りきせつ 力説 ── 力説する 動 (=経済の重要性を力説(=強調)する) *emphasize* [*put emphasis on*, *stress*, *lay stress on*, (熱心に説く) *urge*] the importance of economy.

りきそう 力走 ── 力走する 動 run as hard [(速く) *fast*] as one can.

りきそう 力漕 ── 力漕する 動 (力いっぱいこぐ) row with all one's strength [powerful strokes]; pull hard.

リキッド (a) liquid. (⇨液)
• リキッドファンデーション (a) liquid foundation.

りきてん 力点 (重点) (米) emphasis (米) emphases /-si:z/; (強調) (a) stress. ▶力点を置く put *emphasis* [*stress*] 《*on*》.

りきとう 力投 ── 力投する 動 (力強く投げる) pitch (a ball) with all one's strength; (がんばる) bear down. • 力投して三球三振に打ち取る *bear down* to strike 《him》out on three pitches.

りきむ 力む (精一杯努力する)《やや書》 exert oneself

りきゅう (力を入れすぎる) overpower. ●いくらがんこでみても for all one's efforts. ●力みかえる《書》 *exert oneself* unduly /ʌndjúːli/. ●(打者が)力んで振る overswing. ●(投手が)力んで投げる overthrow.
▶彼は重い岩を動かそうとして力んだ《やや書》 He *exerted himself* [*used all his strength*] to move the heavy rock. ●あんまり力むなよ Don't try so hard./Take it easy.

りきゅう 離宮 a detached palace; an imperial villa. ●桂離宮 the Katsura *Detached Palace*.

りきゅうねずみ 利休鼠 (緑がかったねずみ色) greenish gray.

リキュール [<フランス語] (a) liqueur /likɔ́ːr/.

りきりょう 力量 (能力) (an) ability; (適性, 資格) competence; (受容能力) (a) capacity. (⇨能力)
●力量を発揮する show (one's) *ability* [*competence*]《*for*, *in*》. ▶彼にはその仕事をする力量がある He has the *ability* to do the job./He is *competent* for the job [*to do the* job].

***りく** 陸 land (**!** しばしば the ~); (海岸) shore. ●陸に(たどり)着く come to [reach, touch] land; 《海事》make *land*. ●(船を降りて)陸に上がる [上がっている] go [be] *on shore*. (⇨上陸する) ▶船が陸を離れた [陸に接近した] The ship cleared [approached] the *land*. ▶カエルは陸と水中の両方にすめることができる Frogs can live both *on land* and in water.
●陸の孤島 ▶そこはまさに陸の孤島のような所であった That was exactly what you might call an isolated island *on land*.

りくあげ 陸揚げ 图 unloading.
━━ **陸揚げする** 動 ●マグロを陸揚げする (船が主語) unload [《主に米》discharge] tunnies;《人が主語》unload tunnies from a ship.
●陸揚げ港《書》a port of discharge. ●陸揚げ場 a landing plàce.

りぐい 利食い 图 profit-taking. ▶多くの投資家が利食いに出している Most investors are *taking profits* [(現金化している) cashing in, realizing].
━━ **利食いする** 動 take [make] a profit by selling or buying stocks.

りくうん 陸運 land [ground] transportation 《主に米》[transport 《主に英》].
●陸運会社 a land transportation company.

りくえい 陸影 ●陸影を見る sight land.

リクエスト 图 a request.
━━ **リクエストする** 動 ●歌をリクエストする *request* [*make a request for*] a song.

りくかいくう 陸海空 land, sea, and air. ●陸海空の3軍 the army, navy and air forces; the (armed) forces.

りくぐん 陸軍 the army. (**!** 1 国の陸軍の総称は the Army. 単・複両扱い (⇨海軍))
●陸軍軍人 a soldier. (**!** 兵士も士官も全部含む) ●陸軍士官学校 the Military Academy. ●陸軍将校 an army [a military] officer.

りくさんぶつ 陸産物 land products.

りくし 陸士 (「陸軍士官学校」の略)(⇨陸軍)
●陸士長 Lance Corporal.

りくしょう 陸相 (陸軍大臣) the Minister of the Army.

りくじょう 陸上 the land. ●陸上勤務をする on *shore* [*ground*] duty. (**!** shore は海上に対して, ground は機上に対して) ●陸上でも海上でも *on land* and at [x*on*] sea. ●陸上輸送する transport 《it》by *land*.
●陸上自衛隊 the Ground Self-Defense Force. ●陸上部 (陸上競技部) (⇨陸上)

りくじょうきょうぎ 陸上競技 track and field;《英》athletics (**!** 単・複両扱い); (種目) track-and-field events. ●陸上競技のコーチ a *track-and-field* coach. ●世界陸上(競技)選手権大会 the World *Athletics* Championships.
●陸上競技会《米》a track meet;《英》an athletics meeting. ●陸上競技場 an athletic field. ●陸上競技部 a track-and-field club;《英》an athletics clùb.

りくせいどうぶつ 陸生動物 a land [a terréstrial] animal.

りくせん 陸戦 a land battle [fight].
●陸戦隊 a landing force.

りくそう 陸送 ━━ **陸送する** 動 transport by [on] land.

りくそう 陸曹 Sergent.

りくぞく 陸続 (⇨ひっきりなし, 続々)

りくだな 陸棚 (⇨大陸 [大陸棚])

りくち 陸地 land. (⇨陸) ●陸地を旅行する travel on *land*.

***りくつ** 理屈 [道理] reason,《話》logic (**!** reason は理性的, logic は理性にかなっていること); 『理論』(a) theory;『論拠』an argument;『言い訳』(an) excuse /ikskjúːs/;『口実』a prétext (**!** 偽りの理由);『へ理屈』a quibble 《*over*》.
①【理屈=】 ▶理屈抜きで without demur; perfectly. ▶彼は理屈屋だ(=議論好きだ) He is *arguméntative*./He is fond of *arguing*. ●物事は理屈(=理論)どおりには行かないものだ Things do not always go according to *theory*.
②【理屈】 ▶理屈は抜きにして putting *logic* aside. ▶むだに時間を使ってよいという理屈はない There's no reason to waste your time.
③【理屈の】 ▶理屈の分かった(=分別のある)人 a *reasonable* [a *sensible*] person. ●理屈の上では *in theory*. (⇨理論) ●理屈の通らない (⇨④ [理屈に合わない])
④【理屈に】 ●理屈に合う be reasonable; be logical. (⇨⑥) ●理屈に合わない (理にかなわない) be unreasonable; (筋の通らない) be illogical.
⑤【理屈を】 ●理屈を言う[つける, こねる] (論じる) argue; (理論を立てる) 『理論』theorize; (言い訳をする) make an *excuse*; (口実をつくる) make a *pretext* (へ理屈を言う) quibble. ●何とか理屈をつけて (理由) for one *reason* or another; (言い訳) on one *excuse* or another.
⑥【理屈だ】 ▶それは理屈だ (実践的ではない) That's a mere *theory*./(言い訳) That's just an *excuse* [x*reason*]./(理屈に合っている) That's *reasonable* [*logical*].

りくつづき 陸続き ▶スイスとイタリアは陸続きである(=隣接している) Switzerland *borders* Italy.

りくつっぽい 理屈っぽい (議論好きな) argumentative; (論争好きな) disputatious. ●理屈っぽい人 an *argumentative* person.

りくとう 陸稲 a dry-field rice plant.

りくふう 陸封 陸封された landlocked.

りくふう 陸風 a land breeze.

りくへい 陸兵 (陸軍の兵) land troops.

リクライニングシート a reclíning sèat [chàir].

リクリエーション recreation /rèkriéiʃən/. ●リクリエーションにテニスをする play tennis *for recreation*.

リクルーター a recruiter.

リクルート (新人募集) recruitment; (新入者) a recruit.
●リクルートスーツ (説明的に) a typical dark (gray) suit which college students usually wear when they have a job interview;《和製語》a recruit suit.

りくろ 陸路 ●陸路を行く go *by land*; go *overland*; take an *óverland róute*.

りけい 理系 the science course. (⇨文系) ●理系の大学生 a college student majoring 《米》[specializing 《英》] in *science*. ●理系の大学 a college of *science*.

リケッチア 〖生物〗a rickettsia. (参考 細菌とウイルスの中間の大きさの微生物)

りけん 利権 （特に採掘権）a concession; （権益）an interest; （権利）a right. ●鉱山の利権を与えられる be granted a mining *concession*. ●利権をあさる hunt for *concessions*. ●事業に利権を持っている have an *interest* in business.
●利権屋 a concession hunter; a profiteer.

りげん 俚諺 a proverb; a (popular) saying. (! saying には成句も含まれる)

*** りこう 利口 —— 利口な** 形 ❶ 〖聡明な〗clever, 《主に米》smart; （判断の賢明な）wise; （知能の高い）intelligent; （頭のよい）bright; （並外れて頭のよい）brilliant. (⇨賢い 【類語】) ●彼が即答を避けたのは利口だった *It was wise [clever, smart] of him not to give a ready answer*. (! (1) He was wise [clever, smart] (enough) not .... の言い方より客観的。(2) clever と smart は文脈によってずるさや抜け目のなさを含意することもある) ●犬にはとても利口なのがいる Some dogs are very *intelligent [clever, smart]*. ●彼は利口ぶって(=知ったかぶりで)政治を論じた He discussed politics *knowingly*.
会話 「パパ，そればく 1 人で塗ったんだよ」「お利口だね え」"I painted it myself, Daddy." "There's a *clever boy*!"
❷ 〖行儀のよい〗（特に子供が）good. ●おじさんの家に行ったらお利口にしなさいよ Be *good* [（行儀よくしなさい）*Behave* (*yourself*)] when we visit your uncle. (! *oneself* は省略されることもある) ●お利口さんねそっとはこが良い[girl]"

りこう 理工 ●理工学部 the college [department] of science and engineering. (⇨理系)

りこう 履行 名 （計画・約束・計画などの）fulfillment; （契約・遺言などの）execution; （債務などの）performance. ●契約の履行[不履行] *fulfillment [nonfulfillment]* of a contract.
—— **履行する** 動 ●約束を履行する *fulfill [carry out, （公約などを）deliver]* a promise.
●履行期限[期] the term [date] of performance. ●履行不能 （債務の）impossibility of performance.

りごうしゅうさん 離合集散 ●政界における離合集散 changes in political alignment. (! alignment は「協力関係」の意) ●人は離合集散を重ねて成長する People will grow up by mixing with various kinds of people. (! 「人はいろいろな人と接することにより精神的に大人になるものだ」の意)

リコーダー 〖縦笛〗〖音楽〗a recorder. ●リコーダーを演奏する play the *recorder*. ●リコーダー演奏家 a recorder player.

リコール 名 a recall. (! 通例単数形で.「(公職者への)解職請求」の意で用いるのは 《米》)
—— **リコールする** 動 ●そのメーカーは安全性の理由から自社のチャイルドシートをすべてリコールすると発表した The manufacturer issued a *recall* of all their child's car seats for safety reasons.
●リコール運動 a recall campaign.

りこしゅぎ 利己主義 （自分勝手）selfishness (! 最も日本語に近い概念); （私利中心主義）egoism (! 特に倫理学・哲学で用いられるが，一般には egoism と同義に用いる); (自己中心癖) egotism. (! egoism より一層軽蔑的の)

●利己主義者 a selfish person; an egoist; an egotist.

りこてき 利己的 —— **利己的な** 形 selfish; egoistic.
●彼は利己的だ He is *selfish [egoistic]*./(自己中心的だ) He is *self-centered*.
—— **利己的に** 副 selfishly.

りこん 離婚 名 (a) divorce 《*from*》. ●協議離婚 a *divorce* by agreement [mutual consent]; a no-fault *divorce*. ●離婚(件数)が増えている *Divorce* is on the increase. ●彼らの結婚生活は結局離婚に終わった Their marriage ended in *divorce*. ●彼女は(裁判所へ)離婚を申し立てている She is petitioning [asking, suing, filing] for *divorce*. (! 「離婚の申し立て」は a *divorce* petition)
—— **離婚する** 動 get a divorce 《*from*》; be [get] divorced 《*from*》; divorce. (! 最後の言い方は主語が離婚を望んだことを暗示するが，他の二つは不明) ●離婚した男性 a *divorced* man; a divorcé /-séi/ 《女性は a divorcée /-séi/. 《英》では divorcée はしばしば軽度的な含意を伴うので，男性形の divorcé が好まれる. 《英》では男女両用に divorcee /-siː/》●彼は妻と離婚し秘書と結婚した He *divorced* his wife and married his secretary. ●両親が離婚した時私は5歳でした When my parents *divorced*, I was five years old.
●離婚訴訟 divorce proceedings 《*against*》. ●離婚届 a divorce notice.

リサーチ 〖調査, 研究〗research. (⇨調査, 研究)

リザーブ —— **リザーブする** 動 ●席をリザーブする *reserve* 《英》a seat (*on* the train).

りさい 罹災 —— **罹災する** 動 （被る）suffer 《*from*》.
●罹災者 a sufferer; （犠牲者）a victim. (! 災害の種類を示して a flood [a fire] *victim* (水害[火事]の罹災者)のように使うのが普通) ●罹災地 a disaster [a stricken] area.

りざい 理財 economy; finance.

リサイクル 名 〖再生利用〗recycling. (⇨リデュース)
参考 ●ビンやカンのリサイクル the *recycling* of bottles and cans.
—— **リサイクルする** 動 recycle. (⇨再生 [再生利用する], 再利用) ●空きびんをリサイクルする *recycle* empty bottles.
●リサイクル工場 a recýcling plànt. ●リサイクルショップ（中古品店）a secondhand shop; （慈善のための）《米》a thrift shòp. 《和製語》a recycle shop.

リサイタル a recital. ●ピアノリサイタルを開く give [*xopen*] a piano *recital*.

りさげ 利下げ 名 a reduction in interest.
—— **利下げする** 動 lower the rate of interest [the interest rate].

りざや 利鞘 a (profit) margin. ●利ざやを稼ぐ make a profit; 《米話》scalp 《theater tickets》 (! 「転売して利益をかせぐ」の意)

りさん 離散 —— **離散する** 動 ●父の事業の失敗のために一家は離散した Our family broke up after the failure of my father's business.

りし 利子 interest 《*on*》. ●利子をつけて返す pay back 《the money》 with 《15 percent》 *interest*.
●高い[低い]利子で貸し付けを受ける get a loan at high [low] *interest*. ●その社債は年6パーセントの利子がつく The bond yields [bears] six percent *interest* a year. ●銀行は預金の利子を支払う Banks pay *interest* on [x*of*] savings. ●100万円借りたらいくら利子を払うことになるのですか What's the *interest* I'll have to pay if I borrow one million yen?/How much *interest* will there be *on* a loan of one million yen? ●ローンには利子が

りじ　〈 Loans carry *interest*.
- 利子所得 income from interest. ● 利子税 interest tax.

りじ　理事　a director; (会社・大学などの) a trustee.
- 理事会　a board of directors [trustees].
- 理事長 the chief director; the director general; the chairperson of the board of directors [trustees].

りしゅう　履修　── **履修する** 動　(単位を得る) earn 《a credit》;(講座を取る) take 《a course》; (学科を勉強する) study. ● 化学を履修する take a course in [×of] chemistry; take [study] chemistry. ● 英文学を履修する(=修める) complete English literature.
- 履修科目 a subject to be studied. ● 履修単位 a credit. ● 履修届 the registration for a course.

りじゅん　利潤　(a) profit. (⇨利益❶) ● 利潤の追求 the pursuit of *profits*; *profit* seeking. ● 利潤を上げる make [yield] a *profit* 《on the deal》. (❗ yield では事業が主語)

りしょう　離床　── **離床する** 動　(病気が治って) one's bed (sickbed]; recover from one's illness; (起床する) get out of bed, get up.

りしょう　離礁　── **離礁する** 動　満潮になって離礁することができた At high tide *our boat was set afloat off the rocks*./At full tide there was enough water to *float our boat off the reef*.

りしょく　利殖　(金もうけ) moneymaking. ● 利殖のために金を買う buy gold to *make money*.

りしょく　離職 图　● 高い離職率 a high turnover. ● あの会社は離職率が高い The *turnover* at that company is high./That company has a high *turnover*.
── **離職する** 動　leave a company; leave [《話》quit] one's job.
- 離職者 a person who leaves a company; (失業者) a jobless [an unemployed] person.

りす　栗鼠　[動物] a squirrel.

りすい　利水　the use of water. ● 農業用利水計画 the plan *to use the* 《river》 *water for* agriculture.

りすい　離水　── **離水する** 動　take off 《from the lake》.

りすう　理数　● (高校の)理数コース [科] a *science and mathematics* course. ● 彼女は理数系の頭をしている She thinks scientifically.

リスク　(a) risk. (⇨危険) ● ハイリスク high-risk. (⇨ハイリスク) ● すべてのリスクを負う bear [assume] all the *risk*. ● 大きなリスクを伴う事業 a project involving a great [a lot of] *risk*.
- リスク回避 risk aversion. ● リスクファクター [危険因子] [医学] a risk factor. ● リスク分散 risk diversification [sharing]; diversification of risk. ● リスクマネジメント [危機管理] risk management.

リスタート　restart.

リスト　[目録] a list. (⇨表, 名簿) ● 買いたい本をリストアップする (=のリストを作る) *list* [*make a list of*] the books one wants to buy. (❗ ×list up は和製英語)

リスト　[手首] a wrist. (⇨手首)
- リストバンド (時計用・スポーツ選手の汗止め用) a wristband.

リスト　[ハンガリーの作曲家・ピアニスト] Liszt /list/ (Franz ～).

リストラ　(組織の再編) rèstrúcturing, (縮小) downsizing. ● リストラを実施する carry out [implement] *restructuring* [a *restructuring* program]. ● 彼はリストラされた(=首になった) He was *restructured* out of his job. (❗単に He was restructured. だけでは不可)/He was fired [《婉曲》was laid off]. (⇨レイオフ)

リスナー　[聴取者] a listener.

リスニング　listening.
- リスニングルーム a listening ròom.

リスボン　[ポルトガルの首都] Lisbon /lízbən/.

リズミカル　── **リズミカルな** 形　rhythmic(al). ● 音楽のリズムな拍子に合わせてひざを叩く tap one's knee to the *rhythmic* beat of music.
── **リズミカルに** 副　● リズムに動く move *rhythmically*.

***リズム**　[音楽] (a) rhythm /ríðm/; [テンポ] a tempo (働 ～s; tempi /témpi:/); a pace. ● 3 拍子のリズムで演奏する play in triple *rhythm*. ● タンゴのリズムにのって踊る dance *in* tango *rhythm* [(リズムに合わせて) *to* the *rhythm* of the tango]. ● 足でリズムをとる keep *rhythm* with one's foot. ● リズムをつかむ(スポーツ) find a [one's] *rhythm*. ● (投手が)リズムに乗る get [find] one's *rhythm*. ● (投手が)リズムを失っている [を失っている] be in the *rhythm* [out of *rhythm*]. ● 彼はリズム感がいい[悪い] He has good [poor] *rhythm*./He has a (good) sense [no sense] of *rhythm*. (❗ no sense of rhythm は「リズム音痴」の意)

リズムアンドブルース　[音楽] rhythm and blues 《略 R&B》.

リスリン　(⇨⦿ グリセリン)

りする　利する 動 ❶[利益を得る・与える] profit [benefit] (by [from]); be profitable [beneficial]; (ためになる) be rewarding; be worthwhile 《*to* do, doing》. ● 海外旅行は利するところが大きい We will *profit* greatly *by* traveling abroad. ● 軍の情報漏えいが敵を利することになった The leak of military information *helped* [*profited*] the enemy.
❷[利用する] (役立たせる) utilize; be useful [helpful]; (うまく用いる) make good use of; (巧みに使う) take advantage of. (⇨利用する) ● 地勢を利してダムを建設する build a dam by *making good use of* the natural lie of the land.

りせい　理性 图　《やや書》reason; rationality; (感情・意志に対する理知) intellect. ● 理性に訴える appeal to 《one's》 *reason* [*intellect*]. ● 理性に従って行動する act according to *reason*. ● 理性を失う lose (control of) one's *reason*. ● 人間には理性がある A human being is *rational* [理性的な生き物だ] a *rational* creature]./People have (the power of) *reason*. ● もっと理性を働かせなさい Be more *reasonable*./Why don't you be more *reasonable*?
── **理性的な** 形　rational; reasonable. (❗ 後の方がくだけた語)

りせき　離籍　── **離籍する** 動　leave 《the Tigers》.

リセット 图　(a) reset.
── **リセットする** 動　reset. ● 人生をリセットしたい(=再出発したい)と思う人は少なくない Quite a number of people want to *make a fresh start* in their life.
- リセットボタン 《press》a reset button.

りせん　離船　── **離船する** 動　leave [(沈みゆく船から) abandon] the ship.

＊りそう　理想 图　an ideal (↔reality). ● 理想を実現する realize one's *ideal*. ● 理想にかなう live up to 《his》 *ideals*. ● 理想と現実のギャップに悩む be tormented by the gap between the *ideal* and reality. ● 彼は理想が高い He has high *ideals*./He is a man of high *ideals*. ● 理想を高く持て Hitch your wagon to a star. (❗ Emerson の言

— 理想の, 理想的な [形] ideal. ●理想の夫[妻] one's ideal husband [wife]. ▶彼は私の理想の男性です He's my *ideal* (man) [the man of my *dreams*]. (⚠ *ideal*は名詞で「理想の人[物]」の意味がある) ●彼はその仕事には理想的な人物だ He is the *ideal* person *for* the job.
● 理想化 idealization. ● 理想化する idealize. ● 理想郷 a utopia. (⚠ しばしば U-) ● 理想主義 ⇨ 理想主義 ● 理想像 an ideal image. ● 理想論 an idealistic thought [view].

りそうしゅぎ 理想主義 [名] idealism.
— 理想主義的な [形] idealistic.
● 理想主義者[家] an idealist.

リソース [[資源, 財源]] resources.

リゾート a resort.
● リゾートウェア resort wear [clothing]. ● リゾート開発 resort development; the development of resort areas. ● リゾート施設 resort facilities. ● リゾート地 (海辺の) a seaside resort; (山の) a mountain resort. ● リゾート地でバイトする work part-time at a resort. ● リゾートホテル a resort hotel. ● リゾートマンション 《米》a resort condominium; 《英》a resort condo flat.

りそく 利息 ●利子. (⇨利子)
● 利息計算 computing of interest.

リゾット [<イタリア語] [[イタリア風雑炊]] rizotto.

りそん 離村 [見限って] desert] one's village.

りた 利他 — 利他的な [形] altruistic; unselfish.
● 利他主義 altruism. ● 利他主義者 an altruist.

リターナブル [[再利用のために回収する]] returnable (bottles).

リターン — リターンキー [コンピュータ] a return key.
● リターンマッチ (play) a return match.

リタイア — リタイアする [動] [退職する] retire (⇨退職); [レースなどで] drop out (*of*) (⇨脱落). ●レースからリタイアする *retire* from a race.

りだつ 離脱 — 離脱する [動] ●政党を離脱する(=出て行く) leave [[分離独立する]] break away from, [[書]] secede from] a political party.

りち 理知 [名] [知性] intellect.
— 理知的な [形] intellectual. ●とても理知的な人 a very *intellectual* person; a person of great *intellect*.

リチウム [化学] lithium (元素記号 Li).
● リチウムイオン電池 a lithium-ion battery. ● リチウム電池 a lithium battery. ● リチウムポリマー電池 a lithium-polymer battery.

りちぎ 律義 — 律義な [形] (良心的な) conscientious; (義務を果たす) dutiful; (実直な) faithful, honest.

りちゃくりく 離着陸 — 離着陸する [動] take off and land.

*りつ 率 [[比率]] a rate; [[割合]] (a) proportion; [[百分率]] (a) percentage. (⇨割合) ●競争率(=志願者に対する合格率) an acceptance *rate*. ●高い[低い]率 a high [low] birth [death] *rate*. ●率のいい[悪い] (⇨割❸) ▶その報告書によると, 肺がんの発生率は非喫煙者よりも喫煙者の方が高い The report notes that there is a higher *incidence* of lung cancer in smokers than in nonsmokers. ●大学に進学する高校生の率は高い A high [A large] *percentage* of high school students go (on) to college.

りつ 律 [[法律, おきて]] a rule; a law; a code; [[韻律]] a rhythm. ●黄金律 the golden *rule*. ●不文律 an unwritten *law*. ●道徳律 the moral *code*.

りつあん 立案 [名] planning.

— 立案する [動] plan; (草案を) draft; (練る) draw ... up. ▶このパーティーを立案したのはだれですか Who *planned* this party?
● 立案者 a planner.

りっか 立花 a large-scale flower arrangement.

りっか 立夏 the first day of summer.

りつがん 立願 — 立願する [動] pray (*for*).

りっきゃく 立脚 — 立脚する [動] ▶これらの結論は事実に立脚している(=基づいている) These conclusions *are based on* facts.
● 立脚点 a foothold; (見方) a standpoint; a viewpoint, a point of view.

りっきょう 陸橋 《主に米》 an overpass, 《英》 a flyover; (谷間・山峡にかかる) a viaduct /vǽiədʌ̀kt/.

りっけん 立件 ●過失傷害で立件される *be prosecuted for* accidental inflliction of injury.

りっけん 立憲 — 立憲君主 a constitutional monarch. ● 立憲君主国 a constitutional monarchy. ● 立憲君主制 constitutional government.

りっこう 力行 ●苦学力行の士 (苦しい環境の中, 初志を貫徹して学を修めた人) a person who, under adverse circumstances, *fought* his [her] *way through* college [high school, etc.].

りっこう 立項 — 立項する [動] make an entry (*of* a slang word in a dictionary).

りっこうほ 立候補 [名] (a) candidacy, 《主に英》 (a) candidature. ● 立候補を表明する [断念する] announce [give up] one's *candidacy*.
— 立候補する [動] 《主に米》 run*, 《英》 stand* (*for*). ●彼に対抗して市長職に立候補する *run against* him *for* mayor [(市長職に)*for* the mayoralty, (市長選に) *in* the mayoral election]. ▶彼は衆議院に立候補する He will *run* [*be a candidate*] *for* the House of Representatives. ▶彼は自民党から立候補している He is a Liberal Democratic *candidate*.
● 立候補者 a candidate (*for*).

りっこく 立国 (国を造ること) the founding of a nation. ●立国の精神 the spirit with which (this) *nation is* [*was*] *founded*. ▶日本は貿易立国である Japan is a trading *nation*./(繁栄は貿易にある) The prosperity of Japan depends upon trade with other countries.

りっしき 立志式 (説明的に) a ceremony for fixing one's aim in life.

りっしでん 立志伝 (出世物語) a success story; (自力で出世した人の) a story of a self-made man [woman]. ●立志伝中の人 a *self-made* person.

りっしゅう 立秋 the first day of autumn [《米》 fall].

りっしゅん 立春 the first day of spring.

りっしょう 立証 [名] (a) proof (優 ~s). (⇨証明) ▶立証責任は君にある The burden of *proof* is on you.
— 立証する [動] 有罪 [無罪] を立証する *prove* 《him》 guilty [not guilty].

りっしょく 立食 a stand-up [a buffet] meal.
● 立食パーティー a buffet(-style) party.

りっしんしゅっせ 立身出世 [名] success in life.
— 立身出世する [動] succeed in life. (⇨出世)
● 立身出世主義 the cult of success, careerism. ● 立身出世主義者 (軽蔑的) a (social) climber; a careerist. ● 立身出世物語 a success story.

りっすい 立錐 ●立錐の余地もない (会場などが一杯である) be filled to capacity; (人でかかる) be (jam-)packed (*with*), 《主に英》 be packed-out.

りっする 律する ●自分の基準で他人を律する *judge* other people by one's own standards. ●自己

りつぜん 慄然　▶その光景に慄然とした(=ぞっとした) I *was horrified* [*was terrified*, *was struck with horror*] *at* [*by*] *the sight*./〖話〗The sight *gave me the creeps*. (⇨ぞっと)

りつぞう 立像　a statue.

リッター a liter. (⇨リットル)

りったい 立体　━━立体的な 形 〖画像などが〗three-dimensional; 〖話〗3-D; 〖数学〗solid; 〖音響が〗stereo, 〖書〗stereophonic. (⇨ステレオ) ● 絵に立体感を出す give a painting a *three-dimensional effect*.
● 立体映画 a three-dimensional film; a 3-D picture. ● 立体幾何学 solid geometry. ● 立体鏡 a stereoscope. ● 立体交差 a two-level [multi-level] crossing. ● 立体写真 a three-dimensional photo; a 3-D picture. ● 立体駐車場 a párking strùcture [〖米〗gàràge]. ● 立体派 〖美術〗cubism.

りったいし 立太子　● 立太子礼 [の礼]〈hold〉the investiture of the Crown Prince.

りっち 立地　▶その家は立地条件がよい The house *is* favorably [↔unfavorably] *situated* [*located*]./The house has a good (↔a bad) *situation* [*location*].

りっとう 立冬　the first day of winter.

りっとう 立党　━━立党する 動 form [establish] a political party.

りつどう 律動 图　a rhythmic /ríðmik/ movement, (a) rhythm.
━━律動的, 律動感のある 形 rhythmic; rhýthmical. ● 律動感あふれる彼女の床運動 her *rhythmic* floor exercise.

リットル a liter /líːtər/ 〈記号 l., lit.〉.

__りっぱ__ 立派　━━立派な 形 ❶〖すぐれた〗excellent; 〈よい〉good; 〖すばらしい〗wonderful; 〈見事な〉fine; 〈注目に値する〉remarkable; 〈輝かしい〉splendid. ⇨見事な ● 立派な学者 an *excellent* [a *fine*, 〈著名な〉a *distinguished*] scholar. ● 立派な家具 *wonderful* [*fine*] furniture. ● 立派な家柄の男 a man of *good* [*honorable*] family. ● 立派な業績 a *remarkable* [a *splendid*, a *great*, 〈傑出した〉an *outstanding*] achievement. ● 彼は試験で立派な成績をとった He got *excellent* results [〖高得点〗*high marks*] on [〖主に英〗in] the exam./He did *very well* on [〖主に英〗in] the exam.
❷〖賞賛に値する〗praiseworthy, ádmirable; 〖尊敬すべき〗honorable; 〖ちゃんとした〗respectable (▶通例「恥ずかしくない程度の」という消極的な意味で用いられる). ● 立派な行為 a *good* [a *praiseworthy*, an *admirable*] deed. ● 立派な名誉ある男 an *honorable* man; 〈偉大な男〉a *great* man. ● 立派な一生を送る lead an *honorable* [〖高潔な〗a *virtuous*] life. ▶じゃ, たばこをやめたのね. それは立派だわ (=それは感心だわ) So you've quit smoking. I *admire* you for it.
❸〖十分な〗sufficient; 〖正当な〗good*. ● 立派な証拠 *sufficient* evidence. ● 立派な理由 a *good* reason. ● 立派な言い訳をする make a *fine* excuse. (▶しばしば皮肉を表す) ▶彼はもう立派な大人だ He is *fully* [*quite*] *a man* now.
━━立派に 副　〖うまく〗very well, nicely; 〖よく〗excellently; 〖すばらしく〗wonderfully, splendidly. ● 立派にふるまう behave *well*. ● 彼は立派に成し遂げた He achieved it *very* [*wonderfully*] *well*.

りっぷく 立腹 图　▶ご立腹はもっともです You have good reason to *be* [*get*] *angry*./You may well *be* [*get*] *angry*.

━━立腹する 動　get angry. (⇨怒る)

リップクリーム　〈医薬用〉〖米〗lip-balm, 〖米・英商標〗Chap Stick; 〖英〗lipsalve; 〈日常用〉lip cream.

リップサービス　▶リップサービスをする pay [give] (×a) *lip service* (*to* it [×him]).

リップスティック　(a) lipstick.

りっぽう 立方　〖数学〗cube. ▶箱の体積は 1 立方メートルです The volume of the box is a *cubic* meter.
● 立方根 a cube root. (⇨根（ね）) ● 立方体 a cube.

りっぽう 立法　legislation, lawmaking. (▶後の方が口語的) ● 立法の legislative. (▶通例前置される) ▶国会が立法権を持っている The Diet has (×a) *legislative* power.
● 立法機関 a legislative [a lawmaking] organ [body]. ● 立法府 the legislature. (▶単・複両扱い)

りづめ 理詰め 图　● 理詰めで説き伏せる〈説得して…させる〉reason 《him *into* doing》; persuade 《him *to* do》; 〈説得しても聞かない〉reason 《him *out of* doing》; 〈議論でやりこめる〉argue 《him》down.
━━理詰めの 形　〈論理的な〉logical; 〈理論的な〉theoretical.

りつめんず 立面図　an elevation.

りつりょう 律令 〖歴史〗the *ritsuryo* legal codes; (説明的に) the legal codes of the Nara and Heian periods.
● 律令制 the administrative system based on the *ritsuryo* legal codes; the centralized government system in the Nara and Heian periods.

りつろん 立論　━━立論する 動　argue; make an argument. ▶君の立論の根拠を示してください I'd like to know how you built up your *argument*. ▶彼女の立論には論理の破たんがある Her *argument* has some logical inconsistencies.

りてい 里程　(a) distance (measured by *ri*); mileage /máilidʒ/.
● 里程標 a milestone; 〈主に米〉a milepost.

りてきこうい 利敵行為　an act that profits the enemy. ▶それは利敵行為だ It *profits* [*helps*] *the enemy*.

リデュース　〖減らす〗reduce 《garbage》. 〖参考〗循環型社会を実現するために必要な三つの要素 (reduce〈ごみを減らす〉, reuse〈再利用する〉, recycle〈再資源化する〉を 3R という)

リテラシー　〖読み書き能力, 活用能力〗literacy (↔illiteracy). ● コンピュータリテラシー computer *literacy*.

りてん 利点　an advantage; 〖長所〗a good [a strong] point, a merit. ● 多機能という利点 the [an] *advantage of* being versatile. ▶その方法には他に比べていくつかの利点がある The method has some *advantages over* the others. 〈長所〉▶テレビがあることの利点は数多くある There are lots of *advantages in* having a TV.

━━━ **DISCOURSE** ━━━
紙の辞書を使う利点は明らかだ The *advantages* of using paper dictionaries are **obvious**. (▶The advantages of ... are obvious [clear] (…の利点は明らかだ)は二者択一を表すディスコースマーカー)

リトアニア 〖国名〗Lithuania /lìθjuéiniə/; 〈公式名〉the Republic of Lithuania. 〈首都 Vilnius〉● リトアニア人 a Lithuanian. ● リトアニア語 Lithuanian. ● リトアニア(人[語])の Lithuanian.

りとう 離党 图　(脱党) defection.
━━離党する 動　〈離反する〉defect 《*from*》; 〈去る〉leave 《a party》. ● その党を離党する *defect from* [*leave*] the party.

- 離党者 a defector.
- **りとう** 離島 (孤立した) an isolated [(中心地から遠く離れた) a remote, an outlying] island.
- **りとく** 利得 (a) profit; gains. (⇨利益)
- **リトグラフ** 〖印刷〗a lithograph /líθəgræf/.
- **リトマスしけんし** リトマス試験紙 ●リトマス試験紙で調べる test it with (a strip of) *litmus paper*.
- **リトルリーガー** 〖野球〗a Little Leaguer.
- **リトルリーグ** 〖野球〗the Little League. ●リトルリーグのワールドシリーズ the *Little League* World Series.
- **リナックス** 〖コンピュータ〗Linux.
- **リニアモーター** a linear motor.
  - リニアモーターカー a linear-motor car, a maglev (car).
- **りにち** 離日 —— 離日する 動 leave Japan.
- **りにゅう** 離乳 —— 離乳する 動 wean 《one's baby》 from breast.
  - 離乳期 the weaning period. ●離乳食 báby fóod.
- **リニューアル** 名 〖印刷, 新装〗renewal.
  —— リニューアルする 動
  - リニューアルオープン (新装開店) reopening after redecoration [remodeling]. (⇨新装 [文例])
- **りにょう** 利尿 diuresis /dàɪjʊrí:sɪs/. ▶ハーブには利尿作用のあるものがある Some herbs have a diuretic /dàɪjərétɪk/ effects.
  - 利尿剤 a diuretic.
- **りにん** 離任 名 (a) resignation. (⇨辞職)
  —— 離任する 動 resign 《one's post》.
- **りねん** 理念 (原理) a philosophy; (考え) an idea; (観念) an ideology /àɪdɪάlədʒɪ/. ●彼の政治理念は世界平和を築くことである His political *philosophy* is to build world peace. ▶理念を掲げて戦う者はやっかいだ People who fight for a *principle* are the real problem.
- **リネン** (⇨リンネル)
- **りのう** 離農 —— 離農する 動 give up farming. ▶離農者は増加の一途をたどっている More and more *farmers are giving up* their *jobs*./The number of farmers *leaving* their (hereditary) *farms* has been on the increase.
- **リノールさん** リノール酸 〖生化学〗linoleic /lìnəlí:ɪk/ acid.
- **リノリウム** (床敷き剤) linoleum /lɪnóʊlɪəm/, 《英》lino /láɪnoʊ/.
- **リハーサル** a rehearsal. ●リハーサルをする rehearse 《a play》.
- **リバーシブル** —— リバーシブルの 形 reversible.
- **リバース** 名 〖逆〗the reverse.
  —— リバースする 動 reverse.
- **リパーゼ** 〖生化学〗lipase /láɪpeɪs/.
- **リバイバル** a revival 《of a movie》. ▶今週からスターウォーズがリバイバル上映されている *Star Wars has been rereleased* since this week.
- **リバウンド** 名 〖跳ね返り〗〖バスケ・ラグビー〗a rebound. 〖関連〗リバウンドの扱いがうまい選手は rebounder という) ●リバウンドをとる grab a *rebound*.
  —— リバウンドする 動 〖跳ね返る〗rebound. ▶ダイエットを中断したらすぐにもとの体重にリバウンドした I stopped the diet and *went back the same weight* soon.
- **りはつ** 利発 —— 利発な 形 clever; intelligent. (⇨賢い)
- **りはつ** 理髪 (散髪) haircutting, (整髪) hairdressing.
  - 理髪師 (カット・ひげそりをする) a barber (!通例男性で, 客も男性); (カット・セット・毛染めなどをする) a hairdresser, a hairstylist. ●理髪店 《米》a barbershop, 《英》a barber's.
- **りはっちゃく** 離発着 ●夜間の離発着を禁止する prohibit late-night *arrivals and departures*.
- **りはば** 利幅 ●利幅が大きい have *a* large [a high] *profit margin*. (⇨儲け)
- **リハビリ(テーション)** rehabilitation, 《話》rehab.
  ●リハビリを施す rehabilitate 《a patient》. ▶彼は卒中になって今リハビリ中だそうだ I've heard he had a stroke and now *is in rehab*. 〖事情〗米英では何のためのリハビリかを明確にいわないと, 麻薬中毒やアル中の患者, 犯罪者などの社会復帰訓練と解釈されやすい)
  ●リハビリ施設 rehabilitation facilities.
- **リバプール** 〖英国名〗Liverpool.
- **りばらい** 利払い interest payment.
- **りはん** 離反 名 alienation.
  —— 離反する 動 (見捨てる) desert /dɪzə́:rt/; (運動・団体から敵側へ) defect 《*from*; *to*》. ●人心が離反する lose public support.
- **りひ** 理非 (⇨是非 名)
- **リビア** 〖国名〗Libya; (公式名) the Great Socialist People's Libyan Arab Jamahiriya. (首都 Tripoli) ●リビア人 a Libyan. ●リビア(人)の Libyan.
- **リピーター** 〖繰り返す人〗a repeater; 〖何度も来る人〗a frequent visitor 《*to*》.
- **リピート** 名 〖繰り返し〗a repeat.
  —— リピートする 動 repeat.
- **リビエラ** 〖地中海沿岸地方〗Riviera. ●リビエラで on the Riviera.
- **リヒテンシュタイン** 〖国名〗Liechtenstein /líktənstàɪn/; (公式名) the Principality of Liechtenstein. (首都 Vaduz) ●リヒテンシュタイン人 a Liechtensteiner. ●リヒテンシュタイン(人)の Liechtenstein.
- **リビドー** 〖性的衝動〗libido.
- **りびょう** 罹病 —— 罹病する 動 contract [get, catch] a disease; get sick; (伝染病に) be infected 《*with*》.
  - 罹病率 (an) incidence 《*of*》; (a) morbidity. ▶肺がんの罹病率は増加の一途をたどっている The *incidence* of lung cancer is ever on the increase.
- **リビングウィル** 〖尊厳死の宣言書〗《sign [prepare, write]》a living will.
- **リビングキッチン** a living room with a kitchen; a living-room-cum-kitchen; 《和製語》a living kitchen.
- **リビングルーム** a líving ròom, 《主に英》a sítting ròom.
- **リフォーム** —— リフォームする 動 ●服をリフォームする *make* a dress *over*; (部分的に) *alter* a dress. (! reform は「改正する, 改心させる」の意) ●台所をリフォームする *remodel* [《話》*redo*] the kitchen; *make* some *alterations to* the kitchen; (してもらう) *have* the kitchen *remodeled* [《話》*redone*]; *have* some *alterations done to* the kitchen. (⇨改装する)
- **りふじん** 理不尽 —— 理不尽な 形 (道理に合わない) unreasonable; (不合理な) absurd. ●理不尽な要求 an *unreasonable* demand.
- **リフティング** 〖サッカー〗ball-lifting, kick-up.
- **リフト** ❶〖スキー場の〗a (ski [chair]) lift. ●高いリフト a high *lift*. ●リフトで降りる take a (chair) *lift* down.
  ❷〖シンクロナイズドスイミングなどの浮揚力〗a lift.
- **リフトバック** a liftback. 〖参考〗後部ドアが上に開く乗用車)
- **リプリント** (重版本) a réprint, a reprinted book.
  ●本をリプリントする(=重版する) *reprint* a book.
- **リフレーン** 〖反復句〗a refrain.
- **リフレッシュ** —— リフレッシュする 動 refresh 《one-

self).
リプロダクション [再生産; 生殖] reproduction.
リプロダクティブ [再生の; 生殖の] reproductive.
• リプロダクティブヘルス [性と生殖に関する健康] reproductive health. • リプロダクティブライツ [性と生殖に関する女性の自己決定権] reproductive rights.
リベート ❶ [払い戻し] a rebate. (⚠英語には日本語のような悪い意味はない)
❷ [手数料] a commission; (不正な)《話》a rake-off; (びんはね)《話》a kickback. • 10万円のリベートを受け取る get a *kickback* of 100,000 yen.
りべつ 離別 (a) separation.
—— **離別する** 動 separate. (⇒別れる, 離婚)
リベラリスト a liberal, a liberalist. (⚠ 前の方が普通)
リベラル —— **リベラルな** 形 liberal.
リベリア [国名] Liberia /laibíəriə/; (公式名) the Republic of Liberia. (首都 Monrovia) • リベリア人 a Liberian. • リベリア(人)の Liberian.
リベロ [<イタリア語] [競技] a libero.
りべん 利便 convenience. (⇒便(2)) • 交通の利便が悪い be *inconvenient* to transportation [for trains, buses, etc.]. • 利便(=便宜)をはかる (⇒便宜)
リベンジ • リベンジ (=雪辱)する repay, 《話》get back ⟨at, on⟩, revenge. (⚠日本語の「雪辱」にはrevengeほど深刻な含意はない).
りほう 理法 a law. • 自然の理法にかなう be in accordance with the *law* of nature.
リポーター (⇒レポーター)
リポート (⇒レポート)
リボかくさん リボ核酸 ribonucleic /ràiboun(j)u:klí:ik/ acid (略 RNA).
リボばらい リボ払い [「リボルビング払い」の略] (⇒リボルビング)
リボルバー [回転式連発拳銃] a revolver.
リボルビング revolving. (⇒回転)
• リボルビング払い revolving repayment.
リボン a ribbon; [帽子の] a band; [タイプライターの] (typewriter) ribbon. • 彼女はいつも髪にピンクのリボンをつけている She always wears a pink *ribbon* in [×on] her hair. ▶ 贈り物にはきれいなリボンがかけてあった The present was tied with pretty *ribbons*.
リマ [ペルーの首都] Lima /lí:mə/.
りまわり 利回り [利潤] [利益] a yield; a return; [利子] interest. • 債券の利回りが yields on bonds. • 利回りがよい[悪い] yield [give] a good [a poor] *return*. • 高利回りの金融商品 a high *yield* financial product. • その債券は年6分の利回りがよい The bond *yields* 6 percent *interest* a year.
リミット [限度, 限界] a limit.
リムジン (リムジン車) a limousine /líməzi:n/, 《米話》a limo (複 ~s); (空港送迎バス) an áirport bùs [《主に米》limousine] (⚠ホテルなどの無料の送迎車[バス]は a cóurtesy càr [bùs]).
リメイク 名 [映画・古着などの作り直し] a remake.
—— **リメイクする** 動 remake 《an old movie》.
りめん 裏面 ❶ [物の裏側] the back; the reverse (side). (⇒裏❶) • レコードの裏面(=B面)the *flip side* of a record. • 裏面へ続く Please turn over. 《略 P.T.O.》《米》Over.
❷ [表に現れない部分] • 人生[社会]の裏面 the *dark side* of life [society]. • 裏面で操る《話》pull strings 《米》wires》. ▶ その裏面の経済が (=好ましくない面) が見え始めた We're seeing the *flip side* of the economic policy.
• 裏面工作 behind-the-scene maneuvering [maneuvers]. • 裏面史 an inside history.
リモートコントロール (⇒リモコン)

リモコン (a) remote control (⚠装置は ©, 操作は Ⓤ), 《話》 a remote; (テレビの) a zapper. • リモコン(式)の remote-controled. • リモコンのミュートボタンを押す push the mute button on the (TV) *remote*.
リヤカー (説明的に) a two-wheeled cart (designed to be pulled by a bicycle or a motorcycle); (和製語) a rear car.
りやく 利益 (⇒御利益)
りゃく 略 (an) omission. (⇒省略)
りゃくが 略画 a rough drawing; a sketch. • 略画を描く make a *rough drawing* 《of a dog》; sketch.
りゃくぎ 略儀 ▶ 右略儀ながら書面にてお礼申し上げます 'I would like to express my gratitude to you 《for your valuable help》, though I am well aware that a letter is not good enough as a testimony of my gratitude.' [事情] 米英にはこのような手紙の書式はない)
りゃくげん 略言 a brief statement; a sketch 《of the fact》. • 略言すれば in short [brief]; in a few words;《話》in a nutshell.
りゃくご 略語 an abbreviation 《of, for》, an abbreviated form 《of》. ▶ TPO は何の略語ですか What does TPO stand for?
りゃくごう 略号 (符号) a mark; a symbol; (電信用の) a (telegraphic) code [address].
りゃくし 略史 [印刷技術略史 A *short* [An *Outline*] *History* of Printing Technology.
りゃくじ 略字 a simplified form of a Chinese character.
りゃくしき 略式 —— **略式の** 形 informal (↔formal). • 略式の服装で in *informal* [普通の《ordinary》] clothes. • 略式で informally; without formality.
• 略式起訴 [法律] (file) a summary indictment /indáitmənt/. • 略式裁判 [書] a summary trial. (⚠「手続きが略式の」の意) • 略式命令 《issue》a summary order.
りゃくじゅつ 略述 名 a summary; a short [a brief] account 《of》.
—— **略述する** 動 summarize《complicated facts》; give a short [a brief] account 《of》.
りゃくしょう 略称 (省略形) an abbreviation. ▶ 国連は国際連合の略称である "Kokuren" is an *abbreviation* [is *short*] *for* Kokusairengo." (⚠ abbreviation の場合 for の代わりに of も可)
りゃくしょう 略章 a miniature decoration [medal]. [参考] 正式の勲章の代わりにつける同色で小型のもの)
りゃくす 略す [省く] omit (-tt-), leave... out; [短縮する] shorten; (語句を) abbreviate; (書物・話を) abridge. • その前置詞を略す *omit* the preposition. • 'page' を 'p' と略す *abbreviate* [*shorten*] 'page' to 'p'. • 略さずに名前を書く write one's name *in full*; spell out one's *full* name. ▶ 山田を略して彼を山と呼んでいます We call him Yama, *short for* Yamada.
りゃくず 略図 a sketch; (略地図) a rough map. • 略図を書く sketch; draw a *rough map*.
りゃくせつ 略説 ❶ an outline; a summary. • 略説 20世紀の音楽 a *brief outline* of the twentieth-century music.
—— **略説する** 動 summarize; sum ... up.
りゃくそう 略装 (略式の服装) informal [《ordinary》] clothes.
りゃくだつ 略奪 名 plunder.
—— **略奪する** 動 plunder. • 町[市民]からめぼしいものをすべて略奪する *plunder* [*loot*] the town [the citi-

りゃくでん 略伝 a short biography; a biographical sketch.

りゃくねんぴょう 略年表 an abridged chronological table.

りゃくひょう 略表 an abridged table.

りゃくふ 略譜 ❶ [簡単に書いた系譜] a brief account of one's genealogy; (図) a sketch of one's family tree.
❷ [略式の楽譜] simplified music.

りゃくふく 略服 (略式の服装) informal [(普通の) ordinary] clothes.

りゃくぼう 略帽 (戦闘帽) a combat cap.

りゃくれいそう 略礼装 semiformal wear [clothes].

りゃくれいふく 略礼服 (⇨礼装)

りゃくれき 略歴 one's brief personal history.

りゃっかい 略解 concise comments [commentary] 《on The Tale of Genji》.

りゃっき 略記 ── **略記する** 動 give a brief account [an outline] 《of》.

リヤド [[サウジアラビアの首都]] Riyadh /ríːjɑːd/.

‡りゆう 理由 (a) reason 《for; to do; why 節》; (根拠) (a) ground 《for》(🚨 しばしば複数形で); (過失などの理由・言い訳) (an) excuse /ikskjúːs/《for》; (偽りの理由) a prétext 《of, for》; (動機) a motive 《for, of》.
①【~理由もなく】▶ちゃんとした理由もなく学校を休んではいけない You should not be absent from school without (a) good reason. ▶これという理由もなく彼は私に電話をしてきた For no particular reason, he called me on the telephone.
②【理由が[は]】▶彼には苦情を言うだけの十分な理由がある He has good [every] reason to complain./There is good [every] reason for his complaining. ▶それで彼女が来なかった理由が分かった That explains why she never showed up. ▶彼が遅刻したのは電車に乗り遅れたためです The reason (that) he was late is that [《話》 because] he missed the train. ▶彼を手伝うつもりはないわ。手伝わなくちゃならない理由なんてないもの I'm not going to help him. Is there any reason (why) I should [Why should I]? (🚨 後の方は反語疑問文)▶理由はどうあれそこへ行ってはいけません Whatever the reason (is [《書》may be]), you should not go there.
③【理由に】▶彼は病気を理由にその会議に出席しなかった He didn't attend the meeting because [on the grounds that] he was sick. (🚨 because の方が普通)/He didn't attend the meeting because [on (the)] grounds of, on account of, owing to, by reason of] ill health. (🚨 because of が最も普通)/He didn't attend the meeting on [under] the pretext of being sick [that he was sick]. (🚨 実際は病気ではなかったことを含意) ▶そんなことは遅刻の理由にならない That is no excuse for being late.
④【理由を】▶彼に欠席の理由を尋ねる ask him the reason for his absence. ▶今日ここへいらっしゃった理由をおっしゃってください Tell [Give] me the reason why you've come [for your coming, for you to have come] here today./Tell me why you've come here [what you've come here for, what brought you here] today. ▶遅れた理由を説明してくれませんか Could you explain the reason for this delay? ▶彼は何かと理由をつけて学校を休んでは彼は学校を休んでいる He was absent from school on one pretext or another.
⑤【理由で】▶彼は健康上の理由で辞職した He resigned for reasons of [by reason of] ill health./He resigned for health reasons. ▶どういう理由で彼はそれをしたのか For what reason [motive] did he do that? (🚨 やや堅い言い方)/What made him do that? [《話》 What did he do that for?/Why did he do that? (🚨 後の二つの言い方は直接的な表現なので前の二つの方が好まれる)

りゅう 竜 a dragon.

-りゅう -流 ❶ [やり方] a fashion; a way; [方法] a manner; [様式] a style. ●自己流でやる do a thing in one's own fashion [way, manner, style].
❷ [流派] a school. ●小原流の生け花 the Ohara school of flower arrangement.
❸ [階級] a class; [地位] a rank; [等級] rate. (🚨 通例序数を伴う) (⇨一流)

りゅうあん 硫安 [[「硫酸アンモニウム」の略]] (⇨硫酸)

りゅうい 留意 ── **留意する** 動 pay [give] attention 《to》; (書) pay [give] heed 《to》, take heed 《of》; (心に留める) keep [bear] ... in mind.

りゅういき 流域 a basin; (大河の) a valley. ●淀川流域 the Yodo basin. ●ナイル川流域 the Nile valley; the valley of the Nile.

りゅういん 留飲 ●**留飲が下がる** get rid of one's frustration. ▶その男の心からの謝罪を聞いて留飲が下がった The man's sincere apology got rid of my frustration.

りゅうおう 竜王 ❶ [竜神] a dragon king; (説明的に) the controller of water and rain.
❷ [将棋] (成り飛車) a promoted hisha; (説明的に) a hisha with an added movement of a gin [one square].

りゅうか 硫化 图 sulfuration. ── **硫化する** 動 sulfurize.
●硫化カドミウム cadmium sulfide. ●硫化銀 mercury sulfide. ●硫化水素 hydrogen sulfide. ●硫化物 sulfide.

りゅうかい 流会 ▶定数不足のために流会になった The meeting was canceled [was called off] for want of a quorum.

‡りゅうがく 留学 图

DISCOURSE
海外留学は，若い人だけでなく，年配の人にとっても実り多い経験になるだろう Studying abroad will be a rewarding experience for the elderly **as well as** for the young. (🚨 as well as (...だけでなく) は追加するときに用いるディスコースマーカー)

── **留学する** 動 (外国で勉強する) study abroad; (勉強のために外国に行く) go* abroad to study [for study]. ▶彼は2年間フランスに留学している He has studied in France for two years. ▶私は英国文学研究のため来年イギリスに留学するつもりです I'll go to England to study English literature next year.
●留学生 (⇨留学生)

りゅうがくせい 留学生 a student studying abroad; (海外からの) an overseas student (🚨 a student from overseas ともいう); an international student; (海外への) a student overseas. ●イギリスからの交換留学生 an exchange student from Britain. ●日本の外国人留学生 an overseas [a foreign] student in Japan. (🚨 overseas の方が丁寧)

りゅうかん 流感 《話》 (the) flu; 《書》 influénza. ●流感にかかる come down with (the) flu; get (the)

りゅうき 隆起 an upheaval; (樹木のこぶ) a protuberance /prət(j)úːbərəns/; (道路の) a bump.
— **隆起する** 動 upheave. ▶火山活動で隆起した土地 the land *upheaved* by volcanic activity.

りゅうぎ 流儀 〖やり方〗 a way; 〖独特のやり方〗 a manner; 〖様式〗 a style; 〖流派〗 a school. ▶吉流儀の考え old-fashioned ideas. ▶彼女は何でも自分の流儀でやりたがる She wants to do everything in her (own) *way*.

りゅうきへい 竜騎兵 a dragoon /drəɡúːn/.
りゅうきゅう 琉球 ▷琉球列島 the Ryukyu Islands.
りゅうぐう(じょう) 竜宮(城) the Dragon King's Palace.
りゅうけい 流刑 ⇨流刑(るけい)
りゅうけつ 流血 ▷流血を避ける prevent *bloodshed*. ▶流血の惨事にいたる lead to *bloodshed*.
● 流血事件 a case of bloodshed. ● 流血事件の現場 a *bloody* crime scene.

りゅうげんひご 流言飛語 ▷流言飛語を放つ (根も葉もない) spread a *groundless* [(でたらめな) a *wild*] *rumor*. (⇨デマ)

りゅうこ 竜虎 ● 竜虎相打つ Two strongest [most powerful] rivals try to beat [defeat] one another.

*りゅうこう 流行 图 ❶〖服などの〗 (a) fashion; (a) trend; 〖やや書〗 (a) vogue (▪ vogue は一時性を強調する。また時におとけて用いる); (流行の型) a style, a mode (▪ 後の語は少し気取った語で高級な感じを与える); (一時的大流行) a craze.
①【流行〜】 ▶流行遅れの服 *old-fashioned* [*unfashionable*] clothes.
②【流行は】 ▶婦人服の流行ははやりすたりが激しい Women's *fashions* [*Fashions*] in women's clothing] come and go quickly. ▶コンピュータゲームの流行は全国に広がった A *craze* [A *vogue*] *for computer games* spread all over the country.
③【流行に】 ▶流行にとらわれる conform to (the) *fashion*. ▶流行に遅れないようにする keep up with (the) *fashion*. ▶最新の流行に敏感である be sensitive to the latest *fashion*.
④【流行を】 ▶流行を作り出す set a *fashion* [a *trend*] (*for pantsuits*). ▶彼女はいつも流行を追っている She is always following (the) *fashion*. ▶〖話〗 She is a *trendy* girl. (▪ 時に軽蔑的に)
⑤【流行だ】 ▶これが今年の流行だ This is the *fashion* [*style*] this year. ▶当時女性はひざまである革のブーツをはくのが流行だった It was the *fashion* of the time for women to wear knee-length leather boots.
❷【病気などの】an epidemic. ▶コレラの流行 a cholera *epidemic*; an *epidemic* of cholera.
— **流行の** 〖服などの〗 fashionable, trendy; (人気のある) popular. ▶彼女は流行の髪型をしている She wears a *fashionable* [a *trendy*, a *popular*] hairdo. ▶彼女は最新の流行の服を着ている She is dressed in the latest *fashion* [*style*, *mode*].
— **流行する** 動 ❶〖服などに〗come* into [⇔go* out of] fashion [〖やや書〗 vogue], become* fashionable; (流行している) be in [⇔out of] fashion [〖やや書〗 vogue], be fashionable. ▶ロングスカートの流行はいつのでしたか When did long skirts *come into fashion* [*become fashionable*]? ▶この春はかかとの低い靴が流行しそうです Flat shoes are

going to *be in fashion* [*vogue*] this spring.
❷【病気などが】(広く広まる) spread* quickly; (広まっている) be widespread. ▶今風邪が生徒の間で流行している Colds *are widespread* [(猛威をふるって) *raging*] now among the pupils.
● 流行歌 a popular song. ● 流行歌手 a pop singer. (〈関連〉 a popular singer 人気歌手)
● 流行語 a vogue word, a word in vogue; 〖話〗 an in [a trendy] word; a word that's going around. (▪ 2語以上からなる場合には word の代わりに expression を用いる) ● 流行作家 a popular writer.

りゅうこうせいかんぼう 流行性感冒 〖話〗 (the) flu; 〖書〗 influenza. (⇨流感)
りゅうこつ 竜骨 a keel.
りゅうさ 流砂 ⇨流砂(るさ).
りゅうざい 粒剤 【薬剤】 granulated medicine.
りゅうさん 硫酸 sulfùric ácid. ▶濃硫酸 concentrated *sulfuric acid*.
● 硫酸アンモニウム ammonium sulfate. ● 硫酸塩 sulfate. ● 硫酸紙 parchment paper. (▪ sulfate paper は「クラフト紙」) ● 硫酸銅 copper sulfate. ● 硫酸バリウム 【化学】 barium sulfate.

りゅうざん 流産 图 (a) miscarriage. ▶戦争が始まってその計画は流産に終わった(= 立ち消えになった) The project *went up in smoke* with the war on.
— **流産する** 動 ▶彼女は妊娠3か月[12週]で流産した She *had a miscarriage* [*miscarried*] in the third month [the twelfth week] of pregnancy. (⇨妊娠) (〈参考〉 米国では週単位でいうのが普通)
りゅうさんだん 榴散弾 a shrapnel. (▪ 集合的に扱うと U) ▶榴散弾にあたる be hit by *shrapnel*.
りゅうし 粒子 a particle.
りゅうしつ 流失 ▷流失する 動 ▶橋が洪水で流失した The bridge *was washed* [*was carried*] *away* by the flood.
● 流失家屋 the houses (which were) washed away (by the flood).
りゅうしゃ 流砂 water-carried sand.
リュージュ 流砂 [<フランス語] 【競技用そり】 a luge /lúːʒ/, a toboggan /təbɑ́ɡən/. (▪ 米英では後の方が一般的); 〖競技〗 (the) luge, tobogganing.
りゅうしゅつ 流出 图 an óutflow; (財産などの) a drain. ▶金(%)の国外流出 an *outflow* [a *drain*] of gold *from* a country. ▶頭脳流出 a brain *drain*. ▶座礁したタンカーからの大量の石油流出 a massive oil *spill* from a stranded tanker.
— **流出する** 動 flow [run] out (*of*); (秘密などが漏れる) leak out. ▶溶岩が噴火口から流出し続けた The lava continued to *flow out of* the crater. ▶コンピュータウイルスにより会社の内部資料が流出した The internal information of the company *leaked out* because of infection by computer viruses.
りゅうじょう 粒状 ▷粒状の 图 gránular.
りゅうじん 竜神 (⇨竜王 ❶)
リユース 图 [再使用] reuse. (⇨リデュース [参考])
— **リユースする** 動 reuse.
りゅうず 竜頭 a crown, a button.
りゅうすい 流水 running [flowing] water.
りゅうせい 隆盛 prosperity. ▶彼の事業は当時隆盛をきわめた His business *flourished* at that time. (⇨栄える)
— **隆盛な** 图 prosperous; flourishing; thriving.
りゅうせい 流星 a shooting [a falling] star; a meteor /míːtiər/. (▪ 前の方は日常語)
● 流星雨 a meteor(ic) shower. ● 流星群 a meteor swarm.
りゅうぜつらん 竜舌蘭 【植物】 an agave /əɡáːvi/.

りゅうせんけい 流線型 —— 流線型の 形 streamline(d). ● 流線型にする streamline.

りゅうぜんこう 竜涎香 ambergris.

りゅうそく 流速 the speed [velocity] of a moving fluid. ▶ジェット気流はしばしば流速400キロを超える The *speed* of a jet stream often exceeds 400 km per hour.

りゅうたい 流体 fluid /flúːid/. (参考) 流体は液体 (liquid /líkwid/) と気体 (gas) の総称 ● 流体力学 hydrodynamics. (!単数扱い)

りゅうだん 流弾 (⇨流れ弾)

りゅうち 留置 名 detention.
—— 留置する 動 detain. ▶数人の過激派が留置されている Some radicals *are detained* [*in detention*]. ● 留置所 a detention [a police] cell, (小さな町の) a lockup.

りゅうちょう 流暢 —— 流暢な 形 fluent.
—— 流暢に 副 fluently. ▶日本語を流暢に話す speak Japanese *fluently* [*with fluency*]; speak *fluent* Japanese; be *fluent* in Japanese; be a *fluent* speaker of Japanese.

りゅうちょう 留鳥 a resident bird.

りゅうつう 流通 名 〖貨幣の〗 circulation; 〖物資の〗 distribution; 〖空気の〗 ventilation (⇨換気).
—— 流通する 動 circulate. ● 流通させる circulate; put ... into circulation. ▶100円札は今はもう流通していない 100-yen bills *are not in* [are out of] *circulation* now.
● 流通革命 a distribution revolution. ● 流通貨幣 currency in circulation. ● 流通機構 a distribution system. ● 流通経路 a distribution channel. ● 流通コスト distribution [marketing] cost. ● 流通在庫 distributor's stock. ● 流通産業 [業界] the distribution industry. ● 流通網 a distribution network.

リュート 〖楽器〗 a lute.

りゅうどう 流動 —— 流動的な 形 fluid; (移動しやすい) mobile; (固定していない) not fixed. ● 流動的な a *mobile* society. ▶その問題についての我々の考えは流動的だ Our ideas on the subject are *fluid* [are *not fixed*].
● 流動資産 current liquid assets. ● 非流動資産 non-current [non-liquid] assets; (固定資産) fixed assets. ● 流動資本 circulating [floating, liquid] capital. ● 流動食 a liquid diet; liquid food. ● 流動性 (液体・社会などの) mobility; (資産などの) liquidity. ● 流動体 (a) fluid; (液体) (a) liquid. ● 流動比率 the current ratio; the liquidity ratio. ● 流動負債 (短期負債) current [circulating, floating] liabilities. ● 流動物 (流動性のあるもの) a fluid; (流動食) liquid food.

りゅうとうだび 竜頭蛇尾 (an) anticlimax. ▶彼の演説は竜頭蛇尾だった(=初めはよかったが、最後はつまらなかった) His speech *began with a bang and ended with a whimper*./His speech was very anticlimactic after its attractive [powerful] beginning.

りゅうとした ▶りゅうとした身なりで *smartly* [*stylishly, fashionably*] dressed; in a *smart* [*stylish, a fashionable*] suit [dress].

りゅうにゅう 流入 名 (流れ込むこと) (an) inflow; (突然大量に) (an) influx. ▶難民の大量の流入 a big *inflow* [an *influx*] of refugees. ● 資本の流入 an [the] *inflow* of capital; capital inflow. ● 流入を制限する restrict an *inflow* [(急激な) an *influx*] (*of*).
—— 流入する 動 (流れ込む) flow in [into ...]; (入る) come in [into ...].

りゅうにん 留任 名 ▶彼に委員長留任をお願いする ask him to *remain in office* as chairman.
—— 留任する 動 remain in office.

りゅうねん 留年 —— 留年する (進級できない) fail to pass on to the next grade; (同じ学年に残る) remain in the same grade.
● 留年者 〖生〗 (落第生) a repeater, 《米》 a holdover; (婉曲的) a long-stay student.

りゅうのう 竜脳 borneol /bɔ́ːrniɒl/.

りゅうのひげ 竜の髭 〖植物〗 a dwarf lily-turf; a Japanese snake's beard.

りゅうは 流派 a school. ▶華道には流派がいろいろある There are a lot of *schools* in flower arrangement.

りゅうび 柳眉 ● 柳眉を逆立てる (怒ってまゆをつり上げる) raise one's eyebrows /áibràuz/ angrily [in anger].

りゅうびじゅつ 隆鼻術 cosmetic surgery to heighten the bridge of the nose.

りゅうひょう 流氷 drift ice; (浮氷) floating ice; (浮氷塊) (ice) floes.

りゅうほ 留保 名 (a) reservation; (a) suspension. (⇨保留)
—— 留保する 動 reserve. ▶本書の翻訳権は留保されている All translation rights of this book *are reserved*.

りゅうぼく 流木 driftwood.

リューマチ rheumatism; 《英話》 the rheumatics (! 複数扱い). ● 関節リューマチ articular *rheumatism*. ● リューマチを患う have [suffer from] *rheumatism*. ● リューマチ患者 a rheumatic. ● リューマチ熱 rheumatic fever.

りゅうめ 竜馬 〖足の速いいい馬〗 a swift [a fast] horse; 〖将棋〗 (成り角) a promoted *kaku*.

りゅうよう 流用 名 〖書〗 appropriation (! 不正でなく他の用途に当てることにもいう), 《書》 misappropriation.
—— 流用する 動 appropriate; misappropriate; (転用する) divert. ▶彼は組合の金を私的に流用して免職になった He was discharged for *misappropriating* the union funds [*diverting* the union funds *to* private use].

りゅうり 流離 名 wanderings.
—— 流離する 動 wander (foreign countries [far and wide]).

りゅうりゅう 隆々 ▶筋骨隆々たる男 a *brawny* [a *strong-muscled, a very muscular*] man.

りゅうりゅうしんく 粒々辛苦 ▶粒々辛苦して築いた富 a fortune built by one's hard work over the years [by the sweat of one's brow].

りゅうりょう 流量 (the volume of) flow; 〖物理〗 flux. ▶毎時2万リットルの水の流量 a *flow* of 20,000 liters of water per hour.

りゅうれい 流麗 —— 流麗な 形 (流れるような) flowing; (優雅な) elegant, graceful; (品格のある) refined. ● 流麗な文章を書く write in a *flowing and elegant* [*refined*] style.

りゅうろ 流露 名 (心の内が自然と外に出ること) an expression (*of* feelings).
—— 流露する 動 express itself; overflow. ▶我が子への愛情が流露している彼女の手紙 her letter *overflowing* [*brimming*] *with* her affection for [toward] her son [daughter].

リュック(サック) <ドイツ語> 《米》 a backpack, 《米やや古》 a knapsack /nǽpsæk/; 《英》 a rucksack /rʌ́ksæk/; (小型の) a daypack. ● リュックサックを背負う wear a *backpack*.

:りよう 利用 名 use /júːs/ (❗「用途」の意ではしばしば ⓒ); utilization.
① 【〜利用】 ● 廃物利用 the *recycling* [*utilization*] of waste. ● 原子力の平和的利用 the peaceful *use* of atomic energy; the *use* of atomic energy for peaceful purposes. ● エネルギーの有効利用を図る make the efficient *use* of energy.
② 【利用〜】 ● 利用価値がない [大いにある] be *useless* [very *useful*]; be of no [great] *utility*. ▶ この道具には多くの利用方法がある This tool has a lot of *uses*./There are a lot of *uses* for this tool.

── **利用する** 動 ❶ [役立たせる] use /júːz/, make use /júːs/ of ..., put* ... to use /júːs/; (うまく) take* advantage of ...; (実用的に) 《書》utilize (❗ おおげさに響くことがある); (自然の力を) harness. (❗ 《使う》[類語]) ● 勉強するのに図書館を利用する use [*make use of, take advantage of*] the library to study. ● 倉庫を実験室として利用する use [《書》*employ*] the warehouse *as* a laboratory. ● 施設をよりよく [十分] 利用する make better [full] *use of* the facilities; put the facilities *to* better [full] *use*. ● 川のエネルギーを動力源として利用する *harness* [*utilize*] the energy of the river *as* a source of power [*for* power]. ● あらゆる機会を利用して英語の上達をはかる take [*take advantage of*] every opportunity to improve one's English. ● 休暇を利用して (= 取って) ハワイに行く go to Hawaii *on vacation*. ▶ コンピュータを無断利用する use [*make use of*] the computer without permission. ▶ 余暇を最大限に利用しなさい Make the best *use* [*Make the most*] of your spare time. (❗ 前の方が特に不利な条件について用いる)
❷ [不当に利用する] (自己本位に) use; (弱みにつけ込んで) take* advantage of ...; (不正に) exploit. ● 子供を安い労働力として利用する *exploit* children *as* cheap labor. ● 友人を利用する use [*take advantage of*] one's friends. ▶ 人に利用されるのはいやだ I don't like *being used* by anyone.
❸ [乗り物を] use; (乗って行く) take*. ● よくバスを利用する use buses a lot. ● 渋谷まで地下鉄を利用する *take* the subway to Shibuya. (❗ go to Shibuya by subway より普通の言い方)

── **利用できる** 形 available. ● 利用できるすべての金 all the *available* money; all the money *available*. ▶ このプールは会員だけが利用できる This swimming pool is *available for* members only.
● 利用者 a user /júːzər/.

りよう 理容 (⇨理髪)
● 理容学校 a barbers' school, 《米》 a barber college. ● 理容師 (理髪師) a barber; a hairdresser, a hairstylist. (⇨理髪)

:りよう 量 (a) quantity; (an) amount.

┌─────────────── 使い分け ───────────────┐
quantity 物が全体でどのくらいあるかということに重点があり, quality (質) に対する語.
amount しばしば quantity と同様に用いるが, よりくだけた語で, その物がまとまった単位に分別できることを暗示する. number (数) に対する語.
いずれも通例不可算名詞について用いる.
└─────────────────────────────────────┘

▶ 仕事の量が着実に増えている The *amount of* work [The number of jobs] is [×are] steadily increasing. (❗ (1) 通例, 不可算名詞には amount, 複数可算名詞には number を用いる. ただし, 大量に扱われる商品などには複数可算名詞と続く場合でも amount を用いる: 今年はどれくらいの量のオレンジが輸入されましたか What [×How much, ×How many] is the *amount* of oranges that has been imported this year? (2) 「総量」の意では the [×an] amount) ▶ 私にはその 3 倍 [2 倍] の量が必要です I need three times [double, twice] the *amount* [*quantity*]. ▶ 膨大な [相当な; ある程度の; 一定の] 量のガソリンがこれらのタンクに貯蔵されています There is a huge [a considerable; some; a fixed] *amount of* gasoline stored in these tanks. (⇨大量, 多量, 少量) ● 今年は雨の量が多かった [少なかった] We had *a lot of* [*a little*] rain this year./We had a large [a small] *amount* [*quantity*] of rain this year. (❗ 日常会話では前の方が普通) ▶ こちらのコップの方があちらのより水の量が多い [少ない] There is *more* [*less*] water in this glass than in that one. (❗ ice cubes (角氷) のように複数可算名詞を従える場合は There are *more* [*fewer*, 《話》 *less*] ice cubes ....) ▶ IC の生産は量的にも質的にもずいぶん伸びた The production of ICs [integrated circuits] has grown a great deal *in terms of* both *quantity* and *quality* [both *quantitatively* and *qualitatively*].

[会話] 「どのくらいの量のミルクが必要ですか」「少しでいいです」 "How much [What *amount* of, What *quantity* of] milk do you want?" "Just a little." (❗ 複数可算名詞には How many, a few を用いる: "How many eggs do you want?" "Just a few.")

*りよう 猟 (狩猟一般) hunting; (銃猟) shooting. (⇨狩猟, 狩り) ● 猟をする hunt; shoot. ● 猟に行く go *hunting* [*shooting*] 《*for*》. (❗ 《英》 では銃を使って猟をするは shoot, 銃を使わないで猟犬でウサギ・キツネなどを狩る場合は hunt を用いる. 《米》 では hunt は両方の意で用いられる)
● 猟区 a hunting àrea. ● 猟具 hunting gèar. ● 猟犬 a húnting dòg; a hound. ● 猟場 a húnting gròund. ● 猟鳥 a game bird.

*りよう 漁 (魚採り全般) fishing; (漁業) fishery; (漁獲高) a catch, a take. ● 漁をする catch fish. ● 漁に行く go *fishing*.

*りよう 寮 (大学院などの) 《米》 a dormitory, 《米話》 a dorm, 《英》 a hall (of residence); (学生・青年労働者用の) a hostel. ● 独身寮 a bachelor apartment house. ● (申し込んでいた寮に入れることになりました I've got a place in the *dormitory*.
● 寮歌 a college [a high school] dormitory song. ● 寮生 a boarder; (学生) a dormitory student. ● 寮則 dormitory regulations. ● 寮長 a dormitory superintendent, (低学年の寄宿生のための) a house master. ● 寮費 (a) room and board charge. (❗ しばしば複数形で) ● 寮母 a matron of a dormitory.

りよう 了 ❶ 【終わり】an end; a finish. ● 上巻了 the *end* of the first volume.
❷ 【了承】了とする understand.

りよう 良 (成績の) a B; Good. (⇨優)

りよう 涼 ● 涼を入れる let in cool air.
● 涼をとる (⇨涼(すず))

りよう 陵 a mausoleum /mɔːsəliːəm/. ● 仁徳陵 the *mausoleum* of Emperor Nintoku. ● 御陵 an Imperial *mausoleum*.

りよう 稜 an edge; a line; (尾根) a ridge. ● エベレストの北稜 the North *ridge* of Everest.

りよう- 両- ● 両サイド *both* sides; *either* side. ● 両端に at *both* ends 《*of*》; at *either* side 《*of*》. ● 両 3 日 (*in*) two or three days.

-りよう -両 ● 10 両編成の急行 a 10-*car* express; an express made up of [composed of] 10 *cars*. ● 前から 3 両目の車両に乗る get on the third *car* from the front.

- **−りょう −料** (サービスなどの料金) (a) charge; (単位当たりの料金) a rate; (授業料・入場料など) a fee; (通行料) a toll. ● (1回の)通話料 a télephone chàrge. ● 劇場の入場料 an admission (fee) to a theater.
- **−りょう −領** (領土) ● 南米のフランス領 the French possessions in South America.
- **りょうあん 良案** a good idea [(計画) plan, (提案) suggestion].
- **りょういき 領域** (知識・活動などの分野) a domain; a territory; 《やや書》a realm /rélm/; (研究などの分野) a field; (活動などの範囲) an area. ● 科学の領域 the domain [territory, realm, field] of science. ▶ それは私の領域外だ That's outside my domain [territory, field].
- **りょういん 両院** both [the two] Houses. ▶ 法案は両院を通過した The bill passed both Houses.
  ● 両院議員 members of both Houses. ● 両院協議会 a joint conference of the two Houses.
- **りょうえん 良縁** a good match. ● 良縁に恵まれる find the right man for her; find the right woman for him; make a good match.
- **りょうか 良貨** good money. ▶ 悪貨は良貨を駆逐する (⇨悪貨 [成句])
- **りょうが 凌駕 —— 凌駕する 動** 《書》surpass. (⇨凌ぐ ❶)
- ***りょうかい 了解 图** 〖理解〗(an) understanding 《on, about》; 〖同意〗(an) agreement 《on, about》, consent 《to》. ● 了解を得て with 《his》 consent. ● 了解を得る[求める] get [ask for] 《his》 consent. ● (…であるという)了解のもとに on the understanding 《that 節》. ● 口頭[文書]での了解 a verbal [a written] understanding. ▶ だれが我々のチームの主将をつとめるかということで彼らと暗黙の了解があった We had a tacit understanding [暗黙の約束] an unspoken agreement] with them about who would act as captain of our team.
  会話「明朝6時に迎えに行くよ. 飛行機は8時発だから, 遅れないようにね」「了解. スーツケースを持って玄関に出ているわ」"I'll pick you up at 6:00 a.m. Our flight leaves at 8 o'clock. We don't want to be late." "Roger. I'll be out at the front door with my suitcase." (❗Roger. を電波通信以外で用いるのは《話》)
  —— **了解する 動** understand*; agree 《on, about》, consent 《to; to do》; reach [come*] to an agreement [an understanding] 《on》. ▶ もう一度やってみるということなら了解した All of us agreed [consented] to try [(that) we 《主に英》should] try] again. ▶ 彼は日曜日に来ると私は了解している My understanding is that he'll come on Sunday.
- **りょうかい 領海** territorial waters, a closed sea. ▶ その船は日本の領海12海里内にいた The ship was within the 12-sea-mile limit of the territorial waters of Japan.
  ● 領海侵犯 violation of territorial waters.
- **りょうがえ 両替 图** exchange. ● 両替は空港でもできます You can change money at the airport, too.
  —— **両替する 動** ● 円をドルに両替する exchange yen for [×into] dollars; change yen into [for] dollars. ● 1万円札を両替する (=くずす) change [break] a 10,000 yen bill. ▶ ホテルで両替するとレートが悪い You get a bad rate of exchange in [at] a hotel.
  ● 両替機 a change machine, 《主に米》a money changer. ● 両替所 (空港などの) a money exchange counter; (店) an exchange shop.

- **両替商** a money changer.
- **りょうがわ 両側** ● 通りの両側に on both sides [either side, each side] of the street.
- **りょうかん 涼感** ● 涼感あふれる風鈴の音 the cool-sounding tinglalings of a wind-bell. ● 涼感を呼ぶ(=涼しそうな)ドレス a cool-(looking) dress.
- **りょうかん 猟官** ● 猟官運動 office hunting; hunting for the government office. ● 猟官者 an office hunter.
- **りょうかん 量感** ● 量感のある massive.
- **りょうかん 僚艦** a consort ship [vessel].
- **りょうがん 両岸** ● 川の両岸に on both banks [either bank] of the river.
- **りょうがん 両眼** ● 両眼を失う lose sight of both eyes; (失明する) lose one's sight.
- **りょうき 猟奇 —— 猟奇的な 形** bizarre, weird /wíərd/; (変態的な) abnormal.
- **りょうき 猟期** a hunting [a shooting] season; an open season 《on [for] deer》.
- **りょうき 僚機** a consort plane.
- **りょうき 漁期** the fishing season. ● サケの漁期 the fishing season for salmon /sǽmən/.
- **りょうきょく 両極** the two poles.
- **りょうきょく(たん) 両極(端)** both extremities. ● 愛と憎しみの両極端 the extremes of love and hate. ▶ 彼らの意見は両極(端)に立っている Their opinions are at opposite poles [are extremely different]./ They are poles apart in their opinions.
- **りょうぎり 両切り** ● 両切りの(=フィルターなしの)たばこ a cigarette without a filtertip, a filterless cigarette.
- ***りょうきん 料金** (a) charge; a rate; a fare; a toll; a fee; (価格) a price

  使い分け **charge** 電話代やホテル代などサービスを利用したことに対する料金.
  rate 夜間料金など, 何らかの単位当たりの基準料金.
  fare 人を運ぶことによって発生する料金. 主に交通機関の料金をさす.
  toll 道路や橋などの通行料. 《米》では時に(長距離)電話の料金をさす.
  fee 弁護士などの専門職に対する報酬. 入会金・入学金・授業料・解約金・手数料などを表す.

  ① 【～料金】 ● 公共料金 public utility charges; 《話》utilities. ● 水道[ガス, 電気]料金 the wáter [gás, electricity] chàrge 《英》ràte. (❗料金の請求書は a water [a gas] bill などという) ● 郵便[電話]料金 a postal [a telephone] rate. (❗a telephone charge であれば1回の通話料のこと) ● バス料金 a bús fàre. ● 特急料金 an exprèss fàre. ● 深夜料金 a late-night rate. ● 特別料金 a special rate; (割増料金) an extra charge; (割引料金) a reduced rate. ● 10パーセントのサービス料金 a ten percent service charge.
  ② 【料金は】 ● 配達の料金はいくらですか How much [What] is the charge for delivery?/How much do they charge for delivery? ● 博多までの料金はいくらですか How much is the fare to Hakata?/How much will it cost to Hakata?/What's the fare to Hakata? ● タクシー料金は高い[来月値上げになる] Taxi fares are high (↔low) [will be raised (↔lowered) next month].
  ③ 【料金を】 ● 料金を前払いする pay the charge in advance. ▶ 彼はバスに乗ってから料金を払った He got on the bus and paid his fare. ▶ その修繕で5,000円の料金を請求された They charged (me) 5,000 yen for repairing it. ▶ 橋を渡るのに料金を払わねばならなかった We had to pay a toll when we

りょうくう crossed the bridge. ❹【料金で】▶6歳未満の子供は割引料金でバスに乗れる Children under six are allowed to ride on buses at a reduced [a discounted] *fare*.
- 料金所 a toll gate [booth]. • 料金徴収員 a toll collector • 料金箱 (バスなどの) a fare box. • 料金表 a price list; a list of charges.

りょうくう 領空 airspace, 《書》territorial air. • 中国の領空を侵犯する violate China's *airspace* [the *territorial air* of China].
- 領空権 territorial air rights.

りょうぐん 両軍 opposing armies [(チーム) teams]. ▶両軍ともに多数の死傷者が出た There were heavy casualties on *both sides*. ▶両軍の投手力は互角だ *Both teams* are equal in pitching strength.

りょうけ 両家 both families.

りょうけ 良家 a good family. (❗この good は「上流社会階層に属する」の意) • 良家の子女 sons and daughters of a *good family*.

りょうけん 了見 (考え) an idea; (意図) (an) intention. • 了見の狭い人 a *narrow-minded* person. • 悪い了見を起こす get [conceive] evil *ideas*. ▶勝手に私の部屋を使うとはどういう了見だい What's the *idea* of using my room without asking? ▶それは君の了見違いだ You are *wrong* [*mistaken*].

りょうげん 燎原 • 燎原の火のように燃え広がる spread [run, travel] like *wildfire*.

りょうこう 良好 形 (よい) good*; (立派な) fine; (非常によい) excellent; (申し分ない) satisfactory. • 良好な関係 *good* relations.

りょうこう 良港 • 天然の良港 a *good* natural *harbor*.

りょうこく 両国 the two countries [nations]. • 日ロ両国で解決すべき問題 an issue (which is) to be solved between Russia and Japan.

りょうごく 領国 a king's territory; a kingdom; (封土) a fief (魚〜s).

りょうざい 良材 ❶【材料】good material; (木材) good timber. ❷【人材】(才能ある人) a talented person; (能力ある人) a man of ability. • 天下に良材を求める look for *talented people* far and wide [all over the country].

りょうさいけんぼ 良妻賢母 a good wife and wise mother.

りょうさく 良策 (良い考え) a good idea; (良い政策) a good policy. (⇨良案)

りょうさつ 了察 • その何卒ご了察いただきたいと存じます I ask about your kind *consideration* about that.

りょうさん 量産 名 mass production.
—— 量産する 動 mass-produce 《bicycles》.
- 量産車 mass-produced cars.

りょうし 良師 • 私はいつも良師に恵まれてきました I've always had (good luck to study under) *good teachers*.

りょうし 猟師 a hunter, a huntsman (覆〜men).

りょうし 量子 【物理】a quantum (⦅履〜ta).
- 量子物理学 quantum physics. • 量子力学 quantum mechanics. • 量子論 (the) quantum theory.

りょうし 漁師 (男) a fisherman (覆〜men); (男・女) a fisher.

りょうじ 領事 a consul /kánsl/. • 総領事 a *consul* general. • 副領事 a vice *consul*. • ベルリン駐在英国領事 the British *Consul* in Berlin.
- 領事館 a consulate. • 総領事館 a consulate general. • 領事館員 (1人) a consular attaché; (全体) the staff of a consulate.

りょうじ 療治 (⇨治療)

りょうしき 良識 good sense. • 良識のある人 a person of *good sense* [(正しい判断力) *sound judgment*]; a sensible man [woman]. • 良識のある [ない] 行動をとる act *sensibly* [*foolishly*]. ▶そんなことをしないだけの良識はある I have enough *good sense* [I am *sensible* enough] not to do that. ▶良識をわきまえられないの? Can't you be *sensible*?

りょうしつ 良質 名 good [high] quality.
—— 良質の 形 of (good) quality; quality. • 良質紙 paper of good quality; (good) quality paper.

りょうじつ 両日 (2日) two days; (両方の日) both days. (⇨一両日) ▶文化祭は両日とも天候に恵まれた The school festival had good weather for *two days*.

りょうしゃ 両者 both. (⇨両方) ▶両者の実力は互角だ *The two of* them are equally matched./*Both of* them are equally matched. (❗×both them は不可) ▶両者新しい労働契約に関して対立している *The two sides* are in conflict with each other over a new labor contract.

りょうしゅ 領主 the lord of the manor /mǽnər/; (封建時代の諸侯) a feudal lord.

りょうしゅう 領収 名 receipt /risíːt/. • 領収書 (⇨領収書) • 領収済み Paid. (❗ゴム印などに)/*Received* with thanks. (❗送り状などに)
—— 領収する 動 receive. ▶100万円確かに領収しました I certainly *received* one million yen.

りょうしゅう 領袖 a leader; a head. • 派閥の領袖 the *leader* of a faction; a faction *leader*.

りょうじゅう 猟銃 a sporting [a hunting] rifle, a húnting gùn; (散弾銃) a shotgun.

りょうしゅうしょ 領収書 a receipt. • 領収書を書く[もらう] make out [get] a *receipt* 《for the money》. • 領収書をください Can I have a *receipt*?/(書いてください) Write a *receipt* for me?

りょうしょ 良書 a good book.

りょうしょう 了承 【承認】approval; 【理解】(an) understanding; 【同意】consent.
—— 了承する 動 • その計画を了承する *approve* the plan; (同意する) *consent* to the plan.

りょうしょく 糧食 food; provisions (❗複数形で). • 糧食が尽きる run short of *provisions*.

りょうじょく 陵辱 名 ❶【侮辱】(an) indignity; (an) insult (to); (a) humiliation. (❗いずれも具体的行動は C) • 陵辱を受ける suffer *insults* [*indignities*, *humiliation*]; be insulted [humiliated]. ❷【暴力で女性を犯すこと】(a) sexual assault; (a) rape. (⇨暴力, レイプ)
—— 陵辱する 動 ❶【侮辱】insult; humiliate. ❷【暴力で女性を犯す】• 女性を陵辱する *assault* [*rape*] a woman.

*りょうしん 両親 (one's) parents (❗「両方の」と強調する場合は both をつけることもある); (父母) one's mother and father (❗one's father and mother より普通). (⇨親) ▶私の両親は神戸に住んでいます My *parents* live in Kobe. ▶両親のどちらがよくPTAに出ますか Which of your *parents* often attends the PTA?/Who attends the PTA more often, your mother or father?

*りょうしん 良心 名 (a) conscience /kánʃəns/. (❗修飾語を伴うときや, 個人の「良心」というときは通例 a がつく)
❶【良心が】▶彼には良心がない He has no *con-*

りょうじんひしょう

science. ▶そのことでは良心がとがめた I had a bad [a guilty] *conscience* about it./I had it *on* my *conscience*. (**!** have ... on one's conscience は「…で気がとがめる」の意)/(やましく思った)I felt guilty about it. ▶盗みは彼の良心がどうしても許さなかった His *conscience* would not let him [allow him to] steal.

② 【良心の】 ▶それは良心の問題だ That's a matter of *conscience*.

③ 【良心に】 ▶良心に従う[従って行動する] follow [act according to] one's (own) *conscience*. ▶良心に反する命令には従いません I shall [will] never obey orders that go against my *conscience*. (**!** shall の方が強い意志を表す) ▶良心に恥じる[やましい]ところがない I have a clear *conscience*./My *conscience* is clear. ▶私は良心にかけてそんなことはできない I cannot, *in all conscience*, do such a thing.

● **良心の呵責**(かしゃく) ▶良心の呵責にさいなまれて彼はついに警察に自首した Troubled [Tortured] by *conscience*, he finally turned himself in to the police. ▶私は彼との約束を破ったことに良心の呵責を感じた I felt guilty [felt a pang] *about* having broken my promise to him. (● 後の方は「良心の痛みを感じる」の意の比喩表現で, 主に書き言葉. (⇨呵責))

── **良心的な** 形 conscientious /kànʃiénʃəs/; (正直な) honest. ▶良心的な商取引 *honest* dealings. ▶彼は良心的な仕事をする人だ He is a *conscientious* worker./(仕事に良心的だ) He is *conscientious about* his work./(良心的に仕事をする) He works *conscientiously*. ▶あの店はとても良心的だ They're very *honest* [*conscientious*] at that store.

りょうじんひしょう 『梁塵秘抄』 *The Dance of the Dust on the Rafters*. (【参考】後白河法皇撰の歌謡集)

りょうすい 量水 ● **量水器** a water gauge /géidʒ/ [meter].

りょうすい 領水 territorial waters.

りょうする 領する (領土を所有する) own 《a territory》; (支配する) reign /réin/.

りょうせい 両性 图 both [the two] sexes. ● **両性の合意** an agreement between the (*two*) *sexes*.

── **両性の** 形 bisexual.

● **両性花** a bisexual flower. ● **両性生殖** 『生物』 bisexual reproduction.

りょうせい 良性 ── **良性の** 形 benign /bináin/ (↔ malignant). ● **良性の腫瘍**(しゅよう) a *benign* tumor.

りょうせい 寮生 (⇨寮)

りょうせいぐゆう 両性具有 ── **両性具有の** 形 androgynous /ændrɑ́dʒənəs/. ● **両性具有者** an androgyne; a hermaphrodite.

りょうせいばい 両成敗 ▶けんか両成敗 (⇨喧嘩)

りょうせいるい 両生類 (両生動物) an amphibian.

りょうせん 稜線 (山の尾根) the (mountain) ridge.

りょうせん 僚船 a consort ship.

りょうぜん 両全 ▶両全を図る try to both 《sports and study》 equally well.

りょうぞく 良俗 public decency [(風紀) morals]. ● **良俗に反する** offend [be an offense against] *public decency*.

りょうたん 両端 both ends, either end.

りょうだん 両断 ▶一刀両断 (⇨一刀[成句])

りょうち 領地 (a) territory; 《書》a domain; (封建時代の領土の) a fief. (⇨領土)

りょうちょ 良著 a good books.

りょうちょう 寮長 (⇨寮)

りょうて 両手 both hands; 【両腕】 both arms. (⇨手

りょうひん

❶ ⑤) ▶両手で人の首に抱きつく throw 《*both*》 one's *arms* around 《his》 neck. ▶両手を広げる (手を) open *both hands*; (腕を) spread one's *arms*. ● 両手を使って箱を持ち上げる use *both hands* to lift a box. ▶鳥を両手に包むように持つ cup a bird in one's *hands*.

会話「塩味のポテトチップが好きなの」「両手にいっぱいどうぞ」"I love salted potato chips《米》[crisps《英》]." "Take *a couple of handfuls*(, please)." (**!** 相手に利益になるような場合には必ずしも please をつけなくてもよい)

● **両手に花** ▶彼は両手に花だ(=美人の間にいる) He *is* (*seated*) *between the two beauties*.

りょうてい 料亭 a high-class Japanese-style restaurant.

りょうてい 量定 〖法律〗 determination 《*of*》.

りょうでん 良田 a rich [a fertile] paddy (field).

りょうてんびん 両天秤 ● **両天秤にかける** (両方を獲得[達成]しようとする) try for both; (対立する双方から利を得る) have it both ways; sit on the fence. ▶彼は両天秤をかけて失敗した(=あぶはちとらずになった) He *fell between two stools*.

りょうど 領土 图 (領海を含む) (a) territory; (属領) a possession; (王などの) 《書》a domain. ● **北方領土** the Northern *Territories*; the four northern islands. ● **昔の英国の領土** Britain's former *possessions*. ● **領土を保全する** preserve the *territorial* integrity. ▶この島は日本の領土だ This island is a Japanese *territory* [(日本に属する) *belongs to* Japan].

── **領土(の)** 形 territorial.

● **領土権** territorial rights. ● **領土問題** a territorial issue.

りょうとう 両頭 ▶両頭のヘビ a two-headed snake; a snake *with tow heads*.

りょうどう 両道 文武両道 (⇨文武)

りょうどう 糧道 ▶糧道を断つ cut off (the route of) 《enemy's》 food supply.

りょうどうたい 良導体 a good conductor 《*of* electricity》.

りょうとうづかい 両刀使い ── **両刀使いの** 形 (異性・同性愛者の) bisexual. ▶彼は甘辛の両刀使い(=酒も甘いものも好きだ) He likes sweets as well as *sake* [beer, etc.].

りょうとく 両得 ▶一挙両得 (⇨一挙両得)

りょうどなり 両隣 ● **両隣の人** one's next-door neighbors. ▶昔は「向こう三軒両隣」といって近所の人たちを大切にしたものだ We used to try to live amiably together with our neighbors, with a motto "Be friendly with your neighbors." ▶新幹線の両隣の席は空いていた The seets *on my right and left* were empty on the Shinkansen.

りょうにん 両人 (話題にしている2人) both of them; the two. ▶よう, ご両人! A nice couple you are!

りょうば 両刃 ── **両刃の** 形 two-[double-]edged. ● **両刃の剣** (⇨諸刃(もろは))

りょうば 良馬 a fine horse; (駿馬) a swift horse.

りょうば 漁場 fishing grounds; (魚の豊富な) fishing banks.

りょうはん 量販 图 mass sales.

── **量販する** 動 mass-market; sell mass-market goods [products].

● **量販店** a mass retailer. ● **家電量販店** a mass home electronics retailer.

りょうひ 良否 (質) quality. ▶油の品質の良否を調べる check the *quality* of oil.

りょうびらき 両開き ● **両開きの戸** double doors.

りょうひん 良品 a good product.

りょうふう 良風 ▶昔ながらの良風が次々と絶えていくのはさびしい It's regrettable that *good old customs* have been dying out one after another.
りょうふう 涼風 a cool breeze.
りょうぶん 領分 (活動の領域) one's territory; (分野)《書》one's domain; (範囲) one's sphere. ●人の領分をかってに他国人 encroach on other people's *territory*. ▶それは私の領分ではない That is outside 《*in*》 my *domain*.
りょうぼ 陵墓 a mausoleum /mɔːsəliːəm/. (⇨陵)
:**りょうほう 両方** both 《*of*》. (■複数扱い. 物も人も受ける) (⇨二人, 二つ, どちら)
① 【両方の[とも]】 ●両方の手 *both* hands. (⇨手) ▶その答えは両方とも正しい *Both* 《*of*》 the answers are correct. (■(1) of は省略可. (2) the two answers とするより意味が強い)/The answers are *both* correct. (■主語と同格の both は通例 be 動詞, 助動詞の後に置かれる. ただし短い答えのときは前にくる:「終わりましたか」「はい両方とも終わりました」"Are you through [Have you finished]?" "Yes, we *both* are [have]."次例参照) ▶彼らの家は両方とも庭付きだ *Both* 《*of*》 their houses [×Their both houses] have gardens./Their houses *both* have gardens. (■同格の both は一般動詞の前に置く) ▶両方とも食べた I ate *both*. (■both は単独で用いることもある)/I ate *both* of them [them *both*, ×both them]. (■後の人称代名詞となるときは of は省略できない) ▶両方とも互いに相手をよく知っている Each knows the other well. (■×Both know each other. は不可) (⇨それぞれ, 両者) ▶この前の日曜日に列車の中で手袋を両方ともなくした I lost *a pair of* gloves on [in] the train last Sunday.
② 【AとBの両方ている】 (肯定) both A and B. (■A, B は文法上対等のもの) ▶君とぼくの両方が行かなくてはならない *Both* you *and* I [You *and* I *both*] have to go. (■(1) 日常会話では特に「両方」を強調しないときは単に You *and* I have to go. ということも多い. (2) both of の後は A and B の形はこないので ×Both of you and I [me]....は不可) ▶彼は野球とサッカーの両方とも得意だ He is good *both* at baseball *and* at soccer [×*both* at *both* baseball *and* soccer, ×both at baseball and soccer].
③ 【(AとBの)両方とも...でない】 (全部否定) neither (A nor B). ▶両方ともよくない *Neither* 《of them》is good. (■(1) A, B がともに単数のときは neither は単数扱い. (2) either は any と同じく not より前に置けないので, ×Either is not good. の語順は不可) ▶彼と私の両方とも責任はない *Neither* he nor I am [《話》are] responsible. (■neither A nor B が主語の場合原則として動詞は B に一致させるが, 《話》では複数動詞を用いる方が普通) ▶それらの本は両方とも必要でない I need *neither* book [*neither* of the books]./I don't need *either* book [*either* of the books]. (■後の方が口語的)
④ 【両方とも...というわけではない】 (部分否定) not (...) both. ▶両方とも喜んでいるわけではない *Not both of* them are pleased./*Both of* them are *not* pleased. (■後の方は下げ調子でいうと全部否定になりあいまいなので, 前の方が普通) ▶これらの詩の両方とも好きなわけではない I don't like *both of* these poems.
りょうほう 療法 風邪の民間療法 a folk *remedy for* colds. ●ショック[音楽]療法 《be in [go into]》 shock [music] *therapy*. ●温泉[食事; 断食]療法 a hot spring [a dietary; a fasting] *cure*. ●食事療法をしている[始める] be [go] on a *diet*. (⇨治療) ●電気療法 electrotherapy. ●放射線療法 radiotherapy.

りょうまつ 糧秣 (軍隊で) provisions and fodder.
りょうみ 涼味 (a feeling of) coolness. ●緑の木陰で涼味を満喫する enjoy the *cool air* [*the cool*] under the shade of trees. ●涼味満点のドレス a very *cool-looking* dress.
りょうめ 両目 both eyes. ●両目を閉じる close [shut] your *eyes*.
●両目が明く (やっと 2 勝する) get a second win at last; get a long-awaited second win.
りょうめ 量目 weight. ●量目が足りない be short of *weight*. ●量目をごまかす give short *weight*.
りょうめん 両面 both sides. ●物事の両面を見る look at *both sides* of things.
●両面テープ (a) double-sided (adhesive) tape.
りょうや 良夜 a moonlight night; a night with a full moon.
りょうや 涼夜 a cool evening [night].
りょうやく 良薬 (a) good* medicine.
●良薬は口に苦し 《ことわざ》 (A) good medicine tastes bitter [is bitter to the taste]./Good advice sounds harsh to the ear.
りょうゆう 両雄 two great men.
●両雄並び立たず 'Two great men do not want to stand side by side.'/《ことわざ》If two men ride upon a horse one must sit behind.
りょうゆう 僚友 a friend at work; (職場の同僚) a colleague.
りょうゆう 領有 ― 領有する 動《書》possess. ▶日本はこの島を領有(=所有)している Japan *possesses* [*is in possession of*] this island.
りょうよう 両用 ●水陸両用の戦車 an *amphibious* tank. ●裏表両用の reversible 《coats》. ●遠近両用メガネ bifocals.
りょうよう 両様 ●この文章は両様の解釈が可能である This sentence can be interpreted *in two ways*.
りょうよう 療養 [名] (治療) medical treatment; (病後の)《書》recuperation (⇨保養). ●自宅療養 home *treatment*. ●転地療養に行く go to 《Izu》 for a change 《of air》.
―**療養する 動** receive medical treatment;《書》recuperate.
●療養所 a sanatorium; a rest home.
りょうよく 両翼 both wings; (野球場の) right and left fields; (進撃軍の) both wings [flanks]. ●両翼が狭い球場 a ball park with short foul lines.
りょうらん 繚乱 ●百花繚乱 (⇨百花繚乱)
:**りょうり 料理** [名] [調理すること] cooking; [料理法] cookery, (国・地方独特の)《やや書》cuisine /kwiːziːn/; [料理品] (食べ物) food; (皿に盛った特定の種類の) a dish (■通例修飾語を伴う).
① 【～料理】 ●家庭料理 home *cooking*. ●郷土料理 local [country] *dishes*. ●おいしい料理 a delicious [a nice] *dish*. ●奥さんの手料理 home *cooking* of one's wife. ●1 皿の肉[野菜]料理 a meat [a vegetable] *dish*. ●お魚料理 《御前》. ▶若い女性はフランス料理が好きだ Young women like French *food* [*cuisine*,《主に米》 *dishes*]. (■《米》では dish を国名・地名と共に用いることはあまりない)
② 【料理～】 ●テレビで料理教室をする give a *cookery* class on TV.
③ 【料理が】 ●彼女は料理が上手だ[へた]だ She is a good [a poor] *cook*. (■文脈により「腕のいい[悪い]コック」の意になる. poor は「貧しい」の意にはならない)/She is good [poor] at *cooking*./She *cooks* [doesn't *cook*] (very) well. ▶料理ができた(=ごはんですよ) Dinner is ready. (■×The food is [The dishes are] ready. は不可) ▶この種の魚は料理がし

にくい It's hard to cook this kind of fish./This kind of fish doesn't cook well.
④【料理を】● 料理をする(⇨動) ● 料理を習う learn cooking [cookery]; learn how to cook. ● 料理を並べる arrange [出す] serve; (整える) set] food. ● あの店はうまい料理を出す They serve good food [dishes] at that restaurant.
── 料理する 動 [調理する] cook, do* the cooking; prepare,《米話》fix; dress.

> 使い分け cook 料理することを意味する最も一般的な語. 通例加熱して調理することをさし, 火を使わないサラダなどに対しては用いない.
> prepare 食事を用意[支度]することに焦点を当てた語. cookと異なり, 火を使わないサラダやサンドイッチなどを作る際にも用いる.
> dress 主にサラダなどにドレッシングをかけることをさす. 肉や魚を cook できるように下ごしらえすることも表す.

> 関連 cook に含まれる料理法には次のようなものがある: boil (煮る, 炊く, ゆでる)/fry (フライパンを用いて油で揚げる, 炒(いた)める, 焼く)/deep-fry (たっぷりの油で揚げる)/bake (パン・ケーキ類を天火などで焼く)/toast (すでに調理してあるパンなどを軽く焼く)/grill (肉などを焼き網・鉄板などの上で焼く. ただし, (英) では直火で焼くときにも用いる《(米) broil》)/roast (天火で焼く, あぶる, 豆などをいる)

● 魚を料理する cook fish; (カニ) dress crab (❗カニの内身を取り出し, crab shell に盛りつける料理. ×dress fish の場合は make [prepare] sashimi という). ● 煮て[焼き網にのせて; 弱火で; オーブンで]料理する cook by boiling [on a gridiron; over low heat; in an oven]. ▶ 彼女は手際よくその肉を私たちに料理してくれた She skillfully cooked the meat for us [cooked us the meat].
● 料理学校 a cóokery [a cóoking] schòol; a cooking school. (❗前の方が普通) ● 料理長 a chef /ʃéf/. ● 料理店 a《Chinese》restaurant. ● 料理人 a cook /kúk/. (❗ cooker は調理器具のこと) ● 料理法 cooking; cookery; how to cook; (個々の料理の) a recipe /résipi(ː)/《for roast beef》. ● 料理本 a cookbook; a cookery book.

りょうりつ 両立 ── 両立する 動 (一致する) be consistent《with》; (矛盾しない) be compatible《with》. ▶ その二つの考えは両立する[しない] The two ideas are compatible [incompatible]《with each other》. ▶ 彼女はどうにか仕事と家庭を両立させた She managed to do her job and housework at the same time./She managed to balance her work and [with] family life.

りょうりょう 両々 ▶ 彼らは両々相譲らない They are evenly matched.
● 両々相まって ▶ この二つが両々相まって更なる力となっている These two factors help each other to produce further effects.

りょうりょう 喨々 ── 喨々たる 形 ● 喨々たるラッパの音 the clear sound of a trumpet [(軍隊のラッパ) a bugle]/a clear trumpet [bugle]/(高らかに鳴り響く) the blares of a trumpet [a bugle].

りょうりょう 寥々 ── 寥々たる 形 (ものさびしい) desolate; dreary; (極めて少ない) only a few; (ほとんどない) hardly [scarcely] any .... ● 人家寥々たる山村 a mountain village spare with houses. ▶ 彼の哲学を真に理解している者は寥々たるものだ Hardly [Scarcely] anybody really understands his philosophy.

りょうりん 両輪 ● 車の両輪(＝互いに補い合っていい成果を得る関係) a cooperative relationship. ▶ 彼らは車の両輪となって組織を支えた They helped each other to keep the organization going./They worked in cooperation to run the organization smoothly.

りょうろん 両論 ▶ 賛否両論が相半ばした The pros and cons were almost equal in number.

りょうわき 両脇 ● 両脇に on both sides. ▶ 彼は両脇を警官にかかえられ連行された Flanked by two police officers, he was taken to the police station. (❗ flank は「(両)側面に配置する」の意)

りょかく 旅客 [旅行者] a traveler;[乗客] a passenger. (⇨乗客)
● 旅客機 a passenger plane. ● 旅客列車 a passenger train.

****りょかん 旅館** a Japanese(-style) hotel /houtél/ [inn] (❗ hotel は近代的な, inn は古風な感じを与える); a ryokan (❗(1) 単・複同形. (2) a ryokan, a Japanese(-style) hotel [inn] とする方が分かりやすい). ● 温泉旅館 a Japanese-style inn with hot springs. ▶ その夜は増屋旅館に泊まった I put up at the Masuda Hotel [Inn] for the night. (❗ for は「…を過ごすために」の意)

りよく 利欲 greed [強欲]《書》avarice) for gain.
● 利欲に目がくらむ be blinded by greed for gain.

りょくいん 緑陰 ● 緑陰で in [under] the shade of a tree; in the leafy shade.

りょくおうしょく 緑黄色 ● 緑黄色野菜 green and yellow vegetables.

りょくか 緑化 (⇨緑化(ロ*))

りょくじゅ 緑樹 a green tree.

りょくじゅうじ 緑十字 ● 緑十字運動 a tree planting campaign [movement].

りょくじゅほうしょう 緑綬褒章 the Medal with Green Ribbon. (⇨褒章 関連)

りょくそう 緑藻 green algae /ǽldʒiː/.

りょくち 緑地 a green tract of land; a wooded area.
● 緑地帯 (a) green belt; (車道と歩道の間の) a tree lawn.

りょくちゃ 緑茶 green tea.

りょくど 緑土 land covered with verdure.

りょくないしょう 緑内障 [医学] glaucoma /glɔː-kóumə/. ● 緑内障である have glaucoma《in one's left eye》.

りょくふう 緑風 a pleasant breeze in early summer; a pleasant wind blowing through green trees in May.

りょけん 旅券 a pássport. ● 旅券を申請する[とる; 更新する] apply for [get; renew] a passport. ● 旅券を査証してもらう get [have] one's passport visaed; get a visa on one's passport. (❗「中国へ入国する査証を受ける」は get a visa for China [a Chinese visa] という) ● IC 旅券を発行する issue an IC passport.

****りょこう 旅行** 名 a trip; a journey; travel; a tour.

> 使い分け trip ちょっとした距離の短い旅行から長期の海外旅行にまで幅広く用いられる一般的な語.
> journey 通例陸上の比較的長い旅行を表す.《米》では文語的に響く.
> travel 主に長距離の旅行を表す. 目的地より移動や旅行自体に重点がある. 海外旅行を示す際には複数形で用いることが多い.
> tour 見学や視察などを目的とし, 各地を巡り元の場所へ戻るような旅行を表す. また, コンサートツアーの意でも用いられる.

①【〜旅行】● 小旅行 a short trip; (日帰りの) a day trip (❗ 日帰りの小旅行をする人を a tripper とい

う). ●海外旅行 a trip abroad; an overseas *trip*; foreign *travel*. ●修学旅行 a 《three-day》 school trip [《やや書》 excursion]. ●見学旅行 a field trip. (⇨見学) ●自転車旅行 a bicycle *trip*. ●団体旅行 a group *tour*. (●添乗員同行する場合は a guided [a conducted] *tour* としてもよい) ●世界一周旅行 an around-the-world *trip* [*tour*]. (⇨⑥)
▶月旅行 *travel* [a *trip*] to the moon. ▶私は京都へ1泊のバス旅行に出かけます I'm going to take an overnight [a two-day, two days'] bus *trip to Kyoto*. (**!** two-days は不可) ▶私はパック旅行より一人旅がしたい I'd rather travel on my own [alone] than go on a package [×a pack] *tour*.
② 【旅行する～】 ▶彼は旅行中病気になった He fell sick during a *trip*.
③ 【旅行が[は]】 ▶アメリカ人は旅行が好きだ Americans [American people] like to *travel*. ▶日本への旅行はどうでしたか How was your *trip* [×travel] to Japan? (**!** travel は特定の旅行には用いない (⇨[類語])) / How did you like your *trip* to Japan? ▶私たちの旅行は1週間半でした Our *trip* was a week and a half.
④ 【旅行の】 ▶旅行の準備をする get ready for a *trip*. ▶彼は旅行の経験が豊富だ(＝よく旅行をしている) He has made [taken] a lot of *trips*. ▶彼は世界中を旅行している He is a *well-traveled* [a *widely-traveled*, a *much-traveled*] man. ▶今回の旅行の目的は何ですか What is the purpose [aim] of your *trip* this time?
⑤ 【旅行に】 ▶ヨーロッパ旅行に彼を連れていく take him *on a tour* of Europe [*on* an European *tour*]. ●九州旅行に出かける go to Kyushu *on* [*for*] *a trip*; go on *a trip* to Kyushu. ▶彼は今旅行に出ていて家にいません He's away *on a trip*. / (旅行中です) He's *on a trip* now. ▶母は14日間のヨーロッパ旅行に出かけている My mother is *on a 14-day tour* of Europe.
⑥ 【旅行を】 ▶世界一周旅行を計画しています I am planning to *take a trip* [*make a tour*, *travel around*] the world. (⇨①) ▶どうぞ楽しいご旅行を Have a nice *trip* [*journey*, ×*travel*]. (**!** (1) 前に I hope you will が省略された言い方. (2) Thank you, I will. などと答える)
⑦ 【旅行から[で]】 ▶彼は旅行でみやげ物をたくさん買った He bought a lot of souvenirs *on his trip*. ▶彼はきのう北海道旅行から帰って来た He came back [《やや書》 returned] from his *trip to Hokkaido* yesterday.
━━旅行する 動 travel (**!** 最も一般的な語だが,《米》ではやや文語的); make* [take*, go* on] a trip [a journey] (*to*) (**!** make は仕事上の旅行, take は遊びの旅行を含意し, go on は「出かける」の意); (周遊する) make [take, go on] a tour (*of*). ●身軽に [1か月の旅行なら] *take a trip* with as little baggage as possible [for a month]; *travel light* [(for) a month].
会話 「よく旅行されるのですか」「いいえ, お金がないものですから」"You often *go on trips*?/You *travel* a lot?" "No. There's so little money."
●旅行案内 (本) a guidebook (**!** 単に a guide ともいう); (パンフレット) a travel brochure /brouʃάːr/, a travel pamphlet. ●旅行案内所 a 《travel》 [travel] information office. ●旅行かばん a *tra*veling bàg; (スーツケース) a suitcase; (1泊旅行向きの) an overnight bag. ●旅行記 a travel record; a record of one's travels. ●旅行代理店 [会社] a travel agency [bureau]. (**!** 業者には a travel agent) ●旅行シーズン the tourist season.
●旅行者 (観光客) a tourist; (旅人) 《書》 a traveler.

りょしゅう 旅愁 loneliness on a journey. ●旅愁を慰める relieve the *loneliness on* one's *journey*.

りょしゅう『旅愁』 *Travel Nostalgia* [*Weariness*]. (**[参考]** 横光利一の小説)

りょしゅう 虜囚 a prisoner of war (廸 prisoners-).

りょじゅん 旅順 〖中国大連市の一地区〗 Lüshun /lúːʃún/.

りょじょう 旅情 ▶旅情をかきたてる arouse the *traveler's sentiment*.

りょだん 旅団 a brigade /brigéid/.
●旅団長 《米》 a brigade commander; 《英》 a brigadier /brigədíər/.

りょっか 緑化 ━━緑化する 動 plant trees 《*in* an area》; plant 《an area》 with trees.
●緑化運動 a tree-planting campaign.

りょてい 旅程 (日程) an itinerary /aitínərèri/.

りょひ 旅費 tráveling expènses, 《主に英》 trável expènses. (**!** ホテルなどの宿泊費を含めた出張旅費をいう); 〖支給される手当〗 a tráveling allòwance. ▶旅費は会社に請求できる We can charge the *traveling expenses* to the company('s account)./(…が負担することになる) The *traveling expenses* are chargeable to the company.

リヨン 〖フランスの都市〗 Lyons /líáianz/.

リラ 〖トルコ・マルタなどの通貨単位〗 a lira (廸 ～s, lire /líərei/). (〖記号 L〗)

リラ 〖植物〗 a lilac. (**!** 花は Ⓤ)

リラックス ━━リラックスする 動 ▶家ではリラックスできる We can *relax* [*feel relaxed*, *feel comfortable*] at home. ▶そんなに神経質にならないで. リラックスしなさいよ Don't be so nervous. Just *loosen up* a bit. ▶深呼吸をすると体がリラックスしてくる It is *relaxing* to do deep-breathing exercises.

リリース 名 〖発表〗 release.
━━リリースする 動 ▶その歌手は3か月連続で CD をリリースした The singer *has released* CDs for three consecutive months.
●リリース版 (製品版) a release version.

リリーフ 名 〖野球〗 (投手) a relief pitcher, a reliever; (火消し役) a fireman; (リリーフ専門の) a relief specialist. (**!** 単に ×a relief とはいわない)
●ショート [ロング] リリーフ投手 a short [a long] *reliever*. ●ワンポイントリリーフ投手 a spot *reliever*. ●リリーフ登板する make a *relief* appearance; take over *in relief*. ●リリーフで好投する pitch well *in relief*.
━━リリーフする 動 relieve 《him *in* the ninth inning》.
●リリーフエース an ace reliever. ●リリーフカー a relief truck; 《和製語》 a relief car. ●リリーフ投手陣 a relief corps; a bullpen squad; the bullpen.

りりく 離陸 名 (a) takeoff (廸 ～s). ▶事故は離陸20分後に起こった The accident occurred twenty minutes after *takeoff*.
━━離陸する 動 take off. ▶飛行機は3時に離陸した The plane *took off* (×landed) at three.
●離陸時間 a takeoff time.

りりしい 凛々しい gallant; (男らしい) manly. ●りりしい姿 a *manly* figure.

りりつ 利率 an interest rate. ●年利率 annual *interest rate*. ●利率を上げる[下げる] raise [lower] the *interest rate*. ●定期預金の利率はいくらですか What is the *interest rate* on fixed deposits?

リリック 〖叙情詩〗 a lyric; 〖歌詞〗 lyrics.

リレー a 《800-meter [4×200]》 relay 《race》. (**!** 時

に 4×200 meters relay ともいう. ×は by と読む
- リレーの選手 a *relay* runner. ▶ バケツリレーで水を運ぶ pass buckets of water from one person to another.

りれき 履歴 one's personal history;（家族, 学歴, 職歴）one's background;（職歴）one's career /kəríər/; (履歴書の職歴欄) work experience(s).

りれきしょ 履歴書 a curriculum vitae /kəríkjuləm víːtaɪ/ (徴 -cula vitae) 《略 CV》(!通例単数形で);《米》a résumé /rézj)uméɪ/.（履歴書のタイトルに用いるときは無冠詞・大文字で）(⇨巻末 [履歴書の書き方]) ▶ 履歴書を同封いたしますので, よろしくお願いたします I am enclosing my *résumé* for your perusal.

りろせいぜん 理路整然 —— 理路整然とした 形（論理的な）, (一貫性のある) (logically) consistent. ▶ 彼の意見は理路整然としている His opinion is *logical*.

****りろん 理論** 名 (a) theory (! 立証された理論・学説から実践に対する理論・理屈・空論まで意味が広い. 個々の理論をいうときは C ⟨⟩学説⟩) ● 音楽理論 the *theory* of music; músical *thèory*. ▶ 彼が展開した理論はまだれもいまだにくつがえされていない None of the *theories* he developed have [has] yet been overthrown [disproved].

—— **理論(上)の, 理論的な** 形 theoretical.

—— **理論上, 理論的に** 副 theoretically; in theory. ▶ あなたの案は理論的にはよくできているが, 実行しにくい Your plan, though excellent *in theory*, is difficult to put into practice.

- 理論家 a theorist. ● 理論物理学 theoretical physics.

りん 厘 ❶ 【銭の十分の一】 a *rin*. (!単・複同形) ● 日歩 3 厘で at an daily interest rate of three *rin*.
❷【比率】▶ 打率 2 割 2 分 5 厘では好打者とはいえない You cannot call him a good hitter with a batting average .225. (!.225 is two twenty-five と読む)

りん 鈴 a bell《鈴(チ), ベル》.
りん 燐 phosphorus《元素記号 P》.
-りん -輪 《花・車輪を数える単位語》 ▶ 花 1[2]輪 a flower [two flowers].
りんう 霖雨 a long rain in autumn [《米》the fall].
りんか 隣家 ⟨⇨隣(ミ⁺)⟩.
りんか 燐火 phosphorous light;（鬼火）a will-o'-the-wisp.
リンカーン [米国の政治家・大統領] Lincoln /líŋkn/《Abraham ~》.
りんかい 臨海 —— 臨海の 形 coastal, seaside.
- 臨海学校 a seaside (summer) school. ● 臨海工業地帯 a coastal industrial region.

りんかい 臨界 —— 臨界の 形【理学】critical.
- 臨界事故 a criticality [×a critical] accident. ● 臨界点 (reach) the critical point.

****りんかく 輪郭**【物の外形】an outline;【物事のあらまし】a rough [a general] idea. ● 計画の輪郭を述べる give a *rough idea* [an *outline*] of a project. ▶ 顔の輪郭が [鼻筋立ちが] 整っている have regular *features* [a good and strong *profile*]; be good-looking. ▶ 濃霧で塔の輪郭だけしか見えなかった Only the *outline* of the tower could be seen in the thick fog.

りんがく 林学 forestry.
- 林学者 a forester.

りんかん 輪姦 名 (a) gang rape.
—— **輪姦する** 動 gang-rape. ▶ 輪姦される be gang-raped; be raped. (!複数形で)

りんかんがっこう 林間学校 a camp(ing) [an open-air] school.

りんき 悋気 名 jealousy.
—— **悋気する** 動 be [feel] jealous 《of, that 節》.

りんぎ 稟議 • 稟議書 a round robin.
りんきおうへん 臨機応変 • 臨機応変の処置をとる take *ad hoc* measures; take measures *suited to the occasion*. ● 臨機応変に処理する handle (a matter) *on an ad hoc basis* [*flexibly, according to circumstances*]; do whatever the situation calls for. (!本は「そのときそのときの」の意)

りんぎょう 林業 forestry.
りんきん 淋菌【医学】a gonococcus.
- 淋菌性結膜炎 gonococcal conjunctivitis.

リンク ❶【くさりの輪】a link.
❷【他の文書・画像などの位置情報】【コンピュータ】a link.
- リンク集【コンピュータ】a collection of links 《about》.

リンク スケートの a (skating) rink.
リング【輪】⟨⇨輪⟩;【指輪】a ring;【ボクシングなどの】the ring.
- リングサイド the ringside;（座席）a ringside seat. ● リングネーム (ボクシングなどの) a ring name.

りんけい 鱗茎 a scaly bulb.
りんげつ 臨月 ▶ 彼女は臨月だ She *is in her last month of pregnancy.*/She is going to *have a baby this month*.

リンゲルえき リンゲル液【医学】Ringer's solution.
- リンゲル液を注射する give an injection of *Ringer's solution*.

りんけん 臨検 名 (立ち入り検査) an on-the-spot inspection, (船の) a visitation.
—— **臨検する** 動 inspect; make an on-the-spot inspection 《of》.

りんげん 綸言 Emperor's words; an Imperial message [speech, statement, etc.].
- 綸言汗のごとし Emperor's words cannot be taken back [canceled].

****りんご 林檎**【植物】(実) an apple;（木）an apple (tree). ● リンゴの皮をむく [をかじる;をむしゃむしゃ食べる] peel [bite into; munch on] an *apple*. ▶ リンゴのような赤いほお rosy [apple-red] cheeks. [語源] 米英人は健康的で愛らしい少女の赤いほおの色をバラの赤さで表す方が一般的. リンゴは必ずしも赤を連想させるものではない. cf. apple green (青リンゴの淡い緑色) ▶ リンゴ 1 日 1 個で医者いらず (ことわざ) An *apple* a day keeps the doctor away.
- リンゴ飴 a candied apple. ● リンゴ園 an apple orchard. ● リンゴジャム apple butter. ● リンゴ酒《米》hard cider [! (sweet) cider (リンゴジュースに対して),《英》cider. ● 日本のサイダー (soda pop) とは別物] ● リンゴ酢 cider vinegar.

りんこう 燐光 phosphorescence. ● 燐光を発する物質 a phosphorescent substance.
りんこう 鉱鉱 mineral phosphate.
りんこう 臨港 • 臨港線 (桟橋への引き込み線)《米》harbor railroad,《英》a harbor railway. ● 臨港列車 (船の入出港に合わせて運行する列車) a boat [×a ship] train.

りんごく 隣国 a neighboring [《書》(隣接した) an adjacent /ədʒéɪsnt/] country.
りんさく 輪作 名 crop rotation, the rotation of crops.
—— **輪作する** 動 • 作物を輪作する *rotate* crops.

りんさん 燐酸 phosphoric acid.
- 燐酸カルシウム【化学】calcium phosphate. ● 燐酸肥料 phosphates /fásfeɪts/.

りんさんぶつ 林産物 forest products.

りんじ 臨時 ── 臨時の 形 [特別の] special; [一時的な] temporary; [余分の] extra; (通常に加えての) や や書 extraordinary; [当座の] provisional. ▶今日は臨時休業します We have a *special* [an *extra*] *holiday* today. ▶[掲示] No business today. ▶台風のため多くの学校は臨時(=一時的)に休校した A number of [やや書 Many] schools were *temporarily* closed because of the typhoon.
●臨時国会 an extraordinary (session of the) Diet. ●臨時収入 extra [extraordinary] income. ●臨時昇給 a special (pay) raise [米][rise [英]]. ●臨時召集 (緊急召集) an emergency call. ●臨時政府 a provisional government. ●臨時手当 extra [special] pay. ●臨時ニュース a news flash. ●臨時便 a special flight. (⇨臨時列車) ●臨時雇い(事) temporary employment; (人) a temporary [(時間ぎめの)] a part-time, (不定期の) a casual worker; a part-timer. ●臨時予算 a provisional budget. ●臨時列車 (⇨臨時列車)

りんしたいけん 臨死体験 a near-death-experience 《略 NDE》.

りんしつ 隣室 the next room.

りんじゅう 臨終 (死の床) 《やや書》 one's deathbed; (最後の時) one's last moment. ●臨終の言葉 one's *dying* [*last*] words. ●臨終の際 一に[臨終]の one's *deathbed*. ●臨終の席に呼ばれる be called [《書》summoned] to (his) *deathbed*. ▶彼は母親の臨終に間にあった He arrived after his mother *died*. ▶ご臨終です(医者の発言) This is death.

りんしょ 臨書 ── 臨書する 動 (説明的に) (try to) write exactly like Chinese characters [*kana*] given a model calligraphy book.

りんしょう 輪唱 图 (おのおのの声部が繰り返し歌われる) a round; (こっけいな歌の内容の) a catch; (次々と後を続けて歌う) a trail.
── 輪唱する 動 troll.

りんしょう 臨床 ── 臨床の 形 clinical. ●臨床的に診断する diagnose (his illness [×*him*]) *clinically*.
●臨床医 a clinician. ●臨床医学 clinical medicine. ●臨床試験 a clinical test. ●臨床心理学 clinical psychology. ●臨床心理学者 a clinical psychologist. ●臨床心理士 a clinical psychotherapist.

りんじょうかん 臨場感 ▶このステレオは生演奏の臨場感が味わえる This stereo gives us *the feeling of being at a live performance*.

りんしょく 吝嗇 图 《書》parsimony.
── 吝嗇の 形 《書》parsimonious. ●吝嗇家である be a *parsimonious* person; be (very) *parsimonious*.

りんしるい 鱗翅類 [昆虫] a lepidopteran.

りんじれっしゃ 臨時列車 ▶海水浴客用の臨時(=特別)の列車が数本出ている They're running [There are] several *special* [(追加の) *extra*] *trains* for swimmers.

りんじん 隣人 a (next-door) neighbor; 《集合的》the (whole) neighborhood (!単・複両扱い), the neighbors (!複数扱い). ▶彼らのよき隣人となる be a good *neighbor* to them. ▶隣人を助けるべきだ We should help our ＼*neighbors*.
●隣人愛 love of one's neighbors.

リンス 图 (a) conditioner; (a) rinse.
── リンスする 動 condition (one's hair); (! rinse one's hair は「髪をすすぐ; 毛染めする」の意); treat one's hair with rinse.

りんず 綸子 ●綸子ちりめん figured satin.

りんせい 林政 forestry administration.

りんせい 輪生 (葉や花のつき方が) verticillation.
●輪生葉 verticillate leaves.

りんせき 隣席 the next seat; (隣のテーブル) the next table. ●隣席の女性 a woman at *the next table*.

りんせき 臨席 in attendance. ●市長臨席のもとに with the Mayor *in attendance*. ▶ご臨席の栄をたまわりますようお願い申し上げます 《やや書》We request the honor of your *attendance*.

りんせつ 隣接 ── 隣接する 動 ●隣接する国々 adjoining [《書》adjacent /ədʒéɪsnt/, (近隣の) neighboring] countries. ●学校に隣接した公園 a park next [*adjacent*] *to* the school. ▶私の家はその事務所に隣接している My house *adjoins* [*is adjacent to*] the office. ▶その二つの村は隣接している The two villages *adjoin*.

りんぜん 凛然 ── 凛然たる 形 [寒気が] biting cold; [威光が] imposing; commanding.

りんせんたいせい 臨戦態勢 ●臨戦態勢をとる be prepared [ready] for military action.

りんそん 隣村 the next village, a village next to 《our town》.

リンチ (a) lynching. ●リンチを受ける be beaten up; (仲間による) receive *illegal punishment by the group members*; (群衆による縛り首の) be subjected to *lynch law*, be lynched. ▶彼は態度が生意気だという口実でクラスの者たちからリンチを受けた His classmates *gave him a hard time* [×*lynched him*] on the pretext of having an impudent manner.

りんてんき 輪転機 a rotary press.

りんと 凛と ●凛とした(=威厳に満ちた)態度 a dignified [(威圧するような) an imposing, (堂々とした) a commanding] attitude. ▶シテが登場すると能舞台に凛とした空気が張りつめた As the leading actor appeared on the *Noh* stage, the atmosphere got tense.

りんどう 林道 (林の中の) a path through a forest; (材木運搬の) a forestry path.

りんどう 竜胆 [植物] a gentian /dʒénʃən/.

りんどく 輪読 ── 輪読する 動 read 《a book》in turn.
●輪読会 (サークル) a reading circle; (会合) a meeting of the reading circle.

りんね 輪廻 [宗教] (仏教で) transmigration (of the soul); metempsychosis (複 -ses /siːz/); (特にヒンズー教で) samsara.

リンネル [＜フランス語] linen /línən/.
●リンネル類 linen (goods); linens.

リンパ [＜ドイツ語] 图 [生理] lymph /límf/.
── リンパ(液)の 形 lymphatic.
●リンパ液 lymph (fluid). ●リンパ管 a lymph vessel; a lymphoduct. ●リンパ球 a lymphocyte. ●リンパ系 the lymphatic system. ●リンパ細胞 a lymph cell. ●リンパ腫 a lymphoma. ●リンパ腺 a lymph gland [(節) node]. ●高い熱のためリンパ腺をはらす develop swollen *lymph nodes* because of a high fever. ●リンパ組織 lymphatic tissue.

りんばん 輪番 ── 輪番で 副 (順に) in rotation; (次々に) by turns, in *turn*. ▶彼らは輪番で通りの見回りをした They patrolled the streets *in rotation* [*by turns*].

りんびょう 淋病 gonorrh(o)ea /ɡɑ̀nərí:ə/; 《俗》the clap.
●淋病患者 a gonorrheal patient.

りんぶ 輪舞 a round dance.

りんぷん 鱗粉 (チョウなどの) scales.

りんぺん 鱗片 a scale.

りんもう 厘毛 ― **厘毛の** 形 (きわめてわずかの) minimal; very little. ● 厘毛の利を争う compete to get *very little* profit.

りんや 林野 forests and open fields. ● 林野庁 the Forestry Agency.

りんらく 淪落 (⇨堕落)

りんり 倫理 名 (特定の集団・職業における善悪の判断基準) ethics (❗複数扱い); (社会的行動・慣習の基準) morals. (❗ethics ほど客観性を重視しない) (⇨道徳)
● 医師の倫理 medical *ethics*.
― **倫理的な, 倫理上の** 形 ethical (↔unethical).
● 倫理上の問題 an *ethical* problem; a matter of *ethics*.
― **倫理的に** 副 ethically.
● 倫理学 ethics (❗単数扱い); moral philosophy.

りんり 淋漓 ● 流汗淋漓(＝汗がしたたり落ちる) perspire profusely [heavily, freely]; be dripping with perspiration [sweat].

りんりつ 林立 ― **林立する** 動 ● 林立する煙突 *a forest of* chimneys. ▶その港はマストが林立していた The harbor *bristled with* masts.

りんりん ● (ベルなどが)りんりん鳴る ring. ● (鈴虫などが)りんりん鳴く chirp. ▶電話がりんりん鳴っている The telephone *is ringing*.

りんりん 凛々 ❶ [身にしみる様子] (⇨凛然)
❷ [勇ましい様子] ● 勇気凛々たる若者 a very *courageous* [*bold*] young man; an *intrepid* [a *bold-spirited*] young man.

りんれつ 凛冽 ― **凛冽な** 形 piercing; keen. ● 早春の凛冽な寒気 *piercing* coldness in early spring.

る

ルアー [疑似餌(ﾙｱ)] a lure.
● ルアーフィッシング lure fishing.
＊るい 類 ❶ [種類] a kind; a sort; [部類] a class; [生物学分類上の属] a genus /dʒíːnəs/ (圏 genera). (⇨種類) ● 類に分ける divide 《them》 into *classes*. ▶猫とトラは同じ類です Cats and tigers belong to the same *kind* [*genus*].
❷ [比類] ● 他に類を見ない(=並ぶものがない)偉業 an *unparalleled* achievement. ▶きのうこれに類(=似)た事件が起こった An incident *similar to* this one occurred yesterday. ▶この戦いは歴史上類をみないものだ This battle has no *parallel* in history.
● 類は友を呼ぶ(ことわざ) Birds of a feather flock together. (⚠ a は「同じ (the same)」の意)
るい 累 ● 累を及ぼす (迷惑をかける) get 《him》 into trouble; trouble; (悪影響を及ぼす) have a bad influence [effect] 《on》.
るい 塁 [野球] a base. (⇨一塁, 二塁, 三塁, 本塁) ● 塁を離れて off *base*. ● あいている塁 (作戦上埋める場合の) an open *base*; (走者がいない) an empty [an unoccupied] *base*; (野手がカバーしていない) an uncovered [an undefended] *base*. ● 二塁を回って三塁に進む round second 《base》 and move to third 《base》. ● 塁に(=一塁に)出る get to first 《base》.
● 塁打数 total bases; the total number of bases reached on hits.
るいえん 類縁 a close relation [relationship] 《between; with》. ● 類縁関係にある be closely related 《to》; be in close relation 《with》.
るいか 累加 图 ▶借入金の累加が市の財政を圧迫している The *accumulation* of debts has brought pressure to bear on the finances of the city.
— 累加的 形 cumulative 《effects of drinking》.
— 累加する 動 increase [add up] cumulatively.
るいぎご 類義語 a synonym. (⚠ 類似した意味の語句で文も含めることがある) ▶pretty は beautiful の類義語だ "Pretty" is a *synonym for* [is *synonymous* with] "beautiful."/"Pretty" and "beautiful" are *synonyms* [are *synonymous*].
るいく 類句 a similar *haiku* [*senryu*] poem; (成句) a similar phrase [expression].
るいけい 累計 (合計) the cumulative total. ● 累計で in *total*. ▶私の借金は累計で100万円になる My debts *amount* to a million yen.
るいけい 類型 图 a type; a páttern. (⇨型 ❸)
— 類型的な 形 típical 《=型にはまった》表現 a stereotyped expression. ● 近代文学の類型的な(=類型を代表する)例 a *typical* example of modern literature.
— 類型化する 動 stereotype.
るいご 類語 a synonym. (⇨類義語)
＊るいじ 類似 图 [形・性質などがよく似た] similarity; [[主に外観が] resemblance, likeness. (⚠ いずれも「類似点」の意では C])
— 類似する 動 ▶今のあなたの状況は私のと類似している Your present situation is *similar to* mine. ▶それらの間にはかなり類似したところがある There's a strong similarity [resemblance] between them.
● 類似品 an imitation.
ルイジアナ [米国の州] Louisiana /luːzíænə/ 《略 La. 郵便略 LA》.
るいしょ 類書 similar books.
るいしょう 類焼 ▶幸いにも彼の家は類焼を免れた Fortunately his house escaped the (spreading) *fire*.
るいじょう 累乗 [数学] involution.
● 累乗根 a radical root.
るいしん 累進 ● 累進課税 progressive taxation; graduated taxation. ● 累進税 progressive tax; graduated tax. ● 累進税率 the progressive (tax) rate.
るいしん 塁審 a base umpire. ● 一塁塁審 the *umpire* at first *base*; a first-base *umpire*.
るいじんえん 類人猿 an ánthropoid 《ape》.
るいすい 類推 图 analogy; analogical reasoning. ● …の類推に基づいて on the *analogy* of …; by *analogy* with ….
— 類推する 動 reason by analogy; analogize.
るいする 類する [[似よう] be similar 《to》; [[同じ程度の] be on a par 《with》. (⇨類 ❷) ▶これに類する話はほかにもある There *are similar* stories *to* this one. ▶ベートーベンには類する作曲家はいないという人もいる Some people say that Beethoven *has no equal* [*match*, *rival*] as a composer.
るいせき 累積 图 accumulation.
— 累積(の), 累積的な 形 cumulative; accumulative. ● 100万円の累積赤字 a *cumulative* deficit of one million yen. ● 累積債務を削減する reduce *accumulated* debts [*commulative* debts, debt *accumulation*].
— 累積する 動 accumulate.
● 累積投票 cumulative voting. (参考) 株主総会での取締役選任制度) ● 累積配当 a cumulative dividend.
るいせん 涙腺 [解剖] a lachrymal /lækrəml/ gland.
るいぞう 累増 图 cumulation.
— 累増する 動 cumulate; increase cumulatively.
るいだい 累代 successive generations. ● 先祖累代の墓地 a family graveyard.
るいねん 累年 successive years; (年を重ねるごとに) year after year. ▶高校の中途退学者数が累年増加している The number of high school dropouts is ever on the increase *every year*.
るいはん 累犯 a repeated offense.
● 累犯者 a repeater.
るいひ 類比 图 (a) comparison.
— 類比する 動 compare. (⇨類推)
るいへき 塁壁 a rampart.
るいべつ 類別 图 classification.
— 類別する 動 classify 《into five groups》.
るいらん 累卵 ● 累卵の危うきにある be in imminent danger; be fraught with danger.
るいるい 累々 ▶戦場は死屍(ｼｶﾊﾞﾈ)累々たる有り様であった The battlefield was covered with *heaps* of dead soldiers./*Innumerable* dead soldiers were left on the battlefield.
るいれい 類例 a similar example [(引用例) citation, (事例) case]. ● 類例のない(類似するもののない) unparalleled; (きわめて異例の) most extraordinary.

るいれき 瘰癧 〘医学〙tuberculous lymphadenitis.

ルー (a)《curry》roux /rúː/.《働 〜》.

ルーキー 《米話》a rookie.

ルージュ [<フランス語] rouge. ●ルージュを塗る (⇨紅(に))[紅をさす].

ルーズ ●ルーズな生活をする lead a *slovenly* /slʌ́vənli/ life. ●slovenly は「だらしない,無精な」より広いルーズな性格をしている have a *loose* /lúːs/ character. ▶彼は金にルーズだ He is *careless with* money. ▶彼は時間にルーズだ He is *not punctual*.
● ルーズソックス baggy socks that hang loosely.
● ルーズボール 〘サッカー〙 a loose ball.

ルーズベルト ❶〘米国の第32代大統領〙Roosevelt /róuzəvèlt/ (Franklin Delano 〜). ❷〘米国の第26代大統領〙Roosevelt (Theodore 〜).

ルーズリーフ 《ノート》a loose-leaf notebook; 《紙》《a sheet of》 loose-leaf paper. ●loose の発音は /lúːs/.

ルーツ (祖先, 始祖) roots; one's ancestors; (起源) an origin. ●自分のルーツを探る search for one's *roots*.

ルート [平方根]〘数学〙a square root. ▶ルート36 は6です The *square root* of 36 is 6.

ルート ❶[道, 路線] a route. ●観光ルート a sightseeing [a tóurist] ròute.
❷[経路] a channel. (❗しばしば複数形で単数扱い) ●公式の[秘密の; 外交]ルートを通じての情報を得る get the information through official [secret; diplomatic] *channels*.

ルーバー 〘よろい窓〙a louver.

ルービックキューブ 《商標》Rubik('s) Cube.

ループ ●ループアンテナ a loop antenna. ●ループ線〘鉄道〙a loop line. ●ループタイ (留め具付きひもタイ) a bolo [a bola] tie; 《和製語》 a loop tie.

ルーフガーデン 〘屋上庭園〙 a roof garden.

ルーブル 〘ロシアの貨幣単位〙a r(o)uble /rúːbl/《記号R, r.》.

ルーブル 〘パリの美術館〙the Louvre /lúːvrə/.

ルーペ [<ドイツ語] a loupe /lúːp/, a mágnifying glàss. (❗後の方が普通)

ルーベンス 〘フランドルの画家〙Rubens /rúːbənz/ (Peter Paul 〜).

ルーマニア 〘国名〙Romania /ruːméiniə/ (❗公式名も同じ) (首都 Bucharest). ●ルーマニア人 a Romanian. ●ルーマニア語 Romanian. ●ルーマニア(人[語])の Romanian.

ルーム 〘部屋〙 a room.
● ルームクーラー an air conditioner; 《和製語》 a room cooler. ●ルームサービス (⇨ルームサービス) ●ルームチャージ a róom ràte. ●ルームメイト a roommate. ●ルームライト (室内灯) a róom lìght. ●(自動車の) an interior light (of a car).

ルームサービス 《call》 room service. ▶このホテルにはルームサービスがない This hotel has [provides] no *room service*.

* **ルール** a rule. (❗しばしば複数形で)(⇨規則) ●野球のルール the *rules* of baseball. ▶ルールは知っていなければならない守らなければならない You must know the *rules* and (must) abide by them.
● ルールブック a rulebook.

ルーレット [<フランス語] (とばく) 《play》 roulette; (用具) a roulette (wheel).

ルクス a lux /lúks, lʌ́ks/ (働 〜, 〜es, luces /lúːsiːz/) (略 lx).

ルクセンブルク 〘国名〙Luxembourg /lʌ́ksəmbəːrɡ/; (公式名) the Grand Duchy of Luxembourg. (首都 Luxembourg). ●ルクセンブルク人 a Luxembourger. ●ルクセンブルク語 Luxembourg. ●ルクセンブルク(人[語])の Luxembourg.

るけい 流刑 exile /éɡzail, éksail/. ●流刑に処する exile; send 《him》 into *exile*. ●その島に流刑になる be exiled to the island.

ルゴールえき ルゴール液 〘薬剤〙Lugol's solution.

るざい 流罪 (⇨流刑)

* **るす** 留守 (an) absence. (❗留守の期間・回数を表すときは 〖C〗) ●留守である[にする] (家にいない) be not (at) home (❗at を省略するのは《米》); be not in; (外出している) be out; (休暇で家を離れている) be away; (どこかへ行って) be gone. (⇨不在, 外出) ●留守(=居留守)を使う pretend to be out; pretend not to be in. ▶彼が訪ねてくれたとき私は留守にしていた I was *not at home* [*not in*, *out*] when he came to see me. (❗約束しておきながら留守にした以外は XI was absent when …. とはいわない) ▶兄は東京に[旅行]に出かけて1週間留守にしている My brother *is away* in Tokyo [on a trip] for a week. ▶彼女は買い物に出かけて留守だった She *was out* shopping. ▶私は彼に留守番を(=留守中の家の世話を)頼んだ I asked him to look after my house while I *was out* [while I *was away*, 《書》during my *absence*]. ▶山田さんの留守宅が(=留守の間に)何者かに荒らされた Someone robbed [broke into] Mr. Yamada's house *while* they were *away*.
● お留守になる ▶彼はサッカーに熱中して勉強がすっかりお留守に(=なおざりに)なった He was so absorbed in soccer that he totally *neglected* his studies.
● 留守電 〘「留守番電話」の略〙(⇨留守番電話)

るすばんでんわ 留守番電話 《主に米》an ánswering machine; 《主に英》an answerphone. (関連) 「(トマス)ブラウンですがただ今留守です。…」は "Hello, this is (Thomas) Brown. I'm sorry I'm not at home now."/"Hi, this is (T.) Brown. I can't come to the phone just now." などという) ●留守番電話をセットする put the *answering machine* on. ▶彼は留守番電話に吹き込まれた用件(=来信)に返事をしためしがない He never returned the calls monitored on his *answering machine*.

ルソン ●ルソン島 Luzon /luːzɑ́n/.

ルチン 〘薬剤〙 rutin /rúːtin/

ルックス 〘容貌(ぼう)〙(顔立ち, 外見) looks; (顔立ち) features. ●ルックスがいい have good *looks*; be good-looking.

ルックス 〘照度の単位〙a lux. (⇨ルクス)

ルッツ 〘フィギュアスケート〙 a lutz. ●トリプルルッツ a triple *lutz*.

るつぼ 坩堝 a crucible; (人種などの) a melting pot (❗各人種は固有の文化をも捨てて融合する); 《米》a salad bowl (❗各人種は融合するが固有の文化は失わない); a kaleidoscope /kəláidəskòup/ (of people [ethnic groups]) (❗各人種が混じり合って万華(げ)鏡のような状態になっている). ●人種のるつぼ a *melting pot* of races. ▶彼らサヨナラホームランを打つと球場は興奮のるつぼと化した(=興奮して手がつけられない状態になった) The crowd *went wild with excitement* when he slugged a game-ending home run.

るてん 流転 图 〘絶えず移り変わること〙 continuous [constant] change; flux; 〘人生などの浮沈〙《書》 vicissitudes. ●運命の流転 the *vicissitudes* of fate [fortune].
—— 転する 動 ▶万物は流転する Everything *is continually changing.*/All things are in a state of *flux*.

るにん 流人 an exile /éɡzail/

ルネサンス the Renaissance /rènəsɑ́ːns/. ●ルネサンスの芸術[画家] *Renaissance* art [painters].

ルノアール 〘フランスの画家〙Renoir /rənwɑ́ːr/ (Pierre

Auguste ~).

ルビ ●ルビを振る give [print] *kana* alongside *kanji* [Chinese characters] (to show the letters' readings).

ルピア 〘インドネシアの貨幣単位〙a rupiah /ruːpíːə/.

ルビー a ruby. ●ルビー色の ruby. ●ルビーの指輪 a *ruby* ring.

ルピー 〘インド・パキスタンなどの貨幣単位〙a rupee 《略 R, Re》.

ルビコン ●ルビコン川 the Rubicon.
●ルビコン(川)を渡る (重大な決断をする) cross the Rubicon.

ルピナス 〘植物〙a lupin(e).

るふ 流布 图 circulation.
── **流布する** 動 ●うわさを流布させる *circulate* [*spread*] a rumor.
●流布本 a popular edition (of a book).

ルポ 〘「ルポルタージュ」の略〙(⇨ルポルタージュ)

ルポライター a reporter.

ルポルタージュ [＜フランス語] (報道, 報告) a report (*on*); (現地報告) reportage /ripɔ́ːrtidʒ/; (記録もの) a documentary.

ルミノール ●ルミノール反応 a luminol reaction.

るみん 流民 (難民) refugees; (流浪の民) (⇨流浪)

るり 瑠璃 lápis lázuli. ●るり色 lapis lazuli. (**!** 今では ultramarine (群青(ぐんじょう)色)で同じ色を表す)

るりびたき 瑠璃鶲 〘鳥〙a Siberian bluechat; a red-flanked bluetail.

るる 縷々 ●縷々(=詳しく)説明する explain ... *in detail*; dwell on .... 縷々と(=長々と)語る speak *at* (*great*) *length* 《*about*》.

るろう 流浪 (⇨放浪) ●流浪の民 wanderers; wandering tribes [people].

ルワンダ 〘国名〙Rwanda; (公式名) the Republic of Rwanda. (首都 Kigali) ●ルワンダ人 a Rwandan.
●ルワンダ(人)の Rwandan.

ルンバ [＜スペイン語] 〘音楽〙a rumba /rʌ́mbə/. ●ルンバを踊る dance the rumba.

ルンペン [＜ドイツ語] (浮浪者) 《米》a hobo /hóubou/, 《英》a tramp.

るんるん ●るんるんしている be in a (very) happy mood; (舞い上がるような気持ちで) be in a buoyant /bɔ́iənt/ mood; be on top of the world; (自然と足がはずむ気持ちで) 《話》walk on air. ▶今日で学校が終わると思うと彼女はるんるんするのでした When she thought today was the last day of school, she *was walking on air*.

れ

レア [ステーキなどの生焼けの] rare. (⇒ステーキ)
- レアチーズケーキ a gelatin [an unbaked] cheesecake. ● レアメタル [希少金属] (a) rare metal.

＊れい 礼 ❶ [感謝] (言葉) thanks; (気持ち) gratitude.
- 礼を言う thank. (⇒感謝, ありがとう, お礼) ● お礼の手紙 a letter of *thanks*; a *thank-you* [a *grateful*] letter. (⇒礼状) ● 心から礼を述べる express one's sincere [cordial] *thanks* 《*to* him *for* his help》. ● 礼の気持ちを表す show one's *gratitude* 《*for* his help》. ● 礼を言って贈り物を受け取る accept the present *with thanks*. ▶ 彼女にくれぐれもお礼を言っておいてください Please give my best *thanks* to her. ▶ 彼女は私の親切に対して礼を言った He *thanked* me *for* my kindness. (!xHe thanked my kindness. としない) ▶ お礼の申し上げようもありません I can't *thank* you enough. (!(1) enough の代わりに too much はあまり用いない. (2) Can I éver *thánk* you ＼*enough*! の方が強意的)/I don't know how to *thank* you./Hów can I ＼*thank* you enough? How cán...? の方が強意的) ▶ 和也にお礼の電話をした I phoned Kazuya to *thank* him. ▶ ご親切に対し深くお礼申し上げます I wish to express my deep *gratitude to* you *for* your kindness./I am deeply *grateful to* you *for* your kindness./*Thank* you very much *for* your kindness. (!最後はややくだけた言い方) ▶ お礼を申し上げなければならないことがたくさんあります I have so much to *thank* you *for*.
❷ [返礼] (a) return; [報酬] (a) reward; [医師や弁護士に対する謝礼] a fee. ● 彼の好意に対して相応の礼をする make a proper *return for* his favors.
- 彼の援助に礼をする *reward* [*repay*] (him *for*) his help. (⇒報いる) ● 彼の骨折りに対する礼に金を送った I sent him some money *in return* [*reward*] *for* his labor. ▶ 財布を拾ってくれた礼に彼に 1 万円渡した I offered [gave] him a *reward* of 10,000 yen *for* finding my wallet./I *rewarded* him *with* 10,000 yen *for* finding my wallet.
❸ [礼儀] (礼儀正しい言動) courtesy /kə́ːrtəsi/; (行動面で守るべき決まり) étiquette. (⇒礼儀, 失礼) ● 礼にかなった (=礼儀正しい) あいさつ a *polite* greeting.
- 礼を尽くして客を待遇する treat the guest *with* the utmost *courtesy* [most *courteously*]. ● 目上の人への礼をわきまえている know how to *behave respectfully* toward one's seniors; be *respectful* toward [*to*] one's seniors.
❹ [お辞儀] a bow /báu/. ● 先生に軽く礼をする *bow* slightly [*make* a slight *bow*] to the teacher.

＊れい 例 ❶ [実例] (代表的な実例) an example; (個別的な証拠) an instance, (証明・説明のための) an illustration; [事例] a case. ● 具体的 [典型的] な例をあげて説明する explain (it) by (giving) *examples*; illustrate (it). ● 例をあげて give ... as an *example* [by way of (×an) *illustration*]; take ... for *instance*. ▶ これはほんの 1 例にすぎない This is only one *example*. ▶ 彼がした仕事の例を 2-3 あげてみよう I'll give a few *examples* [*instances*] of his work. ▶ これは「早起きは三文の得」という例だ This is an *instance* in which [×that] "The early bird catches the worm." (!instance は同格の that 節を従えない) ▶ 彼は自らのヨーロッパでの生活の例を引いた He took *illustrations* from his own life in Europe. ▶ 同様の例をご存じですか Do you know any similar *cases*?
❷ [慣例] (個人的な習慣) a habit; (社会的な習慣) a custom (!後者は個人的な固定した習慣の意でも用いる). ▶ 彼は夏休みは海辺で過ごすのが例になっている He has the *habit* [*custom*] of spending his summer vacation by [at] the seaside. (!日常会話では He *usually* spends his summer vacation by [at] the seaside. の方が普通) ▶ 例の道を通って学校へ行くのですか Are you going to school by the *usual* route?
❸ [先例] (a) precedent. ▶ そんなストライキは例がない There is no *precedent* for such a strike./Such a strike is unprecedented [quite without *precedent*].
❹ [その他の表現] ● 人の例 (=模範) にならう follow 《*his*》 *example*. ▶ 例の (=当該の) 問題は来週までそのままにしておいてよい The matter *in question* can be left till next week. ▶ 昨日電話してきた例のジョージという人から電話です The George that called yesterday wants you on the phone. ▶ 美津子の例の (=あの) 作り笑いにはうんざりしているところだ We are tired of *that* forced smile of Mitsuko's [×Mitsuko's *that* forced smile]. (!この that にははしばしば軽蔑などの感情がこもる)
- 例になく ▶ 彼女は近ごろ例になく (=いつになく) 明るい She is *unusually* cheerful these days.
- 例によって ▶ 例によって (=いつもそうであるように) 彼は 1 時間遅れてやって来た He arrived, as *usual* [as is *usual with* him], an hour late. (!as 句[節]は文頭・文尾に置いてもよい) ▶ 彼らは例によって (=いつもの) 悪天候に悩まされた They had the *usual* trouble with bad weather.

れい 零 (a) zero /zíərou/; (梵) ~(e)s; 《英》 (a) nought. (⇒ゼロ) ● 0.2 zero [nought] point two.
- 0.025 point *zero* [*nought*] two five.

れい 霊 the spirit; [霊魂] the soul. (!soul の方が spirit より宗教的色彩が濃い) ● 聖霊 the Holy Spirit. ● 先祖の霊 the *souls* of the departed ancestors. ▶ 彼女は故人の霊に花を捧げた She offered flowers to the departed *spirit* [*soul*]. ▶ 彼の霊が安らかでありますように May his *spirit* rest in peace. ▶ あらゆるものに霊がある There is a *spirit* in everything.

レイ [首にかける花輪] a lei. ● 彼の首にレイをかける put on a *lei* around his neck.

レイアウト [レイアウト] a layout. ● 具体的には C ● 新聞のレイアウトをする *lay out* [do the *layout* of] the newspaper. ● レイアウトがよい be *laid out* beautifully.

れいあんしつ 霊安室 a mortuary.

れいあんしょ 冷暗所 a cool place not exposed to direct sunlight. ● 冷暗所 = 直射日光を避けた冷たい場所) に貯蔵してください Keep [Store] this in a *cool*(, *sunless*) *place*, avoiding direct sunlight.

れいい 霊位 ❶ [死者の魂] a dead person's soul; the soul of the dead. ❷ [位牌(いはい)] a Buddhist memorial tablet. (⇒位牌)

れいいき 霊域 a sacred [a holy] place.

れいう 冷雨 a cold rain.

れいえん 霊園 (共同墓地) a cemetery.

レイオフ 图 〖一時解雇〗 a layoff; 《米》 a furlough /fɔːrlou/. ▶彼はレイオフ中で再雇用されるのを待っている He is awaiting recall from a *layoff*.
—**レイオフ(に)する** 動 lay 《him》 off. ▶従業員の半数を1か月のレイオフにした We *laid off* half our work force for one month.

れいおん 低温 (低温) a low temperature. ●低温で貯蔵されている be preserved at a *low temperature*; be in *cold* storage.

れいか 冷夏 a cool summer.

れいか 冷菓 (シャーベット・アイスクリームなどの氷菓) frozen desserts [《英》sweets]; (バニラなどの冷やして食べる菓子) chilled desserts [《英》sweets].

れいか 零下 ▶温度は零下10度に下がった The temperature fell [dropped] to ten degrees *below zero* [*below the freezing point*].

れいかい 例会 ●例会を開く hold a *regular meeting*. ●月例会 a monthly meeting.

れいかい 例解 —**例解する** 動 explain 《the meanings of a word》by (using) examples.

れいかい 霊界 (精神界) the spirit world; (死者の霊の住むところ) the world of the departed.

*****れいがい** 例外 an exception. ●例外とする[を認める] make an *exception* 《of》. ▶この規則には一つの例外があります There is an [one] *exception to* [×of] this rule. ▶例外のない規則はない Every rule has some *exception*./There is no rule but has some *exception*. (❗(1) but は関係代名詞. ... that does not have some exception と言い換えて可. (2) some は「何らか」の意) ▶彼らは皆例外なく罰せられるだろう They will all be punished without 《an》 *exception*. ▶私たちは毎朝早く起きるが, 日曜日は例外だ We get up early every morning, but Sunday is an *exception*./(日曜日を除いて毎朝早く起きる) We get up early every morning *except* on Sunday. ▶全員9時までに寮に戻ってください. 例外は認められません All be back to the dorm by nine o'clock. No *exceptions*. (❗掲示や放送でよく用いられる) ▶別にあなただけが例外なのではありません You're not *uncommon*.

れいがい 冷害 damage to crops from [by] cold weather. ▶北海道の冷害は深刻だ The crops in Hokkaido have suffered serious *damage from* [*have* seriously *been damaged by*] *cold weather*.

れいかん 冷汗 (a cold) sweat. (⇨冷や汗) ●冷汗三斗(と)の思い (非常に恥ずかしい思いをする) feel extremely ashamed of oneself.

れいかん 冷寒 ●冷寒の very [freezing] cold.

れいかん 冷感 ●冷感症 (不感症) frigidity.

れいかん 霊感 (an) inspiration. ●霊感が(とても)強いbe (very [highly]) sensitive to the spirit world. ▶自然から霊感を受けている詩人は多い A lot of poets have drawn their *inspiration from* [*have been inspired by*] nature.

れいき 冷気 〖寒さ〗 cold; 〖冷たさ〗 chill. ●朝の冷気を感じる feel the morning *chill* [*chilly morning air*].

れいき 例規 ●例規に従う follow the *precedent*. ●例規集 a book of precedents.

れいき 霊気 something mysterious; supernatural power; (超自然的な雰囲気) transcendental atmosphere. ●山の霊気を感じる feel the existence of *something mysterious* in the mountains.

*****れいぎ** 礼儀 〖丁重な言動〗 courtesy /kɚːrtəsi/; 〖礼儀作法〗 manners (❗複数扱いが普通だが単数扱いも可) (⇨礼儀); 〖行動面の正しいルール〗 etiquette. ●礼儀正しい (礼儀作法をわきまえた) polite; (丁寧な) courteous /kɚːrtəs/; (行儀のよい) well-mannered; (失礼にならない程度に) civil. ▶彼は私たちに対して礼儀正しい He is *polite* (*courteous*) *to* us. ▶彼は礼儀知らずだ He has [×knows] no *manners*./He is *rude* [*impolite, ill-mannered*]. (⇨失礼, 行儀) ▶スープを音を立てて飲むのは礼儀 (作法) にかなっていない It's *bad* (↔*good*) *manners* to slurp your soup./Slurping your soup is *against* (the rules of) *etiquette*. ▶間違い電話をしたときは謝るのが礼儀だ When you dial the wrong number, it's common *courtesy* [a matter of *etiquette*] to apologize. ▶親しき中にも礼儀あり (ことわざ) *Courtesy* should exist even among close friends./*Politeness* is not just for strangers.

れいきゃく 冷却 cooling; refrigeration. ●冷却期間をおいて after a *cooling-off* period.
—**冷却する** 動 cool; refrigerate. (⇨冷やす)
●冷却装置 a cóoling device.

れいきゅうしゃ 霊柩車 a hearse, a funeral car.

れいきん 礼金 (アパートなどの)《話》key money. (⇨謝礼)

れいぐう 礼遇 —**礼遇する** 動 give 《him》 a courteous reception; (敬意をもって扱う) treat 《him》 with respect.

れいぐう 冷遇 图 cold treatment.
—**冷遇する** 動 ▶彼を冷遇する *give* him *cold treatment*; *treat* him *coldly*. ▶その客は冷遇された(=冷ややかな応対を受けた) The guest *received* [*met with*] *a cold reception*.

れいけつ 冷血 ●冷血漢 a cold-blooded [a coldhearted, a heartless] fellow. ▶さらに冷酷さを強調するときは a cold-blooded beast) ●冷血動物 a cold-blooded animal.

れいげつ 例月 ●例月のように like other months; as usual. (⇨月例, 月々)

れいげん 冷厳 —**冷厳な** 形 ❶〖冷静かつ厳格な〗 very stern; imperturbable. ●冷厳な態度 an *imperturbable* attitude.
❷〖重大で厳しい〗 severe; extremely serious; (厳然たる) grim (-mm-). ●母の死という冷厳な事実 a *grim* fact that 《one's》 mother is dead.

れいげん 例言 (⇨❾ 凡例(はん))

れいげん 霊験 ●霊験あらたか▶霊験あらたかである be responsive to one's prayers; work [do] wonders. ●霊験あらたかな水 *wonder-working* water.

れいこう 励行 —**励行する** 動 ▶早起きを励行する(=習慣とする) practice early rising; make a *practice of* getting up early (❗前の方が強い言い方); (必ずするよう努力する) *make a point of* rising early ●校則を励行する(=厳守する) *observe* school rules *strictly*.

れいこく 冷酷 图 cold-bloodedness.
—**冷酷な** 形 (血も涙もない) cold-blooded; (冷淡な) cold-hearted; (無情な) heartless; (残酷な) cruel.
●冷酷な殺し屋 a *cold-blooded* [a *heartless*, a *cruel*] killer.

れいこく 例刻 ●例刻に at the *usual time* [*hour*].

れいこん 霊魂 ▶霊魂は不滅だ The soul [spirit] is immortal [never dies]. ▶死ぬと霊魂は体から離れるのだろうか Does the *soul depart* [*leave*] the body at death? (❗このような場面での文体では depart の方が適切)

れいさい 例祭 (毎年の) an annual [(毎月の) a monthly, (定例の) a regular] festival. ●明治神宮の秋の例祭 the *autumn festival* of the Meiji Shrine.

れいさい 零細 ● 零細企業 a small business. ● 零細農家 (小規模農家) a small-scale farmer.

れいさい 零歳 ● 零歳児 a baby less than [under] twelve months. (**事情**) 米英では乳幼児の年齢は月齢でいうのが普通。

れいざん 霊山 a sacred mountain (with a temple shrine).

れいし 荔枝 (⇒⑩ ライチー)

れいし 霊視 ── 霊視する 動 see《what ordinary people cannot see》with extrasensory perception (略 ESP); have extrasensory perception to see《what nobody else can see》.

れいじ 例示 图 an example; (図をともなったもの) an illustration. (⇒例)
── 例示する 動 give an example [an illustration] 《of》; exemplify; illustrate (by giving an example).

れいじ 零時 ● 午前 0 時に at *midnight* [12:00 p.m.]. ● 午後 0 時に at noon [12:00 a.m.]. ● 0 時 50 分に at 50 after《米》[past《英》] *noon* [*midnight*]. ● 0 時 1 秒に新しい日が始まる A new day begins at one second after *midnight*.

れいしき 礼式 (social) etiquette; (good) manners. ● 礼式にかなっている conform to *etiquette*.

れいしつ 令室 (⇒⑩ 令夫人)

れいしゅ 冷酒 *sake* to be served chilled; (ひや酒) cold *sake*.

れいじゅう 霊獣 a lucky beast with superhuman abilities.

れいしょ 令書 official [administrative] papers.

れいしょ 隷書 (説明的に) a simplified form of ancient Chinese seal characters similar to the modern print style.

れいしょう 冷笑 图 a sneer. (⇒笑い)
── 冷笑する 動 sneer《*at*》. (⇒笑い ❷)

れいしょう 例証 (絵・実例などによる説明) (an) illustration (**!** 具体的な例は Ⓒ); (実例) an example. ● 例証として by way of 《×an》 *illustration*; as an *example*.
── 例証する 動 illustrate; exemplify. ● 要点を例証する *illustrate* the point.

れいじょう 令状 a warrant /wɔ́ːrənt/, a writ. ● 捜査令状を執行する execute a search *warrant*《for+場所》. ● 彼に逮捕令状を出す issue a *warrant* for his arrest.

れいじょう 令嬢 《his》daughter. ● ご令嬢 your *daughter*. ● 中田氏令嬢 Mr. Nakata's *daughter*; *Miss* Nakata.

れいじょう 礼状 a letter of thanks; a thank-you letter [(短い) note, (はがき) card]; (もてなしに対する) a bread-and-butter letter. ● 彼に礼状を書く[送る] write [send] a *thank-you letter* to him.

れいじょう 霊場 a sacred place; holy precincts. (⇒霊域) ● 霊場巡りをする go on [make] a pilgrimage (*to* the temples in Shikoku).

れいしょく 令色 ● 巧言(ミミ)令色鮮(ミ)なし仁(シ) (⇒巧言[成句])

れいしょく 冷色 (⇒⑩ 寒色)

れいじん 麗人 a beautiful woman (🐸 ～ women).

れいすい 冷水 cold water. ● 冷水を浴びせる throw [pour] *cold water* on [over]…. ● 冷水域 a cold water mass.

れいすい 霊水 (神聖な水) holy [sacred] water; (霊験のある水) wonder-working water; water with magic power 《*for* longevity, *for* the cure of cancer》.

れいすいまさつ 冷水摩擦 ● 冷水摩擦をする rub oneself [have a rubdown] with a cold wet towel.

れいすいよく 冷水浴 ● 冷水浴をする take《米》[have《英》] a cold bath; bathe /béið/《米》[bath《英》] in cold water.

***れいせい 冷静** 图 (平静) calmness; (沈着) (やや書) composure. ● 彼女は危機に直面しても冷静さを失わなかった She didn't lose (↔keep) her *composure* [her *presence of mind*, her *head*] in the face of danger./(冷静だった) She *kept calm* [*kept her wits about* her] in the face of danger./(うろたえなかった) She did*n't panic* even when she faced danger.
── 冷静な 形 calm; (落ち着いた) cool, cool-headed. ● 冷静な判断を下す make a *cool* [a *cool-headed*] judgment《on》. ● 冷静な態度で危機に対処した I met the crisis with a *calm* attitude.
── 冷静に 副 calmly. ● 彼は危機に際しても冷静に行動した He acted *calmly* in a crisis. ● 少し冷静になれ Calm down a (little) bit./Cool down [*off*] a bit.

れいせい 冷製 ● カモ肉の冷製 *chilled* duck meat.

れいせつ 礼節 manners. (⇒礼儀) ● 衣食足りて礼節を知る《ことわざ》Well fed, well bred.

れいせん 冷泉 a cold mineral spring.

れいせん 冷戦 a cold war (↔a hot war).

れいせん 霊泉 wonder-working spring water.

れいぜん 冷然 ● 冷然たる態度 a *cold* [(冷酷な) a *cold-blooded*, (一片の同情もない) an *unsympathetic*] attitude. ● 倒れている人を冷然と見る watch a person lying on the ground *coldly* [*with unfeeling coldness*].

れいぜん 霊前 (仏前) before the memorial tablet of the deceased. ● 父の霊前に果物を供える offer fruit [*fruits*] *before the tablet of* one's dead father.

れいそう 礼装 [礼服] a ceremonial dress; [正装] full [formal] dress. (⇒正装) ● 礼装用の靴 *dress* shoes.

れいぞう 冷蔵 图 [食物・薬品などの] cold storage. ● 要冷蔵 (標示) Keep *refrigerated*.
── 冷蔵する 動 ● 魚を冷蔵する *keep* fish *in cold storage*; *refrigerate* fish.
● 冷蔵庫 a refrigerator, 《話》a fridge. ● 冷蔵室 a cold room. ● 冷蔵倉庫 a cold store.

れいそく 令息 《his》son. ● ご令息 your *son*. ● 羽田氏令息 Mr. Hada's *son*; Hada junior.

れいぞく 隷属 图 (従属) subordination.
── 隷属する 動 ● ギリシャ人は当時ローマ人に隷属していた《やや書》Greeks *were* subordinate [*subject*] *to* Romans at that time.

れいだい 例題 an exercise. ● 例題 5 を解く do *exercise* 5.

れいたいさい 例大祭 an annual grand festival.

***れいたん 冷淡** 图 coldness; [冷ややかさ] coolness; [冷たい心] cold-heartedness; [無関心さ] indifference.
── 冷淡な 形 cold; cool; cold-hearted; indifferent. ● 冷淡な役人 a *cold-hearted* public official. ● 彼は他人の苦しみに冷淡だ He is *indifferent to* the sufferings of other people.
── 冷淡に ● 彼女はその子を冷淡にあしらった She *treated* the boy *coldly*./She *was cold to* [*toward*] the boy./(話) She *gave* the boy *the cold shoulder*.

れいだんぼう 冷暖房 air-conditioning (and heating). ● 冷暖房の付いた部屋 a room with *air-conditioning*.
● 冷暖房装置 an air conditioner.

れいち 霊地 a sacred [a holy] place.

れいちゃ 冷茶 cold tea; tea brewed in cold water.
れいちょう 霊長 ▶人間は万物の霊長(=支配者)である A human being is the *lord* of creation. ●霊長類 the primates.
れいちょう 霊鳥 (神聖な鳥) a sacred [holy] bird.
れいてき 霊的 ― 霊的な 圈 spiritual. ●霊的な(=神聖で清らかな)美しさ *sanctified* beauty. ●霊的交感(テレパシー) telépathy. ●霊的存在 spiritual beings.
レイテせんき 『レイテ戦記』 *Chronicles of the Battle of Leyte*. (参考) 大岡昇平の小説)
れいてつ 冷徹 ― 冷徹な 圈 (冷静な) cool-headed; (現実的な) realistic; (情に動かされない)《話》 hard-boiled.
れいてん 零点 ▶試験で零点を取った I got *zero* [*no points*,《英》*nought*,《米話》*a goose egg*] in the exam. ▶彼は父親として零点だ(=落第だ) He is a *failure* as a father.
れいど 零度 zero; (氷点) the frèezing pòint. ▶気温が零度以下に下がった It [The temperature] fell below *zero*.
れいとう 冷凍 图 freezing;(食料品の) refrigeration. ●急速冷凍 deep-*freeze*.
― 冷凍する 動 freeze*. ●魚を急速に冷凍する *freeze* [*refrigerate*] fish quickly. ●肉をかちかちに冷凍しておく *keep* meat *frozen* hard. ●肉を冷凍輸送する transport meat *frozen*.
●冷凍機 a frèezing machíne; a refrigerator. ●冷凍庫 a freezer. ●冷凍肉 *frozen meat*; refrigerated meat. ●冷凍冷蔵庫 a refrigerator-freezer.
れいとうほぞん 冷凍保存 ― 冷凍保存する 動 freeze (meat).
れいねつ 冷熱 air conditioning; (冷房と暖房) cooling and heating.
れいねん 例年 ▶例年(=年1回)の催し an *annual event*. (⇒毎年(蒜))) ▶例年このころは天気がいい It's *usually* clear about this time of (the) year. ▶祭りは例年どおり行われた We had [held] the festival *as in other years* [(いつものように) *as usual*]. ▶彼は例年のように息子をキャンプに連れて行った He took his boy camping *as he did each year*. ▶今年の冬は例年になく(=異常に)寒い It is *unusually cold* [(いつもより) *colder than usual*] this winter. ▶今年の収穫高は例年並みだ[例年以上]だ The crops this year are *about the average* [*above average*]./This year we've had *average* crops [*bigger crops than in the average year*].
れいの 例の 〖いつもの〗usual;〖あの〗that;〖問題の〗in question. (⇒例)
れいのうし 霊能師 a (psychic) medium.
れいぞく 冷属 ― (an) indignity.
― 冷属する 動 treat《him》with indignity; scoff《at》.
れいはい 礼拝;〖教会の〗a (church) service. ●早朝礼拝 an early morning *service*. ●礼拝に出る attend *worship* [*a church service*]; (教会へ行く) go to *church* (〖この教会が目的なので church は無冠詞〗. ▶この教会では毎日3回礼拝する This church has three *services* every day.
― 礼拝する 動 worship.
●礼拝所 a place [a house] for [of] worship.
●礼拝堂 a chapel.
れいはい 零敗 ▶我がチームは零敗した Our team was shut out [〖スポーツ〗was whitewashed].
れいばい 霊媒 a medium (複) 〜s).(! 複数形を ×media としない)
れいひつ 麗筆 a beautiful [an artistic] stroke of the brush.
●麗筆をふるう write [paint] beautifully [artistically]; (字を) write a good hand.
れいひょう 冷評 图 unkind [unsympathetic] criticism. (⇒批評)
― 冷評する 動 make unkind comments 《on》.
れいびょう 霊廟 a mausoleum /mɔːˈsəliəm/ (複 〜s, -lea).
レイプ 图 (a) rape. ― レイプする 動 rape.
れいふく 礼服 full [formal] dress.
れいふじん 令夫人 ▶山田一郎様, 令夫人様 (招待状などで) Mr. and Mrs. Ichiro Yamada (! 格式ばった書き方) ●木村氏ご夫人 Mrs. Kimura.
れいぶん 例文 an example (sentence);(説明用の) an illustrative sentence, an illustration. ●例文を挙げる give an *example* sentence.
れいほう 礼法 ▶礼法にかなう conform to the *rules of etiquette*.
れいほう 礼砲 a salute. ●21発の礼砲を放つ fire [give] a 21-gun *salute*. (参考) 国家元首に対する礼砲数)
れいほう 霊峰 a sacred mountain. ●霊峰富士 *Sacred* Mt. Fuji.
れいぼう 冷房 air conditioning. ▶この部屋は冷房がきき過ぎている The *air conditioning* in this room is too strong (←weak, low). ▶この建物には冷房がある This building *has* [*is equipped with*] *an air conditioner*./This building *is air-conditioned*. (! 最後の例文は「冷房されている」の意にもなる)
●冷房車 an air-conditioned car. ●冷房装置 an air conditioner; an air conditioning system; a cooling system. ●冷房病 air conditioning sickness.
れいぼく 霊木 a sacred tree.
れいみょう 霊妙 ― 霊妙な 圈 (不可思議な) miraculous; (この世のものとは思えない) heavenly; supernatural.
れいめい 令名 ●令名が高い be famous 《as》; be held in high repute. ●彼女はモーツァルト弾きとして国際的に令名をはせている She *is* world-*famous* [*internationally held in high repute*] as a Mozart player.
れいめい 黎明 dawn. ●新しい日本の黎明 the *dawn* of a new era of Japan.
れいやく 霊薬 a wonder [a miracle] drug.
れいよう 羚羊 〖動物〗an antelope.
れいよう 麗容 a beautiful shape. ●富士の麗容 the *beautiful shape* of Mt. Fuji.
れいらく 零落 ― 零落する 動 (没落する) go [come, be brought] to ruin; go [come] down in the world. (⇒落ちぶれる)
れいり 怜悧 ― 怜悧な 圈 (聡明な) clever;(判断のよい) wise. ●怜悧そうな顔立ちをしている have a *clever-looking* face; have a *wise-looking* face.
れいりょう 冷涼 ― 冷涼な 圈 cool; (すがすがしい) refreshing; bracing; (ひんやりとする) chilly.
れいれいしい 麗々しい 圈 (これ見よがしの) showy; ostentatious. ― 麗々しく 副 showily; ostentatiously.
れいれいと 麗々と (⇒麗々しい)
れいろう 玲瓏 ●玲瓏たる月夜 a *clear and bright* moon. ●玲瓏たる声 a *clear and beautiful*《singing》voice.
レイン 〖雨〗(a) rain. (⇒雨)
レインコート a raincoat. ●レインコートを着る[着ている] put on [wear] a *raincoat*.
レインシューズ 《a pair of》ráin bòots;《和製語》rain shoes.

レインボー 〖虹〗a rainbow.
レーク 〖湖〗a lake.
・レークサイド 〖湖畔〗the lakeside.
レーサー 〖レース出場選手〗a racer; 〖自動車レースの〗a rácing driver.
レーザー a laser.
・レーザー光線 láser bèams. ・レーザー手術 laser surgery. ・レーザーディスク a láser dìsk 《略 LD》.
・レーザープリンター a láser printer. ・レーザーメス a laser knife.
レーシングカー a rácing càr,《米》a ráce càr.
レース 〖レース編み〗lace, lacework. ・レースのカーテン a lace curtain. ・レースをつける trim (a dress) with lace. ・レースの(縁飾りの)ついたテーブルクロス a lace-trimmed tablecloth.
・レース編み機 a lace frame. ・レース糸 cotton thread.
レース 〖競走〗a race.(⇨競走) ペナントレース a pennant race. ・ボートレース a boat race. ・レースに勝つ [負ける] win [lose] a race.
・レースクイーン 'a race queen'; (説明的に) a type of campaign girl found as part of a pit crew in certain kinds of motor racing.
レーズン 〖干しブドウ〗a raisin.
レーダー radar. ▶レーダーに何か映っている There's [I see] something on the radar screen.
レート 〖率〗a rate. ・為替レート the exchánge ràte; the rate of exchange. ・公定レート the official rate. ▶きのうの銀行へ行ったけど、交換レートはこのホテルよりずっとよかった Yesterday I went to the bank. You get a much better rate there than you do in this hotel.
レーニン 〖ロシアの革命家・政治家〗Lenin /lénin/ (Vladimir Ilyich 〜).
レーヨン rayon. ・レーヨンのワイシャツ a rayon shirt.
レール 〖鉄道の〗a rail (❗通例複数形で); 〖カーテンの〗a curtain rail.
・レールを敷く lay rails; (お膳立てする) pave the way (for).
レーン 〖道路・ボウリングの〗a lane. ・バス優先レーン a bus prioity lane.
レーンコート (⇨レインコート)
レーンジャー (⇨レンジャー)
レーンシューズ (⇨レインシューズ)
レーンボー (⇨レインボー)
レオタード a leotard /líːətɑːrd/.
レオナルド・ダ・ビンチ 〖イタリアの芸術家・科学者〗Leonardo da Vinci /liːɑnɑ́rdou də víntʃi/.
レガース (野球などの) a shin guard.
レガッタ a regatta,《英》a boat race.
-れき -歴 (経験) an experience; (病気などの) a history; (記録) a record; (経歴) a career. ・教員歴 [運転歴] 20 年は (have) twenty years' experience in teaching [driving]. ・職歴 (の職歴); ・犯罪 [逮捕] 歴 a criminal [a police] record.
れきがん 礫岩 〖地学〗a conglomerate.
れきさつ 轢殺 ▶彼は突進してきた列車に轢殺された He was run over and killed by an onrushing train./He was killed under the wheels of an onrushing train.
*****れきし** 歴史 图 history.
① 〖~の歴史〗・日本の歴史 Japanese history; the history of Japan. ・古代の歴史 ancient history.
② 〖歴史~〗・歴史上重要な出来事 an important event in history.
③ 〖歴史が[は]〗・歴史が古い[浅い] have a long [a short] history. ・我が校は 90 年の歴史がある Our school has a history of 90 years. ▶歴史は繰り返す《ことわざ》History repeats itself.
④ 〖歴史の〗・歴史の本 a history book. ・歴史の先生 a history teacher.
⑤ 〖歴史に〗・彼の名は歴史に残るだろう His name will be remembered [go down] in history. ▶首脳会談で 50 年の対立の歴史に幕を下ろした (=対立の歴史を終わりにした) The summit meeting brought an end to the 50-year old history of antagonism.
⑥ 〖歴史から〗▶私たちが歴史から学ぶことは、私たちが歴史から何も学んでいないということだ What we learn from history is that we've learned nothing from history.

── 歴史的な 形 histórric; histórical. (❗前の語は主に「歴史上有名[重要]な」、後の語は「歴史上実在した[起こった]」,「歴史に関する」の意) ・歴史的な事件 (歴史に残る価値のある) a historic [(歴史上起こった) a historical] event. ・歴史的な建物 a historic building ▶大統領は歴史的な演説をした The president made a historic speech. ▶日本が第二次世界大戦で敗れたことは歴史的な事実である It is a historical fact that Japan was defeated in World War Ⅱ [《やや書》the Second World War].

── 歴史的に 副 historically. ▶歴史的に見るとその出来事は大変興味深い Historically, the event is very interesting.

・歴史家 a historian. ・歴史学 history. ・歴史観 a historical view. ・歴史研究家 a history student, a student of history. ・歴史時代 the historical times. (❗ historic times は「歴史上重要な時代」の意) ・歴史小説 a historical novel. (❗ a historic novel は「画期的な小説」の意) ・歴史年表 a historical chart.

れきし 轢死 ── 轢死する (ひかれて死ぬ) be run over and killed (by a train).
れきじつ 暦日 a calendar day. ・暦日制料金のレンタカー a rental car based on a calendar day rate.
れきすう 暦数 ❶ (説明的に) the way of making a calendar by lunar or solar movements.
❷ 〖自然にめぐってくる運命〗one's fate.
れきせい 瀝青 〖地学〗bitumen.
・瀝青炭 bituminous coal.
れきせん 歴戦 ・歴戦の勇士 a soldier with a lot of fighting experiences; a war veteran.
れきぜん 歴然 ・歴然とした (明らかな) obvious, evident, clear,《やや書》positive (⇨明らか); (決定的な) conclusive; (間違えようのない) unmistakable.
・歴然たる事実 an obvious (紛れもない) an unquestionable, an indisputable] fact. ▶両者の違いは歴然としている The difference between the two is quite plain.
れきだい 歴代 ・歴代の 形 (連続する) successive.
・アメリカの歴代大統領 the successive [(過去の) past] presidents of the U.S. ▶彼の 100 メートルの記録は歴代 2 位だ His record for 100 meters ranks second in history.
れきだん 轢断 ── 轢断する run over and cut off the body.
れきてい 歴程 (通ってきた道筋) the route of one's travel.
れきにん 歴任 ── 歴任する 動 (次々に占める) successively hold. ▶安部氏はあまたの要職を歴任しました Mr. Abe has held a number of important positions.
れきねん 暦年 a calendar year.
れきねん 歴年 the passage of years. ▶博士の歴年

れきねんれい (=長年)の研究が実を結んだ The doctor's study *over the years* bore fruit.

れきねんれい 暦年齢 (生活年齢) one's chronological age.

れきほう 暦法 a calendar.

れきほう 歴訪 — 歴訪する 動 make a tour of [a round of] (five Asian countries).

レギュラー ❶ [正規の選手] a regular player, 《米》a regular; (常時出演者) a regular guest. ●そのクラブのレギュラーメンバー a regular member of the club. ●チームのレギュラーから外される be dropped [excluded] from the *regular* lineup of the team.
▶彼はこのチームのレギュラーです He is a *regular* player [a *regular*] of this team./He plays *regularly* for this team.

❷ [標準の品質] regular.
●レギュラーガソリン 《米》regular gasoline [《話》gas]. (❗《米話》では単に regular ともいう) ●レギュラーコーヒー regular coffee. ●レギュラーシーズン (野球の) a regular season. ●レギュラー出演 a regular appearance. ●レギュラー出演する (テレビ番組に) appear regularly (on a TV show); (レギュラーゲストとして) appear as a regular guest (on a TV show). ●レギュラー番組 (テレビ・ラジオなどの) a regular (TV [radio]) program. (❗テレビでは show も可)

れきれき 歴々 (⇨お歴々)

レグ (⇨レッグ)

レクイエム [鎮魂曲] a requiem /rékwiəm/.

レグホン [鳥] a leghorn.

レクリエーション (a) recreation. ▶彼はときどきレクリエーションにゴルフをする He sometimes plays golf for *recreation*.
●レクリエーション施設 recreational facilities.

レゲエ [音楽] reggae /régei/.

レコーダー [記録係, 記録装置] a recorder. ●タイム[テープ]レコーダー a time [a tape] *recorder*.

レコーディング (a) recording. (❗個々の場合は Ⓒ) ●彼女の最新のヒット曲のレコーディングをする make a *recording* of her latest hit song; record her latest hit song (*on* tape).

レコード ❶ [音盤] a récord, 《話》a disk. ●LP レコード an LP [a long-playing] *record*. ●レコードをかける[聞く] play [listen to] a record. ●レコードを作る(=吹き込む) cut a record.

❷ [競技などの記録] a récord. (⇨記録) ●レコードを破る[作る] break [set] a *record*.
●レコード店 a record shop. ●レコードプレーヤー a record player. ●レコード保持者 a record holder.

レザー [かみそり] a razor /réizər/; [皮革] leather. ●レザーのコート a *leather* coat.
●レザークラフト [皮革工芸] leathercraft. ●レザークロス [革布] leathercloth.

レジ [金銭登録機] a cash register; [勘定係] a cashier /kæʃíər/; a checker, checkout clerk (❗ a checkout girl は性差別として避けられる); [スーパーなどの精算台] a checkout (counter). ▶レジで品物の代金を支払った I paid for the goods at the *checkout* (counter). ●お会計はレジでお願いします (レストランなどで) Please pay the *cashier*.
●レジ袋 a plastic shopping bag.

レシート a receipt /risí:t/ (*for*); 《米》(通例レジで受け取る) a sales check [slip]. ●レシートをもらう[とっておく] get [keep] a *receipt* (*for*).

レシーバー (電話・サーブを受ける人) a receiver.

レシーブ — レシーブする receive (a ball).

レジオネラきん レジオネラ菌 [医学] legionella /li:dʒənélə/.

レジオネラしょう レジオネラ症 [医学] Legionnaires' desease.

レジオンドヌール [<フランス語] [最高勲章] the Lègion /líːdʒən/ of Hónor.

レジスター a cash register. (⇨レジ)

レジスタンス resistance. (❗しばしば大文字で) ●フランスのレジスタンスの一員 a member of the French *Resistance*.

レシチン [生化学] lecithin /lésəθin/.

レシピ [調理法] a recipe /résəpi/ (*for*). ●スパゲッティのレシピ a *recipe for* (cooking) spaghetti. ●お菓子のレシピ集 a collection of *recipes for* confectionery.

レシピエント [移植患者] [医学] a recipient (↔a donor).

レジメ a résumé. (⇨レジュメ)

*レジャー leisure /líːʒər, léʒə/. (❗英語の leisure は必ずしも娯楽とは結びつかない (⇨余暇)) ●レジャーにテニスをする play tennis *for recreation* [*as a pastime*, ×*as leisure*].
●レジャー産業 the leisure industry. ●レジャー施設 leisure facilities. ●レジャーセンター a recréation cènter [àrea]. (❗《米》では裕福な退職者を対象にした a leisure world [town] がある); 《英》a leisure centre (❗スポーツ設備のある余暇公共施設). ●レジャーブーム a leisure boom. ●レジャーボート a pleasure boat; 《和製語》a leisure boat. ●レジャー用品 leisure goods. ●レジャーランド 'a leisure land'; a place for enjoyment; (遊園地) an amusement park.

レジュメ [<フランス語] 《やや書》a résumé /rézəmèi/. (❗ resume ともつづる); a summary.

レズ (同性愛の女) a lesbian; (同性愛) lesbianism. (⇨ホモ)

レスキュー レスキュー隊 a rescue tèam [squàd]. ●レスキュー隊員 a réscue wòrker.

レストハウス [休憩所] a resthouse.

レストラン [<フランス語] a restaurant. ●食べ放題のレストラン a smorgasbord *restaurant*. ●和風[洋風]レストラン a Japanese-style [a Western-style] *restaurant*. ▶私たちは夕食を食べにレストランに出かけた We went out to a *restaurant* to have dinner.

レストルーム [休憩室] a lounge; (化粧室・トイレ) 《米》a rest room; 《英》the toilet.

レズビアン (女性の同性愛者) a lesbian /lézbiən/.

レスラー a wrestler.

レスリング wrestling. ●レスリング選手 a wrestler. ●レスリングの試合をする play [have] a *wrestling* match. ●彼とレスリングをする *wrestle* (*with*) him.

レセプション [正式の歓迎会] a reception. ●レセプションを開く hold [give, 《話》throw] a *reception* (*for* him, *in honor of* him).

レソト [国名] Lesotho /ləsóutou/; (公式名) the Kingdom of Lesotho. (首都 Maseru)

レゾンデートル [<フランス語] [存在理由] raison d'être /réizoun détrə/.

レター a letter.
●レターセット stationery for writing letters. ●レターヘッド (a) letterhead. (❗レターヘッドのついた便せんは Ⓤ) ●レターヘッドの付いた便せんで手紙を書く write on a sheet of *letterhead* [*headed* notepaper]. (⇨便箋)

レタス [植物] lettuce. ●レタス 2 個 [2 枚] two head(s) [leaves] of *lettuce*. (❗レタスを数えるときは 《話》では two lettuces という)

レタリング [デザイン文字] lettering.

*れつ 列 [縦の] a line, (主に兵隊の) a file; [横の] a

れつあく

row, (主に兵隊・タクシーの) a rank; [順番待ちの人[車]などの] a queue ／kjúː/.

①【~列】 ●まっすぐ1列に並んで立つ stand *in a straight line*. ●1列に並んでバスを待つ wait *for a bus in line* [*a queue*]. ●7列目に[私の2列前に]座る sit in the seventh *row* [*sit two rows in front of me*]. ▶劇場の前には長い列ができていた There was a long *line* [*queue*] (of people) in front of the theater. ▶机がきちんと3列に並べてあった The desks were arranged in three orderly *rows* [*lines*].

②【列の】 ▶列の最後はここですか Is this the end of the *line*?/Are you the last (in the *line*)? ▶私は列の先頭[いちばん後ろ]だった I was at the head [end] of the *line*.

③【列に】 ●列に並ぶ join the [get in] *line* (❗後の方が口語的); (列の後ろにつく) follow the *line*. ●列に割り込む break [cut] into the *line*; jump the *queue*.

④【列を】 ▶多くの人が切符を買うために列を作った A lot of people *formed a line* [*a queue*] *for* the tickets./A lot of people *lined up* [*queued* (*up*)] to buy the tickets.

れつあく 劣悪 ── **劣悪な** 形 (質の悪い) poor, bad* (❗後の方が口語的); (より劣った) inferior. ●劣悪な品質の商品 goods of *poor* [*inferior*] quality; *inferior* goods.

れつい 劣位 an inferior position.

れっか 劣化 名 ageing, aging; degradation. ●目に見える環境の劣化に驚くbe frightened by the visible environmental *degradation*. ▶このゴムは品質の劣化が進んでいる This rubber *has worsened* in quality.
── **劣化する** 動 worsen (❗悪い状態にあるものがさらに悪化する); age; degrade.
●劣化ウラン depleted uranium. ●劣化ウラン弾 a depleted-uranium shell.

れっか 烈火 ●烈火のごとく怒る be infuriated; fly into a rage; explode with [in] anger; (話) hit the ceiling [roof]. ▶他社に契約を取られたと報告をしたら社長は烈火のごとく怒った When I said I lost the contract to the competitor, my boss *hit the ceiling*.

レッカー(しゃ) レッカー(車) (米) a wrecker, (米) a tow car [truck], (英) a breakdown lorry [truck].

れっき 列記 ── **列記する** 動 list; make [write out] a list (*of*).

れっきとした 歴とした [立派な] (恥ずかしくない程度の) respectable; (十分認められた) well-recognized; [明白な] obvious. ●れっきとした(=論破することができない)証拠 irrefutable evidence. ▶れっきとした(=十分な)理由があって彼にその賞が与えられた The prize was given to him for *good* reasons. ▶君も今やれっきとした(=資格のある)医者です You are now a *qualified* physician.

れっきょ 列挙 名 enumeration.
── **列挙する** 動 enumerate; list. ●彼の欠点を列挙する *enumerate* his faults.

れっきょう 列強 the great [world] powers.

レッグ [足] a leg (⇨足); [同一対戦相手との連戦の1つ][サッカー] a leg.

レッグウォーマー 《a pair of》leg warmers.

れつご 劣後 subordination.
●劣後株 (後配株) a deferred stock. ●劣後債 a subordinated debt [debenture, bond]. ●劣後ローン a subordinated loan.

れっこく 列国 the nations [countries] of the world.

れっし 烈士 a man of integrity [principle].

れつじつ 烈日 a scorching sun.

*れっしゃ 列車 a train. (⇨バス)

①【~列車】 (米) a freight /fréit/ *train*, (英) a goods *train*. ●旅客列車 a passenger *train*. ●コンテナ列車 a container *train*. ●急行列車 an express (*train*). ●普通[直通; 臨時]列車 a local [a through; a special] *train*. ●上り[下り]列車 (英) an up [a down] *train*. (❗米英ともに行先を明示して a Tokyo(-bound) *train*, a *train for Tokyo* という方が一般的) ●満員列車 a crowded [a packed, a jammed, a full] *train*. (⇨満員)

②【列車は】 ▶その列車は6両編成だ The *train* is six cars (米) [*carriages* (英)] *long*./The *train* has [is made up of] six cars (米) [*carriages* (英)]./It's a six-car (米) [six-carriage (英)] *train*. ▶彼の乗る列車は今夜10時3番ホームから出ます His *train* leaves from platform No. 3 at 10:00 tonight.

翻訳のこころ 列車は，内海に沿って東に走っていた (竹西寛子『蘭』) The eastbound train was running along the inland sea. (❗eastbound は「東行きの」の意)

③【列車で】 ●列車で行く go by [*in a*, (米) *on a*] *train*. (⇨バス⑤) ▶私は列車で大阪へ行った I took a *train* to Osaka. (❗(1) take は「利用する」の意. (2) I went to Osaka by *train*. より普通の言い方)

④【列車に[を]】 ●列車に乗る[を降りる] get on [off] a *train*. ●列車に乗り遅れる miss a *train*. ●列車に飛び乗る jump [《話》hop] onto a *train*. ●神戸で列車を乗り換える change trains [×a train] at Kobe.

れつじゃく 劣弱 ── **劣弱な** 形 inferior; weak; low 《intelligence》. ●劣弱な体格 a *poor* [a *weak*] physique.

れつじょ 烈女 a woman of constancy [principle].

れっしょう 裂傷 (a) laceration (❗通例複数形で); a lacerated /lǽsəreitid/ wound. ●腕に裂傷を負う get [receive] *lacerations* on one's arm; have one's arm *lacerated*.

れつじょう 劣情 carnal desires. ●劣情をもよおす be sexually aroused [excited]; lust 《*after* [*for*] women》.

れっしん 烈震 a violent earthquake. (⇨地震)

れっする 列する **①【列席する】** ●会議の席に列する *attend* [*be present at*] a conference.
②【一員となる】 ●先進8か国に列する *become a member of* the Group of Eight. ●一代貴族に列せられる *be made* a life peer.

レッスン a lesson. ●プライベートレッスン a private *lesson*. ●グループレッスン a group *lesson*. ●ピアノのレッスンをする[受ける] give [have, take] piano *lessons*. (❗1回のレッスンなら a piano *lesson*)
●レッスンプロ [ゴルフ] a teaching professional.

れっせい 劣性 recessive.
●劣性遺伝 recessive heredity. ●劣性形質 a recessive (character).

れっせい 劣勢 (不利) a disadvantage. ●劣勢をはね返す overcome a *disadvantage*; (形勢を逆転する) turn the tables 《*on* him》. ▶我が軍は敵に比べて数の上で劣勢である Our army *is inferior to* the enemy in number.

れっせき 列席 名 presence; (特に定期的な) attendance. ▶次の日曜日の式典へのご列席をお願いします I'd like to ask for your *presence* [ask you to *be present*] at the ceremony next Sunday.

れっちゅう

―列席する 動 attend; (している) be present 《*at*》. ● 列席者 an attendant; attendance (**!** 集合的に用い単数扱い. 通例 a large (多い), a small (少ない) などを伴って用いる); those present (**!** 複数扱い).

れっちゅう 列柱 a colonnade. ● 大英博物館のイオニア式の列柱 the Ionic *colonnade* of the British Museum.

レッテル [<オランダ語] a label /léibl/. ● びんに「毒薬」のレッテルを張る label a bottle "Poison"; put a *label* of poison on a bottle; attach a *label* of poison to a bottle. ▶彼はうそつきだというレッテルを張られた He *was labeled* [(烙印(らくいん)を押された) *was branded*] (*as*) a liar.

れつでん 列伝 biographies. ● 英雄列伝 the *biographies* [*lives*] of heroes.

れっとう 列島 (a chain of) islands /áiləndz/; (群島) an archipelago /ɑ̀ːrkəpéləgou/ (種 〜(e)s). ● 千島列島 the Kuril(e) *Islands*. ● 日本列島 the Japanese *Archipelago*.

れっとう 劣等 名 inferiority. **―― 劣等の** 形 inferior. (⇨之項) ● 劣等感 (⇨劣等感). ● 劣等生 a (very) poor [an inferior] student; a slow learner.

れっとうかん 劣等感 an inferiority complex (↔a superiority complex); a sense of inferiority. ▶彼は自分の能力に [友人に対して] 劣等感を持っている He has an *inferiority complex about* his ability [*feels inferior to* his friends].

レッドカード ● レッドカードを出す [サッカー] hold up a *red card* 《*to* him》. ● ボウヤー, 一発レッド(カード)で退場です Bowyer, to get a straight *red card* for that!

レッドキャベツ red cabbage.

レッドデータブック the red data book. (参考 絶滅の恐れのある野生生物のリスト).

レッドパージ [共産主義者の解雇] the Red purge.

レッドペッパー red pepper.

れっぷう 烈風 (強風) a gale. ▶烈風で屋根が吹き飛ばされた The roof was torn off by a *gale*.

れつれつ 烈々 ● 烈々たる気迫 a *firm* [a *great*, a *fierce*] determination; a *fighting* [a *dauntless*] spirit.

レディー [女性, 婦人] a lady /léidi/. ● レディーファースト Ladies first.

レディース ● レディースクリニック a ladies' clinic; a clinic for women. ● レディースコミック [若い女性を対象とした漫画] a comic for young women; 《和製語》 ladies' comic. ● レディースファッション women's fashions.

レディーメード ● レディーメードの背広 a *ready-made* [a *ready-to-wear*] suit. (**!** 前の方は服以外にも使えるが後の方は使わない)

れてん レ点 a reversing mark.

レトリック [修辞(学)] rhetoric /rétərik/.

レトルト ● レトルトカレー retort-packed curry. ● レトルト食品 retort-packed food(s).

レトロ (懐古趣味的な) retro, 《やや書》 retrospective. ● レトロ調バス [電車] a *retro style* [an *old outdated*] bus [streetcar]. ● レトロファッション retro fashion.

レニングラード Leningrad. (参考 現在のサンクトペテルブルク)

レバー [てこ] a lever. ● レバーを引く pull a *lever*. ● レバーを前に倒す throw [push] a *lever* forward.

レバー [(食用としての)肝臓] (a) liver /lívər/. (**!** 臓器としての肝臓は [C]) ● レバーペースト liver paste.

レパートリー a repertoire /répərtwɑ̀ːr/, 《書》 a repertory. ● レパートリーが広い have a *wide* [*wide*] *repertoire* 《*of* songs》. ▶その歌は私のレパートリーにはありません That song is not in my *repertoire*.

レバノン [国名] Lebanon; (公式名) the Republic of Lebanon. (首都 Beirut) ● レバノン人 a Lebanese.

レビュー [評論] a review. ● レビューを投稿する contribute a *review* 《*to*》.

レビュー [<フランス語] [寄席演芸] (a) revue.

レファレンス reference. ● レファレンスサービス a reference service. ● レファレンスブック [参考図書] a reference book. ● レファレンスルーム a reference room.

レフェリー a rèferée. ● レフェリーを務める act as 《x a》 *referee* 《*for* a match》; referee 《a match》. ● 試合はボクサーの負傷でレフェリーストップになった(＝レフェリーがストップした) The *referee* stopped the fight because a boxer was hurt.

レフト [野球の左翼] left field; [野球の左翼手] a left fielder; [思想上の左翼] the left wing. (⇨左翼) ● レフト打ちの打者 a *letf-field* hitter. ● レフトを守る play *left field*. ● レフトにヒットを打つ hit a single to *left* (*field*). ● レフトオーバーの二塁打を打つ hit a double over the *left fielder*. ● レフト線ヘライナーを打つ hit a liner down the *left-field* (foul) line.

レフリー a referee. (⇨レフェリー)

レプリカ [複製] a replica 《*of*》.

レフレックスカメラ a 《single-lens [double-lens]》 reflex camera.

レベル a level; (質・能力の) 《話》 a league; (基準) a standard. ● レベルの高い(＝ハイレベル)の問題 a high-*level* question. ● 事務レベルの交渉 working-*level* negotiations. ● 世界でもトップレベルの設備 the world's top-*level* facilities. ▶彼の走り高跳びはプロのレベルに近い He high-jumps to an almost professional *level*. ▶私も一応ピアノはひけますが, あなたとはレベルが違います I can play the piano anyway, but I'm not in the same *league* as you (are). ▶君は英会話力をもっとレベルアップしなければならない You should *improve* [*raise the level of*] your ability to speak English. (**!** ✕level up は「低位のものを他と同じ水準に上げる」の意でここでは不適) ▶あの学校はレベルが高い That school has a high academic *standard*. ● レベルスイング [野球] a level swing [stroke].

レポーター [報道記者, 報告者] a reporter.

レポート [報告書] a report; [学生の] a paper; (学期末の) a term paper; (小論) an essay. ● レポートを提出する(報告書を) submit [file] a *report*; (学生の論文) turn [hand] in one's *paper*.

レマン ● レマン湖 Lake Leman /líːmən/.

レムすいみん レム睡眠 REM /rém/ sleep (**!** REM is rapid *eye movement* の略); (速波睡眠) fast wave sleep (**!** wave は「脳波」の意). (⇨ノンレム睡眠)

レモネード 《米》 lemonade /lèmənéid/, 《英》 lemon squash.

れもん 『檸檬』 Lemon. (参考 梶井基次郎の小説)

レモン [植物] (a) lemon. ● レモン 1 切れ a slice of *lemon*. ● レモンスカッシュ 《米》 lemon soda; 《英》 lemonade. ● レモンティー tea with lemon. (**!** この意では ✕lemon tea とはいわない)

レモングラス [植物] lemon grass.

レリーフ [浮き彫り] relief. (**!** 作品は [C])

:-れる ❶ [受身] ● 怠けて先生にしかられた I *was told off by* the teacher for being lazy. ▶夕立に降られた I *was* [*got*] *caught in* a shower. (!) be は「巻き込まれてその結果ずぶぬれになった」といった被害や何らかの影響を被ることを伝える場合に、get は予期せぬ出来事に不意に出会うことをいう場合に用いる. cf. be [×get] born) ▶彼は蟹に指をはさまれた He *had* [*got*] his finger *nipped by* a crab. (!) have [get]＋目的語＋過去分詞の型で、過去分詞に強勢を置き、迷惑・被害を表す. get は(不注意による事故など)本人に責任のある場合に、have は(犯罪・災害など)動作主に責任がある場合に通例用いられる： 彼は時計を盗まれた He *got* [×*had*] his watch stolen. ただし、口語では get が多く用いられる. ×He was nipped his finger by a crab. (は不可)/His finger *was nipped by* a crab. (!)「あの人の指どうしたの」といった前提に対して「カニの仕業だ」と教示する言い方)/A crab gave him a nip on the finger. (海辺で遊んでいた時に)何が起こったのかを客観的にいう場合)

❷ [可能] can*; be able to 《do》; be capable of 《doing》. (!) can と be able to はほぼ同じ意味だが、be able to の方が能力を強調し、やや堅い言い方. be capable of は潜在的にある事を遂行する能力があることを表す) ▶5分で駅まで行かれます You *can* go to the station in five minutes. ▶それで君は映画を見に行かれなかったのだね So you *weren't able to* [*couldn't*] go to the movies, were [could] you? ▶このテープレコーダーは遠くの音でもとらえられる This tape recorder *can* catch [*is capable of catching*] even distant sounds. ▶あのホテルの食事は食べられたかい Was the meal *any good* at that hotel?/Was the meal at that hotel *any good*?

❸ [自然にそうなる状態を表す] ▶この写真を見ると中学時代のころが思い出される When I look at this picture, I always remember [I'm reminded of] my junior high school days./This picture reminds me of my junior high school days.

❹ [尊敬を表す] ▶総理はあす北京に向け飛び立たれる The Prime Minister is flying to Beijing tomorrow. (!) (1) 英語では通例尊敬次は特に表さない. (2) この現在進行形はすでに決められた変更不可能な未来の予定を表す)

れん 連 〔紙の量〕 a ream; 〔詩の単位〕 a stanza; 〔ネックレスの〕 a string. ▶2連の真珠のネックレス a double *string* pearl necklace.

*れんあい 恋愛 love. ●自由恋愛 free love. ●精神的な恋愛 platonic [spiritual] *love*. ●恋愛に陥る fall in *love* 《*with*》. ▶彼らは恋愛中です They *are in love with* each other./They love each other. ▶この小説は恋愛事件を扱っている This novel deals with a love affair [a romance].
●恋愛関係 a romance; 〔情事〕 a love affair. ●恋愛結婚 a love marriage. ●恋愛結婚する marry for *love*. ●恋愛小説 a love story; 〔空想的な〕 a romance.

れんか 廉価 ── 廉価な 形 (安い) cheap; inexpensive; (大衆向けの) popular. ▶そこでは廉価でお好みの品が買えます You can buy suitable articles at low [*popular*] prices there./You can buy suitable articles *cheap* there.
●廉価版 a cheap [a popular] edition 《of a book》.

れんが 連歌 a *renga* (poem); (説明的に) a series of *tanka* poems composed by several poets: the first person produces a first half of a *tanka*, and the second person makes a second half to complete it.

れんが 煉瓦 brick. (!) 集合的. 個々には〔C〕. ●煉瓦造りの家 a *brick* house; a house built [made] of *brick*(*s*). ●煉瓦を積む lay *bricks*. ●煉瓦を敷きつめる pave 《a road》 with *brick*(*s*).
●煉瓦職人 a bricklayer. ●煉瓦塀 a brick wall. ●煉瓦舗装 a brick pavement.

れんかん 連関 (⇒関連)

れんき 連記 图 (複数の記載) plural entry.
── 連記する 動 ●2名連記する write two names on a ballot.
●連記制 the plural ballot system. ●連記無記名投票 a secret ballot with plural entry.

れんきゅう 連休 ▶週末は3連休です We have a three-day weekend. (!) We have three *holidays in a row* this weekend. また一般に漠然と We have a *long* weekend. のようにいうこともできる)

れんぎょう 連翹 〔植物〕a forsythia /fɔːrsíθiə/; a Japanese golden bell-tree.

れんきんじゅつ 錬金術 alchemy.
●錬金術師 an alchemist.

れんく 連句 a *renku*, a kind of *renga*.

れんげ 蓮華 ❶ 〔はすの花〕a lotus flower.
❷ 〔ちりれんげ〕a porcelain spoon.

れんげそう 蓮華草 〔植物〕(a) Chinese milk vetch.

れんけい 連係 ●投手と内野手との見事な連係 good *co-ordination* between the pitcher and infielder.
●連係プレー teamwork; (a) combination, coordination. ●見事な連係プレーで試合に勝つ win the game by good *teamwork*.

れんけい 連携 (協力) cooperation. (⇒協力) ▶プロジェクト遂行のために大学との連携を密にする *cooperate* closely *in* a project *with* the University; work *in* close *cooperation* with the University in [in carrying out, to carry out] a project.

れんけつ 連結 图 (a) connection. ●15両連結の列車 a fifteen-car train. ●新幹線は16両連結である The bullet train is 16 cars 《米》[carriages 《英》] *long*. (⇒列車 ❷)
── 連結する 動 connect; link; join; couple; attach. ●(つなぐ) ●(ひと組の)電池を連結する *connect* (*up*) the cells of a battery (*to* [*with*] one another). ●車両を連結する *couple* the cars together. ●寝台車を列車に連結する *couple* [*connect*, *attach*] sleeping cars *to* a train.
●連結売上高 consolidated sales. ●連結器 a coupling; a connector; a coupler. ●連結決算 consolidated accounting; accounting for consolidation. ●連結子会社 a consolidated company [subsidiary]. ●連結財務諸表 consolidated financial sheets [statements]. ●連結納税制度 the consolidated tax payment system. ●連結利益 consolidated profit.

れんけつ 廉潔 ●廉潔の士 a man of rectitude [(great) integrity, 《書》probity].

れんこ 連呼 ●候補者の名前を連呼する *call out* [*shout*] the candidate's name *repeatedly*.

れんご 連語 〔文法〕(成句) a phrase; (複合語) a compound word; (語の連結) (a) collocation.

れんこう 連行 ── 連行する 動 ●容疑者を警察署に連行する *take* a suspect *to* a police station. ●麻薬密売の容疑で連行する *take* 《*him*》*in* on suspicion of drug traffic.

*れんごう 連合 图 〔結合〕(a) union; (a) combination (!) 前の方が一体化を強調する); 〔国家間の同盟〕(an) alliance; 〔政治上の提携〕(a) coalition.
── 連合する 動 unite; combine; ally (!) 主に受身または再帰的に用いる (⇒同盟 [同盟を結ぶ])). ●連合して敵にあたる *unite* [*combine*] *against* the enemy; face the enemy *in combination* [*alliance, coalition*] *with*). ▶これら三つの国が連合して一つの連邦国家になった These three countries *were united*

れんごく into a federal state. ●連合軍 the Allied Forces. 連合国 (第一次・第二次世界大戦時の) the Allied Powers; the Allies. 連合政権 a coalition government.

れんごく 煉獄 〖カトリック〗Purgatory. ── 煉獄の 形 purgatorial.

れんこだい 連子鯛 〖魚名〗a deep-sea porgy.

れんこん 蓮根 〖植物〗a lotus root, a lotus rhizome /ráizoum/.

れんさ 連鎖 ●連鎖的(=連続して発生した)事件 *a chain* [*a series*] *of* events. ●連鎖反応を引き起こす bring [produce] *a chain reaction* 〖(ドミノ効果) *a domino effect*, 《英》 *a knock-on effect*〗. ●連鎖球菌 a streptococcus. ●連鎖球菌感染症 streptococcal infection. ●連鎖店 a chain store;《主に英》a multiple store. ●連鎖倒産 (a) chain-reacting bankruptcy.

れんざ 連座 ── 連座する 動 (関与する) be involved (*in*).

れんさい 連載 名 ●50回完結の連載もの *a serial* in 50 *installments*. ▶その連載は打ち切られた The *serial* was cut short.
── 連載する 動 ●この物語は朝日新聞に連載された This story *appeared serially* in [*was carried in series by*, *was serialized in*] the *Asahi Shimbun*.
●連載小説 a serial (novel) 《*in a magazine*》.
●連載漫画 serial comics; (新聞などの4コマ程度の) a comic strip.

れんさく 連作 ●昔はスイカの連作は不可能でした Years ago it was impossible to *grow* [*cultivate*] water melons *on the same ground in consecutive years* [*consecutively*].

れんざん 連山 a mountain range. (⇨山脈)

レンジ (電子レンジ) a microwave (oven /ʌvn/.(ガス台)《米》a (cooking) stove,《英》a cooker. (1) 下側に大きなオーブン付きのもの. (2) 米英ではガスより電気を熱源とするものが多いので、日本のガス台は a gas stove [cooker] というのが近い (⇨ストーブ) ●レンジでチンする microwave; heat《it》up in a *microwave*;《話》nuke.
●レンジ食品 microwavable foods.

れんじつ 連日 ●連日の猛暑 *a long spell of* very hot weather. ▶展示会は連日(=毎日)盛況だった There were a lot of people in the exhibition *every day*. ▶連日連夜の雨で堤防が決壊した The riverbank broke down because of the rain (*every*) *day and night* [*for the last few days and nights*]. (⇨日夜)

れんじまど 連子窓 a *renji* window; (説明的に) a type of window with closely put thin bars made of wood or bamboo.

れんしゃ 連射 動 shoot in rapid succession; (機関銃を) machine-gun (-nn-).

レンジャー 〖森林などの警備隊〗a《forest》ranger;〖特別兵員隊員〗a commando (日本人をさすこともある);《米》a ranger 〖しばしば R- と書く〗.

れんしゅ 連取 ●あっという間に3ポイントを連取する *get* three points *in quick succession*.

れんじゅ 連珠 (⇨⑩五目並べ)

*れんしゅう 練習 名 (a) practice; (a) drill; (a) training; an exercise 〖しばしば複数形で〗; (a) rehearsal.

〖使い分け〗 **practice** 繰り返して行う定期的な練習. 体や頭などを慣らして習得させることを含意する. **drill** 型の決まった練習を繰り返して体に覚えさせるもの. 集団による防災訓練や軍の演習にも用いる. **training** 運動・楽器・仕事などに必要な技術の訓練. 新たな技術や高度な身体能力の獲得を含意する. **exercise** 体や頭を使うさまざまな練習. 現在獲得している技術を定着・発展させることを含意する. **rehearsal** 芝居などのけいこ.

① 【〜練習】 ●発音練習 a *practice* [*a drill*] *in* pronunciation; a pronunciation *practice* [*drill*]. ●読解練習 reading comprehension. ●自主練習 voluntary training; self-managed [self-organized] sports practice. ●バイオリンの練習 (do) *practice* [*exercises*] *on* the violin.

② 【練習〜】 ●英語の練習問題をする do *exercises in* English; have English *drill*. ▶彼は練習不足だ (練習をしていない) He is out of *practice* (↔*in practice*).〗 He doesn't *practice* enough. ▶私たちが聴衆になってあげるわ. 私たちを練習台にしてスピーチをやってごらん We'll be the audience. You *practice on* us. Give us your presentation now.

③ 【練習に[を]】 ●そのレースに備えて猛練習に入る go into hard *training* [*practice*] *for* the race; start *training* [*practicing*] hard *for* the race.
●サッカーの練習をサボる skip soccer *practice* [*training*]. ▶テニスが上手になるには大いに練習を積む必要がある It takes a lot of *practice* to be a good tennis player./You need a lot of *practice* to play tennis well./Playing tennis well requires a lot of *practice*.
── 練習する 動 practice; drill; train; exercise; rehearse. ●ピアノを練習する *practice* (playing [ˣto play]) the piano; *practice on* the piano.
●彼らにその歌[英語の文型]を練習させる *drill* them in singing the song [English sentence patterns]; have them *practice* singing the song [English sentence patterns]. ●コンテストに備えて猛練習する *train* [*rehearse*] intensively *for* a contest. ●水泳を練習する *exercise* oneself *in* swimming. ▶そのチームはみっちり6時間練習した The team *did* [*had*] 6 hours of grueling *practice*.

●練習機 a training aircraft. ●練習曲 an étude (❗正式演目にもなる); (練習用曲) a practice piece. ●練習試合 a practice game [match]. ●練習所 (劇などの) a practice room. ●練習場 (競技の) a practice [training] field. ●練習生 (訓練生) a trainee; (見習い) an apprentice (❗一般に trainee より apprentice の方が格付けが上とされる). ●練習船 a tráining ship. ●練習帳 an exercise book; (教科書と並行して使う) a workbook. ●練習問題集 a drill book; an exercise book.

れんしょ 連署 名 a joint signature; (副書) a cóuntersìgn. ●我々の連署のもとに under our *joint signature*.
── 連署する 動 sign 《a treaty》jointly; countersign 《a treaty》.

れんしょう 連勝 名 successive [straight, (連続の) a series of] victories; (一連の勝利) a winning streak. ●連勝を10に伸ばす extend [stretch] the *streak* to ten games. ▶きのうの敗北で連勝がストップした Yesterday's defeat broke [ended; stopped] our *winning streak*.
── 連勝する 動 ●12試合に連勝する *win* twelve *successive* games; *win* twelve games *in a row*; *have* a 12-game *winning streak*. ●ダブルヘッダーに連勝する sweep a doubleheader.
●連勝式 〖競馬〗(単式) a perfecta; (複式) a quinella.

れんじょう 恋情 (⇨恋心)

レンズ a lens. ●凹[凸]レンズ a concave [a convex] lens. ●拡大[望遠;広角;魚眼]レンズ a magnifying [a telephoto; a wide-angle; a fish-eye] lens. ●接眼レンズ an eyepiece. ●対物レンズ an object lens. ●(カメラの)レンズを絞る stop down a lens. ●レンズの焦点を合わせる focus a lens.

れんせい 練成 ─ 練成する 動 (心を鍛える) discipline; (技・心身を) train; drill.
●錬成道場 a tráining hàll; a tráining ròom.

れんせん 連戦 图 a series of battles [games]; successive battles. ●3連戦に全勝する sweep a three-game series. ●ホームで行う6連戦 a six-game homestand. ▶5連戦したのでとても疲れた We were very tired after the series of five games.
── **連戦する 動** fight a series of battles. ●連戦連勝[連敗]する(試合で) have a series of victories [defeats]; (戦争で) win [lose] battle after battle.

れんそう 連想 图 (an) association.
── **連想する 動** ▶この写真はいつも私の子供時代を連想させる(この写真から子供時代を連想する) I always connect [associate] this picture with my childhood. (❗(1) 日本語にひかれて with の代わりに ×from を用いない。(2) connect の方が口語的) / (この写真は私に子供時代を思い出させる) This picture always reminds me of my childhood. ▶その旋律はあらしを連想させる(＝暗示する) The melody suggests a storm.
●連想ゲーム an association game.

*れんぞく **連続 图** (a) succession; [[同種類のものの一続き]] a series (❗単・複同形),《書》a sequence 《series より密接な関係の点を強調する》. I always

① **〔～連続〕** ●研究生活は失敗の連続だった My life as a researcher has been a succession of failures. ●現代美術に関する5回連続の講義が K大学で行われた A series of five lectures on modern art was [were] given at K University.

② **〔連続～〕** ●連続通話時間 uninterrupted phone call time. ●連続勝利(＝連勝) consecutive [straight] wins. ●連続試合安打 a consecutive-game hitting streak. ●連続試合出場 a consevutive-game playing streak. ▶衣笠選手は広島カープで 2,215 試合連続出場を果たした Kinugasa appeared in 2,215 consecutive games for the Hiroshima Carp.

③ **【連続して[で]】** ●連続して会議を開く hold successive conferences; hold conferences in succession. ●3日連続して雨が降り続いている It's been raining for three straight [consecutive, successive] days (❗×straight [consecutive, successive] three days の語順は不可) / It's been raining for three days straight [on end, in a row]. ▶火災が連続して(＝次々と)起こった A fire broke out one after another. ▶そのミュージカルは1年間連続で興業された The musical ran for [had a run of] a year.
── **連続的な 形** [[途切れることのない]] continuous, straight(❗後の方が口語的), uninterrupted; [[繰り返される]] continual; [[間を置かず規則的に続く]] consecutive; [[次々と続く]] successive.
── **連続する 動** continue. (⇨続く)
●連続殺人事件 a case of successive murders. ●連続性 continuity. ●連続テレビドラマ a serial TV drama.

れんだ 連打 【ボクシング】 continuous punches [blows]; 【野球】 continuous [consecutive] hits. ●チャンピオンに連打を浴びせる hit the champi-

on repeatedly; pummel the champion. ●5連打で山田(投手)をノックアウトする knock out Yamada with five continuous hits.

れんたい 連体 ●連体形 〖文法〗 the attributive form (of a verb). ●連体詞〖文法〗a prenominal adjective.

れんたい 連帯 图 (結束) solidarity. ●連帯責任を負う assume joint [collective] responsibility 《for》; 〖法律〗 be jointly liable 《for》.
── **連帯の 形** joint; 《やや書》 collective.
── **連帯して 副** jointly. ●彼らはこの計画に連帯してあたった They worked jointly on this project.
●連帯感 a (strong) sense of solidarity [(共同意識) togetherness]; (仲間意識) a (strong) feeling of friendship [(やや古) fellowship]. ●地域住民の連帯感の欠如 the lack of community spirit. ●連帯保証人〖法律〗 (stand) joint surety 《for him》.

れんたい 連隊 a regiment. ▶この連隊の指揮官はだれだ Who is in command [(the) commander] of this regiment?
●連隊長 a regimental commander [leader]. (❗通例 colonel (大佐)がなる)

れんだい 蓮台 a lotus pedestal.

レンタカー 《米》 a rent-a-car, a rental car;《英》a híre càr, a hire-and-drive. ●レンタカーを借りる rent [×borrow] a car. (❗borrow は「無料で借りる」の意)

レンタサイクル a rental [a rented] bicycle.

れんたつ 練達 图 (熟練) skill; (熟達) expertness; (精通) mastery 《of》; proficiency 《in, at》.
── **練達の** skillful; expert; masterly.
── **練達する 動** become [(している) be] skilled [expert] 《in, at》.

レンタル (a) rental;〖期限付き移籍〗a loan. (❗この意で rental を用いるのはまれ (⇨ローン)) ●1日300円のレンタル料で at a rental of 300 yen a day.
●レンタルビデオ a rental video. (❗「レンタル業務」をさすときは video rentals, その店は a video rental shop)

れんたん 連炭 a briquette /brikét/.

れんだん 連弾 图〖音楽〗a four-hand performance.
── **連弾する 動** play a (piano) duet.
●連弾曲 a piano duet; a piano piece for four hands.

レンチ 〖工具〗《米》a wrench;《英》a spanner.

れんちしん 廉恥心 ●廉恥心がない have no sense of honor; (恥知らずである) have no sense of shame (❗「信義・名誉を重んじる気持ちがない」の意); be shameless 《about》.

れんちゅう 連中 〖奴ら〗《話》fellows,《話》guys (⇨奴); 〖仲間〗(ともに時を過ごす) company; (同じ職業・趣味などの) a set;《話》(同類の) a lot. ●以上3語とも集合的で単・複両扱い ●気のいい連中 good-natured fellows [guys]. ●金持ち連中 the wealthy set. ●奇妙な連中 a queer lot. (❗「ゲイ」を暗示) ●悪い連中とつきあう keep bad company. ●酔っ払い連中[の一団] a company of drunkards.

れんちょく 廉直 《書》 rectitude; uprightness. ●廉直の士 a person of rectitude; an upright person.

れんてつ 錬鉄 wrought /rɔ́ːt/ iron.
●錬鉄法 puddling. ●錬鉄炉 a púddling fùrnace.

れんとう 連投 ●3連投する pitch in three successive games.

れんとう 連騰 图 a straight [a consecutive] rise 《in stock prices》.

―― 連騰する 動 rise straight [consecutively].
れんどう 連動 图 a joint movement. ―― 連動する 動 interlóck.
● 連動装置 interlock.
レントゲン [＜ドイツの X 線発見者 Roentgen より] (X 線写真・検査) an X-ray; (X 線) X-rays. ● レントゲン写真を調べる examine [read, interpret] an X-ray (photograph). ▶レントゲンを撮ってもらいに病院へ行く go to the hospital for an X-ray. ▶胸のレントゲンを撮った(＝撮ってもらった) I had my chest X-rayed./I had a chest X-ray [an X-ray on my chest]./(技師が撮った) They X-rayed [took an X-ray of] my chest. ▶レントゲンの結果は異常がなかった The X-ray showed nothing wrong./The X-ray was clear.
● レントゲン技師 a radiologist; a radiographer.
● レントゲン線 (X 線) X rays.
れんにゅう 練乳 condensed milk.
れんねん 連年 ● 連年の (何年にもわたって) for some [many] years; (来る年も来る年も) year after year.
れんぱ 連破 successive victories [wins]. (⇨連勝)
●そのチームを 3 連破する gain [win] three successive victories over the team; defeat [down] the team three times in a row [successively].
れんぱ 連覇 ● 3 連覇する win the championship three seasons running [in succession].
れんばい 廉売 a (bargain) sale. (⇨安売り) ● 廉売合戦をする have [carry on] a price war.
れんぱい 連敗 图 successive [straight, a series of] losses [defeats]; a losing streak. ● 7 連敗を免れる avoid a 7-game losing streak. ● 連敗ストッパー投手 a stopper.
―― 連敗する 動 suffer successive defeats; lose games in a row [successively]. ● 5 連敗する lose five straight games; undergo a 5-game losing streak.
れんぱつ 連発 ―― 連発する 動 (銃・質問などを) fire ... in succession [《やや書》 successively]. ▶その警官は犯人めがけて銃を連発した The police officer fired shots at the suspect in succession. ▶彼はあくびを連発した He gave one yawn after another.
● 連発銃 a six-shooter (という)
れんばん 連判 (連名の署名) a joint signature. 事情 米英にははんこを押す習慣がない) ● 連判を押す sign jointly; sign one's names. ● 連判状 a covenant /kˈʌvənənt/ under joint signature.
れんばん 連番 ● 連番で買う buy 《lottery tickets》 in serial [a consecutive] numbers.
れんびん 憐憫 ● 憐憫の情をもよおす feel pity 《for him》; take pity 《on him》.
レンブラント 〘オランダの画家〙 Rembrandt (〜 van Rijn).
れんぼ 恋慕 ―― 恋慕する 動 be in love 《with》; be attached 《to》.
れんぽう 連邦 图 a federation; a union. ● ロシア連邦 the Russian Federation. ● イギリス連邦 the Commonwealth (of Nations). ● アメリカ連邦政府 the Federal Government of the U.S. ● (アメリカ)連邦捜査局 the Federal Bureau of Investigation (略して FBI).
―― 連邦(政府)の 形 federal.
● 連邦制度 a federal system; federalism.
れんぽう 連峰 (...の峰) the peaks 《of》. ● ヒマラヤ連峰 the peaks of the Himalayas.
れんま 練磨 ● 百戦練磨 ⇨百戦 [成句]
―― 練磨する 動 (⇨練成する) ● 自己を厳しく練磨する discipline oneself strictly.
れんめい 連名 a joint signature. ● 連名で抗議文を出す make a written protest under a joint signature.
れんめい 連盟 a league; (団体の連合体) a federation. ● 日本高等学校野球連盟に加入する enter [join] the Japan High School Baseball Federation.
れんめん 連綿 ―― 連綿たる 形 continuous; (途切れない) unbroken.
―― 連綿と 副 continuously; without a break. ▶我が家系は奈良時代より連綿と続いている Our family has continued without a break ever since the Nara period.
れんや 連夜 图 every night [evening].
―― 連夜の 形 nightly. ▶私は連夜の忘年会でいささか気味が悪い I'm a bit tired from going to year-end parties every night.
れんよう 連用 ● 睡眠薬を連用する continue to take sleeping pills; take sleeping pills without a day's break.
● 連用形 〘文法〙 the continuative form (of a verb). ● 連用修飾語 〘文法〙 a modifier of a verbal, adjectival, or adverbial element.
:れんらく 連絡 图 〘交通機関の接続〙 (a) connection; 〘接触〙 contact, touch, 〘通信〙 communication.
①【連絡～】 ● 連絡便に間に合う[乗り遅れる] catch [miss] one's [the] connection. (❗列車・バスなど) ▶連絡先(＝電話番号)をお教えください Could I have a telephone number where you can be reached [《話》 where we can contact you]?/Do you have a contact phone number?
②【連絡が】 ● 日中はバスと列車との連絡が悪い We have a poor [a bad] bus connection with the train during the daytime. ▶その町との[AB 間の]電話連絡がとだえた The telephone communication with the town [between A and B] has been cut off. ▶古い友人との連絡がとだえてしまった I have lost contact [been out of touch] with my old friend. ▶何度か電話してやっと彼と連絡がとれた I finally made contact with [reached, got] him after calling several times. (❗(1) make contact は特に努力を含意する. (2) 過去の 1 回限りの行為が「とれた」という場合には could (do) は不可) ▶彼が死んだという連絡(＝知らせ)があった We had news [word] of his death./News [Word] came of his death. (❗(1) news, word は無冠詞. 句の代わりに that he had died も可. (2) 前の方が一般的) ▶彼女からまもなく連絡がいくと思います You'll hear from her soon. (⇨(3))
③【連絡を】 ● 連絡をする[とる] (⇨動) ● 連絡をつける (⇨② [第 4 文例]) ● 連絡を取り合う communicate 《with》. ● 連絡をもらう hear from him. (❗手紙・電話などで) ● 連絡を絶つ lose contact 《with》. ▶私は彼女とインターネットで連絡をとりあっている I am [《保っている》 keep] in touch 《with》 her on the Internet. (❗touch と contact は電話・手紙など何らかの通信手段でやりとりをしていること. communication は直接会ったり電話・手紙で情報交換しあうこと)
会話 「そのうちご連絡を差し上げます」「ご連絡をお待ちしております」 "I'll be in touch with you soon." "I'm looking forward to hearing from you." (❗未来形で用いられる be の意で, 動作を表す)
―― 連絡する 動 〘交通機関の接続〙 connect [be connected] 《with》; 〘電話・手紙・メールなどで〙 contact, make* contact 《with》, get* in touch 《with》. (❗最後的が最も口語的の (⇨[第 3 文例])); 〘報

告する]] report; (知らせる) let* 《him》 know. ▶その島は汽船で本土と連絡している The island *is connected with* the mainland by a steamer. ▶この普通列車はA駅で急行と連絡している This local train *connects* [*is connected, makes connection*] *with* the express at A Station. ▶その件で彼に電話で連絡した I *got in touch with* [*made contact with, contacted*] him about the matter by telephone. (⚠ ✕contact with は不可) ▶彼は手がかりを見つけたと連絡してきた He *reported* having found out a clue. ▶あちらに着きしだい連絡します I'll *let* you *know* [(電話する) *call* you (*up*)] as soon as I get there.

• 連絡駅 a junction; a connécting stàtion. • 連絡会 a liaison conference. • 連絡係[窓口] a contact person. • 連絡切符 a connection ticket. • 連絡事務所 (組織間の) a liaison /líéizn/ office. • 連絡船 a ferry(boat)《plying between A and B》. • 連絡網 an emergency call network.

れんりつ 連立 (政治的な提携) a coalition. • 三党立 a three-party *coalition*.
• 連立政権 a coalition government. • 連立内閣 a coalition cabinet. • 連立方程式 〖数学〗 simultaneous equations.

れんれん 恋々 ▶恋々とする (異性に) feel a strong attachment 《*to* him》; (地位などに) cling to one's post.

ろ

ろ 炉 〖溶鉱炉〗a furnace; 〖原子炉〗a (nuclear) reactor.

ろ 絽 (説明的に) high quality silk gauze /gɔ́ːz/ (used for making *kimonos* for high summer).
- 絽の着物 a *kimono* of *silk gauze*.
- 絽刺し embroidery on quality silk gauze.

ろ 櫓 an oar, (小さな) a scull. ●櫓をこぐ pull an *oar*.

ロアール ●ロアール川 the Loire /lwάːr/.

ろあく 露悪 ●あの男には露悪趣味がある He likes to *show off* his *faults* [*shortcomings, bad points*].

ロイター 〖英国などの通信社〗Reuters Trust.

ロイヤリティー (⇨ロイヤルティー)

ロイヤル 〖王(室)の〗royal.
- ロイヤルファミリー the royal family. ●ロイヤルゼリー (⇨ローヤルゼリー) ●ロイヤルボックス the royal box.
- ロイヤルフラッシュ (トランプの) royal flush.

ロイヤルティー 〖特許権・商標などの使用料〗a royalty (**!** 通例複数形で)

ろう 労 〖手数〗trouble, 〖骨折り〗pains; 〖労力〗labor; 〖努力〗(an) effort. (**!** しばしば複数形で) (⇨苦労) ●彼の労に報いる[をねぎらう] reward [thank] him for his *trouble* [*pains, labor*]. ●労せずして (=労なく) He spares no *pains* [*trouble, effort*] for his students.
- 労を取る ●争いを仲裁する労を取る take the *trouble* to reconcile the dispute. (関連 紛争の調停をする人を a troubleshooter という)

ろう 牢 a prison, a jail. 〖刑務所〗●牢を破る break out of *prison*. (⇨脱獄)
- 牢破り a jailbreak.

ろう 楼 a tall building, (塔) a tower. ●三層楼 a three-storied tower; a three-story tower.

ろう 蝋 wax. ●ろうを引く wax 《it》. ●ろうそくのろうがたれている Candle *wax* is running down.
- 蝋紙 《主に米》wax(ed) paper, 《英》greaseproof paper. ●蝋細工 a waxwork. ●蝋人形 a wax doll; (等身大の) a waxwork. ●蝋人形館 a wax museum; a waxworks (**!** 単・複同形).

ろうあ 聾唖 ●聾唖学校 a school for the deaf and (the) mute. ●聾唖者 a deaf-mute; a hearing impaired person.

ろうえい 朗詠 a (melodious) recitation.
— **朗詠する** 動 漢詩[和歌]を朗詠する *recite* a Chinese poem [a *tanka*].

ろうえい 漏洩 ●機密の漏洩 a leak [《やや書》(a) leakage] of secret information.

ろうえき 労役 labor. ●3年の労役を宣告される be sentenced to three years' hard *labor*. ●2年の労役に服する serve a two-year sentence of *labor*.

ろうおう 老翁 a very old man (複 ~ men).

ろうおう 老媼 a very old woman (複 women).

*ろうか 廊下 〖建物の〗a corridor, 《米》a hall, a hallway; 〖通路〗a passage(way).

> **使い分け corridor** 建物の各部をつないだり、あるいはホテル・学校などの各部屋が出入り口を持っている廊下の意。
> **hall** 家の玄関を入ってすぐの広間の意。《米》では corridor の意でも用いられる。

●渡り廊下 a breezeway. ●廊下をさらに行くと弁護士の事務所がもう三つある Down the *corridor* (there) are three more lawyer's offices. (**!** there をつけない場合は廊下を前にして説明するときなどに用いる) ●廊下は静かに歩きなさい Walk along the *corridors* [*halls*] quietly. ●トイレは廊下のつきあたりにあります The bathroom is at the end of [down] the *hall*. (**!** down は「話し手から離れて(向こうに)」の意)

ろうか 老化 图 aging; 〖老衰〗senility.
— **老化する** 動 age; get [grow] old. ●頭の老化を防ぐ prevent one's mind (from) *aging*. ●老化は足からくると言われている People say the legs are the first to be affected by *aging*.
- 老化現象 a symptom of aging.

ろうかい 老獪 ●老獪な 形 (こうかつな) cunning; (ずる賢い) sly, 《やや書》wily /wáili/; (策略にたけた) crafty.

ろうがい 老害 (説明的に) problems caused by the elderly.

ろうかく 楼閣 a tower; a lofty building. ●空中楼閣《build》castles in the air. ●その計画は砂上の楼閣(=非現実的)だ The plan is *unrealistic* [(粗雑で成功しそうもないもの) just *a house of cards*].

ろうがっこう 聾学校 a school for the deaf.

ろうがん 老眼 图 〖医学〗presbyopia; (説明的に) farsightedness due to old age. ●老眼になってきた My eyes are aging.
— **老眼の** 形 presbyopic.
- 老眼鏡 (a pair of) réading glàsses; spectacles for the aged.

ろうきほう 労基法 〖「労働基準法」の略〗the Labor Standards Law.

ろうきゅう 老朽 — **老朽化した** 形 decrepit /dikrépət/, 《やや書》time-worn; (古い) old. ●荒れはてた老朽(化した)建物 a run-down *old* building.
— **老朽化する** 動 get time-worn; become too old for use.

ろうきょう 老境 ●老境に入る attain *advanced age*; get *advanced in years*.

ろうきょく 浪曲 (⇨回 浪花節)

ろうく 老軀 an old body. (⇨老骨, 老体)

ろうく 労苦 trouble. (⇨苦労, 骨折り)

ろうけつぞめ 﨟纈染め ●﨟纈染めの 形 batik /bətíːk/.

ろうこ 牢固 ●牢固たる決意 *firm* [*unyielding, iron*] determination.

ろうご 老後 ●老後に備える prepare [provide] for one's *old age*. ●老後を平和に過ごす live peacefully *in* one's *old age*.

ろうこう 老巧 — **老巧な** 形 experienced; veteran.
- 老巧な政治家 a *veteran* politician.

ろうこう 陋巷 (むさくるしい路地裏) a squalid back alley; (スラム) a slum.
- 陋巷に朽(く)ち果てる ●彼は陋巷に朽ち果てた 'He died a lonely death in the squalid back alley.'/His talent was lost to the world.

ろうごく 牢獄 a prison, a jail. (⇨刑務所)

ろうこつ 老骨 ●老骨に鞭打つ ●老骨にむち打って(=老人ではあるが頑張って)働く work assiduously in spite of *old age* [though *one is old*]. (**!**

ろうさい 労災 workmen's [workwomen's] accidents.
- 労災保険 workmen's compensation insurance. ● 労災補償 workers' compensation.

ろうさく 労作 a painstaking [a laborious] work; (力作) a *tour de force*. ▶彼の超電導に関する論文はなかなかの労作だ His paper on superconductivity is quite a *painstaking work*.

ろうざん 老残 ● 老残の身をさらす live out the rest of one's life doing nothing worthwhile (ℓ「残りの人生を無為に過ごす」の意); be in one's dotage; be weak in body and mind because of old age.

ろうし 老子 [古代中国の思想家] Lao Zi /láuzíə/, Lao-tzu /láutsúː/. (関連) 老子の教えは道教 (Taoism /dáuɪzm, táu-/) という.

ろうし 老師 (僧) an old [an aged] priest; (先生) an old [an aged] teacher.

ろうし 労使 labor and management; management and unions ((主に英) workers). (ℓ いずれも語順の入れ替え可) ● 労使紛争を調停する arbitrate disputes between *management and workers*; arbitrate *labor disputes*. ● 労使交渉が始まった Negotiations started between *labor and management*. ▶労使関係は改善されつつある The relations between *labor and management* are improving./The *labor-management* [The *industrial*] relations are improving.

ろうし 労資 (労働者と資本家) capital and labor.

ろうし 牢死 ── 牢死する 動 die in prison.

ろうし 浪士 a lordless [a masterless] *samurai*.

ろうしゅう 老醜 ● 老醜をさらす look ugly with age; get crabby with age.

ろうしゅう 陋習 a (lingering) bad custom; ● 旧来の陋習を打ち破る do away with [break down] age-old *bad customs*.

ろうじゅう 老中 [歴史] a *roju*, (説明的に) an official of the highest rank in the Shogunate government.

ろうじゅく 老熟 (⇨国 円熟)

ろうしゅつ 漏出 図 (a) leakage; (a) spillage. ▶事故による油の漏出が海洋汚染の主な原因である The accidental *spillage* of oil is a major cause of ocean pollution.
── 漏出する 動 leak [spill] 《*from*》.
● 漏出量 [物] a leakage; (a) spillage.

ろうしょう 老少 (老人と少年少女) the old and the young.

ろうしょう 老将 an old general.

ろうしょう 朗唱 ── 朗唱する 動 read [(暗記で) recite] 《a poem》loudly [in a loud voice].

ろうじょう 楼上 [2 階](米) the second floor; (英) the first floor; [高い建物の上] on the upper floor of a tall building [a tower].

ろうじょう 籠城 ── 籠城する 動 (城を固守する) hold the castle; (包囲されている) be besieged. ● ホテルに籠城して(=閉じこもって)小説を書く shut oneself up in a hotel room and write a novel.
● 籠城軍 a besieged army.

ろうじょう 朗色 a merry [a cheerful] mood.

*ろうじん 老人 (男性)an older [an old, an elderly] man (働men); (女性) an old [an old, an elderly] woman (働women /wímɪn/) (ℓ an old man [woman] は正しい英語だが, 公の場, 特に本人の前では特別の場合を除いて避けて older, elderly を用いる方がよい);(総称) older [old, elderly] people, the old [elderly, (やや様) aged]; (お年寄り) senior citizens (ℓ old people の婉曲語). (お年寄り) ● 老人になる become [grow] old. (ℓ ×become old people とはいわない) ▶若者は老人を敬わなければならない Young people should respect *older* [*elderly*, *senior*] *people*.
- 老人医学 geriatrics. ● 老人学 gèrontólogy.
- 老人性精神病 [医学] senile psychosis. ● 老人性痴呆症 [医学] senile dementia. ● 老人性白内障 [医学] senile cataract. ● 老人大学 a college for the aged; a University of the Third Age.
- 老人パワー the power of the older generation; gray power. ● 老人日帰り介護施設 a day-care center. ● 老人福祉 old people's welfare. ● 老人ホーム (⇨老人ホーム)

ろうじんホーム 老人ホーム a home (やや婉曲的) an institution) for senior citizens; (英) an old people's home; (養護老人ホーム) a nursing home.

ろうすい 老衰 図 senility; infirmity of old age. ● 老衰(=年老いて)で死ぬ die of *old age*.
── 老衰する 動 become senile [infirm with age].

ろうすい 漏水 a water leak; a leak [(やや書) (a) leakage] of water. ● 漏水箇所がつきとめられない We can't find the *leak*./We cannot find out where the *leak* started.

ろうする 労する work hard. (⇨労) ● 労せずして without effort; (簡単に) easily. ▶彼はいつも労せずして何かを得ようとする He always tries to get something *without effort*. ▶ピッチャーの暴投で労せずして三塁に進んだ He advanced to third *easily* on a wild pitch. ▶労せずして得たものは容易になくなる(=悪銭身につかず)《ことわざ》Easy come, easy go.

ろうする 弄する ● 策を弄する use unfair [dirty] means; use dirty tricks. ● 駄弁を弄する talk rubbish; chatter away 《to kill time》.

ろうする 聾する ● 耳を聾するばかりの大音響 a *deafening* [an *earsplitting*] noise.

ろうせい 老成 ● 老成した(=円熟した)人物 a *mature* [(経験豊かな) an *experienced*] person. ▶あの青年はやけに老成している That young man seems too *mature* for his age.

ろうせき 蝋石 figure stone; pagodite; [地学] agalmatolite.

ろうぜき 狼藉 ❶ [乱雑] disorder; a mass. ● 落花狼藉 (⇨落花 [成句])
❷ [乱暴をすること] ● 狼藉をはたらく do violence 《to him》.
● 狼藉者 a rowdy fellow; a wild fellow.

ろうせずして 労せずして (⇨労する)

ろうそ 労組 [『労働組合』の略] a labor union.

ろうそう 老荘 (老子と荘子) Lao Zi and Zhuang Zi.
● 老荘の学 the philosophy of *Lao Zi and Zhuang Zi*.

ろうそく 蝋燭 a candle. 【語法】 米英では現在でもろうそくがパーティーや家庭の夕食などで広く使われている. ● ろうそくに[消す] light [put out, (吹き消す) blow out] *a candle*. ● ろうそくを立てにろうそくを立てる put a *candle* in the candlestick [candle holder]. ● ろうそくの明かりで食事をする have dinner [(書) dine] by *candlelight* [by the light of *candles*].

ろうたい 老体 (老人の体) an old body; (年寄り) an old person, (婉曲的) an elderly man [woman, person]. ● 老体(=高齢)にもかかわらず in spite of one's *old* [*advanced*, *great*] *age*.

ろうたいか 老大家 ● 英文学の老大家(=権威者) an *old authority* on English literature. ● 書道の老大家 an *old master* of calligraphy. (⇨大家[1])

ろうたいこく 老大国 an old great nation [country].

ろうたけた 臈長けた graceful; elegant.

ろうちん 労賃 wages. (⇨賃金)

ろうでん 漏電 图 〖電気〗 a leak; (説明的に) an escape [a loss] of electricity; (ショート) a short (circuit).
── 漏電する 動 short-circuit.

ろうと 漏斗 a funnel.

ろうとう 郎党 (家の子郎党・取り巻き) one's followers; an entourage /ɑ̀ːntərɑ́ːʒ/. (⚠ 単・複両扱い)

***ろうどう** 労働 图 labor; work. (⇨仕事 [類語]) ● 肉体労働 physical *labor*. ● 筋肉労働 manual *work* [*labor*]. ● 頭脳労働 brain [mental] *work*. (⚠ brain work は brainwork のように1語でもつづる) ● 強制労働 forced *labor*. ● 重労働 hard *labor*. ● 日雇い労働 day *work*. ● 単純労働 simple *labor*. ● 時間外労働 overtime *working*. ● 週5日労働 《米》 a five-day *workweek*; 《英》 a five-day *working week*. ● 1日8時間労働(=勤務)をする work (for) eight hours a day; work [have] an eight-hour day.
── 労働する 動 work; labor. (⇨働く)
● 労働委員会 a labor relations commission. ● 労働運動 a labor movement. ● 労働歌 a work song. (⚠ a labor song ともいう) ● 労働関係調整法 the Labor Relations Adjustment Law. ● 労働基準監督署 Labor Standards Inspection Office. ● 労働基準局 the Labor Standards Bureau. ● 労働基準法 the Labor Standards Law. ● 労働基本権 the basic legal rights of labor. ● 労働協約 [契約] a labor contract. ● 労働権 the right to labor [work]. ● 労働災害 a labor accident. ● 労働災害補償 workmen's accident compensation. ● 労働三権 the three major labor rights. (参考) 団結権・争議権・団体交渉権のこと) ● 労働時間 wórking hòurs. ▶彼の1日の労働時間は平均8時間です His average *workday* [*working day*] is eight hours./(彼は1日平均8時間働く) He works (for) eight hours a day on (an [the]) average. ● 労働集約的 [型] 産業 the labor-intensive industry. ● 労働条件 working conditions. ● 労働条件の悪化 deterioration of *working conditions*. ● 労働人口 the working population. ● 労働生産性 labor productivity. ● 労働争議 labor disputes; (スト) (a) strike. ● 労働党 《英国》 the Labour Party. ● 労働法 the Labor Law. ● 労働問題 a labor problem.

ろうどうくみあい 労働組合 《米》 a labor union; 《英》 a trade(s) union. ● 職業別 [産業別; 企業別] 労働組合 a craft [an industrial; an enterprise] union. ● 労働組合を作る [organize] a *labor union*. ● 労働組合を解散する [脱退する] dissolove [leave] a *labor union*. ● 労働組合に加入する join a *labor union*; become a union member.
● 労働組合員 a union member; a member of a labor union. ● 労働組合法 the Labor [Trade] Union Law.

ろうどうしゃ 労働者 a worker; (肉体労働者) a laborer; (集合的) labor, working people. ● 熟練 [非熟練] 労働者 a skilled [an unskilled] *worker*. ● 日雇い労働者 a day *laborer*. ● 臨時雇い [出稼ぎ; 季節] 労働者 a temporary [a migrant /máigrənt/; seasonal] *worker*. ● 外国人労働者 a foreign *worker* [*laborer*]. ● 労働者の権利 the rights of *labor*; *worker*'s rights. ● 労働者と会社側 (⇨労使)
● 労働者階級 the working class(es). ● 労働者派遣業 temporary worker services; manpower displacing business.

ろうどうりょく 労働力 the work force; (資本に対して) labor. ● 労働力不足 a *labor* shortage. ● 潜在的労働力 the potential *labor force*.

ろうどく 朗読 图 〖公開の〗 a reading, a recital. ● 詩の朗読 a poetry *reading*.
── 朗読する 動 自作の詩を朗読する give a reading of one's poetry (⚠ 「朗読会をする」の意にもなる); recite one's poetry.

ろうにゃく 老若 (老いも若きも) young and old. (⚠ 語順に注意)
● 老若男女(なんにょ) men and women of all ages, people of all ages and both sexes. ● 老若男女を問わず without distinction of [regardless of], irrespective of] *age* or *sex*.

ろうにん 浪人 (主君を持たない武士) a masterless *samurai*; (入試に失敗し次の機会に備えて勉強している卒業生)(説明的に) a graduate, usually of a high school, who failed his college entrance exam(s) (*for* the first [second, ...] time) and is studying for the next chance. (⚠ 《 》 内を入れると「一 [二...] 浪」を表せる)

ろうねん 老年 old age. (⇨老齢) ● 老年期にある be *in* (one's) *old age*. ● 老年の男 a man of *old* [*advanced*] *age*; an older [an *aged*] man. (⚠ aged の方が高齢 ⇨老人)
● 老年学 gerontology. ● 老年学の gerontological. ● 老年学者 a gerontologist.

ろうば 老馬 an old horse.

ろうば 老婆 an older [an old] woman (複 women /wímin/). ● 老婆心から (⇨老婆心)

ろうばい 老梅 an old *ume* tree.

ろうばい 狼狽 〖混乱〗 a confusion; 〖狂乱状態〗 (a) panic. ▶彼は狼狽の色をみせた He showed his *confusion*.
── 狼狽する 動 be confused; get into a panic. (⇨慌てる ❶) ▶彼は意外な質問に狼狽した He *was confused* with the unexpected question. ▶私は狼狽して逃げた I fled *in confusion* [*in a panic*].

ろうばい 蝋梅 〖植物〗 a Japanese allspice; a winter sweet.

ろうはいぶつ 老廃物 waste. (⚠ 時に複数形で)

ろうばしん 老婆心 ● 老婆心から out of kindness [goodwill].

ろうひ 浪費 图 (a) waste (↔ thrift); 〖乱費, ぜいたく〗 extravagance. ● 彼の妻の浪費 his wife's *extravagance*. ▶そうすることは時間の浪費だ It is a *waste* of time doing so.
── 浪費する 動 waste 《on》; (はかげたむだ遣いをする) squander 《on》 (⚠ 時に気前よく遺い果たすこともいう); throw*... away. ● とばくに金を浪費する waste [squander] one's money *on* gambling; throw away one's money by gambling. ● プラモデル作りに時間を浪費する *waste* one's time (*on* [*in*]) making plastic models. (⚠ 動名詞の前では前置詞は省略する方が普通) ▶彼らは資源を浪費している They *are wasting* resources./They *are wasteful of* [*with*] resources.
● 浪費家 a wasteful [an extravagant] person (⚠ 前の方は行為に, 後の方は性格・習慣に用いることが多い (⇨むだ)); (金遣いの荒い人) a spendthrift; (将来のことを考えずに浪費する人) 《やや話》 a waster. ● 浪費癖 a wasteful habit.

ろうびょう 老病 (老人病) illnesses of elderly people; (老衰) senility; (全身的に弱る) 〖書〗 de-

ろうふ crepitude.

ろうふ 老父 one's old [aged] father.

ろうへい 老兵 ▶老兵は死なず、ただ消え去るのみ Old soldiers never die; they just fade away. (参考 昔の軍歌のより)

ろうぼ 老母 one's old [aged] mother.

ろうほう 朗報 ─朗報に接する receive the good [happy] news 《of; that 節》.

ろうぼく 老木 an old tree.

ろうむ 労務 labor; work.
● 労務課 the labor section. ● 労務管理 personnél management; labor management. ● 労務者 a laborer, a worker; (日雇いの) a day laborer.

ろうもん 楼門 a two-story gate building; a two-storied gate building; a tower gate.

ろうや 牢屋 a prison. (⇨刑務所)

ろうゆう 老雄 a one-time hero (徽 ~es).

ろうゆう 老優 an old actor [(女優) actress].

ろうよう 老幼 (年寄りと子供) old people and children.

ろうらい 老来 ▶私の祖父は老来いよいよ壮健である My grandfather is enjoying good health in his old age.

ろうらく 籠絡 ── 籠絡する 動 tempt [coax, cajole] 《him into doing》; entice 《him to do》.

＊ろうりょく 労力 (労働) labor; (努力) (an) effort (! しばしば複数形で); (骨折り) pains, trouble; (尽力) a service (! しばしば複数形で). ─労力を費やす spend one's labor [trouble] 《on》; (努力する) make an effort 《to do》. ─労力を提供する offer one's labor [services] 《to him》. ▶その仕事は大変な労力がいる The work needs a lot of labor [effort]./(やや書) The work is very laborious /ləbɔ́ːriəs/. ─この機械は労力の節約になる This machine saves (us) labor./This is a labor-saving machine. ▶我々はそれをするためなら努力を惜しみません We will spare no effort [pains, trouble] to do it./We won't spare ourselves to do it.

ろうれい 老齢 old age (!65 歳程度以上); (婉曲的) the third age, (米) vintage years (! 日本の「熟年」に当たる。その他 sunset years (日没年齢)、twilight years (たそがれ年齢) がある). ● 老齢に達する reach old age; (書) attain advanced age. (! 後の方が高齢) ● 老齢の人 an older (an elderly), (非常に高齢の) an aged] person. (⇨老人) ▶彼は老齢のため足腰が弱っている His legs are weak with (old) age./He has weak legs [He is weak in the legs] because of old age.
● 老齢人口 an aging [an elderly] population. ● 老齢年金 (be on) an old-age [a retirement] pension.

ろうれつ 陋劣 ── 陋劣な 形 (さもしい) mean; (軽蔑すべき) contemptible; (下劣な) degrading. (⇨卑劣な)

ろうれん 老練 ── 老練な 形 (経験を積んだ) véteran, experienced (! 前の語は高齢を暗示する); (熟練した) skilled; (専門的知識・技術のある) expert. (⇨ベテラン) ● 老練な医師 an experienced [a veteran, a skilled, an expert] doctor.

ろうろう 浪々 ● 浪々の(=失業中の)身 out of work [a job], jobless. (⇨失業)

ろうろう 朗々 ─ 朗々と 副 (=澄んでよく響く声で)詩を朗読する 《やや書》 read a poem in a resonant [a sonorous] voice; read a poem resonantly [sonorously].

ろうえい 露営 ── 露営する 動 bivouac /bívuæk/ (! 過去形・過去分詞形は bivouacked); encamp, camp out. (⇨野営)

ローカル [[特定の地方の]] local. (! national (全国)に対する語か、「田舎の」の意はない) ● 放送にローカルカラーを出す show local color in the broadcast.
● ローカル線 (鉄道の) a branch line. (! a local line は「短区間を走る路線」) ● ローカルニュース local news. ● ローカルバス [[コンピュータ]] a local bus. ● ローカル番組 a local program.

ローション lotion. ● アフターシェーブ[スキン]ローション after-shave [skin] lotion.

ロージングバッグ (⇨ロジンバッグ)

ロース a roast; (牛の) sirloin; (豚の) pork loin.

ローズウッド [[紫檀(ん)]] [[植物]] rosewood.

ロースクール [[法科大学校]] a law school.

ロースター [[焼き肉器、焼き網]] a roaster.

ロースト 名 (オーブンなどで焼いた焼き肉) a roast. ── ローストする 動 roast 《coffee beans》.
● ローストチキン roast chicken. ● ローストビーフ roast beef.

ローズマリー [[植物]] a rosemary /róuzməri/. (! 葉は U)

ロータリー (環状交差点) 《米》 a rotary, a traffic circle; 《英》 a roundabout.
● ロータリーエンジン a rotary engine. ● ロータリークラブ the Rotary Club.

ローティーン ● ローティーンの少年 a boy in his early teens [×low teens]. (!(1) ×a low-teen boy などとしない。(2) 13 歳から 15 歳ぐらいまで)(⇨ハイティーン)

ローテーション rotation. ● 先発ローテーション投手 a rotation pitcher. ● 他の 4 人の投手とともにローテーションを組んでいる rotate [be in the rotation] with the other four pitchers. ● ローテーションから外される be put out of [be demoted from] the rotation; lose one's spot in the rotation. ● ローテーションの軸である anchor the rotation. ● 5 人で回すローテーション a five-man rotation. ● ローテーションの谷間の先発投手 a spot starter. ● ローテーションで体育館を使う use the gymnasium in rotation.
● ローテーション(システム) [[サッカー]] rotation (system). (⇨ターンオーバー)

ロード [[野球]] a road. (俺 アウェイ) ● ロードに出る go on [hit] the road. ● 長いロードから戻る get home from a long road trip.

ロードアイランド [[米国の州]] Rhode Island 《略 R.I. 郵便略 RI》.

ロードショー [[新作映画の]] 《米》 a róad shòw (!「(劇・政治家などの)地方公演」「(テレビなどの)現地ロケ」の意もある); [[初演]] a premiere /primíər/.

ロードプライシング [[道路課金]] road pricing.

ロードマップ [[道路地図・工程表]] a road map.

ロードレース (1 回の) a road race; (競技の総称) road racing.

ロードワーク [[スポーツ]] roadwork.

ローヌ ─ ローヌ川 the Rhone /róun/.

ローハス [[健康的で持続可能なライフスタイル]] LOHAS /lóːhæs/ 《Lifestyles of Health and Sustainability の略》.

ローヒール low-heeled shoes.

ロープ [[綱、縄]] (a) rope. (⇨綱、縄) ▶彼はロープに追いつめられて容赦のない連打を浴びた He was mercilessly pummeled against the ropes.

ローファット [[低脂肪の]] low-fat.
● ローファットミルク low-fat milk.

ロープウエー a cable car; an aerial ropeway [cableway, railway]. ▶ロープウエーで山を降りる go down (↔up) a mountain by cable car.

ローボールヒッター [[野球]] a low-ball hitter.

ローマ Rome. ● ローマ人 a Roman. ● ローマ(人)の Roman.

ローマじ

- ローマは1日にして成らず《ことわざ》Rome was not built in a day.
- ローマカトリック教 Roman Catholicism. ● ローマカトリック教会 the Roman Catholic Church. ● ローマカトリック教徒 a (Roman) Catholic. ● ローマ字(⇨ローマ字) ● ローマ数字 Roman numerals. ● ローマ帝国 the Roman Empire. ● ローマ法王[教皇] a pope. (🔲 (1) 通例 the Pope. (2) 名前の前に Pope をつける)

ローマじ ローマ字 ● ローマ字で書く write [spell] in *Roman letters* [*the Roman alphabet*]. ▶プラットホームの駅名には，普通ローマ字が添えてある Station-names on railroad 《米》[railway 《英》] platforms usually have Roman transcription. (🔲 transcription は「(他の言語への)書き替え」の意)

> **参考** 日本語の固有名詞を英語の中で使う場合，ローマ字を使うことになるが，その際注意すべき点を簡単にまとめておく．
> (1) 訓令式とヘボン式： 英語に近いためヘボン式が好まれることが多い．
>
> | 訓令式 | ヘボン式 | | 訓令式 | ヘボン式 |
> |---|---|---|---|---|
> | si | shi | | syo | sho |
> | ti | chi | チャ | tya | cha |
> | tu | tsu | チュ | tyu | chu |
> | hu | fu | チョ | tyo | cho |
> | zi | ji | ジャ | zya | ja |
> | シャ sya | sha | ジュ | zyu | ju |
> | シュ syu | shu | ジョ | zyo | jo |
>
> (2) 長音：長音は母音の上に長音符 (¯) をつけて表すが，特に表記せず無視したり，英語のつづり方をまねて h を添えることも多い：大阪 *Osaka* / 王貞治 *Sada-haru Oh* [*Ō*].
> (3) 撥音(はつおん)：「ン」は一般には n で表されるが，英語のつづりをまねて b, m, p の前では m が用いられることが多い：朝日新聞 the *Asahi Shimbun*.
> (4) 促音：いわゆる「つまる音」は子音字を重ねて表す：札幌 *Sapporo* / 楽器 *gakki*.
> (5) 誤った読み方を避ける工夫：誤った読みを引き起こす恐れのある一部のつづり字の組み合わせでは，アポストロフィー(')やハイフン(-)などを使って誤った読みを避ける工夫がされることが多い：鈴木真一 *Shin-ichi* [*Shin'ichi*] Suzuki (🔲 *Shinichi* では「シニチ」と読まれる恐れがある) / (山陽本線) the *San-yo* [*San'yo*] Line. (🔲 *Sanyo* では「サニョ」と読まれる恐れがある)

ローヤルゼリー ròyal jélly.
ローラー a roller. ● ローラーコースター a roller coaster. ● ローラー作戦 《make [conduct]》 a house-to-house search. ● ローラースケート (⇨ローラースケート)
ローラーカナリヤ 〖鳥〗a roller canary.
ローラースケート roller-skating; 《靴》(a pair of) roller skates. ● ローラースケートをする roller-skate 《on a street》.
ロール ● ロールカーテン (巻き上げブラインド) 《米》a roller shade; 《英》a roller blind. ● ロールキャベツ 《和製語》a roll; 《和製語》a roll cake. ● ロールパン a (bread) roll. (🔲 ×roll bread とはいわない); 《米》a bun. ● ロールフィルム (巻きフィルム) a roll film.
ロールシャッハテスト a Rorschach test.
ロールプレイングゲーム a role-playing game 《略 RPG》.
ローン 〖芝生〗a lawn.
● ローンスキー grass skiing. ● ローンテニス lawn tennis. ● ローンボウリング lawn bowling.
ローン ❶ 〖貸付金〗a loan (⇨借金); 〖信用貸し〗credit. ● 銀行ローン a bank *loan*. ● 住宅ローン a housing [a house, a home] *loan*; a mortgage /mɔ́ːrgidʒ/. ● カードローン a card *loan*. ● 学生ローン a student *loan*. ● ローンの返済 repayment of the *loan*. ● ローンを組む take out a *loan*. ● 20か月ローンでダイヤの指輪を買う buy a diamond ring on a 20-month *loan* [on 20 months' *credit*]. ▶ローンが安く借りられると家が買いやすくなる The low *mortgage* on houses means that they buy easily.
❷ 〖期限付き移籍〗● 1年ローン one-season *loan*; a season-long *loan*. ● 3か月ローン three-month *loan*.

ろか 濾過 图 filtration.
—— 濾過する 動 ● 水を砂で濾過する *filter* water through the sand.
● 濾過器 a filter. ● 濾過紙 filter paper.

ろかた 路肩 the shoulder (of a road); (舗装していない) 《米》a soft shoulder; 《英》a verge. ▶路肩に注意《掲示》Soft Shoulders.

ロカビリー 〖音楽〗rockabilly.

***ろく** 六 six;〖6 番目の〗the sixth. (⇨三)

ろく 禄 a *samurai's* stipend /stáipend/ 《*of* three hundred *koku* of rice》. (🔲 stipend は牧師などの給与)
● 禄を食(は)む receive a stipend.

ログイン 图 〖接続開始〗〖コンピュータ〗log-in (↔log-off).
—— ログインする 動 log-in 《*to*, *from*》. ● 会員ページにログインする *log-in to* the membership web page [the web page of the membership].
● ログイン名 〖接続登録名〗a log-in name.

ろくおん 録音 图 (a) recording. ● 同時録音 a simultaneous *recording*. (⇨同時) ▶その録音は野外で行われた The *recording* took place in the open air.
—— 録音する 動 record, (特にテープに) tape, tape-record. ● 彼の演説をテープに録音する *record* his speech *on tape*; *tape* [*make a tape-recording of*] his speech.
● 録音機 a (tape-)recorder. ● 録音室 a recording studio. ● 録音装置 a recording apparatus.

ログオン (⇨圆 ログイン)

ろくが 録画 图 (videotape) recording.
—— 録画する 動 videotape (a TV program) on video (tape); video [videotape] 《a TV program》. (🔲 文脈上明らかな場合は単に tape も用いられる："Did you see it last night?" "I was out but I *taped* it."(「昨夜のあれ見た？」「出かけていたんだが，録画したよ」))
● 録画放送 a recorded [〖放送〗a transcribed] broadcast 《of the game》. (🔲「録音放送」の意にもなる)

***ろくがつ** 六月 June (略 Jun.). (⇨一月)

ろくさんせい 六三制 ● 六三制の教育制度 'the school education system of six years of primary and three years of middle school'; the 6-3 school education [educational] system.

ろくしゃくぼう 六尺棒 《米》a six-foot nightstick;《英》a six-foot truncheon.

***ろくじゅう** 六十 sixty; 〖60 番目の〗the sixtieth. (⇨二十, 五十)
● 六十の手習い 'One learns how to write at sixty.'/(学問に遅すぎることはない) It is never too late to learn.

ろくしょう 緑青 patina /pətíːnə/, 〖化学〗vérdigris. ▶パイプの表面に緑青が浮いている *Patina* has formed on the surface of the pipe.

ろくすっぽ ● ろくすっぽ考えもしないで thoughtlessly;

ろくだか 禄高 the whole sum of one's stipend /stáipend/.

ろくでなし 《役立たずの人》a góod-for-nòthing;《ぐうたら》《米話》a bum;《価値のない人》a worthless person. ●このろくでなし You *good-for-nothing*.

ろくでもない 《役立たずの》good-for-nothing;《価値のない》worthless. ●ろくでもないやつ a *good-for-nothing* (fellow).●あれはろくでもない(=見る価値がない)番組だ That program is *not worth watching*.

ろくな 〖よい〗 good*;〖満足な〗satisfactory;〖まともな〗decent. ●ろくな返事をしない do not give a *satisfactory* answer. ●ろくな(=これといった)本を持っていない have no books *to speak of* [*worth mentioning*]. ●この町にはろくな本屋も一軒もない There is no *good* [*decent*] bookstore in this city. ●この店にはろくなものは(=つまらないものを除いて)何もない There's *nothing* in this shop *but rubbish*. ▶何かにつけてろくなことがなかった(=万事うまく行かなかった) Everything went [×became] *wrong* for me./Nothing went all right for me.

ろくに 〖よく〗 well*;〖ちゃんと〗 properly;〖十分に〗 enough. ●ろくに眠れないから do not sleep *well*; get *little* sleep. ●ろくに見もしないで without looking at it *well* [*properly*]. ▶君ろくに話をする暇もない I don't have *enough* time to talk with you. ▶今日は調子が出ないね. ろくに(=ほとんど)練習しなかったんでしょう? You're not doing well today. You *hardly* even practiced, did you? (⚠even は強意語)

ろくねんせい 六年生 《小学校の》a sixth-year pupil;《米》a sixth grader;《英》a sixth-former. (⇨年生, 学年)

ログハウス a log house (複 houses /-ziz,《米》-siz/).

ろくぶんぎ 六分儀 a sextant.

ろくぼく 肋木 wall bars.

ろくまく 肋膜 『解剖』the pleura /plúərə/ (複 pleurae /plúəri:/).

● 肋膜炎 〖医学〗pleurisy.

ろくめんたい 六面体 図 a hexahedron /héksəhídrən/ (複 ~s, -dra).

—— 六面体の 動 hexahedral.

ろくよう 六曜 *rokuyo*, 《説明的に》six basic days, each of which is believed to have different workings on human activities.

ろくろ 轆轤 〖滑車〗a pulley;〖旋盤〗a (turning) lathe;〖陶工の〗a potter's wheel. ●ろくろでこけしを作る make [turn] *kokeshi* on a *lathe*. ●ろくろで花びんを作る make a vase *on* [by using] a *potter's wheel*.

● ろくろ首 a long-necked monster.

ろくろく well*. (⇨ろくに)

ロケ (⇨ロケーション)

ロケーション 〖場所〗(a) location. ●ロケーションに金沢へ行く go on *location* in [×to] Kanazawa. ●そのシーンはロケーション(=野外)で撮影された The scene was filmed [was shot] *on location*.

ロケット 〖装身具〗a locket.

ロケット 〖飛行体〗a rocket. (⚠「ロケット弾」の意でも用いる) ●3段[多段]式ロケット a three-stage [a multistage] *rocket*. ●月ロケット a lunar spaceship; a spaceship to the moon. ●宇宙ロケットを打ち上げる launch a space *rocket*. ●ロケット推進の *rocket*-propelled (missiles).

● ロケットエンジン a rócket èngine. ● ロケット工学 rocketry. ● ロケット弾 a rocket (bomb). ● ロケット燃料 rocket fuel. ● ロケット発射台 a rocket launch [launching] pad; a rocket launching site. ● ロケット砲 a rocket launcher.

ろけん 露見 (⇨発覚)

ロゴ (⇨ロゴマーク)

ろこう 露光 (⇨露出)

ロゴタイプ a logotype; a logo (複 ~s).

ろこつ 露骨 —— 露骨な 形 ●露骨な(=あからさまな)冗談 a *crude* [a *broad*] joke. ●露骨な描写[言葉] an *explicit* description [remark].

—— 露骨に 副 ●彼は物を露骨に(=思ったことをはっきり言う)人だ He is very *outspoken* [*straightforward*]./(ぶっきらぼうに) He speaks *bluntly*. ▶彼は露骨に(=包み隠さずに)怒りを表した He showed his anger *plainly* [*openly*]./(隠そうともしなかった) He didn't even try to hide his anger.

ロゴマーク 〖シンボルマーク〗a lógotype;《話》a logo /lóugou/;《和製語》logomark. ●会社のロゴ(マーク) a corporate *logo*.

ろざ 露座 ●露座の大仏 a huge statue of Buddha exposed to the weather [sitting out in the open].

ロザリオ [<ポルトガル語] a rosary /róuzəri/.

ロサンゼルス Los Angeles 《略 LA》.

ろし 濾紙 filter paper.

ろじ 路地 《裏通り》an alley, an alleyway; 《小道》a lane. ●路地裏に逃げ込む run into a back *alley*.

ろじ 露地 a field. ●温室ではなく露地で作ったトマトは本来のトマトのにおいと味がする Tomatoes grown in the *field*, not in the greenhouse, smell and taste like what they really are.

● 露地物野菜 vegetables grown outdoors [in open ground].

ロシア 〖国名〗Russia;《公式名》the Russian Federation. 《首都 Moscow》●ロシア人 a Russian;《総称》Russian people,《やや書》the Russians. ● ロシア語 Russian. ● ロシア(人)の Russian. ● ロシア皇帝 the Czar. ● ロシア正教会 the Russian (Orthodox) Church. ● ロシア文学 Russian literature.

ロシアンルーレット 〖拳銃を用いる死を賭した遊び〗Russian roulette.

ロジスティックス 〖物資の全般的な管理〗〖経済〗logistics.

ロジック 〖論理〗logic.

ろしゅつ 露出 図 (an) exposure. ●《写真の》露出(時間) an *exposure*. ●露出不足[過度]の写真 an underexposed [an overexposed] picture. ●露出度の高い服装 a *revealing* dress.

—— 露出する 動 〖肌などを〗expose;〖鉱脈などが〗crop out (-pp-). ●肌を露出する *expose* one's skin. ●彼の露出した胸 his *exposed* [*bare*] chest. ▶イスラム諸国の中には短パンにタンクトップ姿の女性がみだらに体を露出したという理由で逮捕されるところもある In some Moslem countries, a woman in shorts and a tank top could be arrested for indecent *exposure*.

● 露出狂 an exhibitionist;《俗》a fasher. ● 露出計 an exposure [a light] meter.

ろしょう 路床 《土木》a roadbed.

ろじょう 路上 ●路上(=通り)で遊ぶ play *on* [*in*] *the street*. ●路上で夜を明かしてチケットを手に入れる sleep out [on the sidewalk] all night] for tickets.

● 路上試験 a road test. (⚠「(新型車の)路上テスト」の意でも用いられる) ● 路上事故 《車道での事故》an accident on the road; a road accident. ● 路上駐車 street parking. (⚠「路上駐車をする」は park one's car *on the street*)

ろしん 炉心 (原子炉の) (nuclear) reactor core.
ロジンバッグ 〚野球〛 a rósin [a résin] bàg.
ロス 〚損失〛loss. ●時間のロス loss [(a) waste] of time. ●時間をロスする lose [waste] time.
ロス 〚「ロサンゼルス」の略〛(⇨ロサンゼルス)
ロスタイム 〚スポーツ〛injury time; added [additional] time; stoppage time, 《米》overtime, 《英》extra time (!) injury time は伝統的な表現で, 最近は added [additional] time を用いることが多い; 《和製語》loss time. ▶ロスタイムは3分です There will be three minutes of added [additional] time.
ロストボール 〚ゴルフ〛a lost ball.
ロゼ 〚＜フランス語〛〚ピンク色のワイン〛rosé /rouzéi/.
ろせん 路線 ● a line (!)比喩的にも用いる). (道筋) a route. ●(鉄道[バス]の)赤字路線 a deficit-ridden (railroad [bus]) route [line] ●党の路線に従う[変更する] follow [change] the party lines. ●決まった路線を走る run on regular routes. ●独自の路線を歩む take one's own line. ●路線価 the price of land adjoining a major road. ●路線図 a route map. ●路線バス a route bus.
ろそくたい 路側帯 the edge of a road.
ろだい 露台 (バルコニー) a balcony.
ろだな 炉棚 a mantelshelf 《pl. -shelves》.
ロダン 〚フランスの彫刻家〛 Rodin /roudǽn/ (Auguste 〜).
ロッカー a locker. ●コインロッカー a coin-operated 〔(まれ) a coin〕 locker.
●ロッカールーム a locker room; 〚野球〛a clubhouse.
ろっかく 六角 図 (六角形) a héxagon.
── **六角の** 形 hexágonal; six-sided.
ろっかん 六感. (⇨第六感)
ろっかんしんけい 肋間神経 〚解剖〛 the intercostal nerves.
●肋間神経痛 〚医学〛intercostal neuralgia.
ロッキー ●ロッキー山脈 the Rocky Mountains, the Rockies.
ろっきょくいっそう 六曲一双 a six-panel folding screen [byobu].
ロッキングチェア a rócking chàir.
ロック 〚錠前〛a lock. (⇨鍵(☆)) ▶ドアの開閉がどのようになっていますか. オートロックですか How does the door work? Is it self-locking?
ロック 〚音楽〛rock (music). ●野外ロックフェスティバル an outdoor [an open-air] rock festival.
●ロックミュージシャン a rock musician.
ロックアウト 図 a lockout.
── **ロックアウトする** 動 lock (the workers) out (of a factory).
ロッククライミング rock-climbing. ●ロッククライミングをする人 a rock-climber. ●ロッククライミングをする go rock-climbing.
ロックンロール 〚音楽〛rock'n'roll 《rock-and-roll の略》.
ろっこつ 肋骨 〚解剖〛 (1 本) a rib; (全体) the ribs. (⇨肋骨(ろっこつ))
ろっこん 六根 〚仏教〛six basic things that help make our "perception".
ロッジ a lodge.
ロッシーニ 〚イタリアの作曲家〛 Rossini /rousí:ni/ (Gioacchino 〜).
ロッテルダム 〚オランダの都市〛 Rotterdam /rátərdæ(:)m/.
ロット 〚同一製品の生産単位〛〚経済〛a lot. ●生産ロット a production lot. ●小ロット低コストで生産する produce in small lots and at low cost.
ロッド 〚棒; 釣りざお〛a rod.
●ロッドアンテナ 〚棒状アンテナ〛a rod antenna.
ろっぽう 六方 (東西南北と天地) north, south, east, and west plus heaven and earth.
ろっぽうぜんしょ 六法全書 the Compendium of Laws.
ろてい 露呈 图 (暴露) exposure.
── **露呈する** 動 ▶彼の指導力の限界がついに露呈した The limits of his leadership were exposed [(明らかにされた) were revealed, 《話》came out] [at last.
ロデオ 〚＜スペイン語〛a rodeo /róudiòu/ (複 〜s).
ろてん 露天 ●露天風呂 an open-air [an outdoor] (hot-spring) bath. ●露天掘り《米》strip mining; 《英》open-cast mining. ●露天掘りの炭鉱 a strip [an open-cast] coal mine.
ろてん 露店 a stand; (主に英) a (street) stall. ▶広場には野菜の露店がたくさん出ていた The square was full of vegetable stands.
●露店商 (人) a stand keeper; (街頭商人) a street vendor.
ろとう 路頭 ●路頭に迷う be (left) destitute; be hard up. ●家族を路頭に迷わす leave one's family destitute.
ろとう 露頭 (鉱脈・岩石の) an outcrop.
ろどん 魯鈍 stupidity; (愚鈍) fatuity. ●魯鈍な人 a stupid [a fatuous] person.
ろば 驢馬 〚動物〛a donkey, an ass. (!) 前の方が一般的)
ロハス (⇨ローハス)
ろばた 炉端 a fireside. ●炉端で by the fireside; by the hearth. ●炉端のいす a fireside chair.
●炉端焼き robatayaki, (説明的に) a kind of grilled food. Fish and vegetables are cooked over an open charcoal grill in front of customers.
ろばん 路盤 (道路・鉄道の) a roadbed.
ロビー a lobby. ●ホテルのロビー the lobby of a hotel; a hotel lobby. ●(空港の)出発ロビー the departure lounge [hall]. ●ロビーで待ち合わせる meet in the lobby.
ロビイスト 〚運動者, 陳情者〛 a lobbyist 《for the auto industry》.
ロビング 〚テニス・サッカー〛lobbing.
『ロビンソン・クルーソー』 Robinson Crusoe. (参考) デフォーの小説)
ロビン・フッド 〚英国の伝説上の義賊〛 Robin Hood.
ロブスター 〚魚介〛a lobster.
ろぶつ 露仏 (説明的に) a statue of (the) Buddha exposed to the weather [(out) in the open].
ロフト 〚屋根裏部屋〛a loft, an attic (room); 〚ゴルフ〛a loft.
ろへん 炉辺 (⇨炉端)
ろぼう 路傍 a roadside. ●路傍に at [by] the roadside. ●路傍の花 roadside flowers.
●路傍の人 a stranger; (通行人) a passer-by 《複 passers-》.
『ろぼうのいし』『路傍の石』 A Roadside Stone. (参考) 山本有三の小説)
ロボット a robot /róubət/. ●産業用ロボット an industrial robot. ●人型のロボット a humanoid robot.
●ロボットのオーケストラ a robot orchestra. ●ロボット工学 robotics. (!) 単数扱い)
ロボトミー 〚前頭葉切除術〛〚医学〛(a) lobotomy.
ロマネスク ●ロマネスク(様式の)建築 Romanesque architecture.
ロマン ❶〚物語〛a romance (!)(中世の)空想[伝奇

ロマンしゅぎ

小説); [小説] a novel (❗通例長編小説 (a long novel) をさす).
❷ [冒険的熱情] ▶ロマンに満ちた冒険 a romantic adventure. ▶男のロマン a man's *dream*.

ロマンしゅぎ ロマン主義 romanticism.
● ロマン主義者 a romanticist.

ロマンス (恋愛) a romance; (不倫の情事) a love affair, an affair; (恋愛の話) a love story. (⇨恋愛)
● すてきな男性とのロマンス 《have》 a *romance* [*a love affair*] *with* a handsome man. ▶ロマンスが芽ばえる (=恋をする) fall in love with each other. ▶ロマンスグレーの(愛の)男性 a middle-aged man with silver hair. ▶ロマンスシート a love seat.

ロマンスご ロマンス語 the Romance language. (参考) フランス語・スペイン語・イタリア語など)

ロマンチシズム romanticism. (⇨ロマン主義)

ロマンチスト a romantic (person); a dreamer. (❗この意では a romantist は和製英語)

ロマンチック ▶彼女はロマンチックな気分になった A *romantic* mood came over her.

ロマンは ロマン派 the romantic [Romantic] school; the romanticists, Romanticists.

『ロミオとジュリエット』 *Romeo and Juliet*. (参考) シェイクスピアの悲劇)

ロム [読み出し専用記憶装置] ROM 《read only memory の略》.

ろめい 露命 (はかない命) a transient life; (命のはかなさ) the transience of life.
● 露命をつなぐ (何とか生きていく) keep body and soul together; (細々と生活をする) make a scanty living.

ろめん 路面 a road surface. ▶路面がぬれて[凍結して]すべりやすくなっているから気をつけなさい Be careful. The *roads* are wet [icy, frozen] and slippery.
● 路面改修工事 resúrfacing wòrk. ● 路面電車 a streetcar; 《英》 a tram.

ロリコン (説明的に) the psychology of men's having sexual feelings towards little or very young girls only; 《和製語》 Lolita complex.

ろれつ 呂律 ● ろれつが回らない (言葉を不明瞭(ﾊﾞﾘ)に発音する) slur one's words; can't speak distinctly [articulately]. ▶ろれつの回らない話し方 one's *slurred* speech. ▶彼はアルコールのせいでろれつが回らなくなっていた His voice *was* really very *slurred* with alcohol.

ろんがい 論外 ── 論外の 形 (問題にならない) out of the question (❗× out of question); (不可能な) impossible; (もってのほかの) outrageous. ▶君の賃上げ要求はまったく論外だ Your demand for a pay raise is quite *out of the question*.

ろんぎ 論議 (an) argument; (a) discussion; (a)

ろんしょう

debate. (⇨議論) ▶論議をよんでいる問題 a *much-debated* issue.

ろんきゃく 論客 a controversialist; a dispútant.

ろんきゅう 論及 ── 論及する 動 refer 《*to*》. (⇨言及)

ろんきゅう 論究 ── 論究する 動 make a detailed discussion [study] 《*of*》; research intensively.

ろんきょ 論拠 (しかるべき理由) grounds; (基礎) the basis; (賛成・反対の理由) the argument 《*for*, *against*》. ● 論拠のない申し立て groundless allegations. ▶君の不平には確かな論拠がない You have no real *grounds for* [*basis of*] your complaint.
▶いったいどんな論拠があってそんなことを言ったのか On what *grounds* did you say so?

ロングアイアン [ゴルフ] a long iron.

ロングシュート 『サッカー・バスケ』a long shot; 《和製語》a long shoot. (⇨シュート)

ロングショット [映画などでの遠写し] a long shot.

ロングスカート a long skirt. (⇨スカート)

ロングセラー [息長く売れる商品] a longtime best seller.

ロングパス [スポーツ] a long pass.

ロングビーチ Long Beach.

ロングヒッター a power hitter; a long-ball hitter; a slugger; 《和製語》a long hitter.

ロングヒット a long hit; (二塁打以上の) an extra-base hit. (⇨長打)

ロングヘア long hair. ▶ロングヘアの女の子 a *long-haired* girl; a girl with *long hair*. ▶ロングヘアにしている wear one's *hair long*.

ロングホール [ゴルフ] a long hole; a par-five hole.

ロングラン a long run. ▶ロングラン映画 a *long-run* movie [film]. ▶その劇はロングランを続けている The play has had a *long run*.

ろんご 『論語』the Analects [Discourses] of Confucius. (参考) 孔子の言行録)
● 論語読みの論語知らず The reader of *the Analects of Confucius* doesn't necessarily understand what Confucius taught./(ことわざ) (占星術は真理だが占星術師は右の真理を知らない) Astrology is true, but the astrologers cannot find it.

ろんこう 論考 图 a study 《*of*》; (調査研究) an inquiry 《*into*, *about*》.
── 論考する 動 study; inquire.

ろんこうこうしょう 論功行賞 功行賞を行う give rewards according to 《their》 distinguished services.

ろんこく 論告 the prosecutor's concluding [closing] speech.

ろんし 論旨 (中心点) the main point; (要旨) the gist. (⇨要点, 論点) ▶君の論文の論旨を原稿用紙2枚にまとめてください Please write *the main point* [*the gist*] of your paper on two sheets of manuscript paper.

ろんしゃ 論者 (筆者自身) the present writer; (評者) a reviewer; (本の著者) the author; the writer; (議論をする人) a debater; a disputant; a controversialist.

ろんしゅう 論集 a collection of essays [papers, (学術論文) theses].

ろんじゅつ 論述 图 a statement.
── 論述する 動 state.
● 論述式試験問題 an essay question. ● 論述テスト an essay test. (関連) 客観テスト an objective test)

ろんしょう 論証 图 (a) demonstration.
── 論証する 動 demonstrate, prove. ▶引力の法則を論証する *demonstrate* the law of gravitation.

ろんじる 論じる argue 《about, over》; discuss (⇨議論する); 〖取り扱う〗treat, deal* with .... ● 彼と政治について論じる discuss [talk about, ˟discuss about] politics with him; argue with him about [over] politics. ▶ その本は政治学を論じている The book discusses [treats, deals with] politics.

ろんじん 論陣 ● 賛成[反対]の論陣を張る argue for [against]...; (断固たる立場を取る) take a firm stand for [against].... ● 堂々の論陣を張る argue forcibly; make a strong argument.

ろんせつ 論説 〖意見文〗〖論説記事〗an article; (評論) (a) comment (⚠ しばしば複数形で); 〖社説〗an editorial. (⇨社説)
● 論説委員 an editor; 《米》an editorial writer; 《英》a leader writer.

ろんせん 論戦 〖討論〗(a) debate; 〖論争〗(a) dispúte. (⇨論争) ● 論戦の口火を切る open a debate [a dispute, an argument].

*__ろんそう 論争__ 图 (理由を上げての) (an) argument; (感情的で激しい) (a) dispúte; (紙上などでの公式な) (a) controversy; (賛否に分かれて公の場で) (a) debate. (⇨議論) ▶ 心臓移植はまだ論争中であった Heart transplants were still in [under] dispute. ▶ その問題は広範囲な論争[大論争]を呼んだ The question caused [《書》aroused] widespread [great] controversy.

── **論争する** 動 argue; debate; dispute; have* an argument [a dispute, a controversy]. ▶ その問題について彼と論争する argue [dispute] with him about [on, over] the question. ▶ 我々は何をすべきかで何時間も論争した We disputed for hours what to do [what we should do].

ろんだい 論題 a subject [a topic] 《of [for] discussion》. (⇨論)

ろんだん 論断 ── **論断する** 動 pass judgement [come to a conclusion] after discussion [deliberation].

ろんだん 論壇 〖言論界〗the world of criticism, critical circles; (マスコミ) the press (⚠ 単・複両扱い).

ろんちょう 論調 a tone 《of one's argument》. ▶ 彼は厳しい論調でその小説を批評した He criticized the novel in a severe tone [《厳しく》severely].

ろんてき 論敵 an opponent (in an argument); a disputant.

ろんてん 論点 the point (at issue). ▶ 君の話の論点をはっきりしてくれ Make your point clear.

ロンド [<イタリア語] 〖回旋(旋)曲〗〖音楽〗a rondo /rɑ́ndou/ (《英》～s).

ロンドン London /lʌ́ndən/. ● 旧市内を the City (of London) という. ● ロンドン子[市民] a Londoner.
● ロンドン塔 the Tower of London. 事情 ロンドンで単に the Tower といえば通例ロンドン塔をさす. ● ロンドンなまり cockney; a cockney accent.

ろんなん 論難 ── **論難する** 動 (批判する) criticize; (非難する) censure; (公然と非難する) condemn; (公然と非難する) denounce.

ろんぱ 論破 图 (a) refutation.
── **論破する** 動 (間違いを証明する) refute; (議論で負かす) argue...down. ● 彼を論破するのはやさしい It's easy to argue him down.

ロンパース 〖幼児用の遊び着〗《a pair of》rompers.

ろんばく 論駁 图 〖論破〗(a) refutation, (a) confutation.
── **論駁する** 動 ● 陳述を論駁する refute a statement.

ロンパス (⇨ロンパース).

ろんぴょう 論評 (a) criticism; 〖簡単な批評・意見〗(a) comment 《on, upon》. (⇨批評) ● 論評を加える criticize; comment 《on》.

*__ろんぶん 論文__ (学会・学術誌などで発表される) a paper; (著書などを含めた正式な学術論文) a treatise / 《米》trí:təs, 《英》-tiz/; (学位取得のための) a thesis /θí:sis/ (《複》theses /θí:si:z/); (特に博士論文) a dissertation; (新聞・雑誌などの論説記事) an article. ▶ (軽い小論文) an essay (⚠ 作文などの課題はこれに含まれる); (新聞・雑誌などの論説記事) an article. ● 卒業論文 a graduation thesis. ● 博士論文 a doctoral dissertation. ● 修士論文 a master's thesis. ● 論文を発表する give [offer, 《やや書》deliver] a paper. ▶ 彼は博士号を得るために肺がんに関する論文を大学に提出した He presented [submitted] his dissertation on lung cancer to the university to obtain a doctor's degree.
● 論文集 collected papers.

ろんぽう 論法 (理論; 議論の筋道) reasoning. ● 三段論法 a syllogism. ● 火のない所に煙は立たないという論法 the logic of no fire without smoke. ▶ 君の論法はめちゃくちゃだ Your logic is confused [《やや書》incoherent]./What you say is not logical [is illogical]. ▶ 彼女の論法にはついていけない I can't follow her logic [reasoning]. ▶ 彼女はいつもの論法で母親を言い負かした She argued her mother down through her usual logic.

*__ろんり 論理__ 图 logic. ● 論理に合わない(＝論理的でない) (⇨形) ● 彼の言うことには論理の飛躍がある There is a leap in logic in what he says.
── **論理的な** 形 ● 論理的でない be not logical; be illogical.
── **論理的に** 副 logically.

📖 DISCOURSE
数学を学ぶことで, 論理的思考能力が向上する. すなわち, 数学を学ぶことで思考への理由づけ, 整理, 明確化ができるようになる Studying mathematics will help improve the ability to think *logically*. **That is**, by studying mathematics, you will be better able to reason, organize and clarify your thinking. (⚠ that is, (すなわち)は言い換えに用いるディスコースマーカー. 続けて「論理的」の内容を詳しく言い換えている)

● 論理学 logic. ● 論理学者 a logician.

わ

＊わ 輪 〖円〗a circle;〖環〗a ring (**!** circle は囲まれた部分に，ring は特定の材質・目的・配列などにより形状に重点がある);〖鎖〗a link;〖綱・ひも・針金など〗a loop;〖車輪〗a wheel;〖たが・輪回しの〗a hoop. ●輪になって座る sit in a *circle* [a *ring*]. ●輪にする loop [coil] (a wire); make [form] a *loop* (with a wire). ●輪を作る make a *circle* [a *ring*] (around him). ●友情の輪を広げる widen a *circle* of friendship.
●輪をかける ●輪をかけて言う exaggerate. ▶彼は兄に輪をかけた怠け者だ He is *much* [*far*] *lazier* than his brother. (**!** much, far は比較級を強調)

わ 和 ❶〖合計〗〖数学〗the sum; the total. ●和を求める find the *sum*. ▶6と4の和は10である The *sum* of 6 and 4 is 10./6 plus 4 is [equals] 10. (⇨足す)
❷〖協調〗harmony;〖まとまり〗unity. ●メンバーの間の和を図る try to improve *harmony* [*unity*] among the members. ▶彼はグループの和を乱しがちだ He's apt to disturb the *harmony* of the group.

-わ -羽 ●1羽の鳥 one [a] bird. ●数十羽のスズメ some dozens of sparrows.

-わ -把 ●まき1把(=1束) a *bundle* of firewood. ●枝豆[ホウレンソウ]2把 two *bunches* of green soybeans [spinach]. (⇨束)

わあ 〖歓声〗whoopee;〈やや古〉hurrah;〖驚嘆・歓喜など〗oh (my);〈主に米〉boy (**!** 黒人の前では用いない); say; wow /wáu/;〈主に米語〉gee. ▶わあ, 勝ったぞ *Whoopee!* We've won. ▶わあ, どれもおいしそうだな *Boy* [*Wow*], everything looks so good.

ワーカホリック 〖仕事中毒者〗a workaholic.
ワーキンググループ 〖作業部会〗a wórking gròup.
ワーキングホリデー the Working Holiday.
ワーク work. ●フットワーク footwork.
●ワークシート 〖コンピュータ〗 a worksheet; a spreadsheet. ●ワークシェアリング 〖仕事の分かち合い〗worksharing. ●ワークショップ 〖研究集会〗a workshop (on). ●ワークステーション 〖コンピュータ〗 a workstation. ●ワークステーションを設置する set up a *workstation*. ●ワークブック a workbook.
ワーグナー 〖ドイツの作曲家〗Wagner /vá:gnər/ (Richard -).
ワースト ▶水質汚染度では大和川は日本のワーストスリーに入っていた At the level of water pollution the Yamato River used to be one of the three *worst* [×worst three] rivers in Japan.
●ワースト記録 the worst record. ●ワーストワン the worst one.
ワードプロセッサー a wórd pròcessor. (⇨ワープロ)
ワードラップ(アラウンド) 〖コンピュータ〗wordwrap; wraparound.
ワードローブ a wardrobe.
ワープ 〖SFに登場する宇宙航行法〗a (time [space]) warp. ●ワープする a warp out.
ワープロ a word processor (略WP). ●日本語ワープロ a *word processor* for [×of] Japanese. ●ワープロでビジネスレターを作成する type [write] a business letter *on* [with, ×by] a *word processor*.
ワールドカップ the World Cup. ●ワールドカップの日本代表チーム the Japanese *World Cup* squad. ●ワールドカップを主催する host *the* 〈2010〉*World Cup*. ●ワールドカップを共同開催する co-host the *World Cup*.
ワールドシリーズ 〖野球〗the World Series. ●ワールドシリーズに進出する make it to the *World Series*. ●ワールドシリーズの出場権を得る earn a *World Series* berth [spot]. ▶今年のワールドシリーズを制するのはどこだろう Who [×Which] do you think will win *the World Series* (championship) this year?
ワールドワイド ── ワールドワイドな 形 〖世界的な〗worldwide.
●ワールドワイドウェブ World Wide Web (略WWW).
わあわあ ●わあわあ騒ぐ(陽気に騒ぐ) make merry; (騒がしい声[音]を大いに立てる) make much noise. (**!** noise は make a noise [noises] ともなり数えられる名詞にも扱えるが, この意味で複数形を使うことはまれ)
●わあわあうるさい noisy. ●わあわあうるさく noisily.
●わあわあ文句を言う complain *noisily*; make a *noisy* complaint.
ワイエムシーエー 〖キリスト教青年会〗YMCA, Y.M.C.A.《*Young Men's Christian Association*の略》. (**!** 通例the ～)
ワイオミング 〖米国の州〗Wyoming /waióumiŋ/ (略Wyo. 郵便略WY).
ワイキキ 〖ハワイの海岸〗Waikiki /wáikikí:/.
わいきょく 歪曲 ── 歪曲する 動 (真意をゆがめる) distort, twist; (誤って伝える) misrepresent. ●その事実を歪曲する *misrepresent* [*distort, twist*] the fact. (**!** 後になるほど作為的になる)
わいざつ 猥雑 ── 猥雑な 形 (見苦しい) sordid,〈書〉squalid. ●猥雑でスラムのような地域 a slummy and *sordid* district.
ワイシャツ a shirt /ʃə́:rt/ (**!** 日本語の「シャツ(=肌着)」の意には用いない (⇨シャツ));〖礼装用〗a dress shirt. (〖参考〗「ワイシャツ」は white shirt の発音からしま柄のワイシャツ a striped *shirt*.
わいしょう 矮小 ── 矮小な 形 very small; (小人的な) dwarfish.
── 矮小化する 動 trivialize; (さほど重要でないように思わせる) understate; (最小にする) minimize. ▶政府はその問題を意識的に矮小化した The government *played down* the importance of the problem on purpose.
ワイじろ Y字路 a forked road. (⇨分かれ道)
わいせい 矮性 ── 矮性の 形 dwarfed; (普通以下の大きさの) undersized.
わいせい 矮星 〖天文〗a dwarf (複 ～s); a dwarf star.
わいせつ 猥褻 名 obscenity; indecency. (**!** 後の方が婉曲的. いずれも言葉・行為をさすときは ⓒ (⇨卑猥))
── 猥褻な 形 ●わいせつな映画 an *obscene* [an *indecent*] movie. ●わいせつな冗談 a *dirty* [an *indecent*, a *lewd*] joke.
ワイダブリュシーエー 〖キリスト教女子青年会〗YWCA, Y.W.C.A.《*Young Women's Christian Association*の略》. (**!** 通例the ～)
わいだん 猥談 ●猥談をする tell dirty [bawdy, obscene, indecent,〈話〉smutty] stories [jokes].
ワイド 名 〖サッカー〗wide. (〖参考〗ピッチ上で両タッチライン

—ワイドな 形 [幅の広い] wide; [長い] long.
- ワイドショー a talk 《米》[a chat 《英》] show; (説明的に) a TV program featuring a variety of tabloid-style news; 《和製語》a wide show.
- ワイドスクリーン 〘大型映写幕〙a wide screen.
- ワイド(スクリーン)テレビ 〘横長テレビ〙a wide-screen television. (❗ screen を略さない). ●ワイド番組 〘長時間番組〙a long TV [radio] program. ●ワイドプレーヤー 〘サッカー〙a wide player. ●ワイドの位置でプレーするのが得意なプレーヤー. ●ワイドマン 〘サッカー〙a wideman. ●ワイドレンズ 〘写真〙a wide-angle lens.

ワイナリー 〘ワイン醸造所〙a winery.
ワイパー a windshield 《米》[a windscreen 《英》] wiper, a wiper.
ワイフ 〘自分の妻〙one's wife.
わいほん 猥本 an obscene [a pornographic, a porn] book; 《総称》pornography; 《俗》porno.
ワイヤ(ー) (a) wire. (❗ 個々にいうときは ⓒ)
- ワイヤ(ー)ブラシ a wire brush. ●ワイヤ(ー)ロープ a wire rope.

ワイヤレス 〘無線電信〙wireless.
- ワイヤレスマイク a wireless microphone.

ワイルドカード 〘スポーツ・コンピュータ〙a wild card. (参考 メジャーリーグでは，各リーグの 3 地区の 2 位チーム中の最高勝率チーム). ●ワイルドカード争い a wild-card race. ●ワイルドカード順位表 wild-card standings.
ワイルドスロー 〘野球〙a wild throw. (⇒暴投) ●一塁へワイルドスローを投げる make a wild throw to first.
ワイルドピッチ 〘野球〙a wild pitch. ▶ワイルドピッチでランナーは二塁に進んだ He wild-pitched the runner to second base./The runner advanced to second on his wild pitch.

ワイルびょう ワイル病 Weil's disease.
わいろ 賄賂 a bribe; 《話》a payoff (複 ~s); 《話》a backhander. ●わいろを贈る offer a bribe [to]; bribe; 《話》pay (him) off. ●わいろを受け取る take [accept] a bribe [from]. ▶あの事務官にはわいろがきく The clerk is corruptible [can be corrupted]./He is a corrupt clerk./The clerk takes bribes. (⇒買収する ❷) ▶彼は私にわいろを使って秘密文書の提供をした He bribed me to give [into giving] him the secret documents.
わいわい (⇒わあわあ) ▶たからわいわい言わないで(=口を挟まないで). 決めるのは私なのよ Don't butt in. Let me be the judge of that.
ワイン 《a glass [a bottle] of》wine. (❗ 種類をいうときは ⓒ) ●白[赤] ワイン white [red; rosé /rouzéi/] wine. ●甘口[辛口] ワイン sweet [dry] wine. ●スパークリング[発泡] ワイン sparkling wine. ●貴腐ワイン noble-rot wine. ●ボルドーワインだ Bordeaux is a French wine. (❗ a に注意)
- ワインカラー wine color. ●ワインクーラー a wine cooler. ●ワイングラス a wine glass. ●ワインセラー 〘ワイン貯蔵室〙a wine cellar. ●ワインビネガー wine vinegar. ●ワインレッド wine red. (❗ 単に wine のこと)

ワインドアップ 图 〘投球動作〙〘野球〙a wíndùp. ●ワインドアップする wind up; go into one's windup. ●ワインドアップして投げる work out of the windup.
わえい 和英 ● 和英両文で in Japanese and English. ●和英辞典 a Japanese-English dictionary.
わおん 和音 〘音楽〙a chord /kɔːrd/ (❗「ひも，コード」の意)
わか 和歌 〘短歌〙tanka (poetry); (説明的に) a classical Japanese 31-syllable verse [short poem]

written in a 5-7-5-7-7 meter [pattern]. ●和歌を一首詠む write [compose] a tanka (poem).
わが 我が 〘私の〙my; 〘私たちの〙our. ●我が(=自分自身)の子 one's (own) child. ●我が社 our company (❗ オーナー社長の場合のみ)
わかあゆ 若鮎 a young sweetfish [ayu]. ●〈若者が〉若鮎のように元気だ be (as) fresh as a daisy; be young and lively; be as full of life as a minnow.

:わかい 若い ❶ 〘年齢が〙young /jʌ́ŋ/ (↔old) (❗ 比較変化形は ~er /jʌ́ŋɡər/, ~est /jʌ́ŋɡɪst/ のように /g/ の音が入ることに注意); 〘若々しい〙young, youthful.
① 〘若い〜〙 ▶若い人 a young person; 〘集合的〙 young people, 《やや書》the young (❗ 複数扱い), the youth (❗ 単・複両扱い). (⇒若者) ▶父は若いころ北海道にいた My father was in Hokkaido when (he was) young. (❗ 主節の主語と when 節の主語が同じ場合，when 節の主語と be 動詞は省略可)《書》My father was in Hokkaido in his young days [青春時代に] in his youth]. 〘若いころを北海道で過ごした〙《やや書》He spent his youth in Hokkaido. ▶彼女は 40 歳になるが，若いままだ She is 40 years old now, but she still looks young [has kept her youthful appearance]. ●若いときは二度とない You'll never be young again.
② 〘…は〛〘より〛若い〙 ▶彼は私より 3 歳若い He is three years younger than I am [《話》than me, 《古・まれ》than I]. (❗ 年齢差に重点を置く場合, He is younger than... by three years. も可 (⇒より)) /He is three years my junior. (❗ He is my junior [is junior to me] by three years. ともいう. ×He is junior than me by three years. は不可) ▶彼は若くして死んだ He died young. (❗「die+補語」の文型) ▶彼女のお母さんは年よりずっと若く見える Her mother looks far younger than she is./(年の割にはとても若く見える) Her mother looks really young for her age. (⇒老(ゆ)ける 〘第 2 文例〙) ▶彼は年をとっているが気は若い He is old in years but young in spirit [mind]. (❗ ...but young in [at] heart. ともいう)
会話 「彼はまだ若いんですよ」「若いってどのくらい？はたち？」 "He's still young." "How young? Twenty?" (❗ 文脈から young であるという前提がある場合, how 疑問文も可)

❷ 〘未熟な〙 immature; (経験が浅くだまされやすい); 《話》green; (経験が浅く世間知らずの) naive /naːíːv/ (❗ 日本語と異なり軽蔑的に使われることに注意), 《話》(still) wet [not dry] behind the ears (❗ 子供は耳の裏をふかないことから). ▶そんなことを信じるなんて君もまだ若い If you believe that, you are still immature [green, naive, wet behind the ears]./You are still immature [It is still immature of you, ×It is immature for you] to believe that. (❗ immature の代わりに green, naive も可)

❸ 〘数が〙 ▶若い番号 a low [a small] number. ●若い番号順に並ぶ stand 《米》line (up), 《英》queue up] in numerical order.

わかい 和解 图 (a) reconciliation [between, with]; 〘解決〙(a) settlement; 〘妥協〙(a) compromise. ❗いずれも具体的には ⓒ
—和解する 動 reach a reconciliation; 〘妥協する〙compromise (with a person, on+事). ▶半年に及ぶ調停の末, 両者は和解した A compromise [A reconciliation, A settlement] was finally reached after six months of arbitration. ▶和解して損害賠償金を半分ずつ負担しよう Let's compromise and each pay half the damages.

わかい 〘和解〙 Reconciliation. (参考 志賀直哉の小

わがい 我が意 ●我が意を得る ▶君のその意見を聞いてまさに我が意を得た思いです I *perfectly agree with* you./I *will go along with* your view *wholeheartedly*.

わかいしじんのしょうぞう 『若い詩人の肖像』 *A Portrait of the Poet as a Young Man*. (参考 伊藤整の小説)

わかいひと 『若い人』 *Young People*. (参考 石坂洋次郎の小説)

わかおくさん 若奥さん a young wife (複 -wives).

わかがえり 若返り rejuvenation (若さの回復) (a) restoration of youth. ●経営陣の若返りをはかる《やや書》plan *to rejuvenate* [plan *for rejuvenating*] the management.

わかがえる 若返る ▶かつらをかぶって彼はずいぶん若返ったみたいだ He *looks* very *young again* wearing a wig./Wearing a wig seems to *have taken* years *off* his *age* [him]. (文脈によっては下の目的語を省略して Your new dress *takes* ten years *off*. (新しいドレスで 10 歳は若返って見えますよ)のようにも用いる)

わかぎ 若木 a young tree; (苗木も含めて) a sapling.

わかぎみ 若君 a young lord; (主君の息子) a young prince.

わかくさ 若草 young [fresh] grass. ●若草色 bright green.

わかくさものがたり 『若草物語』 *Little Women*. (参考 オールコットの小説)

わがくに 我が国 this [our] country. (! 自国にいるときは this country の方が一般的)

わかげ 若気 ●若気の至り youthful follies. ●若気の至りで in the folly of youth.

わがこと 我が事 ▶彼は教え子の成長を我が事(=自分自身の事)のように嬉しく思った He was very glad to see the remarkable growth of his former students. Their growth seemed *just his own* growth.

わかさ 若さ youth; youthfulness. ●若さを失う[保つ] lose [keep] one's *youth*. ▶彼は若さが満ちあふれている He is full of *youth*. ▶若さは自然の贈り物. しかし年を重ねるのは芸術作品である *Youth* is a gift from nature, but aging is a work of art.

わかさぎ 公魚 〖魚介〗 a (pond) smelt.

わかさま 若様 a young master.

わかざり 若飾り a *wakazari*; (説明的に) a New Year's (simple) wreath (made of thin ricestraw rope decorated with *urajiro* leaves).

わがし 和菓子 (a) Japanese cake, Japanese-style confectionery. (→菓子)

わかじに 若死に 名 (an) early [(a) premature] death. ── 若死にする 動 die young. (⇒死ぬ)

わかしゆ 沸かし湯 heated water.

わかしらが 若白髪 prematurely gray hair. ▶彼女は心配事が多くて若白髪になった Her hair has turned *prematurely gray* because of a lot of worries.

＊わかす 沸かす (水を) boil; (ふろなどを) heat. (⇒沸く) ●コーヒー[コーヒーポット]を沸かす *boil* coffee [the coffee pot]. ▶コーヒー用のお湯を少し沸かしてください Please *boil* some water [*hot water*] for coffee (in a kettle). ▶ふろを沸かすのは私の仕事だ It's my task to *heat* the bath [ふろの用意をして] *get* the bath *ready*]. ▶彼女はやかんに水を入れてレンジにかけて沸かした She filled a kettle with water and put it on the stove to *heat*.

わかせる 沸かせる (⇒沸かす) ▶久保のファインプレーが球場を沸かせた Kubo's fine play *thrilled* [*excited*] the crowd in the baseball stadium.

わかせる 湧かせる (⇒湧く)

わかぞう 若造 a youngster, a lad. (! いずれもこれだけでは軽蔑的な含みはない) ▶若造のくせに生意気を言うな《話》Don't be cheeky, *young man*! ▶あなたなんか, まだ若造よ You are still green. (! be green は 「若造」 の意の慣用表現)

わかだいしょう 若大将 a young boss; (主家の若い息子) the boss's son.

わかたけ 若竹 a young bamboo (複 ~s).

わかだんな 若旦那 a young master; (大家の若者) a young gentleman (複 -men /-mən/).

わかちあう 分かち合う share 《*with*》. ▶彼と苦しみを分かち合う(=共にする) *share* one's sufferings *with* him.

わかちがき 分かち書き ●分かち書きする write a Japanese sentence leaving some space between words or grammatical units.

わかちがたい 分かち難い inseparable 《*from*》; unable to be separated [treated separately]. ▶音楽と人生は分かちがたく結びついている Music and life is *inseparably* connected./Music and life is inseparable.

わかつ 分かつ (⇒分ける)

わかつ 頒かつ (⇒分ける ❷)

わかづくり 若作り (若々しい服を着る) put on a youthful dress; (若く見えるように化粧する) make oneself up to look young. ▶彼女は年だがいつも若作りしている Although she is old, she always *wears a youthful dress*.

わかづま 若妻 a young wife (複 wives).

わかて 若手 ── 若手の 形 (若い) young; (若い方の) younger. ●若手の選手 *young* players. ●若手の国会議員 a *younger* Diet member. (! 「議員歴の浅い」 の意)

わかどしより 若年寄り ▶勝男は若年寄りだ(=若いのに年寄りのようだ) Katsuo does things as an old man does though he is young.

わかどしより 若年寄 〖歴史〗 *wakadoshiyori*; (説明的に) the second highest position in the Shogunate bureaucracy.

わかとの 若殿 (若い殿様) a young lord; (殿様の息子) a son of a lord.

わかどり 若鳥 〖一人前になっていない鳥〗a young bird; (まだ飛べない鳥) an unfledged bird; (羽の生えたばかりの鳥) a fledgeling; 〖若いニワトリ〗 a (spring) chicken.

わかな 若菜 young greens. (! 複数扱い)

わかなしゅう 『若菜集』 *Seedlings*. (参考 島崎藤村の詩集)

わかねる 綰ねる (曲げて輪にする)(⇒輪)

わかば 若葉 young [fresh, new] leaves. ▶若葉がもえ始めた The *young leaves* have come out./Trees began to sprout *fresh* (*green*) *leaves*. ●若葉マーク (自動車の初心者マーク) a beginning driver's sticker.

わがはい 吾が輩,我が輩 = 私(わたくし)

わがはいはねこである 『吾が輩は猫である』 *I Am a Cat*. (参考 夏目漱石の小説)

わかはげ 若禿げ premature baldness. ●若禿げである[になる] be [go] prematurely bald.

わかふうふ 若夫婦 a young couple. (! 単・複両扱い)

わかぶる 若ぶる act young. ▶若ぶってジーンズをはく wear jeans *to show that* 《one》 *is still young*. ▶若ぶるな. 年には勝てないのだから Don't *act young*. Age will tell.

＊わがまま 我が儘 名 (自分本位) selfishness; (利己主義) egoism; (頑固) willfulness, self-will. ▶彼女のわがままには我慢できない I can't put up with her

わがみ

selfishness [*egoism*]. ▶彼はいつもわがままを通そうとする He always insists on *having his own way*.
── **我が儘** 形 selfish; egoistic; willful, self-willed. ●わがままな子供 a *willful* [(自己中心的な) a *self-centered*, (甘やかされた) a *spoiled*] child. ●わがままな性格を直す get over one's *selfish* [*egoistic*] personality. ▶そんなことをするなんて君はわがままだ It's *selfish* of [✕*for*] you *to* do that./You're *selfish to* do that.
── **我が儘に** 副 selfishly; egoistically; willfully.

わがみ　我が身 oneself. ●我が身を顧みる reflect on [upon] oneself. ▶だれしも我が身がかわいい (=自分のことをいちばん愛する) のは当然です It's natural that everybody loves themselves the most. (❢ everybody が主語のとき、それを受ける代名詞は《話》では複数形をとることが多い) ▶今日は人の身、明日は我が身 Others' misfortune today might fall upon us tomorrow. ▶敏男が首になった。あすは我が身 (=我が運命) だ Toshio was fired. That might be *my fate* tomorrow [might happen to *me* next].

わかみず　若水 *wakamizu*; (説明的に) the first water to be got early in the morning on the New Year's Day.

わかみどり　若緑 fresh green (color);《書》verdure.

わかみや　若宮 ❶ [幼い皇子] an infant prince (of the Emperor); (親王家のあとつぎ) the heir /éər/ to the prince.
❷ [本社の祭神の子をまつった神社] a shrine dedicated to the son of the god of the main shrine.
❸ [新しくまつった神社] a newly-built shrine.

わかむき　若向き ●このセーターは若向きだ This sweater /swétər/ is *suitable* [*designed*] *for* young people.

わかむしゃ　若武者 a young warrior.

わかむらさき　若紫 pale [light] purple; mauve. ●若紫の藤の花 *light purple* wisteria.

わかめ　若布【植物】*wakame*; soft seaweed.

わかめ　若芽 (⇨新芽)

わかもの　若者 a young person;【男性】a young man (複 men), a youth (❢ 後の語はしばしば軽蔑的);【女性】a young woman (複 women /wímin/);《総称》young people, the young, the youth (❢ 単・複両扱い). (⇨青年) ●近ごろの若者は礼儀を知らない *Young people* these days have no manners. ▶若者の失業率が高い There is high unemployment among *young people* [*the youth*]. ▶路上で乱闘していた若者たちが警察に逮捕された The *youths* who were fighting on the road were arrested by the police. ●若者文化《create》youth culture.

わがものがお　我が物顔 ●彼はいつも我が物顔にふるまっている (好きなようにする) He always *does everything just as he likes*./He always *has* (everything) *his own way*./(自分が所有しているかのようにふるまう) He always acts as if he owned the place.

わがや　我が家 my [our] home [house /-ziz, 《米》-siz/]; (家族) my family. (⇨家) ●楽しい我が家 *our* happy [✕*cheerful*] *home*. (❢ 語順に注意) ▶我が家にまさるところはない There's no place like *home*.

わかやぐ　若やぐ (ふるまいが) act young; (外見が) look young; (気分が) feel* young. ▶彼女の声はいつになく若やいでいた Her voice sounded unusually *young* and cheerful. (❢ このように young にもう一つ形容詞を加えると感じがよりよく伝わる)

わがよ　我が世・我が世の春 ▶我が世の春を謳歌するbe *at the peak* [*height*] *of* one's *glory*.

わからずや　分からず屋 [頑固者] an obstinate person; [聞き分けのない人] an unreasonable person.

わからない　分からない (⇨分かる) ▶訳の分からないことを言う talk *nonsense*. ▶あいつは (ものの道理が) 分からない男だ He has no good sense./He is not sensible. ▶分からないもの。あの人が自殺するなんて (夢にも思わなかった) I *never dreamed* (*that*) he would kill himself./(意外で信じられない) I *wonder* (*why*) he killed himself.

わかり　分かり ●分かりのよい [賢明な] sensible; [頭の働きのよい] intelligent (↔stupid); [理解が早い] quick (↔slow) to learn [at understanding], 《話》quick (↔slow) on the uptake.

わかりきった　分かり切った (単純明快な) plain; (見てすぐわかる) obvious; (自明の) self-evident. ●分かり切った事 a *plain* [an *obvious*] fact. ●分かり切った道理 a *self-evident* truth.

わかりにくい　分かりにくい hard to understand; (はっきりしない) obscure; (文字が読みにくい) illegible; (理解できない) incomprehensible. ●分かりにくい説明をする give an *obscure* explanation.

わかりやすい　分かり易い [文章・話・説明などが] (理解しやすい) easy (↔difficult) to understand; (明快な) clear (↔obscure); (単刀明快な) straightforward; [言葉が] plain, simple; [文字が] legible (↔illegible). ▶たいていのコンピュータのマニュアルは初心者には決して分かりやすいものではない Most computer manuals *are* not at all *easy* for the beginners *to understand*. ▶先生は分かりやすい言葉でその話をしてくださった Our teacher told us the story in *plain* [*simple*] language.

:わかる　分かる　　　　　　　　　　　　　**INDEX**

❶ 内容を理解する　　　❷ 知る
❸ 判明する　　　　　　❹ 認める
❺ 区別できる　　　　　❻ 察する
❼ その他の表現

● **WORD CHOICE**　分かる，理解する

understand 物事そのもの、あるいは物事がいかなるものであるかを正しく理解すること、その結果として一定の知識を得ること。●その難しい単語の意味が分かる *understand* the meaning of that hard word.

appreciate 注意深い観察・分析によって、物の価値・利点・必要性・危険性などを十分に理解すること。●問題の奥深さを理解する *appreciate* the depth of the problem.

comprehend 物事を正しく理解しようとすること。understand に比べ、理解に至る途中の心理的過程を強く含意する。●彼の悲しみを完全には分からなかった We couldn't fully *comprehend* his sadness.

● 頻度チャート

understand
▇▇▇▇▇▇▇▇▇▇▇▇▇▇▇▇▇▇

appreciate
▇▇▇

comprehend
▇

　　20　　40　　60　　80　　100 (%)

❶ [内容を理解する] understand* (*wh*- 節・句),《書》comprehend (*that* 節, *wh*- 節・句),《話》see* (*that* 節, *wh*- 節),《話》get* (*wh*- 節); (把握する) grasp (*that* 節, *wh*- 節). ●あなたのおっしゃっていることが分かりません I don't *understand* [*get, see, grasp*] *what* you mean./I don't *understand* [*get*] you. ▶フランス語が分かりますか Do you *understand*

French? (❗Can you ...? は相手の理解能力を疑う言い方で普通はこのようには問わない。ただし I can [can't] understand French. とはいう) ▶あなたのお気持ちは分かりますが支持するわけにはまいりません I *understand* [*know*] how you feel, but I can't support you. (❗「お気持ちはよーく分かります」と深い共感を示す場合は,定型表現で I know exactly what you mean. と言う. cf. 第1文例) ▶彼はなぜそんなばかなことをしたのかさっぱり分からない I just can't *understand* why he did such a foolish thing. (❗just は否定を強調. ×I can't just understand … は不可) ▶(まるで見当がつかない) I don't have *the faintest* [*slightest*] *idea* (*of*) *why* he did such a foolish thing. (❗(1) このように形容詞の最上級を用いて否定の意味を強める場合,成句表現として《米》でも haven't が用いられるのが普通であったが, 今は I haven't the faintest (idea)! のような省略を伴う応答文以外では don't have が一般化しつつある. なお,過去文脈では didn't have the faintest ... が普通. (2) wh-節[句]の前の of などの前置詞は通例省略される) ▶私は英語では自分の考えを分かってもらえなかった I couldn't *make myself understood* in English. ▶私は忙しいってことが分からないの Can't you *see* (*that*) I'm busy? (❗注意深い観察など何らかの努力によって「分かる」という文脈では that は通例省略されやすい)

会話「分かりましたか」「ええ, やっと分かりました」"Do [×Did] you *understand*?" "Yes. Now I *understand*."/"*Have* you *got* (all) that?" "Yes. Now I've *got* it."/(説教などの場面で) "Do I *make* my*self clear*?" "Yes. Perfectly clear."

❷【知る】(すでに知っている) know*; (情報・観察・経験などから) learn*; (はっきり言い切る) tell* (❗通例 can を伴う); 〖発見する〗 (偶然・経験・試みで) find*, (意外にも) discover (*that* 節); 〖悟る, 悟っている〗 realize. ▶駅へ行く道は分かっていますか Do you *know* the way to the station? ▶住所を申します. すぐ分かる道(=分かりやすい)所です I'll *give* you the *address. It's an easy place to find*. ▶彼が正直者であることは分かっています I *know* (*that*) he is honest./I *know* him *to be* honest. ▶(彼の方は堅い表現) ▶君が来ると分かっていたら家にいたのに If I *had known* you were coming, I would have stayed (at) home. ▶何が起こるかだれにも分からない Nobody *knows* [*can tell*] what will happen./Who *can tell what* will happen? (❗反語的な言い方)/There is no *knowing* [*telling*] what will happen. ▶その本を読んで平和の大切さが分かった I *learned* [*realized*, ×*knew*] the importance of peace when I read the book. / I *learned* [*realized*] (*that*) peace is important when I read the book. ▶彼が本当の友であることが分かった I *found* that he was a true friend./I *found* him (*to be*) a true friend. ▶彼女の肺にがんがあることが分かった I *found* that she had lung cancer. ▶アフリカの食糧危機の深刻さは実際にそこに行って初めて分かった I didn't *realize* [*appreciate*] the seriousness of a food crisis in Africa until I went there. ▶だれが来ているのか絶対に分からないわよ(=推測できない) You'll never *guess who's* here.

会話「大学院に進むべきか, 就職活動すべきかどうしたものか本当に分からないの」「助言になるかどうかは分からないけれど, ただ言えることは勉強はできる時にしておくものだということよ」"I just don't *know whether* I should go on to graduate school *or* go out and look for a job." "I don't *know if* it'll help you, but I

say this. Continue to study while you can."
会話「しっかり勉強するのよ」「分かってるよ, 母さん」"Try to study hard, dear." "I *know*, Mother."
会話「すみませんが郵便局はどちらの方でしょうか」「申し訳ありませんが分かりません」"Excuse me. Which way is the post office, please?" "Sorry, I'm not sure./Sorry, I don't (really) *know* [×*understand*]." (❗really を入れたり, 仮定法を用いて I wouldn't know. (さあ分かりかねますが)のように言うとやわらかい表現になる)
会話「あれは彼女のせいだったのよ」「どうして分かるの？」"It was her fault." "How do you *know*?/How *can* you *tell*?"
会話「この間のパーティーでちょっとすてきな男性に出会ったのよ. でももう会うこともないでしょう」「いや, 分からないよ」"I met a nice guy at a party the other day. But I don't think I'll see him again." "You never *know*."
会話「いつ日本をたつんですか」「まだ分かりません(=まだ決めていない)」"When are you leaving Japan?" "I haven't decided yet." (❗×I don't know [*understand*].)

❸【判明する】turn out, prove《*to be*》; (証明される) be proved; (示される) be shown; (身元が) be identified. (⇨判明する) ▶その老人は泥棒であることが分かった It turned out [×*proved*] *that* the old man [woman] was a thief./The old person *turned out* [*proved*] (*to be*) a thief. ▶これらの事実から彼が有罪であることが分かる These facts *prove* his guilt./These facts *prove that* he is guilty. (❗次例より口語的)/These facts *prove* him (*to be*) guilty. ▶それで彼女がいかに取り乱していたかが分かるだろう That *shows how* upset she was. ▶その乗っ取り犯の身元はまだ分かっていない The hijacker *has* not yet *been identified*./The identity of the hijacker *is* not yet *known*. ▶彼が酔っていることが声で分かった His voice *betrayed* (the fact) *that* he was drunk. (❗*betray* は「うっかり暴露する」の意)

❹【認める】(事実として) recognize, know*; 〖真価を認める〗 appreciate; 〖判断する〗《can》tell; judge. ▶あの足音がだれのだか分かりますか Can you *recognize* the footsteps? ▶彼女は近くに来るまで私だとは分からなかった She didn't *recognize* me until she was close. ▶さわってみたら絹だと分かりますよ You'll *recognize* [*know*] silk by its touch./You *can tell* (*that*) it is silk when you touch it. (⇨❷)/You *can tell* by its touch [by touching it] *that* it is silk. (❗この場合 that は通例省略される) ▶私は骨董(ミラ)品のことはあまりよく分かりません I don't fully *appreciate* antiques./I don't *have a (good) eye for* antiques. (❗「音楽のことは...」なら ... a (*good*) *ear for* music. のようにいえる)/I am not a good *judge of* antiques. ▶刺身の味が分かりますか Do you *appreciate* [×*understand*] the taste of sashimi?/(おいしいと思いますか) Do you *enjoy* [*relish*] sashimi? ▶どのネクタイがよいか分かりません I can't *judge which* tie is better.

❺【区別できる】can* tell, know* (❗この *know* は通例否定文・疑問文・条件文で用いる),《やや書》distinguish. ▶彼はトラとライオンの違いが分からない He *can't tell* the difference between tigers and lions./He doesn't *know* [*can't tell*,《やや書》*can't distinguish*] tigers *from* lions.

❻【察する】sense. ▶彼女はその音で彼が何をしているかが分かった She *sensed* from the sound *what* he was doing.

❼【その他の表現】▶へえ, 君にも仲間らの重圧ってのがあるのね. それで(事情が)分かったよ[分かってきたよ]《話》

Really? You got peer pressure, too. *I get* [*I'm getting*] *the picture* now. (!)「それでずっかり分かったよ」なら That clears things up. などという。▶最近の君はどうもよく分からない. 君のあの闘志はどこへ行ってしまったのだ You're a bit of *a puzzlement to me* these days. What has happened to that fighting spirit of yours? (!) a puzzlement は「(人を)困惑させるもの」の意.
会話「タクシーを呼んでくれませんか」「分かりました(=承知しました)」"Will you call a taxi, please?" "All right./(米語) Sùre thíng."
会話「映画は何時に終わりますか」「6 時半です」「分かりました(=結構). ありがとう」"When does the movie end?" "At 6:30." "*Very well*. Thank you very much./*OK*, *Great*. Thank you./*Right*. Thanks a lot."

*わかれ　別れ　〚別れること〛(a) parting, (離別) (a) separation; 〚別れの言葉〛(a) good-by (!) goodbye とつづるのは(主に英), 《書》(a) farewell. (⇨送別)
①〚～別れ〛●けんか別れをする part (*from* him) in anger. ▶家族との別れは悲しかった (My) *separation from* my family made me sad./I was sad when I *was separated from* [*I left*] my family. (⇨別れる) ▶それが(生前の)最後の別れになった That was the last time I ever saw him (alive). ▶私は両親とは戦争で生き別れになったままです My parents and I *were parted* by the war and have never seen each other since then.
②〚別れ(の)～〛●別れ話をする have a talk about *divorce* [*breaking up*]. (!)前の方は「離婚の話」, 後の方は「離婚の話」または「恋人同士の絶交の話」) ▶彼女の別れの言葉 her *parting* words. ▶彼らはお別れのキスを交わした They exchanged *parting* [*farewell*] kisses.
③〚別れを告げる〛say *good-by* [*farewell*] (*to*). ●彼と別れを惜しむ be reluctant to *leave* [*part from*] him.
わかれみち　分かれ道　(枝道) a branch road; (二またに分かれた) a forked road; (分岐点) a fork (in the road); (十字路) crossroads (!) 単・複両扱い). ▶分かれ道を左へ行く take the left fork of the road. ▶人生の分かれ道=岐路)に立つ stand [be] at the *crossroads* of one's life; (転機) be at a *turning point* in one's life.
わかれめ　分かれ目　〚転換期〛a túrning pòint. ▶人生の分かれ目に立つ (⇨分かれ道) ▶戦い[試合]はここが勝敗の分かれ目だ This is the *turning point* in the battle [game].
*わかれる　分かれる　〚分離する〛divide (*into*); 〚川・道などが分岐する〛branch (off), 〚分裂する〛split* (*into*). ▶川は町の向こうで分かれている The river *divides* [*branches off*], (二またに) *forks*] beyond the town. ▶この鉄道はここで二つの路線に[東北線から]分かれる This railroad *divides* here *into* two lines [*from* the Tohoku Line]. (!) This is where the railroad *divides into*.... のようにもいえる) ▶私たちは二つのグループに分かれた We *divided* [*split up*] *into* two groups. ▶その問題では我々の意見は分かれた We *were divided on* [*over*] the matter. (⇨分裂する) ▶この本は 5 章に分かれている(区分されている) This book *is divided into* five chapters./(5 章から成っている) This book *is made up of* five chapters.
わかれる　別れる　〚出会ってのちに〛leave (!)〚口語的に〛(互いに別方向へ) separate, 《主に書》part; 〚別れを告げる〛say* good-by (*to*), 〚離婚する〛divorce, leave, 〚話〛break* [split*] up (!)「恋人同士が別

れる」の意にも用いる. その場合には *break away from* her boyfriend のようにもいう); (別居する) separate. ▶私は彼と駅で別れた He and I *left* each other [*parted*] at the station. (!) ×part each other とはいわない)/I *left* [*parted from*] him at the station. ▶私たちは仲よく別れた We *parted* (*as*) friends. ▶妻は突然「あなたと別れます」と言った My wife said, out of the blue, "I'm leaving you." ▶その夫婦は結局別れた The couple *have divorced* [*split up*, *separated*] after all. (!) separate はしばしば婉曲的に「離婚する」の意で用いられる) ▶私は 5 歳のとき両親と別れた(=引き離された) I *was separated* [*was parted*] *from* my parents when I was five. ▶彼女は親と別れて暮らしている She lives *away* [*apart*] *from* her parents. (!) live *separately* from は「(夫・妻と)別居する」の意) ▶私は手を振って彼と別れた I waved him *good-by* [*good-by to* him]. ▶彼はあのグループとは別れた(=縁を切った) He broke (*up*) [*split* (*up*)] with that group.
わかれわかれ　別れ別れ　●別れ別れに暮らす do not live together; live separately. ▶戦争で母と子は別れ別れになった(=引き離された) The war *separated* the mother *from* her child. ▶彼の家族は別れ別れに(=ちりぢりになっ)た His family *broke up*.
わかわかしい　若々しい　(元気はつらつとした) youthful; (若い) young. ▶彼女は若々しい She has a *youthful* appearance [an appearance of *youthfulness*]./(若々しく見える) She looks *young*. ▶いつまでも若々しくあれ Stay *young*.
わかん　和姦　図 《書》 fornication.
─ 和姦する 動 《書》 fornicate. (⇨姦通)
わかん　和漢　(日本と中国) Japan and China; (日本語と中国語) Japanese and Chinese. ●和漢混交文 writing in a mixed Japanese and classical Chinese style.

*わき　脇　❶〚腕の付け根の下側の部分〛one's síde(s). (⇨脇腹) ●かばんをわきに(=腕の下に)抱えてやって来る come holding [carrying, with] a bag under one's *arm*.
❷〚そば・近くに〛(...のそばに[で]) beside..., by... (!) by と beside は「かたわら」と横の位置をはっきり示す; (近くに) near.... ▶こちらへ来て私のわきに座りなさい Come and sit *beside* me [*by* me, *by* my *side*]. ▶彼は車を道路わきに寄せて止めた He pulled over to the *side* of the road and parked. ▶家のすぐわきに公園がある There is a park right *near* my house.
❸〚中心から外れた方向〛●わきを見る look *aside*. ▶本をわきに置く put *aside* a book; put a book *aside*. ▶彼は彼女を通すためにわきに寄った He stepped [moved] *aside* to let her pass. ▶君の車をわきに動かしなさい/(じゃまにならない所に移動しなさい) Get your car out of the way. ▶彼は私をわきに連れ出してそっと耳打ちした He took me *aside* and whispered in my ear. ▶彼の話はよくわきにそれる He often *strays* [《書》*digresses*] *from* the main topic of his speech. (⇨脇道 ❷)
●脇が甘い　▶彼は脇が甘い His defenses are weak./(油断する) He is off his guard.
●脇明け (服やスカートの) a placket; a slit. ●脇差 a short sword. ●脇師 (能でシテの相手役) the main supporting actor. ●脇丈 (ズボンなどの寸法) hip-to-hem length. ●脇机 a side desk; a small desk placed next to the main desk.
わぎ　和議　peace talks [negotiations]; (商取引で) a composition 《*with*》. ▶和議が成立する conclude

わきあいあい 和気藹藹 — 和気藹々と 副 (仲よく) harmoniously; (楽しくうちとけて) in happy harmony; (うちとけた[友好的な]雰囲気で) in a harmonious [a friendly] atmosphere. ▶彼らは和気あいあいとマージャンをしていた They were playing mah-jong *in a friendly atmosphere*.

わきあがる 沸き上がる ▶サイダーの栓を開けると無数の泡が沸き上がった When I opened a soda bottle, countless small bubbles *went [fizzed] up*. ▶沸き上がる歓声に歌手たちは酔いしれた The singers were in a state of ecstasy at the *loud cheers from the audience*.

わきおこる 沸き起こる [生じる] arise*. ▶観客から拍手かっさいが沸き起こった A storm of applause *broke out* from the audience.

わきが 腋臭 (体臭) body odor (略 BO). ▶ひどいわきがに悩む suffer from a strong *body odor*. ▶あの人はわきがひどい She's got *BO*.
● わきが止め an underarm deodorant.

わきかえる 沸き返る [激しく沸騰する] boil hard; [熱狂する] be excited 《about, by》; (大騒ぎする) be in (an) uproar 《over》. ▶その野球チームの優勝で町中が沸き返っていた The whole town *was excited about* the baseball team's championship.

わきげ 腋毛 underarm hair; hair of the armpit.

わきたつ 沸き立つ (湯が) boil hard; (人々が) be excited 《about》. (⇨沸き返る)

わきでる 湧き出る well (out). (⇨湧く)

わきのした 腋の下 one's armpit, 《婉曲的》 one's underarm. ▶わきの下をかく scratch under one's *armpit*.

わきばら 脇腹 one's side(s); (動物の) the flank(s).
▶脇腹をつつく poke 《him》 *in the ribs*. (▪ ribs は「あばら骨」の意. ひじで横の人が秘かに知らせる動作)
▶左の脇腹がしくしく痛む I have a dull pain *in my left side*. ▶彼は脇腹をおさえてはあはあ息をしていた He was out of breath, clutching his *side*.
● 脇腹肉 (一枚) a flank 《*of* beef》.

わきまえる 弁える [心得る] know*, understand*; [見分ける] distinguish, discriminate; [心にとめる] bear* [keep*]... in mind. ▶礼儀作法をわきまえている *have* 《×know》 good manners. ▶善悪をわきまえる[わきまえている] distinguish [discriminate, can tell] good *from* evil; distinguish [discriminate, can tell the difference] *between* good and evil.

わきみ 脇見 ▶脇見運転しないで Keep your eyes on the road./Don't *take* your eyes *off* the road./ (運転に集中しなさい) Concentrate on your driving. ▶授業中脇見を[=きょろきょろしてはいけません] Don't *look around* during class.

わきみず 湧き水 springwater.

わきみち 脇道 ❶[横道] a side road, a byroad.
● 脇道を通る take [follow] a *side road*. ● 脇道に入る turn into a *side road*. ● (本道からそれて) turn off (a main road) *into* a *side road*.
❷[話などの脱線] ▶先生はよく話が脇道にそれた(=脱線した) Our teacher often *wandered from* [《書》 *digressed from, went off*] the subject./Our teacher often *got sidetracked*.

わきめ 脇目 ▶脇目も振らず (左右を見ずに) (walk) without looking aside [either way]; (必死に) 《run》 for dear life; (全身全霊を打ち込んで) (devote oneself) heart and soul 《to》.

わきやく 脇役 (役割・配役) a suppórting (= a leading) ròle; (役者) a suppórting àctor [àctress].
● 脇役を務める[に回る] play a *supporting role*; play second (↔first) fiddle 《*to* him》.

わぎゅう 和牛 (動物) a Japanese cow [bull]; (肉) Japanese-produced beef; Japanese beef.

わぎり 輪切り ▶大根を輪切りにする *cut* a radish *into round slices*.

わきん 和金 a wakin goldfish.

***わく** 枠 a frame; (眼鏡の縁) frames, rims; (枠組み) a framework; (制限の範囲) a limit. ● 窓枠 a window frame. ● 枠で囲む frame; box... off.
● 伝統文法の枠内でその問題を扱う deal with the problem *within the framework of* traditional grammar. ● 月10万円の枠内で生活する live *within the limits of* 100,000 yen a month.
● 枠にはまる 枠にはまった考え方 a *stereotyped* way of thinking; *limited* ideas.

***わく** 沸く boil. ▶やかんの湯が沸いている (The water in) the kettle *is boiling*. (▪(1) 日本語の「湯」に引かれて, water の代わりに hot water を用いるのは誤り. (2) 容器も主語になるのは日英同じ発想) ▶ふろの湯が沸いている The bathwater's *heated up*./ふろの用意ができている) The bath is ready.

***わく** 湧く ❶[わき出る] (水・涙などが勢いよく流れ出る) gush (out); (どんどん流れる) well (up, out); (急に流れ出る) spring* (up). ● 泉からわき出る水 water *gushing* (out) *from* [《ふくよくと》 *bubbling out of*] a spring. ▶彼女の目に涙がわいてきた Tears *welled up* in her eyes. (▪ 通例 up をつけていう) ▶私の心に希望がわいてきた Hope has begun to *spring up* in my heart.
❷[繁殖する] breed*; (ひな・卵などがかえる) be hatched, hatch. ▶ボウフラがわいた Mosquito larvae (were) *hatched*. ▶その犬はシラミがわいた(=たかっていた) The dog *was infested with* lice. ▶彼は半生焼けの豚肉を食べてサナダ虫がわいた He *got* tapeworms from eating half-roasted pork.
❸[その他の表現] ▶彼の言葉を聞いて自信がわいた I began to feel confident when I heard his words. ▶歴史にはあまり興味がわかない I don't *have* [*take*] much interest in history.

わくぐみ 枠組み a framework. (⇨わく)

わくせい 惑星 a planet. ● 小惑星 an asteroid; 《古》 a minor *planet*.
● 惑星運動 planetary motion.

わくせい 『惑星』 *The Planets*. (参考 ホルスト作曲の組曲)

ワクチン (a) vaccine /væksíːn, væksín/. (▪ 種類は C) ● インフルエンザワクチン influenza *vaccine*.
● ワクチン注射[接種] a vaccine injection, (a) vaccination 《*against, for*》, 《話》 a shot. (⇨注射)
● 子供に小児麻痺(ひ)のワクチン注射をする *vaccinate* a child *against* polio.

わくでき 惑溺 名 the total loss of one's good judgment.
―― 惑溺する 動 be addicted to; be given up to 《drinking》.

わくらん 惑乱 ―― 惑乱する 動 (惑わせる) confuse; upset*; (惑う) be confused; be upset.

わくわく ―― わくわくする 動 be [feel*, get*] excited [thrilled]; (わくわくさせる) excite, thrill. ▶彼女は外国旅行のことを考えるとわくわくする She felt excited at the thought of going abroad. ▶私はその知らせを聞いてわくわくした I *was thrilled to* hear [*at*] the news.
―― わくわくさせる 形 exciting, thrilling.
―― わくわくして 副 excitedly, with excitement.
▶私は旅行をわくわくして待った I looked forward

わくん 和訓 (⇨訓読み)

わけ 訳 ❶【理由】(行動・意見の説明) (a) reason 《*for; to do; why* 節》. (⇨理由) ▸彼らが離婚したのには深い訳があった There was a very good *reason for* their divorce. ▸どういう訳であなたはそこへ行ったのですか What was your *reason for going* [the *reason for* your going] there?/*What* made you go there? (🛈(1) 最初の言い方より口語的. (2) *Why* did you go there?/(話) *How* did you go there *for*? より詰問的ではなく穏やかな表現) ▸そういう訳で彼は来られなかったのです That's (the *reason*) *why* he was unable to come. (🛈 the reason を省略するのが普通)/*For* that *reason* [*Because of* that] he was unable to come. ▸訳あって[どういう訳か知らないが]彼はおじのもとで育てられた He was brought up by his uncle for certain *reasons* [for some *reason* or other]. ▸だからといって彼女が嫌いという訳ではないのだ It is *not because* I don't like her./*Not that* I don't like her. (🛈 後の言い方は ❷の意で, 前に It is が省略されている) ▸私に分かる訳がないでしょう How do I know?
❷【意味】(a) meaning; a sense. ▸彼は訳の分からない(=意味のない)言葉を口走った He uttered some *meaningless* words. ▸この文は訳が分からない(意味をなさない) That sentence doesn't *make sense*./(理解やすい) I can't *understand* [(やや書) *make heads or tails of*] the sentence. ▸だからといってそれが間違っている訳ではない This doesn't *mean* (*that*) it is wrong. (⇨ ❶ 第 5 文例)
❸【道理】(分別) sense; (理性) reason. ●訳の分かった人 a person of *sense*; a *sensible* person. ▸そんな訳の分からないことを言うものではない You shouldn't be so *unreasonable*./Why are you so *unreasonable*?/Be *reasonable*.
❹【事情】(実情) the case; (周囲の状況) circumstances. ▸そういう訳ならごいっしょさせてください If that is *the case* [In] the *circumstances* I decided to stay another night. ▸そういう訳で[以上がその事情で] That's *how it is*. ▸彼らた病気だっていう訳じゃあるまいし It *isn't as if* he were [(話) was] sick. (🛈 (話) では It isn't が省略されることもある)/(米話) *It's not like* he was sick. ▸これとそれとは訳が違う This is very *different from* that. ▸この車はあれと訳が違う(=はずかちいい) This car is *much better* than yours.
❺【当然】 ▸どうりで彼女が私のことを笑うわけだ *It's no wonder that* [*No wonder*] she laughs at me. (🛈以下の例よりも口語的)/It is *natural* that she should laugh [she laughs, ×she laugh] at me./She may well laugh at me./She *has good* [*every*] *reason* to laugh at me. (⇨❶)
❻【面倒】 ▸そんなことは私にはわけのないことだ That's very *easy* for me. (⇨❶)
❼【意図】 ▸自慢するわけではないがまだ学校を休んだことがない I don't *mean* to brag [*Not that* I'm going to brag], but I have not been absent from school yet.
❽【可能】 ▸病気の母親を放っておくわけにはいかない I *can't* leave my sick mother unattended. ▸彼が今そこにいるわけがない(=はずがない) He *can't* be there now. ▸彼の作品を賞賛しないわけにはいかない(=賞賛せざるを得ない) I *can't help* admiring his work.
会話 「どうしてワンセットやらないのだろう」「1 人でテニスをやれるわけないだろ」 "Why didn't you have a set of tennis?" "How *can* I play tennis on my own?/*Can* you play tennis on your own?"
❾【部分否定】(…とは限らない) not all; not everyone. ▸君たちすべてがテストに通るわけではない *Not all* of you will pass the test. ▸だれもが君のように好運だというわけではない *Not everyone* is as lucky as you are. ▸と言っても君は間違っていないというわけはない However, that is *not to* say that you are right./But that does *not mean* [*follow*] that you are not in the wrong.
会話 「物は高くなってるかい」「高くなってるのもあるね. でも全部というわけではないか」 "Are things getting more expensive?" "✓Some things. But *nót* ↘*all*." (🛈 対比の含みがあるため some の方に強勢が置かれる)

わけあう 分け合う share 《*with, between, among*》. ▸もうけを我々 5 人で分け合う *share* the profits *between* the five of us. ▸何でも分けあうのよ You must *share and share alike*. (🛈 平等に分けあうことを強調した言い方)

わけあたえる 分け与える share ... (out) 《*between, among*》. (🛈 本人にも分け前を取る場合も含む); distribute 《*to, among*》. ▸3 人の子供にお金を平等に分け与える *give* one's money equally [*give an equal sum of money*] *to* one's three children; *share* (*out*) one's money equally *among* his three children.

わけあり 訳有り ▸訳ありの with a (special) relationship. ▸訳あり大バーゲン a sale of seconds. ▸彼が突然会社を辞めたのはどうも訳ありだ I think he had a *reason* when he left company in such a hurry.

わけい 和敬 humility and respect.

わけい 話芸 the art of storytelling [(comic) conversation].

わけいる 分け入る ●群衆の中へ分け入る *force* one's *way into* the crowd.

わけぎ 分葱 【植物】a scallion.

わけしり 訳知り (社交好きな人) a man about town; (世慣れた人) a man of the world.

わけても 別けても (⇨特に) ▸学生はわけても(=なかんずく)学問が大事だ Students should, *above all* [*before everything else, among others*], pursue [(やや書) attend to] their studies./What is the most important for students is, *above all*, learning.

わけどり 分け取り ●その日とれた魚を分け取りする *share* the day's catch of fish.

わけない 訳無い 形 (易しい) easy.
── 訳無く 副 easily; without difficulty. ▸わけなく泊まるホテルが見つかった It was *easy* for me to find my hotel./I *easily* found my hotel./I had *no difficulty* (*in*) finding my hotel. (🛈 in は省略するのが普通)

わけへだて 分け隔て [差別] discrimination. ●すべての人を分け隔てなく扱う treat all people without *discrimination* [(書) equally, (公平に) impartially]. ●女子従業員を分け隔てする *discriminate against* women employees. ▸彼らは敵味方の分け隔てなく, 救援活動をした They were engaged in [went about] relief activities without making distinctions between friend and foe. (🛈 friend and foe は「敵味方」の意の慣用表現)

わけまえ 分け前 [取り分] a share, 《話》a cut (いずれも単数形); [割り当て] a portion. ●利益の分け前をもらう have one's *share* [*cut*] of the profits. ●財産の均等の分け前を要求する demand an equal *portion* [*share*] of the property.

わけめ 分け目 (髪の) a part, 《英》a parting; (境界線) a dividing line. ●天下分け目の(=決定的な)戦い a *crucial* [a *decisive*] battle.

‡**わける 分ける** ❶ [[分割する]] divide 《into》; (頭髪を) part. ●ケーキを右と左に三つに分ける *divide* the cake *into* [xin] three equal pieces. (!半分に分ける場合は in half, into halves という) ●髪を真ん中から[横で;左側で] *part* [xdivide] one's hair *in the middle* [*at the side*; *on the left*].
  [翻訳のこころ] 蓑帽子をかぶった専門の猟師か、草をざわざわ分けてやってきました〈宮沢賢治『注文の多い料理店』〉A real [A "professional"] hunter with a straw hat on [wearing a straw hat] approached, plowing through the rustling grass. (!(1) professional (専門の)は通常猟師を修飾させる言葉ではないので、引用符(" ")を付けた。(2) rustling grass は草が"ざわざわ"という音をたてている様子を表す)

❷ [[分配する]] divide; (配る) distribute; (分け合う) share. ●以上のいずれにおいても2者間で分ける場合は between, 3者以上では among が原則であるが、くだけた表現では between も用いられる) ●彼らは現金を自分たちで分けた They *divided* [*distributed*, *shared*] their profits *between* them. ●サンドイッチを弟さんにも分けてあげなさい You must *share* your sandwiches *with* your brother. (!divide も用いられるが、部分に分けたり、自分も分け前にあずかる場合は share が普通) ●砂糖を少々分けてもらえませんか Could you *spare* me some sugar [some sugar *for* me]?

❸ [[分離する]] divide 《from》; separate 《from》 (!divide は分割する、separate は切り離すことに重点がある; (密接な関係にある人・物を切り離す) part. ●病人と他の人を分ける *separate* the sick people *from* the other people; *divide* the sick *from* the others. ●取っ組み合いのけんかをしている生徒を引き分ける *separate* [*part*] the fighting students. ▶多摩川は東京と神奈川を分けている The Tama River *divides* Tokyo *from* Kanagawa.

❹ [[区分する]] separate; (分類する) classify; (えり分ける) sort ... out. ●この本を題目別[三つのグループ]に分ける *classify* the books *according to* subject [*into* three groups]. ●よいリンゴと悪いリンゴを分ける *sort out* [*separate*] the good apples from the bad. ▶先生は生徒を4グループに分けた The teacher *separated* [*divided*] the pupils *into* four groups.

わけん 和犬 a Japanese (breed of) dog.
わご 和語 the Japanese language; Japanese; [[大和言葉]] a native Japanese word.
わこう 倭寇 [[歴史]] Japanese pirates (who had been rife between 14th and 16th centuries).
わごう 和合 (調和) (やや書) harmony; 《書》concord. ●和合して暮らす live in *harmony* [*peace*, *concord*] 《with》. ●夫婦和合の (書) conjugal *harmony*; the *concord* between a husband and his wife.
わこうど 若人 young people; young men and women; the youth. ●若人の祭典 a festival for *young people*.
わこうどうじん 和光同塵 (説明的に) [[仏教]] the appearance of Buddha to this world in many disguises in order to guide people who have lost their ways; (自分の才を隠す) hiding one's light [talent] under a bushel (聖書の言葉).
わこく 倭国 Japan.
わゴム 輪ゴム a rubber [《英》an elastic] band.

●書類を輪ゴムでとめる put a *rubber band* around the papers.
わこん 和魂 ●和魂洋才 trying to develop the national spirit of Japan by learning a lot from Europe; imbibing Western knowledge without being much influenced by it or losing one's identity.
ワゴン [[ワゴン車]] 《米》a station wagon, 《英》an estate car; [車のついた配膳台] 《主に米》a (tea) wagon [cart], 《英》a trolley; [買い物用手押し車] a (shopping) cart 《米》[trolley 《主に英》]. ●ワゴンサービス trolley service. ●ワゴンセール sale on the display stand. ●ワゴンセール wagon sale.
わざ 技 (⇒技術) ●技を磨く polish (up) [improve] one's *skill*. ●(柔道で)寝技[足技]をかける use groundwork [foot] *techniques*. ▶技あり! [柔道] *Waza-ari*!/A half point!
わざ 業 ●それは人間業ではなかった(=人間の能力範囲を超えていた) That was beyond human *power*. ●それは容易な業(=仕事)ではない That's no easy *task*.
わさい 和裁 Japanese dressmaking.
わざし 業師 [[策士]] a schemer; a plotter (!いずれの語もいい意味には用いない); (かけひきのうまい人) a tactician, a strategist; [[スポーツの技にすぐれた人]] a person who has great skill [performs a lot of feats]. ▶あの政治家は業師との評がつきまとっている He is reputed as a *scheming* politician.
*わざと [[故意に]] on purpose, purposely (!前の方が口語的); [[意図的に]] intentionally (↔by accident); [[熟慮の上で]] deliberately. ●わざと彼を侮辱する insult him *intentionally*. ▶それは偶然ではなかった。君がわざとそれをしたのだ It wasn't an accident; you did it *intentionally* [*deliberately*, *on purpose*]. ●彼はわざと私にうそをついた He *deliberately* lied to me./He *deliberately* told me a lie [told me a *deliberate* lie].
  [会話] 「君が窓を割ったんだね」「はい、でもわざとじゃないんです」"You broke the window, didn't you?" "Yes, but (it was) nót on ˅*purpose* [(でもそんなつもりはなかった) but I didn't mean to (do that)]."
わざとらしい [[不自然な]] unnatural; [[意図的な]] intentional; [[無理やりの]] forced; [[気取った]] affected. ●わざとらしい微笑を浮かべる wear [have] an *unnatural* [a *forced*, an *affected*] smile on one's face.
わさび 山葵 [[植物]] a *wasabi*; (おろしたもの) *wasabi*, Japanese mustard; (説明的に) grated Japanese horseradish used as a kind of condiment. ▶ワサビが利き過ぎている There's too much *wasabi* in it./The *wasabi* is too hot. ●このワサビはあまり利かない This *wasabi* doesn't have much bite. (⇒刺身)
●山葵漬け *wasabi* pickles; chopped *wasabi* preserved in sake lees.
わざわい 災い [[不運]] (a) misfortune; (通例軽い) (a) mishap; (ひどい) 《書》(an) evil; [[困った事態]] trouble; [[災難]] (a) disaster; [[破滅の原因]] one's [the] ruin. ●さまざまな災いを経験する suffer various *misfortunes* [*evils*]. ▶彼に災いがふりかかった *Misfortune* [*Evil*] fell on him. ▶あらしの最中に登山するとは自ら災いを招くようなものだ [話] You're asking [looking] for *trouble* by climbing a mountain during a storm./(やや書) You're courting *disaster* by trying to climb a mountain during a storm. ▶酒が彼の災いとなった Drinking was his *ruin*. ▶内気が災いして彼女は友達ができなかった She had no friends because she

わさわさ was shy./《書》Shyness prevented her from making friends. ▶口は災いのもと《ことわざ》Better the foot slip than the tongue.
● 災いを転じて福となす turn a misfortune into a blessing; turn a loss into a gain.

わさわさ ● わさわさしている《落ちつかない様子》be restless;《多くの人が押しかける様子》be crowded.

***わざわざ** ● わざわざ（＝労を取って）お見送りいただくには及びません Don't *bother* [*trouble*,（無理して）*go out of your way*] *to* see me off. ▶「わざわざそんなことしないで」は Don't *bother* [*trouble*]. という》 ● わざわざお手紙をいただきましてありがとうございました Thank you very much for *taking the trouble* to write to me. ▶遠方のところわざわざ（＝はるばる）おいでくださってありがとうございます It's very kind of you to (have) come *all the way* to see me.
会話「山田からだった」「わざわざロンドンから電話してきたのかい」"It was Yamada." "Phoning *all the way* from London?"
会話「田中がそれを引き受けてくれると思うか」「わざわざ彼に頼むほどの事かい」"Would Tanaka take it, do you think?" "Is it worth the *trouble of asking* him?"

わさん 和算 Japanese mathematics (that attained a unique development in the Edo period).

わし (⇨私(ᵂ⁴ᵗ))

わし 鷲【鳥】an eagle;（ひな）an eaglet.
● わし座【天文】the Eagle; Aquila. ● わし鼻 an aquiline [a hooked] nose.

わし 和紙 (a sheet of) (traditional) Japanese [Japan] paper.

わしき 和式 ─ 和式の 形 Japanese-style.

わしつ 和室 a Japanese-style room.

わしづかみ 鷲づかみ ─ 鷲づかみにする 動《不意につかむ》grab;《しっかり握る》clutch. ▶《野手がボールをわしづかみにする》*grab* a ball with all of the fingers. ▶彼は1万円札をわしづかみにして逃げた He *grabbed* 10,000-yen bills and ran away.

わしゃ 話者 a speaker (↔hearer).

わじゅつ 話術 the art of conversation. ● 話術にたけた人（座談が上手な）a good conversationalist;（雄弁な）an eloquent speaker;（口が達者で説得力がある）《話》a person who has *the gift of (the) gab* (𝐈 the を省略するのは《米》).

わしょ 和書《洋書に対し》a Japanese book;（和綴じの本）《和綴じ》

わしょく 和食 Japanese food [dishes];（料理法）Japanese cuisine /kwi(ː)ziːn/.

わしん 和親 両国の友好をはかる endeavor to promote friendly relations between the two countries.
● 和親条約《conclude》a peace treaty.

ワシントン　【米国の地名】（州）Washington《略 Wash. 郵便略 WA》;（首都）Washington, D.C. (𝐈 D.C. is District of Columbia の略)

ワシントン　【米国の初代大統領】Washington (George ～).

『ワシントンポスト』 *The Washington Post*.《参考 米国の新聞名》

***わずか** 僅か ─ 僅かな 形【数が少ない】a few;【量が少ない】a little;【量・程度がわずかな】slight;【数・量・額が小さい】small;【時間・距離が短い】short.（⇨少し）● わずかな金で手に入れる get (it) for a *small* sum [amount] of money; get (it) for very little. ● わずかな収入で暮らす live on a *small* [a *modest*,《やや書》a *meager*] income. ● わずか 2–3 年のうちに in a few *short* years; *only* in a few years. ▶英語の本はほんのわずかしか持っていなかった I had *only a few* [*very few*] English books. ▶冷蔵庫にバターがわずかしか残っていなかった There was only *a little* butter left in the refrigerator. ▶それらにはわずかな違いがある There's a *slight* difference between them./They're *slightly* different. ▶病院までほんのわずか（距離）です It's only *a short distance* to the hospital.

── 僅か(に) 副 slightly;【ただ…だけ】only;【少し】a little;【ようように】barely, narrowly. ● わずか 100円 *only* [*no more than*] one hundred yen. ▶ドアはわずかに開いていた The door was *slightly* open. ▶道はそこでわずかに右に折れている There the road curves *slightly* to the right.

わずらい 患い【病気】(a) sickness, (an) illness;（体の不調）a complaint. ● 長患いをする suffer from a long *sickness* [a *sickness* for a long time].

わずらい 煩い【心配】(a) worry; (a) trouble.

わずらう 患う suffer (*from*). (⇨病む)

わずらう 煩う worry (*about*). (⇨悩む)

わずらわしい 煩わしい【面倒な】troublesome;【やっかいな】annoying;【複雑な】complicated. ● 煩わしい人間関係 *complicated* human relations. ● それをするのを煩わしく思う feel it *troublesome* to do it.

わずらわす 煩わす《面倒をかける》trouble. ● 心を煩わす《心配する》be worried, worry (*about*). ▶お手を煩わせて申し訳ありませんが… I'm sorry to *trouble* [*bother*] you, but….

わすれがたい 忘れ難い《忘れられない》unforgettable;《記憶すべき》memorable. ● 忘れ難い光景 an *unforgettable* scene.

わすれがたみ 忘れ形見《思い出になるもの》《やや書》a memento (轢) ─(e)s;《かたみ》a keepsake;《遺児》a child of the dead《最近亡くなった》the late (actor).

わすれさる 忘れ去る forget* (completely) (𝐈「ころっと忘れる」の意にもなる); 《書》consign to oblivion. ▶事件はうやむやのまま忘れ去られた The incident was forgotten, and remains unresolved.

わすれっぽい 忘れっぽい be forgetful (*of*);（記憶力が足りない）have* a short [a bad, a poor] memory. ● 忘れっぽい人 a *forgetful* person. ● 忘れっぽくなる become *forgetful*.

わすれなぐさ 忘れな草【植物】a fórget-me-nòt.

***わすれもの** 忘れ物 a thing left behind. ▶バスに傘の忘れ物をした I *left* my umbrella in [on] the bus. (⇨忘れる ❶①［第4文例］) ▶忘れ物はありませんか Are you sure you have everything [you haven't *forgotten* anything]? ▶何か忘れ物でも？(Did you) forget something [✕anything]?

***わすれる** 忘れる
WORD CHOICE　忘れる
forget 人が何らかの物事を一時的・永続的に、意識的・非意識的に忘却・失念すること、また、場所を明示したり文脈で明らかな場合、漠然と所持品などを置き忘れること。 ▶過去を忘れてはいけない We must not *forget* the past. ▶携帯電話を置き忘れた I *forgot* my cell phone.
leave 所持品などを特定の場所に置き忘れること。文脈によっては「意図的に残してくる」の意にもなる。 ▶彼の家に携帯電話を置き忘れた I *left* my cell phone in his house.

❶【うっかりして忘れる】forget*;（置き忘れる）leave* … (behind) (𝐈 場所を示す副詞句を伴う);（怠って…しない）neglect (*to* do; do*ing*).
①《…を忘れる》▶あっ、もう少しで忘れるところだった Oh, I almost [nearly] *forgot*! (⇨❷［第1文例］)/《話》I'm *forgetting*. ▶彼の名前を忘れた I *forget* [*have forgotten*] his name. (𝐈 この場合通

例「忘れた」とあっても forgot と過去形を用いない. 現在形で今思い出せない状態, 完了形で一時的に度忘れして思い出せない状態を強調する)/(思い出せない) I *can't remember* his name. ● 忘れないように書きとめておいた方がよい You should write it down before you *forget* [(忘れないように) so that you won't *forget*]. ▶ 車のキーを家に忘れてきた I've *left* my car key (*behind*) at home. (**!** 場所を示す語句を伴う場合は leave を, そうでない場合は forget を用いる) ▶ 人間は忘れることができるので, 生きていくことができる Human beings can continue to live because they can *forget*. ▶ あの刻を忘れない. 1995.1.17.5:46. We shall never *forget* that moment; 5:46 (a.m.) Jan. 17, 1995. (参考) 阪神大震災の碑文)

会話「この傘どなたのですか」「あらいけない, 傘を忘れてたわ. それ, 私のです. ありがとう」 "Whose umbrella is this?" "Oh, no! I *forgot* my umbrella. It's mine. Thanks."

翻訳のこころ せせらぎを作り, 滝をかけ, 池を掘って水を見ることはあれほど好んだ日本人が, 噴水の美だけは近代に至るまで忘れていた (山崎正和『水の東西』) Japanese people have loved watching water so much that we've built small streams, created waterfalls and dug ponds. Until modern times, however, we've failed [×forgotten] to become aware of the beauty of the fountains. (**!** (1)「あれほど好んだ」 is loved so much that... (非常に好んだので...)と表す. (2)「忘れていた」 is have failed to become aware of (気付かなかった)と表す. forgotten とすると「以前には気が付いていたことを忘れていた」の意になるので不適切)

❷ [...(という)ことを忘れる] ▶ 今日彼がやってくることを(すっかり)忘れていた I (completely) *forgot* [×was forgetting] *that* he was coming today. (**!** (1) 忘れていたを思い出した場合は過去形を用いる. (2) この意では進行形は不可. ただし習慣的行為や感情表現では可: She's always *forgetting* things. (彼女はもの忘ればかりしている))(うっかり忘れていた) It (completely) *slipped* my *mind* that he was coming today. ▶ 彼女に会ったときのことは決して忘れません I will [shall] never *forget* (*about*) seeing her./I will [shall] never *forget that* I saw her. (**!** (1) *forget doing* は過去の行為を表す. (2) that 節を用いる方が動名詞を用いるより客観的な表現となる) ▶ 君が魚を嫌いなことを忘れていたよ I was forgetting that you don't like fish. (**!** I had forgotten that ... というより丁寧な表現)

● DISCOURSE
物質的進歩は確かによいものだが, そのために多くを手放す羽目になったことを忘れてはならない Material progress **certainly** is good, but we must not *forget* that we had to give up many things for it. (**!** certainly (たしかに) は譲歩を表すディスコースマーカー)

❸ [...するのを忘れる] ▶ 忘れずに手紙を出してください Please *remember* to mail [*don't forget* to mail, *don't forget* about mailing] the letter. (**!** forget to do は未来の行為を表す) ▶ 彼はドアに鍵をかけるのを忘れた He *forgot* [*didn't remember*] *to* lock the door. (**!** forget に鍵をかけなかった」の意. ×forgot locking と動名詞を用いない)/He *neglected to* lock [lock*ing*] the door. (**!** forget より堅い表現) ▶ 彼女がいること [それをすること] を忘れていたら注意しろよ *Remind* her *about* it [*to do* it]. (**!** remind は「(人に)思い出させる」の意)

❷ [努力して忘れる] ▶ すんだことは忘れよう Let's *forget* (*about*) what happened.

会話「彼女のことがどうしても忘れられないんだ」「旅行でもしてきたら? そうすれば忘れられるかもしれないわ」 "I just can't *get* her *off* my mind." "Well, go on a trip. It'll *take* your *mind off* (*of*) her." (**!** off of は《米話》)

わすれんぼう 忘れん坊 a forgetful person.

わせ 早生, 早稲 図 (稲) an early variety of rice; (一般的に) an early variety.
—— 早生の 形 early; (早なりの) precocious.

わせい 和声 『音楽』 harmony.
● 和声学 harmonics.

わせい 和製 —— 和製の 形 made-in-Japan. ● 和製ベーブルース the Babe Ruth of Japan; a Japanese Babe Ruth.
● 和製英語 Japanese English.

解説 和製英語: 英語にはない単語を使って(または組み合わせて)いるが, 本来の英語には見られない言葉や意味で日本語の中で使用される言葉を和製英語という. マカロニウエスタン((< macaroni + western) 英語では spaghetti western), ミルクコーヒー((< milk + coffee) 英語では coffee with milk) など, 日本でつくり出された, 英語にはない言葉(⇒(**1**)) や, 車のハンドル(英語で handle は「(ドアの取っ手)」, ムーディー(英語で moody は「不機嫌な, むら気な」など, 英語にもある言葉であっても日本語の中ではその意味が異なるもの(⇒(**2**)) などがある(詳しくは該当の項目を参照).

(**1**) 日本でつくり出された, 英語にはない言葉
ガソリンスタンド (< gasoline + stand) a filling station / カンニングペーパー (< cunning + paper) a crib sheet / セールスポイント (< sales + point) a selling point / ダイニングキッチン (< dining + kitchen) a kitchen(-cum-)dining room / チアガール (< cheer + girl) a cheerleader / バックネット (< back + net) a backstop / バックミラー (< back + mirror) a rear-view mirror / フォアボール (< four + ball) a walk / フリーダイヤル (< free + dial) a toll free call / ベッドタウン (< bed + town) a bedroom town.

(**2**) 英語にもあるが日本語では意味が異なるもの
アメリカンコーヒー coffee (**!** American coffee は「アメリカ製のコーヒー」) / コンセント a (wall) socket (**!** consent は「同意」) / シャープペンシル a mechanical pencil (**!** sharp pencil は「鋭い鉛筆」) / トレーニングパンツ sweat pants (**!** training pants は「幼児の排便用しつけパンツ」) / ベビーカー a stroller (**!** baby car は「小型自動車」) / マイカー one's own car (**!** my car は「私の車」) / モーニングサービス breakfast special (**!** morning service は「朝の礼拝」).

ワセリン 《商標》 vaseline /væsəli:n/; petrolatum.
わせん 和船 an old-time Japanese (cargo) boat.
わせん 和戦 peace and war. ● 和戦両様の構えでのぞむ be prepared either for *war or peace*.
わそう 和装 *kimono* [(traditional) Japanese] costume. ● 和装の麗人 a beautiful woman in a *kimono*.
● 和装小物 *kimono* accessories.

***わた** 綿 cotton; 『原綿』 raw cotton, 《米》 cotton wool (**!** 《英》では「精製綿」,「脱脂綿」などの意で用いる); 『詰め綿』 batting, wadding; 『木』 cotton plant; 《集合的》 cotton. ● 綿を打つ whip [willow] *cotton*. ● クッションに綿を詰める stuff *cotton* into a cushion; stuff a cushion with *cotton*; wad a cushion.

● 綿のように疲れる be tired out; be completely exhausted.
● 綿入れ a wadded [a padded] garment.

- 綿菓子 《米》(a) cotton candy; 《英》(a) candyfloss. (!綿菓子売りに「二つちょうだい」と言う場合は C 扱いで "Two cotton candies, please.") ● 綿雲 fleecy clouds. ● 綿ごみ (綿くず)(綿状のごみ) fluff; wooly dust. ● 綿毛 fluff; (鳥などの) down; (植物の) wool; (布地などの) fuzz. ● タンポポの綿毛 the *fluff* of a dandelion. ● 綿帽子 (⇨綿帽子) ● 綿埃(ぼこり)(綿ごみ) fluff; wooly dust. ● 綿雪 large soft flakes of snow. (cf. ぼたん雪)

わた 腸 ● 魚のわた(=内臓)を抜く remove [clean, take out] the *guts* (of a fish); gut a fish.

わだい 話題 [a topic [a subject] (of conversation) (!topic と subject はしばしば同義に用いられるが, 前の方は個別で共通の話題, 後の方は主題, 題目といった広い意味での話題。文脈により of conversation は省略される); [[うわさの種]] the talk (*of*). ● 話題の人 a man [a woman] in the *news*. ● 別の話題に移る turn to another *topic*. ● 車の事故件数が増えたという話題 the *topic of* an increase in the number of car accidents. (!×the topic *that* car accidents increased in number とはいわない) ● 衣服は女性の大好きな話題の一つだ Clothes are one of women's favorite *topics* [*subjects*] *of* conversation. ● 話題を変えよう Let's change the *subject*. ● 話題が尽きた We had nothing more [ran out of things] to talk about. ● その件は話題にもならなかった The subject never came up in our *discussion*.

わだかまり 蟠り (悪感情) bad [ill] feeling; (恨み) a grudge. ● 彼のやさしい言葉を聞いてわだかまりがとれた His kind words dispelled my *bad feeling* [*grudge*] *against* him. ● 彼女は私にわだかまりを持っているようだ She seems to have *bad feeling* [*something personal*] *against* me.

わだかまる 蟠る ● 心にわだかまっている(=ずっともやもやしている)不満 the discontent *rooted* in one's mind; one's *deeply rooted* [*deep-rooted*] discontent; one's *smoldering* discontent.

わたくし 私 图 I. (⇨私(わ)) ● わたくしごと one's *personal* [*private*] affairs [matters].
— **私する** 動 use for personal purposes; (流用する) appropriate; (公金を横領する) misappropriate.

わたくしりつ 私立 ⇨私立(しりつ)

わたし 私 I; my; me; mine; myself. (!英語の人称代名詞は文の中での働きによって表のように変化する)

(a) **[主格]** (!文の主語または主格補語になる場合) ● 私は高校生です I'm a high school student. ● 悪いのは私です It's *me* who is [×am] to blame. (!It is *I* who am [×is] to blame. より普通) ● 彼は私よりよく勉強する He studies harder than I do (《話》than *me*, 《書》than *I*).
会話 「そこにいるのはだれ?」「私です」"Who's there?" "It's *me*./(《書・まれ》It's *I*."
会話 「ゆうべはよく寝た」「私もだ」"I slept well last night." "So did I./(《話》*Me*, too. (⇨も)
会話 「ちょっとお嬢さん.何か落としましたよ」「えっ, 私(のこと)?」"Hi, Miss! I think you dropped something." "*Me*?" (!事典▶相手と距離がある場合などはジェスチャーで日本人なら人指し指で自分の鼻を指すが, 米英人は人差し指や親指で自分の胸を指すことが多い)

(b) **[所有格]** (!所有・所属を表す場合) ● 私のあの[この]新しいカメラ that [this] new camera of *mine*. (×my that [this] new camera. は不可) ● 私の父は教師です My father is a teacher.

(c) **[目的格]** (!動詞・前置詞の目的語になる場合) ● 父は私に自転車を買ってくれた My father bought *me* a bicycle./My father bought a bicycle for *me*. (《略》▶私はコーヒー. あなたは? Coffee for me, and you? (!日本語のように I'm coffee, and you? ということもあるが, 普通ではない)

(d) **[所有代名詞]** (!所有・所属を表すが, 所有格と異なって他の語を修飾しない)
会話 「このカバンだれの」「私のです」"Whose is this bag?" "It's *mine*. (!ここでは It is *my* bag. より普通)

(e) **[再帰代名詞]** (!動詞・前置詞の目的語が主語と同じ場合とか, 主語・目的語を強調する場合とされ, 動詞の目的語は無強勢, 前置詞の目的語と強調用法は強勢を受ける傾向がある) ● 私は私自身に尋ねてみた I tried ↘asking *myself*. ...asking ↘*myself*. では「自分で尋ねてみた」の意 (⇨ [次例]) ● (他の人ではなく)私(自身)が夕食を作りました I ↘*myself* made the dinner./I made the dinner ↘*myself*. (!強調表現. myself の位置は後の文の方が普通) ● 彼と私は同じ学校へ行っています He and I [*myself*] go to the same school. (!(1) 他の(代)名詞と並べる場合, 特にくだけた言い方でない限り, 通例 I は最後におく. ×I and he go... は不自然. (2) myself では「私」が強調される)

(f) **[その他の表現]** ● 私1人で本箱を部屋の中へ運んだ

人称代名詞の格変化

人称	数	格	主 格 …は, が	所有格 …の	目的格 …に, を	所有代名詞 …のもの	再帰代名詞 …自身
一人称	単数	私	I	my	me	mine	myself
	複数	私たち	we	our	us	ours	ourselves
二人称	単数	あなた	you	your	you	yours	yourself
	複数	あなたたち					yourselves
三人称	単数	彼	he	his	him	his	himself
		彼女	she	her	her	hers	herself
		それ	it	its	it		itself
	複数	彼(女)ら, それら	they	their	them	theirs	themselves

わたし

I carried the bookcase into the room 《all》 by myself 《on my own》. ▶私はです,彼ではありません.私には私(自身)のやりたいことをさせてください I'm *me*, not him. Please let *me* do *my own* thing.

会話「もしもし,美智子さんいらっしゃいますか」「はい,私です」"Hello. May I speak to Michiko?" "*Speaking*." (⇨電話での言い方)

わたし 渡し ❶［渡し場］a ferry. ❷［受け渡し］delivery. (⇨受け渡し)
● 渡し船 (⇨渡し船) ● 渡し守り a ferryman.

わたしたち 私たち (私たちは[が]) we; (私たちの) our; (私たちを[に]) us; (私たちのもの) ours; (私たち自身) ourselves. (⇨私)

わたしぶね 渡し船 a ferry; a ferryboat. ●渡し船で川を渡る cross [go across] a river *by ferry* [*on a ferry*].

*****わたす 渡す** ❶［向こう側へ渡す］(人を運ぶ) carry [take*] 《him》 across 《over》... (⇨渡る ❶); (橋などを造る) build*; (かける) span (-nn-); (置く) lay*. ● 彼らを船で川の向こう岸へ渡す carry [*take*] them *across* the river in a boat; (こいで渡す) row them *across* the river. ● 水たまりに板を渡す lay a board *over* [*across*] the puddle. ▶彼らは川に石橋を渡した They *built* a stone bridge *over* [*across*] the river./They *spanned* the river *with* a stone bridge.

❷［手渡す］(与える) give* 《❗渡し方に制限のない最も一般的な語》; (手で渡す) hand... 《over》; (書類などを提出する) hand [give]... in; (回す) pass; (届ける) deliver; (管理をまかせる) turn... over; (そっとすばやく)入れる) slip (-pp-). ● 彼に本を渡す hand a book 《*over*》 to him; hand him a book. ● 彼にボールを渡す pass a ball 《*on*》to him; hand him a ball. ▶上司に辞表を渡す hand [*give*] one's resignation *in to* the boss. ● 金をそっと彼の手に渡す slip some money *into* his hand. ● 彼女に卒業証書を渡す give [*授与する*] *grant*, (発行する) *issue*] her a diploma. ● 妻に給料を渡す turn [*hand*] one's salary *over to* one's wife. ● 強盗は彼女に指輪を渡せと言った The robber told her to *hand over* her ring 《to him》. ▶あなたが着くころには仕事に出ているが思いますが隣の人に鍵(㌍)を渡して(＝預けて)いきます I'll be at work when you arrive, but I'll *leave* a key *with* my next-door neighbor.

会話「それは土曜日ぐらいに持っていくよ」「もう少し早めに渡してもらえないかなあ」"I'll bring them around on Saturday." "Can't you let me *have* them a bit sooner?"

❸［譲り渡す］(権利・所有物を引き渡す) hand... over, (敗北の結果劣勢などに) surrender; (財産などを移管する) transfer (-rr-), 《やや書》make*... over.
● 泥棒を警察に渡す hand [*turn*] the thief *over to* the police. ● 財産を息子に譲り渡す transfer [*make over*] one's property to one's son.

わだち 轍 (車輪の跡) a (tractor [wagon]) rut; (car [tyre]) tracks (❗単数扱い). ● 深いわだちのできた道 a deeply *rutted* road.

わたつみ ❶［海の神］the sea god;『ギリシャ神話』Poseidon /pəsáidn/;『ローマ神話』Neptune /néptj)n/. ❷［海］the sea.

わたぼうし 綿帽子 a floss silk headgear 《worn by a bride traditionally dressed in wedding *kimono* costume》.
● 綿帽子をかぶる ● 綿帽子をかぶった富士山 Mt. Fuji *capped* [*crowned*] with snow.

わたり 渡り ● 渡りの労働者 (＝季節労働者) a migrant /máigrǝnt/ (worker). ● (⇨渡り鳥, 渡り廊下)
● 渡りに船 ▶転勤の話は渡りに船だった (＝時機を得ま

た) The transfer offer was *timely*./The transfer offer came at a perfect time.

わたりあう 渡り合う ❶［剣を交える］cross swords /sɔ́ːrdz/ 《with》.
❷［議論する］argue 《about, over, with》; have* an argument. ● 彼は新税の案について首相と激しく渡り合った He had a heated *argument* with the Prime Minister *over* the new tax bill.

わたりあるく 渡り歩く (場所を) go* [wander] from place to place; (仕事を) change jobs every so often; often switch from one job to another; wander from job to job. ● 町から町へと渡り歩く *wander from town to town*.

わたりいた 渡り板 《船舶》a gangplank; a gangway footplate.

わたりがに 渡り蟹 『動物』a swimming crab.

わたりぞめ 渡り初め (橋の開通式の時の儀式) the first crossing of a new bridge.

わたりどり 渡り鳥 a migratory [a migrant] bird, a migrant; a bird of passage.

わたりろうか 渡り廊下 (別の建物に通じる) a roofed passageway; (ガレージなどに通じる) a breezeway.

*****わたる 亘る** ❶［範囲などが］range; (広範囲に広がる) spread*; (距離・範囲などが伸びる) extend 《及ぶ》; (両端に伸びる) stretch; (包含する) cover. ▶彼らの年齢は6歳から10歳にわたっている Their ages *range from* six *to* ten./They *range* in age *from* six *to* ten. ● その砂漠は数百マイルにわたる The desert /dézərt/ *stretches* [*spreads*, *extends*] (for) hundreds of miles. ● 彼の研究は広範囲にわたる His studies *cover* [*range over*, *extend over*] a wide field.

❷［期間が］(ある期間に延びる) extend; (長期間に広がる) spread*; (続く) continue, last.

解説 上記の動詞のほか,次のような前置詞によっても表せる: 2時間にわたって演説をする make a speech *for* two hours./長期間にわたって *over* a long term of years./4代にわたってここに住む live here *for* [*over*] four generations.

▶試験(期間)は2週間にわたる The exams *extend over* two weeks. ● その軍事政権は30年間にわたって(続いた) The military government *continued* [*lasted*] (for) thirty years. (❗for はしばしば省略される)

*****わたる 渡る** ❶［横断する］(平面の場所を横切る) cross, go* [come*] across...; (高さのあるもの・平面なものの上を越えて) go over...; (歩いて［走って, 泳いで; 車で; 船で; 飛行機で］) walk [run*; swim*; drive*; sail; fly*] across...; (歩いて水の中を渡る) wade 《across...》. ● 橋を渡る cross [go across, go over] the bridge. ● 小川を歩いて渡る *wade 《across》* a brook. ● 道を渡るときは気をつけね Be careful when you *cross* the street. ▶彼は海峡を船[飛行機]で渡った He *sailed across* [*flew over, flew across*] the channel./He *crossed* the channel by ship [plane]. ▶彼は川の対岸まで泳いで渡った He *swam across* (to the other side of) the river. ● 寒風が湖面を渡った(＝さっと通過した) The cold wind *swept over* the lake.

❷［移住する］(人が一時的に, 鳥などが定期的に) migrate; (人が他国へ) emigrate; (人が他国から) immigrate. (⇨移住する) ● 日本から米国へ渡る *migrate* [*emigrate*] from Japan to the United States.

❸［渡来する］(輸入される) be imported; (導入される) be introduced 《into》. ▶ガラスは外国から渡ってきた Glass *was imported* [*brought over*] from abroad. ▶仏教は中国から日本へ渡ってきた Bud-

dhism *was introduced into* Japan from China. ❹[移る](人の手に渡る) pass 《*to, into*》. ▶その家は人手[彼の息子の手]に渡った The house *passed into* other people's hands [*to* his son]. ❺[暮らしていく]●どうにか世を渡ってゆく manage to *get along* [*on*] in the world.
● 渡る世間に鬼はない (親切はどこにでもある) There is kindness to be found everywhere.

わっ ugh /ʌ́(ː)/ 〔嫌悪・恐怖の声〕; boo 〔❗人を不意に驚かすときの声〕.

わっか 輪っか a hoop.（⇨輪）

わづくえ 和机 a Japanese-style table [desk].

ワックス wax.● ワックスを塗る wax 〔a floor〕.

わっしょい（掛け声）yo-heave-ho /jóuhíːvhóu/.

ワッセルマンはんのう ワッセルマン反応〔医学〕the Wassermann /wάːsərmən/ reaction.

わっと（一斉に）all at once; （急に）all of a sudden. ▶人々がわっと(我々の方に)押しかけてきた People came upon us *all at once*. ● 聴衆はわっと笑った The audience *burst* [*broke*] *into* laughter./The audience *burst* [*broke*] *out* laughing. ● 彼女はわっと泣き出した She *burst out* crying./She *burst into* tears. ● 彼のホームランに場内はわっと歓声が上がった The crowd *burst into cheers* [The crowd *cheered*] when he hit a homerun. ● 男の子たちはわっと走り出した The boys *broke into* a run.

ワット a watt（略 W, w）.〔参考〕James Watt の名から）● 60ワットの電球 a 60-*watt* (light) bulb.
● ワット時 a watt-hour〔記号 Wh, WH〕. ● ワット数 wattage ● 時に a ～: 3 キロワット数 *a wattage* of 3 kilowatts [3KW]）

ワッフル（a）waffle.

ワッペン［<ドイツ語］〔記章〕a badge;〔紋章〕an emblem.

わとう 話頭 ● 話頭を転じる change a topic of conversation.

わどく 和独 ● 和独辞典 a Japanese-German dictionary.

わとじ 和綴 old-time Japanese bookbinding. ● 和綴じの本 a book *bound in old-time Japanese style*.

わな 罠 ●〔ばね仕掛けの〕a trap;〔脚が引っ掛かると締まる輪状のもの〕a snare.〔❗(1) ともに人を陥れるわなの意に用いられるが、snare の方が堅い語. (2) snare は時に snares と複数形で用い単数扱い〕● わなで捕える catch 〔a rabbit〕in a *trap* [a *snare*]; trap [snare] 〔a rabbit〕. ● わなをかける set [lay] a *trap* [a *snare*]〔*for* a rabbit〕. ▶その泥棒は警察のわなにはまった The thief was caught in a police *trap*. ▶我々は彼をわなにかけて彼女を殺害したことを認めさせた We *trapped* him *into* admitting that he had murdered her. ▶それが(仕組まれた)わなだと分かったときにはもう遅かった It was too late when I knew it was a *setup* [(何かわなにはめられている) I *was set up for* something].

わなげ 輪投げ ● 輪投げをする play *quoits*.〔❗ a quoit /kwɔ́it, kɔ́it/ は輪投げ遊びの輪〕

わななく（震える）shake*;（小刻みに）tremble.（⇨震える）

わなわな ● 恐ろしさにわなわな(＝がたがた)震える *tremble* all over with fear.

わに 鰐〔動物〕（アフリカ・南アジア産の）a crocodile; (米国南東部・中国東部産の) an alligator.
● ワニ革 crocodile; alligator.

わにぐち 鰐口 ❶〔神社などの大きな鈴〕a flat-shaped gigantic bell (that people ring clankingly several times before offering their prayers to the god).
❷〔幅広の大きな口〕a big mouth like an alligator's; a wide mouth;《英俗》a big gob.

わのり 輪乗り (乗馬で) riding in a circle.● 輪乗りする ride in a circle.

わはは ● わははと大笑いをする roar with laughter; (急に) burst out into loud laughter; (腹をかかえて) double up with laughter;《擬音語》haw-haw /hɔ́ːhɔ́ː/.

わび 侘び *wabi*,〔茶道〕austere refinement, （説明的に）to find enjoyment in a quiet, simple life free from worldly affairs.

わび 詫び (an) apology. ● おわびの手紙 a letter of *apology*. ● わびを聞き入れる accept 〈his〉*apology* [*apologies*].（⇨詫(わ)びる）▶そのグラスを壊してしまっておわびの申し上げようもございません I don't know how to *apologize* [*make an apology*] *to* you *for* breaking the glass.（❗自動詞だから ×apologize you とはいえない）（⇨詫(わ)びる）
〔会話〕「あのう、君におわびしないといけないんだ」「どうして？」「昨日は映画を見に行くことになってたのに、ころっと忘れてたんだ」「それならいいのさ. 実は私の方こそわびないくっちゃ」"You know, I owe you an *apology*." "What for?" "We had planned to see a movie yesterday, but I completely forgot." "Don't worry about it. I owe you an *apology*."

翻訳のこころ わたしの命なぞは、問題ではない. 死んでおり, などと気のいいことは言っておられん (太宰治『走れメロス』) My life is of no value. I don't intend to say naively that I'll trade my life for my apology to you [I offer my life as my apology to you].〔❗〔死んで(あなたに)お詫びする〕は trade my life for my apology to you (私の命を(あなたへの)お詫びとして差し出す) と表す)
● わびを入れる offer [give] 〈him〉an apology.

わびいる 詫び入る （ひたすら詫びる）apologize unreservedly〔(丁寧に) politely; (深く) deeply〕.● 彼は金の件でしきりに詫びいっていた He *was* very *apologetic about* the money problem.

わびごと 詫び言 an apology.

わびしい 侘びしい 〔〔うら悲しい〕dreary,〔寂しい〕lonely. ● わびしい冬の空 a *dreary* winter sky.

わびじょう 詫び状〔write [send]〕a letter of apology.

わびずまい 侘び住まい〔閑静な住まい〕a house in a quiet quarter;（静かで地味な生活）a simple and quiet life;（貧しい家）a humble house;（貧しい生活）a poor man's life; an impoverished life.● 佗び住まいをしている live quietly 《in the country》; live in poverty.

わびる 詫びる apologize, make* [offer] an apology 《*to*＋人, *for*＋事》.〔❗ regret〔遺憾の意を表する〕とは異なることに注意〕（⇨謝る）

わふう 和風 Japanese style [fashion]. ●（純）和風の家 a *Japanese-style* house; a house *in* (*traditional*) *Japanese style*.

わふく 和服 Japanese clothes; (a) *kimono*（複 ～s）.● 和服姿の女性 a woman in *kimono*; a *kimonoed* woman.

わふつ 和仏 ● 和仏辞典 a Japanese-French dictionary.

わぶん 和文 〔〔日本語〕Japanese; 〔日本語の文章〕Japanese writing, (1 文) a Japanese sentence. ● 和文英訳 translation from Japanese into English; Japanese-English translation.

わへい 和平 peace.（⇨平和）
● 和平会談 a peace conference. ● 和平工作 a peace move(ment). ● 和平交渉 peace talks

わほう 話法 ❶ 〖話し方〗(話術) the art of conversation; (話す態度) a manner of speaking.
❷ 〖文法〗speech, narration. ● 描出話法 represented speech.

わぼく 和睦 图 (和解) reconciliation.
── **和睦する** 動 (人と) be reconciled 《with》; (人・国などと) make* peace 《with》.

わめい 和名 a Japanese name. ▶ sea bass の和名を教えてください Please tell me the *Japanese name for* "sea bass."/Please tell me what "sea bass" *is called in Japanese*.

わめきごえ わめき声 a shout, a yell; a scream, a shriek.

わめく 〖大声を出す〗shout, yell; 〖金切り声で〗scream, shriek. (叫ぶ)

わやく 和訳 translation into Japanese; (a) Japanese translation. ● 英文和訳 *translation* from English *into Japanese*; English-Japanese *translation*. ▶ 次の一節を和訳しなさい *Translate* [*Put*] the following passage *into Japanese*.

わよう 和洋 ── **和洋の** 形 Japanese and Western [European].
● 和洋折衷 a compromise between Japanese and Western [European] styles; a semi-Western style. ● 和洋折衷の家 a house of *semi-Western* style. ● 和洋折衷住宅 a *semi-Western* style house.

わら 藁 (1本) a straw; 〖集合的〗straw. ▶ おぼれる者はわらをもつかむ 《ことわざ》A drowning man will grasp [clutch, 《やや古》catch] at a *straw*.
● **わらにもすがる** ▶ 私はわらにもすがる思いで I feel like clutching [grasping] at straws.
● わら打ち (⇨藁打ち) ● わら囲い a protective cover made of straw. ● わら紙 (ざら紙) coarse paper (made from rice straw). ● わらぐつ (a pair of) straw boots. ● わら工品 things made of [from] straw. ● わら細工 straw work. ● わらしべ the pith of rice straw. ● わら人形 a straw figure; a straw doll. ● わら灰 straw ashes. ● わら半紙 coarse writing paper. ● わら葺き (⇨藁葺き)

*****わらい 笑い** 〖笑うこと・その声〗laughter (❗ laugh より大きくて連続的); a laugh; 〖ほほえみ〗a smile; 〖含み笑い〗a chuckle; 〖くすくす笑い〗a giggle; 〖冷笑〗a sneer. (⇨笑う)

〖解説〗**laugh** は laughter と異なり have [give] a loud *laugh* (高笑いする)のように have, give などで始まる動詞句の一部として用いることが多い.

①【笑い～】▶ 隣の部屋から笑い声が聞こえた I heard *laughter* from the next room. ▶ とんだお笑い草だ That's a *laugh* [a *big joke*].
②【笑いが】● 笑いがこみ上げる can't help laughing. ▶ おかしくて笑いがとまらない I can't help [stop] *laughing*. ▶ もうかって笑いがとまらない I'm making so much money that I'm bursting with *smiles*./《古》I *am laughing* all the way to the bank. (❗ 慣用表現) ▶ 笑いが最上の薬 《ことわざ》*Laughter* is the best medicine.
③【笑いを】● 笑いをこらえる suppress [swallow] one's *laughter*; keep from *laughing*. ● 聴衆の笑いを取る get a 《big》*laugh* from the audience. ▶ 彼女はうれしそうな笑いを浮かべていた She had [wore] a happy *smile* on her face./(うれしそうに笑っていた) She *was smiling* happily. ▶ 政治家の方はつくり笑いをなさるんですよ Politicians put on forced *smiles*.
● 笑い顔 a laughing [a smiling] face; a smile. (⇨笑顔) ● 笑い草 (⇨笑い物) ● 笑い声 (the sound of) laughter; a laughing voice. ● 笑い事 (⇨笑い事) ● 笑い上戸 (酒の上の) a happy drunk, a merry drinker (❗ ×a happy drinker とはいわない); (よく笑う人) a (good) laugher. ● 笑いじわ a laugh line. ● 笑い話 (おもしろい話) a funny story; (冗談) a joke.

わらいこける 笑いこける be convulsed with laughter.

わらいごと 笑い事 a laughing matter. ▶ 笑い事ではすまされない That's no *laughing matter* [no *joke*]. (❗ That's not a … より強意的) / That's not *funny*.

わらいころげる 笑い転げる (体をよじらせて笑う) laugh convulsively; (腹をかかえて笑う) 《話》split [hold*, burst*] one's sides (laughing [with laughter]); have* a side-splitting laugh.

わらいたけ 笑い茸 (説明的に) a magic mushroom to make the one who ate it laugh; (学術名) Panaeolus papilionaceus.

わらいとばす 笑い飛ばす ▶ 根も葉もないことと笑い飛ばす *laugh 《it》 away* [*off*] as groundless.

わらいもの 笑い物 〖物笑いの種〗a laughingstock; 〖ばかにされる人〗a fool. ● 町中の笑い物になる become [make oneself] the *laughingstock* of the whole town. ● 彼を笑い物にする make a fool of him; (嘲笑(ちょうしょう)する) laugh at (からかう) make fun of him. (⇨笑う ❷)

ːわらう 笑う

WORD CHOICE 笑う

smile 声を出さずににっこりほほえむこと. at … で人には笑いかけることを, to oneself で一人ではくそ笑むことを表す. ● 彼は周りのみんなにほほ笑みかけた He *smiled* at everyone around him.
laugh 声を出して笑うこと. 面白さ・おかしさによる自然な笑いだけでなく, 悪意をもった嘲笑の意味にもなる. ● 彼の冗談に笑った I *laughed* at his joke.
grin 口を大きく開け, 歯を見せて笑うこと. または, にやりとすること. ● 楽しくて大きな口でにっこり笑う *grin* with pleasure.

頻度チャート

smile
laugh
grin

20　40　60　80　100 (%)

❶ 〖喜び・おかしさなどで〗laugh 《*at, about, over*》(❗ at+人は「嘲笑(ちょうしょう)する」の意 (⇨❷)); smile 《*at*》; grin (-nn-) 《*at*》; chuckle 《*at, over*》(❗ 主に男性が軽く吹き出すようにくすりと笑うこと); giggle 《*at*》(❗ 若い女性や子供が照れ隠しにくすくす笑うこと). ● どっと笑う burst out *laughing*; burst into *laughter*. (❗ 前の方が口語的) ● 1人静かに笑う *chuckle* [*laugh softly*] to oneself. ● 彼のことで[その話を話題にして]笑う *laugh about* him [*over* the story]. ● 大笑いする have [give, 《古》laugh] a good [hearty] *laugh*, *laugh* a lot 《*at, about, over*》. ● (涙が出るほど) *laugh* (*and laugh*) till tears come to one's eyes. ● 笑い転げる ● 笑いながら言う say with a *laugh* [a *smile*]. ● 失敗を笑ってごまかす[すます] *laugh* a mistake *off*. ● 心配を笑って吹き飛ばす *laugh* one's worries *away* [*off*]. ● 笑って承諾の意を表す *laugh* [*smile*] one's consent. ▶ 私の冗談を聞いて彼は大声で笑った He *laughed* [×*smiled*, ×*grinned*] loudly *at* my joke. (❗ loudly がなけれ

ば smiled, grinned も可) / (げらげら笑った) He roared (*with laughter*) when he heard my joke. ▶何を笑っているの? What *are* you *laughing at* [*about*]? ▶彼は子供ににっこり笑った He smiled broadly at [×to] the child./He gave the child *a big smile* [... gave a big smile to the child の語順にも重点がある]. ▶さあ皆さん笑って (集合写真を撮るとき) Everybody, let's *have some smiles*. ▶あの年ごろの女の子はよく笑うものだ Girls of that age *giggle* a lot.

翻訳のこころ 寂しそうに笑った顔が、ジェームズ・ディーンによく似ていた (江國香織『デューク』) When he put on a lonely smile, he looked very much like James Dean. (「寂しそうに笑う」は put on a lonely smile と表す)

❷ [嘲笑(ちょうしょう)する] laugh (*at*), ridicule (**!** 前の方より堅い語); (冷笑する) sneer (*at*); (からかう) make* fun of, 《書》 mock (at ...). ●彼の失敗 [彼が子供っぽいこと] を笑う *laugh* at his mistake [him *for being* childish]. ●彼 [彼の考え] をあざ笑う *mock* (*at*) him [his ideas]; (冷やかに) *sneer* at him [his ideas]. ●面と向かって [腹の中で] 彼をあざ笑う *laugh* in his face [up one's sleeve *at* him]. ▶その問題が解けなかったら人に笑われるよ You'll *be laughed at* if you can't solve the problem. (**!** at を落とさないこと)

● 笑う門には福来たる Happiness will come in to a merry house. / (ことわざ) (楽しく暮らすのが一番) Laugh and grow fat.

わらうち 藁打ち straw beating. ●わら打ちをする *beat straw* to make it flexible.

わらえる 笑える ❶ [自然と笑った状態になる] ●面白くてつい笑えてくるのだった It was so funny that I *couldn't help laughing*.
❷ [笑うことができる] ●笑える話 (おもしろい話) a funny story; (冗談) a joke. ●笑える話ではない It's no *laughing* matter.

● 笑えない喜劇 a comedy you cannot laugh at; (こっけいだがまじめに考えねばならない状況) a comic situation that calls for serious attention.

わらじ 草鞋 《a pair of》 *waraji*; (説明的に) lightweight Japanese sandals made of straw. ●二足のわらじをはく (⇒二足の草鞋) ●長いわらじをはく (⇒長い [成句])
● わらじを脱ぐ (旅を終える) complete [accomplish] one's journey; (宿に泊まる) put up at an inn.

わらしべちょうじゃ 『わらしべ長者』 *The Straw Millionaire*. [参考] 日本の昔話

わらじむし 草鞋虫 [昆虫] a sow bug; a wood louse (⊕ wood lice).

わらび 蕨 [植物] brake; (シダ類) bracken.
● わらび餅 a bracken-starch dumpling [cake].

ワラビー [動物] a wallaby.

わらぶき 藁葺き (straw-)thatched. ●わらぶきの屋根 [家] a (straw-)thatched roof [house (⊕ houses /-ziz/, 《米》/-siz/)].

わらべ 童 a child (⊕ children), a kid.
● 童謡 a traditional children's song; (童謡) a nursery rhyme /ráim/.

わらわせる 笑わせる make* (him) laugh; get* a laugh. (**!** ×be given a laugh とはいわない) (⇒笑う)
● ばかばかしいことをして人を笑わせる *get* a cheap *laugh*. ▶彼は冗談を言って私たちを笑わせた He *made* us *laugh* by telling jokes./His jokes *set* us *laughing*. (楽しませた) *amused* us]. ▶彼が音楽家だって? 笑わせるなよ He is a musician? Don't *make* me *laugh*! [《話》That's a *laugh*./(冗談だろう)《話》You're kidding.]

ワラント [経済] (a) warrant.
● ワラント (付社) 債 a warrant bond; a bond with warrants.

*わり 割 ❶ [割合] a rate; (比率) a ratio /réiʃou/ (⊕ ~s). (⇒割合) ▶1 時間に 4 キロの割で歩いた I walked at the [a] *rate* of four kilometers an hour. ▶世界の人口は毎年どのくらいの割で増加するか知っていますか Do you know at what *rate* the population of the world increases every year?

❷ [百分率] a percént(age). (**!** 通例単数形で) (⇒割合) ▶物価は昨年の今ごろに比較すると約 2 割がた上がっています Prices have risen by about twenty *percent*, (as) compared with those at this time last year. (**!** この by は「...だけ」の意)

会話「何割の学生が自転車通学をしていますか」「約 3 割です」"What *percentage* of the students go to school by bicycle?" "About thirty *percent*." (**!** 動詞の数は of の後の名詞の数に一致する)

❸ [利益] (a) profit; gain. ●割のいい商売 a *profitable* [《書》a *gainful*] business. ●割のいい [よくない] 仕事 a *well-* [a *poorly-*]*paid* job. ▶それは割が合わない It doesn't pay.

❹ [割り当て] 《やや書》 assignment; 《やや書》 allotment. (⇒割り当て) ●作業量 work *assignment*.
● 利益を頭割にする share the profits *equally*.
● 割を食う be put at a disadvantage. ●正直者が割を食う世の中 the world in which honesty doesn't pay.

*わりあい 割合 图 [割合] (a) proportion; [率] a rate; [比率] (a) ratio /réiʃou/ (⊕ ~s); [百分率] a percént(age). (⇒割) ●そのクラスの男女の割合 the *proportion* [*ratio*] of boys to girls in the class. ▶その工場の事故の割合はかなり高い The accident *rate* in the factory is rather high. ▶在校生の大学進学の割合はどのくらいですか What *percentage* [*proportion*] of the students go on to college? (**!** 呼応する動詞の数は of に続く名詞の数に一致する)
▶応募者に対する合格者の割合は 6 対 1 です The *ratio of* the successful candidates *to* the applicants is one to [in] six. (**!** to は「に対して」, in は「...のうちで」の意でいずれも割合を示す) ●油と酢は 3 対 2 の割合で混ぜるべきです Oil and vinegar should be mixed in the *proportion* [*ratio*] of three to two. (**!** A to B では通例 A は B より大) ▶4 人に 1 人の割合で眼鏡をかけている One *out of* four wears glasses.

—— 割合 (に) 副 [比較的に] compáratively; relatively /rélətivli/; [いくぶん] fairly; rather. (⇒幾らか) ▶英語の試験は割合やさしかった The English exam was *comparatively* [*relatively*] easy. ▶今日は割合暖かだ It's *fairly* warm today.

わりあて 割り当て 〖各人に対する仕事・金・時間などの〗《やや書》allotment; (分け前の)《やや書》allocation; [強制的な仕事などの]《やや書》assignment; [生産・販売などの]《やや書》(a) quota (⊕ ~s). ●農民への土地の割り当て *allotment* of the lands to the farmers. ●衣料品の輸入品割当量 an import *quota* on clothings. ●割当量をこなせる fulfill one's *quota*. ●費用の割り当て the *allocation* of expenditure.
● 割り当て制度 the quota system; the allocation system.

わりあてる 割り当てる (仕事・部屋などを) assign; (時間・お金などを) allot (-tt-). (⇒当てる ❻) ●各生徒に一部屋ずつ割り当てる *assign* a room *to* each student; *assign* each student a room. ●割り当てられた仕事をする do one's share of work.

わりいん　割り印　a tally seal; a seal over two pages. ●書類に割り印を押す　put [《書》affix] one's seal at the joining of the papers. ●割り印の押してある(=押印がある)書類　the papers with a *tally impression*.

わりがき　割り書き　(角く書き) a two-lined subtitle.

わりかし　割りかし　(⇨わりに)

わりかん　割り勘　●割り勘にする　split [share] the bill [《米話》tab]; (半々にする) go halves 《on + 費用, with + 人》; go Dutch 《with + 人》. (!) Go Dutch は「費用各自払い」の意にもなる。「割り勘にする食事」などを a Dutch treat ということもある) ●彼らは外で食事をするときはいつも割り勘です　They always *split the bill* when they eat out.

わりきる　割り切る　●割り切った(=理性的な)見方をする　take a *rational* [(情に左右されない) an *unsentimental*] point of view; (非常に単純に考える)《けなして》see things in black-and-white terms [as black or white]. ●彼は何事も割り切っている(実際的[事務的]である) He is *practical* about *businesslike* in everything. (!) 後の方では日本語のもつ冷たい感じはない)/(現実的な態度を取る) He takes a *realistic* attitude toward [about] everything.

わりきれる　割り切れる　▶16 は 2 で割り切れる　16 *can be divided* [*divides, is divisible*] *by* 2. / 2 *divides* [*goes*] *into* 16. / Two is a *factor of* sixteen.
【割り切れない】[数が] cannot be divided 《by》; be indivisible 《by》; [事が] leave* some room for doubt; be unconvincing. ▶彼の説明にはどこか割り切れないところがある　His explanation is still *unsatisfactory* [*unconvincing*]./I'm not quite *satisfied with* his explanation. ▶その問題には何か理屈で割り切れないものがある　There is something in that matter that *cannot be explained by logic* [*reason*].

わりぐり(いし)　割栗(石)　(small) broken stone.

わりご　破り子　a partitioned lunch box.

わりこむ　割り込む　❶[人のじゃまをする] (会話などに口をはさむ) cut* [break*, 《話》butt] in 《on》; (じゃまをする) interrupt; (列に) cut in line, jump the line 《米》[queue 《英》]; (走行車などの前に) cut in 《on, ahead of》(のはぎりぎり前, ahead of は前方をさす); (押し入る) squeeze (oneself) 《into》, force one's way 《into》. ●満員電車に割り込んで乗る　*squeeze* (oneself, one's way) [*push* one's way] *into* a crowded train. ▶人の話に割り込むものではありません　You shouldn't *cut* [*break*] *in on* other people's conversations./You shouldn't *cut in* [*break in, interrupt*] when other people are talking. ▶並んでいる私の前に彼が割り込んだ　He *cut* (*in*) *in front of* me in line. (!) 通例 in は省略される)
❷[下回る] ▶今年度の売上げは前年度の(売り上げ)を大幅に割り込んだ　The sales of this year *have dropped* to a great extent *below* those of the previous year.

わりざん　割り算　division (↔multiplication). ●割り算をする　divide. (⇨割る)

わりだか　割高　(他と比べて値が高い) comparatively expensive (価格が) high]. ●日本の航空運賃はアメリカに比べると割高だ　Airline fares in Japan are *comparatively high* (as) compared with the corresponding ones in America. ●灯油の値段は供給のだぶつきからみて割高(=やや高い)感がある　The price of kerosene is *rather high* [×*expensive* for its oversupply. ▶それでは割高になる(=より費用がかかる) That will *cost* you *more*.

わりだす　割り出す　(算出する) calculate, 《主に米話》figure... out; (推測する) deduce 《from》; (基づく) be based 《on》. ●それを...という事実から割り出す　*deduce it from* the fact that .... ▶この結果はそのアンケートから割り出したものだ　This result *is based on* the questionnaires.

わりちゅう　割り注　(説明的に) two-lined explanatory notes [annotations] given between the lines.

わりつけ　割り付け　图 (a) layout. ●(新聞の)紙面の割り付け　the *layout* of the newspaper.
── **割り付ける**　lay* ... out; make* a layout 《of》. ▶このポスターはうまく割り付けられている　This poster *is well laid out*.

わりに　割に　❶[かなり] rather; fairly;《話》pretty (⇨かなり); (比較的に) comparatively, relatively. ▶きのうは割に疲れた　I was *rather* [*pretty*] tired yesterday. ▶数学の試験は割に簡単だった　The math exam was *fairly* [(他の試験と比べて) *comparatively, relatively*] easy./(予想よりも) The math exam was easier *than* (I had) expected. ▶あちらは割に涼しいんですってよ　They said it was *kind* [*sort*] *of* cool there. (!) kind [sort] of は《話》で「ある程度」の意のぼかし表現) ▶割に多くの人がそれを見に来た　*Quite a few* people came to see it.
❷[割合に] ▶彼は年の割に若く見える　He looks young *for* [*considering*] his age. ▶正直は割に合わない　Honesty doesn't *pay*.

わりばし　割り箸　(使い捨ての木製の箸) disposable wooden chopsticks.

*****わりびき　割引**　a discount (●現金で売買する場合の少額の割引); a price reduction, a reduction in prices. (!) ともにやや改まった言い方。大幅な値引きを指す) ●団体割引　a group *reduction*. ●大量購入割引　a quantity *discount*. ●事前購入割引　a *discount* for advance purchases. ●現金割引　a cash *discount*. ▶1割引で売る　sell 《it》at a 10 percent *discount* [*reduction*]; sell 《it》at 10 percent *off*. ●割引価格で買う　buy 《it》at a *discount* [a *reduced* price]. ▶学生には割引がありますか　Are there any *reductions* for students?/Do we got a student *discount*? ▶10 人以上まとまれば 2 割の割引になるんですね　We can offer a *discount* of 20 percent if there are more than ten of you.
── **割引する**　動　discount; make* [offer, allow, give*] a discount; reduce the price; give [allow] a reduction in price. (!) 動詞の discount, reduce を用いるより名詞の discount, reduction を用いる方が口語的) ▶その車の値段を2割引きする　give [make, allow] a 20 percent *discount on* the car; give [allow] a 20 percent *reduction in* the price of the car. (!) 動詞を用いた *reduce* [*discount*] the price of the car by 20 percent より口語的) ▶少し割引してください　Please give [allow, ×make] me a small *discount*./ Could you make it a little *cheaper*?/Will you take a little *less*? (!) 後の方はぶしつけな言い方) ▶全商品 2 割引に致します　You get a 20 percent *discount* on all goods. ▶5 パーセントの割引をしてもらった　I got a 5 percent *discount*.
●**割引運賃**　a discount fare. ●**割引券**　a discount ticket; (店のちらしなどについている切り取り式の) coupon. ●**割引債**　a discount(ed) bond. ●**割引手形**　a bill [a note] (receivable) discounted. ●**割引発行**　a discount issue. ●**割引率**　a discount rate. (!) 公定歩合の意の時は冠詞の)

わりびく　割り引く　discount /《米》dískaunt;《英》-⁄. (⇨割引) ▶彼の言うことは少し割り引いて聞いた方がよい

You should *discount* a little of his story./《話》 You should *take* what he says *with a grain* [*a pinch*] *of salt*.

わりふ 割り符 a tally; (合い札) a check. ●割り符が合う tally 《*with*》.

わりふり 割り振り assignment. (**!**「達成すべき仕事」の意. 個々の仕事をさすときは 〔C〕) ●彼らに仕事の割り振りをする give them each an *assignment*.

わりふる 割り振る (割り当てる) assign.

わりほぐす 割り解す break* an egg and beat* [whisk] it.

わりまえ 割り前 (⇒分け前)

わりまし 割り増し ─ 割り増しの 形 (余分の) extra; (追加の) additional. ●割増料金を払う pay an *extra* [an *additional*] charge; pay a *premium*.
●超過勤務で割増賃金をもらう get *extra* [(時間外の) *overtime*] pay for extra work.
割増金 a premium.

わりもどし 割り戻し (払い過ぎの) a rebate; (払戻金) a refund, (a) drawback. ●年末に割り戻しを受ける get a tax *rebate* at the end of the year.

わりもどす 割り戻す (払い過ぎの金を) rebate; refund.
●徴収した税金の一部を割り戻す *refund* a part of tax collected.

わりやす 割安 (他と比べて物が安い) comparatively cheap [inexpensive, (価格が) low]. ●その服は割安だ The dress is *comparatively inexpensive* [*cheap*]. (**!** inexpensive は値段の割に質がよいことを暗示) ●その品物は今買うと割安になる If you buy the goods now, you can get them *cheaper*.

:わる 割る ❶ (力を加えて二つ(以上)にする) break*; (粉々に) smash; (音をさせて, ひびを入れて) crack; (おのなどで縦に裂く) split*; (おのなどでぶち割る) chop (-pp-). ●窓ガラスを割る *break* [*smash*] a window.
●皿を粉々に割る *break* [*smash*] a plate (*in*)*to* pieces. ●卵を割る *break* [*crack*] an egg (*into* a frying-pan). ●まきを割る *chop* [*cut*, *split*] wood. ●彼はバットで花びんを割った He *broke* the vase with a bat. (**!** 意識的に割ったのか偶然に割ってしまったのかはあいまい)

❷ (分割する) divide 《*in*, *into*》. ●スイカを六つに割る *divide*(切る) *cut*》a watermelon *in* six [*into* six pieces]. (**!** divide では「分配」のニュアンスが出る. 「スイカを6人に分ける」場合なら *divide* [×*cut*] a watermelon *among* six [the six of us])

❸ (液体を混ぜて薄くする) dilute 《*with*》; (水で薄める) water ... down; (混ぜる) mix 《*with*》. ●このウイスキーを水で割ってください Will you *water down* this whiskey? (**!**「水割り」は whiskey and water)/I'd like a little water with my whiskey, please.

❹ (割り算をする) divide. ●24 割る 4 は 6 です Twenty-four *divided by* four equals [is, makes] six. (**!** 文頭位では数字での表記は避ける)/Four into Twenty-four is [goes] six. (**!**《米》では *Divide* 24 *by* 4 [4 *into* 24] and you get 6. ともいう) ●30 を7で割ると4が立って2が余る 《話》 Seven into thirty is four, remainder two./Seven *divides* [*goes*] *into* thirty four times with two left over [with a remainder of two]. ●20 を5で割ると答えはいくらですか What is the answer if you *divide* 20 *by* 5? (**!** 単に What's 20 *by* 5? ともいう)

❺ (以下になる) ●(温度が)零度を割る *fall* [*drop*] *below* zero. ●ドルが 100 円を割る The dollar *has dropped* below the level of 100 yen.

❻ (その他の表現) ●腹を割って話す talk *frankly* [*openly*]. ●口を割る(=告白する) confess.

わる 悪 〖悪い人〗a rogue; (子供の) a naughty boy, a baddie. ●《ふざけて》a rogue; 《劇中の悪役》《話》a baddie. ●三太郎. あれはたいへんな悪だ Santaro? He's a very *naughty* boy [*a real rogue*].

わるあがき 悪あがき ── 悪あがきをする 動 (むだな努力をする) struggle ineffectively 《*against*》; make* useless efforts 《*to* do》; (むだな抵抗をする) offer [put* up] useless resistance 《*to*》.

:わるい 悪い

INDEX

❶ 道徳上 ❷ 品質・天気・評判など
❸ 有害な ❹ 傷んでいる
❺ 人・体の部位などの調子が ❻ 不運な ❼ 責任がある
❽ 頭・記憶力などが ❾ 姿・容貌(ﾖｳﾎﾞｳ)が
❿ 申し訳ない ⓫ その他の表現

WORD CHOICE 悪い

bad 質・気分・評判・都合・倫理などが悪いこと. ●悪い知らせ[天気] *bad* news [weather].
wrong 機械の調子, 行動の倫理性などが本来のあるべき正しい状態から間違っていること. ●私は何も悪いことはしなかった I didn't do anything *wrong*.
evil 倫理的にひどく悪いこと. また, 人などが悪意に満ちていること. ●悪人[霊] *evil* men [spirits].

■頻度チャート

bad

wrong

evil

20   40   60   80   100 (%)

❶ [道徳上] **bad*** (⇔*good**) (**!** 最も一般的な語); **evil** /íːvl/ (**!** bad より強意的); **wicked** /wíkid/ (**!** evil より強意的で, しばしば意図的な悪を暗示する); **wrong** (⇔*right*) (**!** 通例叙述的に). ●悪い人間 a *bad* [an *evil*, a *wicked*] person. (**!** wicked を人に用いるのは非常に強意的で(やや古).「(うるさくして言うことを聞かない)悪い子」は a *bad* [a *naughty*, ×*wicked*, ×an *evil*] child. たしなめて「悪い子ね」と言う場合は You are a *bad* [*boy* (*girl*)].) ●うそをつくことは悪いことだ It's *bad* [*wrong*] to tell a lie. ●彼に責任を押しつけるなんて君が悪い You are *wrong to* put the blame on him./It's *wrong of* [×*for*] you *to* put the blame on him. (**!** 当人の前で言う場合は後の文の方が好まれる) ●彼は悪いことをしたので罰を受けた He was punished because he did something *bad* [《書》did a *wrong*]. ●彼はまだいいことと悪いことの区別がつかない He still doesn't know right from *wrong*. (⇒善し悪し)

❷ [品質・天気・評判など] **bad***; (貧弱な) **poor**; (質が劣った) **inferior** 《*to*》; (粗悪な) **coarse**; (荒れ模様の) **foul** /fául/. ●質の悪いワイン wine of *poor* [*bad*] quality. ●悪い(=ひどい)風邪をひく catch a *bad* cold. ●あの店では悪い品を高い値段で売っている That store sells *poor quality* [*inferior*] goods at high prices. ●このスープは悪くない This soup isn't *bad*. (**!** not(...) bad は very good ということを控えめにいうくだけた表現) ●このブランデーはあのブランデーより味が悪い This brandy tastes *worse* than that brandy./This brandy is *inferior* (⇔*superior*) *to* that in flavor. ●急に天気が悪くなってしまった The weather has suddenly turned *bad* [*foul*]. ●その先生は生徒の間で評判が悪い The teacher has a *bad* reputation [is *unpopular*] among the

わるがき

students.

❸[有害な] bad*, ill* (**!** ill は通例限定的に); (害になる) harmful, 《書》injurious 《to》. ▶夜ふかしをするのは健康に悪い Keeping late hours is *bad for* you [*for* your health, *for* the health]./《夜ふかしをすることは君にとって悪い》It's *bad for* you to keep late hours. (**!** 話す時は you の後に小休止を置く。書き言葉では「君が夜ふかしをするのは悪いことだ」の意になることもある)/Keeping late hours is *harmful* [*injurious*] *to* your (the) health.

❹[傷んでいる] bad*; (腐っている) rotten; (新鮮でない) stale. ▶この肉は悪くなっている This meat has gone *bad* [*off*, *rotten*]. ▶魚は夏にすぐ悪くなる Fish easily *go bad* [*off*, *rotten*] in (《主に米》the) summer. (**!**「牛乳」などの場合は Milk easily *goes bad* [*off*, *sour*, ×rotten] in (《主に米》the) summer.)/Fish *spoil* quickly in (《主に米》the) summer.

❺[人・体の部位などの調子が] wrong (**!** 通例叙述的に、または something などの不定代名詞の後で); (不健康な) bad*; (病気の) sick, 《主に英》ill*, unwell (**!**《米》では sick を日常語として用い、ill は堅い語。《英》では通例限定用法を除いては ill, unwell を用いる). ▶気分が悪い I feel *bad*./I *don't* feel *well*./I feel *sick*《米》[*ill*《英》]./I feel *terrible*. ▶顔色が悪いですね。どこかお悪いのですか You look *pale*. What's *wrong* [*the matter*] *with* you? ▶彼女は心臓が悪い She has heart *trouble* [*a bad heart*]./She has *problems with* her heart. ▶悪くならないうちに医者に連れて行きます I'll take him to the doctor before he gets any *worse*. ▶事態はさらに悪くなっている Things are going *from bad to worse*. ▶この時計はどこか具合が悪い Something is *wrong* [There is something *wrong*] *with* this watch. ▶この機械は調子が悪い This machine is *not up to par* [*out of order*, ×*wrong*]. (**!** (1) not up to par は「調子がよくない」の意の慣用句。人にも使える。(2) ここに wrong を使うと「違う種類の」「適切でない」の意) / (うまく機能しない) This machine doesn't *work well*.

❻[不運な] unlucky, unfortunate (**!** 後の語は思いもよらぬ不運を暗示); (不快な) bad*, ill* (**!** 通例限定的に). ●悪い前兆 a *bad* [*an ill*] omen. ▶13は縁起の悪い数字であると言われている Thirteen is said to be an *unlucky* number. ▶運の悪いことに彼らは留守だった It was *unfortunate* [*unlucky*] *that* they were out./*Unfortunately* [*Unluckily*, *As* (*bad* [*ill*]) *luck would have it*], they were out. ▶家の中で傘を開くのは縁起が悪いとされている People believe that you'll have *bad* luck if you open an umbrella in your house. ▶私たちはとても疲れていた。そしてさらに悪いことには雨が降り出した We were very tired, and *what was worse* [*to make matters worse*] it began to rain. ▶悪いことに《運悪く》彼は同じ通りに住んでるんだ He lives on 《米》[*in*《英》] the same street, *worse luck*. (**!** worse luck は《英》のように文頭には用いない) ▶悪いことは続くものだ 《ことわざ》*Misfortunes never come singly* [*alone*].

❼[責任がある] (道徳的・法的に責任がある) be in the wrong; (判断などを誤っている) be wrong (↔right); (責めを負うべきだ) be to blame; (…の過失だ) be one's fault. ▶私が悪かった I *am* (《やや書》*in the*) *wrong*./I *am to blame* [×*to be blamed*]./It's my *fault*. ▶遅れたのは私が悪いのではない It's not my *fault* (that) I'm late./I'm not *to blame* for being late.

❽[頭・記憶力などが] (頭の鈍い) slow*; (貧弱の)

わるくすると

poor*. ▶娘は頭がよいが、息子はかなり悪い My daughter is clever, but my son is rather *slow* 《*not quick at learning*》. ▶彼は記憶力が悪い He has a *poor* [*a bad*] memory.

❾[姿・容貌が] (醜い) ugly (↔beautiful); (器量の悪い) plain, 《米》homely. (**!** 女性に対しては通例 plain, homely を用いることが多い) ▶このビルは見た目がひどく悪い The building is so *ugly* to look at. ▶彼女は器量は悪いが性格はよい She is *plain* [*not good-looking*], but she has a fine character.

❿[申し訳ない] be sorry, feel* bad* [terrible]; be afraid. (**!** terrible の方が強意的に) ▶長く待たせて悪かった I'm *sorry to have* [I *feel bad about having*] kept you waiting so long. ▶おじゃましてすいませんだけど、今何時か教えてくれない? *Sorry to bother you* [*Excuse me for bothering you*], but could you tell me the time? ▶悪いけど 1 時にならないとお昼の用意ができないの Lunch won't be ready till one o'clock, *I'm afraid*. (**!** I'm afraid (that) lunch…. のように文頭にも用いられる) ▶悪いんだけど仕事があるのでこれで Now, *if you don't mind*, I have work to do. ▶悪いけどしたらクーペを貸してくれないかい 《悪いけどお願い》 I *hate* to ask, but can I take the coupe /kúːp/ tomorrow? ▶いきなり行くなんて彼に悪い(=思いやりがない) It *wouldn't be nice* to him to come over suddenly.

会話「君のものを全部借りちゃって悪いねえ」「いいんだよ」"I *feel bad*, borrowing all your things." "That's all right."

会話「1 日仕事を休んでドライブに連れて行ってあげるよ」「そんなの悪いわ(=迷惑をかけたくない)」"I'll take a day off from work and take you for a drive." "I don't want to get you in any trouble!"

⓫[その他の表現] ▶彼女は暮らし向きが悪い She is *badly* (↔*well*) *off*. ▶彼女は口が悪い He has a *foul* mouth. ▶人のことを悪く言うな Don't *criticize* [《話》*put down*,《主に米語》*badmouth*] others./You shouldn't *say bad* things [*speak badly*] *about* others. (**!** speak ill of はあまり使われなくなっている) ▶もし彼が来られなくても悪く思わないでください I hope you won't be *offended* if he can't come. ▶悪いことは言いません。安いのはやめになった方が…. あとでがっかりなさいますよ (店員が迷っている客に) Take my advice. Don't buy the cheap one. You'll be disappointed.

会話(けんか・口論のあとの和解として)「悪く思わないでよ」「もちろん」"No *hard* feelings?" "No."

● 悪い虫が付く get involved with a bad guy.

わるがき 悪戯鬼 a bad boy [girl]; a naughty child (❀ children); (しつけの悪い子) a brat; (悪ふざけをする子) an imp;《古》an urchin.

わるがしこい 悪賢い (狡猾(ﾞ)な) cunning, (ずるい) sly; (策略にたけた) crafty, wily /wáili/.

わるぎ 悪気 [悪意] ill will, malice (⇒悪意); [害意] harm. ●悪気のない(=善意の) a *well-meaning* person. ● 悪気のない試み a *well-meant* attempt. ▶すみません、悪気はなかったのです I'm sorry, I didn't mean anything [I didn't mean to hurt you, any *harm*]./(そういうつもりで言ったのではない) I'm sorry, I didn't mean to (say that)./《話》No offense (to you). (**!** I mean を省略した定型表現で、「いいんだよ」と応答するときは No offense was taken. の意で None taken. などという)

わるくすると 悪くすると (最悪の場合には) if (the) worst comes to (the) worst. (**!** the を省くのは《米》) ▶悪くするとストになるかもしれない *If worst comes to worst*, there will be a strike.

わるくち 悪口 abuse /əbjúːs/;《主に米話》(a) bád-mouth;《中傷》(a) slander;《陰口》(a) 悪口を言う say bad things [something bad] about 《him》; speak badly (↔highly) about 《him》;《書》 speak ill (↔well) of 《him》;《非難する》 criticize 《him》;《主に米話》bád-móuth.

わるさ 悪さ 〔〔いたずら〕〕mischief; 〔〔悪ふざけ〕〕a practical joke. ▶いつも何か悪さをしては always up to some *mischief*.

ワルシャワ 〔〔ポーランドの首都〕〕Warsaw /wɔ́ːrsɔː/.

わるずれ 悪ずれ ▶あの男は悪ずれしている He is *too wise in the ways of the world*./He is *too worldly-wise*.

わるだくみ 悪だくみ (計略) a trick; (悪計) a [an evil] design, a [an evil] scheme, a plot. (⇨計画 [類語])

わるだっしゃ 悪達者 ▶あの役者はいかにも悪達者だ He [She] is a skillful actor but his [her] performance lacks refinement. (❗「芸は達者だが心の芸に品がない」の意)

わるぢえ 悪知恵 (こうかつさ) cunning; (悪質さ) slyness; (ずるいこと) 〈やや書〉craft. ▶悪知恵のある男 a *cunning* [a *sly*, a *crafty*] man. ▶悪知恵を働かせる use *cunning* [*craft*].

ワルツ 〔〔音楽〕〕a waltz /wɔ́ːlts/. ▶ワルツを踊る dance a *waltz*; waltz. ● ウィンナーワルツ a Viennese waltz.

わるのり 悪乗り ― 悪乗りする 動 (やりすぎる) overdo*; (調子に乗りすぎる) get* carried away 《with》. ▶彼はわい談を始めると必ず悪乗りする Once he begins to tell dirty jokes, he *gets carried away* (by them).

わるびれずに 悪びれずに (おどおどした様子もなく) without a diffident 〔うしろめたい〕 [a guilty] look. ▶彼女は悪びれずに「私が花びんを割りました」と言った She said *without a diffident look*, "I broke the vase."

わるふざけ 悪ふざけ 图 (人を困らせる) a practical joke; (悪意のない) a trick; 〈やや古〉a prank.
― 悪ふざけをする 動 ▶悪ふざけする play a practical joke [a trick] 《on》. ▶悪ふざけが過ぎる carry a *practical joke too far*.

わるぶる 悪ぶる ▶あの子はそんな悪い子ではない。ちょっと悪ぶっているだけだよ He's not really a bad boy. He's just putting it on. (❗「そんなふりをする」の意で通例進行形で用いる)

わるもの 悪者 (性格の悪い人) a bad* [a wicked] person (⇨悪人); (悪党) a rogue, 〈書〉a villain /vílən/ (❗劇中の悪役の意にもなる(⇨悪(ﾄﾞ))). ▶私だけがいつも悪者にされる(= 他人の罪を負わされる)I'm always made a *scapegoat* [a *whipping boy*]. ▶いない者がいつも悪者にされる(ことわざ) The absent are always *in the wrong*.

わるよい 悪酔い ―悪酔いする 動 (飲んで気持ちが悪くなる) feel* [get*] sick after [from] drinking. ▶安酒は悪酔いする Cheap liquor makes you *feel sick*.

われ 割れ ❶ 〔〔割れること〕〕 ● 仲間割れする be slit (up); be divided. (⇨仲間割れ)
❷ 〔〔かけら〕〕 a fragment; (とがった破片) a splinter. ● ガラスの割れ a *piece* of broken glass; a broken *piece* of glass.
❸ 〔〔相場の〕〕 ● 100 円割れ a *drop* below the 100 yen level.

われ 我 〔〔私〕〕 I; 〔〔自分自身〕〕oneself. ▶我思うゆえに我あり I think, therefore *I* exist [am].
● 我に返る ▶名前を呼ばれて我に返った *I came to myself* when my name was called. ▶我にもなく(思わず)in spite of oneself. ▶我もなく泣いてしまった I cried *in spite of myself*.
● 我も我も ▶そのバーゲン品を買おうと我も我もと押しかける *scramble* to get the bargains.
● 我を忘れる ▶彼らは興奮して我を忘れた They were *beside themselves* with excitement. ▶我を忘れて絵に没頭した I *was completely absorbed in* the painting.

われかえる 割れ返る ▶演奏が終わるとホールは割れ返るような拍手に包まれた When the performance was finished, *a thunder of applause* filled the hall.

われがちに 我勝ちに ▶我勝ちに列車に乗る crush [push] one's *way* onto a train. ▶彼らは我勝ちに外へ出ようと(= 一番に出ようと先を争った) They *scrambled* 〔〔もみ合った〕〕pushed and shoved /ʃʌvd/] to get out first.

われがね 割れ鐘 a cracked bell. ▶男は割れ鐘のような声でどなった The man shouted (out) [called out] in a *thick*, *loud* voice.

われかんせず 我関せず ▶彼女はまったく我関せずといった様子だった She looked very much as if she *had nothing to do with it*.

われこそは 我こそは ▶我こそはと思う人は一歩前へ出なさい Step forward if you think *you are good enough* [*you are the right person*] 《for the job》. ▶彼は我こそは開校以来の秀才だと思っていた He *was conceited enough* to think he was the brightest student in the history of the school.

われさきに 我先に (⇨我勝ちに)

われしらず 我知らず ● 我知らず吹き出す burst out laughing *in spite of oneself*; burst into *involuntary* laughter. (⇨思わず)

われながら 我ながら ▶我ながら恥ずかしい[あきれる]I am ashamed of [am disgusted with] *myself*. ▶我ながら試験はうまくいった I admit that I have done well on the exam.

われなべ 割れ鍋 a cracked pot [pan].
● 割れなべにとじぶた 'There is a cracked cover that is used with a cracked pot.'/(ことわざ) Every Jack has [must have] his Jill.

われめ 割れ目 〔〔地面・コップ・壁などの〕〕a crack; (深い) a chasm /kæzm/; 〔〔長細い〕〕(戸や板の)a chink; (力を加えてできたまっすぐな)(刃物による)a split; (刃物による)a slit; (氷などの) a crevice. ▶壁の大きな割れ目 a wide *crack* in the wall.

われもこう 吾木香 〔〔植物〕〕a great burnet.

われもの 割れ物 fragile /frǽdʒəl, -dʒail/ articles; breakables. ▶割れ物注意《表示》*Fragile*. Handle with care.

***われる 割れる** ❶ 〔〔ものが二つ(以上)に分かれる〕〕break*, be broken; (粉々に) smash, be smashed; (ぱちんとひびが入る) crack, be cracked; (がちゃんと) crash, be crashed; (縦に裂ける) split*, be split. ▶この花びんは割れやすい This vase *breaks* easily [*is fragile*]. (❗be easy to break は「割るのが簡単」の意) ▶買った卵のうち 6 個が割れていた Six of the eggs I bought *were broken*. ▶コップは粉々に割れて床やタイル一面に飛び散った The glass *broke* [*smashed*, *crashed*] *into pieces* all over the tiles. ▶のこぎりを入れるとその板は二つに割れた The board *split* in two when I sawed it. ▶窓が割れた(=ひびが入って)いた There was *a crack in* the window. (❗「割れた窓」は *a broken window* という) ▶足元に気をつけてください 氷が薄くて割れることもありますから Watch your step. The ice is not thick enough and could *give way*. (❗give way は「重力・圧力で崩れる」こと)
❷ 〔〔分裂する〕〕(意見が分かれる) divide (⇨分かれる); (仲間割れする) split* (up). ▶その問題をめぐって党は真

っ二つに割れた The party *divided* [*split*] down the middle over the issue. ▶進歩派と保守派の間で票が割れた(=分割された) The vote *was split* among the liberals and the conservatives. ▶今朝は頭が割れるように痛い I have a *splitting* headache this morning.
❸[明らかになる] ▶脅迫グループの身元が割れた The extortionist group *was identified*.
● 割れるような拍手 聴衆は彼に割れるような拍手を送った The audience gave him a *thunder* of applause [(×a) *thunderous* applause].

:われわれ 我々 (我々は[が]) we; (我々の) our; (我々に[を]) us; (我々のもの) ours; (我々自身) ourselves. (⇨私たち, 私(ぜん))

わん 椀 a (wooden) bowl. ● 吸い物をわんに盛って出す serve soup in a *bowl*.

わん 湾 a bay; a gulf (働 ~s) (**!** bay より大きく奥行きが深い); a cove (**!** bay より小さい); (入り江) an inlet. ● 大阪湾 Osaka *Bay*; the *Bay* of Osaka. (**!** サンフランシスコ近郊は the Bay Area) ● カリフォルニア湾 the *Gulf* of California.

ワンエー [マイナーリーグの] Single A; Class A.

わんがん 湾岸 a coast.
● 湾岸戦争 the (Persian) *Gulf* War. ● 湾岸道路 a highway along the bay; a coast(al) road.

わんきょく 湾曲 图 (曲がり) a curve; a bend. ● 道路の湾曲した所 a *curve* [a *bend*] in a road. ● 背骨の湾曲 the *curve* of the spine.
── 湾曲する 動 curve; bend*. ▶背骨が湾曲している have a *curved* spine.

ワンぎり ワン切り a single-ring cellphone scam.

わんぐち 湾口 the mouth of [entrance to] a bay.

ワンゲル [「ワンダーフォーゲル」の略] (⇨ワンダーフォーゲル)

わんこう 湾口 (⇨湾口(ぐち))

ワンサイドゲーム a one-sided game.

わんさと a lot; (in great numbers; (多人数で) multitudinously; (多量に) plentifully. ● わんさと...する (大勢押しかける) throng; (人でいっぱいにする) crowd, swarm; (洪水のように一気に満たす) flood. ▶わんさと(=掃いて捨てるほどの)金がある have money *to burn*. ▶子供がわんさと集まってきた Children gathered *in great numbers*. ▶若者が会場にわんさと押しかけた Young people *thronged to* the hall.

わんしょう 腕章 (wear) an armband.

ワンストップ [ワンストップサービス] a one-stop service. (参考) 特に行政手続きで, 一度の手続きですべての作業が完了するサービス。● ワンストップショップ a one-stop shop. (参考) 商品・サービスをすべてそろえた総合店舗

ワンスモア [もう一度] once more.

ワンダーフォーゲル [<ドイツ語] a hike, hiking.

ワンタッチ [サッカー] one touch. (参考) ボールを止めずにファーストタッチでパス・シュートなどをすること ● ワンタッチで with [(まれ・英・豪) at] the [a] touch of a button. ▶この傘はワンタッチで開く This umbrella opens *with the* [*a*] *touch of a button*./This umbrella opens *when you touch the button*.
● ワンタッチ操作 one-touch operation [control]. ● ワンタッチフットボール [サッカー] one-touch football. ● ワンタッチパス [サッカー] a one-touch pass.

ワンタン [<中国語] (a) wonton; (説明的に) Chinese flour dumplings with meat stuffing.

ワンツー [サッカー] a one-two; (壁パス) a wall pass.

ワンツーパンチ [ボクシング] a one-two punch.

わんとう 湾頭 ● 湾頭で at [by, near] the head of the bay.

ワンナウト [野球] one out. ▶ワンナウト三塁 It's *one out* and [with] a runner on third.

わんにゅう 湾入 ▶湾入してできた海岸線が絶景をなしている The curved-in coastline made by the *encroachment of the sea* is just magnificent [superb].

ワンバウンド ● ボールをワンバウンドで捕る catch a ball on one bounce. ● ワンバウンドでストライクのバックホームをする throw a one-hop strike to the catcher. ● 一塁へワンバウンドの送球をする bounce a throw to first.

わんぱく 腕白 图 naughtiness.
── 腕白な 形 (言うことを聞かない) naughty; (いたずら好きな) mischievous /mɪ́stʃɪvəs/; (手に負えない) unruly. ▶男の子はたいてい腕白だ Most boys are rather *mischievous*.
● 腕白小僧 a naughty [a mischievous] boy; an urchin; an imp.

ワンパタ(ー)ン ▶彼の話はいつもワンパターンだ His speech always *follows the same pattern*. (**!** ×His speech is always one pattern. は不可)/(どれも似たりよったりだ) His speeches are all the same.

ワンピース a dress; (和製語) one-piece.

ワンペア [トランプ] one pair.

ワンポイント one point. ● 対左打者用のワンポイント左腕投手 a left-handed *specialist* against one left-handed batter.
● ワンポイントアドバイス a (helpful) piece of advice 《*about*, *on*》; a tip 《*on*, *for*》; (和製語) one point advice. ● ワンポイントリリーフ [投手] a spot reliever; (和製語) one point relief.

ワンボックス ● ワンボックスカー a minivan.

ワンマン ❶[独裁的] ▶彼はワンマンだ He's a *dictator* [*dictatorial*, (いばり散らす) [話] *bossy*]. (**!** ×He's one man. とはいわない)
❷[一人だけ] ● ワンマンショーをする put on a *one-person* [(男の) a *one-man*] show; give a *recital*. ● ワンマンカー a bus without a conductor. ● ワンマン社長 a dictatorial company president. ● ワンマンバス a conductorless bus; a one-person [(男の) a *one-man*] bus. (**!** 単に a bus ともいう)

わんりゅう 湾流 [メキシコ湾流] the Gulf Stream.

わんりょく 腕力 ❶[力] (腕の力) strength in one's arms; (筋力) muscle /mʌ́sl/, muscular /mʌ́skjələr/ strength. ▶彼は腕力が強い He has great *strength* in his arms. (**!** 日本語にひかれて ×arm strength といわない)/He is a man of *muscle*. 腕力では私にはかなわない I'm no match for him in *muscle* [(体力) *physical strength*].
❷[暴力] violence. (⇨暴力)
● 腕力を振るう use violence 《*on him*》.

ワンルームマンション (米) a one-room apartment, a studio (apartment); (英) a studio (flat), a bed-sitter, (英話) a bed-sit. (⇨マンション)

わんわん ❶[犬の鳴き声] bowwow /báuwáu/. ● わんわんほえる bark 《*at*》.
❷[人の泣き声] ● わんわん泣く cry one's heart out; wail.
❸[犬] [幼児語] a doggy (**!** a doggie ともつづる); a bówwòw.

を

:―を 《格助詞》 ❶ 【動作の対象】 (**a**) 【他動詞の目的語で表す】 ●水を飲む drink water. ●顔を洗う wash one's face. ●彼の腕をつかむ hold him by the arm; hold his arm (**!** 前の方は人に, 後の方は「腕」に焦点を当てた言い方)
(**b**) 【自動詞(＋副詞)＋前置詞で表す】 ●音楽を聞く listen *to* music. ●私をあざ笑う laugh *at* me. ●彼を待つ wait *for* him. ●睡眠不足を取り戻す catch up *on* one's sleep. ▶そのドレスはとても似合っているけどその髪を何とかしなくちゃね You look so nice in the dress, but we have to do something *with* that hair. (**!** with は「〜に関して」の意. この we は you の持つつっき離した感じを避けるために用いられる)
(**c**) 【他動詞＋副詞で表す】 ●明かりをつける[消す] turn *òn* [*óff*] the líght (**!** 《英》では普通 turn の方に第 2 強勢が移る); tùrn the líght *on* [*off*]. (**!** 目的語が代名詞のときは tùrn it ón [óff] の語順のみ可)
❷ 【動作の起点】 ●席を立つ stand up [《書》rise] *from* one's seat. ●故郷[国]を離れる leave home [one's country].
❸ 【移動を示す】 ●角を曲がる turn the corner. ●山道を登る climb [go up] the mountain path. ●川を渡る cross the river.
❹ 【場所を示す】 ●公園[川岸]を散歩する take a walk *in* a park [*along* a riverbank]. ●国中を旅する travel all *over* the country.
❺ 【経過する時間・通過する場所を示す】 ●銀行のそばを通り過ぎる go *past* a bank. ●雑誌を読んで半日を過ごす spend half a day reading magazines. ▶5 時を回ったところだ It's just *past* five.

巻末付録目次

英語基本文型表	1980
アカデミック・ライティング入門	2062
句読法	2070
自己紹介のポイント	2074
手紙の書き方	2078
カードの書き方	2080
イーメールの書き方	2084
履歴書の書き方	2088
度量衡一覧	2090
不規則動詞変化表	2093
不規則形容詞・副詞変化表	2097

英 語 基 本 文 型 表

ability 名 能力.
① 【~+*in* [*at, for*]+〈事〉】
He has great *ability in* painting. 彼はすぐれた絵画の才がある. (❗前置詞は in が最も普通)
② 【~+*to do*】
He has the *ability to* speak five languages. 彼は5か国語を話せる.

able 形 …できる.
【S〈人〉is ~+*to do*】
You won't be *able to* master English in a year. 英語は1年では習得できないでしょう.

accept 動
❶ 受け取る, (喜んで)受け入れる.
【S〈人〉・V・O〈物・事・人〉】
I *accepted* his gift [offer]. 私は彼の贈り物を受け取った[申し出を受け入れた]. (❗人をOに取る場合はその人の言った内容を受け入れること)
❷ 認める.
① 【S〈人〉・V・O〈物・事〉*as* C〈形・名〉】
We *accepted* his statement *as* true [an excuse]. 私たちは彼の申し立てを正しいと認めた[言い訳と取った]. (❗as true は省略可で, その場合も意味は同じ)
② 【S〈人〉・V・O〈*that* 節〉】
We *accepted that* he was right. 私たちは彼が正しいと認めた.

act 動
❶ 行動する; 役目を務める.
① 【S〈人〉・V+副(句)】
The soldiers *acted* bravely [on his orders]. 兵士たちは勇敢に行動した[彼の命令に従った].
② 【S〈人〉・V・*as* C〈名〉】
He *acted* as go-between [guide]. 彼は仲人[案内]役をした. (❗Cは通例無冠詞)
③ 【S〈人〉・V+*for*+〈人〉】
I *acted for* him while he was out. 私は彼が留守の間彼の代理をした. (❗for の代わりに on behalf of もよく用いられる)
❷ ふるまう.
【S〈人〉・V+副(句・節)】
He *acted* wisely. 彼は賢明にふるまった.
He *acted like* [*as if* he were] a madman. 彼はまるで狂人のようにふるまった.
❸ 動く, 働きをする, 作用する.
【S〈機械・器官・薬など〉・V+副(句)】
The old man's brain *acts* slowly. その老人は頭の働きが遅い.
This box *acts as* a chair. この箱はいす代わりになる.
This medicine *acts on* the liver. この薬は肝臓に効く.
❹ 演じる; 装う, ふりをする.
① 【S〈人〉・V(+副(句))】
She *is acting at* that theater tonight. 彼女は今夜あの劇場で出演している.
② 【S〈人〉・V・O〈役〉】
He *acted* (the part of) Othello. 彼はオセロの役を演じた.
They *are acting* Othello. 「オセロ」を上演中です.

③ 【S〈人〉・V・C〈形〉】
《話》 He *acted* very stupid. 彼はとてもばかみたいなふりをした.

add 動
❶ 加える.
【S〈人〉・V・O〈人・物・事〉+*to*+〈人・物・事〉】
He *added* some sugar *to* his coffee. 彼はコーヒーに砂糖を入れた.
When you *add* 3 *to* 5, you get 8. 5に3を足すと8になる.
❷ 付け加えて言う.
【S〈人〉・V・O〈*that* 節〉】
He *added that* he didn't mind it. 彼はそんなことは気にしていないと付け加えた. (❗直接話法で書くと "I don't mind it," he *added*.)
❸ ふやす.
【S〈人・物・事〉・V+*to*+〈物・事〉】
The news *added to* his worries. その知らせで彼の心配がふえた.
They *added to* the house last year. 彼らは昨年家を増築した.

admit 動
❶ 入ることを許す.
【S〈人・物〉・V・O〈人・物〉(+*to* [*into*]+〈物〉)】
They *admitted* me *to* [*into*] the tennis club. 彼らは私をテニス部に入れてくれた. (❗受身可)
This ticket *admits* two people *to* the show. このチケットで, そのショーに2人入場できる.
❷ 認める.
① 【S〈人〉・V・O〈事〉】
He did not *admit* his fault. 彼は自分の過失を認めなかった.
② 【S〈人〉・V・O〈*doing*〉】
He *admitted* having [×to have] made a mistake. 彼は過ちを認めた.
③ 【S〈人〉・V・O〈(*that*) 節〉】
He *admitted* (*that*) he had made a mistake. 意味は② と同じ. (❗that 節 を用いる方が普通)
④ 【It is admitted+*that* 節】
It *is admitted that* the hotel is the best in this city. あのホテルがこの町でいちばんいいと認められている.
❸ 収容できる.
【S〈建物・場所〉・V・O〈人〉】
The theater *admits* only 300 people. その劇場は300人しか入れない.
❹ 余地がある.
【S〈事〉・V+*of*+〈事〉】《書》
His conduct *admits of* no apology. 彼の行為は弁解の余地がない. (❗通例否定文で)

advantage 名 有利な点.
① 【~+*of*+*doing*】
I have the *advantage of* being younger than he is. 私は彼よりも若いという点で有利だ.
② 【~+*that* 節】
I have the *advantage that* I am younger than he is. 意味は②と同じ.
③ 【~+*over*+〈人・物〉】
He has an *advantage over* us in studying Eng-

lish, because he has an American friend. 彼にはアメリカ人の友人がいるから英語を勉強するには私たちより有利だ.

④ 【It is an ～+*to do*】
For a catcher, it is an *advantage to* have strong arms. キャッチャーにとって, 肩が強いということは強みだ.

advice 图 忠告, 助言.

① 【～+*to do*】
He brushed aside *advice to* remain silent. 黙っていた方がよいという忠告を無視した.

② 【～+*that*】
He brushed aside *advice that* he (should) remain silent. 意味は ① と同じ.

advise 動 忠告する, 助言する.

① 【S〈人〉・V・O〈人〉・C〈*to do*〉】
The teacher *advised* me *to* study harder. 先生は私にもっと勉強するように忠告した. (!③ より一般的. 受身＝I *was advised to* study harder.)

② 【S〈人〉・V・O〈*doing*〉】
I'd *advise* waiting until tomorrow morning. 私なら明日の朝まで待つときを勧めるだろう.

③ 【S〈人〉・V・O〈人〉・O〈*that* 節〉】
The teacher *advised* me *that* I (should) study harder. 意味は ① と同じ. (!① の方が一般的. should を用いるのは《主に英》)

④ 【S〈人〉・V・O〈人〉+*against*+〈*doing*・事〉】
He *advised* me *against* keeping company with them. (＝He *advised* me *not to* keep company with them.) 彼は私に彼らと付き合わない方がよいと忠告した.

⑤ 【S〈人〉・V・O〈人〉+*on*+〈事〉】
He *advised* me *on* my plan. 彼は私の計画に助言をした. (! on の後には wh-句が来るときは on の省略可: He *advised* me (*on*) *how to* do it. ×He *advised how to* do it to me. は不可)

afford 余裕がある. (! 通例 can, could, be able to とともに. 通例否定文, 疑問文で)

① 【S〈人〉・V・O〈時間・金・物〉】
Can you *afford* a week [100,000 yen] for the journey? その旅行のために1週間を取る[10万円を出す]余裕がありますか.

② 【S〈人〉・V・O (*to do*)】
He could not *afford* (*to* buy [×buying]) a car. 彼はとても車を買えなかった. (! to buy を省くと ① の文型)

afraid 形 恐れて, 心配して.

① 【S〈人〉 is ～+*of*+〈人・物・事・*doing*〉】
She is *afraid of* snakes [making mistakes]. 彼女は蛇をこわがっている[間違いをするのではないかと心配している].

② 【S〈人〉 is ～+*to do*】
She is *afraid to* go out alone at night. 彼女はこわくて夜一人で外出できない.

③ 【S〈人〉 is ～+*for*+〈人・事〉】
He is *afraid for* (the safety of) his son. 彼は息子の安否を気づかっている.

④ 【S〈人〉 is ～+(*that*) 節】
He was *afraid* (*that*) she would not pass the exam. 彼女が不合格になるのではないかと彼は心配だった.

agree 動

❶ 意見が一致する.
① 【S〈人〉・V+*with*+〈人・考え・事〉】
He *agreed with* me [my opinion; what I said]. 彼は私[私の意見; 私の言うこと]に賛成した. (!通例受身形, 進行形, 命令形は不可)

② 【S〈複数の人〉・V+*on* [*about*]+〈事〉】
They *agreed on* [*about*] the price. 彼らはその価格で話し合いに達した. (! on は意見が一致し, それに決定するという含みがあるが, about は単に賛成か反対に一致するという意味)

❷ 同意する.
① 【S〈人〉・V+*to*+〈提案・要求〉】
They *agreed to* my proposal [offer]. 彼らは私の提案[申し出]に同意した. (受身＝My proposal [offer] *was agreed to*.) (! to+〈人〉は不可)

② 【S〈人〉・V+*to do*】
We *agreed to* take [×taking] the job. 私たちはその仕事を引き受けることに同意した[意見が一致した]. (!「意見が一致した」の意では主語は常に複数の人. ⇨❶①)

③ 【S〈人〉・V+*to*+〈所有格〉+*doing*〉】
He didn't *agree to* my going there. 彼は私がそこへ行くことを認めてくれなかった.

④ 【S〈人〉・V・O〈(*that*) 節〉】
We *agreed that* we (should) take the job. 意味は ② と同じ. (受身＝It *was agreed that* we (should) take the job.) (! should を用いるのは《主に英》)

❸ 体質に適している.
【S〈物・事〉・V+*with*+〈人〉】
The water there didn't *agree with* him. その水は彼の体には合わなかった. (! (1) 通例否定文で. (2) 通例受身, 進行形, 命令形は不可)

aim 動

❶ ねらう, 目ざす.
① 【S〈人〉・V+*at*+〈人・物・事・*doing*〉】
He *aimed at* the target [*at* perfection]. 彼は的をねらった[完璧を期した].
He *aimed at* pleasing the guests. 意味は ② と同じ.

② 【S〈人〉・V+*to do*】
He *aimed to* please [×pleasing] the guests. 彼は客を喜ばせようとした.

③ 【S〈人〉・V+*for*+〈場所〉】
They *aimed for* the capital. 彼らは首都を目ざして進んだ.

❷ ねらいを向ける.
【S〈人〉・V・O〈物・事〉+*at*+〈人・物〉】
He *aimed* his gun [question] *at* me. 彼は銃[質問]を私に向けた.

aim 图 目的, 志, 計画.

① 【～+*of*+*doing*】
He went on to college with the *aim of* becoming [×to become] a teacher. 彼は教師になるために大学へ進学した. (! with the aim of doing は慣用句)

② 【～+*to do*】
His *aim to* become a politician was frustrated. 政治家になろうとする彼の志は挫折した.

allow 動

❶ 許可する.
① 【S〈人〉・V・O〈人・物・事〉・C〈*to do*〉】
They *allowed* me *to* join [×joining] them. 彼らは私が仲間に加わることを許してくれた. (受身＝I

was allowed to join them.)

② 【S〈人〉・V・O〈事〉】
They don't *allow* smoking here. ここでは喫煙は許されない. (受身＝Smoking *is* not *allowed* here. ×It is not allowed to smoke here. は不可)

❷ 与える.
【S〈人〉・V・O〈人〉・O〈暇・金など〉】
He *allowed* me an hour for lunch. 彼は私に1時間の昼食時間をくれた. (!) He *allowed* an hour to me for lunch. の型はまれ)

❸ 考慮する, 斟酌(しんしゃく)する.
【S〈人〉・V＋for＋〈物・事〉】
We must *allow* for some delay. 少しの遅れを念頭に入れておかなくてはならない.

❹ 認める.
【S〈人〉・V・O〈物・事・that 節〉】
The judge *allowed* his claim. 裁判官は彼の主張を認めた.
He *allowed that* she had the right to appeal. 彼は, 彼女には控訴する権利があることを認めた.

angry 形 怒って.

① 【S〈人〉 is ～(＋at [about]＋〈人・物・事〉/＋with＋〈人〉)(＋for＋〈事・doing〉)】(!) for 以下は原因・理由を表わす) We were *angry at* [*with*] the children *for* their rudeness [*being* rude]. 子供たちが無作法だったので私たちは腹が立った.

② 【S〈人〉 is ～＋about [over, at]＋doing】
He was *angry at* being deceived. 彼はだまされて腹が立った.

③ 【S〈人〉 is ～＋to do】
He was *angry to* hear the news. 彼はその知らせを聞いて怒った.

④ 【S〈人〉 is ～＋that 節】
He was *angry that* he was not invited there. 彼はそこに招待されていなかったので腹を立てた.

announce 動 発表する.

① 【S〈人〉・V・O〈物・事〉(＋to＋〈人〉)】
They *announced* their engagement (*to* their friends). 彼らは(友人に)婚約を発表した.

② 【S〈人〉・V・O〈物・事〉 *as* [*to be*] C〈名・形〉】
They *announced* him *as* [*to be*] heir to the fortune. 彼は彼がその財産の相続人であると発表した. (受身＝He *was announced as* [×to be] (the) heir to the fortune.)

③ 【S〈人〉・V(＋to＋〈人〉)・O〈that 節〉】
They *announced* (*to* the reporters) *that* he was going to resign soon. 彼らは(新聞記者に)彼が間もなく辞任することを発表した. (受身＝It *was announced* (*to* the reporters) *that* he was going to resign soon.) (!) ×They *announced* the reporters *that*.... は不可)

answer 動

❶ 答える, 応答する.
① 【S〈人〉・V・O〈人・物・事〉】
He *answered* me [the question; the telephone; the letter]. 彼は私に返答をした[その質問に答えた; 電話に出た; その手紙の返事を書いた].

② 【S〈人〉・V・O〈that 節〉】
He *answered that* he was not angry. 彼は怒ってはいないと答えた. (受身＝It *was answered that* he was not angry.) (!) いずれの場合も that の省略は不可)

③ 【S〈人〉・V】
He *answered* in a loud voice. 彼は大声で答えた.

❷ 責任を負う.
【S〈人〉・V(＋to＋〈人〉)＋for＋〈人・物・事〉】
He *answered* (*to* me) *for* his mistake. 彼は(私に対して)過ちの責任を取った. (!) 受身は不可)

anticipate 動 予想する.

① 【S〈人〉・V・O〈物・事〉】
They didn't *anticipate* any trouble. 彼らは困難を予想していなかった. (!) expect の堅い語)

② 【S〈人〉・V・O〈doing〉】
We *are anticipating* working with him. 私たちは彼といっしょに働くのを楽しみにしている.

③ 【S〈人〉・V・O〈that 節・wh- 節〉】
We *anticipated that* the weather would turn cold. 私たちは寒くなるだろうと予測した.
Nobody can *anticipate what* he will do. 彼が何をするかだれも予想できない.

④ 【It is anticipated＋that 節】
It is anticipated that interest rates will fall. 利率は下がるだろうと予測されている.

anxious 形

❶ 心配して.
① 【S〈人〉 is ～＋about [for]＋〈事・物・人・doing〉】 He is *anxious about* the results. 彼はその結果を心配している.

② 【S〈人〉 is ～＋(about)＋wh- 節[句]】
I am *anxious* (*about*) *what* has become of her. 私は彼女がどうなったか心配だ.

❷ 切望して.
① 【S〈人〉 is ～＋for＋〈事・物〉】
He is *anxious for* a new car. 彼は新車を欲しがっている.

② 【S〈人〉 is ～＋to do】
He was *anxious to* see her. 彼はしきりに彼女に会いたがっていた.

③ 【S〈人〉 is ～＋for＋〈人・事〉＋to do】
We are *anxious for* him *to* call on us. 私たちは彼に来て欲しいと切望している.

④ 【S〈人〉 is ～＋that 節】
We are *anxious that* he (should) call on us. 意味は ③ と同じ. (!) should を用いるのは《主に英》)

appear 動

❶ 現われる, 姿を現わす.
【S〈人・物・事〉・V】
The sun *appeared* on the horizon [from behind the clouds]. 太陽が地平線上に[雲の後ろから]姿を現した. (!) There *appeared* the sun on the horizon. のようにもいえる)

❷ 出演する.
【S〈人〉・V *as* C〈名〉】
He *appeared as* Macbeth. 彼はマクベスの役で出演した.

❸ 見える, ...らしい. (⇒seem)
① 【S〈人・物〉・V(＋to＋〈人〉)・(to be) C〈形・名〉】
He *appears* (*to be*) tired [a great scholar]. 彼は疲れているように[立派な学者のように]見える.
She *appears to have been* beautiful when she was young. 彼女は若いころ美しかったらしい.

② 【S〈It〉・V(＋to＋〈人〉)＋(that) 節】
It appears that he is tired [a great scholar]. 意味は ① の第1文と同じ.
It appears that she was beautiful when she was young. 意味は ① の第2文と同じ.

③【S〈人・物・事〉・V(+*to*+〈人〉)+*to do*】
He *appears to* know the truth. 彼は真相を知っているように思える.

apply 動

❶ 付ける, 塗る.
【S〈人〉・V・O〈物〉(+*to*+〈物・体〉)】
He *applied* the ointment *to* the wound. 彼は軟膏(なんこう)を傷に塗った.

❷ 応用する, 適用する.
【S〈人〉・V・O〈規則・原理〉(+*to*+〈人・物・事〉)】
He *applied* the theory *to* his research [the rule *to* the case]. 彼はその理論を研究に応用した[その規則をその場合に適用した]. (❗ case の場合は in も可)

❸ 傾注する.
【S〈人〉・V・O〈心・精力〉+*to*+〈事〉】
He *applied* his mind [himself] *to* his studies. 彼は研究に専心した.

❹ 充当する.
【S〈人〉・V・O〈物・事〉+*to*+〈物・事〉】
He *applied* the income from the sales *to* the purchase of a car. 彼はその売り上げの収入を車の購入に当てた.

❺ 申し込む, 志願する.
【S〈人〉・V(+*to*+〈人・機関〉)+*for*+〈仕事・許可・援助など〉】 He *applied* (*to* the company) *for* a job. 彼は(その会社に)就職を申し込んだ./He *applied to* the university. 彼はその大学に出願した.

❻ 当てはまる.
【S〈事〉・V(+*to*+〈人・事〉)】
This rule does not *apply to* children [the particular case]. この規則は子供には[その場合に限って]当てはまらない. (❗ 通例進行形不可)

appoint 動

❶ 任命する, 指名する.
① 【S〈人〉・V・O〈役職〉】
They *appointed* a new governor. 彼らは新しい知事を任命した.
② 【S〈人〉・V・O〈人〉・(*as* [*to be*]) C〈役職〉】
They *appointed* him (*as* [*to be*]) manager of the team. 彼らは彼をそのチームの監督に任命した. (受身=He *was appointed* (*as* [*to be*]) manager of the team.) (❗ C が唯一の役職のときは通例無冠詞)
③ 【S〈人〉・V・O〈人〉+*to*+〈役職〉】
They *appointed* him *to* the job. 彼らは彼をその職に任じた.
④ 【S〈人〉・V・O〈人〉・C〈*to do*〉】
They *appointed* him *to do* the job. 彼らは彼を任命してその仕事をやらせた.

❷ 指定する, 決める.
【S〈人〉・V・O〈時間, 場所〉+*for*+〈事〉】
They *appointed* April 2 *for* a party. 彼らはパーティーの日を4月2日に決めた.

argue 動

❶ 議論する.
① 【S〈人〉・V・O〈事〉】
They *argued* the problem for hours. 彼らはその問題を何時間も論じた.
② 【S〈人〉・V(+*with*+〈人〉)(+*about* [*over*]+〈事・wh-句〉)】
I *argued with* him *about* Japanese economy. 彼と日本経済について論じ合った. (❗「with+〈人〉」と「about [over]+〈事〉」の語順は交換可)
They *argued about* who was responsible for the accident. 彼らはだれにその事故の責任があるかをめぐって言い争った.
③ 【S〈人〉・V+*for* [*against*]+〈事〉】
We *argued for* [*against*] the plan. 私たちはその計画に賛成[反対]の意見を述べた.

❷ 主張する.
【S〈人〉・V・O〈*that* 節〉】
Galileo *argued that* the earth moves around the sun. ガリレオは地球は太陽の周りを回っていると主張した.

❸ 説得する.
【S〈人〉・V・O〈人〉+*into* [*out of*]+〈事・doing〉】 I *argued* him *into* [*out of*] meeting her. 彼が彼女に会うように[会わないように]説得した.

argument 名 議論.

① 【~+*with*+〈人〉+(*over* [*about*]+〈物・事〉)】
I had an *argument with* him *over* [*about*] religion. 私は彼と宗教について議論した.

② 【~+*that* 節】
Can you accept the *argument that* smoking is a necessary evil? 喫煙は必要悪だという議論を受け入れることができますか.

③ 【~+*about*+*wh-*節句】
We had an *argument about* whether to go by bus or by train. 私たちはバスで行くか列車で行くかについて議論した.

arrange 動

❶ 並べる, 整える.
【S〈人〉・V・O〈物・人・事〉】
She *arranged* the flowers in the vase [the books neatly]. 彼女は花を花びんに生けた[本をきちんと整頓(せいとん)した].

❷ 準備する, 手はずを整える.
① 【S〈人〉・V・O〈事〉(+*for*+〈人・事〉)】
He *arranged* everything *for* me [the meeting]. 彼は私のために[会合の]すべての準備をしてくれた.
② 【S〈人〉・V(+*for*+〈人〉)+*to do*】
I *arranged for* him *to* join the team. 彼がそのチームに入れるよう手はずを整えた.
③ 【S〈人〉・V・O〈*that* 節〉】
I *arranged that* he (should) join the team. 意味は ② と同じ. (❗ should を用いるのは《主に英》)

❸ 取り決める.
① 【S〈人〉・V・O〈会合・行事〉+*for*+〈日・時〉】
We *arranged* a meeting *for* next Monday. 私たちは来週月曜日に会合をすることに決めた.
② 【S〈人〉・V・O〈*that* 節・*wh-*節句+*to do*〉】
They *arranged that* they (should) look into the matter. 彼らはその件を調査することに決めた. (受身=It *was arranged that* they (should) look into the matter.) (❗ should を用いるのは《主に英》)
We *arranged to* meet at 6 o'clock. 私たちは6時に会う約束をした.
We have to *arrange where* to meet again. 私たちは今度どこで会うか決めなければならない.

❹ 編曲する.
【S〈人〉・V・O〈音楽〉+*for*+〈物・事〉】
He *arranged* the traditional folk-song *for* the piano. 彼はその伝統的な民謡をピアノ用に編曲した.

arrive 動

❶ 到着する.

【S〈人・乗り物など〉・V+*at* [*in*; *on*]+〈場所〉】
We *arrived at* Osaka Station [*in* Osaka; *on* the shore]. 私たちは大阪駅[大阪; 海岸]に着いた. (❗狭い場所や地理上の一点と考えられるときは at, 広い場所には in, 表面が意識される場合には on が用いられる)

❷ 到達する.
【S〈人・事〉・V+*at*+〈結論・年齢など〉】
At last we *arrived at* a satisfactory conclusion. 私たちはやっと満足できる結論に達した. (受身=At last a satisfactory conclusion *was arrived at*.)

❸ (時が)来る.
【S〈季節など〉・V(+副(句))】
Spring *has arrived* earlier than usual. 春が例年より早くやって来た.

ashamed 形

❶ …を恥じて.
① 【S〈人〉 is ~+*of*+〈人・物・事・*doing*〉】
He is very *ashamed of* his faults [*having* told a lie]. 彼は自分の欠点を[うそをついたことを]非常に恥じている. (❗ of は恥じる対象を示す)

② 【S〈人〉 is ~+*for*】
He was *ashamed for* having betrayed her trust. 彼は彼女の信頼を裏切ったことで恥ずかしく思った. (❗ for は理由を示す)

③ 【S〈人〉 is ~+*that* 節】
I am *ashamed that* I was idle when young. 私は若いとき怠けていたことが恥ずかしい.

❷ 恥ずかしくて…したくない.
【S〈人〉is ~+*to do*】
I'm *ashamed to* let him see my paintings. 私は恥ずかしくて私の絵を彼に見せたくない.

ask 動

❶ 尋ねる.
① 【S〈人〉・V・O〈人〉・O〈物・事〉】
They *asked* me a few questions. 彼らは私に2, 3質問をした. (受身=I *was asked* a few questions by them.)
A few questions *were asked* me by them.) (❗(1) O〈人〉が明らかな場合は省略される. (2)×They asked a few questions to me. は不可)

② 【S〈人〉・V・O〈人〉・O〈*wh*- 節(句)〉】
He *asked* me *if* I knew it [*which* I liked better; *when* to come]. 彼は私にそれを知っているかどうか[どちらの方が好きか; いつ来たらよいか]尋ねた. (❗ O に that 節は不可)

③ 【S〈人〉・V・O〈人〉+*about*+〈物・事〉】
He *asked* (me) *about* my country. 彼は(私に)私の国のことについて尋ねた.

❷ 求める, 頼む.
① 【S〈人〉・V・O〈物・事〉】
He *asked* my help. 彼は私の援助を求めた.
② 【S〈人〉・V・O〈人〉+*for*+〈物・事〉】
He *asked* (me) *for* help. 彼は(私に)援助を求めた.
③ 【S〈人〉・V・O〈人〉・C 〈*to do*〉】
He *asked* me *to* support him. 彼は私に支援してくれと頼んだ.
④ 【S〈人〉・V・O〈*that* 節〉】
He *asked that* I (should) support him. 意味は③と同じ. (❗ should を用いるのは《主に英》)
⑤ 【S〈人〉・V・O〈人〉・O〈事〉】
May I *ask* you a favor? ひとつお願いをしてもよろしいですか.
⑥ 【S〈人〉・V・O〈事〉+*of*+〈人〉】
May I *ask* a favor *of* you? 意味は⑤と同じ. (❗ よりも普通の言い方. of you は省略可.)

❸ 要求する.
【S〈人〉・V・O〈人〉・O〈代金〉+*for*+〈物・事〉】
He *asked* (me) 10,000 yen *for* the watch. 彼はその時計の代金として(私に)1万円を要求した.

❹ 招待する. (❗ invite の方が正式)
【S〈人〉・V・O〈人〉+*to*+〈場所・食事など〉】
We *asked* the neighbors *to* dinner. 私たちは近所の人たちを夕食に招いた.

assume 動

❶ (十分な根拠がなく)当然と思う.
① 【S〈人〉・V・O〈事〉】
We *assume* his innocence. 私たちは当然彼は無罪だと思う.
② 【S〈人〉・V・O〈*that* 節〉】
We *assume that* he is innocent. 意味は①と同じ.
③ 【S〈人〉・V・O〈人・物・事〉・*to be* C〈名・形〉】
We *assume* him *to be* innocent. 意味は①と同じ.

❷ 引き受ける.
【S〈人〉・V・O〈任務・責任など〉】
He *assumed* full responsibility for the action. 彼はその行為の全責任を負った.

assure 動

❶ 保証する.
【S〈人〉・V・O〈人〉+*of*+〈事〉】
He *assured* me *of* its quality. 彼は私にその品質を保証した.

❷ 確信させる.
【S〈人〉・V・O〈人〉・O〈*that* 節〉】
She *assured* me *that* everything would be all right. 彼女は私に万事うまくいくと言って安心させた. (❗受身=I *was assured that* everything would be all right. 私は万事うまくいくと確信していた)

attend 動

❶ 出席する.
【S〈人〉・V・O〈会議・式・学校〉】
He didn't *attend* the meeting. 彼はその会議に出なかった. (❗受身形は通例不可)

❷ 看護する, 世話をする.《書》(❗ look after, take care of の方が一般的)
【S〈人〉・V(+*on* [*to*]+)・O〈人〉】
The nurse *attended* (*on* [*to*]) me. その看護師が私の世話をしてくれた. (受身=I *was attended* (*on* [*to*]) by the nurse.) (❗前置詞を入れた表現は通例一時的な看護を表わす)

❸ 注意して聞く, 専心する.《書》
【S〈人〉・V+*to*+〈人・話・仕事〉】
The students *attended to* the teacher [his speech]. 生徒たちは先生の話[彼の演説]に一生懸命耳を傾けた. (❗受身形は不可)
He *attended to* his business. 彼は仕事に精を出した. (❗受身形は可)

attitude 名 態度.

① 【~+*toward* [*to*]+〈人・物・事〉】
He showed a very positive *attitude to* his work. 彼は自分の仕事にとても積極的な態度を示した.

② 【~+*that* 節】
He takes a negative *attitude that* life is not worth living. 彼は人生は生きる価値がないという消極的な態度を取っている.

③【～+of+doing】
His *attitude of* living aimlessly was annoying. 目的もなく生きている彼の態度は人をいらいらさせるものだった.

avoid 動 避ける.
① 【S〈人〉・V・O〈望ましくない人・事・物〉】
He *avoided* a drunken man [danger]. 彼は酔っ払い[危険]を避けた.
② 【S〈人〉・V・O〈doing〉】
Try to *avoid* mak*ing* [×to make] him angry. 彼を怒らせないようにしなさい.

aware 形 気づいて.
① 【S〈人〉is ～+of+〈周囲の事情〉】
I was *aware of* the danger. 私はその危険に気づいていた.
② 【S〈人〉is ～+of+doing】
He is not *aware of* hav*ing* hurt her feelings. 彼は彼女の感情を害したことに気づいていない.
③ 【S〈人〉is ～+that 節】
Have you been *aware that* he is a spy? 彼はスパイだということに気がついていましたか.
④ 【S〈人〉is ～(+of)+wh-節】
Were you *aware (of) how* dangerous it was to drink and drive? 飲酒運転はどんなに危険か知っていましたか. (!疑問代名詞の場合, 通例 of は省略されるが, 関係代名詞 what の of は省略されない)

bad 形
❶ (道徳的に)悪い, ひどい.
① 【It is ～+to do】
It is *bad to* be unpunctual. 時間を守らないのはよくない.
② 【It is ～+of+〈人〉+to do】
It is *bad of* you *to* betray me. 私を裏切るとはひどいね.
③ 【S〈人〉is ～+to do】
You are *bad to* betray me. 意味は ② と同じ.
❷ 有害な.
① 【S〈事・doing〉is ～+for+〈人・事〉】
Eating too much is *bad for* your health. 食べすぎは体によくない.
② 【It is ～+for+〈人・物・事〉+to do】
It is *bad for* you *to* smoke. 喫煙は君の健康によくない.
❸ 気の毒な.
【It is too ～+(that) 節】
It is too *bad (that)* she had an accident. 彼女が事故にあったのは気の毒だ.
❹ へたな.
【S〈人〉is ～+at+〈事・doing〉】
I am *bad at* skiing. スキーがへただ.
❺ 残念な.
【S〈人〉feel ～+about+〈事・doing〉】
She felt *bad about* not be*ing* able to come last night. 彼女は昨夜来ることができなかったことを残念に思った.

be 動
❶ …である.
【S〈人・物・事〉・V・C〈形・名・to do・doing・that 節・wh-節・句〉】
English *is* difficult [a foreign language to us]. 英語は難しい[私たちにとっては外国語だ].
The difficulty *is to* decide [deciding] what to do. 難しいのは何をすべきかを決めることだ.
The problem *is (that)* you know too much. 問題は君が知りすぎていることだ.
❷ ある, いる.
① 【S〈人・物・事〉・V+副(句)】
His house *is* near the station. 彼の家は駅の近くです. (!(1) 場所・時を表わす副詞(句)を伴う. (2) Sが不特定の名詞の場合には, 通例下の ② のように There is [are, etc.] …. の構文を用いたり, 副詞句を前置して, 主語と述語の語順を倒置することもある. Near the station *was* a large park.)
The election *was* last month. その選挙は先月あった.
② 【There・V・S〈人・物・事〉】
There is a tall tree in the garden. 庭には高い木がある. (!Sには通例特定の名詞や代名詞・固有名詞は不可: ×There was the book on the shelf. The book was on the shelf. (その本は棚の上にあった)とする)

bear 動
❶ 耐える. (!通例 can を伴い, 否定文, 疑問文で)
① 【S〈人〉・V・O〈人・事・行為〉】
I cannot *bear* him [his impudence]. 彼[彼のずうずうしさ]には我慢できない. (!受身は不可)
② 【S〈人〉・V・O〈to do [doing]〉】
I could not *bear* to be [be*ing*] disturbed. じゃまされるのには耐えられなかった.
③ 【S〈人〉・V・O〈所有格+doing〉】
He cannot *bear* your talk*ing* like that. 彼は君がそんなふうに話すのが我慢できない.
④ 【S〈人〉・V・O〈人〉・O〈to do〉】
He cannot *bear* you *to* talk like that. 意味は ③ と同じ.
❷ 支える.
【S〈物〉・V・O〈重さ〉】
The shelf will not *bear* (the weight of) the box. 棚はその箱の(重さ)を支えられないだろう.
❸ 心に抱く.
① 【S〈人〉・V・O〈愛情・悪意など〉+against [for, toward]+〈人〉】
I *bear* no grudge *against* him. 私は彼になんの恨みも抱いていない.
② 【S〈人〉・V・O〈人〉・O〈愛情・悪意など〉】
I *bear* him no grudge. 意味は ① と同じ.
❹ 生まれる. (!受身形で)
【S〈人・組織など〉be born】
He *was born* with a good memory. 彼は生まれつき記憶力がよい.

beat 動
❶ 打つ, たたく.
① 【S〈心臓〉・V(+副)】
His heart *beat* fast. 彼の心臓はどきどき高鳴った.
② 【S〈人・物〉・V+at [on, against]+〈物〉】
The rain *beat against* the window. 雨が窓に打ちつけた.
③ 【S〈人〉・V・O〈人・物〉】
He *beat* the drum loudly. 彼は激しく太鼓をたたいた.
④ 【S〈人・物〉・V・O〈人・物〉+into [to]+名】
He *beat* the dog *to* death. 彼は犬を殴り殺した.
❷ 打ち負かす.
【S〈人・チーム〉・V・O〈人・チーム〉(+前+名)】
Our team *beat* theirs *at* the game (*by* a score of 4-3). 私たちのチームはその試合で彼らのチームを(4対3で)破った.

become 動

❶ なる.
【S〈人・物・事〉・V・C〈名・形〉】
He *has become* a dentist. 彼は歯科医になった.
The town *has become* famous as a tourist resort. その町は観光地として有名になった.

❷ 似合う, ふさわしい.
【S〈衣服・言動など〉・V・O〈人〉】《書》
Those words do not *become* you. そんなことを言うなんて君らしくもない.

beg 動

❶ 請う.
① 【S〈人〉・V(・O〈人〉)+for+〈物〉】
He *begged* (me) *for* some food. 彼は(私に)少し食べ物をくれと言った. (⚠ ×He begged me some food. は不可)
② 【S〈人〉・V・O〈物〉+of [《話》from]+〈人〉】
He *begged* some food *of [from]* me. 意味は ① と同じ.

❷ 頼む.
① 【S〈人〉・V・O〈人〉・C〈to do〉】
He *begged* me *to* change my mind. 彼は私に決心を変えてくれと頼んだ.
② 【S〈人〉・V・O〈that 節〉】
He *begged that* I (should [might]) change my mind. 意味は ① と同じ. (⚠ (1) should [may] を用いるのは《主に英》. (2) ×He begged me that …. は不可)

begin 動

❶ 始まる.
【S〈事〉・V(+副(句))】
School *begins at* eight [*in* April]. 学校は 8 時 [4 月] から始まる. (⚠ from は不可)

❷ 始める.
① 【S〈人・物・事〉・V・O〈物・事〉(+副(句))】
They *began* the meeting *on* time. 彼らは定刻に会議を始めた.
② 【S〈人・物・事〉・V・O〈to do [doing]〉】
The sky *began* to *clear* [*clearing*]. 空が晴れ始めた. (⚠ to do を用いる方が普通. 特に V を進行形にした場合は doing は避ける)

behave 動

❶ ふるまう.
【S〈人など〉・V+副(句)・節](+toward [to]+〈人〉)】
He *behaved* well [badly] *toward* his colleagues. 彼は同僚に対してふるまいがよかった[よくなかった].
He *behaves* like a dictator [as if he were a dictator]. 彼はまるで独裁者のようにふるまう.

❷ 行儀をよくする.
【S〈人〉・V・(O〈oneself〉)】
The child always *behaves* (*himself*) at his grandparents'. その子は祖父母の家ではいつも行儀がよい.

belief 名 信念, 確信.

【～+that 節】
I lent him the book in the full *belief that* he would give it back. 私はきっと返してくれるとばかり思いこんで彼にその本を貸した.

believe 動 信じる. (⚠ 通例進行形では用いない)

① 【S〈人〉・V・O〈人・言葉〉】

I don't *believe* him [his story]. 彼の言うこと[彼の話]は信用しません.
② 【S〈人〉・V・O〈that 節〉】
People *believed that* the earth was flat. 人々は地球は平らだと信じていた. (受身=It *was believed that* the earth was flat.)
③ 【S〈人〉・V・O〈人・物・事〉・(to be) C〈形・名〉】
They *believe* him *to be* efficient [an efficient teacher]. 彼らは彼が有能[有能な教師]であると信じている. (受身=He *is believed* (*to be*) efficient [an efficient teacher].) (⚠ 受身の場合は to be は省略されることが多い)
④ 【S〈人〉・V+in+〈人・物・事〉】
She *believes in* him [his sincerity; ghosts]. 彼女は彼[彼の誠実さ; 幽霊(の存在)]を信じている. (⚠ believe him は彼の言葉を, believe in him は彼の人柄を信じること)

belong 動 属する, …の所有である. (⚠ 進行形, 命令形は不可)

【S〈人・物〉+V+to+〈人・団体・場所〉】
I *belong* [×am belonging] *to* the baseball club. 私は野球部に入っています.
This painting *belongs to* him [the museum]. この絵は彼のものです[その美術館所蔵のものです].

bind 動 縛る.

① 【S〈人〉・V(+up)・O〈人・物〉(+副+名)】
They *bound* (*up*) the captive *with* rope. 彼らは捕虜をロープで縛った. (⚠ up を入れる方が強意的)
② 【S〈人〉・V・O〈人・物〉+to [on]+〈名〉】
He *bound* the boy *to* a post. 彼は少年を柱に縛りつけた.

bite 動 嚙む, 嚙みつく.

① 【S〈人・動物〉・V・O〈人・物〉】
The dog *bit* my arm. その犬は私の腕をかんだ. (⚠ かまれた部分に重点のある表現)
② 【S〈人・動物〉・V・O〈人〉+in [on]+the+〈体の部分〉】 The dog *bit* me *in* [*on*] *the* arm. 意味は ① と同じ. (⚠ かまれた人に重点のある表現)
③ 【S〈人・動物〉・V+at [into]+〈物〉】
He *bit at* the meat [*into* the apple]. 彼は肉[リンゴ]にかぶりついた. (⚠ into の方が深く食い込む感じが強い)

blame 動

❶ 非難する.
【S〈人〉・V・O〈人・団体〉+for+〈事・行為・doing〉】 He *blamed* me *for* the failure [being late]. 彼はその失敗のことで[遅刻したことで]私を非難した.

❷ せいにする.
① 【S〈人〉・V・O〈人・物・事〉+for+〈事・行為・doing〉】 He *blamed* them *for* the accident. 彼はその事故の原因を彼らのせいにした.
② 【S〈人〉・V・O〈事・行為〉+on+〈人・物・事〉】
He *blamed* the accident *on* them. 意味は ① と同じ.

blow 動

❶ 吹く.
【S〈It・風〉・V(+副(句))】
It *blew* hard last night. 昨夜は激しい風が吹いた. (⚠ It を主語にする場合は, 通例強い風をさす)
A strong wind often *blows* in March. 3 月にはしばしば強い風が吹く.

❷ 風で動く.
① 【S〈物〉・V+副】
His umbrella *has blown* off. 彼の傘は風に吹き飛ばされた.
② 【S〈物〉・V・C〈形〉】
The door *blew* open. ドアが風で開いた.

❸ 息を吐く.
① 【S〈人・動物〉・V(+前+名)】
He *blew on* his hands to warm them. 彼は暖めるために手に息を吹きかけた.
② 【S〈人・動物〉・V・O〈息・煙〉(+副(句))】
He *blew* his breath *in* my face. 彼は私の顔に息を吹きかけた.

❹ 鳴る.
【S〈管楽器・サイレン〉・V(+副(句))】
The siren *blows at* five. サイレンは5時に鳴る.

❺ 鳴らす.
【S〈人〉・V・O〈管楽器・警笛〉】
He *blew* the horn at the corner. 彼は曲がり角で警笛を鳴らした.

❻ 吹き消す.
【S〈人・風〉・V+*out*+O〈物〉】
He *blew out* the candle. 彼はろうそくを吹き消した. (❗ *blew* the candle *out* も可)

boast 動 自慢する.
① 【S〈人〉・V+*of* [*about*]+〈人・物・事〉】
He *boasts of* his musical talent. 彼は自分の音楽の才能を鼻にかけている.
② 【S〈人〉・V・O〈*that* 節〉】
He *boasts that* he has musical talent. 意味は ① と同じ.

borrow 動 借りる.
【S〈人〉・V・O〈物・金〉+*from*+〈人・場所〉】
I *borrowed* the book *from* him [the library]. 彼[図書館]からその本を借りた.

bother 動
❶ 悩ませる, 困らせる.
① 【S〈人・物・事〉・V・O〈人〉(+*with* [*about*])+〈原因〉】
He *bothered* me *with* many questions [*about* trifles]. 彼はいろいろと質問をして[つまらないことで]私をわずらわした.
② 【S〈人〉・V・O〈人〉+*for*+〈物〉】
He *bothered* me *for* money. 彼は私にうるさく金をねだった.
③ 【S〈人〉・V・O〈人〉+*to do*】
He *is* always *bothering* me *to* lend him money. 彼はいつも金を貸せといって私を困らせてばかりいる.

❷ 悩む, 気をもむ.
【S〈人〉・V+*with* [*about*]+〈原因〉】
Don't *bother about* it [(*about*) coming to meet me]. そんなこと気にする및迎えに来ていただかなくても結構です]. (❗ 動名詞を用いる場合は about のみを用いるが, しばしば省略される)

❸ わざわざ...する.
【S〈人〉・V+*to do* [*doing*]】
Don't *bother to* write [*writing*] me back. わざわざお返事をいただかなくても結構です. (❗(1) 通例否定文で. (2) to do の方が普通)

brave 形 勇敢な.
① 【S〈人〉・is ~+*to do*】
You were *brave to* jump into the sea to save the child. その子を救助しようと海に飛び込んだとは

君も勇気があるね.
② 【It is ~ *of*+〈人〉+*to do*】
It was *brave of* you *to* jump into the sea to save the child. 意味は ① と同じ.

break 動
❶ こわす.
① 【S〈人〉・V・O〈物〉(+*with*+〈道具〉)】
He *broke* the box *with* a hammer. 彼はハンマーでその箱をこわした.
② 【S〈人〉・V・O〈物〉・C〈open〉】
The burglar *broke* the safe *open*. 泥棒は金庫をこわして開けた. (受身＝The safe *was broken open* by the burglar.) (❗The burglar *broke open* the safe. も可)

❷ 破る.
【S〈人〉・V・O〈約束・法律〉】
He *broke* his promise [the law]. 彼は約束[法]を破った.

❸ こわれる.
【S〈物〉・V(+副(句))】
The glass *broke* easily [*on* the floor; *into* pieces]. コップは簡単に[床の上で; こなごなに]こわれた.

❹ 押し入る.
【S〈人〉・V+*into*+〈場所〉】
The burglars *broke into* the bank. 強盗たちは銀行に押し入った.

❺ 中断する.
【S〈人〉・V・O〈行為〉】
He *broke* his habit of smoking. 彼は禁煙した.

❻ 急に現れる.
【S〈物・事〉・V (+副(句))】
A happy smile *broke over* his face. 幸せそうなほほえみが彼の顔にさっと浮かんだ.

bring 動
❶ 持って来る.
① 【S〈人〉・V・O〈人〉・O〈物〉】
He *brought* me a letter. 彼は私のところへ手紙を持って来た. (❗物に焦点を当てた言い方. (受身＝I *was brought* a letter by him.) ただし, A letter *was brought* me by him. の受身形は不自然)
② 【S〈人〉・V・O〈物〉+*to* [*for*]+〈人〉】
He *brought* a letter *to* [*for*] me. 意味は ① と同じ. (❗(1) 人に焦点を当てた言い方. (2) to は方向を, for は「利益になるように」の意を表わす) (受身＝A letter *was brought to* [*for*] me.)

❷ 連れて来る.
【S〈人・事・乗り物〉・V・O〈人〉(+*to*+〈場所・人〉)】
He *brought* (→took) me *to* the beach. 彼は私を海辺へ連れて来てくれた. (受身＝I *was brought to* the beach by him.)
About fifteen minutes' walk *brought* us *to* the university. 15分ほど歩くとわれわれは大学にやって来た.

❸ もたらす.
【S〈物・事〉・V・O〈物・事〉(+*to*+〈人・場所〉)】
The news *brought* tears *to* her eyes. その知らせで彼女は目に涙を浮かべた.
The heavy snow *brought* disaster *to* the residents. 大雪は住民たちに災害をもたらした.

❹ ...の状態に至らせる.
【S〈人・物・事〉・V・O〈人・物・事〉+*to* [*into*]+名】
The mild weather will *bring* the trees *into* blossom soon. 穏やかな天候はまもなく木々に花を咲かせるだろう.

基本文型

❺ …する気になる.
【S〈人〉・V・O〈oneself〉+to do】
I can't *bring myself to* say "Yes." 私はどうしても「はい」と言う気にはなれない.

build 動 建てる.
① 【S〈人〉・V・O〈建物〉+(out) of+〈材料〉】
They *built* the house (*out*) *of* [×from] brick. 彼らはレンガでその家を建てた. (受身＝The house *was built* (*out*) *of* brick.) (❗out がある方が口語的)
② 【S〈人〉・V・O〈人〉・O〈建物〉】
My father *built* me a new house. 父は私に新しい家を建ててくれた. (受身＝I *was built* a new house by my father.) (❗この文型は「物」に重点があり, ③は「人」に重点がある)
③ 【S〈人〉・V・O〈建物〉+for+〈人〉】
My father *built* a new house *for* me. 意味は② と同じ. (受身＝A new house *was built for* me by my father.)

burn 動
❶ 燃える, 焦げる.
① 【S〈火・物〉・V(+副(句))】
This wood *burns* easily. この木は燃えやすい. Something *is burning in* the kitchen. 台所で何か焦げている.
② 【S〈火・物〉・V・C〈形〉】
This wood *burns* blue. この木は青い火を発して燃える.
❷ 燃やす, 焦がす.
① 【S〈人〉・V・O〈物〉】
He *burned* his old clothes [his toast]. 彼は古着を焼いた[トーストを焦がした].
② 【S〈人・火〉・V・O〈物・人〉+to+〈灰・死〉】
He *burned* all the letters *to* ashes. 彼は手紙をすべて燃やして灰にしてしまった. (受身＝All the letters *were burned to* ashes.) (❗受身形で使うことが多い. 「彼は焼死した」は He *was burned to* death.)
❸ やけどをする.
【S〈人〉・V・O(*oneself*・体の部分)】
He *burned* himself [his finger]. 彼はやけどをした[指にやけどをした].

burst 動
❶ 破裂する.
【S〈物〉・V】
The tire *burst* under great pressure. 高圧がかかってタイヤが破裂した.
❷ 破裂させる.
【S〈人〉・V・O〈物〉】
He *burst* the balloon with a needle. 彼は針で風船を破裂させた.
❸ 突然…し出す.
① 【S〈人・物〉・V+into+〈事〉】
She *burst into* [×in] tears [laughter]. 彼女は突然泣き出した[笑い出した].
② 【S〈人〉・V+out+do*ing*】
She *burst out* crying [laugh*ing*]. 意味は① と同じ.

busy 形 忙しい.
① 【S〈人〉is ～+at [about, on, with]+〈人・物・事〉】
She is *busy with* [*at*] the cooking. 彼女は料理で忙しい.
② 【S〈人〉is ～+do*ing*】
We are now *busy* get*ting* ready for our trip. 私たちは今旅行の支度に忙しい.

buy 動 買う.
① 【S〈人〉・V・O〈物〉+at [in]+〈場所〉】
I *bought* this hat *at* that shop [*in* Paris]. この帽子はあの店[パリ]で買った.
② 【S〈人〉・V・O〈物〉+from+〈人〉】
He *bought* the book *from* her for cash. 彼は彼女からその本を現金で買った.
③ 【S〈人〉・V・O〈物〉+for [at]+〈価格〉】
She *bought* the tie *for* [*at*] 50 dollars. 彼女はそのネクタイを50ドルで買った. (❗price を用いると at [×for] a low *price* となる)
④ 【S〈人〉・V・O〈人〉・O〈物〉】
Mary *bought* Tom the tie. メリーはトムにそのネクタイを買ってやった. (受身＝Tom *was bought* the tie by Mary. ×The tie was bought Tom by Mary. は不可) (❗この文型は「物」に焦点がある. ⑤は「人」に焦点がある)
⑤ 【S〈人〉・V・O〈物〉+for+〈人・物〉】
Mary *bought* the tie *for* Tom. 意味は④ と同じ. (受身＝The tie *was bought for* Tom by Mary.)
I must *buy* a new table *for* this room. この部屋に新しいテーブルを買わなくてはならない. (❗for の後が〈物〉の場合は SVOO の文型は不可. ×…buy this room a new table.)

call 動
❶ 呼ぶ, 呼び出す.
① 【S〈人〉・V・O〈人・名前・警察など〉】
He *called* the police [my name]. 彼は警察[私の名前]を呼んだ.
② 【S〈人〉・V・O〈人〉・O〈車〉】
He *called* me a taxi. 彼は私にタクシーを呼んでくれた. (❗この文型は「物」に重点があり, ③は「人」に重点がある)
③ 【S〈人〉・V・O〈車〉+for+〈人〉】
He *called* a taxi *for* me. 意味は② と同じ.
❷ …と呼ぶ.
【S〈人〉・V・O〈人・物〉・C〈名〉】
They *call* the boy Tony. 彼らはその少年をトニーと呼んでいる. (受身＝The boy *is called* Tony.) (❗C にはその人[物]の愛称などが来る)
❸ 電話をかける.
【S〈人〉・V・O〈人・場所・番号〉】
He *called* me [my office] in the morning. 彼は朝私[私の事務所]に電話してきた.
❹ 訪れる.
【S〈人〉・V+on+〈人〉[at+〈場所〉]】
I *called on* him [*at* his house] last night. 昨夜彼[彼の家]を訪問した. (❗I *called on* him *at* his house last night. も可)

care 動
❶ 気にする, 関心がある.
① 【S〈人〉・V(+副)+about+〈人・物・事〉】
He doesn't *care about* his clothes. 彼は服装に無頓(とん)着だ. (❗否定文・疑問文で用いるのが普通で, 肯定文の場合は very much, a lot, greatly などの副詞を伴う: He *cares* a lot *about* his clothes.)
② 【S〈人〉・V・O〈wh-節・whether節〉】
I don't *care whether* he is angry or not [*what* he says]. 彼が怒っていようがいまいが[何を言おうと]かまうものか. (❗通例否定文, 疑問文で)

❷ 反対する. (! 通例否定文, 疑問文, if 節で)
【S〈人〉・V・O〈if 節〉】
Do you *care* if my sister comes too? 私の妹がいっしょに来てもかまいませんか.

❸ 世話をする.《やや書》
【S〈人〉・V+*for*+〈人・動物〉】
I will *care for* your children while you are away. お留守の間お子さんの面倒を見ましょう.

❹ 好む. (! 通例否定文, 疑問文, 条件節で)
① 【S〈人〉・V+*for*+〈人・物・事・*doing*〉】
He doesn't *care for* golf [bringing work home]. 彼はゴルフ[仕事を家に持ち帰るの]が好きでない.
② 【S〈人〉・V+*to do*〉】
Do you *care to* go to the party? パーティーに行きたいですか.

careful 形 注意深い.
① 【S〈人〉 is 〜+*to do*】
Be *careful* not *to* catch cold. 風邪をひかないように気をつけなさい.
② 【S〈人〉 is 〜+(*that*)節】
You must be *careful* (*that*) you don't [× won't] break the vase. 花びんをこわさないように気をつけるのですよ. (! 従節中では未来形を用いない)
③ 【S〈人〉 is 〜+*about* [*of*]+〈人・物・事〉】
Be *careful about* your health. 健康に注意しなさい.
④ 【S〈人〉 is 〜(+*about* [*of*])+*wh*- 節】
Be *careful* (*about* [*of*]) *what* you say and do. 言動を慎みなさい. (! wh- 節を伴うときは通例前置詞を省略)
⑤ 【S〈人〉 is 〜+*with*+〈人・物・事〉】(! ③ と違って「…の扱いに注意深い」の意味)
He was *careful with* the money. 彼は金の遣い方が慎重だった.
⑥ 【S〈人〉 is 〜+(*in*) *doing*】
He was *careful* (*in*) opening the package. 彼は注意して包みを開けた. (! *in* は省略されることが多い)

careless 形
❶ 不注意な.
① 【S〈人〉 is 〜+*to do*】
I was *careless to* dial the wrong number. 電話をかけ間違うとは私もそそっかしい.
② 【It is 〜 *of*+〈人〉+*to do*】
It was *careless of* me *to* dial the wrong number. 意味は ① と同じ.
③ 【S〈人〉 is 〜+*with*+〈人・物・事〉】
Don't be *careless with* matches. マッチの扱いに注意を怠るな.
④ 【S〈人〉 is 〜+*in*+〈*doing*・事〉】
Don't be *careless in* handling matches. 意味は ③ と同じ.
❷ 無頓着(とんちゃく)な.
【S〈人〉 is 〜 *of* [*about*]+〈物・事〉】
He is *careless of* [*about*] his appearance. 彼は身なりに無頓着だ.

carry 動
❶ 運ぶ.
【S〈人・乗り物・風など〉・V・O〈人・物〉(+副(句))】
He *carried* the box upstairs [*on* his shoulder]. 彼はその箱を2階へ[肩にかついで]運んだ.
The train *carries* a lot of commuters *to* the city. その列車は多くの通勤客を町へ運んでいる.

❷ 持ち歩く.
【S〈人〉・V・O〈物〉(+副=名)】
He always *carries* a phonecard *with* him [*in* his wallet]. 彼はいつもテレホンカードを肌身離さず[財布に入れて]持ち歩いている. (! (1) *with* him は省略可. (2) ×…with himself は不可)

❸ 伝える.
【S〈新聞・雑誌〉・V・O〈記事〉】
Today's newspaper *carries* the story of the accident. 今日の新聞にその事故のことが出ている.

❹ 支える.
【S〈物〉・V・O〈物・重さ〉】
The four pillars *carry* (the weight of) the roof. 4本の柱が屋根(の重み)を支えている. (! 進行形にしない)

catch 動
❶ (動くものを)つかまえる, とらえる.
① 【S〈人・動物〉・V・O〈人・物・動物〉】
The policemen *caught* the thief. 警官たちはその泥棒をつかまえた.
② 【S〈人・動物〉・V・O〈物〉+*in* [*with*]+〈手・口〉】
He *caught* the ball *in* one hand [*with* his naked hands]. 彼はボールを片手で[素手で]取った.
③ 【S〈人〉・V・O〈人〉+*by*+*the*+〈体の部分〉】
He *caught* me *by the* arm. 彼は私の腕をつかんだ. (! I (me)に焦点がある. He *caught* my arm. では(体の部分)に焦点がある)
④ 【S〈人〉・V・O〈人〉・O〈物〉】
We *caught* him some fish. 彼に魚をつかまえてやった. (! (1) この文型では「物」に焦点がある. ⑤ 「人」に焦点がある. (2) 受身形は不可)
⑤ 【S〈人〉・V・O〈物〉+*for*+〈人〉】
We *caught* some fish *for* him. 意味は ④ と同じ. (受身=Some fish *were caught for* him. *for* がなければ不可)

❷ (よくないことをしているところを)見つける.
【S〈人〉・V・O〈人〉+(*in the act of*) *doing*】
I *caught* him (*in the act of*) stealing into the house. 彼がその家にしのび込もうとしているのを見つけた[現場を押さえた]. (受身=He *was caught* (*in the act of*) stealing into the house.) (! 受身形で使うことが多い)

❸ 間に合う.
【S〈人〉・V・O〈乗り物〉】
I couldn't *catch* the train. その列車に間に合わなかった.

❹ 感染する.
【S〈人〉・V・O〈伝染性の病気〉】
He *caught* (a) cold. 彼は風邪をひいた. (! ×A cold was caught by him. の受身は不可)

❺ 襲う.
【S〈あらし・病気〉・V・O〈人〉】
A shower *caught* us on the way. 途中でにわか雨にあった. (受身=We *were caught in* a shower on the way.)

❻ ひっかける.
【S〈人〉・V・O〈服・指など〉+*in* [*on*]+〈物〉】
He *caught* his sweater *on* a nail. 彼はセーターをくぎにひっかけた.

❼ 聞き取る, 理解する.
【S〈人〉・V・O〈事・*wh*-節〉】
I didn't *catch* your idea [what you said]. 君の考えが分からなかった[言うことが聞こえなかった]. (! 通例受身形, 進行形は不可)

cause 動

❶ 引き起こす, 原因となる.
【S〈事・人〉・V・O〈事件・損害・病気〉】
The typhoon *caused* a lot of damage. 台風で大きな被害が出た.
❷ もたらす.
① 【S〈事・物・人〉・V・O〈人〉・O〈損害・苦痛など〉】
He [His failure] *caused* us a lot of trouble. 彼[彼の失敗]のせいで私たちは多大の迷惑をこうむった. (❗ この文型は「事」に焦点があり, ② は「人」に焦点がある)
② 【S〈事・物・人〉・V・O〈損害・苦痛など〉+*to* [*for*] +〈人〉】
He [His failure] *caused* a lot of trouble *to* [*for*] us. 意味は ① と同じ.
❸ …させる.
【S〈事・物・人〉・V・O〈人・事〉・C〈*to* do〉】
What *caused* you *to* change your mind? どうして気持ちが変わったの. (❗ What *made* you change…? の方が普通)

cause 名
❶ 原因.
① 【~+*of* (+所有格)+*doing*】
Drunk driving was the *cause of* his hit*ting* the man. 飲酒運転が彼がその人をはねた原因だ.
② 【~+*that* 節】
Drunk driving was the *cause that* [×*why*] he hit the man. 意味は ① と同じ.
❷ 理由, 動機.
① 【~+*to* do】
You have no *cause to* be angry. 君は何も怒る理由はないじゃないか.
② 【~+*for*+*doing*】
You have no *cause for* being angry. 意味は ① と同じ.
③ 【~+*that* 節】
You have no *cause that* you are angry. 意味は ① と同じ.

certain 形
❶ …を確信して. (❗ 確信する人は S)
① 【S〈人〉is ~+(*that*) 節】
I am *certain* (*that*) he [I] will win. 彼[私]はきっと勝つと私は信じている.
② 【S〈人〉is ~+*of* [*about*]+〈事〉】
Are you *certain of* [*about*] that? それは確かなのですか.
I am *certain of* his success. 彼はきっと成功すると私は信じている.
③ 【S〈人〉is ~+*of* (所有格+) *doing*】
I am *certain of* his win*ning*. 彼はきっと勝つと私は信じている.
I am *certain of* win*ning*. 私はきっと勝つと確信している.
④ 【S〈人〉is ~+*wh*- 節・句】
I am not *certain whether* he will win [*what* to do]. 彼が勝つかどうか[何をすべきか]私にはよくわからない. (❗ 通例否定文, 疑問文で用いる)
❷ 確実な. (❗ 確信する人は話し手)
① 【It is ~+*that* 節】
It is *certain that* he will win. (=That he will win is *certain*.) 彼が勝つことは確かだ. (❗ ×It is *certain for* him *to* win. は不可)
② 【S〈人・物・事〉is ~+*to* do】 He is *certain to* win. The secret is *certain to* leak out. 秘密はきっと漏れるだろう.

challenge 動 挑戦する, 挑む.
① 【S〈人〉・V・O〈人〉+*to*+〈試合・戦い〉】
He *challenged* me *to* a fight [a game of chess]. 彼は私に戦い[チェスの対戦]を申し込んできた.
② 【S〈人〉・V・O〈人〉・C〈*to* do〉】
He *challenged* me *to* beat him. 彼は勝てるものなら勝ってみろ[ぶてるものならぶってみろ]と言った.

chance 名
❶ 見込み, 公算.
① 【~+*of* (+所有格・目的格)+*doing*】
There is a good *chance of* our team win*ning* the game. 我がチームが試合に勝つ見込みは十分ある. (❗ ×There is a good *chance for* our team *to* win the game. の型は通例不可)
② 【~+*that* 節】
There is a good *chance that* our team will win the game. 意味は ① と同じ.
❷ 機会.
① 【~+*to* do】
He never misses a *chance to* use English. 彼は機会を逃さず英語を使う.
② 【~+*of*+*doing*】
He never misses a *chance of* using English. 意味は ① と同じ. (❗ ① の文型の方が普通)

change 動
❶ 変わる.
① 【S〈人・物・事〉・V】
Richard *has changed* since I saw him last. この前会ったときからリチャードは変わってしまった.
Times *have changed*. 時代は変わった.
② 【S〈人・物・事〉・V+*into*+〈人・物・事〉】
The rain *changed into* snow. 雨は雪に変わった.
③ 【S〈人・物・事〉・V+*from*+〈名・形〉+*to*+〈名・形〉】 The wind *has changed from* north *to* west. 風向きが北から西に変わった.
❷ 変える.
① 【S〈人・物・事〉・V・O〈人・物・事〉】
He *changed* his job [mind]. 彼は仕事[心, 考え]を変えた.
② 【S〈人・事〉・V・O〈人・物・事〉+*into*+〈人・物・事〉】 The magician *changed* the stick *into* a rope. 手品師は棒をロープに変えた.
③ 【S〈人〉・V・O〈人・物・事〉+*from*+〈名・形〉+*to*+〈名・形〉】
She *changed* her name *from* Maria *to* Mary. 彼女は名前をマリアからメリーに変えた.
❸ 取り替える.
① 【S〈人〉・V・O〈複数の 名〉(+〈前〉+〈名〉)】
I *changed* seats *with* him [trains *at* Maibara]. 彼と席を入れ替わった[米原で列車を乗り換えた]. (❗ このほか, partners, houses など特定の目的語に限り, それ以外は exchange を用いる)
② 【S〈人〉・V・O〈物〉+*for*+〈物〉】
He *changed* his coat *for* another. 彼はコートを別のと替えた.
❹ 両替する.
【S〈人〉・V・O〈お金〉+*for* [*into*]+〈お金〉】
I *changed* my yen *for* pounds. 私は円をポンドに両替した.

charge 動
❶ 請求する.
【S〈人〉・V・O〈人〉・O〈金額〉+*for*+〈物・事・doing〉】 He *charged* me two hundred

dollars *for* trouble [repair*ing* the machine]. 彼は手数料[機械の修理代]として 200 ドルを私に請求した. (**!** 間接目的語または直接目的語のいずれか一方を省略できる)

❷ 告訴する, 非難する.

① 【S〈人〉・V・O〈人〉+*with*+〈名・*doing*〉】
They *charged* him *with* theft [steal*ing* the money]. 彼らは窃盗の[金を盗んだ]かどで彼を告訴した. (受身=He *was charged with* theft [steal*ing* the money].)

② 【S〈人〉・V・O〈*that* 節〉】
We *charged that* he had violated the contract. 彼が契約違反をしたと告発した.

❸ ゆだねる.
【S〈人〉・V・O〈人〉+*with*+〈仕事・責任〉】
They *charged* me *with* an important duty. 彼らは私に重要な任務を託した. (受身=I *was charged with* an important duty.)

❹ つけにする, つけで買う.
【S〈人〉・V・O〈金・商品〉+*to*+〈人・勘定〉】
He *charged* the expenses *to* me [my account]. 彼はその費用を私の勘定につけた.

check 動

❶ 止める.
【S〈人・物〉・V・O〈人・物・事〉】
I was unable to *check* my laughter. 私は笑いを抑えることができなかった. (**!** stop より堅い語)

❷ 確かめる.
① 【S〈人〉・V・O〈物・事〉(+画(句))】
He *checked* the tyres. 彼はタイヤを点検した.
You must *check* the items *against* the list. あなたは品目をリストと照合しなければならない.

② 【S〈人〉・V・O〈*that* 節〉】
Check that the windows are shut. 窓が閉まっているのを確かめなさい.

③ 【S〈人〉・V・O〈*wh*-節〉】
I *checked whether* the windows were shut. 私は窓が閉まっているかどうか確かめた.

choice 名 選択(の自由).

① 【〈~ *of*+〈物・事・*doing*〉+*or*+〈物・事・*doing*〉】
She was given a *choice of* los*ing* her child or (los*ing*) her own life. 彼女は我が子を失うか自分自身の命を失うかしなかった.

② 【〈~ *between*+〈人・物・事・*doing*〉+*and*+〈人・物・事・*doing*〉】 She was given a *choice between* los*ing* her child *and* (los*ing*) her own life. 意味は ① と同じ.

③ 【〈~+*that* 節〉】
They made a *choice that* Hawaii was where they want to live. ハワイこそ住みたい所だと彼らは選んだのだった.

choose 動

❶ 選ぶ.
① 【S〈人〉・V・O〈人・物〉(+*from* [(*from*) *among*]+〈複数の名〉)】 I *chose* the easiest one *from* [(*from*) *among*] the books. その本の中から一番やさしいものを選んだ.

② 【S〈人〉・V+*between*+〈二つの名〉】
I'll *choose between* this tie and that [these two ties]. このネクタイとあのネクタイ[これら 2 本のネクタイ]のどちらかを選ぼう.

③ 【S〈人〉・V・O〈人〉+(*as* [*for, to be*]) C〈役職〉】
We *chose* him (*as* [*for, to be*]) our leader. 私たちは彼をリーダーに選んだ. (受身=He *was chosen* (*as* [*for, to be*]) our leader.) (**!** 受身形では as [for, to be] は省略可)

④ 【S〈人〉・V・O〈人〉+*to*+〈*to do*〉】
We *chose* him *to* serve as our representative. 私たちは彼を私たちの代表を務めるよう選んだ.

⑤ 【S〈人〉・V・O〈人〉・O〈物〉】
He *chose* me a nice dress. 彼は私にすてきな服を選んでくれた. (受身=I *was chosen* a nice dress./× A nice dress was chosen me. は不可) (**!** この文型では「物」に焦点がある. ⑥ は「人」に焦点がある)

⑥ 【S〈人〉・V・O〈物・人〉+*for*+〈人〉】
He *chose* a nice dress *for* me. 意味は ⑤ と同じ. (受身=A nice dress *was chosen for* me by him.) (**!** ⑤, ⑥ ともに O〈物・人〉には the などのついた特定的な名詞にはこない)

❷ ...することに決める.
【S〈人〉・V・O〈*to do* [*wh*-節句]〉】
She *chose not to* accept his proposal. 彼女は彼のプロポーズを承諾しないことにした.
Have you *chosen where* we should go [*where to* go] for dinner? 夕食にどこへ行くか決めましたか.

claim 動

❶ 要求する, 求める.
【S〈人〉・V・O〈物・事〉】
They *claimed* a pay rise. 彼らは賃上げを要求した.

❷ 主張する.
① 【S〈人〉・V・O〈*that*〉節〉】
He *claims* (*that*) he is the right man for the job. 彼はその仕事には自分が適任だと言い張っている.

② 【S〈人〉・V・O〈*to do*〉】
He *claims to* be the right man for the job. 意味は ① と同じ.

claim 名

❶ 要求.
【~+*for* [*on, to*]+〈賠償など〉】
He made a *claim for* damages against the company. 彼はその会社に対して損害賠償を請求した.

❷ 要求する権利.
【~+*on* [*to*]+〈事〉】
She has a rightful *claim to* her father's land. 彼女には父親の土地を受け継ぐ正当な権利がある.

❸ 主張.
① 【~+*of*+〈事〉】
We believe his *claim of* innocence. 私たちは無実だという彼の主張を信じている.

② 【~+*to do* [*that* 節]】
We believe his *claim to* be innocent [*that* he is innocent]. 意味は ① と同じ.

clear 形

❶ 明らかな.
① 【It is ~+(*to*+〈人〉)+*that* 節】
It is *clear to* me *that* he is not coming. 彼は来ないということが私にははっきりしている.

② 【It is ~+*wh*-節】
It is not *clear what* you want me to do. あなたが私に何をしてもらいたいのかよくわからない.

❷ 確信している.
① 【S〈人〉 is ~+*about* [*on*]+〈事〉】
I am not *clear on* that point. その点について私ははっきりわからない.

② 【S〈人〉 is+*that* 節】
I am *clear* in my mind *that* I should give up

the idea. 私はその考えはすてるべきだとはっきりわかっている.

③ 【S〈人〉 is+wh-節[句]】
He was not *clear which* way *to* go. 彼はどちらの道を行くべきかわからなかった. (!通例否定文, 疑問文で用いる)

clever 形

❶ 利口な.
① 【S〈人〉 is ~+to do】
You were *clever to* solve that difficult problem. その難問が解けたとは君も頭がいいね.
② 【It is ~+of+〈人〉+to do】
It was *clever of* you *to* solve that difficult problem. 意味は①と同じ.

❷ 器用な.
【S〈人〉 is ~+at+〈事〉】
She is *clever at* making excuses. 彼女は言い訳がうまい.

combine 動

❶ 結合させる, 組み[兼ね]合わせる, 両立させる.
【S〈人など〉・V・O〈物・事〉+with [and]+〈物・事〉】 It was difficult for her to *combine* child rearing *with* a career. 子育てと職業とを両立させることは彼女には難しかった.
This TV program *combines* fact *with* [*and*] fiction. このテレビ番組は事実と虚構を結びつけたものである.

❷ 〈物が〉結合する, 〈人が〉団結する.
① 【S〈物・人〉・V(+with+〈物・人〉)】
Hydrogen *combines with* oxygen to form water. (=Hydrogen and oxygen *combine* to form water.) 水素は酸素と化合して水になる.
② 【S〈人〉・V+against+〈人〉】
They *combined* together *against* the enemy. 彼らは敵に対抗して団結した.

come 動

❶ 来る, 〈聞き手の方へ〉行く, 到来する.
【S〈人・物・事〉・V(+副(句))】
He *came* here yesterday. 彼はきのうここへ来た.
I'm afraid I can't *come* [×go] to your party. 残念ながらあなたのパーティーに行くことはできません.
Spring *has come*. 春が来た.

❷ 達する.
【S〈物〉・V+to+〈場所〉】
The water *came to* my waist. 水が腰のところまで来た.

❸ …出身である.
【S〈人〉・V+from+〈場所〉】
"Where do you *come from*?" "I *come from* New Zealand." 「どちらのご出身ですか」「ニュージーランドです」(!生きている人について言うときは現在形で用いる)

❹ 心に浮かぶ.
① 【S〈考え〉・V+to [upon]+〈人〉】
A good idea *came to* [*upon*] me. いい考えが浮かんだ.
② 【S〈考え〉・V+into+〈心〉】
A good idea *came into* my mind. 意味は①と同じ.

❺ 入手できる.
【S〈商品など〉・V+in+〈容器・大きさ・色など〉】
These trousers *come in* two colors [three sizes]. このズボンには2色[3つの大きさが]そろっている. (!進行形は不可)

❻ …になる.
① 【S〈物・事〉・V・C〈形〉】
My dream *has come* true. 夢が実現した.
② 【S〈人・事・物〉・V+to [into]+〈事・状態〉】
The war *has come to* an end. 戦争が終わった.
When did the machine *come into* use? その機械はいつごろから使われるようになりましたか.

❼ …するようになる.
【S〈人〉・V・C〈to do〉】
Soon they *came to* love each other. 間もなく彼らは愛し合うようになった.

command 動

❶ 命じる.
① 【S〈人〉・V・O〈人〉+to do】
The general *commanded* the men *to* advance. 将軍は部下に前進するよう命じた. (受身=The men *were commanded to* advance by the general.)
② 【S〈人〉・V・O〈that 節〉】
The general *commanded that* the men (should) advance. 意味は①と同じ. (!should を用いるのは《主に英》. ①の不定詞構文が好まれる)

❷ 指揮する.
【S〈人〉・V・O〈人・物〉】
The ship's captain *commands* all the officers and crew. 船長はすべての高級船員と乗組員を指揮する.

❸ 見渡す.
【S〈場所〉・V・O〈景色〉】
This hill *commands* a fine view of the lake. この丘からは湖の眺めがすばらしい. (!受身形, 進行形は不可. 人間を主語にすれば command は用いられない. We can get a fine view of the lake from this hill. とする)

common 形 普通の, ありふれた.

【It is ~(+for+〈人・物・事〉)+to do】
It is quite *common for* [×*of*] girls *to* go to college in Japan today. 現代の日本では女性が大学へ行くことはごく普通である. (!×It is common *that* 節 は不可)

compare 動

❶ 比べる.
【S〈人〉・V・O〈人・物・事〉+with [to]+〈人・物・事〉】 They *compared* my pay *with* [*to*, ×*by*] his. 彼らは私の給料を彼のと比較した. (受身=My pay *was compared to* [*with*] his.) (!《話》, 受身では to が好まれる)

❷ たとえる.
【S〈人〉・V・O〈人・物・事〉+to+〈人・物・事〉】
The teacher *compared* man's life *to* a journey. 先生は人の一生を旅にたとえた. (!受身形で使うことが多い)

❸ 匹敵する.
【S〈人・物・事〉・V+with+〈人・物・事〉】
He cannot *compare with* Shakespeare as a writer of tragedies. 悲劇の作家として彼はシェイクスピアにはかなわない. (!通例否定文で用いる)

complain 動 不満を言う.

① 【S〈人〉・V(+to+〈人〉)+about [of]+〈物・人〉】
He *complained* (*to* me) *about* [*of*] his working conditions. 彼は(私に)労働条件のことで不満を言った.
② 【S〈人〉・V(+to+〈人〉)・O〈that 節〉】

He *complained* (to me) *that* the room was too small. 彼は(私に)部屋が狭すぎると文句を言った。(**!** 受身形は不可)

conclude 動
❶ 終える.
【S〈人〉・V・O〈事〉(+副(句))】
She *concluded* her speech *with* an expression of thanks to them. 彼女はスピーチを彼らに対する感謝の言葉でしめくくった.
❷ 結論を下す.
【S〈人〉・V・O〈that 節〉】
They *concluded* from the analysis *that* the accident had been caused by metal fatigue. 彼らは,その分析から事故は金属疲労によってひき起こされたと結論を下した.
❸ 終わる.
【S〈文・会・話など〉・V(+副(句))】
The story *concludes with* the heroine's death. その物語はヒロインの死で終わる.

condition 名
❶ 状態.
【~+*to do*】
I am in no [not in a] *condition to* work hard. 私はとても一生懸命働けるような体じゃない.
❷ 条件.
【*on* ~+(*that*)節】
I will confide the secret *on condition* (*that*) you keep it. だれにもしゃべらないという条件でその秘密を打ち明けよう.

confess 動 白状する, 自白する.
① 【S〈人〉・V・O〈事〉(+*to*+〈人〉)】
He *confessed* his guilt *to* the police. 彼は罪を警察に自白した.
② 【S〈人〉・V(+*to*+〈人〉)・O〈*that* 節〉】
He *confessed to* me *that* he had told a lie. 彼はうそをついたと白状した.
③ 【S〈人〉・V+*to*+〈事・*doing*〉】
He *confessed to* his guilt. 彼は自分の有罪を認めた.
He finally *confessed to* having stolen the money. 彼はとうとうお金を盗んだことを白状した. (**!** ×to have stolen としない)

connect 動
❶ 結びつける, つなぐ.
① 【S〈人・物・事〉・V・O〈複数の物〉】
The bridge *connects* Honshu and Shikoku. その橋は本州と四国を結んでいる.
② 【S〈人〉・V・O〈物〉+*to*+〈物〉】
They *connected* the passenger cars *to* the locomotive. 彼らは客車を機関車に連結した.
The operator *connected* my call *to* the city office. オペレーターは私の電話を市役所につないでくれた.
❷ 関係づける.
【S〈人・物・事〉・V・O〈人・物・事〉+*with*+〈人・物・事〉】
They *connected* his disappearance *with* the accident. 彼らは彼の失踪(しっそう)をその事件と結びつけて考えた. (**!** 受身形, または V+oneself の形で用いることが多い: He *is connected* [He *connects himself*] *with* the company. (彼はその会社と取り引き関係がある))
❸ 接続する.
【S〈交通機関〉・V+*with*+〈交通機関〉】

This train *connects with* the one to Nagano at Nagoya. この列車は名古屋で長野行きと連絡している.

conscious 形 気づいている.
① 【S〈人〉 *is* ~+*of*+〈物・事・*doing*〉】
I was *conscious of* my mistake. 私は自分の誤りに気づいていた.
She was *conscious of* being watched. 彼女は監視されているのに気づいていた.
② 【S〈人〉 *is* ~+*that* 節】
She was *conscious that* she was being watched. 意味は①の第2例と同じ.
③ 【S〈人〉 *is* ~+*wh*-節】
They seem not to be *conscious what* their son is thinking. 彼らは息子が何を考えているか気づいていないようだ.

consider 動
❶ 熟考する.
① 【S〈人〉・V・O〈物・事・*doing*〉】
He *considered* her proposal [put*ting* off his departure]. 彼は彼女の申し込みをよく考えた[出発を延ばそうかと考えた].
② 【S〈人〉・V・O〈*wh*-節(句)〉】
We must *consider whether* we should [*whether to*] carry out the plan. その計画を実行すべきかどうかよく考えねばならない.
I *considered which* was better. どちらがよいかよく考えた.
❷ みなす, 思う. 《書》
① 【S〈人〉・V・O〈人・物・事〉・(*to be*) C〈名・形〉】
We *consider* the report (*to be*) important. その報告は重要だと考えている. (受身=The report *is considered* (*to be*) important.) (**!** (1) to be は省略されることが多い. 受身では省略が普通. (2) to be の代わりに as も可)
I *consider* it (*to be*) necessary to ask him for help. 彼に助けを求めることが必要だと思う.
② 【S〈人〉・V・O〈*that* 節〉】
We *consider that* the report is important. 意味は①の第1例と同じ. (**!** 受身形は It *is considered that* the report is important.)
❸ 考慮に入れる.
① 【S〈人〉・V・O〈物・事〉】
We must *consider* his age. 彼の年齢を考慮に入れなければならない.
② 【S〈人〉・V・O〈*that* 節〉】
He *considered that* I was inexperienced. 彼は私が未経験であることを考慮に入れてくれた. (**!** that 節の前に the fact が入ることもある. その場合は①の文型)
③ 【S〈人〉・V・O〈*wh*-節(句)〉】
He *considered how* difficult the task was. 彼はその仕事がどれほど難しいかを考えてみた.

continue 動
❶ 続ける.
① 【S〈人〉・V・O〈動作・仕事〉】
He *continued* his work. 彼は仕事を続けた. (受身=His work *was continued*.)
② 【S〈人〉・V・O〈*doing*〉】
He *continued* work*ing*. 彼は働き続けた. (**!** 受身形, 進行形は不可)
③ 【S〈人〉・V・O〈*to do*〉】
He *continued to* work. 意味は②と同じ.
❷ 続く.

【S〈状態・動作・出来事〉・V(+副(句))】
The trial *continued* for three years. その裁判は3年間続いた.

❸ 引き続き…である.
【S〈人・物〉・V(*to be*) C〈名・形〉】
She still *continues* (*to be*) healthy. 彼女は依然として健康だ.

convenient 形 便利な, 都合のよい.

① 【S〈物・事〉is ～+*to* [*for*]+〈人・物・事・doing〉】
Please come to see me tomorrow morning if it is *convenient* to [*for*] you [×if you are *convenient*]. ご都合がよろしければあしたの朝お越しください.
My house is *convenient* to [*for*] the station. 私の家は駅に近くて便利だ.

② 【It is ～+*for*+〈人〉+*to do*】
Is it *convenient for* you *to* let me use your telephone now? 今電話お貸しいただいても都合が悪くありませんか.

③ 【It is ～+*to do* [*doing*]】
It is very *convenient to* have [hav*ing*] a supermarket so close. そんなに近くにスーパーマーケットがあるのは便利ですね.

④ 【It is ～+*that* 節】
It is very *convenient that* you have a supermarket so close. 意味は ③ と同じ.

convince 動 納得させる, 確信させる.

① 【S〈人・事〉・V・O〈人〉+*of*+〈事〉】
They *convinced* me *of* the importance of the problem. 彼らは私にその問題の重要性を納得させた. (受身=I was *convinced of* the importance of the problem.)

② 【S〈人・事〉・V・O〈人〉・O〈*that* 節〉】
They *convinced* me *that* the problem was important. 意味は ① と同じ. (受身=I was *convinced that* the problem was important.)

cook 動 料理する.

① 【S〈人〉・V・O〈食物・食事〉】
She *was cooking* the vegetables [the lunch]. 彼女は野菜を料理していた[昼食の支度をしていた].

② 【S〈人〉・V・O〈人〉・O〈食物・食事〉】
She *cooked* her son some meat. 彼女は息子に肉を料理してやった. (!)(1) この文型は「食物・食事」に焦点があり, ③ は「人」に焦点がある. (2) 受身形は ③ のようにする)

③ 【S〈人〉・V・O〈食物・食事〉+*for*+〈人〉】
She *cooked* some meat *for* her son. 意味は ② と同じ. (受身=Some meat *was cooked for* her son by her. for がなければ不可)

④ 【S〈人〉・V(+副(句))】
He *cooks for* himself. 彼は自炊している.
She sometimes *cooks with* her microwave oven. 彼女はときどき電子レンジで料理をする.

cost 動 (!通例受身形, 命令形は不可)

❶ (金が)かかる. (⇒take ❹)
① 【S〈金〉・V・O〈人〉・O〈金額・時間〉】
The taperecorder *cost* (me) fifty thousand yen. そのテープレコーダーは5万円した. (!×The taperecorder *cost* fifty thousand yen *for* [*to*] me. は不可)

② 【S〈*It*〉・V・O〈人〉・O〈金額・時間〉+*to do*】
It will *cost* (you) a lot of money *to* travel abroad. 海外旅行は高くつくでしょう.

③ 【S〈*doing*〉・V・O〈金〉】
Traveling abroad will *cost* a lot of money. 意味は ② と同じ.

④ 【S〈物・事〉・V・O〈金〉+*to do*】
The hotel *cost* 50 million dollars *to* build. そのホテルを建てるのに5,000万ドルかかった.

❷ (犠牲・代償を)払わせる.
【S〈物・事〉・V・O〈人・物〉・O〈犠牲・代償〉】
Swimming in that river may *cost* (you) your life. その川で泳ぐと命取りになりかねない.

count 動

❶ 数える.
① 【S〈人〉・V・O〈数・人・物〉】
He *counted* (the number of) the cars. 彼は車の数を数えた.

② 【S〈人〉・V(+副(句))】
He *counted* (up) *to* twenty. 彼は20まで数えた. (!count の後に up を伴うと「数え上げる」の意味になる)

❷ 勘定に入れる.
【S〈人〉・V・O〈人・物〉】
I didn't *count* the children. 子供たちを数に入れなかった.

❸ みなす. (書)
① 【S〈人〉・V・O〈人・物〉+*among*+〈人・物〉】
We *count* you *among* our family. 私たちは君を家族の一員とみなしている.

② 【S〈人〉・V・O〈人・物・事〉+(*as* [*for*]) C〈名・形〉】
We *count* you *as* a member of our family. 意味は ① と同じ. (!進行形は不可)

❹ 当てにする.
【S〈人〉・V+*on*+〈人・事・doing〉】
I *count on* you [your help]. 君[君の援助]を当てにしている. (!(1) 命令形, 進行形は可. (2) 通例受身形にしない)

courage 名 勇気.

【～+*to do*】 He had no *courage to* tell the truth. 彼は本当のことを言う勇気がなかった.

cover 動

❶ 覆う.
① 【S〈物〉・V・O〈物・人〉】
Snow *covered* the mountain. 雪が山を覆った. (受身=The mountain *was covered with* snow.)

② 【S〈人〉・V・O〈物〉+*with*+〈物〉】
They *covered* the wood *with* a tarpaulin. 彼らは木を防水シートで覆った. (受身=The wood *was covered with* a tarpaulin.)

❷ 含む, 及ぶ.
【S〈本・話〉・V・O〈範囲・問題〉】
This book *covers* Japanese folk tales. この本は日本の民話を取り扱っている.
His farm *covers* two square miles. 彼の農場は2平方マイルに及んでいる.

❸ (距離)行く.
【S〈人・車〉・V・O〈距離〉】
The party *covered* only 5 miles a day. 一行は一日に5マイルしか進まなかった. (!受身形は不可)

cruel 形 残酷な.

① 【S〈人〉 is ～+*to do*】
He was *cruel to* beat his little daughter. かわいい娘をなぐったとは彼もひどい男だ.

② 【It is ～ *of*+〈人〉+*to do*】

It was *cruel of* him *to* beat his little daughter.
意味は ① と同じ.

cry 動

❶ 泣く.
【S〈人〉・V(+*with* [*for*]+〈原因〉)】
The boy *cried with* [*for*] pain. その男の子は痛さのあまり泣いた.

❷ 叫ぶ.
① 【S〈人〉・V(+*out*)(+*for*+〈物・事〉)】
She *cried* (*out*) *for* help. 彼女は大声で助けを求めた. (⚠ ❶ と意味上まぎらわしいときは out を入れる)
② 【S〈人〉・V(+*out*)・O〈*that* 節〉】
He *cried* (*out*) *that* I was very stupid. 彼は私はとてもばかだと大きな声で言った. (⚠(1) 直接話法で書くと He *cried* (*out*), "You are very stupid." (2) 通例受身形にしない)

cure 動 治療する, 治す.

① 【S〈医者・薬〉・V・O〈病人・病気〉】
No medicine can *cure* this disease. どんな薬でもこの病気は治らない.
② 【S〈医者・薬〉・V・O〈病人〉+*of*+〈病気〉】
The doctor *cured* me *of* my appendicitis. 医者は私の虫垂炎を治療した.

curious 形

❶ 知りたがって.
① 【S〈人〉 is ~+*to* do】
I am *curious to* know how he fell in love with her. 彼がどのようにして彼女を見初めたのか知りたい.
② 【S〈人〉 is ~+*about* [*as to*]+〈物・事・人〉】
Children are *curious about* everything. 子供は何でも知りたがる.
③ 【S〈人〉 is ~(+*about* [*as to*])+*wh*- 節】
He is *curious* (*about*) *what* she looks like. 彼は彼女がどのような顔の人か知りたがっている.

❷ 不思議な, 変な.
① 【It is ~(+*for*+〈人〉)+*to* do】
It is *curious for* him *not to* be able to answer such an easy question. 彼がそんなやさしい質問に答えられないのは不思議だ.
② 【It is ~+*that* 節】
It is *curious that* he is [should be] unable to answer such an easy question. 意味は ① と同じ. (⚠ should を用いるのは《主に英》)

cut 動

❶ 切る.
① 【S〈人〉・V・O〈物〉(+*with*+〈道具〉)】
He *cut* his finger *with* a knife. 彼は誤ってナイフで指を切った. (⚠「故意に切った」の意味にもなる)
② 【S〈人〉・V・O〈人〉・O〈物〉】
She *cut* me six slices of bread. 彼女は私にパンを6切れ切ってくれた. (⚠(1) この文型は「物」に焦点があり, ③ は「人」に焦点がある. (2) 受身は ③ のようにする)
③ 【S〈人〉・V・O〈物〉+*for*+〈人〉】
She *cut* six slices of bread *for* me. 意味は ② と同じ. (受身=Six slices of bread *were cut for* me by her. for がなければ不可)
④ 【S〈人〉・V・O〈物〉・C〈形〉】
He *cut* his hair short. 彼は髪を短く刈った.
⑤ 【S〈人〉・V・O〈物〉+*in* [*into*]+〈片〉】
She *cut* the apple *in* two [*into* halves]. 彼女はリンゴを二つ[半分]に切った.

❷ 切れる.
【S〈刃物・物〉・V+副】
These scissors *cut* well. このはさみはよく切れる.
This rope doesn't *cut* easily. このロープは簡単には切れない.

❸ 短縮する, 削減する.
① 【S〈人〉・V・O〈物〉(+副(句))】
I *cut* my essay *from* five *to* four pages. 小論を5ページから4ページに縮めた.
They *cut* my wages *by* five percent. 彼らは私の賃金を5パーセント減らした.
② 【S〈人〉・V・O〈物〉・C〈形〉】
He *cut* his speech short. 彼は演説を短縮した.

danger 名 危険.

① 【~+*of* (+〈所有格〉)+*doing*】
There was a *danger of* his losing his life. (= He was in *danger of* losing his life.) 彼は命が危なかった.
② 【~+*that* 節】
There was a *danger that* he would lose his life. 意味は ① と同じ.

dangerous 形 危険な.

① 【S〈物・事〉 is ~(+*for*+〈人〉)+*to* do】
The lake is *dangerous* (*for* you) *to* swim in. その湖は(君が)泳ぐのは危険だ.
② 【It is ~+(*for*+〈人〉)+*to* do】
It is *dangerous* (*for* you) *to* swim in the lake. 意味は ① と同じ. (⚠ ×It is dangerous *that* you (should) swim in the lake./×You are dangerous *to* swim in the lake. は不可)

dare 動

❶ あえて[大胆にも]...する.
【S〈人〉・V・O(〈*to* do〉)】
I didn't *dare* (*to*) say such a thing to him. そんなことはあえて彼に言わなかった[言う勇気がなかった]. (⚠(1) 否定文, 疑問文では to がしばしば省略される. また否定文, 疑問文, if [whether] 節では dare が助動詞として使われることもあるこれは《主に英》: I *dared* not say such a thing to him. (2) 通例進行形不可)

❷ ...に立ち向かう, 勇敢にいどむ.《書》
【S〈人〉・V・O〈事〉】
He *dared* the danger of the lonely voyage. 彼は孤独な航海の危険を物ともしなかった. (⚠ 受身形は不可)

❸ ...してみろと挑む.
【S〈人〉・V・O〈人〉・C〈*to* do〉】
He *dared* me *to* jump from the roof. 彼は私に屋根から飛び降りれるものなら飛び降りてみろと言った. (⚠ to は省略できない)

deal 動

❶ 分配する, 配る.
① 【S〈人〉・V・O〈人〉・O〈物・事〉】
She *dealt* each player four cards. 彼女は各人にカードを4枚ずつ配った.
② 【S〈人〉・V(+out)・O〈物・事〉+*to*+〈人〉】
She *dealt* out four cards *to* each player. 意味は ① と同じ.

❷ (罰などを)与える.
【S〈人〉・V(+*out*)・O〈物・事〉(+*to*+〈人〉)】
The judge *dealt out* harsh sentences *to* the robbers. 裁判官はその強盗犯に厳しい判決を下した.

❸ (打撃を)与える.

① 【S〈人〉・V・O〈人〉・O〈打撃〉(+前・名)】
He *dealt* me a heavy blow *on* the cheek. 彼は私のほおに強打を見舞った．

② 【S〈人〉・V・O〈打撃〉+*at* [*to*]+〈人〉】
He *dealt* a punch *at* [*to*] me. 彼は私を一発なぐった．

❹ 扱う，処置する．
【S〈人・書物〉・V+*with*+〈問題・事柄〉】
We *dealt with* the difficulty immediately. 私たちはすぐの難局に当たった．(受身＝The difficulty *was dealt with* immediately.)
This book *deals with* Chinese history. この本は中国の歴史を扱っている．(受身＝Chinese history *is dealt with in* this book.)

❺ 取り引きする．
【S〈人・会社〉・V+*with*+〈人・会社〉】
They *deal with* this company. 彼らはこの会社と取り引きがある．(!受身形は不可)

❻ 商う．
【S〈人・店〉・V+*in*+〈商品〉】
That store *deals* mainly *in* stationery. あの店は主に文具を取り扱っている．(!受身形は不可)

decide 動

❶ 決心する．
① 【S〈人〉・V・O〈*to do*〉】
She *decided to* decline [×declining] his offer. 彼女は彼の申し出を断わろうと決心した．

② 【S〈人〉・V・O〈(*that*)節〉】
She *decided* (*that*) she would decline his offer. 意味は１と同じ．

❷ 決定する．
① 【S〈人〉・V・O〈*that*節〉】
They *decided that* the meeting (should) be put off till the next week. 彼らはその会合を翌週まで延期することに決めた．(受身＝It *was decided that* the meeting (should) be put off till the next week. ×The meeting was decided *to* be put off till the next week. は不可)(!*should* を用いるのは《主に英》)

② 【S〈人〉・V・O〈*wh-*節〉】
They *decided whether* or not he should go there [*whether* or not *to* go there]. 彼はそこへ行くかどうか決めた．

③ 【S・V+*on* [*against*]+〈事・物・*doing*〉】
We *have decided on* [*against*] the plan. 私たちはその計画を採用する[しない]ことに決めた．

❸ 判断する．
【S・V・O〈(*that*)節〉】
I *decided* (*that*) I could not do it myself. それは自分だけではできないと判断した．(!*to do* を用いて ×I decided not to do it myself. は不可)

decision 名 決定，結論；決心．

① 【〜+*to do*】
We arrived at [reached] the *decision to* put off the plan. われわれはその計画を延期することに決定した．

② 【〜+*that*】
He altered his *decision that* he would quit drinking. 彼は飲酒を止めようという決心を翻した．

③ 【〜+*wh-*節】
Have you made a *decision when* you should start [*when* to start]? いつ出発すればよいかをもう決めましたか．

delay 動

❶ 遅らせる．
【S〈事〉・V・O〈人・物・事〉】
The storm *delayed* the train for [×*by*] an hour. 暴風雨で汽車が１時間遅れた．(受身＝The train *was delayed* for an hour by the storm.)(!受身形で使われることが多い)

❷ (ある期間・無期限に)延期する．
【S〈人〉・V・O〈事・*doing*〉】
They *delayed* the announcement of [announc*ing*, ×to announce] his death until the next year. 彼らは彼の死の発表を翌年まで延ばした．

❸ 遅れる，ぐずぐずする．
【S〈人〉・V(+*on*+〈事〉)】 He *delayed on* his work. 彼はぐずぐずと仕事をした．(!「故意に」を含意することが多い)

demand 動

❶ 要求する．
① 【S〈人〉・V・O〈物・事〉(+*from* [*of*]+〈人〉)】
He *demanded* an explanation *from* [*of*] me. 彼は私に説明を求めた．

② 【S〈人〉・V・O〈*to do*〉】
He *demanded to* be explained. 彼は説明してくれと要求した．(!×He *demanded* me *to* give an explanation. は不可)

③ 【S〈人〉・V・O〈(*that*)節〉】
He *demanded that* I (should) give an explanation. 彼は私に説明してくれと言った．(受身＝It *was demanded that* I (should) give an explanation. ×I was demanded *to* give an explanation. は不可)(!*should* を用いるのは《主に英》)

❷ 必要とする．《書》
【S〈物・事〉・V・O〈時間・忍耐など〉】
This work *demands* a lot of time [patience]. この仕事は多くの時間[非常な忍耐力]を必要とする．(!通例進行形は不可)

❸ (強制的に)尋ねる．
【S〈人〉・V・O〈事・物・引用文〉】
The policeman *demanded* my name. 警官は私の名を尋ねた．
"What are you doing here?" he *demanded*. 「ここで何をしているのか」と彼は尋ねた．

deny 動

❶ 否定する．
① 【S〈人〉・V・O〈事〉】
He *denied* the rumor. 彼はそのうわさを否定した．

② 【S〈人〉・V・O〈*doing*〉】
They *denied* hav*ing* said anything about it. 彼らはそれについては何も言わなかったと言った．

③ 【S〈人〉・V・O〈*that*節〉】
They *denied that* they had said anything about it. 意味は②と同じ．(受身＝It *was denied that* they had said anything about it.)

❷ 与えない．
【S〈人〉・V・O〈人〉・O〈要求された物・事〉】
He *denied* his daughter nothing. 彼は娘に何でも与えることができるだろう．(＝He could *deny* nothing *to* his daughter.)

depend 動

❶ 頼る，当てにする．
① 【S〈人・国〉・V+*on* [*upon*]+〈人・物・事〉(+*for*+〈物・事〉)】 You can *depend on* him. 彼

当てにできる. (受身＝He can *be depended on*.)
Japan *depends on* Middle Eastern countries *for* oil. 日本は中東諸国に石油を依存している.

② 【S〈人〉・V＋*on*＋〈人〉＋*to do* [do*ing*]】
You may *depend on* him to give you advice [*on* his giving you advice]. 彼が助言してくれることを当てにしていい.

③ 【S〈人〉・V＋*on it*＋*that* 節】
You may *depend on it that* he will give you advice. 意味は②と同じ. (! on it の省略不可. it は that 節と同格)

❷ …次第である. (! 通例受身形, 進行形, 命令形は不可)
【S〈事・*It*〉・V＋*on* [*upon*]＋〈事・物・人・wh-節〉】
Everything *depends on* her intention. すべては彼女の意向による.
Whether you will succeed *depends on* your efforts. 君が成功するかどうかは努力次第だ.
It all *depends on how* much money is needed. すべてはどれくらいのお金がいるかによる. (! It (all) depends＋on＋wh-節 では on は省略可)

dependent 形
❶ 頼っている, 依存する.
【S〈人・国など〉 is ～＋*on*＋〈人・物・事〉(＋*for*＋〈事・物〉)】 I am not financially *dependent on* him. 私は金銭的に彼に頼っていない.
The children are totally *dependent on* their parents *for* support. その子供たちは何から何まで親の扶養に頼っている.
Japan is *dependent on* overseas countries *for* almost all the oil she needs. 日本は必要な石油をほとんど海外諸国に仰いでいる.

❷ …次第である.
【S〈未来の出来事〉 is ～＋*on*＋〈事〉】
Your success [Whether you succeed or not] is *dependent on* your efforts. 君が成功するか否かは努力次第で決まるよ.

describe 動
❶ 述べる, 描写する.
① 【S〈人〉・V・O〈物・事〉(＋*to*＋〈人〉)】
He *described* the present situation *to* me. 彼は私に現在の状況について話した. (! ×He described *about*…. は不可)

② 【S〈人〉・V(＋*to*＋〈人〉)・O〈wh-節句〉】
They *described to* me *what* they had seen. 彼らは私に見たものについて説明した. (受身＝It *was described to* me *what* they had seen.) (! ×They described me *what*…. は不可)

③ 【S〈人〉・V・O〈do*ing*〉】
He *described going* upstairs and find*ing* his father lying on the floor. 彼は2階へ上って父親が床に倒れているのを見つけた時の様子を話した.

④ 【S〈言葉・文章など〉・V・O〈事〉】
Words cannot *describe* the tragic event. 言葉ではその惨劇は言い表わせない. (受身＝The tragic event cannot *be described by* [*in*] words.) (! (1) 進行形, 命令形は不可. (2) ① の文型を用いて We cannot *describe* the tragic event *in words*. ともいえる)

❷ 言う, 評する.
【S〈人〉・V・O〈人・物・事〉・*as*〈形・名〉】
I cannot *describe* him *as* diligent [a scholar]. 彼が勤勉[学者]だとは言えない.

desire 動 (! 通例進行形, 命令形は不可)

❶ 強く望む.
① 【S〈人〉・V・O〈物・事〉】
Her parents *desired* happiness for her. 彼女の両親は彼女の幸福を強く望んでいた.

② 【S〈人〉・V・O〈*to do*〉】
They desperately *desired to* win the game. 彼らは何が何でもその試合に勝ちたかった.

❷ …してほしいと願う[言う].
【S〈人〉・V・O〈人〉＋*to do*】
The President *desired* them *to* reopen negotiations. 大統領は彼らに交渉を再開してほしいと言った.

desire 名 欲望, 願望, 要望.

① 【～＋*to do*】
The government should meet the people's *desire to* have their own houses. 政府はマイホームを持ちたいという国民の要望をかなえるべきだ.

② 【～＋*of*＋*doing*】
The government should meet the people's *desire of* having their own houses. 意味は①と同じ. (! ①の文型の方が普通)

③ 【～＋*that* 節】
The government should meet the people's *desire that* they (should) have their own houses. 意味は①と同じ. (! should を用いるのは《主に英》)

determine 動
❶ 決心する.
① 【S〈人〉・V・O〈*to do*〉】
He *determined to* leave at once. 彼はすぐに出発しようと決心した.

② 【S〈人〉・V・O〈*that* 節〉】
He *determined that* he would leave at once. 意味は①と同じ.

❷ 決心させる.
【S〈物・事〉・V・O〈人〉＋*to do*】
What *determined* you *to* become a teacher? どうして教師になる決心をしたのですか.

❸ 決定する.
① 【S〈人・物・事〉・V・O〈物・事〉】
The exam results could *determine* our career. 試験の結果が私たちの職業を決定することもある.

② 【S〈人・物・事〉・V・O〈*wh-*節句〉】
The board of education *determined what* was to be done first. 教育委員会は最初に何をなすべきかを決めた.

die 動
❶ 死ぬ.
① 【S〈人・動物〉・V(＋*of* [*from*]＋〈原因〉)】
He *died of* cancer [*from* wounds]. 彼はがんで[けががもとで]死んだ. (! (1) 通例 of は病気などの内的原因を, from は外的原因を表わす. with は不可. (2) 「死ぬほど…する」の意味でも用いる: I'm *dying of* thirst. のどが渇いて死にそうだ)

② 【S〈人・動物〉・V・C〈形・名〉】
He *died* young [happy; *as*) a beggar]. 彼は若死にした[幸福のうちに死んだ; 死んだときは乞食であった]. (! (1) He *died* happily. は「幸せな死に方をした」の意. 「老齢が原因で死んだ」は He died *of* old age. とする. (3) C に名詞が来るときには前に as を伴うことがある)

❷ 次第に弱まる, 消える.
【S〈物・事〉・V】

Our traditions will *die*. 私たちの伝統は次第に消えるだろう。
The flame *is dying*. 炎が消えそうだ。

differ 動

❶ 異なる.
【S〈人・物・事〉・V(+*from*+〈人・物・事〉)(+*in*+〈名・doing・that* 節〉)】 My brothers *differ* widely *in* their tastes. 私の兄弟たちは好みがまるで異なっている. (! 進行形は不可)
My brother *differs from* me *in that* he is patient. 兄は忍耐強いという点で私とは違っている.

❷ 意見が違う.
【S〈人〉・V+*with*+〈人〉(+*about* [*on*]+〈物・事〉)】 He *differs with* me *about* that matter. 彼はその問題に関しては私と意見が違う. (! He and I *differ on* that matter. ともいえる)

different 形 異なった, 違った.

【S〈人・物・事〉is ~+*from* [《主に米》*than*, 《英》*to*]+〈人・物・事〉】Rabbits are *different from* [*than, to*] hares. 飼いウサギは野ウサギと違う.
The building was *different* in size *than* [*from* what] I had expected. その建物は私が予期していたのとは大きさが違っていた. (! このような場合は than の方が簡潔に表現できるという利点がある)

difficult 形

❶ 困難な.
① 【It is ~(+*for*+〈人〉)+*to do*】
It is *difficult* (*for* us) *to* learn Russian. 私たちがロシア語を習得するのは難しい. (! ×It is *difficult that* we (should) learn Russian./×We are difficult to learn Russian. は不可)
② 【S〈物・事〉is ~(+*for*+〈人〉)+*to do*】
Russian is *difficult* (*for* us) *to* learn. 意味は ① と同じ.

❷ 気難しい.
【S〈人〉is ~+*to do*】
He is *difficult to* get on with. (=It is *difficult to* get on with him.) 彼はつき合いにくい人だ.

difficulty 名 困難.

① 【~(+*in*)+doing】
I have *difficulty* (*in*) memorizing English words. 私は英単語がなかなか覚えられない. (! この構文では doing の前の in は通例省略される. ただし no, little などの否定詞や great などの限定語がつくときはあまり省略されない)

② 【~+*of*+doing】
It is impossible to exaggerate the *difficulty of* mastering any foreign language. どんな外国語でも, ものにすることはいかに困難かは, 強調しても強調しすぎることはない.

③ 【~+*that* 節】
There is a *difficulty that* the lack of hospital beds obliges us to wait for a vacancy. 病院のベッドが不足しているので空くのを待たざるを得ないという障害がある.

dig 動

❶ 掘る.
① 【S〈人〉・V+副(句)】
He *is digging in* the garden. 彼は庭を掘っている.
② 【S〈人〉・V・O〈地面・穴〉(+前・名)】
They *dug* the ground [a hole *in* the yard]. 彼らは地面[庭に穴]を掘った.

❷ 掘り出す.
【S〈人〉・V(+*up* [*out*])・O〈作物・埋蔵物〉】
He *dug* (*up* [*out*]) potatoes. 彼はジャガイモを掘り出した.

direct 動

❶ 指揮する.
【S〈人〉・V・O〈人・事〉】
He *directed* a research project. 彼は研究計画を指揮した.

❷ 指図する.
① 【S〈人〉・V・O〈人〉・C(*to do*)】
The court *directed* her *to* pay a fine. 裁判官は彼女に罰金を払うよう命令した.
② 【S〈人〉・V・O〈*that* 節〉】
The court *directed that* she (should) pay a fine. 意味は ① と同じ. (! should を用いるのは《主に英》)

❸ 道を教える.
【S〈人〉・V・O〈人〉(+副(句))】
Could you *direct* me *to* the station? 駅への道を教えていただけますか.

❹ 向ける.
【S〈人〉・V・O〈注意・目・歩みなど〉+副(句)】
They *directed* their steps *toward* home. 彼らは家路についた.

disagree 動

❶ 一致しない, 意見が合わない.
① 【S〈人〉・V+*with*+〈人〉+*about* [*on, over, as to*]+〈事〉】 I *disagree with* him *about* what to do [*on* that point]. 私は何をすべきについて[その点に関して]彼と意見が一致しない.
② 【S〈報告・陳述など〉・V+*with*+〈物・事〉】
His answer to the question *disagrees with* hers. 彼のその質問の答えは彼女の答えと一致しない.

❷ 〈風土・食べ物が〉人に合わない.
【S〈風土・食物など〉・V+*with*+〈人〉】
Oysters *disagree with* him. カキは彼の体質には合わない.

disappoint 動

❶ 失望させる.
【S〈人・事〉・V・O〈人〉】
Her answer *disappointed* him. 彼女の返事は彼を失望させた.

❷ 失望する. (! 受身形で)
① 【S〈人〉be ~ed+*at* [*about, in, with*]】
I *was disappointed at* her absence. 彼女が不在なのでがっかりした.
I *was disappointed in* her. 彼女には失望した.
I *am disappointed with* my new car. 私の新車にはがっかりした.
(! at は原因・理由, in は人・人の行為, with は物・人に用いられる)
② 【S〈人〉be ~ed+*that* 節】
He *was disappointed that* he lost the game. 彼は試合に負けてがっかりしていた.
③ 【S〈人〉be ~ed+*to do*】
We *were disappointed to* hear that he lost the game. 私たちは彼がその試合に負けたと聞いてがっかりした.

discover 動 発見する.

① 【S〈人〉・V・O〈人・物〉】
He *discovered* another satellite around

Saturn. 彼は土星の周りにもう一つ衛星があることを発見した.
② 【S〈人〉・V・O〈(that) 節〉】
They *discovered that* the teacher was very strict. 彼らはその先生が大変厳しいことが分かった. (受身＝It *was discovered that* the teacher was very strict.)
③ 【S〈人〉・V・O〈wh- 節・句〉】
Did you *discover how to* solve the puzzle? そのパズルの解決法が分かりましたか.
I *discovered who* had given the present. 私はだれがその贈り物をくれたか分かった.
④ 【S〈人〉・V・O〈人・物〉・*to* be C〈名・形〉】
They *discovered* the teacher *to be* very strict. 意味は ② と同じ. (❗② の文型の方が普通)
⑤ 【S〈人〉・V・O〈人・物〉・C〈*doing*〉[*done*]】
I *discovered* my mother rea*ding* my diary [our house ransack*ed*]. 私は母が私の日記を読んでいるところを[家が荒らされているのを]見つけた.

discuss 動 議論する.

① 【S〈人〉・V・O〈事・物・*doing*〉(＋*with*＋〈人〉)】
He *discussed* the plan *with* his secretary. 彼はその計画について秘書と話し合った. (❗×He discussed *about* [*on*] the plan.... は不可)
We *discussed* sell*ing* [×to sell] the car. 私たちは車を売ることを話し合った.
② 【S〈人〉・V・O〈*wh-* 節・句〉】
We *discussed whether to* [*whether* we should, ×*that* we should] accept the proposal. 私たちはその提案を受け入れるかどうか話し合った. (❗*that* 節 は不可)

divide 動

❶ 分割する, 分ける.
① 【S〈人・物・事〉・V・O〈物・人・事〉(＋*into*＋〈部分〉)】 The teacher *divided* the class *into* [×*in*] three groups. 先生はクラスを 3 つのグループに分けた. (受身＝The class *was divided into* three groups by the teacher.) (❗二つに分けるときは *in* two [*half*] という)
② 【S〈人〉・V・O〈物〉(＋*between* [*among*]＋〈人々〉)】 She *divided* the cookies *between* [*among*] the children. 彼女は子供たちにクッキーを分けた. (❗通例 *between* は 2 人の間で, *among* は 3 人以上の間で分けるときに使う)

❷ 分裂させる.
【S〈物・事〉・V・O〈人・団体・意見〉】
A difference of opinion *divided* the committee. 意見の相違で委員会が分裂した.
The committee *was divided* (*in* opinion) *over* [*on*] the issue. その件について委員会は意見が分かれていた. (❗このように受身形で使うことも多い)

❸ 割る.
【S〈人〉・V・O〈数〉＋*by*＋〈数〉】
Divide 16 *by* 2. 16 を 2 で割りなさい. (❗*Divide* 2 *into* 16. ともいう)

do 動

❶ する, 行なう, 遂行する.
① 【S〈人〉・V・O〈仕事・任務など〉】
He *did* nothing [a lot of work] today. 彼は今日何もしなかった[たくさん仕事をした].
He *did* his duty. 彼は義務を果たした.
② 【S〈人〉・V(＋副(句))】
He *did* as I said. 彼は私の言うとおりにした.

❷ ...を終える. (❗通例完了形で)
【S〈人〉・V・O〈事・*doing*〉】
I *have done* eat*ing*. 食事は済ませた. (受身＝Eat*ing* is *done*.)

❸ もたらす, 与える.
① 【S〈人・物〉・V(・O〈人〉)・O〈利益・害〉】
This medicine will *do* you good. この薬を飲めばよくなるでしょう. (❗(1) この文型は「利益・害」に焦点があり, ② は「人」に焦点がある. (2) O〈人〉は文脈から明らかな場合や一般の人の場合には省略可)
② 【S〈物・事〉・V・O〈利益・害〉＋*to*＋〈人〉】
This medicine will *do* good *to* you. 意味は ① と同じ.

❹ 作る.
【S〈人〉・V・O〈作品・料理など〉】
Can you *do* five copies of this report? この報告書のコピーを 5 部作ってくれますか.
Who *is doing* the food for the party? そのパーティーの食べ物はだれが作ることになっているのですか.

❺ やっていく.
【S〈人・事〉・V＋副】
He *is doing* well in his business [at school]. 彼は事業がうまくいっている[学校の成績がよい]. (❗(1) 前例は His business *is doing* well. ともいえる. (2) 副詞は well, badly が多い)

doubt 動 疑う. (❗通例進行形は不可)

① 【S〈人〉・V・O〈人・事〉】
I *doubt* his sincerity. 彼が誠実であるかどうか疑わしい.
② 【S〈人〉・V・O〈*doing*〉】
I *doubt* his be*ing* sincere. 意味は ① と同じ.
③ 【S〈人〉・V・O *whether* [*if*] 節〉】
I *doubt whether* [*if*] he is sincere. 意味は ① と同じ. (❗(1) 肯定文でのみ用いる. (2) *if* の方が口語的)
④ 【S〈人〉・V・O〈*that* 節〉】
I don't *doubt that* he will keep his promise. 彼はきっと約束を守ってくれると信じて疑わない. (❗主に否定文, 疑問文で用いる. 肯定文中で用いると強い不信を表わす)

doubt 名 疑い.

① 【～＋*of*(＋〈所有格〉)＋*doing*】
I have no *doubt of* his be*ing* sincere (＝his sincerity). 私は彼が誠実であることを疑わない.
② 【～＋*that* 節〉】
I have [There is] no *doubt that* he is sincere. 彼が誠実であることを私は疑わない[ことは疑いない]. (❗*that* 節は否定文, 疑問文で用いられるが, 肯定文で用いると疑いよりも強い不信を表わす)
③ 【There is some ～＋(*about* [*as to*])＋*whether*】 There is some *doubt* (*about* [*as to*]) *whether* he is telling the truth. 彼が本当のことを言っているのかどうか少しあやしい. (❗There is some *doubt if* ... ともいえる)

draw 動

❶ 引く, 引き寄せる.
【S〈人〉・V・O〈人・物〉(＋副(句))】
He *drew* his bed *to* [*toward*] the window. 彼はベッドを窓の方へ引き寄せた.

❷ (線を)引く, (線で)描く.
① 【S〈人〉・V・O〈線・人・物〉】
She *drew* a line [a tree] on the paper. 彼女は紙に線を引いた[木を描いた].
② 【S〈人〉・V・O〈人〉・O〈地図・絵など〉】
The child *drew* me a picture. (＝The child

基本文型　2000

drew a picture *for* me.) その子供は私に絵を描いてくれた.

❸ 引き出す.
【S〈人〉・V・O〈物・事〉(+*from* [*out of*]+〈源〉)】
What conclusion did he *draw from* the report? 彼はその報告からどんな結論を出したのですか.
He *drew* all his money *from* [*out of*] the bank. 彼は金を全額銀行からおろした.

❹ 〈注意・関心を〉引きつける.
【S〈人・物・事〉・V・O〈人・注意・関心など〉(+*to*+〈物・事〉)】The event *drew* people's attention *to* this problem. その事件で人々の関心がこの問題に向いた.

❺ 近づく.
【S〈人・車・時〉・V+副(句)】
The car *drew near* the building. 車は建物に近づいて来た.
The vacation *is drawing to* an end. 休みが終わりに近づいている.

dream 動

❶ 夢を見る.
① 【S〈人〉・V+*about* [*of*]+〈人・物・事〉】
I *dreamed about* [*of*] my school days. 学生時代の夢を見た. (❗単に「夢を見る」は of, 具体的な内容を含む場合は about が普通)
② 【S〈人〉・V+(*that*) 節】
I *dreamed* (*that*) I was flying. 空を飛んでいる夢を見た. (❗that は省略されることが多い)
③ 【S〈人〉・V・O〈a+形+*dream*〉】
I *dreamed* a strange *dream*. 変な夢を見た. (❗形がない場合は不可: ×I dreamed a dream.)

❷ 夢に描く, 空想する.
【S〈人〉・V+*of* [*about*]+〈事・*doing*〉】
He *dreams of* becoming an engineer. 彼は技師になることを夢見ている. (❗この意味では of の方が普通)

❸ 思う. (❗否定文で)
① 【S〈人〉・V+*of*+*doing*】《話》
I wouldn't *dream of* winning the prize. その賞がもらえるなんて夢にも思っていない. (❗現在の考えを述べるときは would [should, could] を伴う)
② 【S〈人〉・V・O〈(*that*) 節〉】
I never *dreamed* (*that*) I would see her again. 彼女にまた会うとは夢にも思わなかった. (❗《書》では Never did I *dream*.... も可)

dream 名

❶ (睡眠中の)夢.
① 【〜+*of* [*about*] (+所有格・目的格)+*doing*】
I had a *dream of* a burglar breaking into my house. 私は泥棒が家に押し入った夢を見た.
② 【〜+*that* 節】
I had a *dream that* a burglar broke into my house. 意味は ① と同じ.
③ 【〜+*in which* [*where*] 節】
I had a *dream in which* [*where*] a burglar broke into my house. 意味は ① と同じ.

❷ 空想, 理想, 願望.
① 【〜+*of*+*doing*】
My *dream of* visiting Peru was fulfilled at last. ペルーを訪れたいという私の夢はついに実現した.
② 【〜+*to do*】
My *dream to* visit Peru was fulfilled at last. 意味は ① と同じ.
③ 【〜+*that* 節】
My *dream that* I would visit Peru was fulfilled at last. 意味は ① と同じ.

drink 動　飲む

① 【S〈人〉・V・O〈飲み物〉】
I *drank* coffee with milk [two glasses of beer]. コーヒーにミルクを入れて[ビールを2杯]飲んだ.
② 【S〈人〉・V・O・C〈形〉】
I *drank* the tea *cold*. 紅茶を冷たくして飲んだ.
③ 【S〈人〉・V(+副(句))】
He *drinks* too much. 彼は飲みすぎる. (❗通例「酒を飲む」の意味)

drive 動

❶ 運転する.
① 【S〈人〉・V・O〈車〉】
Can you *drive* a truck? あなたはトラックを運転できますか.
② 【S〈人〉・V(+副(句))】
He always *drives* carefully. 彼はいつも慎重に運転する.

❷ 車で送る.
【S〈人〉・V・O〈人〉+副(句)】
I'll *drive* him *home* [*to* the station]. 彼を家[駅]まで車で送ろう.

❸ 追いやる.
【S〈人〉・V・O〈動物・人〉+副(句)】
They *drove* the cattle *to* [*out of*] the shed. 彼らは牛を小屋へ駆り立てた[小屋から追い出した].

❹ (ある状態)にする.
【S〈事〉・V・O〈人〉・C〈形〉】
The noisy music *drives* me *mad*. そのやかましい音楽で気が変になりそうだ.

❺ 駆り立てて...させる.
① 【S〈事〉・V・O〈人〉・C〈*to do*〉】
Despair *drove* him *to* commit suicide. 絶望のあまり彼は自殺した.
② 【S〈事〉・V・O〈人〉+*into doing*】
Despair *drove* him *into* committing suicide. 意味は ① と同じ.
③ 【S〈事〉・V・O〈人〉+*to*+〈事〉】
Despair *drove* him *to* suicide. 意味は ① と同じ.

drop 動

❶ 落ちる, したたる.
【S〈物・液体〉・V(+前+名)】
The dictionary *dropped off* the desk. 辞書が机から落ちた.
Blood *dropped from* his finger. 血が彼の指からしたたり落ちた.

❷ 倒れる.
【S〈人〉・V+(*to* [*on*]+〈手足〉)】
The boxer *dropped to* his knees. ボクサーはがっくりとひざをついた.

❸ 下がる, 低下する.
【S〈数量・価値・勢い〉・V】
The wind [His temperature] *dropped*. 風がないだ[彼の体温が下がった].

❹ 落とす, したたらせる.
【S〈人〉・V・O〈物・液体〉】
He *dropped* the pen to the floor. 彼は床にペンを落とした. (❗偶然・故意の両意可能)

❺ 下げる, 低下させる.
【S〈人・事〉・V・O〈数量・価値・勢い〉】
He *dropped* his voice. 彼は声を落とした.
What *has dropped* the water level? どうして水位が下がったのか.

drown 動

❶ 溺(ﾞ)死する.
【S〈人・動物〉・V】
He *drowned* in a pond. 彼は池でおぼれて死んだ.

❷ 溺死させる.
【S〈人〉・V・O〈人・動物〉】
He *was drowned* in a pond. 意味は ❶ と同じ. (**!** 《米》では「彼は(だれかに)溺死させられた」の意味でも用いる) / He *drowned himself* in the river. 彼は川に投身自殺をした.

❸ 浸す.
【S〈人〉・V・O〈物〉+*in* [*with*]+〈物〉】
She *drowned* her pancakes *in* syrup. 彼女はパンケーキをシロップに浸した.

eager 形

❶ 切望して.
① 【S〈人〉 is ~+*for*+〈物・事〉】
He is *eager for* success. 彼は成功を強く望んでいる.
② 【S〈人〉 is ~+*to do*】
He is *eager to* be a doctor. 彼は医師になりたがっている.
③ 【S〈人〉 is ~+*for*+〈名〉+*to do*】
He is *eager for* his son *to* be a doctor. 彼は息子にぜひ医師になってもらいたいと思っている.
④ 【S〈人〉 is ~+*that* 節】《書》
He is *eager that* his son (should) be a doctor. 意味は③と同じ. (**!** should を用いるのは《主に英》)

❷ 熱心な.
【S〈人〉 is ~+*in*+〈事・doing〉】
She is very *eager in* her studies [*in* studying]. 彼女はとても勉強熱心だ.

earn 動

❶ もうける, かせぐ.
【S〈人〉・V・O〈金など〉】
He *earns* 500 dollars a week as a salesperson. 彼は店員として週に500ドルかせぐ.
He *earns* his living [livelihood] by farming. 彼は農業で生計を立てている.

❷ 評価を得る, 得させる.
① 【S〈人〉・V・O〈評価・名声〉】
He *earned* a reputation as a good conductor. 彼は名指揮者としての名声を得た.
② 【S〈事〉・V・O〈人〉・O〈評価・名声〉】
His superb performance *earned* him their praise. 彼の名演奏は彼らの賞賛を得た.

easy 形

❶ (物事が)容易な.
① 【S〈事・物〉 is ~+*for*+〈人〉】
This job is *easy for* me. この仕事は私にはやさしい.
② 【It is ~(+*for*+〈人〉)+*to do*】
It is *easy* (*for* me) *to* learn English. (私には)英語は習得しやすい. (**!** ×It is easy *that* I (should) learn English. は不可)
③ 【It is ~+*doing*】
It is *easy* (×my) learn*ing* English. 英語は習得しやすい.
④ 【S〈物・事〉 is ~(+*for*+〈人〉)+*to do*】
English is *easy* (*for* me) *to* learn. 意味は② と同じ. (**!** ×*I* am easy to learn English. は不可)

❷ (人が)...しやすい.
【S〈人〉 is ~ (+*for*+〈人〉)+*to do*】
She is *easy* (*for* me) *to* get on with. (=It is *easy for* me *to* get on with her.) 彼女は(私には)つき合いやすい人だ.

eat 動 食べる.

① 【S〈人・動物〉・V・O〈食物・食事〉】
He *eats* vegetables [breakfast at seven] every morning. 彼は毎朝野菜を食べる[7時に朝食を取る].
② 【S〈人・動物〉・V(+〈副(句)〉)】
They *ate* out [*with* chopsticks]. 彼らは外食した[はしで食べた].

effect 名

❶ 結果, 効果.
【~+*of*+*doing*】
Her victory had the *effect of* restor*ing* her confidence in herself. その勝利の結果, 彼女は自信を取り戻した.

❷ 趣旨.
【*to the* ~+*that* 節】
I received a letter *to the effect that* he was coming home soon. 間もなく彼が帰国するむねの手紙を受け取った.

elect 動 (投票で)選ぶ.

① 【S〈複数の人〉・V・O〈役職〉】
They *elected* the captain last week. 彼らは先週主将を選んだ.
② 【S〈複数の人〉・V・O〈人〉・(*as* [*to be*])・C〈役職〉】
They *elected* him (*as* [*to be*]) mayor. 彼らは彼を市長に選んだ. (受身=He *was elected* (*as* [*to be*]) mayor. (**!** C が一人の人によって占められる役職の場合は通例無冠詞)
③ 【S〈複数の人〉・V・O〈人〉+*to*+〈議会・役職など〉】
They *elected* him *to* the Diet. 彼らは彼を国会議員に選んだ.

encourage 動 励ます, 勇気づける.

① 【S〈人・物・事〉・V・O〈人〉】
His words *encouraged* me. 彼の言葉で力づけられた.
② 【S〈人・物・事〉・V・O〈人〉・C〈*to do*〉】
The teacher *encouraged* me *to* try again. 先生は私にもう一度やってみるように励ましてくれた. (**!** この文型はこれからすることについて用い, ③は今していることについて用いる)
③ 【S〈人〉・V・O〈人〉+*in*+〈事〉】
He *encouraged* her *in* her studies. 彼は彼女にその調子で研究を続けるように激励した.

end 動

❶ 終わる.
【S〈事〉・V(+*with*+〈事〉[*in*+〈状態・結果〉])】
The story *ends with* the hero's death. その物語は主人公の死で終わっている.
Our plan *ended in* failure. 私たちの計画は失敗に終わった.

❷ 終わらせる.
【S〈人〉・V・O〈物・事〉(+*with*+〈物・事〉[*by*+*doing*])】
He *ended* his speech *with* a joke. 彼は冗談を言って演説をしめくくった.
They *ended* the party *by* sing*ing* a song. 彼らは歌を歌ってパーティーを終えた.

enjoy 動 楽しむ.

① 【S〈人〉・V・O〈物・事〉】
We *enjoyed* the game very much. そのゲームはと

基本文型 2002

ても楽しかった. (! very much の位置は enjoyed の前も可)
② 【S〈人〉・V・O〈doing〉】
We *enjoyed* skating [× to skate] on the lake. 湖の上でスケートを楽しんだ. (! 受身形は不可: × Skating on the lake was enjoyed (by us). ただし, S〈doing〉*is enjoyed* by many people. は可能)

enough 形 十分な.

① 【S〈物・事〉・V・～ (+*for*+〈人・事〉)】
A bottle of whiskey is not *enough for* them all. 彼ら全員でウイスキー 1 本では足りない.
② 【S〈人・動物・事〉・V・～+图 (+*for*+〈人〉)(+*to do*)】 I don't have *enough* time *to* read. 私は読書をするだけの時間がない.
My father sent *enough* money *for* me *to* buy a bicycle. 父は自転車が十分買える金を私に送ってくれた.
③ 【There be+～+图 (+*for*+〈人〉)(+*to do*)】
There are *enough* seats *for* 100 people *to* sit on. 100 人の人が座れるだけのいすがある.

enter 動 入る, 加わる.

① 【S〈人・物〉・V・O〈場所〉】
He *entered* the building. 彼はその建物に入った. (!(1) ここで × enter into は不可. (2) 受身形は可: × The building was entered (by him). ただし,「押し入る」などの場合は可: The Bank *was entered by* robbers. その銀行は強盗に入られた)
② 【S〈人〉・V・O〈団体・職業・競技〉】
He *entered* a university [the teaching profession] last year. 彼は去年大学に入った[教職に就いた]. (! 受身形は不可)
③ 【S〈人・物〉・V (+圖(句))】
He *entered without* knocking. 彼はノックもせずに入ってきた.
A bird *entered at* [*by, through*] the open window. 鳥が開いた窓から入ってきた.
④ 【S〈人〉・V+*into*+〈事〉】
I *entered into* a discussion with them. 彼らと議論を始めた. (! 受身形は可)

envy 動 うらやむ, 羨(ﾔﾏ)望する.

① 【S〈人〉・V・O〈人〉(+*for* [*because of*]+〈物・事〉)】 We *envy* him *for* his success. 彼の成功がうらやましい.
② 【S〈人〉・V(・O〈人〉)・O〈物・事〉】
We *envy* (him) his success. 意味は ① と同じ. (受身=He *is envied* his success.) (!(1) O〈人〉を入れると意味が強くなる. (2) × His success is envied him. の受身形は不可)

escape 動 (! 通例受身形は不可)

❶ 逃げる.
【S〈人・動物〉・V+(*from* [*out of*]+〈場所・人〉)】
He *escaped from* prison [the pursuers]. 彼は脱獄した[追跡者から逃れた]. (! *escape* prison とすれば刑務所入りをまぬがれること)
❷ 漏れる.
【S〈気体・液体〉・V+*from*+〈物〉】
Water *is escaping from* the pipe. 水がパイプから漏れている.
❸ 逃れる.
① 【S〈人・動物〉・V・O〈危険・病気など〉】
He narrowly *escaped* death [the danger]. 彼はあやうく死[危険]をまぬがれた. (! しばしば narrowly, barely などの副詞を伴い,「かろうじて」の意味が加わる)
② 【S〈人・動物〉・V・O〈doing〉】
The baby *escaped being* [× to be] burned to death. 赤ん坊は焼死をまぬがれた. (! doing は通例 being+過去分詞)

examine 動

❶ 調査する, 調べる.
① 【S〈人〉・V・O〈物・事〉】
They *examined* my bag carefully. 彼らは注意深く私のかばんを調べた.
② 【S〈人〉・V・O〈*wh*- 節〉】
He *examined how* the money had been used. 彼はその金がどのように遣われたかを調査した.
❷ 診察する.
【S〈医者〉・V・O〈人・体〉】
The doctor *examined* the patient [injury]. 医者は患者を診察した[傷口を調べた].
❸ 試験をする.
【S〈教師〉・V・O〈学生〉+*in* [*on*]+〈学科〉】
Mr. Kato *examined* the students *in* English [*on* articles]. 加藤先生は生徒に英語[冠詞]の試験をした. (! 通例 in は学科, on はその他)

example 名 模範.

① 【～+*that* 節】
I am a living *example that* the handicapped can enjoy life as much as healthy people. 私は障害者も健常者と同様に人生を楽しめるという生きた手本です.
② 【～+*to*+〈人〉】
His bravery is a good *example to* us all [*for* us *to* follow]. 彼の勇敢さは私たちみんなの[が見習うべき]良い手本だ. (! 不定詞が続くときは for)

exchange 動 交換する.

① 【S〈人同士〉・V・O〈複数の物・事〉】
The newly married couple *exchanged* rings. 新婚の夫婦は指輪を交換した.
② 【S〈人〉・V・O〈複数の物〉+*with*+〈人〉】
I *exchanged* name cards [a few words] *with* him. 彼と名刺を交換した[二言三言言葉をかわした].
③ 【S〈人〉・V・O〈物〉+*for*+〈物〉】
He *exchanged* a one-dollar bill *for* [× with] four 25-cent coins. 彼は 1 ドル札を 25 セント硬貨 4 枚と両替した.

excite 動

❶ 興奮させる.
① 【S〈物・事〉・V・O〈人〉】
The news *excited* all the villagers. その知らせに村人たちはみんな興奮した. (受身=All the villagers *were excited by* [*at, over*] the news.)
② 【S〈人〉・V・O〈人〉+*about*+〈事〉】
I *excited* my children *about* [× with] *going to* the zoo. 動物園へ行くと言うと子供たちはわくわくした. (受身=My children *were excited about* [× with] *going to* the zoo.)
❷ (感情を)起こさせる.
① 【S〈人〉・V・O〈感情〉】
His behavior *excited* her anger. 彼の行動は彼女を怒らせた.
② 【S〈人・物・事〉・V・O〈人〉+*to*+〈感情・行為〉】
His behavior *excited* her *to* anger. 意味は ① と同じ.

③ 【S〈人・物・事〉・V・O〈人〉+*to do*】
His behavior *excited* her *to get* angry. 意味は①と同じ.

excuse 動

❶ 許す.
① 【S〈人〉・V・O〈行為・所有格+do*ing*〉】
I *excused* his mistakes. 私は彼の過ちを大目に見た.
Please *excuse* my disturb*ing* [×excuse *that* I disturb(ed)] you. おじゃましてすみません.
② 【S〈人〉・V・O+*for*+〈行為・do*ing*〉】
I *excused* him *for* his mistakes. 意味は①の第1文と同じ.
Please *excuse* me *for* disturb*ing* [×*to* disturb] you. 意味は①の第2文と同じ.

❷ 言い訳をする. (🗋 通例受身形は不可)
① 【S〈人〉・V・O〈*oneself*〉+*for*+〈行為・do*ing*〉】
He *excused* himself *for* his absence [*for being* late]. 彼は欠席[遅れたこと]の言い訳をした.
② 【S〈人・物・事〉・V・O〈行為・態度〉】
Nothing can *excuse* his rudeness. 彼の無礼を弁解できるものは何もない.

❸ 免除する. (🗋 通例受身形で用いる)
【S〈人〉be ~ed (+*from*)+〈義務など〉】
He *was excused from* military service. 彼は兵役を免除された. (🗋 *from* の省略は《主に英》)

excuse 名 言い訳, 理由.

① 【~+*for*+do*ing*】
What was your *excuse for* leav*ing* early? 君が早退した理由は何でしたか.
② 【~+*to do*】
What was your *excuse to* leave early? 意味は①と同じ.
③ 【~+*that* 節】
She made an *excuse that* she had to do housework for her sick mother. 彼女は病気の母の代わりに家事をしなければならなかったのだと言い訳をした.

expect 動

❶ 予期する, …すると思う.
① 【S〈人〉・V・O〈人・物・事〉】
We didn't *expect* him at the meeting. 私たちは彼が会いに来るとは思っていなかった. (受身=He *wasn't expected* at the meeting.)
We *are expecting* a big typhoon. 大型の台風が来そうだ.
② 【S〈人〉・V・O〈人・物・事〉・C〈*to do*〉】
We *expect* him *to* come [the train *to* be delayed]. 私たちは彼が来るもの[列車が遅れるもの]と思っている. (受身=He *is expected to* come [The train *is expected to* be delayed].)
③ 【S〈人〉・V・O〈(*that*) 節〉】
We *expect* (*that*) he will come [the train will be delayed]. 意味は②と同じ. (受身=It *is expected* (*that*) he will come [the train will be delayed].) (🗋 (1) *that* 節中の時制は未来. (2) *that* はしばしば省略される)
④ 【S〈人〉・V・O〈*to do*〉】
We *expect to* work [×working] with him. 私たちは彼といっしょに働くつもりだ.

❷ 期待する, …して欲しいと思う.
① 【S〈人〉・V・O〈物・事〉+*of* [*from*]+〈人〉】
My mother *expects* too much *of* [*from*] me. 母は私に期待をかけすぎる.
② 【S〈人〉・V・O〈人〉・C〈*to do*〉】
We *expect* the students *to* study harder. 生徒たちにもっと勉強してほしいと思っている. (受身=The students *are expected to* study harder.)
③ 【S〈人〉・V・O〈(*that*) 節〉】
We *expect* (*that*) the students will study harder. 意味は②と同じ. (受身⇒❶③)

experience 名 経験.

① 【~+*of* [*in*]+do*ing*】
I have ten years' *experience of* [*in*] teaching Japanese. 私は10年間日本語を教えた経験がある. (🗋 *in* は特定専門分野における経験を表わす)
② 【~+*to do*】
He doesn't have enough *experience to* set up as a doctor. 彼は医者を開業するには経験不足だ.
③ 【~+*that* 節】
I had the *experience that* I woke up not knowing where I was. 私は目を覚ますと自分がどこにいるのか分からないという経験をした.

explain 動 説明する.

① 【S〈人〉・V・O〈物・事〉(+*to*+〈人〉)】
They *explained* the situation *to* me. 彼らは私に状況を説明した. (受身=The situation *was explained to* me.) (🗋 (1) ×They explained me the situation. は通例不可. (2) O が長いときは *to*+〈人〉が先に来る: They *explained to* me the present situation in teaching Japanese. (彼らは私に日本語教育の現状を説明してくれた))
② 【S〈人〉・V(+*to*+〈人〉)・O〈*that* 節・*wh-* 節/句〉】
They *explained* (*to* me) *that* they could not adopt my plan. 彼らは(私に)私の計画を採用できないと説明した. (受身=It *was explained* (*to* me) *that* they could not adopt my plan.) (🗋 ×They explained me *that*…. は不可)
They *explained* (*to* me) *what to* do with the problem. 彼らは(私に)その問題をどう処理すればよいのかを説明した. (受身=It *was explained* (*to* me) *what to* do with the problem.)

express 動 表現する.

① 【S〈人〉・V・O〈思想・意見・感情〉(+*to*+〈人〉)】
He *expressed* his ideas [thanks] *to* us. 彼は私たちに自分の考え[感謝の言葉]を述べた.
② 【S〈人〉・V(+*to*+〈人〉)・O〈*wh-* 節〉】
I cannot *express how* sad I am [×*that* I am sad, ×"How sad I am!"]. 言葉で言い表わせないくらい悲しい. (🗋 通例否定文で. また *that* 節や引用文は不可)
③ 【S〈人〉・V・O〈*oneself*〉】
He can *express* himself correctly in English. 彼は自分の考えを英語で正確に述べることができる.

fact 名 事実.

① 【~+*that* 節】
The *fact that* the rumor is false cannot be denied. そのうわさがうそであることは否定できない.
② 【~+*of* (+〈所有格・目的格〉)+do*ing*】
The *fact of* the rumor be*ing* false cannot be denied. 意味は①と同じ. (🗋 ×the fact+*for*+名+*to do*… は不可)
③ 【The ~ is (*that*) …】
The *fact* is (*that*) [《話》*Fact* is(,)] the rumor is false. 実はそのうわさはうそだ.

fail 動 (🗋 通例受身形は不可)

❶ 失敗する.
【S〈人〉・V+*in*+〈事業・試験〉】

He *failed in* his business [the examination]. 彼は事業に失敗した[試験に落ちた]. (**!**「試験に落ちる」の場合は in を省略することが多い. ⇒❺)
❷ (健康などが)衰える.
【S〈人・健康・視力〉・V】
My eyesight *is failing*. 視力が落ちてきている.
❸ …しない, …できない.
【S〈人〉・V+*to do*】
He *failed to* do his duty [understand it]. 彼は義務を怠った[それが理解できなかった].
❹ 役に立たない.
【S〈物・事・人〉・V・O〈人〉】
The machine *failed* me when I needed it. その機械は必要なときに動かなかった.
❺ 落第する, (試験に)落ちる.
【S〈人〉・V・O〈学科・試験〉】
He *failed* English and history. 彼は英語と歴史で落第点を取った.

faith 图 信念, 確信.

【~+*that* 節】
I have *faith that* he is innocent. 彼は無罪だと確信している.

fall 動

❶ 落ちる.
【S〈物・人〉・V(+前+名)】
A pen *fell off* the desk. ペンが机から落ちた.
He *fell from* the roof [*into* the pond]. 彼は屋根から[池の中へ]落ちた.
❷ 倒れる, ころぶ.
【S〈人・木・建物〉・V(+副句))】
He *fell* to the floor. 彼は床の上に倒れた.
The tree *fell* (over) *in* the storm. あらしでその木が倒れた.
❸ 垂れ下がる.
【S〈髪など〉・V+*over* [*to*]+〈肩など〉】
Her hair *falls over* her shoulders. 彼女の髪は肩に垂れている.
❹ 下がる, 減る.
【S〈値段・温度・数量〉・V(+副句))】
Prices will *fall*. 物価が下がるだろう.
The temperature *fell* three degrees. 温度が3度下がった.
❺ …になる.
【S〈人・物・事〉・V・C〈形〉】
She *fell* ill [silent; asleep]. 彼女は病気になった[黙った; 寝入った]. (**!** C に比較級は不可: ×She fell more silent.)

familiar 形

❶ よく知られている.
【S〈物・事〉 is ~ *to*+〈人〉】
This proverb is *familiar to* us. このことわざはわれわれにはなじみがある.
❷ …をよく知っている, …に精通している.
【S〈人〉 is ~ *with*+〈事〉】
We are *familiar with* this proverb. われわれはこのことわざをよく知っている.
❸ …と親しい, なれなれしい.
【S〈人〉 is ~ *with*+〈人〉】
I am *familiar with* your father. 君のお父さんをよく知っています.

famous 形 有名な, 名高い.

① 【S〈人・物・事〉 is ~+*for*+〈物・事・*doing*〉】
Kyoto is *famous for* its shrines and temples. 京都は神社仏閣で有名です. (**!**×*It* is famous *that* Kyoto has many shrines and temples./× That Kyoto… is famous. などは不可)
A.G. Bell is *famous for* having invented the telephone. ベルは電話の発明で有名である.
② 【S〈人・物〉 is ~+*as*+〈人・物〉】
He is *famous as* a novelist. 彼は小説家として有名である.
Venice is *famous as* a city built on water. ベニスは水の都として有名である.

fear 動 (**!** 進行形は通例不可)

❶ 恐れる.
【S〈人〉・V・O〈人・物・事・*to do*・*doing*〉】
He didn't *fear* death [*to* die, dy*ing*]. 彼は死を恐れなかった.
❷ こわくて…できない.
【S〈人〉・V・O〈*to do*〉】
He *feared* to go into the cave. 彼はこわくてほら穴の中に入って行けなかった.
❸ 心配する, …ではないかと思う.
【S〈人〉・V・O〈(*that*) 節〉】
They *feared* (*that*) they would have a bad crop. 彼らは不作になるのではないかと心配した. (受身=It *was feared* (that) they would have a bad crop.) (**!** that はしばしば省略される)
I *fear* (*that*) he won't come. 彼は来ないのではないかと思う.

fear 图 不安, 心配.

① 【~+*of*(+所有格)+*doing*】
There is no *fear of* his fail*ing* again. 彼が再度失敗する恐れはない.
② 【~+*that* 節】
There is no *fear that* he will [《書》may] fail again. 意味は ① と同じ.

feed 動

❶ 食物を与える, 養う.
① 【S〈人〉・V・O〈動物・人・家族〉】
She *fed* her baby with a spoon. 彼女はスプーンで赤ん坊に食べ物を与えた.
He *feeds* his parents. 彼は両親を扶養している.
② 【S〈人〉・V・O〈人・動物〉・O〈食べ物・えさ〉】
They *fed* the boy bread and soup. 彼らはその少年にパンとスープを与えた. (受身=The boy *was fed* bread and soup.)
③ 【S〈人〉・V・O〈人・動物〉+*on*+〈食べ物・えさ〉】
They *fed* the dog *on* meat. 彼らはその犬に肉を与えた. (受身=The dog *was fed on* meat.) (**!** 主として《英》) (**!** この文型は「食べ物」に重点があり, ④ は「人・動物」に重点がある)
④ 【S〈人〉・V・O〈食べ物・えさ〉+*to*+〈人・動物〉】
They *fed* meat *to* the dog. 意味は ③ と同じ. (**!** 主として《米》)
❷ 物を食べる.
【S〈動物〉・V】
A horse *was feeding* in the meadow. 馬が草地で草を食べていた.

feel 動

❶ 感じる. (**!** ①, ② は進行形は不可)
① 【S〈人〉・V・O〈痛み・打撃・感情〉(+前+名)】
I *felt* a sharp pain *in* my back. 背中に激しい痛みを感じた.
I *felt* pity *for* the old man. その老人を気の毒に思った.

② 【S〈人〉・V・O〈人・物・事〉・C〈do・doing〉】
I *felt* the building (×to) shake. 建物が揺れるのを感じた. (**!**(1) 揺れの最後までを感じたことを意味する. (2) 受身では to が必要: The building *was felt to* shake.)
I *felt* the building shaking. 建物が揺れているのを感じた. (受身=The building *was felt* shaking.) (**!** 揺れが続いているのを感じたことを意味する)
③ 【S〈人〉・V・O・C〈形〉】
I *feel* happy [better] today. 今日は気分が浮き浮きする[だいぶ気分がよい]. (**!** I'm *feeling*.... としても意味は同じ.)
❷ (物が)...の感じがする. (**!** 進行形は不可)
① 【S〈物〉・V・C〈形〉】
This cloth *feels* soft. この布は肌ざわりがよい.
② 【S〈物〉・V・C〈like+〈物・事〉〉】
This cloth *feels like* silk. この布は絹のような手ざわりがする.
❸ さわる, 触れる. (**!** 進行形は可)
【S〈人〉・V・O〈物・人・事・*if* 節・*wh-* 節〉】
Feel the car seat. It's wet. 車のシートをさわってごらん. ぬれているよ.
Feel how cold this is. これがどんなに冷たいかさわってごらん.
❹ 手探りで捜す. (**!** 進行形は可)
【S〈人〉・V・O [*after*] +〈物〉】
He *felt* [*was feeling*] *for* the keyhole in the dark. 彼は暗がりの中手探りで鍵穴を捜した.
❺ (人が)(何となく)...であると感じる, まるで...のような気がする. (**!** 進行形は不可)
① 【S〈人〉・V・O〈(*that*) 節〉】
I *felt* (*that*) he was not satisfied. 私は彼が満足していないと感じた. (受身=It *was felt that* he was not satisfied.)
② 【S〈人〉・V・O・(*to be*) C〈形〉】
He *felt* the work (to be) difficult. 彼はその仕事は難しいと感じた.

fight 動 戦[闘]う, 争う.
① 【S〈人・国〉・V・*against* [*with*] +〈敵〉】
He *fought against* [*with*] his older brother. 彼は兄とけんかした. (**!** (1) against の方が敵対の意味が強く出る. (2) with の場合は「...に味方して」の意味にもなる. (3) 次のようにも用いる: I *fought with* him *against* the robber. 彼と協力して強盗と戦った.)
② 【S〈人〉・V・O〈病気など〉】
He *is fighting* a serious disease. 彼は難病と戦[闘]っている.
③ 【S〈人〉・V・*for* +〈事〉】
They *fought for* their freedom. 彼らは自由を求めて戦った.
④ 【S〈人〉・V・*to do*】
They always *fight to* win. 彼らは常に勝つために戦う.
⑤ 【S〈複数の人〉・V (+*over* [*about*] +〈物・事・人〉)】 They *are fighting over* trifles. 彼らはつまらないことで争っている.

fill 動
❶ 満たす, あふれる.
① 【S〈人・物〉・V・O〈場所・時間〉(+*with* +〈物・人・事〉)】
Young people *filled* the theater. 若者が劇場を埋め尽くした. (受身=The theater *was filled with* young people.)
He *filled* the bathtub *with* hot water. 彼は浴槽に湯を入れた. (受身=The bathtub *was filled with* hot water.)
② 【S〈人・物・事〉・V・O〈人・心など〉+*with* +〈感情〉】 His story *filled* her *with* admiration. 彼の話を聞いて彼女の心は感嘆の念でいっぱいになった.
❷ 満ちる, いっぱいになる.
【S〈場所・物〉・V (+*with* +〈物・人〉)】
The bottle *filled with* water. びんは水でいっぱいになった.

find 動 (**!** 通例進行形は不可)
❶ 見つける.
① 【S〈人〉・V・O〈物・人〉】
I *found* the missing book. 紛失した本が見つかった.
② 【S〈人〉・V・O〈人〉・O〈物・事〉】
They *found* me a good job. 彼らは私にいい仕事口を見つけてくれた. (**!** (1) この文型は「物・事」に焦点があり, ③ は「人」に焦点がある. (2) 受身⇒ ③)
③ 【S〈人〉・V・O〈物・事〉+*for* +〈人〉】
They *found* a good job *for* [×to] me. 意味は ② と同じ. (受身=A good job *was found for* me. for がなければ不可)
④ 【S〈人〉・V・O〈人〉・O〈C〈形〉・*doing*・*done*〉】
We *found* the man dead [*sleeping*; *killed*]. 私たちはその男が死んでいる[眠っている; 殺されている]のを見つけた. (受身=The man *was found* dead [*sleeping*; *killed*].)
❷ 探り出す.
【S〈人〉・V (+*out*)・O〈事・*wh-* 節句〉】
They *found* (*out*) a good method [*how to* solve the problem]. 彼らはよい方法[問題の解決法]を探り出した.
❸ 分かる.
① 【S〈人〉・V・O〈人・物・事〉・(*to be*)・C〈名・形・*doing*・*done*〉】 We *found* him (*to be*) a liar. 彼がうそつきだと分かった. (受身=He *was found to be* a liar.) (**!** (1) C が doing の場合は to be は省略する. (2) C が名詞の場合の受身形では to be を省略しない)
I *have found* the book interesting [*the door locked*]. その本がおもしろい[ドアに鍵がかかっている]と分かった.
I *found* it difficult to get on with her. 私は彼女と仲良くやっていくのは難しいと分かった. (**!** it は to 以下を受ける形式目的語)
② 【S〈人〉・V・O〈(*that*) 節〉】
We *found* (*that*) he was a liar. 意味は ① の第 1 例と同じ. (受身=It *was found that* he was a liar.)

finish 動
❶ 終える, すます.
【S〈人〉・V・O〈物・事・*doing*〉】
Have you *finished* your work yet? もう仕事を済ませましたか.
I *have* just *finished* cleaning [×to clean] the room. その部屋の掃除をたった今終えた.
❷ 仕上げる.
【S〈人〉・V・O〈物〉】
He *finished* the desk in red paint. 彼は机に赤いペンキを塗って仕上げた.
❸ 終わる.
【S〈人・物・事〉・V (+〈画(句)〉)】
The baseball game *finished at* ten. 野球の試合は 10 時に終わった.

She *finished* first in the 100-meter dash. 彼女は100メートル競争で1等になった.

fit 動

❶ (大きさ・型が)合う.
【S〈物・事〉・V・O〈人・物〉】
This shirt doesn't *fit* me. It's too tight. このシャツは私には合わない. きつすぎる. (!(1) 通例受身形, 進行形は不可. (2) O が明らかな場合は省略可)
He *fits* this task well. 彼はこの仕事にぴったりだ.

❷ 合わせる.
【S〈人〉・V・O〈物〉+*into*+〈物など〉】
We *fitted* the fridge *into* that space. 私たちはあの場所に冷蔵庫をはめ込んだ.

❸ 取り付ける.
【S〈人〉・V・O〈物〉+前+名】
I *fitted* a telephone *in* my room. 私は部屋に電話をつけた.
The room *is fitted with* a carpet. 部屋にはカーペットが敷いてある.

fit 形 適当な, 適した.

① 【S〈物・事・人〉 is ~+*for*+〈人・物・事・doing〉】
This dictionary is *fit for* high school students. この辞書は高校生に適している.
The beach is *fit for* swimming. その海辺は水泳に適している.

② 【S〈人・物・事〉 is ~(+*for*+〈人・物・事〉)+*to do*】 The water is not *fit* (*for* us) *to* drink. その水は(われわれが)飲むのに適さない.

③ 【It is ~ *for*+〈人・物・事〉+*to do*】
It is not *fit for* you *to* scold so much. 君がそんなにがみがみ言うのはよくないよ.

fix 動

❶ 固定する.
【S〈人〉・V・O〈物〉(+*to* [*in*, *on*]+〈物〉)】
He *fixed* a pole *to* the tree [*in* the ground]. 彼はさおを木にしっかりくくりつけた[地面にしっかり立てた].

❷ 定める.
① 【S〈人〉・V・O〈日時・場所〉(+*for*+〈行事〉)】
They *fixed* the date *for* the ceremony. 彼らは式の日取りを決めた.
② 【S〈人〉・V・O〈価格〉(+*at*+〈金額〉)】
We *fixed* the price *at* 10,000 yen. その値段を1万円に決めた.
③ 【S〈人〉・V・O〈*wh*-節句〉】
We *have fixed where* to stay. 私たちはどこに泊まるか決めた.

❸ じっと見つめる.
① 【S〈人〉・V・O〈目・注意など〉+*on* [*upon*]+〈人・物〉】 He *fixed* his eyes *on* the photograph. 彼はその写真をじっと見すえた.
② 【S〈人〉・V・O〈人〉+*with*+〈視線など〉】
He *fixed* me *with* a cold look. 彼は冷たい目で私をじっと見つめた.

❹ 修理する. 《話》
【S〈人〉・V・O〈物〉】
They *fixed* my car. 彼らは私の車を直してくれた.

❺ 用意する.
【S〈人〉・V・O〈人〉・O〈食事・食物・飲み物〉】
I'll *fix* you a drink. (= I'll *fix* a drink *for* you.) あなたに飲み物を用意しましょう.

fly 動

❶ 飛ぶ, 飛行機で行く.
【S〈鳥・飛行機・人など〉・V(+副句)】
Our plane [We] *flew from* London *to* Paris. 私たちが乗った飛行機[私たち]はロンドンからパリまで飛んだ.
The ball *flew over* the fence. ボールは垣根を飛び越えた.

❷ 飛ぶように走る[過ぎる].
【S〈人・時間など〉・V(+副句)】
He *flew down* the stairs. 彼は急いで階段を下りた.
Time *flies*. 光陰矢の如し.

❸ 突然動いて…の状態になる.
【S〈ドアなど〉・V・C〈形〉】
The door *flew* open [shut]. ドアが突然開いた[閉まった].

❹ 飛ばす, 揚げる.
【S〈人〉・V・O〈鳥・旗・気球など〉】
We *flew* a national flag [a balloon]. 私たちは国旗[気球]を揚げた.

follow 動

❶ ついて行く[来る].
【S〈人・動物〉・V・O〈人・動物・動く物〉】
The dog *followed* me into the alley. 犬は私について路地に入って来た.

❷ 続いて起こる.
【S〈事〉・V・O〈事〉】
A fire *followed* the explosion. 爆発に続いて火事が起こった. (受身=The explosion *was followed by* a fire.)

❸ …に従う.
【S〈人〉・V・O〈忠告・指示など〉】
He didn't *follow* my advice [instruction]. 彼は私の忠告[指示]に従わなかった.

❹ 従事する.
【S〈人〉・V・O〈職業〉】
He *follows* teaching profession. 彼は教職にたずさわっている.

❺ 理解する.
【S〈人〉・V・O〈言葉・話など〉】
I don't *follow* the plot at all. 私には話の筋がまったく分からない.

❻ 当然…ということになる.
【S〈*It*〉・V(+*from*+〈事〉)+*that* 節】
It follows from this fact *that* he is innocent. この事実からすれば彼は無実ということになる. (! It は that 節を受ける形式主語)

fond 形 …が好きだ.

【S〈人〉 is ~+*of*+〈人・物・事・doing〉】
He is *fond of* his mother [apples; read*ing*]. 彼は母[リンゴ; 読書]が好きだ.
He grew [became] very *fond of* golf. 彼はゴルフが大好きになった. (! ×(*very*) *much fond of*+O や × *fond of*+O+(*very*) *much* は不可)

foolish 形 愚かな.

① 【S〈人〉 is ~+*to do*】
You were *foolish to* say a thing like that. そのようなことを言うとは君もばかだった.(! You が非難の対象)

② 【It is ~+*of*+〈人〉+*to do*】
It was *foolish of* you *to* say a thing like that. 意味は ① と同じ. (! you と行為の両方が非難の対象)

③ 【It is ~+*for*+〈人〉+*to do*】
It was *foolish for* you *to* say a thing like that. 君がそのようなことを言ったのは愚かだった. (! 行為だ

けが非難の対象)

force 動
❶ 強制して…させる.
① 【S〈人·事〉·V·O〈人〉·C〈to do〉】
They *forced* me *to* help them. 彼らは無理やりに私を手伝わせた. (受身=I *was forced to* help them.) (❗受身形は「…せざるを得ない」の意味になることがある: I *was forced to* sell my house. 私は家を売らざるを得なかった)
② 【S〈人·事〉·V·O〈人〉·*into*+*doing*】
They *forced* me *into* helping them. 意味は①と同じ.
③ 【S〈人〉·V·O〈物〉·C〈形〉】
Robbers *forced* the safe open. 泥棒は金庫をこじあけた. (❗×force the safe to be open は不可)
❷ 強要する, 押しつける.
【S〈人〉·V·O〈事·物〉·*on* [*upon*]+〈人〉】
He *forced* his opinion *on* his friends. 彼は友達に自分の意見を押しつけた.

forget 動
❶ 忘れる.
① 【S〈人〉·V·O〈事〉】
I *forget* his name. 彼の名前を忘れた. (❗「思い出せない」を意味する. I *have forgotten*…. よりこの方が普通)
② 【S〈人〉·V·O〈*doing*〉】
I shall never *forget* visiting [× to visit] New York last spring. この前の春にニューヨークを訪れたときのことはけっして忘れないだろう. (❗(1) 通例否定文, 疑問文で. (2) 過去のことについて「…したことを忘れる」の意味で用いる. ⇨③)
③ 【S〈人〉·V·O〈*to do*〉】
I *forgot to* buy [× buying] the ticket. 切符を買うのを忘れていた. (❗未来のことについて「…するのを忘れる」の意味で用いる. ⇨②)
④ 【S〈人〉·V·O〈(*that*)節·*wh*-節句〉】
I *forgot* (*that*) I had an appointment with him. 彼と会う約束があったのを忘れていた.
I *forget where* I put my glasses. 私はメガネをどこに置いたか思い出せない.
❷ 持って来るのを忘れる.
【S〈人〉·V·O〈物〉】
I *forgot* my handbag. ハンドバッグを忘れてきた. (❗場所を表わす副詞(句)は伴わない. ⇨leave ❸)

forgive 動 許す.
① 【S〈人〉·V·O〈人·言行など〉】
He didn't *forgive* my mistakes. 彼は私の過ちを許してくれなかった.
② 【S〈人〉·V·O〈人〉+*for*+*doing*】
He *forgave* me *for breaking* his watch. 彼は私が時計をこわしたことを許してくれた. (❗この形の方が …*for having* broken his watch より普通)

fortune 名 運.
【~+*to do*】
I had the good *fortune to* find a suitable job. 私は幸運にも適職が見つかった.
He had the bad *fortune to* have a traffic accident. 彼は運悪く交通事故にあった.

free 形
❶ 自由な.
【S〈人〉is ~+*to do*】
You are *free to* ask questions. 君たちは自由に質問してよろしい. (❗× It is *free for* you *to* ask questions. は不可. また × It is *free that* you ask questions. も不可)
❷ …のない.
① 【S〈人·物·事〉is ~+*of*+〈税金·料金など〉】
I am *free of* debt. 私には借金がない.
② 【S〈人·物·事〉is ~+*from*+〈苦痛·不快なもの〉】
This country is *free from* pollution. この国には公害がない.

frighten 動
❶ おびえさせる, ぎょっとさせる.
【S〈人·物·事〉·V·O〈人〉】
The story *frightened* the children. その話を聞いて子供たちはおびえた. (受身=The children *were frightened* by [*at*, × *to hear*] the story.) (❗受身形で用いることが多い)
❷ おどして…させる[やめさせる].
【S〈人·事〉·V·O〈人〉+*into* [*out of*]+*doing*】
He *frightened* me *into* obeying him [*out of* driving a car]. 彼は私をおどして従わせた[車の運転をやめさせた]. (受身=I *was frightened* by him *into* obeying him [*out of* driving a car].)
❸ おびえる. (❗受身形で)
① 【S〈人〉be ~ed+*to do*】
I *was frightened to* see a stranger approach. 私は見知らぬ人が近づいて来るのを見てこわかった.
② 【S〈人〉be ~ed+*that*】
We *were frightened that* the river would flood our house. 私たちは川が氾らんして家が浸水するのではないかと心配した.
③ 【S〈人〉be ~ed+*of*+*doing*】
She *was frightened of* being left by herself in the house. 彼女は1人で家に残されるのがこわかった.

full 形 いっぱいの.
【S〈場所·物·人〉is ~+*of* [*with*]+〈人·物·事〉】
When I arrived at the concert hall, it had already been *full of* [× *with*] an avid audience. 私が演奏会場に着いたときはもう熱心な聴衆で満員だった.
He was *full of* confidence when he started for the entrance examination. 彼が入試を受けに出かけたときは自信満々だった.
The garden was *full* (up) *with* fallen leaves. 庭は落ち葉でいっぱいだった. (❗full with… は内容よりもその状態を強調した言い方. また full up のときは常に with を用いる)

furnish 動
❶ 備えつける, (家具を)入れる.
【S〈人〉·V·O〈家·部屋〉+*with*+〈家具·備品〉】
They *furnished* the room *with* a refrigerator. 彼らはその部屋に冷蔵庫を入れた. (受身=The room *was furnished with* [*by*] a refrigerator.) (❗受身形で「…が備えつけられている」の意味で使われることが多い)
❷ 供給する.
【S〈人〉·V·O〈人〉+*with*+〈物·情報など〉】
We *furnished* the victims *with* food and clothes. (=We *furnished* food and clothes *for* victims.) 私たちは被災者に食料と衣類を供給した.

gain 動
❶ 得る, かせぐ.

【S〈人・物〉・V・O〈物・事〉】
He *gained* a good profit on the stock market [a reputation as a novelist]. 彼は株でかなりもうけた[小説家として名声を得た].
He *gains* his living by working part-time. 彼はアルバイトをして生活費をかせいでいる.

❷ (速度，重量などを)増す.
【S〈人・物〉・V・O〈速度・重量など〉】
The train *gained* speed. 列車は速度を上げた.
I *have gained* two kilograms in weight. 体重が2キロふえた.

❸ (時計が)進む.
【S〈時計〉・V・O〈時間〉】
My watch *gains* two minutes a day. 私の時計は日に2分進む. (⚠ My watch *gains by* two minutes a day. ともいえる)

gather 動
❶ 集める.
【S〈人・物〉・V・O〈人・物〉】
He *gathered* sufficient data. 彼は十分な資料を集めた.

❷ 集まる.
【S〈人・物〉・V(＋前＋名)】
The children *gathered around* the table. 子供たちはテーブルの周りに集まった.

❸ 収穫する，摘む.
【S〈人・物〉・V・O〈作物・花など〉】
They *gathered* strawberries in the field. 彼らは畑でイチゴを摘んだ.

❹ 次第に増す.
【S〈人・車〉・V・O〈速度・勢いなど〉】
The train *was gathering* speed. 列車はしだいにスピードを上げていた.

❺ 推測する.
【S〈人〉・V・O〈(that)節〉】
I *gathered* from his letter (*that*) his mother had been ill. 彼の手紙から，私は彼の母親は病気なのだと推測した. (⚠ 進行形不可)

generous 形 気前がよい，寛大な.
① 【S〈人〉 is ～＋*to*＋〈人〉】
He is always *generous to* poor people. 彼はいつも貧しい人に気前よく物を与える.

② 【S〈人〉 is ～＋*with*＋〈物〉】
He is *generous with* his money. 彼は気前よく金を出す.

③ 【S〈人〉 is ～＋*in*＋(*doing*)】
He is *generous in* giving his money. 意味は②と同じ.

④ 【S〈人〉 is ～＋*to do*】
You are *generous to* let us use your room free. ただで部屋を貸してくださるとは気前がよいですね.

⑤ 【It is ～＋*of*＋〈人〉＋*to do*】
It is *generous of* you to let us use your room free. 意味は④と同じ.

get 動
❶ 得る，手に入れる，買う. (⚠ 受身形は不可)
① 【S〈人〉・V・O〈物・事〉】
He *got* a good job with the company. 彼はその会社でいい職を得た.
Where did you *get* that information? どこからその情報を得たのか.

② 【S〈人〉・V・O〈人〉・O〈物〉】
I *got* my son an interesting book. 息子におもしろい本を買ってやった. (⚠ この文型は「物」に焦点があり，③は「人」に焦点がある)

③ 【S〈人〉・V・O〈物〉＋*for*＋〈人〉】
I *got* an interesting book *for* my son. 意味は②と同じ.

❷ 受け取る. (⚠ 受身形・命令形は不可)
【S〈人〉・V・O〈物・金・許可など〉】
I *got* a letter from him [a lot of money for the work]. 彼から手紙を受け取った[その仕事をしてたくさんのお金をもらった].

❸ 取ってくる. (⚠ 受身形は不可)
① 【S〈人〉・V・O〈物〉】
I'll *get* something to eat. 何か食べ物を取ってこよう.

② 【S〈人〉・V・O〈人〉・O〈物〉】
Will you *get* me the newspaper? 新聞を取ってきてもらえませんか. (⚠ この文型は「物」に焦点があり，③は「人」に焦点がある)

③ 【S〈人〉・V・O〈物〉＋*for*＋〈人〉】
Will you *get* the newspaper *for* me? 意味は②と同じ.

❹ 理解する.
【S〈人〉・V・O〈人・言葉など〉】
He didn't *get* the joke. 彼にはその冗談が分からなかった.
I didn't quite *get* what he said. 私は彼の言うことがよく聞き取れなかった.

❺ …させる，…してもらう. (⚠ 受身形は不可)
① 【S〈人〉・V・O〈人〉・C〈*to do*〉】
I *got* him *to* repair my car. 彼に車を直させた[直してもらった]. (⚠「努力して[説得して]…させる」という意味)

② 【S〈人〉・V・O〈人・物〉・C〈*doing*〉】
I *got* the engine running. エンジンを始動させた.

③ 【S〈人〉・V・O〈物〉・C〈*done*〉】
I must *get* my hair cut. 髪を切ってもらわなくてはならない.

❻ 着く.
【S〈人・乗り物〉・V＋前 [*to*＋〈場所〉]】
We *got* there [home] *at* five. 私たちは5時にそこ[家]に着いた.
We *got to* the station a little before five. 私たちは5時少し前に駅に着いた.

❼ …になる.
【S〈人・物・事〉・V・C〈形・*done*〉】
He *got* angry [tired; drunk]. 彼は怒った[疲れた; 酔った]. (⚠ ❽と違って done は通例形容詞化したもので，受身的意味を持たない)
Things *are getting* better. 事態は好転している.

❽ …される.
【S〈人・物・事〉・V・C〈*done*〉】
He *got* punished [scolded; dismissed]. 彼は罰せられた[しかられた; 解雇された]. (⇒❼)

❾ …するようになる.
【S〈人〉・V・C〈*to do*〉】
Soon they *got to* love each other. すぐに二人は愛し合うようになった.

give 動
❶ 与える，渡す，(助言・祝福を)述べる.
① 【S〈人〉・V・O〈人〉・O〈物・事〉】
They *gave* me some money. 彼らは私にいくらかお金をくれた. (受身＝I *was given* some money. / Some money *was given to* me.) (⚠ (1) この文型は「物・事」に焦点があり，②は「人」に焦点がある. (2) 受身形で前者は「物・事」に，後者は「人」に焦点がある)
Will you *give* him this letter? この手紙を彼に渡し

てもらえませんか.
I'll *give* you my home address. 私の自宅の住所を教えます。(！S・V・O+to+O への書き換えは可)
② 【S〈人〉・V・O〈物・事〉+*to*+〈人〉】
They *gave* some money *to* me. 意味は①の第1例と同じ。(⇨①！)
Please *give* my best wishes *to* your parents. ご両親によろしくお伝えください.
❷ (感情・苦痛などを)生じさせる.
【S〈人・事・物〉・V・O〈人〉・O〈事〉】
His delay *gave* us a lot of trouble. 彼が遅れたことで大変な迷惑をこうむった。(！S・V・O+to+O への書き換えは不可)
❸ (病気を)うつす.
【S〈人〉・V・O〈人〉・O〈病気〉】
He *has given* me his cold. 彼は私に風邪をうつした。(！O〈病気〉が特定されている場合は He *has given* his cold to me. も可。×He *has given* a cold to me. は不可)
❹ (動作を加える.
【S〈人〉・V・O〈人・物〉・O〈行為〉】
I *gave* him a kick [the door a push]. 彼をけった[ドアを押した]。(！S・V・O+to+O への書き換えは不可)
❺ 催す.
① 【S〈人・団体〉・V・O〈人〉・O〈パーティーなど〉】
We *gave* him a welcome party. 私たちは彼のために歓迎会を催した。(！この文型は「物・事」に焦点があり、② は「人」に焦点がある)
② 【S〈人・団体〉・V・O〈パーティーなど〉+*for*+〈人〉】
We *gave* a welcome party *for* him. 意味は①と同じ.
❻ (声・音を)発する.
【S〈人・物〉・V・O〈声・音〉】
She *gave* a cry of joy. 彼女は喜びの叫び声を上げた.

glad 形
❶ うれしい.
① 【S〈人〉 is ～+*to do*】
I'm very *glad to* see you again. 再会できて大変うれしい.
② 【S〈人〉 is ～+*of* [*about*]+〈事〉】
I am *glad of* [*about*] the news of his success. 彼の成功の知らせを聞いて喜んでいる.
③ 【S〈人〉 is ～+(*that*) 節】
I am *glad (that)* you passed the exam. 私はあなたが試験に合格してうれしい.
❷ 喜んで[快く]...する。(！通例 ...will be glad ...で)
【S〈人〉 is ～+*to do*】
I'll be (only too) *glad to* help you. 喜んでお手伝いしましょう.

go 動
❶ 行く, 出かける.
① 【S〈人・車〉・V+画(句)】
He *went* home [*for* a walk]. 彼は家に帰った[散歩に出かけた].
He *has gone to* Tokyo. 彼は東京へ行ってしまった。(！《米》では「東京へ行ったことがある」の意でも用いられる)
② 【S〈人〉・V+*doing*】
He *went* fishing [swim*ming*] in [×to] the lake. 彼は湖に釣り[泳ぎ]に行った.
❷ 去る.
【S〈人・乗り物〉・V】
The bus *has already gone*. バスはもう行ってしまった.
I must *be going* now. もうそろそろ帰らなくてはなりません。(！このように進行形で用いると唐突さを避ける効果がある)
❸ (機械などが)動く.
【S〈機械〉・V(+画(句))】
This machine *goes* well [*by* electricity]. この機械は調子がよい[電気で動く].
❹ (事が)進行する.
【S〈事〉・V+画(句)】
Everything *is going* well [fine] *with* their schedule [him]. 彼らの計画は万事[事態は彼にとって]うまくいっている。(！進行形で用いられることが多い)
❺ (時が)過ぎる.
【S〈時間など〉・V(+画(句))】
The summer *goes* fast. 夏はたちまち過ぎていく.
❻ ...になる.
【S〈人・物〉・V・C〈形・done〉】
He *went* mad [blind]. 彼は気がふれた[目が見えなくなった]。(！C には通例好ましくない状態が来る)

good 形
❶ (判断・行為などが)よい.
【It is ～+(*that*) 節】
It was *good (that)* we didn't buy a loss leader, because it was really of poor quality. 目玉商品を買わなくてよかった。実は粗悪品だったから.
❷ 適した.
① 【S〈物・人〉 is ～+*for*+〈物・人〉】
He is *good for* the job. 彼はその仕事にもってこいだ.
② 【S〈物〉 is ～(+*for*+〈人〉)+*to do*】
This mushroom isn't *good to* eat. このキノコは食用に適さない.
③ 【It is ～(+*for*+〈人〉)+*to do*】
It is not *good (for* us) *to* eat this mushroom. 意味は②と同じ.
❸ 親切な.
① 【S〈人〉 is ～(+*to*+〈人〉)】
He is very *good to* me. 彼は私にとても親切だ.
② 【S〈人〉 is ～+*to do*】
You are very *good to* show me the way. 道案内をしてくださってどうもありがとう.
③ 【It is ～+*of*+〈人〉+*to do*】
It is very *good of* you *to* show me the way. 意味は②と同じ.
❹ 楽しい.
【It is ～+*to do*】
It is *good to* see you again. 君に再会できてうれしい.
❺ 熟達した, 上手な.
① 【S〈人〉 is ～+*at*+〈事・doing〉】
She is *good at* (speak*ing*) English. 彼女は英語(を話すの)が上手だ.
② 【S〈人〉 is ～+*with*+〈道具・人など〉】
She is *good with* children. 彼女は子供の扱いがうまい.

good 名 役立つこと, 利益。(！use と同じ構文だがより口語的。⇨use 名)

① 【It is (no) ～(+〈所有格〉)+*doing*】
It's no *good* (your) complain*ing* about the weather. (君の)天気のことで文句を言っても仕方がない.
② 【*What is* the ～ *of*(+〈所有格〉)+*doing?*】
What's the *good of* (your) complain*ing* about

the weather? (君が)天気のことで文句を言って何になるか.
③ 【*There is* (no) ～ (in) (＋所有格)＋do*ing*】
There's no *good* (*in*) (your) complain*ing* about the weather. 意味は ① と同じ.

grateful 形 感謝して.

① 【S〈人〉 is ～＋*to do*】
I am very *grateful to* get your help. 手伝ってくださったことを大変感謝しています.

② 【S〈人〉 is ～＋*to*＋〈人〉＋*for*＋〈事・do*ing*〉】
I am very *grateful to* you *for* your kindness [*for* helping me]. ご親切に[手伝ってくださったことに]大変感謝しています.

③ 【S〈人〉 is ～ (＋*to*＋〈人〉)＋*that* 節】
I am very *grateful* (*to* you) *that* you were kind [helped me]. 意味は ② と同じ.

ground 名 根拠, 理由.

① 【～＋*for*＋do*ing*】
We have good *grounds* [no *grounds*] *for* doubting it. われわれにはそれを疑う十分な理由がある[理由がない].

② 【～＋*that*】
He resigned on the *grounds that* he was ill. 彼は病気だという理由で辞職した. (**!** on the grounds of ill health. ともいえる)

grow 動

❶ 成長する, 育つ.
① 【S〈人・動植物〉・V (＋副(句))】
He *grew* (*up*) *into* a strong man. 彼は成長してたくましい人間になった.
Bananas don't *grow in* this country. バナナはこの国では育たない.
② 【S〈人・物・事〉・V・C〈*to be*〉】
He *grew to* be a strong man. 意味は ① の上例と同じ. (**!** to be は結果の不定詞)

❷ …になる.
① 【S〈人・事〉・V・C〈形〉】
He *has grown* old. 彼は年をとった.
② 【S〈人・事〉・V・C〈*to do*〉】
She *grew* increasingly *to* rely on me. 彼女はますます私を当てにするようになってきた.

❸ 増大する.
【S〈人・物〉・V (＋副(句))】
The team *has grown in* strength and popularity. そのチームは強くなって人気がでてきた.

❹ 栽培する.
【S〈人〉・V・O〈植物〉】
They *grow* corn in the farm. 彼らはその畑でトウモロコシを作っている.

guarantee 動

❶ 保証する.
① 【S〈人〉・V・O〈商品など〉】
They *guarantee* this watch for one year. この時計は 1 年間の保証付きです.
② 【S〈人〉・V・O〈商品〉・C〈*to do*〉】
She *guaranteed* the jewel *to* be genuine. 彼女はその宝石が本物だと保証した.
③ 【S〈人〉・V・O〈人〉・O〈物〉】
We *guarantee* you delivery within a week. 私たちはあなたに 1 週間以内の配達を保証します.

❷ 約束する.
① 【S〈人〉・V・O〈*that* 節〉】
She *guaranteed that* she would be there. 彼女はそこへ行くと約束した.
② 【S〈人〉・V・O〈*to do*〉】
She *guaranteed to* be there. 意味は ① と同じ.

guard 動

❶ 守る.
【S〈人・動物・物〉・V・O〈人・建物など〉(＋*against* [*from*]＋〈攻撃・危害など〉)】
The dog *is guarding* the house (*against* intruders). 犬がその家を (侵入者から) 守っている.

❷ 用心する.
【S〈人〉・V＋*against*＋〈事・do*ing*〉】
He *guarded against* catching (a) cold. 彼は風邪をひかないように用心した.

guess 動

❶ 推測する.
① 【S〈人〉・V・O〈事〉(＋前＋名)】
I *guess* his age *at* [*as*] 20. 彼は 20 歳だと推測します.
Can you *guess* its weight? その重さはどれくらいだと思いますか.
② 【S〈人〉・V・O〈*that* 節・*wh*- 節〉】
I *guess that* he is 20 (years old). 意味は ① の上例と同じ.
Can you *guess how* much it weighs? 意味は ① の下例と同じ.
③ 【S〈人〉・V・O〈事〉・*to be* C〈名・形〉】
I *guess* him *to be* 20 (years old). 意味は ① の上例と同じ.
④ 【S〈人〉・V (＋副(句))】
I can't *guess at* his age. 彼の年は見当がつかない.

❷ 解き当てる.
【S〈人〉・V・O〈答え・なぞ〉】
Can you *guess* the answer? 答えが分かりますか.

❸ 思う.《米話》
【S〈*I*〉・V・O〈(*that*) 節〉】
I *guess* (*that*) you are responsible. 君に責任があるでしょう. (**!** that は省略されるのが普通)

habit 名 習慣, 癖.

【～＋*of*＋do*ing*】
He is in the *habit* [He has a [the] *habit*] *of* answer*ing* a question with another question. 彼は質問されると別の質問を出して答えるという癖がある. (＝It is a *habit* with him *to* answer a question.…)

hand 動 手渡す.

① 【S〈人〉・V・O〈人〉・O〈物〉】
He *handed* her the postcard. 彼は彼女にその葉書を手渡した. (**!** この文型は「物」に焦点があり, ② は「人」に焦点がある) (受身＝She *was handed* the postcard by him.)
② 【S〈人〉・V・O〈物〉＋*to*＋〈人〉】
He *handed* the postcard *to* her. 意味は ① と同じ. (受身＝The postcard *was handed to* her by him.)

happen 動

❶ 起こる, ふりかかる.
① 【S〈事〉・V (＋副(句))】
A serious accident *happened in* the nuclear power plant. その原子力発電所で重大な事故が発生した.
② 【S〈事〉・V＋*to*＋〈人・物・事〉】
What *happened to* him? 彼に何が起こったのか.

happy 形

❷ たまたま...する. (!通例進行形は不可)
  ① 【S〈人・物・事〉・V・C〈to do〉】
  He *happened to* be at the scene of the accident. 彼はたまたま事故の現場に居合わせた.
  ② 【S〈It〉・V+that 節】
  It happened that he was at the scene of the accident. 意味は ① と同じ.

happy 形

❶ うれしい.
  ① 【S〈人〉 is ~+about+〈事・物・人〉】
  I am *happy about* your present. あなたの贈り物をうれしく思います.
  ② 【S〈人〉 is ~+to do】
  I am *happy to* hear the news [at the news]. その知らせを聞いてうれしく思います.
  ③ 【S〈人〉 is ~ doing】
  I am *happy* working with her. 私は彼女といっしょに働くのが楽しい.
  ④ 【S〈人〉 is ~+(that) 節】
  I am *happy* (*that*) you have got married. あなたが結婚されてうれしい.

❷ 喜んで...する.
  【S〈人〉 is ~+to do】
  I'd be *happy to* help you. 喜んでお手伝いしましょう.

hard 形 難しい.

  ① 【S〈事〉 is ~(+for+〈人〉)】
  Greek is *hard* (*for* me). ギリシャ語は(私には)難しい.
  ② 【It is ~ (+for+〈人〉)+to do】
  It is *hard* (*for* me) *to* learn Greek. ギリシャ語は(私には)習得が難しい. (!×It is *hard that* I (should) learn Greek. は不可)
  ③ 【It is ~ doing】
  It is *hard* learning Greek. ギリシャ語は習得が難しい.
  ④ 【S〈物・事など〉 is ~ (+for+〈人〉)+to do】
  Greek is *hard* (*for* me) *to* learn. 意味は ② と同じ.
  He is *hard* (*for* me) *to* persuade. (=It is *hard* (*for* me) *to* persuade him.) 彼は私には説得しがたい男だ.

hate 動

❶ 憎む, ひどく嫌う.
  【S〈人〉・V・O〈人・物・事〉】
  I *hate* him [fish; injustice]. 私は彼が大嫌いだ[魚が大嫌いだ; 不正を憎む].

❷ ...することをいやがる.
  ① 【S〈人〉・V・O〈to do; doing〉】
  I *hate to* study [study*ing*] on Sundays. 日曜日に勉強するのはいやだ.
  ② 【S〈人〉・V・O〈人・物〉・C〈to do; doing〉】
  I *hate* him *to* talk [talk*ing*] like that. 彼がそんなふうに話すのはいやだ. (!I *hate his* talk*ing*.... ともいえる)

have 動

❶ 持っている, ...がある. (!受身形, 進行形は不可)
  【S〈人・物・事〉・V・O〈物・事・人〉】
  I *have* no money with me [a lot of work to do]. お金の持ち合わせがない[する仕事がたくさんある].
  This envelope *has* no stamps. この封筒には切手が張ってない.

❷ 食べる, 飲む. (!受身形, 進行形は可)
  【S〈人〉・V・O〈物〉】
  I usually *have* bread for breakfast. 朝食にはたいていパンを食べる.

Will you *have* another cup of coffee? コーヒーをもう一杯いかがですか.

❸ 経験する. (!通例受身形, 進行形は不可)
  【S〈人〉・V・O〈病気・困難・楽しみなど〉】
  I *have* a headache. 頭が痛い.
  I *had* great difficulty in mathematics. 数学には大変苦労した.
  We *had* a good time at the party. パーティーは大変楽しかった.
  We (*have*) *had* little snow this winter. この冬は雪が少なかった.

❹ (行為をする. (!受身形まれ, 進行形は可)
  【S〈人〉・V・O〈事〉】 (!O は a+動詞派生名詞)
  He *had* a look at the picture [a good night's sleep]. 彼はその絵を一目見た[一晩ぐっすり眠った].

❺ ...させる, ...してもらう. (!受身形は不可)
  ① 【S〈人〉・V・O〈人〉・C〈do〉】
  I *hád* him *go* there in my place. 彼に私の代わりに行ってもらった[行かせた]. (!(1)《主に米》. (2) *have* に強勢を置く)
  ② 【S〈人〉・V・O〈物・事〉・C〈done〉】
  I *hád* an air-conditioner instal*led* in my room. 部屋にクーラーを取り付けてもらった.

❻ ...される.
  【S〈人〉・V・O〈物〉・C〈done〉】
  I *had* my bag *stólen*. かばんを盗まれた. (!(1) ❺ ①, ② と異なり *done* に強勢を置く. (2) ×I was stolen my bag. としない)

❼ ...させておく. (!通例受身形, 進行形は不可)
  【S〈人〉・V・O〈人・物〉・C〈doing〉】
  I won't *háve* you idl*ing* away your time. 君に時間をむだにさせておくわけにはいかない. (!*have* に強勢を置く)

hear 動

❶ 聞こえる. (!通例進行形, 命令形は不可)
  ① 【S〈人〉・V・O〈声・音など〉】
  I *heard* a loud noise. 大きな音が聞こえた.
  ② 【S〈人〉・V・O〈人・物〉・C〈do〉】
  I *heard* her *cry*. 彼女が叫ぶのが聞こえた. (受身=She *was heard to cry*.) (!この文では叫ぶのが完了しているが, ③ は進行中である)
  ③ 【S〈人〉・V・O〈人・物〉・C〈doing〉】
  I *heard* her *crying*. 彼女が叫んでいるのが聞こえた. (受身=She *was heard crying*.) (⇨②)
  ④ 【S〈人〉・V・O〈人・物〉・C〈done〉】
  I didn't *hear* my name *called*. 私は名前が呼ばれたのが聞こえなかった.

❷ 聞いて知る.
  ① 【S〈人〉・V・O〈事〉】
  I *have* not *heard* the story yet. その話はまだ聞いていない.
  ② 【S〈人〉・V・O〈(that) 節〉】
  Haven't you *heard* (*that*) he was arrested? 彼が逮捕されたことを聞いていないのか.
  ③ 【S〈人〉・V・O〈wh- 節〉】
  Haven't you *heard whether* [*if*] he is all right? 彼がだいじょうぶかどうか聞いていないのか.

❸ ...とうわさに聞いている.
  【S〈I〉・V・O〈(that) 節〉】
  I *hear* (*that*) he's going to marry soon. 彼はもうすぐ結婚すると聞いている. (!*that* は省略されるのが普通)

❹ 耳が聞こえる.
  【S〈人・動物〉・V(+副)】
  My grandmother can't [doesn't] *hear* well. 祖母は耳が遠い.

help 動

❶ 手伝う.
① 【S〈人〉・V・O〈人〉(+*with* [*in*]+〈仕事など〉)】
They *helped* me *with* [*in*] my work. 彼らは私の仕事を手伝ってくれた. (受身=I *was helped with* [*in*] my work.) (❗(1) in の方が困難な仕事を意味する. (2)× They *helped* my work. は不可)
② 【S〈人〉・V・O〈人〉(*to*) do〉】
She *helped* (*to*) wash the dishes. 彼女は皿洗いを手伝った. (❗ to は《話》では《米》では通例,《英》でもしばしば省略される)
③ 【S〈人〉・V・O〈人〉・C〈(*to*) do〉】
They *helped* me (*to*) do my work. 意味は ① と同じ. (受身=I *was helped to* do my work.) (❗受身では to を省略しない)
④ 【S〈人〉・V・O〈人〉(+〈前(句)〉)】
She *helped with* the dishes. 意味は ② と同じ.

❷ 役立つ.
① 【S〈物・事〉・V・O〈(*to*) do〉】
This agreement will *help* (*to*) promote world peace. この協定は世界平和を促進するだろう.
② 【S〈物・事〉・V・O〈人・物・事〉・C〈*to* do〉】
This book will *help* you (*to*) improve your English. この本は君が英語力を伸ばすのに役立つだろう.

hit 動

❶ 打つ, たたく.
【S〈人〉・V・O〈人・物〉(+〈前〉+〈名〉)】
He *hit* the ball with a bat. 彼はバットでそのボールを打った.
He *hit* my head [me *on* the head]. 彼は私の頭をたたいた. (❗前者はたたいた部分に焦点があり, 後者は「人」に焦点がある)

❷ ぶつける.
【S〈人〉・V・O〈物〉+*against* [*on*]+〈物〉】
He *hit* his head *against* [*on*] the pillar. 彼は頭を柱にぶつけた.

❸ ぶつかる.
【S〈人・物〉・V・O〈人・物〉】
The car *hit* an old man. その車は老人をはねた.

❹ 襲う.
【S〈天災など〉・V・O〈場所・人など〉】
A big earthquake *hit* the district. 大地震がその地方を襲った.

hold 動

❶ 持っている, 握って[つかんで]いる.
【S〈人〉・V・O〈物〉(+〈前〉+〈名〉)】
He *was holding* a book under his arm. 彼は本を小わきにかかえていた.
He *held* my arm [me *by* the arm]. 彼は私の腕をつかんでいた. (❗前者はつかんだ部分に焦点があり, 後者は「人」に焦点がある)
He *holds* the world record for the high jump. 彼は高跳びの世界記録を保持している. (❗この場合は進行形不可)

❷ 支える.
【S〈物〉・V・O〈物・人〉】
The branch will not *hold* your weight. その枝はあなたの体重を支えきれないでしょう.

❸ 保つ.
① 【S〈人〉・V・O〈物・人〉・C〈形, done〉】
Please *hold* the door open. ドアを押さえて開けておいてください.
② 【S〈人〉・V・O〈物・人〉+〈前(句)〉】
He *held* his hands up [high]. 彼は両手を上げていた.

❹ 催す.
【S〈人〉・V・O〈会など〉】
They will *hold* an athletic meet next Sunday. 彼らは次の日曜日に運動会を開く.

❺ 〈容器が〉…を入れることができる. (❗通例受身形, 進行形は不可)
【S〈容器など〉・V・O〈液体・容量など〉】
This pot *holds* one liter. このポットは 1 リットル入る.

❻ 思う.
【S〈人〉・V・O〈*that* 節〉】
He *holds that* I am responsible for it. その責任は私にあると彼は思っている.

❼ 持続する, もつ.
【S〈物・事〉・V(+〈前(句)〉)】
This fine weather won't *hold until* the weekend. この好天は週末まで続かないだろう.
The rope didn't *hold* long. そのロープは長くはもたなかった.

honest 形 正直な.

① 【S〈人〉 is ~+*in*+〈事・*doing*〉/*with*+〈人〉】
He is *honest in* everything he does. 彼は何事をするにも正直だ./He is *honest with* everyone. 彼はだれにでも誠実だ.
② 【S〈人〉 is ~+*to* do】
He was *honest* (*enough*) *to* admit his mistake. 彼は正直にも過ちを認めた.
③ 【It is ~+*of*+〈人〉+*to* do】
It was *honest of* him *to* admit his mistake. 意味は ② と同じ.

honor 名 光栄.

① 【~+*of*+*doing*】
Would you do us the *honor of* dining with us tomorrow? あす夕食をごいっしょさせていただけませんでしょうか.
② 【~+*to* do】
I have the *honor to* be president of this association. この協会の会長をさせていただくことは名誉でございます. (=It is an *honor* for me *to* be president….)

hope 動 望む.

① 【S〈人〉・V・O〈*to* do〉】
I *hope to* visit Egypt some day. いつかエジプトに行ってみたい.
② 【S〈人〉・V・O〈(*that*) 節〉】
We *hope* (*that*) everything will go well. すべてうまくいってくれるといいと思います. (受身=《書》It *is hoped that* everything will go well. ×Everything is hoped *to* go well. は不可) (❗that はしばしば省略される)
"Do you think he will come?" "I *hope so* [*not*]." 「彼は来ると思いますか」「来て欲しいね[来て欲しくないね]」. (❗that 節の代わりに肯定文では so, 否定文では not が用いられることがある. ×I don't *hope so*. とはいわない)
③ 【S〈人〉・V+*for*+〈物・事〉】
They *hope for* rain. 彼らは雨を待ち望んでいる. (受身=Rain is *hoped for*.)

hope 名

❶ 希望, 望み.
① 【~+*of*+*doing*】

He went to Paris in the *hope* [in *hope(s)*] of becoming an artist. 彼は画家になろうとしてパリへ行った.

② 【~+*that* 節】
He went to Paris in the *hope* [in *hope(s)*] that he would be an artist. 意味は ① と同じ.

❷ 見込み, 期待.
① 【~+*of* (+所有格)+*doing*】
There was little *hope of* his being saved. 彼が救助される見込みはほとんどなかった.

② 【~+*that* 節】
There was little *hope that* he would be saved. 意味は ① と同じ.

idea 名 考え, 思いつき, 見当.

① 【~+*of doing*】
You will have to give up the *idea of* traveling abroad. 君は海外旅行を断念しなければならないだろう.

② 【~+*that* 節】
I didn't have the slightest *idea that* he would come to see me today. 彼が今日私を訪ねてくるとは少しも思っていなかった.

③ 【~(+*of* [*about, as to*])+*wh*- 節・句】
I have no *idea of* what she is like [*how to* answer it]. 彼女がどのような人か[それにどう答えたらよいか]さっぱり見当がつかない. (❗主に否定文, 疑問文で用いられる. 前置詞はしばしば省略される)

imagine 動

❶ 想像する. (❗通例進行形にしない)
① 【S〈人〉・V・O〈物・事〉】
We cannot *imagine* life without cars. 車のない生活など想像できない.

② 【S〈人〉・V・O〈所有格[目的格]+*doing*〉】
Can you *imagine* his [him] writing novels? 彼が小説を書いているなんて想像できますか.
I can't *imagine* living on a desert island. 無人島で暮らすことなど想像できない. (❗S が所有格・目的格と同一人物の場合, 通例所有格・目的格を省略する)

③ 【S〈人〉・V・O〈*that* [*wh*-] 節〉】
I can't *imagine that* I live on a desert island. 意味は ② の第 2 例と同じ.
I can *imagine why* he got angry. どうして彼が怒ったのか想像できる.

④ 【S〈人〉・V・O〈人・物・事〉・(*to be*) C〈名・形〉[*as* C〈名〉]】 I had *imagined* her (*to be*) a young girl [her *as* a young girl]. 彼女は若い女の子だと想像していた.

❷ 思う. (進行形は不可)
【S〈人〉・V・O〈(*that*) 節・*wh*-節〉】
I *imagine* (*that*) he will agree with us. 彼は私たちに賛成してくれると思います. (❗*that* はしばしば省略される)/I can't *imagine what* she wants. 彼女が何をほしがっているのか推測できない.

importance 名 重要性.

【~+*of doing*】
Doctors stress the *importance of* cultivating new interests. 医者たちは新しい趣味を養うことが重要だと力説している.

important 形 重要な.

① 【S〈物・事〉 is ~+*for* [*to*]+〈人・物・事〉】
His help is *important for* us [our plan]. 私たち[私たちの計画]には彼の援助が大切だ.

② 【It is ~(+*for*+〈人・物・事〉)+*to do*】
It is *important for* him to promote his health. 彼が健康を増進することは大切だ. (❗×He is important *to* promote his health./×It is important promoting his health. は不可)

③ 【It is ~+*that* 節】
It is *important that* he (should) promote [he promotes] his health. 意味は ② と同じ. (❗should を用いるのは〈主に英〉. It is *important to* [*for*] him *that* he promotes his health. も可)

impossible 形

❶ (実行)不可能な.
① 【S〈人・物・事〉 is ~(+*for*+〈人〉)+*to do*】
This problem is *impossible* (*for* me) to solve. この問題を(私が)解くことはできない.

② 【It is ~(+*for*+〈人〉)+*to do*】
It is *impossible* (*for* me) to solve this problem. 意味は ① と同じ. (❗×I am impossible *to* solve this problem./×It is impossible *that* I (should) solve this problem. は不可)

❷ とてもあり得ない.
① 【It is ~+*for*+〈人・物・事〉+*to do*】
It is *impossible for* him *to* have told a lie. 彼がうそをついたはずはない.

② 【It is ~+*that* 節】
It is *impossible that* he told [×*should have* told] a lie. 意味は ① と同じ.

improve 動

❶ 改良する, 進歩させる.
【S〈人〉・V・O〈物・事〉】
He *has improved* his English speaking ability. 彼は英語を話すのがうまくなった.

❷ よくなる, 改良される.
【S〈人・事〉・V(+*in*+〈事・*doing*〉)】
His English speaking ability *is improving*./He *is improving in* English speaking ability. 意味は ❶ と同じ.

independent 形 独立して.

【S〈国・人〉 is ~ *of* [*from*]+〈国・人〉】
India became *independent of* [*from*] Britain in 1947. インドは 1947 年に英国から独立した.
He is not yet economically *independent of* his parents. 彼は経済的にはまだ親から独立していない.

indicate 動

❶ 指し示す.
① 【S〈人・物〉・V・O〈事〉】
The arrow *indicates* the location of the emergency exit. 矢印は非常口の場所を示している.

② 【S〈人・物〉・V・O〈*wh*-節〉】
The arrow *indicates where* the emergency exit is. 意味は ① と同じ.

❷ (物・事が…の)徴候である.
① 【S〈物・事〉・V・O〈物・事〉】
An evening glow often *indicates* fine weather the following day. 夕焼けはしばしば次の日が晴天になる徴候である.

② 【S〈物・事〉・V・O〈*that* 節〉】
Was there any evidence to *indicate that* she intended to return? 彼女が帰って来ることを示す形跡はありましたか.

indifferent 形 無関心な, 冷淡な.

① 【S〈人〉 is ~+*to* [*toward*]+〈人・物・事〉】

He seems *indifferent to* [*toward*] money [others' feelings]. 彼は金[他人の感情]には無関心のようだ.
② 【S〈人〉・**is** ~(+*to*)+*wh-* 節】
I am *indifferent whether* she likes me or not. 私は彼女に好かれようと好かれまいとどうでもいい. (！ *wh-* 節のときはその前の前置詞は略すことがある)

inform 動　知らせる.《書》

① 【S〈人〉・V・O〈人〉】
I will *inform* you when the date is fixed. 日取りが決まったらお知らせします.
② 【S〈人〉・V・O〈人〉+*of* [*about*]+〈事〉】
They *informed* me *of* [*about*] his absence. 彼らは私に彼の欠席を知らせた. (受身＝I *was informed of* [*about*] his absence.)
③ 【S〈人〉・V・O〈人〉・O〈*that* 節〉】
They *informed* me *that* he was absent. 意味は②と同じ. (受身＝I *was informed that* he was absent.)
④ 【S〈人〉・V・O〈人〉・O〈*wh-* 節・句〉】
He *informed* me *where* I should go [*where to go*]. 彼は私にどこへ行けばよいか知らせてくれた.

information 名　情報.

① 【~ +*that* 節】
I have *information that* she is going to marry her boyfriend. 彼女は近く恋人と結婚すると聞いている.
② 【~ *about* [*as to*]+*wh-* 節・句】
We have no *information about* [*as to*] *where* she has gone. 彼女がどこへ行ったか私たちは知らない.

injure 動

❶ 傷つける.
【S〈事・人〉・V・O〈人・身体・動物〉】
He *injured* his health [himself] from overwork. 彼は過労で健康を害した.
He was badly [seriously] *injured* in the accident. 彼は事故で大けがをした.
He *injured* his leg [×He *was injured in* the leg] when he fell off a ladder. 彼ははしごから落ちとき, 脚をけがした.
❷ (感情・名誉などを)害する.
【S〈人・事〉・V・O〈感情・名誉など〉】
The groundless rumor *injured* his reputation. その根も葉もないうわさで彼は評判を傷つけられた.

insist 動

❶ 主張する.
① 【S〈人〉・V+*on*+〈事〉】
He *insisted on* his innocence. 彼は自分が無実だと主張した. (！受身可)
② 【S〈人〉・V・O〈*that* 節〉】
He *insisted* (×on) *that* he was innocent. 意味は①と同じ.
❷ 強く要求する.
① 【S〈人〉・V+*on*+〈物・事+*doing*〉】
He *insisted on* punctuality. 彼は時間厳守を強く求めた. (！受身可)
He *insisted on* attending [×to attend] the meeting. 彼は会議に出ると言ってきかなかった. (！次例および②との意味の違いに注意)
He *insisted on* my [me] attending [×to attend] the meeting. 彼は私がその会議に出席するよう強く要求した. (！受身は不可)
② 【S〈人〉・V・O〈*that* 節〉】
He *insisted that* I (should) attend the meeting. 意味は①第3例と同じ. (！ should を用いるのは《主に英》)

instruct 動

❶ 教える.
【S〈人〉・V・O〈人〉+*in*+〈学科など〉】
He *instructed* us *in* first aid. 彼は私たちに応急手当を教えた.
❷ 指示する.
① 【S〈人〉・V・O〈人〉・O〈*to do*〉】
She *instructed* me *to* buy the book. 彼女は私にその本を買うよう指示した.
② 【S〈人〉・V・O〈人〉・O〈*wh-* 節・句〉】
He *instructed* me *what* I (should) do [*what to do*] next. 彼は私に次に何をするのか指示した. (！ should を用いるのは《主に英》)

intend 動 (！通例進行形にしない)

❶ …するつもりである.
① 【S〈人〉・V・O〈*to do*〉】
I *intend to* persuade him. 彼を説得するつもりだ. (！(1) I *intend* persuading him. はまれ. (2)受身形は不可)
② 【S〈人〉・V・O〈*that* 節〉】《書》
They *intended that* he (should) do the work. 彼らは彼にその仕事をさせるつもりであった. (受身＝It *was intended that* he (should) do the work.) (！(1) should を用いるのは《主に英》, 現在時制では shall を用いる. (2)②より③の文型のほうが普通)
③ 【S〈人〉・V・O〈人〉・C〈*to do*〉】
They *intended* him *to* do the work. 意味は②と同じ. (受身＝He *was intended to* do the work.)
❷ …向けに意図する.
【S〈人〉・V・O〈物・人〉+*for*+〈人・事・*doing*〉】
They *intended* the book *for* high school students. 彼らはその本を高校生向けに書いた. (受身＝The book *was intended for* high school students.) (！受身形で使われることが多い)

intention 名　意図.

① 【~ +*of doing*】
I had no *intention of* insulting him at all. 私は彼を侮辱するつもりは毛頭なかった. (！the [an, any, no, every] ~ のときは *of doing* が普通)
② 【~ +*to do*】
His *intention to* make an exploration of the island seemed absurd. その島を探検しようという彼の意図ははかげているように思えた. (！ intention に何もつかないとき, one's ~ のときは *to do* が普通)

interest 名

❶ 興味, 趣味.
【~ **is** (*in*)+〈事・物・*doing*〉】
His chief *interest* is (*in*) music and collecting stamps. 彼の主な趣味は音楽と切手収集です.
❷ 利害(関係).
【~ +*that* 節】
We have a strong common *interest that* peace and stability should be established throughout the world. 私たちは世界中に平和と安定が確立されるべきだという強い共通の利害関係を持っているのです.

interested 形 興味を持っている.

① 【S〈人〉 is ~+in+〈物・事・doing〉】
He is *interested* [×interesting] *in* dogs [collect*ing* stamps]. 彼は犬[切手収集]に興味がある.

② 【S〈人〉 is ~+to do】
He is very (much) *interested to* know the reason. 彼はその理由をとても知りたがっている.

③ 【S〈人〉 is ~+that 節】
He is *interested that* I am majoring in biotechnology. 彼は私が生物工学を専攻していることに関心を持っている.

interesting 形 興味を引き起こす, おもしろい.

① 【S〈物・事・人〉 is ~+to+〈人〉】
This story is very [×much] *interesting to* me. この話は私にはとてもおもしろい.

② 【S〈物・事・人〉 is ~(+for+〈人〉)+to do】
Baseball is *interesting* (*for* me) *to* watch as well as *to* play. (私には)野球はするのも見るのもおもしろい.

③ 【It is ~(+for+〈人〉)+to do】
It is *interesting* (*for* me) *to* watch baseball as well as *to* play it. 意味は ② と同じ.

④ 【It is ~+that 節】
It is *interesting that* the teacher tells the students to do what he himself cannot do. 面白いことにその先生は自分にもできないことを生徒にせよと言う.

interpret 動

❶ 解釈する.
① 【S〈人〉・V・O〈事・物〉】
She *interpreted* a dream according to Freudian theory. 彼女はフロイトの理論に従って夢を解釈した.
② 【S〈人〉・V・O〈事〉+as+〈事〉】
I *interpreted* your silence *as* acceptance. 私はあなたの沈黙を承諾と解釈した.

❷ 通訳する.
【S〈人〉・V・O〈言葉など〉(+前(句))】
He *interpreted* my remarks *into* English for her. 彼は私の言ったことを彼女に英語に通訳してくれた.

introduce 動

❶ 紹介する.
【S〈人〉・V・O〈人〉(+to+〈人〉)】
He *introduced* his wife *to* his friends. 彼は友人に妻を紹介した. (! 「自己紹介する」では oneself を用いる: May I *introduce* myself? 自己紹介をしてもよろしいですか)

❷ 導入する, もたらす.
【S〈人〉・V・O〈事・物〉(+into [to]+〈国・地方〉)】
Arabs *introduced* coffee *into* Europe. アラビア人がヨーロッパにコーヒーを伝えた. (受身=Coffee was *introduced into* Europe *by* Arabs.)

invite 動

❶ 招待する.
【S〈人〉・V・O〈人〉(+to+〈会など〉)】
They *invited* me *to* the party. 彼らは私をパーティーに招待してくれた. (受身=I *was invited to* the party.)

❷ 勧める, 依頼する.
【S〈人〉・V・O・C〈to do〉】
They *invited* me *to* accept the post. 彼らは私にその地位につくように勧めた[依頼した]. (受身=I *was invited to* accept the post.)

join 動

❶ 加わる, 参加する. (! 通例受身形は不可)
① 【S〈人〉・V・O〈団体など〉】
He *joined* the chorus club [staff]. 彼はコーラス部に入った[そのスタッフの一員となった].
② 【S〈人〉・V・O〈人〉(+in [for]+〈活動・doing〉)】 She *joined* us *in* a walk [*for* lunch; *in* looking for the key]. 彼女は私たちといっしょに散歩をした[昼食をした, 鍵(穽)を捜してくれた].
③ 【S〈人〉・V+in+〈行為〉】
He *joined in* our discussion. 彼は私たちの討論に加わった.

❷ つなぐ.
① 【S〈人〉・V・O〈二つ以上の物〉】
He *joined* the two pipes by cement. 彼は2本のパイプをセメントでつないだ.
② 【S〈人〉・V・O〈物〉+to+〈物〉】
They *joined* the hose *to* the faucet. 彼らはホースを蛇口につないだ.

❸ つながる, 合流する.
【S〈二つ以上の物〉・V(+副(句))】
The two rivers *join* near the town. その二つの川はその町の近くで合流している.

judge 動

❶ 判断する.
① 【S〈人〉・V・O〈人・物・事〉(+by+〈外観など〉)】
You should not *judge* a man *by* his appearance. 人を外見で判断すべきではない.
② 【S〈人〉・V・O〈that 節〉】
From what he said, I *judged that* he was honest. 彼の言うことから彼は正直者であると判断した.
③ 【S〈人〉・V・O〈whether 節〉】
I cannot *judge whether* I should go or stay. 行くべきかとどまるべきか判断がつかない.
④ 【S〈人〉・V・O〈人・物・事〉(+to be) C〈名・形〉】 From what he said, I *judged* him (*to be*) honest. 意味は ② と同じ. (! (1) 受身形では to be は省略されるのが普通: He *was judged* honest. (2) ② の方が普通の言い方)

❷ 裁判する, 判決を下す.
① 【S〈人〉・V・O〈人・事〉】
He *judged* the criminal [case]. 彼がその犯人[事件]を裁いた.
② 【S〈人〉・V・O〈人・事〉・C〈形〉】
The court *judged* him guilty [innocent]. 法廷は彼に有罪[無罪]の判決を下した.

jump 動

❶ 飛[跳]ぶ.
【S〈人・動物〉・V(+前+名)】
He *jumped over* the ditch [*off* the roof; *on* the desk]. 彼は溝を跳び越えた[屋根から飛び降りた; 机に飛び乗った].
The dog *jumped at* me. 犬は私に飛びかかってきた.

❷ 急に上がる.
【S〈価格, 数量など〉・V(+副(句))】
The price of vegetables *has jumped* up. 野菜の値段が急騰した.

❸ 跳び越える.
【S〈人・動物〉・V・O〈障害物など〉】
The horse *jumped* the hurdle. 馬は障害物を跳び越えた.

justify 正当化する.

① 【S〈人・事〉・V・O〈人・言動・行為〉(+副(句))】
Nothing can *justify* her behavior *toward* us.
何と言い訳しても,彼女の私たちに対するふるまいを正当化することはできない.

② 【S〈事〉・V・O〈doing〉】
That doesn't *justify* hav*ing* violated a promise. だからといって約束を破ったことは許されない.

keep 動

❶ 置いておく, 自分のものとする.
【S〈人〉・V・O〈物〉(+副+名)】
He *keeps* all the receipts *in* his safe. 彼は領収書をすべて金庫にしまっておく.
You may *keep* the change. お釣りはいりません.

❷ (家畜を)飼う, (家族を)養う.
【S〈人〉・V・O〈家畜・家族〉】
He *keeps* a lot of cattle [a wife and three children]. 彼はたくさんの牛を飼っている[妻と3人の子供を養っている].

❸ (日記などを)つける.
【S〈人〉・V・O〈日記など〉】
He *keeps* a diary [accounts]. 彼は日記[帳簿]をつけている.

❹ (人を)留置する, 引き留める.
【S〈人・物・事〉・V・O〈人〉+副(句)】
They *kept* him *in* prison. 彼らは彼を刑務所に入れておいた.
The rainy weather *kept* the children indoors. 雨模様の天気のため子供たちは室内にいた.

❺ (商品を)置いておく.
【S〈店〉・V・O〈商品〉】
That store *keeps* all kinds of foods. あの店にはあらゆる食品がそろっている.

❻ (店などを)経営する.
【S〈人〉・V・O〈店・会社など〉】
They *keep* a large restaurant. 彼らは大きなレストランを経営している.

❼ (規則・秘密などを)守る.
【S〈人〉・V・O〈規則・約束など〉】
You should *keep* the traffic rules [your promise; the secret]. 君は交通規則[約束; その秘密]を守るべきだ.

❽ 続ける.
【S〈人など〉・V・O〈状態・動作〉】
He *kept* silence. 彼は沈黙を守った.
My watch *keeps* very good time. 私の腕時計はとても正確だ.

❾ ずっと…である.
【S〈人・事〉・V・C〈形(句)・doing〉】
He *kept* quiet [in good health; sleep*ing*]. 彼は黙っていた[ずっと健康であった; 眠り続けた]. (⚠ 進行形は不可)

❿ …にしておく, …させておく.
【S〈人・物・事〉・V・O〈人・物・事〉・C〈形(句)・名・doing・done〉】 He *kept* the door open [closed]. 彼はドアを開けた[閉めた]ままにしておいた.
They *kept* me wait*ing* [at a distance]. 彼らは私を待たせた[近づかせなかった]. (受身＝I *was kept* wait*ing* [at a distance].)

⓫ …させない.
【S〈物・事・人〉・V・O〈人・物〉+*from*+doing】
Stormy weather *kept* us *from* going further. 荒れ模様の天気のため私たちはそれ以上行けなかった.

kick 動 ける.

① 【S〈人〉・V・O〈人・物〉(+副・名)】
He *kicked* my leg [me *in* the leg]. 彼は私の足をけった. (⚠ 前者はけった場所に, 後者は「人」に焦点がある)

② 【S〈人〉・V(+*at*+〈物〉)】
He *kicked at* the door. 彼はドアをけった. (⚠「ける動作をする」の意味. したがって ① と異なり実際に当たったかどうかは不明)

③ 【S〈人〉・V・O〈物〉・C〈形・done〉】
He *kicked* the door open [shut]. 彼はドアをけって開けた[閉めた].

kind 形 親切な.

① 【S〈人〉is ～+*to*+〈人〉】
My brother is *kind to* everyone. 私の弟はだれにも親切だ.

② 【S〈人〉is ～+*to do*】
He is very *kind to* help me. 彼は私を手伝ってくれるとはとても親切だ. (⚠ この構文は人柄に焦点があり, ③ は人柄と事柄の両方に焦点がある)

③ 【It is ～+*of*+〈人〉+*to do*】
It is very *kind of* him *to* help me. (＝How *kind* (it is) *of* him *to* help me!) 意味は ② と同じ. (⚠ 感嘆文にしたときは通例 it is を省く)

kiss 動 キスする.

① 【S〈人〉・V・O〈人・体の部分〉】
They *kissed* each other passionately [tenderly]. 彼らはお互いに熱烈に[やさしく]キスを交した.
He *kissed* her lips. 彼は彼女の唇にキスをした. (⚠ この文型はキスをした場所に焦点がある. ② は「人」に焦点がある)

② 【S〈人〉・V・O〈人〉+*on*+*the*+〈体の部分〉】
He *kissed* her *on the* lips. 意味は ① の第2例と同じ.

③ 【S〈人〉・V・O〈人〉・C〈別れなど〉】
He *kissed* her good-by [good night]. 彼は彼女にさよなら[おやすみ]のキスをした.

knock 動

❶ たたく.
【S〈人〉・V+*on* [*at*]+〈物〉】
Someone *is knocking on* [*at*] the door. だれかがドアをノックしている.

❷ ぶつかる.
【S〈人・物〉・V+*against* [*into*]+〈物〉】
Her hand *knocked against* the glass. 彼女の手はガラスにぶつかった.

❸ 打つ, たたく.
① 【S〈人〉・V・O〈人・物〉(+副(句))】
He *knocked* my head. 彼は私の頭をなぐった. (⚠ この文型はなぐった場所に焦点があり, ② は「人」に焦点がある)
The boxer *knocked* his opponent down [*to* the floor]. ボクサーは相手をぶちのめした[マットに沈めた].

② 【S〈人〉・V・O〈人〉+*on* [*in*]+*the*+〈体の部分〉】 He *knocked* me *on the* head. 意味は ① の第1例と同じ.

③ 【S〈人など〉・V・O〈人〉・C〈形〉】
The boxer *knocked* his oppnent senseless. ボクサーは相手をなぐって気絶させた.

❹ (うっかり)ぶつける.
【S〈人〉・V・O〈体の部分・物〉+*against* [*on*]+〈物〉】 I *knocked* my head *against* a pillar. 頭を柱にぶつけた.

know 動 (⚠ 通例命令形, 進行形は不可)

❶ 知っている, 分かっている.
  ① 【S〈人〉・V・O・〈人・物・事〉】
  Everyone *knows* his name. だれもが彼の名前を知っている. (受身＝His name *is known to* [*by*] everyone.) (❗受身形で動作主を表わす場合は to が普通)
  We *have known* each other for five years. 私たちは5年間の知り合いである.
  ② 【S〈人〉・V・O〈*that* 節〉】
  He didn't *know* (*that*) I was a policeman. 彼は私が警察官であることを知らなかった.
  ③ 【S〈人〉・V・O〈*wh*- 節・句〉】
  He didn't *know how* much it cost [*what to do*]. 彼はそれがどれくらいするか知らなかった[何をしていいか分からなかった].
  ④ 【S〈人〉・V・O〈人・物・事〉・*to be* C〈形・名〉】
  We *know* him *to be* an honest man. (＝We *know that* he is an honest man.) 私たちは彼が正直者だとわかっている. (受身＝He *is known to be* an honest man.)
  ⑤ 【S〈人〉・V(+*about*+〈事〉)】
  I don't *know* (*about*) it. 私は(それについて)知りません.
❷ 認める, 見て[聞いて]それと分かる.
  【S〈人〉・V・O〈人・物・事〉(+*by*+〈判断基準〉)】
  You'll *know* the house *by* the pointed roof. その家はとがった屋根で分かります. (受身＝The house will *be known by* [×*to*] the pointed roof.)
❸ 見分けがつく.
  【S〈人〉・V・O〈人・物・事〉+*from*+〈人・物・事〉】
  Do you *know* a tiger *from* a leopard? トラとヒョウの見分けがつきますか. (❗否定文, 疑問文, 条件文で)

knowledge 名 知識, 知っていること.
  ① 【〜+*that* 節】
  I took on the job in the full *knowledge that* it wouldn't pay. その仕事は引き合わないことを十分承知で引き受けた.
  ② 【〜+*of*+*wh*- 節・句】
  The *knowledge of how to* do it [*how* it should be done] was not very common. それをどのようにするかあまり知られていない.
  ③ 【〜+*of*+〈人・事・物〉】
  She has a good *knowledge of* Latin. 彼女はラテン語をよく知っている.

late 形 遅れた, 遅い.
  ① 【S〈人〉is 〜+*for* [*to*, *at*]+〈学校・仕事など〉】
  I was *late for* school [the last bus; the meeting]. 授業[最終バス; 会議]に遅れた.
  He was *late to* work because of a traffic jam. 交通渋滞のために彼は仕事に遅れた. (❗この work は名詞)
  Weren't you *late at* the office this morning? 今朝は会社に遅れなかったの? (❗at は場所に重点を置く)
  ② 【S〈人・物〉is 〜(+*in*)+*doing*】
  I was *late* (*in*) handing in my paper. 私はレポートの提出が遅れた.
  Spring is *late* (*in*) coming this year. 今年は春の来るのが遅い. (❗くだけた表現では in は省略されることが多い)
  ③ 【S〈人〉is 〜+*with*+〈事〉】
  I was *late with* my dinner [a reply]. 夕食を食べるのが[返事が]遅れた.

laugh 動
❶ 笑う.
  ① 【S〈人〉・V(+副(句))】
  He *laughed* loud [merrily]. 彼は大声で[楽しそうに]笑った.
  ② 【S〈人〉・V・O〈a+形+*laugh*〉】
  He *laughed* a hearty *laugh*. 彼は心から笑った. (❗He *laughed* heartily. の方が普通)
❷ あざ笑う.
  【S〈人〉・V+*at*+〈人・事〉】
  He *laughed at* me [my idea]. 彼は私[私の考え]をあざ笑った. (受身＝I [My idea] *was laughed at* by him.)

lay 動
❶ 置く, 横たえる.
  【S〈人〉・V・O〈物・人〉(+副(句))】
  He *laid* the bag on the desk [the baby *on* his side]. 彼は机の上にかばんを置いた[赤ん坊を横向きに寝かせた].
❷ 用意する.
  【S〈人〉・V・O〈物・事〉】
  She *laid* the table for dinner. 彼女は夕食の用意をした. (❗テーブルに食器などを並べること)
❸ 敷く.
  ① 【S〈人〉・V・O〈物〉+*in*+〈場所〉】
  They *laid* a carpet *in* the bedroom. 彼らは寝室にカーペットを敷いた.
  ② 【S〈人〉・V・O〈場所〉+*with*+〈物〉】
  They *laid* the bedroom *with* a carpet. 意味は①と同じ.
❹ (卵を)産む.
  【S〈鳥・昆虫など〉・V・O〈卵〉】
  The hen *lays* an egg every other day. そのニワトリは一日おきに卵を産む.

lead 動
❶ 導く, 連れて行く.
  ① 【S〈人〉・V・O〈人・動物〉(+副(句))】
  He *led* me *in* [*across*] the street]. 彼は私を中へ案内した[私の手を取って通りを渡らせてくれた].
  ② 【S〈物〉・V・O+*to*+〈場所〉】
  The light [path] *led* us *to* a small cabin. その光をたどって行くと[その道を歩いて行くと]小さな小屋に着いた.
  ③ 【S〈事〉・V・O〈人〉+*to*+〈事態〉】
  Overwork *led* him *to* illness. 過労で彼は病気になった.
  ④ 【S〈事〉・V+*to*+〈事態〉】
  Overwork *led to* his illness. 意味は③と同じ.
❷ 率いる, 先導する, リードする.
  【S〈人・物・事〉・V・O〈集合体〉】
  The mayor *led* the procession. 市長が行列の先頭に立って歩いた.
  Japan *leads* the world in car production. 日本は自動車の生産では世界一である.
❸ …な生活を送る.
  【S〈人・事〉・V・O〈a+形+*life*〉】
  He *leads* a simple *life*. 彼は質素な生活を送っている.
❹ する気にならせる.
  【S〈人・事〉・V・O〈人〉・C〈*to do*〉】
  What *led* you *to* change your mind? どうして気持ちが変わったのでしょうか.
❺ …に通じる.
  【S〈道・出口〉・V+*to* [*into*]+〈場所〉】

This road *leads to* the station [*into* the town]. この道は駅に[町に]通じている. (❗進行形, 受身形は不可) (⇨❶②)

learn 動

❶ 習得する, 習う.
① 【S〈人〉・V・O〈学科・事/*how to* do〉】
We *are learning* English from Mr. Yasui. 私たちは安井先生に英語を習っている.
I *have learned* the knack of it [*how to* drive a car]. そのコツ[車の運転の仕方]を覚えた.
② 【S〈人〉・V(+副(句))】
He *learns* fast. 彼は物覚えが早い.

❷ ...できる[する]ようになる.
【S〈人〉・V・O〈*to* do〉】
He *learned* to work effectively. 彼は効率よく仕事ができるようになった.

❸ 知る.
【S〈人〉・V・O〈(*that*)節・*wh*-節〉】
I *learned* (*that*) she was ill. 彼女が病気だと知った. (❗受身形は不可: ×*It* was learned *that* she was ill. ×She was learned *to* be ill.)
We have yet to *learn who* will be the new chairman. だれが次の議長になるのかまだわからない.

leave 動

❶ 去る, 離れる.
① 【S〈人〉・V+(*for*+〈行先〉)】
He *left for* Osaka yesterday. 彼はきのう大阪へたった. (❗×*to* Osaka は不可)
What time will the train *leave*? 電車は何時に出ますか.
② 【S〈人〉・V・O〈場所〉(+*for*+〈行先〉)】
He will *leave* Tokyo *for* Osaka tomorrow. 彼はあす東京をたって大阪に向かう. (❗×leave *from* Tokyo... は不可)
③ 【S〈人〉・V・O〈人・団体など〉】
She *has left* me. 彼女は私のもとを去った.
He *left* school last year. 彼は去年学校をやめた[卒業した].

❷ 置いて行く.
【S〈人〉・V・O〈物・人〉+副(句)】
You may *leave* your car here. ここに車を置いて行ってもよろしい.

❸ 置き忘れる.
【S〈人〉・V・O〈物〉+副(句)】
I *left* my umbrella *behind* [*in* the train]. 傘をどこかに[列車の中に]置き忘れた. (⇨forget❷)

❹ 残す.
① 【S〈人・物・事〉・V(・O〈人〉)・O〈物・事〉】
I will *leave* you some food. 食べ物を少し残しておいてあげよう. (❗この文型は物に焦点があり, ②は「人」に焦点がある)
② 【S〈人・物・事〉・V・O〈物・事〉(+*for*+〈人〉)】
I will *leave* some food *for* [×to] you. 意味は①と同じ.

❺ 残して死ぬ.
① 【S〈人〉・V(・O〈人〉)・O〈財産など〉】
He *left* his daughter a large fortune. 彼は娘にばく大な財産を残して死んだ.
② 【S〈人〉・V・O〈財産など〉(+*to*+〈人〉)】
He *left* a large fortune *to* [×for] his daughter. 意味は①と同じ.

❻ 任せる.
① 【S〈人〉・V・O〈物・事〉+*to*+〈人〉】
I *left* the work *to* him. 彼にその仕事を任せた.
② 【S〈人〉・V・O〈人〉・C〈*to* do〉】
I *left* him *to* do the work. 意味は①と同じ.

❼ ...のままにしておく.
① 【S〈人・物・事〉・V・O〈人・物〉・C〈形・名・do-*ing*・done〉】
They *left* the window open. 彼らは窓を開けたままにしておいた. (受身=The window *was left* open.)
She *left* him alone [cry*ing*]. 彼女は彼を一人にしておいた[彼が泣くに任せた].
② 【S〈人〉・V・O〈物・事〉・C〈*as* 節〉】
I *left* the book *as* it was. その本をそのままにしておいた.

lend 動 貸す.

① 【S〈人〉・V(・O〈人〉)・O〈物・金〉】
They *lent* me a large amount of money. 彼らは私に大金を貸してくれた. (❗「金」に焦点がある) (受身=A large amount of money *was lent* (*to*) me./I *was lent* a large amount of money.)
② 【S〈人〉・V・O〈物・金〉(+*to*+〈人〉)】
They *lent* a large amount of money *to* me. 意味は①と同じ. (受身=A large amount of money *was lent to* me.)

lesson 名 教訓.

【〜+*that* 節】
The *lesson that* public health is everyone's business has yet to be learned. 公衆衛生は共同責任だという教訓はまだ学びとられていない.

let 動

❶ ...させる. (❗強制的な使役の意味はなく,「本人が望んだからさせてやる」という消極的な使役を表わす. ⇨ make❷)
① 【S〈人〉・V・O〈人・物〉・C〈do〉】
They didn't *let* me *go* to the party. 彼らはパーティーに行かせてくれなかった. (❗受身形は let を用いず I *wasn't allowed* [*wasn't permitted*] *to* go .... で代用する)
② 【S〈人〉・V・O〈人・物〉+副(句)】
He *let* me out [*into*] his room]. 彼は私を外に出してくれた[彼の部屋に通した].

❷ ...しよう.
【Let's [Let us]・do】
"*Let's* take a rest, shall [×will] we?" "Yes, *let's* [×we shall]." 「一休みしましょうよ」「ええ, そうしましょう」.

❸ 貸す.《英》
【S〈人〉・V・O〈家・部屋〉】
I *let* my spare room for ￡50 a week. 私はあいている部屋を週50ポンドで貸した.

lie 動

❶ 横たわる.
【S〈人・動物〉・V+副(句)】
He *lay* down [*was lying*] *on* the bench. 彼はベンチに横になった[横になっていた]. (❗lie down は動作を, 進行形は一時的な状態を表わす)

❷ 置かれている.
【S〈物〉・V+副(句)】
The books *were lying* neatly on the desk. その本は机の上にきちんと置かれていた. (❗進行形は一時的な状態を表わす)

❸ ...に位置する. (❗通例進行形は不可)
【S〈土地〉・V+副(句)】
Japan *lies in* the east of Asia. 日本はアジアの東

位置する.
④ ...にある.
【S〈事〉・V＋副(句)】
The difficulty *lies* here. 困難はここにある.
⑤ ...の状態にある. (❗通例進行形は不可)
【S〈人・動物・物〉・V・C〈形〉・*doing*・done〉】
He *lay* still. 彼はじっと横になっていた.
The leaves *lay* thick [scatter*ed*] on the garden. 木の葉が庭を厚くおおっていた[庭に散らばっていた].

like 動
❶ 好む.
① 【S〈人〉・V・O〈人・物・事〉】
I *like* English very much. 私は英語がとても好きだ. (❗S が「多数の人」の場合受身形可: He *is* well *liked by* his students. (彼は生徒に好かれている))
I *like* dogs better than cats. 私は猫より犬のほうが好きだ. (❗一般的な好みを述べるときは通例目的語には複数形を用いる)
② 【S〈人〉・V・O〈*to* do・*doing*〉】
I *like to* swim [swim*ming*] in the sea. 海水浴が好きだ. (❗*to* do と *doing* を区別なく用いることが多いが、厳密には *to* do は特定の行為について、*doing* は一般的、または習慣的行為について用いる)
③ 【S〈人〉・V・O〈物・事〉・C〈形〉・done〉】
I *like* my tea hot [ic*ed*]. 茶は熱い[冷たい]のがよい.
❷ ...してほしい.
【S〈人〉・V・O〈人・物〉・C〈*to* do・*doing*〉】
I don't *like* him *to* neglect [neglect*ing*] his duty. 彼には任務を怠ってほしくない. (❗*doing* は否定文でよく使われる)

likely 形 ...しそうである.
① 【S〈人・物・事〉is ～＋*to* do】
He is *likely to* win the election. 彼は当選しそうだ.
② 【It is ～＋*that* 節】
It is *likely that* he will [×should] win the election. 意味は ① と同じ. (❗×It is *likely for* him *to* win the election. は不可)

listen 動
❶ 聞く.
① 【S〈人〉・V(＋*to*＋〈人・話・放送など〉)】
I *listened to* his speech [the news over the radio]. 彼の演説を[そのニュースをラジオで]聞いた.
② 【S〈人〉・V＋*to*＋〈人・物・事〉＋*doing* [do]】
I *listened to* him play*ing* [play] the piano. 彼がピアノを弾いている[弾く]のを聴いた. (❗(1) play*ing* は弾いている途中を、play は最初から最後までを聞いたことを表わす. (2) 受身形は通例不可)
❷ 耳を貸す.
【S〈人〉・V＋*to*＋〈人・忠告など〉】
He wouldn't *listen to* me [my advice]. 彼は私の言うこと[私の忠告]に耳を貸そうとしなかった.

live 動
❶ 生きる.
① 【S〈人・動植物〉・V(＋副(句))】
He *lived* in the 17th century. 彼は 17 世紀に生きていた. (❗進行形は不可)
Very few people *live to* (the age of) 100. 100 歳まで生きる人はきわめて少ない.
② 【S〈人・動植物〉・V＋*to* do】
Very few people *live to* be 100. 意味は ① の第 2 例と同じ. (❗*to* be は結果の不定詞)
❷ 住む.
【S〈人・動物〉・V＋副(句)】
I *live in* Kyoto [*with* my parents]. 京都に[両親といっしょに]住んでいる. (❗進行形は一時的な状態を表わす: I *am* now *living in* Kyoto.)
❸ 暮らす, 生活する.
① 【S〈人〉・V＋副(句)】
They *lived* happily. 彼らは幸せに暮らした.
② 【S〈人〉・V・O〈a＋形＋*life*〉】
They *lived* a happy *life*. 意味は ① と同じ.

look 動
❶ 見る.
① 【S〈人〉・V(＋副)(＋*at*＋〈人・物〉)】
He *looked at* me [up *at* the sky]. 彼は私を見た[空を見上げた].
② 【S〈人〉・V＋*at*＋〈人・物〉＋*doing* [do]】
I *looked at* him danc*ing* [dance]. 彼が踊っている[踊る]のを見た. (❗danc*ing* は踊っている途中を、dance は最初から最後までを見たことを意味する)
❷ ...に見える. (⇒seem)
① 【S〈人・物〉・V・(*to* be) C〈形・名〉】
He *looks* (*to* be) young [his age]. 彼は若く[年相応に]見える. (❗(1) *to* be は通例省略される. *to* be を用いるのは《米》. (2) C に名詞を用いるのは《主に英》.《米》では look like を用いる. (3) 進行形は不可)
② 【S〈人・物〉・V・C〈*like*＋〈人・物・事〉〉】
He *looks like* a policeman. 彼は警官のようだ.
It *looks like* rain. (＝It is likely to rain.) 雨になりそうだ.
③ 【S〈人・物〉・V・C〈*as if* 節〉】
He *looks as if* [*as though*] he didn't know it. 彼はまるでそれを知らないように見える.
❸ 確かめる.
【S〈人〉・V・O〈wh-節〉】
Look where the ball goes. ボールがどこへ行くか確かめなさい. (❗通例命令文で用いる)

lose 動
❶ 失う.
① 【S〈人〉・V・O〈物・人〉】
He *has lost* his purse [his wife]. 彼は財布[妻]を失った.
② 【S〈人〉・V・O〈物・人〉＋*to*＋〈物・人〉】
He *lost* his job *to* alcohol [illness]. 彼は酒[病気]のために失職した.
She *lost* her husband *to* a younger woman. 彼女は夫を自分より若い女に取られた.
❷ 見失う.
【S〈人〉・V・O〈人・物〉】
He *lost* his wife [his way] in the fog. 彼は霧の中で妻を見失った[道に迷った].
❸ 維持できなくなる.
【S〈人〉・V・O〈忍耐・容色・健康・名声〉】
He *lost* his temper. 彼は怒かっとなった.
She *has lost* her beauty [health]. 彼女は容色が衰えた[健康をそこねた].
❹ 負ける.
① 【S〈人・チーム〉・V・O〈試合・戦いなど〉(＋*to*＋〈相手〉)】
We *lost* the game *to* them. 私たちはその試合で彼らに負けた.
② 【S〈人・チーム〉・V(＋*at* [*in*]＋〈試合など〉) [＋*to*＋〈相手〉]】
We *lost at* the match [*to* the Chinese team]. 私たちはその試合に[中国チームに]負けた.
❺ (時計が)遅れる.

【S〈時計〉・V・O〈時間〉】
My watch *loses* a minute a day. 私の時計は日に1分遅れる.

❻ 損をする.
【S〈人〉・V(＋[副(句)])】
They *lost* a lot on that deal. 彼らはその取り引きで大損をした.

love 動
❶ 愛する.
【S〈人〉・V・O〈人〉】
I *love* Mary. メリーを愛している.

❷ 大好きである.
① 【S〈人〉・V・O〈物・事〉】
I *love* his novels. 彼の小説が大好きだ.
② 【S〈人〉・V・O〈*to* do・doing〉】 He *loves to* take [tak*ing*] a walk. 彼は散歩するのが大好きだ. (*to* do と doing の違いは like の場合と同じ. ⇨like ❶ ②)

lucky 形 幸運な.
① 【S〈人〉 *is* ～＋*to do*】
I was *lucky* (enough) *to* draw a prize. くじに当たったのは運がよかった.
② 【S〈人〉 *is* ～＋(*in*)＋〈事・*doing*〉】
I was *lucky* (*in*) drawing a prize. 意味は ① と同じ. (❗ doing の場合は in の省略可)
③ 【S〈人〉 *is* ～＋(*that*) 節】
I was *lucky* (*that*) I drew a prize. 意味は ① と同じ.
④ 【It is ～＋*for*＋〈人〉＋*to do*】
It was *lucky for* me *to* draw a prize. 意味は ① と同じ.
⑤ 【It is ～＋(＋*for*＋〈人〉)＋*that* 節】
It was *lucky* (*for* me) *that* I drew a prize. 意味は ① と同じ.

mad 形
❶ 気が狂う.
① 【S〈人〉 *is* ～＋*to do*】
You are *mad to* refuse such a good proposal of marriage. そんないい縁談を断るなんて君もどうかしているよ.
② 【It is ～＋*of*＋〈人〉＋*to do*】
It is *mad of* you *to* refuse such a good proposal of marriage. 意味は ① と同じ.

❷ 怒って. 《主に米話》(⇨angry)
① 【S〈人〉 *is* ～＋*at* [*with*]＋〈人〉(＋*for doing*)】
He was *mad at* her *for* breaking her promise. 彼は彼女が約束を破ったことで腹を立てた.
② 【S〈人〉 *is* ～＋*about* [*at*] *doing*】
He was *mad about* being kept awake by the dog all night. 彼は夜通し犬のおかげで眠れなくて頭に来た.
③ 【S〈人〉 *is* ～＋*that* 節】
He was *mad that* she had broken her promise. 意味は ① と同じ.

❸ 熱狂して.《話》
【S〈人〉 *is* ～＋*about* [*for*]＋〈事・人〉】
He is *mad about* soccer. 彼はサッカーに夢中になっている.

maintain 動
❶ 維持する.
【S〈人〉・V・O〈状態・行為〉】
We made every effort to *maintain* a high-quality service. 私たちは質の高いサービスを維持するためにあらゆる努力をした.

❷ 保全する.
【S〈人〉・V・O〈物〉】
The engineer *maintained* the machine in good condition. 技師はその機械の調子を良好に整備しておいた.

❸ 主張する.
① 【S〈人〉・V・O〈事〉】
She *maintained* his innocence. 彼女は彼の無罪を主張した.
② 【S〈人〉・V・O＋*that* 節】
She *maintained that* he was innocent. (❗ S・V・O＋*to be* C: She maintained him *to be* innocent. の型も可) 意味は ① と同じ.

make 動
❶ 作る.
① 【S〈人・動物〉・V・O〈物〉】
She *made* a cake. 彼女はケーキを作った.
② 【S〈人〉・V・O〈物〉＋*from* [(*out*) *of*]＋〈物〉】
We *make* paper *from* wood. 紙は木から作る. (受身＝Paper *is made from* wood.)
I *made* a chair (*out*) *of* wood. 木からいすを作った. (❗ from は原材料が化学的変化を起こしてもとの形が分からなくなっている場合, (out) of は材料相をもとの姿を製品に残していて一見して分かる場合. out of は述語動詞が原材料を表わす名詞から離れている場合に多く用いる)
③ 【S〈人〉・V・O〈人〉・O〈物〉】
She *made* him a sweater. 彼女は彼にセーターを作ってやった. この文型は「物」に焦点があり, ④ は「人」に焦点がある.
④ 【S〈人〉・V・O〈物〉＋*for*＋〈人〉】
She *made* a sweater *for* [×to] him. 意味は ③ と同じ.

❷ …させる.(❗ 無理にさせるという強制的な使役を表わす)
【S〈人・物・事〉・V・O〈人〉・C〈do〉】
They *made* him (×to) work all day. 彼らは彼を一日中働かせた. (受身形では to が必要: He *was made to* work all day.)
What *makes* you laugh? どうして笑うのですか.

❸ …にする.
① 【S〈人・物〉・V・O〈人・物〉・C〈形・名・wh- 節〉】
The news *made* him happy [disappointed]. 彼はその知らせを聞いて喜んだ[がっかりした].
My parents *made* me *what* I am today. 私が今日あるのは両親のお陰です. (⇨owe ❶)
He *made* the plan clear. 彼はその計画を明確にした.
② 【S〈人・事〉・V・O〈人〉・C〈名〉】
His parents *made* him a lawyer. 両親は彼を弁護士にした.

❹ 引き起こす.
【S〈人・事〉・V・O〈事〉】
You must not *make* a loud noise. 大きい音を立てるな.
What *made* such a great advance? どうしてこんなに大きな進歩をしたのか.

❺ …になる.
① 【S〈人・物〉・V・C〈人・物〉】
She will *make* a good wife. 彼女はよい奥さんになるだろう. (❗ C は通例良い意味の形容詞を伴う名詞. ×She will make a wife. とは言わない)
② 【S〈人・事〉・V・O〈人〉・C〈名〉】
She will *make* him a good wife. 彼女は彼にとってよい奥さんになるだろう.

③ 【S〈人・物〉・V・O〈人・物〉+*to*+〈人〉】
She will *make* a good wife *to* [《今はまれ》for] him. 意味は ② と同じ.
❻ 行なう, する.
① 【S〈人〉・V・O〈行為・発言など〉】
You must *make* great efforts. 君は大いに努力するべきだ.
② 【S〈人〉・V・O〈人〉・O〈事〉】
We *made* him a concrete proposal. われわれは彼に具体的な提案をした.
③ 【S〈人〉・V・O〈事〉+*to*+〈人〉】
We *made* a concrete proposal *to* [×for] him. 意味は ② と同じ.

manage 動
❶ 経営[管理]する.
【S〈人〉・V・O〈事業など〉】
He *manages* a company [a baseball team]. 彼は会社を経営している[野球チームの監督をしている].
❷ うまく取り扱う.
【S〈人〉・V・O〈物・人〉】
He *manages* the students [money; horse] well. 彼は生徒への対応がうまい[上手に金をやりくりする; その馬を上手に乗りこなす].
❸ 何とかやってゆく.
【S〈人〉・V(+*with*+〈道具・物〉[*on*+〈金〉])】
I can *manage with* this machine [*on* my salary]. この機械[私の給料]で何とかやっていける. (❗ ❸ と ❹ の文型はしばしば can, be able to を伴う)
❹ 何とか…する.
【S〈人〉・V・O〈*to do*〉】
I *managed to* ease his anger. やっとのことで彼の怒りを静めることができた.

marry 動
❶ 結婚する.
① 【S〈人〉・V(+副(句))】
She *married* young [late in life]. 彼女は早婚[晩婚]だった. (❗ (1)×marry old は不可. (2) 主語が二人の場合は Tom and Mary *got married* last year. のようにする)
② 【S〈人〉・V・O〈人〉】
She *married* John. (=She *got married* to John.) 彼女はジョンと結婚した. (❗ (1)×marry *with* [*to*] John は不可. (2) 受身形×John was married by her. は不可. ただし John is *married* (*to* [×with] her). は可で,「ジョンは(彼女と)結婚している」という状態を表わす)
❷ 結婚させる.
【S〈人〉・V・O〈女〉(+*to*〈男〉)】
He *married* his daughter *to* a young lawyer. 彼は娘を若い弁護士に嫁がせた.

match 動
❶ 匹敵する.
① 【S〈人・物〉・V・O〈人・物〉(+*in* [*for*]+〈物・事〉)】
No one can *match* him *in* tennis. テニスではだれ一人彼にかなわない. (受身=He cannot *be matched in* tennis.)
Can any country *match* Brazil *for* good coffee? 良質のコーヒーでブラジルに太刀打ちできる国がありますか.
② 【S〈人・物・事〉・V(+*with*+〈人・物・事〉)】
His record nearly *matches with* the champion's. 彼の記録はチャンピオンの記録とほぼ互角である.

❷ 調和する.
① 【S〈物〉・V・O〈物〉】
Your scarf *matches* your dress. あなたのスカーフは服によく似合っています. (❗ (1) O に人は来ない: ×Your scarf *matches* you. (2) 受身形は不可)
② 【S〈物・人・事〉・V(+*with*+〈物・人・事〉)】
These two colors don't *match* (*with* each other). この二つの色は合わない.
❸ 調和させる.
【S〈人〉・V・O〈物〉+*with* [*to*]+〈物・事〉】
They *matched* the curtains *with* the carpet. 彼らはじゅうたんにカーテンを合わせた. (受身=The curtains *were matched with* the carpet.)
❹ 競争させる, 取り組ませる.
【S〈人〉・V・O〈人・チームなど〉+*against* [*with*]+〈人・チームなど〉】 They *matched* us *against* [*with*] the best team. 彼らは私たちを最強のチームに当てた. (受身=We *were matched against* [*with*] the best team.)

matter 動 重要[重大]である. (❗ 通例否定文, 疑問文で用いる)
【S〈It・事〉・V】
It doesn't *matter* to [with] me whether he comes or not [that he is poor]. 彼が来るかどうか[彼が貧乏だということ]は私にはどうでもよい.
His birth or rank *matters* little. 彼の家柄や地位は大して重要なことではない.
What does it *matter*? そんなことはどうでもよいじゃないか.

mean 動 (❗ 通例進行形は不可)
❶ 意味する. (❗ 受身形は不可)
① 【S〈物・事〉・V・O〈物・事〉】
This traffic sign *means* "No parking." この交通標識は「駐車禁止」という意味だ.
② 【S〈物・事〉・V・O〈(*that*) 節〉】
This traffic sign *means* (*that*) you cannot park here. この交通標識はここでは駐車できないことを意味する.
③ 【S〈物・事〉・V・O〈*doing*〉】
Failing this exam *means* taking another one. この試験に不合格ならもう一度受けなくてはならないことになる.
❷ …のつもりで言う.
① 【S〈人〉・V・O〈事・言葉〉(+前+名)】
What do you *mean by* (saying) that? どういうつもりでそのように言うのですか.
I *mean* it *as* [*for*] a joke. 冗談のつもりでそう言うのです. (❗ I *mean* it. は「本気で言っているのです」の意味)
② 【S〈人〉・V・O〈(*that*) 節〉】
He *means* (*that*) you may go. 彼は君が行ってもいいと言っているのです.
❸ …するつもりである.
① 【S〈人〉・V・O〈*to do*〉】
I *mean to* write him a letter. 彼に手紙を書くつもりです.
I *had meant to* call you. 君に電話をするつもりだったのだが. (❗ (1) 過去完了は実現しなかったことを表わす. (2) I *meant to* have called you. ともいえるが, 前者の方が好まれる)
② 【S〈人〉・V・(+*for*)・O〈人・物〉・C〈*to do*〉】
I *mean* (*for*) my son *to* go to college. 私は息子に大学へ行かせるつもりでいる.
❹ 与えるつもりである.
【S〈人〉・V・O〈物〉+*for*+〈人〉】

I *mean* this watch *for* you. この時計を君にあげたい. (受身＝This watch *is meant for* you.)

❺ 重要性を持つ. (❗受身形は不可)
【S〈人・物・事〉・V・O〈程度〉(+*to*+〈人〉)】
This certificate *means* a lot [nothing] *to* me. この証明書は私にとって大変重要な意味を持つ[まったく意味がない].

meet 動

❶ 会う, (偶然)出会う.
① 【S〈人・物〉・V・O〈人・物〉】
I happened to *meet* him in the park. 私は偶然彼と公園で会った. (❗通例受身形は不可)
② 【S〈複数の人・物〉・V】
We may not *meet* again. 私たちは再会することはないかもしれない.

❷ 面会する, 知り合いになる.
【S〈人〉・V・O〈人〉】
It's nice to *meet* [*meeting*] you. お会いしてうれしいです[お会いできてよかったです]. (❗前者は初対面, 後者は別れるときのあいさつ. 受身形は不可)

❸ 出迎える.
【S〈人〉・V・O〈人・乗り物〉】
I am going to *meet* my uncle at the airport. おじを空港に迎えに行くところです.

❹ 交わる.
① 【S〈道・川・線など〉・V・O〈他の道など〉】
This road *meets* another road in two kilometers. この道は2キロ先で別の道と交差している.
② 【S〈複数の道・川など〉・V】
The two rivers *meet* at this point. その二つの川はここで合流している.

mention 動

❶ ...のことを口にする[書く].
【S〈人〉・V・O〈物・事・人〉(+*to*+〈人〉)】
The teacher *mentioned* the book *to* us. 先生は私たちにその本のことを話した. (❗×...mentioned *about* the book *to* us. は不可)

❷ 述べる.
① 【S〈人〉・V(+*to*+〈人〉)・O〈(*that*)節〉】
He *mentioned to* us (*that*) he was glad to see us. 彼は私たちに会えてうれしいと言った. (受身＝It *was mentioned to* us *that* he was glad to see us.)
② 【S〈人〉・V・O〈wh-節・*doing*〉】
Did he *mention when* he would arrive? 彼はいつ到着するか言いましたか. / He *mentioned losing* his wallet. 彼は財布をなくしたと言った.

message 名 伝言.

① 【〜+*to do*】
Please leave him a *message to* meet me at the airport. 空港へ私を迎えに来てくれるようにとの伝言を彼に伝えてください.
② 【〜+*that*】
I got the *message that* the meeting had been canceled. 会合は中止になったという伝言を受けた.

mind 動 (❗進行形不可)

❶ 注意を払う. (❗命令形で使うことが多い)
① 【S〈人〉・V・O〈人・物・事〉】
Mind your manners. 行儀作法に気をつけよ.
② 【S〈人〉・V・O〈(*that*)節〉】
Mind (*that*) you listen to your teacher. 先生の話をよく聞くようにしなさい. (❗*that*節内は未来形不可)

③ 【S〈人〉・V・O〈wh-節〉】 *Mind what* I tell you. 私の言うことをよく聞きなさい.

❷ いやがる. (❗主に疑問文, 否定文で)
① 【S〈人〉・V・O〈人・物・事・wh-節〉】
I don't *mind* the heat. 暑さは苦にならない.
I don't *mind how* hot it is. 意味は第1例と同じ.
② 【S〈人〉・V・O〈(所有格+)*doing*〉】
"Would [Do] you *mind opening* the window?" "Of course not [Not at all]." 「すみませんが窓を開けていただけませんか」「いいですとも」 (❗ていねいに人に依頼するときの表現. would を用いる方がよりていねい)
Would [Do] you *mind* my *smoking* here? ここでたばこを吸ってもかまいませんか.
③ 【S〈人〉・V】
Would [Do] you *mind if* I smoke here? 意味は②の第2例と同じ.

miss 動

❶ 捕えそこなう, 逃がす.
【S〈人・物〉・V・O〈物・事〉】
He *missed* the ball [the opportunity]. 彼はそのボールを受けそこなった[機会を逸した].
The arrow *missed* the target. 矢は的に当たらなかった.

❷ 乗り遅れる. (❗通例受身形は不可)
【S〈人〉・V・O〈乗り物〉】
I *missed* the bus by three minutes. 3分違いでバスに乗り遅れた.

❸ 見[聞き]そこなう.
【S〈人〉・V・O〈映画・話など〉】
I *missed* the TV program. そのテレビ番組を見逃した.

❹ ...しそこなう.
【S〈人〉・V・O〈*doing*〉】
I *missed watching* the TV program. 意味は❸の例と同じ.

❺ いない[できない]のを寂しく思う.
【S〈人〉・V・O〈人・物〉】
I *miss* you very much. 君がいなくてとても寂しい.
I really *miss driving* in the countryside whenever I want. 私は行きたい時にいつでも田舎をドライブできないのを寂しく思う.

❻ ない[いない]のに気づく.
【S〈人〉・V・O〈人・物〉】
When did you *miss* the key [the boy]? いつ鍵(ぎ)がない[その少年がいない]のに気がつきましたか.

❼ 免れる.
① 【S〈人〉・V・O〈事故・災難など〉】
He *missed* the accident. 彼は事故を免れた.
② 【S〈人〉・V・O〈*doing*〉】
He barely *missed being* injured. 彼はかろうじてけがをしないですんだ.

❽ 抜かす.
【S〈人〉・V+*out*・O〈名前・語など〉】
He *missed out* her name from the list. 彼は名簿から彼女の名前を抜かした. (❗故意に抜かす場合とうっかり抜かす場合の両方を意味する)

mistake 動 間違える, 誤解する.

① 【S〈人〉・V・O〈道・日時・意味など〉】
I *mistook* the road [the date of the meeting; the meaning of the sentence]. 道を間違えた[会議の日を間違えた; 文の意味を取り違えた]. (❗通例受身形不可)
② 【S〈人〉・V・O〈*what*節〉】
He *mistook what* I said. 彼は私の言ったことを誤解

した. (受身=*What* I said *was mistaken*.)
③ 【S〈人〉・V・O〈人・物〉+*for*+〈人・物〉】
He *mistook* Tom *for* his brother. 彼はトムを彼の兄と間違えた. (受身=Tom *was mistaken for* his brother.)

mix 動
❶ 混ぜる.
【S〈人〉・V・O〈物〉(+*with*+〈物〉)】
He *mixed* some paints (together). 彼は幾色かのペンキを混ぜ合わせた.
They *mixed* the cream *with* sugar. 彼らはクリームを砂糖と混ぜ合わせた. (受身=The cream *was mixed with* sugar.)
❷ 混ぜて作る.
【S〈人〉・V・O〈物〉(+*for*+〈人〉)】
He *mixed* some martinis *for* us. 彼は私たちにマティーニを作ってくれた. (❗S・V・O・O=He *mixed* us some martinis. の文型も可)
❸ 混ざる.
① 【S〈二つ以上の物〉・V】
Oil and water don't *mix*. 油と水は混ざらない.
② 【S〈物〉・V+*with*+〈物〉】
Oil doesn't *mix with* water. 油は水とは混ざらない.

move 動
❶ 動かす.
【S〈人〉・V・O〈物〉(+副(句))】
He *moved* the desk *into* his room. 彼はその机を彼の部屋へ移動した.
❷ 動く.
【S〈物・人〉・V(+副(句))】
The earth *moves around* the sun. 地球は太陽の周りを回っている.
This box won't *move* at all. この箱はびくともしない.
❸ 引っ越す.
【S〈人〉・V(+副(句))】
I'll *move* to the suburbs [*into* the apartment]. 郊外へ[そのアパートへ]引っ越すつもりです.
❹ 感動させる.
【S〈人・物・事〉・V・O〈人〉(+副(句))】
His story *moved* me deeply [*to* tears]. 彼の話を聞いて深く感動した[感動して泣いた]. (受身=I *was* deeply *moved* [*was moved* to tears] by his story.)

name 動
❶ 名前をつける.
① 【S〈人〉・V・O〈人・物など〉(・C〈名前〉)】
They *named* the baby (John). 彼らは赤ちゃんに(ジョンという)名前をつけた.
② 【S〈人〉・V・O〈人・物〉(・C〈名前〉)+*after* [(米)*for*]+〈人・物〉】 He *was named* Frank *after* [(米)*for*] his grandfather. 彼は祖父の名をとってフランクと名づけられた.
❷ 正しい名を言う.
【S〈人〉・V・O〈人・物など〉】
Can you *name* the capital of Canada? カナダの首都の名を言えますか.
❸ 任命する.
【S〈人〉・V・O〈人〉・(*as* [*for*; *to be*]) C〈役職・地位など〉】 He *was named* (*as* [*for*; *to be*]) chairman of the committee. 彼は委員長に任命された.

natural 形 当然の.
① 【It is ~(+*for*+〈人〉)+*to do*】
It is *natural for* him *to* fall in love with her. 彼が彼女にほれるのは無理もない.
② 【It is ~+*that* 節】
It is *natural that* he should fall [he falls, ×he fall] in love with her. 意味は ① と同じ.

necessary 形 必要な.
① 【S〈物・事〉 is ~+*for* [*to*]+〈人・物・事〉】
Fresh air is *necessary for* [*to*] health. 新鮮な空気は健康に必要だ.
② 【S〈物・事〉 is ~(+*for*+〈人・物・事〉)+*to do*】
Hard work is *necessary for* you *to* pass the examination. 君が試験に合格するには猛勉強が必要だ.
③ 【It is ~(+*for*+〈人・物・事〉)+*to do*】
It is *necessary for* you *to* take exercise every day. 君は毎日運動する必要がある. (❗× *You are* necessary to take…. ×*Exercise* is necessary (for you) to take. は不可)
④ 【It is ~+*that* 節】
It is *necessary that* you (should) take exercise every day. 意味は ③ と同じ.

need 動 (❗通例進行形不可)
❶ …する必要がある.
【S〈人〉・V・O〈*to do*〉】
You *need to* take it seriously. それはまじめに受け取る必要がある. (❗疑問文・否定文の場合には助動詞 need を用いても表わせる: *Need* you take it seriously?=Do you *need to* take it seriously?)
I didn't *need to* hurry. 急ぐ必要はなかった. (❗「…ので急がなかった」ことを表わす. 「…のに急いだ」は I *need* not have hurried.)
❷ …される必要がある.
【S〈物・人〉・V・O〈*doing*・*to* be done〉】
This sweater *needs* washing [*to* be washed]. このセーターは洗う必要がある.
❸ 必要とする, 要求する.
【S〈人・物・事〉・V・O〈人・物・事〉】
I *need* your help. 君の助けが必要だ.
This job *needs* more people. この仕事にはもっとたくさんの人が必要だ.
❹ …してもらう必要がある
① 【S〈人〉・V・O〈人・物・事〉・C〈過分〉】
I *need* my shoes mended. 靴を修理してもらう必要がある.
② 【S〈人〉・V・O〈人・物〉・C〈*to do*〉】
We *need* volunteers *to* help us. 私たちはボランティアに手伝ってもらう必要がある.

need 名 必要.
① 【~+*of* [*for*]+〈物・事・人・*doing*〉】
I don't see the *need of* [*for*] apology [going there]. 私は弁解の[そこへ行く]必要を認めない.
② 【~+*to do*】
You have no *need to* do it again. 君はもう一度それをやる必要はない.
③ 【~(+*for*+〈人・物・事〉)+*to do*】
There is no *need* (*for* you) *to* do it again. (君は)もう一度それをやる必要はない.

news 名 知らせ.
① 【~+*that* 節】
The *news that* he hadn't succeeded came as a surprise. 彼が不首尾に終わったという知らせは意外

だった.
② 【~+*of* [*about, as to*] *wh-* 節】
Do you have any *news of what* has become of her? 彼女がどうなったのか何か消息がありますか.

nice 形 親切な; 楽しい.
① 【S〈人〉 is ~+*to do*】
You were *nice to* lend me your car. 車を貸してくれてありがとう.
He is *nice to* get on with. 彼はつき合って楽しい人だ.
② 【It is ~ *of*+〈人〉+*to do*】
It was *nice of* you *to* lend me your car. 意味は①の前例と同じ.
③ 【It is ~+*to do* [*doing*]】
It is *nice to* get [get*ting*] on with him. 意味は①の第2例と同じ.
④ 【It is ~+*that* 節】
It is *nice that* we could see again. われわれが再会できたのは楽しい.

nominate 動
❶ 指名する.
【S〈人〉・V・O〈人〉+*for*+〈官職〉】
His party *nominated* him *for* mayor. 党は彼を市長の候補者として指名した.

❷ 任命する.
【S〈人〉・V・O〈人〉+*to be* [*as*] C〈役職〉】
The Prime Minister *nominated* him *to be* an ambassador. 首相は彼を大使に任命した.

notice 動 気づく. (❗進行形不可)
① 【S〈人〉・V・O〈人・物・事〉】
I *noticed* a man in the car [the difference]. 車の中の男 [違い] に気づいた.
② 【S〈人〉・V・O〈(*that*) 節〉】
He didn't *notice* (*that*) his wallet was missing. 彼は財布がなくなっていることに気づかなかった.
③ 【S〈人〉・V・O〈*wh-* 節〉】
Did you *notice whether* he was unwell? 彼が気分が悪いかどうか気がつきましたか. (❗*wh-* 節が続く場合は通例疑問文, 否定文)
④ 【S〈人〉・V・O〈人・物〉・C〈*doing*・*do*〉】
I *noticed* him leaving [leave] the room. 彼が部屋を出て行く [出る] のに気づいた. (❗(1) doing では「…しているのに気づく」, do では「…するのに気づく」の意味. (2) 受身形では do は to do になる: He *was noticed* leaving [*to* leave] the room.)

notion 名
❶ 考え.
① 【~+*that* 節】
You shouldn't have the *notion that* you are too old to learn. 年をとりすぎていて学習できないなどという考えは持つべきではない.
② 【~(+*of*)+*wh-* 節】
I have no *notion* (*of*) *what* they intend to do. 私には彼らが何をするつもりなのかまったく分からない.

❷ 意向.
【~+*to do*】
She had a sudden *notion to* go abroad. 彼女は突然外国へ行きたいと思った.

object 動
❶ 反対する.
【S〈人〉・V+*to* [*against*]+〈物・事・*doing*〉】
He strongly *objected to* my political views. 彼は私の政治についての意見に強く反対した.
We *objected to* his study*ing* abroad. 私たちは彼の留学に反対した.
❷ …だと反対する.
【S〈人〉・V・O〈*that* 節〉】
They *objected that* she was too young for the job. 彼女はその仕事には若すぎると, 彼らは反対した.

observe 動
❶ 観察する, 注意して見守る.
① 【S〈人〉・V・O〈物・事〉】
He *observed* the growth of the insect. 彼はその昆虫の成長を観察した.
② 【S〈人〉・V・O〈*wh-* 節句〉】
He *observed how* I rode a horse [*how to* ride a horse]. 彼はどのようにして馬に乗るか見ていた.

❷ 気づく.
① 【S〈人〉・V・O〈物・事〉】
I *observed* nothing unusual about him. 彼にはふだんと違うところは認められなかった. (受身=Nothing unusual *was observed* about him.)
② 【S〈人〉・V・O〈*that* 節〉】
We *observed that* he was pale. 私たちは彼の顔色が青ざめているのに気づいた. (受身=It *was observed* that he was pale.)
③ 【S〈人〉・V・O〈人〉・C〈*doing*・*do*〉】
We *observed* him entering [enter] the building. 私たちは彼がその建物に入って行く [入る] のに気がついた. (❗(1) doing では「…しているのに気づく」, do では「…するのに気づく」の意味. (2) 受身形では do は to do になる: He *was observed* entering [*to* enter] the building.)

❸ 守る.
【S〈人〉・V・O〈法律・義務など〉】
You should *observe* the traffic rules. 交通規則を守るべきである.

occur 動
❶ 起こる.
【S〈物・事〉・V+副(句)】
An awful car accident *occurred in* the tunnel. トンネルの中で恐ろしい自動車事故が起こった. (❗主語が不特定の名詞の場合は There *occurred* an awful car accident in the tunnel. のようにも表わせる)

❷ (心に) 浮かぶ. (❗進行形不可)
① 【S〈考えなど〉・V+*to*+〈人〉】
A brilliant idea suddenly *occurred to* me. 突然いい考えが浮かんだ.
② 【S〈*It*〉・V+*to*+〈人〉+*that* 節 [*to do*]】
It never *occurred to* me *that* he was telling a lie [*to* ask him]. 彼がうそをついていると [彼に尋ねてみようとは] 思いもよらなかった. (❗It は that 節か to do を受ける形式主語. that の省略は不可)

offend 動 感情を害する.
① 【S〈人・事〉・V・O〈人〉】
His blunt speech *offended* her. 彼のぶしつけな口のきき方は彼女の気分を害した.
② 【S〈人〉 be offended+*at* [*by*]+〈物・事〉】
She *was offended at* [*by*] *his blunt speech*. 彼女は彼のぶしつけは口のきき方に腹を立てていた.
③ 【S〈人〉 be offended+*with* [*by*]+〈人〉】
He *was offended with* the policeman. 彼はその警官に腹をたてていた.

offer 動

❶ 提供する, 申し出る.
① 【S〈人〉・V・O〈物・事〉】
He *offered* his help. 彼は援助を申し出た.
② 【S〈人〉・V・O〈人〉・O〈物・事〉】
They *offered* me a good job. 彼らは私にいい仕事を紹介してくれた. (❗この文型は「事」に焦点があり, ③は「人」に焦点がある) (受身=I *was offered* a good job./A good job *was offered* (to) me.)
③ 【S〈人〉・V・O〈物・事〉+*to*+〈人〉】
They *offered* a good job *to* me. 意味は② と同じ. (受身=A good job *was offered* to me.)
④ 【S〈人〉・V・O〈*to* do〉】
He *offered to* help me. 意味は① と同じ. (❗×He *offered* me to help me. は不可)
❷ 売りに出す.
【S〈人〉・V・O〈物〉+*for* [*at*]+〈価格〉】
He *offered* his house *for* 50 million yen [*at* a low price]. 彼は 5,000 万円[安い価格]で家を売りに出した. (❗price の場合は for も可)
❸ 買うと申し出る.
【S〈人〉・V・O〈金額〉+*for*+〈物〉】
He *offered* 1 million yen *for* the car. 彼はその車に 100 万円出そうと言った.

open 動

❶ 開ける, 広げる.
① 【S〈人〉・V・O〈物〉(+副(句))】
He *opened* the window [envelope]. 彼は窓[封筒]を開けた.
Open your textbook *to* [《英》*at*] page five. 教科書の 5 ページを開けなさい.
② 【S〈人〉・V・O〈戸〉+*for*+〈人〉】
He *opened* the door *for* me. 彼は私に戸を開けてくれた.
❷ 開く.
【S〈物〉・V+副(句)】
The door *opened by* itself [*with* the wind]. ドアがひとりでに[風で]開いた.
❸ 切り開く.
【S〈人〉・V・O〈道・新分野など〉(+副(句))】
They *opened* a road *through* the forest. 彼らは森の中に道を切り開いた.
❹ 始める.
【S〈人〉・V・O〈店・会議など〉(+副(句))】
They *opened* a restaurant *in* the suburbs. 彼らは郊外でレストランを始めた.
They *opened* the ceremony *with* his speech. 彼らは彼の演説で式を始めた.
❺ 始まる.
【S〈店・会議など〉・V(+副(句))】
This shop usually *opens at* ten. この店はたいてい 10 時に開店する.
The ceremony *opened with* his speech. その式は彼の演説で始まった.
❻ 公開する.
【S〈公共機関〉・V・O〈施設〉(+*to*+〈人〉)】
The board of education *opened* the garden *to* the public. 教育委員会はその庭園を一般に公開した.

opinion 名 意見, 見解.

【~+*that* 節】
I am of the *opinion that* he is quite different. 彼はまったく変わっていると私は思う. (❗堅い言い方. I think (that)... などと言う方が普通)

opportunity 名 機会.

① 【~(+*for*+〈人〉)+*to* do】
I don't have much *opportunity* [There are not many *opportunities for* me] *to* go to the movies. 私は映画に行く機会があまりない.
② 【~+*for* [*of*]+*doing*】
I have little [do not have much] *opportunity for* going to the movies. 意味は① と同じ.
I have few *opportunities of* visit*ing* my aunt. 私はおばを訪ねる機会があまりない.

order 動

❶ 命令する.
① 【S〈人〉・V・O〈事〉】
The judge *ordered* silence. 裁判官は静粛にするよう命じた.
② 【S〈人〉・V・O〈人〉・C〈*to* do〉】
They *ordered* me to leave for Tokyo. 彼らは私に東京へたつよう命令した. (受身=I *was ordered to* leave for Tokyo.)
③ 【S〈人〉・V・O〈*that* 節〉】
They *ordered that* I (should) leave for Tokyo. 意味は② と同じ. (受身=It *was ordered that* I (should) leave for Tokyo.) (❗(1)②が直接相手に命令するのに対し, ③は第三者を通じて命令することを示す. (2) should を用いるのは《主に英》. (3) ×They ordered me that.... は不可)
❷ 注文する.
① 【S〈人〉・V・O〈物〉(+*from*+〈注文先〉)】
He *ordered* the book *from* [×to] New York. 彼はその本をニューヨークへ注文した.
② 【S〈人〉・V・O〈人〉・O〈物〉】
He *ordered* me a new suit. 彼は私のために新しいスーツを注文してくれた. (❗この文型は「物」に焦点があり, ③は「人」に焦点がある)
③ 【S〈人〉・V・O〈物〉+*for*+〈人〉】
He *ordered* a new suit *for* [×to] me. 意味は② と同じ. (受身=A new suit *was ordered* by him *for* me.)

order 名 命令.

① 【~(+*for*+〈人・物・事〉)+*to* do】
He gave *orders* (or the, an *order*) *to* clean the room. (=He gave *orders for* the room *to* be cleaned.) 彼は部屋を掃除せよと命じた.
② 【~+*that* 節】
He gave *orders that* we (should) clean the room. 意味は① と同じ. (❗should を用いるのは《主に英》)

owe 動

❶ ...のお陰である.
【S〈人〉・V・O〈事〉+*to*+〈人・事〉】
I *owe* my success *to* my teacher [good luck]. 私が成功したのは先生のお陰である[幸運のたまものである]. (❗(1) 受身形は不可. (2) ×I *owe* my teacher [good luck] my success. は不可)
I *owe* what I am *to* my parents. 私が今日あるのは両親のお陰です. (❗×I *owe to* my parents what I am. は不可) (⇨make ❸)
❷ 義務を負っている.
① 【S〈人〉・V・O〈義務・感情〉+*to*+〈人〉】
We *owe* an apology *to* him. 私たちは彼に謝らなくてはならない. (❗この文型は「人」に焦点があり, ②は義務に焦点がある)
② 【S〈人〉・V・O〈人〉・O〈義務・感情〉】
We *owe* him an apology. 意味は① と同じ. (❗①, ②の文型とも受身形は不可)

❸ 借りがある.
① 【S〈人〉・V・O〈金〉+*to*+〈人〉(+*for*+〈物・事〉)】
We *owe* 100,000 yen *to* him *for* his service. 私たちは彼の業務に対して 10 万円の借りがある. (受身＝100,000 yen *is owed to* him *for* his service.) (❗*to* him の省略可)
② 【S〈人〉・V・O〈人〉・O〈金〉(+*for*+〈物・事〉)】
We *owe* him 100,000 yen *for* his service. 意味は ① と同じ. (❗him, 100,000 yen のいずれかを省略し S・V・O (+for...) の文型でも用いる)

pardon 動 許す, 大目に見る. (❗命令形で用いることが多い)

① 【S〈人〉・V・O〈人・事〉】
Pardon me. ごめんなさい/もう一度おっしゃってください.
② 【S〈人〉・V・O〈所有格+*doing*〉】
Pardon my disturbing you. じゃましてすみません.
③ 【S〈人〉・V・O〈人〉+*for*+〈事・*doing*〉】
Pardon me *for* disturbing you. 意味は ② と同じ.
④ 【S〈人〉・V・O〈人〉・O〈失敗など〉】
We must *pardon* his fault. われわれは彼の落ち度を大目に見てやらなければならない. (❗③ の文型を用いて ...*pardon* him *for* his fault. ともいえる)

pass 動

❶ 通る, 通り過ぎる.
① 【S〈人・車など〉・V(+[副(句)])】
Our bus *passed along* the street. われわれの乗ったバスは街路を通って行った.
② 【S〈人・車など〉・V・O〈人・物〉】
I *passed* him on the street. 通りで彼とすれ違った[彼を追い越した].
❷ (時が)たつ, 過ぎ去る.
【S〈時〉・V】
Ten years have *passed* since we parted. 私たちが別れてから 10 年たつ.
❸ 合格する[させる].
① 【S〈人〉・V(+[副(句)])】
He *passed in* the test. 彼はその試験に合格した.
② 【S〈人〉・V・O〈試験など〉】
He *passed* the test. 意味は ① と同じ.
The teacher *passed* all his students. 先生は生徒全員を合格にした.
❹ (議会などを)通過する, (議案などを)通過させる.
① 【S〈人〉・V(+[副(句)])】
The bill will *pass* within a week. その法案は 1 週間以内に通過するだろう.
② 【S〈人〉・V・O〈議会など〉】
The bill *passed* the Diet. 法案は国会を通過した.
The Diet *passed* the bill. 国会は法案を通過させた.
❺ 渡る, 譲られる.
【S〈地位・財産など〉・V+*to*+人 [*into*+人手]】
A large inheritance *passed to* his children [*into* the hands of his children]. ぼく大な財産が彼の子供たちに渡った.
❻ 過ごす, 送る.
【S〈人〉・V・O〈時〉+[副(句)] [(*in*)+*doing*]】
He *passed* his time (*in* [*by*]) listening to records. 彼はレコードを聴いて時を過ごした.
❼ 手渡す.
① 【S〈人〉・V・O〈物〉(+[副])+*to*+〈人〉】
Would you *pass* the sugar *to* me? 砂糖を回していただけませんか. (❗この文型は「人」に焦点があり, ② は「物」に焦点がある)
② 【S〈人〉・V・O〈人〉・O〈物〉】
Would you *pass* me the sugar? 意味は ① と同じ.

He *passed* me the ball. 彼は私にボールをパスした. (受身＝I *was passed* the ball by him./The ball *was passed* (*to*) me by him.)

pay 動

❶ (金を)支払う.
① 【S〈人〉・V・O〈借金・代金など〉(+*for*+〈物〉)】
He *paid* his debt [bill; tax]. 彼は借金[勘定; 税金]を払った.
He *paid* 3,000 yen *for* the book. 彼はその本に 3,000 円払った.
② 【S〈人〉・V+*for*+〈物〉(+*with*+〈金額〉)】
He *paid for* the book (*with* 3,000 yen). 彼は本代を (3,000 円)払った.
③ 【S〈人〉・V・O〈人〉・O〈金〉(+*for*+〈物〉)】
I *paid* him 3,000 yen (*for* the book). 私は彼に(本代として)3,000 円払った. (受身＝He *was paid* 3,000 yen (*for* the book)./3,000 yen *was paid* (*to*) him (*for* the book).)
④ 【S〈人〉・V・O〈金〉+*to*+〈人〉(+*for*+〈物〉)】
I *paid* 3,000 yen *to* him (*for* the book). 意味は ③ と同じ. (受身＝3,000 yen *was paid* (*to*) him (*for* the book).)
⑤ 【S〈人〉・V・O〈人〉・C〈*to do*〉】
He *paid* his son *to* wash the car. 彼は息子に金を払って車を洗わせた.
❷ (注意・敬意などを)払う; 訪問する.
① 【S〈人〉・V・O〈注意・敬意など〉】
I *pay* my old teacher a visit once a year. 私は年に 1 度以前習った先生を訪問する.
② 【S〈人〉・V・O〈注意・敬意など〉+*to*+〈人・事・物〉】
They *paid* little attention *to* the matter. 彼らはその件にほとんど注意を払わなかった. (受身＝Little attention *was paid to* the matter./The matter *was* little *paid* attention *to*.)
I *pay* a visit *to* my old teacher once a year. 意味は ① と同じ.
❸ (物事が)報いる, 引き合う.
① 【S〈物・事〉・V(・O〈人など〉)】
Crime doesn't *pay* you well. 犯罪はあまり引き合わない.
② 【S〈物・事〉・V(・O〈人〉)・O〈利益など〉】
The job will *pay* (you) 100,000 yen a month. その仕事は月 10 万円になるよ.
③ 【S〈物・事〉・V】
Crime doesn't *pay*. 犯罪は引き合わない.
❹ (人が)報いる, お返しをする.
【S〈人〉・V・O〈人〉(+*with*+〈物〉)(+*for*+〈行為〉)】 I *paid* him *with* a present *for* his help. 手伝ってくれたお礼に彼に贈り物をした.
❺ 償う.
【S〈人〉・V+*for*+〈犯罪・失敗など〉(+*with*+〈事〉)】 He should *pay for* the crime *with* a term in jail. 彼は刑務所に入って罪を償うべきだ.

permission 名 許可.

【〜+*to do*】 The teacher gave her *permission* [✕the permission] *to* go home. 先生は彼女に帰宅してもよいと言われた.

permit 動 許す.

① 【S〈人・規則など〉・V(・O〈人〉)・O〈物・事〉】
Her mother doesn't *permit* her sweets. 彼女の母親は彼女に甘いものを食べさせないことにしている.
② 【S〈人・規則など〉・V・O〈人〉・C〈*to do*〉】
They didn't *permit* their daughter *to* marry

him. 彼らは娘が彼と結婚することを許さなかった.
③ 【S〈人・規則など〉・V・O〈doing〉】
They do not *permit* smok*ing* in the office. 職場での喫煙は許されない. (受身＝Smoking *is* not *permitted* in the office./It *is* not *permitted* to smoke in the office.)
④ 【S〈物・事〉・V＋副(句)】
The situation *permits* of no delay. 事態は遅滞を許さない.

persuade 動

❶ 説得する, 説得して...させる[やめさせる].
① 【S〈人〉・V・O〈人〉・C〈to do〉】
We *persuaded* him *to carry out* the plan. 彼を説得してその計画を実行させた. (受身＝He *was persuaded to carry out* the plan.)
② 【S〈人〉・V・O〈人〉・O〈that 節〉】
We *persuaded* him *that* he (should) carry out the plan. 意味は①と同じ. (受身＝He *was persuaded that* he (should) carry out the plan.) (!) ×*It was persuaded that...*. の受身形は不可. *should* を用いるのは《主に英》)
③ 【S〈人〉・V・O〈人〉＋*into* [*out of*] ＋〈事・doing〉】 We *persuaded* him *into* carry*ing* out the plan. 意味は①と同じ.
We *persuaded* him *out of* carry*ing* out the plan. われわれは彼を説得してその計画の実行をやめさせた.

❷ 確信させる.
① 【S〈人〉・V・O〈人〉＋*of*＋〈事〉】
He *persuaded* me *of* his diligence. 彼は私に彼が勤勉だと納得させた.
② 【S〈人〉・V・O〈人〉＋*of*＋*wh-*節】
He *persuaded* me *of how* diligent he was. 彼は彼がいかに勤勉であるかを私に納得させた.
③ 【S〈人〉・V・O〈人〉＋O〈*that* 節〉】
He *persuaded* me *that* he was diligent. 意味は①と同じ.

pick 動

❶ 摘み取る.
① 【S〈人〉・V・O〈物〉】
She *picked* some daisies. 彼女はヒナギクを摘んだ.
② 【S〈人〉・V・O〈人〉・O〈物〉】
She *picked* me some daisies. 彼女は私にヒナギクを摘んでくれた. (!) この文型は「物」に焦点があり, ③は「人」に焦点がある) (受身＝Some daisies *were picked for* me.)
③ 【S〈人〉・V・O〈物〉＋*for*＋〈人〉】
She *picked* some daisies *for* me. 意味・受身形は②と同じ.

❷ (入念に)選ぶ.
① 【S〈人〉・V・O〈人・物・事〉】
He *picked* this book from my library. 彼は私の蔵書の中からこの本を選び出した.
② 【S〈人〉・V・O〈物〉・O〈人・物〉】
Please *pick* me a nice apple. 私においしいリンゴを選んでください. (!) この文型は「物」に焦点があり, ③は「人」に焦点がある)
③ 【S〈人〉・V・O〈物〉＋*for*＋〈人〉】
Please *pick* a nice apple *for* me. 意味は②と同じ.

plan 動

❶ 計画する.
① 【S〈人〉・V・O〈仕事・行動など〉】
We *are planning* a hike in Hakone. 箱根へハイキングすることを計画中です.
② 【S〈人〉・V・O〈*wh-*節(句)〉】
They *planned* carefully *how* they would build [*how to build*] a bridge. 彼らは橋をかける方法を慎重に計画した.
③ 【S〈人〉・V＋*for*＋〈事〉】
We have to *plan for* our old age. われわれは老後の計画を立てなければならない.

❷ ...するつもりである.
① 【S〈人〉・V・O〈*to do*〉】
I'*m planning to* visit my uncle next Sunday. 私は次の日曜におじを訪ねるつもりです. (!) 堅い言い方)
② 【S〈人〉・V・O〈doing〉】
I *plan* [× am planning] visit*ing* my uncle next Sunday. 意味は①と同じ.
③ 【S〈人〉・V＋*on*＋doing〉】
I'*m planning on* visit*ing* my uncle next Sunday. 意味は①と同じ. (!) くだけた言い方)

plan 名 計画.

① 【〜（＋*for*＋〈人・物・事〉）＋*to do*】
I can't favor your *plan to* study abroad. 私は君の留学の計画には賛成できない.
Have you heard about the *plan for* him *to* study abroad? 彼の留学の計画を聞きましたか.
② 【〜＋*for* [*of*]＋doing】
I can't favor your *plan for* [*of*] study*ing* abroad. 意味は①と同じ. (!) *for* は目的を表わして「...のための」, *of* は同格的に「...という」の意)

plant 動 植える, まく

① 【S〈人〉・V・O〈種など〉（＋*in*＋〈場所〉）】
He *planted* wheat *in* the field. 彼は畑に小麦をまいた.
② 【S〈人〉・V・O〈場所〉（＋*with*＋〈種など〉）】
He *planted* the field *with* wheat. 意味は①と同じ.

play 動

❶ 遊ぶ.
【S〈人〉・V（＋副(句)）】
The girls *are playing with* dolls. 少女たちは人形遊びをしている.

❷ 競技する.
① 【S〈人〉・V（＋副(句)）】
He *played in* goal [*as* goalkeeper]. 彼はゴールキーパーをした.
② 【S〈人〉・V・O〈球技・勝負事など〉】
We *played* baseball yesterday. われわれはきのう野球をした.
The Giants *played* the Dragons. 巨人は中日と対戦した.
The children *played* cards [house; war]. 子供たちはトランプ[ままごと; 戦争ごっこ]をした.

❸ 演奏する.
① 【S〈人〉・V（＋副(句)）】
He *played in* the orchestra. 彼はオーケストラの一員として演奏した.
The CD player *is playing*. CD プレーヤーがかかっている.
② 【S〈人〉・V・O〈楽器・曲など〉（＋副(句)）】
She *played* the piano beautifully. 彼女はピアノをみごとに弾いた.
She *played* Mozart [a tune] *on* the piano. 彼女はピアノでモーツァルトを[一曲]弾いた.
③ 【S〈人〉・V・O〈人〉・O〈曲・レコードなど〉】

She *played* me a Russian folk song. 彼女は私にロシア民謡を一曲弾いてくれた. (❗この文型は「曲」に，④は「人」に焦点がある)
④【S〈人〉・V・O〈曲・レコードなど〉+*for*+〈人〉】
She *played* a Russian folk song *for* me. 意味は③と同じ.

❹ 芝居をする, 上演[上映]される.
① 【S〈人〉・V(+圖(句))】
They *played* to a full house. 彼らは満員の観客の前で芝居をした.
② 【S〈劇・映画など〉・V(+圖(句))】
"Hamlet" *is playing at* that theater. あの劇場で「ハムレット」が上演されている. (❗通例進行形で)

❺ (劇・役などを)演じる; (役割を)演じる.
① 【S〈人〉・V・O〈劇・役など〉】
She *played* (the part of) Juliet. 彼女はジュリエットの役を演じた.
【S〈人〉・V・O〈役割〉】
He *played* an important part [role] in the student council. 彼は生徒会で重要な役割を果たした.

❻ (いたずらなどを)しかける.
① 【S〈人〉・V・O〈人〉・O〈いたずらなど〉】
He *played* me a trick. 彼は私にいたずらをしかけた. (❗この文型はいたずらに焦点があり, ②は「人」に焦点がある) (受身=I *was played* a trick (*on*) by him./A trick *was played on* me by him.)
② 【S〈人〉・V・O〈いたずらなど〉+*on*+〈人〉】
He *played* a trick *on* me. 意味は①と同じ. (受身=A trick *was played on* me by him.)

❼ ふるまう.
【S〈人〉・V・C〈形〉】
The animal *played* dead. その動物は死んだふりをした.
【S〈人〉・V+圖】
They *played* fair. 彼らは正々堂々と勝負した. (❗×play fairly とは言わない)

pleasant 形

❶ 楽しい.
① 【S〈物・事〉 is ~+*to do*】
This novel is *pleasant to* read. この小説は読んで楽しい.
② 【It is ~(+*for*+〈人〉)+*to do*】
It is *pleasant* (*for* me) *to* read this novel. この小説は(私には)読んで楽しい. (❗ ×*I am* pleasant *to* read this novel. は不可)

❷ 愛想のよい.
① 【S〈人〉 is ~+*to do*】
She is *pleasant to* get on with. 彼女はつき合って好感のもてる人だ.
② 【It is ~+*to do* [*doing*]】
It is *pleasant to* get [get*ting*] on with her. 意味は①と同じ.

please 動

❶ 喜ばせる, 楽しませる.
① 【S〈人・物・事〉・V・O〈人〉】
The gift *pleased* her. その贈り物は彼女を喜ばせた. (受身=She *was pleased with* the gift.)
② 【S〈*It*〉・V・O〈人〉+*to do*】
It *pleases* me to listen to music. 音楽を聴くことは楽しい. (❗ It is to 不定詞句を受ける形式主語)
③ 【S〈*It*〉・V・O〈人〉+*that* 圖】
It *pleased* us greatly *that* you were successful. 君が成功したのでわれわれは大いにうれしかった. (❗ It は that 圖 を受ける形式主語) (受身=We *were* greatly *pleased that* you were successful.)

❷ 好む, 気に入る.
【S〈人〉・V】
You may do as you *please*. 好きなようにしてよい.

pleasure 名 喜び, 光栄.

① 【~+*of*+*doing*】
I look forward to the *pleasure of* seeing you on Sunday. 日曜日にお目にかかりますことを楽しみにお待ちしております. (❗社交辞令的な敬意表現)
② 【~+*in*+*doing*】
I take [have] *pleasure in* opening [×to open] this meeting. この会を開かせていただきます. (❗ have the pleasure of doing ほど堅くないが, be pleased [glad, happy] to do より堅い表現)
③ 【~+*to do*】
I have the *pleasure to* welcome you here in Kobe. 皆様をこの神戸にお迎えいたしますことは光栄に存じます.
④ 【~+*that* 圖】
She expressed her *pleasure that* they could come. 彼女は彼らが来られるのはうれしいと喜びを表明した.

point 動

❶ 指し示す, 指さす.
① 【S〈人〉・V・O〈方向〉】
He *pointed* the way to the school. 彼はその学校へ行く道を指さして教えてくれた.
② 【S〈人〉・V・O〈物〉+*at*+〈物・人〉】
He *pointed* his finger *at* the clock on the tower. 彼は人差し指で塔の時計をさした.
③ 【S〈人〉・V+*at* [*to*]+〈物・人〉】
He *pointed at* the top of the mountain. 彼は山の頂上を指さした.
④ 【S〈人・物・事〉・V+圖】
He *pointed* up [down]. 彼は上[下]を指さした.

❷ 向ける.
【S〈人〉・V・O〈物〉(+*at*+〈人・物〉)】
The hijacker *pointed* the gun *at* me. ハイジャック犯人は銃を私に向けた.

❸ とがらせる.
【S〈人〉・V・O〈物〉】
He *pointed* his pencil with a pencil sharpener. 彼は鉛筆削りで鉛筆を削った.

point 名 目的, 意味, 効用.

① 【~+*of doing*】
What's the *point of* giving him advice? 彼に助言して何になるんだ.
② 【~+(*in*) *doing*】
There is no *point* (*in*) giving him advice. (=I don't see any *point in* giving him advice.) 意味は①と同じ.
③ 【~+*that* 圖】
He made the *point that* trying again was necessary. 彼はもう一度やってみることが必要だと主張した.

polite 形 礼儀正しい.

① 【S〈人〉 is ~+*to*+〈人〉】
He is *polite to* his superiors. 彼は目上の人に礼儀正しい.
② 【S〈人〉 is ~+*to do*】
She was very *polite to* write me a letter of thanks. 礼状をくださったとは彼女は何と礼儀正しい

③ 【It is ~+*of*+〈人〉+*to do*】
It was very *polite of* her *to* write me a letter of thanks. 意味は ② と同じ.

popular 形 人気がある, 評判がよい.
① 【S〈人・物・事〉is ~+*with* [*among*]+〈人〉】
That teacher is very *popular with* his students. あの先生は生徒にとても人気がある.
This song is *popular* especially *among* young people. この歌は特に若い人たちの間に人気がある. (❗ with は通例特定の人々に, among は不特定多数の人々に用いる)
② 【S〈人・物・事〉is ~+*as*+〈人・物・事〉】
She is *popular as* a movie actress. 彼女は映画女優として人気が高い.

positive 形 確信のある.
① 【S〈人〉is ~+*about* [*of*]+〈事〉】
He is *positive about* his success. 彼は自分の成功に自信がある.
② 【S〈人〉is ~+(*that*)節】
I am *positive that* somebody stole the money from the safe. だれかが金庫から金を盗んだのは確かだ.

possible 形
❶ 実行可能な.
【It is ~(+*for*+〈人〉)+*to do*】
It is *possible* (*for* me) *to* finish this work in a day. その仕事は(私には) 1 日で仕上げられる. (❗ × *I am* possible to finish…./× *This work* is possible *for* me to finish…./× It is possible *that* I (should) finish…. は不可. ただし 2 番目の構文は(準)否定語が入れば可能: This work is *hardly* [*not*] *possible* (*for* me) *to* finish in a day.)
❷ 起こり得る.
【It is ~+(*that*)節】
It is *possible* (*that*) something happened to him. 彼の身に何かが起こったのかもしれない. (❗ × It is possible *for* something *to* have happened to him. は不可. ❶ と ❷ とでは取り得る構文が異なることに注意)

practice 動
❶ 練習する.
① 【S〈人〉・V・O〈事・*doing*〉】
She *is practicing* a new piece on the flute. 彼女はフルートで新しい曲を練習している.
He *practiced reversing* the car into the garage. 彼は車をバックさせてガレージに入れる練習をした.
② 【S〈人〉・V+*on*+〈楽器〉】
He *practiced on* the flute. 彼はフルートを練習した.
❷ (習慣的に)行う.
【S〈人〉・V・O】
I *practice* yoga every day. 私は毎日ヨガをしている.
❸ 開業する.
【S〈人〉・V・O〈医者・弁護士など〉】
He *practices* law [as a lawyer]. 彼は弁護士をしている.

praise 動 ほめる.
① 【S〈人〉・V・O〈人・行為など〉】
They highly *praised* him [his courage]. 彼らは彼[彼の勇気]を激賞した.

② 【S〈人〉・V・O〈人・物・事〉+*for* [*on*, *upon*]+〈事・*doing*〉】
They highly *praised* him *for* his courage [*for* sav*ing* the child]. 彼らは勇敢だと[その子を救助したことで]彼を激賞した.

pray 動 祈る, 懇願する. (❗ 受身形は不可)
① 【S〈人〉・V】
She knelt down and *prayed*. 彼女はひざまずいて祈った.
② 【S〈人〉・V(+*to*+〈神・人〉)+*for*+〈人・安全・健康・幸福〉】 She *prayed* (*to* God) *for* his safety [good health]. 彼女は彼の安全[健康]を(神に)祈った.
③ 【S〈人〉・V・O〈事〉】
She *prayed* God's mercy. 彼女は神の慈悲を祈った.
④ 【S〈人〉・V・O〈神・人〉+*for*+〈事〉】
She *prayed* God *for* mercy. 意味は ③ と同じ.
⑤ 【S〈人〉・V・O〈神・人〉+*to do*】
She *prayed* God *to* show mercy. 意味は ③ と同じ.
⑥ 【S〈人〉・V(+*to*・O〈神・人〉)・O〈*that* 節〉】
She *prayed* (*to* God) *that* he *would* be safe. 彼女は神に彼が無事であるように祈った. (❗ …*prayed* God *that* he…. も可)

prefer 動
❶ (…の方を)好む.
① 【S〈人〉・V・O〈人・物・事・*doing*・*to do*〉】
Which do you *prefer*, spring or fall? 春と秋とちらの方が好きですか.
He *prefers* traveling [*to* travel] by train. 彼は列車での旅行が好きだ.
② 【S〈人〉・V・O〈人・物・事・*doing*〉+*to*+〈人・物・事・*doing*〉】 I *prefer* spring *to* fall. 私は秋より春の方が好きです.
I *prefer* listen*ing* to the radio *to* watch*ing* television. 私はテレビを見るよりラジオを聞く方が好きです. (❗ × I prefer *to* listen to the radio *to* watch television. は不可)
③ 【S〈人〉・V・O〈*to do*〉+*rather than* do [do*ing*]】 I *prefer to* listen to the radio *rather than* watch [watch*ing*] television. 私はテレビを見るよりラジオを聞きたい.
❷ …してもらいたい.
① 【S〈人〉・V・O〈*that* 節〉】
I *prefer that* you ((英) should) give up the plan. 君にその計画を断念してもらいたい.
② 【S〈人〉・V+O〈所有格(+)*doing*〉】
I *prefer* your giv*ing* up the plan. 意味は ① と同じ.
③ 【S〈人〉・V・(+*for*) O〈人〉・C〈*to do*〉】
I would *prefer* (*for*) you *to* give up the plan. 意味は ① と同じ.
❸ …された方がよい.
【S〈人〉・V・O〈物〉・C〈形・done〉】
She *prefers* coffee iced. 彼女はコーヒーはアイスコーヒーが好きだ.

prepare 動
❶ 準備[用意]する, 調理[調合]する.
① 【S〈人〉・V・O〈物・事〉】
He *is preparing* his lessons. 彼は学科の下調べをしている. (❗ 直接的な準備をすること)
② 【S〈人〉・V+*for*+〈物・事〉】
He *is preparing for* the examination. 彼は受験の準備をしている. (❗ (1) 間接的な準備をすること.

(2) 受身可)
③ 【S〈人〉・V・O〈*to do*〉】
We *prepared* to start. われわれは出発の用意をした.
④ 【S〈人〉・V・O〈物〉+*for*+〈人・物・事〉】
She *prepared* dinner *for* us. 彼女はわれわれに夕食の用意をしてくれた. (**!** この文型は「人」に焦点があり, ⑤ は「物」に焦点がある)
⑤ 【S〈人〉・V・O〈人・物〉・O〈物〉】
She *prepared* us dinner. 意味は ④ と同じ.
❷ 覚悟[支度]させる, ...するように訓練する.
① 【S〈人・物〉・V・O〈人〉+*for*+〈物・事〉】
He *prepared* his students thoroughly *for* the examination. 彼は生徒に受験準備を十分させた. (受身=His students *were* thoroughly *prepared for* the examination.)
② 【S〈人・物〉・V・O〈人〉・C〈*to do*〉】
We *prepared* him *to* start. われわれは彼に出発する支度をさせた. (受身=He *was prepared to* start.) 受身形は「準備[覚悟]ができていた」のほか「喜んで...しようとした」の意もある)

present 動

❶ 贈呈する, 贈る.
① 【S〈人〉・V・O〈人・団体〉(+*with*)+〈物〉】 **!** *with* を省略するのは (主に米))
He *presented* the library (*with*) a lot of rare books. 彼はその図書館にたくさんの希覯(きこう)本を贈った. (受身=The library *was presented* (*with*) a lot of rare books by him.)
② 【S〈人〉・V・O〈物〉+*to*+〈人・団体〉】
He *presented* a lot of rare books *to* the library. 意味は ① と同じ. (受身=A lot of rare books *were presented to* the library by him.)
❷ 提出する, 提案する; 提供する; 引き起こす.
① 【S〈人・物・事〉・V・O〈物・事〉】 The situation will *present* complicated problems. 事態は複雑な問題を引き起こすだろう.
② 【S〈人〉・V・O〈文書など〉+*to*+〈人〉】
He *presented* a detailed report *to* the committee. 彼は詳細な報告書を委員会に提出した.
③ 【S〈人〉・V・O〈人〉(+*with*)・O〈文書など〉】
He *presented* the committee (*with*) a detailed report. 意味は ② と同じ.
❸ 上演[放送]する.
【S〈会社など〉・V・O〈劇・番組〉】
The theater *is presenting* "Macbeth". その劇場は「マクベス」を上演している.

press 動

❶ 押す, 押しつける; アイロンをかける.
① 【S〈人・物〉・V・O〈on [*against*]+〈物〉)】
He *pressed* the button to start the engine. 彼はエンジンをかけるためにボタンを押した.
He *pressed* his face *on* [*against*] the train window. 彼は顔を列車の窓に押しつけた.
I *pressed* my shirt. 私はワイシャツにアイロンをかけた.
② 【S〈人・物〉・V(+*on*+〈物〉)】
He *pressed* hard *on* the accelerator. 彼はアクセルを強く踏みこんだ.
❷ 押し進む.
① 【S〈人〉・V・O〈one's way〉(+副(句))】
He *pressed* his way *through* the crowd. 彼は人込みの中を押しわけて進んだ.
② 【S〈人〉・V+副(句)】
He *pressed through* the crowd. 意味は ① と同じ.
The crowd *pressed toward* the park to see the parade. 群衆はパレードを見物しようと広場へ押し寄せた.
❸ しぼる.
【S〈人〉・V・O〈果汁〉+*from* [*out of*]+〈果物〉】
I *pressed* the juice *from* an orange. 私はオレンジの汁を絞った.
❹ 苦しんでいる. (**!** 受身形で)
【S〈人〉 *be pressed*+*with* [*for*]+〈問題[金・時間]〉】 He *is pressed for* money. 彼は金がなくて困っている. (**!** *with* は問題など, *for* は金・時間などに用いる)
❺ 強く勧める.
【S〈人〉・V・O〈人〉C〈*to do*〉】
She *pressed* me *to* stay a little longer. 彼女は私にもう少し長く滞在するよう強く勧めた.

presume 動

❶ (確信を持って)推定する.
① 【S〈人〉・V・O〈(*that*) 節〉】
We *presume* (*that*) he is innocent. 私たちは彼が無罪であると考える. (受身=It *is presumed that* he is innocent.)
② 【S〈人〉・V・O〈人〉(・*to be*)C〈形・名〉】
We *presume* him (*to be*) innocent. 意味は ① と同じ. (受身=He *is presumed* (*to be*) innocent.)
❷ あえて...する.
【S〈人〉・V+*to do*】
I will not *presume to* argue with you. 私はあえてあなたと議論するつもりはない. (**!** 通例否定文, 疑問文で用いる)

pretend 動

❶ ...のふりをする, 装う.
① 【S〈人〉・V・O〈物・事〉】
He *pretended* sickness. 彼は仮病を使った.
② 【S〈人〉・V+*to do*】
He *pretended to* be sick. 意味は ① と同じ.
③ 【S〈人〉・V・O〈(*that*) 節〉】
He *pretended* (*that*) he was sick. 意味は ① と同じ.
❷ ...するまねをして遊ぶ.
① 【S〈人〉・V・O〈*to do*〉】
The boys *pretended to* be soldiers. 少年たちは兵隊ごっこをして遊んだ.
② 【S〈人〉・V・O〈(*that*) 節〉】
The boys *pretended* (*that*) they were soldiers. 意味は ① と同じ.
❸ あつかましくも...する.
【S〈人〉・V+*to do*】
I can't *pretend to* be an expert on cooking. 私はあつかましくも料理の達人だなどと言うつもりはない. (**!** 通例疑問文, 否定文で用いる)

prevent 動 妨げる.

① 【S〈物・事・人〉・V・O〈人・事〉+*from*+*doing*】
Bad weather [He] *prevented* me *from coming*. 悪天候[彼]のために私は来られなかった.
② 【S〈物・事・人〉・V・O〈所有格〉+*doing*】
Bad weather [He] *prevented* my *coming*. 意味は ① と同じ. (**!** 文語的)
③ 【S〈物・事・人〉・V・O・C〈*doing*〉】
Bad weather [He] *prevented* me *coming*. 意味は ① と同じ. (**!** 口語的)
④ 【S〈物・事・人〉・V・O〈事・人〉】
Rain *prevented* the tennis match. 雨でテニスの試合ができなかった.

probable 形 ありそうな.

【It is ～+*that* 節】
It is *probable that* he will [×should] arrive soon. たぶん彼はもうすぐ到着するだろう。(❗ ×He is probable to arrive soon./× It is probable *for* him *to* arrive soon. は不可)

problem 名 問題.

① 【～+*of*+do*ing*】
We have to tackle the *problem of* preventi*ng* the air pollution of our city. われわれはこの市の大気汚染の防止問題に取り組まなければならない。

② 【～+*of*+*wh*-句】
We have to tackle the *problem of how to* prevent the air pollution of our city. われわれはこの市の大気汚染をいかにして防ぐかという問題に取り組まなければならない。

③ 【～+*in*+do*ing*】
We experienced *problems in* preventi*ng* [×to prevent] accidents. 事故を防止するのにいろいろの問題を経験した。

④ 【The ～ is *that* 節】
The *problem is that* we are short of money. 問題は資金不足だ。

⑤ 【It is a ～+do*ing* [*to* do]】
It is a *problem* do*ing* [*to* do] with radioactive waste. 放射性廃棄物を処理するのは難題だ。

promise 動 約束する.

① 【S〈人〉・V・O〈物・事〉】
He *promised* a reward. 彼は報酬を約束した。

② 【S〈人〉・V・O〈人〉・O〈物・事〉】
They *promised* me a reward. 彼らは私に報酬を約束した。(❗ この文型では物・事に焦点があり，③ は人に焦点がある)(受身＝I *was promised* a reward./A reward *was promised* (to) me.)

③ 【S〈人〉・V・O〈物・事〉+*to*+〈人〉】
They *promised* a reward *to* me. 意味は ② と同じ。(受身＝A reward *was promised to* me.)

④ 【S〈人〉・V・O〈*to* do〉】
He *promised* never *to* be late again. 彼は二度と遅刻しないと約束した。

⑤ 【S〈人〉・V・O〈人〉・O〈*to* do〉】
He *promised* me never *to* be late again. 彼は私に二度と遅刻しないと約束した。(❗ 受身形は不可)

⑥ 【S〈人〉・V・O〈(*that*) 節〉】
He *promised* (*that*) he would never be late again. 意味は ④ と同じ。

⑦ 【S〈人〉・V・O〈人〉・O〈(*that*) 節〉】
He *promised* me *that* he would never be late again. 意味は ⑤ と同じ。(受身＝I *was promised* he would never be late again.)

promise 名 約束.

① 【～+*to* do】
She kept her *promise to* write home every month. 彼女は毎月家に手紙を書き送るという約束を守った。

② 【～+*that* 節】
She kept her *promise that* she would write home every month. 意味は ① と同じ。

proper 形

❶ 礼儀正しい.
① 【It is ～(+*for*+〈人〉)+*to* do】
It is not *proper* (*for* you) *to* answer back to your teacher. 君が先生に口答えするのは無礼だ。

② 【It is ～+*that* 節】
It is not *proper that* you (should) answer back to your teacher. 意味は ① と同じ。(❗ should を用いるのは《主に英》)

❷ 適した, ふさわしい.
① 【S〈人・物・事〉 is ～+*for*+〈人・物・事・do*ing*〉】
He is *proper for* the task. 彼はその任務にふさわしい。
This room is *proper for* study*ing* in. この部屋は勉強に適している。

② 【S〈人・物・事〉 is ～+*to* do】
The house is *proper to* live in. その家は住むのに適している。

propose 動

❶ 提案する.
① 【S〈人〉・V・O〈事〉】
He *proposed* a walk. 彼は散歩しようと提案した。

② 【S〈人〉・V・O〈*to* do〉】
He *proposed to* take a walk. 意味は ① と同じ。

③ 【S〈人〉・V・O〈do*ing*〉】
He *proposed* tak*ing* a walk. 意味は ① と同じ。

④ 【S〈人〉・V・O〈*that* 節〉】
He *proposed that* we (should) take a walk. 意味は ① と同じ。(受身＝It *was proposed* by him *that* we (should) take a walk.)(❗ should を用いるのは《主に英》)

❷ …するつもりである.
【S〈人〉・V・O〈*to* do・do*ing*〉】
He *proposed to* make [mak*ing*] an early start. 彼は早く出発するつもりだった。

❸ 結婚を申し込む.
【S〈男性〉・V+*to*+〈女性〉】
He *proposed to* the professor's daughter. 彼は教授のお嬢さんに結婚を申し込んだ。

prospect 名 見込み.

① 【～+*of* (+所有格)+do*ing*】
There is little *prospect of* his find*ing* a satisfactory solution. 彼が満足のいく解決策を見出す見込みはほとんどない。

② 【～+*that* 節】
There is little *prospect that* he will find a satisfactory solution. 意味は ① と同じ。

proud 形 誇って.

① 【S〈人〉 is ～+*of*+〈人・物・事・do*ing*〉】
He is *proud of* his school [be*ing* of noble birth]. 彼は母校を[貴族の出であることを]誇りにしている。

② 【S〈人〉 is ～(+*that* 節)】
He is *proud* (*that*) he is of noble birth. 彼は貴族の出であることを誇りにしている。

③ 【S〈人〉 is ～+*to* do】
We are *proud to* honor him. 彼を表彰することはわれわれの誇りであります。

prove 動

❶ 証明する, 立証する.
① 【S〈人・事・物〉・V・O〈事〉(+*to*+〈人・法廷〉)】
He [The fact] *proved* her innocence *to* the court. 彼[その事実]が法廷で彼女の無実を証明した。

② 【S〈人・事・物〉・V・O〈(*that*) 節〉】
They *proved* (*that*) I was right. 彼らは私が正しいことを証明してくれた。

③ 【S〈人・事・物〉・V・O〈*wh*-節〉】
I can *prove to* you *where* I was last night. 私が

ゆうべどこにいたかを君に立証できる．
④ 【S〈人・事・物〉・V・O〈人・物〉(to be)C〈形・名〉】
He *proved* himself [The fact *proved* him] (*to be*) innocent. 彼は自分が[その事実は彼が]無実であることを立証した．

❷ ...であると分かる[判明する，となる]．
【S〈人・事〉・V・(to be) C〈名・形〉】
He *proved to be* a good student. 彼がよい生徒だと分かった．
The rumor *proved* (*to be*) groundless. そのうわさは根も葉もないことが判明した．

provide 動
❶ 供給する，与える，提供する．
① 【S〈人・動物・物〉・V・O〈人・場所〉+with+〈必要な物〉】(!)《米》では with を省略し S・V・O・O の型でも用いる)
Bees *provide* us *with* honey. ミツバチは人間にハチミツを与えてくれる．
They *provided* the victims *with* food and medicine. 彼らは被災者に食糧と医薬を用意した．(受身＝The victims *were provided with* food and medicine. (!) この文型は必要な物に焦点があり，② は与えられる人に焦点がある)
② 【S〈人・動物・物〉・V・O〈必要な物〉(+for [《米》 to]+〈人・場所〉)】 They *provided* food and medicine *for* the victims. 意味は ① 例文と同じ．(受身＝Food and medicine *were provided for* the victims.)
③ 【S〈人〉・V+for+〈人・家族〉】
He has to *provide for* his family. 彼は自分の家族を養わなければならない．
❷ 備える．
【S〈人など〉・V+for [against]+名】
We must *provide for* our old age [*against* a flood]. われわれは老後[洪水]に備えなければならない．(!) against は通例悪いことに備える場合に用いる)

pull 動
❶ 引く，引っ張る．
① 【S〈人〉・V・O〈物・人〉(+副(句))】
He *pulled* my jacket. (=He *pulled* me *by* my jacket.) 彼は私の上着を引っ張った．
He *pulled* me *out of* bed. 彼は私をベッドから引きずり出した．
② 【S〈人〉・V+at [on]+〈物〉】
They *pulled at* [*on*] the rope. 彼らはロープをぐっと引いた．(!) 受身形は可)
❷ 引っ張って...にする．
【S〈人〉・V・O〈物〉・C〈形(句)〉】
He *pulled* the door open [shut]. 彼は戸を引っ張って開けた[閉めた]．(!) C が open の場合は pulled open the door の語順になることが多い)
She *pulled* her sweater *out of shape*. 彼女はセーターを引っ張って形をくずしてしまった．
❸ 引き抜く．
【S〈人〉・V・O〈歯・栓・羽毛など〉(+副)】
The dentist *pulled* (out) my decayed tooth yesterday. 歯医者はきのう私の虫歯を抜いてくれた．

punish 動 罰する．
① 【S〈人〉・V・O〈人・悪事など〉】
We should *punish* him [the crime] severely. 彼[その罪]を厳しく罰すべきだ．
② 【S〈人〉・V・O〈人〉+for+〈悪事・doing〉】
They *punished* him *for* his crime [stealing money]. 彼らは彼をその罪のために[金を盗んだために]罰した．(受身＝He *was punished for* his crime [stealing money].)

purpose 名 目的，意図．
① 【~+of doing】
He went to France for [with] the *purpose of* study*ing* fine arts [✕to study fine arts]. 彼は美術研究の目的で渡仏した．
② 【~+in doing】
What is your *purpose in* call*ing* her? どういうつもりで彼女に電話するのだね．

push 動
❶ 押す，突く，押して動かす．
【S〈人〉・V・O〈物・人〉(+副(句))】
He *pushed* the button to shut the elevator. 彼はボタンを押してエレベーターを閉めた．
He *pushed* me *forward* [*away*]. 彼は私を前に押した[押しのけた]．
❷ 押して...の状態にする．
【S〈人〉・V・O〈物〉・C〈形〉】
He *pushed* the door open [shut]. 彼は戸を押して開けた[閉めた]．
❸ 押し進む．
① 【S〈人〉・V・O〈one's way〉(+前+名)】
He *pushed* his way *through* the crowd. 彼は群衆を押し分けて進んだ．
② 【S〈人〉・V+副(句)】
He *pushed through* the crowd. 意味は ① と同じ．
❹ 強いる，強要する．
① 【S〈人〉・V・O〈人〉・C〈to do〉】
She *pushed* her mother *to* buy a necklace. 彼女は母にむりにネックレスを買わせた．
② 【S〈人〉・V・O〈人〉+for [to, into]+〈物・事〉】
They *pushed* me *for* explanation. 彼らは私に釈明を迫った．(受身＝I *was pushed for* explanation.)
She *pushed* her mother *into* buying a necklace. 意味は ① と同じ．

put 動
❶ 置く．
【S〈人〉・V・O〈物・人〉+副(句)】
She *put* the vase there [*on* the table]. 彼女は花びんをそこ[テーブルの上]に置いた．
❷ 入れる，行かせる．
【S〈人〉・V・O〈物・人〉+副(句)】
I *put* too much sugar *in* [*into*] my tea. 紅茶に砂糖を入れすぎた．
He *put* the baby *to* bed. 彼は赤ん坊を寝かしつけた．
❸ ...に課す，...のせいにする．
【S〈人〉・V・O〈税・責任など〉+on [to] +〈人・物〉】
They *put* a heavy tax *on* liquor. 彼らは酒に重い税をかけた．
He *put* the accident *on* me [*to* my carelessness]. 彼はその事故を私[私の不注意]のせいにした．
❹ 記入する，表現する，翻訳する．
① 【S〈人〉・V・O〈考え・気持ちなど〉+in [into]+〈言葉など〉】 He *put* his feelings *into* words. 彼は感情を言葉で表わした．
② 【S〈人〉・V・O〈言葉・文章など〉+into+〈言語〉】
Put the following sentences *into* Japanese. 次の文を和訳しなさい．
❺ 見積もる，評価する．
① 【S〈人〉・V・O〈物〉+at+〈数量〉】
I *put* the weight *at* about 20 kilos. その重さは20

⑤【S〈人〉・V・O〈that 節〉】
The doctor *recommended that* he (should) quit smoking. 医者は彼に禁煙するよう勧めた. (❗ should を用いるのは《主に英》)(受身=He *was recommended to* quit smoking. /It *was recommended that* he (should) quit smoking.)
⑥【S〈人〉・V・O〈(所有格+) doing〉】
The doctor *recommended* his quitt*ing* smoking. 意味は⑤と同じ.
⑦【S〈人〉・V・O〈to do〉】
The doctor *recommended* him *to* quit smoking. 意味は⑤と同じ.

record 名 記録.
①【~+*that* 節】
The *record* was laid out *that* the corporation had made illegal political payments to political parties. その会社が複数の政党に不法な政治献金をしたという記録が暴露された.
②【~+*of*(+所有格・目的格)+*doing*】
The *record* was laid out *of* the corporation hav*ing* made illegal political payments to political parties. 意味は①と同じ.

recover 動
❶ 取り戻す, 回復する.
【S〈人〉・V・O〈損失など〉】
He *recovered* his stolen money [his health]. 彼は盗まれた金[健康]を取り戻した.
❷ 健康を回復する.
【S〈人〉・V(+*from*+〈病気など〉)】
He *recovered* (*from*) illness gradually. 彼は徐々に(病気から)回復した.

refuse 動
❶ 断わる.
【S〈人〉・V・O〈申し出・要求など〉】
He *refused* our offer [invitation]. 彼は私たちの申し出[招待]を断わった.
❷ …を与えることを断わる.
①【S〈人〉・V・O〈助力・許可など〉】
They *refused* permission to use the hall. 彼らは会館の使用許可を与えなかった.
②【S〈人〉・V・O〈人〉・O〈助力・許可など〉】
They *refused* me permission to enter. 彼らは私の入場を許可しなかった. (受身=I *was refused* permission to enter.)
③【S〈人〉・V・O〈助力・許可など〉+*to*+〈人〉】
They *refused* entry *to* me. 私は入場を断わられた. (受身=Entry *was refused to* me.)
❸ (人が)…することを拒む; (物・動物が)どうしても…しようとしない.
【S〈人・物〉・V・O〈to do〉】
He *refused to* reveal his identity. 彼は身元を明かすことを拒んだ.
The cork *refused to* come out. コルク栓はどうしても抜けなかった.

regard 動
❶ …と見なす[思う]. (❗ 進行形は不可)
【S〈人〉・V・O〈人・物・事〉+*as* (*being*) C〈名・形〉】
His mother *regards* him *as* a genius. 彼の母は彼を天才だと思っている.
❷ 尊敬する, 評価する.
【S〈人〉・V・O〈人・物・事〉(+〈副(句)〉)】
His friends *regard* him [his achievements] highly. 彼[彼の業績]は友人から大いに尊敬[高く評価]されている.
❸ (ある感情をもって)…を見る.
【S〈人〉・V・O+〈副(句)〉[*with*+〈名〉]】
The students *regard* him *with* affection. 生徒たちは彼を慕っている.

regret 動
❶ 後悔する, 残念に思う.
①【S〈人〉・V・O〈事〉】
I *regret* my foolish conduct. 愚かなふるまいを後悔している.
②【S〈人〉・V・O〈(所有格+)doing〉】
I *regret* miss*ing* [hav*ing* missed] the only chance. 唯一のチャンスを逃して残念だ.
③【S〈人〉・V・O〈that 節〉】(書)
I *regret that* I missed the only chance. 意味は②と同じ. (受身=It *is regretted that* I missed the only chance.)
❷ 残念ながら…する.
【S〈人〉・V・O〈to do〉】
I *regret to* say that he is sick. 残念ながら彼は病気です.

remain 動
❶ とどまる, 残る.
【S〈人・物・事〉・V(+〈副(句)〉)】
I *remained* at home while my wife went shopping. 妻が買い物に行っている間私は家にいた.
❷ 相変わらず…(のまま)である.
【S〈人・物〉・V・C〈形・名・done〉】(❗ 進行形は不可)
She *remained* single all her life [a widow for the rest of her life]. 彼女は生涯独身だった[夫の死後再婚することはなかった]. (❗ ×remained to be single [a widow].… は不可)
The pollution problems of this city *remain* unsolved. 本市の公害問題は未解決のままである.
❸ 残存している, 残っている. (❗ 進行形は不可)
①【S〈物・事〉・V】
Only the main hall of the temple *remained* after the fire. 火事の後本堂しか残らなかった.
②【S〈物・事〉・V+*of*+〈物・事〉】
Nothing *remained of* the village after the flood. 洪水のあと村は跡形もなくなった.
③【S〈事〉・V+*to* be done】
A lot of work *remains to* be done. まだしなければならない仕事がたくさん残っている.
It *remains to* be seen whether he will keep his promise. 彼が約束を守るかどうかはまだ分からない.

remember 動
❶ 思い出す.
①【S〈人〉・V・O〈人・物・事〉】
I *remembered* her name at last. やっと彼女の名前を思い出した.
②【S〈人〉・V・O〈(*that*) 節〉】
I suddenly *remembered* (*that*) I had owed him some money. 突然私は彼に借金があるのを思い出した.
③【S〈人〉・V・O〈wh- 節(句)〉】
He can't *remember where* he met her before. 彼は以前にどこで彼女に会ったのか思い出せない.
Can you *remember how to* get to his house? どのようにしたら彼の家へ行けるか思い出せますか.
❷ 覚えている, 忘れないで…する. (❗ 進行形不可)
①【S〈人〉・V・O〈人・物・事〉】

I don't *remember* his name. 彼の名を覚えていない。
② 【S〈人〉・V・O〈(that)節〉】
I *remember* (*that*) I read this novel when young. この小説を若いころ読んだ覚えがある。
③ 【S〈人〉・V・O〈wh-節〉】
Do you *remember* *when* and *where* we met first? 私たちが初めていつどこで会ったか覚えていらっしゃいますか。
④ 【S〈人〉・V・O〈to do〉】
Remember *to* take an umbrella with you. 傘をもって行くことを忘れないように。(! 将来のことを「覚えている」意)
⑤ 【S〈人〉・V・O〈(所有格・目的格+)doing〉】(! having done の形はまれ)
I *remember* reading this story in English. この話を英語で読んだ覚えがある。(! 過去のことを「覚えている」意)
I *remember* his [him] being very kind. 彼がとても親切だったのを覚えている(≒似ている)。
⑥ 【S〈人〉・V・O〈人・物・事〉*as* [*to be*] C〈名・形・分詞〉】 I *remember* him *as* [*to be*] a humorous man. 私は彼をこっけいな男だと記憶している。
⑦ 【S〈人〉・V】
If I *remember* correctly [rightly],... 私の記憶に間違いなければ....
❸ よろしく伝える. 《書》
【S〈人〉・V・O〈人〉+*to*+〈人〉】
Please *remember* me *to* all your family. お家の皆様方によろしく。

remind 動
❶ 気づかせる, 念を押す.
① 【S〈人〉・V・O〈人〉+*of* [*about*]+〈人・物・事〉】
He *reminded* me *of* my promise. 彼は私に約束を忘れないようにと言った。(受身=I *was reminded of* my promise.)
② 【S〈人〉・V・O〈人〉・O〈to do〉】
Remind me *to* mail [× of mailing] the letter. 手紙を出すのを忘れないように注意してね。
③ 【S〈人〉・V・O〈人〉・O〈*that* 節〉】
Remind him *that* we have no school tomorrow. あす授業がないことを忘れないように彼に念を押してください。
④ 【S〈人〉・V・O〈人〉・O〈wh- 節〉】
Our teacher *reminded* us *how* important it is to read when young. 先生は私たちに若いときの読書の大切さを忘れないようにと言われた。
❷ 思い出させる. (! 進行形, 命令形は不可)
① 【S〈物・事・人〉・V・O〈人〉+*of*+〈人・事・物〉】
This photo *reminds* me *of* my happy school days. この写真を見ると楽しかった学生時代を思い出す。(受身=I *am reminded of* my happy school days by this photo [when I see this photo].)
His father *reminded* me *of* Chaplin. 彼の父はチャップリンを連想させた(≒似ていた)。
② 【S〈物・事・人〉・V・O〈人〉・O〈to do〉】
His talk *reminded* me *to* visit her in the hospital. 彼の話を聞いて彼女の見舞いに病院へ行くことを思い出した。
③ 【S〈物・事・人〉・V・O〈人〉・O〈*that* 節〉】
His talk *reminded* me *that* I should visit her in the hospital. 意味は②と同じ。
④ 【S〈物・事・人〉・V・O〈人〉・O〈wh- 節〉】
The note *reminded* me *when* I bought the book. 私はメモを見ていつその本を買ったかを思い出した。

reply 動
❶ 答える, 返事をする.
【S〈人〉・V(+*to*+〈人・事・物〉)】
I asked him why he was absent, but he didn't *reply*. 私は彼になぜ欠席したのかと尋ねたが, 彼は返事をしなかった。
He didn't *reply to* me [my letter]. 彼は私[私の手紙]に返事をしなかった。(受身=I [My letter] wasn't *replied to*.)
❷ ...と答える.
① 【S〈人〉・V・O〈返答の内容〉】(! 通例否定文で)
He *replied* nothing. (=He didn't *reply* anything.) 彼は何も返事をしなかった。(! × He didn't *reply* me [my letter]. は不可)
② 【S〈人〉・V・O〈*that* 節・引用文〉】
She *replied that* she didn't like smoking. (="I don't like smoking," she *replied*.) 彼女は喫煙は嫌いだと答えた。(前文の受身=It *was replied that* she didn't like smoking.)

report 動
❶ 報告する, 知らせる.
① 【S〈人・団体〉・V・O〈物・事〉(+*to*+〈人・団体〉)】
He *reported* the accident *to* the police. 彼はその事故を警察に届け出た。(受身=The accident *was reported to* the police.)
② 【S〈人〉・V・O〈doing〉】
He *reported* having seen the wanted criminal. 彼はその指名手配者を見たと報告した。
③ 【S〈人〉・V・O〈(*that*)節〉】
He *reported* (*that*) he had seen the wanted criminal. 意味は②と同じ。(受身=It *was reported that* he had seen the wanted criminal./He *was reported to* have seen the wanted criminal.) (! 引用文は目的語にできない)
④ 【S〈人〉・V・O〈人・物〉・(*to be*) C〈名・形・分詞〉】
He *reported* the boy to have been kidnapped. 彼はその少年が誘拐されたと報告した。(受身=The boy *was reported to* have been kidnapped.) (! *to be* を省略するのは《主に米》)
⑤ 【S〈人など〉・V(+*on*+〈事〉)】
He *reported on* the accident. 彼はその事故について報告した。
❷ 報道する, 伝える.
① 【S〈新聞など〉・V・O〈人・事・物〉】
Today's paper *reports* the outbreak of a war. 今日の新聞は戦争の勃発(ぼっぱつ)を報じている。(受身=The outbreak of a war *is reported* in today's paper.)
② 【S〈新聞など〉・V・O〈*that* 節〉】
Today's paper *reports that* a war broke out. 意味は①と同じ。(受身=It *is reported* in today's paper *that* a war broke out.)
③ 【S〈新聞など〉・V・O〈人・物〉・(*to be*) C〈形・分詞〉】 The newspaper *reports* the flu *to be* going around the Kanto area. 流感が関東方面で蔓(まん)延していると報じられている。(受身=The flu *is reported to be* going around the Kanto area.)
④ 【S〈新聞など〉・V+*on*+〈人・事〉】
Today's paper *reports on* the accident. 今日の新聞はその事故について報道している。
❸ 記事を書く, 取材する.
① 【S〈記者など〉・V・O〈事件など〉(+*for*+〈新聞など〉)】 He *reported* the coup d'état *for* the

newspaper. 彼は新聞にクーデターの記事を書いた.
② 【S〈記者など〉・V+*for*+〈新聞社など〉】
He *reports for* the Asahi. 彼は朝日新聞の記者である.
❹ 告げ口する.
【S〈人〉・V・O〈人・事〉(+*副(句)*)】
She *reported* him to the headmaster for smoking in school. 学校でたばこを吸ったと彼女は彼を校長に言いつけた.

request 頼む, 懇願する, 要請する.
① 【S〈人〉・V・O〈物・事〉】
He *requested* silence. 彼は静かにしてほしいと頼んだ.
② 【S〈人〉・V・O〈物・事〉+*from* [*of*]+〈人・団体・施設〉】 He *requested* a loan *from* [×to] the bank. 彼は銀行にローンを頼んだ.
③ 【S〈人〉・V・O〈人〉・C〈*to do*〉】
He *requested* me *to* lend him some money. 彼は私に金を貸してほしいと頼んだ. (受身＝I *was requested to* lend him some money.)
④ 【S〈人〉・V(+*of*+人)・O〈*that* 節〉】
He *requested* me *that* I (should) lend him some money. 意味は ③ と同じ. (受身＝It *was requested of* me *that* I (should) lend him some money.) (❗should を用いるのは《主に英》) ❗引用文は目的語にできない)

require 動
❶ 必要とする.《やや書》(❗進行形, 命令形は不可)
① 【S〈人・物・事〉・V・O〈人・物・事〉】
This matter *requires* careful study. この問題は慎重に研究する必要がある.
② 【S〈物・事〉・V・O〈*doing*〉】
This fence *requires* repair*ing*. この柵は修理する必要がある. (❗この構文は need, want の方が普通)
③ 【S〈人・物・事〉・V・O〈*that* 節〉】
The situation *requires that* it (should) be treated secretly. その事態は秘密に処理する必要がある. (❗should を用いるのは《主に英》)
❷ 要求する.《書》
① 【S〈人〉・V・O〈物・事〉】
We *required* his attendance. 彼の出席を求めた.
② 【S〈人〉・V・O〈物・事〉+*of*+〈人〉】
They *required* silence *of* everyone during the lecture. 彼らは全員に講演中は静かにするよう求めた. (受身＝Silence *was required of* everyone during the lecture.)
③ 【S〈人・法律など〉・V・O〈人〉・C〈*to do*〉】
They *required* everyone *to* show his ID card. 彼らは全員に身分証明書を見せるよう要求した.
④ 【S〈人・法律など〉・V・O〈*that* 節〉】
They *required that* everyone (should) show his ID card. 意味は ③ と同じ. (受身＝It *was required that* everyone (should) show his ID card.) (❗should を用いるのは《主に英》)

resolve
❶ 決心する.
① 【S〈人〉・V・O〈*that* 節〉】
He *resolved that* he would never see her again. 彼は彼女と二度と会うまいと決心した.
② 【S〈人〉・V・O〈*to do*〉】
He *resolved* never *to* see her again. 意味は ① と同じ.
③ 【S〈人〉・V+*on*+*doing*】
She *resolved on* becoming an English teacher.
彼女は英語の教師になることに決めた.
④ 【S〈人〉・V+*against*+*doing*】
He *resolved against* seeing her again. 意味は ① と同じ.
❷ 解決する.
【S〈人・物・事〉・V・O〈問題・困難など〉】
I can't *resolve* my anger toward them. 私は彼らに対する怒りを解消することはできない.
❸ 分解する.
【S〈人・物・事〉・V・O〈物〉+*副(句)*】
Ammonia can *be resolved* into nitrogen and hydrogen. アンモニアは窒素と水素に分解される.

responsibility 名 責任.
① 【〜+*for*+*doing*】
I will accept full *responsibility for* causing damage to you. あなたに損害をおかけしましたら, 私が全責任を取ります.
② 【〜+*of*+*doing*】
She has the *responsibilities of* taking care of her old mother. 彼女は年をとった母の面倒を見る責任がある.
③ 【〜+*to do*】
We have the *responsibility to* compensate him for the loss. われわれは彼の損害に対して彼に弁償する責任がある.
④ 【〜+*that* 節】
It is her *responsibility that* she (should) take care of her old mother. (＝It is her *responsibility to* take care of her old mother.) 意味は ② と同じ. (❗should を用いるのは《主に英》)

responsible 形 責任がある.
【S〈人〉 is 〜 (+*to*+〈人・団体〉)(+*for*+〈事・物・*doing*〉)】 You are *responsible for* (having caused) the accident. 君はその事故(を起こしたこと)に責任がある.
The teachers are *responsible to* the parents *for* the safety of their children in the school. 校内では教師は親に対して子供の安全を守る責任がある.

rest 動
❶ 休む, 休憩[休養]する.
【S〈人〉・V】
I *rested* for a while. 私はしばらく休憩した.
❷ 休ませる
【S〈人〉・V・O〈人・物〉】
The teacher *rested* the pupils for ten minutes. 先生は生徒を 10 分間休憩させた.
❸ 静止する
【S〈物・事〉・V】
His eyes *rested* on her. 彼の目は彼女に注がれた.
❹ 当てにする.
【S〈人〉・V+*on* [*upon*]+〈人・事〉】
You can't *rest on* him [his help]. 彼[彼の援助]は当てにならないよ.
❺ …次第である.
【S〈決定・選択など〉・V+*with* [*on*]+〈人〉】
The choice *rests with* you. 選択は君次第だ.
❻ 置く, のせておく.
【S〈人〉・V・O〈人・物〉+*on*+〈物〉】
He *rested* his hand *on* his knee. 彼は手をひざにのせていた.

return 動
❶ 戻る, 帰る.

【S〈人〉・V(+副(句))】
He *returned* home from the U.S. 彼は米国から帰国した.
❷ 戻す, 返す.
① 【S〈人〉・V・O〈物〉】
I *returned* the money. 私はお金を返した.
② 【S〈人〉・V・O〈人〉・O〈物〉】
《英》I *returned* him the money. 私は彼にお金を返した. (⚠ この文型は「物」に焦点があり, ③ は「人」に焦点がある)(受身=The money *was returned* to him.)
③ 【S〈人〉・V・O〈物〉+*to*+〈人〉】 I *returned* the money *to* him. 意味, 受身形は ② と同じ.
❸ 報いる, 応じる.
① 【S〈人〉・V・O〈物・事〉+*for*+〈人・物〉】
He *returned* evil *for* good. 彼は恩を仇で返した.
② 【S〈人〉・V・O〈人・物〉+*with*+〈物・事〉】
He *returned* good *with* evil. 意味は ① と同じ.

reveal 動 明らかにする.
① 【S〈人〉・V・O〈事〉】
The doctor did not *reveal* the truth to her. 医者は彼女に真実を明かさなかった.
② 【S〈人〉・V・O〈*that* 節〉】
He *revealed that* he had cancer. 彼はガンにかかっていることを明らかにした.
③ 【S〈人〉・V・O〈*wh*-節〉】
I can't *reveal* who did it. 私はだれがそれをしたのか明らかにすることはできない.
④ 【S〈物・事〉・V・O〈人・物・事〉+*to be* [*as*] C】
The evidence *revealed* the man *to be* innocent. その証拠はその男が無実であることを明らかにした.
⑤ 【S〈物・事〉・V・O〈*that* 節〉】
The evidence *revealed that* the man was innocent. 意味は ④ と同じ.

ride 動 (乗り物に)乗る, 乗って行く.
① 【S〈人〉・V(+*on* [*in*]+〈乗り物〉】
He *rode in* a car [*on* a bus; *on* a train] to his office. 彼は車[バス; 列車]に乗って会社に行った.
② 【S〈人〉・V・O〈乗り物〉】
He *rode* a bicycle [a bus] to school. 彼は自転車[バス]に乗って学校へ行った. (⚠ より ② の構文の方が普通)

right 形
❶ (道徳的に, 社会通念上)正しい.
① 【It is ~ (*for*+〈人〉)+*to do*】
It is *right for* you to respect your parents. 君が両親を尊敬するのは正しい.
② 【It is ~ *that* 節〉】
It is *right that* you should respect [× you respect] your parents. 意味は ① と同じ. (⚠ should は省略不可)
❷ (行動・判断・意見などが)正しい.
① 【S〈人〉 is ~+*to do*】
You were *right to* refuse the request. 君がその要求を拒絶したのは正しかった.
② 【S〈人〉 is ~+*in*+〈事・do*ing*〉】
You were *right in* refusing the request. 意味は ① と同じ.
③ 【It is ~ *of*〈人〉+*to do*】
It was *right of* you *to* refuse the request. 意味は ① と同じ.

rise 動
❶ 出る, 昇る.
【S〈太陽・月・星など〉・V(+副(句))】
The sun *rises in* [× from] the east. 太陽は東から昇る.
❷ 上がる.
【S〈煙・風船など〉・V(+副(句))】
Smoke *rose* up *from* the chimney [*into* the sky]. 煙が煙突から立ち登った[空へ上って行った].
❸ そびえ立つ. (⚠ 進行形は不可)
【S〈山・建物など〉・V(+副(句))】
Look at the mountain which *rises* in the distance. 遠くにそびえるあの山を見てごらん.
❹ 地位が上がる, 出世する.
① 【S〈地位など〉・V(+副(句))】
His status *has risen*. 彼の地位が上がった.
② 【S〈人〉・V(+*in*+〈地位など〉)】
He *has risen in* his status. 意味は ① と同じ.
③ 【S〈人〉・V(+*from*+〈地位など〉+*to*+〈地位など〉)】 He *rose from* chief clerk *to* manager. 彼は係長から課長に出世した.
❺ (水かさが)増す.
【S〈川など〉・V(+副(句))】
The river *has risen* three feet. 川は 3 フィート増水した.
❻ (数・量・程度が)増す, 高まる.
【S〈物・事〉・V(+副(句))】
The yen *has risen against* the dollar. ドルに対して円高になった.
The thermometer *is rising* steadily. 寒暖計は上がる一方だ.
Her voice *rose* to a scream. 彼女の声は高くなって悲鳴になった.
❼ (感情が)高まる.
【S〈感情など〉・V(+副(句))】
Her anger *rose* (*up*) within her. 彼女は内に怒りがこみあげてくるのを感じた.
❽ 立ち上がる.
【S〈人〉・V(+副(句))】
He *rose* to his feet. 彼は立ち上がった.
She *rose from* the chair to greet him. 彼女はいすから立ち上がって彼を迎えた.
❾ 起床する.
【S〈人〉・V(+副(句))】
He *rises* early every morning except on Sundays. 彼は日曜以外毎朝早起きだ.
❿ 反抗して立ち上がる.
【S〈人々〉・V+副(句)】
Democrats *rose against* the bill. 民主党はその法案に反対した.
⓫ 源を発する.
【S〈川〉・V+*from* [*in*]+〈場所〉】
This river *rises in* the Japan Alps. この川は日本アルプスに源を発している.

rob 動
❶ (人から)奪う.
【S〈人〉・V・O〈人〉+*of*+〈金・物〉】
He *robbed* her *of* her wallet. 彼は彼女からさいふを奪った. (受身=She *was robbed of* her wallet.) (⚠ ×Her wallet was robbed./× She had her wallet robbed. の受身形不可)
❷ (場所から)奪う.
【S〈人〉・V・O〈場所〉(+*of*+〈金・物〉)】
The gang *robbed* the bank (*of* its money and precious metals). 犯罪者の一団が銀行を襲ってお金と貴金属を強奪した. (受身=The bank *was robbed* (*of* its money...).)

roll 動

❶ 転がる.
【S〈人・物〉・V(+副(句))】
The children *are rolling in* the sandbox. 子供たちは砂場で転がっている.
A ball *rolled down* the slope. ボールが坂をころがり落ちた.

❷ 鳴る.
【S〈雷・大鼓など〉・V(+副(句))】
A thunder *is rolling in* the distance. 遠くで雷が鳴っている.

❸ 進む, 走る.
【S〈車〉・V(+副(句))】
The taxi *rolled along* an unpaved road. タクシーは舗装されていない道を進んだ.

❹ 転がす.
【S〈人〉・V・O〈球・車など〉(+副(句))】
I *rolled* the ball *along* the road. 私は道にボールを転がした.

❺ 巻く, くるむ.
① 【S〈人〉・V・O〈物〉(+副(句))】
He *rolled* the bandage *around* his arm. 彼は腕に包帯を巻いた.
② 【S〈人〉・V・O〈物〉(+*into*+〈球〉)】
She *rolled* the yarn *into* a ball. 彼女は編み物用糸を巻いて玉にした.
③ 【S〈人〉・V・O〈物〉(+*in*+〈くるむ物〉)】
She *rolled* her baby *in* a bath towel. 彼女は赤ん坊をバスタオルにくるんでやった.

❻ うねる.
【S〈波・雲など〉・V(+副(句))】
Waves *rolled onto* the beach. 波が砂浜に打ち寄せた.

rude 形 無礼な.

❶ 【S〈人〉 is ~+*to*+〈人〉】
He is *rude to* his teacher. 彼は先生に対して失礼だ.

❷ 【S〈人〉 is ~+*to do*】
He was *rude to* take French leave. 無断退出をしたなんて彼も無礼な男だ.

❸ 【It is ~+*of*+〈人〉+*to do*】
It was *rude of* him *to* take French leave. 意味は❷と同じ.

rule 名 規則, 習慣.

① 【~+*that*節】
He is an exception to the *rule that* lean people are generally nervous. 彼はやせた人は概して神経質だという規則の例外だ.

② 【~+*of*+*doing*】
He makes a *rule of* writing in his diary before going to bed. (=He makes it a rule to write in his diary….) 彼は寝る前に日記を書くことにしている.

rumor 名 うわさ.

① 【~+*that*節】
There is a *rumor* [*Rumor* has it] *that* our homeroom teacher is getting married this spring. 私たちの担任の先生はこの春結婚されるといううわさがある.

② 【~+*of*(+所有格・目的格)+*doing*】
There is a *rumor of* our homeroom teacher *getting* married this spring. 意味は①と同じ.

run 動

❶ 走る, 急いで行く.
【S〈人〉・V(+副(句))】
He *ran for* a mile [*to* school]. 彼は1マイル[学校まで]走った.

❷ 逃げる.
【S〈人〉・V+副(句)】
On seeing a policeman, the thief *ran* (*away*). 警官を見て泥棒は逃げた.

❸ (乗り物が)走る, 運行されている.
【S〈乗り物〉・V(+副(句))】
The train *runs* 90 kilometers an hour. 列車は時速90キロで走る. (❗ただし, 今走っているような場合には run を用いない: Our car *is traveling* [*moving, going*] at a speed of 90km an hour. (われわれの乗っている車は時速90キロで走っている.))
The bus *runs* [✕ is running] every thirty minutes *between* Kyoto and Osaka. そのバスは京都・大阪間を30分ごとに運行している. (❗「運行されている」の意では進行形不可)

❹ 競走に出る.
① 【S〈人・動物〉・V(+*in*+〈競技〉)】
He *ran in* the 100-meter dash. 彼は100メートル競走に出た.
② 【S〈人・動物〉・V・C〈序数〉】
He *ran* first [second; last] in the race. 彼は競走で1着[2着; びり]だった.

❺ 競走する.
【S〈人〉・V・O〈競走〉】
I *ran* a race with him in the playground. 運動場で彼と競走した.

❻ 走らせる.
【S〈人〉・V・O〈人・動物・乗り物〉(+副(句))】
He *ran* the horse [car] *along* the river. 彼は馬[車]を川に沿って走らせた.

❼ 流れる.
【S〈川・液体など〉・V(+副(句))】
The Thames *runs* [✕ is running] *through* London. テムズ川はロンドンを貫流している.
Tears *were running from* her eyes. (=Her eyes *were running with* tears.) 彼女の目から涙が流れていた.

❽ 流す.
【S〈人〉・V・O〈液体など〉】
She *ran* the water for a bath. 彼女は浴槽に水を入れた.
She *ran* a hot bath for me. 彼女は私のために熱い風呂を入れてくれた. (❗ She ran me a hot bath. も可)

❾ 延びている, 及ぶ. (❗通例進行形不可)
【S〈物・事〉・V+副(句)】
The road *runs along* the river. 道路は川に沿って延びている.
This book *runs to* nearly 500 pages. この本ははぼ500ページに及ぶ.

❿ …になる.
【S〈物・事〉・V・C〈形〉】
The river *ran* dry. 川が涸れた.
Our sugar *is running* short. うちの砂糖が切れかかっている. (❗ C は通例悪い状態を表わす形容詞)

⓫ 続く.
【S〈物・事〉・V+副(句)】
The play *ran for* three months. その劇は3ヵ月間上演された.
The contract *runs for* two years. その契約は2

基本文型

⑫ (機械が)動く.
【S〈機械など〉・V(+副(句))】
The machine *is running* well. 機械は調子よく動いている.

⑬ (機械を)動かす.
【S〈人・動力〉・V・O〈機械など〉】
They *run* the motor by electricity. (=Electricity *runs* the motor.) その機械は電気で動いている.

⑭ 経営する.
【S〈人〉・V・O〈会社など〉】
He *runs* a large restaurant. 彼は大きなレストランを経営している.

rush 動

❶ 急ぐ, 突進する.
【S〈人・車など〉・V(+副(句))】
He *rushed out of* the house [*into* the garden]. 彼は家から飛び出した[庭へ飛び込んできた].

❷ 勢いよく流れる.
【S〈川など〉・V(+副(句))】
The river *rushed along*. 川は勢いよく流れていた.

❸ 急に現れる.
【S〈人など〉・V(+副(句))】
A good idea *rushed into* my mind. 良い考えが突然私の心に浮かんだ.

❹ 急いで送る.
【S〈人〉・V・O〈人・物〉(+*to*+〈場所など〉)】
They *rushed* the injured *to* a hospital. 彼らはけが人を病院へかつぎ込んだ.

❺ 急がせる, せき立てる.
【S〈人〉・V・O〈人〉(+*into*+〈事・*doing*〉)】
She *rushed* him *into* buying an expensive necklace. 彼女は彼をせき立てて高価なネックレスを買わせた.

sad 形

❶ (人が)悲しい, 悲しむ.
① 【S〈人〉is ~+*about*+〈事〉】
He was [felt] *sad about* his brother's death. 彼は兄の死を悲しんでいた.

② 【S〈人〉is ~+*to do*】
He was *sad to* have lost his brother. 彼は兄を失って悲しかった.

③ 【S〈人〉is ~+*that* 節】
He was *sad that* he had lost his brother. 意味は②と同じ.

❷ (物・事が)悲しませる, 悲しむべき.
① 【It is ~(+*for*+〈人・物・事〉)+*to do*】
It is *sad to* lose your best friend. 親友を失うのは悲しい.
It is *sad for* the actress not *to* make a comeback. その女優にとって復帰できないのは悲しいことだ.

② 【It is ~+*that* 節】
It is *sad that* the actress cannot [should be unable to] make a comeback. 意味は①の第2例と同じ.

safe 形 安全な. (⇨dangerous)

① 【S〈物・事〉is ~ (*for*+〈人・事・*doing*〉)(+*to do*)】 The mushroom is *safe for eating*. そのキノコは食べても安全だ.
This pond is *safe (for* you) *to* swim in. この池で泳いでも安全です.

② 【It is ~ (*for*+〈人〉)+*to do*】
It is *safe (for* you) *to* swim in this pond. 意味は①の第2例と同じ. (⚠ ×It is safe *that* you swim in this pond./× *You* are safe *to* swim in this pond. は不可)

satisfy 動 (⚠ 通例進行形不可)

❶ 満たす, 充足させる.
【S〈物・事〉・V・O〈欲望・必要など〉】
No amount of money *satisfied* his greed. どれだけお金があっても彼の貪欲(どん)は満たされなかった.

❷ 満足させる.
① 【S〈物・事〉・V・O〈人〉】
His superb performance *satisfied* the whole audience. 彼のみごとな演奏に聴衆は全員満足した. (受身=The whole audience *was satisfied with* his superb performance.)

② 【S〈人・物・事〉・V・O〈人・事〉+*with*+〈事・物〉[*by*+*doing*]】 I *satisfied* my hunger *with* [*by* having] a good meal. 私はたっぷり食事をして空腹を満たした.

save 動

❶ 救う.
① 【S〈人・物・事〉・V・O〈人・物〉】
The doctor *saved* his life. 医師は彼の命を救った.

② 【S〈人・物・事〉・V・O〈人・物〉+*from*+〈危険・困難など・*doing*〉】 He *saved* the boy *from* starvation. 彼はその少年を飢えから救った.

❷ 蓄える, とっておく.
① 【S〈人〉・V・O〈物〉(+*for*+〈人・将来など〉)】
I am *saving* (up) money *for* a new car [my old age]. 私は新車を買うために[老後に備えて]お金をためている.
Save some cake *for* me. 私にケーキをとっておいてください. (⚠ この文型は「人」に焦点があり, ② は「物」に焦点がある)

② 【S〈人〉・V・O〈人〉・O〈物〉】
Save me some cake. 意味は①の後例と同じ.

③ 【S〈人〉・V(+*up*)(+*for*+〈物・将来など〉)】
I'm *saving* (*up*) *for* a new car. 意味は①の第1例と同じ. (⚠ ...saving (up) *to* buy a new car. ともいえる)

❸ 節約する, 省く.
① 【S〈人・物・事〉・V・O〈労力・時間など〉】
I *saved* a lot of time by using the computer. コンピュータを使って多くの時間が節約できた.

② 【S〈人・物・事〉・V・O〈人〉・O〈労力・時間など〉】
The computer will *save* you a lot of time and trouble. コンピュータを使えば多くの時間と手間が省ける. (受身=You will *be saved* a lot of time and trouble by using the computer.) (⚠ この場合 a lot of time and trouble を主語にした受身は不可)

say 動

❶ 言う, 話す.
① 【S〈人〉・V・O〈言葉など〉(+*to*+〈人〉)】
What did he *say to* you (*about* the accident)? (その事故について)彼は君に何と言ったのか.

② 【S〈人〉・V・O〈(*that*) 節・引用文〉】
He *said* (*that*) he would come the next day. (=He *said*, "I will come tomorrow.") 彼はあす来ると言った.

③ 【S〈人〉・V・O〈*wh*-節・句〉】
She *said how* happy she was. (=She *said*, "How happy I am!") 彼女はとても幸せだわと言った.

不可)
⑤【S〈人・動物〉・V】
Cats can *see* in the dark. 猫は暗い所で目が見える.
There was no house as far as I could *see*. 見渡す限り家は一軒もなかった.

❷ 会う.
【S〈人〉・V・O〈人〉】
I *saw* him on the street yesterday. きのう道で彼に会った.

❸ 見物する.
【S〈人〉・V・O〈場所・劇など〉】
Have you *seen* (the sights of) Paris? パリを見物されたことがありますか.

❹ 見て知る. (❗進行形は不可)
① 【S〈人〉・V・O〈事〉】
I *saw* his arrest in the paper. 彼が逮捕されたことを新聞で知った.
② 【S〈人〉・V・O〈*that* 節〉】
I *saw* (it) in the paper *that* he was arrested. 意味は①と同じ.

❺ 調べる.
【S〈人〉・V・O〈*wh*-節・句〉・*if* 節〉】
Could you go and *see* if the door is locked? ドアに鍵がかかっているか確かめに行ってくれますか.

❻ 経験する. (❗通例進行形は不可)
【S〈人〉・V・O〈事・時〉】
She *has seen* a great deal in her long life. 彼女は長い人生でたくさんの経験をしてきた.

❼ 分かる, 理解する. (❗進行形は不可)
① 【S〈人〉・V・O〈事〉】
Do you *see* the point of his argument? 彼の議論の要点が分かりますか.
② 【S〈人〉・V・O〈*that* 節〉】
I didn't *see that* the door was unlocked. ドアに鍵がかかっていないのは分からなかった. (受身＝It *was* not *seen that*....)
③ 【S〈人〉・V・O〈*wh*-節・句〉】
I don't *see why* he got angry. なぜ彼が怒ったのか私には分からない.
④ 【S〈人〉・V】
You'll *see*. 今に分かるよ.

❽ (...を...と)考える[みなす]. (❗進行形は不可)
① 【S〈人〉・V・O〈人・事〉＋副(句)】
Try to *see* things differently. 物事を違ったふうに考えてみてごらん.
② 【S〈人〉・V・O〈人・事〉・*as* C〈名〉】
Can you *see* happiness *as* your aim in life? あなたは幸福を人生の目的とみなせますか.

❾ ...するように気をつける.
① 【S〈人〉・V(＋*to it*)・O〈*that* 節〉】
See (to it) [*See* to] *that* the door is locked. ドアに鍵を必ずおろしておきなさい. (❗See that... の構文がほかの表現よりし口語的)
② 【S〈人〉・V・O〈事〉・C〈done〉】
See the work *done* carefully. 監督してその仕事を気をつけてやらせなさい.

❿ 見送る.
【S〈人〉・V・O〈人〉＋副(句)】
He *saw* her home [back to her house]. 彼は彼女を家まで送った.

seem 動 ...のように思われる. (❗進行形は不可)
① 【S〈人・事〉・V(＋*to* ‹・〉)・(*to be*) C〈形・名・doing・done〉】 Mary *seems* (*to be*) nice [a nice girl]. メリーはよい人のようだ.
The man *seems to be* the store keeper. その人は店主のようだ. (❗C が形を伴わない名の場合, 通

---

o take. 私はどっちの列車
I can't *say which* 乗ったらよいのかわ
からない.
④ 【S〈They, People〉ng young people. 海外旅
They [People]ling abroad ....(受身＝It *is*
行は人気があるそうです.
said to be very popular among
very po
saiy are very popular.... の受身形
×Traveling abroad is

I said. 彼は私が言ったとおりにした.
表わす. (❗受身形, 進行形は不可)
掲示・表情など〉・V・O〈*that* 節〉】
wspaper *says* (*that*) the actor committed suicide. その俳優が自殺をしたと新聞に出
clock on the wall *says* (it's) 10:00. 壁にかかっている時計では10時だ.
His look *says* (*that*) he was successful. 彼の表情ではうまくいったようだ.
② 【S〈本・表情など〉・V・O〈*wh*- 節〉】
Her eyes *say how* sad she is. 彼女はとても悲しそうな目をしている.

scold 動 しかる.
① 【S〈人〉・V・O〈人〉(＋*for*＋〈事・*doing*〉)】
The teacher *scolded* the student *for* coming late. 先生は生徒を遅刻したと言ってしかった. (受身＝The student *was scolded* by the teacher *for* coming late.)
② 【S〈人〉・V(＋副(句))】
Don't *scold* so severely. そんなに厳しくしかるな.

search 動 捜す.
① 【S〈人〉・V・O〈場所・人〉(＋*for*＋〈人・物〉)】
The police *searched* the suspect. 警察は容疑者のボディーチェックをした.
I *searched* the drawer *for* the key. 私は鍵はないかと引き出しを捜した.
② 【S〈人〉・V(＋*for*＋〈人・物〉)】
They *searched for* the lost child. 彼らは迷子を捜した.

see 動
❶ 見える, 見る. (❗進行形は不可)
① 【S〈人〉・V・O〈人・物〉】
I (can) *see* several ships in the offing. 沖に船が数隻見える.
② 【S〈人〉・V・O〈人・物〉・C〈do〉】
I *saw* him cross the road. 彼が道を横切るのを見た. (❗(1) 行為の全体を見たことを表わし, 「渡り切るのを見た」の意味. (2) 受身形では to が必要: He *was seen* to cross the road. この場合, 通例話し手は直接見たのではなく, 聞いて知っているという含みになる. したがって「彼は道を横切ったようだ」のような訳になる)
③ 【S〈人〉・V・O〈人・物〉・C〈*doing*〉】
I *saw* him *crossing* the road. 彼が道を横切っているのを見た. (❗(1) ②と違って行為の途中を見たことを表わし, 渡りきったかどうか不明. (2) 受身形にしても②のような意味の変化は生じない: He *was seen crossing* the road.)
④ 【S〈人〉・V・O〈人・物〉・C〈*done*〉】
I *saw* an old man *knocked* down by a car. 一人の老人が車にはねとばされるのを見た. (❗受身

基本文型

例 to be を省略しない)
　It *seems to be* snowing outside. (＝It *seems* that it is snowing outside.) 外は雪が降っているようだ. (! ×It seems snow*ing* outside./×It seems *to* snow outside. は不可. Cに現在分詞が来るときは形容詞化したものを除き通例 to be は省略しない)

② 【S〈人・物・事〉・V(+*to*+〈人〉)+*to do*】
　He doesn't *seem to* know the fact. 彼はその事実を知らないようだ. (! do は通例 know, hear, think など状態を表わす動詞. 動作を表わす動詞の場合は完了形・進行形にするか, 助動詞または時・程度の副詞句を伴う: He *seems to be* learning [×*to learn*] English. 彼は英語を習っているようだ)

③ 【S〈*It*〉・V (*to*+〈人〉)+*that* 節】
　It seems (*to* me) *that* he knows everything about it. 彼はそのことについては何でも知っているように(私には)思われる. (! ②の文型を使って He *seems to* know…. ともいえる)

④ 【S〈人・物・事〉・V+*as if* 節】
　It seems as if he knew [〈話〉knows] nothing about it. 彼はそのことについてはまるで何も知らないようだ.

⑤ 【S〈人・物・事〉・V・C〈*as if* 節〉】
　He *seems as if* he knew [〈話〉knows] nothing about it. 意味は ④ と同じ.

⑥ 【*There*・V(+*to*+〈人〉)・(*to be*) S〈事・物・人〉】
　There seems (*to* me) (*to be*) no hope of her coming back. (＝*It seems* (*to* me) *that* there is no hope of her coming back.) 彼女が帰ってくる見込みはないように(私には)思える.

⑦ 【S〈*It*〉・V・C〈形・名〉+*that* 節】
　It seemed impossible *that* he would succeed. (＝*It seemed that* it was impossible for him to succeed.) 彼が成功するのは不可能のように思われた. (! It is that 以下を受ける形式主語)

⑧ 【S〈*It*〉・V・C〈形・名〉+*for*+名+*to do*】
　It seemed impossible *for* him *to* succeed. 意味は ⑦ と同じ. (! (1) It is for 以下を受ける形式主語. (2)×He seemed impossible to succeed. は不可)

sell 動
❶ 売る, 販売する.
① 【S〈人・店〉・V(+副(句))】
　We don't *sell to* minors. 未成年者には販売していません.

② 【S〈人・店〉・V・O〈物〉(+副(句))/+*for* [*at*]+〈価格など〉】
　They *sell* fruits *at* that shop, not vegetables. その店は野菜ではなく果物を売っている.
　I *sold* the painting cheaply [*for* a million yen]. 私はその絵を安く[100万円で]売った.
　This shop *sells* records *at* 10 percent discount. 当店はレコードを10%引きで売っています.

③ 【S〈人〉・V・O〈人〉・O〈物〉】
　He *sold* me the camera (*for* 5,000 yen). 彼は私に(5,000円で)そのカメラを売ってくれた. (受身＝The camera *was sold* (*to*) me (*for* 5,000 yen)./I *was sold* the camera (*for* 5,000 yen).) (! この文型は「物」に, ④ は「人」に焦点がある)

④ 【S〈人〉・V・O〈物〉+*to*+〈人〉】
　He *sold* the camera *to* me (*for* 5,000 yen). 意味は ③ と同じ. (受身＝The camera *was sold to* me (*for* 5,000 yen).)

❷ 売れる, 売れ行きが…である.
① 【S〈物〉・V+*for* [*at*]+〈価格など〉】

　This magazine *sells* 500 円だ.
　1,500 yen. この雑誌は1,500円で売られている[あまり売れない].

　The apples are low-[high-] *sell well*
　[badly]. (そのリンゴは安い[悪い]). (! ×are sold w...)

send 動
❶ 送る, 発送する.
① 【S〈人〉・V・O〈物〉】
　He *sent* a parcel by mail. 彼は小包を...

② 【S〈人〉・V・O〈人〉・O〈物・伝言〉】
　He *sent* me a Christmas card. 彼は私に...カードを送ってくれた. (! この文型は「物」に焦点, ③ は「人」に焦点がある) (受身＝I *was sent* a Christmas card by him./A Christmas card *was sent* (*to*) me.)

③ 【S〈人〉・V・O〈物〉+*to*+〈人・場所〉】
　He *sent* a Christmas card *to* me. 意味は ② と同じ. (受身＝A Christmas card *was sent to* me.)
　He *sent* a parcel *to* London [×sent London a parcel]. 彼は小包をロンドンへ送った. (! 場所へ送る場合は SVOO の文型は不可)

❷ 行かせる, 派遣する.
　【S〈人〉・V・O〈人〉+*to*+〈人・場所〉 [*for*+〈目的物〉/*to do*]】 They *sent* their son *to* college. 彼らは息子を大学へ行かせた.
　Mother *sent* me *for* [*to* buy] some bread. 母は私にパンを買いにやらせた.

❸ …にする.
① 【S〈人・物・事〉・V・O〈人・物〉・C〈形〉*doing*〉】
　The blow *sent* him *flying*. その一撃で彼はふっ飛んだ.

② 【S〈人・物・事〉・V・O〈人〉+*into* [*to*]+名】
　The news *sent* her *into* a depression. その知らせは彼女を落ち込ませた.

sense 名
❶ 感じ, 意識.
① 【～+*that* 節】
　I have a *sense that* there is someone in the next room. 隣の部屋にだれかいるような感じがする.

② 【～+*of* (+所有格)+*doing*】
　I have a *sense of* there being someone in the next room. 意味は ① と同じ.

❷ 思慮, 分別.
　【～+*to do*】
　They don't have the *sense to* admit defeat. 彼らは負けを認めるだけの分別がない.

❸ 意義, 価値.
　【～+*of* [*in*]+*doing*】
　What is the *sense of* [*in*] learning a foreign language? 外国語を学ぶ意義はどこにあるか.

separate 動
❶ (引き)離す, 分ける, 隔てる.
① 【S〈人・事〉・V・O〈複数の人・物〉】
　We *separated* the men who were fighting. われわれはけんかをしている男たちを引き離した.

② 【S〈人・物・事〉・V・O〈人・物〉+*from* [*into*]+〈人・物〉】 The river *separates* this town *from* that one. その川はこの町とあの町を隔てている. (受身＝This town *is separated from* that one by the river.)
　The teacher *separated* the students *into* four groups. 先生は生徒を4グループに分けた.

❷ 分か[別]れる, 分離する